BIOGRAPHICAL BOOKS 1950–1980

This edition of BIOGRAPHICAL BOOKS 1950-1980 was prepared by the R. R. Bowker Company's Department of Bibliography in collaboration with the Publication Systems Department.

Senior staff of the Department of Bibliography includes:
Gertrude Jennings, Editor-In-Chief, Department of Bibliography.
Peter Simon, Senior Database Production Manager.
Debra K. Brown, Manager, Product Development.
Dean Hollister, Project Manager.

Michael B. Howell, Manager, Systems Development.

Andrew H. Uszak, Vice President, Data Services/Systems.

WITHDRAWN

BIOGRAPHICAL BOOKS 1950–1980

VOCATION INDEX

NAME/SUBJECT INDEX

AUTHOR INDEX

TITLE INDEX

BIOGRAPHICAL BOOKS IN PRINT INDEX

R.R. BOWKER COMPANY

New York & London

Published by the R. R. Bowker Company (a Xerox Publishing Company)
1180 Avenue of the Americas, New York, N.Y. 10036

International Standard Book Number 0-8352-1315-3
Printed and bound in the
United States of America

CONTENTS

PREFACE

In our discussions with librarians to determine areas of reference materials where there remained gaps, we frequently were asked to produce a listing of biographical books. BIOGRAPHICAL BOOKS 1950-1980 began with a survey of over 1150 potential users in public libraries, college and university libraries, school libraries, and bookstores, who contributed to the final design. This bibliography is a comprehensive compilation of information on biographical and autobiographical works published or distributed in the United States since 1950, which derives from the Bowker databases of cataloging records.

This publication includes cataloging and in-print information for biographies, autobiographies, collective biographies, letters, diaries, journals, and other biographical materials, such as dictionaries and directories.

SELECTION OF INFORMATION

This edition of BIOGRAPHICAL BOOKS 1950-1980 was produced from records stored on magnetic tape, edited by computer programs, and set in type by computer-controlled photocomposition.

In the preparation of the name/subject, author and title indexes, we examined Bowker's cataloging database used to produce the AMERICAN BOOK PUBLISHING RECORD CUMULATIVE 1950-1977, AMERICAN BOOK PUBLISHING RECORD CUMULATIVEs 1978 and 1979, and all published monthly issues of the AMERICAN BOOK PUBLISHING RECORD 1980. Utilizing catalog record characteristics, which include Dewey Decimal and Library of Congress classification numbers and subdivisions associated with biographical materials, the presence of name headings when used as subject tracings, and codes contained within the MARC (machine-readable cataloging) entries issued by the Library of Congress, some 42,152 entries were selected from these combined databases, which represent in excess of one million cataloging records. In the fall of 1980, the AMERICAN BOOK PUBLISHING RECORD CUMULATIVE 1876-1949 will be completed, which will add over 600,000 entries to this database, and which will supply the potential to publish information on biographies retrospectively to 1876.

An in-print index, containing over 13,300 titles, was produced from the BOOKS IN PRINT database. A code, BIP, appears on those cataloged entries, in the *Name/Subject Index,* which were identified on the BOOKS IN PRINT database.

CONTENT AND ARRANGEMENT OF ENTRIES

The *Name/Subject Index,* arranged by main entry within headings for personal names and subjects, contains a full entry for each title. Some 42,152 entries are classified under 17,450 personal name headings, and 4,400 Library of Congress subject headings, resulting in a total of 21,850 headings in the entire index. Items cataloged with name headings appear under those, with collective biographies appearing under headings for each of the biographees, when so identified in cataloging. Entries under subjects only are primarily for collective biographies, reference books, and works on the subject of biography. Titles have been located, to appropriate name or subject headings, which received no tracings in original cataloging. The author and title indexes contain page number references to the full entries in the *Name/Subject Index*. Descriptions of all indexes can be found in the ''How To Use'' section, following this preface.

SPECIAL FEATURES

BIOGRAPHICAL BOOKS 1950-1980 contains several features to enhance its usefulness.

The first is the *Vocation Index*. This index gives subject access, using Library of Congress subject headings, to the 10,000 unique personal names contained within the *Name/Subject Index*. Some 2,340 subject headings were used, along with 3,100 cross-references. Wherever possible, the most specific heading available for the vocation or area of interest of a biographee was used. In cases where persons had no discernable vocational area, headings for types of persons or country of origin may have been used. Persons prominently active in more than one vocational area may appear under more than one heading. Subject information within the cataloging entries, as well as numerous standard reference works, were used to compile this index. If information on a specific biographee is being sought by a user, direct access may be obtained by searching in the *Name/Subject Index*.

Another feature of BIOGRAPHICAL BOOKS 1950-1980 is the *Biographical Books In Print* index. This index, arranged by title, was prepared after a computer-controlled comparison between the cataloging information selected from the AMERICAN BOOK PUBLISHING RECORD databases, and the BOOKS IN PRINT database. A code, BIP, identifies cataloging entries for which current acquisitions information can be found in the in-print index. While multiple editions of a title may appear together, this symbol may appear on only one. Complete acquisitions information is provided with each in-print entry: title, subtitle, edition statements, price with binding if other than cloth over boards, International Standard Book Number, publisher's order number, and publisher's or distributor's name abbreviation. A key to these abbreviations, with complete editorial and ordering addresses, is included.

Gertrude Jennings, Editor-In-Chief, Department of Bibliography, Data Services/Systems, developed the concept of BIOGRAPHICAL BOOKS 1950-1980. She and Peter Simon, Senior Database Production Manager, were responsible for the design and planning of this project. Support was received from Debra K. Brown, Manager, Product Development. Dean Hollister, Project Manager, Subject Guide, made a significant contribution in the preparation of all indexes.

We extend our thanks to all of the editors of the Subject Guide and Weekly Record staffs who participated in various phases of preparation of this first edition, as well as to the members of the library and bookseller community who provided guidance in the product design process. We invite users of BIOGRAPHICAL BOOKS 1950-1980 to offer comments and suggestions for subsequent editions.

Peter Simon
Senior Database Production Manager
Department of Bibliography

HOW TO USE BIOGRAPHICAL BOOKS 1950–1980

GENERAL EDITORIAL POLICIES

Original Library of Congress cataloging is provided in the *Name/Subject Index,* with the following editorial policies:

Entries are listed under name tracings, or by primary subject for titles without name tracings.

Multiple listings are provided when an entry contains more than one name tracing.

Entries without name or subject tracings in the original cataloging were assigned to appropriate name or subject headings.

Entries for which acquisitions information can be found in the *Biographical Books In Print Index* contain the symbol *BIP.* This was placed at the end of the entry to preserve the original format of the cataloged entries. The BIP symbol may not necessarily refer to the precise edition of a title identified in the cataloged entry, and multiple purchase options for titles may at times be found in the In Print index.

To insure that critical information can be found in the *Biographical Books In Print Index,* editorial policies consistent with *Books In Print* have been maintained. Every effort is made by most contributing publishers and distributors to prepare their material with consideration for its accuracy throughout the life of this edition of BIOGRAPHICAL BOOKS 1950-1980. In spite of these efforts, a number of changes in price will occur, and a number of titles in this edition will become unavailable before the new edition is published. All prices are subject to change without notice.

Most prices are list prices. Lack of uniformity in the individual catalogs prohibits indicating trade discounts. A lower case "t" indicates a tentative price; a lower case "x" indicates a short discount, 20% or less.

The names of publishers and distributors, in most cases, are abbreviated. A key to these abbreviations, with the addresses of the publishing or distributing firms whose titles are listed in the *Biographical Books In Print Index* will be found in the "*Key to Publishers' and Distributors' Directory,*" at the end of this volume. Here is an example of an entry in this key:

> Bowker, (Bowker, R.R., Co.; 0-8352), A Xerox Publishing Co., 1180 Ave. of the Americas, New York, NY 10036 Tel 212-764-5100; Orders to: P.O. Box 1807, Ann Arbor, MI 48106.

Entries in this "Key" are arranged alphabetically by the abbreviations used in the Biographical Books In Print entries. The full name, ISBN prefix, editorial address, telephone number, ordering address (if different from the editorial address), and imprints follow the abbreviation.

NAME/SUBJECT INDEX

Entries are arranged alphabetically by main entry within name or subject.

Headings were derived from the name and primary subject tracings in the original cataloging entries. Some of these headings were made uniform due to variances in the styling of tracings in these entries.

Name and subject headings are arranged alphabetically.

> *Artists*
> *Ashe, Arthur*
> *Audubon, John James, 1785-1851*

Many of the headings are broken down still further:

> *Artists*
> *Artists,* British
> *Artists* - Dictionaries
> *Audubon, John James, 1785-1851*
> *Audubon, John James, 1785-1851* -
> Juvenile Literature

Headings, as used in Library of Congress cataloging practice, are explicit rather than general. Thus, books on Arthur Ashe are under his name and books on baseball players are under *Baseball*, not *Sports*.

VOCATION INDEX

The *Vocation Index* is designed to provide subject access to the name headings in the *Name/Subject Index,* and can be used to discern the vocational relationships between specific persons.

AUTHOR AND TITLE INDEXES

The author and title indexes are alphabetically arranged by their authors and titles respectively. Page references are provided to the main entries in the *Name/Subject Index*.

BIOGRAPHICAL BOOKS IN PRINT INDEX

The *Biographical Books In Print Index* is alphabetically arranged by title. Entries include the following bibliographic information, when available: title, subtitle, edition statement, price with type of binding if other than cloth over boards, International Standard Book Number, publisher order number and publisher's or distributor's name abbreviation.

KEY TO ABBREVIATIONS

GENERAL

a	after price, specially priced library edition available
a.	annual
abr.	abridged
abstr.	abstracts
adpt.	adapted
adv.	advertising
Amer.	American
annot.	annotation(s), annotated
ans.	answer(s)
app.	appendix
approx.	approximately
assn.	association
auth.	author
bd.	bound
bdg.	binding
bds.	boards
bi-m.	every two months
bibl(s).	bibliography (ies)
bk(s).	book, books
bk. rev.	book reviews
bklet(s)	booklets
Bro.	Brother
c/o	care of
charts	charts (diagrams, graphs, tables)
circ.	circulation
coll.	college
comm.	commission, committee
co.	company
comp(s).	compiler(s)
cond.	condensed
contr.	controlled
corp.	corporation
cum. ind.	cumulative index
Cy.	county
d.	daily
dept.	department
diag(s).	diagram(s)
dir.	director
dist.	distributed
Div.	Division
doz.	dozen
ea.	each
ed.	editor, edited, edition
Ed. Bd.	Editorial Board
eds.	editions, editors
educ.	education
elem.	elementary
ency.	encyclopedia
Eng.	English
enl.	enlarged
exp.	expurgated
fac.	facsimile
fasc.	fascicle
fict.	fiction
fig(s).	figure(s)
film rev.	film reviews
for.	foreign
fortn.	fortnightly
Fr.	French
frwd.	foreword
g	after price, guaranteed juvenile binding
gen.	general
Ger.	German
Gr.	Greek
gr.	grade, grades
hdbk.	handbook
Heb.	Hebrew
i.t.a.	initial teaching alphabet
Illus.	illustrated, illustration(s), illustrator(s)
in prep.	in preparation
incl.	includes, including
inst.	institute
intro.	introduction
ISSN	International Standard Serial Number
irreg.	irregular
It.	Italian
Jr.	Junior
jt. auth.	joint author
jt. ed.	joint editor
k	kindergarten audience level
l.p.	long playing
ltd. ed.	limited edition
lab.	laboratory
lang(s).	language(s)
Lat.	Latin
lea.	leather
lib.	library
lit.	literature, literary
m.	monthly
math.	mathematics
mkt.	market prices
mod.	modern
mor.	morocco
MS, MSS	manuscript, manuscripts
music rev.	music reviews
N.S.	New Series
natl.	national
no., nos.	number, numbers
o.p.	out of print
orig.	original text, not a reprint
pap.	paper
pat.	patents
photos	photographs, photographer
play rev.	play reviews (theatre reviews)
PLB	publisher's library binding
Pol.	Polish
pop. ed.	popular edition
Port.	Portuguese
prep.	preparation
probs.	problems
Prof.	Professor
prog. bk.	programmed book
ps	preschool audience level
pseud.	pseudonym
pt(s).	part, parts
pub.	published, publisher, publishing
pubn.	publication
q.	quarterly
record rev.	record reviews
ref(s).	reference(s)
repr.	reprint
reprod(s).	reproduction(s)
rev.	revised

rpm.	revolution per minute (phono records)
Rus.	Russian
s-a.	twice annually
s-m.	twice monthly
s-w.	twice weekly
s.p.	school price
sec.	section
sel.	selected
ser.	series
s & l	signed & limited
Soc.	Society
sols.	solutions
Span.	Spanish
Sr. (after given name)	Senior
Sr. (before given name)	Sister
St.	Saint
stat.	statistics
subs.	subsidiary
subscr.	subscription
suppl.	supplement
t	after price, tentative price
tech.	technical
tele. rev.	television reviews
text ed.	text edition
3/m.	3 times a month
3/yr.	3 times a year
tr.	translator, translated, translation
tr. lit.	trade literature (manufacturers' catalogues, etc.)
tr. mk.	trade marks
univ.	university
vol(s).	volume, volumes
w.	weekly
wkbk.	workbook
x	after price, short discount (20% or less)
YA	young adult audience level
yrbk.	yearbook
‡	not available from a subscription agency

VOCATION INDEX

The *Vocation Index* is designed to provide subject access, by headings for vocation or area of interest, to the personal names listed in *Biographical Books 1950-1980*. More than 10,000 personal names are classified under 2,340 Library of Congress subject headings. Headings as specific as possible were assigned, with cross-references provided to show the interrelatedness of vocational areas. Personal name headings within *Biographical Books 1950-1980* for *Actors and Actresses*, or *Presidents*, for instance, would be alphabetically arranged under their respective topic. Where biographees have no apparent vocational area, headings for types of persons or country of origin may have been used. Persons active in more than one vocational area may often be listed under multiple headings.

A

Loy, Myrna, 1905-
Lugosi, Bela, 1882-1956.
Lunt, Alfred.
Lupino, Ida, 1918-
McGregor, Charlie.
MacKaye, Steele, 1842-1894.
McQueen, Steve, 1930-
Mansfield, Jayne.
Mansfield, Richard, 1857-1907.
Marlowe, Julia, 1865-1950.
Martin, Mary, 1913-
Massey,Raymond.
Menken, Adah Isaacs, 1835-1868.
Milland, Ray.
Mitchell, Grant, 1874-
Mitchum, Robert, 1917-
Mix, Tom, 1880-1940.
Monroe, Marilyn,1926-1962.
Moore, Mary Tyler.
Moorehead, Agnes, 1906-1974.
Mostel, Kate.
Muni, Paul, 1895-1967.
Nelson, Ozzie, 1906-
Newman, Paul, 1925-
Novak, Kim.
Oakie, Jack, 1903-
Ostrow, Sarah.
Payne, John Howard, 1791-1852.
Peck, Gregory, 1916-
Peters, Jean, 1927-
Peters, Lloyd, 1902-
Pickford, Mary, 1893-
Picon, Molly.
Poitier, Sidney.
Power, Tyrone, 1914-
Price, Vincent, 1911-
Raft, George.
Redford, Robert-Juvenile Literature.
Reynolds, Burt.
Ritchie, Anna Cora (Ogden) Mowatt, 1819-1870.
Robinson, Edward G., 1893-1973.
Ross, Frederick G., 1858-1942.
Russell, Lillian, 1861-1922.
Russell, Rosalind.
Seldes, Marian.
Sharif, Omar, 1932-
Shields, Brooke, 1965-
Stallone, Sylvester-Juvenile Literature.
Stanwyck, Barbara, 1907-
Stewart, Jackie.
Swanson, Gloria.
Talmadge, Constance, 1900-
Taylor, Elizabeth Rosemond, 1932-
Taylor, Laurette, 1884-1946.
Taylor, Robert, 1911-1969.
Temple, Shirley, 1928-
Tierney, Gene.
Tracy, Spencer, 1900-1967.
Travolta, John, 1954-
Turner, Lana, 1920-
Valentine, Rudolph, 1895-1926.
Wagner, Landsay-Juvenile Literature.
Wayne, John, 1907-
Weissmuller, John.
Welles, Orson, 1915-
West, Mae.
White, Pearl, 1889-1938.
Winkler, Henry, 1945-
Wood, Joan, 1945-

ACTRESSES
see Actors and Actresses

ADMINISTRATION
see Civil Service; Management
also subdivision Politics and Government under names of countries, states, cities, etc.

ADMIRALS
Banning, Phineas, 1830-1885.
Barbarossa, Khayr Al-Din, D. 1546.
Beaufort, Francis, Sir, 1774-1857.
Blake, Robert, 1598-1657.
Bligh, William, 1754-1817.
Canaris, Wilhelm.
Cunningham, Andrew Browne Cunningham, 1st Viscount, 1883-1963.
Decker, Benton Weaver, 1899-
Dundonald, Thomas Cochrane, 10th Earl of, 1775-1860.
Ellery, William, 1727-1820.
Farragut, David Glasgow, 1801-1870.
Fisher, John Arbuthnot Fisher, Baron, 1841-1920.
Fiske, Bradley Allen, 1854-1942.
Hawkins, John, Sir, 1532-1595.
Kanhoji Angri, D. 1731.
Mountbatten, Louis Mountbatten, Earl, 1900-
Mountevans, Edward Ratcliffe Garth Russell Evans, Baron, 1880-1957.
Nimitz, Chester William, 1885-1966.
North, Dudley Burton Napier, Sir, 1881-1961.
Rodney, George Brydges Rodney, Baron, 1719-1792.
Ruyter, Michiel Adriaanszoon De, 1607-1676.
Spruance, Raymond Ames, 1886-1969.
Tog- O, Heihachir O, Count, 1848-1934.

ADVENTISTS
see also Seventh-Day Adventists
Haskell, Stephen Nelson.

ADVENTURE AND ADVENTURERS
see also Explorers; Frontier and Pioneer Life; Heroes; Shipwrecks; Voyages and Travels

Aguirre, Lope De, D. 1561.
Bomband, Alain.
Browne, John Ross, 1821-1875.
Cagliostro, Alessandro, Conte Di, Assumed Name of Giuseppe Balsamo, 1743-1795.
Chichester, Francis Charles, Sir, 1901- -Juvenile Literature.
Chudleigh, Elizabeth, Countess of Bristol, Calling Herself Duchess of Kingston, 1720-1788.
Judson, Edward Zane Carroll, 1823-1886.
Lynch, Eliza Alicia, 1835?-1886.
Munroe, Kirk, 1850-1930-Biography.
Schoultz, Nils Gustaf Von, 1807-1838.
Scott, John, 1632-1704.
Selkirk, Alexander, 1676-1721.
Stanhope, Hester Lucy, Lady, 1776-1839.
Vidocq, Eugene Francois, 1775-1857.

ADVERTISING
see also Public Relations; Salesmen and Salesmanship

Caples, John.
Flury, Godfrey, 1864-1936.
Mellors, John, 1920-
Ogilvy, David, 1911-
Sackheim, Maxwell, 1890-
Yoxall, Harold Waldo.

ADVERTISING-RETAIL TRADE
see Advertising

ADVERTISING, CONSUMER
see Advertising

ADVERTISING, RETAIL
see Advertising

ADVOCATES
see Lawyers

AERONAUTICS
see also Air Pilots; Balloon Ascensions; Balloons
Moffett, William Adger, 1869-1933.
Montgomery, John Joseph, 1858-1911.
Sikorsky, Igor Ivan, 1889- -Juvenile Literature.

AFFREIGHTMENT
see Freight and Freightage

AFGHANISTAN

Dost Muhammad, Amir of Afghanistan, 1793-1863.

AFRICA-BIOGRAPHY
Ashmun, Jehudi, 1794-1828.
Azikiwe, Noamdi, 1904-
Chaka, Zulu Chief, 1787-1828.
Eberhardt, Isabelle, 1877-1904.
Jingoes, Stimela Jason, 1895-
Kabiro, Ngugi, 1929-
Kabongo, Kikuyu Chief.
Kaunda, Kenneth David, Pres. Zambia, 1921-
Nu, U.
Smuts, Jan Christiaan, 1870-1950.
Wenning, Pieter, 1873-1921.

AFRICA-COMMERCE
Premorel, Raoul De.

AFRICA-KINGS AND RULERS
Dogho, Chief of Warri, D. 1932-Juvenile Literature.
Edmund, Saint, King of East Anglia, 841-870.
Kenyatta, Jomo.
Nyerere, Julius Kambarage, Pres. Tanzania, 1922-
Osei Tutu, King of Ashanti, 1636-1712-Juvenile Literature.

AFRICA-POLITICS AND GOVERNMENT
Rhodes, Cecil John, 1853-1902.

AFRICA, WEST-RELIGION
Kivengere, Festo.

AFRICAN AMERICANS
see Afro-Americans

AFRICAN AUTHORS
see Authors, African

AFRO-AMERICAN ACTORS

Aldridge, Ira Frederick, D. 1867.
Davis, Ossie-Juvenile Literature.
Robeson, Paul, 1898-1976.
Walker, Jimmy-Juvenile Literature.

AFRO-AMERICAN AUTHORS

Angelou, Maya.
Avery, Burniece, 1908-
Haley, Alex.
Hansberry, Lorraine, 1930-1965-Biography-Juvenile Literature.
Hughes, Langston.

AFRO-AMERICAN CLERGY

Allen, Richard, Bp., 1760-1831.
Bacon, Samuel, 1781-1820.
Borders, William Holmes, 1905-

AFRO-AMERICAN ENTERTAINERS

see also Afro-American Actors; Afro-American Musicians
Baker, Josephine, 1906-1975.
Kitt, Eartha.
Waters, Ethel, 1900-1977.

AFRO-AMERICAN LEGISLATORS
Brooke, Edward William, 1919-

AFRO-AMERICAN MUSICIANS
Armstrong, Louis, 1900-1971.
Calloway, Cab, 1908-
Hendrix, Jimi.
Waller, Fats, 1904-1943.

AFRO-AMERICAN NURSES
Davis, Frances Elliott-Juvenile Literature.

AFRO-AMERICAN PHYSICIANS
Drew, Charles Richard, 1904-1950.
Still, James, 1812-1885.

AFRO-AMERICAN TEACHERS
Bethune, Mary Jane McLeod, 1875-1955.
Stephens, Charlotte, 1854-1951.

AFRO-AMERICAN WOMEN

Brown, Clara, 1800-1885.
Derricotte, Juliette Aline, 1897-1931-Juvenile Literature.
Dunnigan, Alice Allison, 1906-
Goodwin, Ruby Berkley.
Lee, Helen Jackson.
Liddell, Viola Goode, 1901-
Walker, Mary Hardway, 1848-1969.
Webb, Sheyann.

AFRO-AMERICANS

see also Slavery in the United States; United States-History-Civil War, 1861-1865-Afro-Americans
also subdivision Afro-Americans under names of wars, e.g. World War, 1939-1945-Afro-Americans; and headings beginning with Afro-American
Barnett, Ida B. Wells, 1862-1931.
Black Panther Party.
Bollinger, James.
Bond, Scott.
Brown, William Wells, 1815-1884.
Browne, Rose Butler.
Bunche, Ralph Johnson, 1904-1971.
Carver, George Washington, 1864?-1943.
Champion, Jackson R.
Cleaver, Eldridge, 1935-
Craft, Ellen.
Cullen, Countee, 1903-1946.
Davis, Noah, 1803 or 4-
Early, Jordan W., B. 1814.
Garvey, Marcus, 1887-1940.
Gordy, Berry, 1888-1978-Juvenile Literature.
Griffin, John Howard, 1920-
Grimke, Archibald Henry, 1849-1930-Juvenile Literature.
Norris, Clarence.
Seale, Bobby, 1936-
Shackelford, Otis M., 1871- -Biography.
Shivers, Clarence L., 1924-
Stokes, Carl.
Trotter, William Monroe, 1872-1934.
Van DerZee, James-Juvenile Literature.
Walker, Charles Thomas, 1858-1921.
Walls, Josiah T., 1842-1905.
Washington, Booker Taliafero, 1859?-1915.
Wright, Richard Robert, 1855-1947.

AGED
see also Retirement
Cornaro, Luigi, 1475-1566.

AGRICULTURAL WORKERS
Lee, Daniel.
MacDowell. Charles Henry, 1867-
Young, Arthur, 1741-1820.

AGRICULTURE
see also Dairying; Farm Life; Farmers; Food Industry and Trade; Reclamation of Land
also headings beginning with the word Agricultural, and names of agricultural products
Peterson, Elmer George.
Wallace, Henry Agard, 1888-1965.
Wallace, Henry Cantwell, 1866-1924.

AGRICULTURE-UNITED STATES-HISTORY
Knapp, Seaman Asahel, 1833-1911.

AGRICULTURISTS
see also Farmers; Horticulturists
Jasny, Naum, 1883-1967.
McKay, Cecil Newton, 1899-1968.

AGRONOMISTS
see Agriculturists

AGRONOMY
see Agriculture

AIR ATTACHES
see Military Attaches

AIR HOSTESSES
see Air Lines-Flight Attendants

AIR LINE HOSTESSES
see Air Lines-Flight Attendants

AIR LINES-FLIGHT ATTENDANTS
Hillinger, Brad.

AIR LINES-HOSTESSES
see Air Lines-Flight Attendants

AIR NAVIGATION
see Aeronautics

AIR PILOTS
see also Astronauts; Women in Aeronautics

Ardery, Philip, 1914-
Bader, Douglas, 1910-
Balchen, Bernt, 1899-
Barclay, George, 1919-1942.
Barry, Robert Smith, 1886-1949.
Biggs, Dewey.
Bishop, William Avery, 1894-1956.
Bong, Richard Ira, 1920-1945.
Brackley, Herbert George, 1894-1948.
Brereton, Lewis Hyde, 1890-1967.
Calhoun, Jack, 1923-1945.
Chennault, Claire Lee, 1890-
Curtiss, Glenn Hammond, 1878-1930.
Czernin, Manfred, 1913-1962.
Earhart, Amelia, 1898-1937.
Eatherly, Claude.
Elelson, Carl Benjamin, 1897-1929-Juvenile Literature.
Eytinge, Bruce Swomley, 1893-
Foss, Joseph Jacob, 1915-
Gann, Ernest Kellogg, 1910- -Biography.
Gunn, Paul Irvin, 1900-1957.
Guynemer, Georges Marie Ludovic, 1894-1917.
Hackett, John Winthrop, Sir, 1910-
Harker, Ronald W.
Hawker, Lanoe George, 1890-1916.
Johnson, Bob, 1893-
Julian, Hubert Fauntleroy, 1897-
Kingsford-Smith, Charles Edward, Sir, 1897-1935.
Lear, William Powell, 1902-
Leigh-Mallory, George Herbert, 1886-1924.
Lewis, Gwilym Hugh.
Lindberg, Charles Augustus, 1902-1974.
Merritt, Charles E.
Mosley, Zack.
Preddy, George Earl, 1919-1944.
Raymond, Robert S.
Richthofen Family.
Richthofen, Manfred Albrecht, Freiherr Von, 1892-1918.
Rickenbacker, Edward Vernon, 1890-1973.
Saint Exupery, Antoine De, 1900-1944.
Santos-Dumont, Alberto, 1873-1932.
Schneider, Hans J., 1935-
Sheldon, Donald Edward, 1921-
Solomon, Samuel Joseph, 1899-
Spencer, Chauncey E., 1906-
Stover, Elisha Terrill, 1920-1944.
Todd, Robert M., 1897-
Turner, Dick, 1911-
Vampatella, Philip Victor, 1940-
Wallis, Barnes Neville, 1887-
Wien, Noel.
Winfield, Roland, 1910-1970.
Wright, Orville, 1871-1918.
Wright, Wilbur, 1867-1912.
Zeppelin, Ferdinand Adolf August Heinrich, Graf Von, 1838-1917.

AIR STEWARDESSES
see Air Lines-Flight Attendants

AIR STEWARDS
see Air Lines-Flight Attendants

AIRPLANES-DESIGN AND CONSTRUCTION
Fokker, Anthony Herman Gerard, 1890-1939.
Piper, William Thomas, 1881-1970.

AIRPLANES-PILOTS
see Air Pilots

ALABAMA
Crumpton, Howard Ulmer, 1878-1960.

ALASKA
Burke, Margaret Knudsen.

ALCHEMY
see also Medicine, Magic, Mystic, and Spagiric
Paracelsus, 1493-1541.

ALCOHOLIC BEVERAGE INDUSTRY
see Wine and Wine Making

ALCOHOLICS
Allen, Chaney.
Duren, Ryne.
Mehl, Duane.
Patten, George Zeboim, 1929-
Terry, Ronald.
W., Bill.

ALIBAMU INDIANS
see Indians of North America-Eastern States

ALIENISTS
see Psychiatrists

ALIMENTATION
see Nutrition

ALLIED HEALTH PERSONNEL
Cutler, G. Ripley.

ALUMNI
see Universities and Colleges-Alumni

Agam, Yaacov, 1928-
Audubon, John James, 1785-1851.
Ault, George, 1891-1948.
Bacigalupa, Andrea, 1923-
Barchus, Eliza Rosanna, 1857-1959.
Beard, Daniel Carter, 1850-1941.
Beeler, Joe.
Bellows, George Wesley, 1882-1925.
Benbridge, Henry, 1743-1812.
Benton, Thomas Hart, 1889-1975.
Benziger, August, 1867-1955.
Bertoia, Harry.
Bingham, George Caleb, 1811-1879.
Bishop, Isabel, 1902-
Bissier, Julius, 1893-1965.
Blegvad, Erik.
Bolotowsky, Ilya, 1907-
Borein, Edward, 1873-1945.
Brasher, Rex, 1869-1960.
Brinley, Putnam.
Brodetsky, Julian, D. 1962.
Burchfield, Charles Ephraim, 1893-1967.
Burr, George Elbert, 1859-1939.
Carvalho, Solomon Nunes, 1815-1897.
Cary, Freeman Grant.
Castleden, George Frederick, 1861-1945.
Catlin, George, 1796-1872.
Cole, Thomas, 1801-1848.
Danby, Ken, 1940-
DeForest, Lockwood, 1850-1932.
DeGrazia, Ted Ettore, 1909-
Deming, Edwin Willard, 1860-1942.
Dunn, Harvey, 1884-1952.
Fisher, Jonathan, 1768-1847.
French, Daniel Chester, 1850-1931.
Fulton, Robert, 1765-1815.
Goddard, George Henry, 1817-1906.
Gotsch, Friedrich Karl, 1900-
Henry, Edward Lamson, 1841-1919.
Inness, George, 1825-1894.
Minor, Robert, 1884-1952.
Morris, Thomas Francis, 1852-1898.
Morse, Samuel Finley Breese, 1791-1872.
Nesbitt, Lowell, 1933-
New York University. Hall of American Artists.
Newman, Barnett, 1905-1970.
Njau, Elimo, 1932-
Ossorio, Alfonso, 1916-
Porter, Russell Williams, 1871-1959.
Quinn, John, 1870-1924.
Rackham, Arthur, 1867-1939.
Remington, Frederic, 1861-1909.
Rimmer, William, 1816-1879.
Strother, David Hunter, 1816-1888.
Tanner, Henry Ossawa, 1859-1937.
Tiffany, Louis Comfort, 1848-1933.
Warhol, Andy, 1928-
Westermann, Horace Clifford, 1922-

ARTISTS, WOMEN
see Women Artists

ARTS, THE–CRITICISM
see Art Criticism

ARTS, DECORATIVE
see Art Industries and Trade
also subjects referred to under these headings

ARTS, GRAPHIC
see Graphic Arts

ASHANTI–HISTORY
Prempeh, King of Ashanti.

ASIA, SOUTH–HISTORY
Khan, Zarak.

ASIAN STATESMEN
see Statesmen–Asia

ASSASSINATION
see also Terrorism
Czolgosz, Leon Franz, 1873?-1901.
Oswald, Lee Harvey.
Oswald, Marina, 1941-
Sirhan, Sirhan Bishara, 1944-

ASSINIBOIN INDIANS
see Indians of North America–The West

ASSOCIATION FOOTBALL
see Soccer

ASSOCIATIONS, INSTITUTIONS, ETC.
Church of England-Biography.

ASTROLOGY
see also Occult Sciences
Forman, Simon, 1552-1616.
Omarr, Sydney.

ASTRONAUTICS–RUSSIA
Gagarin, IUrii Alekseevich, 1934-1968-Juvenile Literature.

ASTRONAUTS
Armstrong, Neil, 1930- -Juvenile Literature.
Glenn, John Herschel, 1921-
Grissom, Virgil I.
Nikolaeva, Valentina Vladimirovna Tereshkova, 1937--Juvenile Literature.
Shepard, Alan Bartlett, 1923-

ASTRONOMERS
see also Astronomy As a Profession
Bailly, Jean Sylvain, 1736-1793.
Banneker, Benjamin, 1731-1806.
Brahe, Tyge, 1546-1601.
Copher, Glover Hancock, 1893 --
Davidson, George, 1825-1911.
Eddington, Arthur Stanley, 1882-1944.
Eratosthenes.
Folger, Walter, 1765-1849.
Galilei, Galileo, 1564-1642.
Gregory, Sir Richard Arman, Bart., 1864-1952.
Herschel, Caroline Lucretia, 1750-1848-Juvenile Literature.
Herschel, John Frederick William, Sir, Bart., 1792-1871.
Herschel, William, Sir 1738-1822.
Kepler, Johann, 1571-1630.
Langley, Samuel Pierpont, 1834-1906.
Lilly, William, 1602-1618.
Mitchell, Maria, 1818-1889-Juvenile Literature.
Quetelet, Lambert Adolphe Jacques, 1796-1874.
Rittenhouse, David, 1732-1796.
Tombaugh, Clyde William, 1907-

ASTRONOMY–VOCATIONAL GUIDANCE
see Astronomy As a Profession

ASTRONOMY AS A PROFESSION
Hale, George Ellery, 1868-1938.
Halley, Edmond, 1656-1742.

ATHEISM
see also Rationalism
Bradlaugh, Charles, 1833-1891.

ATHLETES
Campbell, Robin, 1959- -Juvenile Literature.
Grange, Harold Edward, 1903- -Juvenile Literature.
Grey, Beryl, 1927-
Hemery, David.
Jenner, Bruce, 1949-
Justice, Charlie, 1924-
Kiick, Jim.
Mathias, Robert Bruce, 1930-
Owens, Jesse, 1913-
Prefontaine, Steve.
Shantz, Bobby, 1925-
Skuthorpe, Lance, 1870-1958.
Thorpe, Jim, 1888-1953.

ATHLETES, WOMEN
Berig, Karen-Juvenile Literature.
Hamill, Dorothy-Juvenile Literature.
Rudolph, Wilma, 1940- -Juvenile Literature.
Zaharias, Mildred Babe (Didrikson) 1913-1956.

ATTACHES
see Military Attaches

ATTORNEYS
see Lawyers

ATTORNEYS-GENERAL
Lee, Howard Burton, 1879-

AUSTRALIA–BIOGRAPHY
Angas, George Fife, 1789-1879.
Archibald, Jules Francois, 1856-1919.
Australia. Constitutional Convention, 1973.
Bates, Daisy, 1861-1951.
Batman, John, 1800-1839.
Bennett, Henry Gordon, 1887-1962.
Bjelke-Petersen, Johannes, 1911-
Bosisto, Joseph, 1827-1898.
Bridges, William Throsby, Sir, 1861-1915.
Brookes, Herbert, 1867-1963.
Brookes, Mabel Emmerton, Dame, 1894-
Bunny, Rupert Charles Wulsten, 1864-1947.
Campbell, Robert, 1769-1846.
Cropley, Ruve.
Dalrymple, George Elphinstone, 1826-1876.
Deakin, Alfred, 1856-1919.
Evatt, Herbert Vere, 1894-1965.
Grimwade, Russell, Sir, 1879-1955.
Holt, Harold Edward, 1908-1967.
Isaacs, Isaac Alfred, Sir, 1855-1948.
Kelly, Edward, 1854-1880.
Kelly, James, 1791-1859.
King, Anna Josepha (Coombe)
Murray, John Hubert Plunkett, Sir, 1861-1940.
Nicholson, Charles, Sir, 1808-1903.
Ogilvie Family.
Scullin, J. H. 1876-1953.
Streeton, Arthur, Sir, 1867-1943.
Thomson, Edward Deas, 1800-1879.
Wentworth, William Charles, 1793-1872-Juvenile Literature.
Wood, George Arnold, 1865-1928.
Worrell, Eric-Juvenile Literature.

AUSTRALIAN AUTHORS
see Authors, Australian

AUSTRIA
see also names of cities, regions, etc. in Austria, e.g. Vienna
Dollfuss, Engelbert, 1892-1934.
Elisabeth, Consort of Francis Joseph I, Emperor of Austria, 1837-1898.
Eugene, Prince of Savoie-Carignan, 1663-1736.
Figl, Leopold, 1902-1965.
Franz Joseph I, Emperor of Austria, 1830-1916.
Schwarzenberg, Felix, Furst Zu, 1800-1852.

AUSTRIAN ART
see Art, Austrian

AUTHOR AND PUBLISHER
see Authors and Publishers

AUTHORS
see also Litterateurs; Women Authors
also particular classes of writers, e.g. Dramatists,

Boston Authors Club-Biography.
Chapin, Henry-Biography.
Clark, Eleanor, 1913- -Biography.
Clemens, Jane (Lampton) 1803-1890.
Compton-Burnett, Ivy, Dame, 1892-1969.
Conroy, Frank, 1936- -Biography.
Cooke, Harry, 1894-
Cowen, Evelyn-Biography-Youth.
Crapsey, Adelaide, 1878-1914.
Craven, Margaret-Biography.
Crews, Harry, 1935- -Biography-Youth.
Curtiss, Mina Stein Kirstein, 1896- -Biography.
Gruffydd, William John, 1881-1954-Biography.
Jones, David James Gwenallt.
Kelkar, Narsinha Chintaman, 1872-1947-Biography.
Krmpotic, Vesna, 1932- -Biography.
Lattimore, Owen, 1900-
MacVicar, Angus, 1908- -Biography.
Maeterlinck, Maurice, 1862-1949.
Momaday, N. Scott,1934-Biography-Youth.
Nagal, Kafu, 1879-1959.
Ocampo, Victoria, 1891- -Biography.
Peretz, Isaac Loeb, 1851-1915.
Senapati, Fakir Mohan, 1843-1918-Biography.
Stevenson, Fanny (Van De Grift) 1840-1914.
Vining, Elizabeth Gray, 1902- -Diaries.

AUTHORS–WIVES
Dickens, Catherine Thomson Hogarth, 1815-1879.
Fitzgerald, Zelda Sayre-Biography.

AUTHORS, AFRICAN
Bleek, Wilhelm Heinrich Immanuel, 1827-1875.
Blyden, Edward Wilmot, 1832-1912.
Bosman, Herman Charles, 1905-1951-Biography.
Burgess, Thornton Waldo, 1874-1965-Homes and Haunts-Sandwich, Mass.
Millin, Philip, 1888-1952.
Stubbs, Thomas, 1808-1877.

AUTHORS, AFRO-AMERICAN
see Afro-American Authors

AUTHORS, AMERICAN
Abbott, Lyman, 1835-1922.
Ade, George, 1866-1944.
Agee, James, 1909-1955.
Aldrich, Thomas, Bailey, 1836-1907.
Alexander, Edward Porter, 1835-1910.
Alger, Horatio, 1832-1899.
Allen, Devere, 1891-1955.
Anderson, Rasmus Bjorn, 1846-1936.
Anderson, Sherwood, 1876-1941.
Andrews, Roy Chapman, 1884-1960.
Arnow, Harriette Louisa Simpson, 1908- -Homes and Haunts-Burnside, Ky.
Asawa, Ruth.
Asimov, Isaac, 1920- -Biography.
Atkinson, Edward, 1827-1905.
Auchincloss, Louis-Biography.
Bacon, Delia Salter, 1811-1859.
Balch, Frederic Homer, 1861-1891.
Barry, Philip, 1896-1949.
Bates, Katherine Lee, 1859-1929.
Baum. Lyman Frank, 1856-1919.
Baxter, George, 1804-1867.
Beebe, Charles William, 1877-1962.
Behrman, Samuel Nathan, 1893-1973.
Bell, William Abraham-Manuscripts.
Bellamy, Edward, 1850-1898.
Bellow, Saul.
Benet, Laura-Biography-Youth-Juvenile Literature.
Benet, Stephen Vincent, 1898-1943-Biography.
Bernstein, Aline Frankau, 1881-1955-Biography.
Bernstein, Burton.
Bessie, Alvah Cecil, 1904- -Journeys-Spain.
Bethell, Pinckney C.-Archives.
Bierce, Ambrose, 1842-1914?
Bigelow, John, 1817-1911.
Binney, Horace, 1780-1875.
Blythe, David Gilmour.
Boker, George Henry, 1823-1890.
Bourne, Randolph Silliman, 1886-1918.
Bowditch, Henry Ingersoll, 1808-1892.
Bowles, Paul Frederic, 1911-
Brackenridge, Hugh Henry, 1748-1816.
Brandes, Georg Morris Cohen, 1842-1927.
Brenan, Gerald.
Bromfield, Louis, 1896-1956.
Brooks, Van Wyck, 1886-1963.
Broun, Heywood Campbell, 1888-1939.
Brown, Charles Brockden, 1771-1810.
Brown, John Mason, 1900-1969.
Buck, Pearl (Sydenstricker) 1892-1973.
Burns, John Horne, 1916-1953.
Burritt, Elihu, 1810-1879.
Burroughs, Edgar Rice, 1875-1950.
Burton, Clarence Monroe, 1853-1932.
Byles, Mather, 1707-1788.
Cabell, James Branch, 1879-1958-Correspondence.
Cable, George Washington, 1844-1925.
Caldwell, Erskine, 1903-
Callaghan, Morley, 1903-
Canby, Henry Seidel, 1878-1961.
Canzoneri, Robert-Biography.
Carson, Rachel Louise.
Caruthers, William Alexander, 1800 (Ca.)-1846.
Caspary, Vera, 1904- -Biography.
Castaneda, Carlos.
Chandler, Raymond, 1888-1959.
Channing, William Ellery, 1818-1901.
Chapman, John Jay, 1862-1933.
Chesnutt, Charles Waddell, 1858-1932.
Clark, Charles Badger, 1883-1957.
Clemens, Samuel Langhorne.
Coatsworth, Elizabeth Jane, 1893- -Biography.
Cooper, James Fenimore, 1789-1851.
Cowley, Malcolm, 1898- -Biography-Youth.
Crane, Stephen, 1871-1900.
Curtis, George William, 1824-1892.
Dana, Richard Henry, 1815-1882.
Daniels, Jonathan, 1902-
Davis, Elmer Holmes, 1890-1958.
Davis, Richard Harding, 1864-1916.
De Forest, John William, 1826-1906.
De Voto, Bernard Augustine, 1897-1955.
Delany, Samuel R.-Addresses, Essays, Lectures.
Derleth, August William, 1909-1971-Friends and Associates.
Dodge, Mary Abigail, 1833-1896.
Dolben, Digby Mackworth, 1848-1867-Biography.
Dos Passos, John, 1896-1970.
Dreiser, Theodore, 1871-1945.
Eaton, Evelyn Sybil Mary, 1902- -Religion and Ethics.
Empson, William, 1906-
Faulkner, William, 1897-1962.
Ferber, Edna, 1887-1968-Biography.
Field, James Thomas, 1816-1881.
Fisher, Dorothea Frances (Canfield) 1879-1958.
Fitzgerald, Francis Scott Key, 1896-1840.
Foote, Mary (Hallock) 1847-1938.
Fowler, Gene, 1890-1960.
Fox, John, 1862-1919.
Frank, Waldo David, 1889-1967.
Freeman, Mary Eleanor (Wilkins) 1852-1930.
Fremont, Jessie (Benton) 1824-1902 -- Juvenile Literature.
French, Alice, 1850-1934.
Gag, Wanda, 1893-1946-Juvenile Literature.
Gardner, Erle Stanley, 1889-1970-Biography.
Garland, Hamlin, 1860-1940.
Gill, Brendan, 1914- -Biography.
Glasgow, Ellen Anderson Gholson, 1873-1945.
Green, Julien, 1900- -Biography.
Grey, Zane, 1872-1939.
Grove, Frederick Philip, 1879-1948-Correspondence.
Guess, George, or Sequoyah, Cherokee Indian, 1770?-1843.
Guest, Edgar Albert, 1881-
Guiney, Louise Imogen, 1861-1920.
Haggard, Henry Rider, Sir 1856-1925.
Hale, Edward Everett, 1822-1909.
Hale, Sarah Josepha Buell, 1788-1879.
Hall, James, 1793-1868.
Halliburton, Richard, 1900-1939.
Hammett, Dashiell, 1894-1961.
Harris, Corra May (White), 1869-1935.
Harris. Frank, 1855-1931.
Harris, Joel Chandler, 1848-1908.
Harrison, Pat, 1881-1941.
Hawthorn, Nathaniel, 1804-1864.
Hawthorne, Julian, 1846-1934.
Hearn, Lafacadio, 1850-1904-
Helper, Hinton Rowan, 1829-1909.
Hemingway, Ernest, 1898-1961.
Hemphill, Paul, 1936-
Heyward, Du Bose, 1885-1940.
Hodgins, Eric, 1899-
Hoffman, Charles Fenno, 1806-1884.
Holmes, Oliver Wendell, 1809-1894.
Horgan, Paul, 1903-
Hovey, Richard, 1864-1900.
Howard, Dorothy, 1902-
Howard, Robert Ervin, 1906-1936-Bibliography.
Howe, Julia (Ward) 1819-1910.
Howe. Mark Antony De Wolfe, 1864-1960.
Howells, William Dean, 1837-1920.
Hubbard, Elbert, 1856-1915.
Hughes, Emmy, 1863-1934.
Humphrey, William.
Huneker, James Gibbons, 1857-1921-Addresses, Essays, Lectures.
Huntington, Archer Miltob, 1870-1955.
Irving, Washington, 1783-1859.
Jackson, Helen Maria (Fiske) Hunt, 1831-1885-Biography.
James, Henry, 1843-1916.
Janson, Kristofer Nagel, 1841-1917-Biography.
Jarrell, Randall, 1914-1965.
Jewett, Sarah Orne.
Johnson, James Weldon, 1871-1938.
Johnson, Nunnally-Biography.
Johnston, Richard Malcolm, 1822-1898.
Jones, Howard Mumford, 1892- -Biography.
Jones, James, 1921-
Judson, Eii, 1770-1821.
Kampen, Irene-Biography.
Kazin, Alfred, 1915-
Keller, Helen Adams, 1880-1968.
Kenaga, R. F., 1898-
Kennedy, John Pendleton, 1795-1870.
Kerouac, John, 1922-1969.
Kostelanetz, Richard.
La Farge, Oliver, 1901-1963.
La France, Marston.
Lane, Rose (Wilder) 1887-1968.
Larcom, Lucy, 1824-1893.
Lardner, Ring Wilmer, 1885-1933.
Lester, Julius-Biography.
Lindbergh, Anne Morrow, 1906-
London, Jack, 1876-1916.
Loos, Anita, 1894- -Biography.
Lovecraft, Howard Phillips, 1890-1937.
Lowry, Malcolm, 1909-1957.

Luhan, Mabel Ganson Dodge, 1879-1962.
Lummis, Charles Fletcher, 1859-1928.
Lyons, Barbara-Biography-Youth.
Lytle, Andrew Nelson, 1902- -Biography.
McCarthy, Mary Therese, 1912- -Bibliography.
McCullers, Carson (Smith) 1917-1967.
Mack, Maynard, 1909-
Mailer, Norman-Biography.
Manfred, Frederick Feikema, 1912- -Interviews.
Mangione, Jerre Gerlando, 1909- -Biography.
Marquand, John Phillips, 1893-1960.
Martin, Frederick Townsend, 1849-1914.
Melville, Herman, 1819-1891.
Mendoza, George-Biography.
Merton, Thomas, 1915-1968.
Meyer, Edith Patterson.
Millay, Edna St. Vincent, 1892-1950.
Miller, Bertha E. (Mahony)
Miller, Henry, 1891-
Millet, Kate.
Mitchell, Margaret, 1900-1949.
Moore, Clement Clarke, 1779-1863.
Moore, John Trotwood, 1858-1929.
More, Paul Elmer, 1864-1937.
Morley, Christopher Darlington, 1890-1957.
Morris, Edita, 1902- -Biography-Youth.
Morris, Wright, 1910-
Motley, Willard, 1909-1965-Diaries.
Mumford, Lewis, 1895-
Murfree, Mary Noailles, 1850-1922.
Murry, Colin, 1926- -Biography.
Nathan, George Jean, 1882-1958-Biography-Addresses, Essays, Lectures.
Neal, John, 1793-1876.
Nemerov, Howard.
Norris, Frank, 1870-1902.
Norton, Charles Eliot, 1827-1908.
O'Connor, Flannery
O'Connor, William Douglas, 1832-1889.
O'Hara, John, 1905-1970.
Orwell, George, 1903-1950.
Parton, James, 1822-1891.
Percy, Walker, 1916-
Perkins, Lucy Fitch, 1865-1937.
Perry, George Sessions, 1910-1956.
Perry, Thomas Sergeant, 1845-1928.
Plimpton, George.
Poe, Edgar Allan, 1800-1849.
Pohl, Frederik.
Porter, Gene Stratton, 1863-1924.
Porter, William Sydney, 1862-1910.
Post, Emily Price, 1873-1960.
Post, Melville Davisson, 1871-1930.
Price, George McCready, 1870-
Pyle, Howard, 1853-1911.
Ransom, John Crowe, 1888-1974-Biography.
Rasmussen, Anne-Marie.
Redfield, Malissa-Homes and Haunts-Vermont.
Rennert, Maggie-Homes and Haunts-Israel-Beersheba.
Richter, Conrad, 1890-
Rider-Kelsey, Corinne, 1877-1947.
Rinehart, Mary Roberts, 1876-1958.
Roberts, Elizabeth Madox, 1886-1941.
Rodgers, Dorothy F., 1909-
Roethke, Theodore, 1908-1963.
Rogers, Earl, 1870-1922.
Runyon, Damon, 1880-1946.
Salinger, Jerome David, 1919-
Saltus, Edgar Evertson, 1855-1921.
Sampter, Jessie Ethel, 1883-1938.
Sandburg, Carl, 1878-
Saroyan, William, 1908- -Biography.
Sarton, May, 1912- -Diaries.
Saunders, Stephen, 1820-1859.
Schlesinger, Marian Cannon-Biography.
Schmitt, Gladys, 1909-1972-Biography-Addresses, Essays, Lectures.
Serpico, Frank.
Simms, William Gilmore, 1806-1870.
Sinclair, Upton Beall, 1878-1968.
Singer, Isaac.
Smith, Arthur James Marshall, 1902-
Smith, Clark Ashton, 1893-1963.
Smith, Russell, 1812-1898.
Stallings, Laurence, 1894-1968.
Stanford, Jane Lathrop, 1828-1905.
Stanley, William, 1858-1916.
Starrett, Vincent, 1886-
Stein, Benjamin, 1944- -Diaries.
Steinbeck, John, 1902-1968.
Stephens, Charles Asbury, 1844-1931.
Stewart, Donald Ogden, 1894- -Biography.
Stockton, Frank Richard, 1834-1902.
Stout, Rex, 1886-1975-Biography.
Strom, Erling, 1897-
Stuart, Jesse, 1907-
Suckow, Ruth, 1892-1960.
Swarthout, Glendon Fred-Biography-Youth.
Tarbell, Ida Minerva, 1857-1944-Biography.
Tarkington, Booth, 1869-1946.
Taylor, Bayard, 1825-1878.
Taylor, Peter Hillsman, 1917-
Terhune, Albert Payson, 1872-1942.
Thane, Elswyth, 1900- -Biography.
Thoreau, Henry David, 1817-1862.
Thurber, James, 1894-1961.
Toklas, Alice B.
Townsend, John Wilson, 1885-1968.
Trevino, Elizabeth Borton, 1904- -Biography.
Trumbo, Dalton, 1905- -Biography.
Updike, John.
Van Doren, Carl Clinton, 1885-1950-Biography.
Van Dyke, Henry, 1852-1933-Journeys-Palestine.
Van Vechten, Carl, 1880-1964.
Van Vogt, Alfred Elton, 1912- -Biography.
Vbenet, William Rose, 1886-1950.
Vesey, Denmark, 1769 (Ca.)-1822-Juvenile Literature.
Wallace, Edgar, 1875-1932.
Wallace, Irving, 1916- -Biography.
Ward, Andrew, 1946-
Ward, Lester Frank, 1841-1913.
Warner, Charles Dudley, 1829-1900.
Webster, Noah, 1758-1843.
Weems, Mason Locke, 1759-1825.
Weingarten, Violet-Diaries.
Weingartner, Felix, 1863-1942.
Welch, Lew-Friends and Associates.
Welty, Eudora, 1909-
Wescott, Glenway, 1901-
West, Nathanael, 1902-1940.
Wharton, Edith Newbold (Jones) 1862-1937.
White, Elwyn Brooks, 1899- -Correspondence.
White, Walter Francis, 1893-1955.
White, William Allen, 1868-1944.
Whiteley, Opal Stanley.
Wiggin, Kate Douglas Smith, 1856-1923.
Wilbur, Richard, 1921-
Wilder, Laura (Ingalls), 1867-1957.
Willeford, Charles Ray, 1919- -Biography.
Williams, William Carlos, 1883-1963.
Willis, Nathaniel Parker, 1806-1867.
Wilson, Edmund, 1895-1972-Biography.
Wilson, Sloan, 1920- -Biography.
Winthrop, Theodore, 1828-1861.
Wister, Owen, 1860-1938.
Wolfe, Thomas, 1900-1938.
Woolson, Constance Fenimore, 1840-1894.
Wright, Richard, 1908-1960-Biography.
Wylie, Elinor Hoyt, 1885-1928-Biography.
Youmans, Edward Livingston, 1821-1887.
Zweig, Paul-Biography.

AUTHORS, AUSTRALIAN

Bedford, Randolph, 1868-1941-Biography.
Clarke, Marcus Andrew Hislop, 1846-1881.
Davis, Arthur Hoey, 1899-1935-Biography.
Davison, Frank Dalby, 1893-1970-Biography.
Egestorff, Georg, 1802-1868.
Murdoch, Walter, Sir, 1874-1970.
Praed, Rosa Caroline (Murray-Prior) 1851-1935-Juvenile Literature.
Richardson, Henry Handel, Pseud.
Robinson, Roland E.-Biography.

AUTHORS, AUSTRIAN

Canetti, Elias, 1905-
Kafka, Franz, 1883-1924.
Zweig, Stefan, 1881-1942.

AUTHORS, CANADIAN

Aitken, John, 1936-
Blaise, Clark.
Burt, Alfred LeRoy, 1888-1971
De La Roche, Mazo, 1885-1961.
Hailey Arthur-Biography-Marriage.
Joudry, Patricia, 1921- -Biography.
Laurence, Margaret-Journeys.
MacPhail, Margaret, 1887- -Biography.
Marty, Sid, 1944--Homes and Haunts-Canada-Rocky Mountains.
Montgomery, Lucy Maud, 1874-1942-Biography.
Raddall, Thomas Head, 1903- Biography.
Richler, Mordecai, 1931- -Biography-Youth.
Service, Robert William, 1874-1958-Biography.

AUTHORS, CHINESE

Tung, Yueh, 1620-1686.
Yang, Wan-Li, 1127-1206.
Yuan, Chen, 779-831.

AUTHORS, ENGLISH

Agate, James Evershed, 1877-1947-Diaries.
Ainsworth, William Harrison, 1805-1882-Biography.
Aldington, Richard, 1892-1962.
Allies, Thomas William, 1813-1903.
Andrews, Charles Freer, 1871-1940.
Angell, Norman, Sir, 1874-1967.
Arblay, Frances (Burney) D', Mme., 1752-1840.
Arlen, Michael, 1895-1956.
Astell, Mary, 1666-1731.
Backhouse, Edmund Trelawny, Sir, Bart., 1873-1944.
Bacon, Francis, Viscount of Albans, 1561-1626.
Baillie, Joanna, 1762-1851.
Baker, Augustine, 1575-1641.
Barbauld, Anna Letitia (Aikin) 1743-1825.
Barber, John, D. 1741.
Barber, Margaret Fairless, 1869-1901.
Barnes, Barnabe, 1569?-1609.
Barrie, James Matthew, Bart., Sir 1860-1937.
Bartlett, William Henry, 1809-1854.
Beckford, William, 1750-1844.
Beda Venerabilis, 673-735.
Beerbohm, Max, Sir, 1872-1956.
Beeton, Isabella Mary Mayson, 1836-1865.
Behn, Aphra (Amis) 1640-1689.
Belloc, Hilaire, 1870-1953.
Bennett, Arnold, 1867-1931.
Bentley, Richard, 1662-1742.
Betjeman, John, Sir, 1906- in Fiction, Drama, Poetry, Etc.
Bishop, Isabella Lucy (Bird) 1831-1904.
Blackmore, Richard Doddridge, 1825-1900-Biography.
Blake, George, 1922-
Bloom, Ursula.
Borrow, George Henry, 1803-1881.
Boston, Lucy Maria, 1892- -Biography-Youth.
Boswell, James 1740-1795.
Bowen, Elizabeth, 1899-1973.
Brazil, Angela-Biography.
Bronte, Anne, 1820-1849.
Bronte, Charlotte, 1816-1855.
Bronte, Emily Jane, 1818-1848.
Bronte Family.
Bronte, Patrick Branwell, 1817-1848.
Bunyan, John, 1628-1688.
Burnett, Frances Hodgson, 1849-1924-Biography.
Burney, Charles, 1726-1814.
Burns, Robert, 1759-1796.
Burton, Richard Francis Sir 1821-1890.
Butler, Samuel, 1835-1902.
Byrd, William, 1674-1744.
Byrne, John Francis, 1880-
Carlyle, Jane Baillie (Welsh) 1801-1866.
Carlyle, Thomas, 1795-1881.
Carter, Elizabeth, 1717-1806.
Cartland, Barbara, 1902
Christie, Agatha Miller, Dame, 1891-1976.
Chubb, Thomas, 1679-1747.
Clarke, Arthur Charles, 1917-
Cleland, John, 1709-1789.
Coleridge, Hartley, 1796-1849.
Coleridge, Samuel Taylor, 1722-1834.
Coleridge, Sara Coleridge, 1802-1852.
Collins, Wilkie, 1824-1889.
Conrad, Joseph, 1837-1924.
Cowper, William, 1731-1800.
Crashaw, Richard, 1613?-1649.
Crowley, Aleister.
Crowne, John --
Darby, John Fletcher, 1803-1882.
Day, Thomas, 1748-1789.
De La Mare, Walter John, 1873-1956.
De Quincey, Thomas, 1785-1859.
Defoe, Daniel, 1661-1731.
Dennis, John, 1657-1734.
Dickens, Charles, 1812-1870.
Dodgson, Charles Lutwidge, 1832-1808.
Douglas, Lord Alfred Bruce, 1870-1945.
Douglas, Norman, 1868-1952.
Dowson, Ernest Christopher, 1867-1900.
Doyle, Arthur Conan, Sir 1859-1930.
Du Maurier, Daphne, Dame, 1907- -Biography-Youth.
Durrell, Lawrence.
Edgeworth, Maria, 1767-1849.
Eliot, George, Pseud., I.E. Marian Evans, Afterwards Cross, 1819-1880.
Farjeon, Eleanor, 1881-1965.
Field, Michael, Pseud.-Addresses, Essays, Lectures.
Fielding, Henry, 1707-1754.
Firbank, Arthur Annesley Ronald, 1886-1926.
Fitz Gerald, Edward, 1809-1883-Biography.
Fleming, Ian, 1908-1964.
Florio, John, 1553? 1625
Ford, Ford Madox, 1873-1939.
Forster, Edward Morgan, 1879-
Freeman, Richard Austin, 1862-1943.
Fuller, John Frederick Charles, 1878-1966.
Galsworthy, John, 1867-1933.
Gaskell, Elizabeth Cleghorn (Stevenson) 1810-1865.
Gay, John, 1685-1732.
Gilchrist, Anne (Burrows) 1828-1885.
Gillies, Robert Pearse, 1788-1858.
Gilpin, William, 1724-1804.
Gissing, George Robert, 1857-1903.
Glyn, Elinor (Sutherland) 1864-1948.
Godwin, Mary Wollstonecraft, 1759-1797.
Goldsmith, Oliver, 1728-1774.
Goudge, Elizabeth, 1900- -Biography.
Grahame, Kenneth, 1859-1932.
Greene, Graham, 1904-
Griffiths, Ann Thomas, 1776-1805.
Hannay, James, 1827-1873.
Hardy, Thomas, 1840-1928.
Hare, Augustus John Cuthbert, 1834-1903.
Hawkins, Anthony Hope, Sir, 1863-1933.
Hawkins, John, Sir, 1719-1789.
Hazlitt, William, 1778-1830.
Henrey, Robert, Mrs., 1906- Biography.
Herbert, Alan Patrick, Sir, 1890-1971-Biography.
Heywood, John 1497?-1580?
Hobbes, Thomas, 1588-1679.
Hodgson, Francis, 1781-1852.
Hone, William, 1780-1842.
Hook, Theodore Edward, 1788-1841.
Hooker, Richard, 1553 or 4-1600.
Hoskins, John, 1566-1638.
Howard, Maureen, 1930- -Biography.
Howitt, Mary (Botham) 1799-1888.
Howitt, William, 1792-1879.
Hunt, Violet, 1866-1942-Biography.
Huxley, Aldous Leonard, 1894-1963.
Inchbald, Elizabeth (Simpson) Mrs., 1753-1821.
Isherwood, Christopher, 1904-
Jefferies, Richard, 1848-1887.
Jerdan, William, 1782-1869-Biography.
Jerome, Jerome Klapka, 1859-1927.
Jerrold, Douglas William, 1803-1857.
Johnson, Joseph, 1738-1809.
Johnson, Pamela Hansford, 1912- -Biography.
Jones, Thomas H.
Jones, Thomas Henry, 1921-1965.
Jonson, Ben, 1572-1637.
Kempe, Margery Burnham, B. Ca. 1373.
Kennedy, Richard, 1910-
Kiely, Benedict.
Kingsley, Charles, 1819-1875.
Kingsley, Henry, 1830-1876.
Kipling, Rudyard, 1865-1936.
Koestler, Arthur, 1905-
Lamb, Caroline Ponsonby, Lady, 1785-1828.
Lamb, Charles, 1775-1834.
Landon, Letitia Elizabeth, 1802-1838.
Landor, Robert Eyres, 1781-1869.
Landor, Walter Savage, 1775-1864.
Law, William, 1686-1761.
Lawrence, David Herbert, 1885-1830.
Lehmann, John, 1907- -Biography.
Lewis, Clive Staples, 1898-1963.
Lockhart, John Gibson, 1794-1854.
Lyly John, 1554?-1606.
Lytton, Edward George Earle Lytton Bulwer-Lytton, 1st Baron, 1803-1873.
Macaulay, Thomas Babington Macaulay, Baron, 1800-1859.
McFee, William, 1881- -Addresses, Essays, Lectures.
Machen, Arthur, 1863-1947.
Maddocks, Margaret Kathleen Avern-Biography-Youth.
Maitland, Frederic William, 1850-1906.
Malory, Thomas, Sir, 15th Century.
Mannin, Ethel Edith, 1900- -Biography.
Mansfield, Katherine, 1888-1923.
Marryat, Frederick, 1792-1848.
Marsh, Edward Howard, Sir, 1872-1953.
Martineau, Harriet, 1802-1876.
Maugham, William Somerset, 1874-1965.
Maxwell, Mary Elizabeth Braddon, 1837-1915.
Medwin, Thomas, 1788-1869.
Meredith, George, 1828-1909.
Milne, Alan Alexander, 1882-1956.
Mitchell, Henry Laurens, 1831-1903.
Mitford, Jessica, Hon., 1917-
Mitford, Mary Russell, 1787-1855-Correspondence.
Mitford, Nancy, 1904-1973-Biography.
Monro, Harold, 1879-1932.
Montagu, Elizabeth (Robinson) 1720-1800.
Moore, Thomas Sturge, 1870-1944.
More, Hannah, 1745-1833.
Mortimer, Penelope, 1918- -Biography-Youth.
Muir, Edwin, 1887-1959.
Murry, John Middleton, 1889-1957.
Narayan, R. K., 1906- -Biography.
Nelson, Michael, 1921- -Biography.
Norton, Caroline Sheridan, 1808-1877-Correspondence.
Norway, Nevil Shute, 1899-1960.
Opie, Amelia Alderson, 1769-1853-Biography.
Orage, Alfred Richard, 1873-1934.
Paget, Violet, 1856-1935.
Pater, Walter Horatio, 1839-1894
Peacock, Thomas Love 1785-1866.
Peake, Mervyn Laurence, 1911-1968-Biography.
Pepys, Samuel, 1633-1703.
Piozzi, Hester Lynch (Salusbury) Thrale, 1741-1821.
Polidori, John William, 1795-1821-Diaries.
Pope, Alexander, 1688-1744.
Powell, Anthony, 1905--Biography.
Priestley, John Boynton, 1894-
Procter, Bryan Waller, 1787-1874-Friends and Associates.
Quennell, Peter, 1905- -Biography.
Radcliffe, Ann (Ward) 1764-1823.
Raine, Kathleen Jessie, 1908- -Biography.
Ransome, Arthur, 1884-1967.
Reid, Forrest, 1875-1947-Biography.
Rich, Barnabe, 1540?-1617.
Rich, Bernard, 1917-
Richardson, Dorothy Miller, 1873-1957.
Richardson, Samuel, 1689-1761.
Rolfe, Frederick William, 1860-1913.
Sayers, Dorothy Leigh, 1893-1957.
Scott, Sir Walter, Bart., 1771-1832.
Shears, Sarah.
Shelley, Harriet Westbrook, D. 1816.
Shelley, Mary Wollstonecraft (Godwin), Mrs., 1797-1851-Biography.
Sheridan, Clare Consuelo Frewen, 1885-1970-
Sherwood, Mary Martha Butt, 1775-1851.
Simcox, Edith Jemima-Relationship with Women-George Eliot.
Sitwell, Constance Talbot, 1887- -Diaries.
Sitwell, George Reresby, Sir Bart., 1800-1943.
Smollett, Tobias George, 1721-1771.
Snow, Sir Charles Percy, 1905-.
Stephen, Leslie, Sir, 1832-1904.
Sterling, John, 1806-1844.
Sterne, Laurence, 1713-1768.
Stevenson, Robert Louis, 1850-1894.
Stoker, Bram, 1847-1912.
Strachey, Giles Lytton, 1880-1932.
Surtees, Robert Smith, 1805-1864.
Swift, Jonathan, 1667-1743.

Swinnerton, Frank Arthur, 1884-
Symons, Arthur, 1865-1945.
Taylor, Henry, Sir, 1800-1886-Correspondence.
Thackeray, William Makepeace, 1811-1863.
Thirkell, Angela (Mackai) 1890-1961.
Thomas, Edward, 1878-1917.
Tibble, Anne (Northgrave)
Tolkien, John Ronald Reuel, 1892-1973.
Tomkins, Thomas, 1575 (Ca.)-1656.
Trevelyan, Paulina Jermyn (Jermyn), Lady, 1816-1866-Biography.
Trillin, Calvin.
Trollope, Anthony, 1815-1882.
Trollope, Frances Milton, 1780-1863.
Urquhart, Thomas, Sir, 1611-1660.
Walpole, Sir Hugh, 1884-1941.
Walton, Izaak, 1593-1683.
Ward, Arthur Sarsfield, 1883-1959.
Ward, Mary Augusta Arnold, 1851-1920-Biography.
Watts-Dunton, Theodore, 1832-1914.
Waugh, Evelyn, 1903-1966.
Webb, Mary Gladys Meredith, 1881-1927.
Wells, Herbert George, 1866-1946.
West, Rebecca, Pseud.
White, Terence Hanbury, 1906-1964.
Wilson, Augusta Jane (Evans) 1835-1909.
Wodehouse, Pelham Grenville, 1881-
Wollstonecraft, Mary, 1750-1797.
Woodward, John, 1665-1728.
Woolf, Virginia Stephen, 1882-1941.
Wordsworth, Dorothy, 1771-1855.
Yonge, Charlotte Mary, 1823-1901.
Young, Francis Brett, 1884-1954.

AUTHORS, EUROPEAN
Almquist, Carl Jonas Love, 1793-1866.
Amiel, Henri Frederic, 1821-1881.
Biaoszewski, Miron-Biography.
Charriere, Isabella Agneta (Van Tuyll) De, D. 1805.
Comnena, Anna, B. 1083.
Cuyp, Aelbert, 1620-1691.
Frisch, Max, 1911- -Biography.
Kazantzak Es, Nikos, 1883-1957.
Pontoppidan, Henrik, 1857-1943.
Rod, Edouard, 1857-1910.
Sienkiewicz, Henryk, 1846-1916.
Wojciechowska, Maia, 1927--Juvenile Literature.

AUTHORS, FRENCH
Apollinaire, Guillaume, 1880-1918.
Artaud, Antonin, 1896-1948.
Balzac, Honore De, 1799-1850.
Baudelaire, Charles Pierre, 1821-1867.
Bazin, Andre, 1918-1958.
Beaudin, Andre, 1895-
Beauvoir, Simone De, 1908-
Benserade, Isaac De, 1613-1671-Biography.
Bernanos, Georges, 1888-1948-Biography.
Beyle, Marie Henri, 1783-1842.
Calvocoressi, Michel D., 1877-1944.
Champmesle, Charles Chevillet, Sieur De, 1642-1701.
Chateaubriand, Francois Auguste Rene, Vicomte De, 1768-1848.
Claudel, Paul, 1868-1955.
Cocteau, Jean, 1889-
Colette, Sidonie Gabrielle, 1873-1954.
Daudet, Alphonse, 1840-1897.
Destouches, Louis Ferdinand, 1894-1961.
Drieu La Rochelle, Pierre, 1893-1945-Biography.
Dudevant, Amadine Aurore Lucie Dupin, Baroness, 1804-1876.
Dumas, Alexandre, 1802-1870.
Flaubert, Gustave, 1821-1880.
France, Anatole, 1844-1924.
Gautier, Theophile, 1811-1872.
Genlis, Stephanie Felicite Ducrest De Saint-Aubin, Comtesse De, Afterwards Marquise De Sillery, 1746-1830.
Gide, Andre Paul Guillaume, 1869-1951.
Giono, Jean, 1895-
Giraudoux, Jean, 1882-1944.
Goncourt, Edmond Louis Antoine Huot De, 1822-1896.
Halevy, Daniel, 1872-1962.
Hugo, Victor Marie, Comte, 1802-1885.
Huysmans, Joris-Karl, 1848-1907.
Larteguy, Jean, 1920- -Biography.
Leroux, Pierre, 1797-1871.
Louys, Pierre, 1870-1925-Biography.
Maritain, Raissa.
Maupassant, Guy De, 1850-1893.
Moncrif, Francois Augustin Paradis De, 1687-1770.
Montaigne, Michel Eyquem De, 1533-1592.
Montesquiou-Fezensac, Robert, Comte De, 1855-1921.
Montherlant, Henry De, 1896-
Mount Cashell, Margaret Jane (King) Moore, Countess of, 1772- 1835.
Nin, Anais, 1903-1977-Diaries.
Nodier, Charles, 1780-1844-Bibliography.
Pascin, Jules, 1885-1930.
Peguy, Charles Pierre, 1873-1914.
Prevost, Antoine Francois, Called Prevost D'Exiles, 1697-1763.
Proust, Marcel, 1871-1922.
Rabelais, Francois, Ca. 1490-1553?
Radiguet, Raymond, 1903-1923-Biography.
Rolland, Romain, 1866-1944.
Sade, Donatien Alphonse Francois, Comte, Called Marquis De, 1740-1814.
Sainte-Beuve, Charles Augustin, 1804-1869.
Sand, George, Pseud. of Mme Dudevant, 1804-1876.
Scudery, Madeleine De, 1607-1701.
Sevigne, Marie De Rabutin Chantal, Marquise De, 1626-1696.
Stael-Holstein, Anne Louise Germaine (Necker) Baronne De, 1766-1817.
Valery, Paul, 1871-1945.
Verne, Jules, 1828-1905.
Viaud, Julien, 1850-1923.
Villiers De L'Isle-Adam, Jean Marie Mathias Philippe Auguste, Comte De, 1838-1889.
Voltaire, Francois Marie Arouet De, 1694-1778.
Wiesel, Elie, 1928- -Biography.
Zola, Emile, 1840-1902.

AUTHORS, GERMAN
Arnim, Bettina (Brentano) Von, 1785-1859.
Brecht, Bertolt, 1898-1956.
Feuchtwanger, Lion, 1884-1958.
Fontane, Theodor, 1819-1898.
Forster-Nietzsche, Elisabeth, 1846-1935.
Forster, William Edward, 1818-1886.
Hesse, Hermann, 1877-1962.
Lewisohn, Ludwig, 1882-1955-Biography.
Mann, Klaus, 1906-1949.
Mann, Thomas, 1875-1955.
May, Karl Friedrich, 1842-1912-Biography.
Moritz, Karl Philipp, 1757-1793.
Puckler-Muskau, Hermann Ludwig Heinrich, Furst Von, 1785-1871.
Sacher-Masoch, Leopold, Ritter Von. 1835-1895.
Stefan, Verena, 1947- -Biography.
Thoma, Ludwig, 1867-1921.
Tieck, Johann Ludwig, 1773-1853.
Tucholsky, Kurt, 1890-1935.
Varnhagen Von Ense, Rahel Antonie Frederike Levin, 1771-1833-Biography.
Wieland, Christoph Martin, 1733-1813.

AUTHORS, GREEK
Plutarchus.

AUTHORS, HEBREW
Luzzatto, Moses Hayyim, 1707-1747.

AUTHORS, HUNGARIAN
Herzl, Theodor, 1860-1904.
Illyes, Gyula, 1902-

AUTHORS, INDIC
Abbas, Khwaja Ahmad-Biography.
Amrita Pritam, 1919-
Khv Ajah M Ir, 1719?-1785?-Religion and Ethics.
Naipaul, Vidiadhar Surajprasad.

AUTHORS, IRISH
Allingham, William, 1824-1889.
Griffin, Gerald, 1803-1840.
Joyce, James, 1882-1941.
Kavanagh, Peter-Biography.
Kickham, Charles Joseph, 1826 (Ca.)-1882.
Moore, George, 1852-1933-Biography.
Moore, Thomas, 1779-1852.
Morgan, Sydney (Owenson) Lady, 1783?-1859.
O'Donovan, Michael, 1903-1966.
O'Kelly, Seumas, 1881-1918.
Russell, George William, 1867-1935.
Ryan, John, 1925-
Stuart, Francis, 1902-

AUTHORS, ITALIAN
Alfieri, Vittorio, 1749-1803.
Annunzio, Gabriele D', 1863-1938.
Aretino, Pietro, 1492-1556.
Beltrami, Giacomo Costantino, 1779-1855.
Boccaccio, Giovanni, 1313-1375.
Capuana, Luigi, 1839-1917.
Cardano, Girolamo, 1501-1576.
Casanova De Seingalt, Giacomo Girolamo, 1725-1796.
Dante Alighieri, 1265-1321.
Deledda, Grazia, 1871-1936-Biography-Juvenile Literature.
Fogazzaro, Antonio, 1842-1911.
Foscolo, Ugo, 1778-1827-Homes and Haunts-England.
Gallenga, Antonio Carlo Napoleone, 1810-1895.
Manzoni, Alessandro, 1785-1873-Biography.
Moravia, Alberto, 1907-
Schmitz, Ettore, 1861-1928.
Vico, Giovanni Battista, 1668-1744.

AUTHORS, JAPANESE
Ishikawa, Takuboku, 1886-1912.
Masamune, Hakuch O, 1879-1962.
Mishima, Yukio, Pseud.
Miura, Ayako, 1922- -Biography.
Okakura, Kakuzo, 1862-1913.

AUTHORS, JEWISH
Ben-Avi, Ittamar, 1884-1943.
Ben-Yehudah, Eliezer, 1858-1922.
Bercinsky Family.
Blumgarten, Solomon, 1871-1927.
Ginzberg, Asher, 1856-1927.
Ginzberg, Louis, 1873-1953.
Rabinowitz, Shalom, 1859-1916.

AUTHORS, LATIN
Frontinus, Sextus Julius.

AUTHORS, LATIN-AMERICAN
Bello, Andres, 1781-1865.
Borges, Jorge Luis, 1899-
Brant, Alice Dayrell.
Isaacs, Jorge, 1837-1895.
Machado De Assis, Joaquim Maria, 1839-1908.
Marti, Jose, 1853-1895.

AUTHORS, LITHUANIAN
Berenson, Bernhard, 1865-1959.

AUTHORS, NEW ZEALAND
Ashton-Warner, Sylvia.
Sargeson, Frank-Biography.

AUTHORS, NORWEGIAN
Goldschmidt, Meir, 1819-1887.
Hamsun, Knut, 1859-1952.
Janson, Kristofer Nagel, 1841-1917-Biography.
Undset, Sigrid, 1882-1949.

AUTHORS, PORTUGESE
Migueis, Jose Rodrigues, 1901- -Bibliography.

AUTHORS, RUSSIAN
Aksakov, Ergei Timofeevich, 1791-1859.
Andreev, Leonid Nikolaevich, 1871-1919.
Belinskii, Vissarion Grigorevich, 1811-1848.
Berdiaev, Nikolai Aleksandrovich, 1874-1948.
Besedovskii, Grigorii Zinovevich.
Bulgakov, Mikhail Afanasevich, 1891-1940.
Dostoevskii, Fedor Mikhailovich, 1821-1881.
Gladilin, Anatolii Tikhonovich-Biography.
Gogol', Nikolai Vasil Evich, 1809-1852.
Goncharov, Ivan Aleksandrovich, 1812-1891.
Gorkii, Maksim, 1868-1936.
Hertzen, Aleksandr Ivanovich, 1812-1870.
Kataev, Valentin Petrovich, 1897- -Biography.
Kuprin, Aleksandr Ivanovich, 1870-1938.
Lermontov, Mikhail IUrevich, 1814-1841-Biography.
Leskov, Nikolai Semenovich, 1831-1895.
Maiakovskii, Vladimir Vladimirovich, 1894-1930-Relationship with Women-Lili Brik.
Nabokov, Vladimir Vladimirovich, 1899-
Navrozov, Lev.
Nikitenko, Aleksandr Vasilevich, 1804?-1877-Biography.
Olesha, IUrii Karlovich, 1899-1960-Biography-Addresses, Essays, Lectures.
Pasternak, Boris Leonidovich, 1890-1960-Biography.
Pushkin, Aleksandr Sergieevich, 1799-1837.
Radishchev, Aleksandr Nikolaevich, 1749-1802-Biography.
Sekowski, Jozef, 1800-1858. (Series: California. University. University of California Publications in Modern Philology, V.73)
Siniavskii, Andrei Donatevich, 1925-
Solzhenitsyn, Aleksandr Isaevich, 1918-
Sutzkever, Abraham, 1913- -Criticism and Interpretation.
Tolstoi, Lev Nikolaevich, Graf, 1828-1910.
Turgenev, Ivan Sergeevich, 1818-1883.
Voinovich, Vladimir, 1932- -Biography.
Zamiatin, Evgenii Ivanovich, 1884-1937.

AUTHORS, SCANDINAVIAN
Andersen, Hans Christian, 1805-1875.
Blixen, Karen, 1885-1962.
Gyllensten, Lars Johan Wictor, 1921-
Johnson, Eyvind, 1900-
Lagerlof, Selma Ottiliana Lovisa, 1858-1940.
Morris, Edita, 1902- -Biography-Youth.

AUTHORS, SCOTTISH
Arbuthnot, John, 1667-1735.
Ballantyne, John, 1774-1821.
Ballantyne, Robert Michael, 1825-1894.
Buchan. John, 1875-1940.
Galt, John, 1779-1839-Biography.
Gunn, Neil Miller, 1891-1973.
Molesworth, Mary Louisa (Stewart) 1842-1921.
Motherwell, William, 1797-1835-Addresses, Essays, Lectures.
Ramsay. Andrew Michael, 1686-1743.
Somerville, Mary Fairfax, 1780-1872.
Thomson, David, 1914- -Biography.
Wall, Mervyn, 1908-

AUTHORS, SPANISH
Alberti, Rafael, 1902-
Calderon, Miguel G., 1885-
Cervantes Saavedra, Miguel De, 1547-1616.
Espinel, Vincente, 1550?-1624.
Jardiel Poncela, Enrique, 1901-1952.
Jarnes, Benjamin, 1888-
Saavedra Fajardo, Diego De, 1584-1648.
Valle-Inclan, Ramon Del. 1870-1936--Bibl.

AUTHORS, WOMEN
see Women Authors

AUTHORS AND PUBLISHERS
see also Literary Agents
Almon, John, 1737-1805.
Ballantyne, James, 1772-1833.
Ballantyne, John, 1774-1821.
Bancroft, Hubert Howe, 1832-1918.
Knopf, Alfred A., 1892-

AUTOMOBILE DRIVERS
Campbell, Donald, 1921-1967.
Mortimer, Charles K.

AUTOMOBILE ENGINEERING
Lancia, Vincenzo.

AUTOMOBILE INDUSTRY AND TRADE
Porsche, Ferdinand, 1875-1951.

AUTOMOBILE INDUSTRY AND TRADE-FRANCE
Renault, Louis, 1877-1944.

AUTOMOBILE INDUSTRY AND TRADE-GREAT BRITAIN
Allard, Sydney Herbert, 1910-1966.

AUTOMOBILE RACING
Andretti, Mario, 1940-
Caruthers, Jimmy.
Clark, Roger, 1939-
De Palma, Ralph-Juvenile Literature.
Foyt, A. J., 1935-
Hill, Graham, 1929-1975.
Hill, Philip Toll, 1927-
Hunt, James, 1947-
Kenyon, Mel, 1933-
Lauda, Niki, 1949-
Moss, Stirling, 1929-
Oldfield, Barney, 1878-1946.
Petty, Richard.
Revson, Peter.
Unser, Bobby.
Ward, Rodger-Juvenile Literature.

AUTOMOBILES-CONSTRUCTION
see Automobiles-Design and Construction

AUTOMOBILES-DESIGN AND CONSTRUCTION
Ferrari, Enzo, 1898-

AVIATION
see Aeronautics

AVIATORS
see Air Pilots
Skelton, Marvin L.

B

BACKWARD CHILDREN
see Mentally Handicapped Children

BACTERIOLOGISTS
Pasteur, Louis, 1822-1895.
Winogradsky, Serge, 1856-1953.

BACTERIOLOGY
Haffkine, Waldemar Mordecai Wolff, 1860-1930.

BALANCING (GYMNASTICS)
see Acrobats and Acrobatism

BALLET DANCERS
see Dancers

BALLET DANCING
Makarova, Natalia, 1940-

BALLOON ASCENSIONS
Van Orman, Ward Tunte, 1894-1978.

BALLOONS
see also Aeronautics; Balloon Ascensions
Piccard, Auguste, 1884-1962-Juvenile Literature.
Piccard, Jean Felix, 1884-1963.

BANDITS
see Brigands and Robbers

BANDMASTERS
see Conductors (Music)

BANK ROBBERIES
see Brigands and Robbers

BANKERS
Blount, Edward Charles, Sir, 1809-
Davison, Henry Pomeroy, 1867-1922.
Driscoll, Robert Henry.
Eccles, Marriner Stoddard, 1890-
Forgan, James Berwick, 1852-1924.
Forrestal, James, 1892-1949.
Giannini, Amadeo Peter, 1870-1949.
Johnston, Percy Hampton, 1881-
Little, Karl St. Clair, 1898-
Morrow, Dwight Whitney, 1873-1931.
Morton, Levi Parsons, 1824-1920.
Norman, Joyce.
Peabody, George Foster, 1852-1938.
Ralston, William Chapman, 1826-1875.
Rockefeller, David, 1915-
Stillman, James, 1850-1918.
Strong, Benjamin, 1872-1928.
Trowbridge, Charles Christopher, 1800-1883.
Warburg, Fredric, 1898-

BAPTISTS
see also Mennonites
Alderman, Rosalie Givens.
Graham, Morrow C., 1892-
Grant, Wilson W., 1941-
Hagstrom, Gustave Arvid, 1867-1953.
Hall, William Henry Harrison, 1823-1907.
Johnson, Carole, 1939-1962.
Jureidini, Said M., 1866-1952.
Mattix, Velva.
Mitson, Eileen Nora.
Nyein Tha, Daw.
Peerman, Frank.
Sargeant, Genevieve (Gildersleeve)
Smith, David H., 1921-
Southern Baptist Convention-History.
Spilman, Bernard Washington, 1871-
Stanley, Clarence Ballard, 1889-1969.
Toles, E. B.
Truett, George Washington, 1867-1944.
Vins, Georgii Petrovich, 1928-
Wallace, William L., 1908-1951.
Warfield, Bernis.
Wieand, Albert Cassel, 1871-1954.

BAPTISTS-CLERGY
Backus, Isaac, 1724-1806.

BAPTISTS-MISSIONS
American Baptist Home Mission Societies.

BAR
see Lawyers

BARBARY CORSAIRS
see Pirates

Jacquemont, Victor, 1801-1832.
Mendel, Gregor, 1822-1884.
Nuttall, Thomas, 1786-1859.
Palmer, Edward, 1831-1911.
Rauwolf, Leonhard, D. 1596.
Solander, Daniel Charles, 1733-1782.
BOXING
Ali, Muhammad, 1942- -Juvenile Literature.
Carter, Rubin, 1937-
Considine, Robert Bernard, 1960-
Darcy, James Leslie. 1895-1917.
Dempsey, Jack, 1895-
Donnelly, Dan, 1786-1820.
Frazier, Joe, 1944-
Gains, Larry, 1900-
Johnson, John Arthur, 1878-1946.
Liston, Sonny.
Louis, Joe, 1914-
McCoy, Kid, 1873-1940.
Marciano, Rocky, 1923-1969.
Muhammad Ali, 1942-
Patterson, Floyd.
Rickard, George Lewis, 1875-1929.
Robinson, Peter, B. 1821.
Robinson, Ray, 1920-
Sullivan, John Lawrence, 1858-1918.
Young, Jimmy.
BOY SCOUTS
Baden-Powell, Robert Stephenson Smyth Baden-Powell, Baron, 1857-1941.
BRACKISH WATER BIOLOGY
see Marine Biology

BRAIN DAMAGE
Lerner, Gerda, 1920-

BRAIN-DAMAGED CHILDREN
Collins, Mary, 1973-
Greenfeld, Noah Jiro, 1966-
Napear, Jane Emerson, 1962-

BRAZIL
see also names of cities, towns and areas in Brazil, e.g. Rio de Janeiro; Amazon River and Valley
Bagby, William Buck, 1855-1939.
Pedro II, Emperor of Brazil, 1825-1891.

BREAST-CANCER
Simpson, Margaret Massie, 1913-

BRETHREN OF THE COMMON LIFE
see Brothers of the Common Life

BRIGANDS AND ROBBERS
see also Outlaws
Ferreira Da Silva, Virgolino, Known As Lampeao, 1900-1938.

BROADCASTERS
Franklin, Joe.
Godfrey, Arthur, 1903-
Julian, Joseph.
May, Earl.
Miller, Bill, 1932-
Murrow, Edward R.
Nebel, Long John.
Pauley, Jane, 1950- -Juvenile Literature.
Reese, Harold Henry, 1919-
Rivera, Geraldo-Juvenile Literature.
Rizzuto, Philip Francis, 1918-
Rose, Hilly.
Ruby, Bob.
Sevareid, Arnold Eric, 1912-
Terkel, Louis.
Thomas, Lowell Jackson, 1892-
Toobin, Jerome, 1922-
Winchell, Walter, 1897-1972.
BROEDERS DES GEMEENEN LEVENS
see Brothers of the Common Life
BROTHELS
see Prostitution
BROTHERS AND SISTERS
see also Twins
Dionne Quintuplets.
BROTHERS OF THE COMMON LIFE
Maurelian, Brother.
BRUDER DES GEMEINSAMEN LEBENS
see Brothers of the Common Life
BUCCANEERS
see also Brigands and Robbers; Pirates
Dampier, William, 1652-1715.
Morgan, Henry, Sir, 1635?-1688.
BUDDHISM
see also Lamaism; Zen Buddhism
also headings beginning with the word Buddhist
Asoka, King of Magadha, Fl. 250 B. C. (Series)
Gautama Buddha.
Hsuan-Tsang, 596 (Ca.)-664.
Humphreys, Christmas, 1901-
Shinran, 1173-1263.
Subrahmanya Bharati, C., 1882-1921.
Vajiran Ana Varoros, Prince, Supreme Patriarch, 1859-1921.
Vivekananda, Swami, 1863-1902.
BUDDHISM-CHINA
Han-Shan, 1546-1623.
BUDDHISM-EAST (FAR EAST)
Asoka, King of Magadha, Fl. 259 B.C.
BUILDING
Young, William Stewart, 1859-1937.
BULL-FIGHTERS
Cintron, Conchita, 1924-
BURNS AND SCALDS
McBride, Michele, 1945-
BUSHWHACKERS
see Guerrillas
BUSINESS CONSULTANTS
Taylor, Frederick Winslow, 1856-1915.
BUSINESS EXECUTIVES
see Executives
BUSINESS MEN
see Businessmen
BUSINESS PATRONAGE OF THE ARTS
see Art Patronage
BUSINESSMEN
see also Capitalists and Financiers; Merchants
Ball, Edward, 1888-
Batchelor, Charles, 1845-1910.
Bearsted, Marcus Samuel, 1st Viscount, 1853-1927.
Bobst, Elmer Holmes, 1884-
Bourne, George Washington, 1801-1856.
Bransten, Manfred.
Brown, Moses, 1738-1836.
Bullis, Harry Amos, 1890-
Cabot, Thomas Dudley, 1897-
Cassatt, Alexander Johnston, 1839-1906.
Cist, Jacob, 1782-1825.
Corcoran, William Wilson, 1798-1888.
Cullen, Hugh Roy, 1881-
Danforth, William Henry, 1870-1955.
Florsheim, Richard, 1924-
Forbes, Malcolm S.
Galvin, Paul, 1885-1959.
Gardner, William Alexander, 1859-1916.
Getty, Jean Paul, 1892-1976.
Goldman, Sylvan Nathan, 1898-
Gordon, George, 1818-1869.
Gumberg, Alexander, 1887-1939.
Gusman, Maurice, 1888-
Hanna, Marcus Alonzo, 1837-1904.
Heintzelman, Samuel Peter, 1805-1880.
Heinz, Henry John, 1844-1919.
Helms, Edgar James, 1863-
Hill, James Jerome, 1838-1916.
Hilton, Conrad Nicholson.
Hirsch, Moritz, Freiherr Auf Gereuth, 1831-1896.
Hook, Charles Ruffin, 1880-.
Hudson, George, 1800-1871.
Huntington, Collis Potter, 1821-1900.
Insull, Samuel, 1859-1938.
Ives. Edward Riley, 1839-1918.
Jansson, Erik, 1808-1850.
Jarvis, Howard.
Kerkorian, Kirk, 1917-
Keys, Brady-Juvenile Literature.
Killam, Izaak Walton, 1885-1955.
Knott, Walter.
Kreuoger, Ivar, 1880-1932.
Ladd, Daniel, 1817-1872.
Lord, Simeon, 1771-1840.
McFarlin, Robert Martin, 1866-1942.
McKay, David Oman, 1873-
McKnight, William Lester, 1887-
Marcus, Stanley, 1905-
Marks, Jeannette Augustus, 1875-1964.
Mears, Norman B., 1904-
Moody, Sewell Prescott, D. 1875.
Morison, George Abbot, 1879-1966.
Murdoch, Rupert, 1931-
Newell, Alton S., 1913- -Juvenile Literature.
Nuffield, William Richard Morris, 1st Viscount, 1877-1963.
Olds, Ransom Eli, 1864-1950.
Penney, James Cash, 1875-
Perkins, George Walbridge, 1862-1920.
Philips, Frits, 1905-
Porter, Lewis B., 1895-
Revson, Charles, 1906-1975.
Rogers, Henry Huttleston, 1840-1909.
Rosenstock, Fred, 1895-
Sanders, Harland.
Scully, William, 1821-1906.
Self, James Cuthbert, 1876-1955.
Stettinius, Edward Reilly, 1865-1925.
Steuber, Roy Edward, 1892-1954.
Swift, Gustavus Franklin, 1839-1903.
Swope, Gerard, 1872-1957.
Taylor, Edward Plunkett, 1901-
Teagle, Walter Clark, 1878-1962.
Tucker, Preston, 1903-1956.
Van Sweringen, Mantis James, 1881-1935.
Wanamaker, John, 1838-1922.
Ward, Aaron Montgomery, 1844-1913.
Watson, Emile Emdon, 1885-
Watson, Thomas John, 1874-1956.
Weintraub, Julie.
Whitsett, William Paul, 1875-
Wier, Robert, 1886-1974.
Williams, Allan.
Williams, George Walton, 1820-1903.
Woolworth, Frank Winfield, 1852-1919.
BUSINESSWOMEN
see Women in Business
BUTCHER SHOPS
see Butchers
BUTCHERS
Gorman, Patrick Emmet, 1892-
BYZANTINE EMPIRE
Alexius I Comnenus, Emperor of the East, 1048-1118.

C

CABINET OFFICERS
see also Prime Ministers
Cheke, John, Sir, 1514-1557.
Dulles, John Foster, 1888-1959.
CABINET-WORKERS
Adam, Robert, 1728-1792.
CAESARS
see Roman Emperors
CALIFORNIA-BIOGRAPHY
Anza, Juan Bautista De, 1735-1788.
Bagley, Helen.
Baker, Dorsey Syng, 1823-1888.
Bard, Thomas Robert, 1841-1915.
Bell, Horace, 1830-1918.
Bowers, Eilley (Orrum) 1826-1903.
Davis, Stephen Chapin, 1833-1856.
Hewes, David, 1822-1915.
Merideth, Robert.
Reinhardt, Aurelia (Henry) 1877-1948.
Shumway, Nina Paul.
CALIFS
see Caliphs
CALIPHS
Ab U Bakr, Caliph, D. 634.
Abreu Gomez, Ermilo, 1894-1971.
CALLIGRAPHERS
Johnston, Edward, 1872-1944.
CANADA-ARMY
Talbot, Matthew, 1856-1925.
Talbot, Thomas, 1771-1853.
CANADA-BIOGRAPHY
Alline, Henry, 1748-1784.
Allison, Susan, 1845-1937.
Angier, Bradford.
Angier, Vena.
Argyll, John George Edward Henry Douglas Sutherland Campbell, 9th Duke of, 1845-1914.
Ashlee, Ted, 1914-
Bayfield, Henry Wolsey, 1795-1885.
Brown, George, 1818-1880.
Cartier, George Etienne, Sir, Bart., 1814-1873.
Foster, Malcolm Cecil.
Hallwas Family.
Mowat, Farley.
Mowat, Oliver, Sir, 1820-1903.
Moyer, Kenneth Allan, 1913-
Ogden, Peter Skene, 1794-1854.
Pickersgill, J. W., 1905-
Trumble, David, 1867-
CANADIAN AUTHORS
see Authors, Canadian
CANADIANS
Lemieux, Jean Paul, 1904-
CANCER
Banks, Graham.
Barron, Dick.
Bayh, Marvella.
Beatty, Robert O.
Davison, Jaquie, 1938-
Hill, Rick.
Kelly, Orville E., 1930-
McGrail, Joie.
Parker, Joan H.
Pond, Jean, 1929-
Robin, 1944-1975.
Rollin, Betty.
Rosenfeld, Jay C.
Seale, Albert B.
Simpson, Margaret Massie, 1913-
Wallin, Bernice.
Zalon, Jean.
CAPITALISTS AND FINANCIERS
see also Businessmen
Bacon, Robert, 1860-1919.
Barker, Jacob, 1779-1871.
Brady, James Buchanan, 1856-1917.
Bronson, Isaac, 1760-1838.
Brooks, Joshua Loring, 1868-1949.
Byrd, David Harold, 1900-
Carnegie, Andrew, 1835-1919.
Cooke, Jay, 1821-1905.
Cornell, Ezra, 1807-1874.
Deterding, Henri, Sir, 1866-1939.
Fanon, Frantz, 1925-1961.
Ferry, Dexter Mason, 1833-1907.
Field, Cyrus West, 1819-1892.
Fisk, James, 1835-1872.
Fox, Stephen, Sir, 1627-1716.
Fugger, Jakob, 1459-1525.
Gallatin, Albert, 1761-1849.
Goldie, George Dashwood Taubman, Sir, 1846-1925.
Green, Hetty Howland (Robinson) 1834-1916.
Greenwood, Harold W.
Gresham, Sir Thomas, 1519?-1579.
Guggenheim Family.
Guggenheimer, Minnie (Schaefer).
Gulbenkian, Calouste Sarkis.
Harriman, Edward Henry, 1848-1909.
Kennedy Family.
Kennedy, Joseph Patrick, 1888-1969.
Law, John, 1671-1729.
Lawson, Thomas William, 1857-1925.
Lefevre, Edwin, 1871-1943.
Lehmann, Herman, 1859-1932.
Little, Royal, 1896-
Loeb, Gerald M.
Mellon, Paul.
Mercer, George, 1733-1784.
Moody, John, 1868-1958.
Morgan, John Pierpont, 1837-1913.
Morris, Robert, 1734-1806.
Necker, Jacques, 1732-1804.
Peabody, George, 1795-1869.
Prochnow, Herbert Victor, 1897-
Rothschild Family.
Saenz, Aaron.
Sage, Russell, 1816-1906.
Schacht, Hjalmar Horace Greeley, 1877-1970.
Stanford, Leland, 1824-1893.
Taylor, Moses.
Vanderbilt, Cornelius, 1794-1877.
Vaughan, Stephen, D. 1549.
Wertheimer, Samson, 1658-1724.
Whitney, William Collins, 1841-1904.
CAPTAINS OF SHIPS
see Shipmasters
CAPTURE AT SEA
see Privateering
CAR WORKERS
see Railroads-Employees
CARCINOMA
see Cancer
CARDIAC ARREST
see Heart Failure
CARDIAC DISEASES
see Heart-Diseases
CARDIAC PATIENTS
see Cardiacs
CARDIACS
Dossick, Philip.
Keiser, Bea.
Poole, Sam.
CARDINALS
Borromeo, Federico, Cardinal, 1564-1631.
Furstenberg, Wilhelm Egon, Graf Von, Cardinal, 1629-1704.
Gasquet, Francis Aldan, Cardinal, 1846-1929.
Newman, John Henry, Cardinal, 1801-1890.
Nicolaus Cusanus, Cardinal, 1401-1464.
O'Connell, William Henry, Cardinal, 1859-1944.
Richelieu, Armand Jean De Plessis, Cardinal, Duc De, 1585-1642.
Stepinac, Aloysius, Cardinal, 1898-1960.
Stritch, Samuel Alphonsus, Cardinal, 1887-1958.
Suenens, Leon Joseph, Cardinal, 1904-
Wiseman, Nicholas Patrick Stephen, Cardinal, 1802-1865.
CARIBBEAN AREA
Eggleston, Hazel.
CARIBBEAN AREA-DISCOVERY AND EXPLORATION
see America-Discovery and Exploration
CARICATURISTS
see Cartoonists
CARTOGRAPHY
Romans, Bernard, Ca. 1720-Ca. 1784.
CARTOONISTS
Crosby, Percy Leo, 1891-1964.
Cruikshank, George, 1792-1878.
Darling, Jay Norwood, 1876-1962.
Davenport, Homer Calvin, 1867-1912.
Fleischer, Max, 1888-
Hartley, Al.
Hubbard, Frank McKinney, 1868-1930.
Lindsay, Norman, 1879-1969.
Tournachon, Felix, 1820-1910.
Young, Arthur Henry, 1866-1943.
CARVING (ART INDUSTRIES)
Ward, Lemuel T.
CATAWBA INDIANS
see Indians of North America-Eastern States
CATHOLIC CHURCH
Lambertini, Imelda, 1321-1333.
CATHOLIC CHURCH-CLERGY
see also Bishops; Cardinals; Priests
Baker, Nelson Henry.
Hecker, Isaac Thomas, 1819-1888.
Manyanet, Joseph, 1833-1901.
CATHOLIC CHURCH-CONVERTS
see Converts, Catholic
CATHOLIC CONVERTS
see Converts, Catholic
CATHOLICS
Conchita, 1862-1937.
Jacques, Father, 1900-1945.
Janssoone, Frederic, 1838-1916.
Lebbe, Vincent, 1877-1940.
Legere, J. Roy, 1922-
Merry Del Val, Raphael, Cardinal, 1865-1930.
Nauer, Barbara.
CATHOLICS IN ENGLAND
Ward, William George, 1812-1882.

CATHOLICS IN THE UNITED STATES
Bloomingdale, Teresa, 1930-
CENTRAL AMERICA-DISCOVERY AND EXPLORATION
see America-Discovery and Exploration
CEREBRAL PALSY-PERSONAL NARRATIVES
Killilea, Karen, 1940-
CERTIFICATION OF SCHOOL SUPERINTENDENTS AND PRINCIPALS
see School Superintendents and Principals
CERTIFIED PUBLIC ACCOUNTANTS
see Accountants
CHANGE OF SEX
Hunt, Nancy.
Martino, Mario.
Morris, Jan, 1926-
CHAPLAINS
Erwin, John Robert, 1930-
Graham, Jerry.
Rogers, Peter V.
CHARLATANS
see Impostors and Imposture
CHASIDISM
see Hasidism
CHEMISTS
see also Pharmacists
Berzelius, Jons Jakob, Friherre, 1779-1848.
Boyle, Hon. Robert, 1627-1691.
Cavendish, Henry, 1731-1810.
Curie, Marie (Sklodovska) 1867-1934.
Curie, Pierre, 1859-1906.
Davy, Humphry, Sir, Bart., 1778-1829.
Dow, Herbert Henry, 1866-1930.
Fleming, Alexander, Sir, 1881-1955.
Florey, Howard Walter, Sir, 1898-1968.
Freund, Ernst, 1864-1932.
Gay-Lussac, Joseph Louis, 1778-1850.
Haber, Fritz, 1868-1934.
Laves, Georg Ludwig Friedrich, 1788-1864.
Lewis, Gilbert Newton, 1875-1946.
Liebig, Justus, Freiherr Von, 1803-1873-Juvenile Literature.
Mendeleev, Dmitrii Ivanovich, 1834-1907.
Neckers, James Winfred, 1902-
Nef, John Ulric, 1899-
Ostwald, Wilhelm, 1853-1932.
Prigogine, Ilya.
Pasteur, Louis, 1822-1895.
Richards, Ellen Henrietta (Swallow) 1842-1911.
Riley, Vincent, 1891-1951?
Robinson, Robert, Sir, 1886-1975.
Silliman, Benjamin, 1779-1864.
Thomson, Tom, 1877-1917.
Urey, Harold Clayton, 1893- -Juvenile Literature.
Werner, Alfred, 1866-1919.
Whitney, Willis Rodney, 1868-1958.
CHERAW INDIANS
see Indians of North America-Eastern States
CHEROKEE INDIANS
see Indians of North America-Eastern States
CHESS
Collins, John W.
Fischer, Bobby, 1943-
Korchnoi, Viktor, 1931-
Lasker, Emanuel, 1868-1941.
Pachman, Ludek.
CHEYENNE INDIANS
see Indians of North America-The West
CHICANOS
see Mexican Americans
CHICKASAW INDIANS
see Indians of North America-Eastern States
CHIEF JUSTICES
see Judges
CHILD AND MOTHER
see Mother and Child
CHILD BEHAVIOR
see Child Psychology
CHILD BIRTH
see Childbirth
CHILD PSYCHOLOGY
Parker, Bob.
Piaget, Jean, 1896-
CHILD STUDY
see Child Psychology
CHILDBIRTH
Brown, Lesley, 1947-
CHILDREN-BIOGRAPHY
see also Presidents-United States-Wives and Children
Cauthen, Steven, 1960- -Juvenile Literature.
Cohen, Ephraim Leo, 1941 or 2-1956.
CHILDREN-PSYCHOLOGY
see Child Psychology
CHILDREN, ABNORMAL AND BACKWARDS
see Handicapped Children; Mentally Handicapped Children
CHILDREN, RETARDED
see Mentally Handicapped Children
CHILDREN, RUNAWAY
see Runaway Children
CHILE

Allende Gossens, Salvador, 1908-1973.
Frei Montalva, Eduardo, Pres. Chile, 1911-
CHILE-POLITICS AND GOVERNMENT
O'Higgins, Bernardo, Supreme Director of Chile, 1778-1842.
CHINA-ARMED FORCES
Feng, Yu-Hsiang, 1882-1948.
CHINA-BIOGRAPHY
Angus, Fay.
Chinn Family.
Chou, En-Lai, 1898-
Su. Ch O. 498-546.
Su, Hsuan-Ying, 1884-1918.
Su, Shih, 1036-1101.
Sun, Ching-Ling (Sung) 1890-
CHINA-KINGS AND RULERS
Tang Tai-Tsung, Emperor of China, 597-649.
CHINA-OFFICIALS AND EMPLOYEES
King, Paul Henry, 1853-
CHIPPEWA INDIANS
see Indians of North America-Northwest, Old
CHIROPRACTIC
Kersten, Felix, 1898-1960.
Palmer, Daniel David, 1842-1913.
Shaklee, Forrest Clell.
CHOCTAW INDIANS
see Indians of North America-Eastern States
CHOREOGRAPHY
Ashton, Frederick, Sir, 1906-
Balanchine, George.
Bournonville, Auguste, 1805-1879.
De Mille, Agnes.
Didelot, Charles Louis, 1767-1838.
Graham, Martha.
Holm, Hanya, 1893-
CHORIONITIS
see Scleroderma (Disease)
CHRISTIAN BIOGRAPHY
see also Bishops; Cardinals; Clergy; Fathers of the Church; Hermits; Missionaries; Popes; Puritans; Reformers; Saints; Theologians
Andes, Florence.
Andre, Brother, 1845-1937.
Anne Marie De Jesus, Sister, 1624-1701.
Apostolic Church of John Maranke.
Armer, Dolores, Mother, 1851-1905.
Armstrong, Annie W., D. 1938-
Arnaldo Da Brescia, D. 1155.
Assimakopoulos, Pat.
Aull, Roger.
Ayer, William Ward.
Bailey, Ney.
Bainton, James Herbert, 1867-1942.
Baker, George, Self-Named Father Divine.
Bakker, Jim.
Barnard, Jerry.
Barnes, John Richard,1833-1919.
Beauraing, Notre Dame De
Benedictus XIII, Antipope, 1342-1423?
Berggrav, Eivid Josef, Bp., 1884-1959.
Berven, Ken.
Billiart, Julie, 1751-1816.
Boom, Casper Ten, 1859-1944.
Boone, Shirley.
Booth-Clibborn, Catherine, 1860-1955.
Boros, Ladislaus, 1927-
Bosco, Margherita (Occhiena) 1788-1856.
Bowen, Charles O.
Brainerd, David, 1718-1747.
Brasted, Alva Jennings, 1876-1965.
Bresee, Phineas Franklin, 1838-1915.
Bringgold, Diane.
Brougher, Mahlon J., 1885-1952.
Brown, John Richards, 1837-1922.
Buckingham, Jamie.
Burke, John Joseph, 1875-1936.
Campbell, Alexander 1788-1866.
Campion, Edmund, 1540-1581.
Cardyn, Leon Joseph Marie, 1882-
Carroll, Julian Morton, 1931-
Cash, June Carter, 1929-
Cutler, Julian Stearns, B. 1854.
Doherty, Catherine De Hueck, 1900-
Durham, Betty.
Edwards, George, 1950-
Elliot, Elisabeth.
Elmslie, John, 1831-1907.
Fahs, Sophia Blache (Lyon) 1876-
Fathers of the Church.
Flesche, Mary Rose, 1824-1906.
Fontbonne, Jeanne, 1759-1843.
Fotedar, S. N.
Friend, J. B. B.
Fuller, Charles Edward, 1887-1968.
Fulton, John Edwin, 1869-1945.
Funkhouser, Lloyd.
Gaffney, Evangelista, 1855-1920.
Gaither, Gloria.
Gillespie, Janet.
Gonzaga, Brother, 1912?-1952.
Gorham, Ethel Bloehm, 1912-
Grieve, Alexander James, 1874-1952.
Griffin, Robert.
Haggai, John Edmund, 1950-1975.
Ham, Mordecal Fowler, 1877-
Henry, Sarepta Myrenda (Irish) 1839-1900.
Hügel, Friedrich, Freiherr Von, 1852-1925.
Hodge, Charles, 1797-1878.
Holmes, Ernest Shurtleff.
Irwin, Mary, 1938-
Jackson, Raymond Samuel, 1892-
Jesus Christ.
Johnson, James E., 1926-
Johnson, Lois Walfrid.
Johnston, John Young, 1857-1931.
Johnstone, Mildred T.
Jones, Margaret Jean.
Jordan, Mickey.
Joyeuse, Henri, Duc De, 1567-1608.
Juniperus, of Assisi, Brother, 13th Cent.
Kelley, Frances.
Kiemel, Ann-United States.
Kline, John, 1797-1864.
Knapp, Bliss, 1877-
Krauth, Charles Porterfield, 1823-1883.
Larson, Melvin Gunnard, 1916-1972.
McAstocker, David Plante, 1884-1958.
McAuley, Mary Catherine, 1778-1841.
McLaughlin, Henry Woods, 1869-1950.
McLeod, Ceil.
McQuilkin, Robert Crawford, 1886-1952.
Marto, Francisco, 1908-1919.
Mather, Increase, 1639-1723.
Matheson, George, 1812-1906.
Matsuda, Kiyoko.
Mattingly, Edward Raymond, 1919-1942.
Maurin, Peter.
Mayhew, Jonathan, 1720-1766.
Meacham, Joseph, 1742-1796.
Mead, Eleanor Tyler.
Mears, Henrietta Cornella, 1890-
Meeks, Cathy.
Megan, Thomas M., 1899-1951.
Mehegan, Mary Xavier, Mother, 1825-1915.
Melton, Sparks White, 1870-1957.
Menno Simons, 1496-1561.
Merlo, Thecla, 1894-1964.
Monson, Todd.
Morrison, Henry Clay, 1857-1942.
Murch, James DeForest, 1892-
Nason, Tara.
Nelson, Reuben Emmanuel, 1905-1960.
Nordtvedt, Matilda.
Nussbaum, Jean, 1888-1967.
Olson, Lois Ellen, 1941-
Paddock, Robert Lewis, Bp., 1869-1939.
Payton, Everett Lee.
Perkins, Carl.
Phillips, Benjamin Dwight, 1885-1968.
Pickett, Clarence Evan, 1884-1965.
Price, Eugenia.
Pulkingham, Betty.
Raines, Robert Arnold.
Rees, Seth Cook, 1854-1933.
Reid, James Seaton, 1793-1851.
Reynolds, Bede, 1892-
Rice, John Holt, 1777-1831.
Rice, John R., 1895-
Rice, Merton Stacher, 1872-1943.
Richards, Theodore, 1867-1948.
Rinker, Rosalind.
Robertson, Dede.
Romano, Juanita Napoles.
Rushmore, Jane Palen.
Russell, Mary Baptist, 1829-1898.
Schervier, Franziska.
Scheuring, Tom.
Sealy, Gayle Burch.
Seelos, Franz Xaver, 1819-1867.
Sharian, Bedros, 1892?
Sheetz, Ann Kindig.
Shelton, Elwood, 1926-1975.
Siedliska, Maria Franciszka, Mother, 1842-1902.
Sihler, Wilhelm, 1801-1885.
Smet, Eugenie Marie Josephe, 1825-1871.
Stamps, Ellen De Kroon, 1940-
Steelberg, Wesley Rowland.
Stein, Edith, 1891-1942
Suttle, John William, 1872-
Taigi, Anna Maria, 1769-1837.
Tanner, Annie Clark, 1864-1941.
Taylor, John, 1808-1887.
Temple, Exra, 1865 or 6-1946.
Ten Boom, Corrie.
Teresa, Mother, 1910-
Tettemer, John Moyniahn, 1876-1949.
Thomas, Tay.
Warde, Mary Francis Xavier, 1810?-1884.
Warnshuis, Abbe Livingston, 1877-1958.
Weatherhead, Leslie Dixon, 1893-
Weigel, Gustave, 1906-1964.
Wolfe, Leslie E.
Zanta, Leontine.
CHRISTIAN CONVERTS
see Converts
CHRISTIAN LEADERSHIP
Mott, John Raleigh 1865-1955.

CHRISTIAN LIFE
see also Monastic and Religious Life; Spiritual Life

Criswell, Wallie A.
Hiebert, Paul Gerhardt, 1892-
Hill, Harold, 1905-
Horton, Marilee.
Huff, James A.
Hughes, Allison.
Jefferson, Ted, 1932-
Lavender, Lucille.
Lawson, William A., 1927-
Loman, Mini.
Longacre, Charles Smull, 1871-1958.
Lovasik, Leo Edward, 1921-1943.
Magruder, Jeb Stuart, 1934-
Mallory, Kathleen Moore, 1879-1954.
Malz, Betty.
Nobili, Roberto De', 1577-1656.
Potterbaum, Charlene.
Ryken, Theodore James, 1797-1871.
Satre, Ellen.
Smith, Oswald J.
Smith, Susy.
Snowden, James Henry, 1852-1936.
Son, Yang-Won.
Spurling, Richard G., 1858-1935.
Tsai, Christiana.
Turner, Taos Lee, 1972-
Van Raalte, Albertus Christiaan, 1811-1876.
Vereide, Abraham, 1886-
Vinet, Alexandre Rodolphe, 1797-1847.
Wesson, Laurence Goddard, 1888-1963.
White, Christopher, 1949-
Workswick, David Jay, 1958-
Zorzano, Isidoro.
Zuck, Barb.
CHRISTIAN LIFE-BIOGRAPHY
see Christian Biography
CHRISTIAN SCIENCE
see also Faith-Cure; Mental Healing
Eddy, Mary (Baker), 1821-1910.
Knapp, Bliss, 1877-
CHRISTIAN THEOLOGIANS
see Theologians
CHRISTIANITY-BIOGRAPHY
see Christian Biography
CHRISTIANITY IN (AFRICA, ASIA, ETC.)
see Christians in (Africa, Asia, etc.)
CHURCH BIOGRAPHY
see Christian Biography
CHURCH FATHERS
see Fathers of the Church
CHURCH HISTORY-REFORMATION, 1517-1648
see Reformation
CHURCH LEADERSHIP
see Christian Leadership
CHURCH OF CHRIST OF LATTER-DAY SAINTS
see Mormons and Mormonism
CHURCH OF ENGLAND CLERGY
Fuller, Thomas, 1608-1661.
Henry, Philip, 1631-1696.
Johnson, Samuel, 1696-1772.
Morse, Henry, 1595-1645.
Priestley, Joseph, 1733-1804.
Ridley, Nicholas, Bp. of London, 1500?-1555.
Simeon, Charles, 1759-1836.
CHURCH OF THE NEW JERUSALEM
see New Jerusalem Church
CINEMA
see Moving-Pictures
CIRCUS
see also Acrobats and Acrobatism; Animals, Training of; Clowns
Beatty, Clyde, 1903-1965-Juvenile Literature.
Ducrow, Andrew, 1793-1842.
Farfan, Armando-Juvenile Literature.
Fulkerson, Jasbo, 1904-1949.
Ringling Brothers.
Ringling, John, 1866-1936.
CIRCUS COLLECTING
see Wild Animal Collecting
CISTERCIANS
see also Trappists
Adam De Perseigne, D. 1221.
CITIES AND TOWNS PLANNING
see City Planning
CITY MANAGER
see Municipal Government by City Managers
CITY PLANNING
L'Enfant, Pierre Charles, 1755-1825.
CITY PLANNING-UNITED STATES
Draper, Stanley Carlyle, 1889-1976.
CIVIC PLANNING
see City Planning
CIVIL ENGINEERS
Cubitt, Thomas, 1788-1855.
Latrobe, Charles Joseph, 1801-1875
O'Connor, C. Y., 1843-1902.
Roebling, John Augustus, 1805-1869.
Roebling, Washington Augustus, 1837-1926.
Steinman, David Barnard, 1886-
Stephens, James, 1825-1901.
Telford, Thomas, 1757-1834.
CIVIL LAW-ROME
see Roman Law
CIVIL LAW (ROMAN LAW)
see Roman Law
CIVIL RIGHTS-UNITED STATES
Aronson, Henry M.-Juvenile Literature.
Bond, Julian, 1940-
King, Coretta Scott, 1927-
King, Martin Luther, 1929-1968.
Parks, Rosa, 1913- -Juvenile Literature.
Webb, Sheyann.
CIVIL RIGHTS WORKERS
Evers, Medgar Wiley, 1925-1963.
Hancock, Gordon Blaine, 1884-1970.
Jackson, Jesse, 1941-
Randolph, Asa Philip, 1889-
Spike, Robert Warren.
Young, Whitney M.-Juvenile Literature.

CIVIL SERVICE
see also Municipal Officials and Employees
Howard, Katherine Graham, 1898-
Lee, Ettie.

CIVIL SERVICE-FRANCE
LeBlanc, Claude, 1669-1728.

CIVIL SERVICE-UNITED STATES
Lowry, Thomas, 1843-1909.

CIVIL WAR-UNITED STATES
see United States-History-Civil War, 1861-1865

CLAIRVOYANCE
Cayce, Edgar, 1877-1945.

CLASSICAL BIOGRAPHY
see also Greece-Biography; Rome-Biography
Agricola, Cn. Julius, 37-93.
Agrippa I, King of Judea, B.C. 10 (Ca.)-A.D. 44.
Alcibiades.
Alexander the Great, B.C. 356-323.
Antonius, Marcus, 83?-30 B.C.
Aratus of Sicyon, 271-213 B.C.

CLERGY
see also Bishops; Chaplains; Priests; Rabbis; Theologians; Women Clergy
also subdivision Clergy under church denominations, e.g. Church of England-Clergy
Abeel, David, 1804-1846.
Ballou, Adin, 1803-1890.
Ballou, Hosea, 1771-1852.
Beecher, Henry Ward, 1813-1887.
Beecher, Lyman, 1775-1863.
Beissel, Johann Conrad, 1690-1768.
Bentley, William, 1759-1819.
Blake, Eugene Carson, 1906-
Boisen, Anton Theophilus, 1876-1975.
Bonsack, Charles Daniel, 1870-1953.
Bowman, Earl McKinley, 1896-
Boyd, Malcolm, 1923-
Bradley, Preston, 1888-
Brownlow, William Gannaway, 1805-1877.
Brownson, Orestes Augustus, 1803-1876.
Buchanan, Jerreal B.
Burtsell, Richard Lalor, 1840-1912.
Bushnell, Horace, 1802-1876.
Campbell, Will D.
Carlsson, Erland, 1822-1893.
Carothers, Merlin R.
Cartwright, Peter, 1785-1872.
Cauthen, Baker James.
Chambers, Stanley Warren, 1915-
Channing, William Ellery, 1780-1842.
Chappell, Clovis Gillham, 1882-1972.
Chauncy, Charles, 1705-1787.
Claassen, Johann, 1820-1876.
Clark, Columbus Andrew.
Clark, John Kenneth.
Clarke, Adam, 1760?-1832-Addresses, Essays, Lectures.
Claus, Tom, 1929-
Clayton, Geoffrey Hare, Abp., 1884-1957.
Cleobury, F. H.
Clergue, Francois Auguste Leon, 1825-1907.
Clifford, Richard L.
Coggan, Jean, 1908-
Cohen, Henry, 1863-1952.
Cohen, Jacob Xenab, 1889-1955.
Colman, Benjamin, 1673-1747.
Colombiere, Claude De la, 1641-1682.
Colton, Walter, 1797-1851.
Compton, Henry, Bp. of London 1632-1713.
Conaty, Thomas James, Bp., 1847-1915.
Conley, Lawrence Alden, 1908-1947.
Contarini, Gasparo, Cardinal, 1484-1542.
Corbly Family.
Corbly, John.
Corrigan, Michael Augustine, Abp., 1839-1902.
Cotton, John, 1584-1652.
Courtenay, William, Abp. of Canterbury, 1342?-1396.
Cranch, Christopher Pearse.
Cranmer, Thomas, Abp., 1489-1556.
Crawford, Raymond Robert, 1891-1965.
Croke, Thomas William, 1823-1902.
Crombruggbe, Constant William Van, 1789-1865.
Cronin, Patrick, 1913-
Culpepper. Burke.
Cushing, Richard James, Cardinal, 1895-
Dabney, Robert Lewis, 1820-1898.
Dahlberg, Edwin Theodore, 1892-
Damon, Samuel Chenery, 1815-1885.
Day, Frank, 1862-
Denman, Harry, 1893-1976.
Dibelius, Otto, Bp., 1880-
Dickinson, Jonathan, 1663-1722.
Dixon, Thomas, 1864-1946.
Dominic of the Mother of God, Father, 1792-1849.
Donders, Petrus, 1809-1887.
Douglas, Lloyd Cassel, 1877-1951.
Duffy, Francis Patrick, 1871-1932.
Duncan, William Asa, 1891-
Dwight, Timothy, 1752-1817.
Dwight, Timothy, 1828-1916.
Eliot, Samuel Atkins, 1862-1950.
Elkins, Opie Eldridge, 1894-1958.
Everett, Edward, 1794-1865.
Falwell, Jerry.
Fiske, John, 1601-1677.
Flagler, Henry Morrison, 1830-1913.
Flanagan, Edward Joseph, 1886-1948.
Foucauld, Charles Eugene, Vicomte De, 1858-1916.
Fowler, James Lowry.
Fox, Emmet.
Frakes, Hiram, 1888-
Fritchman, Stephen Hole, 1902-
Frothingham, Octavius Brooks, 1822-1895.
Fulco.
Fullman, Terry.
Furman, James Clement.
Gates, Frederick Taylor, 1853-1929.
Glanvill, Joseph, 1636-1680.
Glennon, John Joseph, 1862-1946.
Gordon, Philip B., 1885-1948.
Gothard, Bill.
Greeley, Andrew M., 1928-
Gross, Fred W., 1895-
Guanella, Luigi, 1842-1915.
Guiseppe, Francesco, 1887-
Hale, Edward Everett, 1822-1909.
Hannington, James, Bp., 1847-1885.
Hare, Julius Charles, 1795-1855.
Harris, Howel, 1714-1773.
Hauge, Hans Nielsen, 1771-1824.
Haygood, Atticus Greene, Bp., 1839-1896.
Haynes, Lemuel, 1753-1833.
Hewitt, Joe.
Hidalgo y Costilla, Miguel, 1753-1811.
Higginson, Thomas Wentworth, 1823-1911.
Hollings, Michael.
Honcharenko, Ahapius, 1832-1916.
Hooker, Thomas, 1586-1647.
Howson, John, 1865-1956.
Hoyos, Bernardo Francisco De, 1711-1735.
Hus, Jan. 1309-1415.
Huvelin, Henri, 1838-1910.
Hyde, Charles McEwen, 1832-1899.
Jacques, Father, 1900-1945.
Janssoone, Frederic, 1838-1916.
Jarrett, Bede, Father, 1881-1934.
Jesuits-Mexico-Baja California.
John of Salisbury, Bp. of Chartres, D. 1180.
Johnosn, Charles Oscar, 1886-
Johns, John, Bp., 1796-1876.
Josselin, Ralph, 1617-1683.
Judd, Sylvester, 1813-1853.
Kauffman, Daniel, Bp.
Keble, John, 1792-1866.
Keck, L. Robert, 1935-
Kemper, Robert G.
Kilvert, Robert Francis, 1840-1879.
King, Martin Luther, 1929-1968.
King, Thomas Starr, 1824-1864.
Knox, Ronald Arbuthnott, 1888-1957.
Kolbe, Maximilian, Father, 1894-1941.
Kopf, Carl Heath, 1902-1958.
Kuac, Moses.
La Farge, John, 1835-1910.
La Farge, John, 1880-1963.
LaCloche, James, B. 1647.
Lacombe, Albert, 1827?-1916.
Lagrange, Albert, 1855-1938.
Lamb, Burley Frank, 1886-
Lamennais, Hugues Felicite Robert De, 1782-1854.
Lamy, Jean Edouard, 1853-1931.
Lamy, John Baptist, Abp., 1814-1888.
Lanfranc, Abp. of Canterbury, 1005?-1089.
Latimer, Hugh, Bp. of Worcester, 1485?-1555.
Le Clerc Du Tremblay, Francois, 1577-1638.
Leavell, Frank Hartwell, 1884-1949.
Leisner, Karl, 1915-1945.
Lilje, Hanns, Bp., 1899-
McCabe, Herb, 1936-
McCulloch, Oscar C., 1843-1891.
McGlynn, Edward, 1837-1900.
McKinstry, Arthur R.
McMillan, John, 1752-1833.
McNabb, Vincent Joseph, 1868-1943.
Mahan, Asa, 1800-1889.
Mainse, David.
Makhluf, Sharbal, Father, 1828-1896.
Mannix, Daniel, Abp., 1864-1963.
Marshall, Peter, 1902-1949.
Martin, Greg.
Martin, Luther, 1748-1826.
Martin, Paul Elliott, 1897-
Martinez, Antonio Jose, 1793-1867.
Martinez, Luis Maria, Abp., 1881-1956.
Maston, Thomas Bufford, 1897- -Addresses, Essays, Lectures.
Mather, Cotton, 1663-1728.
Mather, Richard, 1596-1669.
Matthews William, 1770-1854.
Mazzuchelli, Samuel Charles, 1806-1864.
Metzger, Max Josef, 1887-1944.
Middleton, Samuel Henry, 1884-1964.
Moody, Howard-Addresses, Essays, Lectures.
Moore, Paul, 1942-
Moreau, Basile Antoine Marie, 1799-1873.
Moyer, Kenneth Allan, 1913-
Muse, Dan Thomas, Bp., 1882-
Muzorewa, Abel Tendekayi, 1925-
Naude, Beyers.
Nerinckx, Charles.
Niccacci, Rufino.
Nicolson, William, Abp. of Cashel, 1655-1727.
Niebuhr, Reinhold, 1892-1971.
Niemoller, Martin, 1892-
Nikolai, Metropolitan of Krutitsy and Kolomna, 1892-1961.
Niles, John, 1775-1812.
O'Connell, Eugene, 1815-1891.
Oldham, Dale.
Olivieri, Umberto, 1884-1973.
Orione, Luigi,1872-1940.
Orsini, Joseph E.
Otterbein, Philip William, Bp., 1726-1813.
Palfrey. John Gorham, 1796-1881.
Parker, Theodore, 1810-1860.
Paul James Francis, Father, 1863-1940.
Peale, Norman Vincent, 1898-
Perrella, Robert.
Perry, Charies, 1807-1891.
Pio Da Pietralcina, Father.
Pirc, Franc, 1785-1880.
Price, Thomas Frederick, 1860-1919.
Pro Juarez, Miguel Agustin, 1891-1927.
Pruden, Edward Hughes.
Radini Tedeschi, Giacomo Maria, 1857-1914.
Ratiu, Alexander.
Reyes, Antonio De los, Bp., 1729-1786.
Richard. Gabriel, 1767-1832.
Robb, James Henry.
Roberts, Benjamin Titus, 1823-1893.
Roe, Edward Payson, 1838-1888.
Ronsisvalle, Daniel.
Rosmini Serbati, Antonio, 1797-1855.
Ryan, John Augustine, 1869-1945.
Sarpi, Paolo, 1552-1623.
Saunders, Albert Edward.
Scalabrini, Giovanni Battista, Bp., 1839-1905.
Schwerdtfeger, Johann Samuel William, 1734-1803.
Seabury, Samuel, 1873-1958.
Sempangi, F. Kefa.
Serra, Junipero, Father, 1713-1784.
Sharp, John Kean, 1892-
Sheffey, Robert Sayers, 1820-1902.
Skattebl, Olaf, 1847-1930.
Smith, Angie Frank, 1889-1962.
Smith, Malcolm, 1938-
Smith, Sydney, 1771-1845.
Snow, Jimmy.
Spellman, Francis Joseph, Cardinal, 1889-
Spencer, Robert Nelson, Bp., 1877-
Spurgeon, Charles Haddon, 1834-1892.
Stagg, Harry P., 1898-
Stiles, Ezra, 1727-1795.
Stiles, James Esmond, 1889-
Storey, Del.
Strickland, Henry Benjamin, 1884-1944.
Sweeney, Zachary Taylor, 1849-1926.
Swieson, Eddy, 1932-
Sykes, Norman, 1897-1961.
Talbot, Louis Thompson, 1889-1976.
Taylor, Graham, 1851-1938.
Temple, William, Abp. of Canterbury, 1881-1944.
Thomas, Joshua, 1776-1853.
Thorwall, Axel Johnson, 1890-1960.
Thurman, Howard, 1899-
Tolton, Augustine, 1854-1897.
Torres Restrepo, Camilo.
Torrey, Charles Turner, 1813-1846.
Turner, Thomas Trussler, 1927-
Twichell, Joseph Hopkins, 1838-1918.
Twitchell, Thomas Donn.
Vale, Roy Ewing, 1885-1959.
Van Orsdel, William Wesley, 1848-1919.
Vaughan, Curry N.
Vogel, Traugott, 1930-
Walsh, Edmund Aloyslus, 1885-1956.
Walsh, John C.
Walsh, Mary, Mother, 1850-1922.
Walther, Carl Ferdinand Wilhelm, 1811-1887.
Waltmire, Baily, 1896-1962.
Ward, C. M.
Ward, Joseph, 1838-1889.
Weems, Mason Locke, 1759-1825.
Wesker, Arnold, 1932-
Wesley, Charles, 1707-1788.
Wesley, Samuel, 1662-1735.
West, Daniel, 1893-1971.
Wheelock, Eleazar, 1711-1779.
Whipple, Henry Benjamin, Bp., 1822-1901.
White, William Charles, Bp., 1873-1960.
Wigglesworth, Michael, 1631-1705.
Wilberforce, Samuel, Bp. of Winchester, 1805-1873.
Willard, Samuel, 1640-1707.
Williams, Daniel Jenkins, 1874-1952.
Williams, Elisha, 1694-1775.
Williams, Lacey Kirk, 1871-1940.
Williams, Roger, 1604-1683.
Winans, William, 1788-1857.
Winchester, Elhanan, 1751-1797.
Wise, John, 1652-1725.
Witherspoon, John, 1723-1794.
Wolsey, Thomas, Cardinal 1475?-1530.
Woodforde, James, 1740-1803.

CLERGY-MAJOR ORDERS
see Bishops; Clergy

CLERGY-GREAT BRITAIN
Barnabas Fellowship.
Dearing, Trevor, 1933-
Dykes, John Bacchus, 1823-1876.
Hale, Matthew Blagdon.
Hall, Joseph, Bp. of Norwich, 1574-1656.
Henley, John, 1692-1756.
Henley, William Ernest, 1849-1903.
Henry, Matthew, 1662-1714.
Laud, William, Abp. of Canterbury, 1573-1645.
Manning, Henry Edward, Cardinal, 1808-1892.
Newton, John, 1725-1807.
Owen, John, 1616-1683.
Rose, Robert, 1704-1751.

CLERGY-RUSSIA
Bissonnette, Georges.

CLERGY, AFRO-AMERICAN
see Afro-American Clergy

CLERGYMEN'S WIVES
Huffman, Carolyn.

CLERKS OF COURT
French, Stanley.

CLOCK AND WATCH MAKERS
Eberhardt, Johann Ludwig, 1758-1839.
Harrison, John, 1693-1776.
Tompion, Thomas, 1639-1713.

CLOWNS
see also Comedians
Grimaldi, Joseph, 1779-1837.
Grimke, Angelina Emily, 1805-1879.
Kelly, Emmett, 1898- -Juvenile Literature.

COACHES (ATHLETICS)
Evans, Jerome, 1930-

COAL MINERS
Mitchell, John, 1870-1919.

COCHITI INDIANS
see Indians of North America-Southwest, New

COHABITATION
see Unmarried Couples

COINING, ILLICIT
see Counterfeits and Counterfeiting

COLITIS
Trachtenberg, Susan.

COLLEGE ADMINISTRATORS
Clap, Thomas, 1703-1767.
Lowell, Abbott Lawrence, 1856-1943.

COLLEGE ATHLETICS
see Track-Athletics

COLLEGE FACULTY
see College Teachers

COLLEGE PRESIDENTS
see Universities and Colleges-Administration

COLLEGE TEACHERS
Baker, George Pierce, 1866-1935.
Langer, William Leonard, 1896-

COLOMBIA
Gaitan, Jorge Eliecer, 1902-1948.

COLONIES-ADMINISTRATION
Winthrop, John, 1588-1649.

COLONIES IN AMERICA
Mayer, Tom.
Mayhew, Thomas, 1593?-1682.

COLONITIS
see Colitis

COLORED PEOPLE (U. S.)
see Afro-Americans

COLUMNISTS
see Journalists

COMANCHE INDIANS
see Indians of North America-The West

COMEDIANS
see also Clowns
Abbott, Bud, 1895-1974.
Allen, Gracie, 1905-
Allen, Woody.
Ball, Lucille Desiree, 1911-
Benny, Jack, 1894-1974.
Berle, Milton.
Brooks, Mel.
Bruce, Lenny.
Chaplin, Charles, 1889-
Cosby, William H.-Juvenile Literature.
Durante, Jimmy.
Fields, W. C., 1879-1946.
Handley, Thomas, 1894-1949.
Hope, Bob, 1903-
Hoyland, Eric.
Kaplan, Gabriel-Juvenile Literature.
Katz, Myron.
Keaton, Buster, 1895-1966.
Laurel, Stan.
Levenson, Samuel, 1911-
Lewis, Joe E.
Lloyd, Harold Clayton, 1894-1971.
Newhart, Robert, 1929- -Juvenile Literature.
Randle, Frank, 1901-1957.
Sanford, John Elroy, 1922-
Silvers, Phil, 1911-
Skelton, Richard Bernard, 1913-
Wynn, Ed.
Youngman, Henny.

COMIC OPERA
see Opera

COMMENTATORS
see Journalists

COMMISSION GOVERNMENT WITH CITY MANAGER
see Municipal Government by City Managers

COMMONS (SOCIAL ORDER)
see Labor and Laboring Classes

COMMUNIST PARTY OF POLAND
Polska Zjednoczona Partia Robotnicza-History.
COMMUNISTS
Budenz, Margaret R.
Buller, Annie, 1896-1973.
Cacchione, Peter V.
Communist International-Biography.
Communist Party of Australia.
Dennis, Peggy.
Gramsci, Antonio, 1891-1937.
Haywood, Harry, 1898-
Lenin, Valdimir Il'ich, 1870-1924.
Partido Comunista De Espana.
Pollitt, Harry, 1890-1960.
Weisbord, Vera Buch, 1895-

COMPOSERS
Arlen, Harold, 1905-
Balfe, Michael William, 1808-1870.
Bartok, Bela, 1881-1945.
Chopin, Fryderyk Francisnek, 1810-1849.
Chotzinoff, Samuel, 1889-1964.
Clark, Eugene Lincoln, 1925-
Collins, Lee, 1901-1960.
Converse, Frederick Shepherd, 1871-1940.
Coslow, Sam, 1902-
Crouch, Andrae.
Falla, Manuel De, 1876-1946.
Gurney, Ivor, 1890-1937-Biography.
Heseltine, Philip, 1894-1930.
Hoffman, Richard, 1831-1909.
Hofmann, Josef, 1876-1957.
Holt, John Caldwell, 1923-
Homer, Sidney, 1864-1953.
Hummel, Johann Nepomuk, 1778-1837.
Joachim, Joseph, 1831-1907.
Kodaly, Zoltan, 1882-1967.
Lehar, Ferenc, 1870-1948.
Leschetitzki, Theodor, 1830-1915.
Liszt, Franz, 1811-1886.
Nairne, Carolina Oliphant Nairne, Baroness, 1766-1845-Biography.
Paderewski, Ignacy Jan, 1860-1941.
Sankey, Ira David, 1840-1908.
Sibelius, Jean, 1865-1957.
Styne, Jule, 1905-
Van Alstyne, Frances Jane Crosby, 1820-1915.
Varese, Edgard, 1883-1965.
COMPOSERS, AMERICAN
Barnard, Charlotte (Alington) 1830-1869.
Berlin, Irving, 1888-
Bernstein, Leonard, 1913-
Billings, William, 1746-1800.
Bloch, Ernest, 1880-1959.
Copland, Aaron, 1900-
Croce, Jim-Juvenile Literature.
Dett, Robert Nathaniel, 1882-1943.
Dietz, Howard, 1896-
Foote, Arthur William, 1853-1937.
Foster, Stephen Collins, 1826-1864.
Fry, William Henry, 1813-1864.
Gershwin, George, 1898-1937.
Gorman, Lawrence, 1846-1917.
Grainger, Percy Aldridge, 1882-1961.
Herbert, Victor, 1859-1924.
Ives, Charles Edward, 1874-1954.
Joplin, Scott, 1868-1917.
Kern, Jerome, 1885-1945.
King, Carole-Juvenile Literature.
Medema, Ken.
Menotti, Gian Carlo, 1911-
Menuhin Family.
Menuhin, Yehudi, 1916-
Ornstein, Leo, 1895-
Porter, Cole, 1891-1964.
Rodgers, Richard, 1902-
Rorem, Ned, 1923-
Schuman, William Howard, 1910-
Sondheim, Stephen.
Sousa, John Philip, 1854-1932.
Thomson, Virgil, 1896-
Waller, Fats, 1904-1943.
Willson, Meredith, 1902-
COMPOSERS, AUSTRIAN
Berg, Alban, 1885-1935.
Bruckner, Anton, 1824-1896.
Haydn, Joseph, 1732-1809.
Mahler, Gustav, 1860-1911.
Mozart, Johann Chrysostom Wolfgang Amadeus, 1756-1791.
Schonberg, Arnold, 1874-1951.
Schubert, Franz Peter, 1797-1828.
Straus, Oscar, 1870-1954.
Strauss, Johann, 1804-1849.
Strauss, Richard, 1864-1949.
Webern, Anton Von, 1883-1945.
Wechsberg, Joseph, 1907-
Wolf, Hugo, 1800-1903.
COMPOSERS, BRITISH
Bliss, Arthur, Sir, 1891-1975.
Brian, Havergal, 1876-1972.
Britten, Benjamin, 1913-
Byrd, William, 1542 or 3-1623.
Coleridge-Taylor, Samuel, 1875-1912.
Delius, Frederick, 1862-1934.
Elgar, Edward William, Sir, 1857-1934.
Handel, Georg Friedrich, 1685-1759.
Hess, Myra, 1890- 1965.
Holst, Gustav, 1874-1934.
Milton, John, 1563 (Ca.)-1647.
Purcell, Henry, 1658 or 9-1695.
Sargent, Malcolm, Sir, 1895-1967.
Smyth, Dame Ethel Mary, 1858-1944.
Stanford, Charles Villiers, Sir, 1852-1924.
Sullivan, Arthur Seymour, Sir 1842-1900.
Tallis, Thomas, 1505(Ca.)-1585.
Taverner, John, 1495 (Ca.)-1545.
Tovey, Donald Francis, Sir, 1875-1940.
Vaughan Williams, Ralph, 1872-
Weelkes, Thomas, 1575 (Ca.)-1623.
Wilder, Alec.
Wynne, David.
COMPOSERS, CZECH
Dvorak, Anton, 1841-1904.
Janacek, Leos, 1854-1928.
Martinu, Bohuslav, 1890-1959.
COMPOSERS, DANISH
Nielsen, Carl, 1865-1931.
COMPOSERS, FRENCH
Alkan, Charles Henri Valentin, 1813-1888.
Berlioz, Hector, 1803-1869.
Bizet, Georges, 1838-1875.
Boulanger, Lili, 1893-1918.
Boulez, Pierre, 1925-
Chaminade, Cecile Louise Stephanie, 1861-1944.
Chausson, Ernest, 1855-1899.
Debussy, Claude, 1862-1918.
Faure, Gabriel Urbain, 1845-1924.
Franck, Cesar Auguste, 1822-1890.
Grandjany, Marcel, 1891-1975.
Guillaume De Machaut, D. 1377.
Indy, Vincent D', 1851-1931.
Massenet, Jules Emile Frederic, 1842-1912.
Offenbach, Jacques, 1819-1880.
Poulenc, Francis, 1899-1963.
Ravel, Maurice, 1875-1937.
Roussel, Albert Charles Paul, 1869-1937.
Satie, Erik, 1866-1925.
COMPOSERS, GERMAN
Bach, Johann Sebastian, 1685-1750.
Beethoven, Ludwig Van, 1770-1827.
Brahms, Johannes, 1833-1897.
Gluck, Christoph Willibald, Ritter Von, 1714-1787.
Handel, Georg Friedlich, 1685-1759.
Hauptmann, Moritz, 1792-1868.
Hindemith, Paul, 1895-1963.
Hoffmann, Ernst Theodor Amadeus, 1776-1822.
Mendelssoh-Bartholdy, Felix, 1809-1847.
Moscheles, Ignaz, 1794-1870.
Orff, Carl, 1895-
Schumann, Clara Josephine Wieck, 1819-1896
Schutz, Heinrich, 1585-1672.
Telemann, Georg Philipp, 1681-1767.
Wagner, Richard, 1813-1883.
Weber, Karl Maria Friedrich Ernst, Freiherr Von, 1786-1826.
COMPOSERS, ITALIAN
Bellini, Vincenzo, 1801-1835.
Boccherini, Luigi, 1745-1805.
Cavalli, Pier Francesco, 1602-1676.
Cherubini, Luigi, 1760-1842.
Clementi, Muzio, 1752-1832.
Corelli, Arcangelo, 1653-1713.
Donizetti, Gaetano, 1797-1840.
Monteverdi, Claudio, 1567-1643.
Paisiello, Giovanni, 1740-1816.
Palestrina, Giovanni Pierluigi Da, 1525?-1594.
Puccini, Giacomo, 1858-1924.
Rossini, Gioacchino Antonio, 1792-1868.
Veracini, Francesco Maria, 1690-1768.
Verdi, Giuseppe, 1813-1901.
Vicentino, Nicola, 1511-1572.
Vivaldi, Antonio, 1678-1741.
COMPOSERS, NORWEGIAN
Grieg, Edvard Hagerup, 1843-1907.
COMPOSERS, RUSSIAN
Borodin, Aleksandr Porfir'evich, 1834-1887.
Chaikovskii, Petr Ilich, 1840-1893.
Glinka, Mikhail Ivanovich, 1804-1857.
Prokofev Sergel Sergeevich, 1891-1953.
Rachmaninoff, Sergei, 1873-1943.
Rimskii-Korsakov, Nikolai Andreevich, 1844-1908.
Skriabin, Aleksandr Nikolaevich, 1872-1915.
Stravinskii, Igor Fedorovich, 1882-1971.
CONDUCTORS (MUSIC)
Barbirolli, John, Sir, 1899-1970.
Beecham, Thomas, Bart., 1879-1961.
Bernstein, Leonard, 1913-
Davis, Colin, 1927-
Fiedler, Arthur, 1894-
King, Karl, 1891-1971.
Koussevitzky, Serge, 1874-1951.
Last, James.
Lombardo, Guy, 1902-
Mehta, Zubin.
Miller, Glenn, 1909-1944-Discography.
Mitropoulos, Dimitri, 1896-1960.
Monteux, Pierre, 1875-
Nichois. Loring.
Shaw, Robert Lawson, 1916-
Thomas, Theodore, 1835-1905.
Toscanini, Arturo, 1867-1957.
Welk, Lawrence, 1904-
Wood, Henry Joseph, Sir, 1869-1944.
CONFEDERATE STATES OF AMERICA–ARMY
Shelby, Joseph Orville, 1830-1897.
CONFEDERATE STATES OF AMERICA–BIOGRAPHY
Barrow, James, 1841-1864.
Beauregard, Pierre Gustave Toutant, 1818-1893.
Benjamin, Judah Philip, 1811-1884.
Brown, Albert Gallatin, 1813-1880.
Cabell, William Lewis, 1827-1911.
Confederate States of America. Army-Biography-Addresses, Essays, Lectures.
Heth, Henry, 1825-1899.
Hindman, Thomas Carmichael, 1818-1868.
Holmes, Emma, 1838-1910.
Inzer, John Washington, 1834-1928.
Jackson, Thomas Jonathan, 1824-1863.
Newman, Howard Walker, 1840-1904.
CONFEDERATE STATES OF AMERICA–NAVY
Alabama (Confederate Cruiser)
Kell, John McIntosh, 1823-1900.
CONFUCIANISM
Hsun, Yueh, 148-209.
CONGRESSMEN
see Legislators
CONNECTICUT–BIOGRAPHY
Davenport, Abraham, 1715-1789.
CONQUISTADORS
see America–Discovery and Exploration
CONSERVATIONISTS
see also Ecologists
Barker, Elliott Speer, 1886-
Bennett, Hugh Hammond, 1881-
Pinchot, Gifford, 1865-1946.
CONSTRUCTION
see Building
CONSULTANTS, BUSINESS
see Business Consultants
CONSUMER ADVERTISING
see Advertising
CONSUMER PROTECTION
Nader, Ralph.
CONTORTION
see Acrobats and Acrobatism
CONTRABAND TRADE
see Smuggling
CONVERTS
see also Buddhist converts, Muslim converts, etc. for works on converts to religions other than Christianity
Basansky, Bill.
Braemer, Alice.
Brannaka, Marjorie, 1927-
Bullock, Randy.
Collins, Dan.
Converts, Mormon.
Coss, Richard David, 1944-
Hayes, Raymond Lee.
Levitt, Zola.
Maharaj, Rabindranath R.
Maweja Apollo.
Norman, Joyce.
Robinson, Jay, 1930-
Schiffman, Steve.
Stanchfield, Wilma.
Tarrants, Thomas A.
Walter Hoving Home.
Warnke, Mike.
York, Thomas Lee.
CONVERTS, CATHOLIC
Antony, Judith.
CONVERTS FROM JUDAISM
Frydland, Rachmiel.
Philip, Scotty, 1858-1911-Juvenile Literature.
CONVICTS
see Prisoners
COOK-BOOKS
see Cookery
COOKERY
Escoffier, Auguste, 1846-1935-Juvenile Literature.
COOKERY, AMERICAN
Darden Family.
COOKERY, AMISH
see Cookery, American
COOKERY, PENNSYLVANIA GERMAN
see Cookery, American
COOKERY, SOUTHERN
see Cookery, American
CORPORATION EXECUTIVES
see Executives
CORRECTION OFFICER
see Correctional Personnel
CORRECTIONAL PERSONNEL
Jimenez, Janey.
Price, John Giles, 1808-1857.
Sturgis, Margie.
CORRECTIONS EMPLOYEES
see Correctional Personnel
CORRESPONDENTS, FOREIGN
see Journalists
CORSAIRS
see Pirates; Privateering
COSMETOLOGY
see Beauty Culture
COSMONAUTS
see Astronauts
COSTUME DESIGN
Poiret, Paul.
Sharaff, Irene.
COSTUME DESIGNERS–BIOGRAPHY
Saint Laurent, Yves.
COUNSELING
see also Interviewing
Lennhoff, F. G.
COUNTERFEITS AND COUNTERFEITING
Baudin, Robert.
COUNTRY MUSICIANS
Acuff, Roy.
Davis, Jimmie, 1900-
Denver, John.
Harkreader, Sidney J.
Jennings, Waylon.
Parton, Dolly.
Pride, Charley-Juvenile Literature.
Stricklin, Al, 1908-
Williams, Hank, 1923-1953.
Wynette, Tammy.
COUPLES, UNMARRIED
see Unmarried Couples
COURT AND COURTIERS
see Courts and Courtiers
COURT CLERKS
see Clerks of Court
COURT FAVORITES
see Favorites, Royal
COURTIERS
see Courts and Courtiers
COURTS AND COURTIERS
see also Favorites, Royal; Kings and Rulers; Princes
also subdivision Courts and Courtiers under names of countries, e.g. Great Britain–Court and Courtiers
Castiglione, Baldassare, Conte, 1478-1529.
Dyer, Edward, Sir, 1543-1607.
Hamilton, James, 1st Duke of, 1606-1649.
Hanover, House of.
Leicester, Robert Dudley, Earl of, 1532?-1588..
Lenclos, Anne, Called Ninon De, 1620-1705.
Marie Adelaide De Savoie, Duchess of Burgundy, Dauphine of France, 1685-1712.
Somerset, Edward Seymour, 1st Duke of, 1506?-1552.
Somerset, Frances (Howard) Carr, Countess of, 1593-1632.
Sophia Dorothea, Consort of George I, King of Great Britain, 1666-1726.
Sophie, Consort of Ernest Augustus, Elector of Hanover. 1630-1714.
Verney, Edmund, Sir 1590-1642.
Victoria, Consort of Frederick III, German Emperor, 1840-1901.
Worth, Charles Frederick, 1825-1895.
COWBOYS
see also Ranch Life; Rodeos
Alford, Ed., 1901-
Autry, Gene, 1907-
Blanton, Henry.
Bond, J. T., 1866-1947.
Glass, Charlie, D. 1937.
McJunkin, George-Juvenile Literature.
Mossman, Burton C., 1867-
Pickett, Bill, 1860 (Ca.)-1932.
Polk, Frank, 1908-
Randall, Dick.
Schmedding, Joseph, 1887-
Siringo, Charles A., 1855-1928.
Thorp, Nathan Howard, 1867-1940.
CRAFTSMEN
see Artisans
CREEK INDIANS
see Indians of North America–Eastern States
CRICKET
Amiss, Dennis.
Dodds, Thomas Carter, 1919-
Jai, L. P., 1902-1968.
Tate, Maurice, 1895-1956.
Trueman, Freddie, 1931-
Wadekar, Ajit, 1941-
CRIME AND CRIMINALS
Here are entered general works. For books dealing with crime and criminals in specific areas see the appropriate geographic subdivision, e.g. Crime and Criminals–United States.
see also Anarchism and Anarchists; Assassination; Brigands and Robbers; Criminologists; Delinquents; Gangs; Impostors and Imposture

Clouser, John William.
Clower, Jerry, 1926-
Cohen, Michael Mickey.
Coppola, Ann Drahmann, 1921-1962.
Corona, Juan Vallejo.
Costello, Frank.
Crimaldi, Charles.
Crippen, Hawley Harvey, 1862-1910.
Fish, Albert.
Gregg, Troy.
Hill, Joan Olive Robinson, 1931-1969.
Hill, Virginia.
Horsley, Albert E., 1866-1954.
Leibowitz, Samuel Simon, 1893-
Leopold, Nathan Freudenthal, 1904 or 5-1971.
Linda Marie, 1943-
Logan, Harvey, Ca. 1867-Ca. 1910.
Luciano, Charles.
Luparelli, Joseph.
Madsen, Christian, 1852-1944.
Rubinstein, Serge, 1908-1955.

Scolnick, Sylvan.
Smith, Thomas James, 1840-1870 -- Juvenile Literature.
Spaggiari, Albert.
Taylor, Leslie Joseph Theodore, 1888-1927.
Vasquez, Tiburcio, 1835-1875.
Vaus, James Arthur.
White, Harry Dexter,1892-1948.
Wolfe, Willy, 1951-1974.
CRIME AND CRIMINALS–BIOGRAPHY
Markel, Robert.
Meegeren, Han Van, 1889-1947.
Merrett, John Donald, 1908-1954.
CRIME AND CRIMINALS–CANADA
Caron, Roger, 1938-
Morrison, Donald.
Pollock, Donald.
CRIME AND CRIMINALS–FRANCE
Brinvilliers, Marie Madeleine (D'Aubray) Gobelin, Marquise De, 1630-1676.
Goldman, Pierre, 1944-
Lustig, Victor, 1890-1947.
Manolescu, Georges, 1871-1911.
Milani, Felix, 1905-
CRIME AND CRIMINALS–GREAT BRITAIN
Biggs, Ronald Arthur, 1929-
Kray, Charles, 1927-
O'Connor, Jimmy.
Probyn, Walter, 1931-
Rais, Gilles De Laval, Seigneur De, 1404-1440.
Sheppard(Jack, 1702-1724.
CRIME AND CRIMINALS–RUSSIA
Demin, Mikhail.
CRIME AND CRIMINALS–UNITED STATES
Allen, John, 1942-
Atkins, Susan, 1948-
Baca, Elfego, 1864-1945.
Baker, Robert Gene.
Barrow, Clyde, 1909-1934.
Barry, Arthur, 1896-
Baudin, Robert.
Bergdoll, Grover Cleveland.
Berkowitz, David Richard, 1953-
Black Jack, 1871-1897?
Borden, Lizzie Andrew, 1860-1927.
Capone, Alphonse, 1899-1947.
Carr, Robert Frederick, 1943-
Carrasco, Fred Gomez.
Cassidy, Butch, B. 1866 or 7.
Colson, Charles W.
Dalton Family.
De La Roche, Harry, 1958-
DeAutremont, Hugh.
DeAutremont, Ray.
Diamond, John, 1895 or 6-1931.
Dillinger, John, 1902-1934.
Donato, Joe.
Flegenheimer, Arthur, 1900 or 1-1935.
Fugate, Caril Ann.
Gacy, John Wayne.
Gallo, Joey, 1929-1972.
Geraway, William R.
Giancana, Sam, 1908-1975.
Giuliano, Salvatore, 1922-1950.
Golden, Jerry.
Grivas, George, 1898-
Hall, Loran.
Hellerman, Michael.
Holliday, John Henry, 1825?-1887.
James, Frank, 1844-1915.
James Jesse Woodson, 1847-1882.
Jennings, James S.
Jones, Jim, 1931-1978.
Ketchum, Thomas Edward, 1865 or 6-1901.
Knowles, Paul John.
Lansky, Meyer, 1902-
McCrary, Sherman.
Mann, William D'Alton.
Manson, Charles, 1934-
Middleton, David C., 1851-1913.
Mullen, Herbert William.
Murrieta, Joaquin, 1828 or 9-1853.
Palliko, Alan Joseph, 1937-
Panzram, Carl, 1891-1930.
Parker, George LeRoy, 1867-
Powers, Jack, D. 1860.
Quick, Thomas, 1734-1796.
Ray, James Earl, 1928-
Reed, Nathaniel, 1862-1950.
Rogers, Kenneth Paul.
Ruby, Jack.
Selmier, Dean.
Sherbondy, James Bryan, 1919-1969.
Slade, Joseph Alfred, 1829-1864.
Speck, Richard, 1941-
Starr, Belle (Shirley) 1848-1889.
Stroud, Robert.
Swaggi, Vincent Norfior, 1914-
Thatcher, Philip.
Thorson, Ralph Edgar.
Torres, Manual J.
Torres, Victor.
Trapnell, Garrett Brock, 1938-
Wainewright, Thomas Griffiths, 1794-1847.
Watson, Frank, 1921-
Weil, Joseph R.
Younger, Cole, 1844-1916.
CRIME AND CRIMINALS–WEST
Bonney, William H., 1839-1881.
Warner, Matt, 1864-1938.

CRIME SYNDICATES
see Gangs
CRIMINALS
see Crime and Criminals
CRIMINOLOGISTS
Glueck, Eleanor Touroff, 1898-1972.
CRIMINOLOGY
see Crime and Criminals
CRIPPLES
see Physically Handicapped
CRITICISM
see also Hermeneutics; Literature–History and Criticism
also Criticism in specific fields e.g. Art Criticism; English Literature–History and Criticism; also names of individuals, with or without the subdivision Criticism and Interpretation
Johnson, Samuel 1709-1784.
Kazin, Alfred, 1915-
Sherman, Stuart Pratt, 1881-1926.
CRITICISM–GERMANY
Heine, Heinrich, 1797-1856.
CRITICISM–UNITED STATES
Gayle, Addison, 1932-
CRITICISM, TEXTUAL
Lamb, Charles, 1775-1834.
CROPS
see Agriculture
CROSS-COUNTRY RUNNING
see Running
CROW INDIANS
see Indians of North America–The West
CRUSADES
Here are entered works on the crusades in general. Specific crusades are listed chronologically at the end of this entry.
Raymond III, of Tripolis, 1140 (Ca.)-1187.
CRUSADES–FIRST, 1096-1099
Tancred, 1075 (Ca.)-1112.
CRYPTANALYSIS
see Cryptography
CRYPTOGRAPHY
Friedman, William Frederick, 1891-1969.
CUB SCOUTS
see Boy Scouts
CUBAN REFUGEES
see Refugees–Cuba
CUBANS IN THE UNITED STATES
Versalles, Zoilo, 1940-
CUBO-FUTURISM
see Futurism
CULTURAL ANTHROPOLOGY
see Ethnology
CYCLING
see also Motorcycles; Motorcycling
Loher, George T.
CZECH COMPOSERS
see Composers, Czech

D

DAIRIES
see Dairying
DAIRY INDUSTRY
see Dairying
DAIRYING
Borden, Gail, 1801-1874.
DAKOTA INDIANS
see Indians of North America–The West
DANCERS
Adam, Adolphe Charles, 1803-1856.
Alonso, Alicia.
Astaire, Fred.
Baryshnikov, Mikhail, 1948-
Bruhn, Erik.
Castle, Vernon, 1887-1918.
Cecchetti, Enrico, 1850-1928.
Duncan, Irma.
Duncan, Isadora, 1878-1927.
Dunham, Katherine.
Enters, Angna, 1907-
Fonteyn, Margot, Dame, 1919-
Frankel, Emily.
Greco, Jose.
Haller, Lelia.
Hayden, Melissa.
Horton, Lester, 1906-1953.
Hughes, Russell Meriwether, 1898-
Humphrey, Doris, 1895-1958.
Ivanov, Lev Ivanovich, 1834-1901.
Kain, Karen.
Karsavina, Tamara.
Kelly, Gene, 1912-
Kshesinskaia, Matilda Feliksovna, 1872-1971.
Kyasht, Lydia.
Laban, Rudolf Von, 1879-1958.
Legat, N Ikolai Gustavovich, 1869-1937.
Leningrad. Gosudarstvennoe Khoreograficheskoe Uchilische.
Mitchell, Arthur, 1934- -Juvenile Literature.
Montez, Lola, 1818-1861.
Murray, Arthur, 1895-
Nijinsky, Waslaw, 1890-1950.
Nureyev, Rudolf Hametovitch, 1938-
Page, Ruth.
Panov, Valery, 1938-
Pavlova, Anna, 1881-1931.
Plisetskaia, Maiia Mikhailovna, 1926-
Preobrazhenskaia, Olga Osipovna, 1870-1962.
Shawn, Ted, 1891-1972.
Shearer, Moira, 1926-
Sibley, Antoinette.
Talbot, William Henry Fox, 1800-1877.
Tallchief, Maria.
Tamiris, Helen, 1905-1966.
Ulanova, Galina Sergeevna, 1910-
Zucchi, Virginia, 1849-1930.
DANCING, BALLET
see Ballet Dancing
DANDIES
Brummell, George Bryan, 1778-1840.
DANDYISM
see Dandies
DANISH COMPOSERS
see Composers, Danish
DAUGHTERS OF THE AMERICAN REVOLUTION
Daughters of the American Revolution. Georgia. Nancy Hart Chapter, Milledgeville-History.
DEAF
Dowdy, Leonard, 1927-
Kinney, Richard, 1923-
DEAF MUTES
see Deaf
DECENNALIA
see Roman Emperors
DECORATION AND ORNAMENT–GREAT BRITAIN
Klimsch, Karl, 1812-1890.
DECORATIVE ARTS
see Art Industries and Trade
also the specific subjects referred to under these headings
DECOYS (HUNTING)
Ward, Lemuel T.
DEEP-SEA EXPLORATION
see Marine Biology
DELAWARE INDIANS
see Indians of North America–Eastern States
DELINQUENCY, JUVENILE
see Juvenile Delinquency
DELINQUENTS
see also Crime and Criminals; Juvenile Delinquency
Torrio, Johnny.
DELUSIONS
see Impostors and Imposture; Swindlers and Swindling; Witchcraft
DEMENTIA PRAECOX
see Schizophrenia
DEMOCRACY
see also Aristocracy; Suffrage
Friedenwald, Hary, 1864-1950.
DEMOCRATIC PARTY
O'Brien, Lawrence F.
DENTISTS
Morton, William Thomas Green, 1819-1868.
National Dental Association (Founded 1932)-Biography.
DEPENDENTS OF MILITARY PERSONNEL
see Army Wives
DERMATOLOGY
Duhring, Louis Adolphus, 1845-1913.
DESTRUCTION OF THE JEWS (1939-1945)
see Holocaust, Jewish (1939-1945)
DETECTIVES
see also Police; Secret Service
Blye, Irwin.
Bonora, Matt.
Burns, William John, 1861-1932.
Canter, Louis, 1797-1865.
Cirile, Marie.
Covelli, Pat.
Franklin, Lyn.
Hume, James B., 1827-1904.
Pinkerton, Allan, 1819-1884.
Ponzi, Tom.
Smith, George Gordon, 1905-1970.
DEVIATION, SEXUAL
see Sexual Deviation
DHYANA (SECT)
see Zen Buddhism
DIASPORA OF THE JEWS
see Jews–Diaspora
DICTATORS
Amin, Idi, 1925-
Franco Bahamonde, Francisco, 1892-
Mussolini, Benito, 1883-1945.
DIETETICS
see Nutrition
DIPLOMATS
see also Ambassadors; Military Attaches
Barmine, Alexandre.
Barrett, John, 1866-1938.
Clay, Cassius Marcellus, 1810-1903.
Clay, John Randolph, 1808-1885.
Coolidge, Archibald Cary, 1866-1928.
Cremer, William Randal, Sir, 1828-1908.
Emmerson, John K.
Eon De Beaumont, Charles Genevieve Louis Auguste Andre Timothee D'. 1728-1810.
Eulenburg-Hertefeld, Philipp, Furst Zu, 1847-1921.
Gallatin, James, 1796-1876.
Gentz, Friedrich Von, 1764-1832.
Grew, Joseph Clark, 1880-1965.
Hammarskjold, Dag, 1905-1961.
Harris, Townsend, 1804-1878.
Harsono, Ganis.
Haymerle, Heinrich, Freiherr Von, 1828-1881.
Hope, Ashley Guy, 1914-
Houghton, Aianson Bigelow, 1863-1941.
Humphreys, David, 1752-1818.
Huygens, Constantijn, Heer Van Zullichem, 1596-1687.
Jaisohn, Philip, 1868-1951.
Jensen, Povl Bang, 1909-1959.
Jones, John Coffin.
Kiep, Otto, 1886-1944.
Lane, Arthur Bliss, 1894-1956.
Lebec, Peter, D. 1837.
Lee, Arthur, 1740-1792.
Lee, William, 1740-1784.
Lesseps, Ferdinand Marie, Vicomte De, 1805-1894.
Lind, John, 1854-1930.
Madariaga, Salvador De, 1886-
Masaryk, Jan Garrigue, 1886-1948.
Masaryk, Tomas Garrigue, Pres. Czechoslovak Republic, 1850-1937.
Metternich-Winneburg, Clemens Lothar Wenzel, Furst Von, 1773-1859.
Morland, Samuel, Sir, Bart., 1625-1695.
Morrison, DeLesseps Story, 1912-1964.
Motley, John Lothrop, 1814-1877.
Murray, William Vans, 1760-1803.
Nabuco, Joaquim, 1849-1910.
Page, Thomas Nelson, 1853-1922.
Panikkar, Kavalam Madhava.
Parrott, Cecil, Sir, 1909-
Perth, James Eric Drummond, 16th Earl of, 1876-
Pestalozzi, Johann Heinrich, 1746-1827.
Reinsch, Paul Samuel, 1869-1923.
Rockhill, William Woodville, 1854-1914.
Ros, Herbert Spencer, 1909-
Urquhart, David, 1805-1877.
Walters, Vernon A.
Washburne, Elihu Benjamin, 1816-1887.
Wotton, Henry, Sir, 1568-1639.

DIPLOMATS' WIVES
Chandler, Zachariah, 1813-1879.
Churchill, Clementine Ogilvy Hozier, Lady, 1885-
Cowles, Anna (Roosevelt) 1855-1931.
DIRECTORS, MOVING-PICTURE
see Moving-Picture Producers and Directors
DISABILITIES, POLITICAL (GREAT BRITAIN)
see Dissenters, Religious–England
DISABLED
see Handicapped
DISCIPLESHIP
see Christian Life
DISCOURSES
see Lectures and Lecturing
DISCOVERERS
see Explorers
DISEASES, MENTAL
see Mental Illness
DISEASES OF THE BLOOD, DISEASES OF THE BRAIN, DISEASES OF THE HEART
see subdivision Diseases under specific subjects, e.g. Blood–Diseases; Brain–Diseases
DISPERSION OF THE JEWS
see Jews–Diaspora
DISSENTERS
Bukovskii, Vladimir Konstantinovich, 1942-
Nekipelov Viktor, 1928-
Simons, Algie Martin, 1870-1950.
DISSENTERS, RELIGIOUS–ENGLAND
Ambrose, Isaac, 1604-1664.
DISTRICT NURSES
see Nurses and Nursing
DIVERS
Mikimoto, K Okichi, 1858-1954.
DIVINE HEALING
see Christian Science; Faith-Cure
DIVING, SKIN
see Skin Diving
DIVORCEES
Braudy, Susan.
Hunter, Brenda.
Hurst, Gloria, 1928-
Willison, Marilyn Murray.
Young, Amy Ross.
DO-IT-YOURSELF WORK
see specific fields of activity for do-it-yourself manuals in such fields, e.g. House Painting; Interior Decoration
DOCTORS
see Physicians
DOG BREEDING
Bryant, Traphes.
DOGS–BREEDING
see Dog Breeding

E

F

G

Johnston, Joseph Eggleston, 1807-1891.
Keitel, Wilhelm, 1882-1946.
Kosciuszko, Tadeusz Andrzej Bonawentura, 1746-1817.
Koxinga, 1624-1662.
Kutuzov, Mikhail Illarionovich Svetleishii Kniaz Smolenskii, 1745-1813.
Lawrence, Henry Montgomery, Sir, 1806-1857.
Lee, Henry, 1756-1818.
Lee, Robert Edward, 1807-1870.
Lowell, Charles Russell, 1835-1864.
MacArthur, Douglas, 1880-1964.
Marion, Francis, 1732-1795.
Marius, C.
Meade, George Gordon, 1815-1872.
Means, Gaston Bullock, 1879-1938.
Mercer, Hugh, 1725 (Ca.)-1777.
Mihailovic, Draza, 1893-1946.
Miles, Nelson Appleton, 1839-1925.
Milne, George Francis Milne, Baron, 1866-1948.
Moore, John, Sir, 1761-1809.
Morillo y Morillo, Pablo, Marques De la Puerta, 1778-1837.
Mouton, Alfred, 1829-1864.
Newcastle, William Cavendish, Duke of, 1592-1676.
Patton, George Smith, 1885-1945-
Paxton, Harry T.
Pender, William Dorsey, 1834-1863.
Pershing, John Joseph, 1860-1948.
Petain, Henri Philippe Benoni Omer, 1856-1951.
Pickens, Andrew, 1739-1817.
Pope, Vyvyan Vavasour, 1891-1941.
Pryor, Roger Atkinson, 1828-1919.
Puller, Lewis Burwell, 1898-
Putnam, Israel, 1718-1790.
Quiroga, Juan Facundo, 1790-1835.
Ravenstein, Johann Theodore Von, B. 1889.
Roe, John Septimus, 1797-1878.
Rosecrans, William Starke, 1819-1898.
Santa Anna, Antonio Lopez De, Pres. Mexico, 1794?-1876.
Scharnhorst, Gerhard Johann David Von.
Sheridan, Philip Henry, 1831-1888.
Sherman, William Tecumseh, 1820-1891.
Slim, William Slim, 1st Viscount, 1891-1970.
Smith, Sam G., 1794-1835.
Stark, John, 1728-1822.
Steele, Frederick, 1819-1868-Manuscripts-Exhibitions.
Sternberg, George Miller, 1838-1915.
Stewart, Alexander Peter, 1821-1908.
Sullivan, John, 1740-1795.
Sumner, Edwin Vose, 1797-1863.
Te Kooti, 1830?-1893.
Thomas, George Henry, 1816-1870.
Tran Van On, 1917-
Van Dorn, Earl, 1820-1863.
Waldersee, Alfred Heinrich Karl Ludwig, Graf Von, 1832-1904.
Wallenstein, Alberecht Wenzel Eusebius Von. Herzog Zu Friendland. 1583-1634.
Ward, Artemas, 1727-1800.
Wauchope, Andrew Gilbert, 1846-1899.
Weedon, George, 1734-1793.
Weizman, Ezer, 1924-
Wellington, Arthur Wellesley, 1st Duke of, 1769-1852.
Wellington, Gerald Wellesley, 7th Duke of, 1885-
Westmoreland, William Childs, 1914-
Wilson, James Harrison, 1837-1925.
Wilson, Robert Thomas, Sir, 1777-1849.
Wolfe, James, 1727-1759.
Worth, William Jenkins, 1794-1849.
Worthington, Frederic Franklin.
Yadin, Yigael, 1917-
Zizka, Jan, 1360 (Ca.)-1424.

GENETICS
Morgan, Thomas Hunt, 1866-1945.

GEOGNOSY
Jefferson, Mark Sylvester William, 1863-1949.

GEOGRAPHERS
Al-Muqaddas I, Muhammad Ibn Ahmad, B. Ca. 946.
Davidson, George, 1825-1911.
Erskine, Robert, 1735-1780.
Kropotkin, Petr Alekseevich, Kniaz, 1842-1921.
Letchworth, William Pryor, 1823-1910.
Ratzel, Friedrich, 1844-1904.

GEOGRAPHICAL DISTRIBUTION OF MAN
see Ethnology

GEOLOGISTS
Hall, James, 1811-1898.
Hooke, Robert.
Houghton, Douglass, 1809-1845.
King, Clarence, 1842-1901.
Lawson, Andrew Cowper, 1861-1952.
Leith, Charles Kenneth, 1875-1956.
Lorenz, Konrad.
Lyell, Charles, Sir, Bart., 1797-1875.
Mallowan, Max Edgar Lucien.
Powell, John Wesley, 1834-1902.
Rominger, Carl Ludwig, 1820-1907.
Silliman, Benjamin, 1779-1864.
Smith, William, 1769-1839.
Sorby, Henry Clifton, 1826-1908.
Udden, Johan August, 1859-1932.

GEORGIA
Graham, Brenda Knight.

King, Thomas Butler, 1800-1864.
McKay, Frances Peabody.

GEORGIA-GENEALOGY
Fraser Family.

GERMAN AUTHORS
see Authors, German

GERMAN REFORMED CHURCH (U. S.)
see Reformed Church in the United States

GERMAN RESISTANCE MOVEMENT
see Anti-Nazi Movement

GERMANS IN THE UNITED STATES
Crouch, John Russell, 1916-
Krueger, Max, 1851-1927.

GERMANY-ARMY
Riedesel, Friedrich Adolf, Freiherr Von, 1738-1800.

GERMANY-BIOGRAPHY
Beck, Ludwig August Theodor, 1880-1944.
Bonhoeffer Family.
Bormann, Martin, 1900-
Braun, Eva.
Friedrich I, Barbarossa, Emperor of Germany, 1121-1190.
Friedrich II, Emperor of Germany, 1194-1250.
Friedrich III, German Emperor, 1831-1888.
Friedrich Wilhelm, Elector of Brandenburg, Called the Great Elector, 1620-1688.
Friesen, Heinrich B., 1837-1926.
Hartmann, Erich, 1922-
Paul Wilhelm, Duke of Wurtemberg, 1797-1860.
Riedesel, Friederike Charlotte Luise (Von Massow) Freifrau Von. 1746-1808.

GERMS
see Bacteriology

GERONTOLOGY
see Aged

GHOSTS
see also Psychical Research; Spiritualism
Bartell, Jan Bryant.

GOLF
Argea, Angelo.
Baugh, Laura, 1955-
Blalock, Jane.
Casper, Billy, 1931-
Elder, Lee, 1934- -Juvenile Literature.
Jones, Robert Tyre, 1902-
Lazaro, Joe.
Miller, Johnny, 1947- -Juvenile Literature.
Nicklaus, Jack.
Palmer, Arnold, 1929-
Player, Gary.
Sanders, George Douglas, 1933-
Trevino, Lee-Juvenile Literature.

GOSPEL MUSIC
Rhea, Claude H.
Sego, James, 1927-
Wilkin, Marijohn.

GOVERNMENT EMPLOYEES
see Civil Service

GOVERNMENT INFORMATION SERVICES
see Government Publicity

GOVERNMENT PUBLICITY
see also Radio Broadcasting
Gentz, Friedrich Von, 1764-1832.

GOVERNORS-UNITED STATES
Allen, Henry Watkins, 1820-1866.
Alston, Joseph, 1778-1816.
Bates, Frederick, 1777-1825.
Brown, Edmund Gerald, 1938-
Brown, Joseph Emerson, 1821-1894.
Catts, Sidney Johnston, 1863-1936.
Crane, Winthrop Murray, 1853-1920.
Crawford, Samuel Johnson, 1835-1913.
Darden, Colgate Whitehead, 1897-
Exon, John James, 1921-
Gardner, Oliver Max, 1882-1947.
Goebel, William, 1856-1900.
Hamilton, Andrew Jackson, 1815-1875.
Hobby, William Pettus, 1878-
Longley, James B.
Mitchell, Henry Laurens, 1831-1903.
Moore, Thomas Overton, 1804-1876.
Pacheco, Romualdo, 1831-1899-Juvenile Literature.
Penalosa, Diego Dionisio De, 1624-1687.
Reagan, Ronald.
Rockefeller, Winthrop, 1912-
Russell, Daniel Lindsay, 1845-1908.
Salcedo, Manuel Maria De, D. 1813.
Spry, William, 1864-1929.
Stevens, Isaac Ingalls, 1818-1862.
Swain, David Lowry, 1801-1868--Juvenile Literature.
Thompson, James R., 1936-
Williams, William Frank, 1877-1963.

GRANDPARENTS
Kaye, Morris, 1901- -Juvenile Literature.
Seaman, SylviaS.

GRAPHIC ARTS
see also Bookbinding
Eyerly, Ray, 1894-

GRAY FRIARS
see Franciscans

GREAT BRITAIN-ADMIRALTY
Mountbatten, Louis Mountbatten, Earl, 1900-
Mountevans, Edward Ratcliffe Garth Russell Evans, Baron, 1880-1957.

GREAT BRITAIN-ARMED FORCES
Dowding, Hugh Caswall Tremenheere Dowding, Baron, 1882-1970.

GREAT BRITAIN-ARMY
see also Great Britain-History, Military
Fuller, John Frederick Charles, 1878-1966.
Pownall, Henry, Sir, 1887-1961.
Rich, Barnabe, 1540?-1617.
Rich, Bernard, 1917-
Wingate, Francis Reginald, Sir, Bart., 1861-1953.

GREAT BRITAIN-BARONETAGE
Simon, Ernest Darwin Simon, Baron, 1879-1960.

GREAT BRITAIN-BIOGRAPHY
Albemarle, George Monk, 1st Duke of, 1608-1670.
Albert Victor, Duke of Clarence and Avondale, 1864-1892.
Ali, Beatrice.
Amherst, Jeffery John Archer, Earl Amherst, 1896-
Anglesey, Henry William Paget, 1st Marquis of, 1768-1854.
Anson, George Anson, Baron, 1697-1762.
Appleton, Edward Victor, Sir 1892-1965.
Armstrong, William George Armstrong, Baron, 1810-1900.
Atkins, Evelyn E.
Baker, Daisy, 1894-
Banks, John, Sir, Bart., 1627-1699.
Bannerman, Margaret (Gordon) Lady, 1798-1878.
Bannerman of Kildonan, John MacDonald Bannerman, Baron, 1901-1969.
Barfield, Tony.
Barrington, William Wildman Barrington, 2d Viscount, 1717-1793.
Baskerville, John, 1706-1775.
Baxter, Alida.
Beckett, Ronald Brymer, Ed.
Bedford, Nicole Russell, Duchess of.
Bell, Gertrude Lowthian, 1868-1926.
Bentinck, George, Lord, 1802-1848.
Bentinck, William Henry Cavendish, Lord, 1774-1839.
Beresford, Delaval James De La Poer, Lord, 1862-1906.
Birch, James Wheeler Woodford, 1826-1875.
Birch, John, 1616-1691.
Birkenhead, Frederick Edwin Smith, 1st Earl of, 1872-1930.
Birkenhead, John, Sir, 1616-1679.
Bourke, Richard, Sir, 1777-1855.
Bourne, Hugh, 1772-1852.
Boycott, Charles Cunningham, 1832-1897.
Bray, Thomas, 1658-1730.
Brook, Sir Isaac, 1769-1812.
Brooke, Fulke Greville, Baron, 1554-1628.
Brooke, James Rajah of Sarawak, Sir 1803-1868.
Brooke, Robert Greville, Baron, 1608?-1643.
Broughton, John Cam Hobhouse, Baron, 1786-1869.
Brown, George Alfred, 1914-
Bull, Alec.
Burgoyne, John, 1722-1792.
Burnaby, Frederick Gustavus, 1842-1885.
Burnes, Alexander, Sir, 1805-1841.
Byron, Anne Isabella Milbanke Byron, Baroness, 1792-1860.
Campbell-Bannerman, Henry, Sir, 1836-1908.
Campbell, Duncan, 1680?-1730.
Campbell, John Charles, 1867-1919.
Cardus, Neville, Sir, 1889-1975.
Carlisle, Rosalind Frances (Stanley) Howard, Countess of, 1845-1921.
Carnegie, Mary Crowninshield (Endicott) 1864-1957.
Carson, Edward Henry Carson, Baron, 1854-1935.
Catnach, James, 1792-1841.
Cecil Family.
Chamberlain Family.
Churchill Family.
Davies, Cclia, 1902-
De la Itamee, Louise, 1839-1908.
Dilke, Sir Charles Wentworth, Bart., 1843-1911.
Doust, W. A., 1895-
Durrell, Jacquie, 1929-
Easton, Tom.
Evans, Kay.
Ferguson, Sarah.
Fitzpatrick, James Percy, Sir 1862-1931.
French, Stanley.
Hamilton, Anne, Duchess of, 1632-1716.
Hamilton, Emm, Lady, 1761-1815.
Hastings, Beatrice.
Hattersley, Roy.
Haynes, Eliza, 1850-1930.
Hickey, William, B. 1749.
Huxley, Elspeth Joscelin Grant, 1907- -Biography.
Maugham, Frederic Herbert Maugham, 1st Viscount, 1866-1958.
Maugham, Robin, 1916- -Biography.
Milne, Christopher, 1920-
Milner Family.
Mitchelhill, John Percy, 1879-1966.
Monmouth, James Scott, Duke of, 1649-1685.
Montagu, Edwin Samuel, 1879-1924.
Newcastle, Margaret (Lucas) Cavendish, Duchess 66, 1624?-1674.
Nichols, John Gough, 1806-1873, Ed.
Northumberland, John Dudley, 1st Duke of, 1502-1553.
Oastler, Richard, 1789-1861.
Oldcastle, John, Styled Lord Cobham, D. Sir 1417.
Powell, Violet Georgiana, Lady, 1912- -Biography.
Roberts, Robert, 1905-1974.
Robinson, Robbie.
Roehenstart, Charles Edward Stuart, Called Count, 1784?-1854.
Rogers, Woodes, D. 1732.
Rossetti Family.
Suffolk, Katharine (Willoughby) Brandon, Duchess of, 1519-1580.
Travers, Austin.
Wolveridge, Jim, 1920-

GREAT BRITAIN-COLONIAL OFFICE
Kitchener, Horatio Herbert Kitchener, 1st Earl, 1850-1916.

GREAT BRITAIN-COLONIES
Pownall, Thomas, 1722-1805.

GREAT BRITAIN-COLONIES-ADMINISTRATION
Head, Edmund Walker, Sir, Bart., 1805-1868.

GREAT BRITAIN-COURT AND COURTIERS
see also Great Britain-Kings and Rulers
Antrim, Louisa Jane McDonnell, Countess of, 1855-1949.
Ingram, Arthur, Sir, 1565 (Ca.)-1642.
Wilsingham, Francis,Sir 1530? 1590.

GREAT BRITAIN-HISTORY, MILITARY
see also Great Britain-Army
Pope, Vyvyan Vavasour, 1891-1941.

GREAT BRITAIN-HISTORY, NAVAL
see also Great Britain-Navy
Hawkins, Sir John, 1719-1789.

GREAT BRITAIN-KINGS AND RULERS
Albert, Consort of Queen Victoria, 1819-1861.
Alfred the Great, King of England, 840-901.
Anne Boleyn, Queen Consort of Henry 8th, King of England, 1507-1536.
Anne, Consort of Richard III, King of England, 1456-1485-Juvenile Literature.
Anne, Princess of Great Britain, 1950-
Anne, Queen of Great Britain, 1665-1714.
Arthur, King.
Canute, the Great, King of England and Denmark, 995?-1035.
Charles I, King of Great Britain, 1600-1649.
Charles II, King of Great Britain, 1630-1685.
Edward I, King of England, 1239-1307.
Edward II, King of England, 1284-1327.
Edward III, King of England, 1312-1377.
Edward IV, King of England, 1442-1483.
Edward, the Confessor, King of England, Saint, D. 1066.
Edward V, King of England, 1470-1483.
Edward VI, King of England, 1537-1553.
Edward VII, King of Great Britain, 1841-1910.
Edward VIII, King of Great Britain, 1894-1972.
Elizabeth II,Queen of Great Britain-1926-
Elizabeth, Queen of England, 1533-1603.
George I, King of Great Britain, 1660-1727.
George II, King of Great Britain, 1683-1760.
George III, King of Great Britain, 1738-1820.
George IV, King of Great Britain, 1762-1830.
George V, King of Great Britain, 1865-1936.
George VI, King of Great Britain, 1895-1952.
Glendower, Owen, 1359?-1416?
Henry II, King of England, 1133-1189.
Henry IV, King of England, 1367-1413.
Henry, King of England, 1491-1547-Juvenile Literature.
Henry V, King of England, 1387-1422.
Henry VIII, King of England, 1491-1547.
James I, King of Great Britain, 1566-1625.
James II, King of Great Britain, 1633-1701.
John, King of England, 1167?-1216.
Margaret of Anjou, Consort of Henry VI, King of England, 1430-1482.
Mary, of Modena, Consort of James II, King of Great Britain, 1658-1718.
Richard I, King of England, 1157-1199.
Richard II, King of England, 1367-1400.
Richard III, King of England, 1452-1485.
Stephen, King of England, 1097?-1154.
Victoria, Queen of Great Briatian, 1819-1901.
William I, the Conqueror, King of England, 1027?-1087.
William III, King of Great Britain, 1650-1702.

GREAT BRITAIN-NAVY
see also Great Britain-History, Naval
Nelson, Horatio Nelson, Viscount, 1758-1805.
Phillip, Arthur, 1738-1814-Juvenile Literature.
Warren, Peter, Sir, 1703-1752.

GREAT BRITAIN-NOBILITY
see also Great Britain-Baronetage
Augustus Frederick, Duke of Sussex, 1773-1843.
Birkett, Norman Birkett, Baron, 1883-1962.
Cardigan, James Thomas Brudenell, 7th Earl of, 1797-1868.
Curzon, Mary, 1870-1906.
Dorset, Charles Sackville, 6th Earl of, 1643-1706.

I

Evans, Oliver, 1755-1819.
Eytinge, Bruce Swomley, 1893-
Ferguson, Harry, 1884-1960.
Fitch, John, 1743-1798.
Friese-Greene, William, 1855-1921.
Fuller, Richard Buckminster, 1895-
Geiser, Peter, 1826-1901.
Goldberg, Reuben Lucius, 1883-1970.
Goldman, Sylvan Nathan, 1898-
Holland, John Philip, 1842-1914.
Jones, Frederick McKinley, 1893-1961-Juvenile Literature.
Lee, William, D. 1610?
Leverone, Nathaniel.
McCormick, Cyrus Hall, 1809-1884.
Marconi, Guglielmo, Marchese, 1874-1937.
Morland, Samuel, Sir, Bart., 1625-1695.
Morse, Samuel Finley Breese, 1791-1872.
Riddell, John Leonard, 1807-1867.
Ries, Elias Elkan, 1862-1928.
Saunders, Charles, Fl. 1763.
Sperry, Elmer Ambrose, 1860-1930.
Stanmore, Arthur Hamilton-Gordon, Baron, 1829-1912.
Stephenson, George, 1781-1848.
Stevens, John, 1749-1838.
Thurber, Charles S., 1864-
Watt, James, 1736-1819.
Westinghouse, George, 1846-1914.
Whitney, Eli, 1765-1825.
Willard, Theodore Arthur, 1862-1943.

INVENTORS-JUVENILE LITERATURE
Gutenberg, Johann, 1397?-1468.

INVESTORS
see Capitalists and Financiers

IOWA
see also names of cities, counties, towns, etc. in Iowa
Dolliver, Jonathan Prentiss, 1858-1910.
Yoseloff, Thomas, 1913-

IRAN-BIOGRAPHY
Kidwai, Rafi Ahmad, 1894-1954.
Reza Shah, Shah of Iran, 1878-1944.

IRELAND
Hare, Robert, 1850-1953.
Parnell, Charles Stewart, 1846-1891.
Parnell, Katharine Wood.

IRISH AUTHORS
see Authors, Irish

IRISH IN FOREIGN COUNTRIES
Curley, James Michael, 1874-1958.

IRISH MISSIONARIES
see Missionaries, Irish

IRISH REPUBLICAN ARMY
McGuire, Maria.

IRON AND STEEL WORKERS
Hudson, Hosea.
Krupp Family.
Krupp Von Bohlen und Halbach, Alfried, 1907-1967.

IRON WORKERS
see Iron and Steel Workers

IROQUOIS INDIANS
see Indians of North America-Eastern States

ISLAM
see also Muslims
also special headings with Islam added in parentheses; subdivision Islam under special topics, e.g. Marriage-Islam; headings beginning with the words Islamic and Muslim
Muhammed, the Prophet.
Zwemer, Samuel Marinus, 1867-1952.

ISLAMIC WOMEN
see Women, Muslim

ISRAEL-ARMED FORCES
Dayan, Moshe, 1915-

ISRAEL-BIOGRAPHY
Allon, Yigal, 1918-
Arad, Yitshak.
Begin, Menachem, 1913-
Ben-Gurion, David, 1886-1973.
Eban, Abba Solomon, 1915-
Eshkol, Levi, 1895-1969.
Meir, Golda (Mabovitz), 1898-
Rabin, Yitzhak, 1922-
Weisgal, Meyer Wolfe, 1894-

ISRAEL-POLITICS AND GOVERNMENT
Weizmann, Chaim Pres. Israel, 1874-1952.

ITALIAN AMERICANS
Della Femina, Jerry.
Panella, Vincent.

ITALIAN AUTHORS
see Authors, Italian

ITALIAN COMPOSERS
see Composers, Italian

ITALY-BIOGRAPHY
Beatrice D'Este, Consort of Lodovico Sforza, Il Moro, Duke of Milan, 1475-1497.
Borghese, Maria Paolina Bonaparte, Principessa, 1780-1825.
Borgia Family.
Ciano, Edda Mussolini, Contessa.
Dolci, Danilo.
Garibaldi, Giuseppe, 1807-1882.
Gian Galeazzo Visconti, Duke of Milan, 1351-1402.
Medici, House of.
Tasso, Torquato, 1544-1595.

ITALY-KINGS AND RULERS
Borgia, Lucrezia, 1480-1519.

J

JACOBITES
Macdonald, Flora (Macdonald) 1722-1790.

JAMAICA
McKay, Claude, 1890-1948-Biography-Youth.

JAPAN-ARMED FORCES
Toio, Hideki. 1884-1948.

JAPAN-BIOGRAPHY
Hatano, Satomi, 1931-
Kishi, Nobusuke.
Matsuoka, Y Oko, 1916-
Miyamoto, Musashi, 1584-1645.
Nakahama, Manjir O, 1827-1898.
Nakanoin Masatada No Musume, B. 1258-Biography.
Okuma, Shigenobu, 1838-1922.
Toyama, Kyuzo, 1868-1910.

JAPAN-EMPERORS
Akihito, Crown Prince of Japan, 1933-

JAPAN-KINGS AND RULERS
see Japan-Emperors

JAPANESE EMPERORS
see Japan-Emperors

JAPANESE IN THE UNITED STATES
Sone, Monica Itoi, 1919-
Takahashi, Shixu (Higuchi)
Toguri, Ikuko, 1916-
Uyesugi, Ruth Farlow.

JAZZ MUSICIANS
Armstrong, Louis, 1900-1971.
Austin, Bill Joe.
Beiderbecke, Bix, 1903-1931.
Charles, Ray, 1930-
Coltrane, John, 1926-1967.
Davis, Miles, 1926-
Doods, Johhny, 1892-1940.
Ellington, Duke, 1899-
Hines, Earl, 1905-
Johnson, William Geary, 1880-1949.
Laine, Cleo.
Lewis, George, 1900-1968.
Morton, Ferdinand Joseph, 1885-1941.
Parker, Charles Christopher, 1920-1955.
Pepper, Art, 1925-
Scobey, Bob, 1916-1963.
Shaw, Artie, 1910-
Smith, Bessie, 1894-1937.
Smith, Willie, 1897-1973.
Waller, Fats, 1904-1943.

JEHOVAH'S WITNESSES
Jehovah's Witnesses-History.

JESUITS
Garnet, Henry, 1555-1606.

JESUITS IN CHINA
Attwater, Rachel, Tr.

JESUS, SOCIETY OF
see Jesuits

JEWISH AUTHORS
see Authors, Jewish

JEWISH CONVERTS TO CHRISTIANITY
see Converts from Judaism

JEWISH HOLOCAUST (1939-1945)
see Holocaust, Jewish (1939-1945)

JEWISH RABBIS
see Rabbis

JEWISH SOLDIERS
Marcus, David, 1901-1948.

JEWISH WOMEN
see Women, Jewish

JEWS
see also Patriarchs (Bible); Prophets
Abraham Ben David, of Pasquieres, 1125(Ca.)-1198.
Cresson, Warder, 1798-1860.
Czerniakow, Adam, 1880-1942.
Harzfeld, Abraham, 1888-
Joshua.
Kohut, Rebekah Bettelheim, 1864-1951.

JEWS-CONVERTS TO CHRISTIANITY
see Converts from Judaism

JEWS-DIASPORA
Gray, Martin.
Ibn Abi Zimra, David Ben Solomon, 1479 (Ca.)-1589.
Manasseh Ben Joseph Ben Israel, 1604-1657.
Solomon Ben Isaac, Called RaSHI, 1040-1105.
Spanier, Ginette.
Tulman, David.

JEWS-DISPERSION
see Jews-Diaspora

JEWS-KINGS AND RULERS
Josel, of Rosheim, 1480 (Ca.)-1554.

JEWS-LITERATURE
see Hebrew Literature

JEWS-WOMEN
see Women, Jewish

JEWS AS SOLDIERS
see Jewish Soldiers

JEWS IN AUSTRIA
Bloch, Josef Samuel, 1850-1923.
Ross, Martin H., 1918-

JEWS IN CANADA
Dunkelman, Ben, 1913-

JEWS IN ENGLAND
see Jews in Great Britain

JEWS IN EUROPE
Pilon, Juliana Geran, 1947-

JEWS IN FOREIGN COUNTRIES
see Jews-Diaspora

JEWS IN GERMANY
Frank. Anne, 1929-1945.
Hameln, Gluckel of, 1646-1724.
Hanpam, Charles.
Katz, Josef, 1918-
Senger, Valentin.

JEWS IN GREAT BRITAIN
Bermant, Chaim I.-Biography.

JEWS IN PALESTINE
Shorrosh, Anis.
Trepman, Paul.

JEWS IN POLAND
Kaplan, Chaim Aron, 1880-Ca. 1942.
Miedzyrzecki, Feigele Peltel.

JEWS IN RUSSIA
Bickermann, Joseph, 1867-1942.
Shcharansky, Avital.

JEWS IN THE UNITED STATES
Gratz, Rebecca, 1781-1869.
Helmreich, William B.
Levin, Louis Hiram, 1866-1923.
Levy, Aaron, 1742-1815.
Levy, Harriet Lane.
Levy, Uriah Phillips, 1792-1862.
Litman, Ray (Frank) 1864 or 5-1948.
Revel, Bernard, 1885-1940.
Samuel, Maurice, 1895-1972-Addresses, Essays, Lectures.
Sitenhop, Yente (Glaser)
Wise, Jonah Bondi, 1881-1959.

JOCKEYS
Bass, Tom, 1859-1934.
Beasley, Bobby.
Cauthen, Steve, 1960-
Francis, Dick.
Smith, Robyn Caroline-Juvenile Literature.

JORDAN
Abdall Ah, King of Jordan, 1882-1951.

JOURNALISM-BIOGRAPHY
see Journalists

JOURNALISM, SOCIALIST
Ellis, Marc H.

JOURNALISTS
see also War Correspondents; Women Journalists
A Beckett, Gilbert Abbott, 1811-1856.
Anderson, Jack, 1922-
Atkinson, Wilmer, 1840-1920.
Bache, Benjamin Franklin, 1769-1798.
Bacon, James, 1914-
Baker, Dan M., 1842-1902.
Baker, Ray Stannard, 1870-1946.
Barrett, Rona.
Barzini, Luigi Giorgio, 1908-
Baxter, Gordon, 1923-
Befrage, Cedric, 1904-
Begley, Kathleen A.
Behr, Edward, 1926-
Bennett, James Gordon, 1841-1918.
Bernard, George, 1939-
Blair, Frank, 1915-
Blowitz, Henri Georges Stephane Adolphe Opper De, 1825-1903.
Bok, Edward William, 1863-1930.
Bowers, Claude Gernade, 1879-1958.
Bradford, Andrew, 1686-1742.
Brann, William Cowper, 1855-1898.
Brisbane, Arthur, 1864-1936.
Cameron, James, 1911-
Cargill, Morris.
Carter, Hodding, 1907-1972.
Caxton, William, Ca. 1422-1491.
Cerf, Bennett Alfred, 1898-1971.
Chernyshevskii, Nikolai Gavrilovich, 1828-1889.
Cheshire, Maxine, 1930-
Chesterton, Gilbert Keith, 1874-1936.
Church, William Conant, 1836-1917.
Cobb, Irvin Shrewsbury, 1876-1944-Biography.
Cobbett, William, 1763-1835.
Cochrane, Elizabeth, 1867-1922.
Cockerill, John Albert, 1845-1896.
Collier, John Payne, 1789-1883-Biography.
Dabney, Virginius, 1901-
Daniels, Jonathan, 1902-
Daniels, Josephus, 1862-1948.
Davis, Richard Harding, 1864-1916.
De Bow, James Dunwoody Brownson, 1820-1867.
Delavan, James.
Dempsey, Lotta.
Dennie, Joseph, 1768-1812.
Dunne, Finley Peter, 1867-1936.
Eggleston, George Teeple, 1906-
Etienne, Charles Guillaume, 1777-1845.
Fischer, Louis, 1896- Ed.
Fortune, Timothy Thomas, 1856-1928.
Freeman, Miller, 1875-1955.
Freneau, Philip Morin, 1752-1832.
Fuldheim, Dorothy.
Gauvreau, Emile Henry, 1891-1956.
Gibbons, Floyd Phillips, 1887-1939.
Goddard, William, 1740-1817.
Godkin, Edwin Lawrence, 1831-1902.
Gray, Barry, 1916-
Gruening, Ernest Henry, 1887-
Gunther, John, 1929-1947.
Hallock, Gerard, 1800-1866.
Hangen, Welles, 1930-
Hannay, James, 1827-1873.
Harris, Radie.
Harris, Thomas Spencer, 1836-1893.
Haydn, Hiram Collins, 1907-1973.
Haykal, Muhammad Hasanayn.
Healy, George W.
Henderson, Randall.
Hobhouse, Leonard Trelawney, 1864-1929.
Hobson, Joshua, 1810-1876.
Holt, Hamilton, 1872-1951.
Hopper, Hedda.
Hough, Henry Beetle, 1896- -Biography.
Howe, Edgar Watson, 1853-1937.
Hubbell, Ralph, 1909-
Ireland, DeWitt Clinton, 1835-1913.
Kahn, Ely Jacques, 1916-
Keim, De Benneville Randolph, 1841-1914.
Kilgallen, Dorothy.
Lawrenson, Helen.
Lawson, Victor Fremont, 1850-1925.
Lazare, Bernard, 1865-1903.
Leland, Charles Godfrey, 1824-1903.
Lichtenstein, Grace.
Lippmann, Walter, 1889-
Locke, David Ross, 1833-1888.
Lockhart, Robert Hamilton Bruce, Sir, 1887-1970.
Lowe, Frank Gordon, 1921-
McClendon, Sarah.
McClure, Alexander Kelly, 1828-1909.
McIntyre, Oscar Odd, 1884-1938.
Mack, Isaac Foster, 1837-1912.
McWhirter, Alan Ross.
McWilliams, Carey, 1905-
Maeztu, Ramiro De, 1875-1936.
Maier, Walter Arthur, 1893-1950.
Marble, Manton, 1834-1917.
Mariategui, Jose Carlos, 1894-1930.
Marquis, Don, 1878-1937.
Martin, Harold H.
Martin, Kingsley, 1897-1969.
Massingham, Henry William, 1860-1924.
Matthews, Thomas Stanley, 1901-
Meeman, Edward John, 1889-1966.
Mencken, Henry Louis, 1880-1956.
Monroe, Harriet, 1860-1936-Biography-Editing Career.
Montalembert, Charles Forbes Rene De Tryon, Comte De, 1810-1870.
Morley, Felix, 1894-
Morrison, George Ernest, 1862-1920.
Moses, George Higgins, 1869-1944.
Mott, Frank Luther, 1886-1964.
Newman, Cecil E., 1903--Juvenile Literature.
Ng Poon Chew, 1866-1931-Juvenile Literature.
Norman, Henry, Sir Bart 1858-1939.
Northcliffe, Alfred Charles William Harmsworth, 1st Viscount, 1865-1922.
O'Reilly, John Boyle, 1844-1890.
Packard, Reynolds, 1903- -Biography-Journalistic Career.
Page, Walter Hines, 1855-1918.
Paisley, Oldham, 1893-
Paterson, Andrew Barton, 1864-1941.
Phillips, David Graham, 1867-1911.
Pomeroy, Marcus Mills, 1833-1896.
Porter, William Trotter, 1809-1858.
Post, Emily Price, 1873-1960.
Pound, Ezra Loomis, 1885-1972.
Pulitzer, Joseph, 1847-1911.
Read, Herbert Edward, Sir, 1893-1968-Biography.
Reed, John, 1887-1920.
Reedy, William Marion, 1862-1920.
Riis, Jacob August, 1849-1914.
Robinson, Henry Crabb, 1775-1867.
Rowan, Carl Thomas.
Royall, Anne (Newport) 1769-1854.
Ruddiman, Thomas, 1674-1757.
Russwurm, John Brown, 1799-1851-Juvenile Literature.
Ryan, Cornelius.
Schoenstein, Paul.
Schorr, Daniel.
Scripps, Edward Wyllis, 1854-1926.
Seaton, William Winston, 1785-1866.
Sheean, Vincent, 1899-
Shiff, Dorothy.
Shipp, Nelson McLester, 1892-
Shirer, William Lawrence, 1904-
Smalley, George Washburn, 1833-1916.
Snow, John Ben, 1883-1973.
Snowden, Edgar.
Sorel, Georges, 1847-1922.
Steffens, Joseph Lincoln, 1866-1936.
Storey, Wilbur F., 1819-1884.
Sulzberger, Cyrus Leo, 1912-
Swaim, William, 1802-1835.
Swinton, John, 1829-1901.
Swope, Herbert Bayard, 1882-1958.
Tabouis, Genevieve R., 1892-
Talbot, Godfrey Walker.
Timpson, John, 1928-
Trohan, Walter, 1903-
Uhlig, Theodor, 1822-1853.

Uspenskii, Petr Demianovich, 1878-1947-
Addresses, Essays, Lectures.
Van Loon, Hendrik Willem, 1882-1944.
Villard, Oswald Garrison, 1872-1949.
Watterson, Henry, 1840-1921.
Watts, Alaric Alexander, 1797-1864-Biography.
Webb, James Watson, 1802-1884.
Weed, Thurlow, 1797-1882.
White, Horace, 1834-1916.
White, Theodore Harold, 1915-
Whitlock, Brand, 1869-1934.
Whyte, Don, 1926-
Wicker, Tom.
Woollcott. Alexander, 1887-1943.
Young, Rosamond McPherson-Biography-
Addresses, Essays, Lectures.
Young, Stark, 1881-1963-Correspondence.
JOURNEYS
see Voyages and Travels
JUDAICA
see Jews
JUDGES
see also Women Lawyers
Benedict, Kirby, 1810-1874.
Black, Hugo LaFayette, 1886-1971.
Blackmun, Harry Andrew, 1908-
Brandeis, Louis Dembitz, 1856-1941.
Brown, Addison, 1830-1913.
Burke, Thomas, 1849-1925.
Cardozo, Benjamin Nathan, 1870-1938.
Coke, Edward, Sir 1552-1634.
Deady, Matthew Paul, 1824-1893.
Dent, Marmaduke, 1801-1880.
Downie, Edward Blake.
Hawkins, John, Sir, 1719-1789.
Hefner, Robert Alexander, 1874-1971.
Hemphill, John, 1803-1862.
Hughes, Charles Evans,
1862-1945.
Hunter, Samuel McFadden, 1838-1906?
Jackson, Robert Houghwout, 1892-1954.
Jenkins, Warwick Hoxie, 1847-1933.
Johnson, Frank Minis, 1918-
Johnson, William, 1771-1834.
Kenny, Robert Walker, 1901-
Legett, Kirvin Kade, 1857-1926.
McDuffie, John, 1883-1950.
Mack, Julian William, 1866-1943.
McKenna, Joseph, 1843-1926.
McLean, John, 1785-1861.
Medina, Harold Raymond, 1888-
Monboddo, James Burnett, Lord, 1714-1799.
New South Wales. District Courts-Biography.
Parker, Isaac Charles, 1838-1896.
Paterson, William, 1745-1806.
Samson, Judge of Israel-Juvenile Literature.
Stephen, James Fitzjames, Sir, Bart., 1829-1894.
Taney, Roger Brooke, 1777-1864.
Terry, David Smith, 1823-1889.
JUDGING (SPORTS)
see Sports Officiating
JURISPRUDENCE, MEDICAL
see Medical Jurisprudence
JURISTS
see Lawyers
JUSTICES' CLERKS
see Clerks of Court
JUVENILE AUTOMOBILE DRIVERS
see Automobile Drivers
JUVENILE DELINQUENCY
see also Gangs; Runaway Children
Williams, Mark.

K

KASHMIR-POLITICS AND GOVERNMENT
Gulab Singh, Maharajah of Kashmir, 1792-1857.
KENTUCKY
see also names of cities, towns, counties etc. in Kentucky
Garner, John Edwin, 1851-1941.
Kirk, Claude R., 1926-
KENTUCKY-GENEALOGY
Slone, Verne Mae, 1914-
KENYA
Mboya, Tom.
KERESAN INDIANS
see Indians of North America-Southwest, New
KHALIFS
see Caliphs
KICKAPOO INDIANS
see Indians of North America-The West
KIDNAPPING
see also Abduction
Mitrione, Dan.
Ross, Charles Brewster, B. 1870.
KINGS AND RULERS
see also Caliphs; Courts and Courtiers; Dictators; Emperors; Roman Emperors
also subdivision Kings and Rulers under names of countries, e.g. Great Britain-Kings and Rulers
Ab U Bakr, Caliph, D. 634.
Abbas I, the Great, Shah of Iran, 1571-1629.
Abdulhamit II, Sultan of Turkey, 1842-1918.
Ahmad Bey, Bey of Tunis, D. 1855.
Albert I, King of Belgians, 1875-1934.
Amenhetep IV, King of Egypt, 1388-1358 B.C.
Cettiwayo, King of Zululand, Ca. 1826-1884.
Charless, Joseph, 1772-1834.
Christophe, Henri, King of Haiti,
1767-1820.
Chulalong Korn, King of Thailand,
1853-1910.
Cleopatra, Queen of Egypt, D., B.C.30.
Cosimo III, De'Medici, Grand Duke of Tuscany,
1642-1723.
Cyrus, the Great, King of Persia, D.529 B.C.
Franco Bahamonde, Francisco, 1892-
Friedrich August I, der Starke, Elector of Saxony
and King of Poland, 1670-1733.
Friedrich I, Barbarossa, Emperor of Germany,
1121-1190.
Friedrich II, der Grosse, King of Prussia, 1712-
1786.
Friedrich II, Emperor of Germany, 1194-1250.
Friedrich III, German Emperor, 1831-1888.
Friedrich Wilhelm, Elector of Brandenburg,
Called the Great Elector, 1620-1688.
Friedrich Wilhelm I, King of Prussia, 1688-1740.
Gustaf II Adolf, King of Sweden, 1594-1632.
Gustaf V. King of Sweden, 1858-1950.
Haakon VII, King of Norway.
Habsburg, House of-History.
Harald III Haroraoi, King of Norway, 1015-1066.
Hassan II, King of Morocco, 1929-
Hatshepsut, Queen of Egypt.
Herod Antipas, Tetrarch of Galilee.
Herod I, the Great, King of Judea, D. 4 B.C.
Hiero II, King of Syracuse, D. 215? B.C.
Hindenburg, Paul Von, Pres. Germany, 1847-
1934.
Hitler, Adolf.
Ho-Chi-Minh, Pres. Democratic Republic of
Vietnam, 1894?-1969.
Holy Roman Empire-Kings and Rulers-Biography.
Hormizd, Rabban, 7th Cent.
Hortense, Consort of Louis, King of Holland,
1783-1837.
Hussein, King of Jordan, 1935-
Ibn Sa'ud, King of Saudi Arabia, 1880-
Ism a Il I, Shah of Iran, 1487-1524.
Jeanne D'Albret, Queen of Navarre, 1528-1572.
Jeri Z Podebrad, King of Bohemia,1420-1471.
Jimma Abba Jifar.
Jiri Z Podebrad, King of Bohemia, 1420-1471.
Joachim Murat, King of Naples, 1767-1815.
Joao II. King of Portugal, 1455-1495.
John IV, King of Ethiopia, 1839-1889.
Joseph Bonaparte, King of Spain, 1766-1844.
Juliana, Queen of the Netherlands, 1909-
Kaahumanu, Consort of Kamehameha I, the
Great, King of the Hawaiian Islands, 1772-
1832.
Kalakaua, David, King of Hawaii, 1836-1891.
Kamehameha I, the Great, King of the Hawaiian
Islands, D. 1819.
Karl XII, King of Sweden, 1682-1718.
Kolbe, Emma Eliza (Coe) 1850-1913.
Koolau, Fl. 1864.
Leopold I, King of the Belgians, 1790-1865.
Leopold II, King of the Belgians, 1835-1909.
Liliuokalani, Queen of the Hawaiian Islands,
1838-1917-Juvenile Literature.
Ludwig II, King of Bavaria, 1845-1886.
Lupescu, Magda.
Mahmud, Sultan of Ghazni, 971-1030.
Manuel II, King of Portugal, 1889-1932.
Margaret Tudor, Consort of James IV, King of
Scotland, 1489-1541.
Margaretha, of Austria, Regent of the
Netherlands, 1480-1530.
Maria, Consort of Louis II, King of Hungary,
1505-1558.
Maria Theresia, Empress of Austria, 1717-1780.
Mirambo, D. 1884.
Mithridates VI, Eupator, King of Pontus, D. 63 B.
C.
Mohammed Reza Pahlavi, Shah of Iran, 1919-
Montezuma I, Emperor of Mexico, Ca. 1398-Ca.
1468.
Montezuma II. Emperor of Mexico, 1483 (Ca.)-
1520.
Mzilikazi, Matabele King, 1790-1868.
Naimbana, D. 1793.
Nezahualcoyotl, King of Texcoco, Fl. 1400-1470.
Nkrumah, Kwame, Pres. Ghana, 1909-1972.
Norodom Sihanouk Varman, King of Cambodia,
1922-
Pyrrhus, King of Epirus, 318-272 B.C.
Rameses II, King of Egypt.
Ramose-Juvenile Literature.
Robert I, King of Scotland, 1274-1329.
Romanus I Lecapenus, Co-Emperor of the East,
D.948.
Saladin, Sultan of Egypt and Syria. 1137-1193.
Saul, King of Israel-Juvenile Literature.
Shivaji, Raja, 1627-1680.
Sobhuza II, King of Swaziland, 1899-
Solomon, King of Israel.
Suleyman I, the Magnificent, Sultan of the Turks,
1494-1566.
Theodora, Consort of Justinian I, Emperor of the
East, D. 548.
Timur, the Great, 1336-1405.
Tutankhamen, King of Egypt.
Tzu-Hsi, Empress Dowager of China, 1835-1908.
Womunafu, Mukama, 1830?-1906.
Zenobia, Queen of Palmyra.
KIOWA INDIANS
see Indians of North America-The West
KNIGHTS OF LABOR
Knights of Labor.
KOASATI INDIANS
see Indians of North America-Eastern States
KUBO-FUTURISM
see Futurism

L

LABOR, ORGANIZED
see Trade-Unions
LABOR AND LABORING CLASSES
see also Artisans; Servants; Slavery; Trade-Unions also classes of laborers, e.g. Coal-Miners, Railroads-Employees
American Federation of Labor.
Anderson, Mary, 1872-1964.
Chavez, Cesar Estrada.
Cruz, Pablo.
Furuseth, Andrew, 1854-1938.
Meany, George, 1894-
Mooney, Thomas J., 1882-1942.
Perry, Pettis.
Randolph, Asa Philip, 1889-
Schrank, Robert.
LABOR AND LABORING CLASSES-GREAT BRITAIN
Thomas, James Henry, 1874?-1949.
LABOR ORGANIZATIONS
see Trade-Unions
LABOR-UNIONS
see Trade-Unions
LABORERS
see Labor and Laboring Classes
LAMAISM
Mi-la-Ras-Pa, 1038-1122.
Padma Sambhava, Ca. 717-Ca. 762.
Rato Khyongla Nawang Losang.
LAND, RECLAMATION OF
see Reclamation of Land
LAND RECLAMATION
see Reclamation of Land
LAND USE, URBAN-PLANNING
see City Planning
LANDSCAPE ARCHITECTURE
Eliot, Charles, 1859-1897.
Le Notre, Andre, 1613-1700.
Olmsted, Frederick Law, 1822-1903.
LATIN AMERICA-DISCOVERY AND EXPLORATION
see America-Discovery and Exploration
LATIN-AMERICAN AUTHORS
see Authors, Latin-American
LATIN AUTHORS
see Authors, Latin
LATTER-DAY SAINTS
see Mormons and Mormonism
LAUREATES
see Poets Laureate
LAW-BIOGRAPHY
see also Judges; Lawyers
Bechtel, Edwin De Turck, 1880-1957.
LAW, ROMAN
see Roman Law
LAW ENFORCEMENT OFFICERS
Davis, William Hardy.
Pusser, Buford, 1937-
LAWN TENNIS
see Tennis
LAWTON FAMILY
Haliburton, Thomas Chandler, 1796-1865.
Hall, Abraham Oakey, 1826-1898.
LAWYERS
see also Judges; Women Lawyers
American Civil Liberties Union.
American Law Institute. Council.
Arnold, Thurman Wesley, 1891-1969.
Bailey, Francis Lee, 1933-
Bates, Edward, 1793-1869.
Belli, Melvin M.,1907-
Black, Jeremiah Sullivan, 1810-1883.
Borah, William Edgar, 1865-1940.
Calhoun, John Caldwell, 1782-1850.
Caro, Joseph, 1488-1575.
Carroll, Mitchell Benedict, 1898-
Chaudri, Nazir Ahmad Khan.
Choate, Rufus, 1799-1859.
Clark, Grenville, 1882-1967.
Clarke, John Hessin, 1857-1945.
Cobb, Howell, 1815-1868.
Coulomb, Charles Augustin De,
1736-1806.
Crawford, William Harris, 1772-1834.
Crittenden, John Jordan, 1787-1863.
Curtis, Benjamin Robbins, 1809-1874.
Dana, Richard Henry, 1815-1882.
Daniel, Peter Vivian, 1784-1860.
Daugherty, Harry Micajah, 1860-1941.
Davie, William Richardson, 1756-1820.
Davis, John William, 1873-1955.
Dawes, Charles Gates, 1865-1951.
Deane, Silas, 1737-1789.
Dies, Martin, 1901-
Dorr, Thomas Wilson, 1805-1854.
Douglas, William Orville, 1898-
Dulany, Daniel, 1685-1753.
Ellsworth, Oliver, 1745-1807.
Emmet, Thomas Addis, 1828-1919.
Field, Stephen Johnson, 1816-1899.
Filangieri, Gaetano, 1752-1788.
Folk, Joseph Wingate, 1869-1923.
Foreman, Percy, 1902-
Frank, Jerome, 1889-1957.
Fuller, Claude Albert, 1876-
Fuller, Melville Weston, 1833-1910.
Galloway, Joseph, 1731-1803.
Garry, Charles R., 1909-
Gaston, William, 1778-1844 -- Juvenile Literature.
Glesler, Jerry, 1886-1962.
Glieberman, Herbert A.
Gore, Christopher, 1758-1827.
Gresham, Walter Quintin, 1832-1895.
Griffith, Samuel Walker, Sir, 1845-1920.
Halbert, Sara.
Hall, Richard Smith, 1855-1910.
Hamilton, Andrew, 1676 (Ca.)-1741.
Hamlin, James D., 1871-1950.
Hargrave, Lawrence, 1850-1916.
Harlan, John Marshall, 1833-1911.
Hillquit, Morris, 1869-1933.
Hindman, Thomas Carmichael, 1818-1868.
Hoard, Edison, 1933- -Juvenile Literature.
Hogan, Frank S.
Hogg, Thomas Jefferson, 1792-1862.
Hogren, Charles V., 1936-
Holtzmann, Fanny E., 1903-
Hoover, John Edgar, 1895-
Hotman, Francois, Sieur De Villiers Saint Paul,
1524-1590.
Howe, William F.
Hughes, Gerard W.
Hurley, Patrick Jay, 1883-1963.
Ingersoll, Jared, 1722-1781.
Ingersoll, Robert Green, 1833-1899.
Isaac, Godfrey.
Jay, John, 1745-1829.
Jerome, William Travers, 1859-1934.
Johnson, William Samuel, 1727-1819.
Kennedy, Florynce, 1916-
King, Stanley, 1883-1951.
Lamar, Lucius Quintus Cincinnatus, 1825-1893.
Lamb, Edward.
Lindsey, Benjamin Barr, 1869-1943.
Lloyd. David, 1656-1731.
Lockwood, Belva Ann Bennett, 1830-1917-
Juvenile Literature.
Long, Huey Pierce, 1893-1935.
Longworth, Nicholas, 1869-1931.
Lowden, Frank Orren, 1861-1943.
Lowe, Charles John, Sir, 1880-
Lynn, Conrad J.
Macdonald, John Sandfield, 1812-1872.
McGlashan, Charles Fayette, 1847-1931.
Marshall, John, 1755-1835.
Marshall, Thurgood, 1908-
Miller, Ben Robertson.
Moldovsky, Joel.
Morgan, Charles, 1930-
Morrow, Dwight Whitney, 1873-1931.
Moyle, James Henry, 1858-1946.
Murphy, Frank, 1890-1949.
Nizer, Louis, 1902-
O'Dwyer, Paul, 1907-
O'Higgins, Kevin Christopher, 1892-1927.
Petigru, James Louis, 1789-1863.
Pike, Albert, 1809-1891.
Pobedonostsev, Konstantine Petrovich, 1827-
1907.
Post, Melville Davisson, 1871-1930.
Prentiss, Seargent Smith, 1808-1850.
Proskauer, Joseph Meyer, 1877-1971.
Quincy, Josiah, 1772-1864.
Ranade, Mahadev Govind,Rao Bahadur, 1842-
1901.
Reed, Thomas Brackett, 1839-1902.
Rerat, Eugene A.
Robinson, Nelson Lemuel, 1857-1944.
Roff, Charles L., 1894-
Ryan, Edward George, 1810-1880.
Samuels, Thomas W., 1886-
Sewall, Samuel, 1652-1730.
Shaw, Lemuel, 1781-1861.
Shiras, George, 1832-1924.
Steuer, Max, 1871-1940.
Stevens, Thaddeus, 1792-1868.
Stone, Harlan Fiske, 1872-1946.
Story, Joseph, 1779-1845.
Sutherland, George, 1862-1942.
Tribonianus, D. 545?
Trumbull, John, 1750-1831.
Tucker, Nathaniel Beverley, 1784-1851.
Turow, Scott.
Vanderveer, George Francis, 1875-1942.
Walsh, David Ignatius, 1872-1947.
Warren, Earl, 1891-1974.
Wayne, James Moore, 1790-1867.
Webster, Daniel, 1782-1852.
Wheeler, Wayne Bidwell, 1869-1927.
Wigmore, John Henry, 1863-1943.
Woodward, Augustus Brevoort, D. 1827.

N

Snowdon, Anthony Armstrong-Jones, 1st Earl of, 1930-
Steiner, Ralph, 1899-
Stetser, Carol.
Stieglitz, Alfred, 1864-1946.
Sudek, Josef, 1896-1976.
Sutcliffe, Joseph Richard, 1897-
Trubetskoi, Sergei Nikolaevich, Kniaz, 1862-1905.
Weston, Edward, 1886-1958.
White, Clarence H., 1871-1925.
White, Minor.

PHOTOGRAPHY–ANIMATED PICTURES
see Moving-Pictures

PHOTOGRAPHY–MOVING-PICTURES
see Moving-Pictures

PHYSICAL CULTURE
see Physical Education and Training

PHYSICAL EDUCATION AND TRAINING
see also Gymnastics; Sports
also names of sports or exercises, e.g. Football; also apparatus used in gymnasiums
Delsarte, Francois Alexandre Nicolas Cheri, 1811-1871.
Lee, Mabel, 1886-
Naismith, James, 1861-1939.

PHYSICAL THERAPISTS
Bertherat, Therese.

PHYSICAL TRAINING
see Physical Education and Training

PHYSICALLY HANDICAPPED
see also Blind; Deaf
Fox, Debbie Diane, 1955-
Hammett, Minnie Lee, 1915-

PHYSICALLY HANDICAPPED–PERSONAL NARRATIVES
Pole, Hilary.

PHYSICIANS
see also Pathologists; Pediatricians; Surgeons; Women Physicians
Alvarez, Walter Clement, 1884-
American Dermatological Association.
American School of Osteopathy, Kirksville, Mo.
Assali, Nicholas S.
Baldwin, Dwight, 1796-1886.
Barnes, Albert Combs, 1872-1951.
Beaumont, William, 1785-1853-Juvenile Literature.
Behrhorst, Carroll, 1922-
Bellevue Hospital, New York.
Bernard, Claude, 1813-1878.
Beshoar, Michael, 1833-1907.
Bethune, Norman.
Bickers, William, 1908-
Bigelow, Henry Jacob, 1818-1890-Addresses, Essays, Lectures.
Billings, Frank, 1854-1932.
Black, Joseph, 1728-1799.
Blackburn, Luke Pryor, 1816-1887.
Bordes, Ary.
Brinkley, John Richard, 1885-1942.
Brown, James Steven, 1866-1958.
Burnet, Frank Macfarlane, Sir, 1899-
Caldwell, Charles, 1772-1853.
Carlsen, Niels Christian, 1884-1950.
Castle, William Bosworth, 1897-
Chandler, Julian Alvin Carroll, 1872-1934.
Chapman, Nathaniel, 1780-1853.
Cooley, Denton A., 1920-
Cushing, Harvey Williams, 1869-1939.
Davaine, Casimir Joseph, 1812-1882.
Eastman, Charles Alexander, 1858-1939.
Ellot, Jared, 1685-1763.
Fayssoux, Peter Dott, 1745-1795.
Ferguson, John T.
Fischer, Ernest G.
Foerster, Otfrid, 1873-1941.
Friedman, Samuel, 1874 or 5-1947.
Gall, Franz Josef. 1758-1828.
Garden, Alexander, 1730-1791.
Geiger, Jacob Casson, 1885-
Gogarty, Oliver St. John, 1878-1957.
Grant-Whyte, Harry.
Grenfell, Sir Wilfred Thomason, 1865-1940.
Grubbe, Emil Herman, 1875-1960.
Hall, John, 1575-1635.
Hanson, Ola, 1864-1929.
Harris, Clifton.
Herriot, James.
Hertzler, Arthur Emanuel, 1870-1946.
Herz, Max.
Hill, Eva Esther, 1898-
Hilliard, Marion.
Holmes, James, 1804-1883.
Holmes, Oliver Wendell, 1809-1894.
Holt, Luther Emmett, 1855-1924.
Horowitz, Steve.
Hosack, David, 1769-1835.
Huizenga, Lee Sjoerds, 1881-1945.
Jackson, Hall, 1739-1797.
Jacobi, Abraham, 1830-1919.
James, Frank Lowber, 1841-1907.
Jeans, Sir James Hopwood, 1877-1946.
Joslin, Elliott Proctor, 1869-1962.
Kelley, William Dennis, 1825-1888.
Koch, Robert, 1843-1910.
Koch, William Frederick.
Laennec, Rene Theophile Hyacinthe, 1781-1826.
Latham, Edward H.
Latham, John R.
Lewis, Henry Clay.
Li, Khai Fai, 1875-1954.
Lindsay, Catherine.
Lodge, Oliver Joseph, Sir, 1851-1940.
Logan, George, 1753-1821.
Lose, M. Phyllis.
McClenahan, William U., 1899-
McDowell, Ephraim, 1771-1830.
McFarland, George Bradley, 1866-1942.
Mackenzie, James, Sir, 1853-1925.
MacMillan, Carleton Lamont, 1903-
MacNeill, Norman Merle, 1888-1965.
Marat, Jean Paul, 1743-1793.
Mead, Richard, 1673-1754.
Mellon, William Larimer, 1910-
Mesmer, Franz Anton, 1734--1815.
Minot, George Richards, 1885-1950.
Mitchell, Silas Weir, 1829-1914.
Monardes, Nicolas, 1512 (Ca.)-1588.
Montessori, Maria, 1870-1952.
Montezuma, Carlos, 1866-1923.
Mooney, Jesse, 1866-1915.
Moor, Elisabeth.
Morgan, John, 1735-1789.
Munthe, Axel Martin Fredrik, 1857-1949.
Nathanson, Bernard N., 1926-
Nicoll, Maurice, 1884-1953.
Niehans, Paul, 1882-1971.
Nixon, Patrick Ireland, 1883-
Nordau, Max Simon, 1849-1923.
Osler, William, Sir, Bart., 1849-1919.
Peterson, Jim.
Pettus, Winston, 1912-1945.
Phlegar, Orrin King, 1876-
Pinel, Philippe, 1745-1826.
Pritham, Frederick John, 1880-
Read, Grantly Dick, 1890-
Reagan, Green Pryor, 1835-1893.
Richli, William C., 1913-
Rivard, Paul Leon.
Rosen, Samuel, 1897-
Roseveare, Helen.
Ross, Ronald.
Ruggles, Ora, 1894-
Ruse, James, 1760-1837?
Rush, Benjamin, 1745-1813.
Sabin, Florence Rena, 1871-1953.
Salk, Jonas Edward, 1914-
Sassall, John.
Saugrain De Vigni, Antoine Francois, 1763-1820.
Scaliger, Julius Caesar, 1484-1558.
Schulze, Gene.
Schweitzer, Albert, 1875-1965.
Servetus, Michael, 1509 or 11-1553.
Shattuck, Frederick Cheever, 1847-1929.
Sims, James Marlon, 1813-1883.
Spears, Leo Leaston, 1894-
Sptisbury, Sir Bernard Henry, 1877-1947.
Squibb, Edward Robinson, 1819-1900.
Stead, Eugene A.-Addresses, Essays, Lectures.
Strain, Samuel Frederick, 1895-
Tagilacozzi, Gaspare, 1545-1599.
Tankard, John, 1752-1836.
Taylor, Edward Robeson, 1838-1923.
Thacher, James, 1754-1844.
Trudeau, Edward Livingston, 1848-1915.
Verghese, Mary, 1925-
Vernon, Edward, 1946-
Von Herff, Ferdinand Ludwig, 1820-1912.
Wallace, David Richard, 1825-1911.
Warren, Joseph, 1741-1775.
Wier, Johann, 1515-1588.
Willis, Thomas, 1621-1675.
Wu, Hsien, 1803-1950.
Yandell, David Wendell, 1826-1898.
Young, Thomas, 1773-1829.

PHYSICIANS–AUSTRALIA
Browne, David Dorey, 1893-

PHYSICIANS–CANADA
Banting, Frederick Grant, Sir, 1891-1941-Juvenile Literature.
Gingras, Gustave, 1918-
Penfield, Wilder, 1891-

PHYSICIANS–GREAT BRITAIN
Addison, Thomas, 1793-1860.
Akenside, Mark, 1721-1770.
Bach, Edward, 1886-1936.
Barber, Geoffrey, 1904-
Beddoe, Robert Earl, 1882-1952.
Browne, Sir Thomas, 1605-1682.
Darwin, Erasmus, 1731-1802.
Dover, Thomas, 1660-1742.
Drake, Daniel, 1785-1852.
Freeman, Richard Austin, 1862-1943.
Harvey, William, 1578-1657.
Jenner, Edward, 1749-1823.
Kelvin, William Thomson, Baron, 1824-1907.
Le Vay, David.
Manson, Patrick, Sir, 1844-1922.
Mayo, William Worrell, 1819-1911.
Roget, Peter Mark, 1779-1869.
Simpson, James Young, Sir, Bart., 1811-1870.
Wakley, Thomas, 1795-1862.

PHYSICIANS, AFRO-AMERICAN
see Afro-American Physicians

PHYSICIANS, WOMEN
see Women Physicians

PHYSICISTS
Ampere, Andre Marie, 1775-1836.
Bohr, Niels Henrik David,1885-1962.
Born, Max, 1882-1970.
Bose, Satyendranath, 1894-1974.
Bragg, William Henry, Sir, 1862-1942.
Curie, Irene, 1897-1956.
Dyson, Freeman, J.
Einstein, Albert, 1879-1955.
Elsasser, Walter M., 1904-
Faraday, Michael, 1791-1867.
Fermi, Enrico, 1901-1954.
Fessenden, Reginald Aubrey, 1866-1932.
Fourier, Jean Baptiste Joseph, Baron, 1768-1830.
Frisch, Otto Robert, 1904-
Gibbs, Josiah Willard, 1839-1903.
Goddard, Robert Hutchings. 1882-1945.
Helmholtz, Hermann Ludwig Ferdinand Von, 1821-1894.
Honiss, William Henry, 1858-1940.
Infeld, Leopold, 1898-1968.
Korn, Arthur, 1870-1945.
Lande, Alfred, 1888-
Lawrence, Ernest Orlando, 1901-1958.
Mach, Ernst, 1838-1916.
Maxwell, James Clerk, 1831-1879.
Michelson, Albert Abraham, 1852-1931.
Morse, Philip McCord, 1903-
Moseley, Henry Gwyn Jeffreys, 1887-1915.
Newton, Isaac, Sir 1642-1727.
Oppenheimer, J. Robert, 1904-1967.
Peirce, Charles Santiago Sanders, 1839-1914.
Phillips John Aristotle.
Rayleigh, John William Strutt, Baron, 1842-1919.
Rontgen, Wilhelm Conrad, 1845-1923.
Rutherford, Ernest Rutherford, Baron, 1871-1937.
Simon, Francis Eugene, Sir 1893-1956.
Thompson, Benjamin, 1843-1884.
Thomson, Joseph John,Sir 1856-1940.

PHYSIOLOGISTS
Foster, Michael, Sir, 1836-1907.
Hales, Stephen, 1677-1761.
Lampkin-Asam, Julia McCain, 1931-
Moser, Albert, 1870-1903.

PIANISTS
De Bottazzi, Ana Maria Trenchi.
Gabrilowitsch, Ossip, 1878-1936.
Heller, Stephen, 1813-1888.
McCabe, Robin.
Rubinstein, Anton, 1829-1894.
Rubinstein, Artur, 1886-
Schnabel, Artur, 1882-1951.
Sutton, Ralph, 1922-

PIANO ACCORDION
see Accordion

PIANO TRADE
see Music Trade

PILGRIM FATHERS
see Pilgrims (New Plymouth Colony)

PILGRIMS (NEW PLYMOUTH COLONY)
Alden, John, 1599-1687.
Bradford, William, 1588-1657.
Brewster, William, 1566 or 7-1644.
Jones, Christopher, 1570 (Ca.)-1622.
Standish, Myles, 1584?-1656.

PILOTS (AERONAUTICS)
see Air Pilots

PILOTS AND PILOTAGE
Maukar, Daniel.

PIMA INDIANS
see Indians of North America–Southwest, New

PIMPS
Donaldson, William.

PING-PONG
see Table Tennis

PIONEERS
see also Frontier and Pioneer Life
Abrams, William, 1836-
Adam, George, Fl. 1850.
Allen, William, Ca. 1710-1780.
Arny, William Frederick Milton, 1813-1881.
Barclay, Alexander, 1810-1855.
Bent, William, 1809-1889.
Bishop, Joseph, B. 1770.
Boone, Daniel, 1734-1820.
Bowie, James, D. 1836.
Brannan, Samuel, 1819-1889.
Brown, James Stephens, B. 1828.
Brunson, Alfred, 1793-1882.
Carver, William F., 1840-1927.
Chapman, John, 1774-1845.
Cleaveland, Agnes Morley, 1874-
Dalrymple, George Elphinstone, 1826-1876.
Dalton, Henry, 1803-1884.
Denny, David Thomas.
Dixon, Billy, 1850-1913.
Dunn, John, 1857-1953.
Eaton, Frank, 1860-
Engelstad, Peder, 1857-1942.
Ezell, Uberto Desalx, 1867-1952.
Fitzpatrick, Thomas, 1799-1854.
Foster, Nathaniel, 1767?-1840.
Gally, Martha.
Grouard, Frank, 1850-
Haley Family.
Hatfield, Emmanuel, B. 1805.
Horne, Joseph, 1812-1897.
Hughes, Jesse, 1750 (Ca.)-1829.
Hunt, John Wesley, 1772-1849.
Ide, William Brown, 1796-1852.
Jackson, Franklin C., 1917-
Johnson, Joseph Ellis, 1817-1882.
Johnson, Montford T., 1843-1896.
Johnson, Oliver, 1821-1907.
Josselyn, Amos Piatt, 1820-1885.
Kemp, Ben E., 1860-1932.
Kenton, Simon, 1755-1836.
Kirker, James, 1793-1852 or 3.
Lanham, Maude (Nation)
Ligon, Robert Leonard, 1867-1959.
Livermore, Robert, 1799-1858.
Logan, James, 1674-1751.
Love, Nat, 1854-1921-Juvenile Literature.
Mackenzie, Ranald Slidell. 1840-1889.
Manby, Arthur Rochford, 1859?-1929?
Maverick, Samuel Augustus, 1803-1870.
Meek, Joseph Lafayette, 1810-1875.
Melton, Ann Eliza.
Mezieres, Athanase De, D. 1779.
Morton, Laura Elizabeth, 1871-1943.
Mossman, Burton C., 1867-
Munson, Charles J.
Navarro, Jose Antonio, 1795-1871.
Olson, David C. B., 1904-
Otero, Miguel Antonio, 1859-1944.
Pambrum, Andrew Dominique, 1822-1895.
Paradis, Charles Alfred Marie, 1848-1926.
Parrott, John, 1811-1884.
Pierce, William, 1590?-1641.
Pinkerton, Kathrene Sutherland Gedney, 1887-1967.
Pointe De Sable, Jean Baptiste, 1745?-1818-Juvenile Literature.
Porter, Rufus, 1792-1884.
Power, Emily, Mother, 1844-1909.
Price, John Milburn.
Redd, Lemuel Hardison, 1856-1923.
Reeves, Malachiah, 1843-1929.
Rich, Charles Coulson, 1809-1883.
Richards, Walter Scott, 1871-
Rose, Edward, Fl.1811-1834.
Rose, Isaac P., 1815-1899.
Royce, Sarah Bayliss.
Schroder, Fred.
Seymour, Louis, 1832?-1915.
Shaw, Elizabeth Cooper, 1794-1877.
Siringo, Charles A., 1855-1928.
Smet, Pierre Jean De, 1801-1873.
Smith, Coho, 1826-1914.
Smith, David, 1753- 1835.
Smith, John, 1580-1631.
Smith, Joseph, 1805-1844.
Smith T, John, 1770-1836.
Smith, Thomas Long.
Stevenson, William, 1768-1857.
Strait, Treva Adams, 1909- -Juvenile Literature.
Stuart, Granville, 1834-1918.
Sumpter, Jesse 1827-1910.
Sutter, John Augustus, 1803-1880.
Swilling, Jack, 1830-1878.
Swope Family.
Tabor, Elizabeth Bonduel McCourt Doe, D. 1935.
Tanner, Henry Martin, 1852-1935.
Vaughan, Alfred Jefferson, 1800-1871.
Wadsworth, James Wolcott, 1877-1952.
Waerenskjold, Elise Amalie Tvede, 1815-1895.
Wailes, Benjamin Leonard Covington, 1797-1862.
Watt, James W., 1843-1944.
Watt, Maud (Maloney)
Wentworth, John, Sir, 1737-1820.
Wentworth, John W., 1858-1954.
Whitman, Marcus, 1802-1847.
Williams, Slim, 1881 or 2-

PIRATES
see also Buccaneers; Privateering
Cofresi y Ramirez De Arellano, Roberto, 1791-1825-Juvenile Literature.
Glass, Hugh, Ca. 1780-Ca. 1833.
Laffite, Jean, 1782-1854.
Radcliffe, Anne Bonny, B. 1700.
Teach, Edward, D. 1718.
Wakeman, Edgar, 1813-1875.

PLANNING, CITY
see City Planning

PLANTATION LIFE
Peters, Frederick C., 1900-
Pinckney, Eliza (Lucas) 1723-1793.
Pond, Cornelia Jones, B. 1834.
Porter, Alexander, 1785-1844.

PLANTING
see Agriculture

PLAY DIRECTION (THEATER)
see Theater–Production and Direction

PLAY PRODUCTION (THEATER)
see Theater–Production and Direction

PLAYWRIGHTS
see Dramatists

POETS
see also Dramatists; Hymn Writers; Poets Laureate
Addison, Joseph, 1672-1719.
Akenside, Mark, 1721-1770.
Archilochus.
Ariosto, Lodovico, 1474-1533.
Arnold Matthew, 1822-1888.
Auden, Wystan Hugh, 1907-1973.
Barnes, Barnabe, 1569?-1609.
Barnes, William, 1801-1886.
Baudelaire, Charles Pierre, 1821-1867.
Beattie, James, 1735-1803.
Beaver, Bruce-Biography.
Beddoes, Thomas Lovell, 1803-1849.
Behan, Brendan.

PRECISIANS
see Puritans
PREMIERS
see Prime Ministers
PRESBYTERIANISM
Sanford, Charlotte, 1936-
Smith, Daisy, 1891-1972.
PRESIDENTS–UNITED STATES
Adams, John, Pres. U.S., 1735-1826.
Adams, John Quincy, Pres. U.S., 1767-1848.
Arthur, Chester Alan, Pres. U.S., 1830-1886.
Buchanan, James, Pres. U.S., 1791-1868.
Carter, Jimmy, 1924-
Cleveland, Grover, Pres. U.S., 1837-1908.
Coolidge, Calvin, Pres. U.S., 1872-1918.
Eisenhower, Dwight David, Pres., U.S., 1890-1969.
Fillmore, Millard, Pres. U.S., 1800-1874.
Ford, Gerald R., 1913-
Garfield, James Abram, Pres. U.S., 1831-1881.
Grant, Ulysses Simpson, Pres. U.S., 1822-1885.
Harding, Warren Gamaliel, Pres. U.S., 1865-1923.
Harrison, Benjamin, Pres. U.S., 1833-1901.
Harrison, William Henry, Pres. U.S., 1773-1841.
Hayes, Rutherford Birchard, Pres. U.S., 1822-1893.
Hoover, Herbert Clark, Pres., U.S., 1874-1964.
Jackson, Andrew, Pres., U.S., 1767-1845.
Jefferson, Thomas, Pres., U.S., 1743-1826.
Johnson, Andrew, Pres. U.S., 1808-1875.
Johnson, Lyndon Baines, Pres. U.S., 1908-1973.
Kennedy, John Fitsgerald, Pres. U.S., 1917-1963.
Lincoln, Abraham, Pres., U.S., 1809-1865.
McKinley, William, Pres. U.S., 1843-1901.
Madison, James, Pres. U.S., 1751-1836.
Monroe, James, Pres. U.S., 1758-1831.
Nixon, Richard Milhous, 1913-
Pierce, Franklin, Pres. U.S., 1804-1869.
Polk, James Knox, Pres. U.S., 1795-1849.
Roosevelt, Franklin Delano, Pres., U.S., 1882-1945.
Roosevelt, Theodore, Pres. U. S., 1858--1919.
Taft, William Howard, Pres. U.S., 1857-1930.
Taylor, Zachary, Pres. U.S., 1784-1850.
Truman, Harry S., Pres., U.S., 1884-1972.
Tyler, John, Pres. U.S., 1790-1862.
Van Buren, Martin, Pres. U.S., 1782-1862.
Washington, George, Pres., U.S., 1732-1799.
Wilson, Woodrow, Pres., U.S., 1856-1924.
PRESIDENTS–UNITED STATES–BROTHERS AND SISTERS
Carter, Billy.
Coolidge Family.
Cowles, Anna (Roosevelt) 1855-1961.
Kennedy, Ethel Skakel.
Kennedy, Joseph Patrick, 1915-1944.
PRESIDENTS–UNITED STATES–WIVES AND CHILDREN
Adams, Abigail Smith, 1744-1818.
Adams, Louisa Catherine (Johnson) 1775-1852.
Carter, Amy.
Carter, Rosalynn.
Coolidge Family.
Eisenhower, Mamie (Dou 1896-
Ford, Betty, 1918-
Grant, Julia Dent, 1826-1902.
Harrison, Jane Irwin.
Jefferson Family.
Jefferson. Martha (Wayles) Skelton. 1748-1782.
Johnson, Claudia Alta (Taylor) 1912-
Kennedy, Caroline.
Kennedy, Jacqueline (Bouvier) 1929-
Lincoln, Mary (Todd) 1818-1882.
Lincoln, Nancy (Hanks) 1784-1818.
Lincoln, Robert Todd, 1843-1926.
Lincoln, Thomas, 1853-1871.
Longworth, Alice Roosevelt, 1884-
Madison, Dolley Payne Todd, 1768-1849.
Nixon Family.
Nixon, Patricia, 1912-
Onassis, Jacqueline Kennedy,1929-
Polk, Sarah Childress, 1803-1891.
Randolph. Martha (Jefferson) 1772-1836.
Randolph, Thomas Mann, 1768-1828.
Robb, Lynda Bird, 1944-
Roosevelt, Eleanor Roosevelt, 1884-1962.
Roosevelt Family.
Roosevelt, James, 1907-
Stanley-Brown, Mary Garfield, B. 1867.
Washington, Martha Dandridge Custis, 1731-1802.
Wilson, Edith Bolling Galt, 1872-1961.
Wilson, Ellen Louis (Axson)
PRESS
Sabinson, Harvey.
PRETENDERS
see Impostors and Imposture
PRIESTESSES
see Priests
PRIESTS
see also Clergy
also subdivision Clergy under church bodies, e.g. Catholic Church–Clergy; Church of England–Clergy
Badin, Stephen Theodore, 1768-1853.
Braun, Albert, 1889-
Brisson, Louis, 1817-1908.
Casey, Solanus, 1870-1957.
Gibault, Pierre, 1737-1804.
Nichiren, 1222-1282.
O'Neill, Felix J., 1860-1937.
Raskolniks.
PRIME MINISTERS
Bustamante, William Alexander, Sir, 1884.
Chifley, Joseph Benedict, 1885-1951-Juvenile Literature.
Kishi, Nobusuke.
Lumumba, Patrice, 1925-1961.
Mancham, James R., 1939-
PRIME MINISTERS–CANADA
Bracken, John, 1883-
Diefenbaker, John George.
Howe, Joseph, 1804-1873.
King, William Lyon Mackenzie, 1874-1950.
Laurier, Wilfrid, Sir 1841-1919.
Macdonald, John Alexander, Sir 1815-1891.
Mackenzie, Alexander, 1822-1892.
Pearson, Lester B.
Riel, Louis David, 1844-1885.
Trudeau, Pierre Elliott.
PRIME MINISTERS–GREAT BRITAIN
Beaconsfield,Benjamin Disraeli, 1st Earl of, 1804-1881.
Callaghan, James, 1912-
Chamberlain, Neville, 1869-1940.
Churchill, Sir Winston Le Spencer, 1874-
Eden, Anthony, Earl of Avon, 1897-
Gladstone, William Ewart, 1809-1898.
Heath, Edward.
Home, Alexander Frederick Douglas-Home, 14th Earl of, 1903-
Law, Andrew Bonar, 1858-1923.
Lloyd George, David Lloyd George, 1st Earl, 1803-1945.
Melbourne, William Lamb, 2d Viscount, 1779-1848.
North, Frederick North, Baron, 1732-1792.
Thatcher, Margaret.
Wilson, Harold, 1916-
PRINCES
Charles D'Orleans, 1394-1465.
Charles Edward, the Young Pretender, 1720-1788.
Charles, Prince of Wales, 1948-
Harald, Crown Prince of Norway, 1937-
Kaapu, Myrtle King, 1898-
Kaiulani, Princess of Hawaii, 1875-1899.
Vajiran Ana Varoros, Prince, Supreme Patriarch, 1859-1921.
Viktoria Luise, Herzogin Zu Braunschweig und Luneburg, 1892-
Vlad II, Dracul, Prince of Wallachia, D. Ca. 1476.
Wilhelm, Crown Prince of the German Empire and of Prussia, 1882-1951.
Willem I, Prince of Orange, 1533-1584.
PRINCIPALS, SCHOOL
see School Superintendents and Principals
PRINTERS
Cock, Hieronymus, 1510 (Ca.)-1570.
Daye, Stephen, 1611-1668.
Estienne, Robert, 1503?-1559.
Ghormley, James Grant, 1925-1967.
Johnston, James, 1738-1808.
Manuzio, Aldo Pio, 1449 or 50-1515.
Morison, Stanley, 1889-1967.
Murdock, Charles Albert, 1841-1928.
Plantin, Christophe, 1514-1589.
Schmied, Francois Louis, 1873-
Strahan, William, 1715-1785.
Williams, Edward, 1750-1813.
Williams, Thomas E., 1894-
PRISONERS
Dolgun, Alexander.
LaFarge, Marie Fortunee Cappelle Pouch, 1816-1852.
Loebl, Eugen.
New York. State Prison, Attica.
Novak, Frank, 1884-
PRISONERS, POLITICAL
see Political Prisoners
PRISONERS OF WAR
Crouter, Natalie, 1898-
Delbo, Charlotte.
Dengler, Dieter.
Heimler, Eugene.
Linke, Maria Zeitner.
Mynarski, Bronisaw, 1899-1971.
Piasecki, Victor.
Quinn, Michael A., 1895-
Stratton, Richard A., 1931-
Watanabe, Kiyoshi, 1890?-
PRISONS–EMPLOYEES
Schneider, Wilma.
PRISONS–GREAT BRITAIN
Fry, Elizabeth Gurney, 1780-1845.
PRIVATE HOUSEHOLD WORKERS
see Servants
PRIVATEERING
Boyle, Thomas, 1775 or 6-1825.
PRIZE-FIGHTING
see Boxing
PROFESSORS
see College Teachers
PROGRESSIVISM (U. S. POLITICS)
Lane, Franklin Knight, 1864-1921.
PROPHETS
Amos, the Prophet.
Branham, William, 1909-
Daniel, the Prophet.
Frodsham, Stanley Howard, 1882-1969.
Issiah, the Prophet.
Jeremiah, the Prophet.
Jonah, the Prophet.
Moses.
Muhammad, the Prophet.
Nehemiah.
Tozer, Aiden Wilson, 1897-1963.
PROSPECTING
Arthur Zua (Bearss)
Ball, Amos Entheus.
Eide, Harald, 1896-
PROSTITUTION
Cordelier, Jeanne.
PROTECTION OF GAME
see Game Protection
PROTESTANT EPISCOPAL CHURCH IN THE U. S. A.–CLERGY
Bozarth-Campbell, Alla, 1947-
PROTESTANT REFORMATION
see Reformation
PRUSSIA
Friedrich II, der Grosse, King of Prussia, 1712-1786.
Friedrich Wilhelm I, King of Prussia, 1688-1740.
PSEUDOLEUCEMIA
see Hodgkin's Disease
PSYCHIATRISTS
Adler, Alfred, 1870-1937.
Allison, Ralph.
Baruk, Henri, 1897-
Dreikurs, Rudolf, 1897-1972.
Groddeck, Georg Walther, 1866-1934.
Hartman, David, 1949-
Jung, Carl Gustav, 1875-1961.
Kagwa, Benjamin N. H.
Laing, Ronald David.
Perls, Frederick S.
Ritchie, George G., 1923-
Salmon, Thomas William, 1876-1927.
Shepard, Martin, 1934-
Viscott, David S., 1938-
PSYCHIC HEALING
see Mental Healing
PSYCHICAL RESEARCH
see also Clairvoyance; Ghosts; Spiritualism
Dixon, Jeane.
Geller, Uri, 1946-
Kingston, Kenny.
Kreskin, 1935-
Monroe, Robert A.
Price, Harry, 1881-1948.
Wilson, Robert Anton, 1932-
PSYCHOANALYSIS
Erikson, Erik Homburger, 1902-
Freud, Sigmund, 1856-1939.
Fromm, Erich, 1900-
Kardiner, Abram, 1891-
Reich, Wilhelm, 1897-1957.
Ribot, Theodule, 1839-1916.
PSYCHOLOGICAL ASPECTS OF DISABILITY
see Handicapped
PSYCHOLOGISTS
see also Psychiatrists
Allport, Gordon Willard, 1897-1967.
Binet, Alfred, 1857-1911.
Boulding, Kenneth Ewart, 1910-
Cattell, James McKeen, 1860-1944-Bibliography.
Clark, Kenneth Bancroft, 1914- -Bibliography.
Erhard, Werner, 1936-
Hall, Granville Stanley, 1844-1924.
Hirsch, Ernest A., 1924-
Horney, Karen, 1885-1952.
James, William, 1842-1910.
Kopp, Sheldon B., 1929-
Ladd, George Trumbull, 1842-1921.
Lewin, Kurt, 1890-1947.
Maslow, Abraham Harold.
Moser, Tilmann, 1938-
Ogden, Charles Kay, 1889-1957.
Pavlov, Ivan Petrovich, 1849-1936.
Reik, Theodor, 1888-1969.
Rogers, Carl Ransom, 1902-
Rorschach, Hermann, 1884-1922. Psychodiagnostics.
Saller, Alfred, 1870-1937.
Shanahan, Louise, Joint Author.
Sherrington, Charles Scott, Sir., 1857-1952.
Skinner, Burrhus Frederic, 1904-
Stevenson, Yvonne, 1915-
Sullivan, Harry Stack, 1892-1949.
Thurston, Louis Leon.
Watson, John Broadus, 1878-1958.
PSYCHOLOGY, CHILD
see Child Psychology
PSYCHOPATHOLOGISTS
see Psychiatrists
PUBLIC ACCOUNTANTS
see Accountants
PUBLIC ASSISTANCE
see Public Welfare
PUBLIC HEALTH ADMINISTRATION
Brown, Lucius Polk, 1867-1935.
PUBLIC OFFICERS
see also Civil Service; Municipal Officials and Employees
Gruening, Ernest Henry, 1887-
Jocelyn, Stephen Perry, 1843-1920.
Moses, Robert, 1888-
PUBLIC RELATIONS
see also Advertising
Lee, Ivy Ledbetter, 1877-1934.
Meed, Samuel Williams, 1895-
Rogers, Henry C., 1914-
PUBLIC RELATIONS–BUSINESS
see Public Relations
PUBLIC RELATIONS–INDUSTRY
see Public Relations

PUBLIC RELATIONS–PUBLIC ADMINISTRATION
see Government Publicity

PUBLIC RELIEF
see Public Welfare

PUBLIC WELFARE
Here are entered works on tax-supported welfare activities.
see also Medical Social Work; Social Workers
Santana, Carmen,1932-

PUBLICITY, GOVERNMENT
see Government Publicity
PUBLISHERS AND AUTHORS
see Authors and Publishers
PUBLISHERS AND PUBLISHING
see also Booksellers and Bookselling; Newspaper Publishing
Aronson, Charles N., 1913-
Bangs, Samuel, Ca. 1794-Ca. 1853.
Bowker, Richard Rogers, 1848-1933.
Brings, Lawrence Martin, 1897.
Cobden-Sanderson, Thomas James, 1840-1922.
Collier Family.
Cundall, Joseph, 1818-1895.
Dennis, Clyde H.
Dwight, John Sullivan, 1813-1893.
Fields, James Thomas, 1816-1881.
Flynt, Larry.
Harper, John C.
Hart, Abraham, 1810-1885.
Hearst, William Randolph, 1863-1951.
Hefner, Hugh Marston, 1926-
Holt, Henry, 1840-1926.
Johnson, Joseph, 1738-1809.
Leslie, Miriam Florence Folline Squier, D. 1914.
Lewis, Fulton.
Liveright, Horace Brisbin, 1886-1933.
Luce, Henry Robinson, 1898-1967.
McAlmon, Robert, 1896-1956.
McClure, Samuel Sidney, 1857-1949.
Mosher, Thomas Bird, 1852-1923.
Munsey, Frank Andrew, 1854-1925.
Ochs, Adolph Simon, 1858-1935.
Patterson, Eleanor Medill, 1881-1948.
Perkins, Maxwell Evarts, 1884-1947.
Regnery, Henry, 1912-
Swenson, Birger, 1895-
Wallace, Henry Cantwell, 1866-1924.
PUBLISHERS AND PUBLISHING–GREAT BRITAIN
Fry Family.
Murray, John, 1778-1843.
Taylor, John, 1781-1864.
PUBLISHING OF NEWSPAPERS
see Newspaper Publishing
PUEBLO INDIANS
see Indians of North America–Southwest, New
PUERTO RICANS IN THE UNITED STATES
Barretto, Lefty, 1942-
Tapia, Carlos, 1885-1945.
PUERTO RICO–BIOGRAPHY
Barbosa, Jose Celso, 1857-1921.
DeGautier, Felisa Rincon.
Munoz Marin, Luis, 1898- -Juvenile Literature.
Rincon De Gautier, Felisa-Juvenile Literature.
PUGILISM
see Boxing
PUPPETS AND PUPPET-PLAYS
Spathar Es, S Ot Erios Eugeniou.
PURITANS
see also Pilgrims (New Plymouth Colony); Presbyterianism
Ames, William, 1576-1633.
Dell, William, D. 1664.
Peters, Hugh 1598-1660.

Q

QUAKERS
see Friends, Society Of
QUEEN BEES
see Bee Culture
QUEENS
see also Courts and Courtiers; Kings and Rulers; also subdivision Kings and Rulers under names of countries, e.g. Great Britain–Kings and Rulers
Carlota Joaquina, Consort of Joao VI, King of Portugal, 1775-1830.
Carolina Maria, Consort of Ferdinand I, King of the Two Sicilies, 1752-1814.
Caroline Amelia Elizabeth, Consort of George IV, 1768-1821.
Caroline, Consort of George II, 1683-1737.

Caroline Mathilde, Consort of Christian VII, King of Denmark, 1751-1775.
Catharine I, Empress of Russia, D. 1727.
Catharine II, Empress of Russia, 1729-1796.
Catharine of Aragon, Consort of Henry VIII, King of England, 1485-1536.
Catharine Parr, Consort of Henry VIII, King of England, 1512-1548.
Catherine De Medicis, Consort of Henry II, King of France, 1519-1589.
Isabel I, la Catolica, Queen of Spain, 1451-1504.
Isabel II, Queen of Spain, 1830-1904.
Kristina, Queen of Sweden, 1626-1689.
Nefertiti, Queen of Egypt, 14th Cent. B.C.

R

RABBIS
Baeck, Leo, 1873-1956.
Brickner, Barnett Robert, 1892-1958.
Carlebach, Joseph, 1883-1942.
David Ben Samuel, Ha-Levi, 1536 (Ca.)-1667.
Hirsch, Emil Gustav, 1851-1923.
Kahan, Israel Meir, 1838-1933.
Kertzer, Morris Norman, 1910-
Levin, Arieh, 1885-1969.
Moses Ben Maimon, 1135-1204.
Moses Ben Nahman, Ca. 1195-Ca. 1270.
Nahman Ben Simhah, of Bratzlav, 1770?-1810?
Reines, Isaac Jacob, 1839-1915.
Rosenblatt, Samuel, 1902-
Steinberg, Milton, 1903-1950.
Wise, Isaac Mayer, 1819-1900.
RACES OF MAN
see Ethnology
RACING
see also Automobile Racing; Horse-Racing; Racing; Motorcycle Racing; Running
Markel, Bart, 1935-
RADIO–BROADCASTING
see Radio Broadcasting
RADIO BROADCASTING
Davis, Elmer Holmes, 1890-1958.
Lujack, Larry.
Sarnoff, David, 1891-
Whittinghill, Dick.
Zacharias, Ellis M.
RADIO JOURNALISTS
see Journalists
RAILROAD CONSTRUCTION
see Railroads–Construction
RAILROAD WORKERS
see Railroads–Employees
RAILROADS–CONSTRUCTION
Moffatt, David Halliday, 1839-1911.
RAILROADS–EMPLOYEES
Bragg, George Nathan, 1897 or 8-1975.
Desmond, J. Patrick.
Foster, Tom, 1902-
Gresley, Herbert Nigel, Sir, 1876-1941.
Judah, Theodore Dehone, 1828-1863.
Sanders, Donald G., 1899-
Willard, Daniel, 1861-1942.
Williams, George H., 1890-
RAILROADS–SWITCHES
see Railroads–Construction
RAILROADS–TURNOUTS
see Railroads–Construction
RAILROADS–ALASKA
Heney, Michael John, 1864-1910.
RANCH LIFE
see also Cowboys
Beckert, Harriet T.
Crosby, Robert Anderson, 1897-1947.
Lavender, David Sievert, 1910-
Lewis, William J., 1870-1960.
Lopez, Jose Jesus, 1852-1939.
Pacheo, Francisco Perez, 1790-1860.
Pankey, Joe, 1892-
Snipes, Ben E., 1835-1906.
Warner, Juan Jose, 1807-1893.
Woodis, Clark, 1888-1971.
RANGE MANAGEMENT
Payne, John, Fl. 1829-1859.
RAPPAHANNOCK INDIANS
see Indians of North America–Eastern States
RATIONALISM
see also Atheism
Edelmann, Johann Christian, 1698-1767.
REBELS (SOCIAL PSYCHOLOGY)
see Dissenters
RECLAMATION OF LAND
Vermuyden, Cornelius, Sir, 1590-1677.
RECLUSES
see also Hermits
Collyer, Langley.
RECREATIONS
see Sports
RECTORS
see Clergy
RECUSANTS
see Catholics in England
REDEVELOPMENT, URBAN
see City Planning
REFEREEING (SPORTS)
see Sports Officiating
REFORMATION
Jonas, Justus, 1493-1555.
Knox John, 1505-1572.
Luther Martin, 1483-1546.
Tyndale, William, D.1536.
Wycliffe, John, D. 1384.
Zwingli, Ulrich, 1484-1531.
REFORMATION–GERMANY
Philipp I, der Grossmutige, Landgrave of Hesse, 1504-1567.
REFORMED CHURCH IN THE UNITED STATES
DePree, Gladis, 1933-
REFORMERS
see also Social Reformers
Dickinson, Anna Elizabeth, 1842-1932.
Dix, Dorothea Lynde, 1802-1887.
Farel, Guillaume, 1489-1565.
Gracchus, G. Sempronius.
Gracchus, Tiberius Sempronius.
Hapgood, Norman, 1868-1937.
Holyoake, George Jacob, 1817-1906.
Hooper, Johnson Jones, 1815?-1863.
Howard, Ebenezer, Sir, 1850-1928.
Howard, John, 1726?-1790.
Hutten, Ulrich Von, 1488-1523.
Jrgen Eriksen, 1535-1604.
Kagawa, Toyohiko, 1888-
Lewis, Alfred Baker, 1897-
Livermore, Mary Ashton Rice, 1820-1905.
Ludlow, John Malcolm Forbes, 1821-1911.
Ocampo, Melchor, 1814-1861.
Ortiz De Ayala, Tadeo.
Phillips, Wendell, 1811-1884.
Plockhoy, Pieter Corneliszoon, Fl.1659.
Savonarola, Girolamo Maria Francesco Matteo, 1452-1498.
Spengler, Lazarus, 1479-1534.
Wiley, George Alvin, 1931-1973.
Wilkes, John, 1727-1797.
REFUGEES
Crist, Evamae Barton.
Henson, Josiah, 1789-1883.
Kruk, Zofia.
REFUGEES–CUBA
Ramirez, Armando Socarras-Juvenile Literature.
REGISTRATION OF VOTERS
see Voters, Registration Of
RELIEF (AID)
see Public Welfare
RELIGION–PHILOSOPHY
Pannenberg, Wolfhart, 1928-
RELIGIOUS BIOGRAPHY
see also Christian Biography
Donicht, Mark.
Ferron, Marie Rose, 1902-1966.
Griffin, Mary Annarose, Sister.
Guerin, Theodore, Mother, 1798-1856.
Guidry, Mary Gabriella, 1914-
Hachard, Marie Madeleine.
Hallahan, Margaret Mary, 1806-1868.
Hawes, Jerome. 1876-1956.
Healy-Murphy, Margaret Mary, 1833 1907.
Jarieot, Paciline Marie, 1799-1862.
Javouhey, Anne Marie, Mother, 1779-1851.
Jordan of Saxony, D.1237.
Joseph of the Sacred Heart, Mother, 1823-1902.
Kalleel, George.
Kasper, Maria, 1820-1898.
Kevin, Mother, O.S.F., 1875-1957.
Kimbangu, Simon, 1889?-1951.
Kowalska, Faustyna, Sister, 1905-1938.
Kramer, Norbert A., 1910-1959.
Lilburne, John, 1614?-1657.
Long, Mary Ann, 1946-1959.
Longley, Lydia, 1674-1758.
Loukaris, Kurillos, Patriarch of Constantinople, 1572-1638.
Lurana Mary Francis, Mother, 1870-1935.
Luther Martin, 1483-1546.
Mall, E. Jane, 1920-
Mallinckrodt, Pauline Von, 1817-1881.
Maria Assunta, Sister, 1878-1905.
Maria Crocifissa Di Gesu, Madre, 1713-1787.
Maria, De Jesus De Agreda, Mother, 1602-1665.
Maria De Passione, Mere, 1839-1904.
Maria Luisa Josefa of the Most Blessed Sacrament, Mother, 1866-1937.
Marie De Jesus, Mother. 1876-1931.
Marie De Jesus, Mother, 1876-1931.
Marie Rose, Mother, 1811-1849.
Marto, Jacintha, 1910-1920.
Mary Adelaide, Mother, 1874-
Mary Cleophas, Mother.
Mary Euthymia, Sister, 1914-1955.
Mary Faustina, Sister, 1905-1938.
Mary Odilia, Mother, 1823-1880.
Mary Veronica, Mother, 1838-1904.
Mary Zita. Mother. 1844-1917.
Meyers, Harvey, 1940-
Mohammad, the Prophet.
Monchanin, Jules.
Moye, Jean Martin, 1730-1793.
Nestorius, Patriarch of Constantinople, Fl. 428.
Neumann, Therese, 1898-1962.
Neve, Rosemary, 1923-
Noah.
Noble, Margaret Elizabeth, 1867-1911.
Ogilvie, John, 1580?--1615.
Power, Emily, Mother, 1844-1909.
Praxedes Mother.
Roberts, Bill.
Robinson, Edward, 1794-1863.
Rogers, Mary Joseph, 1882-1955.
Rookmaaker, Hendrik Roelof, 1922-1977.
Ross, Xavier, Mother, 1813-1895.
Tommasini, Maria.
Trosse, George, 1631-1713.
Truszkowska, Maria Angela, 1825-1899.
Venard, Jean Theophane, 1829-1861.
Vonier, Anscar, 1875-1938.
Wilkinson, Jemima, 1752-1819.
Xainctonge, Anne De, 1567-1621.
Zervas, Annella, 1900-1926.
Zinzendorf, Nicolaus Ludwig, Graf Von, 1700-1760.
RELIGIOUS LIFE
see Christian Life; Monastic and Religious Life also subdivision Religious Life under classes of persons, e.g. Family–Religious Life
RESCUE WORK
Evans, Dick, 1905-
RESEARCH, MUSICAL
see Musicology
RESIDENT PHYSICIANS
see Hospitals–Staff
RESISTANCE MOVEMENTS (WORLD WAR, 1939-1945)
see Anti-Nazi Movement
RESORTS
Grossinger, Jennie (Grossinger) 1892-
RESTAURANT MANAGEMENT
Childs, William Macbride, 1869-1939.
Gust, Peter.
Kroc, Ray, 1902-
RETAIL ADVERTISING
see Advertising
RETARDED CHILDREN
see Mentally Handicapped Children
RETIREMENT
see also Aged
Olmstead, Alan H.
REVIVALISTS
see Evangelists
REVOLUTION, AMERICAN
see United States–History–Revolution, 1775-1783
REVOLUTIONARY WAR, AMERICAN
see United States–History–Revolution, 1775-1783
REVOLUTIONISTS
Corday D'Armont, Marie Anne Charlotte De, 1768-1793.
Danton, Georges Jacques, 1759-1794.
Dardan, Francois, 1733-1792.
Davis, Angela Yvonne, 1944-
Delcev, Goce, 1872-1903.
Guevara, Ernesto, 1928-1967.
Ho Chi Minh, 1890-1969.
Kano, Aminu, 1920-
Levine, Eugen.
Maceo, Antonio, 1845-1896.
Mifflin, Thomas, 1744-1800.
Miranda, Francisco De, 1750-1816.
Narino, Antonio, 1765-1823.
Orsini, Felice, 1819-1858.
Padmore, George, 1903-1959.
Riel, Louis David, 1844-1885.
Robespierre, Maximilien Marie Isadore De, 1758-1794.
Saint-Just, Louis Antoine De, 1767-1794.
Sandino, Augusto Cesar, 1895-1934.
Shu, Ching-Chun, 1898-1966.
Thirion, Andre, 1907- -Biography.
Tousley, Clare M., 1889-
Zapata, Emiliano, 1879-1919.
REVOLUTIONISTS–IRELAND
Pearse, Padraic, 1879-1916.
REVOLUTIONISTS–RUSSIA
Balabanoff, Angelica, 1878-1965.
Mironov, Filipp Kuzmich, 1872-1921.
Nechaev, Sergei Gennadievich, 1847-1882.
Tkachev, Petr Nikitich, 1844-1886.
RHODE ISLAND
see also names of cities, etc., in Rhode Island
Downer, Silas.
RHODESIA AND NYASALAND–NATIVE RACES
Smith, Ian Douglas, 1919-
RIDING
see Horsemanship
RIGHTS OF WOMEN
see Women's Rights
RIVER LIFE
Smyth, Andrew Farney, 1817-1879.
ROBBERS
see Brigands and Robbers
ROCK MUSICIANS
Alice Cooper (Musical Group)
Bach, Thomas John.
Bachman-Turner Overdrive (Musical Group)
Beach Boys.
Bowie, David.
Chicago (Musical Septet)-Juvenile Literature.
Clapton, Eric.
Ferry, Bryan.
Frampton, Peter.
Harrison, George, 1943-
Hunter, Ian, 1946-
Jackson 5 (Musical Group)
John, Elton.
Kooper, Al.
McCartney, Paul.
Plant, Robert.
Slick, Grace.
Springsteen, Bruce.
Who (Musical Quartet)
Williams, Allan.
Young, Neil.
RODEOS
Latting, Thyrl.
ROLLER-SKATING
Dunn, Natalie, 1956- -Juvenile Literature.
ROMAN CATHOLIC CHURCH
see Catholic Church
ROMAN EMPERORS
Augustus, Emperor of Rome, 63 B.C.-14 A.D.
Aurelius Antoninus, Marcus, Emperor of Rome, 121-180.
Caesar, C Julius.
Caligula, Emperor of Rome, 12-41.
Hadrianus, Emperor of Rome, 76-138.
Julianus, Apostata, Emperor of Rome, 331-363.
Severus Alexander, Emperor of Rome, 208-235.
Severus, Lucius Septimius, Emperor of Rome, 146-211.
Tiberius, Emperor of Rome, 42 B.C.-37 A.D.
Titus, Emperor of Rome, 40-81-Juvenile Literature.
ROMAN LAW
Fronto, Marcus Cornelius.
ROMANS–GREAT BRITAIN
Agricola, Cn. Julius, 37-93.
ROME–ARMY
Marius, C.
ROME–BIOGRAPHY
see also Classical Biography; Roman Emperors
Belisarius, 505 (Ca.)-565.
Cassiodorus Senator, Flavius Magnus Aurelius, Ca. 487-Ca. 580.
Catilina, Lucius Sergius, 108 (Ca.)-62 B.C.
Cato, Marcus Porcius, Censorius.
Cicero, Marcus Tillius.
Crassus, Marcus Licinius.
Frontinus, Sextus Julius.
Fronto, Marcus Cornelius.
Galla Placidia, 389 (Ca.) 450.
Pompeius Magnus, Cn.
Sulla, Lucius Cornelius.
ROME–HISTORY–KINGS, 753-510 B.C.
Tarquinius Superbus, Lucius, Fl. 534-510 B. C.
ROME–NOBILITY
Pilate, Pontius, 1st Cent.
ROME–OFFICIALS AND EMPLOYEES
Frontinus, Sextus Julius.
ROYAL DESCENT, FAMILIES OF
Mountbatten Family.
Sidney Family.
ROYAL FAVORITES
see Favorites, Royal
ROYALTY
see also Kings and Rulers; Princes; also subdivision Kings and Rulers under names of countries, e.g. Great Britain–Kings and Rulers
La Valliere, Louise Francoise De La Baume Le Blanc, Duchesse De, 1644-1710.
Margaret, Princess of Great Britain, 1930-
Marie De Medicis, Consort of Henry IV, King of France, 1573-1642.
Marie Louise, Consort of Napoleon I, 1791-1847.
RUGBY FOOTBALL
see also Football
McBride, William John, 1940-
McCormick, William Fergus.
RUGGER
see Rugby Football
RULERS
see Emperors; Kings and Rulers
RUNAWAY CHILDREN
see also Juvenile Delinquency
Ton, Jill.
RUNNING
see also Marathon Running; Track-Athletics
Decker, Mary, 1958- -Juvenile Literature.
Liquori, Marty.
Matthews, Vincent, 1947-
Wilson, Patty.
RURAL LIFE
see Farm Life; Outdoor Life
RUSSIA
see also names of specific cities, areas, etc. in Russia
Elizabeth, Grand Duchess of Russia, 1864-1918.
RUSSIA–ARMED FORCES
Denikin, Anton Ivanovich, 1872-1947.
RUSSIA–BIOGRAPHY
Allilueva, Svetlana, 1925-
Bazili, Nikolai Aleksandrovich, 1883-1963.
Beriia, Lavrentii Pavlovich, 1899-1953.
Brik, Lili IUrevna.
Bunin, Ivan Alekseevich, 1870-1953.
Fyodorova, Victoria, 1946-
Golitsyn, Dmitril Dmitrievich, Kniaz', 1770-1840.
Heinrich, Prince of Prussia, 1726-1802.
Kollontai, Aleksandra Mikhailovna, 1872-1952.
Kovach, Nora, 1931-
Leontev, Konstantin Nikolaevich, 1831-1891.
Masepa, Ivan Stepanovich, Hetman of the Cossacks, D. 1709.
Mikhail Aleksandrovich, Grand Duke of Russia, 1878-1918.
Poltoratskii, Ellen Sarah (Southee) 1819-1908.

Romanov, House of.
Stolypin, Petr Arkadevich, 1862-1911.
Strakhov, Nikolai Nikolaevich, 1828-1896.
RUSSIA-COURT AND COURTIERS
Galitzine, Irina, Princess, 1900-
RUSSIA-KINGS AND RULERS
Alexander I, Emperor of Russia, 1777-1825.
Alexander II, Emperor of Russia, 1818-1881.
Alexander III, Emperor of Russia, 1845-1894.
Alexandra, Consort of Nichola.
Anastasia Nikolaevna, Grand Duchess of Russia, 1901-1918.
Anne, Empress of Russia, 1693-1740.
Boris Godunov, Czar of Russia, 1551?-1605.
Catharine I, Empress of Russia, D. 1727.
Catharine II, Empress of Russia, 1729-1796.
Demetrius (Pseudo-Demetrius) I, Czar of Russia, 1581-1606.
Elizabeth, Empress of Russia, 1709-1762.
Elizabeth, Empress, 1741-1762.
Ivan Iv, the Terrible, Czar of Russia, 1530-1584.
Nicholas I, Emperor of Russia, 1796-1855.
Nicholas II, Emperor of Russia, 1868-1918.
Paul I, Emperor of Russia, 1754-1801.
Peter I, the Great, Emperor of Russia, 1672-1725.
Stalin, Iosif. 1870-1953.
RUSSIA-NAVY
Nakhimov, Pavel Stepanovich, 1803-1855.
RUSSIA-OFFICIALS AND EMPLOYEES
Barmine, Alexandre.
RUSSIAN AUTHORS
see Authors, Russian
RUSSIAN CHURCH
see Orthodox Eastern Church, Russian
RUSSIAN COMPOSERS
see Composers, Russian
RUSSIAN ORTHODOX CHURCH
see Orthodox Eastern Church, Russian
RUSSIANS
Dashkova, Ekaterina Romanovna (Vorontsova) Kniaginia, 1743-1810.

S

SACRED SONGS
see Gospel Music
SAILORS
see Seamen
Stormalong, Alfred Bulltop.
ST. FRANCIS, ORDER OF
see Franciscans
SAINTS
see also Hermits; Martyrs

Adalard, Saint, Abbott of Corbie, D. 826.
Agobard, Saint, Abp. of Lyons, D. 840.
Alacoque, Marguerite Marie, Saint, 1647-1690.
Albertus Magnus, Saint, Bp. of Ratisbon, 1198?-1280.
Aldheim, Saint, Bp. of Sherborne, 640?-709.
Ambrosius, Saint, Bp. of Milan.
Andrew, Saint, Apostle.
Angela Merici, Saint, 1474-1540.
Anne, Saint, Mother of the Virgin Mary.
Anselm, Saint, Abp. of Canterbury, 1033-1109.
Antonia Da Padova, Saint, 1195-1231.
Antonius, the Great, Saint.
Augustin Marie Du Tres Saint Sacrement Pere, 1821-1871.
Augustinus, Aurelius, Saint, Bp. of Hippo.
Barnabas, Saint, Apostle.
Bellarmino, Roberto Francesco Romolo, Saint. 1542-1621.
Benedetto Da San Filadelfo, Saint, 1526-1589.
Benedictus, Saint, Abbot of Monte Cassino.
Berchmans, Jan, Saint, 1590-1621.
Bernadette Soubirous, Saint, 1844-1879.
Bernard De Clairvaux, Saint, 1091?-1153.
Bernardino Da Siena, Saint, 1380-1444.
Birgitta, Saint, of Sweden, D. 1373.
Bobola, Andrzej, Saint, 1591?-1657.
Bonaventura, Saint, Cardinal, 1221-1274.
Bonifacius, Originally Winfried, Saint, Abp. of Mains, 680-755 -- Juvenile Literature.
Bosco, Giovanni, Saint, 1815-1888.
Botolph, Saint, D. 680.
Boylon, Pascual, Saint, 1540-1592.
Brebeuf, Jean De, Saint, 1593-1649.
Brendan, Saint, 484?-557.
Brigid, Saint, of Ireland, Ca. 453-Ca. 524.
Cabrini, Frances Xavier, Saint, 1850-1917.
Cajetanus, Saint, 1480-1547.
Camillus De Lellis, Saint, 1550-1614.
Canisius, Petrus, Saint, 1521-1597.
Carlo Da Sezze, Saint, 1613-1670.
Catarina De San Juan, D. 1688.
Caterina Da Genova, Saint, 1447-1510.
Caterina Da Siena, Saint, 1347-1380.
Chantal, Jeanne Francoise (Fremiot) De Rabutin, Baronne De, Saint, 1572-1641.
Chrysostomus, Joannes, Saint, Patriarch of Constantinople.
Clara of Assisi, Saint, D. 1253.
Claret y Clara, Antonio Maria, Saint, Abp., 1807-1870.
Columba, Saint, 521-597.
Cyprianus, Saint, Bp. of Carthage.
Cyrillus, Saint, of Thessalonica, 827 (Ca-869.
David, Saint, 6th Cent.
Domingo De Guxman, Saint, 1170-1221.
Dominic, Saint, 1170-1221.
Dunstan, Saint, Abp. of Canterbury, D. 988.
Edmund Rich, Saint, Abp. of Canterbury, D.1240.
Elizabeth, of Hungary, Saint, 1207-1231.
Elzear De Sabran, Saint, 1285-1328.
Eudes, Jean, Saint, 1601-1680.
Felipe De Jesus, Saint, D. 1597.
Filippo Neri, Saint, 1515-1595.
Fisher, John, Saint, Bp. of Rochester, 1469-1535.
Fitzherbert, William, Saint, D. 1154.
Francesca, Saint, 1384-1440.
Francesco D'Assisi, Saint, 1182-1226.
Francisco De Borja, Saint, 1510-1572.
Francisco Xavier, Saint, 1506-1552.
Francoes De Sales, Saint, 8p. of Geneva, 1567-1622.
Gabriele, Saint, 1838-1862.
Galgani, Gemma, Saint, 1878-1903.
George, Saint, D. 303.
Gerardo Majella, Saint, 1726-1755.
Glovanni Da Capistrano, Saint, 1385 or 6-1456.
Gregorius I, the Great, Saint, Pope, 540 (Ca.)-604.
Gregorius Nazianzenus, Saint, Patriarch of Constaninople.
Gregorius VII, Saint, Pope, 1015 (Ca.)-1085.
Helena, Saint, 246 (Ca.)-326?.
Hieronymus, Saint.
Hugh De Avalon, Saint, Bp. of Lincoln, 1135?-1200.
Hugo, of Saint Victor, 1096 or 7-1141.
Ignatius Loyola, Saint, 1491-1556.
Ignatius, Saint, Bp. of Antioch, 1st Cent.
Innokentii, Saint, Metropolitan of Moscow, 1797-1879.
Jan, of Nepomuk, Saint, 14th Cent.
Jeanne D'Arc, Saint, 1412-1431.
Jeanne, Saint, Consort of Louis Xii, King. of France, 1464-1506.
Jogues, Isaac, Saint, 1607-1646.
John the Baptist.
Joseph, Saint.
Juan De Dios, Saint, 1495-1550.
Juan De la Cruz, Saint, 1542-1591.
Justinus Martyr, Saint.
Kazimierz, Saint, 1458-1484.
Kosmas Ho Ait Olos, Saint, 1714-1779.
La Salle, Jean Baptiste De, Saint, 1651-1719.
Labourc, Catherine, Saint, 1806-1876.
Laziosi, Pellegrino, Saint, 1265-1345-Juvenile Literature.
Lewis, David, 1814-1895, Tr.
Liguori, Alfonso Maria De', Saint, 1696-1787.
Lorenzo Da Brindisi, Saint, 1559-1619.
Louis IX, Saint, King of France, 1214-1270.
Louise De Marillac, Saint, 1591-1660.
Lucia Filippini, Saint, 1672-1732.
Lucy, Saint, D. 304?
Luigi Gonzaga, Saint, 1568-1591.
Madeleine Sophie, Saint, 1779-1865.
Makarios, Saint, Metropolitan of Corinth, D. 1805.
Malachy O'Morgain, Saint, 1094?-1148.
Margherita Da Cortona, Saint, 1247-1297.
Maria Goretti, Saint, 1890-1902.
Maria Maddalena De' Pazzi, Saint 1566-1607.
Martin De Porres, Saint, 1579-1639.
Martin, Saint, Bp. of Tours. 4th Cent.
Mary Magdalene, Saint.
Mary Mercy, Sister, 1903-
Mary of Bethany.
Matthew, Saint, Apostle-Juvenile Literature.
Monica, Saint, D. 387.
Nicholas, Saint, Bp. of Myra.
Nikephoros of Chios, Saint.
Nikod Emos Hagioreit Es, 1748 or 9-1809.
Nikolaus Von der Fliie, Saint, 1417-1487.
Odo, Abbot of Cluny, Saint 879 (Ca.)-942.
Oswald, Saint, King of Northumbria, 6057-642.
Pachomius, Saint.
Pallotti, Vincenzo, Saint, 1795-1850.
Paolo Della Croce, Saint, 1694-1775.
Patrick, Saint, 373?--163?
Paul, Saint, Apostle.
Paulus, Thebaeus, Saint.
Pedro De Alcantara, Saint, 1499-1562.
Pelletier, Marie De Sainte Euphrasie, Saint.
Peter, Saint, Apostle.
Petrus Thomasius, Saint, 1305-1306.
Philomena, Saint.
Pius V, Saint, Pope, 1504-1572.
Pius X, Saint, Pope, 1835-1914.
Placidus, Saint, Ca. 515-Ca. 550.
Raymundus De Pennaforte, Saint, 1175?-1275.
Realino, Bernardino, Saint, 1530-1616.
Rita Da Cascia, Saint, 1381?-1457.
Saint Augustine of Canterbury Parish, Hecker, Ill.
St. Denis, Louis Juchereau, Chevalier De, 1676-1744.
St. Denis, Ruth, 1880-
Saint-Germain, Comte De, D. 1784?
St. Innocent, Olga, Marquise De.
St. John, Harold, 1876-1957.
St. Johns, Adela Rogers - Biography.
Saint Joseph, Mother, 1756-1838.
Saint, Nathanael, 1923-1956.
Saint, Philip.
Sava, Saint, Abp., of Serbia, 1169-1237.
Savic, Domenico, Saint, 1842-1857.
Sebastian, Saint.
Serafim, Saint, 1759-1833.
Seton, Elizabeth Ann, Saint, 1774-1821.
Severinus, Saint, D. 482.
Soland, Francisco, Saint, 1549-1610.
Soubirous, Bernadette, Saint, 1844-1879.
Stanislaw Kostka, Saint, 1550-1568.
Strambi, Vincenzo Maria, Saint, 1745-1824.
Theodorus Studita, Saint, 759?-826.
Thomas a Becket, Saint, Abp. of Canterbury, 1118?-1170.
Thomas Aquinas, Saint, 1225?-1274.
Tomas De Villanueva, Saint, 1488-1555.
Vianney, Jean Baptiste Marie, Saint, 1786-1859.
Vincent De Paul, Saint, 1581-1660.
Vincentius Ferrerius, Saint, 1350 (Ca.)-1419.
Vlanney, Jean Baptisic Marie, Satint.
Wilfred, Saint, Bp. of York, 634-709.
Zachariah, Father, 1850-1936.
Zita, Saint, 1218-1278.
SAINTS, ENGLISH
More, Sir Thomas, Saint, 1478-1535.
SAINTS, WOMEN
Agnes, Saint, 3d Cent.
Germaine Cousin, Saint, 1579-1601.
Gertrude, Saint, Surnamed the Great, 1256-1302.
Helena, Saint, 246 (Ca.)-326?-Juvenile Literature.
Rossello, Maria Giuseppa, Saint, 1811-1880.
Seaton, Elizabeth Ann, 1774-1821.
Teresa Margherita Del Sacro Cuore Di Gesu, Saint, 1747-1770.
Teresa, Saint, 1515-1582.
Therese, Saint, 1873-1897.
Winifred, Saint.
SALESMANSHIP
see Salesmen and Salesmanship
SALESMEN AND SALESMANSHIP
see also Advertising; Booksellers and Bookselling
Girard, Joe.
Lum, Ray, 1891-
Sampson, Patricia.
SALUS EXTRA ECCLESIAM
see Universalism
SALVATION ARMY
Booth, Evangeline Cory, 1865-1950-Juvenile Literature.
Booth, William, 1829--1912.
SANITARY ENGINEERING
Fuller, George Warren, 1868-1934.
Waring, George Edwin, 1833-1898.
SATIRISTS
Spence, Joseph, 1699-1768-Correspondence.
SAUDI ARABIA
Abdul Razak Bin Abdul Hussein, Tun Haji, 1922-1976.
Faisal, King of Saudi Arabis, 1906-
SAUK INDIANS
see Indians of North America-Northwest, Old
SAVATE
see Boxing
SCALDS
see Burns and Scalds
SCANDINAVIAN AUTHORS
see Authors, Scandinavian

SCENERY (STAGE)
see Theaters-Stage-Setting and Scenery

SCHIZOPHRENIA
Hawksworth, Henry.
Peters, Christina, 1942-
Sizemore, Chris Costner.

SCHOLARS
Dacier, Anne Lefevre, 1654-1720.
Denon, Dominique Vivant, Baron, 1747-1825.
Dodd, Charles Harold, 1884-1973.
Dodds, Eric Robertson, 1893-
Dowden, Edward, 1843-1913.
Drummond, William, 1585-1649.
Dummer, Jeremiah, 1645-1718.
Erasmus, Desiderius, D. 1536.
Fronto, Marcus Cornelius.
Georgius Trapezuntius, D. 1484.
Glover, Terrot Reaveley, 1869-1943.
Hamilton, Edith, 1867-1963.
Johnson, Alexander Bryan, 1786-1867.
K'ang, Yu-Wei, 1858-1927.
Kircher, Athanasius, 1602-1680.
Klausner, Joseph, 1874-1958.
Lang, Andrew, 1844-1912.
Macdonald, George, 1824-1905.
Morrell, Ottoline Violet Anne Cavendish-Bentinck, Lady, 1873-1938.
Pan, Chao, 1st Century.
Parr, Samuel, 1747-1825.
Plinius Caecilius Secundus, C.-Correspondence.
Porson, Richard, 1759-1808.
Randall, James Garfield, 1881-1953.
Saadiah Ben Joseph, Gaon, 892?-942.
Saussure, Ferdinand De, 1857-1913.
Scholem, Gershom Gerhard, 1897-
Smith, Thomas, Sir 1513-1577.
Stevens, David Harrison, 1884-
Thompson, Sir D'Arcy Wentworth, 1860-1948.
Tubbs, Frank Dean.
Van der Kemp, Francis Adrian(1752-1829.
Wavell, Archibald Percival Wavell, 1st Earl, 1883-1950.
SCHOOL ADMINISTRATORS
see School Superintendents and Principals
SCHOOL PRINCIPALS
see School Superintendents and Principals
SCHOOL SUPERINTENDENTS AND PRINCIPALS
Sutcliffe, Joseph Richard, 1897-
SCIENCES, OCCULT
see Occult Sciences
SCIENTISTS
see also Astronomers; Biologists; Botanists; Chemists; Ecologists; Geologists; Mathematicians; Naturalists; Ornithologists; Paleontologists; Physicists; Psychologists; Zoologists
Agassiz, Louis, 1807-1873.
Altken, Robert Grant, 1864--1951.
Bentley, Wilson Alwyn, 1865-1931.
Boskovic, Rudjer Josip, 1711-1787.
Coolidge, William David, 1873-
Cottrell, Frederick Gardner, 1877-1948.
Dall, William Healey, 1845-1927.
Dana, James Dwight, 1813-1895.
Darwin, Charles Robert, 1809-1882.
Draper, John William, 1811-1882.
Eby, James Brian, 1896-
Ehrlich, Paul, 1854-1915.
Eiseley, Loren C., 1907-
Fisher, Ronald Aylmer, Sir, 1890-1962.
Flick, Lawrence Francis, 1856-1968.
Franklin Benjamin, 1706-1790.
Fuchs, Klaus Emil Julius, 1911-
Galton, Francis, Sir, 1822-1911.
Gunther, Robert William Theodore, 1869-1940.
Hand, William Flowers, 1873-1948.
Horton, James Africanus Beale.
Hunt, Robert, 1807-1887.
Huxley, Thomas Henry, 1825-1895.
Jones, Joseph, 1833-1896.
Kistiakowsky, George Bogdan.
Langmuir, Irving, 1881-1957.
Lecomte Du Nouy, Pierre, 1883-1947.
Oberth, Hermann, 1894-
Oldenburg, Henry.
Pascal, Blaise, 1623-1662.
Pugh, Emerson M.
Ritt, Joseph Fels, 1893-1951. (Series: National Academy of Sciences. Washington, D.C. Biographical Memoirs, V. 29, 10th Memoir)
Rockwell, Cleveland, 1837-1907.
Rumford, Benjamin Thompson, Sir, Count, 1753-1814.
Selye, Hans, 1907-
Shaffer, Cleve F.
Spencer, Herbert, 1820-1903.
Teale, Edwin Way, 1899-
Tizard, Sir Henry Thomas, 1885-1959.
Von Braun, Wernher, 1912-
Wheeler, Robert Eric Mortimer Sir 1890-
Woytinsky, Wladimir S., 1885-1960.
SCLERODERMA (DISEASE)
Richards, Edward, 1936-
SCLEROSIS, MULTIPLE
see Multiple Sclerosis
SCOLIOSIS
Griesse, Rosalie.
SCORING (SPORTS)
see Sports Officiating
SCOTCH IN THE UNITED STATES
Philip, Scotty, 1858-1911.
SCOTLAND-BIOGRAPHY
Barrie, Margaret (Ogilvy)
Fraser, Amy Stewart.
Grenfell, Julian Henry Francis, 1888-1915.
Knox, John, 1505-1572.
SCOTLAND-KINGS AND RULERS
Darnley, Henry Stewart, Lord, 1545-1567.
James I, King of Scotland, 1394-1437.
James IV King of Scotland, 1473-1513.
James V, King of Scotland, 1512-1542.
Mary Stuart, Queen of the Scots., 1542-1587.
SCOTTISH AUTHORS
see Authors, Scottish
SCOTTISH PHILOSOPHERS
see Philosophers-Scotland
SCOUTS AND SCOUTING
see also Boy Scouts
Cody, William Frederick, 1846-1917.
Cooley, Corydon Eliphalet, 1836-1917.
Low, Juliette (Gordon) 1860-1927.
SCULPTORS
Akers, Paul, 1825-1861.
Armstrong, Jane B.
Ball, Thomas, 1819-1911.
Barlach, Ernst, 1870-1938.
Bartholdi, Frederic Auguste, 1834-1904.
Barye, Antoine Louis, 1796-1875.
Boehm, Edward Marshall, 1913-1969.
Bologne, Jean De, 1524-1608.
Borglum, John Gutson De la Mothe, 1867-1941.
Boyd, Guy Martin a Beckett, 1923-
Brancusi, Constantin, 1876-1957.
Bufano, Beniamino, 1898-1970.
Calder, Alexander Milne, 1846-1923.
Calder, Alexander Stirling, 1870-1945.
Caro, Anthony, 1924-
Christy, Howard Chandler, 1873-1952-Exhibitions.

SLUM CLEARANCE
see City Planning
SMUGGLING
Monfreid, Henri De.
SOCCER
Beckenbauer, Franz-Juvenile Literature.
Guthrie, Jimmy.
Macari, Lou.
Messing, Shep.
Moore, Bobby, 1941-
Nascimento, Edson Arantes Do, 1940-
New York Cosmos (Soccer Team)
North American Soccer League-Juvenile Literature.
Rote, Kyle.
Rous, Stanley, Sir.
Shankly, Bill.
SOCIAL ASPECTS
see subdivision Social Aspects under subjects
SOCIAL HYGIENE
see Prostitution

SOCIAL PSYCHOTECHNICS
see Interviewing
SOCIAL REFORMERS
Addams, Jane, 1860-1935.
Ames, Jessie Daniel, 1883-1972.
Anthony, Susan Brownell, 1820-1906.
Aveling, Eleanor (Marx) 1855-1898.
Barton, Clara Harlowe, 1821-1912.
Berrigan, Daniel.
Blaine, Anita McCormick.
Bloomer, Amelia (Jenks) 1818-1894.
Booth, Evangeline Cory, 1865-1950-Juvenile Literature.
Booth, Maud Ballington (Charlesworth) 1865-1948.
Booth, William, 1829--1912.
Borlaug, N. E.
Brentano, Lujo, 1844-1931.
Brisbane, Albert, 1809-1890.
Brook Farm.
Comstock, Anthony, 1844-1915.
Lane, Franklin Knight, 1864-1921.
Muste, Abraham John, 1885-
Noyes, John Humphrey, 1811-1886.
Ossoli, Sarah Margaret Fuller, Marchesa D', 1810-1850.
Ripley, George, 1802-1880.
Rose, Ernestine Louise, 1810-1892.
Stewart, Eliza (Daniel) 1816-1908.
Stone, Lucy, 1818-1893.
SOCIAL SCIENCE RESEARCH
Hanley, Tullah Innes.
SOCIAL SCIENCES-BIOGRAPHY
Marts, Arnaud C.
SOCIAL SCIENCES-RESEARCH
see Social Science Research
SOCIAL SCIENTISTS
Booth, Charles, 1840-1916.
Browning, Orville Hickman, 1806-1881.
Drucker, Peter Ferdinand, 1909-
Ellis, Arthur L.
Fourier, Francois Marie Charles, 1772-1837.
Kingsley, Mary Henrietta, 1862-1900 -- Juvenile Literature.
Reinharz, Shulamit.
SOCIAL SERVICE, MEDICAL
see Medical Social Work
SOCIAL WELFARE
see Public Welfare
SOCIAL WORKERS
Brace, Charles Loring, 1826-1890.
Duncan, E. H.
Fry, Margery, 1874-1958.
Henriques, Basil Lucas Quixano, 1890-1961.
Kaplun, Morris J.
Kelley, Florence, 1859-1932.
Krupskaia, Nadezhda Konstantinovna, 1869-1939.
Lathrop, Julia Clifford, 1858-1932.
Perkins, Frances, 1882-1965.
Sparrow, Jane.
Veblen, Thorstein, 1857-1929.
Woods, Robert Archey, 1865-1925.
SOCIALIST JOURNALISM
see Journalism, Socialist
SOCIALISTS
Aveling, Eleanor Marx, 1855-1898.
Baran, Paul A., 1910-1964.
Blanc, Louis, 1811-1882.
Cannon, James Patrick, 1890-1974-Addresses, Essays, Lectures.
Codreanu, Cornelinu Zelea, 1899-1938.
Cole, George Douglas Howard, 1889-1959.
Connolly, James, 1868-1916.
De Leon, Daniel, 1852-1914.
Debs, Eugene Victor, 1855-1926.
Engels, Friedrich, 1820-1895.
Hardie, James Keir, 1856-1915.
Hess, Moses, 1812--1875.
Hillquit, Morris, 1869-1933.
Hopkins, Mark, 1813-1878.
Howe, Louis McHenry, 1871-1936.
Jaures, Jean Leon, 1859-1914.
Katayama, Sen, 1859-1983.
Kautsky, Karl, 1854-1938.
Lassalle, Ferdinand Johann Gottlieb, 1825-1864.
Luxemburg, Rosa, 1870-1919.
Martin, Victoria (Claflin) Woodhull, 1838-1927.
Medem, Vladimir Davidovich, 1880-1923.
Owen, Robert, 1771-1858.
Proudhon, Pierre Joseph, 1809-1865.
Saran, Mary.
Steinmetz, Charles Proteus.
Webb, Beatrice Potter, 1858-1943.
Weber, Max, 1881-1961.
Wolfe, Bertram David, 1896-1977.
SOCIETY OF JESUS
see Jesuits
SOCIOLOGISTS
Benedict, Ruth Fulton, 1887-1948.
Bernard, Jessie Shirley, 1903-
Cooley, Charles Horton, 1864-1929.
Du Bois, William Edward Burghardt, 1868-1963.
Durkheim, Emile, 1858-1917.
Eddy, Thomas, 1758-1827.
Fei, Hsiao-Tung.
Mills, Charles Wright.
Moynihan, Daniel Patrick.
Park, Robert Ezra, 1864-1944.
Ross, Edward Alsworth, 1866-1951.
Ruskin, John, 1819-1900.
Small, Albion Woodbury, 1854-1926.
Weber, Max, 1864-1920.
SOFISM
see Sufism

SOLDIERS
see also Generals; Jewish Soldiers; Military Biography; Scouts and Scouting

Barton, Edward Cecil, 1896-
Blazina, Thomas, 1893-
Bull, Rice C., 1842-1930.
Bunn, Matthew, B. 1772?
Caldera, Miguel, 1548-1597.
Calley, William Laws, 1943-
Campbell, Alastair Guy Spens, 1919-1944.
Caputo, Philip.
Caulaincourt, Armand Augustin Louis, Marquis De, Duc De Vicence, 1773-1827.
Christian, Fletcher, 1764-1793.
Clausewitz, Karl Von, 1780-1831.
Clemenceau, Georges Eugene Benjamin, 1841-1929.
Clive, Robert Clive, Baron, 1725-1774.
Crillon, Louis Balbis De Berton De, 1543-1615.
Custer, George Armstrong, 1839-1876.
Davout, Louis Nicolas, Duc D'Auerstdt et Prince D'Eckmuhl, 1770-1823.
Dumas, Thomas Alexandre, 1762-1806.
Felt, Jonathan, D. 1800.
Francisco, Peter, D. 1831.
Garcilaso De la Vega, el Inca, 1539-1616.
Green, Thomas, 1814-1864.
Greenman, Jeremiah, 1758-1828.
Hackett, John Winthrop, Sir, 1910-
Haig, Douglas Haig, 1st Earl, 1861-1928.
Hampden, John, 1594-1643.
Hardee, William Joseph, 1815-1873.
Harlan, Silas, 1753-1782.
Harney, William Selby, 1800-1889-Juvenile Literature.
Hershey, Lewis Blaine, 1893-
Hitchcock, Ethan Allen, 1798-1870.
Hood, John Bell, 1831-1879.
Hopkins, Esek, 1718-1802.
Houston, Samuel, 1758-1839.
Howe, William H., D. 1864.
Huff, Edgar R., 1919-
Hull, Isaac, 1773-1843.
Hutchinson, Abijah, 1756-1843.
Johnston, Albert Sidney, 1803-1862.
Jouett, John, 1754-1822-Juvenile Literature.
Kalb. Jean. Baron De., Originally Johann Kalb, 1721-1780.
Kearny, Philip, 1815-1862.
Kearny, Stephen Watts, 1794-1848.
Killigrew, Sir Henry, 1525(Ca.)-1603.
Kitchener, Horatio Herbert Kitchener, 1st Earl, 1850-1916.
Kovic, Ron.
Kulski, Julian Eugene, 1929-
Lattre De Tassigny, Jean Joseph Marie Gabriel De, 1889-1952.
Laurens, John, 1754-1782.
Lauzun, Antonin Nompar De Caumont, Duc De, 1633-1723.
Le Marchant, John Gaspard, 1766-1812.
Le Moyne D'Iberville, Pierre, 1661-1706.
Lee, Charles, 1731-1782.
Leffman, Lewis, 1798?-1885.
Lewis, Norman.
Lillie, Gordon William, 1860-1942.
Logan, John Alexander, 1826-1886.
Longstreet, Augustus Baldwin, 1790-1870.
Loring, William Wing, 1818-1886.
Lugard, Frederick John Dealtry, Baron, 1858-1945.
Lyman, Isaac, 1759-1827.
Lynedoch, Thomas Graham, Baron, 1748-1843.
McClary, Clebe.
Macdonald, James A., 1874-
Maigumeri, Charles.
Marcy, Randolph Barnes, 1812-1887.
Marshall, George Catlett, 1880-1959.
Mier Expedition, 1842.
Moltke, Helmuth Karl Bernhard, Graf Von, 1800-1891.
Monteith, Robert, 1878- 1956.
Montgomery, Joe, 1876-
Montgomery of Alamein, Bernard Law Montgomery, 1st Viscount, 1887-
Morgan, Daniel, 1736?-1802.
Morgan, John Hunt, 1825-1864.
Mowat, Farley.
Murphy, Audie, 1924-1971.
Ney, Michel, Duc D'Elchingen, Prince De la Moskowa, 1769-1815.
Nugent, William Lewis, 1832-1897.
O'Neal, John-Juvenile Literature.
Ospital, John, 1915-
Rogers, Horatio.
Rogers, Robert, 1731-1795-Juvenile Literature.
Saunders, Reginald Walter, 1920-
Saxe, Maurice, Comte De, 1696-1750.
Shakespear, William Henry I., 1878-1914.
Slatin, Rudolf Carl, Freiherr Von, 1857-1932.
Slovik, Edward Donald, 1920-1945.
Smith, Cornelius Cole, 1869-1936.
Smith, E. D.
Smith, Parker F., 1943-
Stedman, John Gabriel, 1744-1797.
Stobo, Robert, 1727-1770.
Tandy, James Napper, 1737-1803.
Tarleton, Sir Banastre, Bart., 1754-1833.
Thompson, Meriwether Jeff, 1826-1876.
Travis, William Barret, 1809-1836.
Vetch, Samuel, 1668-1732.
Voorhis, Aurelius Lyman, 1841-1913.
Wheeler, Joseph, 1836-1906.
Wilkinson, James, 1757-1825.
Willcox, Joseph Morgan, 1791?-1814.
Williams, Mike, 1926-
Wolseley, Garnet Joseph Wolseley, Viscount 1833-1913.
Yeager, Charles E.
Yokoi, Sh Oichi, 1915-
York, Alvin Cullum, 1887-1964.
Zhukov, Georgii Konstantinovich, 1896-
Zumwalt, Elmo R., 1920-
SOLICITORS
see Lawyers
SORCERY
see Witchcraft
SOTHO (AFRICAN PEOPLE)
see Basuto (African People)
SOUTH AFRICA-BIOGRAPHY
Alexander, Morris, 1877-1946.
Cullinan, Thomas Major, Sir, 1862-1936.
Duka, Norman, 1940-
Peace, Judy Boppell.
Robertson Family.
SOUTH AMERICA-DISCOVERY AND EXPLORATION
see America-Discovery and Exploration
SOUTH CAROLINA-BIOGRAPHY
Blatt, Solomon, 1896-
Gregorie, Anne King.
SOUTHERN STATES-BIOGRAPHY
Alcorn, James Lusk, 1816-1894.
SOUTHERN STATES-HISTORY-CIVIL WAR, 1861-1865
see United States-History-Civil War, 1861-1865
SOVEREIGNS
see Emperors; Kings and Rulers; Roman Emperors
also subdivision Kings and Rulers under names of countries

SPAIN-BIOGRAPHY
Carlos II, King of Spain, 1661-1700.
Carlos III, King of Spain, 1716-1788.
Enrique IV, King of Castile and Leon, 1425-1474.
Felipe II King of Spain, 1527-1598.
Fernandez De Cordova y Aguilar, Gonzalvo, Called El Gran Capitan, 1453-1515.
Galvez, Bernardo De Galvez, Conde De, 1746-1786.
Guillot, Luis.
Mendoza, Antonio De, Conde De Tendilla, 1491-1552.
SPANISH AMERICANS IN THE UNITED STATES
Reyes, Alfonso, 1889-1959.
SPANISH ARTISTS
see Artists-Spain
SPANISH PAINTERS
see Painters-Spain
SPARRING
see Boxing
SPASTIC PARALYSIS
see Paralysis, Spastic
SPEAKERS
see Orators
SPEAKING
see Lectures and Lecturing; Preaching
SPECTERS
see Ghosts
SPELEOLOGY
Collins, Floyd, 1890-1925.
SPIES
see also Espionage; Secret Service
Baker, Lafayette Charles, 1626-1868.
Carre, Mathilde Belard, Called La Chatte, 1908-
Edmundson, Sarah Emma, 1841-1898.
Gehlen, Reinhard, 1902-
Greenhow, Rose (O'Neal) 1814-1864.
Hunt, Howard, 1918-
Krivitsky, Walter G., 1899-1941.
Lee, Andrew Daulton, 1953-
Macdonell, Alastair Ruadh, 1725?-1761.
Philby, Kim, 1912-
Senac, Felix, 1815-1866.
Spivey, Larry.
Stieber, Wilhelm, 1818-1882.
Van Lew, Elizabeth-Juvenile Literature.
Winterbotham, Frederick William.
X, Mr.
Zelle, Margaretha Geertruida, 1876-1917.
SPIRITISM
see Spiritualism
SPIRITUAL HEALING
see Faith-Cure
SPIRITUAL LIFE
see also Christian Life; Monastic and Religious Life
Chaitanya, 1486-1534.
Chakravarti, Surath Chandra, 1914-
Chandrasekharendra Saraswati, Jagatguru Sankaracharya of Kamakoti, 1893- -Addresses, Essays, Lectures.
Clayton, Philip Thomas Byard, 1885-
Clitherow, Margaret (Middleton) 1556(Ca.)-1586.
Colin, Jean Claude Marie, 1790-1875.
Connelly, Cornelia Augusta (Peacock)
Connor, Robert, 1950-
Copper, Arnold.
Couderc, Therese, 1805-1885-Juvenile Literature.
Couturier, Paul, 1881-1953.
Crawley-Boevey, Mateo, 1875-1960-Juvenile Literature.
Hession, Roy.
Hirschmann, Maria Anne.
Home, Daniel Dunglas, 1833-1886.
Honorat, Sister, 1898-1961.
Howell, Robert Boyte Crawford, 1801-1868.
Hubmaier, Balthasar, D. 1528.
Hutchinson, Anne (Marbury) 1591-1643.
Lathrop, Rose (Hawthorne) 1851-1926.
Leary, Timothy Francis, 1920-
Lechner, Franziska, 1832 or 3-1894.
Lee, Robert Greene, 1886-
Lee, Y. M., 1871-1951.
Leonie, Mother, 1840-1912.
Lewis, Spencer, 1854-
Leyva, Marianna De, Known As Signora Di Monza, 1575-1650.
Libermann, Francis Mary Paul, 1804-1852.
Linsley, Kenneth Williams.
Maass, Clara Louise, 1876-1901-Juvenile Literature.
Magan, Percy Tilson, 1867-1947.
Marmion, Columba, Abbot, 1858-1923.
Satchidananda, Swami.
Speer, Robert Elliott, 1867-1947.
Vanauken, Sheldon.
SPIRITUALISM
see also Ghosts; Occult Sciences; Psychical Research
Blavatsky, Helen Petrovna Hahn-Hahn, 1831-1891.
Davenport, Ira Erastus, 1839-1911.
Fox, Margaret, 1833-1893.
Garrett, Eileen Jeanette (Lyttle) 1893-1970.
Harris, Thomas Lake, 1823-1906.
Jencken, Catherine Fox, 1836-1892.
Kane, Margaret (Fox) 1836-1893.
Olcott, Henry Steel, 1832-1907.
Worrall, Olga Nathalie Ripich, 1906-
Worth, Patience.
SPORTING JOURNALISM
see Sports Journalism
SPORTS
see also Athletes; Gymnastics; Outdoor Life; Physical Education and Training; Rodeos; Track-Athletics
also names of sports, e.g. Golf
Hoppe, Willie, 1887-1959.
Snider, Edwin Donald, 1926-
SPORTS-BIOGRAPHY
Baker, John, D. 1970.
Clark, Georgie White.
Hogan, Ben, 1912-
Mathews, Eddie, 1931-
SPORTS-ORGANIZATION AND ADMINISTRATION
Glickman, Harry.
SPORTS IN TELEVISION
see Television Broadcasting of Sports
SPORTS JOURNALISM
see also Television Broadcasting of Sports
Cannon, James J.
Cosell, Howard, 1920-
Masterson, William Barclay, 1853-1921.
SPORTS OFFICIATING
Gorman, Tom, 1919-
SPORTS TOURNAMENTS
see Sports-Organization and Administration
SPRINTING
see Running
SPYING
see Espionage; Spies
SQUASH (GAME)
Satterthwaite, Frank.
STAGE GUIDES
see Theaters-Stage-Setting and Scenery

Drayton, William Henry, 1742-1779.
Drew, Daniel, 1797-1879.
Dulles, Eleanor Lansing, 1895-
Dulles Family.
Eden, Robert, Sir, 1741-1784.
Eisenhower Family.
Evers, Charles, 1922-
Fessenden, William Pitt, 1806-1869.
Fitch, Thomas, 1838-1923.
Fitzgerald, John Francis, 1863-1950.
Fletcher, Duncan Upshaw, 1859-1936.
Floyd, William, 1734-1821.
Folsom, James Elisha, 1908-
Fornander, Abraham, 1812-1887.
Forsyth, John, 1780-1841.
Franklin Benjamin, 1706-1790.
Fremont, John Charles, 1813-1890.
Gerry, Elbridge, 1744-1814.
Gibson, John, 1740-1822.
Glass, Carter, 1858-1946.
Gompers, Samuel, 1850-1924.
Gower, Herschel.
Groesbeck, Alexander Joseph, 1873-1953.
Hague, Frank, 1876-1956.
Hale, John Parker, 1806-1873.
Hall, Abraham Oakey, 1826-1898.
Halleck, Charles A., 1900-
Hamilton, Alexander, 1757-1804.
Hamlin, Hannibal, 1809-1891.
Hancock, John, 1737-1793.
Hanna, Marcus Alonzo, 1837-1904.
Hartsfield, William Berry.
Hay, John, 1838-1905.
Hayne, Robert Young, 1791-1839.
Henry, Patrick, 1736-1799.
Herter, Christian Archibald, 1895-1966.
Hill, Benjamin Harvey, 1823-1882.
Hopkins, Hampton Colvard, 1903-1956.
Hopkins, Harry Lloyd, 1890-1946.
Hopkins, Stephen, 1581-1644.
Hubbard, Richard Bennett, 1832-1901.
Izard, Ralph, 1742-1804.
Jay, John, 1745-1829.
Johnson, Reverdy, 1796-1876.
Johnson, Richard Mentor, 1781-1850.
Jones Joseph Russell, 1823-1909.
Judd, Gerrit Parmele, 1803-1873.
Kennedy, John Pendleton, 1795-1870.
Kerr, Robert Samuel, 1896-1963.
Key, David McKendree, 1824-1900.
King, Rufus, 1755-1827.
La Follette, Robert Marion, 1855-1925.
Landon, Alfred Mossman, 1887-
Lane, James Henry, 1814-1866.
Laurens, Henry, 1724-1792.
Lawrence, Amos Adams, 1814-1886.
Lease, Mary Elizabeth (Clyens) 1853-1933-Juvenile Literature.
LeBlanc, Dudley J.
Lemke, William, 1878-1950.
Lindbergh, Charles August, 1859-1924.
Livingston, Edward, 1764-1836.
Maddox, Lester, 1915-
Mansfield, Edward Deering, 1801-1880.
Marcy, William Learned, 1786-1857.
Martin, Joseph William, 1884-1968.
Mason, George, 1725-1792.
Maverick, Maury, 1895-1954.
Michigan. University-Biographies.
Mitchel, John Purroy.
Morgan, Daniel Edgar, 1877-1949.
Morgan, Edwin Denison, 1811-1883.
Morris, Gouverneur, 1752-1816.
Morton, Levi Parsons, 1824-1920.
Moses, Robert, 1888-
Mun, Albert, Comte De, 1841-1914.
Murphy, Charles Francis, 1858-1924.
Muskie, Edmund S., 1914-
Oglethorpe, James Edward, 1696-1785.
Olney, Richard, 1835-1917.
Otis, James, 1725-1783.
Paine, Thomas, 1737-1800.
Palmer, Alexander Mitchell, 1872-1936.
Pearson, Drew, 1897-1969.
Pefley, Peter Jackson, 1830-1906.
Pelham, Benjamin B., 1862-1948.
Pelham, John, 1838-1863.
Penn, William, 1644-1718.
Penrose, Boies, 1860-1921.
Percy, Charles H.
Perez, Leander Henry, 1871-1969.
Phelan, James Duval, 1861-1930.
Pickering, Timothy, 1745-1829.
Pike, James Shepherd, 1811-1882.
Pinckney, Charles Cotesworth, 1746-1825.
Pinkney, William, 1764-1822.
Pittman, Vail M., 1883-1964.
Plumer, William, 1759-1850.
Preston, William, 1729-1783.
Prina, L. Edgar.
Rainey, Henry Thomas, 1860-1934.
Rainey, Joseph H., 1832-1887.
Randolph, Edmund, 1753-1813.
Randolph, John, 1772-1833.
Rapier, James T., 1839-1883.
Rayburn, Sam Taliaferro, 1882-1961.
Reed, Joseph, 1741-1785.
Robinson, Charles, 1818-1894.
Rockefeller, Nelson Aldrich, 1908-
Romney, George W., 1907-
Root, Elihu, 1845-1937.
Rosenman, Samuel Irving, 1896-1973.
Rutledge, John, 1739-1800.
Ryan, Thomas Joseph, 1876-1921.
Schuyler, Philip John, 1733-1804.
Sedgewick, Theodore, 1746-1813.
Semple, Eugene, 1840-1908.
Seward, William Henry, 1801-1872.
Shaw, Albert, 1857-1947.
Sherman, John, 1823-1900.
Sherman, Roger, 1721-1793.
Shivers, Allan, 1907-
Shriver, Robert Sargent.
Sickles, Daniel Edgar, 1819-1914.
Sinclair, Upton Beall, 1878-1968.
Smith, Alfred Emanuel, 1873-1944.
Smith, Walter George, 1854-1924.
Stans, Maurice H., 1908-
Stearns, George Luther, 1809-1867.
Stephens, Alexander Hamilton, 1812-1883.
Stevenson, Adlai Ewing, 1900-1965.
Stimson, Henry Lewis, 1867-1950.
Stone, William Joel, 1848-1918.
Stout, Hosea, 1810-1889.
Straight, Willard Dickerman, 1880-1918.
Stratton, Samuel Studdiford, 1916-
Straus, Jesse Isidor, 1872-1936.
Strong, George Templeton, 1820-1875.
Stuyvesant, Peter, 1592-1672.
Sumner, Charles, 1811-1874.
Swensson, Carl Aaron, 1857-1904.
Symington, William Stuart, 1901-
Talmadge, Eugene, 1884-1946.
Taub, William L.
Taylor, Hannis, 1851-1922.
Thompson, William Hale, 1869-1944.
Thomson, Charles, 1729-1824.
Thurmond, Strom, 1902-
Tilden, Samuel Jones, 1814-1886.
Tillman, Benjamin Ryan, 1847-1918.
Toombs, Robert Augustus, 1810-1885.
Tourgee, Albion Winegar, 1838-1905.
Tweed, William Marcy, 1823-1878.
Upshur, Abel Parker, 1790-1844.
Vance, Zebulon Baird, 1830-1894.
Vardaman, James Kimble, 1861-1930.
Vilas, William Freeman, 1840-1906.
Wade, Bejamin Franklin. 1800-1878.
Walker, James John, 1881-1946.
Walker, Robert James, 1801-1869.
Walker, William, 1824-1860.
Wallace, Henry Agard, 1888-1965.
Walters, Herbert Sanford, 1891-
Ward, Samuel, 1814-1884.
Washburn, Israel, 1813-1883.
Washburne, Elihu Benjamin, 1816-1887.
Watson, Thomas Edward, 1856-1922.
Wayne, Anthony, 1745-1796.
Wearin, Otha Donner, 1903-
Weaver, James Baird, 1833-1912.
Webb, James Watson, 1802-1884.
Webster, Daniel, 1782-1852.
Weed, Thurlow, 1797-1882.
Welch, Robert Henry Winborne, 1899-
Welles, Gideon, 1802-1878.
Wheeler, William Almon, 1819-1887.
Wigglesworth, Richard Bowditch, 1891-1960.
Williams, G. Mennen, 1911-
Willkie, Wendell Lewis, 1892-1944.
Wilmot, David, 1814-1868.
Wilson, Henry, 1812-1875.
Wilson, James, 1742-1798.
Woodsworth, James Shaver, 1874-1942.
Worth, Jonathan, 1802-1869.
Worthington, Thomas, 1773-1827.
Wythe, George, 1726-1806.
Young, Pierce Manning Butler, 1836-1896.
STATISTICIANS
Quetelet, Lambert Adolphe Jacques, 1796-1874.
STEEL WORKERS
see Iron and Steel Workers
STEGANOGRAPHY
see Cryptography
STEWARDESSES (AIR LINES)
see Air Lines-Flight Attendants
STEWARDS (AIR LINES)
see Air Lines-Flight Attendants
STONE, PHILOSOPHERS'
see Alchemy
STONY INDIANS
see Indians of North America-The West
STORY-TELLING
Sawyer, Ruth, 1880-
Smith, Abraham.
STRINGED INSTRUMENTS, BOWED-MAKERS
see Violin Makers
STUD FARMS
see Horse Breeding
STUNT MEN
Canutt, Yakima, 1895-
Knievel, Evel, 1938--Juvenile Literature.
Locklear, Ormer Leslie, 1891-1920.
Wright, Elsie (McColl)
STYLE IN DRESS
see Fashion
SUBVERSIVE ACTIVITIES
see also Espionage; Internal Security; Spies; Terrorism
Hennacy, Ammon, 1893-1970.
SUFFRAGE
see also Voters, Registration Of; Women-Suffrage
Duniway, Abigail Scott, 1834-1915.
SUFISM
Al-Alaw I, Ahmad Ibn Mustaf a, 1869-1934.
Al-Hallaj, Al-Husayn Ibn Mansur, 858 or 9-922.
Farid-Uddin, Shaikh, Called Ganj-I Shakar, 1175?-1265.
Feild, Reshad.
Inayat Khan, 1882-1926.
SUICIDE
Kreuoger, Ivar, 1880-1932.
SULKY RACING
see Harness Racing
SULTANS
see Kings and Rulers
SUPERINTENDENTS OF SCHOOLS
see School Superintendents and Principals
SURGEONS
see also Physicians
Arigo.
Bailey, Hamilton, 1894-1961.
Bankoff, George Alexis, 1903-
Barnard, Christiaan Neethling.
Barry, James, 1795-1865.
Carrel, Alexis, 1873-1944.
Cassidy, Sheila, 1937-
Coulter, Bonna.
DeBakey, Michael Ellis, 1908-
Fahrni, Gordon S., 1887-
Gorgas, William Crawford, 1854-1920.
Hall, Edwin Presley.
Halsted, William Stewart, 1832-1922.
Hunter, John, 1728-1793.
Jascalevich, Mario.
Kovanov, Vladimir Vasilevich, 1909-
Lane, William Arbuthnot, Sir Bart., 1856-1943.
Larrey, Dominique Jean, Baron, 1766-1842.
Lister, Joseph Lister, Baron, 1827-1912.
Matas, Rudolph, 1860-1957.
Mayo, Charles Horace, 1865-1939.
Mayo, William James, 1961-1939.
Moynihan, Donald T.
Pare, Ambroise, 1510?-1590.
Penn, Jack.
Scalia, Joni Lynn.
Smith, Robert S., 1906-
Warren, Jonathan Mason, 1811-1867.
Williams, Daniel Hale, 1856-1931.
Woodward, Henry, 1646?-Ca. 1688-Juvenile Literature.
SWEDENBORGIANISM
see New Jerusalem Church
SWEDES
Mattson, Hans, 1832-1893.
SWIMMING
Cox, Lynne-Juvenile Literature.
Farrell, Jeff.
Lennon, Glenda-Juvenile Literature.
Nyad, Diana.
Spitz, Mark-Juvenile Literature.
SWINDLERS AND SWINDLING
see also Forgery; Impostors and Imposture
Altman, Larry, 1928-
Gregory, Maundy, 1877-1941.
Peroff, Frank.
Savundra, Emil.
Vesco, Robert.
SWISS ARTISTS
see Artists-Switzerland
SWITCHES, RAILROAD
see Railroads-Construction

T

TABLE TENNIS
Reisman, Marty, 1930-
TAOIST MONASTICISM AND RELIGIOUS ORDERS
see Monasticism and Religious Orders, Taoist
TAOS INDIANS
see Indians of North America-Southwest, New
TEACHERS
see also College Teachers; Educators; Teachers of the Deaf
Black, Ebenezer Charlton, 1861-1927.
Bonney, Russell N.
Covello, Leonard.
Eastman, Elaine Goodale, 1863-1953.
Frantz, Adolf Ingram.
Friermood, Elisabeth Hamilton-Biography.
Gould, Ronald, Sir, 1904-
Grisham, Noel.
Hillel, the Elder.
Hobbs, Anne.
Holtzclaw, William Henry, 1870?-1943.
Johnson, Franklin Winslow, 1870-1956.
Jones, Laurence Clifton, 1884-
Keister, William Hampton, 1865-
Keller, May Lansfield.
Libanius.
Macy, Anne Sullivan, 1866-1936.
Marshall, James.
Munzer, Martha E.
Nicholson, Lillie M., 1892-1975.
Perry, Newel Lewis, 1873-1960.
Ritchie, Eveline.
Robinson, Dorothy Redus.
Rorer, Sarah Tyson Heston, 1849-1937.
Ryckmans, Pierre.
Sanford, Maria Louisa, 1836-1920-Juvenile Literature.
Stewart, John L., 1907-
Thaler, Alwin, 1891-
Weniger, Charles Elliott, 1896-1964.
West, Winifred Mary, 1881-1971.
White, Andrew Dickson, 1832-1918.
William Dodge, 1867-1957.
Wood, Stella Louise, 1865-1949.
TEACHERS-GREAT BRITAIN
Bowie, Janetta.
Potts, Abbie Findlay, 1884-1964-Correspondence.
Rendall, Montague John, 1862-1950.
TEACHERS, AFRO-AMERICAN
see Afro-American Teachers
TEACHERS OF THE DEAF
Gallaudet, Edward Miner, 1837-1917.
Gallaudet. Thomas Hopkins, 1787-1851.
TECHNOLOGISTS
Lewis, Sir Samuel, 1843-1903.
TELEVISION
McMahon, Ed.
TELEVISION BROADCASTING-BIOGRAPHY
Douglas, Mike.
TELEVISION BROADCASTING OF SPORTS
Johnson, Blaine, 1944-
Johnston, Brian, 1912-
TELEVISION INDUSTRY
Goldmark, Peter C., 1906-
TEMPERANCE
see also Alcoholics
Gordon, Anna Adams, 1853-1931.
Nation, Carry Amelia Moore, 1846-1911.
TENNESSEE-GENEALOGY
Crockett Family.
TENNIS
see also Table Tennis
All-England Club, Wimbledon, Eng.-Juvenile Literature.
Ashe, Arthur.
Borg, Bjorn, 1956-
Casals, Rosemary, 1948-
Connors, Jimmy, 1952-
Court, Margaret Smith, 1942-
Evert, Chris-Juvenile Literature.
Gonzales, Pancho, 1928- -Juvenile Literature.
Goolagong, Evonne, 1951-
King, Billie Jean.
Kramer, John Albert, 1921-
McEnroe, John, 1959- -Juvenile Literature.
Nastase, Ilie, 1946-
Riggs, Robert Larimore, 1918-
Rosewall, Ken.
Smith, Stan.
Tilden, William Tatem, 1893-1953.
TENURE OF OFFICE
see Civil Service
TERRORISM
Carlos, 1949-
Zheliabov, Andrei Ivanovich, 1851-1881.
TEWA INDIANS
see Indians of North America-Southwest, New
TEXAS-BIOGRAPHY
Austin, Stephen Fuller, 1793-1836.
Baker, Cullen Montgomery, 1835-1869.
Bowle, James, D. 1836.
Brite, Lucas Charles, 1860-1941.
Carter, Amon Giles, 1879-1955.
Dimitt, Philip, 1801-Ca. 1841.
Hogg, Ima.
McCarthy. Glenn Herbert, 1907-
Maxey, Samuel Bell, 1825-1895.
Mersfelder, Nick, 1858-1939.
Morgan, James, 1786-1866.
Nunn, Robert Tipton, 1871-1957.
Owens, William A., 1905-
Owsley, Alvin Mansfield, 1888-1967.
Patterson, Paul, 1909-
Stagg, Henry, 1861-1954.
Ward, Arland Langdon, 1885-1965.
TEXAS-GENEALOGY
Porterfield, Bill.
TEXAS RANGERS
Aten, Ira, 1862-1958.
Gonzaullas, Manuel Trazazas, 1891-1977.
Hays, John Coffee, 1817-1883.

TEXTUAL CRITICISM
see Criticism, Textual

THEATER
see also Actors and Actresses; Puppets and Puppet-Plays
Langley, Francis, 1548-1602.
Shubert, Lee, 1873?-1953.
THEATER-DIRECTION
see Theater-Production and Direction
THEATER-PRODUCTION AND DIRECTION
see also Stage Management
Appia, Adolphe, 1862-1928.
Burrows, Abram S.
Carroll, Earl.

Guthrie, Tyrone, Sir, 1900-1971.
Kennedy, Harold J.
Mamoulian, Rouben.
Papp, Joseph.
Payne, Ben Iden, 1881-1976.
Rose, Billy, 1899-1966.
Ziegfeld, Florenz, 1869-1932.
THEATER–ENGLAND
see Theater–Great Britain
THEATER–GREAT BRITAIN
Garrick, David. 1717-1779.
Planche, James Robinson, 1796-1880-Biography-Theatrical Career.
THEATER–RUSSIA
Meierkhol'd, Vsevolod Emil'evich, 1874-1940.
THEATER–UNITED STATES
Fogerty, Elsie.
THEATER IN ART
see Theaters–Stage-Setting and Scenery
THEATERS–STAGE-SETTING AND SCENERY
Oenslager, Donald, 1902-1975.
THEATRICAL MUSIC
see Opera
THEATRICAL SCENERY
see Theaters–Stage-Setting and Scenery
THEOLOGIANS
see also Christian Biography; also subdivisions Biography or Clergy under names of Christian denominations
Bacon, Benjamin Wisner, 1860-1932.
Bahrdt, Karl Friedrich, 1741-1792.
Barth, Karl, 1886-1968.
Berengarius, of Tours, 1000 (Ca.)-1088.
Bochme, Jakob, 1575-1624.
Bonhoeffer, Dietrich, 1906-1945.
Brunner, Heinrich Emil, 1889-1966.
Bultmann, Rudolf Karl, 1884-
Calvert, Edward, 1799-1883.
Calvin, Jean, 1509-1564.
Comenius, Johann Amos, 1592-1670.
Conger, Arthur Latham, 1872-1951.
Conner, Walter Thomas, 1877-1952.
Downing, Emanuel, 1585-1660.
Duns, Joannes, Scotus, 1265-?-1308?
Edwards, Jonathan, 1703-1758.
Grosseteste, Robert, Bp. of Lincoln, 1175?-1253.
Grundtvig, Nicolai Frederik Severin, 1783-1872.
Hartshorne, Charles, 1897-
Harvey, Charles Thompson, 1829-
Hugel, Friedrich, Freiherr Von, 1852-1925.
Langton, Stephen, Cardinal, D. 1228.
Machen, John Gresham, 1881-1937.
Maurice, Frederick Denison, 1805-1872.
Mohler, Johann Adam, 1796-1838.
Murray, John Courtney.
Nevin, John Williamson, 1803-1886.
Plunket, Oliver. Abp., 1629-1681.
Rahner, Karl, 1904-
Ritschl, Albrecht Benjamin, 1822-1889.
Ruotsalainen, Paavo, 1777-1852.
Schleiermacher, Friedrich Ernst Daniel, 1768-1834.
Strauss, David Friedrich, 1808-1874.
Taylor, Nathaniel William, 1786-1858.
Van Til, Cornelius, 1895-
Wesley, John, 1703-1791.
Whitaker, William, 1776-1840.
THEOLOGY–BIOGRAPHY
see Theologians
THEOLOGY, MYSTICAL
see Mysticism
THEOSOPHY
see also Anthroposophy; Yoga
Arundale. George Sydney. 1878-1945.
Besant, Annie (Wood) 1847-1933.
TIBET–RELIGION
Ngawang Lobsang Yishey Tenzing Gyatso, Dalai Lama, 1935-

TOE DANCING
see Ballet Dancing

TORIES, AMERICAN
see American Loyalists

TORT LIABILITY OF PHYSICIANS
see Malpractice

TOTAL ABSTINENCE
see Temperance
TOWN OFFICERS
see Municipal Officials and Employees
TOWN PLANNING
see City Planning
TOXICOLOGY
Hamilton, Alice, 1869-
TOY-MAKING
Ives. Edward Riley, 1839-1918.
TRACK-ATHLETICS
see also Cycling; Running
Heidenreich, Steve.
TRADE-UNIONS
Here are entered general works on Trade Unions. For works on trade unions of specific countries see appropriate subdivision, e.g. Trade-Unions–Africa.
Beck, Dave, 1894-
Jones, Mary Harris, 1830-1930.
Jordan, Crystal Lee, 1940-
Nestor, Agnes.
Robins, Margaret Dreier.
Roney, Frank, 1841-1925.
Trevellick, Richard F., D. 1895.
TRADE-UNIONS–OFFICIALS AND EMPLOYEES
Citrine, Walter McLennan Citrine, Baron, 1887-
Dronfield, William, 1826-1894.
Dubinsky, David, 1892-
Golden, Clinton Strong, 1888-1961.
Green, William, 1872-
Hillman, Sidney, 1887-1946.
Hillstrom, Joseph, 1879-1915.
Hoffa, James Riddle, 1913-
Lewis, John Llewellyn, 1880-
Loeb, William, 1905-
Macarthur, Mary Reid, 1880-1921.
Reid, Jimmy, 1932-
Reuther, Victor G., 1912-
Reuther, Walter Philip, 1907-1970.
TRADE-UNIONS–GREAT BRITAIN
Reid, Jimmy, 1932-
TRAINED NURSES
see Nurses and Nursing
TRAINING, PHYSICAL
see Physical Education and Training
TRAINING OF ANIMALS
see Animals, Training of
TRAMPS
Bailey, William A., 1895-
Box-Car Bertha.
TRANSEXUALISM
see Change of Sex
TRANSMUTATION OF METALS
see Alchemy
TRANSPORTATION–FREIGHT
see Freight and Freightage
TRAPPING
see also Fur Trade; Hunting
Wolfskill, William, 1798-1866.
Young, Ewing, D. 1841.
TRAPPISTS
see also Cistercians
Raymond, Father, 1903-
TRAVEL BOOKS
see Voyages and Travels also subdivision Description and Travel under names of countries, regions, etc.
TRAVELERS
see also Explorers
Bartlett, William Henry, 1809-1854.
Beltrami, Giacomo Costantino, 1779-1855.
Bruce, James, 1730-1794.
Coryate, Thomas, 1577?-1617.
Estevan, D. 1539
Fisher, Lois.
Fitch, Ralph, Fl. 1583-1606.
Fournier-Aubry, Fernand.
Fox, Josephine Clardy, 1881-1970.
Gates, Adelia.
Gerard De Nerval, Gerard Labrunie, Known As, 1808-1855.
Hahn, Emily, 1905- -Biography.
Holmes, Burton, 1870-
Howes, John.
James, Naomi.
Kingsley, Mary Henrietta, 1862-1900 -- Juvenile Literature.
McPhee, Colin, 1901-1964-Journeys-Bali (Island)
Paoli, Pasquale, 1725-1807.
Polo, Marco, 1254-1323?
Ripley, Robert Le Roy, 1893-1949.
Thielicke, Helmut, 1908-
Tweedy, Maureen.
Whiteley, Bruce.
Willey, Willie R., 1884-1956.
TRAVELS
see Voyages and Travels
TROJAN WAR
Helen of Troy.
TROTTING-RACES
see Harness Racing
TUNISIA
Ahmad Bey, Bey of Tunis, D. 1855.
Bourguiba, Habib, Pres. Tunisia, 1903-
TURKEY
see also names of cities, regions, etc. in Turkey
Ataturk, Kamal, Pres. Turkey, D. 1938.
Midhat, Pasa, 1822-1884.
TURKS
Mehmet II, the Great, Sultan of the Turks, 1430 (Ca.)-1481.
TURNOUTS, RAILROAD
see Railroads–Construction
TUSCARORA INDIANS
see Indians of North America–Eastern States
TWINS
see also Brothers and Sisters
Davis, Clarence Agustus, 1886-1935.
TYRANTS
see Dictators

U

UMPIRING (SPORTS)
see Sports Officiating
UNCONVENTIONAL WARFARE
see Subversive Activities
UNDERGROUND MOVEMENTS, (WORLD WAR, 1939-1945)
see Anti-Nazi Movement
UNDERTAKERS AND UNDERTAKING
McCown, Joseph Albert, 1865-1934.
UNDERWATER SWIMMING
see Skin Diving
UNIONS, TRADE
see Trade-Unions
UNITARIANISM
Channing, William Ellery, 1780- 1842.
UNITED STATES–AIR FORCE
Ketchum, Carlton G., 1892-
UNITED STATES–ARMED FORCES–OFFICERS
Brown, Lew Buford, 1861-1944.
Davidson, John W., 1825-1881.
Davidson, William Lee, 1746-1781.
Dodge, Grenville Mellen, 1831-1916.
Eaton, William H., 1764-1811.
Ellis, James Tandy, 1868 1942.
Middleton, Troy H., 1889-
Parker, Ely Samuel, 1828-1895.
UNITED STATES–ARMY
Hoffmann, Charles, 1891-1971.
Ridgway, Matthew Bunker, 1895-
Slovik, Edward Donald, 1920-1945.
Wayne, James Moore, 1790-1867.
UNITED STATES–ARMY–MILITARY LIFE
Sherman, Thomas Ewing, 1856-1933.
UNITED STATES–ARMY–OFFICERS
Alexander, William, 1726-1783.
Crook, George, 1828-1890.
Ford, Henry Lewis.
Fountain, Albert Jennings, 1838-1896.
Goethals, George Washington, 1858-1928--Juvenile Literature.
Hazen, William Babcock, 1830-1887.
Kirby-Smith, Edmund, 1824-1893.
McClellan, George Brinton 1826-1885.
McCoy, Frank Ross, 1874-1954.
McCulloch, Ben, 1811-1862.
McDougall, Alexander, 1732-1786.
McIntosh, Lachlan, 1725-1806.
McKim, Charles Follen, 1847-1909.
McManus, George Henry, 1867-1954.
Mouton, Alfred, 1829-1864.
Moylan, Stephen, 1734-1811.
Pendleton, Alexander Swift, 1840-1864.
Pryor, Roger Atkinson, 1828-1919.
Q. Howard, Oliver Otis, 1830-1909.
Reynolds, John Fulton, 1820-1863.
Scott, Winfield, 1786-1866.
Terry, Alfred Howe, 1827-1890.
UNITED STATES–BIOGRAPHY
Abbe Family.
Adams Family.
Adams, Marian Hooper, 1843-1885.
Allyn Family.
Allyn, William Noah, 1874-
Ames, Fisher, 1758-1808.
Armstrong, A. Joseph, 1873-
Armstrong, John Nelson, 1870-1944.
Arnold, Oren-Biography.
Arnold, Remmie Le Roy, 1894-
Artley, Bob.
Atkinson, John Robert, 1887-1964
Atkinson, Virginia M., 1861-1941.
Aycock, Charles Brantley, 1859-1912.
Ayer, Harriet Hubbard, 1854-1903.
Baber, Sarah Jane (Nelson) 1852-1942.
Bailes, Marry (Thomson) 1851-1939.
Baker Family.
Baker, Pearl Biddlecome.
Baldwin Family.
Bales, Charles F., 1897-
Balfour, Conrad, 1928-
Ball, Hannah, 1733-1792.
Ballard, Charles Littlepage, 1866-1950.
Banks, Frederick, 1898-1964.
Barber Family.
Barker, Joseph, 1747?-1824?
Barnes, Ben E.
Bartlett Family.
Bass, Sam, 1851-1879.
Bauer, Douglas.
Bean, Ellis Peter, 1783-1846.
Beardsley, Ruth Robbins.
Bell, Thomas Frederick, 1819 or 20-1892.
Bennehan Family.
Bennehan, Richard, 1743-1825.
Bennett, Simmons, 1837-1924.
Benton Family.
Benton, William, 1900-
Berkefeld, Constance (Kirkpatrick)
Bernstein, Ruuh, 1914-1953.
Bersell, Peter Olof Immanuel, 1882-
Bertino, Belvina Williamson.
Bevan, Robert, 1865-1925.
Beveridge, Albert Jeremiah, 1862-1927.
Bevier, Isabel, 1860-1942.
Bevington, Helen Smith, 1906- -Biography.
Biddle, Anthony Joseph Drexel, 1874-1948.
Biddle, Nicholas, 1893-
Bigler, Jacob G., 1813-1907.
Bilbo, Theodore Gilmore, 1877-1947.
Bingham, William, 1752-1804.
Birch, John Morrison, 1918-1945.
Bisbee Family.
Bishop Family.
Bissell, Richard Pike.
Bitzer, G. W., 1872-1944.
Blaker, Eliza Ann (Cooper) 1854-1926.
Blatchford, Eliphalet Wickes, 1826-1914.
Blennerhassett, Harman, 1764?-1831.
Boat, Ellen (Lynch)
Bond Family.
Boone, Rebecca.
Borglum, Solon Hannibal, 1868-1922.
Bothe, Albert Edward, 1891-1955.
Boulding, Elise.
Boyd, David, B. 1743.
Braddock, Ellsworth C.
Brady, Samuel, 1756-1795.
Braude, Michael-Biography-Youth.
Brayton, Matthew, 1818-1862.
Broach, Claude U.
Brossard Family.
Brown, Aycock.
Brown, Clark, 1771-1817.
Brown, Jacob, 1775-1828.
Burns, Harrison, 1836-1925.
Burrows, Silas Enoch, 1794-1870.
Butler, Joyce.
Campbell, James Duncan, 1833-1907.
Carroll, Anna Ella, 1815-1893.
Cassels, Louis.
Castle, William Richards, 1878-1963-Manuscripts.
Catron, Thomas Benton, 1840-1921.
Cowles, Fleur.
Fetridge, William Harrison, 1906-
Fisher, George, 1795-1873.
Fort, Charles, 1874-1932.
Furnas. William Carlyle, 1886-1962.
Gabrielson, Gabrielle.
Gaylord, Katherine Cole, 1745-1840.
Gibbs, Jane DeBow.
Gibson, Walter Murray.
Goff, Nathan.
Gorges, Thomas, 1618-1670.
Green, Robert B., 1865-1907.
Greene, A. C., 1923-
Hanks, Stedman Shumway, 1889-
Harbin Family.
Harbison, Massy White, B. 1770.
Harland, John.
Harrod, James.
Haughery, Margaret (Gaffney) 1813-1882--Juvenile Literature.
Hitch, Henry Charles, 1884-1921.
Hooe Family.
Hoover, Irwin Hood, 1871-1933.
Hubbard, Harlan.
Hubbard, John Clarence, 1884-
Hughes, Edmond Alexander, 1873-
Hugo, Everett Harold, 1910-
Hutchins Family.
Hutson, Alton, 1903-
James, Ed, 1895-
James Family.
Jaynes, Gregory.
Kashishian, Pearl, 1888-1977.
Knox, Henry, 1750-1806.
Last, Clifford, 1918-
Lewis, Isham, D. 1815(?)
Lisa, Manuel, 1772-1820.
Long, Jane Herbert (Wilkinson) 1798-1880
Longley. William Preston. 1851-1878.
Lundborg, Louis B.
McCoy, Tim.
McDonald, Worden.
McFall, Charles H., 1887-
McGovern, Eleanor, 1921-
McKean, Thomas, 1734-1817.
McLaughlin, James, 1842-1923.
McLoughlin, John, 1784-1857.
McMains, O. P.
McNamara, Robert S., 1916-
McNutt, Paul Vories, 1891-1955.
Mickle, Isaac.
Middlesex, Lionel Cranfield, 1st Earl of, 1575-1645.
Mistrot Family.
Mitchell, Burroughs.
Mitchell Family.
Moley, Raymond, 1886-
Moore, Glover, 1859-1930.
Morgan, Ted, 1932-
Mullen, John Joseph.
Mullen, Thomas Richard, 1920-1948.
Murdock, Stephen.
Myers, Carlton H., 1924-
Nelson, Hallie F., 1905-
Newman, Robert, 1752-1804.
Nicholson, Frank J., 1915-
Nicolay, John George, 1832-1901.
Ohrt, Wallace L.
O'Meara, Walter-Biography.
O'Neill, William Owen, 1860-1898.
Packer, Alferd, 1842-1907.
Pell, Herbert Claiborne, 1884-1961.
Pettus, John Jones, 1813-1867.
Pourier, Bat, 1841-1933.

Powell, Lawrence Clarke, 1906--Addresses, Essays, Lectures.
Preus, Herman Amberg, 1825-1894.
Robertson, Frederick Williams, 1819-1870.
Rockefeller Family.
Rockford College, Rockford, Ill.-Biography.
Rolfsrud, Erling Nicolai, 1912- -Biography-Youth-Juvenile Literature.
Rosenblum, Davida, 1927-
Rowley Family.
Sanford, Henry Shelton, 1823-1891.
Sas-Jaworsky, Alexander.
Schoolcraft, Henry Rowe, 1793-1864.
Scoggins, Thomas Barnes, 1873--
Sharpe, Andrew E.
Shepard, Helen Miller Gould, 1868-1938.
Sherwood, Samuel, 1779-1862.
Shipley, Maynard, 1872-1964.
Sleyman, Albert A., 1882-
Sloane, Eric.
Smith, Erastus Almon, 1818-1907.
Smith, Robert C., 1892-
Steele, Jennie Koons, 1870-1955.
Steuck, Judy.
Stockard, Virginia Alice (Cottey) 1848-1940.
Strachey, William, 1572?-1621.
Strafford, John Conrad, 1756-1840.
Strait, Clifford Norman, 1902-
Strauss, Ray, 1886-1977.
Strong, Moses McCure, 1810-1894.
Sullivan, Andrew.
Susce, Andrew J., 1906-
Sutherland, John Bain, 1889-1948.
Swift, Lucius Burrie, 1844-1929.
Swig, Benjamin H., 1893-
Tulloch, James Francis, B. 1848.
Turner, Harry Smith.
Verran, Roger, 1916-
Waddell, Hugh, 1734?-1773.
Weage, Arthur Deane, 1934-1954.
Welch, Robert Alonzo. 1872-1952.
Wetherill, Benjamin Alfred, 1861-1950.
Wheelock, Edwin Miller, 1829-1901.
White, Peter, 1830-1908.
Wilcox, Morris R., 1893-
Willett, Anne Anne (Coddington) 1653-1751.
Winters, Lee Lowell, 1889-
Yates, Hube-Anecdotes.
Zehme, Friedrich Wilhelm Heinrich, 1840-1895.
UNITED STATES–CIVIL SERVICE
see Civil Service–United States
UNITED STATES–CONGRESS
Revels, Hiram Rhoades, 1827?-1901.
UNITED STATES–CONGRESS–HOUSE
Evins, Joe Landon, 1910-
Ingersoll, Charles Jared, 1782-1862.
McCall, Tom, 19132-
McLane, Robert Milligan, 1815-1898.
UNITED STATES–CONGRESS–SENATE
Dial, Nathaniel Barksdale, 1862-1940.
Dirksen, Everett McKinley.
Dixon, Joseph Moore, 1867-1934.
Dorsey, Stephen Wallace, 1842-1916.
Duval, John Crittenden, 1816-1897.
Ervin, Samuel James, 1896-
Fulbright, James William, 1905-
Goldwater, Barry Morris, 1909-
Hemphill, John, 1803-1862.
Ingalls, John James, 1833-1900.
McAdoo, William Gibbs, 1863-1941.
McCarthy, Eugene J., 1916-
McCarthy, Joseph Raymond, 1908-1957.
McGovern, George Stanley, 1922-
McLane, Louis, 1786-1857.
Morse, Wayne Lyman, 1900-
Platt, Orville Hitchcock, 1827-1905.
Schweiker, Richard Schultz, 1926-
Taft, Robert Alphonso, 1889-1953.
UNITED STATES–DISCOVERY AND EXPLORATION
see America–Discovery and Exploration
UNITED STATES–EMIGRATION AND IMMIGRATION
Edgren, August Hjalmar, 1840-1903.
Jastrow, Marie.
UNITED STATES–EMPLOYEES
see United States–Officials and Employees
UNITED STATES–FEDERAL BUREAU OF INVESTIGATION
Payne, Cril.
Villano, Anthony.
UNITED STATES–GOVERNMENT
see United States–Politics and Government
UNITED STATES–GOVERNMENT EMPLOYEES
see United States–Officials and Employees
UNITED STATES–HISTORY–COLONIAL PERIOD, ca. 1600-1775
Arnold, Benedict, 1741-1801.
Arnold, Mrs. Margaret (Shippen) 1760-1804.
Bradstreet, John, 1711-1774.
Dinwiddie, Robert, 1693-1770.
Dobbs, Arthur, 1689- 1765.
Dongan, Thomas, 2d Earl of Limerick, 1634-1715.
Endecott, John, 1588?-1665.
Gwinnett, Button, 1735-1777.
Laussat, Pierre Clement De, 1756-1835.
Phips, William, Sir, 1651-1695.

UNITED STATES–HISTORY–REVOLUTION, 1775-1783
Alexander, William, 1726-1783.
Allen, Ethan, 1738-1789.
Allen, Ira, 1751-1814.
Carroll, Charles, 1737-1832.
Clark, George Rogers, 1752-1818-Juvenile Literature.
Clinton. George, 1739-1812.
Colden, Cadwallader, 1688-1776.
Cornwallis, Charles Cornwallis, 1st Marquis, 1738-1805.
Cresap, Michael, 1742-1775.
Curwen, Samuel, 1715-1802.
Fanning, David, 1756?-1825.
Gannett, Deborah (Sampson) 1760-1827.
Gwinnett, Button, 1735-1777.
Hale, Nathan, 1755-1776.
Hall, Lyman, 1724-1790.
Holt, Thomas, 1811-1888.
Hutchinson, Thomas, 1711-1780.
Montgomery, Richard, 1738-1775.
Willett, Marinus.
Williams, Ephraim, 1715-1755.
Yeardley, George, Sir 1587-1627.
UNITED STATES–HISTORY–REVOLUTION, 1775-1783–AFRO-AMERICAN TROOPS
Hawley, Nero, D. 1817.
UNITED STATES–HISTORY–REVOLUTION, 1775-1783–CAMPAIGNS AND BATTLES
see also names of individual battles and campaigns
Ward, Artemas, 1727-1800.
UNITED STATES–HISTORY–REVOLUTION, 1775-1783–GERMAN MERCENARIES
Ewald, Johann Von, 1744-1813.

UNITED STATES–HISTORY–REVOLUTION, 1775-1783–PRISONERS AND PRISONS
Hayne, Isaac, 1745-1781.

UNITED STATES–HISTORY–CIVIL WAR, 1861-1865
see also Confederate States of America
Beidelman, George Washington.
Carter, Robert Goldthwaite, 1845-1936.
Cumming, Katherine H., 1836-1921.
Ellsworth, Ephraim Elmer, 1837-1861.
Fisk, Clinton Bowen, 1828-1890.
Martin, Robert Hugh, 1858-1939.
UNITED STATES–HISTORY–CIVIL WAR, 1861-1865–AFRO-AMERICANS
Delany, Martin Robison, 1812-1885.
UNITED STATES–HISTORY–CIVIL WAR, 1861-1865–BIOGRAPHY
Davis, Samuel, 1842-1863.
UNITED STATES–HISTORY, NAVAL
King, Ernest Joseph, 1878-1956.
Preble, Edward, 1761-1807.
Pueblo (Ship)
UNITED STATES–HISTORY, POLITICAL
see United States–Politics and Government
UNITED STATES–IMMIGRATION
see United States–Emigration and Immigration
UNITED STATES–LOYALISTS
see American Loyalists
UNITED STATES–MARINE CORPS
Finney, Ben, 1900-
Thomason, John William, 1893-1944.
UNITED STATES–MARINE CORPS–SPECIAL FORCES
see United States–Marine Corps
UNITED STATES–NATIONAL PARK SERVICE
Mather, Stephen Tyng, 1867-1930.
UNITED STATES–NAVY
Barron, James, 1769-1851.
Barry, John, 1745-1803.
Ellyson, Theodore Gordon, 1885-1928.
Halsey, William Frederick, 1882-1859.
Halsey, William Frederick, 1882-1959.
Porter, David Dixon, 1813-1891.
Porter, David, 1780-1843.
Slocum, Joshua, B. 1844.
Tracy, Benjamin Franklin, 1830-1915.
UNITED STATES–NAVY–OFFICERS
Evans, Robley Dunglison, 1846-1912.
McGiffin, Philo Norton, 1860-1897.
Perry, Mathew Calbraith, 1794-1858.
Perry, Oliver Hazard, 1785-1819.
Rickover, Hyman George.
Sims, William Sowden, 1858-1936.
Walker, John Grimes, 1835-1907.

UNITED STATES–OFFICIALS AND EMPLOYEES
DeVito, Anthony.
Eastman, Joseph Bartlett, 1882-1944.
Forrestal, James, 1892-1949.
Frank, Jerome, 1889-1957.
Hiss, Alger.
Moyle, James Henry, 1858-1946.
Perkins, Clifford Alan, 1908-1977.
Reedy, Michael J., 1905-

UNITED STATES–PRESIDENTS
see Presidents–United States

UNITED STATES–SECRET SERVICE
see Secret Service
UNITED STATES–SUPREME COURT
Black, Hugo LaFayette, 1886-1971.
Frankfurter, Felix, 1882-1965.
Jackson, Robert Houghwout, 1892-1954.
Warren, Earl, 1891-1974.
UNITED STATES–VICE-PRESIDENTS
see Vice-Presidents–United States
UNITED STATES PEACE CORPS
Klein, Henry, 1951-
UNIVERSAL SALVATION
see Universalism
UNIVERSALISM
Brooks, Seth R.
UNIVERSITIES AND COLLEGES–ADMINISTRATION
Eliot, Charles William, 1834-1926.
Killian, James Rhyne, 1904-
Laurie, James Woodin, 1903-1970.
UNIVERSITIES AND COLLEGES–ALUMNI
Miami University, Oxford, Ohio-Alumni.
UNIVERSITY OF IOWA
see Iowa, University Of
UNIVERSITY PRESIDENTS
see Universities and Colleges–Administration
UNIVERSITY TEACHERS
see College Teachers
UNMARRIED COUPLES
Amato, Antony.
URBAN DESIGN
see City Planning
URBAN DEVELOPMENT
see City Planning
URBAN PLANNING
see City Planning
URBAN POLICY
see City Planning
UTE INDIANS
see Indians of North America–Southwest, New

V

VAGABONDS
see Tramps
VAGRANTS
see Tramps
VALVULAR DISEASES
see Heart–Diseases
VAQUEROS
see Cowboys
VENEZUELA
Gomez, Juan Vicente, Pres. Venezuela, 1859-1935.
VERMONT–GENEALOGY
Puffer, Celia L.
VETERINARIANS
Beneke, George J.
Bowring, Maurice.
Farrier, Denis, 1921-
Flynn, Wallace J.
Harthoorn, Antonie Marinus.
Klein, Michel, Dr.
Logue, Jeanne.
Lycan, Dixie (Cline)--Juvenile Literature.
Manely, Frank H.
Taylor, David, 1934-
Waddell, William H.
VETERINARY SURGEONS
see Veterinarians
VICE-PRESIDENTS–UNITED STATES
Agnew, Spiro T., 1918-
Dallas, George Mifflin, 1792-1864.
Humphrey, Hubert Horatio, 1911-
King, William, 1812-1895.
Mondale, Walter F., 1928-
VICTIMS OF CRIMES
Barr, Jennifer.
Diment, Eunice.
Dortzbach, Debbie.
Holder, Maryse.
VIOLIN MAKERS
Guarneri, Giuseppe, B. 1686?
Stradivari, Antonio, D. 1737.
VIOLINISTS, VIOLONCELLISTS, ETC.
Bull, Ole Bornemann, 1810-1880.
Mannes, David, 1866-1959.
Szigeti, Joseph, 1892-1973.
Ysaye, Eugene, 1858-1931.
VIRGINIA–BIOGRAPHY
Breckinridge, Lucy, D. 1865.
Carr, Jess.
Carter, John, D. 1669.
Carter, Robert, 1663-1732.
Carter, Robert, 1728-1804.
Fleet, Maria Louisa Wacker.
Old Concord Presbyterian Church, Appomattox Co., Va.
VOCALISTS
see Singers
VOLUNTARY ORGANIZATIONS
see Associations, Institutions, etc.
VOODOOISM
Laveau, Marie, 1794-1881.
VOTERS, REGISTRATION OF
Hamer, Fannie Lou-Juvenile Literature.

VOYAGES AND TRAVELS
see also Adventure and Adventurers; Buccaneers; Explorers; Mountaineering; Pirates; Seamen; Shipwrecks; Travelers; Whaling; Yachts and Yachting
also subdivision Description and Travel (or Description, Geography) and Discovery and Exploration under names of countries, regions, etc., names of regions, e.g. Antarctic Regions; and names of ships
Merrill, Harriet Elizabeth, 1832-1861.

W

WALAPAI INDIANS
see Indians of North America–Southwest, New
WALES
Cradock, Walter, 1606;-1659.
WALKING
Jenkins, Peter, 1951-
WAR, MARITIME
see Naval Art and Science
WAR, PRISONERS OF
see Prisoners of War
WAR CORRESPONDENTS
see also subdivision Journalists under names of wars, e.g. United States–History–Civil War, 1861-1865–Journalists
Oliphant, Laurence, 1829-1888-Biography.
Pyle, Ernest Taylor, 1900-1945.
WAR FILMS
Riefenstahl, Leni.
WAR OF SECESSION (U. S.)
see United States–History–Civil War, 1861-1865
WAR OF THE AMERICAN REVOLUTION
see United States–History–Revolution, 1775-1783
WASHINGTON (STATE)
McEachern, Daniel Victor, 1879-
WASHINGTON (STATE)–HISTORY
Abrams, William, 1836-
Combs, Ann, 1935-
WASHO INDIANS
see Indians of North America–Southwest, New
WATCH MAKERS
see Clock and Watch Makers
WATER TRANSPORTATION
see Shipping
WEAPONS
see Arms and Armor
WEIGHT LIFTING
Schwarzenegger, Arnold.
WELFARE WORK
see Public Welfare
WEST–BIOGRAPHY
Bean, Roy, D. 1903.
Bond, Marshall, 1867-1941.
Bonneville, Benjamin Louis Eulalie De, 1796-1878.
Boyce, Violet.
Bullock, Seth, 1849-1919.
Carson, Christopher, 1809-1868.
Doig, Ivan.
Earp, Josephine Sarah Marcus.
Gilpin, William, 1822-1894.
Girard, Fred.
Holladay, Ben, 1819-1887.
Sublette, William Lewis, 1799?-1845.
WHALING
Allen, Arthur James, 1875-1944.
WHITE-SLAVE TRAFFIC
see Prostitution
WIDOWS
see also Women
Caine, Lynn.
Fabisch, Judith.
WILD ANIMAL CAPTURE
see Wild Animal Collecting
WILD ANIMAL COLLECTING
Perley, Helen Mewer-Juvenile Literature.
WILD CHILDREN
see Wolf Children
WINE AND WINE MAKING
Haraszthy, Agostin, 1812-1869.
Wynn, Samuel, 1892-
WINNEBAGO INDIANS
see Indians of North America–Northwest, Old
WITCHCRAFT
see also Medicine-Man; Occult Sciences; Voodooism
Madixxa, Donna.
WIVES
see also Army Wives; Clergymen's Wives; Presidents–United States–Wives and Children
Cleopatra, Wife of Juba II, King of Mauretania, B. 40 B.C.
Davis, Varina Howell, 1826-1906.
Dayan, Ruth.
Gordon, Huntly.
Hardy, Emma Lavinia Gifford, 1840-1912.
Hershey, Jean, 1902-
Hoover, Lou (Henry)
Houston, Margaret Lea, 1819-1867.
Howard, Linda.
Jay, Sarah (Livingston)
Jebb, Marjorie.
Jenner, Chrystie, 1950-
Kennedy, Joan Bennett.

Lawrence, Frieda Von Richthofen, 1879-1956.
Loud, Pat, 1926-
Luther, Katharina (Von Bora) 1499-1552.
Maintenon, Francoise D'Aubigne, Marquise De, 1635-1719.
Markish, Peretz, 1895-1952-Biography.
Marlborough, Sarah (Jennings) Churchill, Duchess of, 1660-1744.
Mosley, Diana, Lady, 1910-
Otero, Caroline, 1868-1965.
Reagan, Nancy, 1923-
Sayre, Ruth Buxton, 1896-
Tanner, Cora English.
Wallace, Cornelia, 1939-
Wallace, Lurleen, 1926-1968.
WOLF CHILDREN
Kamala, the Wolf Girl, 1912-1929.
WOMAN
see Women
WOMEN
see also Brothers and Sisters; Feminism; Mothers; Queens; Widows; Wives
also subdivision Women under names of ethnic groups, e.g. Indians of North America–Women; and headings beginning with the word Women
Andreas-Salome, Lou, 1861-1937.
Fitzherbert, Maria Anne (Smythe) 1756-1837.
Holley, Mary (Austin) 1784-1846.
McBurney, Laressa Cox, 1883- -Biography.
McCarthy, Kitty (Lynch) 1858-
McCollum, Ruby.
Modotti, Tina, 1896-1942.
Montgomery, Helen (Barrett) 1861-1934.
Moore, Anne Carroll, 1871-1961.
Nice Family.
O'Brien, Edna.
WOMEN–EMANCIPATION
see Women's Rights
WOMEN–ENFRANCHISEMENT
see Women–Suffrage
WOMEN–POLITICAL ACTIVITY
see Women in Politics
WOMEN–RIGHTS OF WOMEN
see Women'S Rights
WOMEN–SUFFRAGE
Blatch, Harriot Stanton, 1856-1940.
Stanton, Elizabeth (Cady) 1815-1902.
WOMEN–AFRICA
Perham, Margery Freda, Dame, 1895-
WOMEN–ASIA
An, I-Suk.
Ihwa Yoja Taehakkyo, Seoul, Korea.
WOMEN–AUSTRALIA
Spence, Catherine Helen, 1825-1910.
Street, Jessie Mary Grey Lillingston, Lady, 1889-
Wallace, Judith Gytha, 1932-
WOMEN–BURMA
Mi Mi Khaing, Daw.
WOMEN–CANADA
Richardson, Evelyn May Fox, 1902-
Trudeau, Margaret, 1948-
WOMEN–CHINA
Hsieh, Ping-Ying, 1906- -Biography.
Kung, Ai-Ling (Sung) 1888
Sai-Chin-Hua, 1874-1936.
Yin, Old Madam.
WOMEN–EGYPT
Trasher, Lillian Hunt, 1887-
WOMEN–ENGLAND
see Women–Great Britain
WOMEN–EUROPE
Garibaldi, Annita, Ca. 1821-1849.
Molloy, Georgiana (Kennedy) 1805-1843
Walewska, Maria Aczynska, 1789-1817.
WOMEN–FRANCE
Lespinasse, Julie Jeanne Eleonore De, 1732-1778.
Prin, Alice, 1901-
Recamier, Jeanne Francoise Julie Adelaide Bernard, 1777-1849.
Sert, Misia Godebska.
WOMEN–GERMANY
Erdody, Anna Maria (Niczky) Grof, 1780?-1837.
Waldersee, Marie Esther Lee, Grafin Von, 1837 or 8- 1914.
WOMEN–GREAT BRITAIN
Delany, Mary Granville Pendarves, 1700-1788.
Devonshire, Elizabeth Hervey Cavendish, Duchess of, 1757-1824.
Foley, Winifred, 1914-
Leigh, Elizabeth Medora, 1814-1849.
Lindon, Frances (Brawne) 1800-1865.
Meredith, Mary Ellen, 1821-1861.
Mitford, Unity, 1914-1948.
Oglethorpe, Anne Henrietta, B. 1683?
Roper Margaret (More), 1505-1544.
Russell, Dora Winifred Black Russell, Countess, 1894-
Sayers, Peig.
Trefusis, Violet Keppel, 1894-1972-Biography.
Tristan y Moscozo, Flore Celestine Therese Henriette, 1803-1844.
Wesley, Martha, 1707-1791.
Wordsworth, Anne Caroline, B. 1792.
WOMEN–INDIA
Mazumdar, Shudha.
Mehta, Shanti Devi.
Nehru, Kamala, 1899-1936.
WOMEN–IRELAND
O'Casey, Eileen.
WOMEN–LATIN AMERICA
Saenz, Manuela, 1796-1859.
WOMEN–PUERTO RICO
Rincon De Gautier, Felisa-Juvenile Literature.
WOMEN–RUSSIA
Karadja, Kyra.
Ol'ga Aleksandrovna, Grand Duchess of Russia, 1882-1960.
WOMEN–UNITED STATES
see also Presidents–United States–Wives and Children
Alston, Theodosia (Burr) 1783-1813.
Canary, Martha, 1852-1903.
Dickenson, Susanna.
Ellis, Anne, 1875-1938.
Exner, Judith, 1934-
Giles, Janice (Holt)
Gray, Mary Montgomery (Dunklin) 1873-
Halsey, Margaret, 1910-
Hubbard, Barbara Marx, 1929-
Hubbard, Bela, 1814-1896.
Huger, Mary Esther, 1820-1898.
Isackson, Maxie Bridgman, 1933-
Jacobs, Victoria, 1838-1861.
Jaffe, Grace Mary Spurway.
James, Alice, 1848-1892.
Kingston, Maxine Hong.
Kraft, Barbara, 1939-
Lamb, Mary Ann, 1764-1847.
Leverson, Ada.
Ludington, Sybil, B. 1761-Juvenile Literature.
MacDonald, Eleanor Davenport.
Mitchell, Martha, 1918-
Moore, Ellen, 1915-
Mumford, Geddes, 1925-1944.
Nance, Berta Hart, 1883-1958-Biography.
Nathan, Maud Nathan, 1862-
Naylor, Phyllis Reynolds.
Norris, Lynne, 1931-
Oakley, Annie, 1860-1926.
Olds, Sarah E., 1875-1963.
O'Neil, Kitty-Juvenile Literature.
Papegoja, Armegott (Printz) 1626-1695.
Philleo, Prudence (Crandall) 1803-1890.
Randall, Margaret (Randall) 1936-
Repplier, Agnes, 1855-1950.
Richard, Hetty Lawrence (Hemenway) 1890-1961.
Roberts, Evelyn, 1917-
Robinson, Elsie Anne (LeBeau)
Ross, Betsy Griscom, 1752-1836.
Sanford, Agnes Mary (White)
Saunders, Mary.
Schaffer, Dori, 1938-1963.
Sloane, Winifred Margaret Riley, 1904-1975.
Soper, Eileen L.
Sprague, Catherine Jane (Chase) 1840-1899.
Stockhausen, Karlheinz, 1928-
Stone, Lucy, 1818-1893.
Stranahan, Frank, Mrs., 1881-
Strong, Hannah K. Russell.
Strong, June.
Stuart, Eleanor (Calvert) Custis, D. 1811.
Sulzberger, Marina.
Summerhayes, Martha, 1846-1911.
Teague, Vera Snider, 1906-
Thornton, Marianne, 1797-1887.
Treudley, Mary Bosworth.
Tucker, Cornelia Dabney, 1881-
Turner, Gladys Davis, 1914-
Van Waters, Miriam.
Vanderbilt, Grace Wilson, 1870-1953.
Verner, Elizabeth O'Neill, 1884-
Vorse, Mary Marvin Heaton.
Wagner, Minna (Planer) 1809-1866.
Wakeley, Margritte Fletcher (Hevry) 1850-Ca. 1920.
Warner, Edith, 1891 or 2-1951.
Warren, Mercy (Otis) 1728-1814.
Washington, Mary (Ball) 1708-1789.
Waters, Phoebe Lingley, 1835-1928.
Webb, Catherine J.
Weber, Nancy, 1942-
Whistler, Anna Mathilda (McNeill) 1804-1881.
Whitman, Narcissa (Prentiss) 1808-1847.
Williams, Alice Cary-Biography.
Williams, Leila.
Wittenmyer, Annie (Turner) 1827-1900.
Woershoffer, Carola, D. 1911.
Wolf, Marguerite Hurrey.
Wood, Christine.
Wright, Nellie (Morse)
WOMEN, AFRO-AMERICAN
see Afro-American Women
WOMEN, ISLAMIC
see Women, Muslim
WOMEN, JEWISH
Berenice, B. Ca. 28.
LaZebnik, Edith.
WOMEN, MUSLIM
Aishah, 614 (Ca.)-678.
WOMEN ACTORS
see Actors and Actresses
WOMEN AIR PILOTS
see Women in Aeronautics
WOMEN ARTISTS
Here are entered works on the attainments of women as artists.
Armstrong, Jane B.
Bonheur, Rosa, 1822-1899.
Brooks, Romaine.
Cassatt, Mary, 1844-1926.

WOMEN AUTHORS
Here are entered works on the attainments of women as authors.
Alcott, Louisa May, 1832-1888.
Austen, Alice, 1866-1952.
Austen, Jane, 1775-1817.
Beauvoir, Simone De, 1908-
Bremer, Frederika, 1801-1865.
Bronte, Anne, 1820-1849.
Bronte, Charlotte, 1816-1855.
Bronte, Emily Jane, 1818-1848.
Cather, Willa Sibert, 1873-1947.
Gilman, Dorothy-Homes and Haunts-Nova Scotia.
Lessing, Doris May, 1919-
Maynard, Joyce, 1953-
Radcliffe, Ann (Ward) 1764-1823.
Raine, Kathleen Jessie, 1908- -Biography.
Rasmussen, Anne-Marie.
Stein, Gertrude, 1874-1946.
Stowe, Harriet Elizabeth (Beecher) 1811-1806.
Straus, Dorothea-Biography.
Summers, Eliza Ann, 1844-1900.
Susann, Jacqueline.
Suttner, Bertha Felicie Sophie (Kinsky) Freifrau Von, 1843-1914.
Taber, Gladys Bagg, 1899- -Biography.
Webb, Mary Gladys Meredith, 1881-1927.

WOMEN CLERGY
Blackwell, Antoinette Louisa (Brown) 1825-1921.
Demarest, Victoria Booth-Clibborn.

WOMEN IN AERONAUTICS
see also Air Lines–Flight Attendants; Air Pilots
Harris, Grace McAdams.

WOMEN IN BUSINESS
Clare, Dollie.
Cochran, Jacqueline-Juvenile Literature.
Coon, Helen L.
Foxworth, Jo.
Marten, Ethel Sexton.
Pinkham, Lydia Estes, 1819-1883.
Rubinstein, Helena, 1870-1965.
Vanderbilt, Gloria, 1924-
WOMEN IN POLITICS
Bailey, Consuelo Northrop, 1899-1976.
Bolton, Frances Payne (Bingham) 1885-
Brookter, Marie.
Chisholm, Shirley, 1924-
Churchill, Jennie Jerome, Lady Randolph Churchill, 1854-1921.
Herz, Alice.
Herzen, Natalie, 1844-1936.
Rankin, Jeannette.
WOMEN IN THE BIBLE
Ruth (Biblical Character)-Juvenile Literature.
WOMEN IN TRADE-UNIONS
see also Trade-Unions
Barrios De Chungara, Domitila.
WOMEN JOURNALISTS
Alexander, Shana.
Schiff, Dorothy.
Thomas, Helen, 1920-
Thompson, Dorothy, 1893-1961.
WOMEN LAWYERS
Frooks, Dorothy, 1899-
Schwartz, Helene E.
WOMEN MINISTERS
see Women Clergy
WOMEN MOVING-PICTURE ACTRESSES
see Moving-Picture Actors and Actresses
WOMEN PHYSICIANS
Adair, Bethenia Angelina Owens, 1840-1926.
Anderson, Elizabeth (Garrett) 1836-1917.
Barringer, Emily (Dunning) 1876-1961.
Barrows, Isabel Chapin, 1845-1913.
Blackwell, Elizabeth, 1821-1910.
Daniels, Anna (Kleegman)
Guion, Connie M., 1882-
Hamilton, Alice, 1869-
Pechey-Phipson, Edith, 1845-1908.
Price, Nina Mae, 1882-1974.
Schick, Bela, 1877-
Swain, Clara A., 1834-1910.
Walker, Mary Edwards, 1832-1919.
WOMEN POLICE OFFICERS
see Policewomen
WOMEN'S LIB
see Feminism
WOMEN'S LIBERATION
see Women's Rights
WOMEN'S LIBERATION MOVEMENT
see Feminism
WOMEN'S RIGHTS
see also Women–Suffrage
Bloomer, Amelia (Jenks) 1818-1894.
Mott, Lucretia (Coffin) 1793-1880.
WOOD-ENGRAVERS
Janel, Emil, 1896-
WORKERS
see Labor and Laboring Classes
WORKING-CLASSES
see Labor and Laboring Classes
WORKING MEN
see Labor and Laboring Classes
WORKING-MEN'S ASSOCIATIONS
see Trade-Unions
WORKINGMEN
see Labor and Laboring Classes
WORLD WAR, 1939-1945–BIOGRAPHY
Winn, Viola Schuldt.
WORLD WAR, 1939-1945–CHILDREN
Schmeling, E. Marianne.
WORLD WAR, 1939-1945–PERSONAL NARRATIVES, JEWISH
Frank. Anne, 1929-1945.
Friedlander, Saul, 1932-
WORLD WAR, 1939-1945–RESISTANCE MOVEMENTS
see Anti-Nazi Movement
WORLD WAR, 1939-1945–UNDERGROUND MOVEMENTS EUROPE
Molden, Fritz.
WORLD WAR, 1939-1945–UNDERGROUND MOVEMENTS–FRANCE
Wake, Nancy, 1917-
WRECKS
see Shipwrecks
WRITERS
see Authors

Y

YACHTS AND YACHTING
Fitzgerald, Edward, 1809-1883.
YANA INDIANS
see Indians of North America–Southwest, New
YOGA
Ghose, Aurobindo, 1872-1950.
YOGIS
Kriyananda, Swami.
Rama, Swami, 1925-
Ramakrishna, 1836-1886.
YUCHI INDIANS
see Indians of North America–Eastern States
YUGOSLAVIA
see also names of cities, geographic areas, etc. in Yugoslavia

Alexander I, King of Yugoslavia, 1888-1934.
Peter II, King of Yugoslavia, 1923-
Tito, Josip Broz, Pres. Yugoslavia, 1892-
YUGOSLAVIA–SOCIAL LIFE AND CUSTOMS
Levski, Vasil Ivanov, 1837-1873.

Z

ZEN BUDDHISM
Hsu-Yun, 1839-1959.
Owens, Claire Myers.
ZIONISTS
Goldmann, Nachum, 1894-
Levin, Shmarya, 1867-1935.
Neumann, Emanuel, 1893-
Rothschild, Edmond, Baron De, 1845-1934.
Sereni, Enzo, 1905-1944.
Sokolow, Nahum, 1859-1936.
Syrkin, Nachman, 1868-1924.
Szold, Henrietta, 1860-1945.
ZOOLOGISTS
see also Naturalists; Ornithologists
Adamson, Joy.
Boveri, Theodor, 1862-1915.
Elgin, Robert, 1921-
Hornaday, William Temple, 1854-1937.
Ionides, Constantine John Philip.
Johnston, Harry Hamilton, Sir, 1858-1927-Juvenile Literature.
Lawick-Goodall, Jane, Barones Van-Juvenile Literature.
Mechn Ikov, Ilia Il Ich, 1845-1916
Murphy, Terry.
Owen, Richard, Sir, 1804-1892.
Say, Thomas, 1787-1834.
Scheffer, Victor B.
Slye, Maud, 1879-1954.
Wheeler, William Morton, 1865-1937.
Yerkes, Robert Mearns, 1876-1956-Congresses.

NAME/SUBJECT INDEX

A Beckett, Gilbert Abbott, 1811-1856.

A BECKETT, Arthur 070'.922
William, 1844-1909.
The A Becketts of Punch; memories of father and sons. Westminister [Eng.] A. Constable, 1903. Detroit, Singing Tree Press, 1969. 333 p. port. 22 cm. [PN5130.P8A1 1969] 69 17341
1. A Beckett, Gilbert Abbott, 1811-1856. 2. A Beckett, Gilbert Arthur, 1837-1891. 3. Punch (London) I. Title. II. Title: Punch; memories of father and sons.

A, Mr.

MONTGOMERY, Ruth 615'.851'0924 B
(Shick) 1912-
Born to heal; the astonishing story of Mr. A and the ancient art of healing with life energies [by] Ruth Montgomery. Introd. by Dena L. Smith. New York, Coward, McCann & Geoghegan [1973] 224 p. 22 cm. [RZ401.M74] 72-87588 ISBN 0-698-10493-5 6.95
1. A, Mr. 2. Mental healing. I. Title.

MONTGOMERY, Ruth 615'.851'0924 B
(Shick) 1912-
Born to heal; the astonishing story of Mr. A and the ancient art of healing with life energies [by] Ruth Montgomery. Introd. by Dena L. Smith. Boston, G. K. Hall, 1973. 357 p. 24 cm. Large print ed. [RZ408.A18M66 1973b] 73-6576 ISBN 0-8161-6109-7 8.95
1. A, Mr. 2. Mental healing. I. Title.

MONTGOMERY, Ruth 615'.851'0924 B
(Shick) 1912-
Born to heal; the astonishing story of Mr. A. and the ancient art of healing with life energies, by Ruth Montgomery. Introd. by Dena L. Smith. New York, Popular Library [1973] 224 p. 18 cm. [RZ401.M74] 1.50 (pbk.)
1. A, Mr. 2. Mental healing. I. Title.
L.C. card no. for the hardbound ed.: 72-87588.

Aalto, Alvar, 1898-

AALTO, Alvar, 1898- 720'.92'4
Alvar Aalto / [edited] by Karl Fleig. New York : Praeger Publishers, 1975, c1974. 208 p. : ill. ; 21 cm. Includes index. [NA1455.F53A239] 74-5568 ISBN 0-275-49660-0 : 10.00. ISBN 0-275-63610-0 pbk. : 4.95
1. Aalto, Alvar, 1898- I. Fleig, Karl, Architekt, ed.

AALTO, Alvar, 1898- 720'.924
Alvar Aalto, 1963-1970. [Editor: Karl Fleig. Translated by Henry A. Frey. New York, Praeger [1971] 248 p. illus. 24 x 29 cm. Published also in Zurich as Alvar Aalto, v. 2 (1971) Text and captions in English, French, and German. "Index of works, 1918-1971": p. 246-247. [NA1455.F53A218132] 73-158095 29.50
I. Fleig, Karl, Architekt, ed.

Aaron ben Moses, ha-Levi, of Starosel'ye. 1766 (ca.)-1828.

JACOBS, Louis. 296.8'33
Seeker of unity; the life and works of Aaron of Starosselje. New York, Basic Books [1967, c1966] 168 p. 23 cm. Includes bibliographical references. [BM755.A1J3 1967] 67-11452
1. Aaron ben Moses, ha-Levi, of Starosel'ye 1766 (ca.)-1828 I. Title

Aaron, Henry, 1934-

AARON, Henry, 796.357'092'4 B
1934-
Aaron, by Henry Aaron with Furman Bisher. Rev. ed. New York, Crowell [1974] 236 p. illus. 21 cm. First ed. published in 1968 under title: "Aaron, r.f." [GV865.A25A3 1974] 74-566 ISBN 0-690-00509-1 7.95
1. Aaron, Henry, 1934- 2. Baseball. I. Bisher, Furman. II. Title.

AARON, Henry, 796.357'092'4 B
1934-
"Aaron, r.f." by Henry Aaron as told to Furman Bisher. [1st ed.] Cleveland, World Pub. Co. [1968] viii, 212 p. ports. 22 cm. Rev. ed. published in 1974 under title: Aaron. [GV865.A25A3 1968] 68-13715
1. Aaron, Henry, 1934- 2. Baseball. I. Bisher, Furman. II. Title.

BALDWIN, Stanley C. 796.357'092'4
Bad Henry, by Stan Baldwin and Jerry Jenkins in collaboration with Hank Aaron. [1st ed.] Radnor, Pa., Chilton Book Co. [1974] 205 p. illus. 22 cm. [GV865.A25B34] 74-5035 ISBN 0-8019-5960-8 6.95
1. Aaron, Henry, 1934- 2. Baseball. I. Jenkins, Jerry B., joint author. II. Aaron, Henry, 1934- III. Title.

MONEY, Don. 796.357'092'4 B
The man who made Milwaukee famous : a salute to Henry Aaron / by Don Money, with Herb Anastor. Milwaukee : Agape Publishers, 1976. 220 p. : ill. ; 23 cm. A biography of Henry Aaron, who broke Babe Ruth's home run record. [GV865.A25M65] 92 76-1812 ISBN 0-914618-03-2 : 7.95
1. Aaron, Henry, 1934- 2. Baseball. I. Anastor, Herb, joint author. II. Title.

*MUSICK, Phil. 796'.357'092'4 [B]
Hank Aaron: the man who beat the Babe. New York, Popular Library [1974] 220 p. illus. 18 cm. (An Associated Features book) [GV865] 1.25 (pbk.)
1. Aaron, Henry, 1934- 2. Baseball. I. Title.

PLIMPTON, George. 796.357'092'4
One for the record : the inside story of Hank Aaron's chase for the home-run record / George Plimpton. New York : Harper & Row, [1974] vi, 153 p., [4] leaves of plates : ill. ; 22 cm. [GV865.A25P57 1974] 74-7026 ISBN 0-06-013373-2 : 6.95
1. Aaron, Henry, 1934- 2. Baseball. I. Title. **BIP**

SHAPIRO, Milton J. 927.96357
The Hank Aaron story. New York, Messner [c.1961] 192p. illus. 61-6371 2.95
1. Aaron, Hank, 1934- I. Title.

Aaron, Henry, 1934-—Juvenile literature.

BURCHARD, 796.357'092'4 B
Marshall.
Sports hero : Henry Aaron / by Marshall and Sue Burchard. New York : Putnam, [1974] 96 p. : ill. ; 22 cm. An easy-to-read biography of the baseball star who broke Babe Ruth's homerun record. [GV865.A25B87 1974] 92 74-76359 ISBN 0-399-20412-1. ISBN 0-399-60903-2 lib. bdg. : 4.69
1. Aaron, Henry, 1934- —Juvenile literature. 2. Baseball—Juvenile literature. I. Burchard, Sue, joint author. II. Title. **BIP**

EPSTEIN, Samuel, 796.357'092'4 B
1909-
Henry Aaron, home-run king / by Sam and Beryl Epstein. Champaign, Ill. : Garrard Pub. Co., [1975] 96 p. : ill. ; 24 cm. [GV865.A25E67] 75-9966 ISBN 0-8116-6674-3 lib.bdg. : 3.28
1. Aaron, Henry, 1934- —Juvenile literature. 2. Baseball—Juvenile literature. I. Epstein, Beryl Williams, 1910- joint author. II. Title.

GUTMAN, Bill. 796.357'092'4 B
Hank Aaron. New York, Grosset & Dunlap [1973] 87 p. illus. 22 cm. (A Thistle book) A biography of the major league baseball star who at the end of the 1972 season had hit more home runs than any player in history except Babe Ruth. [GV865.A25G87 1973] 92 72-92927 ISBN 0-448-21471-7 1.50
1. Aaron, Hank, 1934- —Juvenile literature. I. Title.
Library ed. 3.99; ISBN 0-448-26234-7.

HIRSHBERG, Albert, 796.357'0924 B
1909-
Henry Aaron; quiet superstar, by Al Hirshberg. New York, Putnam [1969] 205 p. illus., ports. 22 cm. Published in 1974 under title: The up-to-date biography of Henry Aaron, quiet superstar. A biography of the baseball player who hit more than 500 home runs during his career. [GV865.A25H5] 92 70-77755 3.64
1. Aaron, Henry, 1934- —Juvenile literature. 2. Baseball—Juvenile literature. I. Title. **BIP**

HIRSHBERG, 796.357'092'4 B
Albert, 1909-1973.
The up-to-date biography of Henry Aaron, quiet superstar. New York, Putnam [1974] 189 p. 22 cm. Published in 1969 under title: Henry Aaron; quiet superstar. A biography of the baseball player who displaced Babe Ruth as the hitter with the greatest number of career home runs. [GV865.A25H5 1974] 92 74-80656 ISBN 0-399-20424-5 4.97 (lib. bdg.).
1. Aaron, Henry, 1934- —Juvenile literature. 2. Baseball—Juvenile literature. I. Title.

SULLIVAN, George, 796.357'092'4 B
1927-
Hank Aaron / by George Sullivan ; illustrated by George Young. New York : Putnam, [1975] 60 p. : ill. ; 23 cm. (A See and read biography) A biography of the baseball player who displaced Babe Ruth as the hitter with the greatest number of career home runs. [GV865.A25S94] 92 74-76357 ISBN 0-399-20413-X. ISBN 0-399-60904-0 lib. bdg. : 3.96
1. Aaron, Henry, 1934- —Juvenile literature. 2. Baseball—Juvenile literature. I. Young, George, 1925- II. Title. **BIP**

YOUNG, Bernice Elizabeth. 796.357'092'4 B
The picture story of Hank Aaron, by B. E. Young. Illustrated with photos. New York, J. Messner [1974] 62 p. illus. 23 cm. A biography of the baseball slugger who in twenty major league seasons has hit 713 home runs—one less than Babe Ruth's career record. [GV865.A25Y68 1974] 92 73-19238 ISBN 0-671-32671-6 1.95 (pbk.)
1. Aaron, Henry, 1934-—Juvenile literature. 2. Baseball—Juvenile literature. I. Title.
Library binding; 4.79, ISBN 0-671-32672-4. BIP

YOUNG, Bernice Elizabeth. 796.357'092'4
The story of Hank Aaron by B. E. Young. New York, Pocket Books [1976 c1974] 80 p. illus. 18 cm. (An Archway Paperback) Original title: The picture story of Hank Aaron. A biography of the baseball slugger who in twenty major leaguer seasons has hit 713 home runs-one less than Bate Ruth's career record. [GV865.A25Y68] ISBN 0-671-29750-3 0.95 (pbk.)
1. Aaron, Henry, 1934-—Juvenile literature. 2. Baseball—Juvenile literature. I. Title.
L.C. card no. of 1974 Messner edition: 73-19238. BIP

Abad Queipo, Manuel, Bp., 1751-1825.

FISHER, Lillian Estelle, 1891-- 922.272
Champion of reform, Manual Abad y Queipo, Champion of Reform New York, Library Publishers [1955] xi, 314p. 22cm. Bibliography: p. 279-301. [F1232.A128F5] 55-8222
1. Abad Queipo, Manuel, Bp., 1751-1825. I. Title.

FISHER, Lillian Estelle, 1891- 282'.0924 B
Champion of reform, Manuel Abad y Queipo. New York, Russell & Russell [1971, c1955] 314 p. 23 cm. Bibliography: p. 279-301. [F123.F57 1971] 76-151549
1. Abad Queipo, Manuel, Bp., 1751-1825. I. Title.

Abailard, Pierre, 1079-1142.

ABAILARD, Pierre, 1079-1142. 921.9
The story of my misfortunes; the autobiography of Peter Abelard, translated by Henry Adams Bellows. Introd. by Ralph Adams Cram. Glencoe, Ill., Free Press, 1958 [c1922] xxi, 96p. facsim. 25cm. Translation of Historia calamitatum. [Z765.A24A33 1958] 59-1661
I. Bellows, Henry Adams, 1885-1939, tr. II. Title.

GILSON. ETIENNE HENRY, 1884- 921.9
Heloise and Abelard. [Authorized translation by L. K. Shook. 1st ed.] Chicago, H. Regnery Co. [1951] xv, 194 p. 22 cm. Bibliographical references included in "Notes" (p. [167]-194) [BX4705.A2G52] 51-10719
1. Abailard. Pierre, 1079-1142. 2. Heloise, 1101-1164. I. Title.

LLOYD, Roger Bradshaigh, 1901- 189'.4 B
The stricken lute; an account of the life of Peter Abelard, by Roger B. Lloyd. Port Washington, N.Y., Kennikat Press [1971] 221 p. 22 cm. Reprint of the 1932 ed. [BX4705.A2L55 1971] 73-118535 ISBN 8-04-611580-
1. Abailard, Pierre, 1079-1142. I. Title.

MCCABE, Joseph, 1867-1955. 189'.4 B
Peter Abelard. Freeport, N.Y., Books for Libraries Press [1971] ix, 352 p. 23 cm. "First published in 1901." [BX4705.A2M3 1971] 74-148889 ISBN 0-8369-5655-9
1. Abailard, Pierre, 1079-'142.

MCCABE, Joseph, 1867-1955 189'.4 B
Peter Abelard. New York, B. Franklin [1972, i.e. 1973] ix, 352 p. 22 cm. (Burt Franklin research and source works series. Philosophy & religious history monographs, 110) Reprint of the 1901 ed. published by Putnam, New York. [BX4705.A2M3 1972] 72-85102 ISBN 0-8337-4244-2 17.50
1. Abailard, Pierre, 1079-1142.

ROBERTSON, Durant Waite. 189.4
Abelard and Heloise [by] D. W. Robertson, Jr. New York, Dial Press, 1972. xvi, 238 p. 22 cm. (Crosscurrents in world history) Bibliography: p. 227-228. [B765.A24R62] 79-163597 7.95
1. Abailard, Pierre, 1079-1142. 2. Heloise, 1101-1164. I. Title.

WORTHINGTON, Marjoire (Muir) 921.9
The immortal lovers: Heloise and Abelard. Garden City, N.Y., Doubleday [c.]1960. 238p. Bibl.: p[237]-238. 22cm. 60-13751 3.95
1. Abailard, Pierre, 1079-1142. 2. Heloise, 1101-1164. I. Title.

WORTHINGTON, Marjorie (Muir) 1900- 921.9
The immortal lovers: Heloise and Abelard. [1st ed.] Garden City, N.Y., Doubleday, 1960. 238 p. 22 cm. Includes bibliography [BX4705.A2W6] 60-13751
1. Abailard, Pierre, 1079-1142. 2. Heloise, 1101-1164. I. Title.

Abailard, Pierre, 1079-1142—Correspondence.

ABAILARD, Pierre, 1079-1142. 189'.4
The letters of Abelard and Heloise / translated from the Latin by C. K. Scott Moncrieff. New York : Cooper Square Publishers, 1974. xiii, 264 p. ; 22 cm. "A Marandell book." Reprint of the 1942 ed. published by Knopf, New York. [PA8201.A4 1974b] 73-86442 ISBN 0-8154-0486-7 lib.bdg. : 7.50
1. Abailard, Pierre, 1079-1142—Correspondence. 2. Heloise, 1101-1164. I. Heloise, 1101-1164. II. Scott-Moncrieff, Charles Kenneth, 1889-1930, tr. III. Title.

ABAILARD, Pierre, 1079-1142. 189'.4 B
The letters of Abelard and Heloise; translated [from the Latin] with an introduction by Betty Radice. Harmondsworth, Penguin, 1974. 309 p. maps. 18 cm. (Penguin classics) Includes Historia calamitatum; Abelard to a friend; the story of his misfortunes. Includes index. Bibliography: p. 296-297. [PA8201.A4 1974] 74-177112 ISBN 0-14-044297-9
1. Abailard, Pierre, 1079-1142—Correspondence. 2. Heloise, 1101-1164. I. Heloise, 1101-1164. II. Abailard, Pierre, 1079-1142. Historia calamitatum. English. 1974. III. Title.
Distributed by Penguin Books, Baltimore, Md; 1.95 (pbk.). BIP

Abbas I, the Great, Shah of Iran, 1571-1629.

ISKANDAR Munshi, 1560or61-1633or4. 955'.03'0924 B
The history of Shah 'Abbas the Great = Tarik-e 'alamara-ye 'Abbasi / by Eskandar Beg Monshi ; translated by Roger M. Savory. Boulder, Colo. : Westview Press, 1978. 2 v. (xxix, 1399 p.) : ill. ; 24 cm. (Persian heritage series ; no. 28) Translation of Tarikh-i 'Alam'ara-yi 'Abbasi. Includes index. [DS292.6.18413] 78-20663 ISBN 0-89158-296-7 lib.bdg.: 55.00
1. Abbas I, the Great, Shah of Iran, 1571-1629. 2. Iran—History—16th-18th centuries. 3. Safavids. 4. Iran—Kings and rulers—Biography. I. Title. II. Title: Tarik-e 'Alamara-ye 'Abbasi. III. Series: UNESCO collection of representative works : Persian heritage series ; no. 28.

Abbas, Khwaja Ahmad—Biography.

ABBAS, Khwaja Ahmad. 954.04'092'4 B
I am not an island : an experiment in autobiography / Khwaja Ahmad Abbas. New Delhi : Vikas Pub. House, c1977. x, 551 p., [8] leaves of plates : ill. ; 22 cm. Includes index. [PK2200.A14Z466] 77-900428 ISBN 0-88386-941-1 : 12.50
1. Abbas, Khwaja Ahmad—Biography. 2. Authors, Indic—20th century—Biography. I. Title.
Distributed by South Asia Books, P. O. Box 502, Columbia, MO 65201 BIP

Abbe family.

ABBE, George Waldo, 1811-1879. 929.2'0974
Letters of George Waldo Abbe and Charlotte Colgate Abbe. Edited and annotated by Elfriede Abbe. Ithaca, N.Y., Arnold Print. Co. [1968] vi, 39 p. facsim. (on lining papers), ports. 24 cm. [CS71.A1 1968] 73-528
1. Abbe family. I. Abbe, Charlotte Colgate, 1817-1885. II. Abbe, Elfriede Martha, 1919- ed. III. Title.

Abbot. William Richardson. 1839-1916.

SOUTHALL, James Powell Cocke, 1871- 920
Memoirs of the Abbots of Old Bellevue. Charlottesville, University of Virginia Press, 1955. 394p. illus. 25cm. [CT275.A154S6] 56-25336
1. Abbot. William Richardson. 1839-1916. I. Title.

Abbott, Bud, 1895-1974.

THOMAS, Bob, 1922- 791.43'028'0922 B
Bud & Lou : the Abbott & Costello story / by Bob Thomas. 1st ed. Philadelphia : Lippincott, c1977. 224 p. : ill. ; 23 cm. Includes index. Filmography: p. 203-209. [PN2287.A217T5] 76-54743 ISBN 0-397-01195-4 : 9.95
1. Abbott, Bud, 1895-1974. 2. Costello, Lou. 3. Comedians—United States—Biography. I. Title. BIP

Abbott, Lyman, 1835-1922.

BROWN, Ira Vernon. 922.573
Lyman Abbott, Christian evolutionist; a study in religious liberalism. Cambridge, Harvard University Press, 1953. ix, 303p. port. 23cm. 'Bibliography and notes': p. [241]-291. [BX7260.A2B7] 53-5065
1. Abbott, Lyman, 1835-1922. I. Title.

BROWN, Ira Vernon. 285'.8'0924
Lyman Abbott, Christian evolutionist; a study in religious liberalism, by Ira V. Brown. Westport, Conn., Greenwood Press [1970, c1953] ix, 303 p. port. 23 cm. Bibliography: p. [243]-255. [BX7260.A2B7 1970] 79-97325
1. Abbott, Lyman, 1835-1922.

'Abd al-Qadir ibn Muhyi al-din, amir, 1807?-1883.

DANZIGER, Raphael. 965'.03
Abd al-Qadir and the Algerians : resistance to the French and internal consolidation, 1832-1839 / Paphael Danziger. New York : Holmes & Meier Publishers 1976. p. cm. Includes index. Bibliography: p. [DT294.D33] 76-18061 ISBN 0-8419-0236-4 : 25.00
1. 'Abd al-Qadir ibn Muhyi al-din, amir, 1807?-1883. 2. Algeria—History—1830-1962. I. Title. BIP

Abdalian, Zabelle.

ABDALIAN, Zabelle. 920.9133
SA PWH, Prince of the Air. [1st ed.] New York, Pageant Press [1955] 49p. 21cm. Story of the author, founder of the Chapel of the Air. [BF1997.A2A3] 55-9044
I. Title.

'Abdallah, King of Jordan, 1882-1951.

'ABDALLAH, King of Jordan, 1882-1951. 956.95
My memories completed / King 'Abdallah of Jordan ; translated from the Arabic by Harold W. Glidden ; with a foreword by His Majesty King Hussein Ibn Talal of Jordan. London : Longman, 1978. p. cm. Translation of al-Takmilah. Includes index. [DS154.52.A3A313 1978] 77-30750 ISBN 0-582-78082-9 : 25.00
1. 'Abdallah, King of Jordan, 1882-1951. 2. Jordan—Kings and rulers—Biography. 3. Jordan—Politics and government. I. Title.

Abdomen—Surgery—History.

STEVENS, Audrey D. 617'.55'00973
America's pioneers in abdominal surgery, written by Audrey D. Stevens. [Melrose, Mass.] American Society of Abdominal Surgeons [1968] xv, 180 p. illus., facsims., ports. 20 cm. Bibliography: p. 167-172. [RD201.S7] 68-54540
1. Abdomen—Surgery—History. 2. Medicine—United States. 3. Surgeons—United States—Biography. I. American Society of Abdominal Surgeons. II. Title.

Abdulhamit II, Sultan of the Turks, 1842-1918.

HASLIP, Joan, 1911- 956.1'01'0924 B
The Sultan; the life of Abdul Hamid II. New York, Holt, Rinehart and Winston [1973, c1958] 309 p. illus. 22 cm. Reprint of the ed. published by Cassell, London. Bibliography: p. 296-299. [DR571.5.H3 1973] 72-91568 ISBN 0-03-006936-X 7.95
1. Abdulhamit II, Sultan of Turkey, 1842-1918. I. Title.

PEARS, Edwin, Sir, 1835-1919. 956.1'01'0924 B
Life of Abdul Hamid. New York, Arno Press, 1973. x, 365 p. port. 23 cm. (The Middle East collection) Reprint of the 1917 ed. published by Constable, London, in series: Makers of the nineteenth century. Bibliography: p. 354a-354c. [DR571.P4 1973] 73-6296 ISBN 0-405-05354-1 19.00
1. Abdulhamit II, Sultan of the Turks, 1842-1918. I. Title. II. Series. BIP

Abduhl Rahahman, 1762?-1829.

REGISTER, James. 917.62'26'034924 B
Jallon; Arabic prince of Old Natchez, 1788-1828. [1st ed. Shreveport, La., Printed by Mid-South Press 1968] 88 p. map. 23 cm. [E444.A15R4] 73-891
1. Abduhl Rahahman, 1762?-1829. I. Title.

Abdul-Jabbar, Kareem, 1947- — Juvenile literature.

BURCHARD, Marshall. 796.32'3'0924
Sports hero: Kareem Abdul Jabbar; the story of Lew Alcindor, by Marshall and Sue Burchard. New York, Putnam [1972] 111 p. illus. 23 cm. Describes the career of basketball star Lew Alcindor who began breaking scoring records in high school. [GV884.A24B87 1972] 92 72-181324 ISBN 0-399-20284-6 4.29
1. Abdul-Jabbar, Kareem, 1947-—Juvenile literature. I. Burchard, Sue, joint author. II. Title.

DEEGAN, Paul J., 1937- 796.32'3'0924 B
Kareem Abdul Jabbar, by Paul J. Deegan. Illustrated by Harold Henriksen. Mankato, Minn., Amecus Street; [distributed by

Children's Press, Chicago, 1974] 31 p. col. illus. 25 cm. (Superstars) A biography of the seven-foot, two-inch Black basketball star whose life has been greatly influenced by his family, basketball, and the religion of Islam. [GV884.A24D43] 92 74-4138 ISBN 0-87191-350-X 4.95 (lib. bdg.)
1. Abdul-Jabbar, Kareem, 1947- —Juvenile literature. 2. Basketball—Juvenile literature. I. Henriksen, Harold, illus. II. Title. **BIP**

HANO, Arnold, 796.32'3'0924 B
1922-
Kareem! : basketball great / by Arnold Hano. New York : Putnam, [1975] 159 p. ; 21 cm. (Putnam sports shelf) Includes index. A biography of the seven-foot two-inch baseball star of the Milwaukee Bucks renowned for his unusual prowess. [GV884.A24H36] 92 74-13503 ISBN 0-399-60917-2 lib. bdg. : 4.97
1. Abdul-Jabbar, Kareem, 1947- —Juvenile literature. 2. Basketball—Juvenile literature. I. Title.

HASKINS, James, 796.32'3'092
1941-
From Lew Alcindor to Kareem Abdul-Jabbar / James Haskins. Rev. ed. 1st ed. New York : Lothrop, Lee & Shepard Co., c1978. 144 p. : ill. ; 22 cm. Includes index. A biography of the star basketball player who converted to the religion of Islam. [GV884.A24H37 1978] 92 78-1016 ISBN 0-688-41821-X : 5.95 ISBN 0-688-51821-4 lib.bdg. : 5.49
1. Abdul-Jabbar, Kareem, 1947- —Juvenile literature. 2. Basketball players—United States—Biography—Juvenile literature. I. Title. **BIP**

JACKSON, Robert 796.32'3'0924 B
B.
Jabbar, giant of the NBA, by Robert B. Jackson. New York, H. Z. Walck [1972] 72 p. illus. 21 cm. A brief biography of the seven-foot, two-inch basketball star who plays center for the Milwaukee Bucks. [GV884.A24J3] 92 72-3206 ISBN 0-8098-2088-9 4.25
1. Abdul-Jabbar, Kareem, 1947- —Juvenile literature. 2. Basketball—Juvenile literature. I. Title.

MAY, Julian. 796.32'3'0924 B
Kareem Abdul Jabbar, cage superstar. Mankato, Minn., Crestwood House [1973] 48 p. illus. 24 cm. (Sports close-up books) A biography of the seven-foot basketball superstar, Lew Alcindor, a convert to the Moslem faith, who won many awards for his unusual prowess. [GV884.A24M38 1973] 92 73-80425 ISBN 0-913940-05-4
1. Abdul-Jabbar, Kareem, 1947- —Juvenile literature. I. Title.

TAYLOR, Paula. 796.32'3'0924 B
Basketball's finest center, Kareem Abdul-Jabbar / by Paula Taylor. [Mankato, Minn.] : Creative Education, [c1977] 30 p. : ill. ; 19 cm. (The Allstars) A brief biography of the tall, black basketball player who has won many honors in that sport. [GV884.A24T38] 92 76-45194 ISBN 0-87191-584-7 lib.bdg. : 4.95
1. Abdul-Jabbar, Kareem, 1947- —Juvenile literature. 2. Basketball players—United States—Biography—Juvenile literature. I. Title.

Abdul Majid bin Zainuddin, Haji, 1887-1943.

ABDUL Majid bin 959.5'1'030924 B
Zainuddin, Haji, 1887-1943.
The wandering thoughts of a dying man : the life and times of Haji Abdul Majid bin Zainuddin / edited with an introd. and notes by William R. Roff. Kuala Lumpur ; New York : Oxford University Press, 1978. xvi, 169 p. ; 23 cm. (Oxford in Asia historical memoirs) Includes index. [DS594.A23 1978] 78-940893 ISBN 0-19-580349-3 : 19.95
1. Abdul Majid bin Zainuddin, Haji, 1887-1943. 2. Malaya—Social life and customs. 3. Educators—Malaysia—Malaya—Biography. I. Roff, William R. II. Title.

Abdul Razak bin Abdul Hussein, Tun Haji, 1922-1976.

SHAW, William, 959.5'05'0924 B
1925-
Tun Razak : his life and times / William Shaw. London ; New York : Longman, 1976. 267 p., [8] leaves of plates : ill. ; 24 cm. Includes index. Bibliography: p. [258]-261. [DS597.2.A633S5 1976b] 77-361678 ISBN 0-582-72414-7 : 14.50
1. Abdul Razak bin Abdul Hussein, Tun Haji, 1922-1976. 2. Prime ministers—Malaysia—Biography. 3. Malaysia—Politics and government. I. Title. **BIP**

Abeel, David, 1804-1846.

ABEEL, David, 266'.5'7320924 B
1804-1846.
Memoir of the Rev. David Abeel, D.D. Williamson. Wilmington, Del., Scholarly Resources [1972] 315 p. port. 23 cm. Reprint of the 1848 ed. published by R. Carter, New York. [BV3427.A3A35 1972] 72-79842 ISBN 0-8420-1353-9
1. Abeel, David, 1804-1846. I. Williamson, G. R., comp. II. Title.

Abel, John Jacob, 1857-1938.

JOHN Jacob Abel, M. D.; v. 12
investigator, teacher, prophet, 1857-1938. Baltimore, Williams & Wilkins, 1957. 8, 80p. illus., table. A collection of papers by and about the father of American pharmacology.
1. Abel, John Jacob, 1857-1938. 2. Pharmacology—History. I. Abel, John Jacob, 1857-1938.

Abel, Niels Henrik, 1802-1829.

ORE, Oystein, 1899- 925.1
Niels Henrik Abel. Mathematician extraordinary. Minneapolis, University of Minnesota Press [1957] 277p. illus. 24cm. Includes bibliography. [QA29.A2O65] 57-10276
1. Abel, Niels Henrik, 1802-1829. I. Title.

ORE, Oystein, 1899-1968. 925.1
Niels Henrik Abel, mathematician extraordinary. Minneapolis, University of Minnesota Press [1957] 277 p. illus. 24 cm. Includes bibliography. [QA29.A2O65] 57-10276
1. Abel, Niels Henrik, 1802-1829.

ORE, ystein, 1899- 510'.92'4 B
1968.
Niels Henrik Abel, mathematician extraordinary. New York, Chelsea Pub. Co. [1974, c1957] 277 p. illus. 24 cm. Reprint of the ed. published by University of Minnesota Press, Minneapolis. Bibliography: p. 273. [QA29.A2O65 1974] 73-14693 ISBN 0-8284-0274-4
1. Abel, Niels Henrik, 1802-1829.

Abel, Rudolf I.

BERNIKOW, Louise, 327'.12'0924
1940-
Abel. With an introd. by Burt Silverman. New York, Trident Press [1970] 347 p. illus., ports. 22 cm. Includes bibliographical references. [UB271.R92A23] 78-101245 7.95
1. Abel, Rudolf I. I. Title. **BIP**

Abernethy, Julius, 1894-

BLYTHE, LeGette, 332.6'0924 B
1900-
Meet Julius Abernethy: trader and philanthropist. Charlotte, W. Loftin, 1970. xiii, 242 p. illus., ports. 24 cm. [HC102.5.A3B55] 78-15506 5.00
1. Abernethy, Julius, 1894- I. Title.

Abington, E. H.

ABINGTON, E. H. 1873- 926.1
Back roads and bicarbonate; the autobiography of an Arkansas country doctor. [1st ed.] New York, Vantage Press [1955] 166p. 21cm. [R154.A133A3] 55-9077
I. Title.

Ablestein, Sadye (Bond) 1900-

STARK, Pearl Lenora 920
One hundred and four years. San Antonio, Tex., Naylor [c.1963] vii,81p. illus., port. 20cm. 63-21895 3.95
1. Ablestein, Sadye (Bond) 1900- I. Title.

STARK, Pearl Lenora. 920
One hundred and four years. San Antonio, Naylor Co. [1963] vii, 81 p. illus., port. 20 cm. [CT275.A174S7] 63-21895
1. Ablestein, Sadye (Bond) 1900- I. Title.

Abner, Vannie.

ABNER, Vannie. 977.8'54
Heir to these hills / by Vannie Abner. 1st ed. Hicksville, N.Y. : Exposition Press, c1978. 95 p. : ill. ; 22 cm. [F474.H15A23] 79-100481 5.95
1. Abner, Vannie. 2. Hahatonka, Mo.—Biography. I. Title.

Abolitionists.

LUTZ, Alma. 326'.0922
Crusade for freedom; women of the antislavery movement. Boston, Beacon Press [1968] 338 p. ports. 21 cm. Bibliography: p. 319-331. [E449.L95 1968] 68-12841 7.50
1. Abolitionists. 2. Women—United States—Biography. I. Title. II. Title: Women of the antislavery movement.

QUARLES, 326*.0973*092*2
Benjamin.
Black abolitionists. New York, Oxford University Press [1969] x, 310 p. 22 cm. "Note on bibliographical literature": p. 251-252. Bibliographical references included in "Notes" (p. 253-292) [E449.Q17] 69-17766 6.75
1. Abolitionists. 2. Slavery in the United States—Anti-slavery movements. I. Title. **BIP**

SORIN, Gerald, 1940- 326'.0922
The New York abolitionists; a case study of political radicalism. Westport, Conn., Greenwood Pub. Corp. [1971] xiii, 172 p. 22 cm. (Contributions in American history, no. 11) Bibliography: p. 139-165. [E449.S7] 73-105981 ISBN 0-8371-3308-4
1. Abolitionists. 2. New York (State)—Biography. I. Title. **BIP**

Abolitionists—Collections.

BRACEY, John H., comp. 326'.0922
Blacks in the abolitionist movement, edited by John H. Bracey, Jr., August Meier [and] Elliott Rudwick. Belmont, Calif., Wadsworth Pub. Co. [1971] 168 p. 22 cm. (A Wadsworth series: explorations in the Black experience) Contents.Contents.—James Forten: forgotten abolitionist, by R. A. Billington.—Abolition's different drummer: Frederick Douglass, by B. Quarles.—John Mercer Langston: Black protest leader and abolitionist, by W. F. Cheek.—William Still and the Underground Railroad, by L. Gara.—The Negro in the organization of abolition, by C. H. Wesley.—The emancipation of the Negro abolitionist, by L. F. Litwack.—The Negro: innately inferior or equal? By J. McPherson.—Anti-slavery ambivalence: immediatism, expediency, race, by W. H. Pease and J. H. Pease.—The role of Blacks in the abolitionist movement, by A. Meier and E. Rudwick.—National Negro conventions of the middle 1840's: moral suasion vs. political action, by H. H. Bell.—The Black phalanx, by W. E. B. Du Bois.—John OBlacks in the abolitionist movement, edited by John H. Bracey, Jr., August Meier [and] Elliott Rudwick. Belmont, Calif., Wadsworth Pub. Co. [1971] 168 p. 22 cm. (A Wadsworth series: explora
1. Abolitionists—Collections. 2. Slavery in the United States—Anti-slavery movements—Collections. I. Meier, August, 1923- joint comp. II. Rudwick, Elliott M., joint comp. III. Title. IV. Series.

Abraham ben David, of Pasquieres, 1125(ca.)-1198.

TWERSKY, Isadore 922.96
Rabad of Posquieres, a twelfth-century Talmudist. Cambridge, Mass., Harvard [c.] 1962. xii, 336p. 24cm. (Harvard Semitic ser., v.18) Bibl. 62-7192 7.50
1. Abraham ben David, of Pasquieres, 1125(ca.)-1198. I. Title. **BIP**

Abraham, the patriarch.

COLE, C. Donald. 222'.11'0924 B
Abraham : God's man of faith / by C. Donald Cole. Chicago : Moody Press, c1977. 223 p. ; 22 cm. [BS580.A3C57] 77-1268 ISBN 0-8024-0033-7 pbk. : 3.95
1. Abraham, the patriarch. 2. Bible. O.T.—Biography. 3. Patriarchs (Bible)—Biography. I. Title. **BIP**

FERGUSON, Ben. 222'.11'0924 B
The shaping of a man of faith / Ben E. Ferguson. Wheaton, Ill. : Victor Books, c1979. 95 p. ; 18 cm. [BS580.A3F47] 78-55178 ISBN 0-88207-516-0 pbk. : 1.75
1. Abraham, the patriarch. 2. Bible. O.T.—Biography. 3. Patriarchs (Bible)—Biography. 4. Christian life—1960- I. Title. **BIP**

GAUBERT, Henri, 222'.11'0924
1895-
Abraham, loved by God. Translated by Lancelot Sheppard. New York, Hastings House [1968] xii, 195 p. illus., maps. 20 cm. (The Bible in history, v. 1) "A Giniger book." Translation of Abraham, l'ami de Dieu. Bibliography: p. 185-186. [BS580.A3G33 1968] 68-55435 5.95
1. Abraham, the patriarch. I. Title. II. Series.

MILLER, Amos W., 1927- 221.9'24 B
Abraham: friend of God; an ethical biography of the founder of the Jewish people, by Amos W. Miller. Middle Village, N.Y., J. David [1973] 213 p. 22 cm. [BS580.A3M5] 73-6406 ISBN 0-8246-0156-4 7.95
1. Abraham, the patriarch. I. Title.

*STIBBS, Alan M. 221.92
God's friend, studies in the life of Abraham. Chicago, Inter-Varsity [1964] 88p. 19cm. .75 pap.,
I. Title.

VAN SETERS, John. 222'.11'0924 B
Abraham in history and tradition / John Van Seters. New Haven : Yale University Press, 1975. xiii, 335 p. ; 25 cm. Includes bibliographical references and index. [BS580.A3V36] 74-20087 ISBN 0-300-01792-8 : 15.00
1. Abraham, the patriarch. 2. Bible. O.T. Genesis XII-XXV—Criticism, interpretation, etc. I. Title. **BIP**

Abraham, the patriarch—Juvenile literature.

†GRIFFITHS, Kitty 222'.11'0924 B
Anna.
Come, meet Abraham, God's friend : the story of Genesis 21-25 / Kitty Anna Griffiths. Grand Rapids : Zondervan Pub. House, 1977. 95 p. : ill. ; 21 cm. (Come, meet series) Retells the events in the life of Abraham. [BS580.A3G68] 76-54670 ISBN 0-310-25201-6 pbk : 1.95.
1. Abraham, the patriarch—Juvenile literature. 2. Bible. O.T.—Biography—Juvenile literature. 3. Patriarchs (Bible)—Biography—Juvenile literature. I. Title.

†GRIFFITHS, Kitty 222'.11'0924 B
Anna.
Come, meet Abraham, the pioneer : the story of Genesis 12-20 / Kitty Anna Griffiths. Grand Rapids : Zondervan Pub. House, 1977. 95 p. : ill. ; 21 cm. (Come, meet series) Discusses the life of Abraham and God's promise to him as found in Genesis 12-20. [BS580.A3G683] 76-54844 ISBN 0-310-25191-5 pbk : 1.95
1. Abraham, the patriarch—Juvenile literature. 2. Bible. O.T.—Biography—Juvenile literature. 3. Patriarchs (Bible)—Biography—Juvenile literature. I. Title.

RIVES, Elsie. 222'.11'0924 B
Abraham, man of faith / Elsie Rives ; illustrated by William N. McPheeters.

Nashville : Broadman Press, c1976. 48 p. : col. ill. ; 24 cm. (Biblearn series) Discusses Abraham's efforts to obey God and establish a new nation in Canaan. [BS580.A3R58] 76-382767 3.95
1. Abraham, the patriarch—Juvenile literature. 2. Patriarchs (Bible)—Biography—Juvenile literature. I. McPheeters, William N. II. Title.

Abraham, William, 1842-1922.

EVANS, Eric Wyn 923.31429
Mabon (William Abraham, 1842-1922) A study in trade union leadership. Pref. by A. Beacham. Cardiff, Univ. of Wales Pr. [Mystic, Conn., Verry, 1965] 115p. illus. 23cm. [HD8393.A3E9] 3.00
1. Abraham, William, 1842-1922. 2. Coal-miners—Wales. I. Title.

Abrams, William, 1836-

†REIMERS, Henry L. 979.7'37 B
The Abrams story / Henry L. Reimers. Fairfield, Wash. : Ye Galleon Press, 1977. p. cm. [F899.S7A257] 78-5584 ISBN 0-87770-181-4 : 7.50
1. Abrams, William, 1836- 2. Spokane—Biography. 3. Pioneers—Washington (State)—Spokane—Biography. I. Title. BIP

Abramson, Ben.

COVINGTON, D. B. 658.8'09'0705730924
The Argus Book Shop : a memoir / D. B. Covington. West Cornwall, Conn. : Tarrydiddle Press, 1977. 114 p. : ill. ; 24 cm. "Limited to three hundred and fifty copies." [Z473.A24C68] 77-358814
1. Abramson, Ben. 2. Book industries and trade—United States—Biography. I. Title.

Abramson, Manya Polevoi—Juvenile literature.

GRAY, Bettyanne. 947'.71 B
Manya's story / Bettyanne Gray ; foreword by Nora Levin. Minneapolis : Lerner Publications Co., c1978. 127 p. : ill. ; 23 cm. [DS135.R95A2754] 77-88522 ISBN 0-8225-0762-5 lib.bdg. : 6.95
1. Abramson, Manya Polevoi—Juvenile literature. 2. Jews in the Ukraine—Biography—Juvenile literature. 3. Ukraine—Biography—Juvenile literature. I. Title. BIP

Abravanel, Isaac, 1437-1508.

NETANYAHU, Benzion. 296'.0924 B
Don Isaac Abravanel, statesman and philosopher, by B. Netanyahu. [2d ed.] Philadelphia, Jewish Publication Society of America [1968] xii, 350 p. 22 cm. Bibliography: p. 327-335. [BM755.A25N4 1968] 68-15789
1. Abravanel, Isaac, 1437-1508. I. Title.

Abrecht, Mary Ellen.

ABRECHT, Mary Ellen. 363.2'092'4 B
The making of a woman cop / by Mary Ellen Abrecht, with Barbara Lang Stern. New York : Morrow, 1976. 275 p. ; 22 cm. [HV7911.A23A34] 75-23255 ISBN 0-688-02982-5 : 8.95
1. Abrecht, Mary Ellen. 2. Policewomen—Washington, D.C.—Correspondence, reminiscences, etc. I. Stern, Barbara Lang, joint author. II. Title. BIP

Abreu Gomez, Ermilo, 1894-1971.

SILVA de Rodriguez, Cecilia. 868
Vida y obras de Ermilo Abreu Gomez / by Cecilia Silva de Rodriguez. Fort Worth : Texas Christian University Press, 1975. 182 p. : port. ; 22 cm. (Mexican monograph series ; no. 2) Reprint of 1971 ed. published by the Secretaria de Hacienda y Credito Publico, Mexico. Introductory material in English. Bibliography: p. 173-178. [PQ7297.A33Z9 1975] 73-89349
1. Abreu Gomez, Ermilo, 1894-1971. I. Title. II. Series.

Abstract expressionism—United States—Exhibitions.

HOBBS, Robert Carleton, 1946- 759.13'074'014771
Abstract expressionism, the formative years / by Robert Carleton Hobbs and Gail Levin. Ithaca, N.Y. : Herbert F. Johnson Museum of Art, Cornell University, c1978. 140 p. : ill. (some col.) ; 28 cm. "Published in conjunction with an exhibition organized by the Herbert F. Johnson Museum of Art and the Whitney Museum of American Art." Includes bibliographical references. [ND212.5.A25H63] 77-29204 ISBN 0-87427-017-0 : 7.50
1. Abstract expressionism—United States—Exhibitions. 2. Painting, American—Exhibitions. 3. Painting, Modern—20th century—United States—Exhibitions. 4. Painters—United States—Biography. I. Levin, Gail, 1948- joint author. II. Herbert F. Johnson Museum of Art. III. Whitney Museum of American Art, New York. IV. Title.

Abu Bakr, Caliph, d. 634.

FEROZE, Muhammad Rashid. 297'.64 B
Abu Bakr : the first caliph / adapted from Arabic by Muhammad Rashid Feroze. Leicester : Islamic Foundation, 1976. 44 p. : ill., col. maps ; 21 cm. (Glimpses of Islamic history) "Based upon Sabir Abduh Ibrahim's book Abu Bakr." [DS38.4.A28F47] 77-356902 ISBN 0-9503954-4-7 : £0.50
1. Abu Bakr, Caliph, d. 634. 2. Caliphs—Biography. I. Ibrahim, Sabir'Abduh. Abu Bakr.

MASUD-UL-HASAN. 953.8'02'0924 B
Sidiq-i-Akbar Hazrat Abu Bakr : being a biography of Abu Bakr, the first caliph and a history of Islam during the caliphate of Abu Bakr / Masudul Hasan. Lahore : Ferozsons, 1976. vi, 241 p. ; 22 cm. [DS38.4.A28M35] 77-938534 Rs20.00
1. Abu Bakr, Caliph, d. 634. 2. Islamic Empire—History—622-661. 3. Caliphs—Biography. I. Title.

Academy awards (Moving-pictures)

†OSBORNE, Robert A. 791.43'028'0922
Best actress Oscar winners / by Robert Osborne. La Habra, Calif. : ESE California, c1977. [72] p. : ill. ; 28 cm. Cover title. Contains excerpts from the author's Academy awards illustrated and new articles on the Oscar winners up to 1977. [PN1993.5.U6O85] 78-103847 ISBN 0-912076-02-X pbk. : 2.95
1. Academy awards (Moving-pictures) 2. Moving-picture actors and actresses—Biography. I. Osborne, Robert A. Academy awards illustrated. II. Title.

Accountants—United States—Biography.

BURNS, Thomas Junior. 657'.092'2 B
The Accounting Hall of Fame : profiles of thirty-six members / by Thomas J. Burns, Edward N. Coffman. [Columbus] : College of Administrative Science, Ohio State University, 1976. vi, 88 p. : ports. ; 23 cm. [HF5604.B87] 77-150716
1. Accountants—United States—Biography. I. Coffman, Edward N., joint author. II. Title.

Acha, Carlos—Juvenile literature.

COOK, Fred J. 363.2'092'4 B
City cop / Fred J. Cook. 1st ed. Garden City, N.Y. : Doubleday, c1979. viii, 105 p. ; 22 cm. (A Doubleday signal book) A policeman tells of his first years on the beat in New York City. [HV7911.A24C66] 78-60284 5.95
1. Acha, Carlos—Juvenile literature. 2. New York (City)—Police—Biography—Juvenile literature. I. Title. BIP

Acheson, Dean Gooderham, 1893-1971.

ACHESON, Dean Gooderham, 1893- 917.3'03
Fragments of my fleece [by] Dean Acheson. [1st ed.] New York, Norton [1971] 222 p. port. 22 cm. [E748.A15A29 1971] 73-152651 ISBN 0-393-08644-5 6.95
I. Title.

ACHESON, Dean Gooderham, 1893- 973.910924
Morning and noon [by] Dean Acheson. Boston, Houghton Mifflin, 1965. xiii, 288 p. ports. 22 cm. Bibliographical references included in "Notes" (p. [231]-278) [E748.A15A3] 65-19308
I. Title.

ACHESON, Dean Gooderham, 1893- 973.910924
Morning and noon [by] Dean Acheson. Boston, Houghton Mifflin, 1965. xiii, 288 p. ports. 22 cm. An autobiographical account of his youth and early career. Bibliographical references includes in "Notes" (p. [231]-278) [E748.A15A3] 65-19308
I. Title.

ACHESON, Dean Gooderham, 1893-1971. 081
Grapes from thorns. [1st ed.] New York, Norton [1972] 253 p. 22 cm. [E748.A15A293] 76-39604 ISBN 0-393-05254-0
I. Title.

ACHESON, Edward Goodrich, 1856-1931. 662.920924 (B)
A pathfinder: inventor, scientist, industrialist. [Port Huron, Mich,] Acheson Industries [1965] 63 p. port. 22 cm. Includes the autobiographical section of the author's A pathfinder: discovery, invention and industry, published in 1910, with the addition of Preface and Addendum by Raymond Szymanowitz. Erratum slip mounted on p. 61. [TP140.A4A33] 65-6006
I. Title.

MCLELLAN, David S. 973.918'092'4 B
Dean Acheson : the State Department years / by David S. McLellan. New York : Dodd, Mead & Co., c1976. xii, 466 p., [12] leaves of plates : ill. ; 24 cm. Includes bibliographical references and index. [E748.A15M32] 76-8482 ISBN 0-396-07313-1 : 15.00
1. Acheson, Dean Gooderham, 1893-1971. 2. United States—Foreign relations—1945-1953. BIP

Acheson, Edward Goodrich, 1856-1931.

SZYMANOWITZ, Raymond, 1898- 660'.0924 B
Edward Goodrich Acheson: inventor, scientist, industrialist; a biography. [1st ed.] New York, Vantage Press [1971] 628 p. illus. 23 cm. Includes bibliographical references. [TP140.A4S97] 78-31687 10.00
1. Acheson, Edward Goodrich, 1856-1931.

Ackerley, Alfred Roger.

PETRE, Diana. 823'.9'14 B
The secret orchard of Roger Ackerley / Diana Petre. New York : G. Braziller, 1975. vii, 182 p., [4] leaves of plates : ill. ; 22 cm. [PR6066.E754Z525 1975] 75-13516 ISBN 0-8076-0799-1 : 6.95
1. Petre, Diana—Biography. 2. Ackerley, Alfred Roger. 3. Scott-Hewitt, Muriel Haidee Perry, 1890-1960. I. Title. BIP

Ackerley, Joe Randolph, 1896-1967.

ACKERLEY, Joe Randolph, 1896-1967. 301.41'5
My father & myself. [1st American ed.] New York, Coward-McCann [1969, c1968] 219 p. ports. 22 cm. [HQ76.A27 1969] 69-16083 5.00
I. Title. BIP

ACKERLEY, Joe Randolph, 1896-1967. 301.41'57'0922
My father & myself / J. R. Ackerley New York : Harcourt Brace Jovanovich, [1975] c1968. p. cm. (A Harvest book ; HB 314) Reprint of the 1st American ed. published in 1969 by Coward-McCann, New York. [HQ76.3.G7A24 1975] 75-6884 ISBN 0-15-662325-0 pbk. : 3.95
1. Ackerley, Joe Randolph, 1896-1967. 2. Ackerley, Alfred Roger. I. Title.

Ackerley, Joe Randolph, 1896-1967—Correspondence.

ACKERLEY, Joe Randolph, 1896-1967. 828'.9'1209 B
The Ackerley letters / edited by Neville Braybrooke. New York : Harcourt Brace Jovanovich, [1975] p. cm. Includes indexes. Bibliography: p. [PR6001.C4Z53 1975] 74-32313 ISBN 0-15-150858-5 : 15.00
1. Ackerley, Joe Randolph, 1896-1967—Correspondence. I. Title. BIP

Ackerman, Carl William, 1890- —Manuscripts—Indexes.

UNITED States. Library of Congress. Manuscript Division. 016.070'92'4
Carl William Ackerman: a register of his papers in the Library of Congress. Washington, Library of Congress, 1973. lii, 78 p. 27 cm. [Z6616.A33U53] 73-4207 ISBN 0-8444-0089-0
1. Ackerman, Carl William, 1890- —Manuscripts—Indexes. 2. United States—History—Sources—Bibliography. I. Title.

Acosta, Mercedes de—Biography.

ACOSTA, Mercedes de. 928.1 B
Here lies the heart. New York, Reynal [1960] 372 p. illus. 23 cm. Autobiographical. [PS3501.C7Z52] 60-6500
I. Title. BIP

ACOSTA, Mercedes de. 818'.5'209 B
Here lies the heart / Mercedes de Acosta. New York : Arno Press, 1975, c1960. 372 p., [8] leaves of plates : ill. ; 22 cm. (Homosexuality) Autobiographical. Reprint of the ed. published by Reynal, New York. Includes index. [PS3501.C7Z52 1975] 75-13709 ISBN 0-405-07360-7 : 16.00
1. Acosta, Mercedes de—Biography. I. Title. II. Series.

Acosta, Oscar Zeta.

ACOSTA, Oscar Zeta. 340'.092'4 [B]
The autobiography of a Brown Buffalo. New York, Popular Lib. [1973] 254 p. 18 cm. [CT275.A186A3] 72-79030 1.25 (pbk.)
I. Title.

Acting.

EUSTIS, Morton Corcoran, 1905-1944 792/.028/0922
Players at work; acting according to the actors. With a chapter on the singing actor, by Lotte Lehmann. Freeport, N.Y., Bks. for Libs. Pr. [1967] 127p. illus. 22cm. (Essay index reprint ser.) First pub. 1937. [PN2065.E8 1967] 67-23216 5.75
1. Acting. 2. Actors, American. I. Lehmann, Lotte. II. Title.

Acton, Harold Mario Mitchell,

ACTON, Harold Mario Mitchell, 1904- 828'.9'1203 B
Memoirs of an aesthete, 1939-1969 [by] Harold Acton. New York, Viking Press [1971, c1970] xv, 388 p. illus., ports. 23 cm. First published in 1970 under title: More memoirs of an aesthete. [PR6001.C7Z52 1971] 74-138490 ISBN 0-670-46816-9 8.95
I. Title.

Acton, John Emerich Edward Dalberg Acton, Baron, 1834-1902.

ACTON, John Emerich Edward Dalberg Acton, Baron, 1834-1902. 914.2'03'81
The correspondence of Lord Acton and Richard Simpson, edited by Josef L. Altholz and Damian McElrath. Cambridge [Eng.] University Press, 1971 [i.e. 1970]-75. 3 v. 24 cm. Includes bibliographical references. [D15.A25A45] 75-112466 ISBN 0-521-07819-9 £5/-/- ($16.00 U.S.)
1. Acton, John Emerich Edward Dalberg Acton, Baron, 1834-1902. 2. Simpson, Richard, 1820-1876. I. Simpson, Richard, 1820-1876. II. Altholz, Josef Lewis, 1933- ed. III. McElrath, Damian, ed. IV. Title.

DREW, Mary (Gladstone) 1847-1927. 914.2'081'0922
Acton, Gladstone, and others. Port Washington, N. Y., Kennikat Press [1968] 147 p. 19 cm. (Essay and general literature index reprint series) Reprint of the 1924 ed. Contents.--Acton and Gladstone.--Mr. Gladstone's books.--Henry Scott Holland.--Mr. Ruskin and Rose.--Tennyson and Laura Tennant.--"Here's me."

Bibliographical footnotes. [DA531.1.D7] 68-16292
1. Acton, John Emerich Edward Dalberg Acton, Baron, 1834-1902. 2. Gladstone, William Ewart, 1809-1898. 3. Holland, Henry Scott, 1874-1918 I. Title.

DREW, Mary (Gladstone) 920.042
1847-1927.
Acton, Gladstone, and others. Freeport, N.Y., Books for Libraries Press [1968] 147 p. 22 cm. (Essay index reprint series) Reprint of the 1924 ed. Contents.—Acton and Gladstone.—Mr. Gladstone's books.—Henry Scott Holland.—Mr. Ruskin and Rose.—Tennyson and Laura Tennant.—Here's me. Bibliographical footnotes. [DA531.1.D7 1968b] 68-20294
1. Acton, John Emerich Edward Dalberg Acton, Baron, 1834-1902. 2. Gladstone, William Ewart, 1809-1898. 3. Holland, Henry Scott, 1847-1918. I. Title. **BIP**

MATHEW, David, 907'.2'024 B
Abp., 1902-
Acton, the formative years. Westport, Conn., Greenwood Press [1974] viii, 196 p. illus. 22 cm. Reprint of the 1946 ed. published by Eyre & Spottiswoode, London. Includes bibliographical references. [D15.A25M3 1974] 73-19308 ISBN 0-8371-7323-X
1. Acton, John Emerich Edward Dalberg Acton, 1st Baron, 1834-1902. **BIP**

MATHEW, David, 907'.2'024 B
Abp., 1902-
Lord Acton and his times. University, University of Alabama Press [1968] 397 p. map, port. 23 cm. Five of the 38 chapters included have previously been published. Bibliography: p. 375-377. [D15.A25M32 1968b] 68-31556 10.00
1. Acton, John Emerich Edward Dalberg Acton, Baron, 1834-1902. I. Title. **BIP**

SCHUETTINGER, Robert 907'.2'024 B
Lindsay, 1936-
Lord Acton : historian of liberty / Robert L. Schuettinger. LaSalle, Ill. : Open Court, [1975] c1974. p. cm. Bibliography: p. [D15.A25S38 1975] 74-20792 ISBN 0-87548-294-5 : 7.95
1. Acton, John Emerich Edward Dalberg Acton, Baron, 1834-1902. **BIP**

Acton, John Emerich Edward Dalberg Acton, Baron, 1834-1902— Addresses, essays, lectures.

CHADWICK, Owen. 907'.2'024
Acton and Gladstone / [by] Owen Chadwick. London : Athlone Press, 1977. 56 p. ; 22 cm. (The Creighton lecture in history ; 1975) Includes bibliographical references. [D15.A25C48] 77-365899 ISBN 0-485-14122-1 pbk. : 3.25
1. Acton, John Emerich Edward Dalberg Acton, Baron, 1834-1902—Addresses, essays, lectures. 2. Gladstone, William Ewart, 1809-1898—Addresses, essays, lectures. 3. Historians—England—Biography—Addresses, essays, lectures. I. Title. II. Series: Creighton memorial lecture on history ; 1975.
Distributed by Humanities Press, Atlantic Highlands, NJ **BIP**

Actors.

APPLETON, William Worthen 927.92
Charles Macklin; an actor's life. Cambridge, Mass., Harvard University Press [c.]1960. vi, 280p. Bibl.: p.239-270 illus. 22cm. 60-13296 5.00
I. Macklin, Charles, 1697?-1797. II. Title.

BEATON, Cecil Walter Hardy, 927
1904-
Persona grata, by Cecil Beaton &Kenneth Tynan. [New York] Putnam [1954] 99p. illus. 25cm. [PN2205] 54-8464
1. Actors. 2. Authors. 3. Biography. I. Tynan, Kenneth, 1927- joint author. II. Title.

MORIN, Edgar 927.92
The stars. Translated by Richard Howard. New York, Grove Press [1960] 189p. illus. 18cm. (Evergreen profile book 7) 59-7540 1.35 pap.,
1. Actors. 2. Moving-pictures. I. Title.

ROSS, Lillian. 927.92
The player; a profile of an art [by] Lillian Ross, Helen Ross. Photos. by Lillian Ross. New York, S. & S. [1968,c.1962] 459p. illus. 24cm. In autobiographical form ... based on interviews [between 55 actors and the authors] [PN2285.R6] 62-16986 2.95 pap.,
1. Actors. I. Ross, Helen. joint author. II. Title.

WINFORD, Edgar Carlton, 927.92
1925-
Femme mimics. 1st ed. Dallas, Winford Co., 1954. 164p. illus. 29cm. [PN2285.W49] 54-35998
1. Actors. 2. Impersonators, Female. I. Title.

Actors—Correspondence, reminiscences, etc.

ABBOTT, George, 1889- 927.92
Mister Abbott. New York, Random [c.1963] 279p. 22cm. 63-16153 4.95
1. Actors—Correspondence, reminiscences, etc. I. Title.

BARRYMORE, Ethel, 1879- 927.92
1959
Memories, an autobiography, by Ethel Barrymore. New York, Kraus Reprint, 1968. 310p. illus. (front. port) 24cm. First pub. in 1955 by Harper [PN2287.B3A3] 55-6565 10.50
1. Actors—Correspondence, reminiscences, etc. I. Title.

BARRYMORE, Ethel, 1879- 927.92
1959.
Memories, an autobiography. [1st ed.] New York, Harper [1955] 310 p. illus. 22 cm. [PN2287.B3A3] 55-6565
1. Actors—Correspondence, reminiscences, etc. I. Title.

BARRYMORE, John, 792'.028'0924 B
1882-1942.
Confessions of an actor. [New York] B. Blom [1971, c1926] 1 v. (unpaged) illus., facsim., ports. 21 cm. [PN2287.B35A3 1971] 70-84506
1. Actors—Correspondence, reminiscences, etc. I. Title. **BIP**

BELMONT, Eleanor Robson, 927.92
1879-
The fabric of memory. New York, Farrar, Straus and Cudahy [1957] 311 p. illus. 22 cm. Reminiscences. [PN2287.B42A4] 57-12412
1. Actors—Correspondence, reminiscences, etc. I. Title.

BROUN, Heywood Hale, 792.0924
1918-
A studied madness. [1st ed.] Garden City, N. Y., Doubleday, 1965. vi, 298 p. 22 cm. Autobiographical. [PN2287.B696A3] 65-17246
1. Actors—Correspondence, reminiscences, etc. I. Title. **BIP**

CAMPBELL, Beatrice 790.2'0924
Stella (Tanner) 1865-1940.
My life and some letters, by Mrs. Patrick Campbell (Beatrice Stella Cornwallis West) ... New York, Dodd, Mead and company, 1922. 5 p. l., 451 p. front., illus., plates, ports. 25 cm. [PN2598,C23A3] 22-22417
1. Actors—Correspondence, reminiscences, etc. I. Title.

CANTOR, Eddie, 1893- 927.92
As I remember them. [1st ed.] New York, Duell, Sloan and Pearce [1963] 144 p. illus., ports. 24 cm. [PN2287.C26A35] 63-16816
1. Actors—Correspondence, reminiscences, etc. I. Title.

CANTOR, Eddie, 1893- 927.92
Take my life [by] Eddie Cantor, with Jane Kesner Ardmore. [1st ed.] Garden City, N. Y., Doubleday, 1957. 288 p. illus. 22 cm. [PN2287.C26A52] 57-7279
1. Actors—Correspondence, reminiscences, etc. I. Ardmore, Jane Kesner Morris. II. Title.

CHAPLIN, Charles, 1889- 927.92
My autobiography. New York, Simon and Schuster [1964] 512 p. illus., ports. 25 cm. [PN2287.C5A32] 64-19937
1. Actors—Correspondence, reminiscences, etc.

CHAPLIN, 791.430280924 (B)
Charles, 1889-
My autobiography. Harmondsworth, Penguin, 1966. 494 p. 64 plates (113 illus.) 18 1/2 cm. 10/6 [PN2287.C5A32 1966] 67-71441
1. Actors — Correspondence, reminiscences, etc. I. Title.

CHAPLIN, Charles, 1889- 927.92
My autobiography. New York, Pocket Bks. [1966, c.1964] 560p. illus., ports. 18cm. (Cardinal ed., 95026) [PN2287.C5A32] .95 pap.,
1. Actors—Correspondence, reminiscences, etc. I. Title. **BIP**

DIBDIN, Thomas 792'.028'0924
John, 1771-1841.
The reminiscences of Thomas Dibdin. New York, AMS Press [1970] 2 v. port. 23 cm. Reprint of the 1827 ed. [PR4549.D5Z5 1970] 70-111769
1. Actors—Correspondence, reminiscences, etc. 2. Theater—England. **BIP**

ELLSLER, John Adam, 1822- 927.92
1903.
The stage memories of John A. Ellsler; edited by Effie Ellsler Weston. [1st ed.] Cleveland, Rowfant Club, 1950. 159 p. ports. 23 cm. "182 copies ... printed." [PN2287.E5A3] 50-2048
1. Actors—Correspondence, reminiscences, etc. I. Title.

FLYNN, Errol Leslie, 1909- 927.92
1959.
My wicked, wicked ways. New York, Putnam [1960, c1959] 438 p. 23 cm. [PN2287.F55A3] 59 7849
1. Actors—Correspondence, reminiscences, etc. I. Title.

FLYNN, Errol Leslie, 1909- 927.92
1959.
My wicked, wicked ways [New York] Dell [1961, c.1959] 512p. (S11) .60 pap.,
1. Actors—Correspondence, reminiscences, etc. I. Title. **BIP**

FLYNN, Errol 791.43'028'0924 B
Leslie, 1909-1959.
My wicked, wicked ways. [New York] Berkley Pub Co. [1974, c1959] 383 p. 18 cm. (A Berkley medallion book) [PN2287.F55A3] ISBN 0-425-02512-8. 1.25 (pbk.)
1. Actors—Correspondence, reminiscences, etc. I. Title.
L.C. card number for original ed.: 59-7849.

GABOR, Eva. 927.92
Orchids and salami. Foreword by Lawrence Langner. [1st ed.] Garden City, N.Y., Doubleday, 1954. 219p. 22cm. Autobiographical. [PN2287.G32A3] 54-5170
1. Actors—Correspondence, reminiscences, etc. I. Title.

GARRICK, David, 1717-1779. 927.92
Letters [3v.] Ed. by David M. Little, George M. Kahrl. Assoc. ed. Phoebe deK. Wilson. Cambridge, Mass., Belknap Pr., Harvard [c.]1963. 3v. (1xxi, 1418p.) illus., ports., map, facsims. 25cm. Bibl. 63-7129 35.00 set bxd.
1. Actors—Correspondence, reminiscences, etc. I. Little, David Mason, 1896-1954, ed. II. Kahrl, George Morrow, 1904- ed. III. Title.

GORDON, Ruth, 792'.028'0924 B
1896-
Myself among others. [1st ed.] New York, Atheneum, 1971. 389 p. 25 cm. [PN2287.G64A3] 74-139309 10.00
1. Actors—Correspondence, reminiscences, etc. I. Title.

GRAHAM, Sheilah. 791.43'028'0922
Confessions of a Hollywood columnist. New York, Morrow, 1969. 309 p. 22 cm. [PN4874.G67A315] 69-16861 5.95
1. Actors—Correspondence, reminiscences, etc. I. Title. **BIP**

GRANLUND, Nils Thor 927.92
Blondes, brunettes, and bullets, by Nils Thor Granlund with Sid Feder and Ralph Hancock. New York, D. McKay Co. [c1957] 300p. 21cm. [PN2287.G67A4] 57-13513
1. Actors —Correspondence, reminiscences, etc. I. Title.

GUTHRIE, Tyrone, 1900- 927.92
A life in the theatre. New York, McGraw [1963, c.1959] 357p. 21cm. (25293) 2.45 pap.,
1. Actors—Correspondence, reminiscences, etc. I. Title.

GUTHRIE, Tyrone, Sir, 927.92
1900-1971.
A life in the theatre. [1st ed.] New York, McGraw-Hill [1959] 357 p. 22 cm. Autobiography. [PN2598.G85A3] 59-14450
1. Actors—Correspondence, reminiscences, etc. I. Title.

HARDWICKE, Cedric, Sir 927.92
1893-
A Victorian in orbit; the irreverent memoirs of Sir Cedric Hardwicke as told to James Brough. [1st ed.] Garden City, N. Y., Doubleday, 1961. 311p. illus. 22cm. [PN2598.H28A32] 61-7652
1. Actors—Correspondence, reminiscences, etc. I. Brough, James, 1918- II. Title.

HARDWICKE, 792'.028'0924 B
Cedric, Sir, 1893-
A Victorian in orbit; the irreverent memoirs of Sir Cedric Hardwicke as told to James Brough. Westport, Conn., Greenwood Press [1972, c1961] 311 p. illus. 22 cm. [PN2598.H28A32 1972] 72-7504 ISBN 0-8371-6516-4 13.75
1. Actors—Correspondence, reminiscences, etc. I. Brough, James, 1918- II. Title.

HARDWICKE, Cedric 927.92
[Webster] Sir 1893-
A Victorian in orbit; the irreverent memoirs of Sir Cedric Hardwicke as told to James Brough. Garden City, N. Y., Doubleday. [c.]1961. 311p. illus. 61-7652 4.50
1. Actors—Correspondence, reminiscences, etc. I. Brough, James, 1918- II. Title.

HART, William 792'.028'0924 B
Surrey, 1874-1946.
My life East and West. New York, B. Blom [1968] vii, 362 p. illus., ports. 20 cm. First published 1929. [PN2287.H3A3 1968] 68-20228
1. Actors—Correspondence, reminiscences, etc. I. Title. **BIP**

HAYDEN, Sterling 927.92
Wanderer. New York, Bantam [1964, c.1963] 407p. 18cm. (W2864) .85 pap.,
1. Actors—Correspondence, reminiscences, etc. I. Title. **BIP**

HAYDEN, Sterling, 1916- 927.92
Wanderer [1st ed.] New York, Knopf, 1963. 434 p. 22 cm. [PN2287.H34A3] 63-20142
1. Actors—Correspondence, reminiscences, etc. I. Title.

HILL, George 792'.028'0924 B
Handel, known as Yankee Hill, 1809-1849.
Scenes from the life of an actor. New York, B. Blom, 1969. vi, 246 p. illus., port. 20 cm. Reprint of the 1853 ed. [PN2287.H5A3 1969] 75-81204
1. Actors—Correspondence, reminiscences, etc. I. Title. **BIP**

HOLLOWAY, Stanley. 790.2'0924
Wiv a little bit o' luck; the life story of Stanley Holloway, as told to Dick Richards. New York, Stein and Day [1967] 223 p. illus., ports. 22 cm. [PN2598.H63A3 1967b] 67-25621
1. Actors—Correspondence, reminiscences, etc. I. Richards, Dick. II. Title.

HOLLOWAY, Stanley. 790.2'0924
Wiv a little bit o'luck; the life story of Stanley Holloway, as told to Dick Richards. New York, Stein and Day [1967] 223 p. illus., ports. 22 cm. [PN2598.H63A3 1967b] 67-25621
1. Actors—Correspondence, reminiscences, etc. I. Richards, Dick. II. Title.

JEFFERSON, Joseph, 1829- 927.92
1905.
Autobiography. Edited by Alan S. Downer. Cambridge, Belknap Press of Harvard University Press, 1964. xxv, 363 p. illus., ports. 25 cm. (The John Harvard library) Bibliographical footnotes. [PN2287.J4A3 1964] 64-16063
1. Actors—Correspondence, reminiscences, etc. I. Series.

KELLY, Walter C., 1873-1939. 927.92
Of me I sing, an informal autobiography. New York, Dial Press, 1953. 246 p. illus. 21 cm. [PN2287.K65A3] 53-12683
1. Actors—Correspondence, reminiscences, etc. I. Title.

LE GALLIENNE, Eva, 1899- 927.92
With a quiet heart, an autobiography. New York, Viking Press, 1953. 311p. illus. 22cm. [PN2287.L3A35] 53-5201
1. Actors—Correspondence, reminiscences, etc. I. Title.

LEMAN, Walter Moore, b.1810. 792'.028'0924
Memories of an old actor. New York, B. Blom [1969] xv, 406 p. port. 21 cm. Reprint of the 1886 ed. [PN2287.L4A3 1969b] 78-91905
1. Actors—Correspondence, reminiscences, etc. I. Title.

LEMAN, Walter Moore, b.1810. 792'.028'0924
Memories of an old actor. San Francisco, A. Roman Co, 1886. St. Clair Shores, Mich., Scholarly Press [1969?] xv, 406 p. port. 21 cm. [PN2287.L4A3 1969] 70-106905
1. Actors—Correspondence, reminiscences, etc. I. Title. BIP

MACLIAMMHOIR, Michael, 1899- 792'.0924 (B)
All for Hecuba; an Irish theatrical autobiography, by Michael MacLiammoir. [1st American ed.] Boston, Branden Press [1967, c1961] 356 p. illus., ports. 23 cm. "This new and revised edition with extra material first published 1961." [PN2601.M3 1967] 67-26024
1. Actors—Correspondence, reminiscences, etc. 2. Dublin. Gate Theatre. I. Title.

MACREADY, William Charles, 1793-1873. 792'.028'0924
The diaries of William Charles Macready, 1833-1851. Edited by William Toynbee. New York, B. Blom [1969] 2 v. ports. 24 cm. Reprint of the 1912 ed. [PN2598.M3A3 1969] 78-84519
1. Actors—Correspondence, reminiscences, etc. I. Toynbee, William, 1849- ed. BIP

MAEDER, Clara (Fisher) 1811-1898. 792'.028'0924 B
Autobiography of Clara Fisher Maeder. Edited by Douglas Taylor. New York, B. Franklin [1970] xlviii, 138 p. illus., facsims. (2 fold.), ports. 19 cm. (Burt Franklin research & source works series, 573. Theatre & drama series, 12) Reprint of the 1897 ed. [PN2287.M2A3 1970] 79-130094 ISBN 0-8337-2180-1
1. Actors—Correspondence, reminiscences, etc. I. Taylor, Douglas, ed. BIP

MARX, Harpo 927.92
Harpo speaks! [By] Harpo Marx, Rowland Barber. Illus. by Susan Marx. New York, Avon [1962, c.1961] 384p. (V-2050) .75 pap.,
1. Actors—Correspondence, reminiscences, etc. I. Title.

MATINEZ, Luis Maria Abp. c6 927.92
Harpo speaks! With Rowland Barber. Illus. by Susan Marx [New York] B. Geis Associates, dist. Random House [c.1961] 475p. illus. 61-7834 5.95 bds.,
1. Actors—Correspondence, reminiscences, etc. I. M II. Marx, Harpo III. Title.

NUGENT, Elliot, 1900- 792.0924
Events leading up to the comedy. New York. Pocket Bks. [1966, c.1963] xii, 226p. illus. 18cm. (75182) [PN2287.N78A3] .75 pap.,
1. Actors—Correspondence, reminiscences, etc. I. Title.

O'BRIEN, Pat, 1899- 927.92
The wind at my back; the life and times of Pat O'Brien, by himself. [1st ed.] Garden City, N.Y., Doubleday, 1964. 331 p. illus., ports. 22 cm. [PN2287.O23A3] 64-19327
1. Actors — Correspondence, reminiscences, etc. I. Title.

PICKFORD, Mary, 1893- 927.92
Sunshine and shadow. Foreword by Cecil B. de Mille. [1st ed.] Garden City, N. Y., Doubleday, 1955. 382 p. illus. 22 cm. Autobiography. [PN2287.P5A3] 55-5580
1. Actors—Correspondence, reminiscences, etc. I. Title.

RATHBONE, Basil, 1892- 927.92
In and out of character. [1st ed.] Garden City, N. Y., Doubleday, 1962. 278 p. illus. 22 cm. Autobiography. [PN2598.R35A3] 62-15316
1. Actors—Correspondence, reminiscences, etc. I. Title.

REDFIELD, William Henry, 1927- 792'.028'0924
Letters from an actor [by] William Redfield. New York, Viking Press [1967] xii, 243 p. 22 cm. Letters originally written to Robert Mills between January and August 1964. [PN2287.R28A45] 67-11261
1. Actors—Correspondence, reminiscences, etc. I. Mills, Robert P. II. Title.

TERRY, Ellen, Dame, 1848-1928. 792'.028'0924 B
Ellen Terry's memoirs. With a pref., notes, and additional biographical chapters by Edith Craig and Christopher St. John. London, 1932. New York, B. Blom, 1969. xiii, 367 p. illus., facsims., ports. 24 cm. "A new edition of The story of my life, by Ellen Terry, London, 1908. With a collection of illustrations taken from the first limited edition of 1908." [PN2598.T4A3 1969] 74-77976
1. Actors—Correspondence, reminiscences, etc. I. Craig, Edith, 1869-1947. II. St. John, Christopher Marie. BIP

WALLACK, John Lester, 1820-1888. 792'.028'0922
Memories of fifty years. With an introd. by Laurence Hutton. New York, B. Blom [1969] xiv, 232 p. illus., facsims., ports. 20 cm. Reprint of the 1889 ed. [PN2287.W3A3 1969] 71-81979
1. Actors—Correspondence, reminiscences, etc. I. Title. BIP

WOOD, Peggy, 1892- 927.92
Arts and flowers. New York, Morrow, 1963. 189 p. illus., ports. 22 cm. Autobiographical. [PN2287.W6A33] 63-17686
1. Actors—Correspondence, reminiscences, etc. I. Title.

Actors, American.

GARD, Robert Edward. 792'.0922
America's players, by Robert E. Gard and David Semmes. New York, Seabury Press [1967] 152 p. illus. 22 cm. Bibliography: p. 151-152. [PN2285.G3] 67-24462
1. Actors, American. I. Semmes, David, joint author. II. Title.

WAGNER, Frederick, 1928- 927.92
Famous American actors and actresses, by Frederick Wagner and Barbara Brady. Illustrated by Gerald McCann. New York, Dodd, Mead, 1961. 159 p. illus. 22 cm. (Famous biographies for young people) Includes bibliography. [PN2285.W3] 61-6939
1. Actors, American. I. Brady, Barbara, joint author. II. Title.

WAGNER, Frederick [Reese] 1928- 927.92
Famous American actors and actresses, by Frederick Wagner, Barbara Brady. Illus. by Gerald McCann. New York, Dodd, Mead [c.]1961. 159p. illus. (Famous biographies for young people) Bibl. 61-6939 3.00
1. Actors, American. I. Brady, Barbara, jt. author. II. Title.

ZOLOTOW, Maurice, 1913- 927.92
No people like show people; with an introd. by Brooks Atkinson. New York, Random House [1951] xii, 305 p. 21 cm. Contents.Contents.—Are actors people?—Tallulah Bankhead.—Jimmy Durante.—Oscar Levant.—Jack Benny.—Frank Fay.—Jed Harris.—Fred Allen.—Ethel Merman. [PN2283.Z6] 51-11426
1. Actors, American. I. Title.

Actors, American—Dictionaries.

RIGDON, Walter, ed. 792.0922 B
The Biographical encyclopaedia & Who's who of the American theatre. Introd. by George Freedley. [1st ed.] New York, J. H. Heineman [1966, c1965] xiv, 1101 p. 29 cm. [PN2285.R5] 65-19390
1. Actors, American—Dictionaries. 2. Theater—U.S.—Dictionaries. I. Title.

RIGDON, Walter, ed. 792.0922
The biographical encyclopedia & who's who of the American theatre. Introd by George Freedley. New York, J. H. Heineman [1966, c.1965] xiv, 1101p. 29cm. [PN2285.R5] 65-19390 82.50
1. Actors, American—Dictionaries. 2. Theater—U. S. Dictionaries. I. Title.

Actors, Canadian —Correspondence, reminiscences, etc.

PLUNKETT, Al. 927.92
Al Plunkett, the famous Dumbell, by Patrise Earle, as told by Al Plunkett. [1st ed.] New York, Pageant Press [1956] 107p. illus. 21cm. [PN2308.P5A3] 56-9434
1. Actors, Canadian —Correspondence, reminiscences, etc. I. Earle, Patrise. II. Title.

Actors—Caricatures and cartoons.

GLADDING, W. J. 792'.028'0922 B
A group of theatrical caricatures; being twelve plates by W. J. Gladding. With an introd. and biographical sketches by Louis Evan Shipman. New York, B. Franklin [1970] viii, 78 p. illus. 19 cm. (Burt Franklin research and source works series, 573. Theatre and drama series, 12) Reprint of the 1897 ed. Contents.Contents.—John Brougham.—John Lester Wallace.—Edwin Forrest.—Edwin Booth.—William J. Florence.—John E. Owens.—Francis S. Chanfrau.—George L. Fox.—Charles T. White and Dan Bryant.—William Wheatley.—Antonio Pastor. [PN2285.G6 1970] 72-130095 ISBN 0-8337-1362-0
1. Actors—Caricatures and cartoons. 2. Actors—United States—Biography. I. Title. II. Title: Theatrical caricatures.

Actors—England.

BURTON, Hal, 1908- 792.0922
Great acting: Laurence Olivier, Sybil Thorndike, Ralph Richardson, Peggy Ashcroft, Michael Redgrave, Edith Evans, John Gielgud, Noel Coward. Edited by Hal Burton. [1st American ed.] New York, Hill and Wang [1967] 192 p. ports. 29 cm. Interviews conducted by various persons. [PN2597.B8 1967] 67-23522
1. Actors—England. 2. Theater—England. I. Olivier, Laurence Kerr, Baron Olivier, 1907- II. Title.

Actors—England—Biography.

BROOK, Donald. 792'.0922
A pageant of English actors. Freeport, N.Y., Books for Libraries Press [1972, c1950] 286 p. illus. 23 cm. (Biography index reprint series) Contents.Contents.—Richard Burbage.—Richard Tarlton.—William Kemp.—Edward Alleyn.—Thomas Betterton.—David Garrick.—John Kemble.—Edmund Kean.—William Charles Macready.—Samuel Phelps.—Sir Henry Irving.—Sir Johnston Forbes-Robertson.—Sir Herbert Beerbohm-Tree.—John Gielgud.—Sir Laurence Olivier.—Bibliography (p. 285-286) [PN2597.B7 1972] 71-38315 ISBN 0-8369-8116-2
1. Actors—England—Biography. I. Title. BIP

WATERBURY, Ruth 927.92
Richard Burton. New York, Pyramid [c.1965] 171p. illus., ports. 18cm. [PN2598.B795W3] 65-2089 .60 pap.,
I. Title.

Actors—England—Correspondence, reminiscences, etc.

BENSON, Francis Robert, Sir, 1858-1939. 792'.028'0924 B
My memoirs. New York, B. Blom, 1971. ix, 322 p. ports. 21 cm. Reprint of the 1930 ed. [PN2598.B56A3 1971] 70-91473
1. Actors—England—Correspondence, reminiscences, etc. I. Title.

FORBES-ROBERTSON, Johnston, Sir, 1853-1937. 792'.028'0924 B
A player under three reigns. New York, B. Blom, 1971. 291 p. illus. 21 cm. Reprint of the 1925 ed. [PN2598.F6A3 1971] 79-88537
1. Actors—England—Correspondence, reminiscences, etc. I. Title. BIP

HARDWICKE, Cedric, Sir, 1893- 792.028'0924
Let's pretend; recollections and reflections of a lucky actor. New York, B. Blom, 1972. 257 p. illus. 21 cm. Reprint of the 1932 ed. [PN2598.H28A3 1972] 78-93165
1. Actors—England—Correspondence, reminiscences, etc. I. Title.

Actors, English.

PEARSON, Hesketh, 1887- 927.92
The last actor-managers. With illus. from the Raymond Mander and Joe Mitchenson Theatre Collection. New York, Harper [c1950] xii, 83 p. illus., ports. 23 cm. Bibliography (p. 80) [PN2597.P4 1950a] 51-10947
1. Actors, English. I. Title.
Contents omitted. BIP

Actors, English—Correspondence, reminiscences, etc.

HARVEY, John Martin-, Sir, 1863-1944. 792'.028'0924 B
The autobiography of Sir John Martin-Harvey. London, S. Low, Marston. New York, Johnson Reprint Corp., 1971. xix, 563 p. illus. 24 cm. Reprint of the 1933 ed. [PN2598.H34A2 1971b] 78-177275
1. Actors, English—Correspondence, reminiscences, etc. BIP

HARVEY, John Martin-, Sir, 1863-1944. 792'.028'0924 B
The autobiography of Sir John Martin-Harvey. London, S. Low, Marston. St. Clair Shores, Mich., Scholarly Press, 1971. xviii, 563 p. illus., ports. 22 cm. Reprint of the 1933 ed. [PN2598.H34A2 1971] 77-145073 ISBN 0-403-01015-2
1. Actors, English—Correspondence, reminiscences, etc. BIP

SCOTT, Janette, 1938- 927.92
Act one. London, New York, Nelson [1953] 88p. illus. 20cm. Autobiographical. [PN2598.S4A3] 54-1121
1. Actors, English—Correspondence, reminiscences, etc. I. Title.

Actors, French—Correspondence, reminiscences, etc.

SOREL, Cecile, 1875- 927.92
An autobiography. Translated by Philip John Stead. New York, Roy Publishers [1954] 285p. 21cm. Translation of Les belles heures de ma vie. [PN2638.S6A33] 54-7909
1. Actors, French—Correspondence, reminiscences, etc. I. Title.

Actors—Great Britain.

BAIN, Kenneth Bruce Findlater, 1921- 792'.028'0922
The player kings [by] Richard Findlater. New York, Stein and Day [1971] 288 p. illus., ports. 25 cm. Includes bibliographical references. [PN2597.B23] 79-150227 ISBN 0-8128-1363-4 7.95
1. Actors—Great Britain. I. Title.

DAVIES, Thomas, 1712?-1785. 792'.028'0924 B
Memoirs of the life of David Garrick. A new ed. with notes by Stephen Jones. New York, B. Blom, 1969. 2 v. port. 20 cm. Reprint of the 1808 ed. [PN2598.G3D3 1969] 73-82825
I. Garrick, David, 1717-1779. II. Title. BIP

PEARSON, Hesketh, 1887-1964. 792'.028'0922 B
The last actor-managers. With illus. from the Raymond Mander and Joe Mitchenson Theatre Collection. Freeport, N.Y., Books for Libraries Press [1971, c1950] xii, 83 p. illus., ports. 23 cm. (Biography index reprint series) Bibliography: p. 80. [PN2597.P4 1971] 77-148225 ISBN 0-8369-8072-7
1. Actors—Great Britain. I. Title.

Actors—Great Britain—Biography.

ARMSTRONG, Cecil 792'.028'0922
Ferard.
A century of great actors, 1750-1850. New York, B. Blom, 1971. 412 p. illus. 22 cm. Reprint of the 1912 ed. "Books consulted": p. 411-412. [PN2597.A9 1971] 73-91471
1. Actors—Great Britain—Biography. 2. Theater—Great Britain—History. I. Title. BIP

BAIN, Kenneth Bruce 792'.092'2 B
Findlater, 1921-
The player queens / Richard Findlater [i.e. K. B. F. Bain]. London : Weidenfeld and Nicolson, c1976. 250 p., [4] leaves of plates : ports. ; 23 cm. Includes index. Bibliography: p. [238]-243. [PN2597.B24 1976] 77-350005 ISBN 0-297-77158-2 : £6.95
1. Actors—Great Britain—Biography. 2. Actresses—Great Britain—Biography. I. Title.

FINDLATER, Richard, 792'.092'2 B
1921-
The player queens / Richard Findlater. New York : Taplinger Pub. Co., 1977, c1976. p. cm. Includes index. Bibliography: p. [PN2597.F44 1977] 76-53912 ISBN 0-8008-6324-0 : 10.95
1. Actors—Great Britain—Biography. 2. Actresses—Great Britain—Biography. I. Title. BIP

Actors—Great Britain—Correspondence, reminiscences, etc.

GIELGUD, John, 792'.028'0922
Sir, 1904-
Distinguished company. [1st ed. in the U.S.A.] Garden City, N.Y., Doubleday, 1973. xii, 179 p. illus. 22 cm. [PN2597.G5 1973] 72-96237 ISBN 0-385-04563-8 5.95
1. Actors—Great Britain—Correspondence, reminiscences, etc. I. Title.

Actors—Interviews.

OFF camera : 791'.092'2
what it's like to be—Dustin Hoffman ... New York : Stein and Day, [1975] p. cm. Interviews with Dustin Hoffman, Paul Newman, Al Pacino, Shirley MacLaine, George C. Scott, Barbara Walters, Marlo Thomas, Zero Mostel, Dick Cavett, Lynn Redgrave, Gwen Verdon, Edwin Newman, Woody Allen, Elaine May, Angela Lansbury, Mike Nichols, Diana Rigg. [PN2205.O34] 75-15237 ISBN 0-8128-1842-3 : 8.95
1. Actors—Interviews.

Actors—Italy—Correspondence, reminiscences, etc.

SALVINI, Tommaso, 792'.028'0924
1829-1916.
Leaves from the autobiography of Tommaso Salvini. New York, B. Blom, 1971. 240 p. illus. 22 cm. Reprint of the 1893 ed. [PN2688.S3A3 1971] 74-82844
1. Actors—Italy—Correspondence, reminiscences, etc. I. Title.

Actors—United States—Biography.

BECK, Marilyn. 791.43'028'0922
Marilyn Beck's Hollywood. New York, Hawthorn Books [1973] xi, 258 p. illus. 22 cm. [PN2285.B42] 73-355 6.95
1. Actors—United States—Biography. I. Title.

CLAPP, John 792'.028'0922 B
Bouve.
Players of the present, by John Bouve Clapp and Edwin Francis Edgett. New York, B. Blom, 1971. vi, 423 p. facsim., ports. 22 cm. "First published in three parts as the Dunlap Society publications, new series numbers 9, 11, & 13, New York, 1899, 1900, 1901." [PN2285.C5 1971] 72-91897
1. Actors—United States—Biography. I. Edgett, Edwin Francis, 1876-1946, joint author. II. Title. BIP

SHAW, Dale, 1927- 792.028'0922
Titans of the American stage; Edwin Forrest, the Booths, the O'Neills. Philadelphia, Westminster Press [1971] 160 p. illus. 24 cm. Bibliography: p. [155]-156. [PN2285.S43] 73-158123 ISBN 0-664-32501-7 5.95
1. Actors—United States—Biography. I. Title.

STRANG, Lewis 792'.028'0922 B
Clinton, 1869-1935.
Famous actors of the day in America : second series / by Lewis C. Strang. Boston : Longwood Press, 1978. p. cm. Reprint of the 1902 ed. published by L. C. Page and Co., Boston, issued in series: Stage lovers series. [PN2285.S75 1978] 77-92446 ISBN 0-89341-375-5 lib.bdg. : 35.00
1. Actors—United States—Biography. I. Title. II. Series: Stage lovers series.

WINTER, William, 792'.028'0922 B
1836-1917.
Brief chronicles. New York, B. Franklin [1970] xiv, 339 p. port. 19 cm. (Burt Franklin research & source works series 573. Theatre & drama series 12) Reprint of the 1889 ed. Biographies of persons connected with the American stage. Originally published as publications no. 7-8, and 10 of the Dunlap Society. [PN2285.W497 1970] 75-130085 ISBN 0-8337-3826-7
1. Actors—United States—Biography. I. Title. BIP

Actors—United States—Biography—Juvenile literature.

POLSKY, Milton 791.43'028'0922 B
E.
Today's young stars of stage and screen / by Milton E. Polsky. New York : F. Watts, 1979. 120 p. : ill. ; 25 cm. Includes index. Bibliography: p. 118. Spotlights the lives of 12 rising young stars of stage, movies, and television including interviews in which they express their thoughts and attitudes toward their careers. [PN2285.P6] 920 79-13280 ISBN 0-531-02885-2 : 6.90
1. Actors—United States—Biography—Juvenile literature. 2. Children as actors—Juvenile literature. I. Title. BIP

Actors—United States—Correspondence, reminiscences, etc.

COHAN, George Michael, 792.0924
1878-1942.
Twenty years on Broadway, and the years it took to get there; the true story of a trouper's life from the cradle to the "closed shop". Westport, Conn., Greenwood Press [1971, c1925] 264 p. illus. 23 cm. [PN2287.C56A3 1971] 76-138106 ISBN 0-8371-5682-3
1. Actors—United States—Correspondence, reminiscences, etc. I. Title. BIP

RUBIN, Benny. 792'.028'0922
Come backstage with me. Bowling Green, Ohio, Bowling Green University Popular Press [1972?] 218 p. illus. 24 cm. [PN2287.R78A3] 72-189453 ISBN 0-87972-040-9
1. Actors—United States—Correspondence, reminiscences, etc. I. Title.

SKINNER, Otis, 792'.028'0922
1858-1942.
Footlights and spotlights; recollections of my life on the stage. Westport, Conn., Greenwood Press [1972, c1924] 366 p. illus. 22 cm. [PN2287.S5A3 1972] 76-164474 ISBN 0-8371-6216-5 15.50
1. Actors—United States—Correspondence, reminiscences, etc. I. Title.

WINTER, William, 792'.028'0922
1836-1917.
Other days, being chronicles and memories of the stage. Freeport, N.Y., Books for Libraries Press [1970] 389 p. ports. 23 cm. (Essay index reprint series) Contents.Contents.—A royal line.—Joseph Jefferson.—John Brougham.—Dion Boucicault.—Charlotte Cushman.—Edward A. Sothern.—John McCullough.—Lawrence Barrett.—Mary Anderson.—Adelaide Neilson.—Stage conditions—past and present. [PN2285.W5 1970] 77-121513 ISBN 0-8369-1816-9
1. Actors—United States—Correspondence, reminiscences, etc. I. Title.

Actresses.

GILDER, Rosamond 927.92
Enter the actress; the first women in the theatre. [New York] Theatre Arts Bks. [1961, c.1931] 312p. illus. 60-10493 1.95 pap.,
1. Actresses. 2. Dramatists. 3. Theater—Hist. I. Title.

KNEPLER, Henry W. 792'.028'0922
The gilded stage; the years of the great international actresses, by Henry Knepler. New York, W. Morrow, 1968. x, 347 p. illus., ports. 22 cm. Bibliography: p. 322-334. [PN2205.K6] 68-23912 7.50
1. Actresses. 2. Theater—History. I. Title.

MARINACCI, Barbara. 927.92
Leading ladies; a gallery of famous actresses. New York, Dodd, Mead, 1961. 306 p. illus. 21 cm. [PN2205.M35] 61-7169
1. Actresses. I. Title.

WAGENKNECHT, Edward 927.92
Charles, 1900-
Seven daughters of the theater: Jenny Lind, Sarah Bernhardt, Ellen Terry, Julia Marlowe, Isadora Duncan, Mary Garden, Marilyn Monroe. [1st ed.] Norman, University of Oklahoma Press [1964] x, 234 p. illus., ports. 23 cm. Bibliography: p. 217-224 [PN2205.W3] 64-20760
1. Actresses. 2. Singers. 3. Dancers. I. Title.

Actresses—Portraits.

FLORA, Paul 927.92
Viva vamp! A book of photographs in praise of vamps from Mae West to Marilyn Monroe, from Marlene Dietrich to Brigitte Bardot. Illustrated commentary by Paul Flora, with a poetical salute by Ogden Nash. New York, D. McKay Co. [c.1960] unpaged (chiefly illus.) 21cm. 60-14597 2.95 bds.,
1. Actresses—Portraits. I. Title.

Actresses, American—Biography.

PARISH, James Robert. 790.2'092'2
The slapstick queens. Editor: T. Allan Taylor. Research associates: John Robert Cocchi, Florence Solomon. South Brunswick, A. S. Barnes [1973] 297 p. illus. 29 cm. Includes lists of films. [PN1998.A2P4] 71-37815 ISBN 0-498-01007-4 15.00
1. Actresses, American—Biography. 2. Comedy films. I. Title.

ROBBINS, Phyllis. 927.92
The young Maude Adams. Francestown, N. H., M. Jones Co. [c1959] 163p. illus. 21cm. [PN2287.A4R63] 59-15779
I. Adams, Maude, 1872-1953. II. Title. BIP

Actresses—Correspondence, reminiscences, etc.

CAMPBELL, 792'.028'0924 B
Beatrice Stella (Tanner) 1865-1940.
My life and some letters, by Mrs. Patrick Campbell (Beatrice Stella Cornwallis-West) New York, B. Blom [1969] 451 p. ports. 24 cm. Reprint of the 1922 ed. [PN2598.C23A3 1969] 71-83102
1. Actresses—Correspondence, reminiscences, etc. I. Title. BIP

CLAIRON, Claire 792'.028'0924 B
Josephe Hippolyte Legris de Latude, known as Mlle., 1723-1803.
Memoirs of Hyppolite Clairon, the celebrated French actress, with reflections upon the dramatic art, written by herself. London, Printed for G. G. and J. Robinson by S. Hamilton, 1800. New York, B. Blom, 1971. 2 v. in 1. 23 cm. [PN2638.C6A3 1971] 79-82821
1. Actresses—Correspondence, reminiscences, etc. I. Title.

TERRY, Ellen, 792'.028'0924 B
Dame, 1848-1928.
Ellen Terry's memoirs; with a pref., notes and additional biographical chapters, by Edith Craig and Christopher St. John. Westport, Conn., Greenwood Press [1970] xv, 367 p. illus., facsim., ports. 23 cm. Reprint of the 1932 ed. of Ellen Terry's autobiography, first published in 1908 under the title The story of my life. [PN2598.T4A3 1970] 77-100210 ISBN 0-8371-4039-0
1. Actresses—Correspondence, reminiscences, etc. I. Craig, Edith, 1869-1947. II. St. John, Christopher Marie.

Actresses, English—Biography.

FYVIE, John. 792'.028'0922
Tragedy queens of the Georgian era. New York, B. Blom, 1972. x, 316 p. illus. 21 cm. Reprint of the 1909 ed. Contents.Contents.—Elizabeth Barry.—Anne Bracegirdle.—Anne Oldfield.—Mary Porter.—Susannah Maria Cibber.—Hannah Pritchard.—Mary Ann Yates.—Anne Crawford.—Elizabeth Pope.—Elizabeth Inchbald.—Sarah Siddons.—Julia Glover.—Eliza O'Neill (Lady Becher) [PN2597.F82 1972] 78-91503
1. Actresses, English—Biography. I. Title. BIP

SIMPSON, Harold, 792'.028'0922 B
fl.1909-1955.
A century of famous actresses, 1750-1850, by Harold Simpson and Mrs. Charles Braun. New York, B. Blom, 1971. 380 p. illus. 21 cm. Reprint of the 1913 ed. [PN2597.S45 1971] 75-91572
1. Actresses, English—Biography. I. Braun, Charles, Mrs., joint author. II. Title.

Actresses—Great Britain—Biography.

JOHNS, Eric. 792'.028'0922 B
Dames of the theatre / Eric Johns. New Rochelle, N.Y. : Arlington House, [1975] c1974. xii, 179 p., [16] leaves of plates : ill. ; 23 cm. Contents.Contents.—May Whitty.—Genevieve Ward.—Ellen Terry.—Madge Kendal.—Sybil Thorndike.—Marie Tempest.—Irene Vanbrugh.—Lilian Braithwaite.—Edith Evans.—Peggy Ashcroft.—Flora Robson.—Judith Anderson.—Margaret Rutherford.—Gladys Cooper.—Anna Neagle.—Cicely Courtneidge. Includes bibliographical references. [PN2597.J57 1975] 75-1486 ISBN 0-87000-310-0 : 8.95
1. Actresses—Great Britain—Biography. I. Title. BIP

Actresses—Great Britain—Correspondence, remlnlscenes, etc.

NEAGLE, Anna. 791.092'4 B
Anna Neagle says "There's always tomorrow;" an autobiography. London, W. H. Allen, [1975 c1974] 236 p. leaf of plate, [32] p. of plates, ill, facsims, music, ports, 23 cm. Filmography: p.p. 225-226. Ncludes index. [PN2598.N35A28] 75-306373 ISBN 0-491-01941-6
1. Actresses—Great Britain—Correspondence, reminiscences, etc. I. Title. Distributed by Arlington House for 8.95.

Actresses—United States—Biography.

PARISH, James 791.43'028'0922 B
Robert.
Good dames. Associate editor: T. Allan Taylor. Research associates: John Robert Cocchi [and] Florence Solomon. Photo associate: Gene Andrewski. South Brunswick, A. S. Barnes [1973] p. Includes lists of films. [PN2285.P33] 72-5172 ISBN 0-498-01111-9 15.00
1. Actresses—United States—Biography. I. Title.

SPRINGER, John 791.43'028'0922
Shipman, 1916-
They had faces then : super stars, stars, and starlets of the 1930's / by John Springer and Jack Hamilton. 1st ed. Secaucus, N.J. : Citadel Press, [1974] 342 p. : ill. ; 32 cm. [PN2285.S57] 73-90954 ISBN 0-8065-0300-9 : 19.95
1. Actresses—United States—Biography. I. Hamilton, Jack D. II. Title.

Acuff, Roy.

SCHLAPPI, Elizabeth. 784'.092'4 B
Roy Acuff, the Smoky Mountain Boy / Elizabeth Schlappi. Gretna, La. : Pelican Pub. Co., 1977. p. cm. Includes index. Bibliography: [ML410.A168S3] 77-11649 ISBN 0-88289-144-8 : 12.50
1. Acuff, Roy. 2. Country musicians—United States—Biography. I. Title.

Adair, Bethenia Angelina Owens, 1840-1926.

MILLER, Helen Markley. 926.1
Woman doctor of the West, Bethenia Owens-Adair. New York, Messner [1960] 191 p. 22 cm. [R154.A14M5] 60-7054
1. Adair, Bethenia Angelina Owens, 1840-1926. I. Title.

Adair, Fred Lyman,

ADAIR, Fred Lyman, 1877- 610'.924 B
The country doctor and the specialist. Maitland, Fla., Adair Award Fund, 1968. 215 p. illus., ports. 27 cm. Autobiographical. [R154.A145A3] 70-16052
I. Title.

Adalard, Saint, Abbott of Corbie, d. 826.

PASCHASIUS Radbertus, 270 B
Saint, Abbot of Corbie, d.ca.860.
Charlemagne's cousins; contemporary lives of Adalard and Wala. Translated, with introd. and notes, by Allen Cabaniss. [1st ed. Syracuse, N.Y.] Syracuse University Press [1967] vii, 266 p. 24 cm. Translation of Vita sancti Adalhardi and Vita Walae seu Epitaphium Arsenii. Bibliographical references included in "Notes" (p. 205-223) [BX4700.A19P313] 67-26919
1. Adalard, Saint, Abbott of Corbie, d. 826. 2. Wala, Saint, Abbot of Corbie, d. 836. I. Paschasius Radbertus, Saint, Abbot of Corbie, d. ca. 860. Vita Walae. English. 1967. II. Title

Adam, Adolphe Charles, 1803-1856.

MARKOVA, Alicia, 1910- 927.928
Giselle and I. With a foreword by Carl Van Vechten. New York, Vanguard Press [1961, c1960] 193 p. illus. 24 cm. [GV1785.M3A3 1961] 61-14627
1. Adam, Adolphe Charles, 1803-1856. Giselle. I. Title.

Adam (Biblical character)

REED, Gwendolyn E. 221.95
Adam and Eve, by Gwendolyn Reed. Illustrated by Helen Siegl. New York, Lothrop, Lee & Shepard Co. [1968] [28] p. illus. 26 cm. Woodcut illustrations. A retelling of the Biblical story. [BS580.A4R4] AC 68
1. Adam (Biblical character) 2. Eve (Biblical character) I. Siegl, Helen, illus. II. Title. BIP

SANFORD, John A. 221.9'22 B
The man who wrestled with God; a study of individuation (personal growth toward wholeness) based on four Bible stories [by] John A. Sanford. King of Prussia, Pa., Religious Pub. Co. [1974] 126 p. 22 cm. Errata slip inserted. Includes bibliographical references. [BS571.S26] 74-79994 5.95
1. Jacob, the patriarch. 2. Joseph, the patriarch. 3. Moses. 4. Adam (Biblical character) 5. Eve (Biblical character) I. Title.
Publisher's address: 198 Allendale Road, King of Prussia, Pa. 19406.

Adam de Perseigne, d. 1221.

ADAM de Perseigne, d.1221. 271'.12'024 B
The letters of Adam of Perseigne / translated by Grace Perigo ; introduction by Thomas Merton. Kalamazoo, Mich. : Cistercian Publication, c1976- v. ; 23 cm. (Cistercian Fathers series ; no. 21) "The feast of freedom, by Thomas Merton": p. 3-48. Includes index. [BX4705.A27A4313 1976] 76-15486 ISBN 0-87907-621-6 : 12.50.
1. Adam de Perseigne, d. 1221. 2. Cistercians—Biography. I. Merton, Thomas, 1915-1968. The feast of freedom. 1976.

Adam, George, fl. 1850.

ADAM, George, fl.1850. 973'.04'97 S
The dreadful sufferings of emigrants to California / George Adam. New York : Garland Pub., 1978. 60 p., [3] leaves of plates : ill. ; 24 cm. (The Garland library of narratives of North American Indian captivities ; v. 63) Issued with the reprint of the 1848 ed. of Barker, J. Interesting narrative of the sufferings of Joseph Barker and his wife. New York, 1978. Reprint of the 1850 ed. published by Barclay, St. Louis under title: The dreadful sufferings and thrilling adventures of an overland party of emigrants to California. [E85.G2 vol. 63] [F593] 978'.02 76-51253 ISBN 0-8240-1687-4 (set) : 25.00 (set)
1. Adam, George, fl. 1850. 2. Overland journeys to the Pacific. 3. Indians of North America—Captivities. 4. The West—Description and travel—1848-1860. 5. The West—Biography. I. Title. II. Series.

Adam of Orlton, Bp. of Winchester, d. 1345.

HAINES, Roy Martin. 942.03'6'0924 B
The church and politics in fourteenth-century England : the career of Adam Orleton, 1275-1345 / Roy Martin Haines. Cambridge [Eng.] ; New York : Cambridge University Press, 1978. xiv, 303 p. ; 22 cm. (Cambridge studies in medieval life and thought ; 3d ser., v. 10) Includes index. Bibliography: p. 260-274. [DA231.A3H34] 76-54062 ISBN 0-521-21544-7 : 29.50
1. Adam of Orlton, Bp. of Winchester, d. 1345. 2. Statesmen—Great Britain—Biography. 3. Bishops—England—Biography. 4. Great Britain—History—Edward II-III, 1307-1377. I. Title. II. Series.

Adam, Robert, 1728-1792.

FLEMING, John, 1919- 927.2
Robert Adam and his circle, in Edinburgh & Rome. Cambridge, Mass., Harvard [c.] 1962. xxi, 393p. illus. Bibl. 62-2399 7.50
1. Adam, Robert, 1728-1792. 2. Adam family. I. Title.

YARWOOD, Doreen. 720'.924 B
Robert Adam. New York, Scribner [1970] x, 221 p. illus. 26 cm. Bibliography: p. 211-213. [NA997.A4Y3] 73-108198 7.95
1. Adam, Robert, 1728-1792.

Adamic, Louis,

ADAMIC, Louis, 1899-1951. 917.3'03'910924 B
Laughing in the jungle. New York, Arno Press, 1969 [c1932] x, 335 p. 22 cm. (The American immigration collection) [E169.5.A18 1969] 69-18755
I. Title.

Adams, Abigail (Smith) 1744-1818.

ADAMS, Abigail (Smith) 1744-1818. 973.4'3'0924 B
New letters of Abigail Adams, 1788-1801. Edited with an introd. by Stewart Mitchell. Westport, Conn., Greenwood Press [1973, c1947] xlii, 281 p. illus. 23 cm. Letters written to the author's sister, Mary Cranch, reprinted from the Proceedings of the American Antiquarian Society, v. 55, p. [95]-232; [299]-444. Reprint of the ed. published by Houghton Mifflin, Boston. Includes bibliographies. [E322.1.A37 1973] 73-13398 ISBN 0-8371-7055-9
1. Adams, Abigail (Smith) 1744-1818. I. Cranch, Mary (Smith) 1741-1811. II. Title. BIP

AKERS, Charles W. 973.5'5'0924 B
Abigail Adams, an American woman / Charles W. Akers. Boston : Little, Brown, c1980. x, 207 p., [1] leaf of plates : ill. ; 20 cm. (The library of American biography) Includes index. Bibliography: p. [193]-200. [E322.1.A38A35] 79-2241 ISBN 0-316-02040-0 : 9.95
1. Adams, Abigail Smith, 1744-1818. 2. Adams, John, Pres. U.S., 1735-1826. 3. Presidents—United States—Wives—Biography. I. Title. II. Series: Library of American biography.

CRISS, Mildred, 1890- 920.7
Abigail adams: leading lady. New York, Dodd, Mead [1952] 248 p. illus. 21 cm. Includes bibliography. [E322.1.C7] 52-10471
1. Adams, Abigail (Smith) 1744-1818. I. Title.

KELLY, Regina (Zimmerman) 1898- 920
Abigail Adams: the President's lady. Illus. by Robert Frankenberg. Boston, Houghton [c.1962] 191p. col. illus. 22cm. (Piper bks.) 62-9303 1.95; 2.20; 1.16 lib. ed., pap.,
1. Adams, Abigail (Smith) 1744-1818—Juvenile literature I. Title.

MINNIGERODE, Meade, 1887-1967. 973.4'0922
Some American ladies; seven informal biographies. Freeport, N.Y., Books for Libraries Press [1969] viii, 287 p. illus., ports. 23 cm. (Essay index reprint series) "First published 1926." Contents.Contents.—Martha Washington.—Abigail Adams.—Dolly Madison.—Elizabeth Monroe and Louisa Adams.—Rachel Jackson.—Peggy Eaton. [E176.M65 1969] 70-93361
1. Washington, Martha (Dandridge) Custis, 1731-1802. 2. Adams, Abigail (Smith) 1744-1818. 3. Madison, Dolley (Payne) Todd, 1768-1849. 4. Monroe, Elizabeth (Kortright) 1768-1830. 5. Adams, Louisa Catherine (Johnson) 1775-1852. 6. Jackson, Rachel (Donelson) 1767-1828. 7. Eaton, Margaret L. (O'Neale) Timberlake, 1799(?)-1879. I. Title.

RICHARDS, Laura Elizabeth (Howe) 1850-1943. 973.4'4'0924 B
Abigail Adams and her times. Ann Arbor, Mich., Plutarch Press, 1971. 282 p. illus., ports. 22 cm. Facsim. reprint of the ed. published in New York by D. Appleton in 1917. [E322.1.R5 1917a] 78-143631
1. Adams, Abigail (Smith) 1744-1818. I. Title. BIP

WHITNEY, Janet (Payne) 1894- 973.4'4'0924 B
Abigail Adams, by Janet Whitney. Westport, Conn., Greenwood Press [1970, c1947] xii, 357 p. illus., ports. 23 cm. Bibliography: p. [345]-348. [E322.1.W5 1970] 77-100190
1. Adams, Abigail (Smith) 1744-1818. BIP

Adams, Abigail (Smith) 1744-1818—Juvenile literature

BOBBE, Dorothie (du Bear) 92
Abigail Adams. by Dorothie Bobbe. New York, Putnam [1966] 223p. 21cm. (Lives to remember) [E322.1.B66 1966] 66-8226 3.29 lib. ed.,
1. Adams, Abigail (Smith) 1744-1818—Juvenile literature. I. Title.

KELLY, Regina (Zimmerman) 1898- 920
Abigail Adams: the President's lady. Illus. by Robert Frankenberg. Boston, Houghton [c.1962] 191p. col. illus. 22cm. (Piper bks.) 62-9303 1.95; 2.20; 1.16 lib. ed., pap.,
1. Adams, Abigail (Smith) 1744-1818—Juvenile literature I. Title.

LEE, Susan. 973.4'4'0924 B
Abigail Adams / by Susan & John Lee ; illustrated by George Ulrich. Chicago : Childrens Press, c1977. 47 p. :col. ill. ; 24 cm. (Heroes of the Revolution) A biography of the parson's daughter who was the wife of the second President and the mother of the sixth. [E322.1.A38L43 1977] 76-47006 ISBN 0-516-04657-8 lib.bdg. : 6.60
1. Adams, Abigail Smith, 1744-1818—Juvenile literature. 2. Presidents—United States—Wives—Juvenile literaure. I. Lee, John, joint author. II. Ulrich, George. III. Title. BIP

WAYNE, Bennett. 973'.0992 B
Women in the White House : four first ladies / edited, with commentary by Bennett Wayne. Champaign, Ill. : Garrard Pub. Co., c1976. 168 p. : ill. ; 23 cm. (A Target book) Includes indexes. Brief biographies of Martha Washington, Abigail Adams, Dolly Madison, and Mary Lincoln. [E176.2.W38] 920 75-20388 ISBN 0-8116-4915-6 : 4.48
1. Washington, Martha Dandridge Custis, 1731-1802—Juvenile literature. 2. Adams, Abigail Smith, 1744-1818—Juvenile literature. 3. Madison, Dolley (Payne) Todd, 1768-1849—Juvenile literature. 4. Lincoln, Mary Todd, 1818-1882—Juvenile literature. I. Title. BIP

Adams, Brooks, 1848-1927.

ANDERSON, Thornton. 928.1
Brooks Adams, constructive conservative. Ithaca, Cornell University Press [1951] xiv, 250 p. port. 23 cm. Bibliography: p. 229-243. [D15.A3A5] 51-8760
1. Adams, Brooks, 1848-1927. I. Title. BIP

BERINGAUSE, Arthur F 1919- 928.1
Brooks Adams; a biography. [1st ed.] New York, Knopf, 1955. xiii, 404, x p. port. 25cm. Bibliography: p. [392]-404. [D15.A3B4] 55-8357
1. Adams, Brooks, 1848-1927 I. Title.

BERINGAUSE, Arthur F., 1919- 973'.07'2024 B
Brooks Adams : a biography / by Arthur F. Beringause. New York : Octagon Books, 1979, c1955. xiii, 404, x p., [1] leaf of plates : port. ; 24 cm. Reprint of the 1st. ed. published by Knopf, New York. Includes index. Bibliography: p. [392]-404. [D15.A3B4 1979] 78-20822 lib.bdg. : 20.00
1. Adams, Brooks, 1848-1927. 2. Historians—United States—Biography. BIP

Adams, Cedric.

HARDMAN, Benedict E. 070.9'24 B
Everybody called him Cedric, by Benedict E. Hardman. Minneapolis, Twin City Federal Savings and Loan Association [1970] 330 p. illus., ports. 23 cm. [PN1991.4.A4H3] 70-146832 5.95
1. Adams, Cedric. I. Title.

Adams, Charles Francis, 1807-1886.

ADAMS, Charles Francis, 1807-1886 923.273
Diary. Aida DiPace Donald, David Donald, eds. New York, Atheneum, 1967[c.1964] v. illus., facsims., maps, ports. 21cm. (TAP7, 8) Contents.v.1. January 1820-June 1825.--v.2. July 1825-September 1829. Index [to the 1st 2v.] Bibl. [E467.1.A2A15] 3.95 pap., ea.,
I. Donald, Aida DiPace, ed. II. Donald, David Herbert, 1920- ed. III. Title. IV. Series.

ADAMS, Charles Francis, 1807-1886. 923.273
Diary [2v.] Aida DiPace Donald, David Donald, eds. Cambridge, Mass., Belknap Pr. of Harvard [c.]1964. 2v. (469; 514p.) illus., facsims., maps, ports. 26cm. (Adams paps. Ser. I: Diaries) Contents.v.1. January 1820-June 1825.--v.2. July 1825-September 1829. Index [to the 1st 2v.] Bibl. 64-20588 20.00 set,
I. Donald Aida DiPace, ed. II. Donald, David Herbert, 1920- ed. III. Title. IV. Series.

ADAMS, Charles Francis, 1807-1886. 923.273
Diary. Aida DiPace Donald and David Donald, editors. Cambridge, Belknap Press of Harvard University Press, 1964- v. illus., facsims., maps, ports. 26 cm. (The Adams papers. Series i: Diaries) Contents.CONTENTS. -- v. 1. January 1820-June 1825. -- v. 2. July 1825-September 1829. Index [to the 1st 2v.] Bibliography: v. 1, p. ivi-ixiv. [E467.1.A2A15] 64-20588
I. Donald, Alda DiPace, ed. II. Donald, David Herbert, 1920- III. Title. IV. Series.

ADAMS, Charles Francis, 1835-1915. 973.7'0924 B
Charles Francis Adams, by his son. Boston, Houghton, Mifflin. [New York, AMS Press, 1972] vii, 426 p. illus. 19 cm. (American statesmen, v. 29) Reprint of the 1900 ed. [E467.1.A2A2 1972] 72-128955 ISBN 0-404-50879-0
1. Adams, Charles Francis, 1807-1886. I. Title. II. Series.

DUBERMAN, Martin B. 923.273
Charles Francis Adams, 1807-1886. Boston, Houghton Mifflin, 1961 [c1960] 525 p. illus. 22 cm. Includes bibliography. [E467.1.A2D8] 61-5366
1. Adams, Charles Francis, 1807-1886. **BIP**

DUBERMAN, Martin B. 973.7'0924 B
Charles Francis Adams, 1807-1886, by Martin Duberman. Stanford, Calif., Stanford University Press [1968, c1960] xvi, 525 p. illus., ports. 23 cm. Bibliography: p. [401]-421. [E467.1.A2D8 1968] 68-13742
1. Adams, Charles Francis, 1807-1886.

SHEPHERD, Jack. 973'.0992 B
The Adams chronicles : four generations of greatness / Jack Shepherd ; introd. by Daniel J. Boorstin. 1st ed. Boston : Little, Brown, c1975. xxxi, 448 p. : ill. ; 26 cm. "Prepared by arrangement with the Massachusetts Historical Society, The Adams papers, and Harvard University Press." "Prepared in conjunction with the production of a television series of the same name." Includes index. Bibliography: p. 433-436. [E322.1.A28S53] 75-34422 ISBN 0-316-78497-4 : 17.50
1. Adams family. 2. Adams, John, Pres. U.S., 1735-1826. 3. Adams, John Quincy, Pres, U.S., 1767-1848. 4. Adams, Charles Francis, 1807-1886. 5. Adams, Henry, 1838-1918. I. Title. **BIP**

Adams, Charles Francis, 1835-1915.

ADAMS, Charles Francis, 1835-1915. 385'.0924 B
Charles Francis Adams, 1835-1915; an autobiography. With a memorial address delivered November 17, 1915, by Henry Cabot Lodge. New York, Russell & Russell [1968, c1916] lx, 224 p. port. 23 cm. Bibliographical footnotes. [E664.A19A22 1968] 68-10898
1. Adams, Charles Francis, 1835-1915. I. Lodge, Henry Cabot, 1850-1924. **BIP**

ADAMS, Charles Francis, 1835-1915. 385'.092'4 B
Charles Francis Adams, 1835-1915; an autobiography. With a memorial address delivered November 17, 1915, by Henry Cabot Lodge. Westport, Conn., Greenwood Press [1973, c1916] lx, 224 p. port. 22 cm. Reprint of the ed. published by Houghton Mifflin, Boston. [E664.A19A22 1973] 73-10847 ISBN 0-8371-7037-0
1. Adams, Charles Francis, 1835-1915. I. Lodge, Henry Cabot, 1850-1924.

KIRKLAND, Edward Chase 385.0924
Charles Francis Adams, Jr., 1835-1915, the patrician at bay. Cambridge, Mass., Harvard [c.]1965. viii, 256p. illus., ports. 22cm. Bibl. [E664.A19K5] 65-22053 5.95
1. Adams, Charles Francis, 1835-1915. I. Title. **BIP**

KIRKLAND, Edward Chase, 1894- 385.0924 (B)
Charles Francis Adams, Jr., 1835-1915, the patrician at bay. Cambridge, Harvard University Press, 1965. viii, 256 p. illus., ports. 22 cm. Bibliographical references included in "Notes" (p. 225-261) [E664.A19K5] 65-22053
1. Adams, Charles Francis, 1835-1915. I. Title.

Adams, Emma Hildreth.

ADAMS, Emma Hildreth. 917.94'9
To and fro in southern California / Emma H. Adams. New York : Arno Press, 1976, [c1887] p. cm. (The Chicano heritage) Reprint of the ed. published by W.M.B.C. Press, Cincinnati. [F867.A2 1976] 76-1220 ISBN 0-405-09481-7 : 16.00
1. Adams, Emma Hildreth. 2. California, Southern—Description and travel. 3. Arizona—Description and travel. 4. New Mexico—Description and travel. I. Title. II. Series.

Adams family.

THE Adams family. v. 12
New York, Hillary House, 1957. vi, 364p. plate, ports.
1. Adams family. 2. U. S.—Pol. & govt.—1783-1865. I. Adams, James Truslow, 1878-1949. **BIP**

THE Adams family. v. 12
New York, Hillary House, 1957. vi, 364p. plate, ports.
1. Adams family. 2. U. S.—Pol. & govt.—1783-1865. I. Adams, James Truslow, 1878-1949. **BIP**

ADAMS Family. Archives. 929.2
The Adams papers; diary & autobiography of John Adams; 4v. L. H. Butterfield, ed.; Leonard C. Faber, Wendell D. Garrett, asst. ed. New York, Atheneum, 1964 [c.1961] 4v. (various p.) illus, ports., maps. charts, facsims. 21cm. Contents.v.1. Diary 1755-1770.--v.2. Diary 1771-1781.--v.3. Diary 1782-1804. Autobiography, pt.1, To October 1776.--v.4. Autobiography, pts. 2 & 3, 1777-1780. Index. Bibl. 2.65, pap., ea., bxd.
I. Butterfield, Lyman Henry ed. II. Title.

ADAMS, James Truslow, 1878-1949. 929'.2'0973
The Adams family. Westport, Conn., Greenwood Press [1974, c1930] vi, 364 p. illus. 22 cm. Reprint of the ed. published by Little, Brown, Boston. [E176.A23 1974] 73-21487 ISBN 0-8371-6427-3
1. Adams family. 2. Adams, John, Pres. U.S., 1735-1826. 3. Adams, John Quincy, Pres. U.S., 1767-1848. 4. Adams, Charles Francis, 1807-1886. 5. United States—Politics and government—1783-1865. I. Title.

ADAMS FAMILY. ARCHIVES 929.2
Adams family correspondence; 2v. L. H. Butterfield, ed.; Wendell D. Garrett, assoc. ed.; Marjorie E. Sprague. New York, Atheneum, 1965[c.1963] 2v. (lxiii424; xxi, 490p.) illus., ports., maps, charts, facsims. 21cm. (Adams papers, ser. 2) Contents.v.1. December 1761-May 1776.--v.2. June 1776-March 1778. Index. (TAP 5-6) Bibl. ibl. 2.95 pap., ea.,
I. Butterfield, Lyman Henry, ed. II. Title. III. Series.

BRAGDON, Lillian J. 923.2
Meet the remarkable Adams family. Drawings by Frederick Chapman. [1st ed.] New York, Atheneum, 1964. 171 p. illus. 22 cm. [E322.1.B7] 64-11888
1. Adams family — Juvenile literature. I. Title.

BRAGDON, Lillian J. 923.2
Meeting the remarkable Adams family. Drawings by Frederick Chapman. New York, Atheneum [c.]1964. 171p. illus. 22cm. 64-11888 3.75
1. Adams family—Juvenile literature. I. Title.

FRIEDRICH, Otto, 1929- 973'.07'2024 B
Clover / by Otto Friedrich. New York : Simon and Schuster, c1979. 381 p., [8] leaves of plates : ill. ; 24 cm. Includes index. Bibliography: p. 353-368. [CT275.A34F73] 79-12165 ISBN 0-671-22509-X : 10.95
1. Adams, Marian Hooper, 1843-1885. 2. Adams family. 3. Adams, Henry, 1838-1918. 4. United States—Biography. I. Title.

HALL, Eleanor (McAllister) 1910- 929.2
Samuel Lorenzo Adams—stories of his life and of his ancestry. Compiled by Eleanor McAllister Hall. [Salt Lake City?] 1970. 124 p. illus., geneal. tables, maps, ports. 28 cm. [CS71.A2 1970] 78-20370
1. Adams family. 2. Adams, Samuel Lorenzo, 1833-1910.

RUSSELL, Francis, 1910- 973.0992
Adams, an American dynasty / Francis Russell New York : American Heritage : distributed by McGraw-Hill, 1976 374, 10 p. : ill. ; 24 cm. Includes index Bibliography: p. 1 [E322.1.A28R87] 76-924 ISBN 0-07-054302-X 15.00
1. Adams family I. Title.

SHEPHERD, Jack. 973'.0992 B
The Adams chronicles : four generations of greatness / Jack Shepherd ; introd. by Daniel J. Boorstin. 1st ed. Boston : Little, Brown, c1975. xxxi, 448 p. : ill. ; 26 cm. "Prepared by arrangement with the Massachusetts Historical Society, The Adams papers, and Harvard University Press." "Prepared in conjunction with the production of a television series of the same name." Includes index. Bibliography: p. 433-436. [E322.1.A28S53] 75 34422 ISBN 0-316-78497-4 : 17.50
1. Adams family. 2. Adams, John, Pres. U.S., 1735-1826. 3. Adams, John Quincy, Pres, U.S., 1767-1848. 4. Adams, Charles Francis, 1807-1886. 5. Adams, Henry, 1838-1918. I. Title. **BIP**

Adams family—Juvenile literature.

BRAGDON, Lillian J. 923.2
Meet the remarkable Adams family. Drawings by Frederick Chapman. [1st ed.] New York, Atheneum, 1964. 171 p. illus. 22 cm. [E322.1.B7] 64-11888
1. Adams family — Juvenile literature. I. Title.

BRAGDON, Lillian J. 923.2
Meeting the remarkable Adams family. Drawings by Frederick Chapman. New York, Atheneum [c.]1964. 171p. illus. 22cm. 64-11888 3.75
1. Adams family—Juvenile literature. I. Title.

Adams, Hampton, 1897-1965—Archives.

DISCIPLES of Christ Historical Society. 286'.6'09 S
Hampton Adams; a register of his papers in the Disciples of Christ Historical Society. Nashville, 1969. 26 l. 28 cm. (Its Register no. 3) [CD3529.N37D57 no. 3] 216.286'6'0924 B 72-31727
1. Adams, Hampton, 1897-1965—Archives.

Adams, Henry, 1838-1918.

ADAMS, Henry, 1838-1918. 928.1
The education of Henry Adams, and other selected writings. Ed., abridged, introd. by Edward N. Saveth. New York, Washington Sq. [c.1963] xlvii, 304p. 18cm. (Great hists., W1109) Bibl. .90 pap.,
I. Saveth, Edward Norman, 1915- ed. II. Title.

ADAMS, Henry, 1838-1918. 973.07'2'024 B
The education of Henry Adams. Edited with an introd. and notes by Ernest Samuels. Jayne N. Samuels, assistant editor. Boston, Houghton Mifflin [1973, c1918] xxx, 705 p. 21 cm. (Riverside editions) Bibliography: p. 537-538. [E175.5.A174276] 73-6411 ISBN 0-395-16810-4 5.50 (pbk.).
1. Adams, Henry, 1838-1918. I. Samuels, Ernest, 1903- ed. II. Samuels, Jayne N., ed. III. Title. **BIP**

ADAMS, Henry, 1838-1918. 928.1
The education of Henry Adams, an autobiography. With a new introd. by D. W. Brogan. Boston, Houghton Mifflin, 1961. xxiv, 517 p. 21 cm. (Sentry edition, 3) [E175.5.A174275] 61-19373
I. Title.

ADAMS, Henry, 1838-1918. 973'.072'024
Henry Adams and his friends: a collection of his unpublished letters, compiled, with a biographical introd., by Harold Dean Cater. New York, Octagon Books, 1970 [c1947] cxix, 797 p. ports. 24 cm. Includes bibliographical references. [E175.5.A17428 1970] 78-96175
I. Cater, Harold Dean, 1908- ed. II. Title.

ADAMS, Henry, 1838-1918. 818'.4'08
Letters to a niece and Prayer to the Virgin of Chartres. With A niece's memories, by Mabel La Farge. Boston, Houghton Mifflin, 1920. St. Clair Shores, Mich., Scholarly Press, 1970 [c1920] 133 p. 21 cm. [E175.5.A1744 1970] 70-131603 ISBN 0-403-00490-X
I. Adams, Henry, 1838-1918. Prayer to the Virgin of Chartres. 1970. II. La Farge, Mabel (Hooper) 1875- A niece's memories. 1970. III. Title. IV. Title: Prayer to the Virgin of Chartres. V. Title: A niece's memories.

ADAMS, Henry, 1838-1918. 928.1
Selected letters; edited with an introd. by Newton Arvin. New York, Farrar, Straus and Young [1951] xxxiv, 279 p. 22 cm. (Great letters series) [E175.5.A17433] 51-7883
I. Title.

DUSINBERRE, William, 1930- 973'.07'2024 B
Henry Adams, the myth of failure / by William Dusinberre. Charlottesville : University Press of Virginia, [1980] p. cm. Includes index. Bibliography: p. [E175.5.A2D84] 79-16096 ISBN 0-8139-0833-7 : 20.00
1. Adams, Henry, 1838-1918. 2. Adams, Henry, 1838-1918. History of the United States of America. 3. United States—History—1801-1809. 4. United States—History—1809-1817. 5. History—Philosophy. I. Title.

HARBERT, Earl N., 1934- 973'.07'2024
The force so much closer home : Henry Adams and the Adams family / Earl N. Harbert. New York : New York University Press, 1977. xi, 224 p. ; 24 cm. (The Gotham library of the New York University Press) Includes bibliographical references and index. [E175.5.A17488] 76-40744 ISBN 0-8147-3375-1 : 15.00. ISBN 0-8147-3376-X pbk. : 4.95
1. Adams, Henry, 1838-1918. 2. Adams family. 3. Historians United States—Biography. I. Title. **BIP**

JORDY, William H. 928.1
Henry Adams: a scientific historian. New Haven, Conn., Yale [1963, c.1952] xxiii, 327p. 25cm. (16;Y92) Bibl. 1.95 pap.,
1. Adams, Henry, 1838-1918 I. Title. II. Series. **BIP**

JORDY, William H. 928.1
Henry Adams: scientific historian. New Haven, Yale University Press, 1952. xv, 327 p. 25 cm. (Yale historical publications. Studies, 16) Bibliography: p. 291-317. [E175.5.A1755] 52-5362
1. Adams, Henry, 1838-1918. I. Title. II. Series.

JORDY, William H. 973'.072'024 B
Henry Adams: scientific historian, by William H. Jordy. [Hamden, Conn.] Archon Books, 1970 [c1952] xv, 327 p. 23 cm. Bibliography: p. 291-317. [E175.5.A1755 1970] 77-114423
1. Adams, Henry, 1838-1918.

LEVENSON, Jacob Claver, 1922- 928.1
The mind and art of Henry Adams. Boston, Houghton Mifflin, 1957. x, 430p. illus., ports., facsim. 21cm. [E175.5.A1765] 57-6946
1. Adams, Henry, 1838-1918. I. Title. **BIP**

SCHEYER, Ernst, 1900- 709.24 B
The circle of Henry Adams: art & artists. Detroit, Wayne State University Press, 1970. 309 p. illus., ports. 24 cm. "Bibliography of Ernst Scheyer": p. 289-298. [N7483.A3S3 1970] 72-79478 ISBN 0-8143-1418-X 8.95
1. Adams, Henry, 1838-1918. I. Title.

STEVENSON, Elizabeth, 1919- v. 12
Henry Adams, a biography. New York, Collier Books [1961, c1955] 410 p. (Collier Books, BS8) 63-75278
1. Adams, Henry, 1838-1918. I. Title. **BIP**

STEVENSON, Elizabeth, 1919- v. 12
Henry Adams, a biography. New York, Collier Books [1961, c1955] 410 p. (Collier Books, BS8) 63-75278
1. Adams, Henry, 1838-1918. I. Title. **BIP**

STEVENSON, Elizabeth, 1919- 928.1
Henry Adams, a biography. New York, Macmillan, 1955. xiv, 425 p. illus., ports. 22 cm. Bibliography: p. 387-405. [E175.5.A1782] 55-13825
1. Adams, Henry, 1838-1918.

STEVENSON, Elizabeth, 1919- 973'.07'2024 B
Henry Adams : a biography / Elizabeth

Stevenson. New York : Octagon Books, 1977, c1955. xiv, 425 p., [4] leaves of plates : ill. ; 22 cm. Reprint of the ed. published by Macmillan, New York. Includes index. Bibliography: p. 387-405. [E175.5.A1782 1977] 76-56793 ISBN 0-374-97624-4 lib. bdg. : 18.50
1. Adams, Henry, 1838-1918. 2. Historians—United States—Biography.

WAGNER, Vern. 818'.4'08
The suspension of Henry Adams; a study of manner and matter. Detroit, Wayne State University Press, 1969. 268 p. front. 24 cm. Bibliography: p. 249-254. [E175.5.A1784] 68-26875 8.95
1. Adams, Henry, 1838-1918. I. Title. **BIP**

Adams, Hyrum, 1855-1943.

ADAMS, Frank David, 1893- ed. 920
Biography of Hyrum Adams and Annie Laurie Penrod Adams, Layton, Utah. Compiled and edited by Frank D. Adams and Bonnie Adams Kesler. Illus. by Annie Laurie Penrod Adams. [Salt Lake City?] Published by the sons and daughters of Hyrum Adams, 1953. 133p. illus. 24cm. [CT275.A327A5] 55-25798
1. Adams, Hyrum, 1855-1943. 2. Adams, Annie Laurie (Penrod) 1870-1952. I. Kesler, Bonnie (Adams) 1915- joint ed. II. Title.

Adams, James Clyde, 1881-

BISHOP of Heard County: v. 12 the story of J. C. Adams, Georgia circuit rider. [2d ed.] Atlanta, Church and Community Institute [1957] v, 128p. illus., ports. 20cm.
1. Adams, James Clyde, 1881- 2. Methodists in Georgia. I. Byron, Dora.

Adams, James Truslow, 1878-1949.

NEVINS, Allan, 1890-1971. 973'.072'024 B
James Truslow Adams: historian of the American dream. Urbana, University of Illinois Press, 1968. 315 p. illus., ports. 23 cm. "Bibliography of works by James Truslow Adams": p. 305-308. Bibliographical footnotes. [E175.5.A25N4] 68-16627 ISBN 0-252-72452-6 6.95
1. Adams, James Truslow, 1878-1949.

Adams, John, Pres. U.S., 1735-1826.

ADAMS, Charles Francis, 1807-1886. 973.4'4'0924 B
The life of John Adams, begun by John Quincy Adams, completed by Charles Francis Adams. Rev. and corr. New York, Haskell House Publishers, 1968. 2 v. 23 cm. Reprint of the 1871 ed. [E322.A52 1968] 68-24969
1. Adams, John, Pres. U.S., 1735-1826. I. Adams, John Quincy, Pres. U.S., 1767-1848. **BIP**

ADAMS, Charles Francis, 1807-1886. 973.4'4'0924 B
The life of John Adams, begun by John Quincy Adams, completed by Charles Francis Adams. Rev. and corr. Philadelphia, Lippincott, 1871. St. Clair Shores, Mich., Scholarly Press, 1971. 2 v. 22 cm. [E322.A52 1971] 78-108455 ISBN 0-403-00470-5
1. Adams, John, Pres. U.S., 1735-1826. I. Adams, John Quincy, Pres. U.S., 1767-1848.

ADAMS, James Truslow, 1878-1949. 929'.2'0973
The Adams family. Westport, Conn., Greenwood Press [1974, c1930] vi, 364 p. illus. 22 cm. Reprint of the ed. published by Little, Brown, Boston. [E176.A23 1974] 73-21487 ISBN 0-8371-6427-3
1. Adams family. 2. Adams, John, Pres. U.S., 1735-1826. 3. Adams, John Quincy, Pres. U.S., 1767-1848. 4. Adams, Charles Francis, 1807-1886. 5. United States—Politics and government—1783-1865. I. Title.

ADAMS, John. Pres. U. S., 1735-1826. 923.173
The Adams-Jefferson letters; the complete correspondence between Thomas Jefferson and Abigail and John Adams. Edited by Lester. J. Cappon. Chapel Hill. Published for the Institute of Early American History and Culture at Williamsburg. Va., by the University of North Carolina Press [1959] 2v. (li. 638p.) illus., ports. 25cm. [E322.A516] 59-16475
I. Adams. Abigail (Smith) 1744-1818. II. Jefferson, Thomas, Pres. U. S., 1743-1826. III. Cappon. Lester Jesse, 1900- ed. IV. Title. **BIP**

ADAMS, John, Pres. U.S., 1735-1826. 973.4'092'2
Adams to Jefferson & Jefferson to Adams : a dialogue from their correspondence, 1812-1826 / edited by Richard K. Arnold. San Francisco : Jerico Press, 1975. 38 p. ; 22 cm. [E302.A287] 76-352561
1. Adams, John, Pres. U.S., 1735-1826. 2. Jefferson, Thomas, Pres. U.S., 1743-1826. I. Jefferson, Thomas, Pres. U.S., 1743-1826, joint author. II. Title.

ADAMS, John, Pres. U. S., 1735-1826. 923.173
Diary and autobiography. L. H. Butterfield, editor, Leonard C. Faber and Wendell D. Garrett, assistant editors. Cambridge, Belknap Press of Harvard University Press, 1961. 4v. illus., ports., maps. facsims. 26cm. (His Papers. Series i: Diaries) Contents.v.1. Diary, 1755-1770--v. 2. Diary, 1771-1781.--v.3. Diary 1782-1804. Autobiography to October 1776.--v. 4. Autobiography, 1777-1780. [E322.A3] 60-5387
I. Butterfield, Lyman Henry, 1909- ed. II. Title.

ADAMS, John, Pres. U.S., 1735-1826. 973'.0924
The earliest diary of John Adams; June 1753-April 1754, September 1758-January 1759. L. H. Butterfield, editor. Wendell D. Garrett and Marc Friedlaender, associate editors. Cambridge, Belknap Press of Harvard University Press, 1966. xx, 120 p. illus., ports. 26 cm. (The Adams papers. Series I: Diaries) "Diary and autobiography of John Adams, supplement." [E322.A34] 66-14442
I. Adams, John, Pres. U.S., 1735-1826. Diary and autobiography. II. Butterfield, Lyman Henry, ed. III. Garrett, Wendell D., ed. IV. Friedlaender, Marc, 1905- ed. V. Title. VI. Series. **BIP**

ADAMS, John, Pres. U.S., 1735-1826. 973.4'4'0924 B
John Adams: a biography in his own words. Edited by James Bishop Peabody. With an introd. by L. H. Butterfield. Joan Paterson Kerr: picture editor. New York, Newsweek [1973] 2 v. (416 p.) illus. 27 cm. (The Founding Fathers) Bibliography: p. 408. [E322.A35 1973b] 74-159866 ISBN 0-88225-041-8 6.95 ea.
1. Adams, John, Pres. U.S., 1735-1826. I. Peabody, James Bishop, 1922- ed. II. Title.

ADAMS, John, Pres. U.S., 1735-1826. 973.4'4'0924 B
John Adams; a biography in his own words. Edited by James Bishop Peabody. With an introd. by L. H. Butterfield. Joan Paterson Kerr, picture editor. New York, Newsweek; distributed by Harper & Row [1973] 416 p. illus. 27 cm. (The Founding Fathers) Bibliography: p. 408. [E322.A35 1973] 72-92141 ISBN 0-06-013308-2 15.00
1. Adams, John, Pres. U.S., 1735-1826. I. Peabody, James Bishop, 1922- ed. **BIP**

ADAMS, John, Pres. U. S., 1735-1826. 923.173
Diary and autobiography [4.v.] L. H. Butterfield, ed., Leonard C. Faber, Wendell D. Garrett, asst. eds. Cambridge, Mass., Belknap Pr., Harvard [c.]1961. 365;458;449;403p. illus., maps. 26cm. (His Papers. Ser. 1: Diaries) Contents.v.1. Diary, 1755-1770.--v.2. Diary, 1771-1781.--v.3. Diary, 1782-1804. Autobiography to October 1776.--v.4. Autobiography, 1777-1789. Bibl. 60-5387 30.00 set,
I. Butterfield, Lyman Henry, 1909- II. Title.

*ADAMS, John, Pres., U.S., 1735-1826 923.173
Diary and autobiography of John Adams; 4v. L. H. Butterfield, ed. Leonard C. Faber, Wendell D. Garrett, assist eds. New York, Atheneum [1965, c.1961] 4v. (various p.) illus., facsims. 21cm. Orig. pub. by Harvard (Series 1) 2.65, 9.95 pap., ea., bxd. set
I. Butterfield, Lyman Henry, 1909- ed., II. Title.
Contents omitted.

ALLISON, John Murray. 973
Adams and Jefferson: the story of a friendship. [1st ed.] Norman, University of Oklahoma Press [1966] 349 p. ports. 23 cm. Bibliographical footnotes. [E322.A6] 66-13419
1. Adams, John, Pres. U.S., 1735-1826. 2. Jefferson, Thomas, Pres. U.S., 1743-1826. I. Title.

BREMER, Howard F. 973.4'4'0924
John Adams, 1735-1826; chronology, documents [and] bibliographical aids, edited by Howard F. Bremer. Dobbs Ferry, N.Y., Oceana Publications, 1967. v, 88 p. 24 cm. Bibliography: p. 81-86. [E321.B8] 67-19493
1. Adams, John, Pres. U.S., 1735-1826. I. Adams, John, Pres. U.S., 1735-1826. **BIP**

BROWN, Ralph A. 973.4'4'0924 B
The Presidency of John Adams / by Ralph Adams Brown. Lawrence : University Press of Kansas, [1975] x, 248 p., [1] leaf of plates : port. ; 23 cm. (American Presidency series) Includes index. Bibliography: p. 233-243. [E321.B84] 75-5526 ISBN 0-7006-0134-1 : 12.00
1. Adams, John, Pres. U.S., 1735-1826. 2. United States—Politics and government—1797-1801. I. Title. II. Series.

BURLEIGH, Anne Husted, 1941- 973.4'4'0924 B
John Adams. New Rochelle, N.Y., Arlington House [1969] vii, 437 p. 22 cm. (Architects of freedom series) Bibliography: p. [394]-395. [E322.B84] 69-16950 7.00
1. Adams, John, Pres. U.S., 1735-1826.

CHINARD, Gilbert 923.173
Honest John Adams. by Gilbert Chinard. Boston, Little, [c.1933-1964] xiip., 31., [3] -- 359p. front., plates, ports. 20cm. (37) 2.45 pap.,
1. Adams, John, pres. U.S., 1735-1826. I. Title.

CHINARD, Gilbert [Charles Gilbert Chinard] 1881- 923.173
Honest John Adams [Gloucester, Mass., P. Smith, 1965, c.1933-1964] xii, 359p. 20cm. (Little, Brown bk. rebound) Bibl. [E322.C47] 4.50
1. Adams, John, Pres. U.S., 1735-1826. I. Title. **BIP**

COURNOS, Helen Sybil Norton Kestner, 1893- 923.173
John Adams; Independence forever; by Sybil Norton [pseud.] and John Cournos. Illustrated by Jacob Landau. [1st ed.] New York, Holt [1954] 198 p. illus. 21 cm. (Their Pioneers of freedom books) [E322.C75] 54-5740
1. Adams, John, Pres. U.S., 1735-1826. I. Cournos, John, 1881- joint author. II. Title: Independence forever.

IACUZZI, Alfred, 1896- 923.173
John Adams, scholar. New York, S. F. Vanni (Ragusa) [1952] 306 p. 23 cm. "Bibliographical note and references": p. 268-296. [E322.I 15] 52-2528
1. Adams, John, Pres. U. S., 1735-1826. I. Title.

SHAW, Peter, 1936- 973.4'4'0924 B
The character of John Adams / by Peter Shaw. New York : Norton, 1977, c1976. p. cm. Reprint of the ed. published by University of North Carolina Press, Chapel Hill. Includes bibliographical references and index. [E322.S54 1977] 77-9407 ISBN 0-393-00856-8 pbk. : 3.95
1. Adams, John, Pres. U.S., 1735-1826. 2. Presidents—United States—Biography. I. Title. **BIP**

SHAW, Peter, 1936- 973.4'4'0924 B
The character of John Adams / by Peter Shaw. Chapel Hill : Published for the Institute of Early American History and Culture, Williamsburg, Va., by the University of North Carolina Press, c1976. ix, 324 p., [3] leaves of plates : port. ; 21 cm. Includes bibliographical references and index. [E322.S54] 75-14306 ISBN 0-8078-1254-4
1. Adams, John, Pres. U.S., 1735-1826. I. Institute of Early American History and Culture, Williamsburg, Va. II. Title.

SHEPHERD, Jack. 973'.0992 B
The Adams chronicles : four generations of greatness / Jack Shepherd ; introd. by Daniel J. Boorstin. 1st ed. Boston : Little, Brown, c1975. xxxi, 448 p. : ill. ; 26 cm. "Prepared by arrangement with the Massachusetts Historical Society, The Adams papers, and Harvard University Press." "Prepared in conjunction with the production of a television series of the same name." Includes index. Bibliography: p. 433-436. [E322.1.A28S53] 75-34422 ISBN 0-316-78497-4 : 17.50
1. Adams family. 2. Adams, John, Pres. U.S., 1735-1826. 3. Adams, John Quincy, Pres, U.S., 1767-1848. 4. Adams, Charles Francis, 1807-1886. 5. Adams, Henry, 1838-1918. I. Title. **BIP**

SMITH, Page 923.173
John Adams 2v. Garden City, N. Y., Doubleday [c.]1962. 2v. (xx, 1170p.) illus., ports., facsims. 25cm. Contents.v. 1. 1735-1784.--v. 2. 1784-1826. Bibl. 63-7188 14.50 set, bxd.
1. Adams, John, Pres. U. S., 1735-1826. I. Title.

SMITH, Page. 923.173
John Adams. [1st ed.] Garden City, N.Y., Doubleday, 1962. 2 v. (xx, 1170 p.) illus., ports., facsims. 25 cm. Contents.-- v. 1. 1735-1784. -- v. 2 1784-1826. Includes bibliographical references. [E322.S64] 63-7188
1. Adams, John, Pres. U.S., 1735-1826. I. Title. **BIP**

SMITH, Page. 973.4'4'0924 B
John Adams. Westport, Conn., Greenwood Press [1969, c1962-63] 2 v. (xx, 1170 p.) illus., ports., facsims. 23 cm. Contents.Contents.—v. 1. 1735-1784.—v. 2. 1784-1826. Includes bibliographical references. [E322.S642] 77-88941 ISBN 8-371-23305-(v.1)
1. Adams, John, Pres. U.S., 1735-1826.

UMBREIT, Kenneth Bernard. 973.3'0922
Founding fathers; man who shaped our tradition, by Kenneth Umbreit. Port Washington, N.Y., Kennikat Press [1969, c1941] viii, 344 p. ports. 22 cm. (Essay and general literature index reprint series) Contents.Contents.—Thomas Jefferson.—John Adams.—John Hancock.—Samuel Adams.—Patrick Henry.—George Washington. [E302.5.U55 1969] 68-26228
1. Jefferson, Thomas, Pres. U.S., 1743-1826. 2. Adams, John, Pres. U.S., 1735-1826. 3. Hancock, John, 1737-1793. 4. Adams, Samuel, 1722-1803. 5. Henry, Patrick, 1736-1799. 6. Washington, George, Pres. U.S., 1732-1799. I. Title.

Adams, John, Pres. U.S., 1735-1826—Addresses, essays, lectures.

PETERSON, Merrill D. 973.3'092'2 B
Adams and Jefferson : a revolutionary dialogue / Merrill D. Peterson. Athens : University of Georgia Press, c1976. xiv, 146 p. ; 23 cm. (Mercer University Lamar memorial lectures ; no. 19) Includes bibliographical references and index. [E210.P47] 76-1145 ISBN 0-8203-0401-8 : 7.00
1. Adams, John, Pres. U.S., 1735-1826—Addresses, essays, lectures. 2. Jefferson, Thomas, Pres. U.S., 1743-1826—Addresses, essays, lectures. 3. United States—Politics and government—Revolution, 1775-1783—Addresses, essays, lectures. 4. United States—Politics and government—1783-1809—Addresses, essays, lectures. 5. Presidents—United States—Biography—Addresses, essays, lectures. I. Title. II. Series: Mercer University, Macon, Ga. Lamar memorial lectures ; no. 19.

PETERSON, Merrill D. 973.3'092'2
Adams and Jefferson : a revolutionary dialogue / Merrill D. Peterson. Oxford ; New York : Oxford University Press, 1978, c1976. xiv, 146 p. : ports. ; 21 cm. (A Galaxy book ; 533) "Somewhat enlarged version of the Lamar memorial lectures delivered at Mercer University in October 1975." Contents.Contents.—The American Revolution.—The French Revolution.—

"The revolution of 1800."—Retrospect and prospect. Includes bibliographical references and index. [E210.P47 1978] 77-13408 ISBN 0-19-502355-2 pbk. : 2.50
1. Adams, John, Pres. U.S., 1735-1826—Addresses, essays, lectures. 2. Jefferson, Thomas, Pres. U.S., 1743-1826—Addresses, essays, lectures. 3. United States—Politics and government—Revolution, 1775-1783—Addresses, essays, lectures. 4. United States—Politics and government—1783-1809—Addresses, essays, lectures. 5. France—History—Revolution, 1789-1799—Addresses, essays, lectures. 6. Presidents—United States—Biography—Addresses, essays, lectures. I. Title. BIP

Adams, John, Pres. U.S., 1735-1826—Juvenile literature.

BLACKBURN, Joyce. 973.44'0924 B
John Adams: farmer from Braintree, champion of Independence. Illustrated by David Cunningham. Waco, Tex., World Books [1970] 149 p. illus. 23 cm. (Her People you should know) A biography of the man who served as Vice President under George Washington and became the second President of the United States. [E322.B55] 92 70-111962 3.95
1. Adams, John, Pres. U.S., 1735-1826—Juvenile literature. I. Cunningham, David, 1938- II. Title.

FALKNER, Leonard. 973.3'0924 B
John Adams; reluctant patriot of the Revolution. Illustrated by Jerry Contreras. Englewood Cliffs, N.J., Prentice-Hall [1969] 144 p. illus. 22 cm. A Rutledge book. Bibliography: p. 144. A biography of the second President of the United States, the first man in that office to live in the White House. [E322.F3] 92 69-10335 4.50
1. Adams, John, Pres. U.S., 1735-1826—Juvenile literature. I. Contreras, Jerry, illus. II. Title.

KELLY, Regina (Zimmerman) j 92
1898-
The picture story and biography of John Adams [by] Regina Z. Kelly. Illustrated by Aldren Watson. Chicago, Follett Pub. Co. [1965] 144 p. col. illus., col. port. 22 cm. (The Library of American heroes) [E322.K4] 65-14465
1. Adams, John, Pres. U.S., 1735-1826 — Juvenile literature. I. Watson, Aldren Auld, 1917- illus. II. Title.

STEINBERG, Alfred, 973.4'4'0924 B
1917-
John Adams. New York, Putnam [1969] 223 p. port. 22 cm. (Lives to remember) A biography of the lawyer from Braintree, Massachusetts, who became an important public figure in early American history and the second President of the United States. [E322.S83 1969] 73-77756 3.64
1. Adams, John, Pres. U.S., 1735-1826—Juvenile literature. I. Title.

Adams, John Quincy, Pres. U.S., 1767-1848.

ADAMS, James Truslow, 929'.2'0973
1878-1949.
The Adams family. Westport, Conn., Greenwood Press [1974, c1930] vi, 364 p. illus. 22 cm. Reprint of the ed. published by Little, Brown, Boston. [E176.A23 1974] 73-21487 ISBN 0-8371-6427-3
1. Adams family. 2. Adams, John, Pres. U.S., 1735-1826. 3. Adams, John Quincy, Pres. U.S., 1767-1848. 4. Adams, Charles Francis, 1807-1886. 5. United States—Politics and government—1783-1865. I. Title.

ADAMS, John Quincy, 923.173
Pres. U. S., 1767-1848.
Diary, 1794-1845; American diplomacy and political, social, and intellectual life from Washington to Polk, Edited by Allan Nevins New York, Scribner, 1951. xxxv, 586 p. 25 cm. "A selection from 'The memoirs of John Quincy Adams, comprising portions of his diary from 1795 to 1848.'" [E377.A213] 51-10345
1. U. S.—Hist.—1783-1865. 2. U. S.—Pol. & govt.—1783-1865. 3. U. S.—For. rel.—1783-1865. I. Nevins, Allan, 1890- ed. II. Title.

ADAMS, John Quincy, 973.5'0924
Pres. U.S., 1767-1848.
Memoirs of John Quincy Adams, comprising portions of his diary from 1795 to 1848. Edited by Charles Francis Adams. Freeport, N.Y., Books for Libraries Press [1969] 12 v. ports. 24 cm. (Select bibliographies reprint series) Reprint of the 1874-77 ed. [E377.A2 1969] 71-85454
1. U.S.—History—1783-1865—Sources. 2. U.S.—Politics and government—1783-1865. 3. U.S.—Foreign relations—1783-1865. I. Adams, Charles Francis, 1807-1886, ed. II. Title. BIP

BEMIS, Samuel Flagg, 923.173
1891-
John Quincy Adams and the Union. [1st ed.] New York, Knopf, 1956. xix, 546 p. illus., ports. 25 cm. Bibliographical footnotes. [E377.B46] 55-9271
1. Adams, John Quincy, Pres. U.S., 1767-1848.

EAST, Robert Abraham, 923.173
1909-
John Quincy Adams; the critical years: 1785-1794. New York, Bookman Associates [1962] 252 p. 23 cm. Includes bibliography. [E377.E2] 62-15530
1. Adams, John Quincy, Pres. U.S., 1767-1848.

FALKNER, Leonard. 973.6'0924
The President who wouldn't retire. New York, Coward-McCann [1967] 319 p. illus. (on lining papers) 22 cm. Bibliography: p. 307-310. [E377.F3] 67-15277
1. Adams, John Quincy, Pres. U.S., 1767-1848. I. Title.

HECHT, Marie B. 973.5'5'0924 B
John Quincy Adams; a personal history of an independent man [by] Marie B. Hecht. New York, Macmillan [1972] xiv, 682 p. illus. 24 cm. Bibliography: p. 659-665. [E377.H43] 72-77279 12.95
1. Adams, John Quincy, Pres. U.S., 1767-1848.

HOEHLING, Mary (Duprey) 1914- 920
Yankee in the White House: John Quincy Adams. New York, Messner [c.1963] 191p. 22cm. Bibl. 63-8654 3.25; 3.19 lib. ed.,
1. Adams, John Quincy, Pres. U.S., 1767-1848—Juvenile literature. I. Title.

LIPSKY, George A. 923.173
John Quincy Adams, his theory and ideas. Foreword by Allan Nevins. New York, Crowell, 1950. xii, 347 p. ports. 22 cm. Bibliography: p. 334-339. [E377.L5] 50-8112
1. Adams, John Quincy, Pres U S., 1767-1848. I. Title. BIP

LIPSKY, George Arthur, 923.173
1912-
John Quincy Adams, his theory and ideas. Foreword by Allan Nevins. New York, Apollo Eds., [1965, c. 1950] xii, 347p. 20cm. (A-100) Bibl. [E377.L5] 1.95 pap.,
1. Adams, John Quincy, Pres. U.S., 1767-1848. I. Title.

LIPSKY, George Arthur, 923.173
1912-
John Quincy Adams, his theory and ideas. Foreword by Allan Nevins. New York, Crowell, 1950. xii, 347p. ports. 22cm. Bibliography: p. 334-339. [E377.L5] 50-8112
1. Adams, John Quincy, Pres. U. S., 1767-1848. I. Title.

MORSE, John 973.5'5'0924 B
Torrey, 1840-1937.
John Quincy Adams. Boston, Houghton, Mifflin. [New York, AMS Press, 1972] viii, 331 p. illus. 19 cm. (American statesmen, v. 15) Reprint of the 1898 ed. [E377.M88 1972] 77-128967 ISBN 0-404-50866-9
1. Adams, John Quincy, Pres. U.S., 1767-1848. I. Title. II. Series. BIP

SEWARD, William 973.5'5'0924 B
Henry, 1801-1872.
Life and public services of John Quincy Adams, sixth President of the United States, with the eulogy delivered before the Legislature of New York, by William H. Seward. Port Washington, N.Y., Kennikat Press [1971] 404 p. port. 21 cm. (Kennikat Press scholarly reprints. Series in American history and culture in the nineteenth century) Reprint of the 1849 ed. [E377.S513 1971] 75-137926 ISBN 0-8046-1489-X
1. Adams, John Quincy, Pres. U.S., 1767-1848.

SHEPHERD, Jack. 973'.0992 B
The Adams chronicles : four generations of greatness / Jack Shepherd ; introd. by Daniel J. Boorstin. 1st ed. Boston : Little, Brown, c1975. xxxi, 448 p. : ill. ; 26 cm. "Prepared by arrangement with the Massachusetts Historical Society, The Adams papers, and Harvard University Press." "Prepared in conjunction with the production of a television series of the same name." Includes index. Bibliography: p. 433-436. [E322.1.A28S53] 75-34422 ISBN 0-316-78497-4 : 17.50
1. Adams family. 2. Adams, John, Pres. U.S., 1735-1826. 3. Adams, John Quincy, Pres, U.S., 1767-1848. 4. Adams, Charles Francis, 1807-1886. 5. Adams, Henry, 1838-1918. I. Title. BIP

Adams, John Quincy, Pres. U.S., 1767-1848—Juvenile literature.

BOBBE, Dorothie 973.5'5'0924 B
(De Bear)
John Quincy Adams, by Dorothie Bobbe. New York, Putnam [1971] 190 p. 22 cm. (Lives to remember) Bibliography: p. 185-186. A biography of the sixth President, who continued the family's dedication to public service begun by his father, the second President of the United States. [E377.B65 1971] 92 78-132613 3.86
1. Adams, John Quincy, Pres. U.S., 1767-1848—Juvenile literature. I. Title.

CLARKE, Fred G 973.550924 (B)
John Quincy Adams [by] Fred G. Clarke. New York, Collier Books [1966] 216 p. 22 cm. (America in the making) [E377.C65] 65-23072
1. Adams, John Quincy, Pres. U.S., 1767-1848 — Juvenile literature. I. Title.

HOEHLING, Mary (Duprey) 1914- 920
Yankee in the White House: John Quincy Adams. New York, Messner [c.1963] 191p. 22cm. Bibl. 63-8654 3.25; 3.19 lib. ed.,
1. Adams, John Quincy, Pres. U.S., 1767-1848—Juvenile literature. I. Title.

HOYT, Edwin Palmer, 92
John Quincy Adams; a biography of the sixth President of the United States. Chicago, Reilly & Lee, 1963. 152, [1] p. illus., ports. 22 cm. Bibliography. p. [153] [E377.H85] 63-19036
1. Adams, John Quincy, Pres. U.S., 1767-1848—Juvenile literature. I. Title.

HOYT, Edwin Palmer 92
John Quniny Adams; a biography of the sixth President of the United States. Chicago, Reilly [c.]1963. 152,[1]p. illus., ports. 22cm. Bibl. 63-19036 3.95
1. Adams, John Quincy, Pres. U.S., 1767-1848—Juvenile literature. I. Title.

LOMASK, Milton 923.173
John Quincy Adams, son of the American Revolution. New York, Ariel Bks. [dist.] Farrar [c.1965] 147p. 22cm. Bibl. [E377.L83] 65-10513 2.95
1. Adams, John Quincy, Pres. U. S., 1767-1848—Juvenile literature. I. Title.

Adams, John, 1812-1860.

DILLON, Richard H 639.110924
The legend of Grizzly Adams, California's greatest mountain man [by] Richard Dillon. New York, Coward-McCann [1966] 223 p. illus., facsims., 22 cm. 66-14068
1. Adams, John, 1812-1860. I. Title.

HITTELL, 639'.11'744460924 B
Theodore Henry, 1830-1917.
The adventures of James Capen Adams, mountaineer and grizzly bear hunter of California. New ed. Freeport, N.Y., Books for Libraries Press [1972] xiii, 373 p. illus. 23 cm. Reprint of the 1911 ed. [F864.A2 1972] 78-39492 ISBN 0-8369-9914-2
1. Adams, John, 1812-1860. I. Title.

Adams, John, 1812-1860—Juvenile literature.

MUIR, Jean. 639'.11'744460924 B
The adventures of Grizzly Adams. Illustrated by Al Orbaan. New York, Putnam [1970, c1969] 128 p. illus. 23 cm. (Sagas of the West) Biography of a frontiersman who captured and trained wild bears in the Sierras and in his later years became a part of P. T. Barnum's "Greatest Show on Earth." [F864.A225 1970] 92 77-77757 3.49
1. Adams, John, 1812-1860—Juvenile literature. I. Orbaan, Albert, illus. II. Title.

Adams, Julielte (Graves) 1858-1951.

LEMMON, Kathleen. 791.44'5
House in the woods; a biographical sketch of Juliette and Crosby Adams. [Asheville? N. C., c1956] 89p. port. 24cm. [ML406.L4] 61-38394
1. Adams, Julielte (Graves) 1858-1951. 2. Adams, Crosby, 1857-1951. I. Title.

Adams, Kenneth Stanley, 1899-

LOBSENZ, Norman 338.272820924 (B)
M 1919-
The Boots Adams story, by Norman M. Lobsenz. Bartlesville, Okla., Phillips Petroleum Co. [1965] 126 p. illus., ports. 27 cm. [HD9570.A3L6] 65-9687
1. Adams, Kenneth Stanley, 1899- I. Title.

Adams, Louisa Catherine (Johnson) 1775-1852.

MINNIGERODE, Meade, 973.4'0922
1887-1967.
Some American ladies; seven informal biographies. Freeport, N.Y., Books for Libraries Press [1969] viii, 287 p. illus., ports. 23 cm. (Essay index reprint series) "First published 1926." Contents.Contents.—Martha Washington.—Abigail Adams.—Dolly Madison.—Elizabeth Monroe and Louisa Adams.—Rachel Jackson.—Peggy Eaton. [E176.M65 1969] 70-93361
1. Washington, Martha (Dandridge) Custis, 1731-1802. 2. Adams, Abigail (Smith) 1744-1818. 3. Madison, Dolley (Payne) Todd, 1768-1849. 4. Monroe, Elizabeth (Kortright) 1768-1830. 5. Adams, Louisa Catherine (Johnson) 1775-1852. 6. Jackson, Rachel (Donelson) 1767-1828. 7. Eaton, Margaret L. (O'Neale) Timberlake, 1799(?)-1879. I. Title.

Adams, Louisa Catherine Johnson, 1775-1852—Juvenile literature.

KERR, Laura Nowak, 1904- 920.7
Louisa: the life of Mrs. John Quincy Adams [by] Laura Kerr. New York, Funk & Wagnalls Co. [1964] 186 p. illus. 22 cm. [E377.K4] 64-17429
1. Adams, Louisa Catherine Johnson, 1775-1852—Juvenile literature.

Adams, Marian Hooper, 1843-1885.

FRIEDRICH, Otto. 973'.07'2024 B
1929-
Clover / by Otto Friedrich. New York : Simon and Schuster, c1979. 381 p., [8] leaves of plates : ill. ; 24 cm. Includes index. Bibliography: p. 353-368. [CT275.A34F73] 79-12165 ISBN 0-671-22509-X : 10.95
1. Adams, Marian Hooper, 1843-1885. 2. Adams family. 3. Adams, Henry, 1838-1918. 4. United States—Biography. I. Title.

Adams, Maude, 1872-1953.

PATTERSON, Ada, 792'.028'0924 B
d.1939.
Maude Adams; a biography. New York, B. Blom, 1971. 109 p. illus., ports. 23 cm. Reprint of the 1907 ed. [PN2287.A4P3 1971] 72-91558
1. Adams, Maude, 1872-1953.

ROBBINS, Phyllis. 927.92
Maude Adams; an intimate portrait. New York, Putnam [1956] 308 p. illus. 22 cm. [PN2287.A4R6] 56-6625
1. Adams, Maude, 1872-1953.

Adams, Samuel, 1722-1803.

BEACH, Stewart, 1899- 973.270924 B
Samuel Adams; the fateful years, 1764-1776. New York, Dodd, Mead [1965] xiv, 329 p. illus., ports. 22 cm. Bibliography: p. 313-321. [E302.6.A2B4] 65-24251
1. Adams, Samuel, 1722-1803. 2. U.S.—History—Revolution, 1775-1783. I. Title.

CHIDSEY, Donald Barr, 1902- 973.3'092'4 B
The world of Samuel Adams. [1st ed.] Nashville, T. Nelson [1974] 192 p. port. 21 cm. Bibliography: p. 183-189. A biography of the patriot and politician whose speeches, writings, and activities, including the Boston Tea Party, helped stir up the colonists against Great Britain. [E302.6.A2C47] 92 74-698 ISBN 0-8407-6383-2 5.95
1. Adams, Samuel, 1722-1803. 2. United States—History—Revolution, 1775-1783. I. Title. **BIP**

GERSON, Noel Bertram, 1914- 973.3'092'4 B
The grand incendiary; a biography of Samuel Adams, by Paul Lewis. New York, Dial Press, 1973. xi, 403 p. 24 cm. Bibliography: p. 392-394. [E302.6.A2G47] 73-6723 8.95
1. Adams, Samuel, 1722-1803. 2. United States—History—Revolution—Causes. I. Title.

HARLOW, Ralph Volney, 1884-1956. 973.3'092'4 B
Samuel Adams, promoter of the American Revolution : a study in psychology and politics / by Ralph Volney Harlow. New York : Octagon Books, 1975, c1923. x, 363 p. ; 23 cm. Reprint of the ed. published by H. Holt, New York. Includes bibliographical references and index. [E302.6.A2H2 1975] 75-1390 ISBN 0-374-93664-1 :
1. Adams, Samuel, 1722-1803. 2. United States—Politics and government—Revolution, 1775-1783.

HOSMER, James Kendall, 1834-1927. 973.2'7'0924 B
Samuel Adams. Boston, Houghton, Mifflin. [New York, AMS Press, 1972] xv, 405 p. illus. 19 cm. (American statesmen, v. 2) Reprint of the 1898 ed. [E302.6.A2H6 1972] 78-128927 ISBN 0-404-50852-9
1. Adams, Samuel, 1722-1803. I. Title. II. Series. **BIP**

HOSMER, James Kendall, 1834-1927. 300'.8 S
Samuel Adams: the man of the town-meeting. Baltimore, N. Murray, publication agent, Johns Hopkins University, 1884. [New York, Johnson Reprint Corp., 1973] 60 p. 22 cm. Pages also numbered 208-262. Original ed. issued as no. 4 of Institutions and economics, which forms the 2d series of Johns Hopkins University studies in historical and political science. Includes bibliographical references. [H31.I65 no. 4] [E302.6.A2] 973.3'092'4 B 72-12992 ISBN 0-384-24370-3 pap. 4.00
1. Adams, Samuel, 1722-1803. I. Series: Johns Hopkins University. Studies in historical and political science, 2d ser., 4. II. Series: Institutions and economics, no. 4.

MILLER, John Chester, 1907- 923.273
Sam Adams; pioneer in propaganda. Stanford, Calif., Stanford University Press [1960, c1936] 437 p. illus. 24 cm. Includes bibliography. [E302.6.A2M56 1960] 60-7699
1. Adams, Samuel, 1722-1803. 2. United States—History—Revolution, 1775-1783.

UMBREIT, Kenneth Bernard. 973.3'0922
Founding fathers; man who shaped our tradition, by Kenneth Umbreit. Port Washington, N.Y., Kennikat Press [1969, c1941] viii, 344 p. ports. 22 cm. (Essay and general literature index reprint series) Contents.Contents.—Thomas Jefferson.—John Adams.—John Hancock.—Samuel Adams.—Patrick Henry.—George Washington. [E302.5.U55 1969] 68-26228
1. Jefferson, Thomas, Pres. U.S., 1743-1826. 2. Adams, John, Pres. U.S., 1735-1826. 3. Hancock, John, 1737-1793. 4. Adams, Samuel, 1722-1803. 5. Henry, Patrick, 1736-1799. 6. Washington, George, Pres. U.S., 1732-1799. I. Title.

WELLS, William Vincent, 1826-1876. 973.2'7'0924 B
The life and public services of Samuel Adams, being a narrative of his acts and opinions, and of his agency in producing and forwarding the American Revolution, with extracts from his correspondence, State papers, and political essays. 2d ed. Freeport, N.Y., Books for Libraries Press [1969] 3 v. ports. 23 cm. (Select bibliographies reprint series) At head of title: The father of the Revolution. This ed. was first published in 1888. Bibliographical footnotes. [E302.6.A2W4 1969] 76-85458 ISBN 0-8369-5032-1
1. Adams, Samuel, 1722-1803. 2. United States—History—Revolution, 1775-1783. 3. United States—Politics and government—Revolution, 1775-1783. I. Title.

Adams, Samuel, 1722-1803—Juvenile literature.

ALDERMAN, Clifford Lindsey 92
Samuel Adams. son of liberty. New York, Holt. [c.1961] 199p. 61-14606 3.50
1. Adams, Samuel, 1722-1803—Juvenile literature. I. Title.

ALDERMAN, Clifford Lindsey. 92
Samuel Adams, son of liberty. [1st ed.] New York, Holt, Rinehart and Winston [1961] 199p. 22cm. [E302.6.A2A5] 61-14606
1. Adams, Samuel, 1722-1803—Juvenile literature. I. Title.

FRITZ, Jean. 973.3'092'4 B
Why don't you get a horse, Sam Adams? / By Jean Fritz ; illustrated by Trina Schart Hyman. New York : Coward, McCann & Geoghegan, [1974] 47 p. : ill. (some col.) ; 24 cm. A brief biography of Samuel Adams describing his activities in stirring up the revolt against the British and how he was finally persuaded to learn to ride a horse. [E302.6.A2F75] 92 73-88023 ISBN 0-698-20292-9 : 5.95.
1. Adams, Samuel, 1722-1803—Juvenile literature. I. Hyman, Trina Schart, ill. II. Title. **BIP**

GREEN, Margaret. 973.2'7'0924 B
Radical of the Revolution: Samuel Adams. New York, J. Messner [1971] 191 p. 22 cm. Bibliography: p. [187] A biography of the Massachusetts radical whose belief in forceful protest against injustice made him one of the leaders of the Revolution. [E302.6.A2G7] 92 73-160304 ISBN 0-671-32462-4 3.95
1. Adams, Samuel, 1722-1803—Juvenile literature. I. Title.

LEE, Susan. 973.3'092'2 B
Sam and John Adams, by Susan & John Lee. Illustrated by Chuck Mitchell. Chicago, Childrens Press [1974] 47 p. col. illus. 24 cm. (Heroes of the Revolution) A biography of two cousins, one a leader in the American Revolution, the other the second President of the United States. [E302.6.A2L43] 920 74-8937 ISBN 0-516-04656-X
1. Adams, Samuel, 1722-1803—Juvenile literature. 2. Adams, John, Pres. U.S., 1735-1826—Juvenile literature. I. Lee, John, joint author. II. Mitchell, Chuck, illus. III. Title.

RICHARDSON, Fayette, 1923- 973.3'092'4 B
Sam Adams; the boy who became father of the American Revolution. Illustrated by William Sauts Bock. [1st ed.] New York, Crown Publishers [1975] [48] p. col. illus. 24 cm. A brief biography of the Massachusetts radical whose belief in forceful protest against injustice made him one of the leaders of the Revolution. [E302.6.A2R52 1975] 92 74-83211 ISBN 0-517-51847-3
1. Adams, Samuel, 1722-1803—Juvenile literature. I. Bock, William Sauts, 1939- illus. II. Title.

Adams, Sir Grantley Herbert, 1898-

HOYOS, F. A. 917.298
The rise of West Indian democracy; the life & times of Sir Grantley Adams, by F.A. Hoyos. [n.p.] Printed by Advocate Press, 1963. 228 x p. ports. 22 cm. Bibliography: p. i-iv. [F2041.A65H6] 66-83897
1. Adams, Sir Grantley Herbert, 1898- I. Title.

Adams, Vera Mary.

ADAMS, Vera Mary. 994.5
No stranger in Paradise / [by] Vera Mary Adams. Sydney : Australasian Book Society, 1976. 199 p. ; 23 cm. [DU230.P33A33] 77-375079 ISBN 0-909916-74-8
1. Adams, Vera Mary. 2. Paradise, Australia (Victoria)—Social life and customs. 3. Paradies, Australia (Victoria)—Biography. I. Title.

Adams, Willis Seaver, 1844-1921.

BEETHOVEN, Ludwig van, 1770-1827. 780.8
Beethoven, the man and the artist, as revealed in his own words. Compiled and annotated by Friedrich Kerst. Translated into English, and edited, with additional notes, by Henry Edward Krehbiel. New York, Dover Publications [1964] 110 p. 21 cm. "An unabridged and unaltered republication of the work first published by B. W. Huebsch in 1905." Translation of Beethoven im eigenen Wort. [ML410.B4A182 1964] 64-18854
I. Kerst, Friedrich, 1870- comp. II. Krehbiel, Henry Edward, 1854-1923, ed. III. Title.

BEETHOVEN, Ludwig van, 1770-1827. 780'.924 B
Beethoven's letters, with explanatory notes by A. C. Kalischer. Translated withpref. by J. S. Shedlock. Selected and edited by A. Eaglefield-Hull. New York, Dover Publications [1972] xvii, 410 p. illus. 21 cm. Reprint of the 1926 ed, issued in series: Dent's international library of books on music. [ML410.B4A23.S5 1972] 73-159687 ISBN 0-486-22769-3 4.00
I. Kalischer, Alfred Christlieb Salomo Ludwig, 1842-1909. II. Shedlock, John South, 1843-1919, tr. III. Hull, Arthur Eaglefield, 1876-1928, ed. IV. Series: Dent's international library of books on music.

DEERFIELD ACADEMY, Deerfield, Mass. Hilson Gallery. v. 12
Willis Seaver Adams; retrospection. Deerfield, Mass., American Studies Group, 1966. 63 p. illus. 18 x 26 cm. Biography by Roger Black. Includes bibliography. 67-35353
1. Adams, Willis Seaver, 1844-1921. I. Black, Roger. II. Title.

Adamson, Joy.

ADAMSON, Joy. 591'.092'4 B
The searching spirit : Joy Adamson's autobiography / with a foreword by Elspeth Huxley. 1st American ed. New York : Harcourt Brace Jovanovich, 1979, c1978. xii, 244 p., [4] leaves of plates : ill. ; 24 cm. "A Helen and Kurt Wolff book." Includes index. [QL31.A33A3 1979] 78-23764 14.95
1. Adamson, Joy. 2. Zoologists—Kenya—Biography. 3. Zoologists—Czechoslovakia—Biography. I. Title. **BIP**

Adanson, Michel, 1727-1806.

CARNEGIE Institute of Technology, Pittsburgh. Rachel McMasters Hunt Botanical Library. 925.7
Adanson; the bicentennial of Michel Adanson's Familles des plantes. Pittsburgh, Pa., Hunt Botanical Library, Carnegie Institute of Technology, 1963-64. 2 v. (xi, 635 p.) illus., ports., map, facsims. 26 cm. (The Hunt monograph series, no. 1) Full text of papers. English or French, presented in summary at an internatinal symposium held at the Hunt Botanical Library on Aug. 18 and 19, 1963. Includes bibliographies. [QH31.A15A3] 63-21502
1. Adanson, Michel, 1727-1806. I. Title. II. Series.
CONTENTS OMITTED.

Addams, Jane, 1860-1935.

ADDAMS, Jane, 1860-1935. v. 12
Twenty years at Hull-House, with autobiographical notes. With illus. by Norah Hamilton. New York, Macmillan, 1960 [c1938] xvii, 462p. illus., plates, ports. 20cm. 'More than a third of the material in the book has appeared in the American magazine, one chapter of it in McClure's magazine.'
1. Hull House, Chicago. 2. Chicago—Soc. condit. I. Title.

BEAM, Ronald H. 361'.9'73
Cedarville's Jane Addams ... her early influences, compiled and illustrated by Ronald H. Beam. Freeport, Ill., Printed by Wagner Print. Co., c1966. 32 p. illus. 23 cm. [HV28.A35B4] 67-3212
1. Addams, Jane, 1860-1935. I. Title.

FISHWICK, Marshall William. 361'.9'24 B
Jane Addams, by Marshall W. Fishwick and the editors of Silver Burdett. Editor in charge: Sam Welles. Morristown, N.J., Silver Burdett Co. [1968] 240 p. illus. (part col.), facsims. (part col.) ports. (part col.) 27 cm. (Illustrious Americans) Bibliography: p. 232-234. A biography of Jane Addams, highlighting the conditions of the time which were decisive factors in her choice to become a social worker. [HV28.A35F5] 92 AC 68
I. Silver Burdett Company. II. Title.

LEVINE, Daniel, 1934- 361'.9'24 B
Jane Addams and the liberal tradition. Madison, State Historical Society of Wisconsin, 1971. xviii, 277 p. 24 cm. Bibliography: p. 265-272. [HV28.A35L37] 70-634145 ISBN 0-87020-109-3 8.50
1. Addams, Jane, 1860-1935. I. Title.

LINN, James Weber, 1876-1939. 361'.9'24 B
Jane Addams; a biography. New York, Greenwood Press, 1968 [c1935] xi, 457 p. illus., ports. 23 cm. [HV28.A35L5 1968] 69-10120
1. Addams, Jane, 1860-1935.

MEIGS, Cornelia Lynde, 1884- 361'.9'24 B
Jane Addams, pioneer for social justice; a biography, by Cornelia Meigs. [1st ed.] Boston, Little, Brown [1970] 274 p. illus., ports. 22 cm. A history of Hull House and the many social reforms it inspired serve as a background to a biography of the woman who dedicated her life to improving society. [HV28.A35M45] 92 76-91228 5.95
1. Addams, Jane, 1860-1935. I. Title.

OAKLEY, Violet, 1874- 923.673
Cathedral of compassion; dramatic outline of the life of Jane Addams, 1860-1935. [Limited ed.] Philadelphia [1955] xiii, 104p. illus., port. 25cm. [HV28.A35O2] 56-677
1. Addams, Jane, 1860-1935. I. Title.

PETERSON, Helen Stone. 361'.924 B
Jane Addams, pioneer of Hull House. Illustrated by Hobe Hays. Champaign, Ill., Garrard Pub. Co. [1965] 80 p. col. illus. 23 cm. (A Discovery book) A biography of the pioneer in social work who founded the first settlement house in Chicago, campaigned for better social legislation, and won the Nobel Peace Prize. [HV28.A35P4] 92 AC 68
1. Addams, Jane, 1860-1935. I. Hays, Hobart Vance, illus. II. Title.

TIMS, Margaret 923.673
Jane Addams of Hull House, 1860-1935, a centenary study. New York, Macmillan [c.]1961. 166p. (front. port.) 61-16149 4.25 bds.,
I. Title.

TIMS, Margaret, 923.673
1919-
Jane Addams of Hull House, 1860-1935; a centenary study. New York, Macmillan, 1961. 166 p. illus. 23 cm. Includes bibliography. [HV28.A35T5] 61-16149
1. Addams, Jane, 1860-1935. I. Title.

Addams, Jane, 1860-1935—Juvenile literature.

FEUERLICHT, Roberta 001.4'4'0922
Strauss.
In search of peace; the story of four Americans who won the Nobel Peace Prize. New York, J. Messner [1970] 96 p. illus., ports. 22 cm. Bibliography: p. 91. A brief history of the Nobel Prizes and a biography of the man who founded them accompanies biographies of four Americans who received the Nobel Peace Prize. [E176.8.F45 1970] 920 70-123165 3.95
1. Addams, Jane, 1860-1935—Juvenile literature. 2. Bunche, Ralph Johnson, 1904- —Juvenile literature. 3. King, Martin Luther—Juvenile literature. 4. Roosevelt, Theodore, Pres. U.S., 1858-1919—Juvenile literature. 5. Nobel prizes—Juvenile literature. I. Title.

GILBERT, Miriam 923.673
Jane Addams, world neighbor. Illustrated by Corinne Boyd Dillon. Nashville, Abingdon Press [c.1960] 127p. illus. 21cm. (Makers of America) 60-5319 1.75
1. Addams, Jane, 1860-1935—Juvenile literature. I. Title.

GRANT, Matthew G. 361'.92'4 B
Jane Addams, helper of the poor [by] Matthew G. Grant. Illustrated by John Keely. [Mankato, Minn., Creative Education; distributed by Childrens Press, Chicago [1974] 29 p. illus. (part col.) 25 cm. (His Gallery of great Americans series. Women of America) A biography of a rich girl who realized her childhood wish to live and work among the poor. [HV28.A35G7] 92 73-15838 ISBN 0-87191-304-6 3.95
1. Addams, Jane, 1860-1935—Juvenile literature. I. Kelly, John, illus. II. Brude, Dick, illus. III. Title.

JOHNSON, Ann Donegan. 361'.92'4 B
The value of friendship : the story of Jane Addams. 1st ed. La Jolla, Calif. : Value Communications, c1979. p. cm. (ValueTales) Emphasizes the social changes effected by Jane Addams as she worked to improve the lot of the poor people who were her friends. [HV28.A35J63] 92 79-21643 ISBN 0-916392-45-7 : 5.95
1. Addams, Jane, 1860-1935—Juvenile literature. 2. Social workers—United States—Biography—Juvenile literature. I. Title. BIP

KELLER, Gail 361'.924 B
Faithfull.
Jane Addams. Illustrated by Frank Aloise. New York, Crowell [1971] 41 p. illus. 24 cm. (A Crowell biography) An easy-to-read biography of the woman who founded Hull House, one of the first social settlement houses in the United States. [HV28.A35K44] 92 71-139098 ISBN 0-690-45791-X 3.75
1. Addams, Jane, 1860-1935—Juvenile literature. I. Aloise, Frank E., illus. II. Title. BIP

Addison, Joseph, 1672-1719.

ADDISONIANA. 824'.5 B
[Folcroft, Pa.] Folcroft Library Editions, 1973. p. Attributed to Sir Richard Phillips. Cf. Halkett & Laing. Reprint of the 1803 ed. published by R. Phillips, London. [PR3306.A55 1973] 73-9524 ISBN 0-8414-1748-2 (lib. bdg.)
1. Addison, Joseph, 1672-1719. I. Phillips, Richard, Sir, 1767-1840. BIP

DOBREE, Bonamy, 1891- 820.9'004
Essays in biography, 1680-1726 Freeport, N.Y., Books for Libraries Press [1967] x, 362 p. illus., ports. 21 cm. (Essay index reprint series) Reprint of the 1925 ed. Contents.Contents.—His Excellency, Sir George Etherege.—The architect of Blenheim, Sir John Vanbrugh.—The first Victorian, Joseph Addison.—Appendices: Godolphin's warrant to Vanbrugh. Mrs. Yarburgh. Secret. The Frenzy. Pope's letters.—Bibliography (p. [353]-357) [PR433.D6 1967] 67-23203
1. Etherege, George, Sir, 1635?-1691. 2. Vanbrugh, John, Sir, 1664-1726. 3. Addison, Joseph, 1672-1719. 4. Blenheim Palace. I. Title.

Addison, Thomas, 1793-1860.

PALLISTER, George. 610'.92'4 B
Thomas Addison, M.D., F.R.C.P. (1795-1860) / by G. Pallister. [Newcastle upon Tyne] : [The Author], [1975] [2], 32 p. ; 22 cm. Cover title. [R489.A318P34] 75-595762 ISBN 0-9503997-0-1 : £0.40
1. Addison, Thomas, 1793-1860. I. Title.

Ade, George, 1866-1944.

ADE, George, 1866- 818'.4'09 B
1944.
Letters of George Ade. Edited by Terence Tobin. West Lafayette, Ind., Purdue University Studies, 1973. xi, 251 p. illus. 24 cm. [PS1006.A6Z53 1973] 72-619681 ISBN 0-911198-34-2 9.75
1. Ade, George, 1866-1944. BIP

Ade, George, 1866-1944—Biography.

KELLY, Fred Charters, 818'.4'09 B
1882-1959.
George Ade, warmhearted satirist / by Fred C. Kelly Westport, Conn. : Greenwood Press, 1977, c1947. 282 p., [11] leaves of plates : ill. ; 23 cm. Reprint of the ed. published by Bobbs-Merrill, Indianapolis. [PS1006.A6Z7 1977] 76-52441 ISBN 0-8371-9443-1 lib.bdg. : 17.75
1. Ade, George, 1866-1944—Biography. 2. Authors, American—19th century—Biography. I. Title.

Adenauer, Konrad, 1876-1967.

WEYMAR, Paul. 923.243
Adenauer, his authorized biography. Translated from the German by Peter de Mendelssohn. [1st ed.] New York, Dutton, 1957. 509 p. illus. 22 cm [DD259.7.A3W413] 56-6313
1 Adenauer, Konrad, 1876-1967.

WIGHTON, Charles. 923.243
Adenauer, a critical biography. [1st American ed.] New York, Coward-McCann [1964, c1963] 389 p. 23 cm. First published in London in 1963 under title: Adenauer, democratic dictator; a critical biography. [DD259.7.A3W46 1964] 64-13060
1. Adenauer, Konrad, 1876-1967 I. Title.

Adenauer, Konrad, 1876-1967—Juvenile literature.

FINKE, Blythe 943.087'092'4 B
Foote.
Konrad Adenauer, architect of the new Germany. Charlotteville, N.Y., SamHar Press, 1972. 31 p. 23 cm. (Outstanding personalities, no. 23) Bibliography: p. 23-31. A biography of the first Chancellor of the post-World War II Federal Republic of Germany who was known as "Der Alte." [DD259.7.A3F56] 92 79-190241 1.98
1. Adenauer, Konrad, 1876-1967—Juvenile literature. I. Title.
Pap. 0.98

Ader, Clement, 1841-1925.

CLEMENT Ader: his 629.13'0924
flight-claims and his place in history. London, H. M. S. O., 1968. x, 214p. 9 plates, illus., facsims., port. 25cm. At head of title: Science Museum, London. Bibl. foothotes. [TL540.A4G5] (B) 68-103554 5.85
1. Ader, Clement, 1841-1925. I. Gibbs-Smith, Charles Harvard, 1909- II. London. Science Museum.
Available in New York from British Info.

Adirondack Mountains—Social life and customs.

KEITH, Herbert F. 917.47'53
Man of the woods [by] Herbert F. Keith. With introd. and notes by Paul F. Jamieson. [1st ed.] [Syracuse, N.Y.] Syracuse University Press, 1972. xi, 164 p. illus. 24 cm. [F127.A2K4] 78-38507 ISBN 0-8156-0085-2
1. Adirondack Mountains—Social life and customs. I. Title. BIP

Adler, Alfred, 1870-1937.

ALFRED Adler, 921.36
a portrait from life. New York, Vanguard Press [c1957] 300p. illus. 22cm. Published in 1939 under titles: Alfred Adler, a biography, and Alfred Adler, apostle of freedom. [BF109.A4B62 1957a] [BF109.A4B62 1957a] 926.1 58-9249 58-9249
1. Adler, Alfred, 1870-1937. I. Bottome, Phyllis, 1884-

†ALFRED Adler, as we 150'.19'53
remember him / edited by Guy J. Manaster ... [et al.]. [Chicago] : North American Society of Adlerian Psychology, c1977. 122 p. : ill. ; 23 cm. Includes bibliographical references. [BF173.A55A65] 77-99189 7.95
1. Adler, Alfred, 1870-1937. 2. Psychoanalysts—Austria—Biography. I. Manaster, Guy J.
Publisher's address: 159 North Dearborn St., Chicago, IL 60601

TERNER, Janet R. 616.8'9'0924 B
The courage to be imperfect : the life and work of Rudolf Dreikurs / Janet Terner and W. L. Pew ; with the editorial assistance of Robert A. Aird. New York : Hawthorn Books, c1978. xv, 412 p. : ill. ; 24 cm. Includes index. "Rudolf Dreikurs bibliography": p. 377-392. [RC339.52.D73T47 1978] 75-220 ISBN 0-8015-1784-2 : 14.95
1. Dreikurs, Rudolf, 1897-1972. 2. Adler, Alfred, 1870-1937. 3. Dreikus, Rudolf, 1897-1972—Bibliography. 4. Psychiatrists—United States—Biography. 5. Group psychotherapy. I. Pew, W. L., joint author. II. Aird, Robert A. III. Title.

Adler, Felix, 1851-1933.

GUTTCHEN, Robert 370.1'092'4 B
S., 1926 1971.
Felix Adler [by] Robert S. Guttchen. New York, Twayne Publishers [1974] 293 p. port. 21 cm. (Twayne's world leaders series) Bibliography: p. 283-289. [BJ354.A343G87 1974] 73-15952 ISBN 0-8057-3650-6
1. Adler, Felix, 1851-1933. BIP

Adler, Felix, 1851-1933—Biography.

KRAUT, Benny. 296.8'346'0924 B
From Reform Judaism to ethical culture : the religious evolution of Felix Adler / by Benny Kraut. Cincinnati : Hebrew Union College Press, 1979, c1978. p. cm. (Monographs of the Hebrew Union College ; no. 5) "An I. Edward Kiev Library Foundation book." Revision of the author's thesis, Brandeis University. Includes index. Bibliography: p. [BP605.E84K72 1979] 79-14441 ISBN 0-87820-404-0 : 15.00
1. Adler, Felix, 1851-1933—Biography. 2. Ethical culture movement—Biography. 3. Reform Judaism—United States. 4. Jews in New York (City)—Biography. I. Title. II. Series: Hebrew Union College-Jewish Institute of Religion. Monographs ; no. 5. BIP

Adler, Jacob P., 1855-1926.

ROSENFELD, Lulla. 792'.092'4 B
Bright star of exile : Jacob Adler and the Yiddish theatre / Lulla Rosenfeld. New York : Crowell, c1977. 368 p., [4] leaves of plates : ill. ; 24 cm. Includes index. Bibliography: p. 359-360. [PN3035.R6] 76-52988 ISBN 0-690-01446-5 : 12.95
1. Adler, Jacob P., 1855-1926. 2. Theater—Jews. 3. Actors, Jewish—Biography. I. Title.

Adler, Mortimer Jerome, 1902-

ADLER, Mortimer Jerome, 191 B
1902-
Philosopher at large : an intellectual autobiography / by Mortimer J. Adler. New York : Macmillan, c1977. xii, 349 p., [16] leaves of plates : ill. ; 24 cm. Includes index. Bibliography: p. 330-337. [B945.A2864A35] 77-1383 ISBN 0-02-500490-5 : 12.95
1. Adler, Mortimer Jerome, 1902- 2. Philosophers—United States—Biography. I. Title. BIP

Admirals—Biography.

DAVIES, Richard Bell. 359'.00924
Sailor in the air: the memoirs of Vice-Admiral Richard Bell Davies; foreword by Air Chief Marshal Sir Arthur Longmore. London, Davies, 1967. x, 245p. 8 plates (incl. ports., facsim.) 23cm. [V65.D3A3] (B) 67-87329 7.50 bds.,
I. Title.
Distributed by Fernhill House, 162 E. 23 St., New York, N.Y. 10010

JONES, Ken [John Kenneth 923.573
Jones]
Admiral Arleigh (31-knot) Burke; the story of a fighting sailor. by Ken Jones, Hubert Kelley, Jr. Philadelphia, Chilton [c.1962] 203p. illus. 25cm. 62-18614 7.50
I. Title.

WARNER, Oliver, 359.3'31'0922 B
1903-
Command at sea : great fighting admirals from Hawke to Nimitz / Oliver Warner. New York : St. Martin's Press, 1976. xii, 196 p., [6] leaves of plates : ill. ; 23 cm. Includes bibliographical references and index. [V61.W37 1976] 76-376343 8.95
1. Admirals—Biography. I. Title. BIP

Admirals—Correspondence, reminiscences, etc.

CLARK, Joseph 940.544'9'730924
James, 1893-
Carrier admiral, by J. J. Clark with Clark G. Reynolds. New York, D. McKay Co. [1967] xv, 333 p. illus., ports. 22 cm. [E746.C55A3] 67-22006
1. Admirals—Correspondence, reminiscences, etc. I. Reynolds, Clark G. II. Title.

Admirals—Netherlands.

LIEFDE, Jacob B. 359.3'3'10922 B
de, 1847-1878.
The great Dutch admirals. With 11 illus. by Townley Green and others. Freeport, N.Y., Books for Libraries Press [1972] 351 p. illus. 23 cm. (Essay index reprint series) Reprint of the 1873 ed. Contents.Contents.—Jacob van Heemskerk.—Piet Hein.—Marten Harperts Tromp.—Witte Cornelis de With.—Michiel Adrianszoon de Ruyter.—Johan Evertsen.—Cornelis Tromp. [DJ131.L7 1972] 73-37790 ISBN 0-8369-2603-X
1. Admirals—Netherlands. 2. Netherlands—History, Naval. I. Title.

Admirals—United States—Biography.

REYNOLDS, Clark 359.3'3'10922 B
G.
Famous American admirals / Clark G. Reynolds. New York : Van Nostrand Reinhold, c1978. xvii, 446 p. : ports. ; 26 cm. (A Norback book) Includes bibliographical references and index. [V62.R48] 78-9607 ISBN 0-442-26068-7 : 16.95
1. Admirals—United States—Biography. I. Title. BIP

Adnet, Francoise.

ADNET, Francoise. 759.4
Francoise Adnet / par Louis Pauwels. Paris : Editions Art et industrie, [1976?] 79

p. : ill. (some col.) ; 32 cm. French and English. [ND553.A32P37] 76-466920 120F
1. Adnet, Francoise. I. Pauwels, Louis, Aug. 2, 1920-

Adolescence.

KIELL, Norman, ed. 136.7354
The universal experience of adolescence. New York, International Universities Press [1964] 942 p. 24 cm. "Passages ... from more than two hundred autobiographies, diaries, and letters ... dating from about 120 A.D. to the present." Bibliography: p. 884-942. [BF724.K5] 63-22359
1. Adolescence. I. Title. BIP

Adventists—Biog.

PIONEER stories retold; 922.673
a compilation of early experiences in the Advent movement. Illus. by Stanley Dunlap, Jr. Washington, Review and Herald Pub. Association [1956] 192p. illus. 21cm. [BX6191.P5] 56-58615
1. Adventists—Biog.

PIONEER stories retold; a 922.673
compilation of early experiences in the Advent movement. Illus. by Stanley Dunlap, Jr. Washington, Review and Herald Pub. Association [1956] 192p. illus. 21cm. [BX6191.P5] 56-58615
1. Adventists—Biog.

Adventure and adventurers.

ANDERTON, Russ. 910.4
Tic-polonga. [1st ed.] Garden City, N.Y., Doubleday, 1953. 254 p. 21 cm. Autobiographical. [G530.A243] 53-5969
1. Adventure and adventurers. 2. Precious stones. I. Title.

BRIDGES, Thomas Charles, 904
1868-
More heroes of modern adventure, by Thomas Charles Bridges and Hubert Hessell Tiltman. Freeport, N.Y., Books for Libraries Press [1969] xi, 266 p. illus., ports. 23 cm. (Essay index reprint series) Reprint of the 1930 ed. [G525.B84 1969] 76-86735
1. Adventure and adventurers. 2. Explorers. I. Tiltman, Hubert Hessell, 1897- joint author. II. Title. BIP

DAVIS, Hassoldt, 1907- 923.973
World without a roof, an autobiography. [1st ed.] New York, Duell, Sloan and Pearce [1957] 436p. 22cm. [G530.D3] 57-11057
1. Adventure and adventurers. I. Title.

FINGER, Charles Joseph, 1869- 904
1941.
Valiant vagabonds. Freeport, N.Y., Books for Libraries Press [1968, c1936] 315 p. 22 cm. (Essay index reprint series) [G525.F54 1968] 68-58789
1. Adventure and adventurers. 2. Explorers. I. Title. BIP

FREUCHEN, Peter, 1886- 923.9489
Vagrant Viking; my life and adventures. Translated from the Danish by Johan Hambro. New York, J. Messner [1953] 422p. illus. 22cm. [G530.F89] 53-10502
1. Adventure and adventurers. I. Title.

HALL, Daniel Weston, 910.4'5
1841-
Arctic rovings; or, The adventures of a New Bedford boy on sea and land. Edited by Jerome Beatty, Jr. Designed and illustrated by William Hogarth. New York, W. R. Scott, 1968. xiii, 144 p. illus., map, port. 22 cm. [G530.H2 1968] 68-27030 3.95
1. Adventure and adventurers. I. Beatty, Jerome, ed. II. Title. III. Title: The adventures of a New Bedford boy on sea and land.

KERR, Colman. 920
Great adventurers. Original French text by Claude Appell. 8 artists: P. Baur [and others] Chicago, Follett Pub. Co. [1968] c1967. 69 p. col. illus. 31 cm. A survey of history's madcap adventurers and their exploits as conquerors, sea-rovers, crusaders, merchants, explorers, mountaineers, aviators, and astronauts. [G525.K48513] AC 68
1. Adventure and adventurers. I. Appell, Claude, 1919- Grands aventuriers. II. Baur, P., illus. III. Title.

REEMAN, Douglas. 910.4'53
Adventures on the high seas; true sea stories from Captain Bligh to the Nautilus. New York, Walker [1971] 173 p. illus. 21 cm. (Men in action series) [G525.R37 1971] 70-166181 ISBN 0-8027-6088-0 4.50
1. Adventure and adventurers. I. Title.

THORNE, Jim. 923.973
Occupation: adventure. [1st ed.] Garden City, N.Y., Doubleday, 1961. 164 p. illus. 22 cm. Autobiographical. [G530.T45] 61-12590
1. Adventure and adventurers. I. Title.

THORNE, Jim. 923.973
Occupation: adventure. [1st ed.] Garden City, N. Y., Doubleday, 1961. 164 p. illus. 22 cm. Autobiographical. [G530.T45] 61-12590
1. Adventure and adventurers. I. Title.

Adventure and adventurers—Biography.

BESTON, Henry, 1888- 910'.92'2 B
1968.
The book of gallant vagabonds / by Henry Beston. Folcroft, Pa. : Folcroft Library Editions, 1978 [c1925] xi, 231 p. ; 23 cm. Reprint of the ed. published by T. W. Laurie, London. Contents.Contents.—John Ledyard.—Belzoni.—Edward John Trelawny.—Thomas Morton of Merry-Mount.—James Bruce.—Arthur Rimbaud. [CT9970.B44 1978] 78-27411 ISBN 0-8414-9898-9 lib. bdg. : 30.00
1. Adventure and adventurers—Biography. I. Title.

Adventure and adventurers—Juvenile literature.

ARMSTRONG, Richard. 910'.92'2
Themselves alone. Boston, Houghton Mifflin, 1972. 185 p. 22 cm. Includes bibliographical references. Recounts the exploits of such solitary adventurers as Edmund Hillary and Ernest Shackleton and examines their motivations. [G525.A728] 76-184248 ISBN 0-395-13721-7 4.95
1. Adventure and adventurers—Juvenile literature. 2. Explorers—Juvenile literature. I. Title.

HEATTER, Basil, 1918- 904
Against odds. New York, Farrar, Straus & Giroux [1970] 151 p. illus., ports. 21 cm. (An Ariel book) Describes twelve instances, including Lindbergh's transatlantic flight and the evacuation of the British Army from Dunkirk, in which man has attempted extraordinary feats against great odds. [G525.H36 1970] 72-125141 3.95
1. Adventure and adventurers—Juvenile literature. I. Title.

HOGG, Garry. 910'.92'2 B
They did it the hard way; seven astounding journeys. [New York] Pantheon Books [1973] x, 166 p. maps. 22 cm. Seven true adventure stories of people who by choice or necessity made arduous expeditions through desolate places, sometimes totally dependent on their endurance for survival. [G525.H79] 72-7624 ISBN 0-394-82602-7 4.95
1. Adventure and adventurers—Juvenile literature. 2. Voyages and travels—Juvenile literature. I. Title.

VERDICK, Mary. 910'.4
Amazing adventures; real stories of danger and daring, adapted and edited by Mary Verdick. Illustrated by Charles Sovek. Middletown, Conn., American Educational Publications [1972] 96 p. illus. 18 cm. (AEP paperbacks, R1) Eighteen true tales of men, women, and children whose work or recreation has brought them face to face with danger. [G525.V38] 70-185297 0.75
1. Adventure and adventurers—Juvenile literature. I. Sovek, Charles, illus. II. Title.

VERDICK, Mary. 920'.02
Real-life adventures; 13 true tales of courage. Adapted and compiled by Mary Verdick. Illustrated by Hal Ashmead. Middletown, Conn., Xerox Education Publications [1972] 96 p. illus. 18 cm. (A Pal paperback, B1) Contents.Contents.—133 days adrift on the ocean.—Saved from certain death.—Riding a box to freedom.—Young sailor circles the world.—Search for Aztec gold.—Then the buffalo charged again!—Under the Antarctic ice.—Grab onto the skids!—The raft sank slowly into the sea.—Lost in the Maine woods.—Alone across the Atlantic.—Caged for seven months.—Man overboard. [G525.V39] 72-83371 0.75 (pbk)
1. Adventure and adventurers—Juvenile literature. I. Ashmead, Hal, illus. II. Title.

Advertising — Biog.

PETERSON, Eldridge, ed. 926.591
Who's who in advertising. 1st- ed. New York [1963- v. 24 cm. Editor: 1963- E. Peterson. [HF5810.A2W46] 63-18786
1. Advertising — Biog. I. Title.

Advertising, Direct-mail.

SACKHEIM, Maxwell, 1890- 659.13'3
My first sixty years in advertising. Englewood Cliffs, N.J., Prentice-Hall [1970] 224 p. illus. 29 cm. [HF5861.S25] 71-87972
1. Advertising, Direct-mail. I. Title.

Advertising—United States.

DANIELS, Draper. 659.1
Giants, pigmies, and other advertising people. Chicago, Crain Communications [1974] xii, 257 p. 24 cm. [HF5810.D34A3] 73-81492 ISBN 0-87251-013-1 7.95
1. Advertising—United States. I. Title. BIP

OGILVY, David, 1911- 659.112
Confessions of an advertising man. [1st ed.] New York, Atheneum, 1963. 172 p. 24 cm. [HF5810.O34A3] 63-17855
1. Advertising—United States. I. Title. BIP

Advertising—United States—History.

JONES, Howard 659.1'092'4 B
Aldred.
50 years behind the scenes in advertising / by Howard Aldred Jones Philadelphia : Dorrance, [1975] 235 p. : ill. ; 22 cm. [HF5813.U6J63] 75-316608 ISBN 0-8059-2094-3 : 8.95
1. Advertising—United States—History. I. Title.

Aegidius, of Assisi, d. 1262.

BROWN, Beverly Holladay, 922.245
1912-
Franciscan mystic; the life of Blessed Brother Giles of Assisi, companion of St. Francis, by Raphael Brown [pseud. 1st ed.] Garden City, N. Y., Hanover House [1962] 221p. 22cm. Includes bibliography. [BX4705.A319B7] 62-7606
1. Aegidius, of Assisi, d. 1262. I. Title.

SETON, Walter Warren, 271'.3'0924
1882-1927
Blessed Giles of Assisi. Manchester [Eng.] Univ. Pr., 1918. Farnborough, Eng., Gregg Pr., 1966. vii, 94p. 20cm. The short Life of Giles of Assisi which forms the basis of the present work is found in Codex Canonici misc. 528 in the Bodleian Library, Oxford. It is attributed to Brother Leo. 'Text of Canonici misc. 528 and tr.' p. 51-89. Photoreproduction. Bibl. [BX4705.A319S47 1918a] 67-4915 9.80
1. Aegidius, of Assisi, d. 1262. I. Leo, Franciscan, 13th cent. II. Title.
American distributor: Gregg Pr., Ridgewood, N. J.

Aeronautics — Biog.

BRENNAN, Dennis. 629.13'00922
Adventures in courage: the skymasters. Chicago, Reilly & Lee [1968] 159 p. illus., facsims., ports. 24 cm. Cover title: The skymasters. [TL539.B73] 68-18482
1. Aeronautics—Biography. I. Title. II. Title: The skymasters.

CLARK, Ronald 629.13'00922
William.
The air [by] Ronald Clark. Worthington [Ohio] A. Lynn [1967, c1965] 124 p. illus., ports. 21 cm. (The Conquerors series) Contents.Contents.—The Montgolfiers and the early balloonists.—The Lilienthals.—The Wright brothers.—Sir Alan Cobham.—Sir Frank Whittle. [TL539.C55 1967] 67-5806
1. Aeronautics—Biography. I. Title. BIP

DANIEL Guggenheim Medal v. 12
Board of Award.
The Guggenheim medalists; architects of the age of flight [edited by] G. Edward Pendray. New York, 1964. 125 p. illus., ports. 22 cm. A65
1. Aeronautics — Biog. I. Pendray, George Edward, 1901- ed. II. Title.

DANIEL Guggenheim Medal 926.2913
Board of Award.
Pioneering in aeronautics; recipients of the Daniel Guggenheim medal, 1929-1952. New York, Board of Award, 1952. 147p. illus. 24 cm. [TL539.D25] 53-3503
1. Aeronautics—Biog. I. Title.

FEENY, William D 926.2913
In their honor: true stories of fliers for whom United States Air Force bases are named. With pen and ink illus. by the author. [1st ed.] New York, Duell, Sloan and Pearce [1963] xiv, 223 p. illus., ports. 21 cm. Bibliography: p. 205-206. [TL539.F4] 63-16825
1. Aeronautics—Biog. 2. Air bases—U.S.—Names. I. Title.

HOLLAND, Maurice, 629.13'0922 B
1891-
Architects of aviation, by Maurice Holland with Thomas M. Smith. Freeport, N.Y., Books for Libraries Press [1971, c1951] ix, 214 p. illus., ports. 23 cm. (Biography index reprint series) [TL539.H57 1971] 70-148218 ISBN 0-8369-8065-4
1. Aeronautics—Biography. I. Smith, Thomas Motley, 1920- joint author. II. Title.

HOLLAND, Maurice, 1891- 926.2913
Architects of aviation, by Maurice Holland with Thomas M. Smith. New York, Duell, Sloan and Pearce [1951] ix, 214 p. illus., ports. 22 cm. [TL539.H57] 51-10403
1. Aeronautics—Biog. I. Title.
Contents Omitted.

MACMILLAN, Norman, 1896- 926.2913
Great airmen. Illustrated by John Young. New York, St. Martin's Press [1959?] 270p. illus. 20cm. [TL539.M24 1959] 58-8449
1. Aeronautics—Biog. I. Title.

TITLER, Dale 629.13'0922 B
Milton, 1926-
Wings of adventure, by Dale M. Titler. New York, Dodd, Mead [1972] xvi, 364 p. illus. 21 cm. [TL539.T57] 78-175309 ISBN 0-396-06469-8 6.95
1. Aeronautics—Biography. 2. Air pilots. 3. Aeronautics—Flights. I. Title. BIP

WHO'S who in world 926.2913
aviation. v. 1-1955- Washington, American Aviation Publications. v. 24cm. [TL539.W58] 55-1942
1. Aeronautics—Biog.

WHO'S who in world 926.2913
aviation and astronautics. v. 1- 1955- Washington, American Aviation Publications. v. 24 cm. Title varies slightly. [TL539.W58] 55-1942
1. Aeronautics — Biog.

Aeronautics—Biog.—Juvenile literature.

HOYT, Edwin Palmer 920
Heroes of the skies. Illus. by George J. Zaffo. Garden City, N.Y., Doubleday [c.1963] 160p. illus. 25cm. 60-9993 2.95 bds.,
1. Aeronautics—Biog.—Juvenile literature. I. Title.

HOYT, Edwin Palmer. 920
Heroes of the skies. Illustrated by George J. Zaffo. [1st ed.] Garden City, N.Y.,

Doubleday [1963] 100 p. illus. 25 cm. [TL539.H65] 60-9993
1. Aeronautics—Biog.—Juvenile literature. I. Title.

ROSENBAUM, Robert A., 629.13'0922
1926-
*best book of true aviation stories, ed. by Robert A. Rosenbaum. Illus. by Kiyoaki Komoda. [1st ed.] Garden City, N.Y., Doubleday [1967] 284p. illus. (pt. col.) 24cm. (Best bk. ser.) [TL539.R64] 67-15372 3.95; 4.70 lib. ed.,
1. Aeronautics—Biog.—Juvenile literature. I. Title. II. Title: True aviation stories.

Aeronautics—Juvenile literature.

NORRIS, Geoffrey 920
The Wright brothers. Illus. by John Norbury. New York, Roy [1963,c.1961] 159p. illus. 21cm. (People, places and things) 62-21659 2.95 bds.,
1. Aeronautics—Juvenile literature. I. Title.

Aeronautics, Commercial—U.S.—Vocational guidance—Juvenile literature.

LEAK, Zenolia. 301.451'96'024 B
Mission possible, by Zenolia Leak, with George Elrick and Emmett Smith. [Chicago, Childrens Press, 1970] 62 p. illus., ports. 19 cm. (Open door books) A black woman tells of her difficult life and marriage before she got a job as an airline reservation clerk. [HD8039.A4L4] 92 70-123807
1. Aeronautics, Commercial—U.S.—Vocational guidance—Juvenile literature. 2. Air lines—Employees—U.S. I. Elrick, George. II. Smith, Emmett. III. Title.

Aeronautics—Popular works.

COOK, Graeme. 629.13'09'04
Air adventures : landmarks in the true story of flight / Graeme Cook. New York : St. Martin's Press, 1975, c1973. xii, 203 p. : ill. ; 23 cm. [TL546.7.C58 1975] 74-83514 6.95
1. Aeronautics—Popular works. 2. Air pilots—Biography. I. Title.

Aeronautics—United States—History.

VECSEY, George. 629.13'092'2 B
Gotting off the ground : the pioneers of aviation speak for themselves / George Vecsey & George C. Dade. 1st ed. New York : Dutton, c1979. xiii, 304 p. : ill. ; 24 cm. Includes index. [TL539.V4 1979] 78-13106 ISBN 0-525-11333-9 : 12.95
1. Aeronautics—United States—History. 2. Air pilots—United States—Biography. I. Dade, George C., joint author. II. Title.

Africa—Biog.

DICKIE, John, 1923- 920'.06 B
Who's who in Africa; the political, military and business leaders of Africa, by John Dickie and Alan Rake. London, African Development [1973] 602 p. illus. 22 cm. Label mounted on t.p.: Available from: International Publications Service, Collings, Inc. New York. [DT18.D54] 74-155294 ISBN 0-9502755-0-6 27.50
1. Africa—Biography. I. Rake, Alan, joint author. II. Title.

DICTIONARY of African biography. 920'.06 New York : Reference Publications, c1977- v. : ill. ; 29 cm. (The Encyclopaedia Africana) "Editor-in-chief : L. H. Ofosu-Appiah." Contents.Contents.—v. 1. Ethiopia, Ghana. Includes bibliographical references and index. [DT18.D55] 76-17954 ISBN 0-917256-01-8 (v. 1) : 59.95
1. Africa—Biography. I. Ofosu-Appiah, L. H. II. Series.

KAULA, Edna Mason 920.06
Leaders of the new Africa. Illus. by the author. Cleveland, World [1966] 192p. illus., ports. 24cm. [DT18.K3] 66-13906 3.75; 3.61 lib. ed.,
1. Africa—Biog. I. Title.

NIVEN, Cecil Rex, Sir 920.096
1898-
Nine great Africans. New York, Roy [1965, c.1964] xiv, 174p. illus., maps, ports. 23cm. [DT18.N5] 65-10804 6.95 bds.,
1. Africa—Biog. I. Title.

PERHAM, Margery Freda, 920.06
1895- ed.
Ten Africans [2d ed. Evanston, Ill.] Northwestern Univ. Pr. [1964] 356p. illus., ports., fold. map. 23cm. 64-1206 4.95
1. Africa—Biog. 2. Bantus. I. Title.

PERHAM, Margery Freda, 920.06
1895- ed.
Ten Africans. [2d ed.] Evanston, Ill.] Northwestern University Press [1964] 356 p. illus., ports., fold. map. 23 cm. [DT18.P38] 64-1206
1. Africa—Biog. 2. Bantus. I. Title.
Contents omitted BIP

SEGAL, Ronald, 1932- 920.06
African profiles. Baltimore, Penguin [c.1962] 351p. map. 19cm. (Penguin African lib., AP1) 62-51585 1.45 pap.,
1. Africa—Biog. 2. Africa—Politics. I. Title. BIP

SEGAL, Ronald, 920.06
1932-
Political Africa; a who's who of personalities and parties. In collaboration with Catherine Hoskyns [and] Rosalynde Ainslie. New York, Praeger [1961] ix, 475p. map. 25cm. (Books that matter) [DT18.S4] 61-16754
1. Africa—Biog. 2. Political parties—Africa. I. Title. II. Title: A who's who of personalities and parties.

Africa, Central—Biog.

**WHO'S who of Rhodesia,* 920.0689 *Mauritius, Central and East Africa, 1964.* Supplement to the Who's who of Southern Africa. Johannesburg, Wootton & Gibson [New York, Intl. Pubn. Serv., 1964] 240p. illus., ports. 25cm. 15.00
1. Africa, Central—Biog. 2. Africa, E ast—Biog.

**WHO'S who of Rhodesia,* 920.0689 *Mauritius, Central and East Africa, 1965.* Supplement to the Who's Who of Southern Africa Johannesburg, Combined pubns. New York, Intl. Pubns. Serv., 1965 1v. (various p.) illus., ports., 25cm. Pagination numbered as in Who s who of Southern Africa. At head of title: Who's who of Southern Africa (Rhodesia. Central and East Africa) 15.00
1. Africa, Central—Biog. 2. Africa, East—Biog. 3. Rhodesia—Biog 4. Mauritius—Biog.

Africa, Central—Description and travel.

LIVINGSTONE, David, 1813- 916.7 B
1873.
The last journals [of] David Livingstone in Central Africa, from 1865 to his death; continued by a narrative of his last moments and sufferings, obtained from his faithful servants, Chuma and Susi, by Horace Waller. Westport, Conn., Greenwood Press [1970] 2 v. illus., facsims., fold. maps, port. 23 cm. Reprint of the 1874 ed. [DT731.L735 1970] 68-55201 ISBN 0-8371-3899-X
1. Africa, Central—Description and travel. I. Waller, Horace, 1833-1896, ed. II. Title. BIP

LIVINGSTONE, David, 1813- 923.942
1873
The Zambesi doctors; David Livingstone's letters to John Kirk, 1858-1872, ed., introd. by R. Foskett. Edinburgh, Univ. Pr. [Chicago, Aldine, 1965, c.1964] 187p. illus. (pt. col.) facsim., map, ports. 23cm. [DT731.L772] 65-1286 4.75 bds.,
1. Africa, Central—Descr. &trav. I. Kirk, Sir John, 1832-1922. II. Title.

MAUGHAM, Reginald Charles 916
Fulke, 1866-1956.
Africa as I have known it; Nyasaland-East Africa-Liberia-Senegal. New York, Negro Universities Press [1969] xii, 372 p. illus., maps., ports. 23 cm. Reprint of the 1929 ed. [DT351.M4 1969] 76-98726
1. Africa, Central—Description and travel. I. Title. BIP

SCHNITZER, Eduard, 916.7'04
known as Emin Pasha, 1840-1892.
Emin Pasha, his life and work; compiled from his journals, letters, scientific notes and from official documents by Georg Schweitzer, with an introd. by R. W. Felkin. New York, Negro Universities Press [1969] 2 v. fold. map, port. 24 cm. Reprint of the 1898 ed., which was a slight abridgement of the German ed. of the same year. Bibliography: v. 2, p. 313-314. [DT363.S37 1969] 70-82071
1. Africa, Central—Description and travel. I. Schweitzer, Georg, comp. II. Title. BIP

STANLEY, sir Henry 916.7'03
Morton, 1841-1904.
Through the dark continent; or, The sources of the Nile around the great lakes of equatorial Africa and down the Livingstone River to the Atlantic Ocean. New York, Greenwood Press [1969] 2 v. illus. 24 cm. Reprint of the 1878 ed. [DT351.S83 1969] 68-55223
1. Africa, Central—Description and travel. I. Title.

Africa, East—Biog.

WHO'S who in East 920.067 *Africa;* 1965-66. [Nairobi, Marco Pubs. [New York, Intl. Pubns., 1966] 123p. illus. 26cm. [DT433.A2W5] 66-37949 15.00
1. Africa, East—Biog.

Africa, East—Descr. & trav.

LEAKEY, Louis Seymour 916.7 [B]
Bazett, 1903-
White African, an early autobiography, by L. S. B. Leakey. With a foreword by Kirtley F. Mather and a new pref. by the author. New York, Ballantine [1973 c.1966] 274 p. 18 cm. (Ballantine Walden Edition) [DT433.L4A3 1973] 67-7042 1.50 (pbk.)
1. Africa, East—Descr. & trav. 2. Stone age—Africa, East. I. Title. BIP

Africa, East—Description and travel—1951-

SPENCER, Hope Rockefeller. 916.7
The way to Rehema's house; an East African diary, by Hope Spencer. New York, Simon and Schuster [1967] 288 p. 22 cm. [DT426.S6] 67-19820
1. Africa, East—Description and travel—1951- I. Title.

Africa, Eastern—Biography.

BENNETT, Norman Robert, 1932- 960
Leadership in Eastern Africa; six political biographies, edited by Norman R. Bennett. [Boston, Mass.] Boston University Press, 1968. xxvii, 260 p. geneal. table, maps, ports. 22 cm. (Boston University. African research studies, no. 9) Contents.Contents.—Introduction, by D. F. McCall.—Menilek II, by H. G. Marcus.—The poor man of God: Muhammad Abdullah Hassan, by R. L. Hess.—Sheikh Mbaruk bin Rashid bin Salim el Maxrui, by T. H. R. Cashmore.—Mwinyi Kheri, by N. R. Bennett.—Gungunhana, by D. L. Wheeler.—Lobengula, by P. Hassing. Bibliographical footnotes. [DT365.6.A1B4] 68-21921 7.75
1. Africa, Eastern—Biography. I. Title. II. Series: Boston University. African Studies Program. African research studies, no. 9 BIP

Africa—Social life and customs—Juvenile literature.

OJIGBO, A. Okion, 916'.03'08
comp.
Young and Black in Africa, compiled with introductory notes by A. Okion Ojigbo. New York, Random House [1971] 107 p. illus. 22 cm. Cover title: What it means to be young and Black in America. Contents.Contents.—I meet money, by Prince Modupe.—Seized into slavery, by O. Equiano.—My sister is born, by F. Selormey.—Tell Freedom, by P. Abrahams.—Grandfather and granddaughter, by C. Wacjuma.—I am hit by a night stick, by R. M. Gatheru.—An African's adventures in America, by B. Fafunwa.—Homecoming, by L. Kayira.—Bibliography (p. 107) [DT14.O38] 70-158382 ISBN 0-394-82304-4
1. Africa—Social life and customs—Juvenile literature. I. Title. BIP

Africa, South—Biog.

DAVIES, Horton. 922
Great South African Christians. Cape Town, New York, Oxford University Press, 1951. 190 p. 20 cm. [BR1450.D3] 51-14469
1. Africa, South—Biog. 2. Christians in Africa, South. I. Title. BIP

ROSENTHAL, Eric, comp. 920.06803
Southern African dictionary of National biography: comp. by Eric Rosenthal. London, Warne [1966] xxxix, 430p. 20cm. [CT1923.R6] 66-15690 15.00 bds.,
1. Africa, South—Biog. I. Title.
Available from the publisher's New York office.

WHO'S who of Southern 920/.0689 *Africa.* Johannesburg, Combined Pubs. Label pasted on t.p.: Intl. Pubns. Serv., New York, v. illus., ports. 26cm. irregular. Title varies: 1967, Who's who of southern Africa, including Mauritius. Absorbed Who's who of the Federation of Rhodesia and Nyasaland, also Portuguese East Africa in 1959. Incorporates 196- the Central African who's who [DT752.S5] 15-10690 30.00
1. Africa, South—Biog.

WHO'S who of Southern 920.0689 *Africa,* including Mauritius, and incorporating South Africa Who's who, and the Central African Who's who; 1965. An illus. biog. sketchbk. of personalities in Southern Africa, South West Africa, Rhodesia, Zambia (Northern Rhodesia), Malawi (Nyasaland), Central and East Africa and Mauritius. Johannesburg, Combined Pubs. [New York, Intl. Pubns. Serv., 1965] 1v. (various p.) illus., ports. 25cm. 15-10690 30.00
1. Africa, South—Biog. BIP

WHO'S who of Southern 920.W9 *Africa* including Mauritius, and incorporating South African who's who and the Central African who's who, 1966. An illus. biog. sketchbk. of personalities in Southern Africa with separate sects. for the Republic of South Africa South West Africa, Rhodesia, Zambia (Northern Rhodesia), Malawi (Nyasaland), Central and east Africa and Mauritius [50th ed] Johannesburg, Combined Pubs. [1966] v. illus., ports. 25cm. 15-10690 30.00
1. Africa, South—Biog.

WHO'S who of Southern 920.0689 *Africa* including Mauritius, and incorporating South African Who's who and the Central African Who's who, 1964. An illus. biog. sketch bk. of personalities in Southern Africa with separate sects. for the Republic of S. Africa, S-W Africa, Southern Rhodesia, Northern Rhodesia (Zambia), Nysaland, (Malawi), Central and E. Africa and Mauritius. Johannesburg, Wootton & Gibson [New York, Intl. Pubns. Serv. 1964] 1v. (various p.) illus., ports. 25cm. 15-10690 30.00
1. Africa, South—Biog.

WHO'S who of Southern 920.068 *Africa, 1962* (Incorporating South African Who's who and the Who's who of the Federation of Rhodesia and Nyasaland, Central and East Africa) An illus. biog. sketch bk. of personalities in Southern Africa with separate sects. for the Republic of South Africa, South-West Africa and the Federation of Rhodesia and Nyasaland, Central & East Africa. Johannesburg, Wootton & Gibson (PTY) [dist. New York, Intl. Pubns., 1962] various p. illus. 25cm. 15-10609 11.00
1. Africa, South—Biog.

Africa, South—Description and travel—1801-1900.

LEYLAND, J. 916.8'04'4
Adventures in the far interior of South Africa. Cape Town, C. Struik, 1972. xiii, 289 p. illus. 19 cm. (Africana collectanea, v. 40) Reprint of the 1866 ed. [DT756.L68 1972] 72-188829 ISBN 0-86977-014-4
1. Africa, South—Description and travel—1801-1900. 2. Natural history—Africa, South. 3. Hunting—Africa, South. 4. Honduras—Description and travel. I. Title. II. Series.
Available from Verry, 12.60.

SHELDON, Louise (Vescelius) 916.8
Yankee girls in Zulu land, by Louise Vescelius-Sheldon. Illustrated by G. E. Graves. New York, Books for Libraries Press, 1973. p. (The Black heritage library collection) Reprint of the 1888 ed. [DT756.S539 1973] 72-12877 ISBN 0-8369-9237-7
1. Africa, South—Description and travel—1801-1900. I. Title. II. Series.

Africa, South—History.

*TABLER, Edward C. 968 [B]
Pioneers of South West Africa and Ngamiland, 1738-1880. Cape Town, A. A. Balkema, 1973. ix, 142 p. (South African Biographical and Historical Studies, 19) "A biographical dictionary that includes as many as possible of the adult male foreigners who travelled and settled in the defined areas from 1738-1880." Bibliography: p. [133]-140. [DT846] ISBN 0-86961-021-X
1. Africa, South—History. 2. Africa, South—Biography. I. Title. II. Series.
Available from Verry, Mystic, Conn., for 16.50

Africa, Southwest—Biography.

TABLER, Edward C. 916.8'8'030922 B
Pioneers of South West Africa and Ngamiland, 1738-1880, by Edward C. Tabler. Cape Town, Balkema, 1973. ix, 142 p. 26 cm. (South African biographical and historical studies, 19) Bibliography: p. 133-140. [DT715.A2T3] 73-180050 ISBN 0-86961-021-X
1. Africa, Southwest—Biography. 2. Ngamiland, Botswana—Biography. I. Title. II. Series.
Distributed by Verry, 16.50.

Africa, Sub-Saharan—Biography—Juvenile literature.

MITCHISON, Naomi (Haldane) 1897- 967'.00922
African heroes [by] Naomi Mitchison. Illustrated by William Stobbs. [1st American ed.] New York, Farrar, Straus & Giroux [1969, c1968] vii, 205 p. illus., maps. 22 cm. "An Ariel book." Set against tribal customs and traditions, stories of eleven African heroes who lived between 1300 and 1900 give insight into the conflicts of Africans and Europeans. [DT352.6.M5 1969] 920 77-87211 3.95
1. Africa, Sub-Saharan—Biography—Juvenile literature. I. Stobbs, William, illus. II. Title. BIP

POLATNICK, Florence T. 967 B
Shapers of Africa [by] Florence T. Polatnick and Alberta L. Saletan. New York, J. Messner [1969] 184, [8] p. illus. 22 cm. Contents.Contents.—Mansa Musa.—Queen Nzinga.—Samuel Ajayi Crowther.—Moshoeshoe.—Tom Mboya.—Suggested further reading (p. [185]) [DT352.6.P6] 920 76-83149 3.50
1. Africa, Sub-Saharan—Biography—Juvenile literature. I. Saletan, Alberta L., joint author. II. Title.

Africa, West—Description and travel—1851-1950.

KIRK-GREENE, Anthony Hamilton Millard, comp. 916.69'5
West African travels and adventures; two autobiographical narratives from Northern Nigeria. Translated and annotated by Anthony Kirk-Greene and Paul Newman. New Haven, Yale University Press, 1971. vi, 255 p. illus., facsim., map, ports. 21 cm. Includes selections from the original Hausa texts. Contents.Contents.—The life and travels of Dorugu.—The story of Maimaina of Jega, Chief of Askira. Bibliography: p. 241-247. [DT472.K57 1971] 74-151578 ISBN 0-300-01426-0 10.00
1. Africa, West—Description and travel—1851-1950. 2. Northern Nigeria—Description and travel. I. Newman, Paul, 1937- joint comp. II. Dorugu, ca. 1840-1912. The life and travels of Dorugu. 1971. III. Mai Maina, Chief of Askira, 1874-Labarin Mai Maina na jega Sarkin Askira. English. 1971. IV. T

African Methodist Episcopal Church.

HEARD, William Henry, Bp., 1850-1937. 287'.8'0924 B
From slavery to the bishopric in the A.M.E. Church. New York, Arno Press, 1969. vii, 104 p. illus., port. 18 cm. (The American Negro, his history and literature) Reprint of the 1924 ed. Bibliographical references included in "Notes" (p. vii) [BX8449.H4A3] 69-18564
1. African Methodist Episcopal Church. I. Title. II. Series.

PAYNE, Daniel Alexander, Bp., 1811-1893. 287'.8'0924 B
Recollections of seventy years. New York, Arno Press, 1968. 335 p. illus., ports. 21 cm. (The American Negro, his history and literature) Reprint of the 1888 ed. [BX8449.P3A3 1968] 68-29015
1. African Methodist Episcopal Church. I. Title. II. Series.

African Methodist Episcopal Church—Biog.

WRIGHT, Richard Robert, 1878- 922.7873
The bishops of the African Methodist Episcopal Church. [Nashville, African Methodist Episcopal Church] 1963. 389p. illus. 22cm. 63-3919 apply
1. African Methodist Episcopal Church—Biog. 2. Bishops—U.S. I. Title.

African Methodist Episcopal Church—Hist.

MORANT, John J 922.773
Mississippi minister. [1st ed.] New York, Vantage Press [1958] 80p. illus. 21cm. [BX8443.M6] 57-11254
1. African Methodist Episcopal Church—Hist. I. Title.

African Methodist Episcopal Zion Church—Biography.

BROOKS, George Alexander. 287'.83 B
Peerless laymen in the African Methodist Episcopal Zion Church / by George Alexander Brooks, Sr. State College, Pa. : Himes Print. Co., 1974- v. : ports. ; 23 cm. [BX8473.A1B76] 75-324341
1. African Methodist Episcopal Zion Church—Biography. I. Title.

Afro-American actors.

ROLLINS, Charlemae Hill. 792'.028'0922
Famous Negro entertainers of stage, screen and TV, by Charlemae Rollins. New York, Dodd, Mead [1967] 122 p. ports. 22 cm. (Famous biographies for young people) Contents.Contents.—Ira Aldridge.—Marian Anderson.—Louis "Satchmo" Armstrong.—Josephine Baker.—Harry Belafonte.—Nat "King" Cole.—Sammy Davis, Jr.—"Duke" Ellington.—Lena Horne.—Eartha Kitt.—Sidney Poitier.—Leontyne Price.—Paul Robeson.—Bill "Bojangles" Robinson.—"Bert" Williams.—Thomas "Fats" Waller. [PN2286.R6] 67-14305
1. Afro-American actors. I. Title. BIP

Afro-American artists—Biography.

FAX, Elton C. 709'.2'2 B
Black artists of the new generation / Elton C. Fax ; foreword by Romare Bearden. New York : Dodd, Mead, c1977. xiv, 370 p., [8] leaves of plates : ill. ; 22 cm. Includes index. [N6538.N5F29] 77-7053 ISBN 0-396-07434-0 : 8.95
1. Afro-American artists—Biography. 2. Afro-American art. 3. Art, Modern—20th century—United States. I. Title. BIP

Afro-American clergy—Biography—Addresses, essays, lectures.

BLACK apostles : 200'.92'2 B
Afro-American clergy confront the twentieth century / edited by Randall K. Burkett and Richard Newman. Boston : G. K. Hall, c1978. xvi, 283 p. ; 25 cm. Contents.Contents.—Shepperson, G. Introduction.—Pierson, R. M. Alexander Bedward and the Jamaica Native Baptist Free Church.—Henriksen, T. H. African intellectual influences on Black Americans, the role of Edward W. Blyden.—Burnham, K. E. Father Divine and the peace mission movement.—King, K. J. Some notes on Arnold J. Ford and new world Black attitudes to Ethiopia.—Weeks, L. B. Racism, World War I and the Christian life, Francis J. Grimke in the nation's capital.—Gavins, R. Gordon Blaine Hancock.—Roberts, S. K. George Edmund Haynes.—Hayden, J. C. James Theodore Holly, 1829-1911.—Smith, H. M. Harold M. Kingsley.—White, G. Patriarch McGuire and the Episcopal Church.—Wills, D. Reverdy C. Ransom.—Tinney, J. S. William J. Seymour.—Redkey, E. S. Bishop Turner's African dream.—Miller, G. M. The social mission of Bishop Alexander Waltfro-American clergy confront the twentieth century / edited by Randall K. Burkett and Richard Newman. Boston : G. K. Hall, c1978. xvi, 283 p. ; 25 cm. Contents.C
1. Afro-American clergy—Biography—Addresses, essays, lectures. I. Burkett, Randall K. II. Newman, Richard. BIP

Afro-American clergy—Tennessee—Memphis.

TUCKER, David M., 1937- 280'.092'2 B
Black pastors and leaders : Memphis, 1819-1972 / David M. Tucker. [Memphis] : Memphis State University Press, [1975] xi, 158 p. ; 22 cm. Includes bibliographical references and index. [BR563.N4T78] 75-1248 ISBN 0-87870-024-2 : 8.50
1. Afro-American clergy—Tennessee—Memphis. 2. Afro-Americans—Tennessee—Memphis. 3. Memphis—Biography. I. Title.

Afro-American librarians—Southern States—Directories.

HAITH, Dorothy May. 020'.92'2
The southeastern Black librarian / by Dorothy May Haith. Huntsville, AL : IESMP, 1976. v, 63 p. ; 23 cm. [Z720.A45A134] 76-151097 5.95
1. Afro-American librarians—Southern States—Directories. I. Title.

Afro-American musicians—Biography.

HANDY, William Christopher, 1873-1958. 780'.92'2 B
Negro authors and composers of the United States / by W. C. Handy. New York : AMS Press, 1976. 24 p. : port. ; 23 cm. Reprint of the 1938? ed. published by Handy Bros. Music Co., New York. Includes bibliographical references. [ML3556.H23N3 1976] 74-24105 ISBN 0-404-12953-6 : 9.00
1. Afro-American musicians—Biography. 2. Afro-American authors—Biography. BIP

LOVINGGOOD, Penman. 780'.92'2 B
Famous modern Negro musicians / by Penman Lovinggood ; with a new introd. by Eileen Southern. New York : Da Capo Press, 1978 [c1921] viii, 68 p. ; 22 cm. (Da Capo Press music reprint series) Reprint of the ed. published by Press Forum Co., Brooklyn. [ML385.L69 1978] 77-22215 ISBN 0-306-77523-9 : 13.50
1. Afro-American musicians—Biography. I. Title. BIP

Afro-American musicians—Portraits.

WILMER, Valerie. 780'.92'2 B
The face of Black music ; photographs / by Valerie Wilmer ; introduction by Archie Shepp. New York : Da Capo Press, 1976. [118] p. : ill. ; 28 cm. [ML87.W655] 76-18115 ISBN 0-306-80039-X pbk. : 7.95
1. Afro-American musicians—Portraits. 2. Jazz musicians—Portraits. I. Title.

Afro-American scientists—Biography.

CARWELL, Hattie. 509'.2'2 B
Blacks in science : astrophysicist to zoologist / Hattie Carwell. 1st ed. Hicksville, N.Y. : Exposition Press, c1977. 95 p., [4] leaves of plates : ill. ; 22 cm. Includes index. Bibliography: p. 93-94. [Q141.C23] 77-379267 ISBN 0-682-48911-5 : 6.00
1. Afro-American scientists—Biography. I. Title. BIP

Afro-Americans.

RUTLAND, Eva. 301.451 B
The trouble with being a mama. New York, Abingdon Press [1964] 143 p. 21 cm. Autobiographical. [E185.625.R8] 64-21136
1. Afro-Americans. 2. Children—Management. I. Title.

Afro-Americans—Biography.

BAILEY, J. Edward, 1923- 973'.0992 B
Living legends in black / by J. Edward Bailey III. Detroit : Bailey Pub. Co., 1976. 173 p. : ports. ; 28 cm. Includes index. [E185.B22] 75-5063
1. Afro-Americans—Biography. I. Title.

BIRMINGHAM, Stephen. 301.45'19'6073022 B
Certain people : America's black elite / Stephen Birmingham. 1st ed. Boston : Little, Brown, c1977. xv, 301 p., [12] leaves of plates : ill. ; 22 cm. Includes index. [E185.96.B48] 76-56221 ISBN 0-316-09642-3 : 8.95
1. Afro-Americans—Biography. 2. Upper classes—United States. I. Title.

CHRISTOPHER, Maurine. 328.73'092'2 B
Black Americans in Congress / Maurine Christopher. Rev. and expanded ed. New York : c1976. [1976] xvi, 329 p., [11] leaves of plates : ill. ; 24 cm. Published in 1971 under title: America's Black congressmen. Includes index. Bibliography: p. 312-316. [E185.96.C5 1976] 76-8943 ISBN 0-690-01102-4 : 10.00
1. Afro-Americans—Biography. 2. Legislators—United States—Biography. I. Title. BIP

INNIS, Doris Funnye. 920'.073
Profiles in Black : biographical sketches of 100 living Black unsung heroes / edited Doris Funnye Innis, Juliana Wu ; consulting editor, Joyce Duren. 1st ed. New York, N.Y. : CORE Publications, 1976. 240 p. : ill. ; 22 cm. Includes index. Bibliography: p. 232-237. [E185.96.I56] 76-27634 ISBN 0-917354-01-X pbk. : 2.95
1. Afro-Americans—Biography. I. Wu, Juliana, joint author. II. Duren, Joyce. III. Title.

†LEE, George L., 1906- 920'.0092'96073
Interesting people / by George L. Lee. New York : Vantage Press, c1976. 164 p. : chiefly ill. ; 22 cm. Biographical highlights of notable men and women from around the world whose achievements are milestones in black history. [E185.96.L37] 77-363754 ISBN 0-533-02377-7 : 5.95
1. Afro-Americans—Biography. I. Title. BIP

PALMER, Colin A., 1942- 973'.04'96073
Blacks in the age of the American Revolution / by Colin Palmer. [Detroit] : Afro-American Museum of Detroit, c1976. 34 leaves ; 28 cm. Bibliography: leaf 34. [E185.96.P34] 76-359567 2.50
1. Afro-Americans—Biography. 2. Afro-Americans—History—To 1863. I. Title.

TAYLOR, Douglas. 920.073
True Black man's history / by Douglas Taylor and R. P. Powell. New York : Philosophical Library, c1977. xi, 83 p. ; 22 cm. [E185.96.T38] 76-47244 ISBN 0-8022-2192-0 : 8.50
1. Afro-Americans—Biography. I. Powell, Raphael Philemon, joint author. II. Title. BIP

Afro-Americans—Biography—Juvenile literature.

KING, John Taylor, 1921- 920'.073
Famous Black Americans / by John T. King, and Marcet H. King ; ill. by Don Collins. Austin, Tex. : Steck-Vaughn Co., c1975. 126 p. : ill., forms ; 28 cm. Biographical sketches of thirty-three Afro-Americans who, through their contributions to society, have achieved personal success. [E185.96.K49] 920 76-360005 ISBN 0-8114-0449-8
1. Afro-Americans—Biography—Juvenile literature. I. King, Marcet J., joint author. II. Title.

Afro-Americans—Connecticut—New Haven—History.

STEWART, Daniel Y., 1894- 974.6'8'00496073
Black New Haven : personal observations involving colored people, Negroes, Blacks, Afro-Americans (take your choice) / by Daniel Y. Stewart. 1st ed. [s.l. : s.n.], c1977 (New Haven : Advocate Press) 74 p. : ill. ; 22 cm. [F104.N69N337] 77-150704
1. Afro-Americans—Connecticut—New Haven—History. 2. Afro-Americans—Connecticut—New Haven—Biography. 3. New Haven—Race relations. 4. New Haven—Biography. I. Title.

Afro-Americans—Employment—New York (City)

YOUNG Men's Christian Associations. Greater New York. Harlem Branch. 338'.092'2
A salute to Black achievers in industry. 5th ed. New York : Harlem YMCA, 1975. [36] p. : ill. ; 28 cm. Cover title. [F128.9.N3Y68 1975] 75-322332
1. Afro-Americans—Employment—New York (City) I. Title.

Afro-Americans in medicine—Biography—Juvenile literature.

HAYDEN, Robert C. 610'.92'2 B
Nine Black American doctors / by Robert C. Hayden and Jacqueline Harris. Reading, Mass. : Addison-Wesley, c1976. p. cm. "An Addisonian Press book." Includes index. Biographical sketches of nine Afro-Americans who have made significant contributions to medicine. [R153.H39] 920 76-15172 ISBN 0-201-02842-5 lib.bdg. : 6.50
1. Afro-Americans in medicine—Biography—Juvenile literature. I. Harris, Jacqueline L., joint author. II. Title. BIP

Afro-Americans in motion pictures.

SAMPSON, Henry T., 1934- 791.43'092'2 B
Blacks in black and white : a source book on Black films / by Henry T. Sampson. Metuchen, N.J. : Scarecrow Press, 1977. x, 333 p. : ill. ; 23 cm. Includes index. [PN1995.9.N4S2] 77-637 ISBN 0-8108-1023-9 : 13.00
1. Afro-Americans in motion pictures. I. Title. BIP

Afro-Americans—Michigan—Detroit—Biography.

BOONE-JONES, Margaret. 920'.0774'34
To be somebody : portraits of nineteen beautiful Detroiters / by Margaret Boone-Jones. 1st ed. New York : Vantage Press, c1976. ix, 100 p. : ports. ; 22 cm. [F574.D4B54] 76-360170 ISBN 0-533-01871-4 : 4.95
1. Afro-Americans—Michigan—Detroit—Biography. 2. Detroit—Biography. I. Title.

RUSSELL, Anne E. 920'.009296073077434
Builders of Detroit : biographical sketches of 62 outstanding Blacks / Anne D. Russell ; cover design by author ; section dividers by Wendell O. Mason. [1st ed.]. [Pontiac, Mich.] : Russell, [1979, c1978] 152 p. : ports ; 23 cm. [F574.D49N48 1979] 79-65877 ISBN 0-932212-18-2 : 7.00
1. Afro-Americans—Michigan—Detroit—Biography. 2. Detroit—Biography. I. Title.

Afro-Americans—Minnesota—Biography.

MINNESOTA'S Black community. 977.6'004'96073 Minneapolis : Scott Pub. Co., c1976. 216 p. : ill. ; 29 cm. Includes bibliographical references. [E185.93.M55M56] 76-151439
1. Afro-Americans—Minnesota—Biography. 2. Minnesota—Biography. I. Scott Publishing Company, Minneapolis.

Afro-Americans—Mississippi—Biography.

SEWELL, George Alexander. 920'.0092'960730762
Mississippi Black history makers / George Alexander Sewell ; introd. by Margaret Walker. Jackson : University Press of Mississippi, c1977. p. cm. Includes index. Bibliography: p. [E185.93.M6S48] 77-8797 ISBN 0-87805-040-X
1. Afro-Americans—Mississippi—Biography. 2. Mississippi—Biography. I. Title. BIP

Afro-Americans—Segregation.

EAST, P. D. 920.5
The magnolia jungle; the life, times, and education of a southern editor. New York, Simon and Schuster, 1960. 243 p. illus. 22 cm. [PN4874.E3A3] 60-10973
1. The Petal paper. 2. Afro-Americans—Segregation. I. Title.

Afro-Americans—The West—Biography—Juvenile literature.

KATZ, William Loren. 978'.004'96073 B
Black people who made the Old West / by William Loren Katz. New York : Crowell, c1977. x, 181 p. : ill. ; 24 cm. "Juvenile version of ... The Black West: a documentary and pictorial history." Includes index. Bibliography: p. [175]-176. Biographical sketches of thirty-five black people who explored and settled the frontiers of the early United States. [E185.925.K38] 920 76-7051 ISBN 0-690-01253-5 : 7.95
1. Afro-Americans—The West—Biography—Juvenile literature. 2. Frontier and pioneer life—The West Juvenile literature. 3. The West—Biography—Juvenile literature. I. Title. BIP

Agam, Yaacov, 1928-

POPPER, Frank, 1918- 709'.2'4
Agam / by Frank Popper. New York : H. N. Abrams, [1976, i.e.1975] p. cm. Includes index. Bibliography: p. [N7279.A4P66] 75-5580 ISBN 0-8109-0294-X : 7.95
1. Agam, Yaacov, 1928- I. Agam, Yaacov, 1928- II. Title. BIP

Agassiz, Elizabeth Cabot Cary, 1822-1907.

PATON, Lucy Allen. 378.744'4 B
Elizabeth Cary Agassiz; a biography. New York, Arno Press, 1974 [c1919] 423 p. illus. 21 cm. (Women in America: from colonial times to the 20th century) Reprint of the ed. published by Houghton Mifflin, Boston. [QH31.A19P3 1974] 74-3969 ISBN 0-405-06117-X
1. Agassiz, Elizabeth Cabot Cary, 1822-1907. 2. Agassiz, Louis, 1807-1873. I. Title. II. Series. BIP

Agassiz, Louis, 1807-1873.

FORSEE, Aylesa. 925.9
Louis Agassiz: Pied piper of science. Illustrated by Winifred Lubell. New York. Viking Press [1958] 244 p. illus. 22 cm. [QH31.A2F6] 58-10604
1. Agassiz, Louis, 1807-1873.

GUYOT, Arnold Henry, 1807-1884. 925.7
Memoir of Louis Agassiz, 1807-1873. Read before the National Academy, Apr. 1878. [Washington? n. d.] 39-73 p. 24 cm. [QH31.A2G9] 50-48003
1. Agassiz, Louis, 1807-1873. I. Title.

LURIE, Edward, 1927- v. 12
Louis Agassiz: a life in science. Chicago, University of Chicago Press [1966, c1960] of Chicago Press [1966, c1960] xvi, 390 p. (Phoenix books, P248) "First Phoenix ed. (abridged)" 67-100707
1. Agassiz, Louis, 1807-1873. I. Title.

LURIE, Edward, 1927- 500.1'092'4 B
Nature and the American mind: Louis Agassiz and the culture of science. New York, Science History Publications [1974] 121 p. illus. 21 cm. Includes bibliographical references. [QH31.A2L83] 74-933 ISBN 0-88202-011-0 5.00
1. Agassiz, Louis, 1807-1873. 2. Natural history—United States—History. 3. Naturalists—Biography. I. Title.

PEARE, Catherine Owens. 925.9
A scientist of two worlds: Louis Agassiz. [1st ed.] Philadelphia, Lippincott [1958] 188 p. illus. 22 cm. [QH31.A2P4] 58-11882
1. Agassiz, Louis, 1807-1873. I. Title.

ROBINSON, Mabel Louise. 500.1'092'4 B
Runner of the mountain tops; the life of Louis Agassiz. With decorations by Lynd Ward. New York, Random House. Detroit, Grand River Books, 1971 [c1939] 290 p. illus. 22 cm. Bibliography: p. 285-286. [QH31.A2R6 1971] 73-167139
1. Agassiz, Louis, 1807-1873. I. Title. BIP

Agassiz, Louis, 1807-1873 — Juvenile literature.

THARP, Louise (Hall) 1898- 925.9
Louis Agassiz, adventurous scientist. Illustrated by Rafaello Busoni. [1st ed.] Boston, Little, Brown [1961] 200 p. illus. 22 cm. [QH31.A2T53] 61-5332
1. Agassiz, Louis, 1807-1873 — Juvenile literature. I. Title.

Agate, James Evershed, 1877-1947—Diaries.

AGATE, James Evershed, 1877-1947. 792'.092'4 B
The selective Ego : the diaries of James Agate / newly edited by Tim Beaumont. London : Harrap, 1976. xii, 269 p. ; 23 cm. Originally published 1935-1948 in 9 v. under title: Ego. Includes index. [PR6001.G3Z592 1976] 76-383626 ISBN 0-245-52849-0 : £5.75
1. Agate, James Evershed, 1877-1947—Diaries. 2. Authors, English—20th century—Biography. I. Beaumont, Timothy Wentworth. II. Title.

Aged—Biog.

FISCHER, Philip A. 920.020
Beyond three-score and ten. New York, Carlton [dist. Comet, c.]1961. 111p. (Reflection bk.) 61-66548 2.75
1. Aged—Biog. I. Title.

Aged—Biography—Addresses, essays, lectures.

VINTAGE, thirty-eight life stories / 301.43'5'0922 Joan Dufault. New York : Pilgrim Press, c1978. p. cm. [HQ1060.5.V55] 78-17574 ISBN 0-8298-0356-4 : 11.95
1. Aged—Biography—Addresses, essays, lectures. 2. Aged—Pictorial works. I. Dufault, Joan, 1925-

Aged—United States—Biography.

GELLER, Arthur. 301.43'5'0973
Living longer and loving it / by Arthur and Deborah Geller. Maplewood, N.J. : Hammond, c1978. p. cm. [HQ1064.U6G35] 78-5851 ISBN 0-8437-3409-4 : 7.95
1. Aged—United States—Biography. 2. Aged—United States—Attitudes. I. Geller, Deborah, joint author. II. Title. BIP

Aged—United States—Biography—Juvenile literature.

ANCONA, George. 301.43'5'0922 B
Growing older / by George Ancona. 1st ed. New York : Dutton, c1978. p. cm. Presents anecdotal rememberances of older people as told to the author. [HQ1064.U5A648 1978] 920 78-7605 7.95
1. Aged—United States—Biography—Juvenile literature. I. Title. BIP

Agee, James, 1909-1955.

MOREAU, Genevieve. 813'.5'2 B
The restless journey of James Agee / Genevieve Moreau ; translated from the French by Miriam Kleiger, with the assistance of Morty Schiff. New York : Morrow, 1977. 320 p. ; 25 cm. Includes index. Bibliography: p. [281]-289. [PS3501.G35Z786] 76-25832 ISBN 0-688-03141-2 : 10.95
1. Agee, James, 1909-1955. I. Title. BIP

Agee, James, 1909-1955—Biography.

MADDEN, David, 1933- comp. 818'.5'209 B
Remembering James Agee / edited by David Madden. Baton Rouge : Louisiana State University Press, [1974] 172 p. : ports. ; 24 cm. [PS3501.G35Z78] 74-77326 8.95
1. Agee, James, 1909-1955—Biography. I. Title.
Contents omitted. BIP

Aggrey, James Emman Kwegyir, 1875-1927.

AGEE, James, 1909-1955. 818'.5'209
Letters of James Agee to Father Flye. With a new pref. and previously unpublished letters by Father Flye. 2d ed. Boston, Houghton Mifflin, 1971. x, 267 p. 22 cm. [PS3501.G35Z54 1971] 76-146717 ISBN 0-395-12341-0 5.95
I. Flye, James Harold. II. Title. BIP

SMITH, Edwin William, 1876-1957. 370'.924 B
Aggrey of Africa; a study in Black and white, by Edwin W. Smith. Freeport, N.Y., Books for Libraries Press, 1971. xii, 292 p. illus. 23 cm. (The Black heritage library collection) Reprint of the 1929 ed. [LA2387.S6 1971] 70-173617 ISBN 0-8369-8909-0
1. Aggrey, James Emman Kwegyir, 1875-1927. I. Title. II. Series.

Agle, Nan Hayden.

AGLE, Nan Hayden. 813'.5'4 B
My animals and me; an autobiographical story. Photos. by Emily Hayden. New York, Seabury Press [1970] 119 p. illus., ports. 24 cm. An autobiographical account of a little girl's family life and pets in pre-World War 1 Maryland. [PS3551.G55Z5] 92 76-115783 4.95
I. Hayden, Emily, illus. II. Title.

Agnes, Saint, 3d cent.

ANDRE-DELASTRE, Louise 922.237
Saint Agnes. Tr. by Rosemary Sheed. New York, Macmillan [c.]1962. c192p. 18cm. (Your name--Your saint ser.) Bibl. 61-16724 2.50
1. Agnes, Saint, 3d cent. I. Title.

ANDRE-DELASTRE, Louise. 922.237
Saint Agnes. Translated by Rosemary Sheed. New York, Macmillan, 1962. 102p. 18cm. (Your name--your saint series)

Includes bibliography. [BX4700.A3A53] 61-16724
1. Agnes, Saint, 3d cent. I. Title.

CHARLESWORTH, Martin Percival, 1895-1950. 920.037
Five men; character studies from the Roman Empire. Freeport, N.Y., Books for Libraries Press [1967] viii, 170 p. 22 cm. (Essay index reprint series) Martin classical lectures, v.6. Reprint of the 1936 ed. Includes bibliographical references. [PA25.M3 vol. 6 1967] 67-30202
1. Agrippa I, King of Judea, B. C. 10 (ca.)-A. D. 44. 2. Musonius Rufus, C. 3. Josephus, Flavius. 4. Agricola, Cn. Julius, 37-93. 5. Rome—Civilization. I. Title. II. Series: Martin classical lectures, v. 6 BIP

ERNEST, Brother, 1897- 922.137
A story of Saint Agnes. Pictures by Sister Mary Manus. Notre Dame, Dame, Ind., Dujarie Press [1956] unpaged. illus. 22cm. [BX4700.A3E7] 56-42848
1. Agnes, Saint, 3d cent. I. Title.

FLAMES for the bride; a story of Saint Agnes. v. 12 Illustrations by Thekla Ofria. Notre Dame, Ind., Dujarie Press [c1958] 94p. illus. 24cm.
1. Agnes, Saint, 3d century. I. Roberto, Brother, 1927-

KEYES, Frances Parkinson (Wheeler) 1885- 922.22
Three ways of love. New York, Hawthorn, [c1933] 299p. illus. 24cm. Bibl. 63-16770 5.00
1. Agnes, Saint, 3d cent. 2. Francesca, Saint, 1384-1440. 3. Caterina da siena, Saint, 1347-1380. 4. Saints, Italian. I. Title. BIP

KEYES, Frances Parkinson (Wheeler) 1885-1970. 922.22
Three ways of love. [1st ed.] New York, Hawthorn Books [1963] 299 p. illus. 24 cm. Errata slip inserted. Bibliography: p. 286-290. [BX4659.I8K46] 63-16770
1. Agnes, Saint, 3d century. 2. Francesca, Saint, 1384-1440. 3. Caterina da Siena, Saint, 1347-1380. 4. Christian saints—Italy. I. Title.

Agnew, Spiro T., 1918-

AGNEW, Spiro T., 1918- 973.924'0924
The real Spiro Agnew; commonsense quotations of a household word. Edited by James Calhoun. Foreword by Al Capp. Illustrated by Charles Brooks. Gretna [La.] Pelican Pub. Co., 1970. 127 p. illus. 24 cm. [E840.8.A34A56] 73-131935 5.95
I. Title.

AGNEW, Spiro T., 1918- 973.923'0924
Where he stands; the life and convictions of Spiro T. Agnew. With an introd. by Richard M. Nixon. [1st ed.] New York, Hawthorn Books [1968] vii, 116 p. illus. 21 cm. Selections from speeches, interviews, and press releases. [F186.2.A7] 68-57984 1.50
I. Title.

ALBRIGHT, Joseph. 973.924'092'4 B
What makes Spiro run; the life and times of Spiro Agnew. New York, Dodd, Mead [1972] xiii, 295 p. 22 cm. [E840.8.A34A68] 75-38525 ISBN 0-396-06551-1 6.95
1. Agnew, Spiro T., 1918- I. Title.

HOFFMAN, Paul, 1934- 973.924'0924
Spiro! [New York, Tower Publications, 1971] 186 p. 19 cm. (A Tower public affairs book) Includes bibliographical references. [E840.8.A34H6] 76-27309 0.95
1. Agnew, Spiro T., 1918- I. Title.

LIPPMAN, Theo. 973.924'0924 B
Spiro Agnew's America. [1st ed.] New York, Norton [1972] 256 p. 21 cm. [E840.8.A34L5] 71-38950 ISBN 0-393-07470-6
1. Agnew, Spiro T., 1918- I. Title.

LUCAS, Jim Griffing, 1914- 973.924'0924
Agnew: profile in conflict [by] Jim G. Lucas. New York, Award Books; distributed by Scribner [1970] 160 p. 22 cm. [E840.8.A34L8] 70-124445 5.95
1. Agnew, Spiro T., 1918- I. Title.

MARSH, Robert, 1932- 973.924'0924
Agnew: the unexamined man; a political profile. New York, M. Evans and distributed in association with Lippincott, Philadelphia [1971] ix, 182 p. 22 cm. [E840.8.A34M3] 70-150797 5.95
1. Agnew, Spiro T., 1918- I. Title. BIP

PETERSON, Robert W. 973.924'092'4
Agnew: the coining of a household word. Edited by Robert W. Peterson. New York, Facts on File [1972] ii, 181 p. 21 cm. (Interim history) (A Facts on File publication) [E840.8.A34P4] 70-183844 ISBN 0-87196-225-X
1. Agnew, Spiro T., 1918- I. Title.

WITCOVER, Jules. 973.924'0924 B
White knight; the rise of Spiro Agnew. [1st ed.] New York, Random House [1972] xii, 465 p. 25 cm. [E840.8.A34W5] 76-37425 ISBN 0-394-47216-0 10.00
1. Agnew, Spiro T., 1918- I. Title.

Agnew, Spiro T., 1918-—Juvenile literature.

KURLAND, Gerald, 1942- 973.924'092'4 B
Spiro Agnew, controversial Vice-President of the Nixon administration. Charlotteville, N.Y., SamHar Press, 1972. 32 p. 22 cm. (Outstanding personalities, no. 16) Includes bibliographical references. A biography of the Maryland governor who became Vice-President of the United States in the Nixon administration. [E840.8.A34K87] 92 72-190234 ISBN 0-87157-516-7
1. Agnew, Spiro T., 1918-—Juvenile literature. I. Title.
PLB 1.98, pap. 0.98.

Agobard, Saint, Abp. of Lyons, d. 840.

CABANISS, James Allen, 1911- 922.144
Agobard of Luons, churchman and critic. [Syracuse] Syracuse University Press [1953] 137p. 23cm. [BX4700.A33C32] 53-3605
1. Agobard, Saint, Abp. of Lyons, d. 840. I. Title.

Agricola, Cn. Julius, 37-93.

CHARLESWORTH, Martin Percival, 1895-1950. 920.037
Five men; character studies from the Roman Empire. Freeport, N.Y., Books for Libraries Press [1967] viii, 170 p. 22 cm. (Essay index reprint series) (Martin classical lectures, v. 6.) Reprint of the 1936 ed. Includes bibliographical references. [PA25.M3 vol. 6 1967] 67-30202
1. Agrippa I, King of Judea, B.C. 10 (ca.)-A.D. 44. 2. Agricola, Cn. Julius, 37-93. 3. Musonius Rufus, C. 4. Josephus, Flavius. 5. Rome—Civilization. I. Title. II. Series.

Agricultural laborers—California.

[ERICKSON, Bruce] 331.5'44'0924 B
The whole works; the autobiography of a young American couple [by Bruce and Gail Erickson, as recorded and edited by] Starry Krueger. [1st ed.] New York, Random House [1973] xviii, 205 p. 22 cm. [HD1527.C2E7] 73-6874 ISBN 0-394-48691-9 5.95
1. Agricultural laborers—California. 2. Migrant labor—California. I. Erickson, Gail. II. Krueger, Starry. III. Title.

Agriculture—Addresses, essays, lectures.

BUEL, Jesse, 1778-1839. 630'.8
Jesse Buel, agricultural reformer. Selections from his writings, edited, with introd. by Harry J. Carman. New York, Arno Press, 1972 [c1947] xxxvi, 609 p. illus. 23 cm. (Use and abuse of America's natural resources) Original ed. issued as no. 12 of Columbia University studies in the history of American agriculture. Includes bibliographical references. [S523.B925 1972] 72-2835 ISBN 0-405-04503-4 28.00
1. Agriculture—Addresses, essays, lectures. I. Title. II. Series. III. Series: Columbia University studies in the history of American agriculture, no. 12.

Agriculturists.

CANNON, Grant G. 926.3
Great men of modern agriculture. New York, Macmillan [c.1963] 256p. illus., ports. 22cm. Based on articles orig. pub. by the Farm quarterly. Bibl. 63-14540 4.95
1. Agriculturists. I. Title. BIP

DIRLAM, H Kenneth. 926.3
John Chapman, 'by occupation a gatherer and planter of appleseeds.' [Mansfield, Ohio, Richland County Historical Society, 1954] 64p. illus. 28cm. Program of Richland County's tribute to John Chapman, Sept. 25-26, 1953 (4p.) in pocket. [S417.C45D5] 55-16158
I. sChapman, John, 1774-1845. II. Title.

Agriculturists—Biography.

HUTCHINSON, Martin T. 630'.92'2 B
Roster of scientists for the major food crops of the world. Compiled by Martin T. Hutchinson. Washington, Office of Agriculture, Agency for International Development, 1973. 187, [48] p. 27 cm. [S415.H87] 74-600627
1. Agriculturists—Biography. 2. Agriculturists—Directories. I. United States. Agency for International Development. Office of Agriculture. II. Title.

Agriculturists-Kansas.

CALL, Leland Everett, 1881- v. 12
An autobiography. Manhattan, Kan., Kansas State University, 1967.C126 p. 68-32509
1. Agriculturists-Kansas. I. Title.

Agriculturists—United States—Biography.

DIES, Edward Jerome, 1891- 630'.92'2 B
Titans of the soil : great builders of agriculture / Edward Jerome Dies. Westport, Conn. : Greenwood Press, 1976, c1949. ix, 213 p., [18] leaves of plates : ports. ; 23 cm. Reprint of the ed. published by University of North Carolina Press, Chapel Hill. Includes index. Contents.Contents.—Food and freedom.—George Washington, farmer of Mount of Vernon.—Thomas Jefferson, farmer of Monticello.—Elkanah Watson, father of State fairs.—Eli Whitney, immortal mechanical genius.—Henry L. Ellsworth, soldier of the land.—Edmund Ruffin, father of soil chemistry.—John Deere, he turned the prairies.—Cyrus Hall McCormick, man with the reaper.—Justin S. Morrill, he lighted candles of wisdom.—Samuel W. Johnson, genius of the test tube.—Wilbur Olin Atwater, master of nutrition.—Seaman A. Knapp, schoolmaster of agriculture.—Stephen Moulton Babcock, the jolly scientist.—Theobald Smith, conqueror of Texas fever.—Mark A. Carleton, wheat explorer.—Harvey W. Wiley, apostle of pure food.—George HarrOTitans of the soil : great builders of agriculture / Edward Jerome Dies. Westport, Conn. : Greenwood Press, 1976, c1949. ix, 213 p., [18] leaves of plates : ports. ; 2
1. Agriculturists—United States—Biography. I. Title.
Contents omitted BIP

Agrippa I, King of Judea, B.C. 10 (ca.)-A.D. 44.

CHARLESWORTH, Martin Percival, 1895-1950. 920.037
Five men; character studies from the Roman Empire. Freeport, N.Y., Books for Libraries Press [1967] viii, 170 p. 22 cm. (Essay index reprint series) (Martin classical lectures, v. 6.) Reprint of the 1936 ed. Includes bibliographical references. [PA25.M3 vol. 6 1967] 67-30202
1. Agrippa I, King of Judea, B.C. 10 (ca.)-A.D. 44. 2. Agricola, Cn. Julius, 37-93. 3. Musonius Rufus, C. 4. Josephus, Flavius. 5. Rome—Civilization. I. Title. II. Series.

Aguilar, Jeronimo de, d. 1526?

BUTTERFIELD, Marvin Ellis, 1897- 972'.02'0924 B
Jeronimo de Aguilar, conquistador, by Marvin E. Butterfield. University [University of Alabama Press, c1969] 54 p. 23 cm. (University of Alabama studies, no. 10) "Reissued under the sponsorship of the Latin American Studies Program of the University of Alabama." Bibliography: p. [51]-54. [F1230.A44B8 1969] 76-14440
1. Aguilar, Jeronimo de, d. 1526? 2. Mexico—History—Conquest, 1519-1540. I. Series: Alabama. University. University of Alabama studies, no. 10 BIP

Aguirre, Lope de, d. 1561.

LOWRY, Walker. 923.98
Lope Aguirre, the Wanderer. New York, Bookman Associates [c1952] 78p. 23cm. [E125.A35L64] 53-6457
1. Aguirre, Lope de, d. 1561. I. Title.

Ahaz, King of Judah—Fiction.

HEAD, Constance. FIC
Ahaz / Constance Head. Nashville : Broadman Press, c1979. 264 p. ; 22 cm. [PZ4.H4324Ah] [PS3558.E137] 813'.5'4 79-50340 ISBN 0-8054-7309-2 : 7.95
1. Ahaz, King of Judah—Fiction. 2. Bible. O.T.—Biography. I. Title. BIP

Aherne, Brian.

AHERNE, Brian. 791.43'028'0924 B
A proper job. Boston, Houghton Mifflin, 1969. xi, 355 p. illus., ports. 22 cm. Autobiographical. [PN2287.A44A3] 71-80415
I. Title.

Ahmad Bey, Bey of Tunis, d. 1855.

BROWN, Leon Carl, 1928- 961'.1'03
The Tunisia of Ahmad Bey, 1837-1855 [by] L. Carl Brown. [Princeton, N.J.] Princeton University Press [1974] xviii, 409 p. illus. 25 cm. (Princeton studies on the Near East) Bibliography: p. 383-397. [DT264.B76] 73-16770 ISBN 0-691-03100-2 20.00
1. Ahmad Bey, Bey of Tunis, d. 1855. 2. Tunisia—History—1516-1881. 3. Tunisia—Politics and government. I. Title. II. Series. BIP

Ahmad Khan, Syed, Sir, 1817-1898.

MCDONOUGH, Sheila. 297'.0922
The authority of the past; a study of three Muslim modernists. Chambersburg, Pa., American Academy of Religion, 1970. 56 p. 24 cm. (AAR studies in religion, 1970:1) Bibliography: p. 55-56. [BP63.I4M24] 76-141690
1. Ahmad Khan, Syed, Sir, 1817-1898. 2. Iqbal, Muhammad, Sir, 1877-1938. 3. Parwez, Ghulam Ahmad, 1903- 4. Islam—India. I. Title. II. Series: American Academy of Religion. AAR studies in religion, 1970:1

Ahrens family.

BRIDWELL, Margaret 929'.2'0973
Morris, 1905-
The Ahrens story. [Louisville, Ky., 1954] 73p. illus. 25cm. [CS71.A255 1954] 54-12026
1. Ahrens family. I. Title.

Aiken, Conrad Potter,

AIKEN, Conrad Potter, 811'.5'2
1889-
The charnel rose, Senlin: a biography, and other poems, by Conrad Aiken. New York, Haskell House Publishers, 1971. 156 p. 23 cm. [PS3501.I5C5 1971] 79-156910 ISBN 0-8383-1247-0 8.95
I. Title.

AIKEN, Conrad Potter, 1889- 928.1
Ushant, an essay [Gloucester, Mass., P. Smith, 1963,c.1952,1962] 365p. 18cm. (Meridian bk. M148 rebound) 3.75
I. Title.

AIKEN, Conrad Potter, 1889- 928.1
Ushant, an essay. New York, Cleveland. World [c.1952,1962] 365p. 18cm. (Meridian bks., M. 148) 1.75 pap.,
I. Title **BIP**

AIKEN, Conrad Potter, 1889- 928.1
Ushant; an essay. Cleveland, World Pub. Co. [1962] 365 p. 18 cm. (Meridian books, M148) Autobiographical. [PS3501.I5Z53 1962] 62-53419
I. Title.

AIKEN, Conrad 818'.5'209 B
Potter, 1889-
Ushant: an essay, by Conrad Aiken. New York, Oxford University Press, 1971. 365 p. illus., ports. 22 cm. Autobiographical. [PS3501.I5Z53 1971] 72-159980 ISBN 0-19-501452-9 9.50
I. Title.

AIKEN, Conrad Potter, 1889- 928.1
Ushant, an essay. [1st ed.] New York, Duell, Sloan and Pearce [1952] 365 p. 22 cm. Autobiographical. [PS3501.I5Z53] 52-9071
I. Title.

Aikens, Thomas, 1900-

MOLES, Ian, 1935- 994.3'04'0924 B
A majority of one : Tom Aikens and independent politics in Townsville / Ian Moles. St. Lucia, Q. : University of Queensland Press, 1979. xv, 258 p. : ill., maps ; 22 cm. Distributed in the United Kingdom by Prentice-Hall International, Hemel Hempstead, Eng. Includes index. Bibliography: p. [245]-251. [DU272.A45M64] 79-317180 ISBN 0-7022-1285-7 : 18.00
1. Aikens, Thomas, 1900- 2. Queensland—Politics and government. 3. Statesmen—Australia—Queensland—Biography. 4. Queensland—Biography. I. Title.
Dist. by TIC, Lawrence, Mass. **BIP**

Ainsley, Lillian.

DABNEY, Owen P. 973'.04'97 S
The lost shackle / Owen P. Dabney. New York : Garland Pub., 1977, [c1897] 98 p. : ill. ; 23 cm. (The Garland library of narratives of North American Indian captivities ; v. 99) Issued with the reprint of the 1894 ed. of Mrs. J. E. De Camp Sweet's narrative of her captivity ... New York, 1976. Reprint of the ed. published by O. P. Dabney, Salem, Or., under title: True story of the lost shackle. [E85.G2 vol.99] [E87] 970'.004'97 75-7126 ISBN 0-8240-1723-4 lib.bdg. : 25.00
1. Ainsley, Lillian. 2. Bently, Matthew. 3. Indians of North America—Captivities. I. Title. II. Series.

DABNEY, Owen P. 973'.04'97 S
The lost shackle / Owen P. Dabney. New York : Garland Pub., 1977, [c1897] 98 p. : ill. ; 23 cm. (The Garland library of narratives of North American Indian captivities ; v. 99) Issued with the reprint of the 1894 ed. of Mrs. J. E. De Camp Sweet's narrative of her captivity ... New York, 1976. Reprint of the ed. published by O. P. Dabney, Salem, Or., under title: True story of the lost shackle. [E85.G2 vol.99] [E87] 970'.004'97 75-7126 ISBN 0-8240-1723-4 lib.bdg. : 25.00
1. Ainsley, Lillian. 2. Bently, Matthew. 3. Indians of North America—Captivities. I. Title. II. Series.

Ainsworth, William Harrison, 1805-1882—Biography.

ELLIS, Stewart Marsh. 823'.8 B
William Harrison Ainsworth and his friends / by S. M. Ellis. New York : Garland Pub., 1979. p. cm. (The Fiction of popular culture) Reprint of the 1911 ed. published by J. Lane, London and New York. Includes index. "Bibliography of the works of William Harrison Ainsworth": v. 1, p. [PR4003.E5 1979] 78-60905 ISBN 0-8240-9663-0 : 80.00
1. Ainsworth, William Harrison, 1805-1882—Biography. 2. Novelists, English—19th century—Biography. I. Title. II. Series.

Air pilots.

CLARKE, Thomas S M 926.2913
The flying aces of the world. Richmond, Mistral Publications, 1963- v. illus. 28 cm. [TL539.C56] 64-3668
1. Air pilots. 2. Aeronautics, Military — Biog. I. Title.

HIRSCH, Phil, ed. 926.36
Fighting eagles. New York, Pyramid Books [1961] 160p. 19cm. [TL539.H5] 61-65945
1. Air pilots. 2. Aeronautics, Military. I. Title.

Air pilots—Biography.

FORRESTER, Larry. 629.13'092'2
Skymen : heroes of fifty years of flying / by Larry Forrester. New York : St. Martin's Press, [1977] c1961. p. cm. Reprint of the ed. published by Collins, London. [TL539.F6 1977] 76-62765 ISBN 0-312-72782-8 : 7.95
1. Air pilots—Biography. 2. Aeronautics—History. I. Title. **BIP**

ORMES, Ian. 629.13'092'2 B
The sky masters / [by] Ian and Ralph Ormes. London : Kimber, 1976. 224 p., [12] p. of plates : ill., ports. ; 24 cm. Includes index. Bibliography: p. 215-216. [TL539.O39] 76-375369 ISBN 0-7183-0284-2 : £5.50
1. Air pilots—Biography. I. Ormes, Ralph, joint author. II. Title.

Air pilots—Correspondence, reminiscences, etc.

BACH, Richard. 629.13'094
Stranger to the ground. Introd. by Gill Robb Wilson. New York, Harper & Row [1972] xii, 178 p. illus. 22 cm. [TL540.B27A3 1972] 72-193375 ISBN 0-06-010182-2 5.95
1. Air pilots—Correspondence, reminiscences, etc. 2. Fighter planes—Piloting. I. Title. **BIP**

CROSSFIELD, Albert 926.2913
Scott, 1921-
Always another dawn; the story of a rocket test pilot, by A. Scott Crossfield with Clay Blair, Jr. [1st ed.] Cleveland, World Pub. Co. [1960] 421 p. illus. 22 cm. [TL540.C84A3] 60-14641
1. Air pilots—Correspondence, reminiscences, etc. 2. Airplanes—Flight testing. 3. X-15 (Rocket aircraft) I. Blair, Clay, 1925- II. Title. **BIP**

CROSSFIELD, Albert 629.13'092'4 B
Scott, 1921-
Always another dawn; the story of a rocket test pilot, by A. Scott Crossfield, with Clay Blair, Jr. [New York] Arno Press [1972, c1960] 421 p. illus. 23 cm. (Literature and history of aviation) [TL540.C84A3 1972] 73-169413 ISBN 0-405-03758-9
1. Air pilots—Correspondence, reminiscences, etc. 2. Aeroplanes—Flight testing. 3. X-15 (Rocket aircraft) I. Blair, Clay, 1925- II. Title. III. Series.

HODGKINSON, Colin. 926.2913
Best foot forward, the autobiography of Colin Hodgkinson. [1st American ed.] New York, Norton [1957] 269p. 22cm. [TL540.H6A3 1957a] 57-12334
1. Air pilots—Correspondence, reminiscences, Etc. 2. World War, 1939-1945— Personal narratives, British. 3. Amputees. I. Title.

KLOTZ, Alexis 926.2913
Three years off this earth. Garden City, N. Y., Doubleday, 1960[c.1959, 1960] 396p. illus. 24cm. 60-15107 4.95
1. Air pilots—Correspondence, reminiscences, etc. I. Title.

KLOTZ, Alexis, 1905- 926.2913
Three years off this earth. San Francisco, Hooper Pub. Co., 1959. 396 p. illus. 24 cm. Autobiographical. [TL540.K55A3] 59-11358
1. Air pilots—Correspondence, reminiscences, etc. I. Title.

NICHOLS, Ruth, 1901- 926.2913
Wings for life. Foreword by Richard E. Byrd. Edited by Dorothy Roe Lewis. [1st ed.] Philadelphia, Lippincott [1957] 317p. illus. 21cm. Autobiographical. [TL540.N5A3] 57-10874
1. Air pilots—Correspondence, reminiscences, etc. I. Title.

REITSCH, Hanna. 926.2913
Flying is my life. Translated by Lawrence Wilson. New York, Putnam [1954] 246 p. illus. 21 cm. [TL540.R38A314] 54-10502
1. Air pilots—Correspondence, reminiscences, etc. I. Title.

SMITH, Dean C 926.2913
By the seat of my pants, [1st ed.] Boston, Little Brown [1961] 215 p. 22 cm. [TL510.S63A3] 61-12809
1. Air pilots — Correspondence, reminiscences, etc. I. Title.

SMITH, Dean C. 926.2913
By the seat of my pants. [1st ed.] Boston, Little, Brown [1961] 245 p. 22 cm. [TL540.S63A3] 61-12809
1. Air pilots—Correspondence, reminiscences, etc. I. Title.

WRIGHT, Wilbur, 1867-1912. 926.29
Miracle at Kitty Hawk; the letters of Wilbur and Orville Wright, edited by Fred C. Kelly. New York, Farrar Straus and Young [1951] ix, 482 p. illus., ports. 22 cm. [TL540.W7A23] 51-4201
1. Air pilots — Correspondence, reminiscences, etc. I. Wright, Orville, 1871-1948, joint author. II. Title.

WRIGHT, Wilbur, 629.13'092'4 B
1867-1912.
Miracle at Kitty Hawk; the letters of Wilbur and Orville Wright. Edited by Fred C. Kelly. [New York] Arno Press [1972, c1951] ix, 482 p. illus. 23 cm. (Literature and history of aviation) [TL540.W7A23 1972] 74-169424 ISBN 0-405-03769-4
1. Air pilots Correspondence, reminiscences, etc. I. Wright, Orville, 1871-1948. II. Title. III. Series.

WRIGHT, Wilbur, 1867-1912. 926.29
The papers of Wilbur and Orville Wright, including the Chanute-Wright letters and other papers of Octave Chanute. Marvin W. McFarland, editor. New York, McGraw-Hill [1953] 2v. (1v., 1278p.) illus., ports., facsims. 24cm. 'Sponsored by Oberlin College on the Wilbur- Orville Wright Memorial Fund and prepared for the press with notes, appendices, and bibliography by the Aeronautics Division of the Library of Congress.' Contents.v. 1 1899-1905 --v 2. 1906-1948. [TL540.W7A4] 53-9015
1. Air pilots- Correspondence, reminiscences, etc. I. Wright, Orvilley 1871-1948. II. Chanute, Octave. 1832-1910. III. McFarland, Marvin Wilks, 1919- ed. IV. Title.

Air pilots—United States—Biography.

HESS, William N. 358.4'00922
The American aces of World War II and Korea, by William N. Hess. Cover drawing: Richard Groh. New York, Arco Pub. Co. [1968] 64 p. illus., ports. 28 cm. (Famous airmen series) "A Len Morgan book." Bibliography: p. 64. [TL539.H44] 68-22398 2.95
1. Air pilots—United States—Biography. 2. Aeronautics, Military—United States—Biography. I. Title.

Aird, Sir John, bart., 1833-1911.

MIDDLEMAS, Robert Keith, 926.2
1935-
The master builders: Thomas Brassey, Sir John Aird, Lord Cowdray, London, Hutchinson [dist. Chester Springs, Pa., Dufour, 1964, c.1963] 328p. illus., maps, ports. 22cm. Bibl. [TA139.M5] 65-439 6.95
1. Brassey, Thomas, 1805-1870. 2. Aird, Sir John, bart., 1833-1911. 3. Cowdray, Weetman Dickinson Pearson, 1st viscount, 1856-1927. 4. Norton-Griffiths, Sir John, bart., 1871-1930. I. Title.

Airlines—Flight attendants—Correspondence, reminiscences, etc.

BAKER, Trudy. 387.7'42
Coffee, tea, or me? The uninhibited memoirs of two airline stewardesses [by] Trudy Baker and Rachel Jones. Illustrated by Bill Wenzell. [New York] Bartholomew House [1967] 288 p. illus. 22 cm. [D6073.A5B3] 67-17141
1. Airlines—Flight attendants—Correspondence, reminiscences, etc. I. Jones, Rachel, joint author. II. Title.

'A'ishah, 614 (ca.)-678.

ABBOTT, Nabia, 297'.64'0924 B
1897-
Aishah, the beloved of Mohammed. New York, Arno Press, 1973 [c1942] xiii, 230 p. illus. 21 cm. (The Middle East collection) Reprint of the ed. published by the University of Chicago Press, Chicago. Includes bibliographical references. [BP80.A52A62 1973] 73-6264 ISBN 0-405-05318-5 15.00
1. 'A'ishah, 614 (ca.)-678. I. Title. II. Series.

Aitken, John, 1936-

AITKEN, John, 1936- 320.9'71'0644
Conversations : the diary of a worried journalist's trek across a divided & threatened Canada / John Aitken. Scarborough, Ont. : Prentice-Hall of Canada, 1978. 179 p. ; 22 cm. [F1034.2.A6] 78-323996 ISBN 0-13-172056-2 pbk. 7.95
1. Aitken, John, 1936- 2. Nationalism—Canada—Public opinion. 3. Federal government—Canada—Public opinion. 4. Canada—Politics and government—1945-—Public opinion. 5. Public opinion—Canada. I. Title.
Available from Prentice-Hall, Englewood Cliffs, NJ **BIP**

Akana, A'lai A'ii Akamu, 1856-1939.

KAI, Peggy. 996.9'1 B
The story of A'lai : our Hawaiian-Chinese heritage / by Peggy Kai ; design by Marietta Baker Ojha. [s.l.] : Kai, c1976. 53 p., [1] fold. leaf : ill. ; 28 cm. Errata slip inserted. [DU629.H5A384] 77-361257
1. Akana, A'lai A'ii Akamu, 1856-1939. 2. A'ii family. 3. Hilo, Hawaii—Biography. I. Title.

Akeley, Carl Ethan, 1864-1926.

CLARK, James Lippitt, 590'.924
1883-
In the steps of the great American museum collector Carl Ethan Akeley by James L. Clark. Illus by Matthew Kalmenoff. New York, M. Evans; distributed in association with Lippincott, Philadelphia [1968] 127 p. illus. 21 cm. Bibliography: p. 127. [QL31.A5C6] 67-28198
1. Akeley, Carl Ethan, 1864-1926—Juvenile literature. 2. Zoological specimens—Collection and preservation—Juvenile literature. I. Title.

CLARK, James Lippitt, 069'.0924 B
1883-
In the steps of the great American museum collector Carl Ethan Akeley by James L. Clark. Illus. by Matthew Kalmenoff. New York, M. Evans; distributed in association with Lippincott, Philadelphia [1968] 127 p. illus. 21 cm. Bibliography: p. 127. A biography of the museum specialist who invented an inexpensive method of stuffing and displaying animals to make them look natural in a natural setting. [QL31.A5C6] 92 AC 68
1. Akeley, Carl Ethan, 1864-1926. 2. Zoological speciments—Collection and preservation. I. Kalmenoff, Matthew, illus. II. Title.

POND, Seymour Gates, 1896- 925.74
African explorer; the adventures of Carl

Akeley. New York, Dodd, Mead, 1957. 184 p. illus. 21 cm. [QL31.A5P6] 57-8316
1. Akeley, Carl Ethan, 1864-1926. I. Title.

POND, seymour Gates, 1896- 925.74
African explorer; the adventures of Carl Akeley. New York, Dodd, Mead, 1957. 184p. illus. 21cm. [QL31.A5P6] 57-8316
1. Akeley, Carl Ethan, 1864-1926. I. Title.

SUTTON, Felix 925.74
Big game hunter, Carl Akeley. New York, Messner [c.1960] 192p. Bibl.: p.187-188 22cm. 60-13266 2.95
1. Akeley, Carl Ethan, 1864-1926. I. Title.

Akeley, Carl Ethan, 1864-1926—Juvenile literature.

CLARK, James Lippitt, 1883- 590'.924
In the steps of the great American museum collector Carl Ethan Akeley by James L. Clark. Illus by Matthew Kalmenoff. New York, M. Evans; distributed in association with Lippincott, Philadelphia [1968] 127 p. illus. 21 cm. Bibliography: p. 127. [QL31.A5C6] 67-28198
1. Akeley, Carl Ethan, 1864-1926—Juvenile literature. 2. Zoological specimens—Collection and preservation—Juvenile literature. I. Title.

Akenside, Mark, 1721-1770.

HOUPT, Charles Theodore, 1912- 821'.6 B
Mark Akenside; a biographical and critical study. New York, Russell & Russell [1970, c1944] 180 p. 25 cm. Thesis—University of Pennsylvania, 1944. Bibliography: p. 172-180. [PR3313.H6 1970] 70-102504
1. Akenside, Mark, 1721-1770. I. Title. BIP

Akers, Paul, 1825-1861.

CARY, Richard, 1909-. v. 12
The misted prism: Paul Akers and Elizabeth Akers Allen, by Richard Cary. A new review of the career of Paul Akers, 1825-1861, by William B. Miller. Waterville, Me., 1966. [193]-256 p. illus., ports. 21 cm. (Colby library quarterly. ser. 7, no. 5) "Catalogue of works by Paul Akers," p. 253-255. Bibliographical footnotes. 67-19362
1. Akers, Paul, 1825-1861. 2. Allen, Elizabeth Ann (Chase) Akers, 1832-1911. I. Title.

Akihito, Crown Prince of Japan, 1933-

SIMON, Charlie May Hogue, 1897- 923.252
The sun and the birch; the story of Crown Prince Akihito and Crown Princess Michiko. Chapter headings by Grisha. [1st ed.] New York, Dutton, 1960. 192 p. illus. 21 cm. [DS890.A55S5] 60-6014
1. Akihito, Crown Prince of Japan, 1933- 2. Michiko, consort of Akihito, Crown Prince of Japan, 1934- I. Title.

VINING, Elizabeth (Gray) 1902- 952.033
Windows for the Crown Prince. [1st ed.] Philadelphia, Lippincott [1952] 320 p. illus. 22 cm. Autobiographical. [DS889.V5] 52-5098
1. Akihito, Crown Prince of Japan, 1933- 2. Japan—Social life and customs. 3. Education—Japan—1945- I. Title.

Aksakov, Sergei Timofeevich, 1791-1859—Biography—Ancestry.

AKSAKOV, Sergei Timafeevich, 1791-1859. FIC
A Russian gentleman / by Serge Aksakoff ; translated from the Russian by J. D. Duff. Westport, Conn. : Hyperion Press, 1977. 209 p. ; 21 cm. (Classics of Russian literature) (The Hyperion library of world literature) Translation of Semeinaia khronika. Reprint of the 1917 ed. published by E. Arnold, London. [PG3321.A5Z53513 1977] 891.7'3'3 B 76-23869 ISBN 0-88355-469-0 : 10.50.
1. Aksakov, Sergei Timofeevich, 1791-1859—Biography—Ancestry. 2. Aksakov family. 3. Russia—Social life and customs. 4. Russia—Biography. I. Duff, James Duff, 1860-1940.

Aksakov, Sergei Timofeevich, 1791-1859—Biography—Youth.

AKSAKOV, Sergei Timofeevich, 1791-1859. 891.7'3'3 B
A Russian schoolboy / Sergei Aksakov ; translated by J. D. Duff ; illustrated by Kirill Sokolov. Oxford : Oxford University Press, 1978. xii, 193 p. ; 23 cm. Translation of Vospominaniia, originally published together with the author's Semeinaia khronika. Continues The years of childhood. [PG3321.A5Z513 1978] 79-365030 ISBN 0-19-274526-3 : 10.95
1. Aksakov, Sergei Timofeevich, 1791-1859—Biography—Youth. 2. Authors, Russian—19th century—Biography. I. Title.
Available from Oxford University Press, NY, NY. BIP

AKSAKOV, Sergei Timofeevich, 1791-1859. 891.7'3'3 B
A Russian schoolboy / by Serge Aksakoff ; translated from the Russian by J. D. Duff. Westport, Conn. : Hyperion Press, 1977. ix, 216 p. ; 21 cm. (Classics of Russian literature) (The Hyperion library of world literature) Translation of Vospominaniia, originally published together with the author's Semeinaia khronika. Continues the Years of childhood. Reprint of the 1917 ed. published by Longmans, Green, New York. [PG3321.A5Z513 1977] 76-23871 ISBN 0-88355-473-9 : 10.95. ISBN 0-88355-474-7 pbk. : 3.95
1. Aksakov, Sergei Timofeevich, 1791-1859—Biography—Youth. 2. Authors, Russian—19th century—Biography. I. Duff, James Duff, 1860-1940. II. Title.

AKSAKOV, Sergei Timofeevich, 1791-1859 928.917
Years of childhood, by Sergey Aksakov. Newly translated [from the Russian] with an introduction by Alec Brown. Vantage Books [c.]1960. 407p. (Vintage Russian Lib. V-708) 60-51505 1.65 pap.,
I. Title.

AKSAKOV, Sergi Timofeevich, 1791-1859. 891.7'3'3 B
Years of childhood / by Serge Aksakoff ; translated from the Russian by J. D. Duff. Westport, Conn. : Hyperion Press, 1977. xi, 340 p. : port. ; 21 cm. (Classics of Russian literature) (The Hyperion library of world literature) Translation of Detskie gody Bagrova-vnuka. Reprint of the 1916 ed. published by E. Arnold, London. [PG3321.A5Z522 1977] 76-23870 ISBN 0-88355-471-2 : 12.50. ISBN 0-88355-472-0 pbk. : 4.95
1. Aksakov, Sergei Timofeevich, 1791-1859—Biography—Youth. 2. Authors, Russian—19th century—Biography. I. Title.

al-Afghani, Jamal al-Din, 1838-1897.

KEDDIE, Nikki R. 297'.092'4 B
Sayyid Jamal ad-Din "al-Afghani"; a political biography, by Nikki R. Keddie. Berkeley, University of California Press, 1972. xvii, 479 p. port. 24 cm. Bibliography: p. [451]-467. [BP80.A45K43] 74-159671 ISBN 0-520-01986-5 20.00
1. al-Afghani, Jamal al-Din, 1838-1897.

MUHAMMAD Zaki Badawi. 301.24'2'0962
The reformers of Egypt / M. A. Zaki Badawi. London : Croom Helm, c1978. 160 p. ; 23 cm. Includes bibliographical references and index. [BP64.E3M84 1978] 78-312985 ISBN 0-85664-651-2 : 19.00
1. al-Afghani, Jamal al-Din, 1838-1897. 2. Muhammad 'Abduh, 1849-1905. 3. Muhammad Rashid Rida. 4. Muslims in Egypt—Biography. 5. Islam—Egypt—History. I. Title.
Distributed by Biblio Distribution Centre, Totowa, NJ

al-'Alawi, Ahmad ibn Mustafa, 1869-1934.

LINGS, Martin. 297'.4'0924 B
A Sufi saint of the twentieth century: Shaikh Ahmad al-'Alawi; his spiritual heritage and legacy. 2d ed. rev. and enl. Berkeley, University of California Press [1971] 242 p. illus. 23 cm. First ed. published in 1961 under title: A Moslem saint of the twentieth century. Includes bibliographical references. [BP80.A54L5 1971b] 71-182282 ISBN 0-520-02174-6 8.75
1. al-'Alawi, Ahmad ibn Mustafa, 1869-1934. I. Title.

*LINGS, Martin. 297.4'0924 [B]
A Sufi saint of the twentieth century: Shaikh Ahmad al-'Alawi; his spiritual heritage and legacy. 2d ed. rev. and enl. Berkeley, University of California Press [1973, c.1971] 242 p. geneal. port. 21 cm. First published in 1961 by Macmillan under title: A Moslem saint of the twentieth century. Bibliography: p. 230-231. [BP80.A54L5] ISBN 0-520-02486-9 2.95 (pbk)
1. al-Alawi, Ahmad ibn Mustafa, 1869-1934. I. Title.
L.C. card no. for the Allen & Unwin (London) ed.: 77-882819.

al-Hallaj, al-Husayn ibn Mansur, 858 or 9-922.

BREWSTER, David Pearson, 1930- 297'.4'0924 B
Al Hallaj : Muslim mystic and martyr : translated extracts with a short biography and bibliography / D. P. Brewster Christchurch : University of Canterbury, Dept. of Philosophy and Religious Studies, 1976. 51 p. ; 21 cm. (Occasional papers in religious studies) Includes bibliographical references. [BP80.H27B73] 77-366228
1. al-Hallaj, al-Husayn ibn Mansur, 858 or 9-922. 2. Sufism—Biography. I. Title. II. Series.

al-Husari, Abu Khaldun Sati'.

CLEVELAND, William L. 320.5'4'0924 B
The making of an Arab nationalist; Ottomanism and Arabism in the life and thought of Sati' al-Husri, by William L. Cleveland. Princeton, N.J., Princeton University Press, 1971 [i.e. 1972] xvi, 211 p. port. 23 cm. (Princeton studies on the Near East) Bibliography: p. 185-205. [DS61.52.H87C55] 78-155961 ISBN 0-691-03088-X 8.50
1. al-Husari, Abu Khaldun Sati'. I. Title. II. Series. BIP

'Ali ibn 'Isa, Abbasid wazir, 859-946.

BOWEN, Harold. 909'.09'7671 B
The life and times of 'Ali ibn 'Isa, "the Good vizier" / by Harold Bowen. New York : AMS Press, [1975] p. cm. Reprint of the 1928 ed. published by The University Press, Cambridge, Eng. Includes bibliographical references and index. [DS38.4.A53B68 1975] 77-180320 ISBN 0-404-56215-9 : 37.50
1. 'Ali ibn 'Isa, Abbasid wazir, 859-946. 2. Islamic Empire—History—750-1258. I. Title.

al-Kurdufani, Isma'il 'Abd al-Qadir, 1844 or 5-1898 or 9.

SHAKED, Haim. 297'.899 B
The life of the Sudanese Mahdi : a historical study of the unique manuscript of Kitab sa'adat al-mustahdi bi-sirat al-Imam al-Mahdi (The book of the bliss of him who seeks guidance by the life of the Imam the Mahdi by the Sudanese Mahdist adherent Isma'il b. 'Abd al-Qadir. Tel Aviv : Shiloah Center for Middle Eastern and African Studies, Tel Aviv University, 1976. p. cm. "Based on a Ph.D. thesis which was submitted to the School of Oriental and African Studies, University of London, in 1969." Includes index. Bibliography: p. [DT108.3.M84K8737] 76-7552 ISBN 0-87855-132-8 : 19.95
1. al-Kurdufani, Isma'il 'Abd al-Qadir, 1844 or 5-1898 or 9. Sa'adat al-mustahdi bi-sirat al-Iman al-Mahdi. 2. Muhammad Ahmad, calling himself al-Mahdi, 1848-1885. I. Title.
Distributed by Transaction Books.

al-Muqaddasi, Muhammad ibn Ahmad, b. ca. 946.

COLLINS, Basil Anthony. 910'.92'4 B
Al-Muqaddasi : the man and his work : with selected passages translated from the Arabic / by Basil Anthony Collins Ann Arbor : Dept. of Geography, University of Michigan, 1974. xvii, 265 p. ; 26 cm. (Michigan geographical publication ; no. 10) "Translation of selected passages from Ahsan al-taqasim fi ma'rifat al-aqalim": p. 143-265. Bibliography: p. 135-141. [G93.M943C64] 74-623945 5.00
1. al-Muqaddasi, Muhammad ibn Ahmad, b. ca. 946. Ahsan al-taqasim fi ma'rifat al-aqalim. 2. Islamic Empire—Description and travel. I. al-Muqaddasi, Muhammad ibn Ahmad, b. ca. 946. Ahsan al-taqasim fi ma'rifat al-aqalim. Selections. English. 1974. II. Series: Michigan geographical publications ; no. 10.

al-Suhrawardi, Yahya ibn Habash, 1152 or 3-1191.

NASR, Seyyed Hossein. 297'.6 B
Three Muslim sages : Avicenna, Suhrawardi, Ibn 'Arabi / Seyyed Hossein Nasr. Delmar, N.Y. : Caravan Books, [1975] p. cm. Reprint of the 1969 ed. published by Harvard University Press, Cambridge. Bibliography: p. [BP70.N36 1975] 75-14430 ISBN 0-88206-500-9 pbk. : 5.95
1. Avicenna, 980-1037. 2. al-Suhrawardi, Yahya ibn Habash, 1152 or 3-1191. 3. Ibn al-'Arabi, 1165-1240. I. Title.

Alabama—Biography.

GARRETT, William, 1809- 976.1'05'0922 B
Reminiscences of public men in Alabama for thirty years : with an appendix / by William Garrett. Spartanburg, S.C. : Reprint Co., 1975. 809 p. ; 22 cm. Reprint of the 1872 ed. published by Plantation Pub. Co., Atlanta. Includes indexes. [F325.G24 1975] 74-34445 ISBN 0-87152-204-7 : 30.00
1. Alabama—Biography. 2. Alabama—Politics and government. I. Title.

NOTABLE men of Alabama : personal and genealogical, with portraits / Joel C. DuBose, editor. Spartanburg, S.C. : Reprint Co., 1976. 2 v. : ports. ; 24 cm. Reprint of the 1904 ed. published by Southern Historical Association, Atlanta. Includes indexes. [CT221.N67 1976] 75-45385 ISBN 0-87152-225-X(v.1) : 22.50 ISBN 0-87152-226-8(v.2) : 22.50 920.71'09761
1. Alabama—Biography. I. DuBose, Joel Campbell, 1855- BIP

Alabama—Biography—Dictionaries.

MARKS, Henry S. 920'.0761
Who was who in Alabama. Compiled by Henry S. Marks. Huntsville, Ala., Strode Publishers [1972] 200 p. 27 cm. Bibliography: p. [198]-200. [F325.M3] 74-188627 ISBN 0-87397-017-9 10.00
1. Alabama—Biography—Dictionaries. I. Title. BIP

Alabama—Biography—Portraits.

NATIONAL Society of the Colonial Dames of America. Alabama. Historical Activities Committee. 920.0761 B
Alabama portraits prior to 1870. Compiled by the Historical Activities Committee for the National Society of the Colonial Dames of America in the State of Alabama [Mobile? c1969] ix, 417 p. illus. 29 cm. [F325.N37 1969] 71-100904
1. Alabama—Biography—Portraits. I. Title.

Alabama (Confederate cruiser)

DELANEY, Norman C. 973.7'57'0924 B
John McIntosh Kell of the raider Alabama, by Norman C. Delaney. University, University of Alabama Press [1973] 270 p. illus. 24 cm. Bibliography: p. [257]-266.

[E596.K292D44] 72-7349 ISBN 0-8173-5106-X 8.50
1. Kell, John McIntosh, 1823-1900. 2. Alabama (Confederate cruiser) 3. Sumter (Confederate cruiser) 4. United States—History—Civil War—Naval operations—Confederate States. I. Title. BIP

Alabama—Governors—Biography.

STEWART, John Craig. 976.1'00992
The Governors of Alabama / by John Craig Stewart. Gretna, La. : Pelican Pub. Co., 1975. viii, 232 p. : ports. ; 23 cm. (The Pelican governors series) Includes index. Bibliography: p. 227-228. A biography and history of the governors of Alabama from earliest times to the present. [F325.S8] 920 75-8763 ISBN 0-88289-067-0 : 12.95 12.95
1. Alabama—Governors—Biography. I. Title. BIP

Alabama—History—Dictionaries.

OWEN, Thomas McAdory, 976.1'003 1866-1920.
History of Alabama and dictionary of Alabama biography / by Thomas McAdory Owen. Spartanburg, S.C. : Reprint Co., 1978. 4 v. (1867 p.) : ill. ; 24 cm. Reprint of the 1921 ed. published by S. J. Clarke Pub. Co., Chicago; with a new introd. [F326.O9 1978] 78-2229 ISBN 0-87152-259-4 (set) : 150.00
1. Alabama—History—Dictionaries. 2. Alabama—Biography. I. Title. BIP

Alabama—Social life and customs.

CLAYTON, Victoria 917.61'03'5 Virginia (Hunter)
White and Black under the old regime, by Victoria V. Clayton. With introd. by Frederic Cook Morehouse. Freeport, N.Y., Books for Libraries Press [1970] 195 p. illus., ports. 23 cm. Reprint of the 1899 ed. [F326.C62 1970] 70-119928
1. Alabama—Social life and customs. 2. Negroes—Alabama. I. Title. BIP

Alachua Co., Fla.—Biography.

VOICES from the countryside 975.9'79'06 / compiled and edited by Guy Miles ; photos. by Jerry Sherman. Miami, Fla. : Banyan Books, c1977. 112 p. : ill. ; 28 cm. [F317.A4V64] 77-4404 ISBN 0-916224-13-9 : 5.95
1. Alachua Co., Fla.—Biography. 2. Alachua Co., Fla.—Social life and customs 3. Country life—Florida—Alachua Co. 4. Interviews I. Miles, Guy, 1908- II. Sherman, Jerry, 1948- BIP

Alacoque, Marguerite Marie, Saint, 1647-1690.

ALACOQUE, Marguerite 922.244 Marie, Saint, 1647-1690.
The autobiography of Saint Margaret Mary. Newly translated from the French with an introd. by Vincent Kerns. Westminster, Md., Newman Press [1961] 109p. 19cm. Translated from F.L. Gauthey's transcript of the original ms. first published in 1915 in Vie et oeuvres de Sainte Marguerite Marie Alacoque, v.2, p. 20-119. [BX4700.A37A23 1961] 61-10561
I. Title.

ALACOQUE, Marguerite 922.244 Marie, Saint, 1647-1690.
Letters. Translated from the French of the rev. Gauthey ed. of 1920 by Clarence A. Herbst. With an introductory essay by J. Doyle. Chicago, H. Regnery Co., 1954. 286p. 22cm. (Library of living Catholic thought) [BX2179.A6A4] 54-10092
I. Title.

ALACOQUE, Marguerite 922.244 Marie Saint, 1647-1690.
The autobiography of Saint Margaret Mary. Newly tr. from French, introd. by Vincent Kerns. Westminster, Md., Newman [c.1961] 109p. 61-10561 2.50
I. Title.

BOYLE, John, 1922- 922.244
Behold this heart; a story of St. Margaret Mary Alacoque. Illus. by Brother Aloysius Tiedt. Notre Dame, Ind., Dujarie Press [1954] 87p. illus. 24cm. [BX4700.A37B65] 54-41983
1. Alacoque, Marguerite Marie, Saint, 1647-1690. I. Title.

WINDEATT, Mary Fabyan, 922.244 1910-
Mission for Margaret: the story of the first Fridays. Illustrated by Paul A. Grout. St. Meinrad, Ind. [St. Meinrad's Abbey, 1953] 230p. illus. 22cm. 'A Grail publication.' [BX4700.A37W5] 53-13435
1. Alacoque, Marguerite Marie, Saint, 1647-1690. I. Title.

Alacoque, Marguerite Marie, Saint, 1647-1690—Juvenile literature.

HUME, Ruth (Fox) 922.244
St. Margaret Mary, apostle of the Sacred Heart. Illustrated by Johannes Troyer. New York, Farrar, Straus and Cudahy [c.1960] 187p. illus. 22cm. (Vision books, 45) 60-6138 1.95
1. Alacoque, Marguerite Marie, Saint, 1647-1690—Juvenile literature. I. Title.

HUME, Ruth (Fox) 1922- 922.244
St. Margaret Mary, apostle of the Sacred Heart. Illustrated by Johannes Troyer. New York, Vision Books [1960] 187p. illus. 22cm. (Vision books, 45) [BX4700.A37H8] 60-6138
1. Alacoque, Marguerite Marie, Saint, 1647-1690—Juvenile literature. I. Title.

Aladjem, Henrietta, 1917-

ALADJEM, Henrietta, 616.5'4 B 1917-
The sun is my enemy / Henrietta Aladjem. Boston : Beacon Press, [1976] c1972. p. cm. [RC924.5.L85A4 1976] 76-7733 ISBN 0-8070-2171-7 pbk. : 3.95
1. Aladjem, Henrietta, 1917- 2. Lupus erythematosus, Systemic—Biography. I. Title. BIP

Alaska—Biography.

WILLOUGHBY, Florance 917.98'03 (Barrett)
Alaskans all. Freeport, N.Y., Books for Libraries Press [1971, c1961] x, 234 p illus., facsim., ports. 23 cm. (Essay index reprint series) Contents.Contents.—Volcanoes packed in ice: the glacier priest in the smoking valleys of Alaska.—Summering in the moon craters of Alaska: further adventures of the glacier priest.—Ben Eielson: pioneer of the Arctic skies.—Captain Louis Lane: champion ice pilot of the Arctic. Harriet Pullen: mother of the North.—'Stroller' White: the man who invented the ice worm. [F903.W72 1971] 78-134161 ISBN 0-8369-2091-0
1. Alaska—Biography. 2. Alaska—Description and travel—1896-1959. I. Title. BIP

Alaska—Description and travel—1896-1959.

DUFRESNE, Frank. 917.98044
My way was north; an Alaskan autobiography. Introd. by Corey Ford. Drawings by Rachel S. Horne. [1st ed.] New York, Holt, Rinehart and Winston [1966] xiv, 274 p. illus. 22 cm. [F909.D8] 66-21630
1. Alaska—Description and travel—1896-1959. 2. Natural history—Alaska. I. Title.

HEWITT, John Michael. 926.1
The Alaska vagabond, Doctor Skookum; memories of an adventurous life. [1st ed.] New York, Exposition Press [1953] 284 p. 21 cm. [R154.H397A3] 53-6715
1. Alaska—Description and travel—1896-1959. I. Title.

Albany, Louise Maximiliane Caroline Emanuel, Princess of Stolberg, known as countess of, 1752-1824.

CROSLAND, Margaret, 1920- 920.7
Louise of Stolberg, Countess of Albany. Edinburgh, Oliver & Boyd [dist. Chester Springs, Pa., Dufour, 1964, c.1962] 190p. facsims., ports. 23cm. Bibl. 64-9212 5.00
1. Albany, Louise Maximiliane Caroline Emanuel, Princess of Stolberg, known as countess of, 1752-1824. I. Title.

Albee, Edward, 1928-

COHN, Ruby. 812'.5'4
Edward Albee. Minneapolis, University of Minnesota Press [1969] 48 p. 21 cm. (University of Minnesota. Pamphlets on American writers, no. 77) Bibliography: p. 45-48. [PS3551.L25Z6] 78-625288
1. Albee, Edward, 1928- I. Series: Minnesota. University. Pamphlets on American writers, no. 77

Albemarle, George Monk, 1st Duke of, 1608-1670.

ASHLEY, Maurice 941.06'6'0924 B Percy.
General Monck / Maurice Ashley. Totowa, N.J. : Rowman and Littlefield, 1977. 316 p., [1] leaf of plates : ill. ; 23 cm. Includes bibliographical references and index. [DA407.A74A84 1977] 77-150720 ISBN 0-87471-934-8 : 15.00
1. Albemarle, George Monk, 1st Duke of, 1608-1670. 2. Great Britain. Army—Biography. 3. Generals—Great Britain—Biography. 4. Great Britain—History—Puritan Revolution, 1642-1660. 5. Great Britain—History—Restoration, 1660-1688. I. Title. BIP

CORBETT, Julian 942.06'2'0924 Stafford, Sir, 1854-1922.
Monk. Freeport, N.Y., Books for Libraries Press [1971] vi, 221 p. port. 23 cm. Reprint of the 1889 ed. Includes bibliographical references. [DA407.A74C67 1971] 72-154148 ISBN 0-8369-5764-4
1. Albemarle, George Monk, 1st Duke of, 1608-1670. BIP

Albert, consort of Queen Victoria, 1819-1861.

BENNETT, Daphne. 941.081'092'4 B
King without a crown : Albert, Prince Consort of England, 1819-1861 / Daphne Bennett. 1st American ed. Philadelphia : Lippincott, c1977. p. cm. Includes index. Bibliography: p. [DA559.A1B38 1977] 77-22108 ISBN 0-397-01143-1 : 12.50
1. Albert, Consort of Queen Victoria, 1819-1861. 2. Great Britain—Princes and princesses—Biography. 3. Great Britain—History—Victoria, 1837-1901. I. Title. BIP

BERNARDY, Francoise de. 923.142
Albert and Victoria; translated by Ralph Manheim. [1st ed.] New York, Harcourt, Brace [1953] 341p. illus. 21cm. [DA559.A1B44] 53-5655
1. Albert, consort of Queen Victoria, 1819-1861. 2. Victoria, Queen of Great Britain, 1819-1901. I. Title.

BOLITHO, Hector, 1898- 923.142
Albert, Prince consort. Indianapolis, Bobbs [1965, c.1964] xiv, 250p. ports. 22cm. Bibl. [DA559.A1B58] 64-66283 5.95 bds.,
1. Albert, consort of Queen Victoria, 1819-1861. I. Title.

COLSON, Percy, 1873-1952. 920.042
Victorian portraits. Freeport, N.Y., Books for Libraries Press [1968] 256 p. ports. 22 cm. (Essay index reprint series) Reprint of the 1932 ed. Contents.Contents.—The unhappy prince and Baron Stockmar.—The best of both worlds [Bishop Samuel Wilberforce]—Virtue is its own reward [Harriet Martineau]—A fallen idol [Felix Mendelssohn-Bartholdy] Bibliography: p. 255-256. [DA562.C7 1968] 68-16921
1. Albert, Consort of Queen Victoria, 1819-1861. 2. Wilberforce, Samuel, Bp. of Winchester, 1805-1873. 3. Martineau, Harriet, 1802-1876. 4. Mendelssohn-Bartholdy, Felix, 1809-1847. I. Title. BIP

EYCK, Frank. 923.142
The Prince consort; a political biography. Boston, Houghton Mifflin [1959] 269 p. illus. 22 cm. [DA559.A1E9 1959a] 59-8857
1. Albert, consort of Queen Victoria, 1819-1861. I. Title.

POUND, Reginald. 942.081'092'4 B
Albert; a biography of the Prince Consort. New York, Simon and Schuster [1974, c1973] 378 p. illus. 25 cm. Bibliography: p. 359-364. [DA559.A1P68 1974] 73-8429 ISBN 0-671-21659-7 10.00
1. Albert, Consort of Queen Victoria, 1819-1861.

SCHEELE, Godfrey. 941.081'092'4 B
The Prince Consort / Godfrey and Margaret Scheele. New York : Two Continents Pub. Group, [1977] p. cm. (Oresko art book series) Includes index. Bibliography: p. [DA559.A1S33] 77-70921 ISBN 0-8467-0321-1 : 13.95. ISBN 0-8467-0322-X pbk. : 7.95
1. Albert, Consort of Queen Victoria, 1819-1861. 2. Great Britain—Princes and princesses—Biography. 3. Great Britain—History—Victoria, 1837-1901. I. Scheele, Margaret, joint author. II. Title. III. Series. BIP

TISDALL, Evelyn Ernest P 923.142
Restless consort; the invasion of Albert the Conqueror. London, New York, S. Paul [1952] 203 p. illus. 22 cm. [DA559.A1T5] 52-33505
1. Albert, consort of Queen Victoria, 1819-1861. 2. Victoria, Queen of Great Britain, 1819-1901. I. Title.

Albert I, King of Belgians, 1875-1934.

GALET, Emile 949.3'04'0924 B Joseph, 1870-
Albert, king of the Belgians in the great war; his military activities and experiences set down with his approval, by Galet. Translated by Sir Ernest Swinton. Freeport, N.Y., Books for Libraries Press [1973] p. Translation of S. M. le roi Albert. Reprint of the 1931 ed. [DH681.G33 1973] 72-12772 ISBN 0-8369-7136-1
1. Albert I, King of Belgians, 1875-1934. 2. European War, 1914-1918—Belgium.

Albert, Prince of the Hawaiian Islands, 1858-1862.

DUTTON, Meiric Keeler, 923.2969 1900-
Ka Haku o Hawaii (His Royal Highness the Prince of Hawaii) Honolulu, E. et M. Dutton, 1951. unpaged. illus. 16 cm. [DU627.13.D8] 52-25612
1. Albert, Prince of the Hawaiian Islands, 1858-1862. I. Title.

Albert Victor, Duke of Clarence and Avondale, 1864-1892.

HARRISON, Michael. 364.1'523'0924
Clarence: was he Jack the Ripper? New York, Drake Publishers [1974, c1972] viii, 253 p. illus. 22 cm. Bibliography: p. 245-247. [HV6535.G4H28] 73-15968 7.95
1. Albert Victor, Duke of Clarence and Avondale, 1864-1892. 2. Whitechapel murders, 1888. I. Title.

SPIERING, Frank. 364.1'523'0924 B
Prince Jack / Frank Spiering. New York : Doubleday, 1978. p. cm. Bibliography: p. [HV6535.G6L6584] 77-16950 ISBN 0-385-12537-2 : 8.95
1. Albert Victor, duke of Clarence and Avondale, 1864-1892. 2. Whitechapel murders, 1888. I. Title. BIP

Alberti, Leone Battista, 1404-1472.

GADOL, Joan. 709'.24 B
Leon Battista Alberti: universal man of the early Renaissance. Chicago, University of Chicago Press [1969] xv, 266 p. illus. 22 x 23 cm. Bibliography: p. 245-257. [NA1123.A5G3] 72-75811 14.50
1. Alberti, Leone Battista, 1404-1472. I. Title.

Alberti, Rafael, 1902- —Biography—Youth.

ALBERTI, Rafael, 1902- 861'.6'2 B
The Lost Grove / Rafael Alberti ; translated and edited by Gabriel Berns. Berkeley : University of California Press, c1976. 323 p., [1] leaf of plates : ill. ; 23 cm. Translation of La arboleda perdida. [PQ6601.L2A8513] 74-79760 ISBN 0-520-02786-8 : 12.50
1. Alberti, Rafael, 1902- —Biography—Youth. 2. Authors, Spanish—20th century—Biography. I. Title.

Albertus Magnus, Saint, Bp. of Ratisbon, 1198?-1280.

DORCY, Mary Jean, 1914- 922.243
he author. New York, Sheed and Ward [1955] 173p. illus. 21cm. Includes bibliography. [BX4700.A375D66] 55-10500
1. Albertus Magnus, Saint, Bp. of Ratisbon, 1198?-1280. I. Title.

Albion, Robert Greenhalgh, 1896-

THE Atlantic world 909'.09'6308
of Robert G. Albion / edited by Benjamin W. Labaree ; with chapters by William A. Baker ... [et al.] and a bibliography of the works of Robert G. Albion by Joan Bentick-Smith ; drawings by William A. Baker. 1st ed. Middletown, Conn. : Wesleyan University Press, [1975] vii, 263 p. : ill. ; 23 cm. Festschrift for R. G. Albion. "The writings of Robert G. Albicon": p. 218-222. [VK18.A8] 75-21670 ISBN 0-8195-4085-4 : 14.95
1. Albion, Robert Greenhalgh, 1896- 2. Atlantic Ocean—Navigation—History—Addresses, essays, lectures. 3. Shipping—Atlantic Ocean—History—Addresses, essays, lectures. 4. Naval history—Addresses, essays, lectures. I. Albion, Robert Greenhalgh, 1896- II. Labaree, Benjamin Woods. III. Baker, William A. Contents omitted. **BIP**

Albright, Ivan, 1897-

ALBRIGHT, Ivan, 1897- 759.13 B
Ivan Albright / Michael Croydon. New York : Abbeville Press, [c1978] 308 p. : ill. (some col.); 31 cm. Includes index. Bibliography: p. 304-305. [ND237.A32C76] 78-5369 65.00 limited deluxe edition : 1500.00
1. Albright, Ivan, 1897- 2. Painters—United States—Biography. I. Croydon, Michael.

Albright, William Foxwell, 1891-1971.

RUNNING, Leona 950'.07'2024 B
Glidden, 1916-
William Foxwell Albright, a twentieth-century genius / by Leona Glidden Running and David Noel Freedman. New York : Two Continents Pub. Group, [1975] p. cm. Includes index. [BS1161.A39R86] 75-11180 ISBN 0-8467-0071-9 : 20.00
1. Albright, William Foxwell, 1891-1971. I. Freedman, David Noel, 1922- joint author. II. Title.

Alburquerque, Dukes of.

PEARCE, Thomas Matthews, 929.7'6
1902-
"The Dukes of Alburquerque : Albuquerque, New Mexico, old Spain and new Spain" / Thomas M. Pearce. [Albuquerque, N.M.] : Albuquerque Historical Society, c1977. 18 p. ; 23 cm. English and Spanish. Bibliography: p. 17-18. [DP60.A5P4] 77-370963
1. Alburquerque, Dukes of. 2. Spain—Nobility—Biography. 3. Albuquerque, N.M.—History. I. Title.

Alchemists—Biography.

WAITE, Arthur Edward, 1857- 540.1
1942.
Alchemists through the ages; lives of the famous alchemistical philosophers from the year 850 to the close of the 18th century, together with a study of the principles and practice of alchemy, including a bibliography of alchemical and hermetic philosophy. Introd. by Paul M. Allen. Blauvelt, N.Y., Rudolf Steiner Publications, 1970. 315 p. illus., ports. 22 cm. Reprint of the 1888 ed. published under title: Lives of alchemystical philosophers. Based on "The lives of alchemystical philosophers," London, 1815, originally issued anonymously under title: The lives of the adepts in alchemystical philosophy, London, 1814, and generally ascribed to Francis Barrett. [QD24.A1W3 1970] 76-130814 10.00
1. Alchemists—Biography. 2. Alchemy—Bibliography. I. Barrett, Francis. II. Title.

Alchemists—Biography—Juvenile literature.

AYLESWORTH, Thomas G. 540'.1 B
The alchemists: magic into science [by] Thomas G. Aylesworth. [Reading, Mass.] Addison-Wesley [1973] 128 p. illus. 20 cm. "An Addisonian Press book." Traces the history of alchemy and the activities of the alchemists who developed the foundations of modern science. [QD24.A1A94] 72-7495 ISBN 0-201-00143-8 4.75
1. Alchemists—Biography—Juvenile literature. 2. Alchemy—Juvenile literature. I. Title.

Alchisay, Apache chief.

WHARFIELD, H. B. 973.8'0924 B
Alchesay; scout with General Crook, Sierra Blanca Apache chief, friend of Fort Apache whites, counselor to Indian agents, by H. B. Wharfield. [El Cajon, Calif., 1969] v, 53 p. illus., group ports. 22 cm. [E90.A38W45] 76-96756
1. Alchisay, Apache chief.

Alcibiades.

PARRY, Hugh, 1934- 938'.05'0924
The individual and his society: Alcibiades—Greek patriot or traitor? New York, St. Martin's Press [1969] 28 p. illus. 23 cm. (The West and the world, The Greek period, by Hugh Parry) [DF230.A4P3 1969] 70-12127
1. Alcibiades. I. Title.

PLUTARCHUS. [888.8] 920.03
Life stories of men who shaped history, from Plutarch's Lives. Translated by John and William Langhorne, selected and edited by Eduard C. Lindeman. [New York] New American Library [1950] 222 p. 18 cm. (A Mentor book, 55) [DE7.P7L5] 50-38593
1. Alcibiades. 2. Cicero, Marcus Tuillus. 3. Alexander the Great, 356-323 B.C. 4. Lycurgus, orator, 6 BC. 338-326. 5. Solon. 6. Pericles, 499-429 BC. I. Title.

Alcindor, Lew, 1947-

PEPE, Phil. 796.32'3'0924
Stand tall; the Lew Alcindor Story. New York, Grosset & Dunlap [1970] xiv, 206 p. 18 cm. (Tempo books, 5351) [GV884.A4P4] 71-120422 0.95
1. Alcindor, Lew, 1947- I. Title.

Alcoholics—Personal narratives.

BARNES, Horace 362.2'92'0924 B
B., 1904-
The true life story of an alcoholic, by Horace B. (Barney) Barnes. Philadelphia, Dorrance [1974, c1973] 42 p. illus. 22 cm. [HV5293.B37A37] 72-81641 ISBN 0-8059-1722-5 3.00
1. Alcoholics—Personal narratives. I. Title.

PASTOR, Paul. 362.2'92'0924 B
The 13th american. Elgin, Ill., D. C. Cook Pub. Co. [1973] 190 p. 18 cm. [HV5293.P35A5] 73-78711 ISBN 0-912692-12-X 1.50
1. Alcoholics—Personal narratives. I. Title.

Alcoholism—Treatment.

WILLIAMS, 616.86'1'00924 B
Lincoln.
To each his memories: a psychiatrist looks back on his treatment of alcoholics. London, New York, Regency P., 1970. 164 p., 2 plates. illus., port. 23 cm. [RC565.W52] 76-451730 ISBN 0-7212-0071-0 30/-
1. Alcoholism—Treatment. 2. Psychiatrists—Correspondence, reminiscences, etc. I. Title.

Alcorn, James Lusk, 1816-1894.

PEREYRA, Lillian A. 973.80924
James Lusk Alcorn; persistent Whig. [Baton Rouge] La. State Univ. Pr. [c.]1966. xv, 237p. illus., ports. 24cm. (Southern biog. ser.) [F341.A36P4] 66-21756 7.50
1. Alcorn, James Lusk, 1816-1894. I. Title. II. Series. **BIP**

Alcott, Amos Bronson, 1799-1888.

ALCOTT, Amos 917.3'03'80924
Bronson, 1799-1888.
The letters of A. Bronson Alcott. Edited by Richard L. Herrnstadt. [1st ed.] Ames, Iowa State University Press [1969] xxxvii, 846 p. illus., facsims., geneal. table., ports. 26 cm. The letters, are chiefly from the Alcott-Pratt collection of the Harvard College Library. [PS1013.A45H4] 76-76209
I. Herrnstadt, Richard L., 1926- ed. **BIP**

MCCUSKEY, Dorothy. 370'.924 B
Bronson Alcott, teacher. New York, Arno Press, 1969. xiii, 217 p. illus., facsims., ports. 23 cm. (American education: its men, ideas, and institutions) Reprint of the 1940 ed. Thesis—Yale, 1936. Includes bibliographies. [LB695.A3M3 1969] 71-89201
1. Alcott, Amos Bronson, 1790-1888. I. Title. II. Series. **BIP**

SANBORN, Franklin Benjamin, 191
1831-1917
A. Bronson Alcott, his life and philosophy; v. 1 & 2. by F. B. Sanborn, William T. Harris. New York, Biblo & Tannen, 1965. 2 v. (679p.) ports. 22cm. First pub. 1893. [B908.A54S2] 65-23481 12.50 set.,
1. Alcott, Amos Bronson, 1799-1888. I. Harris William Torrey, 1835-1909, joint author. II. Title.

SANBORN, Franklin 370'.92'4 B
Benjamin, 1831-1917.
Bronson Alcott at Alcott House, England, and Fruitlands, New England (1842-1844). [Folcroft, Pa.] Folcroft Library Editions, 1974 [c1908] 103 p. illus. 26 cm. Reprint of the ed. published by Torch Press, Cedar Rapids, Iowa. [B908.A54S22 1974] 74-17078 ISBN 0-8414-7506-7 (lib. bdg.)
1. Alcott, Amos Bronson, 1799-1888. I. Title.

Alcott family—Juvenile literature.

FISHER, Aileen Lucia, 920 (J)
1906-
We Alcotts; the story of Louisa M. Alcott's family as seen through the eyes of "Marmee," mother of Little women [by] Aileen Fisher & Olive Rabe. Decorations by Ellen Raskin. [1st ed.] New York, Atheneum, 1968. 278 p. illus. 22 cm. Bibliography: p. 276-278. [PS1013.F5] 68-18445
1. Alcott family—Juvenile literature. I. Rabe, Olive, joint author. II. Title.

Alcott, Louisa May, 1832-1888.

ALCOTT, Louisa May, 813'.4 B
1832-1888.
Louisa May Alcott; her life, letters, and journals. Edited by Ednah D. Cheney. New York, B. Franklin [1974, c1889] p. cm. Reprint of the 1907 ed. published by Little, Brown, Boston. [PS1018.A4 1974] 72-81926 ISBN 0-8337-5120-4 16.50
I. Cheney, Ednah Dow Littlehale, 1824-1904, ed. **BIP**

MEIGS, Cornelia Lynde, 813'.4 B
1884-
Invincible Louisa; the story of the author of Little women, by Cornelia Meigs. With a new introd. by the author. Boston, Little, Brown [1968] xi, 195 p. illus., ports. 25 cm. "Alcott centennial edition." First published in 1933 under title: The story of the author of Little women: Invincible Louisa, and in 1935 under title: The story of Louisa Alcott. [PS1018.M4 1968] 68-21174 4.95
1. Alcott, Louisa May, 1832-1888. I. Title.

MEIGS, Cornelia Lynde, v. 12
1884-
The story of the author of Little women; Invincible Louisa. Boston, Little, Brown [1961] 260 p. illus. 21 cm. 65-103775
1. Alcott, Louisa May, 1832-1888. I. Title. II. Title: Invincible Louisa.

PEARE, Catherine Owens. 928.1
Louisa May Alcott: her life: illustrated by Margaret Ayer. [1st ed.] New York, Holt [1954] 122 p. illus. 21 cm. [PS1018.P4] 54-5742
1. Alcott, Louisa May, 1832-1888.

STERN, Madeleine Bettina, 928.1
1912-
Louisa May Alcott. London, New York, P. Nevill [1952] xiii, 424p. illus., ports. 22cm. 'Notes on sources': p361-407. 'Bibliography of Louisa M. Alcott's writings': p. 343-360. [PS1018.S75 1952] 52-67803
1. Alcott, Louisa May, 1832-1888. I. Title. **BIP**

WORTHINGTON, Marjorie 928.1
(Muir) 1900-
Miss Alcott of Concord; a biography. [1st ed.] Garden City, N.Y., Doubleday, 1958. 330 p. 22 cm. Includes bibliography. [PS1018.W6] 58-11330
1. Alcott, Louisa May, 1832-1888. I. Title.

Alcott, Louisa May, 1832-1888—Addresses, essays, lectures.

PORTER, Maria S. 811'.3 B
Recollections of Louisa May Alcott, John Greenleaf Whittier, and Robert Browning, together with several memorial poems / by Maria S. Porter. Folcroft, Pa. : Folcroft Library Editions, 1976, c1892. p. cm. Reprint of the 1893 ed. published for the author by the New England Magazine Corp., Boston. [PS121.P64 1976] 76-13453 ISBN 0-8414-6701-3 lib. bdg. : 10.00
1. Alcott, Louisa May, 1832-1888—Addresses, essays, lectures. 2. Whittier, John Greenleaf, 1807-1892—Addresses, essays, lectures. 3. Browning, Robert, 1812-1889—Addresses, essays, lectures. I. Title: Recollections of Louisa May Alcott, John Greenleaf Whittier, and Robert Browning ... **BIP**

Alcott, Louisa May, 1832-1888—Biography.

ANTHONY, Katharine Susan, 813'.4
1877-1965.
Louisa May Alcott / by Katharine Anthony. Westport, Conn. : Greenwood Press, 1977, c1938. xiii, 304, xi p., [15] leaves of plates : ill. ; 22 cm. Reprint of the 1st ed. published by Knopf, New York. Includes index. Bibliography: p. 299-304. [PS1018.A7 1977] 77-2388 ISBN 0-8371-9552-7 : 19.75
1. Alcott, Louise May, 1832-1888—Biography. 2. Novelists, American—19th century—Biography. **BIP**

SEXTON, Martha. 813'.4 B
Louisa May ; a modern biography of Louisa May Alcott / Martha Saxton. Boston : Houghton Mifflin, 1977. viii, 428 p., [6] leaves of plates : ill. ; 25 cm. Includes index. Bibliography: p. [407]-414. [PS1018.S2] 77-23750 ISBN 0-395-25720-4 : 12.50
1. Alcott, Louisa May, 1832-1888—Biography. 2. Novelists, American—19th century—Biography. **BIP**

Alcott, Louisa May, 1832-1888—Juvenile literature.

GRAFF, Polly Anne (Colver) 1908- 813'.4 B
Louisa May Alcott, by Anne Colver. Illustrated by Cary. Champaign, Ill., Garrard Pub. Co. [1969] 142 p. illus., facsims, ports. 22 cm. (Creative arts biographies) A biography of the New England authoress whose own life and family provided much of the material for some of her most famous novels. [PS1018.G7] 92 69-11078 2.49
1. Alcott, Louisa May, 1832-1888—Juvenile literature. I. Cary, Louis F., 1915- illus. II. Title.

MEIGS, Cornelia Lynde, 1884- 813'.4 B
Louisa M. Alcott and the American family story [by] Cornelia Meigs. New York, H. Z. Walck [1971] 127 p. 21 cm. Bibliography: p. 123-127. A biography of the author whose Little Women and other popular books were based on the experiences of her family. [PS1018.M38 1971] 92 76-139860 ISBN 0-8098-3919-9 4.75
1. Alcott, Louisa May, 1832-1888—Juvenile literature. I. Title.

PAPASHVILY, Helen (Waite) 92
Louisa May Alcott. Illus. by Bea Holmes. Boston, Houghton [c.]1965. 183p. illus. 22cm. (North star bks., 39) [PS1018.P3] 65-11024 1.95; 2.20 lib. ed.,
1. Alcott, Louisa May, 1832-1888—Juvenile literature. I. Title.

ROBINSON, Martha 920
The young Louisa M. Alcott. Illus. by William Randell. New York, Roy [1964, c.1963] 133p. illus. 21cm. 64-163530 3.25 bds.,
1. Alcott, Louisa May, 1832-1888—Juvenile literature. I. Title.

Alcuin, 735-804.

DUCKETT, Eleanor Shipley. 923.742
Alcuin, friend of Charlemagne, his world and his work. New York, Macmillan, 1951. xii, 337 p. 22 cm. Bibliography: p. 319-328. [LB125.A4D8] 51-3328
1. Alcuin, 735-804. I. Title.

DUCKETT, Eleanor Shipley 370.924
Alcuin, friend of Charlemagne, his world and his work. Hamden, Conn., Archon [dist. Shoe String] 1965[c.1951] 339p. 22cm. Bibl. [LB125.A4D8] 65-19596 9.00
1. Alcuin, 735-804. I. Title.

ELLARD, Gerald, 1894- 923.742
Master Alcuin, liturgist, a partner of our piety. Chicago, Loyola University Press, 1956. xiii, 266p. 24cm. (Jesuit studies; contributions to the arts and sciences by members of the Society of Jesus) Bibliography. p. 231-249. [BX1979.A6E5] 56-8943
1. Alcuin, 735-804. 2. Catholic Church. Liturgy and ritual—Hist. I. Title.

GASKOIN, Charles Jacinth Bellairs 370.924
Alcuin; his life and his work. New York, Russell & Russell, 1966. xxii, 275p. 23cm. First pub. in 1904. Bibl. [LB125.A4G3] 66-13231 7.50
1. Alcuin, 735-804. I. Title.

WEST, Andrew Fleming, 1853-1943. 370'.924
Alcuin and the rise of the Christian schools. New York, C. Scribner's Sons, 1909. St. Clair Shores, Mich., Scholarly Press [1969?, c1892] vii, 205 p. map. 21 cm. (The great educators) "Books on Alcuin": p. 197-198. Bibliographical footnotes. [LB125.A4W4 1969] 75-7717
1. Alcuin, 735-804. 2. Education, Medieval. I. Title. II. Series. **BIP**

Alden, John, 1599-1687.

BURT, Olive (Woolley) 1894- 974.4'02'0924 B
John Alden, young Puritan. Illustrated by Vic Dowd. Indianapolis, Bobbs-Merrill [1964] 200 p. illus. 20 cm. (Childhood of famous Americans) A biography of Plymouth Colony leader, John Alden, stressing his childhood and his shy courtship of the maid, Priscilla. [PZ7.B9456Jm] 92 AC 68
1. Alden, John, 1599-1687. I. Dowd, Victor, illus. II. Title.

Alderman, Rosalie Givens.

ALDERMAN, Rosalie Givens. 286'.1'0924
Take heart / Rosalie Givens Alderman. Nashville, Tenn. : Broadman Press, c1978. 128 p. : ill. ; 20 cm. [BX6495.A36A7] 78-59782 ISBN 0-8054-5534-5 : 2.95
1. Alderman, Rosalie Givens. 2. Baptists—United States—Biography. 3. Church work with the aged. I. Title. **BIP**

Aldheim, Saint, Bp. of Sherborne, 640?-709.

DUCKETT, Eleanor Shipley. 274.2
Anglo-Saxon saints and scholars Hamden, Conn., Archon Books, 1967 [c1947] x, 484 p. 22 cm. Contents.Contents. -- Aldheim of Malmesbury. -- Wilfrid of York. -- Bede of Jarrow. -- Boniface of Devon. -- Bibliogrpahy and abbreviations (p. 456-473) [BR754.A1D8] 67-11473
1. Aldheim, Saint, Bp. of Sherborne, 640?-709. 2. Wilfrid, Saint, Bp. of York, 634-709. 3. Beda Venerabilis, 673-735. 4. Boniface, originally Winfrid, Saint, Bp. of Mainz, 680-755. I. Title. **BIP**

Aldington, Richard, 1892-1962.

KERSHAW, Alister, ed. 828.91209
Richard Aldington, an intimate portrait, edited by Alister Kershaw and Frederic-Jacques Temple. Carbondale, Southern Illinois University Press [1965] xxi, 186 p. ports. 21 cm. "A chronological checklist of the books by Richard Aldington, prepared by Paul Schlueter": p. 175-186. [PR6001.L4Z65] 65-16539
1. Aldington, Richard, 1892-1962. I. Temple, Frederic Jacques, joint ed. II. Title.

Aldington, Richard, 1892-1962—Correspondence.

ALDINGTON, Richard, 1892-1962. 821'.9'12 B
A passionate prodigality : letters to Alan Bird from Richard Aldington, 1949-1962 / edited with an introd. and notes by Miriam J. Benkovitz. 1st ed. New York : New York Public Library : distributed by Readex Books, 1976 c1975 xv, 361 p., [1] leaf of plates : ports. ; 26 cm. Includes bibliographical references and index. [PR6001.L4Z543] 75-23105 ISBN 0-87104-259-2 : 15.00
1. Aldington, Richard, 1892-1962—Correspondence. 2. Bird, Alan. 3. Authors, English—Correspondence, reminiscences, etc. I. Bird, Alan. II. Title. **BIP**

Aldington, Richard, 1892-1962—Correspondence—Bibliography.

GATES, Norman T. 821'.9'12 B
A checklist of the letters of Richard Aldington / compiled with an introd. by Norman Timmins Gates. Carbondale : Southern Illinois University Press, c1977. xiv, 171 p. ; 24 cm. Includes indexes. [Z8025.4.G28] [PR6001.L4] 76-21638 ISBN 0-8093-0781-2 : 9.85
1. Aldington, Richard, 1892-1962—Correspondence—Bibliography. I. Title.

GATES, Norman T. 821'.9'12 B
A checklist of the letters of Richard Aldington / compiled with an introd. by Norman Timmins Gates. Carbondale : Southern Illinois University Press, c1977. xiv, 171 p. ; 24 cm. Includes indexes. [Z8025.4.G28] [PR6001.L4] 76-21638 ISBN 0-8093-0781-2 : 9.85
1. Aldington, Richard, 1892-1962—Correspondence—Bibliography. I. Title. **BIP**

Aldrich, Doris (Coffin)

MURPHY, Belva (Atkinson) 922.673
Mommie of the mixing bowl; biography of Doris Coffin Aldrich. Chicago. Moody Press [1959] 192p. illus. 22cm. [BX6495.A38M8] 60-467
1. Aldrich, Doris (Coffin) I. Title.

Aldrich, Nelson Wilmarth, 1841-1915.

STEPHENSON, Nathaniel Wright, 1867-1935. 973.8'0924 B
Nelson W. Aldrich, a leader in American politics. Port Washington, N.Y., Kennikat Press [1971, c1930] xii, 496 p. port. 23 cm. (Kennikat Press scholarly reprints. Series in American history and culture in the nineteenth century) [E664.A35S83 1971] 72-137928 ISBN 0-8046-1490-3
1. Aldrich, Nelson Wilmarth, 1841-1915. 2. U.S.—Politics and government—1865-1933.

Aldrich, Thomas, Bailey, 1836-1907.

GREENSLET, Ferris, 1875-1959 811.3
The life of Thomas Bailey Aldrich. Port Washington,N. Y., Kennikat [1965, c.1936] x, 303p. illus., facsims., ports. 22cm. Reissue of 1908 ed. Bibl. [PS1026.G7] 65-21767 8.50
1. Aldrich, Thomas, Bailey, 1836-1907. I. Title. **BIP**

Aldrich, Winthrop Williams, 1885-

JOHNSON, Arthur Menzies, 1921- 332.1'2'0924 B
Winthrop W. Aldrich: lawyer, banker, diplomat [by] Arthur M. Johnson. Boston, Division of Research, Graduate School of Business Administration, Harvard University, 1968. x, 536 p. port. 22 cm. Bibliography: p. [463]-484. [HG172.A4J6] 68-54733 10.00
1. Aldrich, Winthrop Williams, 1885- 2. Finance—U.S. I. Title.

Aldridge, Ira Frederick, d. 1867.

IRA Aldridge, v. 12
the Negro tragedian, by Herbert Marshall and Mildred Stock. New York, Macmillan, 1958. viii, 355p. illus. 23cm. 'References': p.337-342.
1. Aldridge, Ira. I. Marshall, Herbert, 1912- II. Stock, Mildred, joint author.

MARSHALL, Herbert, 1912- 927.92
Ira Aldridge, the Negro tragedian, by Herbert Marshall, Mildred Stock. London, Rockliff [dist. Chester Springs, Pa., Dufour, 1965, c.1958] 355p. illus. 23cm. Bibl. [PN2598.A52M3] 59-22897 6.95
1. Aldridge, Ira Frederick, d. 1867. I. Stock, Mildred, joint author. II. Title.

MARSHALL, Herbert, 1912- 792'.028'0924 B
Ira Aldridge, the Negro tragedian, by Herbert Marshall and Mildred Stock. Carbondale, Southern Illinois University Press [1968, c1958] viii, 355 p. illus., facsims., ports. 21 cm. (Arcturus books) Includes bibliographical references. [PN2598.A52M3 1968] 68-13864
1. Aldridge, Ira Frederick, d. 1867. I. Stock, Mildred, joint author.

Aldridge, Ira Frederick, d. 1867—Juvenile literature.

HARBISON, David. 920'.073
Reaching for freedom: Paul Cuffe, Norbert Rillieux, Ira Aldridge, James McCune Smith. [New York] Scholastic Book Services [1972] 128 p. illus. 22 cm. (Firebird biographies) (Firebird books) Short biographies of four men who overcame racial obstacles to become famous as a sea captain, an inventor, an actor, and a doctor. [E185.96.H33] 920 70-187886
1. Cuffe, Paul, 1759-1817—Juvenile literature. 2. Rillieux, Norbert, 1806-1894—Juvenile literature. 3. Aldridge, Ira Frederick, d. 1867—Juvenile literature. 4. Smith, James McCune—Juvenile literature. I. Title.

MALONE, Mary. 792'.028'0924 B
Actor in exile; the life of Ira Aldridge. Illus. by Eros Keith. [New York] Crowell-Collier Press [1969] vi, 88 p. illus. 21 cm. A biography of the American-barn Negro who went to Europe, became one of the most celebrated actors of his time, and never returned to the United States. [PN2598.A52M28] 92 70-77967
1. Aldridge, Ira Frederick, d. 1867—Juvenile literature. I. Keith, Eros, illus. II. Title. **BIP**

Alekseev, Konstantin Sergeevich,

MAGARSHACK, David. 927.92
Stanislavsky; a life. New York, Chanticleer Press [1951] vii, 411 p. illus., ports. 26 cm. [PN2728.A4M3] 51-2362
1. Alekseev, Konstantin Sergeevich, 2. Moscow. Moskovskii khudozhestvennyl skademicheskii teatr. I. Title.

Alemany, Joseph Sadoc, Abp., 1814-1888.

WEBER, Francis J. 922.244
A biographical sketch of Right Reverend Joseph Sadoc Alemany, Bishop of Monterey, 1850-1853. Van Nuys, California Historical Publications [c1961] 64 p. illus. 22 cm. Includes bibliography. [BX4705.A487W4] 62-9956
1. Alemany, Joseph Sadoc, Bp., 1814-1888. I. Title.

WEBER, Francis J. 282'.092'4 B
Joseph Sadoc Alemany; harbinger of a new era, by Francis J. Weber. Los Angeles, Dawson's Book Shop, 1973. viii, 70 p. illus. 21 cm. "Limited to ... 250 copies." Includes bibliographical references. [BX4705.A487W42] 72-77295
1. Alemany, Joseph Sadoc, Abp., 1814-1888. I. Title.

Alembert, Jean Lerond d', 1717-1783.

VAN TREESE, Glenn Joseph. 194
D'Alembert and Frederick the Great : a study of their relationship / Glenn J. Van Treese. New York : Learned Publications, 1974. 187 p. ; 25 cm. (Philosophical questions series ; 9) Includes index. Bibliography: p. [177]-183. [B1936.V36] 73-82788 ISBN 0-912116-11-0
1. Alembert, Jean Lerond d', 1717-1783. 2. Friedrich II, der Grosse, King of Prussia, 1712-1786. I. Title. **BIP**

Alexander, Archer.

ELIOT, William Greenleaf, 1811-1887. 301.45'22'0924 B
The story of Archer Alexander; from slavery to freedom, March 30, 1863. Westport, Conn., Negro Universities Press [1970] 123 p. illus. 18 cm. Reprint of the 1885 ed. [E444.A37 1970] 72-107506
1. Alexander, Archer. 2. Slavery in the United States—Missouri. I. Title.

Alexander, Edward Porter, 1835-1910.

KLEIN, Maury. 973.78'2
Edward Porter Alexander. Athens, University of Georgia Press [1971] xii, 279 p. port. 25 cm. Bibliography: p. [253]-259. [E467.1.A33K55] 71-90558 ISBN 0-8203-0278-3 11.00
1. Alexander, Edward Porter, 1835-1910.

Alexander, Eveline, 1843-

ALEXANDER, Eveline, 1843- 973.8'1'0924 B
The diary of Eveline M. Alexander, 1866-1867, being a record of her journey from New York to Fort Smith to join her cavalry-officer husband, Andrew J. Alexander, and her experiences with him on active duty among the Indian nations and in Texas, New Mexico, and Colorado / | edited with an introd. by Sandra L. Myres. 1st ed. College Station : Texas A&M University Press, c1977. 175 p. [6] leaves of plates : ill. ; 24 cm. Includes index. Bibliography: p. [163-169] [E83.866.A43] 76-30611 ISBN 0-89096-025-9 : 10.00
1. Alexander, Eveline, 1843- 2. United States. Army—Military life. 3. Indians of North America—Wars—1865-1895. 4. Army wives—United States—Biography. 5. Indians of North America—Southwest, New—Wars. I. Title: The diary of Eveline M. Alexander, 1866-1867 ...

Alexander, Guy B.

ALEXANDER, Guy B. 543'.08
Chromatography : an adventure in graduate school / Guy B. Alexander. Washington : American Chemical Society, 1977. p. cm. (Chemistry in action) Includes index. Bibliography: p. [QD22.A385A34] 77-8637 ISBN 0-8412-0277-X : write for info.
1. Alexander, Guy B. 2. Wisconsin. University—Graduate work. 3. Chemists—Biography. 4. Chromatographic analysis. I. Title. BIP

Alexander, Harold Rupert Leofric George Alexander, 1st Earl, 1891-1969.

NICOLSON, Nigel. 355.3'31'0924 B
Alex, the life of field marshal Earl Alexander of Tunis. [1st American ed.] New York, Atheneum, 1973. xiii, 346 p. illus. 25 cm. Bibliography: p. 324-327. [DA69.3.A57N5 1973b] 72-94244 ISBN 0-689-10552-5 10.00
1. Alexander, Harold Rupert Leofric George Alexander, 1st Earl, 1891-1969. I. Title.

Alexander, Holmes Moss,

ALEXANDER, Holmes Moss, 1906- 813'.5'4 B
Pen and politics; the autobiography of a working writer, by Holmes Alexander. Morgantown, West Virginia University Library, 1970. 212 p. 23 cm. [PS3501.L419Z5] 77-90747 5.00
I. Title. BIP

Alexander I, Emperor of Russia, 1777-1825.

ALMEDINGEN, Martha Edith, 1898- 947.070924
The Emperor Alexander I [by] E. M. Almedingen. New York, Vanguard [1966, c.1964] 257p. geneal. table, ports. 23cm. Bibl. [DK191.A65 1966] 66-16979 5.95
1. Alexander I, Emperor of Russia, 1777-1825. I. Title.

PALEOLOGUE, Georges Maurice, 1859-1944. 947'.07'0924 B
The enigmatic czar; the life of Alexander I of Russia. Translated from the French by Edwin and Willa Muir. [Hamden, Conn.] Archon Books, 1969. 325 p. ports., fold map. 22 cm. Translation of Alexandre 1er. Unabridged and unaltered reprint of the 1938 ed. [DK191.P32 1969] 69-18274 ISBN 0-208-00748-2
1. Alexander I, Emperor of Russia, 1777-1825. I. Title. BIP

PALMER, Alan Warwick. 947'.07'0924 B
Alexander I: Tsar of war and peace [by] Alan Palmer. [1st U.S. ed.] New York, Harper & Row [1974] xviii, 487 p. illus. 24 cm. Bibliography: p. 462-470. [DK191.P348] 74-1844 ISBN 0-06-013264-7 15.00
1. Alexander I, Emperor of Russia, 1777-1825. 2. Russia—History—Alexander I, 1801-1825.

STRAKHOVSKY, Leonid Ivan, 1898-1963. 947'.07'0924 B
Alexander I of Russia; the man who defeated Napoleon Westport, Conn., Greenwood Press [1970, c1947] 302 p. illus., ports. 23 cm. Bibliography: p. 274-292. [DK191.S75 1970] 77-100245 ISBN 0-8371-4034-X
1. Alexander I, Emperor of Russia, 1777-1825.

Alexander I, King of Yugoslavia, 1888-1934.

GRAHAM, Stephen, 1884- 949.7'02'0924 B
Alexander of Yugoslavia; the story of the king who was murdered at Marseilles. [Hamden, Conn.] Archon Books, 1972 [c1939] 329 p. illus. 22 cm. Bibliography: p. [317]-318. [DR368.G7 1972] 73-122414 ISBN 0-208-01082-3 10.00
1. Alexander I, King of Yugoslavia, 1888-1934. I. Title. BIP

MILICEVIC, Vladeta 923.1497
A king dies in Marseilles; the crime and its background. Bad Godesberg, Hahwacht[dist. by Gregory Launz, New York] [1959] 134p. illus. 21cm. 60-2470 3.00
1. Alexander I, King of Yugoslavia, 1888-1934. I. Title.

Alexander II, Emperor of Russia, 1818-1881.

ALMEDINGEN, Martha Edith, 1898- 923.147
The Emperor Alexander II; a study. London, Bodley Head [Chester Springs, Pa.,Dufour, 1964, c.1962] 367p. illus. 23cm. Bibl. 63-2170 6.00
1. Alexander II, Emperor of Russia, 1818-1881. I. Title.

GRAHAM, Stephen, 1884- 947.08'0924 B
Tsar of freedom, the life and reign of Alexander II. [Hamden, Conn.] Archon Books, 1968 [c1963] xii, 324 p. illus., ports. 22 cm. Bibliography: p. [315]-317. [DK220.G7 1968] 68-15345
1. Alexander II, Emperor of Russia, 1818-1881. I. Title.

Alexander III, Emperor of Russia, 1845-1894.

LOWE, Charles, 1848-1931. 947.08'092'4 B
Alexander iii of Russia. Freeport, N.Y., Books for Libraries Press [1972] xii, 370 p. port. 22 cm. Reprint of the 1895 ed. [DK240.L74 1972] 72-4219 ISBN 0-8369-6889-1
1. Alexander III, Emperor of Russia, 1845-1894.

Alexander III, Pope, d. 1181.

BALDWIN, Marshall Whithed, 1903- 262'.13'0924 B
Alexander III and the twelfth century, by Marshall W. Baldwin Glen Rock, N.J., Newman Press [1968] xi, 228 p. maps (on lining papers) 23 cm. (The Popes through history, v. 3) Includes bibliographical references. [BX1226.B3] 67-15715 6.50
1. Alexander III, Pope, d. 1181. 2. Church and state—History. I. Title. II. Series.

SOMERVILLE, Robert, 1940- 262'.5'2
Pope Alexander III and the Council of Tours (1163) : a study of ecclesiastical politics and institutions in the twelfth century / Robert Somerville Berkeley : University of California Press, c1977. xi, 110 p. ; 24 cm. Includes indexes. Bibliography: p. 69-75. [BX1226.S65] 75-46043 ISBN 0-520-03184-9 : 8.50
1. Alexander III, Pope, d. 1181. 2. Council of Tours, 1163—History. 3. Popes—Biography. 4. Tours—Church history. I. Title. BIP

Alexander, Mary Charlotte, 1886-

ALEXANDER, Frances, 1888- 266.6'0924 B
Mary Charlotte Alexander (Au Mo Ling), missionary to China, 1920-1956. [Austin, Tex., Printed by Von Boeckmann-Jones Co., 1968] 93 p. map (on lining papers), ports. 24 cm. Bibliography: p. 93. [BV3427.A42A62] 70-961
1. Alexander, Mary Charlotte, 1886-

Alexander, Morris, 1877-1946.

ALEXANDER, Enid (Baumberg) 301.45'29'6046
Morris Alexander; a biography. Cape Town, Juta, 1953. 256p. illus. 23cm. [DS135.A27A7] 54-35605
1. Alexander, Morris, 1877-1946. I. Title.

Alexander, Richard Henry, 1844-1915.

ALEXANDER, Richard Henry, 1844-1915. 917.11'04'2
The diary and narrative of Richard Henry Alexander in a journey across the Rocky Mountains. Edited and with an introd. by Neil Brearley, map and drawings by Frits Jacobsen. Richmond, B.C., Alcuin Society [1973] iii, 32 p. illus. 20 x 29 cm. Limited ed. of 500 copies. [F1013.A39 1973] 74-169566 ISBN 0-919026-04-4
1. Alexander, Richard Henry, 1844-1915. 2. Canada—Description and travel—1763-1867. 3. Rocky Mountains, Can. I. Brearley, Neil, ed. II. Title.

Alexander, Robert, 1740?-1805.

JOHNSON, Janet Bassett. 973.3'14'0924 B
Robert Alexander, Maryland loyalist. With a new introd. and pref. by George Athan Billias. Boston, Gregg Press, 1972 [c1942] x, xiii, 152 p. illus. 23 cm. (The American Revolutionary series. The Loyalist library.) Reprint of the ed. published by Putnam, New York. Includes bibliographical references. [E278.A3J6 1972] 72-8735 ISBN 0-8398-0960-3 11.00
1. Alexander, Robert, 1740?-1805. I. Series: The Loyalist library. BIP

Alexander, Shana.

ALEXANDER, Shana. 070.4'092'4 B
Talking woman / Shana Alexander. New York : Delacorte Press, c1976. 271 p. ; 24 cm. [PN4874.A36A37] 76-25137 ISBN 0-440-08595-0 : 8.95
1. Alexander, Shana. I. Title. BIP

ALEXANDER, Shana. 070.4'092'4
Talking woman / Shana Alexander. New York : Dell Pub. Co., 1977,c1976. 288p. ; 18 cm. (A Dell Book) [PN4874.A36A37] ISBN 0-440-18596-3 pbk. : 1.95
1. Alexander, Shana. I. Title.
L.C. card no. for 1976 Delacorte ed.: 76-25137.

Alexander the Great, 356-323, B. C.

ALEXANDER of Macedon; v. 12
the journey to the world's end. Garden City, N. Y., Doubleday, 1957 [c1946] 402p. 22cm.
1. Alexander the Great, 356-323, B. C. I. Lamb, Harold, 1892-

ALEXANDER the Great. v. 12
Boston, Beacon [1956] 160p. 21cm.
1. Alexander the Great, 356- 323 B. C. I. Tarn, William Woodthorpe, 1869- BIP

BAUMANN, Hans, 1914- 938'.07'0924 B
Alexander's great march. Translated by Stella Humphries. New York, H. Z. Walck, 1968. 132 p. map. 22 cm. Translation of Der grosse Alexanderzug. An episodic account of the life of the young Macedonian king who conquered half the known world some two hundred years before the birth of Christ. [DF234.B353 1968b] 92 AC 68
1. Alexander the Great, 356-323 B.C. I. Title.

BENOIST-MECHIN, Jacques Gabriel Paul Michel, baron, 1901- 930.40924
Alexander the Great; the meeting of East and West [by] Jacques Benoist-Mechin. Translated from the French by Mary Ilford. [1st English-language ed.] New York, Hawthorn Books [1966] 255 p. illus., map (on lining papers) 22 cm. Bibliographical references included in "Notes" (p. 233-245) [DF234.B413] 65-22909
1. Alexander the Great, 356-323 B.C.

EMMRICH, Kurt, 1897- 930'.4'0924 B
Alexander the Great; power as destiny [by] Peter Bamm. Translated from the German by J. Maxwell Brownjohn. New York, McGraw-Hill [1968] 319 p. illus. (part col.), maps (on lining papers) 25 cm. [DF234.E423] 68-26310 9.95
1. Alexander the Great, 356-323 B.C.

FOX, Robin Lane, 1946- 938'.07'0924 B
Alexander the Great. [New York] Dial Press, 1974 [c1973] 568 p. illus. 25 cm. Bibliography: p. 555-559. [DF234.F69 1973] 73-18880 ISBN 0-8037-0945-5 15.00
1. Alexander the Great, 356-323 B.C.

GREEN, Peter, 1924- 938'.07'0924 B
Alexander of Macedon, 356-323 B.C.; a historical biography. Revised and enlarged ed. Harmondsworth, Penguin, 1974. xxxi, 617 p. 1 illus., geneal. table, maps, plan. 19 cm. (Pelican biographies) Earlier ed. published in 1970 under title: Alexander the Great. Includes index. Bibliography: p. [569]-585. [DF234.G68 1974] 74-166969 ISBN 0-14-021690-1 £1.00
1. Alexander the Great, 356-323 B.C. I. Title.

GREEN, Peter, 1924- 938'.07'0924
Alexander the Great. New York, Praeger Publishers [1970] 272 p. illus. (part col.), geneal. table, maps, ports. 26 cm. Bibliography: p. 261-265. [DF234.G68 1970] 72-100915 12.95
1. Alexander the Great, 356-323 B.C.

GRIFFITH, Guy Thompson, ed. 930.40924
Alexander the Great: the main problems. Cambridge, Eng., Heffer. New York, Barnes & Noble, 1966. xii, 382p. 22cm. (Views and controversies about classical antiquity) Bibl. [DF234.2.G7 1966] 66-72639 8.00
1. Alexander The Great, 356-323 B. C. I. Title. II. Series.

GUNTHER, John, 1901- 938'.07'0924 B
Alexander the Great; illustrated by Isa Barnett. New York, Random House [1953] 183 p. illus. 22 cm. (World landmark books) A life of the warrior who, as a prince, tamed the powerful horse Bucephalus and, during his short reign as king, built an empire that covered almost all of the then-known world, including Greece, India, Egypt, and Persia. [DF234.25.G8] 92 AC 68
1. Alexander the Great, 356-323 B.C. I. Barnett, Isa, illus. II. Title.

LIPSIUS, Frank. 938'.07'0924 B
Alexander the Great / Frank Lipsius ; introd. by Lord Chalfont. New York : Saturday Review Press, [1974] 224 p. : ill. (some col.) ; 26 cm. Includes index. Bibliography: p. 216-217. [DF234.L76] 74-408 14.95
1. Alexander the Great, 356-323 B.C.

MILNS, R. D., 1938- 930'.4'0924 B
Alexander the Great [by] R. D. Milns. New York, Pegasus [1969, c1968] 285 p. illus., maps, plans, ports. 21 cm. Bibliography: p. [274]-278. [DF234.M55 1969] 74-105219 6.00
1. Alexander the Great, 356-323 B.C.

RENAULT, Mary, pseud. 938'.07'0924 B
The nature of Alexander. [1st American ed.] New York, Pantheon Books [1975] 240 p. illus. 26 cm. Bibliography: p. 234. [DF234.R46 1975] 74-15152 ISBN 0-394-49113-0 : 17.95
1. Alexander the Great, 356-323 B.C. I. Title. BIP

ROBINSON, Charles Alexander, 1900- 923.138
Alexander the Great, conqueror and creator of a new world. New York, F. Watts [1963] xii, 158 p. 1 fold. map. 22 cm. (Immortals of history) [DF234.R64] 63-16916
1. Alexander the Great, 356-323 B. C.

ROBINSON, Charles Alexander, 1900- 923.138
The history of Alexander the Great. Providence, R. I., Brown Univ., 1953; New York, Kraus Reprint, 1967- v. map 24cm. (Halftitle: title: Brown Univ. Studies, 16) Kv.1. Pt. 1, An index to the extant

historians.--pt. 2. The fragments [DF234.R66] 52-14222 18.00
1. Alexander the Great, 356-323 B.C. I. Title. II. Series: Brown University. Brown University Studies, v.16

ROBINSON, Charles 938'.07'0924 B
Alexander, 1900-1965.
The history of Alexander the Great. Providence, R.I., Brown University, 1953-63. Millwood, N.Y., Kraus Reprint Co., 1967-72. 2 v. 26 cm. Vol. 2 originally published by Brown University Press. Original ed. issued as v. 16 and 26 of Brown University studies. Contents.Contents.—v. 1. An index to the extant historians. The fragments.—v. 2. The categories. The extant historians. [DF234.R663] 72-5737 Set 30.00
1. Alexander the Great, 356-323 B.C. I. Title. II. Series: Brown University. Brown University studies, v. 16 [etc.]
Vol. 1, 18.00. Vol. 2, 12.00. **BIP**

SAVILL, Agnes Forbes 930.40924 B
(Blackadder) 1876-
Alexander the Great and his time, by Agnes Savill. [2d ed.] New York, Citadel Press [1966, c1959] xx, 300 p. fold. map, plates. 21 cm. Bibliography: p. xv-xviii. [DF234.S2 1966] 66-17199
1. Alexander the Great, 356-323 B.C. I. Title.

SNYDER, John William, 930.40924 B
1924-
Alexander the Great, by John W. Snyder. New York, Twayne Publishers [1966] 223 p. maps. 21 cm. (Twayne's rulers and statesmen of the world series, 4) Bibliography: p. 211-214. [DF234.S65] 66-16126
1. Alexander the Great, 356-323 B.C.

TARN, William Woodthorpe v. 12
Sir 1869-
Alexander the Great. Boston, Beacon [1956] 160 p. 21 cm.
1. Alexander the Great, 356-323 B. C. I. Title. **BIP**

TARN, William, Woodthorpe v. 12
Sir 1869-1957.
Alexander the Great. Boston, Beacon Press [1956] xi, 160 p. 21 cm. (Beacon paperbacks, 26) First published 1948.
1. Alexander the Great, 356-323 B. C. I. Title.

WHEELER, Benjamin 938'.07'0924 B
Ide, 1854-1927.
Alexander the Great; the merging of East and West in universal history. Freeport, N.Y., Books for Libraries Press [1971] xv, 520 p. illus., maps, plans, ports. 23 cm. Reprint of the 1900 ed. [DF234.W56 1971] 77-148907 ISBN 0-8369-5670-2
1. Alexander the Great, B.C. 356-323. 2. Greece—History—To 146 B.C.

Alexander the Great, 356-323 B.C.—Juvenile literature.

BAUMANN, Hans, 930'.4'0924 (B)
1914-
Alexander's great march; translated by Stella Humphries, illustrated by Doreen Roberts. London, Oxford U. P., 1968. vii, 140 p. illus., map. 23 cm. SBN 19-271280-2 Translation of Der Grosse Alexanderzug. [DF234.B353 1968] 68-118520 15/-(B68-12025)
1. Alexander the Great, 356-323 B.C.—Juvenile literature. I. Title.

GRIMAL, Pierre 92
Stories of Alexander the Great. Ed., tr. from French by Barbara Whelpton. Illus. by Rene Peron. Cleveland, World [1966, c.1962-1965] 187p. illus. (pt. col.) 19cm. (Myths legends) Holly bk. [DF234.25.G713] 66-13636 2.50
1. Alexander the Great, 356-323 B.C.—Juvenile literature. I. Title.

MERCER, Charles E. 920
Alexander the Great, by the eds. of Horizon magazine. Author: Charles Mercer. Consultant: Cornelius C. Vermeuel III New York, Harper [c.1962, 1963] 153p. illus. (pt. col.) ports. (pt. col.) maps (pt. col.) 27cm. (Horizon caravel bk.) Bibl. 62-21199 3.95; 3.79 lib. ed.,
1. Alexander the Great—Juvenile literature. I. Horizon (New York 1958-) II. Title.

MITCHISON, Naomi 923.138
(Haldane) 1897-
The young Alexander tHe great. Illustrated by Betty Middleton-Sandford. New York, Roy Publishers [1961, c1960] 118p. illus. 21cm. [DF234.25.M5] 60-14477
1. Alexander the Great, 356-323 B. C.—Juvenile literature. I. Title.

SUGGS, Robert Carl, 1932- 920
Alexander the great, scientist-king. Illus. by Leonard Everett Fisher. New York, Macmillan [1964] 1 v. (unpaged) col. illus., fold. col. map. 24cm. (Sci. story lib.) 63-15664 2.95; 3.15 lib. ed.,
1. Alexander the Great, 356-323 B.C.—Juvenile literature. I. Title.

Alexander the Great, 356-323 B.C. - Campaigns.

DODGE, Theodore 355.3'32'0922
Ayrault, 1842-1909.
Great captains; showing the influence on the art of war of the campaigns of Alexander, Hannibal, Caesar, Gustavus Adolphus, Frederick, and Napoleon. Port Washington, N.Y., Kennikat Press [1968, c1889] xiii, 219 p. illus., maps. 21 cm. [U51.D6 1968] 67-27591
1. Alexander the Great—Campaigns. 2. Hannibal. 3. Caesar, C. Julius. 4. Gustaf II Adolf, King of Sweden, 1594-1632. 5. Friedrich II, der Grosse, King of Prussia, 1712-1821. 6. Napoleon I, Emperor of the French, 1769-1821. 7. Military biography. I. Title.

Alexander the Great, 356-323 B.C.—Campaigns—India.

STEIN, Mark 915.49'12'04350924
Aurel, Sir, 1862-1943.
On Alexander's track to the Indus; personal narrative of explorations on the north-west frontier of India carried out under the orders of H. M. Indian Government. New York, B. Blom, 1972. xi, 182 p. illus. 26 cm. Reprint of the 1929 ed. [DS485.N7S7 1972] 72-79947 18.75
1. Alexander the Great, 356-323 B.C.—Campaigns—India. 2. North-west Frontier Province—Antiquities. 3. North-west Frontier Province—Description and travel. I. Title. **BIP**

DYKEMAN, Wilma 920
Seeds of Southern change: the life of Will Alexander [by] Wilma Dykeman, James Stokely. [Chicago] Univ. of Chic. Pr. [c.1962] 343p. illus. 23cm. Bibl. 62-13923 5.95
1. Alexander, Will Winton, 1884-1956 2. Southern States—Soc. condit. 3. Southern States—Race question I. Stokely, James, joint author. II. Title.

Alexander, Will Winton, 1884-1956.

DYKEMAN, Wilma. 975'.04'0924 B
Seeds of Southern change : the life of Will Alexander / Wilma Dykeman and James Stokely. New York : Norton, [1976], c1962. p. cm. (The Norton library) Reprint of the ed. published by the University of Chicago Press, Chicago. Includes index. Bibliography: p. [F215.A55D9 1976] 76-10712 ISBN 0-393-00813-4
1. Alexander, Will Winton, 1884-1956. 2. Commission of Interracial Cooperation. 3. Afro-Americans—Southern States. 4. Southern States—Race question. I. Stokely, James, joint author. II. Title. **BIP**

Alexander, William, 1726-1783.

VALENTINE, Alan 973.3'0924 B
Chester, 1901-
Lord Stirling [by] Alan Valentine. New York, Oxford University Press, 1969. 299 p. port. 22 cm. Bibliography: p. 282-286. [E207.A3V3] 69-12351 6.50
1. Alexander, William, 1726-1783. I. Title.

Alexandra, consort of Edward VII, King of Great Britain, 1844-1925.

BATTISCOMBE, 942.082'0924 B
Georgina.
Queen Alexandra. Boston, Houghton Mifflin, 1969. 336 p. illus., fold. geneal. table., ports. 24 cm. [DA568.A2B3 1969b] 74-91064 7.50
1. Alexandra, consort of Edward VII, King of Great Britain, 1844-1925.

TISDALL, Evelyn Ernest 923.142
Percy, 1907-
Alexandra, Edward VII's unpredictable queen. New York, J. Day Co. [1954] 308 p. illus. 21 cm. "Published in England, in a slightly different version, as Unpredictable queen." [DA568.A2T57 1954] 54-5887
1. Alexandra, consort of Edward VII, King of Great Britain, 1844-1925.

TISDALL, Evelyn Ernest 923.142
Percy, 1907-
Unpredictable queen; the intimate life of Queen Alexandra. London, New York, S. Paul [1953] 240p. illus. 22cm. [DA568.A2T57 1953] 53-4543
1. Alexandra, consort of Edward VII, King of Great Britain, 1844-1925. I. Title.

Alexandra, consort of Nichola

MAGNIFICO, Meda. 923.147
The human saint; a true biography of the Empress of all the Russians. [1st ed. Springfield, Mass., Boston House Publishers Corp., 1962] 129p. illus. 36cm. [DK254.A5M3] 62-19717
1. Alexandra, consort of Nichola I. Title.

Alexius I Comnenus, Emperor of the East, 1048-1118.

COMNENA, Anna, 949.5'03'0924 B
b.1083.
The Alexiad of Anna Comnena. Translated from the Greek by E. R. A. Sewter. Baltimore, Penguin Books [1969] 560 p. geneal. table, maps. 19 cm. (The Penguin classics) Translation of Alexias. Bibliography: p. 524-525. [DF605.C6 1969] 76-11098 ISBN 0-14-044215-4 3.50
1. Alexius I Comnenus, Emperor of the East, 1048-1118. 2. Byzantine Empire—History—Alexius I Comnenus, 1081-1118. I. Sewter, Edgar Robert Ashton, 1907- tr. II. Title.

COMNENA, Anna, 949.5'03'0924 B
b.1083.
The Alexiad of the Princess Anna Comnena, being the history of the reign of her father, Alexius I, Emperor of the Romans, 1081-1118 A.D. Translated by Elizabeth A. S. Dawes. New York, Barnes & Noble [1967] viii, 439 p. 23 cm. Reprint of the 1928 ed. Translation of Alexias. [DF605.C6 1967a] 67-5910
1. Alexius I Comnenus, Emperor of the East, 1048-1118. 2. Byzantine Empire—History—Alexius I Comnenus, 1081-1118. I. Title.

Alfieri, Dino, 1886-

ALFIERI, Dino, 1886- 940.54'82'45
Dictators face to face / Dino Alfieri ; translated by David Moore. Westport, Conn. : Greenwood Press, 1978, c1954. x, 307 p., [4] leaves of plates : ill. ; 23 cm. Reprint of the ed. published by Elek, London. Translation of Due dittatori di fronte. Includes bibliographical references and index. [D811.5.A533 1978] 78-755 ISBN 0-313-20285-0 : 21.75
1. Alfieri, Dino, 1886- 2. World War, 1939-1945—Personal narratives, Italian. 3. Italy—Foreign relations—Germany. 4. Germany—Foreign relations—Italy. 5. Ambassadors—Italy—Biography. I. Title. **BIP**

Alfieri, Vittorio, 1749-1803.

ALFIERI, Vittorio, 1749- 928.5
1803.
The life of Vittorio Alfieri written by himself. Translated by Sir Henry McAnally. Lawrence, University of Kansas Press, 1953. 288p. port. 24cm. [PQ4681.A3E58] 53-8621
I. Title.

ALFIERI, Vittorio, 1749- 928.5
1803.
Memoirs; the anonymous translation of 1810, revised by E. R. Vincent. London, New York, Oxford University Press, 1961. xix, 310p. 19cm. (The Oxford library of Italian classics) [PQ4681.A3E63 1961] 61-65513
I. Title.

MEGARO, Gaudens, 1903- 852'.6 B
1958.
Vittorio Alfieri : forerunner of Italian nationalism / by Gaudence Megaro. New York : Octagon Books, 1975, c1930. 175 p. ; 24 cm. Originally presented as the author's thesis, Columbia, 1930. Reprint of the ed. published by Columbia University Press, New York, which was issued as no. 336 of Studies in history, economics, and public law. Includes index. Bibliography: p. 161-169. [PQ4681.M4 1975] 78-159246 ISBN 0-374-95557-3 : 9.50
1. Alfieri, Vittorio, 1749-1803. I. Series: Columbia studies in the social sciences ; no. 336.

Alford, Ed., 1901-

GIPSON, Frederick 974'.06'0924 B
Benjamin, 1908-
Cowhand : the story of a working cowboy / by Fred Gipson. College Station : Texas A&M University Press, [1977] p. cm. [F391.A33G56 1977] 77-89509 ISBN 0-89096-040-2 : 7.95
1. Alford, Ed., 1901- 2. Cowboys—Texas—Biography. 3. Ranch life—Texas. I. Title.

Alford, Thomas Wildcat, 1860-

ALFORD, Thomas 970.004'97
Wildcat, 1860-
Civilization, and the story of the Absentee Shawnees / as told to Florence Drake by Thomas Wildcat Alford ; with a foreword by Angie Debo. Norman : University of Oklahoma Press, c1979. 203 p., [5] leaves of plates : ill. ; 22 cm. (The Civilization of the American Indian ; [v. 13]) First published in 1936 under title: Civilization. [E99.S35A453 1979] 79-129832 ISBN 0-8061-1590-4 : 12.50
1. Alford, Thomas Wildcat, 1860- 2. Shawnee Indians—History. 3. Shawnee Indians—Biography. I. Drake, Florence. II. Title. III. Series: Civilization of the American Indian series ; v. 13.

Alfred the Great, King of England, 849-901.

ASSER, Bp. of 942.01'0924
Sherborne, d909?
Life of King Alfred. Translated with introd. and notes by L. C. Jane. New York, Cooper Square Publishers, 1966. lix, 163 p. illus., facsim., geneal. table. 17 cm. (The Medieval library, Translation of De rebus gestis Aelfredi as published in 1848 in Monumenta historica Britannica. [DA153.A88 1966] 66 27658
1. Alfred the Great, King of England, 849-901. I. Jane, Lionel Cecil, 1879-1932, ed. and tr. II. Title.

ASSER, Bp. of 942.01'0924
Sherborne, d.909?
Life of King Alfred. Translated with introd. and notes by L. C. Jane. New York, Cooper Square Publishers, 1966 lix, 173 p. illus., facsim., geneal. table. 17 cm. (The Medieval library) Translation of De rebus gestis Aelfredi as published in 1848 in Monumenta historica Britannica. [DA153.A88 1966] 66-27658
1. Alfred the Great, King of England, 849-901. I. Jane, Lionel Cecil, 1879-1932, ed. and tr. II. Title.

BOWKER, Alfred, ed. 942.01'0924 B
Alfred the Great; containing chapters on his life and times, by Frederic Harrison [and others] Also containing an introd. by Sir Walter Besant and a poem by the Poet Laureate. Edited, with pref., by Alfred Bowker. Freeport, N.Y., Books for Libraries Press [1971] xii, 260 p. illus., map, port. 23 cm. Reprint of the 1899 ed. Contents.Contents.—The spotless king, by A. Austin.—Introduction, by Sir W. Besant.—Alfred as king, by F. Harrison.—Alfred as a religious man and an educationalist, by the Bishop of Bristol [G. F. Browne]—Alfred as a warrior, by C. Oman.—Alfred as a geographer, by Sir C. Markham.—Alfred as a writer, by J. Earle.—English law before the Norman conquest, by Sir F. Pollock.—Alfred and the arts, by W. J. Loftie. Includes

bibliographical references. [DA153.B77 1971] 78-154144 ISBN 0-8369-5760-1
1. Alfred the Great, King of England, 849-901. 2. Gt. Brit.—History—Alfred, 871-901.

DUCKETT, Eleanor Shipley. 923.142
Alfred the Great. [Chicago] University of Chicago Press [1956] 220 p. 22 cm. [DA153.D85] 56-13050
1. Alfred the Great, King of England, 849-901.

DUCKETT, Eleanor Shipley. v. 12
Alfred the Great and his England. [Chicago] University of Chicago Press, Phoenix Books, 1961. 190 p. 65-105102
1. Alfred the Great, King of England. I. Title.

HELM, Peter J., 1916- 923.142
Alfred the Great [by] P. J. Helm. New York, Crowell [1965, c1963] 205 p. illus., map. 22 cm. Bibliography: p. [197] [DA153.H46 1965] 64-25752
1. Alfred the Great, King of England, 849-901.

LEES, Beatrice Adelaide. 942.01'64'0924 B
Alfred the Great, the truth teller, maker of England, 848-899. New York, Lemma Pub. Corp., 1972 [c1915] xv, 493 p. illus. 23 cm. Bibliography: p. 469-471. [DA153.L4 1972] 74-180767 ISBN 0-87696-029-8
1. Alfred the Great, King of England, 849-901. I. Title. BIP

LIFE of King Alfred, v. 12
together with the Annals of Saint Neots erroneously ascribed to Asser; ed., with introduction and commentary by William Henry Stevenson. With article on article on Recent work on Asser's Life of Alfred by Dorothy Whitelock. Oxford, Clarendon Press, 1959. clii, 386p. facsim. 19cm. Latin text.
1. Alfred the Great, King of England, 849-901. I. Asser, Bp. of Sherborne, d. 909? II. Stevenson, William Henry, 1858-1924, ed. III. Whitelock, Dorothy.

LOYN, Henry Royston. 942.01/0924
Alfred the Great, by H. R. Loyn. London, Oxford Univ. Pr., 1967. 64p. 8 plates (incl. facsims.). 21cm. (Clarendon biographies) Maps on endpapers. Bibl. [DA153.L6] (B) 67-108647 1.55 bds.,
1. Alfred the Great, King of England, 849-901. I. Title.
Available from publisher's New York office.

MAPP, Alf Johnson. 942.01'64'0924 B
The golden dragon: Alfred the Great and his times [by] Alf J. Mapp, Jr. La Salle, Ill., Open Court [1974] p. cm. Bibliography: p. [DA153.M25] 74-8983 ISBN 0-87548-293-7 8.95
1. Alfred the Great, King of England, 840-901. 2. Great Britain—History—Alfred, 871-901. I. Title.

PAULI, Reinhold, 1823-1882. 942.01'64'0924 B
The life of Alfred the Great. Translated from the German of Dr. R. Pauli. To which is appended Alfred's Anglo-Saxon version of Orosius, with a literal English translation, and an Anglo-Saxon alphabet and glossary, by B. Thorpe. London, H. G. Bohn, 1853. New York, AMS Press [1968] ix, 582 p. 22 cm. Translation of Konig Aelfred und seine Stelle in der Geschichte Englands. Original ed. issued in series: Bohn's antiquarian library. Includes bibliographical references. [DA153.P3413 1968] 68-57869
1. Alfred the Great, King of England, 849-901. 2. Great Britain—History—Alfred the Great, King of England, 849-901. 3. World history. 4. History, Ancient. I. Orosius, Paulus. Adversus paganos historiarum libri VII. Anglo-Saxon and English. 1968. II. Title. BIP

PLUMMER, Charles, 1851-1927. 942.01'0924 B
The life and times of Alfred the Great. New York, Haskell House, 1970. xi, 232 p. map 23 cm. (Ford lectures, 1901) Reprint of the 1902 ed. Bibliography: p. [x]-xi. [DA153.P73 1970] 68-25261
1. Alfred the Great, King of England, 849-901. I. Title. II. Series: Oxford. University. Ford lectures, 1901 BIP

PLUMMER, Charles, 1851-1927. 942.01'0924 B
The life and times of Alfred the Great. Oxford, Clarendon Press, 1902. St. Clair Shores, Mich., Scholarly Press, 1970. xi, 232 p. 21 cm. (Ford lectures, 1901) Bibliography: p. [x]-xi. [DA153.P73 1970b] 72-131802 ISBN 0-403-00689-9
1. Alfred the Great, King of England, 849-901. I. Title. II. Series: Oxford. University. Ford lectures, 1901

PLUMMER, Charles, 1851-1927. 942.01'64'0924 B
The life and times of Alfred the Great. With an appendix. [Folcroft, Pa.] Folcroft Library Editions, 1973. p. Reprint of the 1902 ed. published by Clarendon Press, Oxford, which was issued as Ford lectures, 1901. Bibliography: p. [DA153.P73 1973] 73-13737 ISBN 0-8414-6723-4 (lib. bdg.)
1. Alfred the Great, King of England, 849-901. I. Series: Oxford. University. Ford lectures 1901.

Alfred the Great, King of England, 849-901—Fiction.

LENANTON, Carola Mary Anima (Oman) 1897- v. 12
Alfred, king of the English, by Carola Oman; illustrated by E. Boye Uden. New York, E. P. Dutton & co. inc. [1962] x, 246 p. incl. plates. col. front. 20 cm. "First published 1939." 68-83197
1. Alfred the Great, King of England, 849-901—Fiction. I. Title.

Alfred the Great, King of England, 849-901—Juvenile literature.

JOHNSON, Eleanor Noyes. 942.01 (J)
King Alfred the Great. Illustrated by Arthur Wallower. Philadelphia, Westminster Press [1966] 176 p. illus., maps. 23 cm. Bibliography: p. 173-176. [DA153.J6] 66-9258
1. Alfred the Great, King of England, 849-901—Juvenile literature. I. Title.

MITCHISON, Naomi mary margaret (Haldane) 1897- 920
The young Alfred the Great. Illus. by Shirley Farrow. New York, Roy [1963] 126p. illus. 21cm. 62-18439 3.00
1. Alfred the Great, King of England, 849-901—Juvenile literature. I. Title.

Alger, Horatio, 1832-1899.

GARDNER, Ralph D., 1923- 928.1
Horatio Alger, or The American hero era. Mendota, Ill., Wayside Pr. [c.1964] 505p. col. illus., facsims. (pt. col.) ports. 23cm. Bibl. 63-11153 5.95
1. Alger, Horatio, 1832-1899. 2. Alger, Horatio, 1832-1899. I. Title. II. Title: The American hero era.

HOYT, Edwin Palmer. 813'.4 B
Horatio's boys; the life and works of Horatio Alger, Jr. [by] Edwin P. Hoyt. [1st ed.] Radnor, Pa., Chilton Book Co. [1974] v, 263 p. illus. 22 cm. Includes bibliographical references. [PS1029.A3Z68] 74-10672 ISBN 0-8019-5966-7 8.95
1. Alger, Horatio, 1832-1899. I. Title. BIP

RUSSELL, Ray. 813'.4 B
Holy Horatio! : the strange life and paradoxical works of the legendary Mr. Algar ; and an afterword chronicling an American success story / by Ray Russell. Santa Barbara, Calif. : Capra Press, 1976, c1966. 50 p. ; 18 cm. (Capra chapbook series ; no 38) [PS1029.A3Z8 1976] 76-14220 ISBN 0-88496-062-5 : 10.00. ISBN 0-88496-061-7 pbk. : 2.50
1. Alger, Horatio, 1832-1899. 2. Authors, American—19th century—Biography. I. Title.

Alger, Horatio, 1832-1899—Biography.

GARDNER, Ralph D., 1923- 813'.4 B
Horatio Alger : or, The American hero era, including Road to success : the bibliography of the works of Horatio Alger / by Ralph D. Gardner. New York : Arco Pub. Co., [1978] p. cm. Includes index. Bibliography: p. [PS1029.A3Z65 1978] 77-28059 ISBN 0-668-04466-7 : 10.00
1. Alger, Horatio, 1832-1899—Biography. 2. Alger, Horatio, 1832-1899—Bibliography. 3. Authors, American—19th century—Biography. I. Gardner, Ralph D., 1923- Road to success. 1978. II. Title: The American hero era.

Alger, Philip Langdon, 1894-

ALGER, Philip Langdon, 1894- 621.3'092'4 B
Tales of my life and family / by Philip L. Alger. [Schenectady? N.Y.] : Alger, [1974] xxx, 261 p. : ill. ; 22 cm. Includes bibliographical references and index. [TK140.A44A32] 74-79024
1. Alger, Philip Langdon, 1894- I. Title.

Algren, Nelson,

ALGREN, Nelson, 1909- 928.1
Conversations with Nelson Algren, by H. E. F. Donohue. New York, Hill & Wang [c.1963,1964] xii, 333p. 21cm. 64-24825 6.50
I. Donohue, H. E. F. II. Title.

ALGREN, Nelson, 1909- 928.1
Conversations with Nelson Algren, by H. E. F. Donohue. New York, Berkeley [1965, c.1963, 1964] 284p. 18cm. (Medallion book, S1134) .75 pap.,
I. Donohue, H. E. F. II. Title.

Ali, Beatrice.

ALI, Beatrice. 942.1'2'0820924
The good deeds of a good woman : recorded between May and September 1975 / Beatrice Ali. London : D. Dobson, 1976. 124 p. ; 23 cm. & disc (33 1/3 rpm. mono. 6 in.). (Ordinary lives ; no. 1) [DA676.8.A4A34 1976] 77-361667 ISBN 0-234-77891-1 : £4.95
1. Ali, Beatrice. 2. London—Biography. I. Title. II. Series.

Ali, Mohamed, Maulana, 1878-1931.

IQBAL, Afzal. 954.03'5 B
The life and times of Mohamed Ali : an analysis of the hopes, fears, and aspirations of Muslim India from 1778-1931 / by Afzal Iqbal. 1st ed. Lahore : Institute of Islamic culture, 1974. xii, 443 p. ; 22 cm. Includes index. Bibliography: p. 423-428. [DS481.A5I65] 75-930033 ISBN 0-88386-630-7 14.00
1. Ali, Mohamed, Maulana, 1878-1931. 2. Muslims in India—History. 3. India—Politics and government—1765-1947. I. Title.
Distributed by South Asia Bks. BIP

Ali, Muhammad, 1942- —Juvenile literature.

LIPSYTE, Robert. 796.8'3'0924 B
Free to be Muhammad Ali / Robert Lipsyte. 1st ed. New York : Harper & Row, c1978. 124 p. ; 21 cm. "An Ursula Nordstrom book." Includes index. A biography of a boxer, twice holder of the title of world heavyweight champion, who has come to be known as "The Greatest." [GV1132.A44L56 1978] 92 77-25640 ISBN 0-06-023901-8 : 5.95. ISBN 0-06-023902-6 lib. bdg. : 5.79
1. Ali, Muhammad, 1942- —Juvenile literature. 2. Boxers (Sports)—United States—Biography—Juvenile literature. I. Title. BIP

Alice Cooper (Musical group)

ALICE Cooper (Musical group). 784'.092'4 B
Me, Alice : the autobiography of Alice Cooper with Steven Gaines. New York : Putnam, c1975. 254 p., [8] leaves of plates : ill. ; 22 cm. [ML421.A4A3] 75-40488 8.95
1. Alice Cooper (Musical group) 2. Rock musicians—Correspondence, reminiscences, etc. I. Gaines, Steven S. II. Title.

Alice, Mother, 1879-1960.

SLOAN, Raymond P. 923.673
On a shoestring and a prayer. [1st ed.] Garden City, N. Y., Doubleday, 1964. vii, 178 p. illus., group ports. 22 cm. [R154.A48S58] 64-11682
1. Alice, Mother, 1879-1960. I. Title.

Alice's Restaurant.

BROCK, Alice May, 1941- 647'.95'0924 B
My life as a restaurant / by Alice May Brock, together with her friends. Woodstock, N.Y. : Overlook Press, 1975. 142 p., [1] leaf of plates : ill. ; 26 cm. [TX945.5.A53B76] 75-4378 ISBN 0-87951-032-3 : 7.95
1. Alice's Restaurant. 2. Brock, Alice May, 1941- 3. Cookery. I. Title. BIP

Alkan, Charles Henri Valentin, 1813-1888.

SMITH, Ronald, 1922- 786.1'092'4 B
Alkan / Ronald Smith. New York : Crescendo Pub., 1977-, c1976- v. : ill. ; 23 cm. Includes index. Contents.Contents.—v. 1. The enigma. Bibliography: v. 1, p. [113]-114. [ML410.A442S6 1977] 78-303347 ISBN 0-87597-105-9 (v. 1) : 7.95 (v. 1)
1. Alkan, Charles Henri Valentin, 1813-1888. 2. Composers—France—Biography.

SMITH, Ronald, 1922- 786.1'092'4 B
Alkan / [by] Ronald Smith. London : Kahn and Averill, 1976- v. : ill., facsims., geneal. table, music, ports. ; 23 cm. Includes index. Contents.—v. 1. The enigma. Bibliography: v. 1, p. [113]-114. [ML410.A442S6] 76-369229 ISBN 0-900707-39-9 (v. 1) : £3.00 (v. 1)
1. Alkan, Charles Henri Valentin, 1813-1888. 2. Composers—France—Biography.

All-England Club, Wimbledon, Eng.—Juvenile literature.

MAY, Julian. 796.34'2'0922 B
Wimbledon / by Julian May. Mankato, Minn. : Creative Education, [1975] p. cm. (Sports classic) A brief history of the world champion tennis tournament at Wimbledon, with brief sketches of some of its singles champions. [GV994.A1M38] 920 75-17779 ISBN 0-87191-444-1
1. All-England Club, Wimbledon, Eng.—Juvenile literature. 2. Tennis—Biography—Juvenile literature. I. Title. BIP

All terrain vehicle racing—United States—History.

JOHNSON, Norman T. 796.7'0973
The off-road racer, 1976 / Norman T. Johnson and Gordon Grimmis. Las Vegas, Nev. : G. & J. Pub. Co., c1976. xiii, 271 p. : ill. ; 29 cm. [GV1029.J65] 77-150576
1. All terrain vehicle racing—United States—History. 2. Automobile racers—United States—Biography. I. Grimmis, Gordon, joint author. II. Title.

Allagash River.

KIDNEY, Dorothy Boone. 917.41'2
Away from it all. South Bunswick [i.e. Brunswick, N.J.] A. S. Barnes [1969] 200 p. illus., map. 22 cm. [F27.A4K5] 68-27204 5.95
1. Allagash River. I. Title. BIP

Allamano, Giuseppe, 1851-1926.

BREEN, Stephen. 266.00924 (B)
The missionary. Somerset, N. J., Consolata Society for Foreign Missions [1965] xii, 156 p. col. port. 23 cm. [BX4705.A523.B7] 66-6030
1. Allamano, Giuseppe, 1851-1926. 2. Missionaries of the Consolata. I. Title.

Allard, Sydney Herbert, 1910-1966.

LUSH, Tom, 1914- 629.22'22
Allard, the inside story / by Tom Lush ; foreword by Bill Boddy. Croydon : Motor

Racing Publications, 1977. 207 p. : ill., ports. ; 19 x 24 cm. On jacket: Sole distributors for the USA, Motorbooks International, Osceola, Wis. [TL140.A36L87] 78-322197 ISBN 0-900549-30-0 : 17.50
1. Allard, Sydney Herbert, 1910-1966. 2. Allard automobile. 3. Automobile industry and trade—Great Britain—Biography. I. Title.

Allen, Arthur James, 1875-1944.

ALLEN, Arthur James, 1875-1944. 639'.28'0924 B
A whaler & trader in the Arctic, 1895 to 1944 : my life with the bowhead / Arthur James Allen. Anchorage : Alaska Northwest Pub. Co., c1978. ix, 213 p. : ill. ; 22 cm. [SH382.A44 1978] 78-2575 ISBN 0-88240-105-X : 5.95
1. Allen, Arthur James, 1875-1944. 2. Whaling—Arctic regions. 3. Whalemen—Biography. I. Title.

Allen, Asa Alonso,

ALLEN, Asa Alonso, 1911-1970. 269'.2'0924 B
Born to lose, bound to win; an autobiography [by] A. A. Allen, with Walter Wagner. [1st ed.] Garden City, N.Y., Doubleday, 1970. 202 p. 22 cm. [BV3785.A43A3] 70-132493
I. Wagner, Walter, 1927- II. Title.

Allen, Cecil John,

ALLEN, Cecil John, 1886- 385.0924
Two million miles of train travel: the autobiography of Cecil J. Allen. London, I. Allan [dist. New Rochelle, N.Y., SportShelf, c.1965] 232p. illus., ports. 24cm. [HE3018.2.A5A3] 65-9811 11.00
I. Title.

Allen, Chaney.

ALLEN, Chaney. 362.2'92'0926 B
I'm Black & I'm sober : a minister's daughter tells her story about fighting the disease of alcoholism—and winning / by Chaney Allen. Minneapolis : CompCare Publications, c1978. xv, 279 p. : ill. ; 21 cm. Published in 1976 under title: I'm Black and I'm drunk, by C. L. Allen and E. L. Mayfield. [HV5232.A54A34 1978] 77-86454 ISBN 0-89638-008-4 : 6.95
1. Allen, Chaney. 2. Alcoholics—United States—Biography. 3. Alcohol and women—United States. 4. Afro-Americans and alcohol—United States. 5. Alcoholics—Rehabilitation—United States—Biography. I. Title.

Allen, Charles Livingstone, 1913-

ALLEN, Charles Livingstone, 1913- 287'.6'0924 B
What I have lived by : an autobiography / Charles L. Allen. Old Tappan, N.J. : F. H. Revell Co., c1976. p. cm. [BX8495.A518A33] 76-40914 ISBN 0-8007-0805-9 : 5.95. ISBN 0-8007-0806-7 gift ed. : 9.95
1. Allen, Charles Livingstone, 1913- 2. Methodist Church—Clergy—Biography. 3. Clergy—United States—Biography. I. Title.
BIP

Allen, Devere, 1891-1955.

ALLEN, Devere, 1891-1955. 327'.172'0924
Devere Allen, life and writings / edited, with an introd., by Charles Chatfield. New York : Garland Pub., 1976. p. cm. (The Garland library of war and peace) Bibliography: p. [JX1937.A47 1976] 75-147691 ISBN 0-8240-0447-7 lib.bdg. : 25.00
1. Allen, Devere, 1891-1955. 2. Peace—Addresses, essays, lectures. I. Title. II. Series.

Allen, Ethan, 1738-1789.

BROWN, Slater, 1896- 923.573
Ethan Allen and the Green Mountain boys; illustrated by William Moyers. New York, Random House [1956] 184p. illus. 22cm. (Landmark books [66]) [E207.A4B84] 56-5457
1. Allen, Ethan, 1737-1789. I. Title.

*HOLBROOK, Stewart. 973.3'092'4
America's Ethan Allen / Stewart Holbrook ; pictures by Lynd Ward. Boston : Houghton Mifflin, 1976c1949. 96p. : ill. (some col.) : 24 cm. (Sandpiper edition) [E207.A4] ISBN 0-395-24908-2 pbk. : 3.95
1. Allen, Ethan, 1738-1789. I. Ward, Lynn, ill. II. Title.
BIP

HOLBROOK, Stewart Hall, 1893-1964. 923.573
Ethan Allen. [1st illustrated ed.] Portland, Or., Binfords & Mort, 1958 [c1940] 283 p. illus. 23 cm. Includes bibliography. [E207.A4H6 1958] 58-11336
1. Allen, Ethan, 1737-1789. **BIP**

HOYT, Edwin Palmer. 974.3'02'0924 B
The damndest Yankees : Ethan Allen & his clan / by Edwin P. Hoyt. Brattleboro, Vt. : S. Greene Press, c1976. viii, 262 p., [2] leaves of plates : ill. ; 24 cm. Includes index. Bibliography: p. 254-255. [E207.A4H65] 74 27455 ISBN 0-8289-0259-3 : 10.95
1. Allen, Ethan, 1738-1789. 2. Allen, Ira, 1751-1814. 3. Allen family. 4. Vermont—History—To 1791. I. Title.

JELLISON, Charles Albert. 973.3'0924 B
Ethan Allen: frontier rebel [by] Charles A. Jellison. [1st ed. Syracuse, N.Y.] Syracuse University Press [1969] viii, 360 p. map. 24 cm. Bibliographical references included in "Notes" (p. 335-350) [E207.A4J4] 73-84582 9.95
1. Allen, Ethan, 1738-1789.

JELLISON, Charles Albert. 973.3'092'4 B
Ethan Allen: frontier rebel [by] Charles A. Jellison. Taftsville, Vt., Countryman Press; [distributed by N. Watson Academic Publications, New York, 1974, c1969] viii, 360 p. map. 23 cm. Reprint of the ed. published by Syracuse University Press, New York. Bibliography: p. 335-350. [E207.A4J4 1974] 74-14632 ISBN 0-914378-03-1 6.95 (pbk.)
1. Allen, Ethan, 1738-1789. I. Title.

PELL, John. 973.3'092'4 B
Ethan Allen. Freeport, N.Y., Books for Libraries Press [1972, c1929] xii, 331 p. illus. 22 cm. "Bibliography and key to Chronology and notes": p. [271]-317. [E207.A4P38 1972] 72-5515 ISBN 0-8369-6919-7
1. Allen, Ethan, 1738-1789. **BIP**

Allen, Ethan, 1738-1789—Juvenile literature.

LENGYEL, Cornel Adam. 92
Ethan Allen and the Green Mountain Boys. Garden City, N. Y., N. Doubleday [1961] 63p. illus. 21cm. (The Living history program) [E207.A4L4] 61-45286
1. Allen, Ethan, 1738-1789—Juvenile literature. I. Title.

RIPLEY, Sheldon N 92
Ethan Allen, Green Mountain hero. Illustrated by Louis F. Cary. Boston, Houghton, Mifflin [1961] 191p. illus. 22cm. (Piper books) [E207.A4R53] 61-8753
1. Allen, Ethan, 1738- 1879—Juvenile literature. I. Title.

Allen, Frank Calvin, 1866-1963.

ALLEN, Robert F., 1906- 630.11'771'55
A rugged man's life, by Robert F. Allen. Philadelphia, Dorrance [1968] 191 p. illus., facsims., ports. 22 cm. [CT275.A5318A7] 68-18880 4.00
1. Allen, Frank Calvin, 1866-1963. I. Title.

Allen, Frederick Lewis, 1890-1954.

ALLEN, Fred, 1894- 927.92
Treadmill to oblivion; with drawings by Hirshfeld. [1st ed.] Boston, Little, Brown [1954] 240p. illus. 21cm. Autobiographical. [PN1991.4.A6A3] 54-11132
I. Title.

ALLEN, Fred, 1894-1956. 927.92
Much ado about me. [1st ed.] Boston, Little, Brown [1956] 380p. illus. 22cm. [PN2287.A48A3] 56-13052
I. Title.

PAYNE, Darwin. 070.4'092'4 B
The man of only yesterday : Frederick Lewis Allen, former editor of Harper's magazine, author, and interpreter of his times / Darwin Payne ; foreword by Russell Lynes. 1st ed. New York : Harper & Row, [1975] xi, 340 p. ; 22 cm. (A Cass Canfield book) Includes bibliographical references and index. [PN4874.A38P3] 74-1847 ISBN 0-06-013296-5 : 10.00
1. Allen, Frederick Lewis, 1890-1954. I. Title.

Allen, George Herbert, 1923-

GILDEA, William. 796.33'2'0924
The future is now; George Allen, pro football's most controversial coach [by] William Gildea & Kenneth Turan. [New York, Dell, 1973 c.1972] 303 p. 18 cm. [GV939.A53G54] 1.25 (pbk.)
1. Allen, George Herbert, 1923- I. Turan, Kenneth, joint author. II. Title.

GILDEA, William. 796.33'2'0924
The future is now; George Allen, pro football's most controversial coach [by] William Gildea & Kenneth Turan. Boston, Houghton Mifflin [1972] xii, 318 p. illus. 22 cm. [GV939.A53G54] 72-2051 ISBN 0-395-14000-5 6.95
1. Allen, George Herbert, 1923- I. Turan, Kenneth, joint author. II. Title.

Allen, George Washington, 1891-

ALLEN, George Washington, 1891- 359.3'31'0924 B
Sails to atoms : from seaman to Admiral / George Washington Allen. Philadelphia : Dorrance, [1975] 169 p. : ill. ; 22 cm. [V63.A44A35] 75-319476 ISBN 0-8059-2141-9 : 5.95
1. Allen, George Washington, 1891- I. Title. **BIP**

Allen, Gracie, 1905-

BURNS, George, 1896- 927.92
I love her, that's why! An autobiography, by George Burns with Cynthia Hobart Lindsay. Prologue by Jack Benny. New York, Simon and Schuster, 1955. 267p. illus. 22cm. [PN1992.4.B4A3] 55-10045
1. Allen, Gracie, 1905- I. Title.

Allen, Henry Tureman, 1859-1930.

TWICHELL, Heath, 1934- 355.3'31'0924 B
Allen: the biography of an army officer 1859-1930 New Brunswick, N.J., Rutgers University Press [1974] xiii, 358 p. illus. 24 cm. Bibliography: p. [327]-340. [U53.A44T94] 74-12224 ISBN 0-8135-0778-2 12.50
1. Allen, Henry Tureman, 1859-1930. I. Title.

Allen, Henry Watkins, 1820-1866.

CASSIDY, Vincent H 923.273
Henry Watkins Allen of Louisiana [by] Vincent H. Cassidy and Amos E. Simpson. Batton Route, Louisiana State University Press [1964] vii, 201 p. port. 24 cm. Bibliographical references included in "Notes" (p. 167-185) [E467.1A4C3] 64-21597
1. Allen, Henry Watkins, 1820-1866. I. Simpson, Amos E., joint author. II. Title.

CASSIDY, Vincent H. 976.3/05/0924
The traveling man; the life story of Henry Watkins Allen, by Vincent H. Cassidy and Amos E. Simpson. Illus. by Wilton G. McIntyre. Baton Rouge, Claitor's Bk. Store, 1967. 79p. illus., port. 23cm. [E467.1A4C33] (B) 66-30722 2.50
1. Allen, Henry Watkins, 1820-1866. I. Simpson, Amos E. joint author. II. Title.

Allen, Ira, 1751-1814.

HOYT, Edwin Palmer. 974.3'02'0924 B
The damndest Yankees : Ethan Allen & his clan / by Edwin P. Hoyt. Brattleboro, Vt. : S. Greene Press, c1976. viii, 262 p., [2] leaves of plates : ill. ; 24 cm. Includes index. Bibliography: p. 254-255. [E207.A4H65] 74-27455 ISBN 0-8289-0259-3 : 10.95
1. Allen, Ethan, 1738-1789. 2. Allen, Ira, 1751-1814. 3. Allen family. 4. Vermont—History—To 1791. I. Title.

Allen, Ivan Earnest, 1877-

WILLIAMS, Eleanor, 1913- 923.373
Ivan Allen, a resourceful citizen. [Limited ed.] Atlanta, I. Allen-Marshall Co., 1950. xiv, 273 p. illus., ports., facsims. 24 cm. [CT275.A532W3] 30-2215
1. Allen, Ivan Earnest, 1877- I. Title.

Allen, John, 1942-

ALLEN, John, 1942- 364.1'092'4 B
Assault with a deadly weapon : the autobiography of a street criminal / John Allen ; edited by Dianne Hall Kelly and Philip Heymann. 1st ed. New York : Pantheon Books, c1977. p. cm. [HV6248.A37A33] 77-5297 ISBN 0-394-41510-8 : 8.95
1. Allen, John, 1942- 2. Crime and criminals—Washington, D.C.—Biography. I. Kelly, Dianne Hall, 1948- II. Heymann, Philip B. III. Title.
BIP

ALLEN, John, 1942- 364.1'092'4
Assault with a deadly weapon : the autobiography of a street criminal / John Allen ; edited by Dianne Hall Kelly and Philip Heymann ; with a foreword by Hylan Lewis. New York : McGraw-Hill, [1978] c1977. p. cm. Reprint of the ed. published by Pantheon Books, New York. [HV6248.A37A33 1978] 78-6883 ISBN 0-07-001073-0 : 3.95
1. Allen, John, 1942- 2. Crime and criminals—Washington, D.C.—Biography. I. Kelly, Dianne Hall, 1948- II. Heymann, Philip B. III. Title.

Allen, John Mills, 1847-1917.

GENTRY, Claude. 923.273
Private John Allen: gentleman, statesman, sage, prophet. Jacket and illus. by the author. [Baldwyn? Miss., 1951] 189 p. illus. 23 cm. [E661.A397G4] 51-5705
1. Allen, John Mills, 1847-1917. I. Title.

Allen, Ralph, 1694-1764.

ALLEN, Ralph H. 365'.66
Flight of a wandering sparrow / by Ralph H. Allen, Jr. [s.l. : s.n.], c1977 (North Newton, KS : Mennonite Press) 116 p. ; 22 cm. [BV4465.A43] 77-88271 2.95
1. Allen, Ralph H. 2. Church work with prisoners—Kansas—Sedgwick Co. 3. Methodists in Wichita, Kan.—Biography. 4. Wichita, Kan.—Biography. I. Title.

BOYCE, Benjamin, 1903- 942.3'8'070924 B
The benevolent man; a life of Ralph Allen of Bath. Cambridge, Mass., Harvard University Press, 1967. xiv, 304 p. illus., map, ports. 25 cm. Bibliographical footnotes. [DA690.B3B6] 67-11667
1. Allen, Ralph, 1694-1764. 2. Bath, Eng.—History. 3. Postal service—Great Britain—History. I. Title. **BIP**

Allen, Richard, Bp., 1760-1831.

MATHEWS, Marcia M. 922.773
Richard Allen. Helicon [dist. New York, Taplinger, c.1963] vi, 151p. 23cm. 63-19403 3.95 bds.,
1. Allen, Richard, Bp., 1760-1831. I. Title.

Allen, Steve [Stephen Valentine Allen]

ALLEN, Steve [Stephen Valentine Allen] 927.914
Mark it and strike it, an autobiography. New York, Holt. Rinehart and Winston [c.1960]. 432p. illus. 22cm. 60-11671 4.95
I. Title.

ALLEN, Steve [Stephen Valentine Allen] 927.914
Mart it and strike it, an autobiography. [New York] Hillman-MacFadden [dist. Bartholomew House, 1961, c.1960] 319p. (60-100) .60 pap.,
I. Title.

Allen, Sydney.

ALLEN, Sydney. 917.93'52'03
Directional signals; memories of a Seventh-day Adventist boyhood in the West. Nashville, Southern Pub. Association [1970] 190 p. 21 cm. [BX6193.A4A3] 74-123335
I. Title.

Allen, William, ca. 1710-1780.

KISTLER, Ruth Moser. v. 12
William Allen, founder of Allentown, colonial jurist, industrialist, and Loyalist; by Ruth Moser Kristler; James Allen and Trout Hall, by John K. Heyl. Allentown, Pa., Lehigh County Historical Society [c1962] 95 p. illus. ([Lehigh County Historical Society, Allentown, Pa.] Proceedings, v. 24) 63-42648
1. Allen, William, ca. 1710-1780. 2. Allen James, 1742-1778. I. Heyl, John K. II. Title.

Allen, William, Cardinal, 1532-1594.

HALLE, Marie. 922.242
An Elizabethan cardinal, William Allen, by Martin Haile [pseud.] London, New York, I. Pitman, 1914. xix, 388 p. illus., ports., fold. map, geneal. table. 23 cm. "Bibliography, by Joseph Gillow": p. 375-379. [BX4705.A53H3] A14
1. Allen, William, Cardinal, 1532-1594. 2. Gt. Brit.—Hist.—Elizabeth, 1558-1603. I. Title.

Allen, Woody.

GUTHRIE, Lee. 791'.092'4 B
Woody Allen, a biography / by Lee Guthrie. New York : Drake Publishers, [1978] p. cm. [PN2287.A53G8] 77-87469 ISBN 0-8473-1702-1 : 9.95
1. Allen, Woody. 2. Comedians—United States—Biography.

LAX, Eric. 791'.092'4
On being funny : Woody Allen and comedy / by Eric Lax. New York : Charterhouse, [1975] 243 p., [4] leaves of plates : ill. ; 22 cm. Includes index. [PN2287.A53L3] 74-25729 ISBN 0-88327-042-0 : 8.95
1. Allen, Woody. I. Title. BIP

Allenby, Edmund Henry Hynman Allenby, 1st viscount, 1861-1936.

GARDNER, Brian. 940.500924 B
Allenby of Arabia Lawrence's general. introd. by Lowell Thomas. 1st American ed. New York, Coward-McCann [1966, c1965] xxxii, 314 p. illus., maps, ports. 22 cm. First published in London in 1965 under title: Allenby. Bibliographical references included in "Notes" (p. 279-292) [DA69.3.A6G3 1966] 66-10426
1. Allenby, Edmund Henry Hynman Allenby, 1st viscount, 1861-1936. 2. Lawrence, Thomas Edward, 1888-1935. I. Title.

Allende Gossens, Salvador, 1908-1973.

VARAS, Florencia. 983'.064'0924 B
Coup! : Allende's last day / Florencia Varas and Jose Manuel Vergara. New York : Stein and Day, 1975, c1974. 182 p. : maps ; 25 cm. [F3100.V34 1975] 74-80900 ISBN 0-8128-1705-2 : 7.95
1. Allende Gossens, Salvador, 1908-1973. 2. Chile—History—Coup d'etat, 1973. I. Vergara, Jose Manuel, joint author. II. Title.

Alleyn, Edward, 1566-1626.

HOSKING, George Llewellyn. 792'.028'0924 B
The life and times of Edward Alleyn. [1st AMS ed.] New York, AMS Press [1970, c1952] 285 p. illus., ports. 23 cm. Bibliography: p. 275-278. [PN2598.A55H6 1970] 78-128935
1. Alleyn, Edward, 1566-1626. 2. Dulwich College, London. 3. Theater—Gt. Brit.—History. I. Title. BIP

Allies, Thomas William, 1813-1903.

DONALD, Gertrude. 283'.43
Men who left the movement: John Henry Newman, Thomas W. Allies, Henry Edward Manning, Basil William Maturin. Freeport, N.Y., Books for Libraries Press [1967] viii, 422 p. 21 cm. (Essay index reprint series) Reprint of the 1933 ed. [BX5100.D6 1967] 67-23207
1. Newman, John Henry, Cardinal, 1801-1890. 2. Allies, Thomas William, 1813-1903. 3. Manning, Henry Edward, Cardinal, 1808-1892. 4. Maturin, Basil William, 1847-1915. 5. Oxford movement. I. Title.

Allilueva, Svetlana, 1925-

ALLILUEVA, Svetlana, 1925- 914.7'03'840924
Only one year [by] Svetlana Alliluyeva. Translated from the Russian by Paul Chavchavadze. [1st ed.] New York, Harper & Row [1969] viii, 444 p. 22 cm. [DK275.A4A33] 79-81883 7.95
I. Title.

ALLILUEVA, Svetlana, 1925- 947.084'2'0924
Twenty letters to a friend. Tr. by Priscilla Johnson McMillan. [New York, Avon, 1968, c.1967] 258p. 18cm. (Discus bks., W129) Tr. of Dvadtsat' pisem k drugu. [DK275.A4A43] 1.25 pap.,
I. Title.

ALVAREZ del Vayo, Julio, 1891- 923.246
The last optimist. [Translation by Charles Duff] New York, Viking Press, 1950. x, 406 p. 22 cm. Autobiography. [DP264.A423A32] 50-5146
I. Title.

BIAGI, Enzo, 1920- 947.084'2'0924
Svetlana; an intimate portrait. Translated by Timothy Wilson. New York, Funk & Wagnalls [1967] 158 p. illus., ports. 22 cm. Translation of Mamma Svetlana. [DK275.A4B53 1967b] 68-23737 4.50
1. Allilueva, Svetlana, 1925- I. Title.

EBON, Martin. 947.084'2'0924 B
Svetlana, the story of Stalin's daughter. [New York] New American Library [1967] 192 p. illus., ports. 18 cm. (A Signet special) (A Signet book.) "Q 3288." Bibliography: p. 185-188. [DK275.A4E2] 67-29699
1. Allilueva, Svetlana, 1925- I. Title.

HUDSON, James A. 947.084/2/0924
Svetlana Alliluyeva: flight to freedom, by James A. Hudson. [New York, Tower Pubns. 1967] 174p. ports. 18cm. (Tower bk.) [DK275.A4H8] 67-31973 .75 pap.,
1. Allilueva, Svetlana, 1925- I. Title.

Allin, Benjamin Casey.

ALLIN, Benjamin Casey. 926.2
Reaching for the sea. Boston, Meador Pub. Co. [1956] 294p. illus. 21cm. Autobiography. [TA140.A43A3] 56-11986
I. Title.

Alline, Henry, 1748-1784.

BUMSTED, J. M. 269'.2'0924 B
Henry Alline 1748-1784. [Toronto] University of Toronto Press [1971] [ix], 116 p. 22 cm. (Canadian biographical studies) Bibliography: p. [107]-112. [BV3785.A46B8] 73-24664 ISBN 0-8020-3247-8 4.50
1. Alline, Henry, 1748-1784. BIP

Allingham, William, 1824-1889.

WARNER, Alan, 1912- 821'.8
William Allingham; an introduction [Dublin] Dolmen Pr. [1972, c.1971] 39 p. 21 cm. Bibl.: p. 39. [PR4004.A5W3] 72-187525 ISBN 0-85105-220-7
1. Allingham, William, 1824-1889.
Dist. by Humanities Pr., New York, for 1.50, pap.

Allison, Bob, 1934-

BUTLER, Hal 796.35764'0924
The Bob Allison story. Illus. with photos. New York, Messner [1967] 192p. ports. 22cm. [GV865.A36B8] 67-21611 3.34 lib. ed.,
1. Allison, Bob, 1934- I. Title.

BUTLER, Hal. 92
The Bob Allison story. Illustrated with photos. New York, J. Messner [1967] 192 p. ports. 22 cm. A biography of "Mr. Clutch" the Minnesota Twins' left fielder and long-ball hitter. [GV865.A36B8] AC 67
1. Allison, Bob, 1934- I. Title.

Allison, John M.

ALLISON, John M. 327'.2'0924 B
Ambassador from the prairie; or, Allison Wonderland [by] John M. Allison. Boston, Houghton Mifflin, 1973. xiv, 400 p. illus. 24 cm. [E748.A197A32] 73-13823 ISBN 0-395-17205-5 7.95
1. Allison, John M. 2. United States—Foreign relations—1933-1945. 3. United States—Foreign relations—1945- I. Title. II. Title: Allison Wonderland.

Allison, Ralph.

ALLISON, Ralph. 616.89'0092'4 B
Minds in many pieces : the making of a very special doctor / by Ralph Allison, with Ted Schwarz. 1st ed. New York : Rawson, Wade Publishers, c1980. p. cm. [PC339.52.A44A35 1980] 79-25565 ISBN 0-89256-097-5 : 9.95
1. Allison, Ralph. 2. Pyschiatrists—United States—Biography. I. Schwarz, Ted, joint author. II. Title. BIP

Allison, Susan, 1845-1937.

ALLISON, Susan, 1845-1937. 971.1'4'030924 B
A pioneer gentlewoman in British Columbia : the recollections of Susan Allison / edited by Margaret A. Ormsby. Vancouver, B.C. : University of British Columbia Press, c1976. xlix, 210 p., [6] leaves of plates : ill. ; 24 cm. (Recollections of the pioneers of British Columbia ; v. 2) Includes index. [F1089.O5A44 1976] 77-354991 ISBN 0-7748-0039-9
1. Allison, Susan, 1845-1937. 2. Okanagan Valley, B.C.—Biography. 3. Frontier and pioneer life—British Columbia—Okanagan Valley. 4. Pioneers—British Columbia—Okanagan Valley—Biography. I. Ormsby, Margaret Anchoretta, 1909- II. Title. III. Series.

Allman, Ruth Cooper.

ALLMAN, Ruth Cooper. 975.4'83
Canaan Valley and the black bear / by Ruth Cooper Allman. Parsons, W. Va. : McClain Print. Co., 1976. viii, 118 p. : ill. ; 22 cm. [F247.T8A43] 75-14530 ISBN 0-87012-220-7 : 5.00
1. Allman, Ruth Cooper. 2. Canaan Valley, W. Va.—Biography. 3. Canaan Valley, W. Va.—History. I. Title. BIP

Allon, Yigal, 1918-

ALLON, Yigal, 1918- 956.94'05'0924 B
My father's house / Yigal Allon ; translated from the Hebrew by Renven Ben-Yosef ; illustrated by Shirley Hirsch. 1st ed. New York : Norton, c1976. 204 p. : ill. ; 22 cm. Translation of Bet avi. [DS126.6.A49A3213] 75-43945 ISBN 0-393-07498-6 : 7.95
1. Allon, Yigal, 1918- 2. Paikovits family. I. Title.

Allport, Gordon Willard, 1897-1967.

EVANS, Richard Isadore, 1922- 155.2'0924
Gordon Allport; the man and his ideas [by] Richard I. Evans. [1st ed.] New York, Dutton [1971] xiii, 157 p. 21 cm. Bibliography: p. [151]-152. [BF698.E84] 74-125908 ISBN 0-525-11602-8 5.95
1. Allport, Gordon Willard, 1897-1967. 2. Personality—Addresses, essays, lectures.

Allred family.

ALLRED, Berten Wendell, 1904- 388.3'22
The life of a horse and buggy stage line operator [by] B. W. Allred. Washington, Potomac Corral, 1972. iv, 18 p. illus. 23 cm. (The Great western series, no. 11) Bibliography: p. 15. [SF307.A44] 72-94396
1. Allred family. 2. Coaching—Utah—History. 3. Utah—Biography. I. Title.

Allston, Washington, 1779-1843.

FLAGG, Jared Bradley, 1820-1899. 759.13
The life and letters of Washington Allston. New York, Kennedy Galleries, 1969 [c1892] xvii, 435 p. illus., ports. 27 cm. (Library of American art) [ND237.A4F5 1969b] 68-27719
1. Allston, Washington, 1779-1843. I. Title.

FLAGG, Jared Bradley, 1820-1899. 759.13
The life and letters of Washington Allston. With reproductions from Allston's pictures. New York, B. Blom [1969] xiii, 435 p. illus., ports. 24 cm. Reprint of the 1892 ed. [ND237.A4F5 1969] 72-82002
I. Allston, Washington, 1779-1843. II. Title. BIP

Allyn family.

ALLYN, Henry, 1794-1880. 929'.2'0973
Henry Allyn autobiography / with parentage and children of Henry Allyn compiled by Jean Allyn Smeltzer. [Portland, Or. : J. A. Smeltzer, 1974] xiv, 84 p. ; 28 cm. Includes indexes. Bibliography: p. xi-xii. [CS71.A43 1974] 74-29538
1. Allyn family. 2. Allyn, Henry, 1794-1880. I. Smeltzer, Jean Allyn, ed.

Allyn, Joseph Pratt, 1833-1869.

ALLYN, Joseph Pratt, 1833-1869. 917.91'04'4
The Arizona of Joseph Pratt Allyn : letters from a pioneer judge—observations and travels, 1863-1866 / John Nicolson, editor. Tucson : University of Arizona Press, [1974] xviii, 284 p. : ill. ; 24 cm. Includes index. Bibliography: p. 263-274. [F811.A44 1974] 73-94117 ISBN 0-8165-0386-9 : 8.50
1. Allyn, Joseph Pratt, 1833-1869. 2. Arizona—Description and travel. I. Nicolson, John, 1927- ed. II. Title.

Allyn, William Noah, 1874-

ALLYN, Helen Rutledge. 001.2
Life & ancestry of William Noah Allyn. Skaneateles, N. Y., Lakeside Print. Co. [1960] 53p. illus. 23cm. [CT275.A62A4] 60-45414
1. Allyn, William Noah, 1874- 2. Allyn family. I. Title.

Alma-Tadema, Lawrence, Sir, 1836-1912.

SWANSON, Vern G. 759.2 B
Alma-Tadema : the painter of the Victorian vision of the ancient world / by Vern G. Swanson. New York : Scribner, 1977. 144 p. : ill. (some col.) ; 31 cm. Includes index. Bibliography: p. 132-134. [ND497.A4S9] 77-77549 ISBN 0-684-15304-1 : 15.95
1. Alma-Tadema, Lawrence, Sir, 1836-1912. 2. Painters—Great Britain—Biography. 3. Egypt in art. 4. Greece in art. 5. Rome in art.

Almada family.

STAGG, Albert. 972'.1
The Almadas and Alamos, 1783-1867 / Albert Stagg Tucson : University of Arizona Press, c1977. p. cm. Includes index. Bibliography: p. [F1391.A4S72] 77-74317 ISBN 0-8165-0609-4 : 11.50 pbk. : 5.95
1. Almada family. 2. Alamos, Mexico—History. I. Title.

Almedingen, Martha Edith,

ALMEDINGEN, Martha Edith, 928.2
1898-
Late arrival [by] E. M. Almedingen. Philadelphia, Westminster Press [1952] 368p. 22cm. Autobiographical. [PR6001.L72Z5] 52-8128
I. Title.

Almeida Soares Portugal Alarcao Eca e Melo, Luis d', marquez de Lavradio, 1727-1790.

ALDEN, Dauril. 981'.03'0924
Royal government in colonial Brazil; with special reference to the administration of the Marquis of Lavradio, viceroy, 1769-1779. Berkeley, University of California Press, 1968. xxvii, 545 p. illus., facsims., maps, port. 25 cm. Bibliography: p. 514-533. Bibliographical footnotes. [F2534.A7] 68-26064 15.00
1. Almeida Soares Portugal Alarcao Eca e Melo, Luis d', marquez de Lavradio, 1727-1790. 2. Brazil—History—1763-1821. I. Title. BIP

Almon, John, 1737-1805.

ALMON, 658.8'09'0705730924 B
John, 1737-1805.
Memoirs of a late eminent bookseller. New York, Garland Pub. [1974] 262 p. 22 cm. (The English book trade, 1660-1853) Reprint of the 1790 ed. published in London under title: Memoirs of John Almon, bookseller, of Piccadilly. [Z325.A5 1974] 74-11173 ISBN 0-8240-0972-X
1. Almon, John, 1737-1805. 2. Booksellers and bookselling—Correspondence, reminiscences, etc. 3. Liberty of the press—Great Britain. I. Title. II. Series. BIP

Almquist, Carl Jonas Love, 1793-1866.

ROMBERG, Bertil. 839.7'8'609
Carl Jonas Love Almqvist / by Bertil Romberg ; translated from the Swedish by Sten Liden. Boston : Twayne Publishers, c1977. 203 p. : port. ; 21 cm. (Twayne's world authors series ; TWAS 401) Includes index. Bibliography: p. 189-197. [PT9729.Z5R6] 76-16859 ISBN 0-8057-6241-8 lib.bdg. 9.95
1. Almquist, Carl Jonas Love, 1793-1866. I. Title. BIP

Alonso, Alicia.

SIEGEL, Beatrice. 792.8'092'4 B
Alicia Alonso, the story of a ballerina / Beatrice Siegel. New York : F. Warne, c1979. x, 182 p. : ill. ; 24 cm. Includes index. Bibliography: p. 175. Follows the career of a Cuban ballerina who continues to dance despite failing eyesight. [GV1785.A63S57] 92 78-15410 ISBN 0-7232-6157-1 : 8.95
1. Alonso, Alicia. 2. Dancers—Biography. I. Title.

Alphonsus Maria, Father, CP, 1884-1949.

VYTELL, Virginia 271'.62'024 B
Marie.
Praise the Lord, ali you nations : Lithuania's historical and cultural development form a background for the life story of Rev. Alphonsus Maria, CP, missionary and founder of the Poor Sisters of Jesus Crucified and of the Sorrowful Mother / Virginia Marie Vytell. Eimhurst [i.e. Elmhurst] Pa. : Sisters of Jesus Crucified and the Sorrowful Mother, c1976. 351 p. : ill. ; 22 cm. Includes bibliographical references and index. [BX4705.A5554V95] 76-21454
1. Alphonsus Maria, Father, CP, 1884-1949. 2. Passionists in Lithuania—Biography. 3. Lithuania—History. I. Title.

Alpuy, Julio, 1919-

JULIO Alpuy. 730'.92'4
[Exhibition held Jan. 26-Mar. 5, 1972, Center for Inter-American Relations] New York, Center for Inter-American Relations [1971] [28] p. illus. (part col.) 26 cm. "In the world and workshop of Julio Alpuy, an interview, by Ronald Christ": p. [5]-[23] "Checklist": p. [26]-[27] [NB429.A4J8] 72-198179
1. Alpuy, Julio, 1919- I. Christ, Ronald J. II. Center for Inter-American Relations.

Alsac, Jacob, 1900-1967.

*BENNETT, 364.1'63'0924 [B]
Thomas J.
Empty pockets lined with gold. With a foreword by Gladys Darling. New York, Exposition Pr. [1973] 126 p. 21 cm. [HV9468] ISBN 0-682-47610-2 5.00
1. Alsac, Jacob, 1900-1967. I. Title.

Alsace — Lorraine question.

LUDMANN, Oscar Henri, 923.544
1900-
Stepchild of the Rhine; an autobiography, by Oscar Ludmann. New York, A. H. King [c1931] x. 276 p. port. 23 cm. [DD801.A397L8] 31-30272
1. Alsace — Lorraine question. 2. European War, 1914-1918. — Alsace. 3. european War, 1914-1918 — Personal narratives. I. Title.

Alston, Joseph, 1778-1816.

DEVEREUX, Anthony 915.57'89'033 B
Q.
The rice princes; a rice epoch revisited, by Anthony Q. Devereux. [Columbia, S.C., State Printing Co., 1973?] viii, 125 p. illus. 24 cm. Bibliography: p. vii-viii. [F273.D54] 73-174829 5.95
1. Alston, Joseph, 1778-1816. 2. Weston, Plowden Charles Jennett. I. Title.

Alston, Theodosia (Burr) 1783-1813.

MINNIGERODE, Meade, 1887- 920.073
1967.
Lives and times; four informal American biographies. Freeport, N.Y., Books for Libraries Press [1970] viii, 215 p. illus., ports. 23 cm. (Essay index reprint series) Reprint of the 1925 ed. Contents.Contents.—Stephen Jumel, merchant.—William Eaton, hero.—Theodosia Burr, prodigy.—Edmond Charles Genet, citizen. [E302.5.M66 1970] 76-121490
1. Jumel, Stephen, 1755-1832. 2. Eaton, William, 1764-1811. 3. Alston, Theodosia (Burr) 1783-1813. 4. Genet, Edmond Charles, 1763-1834. I. Title.

Alston, Walter Emmons, 1911-

ALSTON, Walter 796.357'092'4 B
Emmons, 1911-
A year at a time / Walter Alston, with Jack Tobin. Waco, Tex. : Word Books, c1976. 212 p. : ill. ; 23 cm. [GV865.A4A38] 75-36194 ISBN 0-87680-413-X : 7.95
1. Alston, Walter Emmons, 1911- 2. Baseball managers—United States—Biography. I. Tobin, Jack, joint author. II. Title.

Altamirano, Ignacio Manuel, 1834-1893.

NACCI, Chris N. 868 B
Ignacio Manuel Altamirano, by Chris N. Nacci. New York, Twayne Publishers [1970] 151 p. 21 cm. (Twayne's world authors series, TWAS 124. Mexico) Bibliography: p. 136-138. [PQ7297.A6Z78] 73-110360
1. Altamirano, Ignacio Manuel, 1834-1893. BIP

Altgeld, John Peter, 1847-1902.

BARNARD, Harry, 1906- 923.273
Eagle forgotten; the life of John Peter Altgeld. [Bobbs, dist., New York, Macfadden, 1962, c.1938] 496p. 21cm. (Charter bks., 116) Bibl. 2.85 pap.,
1. Altgeld, John Peter, 1847-1902. I. Title.

Altken, Robert Grant, 1864—1951.

BOS, Willem Hendrik van 509'.22
den, 1896-
Robert Grant Aitken, December 31, 1864--October 29, 1951. (In National Academy of Sciences, Washington, D. C. Biographical memoirs. New York. 24cm. v. 32, (11958) [1st memoir] p. [1]-30. port.) Bibliography of Robert Grant Altken: p. 8-30. [Q141.N2 vol. 32, 1st memoir] 59-690
1. Altken, Robert Grant, 1864—1951. I. Title. II. Series: National Academy of Sciences, Washington, D. C. Biographical memoirs, v. 32, 1st memoir

Altman, Larry, 1928-

ALTMAN, Larry, 364.1'63'0924 B
1928-
The call of the cricket / Irwin Larry Altman. Millbrae, Calif : Celestial Arts, c1978. xiii, 164 p. ; 22 cm. [HV6248.A38A33] 77-90018 ISBN 0-89087-216-3 pbk. : 4.95
1. Altman, Larry, 1928- 2. Swindlers, and swindling—Biography. I. Title. BIP

Alvarez del Vayo, Julio, 1891-

ALVAREZ del Vayo, 946.081'092'4 B
Julio, 1891-
Give me combat; the memoirs of Julio W. Alvarez del Vayo. Foreword by Barbara W. Tuchman. Translation from the Spanish by Donald D. Walsh. [1st ed.] Boston, Little, Brown [1973] xvi, 333 p. illus. 25 cm. [DP264.A423A3] 73-1213 ISBN 0-316-17983-3 12.50
1. Alvarez del Vayo, Julio, 1891- I. Title.

Alvarez, Walter Clement, 1884-

ALVAREZ, Walter 610'.92'4 B
Clement, 1884-
Alvarez on Alvarez / Walter Clement Alvarez. San Francisco : Strawberry Hill Press ; Harrisburg, Pa. : distributed by Stackpole Books, c1977. p. cm. Bibliography: p. [R154.A545A28] 76-47216 ISBN 0-89407-005-3(Strawberry) pbk. : 5.95
1. Alvarez, Walter Clement, 1884- 2. Physicians—United States—Biography. I. Title. BIP

ALVAREZ, Walter Clement, 926.1
1884-
Incurable physician, an autobiography. Englewood Cliffs, N.J., Prentice-Hall [1963] xiii, 274 p. ports. 22 cm. [R154.A545A3] 63-20033
I. Title.

Alvear, Carlos Maria de, 1789-1852.

DAVIS, Thomas Brabson. 923.282
Carlos de Alvear, man of revolution; the diplomatic career of Argentina's first Minister to the United States. Durham, N. C., Duke University Press, 1955. vii, 305p. port. 24cm. 'Bibliographical notes': p. [234]-259. [F2846.A4815D3] 55-6526
1. Alvear, Carlos Maria de, 1789-1852. 2. U. S.—For. rel.—ArgentineRepublic. 3. Argentine Republic—For. rel.—U. S. I. Title.

DAVIS, Thomas 327'.2'0924 B
Brabson.
Carlos de Alvear, man of revolution; the diplomatic career of Argentina's first Minister to the United States, by Thomas B. Davis, Jr. New York, Greenwood Press [1968, c1955] vii, 305 p. port. 24 cm. Includes bibliographical references. [F2846.A4815D3 1968] 69-13878
1. Alvear, Carlos Maria de, 1789-1852. 2. U.S.—Foreign relations—Argentine Republic. 3. Argentine Republic—Foreign relations—U.S. BIP

Alzado, Lyle.

ALZADO, Lyle. 796.33'2'0924 B
Mile high : the story of Lyle Alzado and the amazing Denver Broncos / by Lyle Alzado, with Paul Zimmerman. New York : Atheneum, 1978. 230 p., [4] leaves of plates : ill. ; 21 cm. [GV939.A58A35] 78-52219 ISBN 0-689-10896-6 : 8.95
1. Alzado, Lyle. 2. Denver Broncos (Football team) 3. Football players—United States—Biography. I. Zimmerman, Paul Lionel, joint author. II. Title.

Amadon, George W.

HOOK, Milton Raymond. 286'.73 B
Flames over Battle Creek : the story of George W. Amadon, Review and Herald printer, who shared in the early successes and tragedies of the Seventh-day Adventist Church / Milton Raymond Hook. Washington : Review and Herald Pub. Association, 1978. 128 p : ill. ; 20 cm. Includes bibliographical references. [BX6193.A45H66] 77-78279 pbk. : 3.95
1. Amadon, George W. 2. Seventh-Day Adventists—United States—Biography. I. Title.

Amalu, Sammy.

JIVIDEN, Doris. 364.1'63'0924 B
Sammy Amalu: prince, pauper or phony? Honolulu [Erin Enterprises, 1972] 200 p. illus. 23 cm. [CT2918.A7J58] 73-153530 3.95
1. Amalu, Sammy.

Amat, Thaddeus, Bp., 1811-1878.

WEBER, Francis J. 282.794
California's reluctant prelate; the life and times of Right Reverend Thaddeus Amat, C.M. (1811-1878) Los Angeles, Dawson Book Shop, 1964. xv, 234 p. illus., ports. 22 cm. Bibliography: p. [223]-229. [BX4705.A56/5W4] 63-21211
1. Amat, Thaddeus, Bp., 1811-1878. 2. Catholic Church in California. I. Title.

Amato, Antony.

AMATO, Antony. 301.41'5'0924
Affair / Antony Amato & Katherine Edwards. 1st ed. New York : Putnam, c1978. 228 p. ; 23 cm. [HQ964.A46] 77-20490 7.98
1. Amato, Antony. 2. Edwards, Katherine. 3. Unmarried couples—Biography. I. Edwards, Katherine, joint author. II. Title. BIP

Amberley, John Russell,

AMBERLEY, John 942.0810922
Russell, viscount, 1842-1876.
The Amberley papers; Bertrand Russell's family background. Edited by Bertrand Russell and Patricia Russell. New York, Simon and Schuster [1966] 2 v. port. 22 cm. "First published 1937." [DA565.A45A4 1966] 66-9800
I. Amberley, Katharine Louisa (Stanley) Russell, viscountess, 1842-1874. II. Russell, Bertrand Russell, 3d earl, 1872- ed. III. Russell, Patricia Helen (Spencer) Russell, countess, joint ed. IV. Title. BIP

Ambrose, Isaac, 1604-1664.

GOREHAM, Norman J. 285'.2'0924 B
Isaac Ambrose, Lancashire nonconformist

/ by Norman J. Goreham. Preston : Henry L. Kirby, 1977. [1], 9 p. ; 21 cm. Bibliography: p. [9] [BX5207.A47G67] 77-371584 ISBN 0-9505653-0-X : £0.15
1. Ambrose, Isaac, 1604-1664. 2. Dissenters, Religious—England—Lancashire—Biography. 3. Lancashire, Eng.—Biography. I. Title.

Ambrosius, Saint, Bp. of Milan.

AMBROSIUS, Saint, Bp. of Milan. 230.1'4'0924
Letters. Translated by Mary Melchior Beyenka. [Reprinted with corrections] Washington, Catholic University of America [1967, c1954] xix, 515 p. 22 cm. (The Fathers of the Church, a new translation v. 26) Contents.Contents.—Letters to emperors.—Letters to bishops.—Synodal letters.—Letters to Priests.—Letters to his sister.—Letters to laymen. Bibliography: p. xiv. [BR60.F3A5612] 67-28583
1. Theology—Collected works—Early church, ca. 30-600. I. Title. II. Series.

AMBROSIUS, Saint, Bp. of Milan. 230.1'4'0924
Letters. Translated by Mary Melchior Beyenka. [Reprinted with corrections] Washington, Catholic University of America [1967, c1954] xix, 515 p. 22 cm. (The Fathers of the Church, a new translation, v. 26) Contents.Letters to emperors.--Letters to bishops.--Synodal letters.--Letters to Priests.--Letters to his sister.--Letters to layment. Bibliography: p. xiv. [BR60.F3A5612] 67-28583
1. Theology—Collected works—Early church. I. Title. II. Series.

PAREDI, Angelo 922.137
Saint Ambrose, his life and times. Tr. [from Italian] By M. Joseph Costelloe [Notre Dame, Ind.] Univ. of Notre Dame Pr. [c.]1964. xii, 481p. illus., fold. map. 23cm. Bibl. 63-19325 7.95
1. Ambrosius, Saint, Bp. of Milan. I. Title.

PAREDI, Angelo. 922.137
Saint Ambrose, his life and times. Translated by M. Joseph Costelloe. [Notre Dame, Ind.] University of Notre Dame Press, 1964. xii, 481 p. illus., fold. map. 23 cm. Translation of S. Ambrogio, e la sua eta. Bibliographical references included in "Notes" (p. 379-426) Works of Saint Ambrose": p. 435-440. [BX4700.A425P33] 63-19325
1. Ambrosius, Saint, Bp. of Milan. I. Title.

Amenhetep IV, King of Egypt, 1388-1358 B.C.

COLLIER, Joy. 932'.01'0924
The heretic pharaoh. [1st American ed.] New York, John Day Co. [1972, c1970] vi, 248 p. illus. 24 cm. First published in 1970 in London under title: King Sun. [DT87.4.C63 1972] 71-143407 9.95
1. Amenhetep IV, King of Egypt, 1388-1358 B.C. I. Title.

GILES, Frederick John. 932'.01'0924 B
Ikhnaton: legend and history [by] F. J. Giles. [1st American ed.] Rutherford, [N.J.] Fairleigh Dickinson University Press [1972, c1970] viii, 255 p. illus. 22 cm. Includes bibliographical references. [DT87.4.G5 1972] 76-37800 ISBN 0-8386-1077-3 8.50
1. Amenhetep, IV, King of Egypt, 1388-1358 B.C. I. Title.

SILVERBERG, Robert. 923.132
Akhnaten, the rebel pharaoh. [1st ed.] Philadelphia, Chilton Books [1964] xiv, 234 p. map. 21 cm. Bibliography: p. 223-235. [DT87.4.S5] 64-16520
1. Amenhotep IV, King of Egypt, 1388-1358 B.C. I. Title.

WEIGALL, Arthur Edward Pearse Brome, 1880-1934. 932'.01'0924 B
The life and times of Akhnaton, Pharaoh of Egypt. Port Washington, N.Y., Kennikat Press [1970] xxxi, 255 p. illus. 22 cm. Reprint of the 1922 rev. ed. [DT87.4.W4 1970] 79-115209
1. Amenhetep IV, King of Egypt, 1388-1358 B.C. 2. Egypt—History—To 332 B.C. 3. Egypt—Religion. I. Title. BIP

America—Biography—Dictionaries.

APPLETON'S cyclopaedia of American biography. Edited by James Grant Wilson and John Fiske. New York, Appleton, 1888. Detroit, Gale Research Co., 1968. 7 v. ports. 24 cm. Vol. 7 edited by J. G. Wilson. [E176.A666] 67-14061 168.00 920.07
1. America—Biography—Dictionaries. 2. United States—Biography. I. Wilson, James Grant, 1832-1914, ed. II. Fiske, John, 1842-1901, joint ed. BIP

America—Discovery and exploration—Juvenile literature.

JOHNSTON, Charles Haven Ladd, 1877-1943. 973.1'0924 B
Famous discoverers and explorers of America; their voyages, battles, and hardships in traversing and conquering the unknown territories of a new world. Freeport, N.Y., Books for Libraries Press [1971, c1917] ix, 433 p. illus., ports. 23 cm. (Essay index reprint series) Brief biographies concentrating on the major discoveries of sixteen explorers including Leif Ericson, Hernando Cortes, Giovanni Verrazano, Father Marquette, and Robert Peary. [E101.J73 1971] 920 79-152177 ISBN 0-8369-2230-1
1. America—Discovery and exploration—Juvenile literature. 2. Explorers—Juvenile literature. I. Title.

KEATING, Bern. 917.3'04
Famous American explorers. Line drawings by Lorence Bjorklund. Chicago, Rand McNally [1972] 92 p. illus. (part. col.) 29 cm. Traces the journeys and adventures of those who explored the North American continent including the Spanish conquistadores, the Vikings, French Voyageurs, and mountain men. [E101.K4] 72-4079 ISBN 0-528-82480-5 4.79
1. America—Discovery and exploration—Juvenile literature. I. Bjorklund, Lorence F., illus. II. Title.

America—Discovery and exploration—Spanish—Juvenile literature.

KERBY, Elizabeth Poe. 910.0946
The conquistadors. Illustrated by Jo Polseno. New York, Putnam [1969] 94 p. col illus., col. maps. 24 cm. (A World pioneer biography) Describes the discoveries and explorations of the New World by six Spanish conquistadores—Pizzaro, Cortes, Coronado, Ponce de Leon, Alarcon, and Cabeza de Vaca. [E123.K4] 68-24524 3.29
1. America—Discovery and exploration—Spanish—Juvenile literature. I. Polseno, Jo, illus. II. Title.

American ballads and songs—History and criticism.

LOMAX, John Avery, 1867-1948. 784.4'9'73
Adventures of a ballad hunter. Sketches by Ken Chamerlain. New York, Hafner Pub. Co., 1971 [c1947] xi, 302 p. illus. 22 cm. [ML429.L68A3 1971] 76-152266
1. American ballads and songs—History and criticism. I. Title. BIP

American Baptist Home Mission Societies.

HULL, Eleanor Means. 266'.6'131
Women who carried the good news / Eleanor Hull. Valley Forge, Pa. : Judson Press, [1975] 96 p. ; 22 cm. Includes bibliographical references. [BV2766.B48] 74-22520 ISBN 0-8170-0651-6 pbk. : 2.95
1. American Baptist Home Mission Societies. 2. Missionaries, Women. I. Title. BIP

American Board of Commissioners for Foreign Missions. Oregon Mission.

DRURY, Clifford Merrill, 1897- ed. 922
First white women over the Rockies; diaries, letters, and biographical sketches of the six women of the Oregon Mission who made the overland journey in 1836 and 1838. Glendale, Calif., A. H. Clark Co., 1963-1966. 3 v. illus., facsims., maps, ports. 25 cm. (Northwest historical series, 6-8) Contents.Contents.—v. 1. Mrs. Marcus Whitman, Mrs. Henry H. Spalding. Mrs. William H. Gray, and Mrs. Asa B. Smith.—v. 2. Mrs. Eikanah Walker and Mrs. Cushing Eells.—v. 3. Diary of Sarah White Smith (Mrs. Asa B. Smith). Letters of Asa B. Smith and other documents relating to the 1838 reenforcement to the Oregon Mission. Includes bibliographies. [BV3703.D7] 62-20134
1. American Board of Commissioners for Foreign Missions. Oregon Mission. 2. Missionaries, Women. 3. Missions—Oregon. I. Title. II. Series.

American Civil Liberties Union.

MILNER, Lucille (Bernheimer) 1888- 923.673
Education of an American liberal, an autobiography. Introd. by Alvin Johnson. New York, Horizon Press, 1954. 318p. 22cm. [JC599.U5M5] 54-7897
1. American Civil Liberties Union. I. Title.

American Civil Liberties Union—History.

LAMSON, Peggy. 323.4'092'4 B
Roger Baldwin, founder of the American Civil Liberties Union : a portrait / by Peggy Lamson. Boston : Houghton Mifflin, 1976. xii, 304 p., [8] leaves of plates : ill. ; 24 cm. Includes bibliographical references and index. [JC599.U5L28] 76-25100 ISBN 0-395-24761-6 : 12.50
1. American Civil Liberties Union—History. 2. Baldwin, Roger Nash, 1884- 3. Civil rights—United States—History.

American College of Physicians—Directories.

JAQUES Cattell Press. 610'.92'2 B
Biographical directory of the American College of Physicians, 1979 / compiled for the College by Jaques Cattell Press. New York : R. R. Bowker Co., 1979. xxxi, 1905 p. ; 29 cm. Includes index. [R712.A1J36 1979] 79-90566 ISBN 0-8352-1145-2 : 52.50
1. American College of Physicians—Directories. 2. American College of Physicians—Biography. 3. Internists—United States—Directories. 4. Internists—United States—Biography. 5. Physicians—United States—Directories. 6. Physicians—United States—Biography. I. American College of Physicians. II. Title. BIP

American Dermatological Association—History.

SZYMANSKI, Frederick J., 1915- 616.5'0092'2 B
Centennial history of American Dermatological Association, 1876-1976 / Frederick J. Szymanski. [Philadelphia] : The Association, c1976. 560 p. : ports. ; 24 cm. Includes index. [RL1.A433S94] 76-5974
1. American Dermatological Association—History. 2. Dermatologists—United States—Biography. I. Title.

American Federation of Labor.

GOMPERS, Samuel, 1850-1924. 923.273
Seventy years of life and labor; an autobiography. Revised and edited by Philip Taft and John A. Sessions. With a foreword by George Meany. New York, Dutton, 1957. 334 p. 22 cm. [HD8073.G6A3 1957] 56-8330
1. American Federation of Labor. 2. Labor and laboring classes—U.S. I. Title.

GOMPERS, Samuel, 1850-1924. 331.88'0924
Seventy years of life and labour; an autobiography. New York, A. M. Kelley, 1967 [c1953] 2 v. ports. 22 cm. (Library of American labor history) Reprints of economic classics. [HD8073.G6A3 1967] 66-21674
1. American Federation of Labor. 2. Labor and laboring classes—United States. I. Title.

American fiction—History and criticism.

PRYSE, Marjorie, 1948- 813'.009'27
The mark and the knowledge : social stigma in classic American fiction / Marjorie Pryse. [Columbus] : Published by the Ohio State University for Miami University, c1979. 179 p. ; 24 cm. Includes bibliographical references and index. [PS374.S7P7] 78-23229 ISBN 0-8142-0296-9 : 15.00
1. American fiction—History and criticism. 2. Social problems in literature. 3. Characters and characteristics in literature. I. Title. BIP

American fiction—Women authors—History and criticism.

HARKINS, Edward Francis, 1872- 813'.009 B
Famous authors (women) / by E. F. Harkins. Detroit : Gale Research Co., 1976, c1901. p. cm. Reprint of the 1906 ed. published by L. C. Page, Boston. [PS147.H28 1976] 73-173098 ISBN 0-8103-4306-1 : 14.00
1. American fiction—Women authors—History and criticism. 2. American fiction—19th century—History and criticism. 3. Women authors, American—Biography. I. Title.
Contents omitted

American Fur Company—History.

IRVING, Washington, 1783-1859. 978'.02
Astoria : or, Anecdotes of an enterprise beyond the Rocky Mountains / Washington Irving ; edited by Richard Dilworth Rust. Boston : Twayne Publishers, 1976. xxxiv, 500 p., [3] leaves of plates : ill. ; 24 cm. (His The complete works of Washington Irving ; v. 15) Includes bibliographical references and index. [F884.A8178 1976] 75-44202 ISBN 0-8057-8507-8 lib.bdg. : 25.00
1. American Fur Company—History. 2. Astor, John Jacob, 1763-1848. 3. Astoria, Or.—History. 4. Overland journeys to the Pacific. 5. Voyages to the Pacific coast. I. Rust, Richard Dilworth. II. Title.

American Institute of Certified Public Accountants—History.

WEBSTER, Norman Edward, 1869- 657'.06'273
The American Association of Public Accountants : its first twenty years, 1886-1906 / compiled by Norman E. Webster. New York : Arno Press, 1978, c1954. vi, 402 p. ; 23 cm. (The Development of contemporary accounting thought) Reprint of the ed. published by American Institute of Accountants, New York. [HF5601.A872W4 1978] 77-87292 ISBN 0-405-10919-9 lib.bdg. : 25.00
1. American Institute of Certified Public Accountants—History. 2. Accountants—United States—Biography. I. Title. II. Series. BIP

American Law Institute. Council.

AMERICAN Law Institute. 340'.092'2 B
Minutes in remembrance, 1925-1975 : officers and members of Council deceased 1925-1975. Philadelphia : American Law Institute, c1976. x, 158 p. ; 23 cm. Includes index. [KF372.A53] 76-16455
1. American Law Institute. Council. 2. Lawyers—United States—Biography. I. Title.

American literature.

CLEVELAND, Charles Dexter, 1802-1869. 810.8'002
A compendium of American literature; chronologically arranged, with biographical sketches of the authors, and selections from their works ... Port Washington, N.Y., Kennikat Press [1971] 784 p. 22 cm. (Kennikat Press scholarly reprints. Series on literary America in the nineteenth century) "First published in 1859." Includes

bibliographical references. [PS507.C5 1971] 75-122645 ISBN 0-8046-1293-5
1. American literature. I. Title.

American literature—Afro-American authors—Bio-bibliography.

PAGE, James Allen, 1918- 810'.9'896 B
Selected Black American authors : an illustrated bio-bibliographical dictionary / compiled by James A. Page. Boston : G. K. Hall, c1977. p. cm. (Reference publications in Black studies) Includes indexes. Bibliography: p. [PS153.N5P3] 77-16009 ISBN 0-8161-8065-2 : 30.00
1. American literature—Afro-American authors—Bio-bibliography. 2. Afro-American authors—Biography. I. Title. II. Series. BIP

American literature—Afro-American authors—Handbooks, manuals, etc.

SOUTHGATE, Robert L., 1921- 810'.9'896073
Black plots & black characters : a handbook for Afro-American literature / by Robert L. Southgate. Syracuse, N.Y. : Gaylord Professional Publications, 1978. p. cm. Includes index. Bibliography: p. [PS153.N5S65] 78-14394 ISBN 0-915794-14-4 : 25.00
1. American literature—Afro-American authors—Handbooks, manuals, etc. 2. Afro-Americans—Handbooks, manuals, etc. 3. American literature—Afro-American authors—Bibliography. 4. Afro-Americans—Bibliography. 5. Afro-Americans—Biography. I. Title.

American literature—Bio-bibliography.

ADAMS, Oscar Fay, 1855-1919. 810'.9
A brief handbook of American authors 7th ed., rev. and enl. Boston, Milford House [1973] xi, 210 p. 22 cm. Reprint of the 1884 ed. published by Houghton, Mifflin, Boston. [PS128.A3 1973] 73-4876 ISBN 0-87821-115-2 20.00 Lib. ed.,
1. American literature—Bio-bibliography. I. Title.

ADAMS, Oscar Fay, 1855-1919. 810'.9
A brief handbook of American authors / by Oscar Fay Adams. Boston : Longwood Press, 1977. p. cm. Reprint of the 1884 ed. published by Houghton, Mifflin, Boston. [PS128.A3 1977] 77-21126 ISBN 0-89341-450-6 lib.bdg. : 14.50
1. American literature—Bio-bibliography 2. Authors, American—Biography. I. Title. BIP

ADAMS, Oscar Fay, 1855-1919. 810'.9
A dictionary of American authors / by Oscar Fay Adams. Boston : Longwood Press, 1977. 444 p. ; 22 cm. Originally published in 1897. [Z1224.A22 1977] [PS128] [PS128.A3 1977b] 77-15009 ISBN 0-89341-456-5 lib.bdg. ; 25.00
1. American literature—Bio-bibliography. 2. Authors, American—Biography. I. Title.

American literature—California—History and criticism.

RATHER, Lois, 1905- 810'.9'9794
Bohemians to hippies : waves of rebellion / Lois Rather. Oakland, Calif. : Rather Press, 1977. 166 p. ; 27 cm. "Of an edition of 150 this is no. 44." Includes bibliographical references and index. [PS283.C2R37] 78-300890 20.00
1. American literature—California—History and criticism. 2. Authors, American—California—Biography. 3. Artists—California—Biography. 4. Bohemianism—California. I. Title. BIP

American literature—Dictionaries.

RICHARDS, Robert Fulton, ed. 810'.3
Concise dictionary of American literature. New York, Greenwood Press [1969, c1955] 252 p. 24 cm. [PS21.R5 1969] 74-88927
1. American literature—Dictionaries. 2. American literature—Bio-bibliography. I. Title. BIP

RICHARDS, Robert Fulton, ed. 810.3
Concise dictionary of American literature. Student ed. Ames, Iowa, Littlefield, Adams, 1956 [c1955] 253p. illus. 21cm. (Littzefield college outlines) New students outline series. [PS21] 56-13550
1. American literature—Dictionaries. 2. American literature—Bio-bibl. I. Title.

RICHARDS, Robert Fulton, ed. 810.3
Concise dictionary of American literature. Student ed. Ames, Iowa, Littlefield, Adams, 1956 [c1955] 253p. illus. 21cm. (Littlefield college outlines) New students outline series. [PS21] 56-13550
1. American literature—Dictionaries. 2. American literature—Bio-bibl. I. Title.

American literature—History and criticism.

GOSTWICK, Joseph, 1814-1887. 810.9
Hand-book of American literature, historical, biographical and critical. Port Washington, N.Y., Kennikat Press [1971] xiv, 319 p. 21 cm. (Kennikat Press scholarly reprints. Series on literary America in the nineteenth century) Ascribed also to Margaret E. Foster.—Cf. Brit. Mus. cat. and London Library cat. Reprint of the 1856 ed. [PS85.G6 1971] 78-121942 ISBN 0-8046-1304-4
1. American literature—History and criticism. I. Foster, Margaret E. Hand-book of American literature. II. Title.

LEVIN, David, 1924- 810.92
In defense of historical literature; essays on American history, autobiography, drama, and fiction. [1st ed.] New York, Hill and Wang [1967] x, 144 p. 21 cm. Bibliographical footnotes. [PS169.H5L4] 67-14651
1. American literature—History and criticism. 2. Literature and history. 3. U.S.—Historiography. I. Title.

American literature—Negro authors.

LONG, Richard A., 1927- comp. 810'.8'0352
Afro-American writing: an anthology of prose and poetry. Richard A. Long and Eugenia W. Collier, editors. New York, New York University Press, 1972. 2 v. (xlii, 794 p.) 24 cm. [PS508.N3L6] 72-83827 ISBN 0-8147-4954-2 17.95
1. American literature—Negro authors. 2. American literature—Negro authors—Bio-bibliography. I. Collier, Eugenia, joint comp. II. Title.
pap 7.95. BIP

American literature—Negro authors—Bio-bibliography.

BAILEY, Leaonead Pack. 811'.5'409 B
Broadside authors and artists; an illustrated biographical directory. Compiled and edited by Leaonead Pack Bailey. [1st ed.] Detroit, Mich., Broadside Press [1974] 125 p. illus. 23 cm. [Z1229.N39B34] 70-108887 ISBN 0-910296-25-1 9.95
1. American literature—Negro authors—Bio-bibliography. I. Title.

SHOCKLEY, Ann Allen. 810'.9'896073
Living Black American authors: a biographical directory [by] Ann Allen Shockley and Sue P. Chandler. New York, R. R. Bowker Co., 1973. xv, 220 p. 23 cm. [PS153.N5S5] 73-17005 ISBN 0-8352-0662-9 12.95
1. American literature—Negro authors—Bio-bibliography. 2. American literature—20th century—Bio-bibliography. I. Chandler, Sue P., 1933- joint author. II. Title. BIP

American literature—New England—Bio-bibliography.

THE American renaissance in New England / edited by Joel Myerson. Detroit : Gale Research Co., 1978. p. cm. (Dictionary of literary biography ; v. 1) "A Bruccoli Clark book." Bibliography: p. [PS243.A54] 77-82803 ISBN 0-8103-0913-0 : 35.00 810'.9'003 B
1. American literature—New England—Bio-bibliography. 2. American literature—19th century—Bio-bibliography. 3. New England—Biography. I. Myerson, Joel. II. Series. BIP

American literature—New York (State)—Bio-bibliography.

FLAGG, Mildred (Buchanan) 1886- 808
Profiles of New York authors. New York, Carlton Press [1972] 182 p. 21 cm. (A Hearthstone book) [PS253.N7F57] 72-172765 3.95
1. American literature—New York (State)—Bio-bibliography. I. Title.

American literature—Pennsylvania—Bio-bibliography.

PENNSYLVANIA Council of Teachers of English. 810'.9'9748 B
Biographical companion to the Literary map of Pennsylvania. Rev. [s.l.] : Pennsylvania Council of Teachers of English, 1975, c1965. 36 p. ; 23 cm. [PS253.P4P4 1975b] 76-354057
1. American literature—Pennsylvania—Bio-bibliography. I. Title.

American literature—Southern States—Bio-bibliography.

KNIGHT, Lucian Lamar, 1868-1933. 810'.9'975
Biographical dictionary of Southern authors / [compiled by Lucian Lamar Knight] ; compiled under the direct supervision of Southern men of letters, Edwin Anderson Alderman, Charles Alphonso Smith, editors in chief, John Calvin Metcalf, literary editor. Detroit : Gale Research Co., 1975 [c1910] p. cm. Reprint of the 1929 ed. published by Martin & Hoyt, Atlanta, which was issued as v. 15 of Library of Southern literature, under title: Biographical dictionary of authors. [PS261.K5 1975] 75-26631 ISBN 0-8103-4269-3
1. American literature—Southern States—Bio-bibliography. I. Title. II. Series: Library of Southern literature ; v. 15. BIP

SOUTHERN writers : 810'.9'975 B
a biographical dictionary / edited by Robert Bain, Joseph M. Flora, and Louis D. Rubin, Jr. Baton Rouge : Louisiana State University Press, c1979. p. cm. (Southern literary studies) [PS261.S59] 78-25899 ISBN 0-8071-0354-3 : 30.00 ISBN 0-8071-0390-X pbk. : 7.95
1. American literature—Southern States—Bio-bibliography. 2. Authors, American—Southern States—Biography. I. Bain, Robert. II. Flora, Joseph M. III. Rubin, Louis Decimus, 1923- IV. Series. BIP

American literature—Wisconsin.

TITUS, William A. 810'.8'09775
Wisconsin writers; sketches and studies. Chicago, 1930. Detroit, Gale Research Co., 1974. xi, 433 p. 22 cm. [PS571.W6T5 1974] 74-4303 ISBN 0-8103-3658-8 16.50
1. American literature—Wisconsin. 2. Authors, American—Wisconsin—Biography. I. Title.

TITUS, William A., 1868-1951. 810.8'09775
Wisconson writers; sketches and studies. Ann Arbor, Mich., Plutarch Press, 1971. xi, 433 p. 22 cm. Reprint of the 1930 ed. [PS571.W6T5 1971] 77-145704
1. American literature—Wisconsin. 2. Authors, American—Wisconsin—Biography. I. Title.

American literature—Women authors—History and criticism.

AMERICAN women writers : a critical reference guide from colonial times to the present / edited by Lina Mainiero. New York : Ungar, c1979- v. ; 24 cm. Contents.Contents.—v. 1. A to E. Includes bibliographies. [PS147.A4] 78-20945 ISBN 0-8044-3151-5 : 45.00 (v. 1) 016.810'9'9287
1. American literature—Women authors—History and criticism. 2. Women authors, American—Biography. 3. American literature—Women authors—Bibliography. I. Mainiero, Lina.

American literature—19th century—Bio-bibliography.

ANTEBELLUM writers in New York and the South / edited by Joel Myerson. Detroit : Gale Research Co., 1979. p. cm. (Dictionary of literary biography ; v. 3) "A Bruccoli Clark books." Bibliography: p. [PS128.A5] 79-15481 ISBN 0-8103-0915-7 : 42.00 016.810'9'003
1. American literature—19th century—Bio-bibliography. 2. American literature—New York (State)—Bio-bibliography. 3. American literature—Southern States—Bio-bibliography. 4. Authors, American—19th century—Biography. 5. Authors, American—New York (State)—Biography. 6. Authors, American—Southern States—Biography. I. Myerson, Joel. II. Title. III. Series. BIP

American literature—20th century—Bio-bibliography.

DEKLE, Bernard. 810.9'005 B
Profiles of modern American authors. Rutland, Vt., C. E. Tuttle Co. [1969] 183 p. 18 cm. Includes bibliographies. [PS129.D4] 69-13504 1.95
1. American literature—20th century—Bio-bibliography. I. Title.

LOGGINS, Vernon, 1893- 810.9'005
I hear America ... literature in the United States since 1900. New York, Biblo and Tannen, 1967 [c1937] viii, 378 p. 21 cm. Bibliography: p. 351-357. [PS221.L6 1967] 67-18431
1. American literature—20th century—Bio-bibliography. I. Title.

MANLY, John Matthews, 1865-1940. 810'.9'0052
Contemporary American literature; bibliographies and study outlines, by John Matthews Manly and Edith Rickert. New York, Haskell House Publishers [1974] p. Reprint of the 1921 ed. published by G. C. Harrap, London. 016,810/9/005 [PS221.M3 1974] 74-4436 ISBN 0-8383-2048-1 11.95
1. American literature—20th century—Bio-bibliography. 2. American literature—Outlines, syllabi, etc. I. Rickert, Edith, 1871-1935, joint author. II. Title.

MANLY, John Matthews, 1865-1940. 016.81'09'005
Contemporary American literature : bibliographies and study outlines / by John Matthews Manly and Edith Rickert ; introd. and revision by Fred B. Millett. Westport, Conn. : Greenwood Press, 1975. viii, 378 p. ; 21 cm. Reprint of the 1929 ed. published by Harcourt, Brace, New York. Includes indexes. [PS221.M3 1975] 73-17631 ISBN 0-8371-7254-3 lib.bdg. : 18.25
1. American literature—20th century—Bio-bibliography. 2. American literature—Outlines, syllabi, etc. I. Rickert, Edith, 1871-1938, joint author. II. Title.

MILLETT, Fred Benjamin, 1890- 810.9'005
Contemporary American authors; a critical survey and 219 bio-bibliographies [by] Fred B. Millett. [1st AMS ed.] New York, AMS Press [1970, c1940] xiii, 716 p. 23 cm. Based in part on the author's introd. to the 2d (1929) ed. of J. M. Manly's Contemporary American literature. Bibliography: p. [667]-680. [PS221.M5 1970] 77-128991
1. American literature—20th century—Bio-bibliography. 2. American literature—20th century—History and criticism. I. Title. BIP

American literature—20th century—History and criticism.

COWLEY, Malcolm, 1898- 813'.5'209
A second flowering : works and days of the lost generation / Malcolm Cowley. New York : Penguin Books, [1980] p. cm. Reprint of the 1973 ed. published by

Viking Press, New York. [PS221.C68 1980] 79-25844 ISBN 0-14-005498-7 pbk. : 4.95
1. American literature—20th century—History and criticism. 2. Authors, American—20th century—Biography. I. Title. BIP

KARSNER, David, 1889-1941. 810.9'005
Sixteen authors to one; intimate sketches of leading American story tellers. Illus. by Esther M. Mattsson. Freeport, N.Y., Books for Libraries Press [1968] ix, 290 p. illus., ports. 22 cm. (Essay index reprint series) Reprint of the 1928 ed. Contents.Contents.—Theodore Dreiser.—James Branch Cabell.—Sherwood Anderson.—Sinclair Lewis.—Booth Tarkington.—Eugene O'Neill.—Edgar Lee Masters.—Carl Sandburg.—Christopher Morley.—Clarence Darrow.—Hendrik Willem Van Loon.—Will Durant.—Ben Hecht.—Konrad Bercovici.—Upton Sinclair.—Will Rogers. [PS221.K3 1968] 68-16944
1. American literature—20th century—History and criticism. 2. Authors, American. I. Title. BIP

RANKIN, Thomas Ernest, 1872-1953. 810'.9'0052
American writers of the present day, 1890 to 1920. 2d ed., rev. and enl. [Folcroft, Pa.] Folcroft Library Editions, 1974. p. cm. Reprint of the 1920 ed. published by G. Wahr, Ann Arbor, Mich., which was originally published in 1918 under title: American authorship of the present-day (since 1890) Bibliography: p. [PS221.R3 1974] 74-16098 ISBN 0-8414-7362-5 (lib. bdg.)
1. American literature—20th century—History and criticism. 2. Authors, American—Biography. 3. Canadian literature—History and criticism. 4. Authors, Canadian—Biography. I. Title. BIP

American literature—20th century—History and criticism—Addresses, essays, lectures.

COWLEY, Malcolm, 1898- 810'.9'005
And I worked at the writer's trade : chapters of literary history, 1918-1978 / Malcolm Cowley. New York : Viking Press, c1978. xi, 276 p. ; 23 cm. Includes index. [PS221.C646] 77-28713 ISBN 0-670-12291-2 : 12.50
1. American literature—20th century—History and criticism—Addresses, essays, lectures. 2. Authors, American—20th century—Biography—Addresses, essays, lectures. I. Title. BIP

COWLEY, Malcolm, 1898- 810'.9'005
And I worked at the writer's trade : chapters of literary history, 1918-1978 / Malcolm Cowley. New York : Penguin Books, 1979, c1978. xi, 276 p. ; 20 cm. Includes index. [PS221.C646 1979] 78-24122 ISBN 0-14-005075-2 pbk. : 2.95
1. American literature—20th century—History and criticism—Addresses, essays, lectures. 2. Authors, American—20th century—Biography—Addresses, essays, lectures. I. Title.

American loyalists.

SABINE, Lorenzo, 1803-1877 973.3140922
Biographical sketches of loyalists of the American Revolution, with an historical essay. New introd. by Ralph Adams Brown. Port Washington, N.Y., Kennikat [1966] 2v. (xii, 608; 600p.) 20cm. First pub. in 1864 under title: The American loyalists. [E277.S12] 66-19027 39.50 set.,
1. American loyalists. I. Title.

American loyalists—Biography.

LYNN, Kenneth Schuyler. 973.3'092'2 B
A divided people / Kenneth S. Lynn. Westport, Conn. : Greenwood Press, 1977. 113 p. ; 22 cm. (Contributions in American studies ; no. 30) Includes bibliographical references and index. [E277.L96] 76-25779 ISBN 0-8371-9271-4 lib. bdg. 11.95
1. American loyalists—Biography. 2. United States—History—Revolution, 1775-1783—Biography. 3. United States—History—Revolution, 1775-1783—Causes. I. Title. BIP

American Lutheran Church (1961-)—Clergy—Directories.

A Biographical 284'.131'0922 B
directory of clergymen of The American Lutheran Church. Arnold R. Mickelson, editor; Robert C. Wiederaenders, associate editor. Minneapolis, Augsburg Pub. House, 1972. ix, 1054 p. ports. 24 cm. Published in 1962 under title: A biographical directory of pastors of The American Lutheran Church, compiled by J. M. Jensen, C. E. Linder, and G. Giving. [BX8047.7.B56] 72-80314 ISBN 0-8066-9293-6 15.00
1. American Lutheran Church (1961-)—Clergy—Directories. I. Mickelson, Arnold R., 1922- ed. II. Jensen, John Martin, 1893- comp. A biographical directory of pastors of the American Lutheran Church.

American Ornithologists' Union.

THE Auk. 925.9
Biographies of members of the American Ornithologists' Union, by T. S. Palmer and others. Reprinted from 'The Auk,' 1884-1954. [Edited by Paul H. Oehser] Washington, 1954. 630p. 24cm. [QL671.A476] 55-26967
1. American Ornithologists' Union. 2. Ornithologists. I. Palmer, Theodore Sherman, 1868- II. Title.

American poetry—Connecticut.

EVEREST, Charles William, 1814-1877. 811'.008
The poets of Connecticut; with biographical sketches. Edited by Charles W. Everest. Freeport, N.Y., Books for Libraries Press [1973] p. (Essay index reprint series) Reprint of the 1843 ed. published by Case, Tiffany and Burnham, Hartford, Conn. [PS548.C8E8 1973] 73-4720
1. American poetry—Connecticut. 2. Poets, American—Biography. 3. Connecticut—Biography. I. Title.

American poetry—Women authors.

READ, Thomas Buchanan, 1822-1872. 811'.3'09 B
The female poets of America : with portraits, biographical notices, and specimens of their writings / by Thomas Buchanan Read. Detroit : Gale Research Co., 1976. p. cm. Reprint of the 7th ed., rev. (1857) published by E. H. Butler, Philadelphia. [PS589.R4 1976] 76-9777 ISBN 0-8103-4290-1 : 18.00
1. American poetry—Women authors. 2. American poetry—Women authors—Bio-bibliography. I. Title. BIP

American prose literature—Women authors.

HART, John Seely, 1810-1877. 813'.009 B
The female prose writers of America : with portraits, biographical notices, and specimens of their writings / by John S. Hart. Detroit : Gale Research Co., 1976. p. cm. Reprint of the 1852 ed. published by E. H. Butler, Philadelphia. [PS647.W6H3 1976] 76-9779 ISBN 0-8103-4289-8 : 18.00
1. American prose literature—Women authors. 2. American prose literature—Women authors—Bio-bibliography. I. Title.

American School of Osteopathy, Kirksville, Mo.

STILL, Andrew Taylor, 1828-1917. 615'.533'0924 B
Autobiography of Andrew T. Still, with a history of the discovery and development of the science of osteopathy... New York, Arno Press, 1972 [c1897] 460 p. illus. 21 cm. (Medicine & society in America) [RZ332.S7A5 1972] 78-180591 ISBN 0-405-03973-5
1. American School of Osteopathy, Kirksville, Mo. 2. Osteopathy—History. I. Title. II. Series.

Americans in Paris.

LONGSTREET, Stephen, 1907- 301.45'11'13044361
We all went to Paris; Americans in the City of Light, 1776-1971. New York, Macmillan [1972] 448 p. illus. 24 cm. [DC715.L62] 78-165572 10.95
1. Americans in Paris. I. Title.

Ameringer, Oscar,

AMERINGER, Oscar, 1870-1943. 817'.5'2 B
If you don't weaken; the autobiography of Oscar Ameringer. With a foreword by Carl Sandburg. New York, Greenwood Press [1969, c1940] xviii, 476 p. illus., ports. 23 cm. [PN4874.A45A3] 73-91751
I. Title. BIP

Ames, Adelbert, 1835-1933.

AMES, Blanche (Ames) 973.80924
Adelbert Ames, 1835-1933, general, senator, Governor, the story of his life and times and his integrity as a soldier and statesman in the service of the United States of America throughout the Civil War and in Mississippi in the years of Reconstruction. 1st ed North Easton, Mass., 1964. sviii, 625 p. illus., ports., plans (part col., 1 fold.) 26 cm. "Two hundred and fifty copies ... printed." Bibliography: p. 592-602. [F341.A42] 64-2406
1. Ames, Adelbert, 1835-1933. I. Title.

Ames, Albert Flintoft.

AMES, Edward Carder. 370'.92'4 B
A. F. Ames, village schoolmaster, teacher, administrator, scholar, mathematician, textbook author : a memoir / by Edward C. Ames. 1st ed. Riverside, Ill. : Published for distribution through the Riverside Historical Museum, 1976. 17 p. ; 28 cm. [LA2317.A53A53] 77-670004
1. Ames, Albert Flintoft. 2. Educators—Illinois—Riverside—Biography. I. Title.

Ames, Edward Seribner,

AMES, Edward Seribner, 1870-1958. 922.673
Beyond theology; the autobiography of Edward Scribner Ames. Edited by Van Meter Ames. [Chicago] University of Chicago Press [1959] 223p. illus. 23cm. [BX7343.A64A3] 59-10763
I. Title.

Ames, Fisher, 1758-1808.

BERNHARD, Winfred E. A. 973.410924
Fisher Ames, Federalist and statesman, 1758-1808. Chapel Hill, Pub. for the Inst. of Early Amer. Hist. and Culture at Williamsburg, Va., by the Univ. of N. C. Pr. [c.1965] xiii, 372p. illus., ports. 24cm. Bibl. [E302.6.A5B4] 65-23142 8.75
1. Ames, Fisher, 1758-1808. 2. U. S.—Pol. & govt.—1789-1797. I. Institute of Early American History and Culture, Williamsburg, Va. II. Title.

Ames, Jessie Daniel, 1883-1972.

HALL, Jacquelyn Dowd. 364.6'6'0924
Revolt against chivalry : Jessie Daniel Ames and the women's campaign against lynching / Jacquelyn Dowd Hall. New York : Columbia University Press, 1979. xiv, 373 p. : ill. ; 24 cm. Based on the author's thesis, Columbia University. Includes index. Bibliography: p. [335]-361. [HV6457.H34] 78-11815 ISBN 0-231-04040-7 : 14.95
1. Ames, Jessie Daniel, 1883-1972. 2. Lynching. 3. Social reformers—Biography. I. Title. BIP

Ames, William, 1576-1633.

SPRUNGER, Keith L. 285'.9'0924 B
The learned doctor William Ames; Dutch backgrounds of English and American Puritanism [by] Keith L. Sprunger. Urbana, University of Illinois Press [1972] xi, 289 p. illus. 24 cm. Bibliography: p. [263]-[276] [BX9339.A65S6] 77-175172 ISBN 0-252-00233-4 10.00
1. Ames, William, 1576-1633. I. Title. BIP

Amherst College—Registers.

AMHERST College. 378.744
Amherst College biographical record, 1951; biographical record of the graduates and non-graduates of the classes 1878-1950 inclusive. Amherst, Mass., Trustees of Amherst College, 1951. xi, 568, 63 p. 26 cm. First ed. published 1881-1901 under title: Biographical record of the alumni of Amherst College. [LD152.4.A5 1951] 52-1175
1. Amherst College—Registers. I. Title.

Amherst, Jeffery John Archer, Earl Amherst, 1896-

AMHERST, Jeffery John Archer, Earl Amherst, 1896- 941.082'092'4 B
Wandering abroad : the autobiography of Jeffery Amherst. London : Secker & Warburg, 1976. 223 p., [8] leaves of plates : ill. ; 25 cm. Includes index. [DA566.9.A458A35] 76-366811 ISBN 0-436-01720-2 : £5.50
1. Amherst, Jeffery John Archer, Earl Amherst, 1896- I. Title.

Amiel, Henri Frederic, 1821-1881—Diaries.

AMIEL, Henri Frederic, 1821-1881. 841'.8 B
Amiel's Journal = the Journal intime of Henri-Frederic Amiel / translated with an introd. and notes by Mrs. Humphrey Ward. Westport, Conn. : Hyperion Press, 1977. p. cm. (The Hyperion library of world literature) (Classics of European literature) Translation of Journal intime. Reprint of the 1891 ed. published by Macmillan, London, New York. [PQ2152.A77Z513 1977] 76-48414 ISBN 0-88355-526-3 : 12.95. ISBN 0-88355-527-1 pbk. : 4.95
1. Amiel, Henri Frederic, 1821-1881—Diaries. 2. Authors, Swiss—19th century—Biography. I. Ward, Mary Augusta Arnold, 1851-1920. II. Title. III. Series.

AMIEL, Henri Frederic, 1821-1881. 841'.8 B
Philine : unpublished fragments from the journal of H. F. Amiel / translated from the French by Van Wyck Brooks ; with an introd. by D. L. Murray. Westport, Conn. : Hyperion Press, 1977. p. cm. (The Hyperion library of world literature) (Contemporary European literature) [PQ2152.A77Z513 1977b] 76-48415 ISBN 0-88355-528-X : 13.95. ISBN 0-88355-529-8 : 5.50
1. Amiel, Henri Frederic, 1821-1881—Diaries. 2. Amiel, Henri Frederic, 1821-1881—Relationship with women—Philine. 3. Authors, Swiss—19th century—Biography. I. Title. II. Series.

Amin, Idi, 1925-

LISTOWEL, Judith (Marffy-Mantuano) Hare, Countess of, 1904- 967.6'104
Amin, by Judith Listowel. New York, Drake Publishers [1973] p. [DT433.26.A54L56] 73-3143 ISBN 0-87749-462-2
1. Amin, Idi, 1925-

MELADY, Thomas Patrick. 967.6'104'0924 B
Idi Amin Dada : Hitler in Africa / by Thomas and Margaret Melady. Kansas City, Kan. : Sheed Andrews and McMeel, c1977. p. cm. [DT433.282.A55M44] 77-11706 ISBN 0-8362-0783-1 : 7.95
1. Amin, Idi, 1925- 2. Melady, Thomas Patrick. 3. Melady, Margaret Badum. 4. Uganda—Presidents—Biography. 5. Uganda—Politics and government—1962-

I. Melady, Margaret Badum, joint author. BIP

Amin, Idi, 1925- —Anecdotes.

MOODY, Christopher L. 967.6'1'040924
The wit and wisdom of Idi Amin / by Christopher L. Moody ; with ill. by John Warren. Reno, Nev. : Great Basin Press, [1977] 60 p. : ill. ; 22 cm. (A Ten/foot/pole book) Includes bibliographical references. [DT433.282.A55M66] 77-88611 ISBN 0-930830-01-6 : pbk. : 2.75
1. Amin, Idi, 1925- —Anecdotes. 2. Amin, Idi, 1925- —Quotations. 3. Uganda—President—Biography—Anecdotes, facetiae, satire, etc. I. Amin, Idi, 1925- II. Warren, John. III. Title. BIP

Amiss, Dennis.

AMISS, Dennis. 796.358'092'4 B
In search of runs : an autobiography / [by] Dennis Amiss ; with Michael Carey. London : Paul, 1976. 120 p., [12] p. of plates : ports. ; 23 cm. Includes index. [GV915.A48A34] 77-354430 ISBN 0-09-126780-3 : £3.45
1. Amiss, Dennis. 2. Cricket players—England—Biography. I. Carey, Michael, joint author. II. Title.

Amorim, Enrique, 1900-1960.

MOSE, K. E. A. 863
Enrique Amorim, the passion of a Uruguayan. New York, Plaza Mayor, 1972. 254 p. illus. 21 cm. (Coleccion Scholar, 17) Bibliography: p. 234-254. [PQ8519.A64Z77] 73-163400
1. Amorim, Enrique, 1900-1960. I. Title.

Amos, the prophet.

WOLFF, Hans Walter. 221.9'24 B
Amos, the prophet; the man and his background. Translated by Foster R. McCurley. Edited, with an introd., by John Reumann. Philadelphia, Fortress Press [1973] xii, 100 p. 18 cm. Translation of Amos' geistige Heimat. Bibliography: p. 90-96. [BS580.A6W6513] 72-87062 ISBN 0-8006-0012-6 2.95
1. Amos, the prophet. BIP

Amosov, Nikolai Mikhailovich.

THE open heart, FIC
by N. Amosoff. Tr. from Russian by George St. George. New York. Ballantine [1968,c.1966] 221p. 18cm. (U6123) Tr. of (transliteratcd: Mysli i serdtse) [PZ4.A520p] 617.412 (B) .75 pap.,
I. Amosov, Nikolai Mikhailovich.

Ampere, Andre Marie, 1775-1836—Juvenile literature.

ROBERTO, Brother, 1927- 925.3
The man who tamed a monster; a story of Andre Marie Ampere. Illus. by Carolyn Lee Jagodits. Notre Dame, Ind., Dujarie Press [1959] 95p. illus. 24cm. [QC515.A6R6] 59-65359
1. Ampere, Andre Marie, 1775-1836—Juvenile literature. I. Title.

Ampere, Jean Jacques Antoine, 1800-1864.

HAMERTON, Philip Gilbert, 1834-1894. 920'.044
Modern Frenchmen; five biographies. Freeport, N.Y., Books for Libraries Press [1972] xiv, 422 p. 22 cm. (Essay index reprint series) Reprint of the 1878 ed. Contents.Contents.—Victor Jacquemont.—Henri Perreyve.—Francois Rude.—Jean Jacques Ampere.—Henri Regnault. [CT1012.H3 1972] 72-4579 ISBN 0-8369-2947-0 14.50
1. Jacquemont, Victor, 1801-1832. 2. Perreyve, Henri, 1831-1865. 3. Rude, Francois, 1784-1855. 4. Ampere, Jean Jacques Antoine, 1800-1864. 5. Regnault, Henri, 1843-1871. I. Title. BIP

Amram, David.

AMRAM, David. 780'.92'4 B
Vibrations : the adventures and musical times of David Amram. Westport, Conn. : Greenwood Press, 1980, c1968. p. cm. Reprint of the ed. published by Macmillan Co., New York. [ML410.A534A3 1980] 79-24422 ISBN 0-313-22230-4 lib. bdg. : 29.50
1. Amram, David. 2. Composers—United States—Biography. I. Title. BIP

AMRAM, David. 780'.924
Vibrations; the adventures and musical times of David Amram. New York, Macmillan Co. [1968] 469 p. 22 cm. [ML410.A534A3] 68-23627
1. Musicians—Correspondence, reminiscences, etc. I. Title.

Amrita Pritam, 1919- —Biography.

AMRITA PRITAM, 1919- 891'.42'8'709 B
The revenue stamp : an autobiography / Amrita Pritam ; translated from the Punjabi by Krishna Gorowara. New Delhi : Vikas Pub. House, c1977. 130 p., [8] leaves of plates : ill. ; 23 cm. [PK2659.A44Z52613] 77-903088 7.50
1. Amrita Pritam, 1919- —Biography. 2. Authors, Panjabi—20th century—Biography. I. Title.
Distributed by South Asia Books.

Amshewitz, John Henry, 1882-1942.

AMSHEWITZ, Sarah Briana. [759.2]
The paintings of J. H. Amshewitz, R. B. A. London, New York, Batsford [1951] 66 p. illus. 29 cm. [ND497.A5A58] 927.5 52-42562
1. Amshewitz, John Henry, 1882-1942. I. Title.

Amundsen, Roald Engelbregt Gravning, 1872-1928.

DE LEEUW, Cateau, 1903- 919.8 B
A world explorer: Roald Amundsen. Illustrated by George I. Parrish. Champaign, Ill., Garrard Pub. Co. [1965] 96 p. illus. (part col.) col. maps. 24 cm. (World explorer books) A brief biography of the Norwegian explorer who, in 1911, became the first to conquer the icy elements of the South Pole. [G585.A6D4] 92 AC 68
1. Amundsen, Roald Engelbregt Gravning, 1872-1928. I. Parrish, George I., illus. II. Title.

Amvrosii, Archimandrite of Milkovo, 1894-1933.

ANTONY, Abp. of San Francisco. 271'.8 B
The young elder : a biography of blessed Archimandrite Ambrose of Milkovo / by Archbishop Antony (Medvedev) of San Francisco ; translated from the Russian by Deacon Lev Puhalo and Vasili Novakshonoff. Jordanville, N.Y. : Holy Trinity Russian Orthodox Monastery, 1974. 70 p. ; 23 cm. (Great ascetics of Russia ; book 3) [BX597.A624A5713] 74-79070 pbk. : 1.50
1. Amvrosii, Archimandrite of Milkovo, 1894-1933. I. Title. II. Series.

An, I-suk.

AN, I-suk. 365'.6'0924 B
If I perish / by Mrs. Don M. Kim. Chicago : Moody Press, c1977. p. cm. Translation of Chugumyon chugurira. [CT1848.A49A313] 76-49627 ISBN 0-8024-4001-0 : 6.95
1. An, I-suk. 2. Women—Korea—Biography. I. Title.

Antun, Farah, 1874-1922.

REID, Donald M. 070.4'0924 B
The odyssey of Farah Antun : a Syrian Christian's quest for secularism / by Donald M. Reid. Minneapolis : Bibliotheca Islamica, 1975. xii, 159 p. ; 24 cm. (Studies in Middle Eastern history ; no. 2) Includes index. Bibliography: p. 143-152. [PN5463.A8R4] 74-80598 ISBN 0-88297-009-7 : 12.50
1. Antun, Farah, 1874-1922. I. Title. II. Series.

Anabaptists—Biography.

AUGSBURGER, Myron S. 284'.3 B
Faithful unto death : fifteen young people who were not afraid to die for their faith / Myron S. Augsburger. ; [etchings by Jan Luyken]. Waco, Tex. : Word Books, c1978. 125 p. : ill. ; 22 cm. Presents portraits drawn from court testimony, letters, and other historical records of 16th-century Anabaptist youths, primarily from Holland, Belgium, and Germany, who were persecuted for their religious beliefs. [BX4940.A9] 920 77-92462 ISBN 0-8499-0067-0 : 5.95
1. Anabaptists—Biography. 2. Christian martyrs—Biography. 3. Youth—Religious life. I. Title. BIP

Anarchism and anarchists—France—History.

PATSOURAS, Louis. 320.5'7'0924 B
Jean Grave and French anarchism / by Louis Patsouras. Dubuque, Iowa : Kendall/Hunt Pub. Co., c1978. v, 106 p. ; 23 cm. Bibliography: p. 103-106. [HX893.P37] 78-53639 ISBN 0-8403-1871-5 pbk. : 4.95
1. Anarchism and anarchists—France—History. 2. Anarchism and anarchists—France—Biography. 3. Grave, Jean. I. Title. BIP

Anarchism and anarchists— U. S.—California.

WARREN K. Billings, v. 12
the story of a rebel. A biographical interview conducted by Corinne Gilb, for the Institute of industrial relations oral history project. University of California, on January 9, 16, 29, 31; February 1, 19; and March 12, 29, 1957, in San Francisco, California [A tape recorded interview. Berkeley? 1957] 376l.
1. Anarchism and anarchists— U. S.—California. I. Billings, Warren K 1894-

Anastaise.

MINER, Dorothy Eugenia. 745.6'7
Anastaise and her sisters : women artists of the Middle Ages / Dorothy Miner. Baltimore : Walters Art Gallery, 1974. 24 p. : ill. ; 22 cm. Includes bibliographical references. [ND2920.M54] 75-309852
1. Anastaise. 2. Illumination of books and manuscripts, Medieval. 3. Women painters. I. Title.

Anastasia Nikolaevna, Grand Duchess of Russia, 1901-1918.

ANASTASIA; 920.7
the autobiography of H. I. H. the Grand Duchess Anastasia Nicholaevna of Russia. [1st ed.] New York, R. Speller [1963- v. illus., ports., map. 24 cm. The author claims to be Anastasiia Nikolaevna, Grand Duchess of Russia. [DK254.A7A3] 63-22672
I. Anastasiia Nikolaevna, Grand Duchess of Russia, 1901-

KRUG VON NIDDA, Roland, 1895- 920.7
I am Anastasia; the autobiography of the Grand-Duchess of Russia. With notes by Roland Krug von Nidda. Translated from the German by Oliver Coburn. [1st American ed.] New York, Harcourt, Brace [1959, c1958] 282p. illus. 23cm. Translation of Ich. Anastasia, erziible. Purports to be by Anastasia. [DK254.A7K713] 58-10907
1. Anastasia Nikolaevna, Grand Duchess of Russia, 1901-1918. I. Title.

MAURETTE, Marcelle. 842.91
Anastasia. English adaptation by Guy Bolton. New York, Random House [1955] 180 p. illus. 21 cm. (A Random House play) [PQ2625.A925A78] 55-5419
1. Anastasiia Nikolaevna, Grand Duchess of Russia, 1901-1918—Drama. I. Title.

Anastasoff, Vladimir, 1909-

ANASTASOFF, Vladimir, 1909- 949.5'6
Hang these leaves upon our tree / Vladimir Anastasoff. 1st ed. New York : Vantage Press, c1977. xviii, 281 p. : ill. ; 22 cm. Bibliography: p. 281. [DR701.M15A5] 77-150910 ISBN 0-533-02423-4 : 7.95
1. Anastasoff, Vladimir, 1909- 2. Macedonia—Social life and customs. 3. Macedonia—Biography. 4. Macedonia History. I. Title.

Anatomy—Addresses, essays, lectures.

CORNER, George Washington, 1889- 611
Anatomist at large; an autobiography, and selected essays. Freeport, N.Y., Books for Libraries Press [1969, c1958] 215 p. 23 cm. (Essay index reprint series) Contents.Contents.—Anatomist at large.—Selected essays: Mithridatium and theriac, the most famous remedies of old medicine. Anatomists in search of the soul. The discovery of the mammalian ovum. Quest for a hormone. The gifts of the good physician. Light on the blood capillaries. The focal point in medicine. Benjamin Franklin consults the doctors. A glimpse of incomprehensibles. Science in education. [QM71.C6 1969] 76-86743
1. Anatomy—Addresses, essays, lectures. I. Title.

Anatomy, Artistic.

KNOX, Robert, 1791-1862. 709'.2'2
Great artists and great anatomists : a biographical and philosophical study / by R. Knox. New York : AMS Press, 1977. xii, 213 p. ; 18 cm. Reprint of the 1852 ed. published by J. Van Voorst, London. [N7570.K57 1977] 75-23734 18.00
1. Anatomy, Artistic. 2. Human figure in art. 3. Artists—Biography. I. Title. BIP

Anatomy, Human—History.

STUDIES in pre-Vesalian 081 S
anatomy : biography, translations, documents / L. R. Lind. Philadelphia : American Philosophical Society, 1975. 344 p. : ill. ; 31 cm. (Memoirs of the American Philosophical Society ; v. 104 ISSN 0065-9738s) Includes index.IBibliography: p. 331-336. [Q11.P612 vol. 104] [QM11] 611 74-78093 ISBN 0-87169-104-3 : 18.00
1. Anatomy, Human—History. 2. Anatomy, Human—Early works to 1800. 3. Anatomists—Biography. I. Lind, Levi Robert, 1906- II. Series: American Philosophical Society, Philadelphia. Memoirs ; v. 104.
Contents omitted. BIP

Andersen, Hans Christian, 1805-1875.

ANDERSEN, Hans Christian, 1805-1875. 928.3981
The fairy tale of my life. [English translation by W. Glyn Jones, based on the Danish text of H. Topse-Jensen's annotated edition of 1951] With illus. in colour by Niels Larsen Stevns. New York, British Book Centre [1955, 1954] 350p. col. plates. 35cm. [PT8118.A4 1955a] 55-4864
I. Stevns, Niels Larsen, 1864-1941, illus. II. Jones, W. Glyn, tr. III. Title.

ANDERSEN, Hans Christian, 1805-1875. 928.3981
The mermaid man the autobiography of Hans Christian Andersen. A new abridged translation by Maurice Michael. New York, Library Publishers [1955] 240p. illus. 23cm. Translation of Mit livs eventyr. [PT8118] 55-13537
I. Title.

BOOK, Fredrik [Martin Fredrik Christoffersson Book] 1883- 928.3981
Hans Christian Andersen, a biography. Tr. from Swedish by George C. Schoolfield. Norman, Univ. of Okla. Pr. [c.1962] 260p. illus. 62-10765 4.50
1. Andersen, Hans Christian, 1805-1875. I. Title.

BREDSDORFF, Elias. 839.8'1'36 B
Hans Christian Andersen : the story of his life and work, 1805-75 / Elias Bredsdorff. New York : Scribner, c1975. 376 p. : ill. ; 25 cm. Includes index. Bibliography: p. [366]-372. [PT8119.B6532 1975] 75-23827 ISBN 0-684-14457-3 : 10.00
1. Andersen, Hans Christian, 1805-1875.

GODDEN, Rummer, 1907- 928.3981
Hans Christian Andersen; a great life in brief. [1st ed.] New York, Knopf, 1955 [c1954] 206 p. 19 cm. (Great lives in brief, a new series of biographies) [PT8119.G6] 54-7218
1. Andersen, Hans Christian, 1805-1875.

MANNING-SANDERS, Ruth, 1895- 839.8136
The story of Hans Andersen, Swan of Denmark. With illus. by Astrid Walford. New York, Dutton [1966, c1950] 230 p. illus. 21 cm. First published in 1950 under title: Swan of Denmark. [PT8119.M3 1966] 66-23879
1. Andersen, Hans Christian, 1805-1875. I. Title.

MEYNELL, Esther Hallam (Moorhouse) v. 12
The story of Hans Andersen. New York, H. Schuman [1950] 135 p. illus., ports. 19 cm. 51-9819
1. Andersen, Hans Christian, 1805-1875. I. Title.

MONTGOMERY, Elizabeth Rider. 839.8'1'36 B
Hans Christian Andersen, immortal storyteller. Illustrated by Richard Lebenson. Champaign, Ill., Garrard Pub. Co. [1968] 142 p. illus., ports. 22 cm. ([Creative arts biographies]) A biography of the Danish storyteller who went from an unhappy childhood to become loved and famous for his fairy tales. [PT8119.M6] 92 AC 68
1. Andersen, Hans Christian, 1805-1875. I. Lebenson, Richard, illus. II. Title.

REUMERT, Elith Poul Ponsaing, 1855-1934. 839.8'1'36 B
Hans Andersen the man. Translated from the Danish by Jessie Brochner. Detroit, Tower Books, 1971. xvi, 192 p. illus. 23 cm. Translation of H. C. Andersen som han var. "Facsimile reprint of the 1927 ed." [PT8119.R413 1927a] 71-110811
1. Andersen, Hans Christian, 1805-1875. BIP

ROSSI, Pietro. v. 12
Hans Christian Andersen. Roma, M. Ciranna [1961] 130 p. 17 cm. (I Cirannini) 67-49666
1. Andersen, Hans Christian, 1805-1875. I. Title.

SPINK, Reginald. 839.8'1'36 B
Hans Christian Andersen and his world. New York, Putnam [1972] 128 p. illus. 24 cm. A biography of the nineteenth-century Danish author whose fairy tales brought him world renown. [PT8119.S57 1972] 92 72-77072 6.95
1. Andersen, Hans Christian, 1805-1875. BIP

SPINK, Reginald 920
The young Hans Andersen. Illus. by Anne Linton. New York, Roy [1963, c.1962] 143p. illus. 21cm. 62-18556 3.00 bds.,
1. Andersen, Hans Christian, 1805-1875—Juvenile literature. I. Title.

Andersen, Hans Christian, 1805-1875—Biography.

ANDERSEN, Hans Christian, 1805-1875. 839.8'1'36 B
The fairy tale of my life : an autobiography / Hans Christian Andersen. New York : Paddington Press, [1975] p. cm. Translation of Mit livs eventyr. Reprint of the 1868 ed. [PT8118.A3E5 1975] 75-11175 ISBN 0-8467-0074-3 : 10.95
1. Andersen, Hans Christian, 1805-1875—Biography. I. Title.

ANDERSEN, Hans Christian, 1805-1875. 839.8'1'36 B
The true story of my life / Hans Christian Andersen ; translated by Mary Howitt. Detroit : Gale Research Co., 1976. p. cm. Translation of Mit livs eventyr. Reprint of the 1926 ed. published by the American-Scandinavian Foundation, New York, which was issued as v. 26 of Scandinavian classics. [PT8118.A3E5 1976] 68-21750 ISBN 0-8103-4167-0 : 12.50
1. Andersen, Hans Christian, 1805-1875—Biography. I. Title. II. Series: Scandinavian classics ; v. 26.

Andersen, Hans Christian, 1805-1875—Biography—Juvenile literature.

JOHNSON, Spencer. 839.8'1'36 B
The value of fantasy : the story of Hans Christian Andersen / by Spencer Johnson. 1st ed. La Jolla, Calif. : Value Communications, c1979. p. cm. (Value tales) A brief biography of the 19th-century Danish author of many well-known fairy tales, which stresses the value of personal fantasies and imagination. [PT8119.J6] 79-18237 ISBN 0-916392-43-0 : 5.95
1. Andersen, Hans Christian, 1805-1875—Biography—Juvenile literature. 2. Authors, Danish—19th century—Biography—Juvenile literature. I. Title. BIP

Andersen, Hans Christian, 1805-1875—Juvenile literature.

BROWN, Marion (Marsh) 839.8'1'6 B
The pauper prince; a story of Hans Christian Andersen. Los Angeles, Crescent Publications [1973] vi, 119 p. illus. 22 cm. A biography of the nineteenth-century Danish author whose fairy tales brought him world renown. [PT8119.B69] 92 73-86604 4.95
1. Andersen, Hans Christian, 1805-1875—Juvenile literature. I. Title.

GARST, Doris Shannon, 1899- 92
Hans Christian Andersen: fairy tale author [by] Shannon Garst. Illus. by John Gretzer. Boston, Houghton [c.1965] 191p. illus. 22cm. (Piper bks.) [PT8119.G35] 65-10520 2.20; 1.32 lib. ed., pap.,
1. Andersen, Hans Christian, 1805-1875.—Juvenile literature. I. Title.

GARST, Doris Shannon, 1899- 92 (J)
Hans Christian Andersen: fairy tale author [by] Shannon Garst. Illustrated by John Gretzer. Boston, Houghton Mifflin [1965] 191 p. illus. 22 cm. (Piper books) [PT8119.G35] 65-10520
1. Andersen, Hans Christian, 1805-1875—Juvenile literature. I. Title.

MONTGOMERY, Elizabeth Rider. 92 (J)
Hans Christian Andersen, immortal storyteller. Illustrated by Richard Lebenson. Champaign, Ill., Garrard Pub. Co. [1968] 142 p. illus., ports. 22 cm. ([Creative arts biographies]) [PT8119.M6] 68-10694
1. Andersen, Hans Christian, 1805-1875—Juvenile literature.

SPINK, Reginald 920
The young Hans Andersen. Illus. by Anne Linton. New York, Roy [1963, c.1962] 143p. illus. 21cm. 62-18556 3.00 bds.,
1. Andersen, Hans Christian, 1805-1875—Juvenile literature. I. Title.

Anderson, Abraham Archibald,

ANDERSON, Abraham Archibald, 1847-1940. 759.13 B
Experiences and impressions; the autobiography of Colonel A. A. Anderson. Freeport, N.Y., Books for Libraries Press [1970] xiv, 245 p. illus., facsims., ports. 23 cm. Reprint of the 1933 ed. [ND237.A63A3 1970] 72-124223
I. Title. BIP

Anderson, Alexander,

ANDERSON, Alexander, 1775-1870. 759.13
Autobiography of an early American wood engraver. New York, Traders Press, 1968. [48] p. illus. 63 mm. "Limited to 500 copies ... no. 79." "Alexander Anderson ... a short bibliography": p. [44]-[47] [NE1215.A5A2] 68-5976
I. Title.

Anderson, Alexander Jay, 1832-1903.

ANDERSON, Florence Mary (Bennett) 1883- 923.773
Leaven for the frontier; the true story of a pioneer educator. Boston, Christopher Pub. House [1953] 437p. illus. 21cm. [LA2317.A547A7] 53-3675
1. Anderson, Alexander Jay, 1832-1903. I. Title.

Anderson, Arthur B., 1891-

ANDERSON, Arthur B., 1891- 978.3'03'0924 B
Years of challenge, 1891-1971: the autobiography of Arthur B. Anderson, farmer, mechanic, oil dealer, and State legislator of South Dakota. Edited by Clifford B. Anderson Vermillion, S.D., Dakota Press, 1974. xi, 184 p. illus. 23 cm. [F656.A52A38] 73-84211 ISBN 0-88249-019-2 4.00 (pbk.).
1. Anderson, Arthur B., 1891- 2. South Dakota—Politics and government. I. Title.

Anderson, Carl, 1833-1961.

ANDERSON, Mabel, 1882- 920
The saga of Bodaholm; a true story. Boston, Christopher Pub. House [1955] 421p. illus. 21cm. [CT275.A689A7] 55-3059
1. Anderson, Carl, 1833-1961. I. Title.

Anderson, Colena M.

ANDERSON, Colena M. 177'.6
Friendship's bright shinings / by Colena M. Anderson. Grand Rapids : Zondervan Pub. House, c1976. p. cm. [BJ1533.F8A55] 76-13217 4.95
1. Anderson, Colena M. 2. Friendship. I. Title. BIP

Anderson, Donald Macdougall, 1923-1961.

MCELDOWNEY, Dennis, 1926- 616.83600924
Donald Anderson; a memoir, by Dennis McEldowney. Auckland, Blackwood & J. Paul. San Francisco, Tri-Ocean [1966] 126p. 21cm. Bibl. [CT2888.A5M3] 66-8901 3.00 bds.,
1. Anderson, Donald Macdougall, 1923-1961. 2. Cerebral palsy—Personal narratives. I. Title.

Anderson, Elizabeth (Garrett) 1836-1917.

MANTON, Jo, 1919- 926.1
Elizabeth Garrett, M. D. London, New York, Abelard-Schuman [1960] 159p. 21cm. [R489.A47M3] 60-8077
1. Anderson, Elizabeth (Garrett) 1836-1917. I. Title.

Anderson family.

ANDERSON, Sam. 818.54
Mother's blue hen. With illus. by Elise Healy. New York, Dodd, Mead [1963] 177 p. illus. 21 cm. Autobiographical. [CT275.A728A3] 63-17129
1. Anderson family. 2. Collectors and collecting. I. Title.

SHUMWAY, Anne Anderson, 1891- 929.2'0973
Mother's family; a biography of Ida Russell Anderson. Portsmouth, Ohio [Anderson Newcomb Co.] 1966. 56, viii p. illus., ports. 24 cm. Bibliography: p. 6. [CS71.A55 1966] 68-5561
1. Anderson family. 2. Russell family. I. Title.

Anderson, Guy Irving, 1906-

ROBBINS, Tom. v. 12
Guy Anderson. [Photographed by Bob Peterson and written by Tom Robbins. Seattle, Gear Works Press, 1965] 1 v. (unpaged) illus. (1 col.) ports. 68-62209
1. Anderson, Guy Irving, 1906- I. Title.

Anderson, Harry, 1906-

WOOLSEY, Raymond H. 759.13 B
Harry Anderson : the man behind the paintings / Raymond H. Woolsey and Ruth Anderson. Washington : Review and Herald Pub. Association, c1976. 127 p. : ill. (some col.) ; 26 cm. [ND237.A6423W66] 76-15700 5.95
1. Anderson, Harry, 1906- 2. Painters—United States—Biography. I. Anderson, Ruth, 1911- joint author. II. Title. BIP

Anderson, Hjalmer Andrew,

ANDERSON, Hjalmer Andrew, 1874-1959. 920
The story of my life. Washington, 1962. 89 p. illus., facsims., ports. 24 cm. "Privately published by H. A. Anderson's family ... Printed in Tehran, Iran, by Offset Press [and prepared for publication by Burnett Anderson]" [CT275.A718A3] 65-34680
I. Title.

Anderson Island—History.

CAMMON, Betsey Johnson, 1886- 979.7'78
Island memoir; a personal history of Anderson and McNeil Islands. Introd. by Bruce Le Roy. Drawings by Jane Cammon. Puyallup, Wash., Valley Press [1969] 221 p. illus., maps (on lining papers) 24 cm. [F897.A5C3] 73-83116 5.95
1. Anderson Island—History. 2. McNeil Island, Wash.—History. 3. Anderson Island—Biography. 4. McNeil Island, Wash.—Biography. I. Title.

Anderson, Jack, 1922-

ANDERSON, Jack, 1922- 070.4'3'0924 B
Confessions of a muckraker : the inside story of life in Washington during the Truman, Eisenhower, Kennedy and Johnson years / by Jack Anderson and James Boyd. 1st. ed. New York : Random House, c1979. 354 p. ; 25 cm. Includes index. [PN4874.A48A33] 77-90283 ISBN 0-394-49124-6 : 12.95
1. Anderson, Jack, 1922- 2. Pearson, Drew, 1897-1969. 3. Journalists—United States—Biography. I. Boyd, James, 1929- joint author. II. Title.

Anderson, John, b. 1831?

TWELVETREES, Harper, 1823-1881, ed. 301.44'93'0924 B
The story of the life of John Anderson, the fugitive slave. Freeport, N.Y., Books for Libraries Press [1971] xv, 182 p. port. 23 cm. (The Black heritage library collection) Reprint of the 1863 ed. [E450.A54T9 1971] 72-164378 ISBN 0-8369-8837-X
1. Anderson, John, b. 1831? I. Title. II. Series.

Anderson, Lindsay, 1923-

SUSSEX, Elizabeth. 791.43'023'0924
Lindsay Anderson. [New York] Praeger [1970, c1969] 96 p. illus., ports. 17 cm. ([Praeger film library]) "Filmography": p. 92-96. [PN1998.A3A587 1970] 70-108985 4.95
1. Anderson, Lindsay, 1923-

Anderson, Margaret C.

ANDERSON, Margaret C. 920.5
The fiery fountains. [1st ed.] New York, Hermitage House [1951] 242 p. illus. 22 cm. A continuation of the author's autobiography, My thirty years' war. [PN4874.A5A26] 51-13661
I. Title.

ANDERSON, Margaret C. 070.4'0924
My thirty years' war; an autobiography, by Margaret Anderson. Westport, Conn., Greenwood Press [1971] 274 p. illus.,

facsim., ports. 23 cm. [PN4874.A5A3 1971] 76-136511 ISBN 0-8371-5429-4
I. Title.

ANDERSON, Margaret C. 070.4'0924
My thirty years' war; the autobiography: beginnings and battles to 1930 [by] Margaret Anderson. New York, Horizon Press [1970, c1969] vii, 278 p. illus., ports. 25 cm. [PN4874.A5A3 1970] 76-92706 10.00
I. Title.

ANDERSON, Margaret C. 070.4'0924
The strange necessity; the autobiography: resolutions and reminiscence to 1969 [by] Margaret Anderson. New York, Horizon Press [1970, c1969] 223 p. ports. 25 cm. [PN4874.A5A34 1970] 73-92708 6.95
I. Title.

Anderson, Marian, 1902-

ANDERSON, Marian, 1902- 927.8
My Lord, what a morning; an autobiography. New York, Watts [1966, c.1956] 312p. 29cm. (Keith Jennison large type ed.) [ML420.A6A3] 6.95
1. Musicians—Correspondence, reminiscences, etc. I. Title.

ANDERSON, Marian, 1902- 927.8
My Lord, what a morning. an autobiography. New York, Viking Press, 1956. 312p. illus. 22cm. 'A condensed version ... appeared in serial form in the Woman's home companion.' [ML420.A6A3] 56-10402
1. Musicians—Correspondence, reminiscences, etc. I. Title.

ANDERSON, Marian, 1902- 927.8
My Lord, what a morning; an autobiography. New York, Viking Press, 1956. 312 p. illus. 22 cm. "A condensed version ... appeared in serial form in the Woman's home companion." [ML420.A6A3] 56-10402
1. Musicians—Correspondence, reminiscences, etc. I. Title.

NEWMAN, shirlee Petkin. 927.8
Marian Anderson: lady from Philadelphia. Philadelphia, Westminster [c. 1966] 175p. ports. 22cm. Bibl. [ML420.A6N5] 66-10933 3.75
1. Anderson, Marian, 1902- I. Title.

NEWMAN, Shirlee 782.1'092'4
Petkin.
Marian Anderson: lady from Philadelphia, by Shirlee P. Newman. Philadelphia, Westminster Press [c1965] 175 p. ports. 22 cm. Bibliography: p. 163-165. [ML420.A6N5] 66-10933
1. Anderson, Marian, 1902- I. Title. **BIP**

STEVENSON, Janet JUV
Marian Anderson; singing to the world. Chicago, Ency. Britannica [c.1963] 189p. ports. 22cm. (Britannica bkshelf. Great lives) 63-13517 2.95; 2.36 bds., lib. ed.,
1. Anderson, Marian, 1902- I. Title.

STEVENSON, Janet. 782.1'092'4
Marian Anderson; singing to the world. Chicago, Encyclopaedia Britannica Press [1963] 189 p. ports. 22 cm. (Britannica bookshelf. Great lives) [ML420.A6S8] 63-13517
1. Anderson, Marian, 1902- I. Title.

VEHANEN, Kosti, 1887- 784'.0924 B
Marian Anderson, a portrait. Westport, Conn., Greenwood Press [1970, c1941] 270 p. illus., ports. 23 cm. "Written with the collaboration of George J. Barnett": leaf following t.p. [ML420.A6V4 1970] 74-100184 ISBN 0-8371-4051-X
1. Anderson, Marian, 1902- I. Barnett, George J. **BIP**

Anderson, Marian, 1902- —Juvenile literature.

SPIVEY, Lenore 927.8
Singing heart; a story based on the life of Marian Anderson. Illus. by Howard and Thelma Hogan. Largo, Fla., Community Serv. Found., 1963. 66p. illus. 21cm. Bibl. 63-25308 price unreported
1. Anderson, Marian, 1902- —Juvenile literature. I. Title.

TOBIAS, Tobi. 784'.092'4 B
Marian Anderson. Illustrated by Symeon Shimin. New York, Crowell [1972] 40 p. col. illus. 24 cm. (A Crowell biography) A biography of the Negro concert artist who ultimately triumphed in her struggle for recognition. [ML3930.A5T6] 92 79-139101 ISBN 0-690-51846-3 3.75
1. Anderson, Marian, 1902- —Juvenile literature. I. Shimin, Symeon, illus. **BIP**

Anderson, Mary, 1872-1964.

ANDERSON, Mary, 331.88'092'4 B
1872-1964.
Woman at work; the autobiography of Mary Anderson, as told to Mary N. Winslow. Westport, Conn., Greenwood Press [1973, c1951] p. Reprint of the ed. published by University of Minnesota Press, Minneapolis. [HD6095.A668 1973] 73-13451 ISBN 0-8371-7133-4 12.25
1. Anderson, Mary, 1872-1964. 2. Woman—Employment—United States. I. Winslow, Mary Nelson. II. Title.

Anderson, Maxwell, 1888-1959.

CLARK, Barrett Harper, 812'.5'2 B
1890-1953.
Maxwell Anderson : the man and his plays / by Barrett H. Clark. Brooklyn : Haskell House Publishers, 1977, i.e.1978 p. cm. Reprint of the 1933 ed. published by S. French, New York. "Published work": p. [PS3501.N256Z6 1977] 77-10509 ISBN 0-8383-2212-3 lib.bdg. : 9.95
1. Anderson, Maxwell, 1888-1959. 2. Dramatists, American—20th century—Biography. **BIP**

SHIVERS, Alfred S. 812'.5'2 B
Maxwell Anderson / Alfred S. Shivers. Boston : Twayne Publishers, c1976. p. cm. (Twayne's United States authors series ; TUSAS 279) Includes index. Bibliography: p. [PS3501.N256Z9] 76-24867 ISBN 0-8057-7179-4 lib.bdg. : 7.50
1. Anderson, Maxwell, 1888-1959. **BIP**

Anderson, Olive,

ANDERSON, Olive, 1915- 917.74'6
A wilderness of wonder. Art by Don Wallerstedt. Minneapolis, Augsburg Pub. House [1971] 160 p. illus. 23 cm. Autobiographical. [CT275.A727A3] 76-135218 ISBN 0-8066-1105-7 4.95
I. Title.

Anderson, Rasmus Bjorn, 1846-1936.

HUSTVEDT, Lloyd 973.80924 (B)
Rasmus Bjorn Anderson, pioneer scholar. Northfield, Minn., Norwegian-American Historical Assn. 1966. xi, 381p. illus., ports. 24cm. (Norwegian-Amer. Hist. Assn. Authors ser. v.2) Bibl. [E664.A494H8] 66-31292 6.75
1. Anderson, Rasmus Bjorn, 1846 1936. I. Title. II. Series.

HUSTVEDT, Lloyd. 973.8'092'4 B
Rasmus Bjorn Anderson / Lloyd Hustvedt. New York : Arno Press, 1979, c1966. p. cm. (Scandinavians in America) Reprint of the ed. published by the Norwegian-American Historical Association, Northfield, Minn., which was issued as v. 2 of its Authors series. Includes index. Bibliography: p. [E664.A494H8 1979] 78-15189 ISBN 0-405-11642-X : 26.00
1. Anderson, Rasmus Bjorn, 1846-1936. 2. Intellectuals—United States—Biography. 3. Norwegian Americans—Biography. I. Title. II. Series. III. Series: Norwegian-American Historical Association. Authors series ; v. 2.

Anderson, Richard A., 1891-

ANDERSON, Richard 791.3'4'0924 B
A., 1891-
The most exciting years of show business [by] Richard A. Anderson. Philadelphia, Dorrance [1974] 111 p. illus. 22 cm. [GV1811.A48A35] 73-87469 ISBN 0-8059-1939-2 5.95
1. Anderson, Richard A., 1891- 2. Acrobats and acrobatism. I. Title. **BIP**

Anderson, Robert,

ANDERSON, 917.3'03'80924 B
Robert, 1843-
From slavery to affluence; memoirs of Robert Anderson, ex-slave, by Daisy Anderson Leonard. Steamboat Springs, Colo., Printed by the Steamboat Pilot, c1967. 80 p. illus., ports. 19 cm. "Have you no shame?" by Daisy Anderson Leonard, p. 61-80. [E185.97.A54 1967] 68-2289
I. Leonard, Daisy Anderson. II. Title.

Anderson, Sherwood, 1876-1941.

ANDERSON, Sherwood, 1876- 928.1
1941.
Letters; selected and edited with an introd. and notes by Howard Mumford Jones, in association with Walter B. Rideout. [1st ed.] Boston, Little, Brown [1953] xxv, 479p. ports. 23cm. [PS3501.N4Z54] 52-12649
I. Title.

ANDERSON, Sherwood, 813'.5'209
1876-1941.
Sherwood Anderson/Gertrude Stein: correspondence and personal essays. Edited by Ray Lewis White. Chapel Hill, University of North Carolina Press [1972] 130 p. 2 ports. (on lining papers) 23 cm. Bibliography: p. 121-126. [PS3501.N4Z545 1972] 72-78152 ISBN 0-8078-1197-1 7.95
I. Stein, Gertrude, 1874-1946. II. White, Ray Lewis, ed.

ANDERSON, Sherwood, 811'.5'2 B
1876-1941.
Sherwood Anderson's memoirs; a critical edition. Newly edited from the original manuscripts by Ray Lewis White. Chapel Hill, University of North Carolina Press [1969] xxxix, 579 p. port 27 cm. Bibliography: p. 564-566. [PS3501.N4Z524 1969] 73-80019 15.00
I. White, Ray Lewis, ed. II. Title.

ANDERSON, Sherwood, 1876- 928.1
1941.
A story teller's story. [Gloucester, Mass., Peter Smith, 1960] 442p. (Evergreen Bk. E-109 rebound in cloth) 4.00
I. Title.

ANDERSON, Sherwood, 1876- 928.1
1941.
A story teller's story. New York, Grove Press [1958, c1951] 442p. 21cm. Autobiographical. [PS3501.N4Z5 1958a] 58-8587
I. Title.

ANDERSON, Sherwood, 1876- 928.1
1941.
A story teller's story. New York, Grove Press [1958, c1951] 442p. 21cm. (Evergreen books, E-109) Autobiographical. [PS3501.N4Z5 1958] 58-59461
I. Title.

ANDERSON, Sherwood, 818'.5'203
1876-1941.
A story teller's story; a critical text. Edited with an introd. by Ray Lewis White. Cleveland, Press of Case Western Reserve University, 1968. xix, 360 p. 24 cm. ([His The major fiction of Sherwood Anderson]) Autobiographical. Bibliography: p. [352]-356. [PS3501.N4Z5 1968] 68-19071
I. White, Ray Lewis, ed. II. Title.

ANDERSON, Sherwood, 813'.5'2
1876-1941.
Tar: a Midwest childhood; a critical text. Edited with an introd. by Ray Lewis White. Cleveland, Press of Case Western Reserve University, 1969. xx, 257 p. 24 cm. (His the major fiction of Sherwood Anderson) Autobiographical. Bibliography: p. [245]-253. [PS3501.N4Z52 1969] 69-17680 7.50
I. White, Ray Lewis, ed. II. Title.

DERLETH, August William, 818.52
1909-
Three literary men; a memoir of Sinclair Lewis, Sherwood Anderson. Edgar Lee Masters. New York, Candlelight Press, 1963. 56 p. ports. 22 cm. 63-23595
1. Lewis, Sinclair, 1885-1951. 2. Anderson, Sherwood, 1876-1941. 3. Masters, Edgar Lee, 1969-1950. I. Title. **BIP**

HOWE, Irving 818.5209
Sherwood Anderson. Stanford, Calif., Stanford Univ. Pr. [1966. c.1951] xv. 271p. 23cm. Bibl. [PS3501.N4Z65 1966] 66-26240 6.00; 2.95 pap.,
1. Anderson. Sherwood. 1876-1941. I. Title.

HOWE, Irving. 928.1
Sherwood Anderson. [New York] Sloane [1951] xiii, 271 p. port. 22 cm. (The American men of letters series) "Bibliography": p. 257-260. [PS3501.N4Z65] 51-9927
1. Anderson, Sherwood, 1876-1941. I. Series.

SCHEVILL, James Erwin, 928.1
1920-
Sherwood Anderson, his life and work. [Denver] University of Denver Press [1951] xvi, 360 p. illus., ports. 23 cm. Bibliography: p. 356-357. [PS3501.N4Z8] 51-10225
1. Anderson, Sherwood, 1876-1941. I. Title.

SUTTON, William 813'.5'2 B
Alfred, 1915-
The road to Winesburg; a mosaic of the imaginative life of Sherwood Anderson, by William A. Sutton. Metuchen, N.J., Scarecrow Press, 1972. 645 p. illus. 22 cm. Bibliography: p. 615-629. [PS3501.N4Z854] 73-181997 ISBN 0-8108-0312-7
1. Anderson, Sherwood, 1876-1941. I. Title. **BIP**

Anderson, Sherwood, 1876-1941—Interviews.

DERLETH, August 810'.9'0052
William, 1909-1971.
Three literary men : a memoir of Sinclair Lewis, Sherwood Anderson, Edgar Lee Masters / by August Derleth. Folcroft, Pa. : Folcroft Library Editions, 1978 [c1963] p. cm. Reprint of the ed. published by Candlelight Press, New York. [PS3507.E697Z475 1978] 78-11518 ISBN 0-8414-3686-X lib. bdg. : 10.00
1. Derleth, August William, 1909-1971—Friends and associates. 2. Lewis, Sinclair, 1885-1951—Interviews. 3. Anderson, Sherwood, 1876-1941—Interviews. 4. Masters, Edgar Lee, 1869-1950—Interviews. 5. Authors, American—20th century—Biography. I. Title.

Anderson, Sir John, 1882-1958.

WHEELER-BENNETT, Sir John v. 12
Wheeler, 1902-
John Anderson, Viscount Waverly. London, Macmillan; New York, St. Martin's press, 1962. xv, 430 p. illus. ports. 23 cm. Bibliography, p. 411-414. 63-72000
1. Anderson, Sir John, 1882-1958. I. Title.

Anderson, Sparky, 1934-

ANDERSON, Sparky, 796.357'092'4 B
1934-
The main spark : Sparky Anderson and the Cincinnati Reds / Sparky Anderson and Si Burick. 1st ed. Garden City, N.Y. : Doubleday, 1978. 239 p., [12] leaves of plates : ill. ; 22 cm. [GV865.A48A35] 76-42057 ISBN 0-385-12464-3 : 7.95
1. Anderson, Sparky, 1934- 2. Cincinnati. Baseball club (National League) 3. Baseball managers—United States—Biography. I. Burick, Si, joint author. II. Title. **BIP**

Anderson, Ted, 1952-

ANDERSON, Ted, 248'.2'0924 B
1952-
The God explosion in my life / by Ted Anderson, with David Prudhomme. Wheaton, Ill. : Tyndale House Publishers, 1975. 234 p. ; 18 cm. [BV4935.A58A33] 74-21973 ISBN 0-8423-1040-1 pbk. : 1.95
1. Anderson, Ted, 1952- 2. Conversion. I. Prudhomme, David, 1917-1974, joint author. II. Title.

Anderson, Tom,

ANDERSON, Tom, 1910- 081
Straight talk; the wit and wisdom of Tom Anderson. Selected from editorials and speeches, 1955-1966 by the editors of Western Islands. Boston, Western Islands [1967] viii, 216 p. 22 cm. [AC8.A58] 66-28921
I. Title.

Andersonville, Ga. Military prison.

KELLOGG, Robert H. 973.77'1'0924 B
Life and death in rebel prisons, by Robert H. Kellogg. Freeport, N.Y., Books for Libraries Press, 1971. viii, 398 p. illus. 23 cm. (The Black heritage library collection) Reprint of the 1865 ed. [E612.A5K4 1971] 75-168517 ISBN 0-8369-8869-8
1. Andersonville, Ga. Military prison. 2. Florence, S.C. Military prison. 3. United States—History—Civil War, 1861-1865—Prisons and prisoners. I. Title. II. Series. BIP

Andes, Florence.

TOWNSEND, Elsie Doig. 917.8 B
Always the frontier, by Elsie Townsend. [Independence, Mo., Herald Pub. House, 1970] 256 p. 21 cm. [CT275.A729T68] 75-182433 ISBN 0-8309-0059-4 5.50
1. Andes, Florence. 2. Andes, Sam. I. Title.

Andrade, Victor, 1905—

ANDRADE, Victor, 1905- 327'.2'0924 B
My missions for revolutionary Bolivia, 1944-1962 / by Victor Andrade ; edited and with an introd. by Cole Blasier. [Pittsburgh] : University of Pittsburgh Press, c1976. xv, 200 p. : port. ; 24 cm. (Pitt Latin American series) Includes bibliographical references and index. [F3326.A67] 76-6656 ISBN 0-8229-3320-9 : 11.95
1. Andrade, Victor, 1905- 2. Diplomats—Bolivia—Correspondence, reminiscences, etc. 3. United States—Foreign relations—Bolivia. 4. Bolivia—Foreign relations—United States. I. Title. BIP

Andre, Brother, 1845-1937.

BURTON, Katherine (Kurz), 1890- 922.271
Brother Andre of Mount Royal. [New rev. ed.] Notre Dame, Ind., Ave Maria Press [1952] 197 p. 23 cm. [BX4705.A58B8 1952] 52-41873
1. Andre, Brother, 1845-1937. I. Title.

HATCH, Alden, 1898- 922.271
The miracle of the mountain; the story of Brother Andre and the shrine on Mount Royal. [1st ed.] New York, Hawthorn Books [1959] 223 p. illus. 24 cm. [BX4705.A58H3] 59-6878
1. Andre, Brother, 1845-1887. I. Title.

Andre, Brother, 1845-1937 — Juvenile literature.

WILLETT, Franciscus. j92
A mountain for St. Joseph; the life of Brother Andre, C.S.C., "The miracle man of Montreal" [by] Ian Bond. Illustrated by Gerald Robbins. Valatie, N.Y., Holy Cross Press, 1965. 60 p. illus. 23 cm. [BX4700.A443W5] 65-21805
1. Andre, Brother, 1845-1937 — Juvenile literature. I. Title.

Andre, John, 1751-1780—Juvenile literature.

DUNCAN, Lois, 1934- 973.38'6'0924 B
Major Andre: brave enemy. Illustrated by Tran Mawicke. New York, Putnam [1969] 127 p. illus. 22 cm. (Spies of the world) Bibliography: p. 121. A biography of the British officer executed as a spy by the colonists during the American Revolution. [E280.A5D8] 92 68-24512 3.49
1. Andre, John, 1751-1780—Juvenile literature. I. Mawicke, Tran, illus. II. Title.

NATHAN, Adele (Gutman) 973.38'6'0924 B
Major John Andre, gentleman spy. New York, F. Watts [1969] xiv, 175 p. map. 22 cm. (Hidden heroes series) "A Giniger book." A biography of the British officer who was hanged for treason by colonists for alleged espionage during the Revolution. [E280.A5N3] 92 69-12910 4.95
1. Andre, John, 1751-1780—Juvenile literature. I. Title.

Andreas—Salome, Lou, 1861-1937.

BINION, Rudolph 1927- 838'.809 [B]
Frau Lou; Nietzsche's wayward disciple. With a foreword by Walter Kaufmann. Princeton, N.J., Princeton University Press [1974, c1968] 587 p. 24 cm. Bibliography: p. 557-575. [PT2601.N4Z6] 68-10389 5.95 (pbk.)
1. Andreas—Salome, Lou, 1861-1937. I. Title. BIP

PETERS, Heinz Frederick. 928.3
My sister, my spouse; a biography of Lou Andreas-Salome. [1st ed.] New York, Norton [1962] 320 p. illus. 22 cm. Includes bibliography. [PT2601.N4Z75] 62-10103
1. Andreas-Salome, Lou, 1861-1937. I. Title. BIP

SORELL, Walter, 1905- 920.72
Three women : lives of sex and genius / Walter Sorell. Indianapolis : Bobbs-Merrill, [1975] p. cm. [HQ1123.S67] 74-17644 ISBN 0-672-51750-7 : 7.95
1. Andreas-Salome, Lou, 1861-1937. 2. Werfel, Alma Schindler Mahler. 3. Stein, Gertrude, 1874-1946. I. Title.

Andreas-Salome, Lou, 1861-1937—Biography.

PETERS, Heinz Frederick. 838'.8'09 B
My sister, my spouse; a biography of Lou Andreas-Salome [by] H. F. Peters. With a pref. by Anais Nin. New York, Norton [1974, c1962] 320 p. illus. 20 cm. (The Norton library, N748) "The writings of Lou Andreas-Salome": p. 303-309. [PT2601.N4Z75 1974] 74-14679 ISBN 0-393-00748-0 3.95 (pbk.)
1. Andreas-Salome, Lou, 1861-1937—Biography. I. Title.

Andreasen, Milian Lauritz, 1876-

STEINWEG, Virginia Duffie. 286'.7'0924 B
Without fear or favor / Virginia Duffie Steinweg. Washington : Review and Herald Pub. Association, 1979. p. cm. Includes bibliographical references. [BX6193.A48S76] 79-11906 6.50
1. Andreasen, Milian Lauritz, 1876- 2. Seventh Day Adventists—United States—Biography. I. Title.

Andreev, Leonid Nikolaevich, 1871-1919.

NEWCOMBE, Josephine Marjorie. 891.7'3'3 B
Leonid Andreyev [by] Josephine M. Newcombe. New York, Ungar [1973] ix, 118 p. 20 cm. (Modern literature monographs) Bibliography: p. 107-110. [PG3452.Z5N48 1973] 72-79938 ISBN 0-8044-2657-0 6.00
1. Andreev, Leonid Nikolaevich, 1871-1919. BIP

Andretti, Mario, 1940-

ANDRETTI, Mario, 1940- 796.7'2'0924 B
What's it like out there? [By] Mario Andretti with Bob Collins. Chicago, H. Regnery Co. [1970] 282 p. illus., ports. 22 cm. [GV1032.A5A3] 77-105111 5.95
1. Automobile racing—Biography. I. Collins, Bob, joint author. II. Title. BIP

ENGEL, Lyle Kenyon. 796.7'2'0924 B
Mario Andretti, world driving champion / produced by Lyle Kenyon Engel. New York : Arco Pub., 1979. 159 p. : ill. ; 24 cm. p. cm. [GV1032.A5E52] 79-4176 ISBN 0-668-04739-9 : 8.95 pbk. : 3.95
1. Andretti, Mario, 1940- 2. Automobile racing drivers—United States—Biography. I. Title.

LIBBY, Bill. 796.7'2'0924 B
Andretti. New York, Grossett & Dunlap [1970] 196 p. illus., ports. 22 cm. [GV1032.A5L5] 74-119038 5.95
1. Andretti, Mario, 1940-

Andrew, Saint, apostle.

CAPALDI, Isaias G 225.92
Andrew of Galilee, apostle of Christ. London , New York, Longmans, Green [1955] 276p. illus. 19cm. [BS2451.C36 1955] 55-2321
1. Andrew, Saint, apostle. I. Title.

Andrew, Saint, apostle — Juvenile literature.

DANIELSKI, S E 92
Andrew, the apostle, by S. E. Danielski. Pictures by Carolyn Lee Jagodits. Notre Dame, Ind., Dujarie Press [1966] 1 v. (unpaged) illus. 21 cm. [[BS2451.D3]] 66-3272
1. Andrew, Saint, apostle — Juvenile literature. I. Title.

Andrews, Charles Freer, 1871-1940.

ATTWATER, Donald, 1892- ed. 270.8'1'0922
Modern Christian revolutionaries; an introduction to the lives and thought of: Kierkegaard, Eric Gill, G. K. Chesterton, C. F. Andrews [and] Berdyaev. Edited by Donald Attwater. Freeport, N.Y., Books for Libraries Press [1971, c1947] xiii, 390 p. illus., ports. 23 cm. (Essay index reprint series) Contents.Contents.—Soren Kierkegaard, by M. Chaning-Pearce.—G. K. Chesterton, by F. A. Lea.—Eric Gill, by D. Attwater.—C. F. Andrews, by N. MacNichol.—Nicolas Berdyaev, by E. Lampert.—Bibliography (p. [383]-390) [BR1700.A8 1971] 76-156608 ISBN 0-8369-2304-9
1. Kierkegaard, Soren Aabye, 1813-1855. 2. Chesterton, Gilbert Keith, 1874-1936. 3. Gill, Eric, 1882-1940. 4. Andrews, Charles Freer, 1871-1940. 5. Berdiaev, Nikolai Aleksandrovich, 1874-1948. I. Title.

CHATURVEDI, Benarsidas, 1892- 922.342
Charles Freer Andrews, a narrative by Benarsides Chaturvedi and Marjorie Sykes. With a foreword by M. K. Gandhi. New York, Harper [1950] xiv, 334 p. plate. ports. 22 cm. [BV3269.A65C5 1950] 50-10298
1. Andrews, Charles Freer, 1871-1940. I. Sykes, Marjorie. joint author. II. Title.

Andrews, Grace Eleanor.

ANDREWS, Grace Eleanor. 920.7
The wind that blows. Philadelphia, Dorrance [c1953] 116p. illus. 20cm. Autobiography. [CT275.A7318A3] 53-6012
I. Title.

Andrews, John Nevins, 1829-1883.

ROBINSON, Virgil E. 286'.73 B
John Nevins Andrews, flame for the Lord / Virgil Robinson ; [ill., Kurt Reichenbach] . Washington : Review and Herald Pub. Association, c1975. 122 p. : ill. ; 21 cm. (Penguin series) "Previously printed under the title J. N. Andrews, prince of scholars" in Review and herald, 1975. [BX6193.A5R6] 75-18077
1. Andrews, John Nevins, 1829-1883. I. Title. II. Title: Flame for the Lord.

Andrews, Julie.

WINDELER, Robert. 791'.0924 B
Julie Andrews, a biography. New York, Putnam [1970] 253 p. ports. 22 cm. [PN2598.A65W3] 78-97077 6.95
1. Andrews, Julie.

Andrews, Roy Chapman, 1884-1960.

ARCHER, Jules. 500.9'0924 B
Science explorer: Roy Chapman Andrews. New York, J. Messner [1968] 191 p. map. 22 cm. Bibliography: p. 185-186. [QH31.A55A7] 68-14945
1. Andrews, Roy Chapman, 1884-1960. I. Title.

POND, Alonzo William, 1894- 500.9'2'4 B
Andrews: Gobi explorer, by Alonzo W. Pond. New York, Grosset & Dunlap [1972] viii, 212 p. 21 cm. "A W. W. Norton book." Bibliography: p. 201-206. [QH31.A55P65] 79-182016 ISBN 0-448-21430-X 4.95
1. Andrews, Roy Chapman, 1884-1960. 2. Gobi. 3. Central Asiatic expeditions of the American museum of natural history. I. Title.
Library Binding 4.99.

Andrews, Stephen Pearl, 1812-1886.

STERN, Madeleine Bettina, 1912- 301.15'3'0924 B
The pantarch; a biography of Stephen Pearl Andrews, by Madeleine B. Stern. Austin, University of Texas Press [1968] xviii, 208 p. illus., facsims., ports. 24 cm. Bibliography: p. [180]-197. [HN57.S77] 68-18386
1. Andrews, Stephen Pearl, 1812-1886. I. Title. BIP

Andrews, Thomas, 1873-1912.

BULLOCK, Shan F., 1865-1935. 909'.09'631
"A Titanic hero" Thomas Andrews, shipbuilder. With an introd. by Sir Horace Plunkett. Foreword by Edward S. Kamuda. Riverside, Conn., 7C's Press [1973] xvi, 80 p. illus. 19 cm. Reprint of the 1912 ed. published by Maunsel, Dublin under title: Thomas Andrews, shipbuilder. [VM140.A6B8 1973] 73-158314 ISBN 0-911962-05-0 6.00
1. Andrews, Thomas, 1873-1912. 2. Titanic (Steamship) I. Title.

Andrus, John Emory, 1841-1934.

MORRILL, George P., 1920- 332'.0924 B
The multimillionaire straphanger; a life of John Emory Andrus, by George P. Morrill. [1st ed.] Middletown, Conn., Wesleyan University Press [1971] xiv, 204 p. illus., ports. 24 cm. "Published for Wesleyan University." [CT275.A734M67] 72-146976 ISBN 0-8195-8015-5 10.00
1. Andrus, John Emory, 1841-1934. I. Wesleyan University, Middletown, Conn. II. Title.

Angas, George Fife, 1789-1879.

O'NEILL, Sally. 994.2'3'0924 B
George Fife Angas [by] Sally O'Neill. Melbourne, New York, Oxford University Press, 1972. 30 p. ill., port. 19 cm. (Great Australians) Bibliography: p. 30. A biography of one of the early important colonizers of South Australia. [DU322.A5O53] 92 73-178420 ISBN 0-19-550417-8 0.70
1. Angas, George Fife, 1789-1879.

Angel Falls, Venezuela.

NOTT, David. 918.7'6 B
Angels four. Englewood Cliffs, N.J., Prentice-Hall [1972] 191 p. illus. 25 cm. Autobiographical. [F2331.B6N6] 70-180549 ISBN 0-13-036798-2
1. Angel Falls, Venezuela. I. Title.

Angela Merici, Saint, 1474-1540.

CARAMAN, Philip, 1911- 922.245
Saint Angela; the life of Angela Merici, foundress of the Ursulines (1474-1540).

New York, Farrar [1964] x, 188p. illus. 21cm. Bibl. 64-14687 4.50 bds.,
1. Angela Merici, Saint, 1474-1540. I. Title.

Angela Merici, Saint, 1474-1540.—Juvenile literature.

REIDY, Mary 920
The first Ursuline; the story of St. Angela Merici. Introd. by James Brodrick. Illus. by Marina Hoffer. Westminster, Md., Newman [1962, c.1961] 158p. illus. 21cm. 62-17191 3.25
1. Angela Merici, Saint, 1474-1540—Juvenile literature. I. Title.

[WILLETT, Franciscus] 271.9740924
The promise to Angela; the story of St. Angela Merici [by] Pat McKern. Illus. by Suzanne Atkinson. Valatie, N. Y., Holy Cross Pr. [1966] 82p. illus. 23cm. [BX4700.A45W5] 66-8606 2.50
1. Angela Merici, Saint, 1474-1540.—Juvenile literature. 2. Ursulines—Juvenile literature. I. Title.

Angell, Irma (Rohlfing).

ANGELL, Irma (Rohlfing). 920.7
They put me here. Baltimore, 1951. 71 p. illus. 22 cm. Autobiography. [CT275.A735A3] 52-15529
I. Title.

Angell, Norman, Sir, 1874-1967.

ANGELL, Norman, Sir 1874- 928.2
After all; the autobiography of Norman Angell. New York, Farrar, Straus and Young [1952] 370 p. illus. 23 cm. [JX1962.A6A3] 52-6139
I. Title.

MARRIN, Albert. 327'.172'0924 B
Sir Norman Angell / by Albert Marrin. Boston : Twayne Publishers, 1979. 306 p. : port. ; 21 cm. (Twayne's world leaders series ; TWLS 79) Includes index. Bibliography: p. 290-298. [JX1962.A6M37] 79-10093 ISBN 0-8057-7725-3 : 12.95
1. Angell, Norman, Sir, 1874-1967. 2. Pacifists—Great Britain—Biography. I. Title.

Angelo, Valenti, 1897- —Bibliography.

VALENTI Angelo : 016.709'.2'4
author, illustrator, printer. San Francisco : Book Club of California, 1976. 97 p. : ill., 43 facsims. (some col.) ; 38 cm. (Publication of the Book Club of California ; no. 154) "Four hundred copies." "A bibliographical checklist of the work of Valenti Angelo, edited by Anne Englund" : p. [37]-97. [Z8036.483.V34] [PS3501.N56952] 77-374748
1. Angelo, Valenti, 1897- —Bibliography. I. Angelo, Valenti, 1897- II. Englund, Anne. III. Series: Book Club of California, San Francisco. Publication ; no. 154.

Angelou, Maya.

ANGELOU, Maya. 917.3'06'96073 B
Gather together in my name. [1st ed.] New York, Random House [1974] 214 p. 21 cm. Autobiography. [E185.97.A56A29] 73-20570 ISBN 0-394-48692-7 6.95
1. Angelou, Maya. I. Title.

ANGELOU, Maya. 917.3'06'96073 B
Gather together in my name. New York, Bantam Books [1975, c1974] 181 p. 18 cm. Autobiography [E185.97.A56A29] 1.50 (pbk.)
1. Angelou, Maya. I. Title.
L.C. card number for original ed.: 73-20570. BIP

ANGELOU, Maya. 917.3'09'74960924 B
I know why the caged bird sings. New York, Random House [1970, c1969] 281 p. 22 cm. Autobiography. [E185.97.A56A3 1970] 73-85598 5.95
I. Title. BIP

ANGELOU, Maya. 790.2'092'4 B
Singin' and swingin' and gettin' merry like Christmas / Maya Angelou. 1st ed. New York : Random House, c1976. 269 p. ; 22 cm. Autobiography. [E185.97.A56A33] 76-16580 ISBN 0-394-40545-5 : 8.95
1. Angelou, Maya. I. Title. BIP

Angier, Bradford.

ANGIER, Bradford. 971.23'1
Wilderness neighbors / Bradford Angier. New York : Stein and Day, 1979. p. cm. [F1089.P3A53] 78-26303 ISBN 0-8128-2578-0 : 8.95
1. Angier, Bradford. 2. Peace River region, B.C. and Alta.—Social life and customs. 3. Outdoor life—Peace River region, B.C. and Alta. 4. Peace River region, B.C. and Alta.—Biography. I. Title. BIP

Angier, Vena.

ANGIER, Bradford. 971.1'1 B
Wilderness wife / Bradford & Vena Angier. 1st ed. Radnor, Pa. : Chilton Book Co., c1976. 177 p., [4] leaves of plates : ill. ; 22 cm. [S522.C2A53 1976] 75-15548 ISBN 0-8019-6291-9 : 7.95
1. Angier, Vena. 2. Angier, Bradford. 3. Country life—British Columbia. 4. Outdoor life—British Columbia. I. Angier, Vena, joint author. II. Title.

ANGIER, Bradford. 971.1'1
Wilderness wife / Bradford and Vena Angier. New York : Collier Books, 1977, c1976. 177 p., [4] leaves of plates : ill. ; 21 cm. [S522.C2A53 1977] 76-49489 ISBN 0-02-058230-7 : pbk. : 2.95
1. Angier, Vena. 2. Angier, Bradford. 3. Country life—British Columbia. 4. Outdoor life—British Columbia. 5. British Columbia—Biography. I. Angier, Vena, joint author. II. Title.

Anglesey, Henry William Paget, 1st marquis of, 1768-1854.

ANGLESEY, George Charles 923.242
Henry Victor Paget, 7th marquis of, 1922-
One leg; the life and letters of Henry William Paget, first marquess of Anglesey, K. G., 1768-1854, by the Marquess of Anglesey. New York, Morrow [1961] 428 p. illus. 24 cm. [DA68.12.A45A7] 62-7283
1. Anglesey, Henry William Paget, 1st marquis of, 1768-1854. I. Title.

Anglin, Leslie M., 1882-1942.

ALBUS, Harry James, 1920- 922.651
Twentieth-century Onesiphorus, the story of Leslie M. Anglin and the Home of Onesiphorus. Grand Rapids, Eerdmans, 1951. 160 p. illus., ports. 20 cm. [BV3427.A53A7] 51-10560
1. Anglin, Leslie M., 1882-1942. 2. T'al-an, China. Home of Onesiphorus. I. Title.

Anglin, Timothy Warren, 1822-1896.

BAKER, William M., 328.71'092'4 B
1943-
Timothy Warren Anglin, 1822-96, Irish Catholic Canadian / William M. Baker. Toronto ; Buffalo : University of Toronto Press, c1977. xiv, 336 p., [4] leaves of plates : ill. ; 24 cm. Originally presented as the author's thesis, University of Western Ontario. Includes bibliographical references and index. [F1033.A532B34 1977] 76-49480 ISBN 0-8020-5368-8 : 22.50
1. Anglin, Timothy Warren, 1822-1896. 2. Statesmen—Canada—Biography. I. Title.

Angouleme, Marie Therese Charlotte, duchesse d', 1778-1851.

DAUDET, Ernest, 944.04'092'4
1837-1921.
Madame Royale, daughter of Louis xvi and Marie Antoinette: her youth and marriage. From the French of Ernest Daudet by Mrs. Randolph Stawell. New York, Doran; London, Heinemann, 1913. xii, 263 p. illus., ports. 23 cm. [DC137.2.D3 1913] A16
1. Angouleme, Marie Therese Charlotte, duchesse d', 1778-1851. 2. France — Hist. — Revolution. I. Title.

DESMOND, Alice (Curtis) 1897- FIC
Marie Antoinette's daughter. New York, Dodd, Mead [1967] xvii, 291 p. illus., maps, ports. 22 cm. Bibliography: p. 269-286. A biography of the Duchess of Angouleme, daughter of Marie Antoinette and Louis XVI of France, who was for ten minutes Queen of France and for her entire life a supporter of the Bourbon cause. [PZ4.D462Mar] 944'.035'0924 B 92 AC 68
1. Angouleme, Marie Therese Charlotte, duchesse d', 1778-1851. I. Title. BIP

POWERS, Elizabeth, 944.04'092'4 B
1944-
The journal of Madame Royale / by Elizabeth Powers. New York : Walker, 1976. x, 150 p. : ill. ; 22 cm. Bibliography: p. 149-150. [DC137.2.P68 1976] 75-43990 ISBN 0-8027-6251-4 : 7.50. ISBN 0-8027-6252-2 lib. bdg. : 7.39
1. Angouleme, Marie Therese Charlotte, duchesse d', 1778-1851. 2. France—History—Revolution, 1789-1795. 3. France—Princes and princesses—Biography. I. Title. BIP

Angus, Fay.

ANGUS, Fay. 951.04'2'0924 B
The white pagoda / Fay Angus. Wheaton, Ill. : Tyndale House, c1978. 192 p. : ill. ; 22 cm. [CT1828.A53A38] 77-83555 ISBN 0-8423-8213-5 : 3.95
1. Angus, Fay. 2. China—Biography. 3. China—Social life and customs. I. Title. BIP

Anillo, Rene.

KOZOLCHYK, Boris. 920.07291
The political biographies of three Castro officials. Santa Monica, Calif., Rand Corp., 1966. x, 95 p. 28 cm. ([Rand Corporation. Research] memorandum, RM-4994-RC) Bibliographical footnotes. [Q180.A1R36 no. 4994] 67-2990
1. Grobart, Fabio. 2. Anillo, Rene. 3. Roa, Raul. I. Title. II. Series.

Anjou, House of.

DUGGAN, Alfred 942.03'1'0924 B
Leo, 1903-1961.
Devil's brood : the Angevin family / Alfred Duggan. Bath : Chivers, 1976. 3-278 p., fold. leaf : geneal. table ; 22 cm. Includes index. Bibliography: p. 270. [DC36.8.A6D8 1976] 77-375228 ISBN 0-85997-226-7 : £5.20
1. Anjou, House of. 2. Henry II, King of England, 1133-1189. 3. France Kings and rulers—Biography. I. Title.

Anne Boleyn, consort of Henry VIII, King of England, 1507-1536.

BRUCE, Marie 942.05'2'0924 B
Louise.
Anne Boleyn. [1st American ed.] New York, Coward, McCann & Geoghegan [1972] 380 p. illus. 24 cm. Bibliography: p. [337]-340. [DA333.B6B78 1972] 72-146093 ISBN 0-698-10480-3 10.00
1. Anne Boleyn, consort of Henry VIII, King of England, 1507-1536.

BRUCE, Marie 942.05'2'0924 [B]
Louise.
Anne Boleyn. [New York] Warner Paperback Lib. [1973, c.1972] 382 p. illus. 18 cm. Bibliography: p. 339-343. [DA333.B6B78] 1.75 (pbk.)
1. Anne Boleyn, consort of Henry VIII, King of England, 1507-1536.
L.C. card no. for the hardbound edition: 72-146093.

*CHAPMAN, Hester W. 942.0520924 B
The challenge of Anne Boleyn [by] Hester W. Chapman. New York, Coward, McCann & Geoghegan [1974] 244 p. illus., maps (on lining paper) 22 cm. Bibliography: p. 232-234. [DA333.B6] 74-79681 ISBN 0-698-10612-1 7.95
1. Anne Boleyn, Queen Consort of Henry 8th, King of England, 1507-1536. I. Title. BIP

FRIEDMANN, Paul. 942.05'2'0924 B
Anne Boleyn: a chapter of English history, 1527-1536. London, Macmillan, 1884. [New York, AMS Press, 1973] 2 v. 19 cm. Includes bibliographical references. [DA333.B6F8 1973] 76-161795 ISBN 0-404-09050-8 18.60 (per vol.)
1. Anne Boleyn, consort of Henry VIII, King of England, 1507-1536. 2. Great Britain—History—Henry VIII, 1509-1547.
Set 35.00. BIP

LOFTS, Norah 942.05'2'0924 B
Robinson, 1904-
Anne Boleyn / Norah Lofts. 1st American ed. New York : Coward, McCann & Geoghegan, c1979. p. cm. Includes index. Bibliography: p. [DA333.B6L63 1979] 79-10526 ISBN 0-698-11005-6 : 15.95
1. Anne Boleyn, consort of Henry VIII, King of England, 1507-1536. 2. Great Britain—History—Henry VIII, 1509-1547. 3. Great Britain—Queens—Biography.

STEPHENS, Eve. 923.142
Anne Boleyn, by Evelyn Anthony [pseud.] New York, T. Y. Crowell Co [1957] 310 p. 22 cm. [DA333.B6S8] 57-5634
1. Anne Boleyn, consort of Henry VIII, King of England, 1507-1536. I. Title.

STEPHENS, Eve. 923.142
Anne Boleyn, by Evelyn Anthony [pseud.] New York, T. W. Crowell Co. [1957] 310 p. 22 cm. [DA333.B6S8] 57-5634
1. Anne Boleyn, Queen consort of Henry VIII, King of England, 1507-1536.

STEPHENS, Eve. 923.142
Anne Boleyn, by Evelyn Anthony [New York] New American Library [1974, c1960] 278 p. 18 cm. (A Signet book) [DA333.B6S8] 1.25 (pbk.)
1. Anne Boleyn, consort of Henry VIII, King of England, 1507-1536. I. Title.
L.C. card no. for original edition: 57-5634.

Anne, consort of Richard III, King of England, 1456-1485—Juvenile literature.

WESTCOTT, Jan 942.04'6'0924 B
(Vlachos) 1912-
Set her on a throne, by Jan Westcott. [1st ed.] Boston, Little, Brown [1972] 235 p. 25 cm. Chronicles the life of Anne Neville, daughter of the Earl of Warwick and wife to Richard III, King of England. [DA247.A5W47] 92 72-3804 ISBN 0-316-93126-8 5.95
1. Anne, consort of Richard III, King of England, 1456-1485—Juvenile literature. I. Title.

Anne, Empress of Russia, 1693-1740.

CURTISS, Mina 947'.06'0924 B
Stein Kirstein, 1896-
A forgotten empress: Anna Ivanovna and her era, 1730-1740 [by] Mina Curtiss. New York, Ungar [1974] xii, 335 p. illus. 22 cm. Bibliography: p. 309-320. [DK156.C87] 73-89819 ISBN 0-8044-1213-8 12.50
1. Anne, Empress of Russia, 1693-1740. 2. Russia—History—Anne, 1730-1740. I. Title.

LONGWORTH, Philip, 947'.06'0922 B
1933-
The three empresses: Catherine I, Anne, and Elizabeth of Russia. New York, Holt, Rinehart and Winston [1973, c1972] x, 242 p. illus. 22 cm. Bibliography: p. 231-234. [DK151.L65 1973] 72-78124 ISBN 0-03-001411-5 7.95
1. Catharine I, Empress of Russia, d. 1727. 2. Anne, Empress of Russia, 1693-1740. 3. Elizabeth, Empress of Russia, 1709-1762. I. Title.

Anne Marie de Jesus, Sister, 1624-1701.

EBLANA, Sister. 922.244
The vocation of Lady Christine. Milwaukee, Bruce Pub. Co. [1964] 90 p. 21 cm. [BX4705.A6E2] 64-17408
1. Anne Marie de Jesus, Sister, 1624-1701. I. Title.

Anne (Name)

GLAZER, Tom. 929.4
All about your name, Anne, Anna, Annie, Annette, Hannah, Anita, Nan / by Tom Glazer ; illustrated by Demi. 1st ed. Garden City, N.Y. : Doubleday, c1978. 44 p., [1] leaf of plates : ill. ; 22 cm. Discusses the name Anne and the many interesting people throughtout history who have held that name. [CS2391.A55G57] 77-82444 ISBN 0-385-04279-5 : 4.95 ISBN 0-385-04299-X lib. bdg. : 5.90
1. Anne (Name) 2. Biography—Miscellanea. I. Hitz, Demi. II. Title.

Anne, of Brittany, consort of Louis XII, King of France, 1476-1514.

BUTLER, Mildred Allen. 944'.027'0924
Twice Queen of France: Anne of Brittany. Portraits by Bette Davis. New York, Funk & Wagnalls [1967] 190 p. ports. 22 cm. Bibliographical references included in "Author's note" (p. 7-8) [DC108.3.B8] 67-3022
1. Anne, of Brittany, consort of Louis XII, King of France, 1476-1514. I. Title.

Anne, Princess of Great Britain, 1950-

CATHCART, Helen. 942'.00992 B
Anne and the Princesses Royal. London, New York, W. H. Allen, 1973. x, 205 p. illus. 23 cm. Bibliography: p. 204-205. [DA28.3.C37 1973] 73-177698 ISBN 0-491-01321-3
1. Anne, Princess of Great Britain, 1950- 2. Great Britain—Princes and princesses. I. Title.
Distributed by Transatlantic Arts, Inc. 7.50. **BIP**

MATHESON, Anne. 942.085'092'4 B
Princess Anne; a royal girl of our time [by] Anne Matheson [and] Reginald Davis. New York, Crown Publishers [1973] 155 p. illus. col. ports. 26 cm. [DA591.A34M35 1973b] 73-179295 ISBN 0-517-51398-6 6.95
1. Anne, Princess of Great Britain, 1950- I. Davis, Reginald, illus.

Anne, Queen of Great Britain, 1665-1714.

GREEN, David Bronte, 1910- 942.06'9'0924 B
Queen Anne [by] David Green. New York, Scribner [1971, c1970] 399 p. illus., facsims., ports. 24 cm. Bibliography: p. [343]-347. [DA495.G7 1971] 71-133575 8.95
1. Anne, Queen of Great Britain, 1665-1714. I. Title.

Anne, Queen of Great Britain, 1665-1714—Juvenile literature.

HODGES, Margaret. 942.06'9'0924 B
Lady Queen Anne; a biography of Queen Anne of England. New York, Farrar, Straus & Giroux [1969] vi, 275 p. illus., geneal. tables, ports. 23 cm. "An Ariel book." A biography of the last Stuart monarch to occupy the English throne. [DA495.H58] 92 69-14978 4.95
1. Anne, Queen of Great Britain, 1665-1714—Juvenile literature. I. Title.

Anne, Saint, Mother of the Virgin Mary.

GEARON, Patrick J., D.D., 1890- 232.933
St. Anne, the Mother of Mary. Chicago, Carmelite Third Order Pr. [1961] 172p. illus. 61-66178 2.00 bds.,
1. Anne, Saint, Mother of the Virgin Mary. I. Title.

KEYES, Frances Parkinson (Wheeler) 1885- 232.933
St. Anne, grandmother of Our Saviour. New, rev. ed. New York, Hawthorn [c.1955, 1962] 188p. illus. 26cm. Bibl. 62-8390 5.95
1. Anne, Saint, Mother of the Virgin Mary. I. Title.

KEYES, Frances Parkinson (Wheeler) 1885- 232.933
St. Anne, grandmother of Our Saviour. New and rev. ed. New York, Hawthorn Books [1962] 188p. illus. 26cm. Includes bibliography. [BT685.K4 1962] 62-8390
1. Anne, Saint, Mother of the Virgin Mary. I. Title.

KEYES, Francis Parkinson Wheeler, 1885-1970. 232.933
St. Anne, grandmother of Our Saviour. New York, Messner [1955] 189 p. illus. 26 cm. [BT685.K4] 55-10544
1. Anne, Saint, Mother of the Virgin Mary.

Annesley, Lady Mabel Marguerite,

ANNESLEY, Lady Mabel Marguerite, 1881-1959 927.6
As the sight is bent, an unfinished autobiography. 35 engravings on wood by the author. Ed. by Constance Malleson. London, Museum Pr. [dist. New Rochelle, N. Y., SportShelf, c.1964] 157p. illus., port. 24cm. 64-6446 6.75
I. Title.

Anning, Mary, 1799-1847—Juvenile literature.

BLAIR, Ruth Van Ness. 560'.9 B
Mary's monster / by Ruth Van Ness Blair ; illustrated by Richard Cuffari. New York : Coward, McCann & Geoghegan, [1975] 61, [3] p. : ill. ; 22 cm. Bibliography: p. [62]-[63] A brief biography of the English girl whose discovery of an Ichthyosaurus skeleton in 1811 when she was twelve led to a life-long interest in fossils and other important discoveries. [QE707.A56B55 1975] 74-16651 ISBN 0-698-20304-6 : 5.95.
1. Anning, Mary, 1799-1847—Juvenile literature. 2. Paleontology—England—Juvenile literature. I. Cuffari, Richard, 1925- II. Title.

Annunzio, Gabriele d', 1863-1938.

GRIFFIN, Gerald, 1889- 945.091'0924 B
Gabriele d'Annunzio, the warrior bard. Port Washington, N.Y., Kennikat Press [1970] 288 p. illus., ports. 22 cm. Reprint of the 1935 ed. [PQ4804.G7 1970] 77-113312
1. Annunzio, Gabriele d', 1863-1938.

JULLIAN, Philippe. 858'.8'09 B
D'Annunzio. Translated from the French by Stephen Hardman. New York, Viking Press [1973, c1972] xviii, 366 p. illus. 22 cm. Bibliography: p. 359-360. [PQ4804.J813 1973] 72-78981 ISBN 0-670-25603-X 10.00
1. Annunzio, Gabriele d', 1863-1938.

RHODES, Anthony [Richard Ewart] 928.5
D'Annunzio, the poet as superman. New York, McDowell, Obolensky [1960, c.1959] xx, 299p. (bibl.: p.291-293 and bibl. footnotes) 22cm. 60-8185 4.95
1. Annunzio, Gabriele d', 1863-1938. I. Title. **BIP**

WINWAR, Frances, pseud. 928.5
Wingless victory; a biography of Gabriele d'Annunzio and Eleonora Duse. [1st ed.] New York, Harper [1956] 374 p. illus. 22 cm. Includes bibliography. [PQ4804.W5] 55-11967
1. Annunzio, Gabriele d', 1863-1938. 2. Duse, Eleonora, 1858-1924.

WINWAR, Frances, pseud. 858'.8'09 B
Wingless victory; a biography of Gabriele d'Annunzio and Eleonora Duse. Westport, Conn., Greenwood Press [1974, c1956] x, 374 p. front. 22 cm. Reprint of the ed. published by Harper, New York. Bibliography: p. 357-363. [PQ4804.W5 1974] 74-10363 ISBN 0-8371-7671-9
1. Annunzio, Gabriele d', 1863-1938. 2. Duse, Eleonora, 1858-1924. I. Title.

Annunzio, Gabriele d', 1863-1938—Biography.

ANTONGINI, Tommaso, 1877- 858'.8'09 B
D'Annunzio, by Tom Antongini. Freeport, N.Y., Books for Libraries Press [1971] vi, 591 p. port. 23 cm. Translation of Vita segreta di Gabriele d'Annunzio. Reprint of the 1938 ed. [PQ4804.A84 1971] 75-37327 ISBN 0-8369-6676-7
1. Annunzio, Gabriele d', 1863-1938—Biography. I. Title.

Anonyms and pseudonyms.

FORCE, Helen H. 929.4
Who is who. Helen H. Force, editor. Santa Ana, Calif., Professional Library Service [1967] 109 p. 23 x 9 cm. [Z1045.F6] 67-21461
1. Anonyms and pseudonyms. I. Title.

Anonyms and pseudonyms, American.

ABBATT, William, 1851-1935, comp. 929.4
The colloquial who's who; an attempt to identify the many authors, writers, and contributors who have used pen-names, initials, etc. (1600-1924) Also a list of sobriquets, nicknames, epigrams, oddities, war phrases, etc. Tarrytown, N.Y., 1924-25. Detroit, Gale Research Co., 1974. p. cm. Contents.Contents.—v. 1. The United States and Canada.—v. 2. Great Britain and Colonies. [Z1045.A12 1974] 78-159865 ISBN 0-8103-3956-0 15.00
1. Anonyms and pseudonyms, American. 2. Anonyms and pseudonyms, Canadian. 3. Anonyms and pseudonyms, English. 4. Nicknames. I. Title.

Anouilh, Jean, 1910-

PRONKO, Leonard Cabell. 842.914
The world of Jean Anouilh. Berkeley, University of California Press, 1961. 264 p. illus. 23 cm. (Perspectives in criticism, 7) [PQ2601.N67Z73] 61-6778
1. Anouilh, Jean, 1910- I. Title.

Anselm, Saint, Abp. of Canterbury, 1033-1109.

EADMER, 1124? 922.242
The life of St Anselm, Archbishop of Canterbury. Ed., introd., notes, tr. by R. W. Southern. London Nelson [dist. New York, Oxford, 1963, c.1962] xxxvi, 171, 171, 172-179p. 23cm. (Medieval texts) Added t.p. in Latin: Vita Sancti Anselmi, archiopiscopi Cantuariensis. Latin and Eng. on opposite pages, numbered in duplicate. Bibl. A63 8.00
1. Anselm, Saint, Abp. of Canterbury, 1033-1109. I. Southern, Richard William, ed. and tr. II. Title. III. Series: Medieval classics (London

EADMER, d.1124? 282'.0924 B
The life of St Anselm, Archbishop of Canterbury, edited with introduction, notes and translation by R. W. Southern. Oxford, Clarendon Press [1972, c1962] 1 v. (various pagings) 23 cm. (Oxford medieval texts) Parallel Latin text and English translation. Translation of Vita D. Anselmi archiepiscopi Cantuariensis. Includes bibliographical references. [BX4700.A58E2 1972] 72-190762 ISBN 0-19-822225-4 £4.50
1. Anselm, Saint, Abp. of Canterbury, 1033-1109. I. Title. II. Series.

EADMER, d. 1124? 922.242
The life of St Anselm, Archbishop of Canterbury. Ed., introd., notes, tr. by R. W. Southern. London, Nelson [dist. New York, Oxford, 1963, c 1962] xxxvi, 171, 171, 172-179p. 23cm. (Medieval texts) Added t.p. in Latin: Vita Sancti Anselmi, archiopiscopi Cantuariensis. Latin and Eng. on opposite pages, numbered in duplicate. Bibl. A63 8.00
1. Anselm, Saint, Abp. of Canterbury, 1033-1109. I. Southern, Richard William, ed. and tr. II. Title. III. Series: Medieval classics (London

SOUTHERN, Richard William 922.242
Saint Anselm and his biographer; a study of monastic life and thought, 1059-c. 1130 [New York] Cambridge [c.]1963. xvi, 389p. facsim. 23cm. (Birkbeck lects. 1959) Bibl. 63-4322 9.50
1. Anselm, Saint, Abp. of Canterbury, 1033-1109. 2. Eadmer, d.1124? I. Title. II. Series.

Anson, George Anson, Baron, 1697-1762.

WILCOX, Leslie A. 910.4'1
Anson's voyage. Written and illustrated by L. A. Wilcox. New York, St. Martin's Press [1970] xv, 182 p. illus., maps, ports. 26 cm. [G420.W57 1970] 73-125589 8.95
1. Anson, George Anson, Baron, 1697-1762. 2. Voyages around the world. I. Title.

Antarctic regions.

MOUNTEVANS, Edward Ratcliffe Garth Russell Evans, baron, 1880-1957. v. 12
Happy adventurer, an autobiography. Illus. by S. Drigin. New York, W. Funk, 1951. 130 p. illus. (part col.) 20 cm. A 52
1. Antarctic regions. I. Title.

Antarctic regions—History.

NEIDER, Charles, 1915- comp. 919.8'9'04
Antarctica: authentic accounts of life and exploration in the world's highest, driest, windiest, coldest and most remote continent. Edited with an introd. and notes, by Charles Neider. [1st ed.] New York, Random House [1972] x, 464 p. map (on lining papers) 22 cm. Contents.Contents.—In search of a continent, by J. Cook.—The high latitudes, by G. Forster.—Antarctic seas, by T. Bellingshausen.—Towards the pole, by J. Weddell.—Antarctic cruise, by C. Wilkes.—Farthest south, by J. C. Ross.—At the pole, by R. Amundsen.—The last march, by R. F. Scott.—Boat journey, by E. Shackleton.—Great white south, by H. G. Ponting.—The worst journey in the world, by A. Cherry-Garrard.—Alone, by R. E. Byrd.—Living at the pole, by P. Siple.—Crevasses, by E. Hillary.—Bibliography (p. 461-462) [G870.N36] 79-37072 ISBN 0-394-46831-7 10.00
1. Antarctic regions—History. I. Title.

Anthony, Alba (Riek)

ANTHONY, Alba (Riek) 1879- 922.673
Here am I, a Christian autobiography. [1st ed.] New York, Greenwich Book Publishers, 1957. 171p. 21cm. [BR1725.A74A3] 57-6430
I. Title.

ANTHONY, Alba (Riek) 1879- 922.673
Here am I, a Christian autobiography. [1st ed.] New York, Greenwich Book Publishers, 1957. 171p. 11cm. [BR1725.A.74A3] 57-6430
I. Title.

Anthony, Scott J., 1829 or 30-1903—Manuscripts.

COLORADO. State Historical Society. Library. 016.3553'320924
A calendar of the papers of Scott J. Anthony, 1830-1903; a holding of the Library of the State Historical Society of Colorado. Processed by Jean H. Cramer Denver, 1967. 14 l. 23 x 29 cm. Cover title. [Z6616.A63C6] 72-636571
1. Anthony, Scott J., 1829 or 30-1903—Manuscripts. I. Cramer, Jean H. II. Title.

Anthony, Susan Brownell, 1820-1906.

ANTHONY, Katharine Susan, 1877-1965. 920.7
Susan B. Anthony: her personal history and her era. [1st ed.] Garden City, N. Y., Doubleday, 1954. 521 p. illus. 22 cm. [JK1899.A6A7] 54-8919

1. Anthony, Susan Brownell, 1820-1906. 2. Anthony, Susan Brownell, 1820-1906.

ANTHONY, Katherine 324'.3'0924 B Susan, 1877-1965.
Susan B. Anthony : her personal history and her era / by Katherine Anthony. New York : Russell & Russell, 1975, c1954. x, 521 p., [4] leaves of plates : ill. ; 23 cm. Reprint of the ed. published by Doubleday, New York. Includes index. Bibliography: p. [505]-511. [JK1899.A6A7 1975] 73-84747 ISBN 0-8462-1742-2 : 25.00
1. Anthony, Susan Brownell, 1820-1906. BIP

DORR, Rheta Louise 324'.3'0924 B (Childe) 1872-1948.
Susan B. Anthony, the woman who changed the mind of a nation. New York, AMS Press [1970] xiii, 367 p. illus., ports. 23 cm. Reprint of the 1928 ed. [JK1899.A6D6 1970] 74-100519
1. Anthony, Susan Brownell, 1820-1906. 2. Woman—Suffrage—U.S. BIP

HARPER, Ida Husted, 324'.3'0924 B 1851-1931.
Life and work of Susan B. Anthony. New York, Arno, 1969. 3 v. (xxiv, 1633 p.) illus., ports. 24 cm. Reprint of the 1898-1908 ed. [JK1899.A6H32] 70-79184
1. Anthony, Susan Brownell, 1820-1906. BIP

LUTZ, Alma. 920.7
Susan B. Anthony: rebel, crusader. humanitarian. Boston, Beacon Press [1959] 340p. illus. 24cm. Includes bibliography. [JK1899.A6L8 1959] 59-6164
1. Anthony. Susan Brownell, 1820-1906. I. Title. BIP

MONSELL, Helen Albee, 1895- 920.7
Susan Anthony, girl who dared; illustrated by Paul Laune. [1st ed.] Indianapolis, Bobbs-Merrill [1954] 192p. illus. 20cm. (The Childhood of famous Americans series [81]) [JK1899.A6M6] 54-6062
1. Anthony, Susan Brownell, 1820-1906. I. Title.

Anthony, Susan Brownell, 1820-1906—Juvenile literature.

GRANT, Matthew G. 324'.3'0924 B
Susan B. Anthony, crusader for women's rights [by] Matthew G. Grant. Illustrated by John Keely and Dick Brude. [Mankato, Minn., Creative Education; distributed by Childrens Press, Chicago, 1974] 31 p. illus. (part col.) 25 cm. (His Gallery of great Americans series. Women of America) An easy-to-read biography of the woman who devoted her life to the abolition movement and the fight for equal rights of blacks and women. [JK1899.A6G7] 73-15911 ISBN 0-87191-305-4
1. Anthony, Susan Brownell, 1820-1906—Juvenile literature. I. Keely, John, illus. II. Brude, Dick, illus. III. Title.

GRANT, Matthew G. 324'.3'0924 B
Susan B. Anthony, crusader for women's rights [by] Matthew G. Grant. Illustrated by John Keely and Dick Brude. [Mankato, Minn., Creative Education; distributed by Childrens Press, Chicago, 1974] 31 p. illus. (part col.) 25 cm. (His Gallery of great Americans series. Women of America) An easy-to-read biography of the woman who devoted her life to the abolition movement and the fight for equal rights of blacks and women. [JK1899.A6G7] 73-15911 ISBN 0-87191-305-4 3.95
1. Anthony, Susan Brownell, 1820-1906—Juvenile literature. I. Keely, John, illus. II. Brude, Dick, illus. III. Title.

NOBLE, Iris. 324'.3'0924 B
Susan B. Anthony / by Iris Noble. New York : J. Messner, [1975] 189 p. ; 22 cm. Includes index. Bibliography: p. [179]-182. A biography of one of America's most outspoken crusaders for human rights, particularly those of women. [JK1899.A6N6] 92 74-30230 ISBN 0-671-32714-3 : 5.95 ISBN 0-671-32715-1 lib.bdg. : 5.29
1. Anthony, Susan Brownell, 1820-1906—Juvenile literature. I. Title. BIP

PETERSON, Helen 324'.3'0924 B Stone.
Susan B. Anthony, pioneer in woman's rights. Illustrated by Paul Frame. Champaign, Ill., Garrard Pub. Co. [1971] 96 p. illus. (part col.) 24 cm. (Americans all) A biography of the woman who was one of the pioneers in the movement to gain equal rights for women. [JK1899.A6P4] 92 76-151991 ISBN 0-8116-4570-3 2.79
1. Anthony, Susan Brownell, 1820-1906—Juvenile literature. I. Frame, Paul, 1913- illus. II. Title.

SALSINI, Barbara. 324'.3'0924 B
Susan B. Anthony, a crusader for women's rights. Charlotteville, N.Y., SamHar Press, 1973. 32 p. 22 cm. (Outstanding personalities, no. 49) Bibliography: p. 31-32. A biography of one of the first suffragettes and campaigners for women's rights. [HQ1413.A55S24] 72-89211 ISBN 0-87157-544-2 1.98 (Lib. ed.)
1. Anthony, Susan Brownell, 1820-1906—Juvenile literature. I. Title.
Pbk. 0.98; ISBN 0-87157-044-0. BIP

Anthropologists—Correspondence, reminiscences, etc.

FIELD, Henry, 1902- 925.72
The track of man. Rev. & abridged by the author. [New York, Dell, 1967] 351p. 18cm. (Laurel ed., 9005) [GN21.F5A3] .75 pap.,
1. Anthropologists—Correspondence, reminiscences, etc. I. Title.

FIELD, Henry, 1902- 390.0924 B
The track of man; adventures of an anthropologist. New York, Greenwood Press [1969, c1953] 448 p. illus. 23 cm. [GN21.F5A3 1969] 69-10091
1. Anthropologists—Correspondence, reminiscences, etc. I. Title.

FIELD, Henry, 1902- 925.72
The track of man; adventures of an anthropologist. [1st ed.] Garden City, N. Y., Doubleday, 1953. 448 p. illus. 22 cm. [GN21.F5A3] 53-5594
1. Anthropologists—Correspondence, reminiscences, etc. I. Title. BIP

Anthropologists—Juvenile literature.

HAYS, Hoffman 301.2'092'2 B Reynolds.
Explorers of man; five pioneers in anthropology [by] H. R. Hays. New York, Crowell-Collier Press [1971] 218 p. ports. 24 cm. Contents.Contents.—Henry Rowe Schoolcraft.—Adolph Bastian.—Bronislaw Malinowski.—Claude Levi-Strauss.—Margaret Mead.—Bibliography (p. [209]-211) [GN20.H38] 70-135645 5.95
1. Anthropologists—Juvenile literature. I. Title.

Anthropology—Methodology.

MACNEISH, June Helm, 390'.00922 1924- ed.
Pioneers of American anthropology; the uses of biography, ed. by June Helm. Contribs. by Jacob Gruber [others] Seattle, Univ. of Wash. Pr. [1967, c.1966] xiv, 247p. illus., maps, ports. 23cm. (Amer. Ethnological Soc. Monograph [s]. 43) [E51.A556 vol. 43] 66-19566 5.95
1. Anthropology—Methodology. 2. Anthropologists. I. Gruber, Jacob W. II. Title. III. Series.
Contents omitted.

Antin, Mary,

ANTIN, Mary, 917.3'03'910924 B 1881-1949.
The promised land. With a foreword by Oscar Handlin. 2d ed. Boston, Houghton Mifflin, 1969 [c1912] xxii, 373 p. 22 cm. Autobiographical. [E169.5.A66 1969] 74-2734 5.95
I. Title. BIP

Antioch College, Yellow Springs, Ohio—Biog.

STRAKER, Robert Lincoln 378.77174
Horace Mann and others; chapters from the history of Antioch College. Pref., introd. to the Antiochiana Collection in the Olive Kettering Lib., by Louis Filler. [Yellow Springs, Ohio] Antioch Pr. [c.] 1963. 106p. illus. 24cm. 63-14381 3.00 bds.,
1. Antioch College, Yellow Springs, Ohio—Biog. I. Title.

Antonio da Padova, Saint, 1195-1231.

BEAHN, John Edward, 1910- 922.245
A rich young man: Saint Anthony of Padua. Milwaukee, Bruce Pub. Co. [1953] 250p. 22cm. [BX4700.A6B38] 53-3964
1. Antonio da Padova, Saint, 1195-1231. I. Title.

CLASEN, Sophonius 922.245
St. Anthony, doctor of the gospel. Tr. from German by Ignatius Brady. Chicago, Franciscan Herald Pr., 1961 [c.1960] 136p. illus. 28cm. 61-11200 4.95 bds.,
1. Antonio da Padova, Saint, 1195-1231. I. Title.

ERNEST, Brother, 1897- 922.245
A story of St. Anthony of Padua. Pictures by Carolyn Lee Jagodits. Notre Dame, Ind., Dujarie Press [1957] unpaged. illus. 21cm. [BX4700.A6E72] 57-59265
1. Antonio da Padova, Saint, 1195-1231. I. Title.

HOMAN, Helen (Walker) 922.245 1893-
St. Anthony and the Christ Child. Illustrated by Don Lynch. New York, Vision Books [1958] 185p. illus. 22cm. (Vision books, 30) [BX4700.A6H6] 58-5715
1. Antonio de Padova, Saint, 1195-1231. I. Title.

PAINTING, Norman. 922.245
St. Anthony: the man who found himself, by Norman Painting and Michael Day. Chicago, Franciscan Herald Press [1958?] 188p. 19cm. [BX4700.A6P3] 58-14608
1. Antonia da Padova, Saint, 1195-1231. I. Day, Michael, joint author. II. Title.

PURCELL, Mary 922.245
Saint Anthony and his times. Garden City, N.Y., Hanover House [c.1960] 282p. Includes bibliography. 22cm. 60-5942 3.95 bds.,
1. Antonio da Padova, Saint, 1195-1231. I. Title.

Antonio da Padova, Saint, 1195-1231—juvenile literature.

PROBST, Emile, illus. 92
The life of Saint Anthony of Padua. Pictures by Emile Probst. London, Burns & Oates; New York, Herder & Herder [c.1965] [26]p. col. illus. 19cm. (Men of God, 3) [BX4700.A6B74] 65-21947 1.50 bds.,
1. Antonio da Padova, Saint, 1195-1231—juvenile literature. I. Title. II. Series.

Antonius, Marcus, 83?-30 B.C.

HUZAR, Eleanor 937'.05'0924 B Goltz.
Mark Antony, a biography / Eleanor Goltz Huzar. Minneapolis : University of Minnesota Press, [1978] p. cm. Includes index. Bibliography: p. [DG260.A6H89] 78-53133 ISBN 0-8166-0863-6 : 20.00
1. Antonius, Marcus, 83?-30 B.C. 2. Rome—History—Republic, 265-30 B.C. 3. Statesmen—Rome—Biography. 4. Generals—Rome—Biography.

Antonius, Saint, the Great.

ATHANASIUS, Saint, 922.1 Patriarch of Alexandria, d.373.
The life of Saint Antony; newly translated and annotated by Robert T. Meyer. Westminster, Md., Newman Press, 1950. 154 p. 23 cm. (Ancient Christian writers; the works of the Fathers in transiation. no. 10) Bibliographical references included in "Notes" (p. [90]-136) [BR60.A35 no. 10] 50-3967
1. Antonius, Saint, the Great. I. Meyer, Robert T., 1911- ed. and tr. II. Title. III. Series.

QUEFFELEC, Henri, 1910- 922.1
Saint Anthony of the Desert; translated from the French by James Whitall. [1st ed.] New York, Dutton, 1954. 251 p. 21 cm. [BR1720.A6Q413] 54-5040
1. Antonius, the Great, Saint.

Antonucci, Antonio, 1889-

MAHONEY, Philip Francis. 920
Antonio Antonucci, the pifferaro. [1st ed.] New York, Greenwich Book Publishers [1961] 60p. 21cm. [CT275.A764M3] 61-14014
1. Antonucci, Antonio, 1889- I. Title.

Antony, Judith.

ANTONY, Judith. 248'.246 B
Where time becomes space / Judith Antony. Chicago : Franciscan Herald Press, [1978] p. cm. [BX4668.A56A38] 78-12615 ISBN 0-8199-0699-9 : 7.95
1. Antony, Judith. 2. Jews—Converts to Christianity—Biography. 3. Converts, Catholic—Biography. I. Title. BIP

Antrim, Louisa Jane McDonnell, Countess of, 1855-1949.

ANTRIM, Louisa Jane 941.08'092'4 McDonnell, Countess of, 1855-1949.
Louisa, lady in waiting / compiled and edited by Elizabeth Longford. New York : Mayflower Books, 1979. p. cm. [DA565.A55A3] 78-24247 ISBN 0-8317-5650-0 : 14.95
1. Antrim, Louisa Jane McDonnell, Countess of, 1855-1949. 2. Great Britain—History—Victoria, 1837-1901. 3. Great Britain—History—20th century. 4. Ladies-in-waiting—Great Britain—Biography. I. Longford, Elizabeth Harman Pakenham, Countess of, 1906- II. Title.

Anza, Juan Bautista de, 1735-1788.

POURADE, Richard F. 917.94'04'2
Anza conquers the desert; the Anza expeditions from Mexico to California and the founding of San Francisco, 1774 to 1776, written by Richard F. Pourade. Commissioned by James S. Copley. [San Diego, Calif., Union-Tribune Pub. Co., 1971] viii, 216 p. illus. 29 cm. "A Copley book." [F864.A587] 72-162330 12.50
1. Anza, Juan Bautista de, 1735-1788. 2. California—Description and travel—To 1848. 3. San Francisco—History. I. Title.

Anza, Juan Bautista de, 1735-1788—Juvenile literature.

YOUNG, Bob, 1916- 978.9020924
Anza. hard-riding captain [by] Bob and Jan Young. San Carlos, Calif., Golden Gate [c.1966] 197p. illus. 21cm. Bibl. [F864.A59] 65-17717 3.75; 3.49 bds., lib. ed.,
1. Anza, Juan Bautista de, 1735-1788—Juvenile literature. I. Randall, Janet, joint author. II. Title.

Ao, Longri, 1906-

BEERS, Richard G. 266.6'1'0924 B
Walk the distant hills; the story of Longri Ao, by Richard G. Beers. New York, Friendship Press [1969] 64 p. port. (on cover) 19 cm. (Bold believers series) [BV3269.A67B4] 76-13810 1.50
1. Ao, Longri, 1906- 2. Missions—India. I. Title. BIP

Apache Indians.

CHRIS. 301.29'174'972
Apache odyssey; a journey between two worlds, by Morris E. Opler. New York, Holt, Rinehart and Winston [1969] xvi, 301 p. illus., maps. 24 cm. (Case studies in cultural anthropology) Consists chiefly of the autobiographical narrative of Chris, a Mescalero Apache Indian, with introductory material and notes by M. E. Opler. [E99.A6C46] 79-81690
1. Apache Indians. I. Opler, Morris Edward, 1907- II. Title. III. Series.

COCHISE, Ciye, 1874- 970.3 B
The first hundred years of Nino Cochise; the untold story of an Apache Indian chief, as told by Ciye "Nino" Cochise to A. Kinney Griffith. London, New York, Abelard-Schuman [1971] 346 p. illus. 24 cm. [E99.A6C57] 70-157980 ISBN 0-200-71830-4 9.95 (U.S.)
1. Apache Indians. I. Griffith, A. Kinney. II. Title.

GERONIMO, Apache Chief, 1829-1909. 973.8'0924 B
Geronimo: his own story. Edited by S. M. Barrett. Newly edited with an introd. and notes by Frederick W. Turner, III. New York, Dutton, 1970. 190, [1] p. illus., map, ports. 25 cm. First published in 1906 under title: Geronimo's story of his life. Bibliography: p. [191] [E99.A6G3 1970] 72-113457 ISBN 5-251-13088- 6.95
1. Apache Indians. I. Barrett, Stephen Melvil, 1865- ed. II. Turner, Frederick W., 1937- ed. III. Title.

HORN, Tom, 1860-1903. 923.4173
Life of Tom Horn, Government Scout and interpreter written by himself, together with his letters and statements by his friends; a vindication. With an introd. by Dean Krakel. [New ed.] Norman, University of Oklahoma Press [1964] xviii, 277 p. 20 cm. (The Western frontier library, 26) [F595.H797 1964] 64-20758
1. Apache Indians. 2. Apache Indians—Wars, 1883-1886. 3. Frontier and pioneer life—Arizona. I. Title. BIP

Apache Kid.

HAYES, Jess G 1901- 970.1
Apache vengeance; true story of Apache Kid. Illus. by Horace T. Pierce. Albuquerque, University of New Mexico Press, 1954. 185p. illus. 20cm. [E99.A6A56] 970.2 54-7822
1. Apache Kid. I. Title.

Apollinaire, Guillaume, 1880-1918.

DAVIES, Margaret (Brown) 1923- v. 12
Apollinaire. Edinburgh, Oliver & Boyd, 1964. 312 p. plates (incl. ports., facsims.) 22 cm. (Biography and criticism, 5) Bibliography, p. 305-307. 64-67926
1. Apollinaire, Guillaume, 1880-1918. I. Title. II. Series.

STEEGMULLER, Francis, 1906- 841.912
Apollinaire, poet among the painters. New York, Farrar, Straus [1963] xiii, 365 p. illus., ports. 22 cm. Bibliographical references included in "Notes" (p. 354-358) [PQ2601.P6Z83] 63-17063
1. Apollinaire, Guillaume, 1880-1918.

Apollonius of Tyana.

CAMPBELL, Frederick William Groves, d.1914. 186
Apollonius of Tyana; a study of his life and times. With an introd. by Ernest Oldmeadow. Chicago, Argonaut, 1968. 120 p. 22 cm. Reprint of the 1908 ed. Bibliographical footnotes. [B536.A24C2 1968] 68-7566
1. Apollonius, of Tyana.

THE life of Apollonius of Tyana, the Epistles of Apollonius and the Treatise of Eusebius; with an English translation by F. C. Conybeare ... Cambridge, Mass., Harvard University Press, 1958-1960. 2v. 17cm. (Half- title: The Loeb classical library [Latin authors]) (Greek and English, v. 2, p.484-605) 'The treatise of Eusebius, the son of Pamphilus, against the Life of Apollonius of Tyana, written by Philostratus, occasioned by the parallel drawn by Hierocles between him and Christ' Vol. 1, first printed 1912, reprinted . . . 1948; vol. 2, first printed 1912, rev. and reprinted 1950, reprinted 1960. v. 12
1. Apollonius of Tyana. 2. Hierocles, Sossianus, prooonsul of Bithynia, fl. A. D. 293-303. I. Philostratus, Flavius. II. Eusebius Pamphili, Bp. of Caesarea. Adversus Hierocl.

SCHNUR, Harry C. 109'.22 B
Mystic rebels; Apollonius Tyaneus, Jan van Leyden, Sabbatai Zevi, Cagliostro, by Harry C. Schnur. Freeport, N.Y., Books for Libraries Press [1971, c1949] 316 p. illus. 23 cm. (Biography index reprint series) Includes bibliographical references. [BV5095.A1S3 1971] 74-179741 ISBN 0-8369-8109-X
1. Apollonius, of Tyana. 2. Beukelszoon, Jan, 1509?-1536. 3. Shabbethai Zebi, 1626-1676. 4. Cagliostro, Alessandro, conte di, 1743-1795. I. Title.

WINSTON, Alice. 921.9
Apollonius of Tyana, founder of Christianity. New York, VantagePress [1954] 124p. 22cm. 'Fragments from the life of ... Apollonius of Tyana as taken from the Akashic records by Philo and Celeste; recorded by Alice Winston.' [BF1311.A6W5] 54-9141
1. Apollonius, of Tyana. I. Title.

Apostles.

BAUMGAERTNER, John H 225.92
Meet the twelve. Minneapolis, Augsburg Pub. House [1960] 122p. illus. 21cm. [BS2440.B36] 60-6440
1. Apostles. I. Title. BIP

BAUMGAERTNER, John H. 225.92
Meet the twelve [Rev. ed.] Minneapolis, Augsburg [1966, c.1960] xiii, 130p. illus. 20cm. [BS2440.B36] 60-6440 1.95 pap.,
1. Apostles. I. Title.

BROWNRIGG, Ronald. 225.9'22 B
The twelve apostles. [1st American ed.] New York, Macmillan [1974] 248 p. illus. 26 cm. [BS2440.B68 1974] 73-21569 12.95
1. Apostles. I. Title. BIP

BRUCE, Alexander Balmain, 1831-1899. 232.95
The training of the twelve. Grand Rapids, Kregel Publications [1971] xiv, 552 p. 23 cm. (Kregel reprint library) Includes bibliographical references. [BS2440.B7 1971] 73-129738 6.95
1. Apostles. I. Title. BIP

BRUCE, Alexander Balmain, 1831-1899 232.95
The training of the twelve; or, Passages out of the Gospels, exhibiting the twelve disciples of Jesus under discipline for the apostleship. 3d ed. [3d ed.] Grand Rapids, Mich., Zondervan [1963] xvi, 539p. 23cm. Bibl. 63-2074 6.95
1. Apostles. I. Title. II. Title: Passages out of the Gospels.

BRUCE, Alexander Balmain, 1831-1899. 232.9'5
The training of the twelve : or, Passages out of the Gospels : exhibiting the twelve disciples of Jesus under discipline for the apostleship / by Alexander Balmain Bruce. 4th ed., rev. and improved. New Canaan, Conn. : Keats Pub., 1979. xvii, 552 p., [4] leaves of plates : ill. ; 21 cm. (A Shepherd illustrated classic) Includes bibliographical references and index. [BS2440.B7 1979] 79-88121 ISBN 0-87983-206-1 : 5.95
1. Bible, N.T.—Biography. 2. Apostles. I. Title.

HOMAN, Helen Mary (Walker) 1893- 225.92
By post to the apostles. New York, All Saints [1962, c.1931-1952] 146p. (AS225) .50 pap.,
1. Apostles. I. Title. BIP

HOMAN, Helen (Walker) 1893- 225.9'22
By post to the Apostles. Freeport, N.Y., Books for Libraries Press [1971, c1933] xi, 260 p. 23 cm. (Biography index reprint series) [BS2440.H6 1971] 74-148219 ISBN 0-8369-8066-2
1. Apostles. I. Title.

LOCKYER, Herbert. 225.9'22 B
All the apostles of the Bible; studies in the characters of the apostles, the men Jesus chose, and the message they proclaimed. Grand Rapids, Mich., Zondervan Pub. House [1972] 278 p. illus. 24 cm. Bibliography: p. 271. [BS2440.L6] 70-180837 5.95
1. Apostles. I. Title.

PERRY, Earl. 225.92'2
These first called Him Master. Nashville, Broadman Press [1968] 128 p. 20 cm. Bibliography: p. 128. [BS2440.P4] 68-12131
1. Bible. N.T.—Biograpy. 2. Apostles. I. Title.

SMITH, Woodrow W. 225.9'22 B
The twelve who walked in Galilee: character studies of the members of Jesus' cabinet [by] Woodrow W. Smith. Old Tappan, N.J., Revell [1974] 128 p. 21 cm. Bibliography: p. 126-128. [BS2440.S55] 73-16410 ISBN 0-8007-0636-6 3.95
1. Apostles. I. Title.

Apostles — Juvenile literature.

BATTLE, Gerald N. 225.9'22 B
Armed with love; stories of the disciples [by] Gerald N. Battle. Chapter decorations by Charles Cox. Nashville, Abingdon Press [1973] 222 p. illus. 25 cm. Bibliography: p. 221-222. Biographical profiles of the twelve disciples describing the influence of Christ's teachings on each of them. [BS2440.B35] 73-626 ISBN 0-687-01741-6 4.95
1. Apostles—Juvenile literature. I. Title. BIP

WOOD, Katharine Marie, 1910- 225.92
The twelve apostles. New York, Kenedy [1956] unpaged. illus. 29 cm. [BS2440.W6] 56-3752
1. Apostles — Juvenile literature. I. Title.

Apostles—Biography—Juvenile literature.

ROWELL, Edmon L. 225.9'22 B
Apostles, Jesus' special helpers / Edmon L. Rowell, Jr. ; illustrated by James Padgett. Nashville : Broadman Press, c1979. 48 p. : col. Ill. ; 24 cm. (BibLearn Series) Brief biographies of the 12 men who followed Jesus and spread His teachings. [BS2440.R68] 920 79-111902 ISBN 0-8054-4246-4 : 3.95
1. Bible. N.T.—Biography—Juvenile literature. 2. Apostles—Biography—Juvenile literature. I. Padgett, James. II. Title.

Apostolic Church of John Maranke.

JULES-ROSETTE, Bennetta. 269'.2
African apostles : ritual and conversion in the Church of John Maranke / Bennetta Jules-Rosette. Ithaca, N.Y. : Cornell University Press, 1975. 302 p. : ill. ; 22 cm. (Symbol, myth, and ritual series) Includes index. Bibliography: p. [290]-298. [BX6194.A63J84] 75-8437 ISBN 0-8014-0846-6
1. Apostolic Church of John Maranke. 2. Jules-Rosette, Bennetta. 3. Rites and ceremonies—Africa, Sub-Saharan. I. Title. BIP

Appalachian region, Southern—Social life and customs.

OUR Appalachia : 975 B
an oral history / edited by Laurel Shackelford and Bill Weinberg ; photos. by Donald R. Anderson. 1st ed. New York : Hill and Wang, 1977. ix, 397 p. : ill. ; 22 cm. Includes index. [F217.A65O97 1977] 76-48625 ISBN 0-8090-7462-1 : 12.50
1. Appalachian region, Southern—Social life and customs. 2. Appalachian region, Southern—Biography. I. Shackelford, Laurel, 1946- II. Weinberg, Bill, 1941- III. Anderson, Donald R.

Appalachian Trail.

GARVEY, Edward B. 796.5'22'0974
Appalachian hiker; adventure of a lifetime [by] Edward B. Garvey. Oakton, Va., Appalachian Books [1971] xiii, 397 p. illus. 19 cm. [F106.G29] 76-173289 ISBN 0-912660-01-5
1. Appalachian Trail. 2. Backpacking—Appalachian Trail. I. Title.

Appia, Adolphe, 1862-1928.

VOLBACH, Walther Richard, 1897- 792'.025'0924 B
Adolphe Appia, prophet of the modern theater; a profile, by Walther R. Volbach. [1st ed.] Middletown, Conn., Wesleyan University Press [1968] xviii, 242 p. illus., coat of arms, facsims., map, plans, ports. 26 cm. Bibliography: p. 220-232. [PN2808.A6V6] 68-27547 12.50
1. Appia, Adolphe, 1862-1928. I. Title.

Apple, Arnold.

APPLE, Arnold. 918.8'1'0330924 B
Son of Guyana. London, New York, Oxford University Press, 1973. [7], 128 p. 21 cm. (Three crowns books) [CT418.A66A33] 73-168615 ISBN 0-19-211367-4 9.75
1. Apple, Arnold. I. Title.
Pbk. 3.00; ISBN 0-19-211368-2. BIP

Applegate, Dorothy.

APPLEGATE, Dorothy. 355.1'2'0924 B
Mission a-go-go! / By Dorothy Applegate ; illustrated by Anton Jovick. San Francisco : Apple-Gems, c1979. 233 p. : ill. ; 23 cm. [U766.A66A35] 78-73043 ISBN 0-9602122-2-1 : 9.95 ISBN 0-9602122-1-3 pbk. : 5.95
1. Applegate, Dorothy. 2. United States. Army—Military life. 3. Army wives—United States—Biography. I. Title.
Publisher's address: 63 Stratford DR., San Francisco, CA 94132 BIP

Appleton, Edward Victor, Sir 1892-1965.

CLARK, Ronald William. 551.5'1'0924 B
Sir Edward Appleton, by Ronald Clark. [1st ed.] Oxford, New York, Pergamon Press [1971] xiii, 240 p. 21 cm. Bibliography: p. 221-230. [QC16.A6C55 1971] 74-133009 ISBN 0-08-016093-X
1. Appleton, Edward Victor, Sir 1892-1965.

Appleton, Nathan, 1779-1861.

GREGORY, Frances W. 338.7'67'700924 B
Nathan Appleton, merchant and entrepreneur, 1779-1861 / Frances W. Gregory. Charlottesville : University Press of Virginia, [1975] p. cm. Includes index. Bibliography: p. [HF3023.A6G73] 74-31433 ISBN 0-8139-0561-3 : 12.50
1. Appleton, Nathan, 1779-1861. I. Title.

WINTHROP, Robert Charles, 1809-1894. 677'.21'0924 B
Memoir of the Hon. Nathan Appleton, LL.D. Prepared agreeably to a resolution of the Massachusetts Historical Society. With an introd. and appendix. New York, Greenwood Press [1969] 79 p. 23 cm. On spine: Memoir of Appleton. Reprint of the 1861 ed. [CT275.A78W5 1969] 69-19692
1. Appleton, Nathan, 1779-1861. I. Title. BIP

Appleton, Wis. — Biography.

NELSON, Charles C 1879- v. 12
Biographies of prominent people of Appleton and the Fox River Valley. [Appleton? Wis., 1964] 190 [2] p. ports. 24 cm. 66-86623
1. Appleton, Wis. — Biography. 2. Fox River Valley, Wis. — Biography. I. Title.

Arab countries—Biography.

KHADDURI, Majid, 320.9'17'4927
1909-
Arab contemporaries: the role of personalities in politics. Baltimore, Johns Hopkins University Press [1973] x, 255 p. ports. 23 cm. Includes bibliographical references. [DS39.2.A2K48] 72-12576 ISBN 0-8018-1453-7 8.95
1. Arab countries—Biography. 2. Arab countries—Politics. I. Title. BIP

Arab countries—Biog.—Dictionaries.

WHO'S who in the Arab world. 920.05
2d ed.; 1967/68 Beirut, Publitec Eds. v. 21cm. Companion vol. to Who's who in Lebanon. [D198.3.W5] [PL480:UAR-D-183] NE67 35.00
1. Arab countries—Biog.—Dictionaries. Distributed by Intl. Pubns. Serv., New York.

Arabia—Description and travel.

RASWAN, Carl Reinhard. 915.3'04'4
Black tents of Arabia; my life among the Bedouins, by Carl R. Raswan. Photos. by the author. New York, Farrar, Straus & Giroux [1971, c1935] xvi, 206 p. illus. 22 cm. Translation of Im Land der schwarzen Zelte. [DS207.R32 1971] 71-161365 ISBN 0-374-11416-1 6.95
1. Arabia—Description and travel. 2. Bedouins. I. Title.

Arabic literature—Bio-bibliography.

IBN al-Nadim, 910.03'175'927
Muhammad ibn Ishaq, fl.987.
The Fihrist of al-Nadim; a tenth-century survey of Muslim culture. Bayard Dodge, editor and translator. New York, Columbia University Press, 1970. 2 v. (xxxiv, 1149 p.) facsims., geneal. table. 24 cm. (Records of civilization: sources and studies, no. 83) Bibliography: v. 2, p. [869]-903. [Z7052.I213] 68-8874
1. Arabic literature—Bio-bibliography. I. Dodge, Bayard, ed. II. Title. III. Series.

Arad, Yitshak.

ARAD, Yitshak. 909'.04924'0824
The partisan : from the valley of death to Mt. Zion / Yitzhak Arad ; [cover design by Eric Gluckman]. New York : Holocaust Library : [distributed by Schocken Books], c1979. 241 p., [16] leaves of plates : ill. ; 22 cm. [D810.J4A69] 78-71299 ISBN 0-89604-011-9 : 4.95
1. Arad, Yitshak. 2. Holocaust, Jewish (1939-1945)—Personal narratives. 3. World War, 1939-1945—Underground movements—Jews. 4. Israel-Arab War, 1948-1949—Personal narratives, Israeli. 5. Generals—Israel—Biography. 6. Israel—Armed Forces—Biography. I. Title.

Arakcheev, Alexei Andreevich, graf, 1769-1834.

JENKINS, Michael, 947.07'0924 B
1936-
Arakcheev: grand vizier of the Russian Empire, a biography. New York, Dial Press, 1969. 317 p. illus., map, ports. 24 cm. Includes bibliographical references. [DK190.6.A8J4] 68-29342 5.95
1. Arakcheev, Alexei Andreevich, graf, 1769-1834. I. Title.

Aran Islands.

MULLEN, Pat, 1885- 914.17'4
Man of Aran. Cambridge, Mass., M.I.T. Press [1970, c1935] 286 p. illus., maps. 21 cm. Autobiography. [DA990.A8M8 1970] 77-103890
1. Aran Islands. I. Title. BIP

Arapaho Indians.

BASS, Althea Leah 970.30924[B]
(Bierbower) 1892-
The Arapaho way; a memoir of an Indian boyhood, by Althea Bass. Introd. by Frank Waters. Illus. by Carl Sweezy. [1st ed.] New York, Potter [1966] 80p. illus. (pt. col.) port. 24cm. [[E90.S85A3]] 66-17885 5.95
1. Arapaho Indians. I. Title.

SWEEZY, Carl, 1881- 970.30924 (B)
1953.
The Arapaho way; a memoir of an Indian boyhood, by Althea Bass. Introd. by Frank Waters. Illus. by Carl Sweezy. [1st ed.] New York, C. N. Potter [1966] 80 p. illus. (part col.) port. 24 cm. [E90.S85A3] 66-17885
1. Arapaho Indians. I. Bass, Althea Leah (Bierbower) 1892- II. Title.

Arata family.

ARATA, John Lino. 929.2
The Arata biography. [1st ed. Berkeley, Calif., Arata Biography] 1968. 36 p. geneal. table, maps, group ports. 28 cm. [CS71.A66 1968] 68-6803
1. Arata family. I. Title.

Aratus of Sicyon, 271-213 B.C.

PLUTARCHUS. 938'.7'080924 B
Plutarch's Life of Aratus / with introd., notes, and appendix by W. H. Porter. New York : Arno Press, 1979. cv, 96 p. : map ; 21 cm. (Greek texts and commentaries) Text in Greek; introd. and notes in English. Reprint of the 1937 ed. published by Cork University Press, Dublin and Cork. Includes bibliographical references and indexes. [PA4369.A75 1979] 78-18593 ISBN 0-405-11434-6 : 15.00
1. Aratus of Sicyon, 271-213 B.C. 2. Statesmen—Greece—Biography. I. Porter, William Holt. II. Title. III. Series.

Arberry, Arthur John, 1905- tr.

KORAN, English. 297.12
The Koran interpreted [tr. from Arabic] by Arthur J. Aberry. Combined in one volume. New York, Macmillan [1964, c.1955] 350, 358p. 23cm. Contents.v.1. Suras 1-22.--v.2. Suras 21-114. 64-9828 2.95 pap.,
1. Arberry, Arthur John, 1905- tr. I. Title.

Arblay, Frances (Burney) d', 1752-1840.

ADELSTEIN, Michael E. 823'.6 B
Fanny Burney, by Michael E. Adelstein. New York, Twayne Publishers [1968] 169 p. 22 cm. (Twayne's English authors series, 67) Bibliography: p. 163-166. [PR3316.A4Z58] 68-24282
1. Arblay, Frances (Burney) d', 1752-1840. BIP

ARBLAY, Frances 828'.6'03 B
(Burney) d', 1752-1840.
The early diary of Frances Burney, 1768-1778. Edited by Annie Raine Ellis. Freeport, N.Y., Books for Libraries Press [1971] 2 v. 23 cm. Reprint of the 1889 ed. [PR3316.A4Z53 1971] 70-37331 ISBN 0-8369-6678-3
I. Title. BIP

ARBLAY, Frances (Burney) 823'.6 B
d', 1752-1840.
The journals and letters of Fanny Burney (Madame D'Arblay). Oxford, Clarendon Press, 1972- v. illus., facsim., geneal. table, port. 23 cm. Vol. 2 edited by Joyce Hemlow and Althea Douglas. Contents.Contents.—v. 1. 1791-1792, letters 1-39.—v. 2. Courtship and marriage 1793, letters 40-121.—v. 3. Great Bookham 1793-1797, letters 122-250.—v. 4. West Humble 1797-1801, letters 251-422. [PR3316.A4Z552] 72-189680 ISBN 0-19-811498-2 (v. 1) £3.25 (v. 1) varies
1. Arblay, Frances (Burney) d', 1752-1840.

GERIN, Winifred. 928.2
The young Fanny Burney. London, New York, T. Nelson [1961] 131 p. illus. 23 cm. [PR3316.A4Z643 1961] 61-19480
1. Arblay, Frances Burney d', 1752-1840. I. Title.

HAHN, Emily, 1905- 928.2
A degree of prudery; a biography of Fanny Burney. [1st ed.] Garden City, N. Y., Doubleday, 1950. 340 p. illus., ports. 22 cm. Bibliography: p. [329]-331. [PR3316.A4Z645] 50-6638
1. Arblay, Frances Burney d', 1752-1840. I. Title.

HEMLOW, Joyce. 928.2
The history of Fanny Burney. Oxford, Clarendon Press, 1958. 528p. illus. 23cm. [PR3316.A4Z647] 58-963
1. Arblay, Frances (Burney) d', 1752-1840. I. Title. BIP

MASEFIELD, Muriel Agnes 823'.6 B
Bussell.
The story of Fanny Burney; being an introduction to the Diary & letters of Madame d'Arblay. New York, Haskell House Publishers, 1974. x, 160 p. illus. 23 cm. Reprint of the 1927 ed. published by University Press, Cambridge, Eng. Bibliography: p. [158]-160. [PR3316.A4Z67 1974] 73-21629 ISBN 0-8383-1786-3 13.95
1. Arblay, Frances (Burney) d', 1752-1840. I. Arblay, Frances (Burney) d', 1752-1840. The diary and letters of Madame d'Arblay (Frances Burney). II. Title.

MASEFIELD, Muriel Agnes 823'.6 B
Bussell.
The story of Fanny Burney; being an introduction to the Diary & letters of Madame d'Arblay, by Muriel Masefield. [Folcroft, Pa.] Folcroft Library Editions, 1973. x, 160 p. illus. 23 cm. Reprint of the 1927 ed. published by the University Press, Cambridge, Eng. Bibliography: p. [158]-160. [PR3316.A4Z67 1973] 73-16151 ISBN 0-8414-6089-2 (lib. bdg.)
1. Arblay, Frances (Burney) d', Mme., 1752-1840. I. Arblay, Frances (Burney) d', 1752-1840. The diary and letters of Madame d'Arblay (Frances Burney). II. Title.

Arblay, Frances Burney d', 1752-1840—Diaries.

ARBLAY, Frances Burney d', 823'.6
1752-1840.
The famous Miss Burney : the diaries and letters of Fanny Burney / edited by Barbara G. Schrank and David J. Supino. New York : John Day, c1976.] x, 335 p. ; 24 cm. Bibliography: p. 335. [PR3316.A4Z5235 1976] 75-25622 ISBN 0-381-98285-8 : 9.95
1. Arblay, Frances Burney d', 1752-1840—Diaries. 2. Arblay, Frances Burney d', 1752-1840—Correspondence. I. Schrank, Barbara G. II. Supino, David J. III. Title.

Arbuckle, Roscoe, 1887-1933.

GUILD, Leo, 1911 927.92
The Fatty Arbuckle case. New York, Paperback Library [1962] 156p. 18cm. [PN2287.A67G8] 62-6792
1. Arbuckle, Roscoe, 1887-1933. 2. Rappe, Virginia, 1896-1921. I. Title.

YALLOP, David 791.43'028'0924 B
A.
The day the laughter stopped : the true story of Fatty Arbuckle / by David A. Yallop. New York : St. Martin's Press, [1976] p. cm. Includes index. Filmography: p. [PN2287.A68Y3 1976] 75-40810 10.95
1. Arbuckle, Roscoe, 1887-1933. I. Title.

Arbuthnot, John, 1667-1735.

BEATTIE, Lester 827'.5
Middleswarth.
John Arbuthnot: mathematician and satirist, by Lester M. Beattie. New York, Russell & Russell [1967, c1962] xvi, 432 p. illus., port. 22 cm. (Harvard studies in English, v. 16) Bibliographical footnotes. [PR3316.A5Z6 1967] 66-27038
1. Arbuthnot, John, 1667-1735. I. Series. BIP

Arbuthnot, May Hill, 1884-1969—Bibliography.

HARIG, Katherine 028'.5'0924
Jean.
A bio-bibliography of May Hill Arbuthnot (1884-1969) with selective annotations. Washington, 1971. 93 l. 28 cm. Thesis (M.S. in L.S.)—Catholic University of America. [Z8042.66.H36] 73-29092
1. Arbuthnot, May Hill, 1884-1969—Bibliography. I. Title.

Arceneaux, George, 1895-

ARCENEAUX, George, 1895- 976.3'4
Youth in Acadie : reflections on Acadian life and culture in southwest Louisiana / by George Arceneaux. Baton Rouge, La. : Claitor's Pub. Division, c1974. vii, 100 p. ; 22 cm. Includes bibliographical references and index. [S417.A7A38] 74-16733 4.95
1. Arceneaux, George, 1895- 2. Agriculturists—Correspondence, reminiscences, etc. 3. Acadians in Louisiana. I. Title.

Archaeologists.

POOLE, Lynn. 913.03
Men who dig up history, by Lynn and Gray Poole. New York, Mead [1968] xii, 175 p. illus., ports. 21 cm. (Makers of our modern world books) Professional portraits of ten scientists currently involved in archaeological digs ranging from Masada, Israel, to the Arctic Circle: Yigael Yadin, George F. Bass, Sir Mortimer Wheeler, Gordon Randolph Willey, Oscar Broneer, Nils-Gustaf Gejvall, Max E. L. Mallowan, Willard F. Libby, Douglas Dorland Anderson, and Emil W. Haury. [CC110.P6] AC 68
1. Archaeologists. 2. Archaeology. I. Poole, Gray, joint author. II. Title.

Archaeologists — Correspondence, reminiscences, etc.

JUDD, Neil Merton, 970.1'072'024
1887-
Men met along the trail; adventures in archaeology, by Neil M. Judd. [1st ed.] Norman, University of Oklahoma Press [1968] x, 162 p. illus., ports. 22 cm. [E57.J8A3] 68-10300
1. Archaeologists—Correspondence, reminiscences, etc. I. Title.

WHEELER, Robert Eric 925.71
Mortimer, Sir 1890-
Still digging. [1st American ed.] New York, Dutton, 1956 [c1955] 236 p. illus. 21 cm. [CC115.W58A3 1956] 56-5269
1. Archaeologists — Correspondence, reminiscences, etc. I. Title.

Archaeology—Juvenile literature.

COHEN, Daniel. juv
Secrets from ancient graves; rulers and heroes of the past whose lives have been revealed through archaeology. Illustrated by Eliza McFadden. New York, Dodd, Mead [1968] 158 p. illus., maps. 25 cm. Contents.Contents.—Shub-ad.—Khufu.—Ramses II.—Hattusilis III.—Minos.—Sennacherib.—Ch'in Shih Huang Ti.—Sutton Hoo.—Quetzalcoatl.—Leif Ericsson. Discusses how archaeological discoveries have given credence to legends about ancient rulers and heroes. [D55.C6] 68-26156 3.95
1. Archaeology—Juvenile literature. 2. Kings and rulers, Ancient—Juvenile literature. I. McFadden, Eliza, illus. II. Title.

Archer, Colin, 1832-1921.

LEATHER, John. 623.8'092'4 B
Colin Archer and the seaworthy double-ender / by John Leather. Camden, Me. : International Marine Pub. Co., c1979. 167 p. : ill. ; 29 cm. Includes index. [VM140.A7L4] 78-55782 ISBN 0-87742-086-6 : 17.50
1. Archer, Colin, 1832-1921. 2. Boat-building—Norway—History. 3. Naval architects—Norway—Biography. I. Title. BIP

Archer, John Lee, 1791-1852.

SMITH, Roy, 1924- v. 12
John Lee Archer, Tasmanian architect and engineer. [Hobart] Tasmanian Research Association, 1962. xii, 70 p. illus., plans. 25 cm. 65-60301
1. Archer, John Lee, 1791-1852. I. Title.

Archibald, Jules Francois, 1856-1919.

LAWSON, Sylvia Thomas. 070.9'24 B
J. F. Archibald [by] Sylvia Lawson. Melbourne, New York, Oxford University Press [1971] 30 p. illus., ports. 19 cm. (Great Australians) Bibliography: p. 30. [PN5526.A9L3] 70-865035 ISBN 0-19-550348-1
1. Archibald, Jules Francois, 1856-1919.

Archibald, Nate, 1948- —Juvenile literature.

DEVANEY, John. 796.357'092'4 B
Tiny! : The story of Nate Archibald / by John Devaney. New York : Putnam, c1977. p. cm. (Putnam sports shelf) Includes index. A biography of Nate Archibald who rose from the slums of New York City's South Bronx to become one of the great stars of basketball. [GV884.A7D48 1977] 92 77-3214 ISBN 0-399-61098-7 : 5.29
1. Archibald, Nate, 1948- —Juvenile literature. 2. Basketball players—United States—Biography—Juvenile literature. I. Title. BIP

Archilochus.

RANKIN, H. D. 884'.01
Archilochus of Paros / by H. D. Rankin. Park Ridge, N.J. : Noyes Press, c1977. ix, 142 p. ; 24 cm. (Noyes classical studies) Includes indexes. Bibliography: p. 98-104. [PA3873.A77R3] 77-6157 ISBN 0-8155-5053-7 : 15.00
1. Archilochus. 2. Poets, Greek—Biography. I. Title.

Archimedes.

BENDICK, Jeanne. 510'.924 B
Archimedes and the door of science. Pictures by the author. New York, F. Watts [1962] 143 p. illus. 22 cm. (Immortals of science [IS12]) A biography of one of the important scientists of ancient Greece, and an explanation of his contributions to physics, astronomy, and mathematics. [QA29.A7B4] 92 AC 68
1. Archimedes. I. Title.

Archimedes—Juvenile literature.

GARDNER, Martin, 1914- 925
Archimedes, mathematician and inventor. Illus. by Leonard Everett Fisher. New York, Macmillan [c.1965] 41p. col. illus. 24cm. (Sci. story lib.) [QA29.A7G3] 65-10176 2.95; 3.24 lib. ed.,
1. Archimedes—Juvenile literature. I. Title.

HARVEY, Tad 920
The quest of Archimedes. Illus. by Sam Wisnom. Garden City, N.Y., Doubleday [c.1962] 98p. illus. 24cm. 60-12175 2.75
1. Archimedes—Juvenile literature. I. Title.

JONAS, Arthur 920
Archimedes and his wonderful discoveries. Illus. by Aliki. Englewood Cliffs, N.J., Prentice [1963] 70p. illus. 22cm. (P-H jr. res. bks.) 63-10247 2.95
1. Archimedes—Juvenile literature. I. Title.

Architects.

BLOMFIELD, Reginald Theodore, Sir, 1856-1942. 780'.922
Six architects. Freeport, N.Y., Books for Libraries Press [1969] ix, 198 p. ports. 23 cm. (Essay index reprint series) Reprint of the 1935 ed. Contents.Contents.—Andrea Palladio.—Lorenzo Bernini.—Inigo Jones.—Jacques Francois Mansart.—Ange Jacques Gabriel.—Christopher Wren.—Bibliography (p. 187-189) [NA40.B55 1969] 78-99682
1. Architects. I. Title. BIP

Architects, American.

LAVINE, Sigmund A. 720'.922
Famous American architects, by Sigmund A. Lavine. New York, Dodd, Mead [1967] 158 p. illus. 22 cm. (Famous biographies for young people) Contents.Contents.—Introduction: Amateur architects in early America.—Charles Bulfinch (1763-1844).—Benjamin Henry Latrobe (1764-1820).—Henry Hobson Richardson (1838-1886).—Daniel Hudson Burnham (1846-1912).—Charles Follen McKim [1847-1909).—William Rutherford Mead (1846-1928).—Stanford White (1853-1906.).—Louis Henri Sullivan (1856-1924).—Eliel Saarinen (1873-1950).—Eero Saarinen (1910-1961).—Walter Adolph Gropius (1883-).—Richard Joseph Neutra (1892-).—Richard Buckminster Fuller (1895-).—Marcel Lajos Breuer (1902-) [NA736.L3] 67-14309
1. Architects, American. I. Title. BIP

WITHEY, Henry F v. 12
Biographical Dictionary of American architects (deceased) by Henry F. Withey & Elsie Rathburn Withey. Los Angeles, New Age Pub. Co. [c1956] 678 p. 24 cm. A57
1. Architects, American. I. Withey, Elsie Rathburn, joint author. II. Title.

WITHEY, Henry F v. 12
Biographical dictionary of American architects (deceased) by Henry F. Withey & Elsie Rathburn Withey. Los Angeles, New Age Pub. Co. [c1956] 678p. 24cm. A57
1. Architects, American. I. Withey, Eisie Rathburn, joint author. II. Title.

Architects, American—Biography—Juvenile literature.

LEIPOLD, L. Edmond, 1902- 720'.92'2 B
Famous American architects, by L. E. Leipold. Minneapolis, T. S. Denison [1972] 77 p. 25 cm. (Famous American heroes and leaders series) Contents.Contents.—Charles Bulfinch.—Frank Lloyd Wright.—Louis Sullivan.—Eero Saarinen.—Edward Durell Stone.—Eric Mendelsohn.—Mies van der Rohe.—Paul Williams.—Robert G. Cerny. [NA736.L44] 920 70-178992 ISBN 0-513-01163-3
1. Architects, American—Biography—Juvenile literature. I. Title.

Architects, American—Dictionaries.

KERVICK, Francis William Wynn 927.2
Architects in America of Catholic tradition. Rutland, Vt., Tuttle [1962] 140p. illus. 27cm. 61-14032 10.00
1. Architects, American—Dictionaries. 2. Catholics in the U. S.—Biog.—Dictionaries. 3. Architecture—U. S. I. Title.

Architects—Biography.

WHO'S who in architecture : from 1400 to the present day / edited by J. M. Richards, American consultant, Adolph K. Placzek. 1st ed. New York : Holt, Rinehart and Winston, c1977. 368 p. : ill. ; 26 cm. Includes index. [NA40.W48] 76-44323 ISBN 0-03-017381-7 : 19.95 720'.92'2 B
1. Architects—Biography. I. Richards, James Maude, Sir, 1907-

Architects, British.

BOOTH, Arthur Harold. 720'.924
Sir Christopher Wren [by] Arthur H. Booth; drawings by Charles King. London, Muller, 1967. 125p. illus., plan, facsim., diagrs. 21 cm. (True bks.) Bibl. [NA997.W8B65] (B) 67-96582 3.75 bds.,
I. Wren, Christopher, Sir 1632-1723. II. Title.

COLVIN, Howard Montagu. v. 12
A biographical dictionary of English architects, 1660-1840. [1st ed.] Cambridge, Harvard University Press, 1954. xiv, 821p. 23cm. A54
1. Architects, British. 2. Architecture—Gt. Brit.—Dictionary. I. Title.

Architects—Correspondence, reminiscences, etc.

BENDINER, Alfred. 720'.924
Translated from the Hungarian; notes toward an autobiography. South Brunswick [N.J.] A. S. Barnes [1967] 317 p. illus. 25 cm. [NA737.B45A2] 67-22886
1. Architects—Correspondence, reminiscences, etc. I. Title.

MENDELSOHN, Erich, 1887-1953. 720'.924
Eric Mendelsohn: letters of an architect. Edited by Oskar Beyer. Translated by Geoffrey Strachan. With an introd. by Nikolaus Pevsner. London, New York, Abelard-Schuman [1967] 192 p. illus., ports. 26 cm. Translation of Briefe eins Architekten. [NA1088.M57A313 1967] 66-15598
1. Architects—Correspondence, reminiscences, etc. I. Beyer, Oskar, 1882- ed.

Architecture—Designs and plans.

JEANNERET-GRIS, Charles Edouard, 1887-1965 720.924
Oeuvre complete 1957-1965; Le Corbusier et son atelier, rue de Sevres 35. Ed. by W. Boesiger. New York, Wittenborn [1966, c.1965] 239p. illus. (pt. col.) facsims., plans (pt. col.) ports. 24x29cm. French, English and German. Forms the seventh vol. of Le Corbusier et Pierre Jeanneret, Oeuvres completes; the first vol. includes the period 1910-1929, the second, 1929-1934, the third, 1934-1938, the fourth, 1938-1946, the fifth, 1946-1952, the sixth, 1952-1957. [NA1053.J4A53] 66-7277 18.50
1. Architecture—Designs and plans. 2. Cities and towns—Planning. I. Boesiger, Willy, ed. II. Title.

Architecture—United States—Bibliography.

WODEHOUSE, Lawrence. 016.72'092'2
American architects from the Civil War to the First World War : a guide to information sources / Lawrence Wodehouse. Detroit : Gale Research Co., [1975] p. cm. (Art and architecture information guide series ; v. 3) (Gale information guide library) [Z5944.U5W63] 73-17525 ISBN 0-8103-1269-7 : 18.00
1. Architecture—United States—Bibliography. 2. Architecture, Modern—19th century—United States—Bibliography. 3. Architecture, Modern—20th century—United States—Bibliography. 4. Architects—United States—Bibliography. I. Title. BIP

Arctic regions.

BALCHEN, Bernt, 1899- 926.29
Come north with me, an autobiography. [lst ed.] New York, Dutton, 1958. 313 p. illus. 22 cm. [G585.B3A3] 58-5242
1. Arctic regions. 2. Antarctic regions. 3. Aeronautics—Flights. I. Title.

HENSON, Matthew Alexander, 1866-1955. 919.8 B
A Negro explorer at the North Pole. New York, Arno Press, 1969. xx, 200 p. illus., ports. 20 cm. (The American Negro, his history and literature) Reprint of the 1912 ed. [G670 1909.H4A32] 69-18565 6.00
1. Arctic regions. 2. North Pole. I. Title. II. Series. BIP

STEFANSSON, Vilhjalmur, 1879-1962. 923.973
Discovery; the autobiography of Vilhjalmur Stefansson. [1st ed.] New York, McGraw-Hill [1964] viii, 411 p. illus., ports. 22 cm. [G635.S7A3 1964] 64-16477
1. Arctic regions. I. Title.

Arden, Elizabeth, 1878-1966.

LEWIS, Alfred Allan. 338.7'61'646720924 B
Miss Elizabeth Arden [by] Alfred Allan Lewis and Constance Woodworth. New York, Coward, McCann & Geoghegan, inc. [1972] 320 p. illus. 24 cm. [TP983.A66A7] 72-86464 ISBN 0-698-10479-X 7.95
1. Arden, Elizabeth, 1878-1966. I. Woodworth, Constance, joint author.

Ardery, Philip, 1914-

ARDERY, Philip, 1914- 940.54'49'73
Bomber pilot : a memoir of World War II / by Philip Ardery. Lexington : University Press of Kentucky, c1978. p. cm. Includes index. [D790.A86] 77-92919 ISBN 0-8131-1379-2 : 9.95
1. Ardery, Philip, 1914- 2. United States. Air Force—Biography. 3. World War, 1939-1945—Aerial operations, American. 4. World War, 1939-1945—Personal narratives, American. 5. Air pilots, Military—United States—Biography. I. Title.

Arditi, Luigi, 1822-1903.

ARDITI, Luigi, 1822-1903. 780'.92'4 B
My reminiscences / by Luigi Arditi. New York : Da Capo Press, 1977, [c1896] xxii, 314 p., [10] leaves of plates : ill. ; 24 cm. (Da Capo Press music reprint series) Reprint of the ed. published by Dodd, Mead, New York. [ML410.A67A3 1977] 77-5500 ISBN 0-306-77417-8 : 19.95
1. Arditi, Luigi, 1822-1903. 2. Composers—Biography. BIP

Ardizzone, Edward,

ARDIZZONE, Edward, 1900- 741'.0924 B
The young Ardizzone; an autobiographical fragment. [1st American ed. New York] Macmillan [1970] 144 p. illus. (part col.) 26 cm. Reminiscences of the English author/artist's childhood. [NC978.5.A7A3 1970b] 92 71-125295 7.95
I. Title. BIP

Ardovino, Dominick.

ARDOVINO, Dominick. 796.3576'4'0924
The bat boy. Photography by Gerald Jacobson. New York, McGraw-Hill [1967] 159 p. illus., ports. 22 cm. (A Week with ... series) (A Young pioneer book) Autobiographical. [GV873.A7] 67-19897
I. Title.

Aretino, Pietro, 1492-1556.

ARETINO, Pietro, 1492-1556. 856'.3
The letters of Pietro Aretino [translated] by Thomas Caldecot Chubb. [Hamden, Conn.] Archon Books, 1967. 362 p. 22 cm. [PQ4564.A4 1967] 67-12481
I. Title.

ARETINO, Pietro, 1492-1556. 856'.3
The letters of Pietro Aretino [translated] by Thomas Caldecot Chubb. [Hamden, Conn.] Archon Books, 1967. 362 p. 22 cm. [PQ4564.A4 1967] 67-12481
I. Title.

CLEUGH, James. 858.309
The divine Aretino; a biography. New York, Stein and Day, Pub. [1966, c1965] 256 p. ports. 22 cm. Bibliography: p. 249-251. [PQ4564.C57 1966] 66-14949
1. Aretino, Pietro, 1492-1556. I. Title.

Arfons, Art—Juvenile literature.

KATZ, Frederic 796.720924
Art Arfons, fastest man on wheels; the complete life story of the world's land-speed record holder. New York, Nelson [c.1965] 127p. illus., ports. 22cm. (Champion bks., Rutledge bk.) [GV1032.A7K3] 65-20627 2.75; 2.78 bds., lib. ed.,
1. Arfons, Art—Juvenile literature. 2. Automobiles, Racing—Speed records. I. Title.

KATZ, Frederic, 1938- 796.720924
Art Arfons, fastest man on wheels; the complete life story of the world's land-speed record holder. London, New York, T. Nelson [1965] 127 p. illus., ports. 22 cm. (Champion books) "A Rutledge book." [GV1032.A7K3] 65-20627
1. Arfons, Art—Juvenile literature. 2. Automobiles, Racing—Speed records. I. Title.

Argea, Angelo.

ARGEA, Angelo. 796.352'092'4 B
The Bear and I : the story of the world's most famous caddie / by Angelo Argea, with Jolee Edmondson ; foreword and commentary by Jack Nicklaus. 1st ed. New York : Atheneum/SMI, 1979. p. cm. [GV964.A67A32] 79-63844 ISBN 0-689-10983-0 : 7.95
1. Argea, Angelo. 2. Nicklaus, Jack. 3. Caddies—United States—Biography. I. Edmondson, Jolee, joint author. II. Nicklaus, Jack. III. Title. BIP

Argentes, Eustratios, ca. 1687-ca. 1757.

WARE, Timothy, 1934- 922.1499
Eustratios Argenti; a study of the Greek Church under Turkish rule [New York] Oxford [c.]1964. xii, 196p. 23cm. Bibl. [BX395.A75W3] 65-1331 7.20
1. Argentes, Eustratios, ca. 1687-ca. 1757. I. Title. BIP

Argentine, John, ca. 1442-1507 or. 8.

RHODES, Dennis E. 942.04/0924
John Argentine provost of King's. His life and his library. [By] Dennis E. Rhodes. Amsterdam, Menno Hertzberger, 1967. 40p. with illus. 23cm. Bibl. [LF204.A7R45] (B) 67-101980 4.95 bds.,
1. Argentine, John, ca. 1442-1507 or. 8. I. Title.
Distributed by Abner Schram, 1860 Broadway, New York, N. Y. 10023.

Argentine Republic—Hist.—1817-1860.

SARMIENTO, Domingo 327'.2'0924
Faustino, Pres. Arentine Republic 1811-1888.
Facundo. Selected and edited by Navier A. Fernande [and] Reginald F. Brown. Boston, Ginn [1960] 205p. illus. 22cm. First published in 1843 under title: Civilizacion barbarie. [F2846.S24743] 60-1818
1. Argentine Republic—Hist.—1817-1860. 2. Argentine Republic—Descr. & trav. 3. Quiroga, Juan Facundo, 1790-1837. I. Title.

Argyll, John George Edward Henry Douglas Sutherland Campbell, 9th Duke of, 1845 1914.

MACNUTT, William 971.05'4'0924
Stewart, 1908-
Days of Lorne : impressions of a governor-general, from the private papers of the Marquis of Lorne, 1878-1883 in the possession of the Duke of Argyll at Inveraray Castle, Scotland / by W. Stewart MacNutt. Westport, Conn. : Greenwood Press, 1978, c1955. x, 262 p., [17] leaves of plates : ill. ; 23 cm. Reprint of the ed. published by Brunswick Press, Fredericton, N.B. Includes index. Bibliography: p. 259. [F1033.M145 1978] 77-16170 ISBN 0-313-20021-1 lib.bdg. : 21.00
1. Argyll, John George Edward Henry Douglas Sutherland Campbell, 9th Duke of, 1845-1914. 2. Statesmen—Canada—Biography. 3. Canada—History—1867-1914. I. Title.

Arigo.

FULLER, John 615'.852'0924 B
Grant, 1913-
Arigo: surgeon of the rusty knife, by John G. Fuller. Afterword by Henry K. Puharich. New York, Crowell [1974] viii, 274 p. illus. 24 cm. Bibliography: p. 263-266. [RZ408.A7F84 1974] 74-3492 ISBN 0-690-00512-1 7.95
1. Arigo.

Ariosto, Lodovico, 1474-1533.

GARDNER, Edmund Garratt, 851'.3 B
1869-1935.
The king of court poets; a study of the work, life, and times of Lodovico Ariosto. New York, Greenwood Press [1968] xvi, 395 p. illus., geneal. tables, ports. 23 cm. Reprint of the 1906 ed. Bibliography: p. [369]-376. [PQ4587.G3 1968b] 69-13903
1. Ariosto, Lodovico, 1474-1533. I. Title.

GARDNER, Edmund Garratt, 851'.3 B
1869-1935.
The king of court poets; a study of the work, life, and times of Lodovico Ariosto. New York, Haskell House Publishers, 1968. xix, 395 p. illus., ports. 24 cm. Reprint of the 1906 ed. Bibliography: p. [369]-376. [PQ4587.G3 1968] 68-24954
1. Ariosto, Lodovico, 1474-1533. I. Title. BIP

Aristoteles.

CHROUST, Anton-Herman. 185 S
Some novel interpretations of the man and his life. [Notre Dame, Ind.] University of Notre Dame Press [1973] xxvi, 437 p. 23 cm. (His Aristotle: new light on his life and on some of his lost works, v. 1) Includes bibliographical references. [B481.C56 vol. 1] 185 B 73-8892 ISBN 0-268-00517-6 24.00
1. Aristoteles. I. Title. II. Series.

CHROUST, Anton-Hermann. 185 B
Aristotle: new light on his life and on some of his lost works. [Notre Dame, Ind.] University of Notre Dame Press [1973] 2 v. 23 cm. Includes bibliographical references. [B481.C56] 73-8917 45.00
1. Aristoteles. I. Title. BIP

EDEL, Abraham, 1908- 185
Aristotle. [New York, Dell, 1967] 493p. 18cm. (Laurel great lives and thought) 0272. Bibl. [B485.E3] 67-8852 .95 pap.,
1. Aristoteles. I. Title.

FARRINGTON, Benjamin, 1891- 185
Aristotle: founder of scientific philosophy. New York, Praeger [1969, c1965] vii, 118 p. illus., maps, ports. 22 cm. (Praeger pathfinder biographies) Bibliography: p. 113-114. [B485.F3 1969] 68-16211 3.95
1. Aristoteles. I. Title.

FERGUSON, John, 1921- 185 B
Aristotle. New York, Twayne Publishers [1972] 195 p. 21 cm. (Twayne's world authors series, TWAS 211. Greece) Includes bibliographical references. [B485.F47] 70-186637
1. Aristoteles.

GRAYEFF, Felix. 185
Aristotle and his school; an inquiry into the history of the Peripatos with a commentary on Metaphysics Z, H, and O. New York, Barnes & Noble [1974] 230 p. 23 cm. Bibliography: p. 213-217. [B485.G59 1974b] 73-22545 ISBN 0-06-492531-5 11.50
1. Aristoteles. 2. Aristoteles. Metaphysics. 3. Peripatetics. I. Title.

GRENE, Marjorie (Glicksman) 185
1910-
A portrait of Aristotle. [Chicago] Univ. of Chic. Pr. [c.1963] 271p. illus. 23cm. Bibl. 63-5556 5.00
1. Aristoteles. I. Title. BIP

Aristoteles—Juvenile literature.

DOWNEY, Glanville [Robert 92
Emory Glanville Downey]
Aristotle, dean of early science. New York, Watts [c.1962] 148p. illus. 22cm. (Immortals of sci.) 62-13955 1.95; 2.95 lib. ed.,
1. Aristoteles—Juvenile literature. I. Title.

Arizona—Biog.

WILLSON, Roscoe G 1879- 920.0791
Pioneer cattlemen of Arizona. Phoenix, Ariz., Printed by McGrew Commercial Printery [1951-56] 2v. illus., ports. 23cm. 'Reproduced from a series of Valley National Bank advertisements ... appearing in Arizona cattlelog. official magazine of the Arizona Cattle Growers' Association.' Vol. 2 has title: Pioneer and well known cattlemen of Arizona. [F810.W57] 51-5208
1. Arizona—Biog. 2. Cattle trade—Arizona. I. Valley National Bank, Phoenix, Ariz. II. Title.

WILSON, Roscoe G 1879- 920.0791
Pioneer cattlemen of Arizona. Phoenix, Ariz., Printed by McGrew Commercial Printery [1951- v. illus., ports. 23 cm. "Reproduced from a series of Valley National Bank advertisements ... appearing in Arizona cattlelog, official magazine of the Arizona Cattle Growers' Association." [F810.W57] 51-5208
1. Arizona—Biog. 2. Cattle trade—Arizona. I. Valley National Bank, Phoenix, Ariz II. Title.

Arizona—Hist.—To 1950—Biog.

LOCKWOOD, Francis 979.1'04'0922
Cummins, 1864-1948
Pioneer portraits: selected vignettes, by Frank C. Lockwood. Introd. by John Bret Harte. Tucson, Univ. of Ariz. Pr. [1968] 240p. ports. 20cm. Seven of the sketches appeared orig. in Life in old Tucson, 1854-1864. [F810.L845] 67-30670 5.95
1. Arizona—Hist.—To 1950—Biog. I. Title.

Arizona—Biography.

LOCKWOOD, Francis 920.0791
Cummins, 1864-1948.
Thumbnail sketches of famous Arizona desert riders, 1538-1946 Freeport, N.Y., Books for Libraries Press [1971, c1946] 30 p. 23 cm. (Biography index reprint series) Cover title: Famous Arizona desert riders. "Originally published as vol. XVII, no. 2, University of Arizona bulletin, General bulletin no. 11." Bibliography: p. 30. [F810.L85 1971] 73-148224 ISBN 0-8369-8071-9
1. Arizona Biography. I. Title. II. Title: Famous Arizona desert riders. BIP

PETTICOAT pageant; 920.72'09791
a collection of reports by members of the History Club, Sunnyside High School, Tucson, Arizona. [Tucson] Printed by the Audiovisual Dept., Sunnyside School District [1971] 120 p. illus., ports. 22 cm. (Arizonac, 1971) Includes bibliographies. [F810 P47] 73-159650
1. Arizona—Biography. 2. Women in Arizona—Biography. 3. Frontier and pioneer life—Arizona. I. Sunnyside High School. History Club. II. Title. III. Series.

Arizona—History—Sources.

†THIS land, these voices 979.1
: a different view of Arizona history in the words of those who lived it / [compiled] by Abe Chanin, with Mildred Chanin. 1st ed. Flagstaff [Ariz.] : Northland Press, c1977. xii, 266 p. : ill. ; 25 cm. Includes index. [F811.T45] 78-311177 ISBN 0-87358-164-4 : 12.50
1. Arizona—History—Sources. 2. Arizona—Biography. I. Chanin, Abe. II. Chanin, Mildred. BIP

Arkansas — Biog.

MCNUTT, Walter Scott, 923.273
comp.
Great statesmen of Arkansas. Jefferson, Tex., Four States Pub. House [1954] 142p. 22cm. [F410.M2] 54-27056
1. Arkansas—Biog. I. Title.

WHO is who in 920.0767
Arkansas. v. 1- Little Rock, Ark. [1959- v. ports. 23 cm. [F410.W47] 60-27733
1. Arkansas — Biog.

Arkansas—Biography—Indexes.

PRESLEY, Leister E., Mrs. 917.67
Biographical index to biographical and historical memoirs of Eastern Arkansas [by] Mrs. Leister E. Presley. Searcy, Ark. [1973] 39 p. 29 cm. This index covers the biographical section of a history of Arkansas published 1889-90 by Goodspeed Pub. Co., Nashville, Tenn. [F411.B613P72] 73-159675
1. Biographical and historical memoirs of Eastern Arkansas—Indexes. 2. Arkansas—Biography—Indexes. I. Title.

Arkansas—History—Chronology.

CHRONOLOGY and documentary 976.7
handbook of the State of Arkansas. Ellen Lloyd Trover, state editor. Dobbs Ferry, N.Y., Oceana Publications, 1972. vi, 141 p. 23 cm. (Chronologies and documentary handbooks of the States, v. 4) Bibliography: p. 137. Contains a chronology of historical events from 1541 to 1970, a directory of political figures, an outline of the state constitution, and copies of four historical documents. [F411.C57] 72 5331 ISBN 0-379-16129-X
1. Arkansas—History—Chronology. 2. Arkansas—Biography—Dictionaries. 3. Arkansas—History—Sources. I. Trover, Ellen Lloyd, ed. II. Title. III. Series.

Arlen, Harold, 1905-

JABLONSKI, Edward 927.8
Harold Arlen: happy with the blues. Garden City, N. Y., Doubleday [c.]1961. 286p. illus. discography Bibl. 60-15177 4.95
1. Arlen, Harold, 1905- I. Title.

JABLONSKI, Edward. 927.8
Harold Arlen: happy with the blues. [1st ed.] Garden City, Doubleday, 1961. 286p. illus. 24cm. Includes bibliographies. [ML410.A76J3] 60-15177
1. Arlen, Harold, 1905- I. Title.

Arlen, Michael, 1895-1956.

ARLEN, Michael J. 823'.9'12 B
Exiles [by] Michael J. Arlen. [1st ed.] New York, Farrar, Straus & Giroux [1970] 226 p. 22 cm. [PR6001.R7Z57 1970] 70-109553 6.95
1. Arlen, Michael, 1895-1956. 2. Arlen, Atalanta. I. Title. BIP

Armer, Dolores, Mother, 1851-1905.

TERESITA, Sister. v. 12
Mother Dolores, the story of the foundress of the Sisters of the Holy Family. San Francisco, Sisters of the Holy Family [1956?] 238 246 p. port. 23 cm. "Reprinted from Review for religious, September, 1956." 67-26671
1. Armer, Dolores, Mother, 1851-1905. 2. Sisters of the Holy Family of San Francisco. I. Title.

Armes, Jay J.

ARMES, Jay J. 364.12'092'4
Jay J. Armes, investiator / Jay J. Armes as told to Frederick Nolan. New York : Avon Books, 1977,c1976. 280, [16]p. : ill. ; 18 cm. [HV8083.A75A34] ISBN 0-380-01756-3 pbk. : 1.95
1. Armes, Jay J. 2. Detectives-Correspondence, Reminiscences, etc. I. Nolan, Frederick W., 1931- joint author. II. Title.
L.C. card no. for 1976 Macmillan ed.: 76-18915.

ARMES, Jay J. 364.12'092'4 B
Jay J. Armes, investigator / by Jay J. Armes, as told to Frederick Nolan. New York : Macmillan, c1976. 234 p., [8] leaves of plates : ill. ; 24 cm. [HV8083.A75A34] 76-18915 ISBN 0-02-503200-3 : 8.95
1. Armes, Jay J. 2. Detectives—Correspondence, reminiscences, etc. I. Nolan, Frederick W., 1931- joint author. II. Title.

Armitage, Merle,

ARMITAGE, Merle, 790.20924 (B)
1893-
Accent on life. Foreword by John Charles Thomas. [1st ed.] Ames, Iowa State University Press [1964 c1965] xv. 386 p. illus., ports. 24 cm. Autobiography.

Bibliography of the author's works: p. [ii]-[iii] [CT275.A817A3] 65-10571
I. Title.

Armour, John L

ARMOUR, John L 920
Look what happened to me. New York, Comet Press Books [1958] 153p. illus. 21cm. (A Reflection book) [CT275.A818A3] 58-4097
I. Title.

Armstrong, A. Joseph, 1873-

DOUGLAS, Lois Smith, 1910- 923.773
Through heaven's back door; a biography of A. Joseph Armstrong. Waco, Tex., Baylor University Press [1951] 284p. illus. 22cm. [PR55.A7D6] 54-1552
1. Armstrong, A. Joseph, 1873- I. Title.

Armstrong, Annie W., d. 1938—Juvenile literature.

DURHAM, Jacqueline. j92
Miss Strong Arm; the story of Annie Armstrong. Illus. by Hertha Depper. Nashville, Broadman Press [1966] 174 p. illus. 21 cm. [BX6495.A67-D8] 66-10377
1. Armstrong, Annie W., d. 1938—Juvenile literature. I. Title. BIP

Armstrong, Edwin Howard.

LESSING, Lawrence. 926.21384
Man of high fidelity: Edwin Howard Armstrong, a biography.[1st ed.] Philadelphia, Lippincott [1956] 320p. illus. 22cm. Includes bibliography. [TK6545.A7L4] 56-11677
1. Armstrong, Edwin Howard. I. Title.

LESSING, Lawrence P 926.21384
Man of high fidelity: Edwin Howard Armstrong, a biography. [1st ed.] Philadelphia, Lippincott [1956] 320p. illus. 22cm. Includes bibliography. [TK6545.A7L4] 56-11677
1. Armstrong, Edwin Howard. I. Title.

Armstrong, George Washington,

ARMSTRONG, George Washington, 1866- 923.473
Memoirs. [Austin? Tex., c1958] 414p. illus. 24cm. [HC102.5.A7A3] 59-1908
I. Title.

Armstrong, Gregory, 1931-

ARMSTRONG, Gregory, 1931- 973.92'092'4 B
Wanderers all : an American pilgrimage / Gregory Armstrong. 1st ed. New York : Harper & Row, c1977. 121 p. ; 22 cm. [CT275.A8218A38 1977] 76-26210 ISBN 0-06-010139-3 : 6.95
1. Armstrong, Gregory, 1931- 2. United States—Biography. I. Title. BIP

Armstrong, Henry,

ARMSTRONG, Henry, 1912- 927.9683
Gloves, glory, and God; an autobiography. [Westwood, N.J.] F. H. Revell Co. [1956] 256 p. illus. 22 cm. [GV1132.A7A3] 56-10890
I. Title.

Armstrong, Herbert W.

DELOACH, Charles F. 289.9
The Armstrong error, by C. F. DeLoach. Plainfield, N.J., Logos International [1971] 117 p. 18 cm. On cover: The plain truth on Herbert W. Armstrong. Includes bibliographical references. [BR1725.A77D4] 73-129817 ISBN 0-912106-13-1 0.95
1. Armstrong, Herbert W. I. Title.

HOPKINS, Joseph Martin, 1919- 289.9
The Armstrong empire; a look at the Worldwide Church of God. [Grand Rapids] Eerdmans [1974] 304 p. map. 21 cm. Bibliography: p. 286-291. [BR1725.A77H66] 74-8255 3.95
1. Worldwide Church of God. 2. Armstrong, Herbert W. 3. Armstrong, Garner Ted. I. Title.

SUMNER, Robert Leslie, 1922- 230'.9'9
Armstrongism: the "Worldwide Church of God" examined in the searching light of scripture; (an in-depth study of a false religion) by Robert L. Sumner. Brownsburg, Ind., Biblical Evangelism Press [1974] 424 p. 21 cm. Includes bibliographical references. [BR1725.A77S95] 74-171027 ISBN 0-914012-15-0 5.95
1. Armstrong, Herbert W. 2. Worldwide Church of God. I. Title. BIP

Armstrong, Jane B.

ARMSTRONG, Jane B. 730'.92'4
Discovery in stone / by Jane B. Armstrong. New York : East Woods Press, [1975] [44] p., [24] leaves of plates : ill. ; 21 cm. Autobiographical. [NB237.A75A42] 74-83472 ISBN 0-914788-01-9 : 9.95
1. Armstrong, Jane B. I. Title.

Armstrong, John, 1725-1795.

FLOWER, Milton Embick. 973.3'0924 B
John Armstrong, first citizen of Carlisle, by Milton E. Flower. Carlisle, Pa., Cumberland County Historical Society, 1971. 16 p. 23 cm. Includes bibliographical references. [F152.A75F55] 76-296566
1. Armstrong, John, 1725-1795. I. Title.

Armstrong, John Allen, 1854-1925.

BUXTON, Coburn Allen. 338'.0092'4 B
John Allen Armstrong : man of his day / Coburn Allen Buxton, Sr. 1st ed. New York : Vantage Press, [1974] 144 p. : ill. ; 21 cm. [HC102.5.A73B87] 74-190374 ISBN 0-533-00949-9 : 4.95
1. Armstrong, John Allen, 1854-1925.

Armstrong, John Nelson, 1870-1944.

SEARS, Lloyd Cline, 1895- 378.1'1'0924 B
For freedom; the biography of John Nelson Armstrong [by] L. C. Sears. Austin, Tex., Sweet Pub. Co. [1969] 335 p. illus., ports. 21 cm. [LA2317.A7S4] 79-94236 5.95
1. Armstrong, John Nelson, 1870-1944. I. Title.

Armstrong, Louis, 1900-1971.

ARMSTRONG, Louis, 1900- v. 12
Satchmo; my life in New Orleans. [New York] New American Library [c1954 1961] 191 p. illus. 18 cm. (Signet Book D 1970) NUC66
1. Musicians — Correspondence, reminiscences, etc. 2. Jazz music. I. Title.

ARMSTRONG, Louis, 1900-1971. 788'.1'0924 B
Louis Armstrong—a self-portrait. The interview by Richard Meryman. New York, Eakins Press [1971] 59 p. ports. 19 cm. The major portion of the interview was first published in Life, April 15, 1966. [ML419.A75A7] 70-152507 4.95
I. Meryman, Richard, 1926-

ARMSTRONG, Louis, 1900-1971. 927.8
Satchmo; my life in New Orleans. New York, Prentice-Hall [1954] 240 p. illus. 21 cm. [ML419.A75A3] 54-9628
1. Musicians—Correspondence, reminiscences, etc. 2. Jazz music. I. Title.

EATON, Jeanette. 927.8
Trumpeter's tale; the story of young Louis Armstrong. Illustrated by Elton C. Fax. New York, Morrow, 1955. 191p. illus. 21cm. [ML419.A75E2] 55-5968
1. Armstrong, Louis, 1900- I. Title.

GOFFIN, Robert, 1898- 785.4'2'0924 B
Horn of plenty : the story of Louis Armstrong / by Robert Goffin ; translated from the French by James F. Bezou. New York : Da Capo Press, 1977. 304 p. : port. ; 24 cm. (The Roots of jazz) Reprint of the 1947 ed. published by Allen, Towne & Heath, New York. [ML419.A75G6 1977] 77-8050 ISBN 0-306-77430-5 : 17.50
1. Armstrong, Louis, 1900-1971. 2. Jazz musicians—United States—Biography. I. Bezou, James F. II. Title.

GOFFIN, Robert, 1898- 785.4'2'0924 B
Horn of plenty : the story of Louis Armstrong / by Robert Goffin ; translated from the French by James F. Bezou. Westport, Conn. : Greenwood Press, 1979, c1947. 304 p., [1] leaf of plates : port. ; 23 cm. Reprint of the ed. published by Allen, Towne & Heath, New York. [ML419.A75G6 1978] 78-4838 ISBN 0-313-20398-9 lib. bdg. : 21.00
1. Armstrong, Louis, 1900-1971. 2. Jazz musicians—United States—Biography. I. Title. BIP

JONES, Max. 788'.1'0924 B
Louis; the Louis Armstrong story, 1900-1971 [by] Max Jones & John Chilton. [1st American ed.] Boston, Little, Brown [1971] 256 p. illus. 26 cm. [ML419.A75J625] 76-175031 9.50
1. Armstrong, Louis, 1900-1971. I. Chilton, John, joint author. II. Title.

MCCARTHY, Albert J 927.8
Louis Armstrong. New York, Barnes [1961, c1959] 85p. illus. 21cm. (Kings of jazz) A Prepetua book, P-4033. [ML419.A75M2 1961] 60-16822
1. Armstrong, Louis, 1900- 2. Jazz music. I. Title. BIP

RICHARDS, Kenneth G 1926- 780'.924 (B)
Louis Armstrong, by Kenneth G. Richards. Chicago, Childrens Press [c1967] 95 p. illus., ports. 29 cm. (People of destiny. A humanities series) [ML419.A75R5] 67-26873
1. Armstrong, Louis, 1900- I. Title.

Armstrong, Louis, 1900-1971—Juvenile literature.

CORNELL, Jean Gay. 788'.1'0924 B
Louis Armstrong, Ambassador Satchmo. Illustrated by Victor Mays. Champaign, Ill., Garrard Pub. Co. [1972] 96 p. illus. 24 cm. (Americans all) A biography of the famous jazz trumpeter who began his musical career singing songs on New Orleans street corners. [ML3930.A75C7] 92 75-188567 ISBN 0-8116-4576-2 3.50
1. Armstrong, Louis, 1900-1971—Juvenile literature. I. Mays, Victor, 1927- illus. II. Title.

IVERSON, Genie. 788'.1'0924 B
Louis Armstrong / by Genie Iverson ; illustrated by Kevin Brooks. New York : Crowell, 1976. p. cm. A biography of the famous trumpeter from his childhood in New Orleans to the time when he was known as "Ambassador Satch" and "King of Jazz." [ML3930.A75I9] 92 76-4975 ISBN 0-690-01127-X
1. Armstrong, Louis, 1900-1971—Juvenile literature. I. Brooks, Kevin. II. Title.

MILLENDER, Dharathula H. 788'.1'0924 B
Louis Armstrong; young music maker, by Dharathula H. Millender. Illustrated by Al Fiorentino. Indianapolis, Bobbs-Merrill Co. [1972] 200 p. col. illus. 20 cm. (Childhood of famous Americans) Biography of a trumpeter of humble origin who received international acclaim as a jazz entertainer. [ML3925.A83M5] 92 72-187336 2.75
1. Armstrong, Louis, 1900-1971—Juvenile literature. I. Fiorentino, Al, illus. II. Title.

SANDERS, Ruby (Wilson) 788'.1'0924 B
Jazz ambassador, Louis Armstrong. Illustrated by John Solie. Design by Rolf Zillmer. Chicago, Childrens Press [1973] 79 p. illus. 25 cm. "An Elk Grove book." Bibliography: p. 78-79. A biography stressing the youth and early career of the famous jazz musician from New Orleans who began his career in the Waifs' Home for Boys. [ML3930.A75S25] 92 72-10209 ISBN 0-516-07710-4 5.19
1. Armstrong, Louis, 1900-1971—Juvenile literature. I. Solie, John, illus. II. Title.

Armstrong, Neil, 1930- —Juvenile literature.

WESTMAN, Paul. 629.45'0092'4 B
Neil Armstrong, space pioneer / Paul Westman. Minneapolis : Lerner Publications Co., c1980. p. cm. (The Achievers) Includes index. A biography of Neil Armstrong who, on July 20, 1969, as a member of the three-man Apollo 11 crew, became the first human being to walk on the moon. [TL789.85.A75W47] 92 80-10832 ISBN 0-8225-0479-0 (lib. bdg.) : 5.95
1. Armstrong, Neil, 1930- —Juvenile literature. 2. Astronauts—United States—Biography—Juvenile literature. I. Title. II. Series: Achievers.

Armstrong, Samuel Chapman, 1839-1893.

TALBOT, Edith (Armstrong) 378.1'1'0924 B
Samuel Chapman Armstrong; a biographical study. New York, Negro Universities Press [1969] vi, 301 p. illus. 23 cm. Reprint of 1904 ed. [LC2851.H32T3] 76-79811
1. Armstrong, Samuel Chapman, 1839-1893. 2. Hampton Institute, Hampton, Va.

Armstrong, William George Armstrong, Baron, 1810-1900.

DEUGAN, David, 1936- 338.4'7'62340924 B
The great gun-maker: the story of Lord Armstrong. Newcastle upon Tyne, Graham [1971] 189 p., 16 plates. illus., ports. 23 cm. Bibliography: p. [183]-184. [UF537.A45D68] 76-594552 ISBN 0-902833-31-6 £2.50
1. Armstrong, William George Armstrong, Baron, 1810-1900. I. Title.

Armstrong, William Howard, 1914-

ARMSTRONG, William Howard. 923.773
Through troubled waters. [1st ed.] New York, Harper [c1957] 86p. 20cm. [CT275.A824A3] 56-12060
I. Title.

ARMSTRONG, William Howard. 371.3
Through troubled waters [1st ed.] New York, Harper [c1957] 86p. 20 cm. [CT275.A824A3] 56-6093
I. Title. BIP

ARMSTRONG, William Howard, 1914- 818'.5'403 B
Through troubled waters [by] William H. Armstrong. New York, Harper & Row [1973] 86 p. 20 cm. [PS3551.R483 1973] 73-6335 ISBN 0-06-060303-8 3.95
1. Armstrong, William Howard, 1914- I. Title.

Army wives.

JOHNSON, Virginia Weisel. 355.1'0924
Lady in arms. Boston, Houghton Mifflin, 1967. 181 p. 22 cm. [U766.J58] 67-11827
1. Army wives. I. Title.

Arnaldo da Brescia, d. 1155.

GREENAWAY, George William. 282'.092'4 B
Arnold of Brescia / by George William Greenaway. New York : AMS Press, 1978. xi, 237 p. ; 19 cm. Reprint of the 1931 ed. published by the University Press, Cambridge, Eng. Includes index. Bibliography: p. [222]-227. [BX1256.G7 1978] 77-84710 ISBN 0-404-16116-2 : 23.50
1. Arnaldo da Brescia, d. 1155. 2. Christian biography—Italy. 3. Church history—Middle Ages, 600-1500. 4. Popes—Temporal power. I. Title. BIP

Arnaz, Desi, 1917-

ARNAZ, Desi. 790.2'092' B
A book / by Desi Arnaz. New York : Warner Books, [1977]c1976. 382,[33]p. : ill. ; 18 cm. Autobiography.

[PN2287.A69A32] ISBN 0-446-89153-3 pbk. : 1.95
1. Arnaz, Desi, 1917- I. Title.
L.C. card no. for 1976 Morrow ed. : 75-28040 BIP

ARNAZ, Desi, 1917- 790.2'092'4 B
A book by Desi Arnaz. New York : Morrow, 1976. 322 p., [15] leaves of plates : ill. ; 24 cm. Autobiography. [PN2287.A69A32] 75-28040 ISBN 0-688-00342-7 : 8.95
1. Arnaz, Desi, 1917-

Arnim, Bettina (Brentano) von, 1785-1859.

HELPS, Arthur. 928.3
Bettina, a portrait, by Arthur Helps and Elizabeth Jane Howard. New York, Reynal [1957?] 223p. illus. 23cm. [PT1808.A4H4] 57-14042
1. Arnim, Bettina (Brentano) von, 1785-1859. I. Howard, Elizabeth Jane, joint author. II. Title.

Arnold, Benedict, 1741-1801.

ABBATT, William, 1851-1935. 973.3'092'2 B
The crisis of the Revolution : being the story of Arnold and Andre, now for the first time collected from all sources and illustrated with views of all places identified with it / by William Abbatt ; ill. from original photos. by Edwin S. Bennett ; with an introd. by Jeff Canning. Harrison, N.Y. : Harbor Hill Books, 1976. p. cm. Reprint in re-arranged form of the 1899 ed. published by W. Abbatt, New York, with supplements of 1909 and 1915. Bibliography of Major Andre, by C. A. Campbell (from Magazine of American history, Jan. 1882): p. [E236.A12 1976] 76-2604 16.50
1. Arnold, Benedict, 1741-1801. 2. Andre, John, 1751-1780. I. Title.

BOYLAN, Brian Richard. 973.3'092'4 B
Benedict Arnold: the dark eagle. [1st ed.] New York, Norton [1973] 266 p. illus. 21 cm. Bibliography: p. [258]-262. [E278.A7B69 1973] 73-4235 ISBN 0-393-07471-4 6.95
1. Arnold, Benedict, 1741-1801. 2. Andre, John, 1751-1780. 3. United States—History—Revolution. BIP

FLEXNER, James Thomas 923.41
The Benedict Arnold case. Abridged ed. (Orig. title: The traitor and the spy) New York, Collier [c.1953, 1962] 381p. (BS61) 1.50 pap.,
1. Arnold, Benedict, 1741-1801 I. Title.

FLEXNER, James Thomas, 1908- 923.573
The traitor and the spy: Benedict Arnold and John Andre. [1st ed.] New York, Harcourt, Brace [1953] 431p. illus. 25cm. Includes bibliography. [E278.A7F5] 53-7843
1. Arnold, Benedict, 1741-1801. 2. Andre, John, 1751-1780. I. Title.

FLEXNER, James Thomas, 1908- 973.3'092'2
The traitor and the spy : Benedict Arnold and John Andre / James Thomas Flexner ; newly illustrated and with a new foreword. Boston : Little, Brown, [1975] xxii, 453 p., [12] leaves of plates : ill. ; 24 cm. Includes bibliographical references and index. [E236.F57 1975] 75-11909 ISBN 0-316-28606-0 : 15.00
1. Arnold, Benedict, 1741-1801. 2. Andre, John, 1751-1780. I. Title. BIP

LENGYEL, Cornel Adam. 923.573
I, Benedict Arnold; the anatomy of treason. [1st ed.] Garden City, N. Y., Doubleday, 1960. 237 p. illus. 22 cm. Includes bibliography. [E278.A7L42] 60-15181
1. Arnold, Benedict, 1741-1801.

PAINE, Lauran. 973.3'0924
Benedict Arnold, hero and traitor. New York, Roy Publishers [1967, c1965] 189 p. illus., ports. 23 cm. [E278.A7R3 1967] 67-11259
1. Arnold, Benedict, 1741-1801.

WALLACE, Willard Mosher, 1911- 923.573
Traitorous hero; the life and fortunes of Benedict Arnold. [1st ed.] New York, Harper [1954] xiii, 394p. ports., maps, facsims. 22cm. Bibliography: p. 375-383. [E278.A7W26] 54-6033
1. Arnold, Benedict, 1741-1801. I. Title.

WALLACE, Willard Mosher, 1911- 973.3'0924 B
Traitorous hero; the life and fortunes of Benedict Arnold, by Willard M. Wallace. Freeport, N.Y., Books for Libraries Press [1970, c1954] xiii, 394 p. illus., facsims., maps, ports. 23 cm. Bibliography: p. 375-383. [E278.A7W26 1970] 74-117896
1. Arnold, Benedict, 1741-1801. I. Title. BIP

Arnold, Benedict, 1741-1801—Juvenile literature.

ALDERMAN, Clifford Lindsey. 973.3'092'4 B
The dark eagle : the story of Benedict Arnold / Clifford Lindsey Alderman. New York : Macmillan, c1976. vii, 136 p. : map ; 22 cm. Includes index. Bibliography: p. 128-131. A biography of the ardent patriot and brilliant general who became America's most infamous traitor. [E278.A7A75] 92 75-40087 ISBN 0-02-700210-1
1. Arnold, Benedict, 1741-1801—Juvenile literature. I. Title. BIP

DE LEEUW, Cateau, 1903- 973.3'0924 B
Benedict Arnold: hero and traitor. New York, Putnam [1970] 127 p. illus. 21 cm. (Spies of the world) A biography of the Revolutionary War General describing how he came to be a traitor. [E278.A7D35] 92 77-102396 3.49
1. Arnold, Benedict, 1741-1801—Juvenile literature. I. Title.

DONOVAN, Frank Robert, 1906- 92
The brave traitor. Illus by Arthur Zaidenberg. New York. A. S. Barnes [c.1961] 141p. (Amer. hist. ser.: Wonderful world bk.) Bibl. 61-13919 2.95 bds.,
1. Arnold. Benedict. 1741 1801 Juvenile literature. I. Title.

Arnold, Henry Harley, 1886-1950.

DUPRE, Flint O. 358.4'13'320924 B
Hap Arnold: architect of American air power [by] Flint O. DuPre. New York, Macmillan [1972] xiv, 144 p. illus. 24 cm. (Air Force Academy series) Bibliography: p. 137. [TL540.A69D86] 72-83760 5.95
1. Arnold, Henry Harley, 1886-1950. 2. United States. Air Force—History.

Arnold, Jose.

ARNOLD, Jose. 915.38
Golden swords, and pots and pans. [1st ed.] New York, Harcourt, Brace & World [1963] 240 p. illus. 21 cm. Autobiographical. [TX910.5.A7A3] 63-8097
I. Title.

Arnold, Matthew, 1822-1888.

ALEXANDER, Edward. 821'.8'09
Matthew Arnold, John Ruskin, and the modern temper. Columbus, Ohio State University Press [1973] xviii, 310 p. 23 cm. Bibliography: p. [299]-304. [PR4023.A63] 73-9605 ISBN 0-8142-0188-1 11.00
1. Arnold, Matthew, 1822-1888. 2. Ruskin, John, 1819-1900. I. Title. BIP

ARNOLD, Matthew, 1822-1888. 821'.8 B
The letters of Matthew Arnold to Arthur Hugh Clough. Edited with an introductory study by Howard Foster Lowry. Folcroft, Pa., Folcroft Press [1969] xi, 191 p. 26 cm. Reprint of the 1932 ed. [PR4023.A47C6 1969] 72-196993
I. Clough, Arthur Hugh, 1819-1861. II. Lowry, Howard Foster, 1901-1967, ed. III. Title.

CHAMBERS, Edmund Kerchever, Sir 1866-1954. 928.2
Matthew Arnold, a study. New York, Russell & Russell, 1964. 144p. geneal. table. 23cm. 64-15026 5.00
1. Arnold, Matthew(1822-1888. I. Title. BIP

DUFFIN, Henry Charles, 1884- 821.8
Arnold, the poet. New York, Barnes & Noble [1963, c.1962] 158p. port. 23cm. Bibl. 63-25505 4.50
1. Arnold, Matthew, 1822-1888. I. Title.

HARVEY, Charles H. 828'.6'08
Matthew Arnold, a critic of the Victorian period, by Charles H. Harvey. [Hamden, Conn.] Archon Books, 1969. 256 p. 20 cm. Reprint of the 1931 ed. Includes bibliographies. [PR4023.H34 1969] 69-18273
1. Arnold, Matthew, 1822-1888.

JUMP, John Davies, 1913- 821'.8 B
Matthew Arnold / by J. D. Jump. Folcroft, Pa. : Folcroft Library Editions, 1976. x, 185 p., [2] leaves of plates : ill. ; 26 cm. Reprint of the 1955 ed. published by Longmans, London, in series: Men and books. Includes index. Bibliogrpahy: p. 177-179. [PR4023.J8 1976] 76-7983 ISBN 0-8414-5348-9 lib. bdg. : 15.00
1. Arnold, Matthew, 1822-1888. I. Series: Men and books.

PAUL, Herbert Woodfield, 1853-1935. 821'.8
Matthew Arnold / by Herbert W. Paul. Folcroft, Pa. : Folcroft Library Editions, 1977. viii, 188 p. ; 23 cm. Reprint of the 1925 ed. published by Macmillan, London, in series: English men of letters. Includes index. [PR4023.P3 1977] 77-22490 ISBN 0-8414-6828-1 lib. bdg. : 20.00
1. Arnold, Matthew, 1822-1888. 2. Authors, English—19th century—Biography.

ROWSE, Alfred Leslie, 1903- 821'.8 B
Matthew Arnold : poet and prophet / A. L. Rowse. London : Thames & Hudson, 1976. 208 p., [8] leaves of plates : ill. ; 25 cm. Includes index. Bibliography: p. 204-205. [PR4024.R69] 76-380169 ISBN 0-500-01163-X : £6.50
1. Arnold, Matthew, 1822-1888. 2. Authors, English—19th century—Biography.

RUSSELL, George William Erskine, 1853-1919. 821'.8
Matthew Arnold. [Folcroft, Pa.] Folcroft Library Editions, 1973. xv, 269 p. illus. 21 cm. Reprint of the 2d ed. published in 1904 by Hodder and Stoughton, London, in series: Literary lives. [PR4023.R8 1973] 73-13672 11.75
1. Arnold, Matthew, 1822-1888. I. Series: Literary lives.

RUSSELL, George William Erskine, 1853-1919. 821'.8 B
Matthew Arnold / by G. W. E. Russell. Norwood, Pa. : Norwood Editions, 1976. xv, 269 p., [17] leaves of plates : ill. ; 23 cm. Reprint of the 2d ed. published in 1904 by Hodder and Stoughton, London, in series: Literary lives. [PR4023.R8 1976] 76-8884 ISBN 0-8482-2250-4 lib. bdg. : 15.75
1. Arnold, Matthew, 1822-1888. I. Series: Literary lives.

SAINTSBURY, George Edward Bateman., 1845-1933 828'09
Matthew Arnold. New York, Russell & Russell [1967] vi, 232p. 20cm. Reprint of the 1899 ed. Bibl. (B) 7.50
1. Arnold, Matthew, 1822-1888. I. Title. BIP

SAINTSBURY, George Edward Bateman, 1845-1933. 828'.8'09 (B)
Matthew Arnold. New York, Russell & Russell [1967] vi, 232 p. 20 cm. Reprint of the 1899 ed. Bibliographical footnotes. [PR4023.S3] 66-27143
1. Arnold, Matthew, 1822-1888. I. Title.

TRILLING, Lionel, 1905- 928.2
Matthew Arnold. New York, Meridian Books, 1955 [c1949] 413p. 18cm. (Meridian books, M19) [PR4023] 55-9703
1. Arnold, Matthew, 1822-1888. I. Title.

TRILLING, Lionel, 1905- v. 12
Matthew Arnold. [2d ed.] . . . New York, Columbia University Press [1958, c1949] 465 p. 23 cm. Bibliography: pp. 436-477.
*1. Arnold Matthew, 1822-1888. I. Title.*BIP

TRILLING, Lionel, 1905-1975. 821'.8 B
Matthew Arnold : with an additional essay Matthew Arnold, poet / Lionel Trilling. Uniform ed. New York : Harcourt Brace Jovanovich, c1977. 493 p. ; 21 cm. (The Works of Lionel Trilling) (Series: Trilling, Lionel, 1905-1975. The works of Lionel Trilling.) Includes bibliographies and index. [PR4023.T7 1977] 77-25294 12.95
1. Arnold, Matthew, 1822-1888. 2. Authors, English—19th century—Biography. I. Title. II. Series.

TRILLING, Lionel, 1905-1975. 821'.8 B
Matthew Arnold : with an additional essay, Matthew Arnold, poet / by Lionel Trilling. Uniform ed., 1st Harvest /HBJ ed. New York : Harcourt, Brace, Jovanovich, 1979, c1939. p. cm. (The works of Lionel Trilling) (A Harvest/HBJ book) (Series: Trilling, Lionel, 1905-1975. Works. 1977.) Includes index Bibliography: p. [PR4023.T7 1979] 79-10653 ISBN 0-15-657734-8. : 6.95
1. Arnold, Matthew, 1822-1888. 2. Author, English—19th century—Biography. I. Series.

Arnold, Matthew, 1822-1888—Correspondence.

ARNOLD, Matthew, 1822-1888. 826'.8
Unpublished letters of Matthew Arnold / edited by Arnold Whitridge. Folcroft, Pa. : Folcroft Library Editions, 1977. p. cm. Reprint of the 1923 ed. published by Yale University Press, New Haven. [PR4023.A45 1977] 77-24248 ISBN 0-8414-9490-8 lib. bdg. : 10.00
1. Arnold, Matthew, 1822-1888—Correspondence. 2. Authors, English—19th century—Correspondence. I. Title. BIP

Arnold, Matthew, 1822-1888—Criticism and interpretation.

BICKLEY, Francis Lawrance, 1885- 821'.8
Matthew Arnold & his poetry [by Francis Bickley] London, G. G. Harrap, 1912. [New York, AMS Press, 1972] 116, [1] p. port. 19 cm. (Poetry and life series) Bibliography: p. [117] [PR4023.B5 1972] 77-120977 8.00
1. Arnold, Matthew, 1822-1888—Criticism and interpretation. I. Title. II. Series. BIP

Arnold, Matthew, 1822-1888—Religion and ethics.

COURTNEY, Janet Elizabeth Hogarth, 1865- 192 B
Freethinkers of the nineteenth century / by Janet E. Courtney. Norwood, Pa. : Norwood Editions, 1976. p. cm. Reprint of the 1920 ed. published by Chapman & Hall, London. Contents.Contents.—Frederick Denison Maurice.—Mathew Arnold.—Charles Bradlaugh.—Thomas Henry Huxley.—Leslie Stephen.—Harriet Martineau.—Charles Kingsley. [B1569.C6 1976] 76-17266 ISBN 0-8482-0386-0 : 25.00
1. Maurice, Frederick Denison, 1805-1872. 2. Arnold, Matthew, 1822-1888—Religion and ethics. 3. Bradlaugh, Charles, 1833-1891. 4. Huxley, Thomas Henry, 1825-

1895. 5. Stephen, Leslie, Sir, 1832-1904. 6. Martineau, Harriet, 1802-1876. 7. Kingsley, Charles, 1819-1875. I. Title. BIP

Arnold, Mrs. Margaret (Shippen) 1760-1804 — Juvenile literature.

BEAUTY and the traitor; j92
the story of Mrs. Benedict Arnold. Philadelphia, Macrae Smith [1967] 171 p. 22 cm. Bibliography: p. [167]-171. [E278.A72L6] 67-15062
1. Arnold, Mrs. Margaret (Shippen) 1760-1804 — Juvenile literature. 2. Arnold, Benedict, 1741-1801 — Juvenile literature.

LOMASK, Milton. j92
Beauty and the traitor; the story of Mrs. Benedict Arnold. Philadelphia, Macrae Smith [1967] 171 p. 22 cm. Bibliography: p. [167]-171. [E278.A72L6] 67-15062
1. Arnold, Mrs. Margaret (Shippen) 1760-1804 — Juvenile literature. 2. Arnold, Benedict, 1741-1801 — Juvenile literature. I. Title. BIP

Arnold, Oren—Biography.

ARNOLD, Oren. 818'.5'409 B
A boundless privilege / by Oren Arnold ; introd. by Alan D. LeBaron ; illustrated by Rosemary Detwiler. 1st ed. Austin, Tex. : Madrona Press, [1974] xiv, 159 p. : ill. ; 24 cm. [PS3501.R599Z5] 74-81628 ISBN 0-89052-007-0 : 8.50
1. Arnold, Oren—Biography. I. Title. BIP

Arnold, Remmie Le Roy, 1894-

BROWN, William Moseley, 1894- 920
From these beginnings: the life story of Remmie Le Roy Arnold. [1st ed.] Staunton, Va., McClure Print. Co., 1953. 634p. illus. 24cm. [CT275.A833B7] 54-29653
1. Arnold, Remmie Le Roy, 1894- I. Title.

Arnold, Thomas, 1795-1842.

STANLEY, Arthur 373.1'2'0120924 B
Penrhyn, 1815-1881.
The life and correspondence of Thomas Arnold / by Arthur Penrhyn Stanley. New York : AMS Press, 1978. p. cm. Reprint of the 1845 ed. published by B. Fellowes, London. Includes index. "List of Dr. Arnold's published works": [LF795.R92S7 1978] 75-29624 ISBN 0-404-13980-9 : 38.50
1. Arnold, Thomas, 1795-1842. 2. Superintendents and principals—England—Biography. I. Title.

STRACHEY, Giles Lyton, 920.042
1880-1932
Eminent Victorians: Cardinal Manning, Florence Nightingale, Dr. Arnold, General Gordon. New York [Putnam, 1963] vii, 338p. (Capricorn bk., 83) Bibl. 1.65 pap.,
1. Manning, Henry Edward, cardinal, 1808-1892. 2. Nightingale, Florence, 1820-1910. 3. Arnold, Thomas, 1795-1842. 4. Gordon, Charles George, 1833-1885. I. Title.

STRACHEY, Giles Lytton, 920.042
1880-1932
Eminent Victorians: Cardinal Manning, Florence Nightingale, Dr. Arnold, General Gordon. [Gloucester, Mass., P. Smith, 1964] vii, 338p. 18cm. (Capricorn ed. rebound) Bibl. 3.65
1. Manning, Henry Edward, Cardinal, 1808-1892. 2. Nightingale Florence, 1820-1910. 3. Arnold, Thomas, 1795-1842. 4. Gordon, Charles George, 1833-1885. I. Title.

STRACHEY, Giles Lytton, 920.042
1880-1932.
Eminent Victorians: Cardinal Manning, Florence Nightingale, Dr. Arnold, General Gordon. New York, Capricorn Books [1963] vii, 338 p. 18 cm. Includes bibliographies. [CT782.S8] 64-4150
1. Nightingale, Florence, 1820-1910. 2. Arnold, Thomas, 1795-1842. 3. Gordon, Charles George, 1833-1885. 4. Manning, Henry Edward, Cardinal, 1808-1892. I. Title.

Arnold, Thurman Wesley, 1891-1969.

ARNOLD, Thurman 340'.092'4 B
Wesley, 1891-1969.
Voltaire and the cowboy : the letters of Thurman Arnold / edited by Gene M. Gressley. Boulder : Colorado Associated University Press, c1977. xiv, 552 p. : ill. ; 24 cm. Includes bibliographical references and index. [KF373.A7A4 1977] 76-15772 ISBN 0-87081-073-1 : 15.00
1. Arnold, Thurman Wesley, 1891-1969. 2. Lawyers—United States—Correspondence. I. Gressley, Gene M., 1931- II. Title.

Arnow, Harriette Louisa Simpson, 1908- —Homes and haunts—Burnside, Ky.

ARNOW, Harriette 813'.5'2 B
Louisa Simpson, 1908-
Old Burnside / Harriette Simpson Arnow. Lexington : University Press of Kentucky, c1977. xi, 129 p., [2] leaves of plates : ill., map (on lining paper) ; 21 cm. (The Kentucky Bicentennial bookself) [PS3501.R64Z47] 77-73699 ISBN 0-8131-0208-1 : 4.95
1. Arnow, Harriette Louisa Simpson, 1908- —Homes and haunts—Burnside, Ky. 2. Burnside, Ky.—History. 3. Authors, American—20th century—Biography. I. Title. II. Series. BIP

Arnsdorff. Herman Lovett, 1918-

KNIGHT, Richard 338.7'68'4100924
H
The man in the dream house, a biography. [Savannah?] 1956. 98p. illus. 24cm. [HD9773.U7D73] 57-23077
1. Arnsdorff. Herman Lovett, 1918- 2. Dream House Furniture Company, Savannah. I. Title.

Arny, Mary Travis.

ARNY, Mary Travis. 920.7
Seasoned with salt. Philadelphia, Westminster Press [1954] 230 p. 21 cm. Autobiographical. [CT275.A834A3] 54-9399
I. Title.

Arny, William Frederick Milton, 1813-1881.

MURPHY, Lawrence R., 917.3 B
1942-
Frontier crusader—William F. M. Arny [by] Lawrence R. Murphy. Tucson, University of Arizona Press [1972] xii, 313 p. illus. 23 cm. Bibliography: p. 285-297. [E78.N65M95] 73-184712 ISBN 0-8165-0331-1 5.95 (pbk.)
1. Arny, William Frederick Milton, 1813-1881. I. Title.

Aronson, Charles N., 1913-

ARONSON, Charles N., 338'.092'4 B
1913-
Free enterprise / by Charles N. Aronson. 1st ed. Arcade, N.Y. : C. N. Aronson, c1979. xxxiv, 1655 p. : ill. ; 24 cm. "The Eagle series." [HC102.5.A74A34] 78-73546 ISBN 0-915736-15-2 : 25.00. ISBN 0-915736-16-0 pbk. : 18.00
1. Aronson, Charles N., 1913- 2. Businessmen—United States—Biography. I. Title. BIP

Aronson, Henry M.—Juvenile literature.

COHEN, Tom. 323.4'0922 B
Three who dared. [1st ed.] Garden City, N.Y., Doubleday [1969] 144 p. illus. 22 cm. (A Doubleday signal book) Contents.Contents.—The Henry M. Aronson story.—The John O'Neal story.—The Eric Weinberger story. Describes the activities of three young men who risked their lives to participate in the Freedom Marches and Civil Rights Movement of the early 1960's. [E185.61.C637] 920 69-10998 3.50
1. Aronson, Henry M.—Juvenile literature. 2. O'Neal, John—Juvenile literature. 3. Weinberger, Eric, 1932- —Juvenile literature. 4. Negroes—Civil rights—Juvenile literature. 5. Civil rights—Southern States—Juvenile literature. I. Title. BIP

Aronson, John Hugo,

ARONSON, John 978.6'03'0924 B
Hugo, 1891-
The galloping Swede, by J. Hugo Aronson and L. O. Brockmann. Missoula, Mont., Mountain Press Pub. Co. [1970] xii, 180 p. illus., ports. 28 cm. [F735.2.A7A3] 71-122313 8.50
I. Brockmann, Louis O. II. Title. BIP

Arrows (Musical group)

HARRY, Bill. 784'.092'2
Arrows : the official story / [by] Bill Harry. London : Everest, 1976. 141 p., [8] p. of plates : ill., ports. ; 18 cm. [ML421.A7H4] 77-362482 ISBN 0-903925-61-3 : £0.50
1. Arrows (Musical group) 2. Rock musicians—England—Biography. I. Title.

Art.

EPSTEIN, Jacob, Sir, 709'.24
1880-1959.
The sculptor speaks, Jacob Epstein to Arnold L. Haskell; a series of conversations on art. New York, B. Blom, 1971. xiii, 200 p. illus. 24 cm. Reprint of the 1932 ed. [N7445.2.E6 1971] 73-172922
1. Art. I. Haskell, Arnold Lionel, 1903- II. Title.

Art—Addresses, essays, lectures.

COX, Kenyon, 1856-1919. 709'.22
Painters and sculptors; a second series of old masters and new. Freeport, N.Y., Books for Libraries Press [1970] xi, 187 p. illus., ports. 23 cm. (Essay index reprint series) Reprint of the 1907 ed. Contents.Contents.—The education of an artist.—The Pollaiuoli.—Painters of the mode.—Holbein.—The Rembrandt tercentenary.—Rodin.—Lord Leighton. [N7445.C87 1970] 70-105006
1. Art—Addresses, essays, lectures. I. Title.

Art, American—Dictionaries.

THE Britannica 709'.73
encyclopedia of American art. Chicago, Encyclopaedia Britannica Educational Corp.; distribution by Simon and Schuster, New York [1973] 669 p. illus. (part col.) 29 cm. "A Chanticleer Press edition." Bibliography: p. 638-668. [N6505.B73] 73-6527 ISBN 0-671-21616-3 29.95
1. Art, American—Dictionaries. 2. Artists—United States—Biography—Dictionaries. BIP

THE Britannica 709'.73
encyclopedia of American art : a special educational supplement to the Encyclopaedia Britannica. Chicago : Encyclopaedia Britannica Educational Corp. ; New York : distribution by Simon and Schuster, [1976?] 669 p. : ill. (some col.) ; 29 cm. "A Chanticleer Press edition." Bibliography: p. 638-668. [N6505.B73 1976] 73-80529 ISBN 0-87827-160-0 : write for information
1. Art, American—Dictionaries. 2. Artists—United States—Biography.

Art, American—Exhibitions.

WALKER Art Center, 709'.73
Minneapolis.
Invitation 1974: Joe Breidel, Larry Brown, Carole Fisher, Stuart Nielsen [and] Tom Rose; [catalogue of] an exhibition organized by Walker Art Center, 12 May-23 June, 1974. Essays by Dean Swanson. Biographical commentaries by Gwen Lerner. [Minneapolis, 1974] 1 portfolio (6 pieces) illus. 23 cm. [N6512.W32 1974] 74-80989
1. Art, American—Exhibitions. 2. Art, Modern—20th century—United States. I. Swanson, Dean. II. Lerner, Gwen. III. Title.

Art, American—Indiana—Exhibitions.

MIRAGES of 709'.772'074017252
memory : 200 years of Indiana art : an exhibition ... Indianapolis Museum of Art, November 6, 1976-January 2, 1977, Art Gallery, University of Notre Dame, January 16-March 20, 1977. [s.l. : s.n.], c1977- (South Bend, Ind. : Osthimer) v. : ill. (some col.) ; 28 cm. Catalogue. Includes bibliographies. [N6530.I6M57] 77-153194
1. Art, American—Indiana—Exhibitions. 2. Art—Indiana—Exhibitions. 3. Artists—Indiana—Biography. I. Indianapolis Museum of Art. II. Notre Dame, Ind. University. Art Gallery.

Art—Biography.

INTERNATIONAL who's 709'.2'2 B
who in art and antiques / editorial director, Ernest Kay. 2d ed. Cambridge, Eng. : Melrose Press, 1976. xv, 525 p. ; 25 cm. [N40.I57 1976] 76-373141 ISBN 0-900332-37-9
1. Art—Biography. 2. Artists—Biography. I. Kay, Ernest, ed. BIP

INTERNATIONAL who's 700'.92'2 B
who in art and antiques. Hon. General editor: Ernest Kay. Cambridge [Eng.] Melrose Press [1972] viii, 679 p. illus. 25 cm. [N40.I57] 79-189269 ISBN 0-900332-21-2 32.50
1. Art—Biography. 2. Artists—Biography. I. Kay, Ernest, ed.
Distributed by Rowman & Littlefield.

Art—California, Southern.

MOURE, Nancy Dustin 709'.2'2 B
Wall.
Dictionary of art and artists in Southern California before 1930 / by Nancy Dustin Wall Moure, with research assistance by Lyn Wall Smith ; introd. by Carl Schaefer Dentzel. Glendale, Calif. : Dustin Publications, 1975. xxvi, 306 p. : ill. ; 28 cm. (Publications in Southern California art ; no. 3) "500 copies printed." Bibliography: p. 288-290. [N6530.S7M68] 75-329638
1. Art—California, Southern. 2. Artists—California, Southern—Biography. I. Smith, Lyn Wall, joint author. II. Title. III. Series.

Art—Collectors and collecting.

PRICE, Vincent, 1911- 707.5
I like what I know; a visual autobiography. Illustrated with photos. [1st ed.] Garden City, N. Y., Doubleday, 1959. 313 p. illus. 24 cm. [N8384.P7A3] 59-12830
1. Art—Collectors and collecting. I. Title.

Art dealers.

GIMPEL, Rene. 706.50924
Diary of an art dealer. Translated from the French by John Rosenberg. Introd. by Sir Herbert Read. New York, Farrar, Straus and Giroux [1966] xii, 465 p. illus., ports. 23 cm. [N8660.G5A313] 66-20172
1. Art dealers. 2. Art—Collectors and collecting. I. Title.

Art dealers—France—Correspondence, reminiscences, etc.

KAHNWEILER, Daniel 706'.5 B
Henry, 1884-
My galleries and painters, by Daniel-Henry Kahnweiler, with Francis Cremieux. Translated from the French by Helen Weaver, with an introd. by John Russell. New York, Viking Press [1971] 160 p. illus., ports. 22 cm. (The Documents of

20th-century art) Translation of Mes galeries et mes peintres. "Bibliography, by Bernard Karpel": p. 140-153. [N8660.K3A313 1971] 73-104164 ISBN 0-670-49960-9 8.50
1. Art dealers—France—Correspondence, reminiscences, etc. I. Cremieux, Francis, 1920- II. Title. III. Series.

Art—Dictionaries.

MURRAY, Peter. 703
A dictionary of art and artists / [by] Peter and Linda Murray. 4th ed. Harmondsworth ; New York : Penguin, 1976. 494 p. ; 18 cm. (Penguin reference books) (Open University set book, arts foundation course) [N31.M8 1976] 77-578822 ISBN 0-14-051014-1 pbk. : 3.95
1. Art—Dictionaries. 2. Artists—Biography. I. Murray, Linda, joint author. II. Title. III. Series.

PHAIDON encyclopedia of art and artists. 703 Oxford : Phaidon, 1978. 704 p., [60] p. of plates : ill. (some col.), ports. (some col.) ; 28 cm. "Adapted from the Pall Mall encyclopedia of art." [N31.P48] 77-89312 ISBN 0-7148-1513-6 : 35.00
1. Art—Dictionaries. 2. Artists—Biography. I. Pall Mall encyclopedia of art. Distributed by Dutton, New York Distributed by Dutton, N.Y.

A Visual dictionary of art. 703
[General editor: Ann Hill] Greenwich, Conn., New York Graphic Society [1974] 640 p. illus. (part col.) 27 cm. Bibliography: p. [N33.V56 1974] 73-76181 ISBN 0-8212-0424-6 30.00
1. Art—Dictionaries. 2. Artists Biography—Dictionaries. I. Hill, Ann, ed. BIP

Art, Hungarian.

†PROFESSIONAL 709'.2'2 B
Hungarian artists outside of Hungary / edited by Ernest Gyimesy Kasas and Leslie L. Konnyu ; compiled by Leslie Konnyu. St. Louis : American Hungarian Review, c1977. 264 p. : ill. ; 22 cm. "English version of the Hungarian edition." Bibliography: p. 258-259. [N6820.P76] 77-94982 pbk. : 8.50
1. Art, Hungarian. 2. Art, Modern—20th century—Hungary. 3. Hungarians in foreign countries—Biography. 4. Artists—Hungary—Biography. I. Kasas, Ernest Gy. II. Konnyu, Leslie, 1914-

Art industries and trade, Early American—History.

DYER, Walter Alden, 745.5'0973 1878-1943.
Early American craftsmen. New York, B. Franklin [1971] xv, 387 p. illus., ports. 19 cm. (Burt Franklin research and source works series, 693. American classics in history and social science, 183) Reprint of the 1915 ed. [NK806.D8 1971] 74-154640 ISBN 0-8337-0986-0
1. Art industries and trade, Early American—History. 2. United States—Biography. I. Title. BIP

Art, Modern—20th century—Bio-bibliography.

†CONTEMPORARY artists 709'.2'2 B
/ editors Colin Naylor and Genesis P-Orridge. London : St. James Press ; New York : St. Martin's Press, 1977. 1077 p. : ill. ; 32 cm. [N6490.C6567] 76-54627 ISBN 0-333-22672-0 : 50.00
1. Art, Modern—20th century—Bio-bibliography. I. Naylor, Colin. II. P-Orridge, Genesis, 1950-

Art patrons—England.

GEAR, Josephine. 759.2 B
Masters or servants? : A study of selected English painters and their patrons of the late eighteenth and early nineteenth centuries / Josephine Gear. New York : Garland Pub., 1977. xx, 381, 88 p. : ill. ; 21 cm. (Outstanding dissertations in the fine arts) Originally presented as the author's thesis, New York University, 1976. Bibliography: p. [374]-381. [N5245.G36 1977] 76-23619 ISBN 0-8240-2690-X : 40.00
1. Art patrons—England. 2. Painters—England. 3. Painting—Psychology. 4. Art and society—England. I. Title. II. Series.

GEAR, Josephine. 759.2 B
Masters or servants? : A study of selected English painters and their patrons of the late eighteenth and early nineteenth centuries / Josephine Gear. New York : Garland Pub., 1977. xx, 381, 88 p. : ill. ; 21 cm. (Outstanding dissertations in the fine arts) Originally presented as the author's thesis, New York University, 1976. Bibliography: p. [374]-381. [N5245.G36 1977] 76-23619 ISBN 0-8240-2690-X : 40.00
1. Art patrons—England. 2. Painters—England. 3. Painting—Psychology. 4. Art and society—England. I. Title. II. Series. BIP

Art, Renaissance—Early Renaissance—Italy.

LENGYEL, Alfonz. 709'.45
The Quattrocento; a study of the principles of art and a chronological biography of the Italian 1400's. Dubuque, Iowa, Kendall/Hunt Pub. Co. [1971] xii, 208 p. 23 cm. Bibliography: p. 177-204. [N6915.L4] 79-167841 ISBN 0-8403-0470-6
1. Art, Renaissance—Early Renaissance—Italy. 2. Artists, Italian—Bio-bibliography. I. Title.

Artagnan, Charles de Baatz de Castelmore, styling himself comte d', 1611?-1673.

HALL, Geoffrey Fowler, 923.544 1888-
D'Artagnan, the ultimate musketeer; a biography, by Geoffrey F. Hall and Joan Sanders. Boston, Houghton Mifflin, 1964. xxii, 166 p. geneal. table (on lining papers) port. 21 cm. [DC130.A7H3] 64-17721
1. Artagnan, Charles de Baatz de Castelmore, styling himself comte d', 1611?-1673. I. Sanders, Joan, joint author. II. Title.

Artaud, Antonin, 1896-1948.

ESSLIN, Martin. 841'.9'12
Antonin Artaud / Martin Esslin. New York : Penguin Books, 1977, c1976. 148 p. ; 18 cm. (Penguin modern masters) Includes index. Bibliography: p. [141]-143. [PQ2601.R677Z636 1977] 77-1269 ISBN 0-14-004368-3 pbk. : 2.50
1. Artaud, Antonin, 1896-1948. 2. Authors, French—20th century—Biography. BIP

ESSLIN, Martin. 841'.9'12 B
Artaud / Martin Esslin. Glasgow : Fontana/Collins, 1976. 127 p. ; 18 cm. (Fontana modern masters) [PQ2601.R677Z636 1976b] 77-352447 ISBN 0-00-633831-3 : £0.85
1. Artaud, Antonin, 1896-1948. 2. Authors, French—20th century—Biography. I. Title.

ESSLIN, Martin. 841'.9'12 B
Artaud / Martin Esslin. London : J. Calder, 1976. 127 p. ; 23 cm. Title on spine: Antonin Artaud. Bibliography: p. 125-127. [PQ2601.R677Z636 1976] 77-351571 ISBN 0-7145-3605-9 : £4.95
1. Artaud, Antonin, 1896-1948. 2. Authors, French—20th century—Biography. I. Title.

Artaud, Etienne.

RICKARDS, Colin. 365'.9'882 B
The man from Devil's Island. New York, Stein and Day [1968] 160 p. illus., group port. 22 cm. [HV8947.D4R5] 68-17315
1. Artaud, Etienne. 2. Prisoners—Iles du Salut—Personal narratives. 3. French Guiana—Exiles. I. Title.

Arthur, Chester Alan, Pres. U.S., 1830-1886.

HOWE, George Frederick. 923.173
Chester A. Arthur, a quarter-century of machine New York, F. Ungar Pub. Co. [1957, c1935] xi, 307 p. illus., ports. 24 cm. (American classics) Bibliography: p. 292-295. Bibliographical footnotes. [E692.H67 1957] 57-12324
1. Arthur, Chester Alan, Pres. U.S., 1830-1886. 2. United States—Politics and government—1881-1885.

REEVES, Thomas C., 973.8'4'0924 B 1936-
Gentleman boss: the life of Chester Alan Arthur [by] Thomas C. Reeves. [1st ed.] New York, Knopf; [distributed by Random House] 1975. xvii, 500, xix p. illus. 25 cm. Bibliography: p. [425]-433. [E692.R43 1975] 74-7760 ISBN 0-394-46095-2 15.00
1. Arthur, Chester Alan, Pres. U.S., 1830-1886. I. Title.

Arthur, Chester Alan, Pres. U.S., 1830-1886—Juvenile literature.

†POOLE, Susan D. 973.8'4'0924 B
Chester A. Arthur, the president who reformed / by Susan D. Poole. Reseda, Calif. : M. Bloomfield : distributed by Mojave Books, c1977. ix, 97 p. : port. ; 23 cm. Bibliography: p. 97. A biography of the President known for the honesty and efficiency of his administration during a period of widespread dishonesty in government. [E692.P66] 92 76-40379 ISBN 0-87881-056-0 : 6.95
1. Arthur, Chester Alan, Pres. U.S., 1830-1886—Juvenile literature. 2. Presidents—United States—Biography—Juvenile literature. I. Title.

Arthur, King.

ASHE, Geoffrey. 914.2'03'1
The quest for Arthur's Britain [by] Geoffrey Ashe [and others] New York, Praeger [1968] x, 282 p. illus. (part col.) maps. 26 cm. Bibliography: p. 262-269. [DA140.A74 1968] 68-54498 12.50
1. Arthur, King. I. Title. BIP

BARBER, Richard W. 942.01'4 B
The figure of Arthur [by] Richard Barber. Totowa, N.J., Rowman and Littlefield [1973, c1972] 160 p. map. 23 cm. Bibliography: p. 137-149. [DA152.5.A7B37 1973] 73-6957 ISBN 0-87471-129-0 7.50
1. Arthur, King. I. Title. BIP

BRODEUR, Arthur Gilchrist, 1888- 942.01'4
Arthur, dux bellorum, by Arthur G. Brodeur. [Folcroft, Pa.] Folcroft Library Editions, 1973. p. Reprint of the 1939 ed. published by the University of California Press, Berkeley, which was issued as v. 3, no. 7 of the University of California publications in English. Bibliography: p. [DA152.5.A7B76 1973] 73-16320 5.00
1. Arthur, King. 2. Great Britain—History—Anglo-Saxon period, 449-1066. I. Title. II. Series: California. University. University of California publications in English, v. 3, no. 7. BIP

MARKALE, Jean. 942.01'4
King Arthur, king of kings / Jean Markale ; translated by Christine Hauch. London ; New York : Gordon & Cremonesi, 1977. 242 p. ; 27 cm. Translation of Le roi Arthur et la societe celtique. Includes index. Bibliography: p. [232]-233. [DA152.5.A7M3713] 77-30054 ISBN 0-86033-044-3 : 24.95
1. Arthur, King. 2. Great Britain—Kings and rulers—Biography. 3. Arthurian romances. 4. Civilization, Celtic. I. Title. BIP

SAKLATVALA, Beram. 942.01
Arthur, Roman Britain's last champion. New York, Taplinger Pub. Co. [1967] 221 p. illus., maps, ports. 23 cm. Bibliography: p. 203-207. [DA135.S16 1967b] 67-19281
1. Arthur, King. 2. Great Britain—History—Roman period, 55 B.C.-449 A.D. 3. Great Britain—History—Anglo-Saxon period, 449-1066. I. Title.

Arthur Zua (Bearss)

ARTHUR, Joseph, 1875- 926.22
Broken Hills; the story of Joe Arthur, compuncher and prospector who struck it rich in Nevada [told to] Zua Arthur. [1st ed.] New York, Vantage Press [1958] 220p. illus. 21cm. [CT275.A835A3] 58-2846
1. Arthur Zua (Bearss) I. Title.

Artists.

ATLANTIC brief lives: 700.922 [B] a biographical companion to the arts. Edited by Louis Kronenberger. Assoc. ed.: Emily Morrison Beck. Boston, Little, Brown [1975, c1971] xxii, 900 p. 21 cm. "An Atlantic Monthly Press Book" Includes bibliographical references. [NX90.A73 1975] 73-154960 4.95 (pbk.)
1. Artists—D I. Kronenberger, Louis-1904- ed. II. Title: Brief lives. BIP

CHANCELLOR, 331.7'67'7390922 Valerie E., comp.
Master and artisan in Victorian England. The diary of William Andrews and The autobiography of Joseph Gutteridge. Edited and with an introd. by Valerie E. Chancellor. New York, A. M. Kelley [1969] vii, 238 p. 23 cm. (Documents of social history) The autobiography of Joseph Gutteridge was published in 1893 under title: Lights and shadows in the life of an artisan. [HD8393.A1C52] 69-17619
I. Andrews, William, 1835-1914. The diary of William Andrews. II. Gutteridge, Joseph, 1816-1899. The autobiography of Joseph Gutteridge. Lights and shadows in the life of an artisan. III. Title.

CHANDLER, Anna Curtis. 927
Story-lives of master artists. With 23 reproductions from paintings. 1953 revision. Philadelphia, Lippincott [1953] 255 p. illus. 21 cm. Twenty biographies from the author's Story-lives of master artists, first and second series. Cf. Dust jacket. [N40.C52] 53-5426
1. Artists. I. Title. BIP

FRASNAY, Daniel. 709'.22
The artist's world. Text and photos. by Daniel Frasnay. Pref. by Rene Huyghe. New York, Viking Press [1969] 369 p. illus. (part col.), facsims., ports. 31 cm. (A Studio book) Translation of peintres et sculpteurs, leur monde. [N40.F7613 1969] 69-10630 27.50
1. Artists. I. Title.

KALES, David. 920
Masters of art, by David and Emily Kales. Illustrated by Earl Mayan. New York, Grosset & Dunlap [1967] 128 p. illus., ports. 28 cm. Forty profiles in picture and prose explain the formation and development of the styles of the world's master artists. [N42.K3] AC 67
1. Artists. I. Mayan, Earl, illus. II. Title.

Artists, American.

BIRCHMAN, Willis. 760'.0922
Faces & facts by and about 26 contemporary artists. With an introd. by James Montgomery Flagg & biographies by Willis Birchman. Freeport, N.Y., Books for Libraries Press [1968] 1 v. (unpaged) illus., ports. 24 cm. (Essay index reprint series) Reprint of the 1937 ed. [N6536.B5 1968] 68-25600
1. Artists, American. 2. Caricatures and cartoons—United States. I. Title.

CORTISSOZ, Royal, 1869- 759.13 B 1948.
American artists. New York, Scribner, 1923. Freeport, N.Y., Books for Libraries Press [1970] viii, 363 p. illus. 23 cm. (Essay index reprint series) [N6536.C6 1970] 74-128228
1. Artists, American. 2. Art, American. I. Title. BIP

FREEDGOOD, Lillian. 927
Great artists of America. New York, Crowell [1963] xvii, 253 p. col. plates. 26 cm. "Recommended reading list": p. 237-238. Bibliography: p. 239-245. [N6505.F7] 63-15086
1. Artists, American. I. Title.

LESTER, Charles Edwards, 759.13 B 1815-1890.
The artists of America; a series of biographical sketches of American artists. New York, Kennedy Galleries, 1970. vi, 257 p. ports. 24 cm. (Library of American art) Reprint of the 1846 ed.

Contents.Contents.—Washington Allston.—Henry Inman.—Benjamin West.—Gilbert Charles Stuart.—John Trumbull.—James DeVeaux.—Rembrandt Peale.—Thomas Crawford. [N6536.L6 1970] 68-8689
1. Artists, American. I. Title.

SMITH, Ralph Clifton, 016.709'73
1898-
A biographical index of American artists. Charleston, S.C., Garnier [1967] x, 102 p. 24 cm. "Unabridged and unaltered reproduction of the work originally published ... in 1930." [N6536.S6 1967] 67-30446
1. Artists, American. I. Title. **BIP**

THIEL, Yvonne Greer 927
Artists and people. New York, Philosophical Library [1960, c.1959] vi, 327p. illus. 22cm. 6.00
1. Artists—San Francisco Bay region. 2. Artists— Psychology. I. Title.

TUCKERMAN, Henry Theodore, 709.22
1813-1871.
Book of the artists: American artist life comprising biographical and critical sketches of American artists, preceded by an historical account of the rise & progress of art in America. [2d ed.] New York, J. F. Carr, 1966. 639p. 24cm. First pub. 1867. [N6536.T9] 65-28493 17.50
1. Artists, American. 2. Art, American—Hist. I. Title.

WHO'S who in American art. 927
1962. Ed. by Dorothy B. Gilbert. Pub. under the sponsorship of the Amer. Federation of Arts. New York, Bowker [c] 1962. 761p. 26cm. illus. 36-27014 22.50
1. Artists, American. I. American Federation of Arts.

WHO'S who in American art 709.22
1966 New York Bowker [c.]1966. 600p. 27cm. Biennial. 1936-37--1940-41: irregular 1940-47--1966. Vs. for 1936-37--1940-47 called v. 1-4. Vols. Vols. 1-4 pub. by the Amer. Federation of Arts. Formerly pub. in the American art annual (later American art directory); v.4 issued as pt.2 of v.36 of the annual (NA50.A54) Ed., 1966, Dorothy B. Gilbert [N6536.W5] 36-27014 22.50
1. Artists, American. I. American Federation of Arts.

Artists, American—Biography.

MICHIGAN. State Library, 709'.2'2
Lansing.
Biographical sketches of American artists. Compiled by Helen L. Earle. 5th ed., rev. and enl. Charleston, S.C., Garnier [1972] 370 p. 24 cm. Reprint of the 1924 ed. Bibliography: p. [349]-356. [N6536.M6 1972] 73-155552
1. Artists, American—Biography. I. Earle, Helen L., d. 1925, comp. II. Title.

Artists, American—Correspondence,reminiscences, etc.

CHAMBERLAIN, Samuel, 760'.0924
1895-
Etched in sunlight; fifty years in the graphic arts. [Boston] Boston Public Library, 1968. x, 227 p. illus., facsims., ports. 32 cm. Autobiographical. [N6537.C45A2] 68-29421 20.00
1. Artists, American—Correspondence, reminiscences, etc. I. Title. **BIP**

FORTRESS, Karl E. 709'.22
The preparation of a library of taped interviews with American artists, on problems of professional concern, as resource material for faculty and students of art on the level of higher education [by] Karl E. Fortress. [Washington] U.S. Dept. of Health, Education, and Welfare, Office of Education, Bureau of Research, 1968 [cover 1967] iii, 18 l. 28 cm. Final report, contract no. OEC-1-6-058441-0599, Bureau of Research, U.S. Office of Education. [N6536.F6] 68-66572
1. Artists, American—Correspondence, reminiscences, etc. 2. Art as a profession. 3. Phonotapes. I. Title.

GRUEN, John. 700'.92'2 B
The party's over now; reminiscences of the fifties—New York's artists, writers, musicians, and their friends. New York, Viking Press [1972] 282 p. illus. 22 cm. [NX511.N4G7 1972] 78-170676 ISBN 0-670-54129-X 8.95
1. Artists, American—Correspondence,reminiscences, etc. 2. Artists, American—New York (City) I. Title.

PAVAL, Philip, 1899- 759.13 B
Paval; autobiography of a Hollywood artist. Hollywood, Calif., Gunther Press, 1968. 247 p. illus., ports. 23 cm. [N6537.P3A2] 68-57212 4.95
1. Artists, American—Correspondence, reminiscences, etc.

SIMON, Howard, 1903- 709'.24
Cabin on a ridge. Chicago, Follett [1970] 159 p. illus. 24 cm. Autobiographical. [NC139.S54A2 1970] 69-10267 4.95
1. Artists, American—Correspondence, reminiscences, etc. I. Title.

Artists, American—Dictionaries.

FIELDING, Mantle, 1865- 709'.22
1941.
Dictionary of American painters, engravers, and sculptors. Stratford, Conn., J. Edwards, 1971. vi, 423 p. 24 cm. 1926, 1945, and 1965 editions have title: Dictionary of American painters, sculptors, and engravers. [N6536.F5 1971] 75-31236 15.00
1. Artists, American—Dictionaries. I. Title.

FIELDING, Mantle, 1865- 709.22
1941.
Dictionary of American painters, sculptors, and engravers. With an addendum containing corrections and additional material on the original entries, compiled by James F. Carr. New York, J. F. Carr, 1965. vi, 529 p. 27 cm. 1971 ed. has title: Dictionary of American painters, engravers, and sculptors. Bibliography: p. 528-529. [N6536.F5 1965] 65-27268
1. Artists, American—Dictionaries. I. Carr, James F. II. Title. **BIP**

NEW York Historical 927.5
Society.
Dictionary of artists in America, 1564-1860 by George C. Groce and David H. Wallace New Haven, Yale University Press, 1957. xxvii, 759p. 25cm. Bibliography: p. 713-759. [N6536.M4] 57-6338
1. Artists, American—Dictionaries. I. Groce, George Cuthbert, 1899- II. Wallace, David H. III. Title.

NEW York Historical 927.5
Society.
Dictionary of artists in America, 1564-1860, by George C. Groce and David H. Wallace Dictionary of artists in America fifteen sixty-four eighteen sixty New Haven, Yale University Press, 1957. xxvii, 759p. 25cm. Bibliography: p. 713-759. [N6536.N4] 57-6338
1. Artists, American—Dictionaries. I. Groce, George Outhbert, 1899- II. Wallace, David H. III. Title.

Artists, American—Juvenile literature.

IRWIN, Grace, 1894- 709.22 B
Trail-blazers of American art. Port Washington, N.Y., Kennikat Press [1971, c1930] 228 p. illus., ports. 22 cm. (Essay and general literature index reprint series) Contents.Contents.—Gilbert Stuart.—George Inness.—Winslow Homer.—John Quincy Adams Ward.—James McNeill Whistler.—Edwin Austin Abbey.—Augustus Saint Gaudens.—Joseph Pennell.—Joseph Singer Sargent.—Thomas Nast.—Howard Pyle, and some others. Bibliography: p. 227-228. [N6505.I7 1971] 920 73-122875 ISBN 8-04-613362-
1. Artists, American—Juvenile literature. I. Title.

SMARIDGE, Norah. 700'.922 B
Trailblazers in American arts. Illustrated by Paul Frame. New York, J. Messner [1971] 96 p. illus. 22 cm. Contents.Contents.—Henry Wadsworth Longfellow.—Stephen Foster.—Mark Twain.—Winslow Homer.—Marian Anderson. [NX503.A1S6 1971] 920 72-146487 ISBN 0-671-32397-0 4.50
1. Artists, American—Juvenile literature. I. Frame, Paul, illus. II. Title.

Artists, American—Utah.

KAYSVILLE Art Club. 709.22 B
Pioneers of Utah art. Editors: Elsie S. Heaton, Alice B. Rampton [and] Clover B. Sanders. [Logan, Utah, Educational Printing Service, c1968] xiii, 137 p. ports. 29 cm. [N6530.U8K3] 77-20552
1. Artists, American—Utah. I. Heaton, Elsie S., ed. II. Rampton, Alice B., ed. III. Sanders, Clover B., ed. IV. Title.

Artists—Biography.

KALTENBACH, Gustav 709'.2'2
Emile.
Dictionary of pronunciation of artists' names, with their schools and dates for American readers and students / by G. E. Kaltenbach. 2d ed. Detroit : Gale Research Co., 1976 [i.e.1975] c1938. p. cm. Reprint of the ed. published by the Art Institute of Chicago. [N40.K3 1976] 73-167017 ISBN 0-8103-4190-5 : 9.00
1. Artists—Biography. 2. Names—Pronunciation. 3. Names—Dictionaries. I. Title: Dictionary of pronunciation of artist's names ...

MALLETT, Daniel 709'.2'2 B
Trowbridge, 1862-1944.
Mallett's index of artists, international-biographical : including painters, sculptors, illustrators, engravers, and etchers of the past and present / by Daniel Trowbridge Mallett. Detroit : Gale Research Co., [1975] c1935. p. cm. Reprint of the 1948 ed. published by P. Smith, New York. Bibliography: p. [N40.M3 1975] 79-185365 ISBN 0-8103-4246-4
1. Artists—Biography. I. Title. II. Title: Index of artists, international—biographical.

PERKINS, Michael. 760'.0924
Renie Perkins; the life and work of a young artist who died by her own hand at the age of twenty-five. Text by Michael Perkins. [1st ed.] New York, Croton Press; distributed by Small Publisher's Co., 1969. 57 p. illus., ports. 21 cm. [N6537.P4P4] 70-91411 1.50
I. Perkins, Renie, 1942-1968.

**WHO'S who in art;* 709.22
biographies of leading men and women in the world of art today; artists, designers, craftmen, critics, writers, teachers, collectors and curators, with an appendix of signatures. 13th ed. Havant [Eng.] Art trade Pr. [New York, Intl. Pubns. Serv. 1966, c.1962] xix, 699p. facsims. 20cm. Subtitle varies [N40.W6] 27-14051 15.00
1. Artists—Biog.

WILLARD, Charlotte. 759.06
Famous modern artists; from Cezanne to pop art. New York, Platt & Munk [1971] 119 p. illus. (part col.), ports. 29 cm. "A Chanticleer Press edition." [N40.W64] 72-151241 6.95
1. Artists—Biography. 2. Art, Modern—19th century. 3. Art, Modern—20th century. I. Title.

Artists—Biography—Directories.

HARDMAN, Sammy J. 703
Hardman's Dictionary of artists & estimates. [Atlanta, Ga. : Hardman, 1974] xviii, 258 p. ; 14 cm. Cover title. [N40.H37 1974] 74-189408
1. Artists—Biography—Directories. 2. Art—Prices. I. Title.

Artists—Biography—Indexes.

HAVLICE, Patricia Pate. 709'.2'2
Index to artistic biography. Metuchen, N.J., Scarecrow Press, 1973. 2 v. (viii, 1362 p.) 22 cm. Bibliography: p. v-viii. [N40.H38] 72-6412 ISBN 0-8108-0540-5
1. Artists—Biography—Indexes. I. Title. **BIP**

Artists, British.

ROTHENSTEIN, John 759.2 B
Knewstub Maurice, Sir, 1901-
A pot of paint; the artists of the 1890's, by John K. M. Rothenstein. Freeport, N.Y., Books for Libraries Press [1970] 215 p. 7 illus. 23 cm. (Essay index reprint series) Reprint of the 1929 New York ed. First ed., 1928, has title: The artists of the 1890's. Contents.Contents.—The artist and the industrial world.—Qui nous delivrera des Grecs et des Romains?—Whistler.—Greaves.—Steer.—Sickert.—Conder.—Beardsley.—Ricketts and Shannon.—Rothenstein.—Max. Includes bibliographical references. [N6767.R55 1970] 70-128303 ISBN 8-369-18479-
1. Artists, British. I. Title.

WHITLEY, William Thomas, 709'.22
1858-1942.
Artists and their friends in England, 1700-1799. New York, B. Blom [1968] 2v. illus. 23 cm. Reprint of the 1928 ed. [N6766.W5 1968] 68-56471
1. Artists, British. I. Title. **BIP**

Artists—Canada—Dictionaries.

CREATIVE Canada; 790'.971
a biographical dictionary of twentieth-century creative and performing artists. Compiled by Reference Division, McPherson Library, University of Victoria. [Toronto] Published in association with McPherson Library, University of Victoria, by University of Toronto Press [1971- v. 26 cm. [NX513.A1C7] 71-151387 ISBN 0-8020-3262-1 (v. 1) 15.00 (v. 1)
1. Artists—Canada—Dictionaries. I. British Columbia. University of Victoria. McPherson Library. Reference Division. **BIP**

Artists—Correspondence, reminiscences, etc.

BENTON, Thomas Hart, 759.13 B
1889-
An American in art; a professional and technical autobiography. Lawrence, University Press of Kansas [1969] 197 p. illus. 26 cm. Contents.Contents.—An American in art.—Selected paintings by Thomas Hart Benton (p. [79]-144)—American regionalism; a personal history of the movement. [ND237.B47A28] 69-16060 10.00
1. Artists—Correspondence, reminiscences, etc. I. Title.

BENTON, Thomas Hart, 759.13 B
1889-
An artist in America. 3d [rev. ed.] Columbia, University of Missouri Press [1968] xxii, 369 p. illus. 24 cm. [ND237.B47A3 1968] 68-20096
1. Artists—Correspondence, reminiscences, etc. 2. United States—Description and travel—1920-1940. I. Title. **BIP**

BUONARROTI, Michel Angelo, 927
1475-1564
Letters; 2v. Tr. from the orig. Tuscan, ed., annotated by E. H. Ramsden [Stanford, Calif.] Stanford [c.]1963. 2v. illus., ports., facsims., geneal. tables. 29cm. Contents.v.1. 1496-1534.--v.2. 1537-1563. Bibl. 63-23707 45.00, set, bxd.
1. Artists—Correspondence, reminiscences, etc. I. Ramsden, E. H., ed. II. Title.

CHASE, Joseph Cummings, 927.5
1878-
My friends look better than ever. [1st ed.] New York, Longmans, Green [1950] xv, 300 p. ports. 22 cm. [ND237.C47A49] 50-10901
1. Artists—Correspondence, reminiscences, etc. I. Title.

DAVIDSON, Jo, 1883- 927.3
Between sittings, an informal autobiography. New York, Dial Press, 1951. 369 p. illus. 24 cm. [NB237.D3A2] 51-14393
1. Artists—Correspondence, reminiscences, etc. I. Title.

EPSTEIN, Jacob, 1880- 927.3
Epstein, an autobiography. [Rev. and extended ed.] New York, Dutton [1955] x, 294 p. plates, ports. 24 cm. First published

in 1940 under title: Let there be sculpture. [NB497] 55-4439
1. Artists—Correspondence, reminiscences, etc. 2. Sculpture. I. Title.

FRIEDENTHAL, Richard, 1896- ed. 927
Letters of the great artists [2v.] New York, Random [c.1963] 2v.(287;287p.) illus. (pt. col.) ports. (pt. col.) facsims. 24cm. Contents.1. From Ghiberti to Gainsborough--2. From Blake to Pollock. 15.00; pre-Christmas, 12.95, bxd.
1. Artists—Correspondence, reminiscences, etc. I. Title.

GOGH, Vincent van, 1835-1890. 759.9492
Van Gogh: a self-portrait; letters revealing his life as a painter(selected by W. H. Auden. New York, Dutton, 1963. 398p. illus. 21cm. (Dutton paperback D116) 2.75 pap.,
1. Artist—Correspondence, reminiscences, etc. I. Auden, Wystan Hugh, 1907- II. Title.

GOGH, Vincent van, 1853-1890. v. 12
Van Gogh: a self-portrait; letters revealing his life as a painter, selected by W. H. Auden. New York, E. P. Dutton, 1963. 652 p. illus. (A Dutton paperback D-116) "Newly translated...by Cornelius de Dood and Mrs. J. van Gogh-Bonger." 64-23987
1. Artist — Correspondence, reminiscences, etc. I. Auden, Wystan Hugh, 1907- II. Title.

GREENOUGH, Horatio, 1805-1852. 927.3
The travels, observations, and experience of a Yankee stonecutter (1852) A facsimile reproduction with an introd. by Nathalia Wright. Gainesville, Fla., Scholars' Facsimiles & Reprints, 1958. xvi p., facsim.: 222p. illus. 23cm. 'Reproduced from a copy in the Library of Congress.' [NB237.G8A3 1958] 58-5421
1. Artists— Correspondence, reminiscences, etc. I. Title.

HARVEY, Eli, 1860- 730.924
The autobiography of Eli Harvey, Quaker sculptor from Ohio. Edited by Dorothy Z. Bicker, Jane Z. Vail [and] Vernon G. Wills. Wilmington, Ohio, Clinton County Historical Society [1966] 100 p. illus., ports. 24 cm. [NB237.H34A2] 66-26139
1. Artists—Correspondence, reminiscences, etc. I. Title.

JACKSON, Thomas Graham, Sir bart., 1835-1924. 927.2
Recollections. Arranged and edited by Basil H. Jackson. London, New York, Oxford University Press, 1950. xiv, 283 p. illus., ports. 22 cm. [NA997.J3A3] 50-10153
1. Artists—Correspondence, reminiscences, etc. I. Title.

JACOBS, Michel, 1877- 759.13
Epigramus of an ignoramus; the life of Michel Jacobs by himself. [1st ed. Rumson, N. J., Primatic Art Co., c1953] 241p. illus. 22cm. [ND237.J2A3] 927.5 53-10883
1. Artists—Correspondence, reminiscences, etc. I. Title.

KENT, Rockwell, 1882- 927
It's me, O Lord; the autobiography of Rockwell Kent. New York, Dodd, Mead [1955] x, 617 p. illus. (part col.) 25 cm. [NC139.K4A3] 55-6470
1. Artists—Correspondence, reminiscences, etc. I. Title. **BIP**

KIESLER, Frederick. 720.924
Inside the endless house; art, people, and architecture: a journal. New York, Simon and Schuster [1966] 573 p. illus. 27 cm. [NA737.K5A3] 64-18655
1. Artists — Correspondence, reminiscences, etc. I. Title.

KIESLER, Frederick. 720.924
Inside the endless house; art, people, and architecture: a journal. New York, Simon and Schuster [1966] 573 p. illus. 27 cm. [NA737.K5A3] 65-18655
1. Artists—Correspondence, reminiscences, etc. I. Title.

KLEE, Paul, 1879-1940 927.5
The diaries of Paul Klee. 1898-1918. Ed., introd., by Felix Klee. Berkeley, Univ. of Calif. Pr., 1964. xx, 424p. illus., facsims., ports. 25cm. First complete English-language version based upon the text of the German hardcover ed., pub. in 1957. 64-20693 10.00
1. Artists—Correspondence, reminiscences, etc. I. Klee, Felix, 1907- ed. II. Title.

KLEE, Paul, 1879-1940 927.5
The diaries of Paul Klee, 1898-1918. Ed., introd., by Felix Klee. Berkeley, Univ. of Calif. Pr., 1968. [c.1964] xx, 434p. illus., facsims., ports. 25cm. (Cal 158) First complete English-language version based upon the text of the German hardcover ed., pub. in 1957. [ND588.K5A252] 64-20993 3.45 pap.,
1. Artists—Correspondence, reminiscences, etc. I. Klee, Felix, 1907- ed. II. Title.

KLEE, Paul, 1879-1940. 709'.494
The diaries of Paul Klee, 1898-1918. Edited, with an introd. by Felix Klee. Berkeley, University of California Press, 1968 [c1964] xx, 434 p. illus. 21 cm. "First California paper-bound printing." Translation of Tagebucher. [ND588.K5A252 1968] 68-6958 3.45
1. Artists Correspondence, reminiscences, etc. I. Klee, Felix, 1907- ed. **BIP**

KLEE, Paul, 1879-1940. 927.5
The diaries of Paul Klee, 1898-1918. Edited, with an introd., by Felix Klee. Berkeley, University of California Press, 1964. xx, 424 p. illus., facsims., ports. 25 cm. "First complete English-language version ... based upon the text of the German hardcover edition, published ... in 1957." [ND588.K5A252] 64-20993
1. Artists — Correspondence, reminiscences, etc. I. Klee, Felix, 1907- ed. II. Title.

KOLLWITZ, Kathe (Schmidt) 1867-1945. 927.4
Diary and letters edited by Hans Kollwitz. translated by Richard and Clara Winston Chicago, H. Regnery Co., 1955. vi, 200p. illus., 48plates. 26cm. [NC251.K6A312] 55-9336
1. Artists—Correspondence, reminiscences, etc. I. Title.

MORISOT, Berthe, 1841-1895. 927.5
The correspondence of Berthe Morisot with her family and her friends: Manet, Puvis de Chavannes, Degas, Monet, Renoir, and Mallarme. Compiled and edited by Denis Rouart; translated by Betty W. Hubbard. [1st ed.] New York, G. Wittenborn [1957] 187 p. illus. (part mounted, part col.) facsims. 29 cm. [ND553.M88A313] 759.4 57-9529
1. Artists—Correspondence, reminiscences, etc.

MORISOT, Berthe, 1841-1895. 759.4
The correspondence of Berthe Morisot with her family and her friends: Manet, Puvis de Chavannes, Degas, Monet, Renoir, and Mallarme. Compiled and edited by Denis Rouart; translated by Betty W. Hubbard. [1st ed.] New York, G. Wittenborn [1957] 187p. illus. (part mounted, part col.) facsims. 29cm. [ND553.M88A313] 927.5 57-9529
1. Artists—Correspondence, reminiscences, etc. I. Title.

MOSES, Anna Mary (Robertson) 1860-1961. 927.5
Grandma Moses: my life's history. Edited by Otto Kallir. [1st ed. New York] Harper [1952] xi, 140 p. plates (part col.) ports., facsims. 25 cm. [ND237.M78A22] 51-11940
1. Artists—Correspondence, reminiscences, etc.

NEUHAUS, Eugen, 1879-1963. 927.5
Drawn from memory, a self portrait. Palo Alto, Calif., Pacific Books [1964] 208 p. illus., ports. 22 cm. [ND237.N45A2] 64-23486
1. Artists — Correspondence, reminiscences, etc. I. Title. **BIP**

NEUHAUS, Eugen, 1879-1963 927.5
Drawn from memory, a self portrait. Palo Alto, Calif., Pacific [c.1964] 208p. illus., ports. 22cm. 64-23486 4.95
1. Artists—Correspondence, reminiscences, etc. I. Title.

OROZCO, Jose Clemente, 1883-1949. 927.5
An autobiography. Translated by Robert C. Stephenson. Introd. by John Palmer Leeper. Austin, University of Texas Press [1962] 171 p. illus. 21 cm. (The Texas Pan-American series) [ND259.O7A213] 62-9790
1. Artists—Correspondence, reminiscences, etc.

SPRATLING, William Philip, 1900-1967. 709'.73
File on Spratling; an autobiography. With drawings by the author. Introd. by Budd Schulberg. [1st ed.] Boston, Little, Brown [1967] xiv, 235 p. illus., ports. (1 col.) 20 cm. [N6537.S65A2] 67-21097
1. Artists—Correspondence, reminiscences, etc. I. Title.

VOROBEV, Marevna, 1892- 927.5
Life in two worlds. Tr. by Benet Nash. Pref. by Ossip Zadkine. NewYork, Abelard [c.1962] 309p. illus. 23cm. 62-11783 5.00
1. Artists Correspondence, reminiscences, etc. I. Title.

VOROBEV, Marevna, 1892- 927.5
Life in two worlds. Translated by Benst Nash. With a pref. by Ossip Zadkine. Londeon, New York, Abelard-Schuman [1962] 309 p. illus. 23 cm. Autobiography. []nD553.V67A23 1962] 62-11783
1. Artists — Correspondence, reminiscences, etc. I. Title.

WAUGH, Alfred S d.1856. 927
Travels in search of the elephant; the wanderings of Alfred S. Waugh, artist, in Louisiana, Missouri, and Santa Fe, in 1845-1846. Edited and annotated by John Francis McDermott. St. Louis, Missouri Historical Society, 1951. xxi, 153 p. 24 cm. Bibliography: p. [145]-148. [N6537.W3A3] 51-13469
1. Artists — Correspondence, reminiscences, etc. 2. U.S. — Descr. & trav. — 1783-1848. I. McDermott, John Francis, 1902- ed. II. Missouri Historical Society, St. Louis. III. Title.

ZORACH, William, 1887-1966. 730'.924
Art is my life; the autobiography of William Zorach. Cleveland, World Pub. Co. [1967] ix, 205 p. illus., ports. 26 cm. [NB237.Z6A2] 67-12900
1. Artists—Correspondence, reminiscences, etc. 2. Art—United States. I. Title.

Artists—Dictionaries.

FIELDING, Mantle 927
Dictionary of American painters, sculptors and engravers from Colonial times through 1926. Flushing, N.Y., Paul A. Stroock. [155-06 Sanford Ave., Flushing 55, L. I., N.Y.] 1900 [c.1945] 433p. ports., illus., [This ed. limited to 400 copies] Bibl.: p.424-433 27cm. 25.00
1. Artists-Dictionaries. 2. Artists, American. I. Title.

WATERS, Clara (Erskine) Clement, 1834-1916. 709.22 B
Artists of the nineteenth century and their works [by] Clara Erskine Clement Waters and Laurence Hutton. [7th ed., rev.] New York, Arno Press, 1969 [c1884] 2 v. in 1. 23 cm. Bibliography: v. 1, p. [ix]-x. [N40.W28 1969] 70-88820
1. Artists—Dictionaries. I. Hutton, Laurence, 1843-1904, joint author. II. Title.

Artists, European.

BOLTON, Sarah Knowles, 1841-1916. 709'.22
Famous European artists. Freeport, N.Y., Books for Libraries Press [1972] 423 p. ports. 23 cm. (Essay index reprint series) Reprint of the 1890 ed. Contents.Contents.—Michael Angelo.—Leonardo da Vinci.—Raphael of Urbino.—Titian.—Murillo.—Rubens.—Rembrandt.—Sir Joshua Reynolds.—Sir Edwin Landseer.—Turner. [N40.B64 1972] 74-39676 ISBN 0-8369-2750-8
1. Artists, European. I. Title. **BIP**

SHERWOOD, Ruth, 1890- 927.3
Carving his own destiny; the story of Albin Polasek. Chicago, R. F. Seymour [1954] 466p. illus. 25cm. [NB237.P6S45] 55-18870
I. Polasek, Albin, 1879- II. Title.

Artists—Great Britain—Biography.

JOHNSON, Jane. 709'.2'2 B
The dictionary of British artists, 1880-1940 : an Antique Collectors' Club research project listing 41,000 artists / compiled by J. Johnson and A. Greutzner. [Suffolk, Eng.] : Antique Collectors' Club, c1976. 567 p. ; 29 cm. Bibliography: p. 6. [N6767.J63] 77-357303 ISBN 0-902028-36-7 : £17.50
1. Artists—Great Britain—Biography. 2. Art, Modern—19th century—Great Britain. 3. Art, Modern—20th century—Great Britain. I. Greutzner, A., joint author. II. Antique Collectors' Club. III. Title.

Artists, Italian.

*STONE, Irving, ed. 927
Michelangelo, sculptor; an autobiography through letters. Ed. by Irving and Jean Stone. New York, New Amer. Lib. [1964, c.1962] 256p. ports. 18cm. (Signet T2462) .75. pap.,
I. Title.

TAMARIN, Alfred H. 730'.924 B
The autobiography of Benvenuto Cellini, edited by Alfred Tamarin. Abridged and adapted from the translation by John Addington Symonds. [New York] Macmillan [1969] x, 164 p. illus. 26 cm. [NB623.C3S45 1969] 69-11591
I. Symonds, John Addington, 1840-1893, tr. II. Cellini, Benvenuto, 1500-1571. The autobiography.

VASARI, Giorgio, 1511-1574. 759.5 B
Lives of the most eminent painters. Selected, edited, and introduced by Marilyn Aronberg Lavin. [Translated by Mrs. Jonathan Foster] Verona, Printed for the members of the Limited Editions Club at the Stamperia Valdonega, 1966. 2 v. illus. (part col.), ports. 30 cm. Translations from Le vite de' piu eccellenti pittori, scultori, et architettori. [N6922.V473] 72-185270
1. Artists, Italian. 2. Art, Italian—History. I. Lavin, Marilyn Aronberg, ed. II. Foster, Jonathan, Mrs., tr. III. Limited Editions Club, inc., New York. IV. Title.

VASARI, Giorgio, 1511-1574 927
The lives of the painters, sculptors, and architects; 4v. Ed., introd. by William Gaunt. [Tr. from Italian by A. B. Hinds, newly rev.] London, Dent; New York, Dutton [c.1963] 4v. (various p.) ports. 19cm. (Everyman's lib., no. 784-787) Bibl. 63-5456 1.95 ea.
1. Artists, Italian. 2. Art—Italy—Hist. I. Title.

Artists—Italy—Biography.

VASARI, Giorgio, 1511-1574. 709'.2'2 B
Artists of the Renaissance / Vasari ; translated by George Bull. New York : Viking Press, 1979. p. cm. Translation of parts of Le vite de' piu eccellenti pittori, scultori e architetti. This translation by G. Bull was first published in 1965 under title: The lives of the artists. [N6922.V2213 1979] 78-12467 ISBN 0-670-43445-0 : 17.95
1. Artists—Italy—Biography. 2. Art, Italian. I. Bull, George Anthony. II. Title. **BIP**

VASARI, Giorgio, 1511-1574. 709'.2'2 B
Lives of the most eminent painters, sculptors & architects / by Giorgio Vasari ; newly translated by Gaston du C. de Vere. With five hundred ill. New York : AMS Press, [1976] p. cm. Translation of Le vite de' piu eccellenti pittori. Reprint of the 1912-15 ed. published by Macmillan and the Medici Society, London. Includes indexes. [N6922.V213 1976] 71-153610 ISBN 0-404-09730-8 lib.bdg. : 425.00(set) 42.50 ea.
1. Artists—Italy—Biography. 2. Art, Italian—History. I. De Vere, Gaston du C. II. Title. BIP

Artists—Japan—Biography.

ROBERTS, Laurance P. 709'.2'2 B
A dictionary of Japanese artists : painting, sculpture, ceramics, prints, lacquer / Laurance P. Roberts ; with a foreword by John M. Rosenfield. 1st ed. Tokyo ; New York : Weatherhill, 1976. xi, 299 p. ; 27 cm. Title on spine: Japanese artists. Includes indexes. Bibliography: p. 223-232. [N7358.R6] 76-885 ISBN 0-8348-0113-2 : 22.50
1. Artists—Japan—Biography. I. Title. BIP

Artists' marks—Directories.

CAPLAN, H. H. 760'.092'2
The classified directory of artists signatures, symbols & monograms / [compiled by] H. H. Caplan. London : Prior, 1976. [5], viii, 738 [i.e. 744] p. : chiefly facsims. ; 31 cm. English text; English, French, German, Spanish, and Italian introd. [N45.C36] 77-356200 ISBN 0-86043-004-9 : £29.50
1. Artists' marks—Directories. 2. Monograms—Directories. I. Title. BIP

Artists—Michigan—Biography.

GIBSON, Arthur Hopkin. 709'.2'2 B
Artists of early Michigan : a biographical dictionary of artists native to or active in Michigan, 1701-1900 / compiled by Arthur Hopkin Gibson ; research assistants, Beverly Bassett and Jean Spang. Detroit : Wayne State University Press, 1975. 249 p. : ill. ; 24 cm. Bibliography: p. 19-31. [N6530.M5G52] 74-32480 ISBN 0-8143-1528-3 : 9.95
1. Artists—Michigan—Biography. I. Bassett, Beverly. II. Spang, Jean. III. Title. BIP

Artists—New England—Biography.

ROBINSON, Frank Torrey, 1845-1898. 759.14 B
Living New England artists / Frank T. Robinson. New York : Garland Pub., 1977 [c1888] 200 p., 27 leaves of plates : ill. ; 24 cm. (The Art experience in late nineteenth-century America) Reprint of the ed. published by S. E. Cassino, Boston. [N6515.R6 1977] 75-28880 ISBN 0-8240-2238-6 lib.bdg. : 30.00
1. Artists—New England—Biography. 2. Art, American—New England. 3. Art, Modern—19th century—New England. I. Title. II. Title: New England artists. III. Series.

Artists—Northumberland, Eng.—Biography—Dictionaries.

HALL, Marshall. 760'.092'2 B
The artists of Northumbria: a dictionary of Northumberland and Durham painters, draughtsmen and engravers, born 1647-1900. Newcastle upon Tyne, Marshall Hall Associates, 1973. 72, 32 p. illus., ports. (on lining papers) 29 cm. (Artists of the regions series [1]) Bibliography: p. 72. [N6769.N79H34] 73-178417 ISBN 0-903858-00-2 £3.00
1. Artists—Northumberland, Eng.—Biography—Dictionaries. 2. Artists—Durham, Eng. (County)—Biography—Dictionaries. I. Title.

Artists—United States—Biography.

CUMMINGS, Paul. 709'.22
Dictionary of contemporary American artists / Paul Cummings. 3d ed. New York : St. Martin's Press, 1976. p. cm. Includes index. Bibliography: p. [N6536.C8 1976] 76-10548 35.00
1. Artists—United States—Biography. I. Title. BIP

DAWDY, Doris Ostrander. 709'.2'2
Artists of the American West : a biographical dictionary / Doris Ostrander Dawdy. 1st ed. Chicago : Sage Books, [1974] viii, 275 p. ; 24 cm. Bibliography: p. 261-275. [N6536.D38] 72-91919 ISBN 0-8040-0607-5 : 12.50
1. Artists—United States—Biography. 2. Artists—Biography. 3. The West in art. I. Title. BIP

KIMBROUGH, Sara Dodge. 709'.2'2 B
Drawn from life : the story of four American artists whose friendship & work began in Paris during the 1880s / by Sara Dodge Kimbrough. Jackson : University Press of Mississippi, 1976. 177 p., [16] leaves of plates : ill. ; 24 cm. Includes index. [N6536.K55] 76-5682 ISBN 0-87805-073-6 : 12.00
1. Artists—United States—Biography. 2. Artists—Paris—Biography. 3. Art, Modern—19th century—Paris. 4. Art—Paris. I. Title.

SCHWAB, Arnold T. 709'.2'2 B
A matter of life and death : vital biographical facts about selected American artists / Arnold T. Schwab in cooperation with the Art Libraries Society of North America. New York : Garland Pub., 1977. p. cm. (Garland reference library of the humanities ; v. 90) Includes bibliographical references. [N6536.S35] 76-52694 ISBN 0-8240-9883-8 lib.bdg. : 9.50
1. Artists—United States—Biography. I. Arlis/North America. II. Title. BIP

WHO was who in American history, arts and letters. 700.922B
76 bicentennial ed. Chicago : Marquis Who's Who, c1975. xiii, 604 p. ; 27 cm. [NX503.Z8W48] 75-29617 47.50
1. Artists—United States—Biography. 2. Arts, American. I. Marquis-Who's Who, inc.

Artists—United States—Biography—Dictionaries.

FIELDING, Mantle, 1865-1941. 709'.2'2
Dictionary of American painters, sculptors and engravers / by Mantle Fielding. Enl. ed. with over 2,500 new listings of seventeenth, eighteenth, and nineteenth century American artists / edited by Genevieve C. Doran. Greens Farms, Conn. : Modern Books and Crafts, [1974] vi, 455 p. ; 24 cm. Edition of 1971 published under title: Dictionary of American painters, engravers, and sculptors. [N6536.F5 1974] 74-192539 17.50
1. Artists—United States—Biography—Dictionaries. I. Doran, Genevieve C., ed. II. Title.

Artists—United States—Biography—Indexes.

SMITH, Ralph Clifton, 1898- 709'.2'2 B
A biographical index of American artists / by Ralph Clifton Smith. Detroit : Gale Research Co., [1975] c1930. p. cm. Reprint of the ed. published by Williams & Wilkins, Baltimore. [N6536.S6 1975] 79-167186 ISBN 0-8103-4251-0 : 11.00 11.00
1. Artists—United States—Biography—Indexes. I. Title.

Artists—United States—Biography—Juvenile literature.

SIGNIFICANT American artists and architects. 709'.2'2 B
Chicago : Childrens Press, [1976] p. cm. Includes index. Brief biographies of 166 American artists and architects arranged alphabetically within broad chronological periods of American history. [N6536.S48] 920 75-20688 ISBN 0-516-05303-5 lib. bdg. : 9.25
1. Artists—United States—Biography—Juvenile literature. 2. Architects—United States—Biography—Juvenile literature. I. Title: Artists and architects.

Artists—United States—Interviews.

CUMMINGS, Paul. 709'.2'2 B
Artists in their own words / Paul Cummings. New York : St. Martin's Press, [1979] p. cm. [N6512.C85] 79-16474 ISBN 0-312-05512-9 : 12.95
1. Artists—United States—Interviews. 2. Artists—United States—Biography. 3. Art, Modern—20th century—United States. I. Title. BIP

Artley, Bob.

ARTLEY, Bob. 977.7'03
Memories of a former kid / by Bob Artley ; edited by Floyd Egner. Ames : Iowa State University Press, c1978, 1979 printing. 96 p. : ill. ; 28 cm. [F621.A77] 79-1908 ISBN 0-8138-1070-1 pbk. : 6.95
1. Artley, Bob. 2. Iowa—Social life and customs. 3. Farm life—Iowa. 4. Iowa—Biography. I. Egner, Floyd. II. Title. BIP

Arts, American.

FRYM, Gloria. 700'.92'2 B
Second stories : women artists whose careers began after thirty-five / by Gloria Frym ; photographic ports. by Debra Heimerdinger. San Francisco : Chronicle Books, c1979. p. cm. Contents.Contents.—Helane Aylon, painter.—Beatrice Berlin, printmaker.—Bella Feldman, sculptor.—Bobbie Louise Hawkins, writer.—Cherry Jackson, playwright.—Frances Jaffer, poet.—Eleanor Lawrence, photographer.—Malvina Reynolds, singer and songwriter.—Terry Sendgraff, dancer. [N504.F79] 79-9390 ISBN 0-87701-152-4 : 8.95
1. Arts, American. 2. Arts, Modern—20th century—United States. 3. Women artists—United States—Biography. I. Title.

Arts, Australian.

THOMAS, Laurie. 709'.94
The most noble art of them all : the selected writings of Laurie Thomas / introduced by Charles Blackman, John Olsen. St. Lucia, Australia : University of Queensland Press ; Hemel Hempstead, Eng. : distributed by Prentice-Hall International, 1977,c1976. vi, 321 p. ; 25 cm. [NX590.A1T48] 77-368356 ISBN 0-7022-1370-5 : 15.75
1. Arts, Australian. 2. Artists—Australia—Biography. I. Title.
Distributed by Technical Impex.

Arundale. George Sydney. 1878-1945.

ARUNDALE, George Sydney, 1878-1945. 212.5
Personal memories of G. S. Arundale, third President of the Theosophical Society. by some of his numerous friends and admirers; [ed. by Herbert Staggs, Catharine Mayes]. London, Wheaton, Ill., Theosophical Pub. House. 1967. xiv, 152p. 12 plates (ports.). 23cm. [BP585.A7P.4] (B) 67-93908 5.00
1. Arundale. George Sydney. 1878-1945. I. Title.

Arup, Jens.

HEIN, Piet, 1905- 839.817
Grooks [by] Piet Hein with Jens Arup. [1st English lang. ed.] Cambridge, Mass., M.I.T. Pr. [1967,c.1966] 53p. illus. 16cm. [PT8175.H365G69] 67-13578 1.50 pap.,
1. Arup, Jens. I. Title.

Arwin, Charles Robert,

ARWIN, Charles Robert, 1809-1882 925.9
Autobiography. Ed. by Sir Francis Darwin. With his notes and letters depicting the growth of The origin of species. Introd. essay, 'The meaning of Darwin,' by George Gaylord Simpson. New York, Collier Bks. [1962, c.1950] 254p. (AS94; men of sci. lib.) .95 pap.,
I. Title.

Asa, Katie Maude (Dayton)

ASA, Katie Maude (Dayton) 1880- 001.2
My life's story. Los Angeles, 1960. 125p. illus. 23cm. On cover: Our family. [CT275.A8355A3] 61-21311
I. Title.

Asaf Jah I, Nizam of Hyderabad, 1671-1748.

KHAN, Yusuf Husain. 923.15484
The first Nizam; the life and times of Nizamu'l-Mulk Asaf Jah I. [1st U.S. ed.] New York, Asia Pub. House [1963] viii, 267 p. 22 cm. "First published under the title Nizamu'l-Mulk Asaf Jah I, 1936." Bibliography: p. [251]-253. [DS461.9.N6K5 1963] 64-3476
1. Asaf Jah I, Nizam of Hyderabad, 1671-1748. 2. Hyderabad, India (State) — Hist. 3. Mogul Empire — Hist. I. Title.

Asawa, Ruth.

SAN Francisco. Museum of Art. 730'.92'4
Ruth Asawa : a retrospective view ; [exhibition] organized by the San Francisco Museum of Art, June 29 - August 19, 1973. [San Francisco] : San Francisco Museum of Art, c1973. [28] p. : ill. ; 26 cm. Text by Gerald Nordland. Bibliography: p. [26] [NB237.A82S36 1973] 75-314491
1. Asawa, Ruth. I. Asawa, Ruth. II. Nordland, Gerald. III. Title.

Asbury, Francis, Bp., 1745-1816.

ASBURY, Francis, Bp., 1745-1816. 922.773
Journal and letters. Elmer E. Clark, editor-in-chief, J. Manning Potts [and] Jacob S. Payton. London, Epworth Press; Nashville, Abingdon Press [1958] 3v. illus., ports., maps, facsims. 24cm. Vol. 3: J. M. Potts, editor-in-chief, E. T. Clark, and J. S. Payton. Issued in a case. Contents.v. 1. The journal, 1771 to 1793.--v. 2. The journal, 1794 to 1816.--v.3. The letters. Bibliography: v. 2, p. [809]-815. Bibliographical footnotes. [BX8495.A8A25] 58-4674
I. Title.

COLLINS, John Smiley, 1924- 287'.1'0924 B
Man of devotion, Francis Asbury, by J. Smiley Collins. [Nashville] Upper Room [1971] 86 p. 21 cm. Includes bibliographical references. [BX8495.A8C64] 70-155494
1. Asbury, Francis, Bp., 1745-1816. I. Title.

NYGAARD, Norman Eugene, 1897- 922.773
Bishop on horseback, the story of Francis Asbury. Grand Rapids, Zondervan Pub. House [1962] 183 p. 22 cm. [BX8495.A8N9] 62-52861
1. Asbury, Francis, Bp., 1745-1816. I. Title.

RUDOLPH, L. 287.10924(B)
Francis Asbury [by] L. C. Rudolph. Nashville, Abingdon Press [1966] 240 p. ports. 23 cm. Bibliography: p. 227-234. [BX8495.A8R8] 66-21970
1. Asbury, Francis, Bp., 1745-1816. I. Title.

RUDOLPH, L. C. 287.10924
Francis Asbury [by] L. C. Rudolph. Nashville, Abingdon [1966] 240p. ports 23cm. Bibl. [BX8495.A8R8] 66-21970 5.00
1. Asbury, Francis, Bp., 1745-1816. I. Title.

Ascham, Roger, 1515-1568.

RYAN, Lawrence V. 928.2
Roger Ascham. Stanford, Calif., Stanford University Press, 1963. 352 p. 24 cm. [LB475.A7R9] 63-10735
1. Ascham, Roger, 1515-1568. BIP

Asclepiades Bithynus.

ASCLEPIADES BITHYNUS. 926.1
Asclepiades, a translation of Cocchi's Life of Asclepiades and Gumpert's Fragments of Asclepiades, by Robert Montraville Green. New Haven, E. Licht, 1955. ix, 167p. 24cm. Bibliographical footnotes. [R126.A72A52] 55-14987
1. Cocchi, Antonio, 1693-1738. Life of Asclepiades. II. Gumpert, Christian Gottlieb, 1772-1832, ed. III. Green, Robert Montraville, 1880-1935, tr. IV. Title.

Ashburn, Richie.

ARCHIBALD, Joseph, 1898- 927.96357
The Richie Ashburn story. New York, J. Messner [1960] 192p. illus. 22cm. [GV865.A79A7] 60-12454
1. Ashburn, Richie. I. Title.

Ashby, Turner, 1828-1862.

CUNNINGHAM, Frank, 1911- 923.573
Knight of the Confederacy, Gen. Turner Ashby. San Antonio, Naylor [1960] 225 p. illus. 22 cm. Includes bibliography. [E467.1.A8C8] 60-14904
1. Ashby, Turner, 1828-1862. I. Title.

Ashe, Arthur.

ASHE, Arthur. 796.34'2'0924 B
Arthur Ashe, portrait in motion / Arthur Ashe, with Frank Deford. Boston : Houghton Mifflin, 1975. xii, 272 p., [8] leaves of plates : ill. ; 24 cm. [GV994.A7A32] 74-34465 ISBN 0-395-20429-1 : 8.95
1. Ashe, Arthur. 2. Tennis. I. Deford, Frank, joint author. II. Title.

ASHE, Arthur 796.34'2'0924
Arthur Ashe, portrait in motion. [by] Arthur Ashe, with Frank Deford. New York, Ballantine [1976 c1975] 304 p., 8 leaves of plates illus. 18 cm. [GV994.A7A32] 1.95 (pbk.)
1. Ashe, Arthur. 2. Tennis. I. Deford, Frank, joint author. II. Title.
L.C. card no. of 1975 Houghton Mifflin edition: 74-34465.

ROBINSON, Louie. 796.34'2'0924
Arthur Ashe, tennis champion. New York, Washington Square Press [1969] 135 p. illus., ports. 18 cm. (An Archway paperback) Reprint of the 1967 ed. [GV994.A7R6 1969] 76-7133 0.60
1. Ashe, Arthur. 2. Negro athletes. BIP

ROBINSON, Louie. 796.34'2'0924
Arthur Ashe, tennis champion. [1st ed.] Garden City, N.Y., Doubleday [1967] 136 p. ports. 22 cm. (Doubleday signal books) [GV994.A7R6] 67-1917
1. Ashe, Arthur. 2. Negro athletes.

ROBINSON, Louie. 796.34'2'0924 B
Arthur Ashe, tennis champion. Garden City, N.Y. Doubleday [1970, c1967] 144 p. ports. 22 cm. (Doubleday signal books) [GV994.A7R6 1970] 79-10387 3.50
1. Ashe, Arthur. 2. Negro athletes.

ROBINSON, Louie. 92
Arthur Ashe, tennis champion. [1st ed.] Garden City, N.Y., Doubleday [1967] 136 p. ports. 22 cm. (Doubleday signal books) A biography of the Virginia Negro who smashed his tennis ball across the color line to become the second ranked men's singles player in the United States at age twenty-three. [GV994.A7R6] AC 67
1. Ashe, Arthur. I. Title. BIP

Ashe, Arthur—Juvenile literature.

JACOBS, Linda. 796.34'2'0924 B
Arthur Ashe : alone in the crowd / by Linda Jacobs. St. Paul, Minn. : EMC Corp., 1976. 38 p. : ill. ; 23 cm. (Black American athletes) A biography of the first black man to win at Wimbledon. [GV994.A7J32] 92 76-15 ISBN 0-88436-263-9 lib.bdg. : 4.95 ISBN 0-88436-264-7 pbk. :
1. Ashe, Arthur—Juvenile literature. 2. Tennis—Juvenile literature. I. Title. II. Series. BIP

MORSE, Charles. 796.34'2'0924 B
Arthur Ashe, by Charles and Ann Morse. Illustrated by Harold Henriksen. Mankato, Minn., Amecus Street; [distributed by Childrens Press, Chicago, 1974] 31 p. col. illus. 25 cm. (Superstars) Brief biography concentrating on the career of the Black tennis star. [GV994.A7M67] 92 74-954 ISBN 0-87191-340-2 4.95 (lib. bdg.)
1. Ashe, Arthur—Juvenile literature. I. Morse, Ann, joint author. II. Henricksen, Harold, illus. III. Title. BIP

Ashlee, Ted, 1914-

ASHLEE, Ted, 1914- 971.1'33 B
Gabby, Ernie and me : a Vancouver boyhood / Ted Ashlee. Vancouver : J. J. Douglas, 1976, i.e.1978 129 p. : ill. ; 22 cm. Label mounted on verso of t.p.: Exclusive distributor, ISBS Inc., Forest Grove, Or. [F1089.5.V22A73] 76-48401 ISBN 0-88894-059-9 : 8.95
1. Ashlee, Ted, 1914- 2. Vancouver, B.C.—Biography. I. Title.
Distributed by ISBS BIP

Ashley, Daisy H.

ASHLEY, Daisy H. 917.88'49'0330924 B
A cowgirl's ups and downs, by Daisy H. Ashley. Philadelphia, Dorrance [1972] 107 p. illus. 22 cm. [CT275.A838A3] 76-185576 ISBN 0-8059-1663-6 4.00
I. Title.

Ashley, Elizabeth, 1939-

ASHLEY, Elizabeth, 1939- 792'.028'0924 B
Actress : postcards from the road / Elizabeth Ashley, with Ross Firestone. New York : M. Evans, c1978. 252 p. : ill. ; 22 cm. [PN2287.A77A32] 78-17218 ISBN 0-87131-264-6 : 8.95
1. Ashley, Elizabeth, 1939- 2. Actors—United States—Biography. I. Firestone, Ross, joint author. II. Title. BIP

Ashley, James Monroe, 1824-1896.

HOROWITZ, Robert F. 973.8'092'4 B
The great impeacher : a political biography of James M. Ashley / by Robert F. Horowitz. New York : Brooklyn College Press ; distributed by Columbia University Press, 1979. xii, 227 p. ; 23 cm. (Studies on society in change ; no. 9) Includes index. Bibliography: p. [207]-219. [E415.9.A77H67] 78-62276 ISBN 0-930888-03-0 : 15.00
1. Ashley, James Monroe, 1824-1896 2. Johnson, Andrew, Pres. U.S., 1808-1875—Impeachment. 3. United States. Congress. House—Biography. 4. Reconstruction. 5. Legislators—United States—Biography. I. Title.

Ashley, William Henry, 1778-1838.

CLOKEY, Richard M., 1936- 978'.02'0924 B
William H. Ashley : enterprise and politics in the trans-Mississippi West / by Richard M. Clokey. Norman : University of Oklahoma Press, c1979. p. cm. Includes index. Bibliography: p. [F592.A84C55] 78-21396 ISBN 0-8061-1525-4 : 18.95
1. Ashley, William Henry, 1778-1838. 2. United States. Congress. House—Biography. 3. Fur trade—The West—History. 4. Overland journeys to the Pacific. 5. The West—Discovery and exploration. 6. Pioneers—The West—Biography. 7. Legislators—United States—Biography. BIP

Ashmole, Elias,

ASHMOLE, Elias, 1617-1692. 942.06'0924 (B)
Elias Ashmole (1617-1692): his autobiographical and historical notes, his correspondence, and other contemporary sources relating to his life and work; edited, with a biographical introduction, by C. H. Josten. Oxford, Clarence P. 1966 [i.e. 1967] 5 v. front., plates (incl. diagr.) 22 1/2 cm. 18/18- Contents.v. 1. Biographical introduction. -- v. 2. Texts, 1617-1660. -- v. 3. Texts, 1661-1672. -- v. 4. Texts, 1673-1701. -- v. 5. Index, by M. A. Hennings. Bibliographical footnotes. [DA378.A8A3 1967] 67-78366
I. Josten, Conrad Hermann. II. Hennings, M. A. III. Title.

Ashmun, Jehudi, 1794-1828.

GURLEY, Ralph Randolph, 1797-1872. 326'.0924 B
Life of Jehudi Ashmun, late colonial agent in Liberia. With an appendix containing extracts from his journal and other writings; with a brief sketch of the life of the Rev. Lott Cary. New York, Negro Universities Press [1969] 396, 160 p. 23 cm. Reprint of the 1835 ed. [DT636.A8G8 1969] 76-75532
1. Ashmun, Jehudi, 1794-1828. 2. Cary, Lott, 1780-1828. 3. Negroes—Colonization—Africa. 4. Liberia—History. I. Title.

GURLEY, Ralph Randolph, 1797-1872. 966'.601'0924 B
Life of Jehudi Ashmun, late colonial agent in Liberia. Freeport, N.Y., Books for Libraries Press, 1971 [c1835] vii, 160 p. port. 23 cm. (Black heritage library collection) "With an appendix containing extracts from [Ashmun's] Journal and other writings, with a brief sketch of the life of the Rev. Lott Cary." [DT636.A8G8 1971] 73-149867 ISBN 0-8369-8749-7
1. Ashmun, Jehudi, 1794-1828. 2. Cary, Lott, 1780-1828. 3. Negroes—Colonization—Africa. 4. Liberia—History. I. Title. II. Series. BIP

Ashmun, Jehudi, 1794-1828—Juvenile literature.

ORRMONT, Arthur 326.0924
Fighter against slavery: Jehudi Ashmun. New York, Messner [c.1966] 189p. 22cm. Bibl. [E448A826] 66-14004 3.25; 3.19 lib. ed.,
1. Ashmun, Jehudi, 1794-1828—Juvenile literature. I. Title.

Ashton, Frederick, Sir, 1906-

VAUGHAN, David, 1924- 792.8'092'4 B
Frederick Ashton and his ballets / David Vaughan. 1st American ed. New York : Knopf : distributed by Random House, 1977. xx, 522 p. : ill. ; 26 cm. Chronology: p. 451-494. Includes index. Bibliography: p. 503-509. [GV1785.A8V38 1977] 76-47939 ISBN 0-394-41085-8 : 15.00
1. Ashton, Frederick, Sir, 1906- 2. Choreographers—Great Britain—Biography. I. Title. BIP

Ashton-Warner, Sylvia.

ASHTON-WARNER, Sylvia. 371.1'00973 B
Spearpoint; "teacher" in America. New York, Vintage Books [1974, c1972] 223 p. 19 cm. Autobiographical. [LA2317.A8A3 1974] 73-14780 ISBN 0-394-71997-2 1.95 (pbk.)
1. Ashton-Warner, Sylvia. I. Title.

Ashton-Warner, Sylvia—Biography.

ASHTON-WARNER, Sylvia. 823 B
I passed this way / Sylvia Ashton-Warner. 1st ed. New York : Knopf, 1979. p. cm. [PR9639.3.A8Z47 1979] 79-2133 ISBN 0-394-42612-6 : 15.00
1. Ashton-Warner, Sylvia—Biography. 2. Novelists, New Zealand—20th century—Biography. I. Title. BIP

Ashworth, William, 1942-

ASHWORTH, William, 1942- 796.5'22'097957
The Wallowas : coming of age in the wilderness / by William Ashworth. New York : Hawthorn Books, c1978. ix, 165 p. ; 24 cm. [GV199.42.O72W342 1978] 77-70121 ISBN 0-8015-8371-3 : 8.95
1. Ashworth, William, 1942- 2. Mountaineering—Oregon—Wallowa Mountains. 3. Mountaineers—United States—Biography. 4. Wallowa Mountains—Description. I. Title.

Asia—Biography.

ANTHONY, Joseph 920
The rascal and the pilgrim; the story of the boy from Korea. New York, Farrar. Straus and Cudahy, [c1960] xii, 242p. illus. 22cm. 60-10823 3.75
I. Title.

HALL, Josef Washington, 1894- 950
Eminent Asians; six great personalities of the new East. Portrait drawings by Orre Nobles. Port Washington, N.Y., Kennikat Press [1971, c1929] 510 p. ports. 22 cm. (Essay and general literature index reprint series) [DS32.H3 1971] 77-122876
1. Asia—Biography. I. Title.

Asia—Politics and government.

GUNTHER, John, 1901-1970. 915'.03'41
Inside Asia. Westport, Conn., Greenwood Press [1974, c1942] xii, 637 p. maps. 22 cm. Reprint of the ed. published by Harper, New York. Bibliography: p. 608-611. [DS35.G8 1974] 74-15554 ISBN 0-8371-7825-8
1. Asia—Politics and government. 2. Asia—Biography. I. Title. BIP

Asians in the United States—Biography—Dictionaries.

LO, Samuel E. 920.0973
Asian who? in America. Compiled and edited by Samuel E. Lo. [Roseland, N.J.] East-West Who? [1971] 329 p. 23 cm. [E184.O6L6] 70-155285
1. Asians in the United States—Biography—Dictionaries. 2. United States—Biography—Dictionaries. I. Title.

Asimov, Isaac, 1920- —Biography.

ASIMOV, Isaac, 1920- 813'.5'4 B
In memory yet green : the autobiography of Isaac Asimov, 1920-1954. 1st ed. New York : Doubleday, 1979. vii, 732 p., [12] leaves of plates : ill. ; 24 cm. Includes indexes. "Catalog of books, Isaac Asimov": p. [709]-715. [PS3551.S5Z517] 78-55838 ISBN 0-385-13679-X : 15.95
1. Asimov, Isaac, 1920- —Biography. 2. Authors, American—20th century—Biography. I. Title. BIP

Asoka, King of Magadhe, fl. 259 B.C.

GOKHALE, Balkrishna Govind. 934.040924
Asoka Maurya. New York, Twayne Publishers [1966] 194 p. map. 21 cm. (Twayne's rulers and statesmen of the world series, 3) Bibliography: p. 181-185. [DS451.5.G6] 66-16125
1. Asoka, King of Magadha, fl. 259 B.C.

LENGYEL, Emil, 1895. 934'.04'0924 B
Asoka the Great, India's royal missionary. New York, Watts [1969] ix, 146 p. 22 cm. (Immortals of history) (Immortals of philosophy and religion.) A biography of the maharaja of Magadha in India who converted to Buddhism and made it a major religion of the world through his missionary work. [DS451.5.L45] 92 71-83650
1. Asoka, King of Magadha, fl. 259 B.C.—Juvenile literature. I. Title. BIP

LENGYEL, Emil, 1895- 934'.04'0924 B
Asoka the Great: India's royal missionary. London, New York, Franklin Watts Ltd, [1971]. xii, 146 p. map. 23 cm. Includes index. A biography of the maharaja of Magadha in India who converted to Buddhism and made it a major religion of the world through his missionary work. [DS451.5.L45 1971] 92 73-174540 ISBN 0-85166-319-2 £1.25
1. Asoka, King of Magadha, fl. 259 B.C.—Juvenile literature. I. Title.

SMITH, Vincent Arthur, 1848-1920 934.040924
Asoka, the Buddhist emperor of India. 2d.,

rev., enl. Delhi, S. Chand [1964] 252p. illus., facsim., map. 19cm. (Rulers of India) Rulers of India Reprint of the ed. orig. publ. in 1909. Bibl. [DS451.5.S6 1964] 2.50
1. Asoka, King of Magadha, fl. 250 B. C. (Series) I. Title. II. Series.
Now available from Verry, Mystic, Conn.

Asquith, Cynthia Mary Evelyn (Charteris),

ASQUITH, Cynthia Mary 928.2
Evelyn (Charteris), Lady 1887-
Haply I may remember. New York, Scribner, 1950. xvii, 237 p. illus., ports. 22 cm. [PR6001.S68Z53 1950a] 50-14090
I. Title.

ASQUITH, Cynthia Mary 928.8
Evelyn Charteris, Lady, 1887-
Haply I may remember. New York, Scribner, 1950. xvii, 237 p. illus., ports. 22 cm. [PR6001.S68Z53 1950a] 30-14090
I. Title.

Assali, Nicholas S.

ASSALI, Nicholas S. 618'.092'4 B
A doctor's life / Nicholas S. Assali. New York : Harcourt Brace Jovanovich, c1979. p. cm. Includes index. [RG76.A84A33] 79-1808 ISBN 0-15-126161-X : 12.95
1. Assali, Nicholas S. 2. Gynecologists—United States—Biography. 3. Obstetricians—United States—Biography- 4. Gynecologists—Brazil—Biography. 5. Obstetricians—Brazil—Biography. I. Title. BIP

Assassination—Case studies.

SPARROW, Gerald, 364.15'24'0926
1903-
The great assassins. New York, Arco Pub. Co. [1969] 207 p. 22 cm. [HV6278.S75 1969] 69-16270 3.95
1. Assassination—Case studies. I. Title.

Asser, Bp. of Sherborne, d. 909?

WHITELOCK, Dorothy. 942.01'0924 B
The genuine Asser. Reading, University of Reading, 1968. 21 p. 25 cm. (The Stenton lecture, 1967) Bibliographical footnotes. [DA153.A898] 78-427760 7/6
1. Asser, Bp. of Sherborne, d. 909? De rebus gestis Aelfredi. I. Title. II. Series.

Assimakopoulos, Pat.

ASSIMAKOPOULOS, Pat. 248'.2 B
Both feet in the water / Pat Assimakopoulos. Chappaqua, NY : Christian Herald Books, 1979. p. cm. [BR1725.A82A32] 79-50943 ISBN 0-915684-31-4 : 7.95
1. Assimakopoulos, Pat. 2. Christian biography—United States. I. Title. BIP

Associated Press.

COOPER, Kent, 1880-1965. 920.5
Kent Cooper and the Associated Press; an autobiography. New York, Random House [1959] 334 p. illus. 24 cm. [PN4874.C685A3] 59-6640
1. Associated Press. 2. Journalists—Correspondence, reminiscences, etc.

Astaire, Fred.

ASTAIRE, Fred. 927.933
Steps in time. [1st ed.] New York, Harper [1959] 338p. illus. 22cm. Autobiography. [GV1785.A83A3] 59-8161
I. Title.

ASTAIRE, Fred. 793.3'092'4 B
Steps in time / Fred Astaire. New York : Da Capo Press, 1979, c1959. viii, 327 p., [12] leaves of plates : ill. ; 23 cm. (Da Capo series in dance) Reprint of the 1st ed. published by Harper & Bros., New York. [GV1785.A83A3 1979] 79-9148 ISBN 0-440-01050-0 : 19.50 19.50

1. Astaire, Fred. 2. Dancers—United States—Biography. I. Title. BIP

CROCE, Arlene. 791.43'028'0922
The Fred Astair & Ginger Rogers book / Arlene Croce. New York : Vintage Books, 1977, c1972. 191 p. : ill. ; 21 cmm. Reprint of the ed. published by Galahad Books, New York. [GV1785.A83C76 1977] 77-76588 ISBN 0-394-72476-3 pbk. : 3.95
1. Astaire, Fred. 2. Rogers, Ginger, 1911- 3. Dancers—United States—Biography. I. Title.

FREEDLAND, Michael, 793.3'092'4 B
1934-
Fred Astaire / Michael Freedland. New York : Grosset & Dunlap, 1977, c1976. 183 p. : ill. ; 28 cm. Includes index. [GV1785.A83F73 1977] 77-80371 ISBN 0-448-14079-9 : 14.95 ISBN 0-448-14080-2 pbk. : 7.95
1. Astaire, Fred. 2. Dancers—Biography.

FREEDLAND, Michael, 793.3'092'4 B
1934-
Fred Astaire / Michael Freedland. London : W. H. Allen, 1976. 277 p., [8] leaves of plates : ill. ; 23 cm. Label mounted on t.p.: Transatlantic Arts, Levittown, N.Y. sole distributor for the U.S.A. [GV1785.A83F73] 76-380422 ISBN 0-491-01786-3
1. Astaire, Fred. 2. Dancers—Biography.

GREEN, Stanley. 793.3'092'4
Starring Fred Astaire [by] Stanley Green [and] Burt Goldblatt. New York, Dodd, Mead [1973] 501 p. illus. 29 cm. Discography: p. 470-475. [GV1785.A83G73] 73-13041 ISBN 0-396-06877-4 22.50
1. Astaire, Fred. 2. Musical revue, comedy, etc.—United States. I. Goldblatt, Burt, joint author. II. Title. BIP

HACKL, Alfons. 791.43'028'0924 B
Fred Astaire and his work. ([Auslfg.:] Vienna, Ed. Austria International, 1970.) 120 p. illus., fold. table. 22 cm. Bibliography: p. 114. [GV1785.A83H3] 76-531561 90.00
1. Astaire, Fred. I. Title.

TOPPER, Suzanne. 793.30924
Astaire and Rogers Suzanne Topper. New York : Leisure Books ,1976. 206 p. : ill. ; 18 cm. Filmography: pp. 173-206. [GV1785] pbk. : 1.50
1. Astaire, Fred. 2. Rogers, Ginger, 1911- 3. Dancers. 4. Dancing in moving-pictures, television, etc. I. Title. BIP

Astell, Mary, 1666-1731.

SMITH, Florence Mary, 1877- v. 12
Mary Astell. By Florence M. Smith. New York, AMS Press, 1966. 193 p. 68-22583
1. Astell, Mary, 1666-1731. I. Title. BIP

Astor, Brooke Russell.

ASTOR, Brooke Russell. 920.7
Patchwork child. [1st ed.] New York, Harper & Row [1962] 224 p. illus. 22 cm. Autobiographical. [CT275.A847A3] 62-17083
I. Title.

Astor family.

KAVALER, Lucy. 929.2'0973
The Astors; an American legend. New York, Dodd, Mead [1968] x, 211 p. illus., ports. 22 cm. [CS71.A85 1968] 68-8283 4.00
1. Astor family. I. Title. BIP

Astor, John Jacob, 1763-1848.

KELSEY, Vera. 978
Young men so daring; fur traders who carried the frontier west. [1st ed.] Indianapolis, Bobbs-Merrill [1956] 288 p. illus. 22 cm. [F592.K38] 56-7606
1. Pond, Peter, 1740-1807? 2. Lisa, Manuel, 1772-1820. 3. Astor, John Jacob, 1763-1848. 4. Bridger, James, 1804-1881. I. Title.

MINNIGERODE, Meade, 650'.0922 B
1887-1967.
Certain rich men; Stephen Girard, John Jacob Astor, Jay Cooke, Daniel Drew, Cornelius Vanderbilt, Jay Gould, Jim Fisk. Freeport, N.Y., Books for Libraries Press [1970] xi, 210 p. illus., facsim., ports. 23 cm. (Essay index reprint series) Reprint of the 1927 ed. Bibliography: p. ix-xi. [CT219.M55 1970] 71-121489
1. Girard, Stephen, 1750-1831. 2. Astor, John Jacob, 1763-1848. 3. Cooke, Jay, 1821-1905. 4. Drew, Daniel, 1797-1879. 5. Vanderbilt, Cornelius, 1794-1877. 6. Gould, Jay, 1836-1892. 7. Fisk, James, 1835-1872. I. Title.

Astor, Mary

ASTOR, Mary 927.92
My story: an autobiography. [New York] Dell [1960, c.1959] 382p. 17cm. (F92) .50 pap.,
I. Title.

ASTOR, Mary, 1906- 927.92
My story: an autobiography. [1st ed.] Garden City, N.Y., Doubleday, 1959. 332 p. 22 cm. [PN2287.A8A3] 59-6265

Astor, Nancy Witcher (Langhorne) viscountess.

COLLIS, Maurice [Stewart] 923.242
Nancy Astor, an informal biography. New York, Dutton [c.]1960. 235p. illus. 22cm. 60-5975 5.00
1. Astor, Nancy Witcher (Langhorne) viscountess. I. Title.

HARRISON, Rosina. 942.082'092'4
Rose : my life in service / Rosina Harrison. New York : Viking Press, 1975. x, 237 p., [17] leaves of plates : ill. ; 24 cm. [DA574.A8H37] 75-22428 ISBN 0-670-60814-9 : 8.95
1. Astor, Nancy Witcher (Langhorne) Viscountess. 2. Harrison, Rosina. I. Title.

HARRISON, Rosina. 942.0820924
Rose : my life in service / Rosina Harrison. New York : New American Library, 1976c1975. xiii, 238p. : ill. ; 17cm. (Signet book) [DA574.A8H37] pbk. : 1.95
1. Astor, Nancy Witcher (Langhorne), Viscountess. 2. Harrison, Rosina. I. Title.
L.C. card no. for 1975 Viking Press edition: 75-22428

LANGHORNE, 942.082'092'4 B
Elizabeth.
Nancy Astor and her friends. New York, Praeger [1974] ix, 277 p. illus. 24 cm. Bibliography: p. 268-272. [DA574.A8L36] 72-83006 10.00
1. Astor, Nancy Witcher (Langhorne) Viscountess. I. Title.

SYKES, 942.082'092'4 B
Christopher, 1907-
Nancy; the life of Lady Astor. [1st U.S. ed.] New York, Harper & Row [1972] 543 p. illus. 22 cm. (A Cass Canfield book) Includes bibliographical references. [DA574.A8S95 1972] 79-138766 ISBN 0-06-014184-0 10.00
1. Astor, Nancy Witcher (Langhorne) Viscountess. BIP

Astrology.

LEEK, Sybil. 133.5'0924
My life in astrology. [New York] New American Library [1974, c1972] 188 p. 18 cm. (A Signet book) [BF1408.2L44A3] 72-37290 1.25 (pbk.)
1. Astrology. I. Title. BIP

Astronautics—Biography.

COX, Donald William. 920
America's explorers of space, including a special report on UFO's, by Donald W. Cox. Illustrated by Dwight Dobbins. Maplewood, N.J., Hammond [1967] 93 p. illus. (part col.), maps, ports. 26 cm. (Profile series) Bibliography: p. 89. Biographical profiles of scientists and pilots whose achievements and discoveries will ultimately place man on the moon. Contains a thirteen page report on the creditability of Unidentified Flying Objects. [TL789.85.A1C65] AC 67
1. Astronautics—Biography. 2. Flying saucers. I. Dobbins, Dwight, illus. II. Title.

NEWLON, Clarke 920
Famous pioneers in space. New York, Dodd, [c.1963] 127p. illus. 22cm. (Famous biographies for young people) Bibl. 63-10337 3.00
1. Astronautics—Biog.— Juvenile literature. I. Title.

THOMAS, Shirley. 926.294
Men of space; profiles of the leaders in space research, development, and exploration. [1st ed.] Philadelphia, Chilton Co., Book Division [1960- v. illus. 25 cm. Vol. 5 has imprint: Philadelphia, Chilton Books. [TL789.85.A1T48] 60-15720
1. Astronautics—Biography. 2. Rocketry—Biography. I. Title.

WHO'S who in space. 629.40922
1st- ed.; 1966 67- Washington. D.C., Space Pubns., 1341 G St., N.W. [1966, c.1965] 328p. 26cm Eds.: 1966- Norman L. Baker. ed. in chief: Lynne Weiser, ed. on spine. Who's who in space, 1966-67: v.1 [TL789.85.A1W5] 65-28671 26.00
1. Astronautics—Biog.

Astronautics—Juvenile literature.

THARP, Edgar. 629.4'0922
Giants of space. Illustrated by Charles Gottlieb. New York, Grosset & Dunlap [1968] 128 p. illus., ports. 28 cm. Profiles of the men who challenge gravity, from rocket builder to moon astronaut, provide a survey of progress in space exploration. Includes tables of manned and unmanned orbital flights. [TL793.T43] 920 68-29977 3.95
1. Astronautics—Juvenile literature. 2. Astronautics—Biography—Juvenile literature. I. Gottlieb, Charles, illus. II. Title.

THARP, Edgar. 629.4'0922 B
Giants of space. Illustrated by Charles Gottlieb. New York, Grosset & Dunlap [1970] 128 p. illus., ports. 29 cm. (Illustrated true books) "4079" Profiles of the men who challenge gravity, from rocket builder to moon astronaut, provide a survey of progress in space exploration. Includes tables of manned and unmanned orbital flights. [TL793.T43 1970] 78-98161 3.95
1. Astronautics—Juvenile literature. 2. Astronautics—Biography—Juvenile literature. I. Gottlieb, Charles, illus. II. Title.

Astronautics—U.S.—Biography.

COX, Donald William. 629.4'0922 B
America's explorers of space; including a special report on project Apollo, by Donald W. Cox. Illustrated by Dwight Dobbins. Maplewood, N.J., Hammond [1969] 93 p. illus. (part col.), col. maps, ports. (part col.) 27 cm. (Profile series) Bibliography: p. 89. [TL789.85.A1C68 1969] 70-13740 3.50
1. Astronautics—U.S.—Biography. I. Title.

PANEL on Science 629.4'092'2 B
and Technology.
Biographical briefs of participants, thirteenth meeting, January 25, 26, and 27, 1972. Washington, U.S. Govt. Print. Off., 1972. v, 47 p. 24 cm. "Committee print." "Printed for the use of the [House] Committee on Science and Astronautics." [TL789.85.A1P35] 72-601933
1. Astronautics—United States—Biography. 2. Astronautics—Congresses. I. United States. Congress. House. Committee on Science and Astronautics. II. Title.

Astronautics—United States—Juvenile literature.

CIPRIANO, Anthony 629.4'092'2 B
J.
America's journeys into space : the

astronauts of the United States / portraits by William Joffe Numeroff ; text by Anthony J. Cipriano ; foreword by Gordon Cooper. New York : Wanderer Books, c1979. xi, 212 p. : ill. ; 28 cm. Includes index. Presents biographical sketches of American astronauts from Alan Shepard to Vance Brand and discusses the various space programs in which these men have participated. [TL789.8.U5C56] 920 79-10254 ISBN 0-671-33033-0 pbk. : 4.95
1. Astronautics—United States—Juvenile literature. 2. Astronauts—United States—Biography—Juvenile literature. I. Numeroff, William Joffe. II. Title. **BIP**

Astronauts—Biography.

UNITED States. 629.4'092'2
Library of Congress. Science Policy Research Division.
Astronauts and cosmonauts biographical and statistical data : report / prepared for the Committee on Science and Technology, U.S. House of Representatives, Ninety-fifth Congress, first session, by the Science Policy Research Division, Congressional Research Service, Library of Congress, [prepared by Marcia S. Smith]. Rev. Washington : U.S. Govt. Print. Off., 1977. v, 210 p. : ill. ; 24 cm. "Serial E." [TL789.85.A1U52 1977] 77-604704
1. Astronauts—Biography. I. Smith, Marcia S. II. United States. Congress. House. Committee on Science and Technology. III. Title.

UNITED States. 629.4'092'2 B
Library of Congress. Science Policy Research Division.
Astronauts and cosmonauts biographical and statistical data : report prepared for the Committee on Science and Technology, U.S. House of Representatives, Ninety-fourth Congress, first session by the Science Policy Research Division, Congressional Research Service, Library of Congress / [prepared by Vikki A. Zegel and Marcia S. Smith]. Washington : U.S. Govt. Print. Off., 1975. v, 179 p. : ports. ; 24 cm. At head of title: Committee print. "Serial E." [TL789.85.A1U52 1975] 75-602307
1. Astronauts—Biography. I. Zegel, Vikki A. II. Smith, Marcia S. III. United States. Congress. House. Committee on Science and Technology. IV. Title.

Astronauts—U.S.

O'LEARY, Brian, 629.4'0924 B
1940-
The making of an ex-astronaut. Boston, Houghton Mifflin, 1970. xii, 243 p. illus., ports. 22 cm. Autobiographical. [TL789.85.O4A3] 70-112277 5.95
1. Astronauts—U.S. I. Title.

Astronomers.

BALL, Robert Stawell, 520'.92'2 B
Sir, 1840-1913.
Great astronomers. Plainview, N.Y., Books for Libraries Press [1974] xii, 372 p. illus. 22 cm. (Essay index reprint series) Reprint of the 1895 ed. published by Isbister, London. Contents.Contents.—Ptolemy.—Copernicus.—Tycho Brahe.—Galileo.—Kepler.—Isaac Newton.—Flamsteed.—Halley.—Bradley.—William Herschel.—Laplace.—Brinkley.—John Herschel.—The Earl of Rosse.—Airy.—Hamilton.—Le Verrier.—Adams. [QB35.B18 1974] 74-994 ISBN 0-518-10142-8 18.25
1. Astronomers. 2. Astronomy—History. I. Title. **BIP**

RICHARDSON, Robert 520'922
Shirley, 1902-
The star lovers, by Robert S. Richardson. New York, Macmillan [1967] x, 310p. illus. 22cm. Bibl. [QB35.R5] 67-16714 7.50
1. Astronomers. I. Title.

Astronomers—Juvenile literature.

PICKERING, James Sayre. 520'.922
Famous astronomers, by James S. Pickering. Illustrated with photos. New York, Dodd, Mead [1968] 128 p. illus., ports. 22 cm. (Famous biographies for young people) [QB35.P5] 68-12812
1. Astronomers—Juvenile literature. I. Title.

*SULLIVAN, Navin 925.2
Pioneer astronomers. Illus. by Eric Fraser. New York, Scholastic [1965, c.1964] 154p. illus. 20cm. (TX678) [QB35.S8] .45 pap.,
1. Astronomers—Juvenile literature. I. Title.

SULLIVAN, Navin. 925.2
Pioneer astronomers. Drawings by Eric Fraser. [1st ed.] New York, Atheneum, 1964. 156 p. illus., ports. 24 cm. Bibliography: p. [147]-148. [QB35.S8] 64-11891
1. Astronomers—Juvenile literature. I. Title.

Astronomy—History—Juvenile literature.

SILVERBERG, Robert. 520'.0922
Four men who changed the universe. New York, Putnam's [1968] 255 p. 21 cm. (A Science survey book) Bibliography: p. 251-252. [QB28.S5] 68-15079
1. Astronomy—History—Juvenile literature. 2. Astronomers—Juvenile literature. I. Title.

Ata-ullah, Mohammad,

ATA-ULLAH, Mohammad, 1903- 926.1
Citizen of two worlds, With a foreword by Low Thomas. [1st ed.] New York, Harper [1960] 285 p. 22 cm. Autobiographical. [CT1518.A8A3] 60-13712

Ataturk, Kamal, Pres. Turkey, d. 1938.

ARMSTRONG, Harold 923.156
Courtenay, 1891-
Gray Wolf; the life of Kemal Ataturk. With an introd. and an epilogue by Emil Lengyel. New York, Capricorn Books [1961] 324p. illus. 19cm. (A Capricorn book, CAP 43) First published in 1932 under title: Grey Wolf. Includes bibliography. [DR592.K4A7 1961] 61-65922
1. Atatiirk, Kamal, Pres. Turkey, d. 1938. 2. Turkey Hist. 1909- I. Title.

ARMSTRONG, Harold 923.156
Courtenay 1891-
Gray Wolf; the life of Kemal Ataturk. Introd. and epilogue by Emil Lengyle. New York, [Putnam, c.1933, 1961] 324p. illus., maps. (Capricorn bk., CAP43) 1.45 pap.,
1. Ataturk, Kamal, pres. Turkey, d.1938. 2. Turkey—Hist.—1909- I. Title.

ARMSTRONG, Harold 956.1'02'0924 B
Courtenay, 1891-1943.
Gray Wolf, Mustafa Kemal: an intimate study of a dictator. New York, Minton, Balch, 1933. [New York, AMS Press, 1973] xi, 298 p. illus. 23 cm. First published in 1932 under title: Grey Wolf. Bibliography: p. 289-291. [DR592.K4A7 1973] 75-180317 ISBN 0-404-56212-4 23.50
1. Ataturk, Kamal, Pres. Turkey, d. 1938. I. Title.

ARMSTRONG, Harold 956.1'02'0924 B
Courtenay, 1891-1943.
Grey Wolf, Mustafa Kemal; an intimate study of a dictator. Freeport, N.Y., Books for Libraries Press [1972] 352 p. illus. 23 cm. Reprint of the 1932 ed. Bibliography: p. 343-345. [DR592.K4A7 1972] 72-8397 ISBN 0-8369-6962-6
1. Ataturk, Kamal, Pres. Turkey, d. 1938. I. Title. **BIP**

BALFOUR, Patrick, baron 923.1561
Kinross, 1904-
Ataturk; a biography of Mustafa Kemal, father of modern Turkey, by Lord Kinross. New York, Morrow, 1965 [c.1964] ix, 615p. maps (on lining papers) ports. 25cm. Bibl. [DR592.K4B23] 65-11486 7.50 bds.,
1. Ataturk, Kamal, Pres. Turkey, d. 1938. 2. Turkey—Hist.—1909- I. Title.

FROEMBGEN, Hanns, 956'.102'0924 B
1902-
Kemal Ataturk; a biography. Translated from the German by Kenneth Kirkness. Freeport, N.Y., Books for Libraries Press [1971] 285 p. illus. 23 cm. "First published 1935." [DR592.K4F72 1971] 70-175697 ISBN 0-8369-6612-0
1. Ataturk, Kamal, Pres. Turkey, d. 1938.

HELLER, Deane 956.1'02'0924 B
Fons, 1924-
Hero of modern Turkey: Ataturk. New York, J. Messner [1972] 190 p. 21 cm. Bibliography: p. 184-185. A biography of the first President of the Turkish Republic whose instituted reforms revolutionized every aspect of Turkish life. [DR592.K4H43] 92 70-176379 ISBN 0-671-32541-8
1. Ataturk, Kamal, Pres. Turkey, d. 1938. 2. Turkey—History—1918-1960. I. Title.

KINROSS, John Patrick 923.1561
Douglas Balfour, baron, 1904-
Ataturk: a biography of Mustafa Kemal, father of modern Turkey, by Lord Kinross. New York, Morrow, 1965 [c1964] ix, 615 p. maps (on lining papers) ports. 25 cm. Bibliography: p. [579]-585. [DR592.K4K43 1965] 65-11486
1. Ataturk, Kamal, Pres. Turkey, d. 1938. I. Title.

Atchison, David Rice, 1807-1886.

PARRISH, William Earl, 923.273
1931-
David Rice Atchison of Missouri, border politician. Columbia, Univ. of Missouri Press [c.1961] 271p. illus. (Univ. of Missouri studies, v. 34, no. 1) Bibl. 61-5879 3.95
1. Atchison, David Rice, 1807-1886. I. Title.

Ateah, Michael, 1862-1937.

LESTER, Laela (Ateah). 920
Cedars of Lebanon. Winnipeg, Columbia Press [1951] 159 p. 21 cm. [CT310.A8L4 1951] 51-38991
1. Ateah, Michael, 1862-1937. I. Title.

Aten, Ira, 1862-1958.

PREECE, Harold, 1906- 923.973
Lone Star man: Ira Aten, last of the old Texas Rangers. New York, Hastings House [1960] 256 p. illus. 22 cm. Includes bibliography. [F391.A83P7] 60-14617
1. Aten, Ira, 1862-1958. 2. Frontier and pioneer life—Texas. I. Title.

Athenagoras I, Ecumenical Patriarch of Constantinople, 1886-1972.

†TSAKONAS, 281.9'092'4 B
Demetrios Gr.
A man sent by God : the life of Patriarch Athenagoras of Constantinople / Demetrios Tsakonas ; [translated from the Greek by George Angeloglou]. Brookline, Mass. : Holy Cross Orthodox Press, c1977. x, 99 p., [8] leaves of plates : ill. ; 22 cm. Translation of Athenagoras ho Oikoumenikos ton neon ideon. Includes bibliographical references and index. [BX395.A8T7613] 77-77669 ISBN 0-916586-07-3 pbk. : 3.95
1. Athenagoras I, Ecumenical Patriarch of Constantinople, 1886-1972. 2. Patriarchs and patriarchate—Biography. I. Title.
Publisher's address : 50 Goddard Ave., Brookline, MA 02146 **BIP**

Athletes.

BOYNICK, David King, 1911- 927.96
Champions by setback; athletes who overcame physical handicaps. New York, Crowell [1954] 205 p. 21 cm. [GV697.A1B6] 54-5534
1. Athletes. I. Title.

BROSNAN, Jim. 796
Little League to big league. New York, Random House [1968] xiv, 175 p. illus., ports. 22 cm. (Little League library) Profiles of fourteen record-setting athletes who first learned the fundamentals of good sportsmanship as Little Leaguers. [GV697.A1B76 1968] AC 68
1. Athletes. I. Title. **BIP**

DARDEN, Anne. 796'.092'2 B
The sports hall of fame / by Anne Darden. New York : Drake Publishers, 1976. 236 p. : ill. ; 29 cm. Briefly summarizes the careers and records of outstanding athletes in fourteen sports. [GV697.A1D28] 920 76-28312 ISBN 0-8473-1025-6 : 15.00
1. Athletes. I. Title. **BIP**

DAVIS, Mac, 1905- 927.96
100 greatest sports heroes; illustrated by Samuel Nisenson. New York, Grosset & Dunlap [1954] 145 p. illus. 29 cm. (Illustrated true books) [GV697.A1D3] 54-14204
1. Athletes. I. Title.

FITZGERALD, Edward E., ed. 927.96
Heroes of sport. New York, Bartholomew House, 1960 [c.1955-1960] 256p. 21cm. 60-11978 3.00
1. Athletes. I. Title.

FITZGERALD, Edward E 1919- 927.96
Champions in sports and spirit; illustrated by De Wolfe Hotchkiss. New York, Farrar, Straus & Cudahy [1956] 181p. illus. 22cm. (Vision books, 13) [GV697.A1F5] 56-8651
1. Athletes. I. Title.

LAKLAN, Carli. 796.4
Olympic champions: why they win. New York, Funk & Wagnalls [1968] 168 p. illus., ports. 25 cm. Analyzes the will to win of famous Olympic champions, citing the discipline and training of various athletes, their stamina, sportsmanship, and determination to overcome odds. [GV721.5.L3] AC 68
I. Title.

Athletes, American.

DEMARCO, Mario 927.96
Great American athletes. Menlo Park, Calif., Pacific Coast Pubs. [c.1962] 124p. illus. 22cm. 62-51072 1.00 pap.,
1. Athletes, American. I. Title.

GALLICO, Paul, 1897- 796.0922
The golden people. Garden City, N.Y., Doubleday, 1965[c.1961, 1965] 315p. illus., ports. 25cm. [GV697.A1G3] 65-19889 4.95
1. Athletes, American. I. Title.
Contents omitted.

GALLICO, Paul, 1897- 796.0922
The golden people. [1st ed.] Garden City, N.Y., Doubleday, 1965 315 p illus., ports. 24 cm. Contents.Contents.—The mirror. Babe Ruth.—Gertrude Ederle.—Jack Dempsey.—Gene Tunney.—William T. Tilden 2nd.—Knute Rockne.—Helen Wills.—Tex Rickard.—Ty Cobb.—Johnny Weissmuller.—Babe Didrikson.—Red Grange.—Bob Jones.—Men with the golden pen.—Saint Bambino. [GV697.A1G3] 65-19889
1. Athletes, American. I. Title.

JACOBS, Helen Hull, 1908- 927.9
Famous American women athletes. New York, Dodd, Mead [c1964] 121 p. ports. 22 cm. (Famous biographies for young people) [GV697.A1J3] 63-18781
1. Athletes, American. I. Title.

PRATT, John Lowell, comp. 927.96
Sport, sport, sport; true stories of great athletes and great human beings. New York, J. Lowell Pratt [1962, c.1960] 183p. 18cm. (Amer. Sports lib., 101) .50 pap.,
1. Athletes, American. I. Title.

PRATT, John Lowell, comp. 927.96
Sport, sport, sport; true stories of great athletes and great haman beings. Illustrated by Julio Granda. New York, F. Watts [1960] 212p. illus. 25cm. [GV697.A1P7] 60-8809
1. Athletes, American. I. Title.

WALDMAN, Frank, 1919- 927.96
Famous American athletes of today. Twelfth series. Boston, L. C. Page [1951] 388 p. illus. 21 cm. [GV697.A1F3] 51-5711
1. Athletes, American. I. Title.

Athletes, American—Biography.

DREES, Jack. 796'.092'2
Where is he now? Sports heroes of yesterday—revisited, by Jack Drees and James C. Mullen. With a foreword by Bill Veeck. Middle Village, N.Y., Jonathan David Publishers [1973] viii, 246 p. illus. 24 cm. Errata slip inserted. [GV697.A1D7] 71-188243 ISBN 0-8246-0145-9 7.95
1. Athletes, American—Biography. I. Mullen, James C., joint author. II. Title. BIP

GUTHRIE, Bill. 796'.092'2
Hall of Famers. [New York] Stadia Sports Pub. [1973] 160 p. illus. 20 cm. (Sport-Spectrum classic) [GV697.A1G87] 72-93367 1.50
1. Athletes, American—Biography. I. Title.
Order from Dell.

PORETZ, Art, 1927- 796'.092'2
The super pros. Edited by Art Poretz. [New York] Stadia Sports Pub. [1973] 159 p. illus. 20 cm. (Sport-spectrum classic) On spine: All sports MVPs! [GV697.A1P57] 73-77301 1.50 (pbk.)
1. Athletes, American—Biography. 2. Athletes, Canadian—Biography. I. Title. II. Title: All sports MVPs!
Distributed by Dell.

Athletes, American—Biography—Juvenile literature.

BUTLER, Hal. 796'.092'2
Sports heroes who wouldn't quit. New York, J. Messner [1973] 189 p. illus. 22 cm. Traces the careers of fourteen men and one woman who succeeded or made spectacular combacks in professional sports despite physical handicaps, illness, or injury. [GV697.A1B82 1973] 920 72-11821 ISBN 0-671-32581-7 5.50
1. Athletes, American—Biography—Juvenile literature. 2. Sports—United States—Biography—Juvenile literature. I. Title. BIP

GARFINKEL, Bernard Max, 1929- 796'.092'2
The champions, by Bernard Garfinkel. Illus. by David K. Stone. Photos. by Dan Baliotti. New York, Platt & Munk [1972] 98 p. illus. 29 cm. [GV697.A1G36] 70-185971 3.95
1. Athletes, American—Biography—Juvenile literature. I. Stone, David K., illus. II. Title.

HOLLANDER, Zander, ed. 796'.092'2 B
Great American athletes of the 20th century. Compiled and edited by Zander Hollander. New York, Random House [1972] 174 p. illus. 29 cm. (Landmark giant, 11) Biographical sketches of fifty American athletes who represent eleven different sports. [GV697.A1H6 1972] 72-767 ISBN 0-394-81554-8 3.95
1. Athletes, American—Biography—Juvenile literature. I. Title.

Athletes, American—Juvenile literature.

HEUMAN, William. 927.96
Famous American athletes. New York, Dodd, Mead [1963] 152 p. illus. 22 cm. (Famous biographies for young people) [GV697.A1H4] 63-8236
1. Athletes, American—Juvenile literature. I. Title.

HOLLANDER, Zander, ed. 796.0922
Great American athletes of the 20th century New York, Random House [1966] 172 p. ports. 29 cm. (Landmark giant, 11) [GV697.A1H6] 66-9802
1. Athletes, American—Juvenile literature. I. Title.

HOLLANDER, Zander, ed. 796.0922
Great American athletes of the twentieth century New York, Random [1966] 172p. ports. 29cm. (Landmark giant, 11) [GV697.A1H6] 66-9802 3.95 bds.,
1. Athletes, American—Juvenile literature. I. Title. BIP

Athletes—Australia—Biography.

WHITINGTON, Richard S. 796'.092'2 B
The champions / [by] R. S. Whitington. Melbourne : Macmillan, 1976. 135 p. : ill. ; 26 cm. [GV697.A1W45] 77-352431 ISBN 0-333-21065-4
1. Athletes—Australia—Biography. I. Title.

Athletes—Biography.

CAMPBELL, Gail. 796.4'2'0922 B
Marathon : the world of the long-distance athlete / Gail Campbell. New York : Sterling Pub. Co., 1977. 176 p. : ill. ; 27 cm. Includes index. [GV697.A1C26] 76-58625 ISBN 0-8069-4114-6 : 8.95 ISBN 0-8069-4115-4 lib.bdg. : 7.89
1. Athletes—Biography. I. Title.

CLARY, Jack T. 796'.092'2 B
The captains / Jack Clary. 1st ed. New York : Atheneum, 1978. xiii, 178 p. : ports. ; 22 cm. Spotlights nine professional athletes, captains of their respective teams, focusing on the qualities that make them leaders and the duties and responsiblites that go with job. [GV697.A1C6 1978] 920 77-15830 ISBN 0-689-10871-0 : 7.95 7.95
1. Athletes—Biography. 2. Leadership. 3. Group games. I. Title. BIP

DICKEY, Glenn. 796'.092'2 B
Champs & chumps : an inside look at the sports superstars / by Glenn Dickey. San Francisco : Chronicle Books, [1976] p. cm. [GV697.A1D47] 76-14383 ISBN 0-87701-083-8 : 7.95
1. Athletes—Biography. 2. Athletes—United States—Biography. I. Title.

DOUGLAS, Steve. 796'.092'2 B
Kings of sport / [by] Steve Douglas ; ... text illustrations by Ken Kirkland. London : Pan Books, 1976. 96 p. : ill., ports. ; 18 cm. (Piccolo) [GV697.A1D68] 77-351025 ISBN 0-330-24480-9 : £0.35
1. Athletes—Biography. I. Title.

FOX, Larry. 796'.0922
Little men in sports. [1st ed.] New York, W. W. Norton [1968] xi, 244 p. ports. 21 cm. [GV697.A1F68] 68-16567 4.36
1. Athletes—Biography. I. Title.

*GEMME, Leila B. 796'.092'2
The new breed of athlete, by Leila B. Gemme. New York, Pocket Books [1975] 190 p. illus. 18 cm. [GV697] ISBN 0-671-48150-9 1.25 (pbk.)
1. Athletes—Biography. I. Title. BIP

HEINZ, Wilfred Charles, 1915- 796'.092'2
Once they heard the cheers / W. C. Heinz. 1st ed. Garden City, N.Y. : Doubleday, 1979. 489 p. ; 22 cm. [GV697.A1H375] 78-20076 ISBN 0-385-12609-3 : 12.95
1. Athletes—Biography. I. Title. BIP

LIBBY, Bill. 796.4'8 B
Stars of the Olympics / Bill Libby. New York : Hawthorn Books, [1975] xi, 189 p., [10] leaves of plates : ill. ; 24 cm. Includes index. [GV697.A1L53 1975] 73-21313 ISBN 0-8015-7120-0 : 7.95
1. Athletes—Biography. 2. Athletes—United States—Biography. 3. Olympic games—Biography. I. Title.

LITSKY, Frank. 796'.092'2 B
Superstars / by Frank Litsky ; introd. by Howard Cosell. Secaucus, N.J. : Derbibooks, [1975] 351 p. : ill. ; 29 cm. [GV697.A1L57] 75-7753 ISBN 0-89009-044-0 : 16.95
1. Athletes—Biography. I. Title.

Athletes—Biography—Dictionaries, Juvenile.

THE Lincoln library of sports champions / [editor in chief, Art Berke, chief text editor, William J. Redding]. 2d ed. Columbus, Ohio : Sports Resources Co., 1978. 20 v. : ill. ; 29 cm. Includes index. Bibliography: v. 20, p. 106-111. Includes brief, alphabetically arranged biographies of 500 sports personalities from around the world representing more than 50 sports. Includes an alphabetical table of contents by sport and a glossary of sports terms. [GV697.A1L56 1978] 78-112619 ISBN 0-912168-01-3 : 199.95 (set) 796'.092'2 B
1. Athletes—Biography—Dictionaries, Juvenile. I. Berke, Art. II. Redding, William J.
Published by Frontier Press Co., Columbus, OH 43216 BIP

Athletes—Biography—Juvenile literature.

AASENG, Nathan. 796'.092'2 B
Little giants of pro sports / Nathan Aaseng. Minneapolis : Lerner Publications Co., c1980. p. cm. (The Sports heroes library) Contents.Contents.—Calvin Murphy.—Greg Pruitt.—Tracy Austin.—Pele.—Marcel Dionne.—Joe Morgan.—Fred Patek. [GV697.A1A2 1980] 920 80-12031 ISBN 0-8225-1059-6 (lib. bdg.) : 5.95
1. Athletes—Biography—Juvenile literature. I. Title. BIP

AASENG, Nathan. 796'.092'2 B
Winners never quit : athletes who beat the odds / Nathan Aaseng. Minneapolis: Lerner Publications Co., c1980. p. cm. (The Sports heroes library) Brief biographies of 10 athletes who achieved greatness while overcoming a handicap or misfortune. Includes Bobby Clarke, Wes Unseld, Rocky Bleier, John Hiller, Kitty O'Neill, Lee Trevino, Tom Dempsey, Larry Brown, Ron LeFlore, and Tommy John. [GV697.A1A23 1980] 920 80-12305 ISBN 0-8225-1060-X (lib. bdg.) : 5.95
1. Athletes—Biography—Juvenile literature. 2. Handicapped—Biography—Juvenile literature. I. Title.

ALLEN, Maury, 1932- 796'.0922
The record breakers. Englewood Cliffs, N.J., Prentice-Hall [1968] vii, 213 p. illus., ports. 22 cm. Contents.Contents.—Joe DiMaggio.—Toni Sailer.—Wilt Chamberlain.—Johnny Unitas.—Roger Bannister.—Don Schollander.—Jimmy Clark.—Jim Brown.—Bobby Jones.—Sandy Koufax.—Donald Campbell.—Gordie Howe.—Maureen Connolly.—George Billick.—Roger Maris. [GV697.A1A44] 68-31402 4.95
1. Athletes—Biography—Juvenile literature. I. Title. BIP

BERKOW, Ira. 796'.092'2 B
Beyond the dream : occasional heroes of sports / Ira Berkow ; foreword by Red Smith. 1st ed. New York : Atheneum, 1975. xiv, 221 p. ; 22 cm. Brief biographical sketches of personalities from every aspect of sports. [GV697.A1B47 1975] 920 75-16761 ISBN 0-689-30489-7 : 6.95
1. Athletes—Biography—Juvenile literature. 2. Sports—Biography—Juvenile literature. I. Title.

*GAUTT, Clare S. 927.963
Four stars from the world of sports: Henry Aaron, Roger Staubach, Kareem Abdul Jabbar, Bobby Orr by Clare and Frank Gautt, drawings by Ted Burwell New York, Walker [1975 c1973] 112 p. ill. 21 cm. [GV697.A1] 75-3909 ISBN 0-8027-6221-2 4.95
1. Athletes—Biography—Juvenile literature. I. Gault, Frank M. joint author II. Title.

GUTMAN, Bill. 796'.092'2 B
Superstars of the sports world / by Bill Gutman. New York : J. Messner, c1978. 96 p. : ill. ; 22 cm. Includes index. Career biographies of Bobby Clarke, Julius Erving, Chris Evert, Franco Harris, and Pete Rose. [GV697.A1G89] 920 77-28762 ISBN 0-671-32827-1 lib.bdg. : 7.29
1. Athletes—Biography—Juvenile literature. I. Title. BIP

MCADAM, Robert Everett, 1920- 796'.092'2 B
Climb any mountain / by Robert McAdam ; ill. by Pete Bentovoja. [Los Angeles] : Bowmar, c1976. 58 p. : ill. ; 23 cm. (His Play the game ; book 5) Brief biographies of nine athletes include: Billie Jean King, Tom Dempsey, Rick Wohlhuter, Tony Esposito, Olga Korbut, Marty Riessen, George Blanda, Hank Aaron, and Janet Lynn. [GV697.A1M26 bk. 5] 920 76-13760
1. Athletes—Biography—Juvenile literature. I. Bentovoja, Pete. II. Title.

†MCADAM, Robert Everett, 1920- 796'.092'2 B
More than speedy wheels / by Robert McAdam ; illustrations by Pete Bentovoja. [Los Angeles] : Bowmar, c1976. 56 p. : ill. ; 23 cm. (His Play the game ; book 8) Brief biographies of nine athletes including Micki King, Doug Collins, Henry Baucha, Nolan Ryan, Chi Cheng, Jerry Martin, John Rutherford, Roberto Clemente, and Kyle Rote, Jr. [GV697.A1M26 bk. 8] 76-13762 ISBN 0-8372-2271-0 pbk. : 2.00
1. Athletes—Biography—Juvenile literature. I. Title.

†MCADAM, Robert Everett, 1920- 796'.092'2 B
The skillful rider / by Robert McAdam ; ill. by Pete Bentovoja. Los Angeles : Bowmar, c1976. 56 p. : ill. ; 23 cm. (His Play the game ; book 6) Summarizes special moments and achievements in sports for Larry Wilson, Chris Evert, Jim Ryun, Nate Archibald, Marcia Morey, Jeff Jobe, Bob Lee, Pete Gray, and Robyn Smith. [GV697.A1M26 bk. 6] 920 76-13759 ISBN 0-8372-2269-9 pbk. : 2.00
1. Athletes—Biography—Juvenile literature. I. Bentovoja, Pete. II. Title.

PIZER, Vernon, 1918- 796'.092'2 B
Glorious triumphs : athletes who conquered adversity / Vernon Pizer. Rev. ed. New York : Dodd, Mead, 1980. p. cm. Includes index. Brief biographies of Barney Ross, Babe Didrikson, Gordie Howe, Althea Gibson, Glenn Cunningham, Jerry Kramer, Pete Gray, Tenley Albright, Carol Heiss, Alonzo Wilkins, Ben Hogan, Paul Berlenbach, Sammy Lee, and Jim Hurtubise—all athletes who persevered against great odds to attain prominence in their chosen sport. [GV697.A1P5 1980] 920 79-6648 ISBN 0-396-07793-5 : 6.95
1. Athletes—Biography—Juvenile literature. I. Title.

STAMBLER, Irwin. 796'.092'2 B
Speed kings: world's fastest humans. [1st ed.] Garden City, N.Y., Doubleday, 1973. 161 p. illus. 22 cm. Recounts the efforts of twelve people to set speed records in sprinting, swimming, distance running, flying, and bicycle, motorcycle, power boat, dragster, and automobile racing. [GV697.A1S68 1973] 920 73-79714 ISBN 0-385-09353-5 4.50
1. Athletes—Biography—Juvenile literature. I. Title.

SULLIVAN, George, 1927- 796'.092'2 B
Modern Olympic superstars / George Sullivan. New York : Dodd, Mead, c1979. 111 p. : ill. ; 22 cm. Includes index. Biographies of six Olympic gold medal champions of the 1976 games. [GV697.A1S82] 920 78-23184 ISBN 0-396-07651-3 : 5.95
1. Athletes—Biography—Juvenile literature. 2. Olympic games—Juvenile literature. I. Title. BIP

VASS, George. 796'.0922
Champions of sports: adventures in courage. Chicago, Reilly & Lee Books [1970] 202 p. ports. 24 cm. Brief biographical sketches of ten athletes include Babe Didrikson Zaharias, Jackie Robinson, Johnny Unitas, Mickey Mantle, Jesse Owens, Ben Hogan, Althea Gibson, Jimmy Piersall, Barney Ross, Pete Reiser. [GV697.A1V35] 920 70-106152 4.95
1. Athletes—Biography—Juvenile literature. I. Title.

Athletes—Canada—Biography.

FERGUSON, Bob, 1931- 796'.092'2 B
Who's who in Canadian sport / Bob Ferguson. Scarborough : Prentice-Hall of Canada ; Englewood Cliffs, New Jersey : Prentice-Hall, c1977. 310 p. ; 24 cm. Includes index. [GV697.A1F47] 77-378486 ISBN 0-13-958421-8 pbk. : 10.00
1. Athletes—Canada—Biography. I. Title. BIP

Athletes—Great Britain—Biography.

BRITISH athletes, 1951. 796.4'2'0922 Foreword by the Rt. Hon. the Lord Burghley. Action photos. of more than 200 famous British athletes with biographies by N.D. McWhirker;walkers

by F. W. Blackmore [Rochester, Eng., Athletic and Sporting Publications, 1951?] 1 v. (unpaged) illus. 27 cm. [GV697.A1B754] 74-185333
1. Athletes—Great Britain—Biography. I. McWhirter, Norris Dewar.

Athletes in Action (Basketball team)

ATHLETES in Action 796.32'32
(Basketball team)
One way to play basketball / Athletes in Action ; foreword by John Wooden ; action photos. by Ray Aguirre aand Bob Kofahl. San Diego : Beta Books, c1977. 160 p. : ill. ; 21 cm. [GV885.4.A86 1977] 77-1207 ISBN 0-89293-080-2 : 3.95
1. Athletes in Action (Basketball team) 2. Basketball—History. 3. Basketball players—Biography. I. Title.

ATHLETES in Action 796.32'32
(Basketball team)
One way to play basketball / Athletes in Action ; foreword by John Wooden ; action photos. by Ray Aguirre aand Bob Kofahl. San Diego : Beta Books, c1977. 160 p. : ill. ; 21 cm. [GV885.4.A86 1977] 77-1207 ISBN 0-89293-080-2 : 3.95
1. Athletes in Action (Basketball team) 2. Basketball—History. 3. Basketball players—Biography. I. Title.

Athletes, Jewish.

RIBALOW, Harold Uriel, 927.96
1919-
The Jew in American sports. [2d] rev. ed. New York, Bloch Pub. Co., 1955 [c1948] 356p. illus. 22cm. [GV697.A1R5 1955] 54-11310
1. Athlectes, Jewish. I. Title.

Athletes—Juvenile literature.

PIZER, Vernon, 1918- 796'.0922
Glorious triumphs; athletes who conquered adversity. New York, Dodd, Mead [1968] viii, 209 p. ports. 21 cm. Brief biographies of twelve athletes who persevered against great odds to attain prominence in their chosen sport. Included are Barney Ross, Ben Hogan, Glenn Cunningham, Manolete, Clarence Demar, Alonzo Wilkins, Peter Gray, Paul Berlenbach, Babe Didrikson, Jerry Kramer, Frank Malzone, Althea Gibson. [GV697.A1P5] 920 68-9454 4.50
1. Athletes—Juvenile literature. I. Title. BIP

Athletes—Latin America—Biography—Juvenile literature.

IZENBERG, Jerry. 796'.092'2 B
Great Latin sports figures : the proud people / by Jerry Izenberg. 1st ed. Garden City, N.Y. : Doubleday, c1976. 105 p., [4] leaves of plates : ill. ; 22 cm. Biographies of Latin American athletes who were important in North American sports. [GV697.A1I93] 920 75-36629 ISBN 0-385-11117-7 : 5.95. ISBN 0-385-12060-5 lib. bdg.
1. Athletes—Latin America—Biography—Juvenile literature. 2. Athletes—United States—Biography—Juvenile literature. I. Title. BIP

Athletes—Pennsylvania—Biography.

BEERS, Paul B. 796'.092'2 B
Profiles in Pennsylvania sports : athletic heroes and exploits from past and present in the Commonwealth where sports are almost everyone's passion / Paul B. Beers. Harrisburg, Pa. : Stackpole Books, [1975] 256 p. : ill. ; 23 cm. Includes index. [GV697.A1B43] 75-19234 ISBN 0-8117-2046-2 pbk. : 6.95
1. Athletes—Pennsylvania—Biography. 2. Sports—Pennsylvania—History. I. Title.

Athletes—United States—Biography.

BROSNAN, Jim. 796.3'0922
Little League to big league. New York, Random House [1968] xiv, 175 p. illus., ports. 22 cm. (Little League library) [GV697.A1B76 1968] 68-14486
1. Athletes—United States—Biography. I. Title.

CLARK, Steven, 1951- 796'.092'2 B
Fight against time : five athletes—a legacy of courage / Steven Clark. 1st ed. New York : Atheneum, 1979. xiii, 173 p. : ports. ; 22 cm. Contents.Contents.—Introduction.—Freddie Steinmark.—Danny Thompson.—Joe Roth.—Harry Agganis.—Ernie Davis. [GV697.A1C597 1979] 78-20353 ISBN 0-689-10953-9 : $8.95
1. Athletes—United States—Biography. 2. Cancer Biography. I. Title.

GEMME, Leila B. 796'.092'2 B
The new breed of athlete / by Leila B. Gemme. New York : Washington Square Press, 1975. 190 p. : ill. ; 18 cm. [GV697.A1G45 1975] 75-307190 ISBN 0-671-48150-9 : 1.25
1. Athletes—United States—Biography. I. Title.

GLASS, William. 796.33'2'0922
Don't blame the game; an answer to super star swingers and a look at what's right with sports [by] Bill Glass & William M. Pinson, Jr. With a foreword by Roger Staubach. Waco, Tex., Word Books [1972] 168 p. illus. 23 cm. Includes bibliographical references. [GV697.A1G5] 72-86320 4.95
1. Athletes—United States—Biography. 2. Christian ethics. I. Pinson, William M., joint author. II. Title.

JORDAN, Pat. 796'.092'2 B
After the sundown / Pat Jordan. New York : Dodd, Mead, 1979. p. cm. [GV697.A1J67] 79-9533 ISBN 0-396-07773-0 : 8.95 8.95
1. Athletes—United States—Biography. 2. Athletes—United States—Retirement. I. Title. BIP

PEPE, Phil. 796'.0922
Winners never quit. Englewood Cliffs, N.J., Prentice-Hall [1968] xvi, 272 p. illus., ports. 22 cm. [GV697.A1P4] 67-26079
1. Athletes—United States—Biography. I. Title.

RATLIFF, Harold V., 796'.092'2
1903-
Paths to glory: great men and women in Texas sports history [by] Harold V. Ratliff. Waco, Tex., Word Books [1972] 170 p. illus. 21 cm. [GV697.A1R34] 72-91028 2.95
1. Athletes—United States—Biography. 2. Texas—Biography. I. Title.

SCHAAP, Richard, 1934- 796'.0973
Sport / Dick Schaap. New York : Arbor House, c1975. xiv, 310 p. ; 22 cm. [GV697.A1S36 1975] 75-13407 8.95
1. Athletes—United States—Biography. 2. Sports—Miscellanea. 3. Biography—20th century. I. Title. BIP

SCHAAP, Richard, 1934- 796'.0973
Sport / Dick Schaap. New York : Arbor House, c1975. xiv, 310 p. ; 22 cm. [GV697.A1S36 1975] 75-13407 8.95
1. Athletes—United States—Biography. 2. Sports—Miscellanea. 3. Biography—20th century. I. Title. BIP

STOWERS, Carlton. 796'.092'2 B
Profiles of Christian athletes who became ... the overcomers / Carlton Stowers. Waco, Tex. : Word Books, c1978. 149 p., [1] leaf of plates : ill. ; 21 cm. [GV697.A1S75] 78-58594 ISBN 0-8499-2837-0 pbk. : 3.95
1. Athletes—United States—Biography. 2. Religion and sports. I. Title. II. Title: The overcomers. BIP

Athletes—United States—Biography—Dictionaries.

HICKOK, Ralph. 796'.0922
Who was who in American sports. New York, Hawthorn Books [1971] xlii, 338 p. illus. 24 cm. Includes bibliographical references. [GV697.A1H5] 72-158009 9.95
1. Athletes—United States—Biography—Dictionaries. I. Title.

Athletes—United States—Biography—Juvenile literature.

BORTSTEIN, Larry. 796'.092'3 B
After Olympic glory : the lives of ten outstanding medalists / by Larry Bortstein. New York : F. Warne, c1978. 185 p. : ill. ; 24 cm. Biographies of ten Olympic gold medalists: Micki King, Muhammad Ali, Bob Mathias, Donna de Varona, Jesse Owens, Tenley Albright, Vince Matthews, Benjamin Spock, Nell Jackson, and Bill Bradley. [GV697.A1B578] 920 76-6779 ISBN 0-7232-6135-0 : 7.95
1. Athletes—United States—Biography—Juvenile literature. 2. Olympic games—Juvenile literature. I. Title. BIP

BROWN, Vashti. 796 B
Out in front [by] Vashti Brown, Jack Brown [and] Margaret Lalor. With illus. by Don Miller. Boston, Houghton Mifflin [1971] vii, 150 p. col. illus. 24 cm. Brief biographies of twenty athletes whose performance in various sports made them famous. Includes Jim Thorpe, Peggy Fleming, Eddie Arcaro, Wilma Rudolph, Pancho Gonzales, and Gertrude Ederle. [GV697.A1B78] 920 70-124540 ISBN 0-395-10863-2
1. Athletes—United States—Biography—Juvenile literature. I. Brown, Jack, 1905- joint author. II. Lalor, Margaret, joint author. III. Miller, Don, 1923- illus. IV. Title.

HEFLEY, James C. 796'.0922
The will to win; faith in action in the lives of athletes [by] James C. Hefley. Grand Rapids, Mich., Zondervan Pub. House [1968] 106 p. ports. 22 cm. [GV697.A1H37] 68-27460
1. Athletes—United States—Biography—Juvenile literature. 2. Youth—Religious life. I. Title.

KATZ, Frederic, 1938- 796'.0922 B
American sports heroes of today, by Fred Katz. New York, Random House [1970] x, 174 p. illus., ports. 29 cm. (Landmark giant, 22) Brief biographies of forty contemporary American athletes outstanding in baseball, football, boxing, golf, hockey, automobile racing, and other sports. [GV697.A1K3] 920 70-117545 ISBN 0-394-90287-4
1. Athletes—United States—Biography—Juvenile literature. I. Title.

LEIPOLD, L. Edmond, 796'.0922
1902-
Famous American athletes, by L. Edmond Leipold. Minneapolis, Denison [1969] 83 p. 25 cm. (His Famous American heroes and leaders series) Brief biographies of eight men and two women who have had outstanding careers in sports: Bob Feller, Joe Louis, Babe Ruth, Bill Tilden, Johnny Weissmuller, Bobby Jones, Bob Mathias, Carol Heiss Jenkins, Jack Dempsey, and Shirley Rudolph Garms. [GV697.A1L42] 920 78-91282
1. Athletes—United States—Biography—Juvenile literature. I. Title.

LORIMER, Lawrence 796'.092'2 B
T., comp.
Breaking in: nine first-person accounts about becoming an athlete. Compiled and Edited by Lawrence T. Lorimer. New York, Random House [1974] xvi, 198 p. ports. 22 cm. [GV697.A1L67 1974] 73-18743 ISBN 0-394-82653-1 2.95
1. Athletes—United States—Biography—Juvenile literature. I. Title.

O'CONNOR, Dick, 796'.092'2 B
1930-
American Olympic stars / by Dick O'Connor. New York : Putnam, c1976. 128 p. ; 21 cm. (Putnam sports shelf) Includes index. Briefly traces the winning feats of American athletes in the Olympic Games from 1896 through 1972. [GV697.A1O25 1976] 920 75-44378 ISBN 0-399-61005-7 lib. bdg. : 5.29
1. Athletes—United States—Biography—Juvenile literature. 2. Olympic games—Biography—Juvenile literature. I. Title. BIP

SIGNIFICANT American 796'.092'2 B
sport champions. Chicago : Childrens Press, [1976] p. cm. Includes index. Brief biographies of 177 sports champions arranged in chronological-alphabetical order. [GV697.A1S48] 920 75-20684 ISBN 0-516-05308-6 : 9.25
1. Athletes—United States—Biography—Juvenile literature. I. Title: Sport champions.

Athletes' wives—Biography.

PARR, Jeanne, 1926- 796'.092'2
The superwives / Jeanne Parr. New York : Coward, McCann & Geoghegan, c1976. 287 p. : ports. ; 22 cm. [GV697.A1P33 1976] 75-41348 ISBN 0-698-10716-0 : 7.95
1. Athletes' wives—Biography. I. Title.

PARR, Jeanne, 1926- 796'.092'2
The superwives / [by] Jeanne Parr. New York : Avon Books, 1977,c1976. 328p. : ill. ; 18 cm. [GV697.A1P33 1976] ISBN 0-380-01641-9 pbk. : 1.75
1. Atheletes' wives-Biography. I. Title.
L.C. card no. for 1976 Coward,, McCann and Geoghegan ed.:75-41348. BIP

Athletes, Women—Biography—Juvenile literature.

GUTMAN, Bill. 796'.092'2 B
Modern women superstars / Bill Gutman. New York : Dodd, Mead, c1977. 112 p. : ill. ; 22 cm. Includes index. Brief biographies of six women athletes including, Nadia Comaneci, Dorothy Hamill, and Kathy Kusner, who have excelled in their chosen sport. [GV697.A1G88] 920 77-6503 ISBN 0-396-07489-8 : 5.95
1. Athletes, Women—Biography—Juvenile literature. I. Title. BIP

GUTMAN, Bill. 796'.092'2 B
More modern women superstars / Bill Gutman. New York : Dodd, Mead, c1979. 125 p. : ill. ; 22 cm. Includes index. Brief biographies highlighting the careers of six women athletes including Janet Guthrie, Tracy Austin, Diana Nyad, Joan Joyce, and Carol Blazejowski. [GV697.A1G884] 920 78-22433 ISBN 0-396-07680-7 : 5.95
1. Athletes, Women—Biography—Juvenile literature. I. Title. BIP

†HOLLANDER, 796'.019'40922 B
Phyllis.
100 greatest women in sports / by Phyllis Hollander. New York : Grosset & Dunlap, 1977, c1976 142 p. : ill. ; 28 cm. (Illustrated true books) "An Associated Features book." Includes index. Presents profiles of more than 100 women athletes who have made significant contributions to their respective sports. [GV697.A1H576] 920 76-4254 ISBN 0-448-12506-4 : 4.95. ISBN 0-448-13367-9 lib.bdg. : 5.99
1. Athletes, Women—Biography—Juvenile literature. I. Title.

PHILLIPS, Louis. 796'.092'2 B
Women in sports : records, stars, feats, and facts / by Louis Phillips and Karen Markoe ; ill. by Paul Frame. 1st ed. New York : Harcourt Brace Jovanovich, c1979. p. cm. (A Handy book) Contains brief career biographies of 35 women athletes and a summary of women's achievements in sports. [GV697.A1P45] 79-87527 ISBN 0-15-299186-7 : 2.95
1. Athletes, Women—Biography—Juvenile literature. 2. Sports for women—Records—Juvenile literature. I. Markoe, Karen, joint author. II. Frame, Paul, 1913- III. Title. BIP

ZAHARIAS, Mildred Babe 927.96352
(Didrikson) 1913-
This life I've led: an autobiography, [by] Babe Didrikson Zaharias, as told to Harry Paxton, with an introduction by Joanna Lee. [New York] Dell [1975 c1955] 217 p. 18 cm. [GV964Z3A3] 1.50 (pbk.)
I. Title.
L.C. card no. for original edition: 55-10217

Athletes, Women—Juvenile literature.

HOLLANDER, Phyllis. 796'.092'2
American women in sports. New York, Grosset & Dunlap [1972] 112 p. illus. 21 cm. "An Associated Features book." "A W. W. Norton book." Brief biographies of fifty-two outstanding women athletes in various sports. [GV697.A1H57] 920 73-153920 ISBN 0-448-21412-1
1. Athletes, Women—Juvenile literature. I. Title.

Athletes, Women—Kentucky—Biography.

PARRISH, Margaret Ware. 796'.092'2
Outstanding Kentucky women in sports, 1900-1968. [Midway? Ky., 1968?] 73 p. 22 cm. [GV697.A1P34] 72-194148
1. Athletes, Women—Kentucky—Biography. I. Title.

Athletes, Women—United States—Biography—Juvenile literature.

DAVIS, Mary Lee, 1935- 796'.092'2 B
Women in sports and recreation / by Mary L. Davis. Minneapolis : T. S. Danison, c1976. 15 p. : ill. ; 22 cm. (Women in American life series ; book 5) (Series: Davis, Mary Lee, 1935- Women in American life series ; book 5.) A brief sketch of the history of women's athletics and biographical notes of women noted for outstanding accomplishments in the field. [GV697.A1D37] 920 77-352781 ISBN 0-513-01501-9
1. Athletes, Women—United States—Biography—Juvenile literature. I. Title. II. Series.

JACOBS, Helen Hull. 796'.092'2 B
Famous modern American women athletes / Helen Hull Jacobs ; illustrated with photos. New York : Dodd, Mead, [1975] p. cm. Includes index. Brief biographies of eight American women who have excelled in bowling, skating, diving, golf, skiing, swimming, tennis, or track. [GV697.A1J32] 75-11440 ISBN 0-396-07195-3 : 4.95
1. Athletes, Women—United States—Biography—Juvenile literature. I. Title. **BIP**

RYAN, Joan, 1936- 796'.092'2 B
Sports / by Joan Ryan. Minneapolis : Dillon Press, [1975] 135 p. : ill. ; 23 cm. (Contributions of women) Bibliography: p. [134]-135. Biographies of six women athletes: Babe Didrikson Zaharias, Kathy Kusner, Wilma Rudolph, Billie Jean King, Peggy Fleming, and Melissa Belote. [GV697.A1R92] 920 74-32058 ISBN 0-87518-082-5 lib.bdg. : 6.95
1. Athletes, Women—United States—Biography—Juvenile literature. I. Title.

SABIN, Francene. 796'.092'2
Women who win / by Francene Sabin ; illustrated with photos. New York : Random House, [1975] xiv, 171 p. : ill. ; 22 cm. Includes index. Brief biographies emphasizing the athletic achievements of such women as Billy Jean King, Cathy Rigby, Micki King, Cheryl Toussaint, and others. [GV697.A1S22] 920 74-20835 ISBN 0-394-82832-1 : 3.95 ISBN 0-394-92832-6 lib.bdg. : 4.99
1. Athletes, Women—United States—Biography—Juvenile literature. I. Title. **BIP**

STAMBLER, Irwin. 796'.019'40922 B
Women in sports / Irwin Stambler. 1st ed. Garden City, N.Y. : Doubleday, 1975. 155 p., [12] leaves of plates : ill. ; 22 cm. [GV697.A1S69] 920 74-12713 4.95 ISBN 0-385-07426-3 lib.bdg. : 5.90
1. Athletes, Women—United States—Biography—Juvenile literature. I. Title. Contents omitted. **BIP**

Atkins, Chet.

ATKINS, Chet. 787'.61'0924 B
Country gentleman [by] Chet Atkins with Bill Neely. Chicago, H. Regnery [1974] xiii, 226 p. illus. 21 cm. [ML419.A83A3] 73-21514 ISBN 0-8092-9051-0 7.95
1. Atkins, Chet. I. Neely, Bill. II. Title.

O'DONNELL, Red. 787'.61'0924
Chet Atkins. [1st ed.] Nashville, Athens Music Co. [1967] 46 p. illus., ports. 16 x 24 cm. [ML419.A83O3] 67-6343
1. Atkins, Chet. I. Title.

Atkins, Evelyn E.

ATKINS, Evelyn E. 942.3'74 B
We bought an island / Evelyn E. Atkins. London : Harrap, 1976. 164 p., [4] leaves of plates : ill. ; 23 cm. [CT788.A77A38 1976] 76-373197 ISBN 0-245-52940-3 : £3.25
1. Atkins, Evelyn E. 2. England—Biography. I. Title.

Atkins, Ollie, 1916-

ATKINS, Ollie, 1916- 770'.92'4 B
The White House years : triumph and tragedy / Ollie Atkins. 1st ed. Chicago : Playboy Press, c1977. 244 p. : ill. ; 24 cm. [TR140.A82A38] 77-23545 ISBN 0-87223-494-0 : 12.50
1. Atkins, Ollie, 1916- 2. Nixon, Richard Milhous, 1913- 3. Photographers—United States—Biography. I. Title.

Atkins, Susan, 1948-

ATKINS, Susan, 1948- 248'.246
Child of Satan, child of God / Susan Atkins, with Bob Slosser. Plainfield, N.J. : Logos International, c1977. vii, 290 p., [3] leaves of plates : ill. ; 22 cm. [BV4935.A86A33] 77-81947 ISBN 0-88270-229-7 : 7.95
1. Atkins, Susan, 1948- 2. Converts—California—Biography. 3. California—Biography. I. Slosser, Bob, joint author. II. Title. **BIP**

Atkinson, Donald Taylor,

ATKINSON, Donald Taylor, 1874- 926.1
Texas surgeon; an autobiography. New York, Washburn [1958] 180p. 21cm. [R154.A83A3] 58-11499
I. Title.

Atkinson, Edward, 1827-1905.

WILLIAMSON, Harold Francis, 1901- 330'.92'4 B
Edward Atkinson; the biography of an American liberal, 1827-1905. New York, Arno Press, 1972 [c1934] xiv, 304 p. port. 24 cm. (The Right wing individualist tradition in America) Originally presented as the author's thesis, Harvard. Bibliography: p. [283]-298. [HB119.A8W5 1972] 79-172239 ISBN 0-405-00448-6
1. Atkinson, Edward, 1827-1905. I. Title. II. Series. **BIP**

Atkinson, Henry, 1782-1842.

NICHOLS, Roger L. 355.3320924
General Henry Atkinson, a Western military career. Norman, Univ. of Okla. Pr. [c.1965] xiv, 243p. illus., maps, ports. 23cm. Bibl. [E340.A85N5] 65-11246 5.95
1. Atkinson, Henry, 1782-1842. 2. Indians of North America—Wars—1815-1875. I. Title. **BIP**

NICHOLS, Roger L 355.3320924 (B)
General Henry Atkinson, a Western military career, by Roger L. Nichols. [1st ed.] Norman, University of Oklahoma Press [1965] xiv, 243 p. illus., maps, ports. 23 cm. Bibliography: p. 224-236. [E340.A85N5] 65-11246
1. Atkinson, Henry, 1782-1842. 2. Indians of North America — Wars — 1815-1875. I. Title.

Atkinson, John Robert, 1887-1964.

WESTRATE, Edwin J. 923.673
Beacon in the night. New York, Vantage [c.1964] 244p. illus., ports. 21cm. 64-56423 4.95 bds.,
1. Atkinson, John Robert, 1887-1964. I. Title.

WESTRATE, Edwin J 923.673
Beacon in the night, by Edwin J. Westrate. [1st ed.] New York, Vantage Press [1964] 244 p. illus., ports. 21 cm. [HV1624.A87W4] 64-56423
1. Atkinson, John Robert, 1887-1964. I. Title.

Atkinson, Virginia M., 1861-1941.

WHITE, Mary Culler, 1875- 922.773
Just Jennie; the life story of Virginia M. Atkinson. Atlanta, Tupper and Love [1955] 103p. illus. 22cm. [BV3427.A85W4] 55-8573
1. Atkinson, Virginia M., 1861-1941. I. Title.

Atkinson, Wilmer, 1840-1920.

ATKINSON, Wilmer, 1840-1920. 070.4'092'4 B
Wilmer Atkinson, an autobiography. New York, Beekman Publishers, 1974. xviii, 375 p. illus. 23 cm. (American newspapermen, 1790-1933) Reprint of the 1920 ed. published by W. Atkinson Co., Philadelphia. [PN4874.A6A3 1974] 74-645 ISBN 0-8464-0032-4 20.00
1. Atkinson, Wilmer, 1840-1920. I. Title.

Atlan, Jean Michel, 1913-1960.

RAGON, Michel 759.4
Atlan. [Paris] G. Fall [dist. New York, Efron, c.1962] 91p. illus. (pt. col.) 29cm. 62-52237 6.50
1. Atlan, Jean Michel, 1913-1960. I. Title.

Atlanta—Police.

JENKINS, Herbert T. 363.2'0924 B
Keeping the peace; a police chief looks at his job, by Herbert Jenkins. [1st ed.] New York, Harper & Row [1970] xii, 203 p. 22 cm. Autobiographical. [HV8148.A72J4] 72-95967 5.95
1. Atlanta—Police. I. Title.

Atomic bomb—History—Addresses, essays, lectures.

ALL in our time : 539.7'092'2 B
the reminiscences of twelve nuclear pioneers / edited by Jane Wilson. Chicago : Bulletin of the Atomic Scientists, 1975. 236 p. : ill. ; 19 cm. Includes bibliographical references and index. [QC773.A1A44] 75-12223
1. Atomic bomb—History—Addresses, essays, lectures. 2. Nuclear physics—History—Addresses, essays, lectures. I. Wilson, Jane, 1916-

Atterbury, Francis, Bp. of Rochester, 1662-1732.

BENNETT, Gareth Vaughan. 283'.092'4 B
The Tory crisis in church and state 1688-1730 : the career of Francis Atterbury Bishop of Rochester / G. V. Bennett. Oxford : Clarendon Press, 1975. xvii, 335 p., [5] leaves of plates : ill. ; 23 cm. Includes index. Bibliography: p. [311]-324. [DA501.A8B46] 76-358312 ISBN 0-19-822444-3 : £10.00 ($26.00 U.S.)
1. Atterbury, Francis, Bp. of Rochester, 1662-1732. 2. Church of England—History. 3. Church and state in England. 4. Jacobites. I. Title. **BIP**

Attila, d. 453.

WEBB, Robert N. 936
Attila, King of the Huns, by Robert N. Webb. New York, F. Watts [1965] 113 p. 22 cm. (Masters of infamy) [D141.W4] 65-21643
1. Attila, d. 453. I. Title. II. Series.

Attlee, Clement Richard,

ATTLEE, Clement Richard, 1st earl, 1883-1967. 923.242
As it happened. New York, Viking Press, 1954. viii, 312 p. ports. 22 cm. Autobiography. [DA585.A8A8 1954a] 54-7570
I. Title.

ATTLEE, Clement Richard Attlee, 1st earl, 1883- 923.242
As it happened. New York, Viking Press, 1954. viii, 312p. ports. 22cm. Autobiography. [DA585.A8A8 1954a] 54-7570
I. Title.

FRANCIS-WILLIAMS, Edward Francis Williams, baron, 1903- 923.242
Twilight of Empire: memoirs of Prime Minister Clement Attlee, as set down by Francis Williams. [1st American ed.] New York, Barnes [1962, c1961] 264 p. 22 cm. First published in 1961 under title: A Prime Minister remembers. [DA585.A8F7] 62-14979
1. Attlee, Clement Richard Attlee, 1st earl, 1883- I. Title.

Atwill, Mattie

ATWILL, Mattie 920.7
Thy will be done. New York, Carlton [c.] 1962. 118p. (Reflection bk.) 2.50
I. Title.

Aubry, Francois Xavier, 1824-1854.

CHAPUT, Donald. 978'.02 B
Francois X. Aubry : trader, trailmaker and voyageur in the Southwest, 1846-1854 / by Donald Chaput. Glendale, Calif. : A. H. Clark Co., 1975. 249 p. : ill., maps (1 fold. col.) ; 23 cm. (Western frontiersman series ; 16) Includes index. Bibliography: p. [225]-236. [F786.A892C45] 74-27225 ISBN 0-87062-110-6 : 15.50
1. Aubry, Francois Xavier, 1824-1854. 2. Santa Fe Trail.

Auchincloss, Louis—Biography.

AUCHINCLOSS, Louis. 813'.5'4 B
A writer's capital / by Louis Auchincloss. Boston : Houghton Mifflin, 1979, c1974. 160 p., [4] leaves of plates : ill. ; 20 cm. Includes index. [PS3501.U25Z52 1979] 79-12936 ISBN 0-395-28518-6 pbk. : 4.95
1. Auchincloss, Louis—Biography. 2. Authors, American—20th century—Biography. 3. Lawyers—United States—Biography. I. Title. **BIP**

Auden, Wystan Hugh, 1907-1973.

OSBORNE, Charles, 1927- 821'.9'12 B
W. H. Auden : the life of a poet / Charles Osborne. American 1st ed. New York : Harcourt Brace Jovanovich, c1979. 318 p. ; 28 cm. Includes bibliographical references and index.001(c 79-13116 [PS3501.U55Z83 1979] 79-1840 ISBN 0-15-194286-2 : 15.95
1. Auden, Wystan Hugh, 1907-1973. 2. Poets, American—20th century—Biography. **BIP**

*SPENDER, Stephen, ed. 823'.9'12
W. H. Auden, a tribute New York, Macmillan 1975. 255 p. illus. 26 cm. Includes index [PR6023] 74-15364 14.95
1. Auden, Wystan Hugh, 1907-1973. I. Title.

Audett, James Henry.

AUDETT, James Henry. 923.4173
Rap sheet; my life story, by Blackie Audett (James Henry Audett) Foreword by Gene Lowall. New York, William Sloane Associates [1954] 284 p. illus. 22 cm. [HV6248.A8A3] 54-10085
I. Title.

Audubon, John James, 1785-1851.

ADAMS, Alexander B 598.20924 (B)
John James Audubon; a biography, by Alexander B. Adams. New York, Putnam [1966] 510 p. illus., facsims., ports. 22 cm. Bibliography: p. 475-486. [QL31.A9A6] 66-15573

1. Audubon, John James, 1785-1851. I. Title.

AUDUBON, John James, 598.2'0924 B 1785-1851.
Audubon, by himself; a profile of John James Audubon from writings selected, arranged, and edited, by Alice Ford. [1st ed.] Garden City, N.Y., Published for the American Museum of Natural History [by] the Natural History Press [1969] xi, 276 p. illus., ports. 25 cm. Bibliography: p. [263]-264. [QL31.A9A3] 71-81029 8.95
I. Ford, Alice Elizabeth, 1906- comp. II. American Museum of Natural History, New York.

AUDUBON the 598.2'0924
naturalist; a history of his life and time [Magnolia, Mass., Peter Smith, 1968] 2v. illus., facsims., ports. 22cm. (Dover bk. rebound) Orig. documents, v. 2, p. [313]-379. Bibl. [QL31.A9H4 1968] (B) 11.00 set,
1. Audubon, John James, 1785-1851. I. Herrick, Francis Hobart, 1858-1940

BANNON, Lois. 599'.092'4
Handbook of Audubon prints / Lois Bannon and Taylor Clark. Gretna : Pelican Pub. Co., 1979. p. cm. Includes index. Bibliography: p. [QL31.A9B36] 79-1319 ISBN 0-88289-202-9 pbk. : 4.95
1. Audubon, John James, 1785-1851. 2. Birds in art. 3. Prints, American—Collectors and collecting. 4. Prints—19th century—United States—Collectors and collecting. 5. Ornithologists—United States—Biography. 6. Artists—United States—Biography. I. Clark, Taylor, joint author. II. Title. **BIP**

CHANCELLOR, John. 598.2'092'4 B
Audubon : a biography / by John Chancellor. New York : Viking Press, 1978. 224 p. : ill. ; 26 cm. (A Studio book) Includes index. Bibliography: p. 219. [QL31.A9C43] 78-8465 ISBN 0-670-14053-8 : 16.95
1. Audubon, John James, 1785-1851. 2. Ornithologists—United States—Biography.

FORD, Alice Elizabeth, 925.9 1906-
John James Audubon, by Alice Ford. [1st ed.] Norman, University of Oklahoma Press [1964] xiv, 488 p. illus. (part col.) ports. 25 cm. Bibliography: p. 451-469. [QL31.A9F6] 64-20757
1. Audubon, John James, 1785-1851.

FRIES, Waldemar H , 598.2'973 1889-
The double elephant folio: the story of Audubon's Birds of America [by] Waldemar H. Fries. Chicago, American Library Association, 1973 [i.e. 1974] xxn, 501 p. illus. 27 cm. Includes bibliographical references. [QL674.A953F74] 73-12101 ISBN 0-8389-0103-4 3.50 (pbk.)
1. Audubon, John James, 1785-1851. The birds of America. 2. Audubon, John James, 1785-1851. I. Title.

GORDON, Patricia, 1904- 925.9
The story of John J. Audubon, by Joan Howard [pseud.] Illustrated by Federico Castellon. New York, Grosset & Dunlap [1954] 181p. illus. 22cm. (Signature books, 27cm. [QL31.A9G66] 54-5859
1. Audubon, John James, 1785-1851. I. Title.

HERRICK, Francis 598.2'0924 B Hobart, 1858-1940.
Audubon the naturalist; a history of his life and time. New York, Dover Publications [1968] 2 v. illus., facsims., ports. 22 cm. "Original documents": v. 2, p. [313]-379. Bibliography: v. 2, p. 401-461. [QL31.A9H4 1968] 68-14996
1. Audubon, John James, 1785-1851.

HOGEBOOM, Amy, 1891- 925.9
Audubon and his sons; illustrated with prints by John James Audubon, John Woodhouse Audubon, and others. Supplemented with drawings by Paul Galdone. New York, Lothrop, Lee & Shepard Co. [1956] 210p. illus. 22cm. [QL31.A9H6] 53-6740
1. Audubon, John James, 1785-1851. 2. Audubon, John Woodhouse, 1812-1862. I. Title.

KEATING, Louis 598.2'092'4 B Clark, 1907-
Audubon : the Kentucky years / L. Clark Keating. Lexington : University Press of Kentucky, c1976. viii, 92 p. : port. ; 21 cm. (The Kentucky bicentennial bookshelf) [QL31.A9K4] 75-38216 ISBN 0-8131-0215-4 : 3.95
1. Audubon, John James, 1785-1851. I. Title. II. Series. **BIP**

KEATING, Louis 598.2'092'4 B Clark, 1907-
Audubon : the Kentucky years / L. Clark Keating. Lexington : University Press of Kentucky, c1976. viii, 92 p. : port. ; 21 cm. (The Kentucky bicentennial bookshelf) [QL31.A9K4] 75-38216 ISBN 0-8131-0215-4 : 3.95
1. Audubon, John James, 1785-1851. I. Title. II. Series. **BIP**

KIERAN, Margaret (Ford) 925.9
John James Audubon, by Margaret and John Kieran; illustrated by Christine Price. New York, Random House [1954] 182p. illus 22cm. (Landmark books, 48) [QL31.A9K5] 54-6269
1. Audubon, John James, 1785-1851. I. Kieran, John, 1892- joint author. II. Title.

MUSCHAMP, Edward A. 598.2'092'4 B
Audacious Audubon; the story of a great pioneer, artist, naturalist & man. Freeport, N.Y., Books for Libraries Press [1973] p. Reprint of the 1929 ed. published by Brentano's, New York. [QL31.A9M85 1973] 73-5962 ISBN 0-518-19063-3
1. Audubon, John James, 1785-1851. I. Title.

MUSCHAMP, Edward A. 598.2'092'4 B
Audacious Audubon; the story of a great pioneer, artist, naturalist & man. Freeport, N.Y., Books for Libraries Press [1973] p. Reprint of the 1929 ed. published by Brentano's, New York. [QL31.A9M85 1973] 73-5962 ISBN 0-518-19063-3
1. Audubon, John James, 1785-1851. I. Title.

PEARE, Catherine Owens. 925.9
John James Audubon, his life; illustrated by Margaret Ayer. [1st ed.] New York, Holt [1953] 89p. illus. 21cm. [QL31.A9P36] 52-13070
1. Audubon, John James, 1785-1851. I. Title.

ROURKE, Constance Mayfield, v. 12 1885-
Audubon, by Constance Rourke. Black and white illustrations by James MacDonald. Large type ed. New York, Franklin Watts [1964] 342 p. illus. 29 cm. Pages 319-335, bibliographical references included in "Note." 67-63747
1. Audubon, John James, 1785-1851. I. Title.

Audubon, John James, 1785-1851 — Juvenile literature.

AYARS, James Sterling. j92
John James Audubon: bird artist. Illustrated by George I. Parrish. Campaign, Ill., Garrard Pub. Co. [1966] 80 p. col. illus. 23 cm. (A Discovery book) [QL31.A9A9] 66-10013
1. Audubon, John James, 1785-1851 — Juvenile literature. I. Title. **BIP**

SMARIDGE, Norah. 598.2'0924 B
Audubon: the man who painted birds. Illustrated by Charles Robinson. New York, World Pub. Co. [1970] 77 p. illus. 24 cm. A biography of the nineteenth-century naturalist and artist famous for his accurate paintings of birds and animals. [PZ10.S712Au] 92 71-101849 5.95
1. Audubon, John James, 1785-1851— Juvenile literature. I. Robinson, Charles, 1931- illus. II. Title.

STEVENSON, Janet. 925.9
Painting America's wildlife: John James Audubon. Illustrated by Robert Boehmer. Chicago, Encyclopaedia Britannica Press [1964? c1961] 191 p. illus. (part col.) 22 cm. (Britannica bookshelf: Great lives series) [QL31] 64-57482
1. Audubon, John James, 1785-1851 — Juvenile literature. I. Title.

STEVENSON, Janet. 925.9
Painting America's wildlife. John James Audubon. Illustrated by Robert Boehmer. Chicago, Kingston House; distributed in association with Lippincott, Philadelphia [1961] 191 p. illus. 22 cm. (Bookshelf for young Americans) [QL31.A9S75] 61-13229
1. Audubon, John James, 1785-1851 — Juvenile literature. I. Title.

STEVENSON, Janet. 925.9
John James Audubon, painting America's wildlife. Illustrated by Robert Boehmer. Chicago, Kingston House; distributed in association with Lippincott, Philadelphia [1961] 191 p. illus. 22 cm. (Bookshelf for young Americans) [QL31.A9S75] 61-13229
1. Audubon, John James, 1785-1851 — Juvenile literature. I. Title.

STEVENSON, Janet 925.9
John James Audunon, painting America's wildlife. Illus. by Robert Boehmer. Chicago, Britannica Bks., div. of Ency. Britannica [1963, c.1961] 191p. col. illus. 22cm. (Britannica bkshelf.: Great lives for young Amers. 2.36 lib. ed.,
1. Audubon, John James, 1785-1851— Juvenile literature. I. Title.

Audubon, John James, 1785-1851-Bibl.

JOHN James Audubon. v. 12
[Princeton, 1960] cover-title, 130p. illus. 25cm. 'Volume xxi, numbers 1 &2, Autumn 1959 & Winter, 1960.'
1. Audubon, John James, 1785-1851-Bibl. I. Princeton University Library chronicle. II. Rice, Howard Crosby, 1904-

Auerbach, Arnold, 1917-

AUERBACH, Arnold, 796.32'3'0924 B 1917-
Red Auerbach : an autobiography / by Arnold "Red" Auerbach and Joe Fitzgerald ; foreword by John Havlicek. New York : Putnam, c1977. 331 p., [8] leaves of plates : ill. ; 24 cm. Includes index. [GV884.A8A28 1977] 76-51377 ISBN 0-399-11893-4 : 8.95
1. Auerbach, Arnold, 1917- 2. Boston Celtics (Basketball team) 3. Basketball coaches—United States—Biography. I. Fitzgerald, Joe, joint author. **BIP**

Augustin Marie du Tres Saint Sacrement pere, 1821-1871.

RODINO, Amedeo. 271'3'024 B
Music master; the story of Herman Cohen. Illustrated by the Daughters of St. Paul with the cooperation of Guy B. Pennisi. [Boston, Mass.] St. Paul Editions [1968] 99 p. illus. 22 cm. (Encounter books) A biography of the Jewish boy who became a famous pianist while still a child, but later converted to Catholicism and spent the rest of his life serving in the Carmelite Order. [BX4705.A785R6] 92 AC 68
1. Augustin Marie du Tres Saint Sacrement pere, 1821-1871. I. Title.

Augustin Marie du Tres Saint Sacrement, pere, 1821-1871— Juvenile literature.

RODINO, Amedeo. 92 (J)
Music master; the story of Herman Cohen. Illustrated by the Daughters of St. Paul with the cooperation of Guy R. Pennisi. [Boston] St. Paul Editions [1968] 99 p. illus. 22 cm. (Encounter books) [BX4705.A785R6] 68-20526
1. Augustin Marie du Tres Saint Sacrement, pere, 1821-1871—Juvenile literature. I. Title.

Augustincic, Antun, 1900—

AUGUSTINCIC, Antun, 730'.92'4 1900-
Augustincic / [editors, Boris Kukoc, Igor Prizmic ; photos, Toso Dabac ... [et al.]. Zagreb : Priredni vjesnik, 1976. [168] p. : chiefly ill. (some col.) ; 34 cm. "Published in Croatian or Serbian, English, Russian, and German." [NB953.A8K84] 77-365848
1. Augustincic, Antun, 1900- I. Kukoc, Boris. II. Prizmic, Igor.

Augustinus, Aurelius, Saint, Bp. of Hippo.

AUGUSTINUS, Aurelius, 242'.1 Saint, Bp. of Hippo.
The confessions of Augustine in modern English / translated and abridged by Sherwood E. Wirt. Grand Rapids : Zondervan Pub. House, 1977, c1971. xvi, 143 p. ; 21 cm. Translation of selections from Confessiones. Reprint of the ed. published by Harper & Row, New York, under title: Love song. Includes bibliographical references and index. [BR65.A6E53 1977] 77-13398 ISBN 0-310-34641-X pbk. : 3.95
1. Christian saints—Algeria—Hippo—Biography. 2. Hippo, Algeria—Biography. I. Wirt, Sherwood Eliot. II. Title.

AUGUSTINUS, Aurelius, 922.1 Saint, Bp. of Hippo.
The mind and heart of Augustine, a biographical skectch, compiled from the saint's own writings with explanatory notes by J. M. Flood. With an introd. by M. C. D'Arcy. Fresno, Calif., Academy Guild Press [1960] 108 p. 19 cm. Dublin ed. (Clonmore & Reynolds) has title: St. Augustine, a biographical sketch. [BR1720.A9F5] 61-102
I. Flood, Joseph Mary, 1882- II. Title.

BONNER, Gerald 922.13972
St. Augustine of Hippo. life and controversies. Philadelphia, Westminster [1964, c.1993] 428p. 23cm. (Lib. of Hist. & doctrine) Bibl. 64-10516 8.50
1. Augustinus, Aurelius, Saint, Bp. pf Hippo. I. Title.

BROWN, Peter Robert 270.2'0924 Lamont
Augustine of Hippo; a biography, by Peter Brown. Berkeley. Univ. of Calif. Pr., 1967. 463p. 23cm. Bibl. [BR1720.A9B7 1967b] 67-13137 10.00
1. Augustinus, Aurelius, Saint, Bp. of Hippo. I. Title.

BROWN, Peter Robert 270.2'0924 Lamont.
Augustine of Hippo; a biography, by Peter Brown. Berkeley, University of California Press, 1967. 463 p. 23 cm. Bibliography: p. 435-452. [BR1720.A9B7 1967b] 67-13137
1. Augustinus, Aurelius, Saint, Bp. of Hippo. I. Title. **BIP**

CHABANNES, Jacques, 922.13972 1902-
St. Augustine. Translated by Julie Kernan. [1st American ed.] Garden City, N. Y., Doubleday [1962] 239 p. 22 cm. [BR1720.A9C47] 62-15879
1. Augustinus, Aurelius, Saint, Bp. of Hippo.

FLOOD, Joseph Mary, 1882- 922.1
The mind and heart of Augustine a biographical sketch, complied from the saint s own writings with explanatory notes by J. M. Flood. With an introd. by M. C. D'Arcy. Fresno, Calif., Academy Guild Press [1960] 108p. 61-102 2.45
1. Augustimus, Aurelius, Saint, Bp. of Hippo. I. Title.

FULOP-MILLER, Rene, 1891- 922
The saints that moved the world; Anthony, Augustine, Francis, Ignatius, Theresa. Tr(by Alexander Gode, Erika Fulop-Miller. New York, Collier [1962, c.1945] 511p. 18cm. (AS268 9) Bibl. .95 pap.,
1. Augustinus, Aurelius, Saint, bp. of Hippo. 2. Francesco d'Assisi, Saint, 1182-1226. 3. Loyola, Ignacio de, saint, 1491-1556. 4. Teresa, Saint, 1515-1582. 5. Antonius, Saint, 'the Great.' I. Gode, Alexander, tr. II. Eulop-Miller, Erika, joint tr. III. Title. **BIP**

GNAYALLOOR, Jacob 281.40924
Augustine, saint for today. Milwaukee,

Bruce [c.1965] v, 113p. 22cm. [BR1720.A9G58] 65-21893 2.95
1. Augustinus, Aurelius, Saint, Bp. of Hippo. I. Title.

GNAYALLOOR, Jacob. 281.40924 (B)
Augustine, saint for today. Milwaukee, Bruce Pub. Co. [1965] v. 113 p. 22 cm. [BR1720.A9G58] 65-21893
1. Augustinus, Aurelius, Saint, Bp. of Hippo. I. Title.

GREENWOOD, David. 922.1
Saint Augustine. Foreword by Cardinal Griffin. Archbishop ofWestminster. [1st ed.] New York, Vantage Press [1957] 155p. illus. 21cm. [BR1720.A9G73] 55-11665
1. Augustinus, Aurelius, Saint, Bp. of Hippo. I. Title.

GUARDINI, Romano 922.1
The conversion of Augustine. Translated from the German by Elinor Briefs. Westminster, Md., Newman Press [c.]1960. xviii, 258p. 22cm. 60-10731 3.95
1. Augustinus, Aurelius, Saint, Bp. of Hippo. I. Title.

GUARDINI, Romano, 1885- 922.1
The conversion of Augustine. Translated from the German by Elinor Briefs. Westminster, Md., Newman Press, 1960. 258p. 22cm. Translation of Die Bekehrung des heiligen Aurelius Augustinus. [BR1720.A9G813] 60-10731
1. Augustinus, Aurelius, Saint, Bp. of Hippo. I. Title.

HATZFELD, Adolphe, 270.2'092'4 B
1824-1900.
Saint Augustine / by Ad. Hatzfeld ; translated by E. Holt ; with a pref. and notes by George Tyrrell. New York : AMS Press, 1975. x, 155 p. ; 18 cm. Reprint of the 1903 ed. published by Duckworth, London, in series: The Saints. [BR1720.A9H3413 1975] 71-168252 ISBN 0-404-03155-2 : 11.00
1. Augustinus, Aurelius, Saint, Bp. of Hippo. I. Series: The Saints. **BIP**

LOMASK, Milton. 922.1
St. Augustine and his search for faith. Illustrated by Johannes Troyer. New York, Vision Books [1957] 190p. illus. 22cm. (Vision books, 21) [BR1720.A9L65] 57-7697
1. Augustinus, Aurelius, Saint, Bp. of Hippo. I. Title.

MEER, Frederik Gerben Louis 922.1
van der, 1904-
Augustine the bishop; the life and work of a father of the church. Tr. by Brian Battershaw, G. R. Lamb. New York, Sheed & Ward [1962, c.1961] 679p. illus., maps (pt. col.) 25cm. Bibl. 62-1688 17.50
1. Augustinus, Aurelius. Saint. Bp. of Hippo. I. Title.

O'CONNELL, Robert J. 242'.1
St. Augustine's Confessions; the Odyssey of soul [by] Robert J. O'Connell. Cambridge, Mass, Belknap Press of Harvard University Press, 1969. xiii, 200 p. 24 cm. Includes bibliographical references. [BR65.A9O26] 69-12731 6.50
1. Augustinus, Aurelius, Saint, Bp. of Hippo. Confessiones. I. Title.

O'MEARA, John Joseph. 922.1
The young Augustine; the growth of St. Augustine's mind upto his conversion. London, New York, Longmans, Green [1954] 215p. illus. 22cm. [BR1720.A9O5] 55-1504
1. Augustinus, Aurelius, Saint, Bp. of Hippo. I. Title.

O'MEARA, John Joseph 922.22
The young Augustine: the growth of St. Augustine's mind up to his conversion. Staten Island, N.Y., Alba [c.1965] xv, 215p. illus. 22cm. Bibl. [BR1720.A9O5] 65-4320 4.50
1. Augustinus, Aurelius, Saint, Bp. of Hippo. I. Title.

POPE, Hugh [Secular name: 922.1
Henry Vincent Pope] Father, 1869-1946.
Saint Augustine of Hippo essays dealing with his life and times and some features of his work. Garden City, N.Y., Doubleday [1961] 439p. (Image bk., D119) Bibl. 1.35 pap.,
1. Augustinus, Aurelius, Saint, Bp. of Hippo. I. Title.

SAINT Augustine 922.1
[by] M. C. D'Arcy [others] [Gloucester, Mass., P. Smith, 1963] 367p. 18cm. (Meridian bks., M51 rebound) Bibl. 3.75
1. Augustinus, Aurelius, Saint, Bp. of Hippo. I. D'Arcy, Martin Cyril, 1888-

SAINT Augustine 922.1
[by] M.C. D'Arcy [and others]. New York, Meridian Books, 1957. 367p. 18cm. (Meridian books, M51) 'First published ... in 1930 ... under the title: A Monument to Saint Augustine.' [BR1720.A9M55 1957] 57-11671
1. Augustinus, Aurelius, Saint, Bp. of Hippo. I. D'Arcy, Martin Cyrill, 1888-
Contents omitted.

SCHMID, Evan, 1920- 922.1
The great Saint Augustine. Illus. by Mary K. Rappelli. Notre Dame, Ind., Dujarie Press [1957] 93p. illus. 24cm. [BR1720.A9S3] 57-4983
1. Augustinus, Aurelius, Saint, Bp. of Hippo. I. Title.

SHEED, Francis Joseph, 1897- 242
Our hearts are restless : the prayer of St. Augustine / F. J. Sheed ; photos. by Catharine Hughes. New York : Seabury Press, c1976. 95 p. : ill. ; 23 cm. "A Crossroad book." [BR1720.A9S53] 76-20197 ISBN 0-8164-2127-7 : 4.95
1. Augustinus, Aurelius, Saint, Bp. of Hippo. 2. Christian saints—Hippo, Algeria—Biography. 3. Hippo, Algeria—Biography. 4. Prayer—History. I. Hughes, Catharine, 1935- II. Title. **BIP**

Augustinus, Aurelius, Saint, Bp. of Hippo—Bio-bibliography.

AUGUSTINUS, Aurelius, 281'.4'0924
Saint, Bp. of Hippo.
The retractations. Translated by Mary Inez Bogan. Washington, Catholic University of America Press [1968] xxvi, 321 p. 22 cm. (The Fathers of the church, a new translation, v. 60) Includes bibliographical references. [BR60.F3A8253] 67-30513 7.80
1. Augustinus, Aurelius, Saint, Bp. of Hippo—Bio-bibliography. I. Title. II. Series.

Augustinus, Aurelius, Saint, Bp. of Hippo—Juvenile literature.

HANSEL, Robert R. 270.2'0924 B
The life of Saint Augustine, by Robert R. Hansel. New York, F. Watts [1968, c1969] xii, 116 p. port. 22 cm. (Immortals of religion) Biography of Aurelius Augustinus, who grew up during the decay and fall of the Roman Empire and whose writings had particular significance to Christians and their church at this time. [BR1720.A9H33] 92 69-11687
1. Augustinus, Aurelius, Saint, Bp. of Hippo—Juvenile literature. I. Title.

Augustinus, Aurelius, Saint, Bp. of Hippo—Theology.

TESELLE, Eugene, 230.14'0924
1931-
Augustine, the theologian. [New York] Herder and Herder [1970] 381 p. 22 cm. "Chronological table of Augustine's works": p. [11]-14. Bibliography: p. [351]-360. [BR65.A9T4 1970] 75-87772 12.50
1. Augustinus, Aurelius, Saint, Bp. of Hippo—Theology.

Augustus, Emperor of Rome, 63 B.C.-14 A.D.

CHARLES-PICARD, 937'.06'0922
Gilbert.
Augustus and Nero. Translated from the French by Len Ortzen. New York, T. Y. Crowell Co. [1968] xxviii, 190 p. 19 cm. (Apollo editions A-183) [DG279.C483 1968] 68-19788
1. Augustus, Emperor of Rome, 63 B.C.-14 A.D. 2. Nero, Emperor of Rome, 37-68. I. Title.

GILLIAM, Olive Kuntz 937.050924
The memoirs of Augustus. New York, Vantage [c. 1965] 223p. front., maps (on lining papers) 22cm. Reconstruction of the lost memoirs of Augustus Caesar, based on the texts of early writers. Bibl. [DG279.G5] 65-9482 3.95
1. Augustus, Emperor of Rome, 63 B.C.-14 A.D. 2. Rome—Hist.—Sources. I. Title.

GILLIAM, Olive Kuntz. 937.050924
The memoirs of Augustus. [1st ed.] New York, Vantage Press [1965] 223 p. front., maps (on listing papers) 22 cm. A reconstruction of the lost memoirs of Augustus Caesar, based on the texts of early writers. Bibliographical references included in "Notes" (p. 218-223) [DG279.G5] 65-9482
1. Augustus, Emperor of Rome, 63 B.C.-14 A.D. 2. Rome — Hist. — Sources. I. Title.

JONES, Arnold Hugh 937.05'0924
Martin, 1904-1970.
Augustus [by] A. H. M. Jomes. New York, Norton [1973? c.1970] xi, 196 p. maps, plans. 20 cm. (Ancient culture & society series) (Norton Lib., N584) [DG279.J64 1971] 70-128042 ISBN 0-393-00584-4 pap., 1.95
1. Augustus, Emperorr of Rome, 63 B.C.-14 A.D. **BIP**

Augustus, Emperor of Rome, 63 B.C.-14 A.D.—Juvenile literature.

STEARNS, Monroe. 937'.07'0924 B
Augustus Caesar, architect of empire. New York, F. Watts, 1972. 183 p. illus. 22 cm. (A Franklin Watts biography) Bibliography: p. [175]-178. A biography of the first Emperor of Rome, whose leadership gave rise to the period of prosperity and progress known as the Augustan Age. [DG279.S73] 92 75-182291 ISBN 0-531-00966-1
1. Augustus, Emperor of Rome, 63 B.C.-14 A.D.—Juvenile literature. I. Title.

Augustus Frederick, Duke of Sussex, 1773-1843.

GILLEN, Mollie. 942.07'3'0924 B
Royal duke : Augustus Frederick, Duke of Sussex (1773-1843) / by Mollie Gillen. London : Sidgwick & Jackson, 1976. 268 p., [8] leaves of plates : ill. ; 25 cm. Includes index. Bibliography: p. 246-250. [DA536.A9G54 1976] 77-368140 ISBN 0-283-98316-7 : £6.95
1. Augustus Frederick, Duke of Sussex, 1773-1843. 2. Great Britain—Nobility—Biography. I. Title. **BIP**

Aull, Roger.

CAPORASO, Anthony. 922.273
The miracles of Father Aull. [1st ed.] New York, Pageant Press [1959, c1958] 117p. 21cm. [BX4705.A788C3] 59-134
1. Aull, Roger. I. Title.

Ault, George, 1891-1948.

AULT, Louise. 759.13 B
Artist in Woodstock : George Ault, the independent years / by Louise Ault. Philadelphia : Dorrance, c1978. 176 p., [1] leaf of plates : ill. ; 22 cm. [N6537.A9A9] 78-57264 ISBN 0-8059-2550-3 : 7.95
1. Ault, George, 1891-1948. 2. Ault, Louise. 3. Artists—United States—Biography. 4. Wives—United States—Biography. I. Title.

Aumont, Jean-Pierre.

AUMONT, Jean-Pierre. 791'.092'4 B
Sun and shadow / Jean-Pierre Aumont ; with a foreword by Francois Truffaut ; translated from the French by Bruce Benderson. 1st ed. New York : Norton, c1977. 315 p. : ill. ; 22 cm. Translation of Le soleil et les ombres. Includes index. "The plays and films of Jean-Pierre Aumont": p. 305-307. [PN2638.A88A2913 1977] 76-58878 ISBN 0-393-07511-7 : 9.95
1. Aumont, Jean-Pierre. 2. Actors—France—Biography. I. Title.

Aurelius Antoninus, Marcus, Emperor of Rome, 121-180.

BIRLEY, Anthony 937.060924 (B)
Richard
Marcus Aurelius [by] Anthony Birley. [1st Amer. ed.] Boston, Little [1966] 354p. illus., geneal tables., maps. 22cm. Bibl. [DG297.B5 1966] 66-20802 6.95
1. Aurelius Antonius, Marcus, Emperor of Rome, 121-180. I. Title.

FARQUHARSON, Arthur Spenser v. 12
Loat, 1871-1942.
Marcus Aurelius, his life and his world. Edited by D. A. Rees. New York, W. Salloch, 1951. vi, 154p. illus. 22cm. Chapters dealing with the military and administrative aspects of the Emperor's reign, included in the typescript of the author, have been omitted. 'Additional notes, by D. A. Rees': p.[149]-152. Bibliographical footnotes. A53
1. Aurelius Antoninus, Marcus, Emperor of Rome, 121-180. I. Title.

FARQUHARSON, 937'.07'0924 B
Arthur Spenser Loat, 1871-1942.
Marcus Aurelius : his life and his world / by A. S. L. Farquharson ; edited by D. A. Rees. Westport, Conn. : Greenwood Press, 1975. vi, 154 p., [2] leaves of plates : ill. ; 22 cm. Reprint of the 1951 ed. published by B. Blackwell, Oxford. Includes bibliographical references and index. [DG297.F3 1975] 75-11854 ISBN 0-8371-8139-9 lib.bdg. : 10.50
1. Aurelius Antonius, Marcus, Emperor of Rome, 121-180.

SEDGWICK, Henry 937'.07'0924 B
Dwight, 1861-1957.
Marcus Aurelius; a biography told as much as may be by letters, together with some account of the stoic religion and an exposition of the Roman government's attempt to suppress Christianity during Marcus's reign. New York, AMS Press [1971] 309 p. 19 cm. Reprint of the 1921 ed. Bibliography: p. [273]-278. [DG297.S4 1971] 77-137290 ISBN 0-404-05691-1
1. Aurelius Antoninus, Marcus, Emperor of Rome, 121-180. 2. Stoics.

WATSON, Paul 937'.06'0924 B
Barron, 1861-1948.
Marcus Aurelius Antoninus. Freeport, N.Y., Books for Libraries Press [1971] ix, 338 p. illus., port. 23 cm. Reprint of the 1884 ed. Bibliography: p. [309]-323. [DG297.W3 1971] 76-148904 ISBN 0-8369-5667-2
1. Aurelius Antoninus, Marcus, Emperor of Rome, 121-180. **BIP**

Auriol, Jacqueline.

AURIOL, Jacqueline. 629.13'0924 B
I live to fly. Translated from the French by Pamela Swinglehurst. [1st ed.] New York, Dutton, 1970. 197 p. 21 illus., ports. 25 cm. Translation of Vivre et voler. Autobiography. [TL540.A8A313 1970] 72-95486 ISBN 5-251-30764- 5.95
I. Title.

Austen, Alice, 1866-1952.

NOVOTNY, Ann. 770'.92'4 B
Alice's world : the life and photography of an American original, Alice Austen, 1866-1952 / by Ann Novotny ; pref. by Oliver Jensen. Old Greenwich, Conn. : Chatham Press, c1976. 221 p. : ill. ; 31 cm. [TR140.A83N67] 76-18489 ISBN 0-85699-128-7 : 22.50
1. Austen, Alice, 1866-1952. 2. Photographers—United States—Biography. I. Austen, Alice, 1866-1952. II. Title. **BIP**

Austen, Cassandra, 1773-1845.

AUSTEN, Jane, 1775-1817. 928.2
Jane Austen's letters to her sister Cassandra and others, collected and edited by R. W. Chapman 2d ed. London, New York, Oxford University Press, 1952. xiv, 519, [163]p. illus., ports., maps. 23cm. Bibliography: p. xxxvii-xxxviii. [PR4036.A55 1952] 53-1415
1. Austen, Cassandra, 1773-1845. 2. Austen family. I. Title.

Austen, Jane, 1775-1817.

AUSTEN, Jane, 1775-1817. 928.2
Letters, 1796-1817 selected and edited by R.W. Chapman New York, Oxford University Press [1955] x, 226p. 16cm. (The World's classics, 549) Chiefly letters to her sister Cassandra. [PR4036.A57] 55-13797
I. Austen, Cassandra, 1773-1845. II. Chapman, Robert William, 1881- ed. III. Title.

AUSTEN-LEIGH, William 928.2
Jane Austen; her life and letters, a family record [Reissue] by William Austen-Leigh, Richard Arthur Austen-Leigh. 2d ed. New York, Russell & Russell, 1965. xv, 437p. geneal. table, port. 22cm. Reissue of the 1913 ed. Bibl. [PR4036.A86] 65-13949 8.50
1. Austen, Jane, 1775-1817. I. Austen-Leigh, Richard Arthur, 1872- joint author. II. Title.

BECKER, May (Lamberton), 928.2
1873-
Presenting Miss Jane Austen; illustrated by Edward Price. New York, Dodd, Mead [1952] 204 p. illus. 22 cm. [PR4036.B4] 52-1617
1. Austen, Jane, 1775-1817. I. Title.

BROWN, Ivor John 914.20373
Carnegie, 1891-
Jane Austen and her world [by] Ivor Brown. [1st American ed.] New York, H. Z. Walck, 1966. 44 p. illus., ports. 26 cm. [PR4036.B7 1966a] 67-342
1. Austen, Jane, 1775-1817.

CECIL, David, Lord, 823'.7 B
1902-
A portrait of Jane Austen / David Cecil. New York : Hill and Wang, 1979, c1978. 208 p., [7] leaves of plates : ill. ; 25 cm. Includes index. [PR4036.C4 1979] 78-17317 ISBN 0-8090-7811-2 : 19.95
1. Austen, Jane, 1775-1817. 2. Novelists, English—19th century—Biography. I. Title. BIP

FIRKINS, Oscar W., 1864- 823.7
1932
Jane Austen. New York, Russell & Russell, 1965 [c.1920, 1947] ix, 254p. 23cm. [PR4036.F5] 65-18805 6.50
1. Austen, Jane, 1775-1817. I. Title.

HUBBACK, John Henry, 823'.7 B
b.1844.
Jane Austen's sailor brothers : being the adventures of Sir Francis Austen, G.C.B., Admiral of the Fleet, and Rear-Admiral Charles Austen / by J. H. Hubback and Edith C. Hubback. Folcroft, Pa. : Folcroft Library Editions, 1976. p. cm. Reprint of the 1906 ed. published by J. Lane, London, New York. Includes index. [PR4036.H78 1976] 76-40065 ISBN 0-8414-4717-9 lib. bdg. : 45.00
1. Austen, Jane, 1775-1817. 2. Austen family. 3. Novelists, English—19th century—Biography. I. Brown, Edith Charlotte Hubback, 1876- joint author. II. Title.

JENKINS, Elizabeth, 1907- 928.1
Jane Austen. New York, Farrar, Straus and Cudahy [1959, c1949] 410p. illus. 21cm. [PR4036.J4 1959] 59-16728
1. Austen, Jane, 1775-1817. I. Title.

JOHNSON, Reginald 823'.7 B
Brimley, 1867-1932.
Jane Austen. New York, Haskell House Publishers, 1974. v, 171 p. 20 cm. Reprint of the 1927 ed. published by Sheed & Ward, London. [PR4036.J6 1974] 74-1102 ISBN 0-8383-1746-4 11.95
1. Austen, Jane, 1775-1817.

JOHNSON, Reginald 823'.7 B
Brimley, 1867-1932.
Jane Austen. [Folcroft, Pa.] Folcroft Library Editions, 1972 [i.e. 1974] 171 p. 24 cm. Reprint of the 1927 ed. published by Sheed & Ward, London. [PR4036.J6 1974b] 74-11252 15.00 (lib. bdg.).
1. Austen, Jane, 1775-1817.

JOHNSON, Reginald 823'.7 B
Brimley, 1867-1932.
Jane Austen: her life, her work, her family, and her critics. New York, Haskell House 1974. xiv, 285 p. illus. 22 cm. Reprint of the 1930 ed. published by J. M. Dent, London. [PR4036.J63 1974] 74-6375 ISBN 0-8383-1748-0
1. Austen, Jane, 1775-1817.

LASKI, Marghanita, 1915- 823'.7 B
Jane Austen, and her world. New York, Viking Press [1969] 143 p. illus., geneal. table, map, ports. 24 cm. (A Studio book) Bibliography: p. 138-139. [PR4036.L38 1969] 69-18092
1. Austen, Jane, 1775-1817.

LERNER, Laurence. 823'.009
The truthtellers: Jane Austen, George Eliot, D. H. Lawrence. New York, Schocken Books [1967] 291 p. 23 cm. Bibliographical footnotes. [PR861.L4 1967] 67-12148
1. Austen, Jane, 1775-1817. 2. Eliot, George, pseud., i.e. Marian Evans, afterwards Cross, 1819-1880. 3. Lawrence, David Herbert, 1885-1930. I. Title.

MALDEN, S. F. 823'.7 B
Jane Austen / by Mrs. Charles Malden [i.e. S. F. Malden]. Folcroft, Pa. : Folcroft Library Editions, 1977. p. cm. Reprint of the 1899 ed. published by W. H. Allen, London, which was issued in: Eminent women series. [PR4036.M3 1977] 77-6735 ISBN 0-8414-6188-0 lib. bdg. : 25.00
1. Austen, Jane, 1775-1817. 2. Novelists, English—19th century—Biography. I. Series: Eminent women series.

MITTON, Geraldine Edith. 823'.7
Jane Austen and her times, by G. E. Mitton. With 21 illus. Port Washington, N.Y., Kennikat Press [1970] viii, 334 p. illus., ports. 22 cm. Reprint of the 1905 ed. [PR4036.M5 1970] 74-103206 ISBN 0-8046-0843-1
1. Austen, Jane, 1775-1817. I. Title. BIP

RAWLENCE, Guy, 1888- 823'.7 B
Jane Austen. [Folcroft, Pa.] Folcroft Press [1970] 144 p. 23 cm. Reprint of the 1934 ed., issued in series: Great lives. Bibliography; p. 144. [PR4036.R3 1970] 72-194913
1. Austen, Jane, 1775-1817. BIP

RHYDDERCH, David. 823'.7 B
Jane Austen, her life and art / by David Rhydderch ; with an introd. by Leonard Huxley. Folcroft, Pa. : Folcroft Library Editions, 1976. p. cm. Reprint of the 1932 ed. published by J. Cape, London. [PR4036.R5 1976] 76-8831 ISBN 0-8414-7322-6 lib. bdg. : 20.00
1. Austen, Jane, 1775-1817. I. Title.

SMITH, Goldwin, 1823- 823'.7 B
1910.
Life of Jane Austen. [Folcroft, Pa.] Folcroft Library Editions, 1973. 195, v p. 20 cm. Reprint of the 1890 ed. published by W. Scott, London and New York, in series: Great writers. Bibliography: p. [i]-v. [PR4036.S6 1973] 73-10492 ISBN 0-8414-7574-1 (lib. bdg.)
1. Austen, Jane, 1775-1817. I. Title. BIP

WARRE Cornish, Francis, 823'.7
1839-1916.
Jane Austen. Freeport, N.Y., Books for Libraries Press [1971] xiii, 240 p. 23 cm. Reprint of the 1913 ed., issued in series: English men of letters. Includes bibliographical references. [PR4036.W3 1971] 78-37333 ISBN 0-8369-6680-5
1. Austen, Jane, 1775-1817.

Austen, Jane, 1775-1817—Biography.

ADAMS, Oscar Fay, 1855- 823'.7 B
1919.
The story of Jane Austen's life. [Folcroft, Pa.] Folcroft Library Editions, 1974. p. cm. Reprint of the 1891 ed. published by A. C. McClurg, Chicago. Bibliography: p. [PR4036.A7 1974] 74-14568 ISBN 0-8414-2861-1 (lib. bdg.)
1. Austen, Jane, 1775-1817—Biography. I. Title. BIP

AUSTEN-LEIGH, Mary 823'.7 B
Augusta.
Personal aspects of Jane Austen. [Folcroft, Pa.] Folcroft Library Editions, 1974. viii, 169 p. illus. 24 cm. Reprint of the 1920 ed. published by J. Murray, London. [PR4036.A85 1974] 74-5080 ISBN 0-8414-2972-3 (lib. bdg.)
1. Austen, Jane, 1775-1817—Biography. I. Title. BIP

HILL, Constance, 1844?- 823'.7 B
1929.
Jane Austen : her homes & her friends / by Constance Hill ; ill. by Ellen G. Hill. Folcroft, Pa. : Folcroft Library Editions, 1977. p. cm. Reprint of the 1901 ed. published by J. Lane, London. Includes index. [PR4036.H5 1977] 77-4060 ISBN 0-8414-4903-1 lib. bdg. : 30.00
1. Austen, Jane, 1775-1817—Biography. 2. Novelists, English—19th century—Biography. BIP

REES, Joan. 823'.7 B
Jane Austen : woman and writer / Joan Rees. New York : St. Martin's Press, 1976. 224 p., [4] leaves of plates : ill. ; 23 cm. Includes index. Bibliography: p. [215]-218. [PR4036.R4] 76-2166 ISBN 0-7091-5523-9 : 8.95
1. Austen, Jane, 1775-1817—Biography. 2. Novelists, English—19th century—Biography. BIP

SEYMOUR, Beatrice Kean 823'.7 B
Stapleton.
Jane Austen; study for a portrait, by Beatrice Kean Seymour. [Folcroft, Pa.] Folcroft Library Editions, 1974. p. Reprint of the 1937 ed. published by M. Joseph, London. Bibliography: p. [PR4036.S4 1974b] 74-11437 ISBN 0-8414-7780-9 20.00
1. Austen, Jane, 1775-1817—Biography. I. Title.

Austen, Jane, 1775-1817. Emma.

BRADBROOK, Frank W. 111.8'5
Jane Austen: Emma, by Frank W. Bradbrook. Great Neck, N. Y., Barron's Educational Series, inc. [1961] 64 p. 19 cm. (Barron's studies in English literature, no. 3) Bibliography: p. 62. [PR4034.E52B7] 62-19946
1. Austen, Jane, 1775-1817. Emma. I. Title.

Austen, Jane, 1775-1817—Juvenile literature.

SISSON, Rosemary Anne 920
The young Jane Austen. Illus. by Denise Brown. New York, Roy [1963, c.1962] 134p. illus. 21cm. Bibl. 62-18557 3.00 bds.,
1. Austen, Jane, 1775-1817—Juvenile literature. I. Title.

Austin, Alfred, 1835-1913.

AUSTIN, Alfred, 1835- 821'.8 B
1913.
The autobiography of Alfred Austin, poet laureate, 1835-1910. New York, AMS Press [1973] ix, 325, ix, 308 p. illus. 23 cm. Reprint of the 1911 ed. published by Macmillan, London. [PR4043.A3 1973] 79-148744 ISBN 0-404-08717-5
1. Austin, Alfred, 1835-1913. BIP

CROWELL, Norton B. 928.2
Alfred Austin: Victorian. [Albuquerque] University of New Mexico Press [1953] 296p. illus. 24cm. Includes bibliography. [PR4043.C7] 53-7211
1. Austin, Alfred, 1835-1913. I. Title.

Austin, Bill Joe.

AUSTIN, Bill Joe. 788'.66'0924 B
The beat goes on and on and on / by Bill Joe Austin. [Erwin, N.C. : Carolina Arts and Pub. House, c1976] 170 p., [4] leaves of plates : ill. ; 22 cm. [ML419.A95A3] 76-372710
1. Austin, Bill Joe. 2. Jazz musicians—United States—Biography. I. Title.

Austin, Emily M.

AUSTIN, Emily M. 917.3'03'50924 B
Mormonism; or, Life among the Mormons: being an autobiographical sketch; including an experience of fourteen years of Mormon life [by] Emily M. Austin. Madison, Wis., M. J. Cantwell, Book and Job Printer, 1882. [New York, AMS Press, 1971] 253 p. 22 cm. [BX8695.A95A3] 74-134388 ISBN 0-404-08480-X 10.00
I. Title. II. Title: Life among the Mormons.

Austin, Stephen Fuller, 1793-1836.

BARKER, Eugene 976.4'03'0924 B
Campbell, 1874-1956.
The life of Stephen F. Austin, founder of Texas, 1793-1836; a chapter in the Westward movement of the Anglo-American people. New York, AMS Press [1970] xv, 551 p. 2 fold. maps, ports. 23 cm. Reprint of the 1925 ed. Bibliography: p. 525-534. [F389.A936 1970] 70-111473
1. Austin, Stephen Fuller, 1793-1836. 2. Texas—History—To 1846. BIP

BARKER, Eugene 976.4'03'0924 B
Campbell, 1874-1956.
The life of Stephen F. Austin, founder of Texas, 1793-1836; a chapter of the Westward movement by the Anglo-American people. New introd. by Seymour V. Connor. New York, Da Capo Press, 1968. ix, xv, 551 p. maps, ports. 24 cm. (The American scene) (A Da Capo Press reprint edition.) "An unabridged republication of the first edition published ... in 1925." Includes bibliographical references. [F389.A936 1968] 68-27723 15.00
1. Austin, Stephen Fuller, 1793-1836. 2. Texas—History—to 1846. I. Title.

BEALS, Carleton, 1893- 923.273
Stephen F. Austin, Father of Texas. Drawings by Jay Hyde Barnum. New York, McGraw-Hill [1953] 277p. illus. 21cm. (They made America) Includes bibliography. [F389.A936B4] 52-13446
1. Austin, Stephen Fuller, 1796-1836. 2. Texas—Hist.—Te 1346. I. Title.

GLASSCOCK, Sallie. 923.273
Dreams of an empire; the story of Stephen Fuller Austin and his colony in Texas. [Texas empire ed.] San Antonio, Naylor Co. [1951] x, 213 p. illus., ports. 22 cm. Bibliography: p. 202-206. [F389.A94] 51-2862
1. Austin, Stephen Fuller, 1796-1836. 2. Texas—Hist.—To 1846. I. Title.

HOFF, Carol. 923.273
Wilderness pioneer: Stephen F. Austin of Texas. Illustrated by Robert Todd. Chicago, Follett Pub. Co. [1955] 192 p. illus. 25 cm. [F389.A943] 55-7501
1. Austin, Stephen Fuller, 1793-1836. I. Title.

MCCALEB, Walter Flavius, 923.273
1873-
Stephen F. Austin. San Antonio, Naylor Co. [1957] 90p. illus. 20cm. [F389.A948] 57-295250
1. Austin, Stephen Fuller, 1793-1836. I. Title.

RASBURY, Ruth 976.4'03'0924 B
Grandstaff.
The broad land; the life and times of Stephen Fuller Austin. Philadelphia, Dorrance [1972] 202 p. 22 cm. Bibliography: p. 201-202. [F389.A9495] 72-85382 ISBN 0-8059-1730-6 4.95
1. Austin, Stephen Fuller, 1793-1836. 2. Texas—History—To 1846. I. Title.

STEPHEN F. Austin. 923.273
San Antonio, Naylor Co. [1957] 90p. illus. 20cm. [F389.A948] 57-29525
1. Austin, Stephen Fuller, 1798-1836. 2. cCaleb, Walter Flavius, 1873-

Austin, Tracy, 1962- —Juvenile literature.

HAHN, James. 796.34'2'0924 B
Tracy Austin : powerhouse in pinafore / by James and Lynn Hahn. St. Paul : EMC Corp., 1978. p. cm. (Their Champions and challengers I) A brief biography of the teen-age girl whose participation in the 1977 United States Open tennis championship made her the youngest player ever to compete in that tournament. [GV994.A93H33] 92 78-18902 ISBN 0-88436-439-9 : 5.95
1. Austin, Tracy, 1962- — Juvenile literature. 2. Tennis players—United States—Biography—Juvenile literature. I. Hahn, Lynn, joint author. II. Title. III. Series. BIP

ROBISON, Nancy. 796.34'2'0924 B
Tracy Austin, teenage superstar / by Nancy Robison. New YorK : Harvey

House, c1978. 59 p. : ill. ; 23 cm. A biography of the youngest player to ever compete in the U.S. Open Tennis Championships at Forest Hills. Includes profiles of several other young amateur tennis players. [GV994.A93R62 1978] 92 78-105533 ISBN 0-8178-5807-5 lib.bdg. : 4.99
1. Austin, Tracy, 1962- —Juvenile literature. 2. Tennis players—United States—Biography—Juvenile literature. I. Title.

TALBERT, Peter. 796.34'2'0924 B
Tracy Austin, tennis wonder / by Peter Talbert ; photos. by Bruce Curtis. New York : Putnam, c1979. 46 p. : ill. ; 20 x 28 cm. A career biography beginning with Tracy Austin's childhood and including family background, training, and tournament statistics. [GV994.A93T34 1979] 92 79-11914 ISBN 0-399-20689-2 : 8.95
1. Austin, Tracy, 1962- —Juvenile literature. 2. Tennis players—United States—Biography—Juvenile literature. I. Curtis, Bruce. II. Title.

Australia—Biog.

HETHERINGTON, John 920.094
Aikman, 1907-
Uncommon men [by] John Hetherington. Drawings by Louis Kahan. Melbourne, F. W. Cheshire [1965] xxiv, 200p. illus. 22cm. Profiles orig. pub. in the Age, Melbourne, and other Australian newspapers. [CT2806.H4] 66-31969 4.95
1. Australia—Biog. I. Title.
Dist. by Ginn, Boston.

JOSE, Arthur Wilberforce, 920.094
1863-1934.
Builders and pioneers of Australia. Freeport, N.Y., Books for Libraries Press [1970] xi, 220 p. 23 cm. (Essay index reprint series) Reprint of the 1928 ed. Contents.Contents.—Lachlan Macquarie.—William Charles Wentworth.—Henry Parkes.—Alfred Deakin.—Jan Carstenzoon (explorer).—John Blaxland (farmer).—Gregory Blaxland (farmer and explorer).—Simeon Lord (merchant and manufacturer).—Francis Howard Greenaway (architect).—George Howe (printer and journalist).—William Hilton Hovell (explorer).—James King (inventor and viticulturist) [DU82.J6 1970] 71-107720
1. Australia—Biography. I. Title. BIP

100 famous Australian lives. 920.094
London, New York, Sydney, Hamlyn [1969] 616 p. ports. 23 cm. [CT2803.O5 1969] 75-498299 3.95 Australian dollars
1. Australia—Biography.

THOMPSON, John, 1907- 920.094
Five to remember. Illus. by Noel Counihan [Melbourne] Lansdowne [dist. New Rochelle, N.Y., SportShelf, 1965] 194p. illus. 23cm. Roy Rene: Mo.--Hugh McCrae.--Ben Chifley.--Alf Condon.--Sir Douglas Mawson. [DU82.T44] 65-1545 6.50 bds.,
1. Australia—Biog. I. Title.

THOMPSON, John, 1907- 920.094
On lips of living men. Melbourne, Lansdowne Pr. [New Rochelle, N.Y., Australian Bk. Center, 1964] 164p. illus. 22cm. Based on radio biographies broadcast by the Australian Broadcasting Comm. 6.00 bds.,
1. Australia—Biog. I. Title.
Contents omitted.

TURNBULL, Clive, 1906- 920.094
Australian lives. Melbourne, F. W. Cheshire [Boston, Ginn, 1966] xvi, 158p. 23cm. Six essays, previously pub. separately. Bibl. [DU82.T8] 4.25
1. Australia—Biog. I. Title.
Contents omitted.

WHO'S who in Australia; 920.094
xvith ed; 1959; an Australian biographical dictionary and register of titled persons, with which is incorporated John's notable Australians. Compiled and edited by Joseph A. Alexander. [New York, Collings, 1959] 895p. 23cm. 16.50
1. Australia—Biog.

Australia—Biog.—Dictionaries.

AUSTRALIAN dictionary of biography. 920.094
[General ed.: Douglas Pike. Melbourne] Melbourne Univ. Pr.; London, New York, Cambridge Univ. Pr. [1967] v. 26cm. Contents.v. 2. 1788-1850: I-Z. Section eds.: A. G. L. Clark, 1788-1825; C. M. H. Clark, 1826-1850 [DU82.A9] 66-13723 23.50
1. Australia—Biog.—Dictionaries. I. Pike, Douglas ed.

PIKE, Douglas, ed. 920.094
Australian dictionary of biography. [General editor: Douglas Pike. Melbourne] Melbourne University Press; London, New York, Cambridge University Press [1966] v, 26 cm. v. 1. Contents.CONTENTS -- v. 1.1788-1850, A-H. [DU82.A9] 66-13723
1. Australia — Biog. — Dictionaries. I. Title. BIP

Australia — Biog. — Juvenille literature.

SIX great Australians v. 12
Third series. Melbourne, London [etc.] Oxford U. P., 1965 [i.e. 1966] [196] p. illus. (incl. ports.) map 19 1/2 cm. (B 66-3506) Originally published separately.
1. Australia — Biog. — Juvenille literature.
Contents omitted.

Australia. Constitutional Convention, 1973—Biography.

AUSTRALIA. 342'.94'024
Constitutional Convention, 1973.
Biographical notes of delegates and representatives / Australian Constitutional Convention. [Melbourne] : [Govt. Pr.], 1973. 35 p. ; 24 cm. Cover title. [JQ4015 1973.A313 1973] 75-317002 ISBN 0-7241-0670-7 : free
1. Australia. Constitutional Convention, 1973—Biography. I. Title.

Australia—Description and travel.

CLARK, Anne. 327'.2'0924
Australian adventure; letters from an Ambassador's wife. Foreword by Dame Zara Holt. Austin, University of Texas [1969] 232 p. illus., map, ports. 24 cm. [DU105.C52] 73-97905 7.50
1. Australia—Description and travel. I. Title. BIP

Australia—Foreign relations.

WATT, Alan 327'.2'0924[B]
Stewart, Sir, 1901-
Australian diplomat: memoirs of Sir Alan Watt. Sydney, Angus & Robertson in association with the Australian Institute of International Affairs, [1972] xi, 329 p. plates. 25 cm. Bibliography: p. 317-318. [D413.W35A3] 73-152351 ISBN 0-207-12354-3
1. Australia—Foreign relations. I. Australian Institute of International Affairs. II. Title.
Available from Verry, Mystic, Conn., for 13.00.

Australia—Politics and government.

FADDEN, Arthur 994'.04'0924 B
William, Sir, 1895-
They called me Artie; the memoirs of Sir Arthur Fadden. [Milton, Q.] Jacaranda [1969] 196 p. illus., ports. 23 cm. [DU114.F15A3] 72-498310 4.50
1. Australia—Politics and government. I. Title.

Australian aborigines.

RYAN, W. Michael. 390'.09'1749915
White man, Black man; the true story of a white man who was initiated into an Aboriginal tribe [by] W. Michael Ryan. [Milton, Q.] Jacaranda [1969] 143 p. 23 cm. (Pioneer library, 1) [DU120.R9] 75-519576 ISBN 0-7016-0292-9 3.50
1. Australian aborigines. I. Title.

Austria—Biog.—Dict.

BIOGRAPHISCHES lexikon des kaiserthums Oesterreich, 920/.0436/03
enthaltend de lebensskizzen der denkwurdigen personen, welche seit 1750 in den osterreichischen kronlandern geboren wurden oder darin gelebt und gewirkt haben. Von dr. Constant von Wurzbach. Wien, W. K. Hof- und staatsdruckerei [etc.] 1866-91. New York, Johnson Reprint, 1967. 60v. fold. geneal. tables. 22cm. (v. 1-5: 21cm.)-- Register zu den Nachtragen in Wurbachs Biographischem lexikon d. kaiserthums Osterreich' ... Wien, Gilhofer & Ranschburg, 1923. 16p. 23cm. Index to additions in vols. 9, 11, 14, 22-24, 26 and 28. "Vorrede" signed: Dr. E. F. [CT903.W8] [CT903.W8 Nachtragen Register] 8-30373 950.00 set,
1. Austria—Biog.—Dict. I. Wurzbach, Constantin, ritter von Tannenberg 1818-1893

Authority—Correspondence, reminiscences, etc.

BARNEY, Natalie 848'.9'1209 B
Clifford.
Aventures de l'esprit / Natalie Clifford Barney. New York : Arno Press, 1975. p. cm. (Homosexuality) Reprint of the 1929 ed. published by Editions Emile-Paul freres, Paris. [PQ3939.B3A9 1975] 75-12302 ISBN 0-405-07394-1 : 15.00
1. Authority—Correspondence, reminiscences, etc. I. Title. II. Series. BIP

Authors.

PROFILES of some authors and illustrators published by Walck. 028.52'0922
With a bibliography in the form of a graded catalogue. New York, Henry Z. Walck, inc. [1966?] [48], 65 p. ports. 25 cm. [PN452] 77-7353 1.50 (pbk)
1. Authors. 2. Children's literature—Bibliography—Catalogs. I. Henry Z. Walck, inc.

Authors, American.

ADAMS, Oscar Fay, 1855- 810.9
1919.
A dictionary of American authors. 5th ed. rev. and enl. Boston, Houghton Mifflin, 1904. Detroit, Gale Research Co., 1969. viii, 587 p. 23 cm. [Z1224.A22 1969] 68-21751
1. Authors, American. 2. American literature—Bio-bibliography. I. Title.

ADAMS, Oscar Fay, 1855- 015'.73
1919.
A dictionary of American authors. Kennebunkport, Me., Milford House, 1970. 444 p. 23 cm. Reprint of the 1897 ed., an enlargement of his Brief handbook of American authors. [Z1224.A22 1970] 75-130590
1. Authors, American. 2. American literature—Bio-bibliography. I. Title. BIP

BOLTON, Sarah (Knowles) 928.1
1841-1916.
Famous American authors. Rev. by William A. Fahey. New York, Crowell [1954] 248p. 21cm. [PS121.B6 1954] 54-9770
1. Authors, American. I. Title.

BROOKS, Van Wyck, 1886- 928.1
Days of the phoenix; the nineteen-twenties I remember. [1st ed.] New York, Dutton, 1957. 193p. illus. 22cm. 'A continuation of ... [the author's] Scences and portraits: memories of childhood and youth.' [PS3503.R7297D3] 57-5335
1. Authors, American. 2. Authors—Correspondence, reminiscences, etc. I. Title.

BROOKS, Van Wyck, 1886- 928.1
From the shadow of the mountain; my post-meridian years. [1st ed.] New York, Dutton, 1961. 202p. illus. 22cm. [PS3503.R7297Z5] 61-11417
1. Authors, American. 2. Authors—Correspondence, reminiscences, etc. I. Title.

CANTWELL, Robert, 1908- 928.1
Famous American men of letters; illustrated by Gerald McCann. New York, Dodd, Mead, 1956. 192 p. illus. 22 cm. (Famous biographies for young people) [PS96.C3] 56-7418
1. Authors, American. I. Title.

DELL, Floyd, 1887- 818'.5'209
1969.
Homecoming; an autobiography. Port Washington, N.Y., Kennikat Press [1969, c1933] xi, 368 p. 23 cm. [PS3507.E49Z5 1969] 75-93061 ISBN 8-04-606749-
I. Title. BIP

DODD, Loring Holmes 920.073
Celebrities at our hearthside Boston, Dresser, Chapman & Grimes [c.1959] 402p. illus. 21cm. 59-14846 5.00
1. Authors, American. 2. Actors. 3. Musicians. I. Title.

MELTZER, Milton, 1915- ed. 928.1
A Thoreau profile, by Milton Meltzer and Walter Harding. New York, Crowell [1962] viii, 310 p. illus., ports., map, facsims. 24 cm. "Derived for the most part from Thoreau's own autobiographical writings, supplemented ... by the writings of his friends and contemporaries." Includes bibliographical references. [PS3053.M4] 62-16548
1. Thoreau, Henry David, 1817-1862. II. Harding, Walter Roy. 1917- joint ed. III. Title. BIP

MUIR, Jane. 928.1
Famous modern American women writers. New York, Dodd, Mead, 1959. 171 p. illus. 22 cm. (Famous biographies for young people) Includes bibliography. [PS151.M8] 59-7229
1. Authors, American. 2. Women authors. I. Title.

WILLERT, Arthur, 327'.2'0924 B
Sir, 1882-
Washington and other memories. Boston, Houghton Mifflin, 1972 [c1971] vi, 248 p. 22 cm. [DA566.9.W46A3 1972] 74-162013 ISBN 0-395-12727-0 6.95
1. Title.

Authors, American—Autographs—Facsimiles.

POE, Edgar Allan, 810'.9'003 B
1809-1849.
A chapter on autography / by Edgar Allan Poe ; edited by Don C. Seitz. New York : Haskell House, 1974 [i.e. 1975] 92 p. : ill. ; 20 cm. Reprint of the 1926 ed. published by L. Macveagh, New York. [PS128.P6 1975] 74-30363 ISBN 0-8383-2067-8 : 9.95
1. Authors, American—Autographs—Facsimiles. 2. Authors, American. I. Title.

Authors, American—Biography.

NORMAN, charles. 1904- 928.1
To a different drum; the story of Henry David Thoreau. Pictures by Margaret Bloy Graham. New York, Harper & Row [1962, c.1954] 113p. 22cm. 54-8977 2.44 lib. ed.,
I. Thoreau, Henry David, 1817-1862. II. Title.

RATHER, Lois, 1905- 810'.9'004
Encounters; some incidents of literary history. Oakland [Calif.] Rather Press [1972] 74 p. ports. 22 cm. "80 copies, number 55." Includes bibliographical references. [PS129.R38] 73-153859
1. Authors, American—Biography. I. Title.

RIDEING, William Henry, 820'.9 B
1853-1918.
The boyhood of living authors. Freeport, N.Y., Books for Libraries Press [1973] p. (Essay index reprint series) Reprint of the 1887 ed. published by Crowell, New York. Contents.Contents.—Oliver Wendell Holmes.—Thomas Bailey Aldrich.—John Townsend Trowbridge.—William Clark Russell.—William Ewart Gladstone.—Edward Eggleston.—William Dean Howells.—James Payn.—John Greenleaf Whittier.—Francis Richard Stockton.—Thomas Wallace Knox.—Edward Everett Hale.—James Russell Lowell.—Hjalmar

Hjorth Boyesen.—Thomas Wentworth Higginson.—Edgar Fawcett.—Edmund Clarence Stedman.—Charles Dudley Warner. [PS128.R5 1973] 73-5631 ISBN 0-518-10127-4
1. Authors, American—Biography. 2. Authors, English—Biography. I. Title. BIP

SULLIVAN, Wilson. 810'.9'003 B
New England men of letters. With a foreword by Hyatt H. Waggoner. Drawings by Thomas Evans Hinton. New York, Macmillan [1972] x, 256 p. illus. 23 cm. Contents.Contents.—Ralph Waldo Emerson.—Henry David Thoreau.—Nathaniel Hawthorne.—Richard Henry Dana, Jr., and Herman Melville.—Francis Parkman and William Hickling Prescott.—Henry Wadsworth Longfellow.—James Russell Lowell.—Oliver Wendell Holmes.—Bibliography (p. [243]-250) [PS129.S84] 75-165574 6.95
1. Authors, American—Biography. 2. American literature—New England—History and criticism. I. Title. BIP

TICKNOR, Caroline, 1866- 820.9 B
1937.
Glimpses of authors. Freeport, N.Y., Books for Libraries Press [1972, c1922] xii, 335 p. illus. 23 cm. (Essay index reprint series) [PS128.T5 1972] 70-167429 ISBN 0-8369-2674-9
1. Authors, American—Biography. 2. Authors, English—Biography. I. Title. BIP

Authors, American—Biography—Juvenile literature.

HELMSTADTER, Frances 920
Picture book of American authors. New York, Sterling [c.1962] 64p. illus. 26cm. (Visual hist. ser.) 62-18640 1.00 pap.,
1. Authors, American—Juvenile literature. I. Title.

LEIPOLD, L. Edmond, 813'.009 B
1902-
Famous American fiction writers, by L. E. Leipold. Minneapolis, T. S. Denison [1972] 89 p. 25 cm. (His Famous American heroes and leaders series) Includes ten brief biographies of nineteenth and twentieth-century authors emphasizing their literary contributions. [PS129.L4] 920 72-162688 ISBN 0-513-01197-8
1. Authors, American—Biography—Juvenile literature. 2. American fiction—History and criticism—Juvenile literature. I. Title.

SIGNIFICANT American 810'.9 B
authors, poets, and playrights. Chicago : Childrens Press, [1976] p. cm. Includes index. Brief biographies of 152 prominent American authors, poets, and playwrights arranged in chronological and alphabetical order. [PS106.S45] 920 75-20689 ISBN 0-516-05302-7 : 6.95
1. Authors, American—Biography—Juvenile literature. I. Title: Authors, poets, and playrights.

Authors, American—Correspondence, reminiscences, etc.

SCHULBERG, Budd. 813'.5'209 B
The four seasons of success. [1st ed.] Garden City, N.Y., Doubleday, 1972. 203 p. 22 cm. [PS3537.C7114Z5] 72-76202 ISBN 0-385-00510-5 5.95
1. Authors, American—Correspondence, reminiscences, etc. I. Title.

Authors, American—Homes and haunts.

KRAFT, Stephanie. 810'.9
No castles on Main Street : American authors and their homes / Stephanie Kraft. Chicago : Rand McNally, 1979. p. cm. Includes bibliographical references. [PS141.K7] 79-9816 ISBN 0-528-81828-7 : 9.95
1. Authors, American—Homes and haunts. 2. Literary landmarks—United States. 3. Authors, American—Biography. 4. Historic buildings—United States. I. Title. BIP

Authors, American—Homes and haunts—England—London.

WEINTRAUB, Stanley, 810'.9'94212
1929-
The London Yankees : portraits of American writers and artists in England, 1894-1914 / Stanley Weintraub. 1st ed. New York : Harcourt Brace Jovanovich, c1979. viii, 408 p., [4] leaves of plates : ill. ; 24 cm. Includes index. Bibliography: p. 381-394. [PS144.L6W4] 78-22276 ISBN 0-15-152978-7. : 14.95
1. Authors, American—Homes and haunts—England—London. 2. Authors, American—England—London—Biography. 3. London—Intellectual life. 4. Americans in London. 5. Artists—United States—Biography. 6. Artists—England—London—Biography. I. Title. BIP

Authors, American— Michigan.

HILBERT, Rachel H., ed. 928.1
Michigan poets, with supplement to Michigan authors, 1960. Ed. by Rachel M. Hilbert. Ann Arbor, Michigan Assn. of Sch. Librarians [c.]1964. vii, 77p. illus., ports. 22cm. 64-7686 1.25 pap.,
1. Authors, American— Michigan. 2. Poets, American. I. Hilbert, Rachel M. mIchigan authors. II. Michigan Association of School Librarians. III. Title.

HILBERT, Rachel M ed. 928.1
Michigan authors. Ann Arbor, Michigan Association of School Librarians, 1960. 68p. illus., ports. 22cm. [PS283.M5H5] 60-16690
1. Authors, American—Michigan. I. Title.

HILBERT, Rachel M ed. 928.1
Michigan poets, with supplement to Michigan authors, 1960. Edited by Rachel M. Hilbert. Ann Arbor, Michigan Association of School Librarians, 1964. vii, 77 p. illus., ports. 22 cm. [PS283.M5H53] 64-7686
1. Authors. American — Michigan. 2. Poets, American. I. Hilbert, Rachel M. Michigan authors. II. Michigan Association of School Librarians. III. Title.

Authors, American—Minnesota.

RICHARDS, Carmen Nelson, 928.1
ed.
Minnesota writers; a collection of autobiographical stoies by Minnesota prose writers. Minneapolis, Denison [c.1961] 425p. illus. 61-18646 4.95
1. Authors, American—Minnesota. 2. American literature—Minnesota— Bio-bibl. 3. Minnesota—Biog. I. Title.

Authors, American—New England—Juvenile literature.

BENET, Laura. 810.9 B
Famous New England authors. New York, Dodd, Mead [1970] x, 150 p. ports. 22 cm. (Famous biographies for young people) Contents.Contents.—William Cullen Bryant.—Ralph Waldo Emerson.—Nathaniel Hawthorne.—Henry Wadsworth Longfellow.—John Greenleaf Whittier.—Oliver Wendell Holmes.—Harriet Beecher Stowe.—Richard Henry Dana.—Henry David Thoreau.—James Russell Lowell.—Emily Dickinson.—Louisa May Alcott.—Sarah Orne Jewett.—Mary Eleanor Wilkins Freeman.—Edwin Arlington Robinson.—Amy Lowell.—Robert Frost.—Edna St. Vincent Millay.—John Phillips Marquand.—Thornton Niven Wilder. [PS243.B4] 920 76-127171 3.50
1. Authors, American—New England—Juvenile literature. I. Title. BIP

Authors, American—North Carolina.

WALSER, Richard 810.9'9'756
Gaither, 1908-
Young readers' picturebook of Tar Heel authors, by Richard Walser. 3d ed. rev. and enl. Raleigh, N.C., State Dept. of Archives and History, 1966. iv, 70 p. 23 cm. First ed. published in 1957 under title: Picturebook of Tar Heel authors. Bibliography: p. [3] of cover. [PS266.N8W3 1966] 67-64275
1. Authors, American—North Carolina. 2. American literature—North Carolina—Bio-bibliography. I. North Carolina. State Dept. of Archives and History. II. Title. BIP

Authors, American—Northwest, Pacific.

PACIFIC Northwest 013.9795
Library Association. Reference Section.
Who's who among Pacific Northwest authors. Edited with a pref. by Hazel E. Mills. [Bozeman, Mont., 1957. [Seattle; 1961- 114l. 28cm. no. 28cm. Editor: no. 1- P. M. Harris. No. 1-issued by the association's Reference Division. [Z1251.N7P3] 57-49129
1. Authors, American—Northwest, Pacific. 2. American literature— Northwest, Pacific—Bio-bibl. I. Mills, Hazel E., ed. II. Harris, Phoebe M., ed. III. Pacific Northwest Library Association. Reference Division. IV. Title. V. Title: Supplement.

PACIFIC Northwest 013.9795
Library Association. Reference Section.
Who's who among Pacific Northwest authors. Supplement. 1st- [Seattle? 1961-no. 28 cm. Editor: no. 1- P. M. Harris. No. 1- issued by the association's Reference Division. [Z1251.N7P312]
1. Authors, American—Northwest, Pacific. 2. American literature—Northwest, Pacific—Bio-bibliography. I. Mills, Hazel E., ed. II. Harris, Phoebe M., ed. III. Pacific Northwest Library Association. Reference Division. IV. Title.

WHO'S who among Pacific 810.9'979
Northwest authors. Edited with a pref. by Frances Valentine Wright. 2d ed. [Missoula, Mont.?] Pacific Northwest Library Association, Reference Division, 1969 [c1970] 105 p. 29 cm. (Libri montani) [Z1251.N7W5 1970] 74-16021
1. Authors, American—Northwest, Pacific. 2. American literature—Northwest, Pacific—Bio-bibliography. I. Wright, Frances Valentine, ed. II. Pacific Northwest Library Association. Reference Division.

Authors, American—Southwest, New.

GARD, Wayne, 1899- 636.2'01'0922
Reminiscences of range life. Austin, Tex., Steck-Vaughn Co. [1970] ii, 52 p. 21 cm. (Southwest writers series, no. 30) Biographies. Bibliography: p. 49-52. [PS277.G26] 71-120004 ISBN 8-11-438937-
1. Authors, American—Southwest, New. I. Title. II. Series.

Authors, American—Texas.

BARNS, Florence 810.9'005'2 [B]
Elberta.
Texas writers of today. Foreword by Robert Adger Law. Ann Arbor, Mich., Gryphon Books, 1971. 513, [1] p. 22 cm. Fold. map mounted on inside of back cover. Reprint of the 1935 ed. Biographical sketches with selections from the authors' works. Bibliography: p. [514] [PS266.4B3 1971] 70-157491 23.50
1. Authors, American—Texas. 2. American literature—Texas. I. Title. BIP

Authors, American—Virginia—Biography.

TAYLOR, Welford 810'.9'9755
Dunaway.
Virginia authors, past and present. Welford Dunaway Taylor, general editor, with Maurice Duke, bibliographical editor [and others. Richmond] Virginia Association of Teachers of English, 1972. xiv, 125 p. map (on lining papers) 23 cm. Includes bibliographies. [PS266.V5T3] 72-77884
1. Authors, American—Virginia—Biography. 2. Virginia—Biography. 3. American literature—Virginia—Bio-bibliography. I. Virginia Association of Teachers of English. II. Title.

Authors, American—19th century—Biography—Juvenile literature.

HANCOCK, Carla. 810'.9 B
Seven founders of American literature / by Carla Hancock ; portrait drawings by Ted Trinkaus. Winston-Salem, N.C. : J. F. Blair, c1976. 207 p. : ports. ; 25 cm. Includes bibliographies. Biographies of seven important nineteenth century American authors: Cooper, Irving, Bryant, Poe, Melville, Whitman, and Clemens. [PS128.H27] 920 75-44173 ISBN 0-910244-87-1 : 8.95
1. Authors, American—19th century—Biography—Juvenile literature. I. Trinkaus, Ted. II. Title. BIP

Authors, American—20th century—Bio-Bibliography.

AMERICAN writers in 810'.9'0052 B
Paris, 1920-1939 / edited by Karen Lane Rood ; foreword by Malcolm Cowley. Detroit, Mich. : Gale Research Co., 1980. p. cm. (Dictionary of literary biography ; v. 4) "A Bruccoli Clark book." Bibliography: p. [PS129.A57] 79-26101 ISBN 0-8103-0916-5 : 42.00
1. Authors, American—20th century—Bio-Bibliography. 2. American literature—France—Paris—Bio-Bibliography. 3. Americans in Paris—Biography. 4. Paris—Intellectual life—Bibliography. I. Rood, Karen Lane. II. Title. III. Series.

Authors, American—20th century—Biography.

GAINES, James. 820'.9
Wits end : days and nights of the Algonquin Round Table / by James Gaines. New York : Harcourt Brace Jovanovich, [1977] p. cm. Includes index. [PS129.G34] 77-73050 ISBN 0-15-197521-3 : 12.95
1. Authors, American—20th century Biography. 2. New York (City)—Intellectual life. I. Title. BIP

GAINES, James R. 810'.9'0052
Wit's end : days and nights of the Algonquin Round Table / James R. Gaines. 1st Harvest/HBJ ed. New York : Harcourt, Brace, Jovanovich, 1979, c1977. p. cm. (A Harvest/HBJ book) Includes index. [PS129.G34 1979] 79-10464 ISBN 0-15-697651-X. : 6.95
1. Authors, American—20th century—Biography. 2. New York (City)—Intellectual life. I. Title.

Authors, American—20th century—Correspondence, reminiscences, etc.

THE Beat book / 810'.9'0054 B
[edited by Arthur Winfield Knight and Glee Knight]. [California, Pa. : A W Knight and G. Knight, 1974] 175 p. : ill. ; 28 cm. (The Unspeakable visions of the individual ; v. 4) Cover title. [PS129.B4] 75-310027
1. Authors, American—20th century—Correspondence, reminiscences, etc. 2. American literature—20th century. I. Knight, Arthur Winfield, 1937- II. Knight, Glee, 1947- III. Title. IV. Series. BIP

Authors as artists—United States—Biography—Juvenile literature.

SMARIDGE, Norah. 920
Famous author-illustrators for young people. New York, Dodd, Mead [1973] 159 p. ports. 22 cm. (Famous biographies for young people) Brief biographies of nineteen author-illustrators include Roger Duvoisin, Dr. Seuss, Kate Greenaway, Lois Lenski, and Tomi Ungerer. [NC975.S57] 73-6033 ISBN 0-396-06831-6 3.95
1. Authors as artists—United States—Biography—Juvenile literature. I. Title.

Authors—Biography.

JOHNSON, Rossiter, 1840- 809 B
1931.
A dictionary of biographies of authors represented in the Authors digest series, with a supplemental list of later titles and a supplementary biographical section, edited by Rossiter Johnson and a staff of literary experts. Detroit, Gale Research Co., 1974 [c1927] 467 p. 23 cm. (Series: Johnson, Rossiter, 1840-1931, ed. Authors digest, v. 19.) Reprint of the ed. published by Authors Press, New York, which was

issued as v. 19 of Authors digest series. [PN44.J72 1974] 71-167011 17.50
1. Authors—Biography. I. Title. II. Series.
BIP

QUENNELL, Peter, 1905- 809
Casanova in London. New York, Stein and Day [1971] 198 p. 22 cm. Contents.Contents.—Casanova in London.—Crusoe's island.—The Goncourts.—George Sand.—Ego Hugo.—Oscar Wilde.—Andre Gide.—The secret commonwealth.—'My admirable Margaret.'—The Brontes.—Vanity fair.—Sir John Soane and his museum.—'L'Art sans poitrine.'—'My heart laid bare.'—'Foie gras to the sound of trumpets.'—A literary exile.—La Rochefoucauld.—The magician of pleasure.—Taine in England.—Mayhew's London.—Evelyn Waugh.—'The colour of his hair.'—Robert Graves.—John Falstaff: a biography. [PN452.Q4 1971] 72-150603 ISBN 0-8128-1368-5 6.95
1. Authors—Biography. I. Title.

SAINTE-BEUVE, Charles Augustin, 1804-1869. 809
Portraits of men. Translated by Forsyth Edeveain, with critical memoir by William Sharp. Freeport, N.Y., Books for Libraries Press [1972] xlviii, 223 p. port. 22 cm. (Essay index reprint series) Reprint of the 1891 ed. Contents.Contents.—Goethe and Bettina, 1850.—Alfred de Musset, 1857.—Letters of Lord Chesterfield to his son, 1850.—De Balzac, 1850.—The memoirs of Saint-Simon, 1851.—Camille Desmoulins, 1850.—Diderot, 1851.—La Bruyere, 1836.—L'Abbe de Choisy, 1851.—Fontenelle, 1851. [PN457.S213 1972] 72-4650 ISBN 0-8369-2972-1 11.00
1. Authors—Biography. I. Title.
BIP

Authors—Biography—Indexes.

WRITERS for young adults 016.809
: biographies master index / Adele Sarkissian, editor, 1st ed. Detroit : Gale Research Co., c1979. xxxi, 199 p. ; 24 cm. (Gale biographical index series ; no. 6) [Z1037.A1W74] [PN497] 79-13228 ISBN 0-8103-1083-X : 24.00
1. Authors—Biography—Indexes. I. Sarkissian, Adele.
BIP

Authors—Biography—Marriage.

MEYERS, Jeffrey. 809 B
Married to genius / Jeffrey Meyers. New York : Barnes & Noble Books, 1977. 214 p. : ill. ; 23 cm. Bibliography: p. [211]-214. [PN481.M48] 76-58233 ISBN 0-06-494790-4 : 20.00
1. Authors—Biography—Marriage. I. Title.
BIP

Authors—Correspondence, reminiscences, etc.

*ALEXANDER, Winston M. 928
The joy, the sorrow and denn, by Winston M. Alexander. New York, Vantage Press, [1974] 175 p. 21 cm. [CT25] ISBN 0-533-00901-4 4.50
1. Authors—Correspondance, reminiscences, etc. I. Title.

ARCHER, William, 1856-1924. 825'.9'12
Real conversations. London, W. Heinemann, 1904. [Folcroft, Pa.] Folcroft Library Editions, 1972. xi, 254 p. ports. 24 cm. "Reprinted from the Pall Mall magazine." Contents.Contents.—An imaginary conversation: with the courteous reader.—Real conversations: With Mr. Arthur W. Pinero. With Mr. Thomas Hardy. With Mrs. Craigie (John Oliver Hobbes) With Mr. Stephen Phillips. With Mr. George Moore. With Mr. W. S. Gilbert. With Professor Masson. With Mr. Spenser Wilkinson. With Mr. William Heinemann. With Mr. George Alexander. With Mrs. St. Leger Harrison (Lucas Malet) With Mr. Sidney Lee. [PR4007.A63Z5 1972] 72-195438 15.00
1. Authors—Correspondence, reminiscences, etc. I. Title.
BIP

BROOKS, Van Wyck, 1886-1963. 928.1
An autobiography. Foreword by John Hall Wheelock. Introd. by Malcolm Cowley. [1st ed.] New York, E. P. Dutton, 1965. xxxvi, 667 p. port. 22 cm. A one vol. ed. of the author's 3 books of memoirs originally published in 1954, 1957 and 1961. Contents.Contents.—Scenes and portraits, memories of childhood and youth.—Days of the Phoenix, the nineteen-twenties I remember.—From the shadow of the mountain, my post-meridian years. [PS3503.R7297Z52] 64-19571
1. Authors—Correspondence, reminiscences, etc.

CLOUGH, Arthur Hugh, 1819-1861. 928.2
Correspondence. Edited by Frederick L. Mulhauser. Oxford, Clarendon Press, 1957. 2v. (xxiii, 655p.) 23cm. [PR4458.A4 1957] 57-59593
1. Authors—Correspondence, reminiscences, etc. I. Title.

CONGREVE, William, 1670-1729. 928.2
Letters & documents. Collected & edited by John C. Hodges. [1st ed.] New York, Harcourt, Brace and World [1964] xxii, 295 p. ports., facsim. 24 cm. Bibliography: p. 281-282. [PR3366.A55] 64-11528
1. Authors—Correspondence, reminiscences, etc. I. Hodges, John Cunyus, 1892- ed.

CRANE, Stephen 928.1
Stephen Crane: letters. Edited by R. W. Stallman and Lillian Gilkes. With an introd. by R. W. Stallman. [New York] New York University Press, [c.] 1960. xxx, 366p. port. 25cm. 59-15192 6.50 bds.,
1. Authors—Correspondence, reminiscences, etc. I. Title.

CRICHTON, Kyle Samuel, 1896- 818.52
Total recoil. [1st ed.] Garden City, N. Y., Doubleday, 1960. 308 p. 22 cm. [PS3505.R635Z52] 60-13729
1. Authors—Correspondence, reminiscences, etc. I. Title.

DICKENS, Charles, 1812-1870. 928.2
Selected letters. Edited, with an introd., by F. W. Dupee. New York, Farrar, Straus and Cudahy [1960] xxiv, 293 p. 22 cm. (Great letters series) [PR4581.A3D8] 60-8013
1. Authors—Correspondence, reminiscences, etc. I. Dupee, Frederick Wilcox, 1904- ed. II. Title.

DOMETT, Alfred, 1811-1887. 928.2
The diary of Alfred Domett, 1872-1885, edited by E. A. Horsman. London, New York, Oxford University Press, 1953. 311 p. ports. 23 cm. (University of Durham publications) Bibliographical footnotes. [PR4613.D3Z52] 54-1073
1. Authors—Correspondence, reminiscences, etc. I. Title. II. Series: Durham, Eng. University. Publications

EHRENBURG, Ilia Grigorevich 1891-1967. 891.7'8'4203 B
Selections from People, years, life [by] Ilya Ehrenburg. Oxford, New York, Pergamon Press [1972] xxx, 282 p. front. 20 cm. (The Commonwealth and international library. Pergamon Oxford Russian series) Text in Russian; summaries in English. Bibliography: p. 282. [PG3476.E5Z5 1972] 73-128339 ISBN 0-08-006354-3 Pap. 6.50
1. Authors—Correspondence, reminiscences, etc. I. Moody, C.

FITZGERALD, Edward, 1809-1883. 928.2
Letters. Edited by J. M. Cohen. Carbondale, Southern Illinois University Press [1960] xxii, 275p. 19cm. (Centaur classics) 60-9249 4.75
1. Authors—Correspondence, reminiscences, etc. I. Title.

GIDE, Andre Paul Guillaume, 1869-1951. 928.4
The journals of Andre Gide, 1889-1949. Edited, translated, abridged, and with an introd. by Justin O'Brien. [1st Vintage ed.] New York, Vintage Books, 1956. 2v. 19cm. (A Vintage book, K33A-B) [PQ2613.I2Z527] 56-58321
1. Authors—Correspondence, reminiscences, etc. I. Title.

GLASGOW, Ellen Anderson Gholson, 1874-1945. 928.1
Letters. Compiled and edited with an introd. and commentary by Blair Rouse. [1st ed.] New York, Harcourt, Brace [1958] 384 p. 25 cm. [PS3513.L34Z53] 58-5473
1. Authors—Correspondence, reminiscences, etc.

HARRIMAN, Margaret (Case) 928.1
Blessed are the debonair; illustrated by Mircea Vasiliu. New York, Rinehart [1956] 254p. illus. 21cm. [PS3515.A695Z5] 56-7255
1. Authors—Correspondence, reminiscences, etc. 2. Actors, American. 3. Algonquin Hotel, New York. I. Title.

JOYCE, James, 1882-1941. 928.2
Letters, edited by Stuart Gilbert. New York, Viking Press, 1957-[66] 3 v. facsims., ports 25 cm. Vols. 2-3 edited by Richard Ellmann. "A chronology of the life of James Joyce, by Richard Ellmann": v. 1, p. 43-50. [PR6019.O9Z52] 57-5129
1. Authors — Correspondence, reminiscences, etc. I. Gilbert, Stuart, ed. II. Ellmann, Richard, 1918- ed. III. Title.

KAFKA, Franz, 1883-1924 928.3
Letters to Milena. Ed. by Willi Haas; tr. by Tania and James Stern. New York, Schocken [1962, c.1953] 238p. 21cm. (SB24) 62-13139 1.75 pap.,
1. Authors—Correspondence, reminiscences, etc. I. Jesenska, Milena, 1896-1944. II. Title.

KING, Grace Elizabeth, 1852-1932. 813'.4 B
Memories of a Southern woman of letters. Freeport, N.Y., Books for Libraries Press [1971] 398 p. port. 23 cm. Reprint of the 1932 ed. [PS2178.A4 1971] 76-146863 ISBN 0-8369-5630-3
1. Authors—Correspondence, reminiscences, etc. I. Title.
BIP

LAWRENCE, Arnold Walter, 1900- ed. 923.542
Letters to T. E. Lawrence. London, Cape [dist. Chester Springs, Pa., Dufour, 1964, c.1962] 216p. facsims. 24cm. 63-5213 6.95
1. Authors— Correspondence, reminiscences, etc. I. Lawrence, Thomas Edward, 1888-1935. II. Title.

LAWRENCE, David Herbert, 1885-1930 928.2
Collected letters; 2v. Ed. introd. by Harry T. Moore. NewYork, Viking [c.1962] 2v. (ivi, 1307p.) 62-9685 17.50 set, bxd.
1. Authors—Correspondence, reminiscences, etc. I. Title.

LAWRENCE, David Herbert, 1885-1930. 928.2
Selected letters. Edited with an introd. by Diana Trilling. New York, Farrar, Straus, and Cudahy [1958] xiiii, 322p. 22cm. (Great letters series) [PR6023.A93Z532] 57-11489
1. Authors—Correspondence, reminiscences, etc. I. Title.

LAWRENCE, David Herbert, 1885-1930. 928.2
Selected letters. Edited with an introd. by Diana Trilling. Garden City, N. Y., Anchor books [dist. by Doubleday] 1961 [c.1958, 1961] 352p. 18cm. (Anchor books, A236) Bibl. footnotes. 60-52285 1.45 pap.,
1. Authors—Correspondence, reminiscences, etc. I. Title.

LEHMANN, John, 1907- 928.2
I am my brother. New York, Reynal [1960] 326p. illus. 22cm. 'The continuation of the autobiography...[begun] in The whispering gallery. [PR6023.FAZ518] 59-13418
1. Authors— Correspondence, reminiscences, etc. 2. World War, 1939-1945—Gt. Brit.— London. I. Title.

LEHMANN, John [Rudolph John Frederick Lehmann] 928.2
I am my brother. New York, Reynal [c.1960] 326p. illus. 22cm. 59-13418 5.00
1. Authors—Correspondence, reminiscences, etc. 2. World War, 1939-1945—Gt. Brit.—London I. Title.

LLYOD, Charles, 1775-1839. 928.2
The Lloyd-Manning letters. Edited by Frederick L. Beaty. Bloomington, Indiana University Press, 1957. ix, 95 p. 23 cm. (Indiana University publications. Humanities series, no. 39) [AS36.I 385 no. 39] 58-62698
1. Authors — Correspondence, reminiscences, etc. I. Manning, Thomas, 1772-1840. II. Title. III. Series: Indiana. University. Indiana University humanities series, no. 39

MAUGHAM, William Somerset, 1874- 928.2
The summing up. [New York] New American Library [1951, c1938] 191 p. 19 cm. (A Mentor book, M 60) [PR6025.A86S8 1951] 51-3088
1. Authors—Correspondence, reminiscences, etc. I. Title.
BIP

MONROE, Harriet, 1860-1936. 811'.5'2 B
A poet's life; seventy years in a changing world. New York, AMS Press [1969] viii, 488 p. facsims., ports. 23 cm. Reprint of the 1938 ed. [PS2423.A4 1969] 71-93777
1. Authors—Correspondence, reminiscences, etc. I. Title.

NOCK, Albert Jay, 1872or3-1945. 928.1
Selected letters. Collected and edited by Francis J. Nock, with Memories of Albert Jay Nock, by Ruth Robinson. Caldwell, Idaho, Caxton Printers, 1962. 201p. 22cm. [PS3527.O2Z53] 62-8189
1. Authors—Correspondence, reminiscences, etc. I. Title.

NORRIS, Kathleen (Thompson) 1880- 928.1
Family gathering. [1st ed.] Garden City, N. Y., Doubleday, 1959. 327p. illus. 22cm. Memolrs. [PS3527.O5Z5] 59-12638
1. Authers—Correspondence, reminiscences, etc. I. Title.

PRIESTLEY, John Boynton, 1894- 828.912
Margin released a writer's reminiscences and reflections. New York, Harper [1963, c.1962] 236p. illus. 22cm. 62-20114 4.95
1. Authors—Correspondence, reminiscences, etc. I. Title.

RENARD, Jules, 1864-1910. 928.4
Journal. Edited and translated by Louise Bogan and Elizabeth Roget. New York, G. Braziller [1964] 254 p. 25 cm. [PQ2635.E48Z533 1964] 64-21767
1. Authors—Correspondence, reminiscences, etc. 2. Authors, French.

ROBINSON, Henry Crabb, 1775-1867. 928.2
The diary of Henry Crabb Robinson: an abridgement; edited with an introduction by Derek Hudson. London, New York [etc.] Oxford U.P., 1967. xix, 348 p. front. (port.), plate (port.). 22 1/2 cm. Unabridged ed. originally published as Henry Crabb Robinson on books and their writers. London, Dent, 1938. Bibliography: p. 319-320. [PR5233.R2A83] 828'.7'08 67-86319
1. Authors—Correspondence, reminiscences, etc. 2. Great Britain.—Intellectual life—19th century. I. Hudson, Derek, ed. II. Title.

SINCLAIR, Upton Beall 928.1
My lifetime in letters. Columbia, University of Missouri Press [c.1960] xxi, 412p. port. 24cm. 59-14141 6.50
1. Authors—Correspondence, reminiscences, etc. I. Title.
BIP

THOREAU, Henry David, 1817-1862. 928.1
Correspondence, edited by Walter Harding and Carl Bode. [New York] New York University Press, 1958. xxi, 665 p. port. 24 cm. [PS3053.A3 1958] 58-11447
1. Authors—Correspondence, reminiscences, etc.

THURBER, James, 1894-1961. 818'.5'207
My life and hard times. With an introd. by John K. Hutchens. New York, Harper & Row [1973, c1933] 114 p. illus. 19 cm. (Perennial library, P 290) [PS3539.H94M87 1973] 73-161582 0.95 (pbk.)
1. Authors—Correspondence, reminiscences, etc. I. Title.
BIP

TURGENEV, Ivan Sergeevich, 1818-1883. 928.917
Literary reminiscences and

autobiographical fragments. Translated with an introd. by David Magarshack, and an essay on Turgenev by Edmund Wilson. New York, Farrar, Strauss and Cudahy [1958] 309 p. 22 cm. Translation of (translated: Literaturnye i zhitelskie vospominania) [PG3431.L5E5] 58-7839
1. Authors — Correspondence, reminiscences, etc. I. Title.

UNTERMEYER, Jean (Starr) 928.1
1886-
Private collection. New York, Knopf [c.] 1965. xii, 295p. v.p. facsims., music, ports. 22cm. [PS3541.N715Z5] 65-10063 5.95
1. Authors—Correspondence, reminiscences, etc. I. Title.

*WAGNER, Ruby. 928.1
Hidden riches in secret places; an autobiography. New York, Vantage Press, [1974]. 112 p. 21 cm. [CT25] ISBN 0-533-00702-X. 4.50.
1. Authors—Correspondence, reminiscence, etc. I. Title.

WHARTON, Edith Newbold 928.1
(Jones) 1862-1937.
A backward glance. New York, Scribner [1964] xxvii, 385 p. illus., ports. 21 cm. [PS3545.H16Z5 1964] 64-3270
1. Authors — Correspondence, reminiscences, etc. I. Title.

WIDDEMER, Margaret. 928.1
Golden friends I had; unrevised memories of Margaret Widdemer. [1st ed.] Garden City, N.Y., Doubleday, 1964. xii, 340 p. 22 cm. [PS3545.I175Z5] 64-19258
1. Authors—Correspondence, reminiscences, etc. I. Title.

WILLIAMS, William Carlos, 928.1
1883-
Selected letters. Edited with an introd. by John C. Thirlwall. New York, McDowell, Obolensky [1957] 347p. 22cm. [PS3545.I544Z53] 57-12112
1. Authors— Correspondence, Reminiscences, etc. I. Title.

WOOLF, Leonard Sidney 928.2
Sowing, an autobiography of the years 1880 to 1904. New York, Harcourt, Brace [c.1960] 224p. illus. 21cm. 60-12726 4.50 half cloth,
1. Authors—Correspondence, reminiscences, etc. I. Title. BIP

WOOLF, Leonard Sidney, 928.2
1880-
Sowing, an autobiography of the years 1880 to 1904. [1st American ed.] New York, Harcourt, Brace [1960] 224 p. illus. 22 cm. [PR6045.O68Z5] 60-12726
1. Authors — Correspondence, reminiscences, etc. I. Title.

Authors, Danish—Biography.

HEEPE, Evelyn, 839.8'1'090072 B
comp.
Modern Danish authors, edited by Evelyn Heepe and Niels Heltberg. Translated by Evelyn Heepe. [Folcroft, Pa.] Folcroft Library Editions, 1974 [c1946] 222 p. 24 cm. Reprint of the ed. published by Scandinavian Pub. Co., Copenhagen, Chicago. Contents.—Jensen, J. V. Among the birds.—Jorgensen, J. The legend of my life.—Nexo, M. A. Reminiscences.—Abell, K. Anna Sophie Hedvig.—Branner, H. C. A child and a mouse.—Dons, A. Where all roads meet.—Kristensen, T. In a Japanese railway carriage. The vanished faces.—Munk, K. Spring comes so gently. An idealist. The word.—Paludan, J. Birds around the light.—Rode, E. The three little girls. The eternal adorer.—Malthe-Bruun, K. Two letters. [PT7700.H4 1974] 74-17194 ISBN 0-8414-4879-5 (lib. bdg.)
1. Authors, Danish—Biography. I. Heltberg, Niels, joint comp. II. Title. BIP

Authors, English.

AUTHOR'S and writer's who's who (The) 928.2 [5th ed.] New York, Hafner [c.1960, 1963] xx, 540p. 26cm. 34-38025 8.00 bds.,
1. Authors, English. 2. Literature—Yearbooks.

AUTHOR'S writer's who's who 928.2 *(The)* 4th ed. Ed.: L. G. Pine. New York, Hafner Pub. Co. [c.1960] 454p. 25cm. 34 7.00
1. Authors, English. 2. Literature—Yearbooks.

COURNOS, John, 1881- 928.2
Famous British novelists, by John Cournos and Sybil Norton [pseud.] Illustrated with photos. New York, Dodd, Mead, 1952. 130 p. illus. 23 cm. (Famous biographies for young people) [PR105.C67] 52-10719
1. Authors, English. I. Title.

HINCHMAN, Walter Swain, 820.9 B
1879-
Lives of great English writers; from Chaucer to Browning, by Walter S. Hinchman and Francis B. Gummere. Freeport, N.Y., Books for Libraries Press [1970, c1908] vi, 569 p. fold. map, ports. 23 cm. (Essay index reprint series) Bibliography: p. [551]-555. [PR105.H6 1970] 74-106409 ISBN 0-8369-1930-0
1. Authors, English. 2. English literature—History and criticism. I. Gummere, Francis Barton, 1855-1919, joint author. II. Title.

JONES, Howard 928.2
Men of letters: Johnson, Marryat, Dickens, Borrow, Trollope, Carroll. London, G. Bell, 1959[i.e., 1960; stamped: distributed by SportShelf, New Rochelle, N.Y.] 183p. (bibl.: p. 182-183) illus. 19cm. 60-1599 3.75 bds.,
1. Authors, English. I. Title.

KUNITZ, Stanley Jasspon, 928.2
1905- ed.
British authors before 1800; a biographical dictionary, edited by Stanley J. Kunitz and Howard Haycraft. New York, Wilson, 1952. vi, 584 p. ports. 26 cm. (The Authors series) [PR105.K9] 52-6758
1. Authors, English. I. Haycraft, Howard, 1905- joint ed. II. Title. III. Series.

THE New writer's who's 928.2 *who.* Ilfracombe, N. Devon, A. H. Stockwell, 19 v. 19 cm. [PR105.N48] 51-30857
1. Authors, English.

PEARSON, Hesketh, 1887- 928.2
Lives of the wits. [1st ed.] New York, Harper & Row [1962] 334p. illus. 22cm. [PR931.P37] 62-14543
1. Authors, English. 2. English wit and humor—Hist. & crit. I. Title.

PEARSON, Hesketh [Edward 928.2
Hesketh Gibbons Pearson] 1877-
Lives of the wits. New York, Harper [c.1962] 334p. illus. 22cm. Bibl. 62-14543 5.95
1. Authors, English. 2. English wit and humor—Hist. & crit. I. Title.

POWYS, Llewelyn, 1884-1939 820.9
Thirteen worthies. Freeport, N.Y., Bks. for Libs. Pr. [1966] 221p. 19cm. (Essay index reprint ser.) First pub. 1923. [CT775.P6 1966] 67-22112 6.50
1. Authors, English. I. Title.
Contents omitted. BIP

SAUNDERS, Beatrice 928
Portraits of genius. [dist. Hollywood-by-the-Sea, Fla., Transatlantic Arts, 1960c.1959] 214p. ports. 61-2316 6.25
1. Authors, English. 2. Authors, Russian. I. Title. BIP

SITWELL, Osbert, bart., 928.2
Sir 1892-
Noble essences, a book of characters. New York, Grosset & Dunlap [1957, c1950] 356p. 21cm. (Grosset's universal library, UL14) The final vol. of the autobiography. Earlier vols. were Left hand. right hand! The scarlet tree, Great morning and Laughter in the next room. [PR6037] 57-13643
1. Authors, English. 2. Authors—Correspondence, reminiscences. etc. I. Title.

SITWELL, Sir Osbert, bart. 928.2
1892-
Noble essences a book of characters. New York, Grosset & Dunlap [1957, c1950] 356 p. 21 cm. (Grosset's universal library, UL14) The final vol. of the autobiography.Earlier vols. were Left hand, right hand! The scarlet tree, Great morning and Laughter in the next room. [[PR6037)] 57-13643
1. Authors, English. 2. Authors — Correspondence, reminiscences, etc. I. Title.

Authors, English—Biography.

MASCHLER, Tom, ed. 820.9'009'14
Declaration [by] Colin Wilson [and others] Port Washington, N.Y., Kennikat Press [1972, c1957] 201 p. ports. 23 cm. [PR472.M3 1972] 75-153228 ISBN 0-8046-1538-1
1. Authors, English—Biography. 2. English literature—20th century—History and criticism. I. Wilson, Colin, 1931- II. Title.

MASON, Edward 820'.9'008 B
Tuckerman, 1847-1911, ed.
Personal traits of British authors: Hood—Macaulay—Sydney Smith—Jerrold—Dickens—Charlotte Bronte—Thackeray. [Folcroft, Pa.] Folcroft Library Editions, 1973 [c1884] p. Reprint of the 1891 ed. published by Scribner, New York. First published in 1885 as the last of a four-vol. series covering 27 authors. [PR105.M34 1973] 73-16184 ISBN 0-8414-6081-7 (lib. bdg.)
1. Authors, English—Biography. I. Title.

*RICHARDS, Vyvyan 923.242
Portrait of T. E. Lawrence. New York, Scholastic [1964,c.1939] 147p. 17cm. (T543) Orig. Eng. pubn. appeared under title: T.E. Lawrence in Duckworth's Gt. lives ser. Bibl. .35 pap.,
I. Lawrence, Thomas Edward, 1888 1935. II. Title.

SCOTT, Walter, Sir, 820'.9 B
bart., 1771-1832.
Biographical memoirs of eminent novelists, and other distinguished persons. Freeport, N.Y., Books for Libraries Press [1972] 2 v. ports. 23 cm. (Essay index reprint series) Reprint of the 1834 ed. Contents.Contents.—v. 1. Samuel Richardson. Henry Fielding. Tobias Smollett. Richard Cumberland. Oliver Goldsmith. Samuel Johnson. Laurence Sterne. Horace Walpole. Clara Reeve. Mrs. Ann Radcliffe. Alain Rene Le Sage. Charles Johnstone. Robert Bage.—v. 2. Henry Mackenzie. Charlotte Smith. Sir Ralph Sadler. John Leyden. Miss Anna Seward.—Daniel De Foe. Appendix no. I. Appendix no. II. Charles Duke of Buccleuch and Queensberry. John Lord Somerville. King George III. Lord Byron. The Duke of York. [PR103.S3 1972] 72-377 ISBN 0-8369-2822-9
1. Authors, English—Biography. I. Title.

WALFORD, Lucy 820'.9'9287 B
Bethia (Colquhoun) 1845-1915.
Twelve English authoresses. New ed. Freeport, N.Y., Books for Libraries Press [1972] vi, 200 p. front. 22 cm. (Essay index reprint series) Reprint of the 1893 ed. Contents.Contents.—Hannah More.—Fanny Burney. Maria Edgeworth.—Harriet Martineau.—Jane Austen.—Felicia Hemans.—Mary Somerville.—Jane Taylor.—Charlotte Bronte.—Elizabeth Gaskell.—Elizabeth Barrett Browning.—George Eliot. [PR115.W3 1972] 72-1314 ISBN 0-8369-2871-7
1. Authors, English—Biography. 2. Authors, Women—Biography. I. Title. BIP

WILSON, Mona, 1872- 820'.9'007 B
Jane Austen and some contemporaries. With an introd. by G. M. Young. New York, Haskell House [1973] xvi, 304 p. 23 cm. Reprint of the 1938 ed. [PR111.W54 1973] 72-11645 ISBN 0-8383-1690-5 11.95
1. Authors, English—Biography. 2. Authors, Women—Biography. I. Title. BIP

WOTTON, Mabel E., ed. 820'.9 B
Word portraits of famous writers, edited by Mabel E. Wotton. Freeport, N.Y., Books for Libraries Press [1973] p. (Essay index reprint series) [PR105.W6 1973b] 72-14192 ISBN 0-518-10033-2
1. Authors, English—Biography. I. Title. BIP

Authors, English—Correspondence, reminiscences, etc.

FORD, Ford Madox, 823'.009 B
1873-1939.
Portraits from life; memories and criticisms of Henry James, Joseph Conrad, Thomas Hardy, H. G. Wells, Stephen Crane, D. H. Lawrence, John Galsworthy, Ivan Turgenev, W. H. Hudson, Theodore Dreiser, Algernon Charles Swinburne. Westport, Conn., Greenwood Press [1974, c1937] vi, 227 p. ports. 23 cm. Reprint of the ed. published by Houghton Mifflin, Boston. [PR107.F6 1974] 74-2553 ISBN 0-8371-7405-8
1. Authors, English—Correspondence, reminiscences, etc. 2. Authors, American—Correspondence, reminiscences, etc. I. Title.

Authors, English—Homes and haunts—England—Lake District.

ABRAHAM, Ashley Perry, 821'.7'09
1876-1951.
Some portraits of the Lake Poets, and their homes / by Ashley P. Abraham. Folcroft, Pa. : Folcroft Library Editions, 1975. p. cm. Reprint of the 1914 ed. published by G. P. Abraham, Keswick, Cumberland, Eng. [PR110.L3A2 1975] 75-28026 ISBN 0-8414-2874-3 lib. bdg. : 20.00
1. Authors, English—Homes and haunts—England—Lake District. 2. Lake District, England—Biography. 3. Lake poets—Biography. 4. Authors, English—19th century—Biography. I. Title. BIP

Authors, English—19th century—Biography.

DUNN, Waldo Hilary, 1882- 928.2
R. D. Blackmore, the author of Lorna Doone; a biography. London, Hale, [1956.] 316p. illus. 23 cm. [PR4133.D8 1956a] 56-4728
I. Blackmore, Richard Doddridge, 1825-1900. II. Title.

GRISWOLD, Hattie 820'.9'008 B
(Tyng) 1840-1909.
Personal sketches of recent authors. Freeport, N.Y., Books for Libraries Press [1973] p. (Essay index reprint series) Reprint of the 1898 ed. Contents.Contents.—Alfred Tennyson.—Ernest Renan.—Charles Darwin.—Matthew Arnold.—George Du Maurier.—Elizabeth Barrett Browning.—John Ruskin.—Thomas Henry Huxley.—Harriet Beecher Stowe.—Robert Louis Stevenson.—William Dean Howells.—Louisa May Alcott.—Lyeff Tolstoi.—Rudyard Kipling.—Christiana Rossetti.—Henry David Thoreau.—Bayard Taylor. James Matthew Barrie. [PR105.G75 1973] 72-14193 ISBN 0-518-10010-3
1. Authors, English—19th century—Biography. 2. Authors, American—19th century—Biography. I. Title. BIP

JOHNSON, Reginald 820'.9'008 B
Brimley, 1867-1932.
Story lives of XIXth century authors. London, Wells Gardner, Darton, Ltd. [Folcroft, Pa.] Folcroft Library Editions, 1972. p. Reprint of the 1925 ed. Contents.Contents.—William Makepeace Thackeray.—George Eliot.—Robert Browning.—Alfred, Lord Tennyson.—Matthew Arnold.—Samuel Butler.—Robert Louis Stevenson. [PR106.J6 1972] 72-12917 ISBN 0-8414-1018-6 (lib. bdg.)
1. Authors, English—19th century—Biography. I. Title.

JOHNSON, Wendell 820'.9'353
Stacy, 1927-
Living in sin : the Victorian sexual revolution / Wendell Stacy Johnson. Chicago : Nelson-Hall, c1979. x, 213 p. ; 23 cm. Includes bibliographical references and index. [PR105.J58] 78-26845 ISBN 0-88229-445-8 : 13.95 pbk. : 6.95
1. Authors, English—19th century—Biography. 2. Great Britain—Social life and customs—19th century. 3. Sex customs—Great Britain—History. 4. Sex in literature. 5. English literature—19th century—History and criticism. I. Title. BIP

MASSON, Flora. 820.9'008
Victorians all. Port Washington, N.Y., Kennikat Press [1970] 128 p. 21 cm.

Reprint of the 1931 ed. Contents.Contents.—Mainly about Dickens and Thackeray.—Holman Hunt and Sir Atalanta.—A London childhood.—A philosopher at play.—Evenings at Avenue Road.—Mainly about the Carlyles and Mazzini.—Edinburgh and the Highlands.—Giants of those days.—Mainly about Stevenson and Browning.—Florence Nightingale and later friendships. [PR6025.A7955V5 1970] 75-105806
I. Title. BIP

PATTERSON, Alfred Temple. 914.22'7 S
Portsmouth nineteen-century literary figures [by A. Temple Patterson]. Portsmouth, Portsmouth City Council, 1972. 18 p. illus., ports. 25 cm. (The Portsmouth papers, no. 14) Cover title. Includes bibliographical references. [DA690.P8P85 no. 14] [PR106] 823'.8'09 73-156501 ISBN 0-901559-16-4 £0.30
1. Authors, English—19th century—Biography. 2. Authors, English—Portsmouth, Eng. I. Title. II. Series.

Authors, English—19th century—Portraits.

MACLISE, Daniel, 1806-1870. 820'.9'007 B
A gallery of illustrious literary characters (1830-1838) / drawn by Daniel Maclise ; and accompanied by notices chiefly by William Maginn ; edited by William Bates, with a pref. and copious notes, biographical, critical, bibliographical, and generally illustrative. Detroit : Gale Research Co., 1976. p. cm. "A reproduction of the portraits and groups originally published in Fraser's magazine, 1830-38." Reprint of the 1873 ed. published by Chatto and Windus, London. Includes index. [PR105.M25 1976] 73-89258 ISBN 0-8103-4305-3 : 18.50
1. Authors, English—19th century—Portraits. 2. English literature—19th century—History and criticism. I. Maginn, William, 1793-1842. II. Bates, William, d. 1884. III. Title.

Authors, English—20th century—Biography.

WHO was who in literature, 1906-1934. 820'.9'00912 B Detroit : Gale Research Company, c1979. 2 v. (1299 p.) ; 23 cm. (Gale composite biographical dictionary series ; no. 5) "Based on entries that first appeared in 'Literary yearbook' (1906-1913), 'Literary yearbook and author's who's who' (1914-1917), 'Literary yearbook' (1920-1922), and Who's who in literature' (1924-1934)" [PR106.W5] 78-25583 ISBN 0-8103-0402-3 : 64.00
1. Authors, English—20th century—Biography. I. Title. II. Series. III. An Omnigraphics book

WILKINSON, Louis Umfreville, 1881- 820'.9'0091
Seven friends / Louis Marlow [i.e. L. U. Wilkinson]. Brooklyn : Haskell House, 1977. v, 169 p. ; 21 cm. Reprint of the 1953 ed. published by Richards Press, London. [PR106.W53] 76-52907 ISBN 0-8383-2132-1 lib.bdg. : 11.95
1. Authors, English—20th century—Biography. I. Title.

Authors, English—20th century—Interviews.

WINTLE, Justin. 820'.9'9282 B
The Pied Pipers : interviews with the influential creators of children's literature / by Justin Wintle and Emma Fisher. New York : Paddington Press, [1975] 320 p. : ill. ; 25 cm. [PR106.W55] 74-15918 ISBN 0-8467-0038-7 : 10.95
1. Authors, English—20th century—Interviews. 2. Authors, American—20th century—Interviews. 3. Illustrators—Great Britain—Interviews. 4. Illustrators—United States—Interviews. 5. Children's literature—History and criticism. I. Fisher, Emma, 1949- joint author. II. Title.

Authors, French—Correspondence, reminiscences, etc.

BALDICK, Robert. 848'.8'0308
Dinner at Magny's. [1st American ed.] New York, Coward, McCann & Geoghegan [1971] 253 p. illus. 23 cm. Bibliography: p. [240]-244. [PQ147.B3 1971b] 76-172624 5.95
1. Authors, French—Correspondence, reminiscences, etc. I. Title.

MAURIAC, Francois, 1885- 928.4
Proust's way; translated from the original French "Du cote de chez Proust" by Elsie Pell. New York, Philosophical Library [1950] 105 p. port. 23 cm. [PQ2631.R63Z772] 50-6681
I. Proust,Marcel, 1871-1922. II. Title.

Authors, German.

JOESTEN, Joachim, 1907- v. 12
Who's who in German letters today. Great Barrington, Mass., 1949-50. 2 v. 30 cm. (His New Germany reports, no. 11-12) Contents.v. 1. Western Germany.--v. 2. Eastern Germany. A51
1. Authors, German. I. Title.

STRINDBERG, August, 1849-1912. 839.7'2'6
The Cloister. Edited by C. G. Bjurstrom. Translated and with a commentary and notes by Mary Sandbach. [1st American ed.] New York, Hill and Wang [1969] 160 p. 23 cm. Translation of Klostret. [PT9814.K513 1969b] 69-16839 5.00
I. Bjurstrom, Carl Gustaf, 1919- ed. II. Title.

Authors, German—Biography.

ANDREWS, Wayne. 830'.9
Siegfried's curse; the German journey from Nietzsche to Hesse. [1st ed.] New York, Atheneum, 1972. x, 370 p. illus. 25 cm. [PT155.A5 1972] 72-78283 10.95
1. Authors, German—Biography. 2. Germany—History—Philosophy. I. Title.
Contents omitted.

Authors, German—Correspondence, reminiscences, etc.

KAFKA, Franz, 1883-1924. 928.3
Letters to Milena. Edited by Willy Haas; translated by Tania and James Stern. [New York] Schocken Books [1954, c 1953] 238 p. 21 cm. [PT2621.A26Z553 1954] 54-1529
1. Authors, German—Correspondence, reminiscences, etc. I. Jesenska, Milena, 1896-1944. II. Haas, Willy, 1891- ed. III. Title. BIP

Authors, Irish—20th century—Biography.

GRIFFIN, Gerald, 1889- 820'.9 B
The wild geese : pen portraits of famous Irish exiles / by Gerald Griffin. Folcroft, Pa. : Folcroft Library Editions, 1977. 288 p., [1] leaves of plates : ports. ; 23 cm. Reprint of the 1938 ed. published by Jarrolds, London. Includes index. [PR8753.G7 1977] 77-2922 ISBN 0-8414-4405-6 lib. bdg. : 30.00
1. Authors, Irish—20th century—Biography. 2. Ireland—Biography. I. Title.
Contents omitted Contents omitted

Authors, Japanese—Biography.

BIOGRAPHICAL dictionary of Japanese literature / [edited by] Sen'ichi Hisamatsu. 895.6'09 B 1st ed. Tokyo : Kodansha International in collaboration with the International Society for Educational Information ; New York : distributed by Harper & Row, 1976. 437 p. ; 22 cm. [PL723.B5] 77-350412 ISBN 0-87011-253-8 : 29.50
1. Authors, Japanese—Biography. I. Hisamatsu, Sen'ichi, 1894-1976. BIP

Authors—Juvenile literature.

SMARIDGE, Norah. 823'.9'109 b
Famous modern storytellers for young people. New York, Dodd, Mead [1969] 120 p. ports. 22 cm. (Famous biographies for young people) Contents.Contents.—Laura Ingalls Wilder.—Eleanor Farjeon.—A. A. Milne.—Hugh Lofting.—Elizabeth Enright.—Marguerite de Angeli.—Carol Ryrie Brink.—Elizabeth Coatsworth.—Meindert Dejong.—Rumer Godden.—Joseph Krumgold.—Mary Norton.—Claire Huchet Bishop.—P. L. Travers.—Marguerite Henry.—Astrid Lindgren.—E. B. White. [PN452.S6] 920 70-84087 3.50
1. Authors—Juvenile literature. I. Title. BIP

Authors, Russian.

COULSON, Jessie 928.917
Dostoevsky: a self-portrait. New York, Oxford [1963, c.] 1962. 279p. illus. 23cm. Bibl. 63-305 6.75
I. Dostoevskii, Fedor Mikhailovich, 1821-1881. II. Title. BIP

COULSON, Jessie (Senior) 1903- 928.917
Dostoevsky: a self-portrait. London, New York, Oxford University Press, 1962. 279 p. illus. 23 cm. Includes selections from the letters of Dostoevsky, translated by the author. [PG3328.A3C6] 68-305
I. Dostoevskii, Fedor Mikhailovich, 1821-1881. II. Title.

LAVRIN, Janko, 1887- 928.917
Russian writers: their lives and literature. New York, Van Nostrand [1954] 363 p. illus. 22 cm. [PG2991.L39] 54-7535
1. Authors, Russian. I. Title.

Authors, Russian—Biography.

MUCHNIC, Helen. 891.709
Russian writers: notes and essays. [1st ed.] New York, Random House [1971] xi, 462 p. 22 cm. [PG2933.M8 1971] 72-139240 ISBN 0-394-46007-3 10.00
1. Authors, Russian—Biography. 2. Russian literature—Addresses, essays, lectures. I. Title.

POSELL, Elsa Z. 891.7'09 B
Russian authors [by] Elsa Z. Posell. Boston, Houghton Mifflin, 1970. 253 p. ports. 22 cm. Includes bibliographical references. [PG2991.P6] 70-115453 4.25
1. Authors, Russian—Biography. I. Title.

Authors,Scottish.

PARKER, William Mathie, 1891- 820.9'008
Modern Scottish writers, by W. M. Parker. Freeport, N.Y., Books for Libraries Press [1968] 255 p. 23 cm. (Essays index reprint series) Reprint of the 1917 ed. [PR8550.P3] 68-26463
1. Authors,Scottish. I. Title. BIP

Authors, Women.

MANLEY, Seon. 820'.9'9287 B
O, those extraordinary women! Or the joys of literary lib [by] Seon Manley and Susan Belcher. [1st ed.] Philadelphia, Chilton Book Co. [1972] 330 p. illus. 24 cm. Bibliography: p. 307-321. [PR111.M24] 72-8061 8.95
1. Authors, Women. 2. Authors, English—Biography. 3. Authors, American—Biography. I. Belcher, Susan, joint author. II. Title.

Authors, Women—Biography.

MAYER, Gertrude Townshend. 820'.9 B
Women of letters. Freeport, N.Y., Books for Libraries Press [1973] p. (Essay index reprint series) Reprint of the 1894 ed. Contents.Contents.—v. 1. Margaret, Duchess of Newcastle. Mary, Countess Cowper. Lady Hervey. Lady Mary Wortley Montagu. Mrs. Delany. Mrs. Montagu. Lady Anne Barnard. Mary and Agnes Berry.—v. 2. Elizabeth Inchbald. Amelia Opie. Sydney Owenson, Lady Morgan. Miss Mitford. Mary Wollstonecraft Shelley. Lady Duff Gordon. [PR111.M3 1973] 73-1197 ISBN 0-518-10059-6
1. Authors, Women—Biography. 2. Authors, English—Biography. I. Title. BIP

Authorship.

DAIGH, Ralph. 808'.025
Maybe you should write a book / Ralph Daigh. Englewood Cliffs, N.J. : Prentice-Hall, c1977. 181 p. ; 24 cm. [PN145.D27] 76-54952 ISBN 0-13-566380-6 : 8.95
1. Authorship. 2. Authors, American—20th century—Biography. 3. Authors, English—20th century—Biography. I. Title. BIP

KEYES, Frances Parkinson (Wheeler), 1885- 928.1
The cost of a best seller; illustrated by Susanne Suba. New York, Messner [1950] 126 p. illus. 21 cm. Autobiographical. [PN147.K4 1950] 50-9958
1. Authorship. I. Title.

Authorship—Case studies.

NEWQUIST, Roy. 928
Counterpoint. Chicago, Rand McNally [1964] 653 p. 24 cm. "Sixty-three interviews with authors and columnists and publishers." [PN151.N4] 64-21326
1. Authorship—Case studies. 2. Authors, American. I. Title.

NEWQUIST, Roy 928
Counterpoint. New York, S. & S. [1967, c.1964] 653p. 21cm. Sixty-three interviews with authors and columnists and publishers [PN151 N4] 2.95 pap.,
1. Authorship—Case studies. 2. Authors, American. I. Title. BIP

Autobiographies.

FACE to face (Television program) 920.02
Face to face. Ed., introd. by Hugh Burnett. Portraits by Feliks Topolski. New York, Stein & Day [1965, c.1964] 93p. ports. 28cm. By arrangement with the British Broadcasting Corporation. [CT120.F3] 65-17933 10.00
1. Autobiographies. I. Burnett, Hugh, ed. II. British Broadcasting Corporation. III. Title.

GARIS, Robert, ed. 920.002
Writing about oneself: selected writing. Boston, Heath [c.1965] ix, 143p. 21cm. (Uses of Eng.; a ser. for coll. composition) [CT105.G3] 65-14111 1.50 pap.,
1. Autobiographies. I. Title.

MALLERY, Richard Davis, ed. 920.02
Masterworks of autobiography; digests of 10 great classics. Freeport, N.Y., Books for Libraries Press [1970, c1946] ix, 755 p. 23 cm. (Masterworks series) (Essay index reprint series.) Contents.Contents.—The confessions of Saint Augustine.—The autobiography of Benvenuto Cellini.—The diary of Samuel Pepys.—The autobiography of Benjamin Franklin.—The confessions of Jean Jacques Rousseau.—Truth and poetry, by J. W. von Goethe.—The true story of my life, by H. C. Andersen.—Apologia pro vita sua, by J. H. Cardinal Newman.—Childhood, boyhood, and youth, by L. Tolstoy.—The education of Henry Adams, by H. Adams. [CT101.M3 1970] 70-111848
1. Autobiographies. I. Title.

MILGRAM, Joel I., comp. 920
Childhood revisited. Edited by Joel I. Milgram [and] Dorothy June Sciarra. Foreword by James L. Hymes, Jr. New York, Macmillan [1974] xx, 364 p. 24 cm. [CT120.M54] 73-1038 ISBN 0-02-381120-X 4.95
1. Autobiographies. I. Sciarra, Dorothy June, joint comp. II. Title. BIP

MUSCATINE, Charles, comp. 920
First person singular, edited by Charles Muscatine and Marlene Griffith. [1st ed.] New York, Knopf; [distributed by Random House, 1973] xvi, 343 p. 24 cm. [CT104.M79] 72-12574 ISBN 0-394-31755-6 4.50
1. Autobiographies. I. Griffith, Marlene, comp. II. Title.

PADOVER, Saul Kussiel, 1905- ed. 920.02
Confessions and self-portraits; 4600 years of autobiography, assembled and edited with an introd. and commentaries. New

York, J. Day Co. [1957] 362 p. 22 cm. [CT101.P3] 57-11703
1. Autobiographies. I. Title.

PADOVER, Saul Kussiel, 920.02
1905- ed.
Confessions and self-portraits; 4600 years of autobiography. Assembled and edited with an introd. and commentaries by Saul K. Padover. Freeport, N.Y., Books for Libraries Press [1969, c1957] xx, 362 p. 23 cm. (Essay index reprint series) Bibliographical footnotes. [CT101.P3 1969] 68-58807
1. Autobiographies. I. Title.

REED, Gwendolyn E., comp. 920.02
Beginnings. Compiled by Gwendolyn Reed. [1st ed.] New York, Atheneum, 1971. xii, 258 p. 25 cm. Contents.Contents.—Benvenuto Cellini, 1500-1571.—Michel de Montaigne, 1533-1592.—Johann Dietz, 1665-1738.—William Hutton, 1723-1815.—Francois Rene Chateaubriand, 1768-1848.—Samuel Taylor Coleridge, 1772-1834.—John Tanner, 1780-1846?—Hans Christian Andersen, 1805-1875.—Samuel Langhorne Clemens (Mark Twain), 1835-1910.—Piotr Alekseyevich Kropotkin, 1842-1921.—Tomas O'Crohan, 1856-1937.—Alfred Kazin, 1915- Includes bibliographical references. [CT105.R38 1971] 76-134821 5.95
1. Autobiographies. I. Title.

*STANFORTH, Willa Bare 920
Each blade of grass New Vienna, Ohio 1974 96 p. illus. 21 cm. [CT104] 3.00 (pbk.)
1. Autobiographies. I. Title.
Order from author, Box 124 New Vienna, Ohio

Autobiographies—Bibl.

LILLARD, Richard Gordon, 016.92
1909-
American life in autobiography, a descriptive guide. Stanford, Calif., Stanford University Press [1956] v, 140p. 23cm. [Z5301.L66] 56-8689
1. Autobiographies—Bibl. 2. U.S.—Biog.—Bibl. I. Title.

Autobiography.

BURR, Anna Robeson (Brown) 814'.4
1873-1941.
The autobiography; a critical and comparative study. Boston, Houghton Mifflin, 1909. [Folcroft, Pa.] Folcroft Library Editions, 1973. p. Bibliography: p. [CT25.B8 1973] 73-504 ISBN 0-8414-1468-8
1. Autobiography. I. Title. BIP

COUSER, G. Thomas. 920'.073
American autobiography : the prophetic mode / G. Thomas Couser. Amherst : University of Massachusetts Press, 1979. vi, 222 p. ; 23 cm. Includes index. Bibliography: p. [211]-216 [CT34.U6C68] 78-11835 ISBN 0-87023-263-0 lib. bdg.: 15.00
1. Autobiography. 2. United States—Biography. 3. Biography (as a literary form) I. Title. BIP

MORRIS, John N. 828.803
Versions of the self; studies in English autobiography from John Bunyan to John Stuart Mill [by] John N. Morris. New York, Basic Books [1966] ix, 242 p. 22 cm. Bibliographical references included in "Notes" (p. 225-234) [CT25.M6] 66-13511
1. Autobiography. I. Title.

OLNEY, James. 920
Metaphors of self; the meaning of autobiography. [Princeton, N.J.] Princeton University Press [1972] xi, 342 p. 25 cm. Includes bibliographical references. [CT25.O44] 71-173758 ISBN 0-691-06221-8 12.50
1. Autobiography. 2. Autobiography—History and criticism. I. Title. BIP

PORTER, Roger J., 1936- 920
The voice within: reading and writing autobiography [by] Roger J. Porter [and] H. R. Wolf. [1st ed.] New York, [Knopf; [distributed by Random House, 1973] xiii, 304 p. 24 cm. Includes bibliographical references. [CT25.P67] 72-4520 ISBN 0-394-31661-4 4.50
1. Autobiography. I. Wolf, Howard R., 1936- joint author. II. Title.

SAYRE, Robert F. 920.002
The examined self: Benjamin Franklin, Henry Adams, Henry James. Princeton, N.J., Princeton [c.]1964. xiii, 212p. 22cm. Bibl. 63-23394 4.75
1. Autobiography. I. Title.

SAYRE, Robert F 920.002
The examined self: Benjamin Franklin, Henry Adams, Henry James. Princeton, N. J., Princeton University Press, 1964. xiii, 212 p. 22 cm. "A study of the autobiographies of Benjamin Franklin, Henry Adams, and Henry James." Bibliographical footnotes. [CT25.S2] 63-23394
1. Autobiography. I. Title.

SIMONS, George F. 808'.066'92
Keeping your personal journal / by George F. Simons. New York: Paulist Press, c1978. v, 144 p. ; 21 cm. Includes bibliographical references. [CT22.S55] 77-99299 ISBN 0-8091-2092-5 pbk. : 4.95
1. Autobiography. 2. Diaries. I. Title. BIP

WEINTRAUB, Karl Joachim, 128
1924-
The value of the individual : self and circumstance in autobiography / Karl Joachim Weintraub. Chicago : University of Chicago Press, 1978. xix, 439 p. : ill. ; 24 cm. Includes index. Bibliography: p. 403-429. [CT25.W37] 77-9435 ISBN 0-226-88621-2 : 24.00
1. Autobiography. 2. Individuality. I. Title. BIP

WIEBE, Katie Funk. 808'.066'92
Good times with old times : how to write your memoirs / Katie Funk Wiebe. Scottdale, Pa. : Herald Press, 1979. 175 p. ; 20 cm. [CT25.W45] 79-12864 ISBN 0-8361-1894-4 . 5.95
1. Autobiography. I. Title.

Autobiography—Addresses, essays, lectures.

AUTOBIOGRAPHY, essays 809
theoretical and critical / edited by James Olney. Princeton, N.J. : Princeton University Press, c1980. p. cm. Includes index. [CT25.A95] 79-17556 ISBN 0-691-06412-1 : 36.00 ISBN 0-691-10080-2 (pbk.) : 9.75
1. Autobiography—Addresses, essays, lectures. I. Olney, James.

Autobiography—Bibl.

MATTHEWS, William, 016.920042
1905-
British autobiographies; an annotated bibliography of British autobiographies published or written before 1951. Berkeley, University of California Press, 1955. xiv, 376p. 25cm. [Z2027.A9M3] 55-13593
1. Autobiography—Bibl. 2. Gt. Brit.—Biog.—Bibl. I. Title.

Autograph albums.

TREMAIN, Ruthven. 929.8
My friends; a self-portrait autograph book. New York, Macmillan [1971] [48] p. illus. (part col.) 16 cm. [BJ1818.T73] 70-25261 2.50
1. Autograph albums. I. Title. BIP

Automobile industry and trade—Biography.

GRISCOM, Lloyd 338.4'7'62920922
E.
The automotive pioneers: industrious adventurers, informal history, by Lloyd E. Griscom. Palmyra, N.J., S. J. Publications [1967] 128 p. illus., ports. 23 cm. Bibliography: p. 123. [TL139.G7] 67-2040
1. Automobile industry and trade—Biography. I. Title.

Automobile industry and trade—United States.

FORBES, Bertie 629.2'092'2 B
Charles, 1880-1954.
Automotive giants of America; men who are making our motor industry, by Bertie C. Forbes and Orline D. Foster. Freeport, N.Y., Books for Libraries Press [1972] x, 295 p. 22 cm. (Essay index reprint series) Reprint of the 1926 ed. [HD9710.U52F56 1972] 72-5603 ISBN 0-8369-2989-6
1. Automobile industry and trade—United States. 2. United States—Biography. I. Foster, Orline (Dorman) joint author. II. Title. BIP

WHO'S who among automotive 926.58
executives. 1964. A reference directory. Detroit, Trends Pub. Co. [c.1964] 275p. 23cm. [HD9710.U5W5] 64-7653 14.85
1. Automobile industry and trade—U.S.—Direct.

Automobile racing.

STEWART, Jackie. 796.7'2
Faster! A racer's diary, by Jackie Stewart and Peter Manso. New York, Farrar, Straus and Giroux [1972] 239 p. illus. 22 cm. [GV1032.S74A25 1972] 72-76337 ISBN 0-374-15370-1 7.95
1. Automobile racing. I. Manso, Peter, joint author. II. Title.

STEWART, Jackie. 796.7'2'0924
Jackie Stewart: world champion [by] Jackie Stewart and Eric Dymock. Chicago, Henry Regnery Co. [1970] 191 p. illus., ports. 22 cm. London ed. (Pelham) has title: World champion. [GV1032.S74A3 1970b] 71-126154 5.95
1. Automobile racing. I. Dymock, Eric, joint author. II. Title.

THOMPSON, Mickey, 1928- 927.9672
Challenger, Mickey Thompson's own story of his life of speed by Mickey Thompson with Griffith Borgeson. Englewood Cliffs, N.J., Prentice-Hall [1964] xii, 237 p. illus., ports. 24 cm. [GV1029.T5] 64-12051
1. Automobile racing. I. Title.

THOMPSON, Mickey, 1928- 927.9672
Challenger, Mickey Thompson's own story of his life of speed [by] Mickey Thompson with Griffith Borgeson. [New York] New Amer. Lib. [1965, c.1964] xii, 237p. illus. 18cm. (Signet key bk. KD500) [GV1029.T5] .50 pap.,
1. Automibile racing. I. Title.

Automobile racing—Biography.

ANDRETTI, Mario, 796.7'2'0924 B
1940-
What's it like out there? [By] Mario Andretti with Bob Collins. Chicago, H. Regnery Co. [1970] 282 p. illus., ports. 22 cm. [GV1032.A5A3] 77-105111 5.95
1. Automobile racing—Biography. I. Collins, Bob, joint author. II. Title.

CUTTER, Bob, 1930- 796.7'2'0922 B
The encyclopedia of auto racing greats, by Robert Cutter and Bob Fendell. Englewood Cliffs, N.J. Prentice-Hall [1973] viii, 675 p. illus. 29 cm. [GV1032.A1C87] 73-7541 ISBN 0-13-275206-9 17.50
1. Automobile racing—Biography. I. Fendell, Bob, 1925- joint author. II. Title.

*GAULD, Graham. 796.720924
Jim Clark remembered. Foreword by Jackie Stewart. New York, Arco [1975] 143 p. ill. 24 cm. Includes index. [GV1029] 75-13551 ISBN 0-668-03848-9 10.00.
1. Automobile racing—Biography. I. Title.

GILL, Barrie. 796.7'2
Motor racing; the Grand Prix greats. Edited by Barrie Gill. New York, Drake Publishers [1972] 165 p. illus. 23 cm. [GV1032.A1G52] 78-188802 ISBN 0-87749-229-8 5.95
1. Automobile racing—Biography. I. Title.

HIGDON, Hal. 796.7'2'0922 B
Finding the groove. New York, Putnam [1973] 312 p. illus. 22 cm. [GV1032.A1H53 1973] 73-78583 ISBN 0-399-11144-1 7.95
1. Automobile racing—Biography. 2. Automobile racing. I. Title.

HILL, Graham, 1929- 796.7'2'0924
Life at the limit. [1st American ed.] New York, Coward-McCann [1970, c1969] 255 p. illus., ports. 22 cm. [GV1032.H48A3 1970] 73-117921 5.95
1. Automobile racing—Biography. I. Title.

HODGES, David W., 796.7'2'0922
ed.
Great racing drivers. Edited by David Hodges. New York, Arco Pub. Co. [1967, c1966] viii, 176 p. illus., ports. 29 cm. [GV1032.A1] 66-25872
1. Automobile racing—Biography. I. Title.

KAHN, Mark 796.7'2'0922
The day I died. London, Gentry Books [1974] [7] 145 p. [24] p. of plates ill., ports. 23 cm. Includes index. [GV1032.A1K33] 75-321651 ISBN 0-85614-035-X
1. Automobile racing—Biography. I. Title.
Distributed by International Publications Service for 10.00. BIP

MANSO, Peter. 796.7'2'0922
Vrooom! Conversations with the Grand Prix champions, by Peter Manso. Photography by Alan Heald and the author. New York, Funk & Wagnalls [1969] xvii, 227 p. illus. 27 cm. [GV1032.A1M35] 75-83722 8.95
1. Automobile racing—Biography. I. Title.

MILLER, Peter, 1927- 927.9672
Men at the wheel. New York, Arco [1965, c.1963] 128p. illus., ports. 26cm. (Arco auto. lib.) [GV1032.A1M5] 65-11328 4.95
1. Automobile racing—Biog. I. Title.

MY greatest race 796.7'2'0922 B
/ by twenty of the finest motor racing drivers of all time ; edited by Adrian Ball for the Jim Clark Foundation. New York : Dutton, 1974. xii, 138 p. : ill. ; 26 cm. [GV1032.A1M9 1974] 74-3634 ISBN 0-525-16225-9 : 8.95
1. Automobile racing—Biography. I. Ball, Adrian. II. Jim Clark Foundation.

NOLAN, William F., 796.7'2'0924 B
1928-
Carnival of speed; true adventures in motor racing, by William F. Nolan. New York, Putnam [1973] 191 p. 22 cm. [GV1032.A1N58] 72-87637 ISBN 0-399-20318-4 4.69 (lib. bdg.)
1. Automobile racing—Biography. I. Title. BIP

NOLAN, William F., 1928- 927.9672
Men of thunder, fabled daredevils of motor sport. New York, Putnam [c.1964] 256p. 22cm. Bibl. 64-10404 4.95
1. Automobile racing—Biog. I. Title.

OLNEY, Ross Robert, 796.720922
1929-
Daredevils of the speedway, by Ross R. Olney. Foreword by Johnnie Parsons. New York, Grosset & Dunlap [1966] 151 p. illus., ports. 25 cm. [GV1032.A1O4] 66-11321
1. Automobile racing—Biography. I. Title. BIP

PRITCHARD, Anthony. 796.7'2'0922
The world champions: Giuseppe Farina to Jackie Stewart. [1st American ed.] New York, Macmillan [1974] ix, 253 p. ports. 21 cm. [GV1032.A1P74 1974] 73-15147 ISBN 0-02-599210-4 7.95
1. Automobile racing—Biography. I. Title.

RACING stock : 796.7'2'0922
[interviews / conducted by] Mark Silber. Garden City, N.Y. : Dolphin Books, 1976. p. cm. [GV1032.A1R32] 75-44525 ISBN 0-385-11172-X : 4.95
1. Automobile racing—Biography. 2. Automobile racing—United States. 3. Interviews. I. Silber, Mark.

SCALZO, Joe. 796.7'2'0922 B
The unbelievable Unsers. Chicago, H. Regnery Co. [1971] xii, 307 p. illus., ports. 22 cm. [GV1032.A1S3] 76-143837 6.95
1. Automobile racing—Biography. I. Title.

YATES, Brock W. 796.7'2'0922
Racers and drivers; the fastest men and

cars from Barney Oldfield to Craig Breedlove, by Brock Yates. Illustrated with photos. [1st ed.] Indianapolis, Bobbs-Merrill [1968] 80 p. illus. 19 x 26 cm. [GV1032.A1Y3] 68-29303 4.00
1. Automobile racing—Biography. I. Title.

Automobile racing—Biography—Juvenile literature.

DILLON, Mark. 796.7'2'0922 B
International race car drivers [by] Mark Dillon [and] Frank Haigh. Minneapolis, Lerner Publications Co. [1974] 51 p. illus. (part col.) 20 x 23 cm. (The Racing books) Describes the lives and the racing careers of four well-known international race car drivers: Dan Gurney, Mario Andretti, Jackie Stewart, and Emerson Fittipaldi. [GV1032.A1D55] 920 73-22514 ISBN 0-8225-0413-8 4.95 (lib. bdg.)
1. Automobile racing—Biography—Juvenile literature. I. Haigh, Frank, joint author. II. Title. BIP

HUNTER, Jim. 796.7'2'0922 B
Stock car racing U.S.A. Produced by Lyle Kenyon Engel. Text by Jim Hunter. Edited by George Engel and Marla Ray. New York, Dodd, Mead [1973] 191 p. illus. 24 cm. Includes brief biographies of well-known drivers and a description of the rules, courses, and major events in stock car racing. [GV1032.A1H86] 920 72-12021 ISBN 0-396-06641-0 5.95
1. Automobile racing—Biography—Juvenile literature. I. Engel, Lyle Kenyon. II. Title.

JACKSON, Robert B. 796.7'2'0922 B
Behind the wheel; great road racing drivers, by Robert B. Jackson. New York, H. Z. Walck [1971] 48 p. illus., ports. 23 cm. Brief biographies of twenty-two outstanding sports and Formula One drivers from Australia, New Zealand, Great Britain, the United States, and other countries. [GV1032.A1J35] 920 77-145416 ISBN 0-8098-2076-5 4.25
1. Automobile racing—Biography—Juvenile literature. I. Title. BIP

LIBBY, Bill. 796.7'2'0922 B
Heroes of stock car racing / by Bill Libby. New York : Random House, [1975] 152 p. : ill. ; 22 cm. (Random House sports library ; no. 5) Includes index. Brief biographies of twelve stock car drivers including Lee and Richard Petty, Pops Turner, A. J. Foyt, and Bobby Allison. [GV1032.A1L52] 920 74-24763 ISBN 0-394-82994-8 : 2.50 ISBN 0-394-92994-2 lib.bdg. : 3.99
1. Automobile racing—Biography—Juvenile literature. I. Title. BIP

OLNEY, Ross Robert, 1929- 796.7'2'0922 B
Superstars of auto racing / by Ross R. Olney. New York : Putnam, c1975. 126 p. : ill. ; 24 cm. Includes index. Biographical sketches of eleven international champion auto racers including Roger McCluskey, Jackie Stewart, and A. J. Foyt. [GV1032.A1O44 1975] 920 75-10438 ISBN 0-399-60959-8 lib. bdg. : 5.89
1. Automobile racing—Biography.—Juvenile literature. I. Title. BIP

ORR, Frank. 796.7'2'0922
World's great race drivers. New York, Random House [1972] p. (Random House sports library, 3) Contents.Contents.—Introduction.—A. J. Foyt.—Richard Petty.—Jackie Stewart.—Mario Andretti.—Bruce McLaren.—Don Garlits.—Mark Donohue.—Jimmy Clark.—Parnelli Jones.—Bobby and Al Unser. Profiles of eleven successful auto race drivers in all areas of the sport. [GV1032.A1O7] 920 72-2038 ISBN 0-394-82416-4 1.95
1. Automobile racing—Biography—Juvenile literature. I. Title.
Library ed. $3.37, ISBN0-394-92416-9 BIP

Automobile racing drivers—Biography—Juvenile literature.

ABODAHER, David J. 796.7'2'0922 B
The speedmakers : great race drivers / David J. Abodaher. New York : J. Messner, c1979. 192 p. : ill. ; 22 cm. Includes index. Bibliography: p. 187. [GV1032.A1A23] 78-27649 7.79
1. Automobile racing drivers—Biography—Juvenile literature. I. Title. BIP

CORSON, Richard, 1918- 796.7'2'0922 B
Champions at speed / written and illustrated by Richard Corson. New York : Dodd, Mead, c1979. 47 p. : ill. ; 19 x 23 cm. Briefly describes the racing careers of automobile racing drivers: Tazio Nuwolari, Rudolf Caracciola, Juan Manuel Fangio, Stirling Moss, Phil Hill, Graham Hill, Jim Clark, and Jackie Stewart. [GV1032.A1C67] 920 78-25853 ISBN 0-396-07656-4 : 5.95
1. Automobile racing drivers—Biography—Juvenile literature. I. Title. BIP

JACKSON, Robert B. 796.7'2'0922 B
Road racers : today's exciting driving stars / Robert B. Jackson. New York : H. Z. Walck, c1977. p. cm. A collection of biographical sketches of racing car drivers from all parts of the world. [GV1032.A1J36] 920 76-54902 ISBN 0-8098-0001-2
1. Automobile racing drivers—Biography—Juvenile literature. I. Title.

OLNEY, Ross Robert, 1929- 796.7'2'0922 B
Auto racing's young lions / Ross R. Olney. New York : Putnam, c1977. 127 p. : ill. ; 21 cm. Includes index. Discusses the racing careers of seven fathers and sons who have each won fame in many kinds of auto racing. Includes Bill Vukovich, senior and junior, Lee and Richard Petty, Tony and Gary Bettenhausen, and others. [GV1032.A1O397 1977] 920 76-53824 ISBN 0-399-20579-9 : 5.95.
1. Automobile racing drivers—Biography—Juvenile literature. I. Title. BIP

Automobile racing—History.

ALEXANDER, Jesse. 796.7'2
At speed. [Photos. by] Jesse Alexander. [Introd.: Karl Ludvigsen. Newport Beach, Calif., Bond/Parkhurst Books, 1972] 158 p. (chiefly col. illus.) 37 x 44 cm. [GV1029.15.A44] 72-86767 ISBN 0-87880-013-1 59.50
1. Automobile racing—History. 2. Automobile racing—Biography. I. Ludvigsen, Karl E. II. Title.

SHAPIRO, Harvey, 1937- 796.7'2
Faster than sound / Harvey Shapiro. South Brunswick : A. S. Barnes, [1975] 176 p. : ill. ; 29 cm. Includes index. Bibliography: p. 173. [GV1029.15.S38 1975] 73-22610 ISBN 0-498-01507-6 : 15.00
1. Automobile racing—History. 2. Automobiles, Racing—Speed records. 3. Automobile racing—Biography. I. Title. BIP

Automobile racing—Juvenile literature.

OLNEY, Ross Robert, 1929- 796.7'2'0922
Kings of motor speed, by Ross R. Olney. New York, G. P. Putnam's Sons [1970] 191 p. illus., ports. 21 cm. Brief biographies stressing the racing careers of thirteen of the fastest men in four-and two-wheel speed competitions. [GV1032.A1O43] 920 79-92818 3.64
1. Automobile racing—Juvenile literature. 2. Automobile racing—Biography. I. Title. BIP

Automobile racing—U.S.—History.

LIBBY, Bill. 796.7'0973
Great American race drivers. [1st ed.] New York Cowles Book Co. [1970] ix, 245 p. illus., ports. 24 cm. [GV1033.L5 1970] 79-104361 6.95
1. Automobile racing—U.S.—History. 2. Automobile racing—Biography. I. Title.

WATSON, Dick, 1931- 796.7'2
The glory road. [New York] Stadia Sports Pub. [1973] 160 p. illus. 20 cm. (Sport-spectrum classic) [GV1033.W37] 73-75019 1.50
1. Automobile racing—United States—History. 2. Automobile racing—Biography. I. Title.

Automobiles, Racing—Speed records—Juvenile literature.

ROSS, Frank Xavier, 1914- 796.7'2'0922 B
Car racing against the clock : the story of the world land speed record / by Frank Ross, Jr. New York : Lothrop, Lee & Shepard Co., c1976. p. cm. Includes index. Bibliography: p. A history, emphasizing famous cars and drivers, of the continuing attempts to drive the fastest car in the world from the 1898 record speed of thirty-nine miles per hour to today's speeds of over 600 miles per hour. [GV1030.R67] 920 75-38965 ISBN 0-688-41743-4 : 5.95 ISBN 0-688-51743-9 lib.bdg. : 5.11
1. Automobiles, Racing—Speed records—Juvenile literature. 2. Automobile racing—Biography—Juvenile literature. I. Title. BIP

Automobiles—Trailers.

KIEFER, Charles. 796.7'9'0924
To each his own Philadelphia, Dorrance [1968] ix, 107 p. illus., ports. 22 cm. Autobiographical. [GV1023.K45] 68-24768
1. Automobiles—Trailers. I. Title.

Autry, Gene, 1907-

AUTRY, Gene, 1907- 791.43'028'0924 B
Back in the saddle again / Gene Autry with Mickey Herskowitz. 1st ed. Garden City, N.Y. : Doubleday, 1978. 252 p., [16] leaves of plates : ill. ; 22 cm. Includes index. Discography: p. [191]-206. [PN2287.A9A32] 76-18332 ISBN 0-385-03234-X : 8.95
1. Autry, Gene, 1907- 2. Moving-picture actors and actresses—United States—Biography. 3. Singers—United States—Biography. I. Herskowitz, Mickey, joint author. II. Title. BIP

Auzello, Blanche.

MARX, Samuel, 1902- 647'.944'360922 B
Queen of the Ritz / by Samuel Marx. Indianapolis : Bobbs-Merrill, [1978] p. cm. [TX910.5.A95M37] 78-55639 ISBN 0-672-52316-7 : 10.00
1. Auzello, Blanche. 2. Auzello, Claude. 3. Ritz Hotel, Paris. 4. Hotel management—France—Paris—Biography. I. Title. BIP

Auzello, Claude.

MARX, Samuel, 1902- 647'.944'360922 B
Queen of the Ritz / by Samuel Marx. Indianapolis : Bobbs-Merrill, [1978] p. cm. [TX910.5.A95M37] 78-55639 ISBN 0-672-52316-7 : 10.00
1. Auzello, Blanche. 2. Auzello, Claude. 3. Ritz Hotel, Paris. 4. Hotel management—France—Paris—Biography. I. Title. BIP

Avakian, Elizabeth, 1943-

AVAKIAN, Elizabeth, 1943- 155.6'33
To deliver me of my dreams / Elizabeth Avakian. [1st ed.] Millbrae, Calif. : Les Femmes Pub., 1975. p. cm. [HQ1206.A87] 75-10577 ISBN 0-89087-906-0 : 3.95
1. Avakian, Elizabeth, 1943- 2. Women—Psychology. 3. Self-actualization. I. Title.

Aveling, Eleanor Marx, 1855-1898.

FLORENCE, Ronald. 335.4'0922 B
Marx's daughters : Eleanor Marx, Rosa Luxemburg, Angelica Balabanoff / Ronald Florence. New York : Dial Press, 1975. 258 p., [4] leaves of plates : ill. ; 24 cm. Includes index. Bibliography: p. 237-243. [HX23.F55] 75-9576 ISBN 0-8037-5432-9 : 10.00
1. Aveling, Eleanor Marx, 1855-1898. 2. Luxemburg, Rosa, 1870-1919. 3. Balabanoff, Angelica, 1878-1965. 4. Marx, Karl, 1818-1883. I. Title. BIP

KAPP, Yvonne (Mayer) 1903- 335.4'092'4 B
Eleanor Marx, by Yvonne Kapp. [1st U.S. ed.] New York, International Publishers [1973, c1972- v. illus. 23 cm. Contents.Contents.—v. 1. Family life (1855-1883) Bibliography: v. 1, p. [308]-313. [HD8393.A9K36 1973] 72-92771 12.00 (v. 1)
1. Aveling, Eleanor (Marx) 1855-1898. BIP

KAPP, Yvonne Mayer, 1903- 335.4'092'4
Eleanor Marx / by Yvonne Kapp. 1st American ed. New York : Pantheon Books, [1977] c1972-1976. p. cm. Includes indexes. Bibliography: v. 1, p. [HD8383.7.A93K36 1977] 77-77538 ISBN 0-394-42143-4(v.1) : 17.95
1. Aveling, Eleanor Marx, 1855-1898. 2. Labor and laboring classes—Great Britain—Biography. 3. Socialists—Great Britain—Biography.

TSUZUKI, Chushichi. 335. 4'O924
The life of Eleanor Marx, 1855-1898: a socialist tragedy. Oxford, Clarendon Pr., 1967. xi, 354p. front. 3 plates (ports., facsim.). 23cm. Bibl. (B) 7.20
1. Avelig, Eleanor Marx, 1856-1898. I. Title.
American distributor: Oxford Univ. Pr., New York.

TSUZUKI, Chushichi. 335.4'0924 (B)
The life of Eleanor Marx, 1855-1898; a socialist tragedy. Oxford, Clarendon P., 1967. xi, 354 p. front., 3 plates (ports., facsim.). 22 1/2 cm. 45/- Bibliography: p. [338]-341. [HX243.A9T8] 67-113094
1. Aveling, Eleanor Marx, 1856-1898. I. Title.

Aveling, Eleanor Marx, 1855-1898—Fiction.

CHERNAIK, Judith. FIC
The daughter : a novel based on the life of Eleanor Marx / by Judith Chernaik. 1st ed. New York : Harper & Row, c1979. vii, 216 p. ; 22 cm. [PZ4.C519Dau 1979] [PS3553.H354] 813'.5'4 78-69618 ISBN 0-06-010757-X : 9.95
1. Aveling, Eleanor Marx, 1855-1898—Fiction. I. Title. BIP

Aventinus, Joannes, 1477-1534.

STRAUSS, Gerald, 1922- 928.3
Historian in an age of crisis; the life and work of Johannes Aventinus, 1477-1534. Cambridge, Mass., Harvard University Press, 1963. ix, 296 p. port. 22 cm. Bibliography: p. 263-278. [DD801.B362S7] 63-10875
1. Aventinus, Joannes, 1477-1534. I. Title.

STRAUSS, Gerald, 1922- 928.3
Historian in an age of crisis; the life and work of Johannes Aventinus, 1477-1534. Cambridge, Mass., Harvard University Press, 1963. ix, 296 p. port. 22 cm. Bibliography: p. 263-278. [DD801.B362S7] 63-10875
1. Aventinus, Joannes, 1477-1534. I. Title.

STRAUSS, Gerald, 1922- 928.3
Historian in an age of cristis; the life and work of Johannes Aventinus, 1477-1534. Cambridge, Mass., Harvard [c.]1963. ix, 296p. port. 22cm. Bibl. 63-10875 6.95
1. Aventinus, Joannes, 1477-1534. I. Title.

Averill, Gerald, 1896-

AVERILL, Gerald, 1896- 974.1'04'0924 B
Ridge runner : the story of a Maine woodsman / Gerald Averill. Thorndike, Me. : Thorndike Press, [1979] c1948. p. cm. Autobiography. Reprint of the ed. published by Lippincott, Philadelphia. [SK354.A93A37 1979] 79-14339 ISBN 0-89621-031-6 : 10.50 ISBN 0-89621-030-8 pbk. : 4.95
1. Averill, Gerald, 1896- 2. Maine—Description and travel. 3. Game wardens—Maine—Biography. I. Title.

Avery, Burniece, 1908-

AVERY, Burniece, 1908- 973'.04'96073 B
Walk quietly through the night and cry softly / Burniece Avery. Detroit : Balamp

Pub., c1977. viii, 193 p. : ill. ; 21 cm. Includes index. Bibliography: p. 186. [E185.97.A89A35] 77-2891 ISBN 0-913642-08-8 : 7.00
1. Avery, Burniece, 1908- 2. Afro-Americans—Biography. I. Title. **BIP**

Avicenna, 980-1037.

AVICENNA, 980-1037. 297'.2
Avicenna on theology / by Arthur J. Arberry. Westport, Conn. : Hyperion Press, 1979. 82 p. ; 22 cm. Reprint of the 1951 ed. published by J. Murray, London, in the Wisdom of the East series. Includes index. [BP166.A92 1979] 78-59000 ISBN 0-88355-676-6 : 10.00
1. Avicenna, 980-1037. 2. Islamic theology—Early works to 1800. 3. Muslims—Biography. I. Arberry, Arthur John, 1905-1969. II. Title. III. Series: The Wisdom of the East series. **BIP**

AVICENNA, 980-1037. 189'.5
The life of Ibn Sina; a critical edition and annotated translation, by William E. Gohlman. [1st ed.] Albany, State University of New York Press, 1974. 163 p. 24 cm. (Studies in Islamic philosophy and science) Arabic text and English translation of the author's autobiography, Sirat al-Shaykh al-Ra'is, which was completed by al-Juzajani. Originally presented as the editor's thesis, University of Michigan. Bibliography: p. 155-158. [B751.A5S5 1974] 73-6793 ISBN 0-87395-226-X 15.00
1. Avicenna, 980-1037. I. al-Juzajani, 'Abd al-Wahid ibn Muhammad, 11th cent. II. Gohlman, William E., ed. III. Title. IV. Series. **BIP**

NASR, Seyyed Hossein. 297'.6 B
Three Muslim sages : Avicenna, Suhrawardi, Ibn 'Arabi / Seyyed Hossein Nasr. Delmar, N.Y. : Caravan Books, [1975] p. cm. Reprint of the 1969 ed. published by Harvard University Press, Cambridge. Bibliography. p. [BP70.N36 1975] 75-14430 ISBN 0-88206-500-9 pbk. : 5.95
1. Avicenna, 980-1037. 2. al-Suhrawardi, Yahya ibn Habash, 1152 or 3-1191. 3. Ibn al-'Arabi, 1165-1240. I. Title.

Awolowo, Obafemi,

AWOLOWO, Obafemi, 1909- 929.2669
Awo; the autobiography of Chief Obafemi Awolowo. [New York] Cambridge [1962, c.1960] 315p. 2.45 pap.,
I. Title.

Axford, Joseph.

AXFORD, Joseph. 979.1'77'050924 B
Around Western campfires, by Joseph "Mack" Axford. Tucson, University of Arizona Press [1969] 266 p. 20 cm. ([Southwest chronicle series]) Autobiographical. [CT275.A9525A3] 70-79583 4.95
I. Title.

Axling, William, 1873-1963.

HINE, Leland D. 266.6'1'0924 B
Axling: a Christian presence in Japan [by] Leland D. Hine. Valley Forge [Pa.] Judson Press [1969] 205 p. illus., ports. 23 cm. [BV3457.A9H5] 69-16390 5.95
1. Axling, William, 1873-1963. 2. Missions—Japan. 3. Baptists—Missions.

Aycelin, Gilles, ca. 1250-1318.

MCNAMARA, Jo Ann, 1931- 327'.2'0924 B
Gilles Aycelin; the servant of two masters. [1st ed.] [Syracuse, N.Y.] Syracuse University Press, 1973. ix, 220 p. 23 cm. An expanded and rev. version of the author's thesis, Columbia University. Bibliography: p. 205-215. [DC94.A9M3 1973] 73-6575 ISBN 0-8156-0094-1 8.50
1. Aycelin, Gilles, ca. 1250-1318. I. Title.

Aycock, Charles Brantley, 1859-1912.

ORR, Oliver Hamilton. 923.273
Charles Brantley Aycock. Chapel Hill, University of North Carolina Press [1961] 394p. illus. 24cm. Issued in 1959 in microfilm form, as thesis, University of North Carolina. Includes bibliography. [F252.A74O7 1961] 61-1629
1. Aycock, Charles Brantley, 1859-1912. I. Title.

Ayer, Alfred Jules, Sir, 1910-

AYER, Alfred Jules, Sir, 1910- 192 B
Part of my life / A. J. Ayer. Oxford [Eng.] ; New York : Oxford University Press, 1978. p. cm. (Oxford paperbacks) Includes index. [B1618.A94A36 1978] 78-40191 ISBN 0-19-281245-9 pbk. : 5.95
1. Ayer, Alfred Jules, Sir, 1910- 2. Philosophers—England—Biography. I. Title. **BIP**

AYER, Alfred Jules, Sir, 1910- 192 B
Part of my life : the memoirs of a philosopher / by A. J. Ayer. 1st American ed. New York : Harcourt, Brace, Jovanovich, c1977. 318 p., [4] leaves of plates : ill. ; 24 cm. Includes index. [B1618.A94A36 1977b] 77-73110 ISBN 0-15-170973-4 : 14.95
1. Ayer, Alfred Jules, Sir, 1910- 2. Philosophers—England—Biography. I. Title. **BIP**

Ayer, Frederick.

AYER, Frederick. 363.2'0924
Yankee G-man. Chicago, H. Regnery Co., 1957. 312p. 22cm. Autobiographical. [HV7914.A9] 57-11726
I. Title.

Ayer, Harriet Hubbard, 1854-1903.

AYER, Margaret Hubbard. 920.5
The three lives of Harriet Hubbard Ayer, by Margaret Hubbard Ayer and Isabella Taves. [1st ed.] Philadelphia, Lippincott [1957] 284 p. illus. 22 cm. [PN4874.A9A9] 57-8947
1. Ayer, Harriet Hubbard, 1854-1903. I. Taves, Isabella, joint author. II. Title.

Ayer, William Ward.

LARSON, Melvin Gunnard, 1916- 922.673
God's man in Manhattan, the biography of Dr. William Ward Ayer. Grand Rapids, Zondervan [1950] 168 p. illus., ports. 20 cm. [BX6495.A9L3] 50-11933
1. Ayer, William Ward. I. Title.

Aylward, Gladys.

AYLWARD, Gladys. 266'.023'0924 B
The small woman of the Inn of the Sixth Happiness, by Gladys Aylward as told to Christine Hunter. Chicago, Moody Press [1970] 153 p. 22 cm. [BV3427.A9A32] 79-104818 3.95
I. Hunter, Christine, joint author. II. Title.

BURGESS, Alan. 922
The small woman. [1st ed.] New York, Dutton, 1957. 256 p. illus. 21 cm. Title also in Chinese. [BV3427.A9B8] 57-7603
1. Aylward, Gladys. I. Title.

COWIE, Vera. 266'.023'0924 B
Girl Friday to Gladys Aylward / [by] Vera Cowie. London : Lakeland, 1976. 156 p., [4] p. of plates : ports. ; 18 cm. [HV887.T28C68] 77-370365 ISBN 0-551-00763-X : £0.95
1. Aylward, Gladys. 2. Orphans and orphan asylums—Taiwan. 3. Missionaries—Biography. I. Title.

THOMPSON, Phyllis. 266'.023'0924 B
A transparent woman; the compelling story of Gladys Aylward, "the small woman" of China whose life was portrayed in "The Inn of the Sixth Happiness." Grand Rapids, Zondervan Pub. House [1972, c1971] 190 p. illus. 18 cm. (Zondervan books) First published in 1971 under title: A London sparrow. [BV3427.A9T48 1972] 72-83876 1.25 (pbk)
1. Aylward, Gladys. I. Title.

Ayorinde, James Tanimola, 1907-

EPPERSON, Barbara. 266'.023'0924
Out of Shango's shadow; a biography of James Tanimola Ayorinde. Nashville, Convention Press [1967] 83 p. plates (incl. ports.) 21 cm. (Foreign mission graded series) "Church study course of the Sunday School Board of the Southern Baptist Convention: This book is number 1003 in category 10, section for juniors." 67-16362
1. Ayorinde, James Tanimola, 1907- 2. Missions — Nigeria. I. Title.

Azad, Abul Kalam, maulana, 1888-1958.

MAULANA Abul Kalam Azad; v. 12 a memorial volume. New York, Asia Publishing House [1959] ix, 241p. port.
1. Azad, Abul Kalam, maulana, 1888-1958. I. Humayun Kabir, 1906- ed.

Azikiwe, Noamdi, 1904-

AZIKIWE, Nnamdi, 1904- 966.9'03'0924 B
My odyssey; an autobiography. New York, Praeger [1970] xii, 452 p. ports. 23 cm. [DT515.6.A9A32 1970] 73-134448 12.50
I. Title. **BIP**

JONES-QUARTEY, K A B 966.9030924
A life of Azikiwe [by] K. A. B. Jones-Quartey. Baltimore, Penguin Books [1965] 272 p. maps. 18 cm. (Penguin African series, WA14) Bibliographical footnotes. [DT515.6.A9J6] 66-1652
1. Azikiwe, Noamdi, 1904- I. Title.

Bab, 'Ali Muhammad Shirazi, 1820-1850.

BALYUZI, H. M. 297'.88'0924 B
The Bab; the herald of the day of days, by H. M. Balyuzi. Oxford [Eng.] G. Ronald [1973] xiv, 255 p. illus. 21 cm. Includes bibliographical references. [BP391.B34] 73-167688 ISBN 0-85398-048-9
1. Bab, 'Ali Muhammad Shirazi, 1820-1850.
Distributed by Bahai Publishing Trust, 415 Linden Ave., Wilmette, Ill. 60091; 5.25.

Babar, Emperor of Hindustan, 1483-1530.

EDWARDES, Stephen Meredyth, 1873-1927. 954.02'5'0924 B
Babur, diarist and despot / by S. M. Edwardes. New York : AMS Press, 1975. 138 p., [4] leaves of plates : ill. ; 18 cm. Reprint of the 1926 ed. published by A. M. Philpot, London. [DS461.1.E4 1975] 79-180334 ISBN 0-404-56246-9 : 10.00
1. Babar, Emperor of Hinclustan, 1483-1530. I. Title.

GRENARD, Fernand, 1866- 954'.025'0924 B
Baber, first of the Moguls. Translated and adapted by Homer White and Richard Glaenzer. Freeport, N.Y., Books for Libraries Press [1970] ix, 253 p. illus. 23 cm. Reprint of the 1930 ed. Bibliography: p. 251-253. [DS461.1.G7 1970] 70-124236
1. Babar, Emperor of Hindustan, 1483-1530. 2. Mogul Empire.

LAL, Muni, 1913- 954.02'5'0924 B
Babar : life and times / Muni Lal. New Delhi : Vikas Pub. House, c1977. x, 126 p., [9] leaves of plates : ill., map ; 23 cm. Includes index. [DS461.1.L27] 77-901281 ISBN 0-7069-0484-2 : 9.00
1. Babar, Emperor of Hindustan, 1483-1530. 2. Mogul Empire—Kings and rulers—Biography. I. Title.
Distributed by Lawrence Verry, Inc., P. O. Box 98, Mystic, CT 06355

LAMB, Harold, 1892- 923.154
Babur. the Tiger; first of the great Moguls. [1st ed.] Garden City, N. Y., Doubleday, 1961. 336p. illus. 22cm. [DS461.1.L28] 61-12545
1. Babar, Emperor of Hindustan, 1483-1530. I. Title.

LAMB, Harold Albert 923.154
Babur, the Tiger; first of the great Moguls. New York, Bantam [1964, c.1961] 250p. 18cm. (H2852) .60 pap.,
1. Babar, Emperor of Hindustan, 1483-1530. I. Title.

LAMB, Harold Albert, 1892- 923.154
Babur, the Tiger; first of the great Moguls. Garden City, N.Y., Doubleday [c.]1961. 336p. illus. 61-12545 4.95
1. Babar, Emperor of Hindustan, 1483-1530. I. Title.

LANE-POOLE, Stanley, 1854-1931 954.025
Babar. Delhi, S. Chand [1964] 206p. illus., fold. map. 19cm. (Rulers of India) [DS461.1.L3 1964] SA 66 2.50
1. Babar, Emperor of Hindustan, 1483-1530. 2. Mogul Empire. I. Title. II. Series.
Available from Verry, Mystic, Conn.

Babbage, Charles, 1792-1871.

HALACY, Daniel Stephen, 1919- 621.3819'5'0924 B
Charles Babbage, father of the computer [by] Dan Halacy. [New York] Crowell-Collier Press [1970] 170 p. illus., ports. 24 cm. Bibliography: p. [166] The life and inventions of Charles Babbage, who, along with numerous other creations, came up with the machine that evolved into today's computer. [QA29.B2H35] 92 79-119618
1. Babbage, Charles, 1792-1871. I. Title.

MOSELEY, Maboth. 681'.14'0924 B
Irascible genius; the life of Charles Babbage. Foreword by B. V. Bowden. Chicago, H. Regnery Co. [1970, c1964] 287 p. illus., facsim., ports. 22 cm.

Bibliography: p. 281-282. [T40.B25M6 1970] 74-105121 6.95
1. Babbage, Charles, 1792-1871. 2. Calculating-machines. I. Title.

MOSELEY, Maboth. v. 12
Irascible genius; a life of Charles Babbage, inventor. Foreword by B. V. Bowden. Label: New York, A. M. Kelley, Reprints of economic classics, 1965. 287 p. plates 22 cm. "First published, 1964" by Hutchinson & Co., London. Bibliography: p. 281-282. 67-46997
1. Babbage, Charles, 1792-1871. I. Title. BIP

Babbitt, Elwood, 1922-

HAPGOOD, Charles H. 133.9'3
Voices of spirit : through the psychic experience of Elwood Babbitt / by Charles H. Hapgood. New York : Delacorte Press/S. Lawrence, [1975] p. cm. [BF1283.B25H37] 74-22238 ISBN 0-440-05983-6
1. Babbitt, Elwood, 1922- 2. Psychical research. I. Title.

Babbitt, Irving, 1865-1933.

MANCHESTER, Frederick Alexander, 1882- ed. 378'.00924
Irving Babbitt, man and teacher. Edited by Frederick Manchester [and] Odell Shepard. New York, Greenwood Press [1969, c1941] xiii, 337 p. ports., facsim. 23 cm. [PQ67.B2M3 1969] 69-13985
1. Babbitt, Irving, 1865-1933. I. Shepard, Odell, 1884-1967, joint ed. BIP

Babel', Isaak Emmanuilovich,

BABEL', Isaak Emmanuilovich, 1894-1941. 928.917
Isaac Babel: the lonely years, 1925-1939; unpublished stories and private correspondence. Translated from the Russian by Andrew R. MacAndrew and Max Hayward. Edited and with an introd. by Nathalie Babel. New York, Farrar, Straus [1964] xxviii, 402 p. illus., ports. 21 cm. [PG3476.B2A25] 64-22499
I. Title: The lonely years.

Baber, Sarah Jane (Nelson) 1852-1942.

SANDERS, Lee (Baber) 920
Sarah Jane; reminiscences of a family and a community, by Lee Sanders and Nola Green. Illustrated by Robert Glen Green. [n. p., 1961] 193p. illus. 18cm. [CT275.B133S3] 61-39891
1. Baber, Sarah Jane (Nelson) 1852-1942. I. Green, Nola, joint author. II. Title.

Babeuf, Francois Noel, 1760-1797.

BAX, Ernest Belfort, 1854-1926. 944.04'0924 B
The last episode of the French Revolution; being a history of Gracchus Babeuf and the conspiracy of the Equals. New York, Haskell House Publishers, 1971. 271 p. port. 23 cm. Bibliography: p. 7. [DC187.8.B3 1971] 74-159489 ISBN 0-8383-1282-9
1. Babeuf, Francois Noel, d. 1797. 2. France—History—Revolution, 1789-1799. 3. Socialism in France. I. Title.

ROSE, R. B. 944.04'092'4 B
Gracchus Babeuf : the first revolutionary Communist / R. B. Rose. Stanford, Calif. : Stanford University Press, 1978. viii, 434 p. : ill. ; 24 cm. Includes index. Bibliography: p. [405]-423. [DC187.8.R67 1978] 76-54099 ISBN 0-8047-0949-1 : 18.50
1. Babeuf, Francois Noel, 1760-1797. 2. Revolutionists—France—Biography. BIP

THOMSON, David, 1912- 944.04'092'4
The Babeuf plot : the making of a Republican legend / by David Thomson. Westport, Conn. : Greenwood Press, 1975 [c1952] xi, 112 p. : ill. ; 21 cm. Reprint of the 1947 ed. published by K. Paul, Trench, Trubner, London. Includes index. Bibliography: p. 107-110. [DC187.8.T5 1975] 75-27687 ISBN 0-8371-8466-5
1. Babeuf, Francois Noel, 1760-1797. 2. Socialism in France. I. Title. BIP

Babson, Roger Ward, 1875-

SMITH, Earl L 923.373
Yankee genius; a biography of Roger W. Babson, pioneer in investment counseling and business forecasting who capitalized on investment patience. [1st ed.] New York, Harper [1954] 298p. illus. 24cm. [HB3730.S5] 54-12158
1. Babson, Roger Ward, 1875- I. Title.

Baca, Elfego, 1864-1945.

CRICHTON, Kyle Samuel, 1896-1960. 363.2'0924 B
Law and order, ltd.; the rousing life of Elfego Baco of New Mexico. Glorieta, N.M., Rio Grande Press [1970] viii, 219 p. illus., ports. 24 cm. (A Rio Grande classic) "First published in 1928." [F801.B15C7 1970] 72-115112
1. Baca, Elfego, 1864-1945. 2. Crime and criminals—New Mexico. I. Title.

CRICHTON, Kyle Samuel, 1896-1960. 363.2'092'4 B
Law and order, ltd. New York, Arno Press, 1974 [c1928] viii, 219 p. illus. 23 cm. (The Mexican American) Reprint of the ed. published by New Mexican Publishing Corp., Santa Fe. [F801.B15C7 1974] 73-14200 ISBN 0-405-05674-5 14.00
1. Baca, Elfego, 1864-1945. 2. Crime and criminals—New Mexico. I. Title. II. Series.

Baca, Elfego, 1864-1945—Juvenile literature.

BERNARD, Jacqueline. 978.9'0092'2 B
Voices from the Southwest: Antonio Jose Martinez, Elfego Baca, Reies Lopez Tijerina. New York, Scholastic Book Services [1972] 128 p. illus. 22 cm. (Firebird books) Discusses the struggles of three Mexican Americans in various historical periods to redress the wrongs that their people suffered at the hands of the English-speaking majority. [F805.M5B47] 920 72-77478 ISBN 0-590-024655. 2.97
1. Martinez, Antonio Jose, 1793-1867—Juvenile literature. 2. Baca, Elfego, 1864-1945—Juvenile literature. 3. Tijerina, Reies—Juvenile literature. 4. Mexican Americans—New Mexico—Juvenile literature. I. Title.
pap. 1.24; ISBN 0-590-024477.

Bacall, Lauren, 1924-

BACALL, Lauren, 1924- 791'.092'4 B
Lauren Bacall by myself. 1st ed. New York : Knopf, c1978. p. cm. Includes index. [PN2287.B115A35 1978] 78-54902 ISBN 0-394-41308-3 : 10.00
1. Bacall, Lauren, 1924- 2. Moving-picture actors and actresses—United States—Biography. I. Title. BIP

BACALL, Lauren 1924- FIC
Lauren Bacall by myself / Lauren Bacall. New York : Ballantine Books, 1980, c1978 506 p. : ill ; 18 cm. [PN2287B115A35] 791.B0092'4 B ISBN 0-345-26040-6 pbk. : 2.75
1. Bacall, Lauren, 1924- 2. Moving-picture actors and actresses — United States — Biography I. Title.
L.C. card no. for 1978 Knopf ed.: 78-54902

GREENBERGER, Howard. 791'.092'4 B
Bogey's baby / Howard Greenberger. London : W. H. Allen, 1976. 216 p., [12] leaves of plates : ill. ; 23 cm. [PN2287.B115G7] 76-365993 ISBN 0-491-01953-X : £4.95
1. Bacall, Lauren, 1924- 2. Moving-picture actors and actresses—United States—Biography. I. Title. BIP

Bach, Edward, 1886-1936.

WEEKS, Nora. 615'.532'0924 B
The medical discoveries of Edward Bach, physician / Nora Weeks ; [with an appreciation by John Diamond]. New Canaan, Conn. : Keats Pub., [c1979] 141, [3] p. ; 21 cm. Bibliography: p. [144] [RX66.B33W43] 79-88118 ISBN 0-87983-197-9 pbk. : 4.95
1. Bach, Edward, 1886-1936. 2. Homeopathic physicians—England—Biography. 3. Materia medica, Vegetable. I. Title. BIP

Bach family.

GEIRINGER, Karl, 1899- 927.8
The Bach family; seven generations of creative genius [by] Karl Geiringer in collaboration with Irene Geiringer. New York, Oxford University Press, 1954. xiv, 514 p. illus., 26 plates (incl. ports., facsims.) map, music. 25 cm. Bibliography: p. 490-495. "Index of compositions by members of the Bach family": p. 506-514. [ML410.B1G397] 54-13129
1. Bach family. 2. Bach, Johann Sebastian, 1685-1750. BIP

Bach, Johann Sebastian, 1685-1750.

DAVID, Hans Theodore, 1902- ed. 780.924
The Bach reader; a life of Johann Sebastian Bach in letters and documents, edited by Hans T. David and Arthur Mendel. Rev., with a supplement. New York, W. W. Norton [1966] 474 p. illus., facsims., music, ports. 22 cm. "Bibliographical notes": p. 408-419. [ML410.B1D24 1966] 66-10768
1. Bach, Johann Sebastian, 1685-1750. I. Mendel, Arthur, 1905- joint ed. II. Title.

FORKEL, Johann Nikolaus, 1749-1818. 780'.924 B
Johann Sebastian Bach: his life, art, and work. With notes and appendices by Charles Sanford Terry. New York, Johnson Reprint Corp. [1970] xxxii, 321 p. illus., 8 geneal. tables. 23 cm. Translation of Ueber Johann Sebastian Bachs Leben, Kunst und Kunstwerke. Reprint of the 1920 ed. Bibliography: p. [287]-293. [ML410.B1F83 1970b] 78-18638
1. Bach, Johann Sebastian, 1685-1750.

FORKEL, Johann Nikolaus, 1749-1818. 780'.924 B
Johann Sebastian Bach; his life, art, and work. Notes and appendices by Charles Sanford Terry. New York, Da Capo Press, 1970. xxxii, 321 p. illus., geneal. tables, ports. 24 cm. (Da Capo Press music reprint series) Translation of Ueber Johann Sebastian Bachs Leben, Kunst und Kunstwerke. Reprint of the 1920 ed. [ML410.B1F83 1970] 75-125044
1. Bach, Johann Sebastian, 1685-1750.

FORKEL, Johann Nikolaus, 1749-1818. 780'.92'4 B
Johann Sebastian Bach, his life; art, and work. Translated from the German of Johann Nikolaus Forkel. With notes and appendices by Charles Sanford Terry. New York, Vienna House [1974] xxxii, 321 p. illus. 21 cm. Translation of Ueber Johann Sebastian Bachs Leben, Kunst und Kunstwerke. Reprint of the 1920 ed. Bibliography: p. [287]-293. [ML410.B1F73 1974] 74-77496 ISBN 0-8443-0021-7 4.95
1. Bach, Johann Sebastian, 1685-1750.

[GREW, Eva Mary (Instone)] 927.8
Bach [by] Eva Mary and Sydney Grew. New York, Collier [1962] 253p. 18cm. (Great composers ser., BS133V) Bibl. 1.50 pap.,
1. Bach, Johann Sebastian, 1685-1750. I. Grew, Sydney, 1879- joint author. II. Title.

GREW, Eva Mary (Instone) v. 12
Bach [by] Eva Mary and Sydney Grew. New York, Collier Books [1962] 253 p. music. 19 cm. (Great composers series) Collier books, BS 133V. Includes bibliography. 64-22596
1. Bach, Johann Sebastian, 1685-1750. I. Grew, Sydney, 1879- joint author. II. Title.

GREW, Eva Mary (Instone) 780'.92'4 B
Bach, by Eva and Sydney Grew. New York, McGraw-Hill Book Co. [1972, c1947] xiii, 239 p. music, port. 21 cm. Original ed. issued in series: The Master musicians. New ser. Bibliography: p. 225-227. [ML410.B1G75 1972] 72-188260 ISBN 0-07-024678-5
1. Bach, Johann Sebastian, 1685-1750. I. Grew, Sydney, 1879- II. Series: The Master musicians. New series.

GURLITT, Wilibald, 1889- 927.8
Johann Sebastian Bach; the master and his work. Translated by Oliver C. Rupprecht. St. Louis, Concordia Pub. House [1957] 149p. 19cm. [MI410.B1G972] 56-7496
1. Bach, Johann Sebastian, 1685-1750. I. Title.

GURLITT, Wilibald, 1889- 927.8
Johann Sebastian Bach; the master and his work. Translated by Oliver C. Rupprecht. St. Louis, Concordia Pub. House [1957] 149p. 19cm. [ML410.B1G972] 56-7496
1. Bach, Johann Sebastian, 1685-1750. I. Title.

HOLST, Imogen, 1907- 780.924
Bach. New York, Crowell [c.1965] 94p. illus., facsims., music, ports. 26cm. (Great composers) [ML410.B13H62] 65-20723 3.95 bds.,
1. Bach, Johann Sebastian, 1685-1750. I. Title. BIP

J. S. Bach. v. 12
Translated from the French by Mervyn Savill. [New York, Crown Publishers, 1957] 204p. illus. 18cm. (A Bonanza paperback)
1. Bach, Johann Sebastian, I. Pirro, Andre, 1869-1943.

KLEINHANS, Theodore J. 780'.92'4 B
The music master; the story of Johann Sebastian Bach, by Theodore J. Kleinhans. Westport, Conn., Greenwood Press [1973, c1962] 156 p. 22 cm. Reprint of the ed. published by Muhlenberg Press, Philadelphia. [ML410.B13K6 1973] 73-11856 ISBN 0-8371-7093-1 8.50
1. Bach, Johann Sebastian, 1685-1750. I. Title.

LEE, Robert E. A. 780'.92'4 B
The joy of Bach / Robert E. A. Lee. Minneapolis : Augsburg Pub. House, c1979. 135 p. : ill. ; 20 cm. Bibliography: p. 124-125. [ML410.B1L275] 79-57201 ISBN 0-8066-1776-4 pbk. : 4.95
1. Bach, Johann Sebastian, 1685-1750. 2. Composers—Germany—Biography. I. Joy of Bach. [Motion picture] BIP

MANTON, Jo, 1919- 927.8
A portrait of Bach. Illustrated by Faith Jacques. New York, Abelard-Schuman

[1957] 176p. illus. 21cm. [ML3930.B12M3] 57-11724
1. Bach, Johnson Sebastian, 1685-1750. 2. Music- -Juvenile literature. I. Title.

MILES, Russell Hancock. 927.8
Johann Sebastian Bach; an introduction to his life and works. Englewood Cliffs, N. J., Prentice-Hall [1962] 166 p. illus. 21 cm. (A Spectrum book, S29) Includes bibliography. [ML410.B1M45] 62-9309
1. Bach, Johann Sebastian, 1685-1750.

NEUMANN, Werner. 927.8
Bach; a pictorial biography. [Translated by Stefan de Haan] New York, Viking Press [1961] 143 p. illus. 24 cm. (A Studio book) [ML88.B22N53] 61-8825
1. Bach, Johann Sebastian—Iconography.

PARRY, Charles Hubert 780'.924 B Hastings, Sir, bart., 1848-1918.
Johann Sebastian Bach; the story of the development of a great personalty. Rev. ed. Westport, Conn., Greenwood Press [1970] xi, 584 p. illus., music. 23 cm. Reprint of the 1934 ed. [ML410.B1P18 1970] 73-109818
1. Bach, Johann Sebastian, 1685-1750. I. Title. **BIP**

PIRRO, Andre, 1869-1943. v. 12
J. S. Bach, translated from the French by Mervyn Savill. Illus. with musical examples. [New York, Bonzana Books, 1957] 204 p. 18 cm. Includes bibliography. 68-19503
1. Bach, Johann Sebastian, 1685-1750. I. Title.

PIRRO, Andre, 1869- 780'.92'4 B 1943.
Johann Sebastian Bach, the organist and his works for the organ / by A. Pirro ; with a pref. by Ch. M. Widor ; translated from the Franch by Wallace Goodrich. New York : AMS Press, 1978. xxi, 116 p. : music ; 23 cm. Reprint of the 1902 ed. published by G. Schirmer, New York. Includes index. [ML410.B1P643 1978] 74-24185 ISBN 0-404-13089-5 : 11.50
1. Bach, Johann Sebastian, 1685-1750. 2. Composers—Germany—Biography. I. Title. **BIP**

ROBERTSON, Alec. 780'.92'4 B
Bach : a biography, with a survey of books, editions, and recordings / by Alec Robertson. London : C. Bingley ; Hamden, Conn. : Linnet Books, 1977. 140 p. ; 23 cm. (The Concertgoer's companions) Includes index. Bibliography: p. 53-71. [ML410.B1R54] 77-23211 ISBN 0-208-01055-6 : 7.50
1. Bach, Johann Sebastian, 1685-1750. 2. Composers—Germany—Biography.

SCHRADE, Leo, 1903- 927.8
Bach: the conflict between the sacred and the secular. New York, Merlin Press [1955?] 135p. 17cm. [Merlin music books, 1] 'Reprinted from Journal of the history of ideas, April, 1946, vol. VII, no.2.' [ML410] 55-4165
1. Bach, Johann Sebastian, 1685-1750. I. Title. **BIP**

SCHRADE, Leo, 1903- 780'.92'4 1964.
Bach: the conflict between the sacred and the secular. New York, Da Capo Press, 1973 [c1955] 135 p. 18 cm. (Da Capo Press music reprint series) Reprint of the ed. published by Merlin Press, New York, which was reprinted from the Journal of the history of ideas, v. 7, no. 2., Apr. 1946, and issued as v. 1 of Merlin music books. [ML410.B1S27 1973] 73-4331 ISBN 0-306-70581-8 6.95

1. Bach, Johann Sebastian, 1685-1750. I. Title.

SCHWEITZER, Albert, 784'.092'4 1875-
J. S. Bach. Translated by Ernest Newman. Pref. by C. M. Widor. New York, Macmillan [1950] 2 v. illus., ports., music. 23 cm. Includes bibliographies. [[ML410.B1S] A51
1. Bach, Johann Sebastian, 1685-1750. I. Title. **BIP**

SCHWEITZER, Albert, 1875- v. 12 1965.
J. S. Bach. Translated by Ernest Newman. Pref. by C. M. Widor. New York, Macmillan [1962] 2 v. facsims., music, port. 22 cm. Translation of J. S. Bach le musicien-poete, first published in 1905. 66-22999
1. Bach, Johann Sebastian, 1685-1750. I. Title.

SCHWEITZER, Albert, 780'.924 B 1875-1965.
J. S. Bach. English translation by Ernest Newman. New York, Dover Publications [1966] 2 v. music, port. 22 cm. "An unabridged and unaltered republication of the work originally published by Breitkopf and Hartel in 1911." [ML410.B1S34 1966] 66-20414
1. Bach, Johann Sebastian, 1685-1750.

TERRY, Charles 780'.92'4 B Sanford, 1864-1936.
Dach; a biography. 2d ed. London, New York, Oxford University Press. St. Clair Shores, Mich., Scholarly Press, 1972. xvii, 292 p. illus. 22 cm. Reprint of the 1933 ed. Bibliography: p. xiii-xvii. [ML410.B13T37 1972] 78-181276 ISBN 0-403-01699-1
1. Bach, Johann Sebastian, 1685-1750. **BIP**

Bach, Johann Sebastian, 1685-1750—Juvenile literature.

ARKIN, David. 780'.924
The twenty children of Johann Sebastian Bach. [Los Angeles] W. Ritchie Press [1968] 1 v. (unpaged) illus. 29 cm. [ML3930.B2A7] 67-24458
1. Bach, Johann Sebastian, 1685-1756—Juvenile literature. I. Title.

BISHOP, Claire 780'.92'4 B (Huchet)
Johann Sebastian Bach: music giant. Illustrated by Russell Hoover. Champaign, Ill., Garrard Pub. Co. [1972] 144 p. illus. 22 cm. A biography of the prolific seventeenth-century German composer whose works were unknown outside of Germany until the nineteenth century. [ML3930.B2B6] 92 78-176357 ISBN 0-8116-4513-4
1. Bach, Johann Sebastian, 1685-1750—Juvenile literature. I. Hoover, Russell, illus. II. Title.

REINGOLD, Carmel 780'.924 B Berman.
Johann Sebastian Bach; revolutionary of music. New York, F. Watts [1970] 118 p. illus., facsims., ports. 22 cm. (Immortals of music) The life of the eighteenth-century musician and composer whose music had a great influence on subsequent composers. Bibliography: p. [113] [ML3930.B2R4] 92 72-114927 ISBN 0-531-00956-4
1. Bach, Johann Sebastian, 1685-1750—Juvenile literature. I. Title. **BIP**

WESTCOTT, Frederic. 780.924 B
Bach. [1st American ed.] New York, H. Z. Walck, 1967. 96 p. 21 cm. (Composers and their times) Bibliography: p. [95]-96. [ML3930.B2W48 1967] 67-3433
1. Bach, Johann Sebastian, 1685-1750—Juvenile literature.

Bach, Thomas John.

WATSON, John 266.00924 (B) Thomas.
T. J. Bach; a voice for missions, by Tom Watson, Jr. Chicago, Moody Press [1965] 186 p. 22 cm. [BV2852.B3W3] 65-9729
1. Bach, Thomas John. I. Title.

Bache, Benjamin Franklin, 1769-1798.

FAY, Bernard, 1893- 070'.924 B
The two Franklins: fathers of American democracy. New York, AMS Press [1969] xvi, 397 p. illus., map. 23 cm. Reprint of the 1933 ed. Bibliography: p. 363-377. [E302.6.B14F3 1969] 70-93277
1. Bache, Benjamin Franklin, 1769-1798. 2. Franklin, Benjamin, 1706-1790. 3. Federal Party. 4. Democratic Party. 5. U.S.—Politics and government—Constitutional period, 1789-1809. I. Title.

FAY, Bernard, 1893- 070'.924 B
The two Franklins: fathers of American democracy. Boston, Little, Brown, 1933. St. Clair Shores, Mich., Scholarly Press [1971] xvi, 397 p. illus. 22 cm. Includes bibliographical references. [E302.6.B14F3 1971] 78-145009 ISBN 0-403-00961-8
1. Bache, Benjamin Franklin, 1769-1798. 2. Franklin, Benjamin, 1706-1790. 3. Federal Party. 4. Democratic Party. 5. U.S.—Politics and government—Constitutional period, 1789-1809. I. Title. **BIP**

Bachman-Turner Overdrive (Musical group)

MELHUISH, Martin. 784'.092'2 B
Bachman-Turner Overdrive : rock is my life, this is my song : the authorized biography / by Martin Melhuish. Toronto : Methuen ; New York : Two Continents, c1975. 178 p. : ill. ; 23 cm. [ML421.B27M4] 75-13915 ISBN 0-8467-0104-9 pbk. 4.95
1. Bachman-Turner Overdrive (Musical group)

Bacigalupa, Andrea, 1923-

BACIGALUPA, Andrea, 759.13 B 1923-
Journal of an itinerant artist / Drew Bacigalupa. Huntington, Ind. : Our Sunday Visitor, inc., c1977. 176 p., [4] leaf of plates : ill. ; 24 cm. [BX4705.B10195A34] 77-78739 ISBN 0-87973-887-1 : 9.95
1. Bacigalupa, Andrea, 1923- 2. Catholics—New Mexico—Santa Fe—Biography. 3. Art dealers—New Mexico—Santa Fe—Biography. 4. Santa Fe, N.M.—Biography. I. Title. **BIP**

Backfield play (Football)

OLDERMAN, Murray. 796.332'0922
The running backs. Drawings and diagr. by Murray Olderman. Englewood Cliffs, N.J., Prentice-Hall [1969] xi, 596 p. illus. (part col.), ports. (part col.) 29 cm. [GV951.8.O4] 75-93865 15.95
1. Backfield play (Football) 2. Football—Biography. I. Title.

Backhouse, Edmund Trelawny, Sir, bart., 1873-1944.

TREVOR-ROPER, 951'.007'2024 B Hugh Redwald.
Hermit of Peking : the hidden life of Sir Edmund Backhouse / Hugh Trevor-Roper. 1st American ed. New York : Knopf, 1977. 316 p., [2] leaves of plates : ill. ; 22 cm. First published in 1976 under title: A hidden life. Includes bibliographical references and index. [DS734.9.B3T73 1977] 76-47921 ISBN 0-394-41104-8 : 10.00
1. Backhouse, Edmund Trelawny, Sir, bart., 1873-1944. 2. Sinologists—Great Britain—Biography. I. Title. **BIP**

TREVOR-ROPER, 951'.007'2024 B Hugh Redwald.
Hermit of Peking : the hidden life of Sir Edmund Backhouse / Hugh Trevor-Roper. Harmondsworth, Eng. ; New York : Penguin Books, 1978. 391 p., [4] leaves of plates : ill. ; 18 cm. First published in 1976 under title: A hidden life. Includes bibliographical references and index. [DS734.9.B3T73 1978] 78-320628 ISBN 0-14-004776-X : 2.95
1. Backhouse, Edmund Trelawny, Sir, bart., 1873-1944. 2. Scholars—Great Britain—Biography. 3. Sinologists—Great Britain—Biography. I. Title.

Backus, Isaac, 1724-1806.

BACKUS, Isaac, 286'.1'0924 B 1724-1806.
The diary of Isaac Backus / edited by William G. McLoughlin. Providence, R.I. : Brown University Press, c1979. p. cm. Includes index. Contents.Contents.—v. 1. 1741- Bibliography: p. [BX6495.B32A33] 76-12018 ISBN 0-87057-148-6 (set) : 120.00
1. Backus, Isaac, 1724-1806. 2. Baptists—Clergy—Biography. 3. Clergy—United States—Biography. I. McLoughlin, William Gerald. II. Title. **BIP**

HOVEY, Alvah, 1820- 286'.1'0924 B 1903.
A memoir of the life and times of the Rev. Isaac Backus. New York, Da Capo Press, 1972. 369 p. 23 cm. (The Era of the American Revolution) Reprint of the 1858 ed. [BX6495.B32H6 1972] 73-148598 ISBN 0-306-70415-3 15.00
1. Backus, Isaac, 1724-1806.

Bacon, Benjamin Wisner, 1860-1932.

HARRISVILLE, Roy A. 220'.092'4 B
Benjamin Wisner Bacon, pioneer in American Biblical criticism / Roy A. Harrisville. Missoula, Mont. : Scholars Press for the Society of Biblical Literature, [1976] p. cm. (SBL studies in American Biblical scholarship ; 2) Bibliography: p. [BS501.B3H37] 76-16178 ISBN 0-89130-110-0
1. Bacon, Benjamin Wisner, 1860-1932. I. Title. II. Series: Society of Biblical Literature. SBL studies in American Biblical scholarship ; 2.

Bacon, Delia Salter, 1811-1859.

HOPKINS, Vivian Constance, 928.1 1909-
Prodigal Puritan; a life of Delia Bacon. Cambridge, Mass., Belknap Press, 1959. 362 p. illus. 25 cm. Includes bibliography. [PS1054.B57Z72] 59-10317
1. Bacon, Delia Salter, 1811-1859. I. Title.

Bacon, Francis, viscount St. Albans, 1561-1626.

BOWEN, Catherine (Drinker) 921.2 1897-
Francis Bacon; the temper of a man. Boston, Atlantic-Little [1965, c.1963] 245p. illus. 20cm. [B1197.B6] 1.95 pap.,
1. Bacon, Francis, viscount St. Albans, 1561-1626. I. Title.

BOWEN, Catherine (Drinker) 921.2
1897-
Francis Bacon; the temper of a man. [1st ed.] Boston, Little, Brown [1963] 245 p. illus. 22 cm. [B1197.B6] 63-8960
1. Bacon, Francis, viscount St. Albans, 1561-1626.

CHURCH, Richard William, 192 B
1815-1890.
Bacon. New York, AMS Press [1968] viii, 227 p. 22 cm. (English men of letters) "Reprinted from the edition of 1889, London." Bibliographical footnotes. [B1197.C5 1968] 68-58371
1. Bacon, Francis, Viscount St. Albans, 1561-1626. BIP

CHURCH, Richard William, 192 B
1815-1890.
Bacon. [Folcroft, Pa.] Folcroft Library Editions, 1973. p. Reprint of the 1892 ed. published by Macmillan, London and New York, in series: English men of letters. [B1197.C5 1973] 73-11039 ISBN 0-8414-3404-2 (lib. bdg.)
1. Bacon, Francis, Viscount St. Albans, 1561-1626.

DUMAURIER, Daphne, 942.06'1'0924
Dame, 1907-
Winding stair / Daphne duMaurier. New York : Avon, 1978,c1976. 304p., 4 leaves of plates : ill. ; 18 cm. Includes index. Bibliography: p. 285-292. [DA358.B3D84] ISBN 0-380-01848-9 pbk. : 2.25
1. Bacon, Francis, Viscount St. Albans, 1561-1626. 2. Statesmen — Great Britain — Biography. I. Title.
L.C. card no. for 1976 Doubleday ed.: 76-41557.

DU MAURIER, 942.06'1'0924 B
Daphne, Dame, 1907-
The winding stair : Francis Bacon, his rise and fall / Daphne du Maurier. 1st ed. Garden City, N.Y. : Doubleday, 1977, c1976. x, 224 p., [10] leaves of plates : ill. ; 24 cm. Includes index. Bibliography: p. 210-211. [DA358.B3D84 1977] 76-41557 ISBN 0-385-12383-3 : 10.00
1. Bacon, Francis, Viscount St. Albans, 1561-1626. 2. Statesmen—Great Britain—Biography. I. Title.

EISELEY, Loren C., 1907- 192 B
The man who saw through time [by] Loren Eiseley. Rev. and enl. ed. of Francis Bacon and the modern dilemma. New York, Scribner [1973] 125 p. 21 cm. (The Scribner library. Lyceum editions) Bibliography: p. 119-122. [B1198.E4 1973] 72-12150 ISBN 0-684-13285-0 2.45
1. Bacon, Francis, Viscount St. Albans, 1561-1626. I. Title. BIP

EPSTEIN, Joel J. 942.05'5'0924 B
Francis Bacon : a political biography / by Joel J. Epstein. Athens : Ohio University Press, c1977. xv, 187 p. : port. ; 25 cm. A revision of the author's thesis, Rutgers. Includes bibliographical references and index. [DA358.B3E67 1977] 76-25617 ISBN 0-8214-0232-3 lib.bdg. : 12.00
1. Bacon, Francis, Viscount St. Albans, 1561-1626. 2. Statesmen—Great Britain—Biography. 3. Great Britain—Politics and government—1603-1625. BIP

FARRINGTON, Benjamin, 1891- v. 12
Francis Bacon; philosopher of industrial science. New York, Collier Books [1961, c1949] 157 p. 18 cm. (Collier books...) "AS72." 64-31212
1. Bacon, Francis, Viscount St. Albans, 1561-1626. I. Title.

FARRINGTON, Benjamin, 1891- 921.2
Francis Bacon, Pioneer of planned science. London, Weidenfeld & Nicolson [dist. New Rochelle, N.Y., SportShelf, 1964, c.1963] 127p. illus., facsim., ports. 19cm. (Pathfinder biogs., 10) 64-6057 3.50
1. Bacon, Francis, viscount St. Albans, 1561-1626. I. Title.

FARRINGTON, Benjamin, 1891- 192 B
Francis Bacon, pioneer of planned science. New York, Praeger [1969, c1963] vi, 122 p. illus., facsim., ports. 22 cm. (Praeger pathfinder biographies) [B1197.F3 1969] 74-86512 4.25
1. Bacon, Francis, Viscount St. Albans, 1561-1626. I. Title.

FRANCIS Bacon, v. 12
by Lord Macaulay. Boston, etc., Educational Pub. Co. [n.d.] 192p. Introduction signed: H. M. [i.e. Henry Morley]
1. Bacon, Francis, viscount St. Albans, 1561-1626. I. Macaulay, Thomas Babington Macaulay, 1st baron, 1800-1859.

GREEN, Adwin Wigfall, 1900- 921.2
Sir Francis Bacon, his life and works. Denver, A. Swallow [1952] xv, 296 p. 24 cm. Bibliography: p. [284]-294. [B1197.G72 1952] 52-131
1. Bacon, Francis, Viscount St. Albans, 1561-1626. I. Title.

LEVINE, Israel. 192 B
Francis Bacon, 1561-1626. Port Washington, N.Y., Kennikat Press [1970] 191 p. port. 20 cm. Reprint of the 1925 ed. Bibliography: p. 187-188. [B1197.L48 1970] 72-103200
1. Bacon, Francis, Viscount St. Albans, 1561-1626.

LEVINE, Israel. 192 B
Francis Bacon (1561-1626) London, L. Parsons; Boston, Small, Maynard and Co. [Folcroft, Pa.] Folcroft Library Editions, 1973. p. Reprint of the 1925 ed., issued in The Roadmaker series. [B1197.L48 1973] 73-4386 ISBN 0-8414-2271-0 (lib. bdg.)
1. Bacon, Francis, Viscount St. Albans, 1561-1626. I. Title. BIP

SKEMP, Arthur Rowland, 192 B
1882-1918.
Francis Bacon. Port Washington, N.Y., Kennikat Press [1970] 94 p. port. 19 cm. Reprint of the 1912 ed. [B1197.S5 1970] 77-103212
1. Bacon, Francis, Viscount St. Albans, 1561-1626.

STURT, Mary. 192 B
Francis Bacon; a biography. [Folcroft, Pa.] Folcroft Library Editions, 1972. xvi, 246 p. illus. 24 cm. "Limited to 150 copies." Reprint of the 1932 ed. Bibliography: p. 243-244. [B1197.S86 1972] 72-186837
1. Bacon, Francis, Viscount of Albans, 1561-1626.

WILLIAMS, Charles, 1886- 192 B
1945.
Bacon. [Folcroft, Pa.] Folcroft Library Editions, 1973. v, 318 p. port. 24 cm. Reprint of the 1933 ed. published by A. Barker, London. [DA358.B3W5 1973] 73-3090 20.00
1. Bacon, Francis, Viscount St. Albans, 1561-1626. BIP

Bacon, Francis, Viscount St. Albans, 1561-1626—Addresses, essays, lectures.

ANDERSON, Fulton Henry, 192 B
1895-
Francis Bacon, his career and his thought / Fulton H. Anderson. Westport, Conn. : Greenwood Press, 1978, c1962. 367 p. ; 23 cm. Reprint of the ed. published by the University of Southern California Press, Los Angeles, which was issued as 1957 of the Arensberg lectures. Includes index. [B1197.A5 1978] 77-18070 ISBN 0-313-20108-0 lib.bdg. : 21.75
1. Bacon, Francis, Viscount St. Albans, 1561-1626—Addresses, essays, lectures. 2. Philosophers—England—Biography—Addresses, essays, lectures. I. Title. II. Series: The Arensberg lectures ; 1957.

Bacon, Francis, 1909-

RUSSELL, John, 1919- 759.9415 B
Francis Bacon / John Russell. Rev. ed. New York : Oxford University Press, 1979. 192 p. : ill. (some col.) ; 22 cm. (World of art series) Includes index. Bibliography: p. 153. [ND497.B16R8 1979] 78-13075 ISBN 0-19-520113-2 : 12.95 ISBN 0-19-520114-0 pbk. : 7.95
1. Bacon, Francis, 1909- 2. Painters—Great Britain—Biography.

Bacon, James, 1914-

BACON, James, 1914- FIC
Made in Hollywood / James Bacon. New York : Warner Books, 1978,c1977. 318p [8] leaves of plates : ill. ; 18 cm. Includes index. [PM4874.B22A35] [B] 791.43'092'4 ISBN 0-446-82913-7 pbk. : 2.25
1. Bacon, James, 1914- 2. Journalists — United States — Biography. 3. Moving-picture industry — United States. I. Title.
L.C. card no. for 1977 Contemporary Books ed.: 77-75716

BACON, James, 791.43'092'4 B
1914-
Made in Hollywood / James Bacon. Chicago : Contemporary Books, inc., c1977. 271 p., [8] leaves of plates : ill. ; 24 cm. Includes index. [PN4874.B22A35] 77-75716 ISBN 0-8092-7870-7 : 8.95
1. Bacon, James, 1914- 2. Journalists—United States—Biography. 3. Moving-picture industry—United States. I. Title. BIP

Bacon, Nicholas, Sir, 1509?-1578.

TITTLER, Robert. 942.05'5'0924 B
Nicholas Bacon : the making of a Tudor statesman / Robert Tittler. Athens : Ohio University Press, c1976. 256 p., [2] leaves of plates : ill. ; 23 cm. Includes bibliographical references and index. [DA347.1.B32T57] 75-36976 ISBN 0-8214-0225-0 lib.bdg. : 15.00
1. Bacon, Nicholas, Sir, 1509?-1578. 2. Great Britain—Court and courtiers—Biography. BIP

Bacon, Robert, 1860-1919.

SCOTT, James Brown, 332.1'092'4 B
1866-1943.
Robert Bacon : life and letters / James Brown Scott. New York : Arno Press, 1975 [c1923] xix, 459 p., [18] leaves of plates : ill. ; 24 cm. (Wall Street and the security markets) Reprint of the ed. published by Doubleday, Page, Garden City, N.Y. Includes bibliographical references and index. [HG172.B24S3 1975] 75-2669 ISBN 0-405-07232-5 : 31.00
1. Bacon, Robert, 1860-1919. 2. Capitalists and financiers—United States—Biography. I. Title. II. Series. BIP

Bacon, Roger, 1214?-1294.

BROPHY, Liam. 921.2
The marvelous doctor, Friar Roger Bacon. Chicago, Franciscan Herald Press [1963] 103 p. illus. 21 cm. [B765.B24B74] 63-12856
1. Bacon, Roger, 1214?-1294. I. Title.

EASTON, Stewart Copinger, v. 12
1907-
Roger Bacon and his search for a universal science; a reconsideration of the life and work of Roger Bacon in the light of his own stated purposes. New York, Columbia University Press, 1952. vii, 255p. 23cm. Bibliographiest. p. 236-244. [A52-10007]
1. Bacon, Roger, 1214?-1294. I. Title. BIP

EASTON, Stewart Copinger, 189
1907-
Roger Bacon and his search for a universal science; a reconsideration of the life and work of Roger Bacon in the light of his own stated purposes [by] Stewart C. Easton. Westport, Conn., Greenwood Press [1970, c1952] vii, 255 p. 23 cm. Bibliography: p. 236-244. [B765.B24E28 1970] 70-100159
1. Bacon, Roger, 1214?-1294. I. Title.

EASTON, Stewart Copinger, 189 B
1907-
Roger Bacon and his search for a universal science; a reconsideration of the life and work of Roger Bacon in the light of his own stated purposes [by] Stewart C. Easton. New York, Russell & Russell [1971] vii, 255 p. 23 cm. Reprint of the 1952 ed. Bibliography: p. 236-244. [B765.B24E28 1971] 77-139918
1. Bacon, Roger, 1214?-1294. I. Title.

WESTACOTT, Evalyn, 1888- 921.2
Roger Bacon in life and legend. New York, Philosophical Library [1953] 140p. 19cm. [B765.B24] 53-13314
1. Bacon, Roger, 1214?-1294. I. Title. BIP

WESTACOTT, Evalyn, 1888- 189 B
Roger Bacon in life and legend, by E. Westacott. [Folcroft, Pa.] Folcroft Library Editions, 1974 [c1953] 140 p. 23 cm. Reprint of the ed. published by Rockliff, London. Bibliography: p. 130-131. [B765.B24W4 1974] 74-14623 ISBN 0-8414-9547-5 (lib. bdg.)
1. Bacon, Roger, 1214?-1294.

Bacon, Samuel, 1781-1820.

ASHMUN, Jehudi, 1794- 283'.0924 B
1828.
Memoir of the life and character of the Rev. Samuel Bacon. Freeport, N.Y. Books for Libraries Press, 1971. viii, 288 p. 23 cm. (The Black heritage library collection) On spine: Life of the Rev. Samuel Bacon. Reprint of the 1822 ed. [BX5995.B3A8 1971] 77-154070 ISBN 0-8369-8781-0
1. Bacon, Samuel, 1781-1820. I. Title. II. Title: Life of the Rev. Samuel Bacon. III. Series. BIP

Bacteriology—History.

BULLOCH, William, 1868- 616.01'4
1941.
The history of bacteriology / by William Bulloch. New York : Dover Publications, 1979, c1938. x, 422 p., [8] leaves of plates : ill. ; 21 cm. Reprint of the ed. published by Oxford University Press, London, which was issued as the 1936 University of London Heath Clark lectures. Includes index. Bibliography: p. [285]-348. [QR21.B8 1979] 78-73065 ISBN 0-486-23761-3 : 6.50
1. Bacteriology—History. 2. Bacteriologists—Biography. I. Title. II. Series: London. University. Heath Clark lectures, 1936. BIP

KNIGHT, David C 926.1
Robert Koch, father of bacteriology. Pictures by Gustav Schrotter. New York, F. Watts [1961] 165p. illus. 22cm. (A First biography) [QR31.K6K57] 61-7501
I. Koch, Robert, 1843-1910. II. Title.

Baden-Powell, Robert Stephenson Smyth Baden-Powell, baron, 1857-1941.

HILLCOURT, William, 1900- 923.542
Baden-Powell; the two lives of a hero, by William Hillcourt with Olave, Lady Baden-Powell. [1st American ed.] New York, Putnam [1964] x, 457 p. illus., ports. 24 cm. "Sources and notes": p. [419]-444. [DA68.32.B2H5] 64-24263
1. Baden-Powell, Robert Stephenson Smyth Baden-Powell, baron, 1857-1941.

KIERNAN, Reginald 942.081'0924 B
Hugh, 1900-
Baden-Powell, by R. H. Kiernan. [New York] Argosy-Antiquarian, 1970. 254 p. illus., maps, ports. 23 cm. Reprint of the 1939 ed., except appendix. [DA68.32.B2K5 1970] 78-122477 ISBN 0-87266-045-1
1. Baden-Powell, Robert Stephenson Smyth Baden-Powell, Baron, 1857-1941. 2. Boy scouts. BIP

REYNOLDS, Ernest Edwin, 923.542
1894-
Baden-Powell; a biography of Lord Baden-Powell of Gilwell, O. M., G. C. M. G., G. C. V. O., K. C. B. 2d ed. London, New York, Oxford University Press, 1957. 270p. illus. 23cm. [DA68.32.B2R4 1957] 57-1823
1. Baden-Powell, Robert Stephenson Smyth Baden-Powell, baron, 1857-1941. 2. Boy Scouts. I. Title.

Baden-Powell, Robert Stephenson Smyth Baden-Powell, baron, 1857-1941—Juvenile literature.

BLASSINGAME, Wyatt. 92 (J)
Baden-Powell, chief scout of the world. Illustrated by Gray Morrow. Champaign, Ill., Garrard Pub. Co. [1966] 80 p. col. illus. 23 cm. ([Books for scouts]) [DA68.32.B2B55] 66-10149
1. Baden-Powell, Robert Stephenson Smyth Baden-Powell, baron, 1857-1941—Juvenile literature. I. Title.

Bader, Douglas, 1910-

BRICKHILL, Paul. 926.2913
Reach for the sky; the story of Douglas Bader, legless ace of the Battle of Britain. [1st ed.] New York, Norton [1954] 312p. illus. 22cm. [D786.B716 1954] 54-10994

1. Bader. Douglas, 1910- 2. World War, 1939-1945—Aerial operations, British. I. Title.

BRICKHILL, Paul Chester 923.2913 Jerome
Reach for the sky; the story of Douglas Bader. the legless ace of the Battle of Britain [by] Paul Brickhill. New York, Ballantine [1967, c.1954] 336p. illus. 18cm. (U7059) [D786.B716] .95 pap.,
1. Bader, Douglas, 1910- 2. World War, 1939-1945—Aerial operations—British. I. Title.

Badiali, Craig, 1952-1969.

ASINOF, Eliot, 1919- 959.7'04'31
Craig and Joan; two lives for peace. New York, Viking Press [1971] x, 245 p. 22 cm. [CT275.B157A8 1971] 6.95
1. Badiali, Craig, 1952-1969. 2. Fox, Joan, 1951 or 2-1969. I. Title.

ASINOF, Eliot, 1919- 959.7'04'31
Craig and Joan; two lives for peace. New York, Viking Press [1971] x, 245 p. 22 cm. [CT275.B157A8 1971] ISBN 0-670-24541-0 6.95
1. Badiali, Craig, 1952-1969. 2. Fox, Joan, 1951 or 2-1969. I. Title.

Badillo, Herman, 1929- —Juvenile literature.

ALLYN, Paul, 328.73'092'4 B pseud.
The picture life of Herman Badillo. Illustrated with photos. William Loren Katz, consulting editor. New York, F. Watts, 1972. 48 p. illus. 23 cm. Photographs and brief text trace the life and political career of the first Puerto Rican to become a voting member of Congress. [E840.8.B25A7] 92 79-185925 ISBN 0-531-00985-8 3.50
1. Badillo, Herman, 1929- —Juvenile literature. I. Title. BIP

Badin, Stephen Theodore, 1768-1853.

SCHAUINGER, Joseph 922.273 Herman, 1912-
Stephen T. Badin, priest in the wildenness Milwaukee, Bruce Rub. Co. [1956] 317p. illus. 23cm. [BX4705.B13S35] 56-10608
1. Badin, Stephen Theodore, 1768-1853. I. Title.

Baeck, Leo, 1873-1956.

ALTMANN, Alexander, 910'.03'924 S 1906-
Leo Baeck and the Jewish mystical tradition. [New York, Leo Baeck Institute, 1973] 28 p. 23 cm. (Leo Baeck memorial lecture 17) Includes bibliographical references. [DS135.G3A263 no. 17] [BM755] 296.6'1 B 73-93000
1. Baeck, Leo, 1873-1956. 2. Mysticism—Judaism. I. Title. II. Series.

BAKER, Leonard. 296.6'10924 B
Days of sorrow and pain : Leo Baeck and the Berlin Jews / by Leonard Baker. New York : Macmillan, c1978. xiii, 396 p., [16] leaves of plates : ill. ; 25 cm. Includes index. Bibliography: p. 339-350. [BM755.B32B34 1978] 77-28872 ISBN 0-02-506340-5 : 12.95
1. Baeck, Leo, 1873-1956. 2. Rabbis—Germany—Biography. 3. Jews in Germany—History—1933-1945. 4. Germany—History—1933-1945. I. Title. BIP

FRIEDLANDER, Albert 296.6'1'0924 H.
Leo Baeck: teacher of Theresienstadt, by Albert H. Friedlander. [1st ed.] New York, Holt, Rinehart, and Winston [1968] 294 p. 24 cm. Bibliography: p. [277]-288. [BM755.B32F7] 68-11829 8.95
1. Baeck, Leo, 1873-1956. I. Title.

Baekeland, Leo Hendrik, 1863-1944.

KAUFMANN, Carl B. 660'.0924 B
Grand duke, wizard, and Bohemian: a biographical profile of Leo Hendrik Baekeland (1863-1944) by Carl B. Kaufmann. [Wilmington? Del., 1968] 142, [45] l. illus., geneal. table, ports. 28 cm. Cover title: LHB. Bibliography: leaves [143]-[156] [TP140.B3K3] 68-5775
1. Baekeland, Leo Hendrik, 1863-1944. I. Title. II. Title: LHB.

Baena, Juan Alfonso de, 1406-1454.

FRAKER, Charles F. 861.2
Studies on the Cancionero de Baena, by Charles F. Fraker, Jr. Chapel Hill, University of North Carolina Press [1966] 131 p. 23 cm. (University of North Carolina. Studies in the romance languages and literatures, no. 61) Bibliographical footnotes. [PC13.N67 no. 61] 67-63054
1. Baena, Juan Alfonso de, 1406-1454. El cancionero. I. Title. II. Series: North Carolina. University. Studies in the romance languages and literatures, no. 61. BIP

Baerle, Kaspar van, 1584-1648.

BLOK, Frans Felix. 616.8'52
Caspar Barlaeus : from the correspondence of a melancholic / F. F. Blok ; [translated by H. S. Lake (prose) and D. A. S. Reid (poetry)]. Assen : Van Gorcum, 1976. viii, 197 p. ; 24 cm. (Respublica literaria Neerlandica ; 2) English or Latin. Includes index. Bibliography: p. [185]-191. [RC516.B5613] 77-470755 ISBN 9-02-321348-3 : fl 55.00
1. Baerle, Kaspar van, 1584-1648. 2. Manic-depressive psychoses—Biography. I. Baerle, Kaspar van, 1584-1648. II. Title.

Baez, Joan.

BAEZ, Joan. 818
Daybreak. New York, Dial Press, 1968. 159 p. 21 cm. A collection of reminiscences and thoughts which reflect the philosophy of a well-known folk singer. [ML420.B114A3] AC 68
I. Title.

Bag-eton, 1954-

LUNA, Severino 959.9'3'040924 B N.
Born primitive in the Philippines / by Severino N. Luna ; edited with a foreword by Irene Murphy. Carbondale : Southern Illinois University Press, [1975] p. cm. [DS666.M3L86] 75-23290 ISBN 0-8093-0746-4 : 8.95
1. Bag-eton, 1954- 2. Mangyans. I. Title. BIP

Bagby, William Buck, 1855-1939.

HARRISON, Helen (Bagby) 922.681
The Bagbys of Brazil. Nashville, Broadman Press [1954] 159p. illus. 20cm. [BV2853.B6H33] 54-3981
1. Bagby, William Buck, 1855-1939. 2. Bagby, Anne (Luther) 1859-1942. I. Title.

Bagehot, Walter, 1826 1877.

BUCHAN, Alastair 928.2
The spare chancellor; the life of Walter Bagehot. [East Lansing] Michigan Statte University Press, 1960 [c.1959-1960] 278p. Bibl. and bibl. notes: p.257-272 22cm. 60-11303 5.00
1. Bagehot, Walter, 1826-1877. I. Title. BIP

IRVINE, William, 330'.0924 B 1906-
Walter Bagehot. [Hamden, Conn.] Archon Books, 1970. 303 p. 22 cm. Reprint of the 1939 ed. Bibliography: p. 285-288. [HB103.B217 1970] 70-103989
1. Bagehot, Walter, 1826-1877.

Bagley, Helen.

BAGLEY, Helen. 979.4'95 B
Sand in my shoe : homestead days in Twentynine Palms / by Helen Bagley ; with an introd. by Lucile and Harold Weight. 1st ed. Twentynine Palms, Calif. : Calico Press, c1978. xviii, 268 p. : ill. ; 24 cm. [F869.T9B33] 77-94990 ISBN 0-912714-08-5 : 8.95
1. Bagley, Helen. 2. Twentynine Palms, Calif.—Biography. I. Title.

Bagley, William Chandler, 1874-1946.

KANDEL, Isaac Leon, 1881- 923.773
William Chandler Bagley, stalwart educator. A Kappa Delta Pi publication. New York, Bureau of Publications, Teachers College, Columbia of Publications, Teachers College, Columbia Univ. [c.]1961. 131p. illus. (front por.) 61-7709 3.50
1. Bagley, William Chandler, 1874-1946. I. Title.

KANDEL, Isaac Leon, 1881- 923.773
William Chandler Bagley, stalwart educator. A Kappa Delta Pi publication. New York, Bureau of Publications, Teachers College, Columbia University, 1961. 131p. illus. 23cm. [LB875.B16K3] 61-7709
1. Bagley, William Chandler, 1874-1946. I. Title.

Bagnold, Enid.

BAGNOLD, Enid. 828'.9'1209 B
Enid Bagnold's Autobiography. [1st American ed.] Boston, Little, Brown [1970, c1969] xii, 382 p. illus., facsims., ports. 24 cm. "An Atlantic Monthly Press book." [PR6003.A35Z5] 70-117032 8.95

Bahaism.

CHANLER, Julie (Olin) 922.97 1882-
From gaslight to dawn, an autobiography. [New York? 1956] 413p. illus. 21cm. [BP395.C45A3] 56-27442
1. Bahaism. I. Title.

Bahaism—Biography.

'ABD ul-Baha ibn 297'.89'0922 Baha Ullah, 1844-1921.
Memorials of the faithful. Translated from the original Persian text and annotated by Marzieh Gail. [1st ed.] Wilmette, Ill., Baha' i Pub. Trust [1971] xii, 208 p. port. 23 cm. Translation of Tazkirat al-vafa' fi tarjamat hayat qudama' al-ahibba'. Includes bibliographical references. [BP390.A2313] 77-157797 ISBN 0-87743-041-1
1. Bahaism—Biography. I. Title. BIP

Bahrdt, Karl Friedrich, 1741-1792.

FLYGT, Sten Gunnar, 230'.0924 1911-
The notorious Dr. Bahrdt. Nashville, Vanderbilt, 1963. ix, 428 p. illus. 24 cm. Bibliography: p. 389-402. [BX4827 B25F5] 63-14648
1. Bahrdt, Karl Friedrich, 1741-1792. 2. Enlightenment. I. Title.

FLYGYT, Sten Gunnar, 1911- 922
The notorious Dr. Bahrdt. Nashville, Vanderbilt [c.]1963. ix, 428p. illus. 24 cm. Bibl. 63-146848 6.50
1. Bahrdt, Karl Friedrich 2. Enlightenment. I. Title.

Bailes, Marry (Thomson) 1851-1939.

BROWN, Esther Catherine 920.7 (Bailes)
Scottish mother. [1st ed.] New York, Vantage Press [1958, c1957] 150p. 21cm. [CT2888.B3B7] 58-1020
1. Bailes, Marry (Thomson) 1851-1939. I. Title.

Bailey, Carolyn Sherwin, 1875-1961.

DAVIS, Dorothy R. 818'.5'208
Carolyn Sherwin Bailey, 1875-1961; profile and bibliography, by Dorothy R. Davis. [New Haven, Conn. Printed by Eastern Press, inc.] 1967. [24] p. ports. 23 cm. [PS3503.A416Z6] 68-2618
1. Bailey, Carolyn Sherwin, 1875-1961.

Bailey, Consuelo Northrop, 1899-1976.

BAILEY, Consuelo 974.3'04'0924 B Northrop, 1899-1976.
Leaves before the wind : the autobiography of Vermont's own daughter / Consuelo Northrop Bailey. Burlington, Vt. : G. Little Press, c1976. 376 p. : ill. ; 24 cm. [F55.B344] 76-47361 9.95
1. Bailey, Consuelo Northrop, 1899-1976. 2. Vermont—Lieutenant-governors—Biography. I. Title.

Bailey, Francis Lee, 1933-

WHITTEN, Leslie H. 340'.0092'4 B
F. Lee Bailey [by] Les Whitten. [New York] Avon [1971] 238 p. 18 cm. [KF373.B27W45] 75-25502 0.95
1. Bailey, Francis Lee, 1933-

Bailey, Hamilton, 1894-1961.

HUMPHRIES, Sydney 617'.092'4 B Vernon, 1907-
The life of Hamilton Bailey; surgeon, author and teacher of surgery [by] S. V. Humphries. Beckenham, Ravenswood Publications, 1973. xiii, 72 p. illus., facsims., ports. 23 cm. Includes index. [R489.B14H85] 73-593747 ISBN 0-901812-10-2 10.00
1. Bailey, Hamilton, 1894-1961. I. Title.
Dist. by British Book Centre, New York.

Bailey, John Moran. 1904-

LIEBERMAN, Joseph I. 329.30924
The power broker; a biography of John M. Bailey, modern political boss [by] Joseph I. Liberman. Boston, Houghton, 1966. x, 365p. illus., ports. 22cm. [F101.B3L5] 66-11223 6.00
1. Bailey, John Moran. 1904- 2. Connecticut—Pol. & govt.— 1951- 3. Politics. Practical. I. Title.

Bailey, Joseph Weldon, 1863-1929.

ACHESON, Sam Hanna, 328.73'07'1 B 1900-
Joe Bailey, the last Democrat. Freeport, N.Y., Books For Libraries Press [1970] xvi, 420 p. port. 23 cm. Reprint of the 1932 ed. Bibliography: p. 409-412. [E664.B2A63 1970] 79-124222 ISBN 0-8369-5199-9
1. Bailey, Joseph Weldon, 1863-1929. 2. United States—Politics and government—1865-1933. 3. Texas—Politics and government—1865-1950. I. Title.

Bailey, Josiah William, 1873-1946.

MOORE, John Robert, 328.73'0924 B 1936-
Senator Josiah William Bailey of North Carolina; a political biography. Durham, N.C., Duke University Press, 1968. vi, 255 p. illus., ports. 25 cm. Bibliography: p. [237]-248. [E748.B26M6] 68-24639
1. Bailey, Josiah William, 1873-1946. I. Title. BIP

Bailey, Liberty Hyde, 1858-1954.

DORF, Philip. 926.3
Liberty Hyde Bailey; an informal biography. Ithaca, N.Y., Cornell University Press [1956] 259 p. illus. 23 cm. Includes bibliography [SB63.B3D6] 56-4695
1. Bailey, Liberty Hyde, 1858-1954.

RODGERS, Andrew Denny, 635.0924 1900-
Liberty Hyde Bailey; a story of American plant sciences. New York, Hafner, 1965 [c.1949] 506p. ports. 24cm. Facsim. of the ed. of 1949. [SB63.B3R6 1965] 65-28107 10.00
1. Bailey, Liberty Hyde, 1858-1954. 2. Agricultural research. 3. Horticulture. I. Title. BIP

Bailey, Ney.

BAILEY, Ney. 248'.2 B
Faith is not a feeling / Ney Bailey with Sharon Fischer. San Bernardino, Ca : Here's Life Publishers, c1978. ix, 114 p. ; 21 cm. [BR1725.B327A33] 78-60077 ISBN 0-918956-45-5 : 2.95
1. Bailey, Ney. 2. Christian biography—United States. I. Fischer, Sharon, joint author. II. Title. BIP

Bailey, Percival,

BAILEY, Percival, 1892- 610'.924
Up from Little Egypt. Chicago, Buckskin Press, 1969. xiii, 265 p. ports. (part col.) 24 cm. Autobiographical. "Publications by Percival Bailey": p. 250-265. [R154.B14A3] 75-91635
I. Title.

Bailey, William,

BAILEY, William, 1890- 001.2
Jayhawker boy. [1st ed.] New York, Vantage Press [1962] 141p. 21cm. Autobiographical. [CT275.B232A3] 62-3452
I. Title.

Bailey, William A., 1895-

BAILEY, William A., 1895- 917.96'03'30924
Bill Bailey came home: as a farm boy, as a stowaway at the age of nine, a trapper at the age of fifteen, and a hobo at the age of sixteen, by William A. Bailey. Edited by Austin and Alta Fife. Logan, Utah State University Press [1973] 183 p. illus. 23 cm. [F746.B255A32] 73-79904 ISBN 0-87421-061-5
1. Bailey, William A., 1895- 2. Idaho—Social life and customs. 3. Tramps—United States. I. Title.

Bailie, Joseph, 1860-1935.

BAILIE, Victoria Worley, 1894- 922.573
Bailie's activities in China; an account of the life and work of Professor Joseph Bailie in and for China, 1890-1935 [by] Victoria W. Bailie. Palo Alto, Calif., Pacific Books [1964] viii, 511 p. illus., facsim., map, ports. 29 cm. [BV3427.B3B3] 64-17671
1. Bailie, Joseph, 1860-1935. 2. Missions—China. I. Title.

Baillie, Joanna, 1762-1851.

CARHART, Margaret Sprague, 1877- 821'.7 B
The life and work of Joanna Baillie, by Margaret S. Carhart. [Hamden, Conn.] Archon Books, 1970 [c1923] 215 p. 23 cm. (Yale studies in English, v. 64) Bibliography: p. [207]-215. [PR4056.C3 1970] 74-91178 6.50
1. Baillie, Joanna, 1762-1851. I. Title. II. Series. BIP

Bailly, Jean Sylvain, 1736-1793.

BRUCKER, Gene A. 923.244
Jean-Sylvain Bailly, revolutionary mayor of Paris. Urbana, University of Illinois Press, 1950. vii, 134 p. 27 cm. (Illinois studies in the social sciences, v. 31,no. 3) "Prepared as a thesis for a master's degree at the University of Illinois." Bibliography: p. 130-134. [H31.I 4 vol. 31, no. 2] 50-62867
1. Bailly, Jean Sylvain, 1736-1793. I. Title. II. Series: Illinois. University. Illinois studies in the social sciences, v. 31, no. 3

Bainbridge, Christopher, Cardinal, 1464?-1514.

CHAMBERS, David Sanderson 922.242
Cardinal Bainbridge in the court of Rome, 1509 to 1514 [New York] Oxford [c.]1965. xii, 178p. illus., maps. 23cm. (Oxford historical ser., 2d ser.) Bibl. [BR754.B3C5] 65-3740 4.80
1. Bainbridge, Christopher, Cardinal, 1464?-1514. I. Title.

Baines, Thomas, 1820-1875.

WALLIS, John Peter Richard, 1880-1957. 916.8
Thomas Baines, his life and explorations in South Africa, Rhodesia and Australia, 1820-1875 / J. P. R. Wallis ; illustrated by a selection of Thomas Baines' water-colours, drawings and prints ; with captions and a new introd. by F. R. Bradlow. Cape Town : A. A. Balkema, 1976. xx, 235 p. : ill. ; 27 cm. First published in 1941 under title: Thomas Baines of King's Lynn, explorer and artist, 1820-1875. Includes index. Bibliography: p. 225-227. [G246.B34W34 1976] 77-350158 ISBN 0-86961-059-7
1. Baines, Thomas, 1820-1875. 2. Explorers—England—Biography. 3. Explorers—South Africa—Biography. 4. Explorers—Australia—Biography.

Bainton, James Herbert, 1867-1942.

BAINTON, Roland Herbert, 1894- 922.573
Pilgrim parson; the life of James Herbert Bainton, 1867-1942. New York, Nelson [1958] 166 p. illus. 21 cm. [BX7260.B17B2] 58-11894
1. Bainton, James Herbert, 1867-1942. I. Title.

Baird, Absalom, 1824-1905.

BAIRD, John A., 1918- 973.7'41'0924 B
Profile of a hero : the story of Absalom Baird, his family, and the American military tradition / by John A. Baird, Jr. Philadelphia : Dorrance, c1977. xiii, 234 p., [6] leaves of plates (1 fold.) : ill. ; 22 cm. Includes index. Bibliography: p. 227-228. [E467.1.B15B34] 77-155112 ISBN 0-8059-2460-4 : 7.95
1. Baird, Absalom, 1824-1905. 2. United States. Army—Biography. 3. Baird family. 4. Generals—United States—Biography. 5. United States—History—Civil War, 1861-1865—Campaigns and battles. I. Title.

Baird, John Logie, 1888-1945.

ROWLAND, John, 1907- 621.38800924 B
The television man: the story of John Logie Baird. New York, Roy Publishers [1967, c1966] 143 p. 21 cm. [TK6635.B3R6] 66-9601
1. Baird, John Logie, 1888-1945. I. Title.

TILTMAN, Ronald Frank, 1901- 621.388'0092'4 B
Baird of television, by Ronald F. Tiltman. New York, Arno Press, 1974. 219 p. illus. 23 cm. (Telecommunications) Reprint of the 1933 ed. published by Seeley Service, London. [TK6635.B3T53 1974] 74-4697 ISBN 0-405-06061-0
1. Baird, John Logie, 1888-1945. 2. Television. I. Title. II. Series: Telecommunications (New York, 1974-)

Baird, Spencer Fullerton, 1823-1887.

ALLARD, Dean C., 1933- 591'.092'4 B
Spencer Fullerton Baird and the U.S. Fish Commission / Dean Conrad Allard, Jr. New York : Arno Press, 1978, c1967. p. cm. (Biologists and their world) Reprint of the author's thesis: George Washington University, 1967. Bibliography: p. [QH31.B17A44 1978] 77-81138 ISBN 0-405-10738-2 : 25.00
1. Baird, Spencer Fullerton, 1823-1887. 2. United States. Bureau of Fisheries—Biography. 3. Naturalists—United States—Biography. I. Title. II. Series.

BAIRD, Spencer Fullerton, 1823-1887. 925.9
Correspondence between Spencer Fullerton Baird and Louis Agassiz--two pioneer American naturalists. Collected and edited by Elmer Charles Herber. Washington, Smithsonian Institution, 1963. 237 p. illus., ports., facsims. 24 cm. (Smithsonian Institution. Publication 4515) [QL21.U6B3 1963] 63-61889
1. Zoology—U.S. 2. Science—Hist.—U.S. I. Agassiz, Louis, 1807-1873. II. Herber, Elmer Charles, ed. III. Title.

Baird, William M., 1862-1931.

BAIRD, Richard H., 1898- 266.5'0924 B
William M. Baird of Korea; a profile. [By Richard H. Baird. Oakland, Calif., 1968] A-D, 241 p. illus., facsims., maps, ports. 29 cm. Cover title. Bibliography: p. 211-212. [BV3462.B3B3] 76-2539 4.75
1. Baird, William M., 1862-1931. 2. Missions—Korea. 3. Presbyterian Church—Missions. 4. Missions—Educational work. I. Title.

Baker, Augustine, 1575-1641.

LOW, Anthony, 1935- 282'.0924 B
Augustine Baker. New York, Twayne Publishers [1970] 170 p. 21 cm. (Twayne's English authors series, 104) Bibliography: p. 155-165. [BX4705.B12L68] 74-99527
1. Baker, Augustine, 1575-1641.

Baker, Cullen Montgomery, 1835-1869.

BARTHOLOMEW, Ed Ellsworth. 923.973
Cullen Baker, premier Texas gunfighter; illustrated from the Rose collection. Houston, Frontier Press of Texas, 1954. 139p. illus., ports. 23cm. 'Life of the notorious desperado, Cullen Baker, from his childhood to his death, with a full account of all the murders he committed. Thos. Orr, editor': p. 85-132. [F594.B22B3] 54-2735
1. Baker, Cullen Montgomery, 1835-1869. 2. Texas—Hist. 3. Frontier and pioneer life—The West. I. Orr, Thomas, ed. Life of the notorious desperado, Cullen Baker. II. Title.

Baker, Daisy, 1894-

BAKER, Daisy, 1894- 942.3'52'08570924 B
More travels in a donkey trap / by Daisy Baker ; illustrated by Pamela Mara. London : Souvenir Press, 1976. 191 p., plate : ill., map, col. port. ; 21 cm. [CT788.B244A36 1976b] 76-377880 ISBN 0-285-62217-X : £3.00
1. Baker, Daisy, 1894- 2. England—Biography. I. Title.

BAKER, Daisy, 1894- 942.3'52'08570924 B
More travels in a donkey trap / Daisy Baker : illustrated by Pamela Mara. Boston : G. K. Hall, 1976. 265 p. : ill. ; 24 cm. "Published in large print." [CT788.B244A36] 76-44317 ISBN 0-8161-6430-4 lib. bdg. : 10.95
1. Baker, Daisy, 1894- 2. England—Biography. 3. Sight-saving books. I. Title.

BAKER, Daisy, 1894- 942.3'52'08570924 B
Travels in a donkey trap / Daisy Baker. London : Coronet, 1976. 160 p. : ill. ; 18 cm. [CT788.B244A37 1976] 77-350104 ISBN 0-340-20303-X : £0.60
1. Baker, Daisy, 1894- 2. England—Biography. I. Title.

BAKER, Daisy, 1894- 942.3'52
Travels in a donkey trap / Daisy Baker ; illustrated by Pamela Mara. Boston : G. K. Hall, 1975, c1974. 196 p. : ill. ; 25 cm. "Published in large print." [CT788.B244A37 1975] 75-4831 ISBN 0-8161-6273-5 lib.bdg. : 7.95 6.95
1. Baker, Daisy, 1894- 2. Sight-saving books. I. Mara, Pamela. II. Title.

Baker, Dan M., 1842-1902.

SLEEPER, Jim. 917.94'96'0340924 B
Turn the rascals out : The life and times of Orange County's fighting editor Dan M. Baker / by Jim Sleeper. 1st ed. Trabuco Canyon, Calif. : California Classics, c1973. xiv, 414 p. : ili. ; 23 cm. (California classics) Includes bibliographical references and index. [F868.O6S55] 74-187952
1. Baker, Dan M., 1842-1902. 2. Orange, Co., Calif.—History. I. Title.

Baker, Dorsey Syng, 1823-1888.

REYNOLDS, Helen (Baker) 923.873
Gold, rawhide and iron; the biography of Dorsey Syng Baker. Palo Alto, Calif., Pacific Books [1955] 191p. illus. 23cm. [CT275.B311R4] 55-13766
1. Baker, Dorsey Syng, 1823-1888. I. Title.

Baker, Edward Dickinson, 1811-1861.

BLAIR, Harry C. 923.273
The life of Colonel Edward D. Baker, Lincoln's constant ally, together with four of his great orations, by Harry C. Blair and Rebecca Tarshis. [Portland, Or.] 1960. xiii, 233 p. illus., ports., maps, facsims. 24 cm. "A Civil War memorial publication by the Oregon Historical Society." Bibliographical references included in "Footnotes" (p. 211-223) [E467.1.B16B55] 60-51575
1. Baker, Edward Dickinson, 1811-1861. I. Tarshis, Rebecca, joint author. II. Oregon Historical Society, Portland.

BLAIR, Harry C. 973.273
The life of Colonel Edward D. Baker, Lincoln's constant ally, together with four of his great orations, by Harry C. Blair and Rebecca Tarshis. [Portland, Or.] 1960. xiii, 233 p. illus., ports., maps. 24 cm. "A Civil War memorial publication by the Oregon Historical Society." Bibliographical references included in "Footnotes" (p. 211-223) [E467.1.B16B55] 60-51575
1. Baker, Edward Dickinson, 1811-1861. I. Tarshis, Rebecca, joint author. II. Oregon Historical Society, Portland.

Baker family.

WITTY, Kathryne Baker, 1897- 929'.2'0973
The William Thatcher Baker family, 1830-1971; biography of William Thatcher Baker and genealogical records, compiled 1971 by Kathryne Baker witty and Alma Baker Rea. Coat of arms from the geneaolgy of the Baker family by Albert C. Baker, Decorah, Iowa, 1920 [Lubbock? Tex., 1971?] 185, 22 p. 29 cm. "Supplement: James Jackson Beeman family history": 22 p. (at end) [CS71.B17 1971] 72-186113
1. Baker family. 2. Beaman family. I. Rea, Alma Baker, 1898- joint author. II. Title.

Baker, George Pierce, 1866-1935.

KINNE, Wisner Payne. 927.92
George Pierce Baker and the American theatre. Cambridge, Harvard University Press, 1954. xiv, 348p. illus., ports., facsims. 25cm. Includes bibliographies. [PN2287.B15K5] 54-8632
1. Baker, George Pierce, 1866-1935. 2. Drama—Study and teaching. 3. American drama—20th cent.—Hist. & crit. 4. Theater—U. S. I. Title. BIP

KINNE, Wisner Payne. 792'.0924
George Pierce Baker and the American theatre. New York, Greenwood Press, 1968 [c1954] xiv, 348 p. illus., ports. 24 cm. Includes bibliographies. [PN2287.B15K5 1968] 68-8741
1. Baker, George Pierce, 1866-1935. 2. Drama—Study and teaching. 3. American drama—20th century—History and criticism. 4. Theatre—United States. I. Title.

Baker, George, self-named Father Divine.

HARRIS, Sara. 289.9 B
Father Divine, by Sara Harris, with the assistance of Harriet Crittendon [i.e.] Crittenden. Newly rev. and expanded, and with an introd. by John Henrik Clarke. New York, Collier Books [1971] xxxiv, 377 p. 19 cm. [BX7350.H37 1971] 78-146617
1. Baker, George, self-named Father Divine. I. Crittenden, Harriet, joint author. BIP

HARRIS, Sara. 922
Father Divine, holy husband, by Sara Harris, with the assistance of Harriet Crittenden. [1st ed.] Garden City, N.Y., Doubleday, 1953. 320 p. 22 cm. [BX7350.H37] 53-9989
1. Baker, George, self-named Father Divine.

HOSHOR, John. 289.9 B
God in a Rolls Royce; the rise of Father Divine: madman, menace, or messiah. Freeport, N.Y., Books for Libraries Press, 1971. 272 p. illus., ports. 23 cm. (The Black heritage library collection) Reprint of the 1936 ed. [BX7350.H6 1971] 70-170698 ISBN 0-8369-8888-4

1. Baker, George, self-named Father Divine. I. Title. II. Series.

Baker, Hattie Price,

BAKER, Hattie Price, 362.30924(B)
1882-
My journey of life; written in my golden years. San Antonio, Naylor [1966] xiv, 37p. illus., ports. 20cm. [CT275.B3125A3] 66-25599 3.95
I. Title.

Baker, Hobart Amory Hare, 1892-1918.

DAVIES, John Dunn, 796.3320924 B
1918-
The legend of Hobey Baker [by] John Davies. [1st ed.] Boston, Little, Brown [1966] xxiii, 116 p. illus., facsims., ports. 27 cm. [GV939.B3D3] 66-12874
1. Baker, Hobart Amory Hare, 1892-1918. I. Title.

Baker, John, d. 1970.

BUCHANAN, William J., 796.4'26 B
1926-
A shining season / William Buchanan. New York : Coward, McCann & Geoghegan, c1978. 249 p., [8] leaves of plates : ill. ; 22 cm. [GV697.B25B8] 78-11303 ISBN 0-698-10888-4 : 8.95
1. Baker, John, d. 1970. 2. Runners (Sports)—United States—Biography. 3. Cancer—Biography. I. Title. **BIP**

Baker, Josephine, 1906-1975.

BAKER, Josephine, 793.3'2'0924 B
1906-1975.
Josephine / by Josephine Baker and Jo Bouillon ; translated from the French by Mariana Fitzpatrick. 1st ed. New York : Harper & Row, c1977. p. cm. Includes index. [GV1785.B3A2913 1977] 76-26212 ISBN 0-06-010212-8 : 12.95
1. Baker, Josephine, 1906-1975. 2. Dancers—Biography. I. Bouillon, Joseph, 1908- joint author. II. Title.

PAPICH, Stephen. 793.3'2'0924 B
Remembering Josephine Baker / by Stephen Papich. Indianapolis : Bobbs-Merrill, [c1976.] xviii, 237 p., [16] leaves of plates : ill. ; 27 cm. Includes index. [GV1785.B3P36] 76-16628 ISBN 0-672-52257-8 : 15.00
1. Baker, Josephine, 1906-1975. 2. Dancing. I. Title.

Baker. LaFayette Charles. 1826-1868.

MILLARD, Joseph 920.8
No law but their own. Evanston [Ill.] Regency [c.1963] 158p. 18cm. (RB324) 63-6107 .50 pap.,
1. Baker, Lafayette Charles, 1626-1868. 2. Boyle, Joseph Whiteside. 3. Streeter, George Wellington, 1837-1921. I. Title.

ORRMONT, Arthur 973.70924
Mr. Lincoln's master spy: Lafayette Baker. New York, Messner [1966] 191p. 22cm. Bibl. [E608.B188] 66-7505 3.25; 3.19 lib. ed.,
1. Baker. LaFayette Charles. 1826-1868. 2. U.S.—Hist.—Civil War—Secret service. I. Title.

Baker, Lorenzo Dow, 1840-1908.

BATCHELDER, Charles 923.373
Foster, 1898-
Tropic gold; the story of the banana pioneer, Captain Lorenzo Dow Baker. [Boston?] W. D. Bradstreet, '1951. 105 l. 28 cm. Bibliography: leaves 102-105. [HD9259.B3J33] 51-3170
1. Baker, Lorenso Dow, 1840-1908. 2. Banana. I. Title.

Baker, Lorenzo Dow, 1840-1908—Juvenile literature.

WILSON, Charles 387'.0924 B
Morrow, 1905-
Dow Baker and the great banana fleet; the story of the Yankee skipper who befriended an island and introduced bananas to America. [Harrisburg, Pa.] Stackpole Books [1972] 128 p. illus. 22 cm. A biography of the nineteenth-century sea captain who introduced the banana to the United States by being the first to ship the fruit from Jamaica. [HD9259.B2W53] 92 77-179601 ISBN 0-8117-0532-3
1. Baker, Lorenzo Dow, 1840-1908—Juvenile literature. 2. Banana—Juvenile literature. I. Title.

Baker, Nelson Henry.

ANDERSON, Floyd, 1906- 922.273
Father Baker. Milwaukee*ruce Pub. Co. [1960] 151p. illus. 22cm. [HV885.L3A7] 60-13938
1. Baker, Nelson Henry. 2. Lackawana, N. Y. Our Lady of Victory Homes of Charity. I. Title.

ANDERSON, Floyd [Edward] 922.273
Father Baker. Milwaukee, Bruce Pub. Co. [c.1960] viii, 151p. illus. 22cm. 60-13938 3.00
1. Baker, Nelson Henry. 2. Lackawanna, N. Y. Our Lady of Victory Homes of Charity. I. Title.

Baker, Newton Diehl, 1871-1937.

CRAMER, Clarence H. 923.273
Newton D. Baker, a biography. [1st ed.] Cleveland, World Pub. Co. [1961] 310 p. illus. 22 cm. Includes bibliography. [E748.B265C7] 61-5805
1. Baker, Newton Diehl, 1871-1937.

Baker, Pearl Biddlecome.

BAKER, Pearl 979.2'03'0924
Biddlecome.
Robbers Roost recollections / Pearl Baker. Logan : Utah State University Press, [1976] p. cm. [F826.B169] 76-4915 ISBN 0-87421-083-6
1. Baker, Pearl Biddlecome. 2. Ranch life—Utah. 3. Utah—Biography. I. Title. **BIP**

Baker, Ray Stannard, 1870-1946.

BANNISTER, Robert C., 818.5208
Jr.
Ray Stannard Baker; the mind and thought of a progressive. New Haven, Conn., Yale [c.]1966. xiv. 335p. group ports. 24cm. (Yale pubns. in Amer. studies, 10) [CT275.B313B3] 66-12486 7.50
1. Baker, Ray Stannard, 1870-1946. I. Title. II. Series.

RAND, Frank Prentice, 1889- 928.1
The story of David Grayson. Amherst, Mass., Jones Lib. [c.]1963. ix, 160p. front. 20cm. 63-25097 3.95
1. Baker, Ray Stannard, 1870-1946. I. Title.

SEMONCHE, John E. 070.9'24 B
Ray Stannard Baker; a quest for democracy in modern America, 1870-1918, by John E. Semonche. Chapel Hill, University of North Carolina Press [1969] ix, 350 p. port. 24 cm. Bibliography: p. [319]-338. [CT275.B313S4] 69-16215 8.95
1. Baker, Ray Stannard, 1870-1946.

Baker, Richard St. Barbe,

BAKER, Richard St. Barbe, 926.349
1889-
Dance of the trees (the adventures of a forester) With a foreword by Arthur Bryant. London, Oldbourne Press [1956; covered by label: Belmont, Mass., Wellington Books, 1960] [[SD129]] A62
I. Title.

Baker, Robert Gene.

ROWE, Robert, 1941- 973.923'0924
The Bobby Baker story. [New York] Parallax Pub. Co.; distributed by Simon & Schuster [1967] 157 p. 18 cm. [E840.8.B3R6] 67-7084
1. Baker, Robert Gene. I. Title.

Bakker, Jim.

BAKKER, Jim. 269'.2'0924 B
Move that mountain / by Jim Bakker with Robert Paul Lamb. 1st ed. Plainfield, N.J. : Logos International, 1976. vii, 183 p., [4] leaves of plates : ill. ; 21 cm. [BV3785.B3A35] 76-10532 ISBN 0-88270-164-9 : 5.95
1. Bakker, Jim. 2. Evangelists—United States—Biography. 3. Television in religion. I. Lamb, Robert Paul, joint author. II. Title. **BIP**

Bakst, Lev Samoilovich, 1866-1924.

LEVINSON, Andrei 759.47
IAkovlevich, 1887-1933.
Bakst, the story of the artist's life. New York, B. Blom, 1971. 240 p. illus., 68 plates, ports. 27 cm. "First published 1923." [ND699.B3L36 1971] 68-57182
1. Bakst, Lev Samoilovich, 1866-1924.

Bakunin, Mikhail Aleksandrovich, 1814-1876.

ALDRED, Guy 335'.83'0924 B
Alfred, 1886-1963.
Bakunin. New York, Haskell House Publishers, 1971. 70 p. port. 23 cm. (His "The Word" library, 2d ser., no. 1) Reprint of the 1940 ed. Bibliography: p. 64-68. [HX915.B3A4 1971] 79-179272 ISBN 0-8383-1259-4
1. Bakunin, Mikhail Aleksandrovich, 1814-1876. **BIP**

BAKUNIN, Mikhail 335'.83'0924 B
Aleksandrovich, 1814-1876.
The confession of Mikhail Bakunin : with the marginal comments of Tsar Nicholas I / translated by Robert C. Howes ; introduction and notes by Lawrence D. Orton. Ithaca, N.Y. : Cornell University Press, 1977. 200 p. : port. ; 22 cm. Translation of Ispoved'. Includes bibliographical references and index. [HX915.B22313] 76-25646 ISBN 0-8014-1073-8 : 12.50
1. Bakumin, Mikhail Aleksandrovich, 1814-1876. 2. Anarchism and anarchists—Biography. I. Orton, Lawrence D. II. Title.

CARR, Edward Hallett, 923.347
1892-
Michael Bakunin [Gloucester, Mass., P. Smith, 1965. c.1937] 511p. 19cm. (Vintage Russian lib., V-725 Rebound) [HX915.B3C3] 3.50
1. Bakunin, Mikhail Aleksandrovich, 1814-1876. 2. Anarchism and anarchists. I. Title. **BIP**

CARR, Edward Hallett, 923.347
1892-
Michael Bakunin. [1st ed.] New York, Vintage Books [1961, c1937] 511p. 19cm. (Vintage Russian library, V-725) [HX915.B3C3 1961] 61-2306
1. Bakunin, Mikhail Aleksandrovich, 1814-1876. 2. Anarchism and anarchists. I. Title.

CARR, Edward 335'.83'0924 B
Hallett, 1892-
Michael Bakunin / by E. H. Carr. Reissued with minor alterations. New York : Octagon Books, 1975. x, 501 p. : port. ; 23 cm. "First published in the United Kingdom 1937." Includes index. Bibliography: p. 489-491. [HX915.B3C3 1975] 74-21517 ISBN 0-374-91296-3 : 27.50
1. Bakunin, Mikhail Aleksandrovich, 1814-1876. 2. Anarchism and anarchists.

CARR. EDWARD HALLETT, 923.347
1892-
Michael Bakunin. New York, [dist.] Random House [1961, c.1937] 511p. (Vintage Russian Lib. V725) Bibl. 1.45 pap.,
1. Bakunin, Makhail Aleksandrovich, 1814-1876. 2. Anarchism and anarchists. I. Title.

MASTERS, Anthony, 335'.83'0924 B
1940-
Bakunin, the father of anarchism / Anthony Masters. 1st American ed. New York : Saturday Review Press, 1974. xxiii, 279 p. : ill. ; 24 cm. Includes index. Bibliography: p. 269-271. [HX915.B3M37 1974b] 74-7892 ISBN 0-8415-0295-1 : 9.95
1. Bakunin, Mikhail Aleksandrovich, 1814-1876. I. Title.

Balaban, Majer, 1877-1943.

BIDERMAN, Israel 943.8'07'2024 B
M., 1911-1973.
Mayer Balaban, historian of Polish Jewry : his influence on the younger generation of Jewish historians / by Israel M. Biderman. New York : I. M. Biderman Book Committee, 1976. xxv, 334 p. : ill. ; 24 cm. Includes indexes. Bibliography: p. 309-326. [DS115.9.B3B5 1976] 76-6800 15.00
1. Balaban, Majer, 1877-1943. 2. Historians, Jewish—Poland—Biography. 3. Jews in Poland—Historiography. 4. Poland—Historiography. I. Title.

Balabanoff, Angelica, 1878-1965.

BALABANOFF, 335.43'092'4 B
Angelica, 1878-1965.
My life as a rebel [by] Angelica Balabanoff. Bloomington, Indiana University Press [1973, c1938] ix, 324 p. 21 cm. (Classics in Russian studies) [HX312.B3 1973] 72-88914 ISBN 0-253-15485-5 3.50
1. Balabanoff, Angelica, 1878-1965. 2. Communism—History. 3. Socialism—History. I. Title.

FLORENCE, Ronald. 335.4'0922 B
Marx's daughters : Eleanor Marx, Rosa Luxemburg, Angelica Balabanoff / Ronald Florence. New York : Dial Press, 1975. 258 p., [4] leaves of plates : ill. ; 24 cm. Includes index. Bibliography: p. 237-243. [HX23.F55] 75-9576 ISBN 0-8037-5432-9 : 10.00
1. Aveling, Eleanor Marx, 1855-1898. 2. Luxemburg, Rosa, 1870-1919. 3. Balabanoff, Angelica, 1878-1965. 4. Marx, Karl, 1818-1883. I. Title. **BIP**

Balanchine, George.

TAPER, Bernard, 927.933
Balanchine. [1st ed.] New York, Harper & Row [c1963] 342 p. illus., ports. 26 cm. Appendix (p. 317-332): A chronological list of Balanchine's ballets.--Musicals with choreography by Balanchine.--Motion pictures with choreography by Balanchine. [GV1785.B32T3] 62-14549
1. Balanchine, George. I. Title.

Balboa, Vasco Nunez de, 1475-1519.

ANDERSON, Charles 973.1'7'0924 B
Loftus Grant, 1863-1952.
Life and letters of Vasco Nunez de Balboa, including the conquest and settlement of Darien and Panama, the odyssey of the discovery of the South sea, a description of the splendid armada to Castilla del Oro, and the execution of the adelantado at Acla; a history of the first years of the introduction of Christian civilization on the continent of America. Introd. by Ricardo J. Alfaro. Westport, Conn., Greenwood Press [1970, c1941] 368 p. illus., coat of arms, maps. 23 cm. [E125.B2A5 1970] 70-100140 ISBN 0-8371-3242-8
1. Balboa, Vasco Nunez de, 1475-1519. I. Title.

MIRSKY, Jeannette, 1903- 920
Balboa: discoverer of the Pacific. E. by Walter Lord. Pictures by Hans Guggenheim. New York, Harper [c.1964] 164p. illus., port. 22cm. (Breakthrough bk.) Bibl. 64-11834 2.95;2.92 lib. ed.,
1. Balboa, Vasco Nunez de, 1475-1519—Juvenile literature. I. Title.

ROMOLI, Kathleen. 923.946
Balboa of Darien, discoverer of the Pacific. [1st ed.] Garden City, N. Y., Doubleday, 1953. xv, 431 p. maps. 22 cm. Bibliography: p. 406-416. [E125.B2R6] 53-9142
1. Balboa, Vasco Nunez de, 1475-1519?

STERNE, Emma (Gelders) 1894- 92
Vasco Nunez de Balboa. Illustrated by Leonard Everett Fisher. [1st ed.] New York, Knopf, 1961. 147 p. illus. 21 cm. [E125.B2S88] 60-8600
1. Balboa, Vasco Nunez de, 1475-1549 — Juvenile literature. I. Title.

Balboa, Vasco Nunez de, 1475-1519—Juvenile literature.

EDUCATIONAL 973.1'6'0924 B Research Council of America. Social Science Staff.
Explorers and discoverers, Balboa / prepared by the Social Science Staff of the Educational Research Council of America. Learner-verified ed. 2. Boston : Allyn and Bacon, [1974] 34 p. : col. ill. ; 21 cm. (Concepts and inquiry, the ERC social science program) Briefly relates the travels of the Spanish explorer who found gold in the New World and discovered the Pacific Ocean. [E125.B2E3 1974] 92 73-78339 pbk. : 1.76
1. Balboa, Vasco Nunez de, 1475-1519—Juvenile literature. I. Title. II. Series: Concepts and inquiry: the Educational Research Council social science program.

KNOOP, Faith Yingling. 910'.924 B
A world explorer: Vasco Nunez de Balboa. Illustrated by Victor Dowd. Champaign, Ill., Garrard Pub. Co. [1969] 96 p. col. illus., map (on lining papers) 24 cm. (World explorer books) A biography stressing the honesty and integrity of the Spanish explorer whose explorations of the northern coast of South America led him to discover the Pacific Ocean. [E125.B2K59] 92 69-10372 2.32
1. Balboa, Vasco Nunez de, 1475-1519—Juvenile literature. I. Dowd, Victor, illus. II. Title.

MIRSKY, Jeannette, 1903- 92
Balboa: discoverer of the Pacific. Edited by Walter Lord. Pictures by Hans Guggenheim. New York, Harper & Row [1964] 164 p. illus., port. 22 cm. (A breakthrough book) Bibliography: p. 144-146. [E125.B2M6] 64-11834
1. Balboa, Vasco Nunez de, 1475-1519 — Juvenile literature. I. Title. BIP

NOBLE, Iris. 910'.924 B
The honor of Balboa. New York, J. Messner [1970] 189 p. 22 cm. Bibliography: p. 183-184. A biography of the first European to see the Pacific Ocean. [E125.B2N6] 92 79-100563 3.50
1. Balboa, Vasco Nunez de, 1475-1519—Juvenile literature. I. Title.

ROMOLI, Kathleen 923.946
Balboa of Darien, discoverer of the Pacific. Garden City, N.Y., Doubleday [1961, c.1953] 474p. (Dolphin, C 162) Bibl. .95 pap.,
1. Balboa, Vasco Nunez de, 1475-1519? I. Title.

STERNE, Emma (Gelders) 1894- 92
Vasco Nunez de Balboa. Illustrated by Leonard Everett Fisher. [1st ed.] New York, Knopf, 1961. 147 p. illus. 21 cm. [E125.B2S88] 60-8600
1. Balboa, Vasco Nunez de, 1475-1549 — Juvenile literature. I. Title.

Balch, Emily Greene, 1867-1961.

RANDALL, Mercedes Moritz, 923.373 1896-
Improper Bostonian: Emily Greene Balch, Nobel peace laureate, 1946, by Mercedes M. Randall. New York, Twayne Publishers [1964] 475 p. illus., ports. 22 cm. Bibliography: p. 447-460. [JX1965.R3] 64-25058
1. Balch, Emily Greene, 1867-1961. 2. Women and peace. I. Title.

Balch, Frederic Homer, 1861-1891.

WILEY, Leonard. 813'.4 B
The granite boulder: a biography of Frederic Homer Balch, author of The bridge of the gods. [1st ed.] Portland, Or., 1970. 146 p. illus., facsim., ports. 23 cm. Bibliography: p. 143-146. [BX7260.B175W54] 77-123297
1. Balch, Frederic Homer, 1861-1891. I. Title.

Balchen, Bernt, 1899-

BALCHEN, Bernt, 1899- 926.29
Come north with me, an autobiography. [lst ed.] New York, Dutton, 1958. 313 p. illus. 22 cm. [G585.B3A3] 58-5242
1. Arctic regions. 2. Antarctic regions. 3. Aeronautics—Flights. I. Title.

KNIGHT, Clayton, 1891- 926.29
Hitch your wagon; the story of Bernt Balchen, by Clayton Knight and Robert C. Durham. Decorations by Clayton Knight. Drexel Hill, Pa., Bell Pub. Co. [1950] xi, 332 p. illus., ports., maps (on lining papers) 22 cm. [TL540.B35K6] 50-5788
1. Balchen, Bernt, 1899- I. Durham, Robert C., joint author. II. Title.

Baldaccini, Cesar, 1921—

RESTANY, Pierre. 730'.92'4
Cesar / text by Pierre Restany ; translated by John Shepley. New York : H. N. Abrams, [1975] p. cm. Includes index. Bibliography: p. [NB553.B22R4713] 74-30064 ISBN 0-8109-0358-X : 45.00
1. Baldaccini, Cesar, 1921- I. Title. BIP

Baldrige, Letitia.

BALDRIGE, 917.3'03'920924 Letitia.
Of diamonds and diplomats. Boston, Houghton Mifflin, 1968. 337 p. 22 cm. Autobiographical. [CT275.B316A3] 68-26055 6.95
I. Title.

Baldwin, Dwight, 1796-1886.

ALEXANDER, Mary 922.5969 Charlotte, 1874-
Dr. Baldwin of Lahaina. Berkeley, Calif., 1953. 359p. illus. 24cm. [BV3680.H4B3] 54-17449
1. Baldwin, Dwight, 1796-1886. I. Title.

Baldwin family.

BALDWIN, Thomas, 973'.04'97 b.1750?
Narrative of the massacre of my wife and children / Thomas Baldwin. New York : Garland Pub., 1977. 24 p., [1] fold. leaf of plates : ill. ; 23 cm. (The Garland library of narratives of North American Indian captivities ; v. 52) Issued with the reprint of the 1833 ed. of Priest, J. The captivity and sufferings of Gen. Freegift Patchin. New York, 1977. Reprint of the 1835 ed. published by Martin and Wood, New York, under title: Narrative of the massacre, by the savages, of the wife and children of Thomas Baldwin .... [E85.G2 vol. 52] [E87] 76-51390 ISBN 0-8240-1676-9(set) lib.bdg. : 25.00
1. Baldwin family. 2. Baldwin, Thomas, b. 1750? 3. Indians of North America—Captivities. 4. Frontier and pioneer life—Kentucky. 5. Kentucky—Biography. I. Title. II. Series.

Baldwin, Joseph Clark.

BALDWIN, Joseph Clark. 923.273
Flowers for the judge. New York, Coward-McCann [1950] ix, 210 p. illus. 21 cm. Autobiographical. [E748.B27A3 1950] 50-9894
I. Title.

Baldwin, Joseph, 1827-1899.

KNIGHT, Homer L. 370'.8 S
Joseph Baldwin: pioneer educator, by Homer L. Knight. Kirksville [Northeast Missouri State Teachers College] 1957 [c1959] 41 p. port. 19 cm. (The Baldwin lecture, 1957) [LB1705.B3 1957] [LB1900] 378.1'12'0924 74-184697
1. Baldwin, Joseph, 1827-1899. 2. Missouri. Northeast Missouri State Teachers College, Kirksville. I. Title. II. Series.

Baldwin, Simeon Eben, 1840-1927.

JACKSON, Frederick 923.473 Herbert, 1919-
Simeon Eben Baldwin: lawyer, social scientist, statesman. Foreword by Charles E. Clark. New York, King's Crown Press, Columbia University, 1955. 291p. illus. 24cm. 'Developed from ... [the author's] doctoral dissertation accepted by the University of Pennsylvania in 1950.' 54-12724
1. Baldwin, Simeon Eben, 1840-1927. I. Title.

Baldwin, Stanley Baldwin. 1st earl. 1867-1947.

BALDWIN, Arthur Windham 923.242 3d earl 1904-
My father: the true story. London, Allen Unwin [1955 label Fair Lawn, N. J., Essential books] 360p. illus. 23cm. [DA566.9.B15B3] 56-13643
1. Baldwin, Stanley Baldwin. 1st earl. 1867-1947. I. Title.

MIDDLEMAS, Robert 942.082'0924 B Keith, 1935-
Baldwin; a biography [by] Keith Middlemas [and] John Barnes. [1st American ed. New York] Macmillan [1970, c1969] xvii, 1149 p. illus., facsim., ports. 25 cm. Includes bibliographical references. [DA566.9.B15M5 1970] 70-87902 14.95
1. Baldwin, Stanley, Baldwin, 1st earl, 1867-1947. I. Barnes, Anthony John Lane, joint author.

YOUNG, George 941.083'092'4 B Malcolm, 1882-1959.
Stanley Baldwin / G. M. Young. Westport, Conn. : Greenwood Press, 1979. 266 p., [7] leaves of plates : ill. ; 23 cm. Reprint of the 1952 ed. published by R. Hart-Davis, London. Includes index. [DA566.9.B15Y6 1979] 78-12301 ISBN 0-313-21041-1 lib. bdg. : 21.50
1. Baldwin, Stanley Baldwin, 1st Earl, 1867-1947. 2. Prime ministers—Great Britain—Biography. BIP

YOUNG, Kenneth, 941.083'092'4 B 1916-
Stanley Baldwin / Kenneth Young ; introd. by A. J. P. Taylor. London : Weidenfeld and Nicolson, c1976. xi, 161 p., [4] leaves of plates : ill., ports. ; 23 cm. ([British Prime Ministers]) Includes index. Bibliography: p. 150-151. [DA566.9.B15Y64] 76-372472 ISBN 0-297-77100-0 : £4.75
1. Baldwin, Stanley Baldwin, 1st Earl, 1867-1947. 2. Prime ministers—Great Britain—Biography.

Bales, Charles F., 1897-

BALES, Charles F., 973.9'092'4 B 1897-
Twice a boy / by Charles F. Bales. Terre Haute, Ind. : Sycamore Press, c1976. xi, 127 p. : ill. ; 23 cm. [CT275.B344A37] 77-150224
1. Bales, Charles F., 1897- 2. United States—Biography. I. Title. BIP

Balfe, Michael William, 1808-1870.

†KENNEY, Charles 782.1'092'4 B Lamb, 1821-1881.
A memoir of Michael William Balfe / by Charles Lamb Kenney. New York : Da Capo Press, 1978. x, 309 p. ; 23 cm. (Da Capo Press music reprint series) Reprint of the 1875 ed. published by Tinsley Bros., London. [ML410.B18K3 1978] 77-13360 19.50
1. Balfe, Michael William, 1808-1870. 2. Composers—Ireland—Biography. BIP

Balfour, Arthur James Balfour, 1st Earl of, 1848-1930.

DUGDALE, Blanche 942.082'0924 B Elizabeth Campbell (Balfour)
Arthur James Balfour, first Earl of Balfour, K.G., O.M., F.R.S., etc. Westport, Conn., Greenwood Press [1970] 2 v. illus., geneal. table, ports. 23 cm. Reprint of the 1936 ed. Includes bibliographical references. [DA566.9.B2D8 1970] 70-97328
1. Balfour, Arthur James Balfour, 1st Earl of, 1848-1930. 2. Gt. Brit.—Politics and government—1837-1901. 3. Gt. Brit.—Politics and government—20th century.

ZEBEL, Sydney Henry, 942.08'092'4 1914-
Balfour; a political biography [by] Sydney H. Zebel. Cambridge [Eng.] University Press, 1973. viii, 312 p. 23 cm. (Conference on British Studies. Biographical series) Bibliography: p. 294-299. [DA566.9.B2Z42 1973] 70-190421 ISBN 0-521-08536-5
1. Balfour, Arthur James Balfour, 1st Earl of, 1848-1930. I. Title. II. Series. Distributed by Cambridge University Pr. N.Y.; 14.95.

Balfour, Conrad, 1928-

BALFOUR, Conrad, 977.6'05'0924 B 1928-
A sack full of sun. Minneapolis, Dillon Press [1974] 169 p. facsim. 21 cm. Autobiographical. [E185.97.B2A36] 74-8763 ISBN 0-87518-074-4 6.95
1. Balfour, Conrad, 1928- I. Title.

Ball, Amos Entheus.

BALL, Amos 971.9'1'020924 B Entheus.
Tenderfoot to sourdough : the true adventures of Amos Entheus Ball in the Klondike gold rush as told in his own words / by Hazel T. Procter. New Holland, Pa. : E. C. Procter, 1975. xii, 94 p. : ill. ; 22 cm. [F931.B33] 74-31818
1. Ball, Amos Entheus. 2. Klondike gold fields. I. Procter, Hazel T. II. Title.

Ball, Edward, 1888-

MASON, Raymond K. 338'.092'4 B
Confusion to the enemy : a biography of Edward Ball / Raymond K. Mason and Virginia Harrison ; illustrated with photos. New York : Dodd, Mead & Co., c1975. p. cm. [HC102.5.B34M37] 75-29088 10.00
1. Ball, Edward, 1888- 2. Florida—Industries. I. Harrison, Virginia W., joint author. II. Title.

Ball family.

BALL, Roy Hutton, 929'.2'0973 1898-
Conquering the frontiers; a biography and history of one branch of the Ball family. Oklahoma City, Lithographed by Semco Color Press [1956] 93p. illus., ports. 29cm. [CS71.B2 1956] 58-25412
1. Ball family. I. Title.

Ball, Hannah, 1733-1792.

MCQUAID, Ina DeBord 922.742
Miss Hannah Ball, a lady of High Wycomb. New York, Vantage [c.1964] 160p. illus. 21cm. Bibl. 64-57884 3.75 bds.,
1. Ball, Hannah, 1733-1792. I. Title.

Ball, Lucille Desiree, 1911-

*GREGORY, James. 792'.092'4
The Lucille Ball story. [New York], New American Library, [1974] 210 p., illus., 18 cm. (Signet, W5833) [PN2598] 1.50 (pbk.)
1. Ball, Lucille Desiree, 1911- I. Title.

HARRIES, Elanor. 927.92
The real story of Lucille Ball. New York, Farrar, Straus and Young [1954] 119p. illus. 18cm. (Ballantine books, 78) [PN2287.B16H3] 54-8217
1. Ball, Lucille, 1911- I. Title.

Ball, Lucille, 1911- —Juvenile literature.

PAIGE, David. 791'.092'4 B
Lucille Ball / written by David Paige ; designed by Gene Kohler. [Mankato, Minn.] : Creative Education, [c1977] 31 p. : ill. ; 25 cm. (Stars of stage and screen) A biography of Lucille Ball, a versatile entertainer who has appeared in movie, stage, and television productions. [PN2287.B16P3] 92 76-28776 ISBN 0-87191-557-X lib.bdg. 4.95
1. Ball, Lucille, 1911- —Juvenile literature. 2. Entertainers—United States—Biography—Juvenile literature. I. Title. BIP

Ball, Mary.

EARL, Lawrence 926.1073
She loved a wicked city; the story of Mary Ball, missionary. New York, Dutton [c.] 1962. 240p. illus. 21cm. Pub. in London under title. One foreign devil. 62-7813 4.50
1. Ball, Mary. I. Title.

Ball, Thomas, 1819-1911.

BALL, Thomas, 1819- 730'.92'4 B
1911.
My threescore years and ten : an authobiography / by Thomas Ball. 2d ed. New York : Garland Pub., 1977, c1891. 13, xi, 379 p., [5] leaves of plates ; ill. ; 19 cm. (The Art experience in late nineteenth-century America) Reprint of the 1892 ed. published by Roberts Bros., Boston; with new introd. [NB237.B3A25 1977] 75-28884 ISBN 0-8240-2242-4 : 25.00
1. Ball, Thomas, 1819-1911. 2. Sculptors—United States—Biography. I. Title. II. Series.

Ball, William Watts, 1868-1952.

STARK, John D. 070'.924 B
Damned upcountryman: William Watts Ball; a study in American conservatism, by John D. Stark. Durham, N.C., Duke University Press, 1968. 248 p. 25 cm. (Duke historical publications) Bibliography: p. [236]-239. [PN4874.B27S7] 68-57269 8.50
1. Ball, William Watts, 1868-1952. I. Title. II. Series.

Balla, Giacomo, 1871-1958.

DORAZIO, Virginia Dortch. 759.5
Giacomo Balla; an album of his life and work. Introd. by Giuseppe Ungaretti. New York, Wittenborn [1969?] 1 v. (unpaged) illus., facsims., ports. 23 x 25 cm. [N6923.B27D6] 70-140146 ISBN 0-8150-0405-2
1. Balla, Giacomo, 1871-1958.

Ballantyne, James, 1772-1833.

THE Ballantyne- 828'.7'09 B
Lockhart controversy, 1838-1839. New York, Garland Pub. Inc., 1974. 88, 122, 125, 97 p. 22 cm. (The English book trade, 1660-1853) Reprint of Refutation of the mistatements and calumnies contained in Mr Lockhart's Life of Sir Walter Scott, bart., respecting the Messrs Ballantyne, by the trustees and son of the late Mr James Ballantyne, first published in 1838 by Longman, Orme, Brown, Green, and Longmans, London; of The Ballantyne-humbug handled, in a letter to Sir Adam Fergusson, by J. G. Lockhart, first published in 1839 by R. Cadell, Edinburgh; and of Reply to Mr Lockhart's pamphlet, entitled, "The Ballantyne-humbug handled," by the authors of a Refutation of the mistatements and calumnies contained in Mr Lockhart's Life of Sir Walter Scott, bart., respecting the Messrs Ballantyne, first published in 1839 by Longman, Orme, Brown, Green, and Longmans, London. [PR5338.B35 1974] 74-13211 ISBN 0-8240-0986-X
1. Scott, Walter, Sir, bart., 1771-1832—Friends and associates. 2. Ballantyne, James, 1772-1833. 3. Ballantyne, John, 1774-1821. 4. Lockhart, John Gibson, 1794-1854. Life of Sir Walter Scott. 5. Lockhart, John Gibson, 1794-1854. The Ballantyne-humbug handled. I. Lockhart, John Gibson, 1794-1854. The Ballantyne-humbug handled. 1974. II. Refutation of the mistatements and calumnies contained in Mr Lockhart's Life of Sir Walter Scott, bart., respecting the Messrs. Ballantyne. 1974. III. Reply to Mr. Lockhart's pamphlet, entitled, "The Ballantyne-humbug handled." 1974. IV. Title. V. Series.

Ballantyne, John, 1774-1821.

THE Ballantyne- 828'.7'09 B
Lockhart controversy, 1838-1839. New York, Garland Pub. Inc., 1974. 88, 122, 125, 97 p. 22 cm. (The English book trade, 1660-1853) Reprint of Refutation of the mistatements and calumnies contained in Mr Lockhart's Life of Sir Walter Scott, bart., respecting the Messrs Ballantyne, by the trustees and son of the late Mr James Ballantyne, first published in 1838 by Longman, Orme, Brown, Green, and Longmans, London; of The Ballantyne-humbug handled, in a letter to Sir Adam Fergusson, by J. G. Lockhart, first published in 1839 by R. Cadell, Edinburgh; and of Reply to Mr Lockhart's pamphlet, entitled, "The Ballantyne-humbug handled," by the authors of a Refutation of the mistatements and calumnies contained in Mr Lockhart's Life of Sir Walter Scott, bart., respecting the Messrs Ballantyne, first published in 1839 by Longman, Orme, Brown, Green, and Longmans, London. [PR5338.B35 1974] 74-13211 ISBN 0-8240-0986-X
1. Scott, Walter, Sir, bart., 1771-1832—Friends and associates. 2. Ballantyne, James, 1772-1833. 3. Ballantyne, John, 1774-1821. 4. Lockhart, John Gibson, 1794-1854. Life of Sir Walter Scott. 5. Lockhart, John Gibson, 1794-1854. The Ballantyne-humbug handled. I. Lockhart, John Gibson, 1794-1854. The Ballantyne-humbug handled. 1974. II. Refutation of the mistatements and calumnies contained in Mr Lockhart's Life of Sir Walter Scott, bart., respecting the Messrs. Ballantyne. 1974. III. Reply to Mr. Lockhart's pamphlet, entitled, "The Ballantyne-humbug handled." 1974. IV. Title. V. Series.

Ballantyne, Robert Michael, 1825-1894.

BALLANTYNE the brave: 823'.8
a Victorian writer and his family. London, Hart-Davis, 1967. [13], 316p. front., 8 plates (incl. ports.), facsims. 23cm. [PR4057.B15Z83] (B) 67-85935 7.50 bds.,
1. Ballantyne, Robert Michael, 1825-1894. I. Quayle, Eric.
Distributed by Fernhill House, 162 E. 23d St., New York, N.Y. 10010. BIP

Ballard, Charles Littlepage, 1866-1950.

RICKARDS, Colin. 978.9'04'0924 B
Charles Littlepage Ballard, southwesterner. [El Paso, Texas Western Press] 1966. 40 p. ports. 23 cm. (Southwestern studies, v. 4, no. 4. Monograph no. 16) Cover title. Bibliography: p. 31-39. [F801.B2R5] 67-64689
1. Ballard, Charles Littlepage, 1866-1950. I. Series: Southwestern studies (El Paso, Tex.), v. 4, no. 4.

Ballard, Gussie Alexander.

BALLARD, Gussie Alexander. 920.7
Remember our yesterdays? New Orleans, Pelican Pub. Co. [1960] 84p. illus. 23cm. Autobiographical. [CT275.B3635A3] 61-22895
I. Title.

Ballet.

KARSAVINA, Tamara 927.93
Theatre Street; the reminiscences of Tamara Karsavina. Rev. ed. New York, Dutton, 1961 [c.1931, 1950] 301p. illus., (Everyman paperback D71) 1.45 pap.,
1. Ballet. I. Title.

KARSAVINA, Tamara. 927.93
Theatre Street; the reminiscences of Tamara Karsavina. New ed., rev. and enl. New York, Dutton [1950] xi, 301 p. illus., ports. 22 cm. [GV1785.K3A3 1950] 50-241
1. Ballet. I. Title.

Ballet—Biography.

GRUEN, John. 792.8'092'2
The private world of ballet / John Gruen. New York : Viking Press, 1975. xv, 464 p. : ports. ; 24 cm. Includes index. [GV1785.A1G78 1975] 74-23726 ISBN 0-670-57851-7
1. Ballet—Biography. 2. Ballet—History. I. Title.

GRUEN, John. 792.8'092'2 B
The private world of ballet / John Gruen. New York : Penguin Books, 1976. p. cm. Reprint of the 1975 ed. published by Viking Press, New York. Includes index. [GV1785.A1G78 1976] 76-24890 pbk. : 4.95
1. Ballet—Biography. 2. Ballet—History. I. Title. BIP

Ballet—History.

LIVEN, Petr 792.8'0947
Aleksandrovich, kniaz, 1887-
The birth of ballets-russes [by] Peter Lieven. Translated by L. Zarine. New York, Dover Publications [1973] 377 p. illus. 22 cm. Reprint of the 1936 ed. published by G. Allen & Unwin, London. [GV1787.L5 1973] 73-80556 ISBN 0-486-22962-9 3.50
1. Ballet—History. 2. Dancers—Biography. I. Title. BIP

Ballin, Albert, 1857-1918.

CECIL, Lamar. 943.08'4'0924 B
Albert Ballin; business and politics in imperial Germany, 1888-1918 Princeton, N.J., Princeton University Press, 1967. xxi, 388 p. front. 22 cm. Based on the author's thesis, Johns Hopkins University. "Bibliographical essay": p. 357-369. [DD231.B3C4] 66-21830
1. Ballin, Albert, 1857-1918. 2. Hamburg-American Lines.

Ballinger, Richard Achilles, 1858-1922. Papers, 1907-22 — Indexes.

WASHINGTON (State 016.070'92'4
University. Library)
[Calendar of the Richard A. Ballinger papers, prepared by Alfred E. Norwood for the Manuscripts Section of the University of Washington Library, Seattle. n. p., 1960] 1 v. (various pagings) 29 cm. Binders title: Ballinger papers. Photocopy prepared for limited distribution only. [Z6616.B25W3] 64-55624
1. Ballinger, Richard Achilles, 1858-1922. Papers, 1907-22 — Indexes. 2. U.S. Dept. of the Interior — Inventories, calendars, etc. I. Norwood, Alfred E. II. Title.

Balloon ascensions—Juvenile literature.

DOUTY, Esther Morris. 629.13'0973
The brave ballonists: America's first airmen, by Esther M. Douty. Illustrated by Victor Mays. Champaign, Ill., Garrard Pub. Co. [1974] 95 p. illus. (part col.) 24 cm. (How they lived series) A brief history of balloon flights in the United States from the late eighteenth century until the flight of the first airplane in 1903. [TL620.A1D68] 73-19642 ISBN 0-8116-6926-2 4.25
1. Balloon ascensions—Juvenile literature. 2. Aeronautics—United States—History—Juvenile literature. I. Mays, Victor, 1927- joint author. II. Title.

Ballou, Adin, 1803-1890.

BALLOU, Adin, 1803- 288'.092'4 B
1890.
Autobiography of Adin Ballou, 1803-1890, containing an elaborate record and narrative of his life from infancy to old age : with appendixes / completed and edited by William S. Heywood. Philadelphia : Porcupine Press, 1975. xviii, 586 p. : ports. ; 22 cm. (The American utopian adventure : series two) Reprint of the 1896 ed. published by Vox Populi Press, Lowell, Mass. Includes index. "Published works of Adin Ballou": p. [573]-574. [BX9969.B27A3 1975] 74-26603 ISBN 0-87991-033-X lib.bdg. : 22.50
1. Ballou, Adin, 1803-1890. I. Heywood, William Sweetzer, 1824-1903.

Ballou, Hosea, 1771-1852.

CASSARA, Ernest, 1925- 922.8173
Hosea Ballou; the challenge to orthodoxy. Boston, Universalist Historical Society [1961] 226p. 22cm. Includes bibliography. [BX9969.B3C3] 61-6545
1. Ballou, Hosea, 1771-1852. 2. Universalism. I. Title.

Balmain, Pierre,

BALMAIN, Pierre, 746.90924 B
1914-
My years and seasons. Translated by Edward Lanchberry with Gordon Young. [1st ed.] Garden City, N.Y., Doubleday, 1965. xiv, 216 p. ports. 22 cm. [TT505.B3A313 1965] 65-19913
I. Title.

Balsan, Consuelo (Vanderbilt).

BALSAN, Consuelo 920.7
(Vanderbilt).
The glitter and the gold. [1st ed. New York] Harper [1952] 336 p. illus. 22 cm. Autobiography. [CT3150.B34A3] 52-5419
I. Title.

Balsillie, A. D.

BALSILLIE, A. D. 385'.092'4 B
That was my line / [by] A. D. Balsillie. Ilfracombe : Stockwell, 1976. 34 p. : ill. ; 19 cm [TF140.B34A34 1976] 76-381169 ISBN 0-7223-0894-9 : £0.75
1. Balsillie, A. D. 2. Railroads—Employees—Biography.

Balston, William, 1759-1849.

BALSTON, Thomas. 676'.2'0924 B
William Balston, paper maker, 1759-1849 / by Thomas Balston. New York : Garland Pub., 1979. xii, 171 p., [8] leaves of plates : ill. ; 23 cm. (Nineteenth-century book arts & printing history) Reprint of the 1954 ed. published by Methuen, London. Includes index. [TS1098.B3B3 1979] 78-74387 ISBN 0-8240-3876-2 : 20.00
1. Balston, William, 1759-1849 2. Paper making and trade—Great Britain—History. 3. Paper making and trade Great Britain—Biography. I. Title. II. Series. BIP

Baltimore. Baseball club (American League)

WEAVER, Earl, 1930- 796.357
Winning! Edited by John Sammis. New York, Morrow, 1972. xiii, 202 p. illus. 22 cm. [GV865.W38A38] 76-182452 6.95
1. Baltimore. Baseball club (American League) 2. Baseball. I. Title.

Baltimore. Football club (National League)—Biography.

KLEIN, Dave. 796.33'2'0922 B
The game of their lives / Dave Klein. 1st ed. New York : Random House, c1976. viii, 239 p., [4] leaves of plates : ill. ; 22 cm. [GV939.A1K53] 76-14177 8.95
1. Baltimore. Football club (National League)—Biography. 2. New York (City). Football club (National League)—Biography. 3. Football—Biography. I. Title. BIP

Balzac, Honore de, 1799-1850.

FAGUET, Emile, 1847- 843'.7 B
1916.
Balzac. Translated, with notes, by Wilfrid Thorley. New York, Haskell House Publishers, 1974. 264 p. 22 cm. Reprint of the 1918 ed. published by Constable, London. [PQ2178.F2 1974] 73-21621 ISBN 0-8383-1778-2

1. Balzac, Honore de, 1799-1850. BIP

HUNT, Herbert James. 843.7 B
Honore de Balzac; a biography, by Herbert J. Hunt. New York, Greenwood Press [1969] xii, 198 p. port. 23 cm. Reprint of the 1957 ed. Bibliographical footnotes. [PQ2178.H8 1969] 69-13943
1. Balzac, Honore de, 1799-1850.

PRITCHETT, Victor Sawdon, 843'.7
1900-
Balzac. [by] V. S. Pritchett. [1st American ed.] New York, Knopf; [distributed by Random House] 1973. 272 p. illus. (part col.) 27 cm. Bibliography: p. 264-265. [PQ2178.P74 1973] 72-8681 ISBN 0-394-48357-X 15.00
1. Balzac, Honorede, 1799-1850

SALTUS, Edgar Evertson, 843'.7 B
1855-1921.
Balzac. New York, AMS Press [1969] 199 p. port. 23 cm. Reprint of the 1884 ed. Bibliography: p. [165]-199. [PQ2178.S3 1969] 71-93190
1. Balzac, Honore de, 1799-1850. BIP

SANDARS, Mary Frances, 843'.7
1864-
Honore de Balzac: his life and writings, by Mary F. Sandars. Port Washington, N.Y., Kennikat Press [1970] xv, 396 p. illus., facsim., ports. 22 cm. Reprint of the 1904 ed. Includes bibliographical references. [PQ2178.S4 1970] 75-103209
1. Balzac, Honore de, 1799-1850.

WEDMORE, Frederick, 843'.7 B
Sir, 1844-1921.
Life of Honore de Balzac. Port Washington, N.Y., Kennikat Press [1972] 145, xv p. 22 cm. Reprint of the 1890 ed. Bibliography: p. [i]-xv. [PQ2178.W4 1972] 78-153285 ISBN 0-8046-1592-6
1. Balzac, Honore de, 1799-1850. I. Title. BIP

Balzac, Honore de, 1799-1850—Biography.

GERSON, Noel Bertram, 843'.7 B
1914-
The prodigal genius; the life and times of Honore de Balzac, by Noel B. Gerson. [1st ed.] Garden City, N.Y., Doubleday, 1972. 370 p. illus. 22 cm. Bibliography: p. [355] [PQ2178.G4] 78-175376 8.95
1. Balzac, Honore de, 1799-1850—Biography. I. Title.

KEIM, Albert, 1876-1947. 843'.7 B
Honore de Balzac, by Albert Keim and Louis Lumet. Translated from the French by Frederic Taber Cooper. New York, Haskell House, 1974. x, 250 p. illus. 23 cm. Reprint of the 1914 ed. published by F. A. Stokes Co., New York, in the authors' series: Great men. [PQ2178.K42 1974] 74-1475 ISBN 0-8383-2040-6 10.95
1. Balzac, Honore de, 1799-1850—Biography. I. Lumet, Louis, 1872-1923, joint author. BIP

MAUROIS, Andre, 1885-1967. 843.7
Prometheus; the life of Balzac. Translated by Norman Denny. [1st ed.] New York, Harper & Row [1966, c1965] 573 p. illus., ports. 25 cm. Bibliography: p. 563-564. [PQ2178.M333 1966] 66-13912
1. Balzac, Honore de, 1799-1850—Biography. I. Title.

Bamberger, Ludwig, 1823-1899.

ZUCKER, Stanley, 943.08'092'4 B
1936-
Ludwig Bamberger : German liberal politician and social critic, 1823-1899 / Stanley Zucker. [Pittsburgh] : University of Pittsburgh Press, [1975] xi, 343 p. ; 24 cm. Includes index. Bibliography: p. 315-334. [DD219.B3Z92] 74-17839 ISBN 0-8229-3298-9 : 14.95
1. Bamberger, Ludwig, 1823-1899. 2. Germany—Politics and government—1848-1870. 3. Germany—Politics and government—1871-1918. BIP

Bancroft, George, 1800-1891.

HOWE, Mark Antony 973'.072'024 B
De Wolfe, 1864-1960.
The life and letters of George Bancroft. New York, Da Capo Press, 1970 [c1908] 2 v. in 1. ports. 23 cm. "A bibliography of books and pamphlets by George Bancroft," compiled by Henry C. Strippel: v. 2, p. [329]-341. [E340.B2H8 1970] 78-106990
1. Bancroft, George, 1800-1891. BIP

HOWE, Mark Antony 973'.072'024 B
De Wolfe, 1864-1960.
The life and letters of George Bancroft. Port Washington, N.Y., Kennikat Press [1971] 2 v. ports. 21 cm. (Kennikat Press scholarly reprints. Series in American history and culture in the nineteenth century) Reprint of the 1908 ed. "A bibliography of books and pamphlets by George Bancroft, compiled by Henry C. Strippel": v. 2, p. [329]-341. [E340.B2H8 1971] 71-137917
1. Bancroft, George, 1800-1891. I. Title. BIP

NYE, Russel Blaine, 1913- 928.1
George Bancroft [by] Russel B. Nye. New York, Washington Square Press [1964] x, 212 p. 18 cm. (The Great American thinkers series) "W 879." Bibliography: p. 201-204. [E175.5.B196] 64-6743
1. Bancroft, George, 1800-1891. I. Title. BIP

NYE, Russel 973'.072'024 B
Blaine, 1913-
George Bancroft, Brahmin rebel, by Russel B. Nye. New York, Octagon Books, 1972 [c1944] x, 340, xii p. illus. 24 cm. Bibliography: p. [337]-340. [E175.5.B186 1972] 72-4400 ISBN 0-374-96133-6
1. Bancroft, George, 1800-1891.

Bancroft, Hubert Howe, 1832-1918.

CAUGHEY, John 978'.0072024
Walton, 1902-
Hubert Howe Bancroft, historian of the West. New York, Russell & Russell [1970, c1946] 422 p. illus., facsims., ports. 23 cm. Includes bibliographical references. [E175.5.B199 1970] 77-102475
1. Bancroft, Hubert Howe, 1832-1918. 2. California. University. Bancroft Library. I. Title. BIP

Bancroft, Marie Effie (Wilton) Lady, 1839-1921.

BANCROFT, Marie 792'.028'0924 B
Effie (Wilton) Lady, 1839-1921.
The Bancrofts: recollections of sixty years [by] Marie Bancroft [and] Squire Bancroft. New York, B. Blom [1969] xi, 462 p. illus. 24 cm. Reprint of the 1909 ed. published by Dutton, New York. [PN2598.B3A3 1969] 70-87117
1. Bancroft, Marie Effie (Wilton) Lady, 1839-1921. 2. Bancroft, Squire Bancroft, Sir, 1841-1926. 3. Actors—England—Correspondence, reminiscences, etc. I. Bancroft, Squire Bancroft, Sir, 1841-1926, joint author. II. Title.

Banda, Hastings Kamuzu, 1905-

SHORT, Philip. 968.9'7'040924 B
Banda. London, Boston, Routledge & Kegan Paul [1974] 357 p. 23 cm. Bibliography: p. [317]-320. [DT859.6.B3S53] 73-76089 ISBN 0-7100-7631-2 11.75
1. Banda, Hastings Kamuzu, 1905- 2. Malawi—Politics and government. I. Title. BIP

Bang-Jensen, Povl, 1909-1959.

COPP, DeWitt S 923.273
Betrayal at the UN, the story of Paul Bang-Jensen by DeWitt Copp and Marshall Peck. New York, Devin-Adair Co., 1961. 335 p. 21 cm. [D839.7.J4C6] 61-6796
1. Bang-Jensen, Povl, 1909-1959. 2. United Nations—Hungary. I. Peck, Marshall, joint author. II. Title.

Bangs, Samuel, ca. 1794-ca. 1853.

SPEIL, Lota May (Harrigan) v. 12
1885-
Pioneer printer: Samuel Bangs in Mexico and Texas; Austin, University of Texas Press [1963] 230 p. facsims., maps. 24 cm. Bibliographical footnotes. Bibliography: p. 201-214. 66-63832
1. Bangs, Samuel, ca. 1794-ca. 1853. 2. Printing — History — Mexico. 3. Printing — History — Texas. I. Title.

SPELL, Lota May (Harrigan) 926.55
1885-
Pioneer printer: Samuel Bangs in Mexico and Texas. Austin, Univ. of Tex. Pr. [c.1963] xii, 230p. maps, facsims. 24cm. Bibl. 63-11190 5.00
1. Bangs, Samuel, ca. 1794-ca. 1853. I. Title.

Banis, Josephine (Taft)

BANIS, Josephine (Taft) 920.7
1904-
From bagpipes to foghorns: an orphan's adventures between two worlds. New York, Vantage Press [1953] 239p. 23cm. [CT275.B36525A3] 53-10282
I. Title.

Bankers — U.S. — Direct.

DAHL, Arndt E 332.120924 (B)
1897-
Banker Dahl of South Dakota; an autobiography, by A. E. Dahl. [1st ed.] Rapid City, S.D., Fenske Book Co. [1965] ii, 269 p. illus., ports. 23 cm. [HG2463.D25D3] 65-5778
I. Title.

HAMBELTON, James R., 332.1'092'4
ed.
Who's who in banking. New York, Business Press. 1966. v. 26 cm. Editors: 1966- J. R. Hambleton and F. Stein. [HG2463.A1W55] 66-24372
1. Bankers — U.S. — Direct. 2. Bankers — Direct. I. Stein, Frederick, ed. II. Title.

WHO'S who in banking. 923.3321
1966- New York. Business Pr. [c.1966] ix, 447p. 26cm. Eds.: 1966-J. R. Hambelton, F. Stein. [HG2463.A1W55] 66-24372 25.00
1. Bankers—U.S.—Direct. 2. Bankers—Direct. I. Hambelton, James R., ed. II. Stein, Frederick, ed.

Bankhead, Tallulah, 1902-1968.

BANKHEAD, Tallulah 1902- 927.92
Tallulah: my autobiography. [1st ed.] New York, Harper [1952] 335 p. illus. 22 cm. [PN2287.B17A3] 52-7278
I. Title.

BRIAN, Denis. 791'.092'4 B
Tallulah, darling; a biography of Tallulah Bankhead. New York, Pyramid Books [1972] 285 p. illus. 18 cm. [PN2287.B17B7] 73-173408 1.25
1. Bankhead, Tallulah, 1902-1968. I. Title. BIP

GILL, Brendan, 1914- 791'.092'4
Tallulah. Designed by Marvin Israel. [1st ed.] New York, Holt, Rinehart & Winston [1972] 287 p. illus. 32 cm. "Tallulah Bankhead: a chronology of her professional career, by Hugh Beeson, Jr.": p. 264-283. [PN2287.B17G5] 72-78106 ISBN 0-03-001026-8 25.00
1. Bankhead, Tallulah, 1902-1968. I. Title.

ISRAEL, Lee. 791'.092'4
Miss Tallulah Bankhead. New York, Putnam [1972] 384 p. illus. 22 cm. [PN2287.B17I8] 71-175263 7.95
1. Bankhead, Tallulah, 1902-1968. BIP

ISRAEL, Lee. 791'.092'4
Miss Tallulah Bankhead. [New York, Dell, 1973, c.1972] 381 p. illus. 18 cm. (Dell Book, 9143) [PN2287.B17] pap., 1.75
1. Bankhead, Tallulah, 1902-1968. I. Title.

ISRAEL, Lee. 791'.092'4
Miss Tallulah Bankhead. Boston, G. K. Hall, 1972. 731 p. 25 cm. Large print ed. [PN2287.B17I8 1972b] 72-7431 ISBN 0-8161-6049-X 14.95

1. Bankhead, Tallulah, 1902-1968.

TUNNEY, Kieran. 791.43'028'0924 B
Tallulah: darling of the gods; an intimate portrait. [1st ed.] New York, Dutton, 1973 [c1972] 228 p. ports. 22 cm. [PN2287.B17T8 1973] 72-94689 ISBN 0-525-21395-3 6.95
1. Bankhead, Tallulah, 1902-1968. I. Title.

TUNNEY, Kieran. 791.43'028'0924 B
Tallulah: darling of the gods; an intimate portrait. New York, Manor Books [1974, c1972] 228 p. ports. 18 cm. [PN2287.B17T8 1974] 1.75 (pbk.)
1. Bankhead, Tallulah, 1902-1968. I. Title.
L.C. card number for original ed.: 72-94689

Bankoff, George Alexis, 1903—

BANKOFF, George 617'.092'4 B
Alexis, 1903-
The years of the healing knife : a surgeon's autobiography / [by] George Sava. London : Kimber, 1976. 191 p. ; 23 cm. [R489.B17A38] 77-367787 ISBN 0-7183-0334-2 : £2.95
1. Bankoff, George Alexis, 1903- 2. Surgeons—England—Biography. 3. Surgeons—United States—Biography. 4. Europe—Description and travel—1919- I. Title.

Banks and banking—United States—Case studies.

TWO private banking 332.1'0973
partnerships. New York : Arno Press, 1975. xxxiii, 374, 62 p., [56] leaves of plates : ill. ; 23 cm. (Wall Street and the security markets) Reprint of the 1909 ed. of A hundred years of merchant banking, by J. C. Brown, printed in New York; and of the 1871 ed. of Sketch of the life of J. F. D. Lanier, by J. F. D. Lanier, printed by Hosford, New York. Includes index. [HG2477.T9 1975] 75-2676 ISBN 0-405-07238-4 : 34.00
1. Banks and banking—United States—Case studies. I. Brown, John Crosby, 1838-1909. A hundred years of merchant banking. 1975. II. Lanier, James Franklin Doughty, 1800-1881. Sketch of the life of J. F. D. Lanier. 1975. III. Series.

Banks, Ernie, 1931- —Juvenile literature.

BANKS, Ernie, 796.357'0924 B
1931-
"Mr. Cub," by Ernie Banks and Jim Enright. Chicago, Follett Pub. Co. [1971] 237 p. illus. 22 cm. "A Rutledge book." [GV865.B26A3] 76-149246 ISBN 0-695-80225-9 6.95
I. Enright, Jim, joint author. II. Title.

LIBBY, Bill. 796.357'0924 B
Ernie Banks: Mr. Cub. New York, Putnam [1971] 174 p. 21 cm. (Putnam sports shelf) A biography of the only National League ball player to be voted Most Valuable Player for two consecutive seasons. [GV865.B26L5 1971] 92 77-142465 3.86
1. Banks, Ernie, 1931- —Juvenile literature. I. Title.

MAY, Julian. 796.357'092'4 B
Ernie Banks, home run slugger. Mankato, Minn., Crestwood House [1973] 46 p. illus. 24 cm. (Sports close-up books) A biography of the star batter for the Chicago Cubs, elected by the fans as "Greatest Cub Player of All Time." [GV865.B26M38 1973] 92 73-80420 ISBN 0-913940-00-3
1. Banks, Ernie, 1931- —Juvenile literature. I. Title.

Banks, Frederick, 1898-1964.

BANKS, Ivy 974.9'04'0924 B
Jackson.
Banks of the Delaware; the life and times of Frederick Banks, 1898-1964. Drawings by Mary Grace Johnston. [1st ed.] Trenton, Trenton Historical Society, 1967. 204 p. illus., facsims, maps, ports. 24 cm. [F144.T7B3] 67-25767
1. Banks, Frederick, 1898-1964. 2. Trenton—Social life and customs. I. Title.

Banks, Graham.

BRADY, Mari, 1948- 362.1'9'699400926
Please remember me : a young woman's story of her friendship with an unforgettable fifteen-year old boy / Mari Brady. 1st ed. Garden City, N.Y. : Doubleday, 1977. 104 p. ; 22 cm. [RC263.B63] 76-56268 ISBN 0-385-12913-0 : 6.95
1. Banks, Graham. 2. Cancer—Biography. I. Title.

Banks, John, Sir, bart., 1627-1699.

COLEMAN, Donald Cuthbert 923.342
Sir John Banks, baronet and businessman; a study of business, politics, and society in later Stuart England. Oxford, Clarendon Pr. [dist. New York, Oxford, c.]1963. ix, 215p. plates, ports., map, geneal. table, tables. 23cm. Bibl. 63-24910 6.40
1. Banks, John, bart., Sir I. Title.

COLEMAN, Donald Cuthbert. 923.342
Sir John Banks, baronet and businessman; a study of business, politics, and society in later Stuart England. Oxford, Clarendon Press, 1963. ix, 215 p. plates, ports., map, geneal. table, tables. 23 cm. Bibliographical footnotes. [DA378.B3C6 1963] 63-24910
1. Banks, Sir John, bart., 1627-1699. I. Title.

COLEMAN, Donald Cuthbert. 941.06'092'4 B
Sir John Banks, baronet and businessman : a study of business, politics, and society in later Stuart England / by D. C. Coleman. Westport, Conn. : Greenwood Press, 1975, c1963. ix, 215 p. : ill. ; 22 cm. Reprint of the ed. published by Clarendon Press, Oxford. Includes bibliographical references and index. [DA378.B3C6 1975] 74-30845 ISBN 0-8371-7932-7 lib.bdg. : 13.25
1. Banks, John, Sir, bart., 1627-1699. I. Title.

Banks, Joseph, Sir, bart., 1743-1820.

CAMERON, Hector Charles, Sir 1743-1820. 574.0924
Sir Joseph Banks. [Sydney] Angus & Robertson [San Francisco, Tri-Ocean, 1966] xx, 341p. illus., ports. 23cm. Bibl. [Q143] 66-15930 6.75
1. Banks, Sir Joseph Bank, bart., 1743-1820. I. Title.

SMITH, Edward, 1839-1919. 574'.092'4 B
The life of Sir Joseph Banks / by Edward Smith. New York : Arno Press, 1975, c1911. xvi, 348 p., [16] leaves of plates : ill. ; 23 cm. (History, philosophy, and sociology of science) Reprint of the ed. published by J. Lane, London. Includes bibliographical references and index. [Q143.B3S6 1975] 74-26292 ISBN 0-405-06618-X : 22.00
1. Banks, Joseph, Sir, bart., 1743-1820. I. Title. II. Series. BIP

Banks, Nathaniel Prentice, 1816-1894.

HARRINGTON, Fred Harvey, 1912- 973.7'0924
Fighting politician, Major General N. P. Banks. Westport, Conn., Greenwood Press [1970, c1948] xi, 301 p. maps (on lining papers), port. 23 cm. At head of title: American Historical Association. Bibliography: p. 272-285. [E467.1.B23H28 1970] 73-100228
1. Banks, Nathaniel Prentice, 1816-1894. I. American Historical Association. II. Title.

Banneker, Benjamin, 1731-1806.

AFRICAN-AMERICAN Bicentennial Center. 520'.92'4 B
A chronology of the life of Benjamin Banneker, son of Maryland, 1731-1806 / African-American Bicentennial Center. Baltimore : Commission on Afro-American History and Culture, [1976] [20] p. : ill. ; 23 cm. Cover title. [QB36.B22A37 1976] 77-622250 1.00
1. Banneker, Benjamin, 1731-1806. 2. Astronomers—United States—Biography. 3. Afro-Americans—United States—Biography. I. Title.

ALLEN, Will W. 520'.924 B
Banneker: the Afro-American astronomer. From data collected by Will W. Allen assisted by Daniel Murray. Freeport, N.Y., Books for Libraries Press, 1971. 80 p. port. 23 cm. (The Black heritage library collection) Reprint of the 1921 ed. [QB36.B22A4 1971] 77-168504 ISBN 0-8369-8858-2
1. Banneker, Benjamin, 1731-1806. I. Murray, Daniel Alexander Payne, 1862-1934, joint author. II. Title. III. Series.

ALLEN, William G., comp. 811'.008
Wheatley, Banneker, and Horton; with selections from the poetical works of Wheatley and Horton, by William G. Allen. Freeport, N.Y., 1970. 48 p. 23 cm. (The Black heritage library collection) Reprint of the 1849 ed. [E185.96.A53 1970] 77-133145 ISBN 0-8369-8657-1
1. Wheatley, Phillis, afterwards Phillis Peters, 1753?-1784. 2. Banneker, Benjamin, 1731-1806. 3. Horton, George Moses, 1798?-ca. 1880. I. Title.

BEDINI, Silvio A. 520'.92'4 B
The life of Benjamin Banneker [by] Silvio A. Bedini. New York, Scribner [1971, c1972] xvii, 434 p. illus. 25 cm. Bibliography: p. [377]-406. [QB36.B22B4] 78-162755 ISBN 0-684-12574-9 14.95
1. Banneker, Benjamin, 1731-1806. I. Title.

PATTERSON, Lillie. 520'.92'4 B
Benjamin Banneker, genius of early America / Lillie Patterson ; illustrated by David Scott Brown. Nashville : Abingdon, c1978. 142 p. : ill. ; 21 cm. Bibliography: p. 141-142. A biography of the distinguished eighteenth-century black astronomer, farmer, mathematician, and surveyor whose accomplishments include having published a popular almanac and constructed the first completely American made clock. [QB36.B22P38] 92 77-13216 ISBN 0-687-02900-7 : 5.95
1. Banneker, Benjamin, 1731-1806. 2. Astronomers—United States—Biography. I. Brown, David Scott. II. Title.

Banneker, Benjamin, 1731-1806—Juvenile literature.

CLARK, Margaret Goff. 520'.92'4 B
Benjamin Banneker, astronomer and scientist. Illustrated by Russell Hoover. Champaign, Ill., Garrard Pub. Co. [1971] 96 p. illus. (part col.), map, ports. 24 cm. (Americans all) A biography of the free-born black man who, as a self-taught mathematician and astronomer, helped survey the site of the Nation's Capitol and published several popular almanacs. [QB36.B22C45] 74-131055 ISBN 0-8116-4564-9 2.49
1. Banneker, Benjamin, 1731-1806—Juvenile literature. I. Hoover, Russell, illus. II. Title.

HARRISON, Deloris. 929.2'0973
The Bannekers of Bannaky Springs. Illustrated by David Hodges. [1st ed.] New York, Hawthorn Books [1970] 80 p. illus. 23 cm. A biography concentrating of the family background of the eighteenth-century black man, self-taught natural scientist, astronomer, and mathematician, who helped survey Washington, D.C. [E185.97.B22H3] 920 70-92636 4.25
1. Banneker, Benjamin, 1731-1806—Juvenile literature. 2. Banneker family—Juvenile literature. I. Hodges, David, illus. II. Title.

LEWIS, Claude. 520'.0924 B
Benjamin Banneker: the man who saved Washington. Illustrated by Ernest T. Crichlow. New York, McGraw-Hill [1970] 127 p. illus. 22 cm. (McGraw-Hill Black Legacy) "A Rutledge book." Bibliography: p. 126-127. A biography of the self-taught black mathematician and astronomer who as a surveyor helped determine the boundaries of the District of Columbia. [QB36.B22L47] 92 79-92101
1. Banneker, Benjamin, 1731-1806.—Juvenile literature. I. Crichlow, Ernest T., 1914, illus. II. Title. III. Series.

WILSON, Ruth, 1919- 322.4'4'0922 B
Our blood and tears; black freedom fighters. New York, Putnam [1972] 192 p. 21 cm. Brief biographies of three nineteenth-century black men emphasizing their struggles to free their people from slavery. [E185.96.W58 1972] 920 70-185404 4.69
1. Banneker, Benjamin, 1731-1806—Juvenile literature. 2. Turner, Nat, 1800?-1831—Juvenile literature. 3. Douglass, Frederick, 1817?-1895—Juvenile literature. I. Title. BIP

Bannerman, Margaret (Gordon) Lady, 1798-1878.

ARCHIBALD, Raymond Clare, 1875- 824'.8 B
Carlyle's first love, Margaret Gordon Lady Bannerman; an account of her life, ancestry and homes, her family and friends. New York, Haskell House, 1973. xvi, 213 p. illus. 23 cm. Reprint of the 1910 ed. Bibliography: p. 183-188. [PR4433.A65 1973] 72-3374 ISBN 0-8383-1535-6 12.95
1. Bannerman, Margaret (Gordon) Lady, 1798-1878. 2. Carlyle, Thomas, 1795-1881. I. Title.

Bannerman of Kildonan, John MacDonald Bannerman, Baron, 1901-1969.

BANNERMAN of Kildonan, John MacDonald Bannerman, Baron, 1901-1969. 329.9'41 B
Bannerman: the memoirs of Lord Bannerman of Kildonan; edited by John Fowler. Aberdeen, Impulse Books, 1972. 133, [9] p. illus., ports. 22 cm. [DA822.B36A3] 73-159777 ISBN 0-901311-19-7 £2.80
1. Bannerman of Kildonan, John MacDonald Bannerman, Baron, 1901-1969. I. Fowler, John, ed.

Banning, Phineas, 1830-1885.

KRYTHE, Maymie Richardson. 923.873
Port Admiral: Phineas Banning, 1830-1885. San Francisco, California Historical Society, 1957. xv, 251p. illus., ports. 25cm. ([California Historical Society] Special publication no. 28) Bibliography: p. 237-245. [F867.B3K7] 57-11459
1. Banning, Phineas, 1830-1885. I. Title. II. Series.

Bannister, Harry Ray,

BANNISTER, Harry Ray, 1894- 791.44
The education of a broadcaster [by] Harry Bannister. New York, Simon and Schuster [1965] 351 p. 22 cm. Autobiographical. [PN1991.4.B25A3] 65-15021
I. Title.

Banting, Frederick Grant, Sir, 1891-1941.

ROWLAND, John, 1907- 616.4620610924
The insulin man; the story of Sir Frederick Banting. New York, Roy Publishers [1966, c1965] 140 p. 21 cm. [R464.B3R67] 66-10775
1. Banting, Frederick Grant, Sir, 1891-1941. I. Title.

Banting, Frederick Grant, Sir, 1891-1941—Juvenile literature.

MAYER, Ann Margaret, 1938- 616.4'62'00924 B
Sir Frederick Banting, doctor against diabetes. Illustrated by Harold Henriksen. Mankato, Minn., Creative Education; [distributed by Childrens Press, Chicago, 1974] 36 p. col. illus. 25 cm. (Creative Education close-ups) Recounts the life of the Canadian doctor who discovered the means of keeping the once fatal disease of diabetes under control. [R464.B3M38] 92 74-2048 ISBN 0-87191-323-2 4.95 (lib. bdg.).
1. Banting, Frederick Grant, Sir, 1891-1941—Juvenile literature. I. Henriksen, Harold, illus. II. Title.

SHAW, Margaret Mason. 616.4'62'00924 B
Frederick Banting / Margaret Mason Shaw. Don Mills, Ont. : Fitzhenry & Whiteside, c1976. 61 p. : ill. ; 22 cm. (The Canadians) Includes bibliographical references. [R464.B3S49] 77-371174 ISBN 0-88902-229-1
1. Banting, Frederick Grant, Sir, 1891-1941—Juvenile literature. 2. Physicians—Ontario—Biography—Juvenile literature. I. Title. II. Series.

Baptist standard.

WOOD, Presnall H. 286'.0922
Prophets with pens [by] Presnall H. Wood and Floyd W. Thatcher. Dallas, Baptist Standard Pub. Co. [1969] 158 p. ports. 23 cm. Outgrowth of the author's thesis, Southwestern Baptist Seminary. [BX6201.B72W6] 71-103137 4.25
1. Baptist standard. 2. Baptists—Biography. I. Thatcher, Floyd W., joint author. II. Title.

Baptists— Clergy—Correspondence, Reminiscences, etc.

DOMENICA, Angelo di, 1872- 922.673
Protestant witness of a new American; mission of a lifetime. [1st ed.] Chicago, Judson Press [1956] 172 p. 22 cm. [BX6495.D6A38] 56-8501
1. Baptists— Clergy—Correspondence, Reminiscences, etc. 2. Baptists, Italian. I. Title.

HURT, John Jeter. 922.673
This is my story. Atlanta, [c1957] 251p. 23cm. [BX6495.H83A3] 57-14406
1. Baptists—Clergy— Correspondence, reminiscences, etc. I. Title.

MADDRY, Charles Edward, 1876- 922.673
Charles E. Maddry; an autobiography. Nashville, Broadman Press [1955] 141p. illus. 23cm. [BX6495.M275A3] 55-14632
1. Baptists—Clergy —Correspondence, reminiscences, etc. I. Title.

Baptists—Biography.

ADAMS, Theodore Floyd, 1898- 286.'0922
Baptists around the world [by] Theodore F. Adams. Nashville, Broadman Press [1967] 128 p. 20 cm. [BX6493.A3] 67-10306
1. Baptists—Biography. I. Title.

BROWNE, Benjamin P 922.6
Tales of Baptist daring. Illus. by William Hamilton. [1st ed.] Philadelphia, Judson Press [1961] 175p. illus. 22cm. Includes bibliography. [BX6493.B7] 61-10119
1. Baptists— Biog. I. Title.

HOADLEY, Frank T. 286'.092'2 B
Baptists who dared / Frank T. Hoadley & Benjamin P. Browne ; illustrated by William Hamilton. Valley Forge, PA : Judson Press, c1980. 112 p. : ill. ; 22 cm. Twelve of the stories are adapted from Tales of Baptist daring by B. P. Browne. Bibliography: p. 111-112. [BX6493.H6] 79-21695 ISBN 0-8170-0855-1 pbk. : 3.95
1. Baptists—Biography. I. Browne, Benjamin P., joint author. II. Title. BIP

THATCHER, John. 922.673
Summoned to serve; real-life stories of twelve persons at work in the church vocations. Philadelphia, Judson Press [1960] 140 p. 20 cm. Includes bibliography. [BX6493.T48] 6012264
1. Baptists — Biog. 2. Vocation. I. Title.

THOMPSON, Evelyn Wingo. 286.0924 (B)
Luther Rice: believer in tomorrow. Nashville, Broadman Press [c1967] 234 p. 22 cm. Bibliography: p. 226-228. [BX6495.R55T5] 67-10034
I. Rice, Luther, 1783-1836. II. Title.

VANDERPOOL, Herbert Campbell, 1923- 922.6768
Twentieth century Baptists; biographies of over one hundred ministers. Also sketches in Enon, Wiseman and Siloam Baptist Associations [and] an additional history of other churches. [By] H. C. Vanderpool [and] W. T. Russell. Tompkinsville, Ky., Printed by Monroe County Press, 1962. 322 p. illus. 22 cm. [BX6493.V3] 63-1905

1. Baptists — Biog. 2. Baptists — Tennessee. I. Russell, William Thompson, 1914- II. Title.

VANDERPOOL, Herbert 922.6768
Campbell, 1923-
Twentieth century Baptists; biographies of over one hundred ministers. Also sketches in Enon, Wiseman and Siloam Baptist Associations [and] an additional history of other churches. [By] H. C. Vanderpool, W. T. Russell. Goodlettsville, Tenn., Author, Box 186 [1963] 322p. illus. 22cm. 63-1905 3.50
1. Baptists—Biog. 2. Baptists—Tennessee. I. Russell, William Thompson, 1914- II. Title.

WOOD, Presnall H. 286'.0922
Prophets with pens [by] Presnall H. Wood and Floyd W. Thatcher. Dallas, Baptist Standard Pub. Co. [1969] 158 p. ports. 23 cm. Outgrowth of the author's thesis, Southwestern Baptist Seminary. [BX6201.B72W6] 71-103137 4.25
1. Baptist standard. 2. Baptists—Biography. I. Thatcher, Floyd W., joint author. II. Title.

Baptists—Clergy—Biography.

STROBER, Gerald S. 286'.1'0924 B
Aflame for God / Gerald Strober, Ruth Tomczak. Nashville, TN : T. Nelson Pub. Co., 1979. p. cm. Includes index. [BX6495.F3S8] 79-16248 ISBN 0-8407-5172-9 : 8.95
1. Falwell, Jerry. 2. Baptists—Clergy—Biography. 3. Thomas Road Baptist Church. 4. Clergy—United States—Biography. I. Tomczak, Ruth, joint author. II. Title.

Baptists—Doctrinal and controversial works.

TULL, James E. 286'.092'2 B
Shapers of Baptist thought [by] James E. Tull. Valley Forge [Pa.], Judson Press [1972] 255 p. 24 cm. Includes bibliographical references. [BX6331.2.T84] 72-75359 ISBN 0-8170-0503-X 10.00
1. Baptists—Doctrinal and controversial works. 2. Baptists—Biography. I. Title. BIP

Baptists—Missions.

HEFLEY, James C. 266.6'0924
Intrigue in Santo Domingo; the story of Howard Shoemake, missionary to revolution, by James C. Hefley. Waco, Tex., Word Books [1968] 184 p. illus., map, ports. 23 cm. Bibliography: p. 182-183. [BV2848.D7H4 1968] 68-57016 3.95
1. Baptists—Missions. 2. Missions, Medical—Dominican Republic. I. Title.

Baptists, Negro.

CARTER, Edward R. 286'.0922 B
Biographical sketches of our pulpit, written and collated by E. R. Carter. Chicago, Afro-Am Press, 1969. ix [i.e. xix], 216 p. illus., ports. 22 cm. Reprint of the 1888 ed. [BX6453.C33 1969] 72-99355
1. Baptists, Negro. 2. Baptists—Georgia. I. Title. BIP

Baptists—Relations.

GARRETT, James Leo. 286
Baptist relations with other Christians. Edited by James Leo Garrett. Valley Forge [Pa.] Judson Press [1974] 224 p. 23 cm. Includes bibliographical references. [BX6329.A1G37] 73-16788 ISBN 0-8170-0602-8 12.00
1. Baptists—Relations. I. Title. BIP

Baptists—United States.

ARMSTRONG, O. K. 286'.0973
Baptists who shaped a nation / O. K. and Marjorie Armstrong. Nashville : Broadman Press, [1975] 123 p. ; 18 cm. Excerpts from the authors' The indomitable Baptists, published in 1967 by Doubleday, Garden City, N.Y. Includes bibliographical references. [BX6235.A752 1975] 74-27925 ISBN 0-8054-6517-0 pbk. : 1.95
1. Baptists—United States. 2. Baptists—Bigraphy. I. Armstrong, Marjorie Moore, joint author. II. Title. BIP

ARMSTRONG, Orland Kay, 286'.0973
1893-
The Baptists in America / O. K. Armstrong and Marjorie Armstrong. Garden City, N.Y. : Doubleday, 1979. xvii, 485 p. ; 21 cm. (A Doubleday-Galilee book) Previous ed. (1967) published under title: The indomitable Baptists. Includes bibliographical references. [BX6235.A75 1979] 78-22150 ISBN 0-385-14655-8 : 6.95
1. Baptists—United States. 2. Baptists—Biography. I. Armstrong, Marjorie Moore, joint author. II. Title. III. Series. BIP

Baraga, Frederick, Bp., 1797-1868.

JEZERNIK, 282'.0924 B
Maksimilijan.
Frederick Baraga; a portrait of the first bishop of Marquette, based on the archives of the Congregatio de Propaganda Fide. New York, Studia Slovenica, 1968. 155 p. maps, port. 23 cm. (Studia Slovenica, 7) [BX4705.B18J4] 68-16856
1. Baraga, Frederick, Bp., 1797-1868. I. Title. II. Series.

LAMBERT, Bernard J 282'.0924
Shepherd of the wilderness; a biography of Bishop Frederic Baraga [by] Bernard J. Lambert. L'Anse, Mich., 1967. xiv, 255 p. maps (on lining papers), port. 24 cm. Bibliography: p. 253-255. [BX4705.B18L3] 67-29795
1. Baraga, Friedrich, Bp., 1797-1868. I. Title.

Baraheni, Reza, 1935- —Biography.

BARAHENI, Reza, 1935- 320.9'55'05
The crowned cannibal : writings on repression in Iran / Reza Baraheni. 1st ed. New York : Vintage Books, 1977. p. cm. Includes bibliographical references. [DS318.B335] 76-62496 ISBN 0-394-72357-0 pbk. : 3.95
1. Baraheni, Reza, 1935- —Biography. 2. Iran—Politics and government—1945- 3. Poets, Persian—Biography. 4. Political prisoners—Iran—Biography. 5. Torture—Iran. I. Title.

Baran, Paul A., 1910-1964.

SWEEZY, Paul Marlor, 335.40924
1910-
Paul A. Baran, 1910-1964: a collective portrait, ed. by Paul M. Sweezy, Leo Huberman. New York, Monthly Review [c.1965] vii, 135p. ports. Bibl. [HB119.B3S9] 65-19365 3.50
1. Baran, Paul A., 1910-1964. I. Huberman, Leo, 1903- joint ed. II. Title.

SWEEZY, Paul Marlor, 335.40924
1910- ed.
Paul A. Baran, 1910-1964: a collective portrait, edited by Paul M. Sweezy and Leo Huberman New York, Monthly Review Press [1965] viii, 135 p. 23 cm. Contents.Contents. -- The commitment of the intellectual, by P. A. Baran. -- Social and economic planning, by P. A. Baran. -- An alternative to Marxism? by P. A. Baran. -- Paul Alexander Baran: a personal memoir, by P. M. Sweezy. -- The achievement of Paul Baran, by H. Magdoff. -- Statements, by M. Abramovitz and others. -- A preliminary bibliography of Paul Baran. [HB119.B3S9] 65-19365
1. Baran, Paul A., 1910-1964. I. Huberman, Leo, 1908- joint ed. II. Title.

Baranov, Aleksandr Andreevich, 1745-1819.

CHEVIGNY, Hector, 1904- 923.873
Lord of Alaska; Baranov and the Russian adventure. Portland, Or., Binfords & Mort, 1951 ['1942] 320 p. map (on lining papers) 22 cm. Bibliography: p. 307-311. [F907.B2 1951] 51-4156
1. Baranov, Aleksandr Andreevich, 1745-1819. 2. Alaska—Hist. I. Title.

KHLEBNIKOV, 979.8'02'0924 B
Kirill Timofeevich, 1776-1838.
Baranov, chief manager of the Russian colonies in America, by K. T. Khlebnikov. Translated by Colin Bearne. Edited by Richard A. Pierce. Kingston, Ont., Limestone Press, c1973. xvi, 140 p., [4] l. of plates. ill., maps (on lining papers), ports. 24 cm. ([Materials for the study of Alaska history, no. 3]) Translation of Zhizneopisanie Aleksandra Andreevicha Baranova. First published in Russian, St. Petersburg, 1835. Series statement on label mounted on t.p. Includes bibliographical references and index. [F907.K4913] 74-80853 ISBN 0-919642-50-0
1. Baranov, Aleksandr Andreevich, 1745-1819. 2. Alaska—History—To 1867. 3. California—History—To 1846. I. Title. II. Series.

Barbacena, Afonso Furtado de Castro do Rio de Mendonca visconde de, d. 1675.

LOPES Serra, 981'.03'0924 B
Joao, 17thcent.
A Governor and his image in baroque Brazil : the funereal eulogy of Afonso Furtado de Castro do Rio de Mendoca / by Juan Lopes Sierra ; edited by Stuart B. Schwartz ; translated by Ruth E. Jones. Minneapolis : University of Minnesota Press, c1979. xi, 216 p. : ill. ; 23 cm. Translation of Paneguirico funebre. Includes bibliographical references and index. [F2528.B37L6613] 78-27512 ISBN 0-8166-0879-2 : 15.00
1. Barbacena, Afonso Furtado de Castro do Rio de Mendonca visconde de, d. 1675. 2. Brazil—Governor—Biography. 3. Brazil—History—17th century. I. Schwartz, Stuart B. II. Title.

Barbara, Saint—Juvenile literature.

RICHARDSON, Mary Kathleen, 922.1
1903-
Barbara. Drawings by Jeanyee Wong. New York, Sheed & Ward [1959] unpaged. illus. 21cm. (A Patron saint book) [BX4700.B15R5] 59-10653
1. Barbara, Saint—Juvenile literature. I. Title.

Barbarigo, Andrea, 1398 or 9-1449.

LANE, Frederic Chapin, 382'.0924
1900-
Andrea Barbarigo, merchant of Venice, 1418-1449, by Frederic C. Lane. New York, Octagon Books, 1967 [c1944] 224 p. 24 cm. "Sources for the study of private mercantile enterprise in the Venetian republic": p. 137-152. [HF3590.V4L3] 67-25624
1. Barbarigo, Andrea, 1398 or 9-1449. 2. Venice—Comm.—Hist. I. Title.

Barbarossa, Khayr al-Din, d. 1546.

BRADFORD, Ernle Dusgate 949.6
Selby.
The sultan's admiral; the life of Barbarossa [by] Ernle Bradford [1st ed.] New York, Harcourt, [1968] xiv, 224p. illus., maps., ports. 21cm. Bibl. [DR509.B22B7] (B) 68-24384 5.75
1. Barbarossa, Khayr al-Din, d. 1546. I. Title.

BRADFORD, Ernle 961'.02'0924 B
Dusgate Selby.
The sultan's admiral; the life of Barbarossa [by] Ernle Bradford [1st ed.] New York, Harcourt, Brace & World [1968] xiv, 224 p. illus., maps., ports. 21 cm. Bibliography: p. 209-210. [DR509.B22B7] 68-24384
1. Barbarossa, Khayr al-Din, d. 1546. I. Title.

Barbarossa, Khayr al-Din, d. 1546—Juvenile literature.

GRANT, Neil. 961'.02'0924 B
Barbarossa, the pirate king. New York, Hawthorn Books [1972] v, 85 p. 22 cm. "A note on books": p. 75. A biography of the king of Algiers and Turkish national hero responsible for establishing Turkish dominance of the Mediterranean in the sixteenth century. [DR509.B22G7 1972] 92 75-150837 3.95
1. Barbarossa, Khayr al-Din, d. 1546—Juvenile literature. I. Title.

Barbauld, Anna Letitia (Aikin) 1743-1825.

LE BRETON, Anna 828'.6'09 B
Letitia Aikin, 1808-1885.
Memoir of Mrs. Barbauld, including letters and notices of her family and friends. London, G. Bell, 1874. [New York, AMS Press, 1974] ii, 236 p. port. 19 cm. [PR4057.B7Z7 1974] 73-19902 ISBN 0-404-07397-2 10.00
1. Barbauld, Anna Letitia (Aikin) 1743-1825. I. Title.

LE BRETON, Anna 828'.6'09 B
Letitia (Aikin) 1808-1885.
Memoir of Mrs. Barbauld, including letters and notices of her family and friends. London, G. Bell, 1874. [New York, AMS Press, 1974] p. [PR4057.B7Z7 1974] 73-172311 ISBN 0-404-07397-2 10.00
1. Barbauld, Anna Letitia (Aikin) 1743-1825. I. Title. BIP

Barber, Eunice.

BARBER, Eunice. 973'.04'97 S
Narrative of the tragical death of Darius Barber / Eunice Barber. New York : Garland Pub., 1977. 24 p. : ill. ;23 cm. (The Garland library of narratives of North American Indian captivities ; v. 36) Reprint of the 1818 ed. printed for D. Hazen, Boston, under title: Narrative of the tragical death of Mr. Darius Barber. Issued with the reprint of Shocking murder by the savages of Mr. Darius Barber's family. New York, 1977, the reprint of the 1817 ed. of Lewis, H. Narrative of captivity and sufferings. New York, 1977, the reprint of the 1833 ed. of Lewis, H. Narrative of the captivity of Jane Lewis. New York, 1977, the reprint of the 1957? ed. of Van Horne, J. A narrative of captivity and sufferings. New York, 1977, and the reprint of the 1818 ed. of Steele, Z. The Indian captive. New York, 1977. [E85.G2 vol. 36] [E83.817] 975.8'746'030924 B 77-4089 ISBN 0-8240-1660-2 lib.bdg. : 25.00
1. Barber, Eunice. 2. Seminole Indians—Captivities. 3. Seminole War, 1st, 1817-1818. 4. Indians of North America—Captivities. 5. Georgia—Biography. I. Title. II. Series.

Barber family.

MORGAN, David Wayne, 929'.2'0973
1943-
Captain George Barber of Georgia / by David W. Morgan. [Temple, Okla.] : Morgan, 1975. vi, 170 leaves ; 28 cm. Includes bibliographical references and indexes. [CS71.B24 1975] 75-324184
1. Barber family. I. Title.

Barber, Geoffrey, 1904-

BARBER, Geoffrey, 610'.92'4 B
1904-
Country doctor / Geoffrey Barber. Ipswich : Boydell Press, 1974. [2], x, 98 p., [4] p. of plates : ill., map, ports. ; 23 cm. (The Essex library) [R489.B19A32] 75-594692 ISBN 0-85115-037-3 : £2.50
1. Barber, Geoffrey, 1904- 2. Physicians (General practice)—Correspondence, reminiscences, etc. 3. Essex, Eng.—Biography. I. Title. II. Series. BIP

Barber, John, d. 1741.

AN impartial 352'.00092'4 B
history of the life of Mr. John Barber, 1741. The life and character of John Barber, 1741. New York, Garland Pub., 1974. 1 v. (various pagings) 22 cm. (The English book trade, 1660-1853) Reprint of the ed. printed by E. Curll, London under title: An impartial history of the life, character, amours, travels, and transactions of Mr. John Barber; and of the ed. printed for T. Cooper, London, of the life and character of John Barber, Esq. [DA676.8.B28I45 1974] 74-18362 ISBN 0-8240-0959-2
1. Barber, John, d. 1741. I. The life and character of John Barber, Esq. 1974. II. Title. III. Series.

Barber, Margaret Fairless, 1869-1901.

DOWSON, Mary Emily, 828'.8'09 B
1848-
Michael Fairless : her life and writings / by W. Scott Palmer (M. E. Dowson) and A. M. Haggard ; with two portraits by Elinor Dowson. Brooklyn : Haskell House Publishers, 1977. 137 p. : ports. ; 21 cm. Reprint of the 1913 ed. published by Duckworth, London. [PR6003.A65Z62 1977] 76-30785 ISBN 0-8383-2158-5 lib.bdg. : 10.95
1. Barber, Margaret Fairless, 1869-1901. 2. Authors, English—19th century—Biography. I. Haggard, A. M., joint author.

Barber, Virgil, 1782-1847—Juvenile literature.

BETZ, Eva (Kelly) 1897- 92
Virgil Barber, New England pied piper. Illus. by Bruno Frost. New York, Kenedy [1963] 188p. illus. 22cm. (Amer. background bks., 25) 63-18884 2.50
1. Barber, Virgil, 1782-1847—Juvenile literature. I. Title. II. Series.

Barbirolli, John, Sir, 1899-1970.

REID, Charles, 1900- 785'.0924 B
John Barbirolli: a biography. New York, Taplinger Pub. Co. [1971] xvii, 446 p. ports. 23 cm. Bibliography: p. xvi-xvii. [ML422.B18R4 1971b] 72-163476 ISBN 0-8008-4408-4 12.95
1. Barbirolli, John, Sir, 1899-1970.

Barbosa, Jose Celso, 1857-1921.

STERLING, Philip. 920(J)
The quiet rebels; four Puerto Rican leaders: Jose Celso Barbosa, Luis Munoz Rivera, Jose de Diego, Luiz Munoz Marin, by Philip Sterling and Maria Brau. Illustrated by Tracy Sugerman. [1st ed.] Garden City, N.Y., Doubleday, 1968. 118 p. col. illus., col. map, col. ports. 21 cm. (Zenith books) [F1955.S7] 67-11153 2.95
1. Barbosa, Jose Celso, 1851-1921—Juvenile literature. 2. Munoz Rivera, Luis, 1859-1916—Juvenile literature. 3. Diego, Jose de, 1866-1918—Juvenile literature. 4. Munoz Marin, Luis, 1898- —Juvenile literature. I. Brau, Maria M., 1932- joint author. II. Title.

STERLING, Philip. 920
The quiet rebels; four Puerto Rican leaders Jose Celso Barbosa, Luis Munoz Rivera, Jose de Diego, Luis Munoz Marin by Philip Sterling and Maria Brau. Illus. by Tracy Sugarman [1st ed.] Garden City, N.Y., Doubleday, 1968. 118 p. col. illus., col. map, col. ports. 21 cm. (Zenith books) Profiles of four Puerto Ricans who fought for independence and equal rights for their island people. [F1955.S7] AC 68
1. Barbosa, Jose Celso, 1857-1921. 2. Munoz Rivera, Luis, 1859-1916. 3. Diego, Jose de, 1866-1918. 4. Munoz Marin, Luis, 1898- I. Brau, Maria, joint author. II. Sugarman, Tracy, 1921- illus. III. Title.

Barchus, Eliza Rosanna, 1857-1959.

BARCHUS, Agnes, 1893- 759.13
Eliza R. Barchus, the Oregon artist, 1857-1959 / by Agnes Barchus. 1st ed. Portland, Or. : Binford & Mort, c1974. ix, 166 p., [4] leaves of plates : ill. (some col.) ; 24 cm. [ND237.B2615A46] 74-24495 ISBN 0-8323-0245-7 : 8.95
1. Barchus, Eliza Rosanna, 1857-1959.

Barclay, Alexander, 1810-1855.

HAMMOND, George 978.9'03'0924 B
Peter, 1896-
The adventures of Alexander Barclay, mountain man, from London corsetier to pioneer farmer in Canada, bookkeeper in St. Louis, superintendent of Bent's Fort, fur trader and mountain man in Colorado and New Mexico, builder of Barclay's Fort on the Santa Fe Trail, New Mexico, in 1848 : a narrative of his career, 1810 to 1855, his memorandum diary, 1845 to 1850 / by George P. Hammond. Denver : Old West Pub. Co., 1976. viii, 246 p., [10] leaves of plates : ill., 3 maps (in pocket) ; 23 cm. [F800.B252H35] 74-84294 17.50
1. Barclay, Alexander, 1810-1855. 2. Southwest, New—Biography. 3. Fur trade—Southwest, New. 4. Frontier and pioneer life—Southwest, New. I. Barclay, Alexander, 1810-1855. II. Title: The adventures of Alexander Barclay, mountain man ...

Barclay, George, 1919-1942.

BARCLAY, George, 940.54'49'410924
1919-1942.
Fighter pilot : a self-portrait / by George Barclay ; edited by Humphrey Wynn ; with a foreword by Sir John Grandy. London : Kimber, 1976. 224 p. : ill., facsims., maps, ports. ; 24 cm. Includes index. [D786.B258 1976] 77-353533 ISBN 0-7183-0294-X : £4.50
1. Barclay, George, 1919-1942. 2. Great Britain. Royal Air Force—Biography. 3. World War, 1939-1945—Aerial operations, British. 4. Air pilots—Great Britain—Biography. I. Wynn, Humphrey. II. Title.

Barclay, Robert, 1648-1690.

TRUEBLOOD, David 289.6'0924
Elton, 1900-
Robert Barclay [by] D. Elton Trueblood. [1st ed.] New York, Harper & Row [1967, c1968] xi, 274 p. illus., coat of arms, facsims., port. 22 cm. Bibliography: p. 252-257. Bibliographical footnotes. [BX7795.B343T7] 68-11731
1. Barclay, Robert, 1648-1690.

Barclay, William, lecturer in the University of Glasgow.

BARCLAY, William, 285'.2'0924 B
lecturer in the University of Glasgow.
William Barclay : a spiritual autobiography. [Grand Rapids] : Eerdmans, [1975] 122 p. ; 22 cm. Bibliography: p. 122. [BS2351.B28A37 1975] 73-76528 ISBN 0-8028-3464-7 5.95
1. Barclay, William, lecturer in the University of Glasgow. I. Title. II. Title: A spiritual autobiography. BIP

Bard, Thomas Robert, 1841-1915.

HUTCHINSON, William 923.273
Henry, 1910-
Oil, land, and politics; the California career of Thomas Robert Bard, by W. H. Hutchinson [1st ed.] Norman, University of Oklahoma Press [1965] 2 v. illus., maps, ports. 23 cm. Bibliography: v. 2, p. 363 371. [HD9569.U6H8] 65-10114
1. Bard, Thomas Robert, 1841-1915. 2. Union Oil Company of California. I. Title. BIP

Bardot, Brigitte.

BEAUVOIR, Simone de, 1908- 927.92
Brigitte Bardot and the Lolita syndrome. [Translated from the French by Bernard Fretchman] New York, Reynal [1960] 37p. illus. 19x21cm. 61-476 1.95 pap.,
1. Bardot, Brigitte. I. Title.

BEAUVOIR, Simone 791.43'028'0924
de, 1908-
Brigitte Bardot and the Lolita syndrome. Foreword by George Amberg. New York, Arno Press, 1972 [c1959] 37, [52] p. illus. 21 x 24 cm. (The Literature of cinema) "Brigitte Bardot films": p. [51]-[52] [PN2638.B25B4 1972] 78-169346 ISBN 0-405-03912-3
1. Bardot, Brigitte. I. Title. BIP

CARPOZI, George, Jr. 927.92
The Brigitte Bardot story. [New York 13] Belmont Books [dist. Belmont Productions, 66 Leonard St., c.1961] 157p. illus. (L504) 61-2655 .50 pap.,
1. Bardot, Brigitte. I. Title.

EVANS, Peter, 791.43'028'0924 B
1933-
Bardot; eternal sex goddess. New York, Drake Publishers [1973] 186 p. illus. 24 cm. Filmography: p. [147]-186. [PN2638.B25E9] 73-4316 ISBN 0-87749-497-5 6.95
1. Bardot, Brigitte.

Barela, Casimiro.

FERNANDEZ, 328.788'092'4 B
Jose, 1882-
Cuarenta anos de legislador : biografia del senador Casimiro Barela / Emilio Fernandez. New York : Arno Press, 1976. ca. 400 p. ; 24 cm. (The Chicano heritage) Reprint of the 1911 ed. published in Trinidad, Colo. [F781.B232F47 1976] 76-1254 ISBN 0-405-09501-5 : 29.00
1. Barela, Casimiro. I. Title. II. Series. BIP

Barere de Vieuzac, Bertrand, 1755-1841.

GERSHOY, Leo, 1897- 923.244
Bertrand Barere; a reluctant terrorist. Princeton N. J., Princeton [c.]1962. 459p. illus. Bibl. 61-11848 8.50
1. Barere de Vieuzac, Bertrand, 1755-1841. I. Title. BIP

Barfield, Tony.

BARFIELD, Tony. 385'.36'10922 B
When there was steam : memories of a Western Region fireman / [by] Tony Barfield. Truro : Barton, [1976] 116 p. : ill., map, plan ; 22 cm. [TF140.B37A34] 76-375302 ISBN 0-85153-226-8 : £1.50
1. Barfield, Tony. 2. Great Western Railway (Great Britain) 3. Locomotive firemen—Biography. I. Title.

Barker, Alfred Charles, 1819-1873.

BURDON, Cotsford 770'.92'4 B
Carlton.
Dr. A. C. Barker, 1819-1873, photographer, farmer, physician [by] C. C. Burdon. Dunedin, McIndoe [1972] 88 p., 24 p. of illus. illus., geneal. table, ports. 23 cm. Bibliography: p. 88. [TR140.B27B87] 73-174677 4.50
1. Barker, Alfred Charles, 1819-1873.

Barker, David,

BARKER, David, 1935- 927.98
One thing and another: an autobiography, as told to Kenneth Ligertwood [London] Pelham Bks. [New Rochelle, N.Y., SportShelf, 1965, c.1964] 143p. illus., ports. 23cm. (Pelham champions' lib.) [SF33.B28A3] 65-964 5.75 bds.,
I. Ligertwood, Kenneth. II. Title.

Barker, Elliott Speer, 1886-

BARKER, Elliott 639'.9'0924 B
Speer, 1886-
Ramblings in the field of conservation / by Elliott S. Barker. [Santa Fe, N.M.] : Sunstone Press, c1976. 181 p., [6] leaves of plates : ill. ; 19 cm. [S926.B37A37] 76-150808 4.95
1. Barker, Elliott Speer, 1886- 2. Conservationists—New Mexico—Biography. I. Title.

Barker, Eugene Campbell, 1874-1956.

POOL, William C. 978'.072'2
Eugene C. Barker, historian, by William C. Pool. Austin, Texas State Historical Association [1971] 228 p. illus., ports. 23 cm. Bibliography: p. [217]-218. [E175.5.B32P6] 76-627820 ISBN 0-87611-025-1
1. Barker, Eugene Campbell, 1874-1956.

Barker, Jacob, 1779-1871.

INCIDENTS in the life 917.3'03 B
of Jacob Barker, of New Orleans, Louisiana; with historical facts, his financial transactions with the government, and his courseWon improtant political questions, from 1800 to 1855. Freeport, N.Y., Books for Libraries Press [1970] v, 285 p. ports. 24 cm. Reprint of the 1855 ed. [CT275.B415 1970] 74-121487
1. Barker, Jacob, 1779-1871.

Barker, Joseph, 1747?-1824?

BARKER, Joseph, 973'.04'97 S
1747?-1824?
Interesting narrative of the sufferings of Joseph Barker and his wife. New York : Garland Pub., 1977. p. cm. (The Garland library of narratives of North American Indian captivities ; v. 63) "The history of the captivity and providential release of Mrs. Caroline Harris": p. Reprint of the 1848 ed. published by Cunningham & Brooks, Rochester, N.Y. Issued with the reprint of the 1848 ed. of An Indian tradition, no fiction. New York, 1977. The reprint of the 1850 ed. of Adam, G. The dreadful sufferings and thrilling adventures of an overland party of emigrants to California. New York, 1977. The reprint of the 1851 ed. of Brice, J. R. History of the Revolutionary War. New York, 1977. The reprint of the 1851 ed. of Butterfield, D.C. Life and adventures of David C. Butterfield. New York, 1977. [E85.G2 vol. 63] 973.3'8 B 75-7087 ISBN 0-8240-1687-4(set) lib. bdg. : 25.00
1. Barker, Joseph, 1747?-1824? 2. Harris, Caroline. 3. Plummer, Clarissa. 4. Indians of North America—Captivities. 5. United States—History—Revolution, 1775-1783—Personal narratives. 6. Comanche Indians—Captivities. 7. United States—Biography. I. Harris, Caroline. History of the captivity and providential release therefrom of Mrs. Caroline Harris. 1977. II. Title. III. Series.

Barkley, Alben William, 1877-1956.

BARKLEY, Alben William, 923.273
1877-
That reminds me. [1st ed.] Garden City, N. Y., Doubleday, 1954. 288 p. illus. 22 cm. Autobiography. [E748.B318A3] 54-10775
I. Title.

DAVIS, Polly Ann, 973.918'092'4 B
1931-
Alben W. Barkley, Senate majority leader and Vice President / Polly Ann Davis. New York : Garland Pub., 1979. xviii, 343 p. : ports. ; 21 cm. (Modern American history) Includes index. Bibliography: p. 325-335. [E748.B318D38] 78-62380 ISBN 0-8240-3630-1 28.00
1. Barkley, Alben William, 1877-1956. 2. United States. Congress. Senate—Biography. 3. United States—Politics and government—1933-1945. 4. United States—Politics and government—1945-1953. 5. Legislators—United States—Biography. 6. Vice-Presidents—United States—Biography. I. Title. II. Series.

LIBBEY, James K. 973.918'092'4 B
Dear Alben : Mr. Barkley of Kentucky / James K. Libbey. Lexington : University Press of Kentucky, c1979. vii, 118, [1] p., [4] leaves of plates : ill. ; 21 cm. (The Kentucky Bicentennial bookshelf) Bibliography: p. 117-[119] [E748.B318L5] 78-57391 ISBN 0-8131-0238-3 : 4.95
1. Barkley, Alben William, 1877-1956. 2. United States. Congress—Biography. 3. Legislators—United States—Biography. 4. Vice Presidents—United States—Biography. 5. United States—Politics and government—1901-1953. I. Title. II. Series. BIP

Barlach, Ernst, 1870-1938.

CARLS, Carl Dietrich, 730'.924
1905-
Ernst Barlach. [New, expanded, rev. ed.] New York, Praeger [1969] 216 p. plates. 29 cm. [NB588.B35C313 1969] 78-89602 17.50
1. Barlach, Ernst, 1870-1938.

Barlow, Joel, 1754-1812.

TODD, Charles Burr, 811'.2 B
1849-
Life and letters of Joel Barlow, LL.D., poet, statesman, philosopher, with extracts from his works and hitherto unpublished poems. New York, B. Franklin [1972] iv, 306 p. port. 22 cm. (Burt Franklin research & source works series. American classics in history and social science, 243) Reprint of the 1886 ed. [PS705.T6 1972] 77-179400 ISBN 0-8337-3541-1 14.00

1. Barlow, Joel, 1754-1812. I. Barlow, Joel, 1754-1812. II. Title.

TODD, Charles Burr, 1849- 811'.2 B
Life and letters of Joel Barlow, poet, statesman, philosopher. New York, Da Capo Press, 1970. iv, 306 p. facsim., port. 24 cm. Reprint of the 1886 ed. [PS705.T6 1970] 70-106988
1. Barlow, Joel, 1754-1812. I. Title.

WOODRESS, James Leslie. 811'.2 B
A Yankee's odyssey; the life of Joel Barlow, by James Woodress. New York, Greenwood Press [1968, c1958] 347 p. illus., ports. 23 cm. Bibliographical references included in "Notes" (p. 309-328) [PS705.W6 1968] 69-14157
1. Barlow, Joel, 1754-1812. I. Title. BIP

WOODRESS, James Leslie. 923.273
A Yankee's odyssey; the life of Joel Barlow. [1st ed.] Philadelphia, Lippincott [1958] 347 p. illus. 22 cm. Includes bibliography. [PS705.W6] 58-11128
1. Barlow, Joel, 1754-1812. I. Title.

ZUNDER, Theodore Albert, 1901-1945. 811'.2 B
The early days of Joel Barlow, a Connecticut wit, Yale graduate, editor, lawyer, and poet chaplain during the Revolutionary War; his life and works from 1754 to 1787. [Hamden, Conn.] Archon Books, 1969 [c1934] x, 320 p. port. 22 cm. (Yale studies in English, v. 84) A revision of the author's thesis: Joel Barlow; his life and work to 1790, Yale University, 1927. Bibliographical references included in "Footnotes" (p. [233]-307) Bibliography: p. [308]-311. [PS705.Z8 1969] 69-15696
1. Barlow, Joel, 1754-1812. I. Title. II. Series.

Barlow, Joel, 1754-1812—Biography—Juvenile literature.

DOUTY, Esther Morris. 811'.2 B
Hasty pudding and Barbary pirates : a life of Joel Barlow / by Esther M. Douty. Philadelphia : Westminster Press, [1975] 144 p. : ill. ; 21 cm. Includes index. Bibliography: p. 139-140. A biography of the American poet, minister, and lawyer whose diplomatic skill in foreign affairs served several presidents in the difficult post-Revolutionary period. [E302.6.B197D68] 74-22023 ISBN 0-664-32559-9
1. Barlow, Joel, 1754-1812—Biography—Juvenile literature. I. Title. BIP

Barluzzi, Antonio, 1884-1960—Juvenile literature.

MADDEN, Daniel M. 927.2
Monuments to glory; the story of Antonio Barluzzi, architect of the Holy Land. Illus. by Lili Rethi. New York, Hawthorn [c.1964] 186p. illus., ports. 22cm. (Credo Bks.) Bibl. 64-11245 2.95
1. Barluzzi, Antonio, 1884-1960—Juvenile literature. I. Title.

Barmine, Alexandre.

BARMINE, Alexandre. 327'.2'0924 B
Memoirs of a Soviet diplomat; twenty years in the service of the U.S.S.R. Translated by Gerard Hopkins. Westport, Conn., Hyperion Press [1973] xvi, 360 p. illus. 23 cm. Reprint of the 1938 ed. published by L. Dickson, London. [DK268.B3A4 1973] 73-3736 ISBN 0-88355-040-7 17.50
1. Barmine, Alexandre. 2. Russia—Foreign relations—1917-1945. 3. Russia—Politics and government—1917-1936. I. Title. BIP

Barnabas Fellowship.

†GUNSTONE, John Thomas Arthur. 283'.092'4 B
Living together : the warm and candid story of one man's experience in a Christian community / John Gunstone ; drawings by Sylvia Lawton. 1st American ed. Minneapolis : Bethany Fellowship, 1976. 125 p. : ill. ; 18 cm. (Dimension books) [BX5186.B37G86 1976] 76-57794 ISBN 0-87123-325-8 pbk. : 1.95
1. Barnabas Fellowship. 2. Gunstone, John Thomas Arthur. 3. Church of England—Clergy—Biography. 4. Pentecostalism—Church of England. 5. Clergy—England—Biography. I. Title.

Barnabas, Saint, apostle.

KRAFT, Robert Alan, 1934- v. 12
Barnabas and the Didache, by Robert A. Kraft. New York, T. Nelson [1965] xx, 188 p. 22 cm. (The Apostolic Fathers; a new translation and commentary, v. 3) Includes bibliographical references. 66-81950
1. Barnabas, Saint, apostle. 2. Teaching of the twelve apostles. I. Title.

Barnard, Charlotte (Alington) 1830-1869.

SMITH, Phyllis. 780.924
The story of Claribel (Charlotte Alington Barnard), by the late Phyllis Smith, assisted by Margaret Godsmark. Lincoln, J.W. Ruddock & Sons, 1965. [7] 167 p. col. front., illus. (music) 12 plates (inc. ports., map, facisms.) 25 cm. (B66-995) "Claribel's Songs": p. 162-164; "Other publications by Claribel": p. 165. Illus. on endpapers. [ML410.B248S6] 66-2618
1. Barnard, Charlotte (Alington) 1830-1869. I. Title.

Barnard, Christiaan Neethling.

BARNARD, Christiaan Neethling. 617'.0924 B
Christiaan Barnard: one life [by] Christiaan Barnard and Curtis Bill Pepper. [1st American ed. New York] Macmillan [1970, c1969] 402 p. 24 cm. [RD598.B37 1970] 78-99020
1. Heart—Transplantation. I. Pepper, Curtis Bill, joint author. II. Title.

LEIPOLD, L. Edmond, 1902- 617'.0924 B
Dr. Christiaan N. Barnard, the man with the golden hands, by L. E. Leipold. Minneapolis, Denison [1971] 179 p. 22 cm. (Men of achievement series) A biography of the first surgeon to perform a human heart transplant successfully. [RD598.L38] 92 78-118161 ISBN 0-513-01106-4
1. Barnard, Christiaan Neethling. 2. Heart—Transplantation. I. Title.

Barnard, Daniel Dewey, 1797-1861.

PENNEY, Sherry. 328.73'092'4 B
Patrician in politics : Daniel Dewey Barnard of New York / Sherry Penney. Port Washington, N.Y. : Kennikat Press, 1974. xv, 206 p. : ill. ; 23 cm. (National university publications) Includes index. Bibliography: p. 183-201. [E415.9.B19P46] 74-77652 ISBN 0-8046-9067-7 : 12.50
1. Barnard, Daniel Dewey, 1797-1861. I. Title.

Barnard, Frederick Augustus Porter, 1809-1889.

CHUTE, William Joseph. 378.1'12'0924 B
Damn Yankee! : The first career of Frederick A. P. Barnard / William J. Chute. Port Washington, N.Y. : Kennikat Press, 1977. p. cm. (Series in American studies) (Kennikat Press National university publications) Includes index. Bibliography: p. [LD1245 1864.C48] 77-24383 ISBN 0-8046-9177-0 : 12.50
1. Barnard, Frederick Augustus Porter, 1809-1889. 2. College presidents—United States—Biography. I. Title. BIP

FULTON, John. 378.1'12'0924 B
Memoirs of Frederick A. P. Barnard, tenth president of Columbia College in the city of New York. Freeport, N.Y., Books for Libraries Press [1973] p. Reprint of the 1896 ed. [LD1245 1864.F842] 73-2741 ISBN 0-8369-7160-4
1. Barnard, Frederick Augustus Porter, 1809-1889.

Barnard, Henry, 1811-1900.

DOWNS, Robert Bingham, 1903- 370'.92'4 B
Henry Barnard / by Robert B. Downs. Boston : Twayne Publishers, c1977. 138 p. : port. ; 21 cm. (Twayne's world leaders series ; TWLS 59) Includes index. Bibliography: p. 133-135. [LA2317.B18D68] 77-1775 ISBN 0-8057-7710-5 : 7.50
1. Barnard, Henry, 1811-1900. 2. Educators—United States—Biography. BIP

Barnard, Jerry.

COPPIN, Ezra. 248'.2'0924 B
Turn loose / by Ezra Coppin. San Diego, CA : Faith Outreach International, c1976. 137 p. : ill. ; 21 cm. On cover: The Jerry Barnard story, as told to Ezra Coppin. [BR1725.B344C66] 76-53625
1. Barnard, Jerry. 2. Christian biography—California. I. Title.

Barnes, Albert Combs, 1872-1951.

SCHACK, William. 926.1
Art and argyrol; the life and career of Dr. Albert C. Barnes. New York, T. Yoseloff [1960] 412p. illus. 22cm. [CT275.B446S3] 60-6835
1. Barnes, Albert Combs, 1872-1951. I. Title.

Barnes, Barnabe, 1569?-1609.

SISSON, Charles Jasper, 1885- ed. 820.9003
Thomas Ladge and other Elizabethans. ed. by Charles J. Sisson. New York, Octagon 1966 [c1933] xii, 526p. illus., maps, geneal, tables 24cm. [PR2298.S5 1966] 66-18029 11.00
1. Lodge Thomas, 1558 -1625. 2. Barnes, Barnabe. 1569 -1609. 3. Bruskett, Lodowick, ca. 1545-ca. 1612. 4. Lyly John, 1554?-1606. 5. Buck. George d. Sir 1623. I. Eccles. Mark. II. Jones. Deborah. III. Title.
Contents omitted.

SISSON, Charles Jasper, 1885- ed. 820.9003
Thomas Lodge and other Elizabethans, edited by Charles J. Sisson. New York, Octagon Books, 1966 [c1933] xii, 526 p. illus., maps, geneal. tables. 24 cm. Contents.Contents.—Thomas Lodge and his family, by C. J. Sisson.—Barnabe Barnes, by M. Eccles.—Lodowick Bryskett and his family, by D. Jones.—John Lyly at St. Bartholomew's, or Much ado about washing, by D. Jones.—Sir George Buc, master of the revels, by M. Eccles. [PR2298.S5 1966] 66-18029
1. Lodge, Thomas, 1558?-1625. 2. Barnes, Barnabe, 1569?-1609. 3. Bryskett, Lodowick, ca. 1545-ca. 1612. 4. Lyly, John, 1554?-1606. 5. Buck, George, Sir, d. 1623. I. Eccles, Mark. II. Jones, Deborah. III. Title. BIP

Barnes, Ben E.

BARNES, Ben E. 973.9'092'4 B
The river flows backward / by Ben E. Barnes, with Kathlyn Gay. 1st ed. Port Washington, N.Y. : Ashley Books, [1975] 288 p. ; 22 cm. Autobiographical. [E185.97.B24A37 1975] 74-76645 ISBN 0-87949-027-6 : 8.95
1. Barnes, Ben E. I. Gay, Kathlyn. II. Title.

Barnes, Harry Elmer, 1889-1968.

HARRY Elmer Barnes, 301.15'3'0924
learned crusader; the new history in action. Edited by Arthur Goddard. Colorado Springs, R. Myles, 1968. lxxxvi, 884 p. illus., col. port. 23 cm. "Personalia and bibliography": p. 812-858. [HM22.U6B42] 68-57017 10.00
1. Barnes, Harry Elmer, 1889-1968. I. Goddard, Arthur, ed. II. Barnes, Harry Elmer, 1889-1968. BIP

Barnes, John Richard, 1833-1919.

BARNES, Claude Teancum, 1884- 922.8373
Toward the eternal; or, The life of John R. Barnes. Salt Lake City, Ralton Co., 1954. 98p. illus. 24cm. [BX8695.B34B3] 54-31940
1. Barnes, John Richard,1833-1919. I. Title.

Barnes, Ron.

BARNES, Ron. 942.1'44'082
Coronation cups and jam jars : a portrait of an East End family through three generations / [by] Ron Barnes. London : Centerprise, 1976. 208 p. ; 22 cm. [HD8383.5.B37] 77-365609 ISBN 0-903738-26-0 : £4.00. ISBN 0-903738-27-9 pbk.
1. Barnes, Ron. 2. Labor and laboring classes—England—London—Biography. I. Title.

Barnes, William, 1801-1886.

BAXTER, Lucy E. (Barnes) 1837-1902. 821'.8 B
The life of William Barnes, poet and philologist. London, New York, Macmillan, 1887. St. Clair Shores, Mich., Scholarly Press, 1971. xiv, 358 p. port. 22 cm. "Published works of William Barnes:" p. [350]-356. [PR4065.B3 1971] 72-144868 ISBN 0-403-00855-7
1. Barnes, William, 1801-1886. BIP

JACOBS, Willis D. 928.1
William Barnes, linguist. Albuquerque, University of New Mexico Press, 1952. 87 p. 23 cm. (University of New Mexico publications in language and literature, no. 9) Bibliographical references included in "Notes" (p. 83-87) [PE64.B3J3] 52-62762
1. Barnes, William, 1801-1886. I. Title. II. Series: New Mexico. University. University of New Mexico publications in language and literature, no. 9

Barnett, Ida B. Wells, 1862-1931.

BARNETT, Ida B. Wells, 1862-1931. 323.4'0924 B
Crusade for justice; the autobiography of Ida B. Wells. Edited by Alfreda M. Duster. Chicago, University of Chicago Press [1970] xxxii, 434 p. ports. 23 cm. (Negro American biographies and autobiographies.) Bibliography: p. 421-423. [E185.97.B26A3 1970] 73-108837 ISBN 0-226-89342-1
1. Barnett, Ida B. Wells, 1862-1931. I. Title.

Barnett, Ida B. Wells, 1862-1931—Juvenile literature.

BURT, Olive Wooley, 1894- 920.72'0973 B
Black women of valor, by Olive W. Burt. Illustrated by Paul Frame. New York, J. Messner [1974] 96 p. illus. 22 cm. Contents.Contents.—Juliette Derricotte.—Maggie Mitchell Walker.—Ida Wells Barnett.—Septima Poinsette Clark.—Other Black women of valor. [E185.96.B95] 920 74-7595 ISBN 0-671-32699-6 6.25
1. Derricotte, Juliette Aline, 1897-1931—Juvenile literature. 2. Walker, Maggie Lena—Juvenile literature. 3. Barnett, Ida B. Wells, 1862-1931—Juvenile literature. 4. Clark, Septima (Poinsette) 1898- Juvenile literature. I. Frame, Paul, illus. II. Title.
Library binding; 5.79, ISBN 0-671-32700-3. Contents omitted. BIP

Barney, Natalie Clifford.

BARNEY, Natalie Clifford. 848'.9'1209 B
Aventures de l'esprit / Natalie Clifford Barney. New York : Arno Press, 1975. p. cm. (Homosexuality) Reprint of the 1929 ed. published by Editions Emile-Paul freres, Paris. [PQ3939.B3A9 1975] 75-12302 ISBN 0-405-07394-1 : 15.00
1. Authority—Correspondence, reminiscences, etc. I. Title. II. Series. BIP

WICKES, George. 848'.9'1209 B
The Amazon of letters : the life and loves

of Natalie Barney / by George Wickes. New York : Putnam, c1976. 286 p., [8] leaves of plates : ill. ; 22 cm. Includes index. Bibliography: p. 273-278. [PQ3939.B3Z94 1976] 76-17302 ISBN 0-399-11864-0 : 10.00
1. Barney, Natalie Clifford. I. Title. **BIP**

Barney, Natalie Clifford—Biography.

CHALON, Jean. 841'.9'12
Portrait of a seductress : the world of Natalie Barney / by Jean Chalon ; translated from the French by Carol Barko. New York : Crown Publishers, c1979. p. cm. Translation of Portrait d'une seductrice. Includes bibliographical references and index. [PQ3939.B3Z613 1979] 78-32170 ISBN 0-517-53264-6 : 10.00
1. Barney, Natalie Clifford—Biography. 2. Authors, French—20th century—Biography. 3. Lesbians—Biography. I. Title.

Barnhart family.

BARNHART, Miles Goodwin, 1866- 929'.2'0973
Barnhart memoirs. Long Beach, Calif., Printed by Associated Offices, 1956. 95p., xiv 1. illus., ports. 30cm. [CS71.B2857 1956] 59-20372
1. Barnhart family. I. Title.

Barnum, Phineas Taylor, 1810-1891.

BARNUM, Phineas Taylor, 1810-1891 927.91
Barnum's own story; the autobiography of P. T. Barnum, combined, condensed from the various eds. pub. during his lifetime by Waldo R. Browne. [Gloucester, Mass., Peter Smith, 1962] 452p. (Dover bk. rebound) 3.75
I. Browne, Waldo Ralph, 1876-1954, ed. II. Title.

BARNUM, Phineas Taylor, 1810-1891 927.91
Barnum's own story; the autobiography of P. T. Barnum, combined, condensed from the various editions published during his lifetime by Waldo R. Browne. New York, Dover [1961] 452p. illus. 'An unabridged and unaltered republication of the work first published . . in 1927 . . This Dover edition also includes forty-eight pages of illustrations not included in the 1927 edition. 61-19631 1.65 pap.,
I. Browne, Waldo Ralph, 1876-1954, ed. II. Title.

BARNUM, Phineas Taylor, 1810-1891. 927.91
Barnum's own story; the autobiography of P. T. Barnum, combined & condensed from the various editions published during his lifetime by Waldo R. Browne. Gloucester, Mass., Peter Smith, 1972. 452 p. illus. 21 cm. Reprint of "an unaltered & unabridged republication of the work first published... in 1927..." in turn reprinted from the "Dover edition which also includes 48 pages of illus. not included in the 1927 edition." [GV1811.B3A3] ISBN 0-8446-4001-8 6.75
I. Browne, Waldo Ralph, 1876-1954, ed. II. Title.

BRYAN, Joseph, 1904- 927.91
The world's greatest showman; the life of P. T. Barnum. New York, Random House [1956] 182 p. illus. 22 cm. (Landmark books, 64) [GV1811.B3B7] 56-5460
1. Barnum, Phineas Taylor, 1810-1891. I. Title.

FITZSIMONS, Raymund. 791.1'0924
Barnum in London. New York, St. Martin's Press [1970] 179 p. plates, ports. 23 cm. Bibliography: p. 170-173. [GV1811.B3F53 1970] 73-106205 6.95
1. Barnum, Phineas Taylor, 1810-1891. 2. Stratton, Charles Sherwood, 1838-1883. 3. Haydon, Benjamin Robert, 1786-1846. I. Title.

STEVENSON, Augusta. 791.3'0924 B
P. T. Barnum, circus boy. Illustrated by Al Fiorentino. Indianapolis, Bobbs-Merrill [1964] 200 p. col. illus. 20 cm. (Childhood of famous Americans) The boyhood of the showman, operator of a popular museum in New York and a three ring circus known as "the greatest show on earth." [PZ7.S8467P] 92 AC 68
1. Barnum, Phineas Taylor, 1810-1891. I. Fiorentino, Al, illus. II. Title.

WALLACE, Irving, 1916- 927.91
The fabulous showman; the life and times of P. T. Barnum. [New York] New Amer. Lib. [1962, c.1959] 288p. (Signet bks., T2074) Bibl. .75 pap.,
1. Barnum, Phineas Taylor, 1810-1891. I. Title.

WALLACE, Irving, 1916- 927.91
The fabulous showman; the life and times of P. T. Barnum. [1st ed.] New York, Knopf, 1959. 317 p. illus. 22 cm. [GV1811.B3W3] 59-11239
1. Barnum, Phineas Taylor, 1810-1891. I. Title.

WELLS, Helen, 1910- 927.91
Barnum, showman of America. Illustrated by Leonard Vosburgh. [New York] D. McKay Co. [1957] 239 p. illus. 21 cm. [GV1811.B3W38] 57-5810
1. Barnum, Phineas Taylor, 1810-1891. I. Title.

Barnum, Phineas Taylor, 1810-1891—Juvenile literature.

COOK, Fred J. 920
Entertaining the world: P.T. Barnum. Illus. by Dan Siculan. Chicago, Ency. Britannica [1963,c1962] 192p. col. illus. 22 cm. (Britannica bkshelf: Great lives for young Amers.) 62-10425 lib. ed., 2.36
1. Barnum, Phineas Taylor, 1810-1891—Juvenile literature. I. Title.

EDWARDS, Anne, 1927- 791.3'092'4 B
P. T. Barnum / by Anne Edwards ; pictures by Marylin Hafner. New York : Putnam, c1977. 59 p. : ill. ; 23 cm. (See and read biography) An easy-to-read biography of the man who created "The Greatest Show on Earth." [GV1811.B3E35 1977] 92 76-52993 ISBN 0-399-61083-9 lib.bdg. : 4.29
1. Barnum, Phineas Taylor, 1810-1891—Juvenile literature. 2. Circus owners—United States—Biography—Juvenile literature. I. Hafner, Marylin. II. Title.

SUTTON, Felix. 791.3'0924 B
Master of ballyhoo; the story of P. T. Barnum. New York, Putnam [1968] 191 p. port. 22 cm. (Lives to remember) A biography of the show master who organized the "Greatest Show on Earth" and who sponsored such notables as Tom Thumb, Jenny Lind, and Jumbo, the elephant. [GV1811.B3S9] 92 68-24552 3.49
1. Barnum, Phineas Taylor, 1810-1891—Juvenile literature. I. Title.

Baronio, Cesare, Cardinal, 1538-1607.

PULLAPILLY, Cyriac K. 270'.09 B
Caesar Baronius, Counter-Reformation historian / Cyriac K. Pullapilly. Notre Dame, Ind. : University of Notre Dame Press, [1975] xiv, 222 p. : port., facsim. (on lining papers) ; 24 cm. Includes index. Bibliography: p. 207-216. [BX4705.B2P8] 74-12567 ISBN 0-268-00501-X : 12.95
1. Baronio, Cesare, Cardinal, 1538-1607. I. Title.

Barr, Jennifer.

BARR, Jennifer, 1945- 362.8'8 B
Within a dark wood : the personal story of a rape victim / by Jennifer Barr. 1st ed. Garden City, N.Y. : Doubleday, 1979. 284 p. ; 22 cm. [HV6561.B36] 79-6976 ISBN 0-385-15228-0 : 8.95
1. Barr, Jennifer. 2. Rape—United States—Case studies. 3. Victims of crimes—United States—Biography. 4. Rape victim services—United States. I. Title.

Barrault, Jean Louis.

BARRAULT, Jean Louis. 792'.092'4 B
Memories for tomorrow; the memoirs of Jean-Louis Barrault. Translated by Jonathan Griffin. New York, Dutton, 1974. 336 p. illus. 25 cm. Translation of Souvenirs pour demain. [PN2638.B27A3513] 73-20837 ISBN 0-525-15503-1 10.00
1. Barrault, Jean Louis. 2. Actors—Correspondence, reminiscences, etc. I. Title.

BARRAULT, Jean Louis. 792'.092'4
Reflections on the theatre / Jean-Louis Barrault ; with ill. by Christian Berard ... [et al.]. Westport, Conn. : Hyperion Press, 1979. p. cm. Translation of Reflexions sur le theatre. Reprint of the 1951 ed. published by Rockliff, London. Includes index. [PN2638.B27A313 1979] 78-59003 ISBN 0-88355-679-0 : lib.bdg. : 19.75
1. Barrault, Jean Louis. 2. Actors—France—Biography. I. Title. **BIP**

Barrett, Edward John Boyd,

BARRETT, Edward John Boyd, 1883- 922.273
A shepherd without sheep. Milwaukee, Bruce Pub. Co. [c1956] 143p. 21cm. Autobiographical. [BX8495.B327A3] 56-6719
I. Title.

Barrett, Gary, Sgt.

BARRETT, Ethel. 248'.2'0924 B
Barrett : a street cop who cared / as told by Ethel Barrett. Old Tappan, N.J. : F. H. Revell Co., c1978. 189 p. ill. ; 24 cm. [BB1725.B347A33] 78-710 ISBN 0-8007-0918-7 : 7.95
1. Barrett, Gary, Sgt. 2. Christian biography—California—Los Angeles. 3. Los Angeles—Police—Biography. I. Title. **BIP**

Barrett, John, 1866-1938.

PRISCO, Salvatore. 327'.2'0924 B
John Barrett, progressive era diplomat: a study of a commercial expansionist, 1887-1920, by Salvatore Prisco, III. University, University of Alabama Press [1973] xi, 149 p. 22 cm. Bibliography: p. 132-144. [HF3023.B28P74] 73-3776 ISBN 0-8173-5162-0 5.75
1. Barrett, John, 1866-1938. I. Title. **BIP**

Barrett, Rona.

BARRETT, Rona 791.430924
Miss Rona; an autobiography. New York, Bantam Books [1975, c1974] 250 p. illus. 18 cm. [PN1998.A3B386] 1.75 (pbk.)
I. Title.
L.C. card number for original ed.: 73-93029

BARRETT, Rona. 791.43'092'4
Miss Rona; an autobiography. Los Angeles, Nash Pub. [1974] 281 p. illus. 24 cm. [PN1998.A3B386] 73-93029 ISBN 0-8402-1336-0 7.95
1. Barrett, Rona. I. Title.

Barretto, Lefty, 1942-

BARRETTO, Lefty, 1942- 364.36'3'0924 B
Nobody's hero : a Puerto Rican story / by Lefty Barretto. New York : New American Library, 1977, c1976. xi, 258 p. ; 18 cm. (A Signet book) [HV6248.B28A36 1977] 77-356475 ISBN 0-451-07357-6 pbk. : 1.75
1. Barretto, Lefty, 1942- 2. Delinquents—New York (City)—Biography. 3. Puerto Ricans in New York (City) I. Title.

Barrie, James Matthew, Sir, bart., 1860-1937.

ASQUITH, Lady Cynthia Mary Evelyn (Charteris) 1887- 928.2
Portrait of Barrie. [1st ed.] New York, Dutton, 1955. 230p. illus. 22cm. [PR4076.A8 1955] 55-9648
1. Barrie, James Matthew, bart., 1860-1937. I. Title.

GREEN, Roger Gilbert Lancelyn 928.2
J. M. Barrie. New York, Walck [1961, c.1960] 64p. illus. (Walck monograph) 61-8577 2.50
1. Barrie, James Matthew, bart., Sir 1860-1937. I. Title.

HAMMERTON, John Alexander, Sir, 1871-1949. 828'.9'1209 B
J. M. Barrie and his books; biographical and critical studies. New York, Haskell House Publishers, 1974. 264 p. port. 22 cm. Reprint of the 1900 ed. published by H. Marshall, London. "Barriana": p. 255-257. [PR4076.H33 1974] 73-17096 ISBN 0-8383-1730-8 13.95 (lib. bdg.)
1. Barrie, James Matthews, bart., 1860-1937. I. Title.

MACKAIL, Denis George, 1892- 828'.9'1209 B
Barrie, the story of J. M. B.; a biography by Denis Mackail. Freeport, N.Y., Books for Libraries Press [1972] 736 p. port. 23 cm. Reprint of the 1941 ed. [PR4076.M3 1972] 73-37896 ISBN 0-8369-6734-8
1. Barrie, James Matthew, Sir, bart., 1860-1932—Biography. I. Title.

WRIGHT, Allen. 828'.9'1209 B
J. M. Barrie : glamour of twilight / [by] Allen Wright. Edinburgh : Ramsay Head Press, 1976. 96 p. ; 19 cm. (New assessments) Bibliography: p. [96] [PR4076.W73] 77-363590 ISBN 0-902859-37-4 : £2.50
1. Barrie, James Matthew, Sir, bart., 1860-1937. 2. Authors, Scottish—20th century—Biography.

Barrie, James Matthew, Sir, bart., 1860-1937—Biography.

ASQUITH, Cynthia Mary Evelyn (Charteris) Lady, 1887-1960. 828'.9'1209 B
Portrait of Barrie. Westport, Conn., Greenwood Press [1971, c1955] vii, 230 p. illus. 23 cm. [PR4076.A8 1971] 74-156172 ISBN 0-8371-6115-0
1. Barrie, James Matthew, Sir, bart., 1860-1937—Biography. I. Title. **BIP**

BIRKIN, Andrew. 828'.9'1209 B
J. M. Barrie : Peter Pan and the lost boys / by Andrew Birkin. New York : C. N. Potter : distributed by Crown Publishers, c1979. p. cm. [PR4076.B5 1979] 79-14571 ISBN 0-517-53873-3 : 14.95
1. Barrie, James Matthew, Sir, bart., 1860-1937—Biography. 2. Authors, English—19th century—Biography.

DARLINGTON, William Aubrey, 1890- 828'.9'1209 B
J. M. Barrie, by W. A. Darlington. New York, Haskell House, 1974. xiv, 158 p. illus. 23 cm. Reprint of the 1938 ed. published by Blackie, London. Bibliography: p. [153] [PR4076.D26 1974] 73-20391 ISBN 0-8383-1768-5 12.95 (lib. bdg.).
1. Barrie, James Matthew, Sir, bart., 1860-1937—Biography.

DARTON, Frederick Joseph Harvey. 823'.9'12
J. M. Barrie, by F. J. Harvey Darton. New York, Holt, 1929. St. Clair Shores, Mich., Scholarly Press, 1970. 126 p. 22 cm. Bibliography: p. 119-122. [PR4076.D3 1970] 74-131682 ISBN 0-403-00569-8
1. Barrie, James Matthew, Sir, bart., 1860-1937—Biography. I. Title.

Barrie, Margaret (Ogilvy)

BARRIE, James Matthew, Sir, bart., 1860-1937. 828'.9'1209
Margaret Ogilvy, by her son J. M. Barrie. New York, Scribner, 1896. St. Clair Shores, Mich., Scholarly Press [1969] 207 p. port. 21 cm. [PR4076.A42 1969] 71-9020
1. Barrie, Margaret (Ogilvy) I. Title. **BIP**

Barringer, Emily (Dunning) 1876-1961—Juvenile literature.

BARRINGER, Emily Dunning, 1876-1961. 926.1
Bowery to Bellevue; the story of New York's first woman ambulance surgeon. [1st ed.] New York, Norton [1950] 262 p. port. 22 cm. Autobiography. [R154.B26A3] 50-6665
I. Title.

DUNNAHOO, Terry. 617'.0924 B
Emily Dunning: a portrait. Chicago, Reilly & Lee Books [1970] 142 p. 24 cm. A biography of New York's first woman ambulance surgeon emphasizing her struggle to gain and hold that position in "a man's world." [R154.B26D84] 92 79-125376
1. Barringer, Emily (Dunning) 1876-1961—Juvenile literature. 2. Women physicians—Juvenile literature. I. Title.

Barrington, William Wildman Barrington, 2d Viscount, 1717-1793.

BARRINGTON, William Wildman Barrington, 2d Viscount, 1717-1793. 974.4'02
The Barrington-Bernard correspondence and illustrative matter, 1760-1770. Edited by Edward Channing and Archibald Cary Coolidge. New York, Da Capo Press, 1970 [c1912] xxiii, 306 p. 24 cm. (The Era of the American Revolution) Reprint of the ed. published by Harvard University, Cambridge, which was issued as v. 17 of Harvard historical studies. Includes bibliographical references. [F67.B27 1970] 75-109612 ISBN 0-306-71909-6
1. Barrington, William Wildman Barrington, 2d Viscount, 1717-1793. 2. Bernard, Francis, Sir, bart., 1712-1779. 3. Massachusetts—History—Colonial period, ca. 1600-1775—Sources. 4. Massachusetts—Politics and government—Revolution, 1775-1783—Sources. I. Bernard, Francis, Sir, bart., 1712-1779. II. Title. III. Series: Harvard historical studies, v. 17. BIP

Barrios de Chungara, Domitila.

BARRIOS de Chungara, Domitila. 984
Let me speak! : Testimony of Domitila, a woman of the Bolivian mines / by Domitila Barrios de Chungara with Moema Viezzer ; translated by Victoria Ortiz. New York : Monthly Review Press, c1978. 235 p. : ill. ; 21 cm. Translation of Si me permiten hablar. [HQ1537.B37713] 77-91757 ISBN 0-85345-485-X : 12.50
1. Barrios de Chungara, Domitila. 2. Women in community development—Bolivia—Biography. 3. Women in trade-unions—Bolivia—Biography. 4. Tin mines and mining—Bolivia. 5. Tin miners—Bolivia. 6. Feminists—Bolivia—Biography. I. Viezzer, Moema, joint author. II. Title. BIP

Barron, Dick.

LOCKE, Elisabeth. 616.9'94'00924 B
Comes the whirlwind; the Dick Barron story. Mountain View, Calif., Pacific Press Pub. Association [1969] 192 p. illus., ports. 23 cm. [RC263.L62] 68-59508
1. Barron, Dick. 2. Cancer—Personal narratives. I. Title.

Barron, James, 1769-1851.

STEVENS, William Oliver, 1878-1955. 359.3'32'0924 B
An affair of honor; the biography of Commodore James Barron, U.S.N. Chesapeake, Va., Norfolk County Historical Society, 1969. xvii, 204 p. illus., facsims., geneal. table, ports. 26 cm. [V63.B34S7] 75-6500
1. Barron, James, 1769-1851. I. Title.

Barrow, Clyde, 1909-1934.

FROST, H. Gordon. 363.2'32'0924 B
I'm Frank Hamer; the life of a Texas peace officer, by H. Gordon Frost and John H. Jenkins. Austin, Pemberton Press, 1968. 305 p. illus., ports. 26 cm. Bibliography: p. 295-297. [HV7911.H35F7] 68-31953
1. Hamer, Frank, 1884-1955. 2. Barrow, Clyde, 1909-1934. 3. Parker, Bonnie, 1909-1934. I. Jenkins, John Holmes, joint author. II. Title. BIP

HINTON, Ted, 1904-1977. 364.1'55 B
Ambush : the real story of Bonnie and Clyde / by Ted Hinton as told to Larry Grove. 1st ed. Austin, Tex. : Shoal Creek Publishers, c1978. p. cm. Includes index. [HV6245.H48] 79-11686 ISBN 0-88319-041-9 : 12.50
1. Barrow, Clyde, 1909-1934. 2. Parker, Bonnie, 1910-1934. 3. Crime and criminals—Texas—Biography. I. Grove, Larry, 1923- II. Title. BIP

PARKER, Emma (Krause) 1886- 364.15'0922 B
The true story of Bonnie & Clyde, as told by Bonnie's mother [Emma Parker] and Clyde's sister [Nell Barrow Cowan] With an introd. by Nelson Algren. Compiled, arr., and edited by Jan I. Fortune. [New York] New American Library [1968] 175 p. 18 cm. (A Signet book, P-3437) 1934 ed. published under title: Fugitives. [HV6248.B33P3 1968] 71-13675 0.60
1. Barrow, Clyde, 1909-1934. 2. Parker, Bonnie, 1910-1934. 3. Crime and criminals—Texas. I. Cowan, Nellie (Barrow) 1905- II. Fortune, Jan (Isabelle) 1892- ed. III. Title. IV. Title: Bonnie & Clyde.

Barrow, James, 1841-1864.

COULTER, Ellis Merton, 1890- 923.573
Lost generation: the life and death of James Barrow, C. S. A. Tuscaloosa, Ala., Confederate Pub. Co., 1956. 118p. 22cm. (Confederate contennial studies, no.1) 'Limited edition ... four hundred and fifty sale copies.' Bibliography: p.[107]-110. [E467.1.B28C6] 56-3306
1. Barrow, James, 1841-1864. I. Title. II. Series.

Barrows, Isabel Chapin, 1845-1913.

STERN, Madeleine Bettina, 1912- 926.1
So much in a lifetime; the story of Dr. Isabel Barrows, by Madeleine B. Stern. New York, Messner [1964] 191 p. 22 cm. [RE36.B27S7] 64-20156
1. Barrows, Isabel Chapin, 1845-1913. I. Title.

Barry, Arthur, 1896-

HICKEY, Neil 923.4173
The gentleman was a thief. New York, Collier [1962, c.1961] 190p. (AS13X) .95 pap.,
1. Barry, Arthur, 1896- I. Title.

HICKEY, Neil 923.41731
The gentleman was a thief. New York, Holt, Rinehart and Winston [c.1961] 208p. illus. 3.95
1. Barry, Arthur, 1896- I. Title.

HICKEY, Neil. 923.4173
The gentleman was a thief. [1st ed.] New York, Holt, Rinehart and Winston [1961] 208p. illus. 22cm. [HV6658.B3H5] 61-10731
1. Barry, Arthur, 1896- I. Title.

Barry, Clara (Reasoner)

BARRY, Clara (Reasoner) 1880- 920.7
Preachers' progeny. New York, Vantage Press [1954] 144p. illus. 23cm. Autobiographical. [CT275.B465A3] 53-12121
I. Title.

Barry, Henry M.,

BARRY, Henry M., 1911- 362.41
I'll be seeing you. [1st ed.] New York, Knopf, 1952. 239 p. 21 cm. Autobiographical. [HV1792.B3A3] 51-11979
I. Title.

Barry, James, 1795-1865.

RAE, Isobel, 1902- 926.1
The strange story of Dr. James Barry, army surgeon, inspector-general of hospitals, discovered on death to be a woman. London, New York, Longmans, Green [1958] 124p. illus. 21cm. [UH347.B3R3] 59-2052
1. Barry, James, 1795-1865. I. Title.

Barry, John, 1745-1803.

FINK, Leo Gregory, 1886- 923.573
Barry or Jones, "Father of the United States Navy"; historical reconnaissance. Philadelphia, Jefferies & Manz, 1962. 138 p. illus. 21 cm. Includes bibliography. [E207.B2F5] 63-32263
1. Barry, John, 1745-1803. 2. Jones, John Paul, 1747-1792. I. Title.

WIBBERLEY, Leonard. 923.573
John Barry. father of the Navy. New York, Ariel Books [1957] 157p. 22cm. [E207.B2W5] 57-8506
1. Barry, John, 1745-1803. I. Title.

WIBBERLEY, Leonard Patrick O'Connor, 1915- 923.573
John Barry, father of the Navy. New York, Ariel Books [1957] 157 p. 22 cm. [E207.B2W5] 57-8506
1. Barry, John, 1745-1803. I. Title.

Barry, Philip, 1896-1949.

ROPPOLO, Joseph Patrick 928.1
Philip Barry. New York, Twayne [c.1965] 158p. 21cm. (Twayne's U.S. authors sers, 78) Bibl. [PS3503.A648Z85] 65-12998 3.50 bds.,
1. Barry, Philip, 1896-1949. I. Title.

ROPPOLO, Joseph Patrick 928.1
Philip Barry. New Haven, Conn., Coll. & Univ. Pr. [c.1965] 158p. 21cm. (Twayne's U.S. authors ser., T-78) Bibl. [PS3503.A648Z85] 1.95 pap.,
1. Barry, Philip, 1896-1949. I. Title. BIP

Barry, Rick, 1944- —Juvenile literature.

ARMSTRONG, Robert, 1938- 796.32'3'0924 B
Rick Barry / by Robert Armstrong ; photos. by Vernon J. Biever Mankato, Minn. : Creative Education, c1977. 31 p. : col. ill. ; 25 cm. (Creative education sports superstars) A biography of basketball forward Rick Barry, a consistent top scorer. [GV884.B3A85] 92 76-44355 ISBN 0-87191-539-1 : 4.95
1. Barry, Rick, 1944- —Juvenile literature. 2. Basketball players—United States—Biography—Juvenile literature. I. Biever, Vernon J. II. Title. BIP

BARRY, Rick, 1944- 796.32'3'0924 [B]
Confessions of a basketball gypsy: the Rick Barry story [by] Rick Barry with Bill Libby [New York] [Dell] [1973, c.1972] 299 p. illus. 18 cm. (Dell Book, 1227) [GV884.B3A3] pap., 1.25
I. Libby, Bill. II. Title.

BARRY, Rick, 1944- 796.32'3'0924 B
Confessions of a basketball gypsy: the Rick Barry story, by Rick Barry with Bill Libby. Englewood Cliffs, N.J., Prentice-Hall [1972] 216 p. illus. 24 cm. [GV884.B3A3] 76-173700 ISBN 0-13-167445-5 7.95
I. Libby, Bill. II. Title.

*GOLDAPER, Sam. 796.32'3'0924 B
Rick Barry: Golden State super-star, by Sam Goldaper and Jay Searcy. New York, Grosset & Dunlap [1976] 158 p. 18 cm. (Tempo Books) [GV884] ISBN 0-448-12296-0 1.25 (pbk.)
1. Barry Rick, 1944- Juvenile literature. 2. Basketball—Biography—Juvenile literature. I. Searcy, Jay, joint author. II. Title.

O'CONNOR, Dick, 1930- 796.32'3'0924 B
Rick Barry : basketball ace / by Dick O'Connor. New York : Putnam, c1977. 125 p. : ill. ; 22 cm. (Putnam sports shelf) Includes index. A brief biography concentrating on the career of the star forward of the Golden State Warriors. [GV884.B3O26 1977] 92 76-41690 ISBN 0-399-61060-X lib. bdg. : 5.29
1. Barry, Rick, 1944- —Juvenile literature. 2. Basketball players—United States—Biography—Juvenile literature. BIP

Barry, Robert Smith, 1886-1949.

TREDREY, Frank D. 629.13'092'4 B
Pioneer pilot : the great Smith Barry who taught the world how to fly / [by] F. D. Tredrey. London : P. Davies, 1976. x, 164 p., 8 p. of plates : ill., ports. ; 23 cm. Includes index. Bibliography: p. 151-152. [TL540.B367T73] 76-366353 ISBN 0-432-16515-0 : £4.50
1. Barry, Robert Smith, 1886-1949. I. Title.

Barrymore, Diana,

BARRYMORE, Diana, 1921- 927.92
Too much, too soon, by Diana Barrymore and Gerold Frank. [1st ed.] New York, Holt [1957] 380 p. illus. 22 cm. Autobiography of Diana Barrymore. [PN2287.B28A3] 57-6184
I. Frank, Gerold, 1907- II. Title.

Barrymore,Ethel, 1879-1959—Juvenile literature.

FOX, Mary Virginia. 791'.0924 B
Ethel Barrymore: a portrait. Chicago, Reilly & Lee Books [1970] 133 p. 24 cm. A biography of the stage and screen actress from the well-known theatrical family. [PN2287.B3F6] 92 72-125377
1. Barrymore, Ethel, 1879-1959—Juvenile literature. I. Title.

NEWMAN, Shirlee Petkin 92
Ethel Barrymore, girl actress. Illus. by Al Florentino. Indianapolis, Bobbs [c.1966] 200p. col. illus. 20cm. (Childhood of famous Americans) Bibl. [PN2287.B3N4] 66-18416 2.25 bds.,
1. Barrymore,Ethel, 1879-1959—Juvenile literature. I. Title.

Barrymore family.

ALPERT, Hollis, 1916- 927.9
The Barrymores. New York, Dial Press, 1964. xviii, 397 p. illus., ports. 24 cm. Bibliography: p. xxii-xviii. [PN2285.A45] 64-20278
1. Barrymore family. I. Title.

Barrymore, John, 1882-1942.

BARRYMORE, Elaine (Jacobs) 927.92
All my sins remembered [by] Elaine Barrymore, Sandford Dody. New York, Popular Lib. [1965, c.1964] 240p. 18cm. (M2075) [PN2287.B55B3] .60 pap.,
1. Barrymore, John, 1882-1942. I. Dody, Sandford, joint author. II. Title.

BARRYMORE, Elaine Jacobs. 927.92
All my sins remembered, by Elaine Barrymore and Sandford Dody. [1st ed.] New York, Appleton-Century [1964] 274 p. ports. 24 cm. [PN2287.B35B3] 63-10352
1. Barrymore, John, 1882-1942. I. Dody, Sandford, joint author. II. Title.

BARRYMORE, John, 1882-1942. 792'.028'0924 B
Confessions of an actor. [New York] B. Blom [1971, c1926] 1 v. (unpaged) illus., facsim., ports. 21 cm. [PN2287.B35A3 1971] 70-84506
1. Actors—Correspondence, reminiscences, etc. I. Title. BIP

KOBLER, John. 792'.028'0924 B
Damned in paradise : the life of John Barrymore / John Kobler. 1st ed. New York : Atheneum, 1977. xii, 401 p., [8] leaves of plates : ill. ; 24 cm. Includes index. Bibliography: p. 377-385. [PN2287.B35K58 1977] 77-76752 ISBN 0-689-10814-1 : 12.95
1. Barrymore, John, 1882-1942. 2. Actors—United States—Biography. I. Title. BIP

Barrymore, Lionel, 1878-1954.

BARRYMORE, Lionel, 791'.092'4 B
1878-1954.
We Barrymores, by Lionel Barrymore, as told to Cameron Shipp. Westport, Conn., Greenwood Press [1974, c1951] viii, 311 p. illus. 22 cm. Reprint of the ed. published by Appleton-Century-Crofts, New York. [PN2287.B37A3 1974] 74-6702 ISBN 0-8371-7550-X
1. Barrymore, Lionel, 1878-1954. 2. Barrymore family. 3. Actors—Correspondence, reminiscences, etc. I. Shipp, Cameron. II. Title. **BIP**

Barrymore, Maurice, 1849-1905.

KOTSILIBAS-DAVIS, 792'.028'0924 B
James.
Great times, good times : the odyssey of Maurice Barrymore / James Kotsilibas-Davis. 1st ed. Garden City, N.Y. : Doubleday, 1977. 538 p., [16] leaves of plates : ill. ; 24 cm. Includes index. Bibliography: p. 504-514. [PN2287.B35K6] 72-76182 ISBN 0-385-04953-6 : 12.95
1. Barrymore, Maurice, 1849-1905. 2. Actors—United States—Biography. I. Title.

Barrymore, Richard Barry, 7th Earl of, 1769-1793.

ROBINSON, John 914.2'03'730924 B
Robert, 1850-1910.
The last earls of Barrymore, 1769-1824. New York, B. Blom, [1973 c.1972] xiv, 272 p. illus. 19 cm. Reprint of the 1894 ed. published by S. Low, Marston, London. [DA506.B3R6 1972] 72-80506 12.75
1. Barrymore, Richard Barry, 7th Earl of, 1769-1793. 2. Barrymore, Henry Barry, 8th Earl of, 1770-1823. 3. Theater—England—History. I. Title. **BIP**

Bartell, Jan Bryant.

BARTELL, Jan 133.1'092'4 B
Bryant.
Spindrift: spray from a psychic sea. New York, Hawthorn Books [1974] 245 p. 22 cm. Autobiographical. [BF1408.2.B37A34 1974] 73-10648 7.95
1. Bartell, Jan Bryant. 2. Ghosts. I. Title.

Barth, Karl, 1886-1968.

BARTH, Karl, 1886- 230.420924
How I changed my mind. Introd., epilogue by John D. Godsey. Richmond, Knox [1966] 96p. ports 21cm. Three autobiographical articles which first appeared in issues of the Christian Century. Bibl. [BX4827.B3A3] 66-17277 3.00
I. Title.

BUSCH, Eberhard, 230'.092'4 B
1937-
Karl Barth : his life from letters and autobiographical texts / Eberhard Busch ; translated by John Bowden. Philadelphia : Fortress Press, c1976. xvii, 569 p. : ill. ; 23 cm. Translation of Karl Barths Lebenslauf. Includes bibliographical references and indexes. [BX4827.B3B86313] 76-15881 ISBN 0-8006-0485-7 : 19.95
1. Barth, Karl, 1886-1968. 2. Theologians—Switzerland—Basel—Biography. 3. Basel—Biography. **BIP**

CASALIS, Georges 230
Portrait of Karl Barth. Tr., introd., by Robert McAfee Brown. Garden City, N. Y., Doubleday [c.] 1963. 135p. 22cm. Bibl. 63-7483 3.50
1. Barth, Karl, 1886- I. Title.

CASALIS, Georges 230
Portrait of Karl Barth. Tr. [from French] introd. by Robert McAfee Brown. Garden City, N.Y., Doubleday [1964, c.1963] 114p. 18cm. (Anchor bk. A422) Bibl. .95 pap.,
1. Barth, Karl, 1886- I. Title.

HAMER, Jerome 922.4494
Karl Barth. Tr. [from French] by Dominic M. Maruca. Westminister, Md., Newman [c.]1962. 300p. 24cm. Bibl. 61-16574 4.95
1. Barth, Karl, 1886- I. Title.

MUELLER, David 230'.4'0924 B
Livingstone, 1929-
Karl Barth, by David L. Mueller. Waco, Tex., Word Books [1972] 172 p. 23 cm. (Makers of the modern theological mind) Bibliography: p. 169-172. [BX4827.B3M8] 70-188066 4.95
1. Barth, Karl, 1886-1968.

ODEN, Thomas C. 230.4'0924
The promise of Barth; the ethics of freedom, by Thomas C. Oden. [1st ed.] Philadelphia, Lippincott [1969] 109 p. 22 cm. (The Promise of theology) "Selected bibliography of works by Karl Barth": p. 109. Bibliographical references included in "Notes" (p. 103-107) [BX4827.B3O3] 79-86078 3.50
1. Barth, Karl, 1886-1968. I. Title.

PARKER, Thomas Henry 230.4'0924 B
Louis.
Karl Barth, by T. H. L. Parker. Grand Rapids, Eerdmans [1970] 125 p. 22 cm. Includes bibliographical references. [BX4827.B3P28] 70-103449 2.45
1. Barth, Karl, 1886-1968.

POLMAN, Andries Derk 922.4494
Rietema, 1897-
Barth. Translated by Calvin D. Freeman. Philadelphia, Presbyterian and Reformed Pub. Co., 1960. 68p. 23cm. (International library of philosophy and theology. Modern thinkers series) Includes bibliography. [BX4827.B3P63] 60-6801
1. Barth. Karl, 1886- I. Title.

POLMAN, Andries Derk 922.4494
Rieteme, 1897-
Barth. Tr. by Calvin D. Freeman. Philadelphia, Presbyterian and Reformed Pub. Co. [c.]1960. 68p. (International library of philosophy and theology. Modern thinkers series) Bibl. 60-6801 1.50 pap.,
1. Barth, Karl, 1886- I. Title.

Bartha, Wands, 1908-1947.

MOLNAR, Ferenc, 1878- 894.5118
Companion in exile: notes for an autobiography; translated by Barrows Mussey. New York, Gaer Associates, 1950. 363 p. 22 cm. Translated from the unpublished Hungarian me. [PH3288.A3] 50-5701
1. Bartha, Wands, 1908-1947. I. Title.

Bartholdi, Frederic Auguste, 1834-1904.

GSCHAEDLER, Andre 730.924
True light on the Statue of Liberty and its creator. [1st ed.] Narbertn, Pa., Livingston [1966] xiii, 186p. illus., ports. 23cm. Bibl. [NB553.B3G8] 65-28279 3.95 pap.,
1. Bartholdi, Frederic Auguste, 1834-1904. 2. Statue of Liberty, New York. I. Title.

LUDMANN, Oscar Henry, 730.924
1900-
Quand? Or, Liberty nee Bartholdi, by Oscar H. Ludmann. [1st ed.] New York, Vantage Press [1965] 251 p. ports. 21 cm. [NB553.B3LS] 65-20120
1. Bartholdi, Frederic Auguste, 1834-1904. 2. State of Liberty, New York. I. Title. II. Title: Liberty nee Bartholdi.

Bartholomew, Joseph, 1766-1840.

GARBER, Wesley. 917.7
General Jos. Bartholomew—forgotten warrior. [Perrysville, Ohio, 1962] 22 p. illus. 23 cm. Caption title. One hundred copies printed. [F479.5.G37] 74-152609
1. Bartholomew, Joseph, 1766-1840. 2. Northwest, Old—History. I. Title.

Bartlett, Catherine (Thom)

BARTLETT, 917.52'6'0340924 B
Catherine (Thom)
Three under three; a Baltimore tale. Richmond, Dietz Press, 1970. 70 p. illus., ports. 24 cm. Autobiographical. [CT275.B4679A3] 71-17607
I. Title.

Bartlett family.

OLTORF, Frank Calvert, 917.64'286
1923- comp.
The Marlin compound; letters of a singular family. Austin, University of Texas Press [1968] x, 290 p. illus., facsims., map, ports. 24 cm. "The letters of Zenas Bartlett and his family." Bibliographical footnotes. [CS71.B33 1968] 68-56992 ISBN 0-292-78380-9 7.50
1. Bartlett family. I. Bartlett, Zenas, 1819-1897. II. Title. **BIP**

Bartlett, Robert Abram, 1875-1946.

NORWOOD, Harold 910'.45'0924 B
Andrew, 1923-
Bartlett, the great Canadian explorer / Harold Norwood ; photos. by Bartlett. 1st ed. Garden City, N.Y. : Doubleday, 1977. p. cm. Includes index. Bibliography: p. [G635.B3H67] 76-56304 ISBN 0-385-09984-3 : 7.95
1. Bartlett, Robert Abram, 1875-1946. 2. Explorers—Canada—Biography. I. Title.

SARNOFF, Paul. 910.450924 B
Ice pilot Bob Bartlett. New York, J. Messner [1966] 191 p. 22 cm. Bibliography: p. 181-183. [VK140.B3S3] 66-7372
1. Bartlett, Robert Abram, 1875-1946. I. Title.

Bartlett, William Henry, 1809-1854.

ROSS, Alexander M. 760'.092'4
William Henry Bartlett; artist, author and traveller [by] Alexander M. Ross. Containing a reprint of Dr. William Beattie's Brief memoir of the late William Henry Bartlett. [Toronto, Buffalo] University of Toronto Press [1973] ix, 164 p. illus. 29 cm. Bibliography: p. 151-154. [NX547.6.B37R67] 72-97783 ISBN 0-8020-1986-2 15.00
1. Bartlett, William Henry, 1809-1854. I. Beattie, William, 1793-1875. Brief memoir of the late William Henry Bartlett. 1973. **BIP**

Bartok, Bela, 1881-1945.

FASSETT, Agatha. 785'.0924 B
Bela Bartok - the American years (formerly titled: The naked face of genius) New York, Dover Publications [1970] 367 p. illus., ports. 22 cm. Reprint of the 1958 ed. [ML410.B26F3 1970] 77-127848 3.00
1. Bartok, Bela, 1881-1945.

HALSEY, Halsey, 1908- 927.8
The life and music of Bela Bartok. Rev. ed. London, New York, Oxford Univ. Pr. [1967] c.1964] xvi, 364p. illus., music. 21cm. (Galaxy bk., GB207) Chronological list of works, p. 323-334p. Discography, p. 335-343. Bibl. [ML410.B62S6] 53-5551 2.25 pap.,
1. Bartok, Bela, 1881-1945. 2. Bartok, Bela, 1881-1945— Discography. I. Title.

HELM, Everett Burton, 780'.92'4 B
1913-
Bartok, by Everett Helm. New York, T. Y. Crowell Co. [1972, c1971] 80 p. illus. 26 cm. (The Great composers) Bibliography: p. 77. Biography of a Hungarian musician and collector of folk music who was one of the most prominent composers of the twentieth century. Includes musical examples. [ML410.B26H4 1972] 92 79-154041 ISBN 0-690-11568-7 4.95
1. Bartok, Bela, 1881-1945. I. Title.

LESZNAI, Lajos. 780'.92'4 B
Bartok. Translated from the German by Percy M. Young. London, Dent, 1973. xii, 219, [8] p. illus., music, ports. 20 cm. (The Master musicians series) Translation of Bela Bartok. Includes index. Bibliography: p. 205-207. [ML410.B26L53] 73-180820 ISBN 0-460-03136-8
1. Bartok, Bela, 1881-1945. I. Title. II. Series.
Distributed by Octagon Books, 8.50.

LESZNAI, Lajos. 780'.92'4 B
Bartok. Translated from the German by Percy M. Young. New York, Octagon Books [1973] xii, 219 p. illus. 20 cm. (The Master musicians series) Imprint on mounted label. Translation of Bela Bartok; sein Leben, seine Werke. Bibliography: p. 205-207. [ML410.B26L53 1973b] 73-7004 ISBN 0-460-03136-8 8.50
1. Bartok, Bela, 1881-1945. I. Title. II. Series. **BIP**

MOREUX, Serge. 780'.92'4 B
Bela Bartok. Pref. by Arthur Honegger. Translated from the French by G. S. Fraser and Erik de Mauny. New York, Vienna House [1974] 224 p. 21 cm. Partial reprint of the 1953 ed. published by Harvill Press, London. "Works by Bartok": p. 221-224. [ML410.B26M62 1974] 74-77494 ISBN 0-8443-0105-1 2.95 (pbk.).
1. Bartok, Bela, 1881-1945. **BIP**

STEVENS, Halsey, 1908- 780.92
The life and music of Bela Bartok. Rev. ed. New York, Oxford University Press, 1964. xvi, 364 p. illus., facsim., music, ports. 22 cm. "Chronological list of works": p. 323-335. [ML410.B26S8 1964] 64-24867
1. Bartok, Bela, 1881-1945.

UJFALUSSY, Jozsef. 780'.924 B
Bela Bartok. [Translated by Ruth Pataki. 1st U.S. ed.] Boston, Crescendo Pub. Co. [1972, c1971] 459 p. port. 21 cm. Bibliography: p. 453-459. [ML410.B26U383] 72-200879 ISBN 0-87597-077-X 9.00
1. Bartok, Bela, 1881-1945. **BIP**

Bartok, Eva.

BARTOK, Eva. 927.92
Worth living for. New York, University Books [1959] 181p. illus. 22cm. Autobiographical. [PN2618.B3A3] 59-15874
I. Title.

Barton, Clara Harlowe, 1821-1912.

BARTON, William 361.5'0924 B
Eleazar, 1861-1930.
The life of Clara Barton, founder of the American Red Cross. New York, AMS Press [1969] 2 v. illus., ports. 23 cm. Reprint of the 1922 ed. [HV569.B3B4 1969] 71-86171
1. Barton, Clara Harlowe, 1821-1912. 2. Red Cross. U.S. American National Red Cross. I. Title.

BOYLSTON, Helen Dore, 923.673
1895-
Clara Barton, founder of the American Red Cross; illustrated by Paula Hutchison. New York, Random House [1955] 182 p. illus. 22 cm. (Landmark books, 58) [HV569.B3B6] 55-5824
1. Barton, Clara Harlowe, 1821-1912. **BIP**

GRAHAM, Alberta (Powell) 923.673
Clara Barton, Red Cross pioneer. Illustrated by Clifford N. Geary. New York, Abingdon Press [c1956] 128p. illus. 21cm. (Makers of America) [HV569.B3G7] 56-13770
1. Barton, Clara Harlowe, 1821-1912. I. Title.

PACE, Mildred Mastin. v. 12
Clara Barton. Illustrated by Robert Ball. New York, Scribner's [1965, c1941] 141 p. illus. 22 cm. 68-62319
1. Barton, Clara Harlowe, 1821-1912. I. Title.

PRICE, Olive M. 923.673
The story of Clara Barton; illustrated by Ruth Ives. New York, Grosset & Dunlap [1954] 178 p. illus. 22 cm. (Signature books, 25) [HV569.B3P7] 54-5857
1. Barton, Clara Harlowe, 1821-1912.

RED Cross. U.S. 610.730924
American National Red Cross. Clara Barton Chapter No. 1.
Clara Barton and Dansville: together with supplementary materials. Compiled with the approval of Clara Barton Chapter No. 1, the American National Red Cross. Dansville, N.Y., [F.A. Owen Pub. Co., 1966. xiv, 621 p. illus., facsims., ports. 23 cm. "A limited edition. Copies are not for sale." Bibliographical references inculded in "Introduction." [RT37.B33R4] 67-358
1. Barton, Clara Harlowe, 1821-1912. 2. Dansville, N.Y. I. Title.

ROSE, Mary Catherine. 923.673
Clara Barton: soldier of mercy. Illustrated by E. Harper Johnson. Champaign, Ill.,

Garrard Press [1960] 80p. illus. 23cm. (A Discovery book) [HV569.B3R57] 60-7080
1. Barton, Clara Harlowe, 1821-1912—Juvenile literature. I. Title.

ROSS, Ishbel, 1897- 923.673
Angel of the Battlefield; the life of Clara Barton. [1st ed.] New York, Harper [1956] xi, 305p. illus., ports., facsims. 22cm. Bibliography: p. 291-294. [HV569.B3R6] 56-6033
1. Barton, Clara Harlowe, 1821-1912. I. Title.

STEVENSON, Augusta. 610.73'0924 B
Clara Barton, girl nurse. Illustrated by Frank Giacoia. Indianapolis, Bobbs-Merrill [1962] 200 p. illus. 20 cm. (Childhood of famous Americans) Describes the girlhood of one of the first battlefield nurses, who aided wounded soldiers in the Civil War and founded the American Red Cross. [PZ7.S8467Cl4] 92 AC 68
1. Barton, Clara Harlowe, 1821-1912. I. Giacoia, Frank, illus. II. Title.

Barton, Clara Harlowe, 1821-1912—Juvenile literature.

FISHWICK, Marshall William. 361.50924 B
Clara Barton, by Marshall W. Fishwick and the editors of Silver Burdett. Editor in charge: Sam Welles. Morristown, N.J., Silver Burdett Co. [1966] 240 p. illus. (part col.) 27 cm. (Illustrious Americans) Bibliography: p. 233-234. [HV569.B3F5] 66-20553
1. Barton, Clara Harlowe, 1821-1912—Juvenile literature.

GRANT, Matthew G. 361.7'7 B
Clara Barton, Red Cross pioneer [by] Matthew G. Grant. Illustrated by John Keely. [Mankato, Minn., Creative Education; distributed by Childrens Press, Chicago, 1974] 31 p. illus. (part col.) 25 cm. (His Gallery of great Americans series. Women of America) A biography of the teacher, nurse, and founder of the American Red Cross. [HV569.B3G73] 92 73-15869 ISBN 0-87191-306-2
1. Barton, Clara Harlowe, 1821-1912—Juvenile literature. I. Keely, John, illus. II. Title.

GRANT, Matthew G. 361.7'7 B
Clara Barton, Red Cross pioneer [by] Matthew G. Grant. Illustrated by John Keely. [Mankato, Minn., Creative Education; distributed by Childrens Press, Chicago, 1974] 31 p. illus. (part col.) 25 cm. (His Gallery of great Americans series. Women of America) A biography of the teacher, nurse, and founder of the American Red Cross. [HV569.B3G73] 92 73-15869 ISBN 0-87191-306-2 3.95
1. Barton, Clara Harlowe, 1821-1912—Juvenile literature. I. Keely, John, illus. II. Title.

MANN, Peggy. 610.73'0924 B
Clara Barton, battlefield nurse. Pictures by Angie Culfogienis. New York, Coward-McCann [1969] 124 p. illus. 20 cm. (Famous women biographies) A biography of the teacher, nurse, and founder of the American Red Cross, who became known to the world as "the benefactress of humanity." [RT37.B33M3] 92 69-12664 3.49
1. Barton, Clara Harlowe, 1821-1912—Juvenile literature. I. Culfogienis, Angie, illus. II. Title.

Barton, Edward Cecil, 1896-

BARTON, Edward Cecil, 1896- 355.3'32'0924 B
Let the boy win his spurs : an autobiography / E. C. Barton. London : Research Pub. Co., c1976. 447 p., [4] leaves of plates : ill. ; 22 cm. [U55.B26A33] 76-377861 ISBN 0-7050-0035-4 : £3.90
1. Barton, Edward Cecil, 1896- 2. Great Britain. Army—Biography. 3. Soldiers—Great Britain—Biography. I. Title.

Barton, Robert, d.1540.

REID, William Stanford, 1913- 923.841
Skipper from Leith; the history of Robert Barton of Over Barnton. Philadelphia, University of Pennsylvania Press [1962] 334p. illus. 22cm. Includes bibliography. [HF3524.5.B3R4] 61-6623
1. Barton, Robert, d.1540. I. Title.

Bartram, William, 1739-1823—Juvenile literature.

SANGER, Marjory (Bartlett) 574'.092'4 B
Billy Bartram and his green world; an interpretative biography. [1st ed.] New York, Farrar, Straus & Giroux [1972] 207 p. plates. 24 cm. Bibliography: p. [197]-202. A biography of the eighteenth-century man who devoted his life to studying and drawing birds, animals, and plants in America's wilderness. [QL31.B33S35 1972] 92 78-175822 ISBN 0-374-30707-5 6.50
1. Bartram, William, 1739-1823—Juvenile literature. 2. Ornithologists—United States—Juvenile literature. I. Title.

Barua, Devakanta, 1914-

NAIDU, M. A., 1925- 954.04'092'4 B
Dev Kant Borooah : a political biography / M. A. Naidu. Hyderabad, [India] : Naidu : distributors, Booklinks Corp., 1976. 76 p., [3] leaves of plates : ill. ; 23 cm. [DS481.B3628N34] 76-902434 Rs30.00
1. Barua, Devakanta, 1914- 2. Statesmen—India—Biography. 3. India—Politics and government—20th century. I. Title.

Baruch, Bernard Mannes, 1870-1965.

BARUCH, Bernard Mannes, 1870- 923.273
Baruch. 1st ed. New York, Holt [1957-60] 2v. illus. 22cm. Vol. 2 published by Holt, Rinehart and Winston. Contents.[1] My own story.--[2] The public years. [E748.B32A3] 57-11982
I. Title.

BARUCH, Bernard Mannes, 1870- 923.273
Baruch, the public years. New York, Pocket Bks. [1962, c.1960] 415p. illus. (Giant Cardinal ed. GC135) .50 pap.,
I. Title.

BARUCH, Bernard Mannes, 1870-1965. 923.273
Baruch. [1st ed.] New York, Holt [1957-60] 2 v. illus. 22 cm. Vol. 2 published by Holt, Rinehart and Winston. Contents.Contents.—[1] My own story.—[2] The public years. [E748.B32A3] 57-11982

COIT, Margaret L. 923.273
Mr. Baruch. Illustrated with photos. Boston, Houghton Mifflin, 1957. xiv, 784 p. illus., ports. 22 cm. Bibliography: p. 767-772. [E748.B32C6] 56-10289
1. Baruch, Bernard Mannes, 1870- I. Title.

COIT, Margaret L. 973.91'3'0924 B
Mr. Baruch / by Margaret L. Coit. Westport, Conn. : Greenwood Press, 1975, c1957. p. cm. Reprint of the ed. published by Houghton Mifflin, Boston. Includes index. Bibliography: p. [E748.B32C6 1975] 75-19132 ISBN 0-8371-8251-4
1. Baruch, Bernard Mannes, 1870-1965. I. Title. **BIP**

COIT, Margaret L. 973.91'3'0924 B
Mr. Baruch / by Margaret L. Coit. Westport, Conn. : Greenwood Press, 1975, c1957. xii, 784 p., [8] leaves of plates : ill. ; 22 cm. Reprint of the ed. published by Houghton Mifflin, Boston. Includes index. Bibliography: p. 764-772. [E748.B32C6 1975] 75-19132 ISBN 0-8371-8251-4 lib.bdg. : 33.50
1. Baruch, Bernard Mannes, 1870-1965. I. Title.

ROSENBLOOM, Morris Victor, 1915- 923.273
Peace through strength; Bernard Baruch and a blueprint for security. Foreword by Eleanor Roosevelt; afterword by Charles E. Wilson. [1st trade ed.] Washington, American Surveys in association with Farrar, Straus and Young, New York, 1953 [c1952] 325p. illus. 23cm. [E748.B32R6 1953a] 53-3253
1. Baruch, Bernard Mannes, 1870- 2. U. S.—Defenses. I. Title.

ROSENBLOOM, Morris Victor, 1915- 923.273
Peace through strength; Bernard Baruch and a blueprint for security. Foreword by Eleanor Roosevelt; afterword by Charles E. Wilson. [Limited first ed.] Washington, American Surveys in association with Farrar, Straus and Young, New York, 1953 [c1952] 325p. col. port. 23cm. 'Each copy numbered and signed by the author ... Number 197.' Bibliography: p. 315-319. [E748.B32R6] 53-1566
1. Baruch, Bernard Mannes, 1870- 2. U. S.— Defenses. I. Title.

WHITE, William Lindsay, 1900- 923.273
Bernard Baruch, portrait of a citizen. [1st ed.] New York, Harcourt, Brace [1950] 158 p. 21 cm. Bibliography: p. 157-158. [E748.B32W48] 50-9610
1. Baruch, Bernard Mannes, 1870- I. Title.

WHITE, William Lindsay, 1900- 973.91'3'0924 B
Bernard Baruch, portrait of a citizen [by] W. L. White. Westport, Conn., Greenwood Press [1970, c1950] 155 p. 23 cm. [E748.B32W48 1970] 79-104231 ISBN 0-8371-3348-3 9.00
1. Baruch, Bernard Mannes, 1870-1965. I. Title. **BIP**

Baruch, Bernard Mannes, 1870-1965—Juvenile literature.

FINKE, Blythe Foote. 973.91'3'0924 B
Bernard M. Baruch, speculator and statesman. Charlotteville, N.Y., SamHar Press, 1972. 28 p. 22 cm. (Outstanding personalities, no. 32) Bibliography: p. 23-28. A biography of the self-made millionaire known as Baruch of Wall Street, emphasizing his stock market philosophy and his influence on United States economic policy during his lifetime. [E748.B32F55] 92 78-190249
1. Baruch, Bernard Mannes, 1870-1965—Juvenile literature. I. Title.

HENRY, Joanne Landers. 973.91'3'0924 B
Bernard Baruch, boy from South Carolina. Illustrated by Al Fiorentino. Indianapolis, Bobbs-Merrill [1971] 200 p. col. illus. 20 cm. (Childhood of famous Americans) Bibliography: p. 198. Stresses the childhood of the boy who became a financier and statesman and served as an unpaid adviser to every President from Woodrow Wilson to Dwight Eisenhower. [E748.B32H4] 92 78-146329
1. Baruch, Bernard Mannes, 1870-1965—Juvenile literature. I. Fiorentino, Al, illus. II. Title.

Baruch, of Tul'chin, 1757 (ca.)-1811.

WIESEL, Elie, 1928- 296.8'33
Four Hasidic masters and their struggle against melancholy / by Elie Wiesel ; foreword, Theodore M. Hesburgh. Notre Dame [Ind.] : University of Notre Dame Press, c1978. xix, 131 p., [1] leaf of plates : ill. ; 21 cm. (Ward-Phillips lectures in English language and literature ; v. 9) [BM198.W5125] 78-1419 ISBN 0-268-00944-9 : 7.95
1. Phinehas ben Abraham, of Korets, 1726 or 8-1791. 2. Baruch, of Tul'chin, 1757 (ca.)-1811. 3. Horowitz, Jacob Isaac, d. 1815. 4. Horowitz, Naphtali Zebi, 1760-1827. 5. Hasidim—Biography. I. Title. II. Series. **BIP**

Baruk, Henri, 1897-

BARUK, Henri, 1897- 616.8'9'00924 B
Patients are people like us : the experiences of half a century in neuropsychiatry / by Henri Baruk, with the assistance of Jean Laborde ; translated from the French by Eileen Finletter and Jean Ayer. New York : Morrow, 1978, c1977. 318 p. ; 25 cm. Translation of Des hommes comme nous. Includes index. "Principal publications by the same author": p. [305]-308. [RC339.52.B37A3312 1977] 77-13692 ISBN 0-688-03271-0 : 10.95
1. Baruk, Henri, 1897- 2. Psychiatrists—France—Biography. I. Laborde, Jean, 1918- joint author. II. Title. **BIP**

Barye, Antoine Louis, 1796-1875.

DEKAY, Charles, 1848-1935. 730'.92'4
Barye: life and works of Antoine Louis Bayre, sculptor; with eighty-six wood-cuts, artotypes, and prints, in memory of an exhibition of his bronzes, paintings, and water-colors, held at New York in aid of the fund for his monument at Paris. New York, Barye Monument Association, 1889. [New York, AMS Press, 1974] xi, 158 p. illus. 23 cm. [NB553.B4D3 1974] 73-163696 ISBN 0-404-02068-2
1. Barye, Antoine Louis, 1796-1875.

Baryshnikov, Mikhail, 1948-

LEMOND, Alan. 792.8'092'4 B
Bravo, Baryshnikov! / Alan LeMond ; with photos. by Lois Greenfield and others. New York : Grosset & Dunlap, 1978. 96 p. : ill. ; 28 cm. Includes index. [GV1785.B348L45] 78-60460 ISBN 0-448-16386-1. ISBN 0-448-16388-8 pbk. : 5.95
1. Baryshnikov, Mikhail, 1948- 2. Dancers—Russia—Biography. I. Greenfield, Lois. II. Title. **BIP**

Barzini, Luigi Giorgio, 1908-

BARZINI, Luigi Giorgio, 1908- 070'.92'4 B
O America, when you and I were young / Luigi Barzini. 1st ed. New York : Harper & Row, c1977. 329 p. ; 22 cm. [PN5246.B33A36] 76-5110 ISBN 0-06-010226-8 : 10.95
1. Barzini, Luigi Giorgio, 1908- 2. Journalists—Italy—Biography. 3. Journalists—United States—Biography. I. Title.

Basansky, Bill.

BASANSKY, Bill. 248'.246 B
The land of milk and honey / Bill Basansky, with David Manuel. Orleans, Mass. : Rock Harbor Press, 1978, c1977. 205 p. : ill. ; 22 cm. [BV4935.B23A34] 77-81266 5.95
1. Basansky, Bill. 2. Converts—United States—Biography. I. Manuel, David, joint author. II. Title.

Baseball.

ARDOVINO, Dominick. 796.357
The bat boy. Photography by Gerald Jacobson. New York, McGraw-Hill [1967] 159 p. illus., ports. 22 cm. (A Week with ... series) (A Young pioneer book.) Autobiographical. A batboy for the New York Mets tells about baseball in the major leagues and his three years with the team. [GV873.A7] AC 67
1. Baseball. I. Title.

BOUTON, Jim. 796.357'0924
Ball four; my life and hard times throwing the knuckleball in the Big Leagues. Edited by Leonard Shecter. New York, World Pub. Co. [1970] xiii, 400 p. illus., ports. 24 cm. [GV865.B69A3 1970] 78-120125 6.95
1. Baseball. I. Shecter, Leonard, ed. II. Title.

DAVIDSON, Donald, 1925- 796.357
Caught short, by Donald Davidson with Jesse Outlar. [1st ed.] New York, Atheneum, 1972. xii, 177 p. illus. 22 cm. [GV865.D29A3 1972] 74-190406 5.95
1. Baseball. I. Outlar, Jesse, joint author. II. Title.

KOUFAX, Sanford, 1935- 796.3570924 B
Koufax, by Sandy Koufax with Ed Linn. New York, Viking Press [1966] 294 p. port. 22 cm. [GV865.K67A9] 66-19162
1. Baseball. I. Linn, Edward. II. Title. **BIP**

*LEWIS, Jerry D. 796.357'092'2
Great Baseball stories / Jerry D. Lewis

New York Grosset & dunlap, c1979 309 p. ; 18cm. (tempo books) [GV865.A1] ISBN 0-448-17018-3 pbk.: 1.95
1. Baseball. 2. Baseball players — United states — Biography. I. Title. **BIP**

Baseball—Biography.

BASEBALL stars 927.96357
New York, Pyramid. v. ports. 19cm. Annual. Ed.: R. Robinson. [GV865.A1B36] 61-16051 .50 pap.,
1. Baseball—Biog. I. Robinson, Ray, Dec. 4, 1920- ed.

BASEBALL when the 796.357'092'2 *grass was real* : baseball from the twenties to the forties told by the men who played it / Donald Honig. New York : Coward, McCann & Geoghegan, [1975] 320 p. : ill. ; 25 cm. Includes index. [GV865.A1B37] 74-30610 ISBN 0-698-10660-1 : 12.50
1. Baseball—Biography. I. Honig, Donald.

BASEBALL when the 796.357'092'2 *grass was real* : baseball from the twenties to the forties told by the men who played it / Donald Honig. New York : Berkley Publishing Corp., 1976c1975. 304p. : ill. ; 18 cm. (A Berkley Medallion Book) Includes index. [GV865.A1B37] ISBN 0-425-03138-1 pbk. : 1.95
1. Baseball-Biography. I. Honig, Donald.
L.C. card no. of 1975 Coward, McCann &Geoghegan edition: 74-30610.

BONNER, Mary Graham, 927.96357 1890-
Baseball rookies who made good. Foreword by Joe Reichler. [1st ed.] New York, Knopf, 1954. 173p. illus. 21cm. [GV865.A1B6] 54-5303
1. Baseball—Biog. I. Title.

BOUTON, Jim, 796.357'092'2 B comp.
"I managed good, but boy did they play bad." Written and edited by Jim Bouton, with Neil Offen. [1st ed. Chicago] Playboy Press [1973] xxiii, 325 p. illus. 22 cm. [GV865.A1B63] 73-76276 7.95
1. Baseball—Biography. 2. Baseball managing. I. Offen, Neil. II. Title.
Contents Omitted.

BOUTON, Jim., 796.357'092'2 [B] comp.
"I managed good, but boy did they play bad." Written and edited by Jim Bouton, with Neil Offen. [New York, Dell, 1974, c1973] 300 p. illus. 18 cm. [GV865.A1B63] 1.50 (pbk.)
1. Baseball—Biography. 2. Baseball managing. I. Offen, Neil. II. Title.
L.C. card number for hardbound ed.: 73-76276.

BROEG, Robert M. 796.357'0922 B
Super stars of baseball; their lives, their loves, their laughs, their laments, by Bob Broeg. St. Louis, Mo., Sporting News [1971] xiii, 329 p. illus., ports. 29 cm. (A Spink sports publication) [GV865.A1B66] 79-26472 8.95
1. Baseball—Biography. I. Title.

CONIGLIARO, Tony, 796.357'0924 B 1945-
Seeing it through, by Tony Conigliaro with Jack Zanger. [New York, Macmillan [1970] 238 p. illus. 21 cm. [GV865.C66A3] 72-124869
1. Baseball—Biography. I. Zanger, Jack. II. Title.

DALEY, Arthur. 796.35708
Kings of the home run. New York, Putnam [1962] 253 p. illus. 21 cm. [GV865.A1D3] 62-10964
1. Baseball—Biography. I. Title.

DAVIS, Mac 796.3570922
Baseball's unforgettables. New York, Bantam [1966] 156p. illus. 18cm. (Bantam pathfinder eds., FP139) [GV865.A1D35] 66-14717 .50 pap.,
1. Baseball—Biog. I. Title.

DAVIS, Mac, 1905- 796.357'092'2 B
100 greatest baseball heroes / by Mac Davis. New York : Grosset & Dunlap, [1974] 151 p. : ill. ; 29 cm. (Illustrated true books) Biographical sketches of such baseball stars as Babe Ruth, Pete Gray, Connie Mack, Jackie Robinson, Warren Spahn, and ninety-five others. [GV865.A1D368] 920 73-19192 ISBN 0-448-11742-8 : 4.95. ISBN 0-448-13208-7 lib.bdg. : 5.59
1. Baseball—Biography. I. Title.

DAVIS, Mac, 1905- 796.3570922
Baseball's all-time greats: the top fifty players. Toronto, New York, [Bantam Books, 1970] 149 p. ports. 18 cm. (Bantam pathfinder editions) [GV865.A1D33] 71-18821 0.75 (pbk.)
1. Baseball—Biography. I. Title.

DAVIS, Mac, 1905- 796.3570922
Baseball's unforgettables. New York, Bantam Books [1966] 156 p. illus. 18 cm. (Bantam pathfinder editions, FP139) [GV865.A1D35] 66-14717
1. Baseball—Biog. I. Title.

DAVIS, Mac Samuel, 927.96357 1905-
The greatest in baseball. New York, Scholastic Bk. Servs. [c.1962] 96p. illus. 20cm. A62 .50 pap.,
1. Baseball—Biog. I. Title.

FREEHAN, Bill, 1941- 796.357'0924
Behind the mask; an inside baseball diary. Edited by Steve Gelman and Dick Schaap. New York, [Maddick Manuscripts, Inc.; distributed by] World Pub. Co., Cleveland [1970] 225 p. ports. 22 cm. (A Maddick manuscripts book) [GV865.F67A3 1970] 71-115798 5.95
1. Baseball—Biography. I. Title.

GRAHAM, Frank, 796.357'0922 B 1925-
Great hitters of the major leagues. [New York, Random House, 1969] 171 p. ports. 22 cm. (Little League library, 11) Contents.Contents.—Ty Cobb.—Babe Ruth.—Rogers Hornsby.—Lou Gehrig.—Hank Greenberg.—Joe DiMaggio.—Ted Williams.—Stan Musial.—Willie Mays.—Mickey Mantle.—Henry Aaron. [GV865.A1G683] 69-19289
1. Baseball—Biography. 2. Baseball—Juvenile literature. I. Title. **BIP**

GRAYSON, Harry, 796.357'0922 B d.1968.
They played the game; the story of baseball greats. Freeport, N.Y., Books for Libraries Press [1972, c1945] xiii, 153 p. illus. 24 cm. (Essay index reprint series) [GV865.A1G7 1972] 77-167349 ISBN 0-8369-2692-7
1. Baseball—Biography. I. Title. **BIP**

HARRELSON, Ken, 796.357'0924 B 1941-
Hawk, by Ken Harrelson with Al Hirshberg. New York, Viking Press [1969] 244 p. ports. 22 cm. [GV865.H28A3] 69-18805 5.95
1. Baseball—Biography. I. Hirshberg, Albert, 1909- joint author. II. Title.

HIRSHBERG, Albert, 796.3570922 1909-
Baseball's greatest catchers. New York, Putnam [c.1966] 190p. 21cm. [GV865.A1H5] 66-14324 3.50; 3.29 lib. ed.,
1. Baseball—Biog. I. Title.

HOLWAY, John. 796.357'092'2 B
Voices from the great Black baseball leagues / John Holway. New York : Dodd, Mead, [1975] p. cm. [GV865.A1H615] 75-11931 ISBN 0-396-07124-4 : 9.95
1. Baseball—Biography. 2. Negro athletes—Biography. I. Title. **BIP**

HONIG, Donald. 796.357'092'2
Baseball between the lines : baseball in the '40s and '50s as told by the men who played it / Donald Honig ; introd. by Red Smith. New York : Coward, McCann & Geoghegan, c1976. 252 p. : ill. ; 25 cm. Includes index. [GV865.A1H618 1976] 75-34477 12.50
1. Baseball—Biography. I. Title.

JONES, Cleon, 796.357'0924 B 1942-
Cleon, by Cleon Jones with Ed Hershey. New York, Coward-McCann [1970] 191 p. plates, ports. 22 cm. [GV865.J64A3 1970] 78-113524 5.95
1. Baseball—Biography. I. Hershey, Ed, joint author. II. Title. **BIP**

JORDAN, Pat. 796.357'092'2
The suitors of spring. New York, Dodd, Mead [1973] xi, 211 p. illus. 22 cm. [GV865.A1J67 1973] 72-9933 ISBN 0-396-06711-5 6.95
1. Baseball Biography. 2. Pitchers (Baseball)—Biography. I. Title. **BIP**

KARST, Gene, 796.357'64'0922 B 1906-
Who's who in professional baseball [by] Gene Karst [and] Martin J. Jones, Jr. New Rochelle, N.Y., Arlington House [1973] 919 p. 24 cm. [GV865.A1K37] 73-11870 ISBN 0-87000-220-1 12.95
1. Baseball—Biography. I. Jones, Martin J., 1943- joint author. II. Title.

MEANY, Thomas 927.96357
Baseball's best: the all-time major league baseball team, by Tom Meany, Tommy Holmes. New York, Watts [c.1964] vi, 260p. ports. 25cm. 64-20261 5.95
1. Baseball—Biog. I. Holmes, Tommy, 1903- joint author. II. Title.

MEANY, Thomas. 927.86357
Baseball's greatest players. Rev. ed. [New York, Dell Pub. Co., 1955] 288p. 17cm. (A Dell book, 839) [GV865.A1M43 1955] 55-3904
1. Baseball—Biog. I. Title.

MEANY, Thomas 927.96357
Baseball's greatest players. Foreword by Ford C. Frick. New York, Grosset [1964, c.1953] 295p. 20cm. (Big league baseball lib.) 53-8312 1.95 bds.,
1. Baseball— Biog. I. Title.

MEANY, Thomas. 927.96357
Baseball's greatestplayers. With a foreword by Ford C. Frick. New York, Grosset Dunlap [1953] 295p. illus. 20cm. (The Big league baseball library [GV865.A1M43] 53-8312
1. Baseball—Biog. I. Title.

NEWCOMBE, Jack. 927.96357
The fireballers; baseball's fastest pitchers. New York, Putnam [1964] 187 p. ports. 21 cm. [GV865.A1N4] 64-13053
1. Baseball—Biography. I. Title. II. Title: Baseball's fastest pitchers.

ORR, Jack, ed. 927.96357
Baseball's greatest players today [the contemporary 'Who's who' of baseball] New York, Watts [c.1963] 150p. 24cm. 3.95
1. Baseball—Biog. I. Title. II. Title: Who's who of baseball.

ORR, Jack, ed. 927.96357
Baseball's greatest players today; [the contemporary 'Who's who' of baseball] New York, Part [dist. by Kable News Co., c.1953] 150p. 19cm. (Amer. sports lib., 105) 63-12509 .50 pap.,
1. Baseball—Biog. I. Title. II. Title: Who's who of baseball.

POPE, Edwin. 927.96357
Baseball's greatest managers. [1st ed.] Garden City, N. Y., Doubleday, 1960. 286p. 22cm. [GV865.A1P66] 60-7881
1. Baseball—Biog. I. Title.

PRATT, John 796.3576'4'0922 Lowell.
Baseball's all-stars, edited by J. Lowell Pratt. Introd. by Lee MacPhail. [1st ed.] Garden City, N.Y., Doubleday [1967] x, 151 p. ports. 24 cm. [GV865.A1P7] 67-17264
1. Baseball—Biography. I. Title.

RITTER, Lawrence S. 796.3570922
The glory of their times; the story of the early days of baseball told by the men who played it [by] Lawrence S. Ritter. With a foreword by John K. Hutchens. New York, Macmillan [1966] xviii, 300 p. illus., facsims., ports. 24 cm. [GV865.A1R5] 66-17905
1. Baseball—Biography. I. Title.

ROBINSON, Ray, ed. 927.96357
Baseball stars of 1965. New York, Pyramid [c.1965] 172p. illus. 18cm. annual. (R1148) .50 pap.,
1. Baseball—Biog. I. Title.

ROBINSON, Ray, 796.357'0922 B Dec.4,1920-
Baseball's most colorful managers. New York, Putnam [1969] 191 p. 21 cm. Contents.Contents.—Leo Durocher.—Casey Stengel.—Miller Huggins.—Connie Mack.—Wilbert Robinson.—John J. McGraw. [GV865.A1R57] 920 69-13328 3.64
1. Baseball—Biography 2. Baseball—Juvenile literature. I. Title. **BIP**

ROBINSON, Ray, Dec. 4, 927.96357 1920- ed.
Baseball stars. New York, Pyramid Publications [etc.] v. ports. 19 cm. annual. Editor: R. Robinson. [GV865.A1B36] 61-16051
1. Baseball — Biog. I. Title.

ROSE, Pete, 1942- 796.357'0924 B
The Pete Rose story: an autobiography. Introd. by Joe Garagiola. New York, World [1970] 202 p. illus., ports. 22 cm. [GV865.R65A3 1970] 71-120126 6.95
1. Baseball—Biography. I. Title.

ROSENTHAL, Harold. 927.96357
Baseball's best managers. New York, T. Nelson [1961] 160p. 23cm. (A Sport magazine library book) [GV865.A1R67] 61-10432
1. Baseball—Biog. I. Title.

RUST, Art, 1927- 796.357'092'2 B
"Get that nigger off the field!" : A sparkling, informal history of the Black man in baseball / by Art Rust, Jr. New York : Delacorte Press, c1976. 228 p. : ill. ; 24 cm. Includes index [GV865.A1R87] 75-38513 ISBN 0-440-02791-8 : 7.95
1. Baseball—Biography. 2. Negro athletes—Biography. I. Title.

SEAVER, Tom, 796.357'092'2 B 1944- comp.
How I would pitch to Babe Ruth, by Tom Seaver with Norman Lewis Smith. [Chicago] Playboy Press [1975, c1974] xix, 268 p. 18 cm. [GV865.A1537] 1.50 (pbk.)
1. Baseball—Biography. 2. Pitching (Baseball) 3. Batting (Baseball) I. Smith, Norman Lewis, joint comp. II. Title.

SEAVER, Tom, 796.357'092'2 B 1944- comp.
How I would pitch to Babe Ruth; Seaver vs. the sluggers. Written and edited by Tom Seaver, with Norman Lewis Smith. [1st ed. Chicago] Playboy Press [1974] xix, 268 p. illus. 22 cm. [GV865.A1S37] 73-91660 ISBN 0-87223-405-3 8.50
1. Baseball—Biography. 2. Pitching (Baseball) 3. Batting (Baseball) I. Smith, Norman Lewis, joint comp. II. Title.

SHAPIRO, Milton J. 920
The day they made the record book, by Milton J. Shapiro. New York; J. Messner [1968] 191 p. illus. 22 cm. Brief biographies of seven baseball players whose accomplishments may never be surpassed: Babe Ruth, Lou Gehrig, Joe DiMaggio, Don Larsen, Roger Maris, Maury Wills, and Sandy Koufax. [GV865.A1S45] AC 68
1. Baseball—Biography. I. Title.

SHAPIRO, Milton J. 796.3570922
The year they won the Most Valuable Player Award. New York, Messner [c.1966] 189p. ports. 22cm. [GV865.A1S48] 66-14009 3.95; 3.64 lib. ed.,
1. Baseball—Biog. I. Title.

SMITH, Ira Lepouce, 927.96357 1895-
Baseball's famous first basemen. Illustrated by Leo Hershfield. New York, Barnes [1956] 310 p. illus. 20 cm. (Baseball's famous players library) [GV865.A1S53] 56-5559
1. Baseball—Biography. I. Title.

SMITH, Ira Lepouce, 927.96357 1895-
Baseball's famous outfielders; illustrated by Leo Hershfield. New York, Barnes [1954] 312 p. illus. 20 cm. (Baseball's famous players library) [GV865.A1554] 54-10347
1. Baseball—Biography.

WAYNE, Bennett. 796.357'092'2 B
Heroes of the home run. Edited, with commentary, by Bennett Wayne.

Champaign, Ill., Garrard Pub. Co. [1973] 168 p. illus. 22 cm. (A Target book) Brief biographies of ten major league baseball stars well known for their outstanding batting records. [GV865.A1W35] 73-6750 ISBN 0-8116-4903-2 4.75
1. Baseball—Biography. I. Title. BIP

Baseball—Biography—Juvenile literature.

BERKE, Art. 796.357'092'2 B
Unsung heroes of the major leagues / by Art Berke. New York : Random House, c1976. 152 p. : ill. ; 22 cm. (Major league library ; 24) Includes index. Contents.Contents.—Joe Rudi.—Doug Rader.—Phil Niekro.—Thurman Munson.—Cookie Rojas.—Billy Williams.—Mike Cuellar.—Bill Melton.—Ron Fairly.—Tony Perez. [GV865.A1B47] 920 75-34909 ISBN 0-394-83096-2. lib.bdg. : 2.50
1. Baseball—Biography—Juvenile literature. I. Title.
Contents omitted BIP

BRAUN, Thomas, 1944- 796.357'092'2 B
The hitters / by Thomas C. Braun. Mankato, Minn. : Creative Education, [1976] p. cm. (Stars of the NBL and ABL) Brief biographies of Rod Carew, Lou Brock, Reggie Jackson, Pete Rose, and Hank Aaron—all outstanding hitters for the NBL or ABL. [GV865.A1B65] 920 76-8422 ISBN 0-87191-515-4 lib.bdg. : 5.95
1. Baseball—Biography—Juvenile literature. 2. Batting (Baseball)—Biography—Juvenile literature. I. Title. BIP

BROSNAN, Jim. 796.357640922
Great rookies of the major leagues. Illustrated with photos. New York, Random House [1966] 186 p. illus., ports. 22 cm. (Little League library 6) [GB865.A1B73] 66-9801
1. Baseball — Biog. — Juvenile literature. I. Title.

BUTLER, Hal. 796.357'092'2 B
Baseball's champion pitchers: the Cy Young Award winners. New York, J. Messner [1974] 96 p. illus. 22 cm. Biographies of the six pitchers who won the Cy Young award in 1971, 1972, and 1973: Vida Blue, Ferguson Jenkins, Gaylord Perry, Steve Carlton, Jim Palmer, and Tom Seaver. [GV865.A1B87] 920 74-7594 ISBN 0-671-32697-X 6.95
1. Baseball—Biography—Juvenile literature. 2. Pitchers (Baseball)—Biography—Juvenile literature. I. Title. II. Title: The Cy Young Award winners.
Library binding 5.79; ISBN 0-671-32698-8. BIP

DALEY, Arthur. 796.357'092'2
All the home run kings. New York, Putnam [1972] 223 p. illus. 21 cm. Brief biographies concentrating on the special feats of twenty-three baseball players noted for their home runs. [GV865.A1D28 1972] 920 74-188722 5.95
1. Baseball—Biography—Juvenile literature. I. Title. BIP

DAVIS, Mac, 1905- 796.3 B
The greatest in sports; all time heroes of baseball, football & track. Illustrated by Sam Nisenson. New York, World Pub. [1972] 160 p. illus. 29 cm. Brief biographies emphasizing the achievements of thirty-eight star performers in baseball, football, and track. [GV865.A1D36 1972] 920 78-184026 ISBN 0-529-04469-2 4.95
1. Baseball—Biography Juvenile literature. 2. Football—Biography—Juvenile literature. 3. Track-athletics—Biography—Juvenile literature. I. Nisenson, Samuel, illus. II. Title.

DAVIS, Mac, 1905- 796.357'64'0922
Pacemakers in baseball. Illustrated by Sam Nisenson. Cleveland, World Pub. Co. [1968] 128 p. illus. 29 cm. "A Holly book." Brief biographies of thirty major league players who made important contributions to the game of baseball. [GV865.A1D37] 920 68-13705
1. Baseball—Biography—Juvenile literature. I. Nisenson, Samuel, illus. II. Title.

EPSTEIN, Samuel, 1909- 920 (J)
Stories of champions; Baseball Hall of Fame by Sam and Beryl Epstein. Illustrated by Ken Wagner. Champaign, Ill., Garrard Pub. Co. [1965] 96 p. illus. (part col.) ports. 23 cm. ([Garrard sports library]) [GV865.A1E6] 65-10091
1. Baseball—Biography—Juvenile literature. I. Epstein, Beryl (Williams) 1910- joint author. II. Title.

GELMAN, Steve. 796.3570922
Young baseball champions. [1st ed.] New York, Norton [1966] 188 p. ports. 21 cm. Contents.--Introduction.--Joe DiMaggio.--Hank Aaron.--Bob Feller.--Willie Mays.--Babe Ruth.--Mickey Mantle.--Ty Cobb.--Mel Ott.--Don Drysdale.--Ted Williams. [GV865.A1G4] 66-15467
1. Baseball—Biog.—Juvenile literature. I. Title.

GLUCK, Herb. 796.357'092'2 B
Baseball's great moments / by Herb Gluck. New York : Random House, [1975] 152 p. : ill. ; 22 cm. (Major league library ; 23) Includes index. Presents major league baseball highlights from the early 1900's to the present. [GV865A1G58] 74-23539 ISBN 0-394-83030-X : 2.50 ISBN 0-394-93030-4 lib.bdg. : 3.69
1. Baseball—Biography—Juvenile literature. 2. Baseball—History—Juvenile literature. I. Title. BIP

GUTMAN, Bill. 796.357'092'2 B
Famous baseball stars. Illustrated with photos. New York, Dodd, Mead [1973] x, 208 p. ports. 22 cm. (Famous biographies for young people) Profiles of sixteen baseball greats including Ty Cobb, Babe Ruth, Joe DiMaggio, Willie Mays, and Sandy Koufax. [GV865.A1G87] 920 72-12542 ISBN 0-396-06776-X 4.95
1. Baseball—Biography—Juvenile literature. I. Title.

GUTMAN, Bill. 796.357'092'2 B
Modern baseball superstars. New York, Dodd, Mead [1973] 112 p. ports. 22 cm. Introduces six "greats of the diamond:" Willie Mays, Johnny Bench, Henry Aaron, Tom Seaver, Dick Allen, and Roberto Clemente. [GV865.A1G877] 73-1649 ISBN 0-396-06805-7 3.95
1. Baseball—Biography—Juvenile literature. I. Title. BIP

GUTMAN, Bill. 796.357'092'2 B
New breed heroes in pro baseball. New York, Messner [1974] 190 p. ports. 21 cm. Brief biographies concentrating on the careers of twelve baseball players, including Bobby Murcer, Pete Rose, and Carleton Fisk. [GV865.A1G88 1974] 920 73-19232 ISBN 0-671-32667-8 6.95
1. Baseball—Biography—Juvenile literature. I. Title.
Library binding 5.79; ISBN 0-671-32668-6. BIP

HIRSHBERG, Albert, 1909- 796.357'0922
The greatest American leaguers [by] Al Hirshberg. New York, Putnam [1970] 223 p. 21 cm. Briefly traces the baseball careers of twenty outstanding American League players including four pitchers and two men in each of the other eight positions. [GV865.A1H52 1970] 920 70-92810 3.64
1. Baseball—Biography—Juvenile literature. I. Title.

HONIG, Donald. 796.3576'4'0922
Up from the minor leagues. [1st ed.] New York, Cowles Book Co. [1970] xiii, 129 p. illus. 22 cm. Seven major league baseball players relate the trials and rewards of their minor league experiences that culminated in the thrill of being called to the majors. [GV865.A1H62 1970] 920 76-104363 3.95
1. Baseball—Biography—Juvenile literature. I. Title.

KLEIN, Dave. 796.357'0922
Great infielders of the major leagues. Illustrated with photos. New York, Random House [1972] ix, 140 p. illus. 22 cm. (Major league library, 17) Profiles of twelve outstanding major league infielders since World War II. [GV865.A1K56] 920 70-37410 ISBN 0-394-82383-4 3.37
1. Baseball—Biography—Juvenile literature. I. Title. BIP

KLEIN, Dave. 796.357'092'2 B
Stars of the major leagues. Illustrated with photos. New York, Random House [1974] 152 p. illus. 22 cm. (Major league library, 21) Profiles of nine major league baseball stars: Johnny Bench, Cesar Cedeno, Jim "Catfish" Hunter, Bobby Murcer, Nate Colbert, John Mayberry, Carlton Fisk, Bobby Bonds, and Ferguson Jenkins. [GV865.A1K57 1974] 73-18739 ISBN 0-394-82762-7 3.37 (lib. bdg.)
1. Baseball—Biography—Juvenile literature. I. Title.
Pbk. 1.95; ISBN 0-394-92762-1. BIP

LIBBY, Bill. 796.357'092'2
Baseball's greatest sluggers. Illustrated with photos. New York, Random House [1973] 153 p. illus. 22 cm. (Major league library, 19) Profiles of five home run heroes: Babe Ruth, Hank Aaron, Jimmy Foxx, Ted Williams and Willie Mays. [GV865.A1L47] 920 72-11715 ISBN 0-394-82538-1 3.37
1. Baseball—Biography—Juvenile literature. 2. Batting (Baseball)—Juvenile literature. I. Title. BIP

LIBBY, Bill. 796.357'092'2
Heroes of the hot corner; great third basemen of the major leagues. New York, F. Watts, 1972. xiii, 145 p. illus. 21 cm. (The Franklin Watts sports library) Briefly traces the careers of some of baseball's outstanding third basemen of the past, present, and, potentially, of the future. [GV865.A1L48] 920 72-2889 ISBN 0-531-02573-X
1. Baseball—Biography—Juvenile literature. I. Title.

LISS, Howard. 796.357'0922 B
Baseball's zaniest stars. New York, Random House [1971] vii, 144 p. illus., ports. 22 cm. (Major league library, 15) Biographical profiles stressing the antics of some of baseball's more colorful players including Babe Ruth, Casey Stengel, Germany Schaefer, and others. [GV865.A1L56] 920 71-146650 ISBN 0-394-92142-9 (Library)
1. Baseball—Biography—Juvenile literature. I. Title. BIP

RAINBOLT, Richard. 796.357'092'2 B
Baseball's home-run hitters / Richard Rainbolt. Minneapolis : Lerner Publications Co., [1975] 71 p. : ill. ; 23 cm. (The Sports heroes library) Brief biographies emphasizing the careers of ten famous home-run hitters: Babe Ruth, Lou Gehrig, Jimmy Foxx, Ted Williams, Ralph Kiner, Mickey Mantle, Willie Mays, Roger Maris, Henry Aaron, and Harmon Killebrew. [GV867.5.R34 1975] 920 74-27473 ISBN 0-8225-1055-3 lib.bdg. : 4.95
1. Baseball—Biography—Juvenile literature. 2. Batting (Baseball)—Juvenile literature. I. Title. BIP

ROBINSON, Ray, Dec.4,1920- 927.96357
Speed kings of the base paths; baseball's greatest runners. New York, Putnam [1964] 191 p. ports. 21 cm. [GV865.A1R6] 64-14218
1. Baseball—Biography—Juvenile literature. I. Title. II. Title: Baseball's greatest runners.

SABIN, Louis. 796.357'092'2 B
Record-breakers of the major leagues, by Lou Sabin. Illustrated with photos. New York, Random House [1974] 151 p. illus. 22 cm. (Major league library) Traces the careers of baseball players who have broken major league records. [GV865.A1S22 1974] 920 73-18740 ISBN 0-394-82769-4 1.95
1. Baseball—Biography—Juvenile literature. I. Title.
Library binding; 3.37, ISBN 0-394-92769-9. BIP

SHAPIRO, Milton J. 796.357'0922 B
All stars of the outfield, by Milton J. Shapiro. New York, J. Messner [1970] 191 p. ports. 22 cm. Brief biographies stressing the major league careers of ten of baseball's great outfielders include six from the post-World War II era and four from the prewar era. [GV865.A1S42] 920 79-107398 3.95
1. Baseball—Biography—Juvenile literature. I. Title.

SHAPIRO, Milton J 796.357'0922
Champions of the bat: baseball's greatest sluggers, by Milton J. Shapiro. New York, Messner [1967] 222 p. ports. 22 cm. [GV865.A1S44] 67-21627
1. Baseball—Biog.—Juvenile literature. I. Title.

SHAPIRO, Milton J. 796.357'0922
Champions of the bat: baseball's greatest sluggers, by Milton J. Shapiro. New York, Massner [1967] 222 p. ports. 22 cm. [GV865.A1S44] 67-21627
1. Baseball—Biography—Juvenile literature. I. Title.

SHAPIRO, Milton J. 796.357'0922
The day they made the record book, by Milton J. Shapiro. New York, J. Messner [1968] 191 p. illus. 22 cm. [GV865.A1S45] 68-14949
1. Baseball—Biography—Juvenile literature. I. Title.

SHOEMAKER, Robert Hilles, 1911- 796.357'092'2 B
The best in baseball, by Robert H. Shoemaker. 3d ed., rev. New York, Crowell [1974] 274 p. 21 cm. Profiles of twenty-two baseball greats provide an outline of baseball history. [GV865.A1S513 1974] 920 73-20442 ISBN 0-690-00314-5 5.50
1. Baseball—Biography—Juvenile literature. I. Title. BIP

SMITH, Jay H. 796.357'092'2 B
The infielders / by Jay H. Smith. Mankato, Minn. : Creative Education, [1976] p. cm. (Stars of the NBL and ABL) Brief biographies of Joe Morgan, Steve Garvey, Bert Campaneris, Brooks Robinson, and Robin Yount—all infielders for the NBL or ABL. [GV865.A1S558] 920 76-8465 lib.bdg. : 5.95
1. Baseball—Biography—Juvenile literature. 2. Fielding (Baseball)—Biography—Juvenile literature. I. Title. BIP

SMITH, Jay H. 796.357'092'2 B
The managers / by Jay H. Smith. Mankato, Minn. : Creative Education, [1976] p. cm. (Stars of the NBL and ABL) Biographical sketches of five NBL and ABL team managers: Danny Murtaugh, Sparky Anderson, Frank Robinson, Walt Alston, and Billy Martin. [GV865.A1S559] 920 76-8905 ISBN 0-87191-516-2 lib. bdg. : 5.95
1. Baseball—Biography—Juvenile literature. 2. Baseball managing—Biography—Juvenile literature. I. Title. BIP

SMITH, Jay H. 796.357'092'2 B
The pitchers / by Jay H. Smith. Mankato, Minn. : Creative Education, [1976] p. cm. (Stars of the NBL and ABL) Brief biographies of Mike Marshall, Nolan Ryan, Catfish Hunter, Tom Seaver, and Gaylord Perry—all catchers with the NBL or ABL. [GV865.A1S56] 920 76-8485 ISBN 0-87191-518-9 lib.bdg. : 5.95
1. Baseball—Biography—Juvenile literature. 2. Pitchers (Baseball)—Biography—Juvenile literature. I. Title. BIP

TUTTLE, Anthony. 920
The catchers / by Anthony Tuttle. Mankato, Minn. : Creative Education, [1976] p. cm. (Stars of the NBL and ABL) Brief biographies of Johnny Bench, Ted Simmons, Carlton Fisk, Manny Sanguillen, and Jerry Grote—all catchers with the NBL or ABL. [GV865.A1T87] 76-8456 ISBN 0-87191-519-7 lib.bdg. : 5.95
1. Baseball—Biography—Juvenile literature. 2. Catchers (Baseball)—Biography—Juvenile literature. I. Title. BIP

WAYNE, Bennett. 796.357'092'2 B
Big league pitchers and catchers. Edited, with commentary, by Bennett Wayne. Champaign, Ill., Garrard Pub. Co. [1974] 168 p. illus. 21 cm. (A Target book) Profiles of such pitchers and catchers as Cy Young, Christy Mathewson, and Howard Ehmke and their unusual careers in professional baseball. [GV865.A1W34] 920 73-17166 ISBN 0-8116-4907-5
1. Baseball—Biography—Juvenile literature. 2. Pitchers (Baseball)—Biography—Juvenile literature. 3. Catchers (Baseball)—Biography—Juvenile literature. I. Title. BIP

Baseball—History.

HORNSBY, Rogers, 1896- 796.357
My kind of baseball; edited by J. Roy Stockton. New York, D. McKay [1953] 185 p. illus. 21 cm. Autobiographical. [GV865.H6A3] 53-7543
1. Baseball—History. I. Title.

STENGEL, Casey. 927.96357
Casey at the bat; the story of my life in baseball as told to Harry T. Taxton. New York, Random House [1962] 354 p. illus. 21 cm. [GV865.S8A3] 62-8465
1. Baseball — Hist. I. Paxton, Harry T. II. Title.

Baseball—Juvenile literature.

DEVANEY, John. 796.357'0922
Baseball's youngest big leaguers. [1st ed.] New York, Holt, Rinehart, and Winston [1969] 139, [4] p. illus. 22 cm. (Pacesetter) Bibliographical references included in "Author's note" (p. [141]) Traces the careers of six baseball players who made the majors before their twenty-second birthday: Ted Williams, Bob Feller, Joe DiMaggio, Dean Chance, Carl Yastrzemski, and Willie Mays, the Say-Hey kid. [GV865.A1D38] 920 68-11824 2.95
1. Baseball—Juvenile literature. 2. Baseball—Biography. I. Title.

LISS, Howard. 796.357'0922 B
Triple-crown winners. New York, J. Messner [1969] 95 p. illus., ports. 23 cm. Briefly traces the baseball careers of the six major league baseball players who have earned the Triple Crown: Lou Gehrig, Joe Medwick, Ted Williams, Mickey Mantle, Frank Robinson, and Carl Yastrzemski. [GV865.A1L57] 920 78-81391 3.95
1. Baseball—Juvenile literature. 2. Baseball—Biography. I. Title.

Baseball managers—United States—Biography.

HONIG, Donald. 796.357'092'2 B
The man in the dugout : fifteen big league managers speak their minds / by Donald Honig. Chicago : Follett Pub. Co., c1977. xiii, 305 p. : ports. ; 24 cm. Includes index. [GV865.A1H619] 75-25419 ISBN 0-695-80633-5 : 8.95
1. Baseball managers—United States—Biography. I. Title.

SCHOOR, Gene 927.96357
Casey Stengel, baseball's greatest manager, by Gene Schoor, Henry Gilfond. New York, Messner [1961, c.1958, 1961] 186p. front port. 61-3127 2.95
I. Title.

Baseball managers—United States—Biography—Juvenile literature.

SMITH, Jay H. 796.357'092'2 B
Meet the managers / by Jay H. Smith. [Mankato, MN] : Creative Education, 1976i.e.1977 30 p. : ill. (some col.) ; 20 cm. (Creative Education early sports books) Brief biographies concentrating on the careers of managers Walt Alston, Frank Robinson, Danny Murtaugh, Billy Martin, and Sparky Anderson. [GV865.A1S5592] 920 76-28376 ISBN 0-87191-577-4 lib.bdg. : 4.95
1. Baseball managers—United States—Biography—Juvenile literature. I. Title. II. Series. BIP

Baseball players—United States—Biography.

BRUNO, Joseph. 796.357'092'2 B
Baseball's golden dozen / Joseph Bruno. 1st ed. Hicksville, N.Y. : Exposition Press, c1976. 184 p. ; 22 cm. (An Exposition-Banner book) [GV865.A1B77] 76-20029 ISBN 0-682-48564-0 : 8.50
1. Baseball players—United States—Biography. I. Title.

CLARK, Tom, 1941- 796.357'092'2 B
Baseball / by Tom Clark. Berkeley, CA : Th Figures : distributed by Serendipity Books, c1976. 73 p. : 34 ports. (some col.) ; 25 cm. "Edition of 2000 copies, of which 50, with a special color photograph tipped in, are numbered and signed by the artist." No. 7. [GV865.A1C47] 77-367756
1. Baseball players—United States—Biography. I. Title.

†GUTMAN, Bill. 796.357'092'2 B
At bat / by Bill Gutman. New York : Grosset & Dunlap, c1976 v. ; 18 cm. (Tempo books) Contents.Contents.— —v. 3. Munson, Garvey, Brock, Carew. [GV865.A1G86] 920 75-39515 ISBN 0-448-12270-7 pbk. : 1.25.
1. Baseball players—United States—Biography. I. Title.

HONIG, Donald. 796.357'092'2 B
The October heroes : great world series games remembered by the men who played them / by Donald Honig. New York : Simon and Schuster, c1979. 285 p. : ill. ; 24 cm. Includes index. [GV865.A1H6193] 78-12134 ISBN 0-671-23059-X : 10.95
1. Baseball players—United States—Biography. 2. World series (Baseball)—History. I. Title.

Baseball players—United States—Biography—Addresses, essays, lectures.

MUSIAL, Stanley Frank, 1920- 796.357'092'2 B
We saw stars / Stan Musial, Jack Buck, Bob Broeg. St. Louis : Bethany Press, c1976. 79 p. : ill. ; 26 cm. [GV865.A1M87] 76-27220 ISBN 0-8272-4211-5 pbk. : 3.95
1. Baseball players—United States—Biography—Addresses, essays, lectures. I. Buck, Jack, joint author. II. Broeg, Robert M., joint author. III. Title. BIP

Baseball players—United States—Biography—Juvenile literature.

BRAUN, Thomas, 1944- 796.357'092'2 B
Meet the hitters / by Thomas Braun. [Mankato, Minn] : Creative Education/Children's Press, [c1977]. 31 p. : ill. (some col.) ; 19 cm. (Creative Education early sports books) Brief biographies concentrating on the careers of star hitters Rod Carew, Lou Brock, Reggie Jackson, Steve Garvey, and Robin Yount. [GV865.A1B654] 920 76-28386 ISBN 0-87191-579-0 lib.bdg. 4.95
1. Baseball players—United States—Biography—Juvenile literature. I. Title. BIP

GUTMAN, Bill. 796.357'092'2
More modern baseball superstars / Bill Gutman ; illustrated with photos. New York : Dodd, Mead, c1978. 128 p. : ill. ; 22 cm. Includes index. Career biographies of Thurman Munson, Steve Garvey, Rod Carew, Nolan Ryan, George Foster, and Greg Luzinski. [GV865.A1G878] 920 B 78-7741 ISBN 0-396-07616-5 : 5.95
1. Baseball players—United States—Biography—Juvenile literature. I. Title. BIP

PHILLIPS, Louis. 796.357'092'2 B
Baseball : records, stars, feats, and facts / by Louis Phillips ; ill. by Paul Frame. 1st ed. New York : Harcourt Brace Jovanovich, c1979. p. cm. (A Handy book) Brief biographies of 35 "great" players plus a potpourri of feats, facts, and records about baseball. [GV865.A1P46] 920 79-87525 ISBN 0-15-205718-8 : 2.95
1. Baseball players—United States—Biography—Juvenile literature. 2. Baseball—United States—Records—Juvenile literature. I. Frame, Paul, 1913- II. Title. BIP

SMITH, Robert, 1905- 796.357'092'2 B
Pioneers of baseball / by Robert Smith. 1st ed. Boston : Little, Brown, c1978. 180 p. : ill. ; 22 cm. Contents.—Alexander Joy Cartwright, real father of the game.—William Henry (Harry) Wright, father of professional baseball.—Albert Goodwill (A. G.) Spalding, father of the National League.—Michael J. (King) Kelly, the ten-thousand-dollar beauty.—John Montgomery (Monte) Ward, Gentleman John.—Charles Comiskey, father of the American League.—Lewis Rogers (Pete) Browning, the original Louisville slugger.—Cornelius McGillicuddy, the indestructible Connie Mack.—Louis Sockalexis, the first Cleveland Indian.—Joe Williams, the Texas Cyclone.—Harold (Hal) Chase, prince of first basemen.—Jay Hanna Dean, the original "Dizzy."—George Herman (Babe) Ruth, the one and only.—Leroy (Satchel) Paige, Old Man Mose.—Jack Roosevelt (Jackie) Robinson, first Black across the line.—Theodore Samuels (Ted) Williams, doctor of hitting. [GV865.A1S583] 920 77-18820 ISBN 0-316-80156-9 : 7.95
1. Baseball players—United States—Biography—Juvenile literature. 2. Baseball—United States—History—Juvenile literature. I. Title.
Contents omitted. BIP

Baseball stories.

GUTMAN, Bill. 796.357'092'2 B
Great baseball stories : today and yesterday / Bill Gutman. New York : J. Messner, c1978. 191 p. : ill. ; 22 cm. Includes index. [GV873.G87] 78-480 ISBN 0-671-32881-6 lib.bdg. : 7.79
1. Baseball stories. 2. Baseball players—United States—Biography. I. Title.

Baseball—Yearbooks.

BASEBALL stars. 927.96357
v. 1- 1949- [New York, Dell Pub. Co.] v. ports. 28 cm. annual. [GV877.B336] 51-269
1. Baseball—Yearbooks.

Bashkirtseva, Maria Konstantinova, 1860-1884.

MOORE, Doris (Langley-Levy) 1903- 891.78900303
Marie & the Duke of H.; the daydream love affair of Marie Bashkirtseff [by] Doris Langley Moore. Philadelphia, Lippincott [c.1966] xxvii, 304p. illus., ports. 22cm. Bibl. [CT128.B3M66] 66-22114 6.50
1. Bashkirtseva, Maria Konstantinova, 1860-1884. 2. Hamilton, William Alexander Louis Stephen Douglas-Hamilton, 12th duke of, 1845-1895. I. Title.

MOORE, Doris (Langley-Levy) 1903- 891.78900303
Marie & the Duke of H.; the daydream love affair of Marke Bashkirtseff [by] Doris Langley Moore. Philadelphia, J. B. Lippincott Co. [1966] xxvii, 304 p. illus., ports. 22 cm. Bibliography: p. 293-295. [CT1218.B3M66] 66-22114
1. Bashkirtseva, Maria Konstantonova, 1860-1884. 2. Hamilton, William Alexander Louis Stephen Douglas-Hamilton, 12th duke of, 1845-1895. I. Title.

Basilius,

BASILIUS, Saint, the Great, Abp. of Caesarea, 330(ca.)-379. 922.1
Letters, translated by Sister Agnes Clare Way, with notes by Roy J. Deferrari. New York, Fathers of the Church, inc., 1951- v. 22 cm. (The Fathers of the Church, a new translation. v. 13) Bibliography: v. 1, p. xviii. [BR60.F3B28] 52-7758
I. Title. II. Series.

BASILIUS Saint, the Great, Abp. of Caesarea 330(ca.)-379. 922.1
Letters, translated by Sister Agnes Clare Way, with notes by Roy J. Deferrari. New York, Fathers of the Church, inc., 1951-55. 2v. 22cm. (The Fathers of the Church, a new translation, v. 13, 28) Bibliography: v. 1, p. xviii. [BR60.F3B28] 52-7758
I. Title.

Baskerville, John, 1706-1775.

BENTON, Josiah Henry, 1843-1917. 655.1'42 B
John Baskerville, type-founder and printer, 1706-1775. New York, B. Franklin [1968] 78 p. illus., facsim., port. 23 cm. (Burt Franklin bibliography and reference series, 230) Reprint of the 1914 ed. Includes bibliographical references. [Z232.B2B4 1968] 68-56593
1. Baskerville, John, 1706-1775.

Basketball—Biography.

BERGER, Phil. 796.32'3'0922
Heroes of pro basketball. New York, Random House [1968] xiv, 173 p. illus. 22 cm. (Pro basketball library, 1) Contents.Contents.—Nat Holman.—George Mikan.—Dolph Schayes.—Bob Cousy.—Bob Pettit.—Bill Russell.—Elgin Baylor.—Wilt Chamberlain.—Jerry West.—Oscar Robertson.—Willis Reed.—Dave Bing. [GV884.A1B4] 920 68-29583 1.95
1. Basketball—Biography. 2. Basketball—Juvenile literature. I. Title. BIP

DAVIS, Mac. 796.32'3'0922
Basketball's unforgettables. Toronto, New York [Bantam Books, c1972] 137 p. illus. 18 cm. (Bantam pathfinder editions) [GV884.A1D38] 72-10109 0.75
1. Basketball—Biography. I. Title.

HARRIS, Merv. 796.32'3'0922 B
The lonely heroes : professional basketball's great centers / Merv Harris. New York : Viking Press, [1975] 230 p. : ill. ; 22 cm. [GV884.A1H35] 75-8977 ISBN 0-670-43764-6 : 7.95
1. Basketball—Biography. I. Title.

HIRSHBERG, Albert, 1909- 927.96323
Basketball's greatest stars. New York, Putman [1963] 191 p. illus 21 cm. [GV885.H575] 63-7741
1. Basketball—Biography. I. Title. BIP

HOLLANDER, Zander. 796.32'3'0922
Great rookies of pro basketball. Compiled by Zander Hollander. New York, Random House [1969] viii, 172 p. illus., ports. 22 cm. (Pro basketball library, 3) Contents.Contents.—Introduction, by Z. Hollander.—Westley Unseld, by B. Rubin.—Don Meineke, by S. Burick.—Ray Felix, by B. Rubin.—Maurice Stokes, by N. Amdur.—Tom Heinsohn, by B. Sales.—Walt Bellamy, by N. Amdur.—Terry Dischinger, by J. Zanger.—Jerry Lucas, by J. Zanger.—Rick Barry, by E. Hershey.—Earl Monroe, by B. Rubin.—Official NBA rookie-of-the-year list. [GV884.A1H6] 920 75-86941 1.95
1. Basketball—Biography. 2. Basketball—Juvenile literature. I. Title.

KLEIN, Dave. 796.32'3'0922
Rookie: the world of the NBA [by] David Klein. [Chicago] Cowles Book Co. [1971] x, 166 p. illus. 22 cm. [GV884.A1K57] 71-163264 5.95
1. Basketball—Biography. I. Title.

MENDELL, Ronald L., 1943- 796.32'3'0922 B
Who's who in basketball [by] Ronald L. Mendell. New Rochelle, N.Y., Arlington House [1973] 248 p. 25 cm. [GV884.A1M46] 73-11871 7.95
1. Basketball—Biography. I. Title. BIP

MOKRAY, William George. 927.96323
Basketball stars. New York, Pyramid Books. v. illus. 19 cm. (Pyramid [GV885.M58] 61-65943
1. Basketball — Biog. I. Title.

MOKRAY, William George 927.96323
Basketball stars of 1962. New York, Pyramid Bks. [c.1961] 160p. illus. (Pyramid F675) 61-65943 .40 pap.,
1. Basketball—Biog. I. Title.

MOKRAY, William George 927.96323
Basketball stars of 1963. New York, Pyramid [c.1962] 160p. illus. 19cm. (F-797) .40 pap.,
1. Basketball—Biog. I. Title.

PADWE, Sandy. 796.357'0922
Basketball's hall of fame. Englewood Cliffs, N.J., Prentice-Hall [1970] 193 p. illus., ports. 24 cm. "An Associated Features book." [GV884.A1P3] 76-99451 6.95
1. Basketball—Biography. I. Title.

SABIN, Louis. 796.32'3'0922
Basketball stars of 1970. New York, Pyramid Books [1969] 128 p. illus. 18 cm. [GV884.A1S2] 74-8939 0.60
1. Basketball—Biography. I. Title.

*STAINBACK, Barry 796.323640922
Basketball stars of 1968 New York. Pyramid [1967] v. illus. ports. 18cm. (R-1725) [GV884.A1S7] .50 pap.,

1. Basketball—Biog. I. Title.

STAINBACK, Berry 796.323640922
Basketball stars of 1967. New York, Pyramid [1966] 159p. illus., ports. 18cm. [GV884.A157] 66-31678 .50 pap.,
1. Basketball—Biog. I. Title.

STAINBACK, Berry 796.323640922
Basketball stars of 1966 [by] Berry Stainback: Steve Gelman. New York, Pyramid [1965] 176p. illus., ports. 18cm. [GV885.S79] 65-29837 .50 pap.,
1. Basketball—Biog. I. Gelman, Steve, joint author. II. Title.

Basketball—Biography—Juvenile literature.

GUTMAN, Bill. 796.32'3'0922 B
Modern basketball superstars / Bill Gutman. New York : Dodd, Mead, [1975] 124 p. : ill. ; 22 cm. Includes index. Profiles of six outstanding basketball players: Wilt Chamberlain, John Havlicek, Walt Frazier, Kareem Abdul-Jabbar, Dave Cowens, and Julius Erving. [GV884.A1G87] 920 75-11439 ISBN 0-396-07192-9
1. Basketball—Biography—Juvenile literature. I. Title.

HILL, Ray. 796.32'3'0922 B
Pro basketball's little men. Illustrated with photos. New York, Random House [1974] 152 p. illus. 22 cm. (Pro basketball library #10) Traces the success stories of nine shorter-than-usual pro basketball stars who made up for in skill what they lacked in height. [GV884.A1H49 1974] 920 74-4933 ISBN 0-394-82768-6 1.95
1. Basketball—Biography—Juvenile literature. I. Title.
Library binding; 3.77, ISBN 0-394-92768-0. BIP

HILL, Ray. 796.32'3'0922
Unsung heroes of pro basketball. New York, Random House [1973] 153 p. illus. 22 cm. (Pro basketball library) Brief biographies of nine basketball players including Mel Daniels, Bob Love, Dan Issel, Hal Greer, Dave DeBusschere, Roger Brown, Lenny Wilkins, Charlie Scott, and Gus Johnson. [GV884.A1H5] 920 73-4233 ISBN 0-394-82415-6 1.95
1. Basketball—Biography—Juvenile literature. I. Title. BIP

RAINBOLT, Richard. 796.32'3'0922 B
Basketball's big men / Richard Rainbolt. Minneapolis : Lerner Publications Co., [1975] 77 p. : ill. ; 23 cm. (The Sports heroes library) Brief biographies emphasizing the careers of ten basketball stars: George Mikan, Dolph Schayes, Bob Pettit, Bill Russell, Elgin Baylor, Jerry Lucas, Wilt Chamberlain, Willis Reed, Rick Barry, Kareem Abdul-Jabbar. [GV884.A1R34 1975] 920 74-27472 ISBN 0-8225-1054-5 lib.bdg. : 4.95
1. Basketball—Biography—Juvenile literature. I. Title. BIP

SABIN, Louis. 796.32'3'0922 B
Hot shots of pro basketball, by Lou Sabin. Illustrated with photos. New York, Random House [1974] 152 p. illus. 22 cm. (Pro basketball library, 9) Profiles of nine professional basketball superstars with exceptional scoring records. [GV884.A1S214 1974] 920 74-4932 ISBN 0-394-82901-8 1.95
1. Basketball—Biography—Juvenile literature. I. Title.
Library binding; 3.77, ISBN 0-394-92901-2. BIP

SABIN, Louis. 796.32'3'0922 B
Pro basketball's greatest : selected all-star offensive and defensive teams / by Louis Sabin. New York : Putnam, c1976. 127 p. ; 22 cm. (Putnam sports shelf) Includes index. Profiles the lives and careers of ten outstanding offensive and defensive basketball players from both the N.B.A. and the A.B.A. [GV884.A1S2166 1976] 920 75-45485 ISBN 0-399-20509-8. ISBN 0-399-60999-7 lib. bdg. : 5.29
1. Basketball—Biography—Juvenile literature. I. Title. BIP

SABIN, Louis. 796.32'3'0922
Stars of pro basketball, by Lou Sabin and Dave Sendler. New York, Random House [1970] 144 p. illus., ports. 22 cm. (Pro basketball library, 4) Brief biographies of nine pro basketball players: Lew Alcindor, Billy Cunningham, Walt Frazier, John Havlicek, Connie Hawkins, Elvin Hayes, Spencer Haywood, Lou Hudson, Jimmy Walker. [GV884.A1S22] 920 73-117546
1. Basketball—Biography—Juvenile literature. I. Sendler, Dave, joint author. II. Title. BIP

SABIN, Louis. 796.32'3'0922
Stars of pro basketball, by Lou Sabin and Dave Sendler. [Rev. ed.] New York, Random House [1973, c1970] 144 p. illus. 22 cm. (Pro basketball library, 4) Brief biographies of nine basketball stars: Kareem Abdul-Jabbar, Billy Cunningham, Walt Frazier, John Havlicek, Connie Hawkins, Elvin Hayes, Spencer Haywood, Lou Hudson, Jimmy Walker. [GV884.A1S22 1973] 920 73-8724 ISBN 0-394-80621-2
1. Basketball—Biography—Juvenile literature. I. Sendler, Dave, joint author. II. Title.

Basketball coaches—United States—Biography—Juvenile literature.

O'REILLY, Sean, 1922- 796.32'3'0922 B
Meet the coaches / by Sean O'Reilly. Mankato, Minn. : Creative Education, c1977. 30 p. : col. ill. ; 19 cm. (Creative Education early sports books) A brief description of the character and triumphs of basketball coaches Al Attles, Red Holzman, Bill Fitch, and Bill Sharman. [GV884.A1O74] 920 76-54899 ISBN 0-87191-600-2 lib.bdg. : 4.95
1. Basketball coaches—United States—Biography—Juvenile literature. I. Title. BIP

Basketball coaching.

LAPCHICK, Joe, 1900- 796.32'364
50 years of basketball. Englewood Cliffs, N.J., Prentice-Hall [1968] xvii, 251 p. illus., plans, ports. 24 cm. [GV885.3.L34] 68-31767
1. Basketball coaching. I. Title.

Basketball—Hist.

COUSY, Robert, 1928- 927.96357
Basketball is my life, as told to Al Hirshberg. Rev. ed. New York, J.L. Pratt [c.1957-1963] 186p. 18cm. (Amer. lib., 109) 63-21861 .50 pap.,
1. Basketball—Hist. I. Hirshberg, Albert. 1909- II. Title.

Basketball—History—Juvenile literature.

DEVANEY, John. 796.32'3'0973
The story of basketball / by John Devaney. New York : Random House, c1976. 150 p. : ill. ; 29 cm. Includes index. Traces the history of basketball including biographical sketches of fourteen players and coaches. [GV883.D48] 76-8129 ISBN 0-394-82806-2 : 4.95. ISBN 0-394-92806-7 lib. bdg. : 5.99
1. Basketball—History—Juvenile literature. 2. Basketball—United States—History—Juvenile literature. 3. Basketball—Biography—Juvenile literature. I. Title. BIP

Basketball—Juvenile literature.

HEUMAN, William. 796.32'3'0922
Famous pro basketball stars. New York, Dodd, Mead [1970] 121 p. ports. 22 cm. (Famous biographies for young people) Contents.Contents.—Nat Holman.—George Lawrence Mikan.—Slater Martin.—Adolph Schayes.—Robert Cousy.—Robert E. Lee Pettit.—Elgin Baylor.—William Fenton Russell.—Wilton Norman Chamberlain.—Jerry West.—Oscar Robertson.—Jerry Lucas. [GV884.A1H4] 920 70-95910 3.50
1. Basketball—Juvenile literature. 2. Basketball—Biography. I. Title. BIP

Basketball players—United States—Biography—Juvenile literature.

ARMSTRONG, Robert, 1938- 796.34'2'0922 B
The forwards / by Robert Armstrong. Markato, Minn. : Creative Education, c1977. 46 p. : col. ill. ; 28 cm. (Stars of the NBA) Brief biographies emphasizing the careers of five star forwards: Rick Barry, Julius Erving, David Thompson, George McGinnis, and John Havlicek. [GV884.A1A74] 920 76-28378 ISBN 0-87191-563-4 lib.bdg. : 5.95
1. Basketball players—United States—Biography—Juvenile literature. I. Title. BIP

Bass, Dick, 1937- —Juvenile literature.

LIBBY, Bill. 796.332'0924 B
The Dick Bass story. New York, J. Messner [1969] 191 p. illus., ports. 22 cm. A biography stressing the football career of the California star who set many high school, college, and professional records. [GV939.B37LS] 92 71-79704 3.95
1. Bass, Dick, 1937- —Juvenile literature. I. Title.

Bass, George Fletcher.

BASS, George Fletcher. 930'.1'02804
Archaeology beneath the sea / George F. Bass. New York : Walker, 1975. 238 p., [4] leaves of plates : ill. ; 24 cm. Includes index. [DS56.B33 1975] 74-24795 ISBN 0-8027-0477-8 : 12.95
1. Bass, George Fletcher. 2. Near East—Antiquities. 3. Underwater archaeology. I. Title. BIP

Bass, George, 1771-1803.

BOWDEN, Keith Macrae. 923.994
George Bass, 1771-1803 his discoveries, romantic life and tragic disappearance. Melbourne, Oxford University Press [1952] xi, 171p. illus., port., maps. facsims. 22cm. 'Principle sources of information': p. [158]-164. [DU114.B34B6] 53-2355
1. Bass, George, 1771-1803. I. Title.

Bass, Sam, 1851-1879.

GRISHAM, Noel. 364.1'0924
Tame the restless wind; the life and legends of Sam Bass. Illus. by Gene Fallwell. Austin, San Felipe Press, 1968. xiv, 100 p. illus. 23 cm. Bibliography: p. 97. [HV6452.T4B3 1968] 68-26910
1. Bass, Sam, 1851-1879. I. Title. BIP

Bass, Tom, 1859-1934.

DOWNEY, Bill. 798'.23'0924 B
Tom Bass, Black horseman / by Bill Downey. St. Louis : Saddle and Bridle, c1975. 211 p. : ill. ; 24 cm. Bibliography: p. 4. [SF287.D68] 75-32101 11.95
1. Bass, Tom, 1859-1934. 2. Horse-training. 3. American saddle horse. 4. Mexico, Mo.—Biography. I. Title. II. Title: Black horseman.

Bastiat, Frederic, 1801-1850.

ROCHE, George Charles. 330'.0924 B
Frederic Bastiat; a man alone [by] George Charles Roche III. New Rochelle, N.Y., Arlington House [1971] 256 p. port. 24 cm. (Architects of freedom series) [HB105.B3R62] 71-139891 ISBN 0-87000-116-7 6.95
1. Bastiat, Frederic, 1801-1850.

Batchelor, Charles, 1845-1910.

WELCH, Walter Leslie, 1901- 621.3'092'4 B
Charles Batchelor; Edison's chief partner, by Walter L. Welch. [Syracuse, N.Y.] Syracuse University, 1972. x, 118 p. illus. 24 cm. Includes bibliographical references. [TK140.B32W44] 77-176129
1. Batchelor, Charles, 1845-1910.

Bates, Daisy, 1861-1951.

SALTER, Elizabeth. 994'.04'0924 B
Daisy Bates. [1st American ed.] New York, Coward, McCann & Geoghegan [1972, c1971] xvi, 266 p. illus. 22 cm. Bibliography: p. [251]-253. [GN21.B38S25 1972] 73-175277 6.95
1. Bates, Daisy, 1861-1951. 2. Australian aborigines.

Bates, Edward, 1793-1869.

BATES, Edward, 1793-1869. 973.71'0924
The diary of Edward Bates, 1859-1866. Edited by Howard K. Beale. New York, Da Capo Press, 1971. xvi, 685 p. 24 cm. Reprint of the 1933 ed. Originally published as Annual report of the American Historical Association for the year 1930, v. 4. [E415.9.B2A3 1971] 75-75304 ISBN 0-306-71260-1
1. United States—Politics and government—Civil War, 1861-1865. 2. Reconstruction—Missouri. I. Title.

CAIN, Marvin R. 973.70924
Lincoln's Attorney General: Edward Bates of Missouri. Columbia, Univ. of Mo. Pr. [c.1965] x, 361p. ports. 23cm. Bibl. [E415.9.B2C3] 65-13690 7.00
1. Bates, Edward, 1793-1869. I. Title. BIP

Bates, Frederick, 1777-1825.

BATES, Frederick, 1777-1825. 977.8'03'0924 B
The life and papers of Frederick Bates / edited by Thomas Maitland Marshall. New York : Arno Press, 1975, c1926. p. cm. (The Mid-American frontier) Reprint of the ed. published by the Missouri Historical Society, St. Louis, issued in the series: Publications of the Missouri Historical Society. Includes bibliographical references and index. [F466.B3 1975] 75-109 ISBN 0-405-06876-X : 39.00
1. Bates, Frederick, 1777-1825. 2. Missouri—Politics and government—To 1865. I. Title. II. Series. III. Series: Missouri Historical Society, St. Louis. Publications. BIP

Bates, Henry Walter, 1825-1892.

WOODCOCK, George, 1912- 509'.24 B
Henry Walter Bates, naturalist of the Amazons. New York, Barnes & Noble [1969] 269 p. illus., maps, ports. 21 cm. (Great travellers) Bibliography: p. 262-264. [QH31.B26W6 1969b] 72-8460 5.50
1. Bates, Henry Walter, 1825-1892.

Bates, Henry Walter, 1825-1892—Addresses, essays, lectures.

BATES, Henry Walter, 1825-1892. 595.7'89'09811
The principal contributions of Henry Walter Bates to a knowledge of the butterflies and longicorn beetles of the Amazon Valley / edited by E. Gorton Linsley ; with an introd. by Keir B. Sterling. New York : Arno Press, 1978. p. cm. (Biologists and their world) Reprint of articles originally published between 1859 and 1892. [QL554.A4B37 1978] 77-81106 ISBN 0-405-10690-4 : 50.00
1. Bates, Henry Walter, 1825-1892—Addresses, essays, lectures. 2. Butterflies—Amazon Valley—Addresses, essays, lectures. 3. Cerambycidae. 4. Entomologists—Great Britain—Biography—Addresses, essays, lectures. I. Linsley, Earle Gorton, 1910- II. Title. III. Series.

Bates, Herbert Ernest,

BATES, Herbert Ernest, 1905- 823'.9'12 B
An autobiography [by] H. E. Bates. Illustrated by John Ward. [U.S. ed.] Columbia, University of Missouri Press [1969?-72] 3 v. illus. 24 cm. Contents.Contents.—[1] The vanished world.—v. 2. The blossoming world.—v. 3. The world in ripeness. [PR6003.A965Z5 1969b] 77-130667 ISBN 0-8262-0096-6 (v. 1) varies 6.50 (v. 1-2) 7.50 (v. 3)
I. Title: The vanished world. II. Title: The blossoming world. III. Title: The world in ripeness.

Bates, Joseph, 1792-1872.

ANDERSON, Godfrey 286'.7'0924 B Tryggve, 1909-
Outrider of the apocalypse: life and times of Joseph Bates, by Godfrey T. Anderson. Mountain View, Calif., Pacific Press Pub. Association [1972] 143 p. illus. 22 cm. (Dimension 112) Bibliography: p. 130-137. [BX6193.B3A83] 76-182495
1. Bates, Joseph, 1792-1872. I. Title.

BATES, Joseph, 286'.7'0924 B 1792-1872.
The autobiography of Elder Joseph Bates; embracing a long life on shipboard, with sketches of voyages on the Atlantic and Pacific Oceans, the Baltic and Mediterranean Seas; also impressment and service on board British war ships, long confinement in Dartmoor Prison, early experience in reformatory movements; travels in various parts of the world and a brief account of the great Advent movement of 1840-44. Battle Creek, Mich., Steam Press of the Seventh-day Adventist Pub. Association, 1868. [Nashville, Southern Pub. Association, 1970] 306 p. port. 21 cm. (Heritage library) [BX6193.B3A3 1970] 73-20192

Bates, Katherine Lee, 1859-1929.

BURGESS, Dorothy 923.773 Whittemore Bates.
Dream and deed; the story of Katherine Lee Bates. [1st ed.] Norman, University of Oklahoma Press [1952] 241 p. illus. 22 cm. [PS1077.B4Z58] 52-10500
1. Bates, Katherine Lee, 1859-1929. I. Title.

Bates, Katharine Lee, 1859-1929—Juvenile fiction.

MYERS, Elisabeth P. 920
Katharine Lee Bates, girl poet. Illus. by Maurice Rawson. Indianapolis, Bobbs [c.1961] 200p. col. illus. (Childhood of famous Americans) 61-12320 2.25
1. Bates, Katharine Lee, 1859-1929—Juvenile fiction. I. Title.

Batheaston, Eng.—Biography.

VILLAGE life, 1883-1940 942.3'97
: Batheaston remembers / [edited by B. M. Willmott Dobbie]. [Bath] : The Batheaston Society, 1976. [7], 79 p., [4] p. of plates : ill., map, ports. ; 22 cm. Includes index. [DA690.B313V54] 77-358233 ISBN 0-9505390-0-7 : £1.50
1. Batheaston, Eng.—Biography. 2. Batheaston, Eng.—Social life and customs. I. Dobbie, Beatrice Marion Willmott, 1903-

Batista y Zaldfvar, Fulgenclo, Pres. Cuba, 1901-

CHESTER, Edmund A 923.17291
A sergeant named Batista. [1st ed.] New York, Holt [c1954] 276p. illus. 22cm. [F1787.B27C5] 53-10728
1. Batista y Zaldfvar, Fulgenclo, Pres. Cuba, 1901- 2. Cuba—Pol. & govt.—1900- I. Title.

Batman, John, 1800-1839.

BONWICK, James, 994.502'092'4 B 1817-1906.
John Batman the founder of Victoria / by James Bonwick ; edited, with an introduction and notes by C. E. Sayers. Melbourne : Wren Pub., 1973. xxxi, 127 p. ; 19 cm. (Link history series) Original ed. published in 1867 by S. Mullen, Melbourne. Includes bibliographical references. [DU222.B35B66 1973] 74-196559 ISBN 0-85885-022-2
1. Batman, John, 1800-1839. 2. Fawkner, John Pascoe, 1792-1869. 3. Victoria, Australia—History.

Battiss, Walter, 1906-

BATTISS, Walter, 1906- 760'.092'4
Walter Battiss / [text] by Murray Schoonraad. Cape Town : Struik (C.), 1976. 66 p. : chiefly ill. (some col.) ; 25 x 28 cm. (South African art library) Includes index. Bibliography: p. 63. [N7396.B28S36] 77-368762 ISBN 0-86977-071-3 : R9.75
1. Battiss, Walter, 1906- I. Schoonraad, Murray. II. Title. III. Series.

Battistella, Annabel.

*BATTISTELLA, Annabel. 792.7 B
Fanne Foxe, by Annabel "Fanne Foxe" Battistella with Yvonne Dunleavy. New York, Pinnacle Books [1975] 178 p. illus. 18 cm. [PN1949] ISBN 0-523-00752-3 1.75 (pbk.)
I. Dunleavy, Yvonne. II. Title.

Baudelaire, Charles Pierre, 1821-1867.

BAUDELAIRE, Charles Pierre, 928.4 1821-1867.
Baudelaire: a self-portrait. Selected letters translated and edited with a running commentary, by Lois Boe Hyslop and Francis E. Hyslop, Jr. London, New York, Oxford University Press, 1957. viii, 259 p. 23 cm. Bibliography: p. 241-242. Bibliographical references included in "Notes" (p. 243-252) [PQ2191.Z5A28] 57-1906

BAUDELAIRE, Charles 841'.8 B Pierre, 1821-1867.
The letters of Charles Baudelaire to his mother, 1833-1866, translated by Arthur Symons. New York, Haskell House Publishers, 1971. xii, 302 p. port. 23 cm. Reprint of the 1928 ed. Translation of Lettres a sa mere. [PQ2191.Z5A3313 1971] 73-153490 ISBN 0-8383-1241-1
I. Aupick, Caroline (Archimbault-Dufays) Baudelaire, 1793-1871. II. Title.

BAUDELAIRE, Charles 841'.8 B Pierre, 1821-1867.
The letters of Charles Baudelaire to his mother, 1833-1866. Translated by Arthur Symons. New York, B. Blom, 1971. xii, 302 p. port. 22 cm. Reprint of the 1927 ed. Translation of Lettres a sa mere. Includes bibliographical references. [PQ2191.Z5A3313 1971b] 70-173184
I. Aupick, Caroline (Archimbault-Dufays) Baudelaire, 1793-1871. II. Title. BIP

EMMANUEL, Pierre. 841'.8
Baudelaire; the paradox of redemptive satanism. Translated by Robert T. Cargo. University, Ala., University of Alabama Press [1970] 189 p. 21 cm. Bibliography: p. [179]-180. [PQ2191.Z5E413] 78-104929 7.50
1. Baudelaire, Charles Pierre, 1821-1867. BIP

MORGAN, Edwin. 841'.8 B
Flower of evil; a life of Charles Baudelaire. Freeport, N.Y. Books for Libraries Press [1970, c1943] 179 p. port. 23 cm. "Works of Baudelaire": p. 176. Bibliography: p. 177-179. [PQ2191.Z5M6 1970] 75-114889
1. Baudelaire, Charles Pierre, 1821-1867. I. Title. BIP

PEYRE, Henri, 1901- ed. 841.8
Baudelaire, a collection of critical essays. Englewood Cliffs, N.J., Prentice-Hall [1962] vi, 184 p. 21 cm. (A Spectrum book: Twentieth century views S-TC-18) Bibliography: p. 183-184. [PQ2191.Z5P39] 62-18082
1. Baudelaire, Charles Pierre, 1821-1867. BIP

RUFF, Marcel A., 1896- 841.8
Baudelaire, by M. A. Ruff. Translated and slightly abridged by Agnes Kertesz. [New York] New York University Press, 1966. v, 205 p. 22 cm. "Bibliographical notes": p. 174-194. [PQ2191.Z5R783] 65-10767
1. Baudelaire, Charles Pierre, 1821-1867. BIP

SARTRE, Jean Paul, 1905- 928.4
Baudelaire. Tr. from French by Martin Turnell. New Directions, [1967, c.1950] 192p. 19cm. (New Directions paperbk., NDP 233) [PQ2191.Z5S32] 1.75 pap.,
1. Baudelaire, Charles Pierre, 1821-1867. I. Title.
Distributed by Lippincott, Philadelphia.

SHANKS, Lewis Piaget, 841'.8 1878-1935.
Baudelaire : flesh and spirit / by Lewis Piaget Shanks. New York : Haskell House, 1974. viii, 263 p. : port. ; 22 cm. Reprint of the 1930 ed. published by Little, Brown, Boston. Includes index. [PQ2191.Z5S5 1974] 74-34363 ISBN 0-8383-2058-9 lib.bdg. : 14.95
1. Baudelaire, Charles Pierre, 1821-1867. I. Title. BIP

STARKIE, Enid. 928.4
Baudelaire. [Norfolk, Conn.] New Directions [1958] 622 p. illus. 21 cm. Includes bibliography. [PQ2191.Z5S8 1958] 57-13080
1. Baudelaire, Charles Pierre, 1821-1867. BIP

Baudelaire, Charles Pierre, 1821-1867—Biography.

BAUDELAIRE, Charles 841'.8 B Pierre, 1821-1867.
Intimate journals / Charles Baudelaire ; translated by Ch. Isherwood ; introd. by T. S. Eliot. Westport, Conn. : Hyperion Press, 1977, c1930. p. cm. (Hyperion library of world literature) (Classics of European literature) Translation of Journaux intimes. Reprint of the ed. published by Blackmore Press, London, Random House, New York. [PQ2191.Z5A42 1977] 76-48417 ISBN 0-88355-532-8 lib.bdg. : 10.50. ISBN 0-88355-533-6 pbk. : 2.95
1. Baudelaire, Charles Pierre, 1821-1867—Biography. 2. Authors, French—19th century—Biography. I. Title. II. Series. BIP

DE JONGE, Alex, 1938- 841'.8 B
Baudelaire, Prince of Clouds : a bibliography / by Alex de Jonge. New York : Paddington Press, c1976. 240 p. ; 24 cm. Includes index. Bibliography: p. 236. [PQ2191.Z5D44 1976] 76-3804 ISBN 0-8467-0137-5 : 10.95
1. Baudelaire, Charles Pierre, 1821-1867—Biography. I. Title.

PORCHE, Francois, 1877- 841'.8 1944.
Charles Baudelaire. Translated by John Mavin. [Folcroft, Pa.] Folcroft Library Editions, 1974. 235 p. illus. 24 cm. Translation of La vie douloureuse de Charles Baudelaire. Reprint of the 1928 ed. published by Wishart, London. [PQ2191.Z5P62 1974] 74-17204 ISBN 0-8414-6789-7 (lib. bdg.)
1. Baudelaire, Charles Pierre, 1821-1867—Biography. BIP

Baudelaire, Charles pierre, 1821-1867—Biography—Character.

LAFORGUE, Rene. 841'.8
The defeat of Baudelaire : a psycho-analytical study of the neurosis of Charles Baudelaire / by Rene Laforgue ; translated from the French by Herbert Agar. Folcroft, Pa. : Folcroft Library Editions, 1977. p. cm. Translation of L'echec de Baudelaire. Reprint of the 1932 ed. published by the Hogarth Press, London, which was issued as no. 21 of the International psycho-analytical library. Includes indexes. Bibliography. p. [PQ2191.Z5L2713 1977] 77-377 ISBN 0-8414-5812-X lib. bdg. : 20.00
1. Baudelaire, Charles pierre, 1821-1867—Biography—Character. 2. Poets, French—19th century—Biography. I. Title. II. Series: The International psycho-analytical library ; no. 21. BIP

Baudelaire, Charles Pierre, 1821-1867—Correspondence.

BAUDELAIRE, Charles 841'.8 Pierre, 1821-1867.
Letters from his youth. Translated by Simona Morini and Frederic Tuten. Garden City, N.Y., Doubleday, 1970. xii, 143 p. 22 cm. Translation of Lettres inedites aux siens. [PQ2191.Z5A193] 69-10975 4.95
1. Baudelaire, Charles Pierre, 1821-1867—Correspondence.

Baudin, Robert.

BAUDIN, Robert. 364.1'33 B
Confessions of a promiscuous counterfeiter / Robert Baudin. 1st American ed. New York : Harcourt Brace Jovanovich, c1979. 330 p. ; 25 cm. [HG336.U5B382 1979] 78-22243 9.95
1. Baudin, Robert. 2. Counterfeiters—Biography. I. Title. BIP

Bauer, Douglas.

BAUER, Douglas. 977.7'594
Prairie City, Iowa : three seasons at home / Douglas Bauer. New York : Putnam, c1979. 330 p. ; 23 cm. [F629.P75B38] 79-10314 ISBN 0-399-12359-8 : 9.95
1. Bauer, Douglas. 2. Prairie City, Iowa—Biography. 3. Prairie City, Iowa—Social life and customs. I. Title.

Bauer, Evelyn (Showalter)

BAUER, Evelyn (Showalter) 922.654
Through sunlight and shadow. Scottdale, Pa., Herald Press, [1959] 221p. illus. 20cm. Autobiographical. [BV3269.B37A3] 59-11040
I. Title.

Baugh, Laura, 1955-

JACOBS, Linda. 796.352'092'4 B
Laura Baugh : golf's golden girl / by Linda Jacobs. St. Paul, Minn. : EMC Corp., [1975] p. cm. (Women who win 2) A biography of the youngest winner in the history of the U.S. Women's Amateur Championship who was also voted Most Beautiful Golfer of 1971. [GV964.B38J32] 92 74-31187 ISBN 0-88436-160-8 lib.bdg. : 4.95 ISBN 0-88436-161-6 pbk. : 2.95
1. Baugh, Laura, 1955- Juvenile literature. 2. Golf—Juvenile literature. I. Title. BIP

Baugh, Laura, 1955- —Juvenile literature.

O'SHEA, Mary Jo. 796.352'092'4 B
Laura Baugh / by Mary Jo O'Shea ; illustrated by John Keely. Mankato, Minn. : Creative Education, [1976] p. cm. A brief biography emphasizing the career of professional golfer Laura Baugh. [GV964.B38O83] 92 75-38826 ISBN 0-87191-501-4
1. Baugh, Laura, 1955- —Juvenile literature. 2. Golf for women—Juvenile literature. I. Keely, John. II. Title. BIP

Baum ann, Charly.

BAUMAN, Charly. 791.3'2'0924
Tiger, tiger / byCharly Baumann, with Leonard A. Stevens. Chicago : Playboy Press, 1977c1975. 279p. ; 18 cm. [GV1811.B33A37] 75-18264 pbk. : 1.95
1. Baum ann, Charly. 2. Circus. 3. Tigers. 4. Animals, Training of. I. Title.

Baum. Lyman Frank, 1856-1919.

BAUM, Frank Joslyn, 1883- 928.1 1958
To please a child; a biography of L. Frank Baum, royal historian of Oz [by] Frank Joslyn Baum and Russell P. MacFall. Chicago, Reilly & Lee Co., 1961. 284p. illus. 21cm. [PS3503.A923Z58] 61-12110
1. Baum. Lyman Frank, 1856-1919. I. MacFall, Russell P. II. Title.

Baumann, Arthur Anthony,

BAUMANN, Arthur Anthony, 920.042 1856-1936.
Personalities; a selection from the writings of A. A. Baumann. Freeport, N.Y., Books for Libraries Press [1968] xvi, 271 p. 22 cm. (Essay index reprint series) Reprint of the 1936 ed. Contents.Contents.—The Victorian tradition.—Portrait of a college friend.—Benjamin Jowett.—Mr. "Jim" Lowther.—Lord Randolph Churchill.—Lord Curzon.—Sir Henry Fowler.—Sir John Gorst.—Henry Labouchere.—Mr. Speaker Peel.—The Marquis of Salisbury.—Lord Chesterfield.—An Irish triumvirate.—Anthony Trollope.—Frank Harris.—Queen Victoria's middle years.—Disraeli's meridian.—Burke: the founder of conservatism. [DA550.B32 1968] 68-54323
I. Title.

Baumann, Charly.

BAUMANN, Charly. 791.3'2'0924 B
Tiger, tiger : my 25 years with the big cats / Charly Baumann with Leonard A. Stevens. 1st ed. Chicago : Playboy Press, c1975. 279 p. : ill. ; 22 cm. [GV1811.B33A37] 75-17264 ISBN 0-87223-437-1
1. Baumann, Charly. 2. Circus. 3. Tigers. 4. Animals, Training of. I. Stevens, Leonard A., joint author. II. Title.

Baxter, Alida.

BAXTER, Alida. 301.42'8 B
Out on my ear / [by] Alida Baxter ; illustrated by Bill Tidy. London : W. H. Allen, 1976. [5], 202 p. : ill. ; 23 cm. [CT788.B348A36] 76-383569 ISBN 0-491-01776-6 : £3.50
1. Baxter, Alida. 2. England—Biography. I. Title.

Baxter, Anne.

BAXTER, Anne. 791.43'028'0924 B
Intermission : a true story / Anne Baxter. New York : Putnam, c1976. 384 p. ; 23 cm. [PN2287.B39A32] 75-45285 ISBN 0-399-11577-3 : 10.00
1. Baxter, Anne. 2. Actors—United States—Biography. I. Title. BIP

Baxter, George, 1804-1867.

LEWIS, Charles Thomas Courtney. 769'.92'4
George Baxter—his life and work, by C. T. Courtney Lewis. [1st ed., reprinted with a new foreword by Helen Courtney Lewis. Wakefield, E.P. Publishing, 1972. vi, xviii, 276 p., 31 leaves. illus., ports. 20 cm. Bibliography: p. 236-254. [NE1860.B2L7 1972] 73-167780 ISBN 0-85409-918-2 £3.15
1. Baxter, George, 1804-1867.

Baxter, Gordon, 1923-

BAXTER, Gordon, 1923- 070'.9'24 B
Village Creek : the first and only eyewitness account of the second life of Gordon Baxter / by himself, Gordon Baxter. New York : Summit Books, c1979. p. cm. [PN4874.B336A38] 79-18758 ISBN 0-671-40088-6 : 10.95
1. Baxter, Gordon, 1923- 2. Journalists—United States—Biography. I. Title.

Baxter, Sir Thomas, 1878-

PEPPERALL, Robert Augustus. 926.3
A biography of Sir Thomas Baxter. [Wells, Somerset, Clare, Son] 1950. 242 p. group port. 22 cm. [S417.B28P4] 51-4018
1. Baxter, Sir Thomas, 1878- I. Title.

Bayfield, Henry Wolsey, 1795-1885.

MCKENZIE, Ruth. 526.9'9'0924 B
Admiral Bayfield, pioneer nautical surveyor / Ruth McKenzie. Ottawa : Canada, Fisheries and Marine Service, 1976. 13, 13 p. : ill., map (fold. in pocket) ; 22 x 28 cm. (Miscellaneous special publication - Canada, Fisheries and Marine Service ; 32) Added t.p.: L'amiral Bayfield, pionnier de l'hydrographie marine. English and French. Includes bibliographies. [VK597.C22M3] 76-375032
1. Bayfield, Henry Wolsey, 1795-1885. 2. Surveyors, Marine—Canada—Biography. I. Title. II. Title: L'amiral Bayfield, pionnier de l'hydrographie marine. III. Series: Canada. Fisheries and Marine Service. Miscellaneous special publication — Canada, Fisheries and Marine Service ; 32.

Bayh, Marvella.

BAYH, Marvella. 362.1'9'6994490924 B
Marvella, a personal journey / by Marvella Bayh, with Mary Lynn Kotz ; introd. by Lady Bird Johnson ; epilogue by Birch Bayh. 1st ed. New York : Harcourt Brace Jovanovich, c1979. ix, 309 p., [8] leaves of plates : ill. ; 24 cm. Includes index. [RC280.B8B39] 79-1809 ISBN 0-15-157557-6 : 11.95
1. Bayh, Marvella. 2. Breast—Cancer—Biography. I. Kotz, Mary Lynn, joint author. II. Title.

Bayle, Pierre, 1647-1706.

REX, Walter 230.0924
Essays on Pierre Bayle and religious controversy. The Hague, M. Nijhoff [New York, Humanities, c.1965] xv,271p. port. 24cm. (Intl. archives of the hist. of ideas, 8) Bibl. [BX9419.B3R4] 66-1628 9.50
1. Bayle, Pierre, 1647-1706. 2. Theology—Hist.—17th cent. I. Title. II. Title: Title. (Series: Archives internationales d'histoire des idees, 8)

Baylor Co., Tex.—History.

BAYLOR County Historical Society. 917.64'744'036
Salt pork to sirloin: the history of Baylor County, Texas, from 1879 to 1930. Illus. by Mark Tucker. [Quanah, Tex.] Nortex Offset Publications, 1972. 227, 179 p. illus. 29 cm. [F392.B25B38] 73-159343
1. Baylor Co., Tex.—History. 2. Baylor Co., Tex.—Biography. I. Title.

Baylor, John Robert, 1822-1894.

THOMPSON, Jerry Don. 978'.02'0924 B
Colonel John Robert Baylor: Texas Indian fighter and Confederate soldier. [Hillsboro, Tex., Hill Junior College Press] 1971. viii, 114 p. illus. 23 cm. (Hill Junior College monographs in Texas and Confederate history, no. 5) Bibliography: p. 104-109. [E470.9.T45] 70-187492 ISBN 0-912172-14-2
1. Baylor, John Robert, 1822-1894. 2. United States—History—Civil War, 1861-1865—Campaigns and battles. 3. Southwest, New—History—Civil War, 1861-1865, 1861-1865. I. Series: Hill Junior College, Hillsboro, Tex. Monographs in Texas and Confederate history, no. 5.

Bayreuth, Ger. (City). Festspiele.

SKELTON, Geoffrey 780.924
Wagner at Bayreuth: experment and tradition. Foreword by Wieland Wagner. [1st Amer. ed.] New York, Braziller [c.1965] 239p. illus. (pt. col.), ports. 22cm. Bibl. [ML410.W2S55 1966a] 66-20191 6.50
1. Wagner, Richard, 1813-1883—Performances—Bayreuth, Ger. (City) 2. Bayreuth, Ger. (City) Festspiele. 3. Wagner family. I. Title.

SKELTON, Geoffrey. 782.1'092'4
Wagner at Bayreuth : experiment and tradition / [by] Geoffrey Skelton ; foreword by the late Wieland Wagner. New and revised ed. London ; New York : White Lion Publishers, 1976. 251 p., [16] p. of plates : ill., ports. ; 22 cm. Includes index. Bibliography: p. 241-242. [ML410.W2S55 1976] 76-369181 ISBN 0-85617-068-2 : £5.75
1. Bayreuth, Ger. (City). Festspiele. 2. Wagner family. 3. Musicians—Bayreuth, Ger. (City)—Biography. I. Title.

WAGNER, Richard, 1813-1883. 782.1'079'4331
The story of Bayreuth as told in the Bayreuth letters of Richard Wagner. Translated and edited by Caroline V. Kerr. New York, Vienna House, 1972. 364 p. illus. 21 cm. Reprint of the 1912 ed. [ML410.W1A325 1972] 78-163795 ISBN 0-8443-0015-2
1. Bayreuth, Ger. (City). Festspiele.

Bazili, Nikolai Aleksandrovich, 1883-1963.

DE BASILY, Lascelle Meserve 947.08'092'4 B
Memoirs of a lost world / Lascelle Meserve de Basily. Stanford, Calif. : Distributed by Hoover Institution Press, 1975. vii, 308 p. : ill. ; 24 cm. [DK254.B37D4] 75-29793 ISBN 0-9600928-1-1 : 8.00
1. Bazili, Nikolai Aleksandrovich, 1883-1963. 2. De Basily, Lascelle Meserve. I. Title.

Bazin, Andre, 1918-1958.

ANDREW, Dudley. 791.43'092'4 B
Andre Bazin / Dudley Andrew ; foreword by Francois Truffant. New York : Oxford University Press, 1978. xi, 253 p. : ill. ; 22 cm. Includes bibliographical references and index. [PN1998.A3B3972] 77-9409 ISBN 0-19-502165-7 : 11.95
1. Bazin, Andre, 1918-1958. 2. Moving-picture critics—France—Biography. I. Title. BIP

Beach Boys.

GOLDEN, Bruce, 1933- 784'.092'2 B
The Beach Boys : Southern California pastoral / by Bruce Golden. San Bernardino, Calif. : Borgo Press, 1976. 59 p. ; 21 cm. (The Woodstock series ; v. 1) "A Newcastel/Borgo Press original." Discography: p. 40-52. [ML421.B38G6] 76-5902 ISBN 0-87877-202-2 pbk. : 1.95
1. Beach Boys. BIP

LEAF, David. 784'.092'2 B
The Beach Boys and the California myth / David Leaf. New York : Grosset & Dunlap, c1978. 192 p. : ill. ; 28 cm. [ML421.B38L4] 77-88432 ISBN 0-448-14625-8 : 14.95 ISBN 0-448-14626-6 pbk. : 6.95
1. Beach Boys. 2. Rock musicians—California—Biography. I. Title. BIP

Beach, Charles Lewis, 1866-1933.

BARNETT, James Harwood, 1906- 378.1'12'0924 B
"Mr. Beach"; a profile of Charles Lewis Beach, president, Connecticut Agricultural College, 1908-1928, by James H. Barnett. [Storrs, Conn., c1969] 36 p. illus., ports. 24 cm. (The University of Connecticut publications series) [LD1281.C3317 1908.B3] 78-634991
1. Beach, Charles Lewis, 1866-1933. 2. Connecticut University—History. I. Title.

Beaconsfield, Benjamin Disraeli, 1st Earl of, 1804-1881.

BEACONSFIELD, Benjamin Disraeli, 1st Earl of, 1804-1881. 941.081'092'4 B
Notes for an autobiography / by Benjamin Disraeli ; edited by Helen M. Swartz and Marvin Swartz. New York : Stein and Day, [1975] p. cm. [DA564.B3A125] 75-16287 ISBN 0-8128-1867-9 : 10.00
1. Beaconsfield, Benjamin Disraeli, 1st Earl of, 1804-1881. I. Title.

BLAKE, Robert, 1916- 942.081'0924 B
Disraeli. New York, St. Martin's Press [1967, c1966] xxiv, 819 p. illus., ports. 24 cm. Bibliography: p. 781-786. [DA564.B3B6 1967] 67-11837
1. Beaconsfield, Benjamin Disraeli, 1st earl of, 1804-1881.

BLAKE, Robert, 1916- 942.081'0924 B
Disraeli. London, Oxford U.P., 1969. 64 p. 8 plates, illus., 3 maps, ports. 21 cm. (The Clarendon biographies, [23]) Bibliography: p. [61] [DA564.B3B6 1969] 74-390417 9/6
1. Beaconsfield, Benjamin Disraeli, 1st Earl of, 1804-1881.

BRANDES, Georg Morris Cohen, 1842-1927 942.0810924
Lord Beaconsfield; a study. Introd. by Salo W. Baron. [Tr. from Danish by Mrs. George Sturge] New York. Crowell [c1966] xvi, 238p. 21cm. (Crowell hist. classics ser.) printed from the 1880 edition. Bibl. [DA564.B3B8] 66-14618 2.45 pap.,
1. Beaconsfield, Benjamin Disraeli, 1st earl of, 1804-1881. I. Title.

DAVIS, Richard W. 941.081'092'4 B
Disraeli / by Richard W. Davis. 1st ed. Boston : Little, Brown, c1976. p. cm. (The Library of world biography) Includes index. Bibliography: p. [DA564.B3D38] 76-10289 ISBN 0-316-17660-5
1. Beaconsfield, Benjamin Disraeli, 1st Earl of, 1804-1881.

FROUDE, James Anthony, 1818-1894. 942.081'0924
Lord Beaconsfield. Freeport, N.Y., Books for Libraries Press [1971] x, 267 p. port. 23 cm. Reprint of the 1890 ed. [DA564.B3F9 1971] 76-157333 ISBN 0-8369-5793-8
1. Beaconsfield, Benjamin Disraeli, 1st Earl of, 1804-1881. I. Title. BIP

GRANT, Neil. 942.081'0924 B
Benjamin Disraeli: Prime Minister extraordinary. New York, F. Watts [1969] ix, 245 p. illus., map, ports. 22 cm. (Immortals of history) [DA564.B3G7] 69-11143
1. Beaconsfield, Benjamin Disraeli, 1st earl of, 1804-1881. I. Title.

HIBBERT, Christopher, 1924- 941.081'092'4 B
Disraeli and his world / Christopher Hibbert. New York : Scribner, c1978. 128 p. : ill. ; 24 cm. Includes index. Bibliography: p. 126. [DA564.B3H52 1978b] 78-59111 ISBN 0-684-15915-5 : 10.95
1. Beaconsfield, Benjamin Disraeli, 1st Earl of, 1804-1881. 2. Great Britain—Politics and government—1837-1901. 3. Prime ministers—Great Britain—Biography. I. Title. BIP

JERMAN, B R 923.242
The young Disraeli. Princeton, N. J., Princeton University Press, 1960. 327p. illus. 23cm. [DA564.B3J42] 60-5750
1. Beaconsfield, Benjamin Disraell, 1st earl of, 1804-1881. I. Title.

JERMAN, B R 923.242
The young Disraeli. Princeton, N. J., Princeton University Press, 1960. 327p. illus. 23cm. [DA564.B3J42] 60-5750
1. Beaconsfield, Benjamin Disraell, 1st earl of, 1804-1881. I. Title.

KOMROFF, Manuel, 1890- 942.081'0924 B
Disraeli. New York, J. Messner [1963] 191 p. 22 cm. Bibliography: p. 183-184. A biography of England's Prime Minister during Victoria's reign, who studied law, published a newspaper, wrote successful novels, and served in Parliament before becoming a Prime Minister known for domestic reforms and an imperialistic foreign policy. [DA564.B3K6] 92 AC 68
1. Beaconsfield, Benjamin Disraeli, 1st earl of, 1804-1881. I. Title.

MONYPENNY, William Flavelle, 1866-1912. 942.081'0924 B
The life of Benjamin Disraeli, Earl of Beaconsfield, by William Flavelle Monypenny and George Earle Buckle. New and rev. ed. New York, Russell & Russell [1968] 4 v. illus., port. 23 cm. Reprint of the 1929 ed. Bibliographical footnotes. [DA564.B3M9 1968] 68-25044 85.00
1. Beaconsfield, Benjamin Disraeli, 1st Earl of, 1804-1881. 2. Gt. Brit.—Politics and government—1837-1901. I. Buckle, George Earle, 1854-1935. II. Title. BIP

PEARSON, Hesketh 923.242
Disraeli: his life and personality. (original title: Dizzy.) New York, Grosset [1960, c.1951] 310p. (Universal lib., UL78) 1.45 pap.,
1. Beaconsfield,Benjamin Disraeli, 1st earl of, 1804-1881. I. Title.

PEARSON, Hesketh, 1887- 923.242
Dizzy; the life & personality of Benjamin Disraeli, earl of Beaconsfield. [1st ed.] New York, Harper [1951] ix, 310 p. illus., ports. 22 cm. [D[ano4.B3P4] 51-12064
1. Beaconfield, Benjamin Disraeli, 1st earl of, 1804-1881. I. Title.

PEARSON, Hesketh, 1887-1964. 942.081'092'4 B
Dizzy; the life and personality of Benjamin Disraeli, Earl of Beaconsfield. London, New York, White Lion Publishers, 1974. iii-ix, 284 p., [15] p. of plates. illus., ports. 23 cm. Includes index. Bibliography: p. [279] [DA564.B3P4 1974] 74-181833 ISBN 0-85617-397-5 £3.25

1. Beaconsfield, Benjamin Disraeli, 1st Earl of, 1804-1881. I. Title.

PEARSON, Hesketh, 1887-1964. 942.081'092'4 B
Dizzy : the life and nature of Benjamin Disraeli, Earl of Beaconsfield / by Hesketh Pearson.—With 22—ill. Westport, Conn. : Greenwood Press, 1974, c1951. xi, 284 p., [8] leaves of plates : ill. ; 22 cm. Reprint of the ed. published by Methuen, London. Includes index. Bibliography: p. [279] [DA564.B3P4 1974b] 74-12579 ISBN 0-8371-7729-4 : 15.50
1. Beaconsfield, Benjamin Disraeli, 1st Earl of, 1804-1881. I. Title. **BIP**

WHIBLEY, Charles, 1859-1930. 942 B
Political portraits, second series. Freeport, N.Y., Books for Libraries Press [1970] viii, 293 p. 23 cm. (Essay index reprint series) Reprint of the 1923 ed. Contents.—Portraits: Bolingbroke. Bubb Dodington. Lord Castlereagh. A maker of colonies. Benjamin Disraeli.—Outlines: James Harrington. The trimmer. George Jeffreys. An elderly Tory. Jean-Jacques Rousseau. Chamfort. Mirabeau. William Windham. Landor on Fox. Stendhal's Napoleon. Includes bibliographical references. [DA28.4.W46 1970] 76-117859 ISBN 0-8369-1734-0
1. Beaconsfield, Benjamin Disraeli, 1st Earl of, 1804-1881. 2. Statesmen—Great Britain—Biography. 3. Statesmen—France—Biography. I. Title. **BIP**

Beaconsfield, Benjamin Disraeli, 1st Earl of, 1804-1881—Journeys.

SULTANA, Donald. 823'.8
Benjamin Disraeli in Spain and Malta : a monograph / by Donald Sultana. Salzburg : Institut fur Englische Sprache und Literatur, Universitat Salzburg, 1975. xvi, 101 p. : ill. ; 21 cm. (Romantic reassessment ; 51) Bibliography: p. 100-101. [PR4086.S9] 76-370407 pbk. : 17.50
1. Beaconsfield, Benjamin Disraeli, 1st Earl of, 1804-1881—Journeys. 2. Authors, English—19th century—Biography. I. Title. II. Series. III. Salzburg studies in English literature
Distributed by Humanitics.

SULTANA, Donald. 823'.8 B
Benjamin Disraeli in Spain, Malta, and Albania 1830-32 : a monograph / Donald Sultana. London : Tamesis Books, 1976. ix, 78 p., [4] leaves of plates : ill. ; 24 cm. (Coleccion Tamesis : Series A, Monografias ; 55) Includes index. Bibliography: p. 73-74. [PR4086.S93] 77-364509 ISBN 0-7293-0019-6 : £6.00
1. Beaconsfield, Benjamin Disraeli, 1st Earl of, 1804-1881—Journeys. 2. Authors, English—19th century—Biography. I. Title.

Beaconsfield Benjamin Disraeli, 1st earl of, 1804-1881—Juvenile literature

KOMROFF, Manuel, 1890- 92
Disraeli. New York, J. Messner [1963] 191 p. 22 cm. Bibliography. p. 183-184. [DA564.B3K6] 63-16787
1. Beaconsfield Benjamin Disraeli, 1st earl of, 1804-1881—Juvenile literature

Beaconsfield, Mary Anne (Evans) Disraeli, Viscountess, 1792-1872.

HARDWICK, Mollie. 942.081'092'4
Mrs Dizzy; the life of Mary Anne Disraeli, Viscountess Beaconsfield. New York, St. Martin's Press [1973, c1972] 218 p. illus. 22 cm. Bibliography: p. 205-206. [DA564.B31H37 1972b] 72-89422 7.95
1. Beaconsfield, Mary Anne (Evans) Disraeli, Viscountess, 1792-1872. I. Title.

Beagle Expedition, 1831-1836.

THE Beagle record : 500.9'8
selections from the original pictorial records and written accounts of the voyage of H.M.S. Beagle / edited by Richard Darwin Keynes. Cambridge ; New York : Cambridge University Press, c1978. p. cm. [QH11.B43] 77-82500 ISBN 0-521-21822-5 : 75.00
1. Beagle Expedition, 1831-1836. 2. Darwin, Charles Robert, 1809-1882. 3. Naturalists—England—Biography. 4. Naturalists—England—Correspondence. I. Keynes, R. D.

Beals, Jessie Tarbox.

ALLAND, Alexander. 770'.92'4 B
Jessie Tarbox Beals, first woman news photographer / Alexander Alland, Sir. New York : Camera/Graphic Press, [1978] p. cm. Includes index. [TR140.B38A65] 78-4406 ISBN 0-918696-08-9 : 25.00
1. Beals, Jessie Tarbox. 2. News photographers—United States—Biography. I. Title. **BIP**

Bean, Ellis Peter, 1783-1846.

LAY, Bennett. 923.973
The lives of Ellis P. Bean. Austin, University of Texas Press [1960] 227p. illus. 22cm. Includes bibliography. [F1232.B39] 60-7668
1. Bean, Ellis Peter, 1783-1846. I. Title.

LAY, Bennett Clayton 923.973
The lives of Ellis P. Bean. Austin, University of Texas Press [c.1960] x, 227p. Bibl. notes p.179-201 illus., endpaper map 22cm. 60-7668 4.50
1. Bean, Ellis Peter, 1783-1846. I. Title.

Bean, Roy, d. 1903.

LLOYD, Everett. 974'.06'0924
Law west of the Pecos; the story of Roy Bean. [Rev. and enl. ed.] San Antonio Naylor Co. [1967] vii, 103 p. illus., ports. 20 cm. [F391.B323 1967] 67-13397
1. Bean, Roy, d. 1903. I. Title.

LLOYD, Everett 976.4'06'0924(B)
Law west of the Pecos; the story of Roy Bean. [Rev., enl. ed.] San Antonio, Naylor [1967] vi, 106p. illus., ports. 20cm. [F391.B323 1967] 67-13397 2.95
1. Bean, Roy, d. 1903. I. Title.

SONNICHSEN, Charles Leland, 1901- 923.473
Roy Bean; law west of the Pecos. New York, Devin-Adair Co., 1958 [c1943] 207 p. illus. 22 cm. [F391.B328 1958] 58-9755
1. Bean, Roy, d. 1903. **BIP**

Bear's Heart, 1851-1882—Juvenile literature.

SUPREE, Burton. 970'.004'97 B
Bear's Heart : scenes from the life of a Cheyenne artist of one hundred years ago with pictures by himself / text by Burton Supree, with Ann Ross. 1st ed. Philadelphia : Lippincott, c1977. p. cm. A biography of Bear's Heart illustrated with his own drawings done while he and seventy-one other Indians were imprisoned in Florida. [E99.C53B427] 76-48952 ISBN 0-397-31746-8 : 8.95
1. Bear's Heart, 1851-1882—Juvenile literature. 2. Castillo de San Marcos, St. Augustine—Juvenile literature. 3. Cheyenne Indians—Biography—Juvenile literature. I. Ross, Ann, joint author. II. Bear's Heart, 1851-1882. III. Title. **BIP**

Beard, Charles Austin, 1874-1948.

BEARD, Mary (Ritter) 1876- 928.1
The making of Charles A. Beard, an interpretation. With Chapters by Arthur W. Macmahon and George Radin, and reports from Japanese correspondents. [1st ed.] New York, Exposition Press [c1955] 104p. 21cm. Bibliographical footnotes. [E175.5.B375] 55-12123
1. Beard, Charles Austin, 1874-1948. I. Title.

HOFSTADTER, Richard, 1916-1970. 973'.07'2022
The progressive historians—Turner, Beard, Parrington / Richard Hofstadter. Chicago : University of Chicago Press, 1979, c1968. p. cm. Reprint of the ed. published by Knopf, New York. Includes index. Bibliography: p. [E175.45.H6 1979] 79-12591 ISBN 0-226-34818-0 : 7.95
1. Turner, Frederick Jackson, 1861-1932. 2. Beard, Charles Austin, 1874-1948. 3. Parrington, Vernon Louis, 1871-1929. 4. Historians—United States—Biography. 5. United States—Historiography. I. Title.

KENNEDY, Thomas C., 1932- 327.73
Charles A. Beard and American foreign policy / Thomas C. Kennedy. Gainesville : University Presses of Florida, 1975. xi, 199 p. ; 23 cm. "A University of Florida book." Includes index. Bibliography: p. 175-191. [E175.5.B385] 77-186324 ISBN 0-8130-0354-7 : 8.50
1. Beard, Charles Austin, 1874-1948. 2. United States—Foreign relations—20th century—Historiography. I. Title. **BIP**

Beard. Daniel Carter, 1850-1941—Juvenile literature.

BLASSINGAME, Wyatt. 369.43'092'4 B
Dan Beard, scoutmaster of America. Illustrated by Dom Lupo. Champaign, Ill., Garrard Pub. Co. [1972] 80 p. col. illus. 24 cm. A biography of the writer, artist, and naturalist who began a boys' club called Sons of Daniel Boone and later became one of the founders of the Boy Scouts of America. [CT275.B5418B53] 92 72-76325 ISBN 0-8116-6754-5 3.50 (lib. bdg.)
1. Beard, Daniel Carter, 1850-1941—Juvenile literature. I. Lupo, Dom, illus. II. Title.

SEIBERT, Jerry. 92
Dan Beard, Boy Scout pioneer. Illustrated by Lorence Bjorklung. Boston, Houghton Mifflin [1963] 191 p. col. illus. 22 cm. (Piper books) [CT275.B5418S4] 63-15654
1. Beard. Daniel Carter, 1850-1941—Juvenile literature. I. Title.

Beardsley, Aubrey Vincent, 1872-1898.

BEARDSLEY, Aubrey Vincent, 1872-1898. 760'.092'4
Last letters of Aubrey Beardsley. With an introductory note by the Rev. John Gray. [Folcroft, Pa.] Folcroft Library Editions, 1973, [i.e.1974] p. Reprint of the 1904 ed. published by Longmans, Green, London. [NC242.B3A2 1973] 73-12999 20.00
1. Beardsley, Aubrey Vincent, 1872-1898. I. Gray, John, 1866-1934. II. Title. **BIP**

BEARDSLEY, Aubrey Vincent, 1872-1898. 741'.0924
The letters of Aubrey Beardsley, edited by Henry Maas, J. L. Duncan and W. G. Good. Rutherford, Fairleigh Dickinson University Press [1970] 472 p. illus., facsims., ports. 27 cm. [NC242.B3M28] 68 11571 ISBN 8-386-68844- 20.00
I. Maas, Henry, ed. II. Duncan, John, 1937- ed. III. Good, W. G., 1909- ed. **BIP**

BROPHY, Brigid, 1929- 741'.092'4 B
Beardsley and his world / by Brigid Brophy. New York : Harmony Books, 1976. p. cm. [NC242.B3B68 1976] 76-5969 ISBN 0-517-52628-X
1. Beardsley, Aubrey Vincent, 1872-1898. I. Title.

BROPHY, Brigid, 1929- 741'.092'4 B
Beardsley and his world / Brigid Brophy. London : Thames and Hudson, c1976. 128 p. : ill. ; 24 cm. Includes index. Bibliography: p. 118. [NC242.B3B68 1976b] 76-366635 ISBN 0-500-13057-4 : £3.50
1. Beardsley, Aubrey Vincent, 1872-1898. I. Title.

BROPHY, Brigid, 1929- 741'.0924 B
Black and white; a portrait of Aubrey Beardsley. New York, Stein and Day [1969, c1968] 95 p. 44 illus. 24 cm. Bibliography: p. 95. [NC242.B3B7 1969] 69-15906 4.95
1. Beardsley, Aubrey Vincent, 1872-1898. I. Title. **BIP**

MACFALL, Haldane, 1860-1928. 741.0924 B
Aubrey Beardsley, the man and his work. Freeport, N.Y., Books for Libraries Press [1972] xiv, 109 p. illus. 29 cm. Reprint of the 1928 ed. [NC242.B3M32 1972] 73-39472 ISBN 0-8369-9918-5
1. Beardsley, Aubrey Vincent, 1872-1898. I. Title.

MACFALL, Haldane, 1860-1928. 741.0924 B
Aubrey Beardsley, the man and his work. Freeport, N.Y., Books for Libraries Press [1972] xiv, 109 p. illus. 29 cm. Reprint of the 1928 ed. [NC242.B3M32 1972] 73-39472 ISBN 0-8369-9918-5
1. Beardsley, Aubrey Vincent, 1872-1898. I. Title.

MACFALL, Haldane, 1860-1928. 741'.092'4 B
Aubrey Beardsley, the man and his work / by Haldane Macfall. Norwood, Pa. : Norwood Editions, 1975. xiv, 109 p., [11] leaves of plates : ill. ; 28 cm. Reprint of the 1928 ed. published by John Lane, London. [NC242.B3M32 1975] 75-33095 ISBN 0-88305-443-4 : 30.00
1. Beardsley, Aubrey Vincent, 1872-1898.

MACFALL, Haldane, 1860-1928. 741'.092'4 B
Aubrey Beardsley, the man and his work / by Haldane Macfall. Norwood, Pa. : Norwood Editions, 1975. xiv, 109 p., [11] leaves of plates : ill. ; 28 cm. Reprint of the 1928 ed. published by John Lane, London. [NC242.B3M32 1975] 75-33095 ISBN 0-88305-443-4 : 30.00
1. Beardsley, Aubrey Vincent, 1872-1898.

READE, Brian. v. 12
Aubrey Beardsley. Introd. by John Rothenstein. New York, Viking Press [1967] 372 p. illus. (part col.) (A Studio book) 68-64672
1. Beardsley, Aubrey Vincent, 1872-1898. I. Title.

WEINTRAUB, Stanley, 1929- 741'.0924 B
Beardsley; a biography. New York, G. Braziller [1967] xv, 285 p. 16 illus., port. 22 cm. Bibliographical references included in "Notes" (p. 265-279) [NC242.B4W4] 67-19874
1. Beardsley, Aubrey Vincent, 1872-1898.

WEINTRAUB, Stanley, 1929- 741'.092'4 B
Beardsley. Revised ed. Harmondsworth, Penguin, 1972. 287, 16 p. illus. 18 cm. (Pelican biographies) Includes bibliographical references. [NC242.B3W4 1972] 73-161896 ISBN 0-14-021555-7 £0.50
1. Beardsley, Aubrey Vincent, 1872-1898.

Beardsley, Helen (Brandmeir).

BEARDSLEY, Helen (Brandmeir). 920.073
Who gets the drumstick? The story of the Beardsley family. New York, Bantam [1960, c.1965] 122p. 18cm. (H3675) [CT275.B543A3] .60 pap.,
I. Title.

BEARDSLEY, Helen (Brandmeir) 920.073
Who gets the drumstick? The story of the Beardsley family [by] Helen Beardsley. New York, Random House [1965] 215 p. illus., ports. 22 cm. [CT275.B543A3] 65-11262
I. Title.

Beardsley, Ruth Robbins.

BEARDSLEY, Ruth Robbins. 917.59'39'0360924 B
Pioneering in the Everglades. Illustrated by Emma Bates Robbins Nordlie. Fort Myers Beach, Fla., Island Press [1973] 79 p. illus. 22 cm. Autobiographical. [F317.E9B42] 73-92355 ISBN 0-87208-028-5
1. Beardsley, Ruth Robbins. 2. Everglades, Fla.—Description and travel. I. Title.

Beardsworth, Susanna Mary, 1871-

PARENTE, Pascal P 1890- 922.2
Susanna Mary Beardsworth, the white dove of peace; life, conversion, mysticism. St. Meinrad, Ind. [1950] vii, 195 p. illus. 22 cm. "Grall publication." [BV5095.B4P3] 51-48
1. Beardsworth, Susanna Mary, 1871- I. Title.

Bearsted, Marcus Samuel, 1st Viscount, 1853-1927.

HENRIQUES, Robert David Quixano, 1905- 923.842
Bearsted; a biography of Marcus Samuel, first viscount Bearsted, and founder of 'Shell' Transport and Trading Company. New York, Viking Press [c.1960] 676p. illus. gIncludes bibl. 60-12462 7.50
1. Bearsted, Marcus Samuel, 1st viscount, 1853-1927. 2. 'Shell' Transport and Trading Company, ltd. I. Title.

HENRIQUES, Robert David Quixano, 1905-1967. 338.7'62'233820924 B
Bearsted; a biography of Marcus Samuel, First Viscount Bearsted, and founder of 'Shell' Transport and Trading Co. New York, A. M. Kelley, 1970 [c1960] xi, 676 p. illus., map, ports. 22 cm. (Library of early American business and industry, 48) (Viking reprint editions) Bibliography: p. 651-652. [HD9571.9.S47H45 1970] 73-122071
1. Bearsted, Marcus Samuel, 1st Viscount, 1853-1927. 2. "Shell" Transport and Trading Company, ltd., London.

Beasley, Bobby.

BEASLEY, Bobby. 798'.45'0924 B
Second start / [by] Bobby Beasley. London : W. H. Allen, 1976. 234 p., [24] p. of plates : ill., ports. ; 23 cm. [SF336.B37A37 1976] 76-375965 ISBN 0-491-01985-8 : £4.95
1. Beasley, Bobby. 2. Jockeys—Ireland—Biography. 3. Alcoholics—Ireland—Biography. I. Title.

Beaton, Cecil Walter Hardy, Sir, 1904-

BEATON, Cecil Walter Hardy, 1904- 779'.092'4 B
Cecil Beaton: memoirs of the 40's, by Cecil Beaton. New York, McGraw-Hill Book Co. [1972] 310 p. illus. 24 cm. London ed. (Weidenfeld & Nicolson) has title: The happy years. [TR140.B4A28 1972b] 72-5857 ISBN 0-07-004225-X 10.00
I. Title. II. Title: Memoirs of the 40's.

BEATON, Cecil Walter Hardy, 1904- 927.7
Photobiography. [1st ed.] Garden City, N. Y., Doubleday, 1951. 255 p. illus., ports. 26 cm. [TR140.B4A3] 51-11655
1. Photographers—Correspondence, reminiscences, etc. I. Title.

BEATON, Cecil Walter Hardy, Sir, 1904- 770'.92'4 B
The restless years : diaries, 1955-63 / Cecil Beaton. London : Weidenfeld and Nicolson, c1976. 190 p., [6] leaves of plates : ill. ; 23 cm. [TR140.B4A32] 76-377856 ISBN 0-297-77155-8 : £4.95
1. Beaton, Cecil Walter Hardy, Sir, 1904- 2. Photographers—England—Biography. I. Title.

BEATON, Cecil Walter Hardy, Sir, 1904- 770'.92'4 B
Self portrait with friends : the selected diaries of Cecil Beaton, 1926-1974 / edited by Richard Buckle. New York : Times Books, c1979. p. cm. Includes index. [TR140.B4A325 1979] 79-51451 ISBN 0-8129-0859-7 : 14.95
1. Beaton, Cecil Walter Hardy, Sir, 1904- 2. Photographers—England—Biography. I. Buckle, Richard. II. Title. BIP

BEATON, Cecil Walter Hardy, 1904- 927.7
The wandering years; diaries, 1922-1939. Boston, Little, Brown [1962, c1961] 387 p. illus. 23 cm. [TR140.B4A34 1962] 62-8059
I. Title.

BEATON, Cecil Walter Hardy, 1904- 940.548142
The years between; diaries 1939-44 [by] Cecil Beaton. [1st ed.] New York, Holt, Rinehart and Winston [1965] 352 p. illus., ports. 22 cm. [D811.5.B32 1965a] 65-22457
1. World War, 1939-1945—Personal narratives, English. I. Title.

Beatrice d'Este, consort of Lodovico Sforza, il Moro, Duke of Milan, 1475-1497.

ADY, Julia Mary (Cartright) d.1924. 945'.05'0924 B
Beatrice d'Este, Duchess of Milan, 1475-1497; a study of the Renaissance. Freeport, N.Y., Books for Libraries Press [1972] xx, 387 p. illus. 23 cm. Reprint of the 1899 ed. [DG657.9.B4A65 1972] 73-38345 ISBN 0-8369-6762-3
1. Beatrice d'Este, consort of Lodovico Sforza, il Moro, Duke of Milan, 1475-1497. 2. Italy—History—1268-1492.

ADY, Julia Mary Cartwright, d.1924. 945'.05'0924 B
Beatrice d'Este, Duchess of Milan, 1475-1497; a study of the Renaissance. New York, Dutton, 1905. [New York, AMS Press, 1973] xx, 387 p. illus. 23 cm. Bibliography: p. ix-xi. [DG657.9.B4A65 1973] 71-154137 ISBN 0-404-09204-7 17.50
1. Beatrice d'Este, consort of Lodovico Sforza, il Moro, duke of Milan, 1475-1497. 2. Italy—History—1268-1492.

Beattie, James, 1735-1803.

KING, Everard H. 821'.6 B
James Beattie / by Everard H. King. Boston : Twayne Publishers, c1977. 190 p. : port. ; 21 cm. (Twayne's English authors series ; TEAS 206) Includes index. Bibliography: p. 181-186. [PR3316.B4K5] 76-54693 ISBN 0-8057-6653-7 lib.bdg. : 8.50
1. Beattie, James, 1735-1803. 2. Authors, Scottish—18th century—Biography. BIP

Beatty, Clyde, 1903-1965—Juvenile literature.

WILKIE, Katharine Elliott, 1904- JUV
Clyde Beatty: boy animal trainer, by Katharine E. Wilkie. Illustrated by James Cummins. Indianapolis, Bobbs-Merrill [1968] 200 p. col. illus., port. 20 cm. (Childhood of famous Americans) Concentrates on the boyhood and youth of Clyde Beatty as he ventured into situations that helped him become a famous animal trainer and circus owner. [GV1811.B4W5] 791.3'0924 B 92 68-55145
1. Beatty, Clyde, 1903-1965—Juvenile literature. I. Cummins, James, illus. II. Title.

Beatty, Erkuries, 1759-1823.

WEISS, Harry Bischoff, 1883- 923.573
Colonel Erkuries Beatty, 1759-1823. Pennsylvania Revolutionary soldier, New Jersey judge, senator, farmer, and prominent citizen of Princeton, by Harry B. Weiss and Grace M. Ziegler. Trenton, Past Times Press, 1958. 80 p. illus. 23 cm. Includes bibliography. [F138.B4W4] 58-11354
1. Beatty, Erkuries, 1759-1823. I. Title.

Beatty, Robert O.

BEATTY, Robert O. 362.1'9'699400926 B
Still a lot of living : coping with cancer / Robert O. Beatty, with his family ; foreword by Elliot L. Richardson ; introd. by Charles D. Steuart. New York : Macmillan, c1978. xviii, 196 p. ; 22 cm. Bibliography: p. 195-196. [RC280.P7B42] 78-12543 ISBN 0-02-508100-4 : 8.95
1. Beatty, Robert O. 2. Prostate gland—Cancer—Biography. I. Title.

Beatty, Warren.

BURKE, Jim. 791.430280924
Warren Beatty Jim Burke. New York : Belmont Tower Books ,1976. 182 p. : ill. ; 18 cm. [PN1998] pbk. : 1.50
1. Beatty, Warren. I. Title.

Beaucharnais, Eugene de, prince d'Eichstatt, 1781-1824.

LENANTON, Carola Mary Amina (Oman) 1897- 944.05'0924 B
Napoleon's Viceroy: Eugene de Beauharnais, by Carola Oman. New York, Funk and Wagnalls [1968, c1966] 528 p. illus., geneal. tables, map, ports. 22 cm. Bibliographical references included in "Notes on the chapters" (p. 471-[487]) [DC216.35.L4 1968] 68-18161
1. Beaucharnais, Eugene de, prince d'Eichstatt, 1781-1824. I. Title.

Beaudin, Andre, 1895—

BEAUDIN, Andre, 1895- 709'.2'4
Andre Beaudin / text by Georges Limbour ; [translated by Stuart Gilbert]. New York : Harcourt, Brace and World, [1961] ca. 150 p., [20] leaves of plates : chiefly ill. (some col.) ; 30 cm. "Planned and produced by Editions Verve." Includes bibliography. [ND553.B46L513] 75-303482
1. Beaudin, Andre, 1895- I. Limbour, Georges, 1902-1970.

LIMBOUR, Georges, 1902- v. 12
Andre Beaudin. Text by Georges Limbour. [Translated by Stuart Gilbert] New York Harcourt, Brace, and World [1961] 1 v. illus. Includes bibliography. 65-47071
1. Beaudin, Andre, 1895- I. Title.

Beauduin, Lambert, 1873-1960.

QUITSLUND, Sonya A. 282'.092'4 B
Beauduin, a prophet vindicated [by] Sonya A. Quitslund. New York, Newman Press [1973] xvii, 366 p. illus. 24 cm. Bibliography: p. 338-358. [BX4705.B2595Q5] 72-86594 ISBN 0-8091-0168-8 10.00
1. Beauduin, Lambert, 1873-1960. I. Title.

Beaufort, Francis, Sir, 1774-1857.

FRIENDLY, Alfred. 526.9'9'0924 B
Beaufort of the Admiralty : the life of Sir Francis Beaufort, 1774-1857 / Alfred Friendly. 1st American ed. New York : Random House, c1977. 362 p. : ill. ; 25 cm. Includes index. Bibliography: p. [347]-352. [VK597.G72F74 1977] 77-6022 ISBN 0-394-41760-7 : 15.00
1. Beaufort, Francis, Sir, 1774-1857. 2. Surveyors, Marine—Great Britain—Biography. 3. Admirals—Great Britain—Biography. I. Title.

FRIENDLY, Alfred. 526.9'9'0924 B
Beaufort of the Admiralty : the life of Sir Francis Beaufort, 1774-1857 / Alfred Friendly. 1st American ed. New York : Random House, c1977. 362 p. : ill. ; 25 cm. Includes index. Bibliography: p. [347]-352. [VK597.G72F74 1977] 77-6022 ISBN 0-394-41760-7 : 15.00
1. Beaufort, Francis, Sir, 1774-1857. 2. Surveyors, Marine—Great Britain—Biography. 3. Admirals—Great Britain—Biography. I. Title.

Beaumarchais, Pierre Augustin Caron de, 1732-1799.

COX, Cynthia. 928.4
The real Figaro; the extraordinary career of Caron de Beaumarchais. [1st American ed.] New York, Coward-McCann [1963, c1962] 212 p. illus. 23 cm. Includes bibliography. [PQ1956.C6 1963] 63-18401
1. Beaumarchais, Pierre Augustin Caron de, 1732-1799. I. Title.

RUSKIN, Ariane. 928.4
Spy for liberty; the adventurous life of Beaumarchais, playwright and secret agent for the American Revolution. [New York] Pantheon Books [1965] 178, [1] p. illus., ports. 22 cm. Bibliography: p. [179] [PQ1956.R8] 65-11442
1. Beaumarchais, Pierre Augustin Caron de, 1732-1799. 2. U.S.—History—Revolution, 1775-1783—French participation. I. Title.

Beaumarchais, Pierre Augustin Caron de, 1732-1799—Biography.

FRISCHAUER, Paul, 1898- 842'.5
Beaumarchais, adventurer in the century of women. Port Washington, N.Y., Kennikat Press [1970] xii, 312 p. 22 cm. Originally published in 1935. Bibliography: p. 307-308. [PQ1956.F73 1970] 70-113310 ISBN 0-8046-0993-4
1. Beaumarchais, Pierre Augustin Caron de, 1732-1799—Biography.

Beaumont, Francis, 1584-1616.

GAYLEY, Charles Mills, 1858-1932. 822'.3 B
Beaumont, the dramatist; a portrait with some account of his circle, Elizabethan and Jacobean, and of his association with John Fletcher. New York, Russell & Russell [1969] 423 p. illus., geneal. tables, ports. 20 cm. Reprint of the 1914 ed. Bibliographical footnotes. [PR2433.G3 1969] 68-15125
1. Beaumont, Francis, 1584-1616. 2. Fletcher, John, 1579-1625. BIP

Beaumont, George Hawland, Sir, bart., 1753-1827.

KNIGHT, William Angus, 1836-1916, ed. 821'.7'09 B
Memorials of Coleorton; being letters from Coleridge, Wordsworth and his sister, Southey, and Sir Walter Scott to Sir George and Lady Beaumont of Coleorton, Leicestershire, 1803 to 1834. Edited, with introd. and notes, by William Knight. [Folcroft, Pa.] Folcroft Library Editions, 1974. 2 v. 23 cm. Reprint of the 1887 ed. published by Houghton, Mifflin, Boston. [PR1346.K5 1974] 74-6115 ISBN 0-8414-5491-4 (lib. bdg.)
1. Beaumont, George Hawland, Sir, bart., 1753-1827. 2. Beaumont, Margaret (Willes) lady, d. 1829. 3. Lake poets—Correspondence, reminiscences, etc. I. Title.

Beaumont, William, 1785-1853—Juvenile literature.

EPSTEIN, Samuel, 1909- 612'.3
Dr. Beaumont and the man with a hole in his stomach / by Sam and Beryl Epstein ; illustrated by Joseph Scrofani. New York : Coward, McCann & Geoghegan, [1977] p. cm. (A Science discovery book) Bibliography: p. A biography of a curious physician and the unusual patient who enabled him to carry out experiments concerning digestion. [QP145.E67] 920 77-8236 ISBN 0-698-30680-5 lib. bdg. : 4.99
1. Beaumont, William, 1785-1853—Juvenile literature. 2. United States. Army—Surgeons—Biography—Juvenile literature. 3. St. Martin, Alexis, 1797?-1880—Juvenile literature. 4. Digestion—Juvenile literature. 5. Fur traders—Canada—Biography—Juvenile literature. I. Epstein, Beryl Williams, 1910- joint author. II. Scrofani, Joseph. III. Title. BIP

Beaumount. S. George Howland 1753-1827.

GREAVES. MARGARET 704.360924
Regency Patron: Sir George Beaumont. London Methuen, 1966. 3-163p. front. 14 plates (incl. ports) 23cm. Bibl. [CT788.B353G7] 66-76165 6.50 bds.,
1. Beaumount. S. George Howland 1753-1827. I. Title.
Available from Barnes & Noble.

Beauraing, Notre-Dame de.

SHARKEY, Donald C. 1912- 231.73
Our Lady of Beauraing [by] Don Sharkey and Joseph Debergh. Garden City, N.Y., Hanover House, 1958. 239 p. illus. 22 cm. Includes bibliography. [BT660.B4S45] 57-12474
1. Beauraing, Notre-Dame de. I. Debergh, Joseph, joint author. II. Title.

Beauregard, Pierre Gustave Toutant, 1818-1893.

WILLIAMS, T. Harry 923.573
P. G. T. Beauregard; Napoleon in gray. New York, Collier [1962, c.1955] 416p. illus., maps. 18cm. (BS71) Bibl. 1.50 pap.,
1. Beauregard, Pierre Gustave Toutant, 1818-1893. I. Title.

WILLIAMS, Thomas Harry, v. 12
1909-
P.G.T. Beauregard: Napoleon in gray. New York, Collier [1962, c1955] 416 p. illus. 67-72535
1. Beauregard, Pierre Gustave Toutant, 1818-1893. I. Title. BIP

WILLIAMS, Thomas Harry, 923.573
1909-
P. G. T. Beauregard; Napoleon in gray. Baton Rouge, Louisiana State University Press [1955, c1954] xiii, 345 p. illus., ports., maps. 23 cm. (Southern biography series) "Critical essay on authorities": p. 330-338. "Autographed by the author for the members of the Civil War Book Club." [E467.1.B38W5] 55-7362
1. Beauregard, Pierre Gustave Toutant, 1818-1893. I. Series.

Beauty operators.

PORTER, Gladys L. 646.720922
Three Negro pioneers in beauty culture. New York, Vantage [c.1966] 48p. ports. 21cm. Bibl. [TT955.A1P6] 65-28002 2.95 bds.,
1. Beauty operators. I. Title.

PORTER, Gladys L 646.720922
Three Negro pioneers in beauty culture, by Gladys L. Porter. [1st ed.] New York, Vantage Press [1966] 48 p. ports. 21 cm. Bibliography: p. 48. [TT955.A1P6] 65 28002
1. Beauty operators. I. Title.

Beauty, Personal.

AXUM, Donna 646.7
The outer you ... the inner you / Donna Axum. Waco, Tex. : Word Books, c1978. 155 p. : ill. ; 23 cm. [RA778.A878] 77-83345 ISBN 0-8499-0055-7 : 5.95
1. Beauty, Personal. 2. Charm. 3. Axum, Donna. 4. Beauty contestants—United States—Biography. 5. Television personalities—Texas—Biography. I. Title. BIP

Beauvoir, Simone de, 1908-

COTTRELL, Robert D. 848'.9'1409 B
Simone de Beauvoir / Robert D. Cottrell. New York : F. Ungar Pub. Co., [1975] 168 p. ; 21 cm. (Modern literature monographs) Includes index. Bibliography: p. 157-160. [PQ2603.E362Z63] 74-34131 ISBN 0-8044-2132-3 : 7.00
1. Beauvoir, Simone de, 1908- BIP

MADSEN, Axel. 848'.9'1409
Hearts and minds : the common journey of Simone de Beauvoir and Jean-Paul Sartre / by Axel Madsen. New York : Morrow, 1977. 320 p. : ill. ; 25 cm. Includes index. "Works by Sartre and Beauvoir": p. [297]-303. [PQ2603.E362Z84] 77-2896 ISBN 0-688-03206-0 : 10.95
1. Beauvoir, Simone de, 1908- 2. Sartre, Jean Paul, 1905- 3. Authors, French—20th century—Biography. I. Title.

Beauvoir, Simone de, 1908- — Biography.

BEAUVOIR, Simone de, 848'.9'1409
1908-
All said and done / Simone de Beauvoir ; translated by Patrick O'Brian. 1st American ed. New York : Putnam, 1974. 463 p. ; 24 cm. Translation of Toute compte fait. Includes bibliographical references. [PQ2603.E362Z52513 1974b] 73-93722 ISBN 0-399-11251-0 : 10.00
1. Beauvoir, Simone de, 1908- — Biography. I. Title. BIP

Beaver, Bruce—Biography—Youth.

BEAVER, Bruce. 821 B
As it was / [by] Bruce Beaver. St. Lucia, Q. : University of Queensland Press, 1979. 110 p. : ill. ; 22 cm. Distributed by Prentice-Hall International, International Book Distributors ltd., Hemel Hempstead, Eng. [PR9619.3.B44Z46] 79-314837 ISBN 0-7022-1278-4 : 12.00 ISBN 0-7022-1279-2 pbk. : 5.50
1. Beaver, Bruce—Biography—Youth 2. Beaver, Bruce, in fiction, drama, poetry, etc. 3. Poets, Australian—20th century—Biography. I. Title.
Dist. by TIC, Lawrence MA Distributed by TIC Lawrence MA BIP

Beaverbrook, William Maxwell Aitken, baron, 1879-1964.

FARRER, David, 1906- 942.084'0924
G—for God Almighty; a personal memoir of Lord Beaverbrook. New York, Stein and Day [1969] 176 p. 25 cm. Bibliographical footnotes. [DA566.9.B37F3 1969b] 77-81991 5.95
1. Beaverbrook, William Maxwell Aitken, Baron, 1879-1964. I. Title.

TAYLOR, Alan John 070.5'092'4 B
Percivale, 1906-
Beaverbrook [by] A. J. P. Taylor. New York, Simon and Schuster [1972] xvii, 712 p. illus. 25 cm. Includes bibliographical references. [DA566.9.B37T39 1972b] 72-80688 ISBN 0-671-21376-8 12.95
1. Beaverbrook, William Maxwell Aitken, baron, 1879-1964.

Bebel, August,

BEBEL, August, 335'.0092'4 B
1840-1913.
My life. New York, H. Fertig, 1973. 343 p. port. 22 cm. Translation of Aus meinem Leben. Reprint of the 1912 ed. [HX273.B42 1973] 74-80614 11.50
I. Title.

Beccaria, Cesare Bonesana, marchese di, 1738-1794.

PHILLIPSON, Coleman, 343'.0924
1878-
Three criminal law reformers: Beccaria, Bentham, Romilly. Montclair, N.J., P. Smith, 1970. xvi, 344 p. 22 cm. (Patterson Smith reprint series in criminology, law enforcement, and social problems. Publication no. 113) Reprint of the 1923 ed. Bibliography: p. xv-xvi. [LAW] 77-17157
1. Beccaria, Cesare Bonesana, marchese di, 1738-1794. 2. Beccaria, Cesare Bonesana, marchese di, 1738-1794. Dei delitti e delle pene. 3. Bentham, Jeremy, 1748-1832. 4. Romilly, Samuel, Sir, 1757-1818. 5. Criminal law. 6. Criminal procedure. 7. Law reform. 8. Punishment. 9. Capital punishment. 0. Crime and criminals. I. Title. BIP

Bechet, Sidney.

BECHET, Sidney. 788'.66'0924 B
Treat it gentle : an autobiography / by Sidney Bechet ; with a new preface by Rudi Blesh. 1st paperback ed. New York : Da Capo Press, 1978, c1960. 240 p., [8] leaves of plates : ill. ; 22 cm. (A Da Capo paperback) Reprint of the 1st ed., published by Cassell, London. "A catalogue of the recordings of Sidney Bechet, compiled by David Myline": p. 221-240. Includes index. [ML419.B23A3 1978] 78-17561 ISBN 0-306-80086-1 pbk. : 5.95
1. Bechet, Sidney. 2. Jazz musicians—United States—Biography. I. Blesh, Rudi, 1899- II. Title. BIP

Bechtel, Edwin De Turck, 1880-1957.

BECHTEL, Louise (Seaman) 923.473
1894-
The boy with the star lantern; Edwin De Turck Bechtel, 1880-1957: aMemoir. New York, 1960. 124p. illus. 24cm. [CT275.B545B4] 60-9808
1. Bechtel, Edwin De Turck, 1880-1957. I. Title.

Beck, Daisy (Woodward),

BECK, Daisy (Woodward), 920.7
1876-
All the years were grand; with drawings by Rosemary Emerson. Chicago, Erle Press [1951] 257 p. illus. 22 cm. Autobiography. [CT275.B546A3] 51-11565
I. Title.

Beck, Dave, 1894-

MCCALLUM, 331.88'11'3883240924 B
John Dennis, 1924-
Dave Beck / by John D. McCallum. Mercer Island, Wash. : Writing Works, c1978. p. cm. Includes index. [HD6509.B42A35 1978] 78-11819 ISBN 0-916076-27-X : 9.95
1. Beck, Dave, 1894- 2. International Brotherhood of Teamsters, Chauffeurs, Warehousemen and Helpers of America. 3. Trade-unions—United States—Officials and employees—Biography. BIP

Beck, Frank, 1888-1969.

BARDER, Natalie. 610'.924 B
Dr. and Mrs. Fix-it; the story of Frank and Bessie Beck. New York, Friendship Press [1970] 96 p. 18 cm. (Bold believers series) [R154.B357B37] 79-130776 ISBN 0-377-84181-1 1.50
1. Beck, Frank, 1888-1969. 2. Beck, Bessie Dunn, 1891- 3. Missions, Medical—Bolivia. I. Title.

Beck, James Montgomery,

BECK, James Montgomery, 818.5403
1892-
The years that were, by James M. Beck, [1st ed. New York] Pageant Press [c1965] vii, 284 p. ports. 21 cm. Autobiographical. [CT275.B5465A3] 65-27307
I. Title.

Beck, Ludwig August Theodor, 1880-1944.

REYNOLDS, 943.086'092'4 B
Nicholas.
Treason was no crime ; Ludwig Beck, Chief of the German General Staff / [by] Nicholas Reynolds ; introduction by Sir John Wheeler-Bennett. London : Kimber, 1976. 317 p., [12] p. of plates : 2 ill., ports. ; 24 cm. Includes index. Bibliography: p. [281]-287. [DD247.B4R49] 76-378963 ISBN 0-7183-0014-9 : £5.95
1. Beck, Ludwig August Theodor, 1880-1944. 2. Hitler, Adolf, 1889-1945 Assassination attempt, July 20, 1944. 3. Generals—Germany—Biography. 4. Anti-Nazi movement—History. I. Title.

Beck, Robert,

BECK, Robert, 1918- 814'.5'4 B
The naked soul of Iceberg Slim, by Robert Beck. Los Angeles, Holloway House Pub. Co. [1971] 248 p. 18 cm. Autobiographical. [PS3552.E25Z5] 70-30346 ISBN 0-87067-414-5 1.50
I. Title. BIP

Beckenbauer, Franz—Juvenile literature.

HAHN, James. 796.33'4'0924 B
Franz Beckenbauer : soccer superstar / by James and Lynn Hahn. St. Paul : EMC Corp., 1978. p. cm. (Their Champions and challengers I) A biography of the star German soccer player. [GV942.7.B4H34] 92 78-18736 ISBN 0-88436-445-3 : 5.95
1. Beckenbauer, Franz—Juvenile literature. 2. Soccer players—Germany, West—Biography—Juvenile literature. I. Hahn, Lynn, joint author. II. Title. III. Series.

Becker, Carl Lotus, 1873-1945.

BECKER, Carl 973.3'072'024 B
Lotus, 1873-1945.
"What is the good of history?" Selected letters of Carl L. Becker, 1900 -1945, edited with an introd. by Michael Kammen. Ithaca, Cornell University Press [1973] xlii, 372 p. illus. 23 cm. Bibliography: p. [359]-363. [D15.B33A4 1973] 73-2849 ISBN 0-8014-0778-8 12.50
1. Becker, Carl Lotus, 1873-1945. I. Kammen, Michael G., ed. II. Title.

STROUT, Cushing. 973'.01
The pragmatic revolt in American history : Carl Becker and Charles Beard / Cushing Strout. Westport, Conn. : Greenwood Press, [1980] c1958. p. cm. Reprint of the ed. published by Yale University Press, New Haven, Conn., as no. 3 of the Wallace Notestein essays. Bibliography: p. [E175.9.S8 1980] 79-26417 ISBN 0-313-22203-7 lib. bdg. : 17.25
1. Becker, Carl Lotus, 1873-1945. 2. Beard, Charles Austin, 1874-1948. 3. United States—History—Philosophy. 4. Historians—United States—Biography. I. Title. II. Series: Wallace Notestein essays ; no. 3. BIP

WILKINS, Burleigh Taylor 928.1
Carl Becker; a biographical study in American intellectual history. Cambridge, M.I.T. Pr. [1967, c.1961] 246p. illus. 21cm. (MIT 77) [D15.B33W5] 61-7870 3.45 pap.,
1. Becker, Carl Lotus, 1873-1945. I. Title. BIP

Beckert, Harriet T.

WALLACE, Irving 978.4'82'00994 B
Speed.
Stardust to prairie dust / by Irving Wallace. 1st ed. Brooklyn : T. Gaus' Sons, c1976. ix, 234 p., [4] leaves of plates : ill. ; 23 cm. [F636.B37W34] 76-11324 8.95
1. Beckert, Harriet T. 2. Ranchers—North Dakota—Biography. 3. North Dakota—Biography. I. Title.

Beckett, Ronald Brymer, ed.

CONSTABLE, John, 1776-1837 927.5
Correspondence: the family at East Bergholt, 1807-1837. Ed., introd., notes by R. B. Beckett. London H. M. Stationery Off. [dist. New York, British Info. c.]1962. 337p. illus., map. 25cm. ([Gt. Brit.] Historical Mss. Commission. JP3) 62-5245 9.00
1. Beckett, Ronald Brymer, ed. I. Title. II. Series: Gt. Brit. Historical Manuscripts Commission. Joint publication. III. Series: Suffolk Records Society, Ipswich. Publications, v.4

Beckett, Samuel, 1906-

COE, Richard N v. 12
Beckett. Edinburgh, Oliver and Boyd [1964] 118 p. (Writers and critics, 40) 65-40859
1. Beckett, Samuel, 1906- I. Title.

TINDALL, William 828'.9'14 [B]
York, 1903-
Samuel Beckett. New York, Columbia University Press, 1964. 48 p. 21 cm. (Columbia essays on modern writers, no. 4) Bibliography: p. 46-48. [PR6003.E282Z85] 64-22640
1 Beckett, Samuel, 1906- I. Title. II. Series. BIP

Beckett, Samuel, 1906- —Biography.

BAIR, Deirdre. 848'.9'1409 B
Samuel Beckett : a biography / Deirdre Bair. 1st ed. New York : Harcourt Brace Jovanovich, c1978. xiv, 736 p., [12] leaves of plates : ill. ; 24 cm. Includes bibliographical references and index. [PR6003.E282Z564 1978] 77-92527 ISBN 0-15-179256-9 : 19.95
1. Beckett, Samuel, 1906- —Biography. 2. Authors, Irish—20th century—Biography. BIP

Beckford, William, 1760-1844.

BECKFORD, WILLIAM, 1760- 928.2
1844
Life at Fonthill, 1807-1822, with interludes in Paris and London, from the correspondence of William Beckford. Tr. [from Italian] ed. by Boyd Alexander. London, R. Hart-Davis [Chester Springs, Pa., Dufour, 1966] 352p. illus., ports., facsims. 23cm. [PR4092.A43] A57 7.50
I. Alexander, Boyd, ed. and tr. II. Title.

BENJAMIN, Lewis Saul, 828'.6'09 B 1874-1932.
The life and letters of William Beckford of Fonthill, by Lewis Melville. [Folcroft, Pa.] Folcroft Library Editions, 1970. xv, 391 p. illus. 26 cm. On spine: William Beckford. Reprint of the 1910 ed. Bibliography: p. 367-376. [PR4092.B4 1970] 72-190716
1. Beckford, William, 1750-1844. I. Title.

CHAPMAN, Guy 928.2
Beckford [2d ed.] London, R. Hart-Davis [dist. Chester Springs, Pa., Dufour, 1964] 365p. port. 21cm. Bibl. [PR4092.C5] 52-9709 4.50
1. Beckford, William, 1760-1844. I. Title.

Beckford, William, 1760-1844— Biography.

CHAPMAN, Guy. 828'.6'09 B
Beckford / by Guy Chapman. Folcroft, Pa. : Folcroft Library Editions, 1977. 361 p., [8] leaves of plates : ill. ; 23 cm. Reprint of the 1937 ed. published by Scribner, New York. "The works of William Beckford": p. 357-358. Includes index. Bibliography: p. 19-24. [PR4092.C5 1977] 77-919 ISBN 0-8414-3448-4 lib. bdg. : 30.00
1. Beckford, William, 1760-1844—Biography. 2. Authors, English—19th century—Biography. I. Title. **BIP**

FOTHERGILL, Brian. 828'.6'09 B
Beckford of Fonthill / Brian Fothergill. London ; Boston : Faber and Faber, 1979. 387 p., [6] leaves of plates : ill. ; 22 cm. Includes index. Bibliography: p. [376]-380. [PR4092.F67] 79-670151 ISBN 0-571-10794-X : 27.50
1. Beckford, William, 1760-1844—Biography. 2. Authors, English—18th century—Biography. 3. Eccentrics and eccentricism—England—Biography. I. Title. **BIP**

LEES-MILNE, James. 828'.6'09 B
William Beckford / James Lees-Milne. Tisbury, Wiltshire : Compton Russell, 1976. 124 p. : ill. ; 26 cm. Includes index. Bibliography: p. 123-124. [PR4092.L4] 76-376542 ISBN 0-85955-036-2 : £5.50
1. Beckford, William, 1760-1844—Biography. 2. Authors, English—19th century—Biography.

LEES-MILNE, James. 828'.6'09 B
William Beckford / James Lees-Milne. Montclair, N.J. : Allanheld and Schram, [1979], c1976. p. cm. Includes index. Bibliography: p. [PR4092.L4 1979] 78-73616 ISBN 0-8390-0227-0 : 18.50
1. Beckford, William, 1760-1844—Biography. 2. Authors, English—19th century—Biography.

OLIVER, John Walter. 828'.6'09 B
The life of William Beckford / by J. W. Oliver. Folcroft, Pa. : Folcroft Library Editions, 1974. x, 343 p., [1] leaf of plates : port. ; 23 cm. Based on biographical material taken from Beckford's unpublished manuscripts in the Hamilton papers. Reprint of the 1932 ed. published by Oxford University Press, London. Includes bibliographical references and index. [PR4092.O4 1974] 74-31095 ISBN 0-8414-6530-4 lib. bdg. : 25.00
1. Beckford, William, 1760-1844—Biography. I. Title. **BIP**

Beckley, John James, 1757-1807.

BERKELEY, Edmund. 081 S
John Beckley; zealous partisan in a nation divided [by] Edmund Berkeley and Dorothy Smith Berkeley. Philadelphia, American Philosophical Society, 1973. xiii, 312 p. illus. 24 cm. (Memoirs of the American Philosophical Society, v. 100) Bibliography: p. 290-300. [Q11.P612 vol. 100] [E302.6.B37] 973.4'092'4 B 73-86616 ISBN 0-87169-100-0 6.00 (pbk.)
1. Beckley, John James, 1757-1807. I. Berkeley, Dorothy Smith, joint author. II. Series: American Philosophical Society, Philadelphia. Memoirs, v. 100. **BIP**

Beckmann, Max, 1884-1950.

FISCHER, Friedhelm Wilhelm. 759.3
Max Beckmann [by] Friedhelm W. Fischer. Translated by P. S. Falla [London] Phaidon [distributed in U.S.A. by Praeger Publishers, Inc., 1973] 96 p. illus. (part col.) 30 cm. Translation of Der Maler Max Beckmann. Bibliography: p. 96. [ND588.B37F49513 1973] 72-83182 ISBN 0-7148-1577-2 25.00 (U.S.)
1. Beckmann, Max, 1884-1950.

LACKNER, Stephan. 759.3
Max Beckmann; memories of a friendship. Coral Gables, Fla., University of Miami Press [1969] 126 p. illus. (part col.) 23 cm. Translation of Ich erinnere mich gut an Max Beckmann. [ND588.B37L293] 75-81622 7.95
1. Beckmann, Max, 1884-1950. I. Title. **BIP**

LACKNER, Stephan. 759.3
Max Beckmann / text by Stephan Lackner. New York : H. N. Abrams, 1977. 175 p. : ill. (some col.) ; 34 cm. (The Library of great painters) Includes index. Bibliography: p. 169-170. [ND588.B37L297] 74-22446 ISBN 0-8109-0269-9 : 22.50
1. Beckmann, Max, 1884-1950. 2. Painters—Germany, West—Biography. **BIP**

Beckwourth, James Pierson, 1798-1866.

CORTESI, 917.8'03'20924 B Lawrence.
Jim Beckwourth; explorer-patriot of the Rockies. New York, Criterion Books [1971] 224 p. 22 cm. A biography of the Negro blacksmith from St. Louis who became a trapper, mountain man, adopted Crow chief, and a guerilla fighter in the Mexican War. [F592.B395] 92 78-134563 ISBN 0-200-71788-X 4.95
1. Beckwourth, James Pierson, 1798-1866. 2. Frontier and pioneer life—The West. 3. Crow Indians. I. Title.

MUMEY, Nolie, 1891- 923.973
James Pierson Beckwourth, 1856-1866, an enigmatic figure of the West; a history of the latter years of his life. Denver, F. A. Rosenstock, 1957. 188p. illus. ports., fold. map. 25cm. 'Edition limited to five hundred numbered and signed copies.' No. 60. Bibliographical footnotes. [F592.B397] 59-48039
1. Beckwourth, James Pierson, 1798-1866. 2. Frontier and pioneer life—The West. I. Title.

WILSON, Elinor, 917.8'03'20924 B 1914-
Jim Beckwourth: Black Mountain man and war chief of the Crows. [1st ed.] Norman, University of Oklahoma Press [1972] xvi, 248 p. illus. 22 cm. Bibliography: p. 221-235. [F592.B3975] 72-931 ISBN 0-8061-1012-0
1. Beckwourth, James Pierson, 1798-1866.

Beckwourth, James Pierson, 1798-1866—Juvenile literature.

BLASSINGAME, 917.8'032'0924 B Wyatt.
Jim Beckwourth: Black trapper and Indian chief. Illustrated by Herman Vestal. Champaign, Ill., Garrard Pub. Co. [1973] 80 p. col. illus. 23 cm. (A Discovery book) Biography of the nineteenth-century hunter, trapper, Indian chief, trader, gold seeker, innkeeper, and rancher who discovered a pass in the Sierra Nevadas which bears his name. [F592.B394] 92 73-5698 2.84
1. Beckwourth, James Pierson, 1798-1866—Juvenile literature. I. Vestal, Herman B., illus. II. Title.

Beda Venerabilis, 673-735.

BLAIR, Peter Hunter. 230'.924
The world of Bede. New York, St. Martin's Press [1971, c1970] x, 340 p. 23 cm. Bibliography: p. 310-327. [PR1578.B6 1971] 73-135524 10.00
1. Beda Venerabilis, 673-735. 2. Great Britain—History—To 1066. I. Title. **BIP**

DUCKETT, Eleanor Shipley. 274.2
Anglo-Saxon saints and scholars Hamden, Conn., Archon Books, 1967 [c1947] x, 484 p. 22 cm. Contents.Contents. -- Aldheim of Malmesbury. -- Wilfrid of York. -- Bede of Jarrow. -- Boniface of Devon. -- Bibliogrpahy and abbreviations (p. 456-473) [BR754.A1D8] 67-11473
1. Aldheim, Saint, Bp. of Sherborne, 640?-709. 2. Wilfrid, Saint, Bp. of York, 634-709. 3. Beda Venerabilis, 673-735. 4. Boniface, originally Winfrid, Saint, Bp. of Mainz, 680-755. I. Title. **BIP**

PRICE, Mary Roper. 942.01'0922
Bede and Dunstan, by Mary R. Price. London, Oxford U.P., 1968. 64 p. 8 plates, 9 illus., 2 facsims., map. 21 cm. (Clarendon biographies, 21) Bibliography: p. [62]-63. [PR1578.P7] 76-405248 ISBN 1-9831595-3- 9/6
1. Beda Venerabilis, 673-735. 2. Dunstan, Saint, Abp. of Canterbury, d. 988.

THOMPSON, Alexander 878.02 Hamilton, 1873-1952, ed.
Bede; his life, times, and writings; essays in commemoration of the twelfth centenary of his death, edited by A. Hamilton Thompson. With an introd. by the Lord Bishop of Durham. New York, Russell & Russell, 1966. xvi, 277 p. illus. 23 cm. First published in 1932. Contents.Contents.—Select bibliography (p. [ix]-xii)—The life of the Venerable Bede, by C. E. Whiting.—The age of Bede, by E. W. Watson.—Northumbrian monasticism, by A. H. Thompson.—Monkwearmouth and Jarrow, by C. Peers.—Bede as historian, by W. Levison.—Bede as exegete and theologian, by C. Jenkins.—Bede's miracle stories, by B. Colgrave.—The manuscripts of Bede, by M. R. James.—The library of the Venerable Bede, by M. L. W. Laistner. [PR1578.T5 1966] 65-17923
1. Beda Venerabilis, 673-735.

Beddoe, Robert Earl, 1882-1952.

RALEY, Helen 266.6'1'0924 B Thames.
Doctor in an old world; the story of Robert Earl Beddoe, medical missionary to China. Waco, Tex., Word Books [1969] 156 p. illus. 23 cm. [BV3427.B38R3 1969] 69-20222 3.95
1. Beddoe, Robert Earl, 1882-1952. 2. Missions, Medical—China. I. Title.

Beddoes, Thomas Lovell, 1803-1849.

BEDDOES, Thomas Lovell, 821'.7 B 1803-1849.
The letters of Thomas Lovell Beddoes. Edited, with notes, by Edmund Gosse. New York, B. Blom, 1971. 270 p. 21 cm. Reprint of the 1894 ed. Includes bibliographical references. [PR4098.A3 1971] 70-173168 201 A0003015SNOW, Royall Henderson,

SNOW, Royall Henderson, 821'.7 1898-
Thomas Lovell Beddoes; eccentric & poet, by Royall H. Snow. [Folcroft, Pa.] Folcroft Library Editions, 1970 [c1928] ix, 227 p. front. 24 cm. "Limited to 150 copies." Bibliography: p. 222-227. [PR4098.S6 1970] 72-193743
1. Beddoes, Thomas Lovell, 1803-1849. **BIP**

Bedell, Harriet M., 1875-

HARTLEY, William B 922.373
A woman set apart [by] William and Ellen Hartley. New York, Dodd, Mead [1963] 275 p. 22 cm. [BX5974.B4H3] 62-17921
1. Bedell, Harriet M., 1875- I. Hartley, Ellen, joint author. II. Title.

Bedell, William, bp. of Kilmore, 1571-1642.

BEDELL, William, d.1670. v. 12
A true relation of the life and death of the Right Reverend father in God William Bedell, lord bishop of Kilmore in Ireland. Ed. from a ms. in the Bodleian library, Oxford, and amplified with genealogical and historical chapters, comp. from original sources, by the representative of the bishop's mother's family of Elliston, Thomas Wharton Jones, F.R.S. [Westminster] Printed for the Camden society, 1872. [Reprinted by Johnson Reprint Corp., New York, 1965] 268 p. (Camden society. Publications, n.s.,IV) NUC68
1. Bedell, William, bp. of Kilmore, 1571-1642. I. Jones, Thomas Wharton, 1808-1891, ed. II. Title. III. Series. **BIP**

[BEDELL, William] d. 282.41509 1670
A true relation of the life and death of the Right Reverend father in God William Bedell, lord bishop of Kilmore in Ireland. Ed. from a ms. in the Bodleian Lib., Oxford. Amplified with genealogical and historical chapters, comp. from orig. sources, by the representative of the bishop's mother's family of Elliston, Thomas Wharton Jones, F.R.S. [Westminster] Printed for the Camden Society, 1872. New York, Johnson Reprint, 1965. [2],xvii, 268p. 22cm. [Camden soc. Pubns., new ser., 4) [DA20.C17 new ser., vol. 4] A17 13.50
1. Bedell, William, bp. of Kilmore, 1571-1642. I. Jones, Thomas Wharton, 1808-1891, ed. II. Title.

Bedford, Nicole Russell, Duchess of.

BEDFORD, Nicole 914.2'03'840924 B Russell, Duchess of.
Nicole Nobody; the autobiography of the Duchess of Bedford. London, New York, W. H. Allen, 1974. ix, 377 p., [32] p. of plates. illus., geneal. table (on lining papers), ports. 24 cm. Includes index. [CT788.B358A34] 74-176479 ISBN 0-491-01472-4 £3.50
1. Bedford, Nicole Russell, Duchess of. I. Title.

BEDFORD, Nicole 941.084'092'4 B Russell, Duchess of.
Nicole Nobody : the autobiography of the Duchess of Bedford. 1st ed. in the U.S.A. Garden City, N.Y. : Doubleday, 1975, c1974. x, 397 p., [16] leaves of plates : ill., geneal. table (on lining papers) ; 25 cm. Includes index. [CT788.B358A34 1975] 74-14378 ISBN 0-385-09773-5 : 10.95
1. Bedford, Nicole Russell, Duchess of. I. Title.

Bedford, Randolph, 1868-1941— Biography.

BEDFORD, Randolph, 070'.92'4 B 1868-1941.
Naught to thirty-three / Randolph Bedford. Carlton : Melbourne University Press, 1976. xii, 335 p. ; 23 cm. Distributed in the U.S.A. and Canada by International Scholarly Book Services, Forest Grove, Or. [PR9619.3.B453Z52 1976] 76-384024 ISBN 0-522-84101-5 22.50
1. Bedford, Randolph, 1868-1941—Biography. 2. Authors, Australian—20th century—Biography. I. Title. **BIP**

Bedichek, Roy, 1878-1959.

JAMES, Eleanor, 500.9'0924 B 1912-
Roy Bedichek. Austin, Tex., Steck-Vaughn Co. [1970] ii, 43 p. 21 cm. (Southwest writers series, no. 32) Bibliography: p. 41-43. [QH31.B38J3] 73-114552
1. Bedichek, Roy, 1878-1959. I. Title. II. Series.

OWENS, William A., 1905- 081
Three friends: Roy Bedichek, J. Frank Dobie, Walter Prescott Webb, by William A. Owens. [1st ed.] Garden City, N.Y., Doubleday, 1969. 335 p. 22 cm. "Acknowledgments, bibliographies, notes": p. [323]-335. [LD5332.2.O95] 70-82957 6.95
1. Bedichek, Roy, 1878-1959. 2. Dobie, James Frank, 1888-1964. 3. Webb, Walter Prescott, 1888-1963. 4. Folk-lore—Texas. I. Title.

Bednarik, Chuck, 1925-

MCCALLUM, Jack, 796.33'2'0924 B 1949-
Bednarik, last of the sixty-minute men / by Jack McCallum, with Chuck Bednarik. Englewood Cliffs, N.J. : Prentice-Hall, c1977. xvi, 210 p., [12] leaves of plates : ill. ; 22 cm. [GV939.B425M3] 77-7800 ISBN 0-13-066753-6 : 8.95
1. Bednarik, Chuck, 1925- 2. Football players—United States—Biography. I.

Bednarik, Chuck, 1925- joint author. II. Title.

Bedouins.

DIQS, Isaak, 1938- 915.694'03'40924 B
A Bedouin boyhood. New York, Praeger [1969, c1967] 177 p. map. 22 cm. [DS219.B4D58 1969] 68-8134 4.95
1. Bedouins. I. Title.

Beebe, Charles William, 1877-1962.

WELKER, Robert Henry. 591'.092'4 B
Natural man : the life of William Beebe / Robert Henry Welker. Bloomington : Indiana University Press, [1975] xiv, 224 p., [8] leaves of plates : ill. ; 25 cm. Includes index. Bibliography: p. 215. [QL31.B37W44 1975] 74-22834 ISBN 0-253-33975-8 : 11.50
1. Beebe, Charles William, 1877-1962. 2. Zoologists—Correspondence, reminiscences, etc. I. Title. BIP

Beebe, Charles William, 1877-1962—Bibliography.

BERRA, Tim M., 1943- 016.591'092'4
William Beebe : an annotated bibliography / Tim M. Berra. Hamden, Conn. : Archon Books, 1977. 157 p. : ill. ; 23 cm. Includes indexes. [Z8086.49.B46] [QH31.B39] 76-30857 ISBN 0-208-01608-2 : 15.00
1. Beebe, Charles William, 1877-1962—Bibliography. BIP

Beebe, Charles William, 1877-1962—Juvenile literature.

BLASSINGAME, Wyatt. 591'.092'4 B
William Beebe, underwater explorer / by Wyatt Blassingame ; illustrated by Victor Mays. Champaign, Ill. : Garrard Pub. Co., c1976. 96 p. : ill. (some col.) ; 24 cm. (Americans all) Includes index. A biography of the naturalist, explorer, and writer emphasizing his underwater explorations and discoveries about marine life. [QL31.B37B45] 92 75-29069 ISBN 0-8116-4584-3 lib.bdg. : 3.58
1. Beebe, Charles William, 1877-1962—Juvenile literature. I. Mays, Victor, 1927- II. Title.

Beecham, Thomas, Sir, bart., 1879-1961.

BEECHAM remembered 785'.092'4 B / [compiled and edited by] Humphrey Procter-Gregg. London : Duckworth, 1976. viii, 212 p., [3] leaves of plates : ill., music ; 23 cm. Prelim. ed. published in 1973 under title: Sir Thomas Beecham, conductor and impresario, as remembered by his friends and colleagues, and entered under the editor, H. Procter-Gregg. Includes index. "Recordings, concerts and operas": p. [196]-203. [ML422.B33B4 1976] 77-350686 ISBN 0-7156-1117-8 : £5.95
1. Beecham, Thomas, Sir, bart., 1879-1961. 2. Conductors (Music)—England—Biography. I. Procter-Gregg, Humphrey. BIP

BEECHAM, Thomas, Sir, bart., 1879-1961. 785'.092'4 B
A mingled chime : an autobiography / by Sir Thomas Beecham, bart. Westport, Conn. : Greenwood Press, 1976. p. cm. Reprint of the 1943 ed. published by Putnam, New York. [ML422.B33A2 1976] 76-40238 ISBN 0-8371-9274-9 lib.bdg. : 18.75
1. Beecham, Thomas, Sir, bart., 1879-1961. 2. Conductores (Music)—England—Biography. I. Title. BIP

BEECHAM, Thomas, Sir, bart., 1879-1961. 785'.092'4 B
A mingled chime : an autobiography/ by Sir Thomas Beecham, bart. New York : Da Capo Press, 1976, c1943. p. cm. (The Lyric stage) Reprint of the ed. published by Putnam, New York. [ML422.B33A2 1976b] 76-40182 ISBN 0-306-70791-8 lib.bdg. : 18.75 lib.bdg. : 18.75
1. Beecham, Thomas, Sir bart., 1879-1961. 2. Conductors (Music)—England—Biography. I. Title.

REID, Charles, writes on music 927.8
Thomas Beecham; an independent biography. [1st ed.] New York, Dutton, 1962 [c1961] 256 p. illus. 22 cm. [ML422.B33R4 1962] 62-7810
1. Beecham, Thomas, bart., 1879-1961.

Beecher, Catharine Esther, 1800-1878.

HARVESON, Mae Elizabeth, 1895- 376'.9'24 B
Catharine Esther Beecher (pioneer educator). New York, Arno Press, 1969. x, 295 p. illus., facsim., ports. 24 cm. (American education: its men, ideas, and institutions) Reprint of the 1932 ed. Bibliography: p. 266-284. [LA2317.B35H3 1969] 70-89189
1. Beecher, Catharine Esther, 1800-1878. 2. Education of women—U.S.

SKLAR, Kathryn Kish. 301.41'2'0924 B
Catharine Beecher; a study in American domesticity. New Haven, Yale University Press, 1973. xv, 356 p. illus. 25 cm. Bibliography: p. 331-344. [HQ1413.B4S54] 73-77166 ISBN 0-300-01580-1 12.50
1. Beecher, Catharine Esther, 1800-1878.

SKLAR, Kathryn Kish. 301.41'2'0924 B
Catharine Beecher : a study in American domesticity / Kathryn Kish Sklar. New York : Norton, 1976, c1973. p. cm. (The Norton library) Includes index. Bibliography: p. [HQ1413.B4S54 1976] 76-15292 ISBN 0-393-00812-6 pbk. : 4.95
1. Beecher, Catharine Esther, 1800-1878. BIP

Beecher, George Allen,

BEECHER, George Allen, Bp., 1868- 922.373
A bishop of the Great Plains. Philadelphia, Church Historical Society, 1950. 218 p. illus. ports. 24 cm. Autobiography. [BX5995.B389A3] 50-58132
I. Title.

Beecher, Henry Ward, 1813-1887.

ABBOTT, Lyman, 1835-1922. 285.8'0924 B
Henry Ward Beecher. Cambridge, Riverside Press, 1904. Miami, Fla., Mnemosyne Pub. Co. [1969] xxxviii, 457 p. ports. 23 cm. Bibliography: p. [xvii]-xxxviii. [BX7260.B3A65 1969] 78-89428
1. Beecher, Henry Ward, 1813-1887. BIP

CLARK, Clifford E., 1941- 285'.8'0924 B
Henry Ward Beecher : spokesman for a Middle-class America / Clifford E. Clark, Jr. Urbana : University of Illinois Press, c1978. 288 p., [2] leaves of plates : ill. ; 24 cm. Includes bibliographical references and index. [BX7260.B3C6] 78-1721 ISBN 0-252-00608-9 : 11.95
1. Beecher, Henry Ward, 1813-1887. 2. Congregational churches—Clergy—Biography. 3. Clergy—United States—Biography. BIP

ELSMERE, Jane Shaffer. 285'.8'0924 B
Henry Ward Beecher; the Indiana years, 1837-1847. Indianapolis, Indiana Historical Society, 1973. xiii, 317 p. illus. 24 cm. Bibliography: p. 303-306. [BX7260.B3E47] 74-156947
1. Beecher, Henry Ward, 1813-1887.

HIBBEN, Paxton, 1880-1928. 285'.8'0924 B
Henry Ward Beecher: an American portrait. Foreword by Sinclair Lewis. New York, Beekman Publishers, 1974. xiv, 361 p. 23 cm. (American newspapermen, 1790-1933) Reprint of the 1942 ed. published by the Press of the Readers Club, New York. Bibliography: p. 317-329. [BX7260.B3H5 1974] 73-23116 ISBN 0-8464-0019-7 17.50
1. Beecher, Henry Ward, 1813-1887. BIP

HIGGINS, Paul Lambourne. 922
Preachers of power; Henry Ward Beecher, Phillips Brooks, [and] Walter Rauschenbusch. New York, Vantage Press ['1950] 72 p. ports. 23 cm. [BV4208.U6H5] 51-787
1. Beecher, Henry Ward, 1813-1887. 2. Brooks, Phillips, 1835-1898 3. Rauschenbusch, Walter, 1861-1918. 4. Preaching—U. S.—Hist. I. Title.

Beecher, Lyman, 1775-1863.

BEECHER, Lyman, 1775-1863. 922.573
Autobiography. Edited by Barbara M. Cross. Cambridge, Belknap Press of Harvard University Press, 1961. 2v. illus., ports. 24cm. (The John Harvard library) First published in 1804 under title: Autobiography, correspondence, etc. Bibliography: v. 1, p. xxxix. [BX7260.B33A3 1961] 61-6348
I. Title. II. Series.

HENRY, Stuart Clark. 285'.9'0924 B
Unvanquished Puritan; a portrait of Lyman Beecher, by Stuart C. Henry. Grand Rapids, Mich., W. B. Eerdmans Pub. Co. [1973] 299 p. illus. 23 cm. Includes bibliographical references. [BX7260.B33H4] 72-94608 ISBN 0-8028-3426-4 7.95
1. Beecher, Lyman, 1775-1863. I. Title.

Beekman family.

WHITE, Philip L 929'.2'0973
The Beekmans of New York in politics and commerce, 1647-1877. With an introd. by Fenwick Beekman. New York, New York Historical Society under a grant from the Beekman Family Association, 1956. xxxi, 705p. illus., ports., maps, geneal. table. 25cm. Bibliographical footnotes. 'Bibliographical note': p. 656-657. [CS71.B441 1956] 56-14653
1. Beekman family. I. Title.

Beekman, John.

HEFLEY, James C. 266'.023'0924
Peril by choice; the story of John and Elaine Beekman, Wycliffe Bible translators in Mexico [by] James C. Hefley. Foreword by W. Cameron Townsend. Introd. by William Culbertson. Grand Rapids, Zondervan Pub. House [1968] 226 p. illus., col. map (on lining papers), ports. 23 cm. [BV2836.B4H4] 68-22837 4.95
1. Beekman, John. 2. Beekman, Elaine. 3. Missions—Mexico. 4. Indians of Mexico. I. Title.

STEVEN, Hugh. 266'.023'0924 B
The man with the noisy heart / Hugh Steven Chicago : Moody Press, c1979. 125 p. : ill. ; 22 cm. Includes bibliographical references. [BV2836.B4S73] 78-21038 ISBN 0-8024-5171-3 : 6.95
1. Beekman, John. 2. Missionaries—Mexico—Biography. 3. Missionaries—United States—Biography. 4. Aortic valve—Surgery—Biography. I. Title. BIP

Beeler, Joe.

HEDGPETH, Don. 709'.73 B
Cowboy artist : the Joe Beeler story / by Don Hedgpeth ; with a foreword by Paul Weaver. 1st ed. Flagstaff, Ariz. : Northland Press, c1979. xv, 115 p. : ill. (some col.) ; 24 x 25 cm. [N6537.B44H42] 78-65926 ISBN 0-87358-196-2 : 22.50 ISBN 0-87358-195-4 pbk. : 10.00
1. Beeler, Joe. 2. Artists—United States—Biography. 3. Indians of North American—Pictorial works. 4. The West in art. I. Beeler, Joe. II. Title.

Beene, William Virgil,

BEENE, William Virgil, 1882- 923.773
In retrospect; reminiscencies [sic] and observations of a Hamilton County, Tennessee, retired teacher. [Chattanooga, Taget Print. Lithographing Co., 1958] 158p. illus. 23cm. [LA2317.B36A3] 58-12653
1. Title.

Beerbohm, Max, Sir, 1872-1956.

BEERBOHM, Max, Sir, 1872-1956. 928.2
Max Beerbohm's letters to Reggie Turner. Edited by Rupert Hart Davis. Philadelphia, Lippincott, 1965 c. 1964 312 p. illus., facsims., ports. 22 cm. "200 of the letters are here printed in whole or in part; 183 of them from the originals, which are now in the Houghton Library at Harvard, the other seventeen from ... transcripts of originals which were later destroyed." First published in 1964 under title: Letters to Reggie Turner. Includes bibliographical references. [PR6003.E4Z53 1965] 65-15124
I. Hart-Davis, Rupert, ed. II. Turner, Reginald, 1869?-1938.

BEHRMAN, Samuel Nathaniel, 1893- 928.2
Portrait of Max; an intimate memoir of Sir Max Beerbohm. New York, Random House [1960] 317 p. illus., port. 24 cm. "Originated in the New Yorker as a series of articles." [PR6003.E4Z56] 60-5529
1. Beerbohm, Max, Sir, 1872-1956. I. Title.

928.2
Max, a biography [1st Amer. ed.] Boston, Houghton, 1965[c.1964] xiv, 507p. illus., ports. 22cm. [PR6003.E4Z6] 65-10676 6.95
1. Beerbohm, Sir Max, 1872-1956. I. Cecil, David, Lord, 1902- II. Title.

CECIL, David, Lord, 1902- 928.2
Max, a biography. [1st American ed.] Boston, Houghton Mifflin, 1965 [c1964] [PR6003.E4Z6 1965] 65-10676
1. Beerbohm, Max, Sir, 1872-1956. I. Title.

RIEWALD, Jacobus Gerhardus 824.91
Sir Max Beerbohm, man and writer; a critical analysis with a brief life and a bibl. With a prefatory letter by Sir Max Beerbohm. [dist. Brattleboro, Vt., Stephen Greene Press, 1961] xxxii, 369p. illus. 25cm. Bibl. 54-593 12.00
1. Beerbohm, Sir Max, 1872- I. Title.

Beethoven, Ludwig van, 1770-1827.

BARTLETT, Henry Leigh. 780'.92'4 B
Beethoven, democratic friend. San Antonio, Naylor Co. [1973] xxi, 223 p. illus. 22 cm. Bibliography: p. 221-223. [ML410.B4B278] 72-13570 ISBN 0-8111-0469-9 7.95
1. Beethoven, Ludwig van, 1770-1827. I. Title.

BEETHOVEN. v. 12
London, J. M. Dent. New York, Pelligrini and Cudahy [1956] viii, 342p. illus. 19cm. (Master musicians) 'Catalogue of works': p. 294-314. Bibliography: p. 323-332.
1. Beethoven, Ludwig van, 1770-1827. I. Scott, Marion Margaret, 1877-

BEETHOVEN. v. 12
[Rev. ed.] London, Duckworth; New York, Macmillan [1958] 118p. front. (port.) 19cm. (Great lives [12]) 'Revised edition 1948; reprinted 1958.' Includes bibliography.
1. Beethoven, Ludwig van, 1770-1827. I. Pryce-Jones, Alan, 1908-

BEETHOVEN. v. 12
[4th ed.] London, Dent; New York, Farrar,

Straus and Cudahy [1960] viii, 342p. illus., ports., facsims., music. 19cm. (The Master musicians, new ser.) 'Catalogue of works': p. 294-314. Bibliography: p. 323-332.
1. Beethoven. Ludwig van, 1770-1827. I. Scott, Marion Margaret, 1877-

BEETHOVEN: impressions by his contemporaries. 780/.924 Ed. by O. G. Sonneck [Magnolia, Mass., P. Smith, 1968,c.1964] vi, 231p. music, ports., 21cm. (Dover bk. rebound) Unabridged, unaltered repubn. of the work orig. pub. in 1926 under the title Beethoven: impressions of contemporaries [ML410.B4B28 1967] 4.25
1. Beethoven, Ludwig van, 1770-1827. I. Sonneck, Oscar George Theodore, 1873-1928, comp.

BEETHOVEN, Ludwig van, 1770-1827. 780'.924
Beethoven's letters (1790-1826) from the collection of Dr. Ludwig Nohl, also his letters to the Archduke Rudolph, Cardinal-Archbishop of Olmutz, K. W., from the collection of Dr. Ludwig Ritter von Kochel. Translated by Lady Wallace. Freeport, N.Y., Books for Libraries Press [1970] 2 v. in 1. fold. facsim., music, port. 23 cm. "First published 1868." [ML410.B4A4377 1970] 77-114868 ISBN 8-369-52731-

BEETHOVEN, Ludwig van, 1770-1827. 780'.92'4 B
Beethoven's letters (1790-1826) from the collection of Dr. Ludwig Nohl. Also his letters to the Archduke Rudolph, cardinal-archbishop of Olmutz, K. W., from the collection of Dr. Ludwig ritter von Kochel. Translated by Lady Wallace. Boston, Milford House [1973] p. Reprint of the 1867 ed. published by Hurd and Houghton, New York. [ML410.B4A23.N6 1973] 73-10271 ISBN 0-87821-055-5 45.00
1. Beethoven, Ludwig van, 1770-1827. 2. Rudolph, Archduke of Austria, Abp. of Olmutz, 1788-1831. I. Nohl, Ludwig, 1831-1885, ed. II. Kochel, Ludwig, ritter von, 1800-1877, ed. III. Wallace, Grace (Stein) Don, lady, d. 1878, tr.

BEETHOVEN, Ludwig van, 1770-1827. 780.92'4
Beethoven's letters (1790-1826) from the collection of Dr. Ludwig Nohl : also his letters to the Archduke Rudolph, Cardinal Archbishop of Olmutz, K. W., from the collection of Dr. Ludwig Ritter von Kochel / translated by Lady Wallace Portland, Me. : Longwood Press, 1976. p. cm. Reprint of the 1867 ed. published by Hurd and Houghton, New York. Includes index. [ML410.B4A23N6 1976] 76-22344 ISBN 0-89341-022-5 lib.bdg. : 50.00
1. Beethoven, Ludwig van, 1770-1827. 2. Rudolph, Archduke of Austria, Abp. of Olmutz, 1788-1831. 3. Composers—Germany—Correspondence. I. Nohl, Ludwig, 1831-1885. II. Kochel, Ludwig, Ritter von, 1800-1877. III. Wallace, Grace Stein Don, Lady, d. 1878. IV. Title.

BEETHOVEN, Ludwig van, 1770-1827. 927.8
Letters. Collected, translated and edited with an introduction, appendixes, notes and indexes by Emily Anderson. New York, St. Martin's Press, 1961. 3v. (1489, [1] p.) ports., facsims., music. 23cm. 'List of letters': v. 1, p. xxiii-xiii: 'Classified index of works': v. 3, p. 1473-1481: 'Index of works arranged according to the Kinsky-Halm thematic catalogue (1955) : v. 3, p. 1483-[490] [ML410.B4A43] 61-65707
I. Anderson, Emily, ed. and tr. II. Title.

BEETHOVEN, Ludwig van, 1770-1827. 927.8
Letters, journals, and conversations. Edited, translated, and introduced by Michael Hamburger. [1st ed.] Garden City, N. Y., Doubleday, 1960. xxviii, 290p. music. 18cm. (Anchor books, A206) [ML410.B4A4368 1960] 60-3189
I. Title.

BEETHOVEN, Ludwig van 1770-1827. 927.8
New Beethoven letters. Translated and annotated by Donald W. MacArdle and Ludwing Misch. Norman, University of Okiahoma Press [1957] xxxix, 577p. facsims. 25cm. [ML410.B4A4376] 57-7331
I. Title.

BEETHOVEN, Ludwig van, 1770-1827 780.924
Selected letters of Beethoven; tr. [from German] by Emily Anderson, ed. by Alan Tyson. London, Melbourne [etc.] Macmillan; New York, St. Martin's 1967. xx, 284p. illus. (music). 18cm. (Papermacs, p. 174) Bibl. [ML410.B4A4385] 67-82837 2.65
I. Tyson, Alan, ed. II. Title.

BEETHOVEN, Ludwig von, 1770-1827 927.8
Letters. 3 vs. Collected, tr., ed., introd., appendixes, notes, indexes by Emily Anderson. New York, St. Martin's [c.] 1961. 3 v. (1489,p.) illus., music List of letters : v. 1, p.xxiii-xliii Classified index of works : v. 3, p.1473-1481; 'Index of works arranged according to the Kinsky-Halm thematic catalogue (1955)': v. 3, p.1483-[1490] 61-65707 37.50 set, bxd.; after Jan. 1,
I. Anderson Emily, ed. and tr. II. Title.

BEKKER, Paul, 1882-1937. 780'.924 B
Beethoven. [Translated and adapted from the German by M. M. Bozman] New York, AMS Press [1971] ix, 391 p. port. 23 cm. Reprint of the 1925 ed. [ML410.B4B323 1971] 75-175938 ISBN 0-404-00728-7
1. Beethoven, Ludwig van, 1770-1827.

BERLIOZ, Hector, 1803-1869. 785.1'1'0924
Beethoven : a critical appreciation of Beethoven's nine symphonies and his only opera, Fidelio, with its four overtures / by Berlioz ; compiled and translated by Ralph De Sola. Boston : Crescendo Pub. Co., [1975] 62 p. ; 24 cm. Selections from the author's A travers chants. [ML410.B5A543 1975] 74-84541 ISBN 0-87597-094-X pbk. : 6.00
1. Beethoven, Ludwig van, 1770-1827. Symphonies. 2. Beethoven, Ludwig van, 1770-1827. Fidelio. I. De Sola, Ralph, 1908-

BORY, Robert 927.8
Ludwig van Beethoven; his life and his work in pictures. [Tr. from French by Winifred Glass, Hans Rosenwald] New York, Atlantis Bks. [dist. Taplinger, 1964, c.1960] 228p. illus., ports., facsims. (incl. music) 33cm. Trs. of Beethoven's letters and various documents reproduced in this vol. [4] p. laid in. 64-1734 18.75
1. Beethoven, Ludwig van—Iconography. I. Title.

COOPER, Martin, 1910- 780'.924
Beethoven; the last decade 1817-1827, with a medical appendix by Edward Larkin. London, New York, Oxford University Press, 1970. x, 483, p. facsim., music, port. 23 cm. Bibliography: p. [469]-470. [ML410.B4C75] 76-116137 12.75
1. Beethoven, Ludwig van, 1770-1827.

CROWEST, Frederick James, 1850-1927. 780'.92'4 B
Beethoven / by Frederick J. Crowest. Boston : Longwood Press, 1977. p. cm. Reprint of the 1921 ed. published J. M. Dent, London, in series: The Master musicians. Includes index. Bibliography: [ML410.B4C95 1977] 77-6177 ISBN 0-89341-128-0 lib.bdg. : 35.00
1. Beethoven, Ludwig van, 1770-1827. 2. Composers—Germany—Biography. I. Series: The Master musicians.

HUGHES, Rosemary. 780'.924 B
Beethoven: a biography, with a survey of books, editions, and recordings. [Hamden, Conn.] Archon Books [1970] 114 p. 23 cm. (The Concertgoer's companions) [ML410.B4H92] 79-13492 4.00
1. Beethoven, Ludwig van, 1770-1827.

INDY, Vincent d', 1851-1931. 780'.924 B
Beethoven; a critical biography. Translated by Theodore Baker. New York, Da Capo Press, 1970. v, 127 p. illus., facsims., ports. 23 cm. (Da Capo Press music reprint series) Reprint of the 1913 ed. [ML410.B4I62 1970b] 72-125054
1. Beethoven, Ludwig van, 1770-1827.

INDY, Vincent d', 1851-1931. 780'.924 B
Beethoven; a critical biography. Translated from the French by Theodore Baker. Freeport, N.Y., Books for Libraries Press [1970] 127 p. illus., facsims., ports. 23 cm. "First published 1913." [ML410.B4I62 1970] 74-107808 ISBN 8-369-51840-
1. Beethoven, Ludwig van, 1770-1827.

JAMES, Burnett 927.8
Beethoven and human destiny. New York, Roy [1961, c.1960] 191p. illus. Bibl. 61-11045 6.50
1. Beethoven, Ludwig van, 1770-1827. I. Title.

KAUFMANN, Helen (Loeb) 927.8
The story of Beethoven. Illustrated by Fritz Kredel. Enid Lamonte Meadowcroft, Supervising editor. New York, Grosset & Dunlap [1957] 181p. illus. 22cm. (Signature books, 41) [ML3930.B4K4] 57-10103
1. Beethoven, Ludwig van, 1770-1827. 2. Music— Juvenile literature. I. Title.

KLINGER, George, ed. 927.8
Ludwig van Beethoven: a booklet presented by the High Fidelity Board casting Corporation and prepared especially for subscribers to program guide of radio station WFMR 96.5 fm, Milkwaukee, Wisconsin High Fidelity Broadcasting Corporation, 606 W. Wisconsin Ave. [Milwaukee] c.1960. 46 p. illus. 23 cm 60-2390 pap. 1.00
1. Beethoven, Ludwig van 1770-1827. I. Title.

KNIGHT, Frida. 780'.92'4 B
Beethoven & the age of revolution. New York, International Publishers [1974, c1973] 206 p. 21 cm. (New World paperbacks, NW 182) Bibliography: p. [193]-195. [ML410.B4K66 1974] 74-8247 2.75 (pbk.)
1. Beethoven, Ludwig van, 1770-1827. I. Title. **BIP**

KOLODIN, Irving, 1908- 780'.92'4
The interior Beethoven; a biography of the music. [1st ed.] New York, A. A. Knopf; distributed by Random House 1975. xv, 341, xvi p. music. 24 cm. [ML410.B42K64] 74-7741
1. Beethoven, Ludwig van, 1770-1827. Works. I. Title. **BIP**

KOMROFF, Manuel, 1890- 927.8
Beethoven and the world of music. New York, Dodd, Mead, 1961. 183 p. 22 cm. Includes bibliography and discography. [ML410.B4K715] 61-14418
1. Beethoven, Ludwig van, 1770-1827. I. Title. **BIP**

KOMROFF, Manuel, 1890- 780'.92'4 B
Beethoven and the world of music. Westport, Conn., Greenwood Press [1973, c1961] viii, 183 p. 22 cm. Reprint of the ed. published by Dodd, Mead, New York. Bibliography: p. 173. [ML410.B4K715 1973] 73-2344 ISBN 0-8371-6845-7 9.25
1. Beethoven, Ludwig van, 1770-1827. I. Title.

LANDON, Howard Chandler Robbins, 1926- comp. 780'.92'4 B
Beethoven : a documentary study / compiled and edited by H. C. Robbins Landon ; [translated from the German by Richard Wadleigh and Eugene Hartzell]. Abridged ed. New York : Macmillan, 1975, c1974. p. cm. Includes index. [ML410.B4L287 1975] 74-22052 ISBN 0-02-567830-2 : 9.95. ISBN 0-02-004500-X pbk. : 5.95
1. Beethoven, Ludwig van, 1770-1827.

MAREK, George Richard, 1902- 780'.924 B
Beethoven; biography of a genius, by George R. Marek. New York, Funk & Wagnalls [1969] xix, 696 p. illus., facsims., ports. (part col.) 26 cm. Bibliography: p. 669-672. [ML410.B4M227] 72-85745 10.00
1. Beethoven, Ludwig van, 1770-1827. **BIP**

MAREK, George Richard, 1902- 780'.92'4 B
Beethoven: biography of a genius, by George R. Marek. New York, T. Y. Crowell Co. [1972, c1969] xix, 696 p. illus. 23 cm. (Apollo editions, A-331) Bibliography: p. 669-672. [ML410.B4 M227 1972] 73-159395 4.95
1. Beethoven, Ludwig van, 1770-1827. I. Title.

MIRSKY, Reba Paeff. 927.8
Beethoven. Illustrated by W. T. Mars. Chicago, Follett Pub. Co. [1957] 176 p. illus. 25 cm. [ML3930.B4M5] 57-11032
1. Beethoven, Ludwig van, 1770-1827. 2. Music—Juvenile literature.

NASH, Roy, 1929- 927.8
The thundering silence; a story of Ludwig van Beethoven. Illus. by Brother Harold Ruplinger. Notre Dame, Ind., Dujarie Press [1954] 102p. illus. 24cm. [ML3930.B4N3] 55-672
1. Beethoven, Ludwig van, 1770-1827. 2. Music— Juvenile literature. I. Title.

NOTTEBOHM, Gustav, 1817-1882. 784'.092'4
Beethoveniana. With a new introd. in English by Paul Henry Lang. New York, Johnson Reprint Corp., 1970- v. music. 23 cm. In German. Reprint of the 1872, 1865, 1880, editions. Contents.Contents.—v. 1. Beethoveniana: Aufsatze und Mittheilungen. Ein Skizzenbuch von Beethoven. Ein Skizzenbuch von Beethoven aus dem Jahre 1803. [ML410.B4N89] 68-29518
1. Beethoven, Ludwig van, 1770-1827. I. Beethoven, Ludwig van, 1770-1827. Skizzenbucher. 1970. II. Title.

PRYCE-JONES, Alan, 1908- 927.8
Beethoven. New York, Collier [1962, c.1957] 125p. 18cm. (AS59Y) .95 pap.,
1. Beethoven, Ludwig van, 1770-1827. I. Title. **BIP**

*RIEZLER, Walter. 780'.924 [B]
Beethoven. With an introduction by Wilhelm Furtwangler. Translated from the German by G. D. H. Pidcock. New York, Vienna House [1974, c1972] 312 p. 21 cm. Bibliography: p. 299-302. [ML410] 72-80708 ISBN 0-8443-0076-4. 3.95 (pbk.)
1. Beethoven, Ludwig van, 1770-1827. I. Title.

RIEZLER, Walter, 1878-1965. 780'.92'4 B
Beethoven / Walter Riezler ; with an introd. by Wilhelm Furtwangler ; translated from the German by G. D. H. Pidcock. New York : Haskell House, [1975] p. cm. Reprint of the 1938 ed. published by Dutton, New York. Includes index. Bibliography: p. [ML410.B4R452 1975] 74-30059 ISBN 0-8383-1866-5 : 16.95
1. Beethoven, Ludwig van, 1770-1827.

RODMAN, Selden, 1909- 927.8
The heart of Beethoven [by] Selden Rodman [and] James Kearns. New York, Shorewood Pub. Co. [1962] 157p. illus. 27cm. Illus. by J. Kearns. [ML410.B4R53] 61-15486
1. Beethoven, Ludwig van, 1770-1827. I. Kearns, James. II. Title.

ROLLAND, Romain, 1866-1944. 780'.924
Beethoven. Translated by B. Constance Hull. With a brief analysis of the sonatas, the symphonies, and the quartets, by A. Eaglefield Hull. Introd. by Edward Carpenter. 3d ed. rev. Freeport, N.Y., Books for Libraries Press [1969] xix, 244 p. facsim., music, ports. 23 cm. (Select bibliographies reprint series) "Third edition first published 1919." Bibliography (including list of portraits and list of Beethoven's compositions): p. [193]-235. [ML410.B4R652 1969] 76-95077
1. Beethoven, Ludwig van, 1770-1827. I. Hull, Bertha Constance (Barrett) tr. II. Hull, Arthur Eaglefield, 1876-1928.

ROLLAND, Romain, 1866-1944. 780.92
Beethoven the creator; the great creative epochs: from the Eroica to the Appassionata. Translated by Ernest Newman. New York, Dover Publications [1964] xviii, 392 p. illus., ports., facsims., music. 22 cm. (Dover books on music) Translation of Beethoven: les grandes epoques creatrices. "References" (p. [295]-392) include bibliographical material. [ML410.B4R642 1964] 64-17313
1. Beethoven, Ludwig van, 1770-1827. I. Newman, Ernest, 1868-1959, tr. II. Title. **BIP**

SCHINDLER, Anton Felix, 1795-1864 780.924
Beethoven as I knew him; a biography by Anton Felix Schindler. Ed. by Donald W.

MacArdle. Tr. by Constance S. Jolly. Chapel Hill, Univ. of N.C. Pr. [1966] 547p. facsims. music, plates. 26cm. Tr. of Biographie von Ludwig van Beethoven (Munster, Aschendorff, 1860) [ML410.B4S3333 1966a] 66-7988 12.50
1. Beethoven, Ludwig van, 1770-1827. I. MacArdle, Donald W., ed. II. Title.

SCHINDLER, Anton 780'.92'4 B
Felix, 1795-1864.
Beethoven as I knew him, a biography. New York, W. W. Norton [1972, c1966] 547 p. illus. 20 cm. Translation of Biographie von Ludwig van Beethoven (Munster, Aschendorff, 1860) Reprinted from the University of North Carolina Press ed., 1966. [ML410.B4S3333 1972] 72-6980 ISBN 0-393-00638-7 4.45
1. Beethoven, Ludwig van, 1770-1827. I. MacArdle, Donald W., ed. **BIP**

SCHMIDT-GORG, 780'.924 B
Joseph, 1897-
Ludwig van Beethoven. Edited by Joseph Schmidt-Gorg and Hans Schmidt. New York, Praeger [1970, c1969] 275 p. col. illus, facsims., ports. 32 cm. Translated from the German by the editorial depart. of the Deutsche Grammophon Gesellschaft. Bibliography: p. 269-270. [ML410.B43S253] 70-100925 25.00
1. Beethoven, Ludwig van, 1770-1827.

SCOTT, Marion Margaret, 780.924
1877-
Beethoven, by Marion M. Scott. London, J. M. Dent; New York, Farrar, Straus and Giroux [1965] viii, 342 p. illus., facsims., music, ports. 20 cm. (The Master musicians series) "Catalogue of works": p. 294-314. Bibliography: p. 323-332. [ML410.B4S43] 66-883
1. Beethoven, Ludwig van, 1770-1827. I. Title. II. Series.

SOLOMON, Maynard. 780'.92'4 B
Beethoven / Maynard Solomon New ork : Schimer Books, 1979, c1977 400 p. : ill. ; 24 cm. Includes bibliographic references and index. [ML410.B4S64] ISBN 0-02-872240-X. pbk.: 15.00
1. Beethoven, Ludwig van, 1770-1827 2. Composers — biography I. Title.
L.C. card no. for 1977 Schirmer Books ed.:77-5242

STEICHEN, Dana, 1894-1957. 927.8
Beethoven's beloved. [Ridgefield? Conn.] 1958-59 [v. 4, 1958] 4 x. (1330 l.) ports, facsims., music. 29 cm. q Edrody, Anna Maria (Nckzky) grof. 1780?-1837. [ML410.B4S74] 59-65044
1. Beethoven, Ludwig van. 1770-1827. I. Title.

STERBA, Editha. 927.8
Beethoven and his nephew; a psychoanalytic study of their relationship, by Editha Sterba and Richard Sterba. Translated by Willard R. Trask. [New York] Pantheon [1954] 351p. illus., ports. 22cm. Bibliographical notes: p. 335-351. [ML410.B4S757] 54-11738
1. Beethoven, Ludwig van, 1770-1827. 2. Beethoven, Karl van, 1806-1858. I. Sterba, Richard, joint author. II. Title.

STERBA, Editha. 780'.924 B
Beethoven and his nephew; a psychoanalytic study of their relationship, by Editha Sterba and Richard Sterba. Translated by Willard R. Trask. New York, Schocken Books [1971, c1954] 351 p. illus., ports. 22 cm. Translation of Ludwig van Beethoven und sein Neffe. Includes bibliographical references. [ML410.B4S757 1971] 74-22437
1. Beethoven, Ludwig van, 1770-1827. 2. Beethoven, Karl van, 1806-1858. I. Sterba, Richard, joint author. II. Title.

STERBA, Editha 780.92
Ludwig van Beethoven und sein Neffe, Tragodie eines Genies; eine psychoanalytische Studie [von] Editha und Richard Sterba. Munchen, Szczesny Verlag [dist. New York, Heinman, 1965, c.1964] 350p. facsim., ports. 21cm. Bibl. [ML410.B4S754] 65-51490 7.50
1. Beethoven, Ludwig van, 1770-1827. 2. Beethoven, Karl van, 1806-1858. I. Sterba, Richard, joint author. II. Title.

SULLIVAN, John William 927.8
Navin
Beethoven; his spiritual development. New York, Vintage Books 1960[c.1927] viii, 173p. 19cm. K-100) 1.10 pap.,
I. Beethoven, Ludwig, Van. 1770-1827. II. Title. **BIP**

SULLIVAN, John William 927.8
Navin
Beethoven; his spiritual development. New York, Vintage Books 1960[c.1927] viii, 173p. 19cm. K-100) 1.10 pap.,
I. Beethoven, Ludwig, Van. 1770-1827. II. Title. **BIP**

THAYER, Alexander Wheelock, 927.8
1817-1897
Life of Beethoven. 2v. Rev., ed. by Elliot Forbes. Princeton, N.J., Princeton, 1964[c.1921-1964] 2v. (1136p.) ports., music. 25cm. Although some portions of Thayer's orig. text have been deleted because recent Beethoven res. has proved them inaccurate, 'the majority of the text used consists of the coordinated treatment of Thayer's notes and manuscript by these three editors [H. Deiters, H. Riemann, H. Krehbiel]' with additions and corrections by the present ed. Bibl. 63-16239 25.00 bxd. set,
1. Beethoven, Ludwig van, 1770-1827. I. Forbes, Elliot, ed. II. Deiters, Hermann, 1833-1907, ed. III. Riemann, Hugo, 1849-1919, ed. IV. Krehbiel, Henry Edward, 1854-1923, ed. V. Title.

THAYER, Alexander Wheelock, 927.8
1817-1897.
The life of Ludwig van Beethoven. [translated from German] with and introd. by Alan Pryce-Jones. Carbondale, Southern Illinois, University Press 1960. 3 v. various pages, ports., muscis. 22 cm (Centaur classics) "Unabridged reprint of the Krehbiel edition [published in 1921] 59-15573 17.50
1. Beethoven, Ludwig van, 1770-1827 I. Title.

THAYER, Alexander 780'.924 B
Wheelock, 1817-1897.
Thayer's life of Beethoven Rev. and edited by Elliot Forbes. Princeton, N.J., Princeton University Press, 1967. 2 v. (1141 p.) ports., music. 25 cm. Although some portions of Thayer's original text have been deleted because recent Beethoven research has proved them inaccurate, "the majority of the text used consists of the coordinated treatment of Thayer's notes and manuscript by these three editors [H. Deiters, H. Riemann, and H. Krehbiel]" with additions and corrections by the present editor. "First publication of works after Beethoven's death": v. 2, p. 1077-1084. Bibliography: v. 1, p. xxiii-xxv. [ML410.B4T33 1967] 66-29831
1. Beethoven, Ludwig van, 1770-1827. I. Forbes, Elliot, ed. II. Deiters, Hermann, 1833-1907, ed. III. Riemann, Hugo, 1849-1919, ed. IV. Krehbiel, Henry Edward, 1854-1923, ed.

TURNER, Walter James, 780'.924 B
1889-1946.
Beethoven; the search for reality. Freeport, N.Y., Books for Libraries Press [1971] 343 p. music. 23 cm. Reprint of the 1927 ed. [ML410.B4T9 1971] 75-157357 ISBN 0-8369-5818-7
1. Beethoven, Ludwig van, 1770-1827. **BIP**

VALENTIN, Erich, 1906- 927.8
Beethoven: a pictorial biography. [Translated by Norma Deane] New York, Studio publications [1958] 147 p. illus. 24 cm. [ML88.B4V3] 58-10736
1. Beethoven, Ludwig van — Iconography. I. Title.

YOUNG, Percy Marshall, 780'.92'4
1912-
Beethoven : a victorian tribute based on the papers of Sir George Smart / by Percy M. Young. London : D. Dobson, 1976. x, 125 p., [8] leaves of plates : ill. ; 24 cm. Includes index. Bibliography: p. 119-120. [ML410.B43Y7] 76-377833 ISBN 0-234-77672-2
1. Beethoven, Ludwig van, 1770-1827. 2. Smart, George Thomas, Sir, 1776-1867. I. Smart, George Thomas, Sir, 1776-1867.

ZOBELEY, Fritz. 780'.924 B
Portrait of Beethoven; an illustrated biography. Translated by Ann O'Brien. [New York] Herder and Herder [1972] 176 p. illus. 21 cm. Translation of Ludwig van Beethoven in Selbstzeugnissen und Bilddokumenten. Bibliography: p. 176. [ML410.B4Z63] 77-181013 ISBN 0-07-073225-6 6.95
1. Beethoven, Ludwig van, 1770-1827.
pap. $2.95, ISBN 0-665-00030-8

Beethoven, Ludwig van, 1770-1827— Dictionaries, indexes, etc.

NETTL, Paul, 1889- 927.8
Beethoven encyclopedia. New York, Philosophical Library [1956] 325p. 24cm. (Midcentury reference library) [ML410.B42N4] 56-2483
1. Beethoven, Ludwig van—Dictionaries. I. Title.

NETTL, Paul, 1889- 780'.924
Beethoven handbook. New York, F. Ungar Pub. Co. [1967] 335 p. 23 cm. First published in 1956 under title Beethoven encyclopedia. [ML410.B42N4 1967] 66-26506
1. Beethoven, Ludwig van, 1770-1827— Dictionaries, indexes, etc. I. Title. **BIP**

Beethoven, Ludwig van, 1770-1827— Juvenile literature.

GIMPEL, Herbert J. 780'.924 B
Beethoven, master composer [by] Herbert J. Gimpel. New York, F. Watts [1970] viii, 250 p. illus. 22 cm. (Immortals of music) The life of the musician who composed some of his greatest works after he became deaf. [ML3930.B4G5] 92 71-95641
1. Beethoven, Ludwig van, 1770-1827— Juvenile literature. I. Title.

HARRIS, Paula 927.8
Introducing Beethoven. Drawings by J. J. Crockford. New York, Roy [1965, c.1963] 98p. illus. 19cm. [ML3930.B4H4] 65-12567 2.95 bds.,
1. Beethoven, Ludwig van, 1770-1827— Juvenile literature. I. Title.

JOHNSON, Ann Donegan. 780'.92'4 B
The value of giving : the story of Beethoven / by Ann Donegan Johnson : illustrated by Pileggi. La Jolla, Calif. : Value Communications, c1979. 63 p. : col. ill. ; 29 cm. (ValueTales) A brief biography of Ludwig van Beethoven, emphasizing the importance of giving in his life. [ML3930.B4J6] 92 78-31545 ISBN 0-916392-34-1 : 5.95
1. Beethoven, Ludwig van, 1770-1827— Juvenile literature. 2. Composers— Germany—Biography—Juvenile literature. I. Pileggi, Steve. II. Title.
Distributed by Oak Tree Pubns., San Diego, CA

YOUNG, Percy Marshall, 1912- 92
Beethoven [by] Percy M. Young. New York, D. White [c1966] viii, 69 p. illus., music. 23 cm. (Masters of music.) [ML3930.B4Y7] 67-16968
1. Beethoven, Ludwig Van, 1770-1827 — Juvenile literature. I. Title. **BIP**

Beeton, Isabella Mary Mayson, 1836-1865.

FREEMAN, Sarah. 640'.92'4 B
Isabella and Sam : the story of Mrs. Beeton / Sarah Freeman. 1st American ed. New York : Coward, McCann & Geoghegan, 1978, c1977. 336 p. ; 22 cm. Includes index. Bibliography: p. [325]-327. [TX140.B4F73 1978] 77-11157 ISBN 0-698-10711-X : 9.95
1. Beeton, Isabella Mary Mayson, 1836-1865. 2. Beeton, Samuel Orchart, 1831-1877. 3. Home economics—Great Britain—Biography. I. Title. **BIP**

Befrage, Cedric, 1904-

BELFRAGE, Cedric, 1904- 071
Something to guard : the stormy life of the National guardian, 1948-1967 / Cedric Belfrage, James Aronson. New York : Columbia University Press, [1978] p. cm. Includes bibliographical references and index. [PN4900.N32B44] 78-3530 ISBN 0-231-04510-7 : 19.95
1. Befrage, Cedric, 1904- 2. Aronson, James. 3. National guardian. 4. Journalists—United States—Biography. I. Aronson, James, joint author. II. Title.

Begin, Menahem, 1913-

GERVASI, Frank 956.94'05'0924 B
Henry, 1906-
The life and times of Menahem Begin : rebel to statesman / by Frank Gervasi. New York : Putnam, c1978. p. cm. Includes index. Bibliography: p. [DS126.6.B33G47] 78-11555 ISBN 0-399-12299-0 : 10.95
1. Begin, Menahem, 1913- 2. Prime ministers—Israel—Biography. I. Title. **BIP**

HABER, Eitan. 956.94'05'0924 [B]
Menachem Begin : the legend and the man / Eitan Haber. New York : Dell Pub. Co., 1979, c1978. 479p., 8 leaves of plates : ill. ; 18 cm. (A Dell book) [DS126.6B33H3213] ISBN 0-440-16107-X pbk. : 2.25
1. Begin, Menachem, 1913- 2. Prime Ministers — Israel — Biography. I. Title.
L.C. card no. for 1978 Delacorte Press ed.: 78-4649. **BIP**

HABER, Eithan. 956.94'05'0924 B
Menahem Begin : the legend and the man / Eitan Haber ; translated by Louis Williams. New York : Delacorte Press, c1978. vi, 321 p., [8] leaves of plates : ill. ; 24 cm. Includes index. Bibliography: p. [311]. [DS126.6.B33H3213] 78-4649 ISBN 0-440-05553-9 : 9.95
1. Begin, Menahem, 1913- 2. Prime ministers—Israel—Biography. **BIP**

HIRSCHLER, 956.94'05'0924 B
Gertrude.
Menahem Begin, from freedom fighter to statesman / by Gertrude Hirschler and Lester S. Eckman ; introd. by Howard L. Adelson. New York : Shengold Publishers, c1979. 377 p., [3] leaves of plates : ill. ; 24 cm. Includes bibliographical references and index. [DS126.6.B33H57] 78-54565 ISBN 0-88400-051-6 : 11.95
1. Begin, Menahem, 1913- 2. Prime ministers—Israel—Biography. 3. Israel— Politics and government. I. Eckman, Lester Samuel, joint author. II. Title.

Begin, Menahem, 1913- —Political career before 1977.

BEGIN, Menahem, 947.084'2'0924
1913-
White nights : the story of a prisoner in Russia / by Menachem Begin ; translated from the Hebrew by Katie Kaplan. 1st U.S. ed. New York : Harper & Row, [1979] c1977. 240 p. ; 22 cm. Translation of Be-lelot levanim. [DS126.6.B33A313 1979] 78-69610 ISBN 0-06-010289-6 : 8.95
1. Begin, Menahem, 1913- —Political career before 1977. 2. Prime ministers— Israel—Biography. 3. Political prisoners— Russia—Biography. 4. Zionists—Poland Biography. I. Title. **BIP**

Begley, Kathleen A.

BEGLEY, Kathleen A. 070'.92'4 B
Deadline / Kathleen A. Begley. New York : Dell Pub. Co., 1979, c1977. 169p. ; 18 cm. (Laurel-Leaf library) [PN4874.B364A33] ISBN 0-440-91718 2 pbk. : 1.50
1. Begley, Kathleen A. 2. Journalists — United States — Biography — Juvenile literature. I. Title.
L.C. card no. for 1977 Putnam ed.: 77-2550. **BIP**

BEGLEY, Kathleen A. 070'.92'4 B
Deadline / Kathleen A. Begley. New York : Putnam, c1977. 148 p. ; 23 cm. Autobiographical. Includes index. The author relates how she came to be a news reporter and her early experiences on the job. [PN4874.B364A33] 92 77-2550 ISBN 0-399-20611-6 : 6.95.
1. Begley, Kathleen A. 2. Journalists— United States—Biography—Juvenile literature. I. Title.

Behan, Brenda.

BEHAN, Brendan. 822'.9'14 B
Confessions of an Irish rebel. [New York] B. Geis Associates; distributed by Random House [1966, c1965] 245 p. 22 cm. "The second part of [the author's] autobiography." [PR6003.E417Z55 1966] 66-13706

I. Title.

O'CONNOR, Ulick. 822'.9'14 B
Brendan. [1st American ed.] Englewood Cliffs, N.J., Prentice-Hall [1971, c1970] 328 p. illus. 22 cm. Bibliography: p. 9-12. [PR6003.E417Z8 1971] 74-151192 ISBN 0-13-081851-8 6.95
1. Behan, Brenda.

Behan, Brendan—Biography.

BEHAN, Beatrice. 822'.9'14 B
My life with Brendan / Beatrice Behan, with Des Hickey and Gus Smith. Los Angeles : Nash Pub., [1974] 253 p. : ill. ; 25 cm. [PR6003.E417Z58 1974] 74-83034 ISBN 0-8402-1354-9 : 8.95
1. Behan, Brendan—Biography. 2. Behan, Beatrice. I. Hickey, Des, joint author. II. Smith, Gus, joint author. III. Title.

Behn, Aphra (Amis) 1640-1689.

DUFFY, Maureen. 822'.4 B
The passionate shepherdess: Aphra Behn 1640-89 / Maureen Duffy. New York : Avon Books, 1979, c1977. 328p., [4] pages of plates : ill. ; 18 cm. (A Discus book) Includes index. Bibliography: p. [305]-307. [PR3317.Z5D8] ISBN 0-380-41863-0 pbk. : 2.95
1. Behn Aphra Amis, 1640-1689 — Biography. 2. Authors, English — Early modern, 1500-1700 — Biography. I. Title.
L.C. card no. for 1977 London, Cape ed.: 78-301563.

LINK, Frederick M. 828'.4'09
Aphra Behn, by Frederick M. Link. New York, Twayne Publishers [1968] 183 p. 21 cm. (Twayne's English authors series, no. 63) Bibliography: p. 171-177. [PR3317.Z5L5] 68-17246
1. Behn, Aphra (Amis) 1640-1689. **BIP**

SACKVILLE-WEST, Victoria 822'.4
Mary, Hon., 1892-1962.
Aphra Behn, the incomparable Astrea. New York, Russell & Russell [1970] 92, [1] p. port. 20 cm. Reprint of the 1927 ed. "The works of Aphra Behn": p. [90]-92. Bibliography: p. [93] [PR3317.Z5S3 1970] 75-102540
1. Behn, Aphra (Amis) 1640-1689. **BIP**

Behn, Aphra Amis, 1640-1689—Biography.

DUFFY, Maureen. 822'.4 B
The passionate shepherdess : Aphra Behn, 1640-89 / Maureen Duffy. London : Cape, 1977. 324 p., [4] leaves of plates : ill. ; 23 cm. Includes index. Bibliography: p. [305]-307. [PR3317.Z5D8] 78-301563 ISBN 0-224-01349-1 : 15.00
1. Behn, Aphra Amis, 1640-1689—Biography. 2. Authors, English—Early modern, 1500-1700—Biography. I. Title.

Behr, Edward, 1926-

BEHR, Edward, 1926- 070.4'092'4 B
Bearings : a foreign correspondent's life behind the lines / Edward Behr. New York : Viking Press, 1978, c1969. p. cm. [PN5123.B36A33 1978] 78-15209 ISBN 0-670-15149-1 : 10.95
1. Behr, Edward, 1926- 2. Foreign correspondents—Biography. I. Title. **BIP**

Behrhorst, Carroll, 1922-

BARTON, Edwin, 1917- 610'.924
Physician to the Mayas; the story of Dr. Carroll Behrhorst. Philadelphia, Fortress Press [1970] 208 p. illus., map (on lining papers), ports. 23 cm. [RA454.G8B3] 76-126131 5.95
1. Behrhorst, Carroll, 1922- 2. Indians of Central America—Guatemala. 3. Indians of Central America—Health and hygiene. 4. Cakchikel Indians. I. Title.

Behrman, Daniel.

BEHRMAN, Daniel. 301.31
The man who loved bicycles; the memoirs of an autophobe. [1st ed.] New York, Harper's Magazine Press [1973] 130 p. illus. 24 cm. [CT275.B5565A3] 72-12095 ISBN 0-06-120350-5 6.95
1. Behrman, Daniel. I. Title.

Behrman, Martin, 1864-1926.

BEHRMAN, 976.3'35'060924 B
Martin, 1864-1926.
Martin Behrman of New Orleans : memoirs of a city boss / edited, with an introd., by John R. Kemp. Baton Rouge : Louisiana State University Press, c1977. p. cm. Includes index. Bibliography: p. [F379.N553B443] 77-6781 ISBN 0-8071-0275-X : 20.00
1. Behrman, Martin, 1864-1926. 2. New Orleans—Mayors—Biography. 3. New Orleans—Politics and government. I. Kemp, John R., 1945- II. Title. **BIP**

Behrman, Samuel Nathan, 1893-1973.

BEHRMAN, Samuel 812'.5'2 B
Nathaniel, 1893-
People in a diary; a memoir, by S. N. Behrman. [1st ed.] Boston, Little, Brown [1972] 338 p. illus. 24 cm. [PS3503.E37Z5] 70-186968 10.00
I. Title.

BEHRMAN, Samuel 812'.5'2 B
Nathaniel, 1893-
People in a diary; a memoir, by S. N. Behrman. [1st ed.] Boston, Little, Brown [1972] 338 p. illus. 24 cm. [PS3503.E37Z5] 70-186968 10.00
I. Title.

REED, Kenneth T. 812'.5'2 B
S. N. Behrman / by Kenneth T. Reed. Boston : Twayne Publishers, [1975] p. cm. (Twayne's United States authors series) Includes index. Bibliography: p. [PS3503.E37Z85] 75-2085 ISBN 0-8057-7154-9 lib.bdg. : 6.95
1. Behrman, Samuel Nathan, 1893-1973. **BIP**

Beidelman, George Washington.

BEIDELMAN, George 973.7'81
Washington, ca.1839-1864.
The Civil War letters of George Washington Beidelman / [edited] by Catherine H. Vanderslice. 1st ed. New York : Vantage Press, c1978. 212 p. : ill. ; 21 cm. Bibliography: p. 211-212. [E527.57 2d.B44] 79-108846 ISBN 0-533-03389-6 : 8.95
1. Beidelman, George Washington. 2. Pennsylvania Infantry. 72d Regiment, 1861-1864—Biography. 3. United States—History—Civil War, 1861-1865—Personal narratives. 4. United States—History—Civil War, 1861-1865—Regimental histories—Pennsylvania Infantry—72d Regiment. I. Vanderslice, Catherine H. II. Title.

Beiderbecke, Bix, 1903-1931.

BERTON, Ralph. 788'.1'0924 B
Remembering Bix; a memoir of the jazz age. [1st ed.] New York, Harper & Row [1974] p. Includes bibliographical references. [ML419.B25B5] 72-9108 ISBN 0-06-010304-3 10.00
1. Beiderbecke, Bix, 1903-1931. 2. Jazz music. I. Title.

*SUDHALTER, Richard 788'.1'0924 B
M.
Bix: man & legend, by Richard M. Sudhalter & Phillip R. Evans, with William Dean-Myatt. New York, Schirmer Books [1975 c1974] 512 p. ill. 21 cm. Includes indexes Discography: p. 401-472. [ML419.B25S8] 4.95 (pbk.)
1. Beiderbecke, Bix, 1903-1931 2. Jazz music. I. Evans, Phillip R. joint author II. Dean-Myatt, William joint author III. Title.
L.C. card no. for original Arlington house edition: 74-6326. **BIP**

SUDHALTER, Richard 788'.1'0924 B
M.
Bix: man & legend, by Richard M. Sudhalter & Philip R. Evans, with William Dean-Myatt. New Rochelle, N.Y., Arlington House [1974] 512 p. illus. 24 cm. Discography: p. 401-472. [ML419.B25S8] 74-6326 12.95
1. Beiderbecke, Bix, 1903-1931. 2. Beiderbecke, Bix, 1903-1931—Discography. 3. Jazz music. I. Evans, Philip R., 1935- joint author. II. Title.

Beissel, Johann Conrad, 1690-1768.

KLEIN, Walter 286'.5'0924 B
Conrad, Bp., 1904-
Johann Conrad Beissel, mystic and martinet, 1690-1768, by Walter C. Klein. Philadelphia, Porcupine Press, 1972. ix, 218 p. 22 cm. (The American utopian adventure) Reprint of the 1942 ed., issued in series: Pennsylvania lives. Bibliography: p. 207-211. [F159.E6K55 1972] 74-187453 ISBN 0-87991-012-7
1. Beissel, Johann Conrad, 1690-1768. 2. Ephrata Community. I. Series: Pennsylvania lives. **BIP**

Bek, Antony, Bp. of Durham, d. 1311.

FRASER, C M 922.242
A history of Antony Bek, Bishop of Durham, 1283-1311. Oxford, C'arendon Press, 1957. 266p. front., map. 23cm. Bibliography: p. [250]-257. [BR754.B4F7] 57-1917
1. Bek, Antony, Bp. of Durham, d. 1311. I. Title.

Belafonte, Harold, 1927-

SHAW, Arnold 927.8
Belafonte, an unauthorized biography. New York, Pyramid Bks. 338p. illus. (R556) .50 pap.,
1. Belafonte, Harold, 1927- I. Title.

SHAW, Arnold. 927.8
Belafonte, an unauthorized biography. [1st ed.] Philadelphia, Chilton Co., Book Division [1960] 338 p. illus. 21 cm. [ML420.B14S5] 60-9123
1. Belafonte, Harold, 1927-

STEIRMAN, Hy, ed. 927.8
Harry Belafonte: his complete life story. [Associate editor: Anne E. Knoll; art director: Conrad W. Wienk. Dunellen, N. J., Hillman Perodicals, 1957] 74p. illus. 28cm. [ML420.B14S8] 57-1768
1. Belafonte, Harold, 1927- I. Title.

STEIRMAN, Hy, ed. 927.8
Harry Belafonte: his complete life story. [Associate editor: Anne E. Knoll; art director: Conrad W. Wienk. Dunellen, N.J., Hillman Periodicals, 1957] 74 p. illus. 28 cm. [ML420.B14S8] 57-1768
1. Belafonte, Harold, 1927- I. Title.

Belasco, David, 1853-1931.

BELASCO, David, 1853-1931. 792
The theatre through its stage door. Edited by Louis V. Defoe. New York, B. Blom [1969] 245 p. illus., ports. 21 cm. Reprint of the 1919 ed. [PN2287.B4A3 1969] 68-56534
I. Title. **BIP**

WINTER, William, 792'.0232'0924 B
1836-1917.
The life of David Belasco. New York, B. Blom, 1972. 2 v. illus. 21 cm. Completed after the author's death by William Jefferson Winter. Reprint of the 3rd ed., 1925. [PN2287.B4W5 1972b] 72-91590
1. Belasco, David, 1853-1931. 2. Theater—United States. I. Winter, William Jefferson, 1878-

WINTER, William, 792'.0232'0924 B
1836-1917.
The life of David Belasco. Westport, Conn., Greenwood Press [1972] p. Completed after the author's death by his son, Jefferson Winter. Reprint of the 1918 ed. [PN2287.B4W5 1972] 74-100212 ISBN 0-8371-4085-4
1. Belasco, David, 1853-1931. 2. Theater—United States. I. Winter, William Jefferson, 1878- **BIP**

WINTER, William, 792'.0924 B
1836-1917.
The life of David Belasco. Freeport, N.Y., Books for Libraries Press [1970] 2 v. illus., facsims., ports. 23 cm. Completed after the author's death by William Jefferson Winter. Reprint of the 1918 ed. [PN2287.B4W5 1970] 72-107837
1. Belasco, David, 1853-1931. 2. Theater—U.S. I. Winter, William Jefferson, 1878- II. Title.

Belden, George P.

BELDEN, George P. 970.3
Belden, The white chief; or, Twelve years among the wild Indians of the Plains. From the diaries and manuscripts of George P. Belden. Edited by James S. Brisbin. Introd. by Jack Matthews. Athens, Ohio University Press [1974] xxvi, 513 p. illus. 21 cm. Reprint of the 1870 ed. published by C. F. Vent, Cincinnati. [E78.G73B44 1974] 73-92900 10.00
1. Belden, George P. 2. Indians of North America—Great Plains. 3. Dakota Indians. I. Title. II. Title: Twelve years among the wild Indians of the Plains.

Belden, Jack, 1910-

BELDEN, Jack, 1910- 940.54'81
Still time to die / by Jack Belden. New York : Da Capo Press, 1975, c1944. 322 p. ; 22 cm. (China in the 20th century.) Reprint of the ed. published by Blakiston Co., Philadelphia. [D811.5.B34 1975] 74-34459 ISBN 0-306-70735-7 : 16.50
1. Belden, Jack, 1910- 2. World War, 1939-1945—Personal narratives, American. 3. World War, 1939-1945—China. 4. China—History—1937-1945. I. Title. **BIP**

Belgian Americans—Texas—Biography.

INSTITUTE of Texan 976.4'004'3932
Cultures.
The Belgian Texans. [San Antonio] : University of Texas at San Antonio, Institute of Texan Cultures, [1975]. 32 p. : ill. ; 22 x 28 cm. (The Texians and the Texans) Cover title. [F395.B2I57 1975] 76-356238
1. Belgian Americans—Texas—Biography. 2. Texas—Biography. I. Title. II. Series.

Belgium—Politics and government—1914-1951.

SPAAK, Paul Henri 327.493
Charles, 1899-
The continuing battle; memoirs of a European, 1936-1966 [by] Paul-Henri Spaak. Translated from the French by Henry Fox. [1st American ed.] Boston, Little, Brown [1971] 512 p. 25 cm. Translation of Combats inacheves. [DH689.S6A3132 1971b] 78-175471 12.50
1. Belgium—Politics and government—1914-1951. 2. Belgium—Politics and government—1951- I. Title.

Belinskii, Vissarion Grigor'evich, 1811-1848—Political and social views.

BOWMAN, Herbert 891.7'8'308
Eugene, 1917-
Vissarion Belinski, 1811-1848; a study in the origins of social criticism in Russia [by] Herbert E. Bowman. New York, Russell & Russell [1969, c1954] 220 p. 23 cm. (Harvard studies in comparative literature, 21) An outgrowth of the author's thesis, Harvard University. Bibliographical references included in "Notes" (p. [209]-213) [PG2947.B5B6 1969] 68-27052
1. Belinskii, Vissarion Grigor'evich, 1811-1848—Political and social views. I. Title. II. Series. **BIP**

Belinsky, Bo, 1936-

ALLEN, Maury, 796.357'092'4 B
1932-
Bo: pitching and wooing. With the uncensored cooperation of Bo Belinsky. New York, Dial Press, 1973. x, 308 p. illus. 24 cm. [GV865.B34A79] 73-3047 6.95
1. Belinsky, Bo, 1936- I. Title.

ALLEN, Maury, 796.357'092'4 B
1932-
Bo: pitching and wooing. With the uncensored cooperation of Bo Belinsky.

New York, Bantam Books [1974, c1973] 343 p. 18 cm. [GV865.B34A79] 1.50 (pbk.)
1. Belinsky, Bo, 1936- I. Title.
L.C. card number for hardbound ed.: 73-3047.

Belisarius, 505 (ca.)-565—Juvenile literature.

DOWNEY, Glanville [full name: Robert Emory Glanville Downey] 923.5495
Belisarius, young general of Byzantium. New York, Dutton [c.]1960. 192p. Bibl.: p.191-192. map. 22cm. 60-11870 3.00
1. Belisarius, 505 (ca.)-565—Juvenile literature. I. Title.

Belk, William Henry, 1862-1952.

BLYTHE, Le Gette, 1900- 926.58
William Henry Belk, merchant of the South. [Enl. ed.] Chapel Hill. University of North Carolina Press [1958] 269p. illus. 23cm. [HF5468.B45B55 1958] 58-14574
1. Belk, William Henry, 1862-1952. I. Title.

Bell, Alexander Graham, 1847-1922.

BRUCE, Robert V. 384.6'092'4 B
Bell: Alexander Graham Bell and the conquest of solitude [by] Robert V. Bruce. [1st ed.] Boston, Little, Brown [1973] xi, 564 p. illus. 25 cm. Bibliography: p. 501-503. [TK140.B37B78] 72-11572 ISBN 0-316-11251-8 12.50
1. Bell, Alexander Graham, 1847-1922. I. Title.

COSTAIN, Thomas B. 926.2
The chord of steel. New York, Pocket Bks. [1963, c.1960] 192p. 17cm. (Permabk., M5055) .50 pap.,
1. Bell, Alexander Graham, 1847-1922. I. Title.

COSTAIN, Thomas Bertram, 1885-1965. 926.2
The chord of steel; the story of the invention of the telephone. [1st ed.] Garden City, N. Y., Doubleday, 1960. 238 p. illus. 22 cm. [TK6143.B4C6] 60-10085
1. Bell, Alexander Graham, 1847-1922. 2. Brantford, Ont. I. Title.

MACKENZIE, Catherine Dunlop. 621.385'0924 B
Alexander Graham Bell, the man who contracted space. Freeport, N.Y., Books for Libraries Press [1971] xiii, 382 p. illus., facsims., ports. 23 cm. Reprint of the 1928 ed. [TK6143.B4M3 1971] 77-150193 ISBN 0-8369-5706-7
1. Bell, Alexander Graham, 1847-1922. **BIP**

RHODES, Frederick Leland, 1870-1933. 621.385
Beginnings of telephony. New York, Arno Press, 1974 [c1929] xvii, 261 p. illus. 24 cm. (Telecommunications) Reprint of the ed. published by Harper, New York. Includes bibliographical references. [TK6015.R5 1974] 74-4694 ISBN 0-405-06057-2
1. Bell, Alexander Graham, 1847-1922. 2. Telephone—History. I. Title. II. Series: Telecommunications (New York, 1974-) **BIP**

WAITE, Helen Elmira. 926.2
Make a joyful sound; the romance of Mabel Hubbard and Alexander Graham Bell, an authorized biography. Philadelphia, Macrae Smith Co. [1961] 284 p. illus. 22 cm. Includes bibliography. [TK6143.B4W3] 61-14958
1. Bell, Alexander Graham, 1847-1922. 2. Bell, Mabel Gardiner Hubbard, 1859-1923. I. Title.

Bell, Alexander Graham, 1847-1922—Juvenile literature.

MONTGOMERY, Elizabeth Rider. 92 (J)
Alexander Graham Bell, man of sound. Illustrated by Gray Morrow. Champaign, Ill., Garrard Pub. Co. [1963] 80 p. illus. 23 cm. (A Discovery book) [TK6143.B4M6] 63-9217
1. Bell, Alexander Graham, 1847-1922—Juvenile literature.

Bell, Charles Jasper,

BELL, Charles Jasper, 1885- 328.73'0924 B
The story of a Missourian, by C. Jasper Bell. [Kansas City? Mo., 1971] 419 p. illus. 24 cm. [E748.B37A3] 74-30027
I. Title.

Bell, George Kennedy Allen, Bp. of Chichester 1883-1958.

JASPER, Ronald Claud Dudley. 283/0924
George Bell. Bishop of Chichester [by] Ronald C D. Jasper. London, New York Oxford Univ. Pr., 1967. xi, 401p. front., 13 plates (incl. ports.). 23cm. Bibl. [BX5199.B355J3] (B) 67-10893 11.20
1. Bell, George Kennedy Allen, Bp. of Chichester 1883-1958. I. Title.

Bell, Gertrude Lowthian, 1868-1926.

BURGOYNE, Elizabeth 920.72
Gertrude Bell, from her personal papers, v.1&2 London, E. Benn [dist. Mystic, Conn., Verry, 1965, c.1958-1961] 2v. (320; 399p.) illus. 23cm. [DA566.9.B39B8] 58-3415 10.00 bds., set,
1. Bell, Gertrude Lowthian, 1868-1926. I. Title.
Contents omitted.

KAMM, Josephine. 920.7
Gertrude Bell, daughter of the desert. Pref. by Sir John Glubb. Foreword by Lady Richmond. New York, Vanguard Press [c1956] 191p. 22cm. London ed. (Bodley Head) has title: Daughter of the desert; the story of Gertrude Bell. [DA566.9.B39K3 1956a] 57-8407
1. Bell, Gertrude Lowthian, 1868-1926. I. Title.

Bell, Horace, 1830-1918.

HARRISON, Benjamin Samuel, 1890- 923.973
Fortune favors the brave; the life and times of Horace Bell, pioneer Californian. Los Angeles, W. Ritchie Press, 1953. 307p. illus. 25cm. Includes bibliography. [CT275.B5594H3] 53-10129
1. Bell, Horace, 1830-1918. I. Title.

Bell, John, 1797-1869.

PARKS, Joseph Howard. 923.273
John Bell of Tennessee. Baton Rouge, Louisana State University Press [1950] viii, 435 p. illus., port. 23 cm. (Southern biography series) "Critical essay on authorities": p. [408]-422. [E415.9.B4P28] 50-7790
1. Bell, John, 1797-1869. I. Series.

Bell, Melvin M., 1907-

WALLACE, Robert, 1919- 923.473
Life and limb; an account of the career of Melvin M. Belli, personal injury trial lawyer. 1st ed Garden City, N.Y., Doubleday, 1955. 250p. 22cm. 55-5572
1. Bell, Melvin M., 1907- 2. Personal injuries—U.S. I. Title.

Bell, Thomas Frederick, 1819 or 20-1892.

HOLDREDGE, Helen (O Donnell) 920
Mammy Pleasant's partner. New York, Putnam [1954] 300p. illus. 22cm. [F869.S3B4 1954] 54-12807
1. Bell, Thomas Frederick, 1819 or 20-1892. 2. Pleasant, Mary Ellen. I. Title.

Bell, Vanessa Stephen, 1874-1961.

SHONE, Richard. 759.21'42
Bloomsbury portraits : Vanessa Bell, Duncan Grant, and their circle / Richard Shone. Oxford : Phaidon ; New York : E. P. Dutton, 1976. 272 p., [4] leaves of plates : ill. (some col.) ; 26 cm. Includes index. Bibliography: p. 266-269. [ND497.B44S56] 76-5354 ISBN 0-7148-1628-0 : 18.95
1. Bell, Vanessa Stephen, 1874-1961. 2. Grant, Duncan James Corrowr, 1885- 3. Painters—England—Biography. 4. Bloomsbury group. I. Title.

Bell, William Abraham—Manuscripts.

COLORADO. State Historical Society. Library. 016.385'0924
A calendar of the papers of William Abraham Bell, 1841-1921; a holding of the Library of the State Historical Society of Colorado. Processed by Lee Scamehorn. Denver, 1970. iv, 84 l. 23 x 29 cm. Cover title. [Z6616.B463C6] 76-636564
1. Bell, William Abraham—Manuscripts. I. Scamehorn, Howard Lee, 1926- II. Title.

Bellamy, Edward, 1850-1898.

BELLAMY, Edward, 1850-1898. 191 B
The religion of solidarity. With a discussion of Edward Bellamy's philosophy, by Arthur E. Morgan. [Folcroft, Pa.] Folcroft Library Editions, 1973 [c1940] 43 p. 23 cm. Reprint of the ed. published by Antioch Bookplate Co., Yellow Springs, Ohio. [B945.B43R44 1973] 73-9680 ISBN 0-8414-3139-6 6.50
I. Title.

BOWMAN, Sylvia E 923.373
The year 2000; a critical biography of Edward Bellamy. New York, Bookman Associates [1958] 404p. illus. 24cm. Includes bibliography. [HX84.B37B6] A58
1. Bellamy, Edward, 1850-1898. I. Title.

BOWMAN, Sylvia E. 813'.4 B
The year 2000 : a critical biography of Edward Bellamy / by Sylvia E. Bowman. New York : Octagon Books, 1979, c1958. 404 p., [4] leaves of plates : ill. ; 24 cm. Reprint of the ed. published by Bookman Associates, New York. Includes index. Bibliography: p. 345-393. [PS1087.B6 1979] 79-17696 ISBN 0-374-90879-6 lib. bdg. : 20.00
1. Bellamy, Edward, 1850-1898. 2. Authors, American—19th century—Biography. I. Title.

MORGAN, Arthur Ernest, 1878- 191 B
Edward Bellamy, by Arthur E. Morgan. Philadelphia, Porcupine Press, 1974 [c1944] xvii, 468 p. illus 22 cm. (Perspectives in American history, no. 18) Reprint of the ed. published by Columbia University Press, New York, which was issued as no. 15 of Columbia studies in American culture. Bibliography: p. [421]-439. [HX84.B37M6 1974] 73-16308 ISBN 0-87991-346-0 17.50
1. Bellamy, Edward, 1850-1898. I. Series: Perspectives in American history (Philadelphia) no. 18. II. Series: Columbia studies in American culture, no. 15. **BIP**

Bellamy, Ralph, 1904-

BELLAMY, Ralph, 1904- 791'.092'4 B
When the smoke hit the fan / Ralph Bellamy. 1st ed. Garden City, N.Y. : Doubleday, 1979. 276 p., [16] leaves of plates : ill ; 22 cm. Includes index. [PN2287.B417A38] 78-14693 ISBN 0-385-14860-7 : 10.95
1. Bellamy, Ralph, 1904- 2. Actors—United States—Biography. I. Title. **BIP**

Bellarmino, Roberto Francesco Romolo, Saint. 1542-1621.

BRODRICK, James, 1891- 922.245
Robert Bellarmine, saint and scholar. Westminster, Md., Newman Press [1961] 430p. illus. 23cm. 'A condensed and largely rewritten version of a biography of St. Robert Bellarmine in two volumes published in 1928.' [BX4700.B25B73] 61-19102
1. Bellarmino, Roberto Francesco Romolo, Saint, 1542-1621. I. Title.

BRODRICK, James, 1891- 922.245
Robert Bellarmine, 1542-1621. London, New York, Longmans, Green [1950] 2 v. plates, ports., fold. map, facsims. 22 cm. First published 1928 under title: The life and work of Blessed Robert Francis Cardinal Bellarmine, s. j., 1542-1621. [BX4700.B25B7 1950] 50-14034
1. Bellarmino, Roberto Francesco Romolo, Saint. 1542-1621. I. Title.

Bellarmino, Robert Francesco Romolo, Saint, 1542-1621—Juvenile literature.

RICHARDSON, Mary Kathleen, 1903- 92
Robert. Drawings by R. M. Sax. New York, Sheed & Ward [1961] unpaged. illus. 21cm. (A Patron saint book) [BX4700.B25R5] 61-11802
1. Bellarmino, Robert Francesco Romolo, Saint, 1542-1621—Juvenile literature. I. Title.

Bellevue Hospital, New York.

KARP, Laurence E. 610'.92'4 B
The view from the Vue / by Laurence E. Karp. Middle Village, N.Y. : Jonathan David Publishers, c1977. p. cm. [RA982.N5B517] 77-2628 ISBN 0-8246-0215-3 : 8.95
1. Bellevue Hospital, New York. 2. Karp, Laurence E. 3. Physicians—New York (City)—Biography. I. Title. **BIP**

LEEK, Sybil. 362.1'9'699500926 B
Inside Bellevue / Sybil Leek and Glen A. Hilken. New York : Mason/Charter, 1976. ix, 210 p. ; 24 cm. [RA982.N5B518] 76-18161 ISBN 0-88405-143-9 : 8.95
1. Bellevue Hospital, New York. 2. Hilken, Glen A. 3. Hospital patients—New York (City)—Biography. 4. Neurofibroma—Biography. I. Hilken, Glen A., joint author. II. Title.

Belli, Melvin M., 1907-

BELLI, Melvin M., 1907- 345'.73'00924 B
Melvin Belli : my life on trial : an autobiography / by Melvin M. Belli with Robert Blair Kaiser. New York : Morrow, 1976. p. cm. Includes index. [KF373.B44A34] 76-12475 ISBN 0-688-03085-8 : 10.00
1. Belli, Melvin M., 1907- 2. Lawyers—United States—Correspondence, reminiscences, etc. I. Kaiser, Robert Blair, joint author.

BELLI, Melvin M., 1907- 345'.73'00924
Melvin Belli : my life on trial / by Melvin Belli with Robert Blair Kaiser. New York : Popular Library, 1977,c1976. 413[16]p. : ill. ; 18 cm. Includes index. [KF373.B44A34] ISBN 0-445-04025-4 pbk. : 1.95
1. Belli, Melvin M.,1907- 2. Lawyers-United States-Correspondence, reminiscences, etc. I. Kaiser, Robert Blair, joint author. II. Title.
L.C. card no. for 1976 Morrow ed.:76-12475. **BIP**

Bellievre, Pompone de, seigneur de Grignon, 1529-1607.

DICKERMAN, Edmund H., 1935- 320.9'44'029
Bellievre and Villeroy; power in France under Henry III and Henry IV [by] Edmund H. Dickerman. Providence, Brown University Press [1971] x, 200 p. 24 cm. A revision of the author's thesis, Brown University. Bibliography: p. [189]-195. [DC112.B4D5 1971] 70-127365 ISBN 0-87057-131-1 10.00
1. Bellievre, Pompone de, seigneur de Grignon, 1529-1607. 2. Villeroy, Nicholas de Neufville, seigneur de, 1543?-1617. 3. France—Politics and government—16th century. 4. France—Politics and government—17th century. I. Title.

Bellini, Vincenzo, 1801-1835.

WEINSTOCK, Herbert, 1905- 782.1'0924 B
Vincenzo Bellini; his life and his operas. [1st ed.] New York, A. A. Knopf, 1971. xx, 554, xxxvii p. illus. 25 cm. Bibliography: p. [549]-554. [ML410.B44W4] 70-111256 ISBN 0-394-41656-2 15.00
1. Bellini, Vincenzo, 1801-1835. **BIP**

Bello, Andres, 1781-1865—Biography.

CALDERA Rodriguez, Rafael. 300'.92'4 B
Andres Bello : philosopher, poet, philologist, educator, legislator, statesman / by Rafael Caldera ; translated by John Street. London : G. Allen & Unwin, 1977. 165 p., [2] leaves of plates : ill. ; 23 cm. Includes index. Bibliography: p. [161]-165. [PQ8549.B3Z6313] 77-371735 ISBN 0-04-920049-6 : 18.75
1. Bello, Andres, 1781-1865—Biography. 2. Authors, Venezuelan—19th century—Biography. 3. Scholars—Venezuela—Biography. 4. Statesmen—Venezuela—Biography.
Distributed by Allen & Unwin, 198 Ash St., Reading, MA 01867

Belloc, Hilaire, 1870-1953.

BELLOC, Hilaire, 1870-1953. 828'.9'1209
Belloc; a biographical anthology. Edited by Herbert van Thal. [1st American ed.] New York, Knopf, 1970. xv, 386 p. illus., port. 23 cm. Bibliography: p. 381-386. [PR6003.E45A6 1970b] 71-126292 8.95
I. Van Thal, Herbert Maurice, 1904- ed. II. Title.

BELLOC, Hilaire, 1870-1953. 928.2
Letters; selected and edited by Robert Speaight. New York, Macmillan, 1958. xi, 313p. 23cm. [PR6003.E45Z53 1958] 58-4876
I. Title.

BELLOC, Hilaire [Joseph Hilaire Pierre Belloc] 1870-1953 928.2
Letters. Selected, ed. by Robert Speaight. London, Hollis & Carter [dist. Chester Springs, Pa., Dufour, 1964, c.1958] 313p. 22cm. A58 6.00
I. Speaight, Robert, 1904- ed. II. Title.

JEBB, Eleanor (Belloc) 928.2
Belloc, the man, by Eleanor and Reginald Jebb. Westminster, Md., Newman Press, 1957. 171p. illus. 20cm. First published in London in 1956 under title: Testimony to Hilaire Belloc. [PR6003.E45Z73 1957] 57-6692
1. Belloc. Hilaire, 1870-1953. I. Jebb, Reginald. II. Title.

LOWNDES, Maria Adelaide (Belloc) 1868-1947. 928.2
The young Hilaire Belloc. New York, P. J. Kenedy [1956] 182p. illus. 21cm. [PR6003.E45Z75] 56-5746
1. Belloc. Hilaire, 1870- 1953. I. Title.

LOWNDES, Marie Adeladie (Belloc) 1868-1947. 928.2
The young Hilaire Belloc. New York, P. J. Kenedy [1956] 182p. illus. 21cm. [PR6003.E45Z75] 56-5746
1. Belloc, Hillaire, 1870-1953. I. Title.

MORTON, John Bingham, 1893- 928.2
Hilaire Belloc, a memoir. New York, Sheed & Ward [1955] 185p. 21cm. [PR6003.E45Z8 1955a] 55-10499
1. Belloc, Hilaire, 1870-1953. I. Title. **BIP**

SPEAIGHT, Robert, 1904- 928.2
The life of Hilaire Belloc. New York, Farrar, Straus & Cudahy [1957] 552 p. illus. 22 cm. Includes bibliography. [PR6003.E45Z85 1957a] 57-1391
1. Belloc, Hilaire, 1870-1953. I. Title. **BIP**

Belloc, Hilaire, 1870-1953—Biography.

MORTON, John Bingham, 1893- 828'.9'1209 B
Hilaire Belloc; a memoir, by J. B. Morton. [Folcroft, Pa.] Folcroft Library Editions, 1974. p. cm. Reprint of the 1955 ed. published by Hollis & Carter, London. [PR6003.E45Z8 1974] 74-19265 15.00
1. Belloc, Hilaire, 1870-1953—Biography.

SPEAIGHT, Robert, 1904- 828'.9'1209
The life of Hilaire Belloc. Freeport, N.Y., Books for Libraries Press [1970, c1957] xv, 552 p. illus., ports. 23 cm. (Biography index reprint series) Bibliography: p. 539-544. [PR6003.E45Z85 1970] 78-136655 ISBN 0-8369-8050-6
1. Belloc, Hilaire, 1870-1953—Biography. I. Title.

Bellow, Saul—Journeys—Israel.

BELLOW, Saul. 915.694'4'0448
To Jerusalem and back : a personal account / Saul Bellow. New York : Viking Press, 1976. 182 p. ; 24 cm. [DS107.4.B37 1976] 76-42198 ISBN 0-670-71729-0 : 7.95
1. Bellow, Saul—Journeys—Israel. 2. Israel—Description and travel. 3. Authors, American—20th century—Biography. 4. Jewish-Arab relations—1973- —Addresses, essays, lectures. I. Title.

BELLOW, Saul. 956.694'4'050924 B
To Jerusalem and back : a personal account / [by] Saul Bellow. London : Alison Press : Secker and Warburg, 1976. [4], 182 p. ; 23 cm. Includes bibliographical references. [DS107.4.B37 1976b] 77-362959 ISBN 0-436-03951-6 : £3.90
1. Bellow, Saul—Journeys—Israel. 2. Israel—Description and travel. 3. Authors, American—20th century—Biography. I. Title. **BIP**

Bellows, George Wesley, 1882-1925.

MORGAN, Charles Hill, 1902- 759.13
George Bellows, painter of America. Introd. by Daniel Catton Rich. New York, Revnal [dist. Morrow, 1966, c.]1965. 381p. illus., (pt. col.) ports. (pt. col.) 25cm. Bibl. [ND237.B45M6] 65-23569 8.50
1. Bellows, George Wesley, 1882-1925. I. Title.

Bellows, George Wesley, 1882-1925 — Juvenile Literature.

NUGENT, Francis Roberts. j92
George Bellows, American painter, written and illustrated by Frances Roberts Nugent. With some reproductions of the work of George Bellows. Chicago, Rand McNally [1963] 64 p. illus. (part col.) port. 24 cm. [ND237.B45N8] 63-12332
1. Bellows, George Wesley, 1882-1925 — Juvenile Literature. I. Title.

Belmont, August, 1813-1890.

KATZ, Irving, 1932- 973.6'6'0924
August Belmont; a political biography. New York, Columbia University Press, 1968. xiv, 296 p. illus., ports. 24 cm. Bibliography: p. [279]-285. [E415.9.B45K3] 68-19751 10.00
1. Belmont, August, 1813-1890.

Belmont, Mass.—Biography.

ROBBINS, Samuel Dowse, 1887-1968. 920'.0744'4
Who's who in Belmont; biographical and autobiographical sketches of residents of Belmont, Massachusetts. Edited by Samuel Dowse Robbins. Belmont, Mass., 1972. xiv, 432 p. 24 cm. [F74.B22R62 1972] 72-85346
1. Belmont, Mass.—Biography. I. Title.

Belton, Howard C.

BELTON, Howard C. 328.73'092'4 B
Under eleven governors / by Howard C. Belton. 1st ed. Portland, Or. : Binford & Mort, 1977. xii, 90 p. : ill. ; 23 cm. [F881.B34] 77-20632 ISBN 0-8323-0296-1 : 5.50. ISBN 0-8323-0297-X pbk. : 3.95
1. Belton, Howard C. 2. Legislators—Oregon—Biography. 3. Oregon—Politics and government—1859-1950. 4. Oregon—Politics and government—1951- I. Title. **BIP**

Beltrami, Giacomo Costantino, 1779-1855.

MICELI, Augusto P. 917.7'04'20924
The man with the red umbrella: Giacomo Costantino Beltrami in America, by Augusto P. Miceli. Baton Rouge, La., Claitor's Pub. Division [1974] ix, 183 p. illus. 23 cm. Bibliography: p. 167-174. [F597.B453M52] 73-93581 7.95
1. Beltrami, Giacomo Costantino, 1779-1855. 2. Mississippi River—Sources. 3. Mississippi River—Discovery and exploration. I. Title.

Beltz, William, 1912-1960—Juvenile literature.

WOLFE, Ellen. 328.798'092'4 B
William Beltz / by Ellen Wolfe. Minneapolis : Dillon Press, [1975] 58 p. : ill. ; 24 cm. A biography of the American Eskimo who became president of the first Alaskan state senate. [F909.B45W64] 92 75-17744 ISBN 0-87518-044-2 lib.bdg. : 4.95
1. Beltz, William, 1912-1960—Juvenile literature. 2. Alaska—Politics and government—1867-1959—Juvenile literature. 3. Eskimos—Alaska—Juvenile literature. **BIP**

Ben-Avi, Ittamar, 1884-1943—Juvenile literature.

OMER, Devorah, 1932- 956.94'001'0924 B
Rebirth; the story of Eliezer Ben-Yehudah and the modern Hebrew language, by Dvorah Omer. Translated from the Hebrew by Ruth Rasnic. [1st English ed.] Philadelphia, Jewish Publication Society of America, 1972. 199 p. illus. 22 cm. Translation of ha-Bekhor le-vet Avi. A biography of the turn-of-the-century Jewish scholar and his son who were instrumental in reviving Hebrew and establishing it as a living language in Palestine. [DS125.3.B35O413] 920 79-188584 2.95
1. Ben-Avi, Ittamar, 1884-1943—Juvenile literature. 2. Ben-Yehudah, Eliezer, 1858-1922—Juvenile literature. I. Title. **BIP**

Ben-Gurion, David, 1886-1973.

AVI-HAI, Avraham, 1931- 956.94'05'0924 B
Ben Gurion, State-builder; principles and pragmatism, 1948-1963. New York, Wiley [1974] xi, 354 p. 23 cm. "A Halsted Press book." Bibliography: p. 326-341. [DS125.3.B37A97 1974] 74-557 ISBN 0-470-03836-5 12.50
1. Ben-Gurion, David, 1886-1973. 2. Israel—Politics and government.

AVI-HAI, Avraham, 1931- 320.9'5694'05
David Ben Gurion; principles, pragmatism, and state-building, 1948-1963. [New York] 1972. 404 l. 29 cm. Thesis—Columbia University. Bibliography: leaves 395-404. [DS125.3.B37A97 1972] 74-185056
1. Ben-Gurion, David, 1886-1973. 2. Israel—Politics and government.

BAR-ZOHAR, Michel. 956.94'05'0924 B
Ben-Gurion; the armed prophet [by] Michael Bar-Zohar. Translated from the French by Len Ortzen. [1st American ed.] Englewood Cliffs, N.J., Prentice-Hall [1968, c1967] viii, 296 p. col. maps (on lining papers), ports. 24 cm. Published in London in 1967 under title: The armed prophet. Bibliography: p. 283-288. [DS125.3.B37B283 1967] 68-13398
1. Ben-Gurion, David, 1886-

BAR-ZOHAR, Michel. 956.94'05'0924 B
Ben-Gurion / Michael Bar-zohar ; translated by Peretz Kidron. New York : Delacorte Press, [1979] p. cm. Includes index. [DS125.3.B37B285513] 78-11055 ISBN 0-440-00987-1 : 12.95
1. Ben-Gurion, David, 1886-1973. 2. Prime ministers—Israel—Biography. I. Title.

BEN-GURION, David, 1886- 956.94050924
Ben Gurion looks back in talks with Moshe Pearlman. New York, S. & S. [c.1965] 260p. 23cm. [DS125.3.B37A33] 65-25283 5.00 bds.,
I. Pearlman, Moshe, 1911- II. Title. **BIP**

BEN-GURION, David, 1886- 300'.8
David Ben-Gurion, in his own words, by Amram Ducovny. New York, Fleet Press Corp. [1969, c1968] 152 p. 21 cm. [DS125.3.B37A34] 68-31018 5.95
I. Ducovny, Amram M. II. Title.

BEN-GURION, David, 1886- 956.94'05'0924 B
Letters to Paula. Translated from the Hebrew by Aubrey Hodes. [Pittsburgh] University of Pittsburgh Press [1972, c1971] x, 259 p. illus. 23 cm. Translation of Mikhtavim el Polah ve-el ha-yeladim. [DS125.3.B37A433 1972] 72-164702 ISBN 0-8229-1102-7 5.95
I. Ben-Gurion, Paula (Munwess) 1892-1968. II. Title.

COMAY, Joan. 92
Ben-Gurion and the birth of Israel. New York, Random House [1967] 178 p. illus., map, ports. 22 cm. (World landmark books, W-62) A biography of the first Prime Minister of Israel who's life and activities parallel the establishment and history of Israel. [DS125.3.B37C6] AC 67
1. Ben-Gurion, David, 1886- 2. Israel—History. I. Title. **BIP**

EDELMAN, Maurice, 1911- 923.25694
David; the story of Ben Gurion. [1st American ed.] New York, Putnam [1965, c1964] 214 p. ports. 22 cm. Bibliography: p. [204]-206. [DS125.3.B37E3 1965] 65-10850
1. Ben-Gurion, David, 1886- I. Title.

LITVINOFF, Barnet 923.2569
The story of David Ben-Gurion. New York, Oceana Publications, 1959[ ] 160p. illus. (por.) 19cm. 59-14273 2.95
1. Ben-Gurion, David. I. Title.

ST. John, Robert, 1902- 923.2569
Ben-Gurion: the biography of an extraordinary man. [1st ed.] Garden City, N.Y., Doubleday, 1959. 336 p. 22 cm. [DS125.3.B37S3] 59-6273
1. Ben-Gurion, David, 1886-

ST. JOHN, Robert, 1902- 923.2569
Ben-Gurion; the biography of an extr1or49n1ry m1n•531st ed.] Garden City, N. Y., Doubleday, 1959. 336p. 22cm. [DS125.3.B37S3] 59-6273
1. Ben-Gurion, David, 1887- I. Title.

SAMUELS, Gertrude. 956.94
B-G, fighter of Goliaths; the story of David Ben-Gurion. Photos. by the author. New York, Crowell [1961] 275 p. illus. 21 cm. Includes bibliography. [DS125.3.B37S35] 61-8209
1. Ben-Gurion, David, 1886- I. Title.

SAMUELS, Gertrude. 956.940500924
B-G, fighter of Goliaths; the story of David Ben-Gurion. Photos. by the author. New York, Crowell [c1965] 279 p. illus., maps, ports. 21 cm. Bibliography: p. 269-273. [DS125.3.B37S35] 65-28174
1. Ben-Gurion, David, 1886- I. Title.

Ben-Gurion, David, 1886-1973—Juvenile literature.

ST. JOHN, Robert, 1902- 923.2569
Builder of Israel; the story of Ben-Gurion. [1st ed.] Garden City, N. Y., Doubleday, 1961. 185p. illus. 22cm. [DS125.3.B37S32] 61-7435
1. Ben-Gurion, David, 1887- —Juvenile literature. I. Title.

SAMUELS, Gertrude. 956.94'04'0924 B
B-G: fighter of Goliaths; the story of David Ben-Gurion. Photos. by the author. New rev. ed. New York, Crowell [1974] 309 p. illus. 21 cm. Bibliography: p. 298-303. A biography of the Israeli statesman which is also an account of modern Israel's fight for recognition, independence, and survival. [DS125.3.B37S35 1974] 92 74-13659 ISBN 0-690-00630-6 5.50

1. Ben-Gurion, David, 1886-1973—Juvenile literature. I. Title.

Ben-Yehudah, Eliezer, 1858-1922.

ST. John, Robert, 1902- 922.96
Tongue of the prophets: the life story of Eliezer Ben Yehuda. [1st ed.] Garden City, N. Y., Doubleday, 1952. 377 p. 22 cm. [DS151.B4S3] 52-5233
1. Ben-Yehudah, Eliezer, 1858-1922. I. Title.

ST. John, Robert, 1902- 956.94'001'0924 B
Tongue of the prophets; the life story of Eliezer Ben Yehuda. Westport, Conn., Greenwood Press [1972, c1952] 377 p. 22 cm. [DS151.B4S3 1972] 77-97303 ISBN 0-8371-2631-2
1. Ben-Yehudah, Eliezer, 1858-1922. I. Title.

ST. JOHN, Robert, 1902- 922.96
Tongue of the prophets; the life story of Eliezer Ben Yehuda. Garden City, N. Y., Doubleday [1961, c.1952] 349p. (Dolphin, C 118) .95 pap.,
1. Ben-Yehudah, Eliezer, 1858-1922. I. Title. BIP

Benbridge, Henry, 1743-1812.

NATIONAL Portrait Gallery, Washington, D.C. 759.13
Henry Benbridge (1743-1812): American portrait painter. Robert G. Stewart, curator. Washington, Published for the National Portrait Gallery by the Smithsonian Institution Press, 1971. 93 p. illus., ports. (1 col.) 28 cm. Catalog of an exhibition. Bibliography: p. 89-90. [ND1329.B45N3] 75-608905
1. Benbridge, Henry, 1743-1812. I. Stewart, Robert G. II. Title.

Bench, Johnny, 1947-

BENCH, Johnny, 1947- 796.357'092'4 B
Catch you later : the autobiography of Johnny Bench / by Johnny Bench and William Brashler. 1st ed. New York : Harper & Row, c1979. viii, 245 p., [8] leaves of plates : ill. ; 22 cm. Includes index. [GV865.B35A33 1979] 78-69616 ISBN 0-06-010324-8 : 10.00
1. Bench, Johnny, 1947- 2. Baseballplayers—United States—Biography. I. Brashler, William, joint author. II. Title. BIP

Bench, Johnny, 1947- —Juvenile literature.

BURCHARD, Marshall. 796.357'092'4 B
Sports hero Johnny Bench, by Marshall and Sue Burchard. New York, Putnam [1973] 96 p. illus. 22 cm. A biography of baseball catcher Johnny Bench who at nineteen joined the Cincinnati Reds. [GV865.B35B87 1973] 92 79-179378 ISBN 0-399-20246-3 3.86 (Lib. bdg.)
1. Bench, Johnny, 1947-—Juvenile literature. I. Burchard, Sue, joint author. II. Title.
Available only in Library Binding.

HEASLIP, George. 796.357'092'4 B
Johnny Bench; the young pro. Illustrated by Harold Henriksen. [Mankato, Minn., Creative Education; distributed by Childrens Press, Chicago [1974] 30 p. illus. (part col.) 25 cm. (Creative's superstars) Biography of the Cincinnati Red who recovered from major surgery and won the National League's Most Valuable Player award for the second time. [GV865.B35H42] 92 73-13862 ISBN 0-87191-289-9 4.95
1. Bench, Johnny, 1947- —Juvenile literature. I. Henriksen, Harold, illus.

ITZKOWITZ, Leonore K., 1933- 796.357'092'4 B
Bench of the Reds—the Johnny Bench story [by] Lenore K. Itzkowitz. [New York] Random House [1974] p. cm. A brief biography of the star catcher for the Cincinnati Reds. [GV865.B35I89] 925 74-1257 ISBN 0-394-12314-X
1. Bench, Johnny, 1947- —Juvenile literature. I. Title.

JACKSON, Robert B. 796.357'0924 B
Johnny Bench, by Robert B. Jackson. New York, H. Z. Walck [1971] 60 p. ports. 22 cm. A biography of a baseball catcher covering his career from the Minors to the Majors. [GV865.B35J3] 92 70-145417 ISBN 0-8098-2077-3 4.25
1. Bench, Johnny, 1947- —Juvenile literature. I. Title. BIP

LIBBY, Bill. 796.357'092'4 B
Johnny Bench, the little general. New York, Putnam [1972] 159 p. 21 cm. A biography of the Cincinnati Reds star catcher, considered by many to be one of the greatest catchers in baseball history. [GV865.B35L5 1972] 92 72-170069 4.95
1. Bench, Johnny, 1947- —Juvenile literature. I. Title.

SABIN, Louis. 796.357'092'4 B
Johnny Bench, king of catchers / by Louis Sabin. New York : Putnam, c1977. p. cm. (Putnam sports shelf) Includes index. A biography of Johnny Bench focusing on his climb to the job of number one catcher for the Cincinnati Reds. [GV865.B35S2 1977] 92 76-41906 ISBN 0-399-61072-3 lib. bdg. : 5.29
1. Bench, Johnny, 1947- —Juvenile literature. 2. Baseball players—United States—Biography—Juvenile literature. I. Title.

SMITH, Jay H. 796.357'092'4 B
Baseball's greatest catcher, Johnny Bench / by Jay H. Smith. Mankato, Minn] : Creative Education/Childrens Press, [c1977] 30 p. : ill. ; 19 cm. (The Allstars) A biography of the outstanding baseball catcher known as the Little General because of his team leadership and strategy. [GV865.B35S63] 92 76-46283 lib.bdg. : 4.95
1. Bench, Johnny, 1947- —Juvenile literature. 2. Baseball players—United States—Biography—Juvenile literature. I. Title.

Benchley, Robert Charles, 1889-1945.

BENCHLEY, Nathaniel, 1915- 928.1
Robert Benchley, a biography. Foreword by Robert E. Sherwood. New York, McGraw-Hill [1955] 256p. illus. 21cm. [PS35.3.E49Z6] 55-10402
1. Benchley, Robert Charles, 1889-1945. I. Title.

REDDING, Robert, 1930- 791.43'028'0924 B
Starring Robert Benchley; "those magnificent movie shorts." [1st ed.] Albuquerque, University of New Mexico Press [1973] xviii, 209 p. illus. 24 cm. Bibliography: p. 198-205. [PN2287.B425R4] 73-82771 ISBN 0-8263-0300-5 7.95
1. Benchley, Robert Charles, 1889-1945. I. Title. BIP

ROSMOND, Babette. 817'.5'2 B
Robert Benchley: his life and good times. [1st ed.] Garden City, N.Y., Doubleday, 1970. 239 p. plates, ports. 22 cm. [PS3503.E49Z8] 70-97686 6.95
1. Benchley, Robert Charles, 1889-1945. I. Title.

Benda, Julien, 1867-1956.

NIESS, Robert Judson. 928.4
Julien Benda. Ann Arbor, University of Michigan Press [1956] x, 361p. port. 24cm. Bibliography: p. [337]-354. [B2430.B354N5] 56-11812
1. Benda, Julien, 1867-1956. I. Title.

Bender, Albert Maurice, 1866-1941.

LEWIS, Oscar, 1893- 704'.361
To remember Albert M. (Micky) Bender; notes for a biography. With an appreciation by Elise S. Haas. [Oakland? Calif., Printed by R. Grabhorn & A. Hoyem, 1973] 37 p. port. 27 cm. Limited ed.: 200 copies. [NX712.B46L48] 73-180357
1. Bender, Albert Maurice, 1866-1941. I. Title.

Bender, Harold Stauffer, 1897-1962.

THE Mennonite quarterly review. 922.8773
Harold S. Bender, educator, historian, churchman, by John C. Wenger [and others] Scottdale, Pa., Herald Press [1964] 141 p. ports. 23 cm. "Reprinted ... from the April, 1964, issue of the Mennonite quarterly review ...a memorial to its former editor, Harold S. Bender." Bibliographical footnotes. [BX8143.B4M4] 64-7835
1. Bender, Harold Stauffer, 1897-1962. I. Bender, Harold Stauffer, 1897-1962. II. Wenger, John Christian, 1910- III. Title.
Contents omitted.

MENNONITE quarterly review Harold S. Bender, 922.8773 educator, historian, churchman, by John C. Wenger [others] Scottdale, Pa., Herald Pr. [c.1964] 141p. ports. 23cm. Reprinted from the April, 1964, issue of th Mennonite quarterly review, a memorial to its former ed., Harold S. Bender. Bibl. 64-7835 3.50
1. Bender, Harold Stauffer, 1897-1962. I. Mennonite quarterly review II. Bender, Harold Stauffer, 1897-1962.

Benedetto da San Filadelfo, Saint, 1526-1589.

[CARLETTI, Giuseppe] 271'.3'024 B
Life of St. Benedict. Translated from the French of M. Allibert. Freeport, N.Y., Books For Libraries Press, 1971. 213 p. 23 cm. (The Black heritage library collection) "First published 1835." Translation of Vita di S. Benedetto da S. Filadelfo, detto il moro. [BX4700.B33C32 1971] 70-168505 ISBN 0-8369-8859-0
1. Benedetto da San Filadelfo, Saint, 1526-1589. I. Title. II. Series.

Benedict, Claude A

BENEDICT, Claude A 1895- 923.873
The runaway redhead, by Claude A. "Red" Benedict. [1st ed.] New York, Vantage Press [1965] 57 p. illus., ports. 21 cm. Autobiographical. [CT275.B5613] 65-4163
I. Title.

Benedict Joseph Labre, Saint, 1748-1783—Juv. lit.

I am a beggar; v. 12
a story of St. Benedict Joseph Labre. Illus. by Carolyn Lee Jagodits. Notre Dame, Ind., Dujarie Press [1961] 94p. illus. 24cm.
1. Benedict Joseph Labre, Saint, 1748-1783—Juv. lit. I. Pelous, Donald.

Benedict, Kirby, 1810-1874.

HUNT, Aurora. 923.473
Kirby Benedict, frontier Federal judge; an account of legal and judicial development in the Southwest, 1853-1874, with special reference to the Indian, slavery, social and political affairs, journalism, and a chapter on circuit riding with Abraham Lincoln in Illinois. Glendale, Calif., A.H. Clark Co., 1961. 268 p. illus., ports., fold. map. 25cm. (Western frontiersmen series, 8) Bibliography: p. [247]-255. [KF368.B39H8] 61-7175
1. Benedict, Kirby, 1810-1874. I. Title. II. Series.

Benedict, Ruth Fulton, 1887-1948.

BENEDICT, Ruth Fulton, 1887-1948. 301.2'08
An anthropologist at work : writings of Ruth Benedict / by Margaret Mead. Westport, Conn. : Greenwood Press, 1977, c1959. xxii, 583 p., [4] leaves of plates : ill. ; 23 cm. Reprint of the 1966 ed. published by Houghton Mifflin, New York. Includes bibliographical references and indexes. [GN6.B4 1977] 77-3017 ISBN 0-8371-9576-4 lib.bdg. : 29.50
1. Benedict, Ruth Fulton, 1887-1948. 2. Anthropology—Collected works. 3. Anthropologists—United States—Biography. I. Mead, Margaret, 1901- II. Title. BIP

MEAD, Margaret, 1901- 301.2'092'4 B
Ruth Benedict. New York, Columbia University Press, 1974. viii, 180 p. illus. 23 cm. (Leaders of modern anthropology series) Bibliography: p. 177-180. [GN21.B45M42 1974] 74-6400 ISBN 0-231-03519-5 9.95
1. Benedict, Ruth Fulton, 1887-1948. 2. Ethnology. I. Title.
Pbk. 2.95, ISBN 0-231-03520-0 BIP

Benedictus, Saint, Abbot of Monte Cassino.

CHAPMAN, John, Father, 1865-1933. 271'.1'024 B
Saint Benedict and the sixth century. Westport, Conn., Greenwood Press [1971] vi, 239 p. 23 cm. Reprint of the 1929 ed. Includes bibliographical references. [BX4700.B3C5 1971] 79-109719 ISBN 0-8371-4209-1
1. Benedictus, Saint, Abbot of Monte Cassino. 2. Benedictus, Saint, Abbot of Monte Cassino. Regula. 3. Monasticism and religious orders. I. Title. BIP

MCCANN, Justin, 1882- 922.245
Saint Benedict. Rev. ed. Garden City, N. Y., Image Books [1958] 233p. 19cm. (A Doubleday image book, D68) [BX4700.B3M3 1958] 58-10194
1. Benedictus, Saint, Abbot of Monte Cassino. 2. Benedictines. I. Title.

MATT, Leonard von 922.245
Saint Benedict [by] Leonard von Matt, Stephen Hilpisch. Tr. from German by Ernest Graf. Chicago, Regnery [c.1961] 226p. illus. 25cm. 61-16240 7.00
1. Benedictus, Saint, Abbot of Monte Cassino. I. Hilpisch, Stephanus, 1894- joint author. II. Title.

MISEREY, Marie de 922.245
Saint Benedict. Tr. by Julie Kernan. New York, Macmillan, 1962[c.1960-1962] 112p. 18cm. (Your name--your saint ser.) Bibl 62-13439 2.50
1. Benedictus, Saint, Abbot of Monte Cassino. I. Title.

Benedictus, Saint, Abbot of Monte Cassino — Juvenile literature.

WILLETT, Franciscus. j92
The mountain of God; a life of St. Benedict [by] Orrin Primm. Illustrated by Leslie Johnson. Valatie, N.Y., Holy Cross Press, 1965. 104 p. illus. 23 cm. (Saints who changed history series) [BX4700.B3W47] 65-21804
1. Benedictus, Saint, Abbot of Monte Cassino — Juvenile literature. I. Title.

Benedictus, Saint, Abbot of Monte Cassino. Regula—Commentaries.

BENEDICTUS, Saint, Abbot of Monte Cassino. v. 12
The rule of St. Benedict. With an introduction, a new translation...and a commentary, all reviewed in the light of an earlier monasticism, by Basilius Steidle. Translated [from German] by Urban J. Schnitzhofer. Canon City, Colo., Holy Cross Abbey, 1967. 307 p. 19 cm. 68-85720
1. Benedictus, Saint, Abbot of Monte Cassino. Regula—Commentaries. 2. Monasticism and religious orders—rules. I. Steidle, Basilius, 1903- tr. II. Schnitzhofer, Urban J., 1887- tr. III. Title.

Benedictus XIII, antipope, 1342-1423?

GLASFURD, Alexander Lamont, 1907- 270.50924
The antipope, Peter de Luna, 1342-1423; a study in obstinacy [by] Alec Glasfurd. New York, Roy [1966, c.1965] 287p. illus., map (on lining papers) ports. 23cm. Bibl. [BX1286.G5 1966] 66-21800 6.95
1. Benedictus XIII, antipope, 1342-1423? I. Title.

Benedictus xv, Pope, 1854-1922.

PETERS, Walter H 922.21
The life of Benedict xv. Milwaukee, Bruce Pub. Co. [1959] 321p. illus. 23cm. Includes

bibliography. [BX1376.P46] 59-13565
1. Benedictus xv, Pope, 1854-1922. I. Title.

Beneke, George J.

MCPHEE, Richard B. 636.089
Rounds with a country vet / text and photos. by Richard B. McPhee. New York : Dodd, Mead, c1977. 74 p. : ill. ; 24 cm. Text and photos follow a country veterinarian as he cares for the animals of his rural area. Describes various animal diseases and their treatment. [SF756.M3] 77-6496 ISBN 0-396-07482-0 : 6.95
1. Beneke, George J. 2. Veterinary medicine—Pictorial works—Juvenile literature. 3. Veterinarians—New York (State)—Biography—Juvenile literature. I. Title. BIP

Benet, Laura—Biography—Youth—Juvenile literature.

BENET, Laura. 810'.9'0052 B
When William Rose, Stephen Vincent, and I were young / Laura Benet, illustrated with photos. New York : Dodd, Mead, c1976. lll p. : ill., ; 24 cm. Includes index. An author reminisces about her childhood and that of her two famous brothers. [PS3503.E528Z52] 920 75-38366 ISBN 0-396-07289-5 : 5.95
1. Benet, Laura—Biography—Youth—Juvenile literature. 2. Benet, William Rose, 1886-1950—Biography—Youth—Juvenile literature. 3. Benet, Stephen Vincent, 1898-1943—Biography—Youth—Juvenile literature. I. Title. BIP

Benet, Stephen Vincent,

BENET, Stephen Vincent, 928.1
1898-1943.
Selected letters. Edited by Charles A. Fenton. New Haven, Yale University Press, 1960. 436p. illus. 21cm. [PS3503.E5325Z54] 60-11231
I. Title.

Benet, Stephen Vincent, 1898-1943—Biography.

FENTON, Charles A. 818'.5'209
Stephen Vincent Benet : the life and times of an American man of letters, 1898-1943 / by Charles A. Fenton. Westport, Conn. : Greenwood Press, 1978, c1958. xv, 436 p., [7] leaves of plates : ill. ; 23 cm. Reprint of the ed. by Yale University Press, New Haven, Conn. Includes bibliographical references and index. [PS3503.E5325Z62 1978] 77-19015 ISBN 0-313-20200-1 : 26.00
1. Benet, Stephen Vincent, 1898-1943—Biography. 2. Authors, American—20th century—Biography. BIP

Benet, Stephen Vincent, 1898-1943—Biography—Addresses, essays, lectures.

BENET, William Rose, 818'.5'209
1886-1950.
Stephen Vincent Benet. Folcroft, Pa. : Folcroft Library Editions, 1976. 39 p. ; 26 cm. Reprint of the 1943 ed. published by the Saturday review of literature, New York. Contents.Contents.—Benet, W. R. My brother Steve.—Farrar, J. For the record. Bibliography: p. 37-39. [PS3503.E5325Z53 1976] 76-52937 ISBN 0-8414-1773-3 lib. bdg. : 10.00
1. Benet, Stephen Vincent, 1898-1943—Biography—Addresses, essays, lectures. 2. Benet, Stephen Vincent, 1898-1943—Dramatic production—Addresses, essays, lectures. 3. Authors, American—20th century—Biography—Addresses, essays, lectures. I. Farrar, John Chipman, 1896- For the record. 1976. BIP

Benet, William Rose, 1886-1950—Biography—Youth—Juvenile literature.

BENET, Laura. 810'.9'0052 B
When William Rose, Stephen Vincent, and I were young / Laura Benet, illustrated with photos. New York : Dodd, Mead, c1976. lll p. : ill., ; 24 cm. Includes index. An author reminisces about her childhood and that of her two famous brothers. [PS3503.E528Z52] 920 75-38366 ISBN 0-396-07289-5 : 5.95
1. Benet, Laura—Biography—Youth—Juvenile literature. 2. Benet, William Rose, 1886-1950—Biography—Youth—Juvenile literature. 3. Benet, Stephen Vincent, 1898-1943—Biography—Youth—Juvenile literature. I. Title. BIP

Benezet, Anthony, 1713-1784.

ARMISTEAD, Wilson, 361'.924 B
1819?-1868.
Anthony Benezet; from the original Memoir. Rev., with additions, by Wilson Armistead. Freeport, N.Y., Books for Libraries Press, 1971. xv, 144 p. 23 cm. (Black heritage library collection) Revision of R. Vaux' Memoirs of the life of Anthony Benezet. Reprint of the 1859 ed. Includes bibliographical references. [HV28.B4A73 1971] 77-152916 ISBN 0-8369-8760-8
1. Benezet, Anthony, 1713-1784. I. Vaux, Roberts, 1786-1836. Memoirs of the life of Anthony Benezet. II. Title. III. Series.

VAUX, Roberts, 1786-1836. 370.924
Memoirs of the life of Anthony Benezet. New York, B. Franklin [1969] v, 136 p. 19 cm. (American classics in history and social science 88) (Burt Franklin research and source works series 384.) Reprint of the 1817 ed. Title on spine: Memoirs of Anthony Benezet. [LA2317.B37V3 1969] 72-80241
1. Benezet, Anthony, 1713-1784. BIP

Bengal—Biography.

SANYAL, Ram Gopal. 920'.054'14
A general biography of Bengal celebrities, both living and dead / Ram Gopal Sanyal ; edited by Swapan Majumdar. Rddhi ed. Calcutta : Rddhi, 1976. xvi, 183 p. ; 23 cm. Title on spine: Bengal celebrities. Includes a reproduction of the t.p. of the original ed., first published by U. C. Chuckerbutty, Calcutta, 1889. Includes index. [DS485.B395S25 1976] 77-901694 Rs30.00
1. Bengal—Biography. I. Title.

Benjamin, Judah Philip, 1811-1884.

GOODHART, Arthur 340'.57'0922 B
Lehman, Sir, 1891-
Five Jewish lawyers of the common law [by] Arthur L. Goodhart. With a new pref. to this ed. and a suppl. on Mr. Justice Felix Frankfurter. Freeport, N.Y., Books for Libraries Press [1971, c1949] vii, 81 p. 23 cm. (Biography index reprint series) Includes bibliograhical references. [KF299.J4G65 1971] 79-148212 ISBN 0-8369-8059-X
1. Benjamin, Judah Philip, 1811-1884. 2. Jessel, George, Sir, 1824-1883. 3. Brandeis, Louis Dembitz, 1856-1941. 4. Reading, Rufus Daniel Isaacs, 1st Marquis of, 1860-1935. 5. Cardozo, Benjamin Nathan, 1870-1938. I. Title. BIP

MEADE, Robert 973.7'13'0924 B
Douthat, 1903-
Judah P. Benjamin : Confederate statesman / Robert Douthat Meade. New York : Arno Press, 1975, c1943. ix, 432 p., [3] leaves of plates : ill. ; 23 cm. (The Modern Jewish experience) Reprint of the ed. published by Oxford University Press, New York. Includes index. Bibliography: p. 415-417. [E467.1.B4M4 1975] 74-29506 ISBN 0-405-06733-X : 27.00
1. Benjamin, Judah Philip, 1811-1884. I. Title. II. Series. BIP

NEIMAN, Simon I 1904- 923.273
Judah Benjamin. With a foreword by Otto Eisenschiml. Indianapolis, Bobbs-Merrill [1963] 220 p. 22 cm. [E467.1.B4N4] 61-15540
1. Benjamin, Judah Philip, 1811-1884. I. Title.

Benjamin, Mary.

ANDERSON, Peggy. 610.73'092'4 B
Nurse / by Peggy Anderson. New York : St. Martin's Press, [1978] p. cm. [RT37.B34A63] 78-3994 ISBN 0-312-58021-5 : 10.95
1. Benjamin, Mary. 2. Nurses—United States—Biography. I. Title.

ANDERSON, Peggy. 610.73'092'4 B
Nurse / by Peggy Anderson. New York : Berkley Publishing Corp., 1979, c1978. 344p. ; 18 cm. [RT37.B34A63] pbk. : 2.50
1. Benjamin, Mary. 2. Nurses — United States — Biography. I. Title. L.C. card no. for 1978 St. Martin's Press ed.: 78-3994 BIP

Benjrox, Benjamin Phillips, 1886-

OSLIN, James Calvin, 1886- 920
Benben. [Rev. ed.] Boston, Christopher Pub. House [1952] 286 p. 21 cm. First ed. published in 1948 under title: Benbenjrox. [CT275.B56215O8 1952] 52-4598
1. Benjrox, Benjamin Phillips, 1886- I. Title.

Bennehan family.

SANDERS, 975.6'565'030924 B
Charles Richard, 1904-
The Cameron Plantation in central North Carolina (1776-1973) and its founder Richard Bennehan / by Charles Richard Sanders. Durham, N.C. : Sanders, 1974. viii, 79 p., [1] leaf of plates : ill. ; 28 cm. Includes bibliographical references and index. [F258.B45S26] 75-326797
1. Bennehan, Richard, 1743-1825. 2. Bennehan family. 3. North Carolina. University. 4. Cameron Plantation, N.C. I. Title: The Cameron Plantation in central North Carolina (1776-1973) ...

Bennehan, Richard, 1743-1825.

SANDERS, 975.6'565'030924 B
Charles Richard, 1904-
The Cameron Plantation in central North Carolina (1776-1973) and its founder Richard Bennehan / by Charles Richard Sanders. Durham, N.C. : Sanders, 1974. viii, 79 p., [1] leaf of plates : ill. ; 28 cm. Includes bibliographical references and index. [F258.B45S26] 75-326797
1. Bennehan, Richard, 1743-1825. 2. Bennehan family. 3. North Carolina. University. 4. Cameron Plantation, N.C. I. Title: The Cameron Plantation in central North Carolina (1776-1973) ...

Bennett, Abram Elting, 1898-

BENNETT, Abram 616.8'092'4 B
Elting, 1898-
Fifty years in neurology and psychiatry. New York, Intercontinental Medical Book Corp. [1972] ix, 166 p. ports. 23 cm. Includes bibliographies. [R154.B44A3] 72-86853 ISBN 0-913258-03-2 9.75
1. Bennett, Abram Elting, 1898- 2. Neuropsychiatry—History. I. Title. BIP

Bennett, Arnold, 1867-1931.

BARKER, Dudley 823.912
Writer by trade: a portrait of Arnold Bennett. [1st Amer. ed.] New York, Atheneum, 1966. 260p. illus., ports. 22cm. Bibl. [PR6003.E6Z556 1966a] 66-23025 6.50
1. Bennett. Arnold. 1867-1931. I. Title.

BENNETT, Arnold, 828'.9'1203 B
1867-1931.
The journal of Arnold Bennett. Plainview, N.Y., Books for Libraries Press [1974, c1932-33] p. cm. (The collected works of Arnold Bennett) Reprint of the ed. published by Viking Press, New York. Contents.Contents.—v. 1. 1896-1910.—v. 2. 1911-1920.—v. 3. 1921-1928. [PR6003.E6Z4 1974] 74-5371 ISBN 0-518-19118-4 (v. 1)
1. Bennett, Arnold, 1867-1931. BIP

BENNETT, Arnold, 828'.9'1203 B
1867-1931.
The journals; selected and edited by Frank Swinnerton. Harmondsworth, Penguin, 1971. 599 p. 18 cm. (Penguin modern classics) The Journals originally published London, Cassell, 1930-1933. "Now published with the addition of Journal volume 6, newly discovered, covering the period 21 September 1906-18 July 1907, and Florentine journal, covering the period 1 April 1910 - 25 May 1910." [PR6003.E6Z45 1971] 70-874485 ISBN 0-14-003284-3 £0.75
1. Bennett, Arnold, 1867-1931. I. Swinnerton, Frank Arthur, 1884-

POUND, Reginald. 928.2
Arnold Bennett, a biography. [1st American ed.] New York, Harcourt, Brace [1953] 385 p. illus. 22 cm. [PR6003.E6Z784 1953] 52-9859
1. Bennett, Arnold, 1867-1931. BIP

Bennett, Arnold, 1867-1931—Biography.

BENNETT, Arnold, 823'.9'12 B
1867-1931.
The truth about an author. New ed., with pref. Plainview, N.Y., Books for Libraries Press [1974, c1911] p. cm. (The Collected works of Arnold Bennett) Reprint of the ed. published by G. H. Doran, New York. [PR6003.E6T7 1974] 74-17055 ISBN 0-518-19165-6
1. Bennett, Arnold, 1867-1931—Biography. I. Title. BIP

BENNETT, Dorothy 823'.9'12 B
Cheston.
Arnold Bennett: a portrait done at home, together with 170 letters from A. B. Plainview, N.Y., Books for Libraries Press [1974, c1935] p. cm. (The collected works of Arnold Bennett) Reprint of the ed. published by C. Kendall & W. Sharp, New York. [PR6003.E6Z56 1974] 74-5388 ISBN 0-518-19083-8
1. Bennett, Arnold, 1867-1931—Biography. 2. Bennett, Arnold, 1867-1931—Correspondence. I. Bennett, Arnold, 1867-1931.

POUND, Reginald. 823'.9'12 B
Arnold Bennett, a biography. Port Washington, N.Y., Kennikat Press [1972] x, 385 p. illus. 22 cm. Reprint of the 1952 ed. [PR6003.E6Z784 1972] 76-153239 ISBN 0-8046-1549-7
1. Bennett, Arnold, 1867-1931—Biography. I. Title.

SWINNERTON, Frank 823'.9'12 B
Arthur, 1884-
Arnold Bennett : a last word / Frank Swinnerton. 1st ed. in the USA. Garden City, N.Y. : Doubleday, 1978. 120 p., [4] leaves of plates : ill. ; 22 cm. Includes index. [PR6003.E6Z816 1978b] 78-8204 ISBN 0-385-14545-4 : 7.95
1. Bennett, Arnold, 1867-1931—Biography. 2. Authors, English—20th century—Biography. BIP

Bennett, Forster.

CRAPANZANO, Vincent, 970.3 B
1939-
The fifth world of Forster Bennett; portrait of a Navaho. New York, Viking Press [1972] vii, 245 p. 23 cm. Includes bibliographical references. [E99.N3B463 1972] 77-184547 ISBN 0-670-31220-7 7.95
1. Bennett, Forster. 2. Navaho Indians. I. Title.

Bennett, Henry Gordon, 1887-1962.

LEGG, Frank, 1906- 923.594
The Gordon Bennett story [Sydney] Angus & Robertson [San Francisco, Tri-Ocean, c.1965*Cx, 309p. illus., ports. 25cm. x, 309p. illus., ports. 25cm. [U55.B44L4] 65-8888 6.30
1. Bennett, Henry Gordon, 1887-1962. 2. Australia. Army—Biog. I. Title.

Bennett, Henry H.

RATH, Sara. 770'.92'4 B
Pioneer photographer, Wisconsin's H. H. Bennett / by Sara Rath ; photos. selected by Rick Smith. Madison, Wis. : Tamarack Press, c1979. p. cm. Includes index. Bibliography: p. [TR140.B443R37] 79-9502 ISBN 0-915024-23-3 : 14.95
1. Bennett, Henry H. 2. Photographers—Wisconsin—Wisconsin Dells—Biography. 3. Wisconsin Dells, Wis.—Biography. I. Bennett, Henry H. II. Title.

Bennett, Hugh Hammond, 1881-

BRINK, Wellington, 1895- 926.3
Big Hugh, the father of soil conservation; with a pref. by Louis Bromfield. New York, Macmillan, 1951. xii, 167 p. port. 21 cm. Bibliography: p. 164-167. [S417.B36B7] 51-256
1. Bennett, Hugh Hammond, 1881- 2. Soil conservation—U.S. I. Title.

Bennett, James Gordon, 1841-1918.

O'CONNOR, Richard, 1915- 920.5
The scandalous Mr. Bennett. [1st ed.] Garden City, N. Y., Doubleday, 1962. 335 p. illus. 22 cm. Includes bibliography. [PN4874.B41O3] 62-11314
1. Bennett, James Gordon, 1841-1918. 2. New York herald. I. Title.

Bennett, Joan,

BENNETT, Joan, 791.43'028'0924 B
1910-
The Bennett playbill, by Joan Bennett and Lois Kibbee. [1st ed.] New York, Holt, Rinehart and Winston [1970] xi, 332 p. ports. 22 cm. [PN2287.B432A3] 78-80351 6.95
I. Kibbee, Lois, joint author. II. Title.

Bennett, John G

*BENNETT, John G 922.919
Witness the autobiography of John G. Bennett. Tucson, Arizona, Omen Press, [1974] lx., 380 p. illus. 21 cm. [BP605.B38] ISBN 0-912358-48-3 5.95 (pbk.)
I. Title.

Bennett, John Godolphin,

BENNETT, John Godolphin, 922.912
1897-
Witness; the story of a search. New York, Dharma Book Co. [1962] 381p. illus. 21cm. Autobiographical. [BP605.B38] 62-51805
I. Title.

Bennett, Robert LaFollette, 1912- — Juvenile literature.

NELSON, Mary 970'.004'97 B
Carroll.
Robert Bennett / by Mary Carroll Nelson. Minneapolis : Dillon Press, c1976. 74 p. : ill. ; 24 cm. (The Story of an American Indian) A biography of the Oneida Indian who became head of the Bureau of Indian Affairs. [E99.O45N44] 92 75-43539 ISBN 0-87518-108-2 : 4.95
1. Bennett, Robert LaFollette, 1912- — Juvenile literature. 2. United States. Bureau of Indian Affairs—Juvenile literature. 3. Oneida Indians—Juvenile literature. I. Title. BIP

Bennett, Simmons, 1837-1924.

HEBEL, Ianthe 975.9'21'040924
Bond, 1884-
Captain Simmons Bennett, an early pioneer, and the Halifax River. Daytona Beach, Fla. [1967?] 5 l. 29 cm. [F317.V7H395] 75-317117
1. Bennett, Simmons, 1837-1924. 2. Halifax River region, Fla.—History. I. Title.

Benny, Jack, 1894-1974.

BENNY, Mary 791.4'092'4 B
Livingstone.
Jack Benny / Mary Livingstone Benny and Hilliard Marks, with Marcia Borie. 1st ed. Garden City, N.Y. : Doubleday, 1978. xi, 322 p., [24] leaves of plates : ill. ; 22 cm. Includes index. [PN2287.B4325B4] 77-80902 ISBN 0-385-12497-X : 10.00
1. Benny, Jack, 1894-1974. 2. Comedians—United States—Biography. I. Marks, Hilliard, joint author. II. Borie, Marcia, joint author.

FEIN, Irving A., 791.4'092'4 B
1911-
Jack Benny : an intimate biography / Irving A. Fein ; introd. by George Burns. New York : Putnam, c1976. 319 p., [8] leaves of plates : ill. ; 22 cm. Includes index. [PN2287.B4325F4] 75-30975 ISBN 0-399-11640-0 : 8.95
1. Benny, Jack, 1894-1974.

FEIN, Irving A., 791.4'092'4 B
1911-
Jack Benny : an intimate biography / Irving A. Fein ; introd. by George Burns. Boston : G. K. Hall, 1976. 2 v. (xvii, 642 p.) ; 24 cm. "Published in large print." [PN2287.B4325F4 1976b] 76-16091 16.95
1. Benny, Jack, 1894-1974. 2. Sight-saving books. BIP

JOSEFSBERG, Milt, 791.4'0924 B
1911-
The Jack Benny show / Milt Josefsberg. New Rochelle, N.Y. : Arlington House, 1977. 496 p. : ill. ; 24 cm. Includes index. [PN2287.B4325J6] 76-56172 ISBN 0-87000-347-X : 12.95
1. Benny, Jack, 1894-1974. 2. Comedians—United States—Biography. I. Title. BIP

Benois, Alexandre, 1870-1960.

BENOIS, Alexandre, 792.8'0947
1870-1960.
Reminiscences of the Russian ballet / by Alexandre Benois ; translated by Mary Britnieva. New York : Da Capo Press, 1977. xiv, 414 p., [17] leaves of plates : ill. ; 23 cm. (Da Capo series in dance) Translation of Vospominaniia o balete. Reprint of the 1941 ed. published by Putnam, London. Includes index. [GV1785.B39A3813 1977] 77-7791 ISBN 0-306-77426-7 lib.bdg. : 29.50
1. Benois, Alexandre, 1870-1960. 2. Artists—Russia—Biography. 3. Ballets russes de Serge de Diaghilew. 4. Dancing—Russia—History. 5. Ballet—History. I. Title. BIP

Benserade, Isaac de, 1613-1671—Biography.

SILIN, Charles 841'.4 B
Intervale, 1897-
Benserade and his ballets de cour / by Charles I. Silin. 1st ed. New York : AMS Press, 1978. 435 p. ; 23 cm. (Music and theatre in France in the 17th and 18th centuries) Reprint of the 1940 ed. published by Johns Hopkins Press, Baltimore, which was issued as Extra volume 15 of The Johns Hopkins studies in Romance literatures and languages. Originally presented as the author's thesis, Johns Hopkins University, 1934. Includes index. Bibliography: p. 405-421. [PQ1715.S5 1978] 76-43940 ISBN 0-404-60195-2 : 30.00
1. Benserade, Isaac de, 1613-1671—Biography. 2. Benserade, Isaac de, 1613-1671. Metamorphoser d'Ovide. 3. Authors, French—17th century—Biography. 4. Ballet. 5. France—Court and courtiers. I. Title. II. Series. III. Series: The Johns Hopkins studies in Romance literatures and languages : Extra volume ; 15. BIP

Benson, Elmer Austin, 1895-

SHIELDS, James M. 977.6'05'0924 B
Mr. Progressive; a biography of Elmer Austin Benson, by James M. Shields. Minneapolis, Denison [1971] 346 p. illus., facsims., ports. 24 cm. Bibliography: p. [8] [HX84.B38S34] 71-160735 6.95
1. Benson, Elmer Austin, 1895- 2. Minnesota—Politics and government—1858-1950. I. Title.

Benson, Francis Robert, Sir 1858-1939.

BENSON, Francis 792'.028'0924 B
Robert, Sir, 1858-1939.
My memoirs. New York, B. Blom, 1971. ix, 322 p. ports. 21 cm. Reprint of the 1930 ed. [PN2598.B56A3 1971] 70-91473
1. Actors—England—Correspondence, reminiscences, etc. I. Title.

TREWIN, John Courtenay, 927.92
1908-
Benson and the Bensonians. Foreword by Dorothy Green. London, Barrie & Rockliff [1960] 302p. illus. 23cm. [PN2598.B56T7] 61-430 7.50
1. Benson, Francis Robert, Sir 1858-1939. 2. Shakespeare, William—Stage history—1800- I. Title.
Available from Humanities in New York.

Benson, George, 1699-1762.

TRAVIS, George, 907'.2'024 S
1741-1797.
Letters to Edward Gibson, esq., 1785. New York, Garland Pub., 1974. p. cm. (The Life & times of seven major British writers. Gibboniana 13) Reprint of the 1785 ed. printed by C. F. and J. Rivington, London. [DG206.G5G52 vol. 13] [BT112] 231 74-14851 ISBN 0-8240-1349-2 22.00
1. Gibbon, Edward, 1737-1794. History of the decline and fall of the Roman empire. 2. Benson, George, 1699-1762. 3. Newton, Isaac, Sir, 1642-1727. 4. Bible. N.T. 1 John V, 7—Criticism, Textual. 5. Trinity—Biblical teaching. I. Gibbon, Edward, 1737-1794. II. Title. III. Series: Gibboniana 13.

Benson, Simon, 1851-1942.

ALLEN, Alice 634.9'82'0924 B
Benson, 1881-
Simon Benson: Northwest lumber king. Photos. compiled by Benson Allen. [1st ed.] Portland, Or., Binfords & Mort, 1971. 144 p. illus. 29 cm. [SD129.B42A64] 77-157143 ISBN 0-8323-0047-0 8.95
1. Benson, Simon, 1851-1942. 2. Lumbering—Northwest, Pacific. I. Title.

Bent, William, 1809-1889.

GARST, Doris Shannon, 923.973
1899-
William Bent and his Adobe empire. New York, Messner [1957] 192p. 22cm. (The Julian Messner shelf of biographies) Includes bibliography. [F782.A7G3] 57-6588
1. Bent, William, 1809-1889. 2. Bent's Fort, Colo. I. Title.

Bentham, George, 1800-1884.

JACKSON, Benjamin 581'.092'4 B
Daydon, 1846-1927.
George Bentham / by B. Daydon Jackson. New York : AMS Press, 1976. xii, 292 p. : port. ; 19 cm. Reprint of the 1906 ed. published by J. M. Dent, London and Dutton, New York, in series: English men of science. "EMS 5." Includes index. Bibliography: p. 269-284. [QK31.B5J2 1976] 78-170834 ISBN 0-404-07895-8 : 12.00
1. Bentham, George, 1800-1884. 2. Botanists—England—Biography. I. Series: English men of science. BIP

Bentham, Jeremy, 1748-1832.

ATKINSON, Charles Milner, 192 B
1854-1920.
Jeremy Bentham; his life and work. Westport, Conn., Greenwood Press [1970] xii, 247 p. 23 cm. Reprint of the 1905 ed. Includes bibliographical references. [B1574.B34A7 1970] 78-98208
1. Bentham, Jeremy, 1748-1832. BIP

ATKINSON, Charles Milner, 192 B
1854-1920.
Jeremy Bentham; his life and work. New York, A. M. Kelley, 1969. xii, 247 p. 22 cm. (Reprints of economic classics) Reprint of the 1905 ed. Bibliographical footnotes. [B1574.B34A7 1969] 68-55464
1. Bentham, Jeremy, 1748-1832. I. Title. BIP

BAUMGARDT, David, 1890- 192
Bentham and the ethics of today, with Bentham manuscripts hitherto unpublished. New York, Octagon Books, 1966. xiv, 584 p. 25 cm. Reprint of the 1952 ed. Bibliographical footnotes. [BJ604.B4B3 1966] 66-28381
1. Bentham, Jeremy, 1748-1832. 2. Ethics. I. Title.

EVERETT, Charles Warren, 192
1895-
Jeremy Bentham [New York, Dell c.1966] 256p. 19cm. (Laurel great lives and thought, 4211) Bibl. [B1574.B34E83] 66-997 .75 pap.,
1. Bentham, Jeremy, 1748-1832. I. Title.

PHILLIPSON, Coleman, 343'.0924
1878-
Three criminal law reformers: Beccaria, Bentham, Romilly. Montclair, N.J., P. Smith, 1970. xvi, 344 p. 22 cm. (Patterson Smith reprint series in criminology, law enforcement, and social problems Publication no. 113) Reprint of the 1923 ed. Bibliography: p. xv-xvi. [LAW] 77-17157
1. Beccaria, Cesare Bonesana, marchese di, 1738-1794. 2. Beccaria, Cesare Bonesana, marchese di, 1738-1794. Dei delitti e delle pene. 3. Bentham, Jeremy, 1748-1832. 4. Romilly, Samuel, Sir, 1757-1818. 5. Criminal law. 6. Criminal procedure. 7. Law reform. 8. Punishment. 9. Capital punishment. 0. Crime and criminals. I. Title. BIP

Bentinck, George, Lord, 1802-1848.

BEACONSFIELD, 828'.8'09 S
Benjamin Disraeli, 1st Earl of, 1804-1881.
The young duke : "a moral tale, though gay" / by Benjamin Disraeli, Earl of Beaconsfield. New York : AMS Press, 1976. 2 v. : ill. ; 19 cm. (The Works of Benjamin Disraeli, Earl of Beaconsfield ; v. 3-4) Vol. 2 also includes the author's Ixion in heaven, The rise of Iskander, and Biography of Lord George Bentinck. Reprint of the 1904 ed. published by M. W. Dunne, New York. [PR4080.F76 vol. 3-4] [PR4081.5] 823'.8 76-12450 ISBN 0-404-08800-7 (set)
1. Bentinck, George, Lord, 1802-1848. I. Title.

Bentinck, William Henry Cavendish, Lord, 1774-1839.

THE Correspondence 954.03'1'0924
of Lord William Cavendish Bentinck, Governor-General of India, 1828-1835 / edited with an introd. by C. H. Philips. Oxford ; New York : Oxford University Press, 1977. 2 v. ; 24 cm. "Published for the School of Oriental and African Studies." Contents.Contents.—v. 1. 1828-1831.—v. 2. 1832-1835. Includes bibliographical references and index. [DS475.8.C67] 78-300067 ISBN 0-19-713571-4 : 115.00
1. Bentinck, William Henry Cavendish, Lord, 1774-1839. 2. India—Politics and government—19th century—Sources. 3. India—Governors—Correspondence. I. Bentinck, William Henry Cavendish, Lord, 1774-1839. II. Philips, Cyril Henry, 1912- III. London. University. School of Oriental and African Studies.

Bentley, Phyllis Eleanor,

BENTLEY, Phyllis Eleanor, 928.2
1894-
"O dreams, O destinations"; an autobiography. New York, Macmillan, 1962. 272 p. illus. 22 cm. [PR6003.E725Z5] 62-10634
I. Title.

Bentley, Richard, 1662-1742.

JEBB, Richard 828'.5'09
Claverhouse, Sir, 1841-1905.
Bentley. New York, AMS Press [1968] xi, 224 p. 22 cm. (English men of letters)

Reprint of the 1889 ed. [PA85.B4J4 1968] 68-58384
1. Bentley, Richard, 1662-1742. **BIP**

Bentley, Walter Edmund, 1864-1962.

BURGGRAAFF, Winfield. 283'.092'4 B
Walter Edmund Bentley: actor, priest, missioner, 1864-1962, founder of the Actors' Church Alliance. [Staten Island? N.Y., 1970?] 31 p. illus. 23 cm. [PN2287.B4327B8] 72-178356
1. Bentley, Walter Edmund, 1864-1962. 2. Actors' Church Alliance of America.

Bentley, Walter Owen,

BENTLEY, Walter Owen, 1888- 338.7'62'920924 B
My life and my cars [by] W. O. Bentley. [1st American ed.] South Brunswick [N.J.] A. S. Barnes [1969, c1967] 239 p. illus., ports. (part col.) 22 cm. [HD9710.G72B4 1969] 69-14889 5.95
I. Title.

Bentley, William, 1759-1819.

DR. Bentley's Salem : 974.4'5 B
diary of a town : a special exhibition, 23 June-30 October 1977, Essex Institute, Salem, Massachusetts. Salem, Mass. : Essex Institute, c1977. vi, 86 p., [8] leaves of plates : ill. ; 23 cm. "Checklist [i.e. catalog] of the exhibition": p. 70-86. Includes bibliographical references. [F74.S1B4633] 77-366805 ISBN 0-88389-069-0 : 4.00
1. Bentley, William, 1759-1819. The diary of William Bentley—Exhibitions. 2. Bentley, William, 1759-1819—Exhibitions. 3. Salem, Mass.—History—Exhibitions. 4. Unitarian churches—Clergy—Biography—Exhibitions. 5. Clergy—Massachusetts—Salem—Biography—Exhibitions. I. Essex Institute, Salem, Mass.

Bentley, Wilson Alwyn, 1865-1931—Juvenile literature.

STODDARD, Gloria May, 1942- 551.5'7841
Snowflake Bentley : man of science, man of God / written by Gloria May Stoddard. St. Louis : Concordia Pub. House, c1979. 128 p. : ill. ; 23 cm. Bibliography: p. 123-128. A biography of a self-taught scientist who photographed thousands of individual snowflakes in order to study their unique formations. [QC929.S7S76] 92 79-11525 ISBN 0-570-03620-8 : 3.95
1. Bentley, Wilson Alwyn, 1865-1931—Juvenile literature. 2. Snow crystals—Juvenile literature. 3. Scientists—United States—Biography—Juvenile literature. 4. Photography of water—Juvenile literature. I. Title.

Benton family.

BENTON, Jesse W., 1898- 929.2'0973
Portrait; Joseph Pinkney Benton 1777-1966 [by] Jesse W. Benton, Sr. Danville, Va. [1967] ix, 103 p. illus., maps, ports. 24 cm. [CS71.B48 1967] 73-290765
1. Benton family. I. Title.

Benton, Joseph, 1898-

BENTON, Joseph, 1898- 782.1'092'4 B
Oklahoma tenor; musical memories of Giuseppe Bentonelli, by Joseph Benton. Foreword by Eva Turner. Introd. by B. A. Nugent. [1st ed.] Norman, University of Oklahoma Press [1973] xiii, 150 p. illus. 20 cm. [ML420.B344A3] 73-19393 2.95 (pbk.)
1. Benton, Joseph, 1898- 2. Musicians—Correspondence, reminiscences, etc. I. Title.

Benton, Thomas Hart, 1782-1858.

CHAMBERS, William Nisbet, 1916- 923.273
Old Bullion Benton, Senator from the new West: Thomas Hart Benton, 1782-1858. [1st ed.] Boston, Little, Brown [1956] 517 p. illus. 22 cm. (An Atlantic Monthly Press book) Includes bibliography. [E340.B4C5] 56-9067
1. Benton, Thomas Hart, 1782-1858. I. Title.

CHAMBERS, William Nisbet, 1916- 973.5'0924 B
Old Bullion Benton, Senator from the new West: Thomas Hart Benton, 1782-1858. New York, Russell & Russell [1970, c1956] xv, 517 p. port. 23 cm. Bibliography: p. [487]-503. [E340.B4C5 1970] 70-102476
1. Benton, Thomas Hart, 1782-1858. I. Title.

MEIGS, William Montgomery, 1852-1929. 973.5'0924 B
The life of Thomas Hart Benton. New York, Da Capo Press, 1970. 535 p. illus., ports. 23 cm. (The American scene) Reprint of the 1904 ed. Includes bibliographical references. [E340.B4M5 1970] 71-126599
1. Benton, Thomas Hart, 1782-1858. I. Title. **BIP**

ROOSEVELT, Theodore, Pres. U.S., 1858-1919. 973.5'0924 B
Thomas H. Benton. Boston, Houghton-Mifflin. [New York, AMS Press, 1972] vii, 344 p. illus. 19 cm. (American statesmen, v. 23) First published in 1887 under title: Life of Thomas Hart Benton. Reprint of the 1899 ed. [E340.B4R77 1972] 79-128962 ISBN 0-404-50873-1
1. Benton, Thomas Hart, 1782-1858. I. Title. II. Series. **BIP**

ROOSEVELT, Theodore, Pres. U.S., 1858-1919. 973.5'0924 B
Thomas Hart Benton. Boston, Houghton Mifflin, 1894. St. Clair Shores, Mich., Scholarly Press, 1970. vi, 372 p. 22 cm. (American statesmen [v. 23]) [E340.B4R77 1970] 78-108534
1. Benton, Thomas Hart, 1782-1858. I. Title. II. Series.

ROOSEVELT, Theodore, Pres. U.S., 1858-1919. 973.5'0924 B
Thomas Hart Benton. New York, Haskell House, 1968. vi, 372 p. 23 cm. Reprint of the 1887 ed., published under title: Life of Thomas Hart Benton. "Haskell House catalogue item #275." [E340.B4R77 1968] 68-24995
1. Benton, Thomas Hart, 1782-1858. **BIP**

SMITH, Elbert B 923.273
Magnificent Missourian; the life of Thomas Hart Benton.[1st ed.] Philadelphia, Lippincott, 1958 [c1957] 351 p. 22 cm. Bibliographical references included in "Notes" (p. 327-344) [E340.B4S56] 57-12384
1. Benton, Thomas Hart, 1782-1858. I. Title.

SMITH, Elbert B. 973.5'092'4 B
Magnificent Missourian; the life of Thomas Hart Benton, by Elbert B. Smith. Westport, Conn., Greenwood Press [1973, c1957] 351 p. 22 cm. Reprint of the ed. published by Lippincott, Philadelphia. Includes bibliographical references. [E340.B4S56 1973] 73-7459 ISBN 0-8371-6933-X 13.75
1. Benton, Thomas Hart, 1782-1858. I. Title. **BIP**

Benton, Thomas Hart, 1889-1975.

BENTON, Thomas Hart, 1889- 759.13 B
An American in art; a professional and technical autobiography. Lawrence, University Press of Kansas [1969] 197 p. illus. 26 cm. Contents.Contents.—An American in art.—Selected paintings by Thomas Hart Benton (p. [79]-144)—American regionalism; a personal history of the movement. [ND237.B47A28] 69-16060 10.00
1. Artists—Correspondence, reminiscences, etc. I. Title.

BENTON, Thomas Hart, 1889- 759.13 B
An artist in America. 3d [rev. ed.] Columbia, University of Missouri Press [1968] xxii, 369 p. illus. 24 cm. [ND237.B47A3 1968] 68-20096
1. Artists—Correspondence, reminiscences, etc. 2. United States—Description and travel—1920-1940. I. Title. **BIP**

YEO, Wilma. 759.13 B
Maverick with a paintbrush : Thomas Hart Benton / by Wilma Yeo & Helen K. Cook. 1st ed. Garden City, N.Y. : Doubleday, 1977. 125 p., [4] leaves of plates : ill. ; 25 cm. [ND237.B47Y46] 73-11639 ISBN 0-385-00421-4 : 6.95. ISBN 0-385-08017-4 lib.bdg. : 7.90
1. Benton, Thomas Hart, 1889-1975. 2. Painters—United States—Biography. I. Cook, Helen K., joint author. II. Title. **BIP**

Benton, William, 1900-

HYMAN, Sidney. 030.924 B
The lives of William Benton. Chicago, University of Chicago Press [1969] xviii, 625 p. illus., ports. 24 cm. [E748.B337H9] 72-88231 10.00
1. Benton, William, 1900- I. Title. **BIP**

Bentwich, Norman De Mattos,

BENTWICH, Norman De Mattos, 1883- 923.25693
My seventy-seven years an account of my life and times, 1883-1960. [1st ed.] Philadelphia, Jewish Publication Society of America, 1961. 344p. 22cm. [DS125.3.B38A3] 61-11704
I. Title.

Benzi, Ugo, 1376-1439.

LOCKWOOD, Dean Putnam, 1883- 926.1
Ugo Benzi, medieval philosopher and physician, 1376-1439. [Chicago] University of Chicago Press [1951] xvi, 441 p. 24 cm. Bibliographical footnotes. [R147.B4L6] 51-10990
1. Benzi, Ugo, 1376-1439. I. Title.

Benziger, August, 1867-1955.

BENZIGER, Marieli G 927.5
August Benziger, portrait painter, by Marieli Benziger, with the assistance of Rita Benziger. Glendale, Calif., A. H. Clark Co., 1958. 485p. illus., ports., facsims. 27cm. Bibliography: p. p.[471]-474. [ND853.B4B4] 58-11787
1. Benziger, August, 1867-1955. I. Title.

Berardelli, Alessandro, d. 1920.

SACCO, Nicola, 1891-1927, defendant. 343'.5'230922
The Sacco-Vanzetti case; transcript of the record of the trial of Nicola Sacco and Bartolomeo Vanzetti in the courts of Massachusetts and subsequent proceedings 1920-7. Prefatory essay by William O. Douglas. 2d ed. Mamaroneck, N.Y., P. P. Appel, 1969. 5 v. (L, 5621 p.) illus., fold. plans, ports. 27 cm. Sacco and Vanzetti were tried at Dedham, in the Superior Court of Massachusetts for Norfolk County, May 31-July 14, 1921, for the murder of F. A. Parmenter and A. Berardelli at South Braintree, Apr. 15, 1920. An explanatory title page, not included in the paging, introduces the various sections of the text. [KF224.S2D6 1969] 68-56904
1. Parmenter, Frederick Albert, 1874-1920. 2. Berardelli, Alessandro, d. 1920. 3. Cox, Alfred Elmer, 1887?- 4. Sacco-Vanzetti case. I. Vanzetti, Bartolomeo, 1888-1927, defendant. II. Massachusetts. Superior Court (Norfolk Co.) III. Massachusetts. Supreme Judicial Court. IV. Massachusetts. Superior Court (Plymouth Co.) **BIP**

Beraud-Villars, Jean Marcel Eugene.

BERAUD-VILLARS, Jean Marcel Eugene. 940.4'49'44 B
Notes of a lost pilot, by Jean Beraud Villars. Translated and edited, with foreword and notes, by Stanley J. Pincetl, Jr., & Ernest Marchand. Illus. by Charles Faust. [Hamden, Conn.] Archon Books, 1975. 285 p. illus. 23 cm. Translation of Notes d'un pilote disparu. [D603.B4713] 74-2112 ISBN 0-208-01437-3
1. Beraud-Villars, Jean Marcel Eugene. 2. European War, 1914-1918—Aerial operations, French. 3. European War, 1914-1918—Personal narratives, French. I. Title. **BIP**

Berberova, Nina Nikolaevna.

BERBEROVA, Nina Nikolaevna. 891.7'3'42 B
The italics are mine [by] Nina Berberova. Authorized translation by Philippe Radley. [1st ed.] New York, Harcourt, Brace & World [1969] 606 p. plan, ports. 24 cm. Autobiographical. [PG3476.B425Z513] 68-12564
I. Title.

Berchmans, Jan, Saint, 1599-1621.

ERNEST, Brother, 1897- 922.2493
A story of Saint John Berchmans. Illus. by James O. Christiansen. Notre Aame, Ind., Dujarie Press [1957] unpaged. illus. 21cm. [BX4700.B4E7] 57-30286
1. Berchmans, Jan, Saint, 1590-1621. I. Title.

FOLEY, Albert Sidney, 1912- 282'.092'4 B
A modern Galahad, St. John Berchmans, by Albert S. Foley. Mobile, Spring Hill College Press [1973] xvii, 241 p. illus. 18 cm. Reprint of the 1937 ed. published by The Bruce Pub. Co., Milwaukee in series: Science and culture series. "Berchmansiana": p. 231-235. [BX4700.B4F6 1973] 73-176466
1. Berchmans, Jan, Saint, 1599-1621. I. Title.

ROBERTO, Brother, 1927- 922.2493
A crown for the schoolboy; a story of St. John Berchmans, s. j. Illus. by Thekla Ofria. Notre Dame, Ind., Dujarie Press [1957] 95p. illus. 24cm. [BX4700.B4R6] 58-258
1. Berchmans, Jan. Saint, 1599-1621. I. Title.

Bercinsky family.

ZUNSER, Miriam Shomer. 947'.652
Yesterday : a memoir of a Russian Jewish family / by Miriam Shomer Zunser ; as edited by her granddaughter Emily Wortis Leider. 1st ed. New York : Harper & Row, c1978. p. cm. [DS135.R93P56 1978] 78-2150 ISBN 0-06-012553-5 : 11.95
1. Bercinsky family. 2. Shaikewitz, Nahum Meir, 1849-1905—Biography. 3. Zunser, Miriam Shomer. 4. Jews in Pinsk, White Russia—Biography. 5. Authors, Yiddish—Biography. 6. Pinsk, White Russia—Biography. I. Leider, Emily Wortis. II. Title. **BIP**

***Berczeller, Richard**

*BERCZELLER, Richard 926.1
Displaced doctor [New York] Avon [1965, c.1964] 223p. 18cm. (V2129) .75 pap.,
I. Title.

BERCZELLER, Richard. 926.1
Displaced doctor. New York, Odyssey Press [1964] 238 p. 24 cm. Autobiographical. [R154.B45A3] 64-14670
I. Title.

Berdiaev, Nikolai Aleksandrovich, 1874-1948.

LOWRIE, Donald Alexander 921.7
Rebellious prophet; a life of Nicolai Berdyaev. New York, Harper [c.1960] x, 310p. (bibl.: p. 301-303, 10p. bibl. notes) illus. 22cm. 60-5296 6.00
1. Berdiaev, Nikolai Aleksandrovich, 1874-1948. I. Title.

LOWRIE, Donald Alexander. 197'.2
Rebellious prophet; a life of Nicolai Berdyaev, by Donald A. Lowrie. Westport, Conn., Greenwood Press [1974, c1960] 310 p. illus. 22 cm. Reprint of the ed. published by Harper, New York. Bibliography: p. 301-303. [B4238.B44L6 1974] 73-11867 ISBN 0-8371-7095-8 13.50
1. Berdiaev, Nikolai Aleksandrovich, 1874-1948. I. Title.

VALLON, Michel Alexander 197
An apostle of freedom: life and teachings of Nicolas Berdyaev. New York, Philosophical Library [c.1960] 370p. (17p. bibl. and 28p. bibl. notes) 23cm. 60-2352 6.00
1. Berdiaev, Nikolai Aleksandrovich, 1874-1948. I. Title.

Berengarius, of Tours, 1000 (ca.)-1088.

MACDONALD, Allan John Macdonald, 1887- 230'.2'0924 B
Berengar and the reform of sacramental doctrine / by A. J. Macdonald. Merrick,

N.Y. : Richwood Pub. Co., [1977] xii, 444 p. ; 23 cm. Reprint of the 1930 ed. published by Longmans, Green, London. Includes index. Bibliography: p. [415]-430. [BX4705.B32M3 1977] 77-10031 ISBN 0-915172-25-9 lib.bdg. : 28.50
1. Berengarius, of Tours, 1000 (ca.)-1088. 2. Theologicans—France—Tours—Biography. 3. Tours—Biography. 4. Lord's Supper—History. I. Title.

Berenice, b. ca. 28.

JORDAN, Ruth. 933'.00994 B
Berenice / Ruth Jordan. New York : Barnes & Noble Books, 1974. xix, 248 p., [5] leaves of plates : ill. ; 23 cm. Includes index. Bibliography: p. 235-239. [DS122.8.B47J67] 74-4794 ISBN 0-06-493402-0 : 12.50
1. Berenice, b. ca. 28.

Berenson, Bernhard, 1865-1959.

BERENSON, Bernhard, 1865- 927
Sketch for a self-portrait. Bloomington, Indiana University Press [1958, c1949] 184p. illus. 20cm. (A Midland book, MB11) [N8370] 58-12203
I. Title.

BERENSON, Bernhard, 1865- 927
Sketch for a self-portrait [Gloucester, Mass., Peter Smith. 1960, c.1949] 184p. illus. 21cm. (Indiana University Press Midland book, MB11, rebound in cloth) 3.50
I. Title.

BERENSON, Bernhard, 1865- 927
1959.
Rumor and reflection. New York, Simon and Schuster, 1952. xi, 461 p. port. 24 cm. The author's diary for the years 1941-44. [N8375.B46A3] 52-13219
I. Title.

BERENSON, Bernhard, 1865-1959 927
The selected letters of Bernard Berenson, ed. by A. K. McComb. Epilogue by Nicky Mariano. Boston, Houghton, 1964[c.1963] xvi, 310p. port. 22cm. 63-17241 5.00
I. McComb, Arthur Kilgore, 1895- ed. II. Title.

BERENSON, Bernhard, 1865- 927
1959.
Sunset and twilight; from the diaries of 1947-1958. Ed., epilogue by Nicky Mariano. Introd. by Iris Origo. New York, Harcourt [c.1963] xxv, 547p. illus., ports. 24cm. 63-15313 8.75
I. Title.

SAMUELS, Ernest, 1903- 709'.2'4 B
Bernard Berenson : the making of a connoisseur / Ernest Samuels. Cambridge, Mass. : Belknap Press, 1979. xvi, 477 p., [10] leaves of plates : ill. ; 24 cm. Includes index. Bibliography: p. 435-442. [N7483.B4S25] 78-26748 ISBN 0-674-06775-4 : 15.00
1. Berenson, Bernhard, 1865-1959. 2. Art critics—United States—Biography. **BIP**

SECREST, Meryle. 709'.2'4 B
Being Bernard Berenson : a biography / Meryle Secrest. 1st ed. New York : Holt, Rinehart and Winston, c1979. xxii, 473 p. : ill. ; 24 cm. Includes bibliographical references and index. [N7483.B47S42] 78-31433 14.95
1. Berenson, Bernhard, 1865-1959. 2. Art historians—United States—Biography. I. Title.

SPRIGGE, Sylvia (Saunders) 927
Berenson; a biography. Boston, Houghton Mifflin [c.]1960. 287p. illus. 25cm. 60-7386 5.00 half cloth,
1. Berenson, Bernhard, 1865-1959. I. Title.

Beresford, Delaval James De La Poer, Lord, 1862-1906.

PORTER, Eugene 917.64'96'0360922
Oliver, 1899-
Lord Beresford and Lady Flo, by Eugene O. Porter. [El Paso] University of Texas at El Paso, 1970. 44 p. illus., ports. 23 cm. (Southwestern studies, monograph no. 25) Includes bibliographical references. [CT558.B44P6] 76-631060 2.00
1. Beresford, Delaval James De La Poer, Lord, 1862-1906. 2. Wolfe, FLorida J., 1870 or 1-1913. I. Texas. University at El Paso. II. Title. III. Series.

Berg, Alban, 1885-1935.

CARNER, Mosco. 780'.92'4 B
Alban Berg : the man and the work / Mosco Carner. New York : Holmes & Meier Publishers, 1977, c1975. xv, 255 p., [4] leaves of plates : ill. ; 25 cm. Includes indexes. Bibliography: p. [246]-247. [ML410.B74C4 1977] 76-30457 ISBN 0-8419-0301-8 : 22.00
1. Berg, Alban, 1885-1935. 2. Composers—Austria—Biography. **BIP**

MONSON, Karen. 780'.92'4 B
Alban Berg / Karen Monson. Boston : Houghton Mifflin Co., 1979. xvi, 396 p., [4] leaves of plate : ill. ; 22 cm. Includes index. Bibliography: p. [374]-375. [ML410.B47M6] 79-10174 ISBN 0-395-27762-0 : 15.00
1. Berg, Alban, 1885-1935. 2. Composers—Austria—Biography. **BIP**

Berg, Gertrude,

BERG, Gertrude, 1899- 927.92
Molly and me [by] Gertrude Berg with Cherney Berg. New York, McGraw-Hill [c.1961] 278p. 61-10713 4.95 bds.,
I. Title.

Berg, Moe, 1902-1972.

KAUFMAN, Louis, 796.357'092'4 B
1926-
Moe Berg : athlete, scholar, spy / Louis Kaufman, Barbara Fitzgerald, Tom Sewell. 1st ed. Boston : Little, Brown, [1975] c1974. x, 274 p. : ill. ; 22 cm. Includes index. [GV865.B38K38 1975] 74-20540 ISBN 0-316-48348-6 : 7.95
1. Berg, Moe, 1902-1972. 2. Baseball. I. Fitzgerald, Barbara, 1932- joint author. II. Sewell, Tom, joint author. **BIP**

Berg, Norah (Sullivan),

BERG, Norah (Sullivan), 917.9795
1897-
Lady on the beach, by Norah Berg, with Charles Samuels. New York, Prentice-Hall [1952] 251 p. 21 cm. Autobiographical. [CT275.B564A3] 52-10834
I. Title.

Bergdoll, Grover Cleveland.

DELL, Roberta E., 1946- 364.1'3 B
The United States against Bergdoll : how the Government spent twenty years and millions of dollars to capture and punish America's most notorious draft dodger / Roberta E. Dell. South Brunswick [N.J.] : A. S. Barnes, c1977. p. cm. [UB343.D4] 76-55819 ISBN 0-498-02070-3 : 12.95
1. Bergdoll, Grover Cleveland. 2. Military service, Compulsory—United States—Draft resisters—Biography. 3. European War, 1914-1918—Draft resisters—Biography. I. Title. **BIP**

Berger, Victor L., 1860-1929.

MILLER, Sally M., 335'.0092'4 B
1937-
Victor Berger and the promise of constructive socialism, 1910-1920 [by] Sally M. Miller. Westport, Conn., Greenwood Press [1973] xii, 275 p. port. 22 cm. (Contributions in American history, no. 24) Bibliography: p. 253-266. [HX86.M493] 72-175609 ISBN 0-8371-6264-5 11.50
1. Berger, Victor L., 1860-1929. 2. Socialist Party (U.S.) I. Title. **BIP**

Berggrav, Eivind Josef, Bp., 1884-1959.

JOHNSON, Alex, 1910- 922.4481
Eivind Berggrav, God's man of suspense. Tr. by Kjell Jordheim, Harriet L. Overholt. Minneapolis, Augsburg Pub. House [c.1960] 222p. Bibl. 60-16800 3.50
1. Berggrav, Eivind Josef, Bp., 1884-1959. I. Title.

JOHNSON, Alex, 1910- 922.4481
Eivind Berggrav, God's man of suspense. Translated by Kjell Jordheim with Harriet L. Overholt. Minneapolis, Augsburg Pub. House [1960] 222p. 21cm. Includes bibliography. [BX8080.B43J63] 60-16800
1. Berggrav, Eivid Josef, Bp., 1884-1959. I. Title.

Bergman, Ingmar, 1918-

DONNER, Jorn. 791.43'0233'0924 B
The personal vision of Ingmar Bergman. Translated by Holger Lundbergh. Freeport, N.Y., Books for Libraries Press [1972, c1964] 276 p. illus. 23 cm. (Biography index reprint series) Translation of Djavulens ansikte: Ingmar Bergmans filmer. Bibliography: p. 255-265. [PN1998.A3B46153 1972] 73-38310 ISBN 0-8369-8119-7
1. Bergman, Ingmar, 1918- I. Title. **BIP**

Bergman, Ingrid, 1915-

STEELE, Joseph Henry. 927.92
Ingrid Bergman, an intimate portrait. New York, D. McKay Co. [195 9/] [PN2287.B435S8] 59-9389
1. Bergman, Ingrid, 1915- I. Title.

STEELE, Joseph Henry 927.92
Ingrid Bergman, an intimate portrait. New York, Popular Library [1960, c.1959] 332p. 18cm. (SP60) .50 pap.,
1. Bergman, Ingrid. I. Title.

Bergman, Paul.

BERGMAN, Paul. 940.54'81'47
I begged for bread in Russia : an autobiography / Paul Bergman, with Henry Fitts. 1st ed. Hanover, Mass. : Triumph Books, 1976. 284 p. ; 18 cm. [D805.R9B47] 76-372433 pbk. : 1.95
1. Bergman, Paul. 2. World War, 1939-1945—Prisoners and prisons, Russian. 3. Prisoners of war—Russia—Biography. 4. Prisoners of war—Germany—Biography. 5. World War, 1939-1945—Personal narratives, German. I. Fitts, Henry, joint author. II. Title.
Publisher's address: Box 2049, 02339

Bergson, Henri Louis, 1859-1941.

CHEVALIER, Jacques, 1882- 194
1962.
Henri Bergson. Authorized translation by Lilian A. Clare. New York, AMS Press [1969] xxi, 351 p. 23 cm. Reprint of the 1928 ed. Bibliography: p. 333-335. [B2430.B43C6 1969] 70-93774
1. Bergson, Henri Louis, 1859-1941. **BIP**

CHEVALIER, Jacques, 1882- 194
1962.
Henri Bergson. Authorized translation by Lilian A. Clare. Freeport, N.Y., Books for Libraries Press [1970] xxi, 351 p. 23 cm. Translation of Bergson. Includes bibliographical references. [B2430.B43C6 1970] 78-107797
1. Bergson, Henri Louis, 1859-1941. I. Clare, Lilian Ada (Long) 1865-

GUNTER, Pete Addison 530'.0924 B
Y., 1936- comp.
Bergson and the evolution of physics, edited and translated by P. A. Y. Gunter. [1st ed.] Knoxville, University of Tennessee Press [1969] xi, 348 p. port. 24 cm. Includes bibliographical references. [QC16.B45G8] 77-77844 10.50
1. Bergson, Henri Louis, 1859-1941. I. Title. **BIP**

SLOSSON, Edwin Emery, 920.04
1865-1929.
Major prophets of to-day, by Edwin E. Slosson. Freeport, N.Y., Books for Libraries Press [1968] xii, 299 p. ports. 23 cm. (Essay index reprint series) Reprint of the 1914 ed. "The chapters of this volume have appeared in the Independent ... in a series under the general title of Twelve major prophets of to-day." Contents.Contents.—Maurice Maeterlinck.—Henri Bergson.—Henri Poincare.—Elie Metchnikoff.—Wilhelm Ostwald.—Ernst Haeckel. [CT119.S6 1968] 68-8493
1. Maeterlinck, Maurice, 1862-1949. 2. Bergson, Henri Louis, 1859-1941. 3. Poincare, Henri, 1854-1912. 4. Mechnikov, Il'ia Il'ich, 1845-1916. 5. Ostwald, Wilhelm, 1853-1932. 6. Haeckel, Ernst Heinrich Philipp August, 1834-1919. I. Title. **BIP**

SOLOMON, Joseph. 194
Bergson. Port Washington, N.Y., Kennikat Press [1970] 128 p. 18 cm. "First published in 1912." Includes bibliographical references. [B2430.B43S63 1970] 75-102583
1. Bergson, Henri Louis, 1859-1941. **BIP**

Berig, Karen—Juvenile literature.

FAULKNER, 796.9'1'0924 B
Margaret.
I skate! / By Margaret Faulkner. 1st ed. Boston : Little, Brown, c1979. p. cm. Text and photographs follow the activities of an 11-year-old aspiring skater from her daily training sessions to her participation in competitions and an ice show. [GV850.B44F38] 79-15932 ISBN 0-316-26002-9 lib.bdg. : 8.95
1. Berig, Karen—Juvenile literature. 2. Skaters—United States—Biography—Juvenile literature. I. Title. **BIP**

Beriia, Lavrentii Pavlovich, 1899-1953.

WITTLIN, 947.084'2'0924 B
Tadeusz.
Commissar; the life and death of Lavrenty Pavlovich Beria [by] Thaddeus Wittlin. New York, Macmillan [1972] xxxiv, 566 p. illus. 24 cm. Bibliography: p. 537-545. [DK268.B384W57] 74-189683 12.95
1. Beriia, Lavrentii Pavlovich, 1899-1953. I. Title.

Bering's Expedition, 1st, 1725-1730.

FISHER, Raymond 910'.92'4 B
Henry, 1907-
Bering's voyages : whither and why / Raymond H. Fisher. Seattle : University of Washington Press, [1977] p. cm. Includes index. Bibliography: p. [G296.B4F57] 77-73307 ISBN 0-295-95562-7 : 17.95
1. Bering, Vitus Jonassen, 1681-1741. 2. Bering's Expedition, 1st, 1725-1730. 3. Bering's Expedition, 2nd, 1733-1743. I. Title.

FISHER, Raymond 910'.92'4 B
Henry, 1907-
Bering's voyages : whither and why / Raymond H. Fisher. Seattle : University of Washington Press, [1977] p. cm. Includes index. Bibliography: p. [G296.B4F57] 77-73307 ISBN 0-295-95562-7 : 17.95
1. Bering, Vitus Jonassen, 1681-1741. 2. Bering's Expedition, 1st, 1725-1730. 3. Bering's Expedition, 2nd, 1733-1743. I. Title. **BIP**

Bering, Vitus Jonassen, 1681-1741.

FISHER, Raymond 910'.92'4 B
Henry, 1907
Bering's voyages : whither and why / Raymond H. Fisher. Seattle : University of Washington Press, [1977] p. cm. Includes index. Bibliography: p. [G296.B4F57] 77-73307 ISBN 0-295-95562-7 : 17.95
1. Bering, Vitus Jonassen, 1681-1741. 2. Bering's Expedition, 1st, 1725-1730. 3. Bering's Expedition, 2nd, 1733-1743. I. Title.

FISHER, Raymond 910'.92'4 B
Henry, 1907-
Bering's voyages : whither and why / Raymond H. Fisher. Seattle : University of Washington Press, [1977] p. cm. Includes index. Bibliography: p. [G296.B4F57] 77-73307 ISBN 0-295-95562-7 : 17.95
1. Bering, Vitus Jonassen, 1681-1741. 2. Bering's Expedition, 1st, 1725-1730. 3. Bering's Expedition, 2nd, 1733-1743. I. Title. **BIP**

LAURIDSEN, Peter, 915.7*0924
1846-1923.
Vitus Bering: the discoverer of Bering Strait. Rev. by the author, and translated from the Danish by Julius E. Olson. With an introd. to the American ed. by Frederick Schwatka. Freeport, N.Y., Books for Libraries Press [1969] xvi, 223 p. 23

cm. (Select bibliographies reprint series) At head of title: Russian explorations, 1725-1743. Translation of Vitus J. Bering og de russiske Opdagelsesrejser fra 1725-43. Reprint of the 1889 ed. Bibliographical references included in "Notes" (p. 202-215) [G296.B4L3 1969] 70-94274
1. Bering, Vitus Jonassen, 1681-1741. 2. Bering's Expedition, 1st, 1725-1730.

Berkefeld, Constance (Kirkpatrick)

KIRKPATRICK, Eliza (Atchison) 1841- 920.7
Days gone by, an autobiography, by Eliza Atchison Kirkpatrick as told to Constance Kirkpatrick Berkefeld. Berkeley, Calif., 1956. 93p. 23cm. [CT275.K5933A3] 57-18362
1. Berkefeld, Constance (Kirkpatrick) I. Title.

KIRKPATRICK, Eliza (Atchison) 1841- 920.7
Days gone by, an autobiography, by Eliza Atchison Kirkpatrick as told to Constance Kirkpatrick Berkefeld. Berkeley, Calif., 1956. 93p. 23cm. [CT275.K5933A3] 57-18362
1. Berkefeld, Constance (Kirkpatrick) I. Title.

Berkeley, George, Bp. of Cloyne, 1685-1753.

COLLINS, James Daniel. 146'.4
The British empiricists: Locke, Berkeley, Hume, by James Collins. Milwaukee, Bruce Pub. Co. [1967] viii, 152 p. 22 cm. Includes bibliographical references. [B1297.C6] 67-26506
1. Locke, John, 1632-1704. 2. Berkeley, George, Bp. of Cloyne, 1685-1753. 3. Hume, David, 1711-1776. 4. Empiricism. I. Title.

LUCE, Arthur Aston, 1882- 192
The life of George Berkeley, Bishop of Cloyne, by A. A. Luce. New York, Greenwood Press, 1968. xi, 260 p. illus., facsims., ports. 24 cm. (Bibliotheca Britannica philosophica) Reprint of the 1949 ed. Bibliographical footnotes. [B1347.L8 1968] 68-23309
1. Berkeley, George, Bp. of Cloyne, 1685-1753. I. Title. II. Series. BIP

LUCE, Arthur Aston, 1882- 192
The life of George Berkeley, Bishop of Cloyne, by A. A. Luce. New York, Greenwood Press, 1968. xi, 260 p. illus., facsims., ports. 24 cm. (Bibliotheca Britannica philosophica) Reprint of the 1949 ed. Bibliographical footnotes. [B1347.L8 1968] 68-23309
1. Berkeley, George, Bp. of Cloyne, 1685-1753. I. Title. II. Series. BIP

WARNOCK, Geoffrey James, 1923- 192
Berkeley [by] G. J. Warnock. [1st ed., reprinted with a new bibliography] Harmondsworth, Penguin, 1969. 240 p. 20 cm. (Peregrine books Y80) Bibliography: p. [236] [B1348.W37 1969] 77-405539 12/6
1. Berkeley, George, Bp. of Cloyne, 1685-1753.

WILD, John Daniel, 1902- 192
George Berkeley: a study of his life and philosophy. New York, Russell & Russell, 1962 [c1936] ix, 552 p. 22 cm. Bibliography: p. [531]-546. [B1347.W5 1962] 61-13938
1. Berkeley, George, Bp. of Cloyne, 1685-1753.

Berkeley, George, Bp. of Cloyne, 1685-1753—Homes and haunts—Rhode Island—Newport.

GAUSTAD, Edwin Scott. 192 B
George Berkeley in America / Edwin S. Gaustad. New Haven : Yale University Press, 1979. p. cm. Includes bibliographical references and index. [B1347.G38 1979] 79-64076 ISBN 0-300-02394-4 : 15.00
1. Berkeley, George, Bp. of Cloyne, 1685-1753—Homes and haunts—Rhode Island—Newport. 2. Philosophers—England—Biography. 3. United States—Civilization—To 1783. I. Title. BIP

Berkowitz, David Richard, 1953-

CARPOZI, George. 364.1'523
Son of Sam : the .44-caliber killer / George Carpozi, Jr. New York : Manor Books, 1977. 320 p. : ill. ; 18 cm. [HV6248.B483C37] 77-153177 ISBN 0-532-22112-5 pbk. : 2.25
1. Berkowitz, David Richard, 1953- 2. Crime and criminals—New York (City)—Biography. 3. Murder—New York (City)—Case studies. I. Title. BIP

Berkshire, Eng.—Biography.

DAVIES, Peter. 920'.0425'79
Colourful characters of North Berkshire / [by] Peter Davies. [Wallingford] : [The author], 1974. 44 p. : ill., ports. ; 21 cm. Limited ed. of 500 signed and numbered copies. No. 490. "These six stories originally appeared in various editions of the Wallingford herald." [CT785.B47D38] 76-358083 £0.50
1. Berkshire, Eng.—Biography. I. Title.

Berle, Milton.

BERLE, Milton. 791'.092'4 B
Milton Berle, an autobiography, with Haskel Frankel. New York, Delacorte Press [1974] viii, 337 p. 24 cm. [PN2287.B436A52] 74-9720 ISBN 0-440-05609-8 8.95
1. Berle, Milton. I. Frankel, Haskel.

Berlin—Hist.—Allied occupation, 1945—

BRANDT, Willy 923.243
My road to Berlin [by]Willy Brandt, as told to Leo Lania [pseud.] Garden City, N.Y., Doubleday, [c.] 1960. 287p. illus. 22cm. 60-10666 4.50 half cloth
1. Berlin—Hist.—Allied occupation, 1945- I. Herrmann, Lazar II. Title.

BRANDT, Willy, 1913- 923.243
My road to Berlin [by] Willy Brandt, as told to Leo Lania [pseud. 1st ed.] Garden City, N. Y., Doubleday, 1960. 287p. illus. 22cm. [DD857.B7A3] 60-10666
1. Berlin—Hist. —Allied occupation, 1945- I. Herrmann, Lazar, 1896- II. Title.

Berlin, Irving, 1888-

EWEN, David, 1907- 927.8
The story of Irving Berlin; illustrated by Jane Castle. New York, Holt [1950] viii, 179 p. illus. 22 cm. [ML410.B499E9] 50-6695
1. Berlin, Irving, 1888-

FREEDLAND, Michael, 1934- 784'.092'4 B
Irving Berlin. London, New York, W. H. Allen, 1974. ix, 307 p. illus. 23 cm. [ML410.B499F74] 74-159121 ISBN 0-491-01112-1 £3.50
1. Berlin, Irving, 1888-

FREEDLAND, Michael, 1934- 784'.092'4 B
Irving Berlin. New York, Stein and Day [1974] 224 p. illus. 25 cm. [ML410.B499F74 1974b] 73-90699 ISBN 0-8128-1659-5 8.95
1. Berlin, Irving, 1888- BIP

Berlin. Alliiertes Gefangnis, Spandau.

FISHMAN, Jack. 923.243
The seven men of Spandau. New York, Rinehart [1954] 276 p. illus. 22 cm. [DD244.F5 1954] 54-7073
1. Berlin. Alliiertes Gefangnis, Spandau. 2. War criminals—Germany. I. Title.

Berliner, Emile, 1851-1929.

WILE, Frederic William, 1873-1941. 621.38'0282'0924 B
Emile Berliner, maker of the microphone. New York, Arno Press, 1974 [c1926] 353 p. illus. 23 cm. (Telecommunications) Reprint of the ed. published by Bobbs-Merrill, Indianapolis. [TK140.B39W54 1974] 74-4699 ISBN 0-405-06062-9
1. Berliner, Emile, 1851-1929. 2. Microphone. I. Series: Telecommunications (New York, 1974-)

Berlioz, Hector, 1803-1869.

BARZUN, Jacques, 1907- 927.8
Berlioz and his century; an introduction to the age of romanticism. [Rev. ed.] New York, Meridian Books, 1956. 448 p. 18 cm. (Meridian books, M30) Previous editions published under title: Berlioz and the romantic century. [ML410.B5B2 1956] 56-6566
1. Berlioz, Hector, 1803-1869. I. Title. BIP

BARZUN, Jacques, 1907- 780'.924 B
Berlioz and the romantic century. 3d ed. New York, Columbia University Press, 1969. 2 v. illus., ports. 24 cm. "Errors in the 'complete' edition of the scores": v. 2, p. [358]-381. Bibliography: p. [383]-458. [ML410.B5B2 1969] 77-97504
1. Berlioz, Hector, 1803-1869. I. Title. BIP

BARZUN, Jacques, 1907- 927.8
Berlioz and the romantic century. [1st ed.] Boston, Little, Brown, 1950. 2 v. illus., ports. 25 cm. "An Atlantic Monthly Press book." "Errors in the 'complete' edition of the scores": v. 2, p. 336-359. Classified bibliography: v. 2, p. 377-450. [ML410.B5B2 1950] 50-7935
1. Berlioz, Hector, 1803-1869. I. Title.

BARZUN JACQUES MARTIN, 1907- 927.8
Berlioz and his century; an introduction to the age of romanticism [Rev. ed.] Gloucester, Mass., P. Smith, 1964, c.1949-1956] 448p. 18cm. Previous eds. pub. under title: Berlioz and the romantic century. (Meridian bks. M30 rebound) Bibl. 3.85
1. Berlioz, Hector, 1803-1869. I. Title.

BERLIOZ, Hector, 1803-1868. 780'.924 B
Memoirs of Hector Berlioz, member of the French Institute, including his travels in Italy, Germany, Russia, and England, 1803-1865. Translated and edited by David Cairns. [1st American ed.] New York, A. A. Knopf, 1969. 636 p. illus., facsims., maps, ports. 25 cm. Bibliography: p. [615]-616. [ML410.B5A243 1969b] 69-10712 12.50
I. Cairns, David, ed.

BERLIOZ, Hector, 1803-1869 780.924
Hector Berlioz: a selection from his letters; selected, edited, and translated by Humphrey Seale. New York, Vienna House, 1973 224 p. illus., 21 cm. Bibliography: p. [217]-218. [ML410.B5A517] 73-87555 ISBN 0-8443-0114-0 2.95 (pbk.)
1. Musicians—Correspondence, reminiscences, etc. I. Seale, Humphrey, ed. and tr. II. Title.

BERLIOZ, Hector, 1803-1869 780.924(B)
Memoirs of Hector Berlioz from 1803 to 1865, comprising his travels in Germany, Tialy, Russia, and England. Tr. by Rachel (Scott Russell) Holmes, Eleanor Holmes, Annotated and tr. rev. by Ernest Newman [Magnolia, Mass., P. Smith, 1967, c.1960] xxi, 533p. illus., music, ports. 22cm. (Dover bk. rebound) Unabridged repubn. of work orig. pub. by Knopf in 1932 [ML410.B5A2434 1966] 5.00
I. Russell, Rachel Holmes Scott, tr. II. Holmes, Eleanor, tr. III. Newman, Ernest, 1868-1959, ed. IV. Title.

BERLIOZ, Hector, 1803-1869. 780.924 (B)
Memoirs of Hector Berlioz, from 1803 to 1865, comprising his travels in Germany, Italy, Russia, and England. Translated by Rachel(Scott Russell) Holmes and Eleanor Holmes. Annotated, and the translation rev. by Ernest Newman. New York, Dover Publications [1966, c1960] xxi, 533 p. illus., music, ports. 22 cm. "This Dover ed., first published in 1966, is an unabridged republication of the work originally published ... in 1932." [ML410.B5A243 1966] 66-10735 MN
I. Russell, Rachel Holmes Scott, tr. II. Holmes, Eleanor, tr. III. Newman, Ernest, 1868-1959. ed IV. Title.

BERLIOZ, Hector, 1803-1869. 780'.92'4 B
The memoirs of Hector Berlioz, member of the French Institute : including his travels in Italy, Germany, Russia, and England, 1803-1865 / translated and edited by David Cairns. Corr. ed. New York : Norton, 1975. 636 p., [12] leaves of plates : ill. ; 20 cm. (The Norton library ; N698) Includes index. Bibliography: p. [615]-616. [ML410.B5A42 1975] 74-32133 ISBN 0-393-00698-0 6.95 (pbk.)
1. Berlioz, Hector, 1803-1869. 2. Composers—Correspondence, reminiscences, etc. I. Cairns, David, ed.

BERLIOZ, Hector, 1803-1869. 780'.92'4 B
New letters of Berlioz, 1830-1868. With introd., notes, and English translation by Jacques Barzun. [2d ed.] Westport, Conn., Greenwood Press [1974] xxxi, 322 p. illus. 22 cm. (Columbia bicentennial editions and studies) French and English; added t.p. in French. Bibliography: p. 310-312. [ML410.B5A33 1974] 75-100144 ISBN 0-8371-3251-7 14.50
1. Musicians—Correspondence, reminiscences, etc. I. Barzun, Jacques, 1907- ed. II. Title. BIP

ELLIOT, John Harold, 1900- v. 12
Berlioz, by J.H. Elliot. [3. ed.] London, Dent; New York, Farrar Straus and Cudahy [1959] xi, 243 p. front., illus. (music) 7 plates (incl. ports.), tables. 18 cm. (The Master musicians series) Bibliography; p. 235-236. 68-100306
1. Berlioz, Hector, 1803-1869. I. Title.

ELLIOT, John Harold, 1900- 780'.924 (B)
Berlioz, by J. H. Elliot. Revised ed. London, Dent; New York, Farrar, Straus & Giroux, 1967. xi, 243 p. front., illus. (music), 7 plates (incl. ports.), tables, 18 cm. (The Master muscians series) 21/- (B 67-1653) Bibliography: p. 235-236. [ML410.B5E37] 67-91654 MN
1. Berlioz, Hector, 1803-1869. I. Title. II. Series. III. Series: The Master musicians

GANZ, A. W. 780'.92'4 B
Berlioz in London / by A. W. Ganz. Westport, Conn. : Hyperion Press, 1979. p. cm. (Encore music editions) Reprint of the 1950 ed. published by Quality Press, London. Includes index. [ML410.B5G24 1979] 78-67015 ISBN 0-88355-740-1 : 22.50
1. Berlioz, Hector, 1803-1869. 2. Composers—England—London—Biography. I. Title. BIP

SEROFF, Victor Ilyitch, 1902- 780'.924 (B)
Hector Berlioz, by Vicgor Seroff. New York, Macmillan [1967] 168p. illus., facsims., ports. 26cm. Discography: p. [162]-163. [ML410.B5S46] 67-21253 4.95
1. Berlioz, Hector, 1803-1869. I. Title.

SEROFF, Victor Ilyitch, 1902- 785.0924 B
Hector Berlioz, by Victor Seroff. New York, Macmillan Co. [1967] 168 p. illus., facsims., ports. 26 cm. Discography: p. [162]-163. A biography of the avant-garde French musician who learned to play only the flute, guitar, and drum, but who wrote operas, oratorios, and symphonies, and was well-known as a composer, critic, and conductor. [ML410.B5S46] 92 AC 68
1. Berlioz, Hector, 1803-1869. I. Title. BIP

TURNER, Walter James, 1889-1946. 780'.92'4 B
Berlioz; the man and his work [by] W. J. Turner. New York, Vienna House [1974, c1934] viii, 374 p. ports. 21 cm. "Chronological list of works": p. 356-364. Bibliography: p. viii. [ML410.B5T8 1974] 72-93826 ISBN 0-8443-0096-9 4.95 (pbk.)
1. Berlioz, Hector, 1803-1869.

WOTTON, Tom S. 780'.924
Hector Berlioz, by Tom S. Wotton. Freeport, N.Y., Books for Libraries Press [1970] x, 224 p. music. 23 cm. Reprint of the 1935 ed. Bibliography: p. [208]-211. [ML410.B5W62 1970] 70-114902
1. Berlioz, Hector, 1803-1869. BIP

Bermant, Chaim I.—Biography.

BERMANT, Chaim I. 823'.9'14 B
Coming home / Chaim Bermant. London : Allen & Unwin, 1976. 220 p. ; 23 cm. [DS135.E6B443] 76-374335 ISBN 0-04-920047-X : £5.50
1. Bermant, Chaim I.—Biography. 2. Jews in Great Britain—Biography. 3. Authors, English—Biography. 4. Israel—Emigration and immigration—Personal narratives. 5. Great Britain—Biography. I. Title. **BIP**

Bern—Description.

CARTER, Vincent O., 1924- 914.94'5
The Bern book; a record of a voyage of the mind, by Vincent O. Carter. New York, John Day Co. [1973] xix, 297 p. 22 cm. [E185.97.C3A32] 72-12668 ISBN 0-381-98237-8 8.00
1. Bern—Description. I. Title.

Bernadette Soubirous, Saint, 1844-1879.

BERNADETTE. v. 12
[Translated by Kathryn Sullivan, R. S. C. J. New York, Desclee, 1958] 204p. illus. 21cm.
1. Bernadette Soubirous, Saint, 1844-1879. I. Auclair, Marcelle, 1899-

Bernadotte af Wisborg, Folke, greve, 1895-1948.

BERNADOTTE af Wisborg, Folke, greve, 1895-1948. 956'.042
To Jerusalem / Folke Bernadotte ; translated from the Swedish by Joan Bulman. Westport, Conn. : Hyperion Press, 1976. viii, 280 p. : port. ; 23 cm. (The Rise of Jewish nationalism and the Middle East) Translation of Till Jerusalem. Reprint of the 1951 ed. published by Hodder and Stoughton, London. Includes index. [DS126.92.B4713 1976] 75-6424 ISBN 0-88355-311-2 : 19.00
1. Bernadotte af Wisborg, Folke, greve, 1895-1948. 2. Israel-Arab War, 1948-1949—Diplomatic history. I. Title. II. Series. **BIP**

HEWINS, Ralph. 923.2485
Count Folke Bernadotte, his life and work. London, New York, Hutchinson [1950] 264 p. plates, ports. 24 cm. Bibliography: p. 253. [DL870.B47H4] 50-14077
1. Bernadotte af Wisborg, Folke, greve, 1895-1948. I. Title.

HEWINS, Ralph. 923.2485
Count Folke Bernadotte, his life and work. Minneapolis, T. S. Denison [1950] 279 p. plates, ports. 24 cm. Bibliography: p. 279. [DL870.B47H4 1950a] 51-401
1. Bernadotte af Wisborg, Folke, greve, 1895-1948. I. Title.

Bernanos, Georges, 1888-1948—Biography

SPEAIGHT, Robert, 1904- 843'.9'12 B
Georges Bernanos; a study of the man and the writer. New York, Liveright [1974] 285 p. illus. 24 cm. Bibliography: p. [275]-276. [PQ2603.E5875Z8 1974] 73-93126 ISBN 0-87140-583-0 8.95
1. Bernanos, Georges, 1888-1948—Biography.

Bernard, Claude, 1813-1878.

HOLMES, Frederic Lawrence. 612'.0092'4 B
Claude Bernard and animal chemistry : the emergence of a scientist / Frederic Lawrence Holmes. Cambridge : Harvard University Press, 1974. xx, 541 p. : ill. ; 25 cm. "A Commonwealth Fund book." Includes index. Bibliography: p. 467-483. [QP26.B5H64] 73-88497 ISBN 0-674-13485-0 : 18.00
1. Bernard, Claude, 1813-1878. 2. Physiology, Experimental—History. I. Title.

OLMSTED, James Montrose Duncan, 1886- 926.1
Claude Bernard & the experimental method in medicine. by J. M. D. Olmsted & E. Harris Olmsted. New York, H. Schuman [1952] 277 p. illus. 22 cm. (Life of science library, no. 23) [QP26.B5O39] 52-12430
1. Bernard, Claude, 1813-1878. I. Title.

TARSHIS, Jerome, 1936- 612'.00924 B
Claude Bernard; Father of Experimental Medicine. New York, Dial Press [1968] x, 182 p. port. 22 cm. A biography of the French doctor who devoted his life to research in physiology, especially on the pancreas, liver, and vasomotor nervous system. [QP26.B5T34] 92 AC 68
1. Bernard, Claude, 1813-1878. I. Title.

VIRTANEN, Reino. 926.1
Claude Bernard and his place in the history of ideas. Lincoln, University of Nebraska Press, 1960. 156 p. 24 cm. Includes bibliography. [B2192.B44V5] 60-5494
1. Bernard, Claude, 1813-1878. I. Title.

Bernard de Clairvaux, Saint, 1091?-1153

BERNARD Of Clairvaux [St.]: 922.244
he story of his life as recorded in the Vita prima Bernardi by certain of his contemporaries, William of St. Thierry, Arnold of Bonnevaux, Geoffrey and Philip of Clairvaux, and Odo of Deuil. A first translation into English by Geoffrey Webb and Adrian Walker. Westminster, Md., Newman Press [c.1960] 130p. port. 19cm. 60-16134 2.75
1. Bernard de Clairvaux, Saint, 1091?-1153. I. Guillaume de Saint-Thierry, 1085 (ca.)-1148? II. Webb, Geoffrey, jr. III. Walker, Adrian, tr. IV. Title.

BERNARD DE CLAIRVAUX, Saint 1091?-1153. 922.22
Letters. Newly translated by Bruno Scott James. Chicago, H. Regnery, 1958. xx, 530p. 25cm. Bibliographical footnotes. [BX4700.B] A54
I. Title.

COULTON, George Gordon, 1858-1947. 282'.092'2 B
Two saints: St. Bernard & St. Francis. [Folcroft, Pa.] Folcroft Library Editions, 1974. p. cm. Reprint of the 1932 ed. published by the University Press, Cambridge, which was issued as v. 4 of The Cambridge miscellany. Originally published as v. 1-2 of the author's Five centuries of religion. Includes bibliographical references. [BX4700.B5C6 1974] 74-9549 10.00
1. Bernard de Clairvaux, Saint, 1091 1153. 2. Francesco d'Assisi, Saint, 1182-1226. I. Title. II. Series: The Cambridge miscellany, v. 4.

COULTON, George Gordon, 1858-1947. 282'.092'2 B
Two saints, St. Bernard & St. Francis / by G. G. Coulton. Norwood, Pa. : Norwood Editions, 1976. vii, 129 p. : ill. ; 24 cm. Originally published as v. 1-2 of the author's Five centuries of religion. Reprint of the 1932 ed. published by the University Press, Cambridge, which was issued as v. 4 of the Cambridge miscellany. Includes bibliographical references and index. [BX4700.B5C6 1976] 76-11806 ISBN 0-8482-0355-0 lib. bdg. : 12.50
1. Bernard de Clairvaux, Saint, 1091?-1153. 2. Francesco d'Assisi, Saint, 1182-1226. I. Title. II. Series: The Cambridge miscellany ; v. 4.

CRISTIANI, Leon, 1879- 271'.12'024 B
St. Bernard of Clairvaux, 1090-1153 / by Leon Cristiani ; translated from the french by M. Angeline Bouchard. Boston : St. Paul Editions, c1977. 172 p. ; 21 cm. Tranlation of Saint Bernard de Clairvaux. [BX4700.B5C6913] 77-4942 3.95 pbk. : 2.95
1. Bernard de Clairvaux, Saint, 1091?-1153. 2. Christian saints—France—Clairvaux—Biography. 3. Clairvaux, France—Biography. **BIP**

DANIEL-ROPS, Henry, 1901-1965. 922.244
Bernard of Clairvaux. With a foreword by Thomas Merton. Translated from the French by Elisabeth Abbott. [1st American ed.] New York, Hawthorn Books [1964] 230 p. illus. 24 cm. Translation of Saint Bernard et ses fils. Bibliography: p. 225-228. [BX4700.B5D293] 64-12419
1. Bernard de Clairvaux, Saint, 1091?-1153. I. Title.

HOEVER, Hugo Henry, Father, 1883- 922.244
Saint Bernard, the oracle of the 12th century. New York, Catholic Book Pub. Co. [1925] 128p. illus. 16cm. [BX4700.B5H6] 53-29143
1. Bernard de Clairvaux, Saint, 1091?-1153. I. Title.

JAMES, Bruno Scott. 922.244
Saint Bernard of Clairvaux; an essay in biography. New York, Harper [c1957] 192p. illus. 20cm. Includes bibliography. [BX4700.B5J3 1957a] 58-7095
1. Bernard de Clairvaux, Saint, 1091?-1153. I. Title.

MERTON, Thomas, 1915-1968. 271'.12'024 B
The last of the Fathers; Saint Bernard of Clairvaux and the encyclical letter, Doctor Mellifluus. Westport, Conn., Greenwood Press [1970, c1954] 123 p. 23 cm. Bibliography: p. 119. [BX4700.B5M4 1970] 77-110049 ISBN 0-8371-4434-5
1. Bernard de Clairvaux, Saint, 1091?-1153. I. Title. **BIP**

ST. Bernard of Clairvaux: 922.244
the story of his life as recorded in the Vita prima Bernardi by certain of his contemporaries, William of St. Thierry, Arnold of Bonnevaux, Geoffrey and Philip of Clairvaux, and Odo of Deuil. A first translation into English by Geoffrey Webb and Adrian Walker. Westminster, Md., Newman Press [1960] 130p. port. 19cm. [BX4700.B5V563 1960] 60-16134
1. Bernard de Clairvaux, Saint, 1091?-1153. I. Guillaume de Saint-Thierry, 1085 (ca.)-1148? II. Webb, Geoffrey, jr. III. Walker, Adrian, tr.

WILLIAMS, Watkin Wynn, 1859- 922.244
Saint Bernard of Clairvaux. Westminster, Md., Newman Press, 1952[i. e. 1953] 423p. illus. 22cm. [BX4700.B5W487 1953] 53-6965
1. Bernard de Clairvaux, Saint, 1091?-1153. I. Title.

Bernard de Clairvaux, Saint, 1091?-1153—Juvenile literature.

SCHMID, Evan, 1920- 922.244
The mighty Bernard; a story of St. Bernard of Clairvaux. Notre Dame, Ind., Dujarie Press [1959] 142p. illus. 22cm. [BX4700.B5S27] 59-3314
1. Bernard de Clairvaux, Saint, 1091?-1153—Juvenile literature. I. Title.

WILLETT, Franciscus. 922.244
The thunder of silence; the life of St. Bernard of Clairvaux. Valatie, N.Y., Holy Cross Press, 1964. 128 p. 23 cm. (Saints who changed history series) [BX4700.B5W47] 64-2872
1. Bernard de Clairvaux, Saint, 1091?-1153 — Juvenile literature. I. Title.

WILLIAMS, Walkin Wynn, 1859- 922.244
Saint Bernard of Clairvaux. Westminster, Md., Newman Press, 1952 [i. e. 1953] 423p. illus. 22cm. [BX4700.B5W487 1953] 53-6965
1. Bernard de Clairvaux. Saint, 1001?-1153. I. Title.

Bernard de Menthon, Saint, 923-1006 — Juvenile literature.

SMARIDGE, Norah. 922.244
Bernard. Drawings by Salem Tamer. New York, Sheed & Ward [1960] unpaged. illus. 21 cm. (A Patron saint book) [BX4700.B53S5] 60-11679
1. Bernard de Menthon, Saint, 923-1006 — Juvenile literature. I. Title.

Bernard, George, 1939-

BERNARD, George, 1939- 070.4'3'0924 B
Inside the National enquirer : confessions of an undercover reporter / by George Bernard. 1st ed. Port Washington, N.Y. : Ashley Books, c1977. 354 p. : ill. ; 23 cm. [PN4874.B43A34] 76-44613 ISBN 0-87949-089-6 : 7.95
1. Bernard, George, 1939- 2. National enquirer. 3. Journalists—United States—Biography. I. Title. **BIP**

Bernard, Jessie Shirley, 1903-

BERNARD, Jessie Shirley, 1903- 301.42'7
Self-portrait of a family : letters by Jessie, Dorothy Lee, Claude, and David Bernard : with commentary by Jessie Bernard. Boston : Beacon Press, c1978. xxiii, 344 p. : ill. ; 21 cm. Includes bibliographical references. [HM22.U6B472 1978] 77-88361 ISBN 0-8070-3798-2 : 12.95
1. Bernard, Jessie Shirley, 1903- 2. Sociologists—Biography. 3. Mothers—Biography. 4. Single-parent family—United States—Case studies. 5. Mother and child. I. Title. **BIP**

Bernardi, Berel, 1872 or 3-1932.

BERNARDI, Jack. 792.028'0922 B
My father, the actor. Foreword by Herschel Bernardi. [1st ed.] New York, Norton [1971] 233 p. illus., music, ports. 22 cm. [PN2287.B437B4] 70-137835 ISBN 0-393-07457-9 6.50
1. Bernardi, Berel, 1872 or 3-1932. 2. Bernardi family. I. Title.

Bernardino da Siena, Saint, 1380-1444.

ALLIES, Mary Helen Agnes, 1852-1927. 282'.0922 B
Three Catholic reformers of the fifteenth century. Freeport, N.Y., Books for Libraries Press [1972] xii, 235 p. 23 cm. (Essay index reprint series) Reprint of the 1878 ed. Includes bibliographical references. [BX1302.A63 1972] 73-38755 ISBN 0-8369-2633-1 9.75
1. Vincentius Ferrerius, Saint, 1350 (ca.)-1419. 2. Bernardino da Siena, Saint, 1380-1444. 3. Giovanni da Capistrano, Saint, 1385 or 6-1456. 4. Church history—15th century. I. Title. **BIP**

ERNEST, Brother, 1897- 922.245
The monogram saint; the story of St. Bernardine of Siena. Illus. by Elise Curtis. Notre Dame, Ind., Dujarie Press [1955] 94p. illus. 24cm. [BX4700.B55E7] 55-38172
1. Bernardino da Siena, Saint, 1380-1444. I. Title.

Bernays, Edward L

BERNAYS, Edward L 1891-- 659.20924 (B)
Biography of an idea memoirs of public relations counsel Edward L. Bernays. New York, Simon and Schuster [1965] 849 p. illus., ports. 23 cm. Bibliographical footnotes. [HM263.B394] 65-15030
I. Title.

Berne, N.Y.—History.

†OUR heritage. 974.7'42 B
Cornwallville, N.Y. : Hope Farm Press, 1977. 144 p., [3] leaves of plates : ill. ; 23 cm. Label mounted on t.p.: Town of Berne Bicentennial Commission. Bibliography: p. 133-134. [F129.B39O94] 77-374217 pbk. : 5.95
1. Berne, N.Y.—History. 2. Berne, N.Y.—Biography. I. Berne Bicentennial Commission.
Publisher's address : Strong Rd., Cornwallville, NY 12418

Bernhard Leopold, consort of Juliana, Queen of the Netherlands, 1911-

HATCH, Alden, 1898- 923.1492
Bernhard, Prince of the Netherlands. [1st

American ed.] Garden City, N. Y., Doubleday, 1962. 312p. illus. 22cm. [DJ289.A3H3] 62-15905
1. Bernhard Leopold, consort of Jullana, Queen of the Netherlands, 1911- I. Title.

Bernhardt, Sarah, 1844-1923.

AGATE, May, 1892- 792'.028'0924
Madame Sarah. New York, Blom [1969] 223 p. port. 22 cm. Reprint of the 1945 ed. [PN2638.B5A64 1969] 73-82817
1. Bernhardt, Sarah, 1844-1923.

ARNOLD, Alan. FIC
The incredible Sarah Alan Arnold. New York : New American Library ,1976. 185 p. : ill. ; 18 cm. (Signet Book) [PN2638] 792.0280924 ISBN 0-451-07215-4 pbk. : 1.50
1. Bernhardt, Sarah, 1844-1923. I. Title.

BARING, Maurice, Hon., 1874-1945. 792'.028'0924
Sarah Bernhardt. New York, B. Blom [1969] 162 p. port. 21 cm. Reprint of the 1933 ed. [PN2638.B5B3 1969] 78-91893
1. Bernhardt, Sarah, 1844-1923. BIP

BARING, Maurice, Hon., 1874-1945. 792'.028'0924 B
Sarah Bernhardt. Westport, Conn., Greenwood Press [1970, c1934] 162 p. port. 23 cm. Includes bibliographical references. [PN2638.B5B3 1970] 70-98809 ISBN 8-371-30182-
1. Bernhardt, Sarah, 1844-1923.

BERNHARDT, Sarah, 1844-1923. 792'.028'0924 B
Memories of my life; being my personal, professional, and social recollections as woman and artist. New York, D. Appleton, 1907. Grosse Pointe, Mich., Scholarly Press, 1968. xvi, 456 p. illus., ports. 23 cm. Translation of Ma double vie. [PN2638.B5A3 1968b] 70-2678
I. Title.

BERNHARDT, Sarah, 1844-1923. 792.0924 B
Memories of my life, being my personal, professional, and social recollections as woman and artist. New York, B. Blom, 1968. xvi, 456 p. illus., ports. 24 cm. Reprint of the 1908 ed. Translation of Ma double vie. [PN2638.B5A3 1968] 68-56475
I. Title. BIP

EMBODEN, William A. 792'.028'0924 B
Sarah Bernhardt / William Emboden ; introd. by John Gielgud. 1st American ed. New York : Macmillan, 1975. 176 p. : ill. (some col.) ; 26 cm. Includes index. Bibliography: p. 172. [PN2638.B5E5 1975] 75-685 12.95
1. Bernhardt, Sarah, 1844-1923. BIP

GELLER, Gyula Gaston, 1905- 792'.028'0924 B
Sarah Bernhardt, divine eccentric, by G. G. Geller. Translated by E. S. G. Potter. New York, B. Blom, 1971. 308 p. illus., ports. 22 cm. Reprint of the 1933 ed. [PN2638.B5G42 1971] 79-96206
1. Bernhardt, Sarah, 1844-1923. I. Title.

NOBLE, Iris. 927.92
Great lady of the theatre, Sarah Bernhardt. New York, Messner [1960] 192 p. 22 cm. [PN2638.B5N6] 60-7052
1. Bernhardt, Sarah, 1844-1923. I. Title.

RICHARDSON, Joanna. 792'.028'0924 B
Sarah Bernhardt and her world / Joanna Richardson. New York : Putnam, c1977. 232 p. : ill. ; 26 cm. Includes index. Bibliography: p. 225. [PN2638.B5R53 1977b] 76-29164 ISBN 0-399-11887-X : 15.95
1. Bernhardt, Sarah, 1844-1923. 2. Actors—France—Biography. I. Title. BIP

ROW, Arthur William. 927.92
Sarah, the divine; the biography of Sarah Bernhardt. New York, Comet Press Books [1957] 169p. illus. 21cm. [PN2638.B5R7] 56-7547
1. Bernhardt, Sarah, 1844-1923. I. Title.

SKINNER, Cornelia Otis., 1901- 792.0280924
Madame Sarah. [New York, Dell, 1968, c. 1966] 352p. illus., ports. 18cm. (5139) Bibl. [PN2638.B5S55] (B) .95 pap.,
1. Bernhardt, Sarah, 1844-1923. I. Title.

SKINNER, Cornelia Otis, 1901- 792.0280924 B
Madame Sarah. Boston, Houghton Mifflin, 1967 [c1966] xxii, 356 p. illus., ports. 24 cm. Bibliography: p. [343]-346. [PN2638.B5S55] 66-12074
1. Bernhardt, Sarah, 1844-1923. I. Title.

TARANOW, Gerda. 792'.028'0924
Sarah Bernhardt: the art within the legend. Princeton, N.J., Princeton University Press [1972] xviii, 287 p. illus. 23 cm. Erratum slip inserted. Bibliography: p. 249-261. [PN2638.B5T3] 70-90962 ISBN 0-691-06181-5 10.00
1. Bernhardt, Sarah, 1844-1923.

VERNEUIL, Louis, 1893-1952. 792'.028'0924 B
The fabulous life of Sarah Bernhardt. Translated from the French by Ernest Boyd. Westport, Conn., Greenwood Press [1972, c1942] 312 p. illus. 23 cm. Translation of La vie merveilleuse de Sarah Bernhardt. [PN2638.B5V42 1972] 70-138134 ISBN 0-8371-5707-2
1. Bernhardt, Sarah, 1844-1923. I. Title. BIP

Bernhardt, Sarah, 1844-1923—Juvenile literature.

HOPE, Charlotte 792.0924
The young Sarah Bernhardt. Illus. by William Randell. New York, Roy [1966, c.1965] 143p. illus. 21cm. [PN2638.B5H6] 65-22982 3.25 bds.,
1. Bernhardt, Sarah, 1844-1923—Juvenile literature. I. Title.

Bernier, Joseph Elzear, 1852-1934.

FAIRLEY, T. C. 919.8
The true North; the story of Captain Joseph Bernier, by T. C. Fairley & Charles E. Israel. Illustrated by James Hill. New York, St. Martin's Press, 1957. 160 p. illus. 22 cm. (Great stories of Canada) [G635.B44F3] 57-13902
1. Bernier, Joseph Elzear, 1852-1934. 2. Arctic regions. 3. Canada—Exploring expeditions. I. Israel, Charles E., joint author. II. Title.

Bernini, Giovanni Lorenzo, 1598-1680.

BALDINUCCI, Filippo, 1624?-1696. 730.924
The life of Bernini. Translated from the Italian by Catherine Enggass. Forword by Robert Enggass. University Park, Pennsylvania State University Press, 1966. xviii, 117 p. illus., port. 23 cm. Translation of Vita del cavaliere Glo. Lorenzo Bernino. [N6923.B5B33] 65-26094
1. Bernini, Giovanni Lorenzo, 1598-1680. I. Title.

HIBBARD, Howard, 1928- 730.924
Bernini. [Baltimore] Penguin [1966, c.1965] 255p. illus., plans, ports. 20cm. (Pelican bk. A701) Bibl. [NB623.B5H5] 66-3256 2.45 pap.,
1. Bernini, Giovanni Lorenzo, 1598-1680. I. Title.

HIBBARD, Howard, 1928- 730.924
Bernini [Magnolia, Mass., P. Smith, 1967, c.1965] 255p. illus., plans, ports. 20cm. (Pelican bk. A701 rebound) Bibl. [NB623.B5H5] 4.50
1. Bernini, Giovanni Lorenzo, 1598-1680. I. Title. BIP

Bernis, Francois Joachim de Pierre de, comte de Lyon, Cardinal, 1715-1794.

CHEKE, Marcus. Sir 923.244
The Cardinal de Bernis. [1st ed.] New York, W. W. Norton [1959, c1958] 310p. illus. 22cm. Includes bibliography. [DC135.B5C5 1959] 58-11106
1. Bernis, Francois Joachim de Pierre de, comte de Lyon, Cardinal, 1715-1794. I. Title.

Bernstein, Aline Frankau, 1881-1955—Biography.

KLEIN, Carole. 792'.025'0924 B
Aline / by Carole Klein. 1st ed. New York : Harper & Row, c1979. xi, 352 p. ; 24 cm. Includes index. Bibliography: p. 345-346. [PS3503.E727Z75] 76-26239 ISBN 0-06-012423-7 : 12.95
1. Bernstein, Aline Frankau, 1881-1955—Biography. 2. Wolfe, Thomas, 1900-1938—Relationship with women—Aline Frankau Bernstein. 3. New York (City)—Intellectual life. 4. Set designers—United States—Biography. 5. Novelists, American—20th century—Biography. BIP

Bernstein, Burton.

BERNSTEIN, Burton. 953'.1
Sinai : the great and terrible wilderness / Burton Bernstein. New York : Viking Press, 1979. xviii, 268 p., [1] leaf of plates : ill. ; 25 cm. Includes index. [DS110.5.B46] 79-12794 ISBN 0-670-34837-6 : 13.95
1. Bernstein, Burton. 2. Sinai Peninsula—Description and travel. 3. Journalists—United States—Biography. I. Title. BIP

Bernstein, Leonard, 1918-

BRIGGS, John, 1916- 927.8
Leonard Bernstein; the man, his work, and his world. [1st ed.] Cleveland, World Pub. Co. [1961] 274 p. illus. 22 cm. [ML410.B566B7] 61-10167
1. Bernstein, Leonard, 1918-

GRUEN, John. 780'.924
The private world of Leonard Bernstein. Photos by Ken Heyman. New York, Viking Press [1968] 191 p. illus., ports. 30 cm. "A Ridge Press Book." [ML410.B566G8] 68-29354 12.50
1. Bernstein, Leonard, 1918- I. Title.

MAKING music: 927.8
Leonard Bernstein. Chicago, Encyclopaedia Britannica [1963] 192 p. illus. 22 cm. (Britannica bookshelf -- Great lives) [ML410.B566B5] 63-13513
1. Bernstein, Leonard, 1918-

REIDY JOHN P 780'.924
Leonard Bernstein, by John P. Reidy and Norman Richards. Chicago, Childrens Press [c1967] 95 p. illus., ports. 29 cm. (People of destiny. A humanities series) [ML410.B566R4] 67-20106
1. Bernstein, Leonard, 1913- I. Title.

Bernstein, Leonard, 1918- —Juvenile literature.

CONE, Molly. 780'.924 B
Leonard Bernstein. Illustrated by Robert Galster. New York, Crowell [1970] 30 p. illus. (part col.) 24 cm. (Crowell biographies) A biography of the composer, musician, and conductor of the New York Philharmonic. [ML3930.B48C7] 92 79-94792
1. Bernstein, Leonard, 1918- —Juvenile literature. I. Galster, Robert, illus. II. Title.

EWEN, David, 1907- 927.8
Leonard Bernstein, a biography for young people. [1st ed.] Philadelphia, Chilton Co., Book Division [1960] 174 p. illus. 22 cm. [ML3930.B48E9] 60-13363
1. Bernstein, Leonard, 1918-—Juvenile literature.

EWEN, David, 1907- 780.924
Leonard Bernstein; a biography for young people. [Rev. ed.] Philadelphia, Chilton Book Co. [1967] vi, 180 p. ports. 21 cm. Bibliography: p. 171. [ML3930.B48E9 1967] 67-3844
1. Bernstein, Leonard, 1918- —Juvenile literature.

GREEN, Diane Huss 920
Lenny's surprise piano. Illus. by Robert Dranko. San Carlos, Calif., Golden Gate [c.1963] unpaged. illus. (pt. col.) 24cm. 63-7222 2.75; 2.83 lib. ed.,
1. Bernstein, Leonard, 1918- —Juvenile literature. I. Title.

Bernstein, Ruuh, 1914-1953.

I'LL be waiting; a memoir, by Benjamin Bernstein with Charles Lee. New York, Exposition Press [1958] 126p. ports. 21cm. v. 12
1. Bernstein, Ruuh, 1914-1953. 2. Cancer. I. Bernstein, Benjamin, 1887?-

Berra, Lawrence Peter, 1925-

TRIMBLE, Joe. 927.96357
Yogi Berra. New York, A. S. Barnes [1952] 184 p. illus. 21 cm. (Most valuable player series) [GV865.B4T7] 52-6334
1. Berra, Lawrence Peter, 1925- I. Title.

TRIMBLE, Joe. 927.96357
Yogi Berra. New York, Grosset & Dunlap [1956] 165p. illus. 20cm. (The Big League baseball library) [GV865.B4T7 1956] 56-58143
1. Berra, Lawrence Peter, 1925- I. Title.

Berra, Yogi, 1925-

BERRA, Yogi, 1925- 927.96357
Yogi; the autobiography of a professional baseball player, by Yogi Berra and Ed Fitzgerald. [1st ed.] Garden City, N.Y., Doubleday, 1961. 234 p. illus. 22 cm. [GV865.B4A3] 61-6504
I. Fitzgerald, Edward E., 1919- joint author.

ROSWELL, Gene. 927.96357
The Yogi Berra story. New York, Messner [1958] 192 p. illus. 22 cm. [GV865.B4R6] 58-10931
1. Berra, Yogi, 1925-

TRIMBLE, Joe 927.96357
Yogi Berra. Foreword by Casey Stengel [Rev. ed.] New York, Grosset [c.1954-1965] 224p. ports. 18cm. (Tempo bks., T84) [GV865.B4T7] 65-18452 .50 pap.,
1. Berra, Yogi, 1925- I. Title.

Berra, Yogi, 1925- —Juvenile literature.

SCHOOR, Gene. 796.357'092'4 B
The story of Yogi Berra / Gene Schoor. 1st ed. Garden City, N.Y. : Doubleday, 1976. 213 p., [6] leaves of plates : ill. ; 22 cm. Includes index. A biography of Yogi Berra, who spent most of his baseball career behind home plate for the New York Yankees. [GV865.B4S36] 92 76-2823 ISBN 0-385-11020-0 : 5.95.
1. Berra, Yogi, 1925- —Juvenile literature. 2. Baseball—Juvenile literature. I. Title. BIP

Berrigan, Daniel.

BERRIGAN, Daniel. 261.7
The dark night of resistance. [1st ed.] Garden City, N.Y., Doubleday, 1971. vi, 181 p. 22 cm. Contains personal narrative, poetry, and prose. [BX4705.B3845A29] 74-150282 5.95
1. U.S.—Social conditions—1960- 2. Government, Resistance to. I. Title.

BERRIGAN, Daniel. 365'.6'0924 B
Lights on in the house of the dead; a prison diary. [1st ed.] Garden City, N.Y., Doubleday, 1974. 309 p. 22 cm. [BX4705.B3845A298] 73-16823 ISBN 0-385-03953-0 7.95
1. Berrigan, Daniel. I. Title.

CURTIS, Richard. 322.4'4'0922 B
The Berrigan brothers; the story of Daniel and Philip Berrigan. New York, Hawthorn Books [1974] 174 p. illus. 21 cm. Bibliography: p. 161-162. [BX4705.B3845C87 1974] 73-5447 6.95
1. Berrigan, Daniel. 2. Berrigan, Philip. I. Title.

Berry, Martha McChesney, 1866-1942.

BLACKBURN, Joyce. 371.9'67'0924 B
Martha Berry, little woman with a big dream; a biography. [1st ed.] Philadelphia, Lippincott [1968] 158 p. 21 cm. The life of Martha Berry, who devoted herself to the establishment of schools for underprivileged children in the rural areas of the South. [LA2317.B38B5] 92 AC 68

1. Berry, Martha McChesney, 1866-1942. I. Title.

BYERS, Tracy. 371.9'67'0924 B
Martha Berry, the Sunday Lady of Possum Trot. New York, Putnam, 1932. Ann Arbor, Mich., Gryphon Books, 1971. 268 p. illus. 22 cm. [LD405.B213B4 1971] 72-159905
1. Berry, Martha McChesney, 1866-1942. 2. Berry Schools, Mount Berry, Ga. I. Title. BIP

KANE, Harnett Thomas, 923.673
1910-
Miracle in the mountains, by Harnett T. Kane with Inez Henry. [1st ed.] Garden City, N. Y., Doubleday, 1956. 320p. 22cm. Biography of Martha Berry and the story of how she built the Berry Schools. [LD405.B213K3] 56-10466
1. Berry, Martha McChesney, 1866-1942. 2. Berry Schools, Mount Berry, Ga. I. Title.

MYERS, Elisabeth 371.9'67'0924 B
P.
Angel of Appalachia; Martha Berry [by] Elisabeth P. Myers. New York, J. Messner [1968] 191 p. 22 cm. Bibliography: p. 187-188. A biography of the founder and director of the self-sustaining Berry Schools of Georgia, where students work instead of paying tuition, and receive practical as well as academic training. [LD405.B213M9] 92 AC 68
1. Berry, Martha McChesney, 1866-1942. I. Title.

Berry, Martha McChesney, 1866-1942—Juvenile literature.

BLACKBURN, Joyce. 92
Martha Berry, little woman with a big dream; a biography. [1st ed.] Philadelphia, Lippincott [1968] 158p. 21cm. [LA23137.B38B5] 68-24414 3.95
1. Berry, Martha McChesney, 1866-1942—Juvenile literature. I. Title.

MYERS, Elisabeth P. 92 (J)
Angel of Appalachia; Martha Berry [by] Elisabeth P. Myers. New York, J. Messner [1968] 191 p. 22 cm. Bibliography: p. 187-188. [LD405.B213M9] 68-14944
1. Berry, Martha McChesney, 1866-1942—Juvenile literature. I. Title.

PHELAN, Mary Kay. 371.9'67'0924 B
Martha Berry. Illustrated by Charles W. Walker. New York, Crowell [1972] [48] p. col. illus. 24 cm. (Crowell biographies) A biography of the young woman whose desire to help Appalachian children resulted in the creation of boarding schools and a college in rural Georgia where youngsters could work as well as study. [LA2311.B38P5 1972] 92 77-158699 ISBN 0-690-52112-X 3.75
1. Berry, Martha McChesney, 1886-1942—Juvenile literature. 2. Education, Rural—Georgia—History—Juvenile literature. I. Walker, Charles W., illus. II. Title. BIP

Berry, Ruth Muirhead.

BERRY, Ruth Muirhead. 922.573
To enjoy God, a woman's adventure in faith. Philadelphia, Muhlenberg Press [1956] 228p. 22cm. [BR1725.B44A3] 56-9340
I. Title.

Bersell, Peter Olof Immanuel, 1882-

BONGFELDT, Gustav 922.473
Lawrence, 1903-
Pen portraits of P. O. Bersell and C. A. Wendell. 1st ed. [Rock Island? Ill., 1950] 115 p. ports. 23 cm. On cover: First series. Includes bibliographies. [BX8080.B45B6] 51-791
1. Bersell, Peter Olof Immanuel, 1882- 2. Wendell, Claus August, 1866-1950. I. Title.

Bertherat, Therese.

BERTHERAT, Therese. 815'.82
The body has its reasons : anti-exercises and self-awareness / Therese Bertherat and Carol Bernstein ; translated from the French. New York : Avon, 1979, c1977. 160p. ; 18 cm. Bibliography: p. 158-160. [RA781.B4413] ISBN 0-380-44321-X pbk. : 2.50
1. Bertherat, Therese. 2. Exercise. 3. Body image. 4. Physical therapists — France — Biography. I. Bernstein, Carol. II. Title.
L.C. card no. for 1977 Pantheon Books ed.: 76-54621. BIP

BERTHERAT, Therese. 815'.82
The body has its reasons : anti-exercises and self-awareness / Therese Bertherat and Carol Bernstein ; translated from the French. 1st American ed. New York : Pantheon Books, c1977. 159 p. : ill. ; 25 cm. Bibliography: p. 157-159. [RA781.B4413 1977] 76-54621 ISBN 0-394-41134-X : 7.95
1. Bertherat, Therese. 2. Exercise. 3. Body image. 4. Physical therapists—France—Biography. I. Bernstein, Carol, joint author. II. Title.

Bertillon, Alphonse, 1853-1914.

RHODES, Henry Taylor 925.73
Fowkes, 1892-
Alphonse Bertillon, father of scientific detection. With 11 plates in half-tone. New York, Abelard-Schuman [1956] 238 p. illus. 21 cm. [GN21.B47R45 1956] 56-13802
1. Bertillon, Alphonse, 1853-1914.

RHODES, Henry 364.12'0924 B
Taylor Fowkes, 1892-
Alphonse Bertillon, father of scientific detection, by Henry T. F. Rhodes. New York, Greenwood Press [1968, c1956] 238 p. illus., ports. 23 cm. Bibliography: p. 229-232. [HV6068.R46 1968] 69-14052
1. Bertillon, Alphonse, 1853-1914. I. Title. BIP

Bertini, Gianni, 1922-

RESTANY, Pierre 759.5
Bertini. [dist. New York, Efron, 1962] 68p. illus. (pt. mounted col.) 19cm. (Le Musee depoche) 62-4283 1.50 pap.,
1. Bertini, Gianni, 1922- I. Title.

Bertino, Belvina Williamson.

BERTINO, Belvina 978.6'16 B
Williamson.
The scissorbills : a true story of Montana's homesteaders / Belvina Williamson Bertino. 1st ed. New York : Vantage Press, c1976. 194 p. : ill. ; 23 cm. Includes bibliographical references. [F739.D6B47] 76-374909 ISBN 0-533-01964-8 : 5.95
1. Bertino, Belvina Williamson. 2. Frontier and pioneer life—Montana—Dodson. 3. Dodson, Mont.—History. 4. Dodson, Mont.—Biography. I. Title.

Bertoia, Harry.

NELSON, June Kompass. 730'.924
Harry Bertoia: sculptor. Detroit, Wayne State University Press, 1970. 137 p. illus., port. 26 cm. Bibliography: p. 129-133. [NB237.B44N4 1970] 70-78546 11.50
1. Bertoia, Harry. I. Title. BIP

Berven, Ken.

BERVEN, Ken. 248'.85'0924 B
I love being married to a grandma / Ken Berven ; foreword by Billy Graham. Nashville : T. Nelson, c1978. 144 p. ; 16 cm. [BR1725.B46A34] 78-530 ISBN 0-8407-5647-X : 5.95
1. Berven, Ken. 2. Christian biography—United States. 3. Grandparents—Religious life. I. Title. BIP

Berzelius, Jons Jakob, friherre, 1779-1848.

JORPES, Johan Erik, 540'.924 B
1894-
Jac. Berzelius: his life and work, by J. Erik Jorpes. Translated from the Swedish manuscript by Barbara Steele. Berkeley, University of California Press, 1970. 156 p. illus. (part fold. col.), col. coat of arms, facsims., maps (1 fold.), ports (part col.) 23 cm. Includes bibliographical references. [QD22.B5J63 1970] 75-91801 ISBN 0-520-01628-9
1. Berzelius, Jons Jakob, friherre, 1779-1848.

Besant, Annie (Wood) 1847-1933.

NETHERCOT, Arthur Hobart 922.91
The first five lives of Annie Besant. [Chicago] University of Chicago Press [c.1960] xii, 418p. Includes bibliography. illus. 24cm. 59-11624 7.50
1. Besant, Annie (Wood) 1847-1933. I. Title.

NETHERCOT, Arthur Hobart, 922.91
1895-
The first five lives of Annie Besant. [Chicago] University of Chicago Press [1960] 418p. illus. 24cm. Includes bibliography. [BP585.B3N4] 59-11624
1. Besant, Annie (Wood) 1847-1933. I. Title. BIP

NETHERCOT, Arthur Hobart, 922.912
1895-
The last four lives of Annie Besant. [Chicago] Univ. of Chic. Pr. [1964, c.1963] 483p. illus., ports., diagrs., facsim. 23cm. 64-710 7.50
1. Besant, Annie (Wood) 1847-1933. I. Title. BIP

Besant, Walter,

BESANT, Walter, Sir, 823'.8 B
1836-1901.
Autobiography of Sir Walter Besant. With a prefatory note by S. Squire Sprigge. New York, Dodd, Mead, 1902. St. Clair Shores, Mich., Scholarly Press, 1971. xxvii, 294 p. port. 22 cm. [PR4106.A6 1971] 76-144877

Besedovskii, Grigorii Zinov'evich.

BESEDOVSKII, 327'.2'0924
Grigorii Zinov'evich.
Revelations of a Soviet diplomat / by Grigory Bessedovsky ; translated by Matthew Norgate. Westport, Conn. : Hyperion Press, [1977] p. cm. Abridged translation of Na putiakh k termidoru. Reprint of the 1931 ed. published by Williams & Norgate, London. [DK268.B4A3 1977] 75-39046 ISBN 0-88355-424-0 : 18.50
1. Besedovskii, Grigorii Zinov'evich. 2. Russia (1923- U.S.S.R.)— Ob'edirennoe gosudarstvennoe politicheskoe upravlenie. 3. Diplomats—Russia—Biography. 4. Russia—Diplomatic and consular service. 5. Russia—Foreign relations—1917-1945. I. Title. BIP

Beshoar, Michael, 1833-1907.

BESHOAR, Barron B. 610'.92'4 B
Hippocrates in a red vest; the biography of a frontier doctor, by Barron B. Beshoar. Palo Alto, American West Pub. Co. [1973] 352 p. illus. 24 cm. Bibliography: p. [346]-349. [R154.B559B47] 72-90945 ISBN 0-910118-31-0 9.95
1. Beshoar, Michael, 1833-1907. 2. Physicians—Biography. 3. Colorado—History. I. Title.

Besnard, Marie (Davaillaud)

BESNARD, Marie 340.0924
(Davaillaud) 1896-
The trial of Marie Besnard. Translated from the French by Denise Folliot and with an introd. by Sybille Bedford. New York, Farrar, Straus [1963] 224 p. 22 cm. Translation of Mes memoires. Full name: Marie Josephine Philippine (Davaillaud) Besnard. [343.52] 63-12075
I. Title.

Bessemer, Henry, Sir, 1813-1898.

JEANS, William T. 669'.142'0922 B
The creators of the age of steel, by W. T. Jeans. Freeport, New York, Books for Libraries Press [1973] p. (Essay index reprint series) "First published 1854." Contents.Contents.—Introduction.—Sir Henry Bessemer.—Sir William Siemens.—Sir Joseph Whitworth.—Sir John Brown.—Mr. S. G. Thomas.—Mr. G. J. Snelus. [TN139.J45 1973] 73-1583 ISBN 0-518-10054-5
1. Bessemer, Henry, Sir, 1813-1898. 2. Siemens, William, Sir, 1816-1896. 3. Whitworth, Joseph, Sir, 1803-1887. 4. Brown, John, Sir, 1816-1896. 5. Thomas, Sidney Gilchrist, 1850-1885. 6. Snelus, George James, 1837-1906. 7. Steel—History. 8. Inventors. I. Title.

Bessie, Alvah Cecil, 1904- —Journeys—Spain.

BESSIE, Alvah Cecil, 813'.5'2 B
1904-
Spain again / Alvah Bessie. San Francisco : Chandler & Sharp, [1975] 228 p. : ill. ; 21 cm. Autobiographical. [PS3503.E778Z52] 74-28742 ISBN 0-88316-516-3 pbk. : 5.95
1. Bessie, Alvah Cecil, 1904- —Journeys—Spain. 2. Espana otra vez. [Motion picture] I. Title. BIP

Besterman, Theodore, 1904-

BESTERMAN, Theodore, 010'.92'4
1904-
Fifty years a bookman / by Theodore Besterman. [New Brunswick, N.J.] : Rutgers University, Graduate School of Library Service, 1974. 20 p. ; 23 cm. (Annual Richard H. Shoemaker lecture ; 3d, 1973) [Z1004.B48A53] 74-188884
1. Besterman, Theodore, 1904- 2. Books. 3. Libraries. I. Title. II. Series: Annual Richard H. Shoemaker lecture ; 1973.

Bethea, James A

BETHEA, James A 926.1
Memoirs of James A. Bethea, by James A. Beathea, and coordinated by Dorothy Bethea Ellis. San Antonio, Naylor [1964] ix, 130 p. port. 22 cm. [E181.B55] 64-7801
I. Title.

Bethell, Pinckney C.—Archives.

COLORADO. State 016.3326'092
Historical Society. Library.
A calendar of the papers of Pinckney C. and William D. Bethell, 1848-1901: a holding of the Library of the State Historical Society of Colorado. Processed by Lee Scamehorn Denver, 1968. 32 l. 23 x 29 cm. Cover title. [Z6616.B55C65] 74-636569
1. Bethell, Pinckney C.—Archives. 2. Bethell, William D., 1840-1906—Archives. I. Scamehorn, Howard Lee, 1926- II. Title.

Bethmann-Hollweg, Theobald von, 1856-1921.

JARAUSCH, Konrad 943.08'4'0924 B
Hugo.
The enigmatic chancellor; Bethmann Hollweg and the hubris of Imperial Germany, by Konrad H. Jarausch. New Haven, Yale University Press, 1973 [c1972] xiv, 560 p. port. 25 cm. Includes bibliographical references. [DD231.B5J37] 72-89101 ISBN 0-300-01295-0 20.00
1. Bethmann-Hollweg, Theobald von, 1856-1921. I. Title. BIP

Bethune, Mary Jane (McLeod) 1875-1955.

HOLT, Rackham. 923.773
Mary McLeod Bethune; a biography. [1st ed.] Garden City, N.Y., Doubleday, 1964. 306 p. illus., ports. 22 cm. [E185.97.B34H6] 64-11040
1. Bethune, Mary Jane (McLeod) 1875-1955. I. Title.

STERNE, Emma (Gelders) 923.773
1894-
Mary McLeon Bethune. Illustrated by Raymond Lufkin. [1st ed.] New York, Knopf, 1957. 268 p. illus. 22 cm. [E185.97.B34S8] 57-9201
1. Bethune, Mary Jane (McLeod) 1875-1955. I. Title.

Bethune, Mary Jane McLeod, 1875-1955—Juvenile literature.

ANDERSON, LaVere. 370'.92'4 B
Mary McLeod Bethune, teacher with a dream / by LaVere Anderson; illustrated by William Hutchinson. Champaign, Ill. : Garrard Pub. Co., c1976. 80 p. : col. ill. ; 23 cm. (A Discovery book) A biography of the black woman who spent her life educating and working to earn basic human rights for her people. [LA2317.B39A62] 92 75-25765 ISBN 0-8116-6321-3 lib.bdg. : 3.58
1. Bethune, Mary Jane McLeod, 1875-1955. I. Hutchinson, William M. II. Title.

BURT, Olive (Woolley) 1894- 378.1'11'0924 B
Mary McLeod Bethune; girl devoted to her people, by Olive W. Burt. Illustrated by James Cummings. Indianapolis, Bobbs-Merrill [1970] 200 p. col. illus. 20 cm. (Childhood of famous Americans) A biography stressing the childhood of the Negro woman who devoted her life to improving educational opportunities for her people. [E185.97.B34B8] 92 74-105941
1. Bethune, Mary Jane (McLeod) 1875-1955—Juvenile literature. I. Cummins, James, illus. II. Title. **BIP**

BURT, Olive (Woolley) 1894- 378.1'11'0924 B
Mary McLeod Bethune; girl devoted to her people, by Olive W. Burt. Illustrated by James Cummings. Indianapolis, Bobbs-Merrill [1970] 200 p. col. illus. 20 cm. (Childhood of famous Americans) A biography stressing the childhood of the Negro woman who devoted her life to improving educational opportunities for her people. [E185.97.B34B8] 92 74-105941
1. Bethune, Mary Jane (McLeod) 1875-1955—Juvenile literature. I. Cummins, James, illus. II. Title. **BIP**

CARRUTH, Ella Kaiser 92
She wanted to read; the story of Mary McLeod Bethune. Illus. by Herbert McClure [Nashville] Abingdon [c.1966] 80p. illus. 21cm. [E185.97.B34C3] 66-10568 2.25
1. Bethune, Mary Jane (McLeod) 1875-1955—Juvenile literature. I. Title.

CARRUTH, Ella Kaiser. 92
She wanted to read; the story of Mary McLeod Bethune. Illustrated by Herbert McClure. New York, Abingdon Press [1966] 80 p. illus. 21 cm. [E185.97.B34C3] 66-10568
1. Bethune, Mary Jane (McLeod) 1875-1955 — Juvenile literature. I. Title. **BIP**

GREENFIELD, Eloise. 370'.92'4 B
Mary McLeod Bethune / by Eloise Greenfield; illustrated by Jerry Pinkney. New York : Crowell, 1976. p. cm. (A Crowell biography) Biography of Mary Jane McLeod Bethune who made numerous contributions to education for Afro-Americans. [E185.97.B34G73] 92 76-11522 ISBN 0-690-01129-6 lib.bdg. : 5.95
1. Bethune, Mary Jane McLeod, 1875-1955—Juvenile literature. I. Pinkney, Jerry. II. Title.

JOHNSON, Jan. 370'.92'4 B
Mary Bethune and her somedays : a story about Mary McLeod Bethune / written by Jan Johnson ; illustrated by Troy Howell. Minneapolis : Winston Press, c1979. [32] p. : ill. (some col.) ; 21 cm. (Christian heroes) [E185.97.B34J63] 78-65511 ISBN 0-03-049421-4 pbk. : 1.50
1. Bethune, Mary Jane McLeod, 1875-1955—Juvenile literature. 2. Afro-Americans—Biography—Juvenile literature. 3. Teachers—United States—Biography—Juvenile literature. I. Howell, Troy. II. Title. III. Series.

PEARE, Catherine Owens. 923.773
Mary McLeod Bethune. New York, Vanguard Press [1951] 219 p. illus. 22 cm. Includes bibliography. [E185.97.B34P4] 51-7652
1. Bethune, Mary Jane McLeod, 1875-1955. **BIP**

RADFORD, Ruby Lorraine, 1891- 378.1'11'0924 B
Mary McLeod Bethune, by Ruby L. Radford. Illustrated by Lydia Rosier. New York, Putnam [1973] 61 p. col. illus. 23 cm. (A See and read beginning to read biography) A biography of the black woman who devoted her life to helping her people achieve education and justice. [E185.97.B34R32 1973] 92 77-170070 77-170070 ISBN 0-399-20322-2 3.39 (lib. bdg.)
1. Bethune, Mary Jane (McLeod) 1875-1955—Juvenile literature. I. Rosier, Lydia, illus. II. Title.

RADFORD, Ruby Lorraine, 1891- 378.1'11'0924 B
Mary McLeod Bethune, by Ruby L. Radford. Illustrated by Lydia Rosier. New York, Putnam [1973] 61 p. col. illus. 23 cm. (A See and read beginning to read biography) A biography of the black woman who devoted her life to helping her people achieve education and justice. [E185.97.B34R32 1973] 92 77-170070 77-170070 ISBN 0-399-20322-2 3.39 (lib. bdg.)
1. Bethune, Mary Jane (McLeod) 1875-1955—Juvenile literature. I. Rosier, Lydia, illus. II. Title.

STERNE, Emma Gelders, 1894- 923.773
Mary McLeod Bethune. Illustrated by Raymond Lufkin. [1st ed.] New York, Knopf, 1957. 268 p. illus. 22 cm. [E185.97.B34S8] 57-9201
1. Bethune, Mary Jane McLeod, 1875-1955. **BIP**

WILSON, Beth P. 920'.073
Giants for justice : Bethune, Randolph, and King / Beth P. Wilson. 1st ed. New York : Harcourt Brace Jovanovich, c1978. viii, 103 p., [26] leaves of plates : ill. ; 22 cm. Includes bibliographies and index. Biographical sketches of three outstanding black leaders who did much to pave the way toward dignity and freedom for their people in education, labor, and civil rights. [E185.96.W65] 920 77-88971 ISBN 0-15-230781-8 : 6.95
1. Bethune, Mary Jane McLeod, 1875-1955—Juvenile literature. 2. Randolph, Asa Philip, 1889- —Juvenile literature. 3. King, Martin Luther—Juvenile literature. 4. Afro-Americans—Biography—Juvenile literature. I. Title. **BIP**

Bethune, Norman.

ALLAN, Ted. 926.1
The scalpel, the sword; the story of Dr. Norman Bethune, by Ted Allan and Sydney Gordon. [1st ed.] Boston, Little, Brown [1952] 336 p. illus. 22 cm. [R464.B4A6] 52-5015
1. Bethune, Norman. I. Title.

ALLAN, Ted. 617'.092'4 B
The scalpel, the sword; the story of Dr. Norman Bethune, by Ted Allan [and] Sydney Gordon. Rev. New York, Monthly Review Press, 1973 [i.e. 1974, c1952] xii, 320 p. 21 cm. [R464.B4A6 1974] 73-21897 ISBN 0-85345-301-2 8.95
1. Bethune, Norman. I. Gordon, Sydney, joint author. II. Title.
Pbk. 3.95; ISBN 0-85345-302-0

STEWART, Roderick. 617'.092'4 B
Bethune / Roderick Stewart. 2nd ed. Hamden, Conn. : Archon Books, 1979, c1973. xiii, 210 p. : ill. ; 24 cm. Includes index. Bibliography: p. 202-204. [RD27.35.B47S73 1979] 78-27744 ISBN 0-208-01776-3 : 15.00
1. Bethune, Norman. 2. Surgeons—Canada—Biography. 3. Surgeons—China—Biography. I. Title. **BIP**

Betjeman, John, Sir, 1906- in fiction, drama, poetry, etc.

BETJEMAN, John, Sir, 1906- 821'.9'12
Summoned by bells / John Betjeman. London ; J. Murray, 1976 115 p. : ill. ; 23 cm. Autobiography in verse. Enlarged and illustrated ed. [PR6003.E77Z52 1976] 77-357700 ISBN 0-7195-3349-X. ISBN 0-7195-3350-3 pbk. : £1.75
1. Betjeman, John, Sir, 1906- in fiction, drama, poetry, etc. I. Title.

Betterton, Thomas, 1635?-1710.

GILDON, Charles, 1665-1724. 822'.4 B
The life of Mr. Thomas Betterton, the late eminent tragedian. Wherein the action and utterance of the state, bar, and pulpit, are distinctly consider'd. With the judgment of de St. Evremond, upon the Italian and French music and opera's; in a letter to the Duke of Buckingham. To which is added, The amorous widow; or, The wanton wife. A comedy. Written by Betterton. New York, A. M. Kelley, 1970. xiv, 176, 87 p. port. 23 cm. (Reprints of economic classics.) (Eighteenth century Shakespeare, no. 4) Reprint of the 1710 ed. [PN2598.B6G4 1970] 72-96345
1. Betterton, Thomas, 1635?-1710. I. Saint-Evremond, Charles de Marguetel de Saint-Denis, seigneur de, 1613?-1703. II. Betterton, Thomas, 1635?-1710. The amorous widow. 1970. III. Title. IV. Title: The amorous widow. V. Series.

LOWE, Robert William, 1853-1902. 792'.028'0924
Thomas Betterton. New York, Longmans, Green, 1891. [New York, AMS Press, 1972] vi, 196 p. 19 cm. [PN2598.B6L6 1972] 77-144652 ISBN 0-404-04038-1 8.00
1. Betterton, Thomas, 1635-1710. **BIP**

Beukelszoon, Jan, 1509?-1536.

SCHNUR, Harry C. 109'.22 B
Mystic rebels; Apollonius Tyaneus, Jan van Leyden, Sabbatai Zevi, Cagliostro, by Harry C. Schnur. Freeport, N.Y., Books for Libraries Press [1971, c1949] 316 p. illus. 23 cm. (Biography index reprint series) Includes bibliographical references. [BV5095.A1S3 1971] 74-179741 ISBN 0-8369-8109-X
1. Apollonius, of Tyana. 2. Beukelszoon, Jan, 1509?-1536. 3. Shabbethai Zebi, 1626-1676. 4. Cagliostro, Alessandro, conte di, 1743-1795. I. Title.

Beuys, Joseph.

ADRIANI, Gotz, 1940- 709'.2'4 B
Joseph Beuys, life and works / Gotz Adriani, Winfried Konnertz, Karin Thomas ; translated by Patricia Lech. Woodbury, N.Y. : Barron's Educational Series, inc., c1979. 308 p. : ill. ; 18 cm. Translation of Joseph Beuys. Bibliography: p. 302-307. [N6888.B463A8413 1979] 79-21831 ISBN 0-8120-2175-4 pbk. : 4.95
1. Beuys, Joseph. 2. Artists—Germany, West—Biography. I. Beuys, Joseph. II. Konnertz, Winfried, 1941- joint author. III. Thomas, Karin, 1941- joint author. IV. Title.

Bevan, Aneurin, 1897-1960.

BROME, Vincent, 1910- 923.242
Aneurin Bevan, a biography. London, New York, Longmans, Green [1953] 244p. illus. 23cm. [DA585.B38B7 1953] 53-4246
1. Bevan; Aneurin, 1897- 2. Gt. Brit— Pol. & govt.—1910-1936. 3. Gt. Brit.—Pol. & govt.—1936- I. Title.

FOOT, Michael, 1913- 942'.084'092'4
Aneurin Bevan, a biography. [1st American ed.] New York, Atheneum, 1963- v. illus. 22 cm. [DA585.B38F62] 63-17846 ISBN 0-689-10587-8 (v. 2)
1. Bevan, Aneurin, 1897-1960. I. Title.

KRUG, Mark M 1915- 923.242
Aneurin Bevan, cautious rebel. New York, T. Yoscloff [1961] 316p. 22cm. [DA585.B38K7 1961] 61-6923
1. Bevan, Aneurin, 1897- 2. Labour Party (Gt. Brit.) I. Title.

KRUG, Mark M., 1915- 923.242
Aneurin Bevan, cautious rebel. New York, T. Yoseloff [c.1961] 316p. Bibl. 61-6923 5.00
1. Bevan, Aneurin, 1897-1960. 2. Labour Party (Gt. Brit.) I. Title.

Bevan, Joseph Vallence, 1798-1830.

COULTER, Ellis Merton, 1890- 928.1
Joseph Vallence Bevan, Georgia's first official historian. Athens, Univ. of Ga. Pr. [c.1964] xvii, 157p. illus., facsim., map (on lining papers) ports. 25cm. (Wormsloe Found. Pubns. no. 7) Bibl. 64-17063 5.00
1. Bevan, Joseph Vallence, 1798-1830. I. Title. II. Series.

Bevan, Robert, 1865-1925.

BEVAN, Robert Alexander 759.2
Robert Bevan, 1865-1925: a memoir by his son [R. A. Bevan] London, Studio Vista [1966] 28p., 88p. of illus. (pt. col.) 33cm. Bibl. [ND497.B48B48] 67-6557 12.00
1. Bevan, Robert, 1865-1925. I. Title.

Beveridge, Albert Jeremiah, 1862-1927.

BRAEMAN, John. 973.91'0924 B
Albert J. Beveridge; American nationalist. Chicago, University of Chicago Press [1971] x, 370 p. 23 cm. Includes bibliographical references. [E748.B48B7] 75-142041 ISBN 0-226-07060-3
1. Beveridge, Albert Jeremiah, 1862-1927. **BIP**

Beveridge, William Henry Beveridge, Baron, 1879-1963.

BEVERIDGE, William Henry baron, 1879- 923.242
Power and influence. New York, Beechhurst Press [1955] 447p. illus. 22cm. Autobiography. [HC252.5.B45A3 1955] 55-14219
I. Title.

HARRIS, Jose. 330.9'2'4 B
William Beveridge : a biography / Jose Harris. Oxford [Eng.] : Clarendon Press, 1977. 488 p., [2] leaves of plates : ports. ; 25 cm. Includes index. Bibliography: p. [477]-479. [HC252.5.B45H37] 77-24344 ISBN 0-19-822459-1 : 22.00
1. Beveridge, William Henry Beveridge, Baron, 1879-1963. 2. Economists—Great Britain—Biography. I. Title.
Dist. by Oxford University Press, New York, NY **BIP**

Bevier, Isabel, 1860-1942.

BANE, Juliet Lita, 1887- 926.4
The story of Isabel Bevier. Peoria, Ill., C. A. Bennett Co. [1955] 191p. illus. 22cm. [TX140.B48B3] 55-579
1. Bevier, Isabel, 1860-1942. I. Title.

Bevington, Helen Smith, 1906- — Biography.

BEVINGTON, Helen Smith, 1906- 811'.5'4 B
Along came the witch : a journal in the 1960's / Helen Bevington. 1st ed. New York : Harcourt Brace Jovanovich, c1976. 223 p. ; 22 cm. Autobiographical. [PS3503.E924Z495] 75-31653 ISBN 0-15-105080-5 : 8.95
1. Bevington, Helen Smith, 1906- —Biography. I. Title. **BIP**

BEVINGTON, Helen (Smith) 1906- 811'.5'4 B
The house was quiet and the world was calm [by] Helen Bevington. [1st ed.] New York, Harcourt Brace Jovanovich [1971] 174 p. 21 cm. Autobiographical. [PS3503.E924Z52] 74-134570 ISBN 0-15-142190-0 5.95
I. Title.

Bewick, Thomas, 1753-1828.

BEWICK, Thomas, 1753-1828 927.6
A memoir of Thomas Bewick written by himself [Abridged ed.] Ed., introd. by Montague Weekley. Wood engravings by Thomas Bewick. London, Cresset Pr. [dist. Chester Springs, Pa., Dufour, 1964, c.1961] 203p. illus. 21cm. (Cresset lib.) 62-52032 3.95
I. Title.

BEWICK, Thomas, 1753- 769'.92'4 B 1828.
A memoir of Thomas Bewick / written by himself. Newcastle upon Tyne : Graham, 1974. [4], ii-xix, 344 p. : ill. ; 24 cm. Reprint of 1st ed. Newcastle upon Tyne, J. Bewick, 1862. [NE1147.6.B47A25 1974] 74-193399 ISBN 0-85983-065-9 : £3.50
1. Bewick, Thomas, 1753-1828. I. Title.

BEWICK, Thomas, 1753- 769'.92'4 B 1828.
A memoir of Thomas Bewick / written by himself ; edited with an introd. by Iain Bain. London ; New York : Oxford University Press, 1975. xliv, 258 p., [4] leaves of plates : ill. ; 25 cm. (Oxford English memoirs and travels) Includes index. Bibliography: p. xl-xli. [NE1147.6.B47A25 1975] 75-326114 ISBN 0-19-255413-1 : 21.00
1. Bewick, Thomas, 1753-1828. I. Title. II. Series.

DOBSON, Austin, 1840- 769'.924 B 1921.
Thomas Bewick and his pupils. London, Chatto and Windus, 1884; Detroit, Singing Tree Press, 1968. xviii, 232 p. illus., ports. 20 cm. [NE1212.B5D64 1968] 69-17340
1. Bewick, Thomas, 1753-1828. 2. Wood-engravers, English. I. Title. BIP

ROBINSON, Robert, 769'.92'4 bookseller, fl.1887-1892.
Thomas Bewick: his life and times. Newcastle upon Tyne, Graham, 1972. xxxviii, 328, [30] p. illus., facsims., ports. 25 cm. Facsimile of 1st ed., Newcastle, R. Robinson, 1887. Bibliography: p. 274-305. [NE1147.6.B47R62 1887a] 72-171487 £4.00
1. Bewick, Thomas, 1753-1828. I. Title.

Beyer, Andrew.

BEYER, Andrew. 798'.401
My $50,000 year at the races / Andrew Beyer. 1st ed. New York : Harcourt Brace Jovanovich, c1978. 163 p. ; 24 cm. [SF332.B49] 78-53918 ISBN 0-15-163693-1 : 8.95
1. Beyer, Andrew. 2. Horse race betting—United States. 3. Gamblers—United States—Biography. I. Title.

ROOSEVELT, 973.917'0924 B Franklin Delano, Pres. U.S., 1882-1945.
Franklin Delano Roosevelt, 1882-1945. Edited by Howard F. Bremer. Dobbs Ferry, N.Y., Oceana Publications, 1971. 220 p. 24 cm. ([The Presidential chronologies]) Bibliography: p. 205-216. [E742.5.R577] 71-116062 ISBN 0-379-12066-6 7.00
1. U.S.—Politics and government—1933-1945. I. U.S. President, 1933-1945 (Franklin D. Roosevelt) II. Bremer, Howard F., ed.

Beyle, Marie Henri, 1783-1842.

BEYLE, Marie Henri, 1783- 928.4 1842.
The life of Henri Brulard, by Stendhal (Henri Beyle) Translated from the French by Catherine Alison Phillips. New York, Vintage Books, 1955 [c1925] 376p. illus. 19cm. (a Vintage book, K-18) [PQ2436.A2V43 1955] 55-14434
I. Title.

BEYLE, Marie Henri, 1783- 928.4 1842.
The life of Henry Brulard [by] Stendhal [pseud.] Translated by Jean Stewart and B. C. J. G. Knight. New York, Noonday Press [1958] viii, 347 p. illus. 22 cm. [PQ2436.A2V43 1958] 58-13192
I. Title.

BEYLE, Marie Henri, 848'.7'03 1783-1842.
The life of Henry Brulard [by] Stendhal. Translated by Jean Stewart and B. C. J. G. Knight. New York, Funk & Wagnalls [1968, c1958] viii, 347 p. illus. 21 cm. Translation of Vie de Henri Brulard. [PQ2436.A2V43 1968] 68-4212
I. Title.

BEYLE, Marie Henri, 1783- 928.4 1842.
Memoirs of an egotist [by] Stendhal [pseud.] Translated & with an introd. by T. W. Earp. New York, Noonday Press [1958] xiii, 143p. illus. 21cm. (Noonday paperbacks, N131) [PQ2436.A2S72 1958] 58-13197
I. Title.

[BEYLE, Marie-Henri] 1783- 928.4 1842
The private diaries of Stendhal. Ed., tr. [from French] by Robert Sage. New York, Norton [1962, c.1954] 556p. 20cm. (Norton lib., N175) 1.95 pap.,
I. Title.

BEYLE, Marie Henri, 1783- 928.4 1842.
The private diaries of Stendhal (Marie-Henri Beyle) Edited and translated by Robert Sage. [1st ed.] Garden City, N. Y., Doubleday, 1954. xiv, 570p. illus., ports. facsims. 24cm. [PQ2436.A2J63] 54-11160
I. Title.

BEYLE, Marie Henri, 1783- 928.4 1842.
To the happy few; selected letters of Stendhal [pseud.] Introduced by Emmanuel Boudot-Lamotte; translated by Norman Cameron. New York, Grove Press [1952] 384p. port. 22cm. Translation of Aux ames sensibles. [PQ2436.A2A82] 51-10891
I. Title.

FINESHRIBER, William 848'.7'09 H., Jr.
Stendhal, the romantic rationalist, by William H. Fineshriber, Jr. [Folcroft, Pa.] Folcroft Library Editions, 1972. ix, 57 p. 26 cm. 150 copies printed. Reprint of the 1932 ed. Originally presented as the author's thesis, Princeton University. [PQ2436.F5 1972] 72-187169 10.00
1. Beyle, Marie Henri, 1783-1842. I. Title.

FOWLIE, Wallace, 1908- 843'.7
Stendhal. [New York] Macmillan [1969] xii, 240 p. 22 cm. (Masters of world literature series) Bibliography: p. [227]-233. [PQ2436.F6] 70-75903
1. Beyle, Marie Henri, 1783-1842. I. Title.

GREEN, Frederick 848'.7'09 B Charles, 1891-1964.
Stendhal. New York, Russell & Russell [1970] viii, 336 p. 23 cm. Reprint of the 1939 ed. Includes bibliographical references. [PQ2436.G7 1970] 76-102499
1. Beyle, Marie Henri, 1783-1842.

HAZARD, Paul, 1878-1944. 843.7 B
Stendhal (Henri Beyle) [Translated from the French by Elenaor Hard] New York, F. Ungar Pub. Co. [1965] 315 p. 21 cm. Translation of La vie de Stendhal. Reprint of the 1929 ed. [PQ2436.H32 1965] 65-23368
1. Beyle, Marie Henri, 1783-1842. I. Title.

JOSEPHSON, Matthew, 848'.7'09 B 1899-
Stendhal; or, The pursuit of happiness. New York, Russell & Russell [1969, c1946] xiii, 489 p. port. 25 cm. Includes bibliographical references. [PQ2436.J6 1969] 68-27066
1. Beyle, Marie Henri, 1783-1842.

MAY, Gita. 848'.7'09 B
Stendhal and the Age of Napoleon / by Gita May. New York : Columbia University Press, 1977. p. cm. Includes index. Bibliography: p. [PQ2436.M35] 77-8379 ISBN 0-231-04344-9 : 14.95
1. Beyle, Marie Henri, 1783-1842. 2. Authors, French—19th century—Biography. I. Title.

RICHARDSON, Joanna. 848'.7'09 B
Stendhal / Joanna Richardson. New York : Coward, McCann & Geoghegan, [1974] 344 p., [4] leaves of plates : ports. ; 24 cm. Includes index. Bibliography: p. 325-334. [PQ2436.R5] 73-93760 ISBN 0-698-10597-4 : 10.00
1. Beyle, Marie Henri, 1783-1842.

TILLETT, Margaret G. 848'.7'09 B
Stendhal: the background to the novels [by] Margaret Tillett. London, New York, Oxford University Press, 1971. xiv, 157 p. 23 cm. Bibliography: p. [150]-153. [PQ2440.T5] 78-584545 ISBN 0-19-212549-4 £2.75
1. Beyle, Marie Henri, 1783-1842.

WOOD, Michael, 1936- 843'.7
Stendhal. Ithaca, N.Y., Cornell University Press [1971] 208 p. 23 cm. Bibliography: p. 204-205. [PQ2436.B47W6] 73-164669 ISBN 0-8014-0680-3 7.50
1. Beyle, Marie Henri, 1783-1842. BIP

Beyle, Marie Henri, 1783-1842—Biography.

BEYLE, Marie Henri, 1783- 843'.7 1842.
The life of Henry Brulard [by] Stendhal, translated [from the French] and with an introduction by Jean Stewart and B. C. J. G. Knight. Harmondsworth, Penguin, 1973. 400 p. illus., facsims., plans. 19 cm. (Penguin classics) Translation of Vie de Henri Brulard. Bibliography: p. [19] [PQ2436.A2V43 1973] 74-168471 ISBN 0-14-044290-1 £0.50
1. Beyle, Marie Henri, 1783-1842—Biography. I. Title.

BEYLE, Marie Henri, 843'.7'09 B 1783-1842.
Memoirs of an egotist = Souvenirs d'egotisme / by Stendhal [i.e. Marie Henri Beyle] ; translated with an introd. and notes by David Ellis. New York : Horizon Press, 1975. 160 p. : ill. ; 21 cm. Includes bibliographical references. [PQ2436.A2S72 1975] 75-311543 ISBN 0-8180-0224-7 : 6.95
1. Beyle, Marie Henri, 1783-1842—Biography. I. Title.

BEYLE, Marie Henri, 848'.7'09 B 1783-1842.
Memoirs of egotism : from the intimate journal of Stendhal [i.e. M. H. Beyle] / edited with an introd. and notes by Matthew Josephson ; translated by Hannah and Matthew Josephson. New York : McGraw-Hill, 1975, c1949. p. cm. Translation of Souvenirs d'egotisme. Reprint of the ed. published by Lear, New York. [PQ2436.A2S72 1975b] 75-26924 ISBN 0-07-061145-9 pbk. : 2.95
1. Beyle, Marie Henri, 1783-1842—Biography. I. Title.

BEYLE, Marie Henri, 848'.7'09 B 1783-1842.
The private journals of Stendhal [i.e. M. H. Beyle] 1811-1817 / edited, selected & newly translated by Francis Carmody. Kentfield, Calif. : L-D Allen Press, 1954. 146 p. : ill. ; 27 cm. "Edition limited to 175 copies." [PQ2436.A2J63 1954b] 75-314030
1. Beyle, Marie Henri, 1783-1842—Biography. I. Title.

Beyler, Cecelia Mae.

BEYLER, Cecelia Mae 923.773
America calls from castle walls. Portland, Or., Metropolitan Press [1957] 128p. illus. 23cm. Autobiographical. [LA2317.B44A3] 57-43337
I. Title.

Bhandarkar, Ramkrishna Gopal, Sir, 1837-1925—Congresses.

RAMAKRISHNA Gopal 954.03'5'0924
Bhandarkar as an indologist : a symposium / edited by R. N. Dandekar. Poona : Bhandarkar Oriental Research Institute, 1976. 200 p., [1] leaf of plates : ill. ; 23 cm. (Research unit publications no. 2) Contents.Contents.—Sircar, D. C. Ramakrishna Gopal Bhandarkar as an indologist (particularly as a historian).—Dandekar, R. N. Vaisnavism and Saivism.—Joshi, S. D. Sanskrit grammar.—Ghatage, A. M. Indo-Aryan linguistics.—Mainkar, T. G. Literature and darsanas, with a postscript by R. N. D.—Bedekar, V. M. Research methodology.—Dandekar, R. N. Appendix I: A brief biographical sketch.—Appendix II: Contents of the collected works of Sir R. G. Bhandarkar. Includes bibliographical references. [DS435.7.B47R35] 77-901816
1. Bhandarkar, Ramkrishna Gopal, Sir, 1837-1925—Congresses. 2. Indic philology—Congresses. 3. Hinduism—Congresses. I. Bhandarkar, Ramkrishna Gopal, Sir, 1837-1925. II. Dandekar, Ramchandra Narayan. III. Series: Bhandarkar Oriental Research Institute, Poona, India. Research Unit. Research Unit publications ; no. 2.

Bhartrhari.

COWARD, Harold G. 891'.2'1 B
Bhartrhari / by Harold G. Coward. Boston : Twayne Publishers, c1976. p. cm. (Twayne's world authors series ; TWAS 403 : India) Includes index. Bibliography: p. [PK3791.B29C6] 76-8940 ISBN 0-8057-6243-4 lib. bdg. : 8.95
1. Bhartrhari. BIP

Bialik, Hayyim Nahman, 1873-1934.

EISENBERG, Azriel Louis, 928.924 1903-
Presenting Bialik: a study of his life and works, by Azriel Eisenberg and Abraham Segal. New York, Jewish Education Committee of New York, [1956.] 113p. 25 cm. Bibliography: p. 106-113. [PJ5053.B52E5] 57-3306
1. Bialik, Hayyim Nahman, 1873-1934. I. Segal, Abraham, 1910- joint author. II. Title.

Bialoszewski, Miron—Biography.

BIAIOSZEWSKI, 940.53'438'40924 B Miron.
A memoir of the Warsaw uprising / Miron Bialoszewski ; edited and translated by Madeline Levine. Ann Arbor, Mich. : Ardis, c1977. 234 p. : ill. ; 24 cm. Translation of Pamietnik z powstania warszawskiego. Title on spine: The Warsaw uprising. [D765.2.W3B513] 78-300379 ISBN 0-88233-275-9 : 14.95.
1. Bialoszewski, Miron—Biography. 2. Warsaw—History—Uprising of 1944—Personal narratives. 3. Authors, Polish—20th century—Biography. I. Title. II. Title: The Warsaw uprising. BIP

Bible Biography.

ANDREASEN, Milian Lauritz, 220.92 1876-
Saints and sinners. Washington, Review and Herald Pub. Association [1951] 192 p. 20 cm. [BS571.A6] 51-35224
1. Bible—Biog. 2. Seventh-Day Adventists—Sermons. I. Title.

BAXTER, James Sidlow. 220.92
Mark these men; practical studies in striking aspects of certain Bible characters. Grand Rapids, Zondervan Pub. House [1960] 192p. 20cm. [BS571.5.B3] 60-50186
1. Bible—Biog. 2. Baptists—Sermons. 3. Sermons, English—Scotland. I. Title.

BARKER, William Pierson. 220.92 B
Saints and swingers; the under-thirties in the Bible [by] William P. Barker. Old Tappan, N.J., F. H. Revell Co. [1971] 160 p. 22 cm. [BS571.B34] 72-149375 ISBN 0-8007-0446-0 3.95
1. Bible—Biography. I. Title.

BARLOW, Fred, 1921- 220.9'2
Heaven's hall of heroes / Fred M. Barlow ; ill. by Doug Chaffee. Schaumburg, Ill. : Regular Baptist Press, c1978. 143 p. : ill. ; 23 cm. Includes bibliographical references. [BS571.B347] 78-16887 ISBN 0-87227-062-9 pbk. : 2.95
1. Bible—Biography. I. Title. BIP

BUECHNER, Frederick, 220.9'2 B 1926-
Peculiar treasures : a biblical who's who / Frederick Buechner ; with ill. by Katherine A. Buechner. 1st ed. San Francisco : Harper & Row, c1979. 181 p. : ill. ; 22 cm. [BS571.B84 1979] 78-20586 ISBN 0-06-061157-X. : 7.95
1. Bible—Biography. I. Title. BIP

BURKE, Carl F. 220.9'2 B
The boy who stayed cool, and other stories of young people in the Bible [by] Carl F. Burke. New York, Association Press [1973] 125 p. 19 cm. Retells in slang forty Biblical tales describing the lives of various people in the Old and New Testament.

[BS551.2.B87] 73-15685 ISBN 0-8096-1877-X 4.95
1. Bible—Biography. 2. Bible stories, English. I. Title.
Pbk. 2.95.

CHAPPELL, Clovis Gillham, 1882- 220.92
Meet these men. New York, Abingdon Press [1956] 156p. 20cm. [BS571.C42] 56-6354
1. Bible—Biog. I. Title. BIP

CHAPPELL, Clovis Gillham, 1882- 225.92'2
Men that count, by Clovis G. Chappell. Grand Rapids, Baker Book House [1967] 164 p. 20 cm. (Ministers paperback library) Reprint of the 1929 ed. Sermons. Contents.Contents.—Needless poverty: James.—Worry and its cure: Paul.—All things new: Paul.—A great believer: Paul.—At the cross: Paul.—A successful service: Peter.—Kept: Peter.—A pilgrim's progress: the man born blind.—The glory of the ordinary: Andrew.—A fighter: Zacchaeus.—A woman's revenge: John the Baptist.—A beautiful vocation: Onesiphorus.—Making life count: author of Hebrews.—A wholehearted saint: Caleb.—Mr. Sorrowful: Jabez.—The spoiled dream: Jeremiah. [BS571.5.C46 1967] 67-18173
1. Bible—Biography. 2. Sermons, American. I. Title. BIP

CHAPPELL, Clovis Gillham, 1882-1972. 220.92
Meet these men: sermons on Bible characters. Grand Rapids, Baker Book House [1974, c1956] 156 p. 20 cm. [BS571.C42] ISBN 0-8010-2354-8 2.50 (pbk.)
1. Bible—Biography. I. Title.
L.C. card no. for original edition: 56-6354.

CHEVILLE, Roy Arthur, 1897- 220.92
Meet them in the Scriptures; a guide to character appreciation through family reading. Independence, Mo., Herald House [c.1960] 224p. 60-51797 2.50
1. Bible—Biog. 2. Reorganized Church of Jesus Christ of Latter-Day Saints—Doctrinal and controversial works. I. Title.

CHUPP, Tommy. 220.9'2 B
Bible characters : sinners, saints and servants / Tommy Chupp. Nashville : T. Nelson, [1975] x, 149 p. : ill. ; 21 cm. Title on spine: Sinners, saints and servants. [BS572.C47] 74-23285 ISBN 0-8407-5589-9 pbk. : 3.50.
1. Bible—Biography. I. Title. II. Title: Sinners, Saints, and servants.

CROWELL, Grace (Noll) 1877- 220.92
God's masterpieces. Nashville, Abingdon [c.1963] 96p. 18cm. 63-7479 1.75 bds.,
1. Bible—Biog. I. Title.

CULLY, Iris V. 220.9'2 B
From Aaron to Zerubbabel : profiles of Bible people / Iris V. Cully and Kendig Brubaker Cully. New York : Hawthorn Books, c1976. vi, 149 p. ; 21 cm. [BS570.C84 1976] 76-7830 ISBN 0-8015-6084-5 : 2.95
1. Bible—Biography. I. Cully, Kendig Brubaker, joint author. II. Title.

DEEN, Edith. 220.9'2 B
All the Bible's men of hope. [1st ed.] Garden City, N.Y., Doubleday, 1974. xxiv, 310 p. 22 cm. Bibliography: p. [297]-299. [BS571.D4] 73-22786 ISBN 0-385-05100-X 7.95
1. Bible—Biography. 2. Hope—Biblical teaching. I. Title.

*EVANS, B. Hoyt 220.92
Youth programs about Bible people. Grand Rapids, Mich., Baker Bk. [c.]1964. 107p. 20cm. 1.50 pap.,
I. Title.

FICKETT, Harold L. 220.92
Profiles in clay. Los Angeles, 747 Seward St., Cowman, 1963 147p. 21cm. 63-12081 2.95
1. Bibl.—Biog. I. Title.

FLETCHER, William C. 220.92
Unlikely saints of the Bible, surprising and dramatic character sketches of familiar and unfamiliar personalities in Scripture. Illus. by Dirk Gringhuis. Grand Rapids, Mich., Zondervan Pub. House [c.1961] 144p. 25cm. 61-33979 2.95
1. Bible—Biog. I. Title.

GIBBS, Paul T. 220.92
Men such as we. Washington, D.C., Review & Herald [c.1963] 192p. illus. 22cm. 63-10403 3.50
1. Bible—Biog. I. Title.

GILLILAND, Dolores Scott. 220.9'505
Selected women of the Scriptures of stamina and courage / by Dolores Scott Gilliland ; illustrated by Gael Scott. Spearfish, SD : Honor Books, c1978. 101 p. : ill. ; 22 cm. [BS575.G47] 78-50069 ISBN 0-931446-02-3 pbk. : 3.95
1. Bible—Biography. 2. Women in the Bible. I. Title. BIP

HARBOUR, Brian L. 301.42'7
Famous couples of the Bible / Brian L. Harbour. Nashville : Broadman Press, c1979. 132 p. ; 18 cm. Includes bibliographical references. [BS680.M35H29] 78-60053 ISBN 0-8054-5630-9 pbk. : 2.25
1. Bible—Biography. 2. Marriage—Biblical teaching. I. Title. BIP

HAVNER, Vance, 1901- 248'.4
Moments of decision / Vance Havner. Old Tappan, N.J. : Revell, c1979. p. cm. [BV4501.2.H3683] 79-20786 ISBN 0-8007-1091-6 : 5.95
1. Bible—Biography. 2. Christian life—1960- 3. Decision-making (Ethics) I. Title. BIP

HEWITT, Charles Edward. 220.92
'Songs in the night' for birds with broken wing. New York, Loizeaux Bros. [1938] 124p. 20cm. [BS572.H48] 55-46598
1. Bible—Biog. I. Title.

HUGHES, Edna Beougher. 220.92
Voices from eternity. [1st ed.]. New York, Pageant Press [1957, c1956] 96). 21cm. [BS571.H76] 56-13121
1. Bible—Biog. I. Title.

KEIPER, Ralph L. 248'.4
The power of Biblical thinking / Ralph L. Keiper. Old Tappan, N.J. : F. H. Revell Co., c1977. 159 p. ; 21 cm. [BV4501.2.K417] 77-2956 ISBN 0-8007-0862-8 : 5.95
1. Bible—Biography. 2. Christian life—1960- I. Title.

KEIPER, Ralph L. 248'.4
The power of Biblical thinking / Ralph L. Keiper. Old Tappan, N.J. : F. H. Revell Co., c1977. 159 p. ; 21 cm. [BV4501.2.K417] 77-2956 ISBN 0-8007-0862-8 : 5.95
1. Bible—Biography. 2. Christian life—1960- I. Title. BIP

KIRBAN, Salem. 248'.4
How to live above & beyond your circumstances / by Salem Kirban. Huntingdon Valley, Pa. : Kirban, c1974. 218 p. : ill. ; 18 cm. [BV4501.2.K498] 74-19641 ISBN 0-912582-20-0 : 3.95
1. Bible—Biography. 2. Christian life—1960- I. Title. BIP

KRUER, A. C. 220.9'2
They also speak / A. C. Kruer. Nashville, Tenn. : Broadman Press, c1979. 126 p. ; 19 cm. [BS571.K78] 78-67453 ISBN 0-8054-1133-X pbk. : 2.95
1. Bible—Biography. I. Title. BIP

LA SOR, William Sanford 220.92
Great personalities of the Bible. Westwood, N. J., Revell [1965, c.1964] 192p. 21cm. Most of the mat. in this bk. was orig. pub. in the two vols. entitled Great personalities of the Old Testament and Great personalities of the New Testament. Bibl. [BS571.L318] 65-10560 5.95 bds.,
1. Bible—Biog. I. Title.

LA SOR, William Sanford. 220.92
Great personalities of the Bible. Westwood, N.J., F.H. Revell Co. [1965] 192 p. 21 cm. "Most of the material in this book was originally published in the two volumes entitled Great personalities of the Old Testament and Great personalities of the New Testament." Bibliography: p. 185-189. [BS571.L318 1965] 65-10560
1. Bible — Biog. I. Title.

LEE, G. Avery. 220.92'2
Great men of the Bible and the women in their lives by G. Avery Lee. Waco, Tex., Word Books [1968] 107 p. 21 cm. Bibliographical footnotes. [BS572.L4] 68-22236
1. Bible—Biography. 2. Women in the Bible. I. Title.

LEESTMA, Harold F. 248'.24
God at my elbow; the meaning of conversion [by] Harold F. Leestma. Waco, Tex., Word Books [1973, c1972] 84 p. 23 cm. [BV4916.L43] 72-84165 2.95
1. Bible—Biography. 2. Conversion. I. Title.

LEHMAN, Louis Paul. 220.92
Tears of the Bible. Grand Rapids, Zondervan Pub. House [1958] 93p. 20cm. [BS571.L45] 58-2477
1. Bible—Biog. I. Title.

LEHMBERG, Ben F. 220.92
Seven tall men. Grand Rapids, Mich., Eerdmans [c.1961] 73p. 60-53089 2.00 bds.,
1. Bible—Biog. I. Title.

LOCKYER, Herbert. 220.92
All the kings and queens of the Bible; tragedies and triumps of royalty in past ages. Grand Rapids, Zondervan Pub. House [1961] 253p. maps. 24cm. Bibliography: p. 249-250. [BS579.K5L6] 61-1477
1. Bible—Biog. I. Title.

LOCKYER, Herbert [Henry John] 220.92
All the kings and queens of the Bible; tragedies and triumphs of royalty in past ages. Grand Rapids, Mich., Zondervan Pub. House [c.1961] 253p. maps. Bibl. 61-1477 3.95 bds.,
1. Bible—Biog. I. Title.

*LOCKYER, Herbert 220.92.
Ancient portraits in modern frames Grand Rapids, Baker Book House [1975] 135p. 20 cm. Contents.Contents: vol. 1: bible biographies [BS571] ISBN 0-8010-5545-8. 2.95 (pbk)
1. Bible-Biography. I. Title.

LOCKYER, Herbert. 220.9'2
Their finest hour : thrilling moments in ancient history / Herbert Lockyer. Old Tappan, N.J. : Revell, c1979. 159 p. ; 22 cm. [BS571.L6] 79-15187 ISBN 0-8007-1056-8 : 6.95
1. Bible—Biography. I. Title.

MACARTNEY, Clarence Edward Noble, 1879- 220.92
Chariots of fire, and other sermons on Bible characters. New York, Abingdon-Cokesbury Press [1951] 192 p. 20 cm. [BS571.M222] 51-13256
1. Bible—Biog. 2. Presbyterian Church—Sermons. 3. Sermons, American. I. Title.

MACARTNEY, Clarence Edward Noble, 1879- 220.92
The man who forgot, and other sermons on Bible characters. New York, Abingdon Press [1956] 140p. 20cm. [BS571.M228] 56-5125
1. Bible—Biog. 2. Presbyterian Church—Sermons. 3. Sermons, American. I. Title.

MACARTNEY, Clarence Edward Noble, 1879- 220.92
The man who forgot, and other sermons on Bible characters. New York, Abington Press [1956] 140p. 20cm. [BS571.M228] 56-5125
1. Bible—Biog. 2. Presbyterian Church—Sermons. 3. Sermons, American. I. Title.

MACARTNEY, Clarence Edward Noble, 1879- 220.92
The woman of Tekoah, and other sermons on Bible characters. Nashville, Abingdon Press [c1955] 160p. 20cm. [BS571.M243] 55-5397
1. Bible—Biog. 2. Presbyterian Church—Sermons. 3. Sermons, American. I. Title.

MACARTNEY, Clarence Edward Noble. 220.92
The woman of Tekoah, and other sermons on Bible characters / Clarence Edward Macartney. Grand Rapids : Baker Book House, 1977. 160p. ; 20 cm. [BS571.M243] ISBN 0-8010-6020-6 pbk. : 2.95
1. Bible — Biography. 2. Presbyterian church — Sermons. 3. Sermons, American. I. Title.
L.C. card no. for 1955 Abingdon press ed. : 55-5397. BIP

MCGEE, John Vernon, 1904- 220.9'2 B
Vessels, vehicles, and victory : unforgettable men of the Bible / J. Vernon McGee. Chicago : Moody Press, c1976. 128 p. ; 18 cm. [BS571.M253] 76-9042 ISBN 0-8024-9157-X pbk. : 0.95
1. Bible—Biography. I. Title.

MEAD, Frank Spencer, 1898- 220.92
Who's who in the Bible; 25o Bible biographies. New York, Harper [1966, c.1934] xi p., 1 1., 250p. 21cm. (Chapel bks., CB25H) Formerly pub. under the title, 250 Bible biographies. [BS571.M376] 38-27349 1.45 pap.,
1. Bible — Biog. I. Title.

MILHOUSE, Paul William, 1910- 220.92
At life's crossroads. Anderson, Ind, Warner Press [1959] 112p. 20cm. [BS572.M5] 59-8790
1. Bible— Biog. 2. Decision-making. I. Title.

MULLIKEN, Frances Hartman, 1924- 220.9'2 B
Women of destiny in the Bible / by Frances Hartman Mulliken and Margaret Salts. Independence, Mo. : Herald Pub. House, c1978. 187 p. ; 18 cm. Bibliography: p. 186-187. Introduces seventeen women who play a significant role in the Bible including Sarah, Esther, Mary Magdalene, and Lydia. [BS575.M83] 78-5132 ISBN 0-8309-0211-2 pbk. : 4.00
1. Bible—Biography. 2. Women in the Bible. I. Salts, Margaret, 1918- joint author. II. Title.
Publisher's address : Drawer HH, Independence, MO 64055 BIP

NEWSHAM, Harold Goad. 220.92
The man who feared a bargain, and other sermons on Bible characters. New York, Abingdon Press [1958] 125p. 20cm. [BS571.N58] 58-5391
1. Bible—Biog. 2. Congregational churches— Sermons. 3. Sermons, American. I. Title.

POWELL, Ivor 220.92
Bible cameos. Grand Rapids, Mich., Zondervan Pub. House [1960, 1951] 173p. 21cm. 60-4695 2.50
1. Bible—Biog. I. Title.

POWELL, Ivor 220.92
Bible pinnacles. With a foreword by F. W. Boreham. Grand Rapids, Mich., Zondervan Pub. House [1960] [viii], 174p. 21cm. 60-4694 2.50
1. Bible—Biog. I. Title.

POWELL, Ivor 220.92
Bible treasures. With a foreword by Lionel B. Fletcher. Grand Rapids, Mich., Zondervan Pub. House [1960] 182p. 21cm. 60-4697 2.50
1. Bible—Biog. I. Title.

REDDING, David A. 209'.22 B
What is the man? [By] David A. Redding. Waco, Tex., Word Books [1970] 169 p. 23 cm. Includes bibliographical references. [BS571.R37] 71-128447 4.50
1. Bible—Biography. 2. Christian biography. I. Title.

REECE, Colleen L. 288.3'092'2 B
The unknown witnesses, by Colleen L. Reece. [Independence, Mo., Herald Pub. House, 1974] 159 p. 18 cm. [BX8693.R43] 73-87642 ISBN 0-8309-0107-8 5.00
1. Bible—Biography. 2. Mormons and Mormonism—Biography. I. Title. BIP

*ROBERTSON, A. T. 225.9'22
Some minor characters in the New Testament / by A. T. Robertson. Grand Rapids : Baker Book House, 1976c1928 182p. ; 20 cm. (His LibraryII) [BS2430] ISBN 0-8010-7637-4 pbk. : 2.95.
1. Bible-Biography. I. Title. BIP

SANDERS, John Oswald, 220.9'2 B

1902-
People just like us / by J. Oswald Sanders. Chicago : Moody Press, c1978. 219 p. ; 22 cm. Includes bibliographical references. [BS571.S233] 78-9481 ISBN 0-8024-6459-9 pbk. : 3.95
1. Bible—Biography. I. Title. **BIP**

SANDERS, John Oswald, 220.92
1902-
Robust in faith: men from God's school. Chicago, Moody [c.1965] 219p. 22cm. (Overseas Missionary Fellowship bk.) [BS571.S23] 65-4898 3.50
1. Bible—Biog. I. Title.

SEAGREN, Daniel. 220.9'2 B
Couples in the Bible; a discussion guide [by] Daniel R. Seagren. Grand Rapids, Baker Book House [1972] 162 p. 18 cm. (Contemporary discussion series) Includes bibliographical references. [BS579.H8S4] 72-90330 ISBN 0-8010-7971-3 1.25
1. Bible—Biography. 2. Marriage—Biblical teaching. I. Title.

SESSIONS, Will. 220.92
Greater men and women of the Bible. St. Louis, Bethany Press [1958] 208 p. 23 cm. [BX571.S44] 58-7478
1. Bible — Biog. I. Title.

SMEAD, Elizabeth. 220.92
Women of the Scriptures, by Elizabeth Smead and Elizabeth Stone. [1st ed] New York, Vantage Press [c1956] 67 p. 21 cm. [BS575.S47] 56-11199
1. Bible — Biog. 2. Women in the Bible. I. Stone, Elizabeth Blinn, joint author. II. Title.

STEVENSON, Herbert F 220.92
A galaxy of saints; lesser known Bible men and women. Foreword by Paul S. Rees. [Westwood, N.J.] Revell [1958] 158 p. 21 cm. [BS571.S83] 58-8650
1. Bible — Biog. I. Title.

STRAUSS, Richard L. 248'.4
Living in love : secrets from Bible marriages / Richard L. Strauss. Wheaton, Ill. : Tyndale House Publishers, c1978. 141 p. ; 21 cm. [BS680.M35S8] 77-93752 ISBN 0-8423-2488-7 pbk. : 3.95
1. Bible—Biography. 2. Marriage—Biblical teaching. I. Title.

VAJDA, Jaroslav. 220.9'2 B
Follow the King : models for heroic living / Jaroslav Vajda. St. Louis : Concordia Pub. House, 1977, c1964. 96 p. : ill. ; 26 cm. Abridged ed. of the author's they followed the King, published in 1964. [BS571.V282] 76-30651 ISBN 0-570-03049-8 : 3.95
1. Bible—Biography. I. Title.

WHITESELL, Faris Daniel 220.92
Sermon outlines on Bible characters. [Westwood, N. J.] Revell [c.1960] 64p. 21cm. (Revell's sermon outline series) 60-8460 1.00 pap.,
1. Bible—Biog. I. Title.

WHITESELL, Faris Daniel, 220.92
1895-
Sermon outlines on Bible characters. [Westwood, N.J.] Revell [1960] 64 p. 21 cm. (Revell's sermon outline series) [BS571.W52] 60-8460
1. Bible — Biog. I. Title.

WOOD, Fred M 220.92
Bible truth in person [by] Fred M. Wood. Nashville, Broadman Press [1965] 126 p. 20 cm. Bibliographical footnotes. [BX571.W58] 65-11767
1. Bible — Biog. I. Title.

WRIGHT, John Stafford. 220.9'2 B
Revell's Dictionary of Bible people / J. Stafford Wright. Old Tappan, N.J. : F. H. Revell Co., c1978. x, 239 p., [3] leaves of plates : maps ; 22 cm. Originally published under title: Dictionary of Bible people. [BS570.W74 1978b] 78-20810 ISBN 0-8007-1038-X : 7.95
1. Bible—Biography. I. Title. **BIP**

Bible—Biography—Addresses, essays, lectures.

GOD demands doctrinal preaching / edited by Thomas B. Warren, Garland Elkins. Jonesboro, Ark. : National Christian Press, c1978. 332 p. ; 22 cm. (Spiritual sword lectureship ; 3) Includes bibliographical references. [BV4222.G6] 78-113413 9.95 pbk. : 7.95 251
1. Bible—Biography—Addresses, essays, lectures. 2. Bible—Criticism, interpretation, etc.—Addresses, essays, lectures. 3. Preaching—Addresses, essays, lectures. I. Warren, Thomas B. II. Elkins, Garland. III. Title. IV. Series. **BIP**

Bible—Biography—Dictionaries.

BARKER, William Pierson. 220.92
Everyone in the Bible [by] William P. Barker. Westwood, N.J., F. H. Revell Co. [1966] 370 p. 24 cm. [BS570.B3] 66-21894
1. Bible—Biography—Dictionaries. I. Title. **BIP**

BARR, George, 1916- 220.9'2
Who's who in the Bible. Middle Village, N.Y., Jonathan David Publishers [1975] 177 p. 22 cm. [BS570.B33] 74-1965
1. Bible—Biography—Dictionaries. I. Title.

DOWLEY Bible atlas; 220.9'2
an historical chronological outline of events from the formation of Adam to the building of Solomon's temple; the divided kingdoms of Judah and Israel, and the prophets after the division ... A biography of more than three thousand persons mentioned in the Bible; one hundred and twelve subjects of the positive and negative powers of life; a list of 3132 Bible names, alphabetically and numerically arranged with key for locating same on the accompanying chart; the Adam family tree with cross keyed index and Bible references. Jackson, Mich., Dowley Bible Atlas Co. [1972] 330 p. illus. 29 cm. [BS570.D68] 78-186595
1. Bible—Biography—Dictionaries. I. Title: Bible atlas.

LOCKYER, Herbert. 220.92
All the men of the library of more than 3000 Biblical characters. Grand Bible; a portrait gallery and reference Rapids, Zondervan Pub. House [1958] 381p. 24cm. Bibliography: p. 373-374. [BS570.L6] 58-4616
1. Bible—Biog.— Dictionaries. I. Title.

SAXON, Kurt. 220.9'2 B
The instant who's who in the Bible / Kurt Saxon. [Eureka, Calif. : Atlan Formularies, 1974] 302 p. ; 28 cm. Cover title. [BS570.S38] 74-11874
1. Bible—Biography—Dictionaries. 2. Bible—Geneaology. I. Title.

SIMS, Albert E., ed. 220.92
Who's who in the Bible: an ABC cross reference of names of people in the Bible, compiled and edited by Albert E. Sims and George Dent. New York, Philosophical Library [c.1960] 96p. 20cm. 60-16209 3.75
1. Bible—Biog.—Dictionaries. I. Dent, George, joint ed. II. Title.

SIMS, Albert E., ed. 220.92
Who's who in the Bible: an ABC cross reference of names of people in the Bible, compiled and edited by Albert E. Sims and George Dent. New York, Philosophical Library [c.1960] 96p. 20cm. 60-16209 3.75
1. Bible—Biog.—Dictionaries. I. Dent, George, joint ed. II. Title.

SIMS, Albert E ed. 220.92
Who's who in the Bible; an ABC cross reference of names of people in the Bible, compiled and edited by Albert E. Sims and George Dent. London, New York, W. Foulsham [1958] 96 p. 20 cm. [BS570.S5] 58-35740
1. Bible — Biog. — Dictionaries. I. Dent, George, joint ed. II. Title.

SIMS, Albert E ed. 220.92
Who's who in the Bible; an ABC cross reference of names of people in the Bible, compiled and edited by Albert E. Sims and George Dent. London, New York, W. Foulsham [1958] 96 p. 20 cm. [BS570.S5] 58-35740
1. Bible — Biog. — Dictionaries. I. Dent, George, joint ed. II. Title.

Bible Biography Dictionaries, Juvenile.

GOUKER, Loice 220.92
Bible people: highlights from their lives. Designed by Tyyne Hakola. Norwalk, Conn., C. R. Gibson Co. [c.1965] 68p. illus. 19cm. [BS539.G6] 65-16437 1.35
1. Bible — Biog. — Dictionaries, Juvenile. I. Title.

Bible Biography, Juvenile Literature.

SMITH, Betty 220.92
Friends of Jesus. Illus. by Cicely Steed. Philadelphia, Westminster [1963, c.1962] 32p. illus. (pt. col.) 21cm. (Stories of Jesus, bk. 4) .75 bds.,
1. Bible—Biog.—Juvenile literature. I. Title.

Bible—Biography—Sermons.

*CULBERTSON, Paul T. 221.922
Contemporary insights from Bible characters [by] Paul T. Culbertson. Grand Rapids, Mich., Baker Book House [1973] 144 p. 20 cm. [BS571.5] ISBN 0-8010-2350-5 2.45 (pbk.)
1. Bible—Biography—Sermons. I. Title.

REDHEAD, John A 220.92
Sermons on Bible characters. New York, Abingdon Press [1963] 144 p. 21 cm. [BS571.5.R4] 63-11380
1. Bible — Biog. — Sermons. 2. Presbyterian Church — Sermons. 3. Sermons, American. I. Title.

REDHEAD, John A 220.92
Sermons on Bible characters. New York, Abingdon Press [1963] 144 p. 21 cm. [BS571.5.R4] 63-11380
1. Bible — Biog. — Sermons. 2. Presbyterian Church — Sermons. 3. Sermons, American. I. Title.

Bible—Criticism, interpretation, etc.

LAYMON, Charles M. 220.6'6
They dared to speak for God [by] Charles M. Laymon. Nashville, Abingdon Press [1974] 176 p. 22 cm. Includes bibliographical references. [BS511.2.L4] 73-17196 ISBN 0-687-41649-3 5.95
1. Bible—Criticism, interpretation, etc. 2. Bible—Biography. 3. Preaching—Biblical teaching. I. Title.

Bible—History of contemporary events.

LEWIS, Jack Pearl, 1919- 220.95
Historical backgrounds of Bible history, by Jack P. Lewis. Grand Rapids, Mich., Baker Book House [1971] 199 p. illus. 22 cm. (University Christian Student Center. Annual lectureship, 1969) Includes bibliographical references. [BS635.2.L49] 79-156594 ISBN 0-8010-5507-5 3.95
1. Bible—History of contemporary events 2. Bible—Antiquities. 3. Bible—Biography. I. Title. II. Series.

Bible. N.T.—Biography.

BARCLAY, William, lecturer 270.1
in the University of Glasgow.
God's young church. Philadelphia, Westminster Press [1970] 120 p. 19 cm. [BR165.B277] 70-110082 ISBN 0-664-24884-5 1.85
1. Bible. N.T.—Biography. 2. Church history—Primitive and early church, ca. 30-600. 3. Christian life—1960- I. Title. **BIP**

BARKER, William Pierson 226.092
Personalities around Jesus [Westwood, N.J.] Revell [c.1963] 156p. 20cm. 63-17108 2.95 bds.,
1. Bible. N.T.—Biog. I. Title.

BORGWARDT, Robert G 225.92
Men who knew Jesus. Minneapolis, T. S. Denison [1958] 115p. 22cm. [BS2430.B6] 58-9507
1. Bible. N. T. —Biog. I. Title.

BRUCE, Alexander Balmain, 232.9'5
1831-1899.
The training of the twelve : or, Passages out of the Gospels : exhibiting the twelve disciples of Jesus under discipline for the apostleship / by Alexander Balmain Bruce. 4th ed., rev. and improved. New Canaan, Conn. : Keats Pub., 1979. xvii, 552 p., [4] leaves of plates : ill. ; 21 cm. (A Shepherd illustrated classic) Includes bibliographical references and index. [BS2440.B7 1979] 79-88121 ISBN 0-87983-206-1 : 5.95
1. Bible, N.T.—Biography. 2. Apostles. I. Title.

CORNELL, George W. 225.92
They knew Jesus. New York, Morrow, 1957. 288 p. illus. 21 cm. Includes bibliography. [BS2430.C55] 57-10930
1. Bible. N. T.—Biography. I. Title.

DAUGHTERS of St. Paul. 220.9'2 B
Women of the Gospel / written by the Daughters of St. Paul ; ill. by Gregori. Boston : St. Paul Editions, 1975. 134 p. : ill. ; 25 cm. [BS2445.D38] 74-32122
1. Bible. N.T.—Biography. 2. Women in the Bible. I. Title. **BIP**

DAVIDSON, Donald. 225.922
God chose them; thirty informative character studies of New Testament men and women. Grand Rapids, Zondervan Pub. House [1965] 142 p. 23 cm. [BS2430.D28 1965] 65-6000
1. Bible. N.T. — Biog. I. Title.

DRUMWRIGHT, Huber L. 225.9'2 B
Saints alive! The humble heroes of the New Testament [by] Huber L. Drumwright. Nashville, Tenn., Broadman Press [1972] 128 p. 21 cm. [BS2430.D78] 72-79169 ISBN 0-8054-8116-8 1.95
1. Bible. N.T.—Biography. I. Title. **BIP**

HILL, David C. 225.922
These met the Master; 40 portraits of persons who encountered the Christ [by] David C. Hill. Minneapolis. Augsburg [c.1967] 95p. 20cm. [BS2430.H5] 67-11716 1.95 pap.,
1. Bible. N.T.—Biog. I. Title.

LA SOR, William Sanford. 225.92
Great personalities of the New Testament: their lives and times. [Westwood, N. J.] Revell [1961] 192p. 21cm. Includes bibliography. [BS2430.L23] 61-9239
1. Bible. N. T.—Biog. I. Title.

LA SOR, William Sanford. 225.9'22
Men who knew Christ. Glendale, Calif., G/L Regal Books [1971] 167 p. illus. 18 cm. Bibliography: p. 162-167. [BS2430.L24] 70-135026 ISBN 0-8307-0086-2 0.95
1. Bible. N.T.—Biography. I. Title. **BIP**

LASOR, Williams Sanford 225.92
Great personalities of the New Testament: their lives and times. Westwood, N. J., Revell [c.1961] 192p. Bibl. 61-9239 3.00
1. Bible. N. T.—Biog. I. Title.

PERRY, Earl. 225.92'2
These first called Him Master. Nashville, Broadman Press [1968] 128 p. 20 cm. Bibliography: p. 128. [BS2440.P4] 68-12131
1. Bible. N.T.—Biograpy. 2. Apostles. I. Title.

POWELL, Terry. 248'.4
Nobody's perfect / by Terry Powell. Wheaton, Ill. : Victor Books, c1979. 116 p. : ill. ; 18 cm. (SonPower youth publication) [BS2430.P68] 78-65556 ISBN 0-88207-577-2 pbk. : 1.75
1. Bible N.T.—Biography. 2. Christian life—1960- I. Title. **BIP**

ROLSTON, Holmes, 1900- 225.92
Personalities around Paul; men and women who helped or hindered the Apostle Paul. Richmond, John Knox Press [1954] 206 p. 21 cm. [BS2430.R63] 54-8504
1. Bible. N. T.—Biography. 2. Paul, Saint, apostle. I. Title.

SEGERHAMMAR, Carl William. 225.92
They talked with God; sermon studies on New Testament characters. Rock Island, Ill., Augustana Book Concern [1954] 190p. 21cm. [BS2430.S4] 54-9965
1. Bible. N. T.—Biog. I. Title.

TURNBULL, Ralph G. 225.92
Personalities of the New Testament. Grand Rapids, Mich., Baker Bk. House [c.]1961. 114p. 61-10000 1.95 bds.,
1. Bible N. T.—Biog. I. Title.

TURNBULL, Ralph G 225.92
Personalities of the New Testaments. Grand Rapids, Baker Book House, 1961. 114 p. 20 cm. [BS2430.T85] 61-10000
1. Bible. N. T. — Biog. I. Title.

Bible. N.T.—Biography—Dictionaries.

BROWNRIGG, Ronald. 225.92'2 B
Who's who in the New Testament. Advisory editors for this volume: Canon E. Every [and] Wolfgang E. Pax. [1st ed.] New York, Holt, Rinehart and Winston [1971] 448 p. illus. 26 cm. [BS2430.B67] 75-153654 ISBN 0-03-086262-0 14.95
1. Bible. N.T.—Biography—Dictionaries. I. Title. BIP

Bible. N.T.—Biography—Juvenile literature.

CALDWELL, Louise. 227'.092'4 B
Timothy, young pastor / Louise Caldwell ; illustrated by Paul Karch. Nashville : Broadman Press, c1978. 48 p. : col. ill. ; 24 cm. (Biblearn series) Tells the story of the pastor and missionary who is thought to have been converted to Christianity by Paul. [BS2520.T5C34] 78-105195 ISBN 0-8054-4239-1 pbk. : 3.95
1. Bible. N.T.—Biography—Juvenile literature. 2. Timothy (Biblical character)—Juvenile literature. I. Karch, Paul. II. Title.

ROWELL, Edmon L. 225.9'22 B
Apostles, Jesus' special helpers / Edmon L. Rowell, Jr. ; illustrated by James Padgett. Nashville : Broadman Press, c1979. 48 p. : col. Ill. ; 24 cm. (BibLearn Series) Brief biographies of the 12 men who followed Jesus and spread His teachings. [BS2440.R68] 920 79-111902 ISBN 0-8054-4246-4 : 3.95
1. Bible. N.T.—Biography—Juvenile literature. 2. Apostles—Biography—Juvenile literature. I. Padgett, James. II. Title.

Bible. N.T.—Biography—Meditations.

MILLER, Louis G. 225.9'2'2 B
Touched by Christ : 12 stories about lesser-known people in the Bible / by Louis G. Miller. Liguori, Mo. : Liguori Publications, c1978. 96 p. : ill. ; 18 cm. [BS2430.M5] 77-90929 ISBN 0-89243-072-9 pbk. : 1.95
1. Bible. N.T.—Biography—Meditations. I. Title.

Bible. N.T.—Biography—Miscellanea.

WISE, Charles C. 225.9'22 B
Picture windows on the Christ / by Charles C. Wise, Jr. ; illustrated by Thom Baker. Penn Laird, Va. : Magian Press, c1979. 354 p. : ill. ; 23 cm. Includes bibliographical references. [BS2430.W57] 78-69928 5.95
1. Bible. N.T.—Biography—Miscellanea. I. Baker, Thom. II. Title.

Bible. N.T. Acts—Biography.

REES, Paul Stromberg 226.60922
Men of action in the book of Acts [by] Paul S. Rees. Westwood, N.J., Revell [1966] ix, 102p. 21cm. [BS2625.4.R4] 66-21903 2.95
1. Bible. N. T. Acts—Biog. I. Title.

REES, Paul Stromberg. 226.60922
Men of action in the book of Acts [by] Paul S. Rees. Westwood, N.J., Revell [1966] ix, 102 p. 21 cm. [BS2625.4.R4] 66-21903
1. Bible. N.T. Acts—Biography. I. Title.

Bible. N.T. Gospels—Biography.

MARY Simeon, Mother 1894- 225.92
Personalities in the Gospel story. Milwaukee, Bruce [c.1963] 140p. 23cm. 63-20156 3.50
1. Bible. N.T. Gospels—Biog. I. Title.

PARMELEE, Alice. 225.92'2
They beheld his glory; stories of the men and women who knew Jesus. [1st ed.] New York, Harper & Row [1967] xii, 275 p. 22 cm. [BS2430.P3] 67-11504
1. Bible. N. T. Gospels—Biog. I. Title.

POLING, David, 1928- 225.9'2'2 B
They walked with Christ; illuminating portraits of the men and women who knew Jesus Christ during His ministry on earth. With illus. by John Lane. Forewords by Norman Vincent Peale and Bishop Fulton J. Sheen. New York, Enterprise Publications [1972] v, 62 p. illus. 28 cm. [BS2430.P64] 74-188521
1. Bible. N.T. Gospels—Biography. I. Title.

Bible. N.T. John—Meditations.

SELF, Jerry M. 226'.5'06
Men & women in John's Gospel / Jerry M. Self. Nashville : Broadman Press, [1974] 126 p. ; 19 cm. [BS2615.4.S44] 74-79487 ISBN 0-8054-8123-0 pbk. : 1.95
1. Bible. N.T. John—Meditations. 2. Bible. N.T. John—Biography. I. Title. BIP

Bible. O.T.—Biography.

AGUILAR, Grace, 1816-1847. 221.9'22 B
The women of Israel; or, Characters and sketches from the Holy Scriptures and Jewish history illustrative of the past history, present duties, and future destiny of the Hebrew females, as based on the Word of God. Plainview, N.Y., Books for Libraries Press [1974] p. cm. (Essay index reprint series) Reprint of the 1879 ed. published by G. Routledge, London, and E. P. Dutton, New York. [BS575.A3 1974] 74-4358 ISBN 0-518-10174-6
1. Bible. O.T.—Biography. 2. Women in the Bible. 3. Women, Jewish. I. Title. II. Title: Characters and sketches from the Holy Scriptures and Jewish history.

BARING-GOULD, Sabine, 1834-1924. 221.9'22 B
Legends of the patriarchs and prophets and other Old Testament characters from various sources. [Folcroft, Pa.] Folcroft Library Editions, 1974. p. cm. Reprint of the 1872 ed. published by Holt & Williams, New York. [BS571.B337 1974] 74-9741 ISBN 0-8414-3205-8 (lib. bdg.)
1. Bible. O.T.—Biography. I. Title. BIP

BARINGGOULD SABINE, 1834-1924. 221.9'22 B
Legends of the patriarchs and prophets and other Old Testament characters from various sources. [Folcroft, Pa.] Folcroft Library Editions, 1974. p. cm. Reprint of the 1872 ed. published by Holt & Williams, New York. [BS571.B337 1974] 74-9741 30.00 (lib. bdg.).
1. Bible. O.T.—Biography. I. Title.

BARRETT, Ethel. 222'.09'505
If I had a wish ... / by Ethel Barrett. Glendale, Calif. : G/L Regal Books, c1974. 140 p. : ill. ; 20 cm. (A Regal venture book) Includes bibliographical references. [BJ1500.W55B37] 74-83139 ISBN 0-8307-0314-4 pbk. : 1.25
1. Bible. O.T.—Biography. 2. Wishes. I. Title. BIP

BARRETT, Ethel. 221.9'22 B
I'm no hero. Glendale, Calif., G/L Regal Books [1974] 150 p. illus. 20 cm. (A Regal venture book) [BS571.B37] 73-85395 ISBN 0-8307-0254-7 0.95 (pbk.).
1. Bible. O.T.—Biography. 2. Christian life—1960- I. Title. BIP

DIGGES, Mary Laurentia, 1910- 221.922
Adam's haunted sons. With a foreword by Barnabas Ahern. New York, Macmillan [1966] xvi, 302 p. 22 cm. Bibliographical references included in "Notes" (p. 289-292) [BS571.D5] 66-21162
1. Bible. O.T. — Biog. I. Title.

GARDINER, George E. 222'.35'0924 B
The romance of Ruth / by George E. Gardiner. Grand Rapids : Kregel Publications, [1977] p. cm. [BS580.R8G37] 77-79187 ISBN 0-8254-2718-5 pbk. : 1.50
1. Bible. O.T.—Biography. 2. Ruth (Biblical character) I. Title. BIP

GILPIN, Richard O. 222'.1'0924 B
Moses—born to be a slave, but God ... / Richard O. Gilpin. 1st ed. Hicksville, N.Y. : Exposition Press, c1977. 119 p. ; 22 cm. [BS580.M6G48] 77-366950 ISBN 0-682-48843-7 : 5.50
1. Bible. O.T.—Biography. 2. Moses. I. Title. BIP

HOBBS, Herschel H 221.92
Moses' mighty men. Nashville, Broadman Press [1958] 108p. 21cm. [BS571.H6] 58-5409
1. Bible. O. T.— Biog. 2. Moses. I. Title.

HUBBARD, David Allan. 221.9'22 B
Strange heroes / David Allan Hubbard. Philadelphia : A. J. Holman Co., c1977. 208 p. ; 18 cm. (Trumpet books) [BS571.H74] 77-1889 ISBN 0-87981-077-7 pbk. : 1.95
1. Bible. O.T.—Biography. I. Title. BIP

JAMES FLEMING, 1877-1959 221.92
Personalities of the Old Testament, [Reissue] Foreword by Julius A. Bewer. New York, Scribners [1965, c.1939] xvi p., 632p. maps. 24cm. (Hale lecs.: 4 40451) Bibl. [BS571.J3] 39-24508 3.95 pap.,
1. Bible. O. T.—Biog. I. Title.

LA SOR, William Sanford. 221.92
Great personalities of the Old Testament: their lives and times. [Westwood, N. J.] Revell [1959] 192p. 21cm. Includes bibliography. [BS571.L32] 59-5500
1. Bible. O. T.—Biog. I. Title.

NADEN, Roy C. 221.9'22 B
Without a doubt / by Roy C. Naden. Mountain View, Calif. : Pacific Press Pub. Association, c1975. 78 p. : ill. ; 19 cm. [BS571.N3 1975] 75-32709
1. Bible. O.T.—Biography. 2. Meditations. I. Title. BIP

PETERSEN, Mark E. 222'.1'0924 B
Moses : man of miracles / Mark E. Petersen. Salt Lake City : Deseret Book Co., 1977. 198 p. ; 24 cm. Includes index. [BS580.M6P445] 77-21553 ISBN 0-87747-651-9 : 4.95
1. Bible. O.T.—Biography. 2. Moses. 3. Mormons and Mormonism—Doctrinal and controversial works.

PONDER, Catherine. 222'.11'0922 B
The millionaires of Genesis, their prosperity secrets for you! / Catherine Ponder. Marina del Rey, Ca. : DeVorss, c1976. 178 p. ; 21 cm. (Her The Millionaires of the Bible) [BJ1611.2.P626] 76-19843 ISBN 0-87516-215-0 pbk. : 3.95
1. Bible. O.T.—Biography. 2. Success. 3. Patriarchs (Bible)—Biography. I. Title.

SANFORD, Agnes Mary (White) 221
The healing power of the Bible [by] Agnes Sanford. [1st ed.] Philadelphia, Lippincott [1970, c1969] 221 p. 21 cm. [BS571.S25] 75-88737 4.95
1. Bible. O.T.—Biography. 2. Miracles. I. Title. BIP

TEULINGS, C. P. 221.92
A gallery of portraits of the Old Testament. New York, Vantage [c.1963] 270p. 22cm. 64-215 3.95 bds.,
1. Bible. O. T.—Biog. I. Title.

TURNBULL, Ralph G. 221.92
Personalities of the Old Testament, by Ralph G. Turnbull. Grand Rapids, Baker Book House, 1964. 151 p. 21 cm. [BS571.T85] 64-15681
1. Bible. O. T.—Biography. I. Title.

Bible. O.T.—Biography—Dictionaries.

COMAY, Jean. 221.9'2'2 B
Who's who in the Old Testament, together with the Apocrypha. London, Weidenfeld and Nicolson, 1971. 448 p. illus. (some col.), facsims., maps. 26 cm. [BS570.C64 1971b] 72-195604 ISBN 0-297-00409-3
1. Bible. O.T.—Biography—Dictionaries. I. Title.
Available from Holt, Rinehart and Winston, 14.95, 0-03-086263-9.

COMAY, Joan. 221.92'2 B
Who's who in the Old Testament, together with the Apocrypha. Advisory editors for this volume: Michael Graetz [and] Leonard Cowie. [1st ed.] New York, Holt, Rinehart and Winston [1971] 448 p. illus. 26 cm. [BS570.C64] 79-153655 ISBN 0-03-086263-9 14.95
1. Bible. O.T.—Biography—Dictionaries. I. Title. BIP

Bible. O.T. Biography—Juvenile literature.

ADCOCK, Roger. 221.95'05
God's early heroes. Rev. by Elsiebeth McDaniel. Illustrated by Gordon King. Wheaton, Ill., Scripture Press Publications, 1971. 77 p. col. illus. 32 cm. London ed. published in 1969 under title: Great stories from the Bible. Nineteen Bible stories involving prominent characters of the Old Testament. [BS551.2.A33 1971] 70-151700 ISBN 0-361-01110-5
1. Bible. O.T. Biography—Juvenile literature. 2. Bible stories, English—O.T. I. McDaniel, Elsiebeth. II. King, Gordon, fl. 1971- illus. III. Title.

MCMINN, Tom. 224'.092'2 B
Prophets, preachers for God / Tom McMinn ; illustrated by H. Don Fields. Nashville : Broadman Press, c1979. 48 p. : ill. ; 24 cm. (Biblearn series) Presents accounts of the lives of five Old Testament prophets: Elisha, Amos, Jeremiah, Jonah, and Micah. Discussion questions accompany each selection. [BS1198.M19] 79-111901 ISBN 0-8054-4250-2 : 3.95
1. Bible. O.T.—Biography—Juvenile literature. 2. Prophets—Biography—Juvenile literature. I. Fields, H. Don. II. Title.

MUNOWITZ, Ken. 222'.1'0924 B
Moses, Moses / pictures by Ken Munowitz ; text by Charles L. Mee, Jr.. 1st ed. New York : Harper & Row, c1977. [32] p. : ill. ; 26 cm. Retells the early events in the life of Moses. [BS580.M6M8 1977] 76-41516 ISBN 0-06-024178-0 : 4.95. lib.bdg. : 4.79
1. Bible. O.T.—Biography—Juvenile literature. 2. Moses—Juvenile literature. I. Mee, Charles L. II. Title.

Bible. O.T. Pentateuch—Criticism, interpretation, etc.

MORAIS, Sabato, 1823-1897. 892.4'09'945
Italian Hebrew literature. Edited by Julius H. Greenstone. With a foreword by Henry S. Morais. New York, Hermon Press [1970] vi, 244 p. port. 24 cm. Reprint of the 1926 ed. "A critical and hermeneutical introduction to the Pentateuch," by S. D. Luzzatto: p. [93]-152. Includes bibliographical references. [PJ5049.I8M6 1970] 70-76171 9.75
1. Bible. O.T. Pentateuch—Criticism, interpretation, etc. 2. Hebrew literature—Italy. 3. Jews in Italy—Biography. I. Luzzatto, Samuele Davide, 1800-1865. II. Title. BIP

Bible. O.T. Prophets—Theology.

RAD, Gerhard von, 1901-1971. 224
The message of the prophets. [1st U.S. ed.] New York, Harper & Row [1972, c1965] 289 p. 22 cm. Translation of Die Botschaft der Propheten, a revised version of material from the author's Theologie des Alten Testaments. Includes bibliographical references. [BS1505.2.R313 1972] 72-183633 3.95
1. Bible. O.T. Prophets—Theology. 2. Prophets. I. Title. BIP

Bible. O.T. 2 Kings—Biography.

ELLUL, Jacques. 222'.54'0922
The politics of God and the politics of man. Translated and edited by Geoffrey W. Bromiley. Grand Rapids, Mich., Eerdmans [1972] 199 p. 21 cm. Translation of Politique de Dieu, politiques de l'homme. [BS1335.4.E413] 76-188247 ISBN 0-8028-1442-5 3.45
1. Bible. O.T. 2 Kings—Biography. I. Title. BIP

Bible stories, English.

BURKE, Carl F. 220.9'2 B
The boy who stayed cool, and other stories of young people in the Bible [by] Carl F. Burke. New York, Association Press [1973] 125 p. 19 cm. Retells in slang forty Biblical tales describing the lives of various people in the Old and New Testament. [BS551.2.B87] 73-15685 ISBN 0-8096-1877-X 4.95

1. Bible—Biography. 2. Bible stories, English. I. Title.
Pbk. 2.95.

HAAN, Sheri Dunham. 220.9'505
A child's storybook of Bible people. Martha Bentley, illustrator. Grand Rapids, Mich., Baker Book House [1973] 239 p. illus., music. and phonodisc (1 s. 7 in. 33 1/3 rpm.) in pocket. 24 cm. Includes hymns with music. Old and New Testament stories about Biblical characters are arranged in three sections: Children of the Bible, Women of the Bible, and Men of the Bible. Includes related songs, plays, and rhythm poems. [BS551.2.H24] 73-76202 ISBN 0-8010-4077-9 5.95
1. Bible stories, English. I. Bentley, Martha, illus. II. Title.

Bible stories, English—O.T.

ADCOCK, Roger. 221.95'05
God's early heroes. Rev. by Elsiebeth McDaniel. Illustrated by Gordon King. Wheaton, Ill., Scripture Press Publications, 1971. 77 p. col. illus. 32 cm. London ed. published in 1969 under title: Great stories from the Bible. Nineteen Bible stories involving prominent characters of the Old Testament. [BS551.2.A33 1971] 70-151700 ISBN 0-361-01110-5
1. Bible. O.T. Biography—Juvenile literature. 2. Bible stories, English O.T. I. McDaniel, Elsiebeth. II. King, Gordon, fl. 1971- illus. III. Title.

WEILERSTEIN, Sadie (Rose) 922.96
1895-
Jewish heroes. Illus. by Lili Cassel. New York, United Synagogue Commission on Jewish Education, 1953- v. illus. 24cm. [BS551.W473] 53-39861
1. Bible stories, English—O.T. I. Title.

Bible—study—Text-books.

BIBLE characters and 220'.07
doctrines. [1st U.S.A. ed.] Grand*1Rapids, [Eerdmans [1972- v. 18 cm. [BS605.2B47] 72-189855 ISBN 0-8028-1460-3 1.50 (pbk.)
1. Bible—study—Text-books. I. Blaiklock, E. M. II. Wright, John Stafford. III. Grogan, Geoffrey.

Bibliographers—Correspondence, reminiscences, etc.

HOLMES, Thomas James, 1874- 920.1
The education of a bibliographer, an autobiographical essay. [Cleveland] Western Reserve University Press, 1957. 54p. 20cm. [Z1004.H6A3] 57-10126
1. Bibliographers—Correspondence, reminiscences, etc. I. Title.

Bibliography—Microscope and miniature editions—Specimens.

FRIEND, John Putnam, 1900- 920.4
Captain Jack; being the reminiscences of a seagoing bookseller [Newtown, Conn.] Seahorse Pr., [70 Main, c.] 1963. 32p. 6cm. 63-21210 lim. ed., price unreported
1. Bibliography—Microscope and miniature editions—Specimens. I. Title.

Bickerdyke, Mary Ann (Ball) 1817-1901—Juvenile literature.

DE LEEUW, Adele 610.73'092'4 B
Louise, 1899-
Civil War nurse, Mary Ann Bickerdyke, by Adele deLeeuw. New York, J. Messner [1973] 158 p. 22 cm. Bibliography: p. 151-152. Biography of a woman who distinguished herself during the Civil War by her care of the wounded, and after the war by her social welfare work. [RT4.D38] 92 73-5383 ISBN 0-671-32617-1 5.25
1. Bickerdyke, Mary Ann (Ball) 1817-1901—Juvenile literature. 2. Nurses and nursing—United States—History—Juvenile literature. 3. United States—History—Civil War—Medical and sanitary affairs—Juvenile literature. I. Title.
Library edition 4.79; ISBN 0-671-32618-X.

Bickermann, Joseph, 1867-1942.

BICKERMANN, 947.08'092'2 B
Joseph, 1867-1942.
Two Bikermans : autobiographies / by Joseph and Jacob J. Bikerman. 1st ed. New York : Vantage Press, c1975. 209 p. ; 22 cm. Joseph Bickermann's autobiography translated from the Russian. Includes bibliographical references. [DS135.R95B52 1975] 76-360316 ISBN 0-533-01595-2 : 6.95
1. Bickermann, Joseph, 1867-1942. 2. Bikerman, Jacob Joseph, 1898- 3. Jews in Russia—Social conditions. 4. Russia—Social conditions. 5. Russia—History—Revolution, 1917-1921—Personal narratives. I. Bikerman, Jacob Joseph, 1898- joint author. II. Title.

Bickers, William, 1908-

BICKERS, William, 618'.092'4 B
1908-
Harem surgeon = [Tabib Jirahi Ikhtisas lil-Nasa' (romanized form)] / by William M. Bickers. [Richmond? Va.] : Bickers, 1976. 199 p. : ill. ; 26 cm. Parallel title romanized: Tabib Jirahi Ikhtisas lil-Nisa'. [RG76.B5A3] 76-27144
1. Bickers, William, 1908- 2. Gynecologists—Lebanon—Biography. 3. Gynecology—Arab countries. 4. Obstetrics—Arab countries. 5. Women—Arab countries—Social conditions. I. Title. II. Title: Tabib Jirahi Ikhtisas lil-Nisa'

Bickford, Elizabeth.

BICKFORD, Elizabeth. 818.5
The little girl of long ago. Boston, Bruce Humphries [1956] 73p. illus. 21cm. Autobiographical. [CT275.B5674A3] 56-9959
I. Title.

Biddle, Anthony Joseph Drexel, 1874-1948.

BIDDLE, Cordelia Drexel. 923.373
My Philadelphia father, by Cordelia Drexel Biddle as told to Kyle Crichton. [1st ed.] Garden City, N.Y., Doubleday, 1955. 256 p. illus. 22 cm. [PS3503.128Z6] 55-5584
1. Biddle, Anthony Joseph Drexel, 1874-1948. I. Crichton, Kyle Samuel, 1896- II. Title.

Biddle, James, 1783-1848.

WAINWRIGHT, Nicholas 359.3320924
B
Commodore James Biddle and his sketch book, by Nicholas B. Wainwright. Philadelphia, Historical Society of Pennsylvania, 1966. 92 p. plates (incl. ports.) 26 cm. "First appeared in the January, 1966, issue of the Pennsylvania magazine of history and biography." Bibliographical footnotes. [E353.1.B5W3] 66-3809
1. Biddle, James, 1783-1848. I. Title. BIP

Biddle, Nicholas, 1893-

BIDDLE, Nicholas, 973.91'092'4
1893-
Personal memoirs : an autobiography, including a personal history and accounts of various cruises and hunting expeditions / Nicholas Biddle. [Philadelphia?] : Biddle, c1975. xii, 353 p. : ill. ; 24 cm. [U53.B53A32] 75-29992
1. Biddle, Nicholas, 1893- I. Title.

Bierce, Ambrose, 1842-1914?

BIERCE, Ambrose, 1842- 813'.4 B
1914?
Twenty-one letters of Ambrose Bierce. Edited with a note by Samuel Loveman. [Folcroft, Pa.] Folcroft Library Editions, 1973. p. Reprint of the 1922 ed. published by G. Kirk, Cleveland. [PS1097.Z5A3 1973] 73-12618 ISBN 0-8414-5652-6 (lib. bdg.)
1. Bierce, Ambrose, 1842-1914? I. Title.

DE CASTRO, Adolphe 813'.4 B
Danziger, 1866-
Portrait of Ambrose Bierce. New York, Beekman Publishers, 1974. xvi, 351 p. illus. 23 cm. (American newspapermen, 1790-1933) Reprint of the 1929 ed. published by Century Co., New York. Bibliography: p. 343-345. [PS1097.Z5D4 1974] 74-610 ISBN 0-8464-0025-1 17.00
1. Bierce, Ambrose, 1842-1914? I. Title.

FATOUT, Paul. 928.1
Ambrose Bierce, the Devil's lexicographer. [1st ed.] Norman, University of Oklahoma Press [1951] xv, 349 p. ports. 22 cm. Bibliography: p. 329-340. [PS1097.Z5F3] 51-10020
1. Bierce, Ambrose, 1842-1914?

FATOUT, Paul. 928.1
Ambrose Bierce and the Black Hills. Norman, University of Oklahoma Press [c1956] 180p. illus. 22cm. [PS1097.Z5F28] 56-5993
1. Bierce, Ambrose, 1842-1914? I. Title.

MORRILL, Sibley S. 813'.4 B
Ambrose Bierce, F. A. Mitchell-Hedges, and the crystal skull, by Sibley S. Morrill. San Francisco, Cadleon Press, 1972. 83 p. illus. 22 cm. Errata slip inserted. Bibliography: p. 83. [PS1097.Z5M6] 72-79466 ISBN 0-9600310-3-0 3.95
1. Bierce, Ambrose, 1842-1914? 2. Mitchell-Hedges, Frederick Albert, 1882-1959. I. Title. BIP

Bierce, Ambrose, 1842-1914?—Biography.

MCWILLIAMS, Carey, 1905- 813'.4 B
Ambrose Bierce, a biography. With a new introd. by the author. [Hamden, Conn.] Archon Books, 1967. xxxi, 358 p. 22 cm. Bibliography: p. [337]-346. [PS1097.Z5M3 1967] 67-25641
1. Bierce, Ambrose, 1842-1914?—Biography. BIP

NEALE, Walter, 1873- 813'.4 B
1933.
Life of Ambrose Bierce. New York, AMS Press [1969] 489 p. illus., ports. 23 cm. Reprint of the 1929 ed. "Collected works of Ambrose Bierce": p. 457-474. [PS1097.Z5N4 1969] 77-93773
1. Bierce, Ambrose, 1842-1914—Biography. BIP

O'CONNOR, Richard, 1915- 813'.4 B
Ambrose Bierce; a biography. [1st ed.] Boston, Little, Brown [1967] 333 p. illus., ports. 22 cm. "Selected bibliography": p. [325]-327. [PS1097.Z5O3] 67-11229
1. Bierce, Ambrose, 1842-1914?—Biography.

Bierce, Ambrose, 1842-1914?—Relationship with women.

RATHER, Lois, 1905- 813'.4 B
Bittersweet : Ambrose Bierce & women / Lois Rather. Oakland [Calif.] : Rather Press, 1975. 133 p. : ill. ; 27 cm. "Of an edition limited to 150, this is no. 143." Includes bibliographical references and index. [PS1097.Z5R3] 76-358493
1. Bierce, Ambrose, 1842-1914?—Relationship with women. I. Title.

Bierman, Elenore C.

†BIERMAN, Elenore 966.9'05'0924
C.
There's an iguana in my plumbing / by Elenore C. Bierman. 1st ed. Port Washington, N.Y. : Ashley Books, c1976. 252 p. ; 22 cm. [DT515.4.B53 1976] 75-777 ISBN 0-87949-050-0 : 7.95
1. Bierman, Elenore C. 2. Nigeria—Social life and customs. 3. Americans in Nigeria—Biography. I. Title. BIP

Big Thicket, Tex.—Social life and customs.

BIG Thicket legacy 976.4'157 B
/ compiled and edited by Campbell and Lynn Loughmiller ; foreword by Francis E. Abernethy. Austin : University of Texas Press, c1977. xxiv, 222 p., [2] leaves of plates : ill. ; 26 cm. [F392.H37B53] 76-46329 ISBN 0-292-70716-9 : 12.95
1. Big Thicket, Tex.—Social life and customs. 2. Big Thicket, Tex.—Biography. I. Loughmiller, Campbell. II. Loughmiller, Lynn. BIP

Bigelow, Henry Jacob, 1818-1890—Addresses, essays, lectures.

[BIGELOW, William 617'.092'4 B
Sturgis] 1850-1926.
A memoir of Henry Jacob Bigelow. Boston : Longwood Press, 1977. p. cm. "Prepared anonymously in 1900 by his son, William Sturgis Bigelow."—DAB. Reprint of the 1900 ed. published by Little, Brown, Boston, which was issued as v. 4 of H. J. Bigelow's Life and writings. [R154.B573B53 1977] 77-81657 ISBN 0-89341-138-8 lib.bdg. : 35.00
1. Bigelow, Henry Jacob, 1818-1890—Addresses, essays, lectures. 2. Surgeons—Massachusetts—Biography—Addresses, essays, lectures. I. Bigelow, Henry Jacob, 1818-1890. Life and writings. BIP

Bigelow, John, 1817-1911.

CLAPP, Margaret 973.72'0924
Antoinette, 1910-
Forgotten first citizen: John Bigelow, by Margaret Clapp. New York, Greenwood Press, 1968 [c1947] x, 390 p. port. 24 cm. Bibliography: p. [365]-377. [E664.B55C5 1968] (B) 69-10075
1. Bigelow, John, 1817-1911. I. Title.

Biggs, Dewey.

MCCULLO, Marion (Biggs) 926.2913
Pioneer with wings; the story of a man who loved tofly; the life of Dewey Biggs by his sister. Elgin, Ill., Brethren Pub. House [c1951] 101p. illus. 21cm. [TL540.B54M3] 56-46302
1. Biggs, Dewey. I. Title.

Biggs, Ronald Arthur, 1929-

MACKENZIE, Colin, 1918- 364.1'55
Biggs : the world's most wanted man / Colin Mackenzie. New York : Avon, 1977,c1975. 290p. ; 18 cm. [HV6248.B55M32] ISBN 0-380-01823-3 pbk. : 1.95
1. Biggs, Ronald Arthur, 1929- 2. Crime and criminals — Great Britain — Biography. 3. Train robberies — Great Britain. I. Title.
L.C. card no. for 1975 Morrow ed.: 75-14218. BIP

MACKENZIE, Colin, 364.1'55 B
1918-
Biggs, the world's most wanted man / by Colin Mackenzie. New York : W. Morrow, 1975. 324 p. ; 22 cm. [HV6248.B55M32] 75-14218 ISBN 0-688-02959-0 : 8.95
1. Biggs, Ronald Arthur, 1929- 2. Crime and criminals—Great Britain—Biography. 3. Train robberies—Great Britain. I. Title.

Biggs, Walter D., 1873-1945.

WINDELL, Roland. 926.1
The brush of angels' wings; the story of the country doctor. San Antonio, Naylor

[1952] 104 p. illus. 22 cm. [R154.B58W5] 52-10645
1. Biggs, Walter D., 1873-1945. I. Title.

Biggs, William, 1755-1827.

BIGGS, William, 1755-1827. 973'.04'97 S
Narrative of William Biggs / William Biggs. New York : Garland Pub., 1977. 121 p. ; 23 cm. (The Garland library of narratives of North American Indian captivities ; v. 37) Issued with the reprint of the 1855 ed. of the Escape of Alexander M'Connel, New York, 1977. Reprint of the 1825 ed. [E85.G2 vol. 37] [E99.K4] 977.3'8 75-7059 ISBN 0-8240-1661-0 : 25.00
1. Biggs, William, 1755-1827. 2. Kickapoo Indians—Captivities. 3. Indians of North America—Captivities. 4. Illinois—Biography. I. Title. II. Series.

Bigler, Clark O.

BIGLER, Clark O. 923.773
Country schoolmaster. Philadelphia, Dorrance [1955] 137p. 20cm. Autobiographical. [LA2317.B48A3] 55-5901
I. Title.

Bigler, Jacob G., 1813-1907.

BROUGH, Franklin Keith, 1923- 922.8373
Freely, I gave; the life of Jacob G. Bigler. Wichita, Kan., Grit Print. Co., 1958. 177p. illus. 22cm. [BX8695.B5B7] 58-3722
1. Bigler, Jacob G., 1813-1907. I. Title.

Biko, B. S.

WOODS, Donald, 1933- 322.4'4'0924 B
Biko / Donald Woods. New York : Paddington Press, c1978. 288 p., [8] leaves of plates : ill. ; 24 cm. Includes index. [DT779.8.B48W66] 78-1882 ISBN 0-448-23169-7 : 10.95
1. Biko, B. S. 2. Woods, Donald, 1933- 3. Political prisoners—South Africa—Biography. 4. Journalists—South Africa—Biography. 5. South Africa—Race relations. I. Title.

WOODS, Donald, 1933- 322.4'4'0924 B
Biko / Donald Woods. 1st Vintage Books ed. New York : Vintage Books, 1979. 438 p. ; 18 cm. Includes index. [DT779.8.B48W66 1979] 78-55525 ISBN 0-394-72654-5 pbk. : 3.95
1. Biko, B. S. 2. Woods, Donald, 1933- 3. Political prisoners—South Africa—Biography. 4. Journalists—South Africa—Biography. 5. South Africa—Race relations. I. Title. BIP

Bilbo, Theodore Gilmore, 1877-1947.

GREEN, Adwin Wigfall, 1900- 923.273
The man Bilbo. Baton Rouge, Louisiana State University Press, 1963. xiii, 150 p. illus., ports. 23 cm. "Critical essay on authorities": p. 139-145. [E748.B5G7] 63-16658
1. Bilbo, Theodore Gilmore, 1877-1947. I. Title. BIP

GREEN, Adwin Wigfall, 1900- 976.2'06'0924 B
The man Bilbo / A. Wigfall Green. Westport, Conn. : Greenwood Press, 1976. p. cm. Reprint of the 1963 ed. published by Louisiana State University Press, Baton Rouge. [E748.B5G7 1976] 76-28416 ISBN 0-8371-9103-3 lib.bdg. : 12.25
1. Bilbo, Theodore Gilmore, 1877-1947. 2. Mississippi—Governors—Biography. 3. Legislators—Mississippi—Biography. 4. Legislators—United States—Biography. I. Title.

Billiart, Julie, 1751-1816.

MCMANAMA, Mary Fidelis, 1886- 922.2493
As gold in the furnace; the life of Blessed Julie Billiart, foundress of the Sisters of Notre Dame de Namur. Milwaukee, Bruce Pub. Co. [1957] 218p. illus. 22cm. [BX4485.3.Z8B54] 57-8935
1. Billiart, Julie, 1751-1816. I. Title.

MARY Fidelis, Sister, 1886- 922.2493
As gold in the furnace; the life of Blessed Julie Billiart, foundress of the Sisters of Notre Dame de Namur. Milwaukee, Bruce Pub. Co. [1957] 218p. illus. 22cm. [BX4705.B5M3] 57-8935
1. Billiart, Julie, 1751-1816. I. Title.

SAINT Joseph, Mother, 1756-1838. 271'.97 B
The memoirs of Mother Frances Blin de Bourdon, S.N.D. / [translated by Sister Mary Godfrey ... et al.]. Westminster, Md. : Christian Classics, [1975] xxxi, 299 p., [1] leaf of plates : ports. ; 23 cm. Bibliography: p. [297]-299. [BX4485.3.Z8B5813 1975] 75-311256 6.50
1. Billiart, Julie, 1751-1816. 2. Saint Joseph, Mother, 1756-1838. I. Title.

Billings, Frank, 1854-1932.

HIRSCH, Edwin Frederick, 1886- 610'.924 B
Frank Billings: the architect of medical education, an apostle of excellence in clinical practice, a leader in Chicago medicine [by Edwin F. Hirsch. Chicago? c1966] xiv, 144 p. illus., ports. 24 cm. "Publications of Frank Billings": p. 135-139. Bibliography: p. 141. [R154.B588H5] 67-2125
1. Billings, Frank, 1854-1932.

Billings, John Shaw, 1838-1913.

LYDENBERG, Harry Miller, 1874-1960. 020'.92'4
John Shaw Billings, creator of the National Medical Library and its catalogue, first director of the New York Public Library. Boston, Gregg Press, 1972 [c1924] 94 p. port. 23 cm. (The Library reference series. Library history and biography) Reprint of the ed. published by American Library Association, Chicago, which was issued as no. 1 of American library pioneers. Bibliography: p. 85-[87] [Z720.B6L9 1972] 72-10139 ISBN 0-8398-1183-7
1. Billings, John Shaw, 1838-1913. I. Title. II. Series: Library history and biography. III. Series: American library pioneers, no. 1.

Billings, William, 1746-1800.

MCKAY, David P., 1927- 783'.092'4 B
William Billings of Boston: eighteenth-century composer, by David P. McKay and Richard Crawford. [Princeton, N.J.] Princeton University Press [1975] xii, 303 p. illus. 24 cm. Bibliography: p. 269-290. [ML410.B588M3] 74-19035 ISBN 0-691-09118-8 15.00
1. Billings, William, 1746-1800. I. Crawford, Richard, 1935- joint author. II. Title.

Billington, Dallas Franklin,

BILLINGTON, Dallas Franklin, 1903- 922.673
God is real; a testament in the form of an autobiography. New York, McKay [c.1962] 298p. 62-13202 4.50
I. Title.

Billy the Kid.

BREIHAN, Carl W., 1915- 364.1'0924
Billy the Kid; a date with destiny, by Carl W. Breihan with Marion Ballert. Seattle, Hangman Press [1970] 141 p. illus., facsims., ports. 26 cm. Bibliography: p. 135. [F786.B58] 75-125899
1. Billy the Kid. I. Ballert, Marion, joint author.

BREIHAN, Carl W., 1915- 364.1'0924 B
Billy the Kid; a date with destiny, by Carl W. Breihan with Marion Ballert. Seattle, Hangman Press [1970] 141 p. illus., facsims., ports. 26 cm. Bibliography: p. 135. [F786.B58] 75-125899
1. Billy the Kid. I. Ballert, Marion, joint author.

BRENT, William, 1899- 923.4173
The complete and factual life of Billy the Kid. New York, F. Fell [1964] 212 p. facsims., geneal. table, ports. 22 cm. Errata slip inserted. [F786.B6] 64-23444
1. Billy the Kid. I. Title.

GARRETT, Patrick Floyd, 1850-1908. 923.4173
The authenic life of Billy, the Kid, the noted desperado of the Southwest, whose deeds of daring and blood made his name a terror in New Mexico, Arizona and northern Mexico. With an introd. by J. C. Dykes. [New ed.] Norman, University of Oklahoma Press [1954] 156 p. illus. 20 cm. (The Western frontier library [v. 3]) [F786.B694 1954] 54-10053
1. Billy the Kid. 2. Crime and criminals—Southwest, New.

GARRETT, Patrick Floyd, 1850-1908. 923.4173
The authentic life of Billy, the kid. With a biographical foreword by Jarvis P. Garrett. Albuquerque, Horn & Wallace, 1964. 49, 139 p. illus., facsims., ports. 24 cm. A reprint of the 1st ed.: The authentic life of Billy, the kid, the noted desperado of the Southwest, whose deeds of daring and blood made his name a terror in New Mexico, Arizona, and northern Mexico. By Pat F. Garrett, by whom he was finally hunted down and captured by killing him. Santa Fe, N.M., New Mexican Print. and Pub. co., 1882. 64-23616
1. Billy the Kid. 2. Crime and criminals — Southwest, New. I. Garrett, Jarvis P., ed. II. Title. BIP

HAMLIN, William Lee, 1878- 923.4173
The true story of Billy the Kid; a tale of the Lincoln County war. Caldwell, Idaho, Caxton Printers, 1959. 364 p. illus. 22 cm. [F786.B6945] 59-5484
1. Billy the Kid. 2. Lincoln Co., N. M.—History. I. Title.

MULLIN, Robert Norville. 978.02'0924
The boyhood of Billy the Kid, by Robert N. Mullin. [El Paso, Texas Western Press] 1967. 26 p. illus., ports. 23 cm. (Southwestern studies, v. 5, no. 1. Monograph no. 17) Cover title. Bibliography: p. 24-26. [F786.B6955] 67-64791
1. Billy the Kid. I. Title. II. Series: Southwestern studies (El Paso, Tex.), v. 5, no. 1.

Binder, Abraham Wolf, 1895-1966.

HESKES, Irene, comp. 780'.92'4
A. W. Binder, his life and work. Edited by Irene Heskes. [New York] National Jewish Music Council, 1965. viii, 63 p. illus., ports. 28 cm. [M410.B589H5] 784'.092'4 79-249137
1. Binder, Abraham Wolf, 1895-1966.

Binder, Joseph, 1898-1972.

BINDER, Joseph, 1898-1972. 760'.092'4 B
Joseph Binder : an artist and a lifestyle : from the Joseph Binder Collection of posters, graphic and fine art, notes, and records / [compiled by Carla Binder]. 1st ed. Vienna : A. Schroll, 1976. 143 p. : ill. (some col.) ; 25 cm. [NC1850.B48B558] 77-366012 ISBN 3-7031-0437-6. ISBN 3-7031-0436-8 pbk.
1. Binder, Joseph, 1898-1972. I. Binder, Carla. II. Title.

Binet, Alfred, 1857-1911.

WOLF, Theta Holmes, 1904- 153.9'3'0924 B
Alfred Binet [by] Theta H. Wolf. Chicago, University of Chicago Press [1973] xiii, 376 p. 23 cm. Bibliography: p. 349-367. [BF109.B5W64] 72-95957 ISBN 0-226-90498-9
1. Binet, Alfred, 1857-1911. 2. Mental tests. BIP

Bingham, George Caleb, 1811-1879.

LARKIN, Lew, 1918- 759.13
Bingham: fighting artist; the story of Missouri's immortal painter, patriot, soldier, and statesman. Point Lookout, Mo., S of O Press, Book Division [1971] 358 p. illus., ports. 21 cm. [ND237.B59L3 1971] 77-29322
1. Bingham, George Caleb, 1811-1879. I. Title.

LARKIN, Lew, 1918- 927.5
Bingham: fighting artist; the story of Missouri's immortal painter, patriot, soldier, and statesman. Illus. from photos. of the original paintings. Kansas City, Mo., Burton Pub. Co. [1954] 358p. illus. 22cm. [ND237.B59L3] 55-19715
1. Bingham, George Caleb, 1811-1879. I. Title.

MCDERMOTT, John Francis 759.13
George Caleb Bingham, river portraitist. Norman, University of Oklahoma Press [c.1959] xxviii, 454p. Bibliography: p.438-446. illus. 27cm. 59-13474 15.00
1. Bingham, George Caleb, 1811-1879. I. Title. BIP

Bingham, Hiram, 1875-1956—Juvenile literature.

SCHMIDT, James Norman, 1912- 980.3 B
The riddle of the Incas; the story of Hiram Bingham and Machu Picchu, by James Norman. Illustrated by Jim Fox. [1st ed.] New York, Hawthorn Books [1968] 160 p. illus. 22 cm. Bibliography: p. 152. [F3429.S3 1968] 68-13201
1. Bingham, Hiram, 1875-1956—Juvenile literature. 2. Machu Picchu, Peru—Juvenile literature. 3. Incas—Juvenile literature. I. Title.

Bingham, William, 1752-1804.

ALBERTS, Robert C. 973.3'0924 B
The golden voyage; the life and times of William Bingham, 1752-1804, by Robert C. Alberts. Boston, Houghton-Mifflin, 1969. xvii, 570 p. illus., map, ports. (part col.) 24 cm. Bibliography: p. [531]-545. [E302.6.B5A4] 69-15005 10.00
1. Bingham, William, 1752-1804. I. Title.

Binney, Horace, 1780-1875.

BINNEY, Charles Chauncey, 1855-1913. 340'.092'4 B
The life of Horace Binney, with selections from his letters. Freeport, N.Y., Books for Libraries Press [1972] xi, 460 p. front. 22 cm. Reprint of the 1903 ed. [E340.B57B5 1972] 72-2577 ISBN 0-8369-6849-2
1. Binney, Horace, 1780-1875.

Binns, Walter Pope.

BINNS, Walter Pope. 286'.1'0924 B
My life story. [Wolfe City, Tex., Southern Baptist Press, 1968] 81 p. facsim., ports. 23

cm. Cover title. [BX6495.B49A3] 68-57708
I. Title.

Bio-bibliography.

CONTEMPORARY authors, 810.9'005'2 *permanent series : a bio-bibliographical guide to current authors and their works /* Clare D. Kinsman, editor. Detroit, Mich. : Gale Research Co., c1975- v. ; 29 cm. [Z1010.C67] 75-13539 ISBN 0-8103-0036-2 : 38.00
1. Bio-bibliography. I. Kinsman, Clare D.

WHO'S who among living 016.928 *authors of older nations,* covering the literary activities of living authors and writers of all countries of the world, except the United States of America, Canada, Mexico, Alaska, Hawaii, Newfoundland, the Philippine [!] islands, the West Indies, and Central America . . . 1928- Rev., enlarged ed. [Los Angeles, Calif.] Golden Syndicate Pub. Co.; Detroit, Gale [1967, c.1931] v. 21cm. biennial. Title varies: Introductory volume, 1928, Who's who among authors of older nations. v. 1-1931/32- Who's who among living authors of older nations- [Z1010.W62] 28-28492 15.00
1. Bio-bibliography. 2. Authors. I. Lawrence, Mrs. Alberta (Chamberlain) 1875- ed. II. Title: Who's who among authors of older nations.

Biochemists—Correspondence, reminiscences, etc.

LIPMANN, Fritz 574.1'92'0924 B Albert, 1899-
Wanderings of a biochemist [by] Fritz Lipmann. New York, Wiley-Interscience [1971] viii, 229 p. illus. 24 cm. Includes bibliographies. [QP26.L49A3] 75-138915 ISBN 0-471-54080-3
1. Biochemists—Correspondence, reminiscences, etc. 2. Biological chemistry—Addresses, essays, lectures. I. Title. BIP

Biograph Company.

NIVER, Kemp R., 016.79143'0973 comp.
Biograph bulletins, 1896-1908. Compiled, with an introd. and notes, by Kemp R. Niver. Edited by Bebe Bergsten. [Los Angeles, Locare Research Group, 1971] 464 p. illus., facsims. 29 cm. [PN1999.B5N5] 76-148466 20.00
1. Biograph Company. I. Bergsten, Bebe, ed. II. Title. BIP

Biographical and historical memoirs of Eastern Arkansas—Indexes.

PRESLEY, Leister E., Mrs. 917.67
Biographical index to biographical and historical memoirs of Eastern Arkansas [by] Mrs. Leister E. Presley. Searcy, Ark. [1973] 39 p. 29 cm. This index covers the biographical section of a history of Arkansas published 1889-90 by Goodspeed Pub. Co., Nashville, Tenn. [F411.B613P72] 73-159675
1. Biographical and historical memoirs of Eastern Arkansas—Indexes. 2. Arkansas—Biography—Indexes. I. Title.

Biography.

100 great thinkers; 920.02 [brief biographies of the great men of thought from Hammurabi to Sartre] Editor: Jay E. Greene. Authors: Murray Bromberg [and others] New York, Washington Square Press; [distributed by Simon & Schuster, c1967] xiv, 620 p. 18 cm. Includes bibliographies. [CT105.O53] 68-527
1. Biography. I. Greene, Jay Elihu, 1914- ed. II. Bromberg, Murray.

ABBOT, Lawrence Fraser, 920.02 1859-1933.
Twelve great modernists. Freeport, N.Y., Books for Libraries Press [1969, c1927] xii, 301 p. 23 cm. (Essay index reprint series) Contents.Contents.—Herodotus, the traveller.—St. Francis of Assisi, the worldling.—Erasmus, the emancipator.—Voltaire, the humanitarian.—Thomas Jefferson, the aristocrat.—John Marshall, the democrat.—Beethoven, the poet.—George Stephenson, the philosopher.—Ralph Waldo Emerson, the humourist.—Charles R. Darwin, the saint.—Jean Francois Millet, the naturalist.—Louis Pasteur, the philanthropist. Bibliographical footnotes. [CT104.A25 1969] 76-84292
1. Biography. I. Title.

BARNETT, Lincoln Kinnear, 920.02 1909-
Writing on life: sixteen close-ups. New York, Sloane [1951] 383 p. 22 cm. Contents.Contents.—A sort of looking glass.—Fred Astaire.—Adele Astaire comes home.—Eisenhower.—General Giraud.—George C. Marshall.—Ernie Pyle.—Mr. Piper of Cub-Haven.—Gissler the lawyer.—Bing, inc.—The happiest couple in Hollywood.—Ingrid of Lorraine.—Tennessee Williams.—Lindsay & Crouse.—Richard Rodgers.—Josh Logen.—Physicist Oppenheimer. [CT120.B27] 51-10590
1. Biography. 2. Biography (as a literary form) I. Title.

BAYLE, Pierre, 1647-1706. 920.02
Selections from Bayle's dictionary. Edited by E. A. Beller and M. du P. Lee, Jr. New York, Greenwood Press [1969, c1952] xxxiv, 312 p. port. 23 cm. "Bibliographical note": p. xxxiii. Bibliographical footnotes. [CT95.B333 1969] 69-13810 ISBN 0-8371-1068-8
1. Biography. I. Title. BIP

BISHOP, Morris, 1893- 920.02
The exotics, being a collection of unique personalities and remarkable characters. New York, American Heritage Press [1969] 272 p. illus., ports. 24 cm. [CT105.B56] 70-83805 6.95
1. Biography. I. Title.

BLACK, Ladbroke Lionel 920'.02 Day, 1877-
Some queer people / by Ladbroke Black. Folcroft, Pa. : Folcroft Library Editions, 1979. p. cm. Reprint of the 1931 ed. published by S. Low, Marston, London. Contents.—King William IV.—Napoleon's first-born.—Margaret Fuller.—Dennis Hird.—The Earl of Peterborough.—Lord Fisher.—Edgar Allan Poe.—Francois Blanc.—J. M. W. Turner.—Dr. Beddoes.—Hetty Green.—Benedict Arnold. [CT105.B58 1979] 79-20146 ISBN 0-8414-9842-3 (lib. bdg.) : 30.00
1. Biography. I. Title. BIP

BOLTON, Sarah (Knowles) 920.02 1841-1916.
Lives of poor boys who became famous. Illustrated by Constance Joan Naar. New York, Crowell [1962] 378p. illus. 21cm. [CT105.B65 1962] 62-5076
1. Biography . I. Title. II. Title: Poor boys who became famous.

BOTTOME, Phyllis, 1884- 920.02 1963.
From the life. Freeport, N.Y., Books for Libraries Press [1971, c1944] 100 p. 23 cm. (Essay index reprint series) Contents.Contents. Alfred Adler.—Max Beerbohm.—The secret of Ivor Novello.—Sara Delano Roosevelt.—Ezra Pound.—Margaret MacDonald Bottome. [CT119.B65 1971] 70-134056 ISBN 0-8369-2215-8
1. Biography. I. Title.

BRADFORD, Gamaliel, 1863- 920.073 1932.
Portraits and personalities. Edited by Mabel A. Bessey. Freeport, N.Y., Books for Libraries Press, [1968] xx, 283 p. port. 23 cm. (Essay index reprint series) Reprint of the 1933 ed. Contents.Contents.—Gamaliel Bradford.—The place of biography in the school curriculum.—George Washington.—Benedict Arnold.—Abraham Lincoln.—Robert E. Lee.—William Shakespeare.—Joseph Jefferson.—Florence Nightingale.—Louisa May Alcott.—Napoleon Bonaparte.—Theodore Roosevelt.—Emily Dickinson.—Mark Twain.—Notes.—Questions and topics for discussion.—Topics for themes.—Bibliography: (p. [277]-283) Bibliography: p. [277]-283. [CT104.B65 1968] 68-8440
1. Biography. 2. United States—Biography. I. Bessey, Mabel Abbott, 1884- ed. II. Title.

BRADFORD, Gamaliel, 1863- 920.02 1932.
Saints and sinners. Port Washington, N.Y., Kennikat Press [1971, c1932] 261 p. illus., ports. 22 cm. (Essay and general literature index reprint series) Biographies. [CT105.B72 1971] 74-118459
1. Biography. I. Title.

BRADLEY, Eileen. 828'.9'1409 B
Mrs. Widgery; [illustrations by Richard Bradley]. Winchester, Winton Publications Ltd, 1972. 110 p. illus. 25 cm. [PR6052.R255M5] 73-158169 ISBN 0-901565-07-5 £1.80
I. Title.

BROCKWAY, Wallace, 1905- 920.02 ed.
High moment; stories of supreme crises in the lives of great men, as told by Bertrand Russell [and others] Edited with an introd. New York, Simon and Schuster, 1955. 273p. 22cm. [CT104.B68] 54-9807
1. Biography. I. Title.

CHAMBERS'S biographical 920'.02 *dictionary.* Edited by J. O. Thorne. Rev. ed. New York, St. Martin's Press [1970, c1968] [23], 1432 p. 25 cm. "Supplement": 13th-22d prelim. pages. [CT103.C4 1970] 73-174147 17.50
1. Biography. I. Thorne, J. O., ed.

D'AMATO, Guy Albert, 1903- 920.02
Portraits of ideas. Illustrated by Arturo Duccini. Freeport, N.Y., Books for Libraries Press [1970, c1947] 220 p. illus., ports. 24 cm. (Biography index reprint series) [CT104.D3 1970] 78-117322
1. Biography. I. Duccini, Arturo, illus. II. Title. BIP

DE FORD, Miriam Allen, 1888- 902
Who was when? A dictionary of contemporaries. 2d ed. New York, Wilson, 1950. 1 v. (unpaged) 27 x 36 cm. [CT103.D4 1950] 51-7967
1. Biography. 2. Chronology, Historical—Tables. I. Title.

DE FORD, Miriam Allen, 902'.02 1888-1975.
Who was when? : A dictionary of contemporaries / compiled and edited by Miriam Allen de Ford and Joan S. Jackson. 3d ed. New York : Wilson, 1976. p. cm. Includes index. Lists 10,000 celebrated individuals from 500 B.C. to the present both by date and by field of activity. An alphabetical listing follows. [CT103.D4 1976] 76-2404 ISBN 0-8242-0532-4
1. Biography. 2. Chronology, Historical—Tables. I. Jackson, Joan S., joint author. II. Title.

DE TREVILLE, Ruth (Saffold) FIC 1892-
Cornelius of Beaufort, by Ruth Saffold. Columbia, S.C., Printed by R. L. Bryan Co., 1969. vii, 180 p. illus. 24 cm. [PZ4.D474Co] [PS3554.E86] 917.57'03'30924 B 70-17636 4.95
I. Title.

DE VOSJOLI, P. L. 327'.12'0924 B Thyraud.
Lamia, by P. L. Thyraud de Vosjoli. [1st ed.] Boston, Little, Brown [1970] 344 p. 22 cm. [UB271.F72D4] 70-121424 6.95

DINGWALL, Eric John 920.8
Very peculiar people; portrait studies in the queer, the abnormal, and the uncanny. New Hyde Park, N. Y., University Bks. [c.1962] 223p. illus. 25cm. 62-14949 6.00
1. Biography. 2. Characters and characteristics. I. Title.

DINGWALL, Eric John. 920
Very peculiar people; portrait studies in the queer, the abnormal, and the uncanny. London, New York, Rider [1950?] 224 p. plates, ports. 24 cm. Includes bibliographies. [CT9990.D55] 50-14839
1. Biography. 2. Characters and characteristics. I. Title.
Contents Omitted.

DONALDSON, Norman. 920
How did they die? / By Norman and Betty Donaldson. New York : St. Martin's Press, [1980] p. cm. [CT105.D6] 79-22871 ISBN 0-312-39488-8 : 12.95
1. Biography. 2. Death—Causes. I. Donaldson, Betty, joint author. II. Title. BIP

EASTMAN, Max, 1883-1969. 920'.02
Heroes I have known; twelve who lived great lives. Freeport, N.Y., Books for Libraries Press [1973, c1942] p. (Essay index reprint series) Contents.Contents.—Introduction: hero worship benign and diabolic.—The hero as parent: my most unforgettable character.—The hero as agitator: a life portrait of Carlo Tresca.—Greek drama in Cleveland: the trial of Eugene Debs.—Heroism plus heroics: difficulties in worshiping Isadora Duncan.—Humor in goodness: the constitutional perfection of Art Young.—Mark Twain's Elmira: the influence of a great preacher and his parish.—France and her man of letters: an enthusiasm involving Anatole France.—Actor of one role: a character study of Charlie Chaplin.—Contribution to an apotheosis: John Reed and the Russian Revolution.—Great in time of storm: the character and fate of Leon Trotsky.—Visit in Vienna: the crochety greatness of Sigmund Freud.—The hero as teacher: the life story of John Dewey.—Epilogue. [CT120.E2 1973] 72-10827 ISBN 0-8369-7215OHero
1. Biography. I. Title. BIP

EDDY, George Sherwood, 920.03 1871-
Makers of freedom; biographical sketches in social progress, by George Sherwood Eddy and Kirby Page. Freeport, N.Y., Books for Libraries Press [1970, c1926] 311 p. 23 cm. (Essay index reprint series) Contents.Contents.—Freedom from slavery: William Lloyd Garrison.—Freedom from ignorance and poverty: Booker T. Washington.—Freedom from materialism: Francis of Assisi.—Freedom from ecclesiastical bondage: Martin Luther.—Freedom from moral and spiritual insensibility: John Wesley.—Freedom from social injustice: J. Keir Hardie.—Freedom from man's domination: Susan B. Anthony.—Freedom from international anarchy: Woodrow Wilson.—The present struggle for freedom.—Bibliography: (p. 311) [CT105.E25 1970] 79-117786
1. Biography. 2. Reformers. I. Page, Kirby, 1890-1957, joint author. II. Title.

EDEL, Leon, 1907-ed. 920.02
5 world biographies [by] Leon Edel, Elizabeth S. White, Madolyn W. Brown. New York, Harcourt [c.1961] 845p. illus. (Adventures in good bks.) 61-4545 3.72
1. Biography. I. Title.
Contents omitted.

ELDRIDGE, Paul 920.02
Seven aginst the night. New York, T. Yoseloff [c.1960]*39p. ports. 25cm. 60-9883 6.00
1. Biography. I. Title.

EMERSON, Ralph Waldo, 814'.3 1803-1882.
Representative men; seven lectures. [1st AMS ed.] Boston, Houghton Mifflin, 1903. New York, AMS Press [1968] 378 p. 23 cm. Original ed. issued as v. 4 of Centenary edition: the complete works of Ralph Waldo Emerson. Contents.Contents.—Uses of great men.—Plato; or, The philosopher.—Plato: new readings.—Swedenborg; or, The mystic.—Montaigne; or, The skeptic.—Shakespeare; or, The poet.—Napoleon; or, The man of the world.—Goethe; or, The writer.—Notes (bibliographical: p. [291]-378) [PS1621.A1 1968] 72-187900
1. Biography. I. Title.

EVANS, Pauline Rush, ed. 920
Best book of heroes and heroines. Color illus. by Charles McCurry. Line illus. by Raphael Busoni. Garden City, N.Y., Doubleday [1964] 283 p. illus. (part col.) 25 cm. First ed. published as: Good housekeeping's best book of heroes and heroines. Selections from the biographies of twenty men and women, including Daniel Boone by John Mason Brown, Pasteur by Sir Arthur T. Quiller-Couch, Lindbergh by Herman Hagedorn, and Amelia Earhart by Shannon Garst. [CT107.E65 1964] AC 68
1. Biography. I. McCurry, Charles, illus. II. Busoni, Rafaello, 1900- illus. III. Title.

EWART, Andrew 920.02
The world's wickedest men; authentic

accounts of lives terrible in their power for evil. New York, Taplinger [1966, c1963] 272p. 22cm. [CT9980.E9 1965] 66-10331 4.50 bds.,
1. Biography. I. Title.

FIRST glance : 920'.02
childhood creations of the famous / [compiled by] Tuli Kupferberg and Sylvia Topp. Maplewood, N.J. : Hammond Inc., c1978. 192 p. : ill. ; 28 cm. [CT105.F47] 77-17424 ISBN 0-8437-3403-5 : 12.95
1. Biography. I. Kupferberg, Tuli. II. Topp, Sylvia.

FORTUNE, William L. 920'.02
The moment / William L. Fortune. 1st ed. Villanova, Pa. : Progeny Press, c1979. xx, 207 p. ; 25 cm. [CT104.F63] 79-87489 ISBN 0-934168-00-8 : 8.95
1. Biography. I. Title.
Publisher's address: PO Box 206, Villanova, PA 19085 **BIP**

FOSTER, Annie H., 1875- 920.02
Makers of history, by Annie H. Foster. Freeport, N.Y., Books for Libraries Press [1972, c1946] vii, 184 p. illus. 23 cm. (Biography index reprint series) Contents.—Discoverers and adventurers: Leif Ericsson; Leif the Lucky. Robert Falcon Scott; in the land of the penguins. Sir Charles Kingsford Smith; the knight of the southern cross.—Scientists and inventors: George Stephenson; the father of railways. Thomas Alva Edison; the wizard of Menlo Park. Gugliemo Marconi; the master of space.—Humanitarian and religious leaders: St. Francis of Assisi; the knight of poverty. Martin Luther; the hero of civilization. William Penn; a ruler of brotherly love. Abraham Lincoln; a sheperd of his people. Sir Wilfred Grenfell; a fisher of men.—National heroes: John Sobieski; a saviour of Christendom. James Wolfe; the hero of Quebec. George Washington; the father of his country. Napoleon Buonaparte; the archangel of war. Giuseppe Garibaldi; the Italian liberator. [CT104.F64 1972] 76-38544 ISOMakers of history,
1. Biography. I. Title. **BIP**

FROTHINGHAM, Paul Revere, 920.02
1864-1926.
All these. Freeport, N.Y., Books for Libraries Press [1969] xii, 314 p. 23 cm. (Essay index reprint series) Reprint of the 1927 ed. Contents.Contents.—Introduction, by M. A. D. Howe.—Memoir, by R. Grant.—John Cotton.—John Fiske again.—John Ruskin.—The historian as preacher.—The mysticism of Maeterlinck.—By way of contrast.—Edward Everett Hale.—William Everett.—George Hodges.—Cromwell's head.—A great character: Charles W. Eliot. [CT104.F75 1969] 70-86752
1. Biography. I. Title. **BIP**

FRY, Thomas A. 920'.02
They dared to dream [by] Thomas A. Fry, Jr. Waco, Tex., Word Books [1972] 170 p. 23 cm. Includes bibliographical references. [CT104.F77] 72-188061 3.95
1. Biography. I. Title.

GLADDEN, Washington, 1836- 920
1918.
Witnesses of the light. Freeport, N.Y., Books for Libraries Press [1969] 285 p. ports. 23 cm. (William Belden Noble lectures, 1903) (Essay index reprint series.) Reprint of the 1903 ed. Contents.Contents.—Dante, the poet.—Michelangelo, the artist.—Fichte, the philosopher.—Victor Hugo, the man of letters.—Richard Wagner, the musician.—Ruskin, the preacher. [CT105.G5 1969] 77-84307 ISBN 8-369-10818-
1. Biography. I. Title. II. Series: William Belden Noble lectures, Harvard University, 1903 **BIP**

*GRAY, Marvin M. 920
Island hero: the story of Ramon Magsaysay. Illus. by Alan Moyler. New York, Hawthorn [c.1965] 188p. 22cm. (Hawthorn jr. biogs.) 65-12736 3.25 pap.,
I. Title.

THE Greatest thinkers / 920'.02
[edited by] Edward de Bono ; diagrams by Edward de Bono with George Daulby. London : Weidenfeld and Nicolson, 1976. 215 p. : ill., chart, facsims., maps, ports. ; 25 cm. Includes index. [CT105.G73 1976b] 77-358880 ISBN 0-297-77198-1 : £5.95
1. Biography. 2. Philosophers—Biography. I. De Bono, Edward, 1933- **BIP**

GRIGGS, Edward Howard, 920.02
1868-1951.
Great leaders in human progress. Freeport, N.Y., Books for Libraries Press [1969] 191 p. 23 cm. (Essay index reprint series) Reprint of the 1939 ed. Contents.Contents.—Socrates.—Marcus Aurelius.—Theodoric, the great.—Saint Francis of Assisi.—Dante.—Savonarola.—Leonardo Da Vinci.—Erasmus.—Giordano Bruno.—Shakespeare.—Spinoza.—Voltaire.—Benjamin Franklin. [CT104.G74 1969] 70-86755
1. Biography. I. Title. **BIP**

GUINAGH, Kevin, 1897- 509.'22
Inspired amateurs. Freeport, N.Y., Bks. for Libs. Pr. [1967,c.1937] xv, 171p. 22cm. (Essay index reprint ser.) [CT104.G8 1967] 67-26746 7.75
1. Biography. 2. Scientist—Biog. I. Title.
Contents Omitted. **BIP**

HAGEDORN, Hermann, 1882-1964. 920
Eleven who dared. Abridged and rev. by Dorothea Hagedorn Parfit. New York, Four Winds Press [1967] 143 p. 20 cm. "Adapted and abridged from The book of courage by Hermann Hagedorn." Short biographies of eleven men and women of heroic spiritual and physical courage: Socrates, Hannibal, Joan of Arc, Martin Luther, Elizabeth of England, Robert E. Lee, Father Damien, Theodore Roosevelt, Edith Cavell, Mahatma Gandhi, and Charles Lindbergh. [CT107.H27] AC 67
1. Biography. 2. Heroes. I. Parfit, Dorothea Hagedorn, ed. II. Hagedorn, Hermann, 1882-1964. The book of courage. III. Title.

HALL, Kenneth, 1926- 920.073
They stand tall; life stories of fifteen great men and women. Anderson, Ind., Warner Press, 1953. 150p. 21cm. [CT106.H3] 53-7025
1. Biography. I. Title.

HALL, Kenneth F 1926- 920.073
They stand tall; life stories of fifteen great men and women. Anderson, Ind., Warner Press, 1953. 150 p. 21 cm. [CT106.H3] 53-7025
1. Biography. I. Title.

HARDY, Edward John, 1849- 920'.02
1920.
Love affairs of some famous men. Freeport, N.Y., Books for Libraries Press [1972] 252 p. ports. 22 cm. (Essay index reprint series) Reprint of the 1897 ed. [CT105.H26 1972] 72-4514 ISBN 0-8369-2948-9 13.75
1. Biography. I. Title. **BIP**

HART, Michael H. 920'.02
The 100 : a ranking of the most influential persons in history / Michael H. Hart. New York : Hart Pub. Co., c1978. 572 p. : ill. ; 27 cm. Includes index. [CT105.H32] 77-77090 ISBN 0-8055-1256-X : 12.50
1. Biography. I. Title.

HAYWARD, Abraham, 1801- 920'.02
1884.
Sketches of eminent statesmen and writers, with other essays. Freeport, N.Y., Books for Libraries Press [1973] p. (Essay index reprint series) Reprint of the 1880 ed. published by J. Murray, London, which was reprinted from the Quarterly journal, with additions and corrections. [CT104.H4 1973] 73-5634 ISBN 0-518-10112-6
1. Biography. I. Title.

HENDERSON, Dorothy 920.02
(McLaughlin) 1900-
Biographical sketches of six humanitarians whose lives have been for the greater glory. Symbol designs by Douglas C. Henderson. [1st ed.] New York, Exposition Press [1958] 188p. illus. 21cm. [CT105.H45] 58-4777
1. Biography. I. Title. II. Title: For the greater glory.

HILLIS, Newell Dwight, 920.04
1858-1929.
Great men as prophets of a new era. Freeport, N.Y., Books for Libraries Press [1968] 221 p. 22 cm. (Essay index reprint series) Reprint of the 1922 ed. Contents.Contents.—Dante, and the dawn after the dark ages.—Savonarola, and the renaissance of conscience.—William the Silent, and brave little Holland.—Oliver Cromwell, and the rise of democracy in England.—John Milton, the scholar in politics.—John Wesley, and the moral awakening of the common people.—Garibaldi, the idol of the new Italy.—John Ruskin, and the diffusion of the beautiful. [CT105.H622] 68-16939
1. Biography. I. Title. **BIP**

HOOK, Donald D., 1928- 920'.02
Madmen of history / by Donald D. Hook. Middle Village, N.Y. : Jonathan David Publishers, [1975] p. cm. [D110.H66] 75-14215 ISBN 0-8246-0202-1 : 9.95
1. Biography. 2. Mental illness—Cases, clinical reports, statistics. I. Title. **BIP**

IVERSON, Nick. 920'.02
Record makers and record breakers / by Nick Iverson. Middle Village, N.Y. : Jonathan David Publishers, c1976. p. cm. Uses biographical sketches to present record performances which have captivated the public in such areas as politics, sports, science, entertainment, daily life, and aviation. [CT105.I9] 920 76-10227 ISBN 0-8246-0208-0 : 9.95
1. Biography. I. Title.

JOHNSON, Dorothy M. 920'.02
The bedside book of bastards [by] Dorothy M. Johnson & R. T. Turner. New York, McGraw-Hill [1973] viii, 311 p. illus. 24 cm. Bibliography: p. [301]-311. [CT104.J64] 73-4615 ISBN 0-07-032585-5
1. Biography. I. Turner, Robert Townley, 1917- joint author. II. Title.

KEMBLE, James, 1900- 920'.02
Idols and invalids. [Folcroft, Pa.] Folcroft Library Editions, 1974. p. Reprint of the 1933 ed. published by Methuen, London, in series: The Fountain library. [CT105.K38 1974] 74-11425 ISBN 0-8414-5506-6 (lib. bdg.)
1. Biography. I. Title. II. Series: The Fountain library.

KENWORTHY, Leonard Stout, 920.02
1912-
Twelve citizens of the world, a book of biographies; illustrated by William Sharp. [1st ed.] Garden City, N. Y., Doubleday [1953] 286 p. illus. 22 cm. [CT120.K45] 53-9130
1. Biography. I. Title.

KLAY, Andor, 1912- 920
The visitor speaks; American freedom viewed from afar, 1800-1950, by Andor Klay and Walter Kamprad. [Souvenir ed.] Washington, Lithographed by Williams & Heintz Co., c1950. 96p. illus., ports. 20cm. [CT105.K55 1950] 50-3759
1. Biography. I. Kamprad, Walter Theodore. 1918- joint author. II. Title.

KLEIN,Alexander, 1918- ed. 920.02
Courage is the key. New York, Twayne Publishers [1953] 287p. 23cm. [CT105.K57] 53-13207
1. Biography. I. Title.

LOWNSBERY, Eloise, 1888- 920.02
Saints & rebels. Illustrated by Elizabeth Tyler Wolcott. Freeport, N.Y., Books for Libraries Press [1971, c1937] ix, 356 p. illus. 23 cm. (Essay index reprint series) Contents.Contents.—Henrietta Szold.—Catherine Breshkovsky, "Baboushka."—Malwida von Meysenbug.—Don Bosco.—Lord Shaftesbury.—Hannah More.—William Wilberforce.—Sarah Josepha Hale.—Thomas Paine.—St. Vincent de Paul.—Christine de Pisan.—Fra Antonino.—Bibliography (p. 343-346) [CT104.L65 1971] 72-156682 ISBN 0-8369-2322-7
1. Biography. I. Title. **BIP**

LUDWIG, Emil, 1881-1948, 902.02
ed.
The torch of freedom, edited by Emil Ludwig and Henry B. Kranz. Twenty exiles of history, illustrated by Esta Cosgrave. Port Washington, N.Y., Kennikat Press [1972, c1943] viii, 426 p. 23 cm. (Essay and general literature index reprint series) [CT105.L8 1972] 71-153251 ISBN 0-8046-1504-7
1. Biography. I. Kranz, Henry B., 1895-1964, joint author. II. Title. **BIP**

MCCARTHY, Colman. 920'.02
Inner companions / Colman McCarthy. Washington : Acropolis Books, [1975] 272 p. ; 24 cm. Includes bibliographies and index. [CT104.M23] 75-31846 ISBN 0-87491-054-4
1. Biography. I. Title.

MACCARTHY, Desmond, Sir, 920.02
1878-1952.
Portraits. New York, Oxford University Press, 1954. xii, 293 p. 23 cm. [CT119.M2 1954] 54-4109
1. Biography. 2. Gt. Brit.—Biography. I. Title.

MACCARTHY, Desmond, Sir 920.02
1878-1952
Portraits. London, Saunders with MacGibbon & Kee [dist. Chester Springs, Pa., Dufour, 1964]. xii, 293p. 23cm. [CT119.M2] 3.50
1. Biography. 2. Gt. Brit.—Biog. I. Title. **BIP**

MACCARTHY, Desmond, Sir, 920'.02
1878-1952.
Portraits. Freeport, N.Y., Books for Libraries Press [1972] xii, 293 p. 22 cm. (Essay index reprint series) "First published 1931." [CT119.M2 1972] 72-5613 ISBN 0-8369-7299-6
1. Biography. 2. Great Britain—Biography. I. Title.

MACCARTHY, Mary (Warre 920.02
Cornish)
Handicaps; six studies, by Mary MacCarthy. Freeport, N.Y., Books for Libraries Press [1967] 225 p. 22 cm. (Essay index reprint series) Contents.—Mary Lamb, 1765-1847.—Ludwig van Beethoven, 1770-1827.—Arthur MacMurrough Kavanagh, 1831-1889.—Henry Fawcett, 1833-1884.—W. E. Henley. 1849-1903.—Robert Louis Stevenson, 1850-1894.—Bibliographical note (p. 225-[226]) [CT105.M2 1967] 67-26756
1. Biography. I. Title. **BIP**

MACDOUGALL, Curtis Daniel, 920.02
1903-
Greater dead than alive. Washington, D.C. Public Affairs Pr. [c.1963] 263p. 24cm. Bibl. 63-22193 4.50
1. Biography. I. Title.

MAKERS of the Western 920'.02
tradition : portraits from history / J. Kelley Sowards, editor. New York : St. Martin's Press, [1975- v. : ill. ; 24 cm. Includes bibliographical references. [CT104.M29] 75-3632 4.95 (v. 1)
1. Biography. 2. Civilization—History. I. Sowards, Jesse Kelley, 1924-

*MORETTI, Darcia. 920
Gente importante. [New York] Plus Ultra Educational Publishers [1973] 219 p. 19 cm. [CT104] 2.95 (pbk.)
1. Biography. I. Title.

MORLEY, John Morley, 920.044
Viscount, 1838-1923.
Biographical studies. Freeport, N.Y., Books for Libraries Press [1969] xii, 435 p. 23 cm. (Essay index reprint series) Reprint of the 1923 ed. Contents.Contents.—Turgot.—Condorcet.—The champion of social reaction.—Robespierre.—Victor Hugo's 'Ninety-three.'—France in the eighteenth century.—An Easter digression. Bibliographical footnotes. [CT1011.M6 1969] 78-86773
1. Biography. I. Title. **BIP**

MYERS, Jay Arthur, 1888- 920
Fighters of fate; a story of men and women who have achieved greatly despite the handicaps of the great white plague. With an introd. by Charles H.Mayo. Freeport, N.Y., Books for Libraries Press [1969] xix, 318 p. 23 cm. (Essay index reprint series) Reprint of the 1927 ed. Contents.Contents.—Nicolo Paganini.—Johann Frederic Schiller.—Xavier Bichat.—Rene Theodore Laennec.—Leigh Hunt.—John Keats.—Elizabeth Barrett Browning.—St. Francis of Assisi.—Frederic Chopin.—Henry David Thoreau.—Fedor Dostoievsky.—Artemus Ward.—Sidney Lanier.—Edward Livingston Trudeau.—Cecil John Rhodes.—Christopher Mathewson.—Aubrey Beardsley.—McDugald McLean.—Harold Bell Wright.—Roger W. Babson.—Lawrason

Brown.—Will Irwin.—Albert Edward Wiggam.—Eugene O'Neill. Includes bibliographies. [CT105.M9 1969] 79-84329
1. Biography. 2. Tuberculosis. I. Title.

NISENSON, Samuel. 920.02
Illustrated minute biographies; 150 fascinating life-stories of famous people from the dawn of civilization to the present day, dramatized with portraits and scenes from their lives. Designed and illustrated by Samuel Nisenson. Text by William A. DeWitt. [Rev. ed.] New York, Grosset & Dunlap [1970] 160 p. illus. 28 cm. (Illustrated true books) "2987." One-page biographies of 150 well-known musicians, scientists, philosophers, writers, artists, soldiers, and political leaders from ancient to present times. [CT103.N48 1970] 920 77-120429 3.95
1. Biography. I. De Witt, William A. II. Title.

OLIVER, Peter. 920.02
Saints of chaos. Illus. by H. Glintenkamp. Freeport, N.Y., Books for Libraries Press [1967] 227 p. port. 22 cm. (Essay index reprint series) Reprint of 1934 ed. Contents.Contents.—Harbingers of change.—Martin Luther.—Galileo Galilei.—Ludwig van Beethoven.—James Watt.—Thomas Hobbes.—The new unity. [CT105.O5 1967] 67-23255
1. Biography. 2. Civilization—Philosophy. I. Title. BIP

ONE hundred great lives; 920.02
revealing biographies of scientists and inventors, leaders and reformers, writers and poets, artists and musicians, discoverers and explorers, soldiers and statesmen, great women. Melbourne, Sun Books [1969] vii, 760 p. 19 cm. [CT104.O5] 78-468017 1.75
1. Biography.

ORCUTT, William Dana, 920.02
1870-1953.
Celebrities off parade. Pen-and-ink portrait sketches, by Dwight C. Sturges. Freeport, N.Y., Books for Libraries Press [1969] 287 p. ports. 23 cm. (Essay index reprint series) Reprint of the 1935 ed. [CT104.O7 1969] 79-93369
1. Biography. 2. Authors—Correspondence, reminiscences, etc. I. Title.

PAFFARD, Michael. 791.8
The unattended moment : excerpts from autobiographies with hints and guesses / Michael Paffard. London : S.C.M. Press, 1976. 128 p. ; 19 cm. Includes bibliographical references. [CT105.P33] 76-368148 ISBN 0-334-01721-1 : £0.80
1. Biography. I. Title. BIP

PARKMAN, Mary Rosetta, 1875- 920
1941.
High adventurers. Freeport, N.Y., Books for Libraries Press [1967] vii, 290 p. illus., ports. 22 cm. (Essay index reprint series) Reprint of the 1931 ed. Eleven biographical sketches of Francis Parkman, Michael Pupin, Charles A. Lindbergh, Richard Evelyn Byrd, Vilhjalmur Stefansson, Edward MacDowell, Edwin Austin Abbey, Harriet Hosmer, Edward William Bok, Margaret Bondfield, and Dorothy Canfield Fisher. [CT107.P25 1967] AC 68
1. Biography. I. Title.

PEATTIE, Donald Culross, 920.02
1898-1964.
Lives of destiny, as told for the Reader's digest. Boston, Houghton Mifflin, 1954. 208 p. illus. 21 cm. [CT106.P4] 54-8136
1. Biography. I. Title.

PEOPLE of purpose. 920.02
Editor-in-chief: Herbert S. Zim. Chicago, Spencer Press [1961] xv, 432 p. illus. 24 cm. (Fact and fiction) [CT106.P46] 61-10560
1. Biography. I. Zim, Herbert Spencer, 1909- ed.

PLUMB, Beatrice, 1886- 920
Lives that inspire. A Christian herald family bookshelf selection. Minneapolis, T. S. Denison [1962] 219p. 22cm. [CT105.P55] 62-9578
1. Biography. I. Title.

POTTER, George L 1890- 920.02
Authentic biographies of the world's greatest people. [St. Augustine] c1955. 189p. illus. 23cm. On cover: Potter's Wax Museum. [CT106.P68] 55-25888
1. Biography. 2. Potter's Wax Museum, St. Augustine. I. Title.

PROCHNOW, Herbert Victor, 920.02
1897- ed.
Great stories from great lives; a gallery of portraits from famous biographies. Edited by Herbert V. Prochnow. Freeport, N.Y., Books for Libraries Press [1971, c1944] xi, 404 p. 23 cm. (Essay index reprint series) Includes bibliographical references. [CT104.P75 1971] 77-111858 ISBN 0-8369-2018-X
1. Biography. I. Title.

RAPIER, Regina. v. 12
Parvenu and the purple. Atlanta, 1965. 247 p. illus. Xerox copy of the original. Bibliography: p. [248] 66-90895
1. Biography. I. Title.

THE Reader's digest. 920.02
Great lives, great deeds. Pleasantville, N.Y., Reader's Digest Association [1964] vi, 576 p. col. illus., col. ports. 20 cm. [CT106.R4] 64-22004
1. Biography. I. Title.

RIDOUT, Albert K., comp. 920
Introducing biography, edited by Albert K. Ridout. New York, Scribner [1968] xii, 429 p. illus., ports. 21 cm. Nineteen excerpts from biographies or autobiographies, designed to introduce high school students to the form, with study guides including topics for discussion, vocabulary, and interpretation of the facts. [CT107.R67] AC 68
1. Biography. 2. Biography (as a literary form) I. Title.

ROBINSON, Donald B 1913- 920.02
The 100 most important people, 1953; illustrated by Howard Simon and Constance Joan Naar. New York, Pocket Books [1953] 439p. illus. 17cm. (A Cardinal edition, 86) [CT120.R62] 53-7065
1. Biography. I. Title.

ROBINSON, Donald B., 1913- 920.02
The 100 most important people in the world today. Boston, Little, Brown [1952] 427 p. illus. 18 cm. [CT120.R6 1952a] 52-8335
1. Biography. I. Title.

ROBINSON, Donald B 1913- 920.02
The 100 most important people in the world today; illustrated by Howard Simon. New York, Pocket Books [1952] 427p. illus. 17cm. (A Cardinal edition, 24) [CT120.R6] 53-7334
1. Biography. I. Title.

ROBINSON, Herbert 920'.02
Spencer.
The dictionary of biography / Herbert Spencer Robinson and a staff of editors. Rev. and enl. ed. Totowa, N.J. : Rowman and Littlefield, 1975. xii, 530 p. ; 21 cm. Includes index. [CT103.R57 1975b] 75-12775 ISBN 0 87471-647-0 : 10.00
1. Biography. I. Title.

RUSSELL, Phillips, 1884- 920.02
Harvesters. Freeport, N.Y., Books for Libraries Press [1971] ix, 302 p. ports. 23 cm. (Essay index reprint series) Reprint of the 1932 ed. Contents.Contents.—Frederick Caesar, foe of popes and cities.—Leonardo da Vinci, God's grandson.—Copernicus, disrupter of creeds.—Luther, former and reformer.—Cortes, the collector.—James Watt, the power maker.—Thomas Jefferson, social architect.—The background. Bibliography: p. 301-302. [CT105.R8 1971] 73-156713 ISBN 0-8369-2295-6
1. Biography. I. Title. BIP

RUSSELL, William. 920'.02
Eccentric personages; memoirs of the lives and actions of remarkable characters, including Beau Brummell, Beau Nash, Daniel Defoe, Dean Swift, Captain Morris, J. M. W. Turner, Chevalier D'Eon, etc. Plainview, N.Y., Books for Libraries Press [1974] p. cm. (Essay index reprint series) Reprint of the 1866 ed. published by E. Avery, London. [CT104.R797 1974] 74-4357 ISBN 0-518-10189-4 19.00
1. Biography. I. Title.

SCHNITTKIND, Henry Thomas, 920.02
1888-
Living biographies of famous men; by Henry Thomas [pseud.] and Dana Lee Thomas [pseud.] Garden City, N.Y., Perma Giants [1950, c1944] viii, 300 p. port. (on cover) 21 cm. [CT104.S348 1950] 50-55978
1. Biography. I. Schnittkind, Dana Arnold, 1918- joint author. II. Title.

SENIOR, Nassau William, 920'.02
1790-1864.
Biographical sketches. Freeport, N.Y., Books for Libraries Press [1972] xv, 517 p. 23 cm. (Essay index reprint series) Reprint of the 1863 ed. Contents.Contents.—Berryer.—Tronson du Coudray.—Lord Campbell's chief justices.—Feuerbach.—Jochim Hinrich Ramcke.—Charles V.—Bacon.—Lord King.—Colonel King.—Anecdotes of monkeys. [CT104.S4 1972] 72-452 ISBN 0-8369-2824-5
1. Biography. I. Title. BIP

SHELSTON, Alan. 808'.066'92
Biography / Alan Shelston. London : Methuen ; New York : distributed by Harper & Row, 1977. 82 p. ; 19 cm. (The Critical idiom ; no. 34) Includes index. Bibliography: p. [75]-77. [CT21.S44] 77-375639 ISBN 0-416-83680-1 : 6.00
1. Biography. 2. English prose literature—History and criticism. I. Title. BIP

SHRADY, Maria. 920'.02
Moments of insight; the emergence of great ideas in the lives of creative men. [1st ed.] New York, Harper & Row [1972] vi, 111 p. 20 cm. (Harper colophon books, CN 273) Bibliography: p. [105]-111. [CT106.S53] 72-6532 ISBN 0-06-090273-6 2.95
1. Biography. 2. Inspiration. I. Title.

SIMPSON, Kemper 811.54
Uncommon men. Washington 5, D.C. Agathon Pr., 454 Washington Bldg. [c.1963] 201p. 27cm. 63-14997 5.00
1. Biography. I. Title.

SMITH, Bradford, 1909-1964. 920
Men of peace. [1st ed.] Philadelphia, Lippincott [1964] 359 p. 22 cm. Bibliography: p. 351-354. [CT105.S67] 64-23478
1. Biography. I. Title.

SMITH, Herbert 920'.02
Greenhough, 1855-1935.
The romance of history. Freeport, N.Y., Books for Libraries Press [1972] 335 p. 22 cm. (Essay index reprint series) Reprint of the 1891 ed. Contents.Contents.—Masaniello.—Prince Rupert.—Benyowsky.—Tamerlane.—Marino Faliero.—Bayard.—Lithgow.—Jacqueline de Laguette.—Vidocq.—Lochiel.—Casanova. [D106.S6 1972] 72-5733 ISBN 0-8369-7285-6
1. Biography. I. Title. BIP

SNYDER, Louis Leo, 1907- 920.02
ed.
A treasury of intimate biographies; dramatic stories from the lives of great men told by those who knew them well and who themselves were men and women of distinction in literature and the arts, and placed in historical continuum and perspective by before-and-after notes concerning the lives, loves, and works of both biographee and biographer, and designed for full enjoyment and reading pleasure. New York, Greenberg [1951] xxiv, 384 p. 24 cm. [CT106.S57] 51-10995
1. Biography. I. Title.

STERN, Michael. 920.02
No innocence abroad. New York, Random House [1953] 312p. illus. 21cm. [CT189.S83] 52-5873
1. Biography. I. Title.

STEWART, George Rippey, 920.02
1895-
Good lives [by] George R. Stewart. Illustrated with photos. Boston, Houghton Mifflin, 1967. xiii, 305 p. illus., ports. 22 cm. Contents.Contents.—William the Marshal.—Heinrich Schliemann.—Joab Ben-Zeruiah.—Francisco Eduardo Tresguerras.—Henry of Portugal.—John Bidwell.—Afterword.—Sources (p. 298-304) [CT105.S728] 67-11832
1. Biography. I. Title.

THEVET, Andre, 1502- 920'.02
1590.
Les vrais pourtraits et vies des hommes illustres (1584) A facsimile reproduction, with an introduction by Rouben C. Cholakian. Delmar, N.Y., Scholars' Facsimiles & Reprints, 1973. p. Original t.p. reads: Les vrais povrtraits et vies des hommes illvstres grecz, latins, et payens, recveilliz de levrs tableavx, liures, medalles antiques, et modernes. Par Andre Thevet Angovmoysin ... A Paris, Par la vefue I. Keruert et Guillaume Chaudiere, 1584. Second ed. published in 1670-71 under title: Histoire des plus illustres et scavans hommes de leurs siecles. Bibliography: p. [CT142.T412] 72-14359 ISBN 0-8201-1112-0 50.00 library binding
1. Biography. I. Title.

THOMAS, Henry, 1886- 920.02
50 great modern lives; inspiring biographies of men and women who have guided mankind to a better world, by Henry Thomas and Dana Lee Thomas. Garden City, N. Y., Hanover House [1956] 502p. 22cm. [CT105.T55] 56-7089
1. Biography. I. Thomas, Dana Lee, 1918- joint author. II. Title.

THOMAS, Henry, 1886- 920.02
50 great modern lives; inspiring biographies of men and women who have guided mankind to a better world, by Henry Thomas and Dana Lee Thomas. Garden City, N.Y., Hanover House [1956] 502 p. 22 cm. [CT105.T55] 56-7089
1. Biography. I. Thomas, Dana Lee, 1918- joint author. II. Title.

THOMAS, Henry, 1886- 920.02
Living biographies of famous men, by Henry Thomas and Dana Lee Thomas. Garden City, N. Y., Perma Giants [1950, c1944] viii. 300p. port. (on cover) 21cm. [CT104.T52 1950] 50-55978
1. Biography. I. Thomas, Dana Lee, 1918- joint author. II. Title.

TULLY, Jim. 920'.02
A dozen and one. Freeport, N.Y., Books for Libraries Press [1972] 242 p. 22 cm. (Essay index reprint series) Reprint of the 1943 ed. [CT106.T85 1972] 72-4513 ISBN 0-8369-2980-2 9.00
1. Biography I. Title. BIP

VAN SINDEREN, Adrian, 920.02
1887-
An illustrious company. New York, 1956. 375 p. illus. 26 cm. [CT104.V3] 57-18360
1. Biography I. Title.

WALLACE, Archer, 1884- 920.02
In spite of all. Freeport, N.Y., Books for Libraries Press [1970, c1944] 122 p. 23 cm. (Essay index reprint series) Contents.Contents.—Ludwig van Beethoven.—William Cowper.—Elizabeth Barrett Browning.—Francis Parkman.—Madam Marie Curie.—Sir Walter Scott.—Friedrich von Schiller.—Baruch Spinoza.—Grey of Fallodon.—Katharine Butler Hathaway. Includes bibliographical references. [CT105.W262 1970] 76-99652 ISBN 8-369-15372-
1. Biography. I. Title. BIP

WATSON, Elizabeth Sophia 920'.02
Fletcher, d.1918.
Poet-toilers in many fields, by Mrs. Robert A. Watson. Freeport, N.Y., Books for Libraries Press [1972] 192 p. illus. 23 cm. (Essay index reprint series) Reprint of the 1884 ed. Contents.Contents.—Lucy Larcom: the factory worker.—Daniel Macmillan: the bookseller.—Henri Perreyve: French priest.—Mary Carpenter: social reformer.—James Clerk Maxwell: scientific investigator.—Toru Dutt: Hindu poetess.—John Duncan: weaver and botanist.—Wives and mothers in the age of homespun.—Oberlin: pastor, road-maker, agriculturist.—Edward Denison: Christian socialist.—Annie Keary: writer and home-keeper.—Alfred Saker: apostle to the Cameroons. [CT104.W43 1972] 72-8528 ISBN 0-8369-7336-4
1. Biography. I. Title. BIP

WEBSTER'S biographical 920'.02
dictionary. Springfield, Mass. : G. & C. Merriam Co., c1976. xxxvi, 1697 p. ; 26 cm. [CT103.W4 1976] 75-20219 ISBN 0-87779-343-3
1. Biography.

WEBSTER'S biographical dictionary; a dictionary of names of noteworthy persons with pronunciations and concise biographies. 1st ed. Springfield, Mass., G. & C. Merriam Co. [1971] xxxvi, 1697 p. 26 cm. "A Merriam-Webster." [CT103.W4 1971] 77-23207 ISBN 0-87779-043-4 920.02
1. Biography.

ZOLOTOW, Maurice, 1913- 920.02
It takes all kinds. New York, Randon House [1952] 304 p. 21 cm. [CT109.Z64] 52-7150
1. Biography. I. Title.

Biography—Juvenile literature.

ADVENTURES with world heroes, by Henry Bamman [and others] Westchester, Ill., Benefic Press [1969] 352 p. illus. (part col.), ports. 24 cm. (Invitation to adventure series) Profiles of twenty-four persons whose contributions to their people or cause had international significance. Also includes twenty-four poems by such poets as R. L. Stevenson, Langston Hughes, and Dag Hammarskjold. [CT107.A35] 920 69-15936 920'.009'04
1. Biography—Juvenile literature. I. Bamman, Henry A.

ALDEN, Carroll Storrs, 1876- 920
Youths destined to make history. [1st ed.] New York, Pageant Press [1961] 118p. 21cm. [CT107.A52] 61-17817
1. Biography—Juvenile literature. I. Title.

ARCHER, Jules. 920'.02
Famous young rebels. New York, Messner [1973] 191 p. 21 cm. Bibliography: p. 185. Biographies of twelve well-known men and women including Nehru, Elizabeth Gurley Flynn, Marcus Garvey, and Margaret Sanger who in their youth were considered the radicals of their day. [CT107.A7] 72-11819 ISBN 0-671-32579-5 4.95
1. Biography—Juvenile literature. I. Title.
Library Edition 4.79. **BIP**

BAILEY, Carolyn Sherwin, 1875- 920.02
A candle for your cake; twenty-four birthday stories of famous men and women. Drawings by Margaret Ayer. [1st ed.] Philadelphia, Lippincott [1952] 248 p. illus. 21 cm. [CT107.B17] 52-7458
1. Biography—Juvenile literature. 2. Birthday books. I. Title.

BOEHM, David Alfred, 1914- 920.073
How they got their start, by Robert V. Masters [pseud.] Drawings by Rowena Huber. New York, Sterling Pub. Co. [1958] 191p. illus. 21cm. [CT107.B6] 58-12537
1. Biography—Juvenile literature. I. Title.

BROWN, Vashti. 920.02
Stronger than the rest [by] Vashti Brown, Jack Brown [and] Margaret Lalor. With illus. by Don Miller. Boston, Houghton Mifflin [1971] vii, 152 p. col. illus. 24 cm. (Houghton Mifflin basic education program. English) Brief biographical sketches of twenty men and women who overcame severe physical handicaps to achieve their goals. [CT107.B76] 920 76-130002 ISBN 0-395-10865-9
1. Biography—Juvenile literature. I. Brown, Jack, 1905- joint author. II. Lalor, Margaret, joint author. III. Miller, Don, 1923- illus. IV. Title.

*CHRIST, Henry I. 920'.02
Short world biographies. [Edited by Tom Maksym. Illus. by Harry Schaare] New York, Globe Book Co. [1973] x, 342 p. illus., ports. 21 cm. [CT107] 3.20 (pbk.)
1. Biography—Juvenile literature. 2. Biography—Readers. I. Title.

CLARK, Leonard. 920.02
When they were children. Illustrated by William Randell. New York, Roy Publishers [1964] 144 p. ports. 21 cm. [CT107.C56] 64-22591
1. Biography — Juvenile literature. I. Title.

COMMAGER, Henry Steele, 1902- 920
Crusaders for freedom. Illus. by Mimi Korach. Garden City, N. Y., Doubleday [c.1962] 240p. 22cm. 62-15876 2.95
1. Biography—Juvenile literature. I. Title.

COTTLER, Joseph, 1899- 920.02
Heroes of civilization, by Joseph Cottler and Haym Jaffe. Rev. ed. Boston, Little, Brown [1969] 393 p. 21 cm. Brief biographies of thirty-four men and women well-known in the fields of science, medicine, invention, and exploration. [CT107.C73 1969] 920 69-10655 5.95
1. Biography—Juvenile literature. 2. Heroes. I. Jaffe, Haym, 1899- joint author. II. Title. **BIP**

EATON, Jeanette. 920.02
Leaders in other lands. Boston, Heath [1950] xi, 322 p. illus. (part col.) 22 cm. (History on the march) [CT107.E2] 50-6358
1. Biography—Juvenile literature. I. Title.

EVANS, Pauline Rush, ed. 920
Best book of heroes and heroines. Color illus. by Charles McCurry. Line illus. by Raphael Busoni. Garden City, N. Y., Doubleday [c.1958, 1964] 283p. illus. (pt. col.) 25cm. First ed. pub. as: Good housekeeping's best book of heroes and heroines. 64-16232 3.50
1. Biography—Juvenile literature. I. Title.

FORSEE, Aylesa 920
My love and I together; the stories of six famous marriages. Decorations by Ruth Macrae. Philadelphia. Macrae [c.1961] 208p. 61-14954 2.95
1. Biography—Juvenile literature. 2. Marriage —Juvenile Literature. I. Title.

GARFINKEL, Bernard Max, 1929- 920'.02
Banners of courage; the lives of 14 heroic men and women, by Robert Elliot. Illus. by Huntley Brown. New York, Platt & Munk [1972] 254 p. illus. 22 cm. Biographical sketches of fourteen men and women whose lives were examples of varied kinds of heroism. Includes Martin Luther King, Rachel Carson, Chief Joseph, Anne Frank, Joan of Arc, Richard Byrd, and others. [CT107.G36] 920 68-21696 3.50
1. Biography—Juvenile literature. I. Brown, Huntley, illus. II. Title.

GILBERT, Ariadne. 920.02
More than conquerors. Freeport, N.Y., Books for Libraries Press [1969, c1914] 423 p. illus., ports. 23 cm. (Essay index reprint series) Contents.Contents.—Beethoven.—Lamb.—Scott.—Irving.—Emerson.—Agassiz.—Thackeray.—Livingstone.—Pasteur.—Brooks.—Booth.—Stevenson.—Saint-Gaudens.—[Lincoln] [CT107.G5 1969] 920 68-58791
1. Biography—Juvenile literature. I. Title. **BIP**

*GREENE, Jay E., ed. 920.073
Five biographies. Ed., abridged by Jay E. Greene. New York, Globe [1967, c.1956] xi, 687p. illus. 21cm. 3.84
1. Biography—Juvenile literature. 2. Biography—U. S.—Juvenile literature I. Title.
Contents omitted.

JENNINGS, Gary. 920'.02
March of the heroes / by Gary Jennings. New York : Association Press, [1975] p. cm. Includes index. Follows the march of heroes, both folk and real, from earliest antiquity to the present day, indicating how each of them has reflected the culture, society, and life-style from which he or she sprang. [CT107.J44] 75-9863 ISBN 0-8096-1895-8 : 7.95
1. Biography—Juvenile literature. 2. Heroes—Juvenile literature. I. Title.

*KIESZAK, Kenneth. 920'.02
Turning point: a collection of short biographies. New York, Learning Trends [a divn. of Globe Book Co., 1973] 280 p. illus. (pt. col.) ports. 23 cm. [CT107] 3.20 (pbk)
1. Biography—Juvenile literature. 2. Biography—Readers. I. Title.

MACKINNON, Cleodie. 920
Stories of courage. Illus. by Peter Branfield. New York, Watts [1968,c.1966] 96p. col. illus., map. 29cm. (Franklin Watts ref. lib., 5) [CT107.M32 1968] 67-29734 4.95
1. Biography—Juvenile literature. I. Title. II. Series.

MCNEER, May Yonge, 1902- 920.02
Armed with courage, by May McNeer and Lynd Ward. New York, Abingdon Press [1957] 112p. illus. 25cm. [CT107.M33] 57-13739
1. Biography—Juvenile literature. I. Ward, Lynd Kendall, 1905- joint author. II. Title.

MODEROW, Gertrude 920.02
People to remember; 16 biographical sketches adapted by Gertrude Moderow. With discussion questions by Frances S. Fitzgerald. Illustrated by Peter Gourfain. Chicago, Scott, Foresman [c.1960] 296p. illus. 22cm. 60-10547 2.40
1. Biography—Juvenile literature. I. Title.

MODEROW, Gertrude. 920.02
People to remember: 16 biographical sketches adapted by Gerturde Moderow. With discussion questions by Frances S. Fitzgerald. Illustrated by Peter Gourfain. Chicago, Scott, Foresman [1960] 296p. illus. 22cm. [CT107.M65] 60-10547
1. Biography— Juvenile literature. I. Title.

MYERS, Rawley. 920.02
People who loved. Notre Dame, Ind., Fides Publishers [1970- v. illus., ports. 21 cm. Profiles of people who tried to lead lives of Christian sacrifice and understanding. [CT107.M9] 920 74-124620 ISBN 0-8190-0447-2(v.1) 2.50 (v. 1)
1. Biography—Juvenile literature. I. Title.

PARKMAN, Mary Rosetta, 1875-1941. 917.3'03'80922
High adventurers. Freeport, N. Y., Books for Libraries Press [1967] vii, 290 p. illus., ports. 22 cm. (Essay index reprint series) Reprint of the 1931 ed. [CT107.P25] 67-26770
1. Biography—Juvenile literature. I. Title.
:Contents omitted **BIP**

PARKMAN, Mary Rosetta, 1875-1941. 917.3'03'80922
High adventurers. Freeport, N.Y., Books for Libraries Press [1967] vii, 290 p. illus., ports. 22 cm. (Essay index reprint series) Reprint of the 1931 ed. Contents.Contents.—Adventures with history: Francis Parkman.—Adventures with science: Michael Pupin.—Wings of adventure: Charles A. Lindbergh.—From pole to pole: Richard Evelyn Bryd.—The poet of intrepid daring: Vilhjalmur Steffansson.—A new-world poet of sound: Edward MacDowell.—A master painter of romance: Edwin Austin Abbey.—The friendly sculptor: Harriet Hosmer.—Adventuring for beauty: Edward William Bok.—A champion of labor: Margaret Bondfield.—Adventures in everyday living: Dorothy Canfield Fisher. [CT107.P25 1967] 67-26770
1. Biography—Juvenile literature. I. Title.

PATON, Graham. 920
Great men and women of modern times; ed. by Graham Paton; illus. by R. S. Embleton. London, Purnell [1967] Stamped on t.p.: Dist. SportShelf, New Rochelle, N.Y. 4-77 p. col. illus. (incl parts). 29 cm col. illus. on end papers (Finding out bks) [Finding out bks] Col. illus. on endpapers. [CT107.P36] 66-23309 4.25
1. Biography—Juvenile literature. I. Title.

PEOPLE and great deeds. 920'.02
Yvonne Beckwith, editor. Chicago, Standard Educational Corp., 1974 [C1971] p. cm. (The Child's world) Brief biographies of twenty-three famous people in history include Galileo, Mozart, Helen Keller, Marie Curie, and Thomas Jefferson. [CT107.B4 1974] 920 74-12252
1. Biography—Juvenile literature. I. Beckwith, Yvonne, ed. II. Title. III. Series.
Sold only as part of a eight volume set, 69.50.

PRINGLE, Patrick. 920.02
When they were boys; sixteen boyhood stories of famous men. New York, Roy Publishers [1954?] 224p. illus. 21cm. [CT107] 54-10467
1. Biography—Juvenile literature. 2. Boys—Biog. I. Title.

REYNOLDS, James Joseph, d.1945. 920.02
Short stories of famous men, by James J. Reynolds, Mary A. Horn, and Phoebe Mizell. New York, Noble and Noble [1953] 309 p. illus. 20 cm. [CT107.R6 1953] 53-1585
1. Biography—Juvenile literature. I. Title.

RHOADS, Bert. 920.02
Keepers of the King's gates. Cover design by Charles Cook. Washington, Review and Herald Pub. Association [1956] 160p. illus. 22cm. [CT107.R64] 56-58726
1. Biography—Juvenile literature. I. Title.

RHOADS, Bert. 920.02
Keepers of the King's gates. Cover design by Charles Cook. Washington, Review and Herald Pub. Association [1956] 160p. illus. 22cm. [CT107.R64] 56-58726
1. Biography—Juvenile literature. I. Title.

RIDOUT, Albert K., comp. 920.02 (j)
Introducing biography, edited by Albert K. Ridout. New York, Scribner [1968] xii, 429 p. illus., ports. 21 cm. [CT107.R67] 68-10636
1. Biography—Juvenile literature. I. Title.

STONE, David, 1929- j920
Heroes and heroines. Pictures by Leonard Everett Fisher. New York, F. Watts [1961] 51 p. illus. 23 cm. [CT107.S792] 59-11487
1. Biography — Juvenile literature. I. Title.

STRONG, Jay. 920.02
Famous heroes of the ages. Illustrated by Harry Fisk. New York, Hart Pub. co. [1958] 191 p. illus. 24 cm. [CT107.S793] 58-4776
1. Biography — Juvenile literature. I. Title.

STRONG, Jay. 920.02
Of courage and valor; heroic stories of famous men and women. Illustrated by Jean Frances. New York, Hart Book Co. [1955] 318p. illus. 25cm. [CT107.S795] 55-3554
1. Biography—Juvenile literature. I. Title.

UNSTEAD, R J 920.02
People in history: from Caractacus to Alexander Fleming. New York, Macmillan [1957] 512p. illus. 23cm. [CT107.U5] 57-14128
1. Biography—Juvenile literature. I. Title.

UNSTEAD, R. J. 920.02
People in history; from Caractacus to Alexander Fleming. New York, Macmillan [1957] 512 p. illus. 23 cm. [CT107.U5] 57-14128
1. Biography — Juvenile literature. I. Title.

Biography

BENNETT, Henry Stanley, 1889- 920.042
Six medieval men and women. New York, Atheneum, 1962. 177p. 19cm. (3) bibl. 1.25 pap.,
1. Biography —Middle Ages. 2. Gt. Brit.—Biog. I. Title. **BIP**

FINES, John. 940.1'092'2 B
Who's who in the Middle Ages. New York, Stein and Day [1971, c1970] xii, 218 p. 27 cm. Includes bibliographical references. [D115.F5 1971] 72-127225 ISBN 0-8128-1339-1 12.50
1. Biography—Middle Ages. I. Title.

Biography

BEALE, T. W. 920.095603
Oriental biographical dictionary. New ed., rev., enl. by H. G. Keene. New York, Kraus Reprint, 1965. 434p. 23cm. Reprint of 1894 ed. 15.00
1. Biography—Oriental—Dictionaries. I. Title.

Biography

MOMMSEN, Theodor Ernst, 1905-1958, tr. 923.143
Imperial lives and letters of the eleventh century. Tr. by Theodor E. Mommsen, Karl F. Morrison. Historical introd. by Karl F. Morrison. Ed. by L. Benson. New York, Columbia, 1962. x, 215p. 25cm. (Records of civilization: sources and studies, no. 67) Bibl. 61-15107 5.00
1. Biography—11th cent. 2. Emperors. I. Morrison, Karl F., joint tr. II. Title. III. Series.
Contents omitted.

Biography—Addresses, essays, lectures.

BRADFORD, Gamaliel, 1863-1932. 810.9'003
Biography and the human heart. Freeport, N.Y., Books for Libraries Press [1969] 283 p. ports. 23 cm. (Essay index reprint series) Reprint of the 1932 ed. Contents.Contents.—Biography and the human heart.—Henry Wadsworth Longfellow.—Walt Whitman.—Charlotte Cushman.—William Morris Hunt.—An American Pepys: John Beauchamp Jones.—Jones Very.—The letters of Horace Walpole.—Biography by mirror. [CT105.B715 1969] 68-58772
1. Biography—Addresses, essays, lectures. I. Title. **BIP**

STRACHEY, Giles Lytton, 1880-1932. 920.04
Biographical essays. New York, Harcourt, Brace & World [1969] [8], 295 p. 21 cm. Companion volume to the author's Literary essays. "Bibliographical note": 5th prelim. page. [CT104.S78 1969] 72-2704
1. Biography Addresses, essays, lectures. I. Title. **BIP**

STRACHEY, Giles Lytton, 1880-1932 920.02
Portraits in miniature, and other essays. New York, Norton [1962, c.1931] 214p. 20cm. (Norton lib.,N181) 62-51067 1.45 pap.,
1. Biography—Addresses, essays, lectures. 2. Historians, British. I. Title.

STRACHEY, Giles Lytton, 1880-1932 920.02
Portraits in miniature, and other essays. New York, Norton [1962, c.1931] 214p. 20cm. (Norton lib.,N181) 62-51067 1.45 pap.,
1. Biography—Addresses, essays, lectures. 2. Historians, British. I. Title.

STRACHEY, Giles Lytton, 1880-1932. 920'.02
Portraits in miniature, and other essays / by Lytton Strachey. Westport, Conn. : Greenwood Press, 1977. p. cm. Reprint of the 1st ed. published in 1931 by Harcourt, Brace, New York. [CT105.S8 1977] 77-10347 ISBN 0-8371-9823-2 lib.bdg. : 16.25
1. Biography—Addresses, essays, lectures. 2. Historians—Great Britain—Biography. I. Title.

Biography (as a literary form)

ALTICK, Richard Daniel, 1915- 828.08
Lives and letters; a history of literary biography in England and America. New York, Knopf, 1965. xvii, 438p. 25cm. [CT31.A4] 64-17699 8.95
1. Biography (as a literary form) I. Title.

ALTICK, Richard Daniel, 1915- 808'.066'92
Lives and letters : a history of literary biography in England and America / by Richard D. Altick. Westport, Conn. : Greenwood Press, 1979, c1965. xvii, 438, xvii p. ; 24 cm. Reprint of the ed. published by Knopf, New York. Includes bibliographical references and index. [CT31.A4 1979] 78-13952 ISBN 0-313-21116-7 lib. bdg. : 27.50
1. Biography (as a literary form) I. Title.

BOWEN, Catherine (Drinker) 1897- 920.002
Adventures of a biographer. [1st ed.] Boston, Little, Brown [1959] 235p. 21cm. [PS3503.O814Z52] 59-11888
1. Biography (as a literary form) I. Title.

BOWEN, Catherine Drinker, 1897- 808'.066'92
Biography : the craft and the calling / by Catherine Drinker Bowen. Westport, Conn. : Greenwood Press, [1978] c1969. xvi, 174 p. ; 23 cm. Reprint of the ed. published by Little, Brown, Boston. Includes index. [CT21.B564 1978] 77-19110 ISBN 0-313-20219-2 lib.bdg. : 14.50
1. Biography (as a literary form) I. Title. **BIP**

BRITT, Albert, 1874-1969. 809
The great biographers. Freeport, N.Y. Books for Libraries Press [1969] xi, 223 p. 23 cm. (Essay index reprint series) Reprint of the 1936 ed. [CT31.B7 1969] 71-84300
1. Biography (as a literary form) 2. English literature—History and criticism. 3. Literature—History and criticism. I. Title. **BIP**

COCKSHUT, A. O. J. 828'.8'0809
Truth to life : the art of biography in the nineteenth century / A. O. J. Cockshut. New York : Harcourt Brace Jovanovich, 1976, c1974. 220 p. ; 21 cm. (A Harvest book ; HB 328) Includes bibliographical references and index. [CT21.C58 1974c] 75-29326 ISBN 0-15-691385-2 pbk. : 3.95
1. Biography (as a literary form) I. Title. **BIP**

EDEL, Leon, 1907- 808'.066'809
Literary biography. Bloomington, Indiana University Press [1973] xvii, 170 p. 22 cm. Reprint of the 1959 ed. published by Doubleday, Garden City, N.Y., with a new foreword by the author. Includes bibliographical references. [CT21.E3 1973b] 74-155253 ISBN 0-253-33540-X 5.95
1. Biography (as a literary form) I. Title.
Pbk. 1.95; ISBN 0-253-20169-19

ELLMANN, Richard, 1918- 808'.066'92
Golden codgers; biographical speculations. New York, Oxford University Press, 1973. x, 193 p. 22 cm. Includes bibliographical references. [CT21.E44] 73-86067 ISBN 0-19-211827-7 7.95
1. Biography (as a literary form) 2. Authors—Biography. I. Title.

GARRATY, John Arthur, 1920- 920
The nature of biography. [1st ed.] New York, Knopf, 1957. 289p. 22cm. [CT21.G3] 57-10559
1. Biography (as a literary form) I. Title.

GARRATY, John Arthur. 1920- 920
The nature of biography. Random [1964, c.1957] 289p. 19cm. (Caravelle ed., Vintage bk. v-520) 1.95 pap.,
1. Biography (as a literary form) I. Title.

GARRATY, John Arthur. 1920- 920
The nature of biography. Random [1964, c.1957] 289p. 19cm. (Caravelle ed., Vintage bk. v-520) 1.95 pap.,
1. Biography (as a literary form) I. Title.

GITTINGS, Robert. 808'.066'92
The nature of biography / Robert Gittings. Seattle : University of Washington Press, [1978] p. cm. (The Jessie and John Danz lectures) [CT21.G5] 78-3136 ISBN 0-295-95604-6 : 7.95
1. Biography (as a literary form) 2. England—Biography. I. Title. II. Series. **BIP**

JOHNSON, Edgar. 920
One mighty torrent: the drama of biography. New York, Macmillan, 1955 [c1937] 591p. 24cm. [CT34] 55-14778
1. Biography (as a literary form) 2. Gt. Brit.—Biog. I. Title.

LEE, Sidney, Sir, 1859-1926. 808'.066'92
Principles of biography. [Folcroft, Pa.] Folcroft Library Editions, 1971. 54 p. 23 cm. "Limited to 150 copies." Reprint of the 1911 ed. Original ed. issued as the 1911 Leslie Stephens lecture. [CT21.L4 1971] 72-186978
1. Biography (as a literary form) I. Title. II. Series: Leslie Stephens lecture, 1911. **BIP**

LEE, Sidney, Sir, 1859-1926. 808'.066'92
Principles of biography / by Sir Sidney Lee. Norwood, Pa. : Norwood Editions, 1975. p. cm. Reprint of the 1911 ed. published at the University Press, Cambridge, Eng., which was issued as the 1911 Leslie Stephen lecture. [CT21.L4 1975] 75-30995 ISBN 0-88305-393-4 lib. bdg. : 6.50
1. Biography (as a literary form) I. Title. II. Series: Leslie Stephen lecture ; 1911.

MERRILL, Dana Kinsman, 1890- 920
American biography: its theory and practice. Portland, Me., Bowker Press [1957] 266p. 24cm. Includes bibliography. [CT34.U6M38] 57-9961
1. Biography (as a literary form) 2. American literature—Hist. & crit. I. Title.

REHKOPF, Donald C., ed. 920.002
Portraits in words; an introduction to the study of biography. New York, Odyssey [c.1962] 386p. (Odyssey texts in types of lit.) (T) Bibl. (T)62 3.00
1. Biography (as a literary form) I. Title.

THAYER, William Roscoe, 1859-1923. 809
The art of biography / by William Roscoe Thayer. Folcroft, Pa. : Folcroft Library Editions, 1977 [c1920] vii, 155 p. ; 23 cm. Reprint of the 1920 ed. published by Scribner, New York, in series: University of Virginia, Barbour-Page Foundation, lectures. Bibliography: p. 149-155. [CT21.T5 1977] 77-24569 ISBN 0-8414-8450-3 lib. bdg. : 17.50
1. Biography (as a literary form) I. Title. II. Series: Virginia. University. Page-Barbour Foundation. Lectures, 1920. **BIP**

YELTON, Donald Charles. 920'.073
Brief American lives : four studies in collective biography / by Donald C. Yelton. Metuchen, N.J. : Scarecrow Press, 1978. ix, 239 p. ; 23 cm. Includes bibliographical references and index. [CT21.Y42] 77-29102 ISBN 0-8108-1114-6 : 10.00
1. Biography (as a literary form) I. Title. **BIP**

Biography (as a literary form)—Addresses, essays, lectures.

STUDIES in biography / 809
edited by Daniel Aaron. Cambridge, Mass. : Harvard University Press, 1978. viii, 200 p. ; 22 cm. (Harvard English studies ; 8) Includes bibliographical references. [CT21.S85] 77-18033 ISBN 0-674-84651-6 : 12.50 ISBN 0-674-84652-4 pbk. : 3.95
1. Biography (as a literary form)—Addresses, essays, lectures. I. Aaron, Daniel, 1912- II. Series.

Biography—Bibliography.

CHICOREL, Marietta. 016.92
Chicorel index to biographies. 1st ed. New York, Chicorel Library Pub. Corp., 1974. 2 v. (898 p.) 26 cm. (Her Chicorel index series, v. 15-15A) [Z5301.C54] 74-175082 49.50 (each).
1. Biography—Bibliography. 2. Autobiographies—Bibliography. I. Title. **BIP**

HEFLING, Helen. 016.92
Hefling & Richards' Index to contemporary biography and criticism. A new ed., rev. and enl., by Helen Hefling and Jessie W. Dyde. With an introd. by Mary Emogene Hazeltine. Boston, Gregg Press, 1972. p. (Library reference series) Reprint of the 1934 ed., which was issued as no. 50 of the Useful reference series. Bibliography: p. [Z5301.H46 1972] 72-10260 ISBN 0-8398-0809-7
1. Biography—Bibliography. 2. Criticism—Bibliography. I. Richards, Eva, d. 1929, joint author. II. Dyde, Jesse Wardrope, 1898- joint author. III. Title: Index to contemporary biography and criticism. IV. Series: Useful reference series, no. 50.

O'NEILL, Edward Hayes, 1898- 016.92
Biography by Americans, 1658-1936; a subject bibliography, by Edward O'Neill. Boston, Gregg Press, 1972 [i.e. 1973, c1939] x, 465 p. 24 cm. (The Library reference series. Basic reference sources) Reprint of the ed. published by the University of Pennsylvania Philadelphia. [Z5301.O58 1972] 72-7496 ISBN 0-8398-1455-0
1. Biography—Bibliography. I. Title. II. Series: Basic reference sources.

SLOCUM, Robert B. 016.92
Biographical dictionaries and related works; an international bibliography of collective biographies ... [by] Robert B. Slocum. Detroit, Gale Research Co. 1978, c1967. xxiii, 1056 p. 24 cm. [Z5301.S55] [CT104] 67-27789 ISBN 0-8103-0974-2 :
1. Biography—Bibliography. I. Title. **BIP**

TREVELYAN, George Macaulay, 1876-1962. 016.92
Biography : a reader's guide / by G. M. Trevelyan. Folcroft, Pa. : Folcroft Library Editions, 1977. p. cm. Reprint of the 1947 ed. published for the National Book League by the Cambridge University Press, London, in series: Reader's guides. Bibliography: p. [Z5301.T8 1977] [CT104] 77-22561 ISBN 0-8414-8565-8 lib. bdg. : 6.50
1. Biography—Bibliography. I. Title. II. Series: National Book League, London. Reader's guides. **BIP**

UNITED States. 016.920'073
Library of Congress. General Reference and Bibliography Division.
Biographical sources for the United States. Compiled by Jane Kline. Boston, Gregg Press, 1972. v, 58 p. 27 cm. (The Library reference series. Basic reference sources) Reprint of the 1961 ed. published by the General Reference and Bibliography Division, Library of Congress, Washington. [Z5301.U53 1972] 72-10135 ISBN 0-8398-1181-0
1. Biography—Bibliography. 2. Reference books—Bibliography. I. Kline, Jane. II. Title. III. Series: Basic reference sources.

Biography—Bibliography—Dictionaries.

NICHOLSEN, Margaret E. 016.92
People in books; a selective guide to biographical literature arranged by vocations and other fields of reader interest, by Margaret E. Nicholsen. New York, H. W. Wilson Co., 1969. xviii, 498 p. 27 cm. [Z5301.N53] 69-15811 ISBN 8-242-03941-
1. Biography—Bibliography—Dictionaries. I. Title.

Biography—Dictionaries.

BAYLE, Pierre, 1647-1706. 920.02
Selections from Bayle's Dictionary; edited by E. A. Beller and M. du P. Lee, Jr. Princeton, Princeton University Press, 1952. xxxiv, 312 p. port. 23 cm. "Bibliographical note": p. xxxiii. Bibliographical footnotes. [CT95.B33] 52-8760
1. Biography—Dictionaries. I. Beller. Kimer Adolph, 1894- ed. II. Title.

**BULLETIN monumental,* 920.008
ou, Collection de memoires et de renseignements pour servir a la confection d'une statistique des monuments de la France, classes chronologiquement; v.1-29. Paris, M. de Caumont, 1834-1854; New York, Johnson Reprint, 1966. Indianapolis, Bobbs [1966, c.1965] 29v. (various p22cm. x1iv, 456p. 21cm. (Lib. of liberal arts) Bibl. [CT95.B333] 920.02 64-16703 set, 600.00 & set, pap., 550.00 ea., pap., 27.50 n3 6.50
1. Biography—Dictionaries. I. Bayle, Pierre, 1647-1706 II. Title: Historical and critical dictionary:

CHAMBERS'S biographical 920.02
dictionary. Edited by J. O. Thorne. New ed. New York, St. Martin's Press [1962] 1432). 25cm. [CT103.C4 1962] 61-15007
1. Biography—Dictionaries. I. Thorne, J. O., ed.

CHAMBERS'S biographical 920.02
dictionary Edited by J. O. Thorne. New ed. New York, St. Martin's Press [1962] 1132 p. 25 cm. [CT103.C4 1962] 61-15007
1. Biography—Dictionaries. I. Thorne, J. O., ed. **BIP**

CHAMBERS'S biographical 920.02'03
dictionary. Edited by J. O. Thorne. Rev. ed. New York, St Martin's Press [1969, c1968] vii, 1432 p. 25 cm. [CT103.C4 1969] 76-85529 17.50
1. Biography—Dictionaries. I. Thorne, J. O., ed.

CHAMBERS'S biographical 920.02
dictionary; the great of all nations and all times. Edited by Wm. Geddie & J. Liddell Geddie. [Latest revision, 1956] New York, MacMillan [1956] xix, 1006p. 21cm. [CT103.C4 1956] 56-14748
1. Biography—Dictionaries. I. Geddle, William, ed. II. Geddie, John Lidoell, 1881- ed.

FITZHUGH, Harriet Lloyd (Le Porte). 920.02
The concise biographical dictionary of famous men and women, by Harriet Lloyd

Fitzhugh, Percy K. Fitzhugh and William Morris. Rev. and enl. New York, Grosset & Dunlap [1950] xiii, 830 p. 22 cm. "Copyright 1935 ... under the title: Concise biographical dictionary. Special contents of this edition copyright, 1949." [CT103.F] A50
1. Biography—Dictionaries. I. Title.

FULLER, Muriel, 1901- ed. 928
More junior authors. New York, Wilson [c.]1963. vi, 235p. ports. 27cm. (Authors ser.) Companion vol. to The junior book of authors, 2d ed., rev., ed. by S. J. Kunitz and H. Haycraft. 63-11816 5.00
1. Biography—Dictionaries. 2. Authors. 3. Children's literature— Hist. & crit. 4. Illustrators. I. Title. II. Series. BIP

FULLER, Muriel, 1901- ed. 928
More junior authors. New York, H. W. Wilson Co., 1963. vi, 235 p. ports. 27 cm. (The Authors series) Companion volume to The junior book of authors, 24 ed., rev., edited by S. J. Kunitz and H. Haycraft. [PN1009.A1F8] 63-11816
1. Biography — Dictionaries. 2. Authors. 3. Children's literature — Hist. & crit. 4. Illustrators. I. Title. II. Series.

GRIGSON, Geoffrey, 1905- ed. 920.02
People: a volume of the good, bad, great & eccentric who illustrate the admirable diversity of man. General editors: Geoffrey Grigson & Charles Harvard Gibbs-Smith. Contributors to this volume include Patrick Anderson [and others] New York, Hawthorn Books [1956?] 469p. illus. (part col.) ports. (part col.) 26cm. Published in London in 1954 as v. 1 of the editors' People, places, and things. [CT103.G73] 55-12436
1. Biography—Dictionaries. I. Gibbs-Smith, Charles Harvard, 1909- joint ed. II. Title.

HAMMERTON, John Alexander, Sir, 1871-1949, ed. 920'.003
Concise universal biography : a dictionary of the famous men and women of all countries and all times, recording the lives of more than 20,000 persons and profusely illustrated with authentic portraits and other pictorial documents / edited by Sir J. A. Hammerton. Detroit : Gale Research Co., 1975. 4 v. in 2 (1452 p.) : ill. ; 23 cm. Reprint of the 1934-35 ed. published by the Educational Book Co., London. [CT103.H262 1975] 74-31444 ISBN 0-8103-4209-X : 58.00
1. Biography—Dictionaries. I. Title.

HYAMSON, Albert Montefiore, 1875- 920.02
A dictionary of universal biography of all ages and of all peoples. 2d ed., entirely rewritten. New York, Dutton, 1951. xii, 679 p. 25 cm. Bibliography: p. xii. [CT103.H9 1951a] 51-14243
1. Biography—Dictionaries. I. Title.

INTERNATIONAL who who 920.01
24th ed. London, Europe Publications, ltd. [dist. New York, International Publications Service, u960] 1037p. 26cm. 35-10257 22.00 lea. cl.,
1. Biography—Dictionaries. I. Europa Publications, ltd. London. II. Title: Who's who, International.

INTERNATIONAL who's who 920.01
(The) London, Europa Pubns. [1967] v. 26 x 20 cm. [CT120.15] 35-10257 25.00
1. Biography—Dictionaries. I. Europa publications, ltd., London.
Distributed by Intl. Pubns. Serv., New York.

KUNITZ, Stanley Jasspon, 1905- ed. 928
The junior book of authors, edited by Stanley J. Kunitz and Howard Haycraft. 2d ed., rev. New York, Wilson, 1951. vii, 309 p. ports. 27 cm. (The Authors series) [PN1009.A1K8 1951] 51-13057
1. Biography—Dictionaries. 2. Authors. 3. Children's literature—History and criticism. 4. Illustrators. I. Haycraft, Howard, 1905- joint ed. II. Title. III. Series. BIP

THE McGraw-Hill 920'.02
encyclopedia of world biography; an international reference work. New York, McGraw-Hill [1973] 12 v. illus. 29 cm. Includes bibliographies. [CT103.M27] 70-37402 ISBN 0-07-079633-5
1. Biography—Dictionaries. I. Title: Encyclopedia of world biography.

NEILSON, William Allan, 1869-1940. ed. 920.02
Webster's biographical dictionary. A Merriam-Webster. A dictionary of names of noteworthy persons, with pronunciations and concise biographies. [William Allan Neilson, editor in chief] 1st ed. Springfield, Mass, G. & C. Merriam Co. [1951] xxxvi, 1607 p. 26 cm. [CT103.W4] 51-8378
1. Biography — Dictionaries. I. Title.

NEILSON, William Allan, 1869-1946, ed. 920.02
Webster's biographical dictionary; a dictionary of names of noteworthy persons with pronounciations and concise biographies. [William Allan Neilson, editor in chief] 1st ed. A Merriam-Webster. Springfield, Mass., G. A. Merriam Co. [c1956] xxxvi, 1697 p. 26 cm. [CT103.W4 1956] 56-3528
1. Biography — Dictionaries. I. Title.

THE New Century 920'.0091'822
handbook of leaders of the classical world. Edited by Catherine B. Avery. New York, Appleton-Century-Crofts [1972] v, 393 p. 21 cm. Selected from The New Century classical handbook, published in 1962. [D55.N48] 71-189007 ISBN 0-390-66948-2
1. Biography—Dictionaries. 2. Classical biography—Dictionaries. I. Avery, Catherine B., ed. II. Title: Leaders of the classical world. BIP

NISENSON, Samuel. 920.02
Illustrated minute biographies; 150 fascinating life-stories of famous people, from the dawn of civilization to the present day, dramatized with portraits and scenes from their lives. Designed and illustrated by Samuel Nisenson; text by William A. De Wit. [Rev. ed.] New York, Grosset & Dunlap [1953] 160p. illus. 20cm. [CT103.N48 1953] 53-2265
1. Biography—Dictionaries. I. De Witt, William A. II. Title.

RANDOM House vest pocket 920.02
dictionary of famous people (The). Ed. by Constance Urdang. New York, Random [1963,c.1962] 320p. 15cm. 62-9868 1.25
1. Biography—Dictionaries. I. Urdang, Constance, ed.

ROBINSON, Herbert Spencer 920.02
The dictionary of biography [by] Herbert Spencer Robinson and a staff of eds. [Magnolia, Mass., P. Smith, 1967, c.] 1966. xii, 500p. 19cm. (Dolphin ref. orig., C472 rebound) [CT103.R57] 4.00
1. Biography—Dictionaries. I. Title.

ROBINSON, Herbert Spencer. 920.02
The dictionary of biography [by] Herbert Spencer Robinson and a staff of editors. [1st ed.] Garden City, N.Y., Doubleday, 1966. xii, 500 p. 18 cm. (A Dolphin reference original. C472) [CT103.R57] 66-17456
1. Biography—Dictionaries. I. Title. BIP

ROBINSON, Herbert Spencer. 920'.02
The dictionary of biography / Herbert Spencer Robinson and a staff of editors. Rev. and enl. ed. Totowa, N.J. : Littlefield, Adams, 1975. xii, 530 p. : 21 cm. (Littlefield, Adams quality paperback, no. 281) Includes index. [CT103.R57 1975] 74-32346 ISBN 0-87471-647-0 : 10.00 ISBN 0-8226-0281-4 pbk. : 4.95
1. Biography—Dictionaries. I. Title.

THOMAS, Joseph, 1811-1891. 920.02
Universal pronouncing dictionary of biography and mythology. 5th ed. New York, AMS Press [1972] 2 v. (xi, 2550 p.) 27 cm. [CT103.T46 1972] 76-137298 ISBN 0-404-06386-1 (set) 97.50 (set)
1. Biography—Dictionaries. 2. Mythology—Dictionaries. I. Title. BIP

VINCENT, Benjamin, 1818-1899. 920'.02
A dictionary of biography, past and present, containing the chief events in the lives of eminent persons of all ages and nations, preceded by the biographies and genealogies of the chief representatives of the royal houses of the world. Edited by Benjamin Vincent. London, Ward, Lock. Detroit, Gale Research Co., 1974. 641 p. geneal. tables. 23 cm. Reprint of the 1877 ed., which was a revision of Haydn's universal index of biography, published in 1870 in series: The Haydn series. [CT103.V45 1974] 77-174132 ISBN 0-8103-3983-8 38.00
1. Biography—Dictionaries. I. Haydn, Joseph Timothy, 1786 or 7-1856. Haydn's universal index of biography from the creation to the present time. II. Title. III. Series: The Haydn series.

WEBSTER s biographical 920.02
dictionary a dictionary of names of noteworthy persons with pronunciations and concise biographies. Springfield, Mass., Merriam [c.1963] xxxvi, 1697p. 26cm. 64-55115 8.50
1. Biography—Dictionaries.

WEBSTER'S biographical 920'.02
dictionary. Springfield, Mass., G & C. Merriam Co. [1972] xxxvi, 1697 p. 26 cm. "A Merriam-Webster." [CT103.W4 1972] 72-85 ISBN 0-87779-143-0
1. Biography—Dictionaries.

WEBSTER'S biographical 920'.02
dictionary. Springfield, Mass., G. & C. Merrian Co. [1974] xxxvi, 1697 p. 26 cm. "A Merriam-Webster." [CT103.W4 1974] 73-14908 ISBN 0-87779-243-7 12.95
1. Biography—Dictionaries.

WEBSTER'S biographical 920.02
dictionary; a dictionary of names of noteworthy persons with pronunciations and concise biographies. Springfield, Mass., G. & C. Merriam [c.1963] xxxvi, 1697p. 26cm. 63-24319 8.50
1. Biography—Dictionaries.

WEBSTER'S biographical 920.003
dictionary: a dictionary of names of noteworthy persons with pronunciations and concise biographies. 1st ed. Springfield. Mass., Merriam [1966] xxxvi, 1697p. 26cm. [CT103.W4 1966] 66-7614 8.50
1. Biography—Dictionaries.

WEBSTER'S biographical 920.02
dictionary; a dictionary of names of noteworthy persons with pronunciations andconcise biographies. A Merriam-Webster. Springfield, Mass., G. & C. Merriam [c.1962] xxvi, 1697p. 26cm. 62-52111 8.50
1. Biography— Dictionaries.

WEBSTER'S biographical 920'.003
dictionary; a dictionary of names of noteworthy persons with pronunciations and concise biographies. 1st. ed. Springfield, Mass., G. & C. Merriam Co [1967] xxxvi, 1697 p. 26 cm. [CT103.W4 1967] 67-66246
1. Biography—Dictionaries.

WEBSTER'S biographical 920.003
dictionary; a dictionary of names of noteworthy persons with pronunciations and concise biographies. 1st ed. Springfield, Mass., G. & C. Merriam Co. [1965] xxxvi, 1697 p. 26 cm. [CT103.W4 1965] 66-375
1. Biography—Dictionaries.

WEBSTER'S biographical 920.02
dictionary; a dictionary of names of noteworthy persons with pronunciations and concise biographies. 1st ed. Springfield, Mass., G. & C. Merriam Co. [1970] xxxvi, 1697 p. 26 cm. "A Merriam-Webster." [CT103.W4 1970] 78-15364
1. Biography—Dictionaries.

WEBSTER'S biographical 920'.003
dictionary; a dictionary of names of noteworthy persons with pronunciations and concise biographies. 1st ed. Springfield, Mass., G. & C. Merriam Co. [1969] xxxvi, 1697 p. 26 cm. "A Merriam-Webster." [CT103.W4 1969] 77-3626
1. Biography—Dictionaries.

WEBSTER'S biographical 920.02
dictionary; a dictionary of names of noteworthy persons with pronunciations and concise biographies. [Editor in chief: William Allan Neilson] 1st ed. Springfield, Mass., G. & C. Merriam Co. [c1958] xxxvi, 1697 p. 26 cm. [CT103.W4 1958] 58-4339
1. Biography — Dictionaries.

WEBSTER'S biographical 920.02
dictionary; a dictionary of names of noteworthy persons with pronounciations and concise biographies. [Editor in chief: William Allan Neilson] 1st ed. Springfield, Mass., G. & C. Merriam Co. [c1957] xxxvi, 1697 p. 26 cm. [CT103.W4 1959] 57-3993
1. Biography — Dictionaries.

WEBSTER'S biographical 920.02
dictionary; a dictionary of names of noteworthy persons with pronunciations and concise biographies. [Editor in chief: William Allan Neilson] A Merriam-Webster. 1st ed. Springfield, Mass., G. & C. Merriam Co. [c1959] xxxvi, 1697 p. 26 cm. [CT103.W4 1959] 59-4087
1. Biography — Dictionaries.

WEBSTER'S biographical 920.02
dictionary; a dictionary of names of noteworthy persons with pronunciations and concise biographies. [Editor in chief: William Allan Neilson] A Merriam-Webster. 1st ed. Springfield, Mass., G. & C. Merriam Co. [c1960] xxxvi, 1697 p. 26 cm. [CT103.W4 1960] 60-4604
1. Biography — Dictionaries.

WEBSTER'S biographical 920.02
dictionary; a dictionary of names of noteworthy persons with pronunciations and concise biographies. [Editor-in-chief: William Allan Neilson] A Merriam-Webster. 1st ed. Springfield, Mass., G. & C. Merriam Co. [c1961] xxxvi, 1697 p. 26 cm. [CT103.W4 1961] 61-3937
1. Biogrpahy — Dictionaries.

WEBSTER'S biographical 920.02
dictionary; a dictionary of names of noteworthy persons with pronunciations and concise biographies. [William Allan Neilson, editor in chief] 1st ed. A Merriam-Webster. Springfield, Mass., G. & C. Merriam Co. [c1956] xxxvi, 1697p. 26cm. [CT103.W4 1956] 56-3528
1. Biography—Dictionaries. I. Neilson, William Allan, 1869-1946, ed.

WEBSTER'S biographical 920.02
dictionary, A Merriam-Webster. A dictionary of names of noteworthy persons, with pronunciations and concise biographies. [William Allan Neilson, editor in chief] 1st ed. Springfield, Mass., G. & C. Merriam Co. [c1953] xxxvi, 1697p. 26cm. [CT103.W4 1953] 53-728
1. Biography— Dictionaries. I. Nellson, William Allan, 1869-1946, ed.

WHO did what; 920'.02
the lives and achievements of the 5000 men and women—leaders of nations, saints and sinners, artists and scientists—who shaped our world. New York, Crown Publishers [1974] 383 p. illus. 27 cm. Brief alphabetically arranged biographical sketches of 5000 men and women representing a variety of professions and nationalities. [CT103.W47 1974] 920 73-81194 ISBN 0-517-50567-3 12.95
1. Biography—Dictionaries.

Biography-Dictionaries and encyclopedias.

PEOPLE: v. 12
a volume of the good, bad, great & eccentric who illustrate the admirable diversity of man. General editors: Geoffrey Grigson & Charles Harvard Gibbs-Smith. Contributors to this volume include Patrick Anderson [and others] New York, HawthornBooks [1957] 437p. illus. (part col.) ports. (part col.) 26cm. 2d American ed. Published in London in 1954 as v. 1 of the editors' People, places, and things.
1. Biography-Dictionaries and encyclopedias. I. Grigson, Geoffrey, 1905- ed. II. Gibbs- Smith, Charles Harvard, 1909- joint ed.

Biography—Dictionaries—Bibl.

SLOCUM, Robert B. 016.92
Biographical dictionaries and related works; an international bibliography of collective biographies ... [by] Robert B. Slocum. Detroit, Gale Research Co. [1967] xxiii, 1056 p. 24 cm. Bibliography: p. xix-xxiii. [Z5301.S55] 67-27789 25.00
1. Biography—Dictionaries—Bibl. I. Title.

Biography—Film catalogs.

EMMENS, Carol A. 016.92'002
Famous people on film / by Carol A. Emmens. Metuchen, N.J. : Scarecrow Press, 1977. x, 35 p. : ill. ; 23 cm. Includes indexes. [CT86.Z9E45] 77-3449 ISBN 0-8108-1051-4 : 13.50
1. Biography—Film catalogs. I. Title. **BIP**

Biography—Juvenile literature—Bibliography.

KERR, Laura J., 1916- 016.92
Who's where in books; an index to biographical material. Compiled by Laura J. Kerr. Ann Arbor, Michigan Association of School Librarians [1971] vi, 313 p. 23 cm. [Z5301.K4] 79-161872
1. Biography—Juvenile literature—Bibliography. 2. Biography—Juvenile literature—Indexes. I. Title.

Biography—Juvenile literature—Indexes.

SILVERMAN, Judith, 1933- 920'.02'016
Index to collective biographies for young readers : elementary and junior high school level / Judith Silverman. 3d ed. New York : R. R. Bowker Co., 1979. xxxii, 405 p. ; 26 cm. First-2d ed. published under title: Index to young readers' collective biographies. [Z5301.S523 1979] [CT107] 79-472 ISBN 0-8352-1132-0 : 17.95
1. Biography—Juvenile literature—Indexes. I. Title.

SILVERMAN, Judith, 1933- 920'.02'016
Index to young readers' collective biographies : elementary and junior high school level / by Judith Silverman. 2d ed. New York : R. R. Bowker Co., 1975. xxv, 322 p. ; 27 cm. [Z5301.S523 1975] 75-834 ISBN 0-8352-0741-2 : 14.95
1. Biography—Juvenile literature—Indexes. I. Title.

Biography—Middle Ages, 500-1500.

DUCKETT, Eleanor Shipley. 913'.035'0922 B
Medieval portraits from East and West [by] Eleanor Duckett. Ann Arbor, University of Michigan Press [1972] 270 p. 24 cm. Contents.Contents.—Theodosius the Great.—The Empress Eudoxia and Saint John Chrysostom.—Synesius and Hypatia.—Honorius and Galla Placidia.—Pulcheria and Theodosius II.—Valentinian III and Honoria.—Dhuoda and Bernard of Septimania.—Abelard and Heloise.—Table of the line of Theodosius I, the Great.—Sources (p. 255-261) [D115.D8 1972] 70-163620 ISBN 0-472-29440-7 10.00
1. Biography—Middle Ages, 500-1500. I. Title.

Biography—Miscellanea.

MCFARLAND, Kevin 920'.02
Incredible people / Kevin McFarland ; illustrated by Luis Dominguez. New York : Hart Pub. Co., [1975] 192 p. : ill. ; 18 cm. [CT105.M26] 74-27695 ISBN 0-8055-0166-5 pbk. : 1.25
1. Biography—Miscellanea. I. Dominguez, Luis, 1923- II. Title.

SHEARER, Lloyd. 920.02
Walter Scott's personality parade. Selected, edited and with a foreword, by Lloyd Shearer. New York, Grosset & Dunlap [1971] vi, 90 p. illus., ports. 21 cm. Selections from the column in Parade, the syndicated Sunday magazine. [CT106.S49] 79-131024 ISBN 0-448-00683-9 1.00 ($1.25 Can)
1. Biography—Miscellanea. I. Title. II. Title: Personality parade.

Biography—World War, 1939-1945.

*TUNNEY, Christopher, 1924- 920.940'53
A biographical dictionary of World War II. New York, St. Martin's Press [1973, c1972] viii, 216 p. 22 cm. [CT120] 72-90763 ISBN 0-460-03868-0 8.95
1. Biography—World War, 1939-1945. I. Title.

Biography—18th century.

WILDING, Peter. 920.04
Adventurers in the eighteenth century. Freeport, N.Y., Books for Libraries Press [1969] 350 p. ports. 23 cm. (Essay index reprint series) Reprint of the 1937 ed. Contents.Contents.—John Law.—Alexandre de Bonneval.—Theodore de Neuhoff.—James Keith.—Giacomo Casanova.—Giuseppe Balsamo.—Epilogue.—Bibliographical notes (p. 331-334) [D285.W5 1969] 76-93387
1. Biography—18th century. I. Title. **BIP**

Biography—19th century.

AYLING, Stanley Edward. 909.81'0922
Nineteenth-century gallery; portraits of power and rebellion [by] S. E. Ayling. New York, Barnes & Noble [1970] 454 p. illus., maps, ports. 23 cm. Bibliography: p. [440]-442. [D352.5.A9] 72-14640 ISBN 0-389-01248-3 8.50
1. Biography—19th century. I. Title.

BRIDGE, James Howard, 1858-1939. 920.07
Millionaires and Grub Street; comrades and contacts in the last half century. Foreword by Don C. Seitz. Freeport, N.Y., Books for Libraries Press [1968] xii, 304 p. illus., facsims., ports. 23 cm. (Essay index reprint series) Reprint of the 1931 ed. Song with music: p. 237. Contents.Contents.—Herbert Spencer.—Andrew Carnegie.—Henry Clay Frick.—The Frick collection.—Elbert H. Gary.—General Sherman and the Stuarts.—Edward L. Youmans and social statics.—The elegant eighties and the genial nineties.—The Overland monthly.—The Authors Club.—Canadian interludes.—An adventure in sanitation.—The father of trusts [Charles Ranlett Flint] and the log-book of the Arrow. Appendix: A playful satire that became a prophecy. [CT119.B7 1968] 68-8441
1. Biography—19th century. I. Title. **BIP**

CANNING, John, 1920- ed. 920'.009'034
100 great modern lives; makers of the world today from Faraday to Kennedy. New York, Hawthorn Books [1966, c1965] 640 p. illus., ports. 23 cm. [CT119.C35 1966] 66-10866
1. Biography—19th century. 2. Biography—20th century. I. Title.

JENKINS, Alan, 1914- 920'.02
The rich rich : the story of the big spenders / Alan Jenkins. 1st American ed. New York : Putnam, 1978, c1977. 192 p. : ill. ; 26 cm. Includes index. Bibliography: p. 191. [CT119.J4 1978] 77-89624 ISBN 0-399-12062-9 : 12.50
1. Biography—19th century. 2. Biography—20th century. 3. Millionaires—Biography I. Title. **BIP**

ORIGO, Iris(Cutting) marchesa, 1902- 920.02
A measure of love. [New York] Pantheon [1958?] 256p. illus. 23cm. Includes bibliography. [CT119.O7] 57-7168
1. Biography—19th cent. I. Title.

PARTON, James, 1822-1891, ed. 920'.009'034
Some noted princes, authors, and statesmen of our time. By Canon Farrar [and others] Edited by James Parton. Freeport, N.Y., Books for Libraries Press [1973] p. (Essay index reprint series) Reprint of the 1885 ed. published by Crowell, New York. [CT119.P3 1973] 73-5624 ISBN 0-518-10120-7
1. Biography—19th century. I. Farrar, Canon. II. Title.

UNTERMEYER, Louis, 1885- 920.02
Makers of the modern world; the lives of ninety-two writers, artists, scientists, statesmen, inventors, philosophers, composers, and other creators who formed the pattern of our century. New York, Simon and Schuster, 1955. 809 p. 22 cm. [CT119.U5] 54-12364
1. Biography—19th century. 2. Biography—20th century. I. Title.

Biography—19th century—Anecdotes, facetiae, satire, etc.

PETER, Laurence J. 920'.02
Peter's people / by Laurence J. Peter ; illustrated by Matt Wuerker. 1st ed. New York : Morrow, 1979. 223 p. : ill. ; 22 cm. Includes bibliographical references. [CT119.P4] 79-12906 ISBN 0-688-03488-8 : 8.95
1. Biography—19th century—Anecdotes, facetiae, satire, etc. 2. Biography—20th century—Anecdotes, facetiae, satire, etc. I. Title. **BIP**

Biography—19th century—Dictionaries.

SANDERS, Lloyd Charles, 1857- 920'.009'034
Celebrities of the century; being a dictionary of men and women of the nineteenth century. Edited by Lloyd C. Sanders. London, Cassell. Ann Arbor, Mich., Gryphon Books, 1971. 2 v. (vi, 1077 p.) 22 cm. Reprint of the 1887 ed. [CT119.S3 1971] 68-27185
1. Biography—19th century—Dictionaries. I. Title. **BIP**

Biiography—19th cent.—Juvenile literature.

EGERMEIER, Elsie Emile, 1890- 920.02
Stories of great men and women; stories for boys and girls. Rev. by Zelpha H. Anderson. Illus. by Bernard Case. Anderson, Ind., Warner Press [dist. Gospel Trumpet Press, 1961,c.1931, 1958] 144p. 61-7371 2.50
1. Biiography—19th cent.—Juvenile literature. 2. Biography—20th cent.—Juvenile literature. I. Title.

Biography 20th Century.

AMORY, Cleveland, ed. 920.02
Celebrity register. 1959- New York, Harper & Row [etc.] v. ports. 27 cm. Title varies: 1959, International celebrity register. U.S. ed. Editor: 1959- C. Amory. [CT120.146] 59-15865
1. Biography — 20th cent. I. Title. II. Title: International celebrity register.

ARENDT, Hannah. 920.02
Men in dark times. [1st ed.] New York, Harcourt, Brace & World [1968] x, 272 p. 22 cm. Contents.Contents.—On humanity in dark times; thoughts about Lessing.—Rosa Luxemburg, 1871-1919.—Angelo Giuseppe Roncalli; a Christian on St. Peter's chair from 1958 to 1963.—Karl Jaspers; a laudatio.—Karl Jaspers: citizen of the world?—Isak Dinesen, 1885-1963.—Hermann Broch, 1886-1951.—Walter Benjamin, 1892-1940.—Bertolt Brecht, 1898-1956.—Waldemar Gurian, 1903-1954.—Randall Jarrell, 1914-1965 Bibliographical footnotes. [CT120.A7 1968] 68-24381
1. Biography—20th century. I. Title. **BIP**

AYLING, S. E. 923.2
Portraits of power; an introduction to twentieth-century history through the lives of seventeen great political leaders. [2d ed.] New York, Barnes & Noble [1963] 432 p. 23 cm. First published in 1961 under title: Twelve portraits of power. Includes bibliography. [D412.6.A9 1963] 63-20011
1. Biography—20th century. I. Title.

AYLING, S. E. 923.2
Twelve portraits of power; an introduction to twentieth-century history. New York, Barnes & Noble, [1962, c.1961] 312p. illus. Bibl. 61-66801 4.50
1. Biography—20th cent. I. Title.

BARTLETT, Robert Merrill, 1898- 920.02
They dared to live. Freeport, N.Y., Books for Libraries Press [1969] xii, 135 p. 23 cm. (Essay index reprint series) Reprint of the 1937 ed. [CT120.B3 1969] 76-90606
1. Biography—20th century. I. Title. **BIP**

BARTLETT, Robert Merrill, 1898- 920'.009'04
They did something about it. Freeport, N.Y., Books for Libraries Press [1969] ix, 146 p. 23 cm. (Essay index reprint series) Reprint of the 1939 ed. Contents.Contents.—Charles Franklin Kettering.—Richard E. Byrd.—Edouard Benes.—Jawaharlal Nehru.—Louis Dembitz Brandeis.—Mary McLeod Bethune.—Thomas Mann.—Madame Chiang Kai-shek.—Chevalier Jackson.—Margaret Sanger.—Sources of quotations (p. 145-146) [CT120.B315 1969] 70-90607 ISBN 8-369-12438-
1. Biography—20th century. 2. Success. I. Title. **BIP**

BARTLETT, Robert Merrill, 1898- 920.02
They stand invincible; men who are reshaping our world. New York, Crowell [1959] 261 p. 21 cm. [HN15.B34] 58-14264
1. Biography—20th century. I. Title.

BOTTOME, Phyllis, 1884-1963. 920'.02
From the life. [Folcroft, Pa.] Folcroft Library Editions, 1974. 100 p. 23 cm. Reprint of the 1944 ed. published by Faber and Faber, London. Contents.Contents.—Alfred Adler.—Max Beerbohm.—The secret of Ivor Novello.—Sara Delano Roosevelt.—Ezra Pound.—Margaret MacDonald Bottome. [CT119.B65 1974] 74-720 ISBN 0-88305-095-1 10.00 (lib. bdg.)
I. Title. **BIP**

CARNEGIE, Dale, 1888-1955. 920.02
Biographical roundup; highlights in the lives of forty famous people. Freeport, N.Y., Books for Libraries Press [1970, c1944] 233 p. 23 cm. (Essay index reprint series) [CT120.C3 1970] 77-117764
1. Biography—20th century. I. Title.

CELEBRITY register. 920.2
Ed. by Cleveland Amory, with Earl Blackwell [new ed.] New York, Harper [c.1963] 640. ports. 28cm. 22.50; 25.00 after Dec. 31,
1. Biography—20th cent. I. Amory, Cleveland, ed.

CHURCHILL, Winston Leonard Spencer, Sir, 1874-1965. 920.02
Great contemporaries. Freeport, N.Y., Books for Libraries Press [1971] x, 299 p. facsims., ports. 24 cm. (Essay index reprint series) Reprint of the 1937 ed. Contents.Contents.—The Earl of Rosebery.—The ex-Kaiser. George Bernard Shaw.—Joseph Chamberlain.—Sir John French.—John Morley.—Hindenburg.—Boris Savinkov.—Herbert Henry Asquith.—Lawrence of Arabia.—"F. E." First Earl of Birkenhead.—Marshal Foch. Leon Trotsky, alias Bronstein.—Alfonso XIII.—Douglas Haig. Arthur James Balfour.—Hitler and his choice.—George Nathaniel Curzon.—Philip Snowden.—Clemenceau.—King George V. [D412.6.C5 1971] 79-156630 ISBN 0-8369-2309-X
1. Biography—20th century. 2. Gt. Brit.—Biography. I. Title.

CHURCHILL, Winston Leonard Spencer, Sir, 1874-1965. 920'.02
Great contemporaries. Chicago, University of Chicago Press [1973, i.e.1974] 386 p. illus. 23 cm. Contents.Contents. The Earl of Rosebery.—The ex-Kaiser.—George Bernard Shaw.—Joseph Chamberlain.—Sir John French.—John Morley.—Hindenburg.—Boris Savinkov.—Herbert Henry Asquith.—Lawrence of Arabia.—'F.E.,' first Earl of Birkenhead.—Marshal Foch.—Leon Trotsky, alias Bronstein.—Alfonso XIII.—Douglas Haig.—Arthur James Balfour.—Hitler and his choice.—George Nathaniel Curzon.—Philip Snowden.—Clemenceau.—King George V.—Lord Fisher and his biographer.—Charles Stewart Parnell.—'B.-P.'—Roosevelt from afar. [D412.6.C5 1973] 73-84188 ISBN 0-226-10630-6 7.95
1. Biography—20th century. 2. Great Britain—Biography. I. Title. **BIP**

CONSIDINE, Robert Bernard, 1906- 920'.02
They rose above it : true stories about men, women, and children who fought back in the face of pain, doubt, and dismay / by Bob Considine. 1st ed. Garden City, N.Y. : Doubleday, 1977. 111 p. ; 22 cm. [CT120.C66] 75-21221 ISBN 0-385-11378-1 : 5.95
1. Biography—20th century. 2. Courage. I. Title.

COOKE, Alistair. 920'.009904
Six men / Alistair Cooke. New York : Berkley Pub. Corp. [1978]c1977. 237p. : ill. ; 18 cm. (A Berkley book) [CT120.C67 1977] ISBN 0-425-03885-8 pbk. : 2.25
1. Biography — 20th century. I. Title.

L.C. card no. for 1977 Knopf ed.: 77-74978.

COOKE, Alistair, 1908- 920'.00904
Six men / by Alistair Cooke. 1st ed. New York : Knopf, 1977. 205 p. : ports. ; 25 cm. [CT120.C67 1977] 77-74978 ISBN 0-394-48434-7 : 8.95
1. Biography—20th century. I. Title.
contents omitted BIP

COOKE, Alistair, 920'.009'04
1908-
Six men / Alistair Cooke. Boston : G. K. Hall, 1978, c1977. 392 p. ; 24 cm. Large print ed. Contents.—A note on fame and friendship.—Charles Chaplin: the one and only.—Edward VIII: the golden boy.—H. L. Mencken: the public and the private face.—Adlai Stevenson: the failed saint.—Bertrand Russell: the lord of reason.—Humphrey Bogart: epitaph for a tough guy. [CT120.C67 1978] 77-27888 ISBN 0-8161-6547-5 lib.bdg. : 11.95
1. Biography—20th century. 2. Large type books. I. Title.
Contents omitted

CURRENT biography yearbook. 920
1961. New York, Wilson [c.1961] 1962 497p. illus. 26cm. Title varies. Ed.: 1961, Charles Moritz. 40-27432 7.00 rev2
1. Biography—20th cent. I. Moritz, Charles, ed. II. Wilson, H. W., firm, publishers.

CURRENT biography Yearbook 920
1960. Ed. by Charles Moritz, New York, H. W. Wilson. 518p. ports. 26cm. annual. Cumulated from monthly numbers. Title varies. 40-27432 6.00
1. Biography—20th cent. I. Block, Maxine, ed. II. Rothe, Ann Hertha, ed. III. Candee, Marjorie Dent, 1904- ed. IV. Wilson, H. W., firm, publishers.

CURRENT biography 920.02
yearbook, 1959. Ed. by Charles Moritz. New York, H. W. Wilson [c.1959, 1960] 543p. ports 26cm. annual. Cumulated from monthly numbers. Title varies: 1940-54, Current biography; who's news and why. Vols. for 1941-50 include indexes cumulative from 1940. Vols. for 1951- include indexes cumulative from 1951. 40-27432 6.00 buck.,
1. Biography—20th cent. I. Block, Maxine, ed. II. Rothe, Anna Hertha, ed. III. Candee, Marjorie Dent, ed. IV. Charles, ed. V. Wilsn, H. W., firm, publishers.

EASTMAN, Max, 1883- v. 12
Einstein, Trotsky, Hemingway, Freud, and other great companions; critical memoirs of some famous friends. New York, Collier Books [1962] 219 p. (Collier Books, AS 137X) Originally published as Great companions. 64-32665
1. Biography—20th cent. I. Title.

EASTMAN, Max Forrester, 920.02
1883-
Einstein, Trotsky, Hemingway, Freud and other great companions; critical memories of some famous friends New York, Collier [1962, c.1942, 1959] 219p. 18cm. (Orig. pub. as: Great companions) (AS137X) .95 pap.,
1. Biography—20th cent. I. Title.

EISENHOWER, Julie Nixon. 920'.02
Special people / by Julie Nixon Eisenhower. New York : Simon and Schuster, c1977. 217 p., [8] leaves of plates : ill. ; 25 cm. [CT120.E37] 77-2129 ISBN 0-671-22708-4 : 8.95
1. Biography—20th century. I. Title. BIP

FALLACI, Oriana. 920.009'04
The egotists; sixteen surprising interviews. Chicago, H. Regnery Co. [1968] xiii, 256 p. ports. 21 cm. Contents.Contents.—Norman Mailer: Why do people dislike America?—Sean Connery: The superman.—H. Rap Brown: I'm all ready to kill.—Ingrid Bergman: The lady in gray.—Nguyen Cao Ky: Man of destiny.—Geraldine Chaplin: In the shadow of Father.—Anna Magnani: Tragic mother.—Hugh Hefner: I am in the center of the world.—Jeanne Moreau: Femme fatale.—Mary Hemingway: My husband Hemingway.—Dean Martin: A very happy man.—Duchess of Alba: The duchess.—Federico Fellini: Famous Italian director.—El Cordobes: Story of a bullfighter.—Sammy Davis, Jr.: The luck to be ugly.—Alfred Hitchcock: Mr. Chastity. [CT120.F33] 68-31460 5.95
1. Biography—20th century. I. Title.

FELLOWES-GORDON, Ian, 1921-920.02
Heroes of the twentieth century. New York, Hawthorn Books [1966] 288 p. illus., ports. 22 cm. [CT120.F38 1966a] 66-22034
1. Biography—20th century. I. Title.

FRUM, Barbara. 920'.009'04
As it happened / Barbara Frum. Toronto : McClelland and Stewart, c1976. 188 p. ; 25 cm. Selections from interviews played on the CBC radio program As it happens. [CT120.F78] 77-354288 ISBN 0-7710-3195-5 : 10.00
1. Biography—20th century. 2. Interviews. I. Title.
Distributed by Humanities Press BIP

GREENWALD, Norman David. 923.2
1925-
Portraits of power. Introd. by Louis M. Lyons. [Cambridge, Mass., Berkshire Pub. Co., 1961] 112p. illus. (Berkshire social studies series) 61-4216 1.50 pap.,
1. Biography—20th cent. 2. Statesmen. I. Title.

GUNTHER, John, 1901- 920.02
Procession. New York, Harper [c.1933-1965] xiv, 514p. 25cm. [CT120.G8] 65-16257 6.95
1. Biography—20th cent. I. Title.

GUNTHER, John, 1901-1970. 920.02
Procession. [1st ed.] New York, Harper & Row [1965] xiv, 514 p. 25 cm. [CT120.G8] 65-16257
1. Biography—20th century. I. Title.

HENDERSON, Archibald, 920.02
1877-1963.
Contemporary immortals. Freeport, N.Y., Books for Libraries Press [1968] xii, 208 p. facsim., ports. 22 cm. (Essay index reprint series) Reprint of the 1930 ed. Contents.Contents.—Albert Einstein.—Mahatma Gandhi.—Thomas Alva Edison.—Benito Mussolini.—George Bernard Shaw.—Guglielmo Marconi.—Jane Adams.—Orville Wright.—Ignace Jan Paderewski.—Marie Sklodowska Curie.—Henry Ford.—Rudyard Kipling. [CT120.H4 1968] 68-16938
1. Biography—20th century. I. Title. BIP

HIRSCH, Richard, 364.15'24'0922
1912-
Crimes that shook the world. Freeport, N.Y., Books for Libraries Press [1971, c1949] 224 p. 23 cm. (Biography index reprint series) [D412.H56 1971] 77-148217 ISBN 0-8369-8064-6
1. Biography—20th century. 2. Murder. 3. Crime and criminals. I. Title. BIP

INTERNATIONAL celebrity 920.02
register. U. S. ed. 1st- ed.; 1959- New York, Celebrity Register. v. ports. 27cm. Editor: 1959- C. Amory. [CT120.I46] 59-15865
1. Biography—20th cent. I. Amory, Cleveland, ed.

LETERMAN, Elmer G. 920.02
They dare to be different, by Elmer G. Leterman and Thomas W. Carlin. [1st ed.] New York, Meredith Press [1968] v, 218 p. ports. 21 cm. Bibliography: p. 209-211. [CT120.L4] 68-9518 5.95
1. Biography—20th century. I. Carlin, Thomas W., joint author. II. Title.

LEWYTZKYJ, Borys, 920'.0091'717
1915-
Who's who in the Socialist countries : a biographical encyclopedia of 10,000 leading personalities in 16 Communist countries / edited by Borys Lewytzkyj and Juliusz Stroynowski ; [translated and edited by Stephen Pringle and Ulla Dornberg]. 1st ed. New York : K. G. Saur Pub., 1978. xi, 736 p. ; 31 cm. [CT120.L44] 78-4068 99.00
1. Biography—20th century. 2. Communist countries—Biography. I. Stroynowski, Juliusz, joint author. II. Title.

MCDOWALL, Roddy. 792.0922
Double exposure. New York, Delacorte Press [1966] 251 p. ports. 32 cm. [PN2217.M3] 66-20997
1. Biography—20th century. 2. Actors—Portraits. I. Title.

MCPHEE, John A. 920.009
A roomful of Hovings and other profiles, by John McPhee. New York, Farrar, Straus and Giroux [1969, c1968] 250 p. 21 cm. [CT120.M35] 68-23746 5.95
1. Biography—20th century. I. Title. BIP

MARCOSSON, Isaac 070.924 B
Frederick, 1876-1961.
Adventures in interviewing. [1st AMS ed.] New York, AMS Press [1971] 314 p. illus., facsims., ports. 23 cm. Reprint of the 1920 ed. [CT119.M25 1971] 70-130996 ISBN 0-404-04186-8
1. Biography—20th century. I. Title. BIP

MARCOSSON, Isaac 920'.009'04
Frederick, 1876-1961.
Turbulent years. Freeport, N.Y., Books for Libraries Press [1969] ix, 497 p. 24 cm. (Essay index reprint series) Companion vol. to the author's Adventures in interviewing. Reprint of the 1938 ed. [CT119.M26 1969] 71-90661
1. Biography—20th century. I. Title. BIP

MEN in the news: 2, 920.02
biographic sketches from the New York Times, men and women who made headlines in 1959. Edited by Robert H. Phelps. Philadelphia, Lippincott, 1960 [c.1959] 320p. 22cm. 59-7787 5.95
1. Biography—20th cent. I. Phelps, Robert H., ed.

MEN of turmoil; 920.02
biographies by leading authorities of the dominating personalities of our day. Freeport, N.Y., Books for Libraries Press [1969] 376 p. 24 cm. (Essay index reprint series) Published in England under title: Great contemporaries. Reprint of the 1935 New York ed. [D412.G7 1969] 71-99711
1. Biography—20th century.

NOMAD, Max. 920.02
Dreamers, dynamiters and demagogues; reminiscences. New York, Waldon Press [c1964] 251 p. 23 cm. [CT101.N6] 64-88126
1. Biography — 20th cent. I. Title.

PARKER, William Robert, 920.71
1930- comp.
Men of courage; true stories of present-day adventures in danger & death. Edited by William Parker. [1st ed. Chicago] P[layboy] P[ress, 1972] xiv, 268 p. illus. 25 cm. Contents.Contents.—Terror in the air, by J. P. Blank.—The race driver who wouldn't die, by C. N. Barnard.—They couldn't break Billy Dean, by J. Dos Passos.—Run to glory, by R. Bannister.—Death on the slopes, by C. W. Casewit.—Escape from Devil's Island, by H. Charriere.—Shot down over Russia, by F. G. Powers, with C. Gentry.—Manolete's last dance with death, by V. E. Pizer.—Bloody road to Usumbura, by J.-P. Hallet.—Survival in Blackett Strait, by J. Hersey.—A hole in the clouds, by E. K. Gann.—Showdown on the one-foot line, by J. Kramer, with D. Schaap.—Search for the white death, by P. Mathiessen.—The raid at Apalachin, by J. M. Ross.—The man who flew like a bat, by M. Caidin.—Straight from the lion's mouth, by B. East.—"Heave to or I will fire!" by L. M. Bucher, with M. Rascovich.—Rumble in Haight-AshburyOMen of courage; true stories of present-day adventures in danger & death. Edited by William Parker. [1st ed. Chicago] P[layboy] P[res
1. Biography—20th century. 2. Courage. I. Title.

PARKINSON, Cyril 920.02
Northcote, 1909-
A law unto themselves; twelve portraits, by C. Northcote Parkinson. Boston, Houghton Mifflin, 1966. xii, 232 p. illus., facsim., ports. 22 cm. Contents.Contents.—William Edward Parkinson.—Marylin Wailes.—Edward Welbourne.—Geoffrey Callender.—Evan John.—Eric Gill.—Arthur Bryant.—Gerald Templer.—Lee Kuan Yew.—Richard Miers.—Sibyl Hathaway. [CT120.P37] 66-12073
1. Biography—20th century. I. Title.

PROCHNIK, Leon. 920'.009'04
Endings : death, glorious and otherwise, as faced by ten outstanding figures of our time / by Leon Prochnik. New York : Crown Publishers, 1980, c1979. p. cm. Includes index. [CT120.P76 1980] 79-19501 ISBN 0-517-53405-3 : 9.95
1. Biography—20th century. 2. Death—Case studies. I. Title. BIP

THE Reader's digest. 920.02
70 most unforgettable characters from Reader's digest. Pleasantville, N. Y., Reader's Digest Association [1967] 528 p. illus. 20 cm. [CT120.S4] 67-20606
1. Biography—20th cent. I. Title.

ROBINSON, Donald B., 1913- 920.02
The 100 most important people in the world today [by] Donald Robinson. New York, Putnam [1970] 384 p. 22 cm. [CT120.R6 1970] 75-81649 6.95
1. Biography—20th century. I. Title.

SCAVULLO, Francesco, 1929- 646.7
Scavullo on men / Francesco Scavullo, with Bob Colacello ; Sean Byrnes, photo editor. 1st ed. New York : Random House, c1977. p. cm. [CT120.S333] 77-5965 ISBN 0-394-41934-0 : 15.00
1. Biography—20th century. 2. Interviews. 3. Grooming for men. 4. Success. I. Colacello, Bob, joint author. II. Title. BIP

SNOW, Charles Percy, 920.71
Baron Snow, 1905-
Variety of men [by] C. P. Snow. New York, Scribner [1967] xii, 270 p. 24 cm. Contents.Contents.—Rutherford.—G. H. Hardy.—H. G. Wells.—Einstein.—Lloyd George.—Winston Churchill.—Robert Frost.—Dag Hammarskjold.— Stalin. [CT120.S6] 67-15212
1. Biography—20th cent. I. Title.

SULZBERGER, Cyrus Leo, 1912- 920
The existentialists. [1st ed.] New York, Harper [1962] 201 p. 22 cm. [CT120.S8] 62-9896
1. Biography—20th cent. I. Title.

SULZBERGER, Cyrus Leo, 1912- 920
The resistentialists. New York, Harper & Row [c.1962] 201p. 22cm. 62-9896 3.95 bds.,
1. Biography—20th cent. I. Title.

SULZBERGER, Cyrus Leo, 1912- 920
Unconquered souls; the resistentialists [by] C. L. Sulzberger. Woodstock, N.Y., Overlook Press [1973] 219 p. 24 cm. First ed. published in 1962 under title: The resistentialists. [CT120.S8 1973] 72-81087 ISBN 0-87951-004-8 7.95
1. Biography—20th century. I. Title.

TO most unforgettable 920.02
characters from Reader's digest. Pleasantville, N.Y., Reader's Digest Assn. [1967] 528p. illus. 20cm. [CT120.S4] 67-20606 5.95
1. Biography—20th cent. I. The Reader's Digest.

WEBB, Robert N 920.02
Leaders of our time; series 2, by Robert N. Webb. New York, F. Watts [1965] v, 152 p. ports. 25 cm. Contents.CONTENTS. -- Queen Elizabeth. -- Ludwig Erhard. -- Emperor Hirohito. -- Lyndon Baines Johnson. -- Martin Luther King. -- Robert Gordon Menzies. -- Pope Paul VI. -- Hyman G. Rickover. -- Sargent Shriver. -- Achmed Sukarno. -- Josip Broz Tito. -- Earl Warren. -- Harold Wilson. [CT120.W4] 65-6029
1. Biography — 20th cent. I. Title.

Biography—20th century—Addresses, essays, lectures.

MEHTA, Ved Parkash. 920.02
John is easy to please; encounters with the written and the spoken word [by] Ved Mehta. New York, Farrar, Straus & Giroux [1971] viii, 241 p. 22 cm. [CT120.M39 1971] 72-154862 ISBN 0-374-17986-7 7.50
1. Biography—20th century—Addresses, essays, lectures. I. Title. BIP

Biography—20th century—Juvenile literature.

DARLING, Edward. 920.073
When sparks fly upward. New York, I. Washburn [1970] v, 137 p. 21 cm. Contents.Contents.—Eleanor Roosevelt.—Pablo Picasso.—Richard Wright.—Adlai Stevenson.—Joseph Priestley.—Susan B. Anthony.—Malcolm X.—W. E. B. DuBois. [CT107.D37] 920 78-128533 3.95

1. Biography—20th century—Juvenile literature. I. Title.

FORTUNATO, Pat. 920'.009'04
When we were young : an album of stars / by Pat Fortunato. Englewood Cliffs, N.J. : Prentice-Hall, c1979. 64 p. : ill. ; 24 cm. Offers profiles of well-known performers in television, popular music, and films, highlighting their accomplishments as adults and their personalities and interests as children. [CT120.F67] 920 79-21544 ISBN 0-13-956482-9 : 8.95
1. Biography—20th century—Juvenile literature. 2. Entertainers—Biography—Juvenile literature. I. Title. **BIP**

KELEN, Emery, 1896- comp. 920.02
Fifty voices of the twentieth century. New York, Lothrop, Lee & Shepard [1970] 192 p. 22 cm. Bibliography: p. [187]-189. Capsule biographies of fifty world figures of the twentieth century accompany quotations from their speeches and writings. [CT120.K44] 920 76-101475 4.25
1. Biography—20th century—Juvenile literature. I. Title. **BIP**

WILLIAMS, Gurney, 910'.453 B
1941-
True escape and survival stories / by Gurney Williams III. New York : F. Watts, 1977. p. cm. Includes index. [CT120.W55] 77-1421 ISBN 0-531-00119-9 lib.bdg. : 5.90
1. Biography—20th century—Juvenile literature. 2. Heroes—Biography—Juvenile literature. 3. Adventure and adventurers—Biography—Juvenile literature. 4. Escapes—Juvenile literature. I. Title. **BIP**

Biologists.

BERGER, Melvin. 920
Famous men of modern biology. New York, Crowell [1968] 224 p. 21 cm. Biographical portraits of fourteen biologists who, in the past 100 years, have pursued research in disease, genetics, and the origin of life: Louis Pasteur, Robert Koch, Paul Ehrlich, Frederick Grant Banting, Alexander Fleming, Charles Darwin, Gregor Johann Mendel, Thomas Hunt Morgan, Hermann J. Muller, Wendell M. Stanley, Jonas E. Salk, Melvin Calvin, and Francis H. C. Crick and James Dewey Watson. [QH26.B4] AC 68
1. Biologists. I. Title.

MANN, Alfred Leonard, 925.74
1930-
Famous biologists, by A. L. Mann, A. C. Vivian. Illus. by Norma Ost. London, Museum P1. [dist. New Rochelle, N.Y., SportShelf, 1965, c.1963] 127p. illus., ports 23cm. (Brompton lib.) [QH26.M25] 64-32154 4.25 bds.,
1. Biologists. I. Vivian, Charles, 1917- joint author. II. Title.

THOMSON, John Arthur, 574'.0922
Sir 1861-1933
The great biologists. Freeport, N. Y, Books for Libraries Press [1967] viii, 176 p. 22 cm. (Essay index reprint series) Reprint of the 1932 ed. Bibliography: p. v. [QH26.T5 1967] 67-23273
1. Biologists. 2. Biology—Hist. I. Title. **BIP**

THOMSON, John Arthur, 574'.0922
Sir, 1861-1933.
The great biologists. Freeport, N.Y., Books for Libraries Press [1967] viii, 176 p. 22 cm. (Essay index reprint series) Reprint of the 1932 ed. Bibliography: p. v. [QH26.T5 1967] 67-23273
1. Biologists. 2. Biology—History. I. Title.

Biologists—Biography.

DISCOVERY process in 574'.092'2 B
modern biology : people and processes in biological discovery / edited by W. R. Klemm. Huntington, N.Y. : R. E. Krieger Pub. Co., 1977. xvi, 338 p., [7] leaves of plates : ill. ; 26 cm. Includes bibliographical references and index. [QH26.D5] 76-20732 ISBN 0-88275-442-4 : 12.50
1. Biologists—Biography. 2. Biology—History. 3. Creative ability in science. I. Klemm, William Robert, 1934-

Birch, Clarence Ellis,

BIRCH, Clarence 371.2'011'0924 B
Ellis, 1875-
Breasting the tape, by Clarence E. Birch. [1st ed. North Newton, Kan., Printed by the Mennonite Press, 1968] 171 p. illus., ports. 22 cm. [LA2317.B488A3] 70-75671
I. Title.

Birch, James Wheeler Woodford, 1826-1875.

BIRCH, James 959.5'1'0924 B
Wheeler Woodford, 1826-1875.
The journals of J. W. W. Birch, first British resident to Perak, 1874-1875 / edited and introduced by P. L. Burns Kuala Lumpur ; New York : Oxford University Press, 1976. xiv, 410 p., [6] leaves of plates (1 fold.) : ill. ; 26 cm. (Oxford in Asia historical reprints) Bibliography: p. [406]-410. [DS598.P4B57 1976] 76-372529 ISBN 0-19-580271-3 : 38.00
1. Birch, James Wheeler Woodford, 1826-1875. 2. Perak—History—Sources. 3. Perak—Biography.

Birch, John Morrison, 1918-1945.

WELCH, Robert Henry v. 12
Winborne, 1889-
The life of John Birch; in the story of one American boy, the ordeal of his age. Boston, Los Angeles, Western Islands [1965] vi, 127 p. 18 cm. (Americanist library) 67-69519
1. Birch, John Morrison, 1918-1945. 2. John Birch Society. I. Title.

Birch, John, 1616-1691.

ROE, secretary to Colonel v. 12
John Birch.
Military memoir of Colonel John Birch, sometime governor of Hereford in the civil war between Charles I. and the Parliament; written by Roe, his secretary; with an historical and critical commentary, notes, and appendix, by the late Rev. John Webb. Edited by his son the Rev. T. W. Webb. [Westminster] Printed for the Camden society, 1873 New York,Johnson Reprint Corp. [1965] xiv, 240, 11, p. 22 cm. (On cover: Royal Historical Society [London] Publications [Camden series, n.s.] v. 7) Members of the Camden society: 11 p. at end. 67-95356
1. Birch, John, 1616-1691. 2. Gt. Brit.—Hist.—Civil war, 1642-1649. I. Webb, John 1776-1869, ed. II. Webb, Thomas William, 1807-1885; ed. III. Title. IV. Series. V. Series: Camden Society, London. Publications, n.s., v. 7

Birds U.S.

MILLER, Love Holmes, 925.982
1874-
Lifelong boyhood; recollections of a naturalist afield. Berkeley, University of California Press, 1950. ix, 226 p. illus., port. 22 cm. Includes selections from the author's scientific writings. [QL.31.M57A3] 50-62871
1. Birds — U.S. I. Title.

Birds—Pictorial works.

POPE, William, 500.9'713'360924 B
1811-1902.
The 19th-century journals & paintings of William Pope / Harry B. Barrett; introd. and commentary by J. Fenwick Lansdowne Toronto : M. F. Feheley, c1976. 175 p. : col. ill. ; 32 cm. Includes index. [QL674.P83 1976] 77-360540 ISBN 0-919880-00-2 : 28.00
1. Birds—Pictorial works. 2. Natural history—Canada. 3. Canada—Description and travel. I. Barrett, Harry B. II. Lansdowne, James Fenwick. III. Title.

Birdwood, William Riddell Birdwood,

BIRDWOOD, William Riddell 923.542
Birdwood, baron, 1865-
Khaki and gown, an autobiography. With a foreword by Winston Churchill. New York, R. Speller, 1957. 456p. illus. 22cm. [DA69.3.B5A33 1957] 57-11883
I. Title.

Birge, Edward Asahel, 1851-1950.

SELLERY, George Clarke, 923.773
1872-
E. A. Birge, a memoir. With an appraisal of Birge the limnologist, An explorer of lakes, by C. H. Mortimer. Madison, University of Wisconsin Press, 1956. vii, 221p. illus., ports. 24cm. Includes bibliographical references. [QH31.B5S4] 56-9305
1. Birge, Edward Asahel, 1851-1950. I. Mortimer, Clifford Biley. An explorer of lakes. II. Title.

SELLERY, George Clarke, 923.773
1872-
E. A. Birge, a memoir. With an appraisal of Birge the limnologist. An explorer of lakes. by C. H. Mortimer. Madison, University of Wisconsin Press, 1956. vii. 221p. illus., ports. 24cm. Includes bibliographical references. [QH31.B5S4] 56-9305
1. Birge, Edward Asahel, 1851-1950. I. Mortimer, Clifford Hiley. An explorer of lakes. II. Title.

Birgitta, Saint, of Sweden, d. 1373.

BUTKOVICH, Anthony, 271'.979 B
1921-
Anima eroica; St. Brigitte of Sweden. [Los Angeles?] Ecumenical Foundation of America, 1968. vii, 87 p. illus., ports. 27 cm. Sequel: Iconography: St. Birgitta of Sweden. Bibliography: p. 87. [BX4700.B6B8] 68-26139
1. Birgitta, Saint, of Sweden, d. 1373. I. Title.

BUTKOVICH, Anthony, 271'.979 B
1921-
Iconography: St. Birgitta of Sweden. [Los Angeles?] Ecumenical Foundation of America, 1969. viii, 102 p. illus., ports. (part col.) 27 cm. Sequel to Anima eroica. Sequel: The revelations. Bibliography: p. 101-102. [BX4700.B6B83] 72-107679
1. Birgitta, Saint, of Sweden, d. 1373. I. Title.

BUTKOVICH, Anthony, 271'.979 B
1921-
Revelations; Saint Birgitta of Sweden. Los Angeles, Ecumenical Foundation of America, 1972. xvi, 110 p. illus. 28 cm. Bibliography: p. 108-110. [BX4700.B6B85] 74-187358
1. Birgitta, Saint, of Sweden, d. 1373. I. Title.

JORGENSEN, Johannes, 922.2485
1866-
Saint Bridget of Sweden. Translated from the Danish by Ingeborg Lund. London, New York, Longmans, Green [1954] 2v. port. 23cm. Contents.v.1. 1303-1349.--v. 2. 1349-1373. Includes bibliographical references. [BX4700.B6J63] 54-14411
1. Birgitta, Saint, of Sweden, d. 1373. I. Title.

Birgitta, Saint, of Sweden, d. 1373—Juvenile literature.

ROBERTO, Brother, 1927- 922.2485
The face in the flames; a story of Saint Bridget of Sweden. Illus. by Carolyn Lee Jagodits. Notre Dame, Ind., Dujarie Press [1959] 94p. illus. 24cm. [BX4700.B6R6] 59-65511
1. Birgitta, Saint, of Sweden, d. 1373—Juvenile literature. I. Title.

Birkenhead, Frederick Edwin Smith, 1st earl of, 1872-1930.

BULMER-THOMAS, Ivor, 923.242
1905-
Our Lord Birkenhead, an Oxford appreciation, by Ivor Thomas. London, New York, Putnam [1930] xiv, 207p. 20cm. [DA566.9.B5B8] 31-12766
1. Birkenhead, Frederick Edwin Smith, 1st earl of, 1872-1930. I. Title.

Birkenhead, John, Sir, 1616-1679.

THOMAS, Peter 942.06'0924 B
William.
Sir John Berkenhead, 1617-1679: a Royalist career in politics and polemics [by] P. W. Thomas. Oxford, Clarendon P., 1969. xvi, 298 p. 23 cm. Revision of the author's thesis, Oxford. Bibliography: p. [267]-279. [DA378.B5T5 1969] 79-438434 55/-
1. Birkenhead, John, Sir, 1616-1679. **BIP**

Birkett, Norman Birkett, baron, 1883-1962.

HYDE, Harford Montgomery, 923.442
1907-
Lord Justice; the life and times of Lord Birkett of Ulverston. New York, Random [1965, c.1964] xii, 638p. map, ports. 22cm. Bibl. 65-15740 7.95
1. Birkett, Norman Birkett, baron, 1883-1962. I. Title.

Birmingham, Ala.—History.

PIONEERS Club, 917.61'781'036
Birmingham, Ala.
Early days in Birmingham; a printing of the original papers of the Pioneers Club whose members were eye-witnesses to the events of the founding of the city. Birmingham [Southern University Press] 1968. xiii, 102 p. 23 cm. [F334.B6P5 1968] 68-57709
1. Birmingham, Ala.—History. 2. Birmingham, Ala.—Biography. I. Title.

Birnbaum, Leon,

BIRNBAUM, 338.7'67'76530924 B
Leon, 1888-
Legacy in lace. [New York, Fairchild Publications, 1968] 92 p. illus., ports. 22 cm. Autobiographical. [HD9933.U65B5] 68-16260
I. Title.

Birrer, Cynthia.

BIRRER, Cynthia. 362.1'9'6834
Multiple sclerosis, a personal view / by Cynthia Birrer ; with a foreword by Lawrence D. Dickey ; illustrated by William Birrer. Springfield, Ill. : Thomas, c1979. xxii, 276 p. : ill. ; 24 cm. Includes indexes. Bibliography: p. 261-268. [RC377.B57] 78-11340 ISBN 0-398-03864-3 : 13.75 ISBN 0-398-03886-4 pbk. : 9.75
1. Birrer, Cynthia. 2. Multiple sclerosis—Biography. 3. Multiple sclerosis. I. Title.

Birth control—U.S.

SANGER, Margaret, 613.94'3'0924
1879-1966.
My fight for birth control. New York, Maxwell Reprint Co. [1969, c1931] vii, 360 p. illus., facsim., ports. 24 cm. [HQ766.5.U5S2 1969] 70-98265
1. Birth control—U.S. I. Title.

Bisbee family.

BISBEE, M. J. 929'.2'0973
Two brothers in the Pennsylvania Triangle : a biographical encyclopedia of the descendants of Reuben Bisbee, born 1776, Massachusetts / M. J. Bisbee. Erie, Pa. : Bisbee, 1974. iii, 62 leaves ; 28 cm. "Cousin chart": [2] p. inserted. Number 33 of 100 copies printed. Includes bibliographical references and indexes. [CS71.B63 1974] 75-301331
1. Bisbee family. I. Title.

Bishop, Charles Reed, 1822-1915.

KENT, Harold Winfield. 923.3969
Charles Reed Bishop, man of Hawaii. Palo Alto, Calif., Pacific Books, 1965. xvi, 365 p. illus., ports. 24 cm. [DU627.17.B45K4] 64-23487
1. Bishop, Charles Reed, 1822-1915.

Bishop family.

BALIAN, Esther M. 929'.2'0973
Captain Daniel Bishop, Jr., a brief genealogy / compiled by Esther M. Balian. Baltimore : Gateway Press, 1974. 45 p. : ill. ; 22 cm. Includes bibliographical references and index. [CS71.B6317 1974] 74-21675
1. Bishop family. I. Title.

Bishop, Isabel, 1902-

BISHOP, Isabel, 1902- 759.13 B
Isabel Bishop [by] Karl Lunde. New York, Abrams [1975] 181 p. illus. (part col.) 28 x 30 cm. Bibliography: p. 176-179. [ND237.B594L86] 73-17122 ISBN 0-8109-0150-1 37.50
1. Bishop, Isabel, 1902- I. Lunde, Karl.

Bishop, Isabella Lucy (Bird) 1831-1904.

BARR, Pat, 1934- 910'.924 B
A curious life for a lady; the story of Isabella Bird, a remarkable Victorian traveller. [1st ed. in the U.S.A.] Garden City, N.Y., Doubleday, 1970. 347 p. illus., maps, ports. 22 cm. Bibliography: p. 341-344. [G246.B5B3 1970] 79-103731 7.95
1. Bishop, Isabella Lucy (Bird) 1831-1904. I. Title.

Bishop, Joseph, b. 1770.

GRAY, John W. 917.68'03'30924 B
The life of Joseph Bishop, the celebrated old pioneer in the first settlements of middle Tennessee, embracing his wonderful adventures and narrow escapes with the Indians, his animating and remarkable hunting excursions. Interspersed with racy anecdotes of those early times. Spartanburg, S.C., Reprint Co., 1974 [c1858] 236 p. port. 22 cm. Reprint of the 1962 private ed. published by J. R. Fleming. [F442.2.B62 1974] 74-582 ISBN 0-87152-157-1
1. Bishop, Joseph, b. 1770. 2. Frontier and pioneer life—Tennessee. I. Title.

GRAY, John W. 917.68'03'30924 B
The life of Joseph Bishop, the celebrated old pioneer in the first settlements of middle Tennessee, embracing his wonderful adventures and narrow escapes with the Indians, his animating and remarkable hunting excursions. Interspersed with racy anecdotes of those early times. Spartanburg, S.C., Reprint Co., 1974 [c1858] 236 p. port. 22 cm. Reprint of the 1962 private ed. published by J. R. Fleming. [F442.2.B62 1974] 74-582 ISBN 0-87152-157-1 12.00
1. Bishop, Joseph, b. 1770. 2. Frontier and pioneer life—Tennessee. I. Title.

Bishop, William Avery, 1894-1956.

BISHIP, William Arthur 940.440924
The courage of the early morning: a frank biography of Billy Bishop, the great ace of World War I. [1st Amer. ed.] New York, McKay [1966,c.1965] 211p. illus., ports. 22cm. [TL540.B552B5] 66-13501 4.95
1. Bishop, William Avery, 1894-1956. I. Title.

BISHOP, William 940.440924 (B)
Arthur.
The courage of the early morning; a frank biography of Billy Bishop, the great ace of World War I. [1st American ed.] New York, D. McKay Co. [1966, c1965] 211 p. illus., ports. 22 cm. [TL540.B552B5] 66-13501
1. Bishop, William Avery, 1894-1956. I. Title.

Bishop, William Howard, 1886-1953.

SANTEN, Herman W. 922.273
Father Bishop, founder of the Glenmary Home Missioners. Milwaukee, Bruce [c.1961] 119p. illus. (Catholic life pubns.) 62-604 3.00
1. Bishop, William Howard, 1886-1953. I. Title.

SANTEN, Herman W 922.244
Father Bishop, founder of the Glenmary Home Missioners. Milwaukee, Bruce Press [c1961] 119p. illus. 22cm. (Catholic life publications) [BX4705.B523S3] 62-604
1. Bishop William Howard, 1886-1953. I. Title.

Bishops—England.

ROSENTHAL, Joel 262'.12'0942
Thomas, 1934-
The training of an elite group: English bishops in the fifteenth century. Philadelphia, American Philosophical Society, 1970. 54 p. 30 cm. (Transactions of the American Philosophical Society, new ser. v. 60, pt. 5) Includes bibliographical references. [BX4666.R65 1970] 78-131553 10.00
1. Bishops—England. I. Title. II. Series: American Philosophical Society, Philadelphia. Transactions, new ser. v. 60, pt. 5

Bismarck, Otto, Furst von, 1815-1898.

APSLER, Alfred. 943.08'0924 B
Iron chancellor: Otto von Bismarck. New York, J. Messner [1968] 189 p. maps. 22 cm. Bibliography: p. [183]-184. [DD218.2.A7] 68-25094 3.50
1. Bismarck, Otto, Furst von, 1815-1898. I. Title.

BISMARCK, Otto, 943'.08'0924 B
Furst von, 1815-1898.
Reflections and reminiscences. Edited with an introd. by Theodore S. Hamerow. New York, Harper & Row [1968] 274 p. 21 cm. (Harper torchbooks, TB 1357) (European perspectives.) Compiled from translations of the author's Gedanken und Erinnerungen. [DD218.A2 1968] 68-25436
1. Germany—History—1789-1900. 2. Germany—Politics and government—1789-1900. 3. Prussia—Politics and government—1815-1870. 4. Europe—Politics and government—1789-1900. I. Title.

BUSCH, Moritz, 943.08'2'0924 B
1821-1899.
Bismarck in the Franco-German War, 1870-1871. New York, H. Fertig, 1973. 2 v. 22 cm. Translation of Graf Bismarck und seine Leute wahrend des Krieges mit Frankreich. Reprint of the 1879 ed. [DC285.B97 1973] 77-80612 25.00 (2. vols.)
1. Bismarck, Otto, Furst von, 1815-1898. 2. Busch, Moritz, 1821-1899. 3. Franco-German War, 1870-1871—Personal narratives. I. Title.

BUSCH, Moritz, 1821- 943.08'0924
1899.
Bismarck; some secret pages of his history, being a diary kept by Moritz Busch during twenty-five years' official and private intercourse with the great chancellor. New York, Macmillan, 1898. St. Clair Shores, Mich., Scholarly Press [1971] 2 v. illus. 21 cm. [DD218.B98 1971] 70-144925 ISBN 0-403-00815-8
1. Bismarck, Otto, Furst von, 1815-1898.

BUSCH, Moritz, 943.08'0924 B
1821-1899.
Bismarck; some secret pages of his history; being a diary kept by Dr. Moritz Busch during twenty-five years' official and private intercourse with the great Chancellor. New York, AMS Press [1970] 2 v. illus., ports. 23 cm. "Reprinted from the edition of 1898, New York." [DD218.B936 1970] 76-112347 ISBN 0-404-01242-6
1. Bismarck, Otto, Furst von, 1815-1898. BIP

BUSCH, Moritz, 943.08'0924 B
1821-1899.
Our chancellor (Bismarck); sketches for a historical picture. Translated from the German by William Beatty-Kingston. Freeport, N.Y., Books for Libraries Press [1970] 2 v. port. 23 cm. Translation of Unser Reichskanzler. [DD218.B9613 1970] 76-109615 ISBN 0-8369-5225-1
1. Bismarck, Otto Furst von, 1815-1898. 2. Prussia—Politics and government—1815-1870. 3. Europe—Politics and government—1789-1900. 4. Germany—History—1789-1900. I. Title.

EYCK, Erich, 1878- 923.243
Bismarck and the German Empire. New York, Norton [1964, c.1958] 327p. 20cm. (N2235) Summary of the 3v. Bismarck, pub. in German. 1.65 pap.,
1. Bismarck, Otto, Furst von, 1815-1898. I. Title. BIP

FLEISCHHAUER, 943.08'092'4
Eckhart.
Bismarcks Russlandpolitik im Jahrzehnt vor der Reichsgrundung und ihre Darstellung in der sowjetischen Historiographie / von Eckart Fleischhauer. Koln ; Wien : Bohlau [in Komm.], 1976. viii, 215 p. ; 21 cm. (Dissertationen zur neueren Geschichte ; 1) Bibliography: p. 199-208. [DD218.2.F53] 77-459484
1. Bismarck, Otto, Furst von, 1815-1898. 2. German Confederation, 1815-1866. 3. Statesmen—Germany—Biography. 4. Prussia—Foreign relations—Russia. 5. Russia—Foreign relations—Prussia. 6. Russia—Historiography. I. Title: Bismarcks Russlandpolitik im Jahrzehnt vor der Reichsgrudung ...

HAAS, Werner, 1928- 438'.2'421
Bismarck. New York, Scribner [1973] ix, 166 p. illus. 23 cm. (The Scribner German series) German text with exercises in English. [PF3127.H5H32] 72-743 3.95 (pbk.)
1. Bismarck, Otto, Furst von, 1815-1898. 2. German language—Readers (History)

HAMEROW, Theodore S., ed. 923.243
Otto von Bismarck, a historical assessment. Boston, Heath [1962] 102 p. 24 cm. (Problems in European civilization) [DD218.H2] 62-19749
1. Bismarck, Otto, Furst von, 1815-1898. BIP

HAMEROW, Theodore 943.08'092'4
S., ed.
Otto von Bismarck. a historical assessment. Edited and with an introd. by Theodore S. Hamerow. 2d ed. Lexington, Mass., Heath [1972] xxii, 169 p. port. 21 cm. (Problems in European civilization) Bibliography: p. 164-169. [DD218.H2 1972] 72-1849 Pap. $2.25
1. Bismarck, Otto, Furst von, 1815-1898. I. Title. II. Series.

HOLLYDAY, Frederic B. 943.08'0924
M., comp.
Bismarck. Edited by Frederic B. M. Hollyday. Englewood Cliffs, N.J., Prentice-Hall [1970] vii, 180 p. 21 cm. (Great lives observed) (A Spectrum book.) Writings by and about Bismarck. Includes bibliographical references. [DD218.H73] 77-126816 5.95
1. Bismarck, Otto, Furst von, 1815-1898.

KENT, George O., 943.08'092'4 B
1919-
Bismarck and his times / George O. Kent. Carbondale : Southern Illinois University Press, c1978. p. cm. Includes index. Bibliography: p. [DD218.K36] 78-2547 ISBN 0-8093-0858-4 : 12.50. ISBN 0-8093-0859-2 pbk. : 4.95
1. Bismarck, Otto, Furst von, 1815-1898. 2. Statesmen—Germany—Biography. 3. Germany—Politics and government—19th century. I. Title. BIP

MORROW, Ian Fitzherbert v. 12
Despard, 1896-
Bismarck. New York, Collier Books [1966, c1962] 125 p. 18 cm. 67-1395
1. Bismarck, Otto, Furst von, 1815-1898. I. Title. BIP

MORROW, Ian Fitzherbert 923.243
Despard, 1896-
Bismarck [by] Ian F. D. Morrow. New York, Collier [1962] 125p. 18cm. (AS60Y) .95 pap.,
1. Bismarck, Otto, Furst von, 1815-1898. I. Title.

PALMER, Alan 943.08'092'4 B
Warwick.
Bismarck / Alan Palmer. New York : Scribner, c1976. x, 326 p., [4] leaves of plates : ill. ; 25 cm. Includes index. Bibliography: p. [301]-307. [DD218.P26 1976b] 76-6021 ISBN 0-684-14683-5 : 12.50
1. Bismarck, Otto, Furst von, 1815-1898. 2. Germany—Politics and government—1871-1918. 3. Statesmen—Germany—Biography.

RICHTER, Werner, 1888- 923.243
Bismarck. Translated from the German by Brian Battershaw. Foreword by F. H. Hinsley. [1st American ed.] New York, Putnam [1965, c1964] 420 p. illus., ports. 22 cm. Bibliography: p. 413-414. [DD218.R513 1965] 64-23090
1. Bismarck, Otto, Furst von, 1815-1898. I. Title.

ROBERTSON, Charles 943.08'0924 B
Grant, Sir, 1869-1948.
Bismarck. New York, H. Fertig, 1969. xii, 520 p. 23 cm. Includes bibliographical references. [DD218.R6 1969] 68-9604
1. Bismarck, Otto, Furst von, 1815-1898. I. Title. BIP

SEMPELL, 943.08'092'4 B
Charlotte.
Otto von Bismarck. New York, Twayne Publishers [1972] 208 p. map. 21 cm. (Twayne's rulers and statesmen of the world series, 16) Bibliography: p. 197-200. [DD218.S45] 78-187620
1. Bismarck, Otto, Furst von, 1815-1898.

SNYDER, Louis Leo, 943.08'0924
1907-
The blood and iron chancellor; a documentary-biography of Otto von Bismarck, by Louis L. Snyder. Princeton, N. J., Van Nostrand [1967] xxii, 423 p. illus. 27 cm. Bibliographical footnotes. [DD218.S675] 67-18058
1. Bismarck, Otto, Furst von, 1815-1898. I. Title.

STERN, Fritz 943.08'092'4 B
Richard, 1926-
Gold and iron : Bismarck, Bleichroder, and the building of the German empire / Fritz Stern. 1st ed. New York : Knopf, 1977. xxiv, 620 p., [8] leaves of plates : ill. ; 25 cm. Includes index. Bibliography: p. [601]-602. [DD218.2.S85 1977] 76-26128 ISBN 0-394-49545-4 : 17.95
1. Bismarck, Otto, Furst von, 1815-1898. 2. Bleichroder, Gerson von, 1822-1893. 3. Statesmen—Germany—Biography. 4. Bankers—Germany—Biography. I. Title.

STERN, Fritz 943.08'092'2 B
Richard, 1926-
Gold and iron : Bismarck, Bleichroder, and the building of the German Empire / Fritz Stern. New York : Vintage Books, [1979] p. cm. Reprint of the 1977 ed. published by Knopf, New York. Includes index. Bibliography: p. [DD218.2.S85 1979] 79-11462 ISBN 0-394-74034-3 pbk. : 8.95
1. Bismarck, Otto, Furst von, 1815-1898. 2. Bleichroder, Gerson von, 1822-1893. 3. Statesmen—Germany—Biography. 4. Bankers—Germany—Biography. I. Title. BIP

TAYLOR, Alan John 923.243
Percivale, 1906-
Bismarck, the man and the statesman. New York, Random [1967, c.1955] 286p. 19cm. (Vantage bk., V-387) Bibl. [DD218.T33 1955a] 1.95 pap., 1.95 pap.,
1. Bismark, Otto, Furst von, 1815-1898. I. Title. BIP

TAYLOR, Alan John 923.243
Percivale, 1906-
Bismarck, the man and the statesman. [1st American ed.] New York, Knopf, 1955. 286 p. illus. 22 cm. Includes bibliographies. [DD218.T33 1955a] 55-10649
1. Bismarck, Otto, Furst von, 1815-1898.

TAYLOR, Alan John v. 12
Percivale, 1906-
Bismarck; the man and the statesman. New York, A.A. Knopf [c1955, 1967] 286 p. illus. 22 cm. 68-68883
1. Bismarck, Otto Furst von, 1815-1898. I. Title.

WALLER, Bruce. 327.43
Bismarck at the crossroads : the reorientation of German foreign policy after the Congress of Berlin, 1878-1880 / Bruce Waller. London : Athlone Press, 1974. viii, 273 p. ; 23 cm. (University of London historical studies ; 35) Distributed by Tiptree Book Services, Tiptree, Eng. and Humanities Press, New York. Includes index. Bibliography: p. [257]-263. [DD221.5.W26 1974] 74-196330 18.00
1. Bismarck, Otto, Furst von, 1815-1898. 2. Berlin. Congress, 1878. 3. Germany—Foreign relations—1871-1888. I. Title. II. Series: London. University. Historical studies ; 35. BIP

Bisno, Abraham,

BISNO, 331.881'1'6870924 B
Abraham, 1866-1929.
Abraham Bisno, union pioneer; an autobiographical account of Bisno's early life and the beginnings of unionism in the women's garment industry. With a foreword by Joel Seidman. Madison, University of Wisconsin Press, 1967. 244 p. port. 22 cm. [HD6515.C6B5] 67-20752
I. Title.

Bison, American.

JONES, Charles 917.8'03'20924 B
Jesse, 1844-1919.
Buffalo Jones' adventures on the Plains, compiled by Henry Inman. Lincoln, University of Nebraska Press [1970] ix, 273 p. illus., port. 21 cm. "A Bison book." "The text ... originally comprised part one of Buffalo Jones' forty years of adventure. It is reproduced from the edition published in 1899." [Sk297.J652] 77-100813 1.95
1. Bison, American. 2. Hunting—The West. I. Inman, Henry, 1837-1899, ed. II. Title.

Bispham, David Scull, 1857-1921.

BISPHAM, David 782.1'092'4 B
Scull, 1857-1921.
A Quaker singer's recollections / David Bispham. New York : Arno Press, 1977, [c1920] ix, 401 p. ; 21 cm. (Opera biographies) Reprint of the 1921 ed. published by Macmillan, New York. Includes index. [ML420.B59A3 1977] 76-29927 ISBN 0-405-09669-0 : 21.00
1. Bispham, David Scull, 1857-1921. 2. Singers—United States—Biography. I. Title. BIP

Bissell, Richard Pike.

BISSELL, Richard 917.7'03'30924 B
Pike.
My life on the Mississippi; or, Why I am not Mark Twain, by Richard Bissell. [1st ed.] Boston, Little, Brown [1973] xvi, 240 p. illus. 22 cm. Bibliography: p. [236]-239. [F354.B63] 73-14537 ISBN 0-316-09674-1 7.95
1. Bissell, Richard Pike. 2. Clemens, Samuel Langhorne, 1835-1910. 3. Mississippi River. I. Title.

Bissier, Julius, 1893-1965.

MESSER, Thomas M. 760'.0924
Julius Bissier, 1893-1965; a retrospective exhibition. [New York, Printed by Sterlip Press, 1968] 62 p. illus. (part col.) 26 cm. Participating institutions: San Francisco Museum of Art and the Solomon R. Guggenheim Museum, New York, and others. Bibliography: p. 60-61. [ND588.B53M4] 68-57008
1. Bissier, Julius, 1893-1965. I. San Francisco. Museum of Art. II. Solomon R. Guggenheim Museum, New York.

SCHMALENBACH, Werner, 1917- 759.3
Bissier. New York, Abrams [1964, c.1963] 73p. illus. (pt. col.) 21x23cm. Bibl. 64-17628 5.95
1. Bissier, Julius, 1893- I. Title.

Bissonnette, Georges.

BISSONNETTE, Georges. 282'.092'4
Moscow was my parish / Georges Bissonnette. Westport, Conn. : Greenwood Press, 1978, c1956. p. cm. Reprint of the ed. published by McGraw-Hill, New York. [BX4705.B5235A34 1978] 78-16489 ISBN 0-313-20594-9 lib.bdg. : 19.50
1. Bissonnette, Georges. 2. Catholic Church—Clergy—Biography. 3. Catholic Church in Russia. 4. Clergy—United States—Biography. I. Title. BIP

Bitzer, G. W., 1872-1944.

BITZER, G. W., 778.5'3'0924 B
1872-1944.
Billy Bitzer; his story. [New York] Farrar, Straus and Giroux [1973] xvii, 266 p. illus. 24 cm. Autobiography. [TR849.B57A3 1973] 72-86780 ISBN 0-374-11294-0 10.00
1. Bitzer, G. W., 1872-1944. I. Title. BIP

Bizet, Georges, 1838-1875.

COOPER, Martin, 1910- 780'.942 B
Georges Bizet. Westport, Conn., Greenwood Press [1971] 136 p. music. 23 cm. Reprint of the 1938 ed. Bibliography: p. 136. [ML410.B62C77 1971] 71-138216 ISBN 0-8371-5571-1
1. Bizet, Georges, 1838-1875. BIP

CURTISS, Mina Stein 780'.92'4 B
Kirstein, 1896-
Bizet and his world / by Mina Curtiss. Westport, Conn. : Greenwood Press, 1977, c1958. xvi, 477, xvii p., [12] leaves of plates : ill. ; 24 cm. Reprint of the ed. published by Knopf, New York. Includes index. Bibliography: p. 475-477. [ML410.B62C87 1977] 76-55412 ISBN 0-8371-9427-X lib. bdg. : 29.50
1. Bizet, Georges, 1838-1875. 2. Composers—France—Biography. I. Title.

CURTISS, Mina Stein 927.8
(Kirstein) 1896-
Bizet and his world. [1st ed.] New York, Knopf, 1958. xvi, 477 p. illus., ports., facsims. 25 cm. Appendices (p. 457-477): 1. Unpublished letters. 2. Works of Georges Bizet chronologically listed with dates of composition and publication.—3. Posthumous presentations of Bizet's dramatic works.—4. Bizet's music library.—5. Selected list of reading on the life and works of George Bizet. "Bibliographical notes": p. 443-455. [ML410.B62C87] 58-10973
1. Bizet, Georges, 1838-1875. 2. Music—France—Paris. I. Title. BIP

CURTISS, Mina Stein 780'.924 [B]
(Kirstein) 1896-
Bizet and his world. New York, Vienna House [1974, c1958] xvi, 477, xvii p. illus., ports., facsims. 21 cm. Appendices (p. 457-477): 1. Unpublished letters.—2. Works of Georges Bizet chronologically listed with dates of composition and publication.—3. Posthumous presentation of Bizet's dramatic works.—4. Bizet's music library.—5. Selected list of reading on the life and works of Georges Bizet. Bibliographical notes: p. 443-455. [ML410.B62C87] ISBN 0-8443-0085-3 5.95 (pbk.)
1. Bizet, Georges, 1838-1875. 2. Music—France—Paris. I. Title.
L.C. card no. for the hardbound edition: 58-10973.

DEAN, Winton 927.8
Bizet. New York, Collier [1962] 287p. 18cm. (Great composers ser., BS116S) Bibl. 1.50 pap.,
1. Bizet, George, 1838-1875. I. Title.

DEAN, Winton. v. 12
Bizet. New York, Collier Books [1962] 287 p. music. 19 cm. (The great composers series) 65-80295
1. Bizet, Georges, 1838-1875. I. Title. BIP

DEAN, Winton. 780'.92'4 B
Bizet / by Winton Dean. Westport, Conn. : Hyperion Press, 1979. p. cm. (Encore music editions) (Reprint of the 1948 ed. published by Dent, London, in series: The Master musicians. New series.) Includes index. [ML410.B62D35 1979] 78-66893 ISBN 0-88355-735-5 : 23.50
1. Bizet, Georges, 1838-1875. 2. Composers—France—Biography. I. Series: The Master musicians. New series.

DEAN, Winton 780.92
Georges Bizet, his life and work London, J. M. Dent [1965] xiv, 304p. illus., facsims., music, ports 22cm. Bibl. [ML410.B62.D355] 65-6938 8.95
1. Bizet, Georges, 1838-1875. I. Title.
Now available from Dufour, Chester Springs, Pa.

PARKER, Douglas Charles, 780'.924
1885-
Georges Bizet; his life and works. Freeport, N.Y., Books for Libraries Press [1969] 278 p. port. 23 cm. (Select bibliographies reprint series) "First published 1926." Bibliography: p. 272-273. [ML410.B62P16 1969] 73-94280
1. Bizet, Georges, 1838-1875. I. Title.

Bjelke-Petersen, Johannes, 1911-

LUNN, Hugh Duncan. 329'.0092'4 B
Joh : the life and political adventures of Johannes Bjelke-Petersen / [by] Hugh Lunn. St. Lucia, Q. : University of Queensland Press, 1978. xvi, 280 p. : ill. ; 23 cm. Distributed by Prentice-Hall International, International Book Distributors, Hemel Hempstead, Eng. Includes index. [DU272.B53L86] 78-321829 ISBN 0-7022-1216-4 : 12.00
1. Bjelke-Petersen, Johannes, 1911- 2. Queensland—Politics and government. 3. Prime ministers—Australia—Queensland—Biography. I. Title.
Available from Technical Impex, Lawrence, MA

Blachly, Mary Adelle Bradley, 1854-1926.

BRADLEY, Ruth, 978.8'03'0924 B
1902-
Dellie; a lotus in the dust. Berkeley, Calif., Ber-Cal Pub. Co. [1967] 192 p. illus., ports. 24 cm. [CT275.B5778B7] 67-24553
1. Blachly, Mary Adelle Bradley, 1854-1926. I. Title.

Black, Davidson, 1884-1934.

HOOD, Dora, 1885- 926.1
Davidson Black, a biography [Toronto] Univ. of Toronto Pr. [c.1964] x, 145p. illus., ports. 24cm. (Distinguished Canadian biogs.) Bibl. 64-3595 5.00
1. Black, Davidson, 1884-1934. I. Title.

Black, Ebenezer Charlton, 1861-1927.

GODDETTE, Marion G, 1893- 923.742
The pen picture of a great teacher. Boston, House of Edinboro [1950] 160 p. illus., ports. 21 cm. [PR55.B5G6] 51-2102
1. Black, Ebenezer Charlton, 1861-1927. I. Title.

Black Elk, Oglala Indian, 1863-1950.

BLACK Elk, Oglala 970'.004'97 B
Indian, 1863-1950
Black Elk speaks : being the life story of a holy man of the Oglala Sioux / as told through John G. Neihardt (Flaming Rainbow) ; introd. by Vine Deloria, Jr. ; illustrated with drawings by Standing Bear and a portfolio of photos. Lincoln : University of Nebraska Press, c1979. xix, 299 p., [6] leaves of plates : ill. ; 23 cm. [E99.O3B49 1979] 79-12367 ISBN 0-8032-3301-9 : 15.00
1. Black Elk, Oglala Indian, 1863-1950. 2. Oglala Indians. 3. Oglala Indians—Biography. 4. Teton Indians. I. Neihardt, John Gneisenau, 1881-1973. II. Title.

Black Hawk, Sauk chief, 1767-1838.

BECKHARD, Arthur J. 970.3 B
Black Hawk. New York, J. Messner [1957] 192 p. 22 cm. Includes bibliography. A biography of Black Hawk, the Sauk Indian who became chief of his tribe in 1788 and whose refusal to yield his tribal lands to the white man resulted in the Black Hawk War. [PZ7.B38172Bl] 92 AC 68
1. Black Hawk, Sauk chief, 1767-1838. I. Title.

BLACK Hawk, Sauk chief, 970.3 B
1767-1838.
Life of Ma-ka-tai-me-she-kia-kiak, or, Black Hawk, dictated by himself, and edited by J. B. Patterson. Fairfield, Wash., Ye Galleon Press, 1974 [c1833] 155 p. illus. 20 cm. Reprint of the ed. published by Russell, Odiorne & Metcalf, Boston. "No. P-120 in Wright Howes' U.S.-iana." "Four hundred copies ... printed ... copy no. 28." [E83.83.B6A34 1974] 74-14929 ISBN 0-87770-139-3
1. Black Hawk, Sauk chief, 1767-1838. 2. Black Hawk war, 1832. I. Patterson, John Barton, 1805-1890, ed.

LAWSON, Marion. 970.3 B
Proud warrior; the story of Black Hawk. Illustrated by W. T. Mars. [1st ed.] New York, Hawthorn Books [1968] 175 p. illus. 22 cm. A biography of the Sauk Indian chief who watched the spirit of his people broken as they lost their fight against the white man's encroachment of the Indians' land. [E83.83.B637] 92 AC 68
1. Black Hawk, Sauk chief, 1767-1838. I. Mars, Witold T., illus. II. Title.

Black Hawk, Sauk chief, 1767-1838—Juvenile literature.

ANDERSON, LaVere. 970.3 B
Black Hawk, Indian patriot. Illustrated by Cary. Champaign, Ill., Garrard Pub. Co. [1972] 80 p. col. illus. 24 cm. A biography of the Sauk chief who fought to protect his country, town, cornfields, and people from the invading white man. [E83.83.A52] 92 72-730 ISBN 0-8116-6610-7
1. Black Hawk, Sauk chief, 1767-1838—Juvenile literature. I. Cary, Louis F., 1915- illus. II. Title.
PLB 2.95.

CUNNINGHAM, Maggi, 970'.004'97 B
1916-
Black Hawk / by Maggi Cunningham. Minneapolis : Dillon Press, c1979. 62 p. : ill. ; 24 cm. (The Story of an American Indian) A biography of the last great war leader of the Sauk whose unsuccessful attempts to keep their homelands ended Indian land holdings in the Illinois region. [E83.83.C86] 92 78-26255 ISBN 0-87518-172-4 : 5.95
1. Black Hawk, Sauk chief, 1767-1838—Juvenile literature. 2. Sauk Indians—Biography—Juvenile literature. I. Title. BIP

LAWSON, Marion. 92 (J)
Proud warrior; the story of Black Hawk. Illustrated by W. T. Mars. [1st ed.] New York, Hawthorn Books [1968] 175 p. illus. 22 cm. [E83.83.B637] 68-27642 3.95
1. Black Hawk, Sauk chief, 1767-1838—Juvenile literature. I. Title.

Black Hawk War, 1832.

BLACK Hawk, Sauk chief, 970.2
1767-1838.
Black Hawk (Ma-ka-tai-me-she-kia-kiak) An autobiography. Edited by Donald Jackson Urbana, University of Illinois Press, 1955. 206 p. illus., ports., maps, facsims. 21 cm. First published in 1833 under title: Life of Ma-ka-tai-me-she-kia-kiak. Bibliography: p. [193]-196. [E83.83.B635] 55-11217
1. Black Hawk War, 1832.

BLACK HAWK, Sauk chief, 970.2
1767-1838
Black Hawk, an autobiography. Ed. by Donald Jackson. Urbana, Univ. of Ill. Pr., 1964 [c.1955] 177p. Illus., ports., maps, facsims. 21cm. First pub. in 1833 under title: Life of Ma-ka-tai-me-she-kia-kiak. (Illini bks. 1B-19) 1.75 pap.,
1. Black Hawk War, 1832. I. Title.

BLACK HAWK, Sauk chief 970.2
1767-1838
Black Hawk; an autobiography. Ed. [by] Donald Jackson [Gloucester, Mass., P. Smith, 1965, c.1955] 177p. 21cm. First pub. in 1833 under title: Life of Ma-ka-tai-me-she-kia-kiak. (Univ. of Ill. Pr. bk. rebound) Bibl. [E83.83B635] 3.75
1. Black Hawk War, 1832. I. Title.

BLACK HAWK, Sauk chief, 970.2
1767-1838.
Black Hawk (Ma-ka-tai-me-she-kia-kiak) An autobiography. Edited by Donald Jackson. Urbana, University of Illinois Press, 1955. 206p. illus. ports., maps, facsims. 21cm. First published in 1833 under title: Life of Ma-ka-tai-me-she-kia-kiak. Bibliography: p. [193]-196. [E83.83.B635] 55-11217
1. Black Hawk War, 1832. I. Title.

Black Hills, S.D. and Wyoming.

ESLING, Dean Arthur, 1908- 917.83'91
My Black Hills story. Rapid City, S.D., Fenwyn Press [1969] 244 p. illus., facsims, maps (1 fold.), ports. 24 cm. Autobiographical. [F657.B6E8] 78-7112
1. Black Hills, S.D. and Wyoming. I. Title.

Black, Hugo LaFayette, 1886-1971.

BALL, Howard, 1937- 340'.0973
The vision and the dream of Justice Hugo L. Balck : an examination of a judicial philosophy / Howard Ball. University : University of Alabama Press, [1975] vii, 232 p. ; 22 cm. Includes bibliographical references and index. [KF8745.B55B3] 74-22710 ISBN 0-8173-5165-5 : 8.50
1. Black, Hugo Lafayette, 1886-1971. I. Title.

BLACK, Hugo, 1922- 347'.73'2634 B
My father, a remembrance / Hugo Black, Jr. 1st ed. New York : Random House, [1975] viii, 273 p., [1] leaf of plates : ill. ; 22 cm. Includes index. [KF8745.B55B55] 75-12410 ISBN 0-394-49631-0 : 8.95
1. Black, Hugo LaFayette, 1886-1971. I. Title.

DUNNE, Gerald T. 347'.73'2634 B
Hugo Black and the judicial revolution / by Gerald T. Dunne. New York : Simon and Schuster, c1977. 492 p., [8] leaves of plates : ill. ; 22 cm. Includes index. Bibliography: p. 469-478. [KF8745.B55D86] 76-44363 ISBN 0-671-22341-0 : 11.95
1. Black, Hugo LaFayette, 1886-1971. 2. Judges—United States—Biography. I. Title. BIP

FRANK, John Paul, 1917- 347'.73'2634 B
Mr. Justice Black: the man and his opinions [by] John P. Frank. Introd. by Charles A. Beard. Westport, Conn., Greenwood Press [1973, c1948] p. Reprint of the ed. published by Knopf, New York. [KF8745.B55F7 1973] 72-6931 ISBN 0-8371-6506-7
1. Black, Hugo Lafayette, 1886-1971. I. Title.

FRANK, John Paul, 1917- 347'.73'2634 B
Mr. Justice Black: the man and his opinions [by] John P. Frank. Introd. by Charles A. Beard. Westport, Conn., Greenwood Press [1973, c1948] p. Reprint of the ed. published by Knopf, New York. [KF8745.B55F7 1973] 72-6931 ISBN 0-8371-6506-7 14.75
1. Black, Hugo Lafayette, 1886-1971. I. Title.

HAMILTON, Virginia Van der Veer. 347'.73'2634 B
Hugo Black; the Alabama years. Baton Rouge, Louisiana State University Press [1972] ix, 330 p. illus. 24 cm. Bibliography: p. [309]-318. [KF8745.B55H34] 75-181566 ISBN 0-8071-0044-7 10.95
1. Black, Hugo Lafayette, 1886-

U.C.L.A. law review. v. 12
Mr. Justice Black: Thirty years in retrospect. Los Angeles, UCLA Law Review, 1967. 397-733 p. 25 cm. In U.C.L.A. Law Review, vol. 14, no. 2, Jan. 1967. 68-109077
1. Black, Hugo Lafayette, 1886- I. Title.

WILLIAMS, Charlotte. 923.473
Hugo L. Black; a study in the judicial process. Baltimore, Johns Hopkins Press, 1950. vii, 208 p. 24 cm. Bibliograhical references included in "Notes" (p. 191-204) 50-10353
1. Black, Hugo Lafayette, 1886- I. Title.

Black Jack, 1871-1897?

BURTON, Jeff. 364.3'0924 (B)
Black Jack Christian: outlaw, being a true and exciting account of the life and death of William Christian ... Time: 1871-1947. [1st ed. Santa Fe, N.M.,] Press of the Territorian [1967] 42 p. 23 cm. (Series of Western Americana, no. 14) Bibliography: p. 86-42. [HV6248.B62B8] 67-28558
1. Black Jack, 1871-1897? I. Title. II. Series.

BURTON, Jeff. 364.3'0924 B
Black Jack Christian: outlaw, being a true and exciting account of the life and death of William Christian ... Time: 1871-1947. [1st ed. Santa Fe, N.M.] Press of the Territorian [1967] 42 p. 23 cm. (Series of Western Americana no. 14) Bibliography: p. 36-42. [HV6248.B62B8] 67-28558
1. Black Jack, 1871-1897? I. Title. II. Series.

Black, Jeremiah Sullivan, 1810-1883.

BRIGANCE, William Norwood, 1896- 340'.0924 B
Jeremiah Sullivan Black, a defender of the Constitution and the Ten commandments, by William N. Brigance. New York, Da Capo Press, 1971 [c1934] ix, 303 p. facsims., ports. 24 cm. (The American scene: comments and commentators) Bibliography: p. 291-298. [KF368.B55B7 1971] 72-139196 ISBN 0-306-70078-6
1. Black, Jeremiah Sullivan, 1810-1883.

Black, Joseph, 1728-1799.

CROWTHER, James Gerald, 1899- 925
Scientists of the industrial revolution: Joseph Black, James Watt, Joseph Priestley [and] Henry Cavendish. Chester Springs. Pa., Dufour, 1963[c.1962] xii, 365p. ports. 23cm. Bibl. 63-21150 6.95
1. Black, Joseph, 1728-1799. 2. Watt, James, 1736-1819. 3. Priestley, Joseph, 1733-1804. 4. Cavendish, Henry, 1731-1810. I. Title.

Black, Martha Louise Munger Purdy, 1866-1957.

BLACK, Martha Louise Munger Purdy, 1866-1957. 971.9'1'020924 B
My ninety years / Martha Louise Black ; edited and updated by Flo Whyard. Anchorage : Alaska Northwest Pub. Co., c1976. ix, 166 p. : ill. ; 22 cm. (Northern history library) Originally published under title: My seventy years. [F1091.B532 1976] 76-3117 ISBN 0-88240-062-2 pbk. : 4.95
1. Black, Martha Louise Munger Purdy, 1866-1957. 2. Frontier and pioneer life—Yukon Territory. 3. Klondike gold fields. 4. Yukon Territory—History. I. Whyard, Flo. II. Title. BIP

Black Mulism—Biography.

*MCNEIL, Mayo. 297.870'.92
Elijah Muhammad the false prophet. [Denver] [1973] 53 p. 14 cm. [BP223.Z8]
1. Black Mulism—Biography. 2. Black Mulism—History and criticism. I. Title. Available from author: Box 7212, Denver, Colorado 80207

Black Muslims.

[LITTLE, Malcolm,] 1925-1965 301.451960730924
The autobiography of Malcolm X. WithAlex Haley. Introd. by M. S. Handler. Epilogue by Alex Haley. New York, Grove [c.1964, 1965] xvi, 455p. illus., ports. 24cm. [E185.97.L5A3] 65-27331 7.50
1. Black Muslims. I. Haley, Alex. II. Title.

Black Panther Party.

LOOK for me in the whirlwind; 301.45'19'6073022 B the collective autobiography of the New York 21, by Kuwasi Balagoon [and others] With an introd. by Haywood Burns. [1st ed.] New York, Random House [1971] xv, 364 p. 22 cm. [E185.96.L65] 74-162955 ISBN 0-394-45343-3 8.95
1. Black Panther Party. 2. Negroes—Biography. 3. Negroes—Social conditions. I. Balagoon, Kuwasi, 1946-

SEALE, Bobby, 1936- 323.2'0924 B
Seize the time; the story of the Black Panther Party and Huey P. Newton. [1st ed.] New York, Random House [1970] xi, 429 p. 22 cm. [E185.615.S37] 74-115816 6.95
1. Black Panther Party. 2. Newton, Huey P. I. Title.

Black power—United States.

JACKSON, George, 1941-1971. 322'.42
Blood in my eye. [1st ed.] New York, Random House [1972] xix, 197 p. 22 cm. [E185.615.J28 1972] 79-37423 5.95
1. Black power—United States. 2. Revolutions—United States. 3. Fascism—United States. 4. United States—Social conditions—1960- I. Title. BIP

Blackburn, Luke Pryor, 1816-1887.

BAIRD, Nancy Disher. 976.9'04'0924 B
Luke Pryor Blackburn, physician, governor, reformer / Nancy Disher Baird. Lexington : University Press of Kentucky, c1979. vii, 127 p., [1] p. : ill. ; 21 cm. (The Kentucky Bicentennial bookshelf) Bibliography: p. 125-[128] [F456.B5B34] 79-888 ISBN 0-8131-0248-0 pbk. : 4.95
1. Blackburn, Luke Pryor, 1816-1887. 2. Prisons—Kentucky—History. 3. Public health—Kentucky—History. 4. Kentucky—Politics and government—1865-1950. 5. Kentucky—Governors—Biography. 6. Physicians—Kentucky—Biography. I. Title. II. Series: Kentucky Bicentennial bookshelf.

Blackford, Mary Berkeley (Minor) 1802-1896.

BLACKFORD, Launcelot Minor, 1894- 920.7
Mine eyes have seen the glory; the story of a Virginia lady, Mary Berkeley Minor Blackford, 1802-1896, who taught her sons to hate slavery and to love the Union. Cambridge, Harvard University Press, 1954. 293p. illus. 22cm. [F230.B65B6] 54-5018
1. Blackford, Mary Berkeley (Minor) 1802-1896. 2. Virginia—Soc. life & cust. I. Title.

Blackman, Marion Cyrenus.

BLACKMAN, Marion Cyrenus. 917.63'76'03 B
Look away! Dixie Land remembered. New York, McCall Pub. Co. [1971] 214 p. 22 cm. Autobiographical. [CT275.B57817A3 1971] 78-139527 ISBN 0-8415-0084-3 5.95
I. Title.

Blackmore, Richard Doddridge, 1825-1900—Biography.

DUNN, Waldo Hilary, 1882-1969. 823'.8 B
R. D. Blackmore: the author of "Lorna Doone"; a biography. Westport, Conn., Greenwood Press [1974] 316 p. illus. 22 cm. Reprint of the 1956 ed. published by Longman's, Green, New York. "Bibliography of Blackmore's writings": p. 292-293; "Uncollected writings of Blackmore": p. 294. [PR4133.D8 1974] 73-19573 ISBN 0-8371-7286-1 14.00
1. Blackmore, Richard Doddridge, 1825-1900—Biography. BIP

Blackmun, Harry Andrew, 1908-

U.S. Congress. Senate. Committee on the Judiciary. 347.99'24 B
Harry A. Blackmun. Hearing, Ninety-first Congress, second session ... April 29, 1970. Washington, U.S. Govt. Print. Off., 1970. iii, 134 p. 24 cm. [KF26.J8 1970a] 79-606995
1. Blackmun, Harry Andrew, 1908-

Blackstone, William, Sir, 1723-1780.

DOUGLAS, d. 347'.42'0234 B
The biographical history of Sir William Blackstone and a catalogue of Sir William Blackstone's works, with a nomenclature of Westminster-Hall, by a gentleman of Lincoln's-Inn. New York, A. M. Kelley, 1971. 1 v. (various pagings) 22 cm. "Authorities" given after pref. Reprint of the 1782 ed. [LAW] 70-112403 ISBN 0-678-04537-2
1. Blackstone, William, Sir, 1723-1780. 2. Blackstone, William, Sir, 1723-1780—Bibliography. 3. Westminster Hall. 4. Judges—Gt. Brit. 5. Lawyers—Gt. Brit. I. A gentleman of Lincoln's Inn. II. Title. III. Title: The nomenclature of Westminster-Hall.

Blackstone, William, Sir, 1723-1780—Bibliography.

DOUGLAS, d. 347'.42'0234 B
The biographical history of Sir William Blackstone and a catalogue of Sir William Blackstone's works, with a nomenclature of Westminster-Hall, by a gentleman of Lincoln's-Inn. New York, A. M. Kelley, 1971. 1 v. (various pagings) 22 cm. "Authorities" given after pref. Reprint of the 1782 ed. [LAW] 70-112403 ISBN 0-678-04537-2
1. Blackstone, William, Sir, 1723-1780. 2. Blackstone, William, Sir, 1723-1780—Bibliography. 3. Westminster Hall. 4. Judges—Gt. Brit. 5. Lawyers—Gt. Brit. I. A gentleman of Lincoln's Inn. II. Title. III. Title: The nomenclature of Westminster-Hall.

Blackwell, Antoinette Louisa (Brown) 1825-1921.

KERR, Laura (Nowak), 1904- 922.8173
Lady in the pulpit. New York, Woman's Press [1951] 239 p. 22 cm. [BX9869.B6K4] 51-10610
1. Blackwell, Antoinette Louisa (Brown) 1825-1921. I. Title.

Blackwell, Elizabeth, 1821-1910.

BAKER, Rachel (Mininberg) 1903- v. 12
The first woman doctor; the story of Elizabeth Blackwell M.D. Illustrated by Evelyn Copelman. New York, Scholastic Book Services [1965, c 1961] 188 p. illus. 20 cm. (SBS, TX 247) NUC66
1. Blackwell, Elizabeth, 1821-1910. I. Title.

BLACKWELL, Elizabeth, 1821-1910. 610'.92'4 B
Pioneer work in opening the medical profession to women : autobiographical sketches / by Elizabeth Blackwell ; new introd. by Mary Roth Walsh. New York : Schocken Books, 1977. xxi, 264 p. ; 21 cm. Cover title: Opening the medical profession to women. Reprint of the 1895 ed. published by Longmans, Green, London & New York, without the bibliography, but with a new introd. [R154.B623A3 1977] 76-48855 ISBN 0-8052-0568-3 pbk. : 5.95
1. Blackwell, Elizabeth, 1821-1910. 2. Physicians—New York (State)—Biography. 3. Women physicians—United States—History. I. Title.

CHAMBERS, Peggy. 926.1
A doctor along; a biography of Elizabeth Blackwell: the first woman doctor, 1821-1910. London, New York, Abelard-Schuman [1958] 183 p. illus. 21 cm. [R154.B623C5 1958] 58-5202
1. Blackwell, Elizabeth, 1821-1910. I. Title.

GREENE, Jay Elihu, 1914- ed. 920.02
Four biographies. [School ed.] New York, Globe Book Co. [1956] 499p. illus. 21cm. [CT106.G65] 56-2582
1. Franklin, Benjamin, 1706-1790. 2. Blackwell, Elizabeth, 1821-1910. 3. Pupin, Michael Idvorsky, 1858-1965. 4. Rogers, Will, 1879-1935. I. Title. Contents omitted.

MCFERRAN, Ann 92
Elizabeth Blackwell, first woman doctor. New York, Grosset [c.1966] 175p. illus. 22cm. (Pioneer bks.) Rutledge bk. [R154.B623M3] 67-4332 2.95
1. Blackwell, Elizabeth, 1821-1910. 2. Women as physicians. I. Title.

WILSON, Dorothy Clarke. 610'.924 B
Lone woman; the story of Elizabeth Blackwell, the first woman doctor. [1st ed.] Boston, Little, Brown [1970] 469 p. illus.,

ports. 24 cm. Bibliography: p. 447-453. [R154.B623W5] 70-97907 8.95
1. Blackwell, Elizabeth, 1821-1910. I. Title. **BIP**

Blackwell, Elizabeth, 1821-1910—Juvenile literature.

CLAPP, Patricia. 610'.92'4 B
Dr. Elizabeth, the story of the first woman doctor. New York, Lothrop, Lee & Shepard Co. [1974] 156, [1] p. 22 cm. Bibliography: p. [157] A biography of the first woman doctor written as if she herself were relating her struggles to become a physician and open the field of medicine to women. [R154.B623C55] 73-17702 ISBN 0-688-40052-3 4.95
1. Blackwell, Elizabeth, 1821-1910—Juvenile literature. 2. Women physicians—Biography—Juvenile literature. I. Title.
Lib. bdg. 4.59, ISBN 0-688-50052-8 **BIP**

GRANT, Matthew G. 610'.92'4 B
Elizabeth Blackwell, by Matthew G. Grant. Illustrated by Nancy Inderieden. [Mankato, Minn., Creative Educational Society, 1973] p. cm. (His Gallery of great Americans series. Women of America) An easy-to-read biography of Elizabeth Blackwell who overcame many difficulties to become the first woman physician in the United States. [R154.B623G7] 92 73-15858 ISBN 0-87191-307-0 3.95
1. Blackwell, Elizabeth, 1821-1910—Juvenile literature. 2. Women physicians—Juvenile literature. I. Inderieden, Nancy, illus. II. Title. **BIP**

GRANT, Matthew G. 610'.92'4 B
Elizabeth Blackwell; pioneer doctor [by] Matthew G. Grant. Illustrated by John Nelson. Mankato, Minn., Creative Education; distributed by Childrens Press, Chicago [1974] 31 p. illus. (part col.) 25 cm. (His Gallery of great Americans series. Women of America) An easy-to-read biography of Elizabeth Blackwell who overcame many difficulties to become the first woman physician in the United States. [R154.B623G7] 92 73-15858 ISBN 0-87191-307-0
1. Blackwell, Elizabeth, 1821-1910—Juvenile literature. 2. Women physicians—Juvenile literature. I. Nelson, John, illus. II. Title.

LATHAM, Jean Lee. 610'.92'4 B
Elizabeth Blackwell, pioneer woman doctor / by Jean Lee Latham ; illustrated by Ethel Gold. Champaign, Ill. : Garrard Pub. Co., [1975] 80 p. : col. ill. ; 23 cm. (A Discovery book) A biography of the first woman doctor in the United States who worked in England and the U.S. to open the field of medicine to women. [R154.B623L37] 92 75-4808 ISBN 0-8116-6319-1 lib.bdg. 3.12
1. Blackwell, Elizabeth, 1821-1910—Juvenile literature. I. Gold, Ethel. II. Title.

Blackwell, Ewell, 1922-

SMITH, Lou. 927.96357
Ewell Blackwell, the Whip. New York, A. S. Barnes [1951] 25 p. illus. 21 cm. (The Barnes all-star library) [GV865.B55S55] 51-12699
1. Blackwell, Ewell, 1922-

Blades, James.

BLADES, James. 789'.01'0924 B
Drum roll / James Blades. London : Faber, 1977. xvi, 275 p., [8] leaves of plates : ill. ; 23 cm. Includes index. [ML419.B55A3] 77-368551 ISBN 0-571-10107-0 : 15.95
1. Blades, James. 2. Musicians—England—Biography. I. Title.
Distributed by Faber and Faber, Salem, NH Distributed by Faber and Faber, Salem, NH

Blades, Joseph Preston.

AYRES, Burt Wilmot, 1865- 922.573
Honor to whom honor is due; the life story of Joseph Preston Blades, especially as related to Taylor University, Upland, Indiana. [Upland] '1951. iv, 71 p. ports. 20 cm. [BX9225.B539A9] 51-22915
1. Blades, Joseph Preston. I. Title.

Blain, Cecil.

WINCHESTER, Barry. 940.4'72'43
Beyond the tumult. With a foreword by Douglas Bader and an introd. by L. G. Nixon. New York, Scribner [1972, c1971] xv, 207 p. illus. 23 cm. [D627.G3W53 1972] 76-38528 ISBN 0-684-12848-9 6.95
1. Blain, Cecil. 2. Gray, David Benjamin. 3. Kennard, Casper. 4. European War, 1914-1918—Prisoners and prisons, German. 5. Escapes. I. Title.

Blaine, Anita McCormick.

HARRISON, Gilbert 301.24'2'0924 B A.
A timeless affair : the life of Anita McCormick Blaine / Gilbert A. Harrison. Chicago : University of Chicago Press, c1979. p. cm. Includes index. [HQ1413.B54H37] 79-15264 ISBN 0-226-31804-4 : 15.00
1. Blaine, Anita McCormick. 2. Social reformers—United States—Biography. 3. United States—Social conditions. I. Title. **BIP**

Blaine, James Gillespie, 1830-1893.

MUZZEY, David Saville, 923.273 1870-
James G. Blaine; a political idol of other days. Port Washington, N. Y., Kennikat Press [1963, c1962] 514 p. illus., ports., facsims. 22 cm. Bibliography: p. 501-504. [E664.B6M8 1963] 63-20592
1. Blaine, James Gillespie, 1830-1893.

STANWOOD, Edward, 973.8'0924 B 1841-1923.
James Gillespie Blaine. Boston, Houghton Mifflin. [New York, AMS Press, 1972] 377 p. illus. 19 cm. (American statesmen, v. 34) Reprint of the 1905 ed. [E664.B6S7 1972] 70-128949 ISBN 0-404-50884-7
1. Blaine, James Gillespie, 1830-1893. I. Title. II. Series. **BIP**

Blair, Charles F.

BLAIR, Charles F. 629.13'0924 B
Red ball in the sky, by Charles F. Blair. Foreword by Lowell Thomas. New York, Random House [1969] xii, 203 p. illus., ports. 22 cm. Autobiographical. [TL540.B557A3] 69-16437 5.95
I. Title.

Blair, Francis Preston, 1791-1876.

SMITH, Elbert B. 973.5'092'4 B
Francis Preston Blair / by Elbert B. Smith. New York : Free Press, c1980. p. cm. Includes bibliographical references and index. [E415.9.B633S64] 79-7380 ISBN 0-02-929510-6 : 15.00
1. Blair, Francis Preston, 1791-1876. 2. Blair family. 3. United States—Politics and government—1815-1861. 4. United States—Politics and government—1849-1877. 5. Politicians—United States—Biography. **BIP**

Blair, Frank, 1915-

BLAIR, Frank, 1915- 070'.92'4 B
Let's be Frank about it / by Frank Blair, with Jack Smith. 1st ed. Garden City, N.Y. : Doubleday, 1979. vi, 377 p., [12] leaves of plates : ill. ; 22 cm. [PN4874.B54A32] 76-53411 ISBN 0-385-11493-1 : 10.95
1. Blair, Frank, 1915- 2. Journalists—United States—Biography. I. Smith, Jack Clifford, 1916- joint author. II. Title. **BIP**

Blair, James, 1656?-1743.

MOTLEY, Daniel Esten. 327.73 S
Life of Commissary James Blair, founder of William and Mary College. Baltimore, Johns Hopkins Press, 1901. [New York, Johnson Reprint Corp., 1973] p. Original ed. issued as no. 10 of Diplomatic and constitutional history, which forms the 19th series of Johns Hopkins University studies in historical and political science. [JA37.D56 no. 10] [LD6051.W513] 378.1'011'0924 B 73-3286 ISBN 0-384-40230-5
1. Blair, James, 1656?-1743. I. Title. II. Series: Johns Hopkins University. Studies in historical and political science, 19th ser., 10. III. Series: Diplomatic and constitutional history, no. 10.

Blair, William Newton, 1876-1970.

BLAIR, William 266'.5'0924 B Newton, 1876-1970.
The Korean Pentecost and the sufferings which followed / William Newton Blair and Bruce F. Hunt. Edinburgh ; Carlisle, Penn. : Banner of Truth Trust, 1977. 159 p., [4] leaves of plates ; 18 cm. [BV3462.B53A3] 78-305678 ISBN 0-85151-244-5 pbk. : 1.95
1. Blair, William Newton, 1876-1970. 2. Missionaries—Korea—Biography. 3. Missionaries—United States—Biography. 4. Presbyterian Church in Korea—History. 5. Korea—Church history. I. Hunt, Bruce F., joint author. II. Title. **BIP**

Blaise, Clark—Journeys—India.

BLAISE, Clark. 813'.5'4 B
Days and nights in Calcutta / Clark Blaise and Bharati Mukherjee. 1st ed. Garden City, N.Y. : Doubleday, 1977. 300 p. ; 22 cm. [PR9199.3.B48Z514] 75-40711 ISBN 0-385-02895-4 : 8.95
1. Blaise, Clark—Journeys—India. 2. Mukherjee, Bharati—Biography. 3. Novelists, Canadian—20th century—Biography. 4. India—Description and travel—1947- I. Mukherjee, Bharati, joint author. II. Title. **BIP**

BLAISE, Clark. 813'.5'4 B
Days and nights in Calcutta / Clark Blaise and Bharati Mukherjee. 1st ed. Garden City, N.Y. : Doubleday, 1977. 300 p. ; 22 cm. [PR9199.3.B48Z514] 75-40711 ISBN 0-385-02895-4 : 8.95
1. Blaise, Clark—Journeys—India. 2. Mukherjee, Bharati—Biography. 3. Novelists, Canadian—20th century—Biography. 4. India—Description and travel—1947- I. Mukherjee, Bharati, joint author. II. Title. **BIP**

Blake, Alma Carwile,

BLAKE, Alma Carwile, 917.54'71 1909-
Of life and love and things. Parsons, W. Va., McClain Print. Co., 1971. 119 p. illus. 23 cm. Autobiographical. [CT275.B5784A3] 70-152066 ISBN 0-87012-075-1
I. Title. **BIP**

Blake, Eubie, 1883-

ROSE, Al. 785.4'2'0924 B
Eubie Blake / by Al Rose. New York : Schirmer Books, c1979. xvi, 214 p., [10] leaves of plates : ill. ; 22 cm. Includes index. Discography: p. 174-188. [ML410.B6247R68] 79-7369 ISBN 0-02-872170-5
1. Blake, Eubie, 1883- 2. Jazz musicians—United States—Biography. **BIP**

Blake, Eugene Carson, 1906-

BRACKENRIDGE, R. 285'.131 B Douglas.
Eugene Carson Blake, prophet with portfolio / R. Douglas Brackenridge. New York : Seabury Press, 1978. xvi, 239 p., [8] leaves of plates: ill. ; 24 cm. (Presbyterian Historical Society publications ; 18) "A Crossroad book." Includes index. Bibliography: p.219-232. [BX9225.B5475B73] 77-25281 ISBN 0-8164-0383-X : 9.95
1. Blake, Eugene Carson, 1906- 2. Presbyterian Church—Clergy—Biography. 3. Clergy—United States—Biography. I. Title. II. Series: Presbyterian Historical Society. Publications ; 18.

Blake, George, 1922-

SPIRO, Edward. 327'.12'0924
The many sides of George Blake, Esq.; the complete dossier, by E. H. Cookridge. Princeton, N.J. [Vertex, 1970] 254 p. illus., facsims., ports. 22 cm. First published in 1967 under title: Shadow of a spy. [UB271.R92B58 1970] 74-123386 6.95
1. Blake, George, 1922- I. Title.

Blake, Robert, 1598-1657.

PHILLIPS, Cecil 942.06'3'0922 B Ernest Lucas, 1898-
Cromwell's captains, by Cecil E. Lucas Phillips. Freeport, N.Y., Books for Libraries Press [1972] ix, 426 p. illus. 23 cm. Reprint of the 1938 ed. Bibliography: p. 399. [DA419.A1P45 1972] 73-37908 ISBN 0-8369-6746-1
1. Hampden, John, 1594-1643. 2. Skippon, Philip, d. 1660. 3. Blake, Robert, 1598-1657. 4. Lambert, John, 1619-1684. 5. Great Britain—History—Puritan Revolution, 1642-1660. I. Title. **BIP**

Blake, William, 1757-1827.

BERGER, Pierre, 1869- 821'.7
William Blake, poet and mystic, by P. Berger. Authorized translation from the French by Daniel H. Conner. New York, Haskell House, 1968. xii, 420 p. 24 cm. Reprint of the 1914 ed. Bibliography: p. [385]-402. [PR4146.B45 1968] 67-31287
1. Blake, William, 1757-1827.

BERGER, Pierre, 1869- 821'.7
William Blake, poet and mystic. Authorized translation from the French by Daniel H. Conner. London, Chapman & Hall, 1914. [Folcroft, Pa.] Folcroft Library Editions, 1973. p. Bibliography: p. [PR4146.B413 1973] 73-3384 ISBN 0-8414-1770-9 13.50
1. Blake, William, 1757-1827. I. Title.

BLACKSTONE, Bernard 828.709
English Blake. Hamden, Conn., Archon 1966. xviii. 454p. illus. 22cm. First pub. 1949. Bibl. [PR4146.B55 1966] 66-20227 11.00
1. Blake, William, 1757-1827. I. Title. **BIP**

BLAKE and the youthful v. 12 *ancients,* being portraits of William Blake and his followers engraved on wood... and with a biographical notice by Bennett Schiff. Northampton, Mass., Gehenna Press, 1956. unpaged. 18 ports. 18cm 'Fifty copies of this book have been printed.'
1. Blake, William, 1757-1827. I. Baskin, Leonard, 1922- II. Schiff, Bennett.

BLAKE, William, 760'.092'4 B 1757-1827.
Letters from William Blake to Thomas Butts, 1800-1803. Printed in facsim. with an introductory note by Geoffrey Keynes. Folcroft, Pa., Folcroft Press [1969] [77] p. 34 cm. Reprint of the 1926 ed. Includes the text of a letter of Butts. [PR4146.A55 1969] 72-194986
I. Keynes, Geoffrey Langdon, Sir, 1887-, ed. **BIP**

BLAKE, William, 1757-1827. 821'.7
William Blake; an introduction. Edited by Anne Malcolmson. With illus. from Blake's paintings and engravings. [1st American ed.] New York, Harcourt, Brace & World [1967] 127 p. illus. 21 cm. Bibliography: p. 123-124. [PR4142.M28 1967] 67-18871
I. Malcolmson, Anne (Burnett) 1910- ed. II. Title.

BLAKE, William 1757-1827. 821.09
William Blake; an introduction. Edited by Anne Malcolmson. With illus. from Blake's paintings and engravings. [1st American ed.] New York, Harcourt, Brace & World [1967] 127 p. illus. 21 cm. Bibliography: p. 123-124. An introduction and critical guide to William Blake's poetry, including a brief biography and fifteen reproductions of his paintings and engravings. [PR4142.M28 1967] AC 68
1. English poetry—History and criticism. I. Malcolmson, Anne (Burnett) 1910- ed. II. Title.

BLAKE WILLIAM, 1757-1827. 759.2
William Blake / William Vaughan. New York : St. Martin's Press, 1978, c1977. [88] p. : chiefly col. ill. ; 28 cm. [N6797.B57A4 1978] 77-9208 ISBN 0-312-88023-5 pbk. : 5.95
1. Blake, William, 1757-1827. I. Vaughan, William, 1943-

CHESTERTON, Gilbert Keith, 1874-1936. 760'.092'4
William Blake / by G. K. Chesterton. Folcroft, Pa. : Folcroft Library Editions, 1976. viii, 210 p. : ill. ; 23 cm. Reprint of the 1910 ed. published by Duckworth, London, and Dutton, New York, in series: The Popular library of art. [ND497.B6C5 1976] 76-7995 ISBN 0-8414-3383-6 lib. bdg. : 17.50
1. Blake, William, 1757-1827. I. Series: The Popular library of art.

CLUTTON-BROCK, Alan Francis. 760'.0924 B
Blake, by Alan Clutton-Brock. New York, Haskell House, 1970. 140 p. 23 cm. (Great lives [14]) Reprint of the 1933 ed. Bibliography: p. 139-140. [PR4146.C6 1970] 77-119438
1. Blake, William, 1757-1827. I. Title. II. Series. BIP

CLUTTON-BROCK, Alan Francis. 760'.092'4 B
Blake, by Alan Clutton-Brock. [Folcroft, Pa.] Folcroft Library Editions, 1973. p. Reprint of the 1933 ed. published by Duckworth, London, which was issued as no. 14 of Great lives. Bibliography: [PR4146.C6 1973] 73-4597 ISBN 0-8414-3353-4 (lib. bdg.)
1. Blake, William, 1757-1827. BIP

DE SELINCOURT, Basil, 1876- 760'.092'4
William Blake. New York, Haskell House Publishers, 1971. xi, 298 p. illus. 23 cm. Reprint of the 1909 ed. [ND497.B6D4 1971b] 70-173850
1. Blake, William, 1757-1827.

DE SELINCOURT, Basil, 1876- 700'.924
William Blake. New York, Cooper Square Publishers, 1971. xi, 298 p. illus. 22 cm. Reprint of the 1909 ed. [ND497.B6D4 1971] 72-162018 ISBN 0-8154-0389-5
1. Blake, William, 1757-1827.

DE SELINCOURT, Basil, 1876- 760'.0924 B
William Blake, by Basil De Selincourt. Port Washington, N.Y., Kennikat Press [1972] xi, 298 p. illus. 21 cm. Reprint of the 1909 ed. [ND497.B6D4 1972] 75-160752 ISBN 0-8046-1568-3
1. Blake, William, 1757-1827.

ELLIS, Edwin John. 700.924 B
The real Blake; a portrait biography, by Edwin J. Ellis. New York, Haskell House Publishers, 1970. xix, 443 p. 13 illus., facsims. 23 cm. Reprint of the 1906 ed. [PR4146.E4 1970] 75-117994 ISBN 0-8383-1049-4
1. Blake, William, 1757-1827. I. Title.

*ESSICK, Robert N., comp. 760'.0924
The visionary hand; essays for the study of William Blake's art and aesthetics, edited and with an introduction by Robert N. Essick. Los Angeles, Hennessey & Ingalls, 1973. 558 p. 23 cm. Includes bibliographical references [ND497] 72-96392 ISBN 0-912158-22-0. 7.95 (pbk.)
1. Blake, William, 1757-1827. I. Title. BIP

GARDNER, Charles, 1874- 760'.092'4
William Blake, the man. London, Dent; New York, Dutton, 1919. [New York, AMS Press, 1973] 202 p. illus. 23 cm. [PR4146.G3 1973] 79-153324 ISBN 0-404-07906-7 9.00
1. Blake, William, 1757-1827. BIP

GARNETT, Richard, 1835-1906. 700'.924
William Blake; painter and poet. New York, Haskell House, 1971. 80 p. illus., port. 23 cm. Reprint of the 1895 ed. [ND497.B6G3 1971] 77-115857 ISBN 0-8383-1074-5
1. Blake, William, 1757-1827. I. Title.

GILCHRIST, Alexander, 1828-1861. 760'.092'4 B
Life of William Blake, with selections from his poems and other writings. A new and enl. ed. illustrated from Blake's own works, with additional letters and a memoir of the author. New introd. by W. A. G. Doyle-Davidson. Totowa, N.J., Rowman and Littlefield, 1973. xxi, 431 p. illus. 24 cm. Reprint of v. 1 of the 1880 ed. published by Macmillan, London. [PR4146.G5 1973] 73-166130 ISBN 0-87471-170-3 16.50
1. Blake, William, 1757-1827.

GILCHRIST, Alexander, 1828-1861. 760'.092'4 B
Life of William Blake, with selections from his poems and other writings. A new and enl. ed. illustrated from Blake's own works, with additional letters and a memoir of the author. New introd. by W. A. G. Doyle-Davidson. Totowa, N.J., Rowman and Littlefield, 1973. xxi, 431 p. illus. 24 cm. Reprint of v. 1 of the 1880 ed. published by Macmillan, London. [PR4146.G5 1973] 73-166130 ISBN 0-87471-170-3 16.50
1. Blake, William, 1757-1827.

JENKINS, Herbert George, 1876-1923. 760'.092'4 B
William Blake; studies of his life and personality. Edited with an introd. by C. E. Lawrence. [Folcroft, Pa.] Folcroft Library Editions, 1974. 110 p. illus. 24 cm. Reprint of the 1925 ed. published by H. Jenkins, London. [PR4146.J4 1974] 73-3386 ISBN 0-8414-2153-6 15.00
1. Blake, William, 1757-1827. I. Lawrence, Charles Edward, 1870-1940, ed. II. Title.

KLONSKY, Milton. 760'.092'4
William Blake, the seer and his visions / by Milton Klonsky. New York : Harmony Books, 1977. p. cm. [N6797.B57K55 1977] 77-3979 ISBN 0-517-52939-4 : 12.00 ISBN 0-517-52940-8 pbk. : 6.95
1. Blake, William, 1757-1827. I. Title. BIP

LISTER, Raymond. 760'.0924 B
William Blake; an introduction to the man and to his work. With a foreword by G. E. Bentley, Jr. [1st American ed.] New York, Ungar [1970, c1968] xi, 200 p. illus. (part col.) 23 cm. Bibliography: p. [191]-193. [PR4146.L5 1970] 70-99289 7.50
1. Blake, William, 1757-1827.

MACDONALD, Greville, 1856-1944. 760'.092'4 B
The sanity of William Blake / by Greville MacDonald ; with six ill. of Blake's drawings. Norwood, Pa. : Norwood Editions, 1975. 59 p., [4] leaves of plates : ill. ; 23 cm. Reprint of the 1920 ed. published by Allen and Unwin, London. [PR4146.M28 1975b] 75-35576 ISBN 0-88305-914-2 : 8.50
1. Blake, William, 1757-1827. I. Title. BIP

MARGOLIOUTH, Herschel Maurice, 1887- v. 12
William Blake. London, New York, Oxford University Press, 1951. 184 p. illus., 17 cm. (The Home university library of modern knowledge, 209) Bibliography: p. [179]-180. A 52
1. Blake, William, I. Title.

MARGOLIOUTH, Herschel Maurice, 1887- 821'.7
William Blake [by] H. M. Margoliouth. [Hamden, Conn.] Archon Books, 1967. 184 p. illus. 17 cm. Reprint of the 1961 ed. Bibliography: p. [179]-180. [PR4146.M3 1967] 67-26654
1. Blake, William, 1757-1827.

PALEY, Morton D. 760'.092'4 B
William Blake / Morton D. Paley. Oxford : Phaidon Press ; New York : E. P. Dutton, 1978. 192 p. : ill. (some col.) ; 29 cm. Includes bibliographical references and index. [N6797.B57P34] 76-62644 ISBN 0-7148-1767-8 19.95
1. Blake, William, 1757-1827. 2. Artists—England—Biography.

PRESTON, Kerrison. 700'.92'2
Blake and Rosetti / by Kerrison Preston. Folcroft, Pa. : Folcroft Library Editions, 1976. p. cm. Reprint of the 1944 ed. published by A. Moring, London. [PR4146.P7 1976] 76-29028 ISBN 0-8414-6782-X lib. bdg. : 17.50
1. Blake, William, 1757-1827. 2. Rossetti, Dante Gabriel, 1828-1882. 3. Poets, English—19th century—Biography. 4. Painters—England—Biography. I. Title.

PRESTON, Kerrison. 700'.922
Blake and Rossetti. New York, Haskell House Publishers, 1971. 111 p. illus., ports. 29 cm. Reprint of the 1944 ed. [PR4146.P7 1971] 73-117999 ISBN 0-8383-1054-0
1. Blake, William, 1757-1827. 2. Rossetti, Dante Gabriel, 1828-1882. BIP

SHORT, Ernest Henry, 1875-1959. 760'.0924
Blake. New York, Haskell House, 1970. vi, 167 p. plates. 23 cm. (British artists) Reprint of the 1926 ed. Bibliography: p. 166-167. [ND497.B6S5 1970] 70-118002
1. Blake, William, 1757-1827. BIP

STORY, Alfred Thomas, 1842-1934. 700'.924 B
William Blake: his life, character, and genius. New York, Haskell House, 1970. 160 p. port. 23 cm. Reprint of the 1893 ed. [PR4146.S7 1970] 77-115183
1. Blake, William, 1757-1827. I. Title.

STORY, Alfred Thomas, 1842-1934. 759.2 B
William Blake: his life, character, and genius. [Folcroft, Pa.] Folcroft Library Editions, 1973. p. Reprint of the 1893 ed. published by S. Sonnenschein, London. [ND497.B6S7 1973] 73-4498 ISBN 0-8414-7537-7
1. Blake, William, 1757-1827.

SWINBURNE, Algernon Charles, 1837-1909. 821'.7
William Blake; a critical essay. With illus. from Blake's designs in facsim. New York, B. Blom [1967] iv, 304 p. facsims. 24 cm. Reprint of the 1868 ed. [PR4146.S77 1967] 67-12468
1. Blake, William, 1757-1827. BIP

SYMONS, Arthur, 1865-1945. 760'.0924
William Blake. New York, Cooper Square Publishers, 1970. [14], 433 p. 23 cm. Reprint of the 1907 ed. "Records from contemporary sources": p. [249]-433. [PR4146.S8 1970] 79-115694
1. Blake, William, 1757-1827. BIP

WITTREICH, Joseph Anthony, comp. 700'.924
Nineteenth century accounts of William Blake, by Benjamin Heath Malkin [and others] Facsim. reproductions, edited, with introd. and headnotes, by Joseph Anthony Wittreich, Jr. Gainesville, Fla., Scholars' Facsimiles & Reprints, 1970. ix, 289 p. 23 cm. [PR4147.W54 1970] 78-133330
1. Blake, William, 1757-1827. I. Malkin, Benjamin Heath, 1769-1842. II. Title.

WRIGHT, Thomas, 1859-1936. 760'.092'4 B
The life of William Blake. New York, B. Franklin [1969] 2 v. in 1. illus. (part col.), facsims., maps, ports. 27 cm. (Burt Franklin research and source works series, 303.) (Selected papers in literature and criticism, 16) Reprint of the 1929 ed. [PR4146.W7 1969] 68-57922
1. Blake, William, 1757-1827. I. Blake, William, 1757-1827. II. Title. III. Series. BIP

Blake, William, 1757-1827—Biography.

BURDETT, Osbert, 1885-1936. 760'.092'4 B
William Blake. [Folcroft, Pa.] Folcroft Library Editions, 1974. viii, 198 p. 24 cm. Reprint of the 1926 ed. published by Macmillan, London, in series: English men of letters. Includes bibliographical references. [PR4146.B8 1974b] 74-3371 ISBN 0-8414-3132-9 20.00 (lib bdg)
1. Blake, William, 1757-1827—Biography.

BURDETT, Osbert, 1885-1936. 760'.092'4 B
William Blake / by Gilbert Burdett. Norwood, Pa. : Norwood Editions, 1976. p. cm. Reprint of the 1926 ed. published by Macmillan, London, in series: English men of letters. Includes bibliographical references. [PR4146.B8 1976] 76-15161 ISBN 0-8482-0159-0 : 15.00
1. Blake, William, 1757-1827—Biography.

DAVIS, Michael. 760'.092'4 B
William Blake : a new kind of man / Michael Davis. Berkeley : University of California Press, 1977. 181 p., [20] leaves of plates : ill. (some col.) ; 25 cm. Includes index. Bibliography: p. 165-170. [PR4146.D34 1977] 77-71059 ISBN 0-520-03443-0 : 12.95
1. Blake, William, 1757-1827—Biography. 2. Poets, English—19th century—Biography. 3. Artists—England—Biography. BIP

GARDNER, Charles, 1874- 700'.924 B
William Blake, the man. New York, Haskell House, 1970. 202 p. illus. 23 cm. Reprint of the 1919 ed. [PR4146.G3 1970] 76-118001 ISBN 0-8383-1056-7
1. Blake, William, 1757-1827—Biography. I. Title.

GILCHRIST, Alexander, 1828-1861. 760'.092'4 B
Life of William Blake, with selections from his poems and other writings. A new and enl. ed., illustrated from Blake's own works, with additional letters and a memoir of the author. New York, Phaeton Press, 1969. 2 v. illus., ports. 24 cm. Reprint of the 1880 ed. "Annotated lists of Blake's paintings, drawings, and engravings": v. 2, p. [207]-307. [PR4146.G5 1969] 72-90368
1. Blake, William, 1757-1827—Biography. I. Title.

JENKINS, Herbert George, 1876-1923. 760'.092'4 B
William Blake : studies of his life and personality / by Herbert Jenkins ; edited with an introd. by C. E. Lawrence. Norwood, Pa. : Norwood Editions, 1975. 110 p., [1] leaf of plates : ill. ; 22 cm. Reprint of the 1925 ed. published by H. Jenkins, ltd., London. [PR4146.J4 1975] 75-31936 ISBN 0-88305-312-8 : 20.00
1. Blake, William, 1757-1827—Biography.

WILSON, Mona, 1872- 700'.924 B
The life of William Blake. New York, Cooper Square Publishers, 1969 [i.e. 1970] xv, 397 p. illus., ports. 27 cm. "This edition has been reproduced from the limited Nonesuch Press edition of 1927, with the last revisions of the 1949 edition." Includes bibliographical references. [PR4146.W5 1970] 68-57020 12.50
1. Blake, William, 1757-1827—Biography. I. Title. BIP

Blake, William, 1757-1827—Biography—Character.

WITCUTT, William Purcell. 760'.092'4 B
Blake : a psychological study / by W. P. Witcutt. [Folcroft, Pa.] : Folcroft Library Editions, 1974. 127 p. ; 24 cm. Reprint of the 1946 ed. published by Hollis & Carter, London. Includes bibliographical references. [PR4148.P8W5 1974] 74-20909 ISBN 0-8414-9574-2 lib. bdg.
1. Blake, William, 1757-1827—Biography—Character. 2. Blake, William, 1757-1827—Criticism and interpretation. I. Title. BIP

Blake, William, 1757-1827—Criticism and interpretation.

MURRY, John Middleton, 1889-1957. 760'.0924
William Blake. New York, Haskell House Publishers, 1971. 380 p. 23 cm. Reprint of the 1933 ed. [PR4147.M8 1971] 71-173845 ISBN 0-8383-1344-2
1. Blake, William, 1757-1827—Criticism and interpretation.

MURRY, John Middleton, 1889-1957. 760'.092'4
William Blake. [Folcroft, Pa.] Folcroft Library Editions, 1974. p. Reprint of the 1936 ed. published by J. Cape, London, which was issued as no. 76 of the Life and letters series. [PR4147.M8 1974] 74-9888 ISBN 0-8414-6142-2 (lib. bdg.)
1. Blake, William, 1757-1827—Criticism and interpretation. I. Series: The Life and letters series (London), no. 76.

RAINE, Kathleen Jessie, 1908- 769'.924
William Blake [by] Kathleen Raine. New York, Praeger [1971, c1970] 216 p. illus. (part col.), ports. 22 cm. (Praeger world of art series) Includes bibliographical references. [PR4146.R32 1971] 70-121081 8.50
1. Blake, William, 1757-1827—Criticism and interpretation.

Blaker, Eliza Ann (Cooper) 1854-1926.

THORNBROUGH, Emma Lou. 923.773
Eliza A. Blaker, her life and work.

Indianapolis, Eliza A. Blaker Club, 1956. 94 p. illus. 24 cm. [LA2317.B52T4] 56-2794
1. Blaker, Eliza Ann (Cooper) 1854-1926. I. Title.

Blalock, Jane.

BLALOCK, Jane. 796.352'092'4 B
The guts to win / Jane Blalock, with Dwayne Netland ; introd. by Billie Jean King. Norwalk, Conn. : Golf digest ; New York : trade book distribution by Simon and Schuster, c1977. 158 p. : ill. ; 24 cm. Autobiographical. [GV964.B54A34] 77-73011 7.95
1. Blalock, Jane. 2. Golfers—United States—Biography. 3. Golf—Psychological aspects. 4. Sports for women. I. Netland, Dwayne, joint author. II. Title.

Blanc, Louis, 1811-1882.

LOUBERE, Leo A 923.244
Louis Blanc: his life and his contribution to the rise of French Jacobin-socialism. [Evanston, Ill.] Northwestern University Press, 1961. xii, 256p. 24cm. (Northwestern University studies in history, no. 1) Bibliography: p. 247-252. [HX263.B54L6] 61-6042
1. Blanc, Louis, 1811-1882. 2. Socialism in France. I. Title. II. Series.

Blanch, Lesley.

BLANCH, Lesley. 914.7'04'842
Journey into the mind's eye; fragments of an autobiography. [1st American ed.] New York, Atheneum, 1969 [c1968] 376 p. group port. 24 cm. [PR6052.L38Z5 1969] 68-27668 6.95
I. Title.

Blanchard, Jonathan, 1811-1892.

KILBY, Clyde S 923.773
Minority of one; the biography of Jonathan Blanchard. Grand Rapids, Eerdmans [1959] 252p. illus. 2icm. Includes bibliography. [LA2317.B54K5] 59-8756
1. Blanchard, Jonathan, 1811-1892. I. Title.

Blanche de Castille, consort of Louis VIII, King of France, 1188-1252.

MORRIS, David D 923.144
The greatest queen of France, her life and times, written and illustrated by David D. Morris. Albion, Mich., c1956. 103 l. illus. 30cm. [DC91.6.B5M6] 56-9535
1. Blanche de Castille, consort of Louis VIII, King of France, 1188-1252. I. Title.

PERNOUD, Regine, 944'.023'0924 B 1909-
Blanche of Castile / Regine Pernoud ; translated by Henry Noel. 1st American ed. New York : Coward, McCann & Geoghegan, 1975. 319 p., [8] leaves of plates : ill., geneal. table (on lining paper) ; 22 cm. Translation of La reine Blanche. Includes index. Bibliography: p. 318-319. [DC91.6.B5P4713 1975] 74-79678 ISBN 0-698-10595-8 : 8.95
1. Blanche de Castille, consort of Louis VIII, King of France, 1188-1252. I. Title.

Blanchet Augustine Magloire Alexander, 1797-1887.

BLANCHET, Augustine 282'.092'4 B Magloire Alexander, 1797-1887.
Journal of a Catholic bishop on the Oregon trail : the overland crossing of the Rt. Rev. A. M. A. Blanchet, Bishop of Walla Walla, from Montreal to Oregon Territory, March 23, 1847 to January 23, 1851. Blackrobe buries Whitmans / J. B. A. Brouillet ; [edited by] Edward J. Kowrach. Fairfield, Wash. : Ye Galleon Press, 1978. 190 p. : ill. ; 29 cm. Translated by E. J. Kowrach from the French mss. Includes index. Bibliography: p. 172-182. [BX4705.B529A33] 78-27768 ISBN 0-87770-166-0 : 14.95
1. Blanchet Augustine Magloire Alexander, 1797-1887. 2. Catholic Church—Bishops—Biography. 3. Whitman, Marcus, 1802-1847. 4. Bishops—United States—Biography. 5. Oregon Trail. 6. Whitman Massacre, 1847. I. Kowrach, Edward J. II. Brouillet, Jean Baptiste Abraham, 1813-1884. Blackrobe buries Whitmans. 1978. III. Title.

Blanchet, Francis Norbert, Abp., 1795-1883.

LYONS, Letitia 266'.2'0924 B Mary, Sister, 1903-
Francis Norbert Blanchet and the founding of the Oregon missions (1838-1848). Washington, Catholic University of America Press, 1940. [New York, AMS Press, 1974] p. Reprint of the author's thesis, Catholic University of America, 1940, which was issued as v. 30 [i.e. 31] of the Catholic University of America. Studies in American church history. Bibliography: p. [BX1415.O7L9 1974] 73-3585 ISBN 0-404-57781-4 9.50
1. Catholic Church in Oregon—History. 2. Blanchet, Francis Norbert, Abp., 1795-1883. 3. Portland, Or. (Ecclesiastical province) I. Title. II. Series: Catholic University of America. Studies in American church history, v. 31.

Blanda, George, 1927-

BLANDA, George, 1927- 613'.04'37
Over forty : feeling great and looking good! / By George Blanda, with Mickey Herskowitz ; introd. by R. Graham Reedy. New York : Simon and Schuster, c1978. 155 p. : ill. ; 23 cm. [RA777.8.B58] 78-1479 ISBN 0-671-22472-7 : 8.95
1. Blanda, George, 1927- 2. Middle aged men—Health and hygiene. 3. Football players—United States—Biography. I. Herskowitz, Mickey, joint author. II. Title.

BLANDA, George, 1927- 613'.04'37
Over forty : feeling great and looking good! / By George Blanda, with Mickey Herskowitz ; introd. by R. Graham Reedy. New York : Simon and Schuster, [1979] c1978. p. cm. (A Fireside book) [RA777.8.B58 1979] 79-13988 ISBN 0-671-25189-9 : 2.95
1. Blanda, George, 1927- 2. Middle aged men—Health and hygiene. 3. Football players—United States—Biography. I. Herskowitz, Mickey, joint author. II. Title.
BIP

TWOMBLY, Wells. 796.33'2'0924 B
Blanda, alive and kicking; the exclusive, authorized biography. Los Angeles, Nash Pub. [1972] 305 p. illus. 24 cm. [GV939.B55T9] 75-186893 ISBN 0-8402-1260-7 6.95
1. Blanda, George, 1927- I. Title.

Blanshard, Paul,

BLANSHARD, Paul, 322.4'4'0924 B 1892-
Personal and controversial: an autobiography. Boston, Beacon Press [1973] 308 p. 22 cm. [BL2790.B5A3] 72-6225 ISBN 0-8070-0514-2 7.95
I. Title. BIP

Blanton, Henry.

KRAMER, Jane. 976.4
The last cowboy / Jane Kramer. 1st ed. New York : Harper & Row, c1977. x, 148 p. ; 22 cm. "This work was originally published in the New Yorker." Portrays the life of a man who strives to be "a proper cowboy" despite radical changes which have propelled the Old West into a New Southwest characterized by industrialized agribusiness. [F391.2.B562] [K73 1977] 77-6150 ISBN 0-06-012454-7 : 8.95
1. Blanton, Henry. 2. Cowboys—Texas—Biography. 3. Texas—Social life and customs. 4. Texas—Biography. I. Title.

KRAMER, Jane. 976.4
The last cowboy / Jane Kramer. New York : Pocket Books, 1980, c1979. 158 p. ; 18 cm. Portrays the life of a man who strives to bea proper cowboy" despite radical changes which have propelled the Old West into a New Southwest characterized by industrialized agribusiness [F391.2.B562] ISBN 0-671-82425-2 pbk. : 1.95
1. Blantor, Henry. 2. Cowboys — Texas — Biography 3. Texas — Social life and customs 4. Texas — Biography. I. Title.
L.C. card no. for 1977 Harper & Row ed.: 77-6150 BIP

Blatch, Harriot Stanton, 1856-1940.

BLATCH, Harriot 324'.3'0924 B Stanton, 1856-1940.
Challenging years : the memoirs of Harriot Stanton Blatch / by Harriot Stanton Blatch and Alma Lutz. Westport, Conn. : Hyperion Press, 1976, c1940. xvi, 347 p., [9] leaves of plates : ill. ; 22 cm. (Pioneers of the woman's movement) Reprint of the ed. published by Putnam, New York. Includes index. [JK1899.B55A4 1976] 74-33933 ISBN 0-88355-256-6 : 22.50
1. Blatch, Harriot Stanton, 1856-1940. 2. Women—Suffrage—History. I. Lutz, Alma, joint author. II. Title.

BLATCH, Harriot 324'.3'0924 B Stanton, 1856-1940.
Challenging years ; the memoirs of Harriot Stanton Blatch / by Harriot Stanton Blatch and Alma Lutz. Washington : Zenger Pub. Co., 1975, c1940. p. cm. Reprint of the 1940 ed. published by Putnam, New York. [JK1899.B55A4 1975] 75-35912 ISBN 0-89201-012-6 : 15.95
1. Blatch, Harriot Stanton, 1856-1940. 2. Women—Suffrage—History. I. Lutz, Alma, joint author. II. Title.

Blatchford, Eliphalet Wickes, 1826-1914.

BLATCHFORD, Charles Hammond. 920
Eliphalet W. Blatchford & Mary E. W. Blatchford & Mary E. W. the story of two Chacagoans. [North Tarrytown N. Y.] 1962. 59p. illus. 26cm. [CT275.B57932B5] 62-43011
1. Blatchford, Eliphalet Wickes, 1826-1914. 2. Blatchfor, Mary Emily (Williams) 1834-1921. I. Title.

Blatt, Solomon, 1896-

CAUTHEN, John 328.757'.092'4 B K., 1906-1973.
Speaker Blatt, his challenges were greater / by John K. Cauthen ; with a new foreword by Jack Bass ; drawings by Gil Petroff, and a new index. Columbia : University of South Carolina Press, 1978. xxxi, 268 p., [10] leaves of plates : ill. ; 24 cm. Reprint of the 1965 ed. published by R. L. Bryan Co., Columbia, S.C. Includes index. [F274.B54C38 1978] 78-109043 ISBN 0-87249-369-5 : 14.95
1. Blatt, Solomon, 1896- 2. South Carolina. General Assembly. House of Representatives—Biography. 3. Legislators—South Carolina—Biography. 4. South Carolina—Politics and government—1865-1950. 5. South Carolina—Politics and government—1950- I. Title.

Blaustein, David, 1866-1912.

BLAUSTEIN, Miriam 361'.0092'4 B Umstadter.
Memoirs of David Blaustein, educator and communal worker / arranged by Miriam Blaustein. New York : Arno Press, 1975 [c1913] 308 p., [11] leaves of plates : ill. ; 23 cm. (The Modern Jewish experience) Reprint of the ed. printed for the author by McBride, Nast, New York. Bibliography: p. 121-122. [JV6895.J6B6 1975] 74-27966 ISBN 0-405-06696-1 : 21.00
1. Blaustein, David, 1866-1912. 2. Jews in the United States. I. Blaustein, David, 1866-1912. II. Title. III. Series.

Blavatsky, Helene Petrovna Hahn-Hahn, 1831-1891.

BLAVATSKY, Helen 212'.52'0924 B Petrovna Hahn-Hahn, 1831-1891.
The letters of H. P. Blavatsky to A. P. Sinnett, and other miscellaneous letters. Transcribed, compiled, and with an introd. by A. T. Barker. Facsim. ed. Pasadena, Calif., Theosophical University Press [1973] xv, 404 p. facsim., port. 23 cm. [BP585.B6A47 1973] 73-84138 10.00
1. Blavatsky, Helen Petrovna Hahn-Hahn, 1831-1891. 2. Theosophy. I. Sinnett, Alfred Parcy, 1840-1921. II. Barker, Alfred Trevor, 1893-1941, ed.

BLAVATSKY, Helene 212'.5 B Petrovna (Hahn-Hahn) 1831-1891.
Personal memoirs. Compiled by Mary K. Neff. Wheaton, Ill., Theosophical Pub. House [1967] 323 p. illus., port. 21 cm. (A Quest book) Bibliography: p. 312. [BP585.B6A32 1967] 67-3800
I. Neff, Mary Katherine, 1877- comp. II. Title.

INCIDENTS in the 212'.52'0924 B *life of Madame Blavatsky* / edited by A. P. Sinnett. New York : Arno Press, 1976. p. cm. (The Occult) Reprint of the 1886 ed. published by G. Redway, London. [BP585.B6I5 1976] 75-36919 ISBN 0-405-07974-5 : 19.00
1. Blavatsky, Helen Petrovna Hahn-Hahn, 1831-1891. I. Sinnett, Alfred Percy, 1840-1921. II. Series: The Occult (New York, 1976-) BIP

LEONARD, Maurice. 212'.52'0924 B
Madame Blavatsky : medium, mystic and magician / by Maurice Leonard. London ; New York : Regency Press, 1977. 115 p. ; 23 cm. [BP585.B6L43] 77-373898 £2.00
1. Blavatsky, Helene Petrovna Hahn-Hahn, 1831-1891. 2. Theosophists—Biography. I. Title.

MURPHET, Howard. 212'.52'0924 B
When daylight comes : a biography of Helena Petrovna Blavatsky / by Howard Murphet. Wheaton, Ill. : Theosophical Pub. House, 1975. xxxi, 277 p., [8] leaves of plates : ill. ; 21 cm. (A Quest book) Includes index. Bibliography: p. [266]-274. [BP585.B6M87] 74-18958 ISBN 0-8356-0461-6 : 8.95 ISBN 0-8356-0459-4 pbk. : 3.50
1. Blavatsky, Helene Petrovna Hahn-Hahn, 1831-1891. I. Title.

OLCOTT, Henry Steel, 133'.092'4 1832-1907.
Inside the occult : the true story of Madame H. P. Blavatsky / by Henry Steel Olcott. Philadelphia : Running Press, c1975. 491 p. ; 21 cm. Reprint, with new introd., of the 1895 ed. published by Putnam, New York, under title: Old diary leaves. Includes index. [BP585.B6O43 1975] 75-17044 ISBN 0-914294-31-8 lib. bdg. : 9.80. ISBN 0-914294-30-X pbk. : 3.95
1. Blavatsky, Helene Petrovna Hahn-Hahn, 1831-1891. I. Title. BIP

SOLOV'EV, Vsevolod 212'.52'0924 B Sergeevich, 1849-1903.
A modern priestess of Isis / Vsevolod Sergyeevich Solovyoff ; abridged and translated by Walter Leaf. New York : Arno Press, 1976. p. cm. (The Occult) Translation of Sovremennaia zhritsa Izidy. Translated on behalf of the Society for Psychical Research. Reprint of the 1895 ed. published by Longmans, Green, London. Appendices (p.): A. Abstract of pamphlet entitled. "II. P. Blavatsky and a modern priest of truth. Reply of Madame Y to Mr. Vs. Solovyoff, "by V. Jelihovsky.—B. Reply to Madame Jelihovsky's pamphlet, by V. S. Solvyoff.—C. The sources of Madame Blavatsky's writings, by W. E. Coleman. [BP585.B6S6 1976] 75-36921 ISBN 0-405-07976-1 : 20.00
1. Blavatsky, Helene Petrovna Hahn-Hahn, 1831-1891. I. Society for Psychical Research, London. II. Title. III. Series: The Occult (New York, 1976-) BIP

SYMONDS, John 922.912
The lady with the magic eyes: Madame Blavatsky. medium and magician. New York, T. Yoseloff [1960, c.1959] 254p. illus. 22cm. First published in London in 1959 under title: Madame Blavatsky, medium and magician. 60-13138 5.00 bds.,
1. Blavatsky, Helene Petrovna (Hahn-Hahn) 1831-1891. I. Title.

SYMONDS, John. 922.912
The lady with the magic eyes: Madame Blavatsky, medium and magician. New York, T. Yosehoff [1960, c1959] 254 p. illus. 22 cm. First published in London in 1959 under title: Madame Blavatsky,

medium and magician. [BP585.B6S9 1960] 60-13138
1. Blavatsky, Helene Petrovna (Hahn-Kahn) 1831-1891. I. Title.

WACHTMEISTER, Constance. 212'.52'0924 B
Reminiscences of H. P. Blavatsky and The secret doctrine / by Countess Constance Wachtmeister et al. Wheaton, Ill. : Theosophical Pub. House, c1976. xiv, 141 p. : map ; 21 cm. (Theosophical classics series) (A Quest book) [BP585.B6W3 1976] 76-44810 ISBN 0-8356-0488-8 pbk. : 3.75
1. Blavatsky, Helene Petrova Hahn-Hahn, 1831-1891. 2. Blavatsky, Helene Petrova Hahn-Hahn, 1831-1891. The secret doctrine. 3. Theosophists—Biography. 4. Theosophy. I. Title.

Blazina, Thomas, 1893-

COBB, Kirkpatrick. 920.8
Ike's Old Sarge. Dallas, Royal Pub. Co. [1964] 200 p. illus., ports. 24 cm. [CT275.B57938C6] 64-23165
1. Blazina, Thomas, 1893- 2. Eisenhower, Dwight David, Pres. U.S. 1890- I. Title.

COBB, Kirpatrick 920.8
Ike's Old Sarge. Dallas, Tex., Royal Pub. [c.1964] 200p. illus., ports. 24cm. [CT275.B57938C6] 64-23165 4.95
1. Blazina, Thomas, 1893- 2. Eisenhower, Dwight David, Pres. U. S., 1890- I. Title.

Bleek, Wilhelm Heinrich Immanuel, 1827-1875.

SPOHR, Otto H v. 12
Wilhelm Heinrich Immanuel Bleek; a bio-bibliographical sketch. Cape Town, University of Cape Town Libraries, 1962. viii, 78 p. illus., port., facsims. 26 cm. (University of Cape Town Libraries. Varia series, no. 6) Bibliography: p. 45-74. [Z8104.5.S65] 63-37682
1. Bleek, Wilhelm Heinrich Immanuel, 1827-1875. 2. African languages — Bibl. I. Title. II. Series: Cape Town. University of Cape Town. Library. Varia series, no. 6

Blegvad, Erik.

BLEGVAD, Erik. 741'.092'4 B
Self-portrait—Erik Blegvad / written and illustrated by Erik Blegvad. Reading, Mass. : Addison-Wesley, c1979. p. cm. A well-known illustrator discourses on himself, his life, and his work. [NC975.5.B55A2 1979] 92 78-23765 ISBN 0-201-00498-4 lib.bdg. : 7.95
1. Blegvad, Erik. 2. Illustrators—United States—Biography. I. Title.

Bleier, Rocky.

BLEIER, Rocky. 796.33'2'0924 B
Fighting back / Rocky Bleier, with Terry O'Neil. New York : Stein and Day, 1975. 224 p. : ill. ; 24 cm. Includes index. [GV939.B57A33] 75-12865 ISBN 0-8128-1845-8 : 8.95
1. Bleier, Rocky. 2. Football. I. O'Neil, Terry, joint author. II. Title. BIP

Blennerhassett, Harman, 1764?-1831.

SAFFORD, William Harrison, 1821-1903. 973.4'8'0924 B
The Blennerhassett papers. [New York] Arno Press [1971] 665 p. ports. 23 cm. (The First American frontier) Reprint of the 1864 ed. [E334.S15 1971] 75-146418 ISBN 0-405-02882-2
1. Blennerhassett, Harman, 1764?-1831. 2. Burr Conspiracy, 1805-1807. I. Title. II. Series.

SAFFORD, William Harrison, 1821-1903. 973.4'0924 B
The life of Harman Blennerhassett; comprising an authentic narrative of the Burr expedition and containing many additional facts not heretofore published. Freeport, N.Y., Books for Libraries Press [1972] 239 p. front. 23 cm. Reprint of the 1850 ed. [E334.B64 1972] 78-39476 ISBN 0-8369-9921-5
1. Blennerhassett, Harman, 1764?-1831. 2. Burr Conspiracy, 1805-1807. I. Title.

Blessitt, Arthur.

BLESSITT, Arthur. 269'.2
A walk with the Cross / Arthur Blessitt, with John Oliver. Plainfield, N.J. : Logos International, c1978. vii, 369 p., [3] leaves of plates : ill. ; 21 cm. [BV3785.B56A35] 78-66414 ISBN 0-88270-302-1 : 6.95
1. Blessitt, Arthur. 2. Evangelists—United States—Biography. I. Oliver, John., 1920- joint author. II. Title.

Bligh, William, 1754-1817.

ALLEN, Kenneth S. 910.92'4 B
"That Bounty Bastard" : the true story of Captain William Bligh / Kenneth S. Allen. London : R. Hale, 1976. 224 p., [6] leaves of plates : ill. ; 23 cm. Includes index. Bibliography: p. [216] [DA87.1.B6A65 1976] 76-363590 ISBN 0-7091-5346-5 : £4.50
1. Bligh, William, 1754-1817. I. Title.

ALLEN, Kenneth S. 359.3'3'10924 B
That Bounty bastard : the true story of Captain William Bligh / Kenneth S. Allen. New York : St. Martin's Press, 1977, c1976. 224 p. [6] leaves of plates : ill. ; 23 cm. Includes index. Bibliography: p. [216] [DA87.1.B6A65 1977] 76-26719 8.95
1. Bligh, William, 1754-1817. 2. Bounty (Ship) 3. Admirals—Great Britain—Biography. 4. New South Wales—Governors—Biography. I. Title.

HOUGH, Richard Alexander, 1922- 359.1'334
Captain Bligh & Mr. Christian; the men and the mutiny [by] Richard Hough. [1st ed.] New York, E. P. Dutton, 1973 [c1972] 320 p. illus. 25 cm. Bibliography: p. 309-314. [DA87.1.B6H68 1973] 72-82713 ISBN 0-525-07310-8 10.00
1. Bligh, William, 1754-1817. 2. Christian, Fletcher, 1764-1793. 3. Bounty (Ship) 4. Pitcairn Island. I. Title.

HUMBLE, Richard. 359.1'334'0924 B
Captain Bligh / Richard Humble. London : A. Barker, c1976. xii, 212 p., [4] leaves of plates : ill. ; 23 cm. Includes index. [DA87.1.B6H85] 76-383726 ISBN 0-213-16584-8 : £4.95
1. Bligh, William, 1754-1817. 2. Great Britain. Navy—Biography. 3. Bounty (Ship) 4. Admirals—Great Britain—Biography. I. Title.

Blind—Biog.

NATIONAL society for the Blind. 920.96177
Who's who among the blind in the business and professional world. [1st- Washington, National Society for the Blind, inc. 1950. v. 23 cm. annual. [HV1792.A3W56] 51-26034
1. Blind—Biog. 2. Blind—U.S. 3. U.S.—Biog. I. Title.

RICHARDS, Norman. 362.4'0924 B
Helen Keller. Chicago, Childrens Press [1968] 94 p. illus. 29 cm. (People of destiny: a humanities series) A biography of Helen Keller that stresses her education and her efforts to aid and encourage the handicapped. [HV1624.K4R5] 92 AC 68
I. Title.

Blind-deaf—Personal narratives.

SMITHDAS, Robert J. 920.96177
Life at my fingertips. [1st ed.] Garden City, N. Y., Doubleday, 1958. 260 p. 22 cm. Autobiographical. [HV1792.S63A3] 58-7369
1. Blind-deaf—Personal narratives. I. Title.

Bliss, Arthur, Sir, 1891-1975.

PALMER, Christopher. 780'.92'4 B
Bliss / [by] Christopher Palmer. Sevenoaks : Novello, 1976. 24 p. ; 19 cm. (Novello short biographies) "List of Bliss' principal works": p. 23-24. [ML410.B644P3] 76-383437 ISBN 0-85360-064-3 : £0.42
1. Bliss, Arthur, Sir, 1891-1975. 2. Composers—England—Biography. I. Title.

Bliss, Tasker Howard, 1853-1930.

PALMER, Frederick, 1873-1958. 355.331'0924 B
Bliss, peacemaker; the life and letters of General Tasker Howard Bliss. Freeport, N.Y., Books for Libraries Press [1970] ix, 477 p. illus., facsims., ports. 24 cm. Reprint of the 1934 ed. Includes bibliographical references. [E181.B68 1970] 70-130562
1. Bliss, Tasker Howard, 1853-1930. 2. Allied and Associated Powers (1914-1920) Supreme War Council. 3. European War, 1914-1918—U.S. I. Title. BIP

Blitzsten, N. Lionel, 1803-1952.

LIONEL Blitzsten Memorial. 926.1
N. Lionel Blitzsten, M.D., psychoanalyst, teacher, friend, 1893-1952. [New York] International Universities Press, 1961. 81p. illus. 21cm. [R154.B68L5] 62-2755
1. Blitzsten, N. Lionel, 1803-1952. I. Title.

Bliven, Bruce,

BLIVEN, Bruce, 1889- 070.4'0924 B
Five million words later; an autobiography. New York, J. Day Co. [1970] 346 p. 24 cm. Includes bibliographical references. [PN4874.B56A3] 78-115955 9.95
I. Title.

Blixen, Karen, 1885-1962.

MIGEL, Parmenia. 839.8'1'372 B
Titania; the biography of Isak Dinesen. New York, Random House [1967] xi, 325 p. illus., geneal. tables, ports. 25 cm. Bibliography: p. [311]-316. [PT8175.B545Z76] 67-14475
1. Blixen, Karen, 1885-1962. I. Title.

Blixen, Karen, 1885-1962—Portraits, etc.

LASSON, Frans, comp. 839.8'1'372 B
The life and destiny of Isak Dinesen. Text by Clara Svendsen. [1st American ed.] New York, Random House [1970] 227 p. illus. 27 cm. Translation of Karen Blixen: en digterskabne i billeder. [PT8175.B545Z75513 1970] 78-117708
1. Blixen, Karen, 1885-1962—Portraits, etc. I. Svendsen, Clara. II. Title.

Bloch, Ernest, 1880-1959.

STRASSBURG, Robert. 780'.92'4 B
Ernest Bloch, voice in the wilderness : a biographical study / Robert Strassburg. [s.l. : s.n.], c1977 (Los Angeles : Trident Shop, California State University, Los Angeles) vii, 192 p. ; 22 cm. Includes bibliographies and index. [ML410.B656S8] 77-152034
1. Bloch, Ernest, 1880-1959. 2. Composers—Biography. I. Title.

Bloch, Josef Samuel, 1850-1923.

BLOCH, Josef Samuel, 1850-1923. 301.45'19'24024 B
My reminiscences [by] Joseph S. Bloch. New York, Arno Press, 1973 [c1922] 576 p. illus. 23 cm. (The Jewish people: history, religion, literature) Translation of Erinnerungen aus meinem Leben. Reprint of the ed. published by R. Lowit, Vienna. "Lawsuit against Dr. Joseph Deckert and Paulus Meyer": p. [357]-570. [DS135.A93B63 1973] 73-2188 ISBN 0-405-05254-5 30.00
1. Bloch, Josef Samuel, 1850-1923. 2. Deckert, Josef, 1843-1901. 3. Meyer, Paulus. 4. Antisemitism—Austria. 5. Blood accusation. I. Title. II. Series.

Blofeld, John Eaton Calthorpe,

BLOFELD, John Eaton Calthorpe, 1913- 294.3'63 B
The wheel of life; the autobiography of a Western Buddhist [by] John Blofeld. 2d ed. Berkeley [Calif.] Shambala, 1972. 291 p. illus. 22 cm. [BQ942.L64A3 1972] 72-189854 3.95
I. Title. BIP

Blom, Frans Ferdinand, 1893-1963.

BRUNHOUSE, Robert Levere, 1908- 972 B
Frans Blom, Maya explorer / Robert L. Brunhouse. 1st ed. Albuquerque : University of New Mexico Press, c1976. xi, 291 p., [9] leaves of plates : ill. ; 24 cm. Includes index. "Chronological bibliography of Frans Blom": p. 273-284. [F1435.B63B78] 75-40833 ISBN 0-8263-0408-7 : 10.00
1. Blom, Frans Ferdinand, 1893-1963. I. Title. BIP

Blondel, Maurice, 1861-1949.

LACROIX, Jean, 1900- 194
Maurice Blondel; an introduction to the man and his philosophy. Translated by John C. Guinness. New York, Sheed and Ward [1968] 158 p. 21 cm. Translation of Maurice Blondel: sa vie, son ouvre, avec un expose de sa philosophie. Bibliography: p. [151]-158. [B2430.B585L313] 67-21910 2.45
1. Blondel, Maurice, 1861-1949.

Blondin, Jean Francois Gravelet, known as, 1824-1897—Juvenile literature.

BONING, Richard A. 791.3'4 B
Blondin; hero of Niagara [by] Richard A. Boning. Illustrated by Jim Sharpe. Baldwin, N.Y., Dexter & Westbrook [1972] 47 p. col. illus. 24 cm. (The Incredible series) Describes a French acrobat's seemingly suicidal stunts on a tightrope over Niagara Falls. [F127.N8B74] 92 70-184887 4.95
1. Blondin, Jean Francois Gravelet, known as, 1824-1897—Juvenile literature. 2. Niagara Falls—Juvenile literature. I. Sharpe, Jim, illus. II. Title.

Blood.

STERNE, Emma (Gelders) 1894- 926.1
Blood brothers: four men of science. Illustrated by Oscar Liebman. [1st ed.] New York, Knopf, 1959. 174 p. illus. 22 cm. [QP91.S773] 59-10025
1. Blood. 2. Physicians. I. Title.

Blood family.

HILL, Ivy Hooper (Blood) 1888- 929'.2'0973
William Blood, his posterity and biographies of their progenitors. Logan, Utah, J. P. Smith, 1962. 195p. illus. 24cm. [CS71.B655 1962] 62-6421
1. Blood family. I. Title.

Bloody Knife, ca. 1840-1876.

INNIS, Ben. 970.3 B
Bloody Knife: Custer's favorite scout. [Fort Collins, Colo.] Old Army Press [1973] 202 p. illus. 23 cm. Bibliography: p. 162-178. [E99.A8B554] 74-158484 8.50
1. Bloody Knife, ca. 1840-1876. 2. Dakota Indians—Wars. 3. Little Boy Horn, Battle of the, 1876.

Bloom, Alan.

BLOOM, Alan. 635.9'092'4 B
Plantsman's progress / by Alan Bloom. Lavenham [Eng.] : T. Dalton, 1976. 142 p. : ill. ; 24 cm. Includes index. [SB63.B57A34] 76-370078 £4.60
1. Bloom, Alan. 2. Nurserymen—England—Biography. 3. Plants, Ornamental. 4. Gardening. I. Title.

Bloom, Ursula—Biography.

BLOOM, Ursula. 828'.9'1209 B
Life is no fairy tale / Ursula Bloom. London : Hale, 1976. 175 p., [6] leaves of plates : ill. ; 23 cm. [PR6003.L58Z499] 76-380772 ISBN 0-7091-5640-5 : £3.95
1. Bloom, Ursula—Biography. 2. Authors, English—20th century—Biography. I. Title.

Bloomer, Amelia (Jenks) 1818-1894.

BLOOMER, Dexter C., 1820-1900. 301.41'2'0924
Life and writings of Amelia Bloomer / by D. C. Bloomer. St. Clair Shores, Mich. : Scholarly Press, 1976, c1895. 387 p., [1] leaf of plates : port. ; 21 cm. Reprint of the ed. published by Arena Pub. Co., Boston. [HQ1413.B6B6 1975b] 72-78650 ISBN 0-403-01994-X
1. Bloomer, Amelia Jenks, 1818-1894. 2. Women's rights—United States. I. Title. BIP

BLOOMER, Dexter C., 1820-1900. 301.41'2'0924 B
Life and writings of Amelia Bloomer / D. C. Bloomer ; with a new introd. by Susan J. Kleinberg. New York : Schocken Books, 1975. xv, 387 p. : port. ; 21 cm. (Studies in the life of women) Originally published in 1895 by Arena Pub. Co., Boston. Includes bibliographical references. [HQ1413.B6B6 1975] 74-26848 ISBN 0-8052-0483-0 : 7.50 pbk. : 3.95
1. Bloomer, Amelia (Jenks) 1818-1894. 2. Women's rights—United States. I. Title.

Bloomer, Harvey W.

SMITH, Gordon S. 639'.54'10924 B
One man and his sea / Gordon S. Smith. New York : Hastings House, [1978] p. cm. [SH380.2.U6S64] 78-17131 ISBN 0-8038-5391-2 : 5.95
1. Bloomer, Harvey W. 2. Lobster fisheries—Massachusetts—Cape Cod. 3. Fishermen—Massachusetts—Biography. 4. Chatham, Mass. I. Title. BIP

Bloomingdale, Teresa, 1930-

BLOOMINGDALE, Teresa, 1930- 282'.092'4 B
I should have seen it coming when the rabbit died / Teresa Bloomingdale. 1st ed. Garden City, N.Y. : Doubleday, 1979. 235 p. ; 22 cm. [BX4705.B5413A34] 78-22304 ISBN 0-385-14057-6 : 7.95
1. Bloomingdale, Teresa, 1930- 2. Catholics—United States—Biography. 3. Family—United States. I. Title. BIP

***Blose, Elcy Marie,**

*BLOSE, Elcy Marie, 1917- 248.2'0924
Hello, God; the life story of Elcy Marie Blose. New York, Exposition [1968] 125p. 21cm. (EP46760) 4.50
I. Title.

Blount, Edward Charles, Sir, 1809-

†BLOUNT, Edward Charles, Sir, 1809- 332.1'092'4 B
Memoirs of Sir Edward Blount / edited by Stuart J. Reid. New York : Arno Press, 1977. p. cm. (European business) Reprint of the 1902 ed. published by Longmans, Green, London. [D400.B6A3 1977] 76-29985 ISBN 0-405-09717-4 lib. bdg. : 19.00
1. Blount, Edward Charles, Sir, 1809- 2. Bankers—Great Britain—Biography. 3. Railroads—France—Finance. I. Title. II. Series. BIP

Blount, F. Nelson, 1918-

ADAIR, James R., 1923- 621.1'3'0924(B)
The man from Steamtown; the story of F. Nelson Blount [by] James R. Adair. Chicago, Moody [1967] 224p. illus., ports. 22cm. [TJ608.A65] 67-17725 3.95
1. Blount, F. Nelson, 1918- I. Title.

Blount, William, 1749-1800.

MASTERSON, William Henry. 973.4'092'2
William Blount, by William H. Masterson. New York, Greenwood Press [1969, c1954] viii, 378 p. illus., fold. map., ports. 23 cm. (Southern biography series) [E302.6.B6M3 1969] 320.50924 79-88904
1. Blount, William, 1749-1800. I. Title. II. Series. BIP

MASTERSON, William Henry. 923.273
William Blount. Baton Rouge, Louisiana State University Press [1954] viii, 378 p. illus., ports., fold. map. 22 cm. (Southern biography series) "Critical essay on authorities": p. [353]-368. [E302.6.B6M3] 54-12289
1. Blount, William, 1749-1800. I. Series.

Blowitz, Henri Georges Stephane Adolphe Opper de, 1825-1903.

GILES, Frank T. R. 070'.92'4 B
A prince of journalists : the life and times of Henri Stefan Opper de Blowitz / by Frank Giles. LaSalle, Ill. : Open Court, [1974] 228 p. : ill. ; 21 cm. "A Library Press book." Includes index. Bibliography: p. 220-221. [PN5183.B55G5 1974] 74-185499 ISBN 0-912050-51-9 : 8.95
1. Blowitz, Henri Georges Stephane Adolphe Opper de, 1825-1903. I. Title.

Bloy, Leon, 1846-1917.

DUBOIS, Elfrieda Theresa. 928.4
Portrait of Leon Bloy. London, New York, Sheed and Ward [1950] 125 p. 19 cm. Includes bibliographies. [PQ2198.B 18Z62] 51-9670
1. Bloy, Leon, 1846-1917. I. Title.

POLIMENI, Emmanuela. 928.4
Leon Bloy, the pauper prophet, 1846-1917. New York, Philosophical Library [1951] 119 p. 19 cm. [PQ2198.B18Z75 1951] 51-13357
1. Bloy, Leon, 1846-1917. I. Title.

Blue-Gray games, Montgomery, Aia.

PICKENS, Champ. 927.96
A rebel in sports; the autobiography of the father of the colorful Blue-Gray football game. New York, Barnes [c1956] 175p. illus. 20cm. [GV957.B55P5] 57-5735
1. Blue-Gray games, Montgomery, Aia. I. Title.

Blue Hill, Neb.—History.

BLUE Hill Bicentennial History Committee. 978.2'374 B
The heritage of Blue Hill / compiled and published by the Blue Hill Bicentennial Committee ; ill. by Dot Alber. Blue Hill, Neb. : The Committee, 1977. viii, 310, [62] p. : ill. ; 28 cm. Includes bibliographical references. [F674.B58B58 1977] 77-76802
1. Blue Hill, Neb.—History. 2. Blue Hill, Neb.—Biography. I. Alber, Dot. II. Title.

Blue Jacket, Shawnee chief, b. ca. 1752.

ECKERT, Allan W. 970.3 B
Blue Jacket, war chief of the Shawnees [by] Allan W. Eckert. [1st ed.] Boston, Little, Brown [1969] x, 177 p. map. 21 cm. [E90.B56E25] 69-10656 4.50
1. Blue Jacket, Shawnee chief, b. ca. 1752.

Blue, Vida, 1949-

BLUE, Vida, 1949- 796.357'092'4 B
Vida: his own story, by Bill Libby and Vida Blue. Englewood Cliffs, N.J., Prentice-Hall [1972] 248 p. illus. 24 cm. [GV865.B57A3] 72-3635 ISBN 0-13-941773-7 6.95
I. Libby, Bill, joint author. II. Title.

DEMING, Richard. 796.357'092'4 B
Vida. New York, Lancer Books [1972] 173 p. illus. 18 cm. (A Lancer sports original) [GV865.B57D4] 72-179443 0.95
1. Blue, Vida, 1949- I. Title.

Blue, Vida, 1949- —Juvenile literature.

KOWET, Don. 796.357'092'4 B
Vida Blue, coming up again / by Don Kowet. New York : Putnam, [1974] 160 p. ; 21 cm. (Putnam sports shelf) Includes index. A biography emphasizing the tumultous career of the star pitcher who was the youngest recipient ever of the Cy Young Award. [GV865.B57K68 1974] ISBN 0-399-60890-7 lib. bdg. : 4.89
1. Blue, Vida, 1949- —Juvenile literature. 2. Baseball—Juvenile literature. I. Title.

Blues (Songs, etc.)—United States—Bio-bibliography.

HARRIS, Sheldon. 784'.092'2 B
Blues who's who : a biographical dictionary of Blues singers / Sheldon Harris. New Rochelle, N.Y. : Arlington House, c1979. 775 p. : ports ; 29 cm. Includes indexes. Bibliography: p. 599-609. [ML102.B6H3] 78-27073 ISBN 0-87000-425-5 : 35.00
1. Blues (Songs, etc.)—United States—Bio-bibliography. I. Title.

Blues (Songs, etc.)—United States—History and criticism.

CHARTERS, Samuel Barclay. 784'.092'2 B
The legacy of the blues : a glimpse into the art and the lives of twelve great bluesmen : an informal study / Samuel Charters. 1st American ed. New York : Da Capo Press, 1977, c1975. 192 p. : ill. ; 22 cm. (The Roots of jazz) Discography: p. 189-192. [ML3556.C475L4 1977b] 76-51809 ISBN 0-306-70847-7 pbk. : 4.95
1. Blues (Songs, etc.)—United States—History and criticism. 2. Afro-American musicians—Biography. I. Title.

CHARTERS, Samuel Barclay. 784
The legacy of the blues : a glimpse into the art and the lives of twelve great bluesmen : an informal study / Samuel Charters. 1st American ed. New York : Da Capo Press, 1977, c1975. 192 p. : ill. ; 22 cm. (A Da Capo paperback) Reprint of the ed. published by Calder & Boyers, London. Bibliography: p. 187-188. [ML3556.C475L4 1977] 76-51399 ISBN 0-306-80054-3 pbk. : 4.95
1. Blues (Songs, etc.) United States—History and criticism. 2. Afro-American musicians—Biography. I. Title.

CHARTERS, Samuel Barclay. 784'.092'2 S B
Sweet as the showers of rain / Samuel Charters. New York : Oak Publications, c1977. 178 p. : ill. ; 26 cm. (His The bluesmen ; v. 2) Includes index. Discography: p. 173-174. [ML3561.B63C5 vol. 2] 784'.092'2 B 76-50484 ISBN 0-8256-0178-9 : 6.95
1. Blues (Songs, etc.)—United States—History and criticism. 2. Afro-American musicians—Biography. I. Title.
Publisher's address: 33 W. 60th street, New York, N.Y 10023 BIP

Blum, Leon, 1872-1950.

COLTON, Joel G., 1918- 944.08150924(B)
Leon Blum. humanist in politics [by] Joel Colton. [1st ed.] New York, Knopf. 1966. xiv, 512p. illus., ports. 25cm. Bibl. [DC37.B5C6] 65-18764 10.00
1. Blum, Leon, 1872-1950. I. Title.

COLTON, Joel G., 1918- 944.081'5'0924 B
Leon Blum: humanist in politics [by] Joel Colton. Cambridge, Mass., MIT Press [1974, c1966] viii, 512, xiv p. illus. 21 cm. Reprint of the ed. published by Knopf, New York. Bibliography: p. 495-512. [DC373.B5C6 1974] 73-21892 ISBN 0-262-53027-9 4.95 (pbk.).
1. Blum, Leon, 1872-1950. I. Title.

DALBY, Louise Elliott. 923.244
Leon Blum; evolution of a socialist. New York, T. Yoseloff [1963] 447 p. 22 cm. Bibliography: p. 424-443. [DC373.B5D3] 63-9377
1. Blum, Leon, 1872-1950.

JOLL, James. 923.24
Three intellectuals in politics. [New York] Pantheon Books [1961, c1960] xiv, 203 p. 23 cm. Published in 1960 under title: Intellectuals in politics. Bibliographical references included in "Notes" (p. 185-197) [D412.6.J64] 61-10030
1. Blum, Leon, 1872-1950. 2. Rathenau, Walther, 1867-1922. 3. Marinetti, Filippo Tommaso, 1876-1944. I. Title.

LOGUE, William, 1934- 944.081'5'0924 B
Leon Blum: the formative years, 1872-1914. DeKalb, Northern Illinois University Press [1973] 344 p. port. 24 cm. Bibliography: p. 293-336. [DC373.B5L64] 72-7515 ISBN 0-87580-030-0 15.00
1. Blum, Leon, 1872-1950. BIP

Blum, Robert, 1807-1848.

NEWMAN, Eugene J. 320.9'43'07 B
Restoration radical : Robert Blum and the challenge of German democracy 1807-48 / by Eugene Newman. Boston : Branden Press, [1974] x, 179 p. ; 22 cm. Based on the author's thesis, University of Wisconsin. Includes index. Bibliography: p. 159-163. [DD205.B6N48] 73-86958 ISBN 0-8283-1530-2 : 8.00
1. Blum, Robert, 1807-1848. I. Title. BIP

Blumgarten, Solomon, 1871-1927—Journeys—Palestine.

BLUMGARTEN, Solomon, 1871-1927. 915.694'04'40924 B
The feet of the messenger / Yehoash (Solomon Bloomgarden). New York : Arno Press, 1977. p. cm. (America and the Holy Land) Translation of Fun Nyu-York biz Rehovot. Reprint of the 1923 ed. published by the Jewish Publication Society, Philadelphia. [DS149.B5513 1977] 77-70682 ISBN 0-405-10229-1 : 20.00
1. Blumgarten, Solomon, 1871-1927—Journeys—Palestine. 2. Palestine—Description and travel. 3. Zionism. 4. Authors, Yiddish—Biography. I. Title. II. Series.

Blumhardt,Johann Christoph, 1805-1880.

ROSENBLUM, Arthur. 284'.1'0924 B
Johann Christoph Blumhardt; a summarized translation of the biography by Friedrich Zundel, with parts added. [Rifton? N.Y., 1967] 125 p. 30 cm. 200 copies. No. Translated by Art Rosenblum. [BX8080.B615R67] 71-12276 3.00
1. Blumhardt,Johann Christoph, 1805-1880. I. Zundel, Friedrich. Johann Christoph Blumhardt. II. Title.

Blunt, Harry L.

STARK, Charles Rathbone, 1885- 926.2913
The Bering Sea Eagle. Caldwell, Idaho, Caxton Printers, 1957. 170 p. illus. 22 cm. [TL540.B62S8] 57-5243
1. Blunt, Harry L. I. Title.

Blunt, Wilfrid Scawen, 1840-1922.

ASSAD, Thomas J. 928.2
Three Victorian travellers: Burton, Blunt, Doughty, London, Routledge & K. Paul [dist. New York, Hillary, 1965, c.1964] x, 154p. ports. 23cm. Bibl. [G245.A8] 65-2934 5.00 bds.,
1. Burton, Sir Richard Francis, 1821-1890. 2. Blunt, Wilfrid Scawen, 1840-1922. 3. Doughty, Charles Montagu, 1843-1926. I. Title.

Blunt, Wilfrid Scawen, 1840-1922—Biography.

LONGFORD, Elizabeth Harman Pakenham, Countess of, 1906- 941.081'092'4 B
A pilgrimage of passion : the life of Wilfrid Scawen Blunt / Elizabeth Longford. 1st American ed. New York : Knopf, 1980, c1979. p. cm. Includes index. Bibliography: p. [PR4149.B8Z73 1980] 79-3486 ISBN 0-394-50944-7 : 15.00
1. Blunt, Wilfrid Scawen, 1840-1922—Biography. 2. Poets, English—19th century—Biography. 3. Arabists—England—Biography. I. Title. BIP

Blyden, Edward Wilmot, 1832-1912.

BENJAMIN, George J. 966.6'202'0924 B
Edward W. Blyden, messiah of Black Revolution / George J. Benjamin. 1st ed.

New York : Vantage Press, c1979. 92 p. ; 22 cm. [DT634.3.B58B46] 78-51609 ISBN 0-533-03651-8 : 6.95
1. Blyden, Edward Wilmot, 1832-1912. 2. Liberia—Intellectual life. 3. Africa, West—Intellectual life. 4. Pan-Africanism. 5. Blacks—Race identity. 6. Intellectuals—Liberia—Biography. 7. Intellectuals—Africa, West—Biography. I. Title.

BLYDEN of 966'.6'020924 (B)
Liberia; an account of the life and labors of Edward Wilmot Blyden, LL. D., as recorded in letters and in print. Foreword by Nnamdi Azikiwe. [1st ed.] New York. Vantage [1967, c.1966] 1040p. illus., facsim. (on lining papers), ports. 22cm. Bibl. [DT636.B4H6] 67-6671 1887- 10.00
1. Blyden, Edward Wilmot, 1832-1912.

HOLDEN, Edith, 1887- 966'.6'020924 B
Blyden of Liberia; an account of the life and labors of Edward Wilmot Blyden, LL.D., as recorded in letters and in print. Foreword by Nnamdi Azikiwe. [1st ed.] New York, Vantage Press [1967, c1966] 1040 p. illus. facsim. (on lining papers), ports. 22 cm. Bibliographical references included in "Notes" (p. 923-1016) "Selected published writings of Dr. Edward Wilmot Blyden": p. 1017-1023. [DT636.B4H6] 67-6671
1. Blyden, Edward Wilmot, 1832-1912. I. Title.

LYNCH, Hollis Ralph 966'.602'0924(B)
Edward Wilmot Blyden: Pan-Negro patriot 1832-1912 [by] Hollis R. Lynch. London, New York, Oxford Univ. Pr., 1967. xvi, 272p. front. (port), plate, 23cm. (West African hist. ser.) Bibl. [CT2750.B4L9] 67-106354 6.70
1. Blyden, Edward Wilmot, 1832-1912. I. Title.

LYNCH, Hollis Ralph. 966'.602'0924 B
Edward Wilmot Blyden; Pan-Negro patriot, 1832-1912 [by] Hollis R. Lynch. London, New York, Oxford University Press [1970] ix, 272 p. 21 cm. (West African history series) (Galaxy book 326.) Bibliography: p. [253]-261. [CT2750.B4L9 1970] 70-509035 1.95
1. Blyden, Edward Wilmot, 1832-1912. BIP

LYNCH, Hollis Ralph 966'.6'020924
Edward Wilmot Blyden: Pan-Negro patriot 1832-1912 [by] Hollis R. Lynch. London, New York [etc.] Oxford U.P., 1967. xvi, 272 p. front. (port.), plate, 22 1/2 cm. (West African history series) 42/- (B67-19910) Bibliography: p. [253]-261. [CT2750.B4L9] 67-106354
1. Blyden, Edward Wilmot, 1832-1912. I. Title.

Blye, Irwin.

PILEGGI, Nicholas. 363.2'092'4 B
Blye, private eye / Nicholas Pileggi. 1st ed. Chicago : Playboy Press, c1976. p. cm. [HV8083.B59P55] 76-55344 ISBN 0-87223-475-4 : 8.95
1. Blye, Irwin. 2. Detectives—United States. I. Title. BIP

Blythe, David Gilmour,

MILLER, Dorothy, 1915- 927.5
The life and work of David G. Blythe. [Pittsburgh] University of Pittsburgh Press [1950] 142 p. illus., ports. 24 cm. Bibliography: p. 135-138. [ND237.B72M5] 50-4228
1. Blythe, David Gilmour, 1815-1865. I. Title.

Boas, Franz, 1858-1942.

HERSKOVITS, Melville Jean, 1895-1963. 301.2'092'4 B
Franz Boas; the science of man in the making. Clifton [N.J.] A. M. Kelley, 1973 [c1953] 131 p. 22 cm. (Scribner reprint editions) Original ed. issued in series: Twentieth century library. Bibliography: p. 123-125. [GN21.B56H4 1973] 70-128058 ISBN 0-678-02761-7 8.50
1. Boas, Franz, 1858-1942.

HERSKOVITS, Melville Jean, 1895-1963. 301.2'092'4 B
Franz Boas; the science of man in the making. Clifton [N.J.] A. M. Kelley, 1973 [c1953] (Scribner reprint editions) Original ed. issued in series: Twentieth century library. Bibliography: p: [GN21.B56H4 1973] 70-127058 ISBN 0-678-02761-7 8.50
1. Boas, Franz, 1858-1942.

Boat, Ellen (Lynch)

BOAT, Father William J. 920.7
A valiant woman; a priest's tribute to his mother. New York, Exposition Press [c.1961] 65p. 2.50
1. Boat, Ellen (Lynch) I. Title.

BOAT, William J 1896- v. 12
A valiant woman; a priest's tribute to his mother. [1st ed.] New York, Exposition Press [1961] 65p. 21cm. [CT848.B6B6] 62-1072
1. Boat, Ellen (Lynch) 1872-1945. I. Title.

Boat, Reverend William J.

BOAT, Reverend William J. 922.273
With gun and cross; a soldier and his angel advance and defend the eternal truths of the church militant. New York, Exposition [c.1962] 511p. (Expositiontestament bk.) 6.00
I. Title.

Boatwright, Frederic William, 1868-1951.

ALLEY, Reuben E. 378.1'12'0924 B
Frederic W. Boatwright [by] Reuben E. Alley. Richmond, Va., University of Richmond [1973] viii, 141 p. port. 25 cm. Includes bibliographical references. [LD4711.R417 1895.A44] 72-96020
1. Boatwright, Frederic William, 1868-1951.

Boaz, Hiram Abiff,

BOAZ, Hiram Abiff, Bp., 1866- 922.773
Eighty-four golden years; an autobiography of Bishop Hiram Abiff Boaz. Nashville, Parthenon Press [1951] 232 p. illus. 24 cm. [BX8495.B58A3] 51-8947
I. Title.

Bobola, Andrsej, Saint, 1591?-1657.

ROBERTO, Brother, 1927- 922.2438
With fire, sword, and whips; a story of St. Andrew Bobola. Illus. by Elaine Smith. Notre Dame, Ind., Dujarie Press [1957] 94p. illus. 24cm. [BX4700.B67R6] 57-37885
1. Bobola, Andrsej, Saint, 1591?-1657. I. Title.

ROBERTO, Brother, 1927- 922.2438
With fire, sword, and whips; a story of St. Andrew Bobola. Illus. by Elaine Smith. Notre Dame, Ind., Dujarie Press [1957] 94p. illus. 24cm. [BX4700.B67R6] 57-37885
1. Bobola, Andrzej, Saint, 1591?-1657. I. Title.

Bobst, Elmer Holmes, 1884-

BOBST, Elmer Holmes. 615'.1 B
Bobst: the autobiography of a pharmaceutical pioneer. New York, McKay [1973] vii, 360 p. illus. 25 cm. [HD9666.95.B6A3] 72-93992 7.95
1. Bobst, Elmer Holmes, 1884- I. Title.

Boccaccio, Giovanni, 1313-1375.

BRANCA, Vittore. 858'.1'09 B
Boccaccio : the man and his works / Vittore Branca ; translated by Richard Monges ; cotranslator and editor Dennis J. McAuliffe ; foreword by Robert C. Clements. New York : New York University Press, 1976. ix, 341 p. ; 24 cm. Based on the author's Boccaccio medievale. Includes bibliographical references and index. [PQ4277.B7] 71-81830 ISBN 0-8147-0953-2 : 12.50
1. Boccaccio, Giovanni, 1313-1375. BIP

CARSWELL, Catherine MacFarlane, 1879-1946. 851'.1 B
The tranquil heart : portrait of Giovanni Boccaccio / by Catherine Carswell. Folcroft, Pa. : Folcroft Library Editions, 1976. p. cm. Reprint of the 1937 ed. published by Lawrence and Wishart, London. Includes index. Bibliography: p. [PQ4277.C3 1976] 76-8895 ISBN 0-8414-3639-8 lib. bdg. : 25.00
1. Boccaccio, Giovanni, 1313-1375. I. Title. BIP

CARSWELL, Catherine MacFarlane, 1879-1946. 851'.1 B
The tranquil heart : portrait of Giovanni Boccaccio / by Catherine Carswell. Folcroft, Pa. : Folcroft Library Editions, 1976. p. cm. Reprint of the 1937 ed. published by Lawrence and Wishart, London. Includes index. Bibliography: p. [PQ4277.C3 1976] 76-8895 ISBN 0-8414-3639-8 lib. bdg. : 25.00
1. Boccaccio, Giovanni, 1313-1375. I. Title. BIP

SYMONDS, John Addington, 1840-1893. 851.1 B
Giovanni Boccaccio as man and author. London, J. C. Nimmo, 1895. New York, AMS Press [1968] xi, 100 p. 22 cm. [PQ4277.S8 1968] 68-54298
1. Boccaccio, Giovanni, 1313-1375.

SYMONDS, John Addington, 1840-1893. v. 12
Giovanni Boccaccio as man and author. Sandoval, N.M., Coronado Press [1961] 100 p. 21 cm. (Coronado classics) "Reprinted from the edition of 1895 published in New York by Charles Scribner's Sons."
1. Boccaccio, Giovanni, 1313-1375. I. Title. BIP

Boccaccio, Giovanni, 1313-1375—Biography.

CHUBB, Thomas Caldecot, 1899- 851'.1 B
The life of Giovanni Boccaccio. Port Washington, N.Y., Kennikat Press [1969] 286 p. facsims. 22 cm. Reprint of the 1930 ed. Bibliography: p. 265-268. [PQ4277.C5 1969] 68-26256
1. Boccaccio, Giovanni, 1313-1375—Biography. BIP

Boccherini, Luigi, 1745-1805.

ROTHSCHILD, Germaine (Halphen) baronne de. 780.924
Luigi Boccherini; his life and work. Pref by Norbert Dufourcq. Tr. by Andreas Mayor. New York, Oxford [c.]1965. xix, 154p. facsims., ports. 23cm. Bibl. [ML410.B66R83] 4.00
1. Boccherini, Luigi, 1745-1805. I. Title.

Bock, August J,

BOCK, August J, 1886- 926.4795
Knight of the napkin; memoirs of fifty years' experiences in many lands. With a foreword by Edward Bryce Bell. New York, Exposition Press [1951] 61 p. illus. 23 cm. [TX910.5.B6A3] 51-11832
I. Title.

Bode, Boyd Henry, 1873-1953.

†SUN, Huai Chin, 1904- 370'.92'4 B
Boyd H. Bode (1873-1953) and the reform of American education : recollections and correspondence / by H. C. Sun. 1st ed. [Hampton, VA] : Sun, c1977. ix, 126 p. : ill. ; 22 cm. Bibliography: p. [71]-75. [LA2317.B554S9] 77-71604 pbk. : 4.00
1. Bode, Boyd Henry, 1873-1953. 2. College teachers—United States—Biography. I. Title.
Publisher's address : H. C. Sun, 1356 Coral Pl., Hampton, VA BIP

Bodine, A. Aubrey, 1907-1970.

WILLIAMS, Harold A., 1916- 779
Bodine; a legend in his time, by Harold A. Williams. [1st ed.] Baltimore, Bodine, 1971. 82 p., [77] p. of illus. 27 cm. "The photography of A. Aubrey Bodine, 1924-1970": p. [1]-[75] (2d group) [TR140.B55W5] 70-169537 ISBN 0-910254-70-2 12.50
1. Bodine, A. Aubrey, 1907-1970. 2. Photography, Artistic. I. Bodine, A. Aubrey, 1907-1970. II. Title.

Boehm, Edward Marshall, 1913-1969.

COSENTINO, Frank J. 738'.0924
Edward Marshall Boehm, 1913-1969, by Frank J. Cosentino. [Chicago, Printed by The Lakeside Press, 1970] 264 p. illus. (part col.), ports. (part col.) 32 cm. Bibliography: p. 264. [NK4210.B6C63] 75-130889
1. Boehm, Edward Marshall, 1913-1969.

†PALLEY, Reese. 738.2'092'4
The porcelain art of Edward Marshall Boehm / by Reese Palley. New York : H. N. Abrams, [1976] p. cm. Includes index. [NK4210.B6P34] 76-20690 ISBN 0-8109-0701-1 : 35.00
1. Boehm, Edward Marshall, 1913-1969. 2. Porcelain, American. I. Title.

Boehme, Jakob, 1575-1624.

STOUDT, John Joseph, 1911- (921.3)
Sunrise to eternity; a study in Jacob Bochme's life and thought. Pref. by Paul Tillich. Philadelphia, University of Pennsylvania Press [1957] 317 p. illus. 22 cm. Includes bibliography. [BV5095.B7S69] [922.91] 56-11804
1. Bochme, Jakob, 1575-1624. I. Title.

Boetie, Dugmore.

BOETIE, Dugmore. 364.1'0924 B
Familiarity is the kingdom of the lost. Edited by Barney Simon. Pref. by Nadine Gordimer. [1st ed.] New York, Dutton, 1969. 189 p. 22 cm. Autobiographical. [HV6248.B645A3 1969b] 79-99819 4.95
I. Simon, Barney, ed. II. Title.

Bogan, Louise,

BOGAN, Louise, 1897-1970. 811'.5'2 B
What the woman lived; selected letters of Louise Bogan, 1920-1970. Edited by Ruth Limmer. [1st ed.] New York, Harcourt Brace Jovanovich [1973] xiv, 401 p. 25 cm. [PS3503.O195Z53 1973] 73-9737 ISBN 0-15-195878-5 14.50
I. Title. BIP

Bogarde, Dirk, 1921-

BOGARDE, Dirk, 1921- 791.43'028'0924 B
A postillion struck by lightning / Dirk Bogarde. New York : Holt, Rinehart and Winston, c1977. 268 p., [6] leaves of plates : ill. ; 22 cm. Includes index. [PN2598.B647A36 1977b] 77-72337 ISBN 0-03-021511-0 : 8.95
1. Bogarde, Dirk, 1921- 2. Actors—Great Britain—Biography. I. Title. BIP

BOGARDE, Dirk, 1921- 791.43'028'0924 B
Snakes & ladders / Dirk Bogarde. New York : Holt, Rinehart and Winston, 1979, c1978. xii, 341 p., [13] leaves of plates : ill. ; 22 cm. Continues A postillion struck by lightning. Sequel to A postillion struck by lightning. Includes index. Filmography: p. 333-334. [PN2598.B647A37 1979] 78-23877 ISBN 0-03-047161-3 : 10.95
1. Bogarde, Dirk, 1921- 2. Actors—Great Britain—Biography. I. Title. BIP

Bogardus, Emory Stephen,

BOGARDUS, Emory Stephen, 1882- 301'.0922
Personal tributes to friends [by] Emory S. Bogardus. Los Angeles, University of Southern California Press [1970] 158 p. 24 cm. [HM22.U6B62] 74-11845
I. Title.

Bogart, Humphrey, 1899-1957.

BARBOUR, Alan G. 791.43'028'0924
Humphrey Bogart, by Alan G. Barbour. New York, Pyramid Publications [1973] 160 p. illus. 20 cm. (A Pyramid illustrated history of the movies) Bibliography: p. 140. [PN2287.B48B3] 72-93667 ISBN 0-515-02930-0 1.45 (pbk.)
1. Bogart, Humphrey, 1899-1957.

BARBOUR, Alan G. 791.43'028'0924 B
Humphrey Bogart / by Alan G. Barbour ; general editor, Ted Sennett. New York : Galahad Books, [1974] c1973. 160 p. : ill. ; 22 cm. (The pictorial treasury of film stars) Originally published by Pyramid Publications, New York. Includes index. Bibliography: p. 140. [PN2287.B48B3 1974] 73-90216 ISBN 0-88365-163-7 : 4.95
1. Bogart, Humphrey, 1899-1957.

BENCHLEY, Nathaniel, 1915- 791.43'028'0924 B
Humphrey Bogart / Nathaniel Benchley. 1st ed. Boston : Little, Brown, [1975] 242 p. : ill. ; 25 cm. [PN2287.B48B45] 75-1384 ISBN 0-316-08886-2 : 15.00
1. Bogart, Humphrey, 1899-1957.

EYLES, Allen. 791.43'028'0924 B
Bogart / Allen Eyles. 1st ed. [New York] : Doubleday, 1975. 128 p. : ill. (some col.) ; 26 cm. (The Movie makers) Includes index. Bibliography: p. 128. [PN2287.B48E9] 74-12683 7.50
1. Bogart, Humphrey, 1899-1957.

GOODMAN, Ezra 791.430280924
Bogey: the good-bad guy. New York, Lyle Stuart [c.1965] 223p. 21cm. [PN2287.B48G6] 65-27893 4.95 bds.,
1. Bogart, Humphrey, 1899-1957. I. Title.

HYAMS, Joe 791.430280924
Bogie; the biography of Humphrey Bogart. Introd. by Lauren Bacall. [New York] New Amer. Lib. [c.1966] xii, 210p. illus., ports 22cm. [PN2287.B48H9] 66-18811 4.95
1. Bogart, Humphrey, 1899-1957 I. Title.

HYAMS, Joseph. 791.43'028'0922 B
Bogart and Bacall a love story. New York : WarnerBooks, 1976c1975 236p. : ill. 18cm. Includes index. [PN2287.B48H88] pbk. : 1.95
1. bogart, Humphrey, 1899-1957. 2. bacall,Lauren, 1924- I. Title.
L.C. card no. of 1975 D. McKay edition:75-9842.

HYAMS, Joseph. 791.43'028'0922 B
Bogart & Bacall : a love story / Joe Hyams. New York : D. McKay, [1975] 245 p., [16] leaves of plates : ill. ; 24 cm. Includes index. [PN2287.B48H88] 75-9842 ISBN 0-679-50549-0 : 7.95
1. Bogart, Humphrey, 1899-1957. 2. Bacall, Lauren, 1924- I. Title.

HYAMS, Joseph. 791.430280924
Bogie; the biography of Humphrey Bogart. Introd. by Lauren Bacall. [New York] New American Library [1966] xii, 210 p. illus., ports. 22 cm. [PN2287.B48H9] 66-18811
1. Bogart, Humphrey, 1899-1957. I. Title.

HYAMS, Joe. 791.43'028'0922
Bogie: the biography of Humphrey Bogart. Introd. by Laureen Bacall. [New York] New American Lib. [1973? c.1966] 174 p. illus. 18 cm. (Signet, Y5404) [PN2287.B48 H9] pap., 1.25
1. Bogart, Humphrey, 1899-1957. I. Title.

Bohm von Bawerk, Eugen, Ritter, 1851-1914.

KUENNE, Robert E. 338.5'21'0924
Eugen von Bohm-Bawerk, by Robert E. Kuenne. New York, Columbia University Press, 1971. 76 p. illus. 21 cm. (Columbia essays on great economists, no. 2) Bibliography: p. 74-76. [HB539.K9] 79-142889 1.45
1. Bohm von Bawerk, Eugen, Ritter, 1851-1914. 2. Interest and usury. **BIP**

Bohme, Jakob, 1575-1624.

HARTMANN, Franz, d. 1912. 230'.092'4 B
Jacob Boehme : life and doctrines / by Franz Hartmann. 1st ed. Blauvelt, N.Y. : Steinerbooks, c1977. xii, 338 p. ; 22 cm. Published in 1891 under title: The life and doctrines of Jacob Boehme; in 1919 and in 1957 under title: Personal Christianity. Reprint of the 1891 ed. published by K. Paul, Trench, Trubner, London. Includes bibliographical references and index. [BV5095.B7H3 1977] 76-53631 ISBN 0-8334-1734-7 : 6.50
1. Bohme, Jakob, 1575-1624. I. Bohme, Jakob, 1575-1624.

LIEM, Ann. 230'.092'4
Jacob Boehme : insights into the challenge of evil / Ann Liem. Wallingford, Pa. : Pendle Hill Publications, 1977. 32 p. ; 19 cm. (Pendle Hill pamphlet ; 214 ISSN 0031-4250s) Includes bibliographical references. [BV5095.B7L53] 77-79823 ISBN 0-87574-214-9 : 0.95
1. Bohme, Jakob, 1575-1624. I. Title. **BIP**

Bohner, Olivine (Nadeau)

BOHNER, Olivine (Nadeau) 922.75952
The long long trail. Illustrated by Vance Locke. Mountain View, Calif., Pacific Press Pub. Association [1960] 167p. illus. 21cm. Autobiographical. [CT275.B5828A3] 60-10103
I. Title.

Bohr, Niels Henrik David, 1885-1962.

MOORE, Ruth E 539.70924 (B)
Niels Bohr: the man, his science, & the world they changed [by] Ruth Moore. With drawings by Sue Richert Allen. [1st ed.] New York, Knopf, 1966. xvi, 436, vii p. ports. 22 cm. [QC16.B63M6] 66-17969
1. Bohr, Niels Henrik David,1885-1962. I. Title.

NIELS Bohr; 530.0924
his life and work as seen by his friends and colleagues. Ed. by S. Rosental New York, Interscience [1968,c.1967] 355p. 23cm. (74423) [QC16B3N53] 67-31932 5.95 pap.,
1. Bohr, Niels Henrik David, 1885 1962. I. Rosental, Stefan. ed.

NIELS Bohr; 530'.0924(B)
his life and work as seen by his friends and colleagues. Ed. by S. Rozental. [1st Eng. ed.] Amsterdam, North-Holland Pub. Co.; New York, Wiley, 1967. 355p. illus., ports. 23cm. [QC16.B63N53] 67-31932 9.00 bds.,
1. Bohr, Niels Henrik David, 1885-1962. I. Rozental, Stefan, ed.
Contents omitted.

Bohr, Niels Henrik David, 1885-1962—Juvenile literature.

SILVERBERG, Robert 92
Niels Bohr; the man who mapped the atom. Philadelphia, Macrae [c.1965] 189p. port. 22cm. Bibl. [QC16.B63S5] 65-16330 3.25
1. Bohr, Niels Henrik David, 1885-1962—Juvenile literature. I. Title.

Bohrod, Aaron

BOHROD, Aaron 759.13
A decade of still life. Madison, Univ. of Wis. Pr., 1966. xiii, 298p. illus. (pt. col.) 32cm. Autobiographical. [ND237.A2B6] 66-10492 20.00
I. Title. **BIP**

Boileau-Despreaux, Nicolas, 1636-1711—Influence.

CLARK, Alexander Frederick Bruce, 1884- 809 B
Boileau and the French classical critics in England (1660-1830) by A. F. B. Clark. New York, B. Franklin [1970] xviii, 534 p. 22 cm. (Burt Franklin research and source works series, 651. Essays in literature and criticism, 111) Reprint of the 1925 ed. Bibliography: p. [507]-522. [PQ1723.C6 1970] 75-147841 ISBN 0-8337-4046-6
1. Boileau-Despreaux, Nicolas, 1636-1711—Influence. I. Title. **BIP**

Boisen, Anton Theophilus, 1876-1975.

POWELL, Robert Charles. 285'.1'0924 B
Anton T. Boisen, 1876-1965 : breaking an opening in the wall between religion and medicine / by Robert Charles Powell. [Buffalo?] : Association of Mental Health Clergy, c1976. 47 p. : ports. ; 23 cm. "A special supplement to the AMHC forum, vol. 29, no. 1, October 1976." Bibliography: p. 38-46. [BX9225.B568P68] 76-151903
1. Boisen, Anton Theophilus, 1876-1975. 2. Presbyterian Church—Clergy—Biography. 3. Chaplains, Hospital—United States—Biography. 4. Clergy—United States—Biography. I. Association of Mental Health Clergy. AMHC forum. II. Title.

Bojer, Johan, 1872-1959.

GAD, Carl, 1890- 839.8'2'372 B
Johan Bojer, the man and his works. Translated from the Norwegian by Elizabeth Jelliffe Macintire. With an introd. by Llewellyn Jones and critiques by John Galsworthy [and others] Westport, Conn., Greenwood Press [1974, c1920] 260 p. port. 22 cm. Reprint of the ed. published by Moffat, Yard, New York. [PT8950.B6Z63 1974] 73-17656 ISBN 0-8371-7263-2
1. Bojer, Johan, 1872-1959. I. Title. **BIP**

Bojnowski, Lucyan, 1868-1960.

BUCZEK, Daniel S. 282'.092'4 B
Immigrant pastor; the life of the Right Reverend Monsignor Lucyan Bojnowski of New Britain, Connecticut [by] Daniel S. Buczek. Waterbury, Conn., Heminway Corp., 1974. ix, 184 p. illus. 23 cm. Bibliography: p. 174-176. [BX4705.B5724B8] 74-81981 2.95
1. Bojnowski, Lucyan, 1868-1960. I. Title.

Bok, Edward William, 1863-1930.

BOK, Edward William, 1863-1930. 070'.92'4 B
The Americanization of Edward Bok; the autobiography of a Dutch boy fifty years after. Westport, Conn., Greenwood Press [1972, c1920] xiii, 461 p. illus. 22 cm. [PN4874.B62A4 1972] 73-137048 ISBN 0-8371-5509-6 19.25
I. Title.

MYERS, Elisabeth P. 070'.924 B
Edward Bok; young editor, by Elisabeth P. Myers. Illustrated by Shannon Sternweis. Indianapolis, Bobbs-Merrill [1967] 200 p. col. illus., col. ports. 20 cm. (Childhood of famous Americans) Concentrates on the childhood of Edward Bok who became the editor of Ladies Home Journal and the first to obtain a magazine circulation of one million copies a month. [PZ7.M9827Ed] 92 AC 68
1. Bok, Edward William, 1863-1930. I. Sternweis, Shannon, illus. II. Title.

STEINBERG, Salme Harju, 1940- 070.4'092'4 B
Reformer in the marketplace : Edward W. Bok and the Ladies' home journal / Salme Harju Steinberg. Baton Rouge : Louisiana State University Press, c1979. xix, 193 p. : port. ; 22 cm. Includes index. Bibliography: p. 179-190. [PN4874.B62S7] 78-23846 ISBN 0-8071-0398-5 : 12.95
1. Bok, Edward William, 1863-1930. 2. The Ladies' home journal. 3. Journalists—United States—Biography. I. Title. **BIP**

Boker, George Henry, 1823-1890.

BRADLEY, Edward Sculley, 1897- 812'.3 B
George Henry Boker; poet and patriot. New York, B. Blom, 1972. xi, 361 p. illus. 26 cm. Reprint of the 1927 ed. Bibliography: p. 343-355. [PS1106.B7 1972] 68-57753 12.50
1. Boker, George Henry, 1823-1890.

BRADLEY, Edward Sculley, 1897- 811'.3 B
George Henry Boker, poet and patriot. New York, AMS Press [1969] xi, 361 p. illus., ports. 23 cm. Reprint of the 1927 ed. Bibliography: p. 343-355. [PS1106.B7 1967] 70-94467
1. Boker, George Henry, 1823-1890. **BIP**

Boland, Joseph M.

BOLAND, Peg, ed. 927.9633
Joe Boland, Notre Dame man. [Hammond, Ind., NSP Pub. Co., 1962] 180p. illus. 22cm. 'The Joe Boland story as told by his wife, friends, and associates. [GV939.B6B6] 62-52737
1. Boland, Joseph M. I. Title.

Bolden, Buddy, 1877-1931.

MARQUIS, Donald M., 1933- 785.4'2'0924 B
In search of Buddy Bolden, first man of jazz / Donald M. Marquis. Baton Rouge : Louisiana State University Press, c1978. xix, 176 p., [12] leaves of plates : ill. ; 24 cm. Includes index. Bibliography: p. 153-170. [ML419.B65M4] 77-10958 ISBN 0-8071-0376-4 : 9.95
1. Bolden, Buddy, 1877-1931. 2. Jazz musicians—Louisiana—New Orleans—Biography. I. Title.

Boldt, Steven.

BOLDT, Steven. 301.41'57
Static creation : a metaphor of metamorphosing lust / by Steven Boldt. 1st ed. Ithaca, N.Y. : Static Creation Press, 1978. 289 p. ; 28 cm. [HQ75.8.B65A37] 78-63615 ISBN 0-932736-00-9 pbk. : 7.95
1. Boldt, Steven. 2. Homosexuals, Male—United States—Biography. I. Title.

Bolingbroke, Henry Saint-John, 1st Viscount, 1678-1751.

BIDDLE, Sheila. 942.06'9'0922
Bolingbroke and Harley. [1st ed.] New York, Knopf, [distributed by Random House] 1974. 307, xv p. 22 cm. Bibliography: p. [295]-307. [DA501.B6B52 1974] 73-20749 ISBN 0-394-46974-7
1. Bolingbroke, Henry Saint-John, 1st Viscount, 1678-1751. 2. Oxford, Robert Harley, 1st Earl of, 1661-1724. I. Title. **BIP**

KRAMNICK, Isaac. 942.07'1
Bolingbroke and his circle; the politics of nostalgia in the age of Walpole. Cambridge, Mass., Harvard University Press, 1968. xiii, 321 p. port. 24 cm. (Harvard political studies) Bibliographical references included in "Notes" (p. 269-313) [DA501.B6K7 1968] 68-15639
1. Bolingbroke, Henry Saint-John, 1st viscount, 1678-1751. I. Title. II. Series.

SICHEL, Walter Sydney, 1855-1933. 942.06'9'0924 B
Bolingbroke and his times. New York, Greenwood Press, 1968. 2 v. illus., ports. 23 cm. Vol. 2 has title: Bolingbroke and his times; the sequel. Reprint of the 1901-02 ed. Bibliographical footnotes. [DA501.B6S63] 68-31003
1. Bolingbroke, Henry Saint-John, 1st Viscount, 1678-1751. I. Title.

SICHEL, Walter Sydney, 1855-1933. 942'.06'90924 B
Bolingbroke and his times. New York, Haskell House, 1968. 2 v. ports. 24 cm. "Haskell House catalogue item #170." Reprint of the 1901-1902 ed. Vol. 2 has subtitle: The sequel. Contents.Contents.—v. 1. [Period I. The reign of Queen Anne] —v. 2. [Period II. March 1715-December 1715] Bibliography: v. 2, p. 456-457. [DA501.B6S62] 68-25265
1. Bolingbroke, Henry Saint-John, 1st Viscount, 1678-1751. 2. Luxborough, Henrietta (Saint-John) Knight, Lady, d. 1756. I. Title. **BIP**

Bolivar, Simon, 1783-1830.

BOLIVAR, Simon, 1783-1830. 980.02'0924 B
The liberator Simon Bolivar, man and image. Edited with an introd. by David Bushnell. New York, Knopf [1970] xxxiv, 218 p. map, port. 20 cm. (Borzoi books on Latin America.) Bibliography: p. [212]-218. [F2235.3.A156] 74-88158
I. Bushnell, David, 1923- comp.

DEL RIO, Daniel A 980.00924 (B)
Simon Bolivar, by Daniel A. del Rio. [New York] Bolivarian Society of the United States, 1965. x, 148 p. illus., map. 21 cm. Bibliography: p. 147-148. [F2235.3.D38] 66-7475
1. Bolivar, Simon, 1783-1830. I. Title.

FRANK, Waldo David, 1889- 923.28
Birth of a world: Bolivar in terms of his peoples. Boston, Houghton Mifflin, 1951. xvi, 432 p. illus., ports., maps. 24 cm. Bibliography: p. 415-425. [F2235.3.F75] 51-12909
1. Bolivar, Simon, 1783-1830. I. Title.

JOHNSON, John J., 1912- 980'.02'0924
Simon Bolivar and Spanish American independence, 1783-1830 [by] John J. Johnson, with the collaboration of Doris M. Ladd. Princeton, N.J., Van Nostrand [1968] 223 p. map. 19 cm. (An Anvil original, 95) Bibliography: p. 218-222. [F2235.3.J72] 68-1890
1. Bolivar, Simon, 1783-1830. 2. South America—History—Wars of Independence, 1806-1830. I. Ladd, Doris M. II. Title.

MADARIAGA, Salvador de, 1886- 370.11
Bolivar. Coral Gables, Fla., University of Miami Press [1967, c1952] xix, 711 p. illus., maps (on lining papers), ports. 24 cm. Bibliography: p. 653-656. [F2235.3.M163 1967] 67-28273
1. Bolivar, Simon, 1783-1830. **BIP**

MADARIAGA, Salvador de, 1886- 980'.02'0924 B
Bolivar / by Salvador de Madariaga. Westport, Conn. : Greenwood Press, [1979] c1952. p. cm. Reprint of the ed. published by Pellegrini & Cudahy, New York. Includes indexes. Bibliography: p. [F2235.3.M163 1979] 79-16763 ISBN 0-313-22029-8 : 39.75
1. Bolivar, Simon, 1783-1830. 2. Heads of state—South America—Biography. 3. South America—History—Wars of Independence, 1806-1830.

MASUR, Gerhard, 1901- 980'.02'0924 B
Simon Bolivar. [Rev. ed.] Albuquerque, University of New Mexico Press [1969] xiv, 572 p. maps. 25 cm. Bibliography: p. 545-562. [F2235.3.M39 1969] 68-56230 15.00
1. Bolivar, Simon, 1783-1830.

SYME, Ronald, 1910- 980'.02'0924 B
Bolivar, the liberator. Illustrated by William Stobbs. New York, Morrow [1968] 190, [2] p. illus. 21 cm. Bibliography: p. [191] A biography of the man who devoted his life to liberating South America and who, at the peak of his career, was president of five South American countries. [F2235.3.S97] 92 AC 68
1. Bolivar, Simon, 1783-1830. I. Stobbs, William, illus. II. Title.

WHITRIDGE, Arnold, 1891- 923.28
Simon Bolivar, the great liberator; illustrated by Dirk Gringhuis. New York, Random House [1954] 180 p. illus. 22 cm. (World landmark books, W-14) [F2235.3.W5] 54-9403
1. Bolivar, Simon, 1783-1830.

WORCESTER, Donald Emmet, 1915- 980'.02'0924 B
Bolivar / Donald E. Worcester. 1st ed. Boston : Little, Brown, c1977. viii, 243 p. ; 21 cm. (The Library of world biography) Includes index. Bibliography: p. [236]. [F2235.3.W67] 76-56616 ISBN 0-316-95390-3 : 8.95
1. Bolivar, Simon, 1783-1830. 2. Heads of state—South America—Biography. 3. South America—History—Wars of Independence, 1806-1830. **BIP**

YOUNG, Bob, 1916- 980'.02'0924 B
Simon Bolivar; the George Washington of South America, by Bob and Jan Young. Illustrated by Don Lambo. [1st ed.] New York, Hawthorn Books [1968] 176 p. illus. 22 cm. Bibliography: p. 169-170. A biography of the man who, enraged by Spain's oppression of the South American countries, vowed to liberate them and spent the rest of his life struggling to fulfill this vow. [F2235.3.Y6] 92 AC 68
1. Bolivar, Simon, 1783-1830. I. Young, Jan, 1919- joint author. II. Lambo, Don, illus. III. Title.

Bolivar, Simon, 1783-1830—Juvenile literature.

RINK, Paul, 1912- 980'.02'0924 B
Quest for freedom; Bolivar and the South American Revolution. Maps and drawings by Barry Martin. New York, J. Messner [1968] 188 p. illus., map. 22 cm. ([Milestones in history]) Bibliography: p. [183] [F2235.3.R565] 68-25100 3.95
1. Bolivar, Simon, 1783-1830—Juvenile literature. I. Title.

SYME, Ronald, 1910- 92 (J)
Bolivar, the liberator. Illustrated by William Stobbs. New York, Morrow [1968] 190, [2] p. illus. 21 cm. Bibliography: p. [191] [F2235.3.S97] 68-16497 3.50
1. Bolivar, Simon, 1783-1830—Juvenile literature. I. Title.

WEBB, Robert N 980.0924 (B)
Simon Bolivar, the liberator, by Robert N. Webb. New York, F. Watts [1966] 133 p. 22 cm. (Immortals of history) [F2235.3.W4] 66-12146
1. Bolivar, Simon, 1783-1830 — Juvenile literature. I. Title.

YOUNG, Bob, 1916- 980'.02'0924 B
Simon Bolivar, the George Washington of South America, by Bob and Jan Young. Illustrated by Don Lambo. [1st ed.] New York, Hawthorn Books [1968] 176 p. illus. 22 cm. Bibliography: p. 169-170. [F2235.3.Y6] 68-13200
1. Bolivar, Simon, 1783-1830—Juvenile literature. I. Young, Jan, 1919- joint author.

Bolivia—History—1938-

JAMES, Daniel, comp. 984'.05'0922
The complete Bolivian diaries of Che Guevara, and other captured documents. Edited and with an introd. by Daniel James. New York, Stein and Day [1968] 330 p. illus., facsims., maps, ports. 21 cm. Contents.Contents.—Chronology of the Bolivian campaign.—Che Guevara's diary.—Rolando's diary.—Pombo's diary.—Braulio's diary.—Appendices (p. 323-330) :1. A list of the querrilla forces.—2. Others mentioned in the diaries. Bibliographical footnotes. [F3326.J3] 68-55642 6.95
1. Bolivia—History—1938- 2. Guerrillas—Bolivia. 3. Subversive activities—Bolivia. I. Guevara, Ernesto, 1928-1967. II. Title.

Bollani, Domenico, 1513-1579.

CAIRNS, Christopher. 189.4
Domenico Bollani, Bishop of Brescia : devotion to church and state in the republic of Venice in the sixteenth century / by Christopher Cairns. Nieuwkoop : De Graaf, 1976. 302 p., [15] leaves of plates : ill. ; 25 cm. (Bibliotheca humanistica et reformatorica ; v. 15) Dutch or Italian. Includes index. Bibliography: p. 278-294. [BX4705.B5754C34] 76-483172 ISBN 9-06-004346-4 : fl 95.00
1. Bollani, Domenico, 1513-1579. 2. Catholic Church—Bishops—Biography. 3. Bishops—Italy—Brescia (Diocese)—Biography. 4. Church and state in Venice. I. Title. II. Series.

Bollinger, James.

SCHOEN, Elin. 301.45'19'6073077389 B
Tales of an all-night town / by Elin Schoen. 1st ed. New York : Harcourt Brace Jovanovich, c1979. 222 p. ; 22 cm. [F549.B88B647] 79-1841 ISBN 0-15-184993-5 : 9.95
1. Bollinger, James. 2. Brooklyn, Ill.—Race relations. 3. East St. Louis, Ill.—Race relations. 4. Crime and criminals—Illinois—Brooklyn. 5. Crime and criminals—Illinois—East. St. Louis. 6. Afro-Americans—Illinois—Brooklyn—Biography. 7. Afro-Americans—Illinois—East. St. Louis—Biography. I. Title. **BIP**

Bologne, Jean de, 1524-1608.

HOLDERBAUM, James. 730'.92'4
The sculptor Giovanni Bologna / James Holderbaum. New York : Garland Pub., 1977. p. cm. (Outstanding dissertations in the fine arts) Originally presented as the author's thesis, Harvard, 1959. Bibliography: p. [NB623.B7H64 1977] 76-23626 ISBN 0-8240-2696-9 lib.bdg. : 46.00
1. Bologne, Jean de, 1524-1608. 2. Sculptors—Italy—Biography. I. Title. II. Series. **BIP**

Bolotowsky, Ilya, 1907-

BOLOTOWSKY, Ilya, 1907- 759.13
Ilya Bolotowsky : the Solomon R. Guggenheim Museum, New York. New York : Solomon R. Guggenheim Foundation, 1974. 133 p. : ill. (some col.) ; 26 cm. "Exhibition 74/5." Bibliography: p. 132-133. [ND237.B725S64] 74-14271 pbk. : 6.95
1. Bolotowsky, Ilya, 1907- I. Solomon R. Guggenheim Museum, New York.

Bolster, Alice (Landon).

BOLSTER, Alice (Landon). 920.7
True adventures of a little country girl; an autobiographical narrative. With 4 illus. by Henry Merchant. New York, Vantage Press [1950] 96 p. illus. 23 cm. [CT275.B58315A3] 50-58332
I. Title.

Bolte, Henry Edward, Sir, 1908-

BLAZEY, Peter Bradford, 1939- 329'.0092'4 B
Bolte: a political biography [by] Peter Blazey. Milton, Q., Jacaranda, 1972. x, 251 p. plates, tables. 22 cm. Bibliographical notes: p. 246-248. [DU222.B6B55] 73-167071 ISBN 0-7016-0618-5 5.95
1. Bolte, Henry Edward, Sir, 1908-

MUIR, Barry. 329.9'945 B
Bolte from Bamganie. Melbourne, Hill of Content, 1973. xvi, 214 p. ill. 25 cm. [DU222.B6M84] 74-174750 ISBN 0-85572-054-9 5.95
1. Bolte, Henry Edward, Sir, 1908- 2. Victoria, Australia—Politics and government. I. Title.

Bolton, Frances Payne (Bingham) 1885-

LOTH, David Goldsmith, 1899- 923.278
A long way forward; the biography of Congresswoman Frances P. Bolton. [1st ed.] New York, Longmans, Green, 1957. 302p. illus. 22cm. [E748.B68L6] 57-7088
1. Bolton, Frances Payne (Bingham) 1885- I. Title.

LOTH, David Goldsmith, 1899- 923.273
A long way forward; the biography of Congresswoman Frances P. Bolton. [1st ed.] New York, Longmans, Green, 1957. 302p. illus. 22cm. [E748.B68L6] 57-7088
1. Bolton, Frances Payne (Bingham) 1885- I. Title.

Bolton, Herbert Eugene, 1870-1953.

BANNON, John Francis, 1905- 978'.007'2024 B
Herbert Eugene Bolton : the historian and the man, 1870-1953 / John Francis Bannon. Tucson : University of Arizona Press, c1977. p. cm. Includes index. Bibliography: p. [E175.B65B36] 77-20951 ISBN 0-8165-0557-8 : 13.50 pbk. : 7.50
1. Bolton, Herbert Eugene, 1870-1953. 2. Historians—United States—Biography. **BIP**

CLARK, Robert Carlton, 1877-1939. 976.4'02
The beginnings of Texas, 1684-1718 / by Robert Carlton Clark ; with the addition of Notes on Clark's "The beginnings of Texas" / by Herbert E. Bolton ; and Letter of Fray Damian Massanet to Don Carlos de Siguenza on the discovery of the Bay of Espiritu Santo. Philadelphia : Porcupine Press, 1976. 94, [34] p. : maps ; 22 cm. (Perspectives in American history; no. 25) Reprint of the 1907 ed. which was issued as no. 98 of the Bulletin of the University of Texas, Humanistic series no. 6; with additions reprinted from the Quarterly of the Texas State Historical Association, v. 12, p. 148-158, and v. 2, p. 281-312, respectively. Includes bibliographical references. [F389.C59 1976] 76-11795 ISBN 0-87991-349-5 : 12.50
1. Bolton, Herbert Eugene, 1870-1953. Notes on Clark's "The beginnings of Texas." 2. Siguenza y Gongora, Carlos de, 1645-1700. 3. Texas—History—To 1846. 4. Espiritu Santo Bay region, Tex.—Discovery and exploration. I. Bolton, Herbert Eugene, 1870-1953. Notes on Clark's "The beginnings of Texas." 1976. II. Title. III. Series: Texas. University. Humanistic series ; no. 6. IV. Series: Perspectives in American history (Philadelphia) ; no. 25.

Bolton, Herbert Eugene, 1870-1953—Addresses, essays, lectures.

JACOBS, Wilbur R. 973'.07'2022
Turner, Bolton, and Webb : three historians of the American frontier / Wilbur R. Jacobs, John W. Caughey, and Joe B. Frantz. Seattle : University of Washington Press, c1965, 1979 printing. xv, 113 p. : ill. ; 21 cm. "Second printing with new preface." "Lectures originally delivered at the 1963 meeting of the Western History Association." Includes bibliographies and index. [E175.45.J3 1965b] 79-129116 ISBN 0-295-95677-1 pbk. : 4.95
1. Turner, Frederick Jackson, 1861-1932—Addresses, essays, lectures. 2. Bolton, Herbert Eugene, 1870-1953—Addresses, essays, lectures. 3. Webb, Walter Prescott, 1888-1963—Addresses, essays, lectures. 4. Historians—United States—Biography—Addresses, essays, lectures. 5. The West—Historiography—Addresses, essays, lectures. I. Caughey, John Walton, 1902- joint author. II. Frantz, Joe Bertram, 1917- joint author. III. Title. **BIP**

Bolz, Frank, 1930-

BOLZ, Frank, 1930- 363.2'32
Hostage cop : the story of the New York City Police Hostage Negotiating Team and the man who leads it / by Frank Bolz and Edward Hershey. New York : Rawson, Wade, c1979. p. cm. [HV7911.B64A34 1979] 79-64199 ISBN 0-89256-102-5 : 10.95
1. Bolz, Frank, 1930- 2. New York (City). Police Dept. Hostage Negotiating Team. 3. Police—New York (City)—Biography. I. Hershey, Edward, joint author. II. Title.

Bombard, Alain—Juvenile literature.

GARIBALDI, Gerald. 910'.92'4 B
He gave himself to the sea / Gerald Garibaldi ; ill., Ken Bachaus. Milwaukee : Raintree Publishers, c1980. p. cm. An account of the actual adventure of a French doctor who crossed the Atlantic on a rubber raft and without provisions. [G530.B676G37] 79-21326 ISBN 0-8172-1561-1 (lib. bdg.) : 7.99
1. Bombard, Alain—Juvenile literature. 2. Survival (after airplane accidents, shipwrecks, etc.)—Juvenile literature. 3. Adventure and adventurers—France—Biography—Juvenile literature. 4. Atlantic Ocean—Juvenile literature. I. Bachaus, Ken. II. Title. **BIP**

Bon Viso, Peter John.

WILLWERTH, James. 363.2'092'4 B
Badge of madness : the true story of Patrolman Pete Bon Viso / James Willwerth. New York : M. Evans ; Philadelphia : distributed in the U.S. by Lippincott, c1977. p. cm. [HV7911.B654W54] 76-56363 ISBN 0-87131-230-1 : 7.95
1. Bon Viso, Peter John. 2. Police—New York (City) 3. Paranoia. I. Title.

Bonaparte family.

DELDERFIELD, Ronald 940.270922
Frederick, 1912-
The golden millstones: Napoleon's brothers and sisters. New York, Harper [1965, c.1964] ix, 246p. ports. 22cm. [DC216.D4] 64-25114 4.95
1. Bonaparte family. I. Title. II. Title: Napoleon's brothers and sisters.

Bonaparte, Francois Charles Joseph, Herzog von Reichstadt, called Napoleon II, 1811-1832.

CASTELOT, Andre. 923.244
King of Rome; a biography of Napoleon's tragic son. Translated from the French by Robert Baldick. [1st ed.] New York, Harper [1960] 396 p. illus. 22 cm. Translation of L'aiglon Napoleon deux. [DC216.3.C363] 59-10574
1. Bonaparte, Francois Charles Joseph, Herzog von Reichstadt, called Napoleon II, 1811-1832. I. Title.

CASTELOT, Andre. 944.06'092'4 B
King of Rome; a biography of Napoleon's tragic son. Translated from the French by Robert Baldick. Westport, Conn., Greenwood Press [1974, c1960] xii, 396 p. illus. 22 cm. Translation of L'aiglon, Napoleon deux. Reprint of the ed. published by Harper, New York. [DC216.3.C363 1974] 74-6778 ISBN 0-8371-7571-2
1. Bonaparte, Francois Charles Joseph, Herzog von Reichstadt, called Napoleon II, 1811-1832. I. Title.

CASTELOT, Andre 923.244
Napoleon's son. Tr. from French by Robert Baldick. London, H. Hamilton [Mystic, Conn., Verry, 1966, c.1959, 1960] 91p. illus. 23cm. [DC216.3.C363] 61-4345 6.00
1. Bonaparte, Francois Charles Joseph, Herzog von Reichstadt, called Napoleon II, 1811-1832. I. Title.

Bonaparte, Maria Letizia (Ramolino) 1750-1836.

STIRLING, Monica, 1916- 920.7
Madame Letizia; a portrait of Napoleon's mother, by Monica Sterling [sic. 1st American ed.] New York, Harper [1962, c1961] 319 p. illus. 22 cm. Published in London in 1961 under title: A pride of lions. Includes bibliography. [DC216.9.S75 1962] 62-7915
1. Bonaparte, Maria Letizia (Ramolino) 1750-1836. I. Title.

Bonaventura, Saint, Cardinal, 1221-1274.

QUINN, Mary Bernetta. 922.245
To God alone the glory; a life of St. Bonaventure. Westminster, Md., Newman Press, 1962. ix, 281 p. 23 cm. Bibliography: p. 265-281. [BX4700.B68Q5] 62-21499
1. Bonaventura, Saint, Cardinal, 1221-1274. I. Title.

Bond family.

WILLIAMS, Roger 917.3'03'80922 B
M., 1934-
The Bonds; an American family [by] Roger M. Williams. [1st ed.] New York, Atheneum, 1971. xvi, 301 p. 25 cm. Bibliography: p. [283]-284. [E185.97.B75W5 1971] 74-165208 10.00
1. Bond family. 2. Bond, Julian, 1940- I. Title.

Bond, J. T., 1866-1947.

BAIRD, Josie. 923.973
Tom Bond brong-buster, cow-poke, and trail driver, illustrated by Delila Baird. Sweetwater, Tex., Printed by Watson-Focht Co. [1960] 135p. illus. 22cm. [F596.B64B3] 60-15708
1. Bond, J. T., 1866-1947. 2. Fronter and pioneer life—The West. 3. Ranch life. 4. Cowboys. I. Title.

Bond, Julian, 1940-

NEARY, John, 1937- 328.758'0924 B
Julian Bond: Black rebel. New York, Morrow, 1971. 256 p. 22 cm. [F291.3.B65N4] 71-142398 5.95
1. Bond, Julian, 1940- I. Title.

Bond, Marshall, 1867-1941.

BOND, Marshall. 622'.342 B
Gold hunter; the adventures of Marshall Bond. [1st ed. Albuquerque] University of New Mexico Press [1969] x, 258 p. illus., facsims., ports. 22 cm. [TN140.B56B6] 68-56231 8.50
1. Bond, Marshall, 1867-1941. I. Title. **BIP**

Bond, Scott,

RUDD, Daniel Arthur, 650'.0924
1854-
From slavery to wealth; the life of Scott Bond, by Daniel A. Rudd and Theophilus Bond. Freeport, N.Y., Books for Libraries Press, 1971. 383 p. illus. 23 cm. (The Black heritage library collection) Reprint of the 1917 ed. [E185.97.B7R8 1971] 73-173615 ISBN 0-8369-8907-4
1. Bond, Scott, I. Bond, Theophilius, 1879- joint author. II. Title. III. Series. **BIP**

Bond, Willard Faroe,

BOND, Willard Faroe, 923.773
1876-
I had a friend, an autobiography. [Jackson? Miss., 1958] 268p. illus. 24cm. [F341.B77] 58-33882
I. Title.

Bonds, Bobby, 1946- —Juvenile literature.

SULLIVAN, George, 796.357'092'4 B
1927-
Bobby Bonds, rising superstar / by George Sullivan. New York : Putnam, c1976. 126 p. ; 21 cm. (Putnam sports shelf) Includes index. A biography of the star Yankee outfielder who has won the Golden Glove award for his fielding. [GV865.B64S84] 92 75-45427 ISBN 0-399-20511-X. lib. bdg. : 5.29
1. Bonds, Bobby, 1946- —Juvenile literature. 2. Baseball—Juvenile literature. I. Title.

Bong, Richard Ira, 1920-1945.

KENNEY, General George 923.573
Churchill, 1889-
Dick Bong, ace of aces. New York, Duell, Sloan and Pearce [c.1960] 116p. illus. 22cm. 60-12832 2.95
1. Bong, Richard Ira, 1920-1945. I. Title.

KENNEY, George Churchill, 923.573
1889-
Dick Bong, ace of aces. [1st ed.] New York, Duell, Sloan and Pearce [1960] 116p. illus. 22cm. [E745.B6K4] 60-12832
1. Bong, Richard Ira, 1920-1945. I. Title.

Bonheur, Rosa, 1822-1899.

PEARE, Catherine Owens. 759.4
Rosa Bonheur, her life Illustrated by Margaret Ayer. [1st ed.] New York, Holt [1956] 126p. illus. 21cm. [Holt books for young people] [ND553.B6P35] 927.5 56-10035
1. Bonheur, Rosa, 1822-1899. I. Title.

PEARE, Catherine Owens. 759.4
Rosa Bonheur, her life. Illustrated by Margaret Ayer. [1st ed.] New York, Holt [1956] 126p. illus. 21cm. [Holt books for young people] [ND553.B6P35] [ND553.B6P35] 927.5 56-10035 56-10035
1. Bonheur, Rosa, 1822-1899. I. Title.

STANTON, Theodore, 1851- 759.4 B
1925, ed.
Reminiscences of Rosa Bonheur / edited by Theodore Stanton. New York : Hacker Art Books, 1976. xvii, 413 p., [23] leaves of plates : ill. ; 25 cm. Reprint of the 1910 ed. published by D. Appleton, New York. Includes indexes. [ND553.B6S8 1976] 74-147039 ISBN 0-87817-096-0 : 30.00
1. Bonheur, Rosa, 1822-1899. 2. Painters—France—Biography. I. Title. **BIP**

Bonheur, Rosa, 1822-1899—Juvenile literature.

PRICE, Olive M. 759.4
Rosa Bonheur, painter of animals, by Olive Price. Illustrated by Cary. Champaign, Ill., Garrard Pub. Co. [1972] 144 p. illus. 22 cm. A biography of a nineteenth-century French artist acclaimed internationally during her lifetime for her realistic animal paintings. [ND553.B6P74] 92 71-190739 ISBN 0-8116-4515-0
1. Bonheur, Rosa, 1822-1899—Juvenile literature. I. Cary, Louis F., 1915- illus. II. Title.

Bonhoeffer, Dietrich, 1906-1945.

BETHGE, Eberhard, 284'.1'0924 B
1909-
Dietrich Bonhoeffer; man of vision, man of courage. Translated from the German by Eric Mosbacher [and others] under the editorship of Edwin Robertson. New York, Harper & Row, 1970. xxiv, 867 p. illus., facsims., ports. 25 cm. [BX4827.B57B43] 70-109075 17.95
1. Bonhoeffer, Dietrich, 1906-1945. I. Title.

BONHOEFFER, Dietrich, 284'.10924
1906-1945.
Letters and papers from prison. Edited by Eberhard Bethge. Rev. ed. New York, Macmillan [1967] 240 p. illus., ports. 22 cm. Translation of Widerstand und Ergebung. [BX4827.B57A43] 67-19951
I. Title. **BIP**

BONHOEFFER, 230'.092'4 B
Dietrich, 1906-1945.
Letters and papers from prison. Edited by Eberhard Bethge. Rev. ed. New York, Macmillan [1967] 240 p. illus., ports. 22 cm. Translation of Widerstand und Ergebung. [BX4827.B57A43 1967a] 67-19951
I. Title.

BONHOEFFER, 230'.092'4 B
Dietrich, 1906-1945.
Letters and papers from prison. Edited by Eberhard Bethge. [1st American] enl. ed. New York, Macmillan [1972, c1971] x, 437 p. maps. 22 cm. Translation of Widerstand und Ergebung. [BX4827.B57A43 1972] 78-184531
I. Title.

BOSANQUET, Mary. 284'.1'0924 B
The life and death of Dietrich Bonhoeffer. [1st ed.] New York, Harper & Row [1969, c1968] 287 p. illus., ports. 22 cm. Bibliographical footnotes. [BX4827.B57B6] 69-17003 5.95
1. Bonhoeffer, Dietrich, 1906-1945. I. Title.

BOSANQUET, Mary. 284'.1'0924 [B]
The life and death of Dietrich Bonhoeffer. New York, Harper [1973, c.1968] 287 p. illus., ports. 21 cm. (Colophon Books, CN294) Bibliographical footnotes. [BX4827.B57B6] 68-17003 ISBN 0-06-090294-9 2.95 (pbk.)
1. Bonhoeffer, Dietrich, 1906-1945. I. Title.

GILL, Theodore 248'.1'0924 B
Alexander, 1920-
Memo for a movie: a short life of Dietrich Bonhoeffer [by] Theodore A. Gill. New York, Macmillan [1971] vi, 268 p. 21 cm. Includes bibliographical references. [BX4827.B57G5] 71-80301
1. Bonhoeffer, Dietrich, 1906-1945. I. Title.

GODDARD, Donald. 230'.092'4 B
The last days of Dietrich Bonhoeffer / Donald Goddard. 1st ed. New York : Harper & Row, c1976. 245 p. ; 24 cm. [BX4827.B57G58 1976] 75-25106 ISBN 0-06-011564-5 : 12.50
1. Bonhoeffer, Dietrich, 1906-1945. I. Title. **BIP**

KUHNS, William. 284'.1'0924
In pursuit of Dietrich Bonhoeffer. With a foreword by Eberhard Bethge. Dayton, Ohio, Pflaum Press, 1967. xiii, 314 p. port. 22 cm. Bibliography: p. [287]-297. [BX4827.B59K8] 67-29763
1. Bonhoeffer, Dietrich, 1906-1945. I. Title.

MARLE, Rene. 230.4'1'0924
Bonhoeffer; the man and his work. Translated by Rosemary Sheed. New York, Newman Press [1968] 141 p. 22 cm. Translation of Dietrich Bonhoeffer. Temoin de Jesus-Christ parmi ses freres. Bibliographical footnotes. [BX4827.B57M33] 68-8395 4.50
1. Bonhoeffer, Dietrich, 1906-1945.

REIST, Benjamin A. 230.4'1'0924
The promise of Bonhoeffer, by Benjamin A. Reist. [1st ed.] Philadelphia, Lippincott [1969] 128 p. 21 cm. (The Promise of theology) Bibliographical references included in "Notes" (p. 122-126) Bibliography: p. 127-128. [BX4827.B57R4] 75-86077 3.50
1. Bonhoeffer, Dietrich, 1906-1945. I. Title.

ROBERTSON, Edwin 230.410924
Hanton.
Dietrich Bonhoeffer, by E. H. Robertson. Richmond, John Knox Press [1966] ix, 54 p. 19 cm. (Makers of contemporary theology) [BX8080.B645R6 1966a] 66-15514
1. Bonhoeffer, Dietrich, 1906-1945. **BIP**

ZIMMERMANN, Wolf 284'.10924
Dieter, 1911- ed.
I knew Dietrich Bonhoeffer. Edited by Wolf-Dieter Zimmermann and Ronald Gregor Smith. Translated from the German by Kathe Gregor Smith. [1st ed.] New York, Harper & Row [1967, c1966] 238 p. illus., ports. 22 cm. Translation of Begegnungen mit Dietrich Bonhoeffer. [BX4827.B59Z513 1967] 67-11502
1. Bonhoeffer, Dietrich, 1906-1945. I. Smith, Ronald Gregor, joint ed. II. Title. **BIP**

Bonhoeffer family.

LEIBHOLZ- 943.086'092'2 B
BONHOEFFER, Sabine, 1906-
The Bonhoeffers; portrait of a family. New York, St. Martin's Press [1972, c1971] xviii, 203 p. illus. 23 cm. Translation of Vergangen, erlebt, uberwunden. [CS629.B5813 1972] 74-183880 7.95
1. Bonhoeffer family. I. Title.

Bonifacius, originally Winfried, Saint, Abp. of Mainz, 680-755.

BONIFACIUS, 270'.2'0924 B
originally Winfried, Saint, Abp. of Mainz, 680-755.
The letters of Saint Boniface Translated with an introd. by Ephraim Emerton. New York, Octagon Books, 1973 [c1940] 204 p. 24 cm. Translation of the author's Epistolae. Reprint of the ed. published by Columbia University Press, New York, which was issued as no. 331 of Records of civilization: sources and studies. Bibliography: p. [193]-195. [BX4700.B7A43 1973] 79-147408 ISBN 0-374-92584-4 10.00
1. Bonifacius, originally Winfried, Saint, Abp. of Mainz, 680-755. I. Emerton, Ephraim, 1851-1935, tr. II. Series: Records of civilization: sources and studies, no. 331. **BIP**

†BONIFACIUS, 270.2'092'4 B
originally Winfried, Saint, Abp. of Mainz, 680-755.
The letters of Saint Boniface / translated with an introd. by Ephraim Emerton. New York : Norton, 1976, c1940. 204 p. ; 20 cm. Reprint of the ed. published by Columbia University Press, New York, which was issued as no. 31 of Records of civilization, sources and studies. Includes index. Bibliography: p. [193]-195. [BX4700.B7A413 1976] 76-18847 ISBN 0-393-09147-3 pbk. : 3.95
1. Bonifacius, originally Winfried, Saint, Abp. of Mainz, 680-755. 2. Christian saints—Germany, West—Mainz—Biography. 3. Mainz—Biography. I. Emerton, Ephraim, 1851-1935. II. Title. III. Series: Records of civilization, sources and studies ; no. 31.

ROBERTO, Brother, 1927- 92
Bring me an ax! A story of St. Boniface of Germany. Illus. by Carolyn Lee Jagodits. Notre Dame, Ind., Dujarie Press, 1964. 95 p. illus. 24 cm. [BX4700.B7R6] 65-852
1. Bonifacius, originally Winfried, Saint, Abp. of Mains, 680-755 — Juvenile literature. I. Title.

Bonifacius, originally Winfried, Saint, Abp. of Mainz, 680-755—Juvenile literature.

ROBERTO, Brother, 1927- 92
Bring me an ax! A story of St. Boniface of Germany. Illus. by Carolyn Lee Jagodits. Notre Dame, Ind. 46556, Dujarie Pr. [c.] 1964. 95p. illus. 24cm. [BX4700.B7R6] 65-852 2.25
1. Bonifacius, originally Winfried, Saint, Abp. of Mainz, 680-755—Juvenile literature. I. Title.

Bonnard, Pierre, 1867-1947.

TERRASSE, Antoine. 759.4
Bonnard; biographical and critical study. Translated from the French by Stuart Gilbert. [Geneva] Skira; [distributed in the U.S. by the World Pub. Co., Cleveland, 1964] 115 p. mounted col. illus. 19 cm. (The Taste of our time, v. 42) Bibliography: p. 103-105. [ND553.B65T423] 64-23256
1. Bonnard, Pierre, 1867-1947. I. Title.

Bonneville, Benjamin Louis Eulalie de, 1796-1878.

IRVING, Washington, 1783-1859. 917.8'04'20924
The adventures of Captain Bonneville / Washington Irving ; edited by Robert A. Rees & Alan Sandy. Boston : Twayne Publishers, 1976. p. cm. (The Complete works of Washington Irving ; v. 10) Includes bibliographical references and index. [F592.I733 1976] 76-4561 ISBN 0-8057-8508-6 lib.bdg. : 25.00
1. Bonneville, Benjamin Louis Eulalie de, 1796-1878. 2. The West—Description and travel—To 1848. 3. Northwestern States—Description and travel. I. Bonneville, Benjamin Louis Eulalie de, 1796-1878. II. Title. BIP

IRVING, Washington, 1783-1859. 917.8'04'20924
The adventures of Captain Bonneville, U.S.A., in the Rocky Mountains and the Far West, digested from his journal and illustrated from various other sources. New York, Putnam. [New York, AMS Press, 1973] 524 p. illus. 19 cm. (The works of Washington Irving, v. 3) At head of title: Hudson edition. "The author's revised edition." Reprint of the 1889 ed. [F592.I733 1973] 73-8740 ISBN 0-404-03513-2 20.00
1. Bonneville, Benjamin Louis Eulalie de, 1796-1878. 2. The West—Description and travel—To 1848. 3. Northwestern States—Description and travel. I. Bonneville, Benjamin Louis Eulalie de, 1796-1878. II. Title. BIP

Bonney, Russell N.

BONNEY, Russell N., 1910- 309.1'73'092
"Indian" : a taxpayer on the warpath / Russell N. Bonney. 1st ed. Hicksville, N.Y. : Exposition Press, c1977. 144 p. ; 22 cm. [LA2317.B556A34] 76-42855 ISBN 0-682-48678-7 : 7.00
1. Bonney, Russell N. 2. Teachers—United States—Biography. 3. Bureaucracy. 4. Taxation—United States. 5. United States—Civilization. I. Title.

Bonney, William H., 1859-1881.

BURNS, Walter Noble, 1872-1932. 923.4173
The saga of Billy the Kid. Graden City, N. Y., Doubleday, 1951 ['1926] 322 p. 22 cm. [F786.B69 1951] 51-1843
1. Bonney, William H., 1859-1881. I. Title. BIP

COE, George Washington, 1856-1941. 923.973
Frontier fighter; the autobiography of George W. Coe, who fought and rode with Billy the Kid, as related to Nan Hillary Harrison. [2d ed.] Albuquerque, University of New Mexico Press [1951] 220 p. illus. 22 cm. [F786.C65 1951] 51-5480
1. Bonney, William H., 1859-1881. I. Harrison, Nannie Hillary. II. Title.

GARRETT, Patrick Floyd, 1850-1908. 923.4173
The authentic life of Billy, the Kid, the noted desperado of the Southwest, whose deeds of daring and blood made his name a terror in New Mexico, Arizona, and northern Mexico. By Pat. F. Garrett ... by whom he was finally hunted down and captured by Killing him ... Santa Fe, New Mexican Pring0pt. and Pub. Co., 1882. Houston, Frontier Press of Texas, 1953. facsim. (137p.), [5] p. illus. 22cm. [F786.B694 1882a] 54-27872
1. Bonney, William H., 1859-1881. 2. Crime and criminals—Southwest, New. I. Title.

GARRETT, Patrick Floyd, 1850-1908. 923.4173
The authentic life of Billy the Kid, the noted desperado of the Southwest, whose deeds of daring and blood made his name a terror in New Mexico, Arizona and northern Mexico. With an introd. by J.C. Dykes. [New ed.] Norman, University of Oklahoma Press [1954] 156 p. illus. 20 cm. (The Western frontier library [v. 3]) 54-10053
1. Bonney, William H., 1859-1881. 2. Crime and criminals — Southwest, New. I. Title.

HUNT, Frazier, 1885- 923.4173
The tragic days of Billy the Kid. Maps by Robert N. Mullin. New York, Hastings House [1956] 316p. illus. 21cm. [F786.B695] 56-8120
1. Bonney, William H., 1839-1881. I. Title.

SONNICHSEN, Charles Leland, 1901- 923.973
Alias Billy the Kid.'... I want to die a free man ...' [By] C. L. Sonnichsen [and] William V. Morrison. Albuquerque, University of New Mexico Press, 1955. xi, 136p. illus., ports. 24cm. [F786.B72] 55-5452
1. Bonney, William H., 1859-1881. 2. Roberts, William Henry, 1859-1950. I. Morrison, William Vincent, 1906- joint author. II. Title.

SPIEGELBERG, Flora (Langerman) v. 12
Billy the Kid, the cowboy outlaw; an incident recalled by Flora Spiegelberg. Edited by Floyd S. Fierman and John O. West. [Philadelphia, Press of M. Jacobs, c1965] 98-106 p. 23 cm. Cover title. "Reprinted from American Jewish historical quarterly, vol. LV, no. 1, September, 1965." 66-40735
1. Bonney, William H., 1859-1881. I. Fierman, Floyd S., ed. II. West, John Oliver, 1925- ed. III. Title.

Bono, Sonny—Juvenile literature.

BRAUN, Thomas, 1944- 784'.092'2 B
Sonny and Cher / by Thomas Braun ; designed by Mark Lankamer. Mankato, Minn. : Creative Education, c1978. 31 p. : ill. ; 25 cm. Relates the rise from poverty to television stardom of singers Sonny and Cher. [ML3930.B593B7] 920 77-24706 ISBN 0-87191-620-7 : 4.95
1. Bono, Sonny—Juvenile literature. 2. Cher, 1946- —Juvenile literature. 3. Singers—United States—Biography—Juvenile literature. I. Title. BIP

Bonomo, Joe,

BONOMO, Joe, 1901- 791.43'0924 B
The strongman; a true life, pictorial autobiography of the Hercules of the screen, Joe Bonomo. [New York, Bonomo Studios, 1968] 352 p. illus., ports. 28 cm. [PN2287.B486A3] 79-559 3.95
I. Title.

Bonora, Matt.

FLUSSER, Martin. 364.12'092'4 B
The squeal man : the true story of Matt Bonora, suburban homicide detective / Martin Flusser. New York : Morrow, 1977. 251 p. ; 22 cm. [HV7911.B656F56] 77-1768 ISBN 0-688-03193-5 : 8.95
1. Bonora, Matt. 2. Detectives—New York (State)—Nassau Co.—Biography. 3. Homicide investigation—New York (State)—Nassau Co. I. Title.

Bonsack, Charles Daniel, 1870-1953.

MINNICH, H Spenser. 922.673
Brother Bonsack. Illus. by Daulat Daniel Chauhan. Elgin, Ill., Brethren Pub. House [1954] 118p. illus. 20cm. [BX7843.B6M5] 55-16553
1. Bonsack, Charles Daniel, 1870-1953. I. Title.

Bonta, Marcia, 1940-

BONTA, Marcia, 1940- 974.8'53'040922 B
Escape to the mountain : a family's adventures in the wilderness. South Brunswick [N.J.] : A. S. Barnes, c1979. p. cm. [F157.C3B662] 78-75299 ISBN 0-498-02365-6 : 9.95
1. Bonta, Marcia, 1940- 2. Bonta, Bruce. 3. Mountain life—Pennsylvania—Centre Co. 4. Natural history—Pennsylvania—Centre Co. 5. Centre Co., Pa.—Biography. I. Title. BIP

Bonzel, Maria Theresia, Mother, 1830-1905.

HARDICK, Lothar. 271'.973'024 B
He leads, I follow; the life of Mother Maria Theresia Bonzel, foundress of the Sisters of St. Francis of Perpetual Adoration. Translated from the German by M. Honora Hau and M. Clarahilda Fischer. Colorado Springs, Sisters of St. Francis of Perpetual Adoration [1971] xi, 344 p. port. 23 cm. [BX4519.Z8H37] 72-177750 8.50
1. Bonzel, Maria Theresia, Mother, 1830-1905. 2. Sisters of the Third order of St. Francis of the Perpetual Adoration. I. Title.

Book collectors—Biography.

ELTON, Charles Isaac, 1839-1900. 020'.75
The great book-collectors, by Charles Isaac Elton & Mary Augusta Elton. Freeport, N.Y., Books for Libraries Press [1972] p. Reprint of the 1893 ed., issued in series: Books about books. [Z989.A1E45 1972] 72-8693 ISBN 0-8369-6972-3
1. Book collectors—Biography. 2. Book collecting—History. I. Elton, Mary Augusta (Strachey) 1838-1914, joint author. II. Title. BIP

Book collectors—United States.

CANNON, Carl Leslie, 1888- 020'.75'0922 B
American book collectors and collecting from colonial times to the present / by Carl L. Cannon. Westport, Conn. : Greenwood Press, 1976, c1941. xi, 391 p. ; 24 cm. Reprint of the ed. published by H. W. Wilson Co., New York. Includes index. [Z989.A1C36 1976] 76-6149 ISBN 0-8371-8841-5 lib.bdg. : 24.00
1. Book collectors—United States. I. Title. BIP

Book design—Addresses, essays, lectures.

SALTER, Stefan. 655.5'3'0924 B
From cover to cover. Englewood Cliffs, N.J., Prentice-Hall [1969] 270 p. 22 cm. Half title: The occasional papers of a book designer. Autobiographical essays. [Z116.A3S27] 76-80486 9.95
1. Book design—Addresses, essays, lectures. I. Title. II. Title: The occasional papers of a book designer.

Book of Mormon—Biography.

LUNDSTROM, Joseph. 289.3'22'0922 B
Book of Mormon personalities. [Salt Lake City] Deseret Book Co., 1969. 111 p. illus. (part col.) 24 cm. "Book of Mormon personalities first appeared in the Deseret news as ... a series on the editorial page of the Church news." [BX8627.L85] 76-102890 3.95
1. Book of Mormon—Biography. I. Title.

MATTHEWS, Robert J. 289.3'22'0922
Who's who in the Book of Mormon / Robert J. Matthews. [Salt Lake City] : Deseret Book Co., c1976. vii, 75 p. ; 23 cm. Includes bibliographical references and index. [BX8622.M37] 76-377261 ISBN 0-87747-613-6 pbk. : 1.95
1. Book of Mormon—Biography. 2. Book of Mormon—Concordances. I. Title. BIP

Book of Mormon—Biography—Juvenile literature.

CHEESMAN, Paul R. 289.3'22'0922 B
Great leaders of the Book of Mormon [by] Paul R. Cheesman. Poetry: Millie Foster Cheesman. Ports.: Stuart Heimdal. Salt Lake City, Utah, Promised Land Publications [1970] 96 p. col. illus. 31 cm. A full-page, color portrait accompanies a brief biographical sketch and poem about each of nineteen leaders of the Book of Mormon. [BX8627.C47] 76-18884
1. Book of Mormon—Biography—Juvenile literature. I. Cheesman, Millie Foster. II. Heimdal, Stuart, illus. III. Title. BIP

GABBOTT, Mabel Jones. 289.3'22'0922 B
Heroes of the Book of Mormon / Mabel Jones Gabbott ; illustrated by Howard Post. Salt Lake City : Deseret Book Co., 1975. 45 p. : ill. ; 29 cm. [BX8627.G27] 75-22770 ISBN 0-87747-570-9
1. Book of Mormon—Biography—Juvenile literature. I. Title.

Books—Reviews.

SPRING, Howard, 1889-1965. 920.02
Book parade. Port Washington, N.Y., Kennikat Press [1970] xvi, 278 p. 20 cm. Reprint of the 1938 ed. A collection of book reviews, originally published in the Manchester guardian, and the Evening standard. [CT104.S66 1970] 70-105837
1. Books—Reviews. 2. Biography. 3. Biography (as a literary form) I. Title. BIP

Booksellers and bookselling—Australia—Biography.

FERGUSON, George, 1910- 658.8'09'0705730994
Some early Australian bookmen / [by] George Ferguson. Canberra : Australian National University Press, 1979. 65 p. : ill. ; 25 cm. Includes bibliographical references. [Z533.3.F47] 78-60698 ISBN 0-7081-0225-5 : 27.50
1. Booksellers and bookselling—Australia—Biography. 2. Publishers and publishing—Australia—Biography. I. Title.
Publisher's address: 25 Van Zant St., Norwalk, CT BIP

Boom, Casper ten, 1859-1944.

TEN Boom, Corrie. 284'.2492 B
Father ten Boom, God's man / Corrie ten Boom. Boston : G. K. Hall, 1979. 218 p. ; 24 cm. Large print ed. [BX9479.B56T46 1979] 79-10857 ISBN 0-8161-6700-1 : 6.95
1. Boom, Casper ten, 1859-1944. 2. Reformed (Reformed Church) in the Netherlands—Biography. 3. Haarlem—Biography. 4. Large type books. I. Title. II. Title: God's man.

TEN BOOM, Corrie. 284'.2492 B
Father ten Boom, God's man / Corrie ten Boom. Old Tappan, N.J. : Revell, [1978] 159 p. : ill. ; 22 cm. [BX9479.B56T46] 78-18713 ISBN 0-8007-0958-6 : 6.95
1. Boom, Casper ten, 1859-1944. 2. Reformed (Reformed Church) in the Netherlands—Biography. 3. Haarlem—Biography. I. Title.

Boone, Daniel, 1734-1820.

BAKELESS, John Edwin, 1894- 976.9020924
Daniel Boone [by] John Bakeless. Harrisburg, Pa., Stackpole Co. [1965, c1939] xii, 480 p. illus., facsims., maps, ports. 23 cm. "Bibliography and notes": p. 425-465. [F454.B724 1965] 65-6283
1. Boone, Daniel, 1734-1820.

BROWN, John Mason, 1900-1969. 923.973
Daniel Boone: the opening of the wilderness. Illustrated by Lee J. Ames. New York, Random House [1952] 181 p. illus. 22 cm. (Landmark books, 21) [F454.B73B7] 52-7223
1. Boone, Daniel, 1734-1820.

*CUNNINGHAM, William 92
The story of Daniel Boone; abridged from The real book about Daniel Boone. Illus. by Wayne Blicken-staff. New York, Scholastic [c.1952, 1964] 159p. 20cm. (TX662) .45 pap.,
I. Title.

CUNNINGHAM, William, 1901- 923.973
The real book about Daniel Boone; illustrated by Deane Cate. [1st ed.] Garden City, N. Y., Garden City Books, by arrangement with F. Watts [New York, 1952] 192 p. illus. 21 cm. (Real books [R24]) [F454.B7328] 52-12470
1. Boone, Daniel, 1734-1820. I. Title.

CUNNINGHAM, William, 1901- v. 12
The story of Daniel Boone; abridged from The real book about Daniel Boone. Illus. by Wayne Blickenstaff. New York, Scholastic Book Services [1965] 159 p. illus., maps. 20 cm. 66-35124
1. Boone, Daniel, 1734-1820. I. Title.

ELLIOTT, Lawrence. 976.9'02'0924 B
The long hunter : a new life of Daniel Boone / Lawrence Elliott. New York : Reader's Digest Press : distributed by Crowell, 1976. xiii, 242 p. : ill. ; 24 cm. Includes index. Bibliography: p. [228]-236. [F454.B736] 75-30688 ISBN 0-88349-066-8 : 12.95
1. Boone, Daniel, 1734-1820. I. Title.

FILSON, John, 1733?-1788. 976.9'02'0924 B
The adventures of Colonel Daniel Boon, formerly a hunter: containing a narrative of the wars of Kentucky. With the discovery, purchase, and settlement of Kentucky; and the Piankashaw Council, 1784; and territory of North American Indians; and the rights of land in Kentucky. New ed. Xenia, Ohio, Old Chelicothe Press, 1968. A4, 37 p. illus., maps, port. 23 cm. Preface signed: Alvin Salisbury. Written in the form of an autobiography of Boone by Filson and first published as an appendix to Filson's Discovery, settlement, and present state of Kentucke (1784, 1st ed.) Cf. DAB. This ed. is from Filson's narrative as reprinted by Gilbert Imlay in his Topographical description, 3d. ed London, 1797. Additions are taken from the source to augment the Boon tale. [F454.B757 1968] 68-5596
1. Boone, Daniel, 1734-1820. I. Salisbury, Alvin. II. Title.

FLINT, Timothy, 1780-1840. 976.9'02'0924 B
Biographical memoir of Daniel Boone, the first settler of Kentucky; interspersed with incidents in the early annals of the country. Edited for the modern reader by James K. Folsom. New Haven, College & University Press [1967] 188 p. 21 cm. (The Masterworks of literature series) [F454.B752] 67-13186
1. Boone, Daniel, 1734-1820. I. Title.

GARST, Doris Shannon, 1899- 976.9'02'0924 B
The picture story and biography of Daniel Boone [by] Shannon Garst. Illustrated by Bill Barss. Chicago, Follett Pub. Co. [1965] 140 p. illus. (part col.) fold map, col. port. 22 cm. (The Library of American heroes) A biography of the frontier scout, hunter, trapper, soldier, and Indian fighter who helped establish the Wilderness Road over which many pioneers traveled westward. [F454.B7585] 92 AC 68
1. Boone, Daniel, 1734-1820. I. Barss, William, illus. II. Title.

LOFARO, Michael A., 1948- 976.9'02'0924 B
The life and adventures of Daniel Boone / Michael A. Lofaro. Lexington : University Press of Kentucky, c1978. p. cm. (The Kentucky Bicentennial bookshelf) Bibliography: p. [F454.B66L63] 78-57389 ISBN 0-8131-0244-8 : 4.95
1. Boone, Daniel, 1734-1820. 2. Pioneers—Kentucky—Biography. 3. Kentucky—Biography. 4. Frontier and pioneer life—Kentucky. I. Title. II. Series. BIP

MOORE, Lilian. 923.973
Daniel Boone; illustrated by William Moyers. Prepared under the supervision of Josette Frank. New York, Random House [1956] c1955. 64p. illus. 29cm. [F454.B7694] 55-6062
1. Boone, Daniel, 1734-1820. I. Title.

SHAPP, Martha. 92
Let's find out about Daniel Boone, by Martha and Charles Shapp. Pictures by Vic Donahue. New York, F. Watts [1967] 61 p. col. illus. 23 cm. An easy-to-read biography of the pioneer who led the first American settlers through the Cumberland Gap into Kentucky. [F454.B824] AC 67
1. Boone, Daniel, 1734-1820. I. Shapp, Charles, joint author. II. Donahue, Vic, illus. III. Title. BIP

SUTTON, Felix. 923.973
Daniel Boone; illustrated by De Witt Whistler Jayne. New York. Grosset & Dunlap [1956] 69 p. illus. 29 cm. [F454.B826] 56-14292
1. Boone, Daniel, 1734-1820. I. Title.

THWAITES, Reuben Gold, 1853-1913. 976.9'02'0924 B
Daniel Boone. Freeport, N.Y., Books for Libraries Press [1971] xv, 257 p. illus. 23 cm. Reprint of the 1902 ed. [F454.B83 1971] 79-165812 ISBN 0-8369-5966-3
1. Boone, Daniel, 1734-1820. BIP

VAN NOPPEN, John James 973.030924
Daniel Boone, backwoodsman; the green woods were his portion, by John James Van Noppen, Ina Woestemeyer Van Noppen. Boone [N.C.] Applachian Pr. [1966] xi, 209p. illus., geneal, table, maps. 24cm. Bibl. [F454.B843] 66-6562 4.95
1. Boone, Daniel, 1734-1820. 2. Boone family. I. Van Noppen, Ina Woestemeyer, 1906- II. Title.

WHITE, Stewart Edward, 1873-1946. 923.973
Daniel Boone, wilderness scout Illustrated by Henry C. Pitz Garden City, N. Y., Junior Deluxe Editions [1957] 254p. illus. 22cm. [F454.B849 1957] 57-788
1. Boone, Daniel, 1734-1820. I. Title.

Boone, Daniel, 1734-1820—Juvenile literature.

MASON, Miriam Evangeline, 1899- 920
Daniel Boone: wilderness trailblazer. Illus. by Harve Stein. Boston, Houghton [c.1961] 191p. col. illus. (Piper bks.) 61-8752 2.24
1. Boone, Daniel, 1734-1820—Juvenile literature. I. Title.

WILKIE, Katharine Elliott, 1904- 923.973
Daniel Boone; taming the wilds. Illus. by E. Harper Johnson. New York, Grosset [1963, c.1960] 72p. col. illus. (Garrard discovery bk., 4165 1.00 bds.,
1. Boone, Daniel, 1734-1820—Juvenile literature. I. Title.

Boone, Daniel, 1734-1820—Juvenile literature.

GARST, Doris Shannon, 1899- 92
The picture story and biography of Daniel Boone [by] Shannon Garst. Illustrated by Bill Barss. Chicago, Follett Pub. Co. [1965] 140 p. illus. (part col.) fold map, col. port. 22 cm. (The Library of American heroes) 65-14480
1. Boone, Daniel, 1734-1820 — Juvenile literature. I. Barss, Bill, illus. II. Title.

GRANT, Matthew G. 976.9'02'0924 B
Daniel Boone in the wilderness [by] Matthew G. Grant. Illustrated by Harold Henriksen. [Chicago, Distributed by Children's Press, 1973, c1974] 31 p. illus. (part col.) 25 cm. (His Gallery of great Americans series. Frontiersmen of America) A brief biography of the famed frontiersman who led settlers into Kentucky, was elected to the Kentucky assembly, and lost his own land there in disastrous legal battles. [F454.G72 1974] 92 73-10070 ISBN 0-87191-256-2 3.95
1. Boone, Daniel, 1734-1820—Juvenile literature. I. Henriksen, Harold, illus. II. Title.

MARTIN, Patricia Miles. 923.973
Daniel Boone. Illustrated by Glen Dines. New York, Putnam [1965] 62 p. col. illus. 23 cm. (A See and read beginning to read biography) [F454.B7683] 65-10873
1. Boone, Daniel, 1784-1820—Juvenile literature. I. Title.

SHAPP, Martha. 920
Let's find out about Daniel Boone, by Martha and Charles Shapp. Pictures by Vic Donahue. New York, F. Watts [1967] 61 p. col. illus. 28 cm. [F454.B824] 67-15732
1. Boone, Daniel, 1734-1820—Juvenile literature. I. Shapp, Charles, joint author. II. Title.

WAYNE, Bennett. 973.5'092'2 B
Men of the wild frontier. Edited, with commentary, by Bennett Wayne. Champaign, Ill., Garrard Pub. Co. [1974] 167 p. illus. (part col.) 22 cm. (A Target book) Brief biographies of four men instrumental in opening up new American frontiers. [F454.B844] 920 73-13615 ISBN 0-8116-4905-9
1. Boone, Daniel, 1734-1820—Juvenile literature. 2. Jackson, Andrew, Pres. U.S., 1767-1845—Juvenile literature. 3. Crockett, David, 1786-1836—Juvenile literature. 4. Houston, Samuel, 1793-1863—Juvenile literature. I. Title. BIP

WILKIE, Katharine Elliott, 1904- 923.973
Daniel Boone; taming the wilds. Illustrated by E. Harper Johnson. Champaign, Ill., Garrard Press [1960] 72 p. illus. 23 cm. (A Discovery book) [F454.B8493] 60-6468
1. Boone, Daniel, 1734-1820—Juvenile literature. BIP

Boone, Debby—Juvenile literature.

ELDRED, Patricia Mulrooney. 784.5'0092'4 B
Debby Boone / by Patricia Mulrooney Eldred. Mankato, Minn. : Creative Education, c1979. 31 p. : ports. ; 23 cm. (Rock 'n pop stars) A profile of singer Debby Boone with a glimpse of her relationship with her family. [ML3930.B6E4] 92 79-52897 ISBN 0-87191-696-7 : 5.95
1. Boone, Debby—Juvenile literature. 2. Singers—United States—Biography—Juvenile literature. I. Title.
Publisher's Address : 123 South Broad St., Mankato, MN 56001

Boone family.

BOONE, Charles Eugene. 784'.092'4 B
Together : 25 years with the Boone family / by Pat Boone ; photos. selected by Shirley and Laury Boone. Nashville : T. Nelson, c1979. 128 p. : ill. ; 29 cm. The well-known singer describes his career and family life from the early days to the present. [ML420.B7A33] 92 79-5243 10.95
1. Boone family. 2. Boone, Charles Eugene. 3. Singers—United States—Biography. I. Title.

Boone, Rebecca — Juvenile literature.

DEGERING, Etta. 917.3030924
Wilderness wife; the story of Rebecca Bryan Boone. Illustrated by Ursula Koering. New York, D. McKay Co. [1966] xx, 138 p. illus. 21 cm. Bibliography: p. 135-138. [F454.B85D4] 66-8401
1. Boone, Rebecca — Juvenile literature. I. Title.

Boone, Shirley.

BOONE, Shirley. 248'.2 B
The honeymoon is over / Shirley and Pat Boone. Carol Stream, Ill. : Creation House, 1978, c1977. 185 p., [7] leaves of plates : ill. ; 23 cm. [BR1702.B58] 77-75818 ISBN 0-88419-130-3 : 6.95
1. Boone, Shirley. 2. Boone, Charles Eugene. 3. Christian biography—United States. I. Boone, Charles Eugene, joint author. II. Title. BIP

BOONE, Shirley. 784'.092'4 B
One woman's liberation. 1st ed. Carol Stream, Ill., Creation House [1972] 230 p. illus. 23 cm. [ML420.B723A3] 72-81113 4.95
I. Title. BIP

Booth, Charles, 1840-1916.

SIMEY, Thomas Spensley, 1906- 923
Charles Booth, social scientist [by] T. S. Simey [and] M. B. Simey. [London] Oxford University Press, 1960. 282 p. illus. 23 cm. [IIV28.B6S5] 61-505
1. Booth, Charles, 1840-1916. I. Simey, Margaret B. joint author. II. Title.

SIMEY, Thomas Spensley, 1906- 923
Charles Booth, social scientist [by] T. S. Simey, M. B. Simey. [New York] Oxford Univ. Press [c.]1960 282p. Front. Bibl. 61-505 4.80
1. Booth, Charles, 1840-1916. I. Simey, Margaret B., joint author. II. Title.

Booth-Clibborn, Catherine, 1860-1955.

STRAHAN, James, 1863-1926. 267'.15'0924 B
The Marechale, by James Strachan. Foreword by Theodore Booth-Clibborn. Minneapolis, Bethany Fellowship [1966] 221 p. ports. 19 cm. "The cross and the glory, by Theodore Booth-Clibborn": p. 198-221. [BX9743.B8S8 1966] 67-6260
1. Booth-Clibborn, Catherine, 1860-1955. I. Booth-Clibborn, Theodore. II. Title.

Booth, Edwin, 1833-1893.

BOOTH, Edwin, 1833-1893. 792'.028'0924 B
Between actor and critic; selected letters of Edwin Booth and William Winter. Edited with an introd. and commentary by Daniel J. Watermeier. Princeton, N.J., Princeton University Press, 1971. ix, 329 p. facsims., ports. 25 cm. Bibliography: p. 310-316. [PN2287.B5A48 1971] 72-113012 ISBN 0 691-06193-9 10.00
I. Winter, William, 1836-1917. II. Watermeier, Daniel J., ed. III. Title. BIP

BOOTH, Edwin, 1833-1893. 792'.028'0924
Edwin Booth; recollections by his daughter Edwina Booth Grossmann, and letters to her and to his friends. New York, B. Blom [1969] vi, 292 p. illus., ports. 24 cm. Reprint of the 1894 ed. Letters: p. [29]-284. [PN2287.B5A4 1969] 70-81199
I. Grossman, Edwina (Booth) 1861- II. Title.

BOOTH, Edwin, 1833-1893. 792'.028'0924
Edwin Booth; recollections by his daughter Edwina Booth Grossmann, and letters to her and to his friends. Freeport, N.Y., Books for Libraries Press [1970] vi, 292 p. illus., ports. 23 cm. Reprint of the 1894 ed. "Letters to his daughter": p. [29]-284. [PN2287.B5A4 1970] 76-114881
I. Grossman, Edwina (Booth) 1861- II. Title.

LOCKRIDGE, Richard, 1898- 792'.028'0924 B
Darling of misfortune: Edwin Booth: 1833-

1893. New York, B. Blom, 1971. xi, 358 p. illus. 21 cm. Reprint of the 1932 ed. Includes bibliographical footnotes. [PN2287.B5L6 1971] 79-91908
1. Booth, Edwin, 1833-1893. I. Title.

POWER-WATERS, Alma 927.92
(Shelley) 1896-
The story of young Edwin Booth. Foreword by Eva Le Gallienne; with photos. [1st ed.] New York, Dutton [1955] 192p. illus. 22cm. [PN2287.B5] 55-5363
1. Booth, Edwin, 1833-1893. I. Title.

RUGGLES, Eleanor, 1916- 927.92
Prince of players: Edwin Booth. [1st ed.] New York, Norton [c1953] xii, 401p. illus., ports. 22cm. 'Notes on sources' : p. 377-386. [PN2287.B5R9] 53-5986
1. Booth, Edwin, 1833-1896. I. Title.

RUGGLES, Eleanor, 792'.028'0924
1916-
Prince of players: Edwin Booth. Westport, Conn., Greenwood Press [1972, c1953] xii, 401 p. illus. 22 cm. Bibliography: p. 377-386. [PN2287.B5R9 1972] 72-7824 ISBN 0-8371-6529-6 15.00
1. Booth, Edwin, 1833-1893. I. Title.

WINTER, William, 792'.028'0924 B
1836-1917.
Life and art of Edwin Booth. New York, Greenwood Press, 1968 [c1893] xii, 308 p. illus., ports. 22 cm. [PN2287.B5W5 1968] 68-8939
1. Booth, Edwin, 1833-1893. I. Title. **BIP**

Booth, Evangeline Cory, 1865-1950—Juvenile literature.

LAVINE, Sigmund A. 267.15'0924 B
Evangeline Booth; daughter of Salvation [by] Sigmund A. Lavine. New York, Dodd, Mead [1970] viii, 143 p. illus., facsim., ports. 22 cm. Bibliography: p. 139-140. A biography of the woman who, as head of the Salvation Army, brought practical assistance to many in need throughout the world. [BX9743.B63L38] 92 74-108044 4.00
1. Booth, Evangeline Cory, 1865-1950—Juvenile literature. I. Title.

Booth, John Wilkes, 1838-1865.

BAUER, Charles J. 973.7'092'4 B
So I killed Lincoln : John Wilkes Booth / by Charles J. Bauer. 1st ed. New York : Vantage Press, c1976. xxi, 225 p. : ill. ; 22 cm. Bibliography: p. 223-225. [E457.5.B38] 76-367677 ISBN 0-533-02035-2 : 6.50
1. Booth, John Wilkes, 1838-1865. 2. Lincoln, Abraham, Pres. U.S., 1809-1865—Assassination. I. Title.

STERN, Philip Van Doren, 927.92
1900-
The man who killed Lincoln. [Rev. ed. New York, Dell Pub. Co., 1955] 319p. illus. 17cm. (A Dell book, D159) [E457.5.S825 1955] [E457.5.S825 1955] 923.4173 55-11978 55-11978
1. Booth, John Wilkes, 1838-1865. 2. Lincoln, Abraham, Pres. U. S.—Association. I. Title.

WEICHMANN, Louis J. 364.1'31'0973
True history of the assassination of Abraham Lincoln and of the Conspiracy of 1865 Louis J. Weichmann ; edited by Floyd E. Risvold. 1st ed. New York : Knopf, 1975. xxxii, 492, xvi p., [8] leaves of plates : ill. ; 25 cm. Includes 23 letters written by A. C. Richards to Weichmann from Apr. 1898 to Nov. 1901. Includes index. Bibliography: p. 461-463. [E457.5.W44] 74-21278 ISBN 0-394-49319-2 : 15.00
1. Lincoln, Abraham, Pres. U.S., 1809-1865—Assassination. 2. Booth, John Wilkes, 1838-1865. 3. United States. Army. Military Commission. Lincoln's assassins. 1865. 4. Weichmann, Louis J. I. Richards, A. C., d. 1907. II. Title.

WEICHMANN, Louis J. 973.7'092'4 B
A true history of the assassination of Abraham Lincoln and of the conspiracy of 1865 / Louis J. Weichmann ; edited by Floyd E. Risvold. New York : Vintage Books, 1977, c1975. xxx, 492, xvi p. ; 24 cm. Includes 23 letters written by A. C. Richards to L. J. Weichmann from Apr. 1898 to Nov. 1901. Includes index. Bibliography: p. 461-463. [E475.5.W44 1977] 76-41211 ISBN 0-394-72260-4 pbk. 5.95
1. Lincoln, Abraham, Pres. U.S., 1809-1865—Assassination. 2. Booth, John Wilkes, 1838-1865. 3. United States. Army. Military Commission. Lincoln's assassins. 1865. 4. Weichmann, Louis J. I. Richards, A. C., d. 1907. II. Title. **BIP**

WILSON, Francis, 973.7'092'4 B
1854-1935.
John Wilkes Booth; fact and fiction of Lincoln's assassination. New York, B. Blom, 1972. xiv, 321 p. illus. 22 cm. Reprint of the 1929 ed. Includes bibliographical references. [E457.5.W75 1972] 74-91588
1. Booth, John Wilkes, 1838-1865. 2. Lincoln, Abraham, Pres. U.S., 1809-1865—Assassination.

Booth, John Wilkes, 1838-1865—Portraits, etc.

GUTMAN, Richard. 973.7'092'4 B
John Wilkes Booth himself / Richard J. S. Gutman, Kellie O. Gutman. Dover, Mass. : Hired Hand Press, 1979. 87 p. : 45 ill. ; 22 cm. Includes bibliographical references. [E457.5.B67G78] 78-71462 ISBN 0-9602256-0-9. : 17.50
1. Booth, John Wilkes, 1838-1865—Portraits, etc. 2. Assassins—United States—Biography. 3. Actors—United States—Biography. I. Gutman, Kellie O., joint author. II. Title. **BIP**

Booth, Maud Ballington (Charlesworth) 1865-1948.

WELTY, Susan Elizabeth 922.89
(Fulton) 1905-
Look up and hope! the motto of the Volunteer Prison League; the life of Maud Ballington Booth. New York, T. Nelson [c.1961] 284p. front. port). Bibl. 61-12423 5.00
1. Booth, Maud Ballington (Charlesworth) 1865-1948. I. Title.

Booth, William, 1829-1912.

BISHOP, Edward 922.89
Blood and fire! The story of General William Booth and the Salvation Army. Chicago, Moody [1965, c.1964] 114p. illus. ports. 20cm. Bibl. [BX9743.B7B5] 65-4089 2.50 bds.,
1. Booth, William, 1829—1912. 2. Salvation Army. I. Title.

COLLIER, Richard, 1924- 267.1509
The general next to God; the story of William Booth and the Salvation Army. [1st ed.] New York, Dutton, 1965. 320 p. illus., ports. 22 cm. Bibliography: p. 293-310. [BX9743.B7C65 1965a] 65-11410
1. Booth, William, 1829-1912. 2. Salvation Army. I. Title.

NYGAARD, Norman Eugene, 922.89
1897-
Trumpet of salvation: the story of William and Catherine Booth. Grand Rapids, Zondervan Pub. House [1961] 180p. 21cm. [BX9743.B7N9] 61-1590
1. Booth, William, 1829-1912. 2. Booth, Catherine (Mumford) 1829-1800. 3. Salvation Army—Hist. I. Title.

ROBINSON, Virgil 267'.15'0924 B
E.
William Booth and his Army / Virgil Robinson. Mountain View, Calif. : Pacific Press Pub. Association, c1976. 112 p. : ill. ; 22 cm. (A Destiny book ; D-163) [BX9743.B7R62] 75-25226 pbk. : 3.50
1. Booth, William, 1829-1912. 2. Salvation Army. 3. Salvationists—England—Biography. I. Title. **BIP**

WATSON, Bernard, 1906- 920
The young William Booth. Illus. by Susan E. Sims. New York, Roy [1964, c.1963] 135p. illus. 21cm. 64-16352 3.25 bds.,
1. Booth, William, 1829-1912. I. Title.

Booth, William, 1829-1912—Juvenile literature.

LUDWIG, Charles, 1918- 92
General without a gun; the life of William Booth, founder of the Salvation Army, for teens. Grand Rapids, Zondervan Pub. House [c1961] 107p. illus. 21cm. [BX9743.B7L78] 62-931
1. Booth, William, 1829-1912—Juvenile literature. I. Title.

LUDWIG, Charles Shelton, 920
1918-
General without a gun; the life of William Booth, founder of the salvation Army, for teens. Grand Rapids, Mch., Zondervan [c.1961] .107p. illus. 62-931 1.95 1.95 bds.,
1. Booth, William, 1829-1912— Juvenile literature. I. Title.

Boots and shoes—Trade and manufacture—Italy.

FERRAGAMO, 685'.31'00924 B
Salvatore, 1898-1961.
Shoemaker of dreams; the autobiography of Salvatore Ferragamo. New York, Crown Publishers [1972] 232 p. illus. 22 cm. Originally published in 1957. [HD9787.I82F47 1972] 72-83406 5.95
1. Boots and shoes—Trade and manufacture—Italy. I. Title.

Borah, William Edgar, 1865-1940.

ASHBY, LeRoy. 320.9'73'0910924 B
The spearless leader; Senator Borah and the progressive movement in the 1920's. Urbana, University of Illinois Press [1972] x, 325 p. 24 cm. Bibliography: p. 295-307. [E748.B7A85] 74-170963 ISBN 0-252-00220-2 10.00
1. Borah, William Edgar, 1865-1940. 2. Progressivism (United States politics) I. Title. **BIP**

BORAH, Mary, 1870- 328.73'092'4 B
1976.
Elephants and donkeys : the memoirs of Mary Borah as told to Mary Louise Perrine. Moscow : University Press of Idaho, c1976. 152 p. [1] leaf of plates : ill. ; 22 cm. (A Gem book) [E748.B699A34] 76-14107 ISBN 0-89301-032-4
1. Borah, William Edgar, 1865-1940. 2. Borah, Mary, 1870-1976. 3. Legislators—United States—Biography. 4. Wives—United States—Biography. 5. United States—Politics and government—1901-1953. I. Perrine, Mary. II. Title.

MCKENNA, Marian Cecilia, 923.273
1926-
Borah. Ann Arbor, University of Michigan Press [1961] 450 p. illus. 23 cm. Includes bibliography. [E748.B7M3] 60-15771
1. Borah, William Edgar, 1865-1940.

MADDOX, Robert James. 327.73
William E. Borah and American foreign policy. Baton Rouge, Louisiana State University Press [1970, c1969] xx, 272 p. illus. 23 cm. Includes bibliographical references. [E748.B7M6] 74-86492 7.50
1. Borah, William Edgar, 1865-1940. 2. U.S.—Foreign relations—20th century. I. Title. **BIP**

Borden, Abby Durfee (Gray) 1828-1892.

RADIN, Edward D. FIC
Lizzie Borden: the untold story. New York, Simon and Schuster, 1961. 269 p. illus. 22cm. [KF223.B6R3 1961b] 920.7 61-9597
1. Borden, Lizzie Andrew, 1860-1927. 2. Borden, Abby Durfee (Gray) 1828-1892. 3. Borden, Andrew Jackson, 1822-1892.

SULLIVAN, Robert, 345'.73'02523
1916-
Goodbye Lizzie Borden. Battleboro, Vt., S. Greene Press [1974] viii, 245 p. illus. 23 cm. Bibliography: p. 238-240. [KF223.B6S9] 73-86037 ISBN 0-8289-0203-8 7.95
1. Borden, Lizzie Andrew, 1860-1927. 2. Borden, Abby Durfee (Gray) 1828-1892. 3. Borden, Andrew Jackson, 1822-1892. I. Title. **BIP**

Borden, Gail, 1801-1874.

BAKER, Nina (Brown) 1888- 926.37
Texas Yankee; the story of Gail Borden. Illustrated by Alan Moyler. [1st ed.] New York, Harcourt, Brace [1955] 129p. illus. 21cm. [HD9282.U6B63] [HD9282.U6B63] 923.973 55-9005 55-9005
1. Borden, Gail, 1801-1874. I. Title.

FRANTZ, Joe B. [926.37]
Gail Borden, dairyman to a nation. [1st ed.] Norman, University of Oklahoma Press [1951] xiii, 310 p. illus., ports., maps. 24 cm. Bibliography: p. 277-294. [HD9275.U82B64] 923.973 51-11349
1. Borden, Gail, 1801-1874. 2. Borden Company. I. Title.

Borden, Lizzie Andrew, 1860-1927.

LINCOLN, 364.15'23'0924 (B)
Victoria, 1904-
A private disgrace; Lizzie Borden by daylight. New York, Putnam [1967] 317 p. illus. 22 cm. [HV6248.B66L5] 67-23132
1. Borden, Lizzie Andrew, 1860-1927. I. Title.

RADIN, Edward D. FIC
Lizzie Borden: the untold story. New York, Simon and Schuster, 1961. 269 p. illus. 22cm. [KF223.B6R3 1961b] 920.7 61-9597
1. Borden, Lizzie Andrew, 1860-1927. 2. Borden, Abby Durfee (Gray) 1828-1892. 3. Borden, Andrew Jackson, 1822-1892.

SULLIVAN, Robert, 345'.73'02523
1916-
Goodbye Lizzie Borden. Battleboro, Vt., S. Greene Press [1974] viii, 245 p. illus. 23 cm. Bibliography: p. 238-240. [KF223.B6S9] 73-86037 ISBN 0-8289-0203-8 7.95
1. Borden, Lizzie Andrew, 1860-1927. 2. Borden, Abby Durfee (Gray) 1828-1892. 3. Borden, Andrew Jackson, 1822-1892. I. Title. **BIP**

Borders, William Holmes, 1905-

ENGLISH, James W. 286'.133'0924
Handyman of the Lord: the life and ministry of the Rev. William Holmes Borders, by James W. English. [1st ed.] New York, Meredith Press [1967] ix, 177 p. 21 cm. Published in 1973 under title: The prophet of Wheat Street. [BX6455.B63E5] 67-12637
1. Borders, William Holmes, 1905- 2. Negroes—Atlanta. I. Title.

ENGLISH, James W. 286'.133'0924 B
The prophet of Wheat Street; the story of William Holmes Borders, a man who refused to fail, by James W. English. Elgin, Ill., D. C. Cook Pub. Co. [1973] 205 p. 18 cm. First ed. published in 1967 under title: Handyman of the Lord. [BX6455.B63E5 1973] 73-78715 ISBN 0-912692-19-7 1.25
1. Borders, William Holmes, 1905- 2. Negroes—Atlanta. I. Title. **BIP**

Bordes, Ary.

BORDES, Ary. 362.8'2
For the people, for a change : bringing health to the families of Haiti / Ary Bordes and Andrea Couture. Boston : Beacon Press, c1978. xv, 299 p. : ill. ; 21 cm. Includes index. [RG963.H2B67 1978] 77-88372 ISBN 0-8070-2166-0 : 11.95
1. Bordes, Ary. 2. Maternal health services—Haiti. 3. Birth control—Haiti. 4. Child health services—Haiti. 5. Haiti—Social conditions. 6. Health-officers—Haiti—Biography. I. Couture, Andrea, joint author. II. Title. **BIP**

Borduas, Paul Emile.

BORDUAS, Paul Emile. 759.11
Paul-Emile Borduas / Francois-Marc Gagnon. Toronto : National Gallery of Canada, 1976. 93 p. : ill. (some col.) ; 24 cm. (Canadian artists series ; no. 3) Bibliography: p. 93-95. [ND249.B6G33] 77-360042 ISBN 0-88884-271-6
1. Borduas, Paul Emile. 2. Painters—Canada—Biography. I. Gagnon, Francois. II. Title. III. Series.

Borein, Edward, 1873-1945.

DAVIDSON, Harold G., 1912- 769'.92'4 B
Edward Borein, cowboy artist; the life and works of John Edward Borein, 1872 [sic]-1945 [by] Harold G. Davidson. [1st ed.] Garden City, N.Y., Doubleday, 1974. 189 p. illus. (part col.) 32 cm. Includes bibliographical references. [N6537.B63D38 1974] 74-2063 ISBN 0-385-09607-0 25.00
1. Borein, Edward, 1873-1945. 2. The West in art. I. Borein, Edward, 1873-1945. II. Title.

Borg, Bjorn, 1956—

BORG, Bjorn, 1956- 796.34'2'0924 B
The Bjorn Borg story / Bjorn Borg ; translated from the Swedish by Joan Tate. Chicago : H. Regnery Co., 1975. 94 p. : ill. ; 22 cm. [GV994.B65A3213 1975] 75-321039 ISBN 0-8092-8184-8 : 6.95
1. Borg, Bjorn, 1956- 2. Tennis. I. Title.

Borg, Bjorn, 1956- —Juvenile literature.

AUDETTE, Larry. 796.34'2'0924 B
Bjorn Borg / Larry Audette. New York : Quick Fox, c1979. 106 p., [1] leaf of plates : ill. ; 26 cm. A career biography of the Swedish tennis player who by the age of 22 has won every major tennis tournament in the world at least once. [GV994.B65A95] 92 78-68485 ISBN 0-8256-3931-X pbk. : 4.95
1. Borg, Bjorn, 1956- —Juvenile literature. 2. Tennis players—Sweden—Biography—Juvenile literature. I. Title. BIP

HAHN, James. 796.34'2'0924 B
Bjorn Borg : the coolest ace / by James and Lynn Hahn. St. Paul : EMC Corp., 1978. p. cm. (Their Champions and challengers 2) A biography of the Swedish tennis player who in 1978 won Wimbledon for the third year in a row. [GV994.B65H33] 92 78-13127 ISBN 0-88436-478-X : 5.95
1. Borg, Bjorn, 1956- —Juvenile literature. 2. Tennis players—Sweden—Biography. I. Hahn, Lynn, joint author. II. Title. III. Series. BIP

LIBMAN, Gary. 796.34'2'0924 B
Bjorn Borg / by Gary Libman. Mankato, MN : Creative Education, [1979] p. cm. A career biography of the record-setting Swedish tennis player. [GV994.B65L52] 92 79-11046 ISBN 0-87191-721-1 : 5.50
1. Borg, Bjorn, 1956- —Juvenile literature. 2. Tennis players—Sweden—Biography—Juvenile literature. I. Title. BIP

Borges, Jorge Luis, 1899-

RODRIGUEZ Monegal, Emir. 868 B
Jorge Luis Borges : a literary biography / Emir, Rodriguez Monegal. 1st ed. New York : Dutton, c1978. ix, 502 p., [4] leaves of plates : ill. ; 24 cm. Includes index. Bibliography: p. 480-487. [PQ7797.B635Z916] 77-26736 ISBN 0-525-13748-3 : 19.95
1. Borges, Jorge Luis, 1899- 2. Authors, Argentine—20th century—Biography.

Borghese, Maria Paolina (Bonaparte) principessa, 1780-1825.

DIXON, Pierson Sir 920.7
Pauline, Napoleon's favourite sister. New York, McKay [c.1964, 1965] 223p. illus., ports. 22cm. Bibl. [DC216.87.D5] 65-18945 5.95
1. Borghese, Maria Paolina (Bonaparte) principessa, 1780-1825. I. Title.

ORTZEN, Len. 944.05'092'4 B
Imperial Venus; the story of Pauline Bonaparte-Borghese. New York, Stein and Day [1974] 224 p. illus. 24 cm. Bibliography: p. [217]-218. [DC216.87.O77 1974b] 73-92186 ISBN 0-8128-1689-7 8.95
1. Borghese, Maria Paolina Bonaparte, principessa, 1780-1825. I. Title.

Borgia, Cesare, 1476?-1507.

BRADFORD, Sarah. 945'.6'060924 B
Cesare Borgia, his life and times / Sarah Bradford. New York : Macmillan, 1976. viii, 327 p., [4] leaves of plates : ill. ; 22 cm. Includes index. Bibliography: p. [303]-311. [DG797.82.B65 1976] 76-18925 ISBN 0-02-514400-6 : 10.95
1. Borgia, Cesare, 1476?-1507. I. Title.

BRADFORD, Sarah. 945'.6'060924 B
Cesare Borgia, his life and times / Sarah Bradford. London : Weidenfeld and Nicolson, c1976. viii, 327 p., [4] leaves of plates : ill. ; 23 cm. Includes index. Bibliography: p. [303]-311. [DG797.82.B65 1976b] 76-374797 ISBN 0-297-77124-8 : £5.95
1. Borgia, Cesare, 1476?-1507. 2. Statesmen—Papal States—Biography. 3. Papal States—Nobility—Biography.

Borgia family.

CHAMBERLIN, Eric Russell. 929.7'5
The fall of the house of Borgia [by] E. R. Chamberlin. New York, Dial Press, 1974. xxx, 347 p. illus. 24 cm. Bibliography: p. 333-337. [DG463.8.B7C45] 73-9703 10.00
1. Borgia family. 2. Italy—History—1492-1559. I. Title.

FUSERO, Clemente. 945'.05
The Borgias. Translated from the Italian by Peter Green. New York, Praeger [1972] 352 p. illus. 25 cm. Bibliography: p. 327-332. [DG463.8.B7F7413 1972] 71-154354 12.50
1. Borgia family. I. Title.

Borgia, Lucrezia, 1480-1519.

BELLONCI, Maria. 923.245
The life and times of Lucrezia Borgia. Translated by Bernard and Barbara Wall. New York, Grosset & Dunlap [1957] 343p. 21cm. (Grosset's universal library, UL-26) Translation of Lucrezia Borgia. [DG797] 57-3441
1. Borgia, Lucrezia, 1480-1519. 2. Italy—Hist.—1492-1559. I. Title.

BELLONCI, Maria. 923.245
The life and times of Lucrezia Borgia. Translated by Bernard and Barbara Wall. New York, Harcourt, Brace [1953, c1939] 343 p. 23 cm. Translation of Lucrezia Borgia. Bibliography: p. 327-335. [DG797.83.B3713] 53-9222
1. Borgia, Lucrezia, 1480-1519. 2. Italy—History—1492-1559.

ERLANGER, Rachel. 945'.06'0924 B
Lucrezia Borgia : a biography / Rachel Erlanger. New York : Hawthorn Books, c1978. xii, 372 p., [4] leaves of plates : ill. ; 24 cm. Includes index. Bibliography: p. [347]-355. [DG797.83.E74] 75-39117 ISBN 0-8015-4725-3 : 13.95
1. Borgia, Lucrezia, 1480-1519. 2. Papal States—Nobility—Biography. BIP

GREGOROVIUS, Ferdinand Adolf, 1821-1891. 945'.06'0924 B
Lucretia Borgia, according to original documents and correspondence of her day. Translated from the 3d German ed., by John Leslie Garner. New York, B. Blom [1968] xxiii, 378 p. illus. 20 cm. Reprint of 1903 ed. [DG797.83.G71 1968] 68-20226
1. Borgia, Lucrezia, 1480-1519. 2. Italy—History—1492-1559. 3. Renaissance—Italy. I. Garner, John Leslie, tr.

Borglum, John Gutson de la Mothe, 1867-1941.

CASEY, Robert Joseph, 1890- 927.3
Give the man room; the story of Gutzon Borglum, by Robert J. Casey and Mary Borglum. [1st ed.] Indianapolis, Bobbs-Merrill [1952] 326 p. illus. 23 cm. [NB237.B6C3] 52-5804
1. Borglum, John Gutson de la Mothe, 1867-1941. I. Title.

Borglum, Solon Hannibal, 1868-1922.

DAVIES, Alfred Mervyn. 730'.92'4 B
Solon H. Borglum, "a man who stands alone"; a biography, by A. Mervyn Davies. [1st ed.] Chester, Conn., Pequot Press [1974] xxi; 285 p. illus. 26 cm. Bibliography: p. [257]-265. [NB237.B62D38] 74-181506 ISBN 0-87106-140-6 18.50
1. Borglum, Solon Hannibal, 1868-1922.

Borhek, Eric.

BORHEK, Mary V., 1922- 301.41'57'0924
My son Eric / by Mary V. Borhek. New York : Pilgrim Press, [1979] p. cm. Includes bibliographical references. [HQ75.8.B67B67] 79-16161 ISBN 0-8298-0372-6 : 8.95
1. Borhek, Eric. 2. Homosexuals, Male—Biography. 3. Homosexuals, Male—Family relationships. I. Title. BIP

Bori, Lucrezia, 1887-1960.

MARION, John Francis. 927.8
Lucrezia Bori of the Metropolitan Opera. New York, P. J. Kenedy [1962] 189p. illus. 22cm. (American background books, 223 [ML420.B74M4] 62-16534
1. Bori, Lucrezia, 1887-1960. I. Title.

Boris Godunov, Czar of Russia, 1551?-1605.

GRAHAM, Stephen, 1884- 947'.04'0924 B
Boris Godunof. With a pref. by George Vernadsky. [Hamden, Conn.] Archon Books, 1970 [c1933] ix, 290 p. ports. 22 cm. Includes bibliographical references. [DK109.G7 1970] 74-120368
1. Boris Godunov, Czar of Russia, 1551?-1605. 2. Russia—History—Boris Godunov, 1598-1605. BIP

GREY, Ian, 1918- 947'.04'0924 B
Boris Godunov; the tragic Tsar. New York, Scribner [1973] 188 p. illus. 24 cm. Bibliography: p. 180-182. [DK109.G73] 72-11119 ISBN 0-684-13339-3 8.95
1. Boris Godunov, Czar of Russia, 1551?-1605. 2. Russia—History—1553-1613. I. Title.

PLATONOV, Sergei Fedorovich, 1860-1933. 947'.04'0924 B
Boris Godunov, Tsar of Russia. Translated from the Russian by L. Rex Pyles. With an introductory essay S. F. Platonov: Eminence and obscurity, by John T. Alexander. [Gulf Breeze, Fla.] Academic International Press, 1973. xlii, 230 p. port., map. 23 cm. (Russian series, v. 10) Translation of Boris Godunov. Bibliography: p. 222-223. [DK109.P513] 73-176467 ISBN 0-87569-024-6 11.00
1. Boris Godunov, Czar of Russia, 1551?-1605. 2. Russia—History—Boris Godunov, 1598-1605. I. Alexander, John T. S. F. Platonov: Eminence and obscurity. 1973.

Borlaug, N. E.

BICKEL, Lennard. 630'.92'4 B
Facing starvation; Norman Borlaug and the fight against hunger. [1st ed. Pleasantville, N.Y.] Reader's Digest Press; distributed by Dutton, New York, 1974. 376 p. 22 cm. [HD9010.B66B5 1974] 74-1078 ISBN 0-88349-015-3 7.95
1. Borlaug, N. E. I. Title.

Bormann, Martin, 1900-1945.

FARAGO, Ladislas. 943.086'092'4 B
Aftermath. [New York] Avon [1975, c1974] ix, 550 p. illus. 18 cm. Bibliography: p. 518-533. [DD247.B6F37] 73-22782 ISBN 0-380-00407-0 1.95 (pbk.)
1. Bormann, Martin, 1900- I. Title. BIP

LANG, Jochen von. 943.086'092'4 B
The secretary : Martin Bormann, the man who manipulated Hitler / Jochen von Lang, with the assistance of Claus Sibyll ; translated from the German by Christa Armstrong and Peter White. 1st American ed. New York : Random House, c1979. x, 430 p., [16] leaves of plates : ill. ; 24 cm. Translation of Der Sekretar. Includes index. Bibliography: p. [415]-421. [DD247.B65L3613 1979] 78-57114 ISBN 0-394-50321-X : 15.95
1. Bormann, Martin, 1900-1945. 2. National socialism—Biography. I. Sibyll, Claus. II. Title. BIP

MCGOVERN, James. 943.086'0924 B
Martin Bormann. New York, Morrow, 1968. viii, 237 p. illus., ports. 22 cm. Bibliography: p. 219-223. [DD247.B65M3] 68-19745
1. Bormann, Martin, 1900- 2. Hitler, Adolf, 1889-1945.

Born, Max, 1882-1970.

BORN, Max, 1882-1970. 530'.092'4 B
My life : recollections of a Nobel prize winner / by Max Born. New York : Scribner, [1978] p. cm. Includes index. [QC16.B643A3213] 78-7868 ISBN 0-684-15662-8 : 17.50
1. Born, Max, 1882-1970. 2. Physicists—Germany, West—Biography. BIP

Borntrager, Karl A.

BORNTRAGER, Karl A. 385'.092'4 B
Keeping the railroads running; fifty years on the New York Central, an autobiography, and a review of the railroad crisis today, by Karl A. Borntrager. New York, Hastings House [1974] 256 p. 21 cm. [HE2754.B76A33] 74-11392 ISBN 0-8038-3941-3
1. Borntrager, Karl A. 2. Railroads and state—United States. I. Title.

Borodin, Aleksandr Porfir'evich, 1834-1887.

DIANIN, Sergei Aleksandrovich. 927.8
Borodin. Translated from the Russian by Robert Lord. London, New York, Oxford University Press, 1963. 356 p. illus., ports., music. 23 cm. Includes bibliography. [ML410.B73D5] 63-24461
1. Borodin, Aleksandr Porfir'evich, 1833-1887. I. Title.

HABETS, Alfred, 1839-1908. 780'.92'4 B
Borodin and Liszt / by Alfred Habets ; translated with a pref. by Rosa Newmarch. New York : AMS Press, 1977. liv, 199 p. : ill. ; 18 cm. Translation of Alexandre Borodine, d'apres la biographie et la correspondance publiees par Wladimir Stassoff. Reprint of the 1895 ed. published by Digby, Long, London. Contents.—Life and works of a Russian composer.—Liszt, as sketched in the letters of Borodin. "Catalogue of the works of Borodin" p. 195-199. [ML410.B73H13 1977] 74-24093 ISBN 0-404-12938-2 ; 17.50
1. Borodin, Aleksandr Porfir'evich, 1834-1887. 2. Liszt, Franz, 1811-1886. 3. Composers—Russia—Biography. BIP

Boros, Ladislaus, 1927-

BOROS, Ladislaus, 1927- 230'.2'0924 B
Open spirit / Ladislaus Boros ; translated by Erika Young. New York : Paulist Press, [1974] 204 p. ; 21 cm. Translation of Denken in der Begegnung. [BX4705.B663A313 1974] 74-192513 ISBN 0-8091-1856-4 pbk. : 3.95.
1. Boros, Ladislaus, 1927- I. Title.

Borromeo, Federico, Cardinal, 1564-1631.

WRIGHT, Anthony David. 274.5
Federico Borromeo and Baronius : a turning-point in the development of the Counter-Reformation Church / by A. D. Wright. [Reading] : University of Reading, Department of Italian Studies, 1974. 27 p. ; 22 cm. (Occasional papers - Centre for the Advanced Study of Italian Society ; no. 6) Includes bibliographical references. [BX4705.B67W74] 75-323797 ISBN 0-7049-0401-2 : £0.80
1. Borromeo, Federico, Cardinal, 1564-1631. 2. Baronio, Cesare, Cardinal, 1538-1607. 3. Counter-Reformation—Italy. I. Title. II. Series: Reading, Eng. University. Centre for the Advanced Study of Italian Society. Occasional papers ; no. 6.

Borromini, Francesco, 1599-1667.

BLUNT, Anthony, Sir, 1907- 720'.92'4
Borromini / by Anthony Blunt. Cambridge, Mass. : Harvard University Press, [1979] p. cm. Includes index. Bibliography: p. [NA1123.B6B56] 78-11320 ISBN 0-674-07925-6 : 15.00
1. Borromini, Francesco, 1599-1667. 2. Architects—Italy—Biography. 3. Architecture, Baroque—italy. **BIP**

Borrow, George Henry, 1803-1881.

BIGLAND, Eileen. 928.2
In the steps of George Borrow. London, New York, Rich and Cowan [1951] 355 p. illus. 19 cm. [PR4156.B53] 52-4904
1. Borrow, George Henry, 1803-1881. I. Title. **BIP**

JENKINS, Herbert George, 1876-1923, comp. 828'.8'09 B
The life of George Borrow, compiled from unpublished official documents, his works, correspondence, etc. Port Washington, N.Y., Kennikat Press [1970] xxviii, 496 p. illus., ports. 22 cm. Reprint of the 1912 ed. "List of Borrow's works": p. 479-480. [PR4156.J4 1970] 71-113316
1. Borrow, George Henry, 1803-1881. I. Title.

MEYERS, Robert Rex, 1923- 828.808
George Borrow, by Robert R. Meyers. New York, Twayne Publishers [1966] 156 p. 21 cm. (Twayne's English authors series, 32) Bibliography: p. 149-153. [PR4156.M4] 66-16114
1. Borrow, George Henry, 1803-1881.

MEYERS, Robert Rex, 1923- 266'.023'0924
George Borrow: God's picaro, by Robert Meyers. Wichita, Kan., Wichita State University, 1969. 9 p. 23 cm. (University studies, no. 78) (Wichita State University bulletin, v. 45, no. 1.) Includes bibliographical references. [AS36.W62 no. 78] 74-12101
1. Borrow, George Henry, 1803-1881. I. Title. II. Series: Kansas. State University, Wichita. University studies, no. 78

Borrow, George Henry, 1803-1881—Biography.

ELAM, Samuel Milton, 1907- 828'.4'09 B
George Borrow. [Folcroft, Pa.] Folcroft Library Editions, 1974 [c1929] p. cm. Reprint of the ed. published by Knopf, New York. Bibliography: p. [PR4156.E5 1974] 74-11134 10.75
1. Borrow, George Henry, 1803-1881—Biography.

Borzocka, Celina, 1833-1913.

KALKSTEIN, Teresa. 271'.979 B
Witness to the resurrection; the servant of God, Mother Celine Borzecka, foundress of the Congregation, Sisters of the Resurrection of our Lord Jesus Christ. Translated by Sisters Celine and Mary Gertrude Maleska. Castleton-on-Hudson, N.Y., Sisters of the Resurrection [1967] xiii, 212 p. illus., facsim., ports. 23 cm. "An enlarged version of the first edition, written by the author, in Polish and Italian." Bibliography: p. 211-212. [BX4705.B675K33] 67-29594
1. Borzocka, Celina, 1833-1913. I. Title.

Bosch, Hieronymus van Aken, known as, d.1516.

BUSSAGLI, Mario. 759.9492
Bosch. [Translated from the Italian by Claire Pace. 1st American ed.] New York, Grosset & Dunlap [1967] 39, [80] p. illus. (part col.) 18 cm. (The New Grosset art library, 3) On cover: Bosch; the life and work of the artist. [ND653.B65B83 1967] 67-24230
1. Bosch, Hieronymus van Aken, known as, 1516, d.

DELEVOY, Robert L. 759.9492
Bosch: biographical and critical study. Translated by Stuart Gilbert. [Lausanne] Skira; [distributed in the U. S. by World Pub. Co., Cleveland, 1960] 141p. mounted col. illus. (The Taste of our time, v. 34) Bibl.: 60-15595 .125-[134] 5.75
1. Bosch, Hieronymus van Aken, known as, d.1516. I. Title.

GIBSON, Walter S. 759.9492
Hieronymus Bosch [by] Walter S. Gibson. New York, Praeger [1973] 180 p., 151 illus. (26 in color) 22 cm. Bibliography: p. 175-176. [ND653.B65G52] 73-6495 10.00
1. Bosch, Hieronymus van aken, known as, d. 1516.

Bosco, Giovanni, Saint, 1815-1888.

DOHERTY, Edward Joseph. 1890- 922.245
Lambs in wolfskins; the conquering march of Don John Bosco. New York, Scribner, 1953. 228p. 22cm. [BX4700.B75D57] 53-9435
1. Bosco, Giovanni, Saint, 1815-1888. 2. Salesians. I. Title.

DON Bosco's mother, v. 12
by Marieli and Rita Benziger. Paterson, N. J., Salesiana Publishers, 1958. vii, 215p. photos. 22cm. Bibliography: p.215.
1. Bosco, Margherita, d.1856. I. Benziger, Marieli G II. Benziger, Rita, joint author.

LAPPIN, Peter. 271.7 B
Give me souls! : Life of Don Bosco / Peter Lappin. Huntington, Ind. : Our Sunday Visitor, c1977. 366 p. ; 22 cm. Bibliography: p. 363-366. [BX4700.B75L26] 77-10350 ISBN 0-87973-749-2 : 9.95
1. Bosco, Giovanni, Saint, 1815-1888. 2. Christian saints—Italy—Biography. I. Title.

LEMOYNE, Giovanni Battista. 922.22
The biographical memoirs of Saint John Bosco. An American ed. New Rochelle, N.Y., Salesiana Publishers, 1964- v. 24 cm. Editor-in-chief: Diego Borgatello. Vols. 11-1875- by E. Ceria. [BX4700.L53133] 65-3104
1. Bosco, Giovanni, Saint, 1815-1888. I. Borgatello, Diego, 1911- ed. II. Ceria, Eugenio, 1870-1957. III. Title. **BIP**

MATT, Leonard von. 271'.79 B
Don Bosco [by] Leonard von Matt and Henri Bosco. [Translated from the Italian by John Bennett. 1st American ed.] New York, Universe Books [1967] 228 p. illus., facsims., ports. 25 cm. [BX4700.B75M343] 67-12505
1. Bosco, Giovanni, Saint, 1815-1888. I. Bosco, Henri, 1888- joint author. II. Title.

PHELAN, Edna Beyer. 922.245
Dan Bosco; a spiritual portrait. Garden City, N.Y., Doubleday [c.]1963 352p. 22 cm. Bibl. 63-8744 4.95
1. Bosco, Giovanni, Saint, 1815-1888. I. Title.

SHEPPARD, Lancelot Capel, 1906- 922.245
Don Bosco Westminster, Md., Newman Press [1957] 196 p. illus 22 cm. [LB675.B725S5] 57-11829
1. Bosco, Glovanni, Saint, 1815-1888 I. Title.

Bosco, Margherita (Occhiena) 1788-1856.

BENZIGER, Marieli G. 282'.092'4 B
Mamma Margherita: St. John Bosco's mother, by Marieli and Rita Benziger. [2d ed.] Altadena, Calif., Benziger Sisters [1973, c1958] ix, 213 p. 21 cm. Bibliography: p. 213. [BX4705.B68B46 1973] 73-84375
1. Bosco, Margherita (Occhiena) 1788-1856. 2. Bosco, Giovanni, Saint, 1815-1888. I. Benziger, Rita, joint author. II. Title.

Bose, Satyendranath, 1894-1974.

CHATTERJEE, Santimay. 530'.092'4 B
Satyendra Nath Bose / Santimay Chatterjee & Enakshi Chatterjee. New Delhi : National Book Trust, India, 1976. vi, 127 p. ; 19 cm. (National biography series) Bibliography: p. [108]-110. [QC16.B645C45] 76-902524 Rs5.00
1. Bose, Satyendranath, 1894-1974. 2. Physicists—India—Biography. I. Chatterjee, Enakshi, joint author. **BIP**

Bose, Subhas Chandra,

BOSE, Subhas Chandra, 1897-1945 954.0350924
An Indian pilgrim; an unfinish & autobiography and collected letters, 1897-1921. [Tr. from Bengali by Sisir Kumar Bose] New York, Asia Pub. [dist. Taplinger, c.1965] viii, 199p. facsims., geneal. tables. port. 23cm [DS481.B6A3] 65-5400 7.00
I. Title.

Bosisto, Joseph, 1827-1898.

STIRLING, Alfred Thorpe, 1902- 615'.19'00924 B
Joseph Bosisto, by Alfred Stirling. Melbourne, Hawthorn Press, 1970. 44 p. port. 23 cm. "Based on an address delivered to the Royal Historical Society of Victoria on 24 February 1970." [TP40.B63S7] 77-588785 ISBN 0-7256-0014-4 4.50
1. Bosisto, Joseph, 1827-1898. I. Royal Historical Society of Victoria.

Boskovic, Rudjer Josip, 1711-1787.

WHYTE, Lancelot Law, 1896- ed. 925
Roger Joseph Boscovich, S.J., F.R.S., studies of his life and work on the 250th anniversary of his birth. Foreword by Harold Hartley. [Dist. New York, Humanities, 1962, c.1961] 230p. illus. 23cm. Bibl. 62-6280 6.50
1. Boskovic, Rudjer Josip, 1711-1787. I. Title.

WHYTE, Lancelot Law, 1896- ed. 509'.2'2
Roger Joseph Boscovich, S.J., F.R.S., 1711-1787; studies of his life and work on the 250th anniversary of his birth. Foreword by Sir Harold Hartley. New York, Fordham University Press [1961] 230 p. illus., facsims., port. 23 cm. Bibliography: p. [214]-226. [Q143.B7W5] 63-21822
1. Boskovic, Rudjer Josip, 1711-1787. I. Boskovic, Rudjer Josip, 1711-1787. II. Title.

Bosman, Herman Charles, 1905-1951—Biography.

ROSENBERG, Valerie. 823 B
Sunflower to the sun / Valerie Rosenberg. Cape Town : Human & Rousseau, 1976. 241 p. ; 22 cm. [PR9369.3.B6Z85] 77-361838 ISBN 0-7981-0711-1
1. Bosman, Herman Charles, 1905-1951—Biography. 2. Authors, South African—Biography. I. Title.

Bossuet, Jacques Benigne, Bp. of Meaux, 1627-1704.

*BOSSUET, Jacques Benigne, 1627-1704 922.24
Correspondance; 15v. Nouvelle ed., augmentee de Lettres Inedites, et publiee avec des Notes et des Appendices sous le patronage le l'Academie Francaise, par Charles Urbain et E. Levesque. New York, Kraus Reprint, 1966. 15v. (various p.) 23cm. (Les Grands Ecrivains de la France) Orig. pub. in Paris, 1909-1925. 297.00 set,
I. Title.

REYNOLDS, Ernest Edwin, 1894- 922.244
Bossuet. [1st ed.] Garden City, N. Y., Doubleday, 1963. 285 p. port. 22 cm. "A note on books": p. [279]-280. Bibliographical footnotes. [BX4705.B7R44] 63-18197
1. Bossuet, Jacques Benigne, Bp. of Meaux, 1627-1704.

Boston Authors Club — Biog.

FLAGG, Mildred (Buchanan) 1886- 810.9
Boston authors now and then; more members of the Boston Authors Club, 1900-1966. With foreword by Erwin D. Canham. Cambridge, Mass., Dresser, Chapman & Grimes [1966] 269 p. illus., ports. 21 cm. "Sequel to Notable Boston authors." [PS128.F49] 66-25985
1. Boston Authors Club—Biography. I. Boston Authors Club. II. Title.

FLAGG, Mildred (Buchanan) 1886- 810.9005
Notable Boston authors; members of the Boston Authors Club, 1900-1966. With foreword by Erwin D. Canham. Cambridge, Mass., Dresser, Chapman & Grimes [1965- v. ports. 21 cm. [PS128.F5] 65-26731
1. Boston Authors Club — Biog. I. Title.

Boston. Baseball club (American League)

YASTRZEMSKI, Carl. 796.35'0924 B
Yaz [by] Carl Yastrzemski with Al Hirshberg. New York, Viking Press [1968] 183 p. illus., ports. 22 cm. [GV875.B62Y3] 68-18115
1. Boston. Baseball club (American League) I. Hirshberg, Albert, 1909- joint author. II. Title.

Boston Celtics (Basketball team)

HENSHAW, Tom. 796.32'364'0974461
The Boston Celtics : a championship tradition / by Tom Henshaw ; photography by Bruce Curtis, Kevin Fitzgerald. Englewood Cliffs, N.J. : Prentice-Hall, [1974] 127 p. : ill. ; 28 cm. (Reward books) "A Stuart L. Daniels book." [GV885.52.B67H46] 74-7518 ISBN 0-13-080267-0 pbk. : 3.95
1. Boston Celtics (Basketball team) 2. Basketball. 3. Basketball—Biography.

Boston, Lucy Maria, 1892- — Biography—Youth.

BOSTON, Lucy Maria, 1892- 823'.914 B
Perverse and foolish : a memoir of childhood and youth / L. M. Boston. 1st American ed. New York : Atheneum, 1979. 139 p., [6] leaves of plates : ill. ; 23 cm. "A Margaret K. McElderry book." [PR6052.O78Z524 1979] 78-71593 ISBN 0-689-50136-6 : 8.95.
1. Boston, Lucy Maria, 1892- —Biography—Youth. 2. Authors, English—20th century—Biography. I. Title.

Boston—Social life and customs.

PEABODY, Marian Lawrence, 1875- 974.4'61'040924
To be young was very heaven. Boston, Houghton Mifflin, 1967. 366 p. illus., ports. 22 cm. Autobiographical. [CT275.P488A3] 67-11756
1. Boston—Social life and customs. I. Title.

WINSLOW, Anna Green, 1759-1779. 309.1'744'6102
Diary of Anna Green Winslow; a Boston school girl of 1771. Edited by Alice Morse Earle. Detroit, Singing Tree Press, 1970. xx, 121 p. illus. 23 cm. "Facsimile reprint of the 1894 edition." [F73.4.W78 1894a] 71-124586
1. Boston—Social life and customs. I. Earle, Alice (Morse) 1851-1911, ed. **BIP**

Bostwick, A C

BOSTWICK, A C 920
Grouping; selections from the events in the life of a boy as seen through the eyes of that same boy when past middle age, as he relives that period of his life in memory. New York, Vantage Press [c1953] 175p. 23cm. [CT275.B58467A3] 53-10287
I. Title.

3. Heroes in literature. 4. Biography (as a literary form) I. Title. BIP

Botanists.

BUSH-BROWN, Louise (Carter) 1897- 925.8
Men with green pens; lives of the great writers on plants in early times, by Louise Bush-Brown. Philadelphia, Dorrance [1964] 161 p. illus., facsims., ports. 24 cm. Bibliography: p. 160-161. [QK26.B8] 64-21798
1. Botanists. I. Title.

BUSH-BROWN, Louise (Charter) 1897- 925.8
Men with green pens; lives of the great writers on plants in early times. Philadelphia, Dorrance [c.1964] 161p. illus., facsims., ports. 24cm. Bibl. 64-21798 5.00
1. Botanists. I. Title.

Botanists, American.

HUMPHREY, Harry Baker, 1873-1955. 925.8
Makers of North American botany. New York, Ronald Press Co. [1961] xi, 265p. 24cm. (Chronica botanica, no. 21) Includes bibliographical references. [QK1.C55 vol. 21] 61-18435
1. Botanists, American. I. Title. II. Series. BIP

Botanists—Biography.

*BARNHART, John Hendley. comp. 925.81
Biographical notes upon botanists. maintained in the New York Botanical Gardens 3v. Boston, G. K. Hall, 1966. 3v. (1667p.& 35cm. 250.00 set,
1. Botanists—Biog. I. Title.

HALL, Norman, 1906- 583.42'0922
Botanists of the eucalypts / Norman Hall. Australia : Commonwealth Scientific and Industrial Research Organization, c1978. v, 160p. : photos. ; 25 cm. Includes bibliographical references and index. [QK26] ISBN 0-643-00271-5 pbk. : 10.00
1. Botanists — Biography. I. Commonwealth Scientific and Industrial Research Organization. II. Title.
Distributed by ISBS BIP

HALL, Norman, 1906- 583'.42
Botanists of the eucalypts : short biographies of people who have named eucalypts, whose names have been given to species or who have collected type material / Norman Hall. Melbourne : Commonwealth Scientific and Industrial Research Orgnization, 1979. v, 160 p. : ports. ; 25 cm. Bibliography: p. 147-148. [QK26.H27] 79-319701 ISBN 0-643-00271-5 : 10.00
1. Botanists—Biography. 2. Plant collectors—Biography. 3. Eucalyptus—Nomenclature. 4. Botany—Nomenclature. 5. Botany—Australia—History. I. Title.
Distributed by International Scholarly Book Services, Inc., P.O. Box 555, Forest Grove, OR 97116

HAWKS, Ellison, 1890- 581'.0922 B
Pioneers of plant study. This book was originally planned, and some parts of it written, in collaboration with the late George Simonds Boulger. Freeport N.Y., Books for Libraries Press [1969] x, 288 p. illus., ports. 23 cm. (Essay index reprint series) Reprint of the 1928 ed. [QK26.H35 1969] 75-86759 ISBN 0-8369-1139-3
1. Botanists—Biography. 2. Botany—History. I. Boulger, George Simonds, 1853-1922. II. Title. BIP

HUNT Institute for Botanical Documentation. 581'.092'2 B
Biographical dictionary of botanists represented in the Hunt Institute portrait collection. Boston, G. K. Hall, 1972. viii, 451 p. 29 cm. Based on the collections of the Hunt Institute for Botanical Documentation, which was the Hunt Botanical Library prior to 1971. [QK26.H83] 72-6496 ISBN 0-8161-1023-9
1. Botanists—Biography. I. Hunt Botanical Library. II. Title.

Botanists—Biography—Dictionaries.

BARNHART, John Hendley, 1871-1949. 581'.092
Biographical notes upon botanists. Compiled by John Hendley Barnhart and maintained in the New York Botanical Garden Library. Boston, G. K. Hall, 1965. 3 v. 37 cm. Bibliography: v. 1, p. vii-xv. [QK26.B38] 581'.092'2 78-241179
1. Botanists—Biography—Dictionaries. I. New York (City). Botanical Garden. Library. II. Title.

Botanists—United States—Biography.

EIFERT, Virginia Louise (Snider) 1911-1966. 581'.0922 B
Tall trees and far horizons; adventures and discoveries of early botanists in America. With photos., maps, and drawings by the author. Freeport, N.Y., Books for Libraries Press [1972, c1965] xvii, 301 p. illus. 24 cm. (Essay index reprint series) Bibliography: p. 287-292. [QK26.E35 1972] 70-39100 ISBN 0-8369-2686-2
1. Botanists—United States—Biography. 2. Botany—United States—History. I. Title. BIP

KELLY, Howard Atwood, 1858-1943. 581'.092'2 B
Some American medical botanists commemorated in our botanical nomenclature. Boston, Milford House [1973] p. "Delivered as a lecture before the Medical Historical Society of Chicago, 1910, and before the University of Nebraska, October 16, 1913." Reprint of the 1914 ed. published by Southworth Co., Troy, N.Y. [QK26.K4 1973] 73-9882 ISBN 0-87821-057-1 20.00 (lib. bdg.)
1. Botanists—United States—Biography. 2. Physicians—United States—Biography. 3. Botany—Nomenclature. I. Title.

KELLY, Howard Atwood, 1858-1943. 580'.92'2
Some American medical botanists commemorated in our botanical nomenclature / by Howard A. Kelly. Portland, Me. : Longwood Press, 1977. 215 p., [42] leaves of plates : ill. ; 22 cm. "Delivered as a lecture before the Medical Historical Society of Chicago, 1910, and before the University of Nebraska, October 16, 1913." Reprint of the ed. published by Southworth Co., Troy, N.Y. Includes index. Includes bibliographical references. [QK26.K4 1977] 77-3485 ISBN 0-89341-145-0 : 25.00
1. Botanists—United States—Biography. 2. Medical botanists—United States—Biography. 3. Physicians—United States—Biography. 4. Botany—Nomenclature. I. Title.

KELLY, Howard Atwood, 1858-1943. 580'.92'2
Some American medical botanists commemorated in our botanical nomenclature / by Howard A. Kelly. Portland, Me. : Longwood Press, 1977. 215 p., [42] leaves of plates : ill. ; 22 cm. "Delivered as a lecture before the Medical Historical Society of Chicago, 1910, and before the University of Nebraska, October 16, 1913." Reprint of the ed. published by Southworth Co., Troy, N.Y. Includes index. Includes bibliographical references. [QK26.K4 1977] 77-3485 ISBN 0-89341-145-0 : 25.00
1. Botanists—United States—Biography. 2. Medical botanists—United States—Biography. 3. Physicians—United States—Biography. 4. Botany—Nomenclature. I. Title.

Botany—Lake States—History.

VOSS, Edward Groesbeck, 1929- 581.9'77
Botanical beachcombers and explorers : pioneers of the 19th century in the upper Great Lakes / Edward G. Voss. Ann Arbor : University of Michigan Herbarium, 1978. viii, 100 p. : ill. ; 26 cm. (Contributions from the University of Michigan Herbarium ; v. 13) Includes index. Bibliography: p. 91-97. [QK21.U5V67] 78-620015 4.00
1. Botany—Lake States—History. 2. Plant collectors—Lake States—Biography. 3. Botanists—Lake States—Biography. I. Title. II. Series: Michigan. University. Herbarium. Contributions from the University of Michigan Herbarium ; v. 13.

Botany—Nomenclature.

ANDERSON, Berta. 582'.13'014
Wild flower name tales / by Berta Anderson ; photography by Bill Anderson. Colorado Springs, Colo : Century One Press, c1976. 124 p. : ill. ; 22 cm. Includes index. Bibliography: p. 109-115. [QK96.A52] 75-41846 6.95
1. Botany—Nomenclature. 2. Botanists—Biography. 3. Wild flowers—Rocky Mountains. 4. Wild flowers—Colorado. 5. Botany—United States—History. I. Anderson, Bill, 1905- II. Title.

Botefuhr, John Henry Lyons.

HEBEL, Ianthe Bond, 1884- 975.9'21'040924
John H. L. Botefuhr, early pioneer of the Halifax area. Daytona Beach, Fla., 1961 [cover 1960] [25] l. 29 cm. Typescript (carbon copy) [F317.V7H44] 75-317120
1. Botefuhr, John Henry Lyons. 2. Halifax River region, Fla.—History. I. Title.

Botein, Bernard.

BOTEIN, Bernard. 347'.747'07
Trial judge; the candid behind-the-bench story of Justice Bernard Botein. New York, Da Capo Press, 1974 [c1952] 337 p. 23 cm. (Da Capo Press reprints in American constitutional and legal history) Reprint of the ed. published by Simon and Schuster, New York. [KF373.B58A3 1974] 74-7340 13.50
1. Botein, Bernard. 2. Judges—New York (State)—Correspondence, reminiscences, etc. 3. Trial practice—New York (State) I. Title.

Botero, Fernando, 1932-

BOTERO, Fernando, 1932- 759.9861
Botero / Klaus Gallwitz ; [translated from the German by John Gabriel]. New York : Rizzoli, 1976. 87, [1] p. : chiefly ill. (some col.) ; 21 x 23 cm. Bibliography: p. 86-[88] [ND379.B6G3413] 76-11502 ISBN 0-8478-0045-8 : 7.95
1. Botero, Fernando, 1932- 2. Painters—Colombia—Biography. I. Gallwitz, Klaus.

Botev, Khristo, 1848-1876—Biography.

UNDZHIEV, Ivan N. 949.77'01'0924 B
Hristo Botev : a biography / Ivan Oundjiev, Tsveta Oundjieva ; [translated by Nikolina Panova]. Sofia : Sofia Press, [1976] 75 p. ; 17 cm. Translated from the authors' unpublished manuscript. [DR83.2.B6U513] 76-464161
1. Botev, Khristo, 1848-1876—Biography. I. Undzhieva, Tsveta Ivanova, joint author.

Bothe, Albert Edward, 1891-1955.

BOTHE, Marion (Bradley) 926.1
Dr. Albert E. Bothe, August 5, 1891-November 11, 1955. [Philadelphia?] 1962. 95 p. illus. 22 cm. [R154.B75B6] 63-6339
1. Bothe, Albert Edward, 1891-1955. I. Title.

Botolph, Saint, d. 680.

RYAN, George E. 271'.1'024 B
Botolph of Boston, by George E. Ryan. Foreword by Richard Cardinal Cushing. [North Quincy, Mass., Christopher Pub. House, 1971] 268 p. illus., facsims. 25 cm. Includes bibliographical references. [BX4700.B76R9] 76-136030 ISBN 0-8158-0252-8 10.00
1. Botolph, Saint, d. 680. 2. Boston. I. Title. BIP

Bott, Henry, 1818-1910.

BOTT, Henry, 1818-1910. 917.48'41'0330924
Reminiscences of an old man in York County, Pennsylvania, during the nineteenth century; diary and recollections of Henry Bott. Edited by Carl E. Hatch and Richard E. Kohler. York, Pa., Strine Pub. Co. [1973] vii, 15 p. 23 cm. (Martin Library publications, no. 2) [F157.Y6B67] 73-173339 1.25
1. Bott, Henry, 1818-1910. 2. York Co., Pa.—Social life and customs. I. Hatch, Carl E., ed. II. Kohler, Richard E., ed. III. Title. IV. Series: Martin Memorial Library, York, Pa. Publications, no. 2.

Botticelli, Sandro, 1447?-1510.

ARGAN, Giulio Carlo. 759.5
Botticelli: biographical and critical study. Translated from the Italian by James Emmons. [New York] Skira [1957] 146 p. mounted col. illus. 19 cm. (The Taste of our time, 19) Bibliography: p. [140] [ND623.B7A713] 927.5 57-7822
1. Botticelli, Sandro, 1447?-1510.

ARGAN, Guilio Carlo. 927.5
Botticelli: Biographical and critical stury. Translated from the Italian by James Emmons. [New York] Skira [1957] 146p. mounted col. illus. 19cm. (The Taste of our time, 19) Bibliography: p. [140] [ND623.B7A713] [ND623.B7A713] 759.5 57-7822 57-7822
1. Botticelli, Sandro, 1447?-1510. I. Title.

ETTLINGER, Leopold David, 1913- 759.5
Botticelli / L. D. and Helen S. Ettlinger. London : Thames and Hudson, c1976. 216 p. : 138 ill. (some col.) ; 22 cm. Includes index. Bibliography: p. 208. [ND623.B7E85] 77-350818 ISBN 0-500-18156-X : £4.50
1. Botticelli, Sandro, 1447?-1510. I. Ettlinger, Helen S., joint author. II. Botticelli, Sandro, 1447?-1510.

EWING, Lucy Elizabeth Lee. 759.2
George Frederick Watts, Sandro Botticelli, Matthew Arnold, by Lucie Lee Ewing. [Folcroft, Pa.] Folcroft Library Editions, 1973 [c1904] 64 p. illus. 22 cm. Reprint of the ed. published by Grafton Press, New York. [ND497.W3E9 1973] 73-8983 15.00
1. Watts, George Frederick, 1817-1904. 2. Botticelli, Sandro, 1447?-1510. 3. Arnold, Matthew, 1822-1888. BIP

LEGOUIX, Susan. 759.5
Botticelli / Susan Legouix. 1st U.S. ed. New York : Two Continents/Oresko, c1977. p. cm. (Oresko art book series) Includes index. Bibliography: p. [ND623.B7L43 1977] 77-10355 ISBN 0-8467-0376-9 : 15.95 pbk. : 9.95
1. Botticelli, Sandro, 1447?-1510. 2. Painters—Italy—Biography. I. Botticelli, Sandro, 1447?-1510. II. Title. III. Series. BIP

LIGHTBOWN, R. W. 759.5 B
Sandro Botticelli / Ronald Lightbown. Berkeley : University of California Press, c1978. 2 v. : ill. (some col.) ; 29 cm. On spine: Botticelli. Contents.Contents.—v. 1. Life and work.—v. 2. Complete catalogue. Includes bibliographies and indexes. [ND623.B7L53 1978b] 76-46237 ISBN 0-520-03372-8 : 120.00
1. Botticelli, Sandro, 1447?-1510. 2. Painters—Italy—Biography. I. Botticelli, Sandro, 1447?-1510. BIP

RIPLEY, Elizabeth 927.5
Botticelli. a biography. Philadelphia, Lippincott [c.1960] 68p. Bibl.: p.[70-71]. illus. 26cm. 60-11361 3.00
1. Botticelli, Sandro, 1447?-1510. I. Title.

SANDRO Botticelli (1444/5-1510) Text by Frederick Hartt. New York, H. N. Abrams in association with Pocket Books [1953] [74]p. 44illus. (part col.) 18cm. (The Pocket library of great art, A9) An Abrams art book. Bibliography: p.[74] [ND623.B7H32] [ND623.B7H32] 927.5 53-4517 53-4517 759.5
I. Botticelli, Sandro, 1447?-1510. II. Hartt, Frederick.

Bottomley, Gordon,

BOTTOMLEY, Gordon, 1874-1948. 928.2
Poet & painter; being the correspondence between Gordon Bottomley and Paul

Nash, 1910-1946, edited by Claude Colleer Abbott and Anthony Bertram. London, New York, Oxford University Press, 1955. 277p. illus. 22cm. [PR6003.O67Z55] 55-14450
1. Nash, Paul, 1889-1946. II. Title.

Boucher, Guillaume, 13th cent.

OLSCHKI, Leonardo, 1885- 709'.24 B
Guillaume Boucher, a French artist at the court of the Khans. New York, Greenwood Press [1969, c1946] viii, 125 p. illus. 23 cm. Includes bibliographical references. [ND553.B7O4 1969] 69-14019
1. Boucher, Guillaume, 13th cent. 2. Art—Mongolia.

Boucher, Jonathan,

BOUCHER, Jonathan, 1738-1804. 973.3'0924 B
Reminiscences of an American loyalist, 1738-1789, being the autobiography of the Revd. Jonathan Boucher, Rector of Annapolis in Maryland and afterwards Vicar of Epsom, Surrey, england. edited by his grandson Jonathan Bouchier Port Washington, N.Y., Kennikat Press [1967] xi, 201 p. facsim., port. 22 cm. Reprint of the 1925 ed. [E277.B75 1967] 67-27577
I. Bouchier, Jonathan, ed. II. Title.

Boucicault, Dion, 1820-1890.

WALSH, Townsend. 822'.8 B
The career of Dion Boucicault. New York, B. Blom [1967] xviii, 224 p. illus., ports. 20 cm. Reprint of the 1915 ed. "Chronological list of Boucicault's dramatic works": p. 220-224. [PN2598.B67W3 1967] 67-28848
1. Boucicault, Dion, 1820-1890. I. Title. BIP

Boudinot, Elias, 1740-1821.

BOUDINOT, Elias, 1740-1821. 973.3'0924 B
The life, public services, addresses, and letters of Elias Boudinot. Edited by J. J. Boudinot. New York, Da Capo Press, 1971 [c1896] 2 v. ports. 23 cm. (The Era of the American Revolution) Includes bibliographical references. [E302.6.B7A45 1971] 72-119059 ISBN 0-306-71946-0
1. United States—History—Revolution, 1775-1783—Personal narratives. 2. United States—History—Constitutional period, 1789-1809. I. Doudinot, Jane J., ed. II. Title.

BOYD, George Adams. 923.273
Elias Boudinot, patriot and statesman, 1740-1821. Princeton, Princeton University Press, 1952. xiii, 321 p. illus., ports., map. 25 cm. Bibliography: p. [297]-304. [E302.6.B7B6] 52-8761
1. Boudinot, Elias, 1740-1821. I. Title.

BOYD, George Adams. 973.3'0924 B
Elias Boudinot; patriot and statesman, 1740-1821. New York, Greenwood Press [1969, c1952] xiii, 321 p. illus., ports, map. 24 cm. Bibliography: p. [295]-304. [E302.6.B7B6 1969] 69-13835
1. Boudinot, Elias, 1740-1821.

CLARK, Barbara Louise. 973.3'092'4 B
E. B. : the story of Elias Boudinot IV, his family, his friends, and his country / Barbara Louise Clark. Philadelphia : Dorrance, c1977. xiv, 472 p. : ill. ; 23 cm. Bibliography: p. 467-472. [E302.6.B7C57] 77-367320 ISBN 0-8059-2246-6 : 10.00
1. Boudinot, Elias, 1740-1821. 2. Legislators—United States—Biography. 3. United States—History—Revolution, 1775-1783. 4. United States—History—1783-1815.

Boudreau, Lou,

BOUDREAU, Lou, 1917- 927.96357
Player-manager, by Lou Boudreau with Ed Fitzgerald. [Rev. ed.] Boston, Little, Brown, 1952. 256 p. illus. 22 cm. [GV865.B68A3 1952] 52-4018
I. Title.

Bougainville, Louis Antoine de, comte, 1729-1811.

ROSS, Michael, 1905- 910'.92'4 B
Bougainville / by Michael Ross ; with drawings by the author. London : Gordon & Cremonesi, 1978. 167 p., [8] leaves of plates : ill. ; 27 cm. Includes index. [G256.B6R67] 77-30500 ISBN 0-86033-059-1 : 24.95
1. Bougainville, Louis Antoine de, comte, 1729-1811. 2. Explorers—France—Biography.
Distributed by Atheneum BIP

Boulee, Etienne Louis, 1728-1799.

LEMAGNY, J. C. 720'.922
Visionary architects: Boulee, Ledoux, Lequeu. [Houston, Tex., Printed by Gulf Print. Co., 1968] 240 p. illus. 23 cm. Catalogue of an exhibition held at the University of St. Thomas, Houston, Tex., Oct. 19, 1967-Jan. 3, 1968, and at four other American museums, Jan. 22-Oct. 29, 1968. Bibliography: p. 235-240. [NA1052.L4] 68-24454
1. Boulee, Etienne Louis, 1728-1799. 2. Ledoux, Claude Nicolas, 1736-1806. 3. Lequeu, Jean Jacques, 1757-ca. 1825. I. Houston, Tex. University of St. Thomas. II. Title.

Boulanger, Georges Ernest Jean Marie, 1837-1891.

HARDING, James. 944.081'0924 B
The astonishing adventure of General Boulanger. London, New York, W. H. Allen, 1971. xiii, 251 p., 8 plates. illus., ports. 23 cm. Bibliography: p. 245-248. [DC342.8.B7H37] 70-852813 ISBN 0-491-00047-2 £3.20
1. Boulanger, Georges Ernest Jean Marie, 1837-1891. I. Title.

Boulanger, Lili, 1893-1918.

ROSENSTIEL, Leonie. 780'.92'4 B
The life and works of Lili Boulanger / Leonie Rosenstiel. Rutherford, N.Y. : Fairleigh Dickinson University Press, c1977. p. cm. Includes index. Bibliography: p. [ML410.B7727R7] 75-18244 ISBN 0-8386-1796-4 : 22.50
1. Boulanger, Lili, 1893-1918. 2. Composers—France—Biography. BIP

Boulder, Utah—History.

LEFEVRE, Lenora Hall. 917.92'52
The Boulder country and its people; a history of the people of Boulder and the surrounding country, one hundred years, 1872-1973. Written and compiled by Lenora Hall LeFevre. Edited by Nethella Griffin Woolsey. [Springville, Utah, Art City Pub., 1973] ix, 294 p. illus. 28 cm. [F834.B68L43] 74-162886
1. Boulder, Utah—History. 2. Boulder, Utah—Biography. I. Title.

Boulding, Elise.

BOULDING, Elise. 289.6'092'4 B
Born remembering / by Elise Boulding. [Wallingford, Pa. : Pendle Hill Publications], 1975. 30 p. ; 19 cm. (Pendle Hill pamphlet ; 200 ISSN 0031-4250) Bibliography: p. 30. [BX7795.B56A33] 74-30805 ISBN 0-87574-200-9 : 0.95
1. Boulding, Elise. I. Title. BIP

Boulding, Kenneth Ewart, 1910-

KERMAN, Cynthia Earl. 300'.92'4 B
Creative tension; the life and thought of Kenneth Boulding. Ann Arbor, University of Michigan Press [1974] xiv, 380 p. illus. 24 cm. Bibliography: p. 371-373. [H59.B65K47] 72-94762 ISBN 0-472-51500-4 12.50
1. Boulding, Kenneth Ewart, 1910- I. Title. BIP

Boulez, Pierre, 1925-

BOULEZ, Pierre, 1925- 780'.92'4 B
Conversations with Celestin Deliege / Pierre Boulez ; foreword by Robert Wangermee. London : Eulenburg Books, 1976. 123 p. ; 24 cm. Translation of Par volonte et par hasard : entretiens avec Celestin Deliege. [ML410.B773A33] 77-374549 ISBN 0-903873-21-4 : £3.00. ISBN 0-903873-22-2 pbk.
1. Boulez, Pierre, 1925- 2. Composers—France—Interviews. 3. Music—History and criticism—20th century. I. Deliege, Celestin. II. Title.

PEYSER, Joan. 780'.92'4 B
Boulez / Joan Peyser. New York : Schirmer Books, c1976. p. cm. Includes index. [ML410.B773P5] 76-20884 ISBN 0-02-871700-7 : 12.95
1. Boulez, Pierre, 1925- 2. Composers—France—Biography. BIP

Boullee, Etienne Louis, 1728-1799.

PEROUSE de Montclos, Jean Marie. 720'.92'4
Etienne-Louis Boullee (1728-1799); theoretician of revolutionary architecture. [Translated from the French by James Emmons.] New York, Braziller [1974] 128 p. illus. 25 cm. Bibliography: p. 119-121. [NA1053.B69P413 1974] 72-92833 ISBN 0-8076-0672-3 6.95
1. Boullee, Etienne Louis, 1728-1799.

Boulton, Matthew, 1728-1809.

DELIEB, Eric. 739.3'72'4
Matthew Boulton: master silversmith, 1760-1790. Research collaboration by Michael Roberts. New York, C. N. Potter; distributed by Crown Publishers [1971] 144 p. illus. 26 cm. Bibliography: p. 139. [NK7198.B66D4 1971] 71-176094 10.95
1. Boulton, Matthew, 1728-1809.

Bourbon, House of.

SEWARD, Desmond, 1935- 944'.03'0922 B
The Bourbon kings of France / Desmond Seward. New York : Barnes & Noble Books, 1976. xiv, 331 p., [7] leaves of plates : ill. ; 23 cm. Includes bibliographical references and index. [DC36.8.B7S48] 75-40528 ISBN 0-06-496185-0 : 18.50
1. Bourbon, House of. I. Title. BIP

Bourgeoys, Marguerite, 1620-1700.

BURTON, Katherine (Kruz) 1890- 922.244
Valiant voyager: Blessed Marguerite Bourgeoys, foundress of the Congregation de Notre Dame of Montreal, by Katherine Burton. With a pref. by Francis Cardinal Spellman. Milwaukee, Bruce Pub. Co. [c1964] xiii, 197 p. illus., port. 23 cm. [BX4331.2.Z8B8] 65-2150
1. Bourgeoys, Marguerite, 1620-1700. 2. Congregation de Notre Dame de Montreal. I. Title.

Bourgeoys, Marguerite, 1620-1700—Juvenile literature.

SAINT MARY GENEVIEVE, Sister 920
Marguerite Bourgeoys, pioneer teacher. Illus. by Harry Barton. London, Burns & Oates; New York, Farrar [c.1963] 176p. illus. 22cm. (Vision bks., 58) 63-9925 2.25
1. Bourgeoys, Marguerite, 1620-1700—Juvenile literature. I. Title.

Bourguiba, Habib, Pres. Tunisia, 1903-

LACOUTURE, Jean. 960
The demigods: charismatic leadership in the third world. [Translated from the French by Patricia Wolf. 1st American ed.] New York, Knopf, 1970. 300, vi p. 22 cm. Translation of Quatre hommes et leurs peuples. Bibliography: p. [295]-300. [D839.5.L2513 1970] 72-111235 7.95
1. Nasser, Gamal Abdel, Pres. United Arab Republic, 1918-1970. 2. Bourguiba, Habib, Pres. Tunisia, 1903- 3. Norodom Sihanouk Varman, King of Cambodia, 1922- 4. Nkrumah, Kwame, Pres. Ghana, 1909- I. Title.

Bourke, Richard, Sir, 1777-1855.

KING, Hazel. 941.58'092'4 B
Richard Bourke. Melbourne, New York, Oxford University Press, 1971. xv, 312 p. illus. 22 cm. Bibliography: p. 293-300. [DU172.B6K5] 72-185578
1. Bourke, Richard, Sir, 1777-1855. BIP

Bourke-White, Margaret, 1906-1971.

BOURKE-WHITE, Margarett, 1905- 927.7
Portrait of myself. New York, Simon and Schuster, 1963. 383 p. illus. 24 cm. [TR140.B6A3] 63-11141
I. Title.

BROWN, Theodore M. 779'.092'4
Margaret Bourke-White, photojournalist [by] Theodore M. Brown. [Ithaca, N.Y.] Andrew Dickson White Museum of Art, Cornell University, 1972. 136 p. illus. 29 cm. "Catalog of the exhibition, Andrew Dickson White Museum of Art, Cornell University, March 15-April 23, 1972:" (p. [127]-131) Bibliography: p. [109]-119. [TR140.B6B76] 76-188882
1. Bourke-White, Margaret, 1905-1971. 2. Photography, Journalistic—Exhibitions. I. Cornell University. Andrew Dickson White Museum of Art. II. Title.

BROWN, Theodore M. 779'.092'4
Margaret Bourke-White, photojournalist [by] Theodore M. Brown. [Ithaca, N.Y.] Andrew Dickson White Museum of Art, Cornell University, 1972. 136 p. illus. 29 cm. "Catalog of the exhibition, Andrew Dickson White Museum of Art, Cornell University, March 15-April 23, 1972:" (p. [127]-131) Bibliography: p. [109]-119. [TR140.B6B76] 76-188882
1. Bourke-White, Margaret, 1905-1971. 2. Photography, Journalistic—Exhibitions. I. Cornell University. Andrew Dickson White Museum of Art. II. Title.

DUNHAM, Montrew. 770'.92'4 B
Margaret Bourke-White, young photographer / by Montrew Dunham ; illustrated by Robert Doremus. Indianapolis : Bobbs-Merrill, c1977. 192 p. : ill. ; 20 cm. (Childhood of famous Americans) A biography of the photographer and writer who was one of the original staff photographers for Life magazine and the first accredited woman war correspondent to be sent overseas during World War II. [TR140.B6D86] 92 75-34512 ISBN 0-672-52225-X : 3.95 ISBN 0-672-71413-2 lib.bdg. : 3.73
1. Bourke-White, Margaret, 1906-1971. 2. Photographers—United States—Biography—Juvenile literature. I. Doremus, Robert. II. Title.

Bourke-White, Margaret, 1906-1971—Juvenile literature.

NOBLE, Iris. 770'.92'4 B
Cameras and courage: Margaret Bourke-White. New York, J. Messner [1973] 191 p. 21 cm. Bibliography: p. 183. Biography of a woman renowned for her photographic interpretations of war, revolution, and poverty and for her personal battle against Parkinsonism. [TR140.B6N6] 92 72-11927 ISBN 0-671-32577-9 4.95
1. Bourke-White, Margaret, 1906-1971—Juvenile literature. I. Title.
Library ed. 4.29.

SIEGEL, Beatrice. 770'.92'4 B
An eye on the world : Margaret Bourke-White, photographer / by Beatrice Siegel. New York : F. Warne, 1980 p. cm. Includes index. Bibliography: p. A biography of a woman renowned for her photographic interpretations of war, revolution, and poverty and for her personal battle against Parkinsonism. [TR140.B6S58] 92 79-2432 ISBN 0-7232-6173-3 : 7.95
1. Bourke-White, Margaret, 1904-1971—Juvenile literature. 2. Photographers—United States—Biography—Juvenile literature. I. Title.

Bourne, George Washington, 1801-1856.

MURPHY, Thomas W. 974.1'95
The Wedding Cake House : the world of

George W. Bourne / by Thomas W. Murphy, Jr. Kennebunk, ME. : Murphy, c1978. 104 p. : ill. ; 22 cm. Includes index. Bibliography: p. 92-94. [F29.W38M87] 78-61276 ISBN 0-932006-07-8 : 5.25
1. Bourne, George Washington, 1801-1856. 2. Wedding Cake House, ME. 3. Kennebunk, ME.—Biography. 4. Kennebunkport, ME.—Biography. 5. Businessmen—Maine—Kennebunk—Biography. 6. Businessmen—Maine—Kennebunkport—Biography. I. Title. **BIP**

Bourne, Hugh, 1772-1852.

WILKINSON, John Thomas, 1893- 922.742
Hugh Bourne, 1772-1852. London, Epworth Press [1952] 203p. illus. 23cm. [BX8379.B6W5] 53-29344
1. Bourne, Hugh, 1772-1852. I. Title.

Bourne, Randolph Silliman, 1886-1918.

FILLER, Louis, 1911- 928.1
Randolph Bourne [Introd. by Max Lerner] New York, Citadel [1966, c.1943] (C217) Bibl. [PS3503.O8Z6] 1.75 pap.,
1. Bourne, Randolph Silliman, 1886-1918. I. Title.

MOREAU, John Adam 818.5209
Randolph Bourne: legend and reality. Washington, D.C., Public Affairs Pr. [c.1966] viii, 227p. port. 24cm. Bibl. [PS3503.O8Z78] 66-17651 5.00
1. Bourne, Randolph Silliman, 1886-1918. I. Title.

Bournonville, Auguste, 1805-1879.

BOURNONVILLE, Auguste, 1805-1879. 792.8'092'4 B
My theatre life / August Bournonville ; translated from the Danish by Patricia N. McAndrew ; introd. by Svend Kragh-Jacobsen. Middletown, Conn. : Wesleyan University Press, c1979. xx, 709 p., [16] leaves of plates : ill. ; 26 cm. Translation of Mit theaterliv. Includes index. [GV1785.B64A3313] 78-27349 ISBN 0-8195-5035-3 : 37.50
1. Bournonville, Auguste, 1805-1879. 2. Kongelige Teater og kapel. 3. Choreographers—Denmark—Biography. I. Title. **BIP**

TERRY, Walter. 792.8'0924 B
The King's ballet master : a biography of Denmark's August Bournonville / Walter Terry. New York : Dodd, Mead, c1979. xv, 173 p. : ill. ; 24 cm. Includes index. Bibliography: p. 167-168. [GV1785.B64T47] 79-55736 ISBN 0-396-07722-6 : 8.95
1. Bournonville, Auguste, 1805-1879. 2. Copenhagen. Kongelige Teater og kapel. Kongelige Ballet. 3. Choreographers—Denmark—Biography. I. Title. **BIP**

Bouscaren, Louis Frederic Gustave, 1840-1904.

BOUSCAREN, Louis Henri Gustave. 620.136
The bridge builder; Louis Frederic Gustave Bouscaren, 1840-1904, written by his son Louis Henri Gustave, for his grandchildren. [Winnetka? Ill., 1964] ix, 83 p. illus., map (on lining papers) ports. 24 cm. [TG140.B6B6] 65-2690
1. Bouscaren, Louis Frederic Gustave, 1840-1904. I. Title.

Bouton, Jim.

BOUTON, Jim. 796.357'0924
Ball four; my life and hard times throwing the knuckleball in the Big Leagues. Edited by Leonard Shecter. New York, World Pub. Co. [1970] xiii, 400 p. illus., ports. 24 cm. [GV865.B69A3 1970] 78-120125 6.95
1. Baseball. I. Shecter, Leonard, ed. II. Title.

BOUTON, Jim, comp. 796.357'092'2 B
"I managed good, but boy did they play bad." Written and edited by Jim Bouton, with Neil Offen. [1st ed. Chicago] Playboy Press [1973] xxiii, 325 p. illus. 22 cm. [GV865.A1B63] 73-76276 7.95
1. Baseball—Biography. 2. Baseball managing. I. Offen, Neil. II. Title.
Contents Omitted.

BOUTON, Jim., comp. 796.357'092'2 [B]
"I managed good, but boy did they play bad." Written and edited by Jim Bouton, with Neil Offen. [New York, Dell 1974, c1973] 300 p. illus. 18 cm. [GV865.A1B63] 1.50 (pbk.)
1. Baseball—Biography. 2. Baseball managing. I. Offen, Neil. II. Title.
L.C. card number for hardbound ed.: 73-76276.

PLUTO, Terry, 1955- 796.357'092'4 B
The greatest summer : the remarkable story of Jim Bouton's comeback to major league baseball / Terry Pluto. Englewood Cliffs, N.J. : Prentice-Hall, c1979. 179 p., [4] leaves of plates : ill. ; 22 cm. [GV865.B69P58] 78-31646 ISBN 0-13-364927-X : 8.95
1. Bouton, Jim. 2. Baseball players—United States—Biography. I. Title.

Bove, Charles F.,

BOVE, Charles F., M.D. 926.1
Diary of a French doctor, by Charles F. Bove, M.D., Dana L. Thomas. New York, Belmont [1962, c.1956] 221p. 18cm. (L92-534) Orig. pub. as: A Paris surgeon's story. .50 pap.,
I. Title.

BOVE, Charles F 1892- 926.1
A Paris surgeon's story [by] Charles F. Bove, with Dana Lee Thomas. Foreword by Leland Stowe. [1st ed.] Boston, Little, Brown [c1956] 306p. 21cm. Autobiographical. [R154.B76A3] 56-5617
I. Title.

Boveri, Theodor, 1862-1915.

BALTZER, Friedrich, 1884- 574.8/7/0924
Theodor Boveri; life and work of a great biologist, 1862-1915 [by] Fritz Baltzer. Tr. from German by Dorothea Rudnick. Berkeley, Univ. of Calif. Pr., 1967. 165p. illus., ports. 23cm. Bibl. [QH31.B77B33] (B) 67-21996 6.00
1. Boveri, Theodor, 1862-1915. I. Title.

BALTZER, Friedrich, 1884- 574.8'7'0924 (B)
Theodor Boveri; life and work of a great biologist, 1862-1915 [by] Fritz Baltzer. Translated from the German by Dorothea Rudnick. Berkeley, University of California Press, 1967. 165 p. illus., ports. 23 cm. Bibliography: p. 143-157. [QH31.B77B33] 67-21996
1. Boveri, Theodor, 1862-1915. I. Title. **BIP**

Bow, Clara, 1905-1965.

MORELLA, Joe. 791.43'028'0924 B
The "It" girl : the incredible story of Clara Bow / Joe Morella and Edward Z. Epstein. New York : Delacorte Press, c1976. 284 p., [13] leaves of plates : ill. ; 22 cm. [PN2287.B65M6] 75-45059 ISBN 0-440-04127-9 : 8.95
1. Bow, Clara, 1905-1965. I. Epstein, Edward Z., joint author. II. Title.

MORELLA, Joe. 791.43'028'0924
The "It" girl : the incredible story of Clara Bow / Joe Morella & Edward Z. Epstein. New York : Dell Pub. Co., 1977c1976. 284p.,[8] leaves of plates : ill. ; 18 cm. (A Dell Book) [PN2287.B65M6] ISBN 0-440-14068-4 pbk. : 1.95
1. Bow, Clara, 1905-1965. I. Epstein, Edward Z., joint author. II. Title.
L.C. card no. for c1976 Delacorte Press ed.: 75-45059.

Bowditch, Henry Ingersoll, 1808-1892.

BOWDITCH, Vincent Yardley, 1852-1929. 610'.924 B
Life and correspondence of Henry Ingersoll Bowditch. Freeport, N.Y., Books for Libraries Press [1970] 2 v. illus., facsim., ports. 23 cm. Reprint of the 1902 ed. [R154.B77B7 1970] 72-121501
1. Bowditch, Henry Ingersoll, 1808-1892. I. Title. **BIP**

Bowditch, Nathaniel, 1773-1838.

RINK, Paul, 1912- 527'.0924 B
To steer by the stars; the story of Nathaniel Bowditch. [1st ed.] Garden City, N.Y., Doubleday [1969] 189 p. port. 24 cm. [VK140.B68R5] 71-79416 3.95
1. Bowditch, Nathaniel, 1773-1838. I. Title.

Bowen, Barbara (Macdonald)

BOWEN, Barbara (Macdonald) 1876- 922
God still guides. New York, Vantage Press [c1954] 57p. 23cm. Autobiography. [BV3785.B65A3 1954] 54-9128
I. Title.

Bowen, Charles O.

†KELLER, Weldon Phillip, 1920- 269'.2'0924 B
Charles Bowen : "Paul Bunyan" of the Canadian West / W. Phillip Keller. Beaverlodge, Alta. : Horizon House, 1977 141 p. : ill. ; 18 cm. (Horizon books) Originally published under title: Bold under God. [BR1725.B673K44 1976] 78-314012 ISBN 0-88965-012-8 : 1.95
1. Bowen, Charles O. 2. Christian biography—Northwest, Canadian. 3. Northwest, Canadian—Biography.

Bowen, Elizabeth, 1899-1973.

KENNEY, Edwin J. 823'.9'12
Elizabeth Bowen [by] Edwin J. Kenney, Jr. Lewisburg [Pa.] Bucknell University Press [1974, c1975] 107 p. 21 cm. (The Irish writers series) Bibliography: p. 105-107. [PR6003.O6757Z675] 74-168810 ISBN 0-8387-7939-5 4.50
1. Bowen, Elizabeth, 1899-1973. **BIP**

Bowen, Elizabeth, 1899-1973 - Biography.

GLENDINNING, Victoria. 823'.9'12
Elizabeth Bowen / by Victoria Glendinning. 1st American ed. New York : Knopf : distributed by Random House, 1978. xvii, 331 p., [8] leaves of plates : ill. ; 22 cm. Includes index. "Books by Elizabeth Bowen": p. 315-316. [PR6003.O6757Z65 1978] 77-10604 ISBN 0-394-40533-1 : 12.50
1. Bowen, Elizabeth, 1899-1973—Biography. 2. Novelists, English—20th century—Biography.

GLENDINNING, Victoria. 823'.9'12
Elizabeth Bowen / Victoria Glendinning. New York : Avon Books, 1979, c1977. xiv, 306 p., [8] leaves of plates : ill. ; 18 cm. (A Discus book) Includes index. "Books by Elizabeth Bowen": p. 285-287. [PR6003.O6757Z65] ISBN 0-380-44354-6 pbk. : 3.50
1. Bowen, Elizabeth, 1899-1973 — Biography. 2. Novelists, English — 20th century — Biography. I. Title.
L.C. card no. for 1978 Knopf ed.: 77-10604. **BIP**

Bowen, Ezra.

BOWEN, Ezra. 070.4'092'4 B
Henry and other heroes; an informal memoir of high dreams and vanished seasons. [1st ed.] Boston, Little, Brown [1974] 246 p. 21 cm. "A Sports illustrated book." [GV719.B68A34] 73-22257 ISBN 0-316-10395-0 6.95
1. Bowen, Ezra. I. Title.

Bower, William Clayton,

BOWER, William Clayton, 1878- 922.673
Through the years; personal memoirs. Lexington, Ky., Transylvania College Press, 1957. 111p. illus. 24cm. [BX7343.B6A3] 57-22216
I. Title.

Bowers, Claude Gernade, 1879-1958.

BOWERS, Claude Gernade, 1879-1958. 983'.064
Chile through embassy windows, 1939-1953 / by Claude G. Bowers. Westport, Conn. : Greenwood Press, [1977] c1958. ix, 375 p. ; 24 cm. Reprint of the ed. published by Simon and Schuster, New York. Includes index. [F3058.B68 1977] 76-56739 ISBN 0-8371-9435-0 lib. bdg. : 22.00
1. Bowers, Claude Gernade, 1879-1958. 2. Chile. 3. Chile—Foreign relations—United States. 4. United States—foreign relations—Chile. 5. Diplomats—Chile—Biography. I. Title.

Bowers, Eilley (Orrum) 1826-1903.

ADDENBROOKE, Alice B. 920.7
The mistress of the mansion. Palo Alto, Calif., Pacific Books [c.1959] 38p. illus. 23cm. 59-3216 pap., apply
1. Bowers, Eilley (Orrum) 1826-1903. I. Title. **BIP**

Bowes, John, 1811-1885.

HARDY, Charles Edwin. 069'.0924 B
John Bowes and the Bowes Museum, by Charles E. Hardy. Newcastle upon Tyne, Graham, 1970. xvi, 288 p., 40 plates. illus. (some col.), facsims., map (on lining papers), ports. (some col.) 23 cm. [CT788.B752H3] 78-529256 ISBN 0-900409-95-9 52/6
1. Bowes, John, 1811-1885. 2. Bowes Museum, Barnard Castle, Eng. I. Title.

Bowie, David.

CLAIRE, Vivian. 784'.092'4 B
David Bowie! The king of glitter rock / by Vivian Claire. New York : Flash Books, c1977. 77 p. : ill. ; 26 cm. [ML420.B754C6] 76-56571 ISBN 0-8256-3911-5 : 3.95
1. Bowie, David. 2. Singers—England—Biography.
Available from Music Sales Corp.

*DOUGLAS, David. 784'.092'4 B
presenting David Bowie! New York, Pinnacle Books [1975] 212 p. 18 cm. [ML420] ISBN 0-523-00724-8 1.75 (pbk.)
1. Bowie, David. I. Title.

TREMELETT, George. 784'.092'4
The David Bowie story / by George Tremlett. New York : Warner Paperback Library, 1975, c1974. 158 p. : ill. ; 18 cm. [ML420.B754T7] 75-314227 ISBN 0-446-78789-2 : 1.50
1. Bowie, David. I. Title.

Bowie family.

BOWIE, Walter Worthington, 1858-1938. 929'.2'0973
The Bowies and their kindred; a genealogical and biographical history. With an introd. by Raymond B. Clark, Jr. Cottonport [La.] Polyanthos, 1971. xix, 523 p. illus. 24 cm. Reprint of the 1899 ed. published by Cromwell Bros., Washington. [CS71.B787 1971] 74-172558
1. Bowie family. I. Title.

Bowie, James, d. 1836.

GARST, Doris Shannon, 1899- 976.4'03'0924 B
James Bowie and his famous knife. New York, J. Messner [1955] 192 p. 22 cm. A biography of a famous Indian fighter and reputed inventor of the defensive Bowie knife, from his childhood on the Louisiana bayou to his death defending the Alamo. [PZ7.G19Jam] 92 AC 68
1. Bowie, James, d. 1836. I. Title.

Bowie, Janetta—Biography.

BOWIE, Janetta. 372.1'1'00924 B
Penny Boss : a Clydeside school in the 'fifties / [by] Janetta Bowie ; illustrations by Anthony Colbert. London : Constable, 1976. 224 p. : ill. ; 23 cm. [LA23.B65 1976] 76-378407 ISBN 0-09-460900-4 : £3.50

1. Bowie, Janetta—Biography. 2. Teaching—Anecdotes, facetiae, satire, etc. 3. Education—Great Britain—Anecdotes, facetiae, satire, etc. 4. Teachers—Great Britain—Biography. I. Title.

Bowie, Walter Russell,

BOWIE, Walter Russell, 1882-1969. 283'.0924 B
Learning to live. Nashville, Abingdon Press [1969] 288 p. 22 cm. Autobiography. Bibliographical footnotes. [BX5995.B63A3] 69-18450 4.95
I. Title.

Bowker, Richard Rogers, 1848-1933.

FLEMING, Edward McClung, 1909- 920.4
R. R. Bowker: militant liberal. [1st ed.] Norman, University of Oklahoma Press [1952] xv, 395 p. illus., ports. 24 cm. Bibliography: p. 363-384. [Z473.B68F55] 52-11604
1. Bowker, Richard Rogers, 1848-1933. I. Title.

Bowie, James, d. 1836.

BAUGH, Virgil E 923.973
Rendezvous at the Alamo; highlights in the lives of Bowie, Crockett and Travis. [1st ed.] New York, Pageant Press [1960] 251p. illus. 24cm. Includes bibliography. [F390.B38] 60-122866
1. Bowie, James, d. 1836 2. Crockett, David, 1786-1836. 3. Travis, William Barret, 1809-1836. 4. Alamo—Siege, 1836. I. Title.

Bowles, Paul Frederic, 1911-

BOWLES, Paul Frederic, 1911- 818'.5'409 B
Without stopping; an autobiography, by Paul Bowles. New York, Putnam [1972] 379 p. illus. 23 cm. [PS3552.O874Z5] 72-175258 7.95
1. Bowles, Paul Frederic, 1911- I. Title.

Bowles, Samuel, 1826-1878.

MERRIAM, George Spring, 1843-1914. 070.4'0924 B
The life and times of Samuel Bowles. New York, Century Co., 1885. St. Clair Shores, Mich., Scholarly Press, 1970. 2 v. port. 22 cm. [PN4874.B63M4 1970] 76-108512
1. Bowles, Samuel, 1826-1878. 2. Springfield Republican. 3. U.S.—Politics and government—1849-1877. I. Title. BIP

MERRIAM, George Spring, 1843-1914. 070.4'0924 B
The life and times of Samuel Bowles. New York, Da Capo Press, 1970. 2 v. port. 23 cm. (A Da Capo Press reprint edition) Reprint of the 1885 ed. [PN4874.B63M4 1970b] 75-87417
1. Bowles, Samuel, 1826-1878. 2. Springfield republican. 3. U.S.—Politics and government—1849-1877. I. Title. BIP

Bowles, William Augustus, 1764-1805.

[BAYNTON, Benjamin] 975'.03'0924 B
Authentic memoirs of William Augustus Bowles. [New York] Arno Press [1971] vi, 79 p. 23 cm. (The First American frontier) Reprint of the 1791 ed. [E99.C9B62 1971] 73-146376 ISBN 0-405-02827-X
1. Bowles, William Augustus, 1764-1805. I. Title. II. Series.

WRIGHT, James Leitch. 975'.03'0924 B
William Augustus Bowles, Director General of the Creek Nation, by J. Leitch Wright, Jr. Athens, University of Georgia Press [1967] viii, 211 p. map, port. 25 cm. Bibliography: p. 197-205. [E99.C9W7] 67-27143
1. Bowles, William Augustus, 1764-1805. 2. Creek Indians—History. I. Title.

Bowman, Earl McKinley, 1896-

BOWMAN, Earl McKinley, 1896- 286'.5 B
An unknown parson / Earl McKinley Bowman. [s.l. : s.n., c1976] ([Verona, Va. : McClure Print. Co.]) viii, 240 p., [2] leaves of plates : ill. ; 23 cm. [BX7843.B67A36] 76-19707
1. Bowman, Earl McKinley, 1896- 2. Church of the Brethren—Clergy—Biography. 3. Church of the Brethren—Sermons. 4. Clergy—United States—Biography. 5. Sermons, American. I. Title.

Bowman, Laura.

ANTOINE, Le Roi, 1905- 927.92
Achievement: the life of Laura Bowman. New York, Pageant [c.1961] 439p. illus. 61-17816 5.00
1. Bowman, Laura. I. Title.

ANTOINE, Le Roi, 1905- 927.92
Achievement: the life of Laura Bowman. [1st ed.] New York, Pageant Press [1961] 439p. illus. 21cm. Written in collaboration with the author's wife, Laura Bowman. [PN2287.B66A65] 61-17816
1. Bowman, Laura. I. Title.

Bowra, Cecil Maurice, Sir, 1898-1971—Addresses, essays, lectures.

BOWRA, Cecil Maurice 1898- 378.1'11'0924
Memories, 1898-1939 [by]C. M. Bowra. Cambridge, Harvard University Press, 1967 [c1966] 869 p. illus., ports. 23 cm. [LF724.B6A3] 67-27994
I. Title.

BOWRA, Cecil Maurice, Sir, 1898-1971. 378.1'11'0924
Memories, 1898-1939 [by] C. M. Bowra. Cambridge, Harvard University Press, 1967 [c1966] 369 p. illus., ports. 23 cm. [LF724.B6A3 1967] 67-27994
I. Title.

MAURICE Bowra, a celebration / edited by Hugh Lloyd-Jones. 378.1'11'0924
New York : Harcourt, Brace, Jovanovich, [1975] p. cm. Contents.Contents.—The Times. A brilliant Oxford figure.—Berlin, I. Memorial address in St. Mary's.—Lloyd-Jones, H. British Academy memoir.—Mercurius Oxoniensis. Glorious reign of Sir Maurice, decd.—Connolly, C. Hedonist and stoic.—Annan, N. A man I loved.—Betjeman, J. A formative friend.—Powell, A. The Bowra world and Bowra lore.—Lancaster, O. A very salutary experience.—Finley, J. H., Jr. Maurice in America: I.—Quinton, A. Maurice in America: II.—Wheare, K. A legendary vice-chancellor.—Wheeler, M. Maurice afloat, and as P.B.A.—Mitchell, L. An undergraduate's view of the warden.—Gardiner, S. Maurice at dinner.—King, F. "Pray you, undo this button."—Bowle, J. A plain way with heroic poetry.—Sparrow, J. C. M. B. [LF724.B6M38 1975] 75-2483
1. Bowra, Cecil Maurice, Sir, 1898-1971—Addresses, essays, lectures. I. Bowra, Cecil Maurice, Sir, 1898-1971. II. Lloyd-Jones, Hugh, ed.

Bowring, Maurice.

BOWRING, Mary. 636.089'092'4 B
The animals come first / Mary Bowring. New York : Simon and Schuster, c1976. p. cm. [SF613.B68B67] 76-27885 ISBN 0-671-22440-9 : 7.95
1. Bowring, Maurice. 2. Bowring, Mary. 3. Veterinarians—England—Biography. 4. Wives—Biography. I. Title. BIP

BOWRING, Mary. 636.089'092'4 B
The animals come first / Mary Bowring ; with a foreword by Philip Wayre. London : Collins & Harvill Press, 1976. 217 p. ; 21 cm. [SF613.B68B67 1976b] 76-380473 ISBN 0-00-262006-5 : £3.50
1. Bowring, Maurice. 2. Bowring, Mary. 3. Veterinarians—England—Biography. 4. Wives—Biography. I. Title.

Box-Car Bertha.

BOX-CAR Bertha 301.44'94'0924 B
Sister of the road : the autobiography of Box-Car Bertha, as told to Dr. Ben L. Reitman. New York : Harper & Row, 1975, c1937. 314 p. ; 21 cm. (Harper colophon books) [HV4505.B65 1975] 75-322753 ISBN 0-06-090417-8 pbk. : 3.45
1. Box-Car Bertha. 2. Tramps—United States—Personal narratives. 3. Female offenders—United States. I. Reitman, Ben Lewis, 1879-1942. II. Title.

Boxers (Sports)-Biography.

WESTON, Stanley. 796.8'3'0922 B
The heavyweight champions / Stanley Weston. New York : Ace Books, c1976. 337p. ; 18 cm. [GV1131.W7 1976] 76-150200 pbk. : 1.75
1. Boxers (Sports)-Biography. 2. Boxing-History. I. Title.

Boxing.

BENNETT, George, 1945- 796.8'3'0922 B
Fighters / photos. by George Bennett ; text by Pete Hamill. 1st ed. Garden City, N.Y. : Dolphin Books, 1978. [126] p. : chiefly ill. ; 28 cm. [GV1133.B424] 77-12839 ISBN 0-385-13524-6 : 7.95
1. Boxing. 2. Boxers (Sports)—Biography. 3. Boxing—Pictorial works. I. Hamill, Pete, 1935- II. Title. BIP

Boxing — Hist.

MENDOZA, Daniel, 1764-1836. 927.9683
The memoirs of the life of Daniel Mendoza; edited, and with an introd. by Paul Magriel. London, New York, Bataford [1951] 115 p. illus. 24 cm. [GV1132.M4A3] 51-13258
1. Boxing — Hist. I. Title. BIP

Boxing—Biography.

CARPENTER, Harry 796.830922
Masters of boxing. New York, A. S. Barnes [1965, c.1964] ix, 245p. ports. 22cm. [GV1131.C32] 65-24577 5.00
1. Boxing—Biog. I. Title.

DEMPSEY, Jack [William Harrison Dempsey] 927.9683
Dempsey, by the man himself, as told to Bob Considine and Bill Slocum. New York, Simon and Schuster, 1960 [c.1959,1960] 249p. illus. 22cm. 60-6719 3.95
I. Considine, Robert Bernard II. Title.

HOUSTON, Graham. 796.8'3'0922
Superfists / by Graham Houston. New York : Bounty Books, c1975. 176 p. : ill. ; 29 cm. [GV1131.H69 1975] 75-13824 ISBN 0-517-52433-3 pbk. : 5.95
1. Boxing—Biography. I. Title.

"IN this corner ... !": forty world champions tell their stories, by Peter Heller. With an introd. by Muhammad Ali. New York, Simon and Schuster [1973] 431 p. illus. 24 cm. [GV1131.I49] 73-8227 ISBN 0-671-21568-X 10.00 796.8'3'0922 B
1. Boxing—Biography. I. Heller, Peter, 1947-

"IN this corner - - - !" Forty world champions tell their stories by Peter Heller. With an introduction by Muhammad Ali. [New York, Dell, 1974, c1973] 430 p. illus. 18 cm. [GV1131.I49] 1.75 (pbk.) 796.8'3'0922
1. Boxing—Biography. I. Heller, Peter.
L.C. card number for original ed.: 73-8227.

JOHNSON, John Arthur, 1878-1946. 796.8'30924 B
Jack Johnson is a dandy; an autobiography. Introductory essays by Dick Schaap and the Lampman. New York, Chelsea House [1969] 262 p. illus., ports. 29 cm. [GV1132.J7A3] 78-79537 8.95
1. Boxing—Biography. I. Title.

LARDNER, Rex. 796.8'3'0922
The legendary champions. Consultants: Turn-of-the-Century Fights, inc., William Cayton, and Jim Jacobs. Pictorial research and commentary by Alan Bodian. New York, American Heritage Press [1972] 289 p. illus. 28 cm. [GV1131.L36] 76-177592 ISBN 0-07-036390-0
1. Boxing—Biography. I. Bodian, Alan. II. Title.

MCCALLUM, John Dennis, 1924- 796.8'3'0922 B
The encyclopedia of world boxing champions since 1882 / John D. McCallum. 1st ed. Radnor, Pa. : Chilton Book Co., [1975] p. cm. [GV1131.M32 1975] 75-19012 ISBN 0-8019-6163-7
1. Boxing—Biography. I. Title.

MCCALLUM, John Dennis, 1924- 796.8'3'0922 B
The encyclopedia of world boxing champions since 1882 / John D. McCallum. 1st ed. Radnor, Pa. : Chilton Book Co., [1975] xix, 337 p. : ill. ; 29 cm. Includes index. [GV1131.M32 1975] 75-19012 ISBN 0-8019-6163-7 : 19.95
1. Boxing—Biography. I. Title.

ODD, Gilbert E. 796.8'3'0922
Boxing, the great champions / [by] Gilbert Odd. London ; New York [etc.] : Hamlyn, 1974. 2-175 p. : ill., ports. ; 31 cm. Includes index. [GV1131.O32] 74-185900 ISBN 0-600-31302-6 : £2.50
1. Boxing—Biography. I. Title.

ROBINSON, Ray, May3,1920- 796.8'3'0924 B
Sugar Ray [by] Sugar Ray Robinson with Dave Anderson. New York, Viking Press [1970] 376 p. 22 cm. [GV1132.R6A3] 69-18799 6.95
1. Boxing—Biography. I. Anderson, Dave, joint author. II. Title.

SANFORD, Harry. 927.9683
Stand up and fight; the fight game and the men who make it. [1st ed.] New York, Exposition Press [c1962] 204 p. 22 cm. [GV1131.S3] 63-732
1. Boxing—Biog. I. Title.

TURPIN, Guy 927.9683
Forgotten men of the prize ring, a reference book of old time boxers. San Antonio, Tex., Naylor [c.1963] 76p. illus. 21cm. 63-13475 3.50 pap.,
1. Boxing—Biog. I. Title.

TURPIN, Guy. 927.9683
Forgotten men of the prize ring, a reference book of old time boxers. San Antonio, Naylor Co. [1963] 76 p. illus. 21 cm. [GV1131.T8] 63-13475
1. Boxing — Biog. I. Title.

Boxing—Biography—Dictionaries.

BURRILL, Bob. 796.8'3'0922
Who's who in boxing. New Rochelle, N.Y., Arlington House [1974] 208 p. 24 cm. [GV1131.B87] 73-13020 ISBN 0-87000-232-5 8.95
1. Boxing—Biography—Dictionaries. I. Title. BIP

Boxing—Biography—Juvenile literature.

RAINBOLT, Richard. 796.8'3'0922 B
Boxing's heavyweight champions / Richard Rainbolt. Minneapolis : Lerner Publications Co., [1975] 70 p. : ill. ; 23 cm. (The Sports heroes library) Biographies of ten heavyweight prize fighters: John L. Sullivan, Jim Corbett, Robert Fitzsimmons, Jim Jeffries, Jack Johnson, Jack Dempsey, Gene Tunney, Joe Louis, Rocky Marciano, and Muhammad Ali. [GV1131.R34 1975] 920 74-27470 ISBN 0-8225-1053-7
1. Boxing—Biography—Juvenile literature. I. Title. BIP

Boxing—History.

FLEISCHER, Nathaniel 796.8'3'09 S.
50 years at ringside [by Nat Fleischer. New York, Greenwood Press [1969, c1940] viii, 296 p. illus., ports. 23 cm. [GV1125.F55 1969] 77-90144 ISBN 0-8371-2164-7
1. Boxing—History. I. Title.

MCCALLUM, John Dennis, 1924- 796.9'62'0922 B
The world heavyweight boxing championship; a history [by] John D. McCallum. Foreword by Charles P. Larson. [1st ed.] Radnor, Pa., Chilton Book Co. [1974] xvi, 393 p. illus. 24 cm. [GV1121.M32 1974] 74-1462 ISBN 0-8019-5951-9 12.00
1. Boxing—History. 2. Boxing—Biography. I. Title.

Boxing—History—Juvenile literature.

MAY, Julian. 796.8'3'0922 B
Boxing's heavyweight championship / by Julian May. Mankato, Minn. : Creative Education, [1976] p. cm. (Sports classic) Discusses boxing in the United States and some of the heavyweight champions of the world. [GV1121.M39] 920 76-4861 ISBN 0-87191-503-0
1. Boxing—History—Juvenile literature. I. Title. BIP

Boyce, Violet.

BOYCE, Violet. 979.2'25
Upstairs to a mine / Violet Boyce, Mabel Harmer. Logan : Utah State University Press, [1976] p. cm. [F834.B56B68] 76-28980 ISBN 0-87421-085-2 : 6.95
1. Boyce, Violet. 2. Bingham Canyon, Utah—Biography. I. Harmer, Mabel, 1894- joint author. II. Title. BIP

Boycott, Charles Cunningham, 1832-1897.

MARLOW, Joyce. 941.58
Captain Boycott and the Irish. [1st American ed.] New York, Saturday Review Press [1973] 319 p. illus. 22 cm. Bibliography: p. [303]-308. [HD625.M35 1973b] 73-78914 ISBN 0-8415-0271-4 8.95
1. Boycott, Charles Cunningham, 1832-1897. 2. Land tenure—Ireland—History. 3. Ireland—Politics and government—19th century. I. Title.

Boyd, David, b. 1743.

HISTORY of the captivity of David Boyd 973'.04'97 S / edited by Marion Morse. New York : Garland Pub., 1977. 42 p., [6] leaves of plates : ill. ; 23 cm. (The Garland library of narratives of North American Indian captivities ; v. 109) Issued with the reprint of the 1927 ed. of Meredith, G. E. Girl captives of the Cheyennes. New York, 1977. Reprint of the 1931 ed. published under title: History of the capture and captivity of David Boyd from Cumberland County, Pennsylvania in 1756. [E85.G2 vol. 109] [E99.D2] 970'.004'97 B 76-51269 ISBN 0-8240-1733-1 lib.bdg. : 25.00 (set)
1. Boyd, David, b. 1743. 2. Delaware Indians—Captivities. 3. Indians of North America—Captivities. 4. Pennsylvania—Biography. I. Davis, Marion Morse. II. Series.

Boyd, David French, 1834-1899.

REED, Germaine M., 1929- 370'.92'4 B
David French Boyd, founder of Louisiana State University / Germaine M. Reed. Baton Rouge : Louisiana State University, c1977. xiv, 315 p., [6] leaves of plates : ill. ; 24 cm. (Southern biography series) A revision of the author's thesis, Louisiana State University. Includes index. Bibliography: p. [LA2317.B567R43 1977] 77-446 ISBN 0-8071-0266-0 : 20.00
1. Boyd, David French, 1834-1899. 2. Louisiana State University and Agricultural and Mechanical College—History. 3. Educators—Louisiana—Biography. 4. Louisiana—Biography. I. Title. II. Series. BIP

Boyd, Frank W.,

BOYD, Frank W., Mrs., 1876- 917.81'03'3
Rode a heifer calf through college, by Mrs. Frank W. Boyd (Mamie Alexander Boyd). Brooklyn, Pageant-Poseidon [1972] xvi, 253 p. illus. 24 cm. [PN4874.B636A3] 79-190643 ISBN 0-8181-0182-2 8.95
I. Title.

Boyd, Guy Martin a Beckett, 1923—

VON BERTOUCH, Ann. 730'.92'4 B
Guy Boyd / [by] Ann von Bertouch [and] Patrick Hutchings. Melbourne : Lansdowne Press, 1976. 136 p. : ill. ; 38 cm. Includes bibliographical references and index. [NB1105.B7V66] 77-350246 ISBN 0-7018-0079-8
1. Boyd, Guy Martin a Beckett, 1923- 2. Sculptors—Australia—Biography. I. Hutchings, Patrick A., joint author. II. Boyd, Guy Martin a Beckett, 1923-

Boyd, Malcolm, 1923-

BOYD, Malcolm, 1923- 283'.0924 B
As I live and breathe; stages of an autobiography. New York, Random House [1970, c1969] xi, 276 p. 22 cm. [BX5995.B66A3] 76-85608 6.95
I. Title.

BOYD, Malcolm, 1923- 301.41'57'0924 B
Take off the masks / Malcolm Boyd. 1st ed. Garden City, N.Y. : Doubleday, 1978. x, 178 p., [4] leaves of plates : ill. ; 22 cm. [BX5995.B66A37] 77-9230 ISBN 0-385-13219-0 : 7.95
1. Boyd, Malcolm, 1923- 2. Protestant Episcopal Church in the U.S.A.—Clergy—Biography. 3. Clergy—United States—Biography. 4. Homosexuals—United States—Biography. I. Title. BIP

Boyer, Kenton Lloyd, 1931-

LIPMAN, David. 92
Ken Boyer. New York, Putnam [1967] 221 p. 22 cm. (Putnam sports shelf) A biography emphasizing the career of a star who, in 1964 as third baseman for the World Series winning St. Louis Cardinals, was named National League Player of the year, National League's most valuable player, Major League Player of the Year, and outstanding athlete of the St. Louis area. [GV865.B7L5] AC 67
1. Boyer, Kenton Lloyd, 1931- I. Title.

ZANGER, Jack 92
Ken Boyer, guardian of the hot corner; the complete life story of baseball's 'most valuable player.' New York, Nelson [c.1965] 128p. illus. ports. 22cm. (Champion bks.; Rutledge bk.) [GV865.B7Z3] 65-16504 2.75;2.78 bds., lib. ed.
1. Boyer, Kenton Lloyd, 1931- I. Title.

Boykin, Frank William, 1885-1969.

BOYKIN, Edward. 328.73'092'4 B
Everything's made for love in this man's world; vignettes from the life of Frank W. Boykin, by Edward Boykin. [Mobile, Ala., 1973] vii, 245 p. illus. 29 cm. [E748.B74B68] 73-83798
1. Boykin, Frank William, 1885-1969. I. Title.

Boyle, Donzella Cross, 1891-

BOYLE, Donzella Cross, 1891- 973'.07
American history was my undoing : a case study of a textbook / by Donzella Cross Boyle. 2d ed. Fullerton, Calif. : Education Information, 1961. v, 150 p. ; 23 cm. [E175.85.B68 1961] 75-317295
1. Boyle, Donzella Cross, 1891- 2. United States—History—Text-books. 3. United States—History—Study and teaching. I. Title.

Boyle, Harry J.

BOYLE, Harry J. 920
Homebrew and patches [by] Harry J. Boyle. With a foreword by Harry Halliwell. Toronto, Clarke, Irwin, 1963. x, 173 p. illus. 24 cm. Autobiographical. Sequel to Mostly in clover. [CT310.B69A28] 64-2859
I. Title.

BOYLE, Harry J. 818.54
With a pinch of sin [by] Harry J. Boyle. [1st ed.] Garden City, N. Y., Doubleday, 1966. 230 p. 22 cm. Autobiographical [CT310.B69A32] 66-11171
I. Title.

Boyle, Hon. Robert, 1627-1691.

PILKINGTON, Roger 925.3
Robert Boyle: father of chemistry. London, Murray [dist. Mystic, Conn., Verry, 1965, c.1959] 179p. illus., port. 23cm. (Men and discoveries lib.) [QD22.B76P5] 64-7488 4.00
1. Boyle, Hon. Robert, 1627-1691. I. Title.

Boyle, Hon. Robert, 1627-1691 — Juvenile literature.

SOOTIN, Harry. j 92
Robert Boyle, founder of modern chemistry. Pictures by Gustay Schrotter. New York, F. Watts [1962] vi. 133 p. illus., port. 22 cm. (Immortals of science, B10) [QD22B76S6] 62-7422
1. Boyle, Hon. Robert, 1627-1691 — Juvenile literature. I. Title.

Boyle, Joseph Whiteside.

MILLARD, Joseph 920.8
No law but their own. Evanston [Ill.] Regency [c.1963] 158p. 18cm. (RB324) 63-6107 .50 pap.,
1. Baker, Lafayette Charles, 1626-1868. 2. Boyle, Joseph Whiteside. 3. Streeter, George Wellington, 1837-1921. I. Title.

RODNEY, William. 971.9'1'020924 B
Joe Boyle : king of the Klondike / William Rodney. Toronto ; New York : McGraw-Hill Ryerson, [1974] xiii, 368 p. ; 24 cm. Includes index. Bibliography: p. 347-354. [D413.B6R6] 74-6562 ISBN 0-07-077763-2 : 11.95
1. Boyle, Joseph Whiteside.

Boyle, Robert, Hon., 1627-1691.

JACOB, J. R. 530'.092'4
Robert Boyle and the English Revolution : a study in social and intellectual change / by J. R. Jacob. New York : B. Franklin, [1977] i.e. 1978 p. cm. (Studies in the history of science ; 3) Includes index. Bibliography: p. [Q127.G4J3] 77-2997 ISBN 0-89102-072-1 : 18.95
1. Boyle, Robert, 1627-1691. 2. Science—History—Great Britain. 3. Science—Social aspects—Great Britain. 4. Scientists—Great Britain—Biography. I. Title. BIP

KUSLAN, Louis I. 530'.0924 B
Robert Boyle, the great experimenter, by Louis I. Kuslan and A. Harris Stone. Illustrated by Henry Gorski. Englewood Cliffs, N.J., Prentice-Hall [1970] iii, 105 p. illus. 22 cm. (History of science series) The life of the seventeenth-century scientist best known for his analysis of pressure and volume in gases and for his example to fellow scientists in sharing his discoveries with them. [QC16.B65K87] 92 71-122321 ISBN 0-13-781468-2 4.25
1. Boyle, Robert, Hon., 1627-1691. I. Stone, A. Harris, joint author.

Boyle, Thomas, 1775 or 6-1825.

HOPKINS, Fred W. 387.5'092'4 B
Tom Boyle, master privateer / by Fred W. Hopkins, Jr. Cambridge, Md. : Tidewater Publishers, 1976. ix, 101 p. : ill. ; 23 cm. Bibliography: p. 99-101. [HE569.B64H64] 76-6026 ISBN 0-87033-218-X : 4.00
1. Boyle, Thomas, 1775 or 6-1825. 2. Shipmasters—United States—Biography. 3. Privateering—History. I. Title. BIP

Boyle, William A.

BROWN, Stuart. 364.1'523'0924 B
A man named Tony : the true story of the Yablonski murders / by Stuart Brown. 1st ed. New York : Norton, [1976] 232 p. : ill. ; 21 cm. Includes index. [KF224.B68B76] 75-20280 ISBN 0-393-08707-7 : 8.95
1. Boyle, William A. 2. Yablonski, Joseph. I. Title.

Boylon, Pascual, Saint, 1540-1592.

ERNEST, Brother, 1897- 922.246
Saint of the Eucharist, a story of Saint Paschal Baylon. Illus. by Rosemary Donatino. Notre Dame, Ind., Dujarie Press [1951] 109 p. illus. 24 cm. [BX4700.B2E7] 51-2985
1. Boylon, Pascual, Saint, 1540-1592. I. Title.

Boys Home Society of Baltimore—History.

BOYS Home Society of Baltimore. 362.7'33'097526
One hundred years of service, 1866-1966 : a history of the Boys Home Society of Baltimore, inc. Baltimore ; The Society, [1964?] v, 94 p. : ill. ; 28 cm. [HV885.B2B72 1964] 922.273 75-316413
1. Boys Home Society of Baltimore—History. I. Title.

Bozarth-Campbell, Alla, 1947-

BOZARTH-CAMPBELL, Alla, 1947- 283'.092'4 B
Womanpriest : a personal odyssey / Alla Bozarth-Campbell. New York : Paulist Press, c1978. ix, 229 p. ; 22 cm. [BX5995.B665A38] 78-58957 ISBN 0-8091-0243-9 : 9.95
1. Bozarth-Campbell, Alla, 1947- 2. Protestant Episcopal Church in the U.S.A.—Clergy—Biography. 3. Clergy—United States—Biography. 4. Ordination of women. I. Title. BIP

Brace, Charles Loring, 1826-1890.

BRACE, Charles Loring, 1826-1890. 361'.92'4 B
The life of Charles Loring Brace / edited by Emma Brace. New York : Arno Press, 1976 [i.e.1975], c1894 p. cm. (Social problems and social policy) Reprint of the ed. published by Scribner, New York. "Chiefly told in his own letters." [HV28.B66A34 1976] 75-17205 ISBN 0-405-07478-6 : 29.00
1. Brace, Charles Loring, 1826-1890. I. Brace, Emma. II. Title. III. Series.

Bracken, John, 1883-

KENDLE, John Edward. 971.27'02'0924 B
John Bracken : a political biography / John Kendle. Toronto ; Buffalo : University of Toronto Press, 1979. xiii, 318 p., [5] leaves of plates : ill. ; 24 cm. Includes index. Bibliography: p. [297]-303. [F1063.B7K46] 79-319961 ISBN 0-8020-5439-0 : 17.50
1. Bracken, John, 1883- 2. Progressive Conservative Party (Canada)—History. 3. Manitoba—Politics and government. 4. Prime ministers—Manitoba—Biography. I. Title. BIP

Brackenridge, Henry Marie, 1786-1871.

KELLER, William F 923.473
The Nation's advocate: Henry Marie Brackenridge and young America. [Pittsburgh] University of Pittsburgh Press [1956] x, 451p. illus., ports., maps. 24cm. Bibliography: p.425-434. [E353.1.B65K4] 56-6426
1. Brackenridge, Henry Marie, 1786-1871. I. Title.

Brackenridge, Hugh Henry, 1748-1816.

NEWLIN, Claude Milton. 818'.2'09 B
The life and writings of Hugh Henry Brackenridge. Mamaroneck, N.Y., P. P. Appel, 1971. vi, 328 p. 23 cm. Reprint of the 1932 ed. Bibliography: p. [309]-322. [PS708.B5Z7 1971] 73-162498 ISBN 0-911858-20-2
1. Brackenridge, Hugh Henry, 1748-1816. I. Title. BIP

Brackley, Herbert George, 1894-1948.

BRACKLEY, Frida H 926.2913
Brackles: memoirs of a pioneer of civil aviation. With a foreword by Lord Mountevans. Research, revision, continuity [by] N. S. B. Miller. [Chatham, W. & J. Mackay, 1952] 695p. illus. 22cm. [TL540.B69B7] 53-21854
1. Brackley, Herbert George, 1894-1948. I. Title.

Braddock, Edward, 1695?-1755.

MCCARDELL, Lee, 1901- 923.542
Ill-starred general: Braddock of the Coldstream Guards. [Pittsburgh] University of Pittsburgh Press, 1958. viii, 335 p. illus., port., maps, geneal. table. 24 cm. Bibliography: p. 315-328. [DA67.1.B7M35] 57-14574
1. Braddock, Edward, 1695?-1755. 2. Braddock's campaign, 1755. I. Title.

Braddock, Ellsworth C.

BRADDOCK, Ellsworth C. 974.4'82 B
Memories of North Carver village / by Ellsworth C. Braddock ; as told to E. J. Snow ; drawings by Doris F. Moore. Marion, Mass. : Channing Books, c1977. x, 118 p. : ill. ; 23 cm. Includes index. Bibliography: p. 115. [F74.C28B72] 76-51098 ISBN 0-9600496-6-5 pbk. : 6.00
1. Braddock, Ellsworth C. 2. Carver, Mass.—Biography. 3. Carver, Mass.—History. I. Snow, Elizabeth Jackson. II. Moore, Doris F. III. Title. BIP

Braddock, William Hallock,

BRADDOCK, William Hallock, 1887- 920
I cannot rest from travel. [1st ed.] New York, Vantage Press [1961] 188p. 21cm. Autobiographical. [CT275.B5925A3] 61-16161
I. Title.

Braden, Thomas Wardell, 1918-

BRADEN, Thomas Wardell, 1918- 070'.92'4 B
Eight is enough / Tom Braden. 1st ed. New York : Random House, [1975] xiv, 201 p. ; 22 cm. [PN4874.B657A33] 75-10281 ISBN 0-394-49583-7 : 6.95
1. Braden, Thomas Wardell, 1918- I. Title.

BRADEN, Thomas Wardell, 1918- 070.924
Eight is enough Ton Braden. Greenwich, Conn. : Fawcett Crest 1976 c1975. 224 p. ; 17 cm. [PN4874.B657A33] ISBN 0-449-23002-3 pbk. : 1.75
I. Title.
L.C. card no. for 1975 Doubleday edition: 75-10281. BIP

Bradford, Andrew, 1686-1742.

DE ARMOND, Anna Janney, 1910- 070.9'24
Andrew Bradford, colonial journalist. New York, Greenwood Press [1969] ix, 272 p. facsims. 23 cm. Reprint of 1949 ed. Bibliography: p. 247-251. [PN4874.B66D4 1969] 79-91758 ISBN 0-8371-2429-8
1. Bradford, Andrew, 1686-1742. 2. The American weekly mercury. 3. The American magazine. 4. Pennsylvania—History—Colonial period, ca. 1600-1775. BIP

Bradford, Eng. (Yorkshire)—Biography.

HIRD, Horace. 914.27'46
Bradford remembrancer: twenty-six essays on people or incidents in their lives which are worthy of remembrance. Bradford, McDonald Book Co. Ltd, 1972. xvi, 232, [32] p. illus., facsim., maps, ports. 24 cm. [DA690.B7H484] 72-172151 ISBN 0-900958-01-4 £3.00
1. Bradford, Eng. (Yorkshire)—Biography. 2. Bradford, Eng. (Yorkshire)—History. I. Title.

Bradford, Geneva

BRADFORD, Geneva 920.7
Hap and Miss Hap. New York, Vantage [c.1963] 510p. 21cm. 4.95
I. Title.

Bradford, William, 1588-1657—Juvenile literature.

GRAVES, Charles Parlin, 1911- 974.4'02'0924 B
A colony leader: William Bradford, by Charles P. Graves. Illustrated by Marvin Besunder. Champaign, Ill., Garrard Pub. Co. [1969] 64 p. col. illus., col. map. 24 cm. (Colony leaders) A biography of the first Governor of Plymouth Colony and a history of the colony's early years. [F68.B8235] 92 69-10371 2.32
1. Bradford, William, 1588-1657—Juvenile literature. I. Besunder, Marvin, illus. II. Title.

HAYS, Wilma Pitchford. 974.4'02'0924 B
Rebel Pilgrim; a biography of Governor William Bradford. Philadelphia, Westminster Press [1969] 96 p. illus., map. 25 cm. A biography of the rebellious Englishman whose association with the Separatists of England led him out of that country and eventually to the New World where he served many years as Governor of the Pilgrim colony of Plymouth. [F68.B824] 92 69-10387 3.95
1. Bradford, William, 1588-1657—Juvenile literature. I. Title.

JACOBS, William Jay. 974.4'02'0924 B
William Bradford of Plymouth Colony [by] W. J. Jacobs. Illustrated with authentic prints, documents, and maps. New York, Watts, 1974. 57 p. illus. 26 cm. (A Visual biography) Bibliography: p. 53. A biography of the first governor of the Plymouth Colony who served in that office for thirty years and greatly influenced the development of the community. [F68.B8243] 92 74-870 ISBN 0-531-02724-4 4.33 (lib. bdg.)
1. Bradford, William, 1588-1657—Juvenile literature. 2. Massachusetts—History—Colonial period (New Plymouth)—Juvenile literature. I. Title. BIP

Bradlaugh, Charles, 1833-1891.

CHAMPION of liberty: Charles Bradlaugh (centenary volume) 942.081'092'4 New York, Arno Press, 1972. xii, 346 p. illus. 23 cm. (The Atheist viewpoint) Reprint of the 1934 ed. Bibliography: p. 337-346. [DA565.B7C5 1972] 75-161323 ISBN 0-405-03626-4
1. Bradlaugh, Charles, 1833-1891. I. Title. II. Series.

COURTNEY, Janet Elizabeth Hogarth, 1865- 192 B
Freethinkers of the nineteenth century / by Janet E. Courtney. Norwood, Pa. : Norwood Editions, 1976. p. cm. Reprint of the 1920 ed. published by Chapman & Hall, London. Contents.Contents.—Frederick Denison Maurice.—Mathew Arnold.—Charles Bradlaugh.—Thomas Henry Huxley.—Leslie Stephen.—Harriet Martineau.—Charles Kingsley. [B1569.C6 1976] 76-17266 ISBN 0-8482-0386-0 : 25.00
1. Maurice, Frederick Denison, 1805-1872. 2. Arnold, Matthew, 1822-1888—Religion and ethics. 3. Bradlaugh, Charles, 1833-1891. 4. Huxley, Thomas Henry, 1825-1895. 5. Stephen, Leslie, Sir, 1832-1904. 6. Martineau, Harriet, 1802-1876. 7. Kingsley, Charles, 1819-1875. I. Title. BIP

TRIBE, David H. 942.081'0924 B
President Charles Bradlaugh, M.P. [by] David Tribe. [Hamden, Conn.] Archon Books, 1971. 391 p. illus., ports. 26 cm. Bibliography: p. 371-375. [DA565.B7T75 1971] 70-27779 ISBN 0-208-01155-2 11.00
1. Bradlaugh, Charles, 1833-1891. BIP

Bradley, Dan Beach, 1804-1873.

LORD, Donald C. 266'.023'0924 B
Mo Bradley and Thailand, by Donald C. Lord. Grand Rapids, Eerdmans [1969] 227 p. 20 cm. (A Christian world mission book) Bibliography: p. 214-220. [BV3317.B7L6] 68-28852 3.95
1. Bradley, Dan Beach, 1804-1873. 2. Missions—Thailand. I. Title.

Bradley, Humphrey, fl. 1584-1625.

HARRIS, Lawrence Ernest. 627.130924
The two Netherlanders: Humphrey Bradley and Cornelis Drebbel. Cambridge [Eng.] W. Heffer, 1961. 227p. illus. 21cm. [TC140.B68H3] 62-51111
1. Bradley, Humphrey, fl. 1584-1625. 2. Drebbel, Cornelis, 1572-1634. I. Title.

Bradley, John Lewis, ed.

NICHOLSON, Renton, 1809-1861. 914.21
Rogue's progress; the autobiography of "Lord Chief Baron" Nicholson. Edited, and with an introd., by John L. Bradley. Boston, Houghton Mifflin, 1965. xiii, 330 p. illus. 21 cm. First published in 1860 under title: The Lord Chief Baron Nicholson. [CT788.N5A3] 65-10328
1. Bradley, John Lewis, ed. I. Title.

Bradley, Katherine Harris, 1846-1914—Biography—Addresses, essays, lectures.

RICKETTS, Charles S., 1866-1931. 821'.9'12 B
Michael Field / by Charles Ricketts ; edited by Paul Delaney. Edinburgh : Tragara Press, 1976. vii, 12 p., [2] leaves of plates : ports ; 24 cm. Limited ed. of 125 numbered copies. No. 106. [PR4699.F5Z77 1976] 77-365380 ISBN 0-902616-32-3 : £6.00
1. Field, Michael, pseud.—Addresses, essays, lectures. 2. Bradley, Katherine Harris, 1846-1914—Biography—Addresses, essays, lectures. 3. Cooper, Edith Emma, 1862-1913—Biography—Addresses, essays, lectures. 4. Authors, English—19th century—Biography—Addresses, essays, lectures.

Bradley, Omar Nelson, 1893-

BRADLEY, Omar Nelson, 1893- 940.54 B
Magazine articles. [Washington, Defense Print. Office, 1970-71] 4 v. illus. 28 cm. Cover title. Contents.Contents.—v. 1. Articles written by General of the Army, Omar N. Bradley, 1947-1969.—v. 2. Articles written about General of the Army, Omar N. Bradley, 1943-1950.—v. 3. Articles written about General of the Army, Omar N. Bradley, 1951-1969.—v. 4. Articles written by and about General of the Army, Omar N. Bradley, 1970-71. [E745.B6915] 74-151153
1. Bradley, Omar Nelson, 1893-

BRADLEY, Omar Nelson, 1893- 940.54'21
A soldier's story / Omar N. Bradley ; foreword by Bill Mauldin. Chicago : Rand McNally, [1978] c1951. xxi, 618 p. [8] leaves of plates : ill. ; 22 cm. Includes index. [D756.B7 1978] 77-14709 ISBN 0-528-81052-9 : 10.00. ISBN 0-528-88133-7 pbk. : 6.95
1. Bradley, Omar Nelson, 1893- 2. United States. Army—Biography. 3. World War, 1939-1945—Campaigns—Western. 4. Warld War, 1939-1945—Personal narratives, American. 5. Generals—United States—Biography. I. Title.

WHITING, Charles, 1926- 940.54 B
Bradley. [New York, Ballantine Books, 1971] 160 p. illus. 21 cm. (Ballantine's illustrated history of the violent century. War leader book no. 5) Bibliography: p. 160. [E745.B7W45] 72-175291 ISBN 0-345-02288-2 1.00
1. Bradley, Omar Nelson, 1893- 2. World War, 1939-1945—Campaigns—France (1944-1945) 3. World War, 1939-1945—Campaigns—Germany.

Bradley, Omar Nelson, 1893- —Juvenile literature.

REEDER, Russell Potter. 355.3'31'0924 B
Omar Nelson Bradley: the soldiers' general, by Red Reeder. Illustrated by Herman B. Vestal. Champaign, Ill., Garrard Pub. Co. [1969] 112 p. illus. (part col.), col. maps, ports. 24 cm. (Defenders of freedom) A biography of "The Soldiers' General" from his years at West Point to his position as Chairman of the Joint Chiefs of Staff. [E745.B7R4] 92 76-78822 ISBN 8-11-646025- 2.69
1. Bradley, Omar Nelson, 1893- —Juvenile literature. I. Vestal, Herman B, illus. II. Title.

Bradley, Preston, 1888-

BRADLEY, Preston, 1888- 922.8173
Along the way, an autobiography [by] Preston Bradley with Harry Bernard. New York, McKay [c.1962] 280p. 21cm. 62-18486 4.95
I. Title.

CHANDLER, Daniel Ross, 1937- 280 B
The official, authorized biography of the Reverend Dr. Preston Bradley. [1st ed.] New York, Exposition Press [1971] 115, [2] p. 21 cm. (An Exposition-testament book) Bibliography: p. [117] [BR1725.B68C48] 78-166186 ISBN 0-682-47333-2 4.50
1. Bradley, Preston, 1888- 2. Sermons, American. I. Title.

Bradley, Stuart B

BRADLEY, Stuart B 920
Candide in calked boots. [Chicago? 1961] 112p. illus. 22cm. Autobiographical. [CT275.B59394A3] 61-33964
I. Title.

Bradley, Will,

BRADLEY, Will, 1868- 926.55
Will Bradley, his chap book; an account, in the words of the dean of American typographers, of his graphic arts adventures: as a boy printer in Ishpeming, art student in Chicago, designer, printer, and publisher at the Wayside Press, the years as art director in periodical publishing, and the interludes of stage, cinema, and authorship. New York, The Typophiles, 1955. vii, 104p. 19cm. (Typophile chap books, 30) [Z232.B812A3] 55-4441
I. Title.

Bradley, Will H. 1868—

BRADLEY, Will H. 1868- 926.55
Will Bradley, his chap book; an account, in the words of the dean of American typographers, of his graphic arts adventures: as a boy printer in Ishpeming, art student in Chicago, designer, printer, and publisher at the Wayside Press, the years as art director in periodical publishing, and the interludes of stage, cinema, and authorship. New York, The Typophiles, 1955. vii, 104 p. 19 cm. (Typophile chap books, 30) [Z232.B812A3] 55-4441
1. Title. II. Series: The Typophiles, New York. Typophile chap books, 30

Bradley, William Warren, 1943-

†BRADLEY, William Warren, 1943- 796.32'3'0924 B
Life on the run / Bill Bradley. New York : Quadrangle/New York Times Book Co., c1976. 229 p. ; 24 cm. [GV884.B7A34 1976] 75-36268 ISBN 0-8129-0623-3 : 8.95
1. Bradley, William Warren, 1943- 2. Basketball. I. Title. BIP

MCPHEE, John A. 796.323630924
A sense of where you are; a profile of William Warren Bradley. New York, Bantam [1967, c.1965] 92p. illus. 18cm. (Pathfinder ed., HP162) [GV885.M28] .60 pap.,
1. Bradley, William Warren. 2. Basketball. I. Title.

MCPHEE, John A. 796.32'3'0924 B
A sense of where you are : a profile of William Warren Bradley / by John McPhee. 2d ed. New York : Farrar, Straus, and Giroux, 1978. xii, 144 p., [30] leaves of plates : ill. ; 19 cm. [GV884.B7M32 1978] 78-110298 ISBN 0-374-51485-2 : 3.95
1. Bradley, William Warren. 2. Basketball players—United States—Biography. I. Title.

Bradley, William Warren, 1943—Juvenile literature.

HALTER, Jon C. 796.32'3'0924 B
Bill Bradley, one to remember / Jon C. Halter. New York : Putnam, [1975] 159 p. ; 21 cm. (Putnam sports shelf) Includes index. A biography emphasizing the career of the basketball star of the New York Knicks. [GV884.B7H35] 92 74-80655 ISBN 0-399-60916-4 lib. bdg. : 4.97
1. Bradley, William Warren, 1943—Juvenile literature. 2. Basketball—Juvenile literature. I. Title.

JACKSON, Robert B. 796.32'3'0924 B
Bradley of the Knicks, by Robert B. Jackson. New York, H. Z. Walck [1970] 64 p. ports. 21 cm. Traces the basketball career of Bill Bradley, the third highest scorer in the history of college basketball, and his association with the New York Knickerbockers. [GV884.B7J3] 92 77-124113 3.75
1. Bradley, William Warren, 1943- —Juvenile literature. I. Title.

Bradshaw, Terry.

BRADSHAW, Terry. 796.33'2'0924 B
Terry Bradshaw, man of steel / Terry Bradshaw, with David Diles ; pref. by Pete Rozelle ; foreword by Roger Staubach. Grand Rapids : Zondervan Pub. House, c1979. 195 p., [8] leaves of plates : ill. ; 23 cm. [GV939.B68A37] 79-16620 ISBN 0-310-39460-0 : 7.95
1. Bradshaw, Terry. 2. Pittsburg Steelers (Football club) 3. Football players—United States—Biography. I. Diles, David L., joint author. II. Title.

Bradshaw, Terry—Juvenile literature.

BENAGH, Jim, 1937- 796.33'2'0924 B
Terry Bradshaw, superarm of pro football / by Jim Benagh. New York : Putnam, c1976. 128 p. : ill. ; 21 cm. (Putnam sports shelf) Includes index. A biography of the quarterback who helped lead his team, the Pittsburgh Steelers, to the Super Bowl. [GV939.B68B46 1976] 92 75-43585 ISBN 0-399-20478-4. ISBN 0-399-20478-4 lib. bdg. : 5.29
1. Bradshaw, Terry—Juvenile literature. 2. Football—Juvenile literature. I. Title.

DEVANEY, John. 796.33'2'0924 B
The picture story of Terry Bradshaw / by John Devaney ; illustrated with photos. New York : Messner, c1977. p. cm. A biography of the quarterback for the Pittsburgh Steelers. [GV939.B68D48] 92 77-22841 ISBN 0-671-32867-0 lib.bdg. : 6.64
1. Bradshaw, Terry—Juvenile literature. 2. Pittsburg Steelers (Football club)—Juvenile literature. 3. Football players—United States—Biography—Juvenile literature. I. Title. BIP

HASEGAWA, Sam. 796.33'2'0924 B
Terry Bradshaw / by Sam Hasegawa. Mankato, Minn. : Creative Education, c1977. 31 p. : col. ill. ; 25 cm. (Creative education sports superstars) A brief biography of the Pittsburgh Steelers' leading quarterback. [GV939.B68H37] 92 76-48909 ISBN 0-87191-542-1 lib.bdg. : 4.95
1. Bradshaw, Terry—Juvenile literature. 2. Football players—United States—Biography—Juvenile literature. I. Title. BIP

Bradstreet, Anne (Dudley) 1612?-1672—Juvenile literature.

DUNHAM, Montrew. 811'.1 B
Anne Bradstreet; young Puritan poet. Illustrated by Paul and Patty Karch. Indianapolis, Bobbs-Merrill [1969] 200 p. col. illus. 20 cm. (Childhood of famous Americans) Bibliography: p. 198. A biography stressing the childhood of America's first woman poet who became known as "The Tenth Muse." [PS712.D8] 92 74-89983
1. Bradstreet, Anne (Dudley) 1612?-1672—Juvenile literature. I. Karch, Paul, illus. II. Karch, Patty, illus. BIP

Bradstreet, John, 1711-1774.

RAHMER, Frederick A. 973.2'6
Dash to Frontenac; an account of Lt. Col. John Bradstreet's expedition to and capture of Fort Frontenac, by Frederick A. Rahmer. Rome, N.Y. [1973] 52 p. illus. 22 cm. Bibliography: p. 50-51. [E199.B823R34] 73-85668 ISBN 0-9600412-3-0 1.50
1. Bradstreet, John, 1711-1774. 2. Frontenac, Fort—Capture, 1758. I. Title.
Publisher's address: P.O. Box 123; Rome, N.Y. 13440.

Brady, James Buchanan, 1856-1917.

MORELL, Parker, 1906-1943. 917.3'03'80924 B
Diamond Jim; the life and times of James Buchanan Brady. New York, AMS Press [1970, c1934] 286 p. illus., ports. 23 cm. [CT275.B5943M6 1970] 78-126693
1. Brady, James Buchanan, 1856-1917. I. Title. BIP

Brady, James, 1928-

BRADY, James, 1928- 746.9'2'0924 B
Superchic. [1st ed.] Boston, Little, Brown [1974] 266 p. 22 cm. Autobiographical. [TT505.B7A34] 74-13303 ISBN 0-316-10593-7 6.95
1. Brady, James, 1928- I. Title.

Brady, Matthew, 1798 or 9-1826—Fiction.

BUTLER, Richard, 1925- FIC
And wretches hang : the true and authentic story of the rise and fall of Matt Brady, bushranger / Richard Butler. New York : St. Martin's Press, 1979, c1977. 225 p., [1] leaf of plates : map ; 21 cm. Bibliography: p. 225. [PZ4.B9868An 1979] [PR6052.U85] 823'.9'14 78-60464 ISBN 0-312-03619-1 : 8.95
1. Brady, Matthew, 1798 or 9-1826—Fiction. I. Title.

Brady, Mathew B., 1823 (ca.)-1896.

BRADY, Mathew B., 1823(ca.)-1896. 779'.2'0973
Mathew Brady's Great Americans : prints from the original glass negatives in the Meserve collection / produced in collaboration with Time-Life Books. [Alexandria, Va.] : Time-Life Books, [1977,c1976] 1 case : ports. ; 30 cm. Title from case. Contains text (6 p.), by P. B. Kunhardt, Jr., 1 photoprint (9 x 11 in.), and 10 contact prints (3 x 4 in.), each mounted on a folder with accompanying descriptive text. [TR681.F3B7 1976] 77-150942 19.95
1. Brady, Mathew B., 1823 (ca.)-1896. 2. Photography—Portraits. 3. United States—Biography—Portraits. I. Time-Life Books. II. Title: Great Americans.

MEREDITH, Roy, 1908- 770'.92'4 B
Mr. Lincoln's camera man, Mathew B. Brady / Roy Meredith. 2d rev. ed New York : Dover Publications, [1974] xiii, 368 p. : ill. ; 29 cm. An unabridged and corrected republication of the work originally published in 1946 by Scribner, New York, with a new index of negative numbers. Bibliography: p. 365-368. [TR140.B7M4 1974] 73-92262 ISBN 0-486-23087-2 : 12.50 ISBN 0-486-23021-X : 6.95
1. Brady, Mathew B., 1823 (ca.)-1896. 2. Photography, Artistic. 3. United States—History—Civil war, 1861-1865—Pictorial works. I. Title.

MEREDITH, Roy, 1908- 973.7'092'2 B
The world of Mathew Brady : portraits of the Civil War period / by Roy Meredith. Los Angeles, Calif. : Brooke House Publishers, c1976. 240 p. : ill. ; 29 cm. [E415.8.M43] 76-45627 ISBN 0-912588-05-5 : 20.00
1. Brady, Mathew B., 1823-1896. 2. United States—History—Civil War, 1861-1865—Biography. 3. United States—Biography. 4. United States—History—Civil War, 1861-1865. I. Title.

Brady, Mathew B., 1823 (ca.)-1896—Juvenile literature.

HOOBLER, Dorothy. 770'.92'4 B
Photographing history : the career of Mathew Brady / by Dorothy and Thomas Hoobler. New York : Putnam, c1977. 143 p. : ill. ; 24 cm. Includes index. A biography of the photographer of famous men and women of his time who left his studio at the zenith of his career to travel with Union troops photographing the Civil War. [TR140.B7H59 1977] 92 77-3009 ISBN 0-399-20602-7 : 8.95.
1. Brady, Mathew B., 1823 (ca.)-1896—Juvenile literature. 2. Photographers—United States—Biography—Juvenile literature. I. Hoobler, Thomas, joint author. II. Title. BIP

KOMROFF, Manuel, 1890- 920
Photographing history: Matthew Brady. Photos. from the Ansco Historical Collection, the Chicago Historical Society, and Kean Archives, Philadelphia. Chicago, [Ency. Britannica, 1963, c.1962] 192p. 22cm. (Britannica bkshelf: Great lives for young Amers.) 62-10424 2.36 lib. ed.,
1. Brady, Mathew B., 1823 (ca.)—1896—Juvenile literature. I. Title.

Brady, Samuel, 1756-1795.

BRADY, William Young. comp. 923.573
Captain Sam Brady, Indian fighter. Washington, Brady Pub. Co. [1950] viii, 184 p. illus. 19 cm. [E85.B8B7] 50-1248
1. Brady, Samuel, 1756-1795. I. Title.

Brady, William, 1825-1878.

DYKES, Jefferson Chenowth, 1900- 978.9'64'040922 B
Law on a wild frontier: four sheriffs of Lincoln County, by Jeff C. Dykes. Washington, Potomac Corral, The Westerners 1969. iv, 25 p. illus., map, ports. 23 cm. (The Great Western series, no. 5) Bibliography: p. 23. [F802.L7D9] 70-86594
1. Brady, William, 1825-1878. 2. Curry, George, 1861-1947. 3. Garrett, Patrick Floyd, 1850-1908. 4. Poe, John William, 1850-1923. I. Title.

Braemer, Alice.

BRAEMER, Alice. 248'.246 B
Cultism to charisma : my seven years with Jeane Dixon / Alice Braemer, with Dolores Hayford ; and with a foreword by Ruth D. Nickel. 1st ed. Hicksville, N.Y. : Exposition Press, c1977. 45 p. ; 22 cm. [BV4935.B65A33] 77-150260 ISBN 0-682-48755-4 : 4.00
1. Braemer, Alice. 2. Dixon, Jeane. 3. Converts—California—Biography. I. Hayford, Dolores. II. Title. BIP

Bragg, Braxton, 1817-1876.

MCWHINEY, Grady. 973.73'0924 B
Braxton Bragg and Confederate defeat. New York, Columbia University Press, 1969- v. illus., maps, ports. 23 cm. Contents.Contents.—v. 1. Field command. Bibliography: v. 1, p. [393]-407. [E467.1.B75M3] 69-19856 10.00 (v. 1)
1. Bragg, Braxton, 1817-1876. I. Title.

SEITZ, Don Carlos, 1862-1935. 973.7'3'0924 B
Braxton Bragg, general of the Confederacy. Freeport, N.Y., Books for Libraries Press [1971] 544 p. port. 23 cm. Reprint of the 1924 ed. [E467.1.B75S4 1971] 72-179537 ISBN 0-8369-6666-X
1. Bragg, Braxton, 1817-1876. I. Title.

Bragg, George Nathan, 1897 or 8-1975.

CLAYBURN, Barbara B., 1930- 385'.092'4 B
Prairie stationmaster : the story of one man's railroading career in Nebraska 1917-1963 / by Barbara B. Clayburn. Detroit : Harlo, c1979. 128 p. : ill. ; 23 cm. [TF140.B6C57] 78-78305 ISBN 0-8187-0034-3 : 6.50
1. Bragg, George Nathan, 1897 or 8-1975. 2. Chicago, Burlington and Quincy Railroad—Employees—Biography. I. Title. BIP

Bragg, William Henry, Sir, 1862-1942.

CAROE, G. M. 530'.092'4 B
William Henry Bragg, 1862-1942 : man and scientist / G. M. Caroe. Cambridge ; New York : Cambridge University Press, 1978. xii, 212 p., [2] leaves of plates : ill. ; 23 cm. Includes bibliographical references and index. [QC16.B66C37] 77-84799 ISBN 0-521-21839-X : 16.95
1. Bragg, William Henry, Sir, 1862-1942. 2. Physicists—England—Biography.

Braggiotti family.

BRAGGIOTTI, Gloria. 929'.2'0973
Born in a crowd. Illustrated by Emlen Etting. New York, Crowell [1957] 311p. illus. 21cm. Autobiographical. [CS71.B8135 1957] 57-5632
1. Braggiotti family. I. Title.

Brahe, Tyge, 1546-1601.

DREYER, John Louis Emil, 1852-1926 925.2
Tycho Brahe a picture of scientific life and work in the scientific century [Gloucester, Mass., P. Smith, 1964] xvi, 405p. illus. 22cm. (Dover bk. rebound) Bibl. 4.00

1. Brahe, Tyge, 1546-1601. I. Title.

GADE, John Allyne, 1875- 520'.924 B
The life and times of Tycho Brahe. New York, Greenwood Press [1969, c1947] xii, 209 p. illus., facsims., ports. 24 cm. Bibliography: p. 195-203. [QB36.B8G2 1969] 69-13899
1. Brahe, Tyge, 1546-1601. I. Title.

Brahmananda, Swami, 1863-1922.

VEDANTA Society 921.9
Memories of Maharaj new reminiscences by disciples and devotees. Hollywood, Calif., Vedanta Press [c.1960] 80p. illus. 18cm. 60-1532 .50 pap.,
1. Brahmananda, Swami, 1863-1922. I. Title.

VEDANTA SOCIETY. 921.9
Memories of Maharaj; new reminiscences by disciples and devotees. Hollywood, Calif., Vedanta Press [1960] 80 p. illus. 18 cm. [B133.B72V4] 60-1532
1. Brahmananda, Swami, 1803-1922. I. Title.

Brahms, Johannes, 1833-1897.

BRAHMS, Johannes, 1833-1897. 780'.92'4 B
Johannes Brahms; the Herzogenberg correspondence. Edited by Max Kalbeck. Translated by Hannah Bryant. Freeport, N.Y., Books for Libraries Press [1972] xix, 425 p. illus. 22 cm. Reprint of the 1909 ed. [ML410.B8A333 1972] 72-5395 ISBN 0-8369-6899-9
I. Herzogenberg, Heinrich, Freiherr von, 1843-1900. II. Herzogenberg, Elisabet (Stockhausen) Freiin von, 1847-1892. **BIP**

BRAHMS, Johannes, 1833-1897. 780'.92'4 B
Johannes Brahms: the Herzogenberg correspondence. Edited by Max Kalbeck. Translated by Hannah Bryant. New York, Vienna House [1971] xix, 425 p. port. 23 cm. Reprint of the 1909 ed. [ML410.B8A333 1971] 78-163787 ISBN 0-8443-0011-X
I. Herzogenberg, Heinrich, Freiherr von, 1843-1900. II. Herzogenberg, Elisabet (Stockhausen) Freiin von, 1847-1892. III. Kalbeck, Max, 1850-1921, ed. IV. Bryant, Hannah, tr.

BRAHMS, Johannes, 1833-1897. 927.8
Johannes Brahms and Theodor Billroth; letters from a musical friendship. Translated and edited by Hans Barkan. Norman, University of Oklahoma Press [1957] xxi, 264p. illus., ports. 24cm. Bibliography: p. 253-257. [ML410.B8A3235] 57-11190
I. Billroth, Theodor, 1829-1894. II. Title. III. Title: Letters from a musical friendship.

CHISSELL, Joan. 780'.92'4 B
Brahms / Joan Chissell. London : Faber, 1977. 104 p. : ill. ; 23 cm. (The Great composers) Includes index. Bibliography: p. 98. [ML410.B8C45] 77-364974 ISBN 0-571-10791-5 : 7.95
1. Brahms, Johannes, 1833-1897. 2. Composers—Germany—Biography.
Distributed by Faber and Faber, Salem, N.H

DALE, Kathleen. 780'.924 B
Brahms; a biography with a survey of books, editions & recordings. [Hamden, Conn.] Archon Books [1970] 118 p. 23 cm. (The Concertgoer's companions) [ML410.B8D2] 77-18024
1. Brahms, Johannes, 1833-1897. **BIP**

FULLER-MAITLAND, John Alexander, 1856-1936. 780'.924 B
Brahms. Port Washington, N.Y., Kennikat Press [1972] xi, 263 p. illus. 23 cm. Reprint of the 1911 ed. [ML410.B8F8 1971] 75-153898 ISBN 0-8046-1598-5
1. Brahms, Johannes, 1833-1897.

GAL, Hans, 1890- 927.8
Johannes Brahms; his work and personality. Tr. from German by Josepj Stein. New York, Knopf, 1963 [c.1961, 1963] 245p. illus. 22cm. Bibl. 63-9122 5.95
1. Brahms, Johannes, 1833-1897. I. Title.

GAL, Hans, 1890- 780'.92'4 B
Johannes Brahms : his work and personality / by Hans Gal ; translated from the German by Joseph Stein. Westport, Conn. : Greenwood Press, [1977] c1963. ix, 245, iv p., [4] leaves of plates : ill. ; 22 cm. Reprint of the ed. published by Knopf, New York. Includes index. "List of compositions" : p. 240-245. [ML410.B8G153 1977] 76-55410 ISBN 0-8371-9367-2 lib. bdg. : 17.50
1. Brahms, Johannes, 1833-1897. 2. Composers—Germany—Biography.

GAL, Hans, 1890- 780'.92'4 B
Johannes Brahms : his work and personality / by Hans Gal ; translated from the German by Joseph Stein. Westport, Conn. : Greenwood Press, [1977] c1963. ix, 245, iv p., [4] leaves of plates : ill. ; 22 cm. Reprint of the ed. published by Knopf, New York. Includes index. "List of compositions" : p. 240-245. [ML410.B8G153 1977] 76-55410 ISBN 0-8371-9367-2 lib. bdg. : 17.50
1. Brahms, Johannes, 1833-1897. 2. Composers—Germany—Biography. **BIP**

GEIRINGER, Karl, 1899- 927.8
Brahms, his life and work. Tr. by H. B. Wiener and Bernard Miall [2d ed., rev. and enl., new appendix of Brahms' letters.] Garden City, N.Y., Dubleday 1961[c.1947] 344p. (Anchor bk. A248) 1.45 pap.,
1. Brahms, Johannes, 1833-1897. I. Weiner, H. B., tr. II. Title.

HENSCHEL, George, Sir, 1850-1934. 780'.92'4 B
Personal recollections of Johannes Brahms : some of his letters to and pages from a journal kept by George Henschel. New York : AMS Press, 1978. 95 p. : ill. ; 19 cm. Reprint of the 1907 ed. published by R. G. Badger, Boston. Includes index. [ML410.B8H3 1978] 74-24110 ISBN 0-404-12963-3 : 11.50
1. Brahms, Johannes, 1833-1897. 2. Composers—Germany—Biography. 3. Composers—Germany—Correspondence. I. Brahms, Johannes, 1833-1897. II. Title.

LEE, Ernest Markham, 1874- 780'.92'4 B
Brahms, the man and his music / by E. Markham Lee. 1st AMS ed. New York : AMS Press, 1978 viii, 183 p., [3] leaves of plates : ports. ; 19 cm. Reprint of the 1916 ed. published by S. Low, Marston, London. Includes index. Bibliography: p. 171-174. [ML410.B8L33 1978] 74-24138 ISBN 0-404-13056-9 : 24.50
1. Brahms, Johannes, 1833-1897. 2. Composers—Germany—Biography. I. Title. **BIP**

NIEMANN, Walter, 1876-1953. 780'.924 B
Brahms. Translated by Catherine Alison Phillips. New York, Cooper Square Publishers, 1969 [c1929] xiii, 492 p. port. 24 cm. Originally published 1929. Bibliography: p. 470-475. [ML410.B8N42 1969] 70-92028 ISBN 0-8154-0310-0 10.00
1. Brahms, Johannes, 1833-1897. I. Phillips, Catherine Alison, 1884- tr. **BIP**

SCHAUFFLER, Robert Haven, 1879-1945. 780'.92'4 B
The unknown Brahms, his life, character and works; based on new material. Westport, Conn., Greenwood Press [1972, c1933] xiv, 560 p. illus. music. 22 cm. Bibliography: p. 513-529. [ML410.B8S23 1972] 70-152602 ISBN 0-8371-6037-5 22.54
1. Brahms, Johannes, 1833-1897. I. Title.

Brahms, Johannes, 1833-1897—Biography.

MURDOCH, William David, 1888-1942. 780'.92'4 B
Brahms : with an analytical study of the complete pianoforte works / by William Murloch. New York : AMS Press, 1978. 394 p., [9] leaves of plates : ill. ; 23 cm. Reprint of the 1933 ed. published by Rich & Cowan, London under title: Brahms, with an analytical study of the complete pianoforte works. Includes index. Bibliography: p. 378-379. [ML410.B8M85 1978] 74-24161 ISBN 0-404-13056-9 : 14.00
1. Brahms, Johannes, 1833-1897—Biography. 2. Brahms, Johannes, 1833-1897. Works, piano. 3. Composers—Biography.

Brahms, Johannes, 1833-1897—Juvenile literature.

MIRSKY, Reba Paeff 780.924(B)
Brahms. Illus. by W. T. Mars. Chicago, Follett [c.1966] 160p. illus., music. 25cm. [ML3930.B75M6] 66-16941 3.95
1. Brahms, Johannes, 1833-1897—Juvenile literature. I. Title.

Braille, Louis, 1809-1852.

DEGERING, Etta. 926.5538
Seeing fingers, the story of Louis Braille. Illustrated by Emil Weiss. New York, D. McKay Co. [1962] 115 p. illus. 21 cm. [HV1624.B65D4] 62-18959
1. Braille, Louis, 1809-1852. I. Title. **BIP**

KUGELMASS, J. Alvin. 920.96177
Louis Braille, windows for the blind. Decorations by Edgard Cirlin. New York, Messner [1951] 160 p. illus., port. 22 cm. Bibliographical references includes in "Author's note": p. [7]-[8] [HV1624.B65K8 1951] 51-9808
1. Braille, Louis, 1809-1852.

ROBERTO, Brother, 1927- 92
Treasures at my finger tips; a story of Louis Braille. Illus. by Carolyn Lee Jagodits. Notre Dame, Ind., Dujarie Press [1961] 94p. illus. 24cm. [HV1624.B65R58] 61-4730
1. Braille, Louis, 1809-1852. I. Title.

ROBLIN, Jean. 926.5538
The reading fingers; life of Louis Braille, 1809-1852. Translated from the French by Ruth G. Mandalian. New York, American Foundation for the Blind [1955] 65p. 25cm. 'This translation... was first published in March 1952 in a slightly abbreviated form.' [HV1624 B65R62 1955] 60-45912
1. Braille, Louis, 1800-1852. I. Title.

Braille, Louis, 1809-1852—Juvenile literature.

ABRAHALL, Clare Constance (Drury) Hoskyns. 92
The young Louis Braille. Illus. by John Bowers. New York, Roy [1965, c.1964] 123p. illus. 21cm. [HV1624.B65A52] 65-18882 3.25 bds.,
1. Braille, Louis, 1809-1852—Juvenile literature. I. Title.

DAVIDSON, Mickie. 371.9'11'0924 B
Louis Braille, the boy who invented books for the blind, by Margaret Davidson. Illustrated by Janet Compere. New York, Hastings House [1972, c1971] 80 p. illus. 22 cm. The life of the nineteenth-century Frenchman who invented an alphabet enabling the blind to read. [HV1624.B65D37] 73-39630 ISBN 0-8038-4281-3 4.95
1. Braille, Louis, 1809-1852 Juvenile literature. I. Compere, Janet, illus. II. Title.

NEIMARK, Anne E. 371.9110924 B
Touch of light; the story of Louis Braille [by] Anne E. Neimark. Illustrated by Robert Parker. [1st ed.] New York, Harcourt, Brace & World [1970] 186 p. illus. 22 cm. Bibliography: p. 185-186. The life of the nineteenth-century Frenchman who invented a system of reading for the blind that is used universally. [HV1624.B65N43] 92 75-96319 4.95
1. Braille, Louis, 1809-1852—Juvenile literature. I. Parker, Robert, 1923- illus. II. Title. **BIP**

Brain, Dennis, 1921-1957.

PETTITT, Stephen, 1945- 788'.41'0924 B
Dennis Brain : a biography / by Stephen Pettitt ; with an appreciation by Benjamin Britten. London : Hale, 1976. 192 p., [4] leaves of plates : ill. ; 23 cm. Includes index. Discography: p. [175]-184. [ML419.B72P5] 77-351044 ISBN 0-7091-5772-X : £5.00
1. Brain, Dennis, 1921-1957. 2. Horn players—England—Biography. **BIP**

Brainerd, David, 1718-1747.

*BRAINERD, David. 266.5'8'0924
David Brainerd, his life and diary, ed. by Jonathan Edwards. With a biographical sketch of President Edwards, by Philip E. Howard, Jr. Chicago, Moody [1968, c.1949] 384p. 21cm. (B) 4.95
I. Edwards, Jonathan, 1703-1758. II. Title.

BRAINERD, David, 1718-1747. 266'.5'10924 B
Journey with David Brainerd : forty days or forty nights with David Brainerd. Downers Grove, Ill. : InterVarsity Press, [1975] 120 p. : ill. ; 21 cm. Selections from the author's An account of the life of the late Reverend Mr. David Brainerd; with a prayer by R. A. Hasler following each selection. Includes bibliographical references. [E98.M6M7864 1975] 74-20100 ISBN 0-87784-640-5 pbk. : 2.50
1. Brainerd, David, 1718-1747. 2. Prayers. I. Hasler, Richard A. II. Title.

DAY, Richard Ellsworth, 1884- 922.573
Flagellant on horseback; the life story of David Brainerd. [1st ed.] Philadelphia, Judson [1950] 253 p. illus., ports., facsims., map (on lining papers) 21 cm. "A broad brim book." [E98.M6D35] 50-6068
1. Brainerd, David, 1718-1747. 2. Indians of North America—Missions. I. Title.

WYNBEEK, David. 922.573
David Brainerd, beloved Yankee. Grank Rapids, Eerdmans [1961] 256 p. illus. 22 cm. Includes bibliographies. [E98.M6B914] 61-18339
1. Brainerd, David, 1718-1747. I. Title.

Braithwaite, Edward Ricardo.

BRAITHWAITE, Edward Ricardo. 301.45'1'0968
Honorary white / E. R. Braithwaite. New York : McGraw-Hill, [1975] 190 p. : map ; 22 cm. Autobiographical. [DT763.B633] 74-30097 ISBN 0-07-007118-7 : 7.95
1. Braithwaite, Edward Ricardo. 2. Africa, South—Race question. I. Title.

BRAITHWAITE, Edward Ricardo. 362.7'0924
Paid servant, by E. R. Braithwaite. [1st U.S. ed.] New York, McGraw-Hill [1968, c1962] 219 p. 21 cm. Autobiographical. [HV250.L8B7 1968] 68-17502
1. Social workers—Correspondence, reminiscences, etc. 2. Child welfare—London. I. Title.

BRAITHWAITE, Edward Ricardo. 813 B
Reluctant neighbors [by] E. R. Braithwaite. New York, McGraw Hill [1972] 184 p. 22 cm. Autobiographical. [PR6052.R267Z5 1972] 72-3425 ISBN 0-07-007115-2
I. Title.

Braly, Malcolm, 1925-

BRALY, Malcolm, 1925- 365'.6'0924 B
False starts : a memoir of San Quentin and other prisons / by Malcolm Braly. 1st ed. Boston : Little, Brown, c1976. 375 p. ; 22 cm. Autobiographical. [HV6248.B718A37] 75-30837 ISBN 0-316-10614-3 : 8.95
1. Braly, Malcolm, 1925- 2. Crime and criminals—United States—Correspondence, reminiscences, etc. I. Title. **BIP**

Bramah, Joseph, 1749-1814.

MCNEIL, Ian. 608.7'24 B
Joseph Bramah; a century of invention, 1749-1851 Joseph Braham a century of invention seventeen forty-nine-eighteen fifty-one New York, A. M. Kelley, 1968. 216 p. illus., plans, ports. 23 cm. Bibliography: p. 203-207. [TA140.B72M3] 68-18647
1. Bramah, Joseph, 1749-1814.

Bramante, Donato, 1444?-1514.

BRUSCHI, Arnaldo. 720'.92'4 B
Bramante / Arnaldo Bruschi ; foreword by Peter Murray ; translated from the Italian. London : Thames and Hudson, c1977. 208 p. : ill. ; 26 cm. Translation of Bramante.

Includes index. Bibliography: p. 198-203. [NA1123.B7B6913 1977] 77-570081 ISBN 0-500-34065-X : 22.50
1. Bramante, Donato, 1444?-1514. 2. Architects—Italy—Biography. 3. Architecture, Renaissance—Italy.
Distributed by W.W. Norton. BIP

Brancusi, Constantin, 1876-1957.

BRANCUSI, Constantin, 1876-1957. 730.9498
Constantin Brancusi, [by] Carola Giedion-Welcker. Translated by Maria Jolas and Anne Leroy. New York, G. Braziller, 1959. 240 p. (p. 45-192 plates (part col)) illus., ports. 31 cm. "Bibliography, by Hans Bolliger": p. 225-234. [NB553.B73G513] 59-9867
I. Giedion-Welcker, Carola, ed.

CONSTANTIN Brancusi. 735.44
New York, Wittenborn, 1957 [i.e. 1958] vi, 50p. 65 plates. 20cm. Bibliography: p. 48-50. [NB553.B73L4] 927.3 58-2232
1. Brancusi, Constantin, 1876-1957. I. Lewis, David, writer on art.

JIANU, Ionel 730.9498
Brancusi. New York, Tudor [c.]1963. 223p. illus., ports. 28cm. Bibl. 63-5890 12.50
1. Brancusi, Constantin, 1876-1957. I. Title. BIP

Brand, Evelyn Constance, 1879-1974.

WILSON, Dorothy Clarke. 266'.023'0924 B
Climb every mountain : the story of Granny Brand / by Dorothy Clarke Wilson. London : Hodder and Stoughton, 1976. 222 p., [8] p. of plates : ill., map, ports. ; 21 cm. American ed. published under title: Granny Brand, her story. [BV3269.B69W54 1976b] 77-356901 ISBN 0-340-20603-9 : £4.50
1. Brand, Evelyn Constance, 1879-1974. 2. Missionaries—India—South India—Biography. 3. Missionaries—England—Biography. I. Title.

WILSON, Dorothy Clarke. 266'.023'0924 B
Granny Brand, her story / Dorothy Clarke Wilson. 1st ed. Chappaqua, N.Y. : Christian Herald Books, c1976. 222 p., [4] leaves of plates : ill. ; 22 cm. [BV3269.B69W54 1976] 76-16721 ISBN 0-915684-11-X : 6.95
1. Brand, Evelyn Constance, 1879-1974. 2. Missionaries—India—South India—Biography. 3. Missionaries—England—Biography. I. Title. BIP

Brand, Paul Wilson, 1914-

WILSON, Dorothy Clarke 617.0924
Ten fingers for God. New York, McGraw [c.1965] viii, 247p. illus., ports. 22cm. [BV3269.B7W5] 65-25554 5.50
1. Brand, Paul Wilson, 2. Missions to Lepers—India. I. Title.

WILSON, Dorothy Clarke. 617.0924 (B)
Ten fingers for God. [1st ed.] New York, McGraw-Hill [1965] viii, 247 p. illus., ports. 22 cm. [BV3269.B7W5] 65-25554
1. Brand, Paul Wilson, 1914- 2. Missions to Lepers — India. I. Title.

Brandeis, Donald,

BRANDEIS, Donald, 1928- 922.673
Fling wide the gates! The life story of Don Brandeis as told to Byron McKissack. [1st ed.] New York, Vantage Press [1958] 105p. 21cm. [BV2623.B7A3] 58-10664
I. McKissack, Byron. II. Title.

Brandeis, Louis Dembitz, 1856-1941.

BRANDEIS, a free man's life. v. 12
[Aniversary ed.] New York, Viking Press, 1956. xii, 713p. port. 24cm. Bibliography: p. 647-684.
1. Brandeis, Louis Dembitz, 1856-1941. I. Mason, Alpheus Thomas, 1899-

BRANDEIS, Louis Dembitz, 1856-1941. 347'.73'2634
Letters of Louis D. Brandeis. Edited by Melvin I. Urofsky and David W. Levy. Albany, State University of New York Press, 1971- v. illus., ports. 22 cm. Vol. 3: 1st ed. Contents.Contents.—v. 1. 1870-1907: Urban reformer.—v. 2. 1907-1912: People's attorney.—v. 3. 1913-1915: Progressive and Zionist.—v. 4. 1916-1921: Mr. Justice Brandeis. [E664.B819A4 1971] 73-129640 ISBN 0-87395-078-X (v. 1) 20.00 (v. 1)
1. Brandeis, Louis Dembitz, 1856-1941. BIP

EISEMAN, Alberta. 973'.04'924 B
Rebels and reformers : biographies of four Jewish Americans : Uriah Phillips Levy, Ernestine L. Rose, Louis D. Brandeis, Lillian D. Wald / by Alberta Eiseman ; illustrated by Herb Steinberg. 1st ed. Garden City, N.Y. : Zenith Books, 1976. 131 p. : ill. ; 22 cm. Includes index. Biographies of four Jewish Americans whose activities in women's rights, abolition, law, nursing, and the military contributed to the growth, development, and needed reform of the country. [E184.J5E34] 920 75-21224 ISBN 0-385-01588-7 : 4.95. ISBN 0-385-09662-3 pbk. : 2.50
1. Levy, Uriah Phillips, 1792-1862. 2. Rose, Ernestine Louise, 1810-1892. 3. Brandeis, Louis Dembitz, 1856-1941. 4. Wald, Lillian D., 1867-1940. 5. Jews in the United States. I. Steinberg, Herbert, 1928- II. Title.

GOODHART, Arthur Lehman, Sir, 1891- 340'.57'0922 B
Five Jewish lawyers of the common law [by] Arthur L. Goodhart. With a new pref. to this ed. and a suppl. on Mr. Justice Felix Frankfurter. Freeport, N.Y., Books for Libraries Press [1971, c1949] vii, 81 p. 23 cm. (Biography index reprint series) Includes bibliographical references. [KF299.J4G65 1971] 79-148212 ISBN 0-8369-8059-X
1. Benjamin, Judah Philip, 1811-1884. 2. Jessel, George, Sir, 1824-1883. 3. Brandeis, Louis Dembitz, 1856-1941. 4. Reading, Rufus Daniel Isaacs, 1st Marquis of, 1860-1935. 5. Cardozo, Benjamin Nathan, 1870-1938. I. Title. BIP

LIEF, Alfred, 1901- 347'.73'2634 B
Brandeis; the personal history of an American ideal. Freeport, N.Y., Books for Libraries Press [1971, c1936] 508 p. illus. 23 cm. Bibliography: p. 489-497. [KF8745.B67L5 1971] 72-169768 ISBN 0-8369-5988-4
1. Brandeis, Louis Dembitz, 1856-1941.

MASON, Alpheus Thomas, 1899- v. 12
Brandeis, a free man's life.Anniversary ed. New York, Viking Press, 1956. xii, 713p. port. 24cm. Bibliography: p. 647-684.
1. Brandeis, Louis Dembitz, 1856-1941. I. Title.

MR. Justice Brandeis. 347'.73'2634 B
Edited by Felix Frankfurter. Introd. by Oliver Wendell Holmes. New York, Da Capo Press, 1972 [c1932] vi, 232 p. 22 cm. (Da Capo Press reprints in American constitutional and legal history) "Published on the fund established in memory of Ganson Goodyear Depew." Contents.Contents.—Introduction, by O. W. Holmes.—Mr. Justice Brandeis, by C. E. Hughes.—The social thought of Mr. Justice Brandeis, by M. Lerner.—Mr. Justice Brandeis and the Constitution, by F. Frankfurter.—The industrial liberalism of Mr. Justice Brandeis, by D. R. Richberg.—Mr. Justice Brandeis and the regulation of railroads, by H. W. Bikle.—The jurist's art, by W. H. Hamilton.—Notes.—List of opinions. [KF210.M55 1972] 73-37766 ISBN 0-306-70430-7
1. Brandeis, Louis Dembitz, 1856-1941. 2. Law—United States—Addresses, essays, lectures. I. Frankfurter, Felix, 1882-1965, ed. II. Yale University. Ganson Goodyear Depew Memorial Fund. BIP

NOBLE, Iris. 347.9924 B
Firebrand for justice: a biography of Louis Dembitz Brandeis. Philadelphia, Westminster Press [1969] 176 p. 23 cm. Bibliography: p. 169-170. [KF8745.B67N6] 69-10867 4.50
1. Brandeis, Louis Dembitz, 1856-1941. I. Title.

PEARE, Catherine Owens. 347.99'24 B
The Louis D. Brandeis story. New York, Crowell [1970] vii, 297 p. 21 cm. Bibliography: p. [279]-288. [KF8745.B67P4] 78-109909 4.50
1. Brandeis, Louis Dembitz, 1856-1941.

POLLACK, Ervin Harold, 1913- ed. 923.473
The Brandeis reader; the life and contributions of Mr. Justice Louis D. Brandies, edited with commentary. Centenary ed. New York, Oceana Publications, 1956. 256p. 21cm. (Docket series, v. 7) 56-12251
1. Brandeis, Louis Dembitz, 1856-1941. I. Title.

RABINOWITZ, Ezekiel, 1890- 956.94'001'0924
Justice Louis D. Brandeis, the Zionist chapter of his life. New York, Philosophical Lib. [1968] 130p. 23cm. Bibl. footnotes. [DS151.B74R3] 68-22350 4.50
1. Brandeis, Louis Dembitz, 1856-1941. 2. Zionism—U. S. I. Title.

RABINOWITZ, Ezekiel, 1890- 492.4'092'4
Justice Louis D. Brandeis, the Zionist chapter of his life. New York, Philosophical Library [1968] 130 p. 23 cm. Bibliographical footnotes. [DS151.B74R3] 68-22350
1. Brandeis, Louis Dembitz, 1856-1941. 2. Zionism—United States. I. Title.

STERN, Ellen Norman. 347'.7326'34 B
Embattled Justice; the story of Louis Dembitz Brandeis. [1st ed.] Philadelphia, Jewish Publication Society of America, 1971. viii, 142, [1] p. ports. 22 cm. (Covenant 23) Bibliography: p. [143] [KF8745.B67S74] 72-136257 2.95
1. Brandeis, Louis Dembitz, 1856-1941. I. Title. BIP

Brandes, Georg Morris Cohen, 1842-1927.

BRANDES, Georg Morris Cohen, 1842-1927. 809 B
Reminiscences of my childhood and youth / by George Brandes. New York : Arno Press, 1975 [c1906] 397 p. ; 23 cm. (The Modern Jewish experience) Translation of Barndom og forste ungdom. Reprint of the ed. published by Duffield, New York. Includes index. [PT8125.B8Z53 1975] 74-27967 ISBN 0-405-06697-X : 25.00
1. Brandes, Georg Morris Cohen, 1842-1927. 2. Jews in Copenhagen—Social life and customs. I. Title. II. Series. BIP

NOLIN, Bertil. 809
Georg Brandes / by Bertil Nolin. Boston : Twayne Publishers, c1976. 208 p. : port. ; 21 cm. (Twayne's world authors series ; TWAS 390) Includes index. Bibliography: p. 199-202. [PT8125.B8Z837] 76-2718 ISBN 0-8057-6232-9 lib.bdg. : 6.50
1. Brandes, Georg Morris Cohen, 1842-1927. BIP

Brando, Marlon.

BRANDO, Anna Kashfi. 791.43'028'0924 B
Brando for breakfast / by Anna Kashfi Brando and E. P. Stein. New York : Crown Publishers, c1979. p. cm. [PN2287.B683B74] 79-11048 ISBN 0-517-53686-2 : 10.00
1. Brando, Marlon. 2. Moving-picture actors and actresses—United States—Biography. I. Stein, E. P., joint author. II. Title. BIP

CAREY, Gary. 791.43'028'0924 B
Brando! New York, Pocket Books [1973] vi, 278 p. illus. 18 cm. [PN2287.B683C3] 73-164000 ISBN 0-671-78655-5 1.50 (pbk.)
1. Brando, Marlon. I. Title.

FIORE, Carlo, 1919- 791.43'028'0924
Bud: the Brando I knew; the untold story of Brando's private life. New York, Delacorte Press [1974] 294 p. ports. 24 cm. [PN2287.B683F5] 73-18286 8.95
1. Brando, Marlon. I. Title.

FIORE, Carlo, 1919- 791.43'028'0924
Bud! the Brando I knew; the untold story of Brando's private life. [New York, Dell, 1975, c1974] 271 p. ports. 18 cm. [PN2287.B683F5] 1.50 (pbk.)
1. Brando, Marlon I. Title.
L.C. card number for original ed.: 73-18286.

MORELLA, Joe. 791.43'028'0924 B
Brando; the unauthorized biography [by] Joe Morella and Edward Z. Epstein. New York, Crown Publishers [1973] 248 p. illus. 25 cm. [PN2287.B683M6] 72-96659 ISBN 0-517-50359-X 6.95
1. Brando, Marlon. I. Epstein, Edward Z., joint author.

OFFEN, Ron. 791.43'028'0924 B
Brando. Chicago, Regnery [1973] xiv, 222 p. illus. 22 cm. [PN2287.B683O3] 72-11186 6.95
1. Brando, Marlon.

SHIPMAN, David. 791.43'028'0924
Brando / David Shipman. 1st ed. in the U.S. Garden City, N.Y. : Doubleday, 1974. 127 p. : ill. (some col.) ; 26 cm. (The Movie makers) Includes index. Filmography: p. 122-125. [PN2287.B683S5 1974] 73-11635 ISBN 0-385-01045-1 : 7.50
1. Brando, Marlon.

THOMAS, Bob, 1922- 791.43'028'0924 B
Brando, portrait of the rebel as an artist. New York, Random House [1974] p. cm. [PN2287.B683T47] 73-21710 ISBN 0-394-48728-1 7.95
1. Brando, Marlon. I. Title.

THOMAS, Bob, 1922- 791.43'028'0924 B
Marlon, portrait of the rebel as an artist. [1st American ed.] New York, Random House [1973] 276 p. illus. 22 cm. [PN2287.B683T47 1973] 73-20573 ISBN 0-394-48728-1 6.95
1. Brando, Marlon. I. Title.

Brando, Marlon—Juvenile literature.

PAIGE, David. 791.43'028'0924 B
Marlon Brando / written by David Paige ; designed by Gene Kohler. [Mankato, Minn.] : Creative Education, [c1977] 39 p. : ill. ; 25 cm. (Stars of stage and screen) A biography of a man who has earned the reputation for being not only a fine actor but a notorious rebel as well. [PN2287.B683P3] 92 76-40690 ISBN 0-87191-552-9 lib.bdg. 4.95
1. Brando, Marlon—Juvenile literature. 2. Moving-picture actors and actresses—United States—Biography—Juvenile literature. I. Title. BIP

Brandt, Inez Denney.

BRANDT, Inez Denney. 917.97'78 B
Just one girl; an autobiography, by Inez D. Brandt. North Quincy, Mass., Christopher Pub. House [1969] 106 p. 21 cm. [CT275.B5974A3] 70-101362 3.95
I. Title.

Brandt, Willy, 1913-

BINDER, David. 943.087'092'4 B
The other German : Willy Brandt's life & times / David Binder. Washington : New Republic Book Co., 1975. viii, 373 p., [6] leaves of plates : ill. ; 24 cm. Includes bibliographical references and index. [DD259.7.B7B5] 75-29024 ISBN 0-915220-09-1 : 12.50
1. Brandt, Willy, 1913- I. Title.

BRANDT, Willy 923.243
My road to Berlin [by]Willy Brandt, as told to Leo Lania [pseud.] Garden City, N.Y., Doubleday, [c.] 1960. 287p. illus. 22cm. 60-10666 4.50 half cloth
1. Berlin—Hist.—Allied occupation, 1945- I. Herrmann, Lazar II. Title.

BRANDT, Willy, 1913- 923.243
My road to Berlin [by] Willy Brandt, as told to Leo Lania [pseud. 1st ed.] Garden City, N. Y., Doubleday, 1960. 287p. illus. 22cm. [DD857.B7A3] 60-10666

1. Berlin—Hist. —Allied occupation, 1945- I. Herrmann, Lazar, 1896- II. Title.

DRATH, Viola Herms. 943.087'092'4
Willy Brandt, a prisoner of his past / Viola Herms Drath. 1st ed. Radnor, Pa. : Chilton Book Co., c1975. p. cm. Includes index. Bibliography: p. [DD259.7.B7D7] 75-24964 ISBN 0-8019-6196-3
1. Brandt, Willy, 1913- 2. Guillaume, Gunter, 1926- 3. Germany, West—Politics and government. I. Title.

DRATH, Viola Herms. 943.087'092'4
Willy Brandt, prisoner of his past / Viola Herms Drath. 1st ed. Radnor, Pa. : Chilton Book Co., c1975. xviii, 364 p., [6] leaves of plates : ill. ; 24 cm. Includes index. Bibliography: p. [356]-358. [DD259.7.B7D7 1975] 75-24964 ISBN 0-8019-6196-3 : 8.95
1. Brandt, Willy, 1913- 2. Guillaume, Gunter, 1926- 3. Germany, West—Politics and government. I. Title.

HARPPRECHT, Klaus. 943.087'092'4 B
Willy Brandt: portrait and self-portrait. Translated by Hank Keller. Los Angeles, Nash Pub. [1971] xiv, 300 p. 23 cm. Includes bibliographical references. [DD259.7.B7H313 1971] 77-167531 ISBN 0-8402-1240-2 8.95
1. Brandt, Willy, 1913-

HOMZE, Alma. 943.087'092'4 B
Willy Brandt, a biography, by Alma and Edward Homze. [1st ed.] Nashville, T. Nelson [1974] 175 p. port. 21 cm. [DD259.7.B7H6] 74-3273 ISBN 0-8407-6391-3 5.95
1. Brandt, Willy, 1913- I. Homze, Edward L., joint author. BIP

PRITTIE, Terence Cornelius Farmer, Hon., 1913- 943.087'092'4 B
Willy Brandt; portrait of a statesman [by] Terence Prittie. New York, Schocken Books [1974] 356 p. illus. 24 cm. Bibliography: p. 333-339. [DD259.7.B7P74 1974b] 74-9229 ISBN 0-8052-3561-2 10.50
1. Brandt, Willy, 1913-

Branham, William, 1909-

LINDSAY, Gordon. 922
William Branham; a man sent from God, by Gordon Lindsay in collaboration with William Branham. Jeffersonville, Ind., W. Branham [1950] 216 p. illus., ports. 21 cm. [BR1716.B7L5] 51-17099
1. Branham, William, 1909- I. Title.

STADSKLEV, Julius. 922
William Branham: a prophet visits South Africa. Minneapolis [1952] 195 p. illus. 23 cm. [BR1716.B7S8] 52-38079
1. Branham, William, 1909- I. Title.

Brann, William Cowper, 1855-1898.

CARVER, Charles. 920.5
Brann and the Iconoclast. Introd. by Roy Bedichek. Austin, University of Texas Press [1957] 196p. illus. 22cm. Includes bibliographies. [PN4874.B663C3] 57-8822
1. Brann, William Cowper, 1855-1898. 2. Liberal. Chicago. I. Title.

Brannaka, Marjorie, 1927-

BRANNAKA, Marjorie, 1927- 286'.73
Sea, sand, & stars / Marjorie Brannaka. Washington : Review and Herald Pub. Co., c1978. 64 p. : ill. ; 21 cm. [BX6193.B7A35] 78-15097 2.95
1. Brannaka, Marjorie, 1927- 2. Brannaka, Charles. 3. Converts, Seventh-Day Adventist—Florida—Biography. 4. Park rangers—Florida—Biography. 5. Caladesi Island State Park, Fla. 6. Florida—Biography. I. Title.
Publisher's address: Takoma Park, Washington, D.C. 20012.

Brannan, Samuel, 1819-1889.

BAILEY, Paul Dayton, 1906- 979.4
Sam Brannan and the California Mormons. Los Angeles, Westernlore Press [1959] 265 p. illus. 21 cm. (Great West and Indian series, v. 1) Includes bibliography. [F865.B8 1959] 59-14042
1. Brannan, Samuel, 1819-1889. 2. Mormons and Mormonism in California.

STELLMAN, Louis John, 1877- 923.973
Sam Brannan, builder of San Francisco; a biography. [1st ed.] New York, Exposition Press [1954, c1953] 254p. illus. 21cm. Exposition-Lochinvar book. [F865.B83] 53-12076
1. Brannan, Samuel, 1819-1889. I. Title.

Brannan, Samuel, 1819-1889— Juvenile literature.

YOUNG, Bob, 1916- 979.4'0924
Empire builder; Sam Brannan, by Bob and Jan Young. New York, Messner [1967] 191p. 22cm. Bibl. [F865.B84] 67-21615 3.34
1. Brannan, Samuel, 1819-1889—Juvenile literature. I. Young, Jan, 1919- joint author. II. Title.

Branscomb, John Warren, 1905-1959.

BLANCHARD, Richard E. 922.773
We remember John; a biography of John W. Branscomb, first bishop elected from Florida Methodism. Commissioned by Bishop James W. Henley and the Cabinet of the Florida Conference of the Methodist Church. [Miami, Fla., Methodist Church, 1964] vii, 104p. illus., ports. 23cm. 64-21420 price unreported
1. Branscomb, John Warren, 1905-1959. I. Title.

Branson, Eugene Cunningham,

BRANSON, Lanier. v. 12
Eugene Cunningham Branson, humanitarian. Charlotte [Heritage Printers] 1967.C183 p. port. 24 cm. 68-34807
1. Branson, Eugene Cunningham, I. Title

Bransten, Manfred.

MCDOUGALL, Ruth Bransten. 338'.092'4 B
Coffee, martinis, and San Francisco / Ruth Bransten McDougall. San Rafael, Calif. : Presidio Press, c1978. p. cm. [HD9199.U48B75] 78-17880 ISBN 0-89141-039-2 pbk. : 7.95
1. Bransten, Manfred. 2. Brandenstein (M. J.) and Company, San Francisco—History. 3. San Francisco—History. 4. Businessmen—United States—Biography. I. Title. BIP

Brant, Alice Dayrell.

BRANT, Alice (Dayrell) 920.7
The diary of 'Helena Morley.' Translated from the Portuguese by Elizabeth Bishop. New York, Farrar, Straus and Cudahy [1957] 281p. illus. 22cm. Translation of Minha vida de menina. [CT688.B7A32] 57-12509
I. Title.

BRANT, Alice Dayrell. 981'.5 B
The diary of "Helena Morley" [i.e. A. D. Brant] / translated from the Portuguese by Elizabeth Bishop. New York : Ecco Press, [1977] p. cm. Translation of Minha vida de menina. [F2651.D5B7213 1977] 77-2327 ISBN 0-912946-46-6 : 4.95
1. Brant, Alice Dayrell. 2. Diamantina, Brazil—Biography.

Brant, Joseph, Mohawk chief, 1742-1807.

HECHT, Robert A. 973.3'43'0924 B
Joseph Brant, Iroquois ally of the British / by Robert A. Hecht, compiled with the assistance of the research staff of SamHar Press. Charlotteville, N.Y. : SamHar Press, 1975. p. cm. (Outstanding personalities of the American Revolution ; #9) (Outstanding personalities ; #83) Bibliography: p. [E99.M8B83] 75-16425 lib.bdg. : 2.29 pbk. : 0.98
1. Brant, Joseph, Mohawk Chief, 1742-1807. 2. Indians of North America—Wars—1775-1783. I. Title. BIP

JAKES, John W., 1932- 970.3 B
Mohawk; the life of Joseph Brant, by John Jakes. Illus. by Roger Hane. [New York] Crowell-Collier Press [1969] vi, 136 p. illus. 21 cm. Bibliography: p. [132] A biography of the Mohawk Indian chief, statesman, and missionary who led the Iroquois forces on the British side during the Revolutionary War. [E176.8.J3] 92 76-75898
1. Brant, Joseph, Mohawk chief, 1742-1807. I. Hane, Roger, illus. II. Title.

PRIEST, Josiah, 1788-1851. 973'.04'97 S
The captivity and sufferings of Gen. Freegift Patchin / Josiah Priest. New York : Garland Pub., 1977. 50 p. ; 23 cm. (The Garland library of narratives of North American Indian captivities ; v. 52) Reprint of the 1833 ed. printed by Packard, Hoffman and White, Albany, N.Y. Issued with the 1835 ed. of United States. Congress. House. Committee on Claims. U.S. Congress report on claims of Samuel Cozad. New York, 1977. Reprint of the 1835 ed. of Baldwin, T. Narrative of the massacre of my wife and children. New York, 1977. Reprint of the 1836 ed. of Baldwin, T. Narrative of the massacre of my wife and children New York, 1977. Reprint of the 1836 ed. of Narrative of the Seminole War and the miraculous escape of Mary Godfrey. New York, 1977. Reprint of an undated broadside, Captivity and sufferings of Mrs. Mason. New York, 1977. Reprint of the 1836 ed. of Priest, J. Stories of the Revolution. New York, 1977. Reprint of articles published in Columbian almanac for 1838, CaptivitiOThe captivity and sufferings of Gen. Freegift Patchin / Josiah Priest. New York : Garland Pub., 1977. 50 p. ; 23 cm. (The Ga
1. Patchin, Freegift, d. 1831. 2. Brant, Joseph, Mohawk chief, 1742-1807. 3. Iroquois Indians—Captivities. 4. United States—History—Revolution, 1775-1783—Personal narratives. 5. New York (State)—Biography. 6. Indians of North America—Captivities. I. Title. II. Series.

STONE, William Leete, 1792-1844. 970.3 B
Life of Joseph Brant-Thayendanegea, including the border wars of the American Revolution and sketches of the Indian campaigns of Generals Harmar, St. Clair, and Wayne; and other matters connected with the Indian relations of the United States and Great Britain, from the peace of 1783 to the Indian peace of 1795. New York, A. V. Blake, 1838. St. Clair Shores, Mich., Scholarly Press, 1970. 2 v. illus., map, ports. 23 cm. [E99.M8B874 1970] 75-108544 ISBN 4-03-002265-
1. Brant, Joseph, Mohawk chief, 1742-1807. 2. Indians of North America—Wars 1750-1815. I. Title.

Braque, Georges, 1882-1963.

BRAQUE, Georges, 1882-1963. 759.4
G. Braque [by] Francis Ponge, Pierre Descargues [and] Andre Malraux. Texts translated by Richard Howard. Biography and captions translated by Lane Dunlop. New York, H N Abrams [1971] 261, [7] p. illus. (part col.) 31 cm. "To the memory of Georges Braque, funeral oration by A. Malraux": p. [263]-[264] [ND553.B86P6313] 78-160123 ISBN 0-8109-0044-0
I. Ponge, Francis. II. Descargues, Pierre.

BRION, Marcel, 1895- 759.4
Braque. [Tr. from French by A. H. N. Molesworth] New York, Abrams [1962] 87p. illus. (pt. col.) (Student's ser. of great artists) 60-11165 1.95
1. Braque, Georges, 1882- I. Title.

DAMASE, Jacques 759.4
Georges Braque. [Tr.: Tony White] New York, Barnes & Noble [c.1963] 90p. illus. (pt. col.) port. 18cm. (Barnes ; Noble art ser. 611) 63-5389 .75 pap.,
1. Braque, George, 1882- I. Title.

LEYMARIE, Jean. 759.4
Braque. Translated by James Emmons. [New York] Skira; [distributed by World Pub. Co., Cleveland, 1961] 133 p. mounted col. illus. 19 cm. (The Taste of our time, v. 35) Bibliography: p. 119-122. [ND553.B86L45] 61-10170
1. Braque, Georges, 1882-1963.

RICHARDSON, John Patrick, 1924- 759.4
G. Braque. Greenwich, Conn., New York Graphic Society [c.1961] 32p. illus., 68 plates (part col.) 36cm. Bibl. 61-8631 12.50
1. Braque, Georges, 1882- I. Title.

Brasher, Rex, 1869-1960.

BRASHER, Milton E. 927.5
Rex Brasher: painter of birds, a biography. New York, Rowman and Littlefield [1962] 345 p. illus. 24 cm. [QL31.B684B7] 61-18827
1. Brasher, Rex, 1869-1960. BIP

Brasset, Edmund A.,

BRASSET, Edmund A., 1907- 926.1
A doctor's pilgrimage. [1st ed.] Philadelphia, Lippincott [1951] 256 p. 21 cm. Autobiographical. [R464.B6A3] 51-11186
I. Title.

Brassey, Thomas, 1805-1870.

HELPS, Arthur, Sir, 1813-1875. 385'.0924 B
Life and labours of Mr. Brassey. [New York] A. M. Kelley [1969] xxviii, 386 p. illus., maps, port. 23 cm. (Documents of social history) Reprint of the 1872 ed. with a new introd. by J. Simmons. [HE3018.2.B7H5 1969] 69-17620
1. Brassey, Thomas, 1805-1870. 2. Railroads—History. I. Title.

MIDDLEMAS, Robert Keith, 1935- 926.2
The master builders: Thomas Brassey, Sir John Aird, Lord Cowdray, London, Hutchinson [dist. Chester Springs, Pa., Dufour, 1964, c.1963] 328p. illus., maps, ports. 22cm. Bibl. [TA139.M5] 65-439 6.95
1. Brassey, Thomas, 1805-1870. 2. Aird, Sir John, bart., 1833-1911. 3. Cowdray, Weetman Dickinson Pearson, 1st viscount, 1856-1927. 4. Norton-Griffiths, Sir John, bart., 1871-1930. I. Title.

Brasted, Alva Jennings, 1876-1965.

BRASTED, Evelyn. 355.3'47'0924 B
Soldier of God. New York, Carlton Press [1971] 338 p. illus., facsims., ports. 21 cm. (A Hearthstone book) [UH23.B683] 73-28462 5.00
1. Brasted, Alva Jennings, 1876-1965. I. Title.

Braude, Michael—Biography—Youth.

BRAUDE, Michael. 808 B
The first 30 odd years : an autobiography / by Michael Braude. New York : Horizon Press, c1976. 220 p. ; 25 cm. [PS3552.R34Z52] 76-372420 ISBN 0-8180-0228-X : 8.95
1. Braude, Michael—Biography—Youth. I. Title.

Braudy, Susan.

BRAUDY, Susan. 301.42'7'0924
Between marriage and divorce : a woman's diary / by Susan Braudy. New York : Morrow, 1975. 252 p. ; 22 cm. [HQ1413.B7A33] 75-16468 ISBN 0-688-02960-4 : 7.95
1. Braudy, Susan. 2. Wives—Biography. 3. Divorcees—Biography. 4. Women—Sexual behavior. I. Title.

Braun, Albert, 1889-

EMERSON, Dorothy. 266'.2'0924 B
Among the Mescalero Apaches; the story of Father Albert Braun, O.F.M. Tucson, Ariz., University of Arizona Press [1973] xiii, 224 p. illus. 24 cm. Bibliography: p. 217-219. [E99.M45E47] 73-76302 ISBN 0-8165-0321-4 7.50
1. Braun, Albert, 1889- 2. Apache Indians—Missions. I. Title.

Braun, Bob.

BRAUN, Bob. 791.45'028'0924 B
Here's Bob. Introd. by Ruth Lyons. Afterword by Dick Clark. [1st ed.] Garden City, N.Y., Doubleday, 1969. 191 p. ports. 22 cm. [PN1992.4.B7A3] 78-86895 5.95
I. Title.

Braun, Eva.

GUN, Nerin E. 943.086'092'4 B
Eva Braun : Hitler's mistress / Nerin E. Gun ; [translated from the German]. [London] : Coronet, 1976. 272 p., [8] p. of plates : ill., ports ; 18 cm. Translation of Eva Braun-Hitler. Includes index. [DD247.B66G813 1976] 77-352216 ISBN 0-340-19932-6 : £0.80
1. Braun, Eva. 2. Hitler, Adolf, 1889-1945. 3. Heads of state—Germany—Biography. 4. Mistresses—Germany—Biography.

GUN, Nerin E. 943.086'0924 B
Eva Braun: Hitler's mistress, by Nerin E. Gun. New York, Meredith Press [1968] xv, 301 p. illus., ports. 24 cm. Translation of Eva Braun—Hitler: Leben und Schicksal. [DD247.B66G813] 67-15018 6.95
1. Braun, Eva. 2. Hitler, Adolf, 1889-1945. I. Title.

Brav, Stanley Rosenbaum,

BRAV, Stanley Rosenbaum, 1908- 296.6'1 B
Dawn of reckoning; self-portrait of a liberal rabbi [by] Stanley R. Brav. [1st ed. Cincinnati, Ohio, Sholom Press, 1971] vi, 390 p. illus., ports. 18 cm. [BM755.B65A3] 71-129180 3.95
I. Title.

Bray, Thomas, 1658-1730.

LAUGHER, Charles T. 021'.00973
Thomas Bray's grand design; libraries of the Church of England in America, 1695-1785, by Charles T. Laugher. Chicago, American Library Association, 1973. x, 115 p. 24 cm. (ACRL publications in librarianship, no. 35) Includes bibliographical references. [Z674.A75 no. 35] [Z731] 73-16332 ISBN 0-8389-0151-4 9.95 (pbk. text ed.)
1. Bray, Thomas, 1658-1730. 2. Church of England in America. 3. Libraries—United States—History. I. Title. II. Series: Association of College and Research Libraries. ACRL publications in librarianship, no. 35.

Brayton, Matthew, 1818-1862.

[BONE, John Herbert A.] 1830-1906. 973'.04'97 S
The Indian captive (Matthew Brayton). New York : Garland Pub., 1977. 68 p. ; 23 cm. (The Garland library of narratives of North American Indian captivities ; v. 76) Reprint of the 1860 ed. published by Fairbanks, Benedict, Cleveland. Issued with the reprint of the 1860 ed. of Page, L. A. Narrative of Larsena A. Page. New York, 1977, the reprint of the 1930 ed. of Kimball, J. P. Short narrative of James Kimball. New York, 1977, the reprint of the 1861 ed. of Persinger, J. The life of Jacob Persinger. New York, 1977, the reprint of the 1896? ed. of Brown, S. J. In captivity. New York, 1977, and the reprint of the 1863 ed. of Abenteuer unter den Indianern. New York, 1977. [E85.G2 vol. 76] [E99.S4] 970'.004'97 B 76-54518 ISBN 0-8240-1700-5 lib.bdg. : 25.00
1. Brayton, Matthew, 1818-1862. 2. Shoshoni Indians—Captivities. 3. Indians of North America—Captivities. 4. United States—Biography. I. Title. II. Series.

Brazil, Angela—Biography.

FREEMAN, Gillian. 823'.8 B
The schoolgirl ethic : the life and work of Angela Brazil / Gillian Freeman. London : Allen Lane, 1976. 160 p., [6] leaves of plates ; 23 cm. Includes index. Bibliography: p. 153-156. [PR6003.R326Z65] 76-375173 ISBN 0-7139-0741-X : £4.50
1. Brazil, Angela—Biography. 2. Authors, English—20th century—Biography. I. Title.

Brebeuf, Jean de, Saint, 1593-1649.

DONNELLY, Joseph Peter, 1905- 282'.092'4 B
Jean de Brebeuf, 1593-1649 / Joseph P. Donnelly. Chicago : Loyola University Press, 1975. xii, 346 p. : maps ; 23 cm. Includes index. Bibliography: p. 313-323. [E99.H9B743] 75-5682 ISBN 0-8294-0233-0 : 5.95
1. Brebeuf, Jean de, Saint, 1593-1649. 2. Huron Indians—Missions. BIP

Brebeuf, Jean de, Saint, 1593-1649—Juvenile literature.

JOHNROE, Donan. 922.271
Gold tried by fire; a story of Saint Jean de Brebeuf. Illus. by Carolyn Lee Jagodits. Notre Dame, Ind., Dujarie Press [1959] 95p. illus. 24cm. [F1030.8.B8J6] 60-310
1. Brebeuf, Jean de, Saint, 1593-1649—Juvenile literature. I. Title.

Brecht, Bertolt, 1898-1956.

ESSLIN, Martin. v. 12
Brecht; the man and his work. Garden City, N.Y., Doubleday, 1961. 370 p. (Anchor books, A 244) 64-70795
1. Brecht, Bertolt, 1898-1956. I. Title. BIP

ESSLIN, Martin. 832.912
Brecht: the man and his work. [1st American ed.] Garden City, N.Y., Doubleday, 1960. 360 p. 22 cm. First published in London in 1959 under title: Brecht: a choice of evils; a critical study of the man, his work, and his opinions. Includes bibliographies. [PT2603.R397Z6 1960] 60-7971
1. Brecht, Bertolt, 1898-1956.

ESSLIN, Martin. 832'.9'12
Brecht: the man and his work. New rev. ed. Garden City, N.Y., Anchor Books [1971] xix, 379 p. 18 cm. First published in London in 1959 under title: Brecht: a choice of evils. Bibliography: p. [333]-351. [PT2603.R397Z6 1971] 77-135718 1.95
1. Brecht, Bertolt, 1898-1956. I. Title.

ESSLIN, Martin. 832'.9'12 B
Brecht; the man and his work. New York, Norton [1974, c1971] xix, 379 p. 20 cm. (The Norton library, N754) First published in London in 1959 under title: Brecht: a choice of evils. Bibliography: p. [333]-351. [PT2603.R397Z6 1974] 74-13885 ISBN 0-393-00754-5 3.95
1. Brecht, Bertolt, 1898-1956. I. Title.

EWEN, Frederic, 1899- 832'.9'12
Bertolt Brecht; his life, his art, and his times. [1st ed.] New York, Citadel Press [1967] 573 p. illus., ports. 22 cm. Bibliography: p. 541-553. [PT2603.R397Z617 1967] 67-25655
1. Brecht, Bertolt, 1898-1956.

Brecht, Bertolt, 1898-1956—Biography.

VOLKER, Klaus, 1938- 832'.9'12 B
Brecht, a biography / Klaus Volker ; translated by John Nowell. New York : Seabury Press, [1978] p. cm. Translation of Bertolt Brecht, eine Biographie. Includes bibliographical references and indexes. [Z8116.5.V58513] [PT2603.R397] 78-12610 ISBN 0-8164-9344-8 : 14.95
1. Brecht, Bertolt, 1898-1956—Biography. 2. Authors, German—20th century—Biography. I. Title.

VOLKER, Klaus, 1938- 832'.9'12 B
Brecht chronicle. Translated by Fred Wieck. New York, Seabury Press [1975] x, 209 p. 21 cm. (A Continuum book) Bibliography: p. [191]-194. [PT2603.R397Z889713] 74-12474 ISBN 0-8164-9231-X 9.50
1. Brecht, Bertolt, 1898-1956—Biography. I. Title. BIP

Brecht, Bertolt, 1898-1956—Diaries.

BRECHT, Bertolt, 1898-1956. 838'.9'1203
Diaries 1920-1922 / Bertolt Brecht ; edited by Herta Ramthun ; translated and annotated with an introductory essay by John Willett. New York : St. Martin's Press, c1979. xxiii, 182 p., [4] leaves of plates : ill. ; 22 cm. Translation of Tagebucher 1920-1922. Includes index. [PT2603.R397Z52513 1979] 78-21345 ISBN 0-312-07703-3 : 10.00
1. Brecht, Bertolt, 1898-1956—Diaries. 2. Authors, German—20th century—Biography. I. Ramthun, Herta. II. Willett, John. III. Title.

Breckinridge, John Cabell, 1821-1875.

DAVIS, William C., 1946- 973.6'8'0924 B
Breckinridge : statesman, soldier, symbol / William C. Davis. Baton Rouge : Louisiana State University Press, [1974] xxii, 687 p., [7] leaves of plates : 18 ill., ; 24 cm. (Southern biography series) Includes index. Bibliography: p. 641-667. [E302.6.B84D38] 73-77658 ISBN 0-8071-0068-4 : 17.50
1. Breckinridge, John Cabell, 1821-1875. I. Title. II. Series. BIP

HECK, Frank Hopkins. 973.6'8'0924 B
Proud Kentuckian, John C. Breckinridge, 1821-1875 / Frank H. Heck. Lexington : University Press of Kentucky, c1976. xi, 171 p. : ill. ; 22 cm. (The Kentucky bicentennial bookshelf) On spine: John C. Breckinridge. Bibliography: p. 169-171. [E353.1.B7H42] 76-9502 ISBN 0-8131-0217-0 : 3.95
1. Breckinridge, John Cabell, 1821-1875. 2. Vice-Presidents—United States—Biography. 3. Legislators—United States—Biography. I. Title. II. Series.

Breckinridge, John, 1760-1806.

HARRISON, Lowell Hayes, 1922- 973.4'6'0924 B
John Breckinridge: Jeffersonian Republican, by Lowell H. Harrison. Introd. by Thomas D. Clark. [1st ed.] Louisville, Ky., Filson Club [1969] x, 243 p. illus., facsim., ports. 24 cm. (Filson Club publications; second series, no. 2) Includes bibliographical references. [E302.6.B84H28] 71-76319 8.50
1. Breckinridge, John, 1760-1806. I. Title. II. Series: Filson Club, Louisville, Ky. Filson Club publication; second series, no. 2 BIP

Breckinridge, Lucy, d. 1865.

BRECKINRIDGE, Lucy, d.1865. 975.5'83 B
Lucy Breckinridge of Grove Hill : the journal of a Virginia girl, 1862-1864 ; edited by Mary D. Robertson. Kent, Ohio : Kent State University Press, c1979. p. cm. Includes index. Bibliography: p. [F234.G816B733] 79-88609 ISBN 0-87338-234-X : 14.00
1. Breckinridge, Lucy, d. 1865. 2. Grove Hill, Va. 3. Plantation life—Virginia—Sources. 4. Botetourt Co., Va.—Biography. 5. Virginia—History—Civil War, 1861-1865—Sources. I. Robertson, Mary D. II. Title.

Breckinridge, Mary, 1881-1965—Juvenile literature.

WILKIE, Katharine Elliott, 1904- 610.73'0924 B
Frontier nurse: Mary Breckinridge, by Katharine E. Wilkie and Elizabeth R. Moseley. New York, Messner [1969] 195 p. 22 cm. Bibliography: p. 189. A biography of the woman who gave up the riches and comfort of her aristocratic birth to serve as a nurse in the Kentucky mountains where she established the Frontier Nursing Service. [RT37.B72W5] 92 69-13047 3.50
1. Breckinridge, Mary, 1881-1965—Juvenile literature. I. Moseley, Elizabeth Robards, joint author. II. Title.

Breech, Ernie, 1897-

HICKERSON, John Melancthon, 1897- 338.7'4'0924 B
Ernie Breech; the story of his remarkable career at General Motors, Ford, and TWA, by J. Mel Hickerson. With a foreword by Henry Ford, II. [1st ed.] New York, Meredith Press [1968] xii, 241 p. illus., ports. 22 cm. [HD9710.U52H53] 68-26499 6.95
1. Breech, Ernie, 1897-

Breig, Joseph Anthony,

BREIG, Joseph Anthony, 1905- 817.5
Life with my Mary. Milwaukee, Bruce Pub. Co. [1955] 202p. 22cm. Autobiography. [CT275.B64A3] 55-10559
I. Title.

Brel, Jacques.

BLAU, Eric. 782.8'1
Jacques Brel is alive and well and living in Paris. [1st ed.] New York, E. P. Dutton, 1971. 191 p. illus., ports. 22 cm. Biography, with the story of the musical's production and complete lyrics, in French and English. [ML410.B8433B6] 70-108898 ISBN 0-525-13586-3 5.95
1. Brel, Jacques. 2. Brel, Jacques. Jacques Brel is alive and well and living in Paris. I. Brel, Jacques. Jacques Brel is alive and well and living in Paris. Texts. English & French. 1971. II. Title. BIP

Bremer, Frederika, 1801-1865—Biography.

BREMER, Fredrika, 1801-1865. 839.7'3'6
Life, letters, and posthumous works of Frederika Bremer / edited by her sister, Charlotte Bremer ; translated from the Swedish by Fredr. Milow ; the poetry marked with an asterisk translated by Emily Nonnen. New York : AMS Press, 1976. x, 439 p. ; 18 cm. (Women of letters) Translation of Sjelfbiografiska anteckningar, bref och efterlemnade skrifter. Reprint of the 1868 ed. published by Hurd and Houghton, New York. [PT9737.Z5A3713 1976] 75-37682 ISBN 0-404-56708-8 : 27.50
1. Bremer, Frederika, 1801-1865—Biography. I. Title. BIP

Brenan, Gerald—Biography.

BRENAN, Gerald. 828'.9'1209 B
Personal record, 1920-1972 / Gerald Brenan. 1st American ed. New York : Knopf : distributed by Random House, 1975. 380 p., [8] leaves of plates : ill. ; 25 cm. Includes index. [PR6003.R3513Z525 1975] 74-21286 ISBN 0-394-49582-9 : 12.50
1. Brenan, Gerald—Biography. I. Title.

Brendan, Saint, 484?-577?—Legends—History and criticism.

CHAPMAN, Paul H. 973.1'1
The man who led Columbus to America, by Paul H. Chapman. Atlanta, Judson Press [1973] xx, 202 p. illus. 24 cm. Bibliography: p. 196-197. [E109.I6C46] 73-84779 ISBN 0-914032-01-1 6.00
1. Brendan, Saint, 484?-577?—Legends—History and criticism. 2. Colombo, Cristoforo. 3. America—Discovery and exploration—Irish. 4. America—Discovery and exploration—Pre-Columbian. I. Title.

Brennan, James McClellan,

BRENNAN, James McClellan, 1871- 922.773
From mine pit to pulpit Boston, Christopher Pub. House [c1954] 226p. illus. 21cm. [BX8495.B755A3] 54-7743
I. Title.

Brennan, Joseph Gerard, 1910-

BRENNAN, Joseph Gerard, 1910- 191 B
The education of a prejudiced man / Joseph Gerard Brennan. New York : Scribner, c1977. x, 302 p. ; 24 cm. [B945.B7444A33] 77-4857 ISBN 0-684-14915-X : 8.95
1. Brennan, Joseph Gerard, 1910- 2.

Philosophers—United States—Biography. I. Title. BIP

Brennan, Terence Aloysius, 1928-

WARNER, Dave. 927.96
Terry Brennan of Notre Dame. Westminster, Md., Newman Press, 1956. 146p. illus. 23cm. [GV939.B7W3] 56-13466
1. Brennan, Terance Aloysius, 1928- I. Title.

WARNER, Dave. 927.96
Terry Brennan of Notre Dame. Westminster, Md., Newman Press, 1956. 146 p. illus. 23 cm. [GV939.B7W3] 56-13466
1. Brennan, Terence Aloysius, 1928- I. Title.

Brentano, Lujo, 1844-1931.

SHEEHAN, James J. 320.510924
The career of Lujo Brentano; a study of liberalism and social reform in imperial Germany. Chicago, Univ. of Chic. Pr. [c.1966] 223p. 22cm. Bibl. [HB107.B6S5] 66-20574 6.95
1. Brentano, Lujo, 1844-1931. I. Title. BIP

Brereton, Lewis Hyde, 1890-1967.

BRERETON, Lewis Hyde, 1890-1967. 940.54'49'73
The Brereton diaries : the war in the air in the Pacific, Middle East, and Europe, 3 October 1941-8 May 1945 / by Lewis H. Brereton. New York : Da Capo Press, 1976, c1946. p. cm. (The Politics and strategy of World War II) Reprint of the ed. published by W. Morrow, New York. [D790.B67 1976] 76-10630 ISBN 0-306-70766-7 : 27.50
1. Brereton, Lewis Hyde, 1890-1967. 2. World War, 1939-1945—Aerial operations, American. 3. World War, 1939-1945—Personal narratives, American. I. Title.

Bresdin, Rodolphe,

BRESDIN, Rodolphe, 1822-1885. 769'.92'4 B
Bresdin to Redon; six letters 1870 to 1881. Edited by Roseline Bacou. Translated by Seymour S. Weiner. [Northampton, Mass.] Gehenna Press, 1969. [21] p. port. 27 cm. Translation of chapter 3 of Lettres de Gauguin, Gide, Huysmans, Jammes, Mallarme, Verhaeren ... a Odilon Redon, 1960. "Four hundred copies have been printed ... A double portrait of Bresdin and Redon, etched by Leonard Baskin, is printed from the plate. The first hundred copies, specially bound, have an additional impression of the etching signed by the artist." No. 33. [NE2049.5.B7A33] 73-83577
I. Redon, Odilon, 1840-1916. II. Baskin, Leonard, 1922- III. Bacou, Roceline. Letters ... a Odilon Redon. IV. Title.

Bresee, Phineas Franklin, 1838-1915.

BRICKLEY, Donald Paul. 922.89
Man of the morning; the life and work of Phileas F. Bresee. Kansas City, Mo., Nazarene Pub. House [1960] 297p. illus. 20cm. Includes bibliography. [BX8699.N38B7 1960] 60-5047
1. Bresee, Phineas Franklin, 1838-1915. I. Title.

Breshko-Breshkovskaia, Ekaterina Konstantinovna Verigo, 1844-1934.

BRESHKO-BRESHKOVSKAIA, Ekaterina Konstantinovna Verigo, 1844-1934. 947.08'092'4 B
The little grandmother of the Russian Revolution; reminiscences and letters of Catherine Breshkovsky. Edited by Alice Stone Blackwell. Westport, Conn., Hyperion Press [1973, c1917] 348 p. port. 23 cm. Reprint of the ed. published by Little, Brown, Boston. [DK254.B7A5 1973] 73-2304 ISBN 0-88355-099-7
1. Breshko-Breshkovskaia, Ekaterina Konstantinovna Verigo, 1844-1934. 2. Political prisoners—Russia—Personal narratives. I. Blackwell, Alice Stone, 1857-1950, ed. II. Title.

Brett, William Howard, 1846-1918.

EASTMAN, Linda Anne, 1867-1963. 020'.92'4
Portrait of a librarian: William Howard Brett. Boston, Gregg Press, 1972 [c1940] 104 p. port. 23 cm. (The Library reference series. Library history and biography) Reprint of the ed. published by the American Library Association, Chicago, which was issued as no. 4 of American library pioneers. Bibliography: p. 101-102. [Z720.B85E2 1972] 72-8742 ISBN 0-8398-0459-8 6.50
1. Brett, William Howard, 1846-1918. I. Title. II. Series: Library history and biography. III. Series: American library pioneers, no. 4.

Breuil, Henri, 1877-1961.

BRODRICK, Alan Houghton. 925.6
Father of prehistory; the Abbe Henri Breuil: his life and times. New York, Morrow, 1963. vii, 306 p. illus., ports. 22 cm. "Bibliographical note": p. 305-306. [CC115.B7B7 1963] 63-17104
1. Breuil, Henri, 1877-1961. I. Title.

BRODRICK, Alan Houghton. 913'.031'0924 B
Father of prehistory; the Abbe Henri Breuil: his life and times. Westport, Conn., Greenwood Press [1973, c1963] vii, 306 p. illus. 22 cm. Reprint of the ed. published by Morrow, New York. Bibliography: p. [305]-306. [CC115.B7B7 1973] 73-2342 ISBN 0-8371-6840-6 14.00
1. Breuil, Henri, 1877-1961. I. Title.

Brewster, William, 1566 or 7-1644.

BREWSTER, Dorothy, 1883- 973.2'2 B
William Brewster of the Mayflower; portrait of a Pilgrim. New York, New York University Press, 1970. xiii, 116 p. illus., map. 22 cm. Bibliography: p. 107-112. [F68.B84B7] 73-133014 ISBN 0-8147-0963-X
1. Brewster, William, 1566 or 7-1644. I. Title.

STEELE, Ashbel, b.1796. 974.4'8
Chief of the Pilgrims: or, The life and time of William Brewster, ruling elder of the Pilgrim company that founded New Plymouth, the parent colony of New England, in 1620. Freeport, N.Y., Books for Libraries Press [1970] xxviii, 416 p. illus. 23 cm. Reprint of the 1857 ed. Includes bibliographical references. [F68.B84 1970] 72-133535 ISBN 0-8369-5567-6
1. Brewster, William, 1566 or 7-1644. 2. Massachusetts—New Plymouth, 1620-1691—Colonial period (New Plymouth) 3. Pilgrim Fathers. I. Title.

Brezhnev, Leonid Il'ich, 1906-

LEONID I. 947.085'092'4 B
Brezhnev : pages from his life / with a foreword by L. I. Brezhnev ; written under the auspices of the Academy of Sciences of the USSR. New York : Simon and Schuster, c1978. p. cm. [DK275.B7L44] 77-25538 ISBN 0-671-24111-7 : 10.00
1. Brezhnev, Leonid Il'ich, 1906- 2. Russia—Presidents—Biography. 3. Heads of state—Russia—Biography. I. Akademiia nauk SSSR. BIP

LEONID Ilyich 947.085'092'4 B
Brezhnev, General Secretary, Central Committee of the Communist Party of the Soviet Union : a short biography. Moscow : Novosti, 1976. 30 p. : ports. ; 23 cm. [DK275.B7L46] 77-358758 0.13rub
1. Brezhnev, Leonid Il'ich, 1906- 2. Statesmen—Russia—Biography.

MOSCOW. Institut marksizma-leninizma. 947.085'092'4 B
Leonid Ilyich Brezhnev : a short biography / by the Institute of Marxism-Leninism, CPSU Central Committee. Oxford ; New York : Pergamon Press, 1978 xii, 240 p., [1] leaf of plates : ill. ; 26 cm. (Biographies of world political leaders) Translation of Leonid Il'ich Brezhnev. Bibliography: p. [DK275.B7M68 1977] 77-30493 ISBN 0-08-022266-8 : 10.00 4.00
1. Brezhnev, Leonid Il'ich, 1906- 2. Russia—Presidents—Biography. 3. Heads of state—Russia—Biography. I. Moscow. Institut marksizma-leninizma. II. Russia (1923- U.S.S.R.) Constitution. English. 1977. III. Title. IV. Series.

Brian, Havergal, 1876-1972.

EASTAUGH, Kenneth. 780'.92'4 B
Havergal Brian : the making of a composer / Kenneth Eastaugh. London : Harrap, 1976. viii, 337 p., [8] leaves of plates : ill. ; 23 cm. Includes index. [ML410.B8447E2] 76-380799 ISBN 0-245-52748-6 : £10.00
1. Brian, Havergal, 1876-1972. 2. Composers—England—Biography.

NETTEL, Reginald, 1899- 780'.92'4 B
Havergal Brian and his music / by Reginald Nettel ; witzza catalogue of works by Lewis Foreman. London : Dobson, 1976. xiii, 223 p., [8] p. of plates : ill., facsims., music, ports. ; 23 cm. (The student's music library . historical and critical studies) Catalog of Brian's compositions: p. [205]-215. Includes bibliographical references and indexes. [ML410.B8447N5] 76-381477 ISBN 0-234-77861-X : £7.50
1. Brian, Havergal. 2. Composers—England—Bibliography. I. Title. II. Series: The student's music library.

Brice, Fanny, 1891-1951.

KATKOV, Norman. 927.914
The fabulous Fanny; the story of Fanny Brice. [1st ed.] New York, Knopf, 1953. 337 p. illus. 22 cm. [PN2287.B69K3] 52-6419
1. Brice, Fanny, 1891-1951. I. Title.

Bricker, Gertrude (DeWeese)

BRICKER, Gertrude (DeWeese) 1876- 920.7
Preacher's girl. Philadelphia, Dorrance [1957] 157p. 20cm. Autobiography. [CT275.B67777A3] 57-13488
I. Title.

Brickner, Barnett Robert, 1892-1958.

SILVER, Samuel M 922.96
Portrait of a rabbi; an affectionate memoir on the life of Barnett R. Brickner. Cleveland, Barnett R. Brickner Memorial Foundation [c1959] 125 p. illus. 21 cm. [BM755.B67S5] 59-12895
1. Brickner, Barnett Robert, 1892-1958. I. Title.

Brickner, Richard P.—Biography.

BRICKNER, Richard P. 813'.5'4 B
My second twenty years : an unexpected life / Richard P. Brickner. New York : Basic Books, c1976. 198 p. ; 22 cm. [PS3552.R45Z52] 76-10972 ISBN 0-465-04773-4 : 7.95
1. Brickner, Richard P.—Biography. I. Title. BIP

Bridger, James, 1804-1881.

ALTER, J Cecil, 1879- 923.973
Jim Bridger. [New and rev.ed.] Norman, University of Oklahoma Press [1962] xi, 358 p. illus., port, maps. 25 cm. First published in 1925 under title: James Bridger, trapper, frontiersman, scout and guide. Bibliography: p. 343-352. [F592.B85 1962] 62-16478
1. Bridger, James, 1804-1881. 2. Frontier and pioneer life — The West. I. Title. BIP

ALTER, J. Cecil, 1879- 923.973
Jim Bridger. [New and rev. ed.] Norman, University of Oklahoma Press [1962] xi, 358 p. illus., port., maps. 25 cm. First published in 1925 under title: James Bridger, trapper, frontiersman, scout and guide. Bibliography: p. 343-352. [F592.B85 1962] 62-16478
1. Bridger, James, 1804-1881. 2. Frontier and pioneer life—The West.

CAESAR, Gene, 1927- 923.973
King of the mountain men; the life of Jim Bridger. [1st ed.] New York, Dutton, 1961. 317 p. illus. 21 cm. Includes bibliography. [F592.B852] 61-6022
1. Bridger, James, 1804-1881. I. Title.

GARST, Doris Shannon, 1899- 923.973
Jim Bridger, greatest of the mountain men. Illustrated by William Moyers. Boston, Houghton Mifflin, 1952. 242 p. illus. 24 cm. Includes bibliography. [F592.B854] 52-1014
1. Bridger, James, 1804-1881. 2. Frontier and pioneer life—The West. 3. The West—Discovery and exploration.

HONIG, Louis O, 1887- 923.973
James Bridger, the pathfinder of the West. [Subscriber's ed.] Kansas City, Mo., Brown-White-Lowell Press, 1951. 152 p. illus. 23 cm. (His It happened in America series) Includes bibliography. [F592.B855] 52-474
1. Bridger, James, 1804-1881. 2. The West—Disc. & explor. I. Title.

VESTAL, Stanley, 1887- 978'.02'0924 B
Jim Bridger, mountain man; a biography. Lincoln, University of Nebraska Press [1970, c1946] x, 333 p. maps, port. 21 cm. "A Bison book." Bibliography: p. 305-309. [F592.B87 1970] 73-108790 1.95
1. Bridger, James, 1804-1881. 2. Frontier and pioneer life—The West. I. Title. BIP

Bridger, James, 1804-1881—Juvenile literature.

GRANT, Matthew G. 978'.02'0924 B
Jim Bridger the mountain man [by] Matthew G. Grant. Illustrated by Nancy Inderieden. [Mankato, Minn., Creative Education; distributed by Childrens Press, Chicago, [1973, c1974] 31 p. illus. (part col.) 25 cm. (His Gallery of great Americans series. Frontiersmen of America) A brief biography of the nineteenth-century trapper, scout, and explorer who helped open the West to settlers. [F592.B8544] 73-10071 ISBN 0-87191-254-6 4.95
1. Bridger, James, 1804-1881—Juvenile literature. I. Inderieden, Nancy, illus. II. Title.

Bridges, William Throsby, Sir, 1861-1915.

COULTHARD-CLARK, Christopher David, 1951- 355.3'31'0924 B
A heritage of spirit : a biography of Major-General Sir William Throsby Bridges / C. D. Coulthard-Clark. Carlton [Australia] : Melbourne University Press ; Forest Grove, Or. : [distributed by] International Scholarly Book Services, 1979. x, 220 p., [2] leaves of plates : ill. ; 23 cm. Includes index. Bibliography: p. 209-212. [U55.B73C68] 76-670229 ISBN 0-522-84170-8 : 20.00
1. Bridges, William Throsby, Sir, 1861-1915. 2. Australia. Army—Biography 3 Generals—Australia—Biography. I. Title.

Bridgewater, Francis Egerton, 3d duke of, 1736-1803.

MALET, Hugh 386.46
The canal duke; a biography of Francis, 3rd duke of Bridgewater. Dawlish, David & Charles [dist. New York, Taplinger, 1965, c.1961] 200p. illus. 19cm. Bibl. [HE435.B68M3] 61-59724 4.75 bds.,
1. Bridgewater, Francis Egerton, 3d duke of, 1736-1803. 2. Canals—Gt. Brit. I. Title.

Bridgman, Laura Dewey, 1829-1889.

LAMSON, Mary Swift, 1822-1909. 362.4'092'4 B
Life and education of Laura Dewey Bridgman, the deaf, dumb, and blind girl / by Mary Swift Lamson. New York : Arno Press, 1975 [c1878] p. cm. (Classics in child development) Reprint of the 1881 ed. published by Houghton Mifflin, Boston. [HV1624.B7L2 1975] 74-21419 ISBN 0-405-06469-1 : 24.00
1. Bridgman, Laura Dewey, 1829-1889. I. Title. II. Series.

Brigands and robbers—Southwestern States—Biography.

CASTILLO, Pedro, comp. 364.1'55 B
Furia y muerte: los bandidos Chicanos, edited and with an introd. by Pedro Castillo and Albert Camarillo. Los Angeles, Aztlan Publications [1973] vii, 171 p. ports. 24 cm. (University of California, Los Angeles. Chicano Studies Center. Monograph no. 4) Contents.Contents.—Tiburcio Vasquez.—Joaquin Murieta.—Elfego Baca.—Juan N. Cortina.—Gregorio Cortez.—Suggested readings (p. 167-168) [HV6448.C37] 73-174077
1. Brigands and robbers—Southwestern States—Biography. 2. Brigands and robbers—Mexico—Biography. I. Camarillo, Albert, joint comp. II. Title. III. Series: California. University. University at Los Angeles. Chicano Studies Center. Monograph no. 4.

Bright, Bill.

QUEBEDEAUX, Richard. 267'.61'0924 B
I found it! : The story of Bill Bright and Campus Crusade / Richard Quebedeaux. 1st ed. San Francisco : Harper & Row, c1979. xiii, 202 p., [8] leaves of plates : ill. ; 22 cm. Includes index. Bibliography: p. [195]-196. [BV3785.B73Q4 1979] 78-20582 8.95
1. Bright, Bill. 2. Campus Crusade for Christ. 3. Evangelists—United States—Biography. I. Title.

Bright, John, 1811-1889.

AUSUBEL, Herman 942.0810924
John Bright. Victorian reformer. New York, Wiley [c.1966] xvi, 250p. illus. 22cm. Bibl. [DA565.B8A9] 66-14126 5.95
1. Bright, John, 1811-1889. I. Title.

AUSUBEL, Herman. 942.0810924(B)
John Bright, Victorian reformer. New York, Wiley [1966] xvi, 250 p. illus. 22 cm. Includes bibliographies. [DA565.B8A9] 66-14126
1. Bright, John, 1811-1889. I. Title.

ROBBINS, Keith. 942.081'092'4 B
John Bright / Keith Robbins. London ; Boston : Routledge & K. Paul, 1979. xvi, 288 p., [8] leaves of plates : ill. ; 23 cm. Includes index. Bibliography: p. 273-278. [DA565.B8R59] 79-309083 ISBN 0-7100-8992-9 : 18.50
1. Bright, John, 1811-1889. 2. Great Britain—Politics and government—1837-1901. 3. Statesmen—Great Britain—Biography. BIP

TREVELYAN, George Macaulay, 1876-1962. 942.081'0924 B
The life of John Bright. Westport, Conn., Greenwood Press [1971] x, [1], 480 p. illus. 23 cm. Reprint of the 1913 ed. Bibliography: p. [xi] [DA565.B8T8 1971] 72-110873 ISBN 0-8371-4552-X
1. Bright, John, 1811-1889. 2. Gt. Brit.—Politics and government—19th century. I. Title. BIP

Brighton Pharmacy, Brooklyn.

LICHTENFELD, Julius. 926.1
A pharmacist's memoirs, fifty years of Ukrainczyk's Brighton Pharmacy. New York, Exposition Press [1952] 108 p. 22 cm. [RS73.L5A3] 51-12341
1. Brighton Pharmacy, Brooklyn. I. Title.

Brigid, Saint, of Ireland, ca. 453-ca. 524.

CURTAYNE, Alice. 922.2415
St. Brigid of Ireland. New York, Sheed and Ward, 1954. 122p. 20cm. [BX4700.B85C8 1954] 54-11140
1. Brigid, Saint, of Ireland, ca. 453-ca. 524. I. Title.

FLAVIUS, Brother, 1927- 922.2415
Miracle for the bride. and a story of Saint Bridget of Ireland. Illustrated by Brother Bernard Howard Notre Dame, Ind., Dujarie Press [1953] 95p. illus. 24cm. [BX4700.B85F5] 53-38206
1. Brigid, Saint, of Ireland, ca. 453-ca. 524. I. Title.

Brigid, Saint, of Ireland, ca. 453-ca. 524 — Juvenile literature.

BETZ, Eva (Kelly) 1897- 92
Saint Brigid and the cows, by Eva K. Betz. Illustrated by Russell Peterson. [1st ed.] Paterson, N.J., St. Anthony Guild Press [1964] 47 p. illus. 21 cm. (Easy reading books of saints and friendly beasts) [BX4700.B854] 63-22679
1. Brigid, Saint, of Ireland, ca. 453-ca. 524 — Juvenile literature. I. Title.

Brik, Lili IUr'evna.

BAROOSHIAN, Vahan D. 891.7'1'42 B
Brik and Mayakovsky / Vahan D. Barooshian. [2514 GC] The Hague, [Noordeinde 41] ; New York : Mouton, 1979. ix, 159 p. ; 24 cm. (Slavistic printings and reprintings ; 301) Bibliography of works by O. Brik: p. [149]-154. [PG3476.B74Z59] 79-348013 ISBN 90-279-7826-3 : 28.25
1. Brik, Osip Maksimovich, 1888-1945. 2. Maiakovskii, Vladimir Vladimirovich, 1894-1930. 3. Brik, Osip Maksimovich, 1888-1945—Relationship with men—Vladimir Maiakovskii. 4. Brik, Lili IUr'evna. 5. Brik, Osip Maksimovich, 1888-1945—Relationship with women—Lili Brik. 6. Maiakovskii, Vladimir Vladimirovich, 1894-1930—Relationship with women—Lili Brik. 7. Poets, Russian—20th century—Biography. 8. Futurism. I. Title. II. Series. BIP

Brik, Osip Maksimovich, 1888-1945.

BAROOSHIAN, Vahan D. 891.7'1'42 B
Brik and Mayakovsky / Vahan D. Barooshian. [2514 GC] The Hague, [Noordeinde 41] ; New York : Mouton, 1979. ix, 159 p. ; 24 cm. (Slavistic printings and reprintings ; 301) Bibliography of works by O. Brik: p. [149]-154. [PG3476.B74Z59] 79-348013 ISBN 90-279-7826-3 : 28.25
1. Brik, Osip Maksimovich, 1888-1945. 2. Maiakovskii, Vladimir Vladimirovich, 1894-1930. 3. Brik, Osip Maksimovich, 1888-1945—Relationship with men—Vladimir Maiakovskii. 4. Brik, Lili IUr'evna. 5. Brik, Osip Maksimovich, 1888-1945—Relationship with women—Lili Brik. 6. Maiakovskii, Vladimir Vladimirovich, 1894-1930—Relationship with women—Lili Brik. 7. Poets, Russian—20th century—Biography. 8. Futurism. I. Title. II. Series. BIP

Brik, Osip Maksimovich, 1888-1945—Relationship with men—Vladimir Maiakovskii.

BAROOSHIAN, Vahan D. 891.7'1'42 B
Brik and Mayakovsky / Vahan D. Barooshian. [2514 GC] The Hague, [Noordeinde 41] ; New York : Mouton, 1979. ix, 159 p. ; 24 cm. (Slavistic printings and reprintings ; 301) Bibliography of works by O. Brik: p. [149]-154. [PG3476.B74Z59] 79-348013 ISBN 90-279-7826-3 : 28.25
1. Brik, Osip Maksimovich, 1888-1945. 2. Maiakovskii, Vladimir Vladimirovich, 1894-1930. 3. Brik, Osip Maksimovich, 1888-1945—Relationship with men—Vladimir Maiakovskii. 4. Brik, Lili IUr'evna. 5. Brik, Osip Maksimovich, 1888-1945—Relationship with women—Lili Brik. 6. Maiakovskii, Vladimir Vladimirovich, 1894-1930—Relationship with women—Lili Brik. 7. Poets, Russian—20th century—Biography. 8. Futurism. I. Title. II. Series. BIP

Brik, Osip Maksimovich, 1888-1945—Relationship with women—Lili Brik.

BAROOSHIAN, Vahan D. 891.7'1'42 B
Brik and Mayakovsky / Vahan D. Barooshian. [2514 GC] The Hague, [Noordeinde 41] ; New York : Mouton, 1979. ix, 159 p. ; 24 cm. (Slavistic printings and reprintings ; 301) Bibliography of works by O. Brik: p. [149]-154. [PG3476.B74Z59] 79-348013 ISBN 90-279-7826-3 : 28.25
1. Brik, Osip Maksimovich, 1888-1945. 2. Maiakovskii, Vladimir Vladimirovich, 1894-1930. 3. Brik, Osip Maksimovich, 1888-1945—Relationship with men—Vladimir Maiakovskii. 4. Brik, Lili IUr'evna. 5. Brik, Osip Maksimovich, 1888-1945—Relationship with women—Lili Brik. 6. Maiakovskii, Vladimir Vladimirovich, 1894-1930—Relationship with women—Lili Brik. 7. Poets, Russian—20th century—Biography. 8. Futurism. I. Title. II. Series. BIP

Brindley, James, 1716-1772.

BOUCHER, Cyril Thomas Goodman. 627'.13'0924 B
James Brindley, engineer, 1716-1772 [by] Cyril T. G. Boucher. Norwich, Goose, 1968. [14], 130 p. illus., facsim., maps, plans, port. 23 cm. Map on lining papers. Bibliography: p. 122-126. [TA140.B735B6] 79-394401 35/-
1. Brindley, James, 1716-1772. BIP

Bringgold, Diane.

BRINGGOLD, Diane. 283'.092'4 B
Life instead / Diane Bringgold. Waco, Tex. : Word Books, c1979. 128 p. : ill. ; 21 cm. [BX5995.B755A34] 79-63931 ISBN 0-8499-0124-3 : 6.95
1. Bringgold, Diane. 2. Anglicans—United States—Biography. 3. Burns and scalds—Biography. I. Title.

Brings, Lawrence Martin, 1897- — Juvenile literature.

ZEHNPFENNIG, Gladys. 070.5'73'0924 B
Lawrence M. Brings, book publisher. Minneapolis, Denison [1973] 253 p. 23 cm. (Men of achievement series) A biography of the author, educator, and publisher who is the editor of the "Men of Achievement" series. [Z473.B797Z44] 92 73-77194 ISBN 0-513-01309-1 4.98
1. Brings, Lawrence Martin, 1897- — Juvenile literature. I. Title.

Brinkley, John Richard, 1885-1942.

CARSON, Gerald. 926.1
The roguish world of Doctor Brinkley. New York, Rinehart [1960] 280p. illus. 22cm. [R730.C36] 60-5989
1. Brinkley, John Richard, 1885-1942. I. Title.

CARSON, Gerald [Hewes] 926.1
The roguish world of Doctor Brinkley. New York, Rinehart [c.1960] vi, 280p. illus. 22cm. 60-5989 4.95 half cloth,
1. Brinkley, John Richard, 1885-1942. I. Title.

Brinley, Putnam.

LODER, Elizabeth M., 1912- 759.13 B
D. Putnam Brinley, impressionist and mural painter / by Elizabeth M. Loder. Ann Arbor : Published for New Canaan Historical Society and the Silvermine Guild of Artists by University Microfilms International, 1979. xii, 90 p., [13] leaves of plates : ill. ; 26 cm. (Monograph publishing : Sponsor series) Includes index. Bibliography: p. 81. [ND237.B866L62] 79-551 ISBN 0-8357-0390-8 pbk. : 8.75
1. Brinley, Putnam. 2. Painters—United States—Biography. I. Title.

Brinton, Mary (Williams).

BRINTON, Mary (Williams). 926.1
My cap and my cape, an autobiography. Philadelphia, Dorrance [1950] 262 p. 20 cm. [RT37.B74A3] 50-11011
I. Title.

Brinvilliers, Marie Madeleine (d'Aubray) Gobelin, marquise de, 1630-1676.

VERNON, Virginia (Fox-Brooks) 1894- 923.4144
Enchanting little lady; the criminal life of the Marquise de Brinvilliers. New York, Abelard [c.1964] 221p. illus., port. 22cm. Bibl. 64-13926 4.50 bds.,
1. Brinvilliers, Marie Madeleine (d'Aubray) Gobelin, marquise de, 1630-1676. 2. France—Soc. life & cust. I. Title.

VERNON, Virginia (Fox-Brooks) 1894- 923.4144
Enchanting little lady; the criminal life of the Marquise de Brinvilliers, by Virginia Vernon. London, New York Abelard-Schuman [1964] 221 p. illus., port. 22 cm. Bibliography: p. 215-217. [HV6555.F7V4 1964] 64-13926
1. Brinvilliers, Marie Madeleine (d'Aubray) Gobelin, marquise de, 1630-1676. 2. France — Soc. life & cust. I. Title.

Brisbane, Albert, 1809-1890.

BRISBANE, Redelia (Bates) 335.2'0924 B
Albert Brisbane; a mental biography, with a character study, by Redelia Brisbane. New York, B. Franklin, New York [1969] xi, 377 p. port. 23 cm. (Burt Franklin research & source works series, 280) (American classics in history & social science, 50.) Reprint of the 1893 ed. [HX653.B68 1969] 68-56790
1. Brisbane, Albert, 1809-1890.

Brisbane, Arthur, 1864-1936.

CARLSON, Oliver, 1899- 070.9'24 B
Brisbane, a candid biography. Westport, Conn., Greenwood Press [1970, c1937] 373 p. illus. 23 cm. Bibliography: p. 354-358. [PN4874.B67C3 1970] 75-98829
1. Brisbane, Arthur, 1864-1936.

Briscoe, Mattie White

BRISCOE, Mattie White 920.7
Dun-Movin, the memoirs of a minister's wife. New York, Exposition [c.1963] 98p. 21cm. 3.00
I. Title.

Brisson, Louis, 1817-1908.

BURTON, Katherine (Kurz) 1890- 922.244
So much, so soon; Father Brisson, founder of the Oblates of St. Francis de Sales. With a pref. by John F. O'Hara. New York, Benziger Bros. [1953] 243p. 21cm. [BX4705.B8467B8] 53-25516
1. Brisson, Louis, 1817-1908. I. Title.

Brissot de Warville, Jacques Pierre, 1754-1793.

ELLERY, Eloise, 1874- 944.04'1'0924 B
Brissot de Warville; a study in the history of the French Revolution. New York, AMS Press [1970] xix, 528 p. 23 cm. Reprint of the 1915 ed. Bibliography: p. [453]-508. [DC146.B85E6 1970] 75-109919
1. Brissot de Warville, Jacques Pierre, 1754-1793. BIP

ELLERY, Eloise, 1874- 944.04'1'0924 B
Brissot de Warville; a study in the history of the French Revolution. New York, B. Franklin [1970] xix, 528 p. 22 cm. (Selected essays in history, economics & social science, 168) (Burt Franklin research & source works series, 536.) Originally presented as the author's thesis, Cornell, 1902. Reprint of the 1915 ed. Bibliography: p. [453]-508. [DC146.B85E6 1970b] 71-130601
1. Brissot de Warville, Jacques Pierre, 1754-1793.

Bristow, Benjamin Helm, 1832-1896.

WEBB, Ross Allan. 973.8'2'0924 B
Benjamin Helm Bristow, border state

politician [by] Ross A. Webb. [Lexington] University Press of Kentucky [1969] xiii, 370 p. illus., ports. 24 cm. Bibliographical footnotes. "Critical essay on authorities": p. [339]-353. [E664.B856W4] 74-80089 8.75
1. Bristow, Benjamin Helm, 1832-1896.

Bristow, Joseph Little, 1861-1944.

SAGESER, Adelbert 973.91'2'0924 B
Bower, 1902-
Joseph L. Bristow: Kansas progressive [by] A. Bower Sageser. Lawrence, University Press of Kansas [1968] 197 p. illus., ports. 23 cm. Bibliography: p. 187-189. [E664.B8563S2] 68-14434 6.50
1. Bristow, Joseph Little, 1861-1944.

Brite, Lucas Charles, 1860-1941.

KEITH, Noel Leonard. v. 12
The Brites of Capote. New ed. Fort Worth, Texas Christian University Press, 1961 [c1950] 294 p. illus. 63-41016
1. Brite, Lucas Charles, 1860-1941. 2. Brite, Edward McMinn (Anderson) 1875- I. Title.

KEITH, Noel Leonard. 926.3
The Brites of Capote. Fort Worth, Texas Christian UniversityPress, 1950. xivi, 272 p. illus., ports., maps. 24 cm.

Briusov, Valerii IAkovlevich, 1873-1924.

RICE, Martin P. 891.7'1'42
Valery Briusov and the rise of Russian symbolism / by Martin P. Rice. Ann Arbor : Ardis, 1975. 155 p., [1] leaf of plates : port. ; 24 cm. On spine: Briusov. Includes index. Bibliography: p. 142-145. [PG3453.B7Z82] 75-306761 8.95
1. Briusov, Valerii IAkovlevich, 1873-1924. 2. Symbolism in literature. 3. Russian poetry—19th century—History and criticism. 4. Russian poetry—20th century—History and criticism. I. Title. **BIP**

British Antarctic ("Terra Nova") Expedition, 1910-1913.

WILSON, Edward Adrian, 919.89'04
1872-1912.
Diary of the Terra Nova Expedition to the Antarctic, 1910-1912. An account of Scott's last expedition edited from the original mss. in the Scott Polar Research Institute and the British Museum by H. G. R. King. New York, Humanities Press [1972] xxiii, 279 p. illus. (part col.) 25 cm. Bibliography: p. 261. [G850 1910.S95] 72-76897 19.50
1. British Antarctic ("Terra Nova") Expedition, 1910-1913. I. King, H. G. R., ed. II. Title. **BIP**

British Guiana—Biog.—Dictionaries.

THE DAILY CHRONICLE, 920.088
Georgetown, British Guiana.
Who is who in British Guiana. Georgetown, The Daily Chronicle. [F2365.W45] 51-15319
1. British Guiana—Biog.—Dictionaries. 2. British Guiana—Direct. I. Title.

British Museum.

EDWARDS, Edward, 1812- 027.5'42
1886.
Lives of the founders of the British Museum, with notices of its chief augmentors and other benefactors, 1570-1870. New York, B. Franklin [1969] x, 780 p. illus., plans. 23 cm. (Burt Franklin bibliography & reference series, 202) Reprint of the 1870 ed. [Z792.B863E1 1969] 68-58473
1. British Museum. 2. Book collectors—Gt. Brit. I. Title.

Britt, Peter, 1819-1905.

MILLER, Alan Clark. 770'.92'4 B
Photographer of a frontier : the photographs of Peter Britt / by Alan Clark Miller. Eureka : Interface California Corp., c1976. 107 p. : ill. ; 27 cm. (Interface monographs on photography) [TR140.B78M54] 76-48832 ISBN 0-915580-05-5 : 20.95
1. Britt, Peter, 1819-1905. 2. Jacksonville, Or.—Description—Views. 3. Photographers—Oregon—Biography. I. Britt, Peter, 1819-1905. II. Title. III. Series. **BIP**

Britten, Benjamin, 1913-

WHITE, Eric Walter, 1905- 927.8
Benjamin Britten, a sketch of his life and works. New ed. rev and enl. London, New York, Boosey & Hawkes [1954] 219p. port., music. 20cm. 'Chronological list of works : p. [198]-196. List of opera productions': p. [197]-206. [ML410.B853W4 1954] 54-29542
1. Britten, Benjamin, 1913- I. Title.

WHITE, Eric Walter, 782.1'0924
1905-
Benjamin Britten, his life and operas. [New ed.] Berkeley, University of California Press, 1970. 256 p. illus., music, ports. 26 cm. Previous editions have title: Benjamin Britten, a sketch of his life and works. Bibliography: p. 244-245. [ML410.B853W4 1970] 73-107655 ISBN 0-520-01679-3 10.00
1. Britten, Benjamin, 1913-

Britten, Benjamin, 1913- —Juvenile literature.

YOUNG, Percy Marshall, 782.1'0924
1912-
Britten [by] Percy M. Young. New York, D. White [1968, c1966] viii, 68 p. illus., music. 23 cm. (Masters of music) [ML3930.B83Y7] 68-14885
1. Britten, Benjamin, 1913- —Juvenile literature. **BIP**

Broach, Claude U.

BROACH, Claude U. 286'.1'0924 B
Before it slips my mind [by] Claude Upshaw Broach. Charlotte, N.C., Delmar Print. Co. [1974] 121 p. 24 cm. [BX6495.B696A32] 74-83798 4.95
1. Broach, Claude U. I. Title.
Publisher's address: 9601 Monroe Rd. Charlotte, N.C. 28212

Brock, Isaac, Sir 1769-1812—Juvenile literature.

GOODSPEED, Donald James, 923.571
1919-
The good soldier; the story of Isaac Brock. Illus. by Jack Ferguson. New York, St Martin's [c.]1964. 156p. illus. (pt. col.) 22cm. (Great stories of Canada, 29) 64-21439 2.95
1. Brock, Isaac, Sir 1769-1812—Juvenile literature. I. Title.

Brock, Jim.

BROCK, Jim. 796.357'092'4 B
The Devils' coach / Jim Brock and Joe Gilmartin. Elgin, Ill. : D.C. Cook Pub. Co., c1977. 168 p., [4] leaves of plates : ill. ; 22 cm. [GV865.B718A33] 77-87255 ISBN 0-89191-103-0 : 6.95
1. Brock, Jim. 2. Arizona. State University, Tempe—Baseball. 3. Baseball coaches—United States—Biography. I. Gilmartin, Joe, joint author. II. Title. **BIP**

Brock, Lou, 1939-

BROCK, Lou, 1939- 796.357'092'4 B
Stealing is my game / by Lou Brock and Franz Schulze. Englewood Cliffs, N.J. : Prentice-Hall, c1976. 206 p. : ill. ; 22 cm. [GV865.B72A33] 76-17051 ISBN 0-13-846378-6 : 7.95
1. Brock, Lou, 1939- 2. Baseball. I. Schulze, Franz, 1927- joint author. II. Title.

Brock, Sir Isaac, 1769-1812 — Juvenile literature.

GOODSPEED, Donald James, 923.571
1919-
The good soldier the story of Isaac Brock, by D. J. Goodspeed. Illustrated by Jack Ferguson. New York, St. Martin's Press, 1964. 156 p. illus. (part col.) 22 cm. (Great stories of Canada, 29) [E353.1.B8G6] 64-21439
1. Brock, Sir Isaac, 1769-1812 — Juvenile literature. I. Title.

Brockenbrough, John W.

PAXTON, M. W. 340'.07'11755852
A judge's school; the story of John White Brockenbrough, by M. W. Paxton, Jr. [Lexington, Va., Washington and Lee University, 1971] 1 v. (unpaged) port. 14 x 22 cm. Cover title. Includes bibliographical references. [LD5872.8.B76P38] 72-194151
1. Brockenbrough, John W. I. Title.

Brockway family.

BUSH, Charles T. 929'.2'0973
Hiel Brockway : the story of Hiel Brockway, founder of Brockport : his life, his descendants, his ancestry / prepared by Charles T. Bush for the Western Monroe Historical Society. Brockport, N.Y. : The Society, c1976. 48 p. : ill., maps (1 fold. in pocket) ; 22 cm. Bibliography: p. [3] of cover. [CS71.B865 1976] 76-370919
1. Brockway family. 2. Brockway, Hiel, 1775-1842. 3. Brockport, N.Y.—History. 4. United States—Genealogy. I. Western Monroe Historical Society. II. Title: The story of Hiel Brockway, founder of Brockport.

Brodetsky, Julian, d. 1962.

WIBBERLEY, Leonard Patrick 927.8
O'Connor, 1915-
Ah, Julian! A memoir of Julian Brodetsky. New York, I. Washburn [1963] 154 p. illus. 21 cm. [ML418.B69W5] 63-16392
1. Brodetsky, Julian, d. 1962. I. Title.

Brodie, John.

BRODIE, John. 796.33'2'0924
Open field. [by] John Brodie and James D. Houston. New York, Bantam Books, 1975. 194 p. illus. 18 cm. [GV939.B73A36] 1.50 (pbk.)
1. Brodie, John. 2. Football. I. Houston, James D., joint author. II. Title.
L.C. card no. for original edition: 74-14627. **BIP**

Brokenshire, Norman,

BROKENSHIRE, Norman, 927.914
1898-
This is Norman Brokenshire, an unvarnished self-portrait. New York, D. McKay Co. [1954] 307p. illus. i1cm. [PN1991.4.B75A3] 53-11368
I. Title.

Bromfield, Louis, 1896-1956.

GELD, Ellen (Bromfield) 928.1
1932-
The heritage: a daughter's memories of Louis Bromfield. New York(Harper [c.1962] 204p. illus. 62-7910 4.50 bds.,
1. Bromfield, Louis, 1896-1956. I. Title.

Bronkie, Virginia Bissell.

BRONKIE, Virginia Bissell. 920.7
It's all in your head. [1st ed.] New York, Vantage Press [1956] 89p. illus. 21cm. Autobiographical. [CT275.B753A3] 56-5522
I. Title.

Bronson, Charles, 1920-

*HARBINSON, W. 791.43'028'0924 B
A.
Bronson! A biographical portrait [by] W. A. Harbinson. New York, Pinnacle Books [1975] 164 p. illus. 18 cm. [PN2287] ISBN 0-523-00696-9 1.50 (pbk.)
1. Bronson, Charles. I. Title.

HARBINSON, 791.43'028'0924 B
William Allen, 1941-
Bronson! : a biographical portrait / W. A. Harbinson. London : W. H. Allen, 1976. 157 p., [12] p. of plates : ill., ports. ; 23 cm. Filmography: p. 151-157. [PN2287.B693H3 1976] 77-355080 ISBN 0-491-01536-4 : £3.00
1. Bronson, Charles, 1920- 2. Moving-picture actors and actresses—United States—Biography.

Bronson, Isaac, 1760-1838.

MORRISON, Grant. 332'.092'4 B
Isaac Bronson and the search for system in American capitalism, 1789-1838 / Grant Morrison. New York : Arno Press, 1978, c1973. p. cm. (Dissertations in American economic history) Originally presented as the author's thesis, City University of New York, 1973. Bibliography: p. [HG172.B76M67 1978] 77-14777 ISBN 0-405-11050-2 : 25.00
1. Bronson, Isaac, 1760-1838. 2. Capitalists and financiers—United States—Biography. 3. United States—Economic conditions—To 1865. I. Title. II. Series.

Bronte, Anne, 1820-1849.

ANNE Bronte. v. 12
London, New York, T. Nelson [c1959] 368p. illus. Includes bibliography.
1. Bronte, Anne, 1820-1849. I. Cerin, Winifred. **BIP**

GERIN, Winifred. 928.2
Anne Bronte. London, New York, Nelson [1959] 368 p. illus. 23 cm. Includes bibliography. [PR4163.G4] 59-4263
1. Bronte, Anne, 1820-1849.

GE'RIN, Winifred. 928.2
Anne Bronte. Totowa, N.J. : distributed by Rowman and Littlefield [1976c1959.] xv,372p. ; 22 cm. Includes index. Bibliography: p. 352-354. [PR4163.G4] ISBN 0-7139-0977-3 : 14.50
1. Bronte, Anne, 1820-1849. I. Title.
L. C. card no. for original edition: 59-4263.

HALE, Will Taliaferro, 823'.8
1880-
Anne Bronte : her life and writings / by Will T. Hale. Norwood, Pa. : Norwood Editions, 1975. 44 p. ; 26 cm. Reprint of the 1929 ed. published by Indiana University, Bloomington, which was issued as v. 16, no. 83 of Indiana University Studies. Includes bibliographical references. [PR4163.H27 1975] 75-31966 ISBN 0-88305-273-3 : 10.00
1. Bronte, Anne, 1820-1849. I. Series: Indiana. University. Indiana University studies ; v. 16, no. 83. **BIP**

HALE, Will Taliaferro, 823'.8 B
1880-
Anne Bronte: her life and writings, by Will T. Hale. [Folcroft, Pa.] Folcroft Library Editions, 1973. p. Reprint of the 1929 ed. published by Indiana University, Bloomington which was issued as v. 16, study no. 83. [PR4163.H27 1973] 73-14717 10.00
1. Bronte, Anne, 1820 1849. I. Series: Indiana. University. Indiana University studies, vol. 16, Study no. 83.

HARRISON, Ada M 928.2
Anne Bronte, her life and work [by] Ada Harrison and Derek Stanford. New York, J. Day Co. [1959] 252p. illus. 23cm. [PR4163.H3] 59-13467
1. Bronte, Anne, 1820-1849. I. Stanford, Derek. II. Title.

HARRISON, Ada M. 823.8 B
Anne Bronte, her life and work [by] Ada Harrison and Derek Stanford. [Unaltered and unabridged ed. Hamden, Conn.] Archon Books, 1970 [c1959] 252 p. port. 23 cm. Bibliography: p. 247. [PR4163.H3 1970] 73-121756 ISBN 0-208-00987-6
1. Bronte, Anne, 1820-1849. I. Stanford, Derek.

Bronte, Anne, 1820-1849—Biography.

GERIN, Winifred. 823'.8 B
Anne Bronte / by Winifred Gerin. New ed. London : Allen Lane, 1976. xv, 372 p., [4] p. of plates : ill., ports. ; 23 cm. Includes index. Bibliography: p. 352-354. [PR4163.G4 1976] 76-360684 ISBN 0-7139-0977-3 : 14.50
1. Bronte, Anne, 1820-1849—Biography.
Distributed by Rowman & Littlfield Totowa, N.J.

Bronte, Charlotte, 1816-1855.

ALLOTT, Miriam 823'.8'09 B
Farris, comp.
The Brontes, the critical heritage / edited by Miriam Allott. London ; Boston : Routledge and Kegan Paul, 1974. xx, 475 p. ; 23 cm. (The Critical heritage series) Includes index. Bibliography: p. 461-463. [PR4168.A7 1974] 73-85426 ISBN 0-7100-7701-7 : £7.50
1. Bronte, Charlotte, 1816-1855. 2. Bronte, Emily Jane, 1818-1848. 3. Bronte, Anne, 1820-1849. I. Title.

BENSON, Edward Frederic, 823'.8 B
1867-1940.
Charlotte Bronte. New York, B. Blom, 1971. xiii, 313 p. illus. 22 cm. Reprint of the 1932 ed. [PR4168.B4 1971] 70-173101
1. Bronte, Charlotte, 1816-1855. BIP

BENSON, Edward Frederic, 823'.8 B
1867-1940.
Charlotte Bronte. [Folcroft, Pa.] Folcroft Library Editions, 1973. p. Reprint of the 1932 ed. published by Longmans, Green, London, New York. [PR4168.B4 1973] 73-15736 13.00
1. Bronte, Charlotte, 1816-1855. BIP

BENSON, Edward Frederic, 823'.8
1867-1940.
Charlotte Bronte. Freeport, N.Y., Books for Libraries Press [1971] xiii, 313 p. illus. 23 cm. Reprint of the 1932 ed. Includes bibliographical references. [PR4168.B4 1971b] 73-175687 ISBN 0-8369-6602-3
1. Bronte, Charlotte, 1816-1855.

BENTLEY, Phyllis Eleanor, 928.2
1894-
The Bronte sisters. London New York, Published for the British Council and the National Book League by Longmans, Green [1950] 44 p. group port. 22 cm. (Bibliographical series of supplements to British Book News) "A select bibliography of the Bronte family": p. 41-44. [PR4168.B425] 51-3395
1. Bronte, Charlotte, 1816-1855. 2. Bronte, Emily Jane, 1818-1848. 3. Bronte, Anne, 1820-1849. I. Title. II. Series. BIP

BIRRELL, Augustine, 823'.8 B
1850-1933.
Life of Charlotte Bronte. [Folcroft, Pa.] Folcroft Library Editions, 1973. 186, vii, p. 19 cm. Reprint of the 1887 ed. published by W. Scott, London, in series: Great writers. "Bibliography, by John P. Anderson": p. [i]-vii. [PR4168.B5 1973b] 73-16464 9.95
1. Bronte, Charlotte, 1816-1855. I. Title. BIP

BRONTE, Charlotte, 823'.8 B
1816-1855.
An hour with Charlotte Bronte : or, Flowers from a Yorkshire moor / by Laura C. Holloway. Folcroft, Pa. : Folcroft Library Editions, 1976. p. cm. Reprint of the 1883 ed. published by Funk & Wagnalls, New York. [PR4166.L3 1976] 76-24882 ISBN 0-8414-4839-6 : 20.00
I. Langford, Laura Carter Holloway, 1848- II. Title.

BYRON, May Clarissa 823'.8 B
Gillington, d.1936.
A day with Charlotte Bronte / by May Byron. Folcroft, Pa. : Folcroft Library Editions, 1975,i.e.1977 47 p., [5] leaves of plates : ill. ; 23 cm. Reprint of the ed. published by Hodder & Stoughton, London. [PR4168.B9 1975] 76-58442 ISBN 0-8414-1653-2 lib. bdg. : 10.00
1. Bronte, Charlotte, 1816-1855. 2. Novelists, English—19th century—Biography. I. Title. BIP

CROMPTON, Margaret. 928.2
Passionate search; a life of Charlotte Bronte. New York, D. McKay Co. [1956, c1955] 252 p. illus. 22 cm. [PR4168.C7 1956] 56-13927
1. Bronte, Charlotte, 1816-1855. I. Title.

[DUNLOP, Agnes Mary Robertson] 92
Girl with a pen, Charlotte Bronte, by Elisabeth Kyle [pseud.] New York, Holt [1964] 211p. 22cm. Bibl. 64-14576 3.50; 3.27 bds., lib. ed.,
1. Bronte, Charlotte, 1816-1855—Juvenile literature. I. Title.

FFRENCH, Yvonne. 920.72'094
Six great Englishwomen : Queen Elizabeth I, Sarah Siddons, Charlotte Bronte, Florence Nightingale, Queen Victoria, Gertrude Bell / by Yvonne Ffrench. Folcroft, Pa. : Folcroft Library Editions, 1976. p. cm. Reprint of the 1953 ed. published by Hamilton, London. [DA28.7.F42 1976] 76-10646 ISBN 0-8414-4219-3 lib. bdg. : 17.50
1. Elizabeth, Queen of England, 1533-1603. 2. Siddons, Sarah Kemble, 1755-1831. 3. Bronte, Charlotte, 1816-1855. 4. Nightingale, Florence, 1820-1910. 5. Victoria, Queen of Great Britain, 1819-1901. 6. Bell, Gertrude Lowthian, 1868-1926. I. Title.

GASKELL, Elizabeth Cleghorn v. 12
(Stevenson) 1810-1865.
The life of Charlotte Bronte, by Elizabeth C. Gaskell; with an introduction by Clement Shorter. London, Oxford University Press [1961] xx, 476 p. 16 cm. (The World's Classics. CCXIV) "First published in 1857. In the World's Classics...first published in 1919." Last reprinted 1961. 64-25437
1. Bronte, Charlotte, 1816-1855. I. Shorter, Clement King, 1857-1926. II. Title. BIP

GASKELL, Elizabeth 823'.8 B
Cleghorn (Stevenson), 1810-1865.
The life of Charlotte Bronte. With an introd. an notes by Clement K. Shorter. New York, Harper. [New York, AMS Press, 1973] xxxvi, 670 p. illus. 23 cm. (Series: Bronte, Charlotte, 1816-1855. Life and works of the sisters Bronte, v. 7.) "The Haworth edition." Reprint of the 1900 ed., which was issued as v. 7 of Life and works of the sisters Bronte. [PR4168.G3 1973] 77-148757 ISBN 0-404-08837-6 8.50
1. Bronte, Charlotte, 1816-1855. I. Title. II. Series.

GERIN, Winifred. 823'.8 B
Charlotte Bronte: the evolution of genius. Oxford, Clarendon P., 1967. xvi, 617 p. front., 10 plates (incl. ports.) 22 1/2 cm. Bibliography: p. [600]-607. [PR4168.G4] 67-92825
1. Bronte, Charlotte, 1816-1855. I. Title. BIP

LANE, Margaret, 1907- 928.2
The Bronte story; a reconsideration of Mrs. Gaskell's Life of Charlotte Bronte. With drawings by Joan Hassall. [1st American ed.] New York, Duell, Sloan & Pearce [1953] 368 p. illus. 22 cm. [PR4168.L27 1953a] 52-12635
1. Bronte, Charlotte, 1816-1855. 2. Gaskell, Elizabeth Cleghorn Stevenson, 1810-1865. The life of Charlotte Bronte.

LANE, Margaret, 1907- 823'.8 B
The Bronte story; a reconsideration of Mrs. Gaskell's Life of Charlotte Bronte. With drawings by Joan Hassall. Westport, Conn., Greenwood Press [1971, c1953] xii, 368 p. illus. 23 cm. Bibliography: p. [359]-360. [PR4168.L27 1971] 75-108394 ISBN 0-8371-3817-5
1. Bronte, Charlotte, 1816-1855. 2. Gaskell, Elizabeth Cleghorn (Stevenson) 1810-1865. The life of Charlotte Bronte. I. Title.

LANGBRIDGE, Rosamond, 823'.8 B
1880-
Charlotte Bronte: a psychological study. New York, Haskell House [1972] 260 p. 23 cm. Reprint of the 1929 ed. [PR4168.L3 1972] 72-3280 ISBN 0-8383-1529-1 11.95
1. Bronte, Charlotte, 1816-1855.

MOGLEN, Helene, 1936- 823'.8 B
Charlotte Bronte : the self conceived / Helene Moglen. 1st ed. New York : Norton, c1976. 256 p. : ill. ; 24 cm. Includes index. Bibliography: p. [243]-247. [PR4168.M575] 76-16010 ISBN 0-393-07505-2 pbk. : 11.95
1. Bronte, Charlotte, 1816-1855. BIP

Bronte, Charlotte, 1816-1855—Biography.

GASKELL, Elizabeth 823'.8 B
Cleghorn Stevenson, 1810-1865.
The life of Charlotte Bronte / [by] Elizabeth Gaskell. [1st ed. reprinted] / edited by Alan Shelston. Harmondsworth : Penguin, 1975. 623 p. : facsims. ; 19 cm. (Penguin English library) Bibliography: p. 39-40. [PR4168.G3 1975] 75-328560 ISBN 0-14-043099-7 pbk. : 3.95
1. Bronte, Charlotte, 1816-1855—Biography. I. Shelston, Alan. II. Title.
Distributed by Penquin, Baltimore, Md.

GOLDRING, Maude. 823'.8 B
Charlotte Bronte, the woman : a study / by Maude Goldring. Folcroft, Pa. : Folcroft Library Editions, 1976. p. cm. Reprint of the 1915 ed. published by E. Mathews, London. [PR4168.G6 1976] 76-26960 ISBN 0-8414-4536-2 lib. bdg. : 20.00
1. Bronte, Charlotte, 1816-1855—Biography. 2. Novelists, English—19th century—Biography. I. Title.

PETERS, Margot. 823'.8
Unquiet soul : a biography of Charlotte Bronte / Margot Peters. 1st ed. Garden City, N.Y. : Doubleday, 1975. xv, 460 p. : ill. ; 24 cm. Includes index. Bibliography: p. [443]-449. [PR4168.P38] 74-9461 ISBN 0-385-06622-8 : 12.50
1. Bronte, Charlotte, 1816-1855—Biography. I. Title. BIP

PETERS, Margot. 823.8
Unquiet soul : a biography of Charlotte Bronte / Margot Peters. New York : Pocket Books, 1976c1975. xviii, 540p. : ill. ; 18 cm. Includes index. Bibliography: pp. 519-526. [PR4168.P38] ISBN 0-671-80712-9 pbk. : 2.75
1. Bronte, Charlotte, 1816-1855-Biography. I. Title.
L.C. card no. for 1975 Doubleday edition: 74-9461.

TERHUNE, Mary Virginia 823'.8 B
Hawes, 1830-1922.
Charlotte Bronte at home / by Marion Harland [i.e. M. V. H. Terhune]. Folcroft, Pa. : Folcroft Library Editions, 1976 [c1899] p. cm. (Series: Terhune, Mary Virginia Hawes, 1830-1922. Literary hearthstones.) Reprint of the ed. published by Putnam, New York, in the author's series: Literary hearthstones. [PR4168.T4 1976] 76-17037 ISBN 0-8414-4820-5 lib. bdg. : 30.00
1. Bronte, Charlotte, 1816-1855—Biography. I. Title. II. Series. BIP

Bronte, Charlotte, 1816-1855—Criticism and interpretation.

KEEFE, Robert, 1938- 823'.8
Charlotte Bronte's world of death / Robert Keefe. Austin : University of Texas Press, c1979. xxi, 224 p. ; 23 cm. Includes index. Bibliography: p. [213]-216. [PR4169.K4] 78-9853 ISBN 0-292-75043-9 : 11.95
1. Bronte, Charlotte, 1816-1855—Criticism and interpretation. 2. Death in literature. 3. Psychology and literature. I. Title. BIP

Bronte, Emily Jane, 1818-1848.

ALLOTT, Miriam 823'.8'09 B
Farris, comp.
The Brontes, the critical heritage / edited by Miriam Allott. London ; Boston : Routledge and Kegan Paul, 1974. xx, 475 p. ; 23 cm. (The Critical heritage series) Includes index. Bibliography: p. 461-463. [PR4168.A7 1974] 73-85426 ISBN 0-7100-7701-7 : £7.50
1. Bronte, Charlotte, 1816-1855. 2. Bronte, Emily Jane, 1818-1848. 3. Bronte, Anne, 1820-1849. I. Title.

BENTLEY, Phyllis Eleanor, 928.2
1894-
The Bronte sisters. London New York, Published for the British Council and the National Book League by Longmans, Green [1950] 44 p. group port. 22 cm. (Bibliographical series of supplements to British Book News) "A select bibliography of the Bronte family": p. 41-44. [PR4168.B425] 51-3395
1. Bronte, Charlotte, 1816-1855. 2. Bronte, Emily Jane, 1818-1848. 3. Bronte, Anne, 1820-1849. I. Title. II. Series. BIP

CRANDALL, Norma 928.2
Emily Bronte, a psychological portrait. Rindge, N. H., R. R. Smith Publisher, 1957. 160 p. illus. 23 cm. [PR4173.C7] 57-10364
1. Bronte, Emily Jane, 1818-1848. BIP

SPARK, Muriel 828.809
Emily Bronte, her life and work, by Muriel Spark, Derek Stanford. [1st Amer. ed.] New York, Coward [1966] 271p. illus. 22cm. Bibl. [PR4173.S66 1966] 66-20161 5.75
1. Bronte, Emily Jane, 1818-1848. I. Stanford, Derek, joint author. II. Title.

SPARK, Muriel. 928.2
Emily Bronte, her life and work, by Muriel Spark and Derek Stanford. New York, London House and Maxwell [British Bk. Centre, 1960] 271p. illus. 23cm. 60-2327 4.95 bds.,
1. Brontie, Emily Jane, 1818-1848 I. Stanford, Derek. II. Title.

STEVENSON, W. H. 823'.8'09
Emily and Anne Bronte, by W. H. Stevenson. New York, Humanities Press [1968] ix, 116, [1] p. 19 cm. (The Profiles in literature series) Bibliography: p. 112-[117] [PR4173.S67 1968b] 68-25994
1. Bronte, Emily Jane, 1818-1848. 2. Bronte, Anne, 1820-1849. I. Title. BIP

Bronte, Emily Jane, 1818-1848—Biography.

DUCLAUX, Agnes Mary 823'.8 B
Frances Robinson, 1857-1944.
Emily Bronte / by A. Mary F. Robinson. Philadelphia : R. West, 1978 [c1883] viii, 315 p. ; 23 cm. Reprint of the ed. published by Roberts Bros., Boston, which was issued as v. 2 of Famous women. Includes bibliographical references. [PR4173.D8 1978] 78-1095 ISBN 0-8492-2381-4 : 27.50
1. Bronte, Emily Jane, 1818-1848—Biography. 2. Authors, English—19th century—Biography. I. Series: Famous women ; v. 2.

DUCLAUX, Agnes Mary 823'.8 B
Francis Robinson, 1857-1944.
Emily Bronte, by A. Mary F. Robinson. [Folcroft, Pa.] Folcroft Library Editions, 1974 [c1883] viii, 315 p. 23 cm. Reprint of the ed. published by Roberts Bros., Boston, which was issued as v. 2 of Famous women. Includes bibliographical references. [PR4173.D8 1974] 74-5031 ISBN 0-8414-7301-3 (lib. bdg.)
1. Bronte, Emily Jane, 1818-1848—Biography. I. Series: Famous women, v. 2.

DUCLAUX, Agnes Mary 823'.8 B
Francis Robinson, 1857-1944.
Emily Bronte / by A. Mary F. Robinson. [Norwood, Pa.] : Norwood Editions, 1976 [c1883] p. cm. Reprint of the ed. published by Roberts Brothers, Boston, which was issued as v. 2 of Famous women. Includes bibliographical references. [PR4173.D8 1976] 76-14943 ISBN 0-8482-2255-5 lib. bdg. : 25.00
1. Bronte, Emily Jane, 1818-1848—Biography. I. Series: Famous women ; v. 2.

GERIN, Winifred. 823'.8 B
Emily Bronte: a biography. Oxford, Clarendon Press, 1971. xviii, 290 p., 10 plates. illus., facsims., ports. 23 cm. Bibliography: p. [278]-284. [PR4173.G4] 79-881328 ISBN 0-19-812018-4 £2.50
1. Bronte, Emily Jane, 1818-1848—Biography. BIP

MOORE, Virginia, 1903- 823'.8 B
The life and eager death of Emily Bronte, a biography. New York, Haskell House Publishers, 1971. xii, 383 p. illus. 23 cm. Reprint of the 1936 ed. Bibliography: p. 370-374. [PR4173.M7 1971] 78-173844 ISBN 0-8383-1345-0
1. Bronte, Emily Jane, 1818-1848—Biography. I. Title.

O'BRIEN, Florence Roma 823'.8
Muir Wilson, 1891-1930.
The life and private history of Emily Jane Bronte, by Romer Wilson. New York, A. and C. Boni, 1928. New York, Haskell House Publishers, 1972. xii, 292 p. illus. 23 cm. [PR4173.O3 1972] 72-3230 ISBN 0-8383-1527-5 11.95

1. Bronte, Emily Jane, 1818-1848—Biography. I. Title.

SIMPSON, Charles Walter, 1885- 823'.8 B
Emily Bronte / by Charles Simpson. Folcroft, Pa. : Folcroft Library Editions, 1977. p. cm. Reprint of the 1929 ed. published by Country Life Ltd, London. [PR4173.S5 1977] 77-22298 ISBN 0-8414-7785-X lib. bdg. : 30.00
1. Bronte, Emily Jane, 1818-1848—Biography. 2. Authors, English 19th century—Biography. BIP

Bronte family.

BENTLEY, Phyllis Eleanor, 1894- 823'.8'09
The Brontes / by Phyllis Bentley. Darby, Pa. : Arden Library, 1978. 114 p. ; 23 cm. Reprint of the 1948 ed. published by A. Swallow, Denver, in series: The English novelists. [PR4168.B43 1978] 78-18864 ISBN 0-8495-0345-0 lib. bdg. : 12.50
1. Bronte family. 2. Authors, English—19th century—Biography. I. Title. II. Series: The English novelists (Denver).

BENTLEY, Phyllis Eleanor, 1894- 823'.8'09 B
The Brontes and their world, by Phyllis Bentley. New York, Viking Press [1969] 144 p. illus., facsims., ports. 25 cm. (A Studio book) [PR4168.B424 1969] 69-17972 6.95
1. Bronte family. I. Title. BIP

BENTLEY, Phyllis Eleanor, 1894- 823'.8'09 B
The Brontes and their world / Phyllis Bentley. New York : Scribner, 1979, c1969. 144 p. : ill. ; 25 cm. Includes index. [PR4168.B434 1979] 78-19213 ISBN 0-684-16023-4 : 10.95
1. Bronte family. 2. Authors, English—19th century—Biography. I. Title.

BENTLEY, Phyllis Eleanor, 1894- 928.2
The young Brontes. Illus. by Marie Hartley. New York, Roy Publishers [1961, c.1960] 136p. 60-14476 3.00 bds.,
1. Bronte family—Juvenile literature. I. Title.

BRAITHWAITE, William Stanley Beaumont, 1878- 928.2
The bewitched parsonage; the story of the Brontes. New York, Coward-McCann [1950] xi, 238 p. illus., ports. 22 cm. Bibliography: p. 235-238. [PR4168.B75] 50-10234
1. Bronte family. I. Title.

BRONTE, Patrick, 1777-1861. 823'.8'09 B
Bronteana. The Rev. Patrick Bronte, A.B.: his collected works and life. The Works; and the Brontes of Ireland. Edited, etc., by J. Horsfall Turner. [Folcroft, Pa.] Folcroft Library Editions, 1974. p. cm. Reprint of the 1898 ed. printed by T. Harrison, Bingley, Eng., for the editor. [PR4174.B2 1974] 74-14840 ISBN 0-8414-8501-1 (lib. bdg.)
1. Bronte family. I. Turner, Joseph Horsfall, 1845- ed. II. Title.

HANSON, Lawrence. 823'.8'09 B
The four Brontes; the lives and works of Charlotte, Branwell, Emily, and Anne Bronte, by Lawrence and Elisabeth Hanson. With a new pref. by the authors. [Hamden, Conn.] Archon Books, 1967. xxxiv, 414 p. illus., facsim., ports. 22 cm. First published in 1949. Includes bibliographical references. [PR4168.H25 1967] 67-11475
1. Bronte family. I. Hanson, Elisabeth M., joint author. II. Title. BIP

LEYLAND, Francis A. 823'.8'09 B
The Bronte family, with special reference to Patrick Branwell Bronte. New York, Haskell House Publishers, 1971. 2 v. 23 cm. Reprint of the 1886 ed. Includes bibliographical references. [PR4168.L4 1971] 70-157554 ISBN 0-8383-1256-X
1. Bronte family. 2. Bronte, Patrick Branwell, 1817-1848.

LOCK, John. 828'.7'09 B
A man of sorrow : the life, letters, and times of the Rev. Patrick Bronte, 1777-1861 / by John Lock and W. T. Dixon ; foreword by the Archbishop of Canterbury (formerly the Archbishop of York). London : I. Hodgkins ; Westport, Conn. : Meckler Books, 1979. xiv, 566 p., [7] leaves of plates : ill. ; 24 cm. Reprint of the ed. published by Nelson, London. Includes index. Bibliography: p. 541-549. [PR4174.B2L6 1979] 78-27130 ISBN 0-930466-15-2 lib. bdg. : 35.95
1. Bronte, Patrick, 1777-1861—Biography. 2. Bronte family. 3. Church of England—Clergy—Biography. 4. Authors, English—19th century—Biography. 5. Clergy—England—Biography. I. Dixon, William Thomas, joint author. II. Title.

MACKAY, Angus Mason. 823'.8'09 B
The Brontes; fact and fiction. London, Service & Paton, 1897. [New York, AMS Press, 1973] 186 p. 19 cm. Includes bibliographical references. [PR4168.M3 1973] 70-148277 ISBN 0-404-08886-4 8.50
1. Bronte family. I. Title.

MASSON, Flora. 823'.8'09 B
The Brontes. Port Washington, N.Y., Kennikat Press [1970] 92 p. port. 18 cm. Reprint of the 1912 ed. Bibliography: p. 92. [PR4168.M37 1970] 73-103203
1. Bronte family. I. Title. BIP

RATCHFORD, Fannie Elizabeth, 1888- 928.2
The Brontes' web of childhood [Reissue] New York, Russell & Russell, 1964 [c.1963] xviii, 293p. illus., facsims. 23cm. Bibl. 64-18601 7.50
1. Bronte family. I. Title.

SHORTER, Clement King, 1857-1926. 823'.8'09 B
Charlotte Bronte and her sisters / by Clement K. Shorter. New York : AMS Press, 1975. xii, 247 p., [8] leaves of plates ; ill. ; 19 cm. Reprint of the 1905 ed. published by Scribner, New York, issued in series: Literary lives. [PR4168.S4 1975] 73-148303 ISBN 0-404-08911-9 : 12.50
1. Bronte family. BIP

SHORTER, Clement King, 1857-1926. 823'.8'09 B
The Brontes; life and letters. Being an attempt to present a full and final record of the lives of the three sisters, Charlotte, Emily, and Anne Bronte, from the biographies of Mrs. Gaskell and others, and from numerous hitherto unpublished manuscripts and letters. New York, Haskell House Publishers, 1969. 2 v. ports. 23 cm. Reprint of the 1908 ed. [PR4168.S38 1969] 68-24918
1. Bronte family. I. Title.

SINCLAIR, May. 823'.8'09
The three Brontes. Port Washington, N.Y., Kennikat press [1967, c1939] xvi, 296 p. illus., facsim., ports. 22 cm. [PR4168.S5 1967] 67-27650
1. Bronte family. I. Title. BIP

SPARK, Muriel, ed. 823.8
The Bronte letters: selected and with an introduction by Muriel Spark. [New ed.] London, Melbourne [etc.] Macmillan, 1966. 208 p. 21 cm. 25/- (B66-20868) Includes letters from Branwell Bronte, Emily Bronte, Anne Bronte and Patrick Bronte. [PR4168.A4S6 1966] 66-68258
1. Bronte family. I. Title.

SPARK, Muriel, ed. 928.2
The letters of the Brontes; a selection. [1st American ed.] Norman, University of Oklahoma Press [1954] 208 p. 21 cm. London ed. (Nevill) has title: The Bronte letters. [PR4168.A4S6 1954a] 54-10062
1. Bronte family. I. Title.

STUART, J. A. Erskine. 823'.8'09 B
The Bronte country; its topography, antiquities, and history, by J. A. Erskine Stuart. New York, Haskell House Publishers, 1971. xiii, 241 p. illus. 23 cm. Reprint of the 1888 ed. [PR4168.S7 1971] 71-179270 ISBN 0-8383-1252-7
1. Bronte family. 2. Yorkshire, Eng.—Description and travel. I. Title.

TRUST, Estelle, 1908- 928.2
Anne Bronte. Dallas, Story Book Press [1954] 247p. illus. 20cm. [PR4163.T7] 54-41599
1. Bronte, Anne, 1820-1849. I. Title.

WILKS, Brian. 823'.8'09 B
The Brontes / Brian Wilks. New York : Viking Press, 1975. 144 p. : ill. (some col.) ; 31 cm. (A Studio book) Includes index. [PR4168.W49 1975] 75-998 ISBN 0-670-19231-7 : 14.95
1. Bronte family. I. Title.

WILKS, Brian. 823'.8'09
The Brontes / [by] Brian Wilks. London ; New York : Hamlyn, 1975. 144 p. : ill. (some col.), facsims., map, ports. (some col.) ; 31 cm. Ill. on lining papers. Includes index. [PR4168.W49 1975b] 75-332836 ISBN 0-600-31269-0 : £2.95
1. Bronte family. I. Title.

WILLIS, Irene Cooper. 823'.8'09
The Brontes / by Irene Cooper Willis. Folcroft, Pa. : Folcroft Library Editions, 1976. p. cm. Reprint of the 1933 ed. published by Duckworth, London, issued in series: Great lives. Bibliography: p. [PR4158.W5 1976] 76-8205 ISBN 0-8414-9435-5 lib bdg. : 8.50
1. Bronte family. I. Title. BIP

WRIGHT, John Charles, 1852- 823.8'09 B
The story of the Brontes / by J. C. Wright. Folcroft, Pa. : Folcroft Library Editions, 1974. 189 p. ; 24 cm. Reprint of the 1925 ed. published by L. Parsons, London. Includes index. [PR4168.W65 1974] 74-30153 ISBN 0-8414-9411-8 lib. bdg. : 20.00
1. Bronte family. I. Title.

WRIGHT, William, 1837-1899. 823'.8'09 B
The Brontes in Ireland; or, Facts stranger than fiction. New York, Haskell House, 1971. xviii, 308 p. illus., facsims., maps, ports. 23 cm. Reprint of the 1893 ed. [PR4168.W7 1971] 70-160161 ISBN 0-8383-1257-8
1. Bronte family. I. Title.

Bronte family—Fiction.

BANKS, Lynne Reid. FIC
Dark quartet : the story of the Brontes / by Lynne Reid Banks. New York : Delacorte Press, c1976. p. cm. [PZ4.B2173Dar3] [PR6003.A528] 823'.8'09 B 76-29727 ISBN 0-440-01657-6 : 10.00
1. Bronte family—Fiction. I. Title. BIP

Bronte, Patrick Branwell, 1817-1848.

GERIN, Winifred. 928.2
Branwell Bronte. London, New York, T. Nelson [1961] xi, 338 p. illus., ports., map, facsims. 23 cm. "Sources of evidence": p. 319-323. [PR4174.B2G4] 61-65127
1. Bronte, Patrick Branwell, 1817-1848.

LAW, Alice, 1886- 823'.8'09 B
Patrick Branwell Bronte / by Alice Law. Folcroft, Pa. : Folcroft Library Editions, 1976. p. cm. Reprint of the 1923 ed. published by A. M. Philpot, London. [PR4174.B2L3 1976] 76-13012 ISBN 0-8414-5721-2 lib. bdg. : 20.00
1. Bronte, Patrick Branwell, 1817-1848.

Bronte, Patrick, 1777-1861—Biography.

HOPKINS, Annette Brown, 1879- 928.2
The father of the Brontes. Baltimore, Published for Goucher College by the Johns Hopkins Press [1958] xi, 179p. port. 23cm. Includes bibliographical references. [PR4174.B2H6] 58-11997
1. Bronte, Patrick, 1777-1861. 2. Bronte family. I. Title. BIP

LOCK, John. 828'.7'09 B
A man of sorrow : the life, letters, and times of the Rev. Patrick Bronte, 1777-1861 / by John Lock and W. T. Dixon ; foreword by the Archbishop of Canterbury (formerly the Archbishop of York). London : I. Hodgkins ; Westport, Conn. : Meckler Books, 1979. xiv, 566 p., [7] leaves of plates : ill. ; 24 cm. Reprint of the ed. published by Nelson, London. Includes index. Bibliography: p. 541-549. [PR4174.B2L6 1979] 78-27130 ISBN 0-930466-15-2 lib. bdg. : 35.95
1. Bronte, Patrick, 1777-1861—Biography. 2. Bronte family. 3. Church of England—Clergy—Biography. 4. Authors, English—19th century—Biography. 5. Clergy—England—Biography. I. Dixon, William Thomas, joint author. II. Title.

Brook Farm.

KIRBY, Georgiana (Bruce) b.1818. 335'.3
Years of experience; an autobiographical narrative. New York, AMS Press [1971] iii, 315 p. 22 cm. Reprint of the 1887 ed. [CT275.K59A3 1971] 79-134373 ISBN 0-404-08421-4 12.50
1. Brook Farm. I. Title.

Brooke, Edward William, 1919-

BLACK Americans in government. 973.92'0922 [Text and exercises by Sheila Hobson and Harvey D. Goldenberg. General editor: Saunders Redding]. Produced by Buckingham Learning Corporation. [Jamaica, N.Y., Buckingham Learning Corp., 1969] 5 v. illus., ports. 28 cm. Cover title. Contents.Contents.—[1] The three wars of Edward Brooke; the story of the first black U.S. Senator since Reconstruction.—[2] Fighting Shirley Chisholm; the story of the first black U.S. Congresswoman.—[3] Ambassador for progress; the story of Patricia Harris, former U.S. Ambassador to Luxembourg.—[4] Equal under the law; the story of Supreme Court Justice Thurgood Marshall.—[5] Robert Weaver sees a new city; the story of the first Secretary of Housing and Urban Development. [E185.96.B53] 79-20085
1. Brooke, Edward William, 1919- 2. Chisholm, Shirley, 1924- 3. Harris, Patricia Roberts, 1924- 4. Marshall, Thurgood, 1908- 5. Weaver, Robert Clifton, 1907- I. Hobson, Sheila. II. Goldenberg, Harvey D.

Brooke, Fulke Greville, Baron, 1554-1628.

REBHOLZ, Ronald A. 821'.3 B
The life of Fulke Greville, first Lord Brooke, [by] Ronald A. Rebholz. Oxford, Clarendon Press, 1971. xxxv, 384 p., 2 plates (1 fold.); geneal. table, port. 23 cm. Bibliography: p. [353]-368. [PR2216.R38] 78-874436 ISBN 0-19-812010-9 £5.50
1. Brooke, Fulke Greville, Baron, 1554-1628. I. Title.

Brooke, James Rajah of Sarawak, Sir 1803-1868.

HAHN, Emily, 1905- v. 12
James Brooke of Sarawak, a biography of Sir James Brooke. London, A Barker [1953] 271p. illus., ports. 22cm. Bibliography: p. 263-265. A55
1. Brooke, James Rajah of Sarawak, Sir 1803-1868. I. Title.

Brooke, Robert Greville, baron, 1608?-1643.

STRIDER, Robert Edward Lee, 1917- 923.242
Robert Greville, Lord Brooke. Cambridge, Harvard University Press, 1958. ix, 252 p. facsims., geneal. table. 24 cm. Bibliography: p. [239]-247. [DA396.B7S75] 58-5599

1. Brooke, Robert Greville, baron, 1608?-1643. I. Title.

Brooke, Rupert, 1887-1915.

HASSALL, Christopher Vernon, 1912-1963. 928.2
Rupert Brooke; a biography. [1st American ed.] New York, Harcourt, Brace & World [1964] 556 p. illus., ports. 25 cm. [PR6003.R4Z67 1964] 63-8099
1. Brooke, Rupert, 1887-1915. BIP

PEARSALL, Robert Brainard, 1920- 821'.9'12 B
Rupert Brooke; the man and poet. Amsterdam, Rodopi, 1974. 174 p. 23 cm. Bibliography: p. [169]-170. [PR6003.R4Z723] 74-180347 ISBN 9-06-203437-3
1. Brooke, Rupert, 1887-1915.
Distributed by International Scholarly Book Services; 10.00 (pbk.) BIP

STRINGER, Arthur John Arbuthnott, 1874-1950. 821'.9'12 B
Red wine of youth; a life of Rupert Brooke. Westport, Conn., Greenwood Press [1972, c1948] 287 p. illus. 22 cm. [PR6003.R4Z75 1972] 72-6211 ISBN 0-8371-6456-7 12.50
1. Brooke, Rupert, 1887-1915. I. Title. BIP

Brooke, Rupert, 1887-1915—Correspondence.

BROOKE, Rupert, 1887-1915. 821'.9'12 B
Letters from Rupert Brooke to his publisher, 1911-1914. New York : Octagon Books, 1975. [63] p. : ill. ; 25 cm. Limited ed. of 400 copies. No. 393. [PR6003.R4Z547 1975] 75-4445 ISBN 0-374-90997-0 lib.bdg. : 25.00
1. Brooke, Rupert, 1887-1915—Correspondence. 2. Sidgwick, Frank. I. Title. BIP

Brooke, Sylvia Leonora (Brett)

BROOKE, Sylvia Leonora (Brett) Lady, Rani of Sarawak, 1885-1971. 959.5'30924 B
Queen of the head hunters; the autobiography of H. H. the Hon. Sylvia Lady Brooke. New York, Morrow, 1972 [c1970] x, 194 p. illus. 22 cm. [DS646.38.B73A28 1972] 70-181030 6.95
I. Title.

Brookes, Herbert, 1867-1963.

RIVETT, Rohan Deakin. 919.4
Australian citizen: Herbert Brookes, 1867-1963 [by] Rohan Rivett. Melbourne, Melbourne U.P.; London, New York, Cambridge U.P., 1965. xiii, 217 p. front., illus., 8 plates (incl. ports.). 22 cm. 65/ -- [DU114.B72R5] 66-13722
1. Brookes, Herbert, 1867-1963. I. Title.

Brookes, Mabel Emmerton, Dame, 1894-

BROOKES, Mabel Emmerton, Dame, 1894- 994.04'092'4 B
Memoirs / by Mable Brooks. Melbourne : Macmillan, 1974. 216 p. : ill. ; 24 cm. Includes index. [CT2808.B68A34] 75-318351 ISBN 0-333-13989-5
1. Brookes, Mabel Emmerton, Dame, 1894-

Brooklyn.

GELMAN, Steve. 796.357
The greatest Dodgers of them all. New York, Putnam [1968] 191 p. ports. 22 cm. Brief biographies of well-known players associated with the Dodger baseball team including Sandy Koufax, Don Drysdale, Dazzy Vance, Burleigh Grimes, Roy Campanella, Gil Hodges, Jackie Robinson, Pee Wee Reese, Maury Wills, Zack Wheat, Babe Herman, Duke Snider, Dixie Walker, and Peter Reiser. [GV865.A1G37] AC 68
1. Brooklyn. Baseball club (National league) 2. Baseball—Biography. I. Title.

Brooklyn. Baseball club (National league)

ALSTON, Walter Emmons, 1911- 796.3570770924
Alston and the Dodgers, by Walter Alston, with Si Burick. [1st ed.] Garden City, N.Y., Doubleday, 1966. 189 p. ports. 22 cm. [GV865.A4A3] 66-20919
1. Brooklyn. Baseball club (National League) 2. Los Angeles. Baseball club (National League) I. Burick, Si. II. Title.

GELMAN, Steve. 796.357'0922
The greatest Dodgers of them all. New York, Putnam [1968] 191 p. ports. 22 cm. [GV865.A1G37] 68-15047 3.49
1. Brooklyn. Baseball club (National league) 2. Baseball—Biography. I. Title.

Brooks, Aubrey Lee,

BROOKS, Aubrey Lee, 1871- 923.473
A southern lawyer; fifty years at the bar. Chapel Hill, University of North Carolina Press [1950] viii, 214 p. 25 cm. 50-10879
I. Title.

Brooks, Gladys.

BROOKS, Gladys. 920.7
Boston and return. [1st ed.] New York, Atheneum, 1962. 272 p. illus. 20 cm. Autobiographical. [CT275.B75612A3] 62-11684
I. Title.

Brooks, Joshua Loring, 1868-1949.

BROOKS, Joshua Loring, 1906- 926.55
"J. L."; a biography. Springfield, Mass., Brooks Bank Note Co. [1952] 127 p. illus. 20 cm. [HG591.B7] 52-34918
1. Brooks, Joshua Loring, 1868-1949. 2. Brooks Bank Note Company, Springfield, Mass. I. Title.

Brooks, Mel.

*ADLER, Bill. 791.4302330924
Mel Brooks : the irreverent funnyman Bill Adler and Jeffrey Feinman. Chicago : Playboy Press ,1976. 190 p. ; 18 cm. [PN1998] 75-36300 pbk. : 1.95
1. Brooks, Mel. I. Feinman, Jeffrey, joint author. II. Title.

ADLER, Bill. 790.2'092'4 B
Mel Brooks : the irreverent funnyman / Bill Adler, Jeffrey Feinman. 1st ed. Chicago : Playboy Press, c1976. 190 p. ; 18 cm. [PN2287.B695A63] 75-36300 pbk. : 1.95
1. Brooks, Mel. 2. Comedians—United States—Biography. I. Feinman, Jeffrey, joint author.

HOLTZMAN, Will. 791'.092'2 B
Seesaw, a dual biography of Anne Bancroft and Mel Brooks / William Holtzman. 1st ed. Garden City, N.Y. : Doubleday, 1979. 300 p., [8] leaves of plates : ill. ; 22 cm. Includes index. [PN2287.B695H6] 78-22616 ISBN 0-385-13076-7 : 10.95
1. Brooks, Mel. 2. Bancroft, Anne, 1931- 3. Actors—United States—Biography. 4. Moving-picture producers and directors—United States—Biography. I. Title.

Brooks, Phillips, Bp., 1835-1893.

ALBRIGHT, Raymond Wolf, 1901- 922.373
Focus on infinity; a life of Phillips Brooks. New York, Macmillan, [c.]1961. 464p. illus. (front port.) Bibl. 61-7603 4.95
1. Brooks, Phillips, Bp., 1835-1893. I. Title.

HIGGINS, Paul Lambourne. 922
Preachers of power; Henry Ward Beecher, Phillips Brooks, [and] Walter Rauschenbusch. New York, Vantage Press ['1950] 72 p. ports. 23 cm. [BV4208.U6H5] 51-787
1. Beecher, Henry Ward, 1813-1887. 2. Brooks, Phillips, 1835-1898 3. Rauschenbusch, Walter, 1861-1918. 4. Preaching—U. S.—Hist. I. Title.

Brooks, Romaine.

SECREST, Meryle. 759.13 B
Between me and life; a biography of Romaine Brooks. [1st ed.] Garden City, N.Y., Doubleday, 1974. xviii, 432 p. illus. 24 cm. Bibliography: p. [417]-422. [ND237.B872S42] 74-6991 ISBN 0-385-03469-5
1. Brooks, Romaine. I. Title.

Brooks, Seth R.

BROOKS, Seth R. 289.1'092'4 B
Recollections and reflections of Seth R. Brooks and Corinne H. Brooks / edited by William Lloyd Fox. Washington : Universalist National Memorial Church, 1977. 106 p. ; 23 cm. [BX9969.B75A35] 77-84948
1. Brooks, Seth R. 2. Brooks, Corinne H. 3. Universalists—Washington, D.C.—Biography. 4. Washington, D.C.—Biography. I. Brooks, Corinne H., joint author. II. Fox, William Lloyd.

Brooks, Van Wyck, 1886-1963.

BROOKS, Van Wyck, 1886- 928.1
Days of the phoenix; the nineteen-twenties I remember. [1st ed.] New York, Dutton, 1957. 193p. illus. 22cm. 'A continuation of ... [the author's] Scences and portraits: memories of childhood and youth.' [PS3503.R7297D3] 57-5335
1. Authors, American. 2. Authors—Correspondence, reminiscences, etc. I. Title.

BROOKS, Van Wyck, 1886- 928.1
An autobiography. Foreword by John Hall Wheelock. Introd. by Malcolm Cowley. [1st ed.] New York, E. P. Dutton, 1965. xxxvi, 667 p. port. 22 cm. A one vol. ed. of the author's 3 books of memoirs originally published in 1954, 1957 and 1961. Contents.Contents.—Scenes and portraits, memories of childhood and youth.—Days of the Phoenix, the nineteen-twenties I remember.—From the shadow of the mountain, my post-meridian years. [PS3503.R7297Z52] 64-19571
1. Authors—Correspondence, reminiscences, etc.

BROOKS, Van Wyck, 1886-1963. 928.1
Scenes and portraits; memories of childhood and youth. [1st ed.] New York, Dutton, 1954. 243 p. port. 22 cm. [PS3503.R7297S4] 54-5828
I. Title.

HOOPES, James, 1944- 818'.5'209 B
Van Wyck Brooks : in search of American culture James Hoopes. Amherst : University of Massachusetts Press, 1977. p. cm. Includes index. Bibliography: p. [PS3503.R7297Z7] 76-8754 ISBN 0-87023-212-6 : 15.00
1. Brooks, Van Wyck, 1886-1963.

Brookter, Marie.

BROOKTER, Marie. 329'.0092'4 B
Here I am - take my hand [by] Marie Brookter, with Jean Curtis. [1st ed.] New York, Harper & Row [1974] viii, 248 p. 22 cm. Autobiography. [E185.97.B83A33] 73-14248 ISBN 0-06-010531-3 7.95
1. Brookter, Marie. I. Curtis, Jean, 1939- joint author. II. Title. BIP

Broom, Robert, 1866-1951.

FINDLAY, George. 560'.9 B
Dr. Robert Broom, F.R.S.; palaeontologist and physician, 1866-1951; a biography, appreciation and bibliography, by G. H. Findlay. Introd. by Raymond A. Dart. Cape Town, A. A. Balkema, 1972. 157 p. illus. 26 cm. (South African biographical and historical studies, no. 15) Bibliography: p. 133-153. [QE707.B75F56] 73-155633
1. Broom, Robert, 1866-1951. I. Title. II. Series.
Distributed by Verry; 16.50.

Brossard family.

BROSSARD, Edgar Bernard, 1889- 929'.2'0973
Alphonse and Mary Hobson Brossard; their life in pioneer America with photographs, stories and genealogies of their families, ancestors and descendants, by Edgar B. Brossard. [Salt Lake City, Lithographed by Wheelwright Lithographing Co., 1972] xiv, 213 p. illus. 24 cm. Part of illustrative matter in pocket. [CS71.B8742 1972] 75-179890
1. Brossard family. I. Title.

Brothers in the Bible.

SAY, David Lester. 252'.05'1
Brothers of the Bible. Parsons, W. Va., McClain Print. Co., 1973. 77 p. 22 cm. [BS579.B7S29] 72-89116
1. Brothers in the Bible. I. Title.

Brothers of the Christian Schools.

LA SALLE, Jean Baptiste de, Saint, 1651-1719. 922.244
Letters and documents edited by W. J. Battersby. London, New York, Longmans, Green [1952] xxxix, 270p. port., facsims. 23cm. French and English. [LB475.L22A4] 52-12332
1. Brothers of the Christian Schools. I. Title.

Brougham and Vaux, Henry Peter Brougham, baron, 1778-1868.

ASPINALL, Arthur, 1901- 320.9'42'0750924 B
Lord Brougham and the Whig Party. [Hamden, Conn.] Archon Books, 1972. xxii, 322 p. illus. 22 cm. "First published 1927." Original ed. issued as no. 179 of Publications of the University of Manchester and no. 47 of Publications of the University of Manchester historical series. "Authorities": p. xiii-xx. [DA536.B7A8 1972] 72-453 ISBN 0-208-01240-0 11.00
1. Brougham and Vaux, Henry Peter Brougham, Baron, 1778-1868. 2. Whig Party (Gt. Brit.) 3. Great Britain—Politics and government—1800-1837. I. Title. II. Series: Victoria University of Manchester. Publications, no. 179. III. Series: Victoria University of Manchester. Publications. Historical series, no. 47. BIP

HAWES, Frances (Richmond) 942.242
Henry Brougham. New York, St. Martin's Press [1958] 325 p. illus. 23 cm. [DA536.B7H3 1958] 58-1087
1. Brougham and Vaux, Henry Peter Brougham, baron, 1778-1868. I. Title.

NEW, Chester William, 1882- 923.242
The life of Henry Brougham to 1830. Oxford, Clarendon Press, 1961. 438p. illus. 23cm. [DA536.B7N4] 61-66248
1. Brougham and Vaux, Henry Peter Brougham, baron, 1778-1868. I. Title.

NEW, Chester William, 1882- 923.242
The life of Henry Brougham to 1830. Oxford, Clarendon Press, 1961. 458 p. illus. 23 cm. [DA536.B7N4] 61-66248
1. Brougham and Vaux, Henry Peter Brougham, baron, 1778-1868.

Brougher, Mahlon J., 1885-1952.

STATLER, Ruth Beeghly, 1906- 922.673
Like a living stone; a biography of Mahlon J. Brougher. Elgin, Ill., Printed for the author by the Brethren Pub. House [1955] 187p. illus. 20cm. [BX7843.B7S8] 55-28629
1. Brougher, Mahlon J., 1885-1952. I. Title.

Broughton, John Cam Hobhouse, Baron, 1786-1869.

JOYCE, Michael. 329'.0092'4 B
My friend H: John Cam Hobhouse, Baron Broughton of Broughton de Gyfford. [Folcroft, Pa.] Folcroft Library Editions, 1973. p. Reprint of the 1948 ed. published

by Murray, London. Bibliography: [DA536.B75J6 1973] 73-16021 25.00
1. Broughton, John Cam Hobhouse, Baron, 1786-1869. I. Title. BIP

JOYCE, Michael. 329'.0092'4 B
My friend H: John Cam Hobhouse, Baron Broughton of Broughton de Gyfford. [Folcroft, Pa.] Folcroft Library Editions, 1973. p. Reprint of the 1948 ed. published by Murray, London. Bibliography: [DA536.B75J6 1973] 73-16021 ISBN 0-8414-5272-5 (lib. bdg.)
1. Broughton, John Cam Hobhouse, Baron, 1786-1869. I. Title.

ZEGGER, Robert E. 329'.0092'4 B
John Cam Hobhouse: a political life, 1819-1852 [by] Robert E. Zegger. Columbia, University of Missouri Press, 1973. vi, 312 p. 25 cm. Bibliography: p. [290]-304. [DA536.B75Z4] 72-93762 ISBN 0-8262-0137-7 11.00
1. Broughton, John Cam Hobhouse, Baron, 1786-1869.

Broun, Heywood Campbell, 1888-1939—Biography.

O'CONNOR, Richard, 1915- 070'.92'4 B
Heywood Broun : a biography / by Richard O'Connor. New York : Putnam, [1975] p. cm. Includes index. Bibliography: p. [PS3503.R76Z74] 75-4612
1. Broun, Heywood Campbell, 1888-1939—Biography. BIP

O'CONNOR, Richard, 1915-1975. 070'.92'4 B
Heywood Broun : a biography / by Richard O'Connor. New York : Putnam, [1975] 249 p., [4] leaves of plates : ill. ; 22 cm. Includes index. Bibliography: p. 240-241. [PS3503.R76Z74] 74-30572 ISBN 0-399-11503-X : 8.95
1. Broun, Heywood Campbell, 1888-1939—Biography.

Broward, Napoleon Bonaparte, 1857-1910.

PROCTOR, Samuel. 923.273
Napoleon Bonaparte Broward, Florida's fighting Democrat. Gainesville, University of Florida Press, 1950. x. 400 p. ports. 24 cm. Bibliography. p. 367-383. [F316.B878P7] 50-11070
1. Broward, Napoleon Bonaparte, 1857-1910. 2. Florida—Pol. & govt—1865- I. Title.

Brown, Addison, 1830-1913.

BROWN, Addison, 1830-1913. 347'.73'2234
Judge Addison Brown: autobiographical notes for his children. Boyce, Va., Printed by Carr Pub. Co., 1972. 193, A5 p. illus. 24 cm. [KF368.B73A34 1972] 74-165061
1. Brown, Addison, 1830-1913.

Brown, Albert Gallatin, 1813-1880.

RANCK, James Byrne. 976.2'05'0924 B
Albert Gallatin Brown, radical Southern nationalist. Philadelphia, Porcupine Press, 1974 [c1937] xiv, 320 p. illus. 22 cm. (Perspectives in American history, no. 20) Reprint of the ed. published by D. Appleton-Century Co., New York. Bibliography: p. 299-306. [F341.R88R36 1974] 73-16349 ISBN 0-87991-347-9 15.00
1. Brown, Albert Gallatin, 1813-1880. 2. Mississippi—Politics and government. 3. Slavery in the United States. I. Title. II. Series: Perspectives in American history (Philadelphia) no. 20.

Brown, Aycock.

AYCOCK Brown's 975.6'175'0924
Outer Banks / edited by David Stick. Norfolk : Donning, c1976. p. cm. [F262.D2A9] 76-28296 ISBN 0-915442-18-3 : 14.95. ISBN 0-915442-17-5 de luxe : 39.95
1. Brown, Aycock. 2. Dare Co., N.C.—Biography. 3. Outer Banks, N.C.—Biography. I. Brown, Aycock. II. Stick, David, 1919- BIP

Brown, Bedford, 1795-1870.

JONES, Houston G 975.6'565'030924
Bedford Brown: state rights unionist. Carrollton, Ga., 1955. 54p. illus. 24cm. [F258.B83J6] 56-45727
1. Brown, Bedford, 1795-1870. I. Title.

Brown, Charles Brockden, 1771-1810.

ALLEN, Paul, 1775-1826. 813'.2 B
The life of Charles Brockden Brown / by Paul Allen ; a facsim. reproduction with an introd. and a biographical sketch of the author by Charles E. Bennett. Delmar, N.Y. : Scholars' Facsimiles & Reprints, 1975. xxxiv, 10-391 p. ; ports. ; 21 cm. From an unpublished printer's press proof found in the collection of the Historical Society of Pennsylvania, erroneously attributed to W. Dunlap. Includes bibliographical references. [PS1136.A4 1975] 75-25800 ISBN 0-8201-1160-0 : 35.00
1. Brown, Charles Brockden, 1771-1810. I. Title. BIP

CLARK, David Lee, 1887- 928.1
Charles Brockden Brown, Pioneer voice of America. Durham, N. C., Duke University Press, 1952. xi, 383p. illus., ports. 24cm. Bibliography: p. [334]-341. [PS1136.C52] 52-14893
1. Brown, Charles Brockden, 1771-1810. I. Title. BIP

CLARK, David Lee, 1887-1956. 813'.2 B
Charles Brockden Brown, pioneer voice of America. New York, AMS Press, 1966 [c1952] xi, 363 p. front. 23 cm. Bibliography: p. [334]-341. [PS1136.C52 1966] 75-181909
1. Brown, Charles Brockden, 1771-1810.

RINGE, Donald A v. 12
Charles Brockden Brown, by Donald A. Ringe. New Haven, College & University Press [1966] 158 p. 21 cm. Bibliography: p. 151-155. 68-16977
1. Brown, Charles Brockden, 1771-1810. I. Title. BIP

WARFEL, Harry Redcay, 1899-1971. 813'.2 B
Charles Brockden Brown, American Gothic novelist. New York, Octagon Books, 1974 [c1949] xi, 255 p. port. 21 cm. Reprint of the ed. published by University of Florida Press, Gainesville. Bibliography: p. 239-243. [PS1136.W3 1974] 73-19931 ISBN 0-374-98244-9 11.00
1. Brown, Charles Brockden, 1771-1810. BIP

Brown, Clara, 1800-1885.

BRUYN, Kathleen, 1903- 917.88'06'96073
"Aunt" Clara Brown; story of a black pioneer. Boulder Colo., Pruett Pub. Co. [1970] xv, 206 p. illus., facsims., ports. 22 cm. Bibliography: p. [194]-202. [E185.97.B84B7] 70-21917 ISBN 0-87108-043-5
1. Brown, Clara, 1800-1885. 2. Negroes in Colorado. I. Title.

Brown, Clark, 1771-1817.

SPOONER, Ella Brown (Jackson) 1880- 922.573
Clark and Tabitha Brown; the first part of their adventures and those of their three children in New England, Washington, and Maryland. [1st ed.] New York, Exposition Press [1957] 182p. illus. 21cm. [BX7260.B7S6] 57-10672
1. Brown, Clark, 1771-1817. 2. Brown, Tabitha (Moffatt) 1780- I. Title.

SPOONER, Ella Brown (Jackson) 1880- 922.573
Clark and Tabitha Brown; the first part of their adventures and those of their three children in New England, Washington, and Maryland. [1st ed.] New York, Exposition Press [1957] 132 p. illus. 21 cm. [BX7260.B7S6] 57-10672
1. Brown, Clark, 1771-1817. 2. Brown, Tabitha (Moffatt) 1780- I. Title.

Brown, Ed, 1908-

BROWN, Ed, 1908- 301.44'43'0924 B
On shares : Ed Brown's story / by Jane Maguire. 1st ed. New York : Norton, [1975] 224 p. ; 21 cm. [HD1478.U6B76 1975] 75-20075 ISBN 0-393-07495-1 : 7.95
1. Brown, Ed, 1908- 2. Share-cropping—Personal narratives. I. Maguire, Jane. II. Title.

Brown, Edmund Gerald, 1938-

BOLLENS, John Constantinus, 1920- 979.4'05'0924 B
Jerry Brown : in a plain brown wrapper / John C. Bollens and G. Robert Williams. Pacific Palisades, CA : Palisades Publishers, c1978. 272 p. : ill. ; 24 cm. Includes bibliographical references and index. [F866.2.B732B64] 78-53641 ISBN 0-913530-12-3 : 9.95
1. Brown, Edmund Gerald, 1938- 2. California—Governors—Biography. 3. California—Politics and government—1951- I. Williams, George Robert, joint author. BIP

PACK, Robert, 1929- 979.4'05'0924 B
Jerry Brown : a biography / Robert Pack. New York : Stein and Day, 1978. p. cm. [F866.2.B732P33] 77-16251 ISBN 0-8128-2437-7 : 8.95
1. Brown, Edmund Gerald, 1938- 2. California—Governors—Biography. 3. California—Politics and government—1951- 4. United States—Politics and government—1974-1977.

SCHELL, Orville. 979.4'05'0924
Brown / Orville Schell. 1st ed. New York : Random House, c1978. 307 p. ; 22 cm. [F866.2.B732S33] 77-90246 ISBN 0-394-41043-2 : 10.00
1. Brown, Edmund Gerald, 1938- 2. California—Governors—Biography. I. Title. BIP

Brown, Edward, 1834-1905.

BROWN, Edna Margaret, 1888- 926
Edward Brown, inventor, 1834-1905. [Philadelphia? 1957] 114p. illus. 23cm. [T40.D7D7] 57-36754
1. Brown, Edward, 1834-1905. I. Title.

Brown, Eleanor Gertrude,

BROWN, Eleanor Gertrude, 1888- 923.773
Corridors of light. Yellow Springs, Ohio, Antioch Press [1958] 186p. illus. 24cm. Autobiography. [HV1792.B84A3] 58-59546
I. Title.

Brown, Ford Madox, 1821-1893.

RABIN, Lucy Feiden. 759.2 B
Ford Madox Brown and the pre-Raphaelite history-picture / Lucy Rabin. New York : Garland Pub., 1979 p. cm. (Outstanding dissertations in the fine arts) Originally presented as the author's thesis, Bryn Mawr College, 1973. Bibliography: p. [ND497.B73R3 1978] 77-94725 ISBN 0-8240-3246-2 : 25.00
1. Brown, Ford Madox, 1821-1893. 2. Painters—England—Biography. 3. Preraphaelitism—Europe. I. Title. II. Series. BIP

Brown, Francis Jacob, 1850-1929.

MCGINNIS, Edith Brown, 1886- 917.64'139 B
The promised land; a narrative featuring the life history and adventures of Frank J. Brown, pioneer, buffalo hunter, Indian fighter, and founder of the Quaker settlement of Friendswood, by Edith B. McGinnis. [3d ed. Friendswood, Tex., 1969, c1947] 166 p. illus. 23 cm. [CT275.B7624 1969] 74-176011
1. Brown, Francis Jacob, 1850-1929. 2. Friendswood, Tex. I. Title.

Brown, George Alfred, 1914-

CONNOR, William N. 923.242
George Brown, a profile and pictorial biography, by Cassandra of the [London] Daily Mirror [Long Island City, N.Y.] Pergamon [1965, c.1964] 96p. illus., ports. 23cm. [DA591.B75C6] 64-8293 2.95 bds.,
1. Brown, George Alfred, 1914- I. Title.

Brown, George Spencer.

BROWN, George Spencer. 828'.9'1407
Only two can play this game [by] James Keys. New York, Bantam Books [1974, c1972] 150 p. 18 cm. [CT788.B86418A36 1974] 1.65 (pbk.)
I. Title.
L.C. card number for original ed.: 72-80667.

Brown, George, 1818-1880.

CARELESS, James Maurice Stockford 923.271
Brown of the Globe; v. 1, The voice of Upper Canada, 1818-1859. [dist., New York, St. Martin's Press] 1959[i.e.1960] viii, 354p. illus. 26cm. 60-30 6.50 buck.,
1. Brown, George, 1818-1880. 2. Canada—Pol. & govt.—1841-1867. I. Title.

Brown, George, 1835-1917.

BROWN, George, 1835-1917. 260'.0092'4 B
George Brown, D. D., pioneer-missionary and explorer, an autobiography : a narrative of forty-eight years' residence and travel in Samoa, New Britain, New Ireland, New Guinea, and the Solomon Islands. New York : AMS Press, [1978] p. cm. Reprint of the 1908 ed. published by Hodder and Stoughton, London. [BV3672.B7A3 1978] 75-32802 ISBN 0-404-14104-8 : 51.00
1. Brown, George, 1835-1917. 2. Missionaries—England—Biography. 3. Missionaries—Oceanica—Biography. 4. Missions—Oceanica. 5. Oceanica—Description and travel. I. Title.

Brown, Jacob, 1775-1828.

LATHAM, Frank Brown, 1910- 973.5'23'0924
Jacob Brown and the War of 1812, by Frank B. Latham. [1st ed.] New York, Cowles Book Co. [1971] x, 161 p. illus., maps, ports. 22 cm. Bibliography: p. [151] A biography of the Quaker schoolteacher who became one of the prominent military leaders of the American forces in the War of 1812. [E353.1.B9L3 1971] 92 B 70-144121 ISBN 0-402-14006-0 4.95
1. Brown, Jacob, 1775-1828. 2. U.S.—History—War of 1812. I. Title. BIP

Brown, James Nathaniel, 1936-

ISAACS, Stan. 796.332'0924
Jim Brown; the golden year 1964. Englewood Cliffs, N.J., Prentice-Hall [1970] vi, 150 p. illus., ports. 22 cm. (The Golden year series) [GV939.B75I8] 74-107962 4.95
1. Brown, James Nathaniel, 1936- I. Title.

TERZIAN, James P 796.33224
The Jimmy Brown story, by James P. Terzian and Jim Benagh. New York, J. Messner [1964] 190 p. ports. 22 cm. [GV939.B75T4] 64-20151
1. Brown, James Nathaniel, 1936- I. Benagh, Jim, 1937- joint author. II. Title.

TERZIAN, James P. 796.33224
The Jimmy Brown story, by James P. Terzian, Jim Benagh. New York, Messner [c.1964] 190p. ports. 22cm. 64-20151 3.25;3.19 lib. ed.,

1. Brown, James Nathaniel, 1936- I. Benagh, Jim, 1937- joint author. II. Title.

TOBACK, James. 791.43'028'0924
Jim: the author's self-centered memoir on the great Jim Brown. [1st ed.] Garden City, N.Y., Doubleday, 1971. 133 p. 22 cm. [PN2287.B717T6] 77-131108 4.95
1. Brown, James Nathaniel, 1936- 2. Negroes—Psychology. I. Title.

Brown, James Nathaniel, 1936- — Juvenile literature.

MAY, Julian. 796.33'2'0924 B
Jim Brown runs with the ball. Mankato, Minn., Crestwood House [1972] 47 p. illus. 24 cm. (Sports close-up books) Traces Jim Brown's rise to stardom with the Cleveland Browns. [GV939.B75M3 1972] 92 72-77301 ISBN 0-87191-201-5
1. Brown, James Nathaniel, 1936- — Juvenile literature. I. Title.

Brown, James Stephens, b. 1828.

BROWN, James Stephens, b.1828. 289.3'0924 B
Life of a pioneer; being the autobiography of James S. Brown. Salt Lake City, G. Q. Cannon, 1900. [New York, AMS Press, 1971] xix, 520 p. illus. 22 cm. [BX8695.B7A3 1971] 78-134389 ISBN 0-404-08432-X 21.00
I. Title.

BROWN, James Stephens, b.1828. 289.3'3 B
Life of a pioneer : being the autobiography of James S. Brown. New York : AMS Press, 1977. p. cm. (Communal societies in America) Reprint of the 1900 ed. published by G. Q. Cannon, Salt Lake City. [BX8695.B7A3 1977] 77-17574 ISBN 0-404-08432-X : 21.00
1. Brown, James Stephens, b. 1828. 2. Mormons and Mormonism—Biography. I. Title.

Brown, James Steven, 1866-1958.

DR. James Steven Brown, M. D.; the country doctor. [Hendersonville, N.C.? 1959?] 1v. (unpaged) ports. v. 12
1. Brown, James Steven, 1866-1958. I. Cameron, Robert Bruce.

Brown, Jeanie Gordon, 1886-1960.

QUINN, Jane, 1916- 271'.976'024 B
The story of a nun : Jeanie Gordon Brown / Jane Quinn. St Augustine, Fla. : Villa Flora Press, c1978. xii, 469 p. : ill. ; 24 cm. Includes bibliographical references. [BX4705.B84653Q56] 78-60323 15.00
1. Brown, Jeanie Gordon, 1886-1960. 2. Nuns—Florida—Biography. 3. Florida—Biography. I. Title.

Brown, Joan Winmill.

BROWN, Joan Winmill. 791'.092'4 B
No longer alone / Joan Winmill Brown. Old Tappan, N.J. : F. H. Revell Co., [1975] 157 p. : ill. ; 21 cm. [PN2287.B719A34] 75-23195 ISBN 0-8007-0749-4 : 5.95
1. Brown, Joan Winmill. 2. Conversion. I. Title. **BIP**

BROWN, Joan Winmill. 791'.092'4 B
No longer alone / Joan Winmill Brown. London : Hodder and Stoughton, 1976. 187 p., [8] p. of plates : ill., ports. ; 18 cm. (Hodder Christian paperbacks) [PN2598.B727A36 1976] 77-367810 ISBN 0-340-20123-1 : £0.90
1. Brown, Joan Winmill. 2. Conversion. 3. Actors—Great Britain—Biography. I. Title.

Brown, John, 1800-1859.

ABELS, Jules, 1913- 973.71*14*0924
Man on fire; John Brown and the cause of liberty. New York, Macmillan [1971] xviii, 428 p. illus., facsims., ports. 24 cm. Bibliography: p. [399]-405. [E451.A2] 72-117961
1. Brown, John, 1800-1859. I. Title.

AMERICAN Anti-slavery Society. 322'.4
The anti-slavery history of the John-Brown year; being the twenty-seventh annual report of the American Anti-slavery Society. New York, Negro Universities Press [1969] 337 p. 23 cm. Reprint of the 1861 ed. [E451.A51 1969] 76-76852
1. Brown, John, 1800-1859. 2. Slavery in the United States. 3. Harpers Ferry, W. Va.—John Brown Raid, 1859. I. Title. **BIP**

BOYER, Richard Owen, 1903- 973.6'8'0924 B
The legend of John Brown: a biography and a history [by] Richard O. Boyer. [1st ed.] New York, Knopf, 1973 [c1972] xxiii, 627, xvii p. illus. 27 cm. Includes bibliographical references. [E451.B77] 69-10672 ISBN 0-394-46124-X 12.50
1. Brown, John, 1800-1859. I. Title. **BIP**

CONNELLEY, William Elsey, 1855-1930. 973.6'8'0924 B
John Brown. Freeport, N.Y., Books for Libraries Press, 1971. 426 p. map, port. 23 cm. (The Black heritage library collection) Reprint of the 1900 ed. Includes bibliographical references. [E451.C75 1971] 71-164383 ISBN 0-8369-8842-6
1. Brown, John, 1800-1859. I. Title. II. Series.

DU BOIS, William Edward Burghardt, 1868- 923.673
John Brown. Centennial ed. New York, International Publishers [1962] 414 p. illus. 21 cm. Includes bibliography. [E451.D81] 62-21668
1. Brown, John, 1800-1859. I. Title.

DU BOIS, William Edward Burghardt, 1868-1963. 923.673
John Brown. Centennial ed. New York, International Publishers [1962] 414 p. illus. 21 cm. Includes bibliography. [E451.D81 1962] 62-21668
1. Brown, John, 1800-1859.

DU BOIS, William Edward Burghardt, 1868-1963. 973.6'8'0924 B
John Brown. New foreword by Blyden Jackson. Northbrook, Ill., Metro Books, 1972. 406 p. illus. 22 cm. (American crisis biographies) Reprint of the 1909 ed., with a new foreword. Bibliography: p. [397]-400. [E451.D8 1972] 79-99370 ISBN 0-8411-0041-1
1. Brown, John, 1800-1859.

DU BOIS, William Edward Burghardt, 1868-1963. 973.6'8'0924 B
John Brown. New introd. by Herbert Aptheker. Millwood, N.Y., Kraus-Thompson Organization [1973] 25, 414 p. port. 24 cm. Reprint of the 1962 ed. published by International Publishers, New York. Bibliography: p. [405]-408. [E451.D8 1973] 73-15643 ISBN 0-527-25285-9
1. Brown, John, 1800-1859.

FRIED, Albert. 973.6'8'0924 B
John Brown's journey : notes and reflections on his America and mine / Albert Fried. 1st ed. Garden City, N.Y. : Anchor Press/Doubleday, 1978. 293 p., [6] leaves of plates : ill. ; 22 cm. Includes index. Bibliography: p. [277]-282. [E451.F75] 72-79388 ISBN 0-385-05511-0 : 10.00
1. Brown, John, 1800-1859. 2. Abolitionists—United States—Biography. 3. Slavery in the United States—Emancipation. I. Title. **BIP**

GOLD, Michael. 923.673
Life of John Brown: centennial of his execution. New York, Roving Eye Press [1960] 60p. illus. 23cm. 60-174 apply pap.,
1. Brown, John, 1800-1859. I. Title.

THE Life, trial, and execution of Captain John Brown, 973.6'8'0924 B known as "Old Brown of Ossawatomie." Compiled from official and authentic sources. New York, Da Capo Press, 1969. 108 p. illus., ports. 24 cm. (A Da Capo Press reprint edition) "An unabridged republication of the revised edition published [by R. M. De Witt] in New York in 1859." Includes report of Brown's trial before the Circuit Court of Jefferson County, Va., Oct. 25-Nov. 2, 1859. [E451.L73 1969b] 69-18827 10.00
1. Brown, John, 1800-1859. 2. Harpers Ferry, W. Va.—John Brown Raid, 1859. I. De Witt, Robert M., 1827-1877. II. Virginia. Circuit Court (Jefferson Co.)

NELSON, Truman John, 1912- 973.6'8'0924 B
The old man; John Brown at Harper's Ferry [by] Truman Nelson. [1st ed.] New York, Holt, Rinehart and Winston [1973] 304 p. illus. 22 cm. [E451.N5] 72-78120 ISBN 0-03-001051-9 8.95
1. Brown, John, 1800-1859. 2. Harpers Ferry, W.Va.—John Brown Raid, 1859. I. Title.

NOBLE, Glenn. 973.6'8'0922 B
John Brown and the Jim Lane trail / by Glenn Noble. 1st ed. Broken Bow, Neb. : Purcells, c1977. 210 p., [10] leaves of plates : ill. ; 23 cm. Includes index. Bibliography: p. 161-175. [F685.B877N63] 76-42113 10.00
1. Brown, John, 1800-1859. 2. Lane, James Henry, 1814-1866. 3. Abolitionists—United States—Biography. 4. Kansas—History—1854-1861. 5. Underground railroad. I. Title. **BIP**

NOLAN, Jeanette (Covert) 1896- v. 12
John Brown. Decorations by Robert Burns. New York, Messner [1962, 1950] 181 p. illus. 22 cm. "Sixth printing." Bibliography: p. 175-176. 68-57791
1. Brown, John, 1800-1859. I. Title. **BIP**

NOLAN, Jeannette (Covert) 1896- 923.673
John Brown. Decorations by Robert Burns. New York, Messner [1950] 181 p. illus. 22 cm. Bibliography: p. 175-176. [E451.N7] 50-9596
1. Brown, John, 1800-1859. I. Title.

OATES, Stephen B. 973.68'0924 B
To purge this land with blood; a biography of John Brown [by] Stephen B. Oates. [1st ed.] New York, Harper & Row [1970] xii, 434 p. illus., maps, ports. 25 cm. Bibliography: p. 417-420. [E451.O17 1970] 77-95979 10.00
1. Brown, John, 1800-1859. I. Title. **BIP**

QUARLES, Benjamin. 973.6'8'0924
Allies for freedom; Blacks and John Brown. New York, Oxford University Press, 1974. xiv, 244 p. illus. 22 cm. Includes bibliographical references. [E451.Q36] 73-90372 ISBN 0-19-501770-6 7.95
1. Brown, John, 1800-1859. 2. Harpers Ferry, W. Va.—John Brown Raid, 1859. 3. Negroes—History—To 1863. I. Title. **BIP**

QUARLES, Benjamin, comp. 973.6'8'0924 B
Blacks on John Brown. Urbana, University of Illinois Press [1972] xv, 164 p. illus. 21 cm. Bibliography: p. 153-155. [E451.Q37] 72-188132 ISBN 0-252-00245-8 6.95
1. Brown, John, 1800-1859. I. Title. **BIP**

REDPATH, James, 1833-1891. 973.6'8'0924 B
The public life of Capt. John Brown. With an auto-biography of his childhood and youth. Freeport, N.Y., Books for Libraries Press [1970] 407 p. port. 23 cm. Reprint of the 1860 ed. [E451.R39] 79-126251 ISBN 8-369-54785-
1. Brown, John, 1800-1859.

ROSS, Alexander Milton, 1832-1897. 322.4'4'0924 B
Recollections and experiences of an abolitionist, from 1855 to 1865. New foreword by Donald Franklin Joyce. Northbrook, Ill., Metro Books, 1972. xv, 224 p. illus. 23 cm. Reprint of the 1875 ed. [E450.R82 1972] 77-99403 ISBN 0-8411-0074-8
1. Brown, John, 1800-1859. 2. Slavery in the United States—Anti-slavery movements. 3. Slavery in the United States—Fugitive slaves. I. Title. **BIP**

RUCHAMES, Louis, 1917- comp. 973.6'8'0924
John Brown: the making of a revolutionary; the story of John Brown in his own words and in the words of those who knew him, edited and with introductions and commentary by Louis Ruchames. New York, Grosset & Dunlap [1969] 315 p. 21 cm. (Grosset's universal library, UL238) 1959 ed. published under title: A John Brown reader. Includes bibliographical references. [E451.R8 1969] 76-75331 2.95
1. Brown, John, 1800-1859.

SANBORN, Franklin Benjamin, 1831-1917. 973.6'8'0924 B
The life and letters of John Brown; liberator of Kansas and martyr of Virginia. New York, Negro Universities Press [1969, c1885] viii, 645 p. illus., facsims., ports. 23 cm. [E451.S19 1969] 69-18658
1. Brown, John, 1800-1859.

SCOTT, Otto J. 973.6'8'0924
The secret six / by Otto J. Scott. New York : Times Books, [1978] p. cm. Includes index. Bibliography: p. [E451.S36] 78-53310 ISBN 0-8129-0777-9 : 15.00
1. Brown, John, 1800-1859. 2. Harpers Ferry, W. Va.—John Brown Raid, 1859. 3. Kansas—History—1854-1861. 4. Abolitionists—United States—Biography. I. Title.

STAVIS, Barrie. 973.6'8'0924 B
John Brown: the sword and the word. South Brunswick, A. S. Barnes [1970] 190 p. illus., facsims., map (on lining papers), ports., plates. 22 cm. Bibliography: p. 175-181. [E451.S84] 76-81676 6.95
1. Brown, John, 1800-1859.

VILLARD, Oswald Garrison, 1872-1949 973.680924
John Brown, 1800-1859; a biography fifty years after. Gloucester, Mass., P. Smith, [1966, c.1910] xiv, 738p. facsims., map, plates, ports. 21cm. First pub. in 1910 by Houghton. Bibl. [E451.V72] 66-2893 9.00
1. Brown, John, 1800-1859. I. Title.

WARCH, Richard, 1939- comp. 973.6'8'0924 B
John Brown, edited by Richard Warch and Jonathan F. Fanton. Englewood Cliffs, N.J., Prentice-Hall [1973] viii, 184 p. 21 cm. (Great lives observed) (A Spectrum book) Bibliography: p. 179-181. [E451.W27] 73-2620 ISBN 0-13-510164-6 6.95
1. Brown, John, 1800-1859. 2. Harpers Ferry, W. Va.—John Brown Raid, 1859—Sources. I. Fanton, Jonathan F., 1943- joint comp. II. Title.
pap. 2.45; ISBN 0-13-510156-5

WARREN, Robert Penn, 1905- 973.6'8'0924
John Brown; the making of a martyr. New York, Payson & Clarke, 1929. St. Clair Shores, Mich., Scholarly Press, 1970. 474 p. illus., map, port. 22 cm. "Bibliographical note": p. 441-462. [E451.W29 1970] 73-145360 ISBN 0-403-01266-X
1. Brown, John, 1800-1859.

WEBB, Richard Davis. 973.6'8'0924 B
The life and letters of Captain John Brown, who was executed at Charlestown, Virginia, Dec. 2, 1859, for an armed attack upon American slavery, with notices of some of his confederates. Edited by Richard D. Webb. Westport, Conn., Negro Universities Press [1972] xiv, 453 p. port. 16 cm. Reprint of the 1861 ed. [E451.W36 1972] 71-82085 ISBN 0-8371-1560-4
1. Brown, John, 1800-1859.

Brown, John Henry, 1820-1895.

HONIG, Lawrence E., 1948- 070.4'1'0924 B
John Henry Brown: Texian journalist, 1820-1895, by Lawrence E. Honig. [El Paso] Texas Western Press, 1973. 55 p. illus. 24 cm. (Southwestern studies. Monograph no. 36) Bibliography: p. 45-55. [PN4874.B775H6] 73-157534 3.00
1. Brown, John Henry, 1820-1895. I. Series: Southwestern studies (El Paso, Tex.) Monograph no. 36.

Brown, John Mason, 1900-1969.

STEVENS, George, 1904- 792'.092'4 B
Speak for yourself, John; the life of John Mason Brown, with some of his letters and many of his opinions [by] George Stevens. New York, Viking Press [1974] xiv, 308 p. 22 cm. "Books by John Mason Brown": p. 293-294. [PN1708.B74S8] 73-17786 ISBN 0-670-66203-8 10.95
1. Brown, John Mason, 1900-1969. I. Brown, John Mason, 1900-1969. II. Title.

Brown, John Richards, 1837-1922.

BROWN, Winfred Q. 920
By reason of strength. [1st ed.] Los Angeles, De Vorss [1951] 222 p. port. 21 cm. Autobiographical. [CT275.B7653B7] 51-756
1. Brown, John Richards, 1837-1922. I. Title.

Brown, John, Sir, 1816-1896.

JEANS, William T. 669'.142'0922 B
The creators of the age of steel, by W. T. Jeans. Freeport, New York, Books for Libraries Press [1973] p. (Essay index reprint series) "First published 1854." Contents.Contents.—Introduction.—Sir Henry Bessemer.—Sir William Siemens.—Sir Joseph Whitworth.—Sir John Brown.—Mr. S. G. Thomas.—Mr. G. J. Snelus. [TN139.J45 1973] 73-1583 ISBN 0-518-10054-5
1. Bessemer, Henry, Sir, 1813-1898. 2. Siemens, William, Sir, 1816-1896. 3. Whitworth, Joseph, Sir, 1803-1887. 4. Brown, John, Sir, 1816-1896. 5. Thomas, Sidney Gilchrist, 1850-1885. 6. Snelus, George James, 1837-1906. 7. Steel—History. 8. Inventors. I. Title.

Brown, Joseph, 1772-1886—Juvenile literature.

JOSEPH Brown : 973'.04'97 S
or, The young Tennessean / [edited by] Thomas Osmund Summers. New York : Garland Pub., 1977. p. cm. (The Garland library of narratives of North American Indian captivities ; v. 67) Reprint of the 1856 ed. published by E. Stevenson & J. E. Evans, Nashville. Issued with the reprint of the 1856 ed. of Jogues, Isaac. Narrative of a captivity among the Mohawk Indians. New York, 1977. Recounts the life of a young boy captured in Tennessee in 1785 by a band of Cherokee and Creek Indians. [E85.G2 vol. 67] [E99.C9] 970'.004'97 B 92 77-7260 ISBN 0-8240-1691-2 lib.bdg. : 25.00
1. Brown, Joseph, 1772-1886—Juvenile literature. 2. Creek Indians—Captivities—Juvenile literature. 3. Indians of North America—Captivities—Juvenile literature. 4. Cherokee Indians—Captivities—Juvenile literature. 5. Tennessee—Biography—Juvenile literature. I. Summers, Thomas Osmund, 1812-1882. II. Series.

JOSEPH Brown : 973'.04'97 S
or, The young Tennessean / [edited by] Thomas Osmund Summers. New York : Garland Pub., 1977. p. cm. (The Garland library of narratives of North American Indian captivities ; v. 67) Reprint of the 1856 ed. published by E. Stevenson & J. E. Evans, Nashville. Issued with the reprint of the 1856 ed. of Jogues, Isaac. Narrative of a captivity among the Mohawk Indians. New York, 1977. Recounts the life of a young boy captured in Tennessee in 1785 by a band of Cherokee and Creek Indians. [E85.G2 vol. 67] [E99.C9] 970'.004'97 B 92 77-7260 ISBN 0-8240-1691-2 lib.bdg. : 25.00
1. Brown, Joseph, 1772-1886—Juvenile literature. 2. Creek Indians—Captivities—Juvenile literature. 3. Indians of North America—Captivities—Juvenile literature. 4. Cherokee Indians—Captivities—Juvenile literature. 5. Tennessee—Biography—Juvenile literature. I. Summers, Thomas Osmund, 1812-1882. II. Series.

Brown, Joseph Emerson, 1821-1894.

HILL, Louise 973.7'13'0924 B
Biles, 1891-
Joseph E. Brown and the Confederacy. Westport, Conn., Greenwood Press [1972] viii, 360 p. 22 cm. Reprint of the 1939 ed. Bibliography: p. [329]-346. [E559.B876 1972] 70-138612 ISBN 0-8371-5722-6
1. Brown, Joseph Emerson, 1821-1894. 2. Confederate States of America—History. 3. Georgia—History—Civil War, 1861-1865. I. Title. **BIP**

PARKS, Joseph 975.8'03'0924
Howard.
Joseph E. Brown of Georgia / Joseph H. Parks. Baton Rouge : Louisiana State University Press, c1977. x, 612 p., [4] leaves of plates : ill. ; 24 cm. (Southern biography series) Includes index. Bibliography: p. [579]-593. [E664.B8613P37] 74-27192 ISBN 0-8071-0189-3 : 35.00
1. Brown, Joseph Emerson, 1821-1894. 2. Legislators—United States—Biography. 3. Georgia—Governors—Biography. 4. Georgia—Politics and government—1775-1865. 5. Reconstruction. I. Title. II. Series. **BIP**

Brown, Lancelot, 1716-1783.

HYAMS, Edward S. 712'.0922 B
Capability Brown and Humphry Repton, by Edward Hyams. New York, Scribner [1971] vii, 248 p. illus., facsims., port. 26 cm. Bibliography: p. 238-239. [SB470.B7H9 1971b] 71-123850 ISBN 0-684-10273-0 7.95
1. Brown, Lancelot, 1716-1783. 2. Repton, Humphry, 1752-1818. 3. Landscape architecture—Gt. Brit.—History. I. Title. **BIP**

STROUD, Dorothy. 712'.092'4 B
Capability Brown / Dorothy Stroud ; with an introd. by Christopher Hussey. New ed. London : Faber, 1975. 262 p. : ill. ; 26 cm. Includes index. Bibliography: p. 248-250. [SB470.B7S7 1975] 75-318594 ISBN 0-571-10267-0 : 24.95
1. Brown, Lancelot, 1716-1783. I. Title.
Distributed by Faber and Faber; Salem, N. H. **BIP**

Brown, Lesley, 1947-

BROWN, Lesley, 1941- 618.1
Our miracle called Louise : a parents' story / by Lesley and John Brown, with Sue Freeman. New York : Paddington Press : distributed by Grosset & Dunlap, c1979. 188 p. : ill. ; 24 cm. [RG135.B76] 79-15292 ISBN 0-448-22073-3 : 8.95
1. Brown, Lesley, 1947- 2. Brown, Louise, 1978- 3. Fertilization in vitro, Human. 4. Sterility, Female—Biography. 5. Infants—England—Biography. I. Brown, John, 1941- joint author. II. Freeman, Sue, joint author. III. Title. **BIP**

Brown, Lew Buford, 1861-1944.

ZAISER, Marion (Brown) 920.5
The beneficent blaze; the story of Major Lew B. Brown. ed.] New York, Pageant Press [1960] 347 p. illus. 21 cm. [PN4874.B78Z3] 60-4749
1. Brown, Lew Buford, 1861-1944. I. Title.

Brown, Lucius Polk, 1867-1935

WOLFE, Margaret 614.3'092'4 B
Ripley, 1947-
Lucius Polk Brown and progressive food and drug control : Tennessee and New York City, 1908-1920 / Margaret Ripley Wolfe. Lawrence : Regents Press of Kansas, c1978. x, 194 p. : port. ; 24 cm. Based on the author's thesis, University of Kentucky. Includes index. Bibliography: p. 155-158. [RA424.5.B76W64 1978] 77-6637 ISBN 0-7006-0163-5 : 12.50
1. Brown, Lucius Polk, 1867-1935. 2. Public health personnel—United States—Biography. 3. Food adulteration and inspection—Tennessee—History. 4. Drug adulteration—Tennessee—History. 5. Food adulteration and inspection—New York (City)—History. 6. Drug adulteration—New York (City)—History. 7. Progressivism (United States politics) I. Title. **BIP**

Brown, Margaret Wise, 1910-1952.

SHEEL, Eugene M. 813'.5'2 B
Margaret Wise Brown, the foremost innovator of contemporary literature for children: her works and life as seen through her writings and friends, by Eugene M. Scheel. Washington, 1969. vi, 211, XIV l. 29 cm. Thesis (M.A.)—Georgetown University. Bibliography: p. IX-XIV (3d group) [PS3503.R82184Z9] 78-16345
1. Brown, Margaret Wise, 1910-1952. I. Title.

Brown, Mary Anne Day, 1816-1884.

ROSENBERG, Daniel, 973.6'8'0924 B
1953-
Mary Brown : from Harpers Ferry to California / by Daniel Rosenberg. [New York : American Institute for Marxist Studies], 1975. 49 p. ; 28 cm. (Occasional paper - American Institute for Marxist Studies ; no. 17) Cover title. Based on the author's senior thesis, State University of New York at Purchase. Includes bibliographical references. [E449.B8815R67 1975] 75-327914 pbk. : 1.50
1. Brown, Mary Anne Day, 1816-1884. 2. Brown, John, 1800-1859. I. Title. II. Series: American Institute for Marxist Studies. Occasional papers ; no. 17. **BIP**

Brown, Mary Moore, d. 1824.

BROWN, James Moore, 973'.04'97 S
1799-1862.
The captives of Abb's Valley / James Moore Brown. New York : Garland Pub., 1979, c1854 168 p., [2] leaves of plates : ill. ; 19 cm. (The Garland library of narratives of North American Indian captivities ; v. 65) Issued with the reprint of the 1853 ed. of Brown, O. Z. A true narrative of Daniel McCollum. New York, 1978. Reprint of the ed. published by Presbyterian Board of Publication, Philadelphia. Includes bibliographies. [E85.G2 vol. 65] [E99.S35] 970'.004'97 78-18466 ISBN 0-8240-1689-0 : 29.50
1. Brown, Mary Moore, d. 1824. 2. Moore family. 3. Shawnee Indians—Captivities. 4. Indians of North America—Captivities. 5. Frontier and pioneer life—Virginia. 6. Virginia—Biography. 7. Abbs Valley, Va.—History. I. Title. II. Series.

Brown, Moses, 1738-1836.

HAZELTON, Robert Morton. 923.273
Let freedom ring! A biography of Moses Brown. New York, New Voices Pub. Co. [1957] 262p. illus. 23cm. [F83.B86] 57-49143
1. Brown, Moses, 1738-1836. I. Title.

THOMPSON, Mack, 1921- 923.273
Moses Brown, reluctant reformer. Chapel Hill, Published for the Institute of Early American History and Culture at Williamsburg, Virginia by the University of North Carolina Press [1962] 316 p. illus. 22 cm. Includes bibliography. [F83.B875] 62-52443
1. Brown, Moses, 1738-1836. I. Title.

Brown, Oliver Madox, 1855-1874.

INGRAM, John Henry, 1842- 759.2 B
1916.
Oliver Madox Brown; a biographical sketch, 1855-1874, by John H. Ingram. London, E. Stock, 1883. [New York, AMS Press, 1972] x, 238 p. illus. 19 cm. [ND497.B7515 1972] 70-148798 ISBN 0-404-03503-5 10.00
1. Brown, Oliver Madox, 1855-1874.

Brown, Pamela, 1816-

BROWN, Sally, 1807- 917.43'65 B
The diaries of Sally and Pamela Brown, 1832-1838 [and] Hyde Leslie, 1887, Plymouth Notch, Vermont. Blanche Brown Bryant [and] Gertrude Elaine Baker, editors. Springfield, Vt., William L. Bryant Foundation, 1970. 176 p. 23 cm. [F59.P7B67] 77-126883
1. Brown, Sally, 1807- 2. Brown, Pamela, 1816- 3. Leslie, Hyde, 1852- 4. Plymouth, Vt.—Social life and customs. I. Brown, Pamela, 1816- II. Leslie, Hyde, 1852- III. Bryant, Blanche (Brown) 1877- ed. IV. Baker, Gertrude Elaine, ed. V. Title.

Brown, Paul E., 1908-

BROWN, Paul E., 796.33'2'0924 B
1908-
PB, the Paul Brown story / Paul Brown with Jack Clary. 1st ed. New York : Atheneum, 1979. 338 p. : ill. ; 24 cm. [GV939.B77A35 1979] 79-7314 ISBN 0-689-10985-7 : 12.95
1. Brown, Paul E., 1908- 2. Cleveland. Football club (National League, Browns) 3. Cincinnati Bengals (Football club) 4. Football coaches—United States—Biography. I. Clary, Jack T., joint author. II. Title.

Brown, Rollo Walter,

BROWN, Rollo Walter, 1880- 928.1
The hills are strong. Boston, Beacon Press [1953, c1952] 244p. 22cm. Autobiography. [PS3503.R82843Z5] 52-13752
I. Title.

Brown, Sally, 1807-

BROWN, Sally, 1807- 917.43'65 B
The diaries of Sally and Pamela Brown, 1832-1838 [and] Hyde Leslie, 1887, Plymouth Notch, Vermont. Blanche Brown Bryant [and] Gertrude Elaine Baker, editors. Springfield, Vt., William L. Bryant Foundation, 1970. 176 p. 23 cm. [F59.P7B67] 77-126883
1. Brown, Sally, 1807- 2. Brown, Pamela, 1816- 3. Leslie, Hyde, 1852- 4. Plymouth, Vt.—Social life and customs. I. Brown, Pamela, 1816- II. Leslie, Hyde, 1852- III Bryant, Blanche (Brown) 1877- ed. IV. Baker, Gertrude Elaine, ed. V. Title.

Brown, Samuel J., 1845-1925.

BROWN, Samuel J., 973'.04'97 S
1845-1925.
In captivity / Samuel J. Brown. New York : Garland Pub., 1977. 16, 8 p. : ill. ; 23 cm. (The Garland library of narratives of North American Indian captivities ; v. 76) Issued with the reprint of the 1860 ed. of Bone, J. H. A. The Indian captive. New York, 1977. Reprint of an article entitled Reminiscenses of the Sioux massacre and war of 1862, originally published in the Daily & weekly review, Mankato, Minn., 1896? [E85.G2 vol. 76] [E83.86] 977.6'04 B 76-54522 ISBN 0-8240-1700-5 : part of 7 vol. set : 29.50 (set)
1. Brown, Samuel J., 1845-1925. 2. Dakota Indians—Wars, 1862-1865. 3. Dakota Indians—Captivities. 4. Indians of North America—Captivities. 5. United States—Biography. I. Title. II. Series.

Brown, Sandy, 1929-1975.

BROWN, Sandy, 1929- 785.4'2'08
1975.
The McJazz manuscripts : a collection of the writings of Sandy Brown / compiled and introduced by David Binns. London ; Boston : Faber and Faber, 1979. 168 p., [4] leaves of plates : ill. ; 23 cm. Includes index. Discography: p. 151-164. [ML419.B77A3] 79-670355 ISBN 0-571-11219-2 : 16.95
1. Brown, Sandy, 1929-1975. 2. Jazz musicians—Great Britain—Biography. 3. Jazz musicians—Great Britain—Correspondence. 4. Jazz music. I. Binns, David. II. Title.

Brown, Thomas, b. 1766.

BROWN, Thomas, b.1766. 289.8
An account of the people called Shakers : their faith, doctrines, and practice, exemplified in the life, conversations, and experience of the author during the time he belonged to the society : to which is affixed a history of their rise and progress to the present day / by Thomas Brown. New York : AMS Press, [1977] p. cm. (Communal societies in America) Reprint of the 1812 ed. published by Parker and Bliss, Troy. [BX9771.B8 1977] 77-17584 ISBN 0-404-08459-1 : 14.50
1. Brown, Thomas, b. 1766. 2. Shakers. 3. Shakers—New York (State)—Biography. 4. New York (State)—Biography. I. Title.

Brown University.

WAYLAND, Francis, 378.1'12'0924 B
1826-1904.
A memoir of the life and labors of Francis Wayland, D.D., LL.D. [by] Francis Wayland and H. L. Wayland. New York, Arno Press, 1972. 2 v. in 1. ports. 22 cm. (Religion in America, series II) Reprint of the 1867 ed. [LD636 1827.W32] 76-38465 ISBN 0-405-04092-X

1. Brown University. 2. Wayland, Francis, 1796-1865. I. Wayland, Heman Lincoln, 1830-1898. II. Title.

Brown, William Theo.

KANSAS, University. Museum of Art. v. 12
William Theo Brown [by William Inge. n.p. Kansas University. Museum of Art, 1967?] 1 v. (unpaged) 21 cm. (Kansas, University. Museum of Art. Miscellaneous publications no. 67) 67-96013
1. Brown, William Theo. I. Inge, William. II. Title.

Brown, William Wells, 1815-1884.

BROWN, William Wells, 1815-1884. 914.2'04'81
The American fugitive in Europe; sketches of places and people abroad. With a memoir of the author. New York, Negro Universities Press [1969] 320 p. port. 23 cm. "Originally published in 1855." An enlarged edition of the author's Three years in Europe, published in London, 1852. [DA625.B881 1969] 72-88424
1. Gt. Brit.—Description and travel—1801-1900. I. Title.

BROWN, William Wells, 1815-1884. 301.45'22'0924
Narrative of William W. Brown, a fugitive slave. Boston, Anti-slavery Office, 1847. New York, Johnson Reprint Corp. [1970] 110 p. port. 19 cm. (Series in American studies) [E444.B88 1970] 70-18940
1. Slavery in the United States—Missouri.

FARRISON, William Edward. 818'.4'09 B
William Wells Brown: author & reformer. Chicago, University of Chicago Press [1969] xii, 482 p. port. 23 cm. (Negro American biographies and autobiographies) Bibliography: p. 458-471. [E185.97.B89F3] 69-19275
1. Brown, William Wells, 1815-1884. I. Title. II. Series.

Brown, William Wells, 1815-1884—Juvenile literature.

CLARK, Margaret Goff. 810'.9'896073 B
Their eyes on the stars: four Black writers. Champaign, Ill., Garrard Pub. Co. [1973] 174 p. illus. 22 cm. (Toward freedom series) Traces the lives of four black writers who wrote of the Negro experience in eighteenth-and nineteenth-century America. [PS153.N5C5] 920 73-3499 ISBN 0-8116-4804-4 3.78
1. Hammon, Jupiter, 1711-ca. 1800—Juvenile literature. 2. Horton, George Moses, 1798?-ca. 1880—Juvenile literature. 3. Brown, William Wells, 1815-1884—Juvenile literature. 4. Chesnutt, Charles Waddell, 1858-1932—Juvenile literature. I. Cary, Louis F., 1915- illus. II. Title. III. Series.

WARNER, Lucille Schulberg. 301.44'93'0924 B
From slave to abolitionist : the life of William Wells Brown / adapted by Lucille Schulberg Warner. New York : Dial Press, c1976. p. cm. Based on The narrative of William W. Brown, published by the Boston Anti-Slavery Society in 1847. Bibliography: p. Autobiography of William Wells Brown who was born and raised a slave but when freed, devoted his life to the abolitionist movement. [E444.B886W37] 92 76-2288 ISBN 0-8037-9519-X : 5.95
1. Brown, William Wells, 1815-1884—Juvenile literature. 2. Slavery in the United States—Personal narratives—Juvenile literature. 3. Slavery in the United States—Missouri—Juvenile literature. I. Brown, William Wells, 1815-1884. Narrative of William W. Brown, a fugitive slave. II. Title. BIP

Browne, Charles Farrar, 1834-1867.

HINGSTON, Edward Peron, 1823(ca.)-1876. 818'.3'03 B
The genial showman, being the reminiscences of the life of Artemus Ward. With an introd. by Walter Muir Whitehill. Barre, Mass., Imprint Society, 1971. xxv, 359 p. illus. 27 cm. [PS1143.H5 1971] 73-142578 ISBN 0-87636-014-2
1. Browne, Charles Farrar, 1834-1867. I. Title.

Browne, Charles Farrar, 1834-1867—Biography.

SEITZ, Don Carlos, 1862-1935. 818'.3'03 B
Artemus Ward (Charles Farrar Browne); a biography and bibliography. New York, Beekman Publishers, 1974 [c1919] 338 p. illus. 23 cm. (American newspapermen, 1790-1933) Reprint of the ed. published by Harper, New York. Bibliography: p. 319-338. [PS1143.S4 1974] 74-622 ISBN 0-8464-0009-X 18.50
1. Browne, Charles Farrar, 1834-1867—Biography. 2. Browne, Charles Farrar, 1834-1867—Bibliography. BIP

Browne, David Dorey, 1893-

BROWNE, David Dorey, 1893- 610'.92'4 B
The wind and the book : memoirs of a country doctor / David D. Browne. Carlton : Melbourne University Press, 1976. ix, 161 p. ; 22 cm. Label mounted on t.p. verso: Exclusive distributor, ISBS, Inc., Forest Grove, Or. [R674.B76A33] 76-379930 ISBN 0-522-84099-X : 16.50
1. Browne, David Dorey, 1893- 2. Physicians (General practice)—Victoria, Australia—Biography. 3. Medicine, Rural—Victoria, Australia. I. Title. BIP

Browne, John Ross, 1821-1875.

DILLON, Richard H. 353.00820924
J. Ross Browne, confidential agent in old California. Norman, Univ. of Okla. Pr. [c.1965] xix, 218p. illus., map, ports. 23cm. Bibl. [F865.B898D5] 65-11243 5.95
1. Browne, John Ross, 1821-1875. 2. California—Descr. & trav. 3. Texas—Descr. & trav. 4. U. S. Treasury Dept.—Offcials and employees. I. Title. BIP

DILLON, Richard H 353.00820924
J. Ross Browne, confidential agent in old California, by Richard H. Dillon. [1st ed.] Norman, University of Oklahoma Press [1965] xix, 218 p. illus., map, ports. 23 cm. Bibliographical footnotes. [F865.B898D5] 65-11243
1. Browne, John Ross, 1821-1875. 2. California — Descr. & trav. 3. Texas — Descr. & trav. 4. U.S. Treasury Dept. — Officials and employees. I. Title.

RATHER, Lois, 1905- 979.4'04'0924 B
J. Ross Browne, adventurer / Lois Rather. Oakland, CA : Rather Press, 1978. 110 p. : ill. ;27 cm. "Of an edition of 150 this is no. 87." Includes bibliographical references and index. [F865.B898R37] 79-103879 20.00
1. Browne, John Ross, 1821-1875. 2. California—Description and travel—1848-1869. 3. Voyages and travels. 4. Pioneers—California—Biography. 5. California—Biography. 6. Businessmen—California—Biography. I. Title. BIP

Browne, Maximilian Ulysses, Reichsgraf von, 1705-1757.

DUFFY, Christopher, 1936- 923.5436
The wild goose and the eagle; a life of Marshal von Browne, 1705-1757. London, Chatto & Windus [dist. Mystic, Conn., Verry, c.]1964. xiii, 278p. maps, 8 plates (incl. ports.) 23cm. Bibl. 64-6454 7.50
1. Browne, Maximilian Ulysses, Reichsgraf von, 1705-1757. I. Title.

Browne, Rose Butler.

BROWNE, Rose Butler. 370'.92'4 B
Love my children : an autobiography / by Rose Butler Browne and James W. English. 2d. ed. Elgin, Ill. : David C. Cook Pub. Co., [1974] 250 p. ; 18 cm. Includes index. [LA2317.B715A34 1974] 74-80406 ISBN 0-912692-43-X pbk. : 1.95
1. Browne, Rose Butler. 2. Negroes—Education. I. English, James W., joint author. II. Title.

Browne, Thomas, Sir 1605-1682.

BENNETT, Joan (Frankau) 828.3
Sir Thomas Browne, a man of achievement in literature [New York] Cambridge [c.] 1962. 254p. 23cm. Bibl. 62-52250 5.50
1. Browne, Thomas, Sir 1605-1682. I. Title.

BENNETT, Joan (Frankau) 828.3
Sir Thomas Browne, a man of achievement in literature. Cambridge [Eng.] University Press, 1962. 254p. 23cm. Includes bibliography. [PR3327.B4] 62-52250
1. Browne, Thomas, Sir 1605-1682. I. Title.

BROWNE, Thomas, Sir, 1605-1682. 828'.4'09
Sir Thomas Browne's works, including his life and correspondence. Edited by Simon Wilkin. London, W. Pickering, 1835-36. [1st AMS ed.] New York, AMS Press [1968] 4 v. illus. 23 cm. Includes bibliographical references. [PR3327.A18 1968] 68-57225
I. Wilkin, Simon, 1790-1862, ed.

FINCH, Jeremiah Stanton, 1910- v. 12
Sir Thomas Browne; a doctor's life of science & faith. New York, Collier Books [1961, c1950] 251 p. 18 cm. (Collier books. Men of science library, BS32) Bibliography: p. 218-244 68-38284
1. Browne, Sir Thomas, 1605-1682. I. Title.

FINCH, Jeremiah Stanton, 1910- 928.2
Sir Thomas Browne; a doctor's life of science & faith. New York, Schuman [1950] viii, 319 p. illus., ports. 22 cm. [The Life of science library] Bibliography: p. 278-308. [R489.B86F5] 50-10750
1. Browne, Sir Thomas, 1605-1682. I. Title.

HUNTLEY, Frank Livingstone, 1902- 928.2
Sir Thomas Browne, a biographical and critical study. Ann Arbor, University of Michigan Press [1962] 283p. 22cm. Includes bibliography. [PR3327.H8] 62-7706
1. Browne, Thomas, Sir 1605-1682. I. Title.

Browne, Virgil, 1877-

BONNIFIELD, Mathew Paul, 1937- 338.4'7'663620924 B
Oklahoma innovator : the life of Virgil Browne / by Mathew Paul Bonnifield ; epilogue by Virgil Browne. 1st ed. Norman : Published for the Oklahoma Heritage Association by the University of Oklahoma Press, c1976. xiv, 240 p. : ill. ; 22 cm. (Oklahoma trackmaker series) Includes index. Bibliography: p. 236-238. [HD9348.U52B65] 75-41452 ISBN 0-8061-1326-X : 7.75
1. Browne, Virgil, 1877- 2. Soft drink industry—United States—History. 3. Oklahoma City—History. I. Title. II. Series.

Browne, William Montague, 1823-1883.

COULTER, Ellis Merton, 1890- 070.924
William Montague Browne, versatile Anglo-Irish American, 1823-1883, by E. Merton Coulter. Athens, University of Georgia Press [1967] viii, 328 p. illus., ports. 25 cm. Bibliography: p. 306-313. [PN4874.B785C6] 67-27138
1. Browne, William Montague, 1823-1883. I. Title. BIP

COULTER, Ellis Merton, 1890- 070.924
William Montague Browne, versatile Anglo-Irish American, 1823-1883, by E. Merton Coulter. Athens, University of Georgia Press [1967] viii, 328 p. illus., ports. 25 cm. Bibliography: p. 306-313. [PN4874.B785C6] 67-27138
1. Browne, William Montague, 1823- I. Title.

Brownell, Sam,

BROWNELL, Sam, 1887- 927.1
Rodeos and Tipperary including the life of Sam Brownell. Denver, Big Mountain Press [1961] 126p. illus. 22cm. [SF33.B73A3] 61-997
I. Title.

Browning, Elizabeth (Barrett) 1806-1861.

BROWNING, Elizabeth (Barrett) 1806-1861. 821.8 B
Diary by E. B. B.; the unpublished diary of Elizabeth Barrett Barrett, 1831-1832. Edited with an introd. and notes by Philip Kelley and Ronald Hudson. Including psychoanalytical observations by Robert Coles. Athens, Ohio University Press, 1969. xlvii, 358 p. illus., facsims., maps (1 fold.), port. 26 cm. Bibliographical footnotes. [PR4193.A2] 68-18390 12.00
I. Kelley, Philip, ed. II. Hudson, Ronald, ed. III. Title.

BROWNING, Elizabeth Barrett, 1806-1861. 928.2
Elizabeth Barrett to Miss Mitford; the unpublished letters of Elizabeth Barrett Browning to Mary Russell Mitford. Edited and introduced by Betty Miller. New Haven, Yale University Press, 1954 [c1953] xviii, 284 p. illus., ports. 23 cm. "The manuscripts of this correspondence are in the ... library of Wellesley College, Massachusetts." [PR4193.A374 1954a] A 54
I. Mitford, Mary Russell, 1787-1855.

BROWNING, Elizabeth (Barrett) 1806-1861. 928.2
Elizabeth Barrett to Mr. Boyd; unpublished letters of Elizabeth Barrett Browning to Hugh Stuart Boyd. Introduced and edited by Barbara P. McCarthy. New Haven, Published for Wellesley College by Yale University Press, 1955. xxxix, 299p. facsim. 24cm. Bibliographical footnotes. [PR4193.A355] 55-8706
I. Boyd, Hugh Stuart, 1781-1848. II. Title.

BROWNING, Elizabeth (Barrett), 1806-1861. 821'.8 B
Invisible friends; the correspondence of Elizabeth Barrett Barrett and Benjamin Robert Haydon, 1842-1845. Edited by Willard Bissell Pope. Cambridge, Harvard University Press, 1972. xviii, 200 p. illus. 24 cm. Includes bibliographical references. [PR4193.A36 1972] 72-80659 ISBN 0-674-46586-5
I. Haydon, Benjamin Robert, 1786-1846. II. Pope, Willard Bissell, ed. III. Title. BIP

BROWNING, Elizabeth (Barrett) 1806-1861. 928.2
Letters of the Brownings to George Barrett. Edited by Paul Landis with the assistance of Ronald E. Freeman. Urbana, University of Illinois Press, 1958. 392p. illus., ports., facsims. 24cm. 'Bibliographical note': p. [35]-36. Bibliographical footnotes. [PR4193.A33] 57-6950
I. Browning, Robert, 1812-1889. II. Landis, Paul Nissley, 1893- ed. III. Barrett, George Goodin, 1816-1896. IV. Title.

BROWNING, Elizabeth (Barrett) 1806-1861. 821'.8 B
Letters to Mrs. David Ogilvy, 1849-1861, with recollections by Mrs. Ogilvy. Edited by Peter N. Heydon and Philip Kelly. New York, Quadrangle [1973] xxxv, 220 p. illus. 22 cm. [PR4193.A38 1973] 72-92081 ISBN 0-8129-0287-4 7.95
1. Browning, Elizabeth (Barrett) 1806-1861. 2. Ogilvy, Eliza Ann Harris (Dick) I. Ogilvy, Eliza Ann Harris (Dick) II. Title.

BROWNING, Elizabeth (Barrett) 1806-1861. 826'.8
Twenty-two unpublished letters of Elizabeth Barrett Browning and Robert Browning addressed to Henrietta and Arabella Moulton-Barrett. New York, Haskell House, 1971. x, 89 p. 23 cm. Reprint of the 1935 ed. [PR4193.A353 1971] 75-163206 ISBN 0-8383-1313-2
I. Browning, Robert, 1812-1889. II. Cook, Henrietta (Barrett) d. 1860. III. Barrett, Arabella, d. 1868. IV. Title. BIP

BROWNING, Elizabeth (Barrett) 1806-1861. 826'.8
Twenty-two unpublished letters of

Elizabeth Barrett Browning and Robert Browning addressed to Henrietta and Arabella Moulton-Barrett. New York, Haskell House, 1971. x, 89 p. 23 cm. Reprint of the 1935 ed. [PR4193.A353 1971] 75-163206 ISBN 0-8383-1313-2
I. Browning, Robert, 1812-1889. II. Cook, Henrietta (Barrett) d. 1860. III. Barrett, Arabella, d. 1868. IV. Title. **BIP**

BURNETT, Constance (Buel) 928.2
The silver answer; a romantic biography of Elizabeth Barrett Browning. Drawings by Susan Foster. [1st ed.] New York, Knopf, 1955. 216p. illus. 22cm. Includes bibliography. [PR4193.B7] 55-6101
1. Browning, Elizabeth (Barrett) 1806-1861. I. Title.

HEWLETT, Dorothy. 821'.8 B
Elizabeth Barrett Browning, a life. New York, Octagon Books, 1972 [c1952] xiii, 388, xi p. illus. 24 cm. Reprint of the 1st ed. Bibliography: p. 385-388. [PR4193.H4 1972] 72-4251 ISBN 0-374-93883-0
1. Browning, Elizabeth (Barrett) 1806-1861.

HEWLETT, Dorothy. 928.2
Elizabeth Barrett Browning, a life. [1st ed.] New York, Knopf. 1952. xiii, 388 p. illus., ports. 25 cm. Bibliography: p. 385-388. [PR4193.H4] 51-13218
1. Browning. Elizabeth (Barrett) 1803-1861. I. Title.

INGRAM, John Henry, 1842-1916. 821'.8 B
Elizabeth Barrett Browning. New York, Haskell House Publishers, 1973. 264 p. 23 cm. Reprint of the 1888 ed. published by Roberts Brothers, Boston, in series: Famous women. Bibliography: p. [7]-[8] [PR4193.I6 1973] 73-16089 ISBN 0-8383-1722-7
1. Browning, Elizabeth (Barrett) 1806-1861. I. Series: Famous women. **BIP**

INNES, Kathleen Elizabeth (Royds) 821'.8
Elizabeth Barrett Browning & her poetry, by Kathleen E. Royds. London, G. G. Harrap. [New York, AMS Press, 1972] 132, [1] p. 19 cm. (Poetry & life series) Reprint of the 1912 ed. Bibliography: p. [133] [PR4193.I65 1972] 73-148799 ISBN 0-404-52531-8 8.00
1. Browning, Elizabeth (Barrett) 1806-1861. I. Title. II. Series. **BIP**

LUBBOCK, Percy, 1879- 821'.8 B
Elizabeth Barrett Browning in her letters. With a portrait. [Folcroft, Pa.] Folcroft Library Editions, 1973. p. Reprint of the 1906 ed. published by J. Murray, London. [PR4193.L77 1973] 73-15778 12.25
1. Browning, Elizabeth (Barrett) 1806-1861.

LUPTON, Mary Jane. 821'.8
Elizabeth Barrett Browning. [Long Island, N.Y.] Feminist Press, 1972 [c1971] 103 p. illus. 18 cm. (Feminist Press biography no. 1) Bibliography: p. 101-103. [PR4193.L8 1972] 72-182984 ISBN 0-912670-02-9 1.50
1. Browning, Elizabeth (Barrett) 1806-1861.

TAPLIN, Gardner B 928.2
The life of Elizabeth Barrett Browning. New Haven, Yale University Press, 1957. 482 p. illus. 25 cm. Includes bibliography. [PR4193.T3] 57-6344
1. Browning, Elizabeth (Barrett) 1806-1861. I. Title.

TAPLIN, Gardner B 928.2
The life of Elizabeth Barrett Browning. New Haven, Yale University Press, 1957. 482p. illus. 25cm. Includes bibliography. [PR4193.T3] 57-6344
1. Browning, Elizabeth (Barrett) 1806-1861. I. Title. **BIP**

TAPLIN, Gardner B. 821'.8 B
The life of Elizabeth Barrett Browning, by Gardner B. Taplin. [Hamden, Conn.] Archon Books, 1970 [c1957] xv, 482 p. illus., facsim., ports. 23 cm. Bibliographical references includes in "Notes" (p. 427-454) Bibliography: p. 455-466. [PR4193.T3 1970] 77-95029
1. Browning, Elizabeth (Barrett) 1806-1861.

WHITING, Lilian, 1859-1942. 821'.8 B
A study of Elizabeth Barrett Browning. London, Gay and Bird, 1899. [New York, AMS Press, 1973] xxii, 191 p. port. 19 cm. Running title: A study of Mrs. Browning. [PR4193.W5 1973] 71-148332 ISBN 0-404-08924-0 9.50
1. Browning, Elizabeth (Barrett) 1806-1861. I. Title. **BIP**

WILLIS, Irene Cooper. 821'.8
Elizabeth Barrett Browning. New York, Haskell House, 1973. 96 p. front. 23 cm. Reprint of the 1928 ed., issued in series: Representative women. [PR4193.W55 1973] 72-6288 ISBN 0-8383-1622-0 7.95
1. Browning, Elizabeth (Barrett) 1806-1861. I. Series: Representative women (London) **BIP**

WINWAR, Frances, pseud. 928.2
Elizabeth, the romantic story of Elizabeth Barrett Browning. Illustrated by Enrico Arno. [1st ed.] Cleveland, World Pub. Co. [1957] 245 p. illus. 22 cm. [PR4193.W58] 57-5899
1. Browning, Elizabeth (Barrett) 1806-1861. 2. Browning, Robert, 1812-1889. I. Title.

WINWAR, Frances, pseud. 928.2
Elizabeth, the romantic story of Elizabeth Barrett Browning. Illustrated by Enrico Arno. [1st ed.] Cleveland, World Pub. Co. [1957] 245 p. illus. 22 cm. [PR4193.W58] 57-5899
1. Browning, Elizabeth Barrett, 1806-1861. 2. Browning, Robert, 1812-1889. I. Title.

WINWAR, Frances, pseud. 928.2
The immortal lovers: Elizabeth Barrett and Robert Browning, a biography. [1st ed.] New York, Harper [1950] Bibliography: p. 327-335. [PR4231.W55] 50-7506
1. Browning, Elizabeth Barrett, 1806-1861. 2. Browning, Robert, 1812-1889. I. Title.

*WOOLF, Virginia (Stephen) 1882-1941 828.912
Flush, a biography. New York, Harcourt [1966, c.1933] 120p. 18cm. (Harbrace paperback, HPL12) .45 pap.,
1. Browning, Elizabeth (Barrett) 1806-1861. 2. Flush (dog) I. Title. **BIP**

Browning, Elizabeth (Barrett) 1806-1861—Biography.

CLARKE, Isabel Constance. 821'.8 B
Elizabeth Barrett Browning; a portrait, by Isabel C. Clarke. Port Washington, N.Y., Kennikat Press [1970] vi, 304 p. illus., ports. 22 cm. "First published in 1929." [PR4193.C6 1970] 73-103175 ISBN 0-8046-0812-1
1. Browning, Elizabeth (Barrett) 1806-1861—Biography.

LUBBOCK, Percy, 1879- 821'.8 B
Elizabeth Barrett Browning in her letters, by Percy Lubbock. London, Smith, Elder, 1906. [New York, AMS Press, 1974] 382 p. port. 19 cm. [PR4193.L77 1974] 75-148814 ISBN 0-404-08879-1 12.50
1. Browning, Elizabeth Barrett, 1806-1861—Biography. I. Title. **BIP**

Browning, Elizabeth Barrett, 1806-1861—Correspondence.

BROWNING, Elizabeth Barrett, 1806-1961. 821'.8 B
Twenty-two unpublished letters of Elizabeth Barrett Browning and Robert Browning addressed to Henrietta and Arabella Moulton-Barrett. Folcroft, Pa. : Folcroft Library Editions, 1975. x, 89 p. ; 23 cm. Reprint of the 1935 ed. published by the United Feature Syndicate, New York. [PR4193.A353 1975] 75-44045 ISBN 0-8414-3236-8 lib. bdg. : 9.00
1. Browning, Elizabeth Barrett, 1806-1861—Correspondence. 2. Browning, Robert, 1812-1889—Correspondence. 3. Cook, Henrietta Barrett, d. 1860. 4. Barrett, Arabella, d. 1868. I. Browning, Robert, 1812-1889. II. Cook, Henrietta Barrett, d. 1860. III. Barrett, Arabella, d. 1868. IV. Title: Twenty-two unpublished letters of Elizabeth Barrett Browning and Robert Browning ...

Browning, Elizabeth Barrett, 1806-1861—Exhibitions.

NEW York (City). 821'.8'09 B
Public Library. Berg Collection.
Joint lives, Elizabeth Barrett and Robert Browning : a selection of works from the Henry W. and Albert A. Berg Collection of English and American Literature / [compiled] by John D. Gordan ; with a foreword by Lola L. Szladits. [New York] : New York Public Library : distributed by Readex Books, [1975] 40 p. : ill. ; 26 cm. [PR4235.N42 1975] 75-8863 ISBN 0-87104-258-4 pbk. : 5.00
1. Browning, Robert, 1812-1889—Exhibitions. 2. Browning, Elizabeth Barrett, 1806-1861—Exhibitions. 3. New York (City). Public Library. Berg Collection. I. Gordan, John Dozier, 1907-1968. II. Title.

Browning, Elizabeth (Barrett) 1806-1861—Juvenile literature.

ABRAHALL, Clare Constance (Drury) Hoskyns 92
The young Elizabeth Barrett Browning. Illus. by Denise Brown. New York, Roy [1963] 141p. illus. 21cm. 62-18438 3.00 bds.,
1. Browning, Elizabeth (Barrett) 1806-1861—Juvenile literature. I. Title.

*WINWAR, Frances. 920.042
Elizabeth, the romantic story of Elizabeth Barrett Browning [by] Frances Winwar. Illus. by Enrico Arno. New York, Avon [1968, c. 1957] 157p. 18cm. (ZS 131) .60 pap.,
I. Title.

*WOOD, James Playsted 973.9220924(B)
The life and words of John F. Kennedy by James Playsted Wood and the eds. of Country Beautiful magazine. New York, Scholastic [1966,c.1964] 79p. illus. 23cm. .60 pap.,
I. Title.

Browning, John Moses, 1855-1926.

BROWNING, John, 1880- 926.7
John M. Browning, American gunmaker; an illustrated biography of the man and his guns, by John Browning & Curt Gentry. [1st ed.] Garden City, N. Y., Doubleday, 1964. ix, 323 p. illus., map, ports. (1 col.) 24 cm. Bibliography: p. [311]-312. [TS535.B68] 64-19275
1. Browning, John Moses, 1855-1926. 2. Firearms, American. I. Gentry, Curt, 1931- joint author.

Browning, John Moses, 1855-1926 — Juvenile literature.

WINDERS, Gertrude (Hecker) 338.4'7'62340924
Browining, world's greatest gunmaker. With sketches by the author. New York, John Day Co. [1961] 157 p. illus. 21 cm. Includes bibliography. [UF537.B79W5] 61-8286
1. Browning, John Moses, 1855-1926 — Juvenile literature. I. Title.

Browning, Meshach, 1781-1859.

BROWNING, Meshach, 1781-1859. 799.2'924 B
"Forty-four years of the life of a hunter," being reminiscences of Meshach Browning, a Maryland hunter, roughly written down by himself. Rev. and illustrated by E. Stabler. Port Washington, N.Y., Kennikat Press [1972] xxiii, 400 p. illus. 21 cm. (Middle Atlantic States historical publications series, no. 14) Reprint of the 1942 ed. [SK17.B76A3 1972] 70-186088 ISBN 0-8046-8614-9 14.50
1. Browning, Meshach, 1781-1859. 2. Hunting—Maryland—Garrett Co. I. Stabler, Edward, 1794-1883. II. Title. III. Series.

Browning, Orville Hickman, 1806-1881.

BAXTER, Maurice Glen, 1920- 923.273
Orville H. Browning, Lincoln's friend and critic. Bloomington, Indiana University Press, 1957. vii, 351p. 23cm. (Indiana University publications. Social science series, no. 16) Bibliographical references included in 'Notes' (p. 287-332) Bibliography: p. 333-343. [E415.9.B88B44] 57-63150
1. Browning, Orville Hickman, 1806-1881. 2. Lincoln, Abraham, Pres. U. S., 1809-1865. I. Title. II. Series: Indiana. University. Indiana University publications. Social science series, no. 16

Browning, Robert, 1812-1889.

BROWNING, Robert, 1812-1889 928.2
Browning to his American friends; letters between the Brownings, the Storys and James Russell Lowell, 1841-1890. Ed., introd., notes by Gertrude Reese Hudson. New York, Barnes & Noble [c.1965] xvi, 382p. ports. 23cm. Bibl. [PR4231.A3] 65-2653 10.00
I. Browning, Elizabeth (Barrett) 1906-1861. II. Story, William Wetmore, 1819-1895. III. Story, Emelyn. IV. Lowell, James Russell, 1819-1891. V. Hudson, Gertrude Reese, ed. VI. Title.

BROWNING, Robert, 1812-1889. 821'.8 B
The Brownings to the Tennysons; letters from Robert Browning and Elizabeth Barrett Browning to Alfred, Emily, and Hallam Tennyson, 1852-1889. Edited with introd. and notes by Thomas J. Collins. Waco, Tex., Armstrong Browning Library, Baylor University, 1971. 59 p. 24 cm. (Baylor Browning interests, no. 22) Bibliography: p. 5. [PR4231.A3 1971] 73-170389
1. Browning, Robert, 1812-1889. 2. Tennyson, Alfred Tennyson, Baron, 1809-1892. I. Tennyson, Alfred Tennyson, Baron, 1809-1892. II. Title. III. Series: Baylor University, Waco, Tex. Baylor University Browning interests, no. 22.

BROWNING, Robert, 1812-1889. 826.8
Learned lady; letters from Robert Browning to Mrs. Thomas FitzGerald, 1876-1889. Edited by Edward C. McAleer. Cambridge, Harvard University Press, 1966. xii, 232 p. illus., port. 22 cm. "Consists of sixty-six letters in The Carl H. Pforzheimer Library, for the most part heretofore unpublished, supplemented by eight letters or portions of letters previously published." Bibliographical footnotes. [PR4231.A34 1966] 66-11358
I. FitzGerald, Sarah Anne Elizabeth Purefoy (Jervoise) 1809-1899. II. McAleer, Edward C., ed. III. Carl H. Pforzheimer Library, New York. IV. Title.

BROWNING, Robert, 1812-1889. 821'.8 B
Letters of Robert Browning. Collected by Thomas J. Wise. Edited with an introd. and notes by Thurman L. Hood. Port Washington, N.Y., Kennikat Press [1973, c1933] xx, 389 p. illus. 22 cm. Includes bibliographical references. [PR4231.A3 1973] 72-85315 ISBN 0-8046-1735-X 17.50
I. Wise, Thomas James, 1859-1937. II. Hood, Thurman Losson, ed. III. Title. **BIP**

BURDETT, Osbert, 1885-1936. 821'.8'09 B
The Brownings. Boston, Houghton Mifflin, 1929. St. Clair Shores, Mich., Scholarly Press, 1971. ix, 345 p. 22 cm. Bibliography: p. 339. [PR4231.B8 1971] 78-144919 ISBN 0-403-00882-4
1. Browning, Robert, 1812-1889. 2. Browning, Elizabeth (Barrett) 1806-1861. I. Title. **BIP**

CARY, Elisabeth Luther, 1867-1936. 821'.8 B
Browning, poet and man : a survey / by Elisabeth Luther Cary. New York : Haskell House Publishers, [1975] c1899. p. cm. Reprint of the ed. published by Putnam, New York. [PR4231.C2 1975] 74-30337 ISBN 0-8383-1876-2 : 19.95
1. Browning, Robert, 1812-1889. I. Title. **BIP**

CLARKE, Helen Archibald, 821'.8 B d.1926.
Browning and his century. New York, Haskell House Publishers, 1974. ix, 374 p. ports. 22 cm. Reprint of the 1912 ed. published by Doubleday, Page, Garden City, N.Y. [PR4231.C5 1974] 73-18248 ISBN 0-8383-1734-0 17.95
1. Browning, Robert, 1812-1889. 2. Nineteenth century. I. Title. BIP

COHEN, John Michael. 928.2
Robert Browning. London, New York, Longmans, Green [1952] 198 p. illus. 20 cm. (Men and books) [PR4231.C57] 52-14066
1. Browning, Robert, 1812-1889.

DOUGLAS, James, 1867- 821'.8 B 1940.
Robert Browning. [Folcroft, Pa.] Folcroft Library Editions, 1972. 36 p. illus. 34 cm. Reprint of the 1903 ed. published by Hodder and Stoughton, London, in series: The Bookman biographies, 7. [PR4231.D6 1972] 72-12897 ISBN 0-8414-1031-3 (lib. bdg.)
1. Browning, Robert, 1812-1889.

DOUGLAS, James, 1867- 821'.8 B 1940.
Robert Browning / by James Douglas. Norwood, Pa. : Norwood Editions, 1976. iv, 36 p., [1] leaf of plates : ill. ; 34 cm. Reprint of the 1903 ed. published by Hodder and Stoughton, London, in series: The Bookman biographies. [PR4231.D6 1976] 76-2632 ISBN 0-88305-499-X lib. bdg. : 6.50
1. Browning, Robert, 1812-1889. I. Series: The Bookman biographies.

DOWDEN, Edward, 1843- 821'.8 B 1913.
Robert Browning. Port Washington, N.Y., Kennikat Press [1970] xvi, 404 p. illus., facsim., ports. 21 cm. Reprint of the 1904 ed. Includes bibliographical references. [PR4231.D7 1970] 70-103185
1. Browning, Robert, 1812-1889.

DOWDEN, Edward, 1843- 821'.8 B 1913.
Robert Browning. [Folcroft, Pa.] Folcroft Library Editions, 1973. p. Reprint of the 1904 ed. published by J. M. Dent, London, and Dutton, New York, in series: The Temple biographies. [PR4231.D7 1973] 73-15887
1. Browning, Robert, 1812-1889. I. Series: The Temple biographies.

DREW, Philip, comp. v. 12
Robert Browning: a collection of critical essays. Boston, Houghton Mifflin [1966] ix, 278 p. Includes bibliographical notes. 67-85729
1. Browning, Robert, 1812-1889. I. Title.

GOSSE, Edmund William, 821'.8 B Sir, 1849-1928.
Robert Browning; personalia. New York, Haskell House Publishers, 1973. 92 p. port. 23 cm. Reprint of the 1890 ed. published by Houghton Mifflin, New York. [PR4231.G5 1973] 73-17095 ISBN 0-8383-1728-6
1. Browning, Robert, 1812-1889. BIP

HERRING, Jack W., 1925- 821'.8
Browning's Old schoolfellow; the artistic relationship of two Robert Brownings, by Jack Herring. [Pittsburgh] Beta Phi Mu, 1972. vi, 78 p. illus. 24 cm. (Beta Phi Mu. Chapbook no. 9) [PR4231.H45] 72-81905 ISBN 0-910230-09-9
1. Browning, Robert, 1812-1889. 2. Browning, Robert, 1781-1866. The old schoolfellow. I. Browning, Robert, 1781-1866. The old schoolfellow. II. Title. III. Series.

MILLER, Betty Bergson 928.2 (Spiro) 1910-
Robert Browning, a portrait. New York, Scribner [1953] xv, 317p. illus., ports. 25cm. Bibliography: p. 305-310. [PR4231.M5 1953] 53-6955
1. Browning, Robert, 1812-1889. 2. Browning, Elizabeth (Barrett) 1806-1861. I. Title.

MILLER, Betty Bergson 821'.8 B (Spiro) 1910-
Robert Browning, a portrait, by Betty Miller. New York, Scribner [1973] xi, 302 p. illus. 23 cm. Originally published in 1953. Bibliography: p. 287-292. [PR4231.M5 1973] 72-4127 ISBN 0-684-13131-5 7.95
1. Browning, Robert, 1812-1889. 2. Browning, Elizabeth (Barrett) 1806-1861.

MILLER, Betty Bergson 928.2 (Spiro) 1910-
Robert Browning, a portrait. London, J. Murray [dist. Chester Springs, Pa., Dufour, 1965] xv, 302p. illus., ports. 22cm. Bibl. [PR4231.M5] 53-228 5.00
1. Browning, Robert, 1812-1889. 2. Browning, Elizabeth (Barrett) 1806-1861. I. Title.

ORR, Alexandra 821'.8 B (Leighton) 1828-1903.
Life and letters of Robert Browning, by Mrs. Sutherland Orr. New ed., rev. and in part rewritten by Frederic G. Kenyon. Westport, Conn., Greenwood Press [1973] xvii, 431 p. ports. 19 cm. Reprint of the 1908 ed. published by Houghton Mifflin, Boston. [PR4231.O6 1973] 74-136942 ISBN 0-8371-5416-2 16.50
1. Browning, Robert, 1812-1889. I. Browning, Robert, 1812-1889. II. Kenyon, Frederic George, Sir, 1863-1952, ed. BIP

PHELPS, William Lyon, 821'.8 1865-1943.
Robert Browning. [Hamden, Conn.] Archon Books, 1968 [c1932] 536 p. 21 cm. [PR4238.P55 1968] 68-26926
1. Browning, Robert, 1812-1889.

RHYS, Ernest, 1859-1946. 821'.8
Browning & his poetry. London, G. G. Harrap, 1914. [New York, AMS Press, 1972] 127, [1] p. port. 19 cm. (Poetry and life series) Bibliography: p. [128] [PR4231.R5 1972] 73-120992 ISBN 0-404-52529-6 8.00
1. Browning, Robert, 1812-1889. I. Title. II. Series. BIP

ROBERT Browning. v. 12
London, Macmillan; New York, St. Martin' press, 1957. 207p. 18cm. (Macmillan's pocket library)
1. Browning, Robert, 1812-1889. I. Chesterton, Gilbert Keith, 1874-1936. BIP

SHARP, William, 1855- 821'.8 B 1905.
Life and writings of Robert Browning. [Folcroft, Pa.] Folcroft Library Editions, 1973. p. Reprint of the 1890? ed. published by W. Scott, London, New York. Bibliography: p. [PR4231.S5 1973] 73-11423 ISBN 0-8414-7591-1 10.00 (lib. bdg.)
1. Browning, Robert, 1812-1889. I. Title.

SHARP, William, 1855- 821'.8 B 1905.
Life of Robert Browning. Freeport, N.Y., Books for Libraries Press [1971] 220, xxii p. 23 cm. Reprint of the 1890 ed. Bibliography, by J. P. Anderson: p. [i]-xxii. [PR4231.S5 1971] 77-165809 ISBN 0-8369-5963-9
1. Browning, Robert, 1812-1889. I. Title. BIP

SIM, Frances Mary 821'.8 B (Walters)
Robert Browning, the poet and the man, 1833-1846, by Frances M. Sim. New York, Haskell House Publishers, 1972. 212 p. 23 cm. Reprint of the 1923 ed. [PR4231.S6 1972] 72-3196 ISBN 0-8383-1538-0 11.95
1. Browning, Robert, 1812-1889. BIP

SKEMP, Arthur Rowland, 821'.8 B 1882-1918.
Robert Browning. [Folcroft, Pa.] Folcroft Library Editions, 1973. 126 p. port. 23 cm. Reprint of the 1920 ed. published by T. C. & E. C. Jack, London, which was issued as no. 86 of The People's books. Includes bibliographical references. [PR4231.S63 1973] 73-12075 ISBN 0-8414-7593-8 (lib. bdg.)
1. Browning, Robert, 1812-1889. BIP

SPRAGUE, Rosemary, 1922- 821.8
Forever in joy: the life of Robert Browning. Philadelphia, Chilton [c.1965] viii, 171p. illus., facsims., ports. 21cm. Bibl. [PR4231.S65] 65-22542 4.95
1. Browning, Robert, 1812-1889. I. Title.

WAUGH, Arthur, 1866- 821'.8 B 1943.
Robert Browning. [Folcroft, Pa.] Folcroft Press, 1970. xiv, 155 p. port. 21 cm. "Limited to 150 copies." Reprint of the 1900 ed., issued in series: The Westminster biographies. Bibliography: p. [153]-155. [PR4231.W3 1970] 72-190928
1. Browning, Robert, 1812-1889. I. Series: The Westminster biographies BIP

WHITING, Lilian, 821'.8'09 B 1859-1942.
The Brownings; their life and art. New York, Haskell House Publishers, [1973, c1972] xiv, 304 p. illus. 23 cm. Reprint of the 1911 ed. published by Hodder and Stoughton, London. [PR4231.W45 1972] 72-1270 ISBN 0-8383-1433-3 15.95
1. Browning, Robert, 1812-1889. 2. Browning, Elizabeth (Barrett) 1806-1861. I. Title.

Browning, Robert, 1812-1889— Addresses, essays, lectures.

†MOXOM, Philip Stafford, 809 1848-1923.
Two masters : Browning and Turgenief / by Philip Stafford Moxom. Folcraft, Pa. : Folcraft Library Editions, 1976 [c1912] 91 p. ; 23 cm. Reprint of the ed. published by Sherman, French, Boston. [PR4231.M6 1976] 76-28217 ISBN 0-8414-6137-6 lib. bdg. : 15.00
1. Browning, Robert, 1812-1889—Addresses, essays, lectures. 2. Turgenev, Ivan Sergeevich, 1818-1883—Addresses, essays, lectures. 3. Authors, Russian—19th century—Biography—Addresses, essays, lectures. I. Title.

Browning, Robert, 1812-1889— Bibliography.

PETERSON, William S. 016.821'8'09
Robert and Elizabeth Barrett Browning : an annotated bibliography, 1951-1970 / by William S. Peterson. New York : Browning Institute, 1974. xiii, 209 p. ; 24 cm. Includes indexes. [Z8124.5.P48] 74-24915
1. Browning, Robert, 1812-1889—Bibliography. 2. Browning, Elizabeth Barrett, 1806-1861—Bibliography. I. Title. BIP

Browning, Robert, 1812-1889— Biography.

WAUGH, Arthur, 1866- 821'.8 B 1943.
Robert Browning / by Arthur Waugh. Folcroft, Pa. : Folcroft Library Editions, 1977, c1963. xiv, 155 p., [1] leaf of plates : port. ; 22 cm. Reprint of the 1899 ed. published by K. Paul, Trench, Trubner, London, issued in series: The Westminster biographies. Bibliography: p. [153]-155. [PR4231.W3 1977] 77-22495 ISBN 0-8414-9396-0 lib. bdg. : 17.50
1. Browning, Robert, 1812-1889—Biography. 2. Poets, English—19th century—Biography. I. Series: The Westminster biographies.

Browning, Robert, 1812-1889— Biography—Youth.

MAYNARD, John, 1941- 821'.8 B
Browning's youth / John Maynard. Cambridge, Mass. : Harvard University Press, 1977. xix, 490 p. : ill. ; 24 cm. Includes bibliographical references and index. [PR4232.M3] 76-16555 ISBN 0-674-08441-1 : 20.00
1. Browning, Robert, 1812-1889—Biography—Youth. 2. Poets, English—19th century—Biography. I. Title. BIP

Browning, Robert, 1812-1889— Correspondence.

BROWNING, Elizabeth 821'.8 B Barrett, 1806-1961.
Twenty-two unpublished letters of Elizabeth Barrett Browning and Robert Browning addressed to Henrietta and Arabella Moulton-Barrett. Folcroft, Pa. : Folcroft Library Editions, 1975. x, 89 p. ; 23 cm. Reprint of the 1935 ed. published by the United Feature Syndicate, New York. [PR4193.A353 1975] 75-44045 ISBN 0-8414-3236-8 lib. bdg. : 9.00
1. Browning, Elizabeth Barrett, 1806-1861—Correspondence. 2. Browning, Robert, 1812-1889—Correspondence. 3. Cook, Henrietta Barrett, d. 1860. 4. Barrett, Arabella, d. 1868. I. Browning, Robert, 1812-1889. II. Cook, Henrietta Barrett, d. 1860. III. Barrett, Arabella, d. 1868. IV. Title: Twenty-two unpublished letters of Elizabeth Barrett Browning and Robert Browning ...

BROWNING, Robert, 1812- 821'.8 B 1899.
Intimate glimpses from Browning's letter file : selected from letters in the Baylor University Browning collection / assembled by A. Joseph Armstrong ; with an introd. by Roland A. Young. Folcroft, Pa. : Folcroft Library Editions, 1976. p. cm. Reprint of the 1934 ed. published by Baylor University, Waco, Tex., which was issued as v. 37, no. 3-4 of the Baylor bulletin and ser. 8 of Baylor University Browning interests. Includes index. [PR4231.A3 1976] 76-28548 ISBN 0-8414-2886-7 lib. bdg. : 20.00
1. Browning, Robert, 1812-1899—Correspondence. 2. Baylor University, Waco, Tex. Library. 3. Poets, English—19th century—Biography. I. Armstrong, A. Joseph, 1873-1954. II. Title. III. Series: Baylor University, Waco, Tex. Baylor University Browning interests ; ser. 8.

KENMARE, Dallas, pseud. 821'.8 B
The Browning love-story / Dallas Kenmare. Folcroft, Pa. : Folcroft Library Editions, 1976. p. cm. Reprint of the 1957 ed. published by P. Owen, London. [PR4231.A343K4 1976] 76-24457 ISBN 0-8414-5509-0 lib. bdg. : 25.00
1. Browning, Robert, 1812-1889—Correspondence. 2. Browning, Elizabeth barrett, 1806-1861—Correspondence. 3. Poets, English—19th century—Biography. I. Title. BIP

Browning, Robert, 1812-1889— Exhibitions.

NEW York (City). 821'.8'09 B Public Library. Berg Collection.
Joint lives, Elizabeth Barrett and Robert Browning : a selection of works from the Henry W. and Albert A. Berg Collection of English and American Literature / [compiled] by John D. Gordan ; with a foreword by Lola L. Szladits. [New York] : New York Public Library : distributed by Readex Books, [1975] 40 p. : ill. ; 26 cm. [PR4235.N42 1975] 75-8863 ISBN 0-87104-258-4 pbk. : 5.00
1. Browning, Robert, 1812-1889—Exhibitions. 2. Browning, Elizabeth Barrett, 1806-1861—Exhibitions. 3. New York (City). Public Library. Berg Collection. I. Gordan, John Dozier, 1907-1968. II. Title.

Browning, Robert, 1812-1889— Religion and ethics.

LAWSON, E. LeRoy, 1938- 821'.8
Very sure of God: religious language in the poetry of Robert Browning [by] E. LeRoy Lawson. Nashville, Vanderbilt University Press, 1974. xiii, 168 p. 24 cm. Bibliography: p. 159-163. [PR4242.R4L3] 73-21617 ISBN 0-8265-1195-3 8.95
1. Browning, Robert, 1812-1889—Religion and ethics. I. Title.

Browning, Russell.

BROWNING, Norma Lee. 770'.92'4 B
He saw a hummingbird / Norma Lee Browning and Russell Ogg. 1st ed. New York : Dutton, c1978. xi, 143 p., [4] leaves of plates : ill. ; 21 cm. [TR140.B785B76] 78-2559 8.95
1. Browning, Russell. 2. Photographers—United States—Biography. 3. Diabetic rutinopathy—Biography. I. Ogg, Russell, joint author. II. Title. BIP

Brownlow, Louis,

BROWNLOW, Louis, 1879- 923.273
The autobiography of Louis Brownlow. [Chicago] University of Chicago Press [1955-58] 2v. illus. 24cm. Contents.[1] A passion for politics--[2] A passion for anonymity. [JA93.B7A3] 55-5114
I. Title. II. Title: A passion for politics. III. Title: A passion for anonymity.

BROWNLOW, Louis, 1879- 923.273
A passion for politics; the autobiography of Louis Brownlow. [Chicago] University of Chicago Press [1955- v. illus. 24cm. [JA93.B7A3] 55-5114
I. Title.

Brownlow, William Gannaway, 1805-1877.

COULTER, Ellis Merton, 1890- 976.8'04'0924 B
William G. Brownlow; fighting parson of the Southern Highlands, by E. Merton Coulter. With an introd. by James W. Patton. Knoxville, University of Tennessee Press [1971] xxii, 432 p. illus., double map, ports. 23 cm. (Tennesseana editions) Bibliography: p. [401]-412. [E415.9.B9C7 1971] 71-136309 ISBN 0-87049-118-0 6.50
1. Brownlow, William Gannaway, 1805-1877. 2. Tennessee, East—History—Civil War, 1861-1865. 3. Tennessee, East—Politics and government. I. Title. II. Series. **BIP**

Brownson, Orestes Augustus, 1803-1876.

LAPATI, Americo D. 282.0924
Orestes A. Brownson. New Haven, Conn., Coll. & Univ. Pr. [1966, c.1965] 159p. 21cm. (Twayne's U.S. authors ser. 88) Bibl. [B908.B64L3] 1.95 pap.,
1. Brownson, Orestes Augustus, 1803-1876. I. Title.

MARSHALL, Hugh, 1926- 282'.0924 B
Orestes Brownson and the American Republic; an historical perspective. Washington, Catholic University of America Press, 1971. vii, 308 p. 23 cm. Bibliography: p. 293-302. [B908.B64M28] 74-142187 ISBN 0-8132-0508-5
1. Brownson, Orestes Augustus, 1803-1876. I. Title.

MAYNARD, Theodore, 1890-1956. 282'.0924 B
Orestes Brownson: Yankee, radical, Catholic. New York, Hafner Pub. Co., 1971 [c1943] xvi, 456 p. port. 21 cm. "Facsimile of the 1943 edition." Bibliography: p. 433-443. [B908.B64M3 1943a] 70-152267
1. Brownson, Orestes Augustus, 1803-1876.

RYAN, Thomas Richard, 1898- 282'.092'4 B
Orestes A. Brownson : a definitive biography / Thomas R. Ryan. Huntington, Ind. : Our Sunday Visitor, c1976. 872p. ; 27 cm. Includes index. Biography:p. 851-763. [B908.B64R78] 76-29141 ISBN 087973-884-7 : 29.95
1. Brownson, Orestes Augustus, 1803-1876. 2. Philosophers-United States-Biography.

SCHLESINGER, Arthur Meier, Jr., 1917- 922.273
Orestos A. Brownson; a pilgrim's progress. New York, Octagon, 1963 [c.1939] 320p. port. 21cm. Bibl. 63-20896 7.50
1. Brownson, Orestes Augustus, 1803-1876. I. Title.

SCHLESINGER, Arthur Meier, 1917 922.273
A pilgrim's progress: Orestes A. Brownson. Boston, Little [1966, c.1939] xii, 320p. 21cm. (71) Orig. pub. in 1939 and 1963 under title: Orestes A. Brownson: a pilgrim's progress. Bibl. [B908.B64S35 1963] 5.95; 2.65 bds., pap.,
1. Brownson, Orestes Augustus, 1803-1876. I. Title.

SCHLESINGER, Arthur Meier, 1917- 282.0924
A pilgrim's progress: Orestes A. Brownson, by Arthur M. Schlesinger, Jr. Boston, Little, Brown [1966] xii, 320 p. 21 cm. Previous editions published under title: Orestes A. Brownson; a pilgrim's progress. Bibliography: p. [299]-305. [B908.B64S35] 66-29050
1. Brownson, Orestes Augustus, 1803-1876. I. Title.

Broyhill, James Edgar, 1892-

STEVENS, William, 1922- 338.7'68'4100924 B
Anvil of adversity; biography of a furniture pioneer. New York, Popular Library [1968] 211 p. illus., ports. 24 cm. [HD9773.U5S73] 70-752 6.95
1. Broyhill, James Edgar, 1892- I. Title.

Broyles, J. Frank, 1924-

BROYLES, J. Frank, 1924- 796.332'0924 B
Hog wild : the autobiography of Frank Broyles / by Frank Broyles with Jim Bailey. Memphis : Memphis State University Press, c1979. xii, 200 p. : ill. ; 24 cm. [GV939.B78A34] 79-124304 ISBN 0-87870-065-X : 12.95
1. Broyles, J. Frank, 1924- 2. Arkansas. University—Football. 3. Football coaches—Biography. I. Bailey, Jim, 1932- joint author. II. Title. **BIP**

Bruce, James, 1730-1794.

REID, James Macarthur, 1901- 916.3'03'3 B
Traveller extraordinary; the life of James Bruce of Kinnaird [by] J. M. Reid. New York, Norton [1968] 320 p. illus., maps, ports. 22 cm. Bibliographical footnotes. [DT8.R4] 68-16563 6.95
1. Bruce, James, 1730-1794. 2. Ethiopia—Description and travel—To 1900. I. Title.

Bruce, James, 1730 1794—Juvenile literature.

SILVERBERG, Robert. 916.3'03'30924 B
Bruce of the Blue Nile. [1st ed.] New York, Holt, Rinehart and Winston [1969] 232 p. illus., map, ports. 22 cm. Bibliography: p. [225]-226. A biography of a pioneer in African exploration whose extraordinary experiences in his quest for the source of the Nile made many of his contemporaries label him a charlatan. [DT115.S55] 92 69-10246 4.95
1. Bruce, James, 1730-1794—Juvenile literature. I. Title.

Bruce, James, 1892-

BRUCE, James, 1892- 327'.2'0924 B
Memoirs / by James Cabell Bruce. Baltimore : Gateway Press, 1975. xx, 382 p. : port. ; 24 cm. [E748.B854A33] 75-13821
1. Bruce, James, 1892-

Bruce, Lenny.

BRUCE, Honey. 792.2'092'4 B
Honey : the life and loves of Lenny's shady lady / Honey Bruce with Dana Benenson ; edited by Bob McKendrick. 1st ed. Chicago : Playboy Press, 1977c1976 309 p. ; 22 cm. Autobiographical. [PN2287.B726B7] 76-50090 ISBN 0-87223-453-3 : 8.95
1. Bruce, Lenny. 2. Bruce, Honey. 3. Comedians—United States—Biography. 4. Wives—United States—Biography. I. Benenson, Dana, joint author. II. Title.

BRUCE, Lenny. 792.7 B
How to talk dirty and influence people; an autobiography. [1st ed. [Chicago] Playboy Press [1965] xiii, 188 p. 24 cm. [PN2287.B726Z5] 65-25274
I. Title.

BRUCE, Lenny. 790.2'092'4 B
How to talk dirty and influence people : an autobiography / Lenny Bruce. Chicago : Playboy Press, 1972. xi, 240 p., [12] leaves of plates : ill. ; 18 cm. "Originally appeared in serial form in Playboy magazine." [PN2287.B726A3 1972] 74-189393 1.25
1. Bruce, Lenny. I. Title.

CABLE, George Washington 928.1
Mark Twain [and] G. W. Cable; the record of a literary friendship [by] Arlin Turner. [East Lansing] Michigan State University Press [c.]1960. xi, 141p. gBibliographical references included in "Notes" (p.137-141) group port. 22cm. 59-15221 3.50
I. Clemens, Samuel Langhorne, 1835—1910. II. Turner, Arlin, ed. III. Title.

*CAREY, Gary 784.0924
Lenny, Janis, and Jimi. New York, Pocket Books, [1975] 299 p. 18 cm. [ML420] ISBN 0-671-78969-4 1.75 (pbk.)
1. Bruce, Lenny 2. Joplin, Janis 3. Hendrix, Jimi I. Title. **BIP**

GOLDMAN, Albert Harry, 1927- 792.2'092'4 B
Ladies and gentlemen - Lenny Bruce!! By Albert Goldman, from the journalism of Lawrence Schiller. [1st ed.] New York, Random House [1974] 565 p. illus. 25 cm. [PN2287.B726G6] 72-11459 ISBN 0-394-46274-2 10.00
1. Bruce, Lenny. I. Schiller, Lawrence. II. Title. **BIP**

KOFSKY, Frank. 792* 028*0924
Lenny Bruce; the comedian as social critic and secular moralist. [1st ed.] New York, Monad Press; distributed by Pathfinder Press [1974] 128 p. port. 22 cm. Includes bibliographical references. [PN2287.B726K6] 73-91401 ISBN 0-913460-31-1 6.00
1. Bruce, Lenny. **BIP**

Brucker, Wilber Marion, 1894-1968.

BRUCKER, Clara H. 973.921'0924
To have your cake and eat it, by Clara H. Brucker. [1st ed.] New York, Vantage Press [1968] 378 p. ports. 21 cm. Autobiographical. [F196.B7] 77-537 4.95
1. Brucker, Wilber Marion, 1894-1968. 2. Washington, D.C.—Social life and customs—1951- 3. Army wives. I. Title.

Bruckner, Anton, 1824-1896.

DOERNBERG, Erwin 927.8
The life and symphonies of Anton Bruckner. Foreword by Robert Simpson. [New York, Heinman, 1961, c.1960] 235p. 8.50
1. Bruckner, Anton, 1824-1896. 2. Bruckner, Anton, 1824-1896. Symphonies. I. Title.

DOERNBERG, Erwin 780.92
The life and symphonies of Anton Bruckner. Foreword by Robert Simpson. London, Barrie & Rockliff [dist. New York, Dover, 1965, c.1960] 235p. illus. 22cm. [ML410.B88D6] 60-50041 6.00
1. Bruckner, Anton, 1824-1896. 2. Bruckner, Anton, 1824-1896. Symphonies. I. Title.

DOERNBERG, Erwin. 780'.924
The life and symphonies of Anton Bruckner. Foreword by Robert Simpson [Magnolia, Mass., Peter Smith, 1968] xii, 235p. illus., facsims., music, ports. 22cm. (Rebound ed. of the Dover paperback, an unabridged, unaltered repubn. of the work orig. pub. in 1960) Bibl. [ML410.B88D6 1968] (B) 4.25
1. Bruckner, Anton, 1824-1896. 2. Bruckner, Anton, 1824-1896. Symphonies. I. Title.

DOERNBERG, Erwin. 780'.924 B
The life and symphonies of Anton Bruckner. With a foreword by Robert Simpson. New York, Dover Publications [1968, c1960] xii, 235 p. illus., facsims., music, ports. 22 cm. "This Dover edition is an unabridged and unaltered republication of the work originally published in 1960." Bibliography: p. [230]-232. [ML410.B88D6 1968] 68-19176
1. Bruckner, Anton, 1824-1896. 2. Bruckner, Anton, 1824-1896. Symphonies. I. Title.

REDLICH, Hans Ferdinand, 1903- 927.8
Bruckner and Mahler. London, J. M. Dent NewYork, Farrar, Straus and Cudahy [1955] xi, 300p. illus., ports., facsims music. 19cm. (The Master musicians. New ser.) Calendar, Catalogue of works, Personalls, and Bibliography: p. 285-290. [ML410.B88P4] 55-13671
1. Bruckner, Anton, 1824-1896. 2. Mahler, Gustav, 1860-1911. I. Title. II. Series.

SCHONZELER, Hans Hubert. 780'.92'4 B
Bruckner. New York, Grossman Publishers, 1970. 190 p. illus. 22 cm. ([Library of composers, 3]) [ML410.B88S24 1970b] 78-114931
1. Bruckner, Anton, 1824-1896. I. Title. II. Series. **BIP**

WOLFF, Werner, 1883- 780'.92'4 B
Anton Bruckner, rustic genius. Introd. by Walter Damrosch. New York, Cooper Square Publishers, 1973 [c1942] 283 p. illus. 22 cm. Reprint of the ed. published by E. P. Dutton, New York. Bibliography: p. 275-276. [ML410.B88W6 1973] 72-91354 ISBN 0-8154-0449-2 7.50
1. Bruckner, Anton, 1824-1896.

Bruegel, Pieter, the Elder, d. 1569.

BRUEGEL, Pieter, the Elder, d.1569. 759.9493
Bruegel / text by Jacques Dopagne. Bourne End, Bucks. : Spurbooks, [1976] [41] p., [95] p. of plates : chiefly col. ill. ; 18 cm. [ND673.B73D66] 77-354821 ISBN 0-904978-18-4 : £2.50
1. Bruegel, Pieter, the Elder, d. 1569. I. Dopagne, Jacques.

Bruegel, Pieter, the Elder, d. 1569—Juvenile literature.

KLEIN, H. Arthur. 760'.0924
Peter Bruegel the Elder, artist of abundance; an illustrated portrait of his life, era, and art, by H. Arthur Klein & Mina C. Klein. New York, Macmillan [1968] xix, 188 p. illus. (part col.) 26 cm. [ND673.B73K42] 68-20616
1. Bruegel, Pieter, the Elder, d. 1569—Juvenile literature. I. Klein, Mina C., joint author.

Bruguiere, Francis.

ENYEART, James. 770'.92'4 B
Bruguiere, his photographs and his life / by James Enyeart. New York : Knopf, [1977] p. cm. Bibliography: p. [TR140.B79E58] 77-75355 ISBN 0-394-40852-7 : 17.50 ISBN 0-394-73385-1 pbk. : 9.95
1. Bruguiere, Francis. 2. Photography, Artistic. 3. Photographers—United States—Biography. I. Title.

ENYEART, James. 770'.92'4 B
Bruguiere, his photographs and his life / by James Enyeart. New York : Knopf, [1977] p. cm. Bibliography: p. [TR140.B79E58] 77-75355 ISBN 0-394-40852-7 : 17.50 ISBN 0-394-73385-1 pbk. : 9.95
1. Bruguiere, Francis. 2. Photography, Artistic 3 Photographers—United States—Biography. I. Title.

Bruhn, Erik.

GRUEN, John. 792.8'092'4 B
Erik Bruhn, danseur noble / John Gruen. New York : Viking Press, 1979. xii, 252 p., [19] leaves of plates : ill. ; 25 cm. Includes index. Filmography: p. 239-240. [GV1785.B78G78] 79-12719 ISBN 0-670-29771-2 : 14.95
1. Bruhn, Erik. 2. Dancers—Denmark—Biography. 3. Choreographers—Denmark—Biography. I. Title.

Brummell, George Bryan, 1778-1840.

COLE, Hubert. 941.07'3'0924 B
Beau Brummell / Hubert Cole. New York : Mason/Charter, 1977. 240 p., [6] leaves of plates : ill. ; 23 cm. Includes index. Bibliography: p. 226-228. [DA538.B6C54 1977] 77-2462 ISBN 0-88405-593-0 : 12.95
1. Brummell, George Bryan, 1778-1840. 2. Great Britain—Court and courtiers—Biography. 3. London—Social life and customs.

COLE, Hubert. 941.07'3'0924 B
Beau Brummell / Hubert Cole. New York : Mason/Charter, 1977. 240 p., [6] leaves of plates : ill. ; 23 cm. Includes index. Bibliography: p. 226-228. [DA538.B6C54 1977] 77-2462 ISBN 0-88405-593-0 : 12.95
1. Brummell, George Bryan, 1778-1840. 2. Great Britain—Court and courtiers—Biography. 3. London—Social life and customs.

FRANZERO, Charles Marie, 1892- 923.942
Beau Brummell, his life and times. New York, J. Day Co. [1958] 256 p. illus. 22 cm. London ed. (A. Redman) has title: The life and times of Beau Brummell. [DA538.B6F7 1958a] 59-5452
1. Brummell, George Bryan, 1778-1840.

TENENBAUM, Samuel, 1902- 942.07'3'0924 B
The incredible Beau Brummell. South Brunswick [N.J.] A. S. Barnes [1967] 285 p. 22 cm. [DA538.B6T4] 67-10697
1. Brummell, George Bryan, 1778-1840. I. Title.

WOOLF, Virginia Stephen, 1882-1941. 941.07'3'0924 B
Beau Brummell / Virginia Woolf. Folcroft, Pa. : Folcroft Library Editions, 1977 [c1930] p. cm. Reprint of the ed. published by Rimington & Hooper, New York. [DA538.B6W6 1977] 77-22436 ISBN 0-8414-9616-1 lib. bdg. : 12.50
1. Brummell, George Bryan, 1778-1840. 2. Great Britain—Court and courtiers—Biography. **BIP**

Brunel, Isambard Kingdom, 1806-1859.

BRUNEL, Isambard, 1837- 624'.092'4 B
The life of Isambard Kingdom Brunel, civil engineer. A reprint with an introd. by L. T. C. Rolt. Rutherford [N.J.] Fairleigh Dickinson University Press [1972] xxviii, 568 p. illus. 22 cm. Reprint of the 1870 edition. Includes bibliographical references. [TA140.B75B6 1972] 72-850 ISBN 0-8386-1201-6 25.00
1. Brunel, Isambard Kingdom, 1806-1859. 2. Civil engineering. I. Title.

HAY, Peter. 624'.092'4 B
Brunel—his achievements in the transport revolution. Reading, Osprey Publishing, 1973. ix, 134, [24] p. illus., map, plans, ports. 22 cm. (The Great innovators) Includes index. Bibliography: p. 130. [TA140.B75H38] 74-152976 ISBN 0-85045-143-4 £2.45
1. Brunel, Isambard Kingdom, 1806-1859.

PUDNEY, John, 1909- 624'.092'4 B
Brunel and his world. London, Thames and Hudson [1974] 128 p. illus. 24 cm. Bibliography: p. 118. [TA140.B75P82] 74-166684 ISBN 0-500-13047-7
1. Brunel, Isambard Kingdom, 1806-1859. I. Title.
Distributed by Transatlantic Arts; 8.75 **BIP**

ROLT, Lionel Thomas Caswell 926.2
Isambard Kingdom Brunel, a biography. New York, St. Martin's Press, 1959[ ] ix, 345p. (bibl.) illus. 23cm. 59-10431 6.0
1. Brunel, Isambard Kingdom, 1806-1859. I. Title.

ROLT, Lionel Thomas Caswell, 1910- 926.2
Isamb ard Kingdom Brunel, a biography. New York, St. Martin's Press, 1959. 345p. illus. 23cm. Includes bibliography. [TA140.B75R6 1959] 59-10431
1. Brunel, Isambard Kingdom, 1806-1859. I. Title.

ROLT, Lionel Thomas Caswell, 1910- 926.2
Isambard Kingdom Brunel, a biography. London, New York, Longmans, Green [1957] 345 p. illus. 23 cm. [TA140.B75R6 1957] 57-3475
1. Brunel, Isambard Kingdom, 1806-1859.

ROLT, Lionel Thomas Caswell, 1910- 926.2
Isambard Kingdom Brunel, a biography. London, New York, Longmans, Green [1957] 345p. illus. 23cm. [TA140.B75R6 1957] 57-3475
1. Brunel, Isambard Kingdom, 1806-1859. I. Title.

ROLT, Lionel Thomas Caswell, 1910- 624'.0924 B
The story of Brunel [by] L. T. C. Rolt. New York, Abelard-Schuman [1968, c1965] 125 p. illus., port. 22 cm. The life of the nineteenth-century English engineer who was responsible for many innovations and advances in the building of bridges, tunnels, and early trans-Atlantic steamships. [TA140.B75R62 1968] 92 68-14298 3.50
1. Brunel, Isambard Kingdom, 1806-1859. I. Title.

Brunelleschi, Filippo, 1377-1446.

MANETTI, Antonio, 1423-1497. 720'.924 B
The life of Brunelleschi, by Antonio di Tuccio Manetti. Introd., notes, and critical text ed. by Howard Saalman. English translation of the Italian text by Catherine Enggass. University Park, Pennsylvania State University Press [1970] vii, 176 p. illus., facsims. 24 cm. English and Italian. Translation of Vita di Filippo di Ser Brunelleschi. [NA1123.B8M33] 68-8183 12.50
1. Brunelleschi, Filippo, 1377-1446. **BIP**

Brunner, Heinrich Emil, 1889-1966.

HUMPHREY, James Edward. 230'.092'4
Emil Brunner / by J. Edward Humphrey. Waco, Tex. : Word Books, c1976. 183 p. ; 23 cm. (Makers of the modern theological mind) Bibliography: p. 180-183. [BX4827.B67H85] 75-36186 ISBN 0-87680-453-9 : 6.95
1. Brunner, Heinrich Emil, 1889-1966. **BIP**

Bruno, Giordano, 1548-1600.

BOULTING, William. 195 B
Giordano Bruno, his life, thought, and martyrdom. Freeport, N.Y., Books for Libraries Press [1972] viii, 315 p. 22 cm. Reprint of the 1914 ed. Includes bibliographical references. [B783.Z7B6 1972] 72-5438 ISBN 0-8369-6898-0
1. Bruno, Giordano, 1548-1600.

SINGER, Dorothea (Waley) 1884- 195
Giordano Bruno; his life and thought. With annotated translation of his work, On the infinite universe and worlds. New York, Greenwood Press, 1968 [c1950] xi, 389 p. illus., charts, maps, ports. 24 cm. Appendices (p. 203-224): List of Bruno's writings.—Printers of Bruno.—Surviving manuscripts of Bruno's works.—Select bibliography of Bruno's philosophy. Includes bibliographical references. [B783.Z7S45 1968] 68-23329
1. Bruno, Giordano, 1548-1600. 2. Infinite. I. Bruno, Giordano, 1548-1600. On the infinite universe and worlds. II. Title.

Bruno, Henry Augustine,

CALITRI, Princine M 659.2'0924 (B)
Harry A. Bruno, public relations pioneer, by Princine M. Calitri. Minneapolis, T. S. Denison [1968] 298 p. 22 cm. (Men of achievement series) [HE9781.C3] 67-31416
1. Bruno, Henry Augustine, 2. Public relations-Air lines. I. Title.

Brunson, Alfred, 1793-1882.

BRUNSON, Alfred, 1793-1882. 287'.1'0924 B
A western pioneer / Alfred Brunson. New York : Arno Press, 1975. 418, 413 p. ; 21 cm. (The Mid-American frontier) Reprint of the 1872-1879 ed. published by Hitchcock and Walden, Cincinnati. [BX8495.B78A3 1975] 75-89 ISBN 0-405-06856-5 : 46.00
1. Brunson, Alfred, 1793-1882. I. Title. II. Series.

BRUNSON, Alfred, 1793-1882. 287'.1'0924 B
A western pioneer / Alfred Brunson. New York : Arno Press, 1975. 418, 413 p. ; 21 cm. (The Mid-American frontier) Reprint of the 1872-1879 ed. published by Hitchcock and Walden, Cincinnati. [BX8495.B78A3 1975] 75-89 ISBN 0-405-06856-5 : 46.00
1. Brunson, Alfred, 1793-1882. I. Title. II. Series.

Brunson, Howard,

BRUNSON, Howard, 1884- 926.22338
The oilman who didn't want to become a millionaire, his own story. [1st ed.] New York, Exposition Press [1955] 83p. illus. 21cm. [HD9570.B7A3] 55-12124
I. Title.

Brushton, N.Y.—Genealogy.

SAXTON, Kermit E., 1923- 929'.2'0973
Life's book of recollections : Gale Rd. settlers, 1825-1975 / [by Kermit E. Saxton]. [Brushton, N.Y.] : Saxton, c1975. 84 p. : ill., ports. ; 23 cm. Cover title. [F129.B76S28] 76-350311
1. Brushton, N.Y.—Genealogy. I. Title.

Bruskett, Lodowick, ca. 1545-ca. 1612.

SISSON, Charles Jasper, 1885- ed. 820.9003
Thomas Ladge and other Elizabethans. ed. by Charles J. Sisson. New York, Octagon 1966 [c1933] xii, 526p. illus., maps, geneal, tables 24cm. [PR2298.S5 1966] 66-18029 11.00
1. Lodge Thomas, 1558 -1625. 2. Barnes, Barnabe. 1569 -1609. 3. Bruskett, Lodowick, ca. 1545-ca. 1612. 4. Lyly John, 1554?-1606. 5. Buck. George d. Sir 1623. I. Eccles. Mark. II. Jones. Deborah. III. Title.
Contents omitted.

Brute de Remur, Simon Guillaume Gabriel, Bp., 1779-1839.

BAYLEY, James Roosevelt, Abp., 1814-1877. 282'.0924 B
Frontier bishop; the life of Bishop Simon Brute. Edited by Albert J. Nevins. Huntington, Ind., Our Sunday Visitor, inc. [1971] 92 p. illus., maps, port. 21 cm. Originally published in 1861 as the introd. to Memoirs of the Right Reverend Simon Wm. Gabriel Brute. [BX4705.B88B34 1971] 70-147935 1.95 (pbk)
1. Brute de Remur, Simon Guillaume Gabriel, Bp., 1779-1839. I. Title. **BIP**

HUGHES, Riley. 922.273
Frontier bishop, Simon Gabriel Brute. Illustrated by Syl Sowinski. Milwaukee, Bruce Pub. Co. [1959] 152p. illus. 22cm. (Catholic treasury books) [BX4705.B88H8] 59-13227
1. Brute de Remur, Simon Guillaume Gabriel, Bp., 1779-1839. I. Title.

Bryan, Charles Valentine,

BRYAN, Charles Valentine, 1885- 926.55
Born to be hung; the devil's own story, by Charles V. Bryan (Paul Pry) [Lynwood, Calif., 1950] 268 p. 23 cm. [Z232.B9A3] 50-58191
I. Title.

Bryan, James Alexander, 1863-1941.

BLAKELY, Hunter Bryson, 1894- 922.573
Religion in shoes; Brother Bryan of Birmingham. With an introd. by Benjamin R. Lacy. [Rev. ed.] Richmond, John Knox Press [1953] 188 p. illus. 21 cm. [BX9225.B764B5 1953] 53-1245
1. Bryan, James Alexander, 1863-1941. I. Title.

Bryan, William Jennings, 1860-1925.

BRYAN, William Jennings, 1860-1925. 973.91'0924 B
The memoirs of William Jennings Bryan, by himself and his wife Mary Baird Bryan. New York, Haskell House, 1971. 560 p. illus., ports. 22 cm. Reprint of the 1925 ed. [E664.B87B8 1971b] 72-130261 ISBN 0-8383-1165-2
I. Bryan, Mary (Baird) 1861-1930, joint author. **BIP**

BRYAN, William Jennings, 1860-1925. 973.91'0924 B
The memoirs of William Jennings Bryan, by himself and his wife Mary Baird Bryan. Port Washington, N.Y., Kennikat Press [1971] 2 v. (560 p.) illus., facsims., ports. 23 cm. (Kennikat Press scholarly reprints. American history and culture in the nineteenth century) Reprint of the 1925 ed. [E664.B87B8 1971] 73-137904 ISBN 0-8046-1472-5
I. Bryan, Mary Baird, 1861-1930.

COLETTA, Paolo Enrico, 1916- 973.91'0924 B
William Jennings Bryan, by Paolo E. Coletta. Lincoln, University of Nebraska Press, 1964-[69] 3 v. 24 cm. Contents.Contents.—1. Political evangelist, 1860-1908.—2. Progressive politician and moral statesman, 1909-1915.—3. Political puritan, 1915-1925. Includes bibliographies. [E664.B87C55] 64-11352
1. Bryan, William Jennings, 1860-1925. **BIP**

GLAD, Paul W. 923.273
The trumpet soundeth; William Jennings Bryan and his democracy, 1896-1912. [Lincoln] University of Nebraska Press [c.] 1960. xii, 242p. Bibl. references included in "Notes" (p.179-217)"Bibliographical essay":p.219-230. illus., ports. 24cm. 60-12259 4.75
1. Bryan, William Jennings, 1860-1925. I. Title. **BIP**

GLAD, Paul W., 1926- comp. 973.91'0924
William Jennings Bryan; a profile, edited by Paul W. Glad. [1st ed.] New York, Hill and Wang [1968] xxi, 251 p. 22 cm. (American profiles) "Bibliographical note": p. 245-248. [E664.B87G56] 68-14784 5.95
1. Bryan, William Jennings, 1860-1925.

HIBBEN, Paxton, 1880-1928. 973.91'0924 B
The peerless leader, William Jennings Bryan. Introd. by Charles A. Beard. New York, Russell & Russell [1967] xvi, 446 p. illus., ports. 22 cm. "The first twenty-one chapters ... were completed by Paxton Hibben before his untimely death. The book ... was completed by C. Hartley Grattan." Reprint of the 1929 ed. Bibliography: p. 409-419. [E664.B87H6 1967] 66-27099
1. Bryan, William Jennings, 1860-1925. I. Grattan, Clinton Hartley, 1902- ed. II. Title. **BIP**

KOENIG, Louis William, 1916- 973.91'0924 B
Bryan; a political biography of William Jennings Bryan, by Louis W. Koenig. New York, Putnam [1971] 736 p. 24 cm. Bibliography: p. [705]-719. [E664.B87K57 1971] 79-97088 14.95
1. Bryan, William Jennings, 1860-1925. 2. U.S.—Politics and government—1865-1933.

LEVINE, Lawrence W. 923.273
Defender of the faith: William Jennings Bryan; the last decade, 1915-1925. New York, Oxford [c.]1965. cix, 386p. port. 22cm. Bibl. [E664.B87L4] 65-12465 7.50
1. Bryan, William Jennings, 1860-1925. I. Title.

LEVINE, Lawrence W. 923.273
Defender of the faith: William Jennings Bryan; the last decade, 1915-1925. New York, Oxford Univ. Pr. [1968, c.1965] ix, 386p. port. 20cm. (GB 254) Bibl. [E664,B87L4] 65-12465 2.25 pap.,
I. Bryan, William Jennings, 1860-1925. II. Title.

POTTERF, Rex M. 973.91'092'4 B
William Jennings Bryan, the great commoner / by Rex M. Potterf ; prepared by the staff of the Allen County-Fort Wayne Historical Society. Fort Wayne : [s.n.], 1961. 96 p. : port. ; 22 cm. "Reprinted from an original paper published by the Allen County-Fort Wayne Historical Society." [E664.B87P67 1961] 75-317100
1. Bryan, William Jennings, 1860-1925.

THOMPSON, Charles Willis, 1871-1946. 973.9'0922
Presidents I've known and two near Presidents. Freeport, N.Y., Books for Libraries Press [1970, c1956] 386 p. 23 cm. (Essay index reprint series) Contents.Contents.—Hanna-McKinley.—Bryan.—Roosevelt.—Taft.—Wilson.—Harding.—Coolidge. [E176.1.T45 1970] 71-93383
1. Hanna, Marcus Alonzo, 1837-1904. 2. McKinley, William, Pres. U.S., 1843-1901. 3. Bryan, William Jennings, 1860-1925. 4. Roosevelt, Theodore, Pres. U.S., 1858-1919. 5. Taft, William Howard, Pres. U.S., 1857-1930. 6. Wilson, Woodrow, Pres. U.S., 1856-1924. 7. Harding, Warren Gamaliel, Pres. U.S., 1865-1923. 8. Coolidge, Calvin, Pres. U.S., 1872-1933. I. Title. **BIP**

Bryan, William Jennings, 1860-1925—Juvenile literature.

KOSNER, Alice. 973.91'0924 B
The voice of the people: William Jennings Bryan. New York, J. Messner [1970] 190 p. 22 cm. Bibliography: p. 185-186. The life of the lawyer, orator, and politician who ran unsuccessfully for the Presidency three times. [E664.B87K6] 92 75-100562 3.50
1. Bryan, William Jennings, 1860-1925—Juvenile literature. I. Title.

Bryant, Anita.

BRYANT, Anita. 784'.092'4 B
Amazing grace. Boston, G. K. Hall, 1973 [c1971] 169 p. 25 cm. Large print ed. [ML420.B84A28 1973] 73-9985 ISBN 0-8161-6136-4 6.95 (lib. bdg.)
1. Bryant, Anita. I. Title.

BRYANT, Anita. 784'.0924 [B]
Amazing grace. New York, Bantam Books [1974, c.1971] 132 p. 18 cm. Autobiographical. [ML420.B84A28] 1.25 (pbk.)
I. Title.
L.C. card no. for the hardbound edition: 73-160276. **BIP**

Bryant, Elizabeth Brimmer (Sohier) 1823-1916.

BRYANT, William Sohier, 1861- 920.7
Elizabeth Brimmer Sohier (Mrs. Henry Bryant) 1823-1916; her biography. New York, 1950. ix, 93 p. illus., ports. 27 cm. "Private edition of 100 copies ... No. 84." [CT275.B7842B7] 50-11385
1. Bryant, Elizabeth Brimmer (Sohier) 1823-1916. I. Title.

Bryant family.

KENDRICK, Mattie (Bryant) 1889- 929'.2'0973
My dearest one. Greenville, S. C., 1955. 126p. illus. 22cm. Autobiographical. [CS71.B885 1955] 56-29818
1. Bryant family. I. Title.

Bryant, James McKinley.

BRYANT, James McKinley. 917.3'03'90924 B
Loves and tragedies; an autobiography. Dallas, Rocket Pub. Co., [1968] 294 p. illus., ports. 24 cm. [CT275.B78415A3] 68-58998 9.95
I. Title.

Bryant, Louise Frances (Stevens) 1885-1956.

BEAM, Lura, 1887- 920.7
Bequest from a life; a biography of Louise Stevens Bryant. Baltimore, Manufactured by Waverly Press [1963] 194 p. illus. 22 cm. Full name: Lura Ella Beam. [R154.B8633B4] 63-3608
1. Bryant, Louis Frances (Stevens) 1885-1956. I. Title.

BEAM, Lura Ella, 1887- 920.7
Bequest from a life; a biography of Louise Stevens Bryant. Baltimore, Author. [dist. Williams & Wilkins. c.1963] 194p. illus. 22cm. 63-3608 5.00
1. Bryant, Louise Frances (Stevens) 1885-1956. I. Title.

Bryant, Paul W.

BRYANT, Paul W. 796.33'2'0924 B
Bear; the hard life and good times of Alabama's Coach Bryant [by] Paul W. Bryant and John Underwood. New York, Bantam Books [1975, c1974] xii, 367 p. illus. 18 cm. [GV939.B79A32 1975] 1.75 (pbk.)
1. Bryant, Paul W. 2. Football. 3. Football coaching. I. Underwood, John, 1934- II. Title.
L.C. card number for original ed.: 74-17177.

BRYANT, Paul W. 796.33'2'0924 B
Bear; the hard life and good times of Alabama's Coach Bryant [by] Paul W. Bryant [and] John Underwood. [1st ed.] Boston, Little, Brown [1975, c1974] xii, 342 p. illus. 22 cm. "A Sports illustrated book." [GV939.B79A32 1975] 74-17177 ISBN 0-316-11325 5 7.95
1. Bryant, Paul W. 2. Football. 3. Football coaching. I. Underwood, John, 1934- II. Title.

BYNUM, Mike. 796.332'.092'4 B
Bryant, the man, the myth / by Mike Bynum. Atlanta, Ga. : Cross Roads Books, c1979. 191 p. : ill. ; 23 cm. [GV939.B79B9] 79-53913 8.95
1. Bryant, Paul W. 2. Football coaches—Biography. I. Title.
Publisher's Address : 2751 Buford Hwy., N.E., Ste. 720, Atlanta, GA 30324

Bryant, Paul W.—Juvenile literature.

LEE, S. C. 796.33'2'0924 B
Young Bear : the legend of Bear Bryant's boyhood / by S. C. Lee. Huntsville, Ala. : Strode Publishers, c1978. 143 p. : ill. ; 23 cm. Presents highlights from the childhood of Paul "Bear" Bryant, who later became football coach at the University of Alabama. [GV939.B79L43] 92 77-14848 ISBN 0-87397-127-2 : 5.95
1. Bryant, Paul W.—Juvenile literature. 2. Football coaches—United States—Biography—Juvenile literature. I. Title. **BIP**

Bryant, Traphes.

BRYANT, Traphes. 973'.0992
Dog days at the White House : the outrageous memoirs of the Presidential kennel keeper / Traphes Bryant, with Frances Spatz Leighton. New York : Macmillan, 1975. 343 p., [16] leaves of plates : ill. ; 24 cm. Includes index. [E840.6.B79] 75-6504 ISBN 0-02-517990-X : 10.95
1. Bryant, Traphes. 2. Presidents—United States—Biography. 3. Presidents—United States—Wives. 4. Washington, D.C. White House. 5. Dogs—Anecdotes, facetiae, satire, etc. I. Leighton, Frances Spatz. II. Title. **BIP**

BRYANT, Traphes. 973.9'092'2
Dog days at the White House : the outrageous memoirs of the Presidential kennel keeper / Traphes Bryant, with Frances Spatz Leighton. New York : Pocket Books, 1976, c1975. xvi, 397 p., [8] leaves of plates : ill. ; 18 cm. Includes index. [E840.6.B79 1976] 77-152546 ISBN 0-671-80533-9 : 1.95
1. Bryant, Traphes. 2. Presidents—United States—Biography. 3. Presidents—United States—Wives. 4. Washington, D.C. White House. 5. Dogs—Anecdotes, facetiae, satire, etc. I. Leighton, Frances Spatz, joint author. II. Title.

Bryant, William Cullen, 1794-1878.

BIGELOW, John, 1817-1911. 811'.3 B
William Cullen Bryant. Detroit, Gale Research Co., 1970. vi, 355 p. port. 23 cm. Reprint of the 1890 ed. [PS1181.B5 1970] 79-78114
1. Bryant, William Cullen, 1794-1878.

BIGELOW, John, 1817-1911. 811'.3 B
William Cullen Bryant. [New York] Arno [1970] vi, 355 p. port. 23 cm. (The American journalists) Reprint of the 1890 ed. [PS1181.B5 1970b] 70-125678 ISBN 0-405-01653-0
1. Bryant, William Cullen, 1794-1878.

BRADLEY, William Aspenwall, 1878-1939. 811'.3 B
William Cullen Bryant. [Folcroft, Pa.] Folcroft Library Editions, 1973 [c1905] p. Reprint of the ed. published by Macmillan, New York, in series: English men of letters. [PS1181.B7 1973] 73-11373 ISBN 0-8414-3200-7 (lib. bdg.)
1. Bryant, William Cullen, 1794-1875. **BIP**

BRADLEY, William Aspenwall, 1878-1939. 811'.3 B
William Cullen Bryant / by William Aspenwall Bradley. Norwood, Pa. : Norwood Editions, 1975 [c1905] viii, 229 p. ; 23 cm. Reprint of the ed. published by MacMillan, New York, in series: English men of letters. Includes index. [PS1181.B7 1975] 75-40239 ISBN 0-88305-897-9 : 18.00
1. Bryant, William Cullen, 1794-1878. I. Title.

BROWN, Charles Henry, 1910- 811'.3 B
William Cullen Bryant [by] Charles H. Brown. New York, Scribner [1971] 576 p. illus. 25 cm. Includes bibliographical references. [PS1181.B74] 79-143949 ISBN 0-684-12370-3 12.50
1. Bryant, William Cullen, 1794-1878. **BIP**

BRYANT, William Cullen, 1794-1878. 811'.3 B
William Cullen Bryant and Isaac Henderson; new evidence on a strange partnership. Twenty-one letters hitherto unprinted, edited with introd. and notes by Theodore Hornberger. New York, Haskell House, 1973. v, 44 p. 23 cm. Reprint of the 1950 ed. Includes bibliographical references. [PS1181.A3 1973] 72-6771 ISBN 0-8383-1645-X 7.95
I. Henderson, Isaac. II. Hornberger, Theodore, 1906- ed. III. Title.

GODWIN, Parke, 1816-1904. 811'.3 B
A biography of William Cullen Bryant, with extracts from his private correspondence. New York, Russell & Russell [1967] 2 v. ports. 22 cm. Reprint of the 1883 ed. [PS1181.G6 1967] 66-27084
1. Bryant, William Cullen, 1794-1878. I. Title.

JOHNSON, Curtiss S 928.1
Politics and a belly-full; the journalistic carrer of William Cullen Bryant, Civil War editor of the New York evening post. [1st ed.] New York, Vantage Press [1962] 209p. ports., facsims. 21cm. Bibliography: p. 191-192. [PN4874.B79J6] 62-52821
1. Bryant, William Cullen, 1794-1878. 2. New York post. I. Title.

JOHNSON, Curtiss S. 070.4'092'4 B
Politics and a belly-full; the journalistic career of William Cullen Bryant, Civil War editor of the New York evening post, by Curtiss S. Johnson. Westport, Conn., Greenwood Press [1974, c1962] 209 p. illus. 22 cm. Reprint of the ed. published by Vantage Press, New York. Bibliography: p. 191-192. [PN4874.B79J6 1974] 73-16948 ISBN 0-8371-7246-2 10.00
1. Bryant, William Cullen, 1794-1878. 2. New York post. I. Title.

PECKHAM, Harry Houston. 811'.3 B
Gotham Yankee; a biography of William Cullen Bryant. New York, Russell & Russell [1971, c1950] 228 p. illus., ports. 22 cm. Bibliography: p. 217-219. [PS1181.P4 1971] 70-139935
1. Bryant, William Cullen, 1794-1878. I. Title.

PECKMAN, Harry Houston. 928.1
Gotham Yankee: a biography of William Cullen Bryant. New York, Vantage Press [c1950] 228 p. illus., ports. 23 cm. Bibliography: p. 217-219. [PS1181.P4] 51-887
1. Bryant, William Cullen, 1794-1878. I. Title.

SYMINGTON, Andrew James, b.1825. 811'.3 B
William Cullen Bryant; a biographical sketch, with selections from his poems and other writings. [Folcroft] Folcroft Library Editions, 1972. 256 p. front. 23 cm. Reprint of the 1880 ed. [PS1181.S8 1972] 72-13257 15.00
1. Bryant, William Cullen, 1794-1878. I. Bryant, William Cullen, 1794-1878.

Bryant, William Cullen, 1794-1878—Biography—Juvenile literature.

CODY, Sherwin, 1868-1959. 811'.3'09
Four American poets : William Cullen Bryant, Henry Wadsworth Longfellow, John Greenleaf Whittier, Oliver Wendell Holmes : a book for young Americans / by Sherwin Cody. Folcroft, Pa. : Folcroft Library Editions, 1977. p. cm. Reprint of the 1899 ed. published by American Book Co., New York, which was issued as v. 4 of The Four great Americans series. Essays discussing the life and work of four major American poets of the nineteenth century. [PS96.C57 1977] 920 77-24729 ISBN 0-8414-1811-X lib. bdg. : 25.00
1. Bryant, William Cullen, 1794-1878—Biography—Juvenile literature. 2. Longfellow, Henry Wadsworth, 1807-1882—Biography—Juvenile literature. 3. Whittier, John Greenleaf, 1807-1892—Biography—Juvenile literature. 4. Holmes, Oliver Wendell, 1809-1894—Biography—Juvenile literature. 5. Poets, American—19th century—Biography—Juvenile literature. I. Title. II. Series: The Four great Americans series ; v. 4.

Bryant, William Cullen, 1794-1878—Correspondence.

BRYANT, William Cullen, 1794-1878. 811'.3 B
The letters of William Cullen Bryant / edited by William Cullen Bryant, II, and Thomas G. Voss. 1st ed. New York : Fordham University Press, 1975- v. : ill. ; 24 cm. Includes index. Contents.Contents.—v. 1. 1809-1836. Bibliography: v. 1, p. [487]-489. [PS1181.A4 1975] 74-27169 ISBN 0-8232-0991-1 : 35.00 (v. 1)
1. Bryant, William Cullen, 1794-1878—Correspondence. I. Bryant, William Cullen, 1908- II. Voss, Thomas G. III. Title. **BIP**

Bryher, Winifred,

BRYHER, Winifred, 1894- 914.21'03'840924 B
The days of Mars; a memoir, 1940-1946, by Bryher. [1st ed.] New York, Harcourt Brace Jovanovich [1971, c1972] xii, 190 p. 21 cm. "A Helen and Kurt Wolff book." [PR6003.R98Z52] 79-174505 ISBN 0-15-124055-8
I. Title.

Bryskett, Lodowick, ca. 1545-ca. 1612.

SISSON, Charles Jasper, 1885- ed. 820.9003
Thomas Lodge and other Elizabethans, edited by Charles J. Sisson. New York, Octagon Books, 1966 [c1933] xii, 526 p. illus., maps, geneal. tables. 24 cm. Contents.Contents.—Thomas Lodge and his family, by C. J. Sisson.—Barnabe Barnes, by M. Eccles.—Lodowick Bryskett and his family, by D. Jones.—John Lyly at St. Bartholomew's, or Much ado about washing, by D. Jones.—Sir George Buc, master of the revels, by M. Eccles. [PR2298.S5 1966] 66-18029
1. Lodge, Thomas, 1558?-1625. 2. Barnes, Barnabe, 1569?-1609. 3. Bryskett, Lodowick, ca. 1545-ca. 1612. 4. Lyly, John, 1554?-1606. 5. Buck, George, Sir, d. 1623. I. Eccles, Mark. II. Jones, Deborah. III. Title. **BIP**

Buber, Martin, 1878-1965.

BRESLAUER, S. Daniel. 181'.3
The chrysalis of religion : a guide to the Jewishness of Buber's I and Thou. / S. Daniel Breslauer. Nashville : Abingdon, 1980. p. cm. Includes bibliographical references and index. [B3213.B831233] 79-20067 ISBN 0-687-08040-1 pbk. : 5.95
1. Buber, Martin, 1878-1965. Ich und du. I. Title. BIP

BUBER, Martin, 1878-1965. 193 B
Encounter; autobiographical fragments. La Salle, Ill., Open Court [1972, c1967] vi, 136 p. port. 22 cm. ([The Open Court classics]) Reprinted from The philosophy of Martin Buber, edited by P. A. Schilpp and M. Friedman. [B3213.B84A28 1972] 70-110213 4.95
I. Title.

FRIEDMAN, Maurice S. 296.3'092'4
Martin Buber : the life of dialogue / Maurice S. Friedman. [3d ed.] Chicago : University of Chicago Press, 1976. xvii, 322 p. ; 21 cm. Includes index. Bibliography: p. 283-309. [B3213.B84F7 1976] 76-369402 ISBN 0-226-26356-8 : 12.50
1. Buber, Martin, 1878-1965. BIP

HODES, Aubrey. 296'.0924 B
Martin Buber; an intimate portrait. New York, Viking Press [1971] xii, 242 p. 23 cm. Revised ed. published in 1972 under title: Encounter with Martin Buber. Bibliography: p. 235-237. [B3213.B84H6 1971] 74-83249 ISBN 0-670-45904-6 7.95
1. Buber, Martin, 1878-1965.

MOORE, Donald J. 296.3'092'4
Martin Buber, prophet of religious secularism : the criticism of institutional religion in the writings of Martin Buber / by Donald J. Moore. 1st ed. Philadelphia : Jewish Publication Society of America, c1974. xxviii, 264 p. ; 22 cm. Bibliography: p. [261]-264. [B3213.B84M66] 74-12888 ISBN 0-8276-0055-0 : 6.00
1. Buber, Martin, 1878-1965.

PANKO, Stephen M. 296.3'092'4 B
Martin Buber / by Stephen M. Panko. Waco, Tex. : Word Books, c1976. 135 p. ; 23 cm. (Makers of the modern theological mind) Bibliography; p. 132-135. [BM755.B8P36] 76-2869 ISBN 0-87680-470-9 : 5.95
1. Buber, Martin, 1878-1965. BIP

Buber, Martin, 1878-1965—Juvenile literature.

SIMON, Charlie May (Hogue) 1897- 296'.0924 B
Martin Buber: wisdom in our time; the story of an outstanding Jewish thinker and humanist, by Charlie May Simon. [1st ed.] New York, Dutton [1969] 191 p. illus., ports. 22 cm. Bibliography: p. 181-183. A biography of the Jewish philosopher and Zionist leader who became noted for his studies of Hasidism, a movement of Jewish mysticism. [B3213.B84S5] 92 74-81725 4.50
1. Buber, Martin, 1878-1965—Juvenile literature. I. Title.

Bubis, Jacob Louis,

BUBIS, Jacob Louis, 1885- 926.1
Women are my problem; the autobiography of an obstetrician and gynecologist. New York, Comet Press Books [1953] 223p. illus. 23cm. [RG76.B8A3] 53-9374
I. Title.

Bublitz, Dorothea E.

BUBLITZ, Dorothea E. 920.7
Life on the dotted line. New York, Vantage Press [c.1960] 110p. 2.00 bds.,
I. Title.

Bubolz family.

BUBOLZ, George C., 1902- 929'.2'0973
Father Julius and Mother Emilie : a personal biography of midwestern pioneers / George C. Bubolz. 1st ed. Hicksville, N.Y. : Exposition Press, c1975. xvi, 172 p., [4] leaves of plates : ill. ; 22 cm. (An Exposition-Lochinvar book) [CS71.B9175 1975] 75-329401 ISBN 0-682-48354-0 : 9.00
1. Bubolz family. 2. Bubolz, Julius, 1862-1956. 3. Bubolz, Emilie. I. Title.

Buca, Edward, 1926-

BUCA, Edward, 1926- 365'.6'0924 B
Vorkuta / [by] Edward Buca ; translated from the Polish [MS.] by Michal Lisinski and Kennedy Wells. London : Constable, 1976. ix, 352 p., leaf of plate, [4] p. of plates : facsims., ports. ; 23 cm. [HV8959.R9B8 1976] 77-364618 ISBN 0-09-460880-6 : £5.95
1. Buca, Edward, 1926- 2. Political prisoners—Russia—Biography. I. Title.

Buchan. John, 1875-1940.

SMITH, Janet Adam 828.91209
John Buchan, a biography [1st Amer. ed.] Boston, Little [1966, c.1965] 524p. illus., facsim., ports. 22cm. Bibl. [PR6003.U13Z78] 65-21358 7.50
1. Buchan. John, 1875-1940. I. Title.

Buchan, John, 1875-1940—Biography.

BUCHAN, John, 1875-1940. 828'.9'1209 B
Pilgrim's way : an essay in recollection / by John Buchan (Lord Tweedsmuir). New York : AMS Press, 1979. p. cm. Reprint of the 1940 ed. published by Houghton Mifflin, Boston. Includes index. [PR6003.U13Z5 1979] 76-6591 ISBN 0-404-15278-3 : 32.50
1. Buchan, John, 1875-1940—Biography. 2. Authors, Scottish—20th century—Biography. 3. Statesmen—Great Britain—Biography. I. Title. BIP

SMITH, Janet Adam. 828'.9'1209 B
John Buchan and his world / Janet Adam Smith. New York : Scribner, c1979. 128 p. : ill. ; 25 cm. Includes index. Bibliography: p. 118-120. [PR6003.U13Z783] 79-84519 ISBN 0-684-16278-4 : 10.95
1. Buchan, John, 1875-1940—Biography. 2. Authors, Scottish—20th century—Biography. 3. Statesmen—Great Britain—Biography. I. Title. BIP

Buchanan, James, Pres. U.S., 1791-1868.

CURTIS, George Ticknor, 1812-1894. 973.68'0924 B
Life of James Buchanan, fifteenth President of the United States. New York, Harper, 1883. Freeport, N.Y., Books for Libraries Press, 1969 [c1883] 2 v. ports. 23 cm. (Select bibliographies reprint series) [E437.C97 1969] 69-16849
1. Buchanan, James, Pres. U.S., 1791-1868. I. Title.

HORTON, Rushmore G., b.1826. 973.6'8'0924
The life and public services of James Buchanan, late minister to England and formerly minister to Russia, senator and representative in Congress, and Secretary of State: including the most important of his state papers. Port Washington, N.Y., Kennikat Press [1971] 428 p. port. 21 cm. (Kennikat Press scholarly reprints. Series in American history and culture in the nineteenth century) Reprint of the 1856 ed. [E437.H82 1971] 78-137916 ISBN 0-8046-1493-8
1. Buchanan, James, Pres. U.S., 1791-1868. 2. Campaign literature, 1856—Democratic. I. Title.

KLEIN, Philip Shriver, 1909- 923.173
President James Buchanan, a biography. Univ. Park, Pa. State Univ. Pr. [c.1962] xviii, 506p. illus. Bibl. 62-12623 7.50
1. Buchanan, james, Pres. U. S., 1791-1868. I. Title. BIP

Buchanan, James, Pres. U.S., 1791-1868.—Juvenile literature.

HOYT, Edwin Palmer. 973.6'8'0924 B
James Buchanan, by Edwin P. Hoyt. Chicago, Reilly & Lee Co. [1966] 150 p. illus., ports. 21 cm. Bibliography: p. 145. [E437.H88] 67-7990
1. Buchanan, James, Pres. U.S., 1791-1868.—Juvenile literature. I. Title.

Buchanan, Jerreal B.

BUCHANAN, Jerreal B. 616.1'23
Who's calling my name? / Jerreal B. Buchanan. Nashville : Broadman Press, c1977. 154 p. ; 19 cm. [RC685.I6B76] 76-58063 ISBN 0-8054-5418-7 pbk. : 2.95
1. Buchanan, Jerreal B. 2. Heart—Infarction—Biography. 3. Baptists—Clergy—Biography. 4. Clergy—United States—Biography. I. Title. BIP

Buchanan, Robert Williams, 1841-1901.

JAY, Harriett, 1857-1932. 828'.8'09 B
Robert Buchanan; some account of his life, his life's work, and his literary friendships. New York, AMS Press [1970] xii, 324 p. illus., facsim., ports. 23 cm. Reprint of the 1903 ed. [PR4263.J3 1970] 72-130237
1. Buchanan, Robert Williams, 1841-1901.

Buchman, Frank Nathan Daniel, 1878-1961.

SPOERRI, Theophil, 1890-1975. 248'.25'0924 B
Dynamic out of silence : Frank Buchman's relevance today / [by] Theophil Spoerri ; [translated from the German by John Morrison and Peter Thwaites]. London : Grosvenor Books, 1976. 219 p. ; 18 cm. Translation of Dynamik aus der Stille. Bibliography: p. 219. [BJ10.M6B83613] 77-366327 ISBN 0-901269-19-0 : £1.30
1. Buchman, Frank Nathan Daniel, 1878-1961. 2. Oxford group. 3. Moral Rearmament—Biography. I. Title.

Buck, Pearl (Sydenstricker) 1892-1973.

BLOCK, Irvin. 813'.5'2 B
The lives of Pearl Buck; a tale of China and America. New York, Crowell [1973] 169 p. illus. 21 cm. (Women of America) Bibliography: p. [161] [PS3503.U198Z6] 73-8891 ISBN 0-690-00165-7 4.50
1. Buck, Pearl (Sydenstricker) 1892-1973. BIP

BUCK, Pearl (Sydenstricker) 1892- 928.1
My several worlds, a personal record. New York, Day [1954] 407 p. 22 cm. [PS3503.U198Z5] 54-10460
I. Title.

BUCK, Pearl (Sydenstricker) 1892- 928.1
My several worlds. Abridged for younger readers [by Cornelia Spencer] New York, J. Day Co. [1957] 192p. 21cm. [PS3503.U198Z52] 57-7416
I. Title.

HARRIS, Theodore F. 813'.5'2 B
Pearl S. Buck; a biography, by Theodore F. Harris in consultation with Pearl S. Buck. New York, John Day Co. [1969-71] 2 v. port. 24 cm. Vol. 2 has subtitle: Her philosophy as expressed in her letters. Bibliography: v. 1, p. [367]-372. [PS3503.U198Z69] 68-9456 8.95 (v. 1) 9.95 (v. 2)
1. Buck, Pearl (Sydenstricker) 1892- —Biography.

Buck, Pearl Sydenstricker, 1892-1973—Biography—Juvenile literature.

MYERS, Elisabeth P. 813'.5'2 B
Pearl S. Buck, literary girl / by Elisabeth P. Myers ; illustrated by Al Fiorentino. Indianapolis : Bobbs-Merrill, 1974. 200 p. : col. ill. ; 20 cm. (Childhood of famous Americans) Bibliography: p. 198. [PS3503.U198Z74] 74-261
1. Buck, Pearl Sydenstricker, 1892-1973—Biography—Juvenile literature. I. Fiorentino, Al. II. Title.

SCHOEN, Scelin V. 813'.5'2 B
Pearl Buck, famed American author of oriental stories, by Celin V. Schoen. Charlotteville, N.Y., SamHar Press, 1972. 32 p. 22 cm. (Outstanding personalities, no. 30) Bibliography: p. 29-32. A biography of the American author whose life and works were greatly influenced by her childhood in China. [PS3503.U198Z8] 92 70-190247
1. Buck, Pearl Sydenstricker, 1892-1972—Biography—Juvenile literature. 2. Buck, Pearl Sydenstricker, 1892-1972—Bibliography. I. Title.

YAUKEY, Grace (Sydenstricker) 1899- 928.1
Pearl S. Buck; revealing the human heart, by Cornelia Spencer [pseud.] Chicago, Encyclopedia Britannica Press [1964] 192 p. illus., ports. 22 cm. (Brittanica bookshelf: Great lives) [PS3503.U198Z973] 63-13521
1. Buck, Pearl (Sydenstricker) 1892- —Juvenile literature. I. Title.

Buckelew, F. M., 1852-

BUCKELEW, F. M., 1852- 973'.04'97 S
Buckelew, the Indian captive / [as related by himself ; written by] S. E. Banta. New York : Garland Pub., 1976. p. cm. (The Garland library of narratives of North American Indian captivities ; v. 107) Reprint of the 1911 ed. printed by the Mason herald, Mason, Tex. Issued with the reprint of the 1925 ed. of Buckelew, F. M. Life of F. M. Buckelew. New York, 1976. The reprint of the 1912 ed. of Babb, T. A. In the bosom of the Comanches. New York, 1976. [E85.G2 vol. 107] [E99.L5] 970'.004'97 B 75-7135 ISBN 0-8240-1731-5 lib.bdg. : 21.00
1. Buckelew, F. M., 1852- 2. Lipan Indians—Captivities. 3. Indians of North America—Captivities. 4. Frontier and pioneer life—Texas. I. Banta, Seth Emmet, 1877- II. Title. III. Series.

BUCKELEW, F. M., 1852- 973'.04'97 S
Life of F. M. Buckelew / [as related by himself ; written by] T. S. Dennis [and Mrs. T. S. Dennis]. New York : Garland Pub., 1976, [c1925] p. cm. (The Garland library of narratives of North American Indian captivities ; v. 107) Issued with the reprint of the 1911 ed. of Buckelew, F. M. Buckelew, the Indian captive. New York, 1976. Reprint of the ed. published by Hunter's Print. House, Bandera, Tex. [E85.G2 vol. 107] [E99.L5] 970'.004'97 B 75-40047 ISBN 0-8240-1731-5 lib.bdg. : 21.00
1. Buckelew, F. M., 1852- 2. Lipan Indians—Captivities. 3. Indians of North America—Captivities. 4. Frontier and pioneer life—Texas. I. Dennis, Thomas S., 1867- II. Dennis, Lucy S. Rea, 1893- III. Title. IV. Series.

Buckingham, George Villiers, 2d Duke of, 1628-1687.

BURGHCLERE, Winifred Anne Henrietta Christina (Herbert) Gardner, Baroness, 1864-1933. 942.06'6'0924
George Villiers, Second Duke of Buckingham, 1628-1687; a study in the history of the restoration. Port Washington, N.Y., Kennikat Press [1971] vii, 414 p. facsim., ports. 22 cm. Reprint of the 1903 ed. Includes bibliographical references. [DA447.B9B9 1971] 74-118511 ISBN 0-8046-1259-5
1. Buckingham, George Villiers, 2d Duke

of, 1628-1687. 2. Gt. Brit.—History—Restoration, 1660-1688. I. Title.

WILSON, John Harold, 1900- 923.242
A rake and his times: George Villiers, 2nd duke of Buckingham. New York, Farrar, Straus and Young [1954] 280 p. illus. 22 cm. [DA447.B9W5] 54-7304
1. Buckingham, George Villiers, 2d duke of, 1628-1687. 2. Gt. Brit.—History—Restoration, 1660-1688. I. Title.

Buckingham, Jamie.

BUCKINGHAM, Jamie. 248'.092'4 B
Risky living : keys to inner healing / Jamie Buckingham. Plainfield, N.J. : Logos International, c1976. ix, 192 p. ; 22 cm. [BV4501.2.B82] 76-12033 ISBN 0-88270-175-4 : 5.95. ISBN 0-88270-177-0 pbk. :
1. Buckingham, Jamie. 2. Christian life—1960- 3. Christian biography—United States. I. Title.

Buckingham, Joseph Tinker,

BUCKINGHAM, Joseph Tinker, 1779-1861. 070.4'0924 B
Personal memoirs and recollections of editorial life. [New York] Arno [1970] 256, 255 p. ports. 23 cm. (The American journalists) Reprint of the 1852 ed. [PN4874.B795A3 1970] 76-125682 ISBN 0-405-01657-3
I. Title. BIP

Buckle, Henry Thomas, 1821-1862.

ST. AUBYN, Giles 928.2
A Victorian eminence; the life and works of Henry Thomas Buckle [London] Barrie [dist. Chester Springs, Pa., Dufour, 1964, c.1958] 229p. illus. 23cm. Bibl. 58-3551 5.00
1. Buckle, Henry Thomas, 1821-1862. I. Title.

Buckner, Emory Roy, 1877-1941.

MAYER, Martin, 1928- 340'.0924 B
Emory Buckner. With an introd. by John M. Harlan. [1st ed.] New York, Harper & Row [1968] xiv, 304 p. group ports. 22 cm. "Published under the auspices of the William Nelson Cromwell Foundation." Bibliographical footnotes. [KF373.B8M3] 68-15965
1. Buckner, Emory Roy, 1877-1941. I. William Nelson Foundation, New York.

Buddha and Buddhism.

GAUTAMA; the story of Lord Buddha. v. 12
Illustrated by Nena von Leyden. New York, Macmillan [1956] 118p. illus. 19cm.
1. Buddha and Buddhism. I. Masani, Shakuntala.

MASANI, Shakuntala. v. 12
Gautama; the story of Lord Buddha. Illustrated by Nena von Leyden. New York, Macmillan [1956] 118p. illus. 19cm.
1. Buddha and Buddhism. I. Title.

Buddha and Buddhism—Korea—Biography.

KAKHUN, Sok, 13thcent., comp. 294.3'657'0922 B
Lives of eminent Korean monks; the Haedong kosung chon. Translated with an introd. by Peter H. Lee. Cambridge, Harvard University Press, 1969. xiii, 116 p. 26 cm. (Harvard-Yenching Institute studies, 25) Bibliography: p. [99]-110. [BL1460.K2613] 69-18037 7.00
1. Buddha and Buddhism—Korea—Biography. I. Title. II. Series. BIP

Budenz, Margaret R.

BUDENZ, Margaret R. 335.43'092'4 B
Streets / Margaret R. Budenz. Huntington, Ind. : Our Sunday Visitor, c1979. xv, 494 p. : ill. ; 22 cm. Includes index. Bibliography: p. 483-487. [HX84.B75A37] 78-71421 ISBN 0-87973-754-9 : 11.95
1. Budenz, Margaret R. 2. Communists—United States—Biography. I. Title. BIP

Budge, John Donald,

BUDGE, John Donald, 1915- 796.34'2'0924
Don Budge: a tennis memoir. New York, Viking Press [1969] 184 p. illus., ports. 23 cm. [GV994.B8A3] 69-15661 5.95
I. Title.

Budgen, Frank Spencer Curtis,

BUDGEN, Frank Spencer Curtis, 1882- 914.2'03'820924 B
Myselves when young [by] Frank Budgen. London, New York, Oxford University Press, 1970. 212 p. illus., ports. 23 cm. [CT788.B8768A3] 79-466634 7.00
I. Title. BIP

Buell, Abel, 1742-1822.

WROTH, Lawrence Counselman, 1884- 927.6
Abel Buell of Connecticut, silversmith, typefounder & engraver. [2d ed. rev.] Middletown, Wesleyan University Press, 1958. xiv, 102 p. illus., facsims. 24 cm. Bibliographical references included in "Notes" (p. 86-96) [NK7198.B8W7 1958] 58-13601
1. Buell, Abel, 1742-1822.

Bufano, Beniamino, 1898-1970.

RATHER, Lois, 1905- 730'.92'4 B
Bufano and the U.S.A. / Lois Rather. Oakland, CA : Rather Press, 1975. 125 p. : ill. ; 24 cm. "An edition of one hundred fifty copies. This is number 13." Includes bibliographical references and index. [NB237.B76R37] 75-322851
1. Bufano, Beniamino, 1898-1970. I. Title. BIP

WILKENING, Howard. 730'.92'4 B
Bufano: an intimate biography, by H. Wilkening and Sonia Brown. Berkeley, Calif., Howell-North Books [1972] 232 p. illus. 24 cm. [NB237.B76W5] 72-79789 ISBN 0-8310-7089-7 6.50
1. Bufano, Beniamino, 1898-1970. I. Brown, Sonia, joint author. II. Title. BIP

Buffalo Bill's Wild West Show.

HAVIGHURST, Walter, 1901- 301.42
Buffalo Bill's great Wild West Show Illustrated by John C. Wonsetler. New York, Random House [1957] 183 p. illus. 22 cm. (Landmark books, 73) [PZ9.H29Bu] 57-7507
1. Buffalo Bill's Wild West Show. I. Title.

Buffalo Bills (Football team)

BAKER, Jim, 1941- 796.33'264'0974797
The Buffalo Bills : O. J. Simpson, rushing champion / by Jim Baker. Englewood Cliffs, N.J. : Prentice-Hall, [1974] 126 p. : ill. ; 28 cm. (Reward books) "A Stuart L. Daniels book." Text and photographs present a brief history of the Buffalo Bills football team with short biographies of the team members and special focus on O. J. Simpson. [GV956.B83B34] 920 74-7522 ISBN 0-13-085803-X pbk. : 3.95
1. Buffalo Bills (Football team) 2. Football—Biography.

Buffalo Sabres (Hockey team)

FISCHLER, Stan. 796.9'62'0974797
The Buffalo Sabres : swashbucklers of the ice / by Stan Fischler ; photography, Melchior Di Giacomo, Joe Bongi, Jr. Englewood Cliffs, N.J. : Prentice-Hall, [1974] 127 p. : ill. ; 28 cm. (Reward books) "A Stuart L. Daniels book." [GV848.B83F57] 74-7520 ISBN 0-13-085845-5 pbk. : 3.95
1. Buffalo Sabres (Hockey team) 2. Hockey. 3. Hockey—Biography.

Buffet, Benard, 1928-

DRUON, Maurice, 1918- 759.4
Bernard Buffet. Text. Maurice Druon [tr. from French by Humphrey Hare] Photos.: Luc Fournol. Captions: Annabel Buffet. Design: Jean Widmer. [New York] October House [1966, c.1964] 1v. (unpaged) illus. (pt. col.) facsims., ports. (pt. col.) 30cm. [ND553.B98D73] 66-14713 17.50
1. Buffet, Benard, 1928- I. Fournol, Luc. II. Title.

Buffon, Georges Louis Leclerc, comte de, 1707-1788.

FELLOWS, Otis Edward, 1908- 574'.092'4 B
Buffon, by Otis E. Fellows and Stephen F. Milliken. New York, Twayne Publishers [1972] 186 p. 21 cm. (Twayne's world authors series, TWAS 243. France) Bibliography: p. 179-181. [QH31.B88F44] 76-39777 5.95
1. Buffon, Georges Louis Leclerc, comte de, 1707-1788. I. Milliken, Stephen F., joint author. BIP

Bugaev, Boris Nikolaevich, 1880-1934.

MOCHUL'SKII, Konstantin Vasil'evich, 1892-1948. 891.7142 B
Andrei Bely : his life and works / Konstantin Mochulsky ; translated by Nora Szalavitz. Ann Arbor [Mich.] : Ardis, c1977. 230 p. ; 24 cm. Translation of Andrei Belyi. Includes bibliographical references. [PG3453.B84Z7813 1977] 76-150858 ISBN 0-88233-122-1 : 13.95
1. Bugaev, Boris Nikolaevich, 1880-1934. 2. Authors, Russian—20th century—Biography.

Bugan nak Manghe.

BARTON, Roy Franklin, 1883-1947. 959.9'1
Philippine pagans : the autobiographies of three Ifugaos / by R. F. Barton. 1st AMS ed. New York : AMS Press, 1979. xxi, 271 p., [20] leaves of plates : ill. ; 22 cm. Reprint of the 1938 ed. published by G. Routledge, London. [DS666.I15B35 1979] 76-44686 ISBN 0-404-15903-6 : 24.50
1. Ngidulu. 2. Bugan nak Manghe. 3. Kumiha. 4. Ifugaos—Biography. 5. Ifugaos—Social life and customs. I. Title. BIP

Bugatti, Ettore, 1881-1947.

BUGATTI, L'Ebe. 629.22'22'0924 B
The Bugatti story. Translated from the French by Len Ortzen. [1st American ed.] Philadelphia, Chilton Book Co. [1967] xii, 196 p. illus., ports. 21 cm. Translation of L'epopee Bugatti. [TL140.B8B83] 67-27858
1. Bugatti, Ettore, 1881-1947. I. Title.

Buh, Joseph F., 1833-1922.

COLEMAN, Bernard, Sister, 1890- 266'.2'0924 B
Masinaigans: the little book; a biography of Monsignor Joseph F. Buh, Slovenian missionary in America, 1864-1922 [by] Sister Bernard Coleman [and] Sister Verona LaBud. Saint Paul, Minn., North Central Pub. Co., 1972. x, 368 p. illus. 25 cm. Bibliography: p. 261-277. [E78.M7C64] 72-85332
1. Buh, Joseph F., 1833-1922. 2. Indians of North America—Minnesota—Missions. 3. Indians of North America—Nortwest, Old—Missions. I. LaBud, Verona, joint author. II. Title.

Buitrago Salazar, Evelio.

BUITRAGO Salazar, Evelio. 986.1'063
Zarpazo the bandit : memoirs of an undercover agent of the Columbian army / by Evelio Buitrago Salazar ; translated by M. Murray Lasley ; edited, with an introd. and explanatory notes, by Russell W. Ramsey. University : University of Alabama Press, 1977c1976 p. cm. Translation of Zarpazo. The experiences of an army intelligence operative who specialized in penetrating bandit gangs during "la violencia," a series of internal wars in Colombia from 1946-1965. [F2278.B813] 76-10678 ISBN 0-8061-1374-X : 14.95
1. Buitrago Salazar, Evelio. 2. Zarpazo, d. 1967. 3. Colombia—History—1946- 4. Brigands and robbers—Colombia. I. Title.

Bukharin, Nikolai Ivanovich, 1888-1938.

COHEN, Stephen F. 947.084'092'4 B
Bukharin and the Bolshevik Revolution: a political biography, 1888-1938 [by] Stephen F. Cohen. [1st ed.] New York, Vintage Books [1975, c1973] xix, 495, xvii p. 21 cm. Bibliography: p. [479]-495. [DK268.B76C63 1975] 74-7047 ISBN 0-394-71261-7 3.95 (pbk.)
1. Bukharin, Nikolai Ivanovich, 1888-1938. 2. Russia—Politics and government—1917-1936. 3. Russia—Economic policy—1917-1928. I. Title. BIP

COHEN, Stephen F. 947.084'092'4 B
Bukharin and the Bolshevik Revolution; a political biography, 1888-1938 [by] Stephen F. Cohen. [1st ed.] New York, A. A. Knopf; [distributed by Random House] 1973. xix, 495, xvii p. 25 cm. Bibliography: p. 479-495. [DK268.B76C63 1973] 73-7288 ISBN 0-394-46014-6 15.00
1. Bukharin, Nikolai Ivanovich, 1888-1938. 2. Russia—Politics and government—1917-1936. 3. Russia—Economic policy—1917-1928. I. Title.

Bukovskii, Vladimir Konstantinovich, 1942—

BUKOVSKII, Vladimir Konstantinovich, 1942- 364.13 B
To build a castle : my life as a dissenter / Vladimir Bukovsky ; translated by Michael Scammell. New York : Viking Press, 1979, c1978. 438 p. ; 24 cm. [DK275.B84A37] 78-12945 ISBN 0-670-71640-5 : 17.50
1. Bukovskii, Vladimir Konstantinovich, 1942- 2. Political prisoners—Russia—Biography. 3. Dissenters—Russia—Biography. I. Title. BIP

Bukowski, Charles.

FOX, Hugh, 1932- 811'.5'4
Charles Bukowski: a critical and bibliographical study. Somerville, Mass., Abyss Publications [1971, c1969] 121 p. 24 cm. [PS3552.U4Z7 1971] 72-129088 ISBN 0-911856-01-3 3.75
1. Bukowski, Charles. 2. Bukowski, Charles—Bibliography.

Bulfinch, Charles, 1763-1844.

BULFINCH, Charles, 1763-1844. 720'.92'4 B
The life and letters of Charles Bulfinch, architect, with other family papers, edited by his granddaughter, Ellen Susan Bulfinch. With an introd. by Charles A. Cummings. New York, B. Franklin [1973] xiv, 323 p. illus. 23 cm. (Burt Franklin research & source works series. Art history & reference series, 45) Reprint of the 1896 ed. published by Houghton Mifflin, Boston. [NA737.B8A3 1973] 78-166963 ISBN 0-8337-0417-6 19.50
1. Bulfinch, Charles, 1763-1844. I. Bulfinch, Ellen Susan, ed.

PLACE, Charles Alpheus, 1866- 720'.924 B
Charles Bulfinch, architect and citizen, by Charles A. Place. New York, Da Capo Press, 1968 [c1925] xiv, 294 p. illus., maps, plans, ports. 26 cm. (Da Capo Press series in architecture and decorative art, v. 16) (A Da Capo Press reprint edition.) [NA737.B8P5 1968] 68-27717
1. Bulfinch, Charles, 1763-1844.

Bulgakov, Mikhail Afanas'evich, 1891-1940.

WRIGHT, Anthony Colin, 1938- 891.7'8'4209
Mikhail Bulgakov : life and interpretations / A. Colin Wright. Toronto ; Buffalo : University of Toronto Press, c1978. viii,

324 p. ; 24 cm. Includes indexes. Bibliography: p. [281]-310. [PG3476.B78Z95] 78-3872 ISBN 0-8020-5402-1 : 25.00
1. Bulgakov, Mikhail Afanas'evich, 1891-1940. 2. Authors, Russian—20th century—Biography. BIP

Bull, Alec.

BULL, Alec. 942.6'48 B
Muck on my boots / by Alec Bull. Lavenham [Eng.] : Dalton, 1976. 148 p., [8] leaves of plates : ill. ; 23 cm. [S522.G7B84] 76-382560 ISBN 0-900963-49-2 : £3.40
1. Bull, Alec. 2. Farm life—England—Hitcham. 3. Hitchan, Eng.—Biography. I. Title.

Bull-fights.

ARRUZA, Carles, 1920- 927.918
My life as a matador; the autobiography of Carlos Arruza, with Barnaby Conrad. Boston, Houghton Mifflin, 1956. 246p. illus. 22cm. [GV1108.A7A3] 56-7446
1. Bull-fights. I. Title.

MCCORMICK, Patricia. 791.8
Lady bullfighter; the autobiography of the North American matador. Illustrated with photos.; line drawings by the author. [1st ed.] New York, Holt [1954] 209 p. illus. 22 cm. [GV1107.M2] 54-10526
1. Bull-fights. I. Title.

Bull, Geoffrey T., 1921-

BULL, Geoffrey T., 1921- 266'.023'0924 B
When iron gates yield / Geoffrey T. Bull. [1st ed. reprinted]. London : Pickering and Inglis, 1976. 254 p. : maps ; 18 cm. [BV3427.B79A3 1976] 77-367631 ISBN 0-7208-0385-3 : £0.90
1. Bull, Geoffrey T., 1921- 2. Missionaries—Tibet—Biography. 3. Missionaries—England—Biography. 4. Missions—Tibet. I. Title.

Bull, Ole Bornemann, 1810-1880.

ACKER, Helen. 920.0481
Four sons of Norway. Illustrated by Nils Hogner. Freeport, N.Y., Books for Libraries Press [1970, c1948] 255 p. illus., ports. 23 cm. (Biography index reprint series) Contents.Contents.—The story of Ole Bull (1810-1880)—The story of Henrik Ibsen (1828-1906)—The story of Edvard Grieg (1843-1907)—The story of Fridtjof Nansen (1861-1930)—Bibliography (p. [256]) [DL504.A2A2] 72-117318
1. Bull, Ole Bornemann, 1810-1880. 2. Grieg, Edvard Hagerup, 1843-1907. 3. Ibsen, Henrik, 1828-1906. 4. Nansen, Fridtjof, 1861-1930. I. Title. BIP

BULL, Inez. 927.8
Ole Bull returns to Pennsylvania; the biography of a Norwegian violin virtuoso and pioneer in the Keystone State 1st. ed. New York, Exposition Press [1961] 124p. illus. 21cm. [ML418.B9B75] 61-16157
1. Bull, Ole Bornemann, 1810-1880. 2. Potter Co., Pa.—Hist. 3. Norwegians in Pennsylvania. I. Title. BIP

BULL, Sara Chapman Thorp, 1850-1911. 787'.1'0924 B
Ole Bull : a memoir / by Sara C. Bull ; with Ole Bull's violin notes and A. B. Crosby's Anatomy of the violinist. Boston : Longwood Press, 1977. p. cm. Reprint of the 1883 ed. published by Houghton Mifflin, Boston. [ML418.B9B9 1977] 77-75211 ISBN 0-89341-112-4 : 45.00
1. Bull, Ole Bornemann, 1810-1880. 2. Violin. I. Bull, Ole Bornemann, 1810-1880. Violin notes, 1977. II. Crosby, Alpheus Benning, 1832-1877. Anatomy of the violinist. 1977. BIP

SMITH, Mortimer Brewster, 1906- 787'.1'0924 B
The life of Ole Bull. Westport, Conn., Greenwood Press [1973, c1943] p. Reprint of the ed. published by Princeton University Press for the American-Scandinavian Foundation, New York. Bibliography: p. [ML418.B9S6 1973] 73-10762 ISBN 0-8371-7035-4 12.00
1. Bull, Ole Bornemann, 1810-1880. I. Title. BIP

Bull, Rice C., 1842-1930.

BULL, Rice C., 1842-1930. 973.7'81'0924 B
Soldiering : the Civil War diary of Rice C. Bull, 123rd New York Volunteer Infantry / edited by K. Jack Bauer. San Rafael, Calif. : Presidio Press, c1977. x, 259 p. : ill. ; 24 cm. Includes index. Bibliography: p. 251-252. [E601.B94 1977] 76-58758 ISBN 0-89141-014-7 : 12.95
1. Bull, Rice C., 1842-1930. 2. United States—History—Civil War, 1861-1865—Personal narratives. 3. Soldiers—United States—Biography. 4. United States—History—Civil War, 1861-1865—Campaigns and battles—Sources. I. Bauer, Karl Jack, 1926- II. Title.

Bullard, Eugene Jacques, 1894-1961.

CARISELLA, P. J. 940.4'49'44
The Black Swallow of Death; the incredible story of Eugene Jacques Bullard, the world's first Black combat aviator, by P. J. Carisella and James W. Ryan. Boston, Marlborough House; distributed by Van Nostrand Reinhold, New York [1972] xii, 271 p. illus. 25 cm. Bibliography: p. 269-271. [TL540.B747C37] 72-75762 6.95
1. Bullard, Eugene Jacques, 1894-1961. I. Ryan, James W., joint author. II. Title.

Bullard, Robert Lee, 1861-1947.

MILLETT, Allan Reed. 355.3'31'0924 B
The general : Robert L. Bullard and officership in the United States Army, 1881-1925 / Allan R. Millett. Westport, Conn. : Greenwood Press, 1975. xi, 499 p. : ill. ; 24 cm. (Contributions in military history ; no. 10) Includes index. Bibliography: p. 475-491. [U53.B78M54] 75-68 ISBN 0-8371-7957-2 lib.bdg. : 19.95
1. Bullard, Robert Lee, 1861-1947. 2. United States. Army—Officers. 3. Military service as a profession. I. Title. II. Series: Contributions in military history.

Bulleid, Oliver Vaughn Snell, 1882-

DAY-LEWIS, Sean 926.211
Bulleid, last giant of steam. Sport Shelf, c.1964 299p. illus., ports. 23cm. 64-56801 10.50
1. Bulleid, Oliver Vaughn Snell, 1882- I. Title.

Buller, Annie, 1896-1973.

WATSON, Louise. 335.43'092'4 B
She never was afraid : the biography of Annie Buller / by Louise Watson. Toronto : Progress Books, 1976. xvi, 129 p., [7] leaves of plates : ill. ; 21 cm. [HX103.B84W37] 76-383780 ISBN 0-919396-31-3
1. Buller, Annie, 1896-1973. 2. Communists—Canada—Biography. 3. Women in trade-unions—Canada. I. Title.

Bullis, Harry Amos, 1890-

ZEHNPFENNIG, Gladys 926.5
Harry A. Bullis, champion American a biography of a business leader who was a champion of human rights. Introd. by Paul G. Hoffman. Minneapolis, Denison [c.1964] 360p. 22cm. (Men of achievement ser.) 63-21944 3.95
1. Bullis, Harry Amos, 1890- 2. General Mills, inc. I. Title.

Bullock, Randy.

BULLOCK, Randy. 248'.2'0924 B
It's good to know / by Randy Bullock, with Dave Balsiger. Milford, Mi. : Mott Media, [1975] 233 p. [4] leaves of plates : ports. ; 20 cm. Autobiographical. [BV4935.B84A34] 74-27321 ISBN 0-915134-00-4 : 5.95 ISBN 0-915134-01-2 pbk. : 2.95
1. Bullock, Randy. 2. Conversion. I. Balsiger, Dave. II. Title.

Bullock, Seth, 1849-1919.

KELLAR, Kenneth C. 363.2'092'4 B
Seth Bullock: frontier marshal, by Kenneth C. Kellar. [Aberdeen, S.D., North Plains Press, 1972] 191 p. illus. 24 cm. [HV7911.B8K4] 72-92726 6.95
1. Bullock, Seth, 1849-1919. I. Title.

Bullock, Wynn.

BULLOCK, Wynn. 779'.092'4
Wynn Bullock photography: a way of life. Edited by Liliane De Cock. Text by Barbara Bullock-Wilson. [Dobbs Ferry, N.Y., Morgan & Morgan, 1973] 160 p. illus. 28 cm. [TR650.B82] 73-77663 ISBN 0-87100-034-2 12.00
1. Bullock, Wynn. 2. Photography, Artistic. I. Bullock-Wilson, Barbara. II. Title.

Bulow, Hans Guido von,

BULOW, Hans Guido von, 1830-1894. 786.1'092'4 B
The early correspondence of Hans von Bulow. Edited by his widow. Selected and translated into English by Constance Bache. New York, Vienna House [1972] xiv, 266 p. ports. 23 cm. Reprint of the 1896 ed. [ML422.B9B94 1972] 71-163788 ISBN 0-8443-0009-8
I. Bulow, Marie (Schanzer) von, Frau, 1857- ed. II. Bache, Constance, 1846-1903, ed.

Bulow, Hans Guido von, 1830-1894.

BULOW, Hans Guido von, 1830-1894. 786.1'092'4 B
Correspondence / Hans von Bulow and Richard Strauss ; edited by Willi Schuh and Franz Trenner ; English translation, Anthony Gishford.. Westport, Conn. : Hyperion Press, 1979. 104 p., [2] leaves of plates : ill. ; 22 cm. (Encore music editions) Reprint of the 1955 ed. published by Boosey & Hawkes, London, New York. [ML422.B9A472 1979] 78-66895 ISBN 0-88355-727-4 : 11.50
1. Bulow, Hans Guido von, 1830-1894. 2. Strauss, Richard, 1864-1949. 3. Conductors (Music)—Germany—Correspondence. 4. Composers—Germany—Correspondence. I. Strauss, Richard, 1864-1949, joint author. II. Schuh, Willi, 1900- III. Trenner, Franz, 1915-

BULOW, Hans Guido von, 1830-1894. 780'.8
Letters of Hans von Bulow to Richard Wagner and others / [edited, with an introd., by Richard Count du Moulin Eckart] ; translated from the German by Hannan Walter ; the translation edited with a pref. by Scott Goddard. New York : Da Capo Press, 1979, c1931. xxx, 434, vi p. ; 24 cm. (Da Capo Press music reprint series) Reprint of the ed. published by Knopf, New York. [ML422.B9B963 1979] 78-31973 ISBN 0-306-79539-6 : 29.50
1. Bulow, Hans Guido von, 1830-1894. 2. Musicians—Germany—Correspondence.

BULOW, Hans Guido von, 1830-1894. 786.1'092'4 B
Letters of Hans von Bulow to Richard Wagner, Cosima Wagner, his daughter Daniela, Luise von Bulow, Karl Klindworth, Carl Bechstein. Edited, with an introd., by Richard Count du Moulin Eckart. Translated from the German by Hannah Walter. The translation edited with a pref. and notes by Scott Goddard. New York, Vienna House, [1973 c1931] xxx, 434, vi p. 24 cm. Translation of Neue Briefe. Reprint of the ed. published by A. A. Knopf, New York. [ML422.B9B963 1972] 72-183503 ISBN 0-8443-0051-9 14.50
1. Bulow, Hans Guido von, 1830-1894. 2. Musicians—Correspondence, reminiscences, etc. I. Du Moulin-Eckart, Richard Maria Ferdinand, Graf, 1864-1938, ed.

Bultmann, Rudolf Karl, 1884-

ASHCRAFT, Morris. 230'.4'10924 B
Rudolf Bultmann. Waco, Tex., Word Books [1972] 123 p. 23 cm. (Makers of the modern theological mind) Bibliography: p. 121-123. [BX4827.B78A83] 74-188059 3.95
1. Bultmann, Rudolf Karl, 1884- BIP

HENDERSON, Ian, 1910- 230.0924
Rudolf Bultmann. Richmond, Va., Knox [1966] viii, 47p. 19cm. (Makers of contemp. theol.) [BX4827.B78H4] 66-11071 1.00 pap.,
1. Bultmann, Rudolf Karl, 1884- I. Title. BIP

LADD, George Eldon, 1911- 230'.0924
Rudolf Bultmann. Chicago, Inter-Varsity Press [c1964] vii, 52 p. 21 cm. (IVP series in contemporary Christian thought, 7) Bibliography: p. 51-52. [BX4827.B78L3] 64-7860
1. Bultmann, Rudolf Karl, 1884- I. Title.

PERRIN, Norman. 230.4'1'0924
The promise of Bultmann. [1st ed.] Philadelphia, Lippincott [1969] 116 p. 21 cm. (The Promise of theology) Bibliography: p. 110-116. [BX4827.B78P4] 70-75174 1.75 (pbk)
1. Bultmann, Rudolf Karl, 1884- I. Title. BIP

RIDDERBOS, Herman N. 922.443
Bultmann. Translated by David H. Freeman. Philadelphia, Presbyterian and Reformed Pub. Co. [c.]1960. 46p. 24cm. (International library of philosophy and theology. Modern thinkers series) 'Appeared originally [in Dutch] as a chapter in the Dutch publication, Modern thinkers (Wever)' Bibl. footnotes 59-15772 1.25 pap.,
1. Bultmann, Rudolf Karl, 1884- I. Title.

Bultmann, Rudolf Karl, 1884- — Addresses, essays, lectures.

O'MEARA, Thomas F., 1935- comp. 230'.0924
Rudolf Bultmann in Catholic thought, edited by Thomas F. O'Meara and Donald M. Weisser. [New York] Herder and Herder [1968] 254 p. 22 cm. Contents.—A prefatory letter from Rudolf Bultmann.—Introduction by the editors.—Demythologizing and theological truth, by H. Fries.—Demythologizing in the school of Alexandria, by J. Danielou.—Form-criticism and the Gospels, by R. Schnackenburg.—Bultmann and the Gospel according to John, by J. Blank.—Bultmann and the Old Testament, by R. Marle.—New insights into faith, by G. Hasenhuttl.—The sacraments in Bultmann's theology, by J. L. McKenzie.—Bultmann on Kerygma and history, by C. Geffre.—Bultmann and Heidegger, by H. Peukert.—Bultmann and tomorrow's theology, by T. F. O'Meara. Bibliographical footnotes. [BX4827.B78O4] 68-55089 5.95
1. Bultmann, Rudolf Karl, 1884- — Addresses, essays, lectures. I. Weisser, Donald M., joint comp. II. Title.

Bunau-Varilla, Philippe, 1859-1940.

ANGUIZOLA, G. A., 1927- 386'.444'09
Philippe Bunau-Varilla / Gustave Anguizola. Chicago : Nelson-Hall, 1980. p. cm. Includes index. Bibliography: p. [TC774.A67] 79-13673 ISBN 0-88229-397-4 : 22.95
1. Bunau-Varilla, Philippe, 1859-1940. 2. Panama Canal—History. 3. Civil engineers—France—Biography.

Bunche, Ralph Johnson, 1904-1971.

KUGELMASS, J. Alvin. 923.273
Ralph J. Bunche, fighter for peace. New York, J. Messner [1952] 174 p. illus. 22 cm. [E748.B885K8] 52-13539
1. Bunche, Ralph Johnson, 1904-

MANN, Peggy. 341.23'3'0924 B
Ralph Bunche, UN peacemaker / by Peggy Mann. New York : Coward, McCann & Geohegan, c1975. 384 p. : ill. ; 22 cm. Includes index. Bibliography: p. 376-378. [E748.B885M35 1975] 72-76708 ISBN 0-698-20204-X : 10.95. lib. bdg.
1. Bunche, Ralph Johnson, 1904-1971. I. Title.

Bunche, Ralph Johnson, 1904-1971— Juvenile literature.

CORNELL, Jean Gay. 341.23'3'0924 B
Ralph Bunche, champion of peace / by Jean Gay Cornell ; illustrated by Victor Mays. Champaign, Ill. : Garrard Pub. Co., c1976. 96 p. : ill. (some col.) ; 24 cm. (Americans all) Includes index. A biography of a man internationally famous for his efforts towards world peace. [E748.B885C67] 92 75-20368 ISBN 0-8116-4583-5 : 3.58
1. Bunche, Ralph Johnson, 1904-1971—Juvenile literature. I. Mays, Victor, 1927- II. Title.

FEUERLICHT, Roberta Strauss. 001.4'4'0922

In search of peace; the story of four Americans who won the Nobel Peace Prize. New York, J. Messner [1970] 96 p. illus., ports. 22 cm. Bibliography: p. 91. A brief history of the Nobel Prizes and a biography of the man who founded them accompanies biographies of four Americans who received the Nobel Peace Prize. [E176.8.F45 1970] 920 70-123165 3.95
1. Addams, Jane, 1860-1935—Juvenile literature. 2. Bunche, Ralph Johnson, 1904-—Juvenile literature. 3. King, Martin Luther—Juvenile literature. 4. Roosevelt, Theodore, Pres. U.S., 1858-1919—Juvenile literature. 5. Nobel prizes—Juvenile literature. I. Title.

HASKINS, James, 1941- 341.23'3'0924 B
Ralph Bunche; a most reluctant hero [by] Jim Haskins. New York, Hawthorn Books [1974] 134 p. illus. 22 cm. Bibliography: p. 127-130. A biography of the first black American to receive a Ph. D. in political science, the first to hold a high position in the State Department, and the first to win the Nobel Peace Prize. [E748.B885H37] 92 73-9311 6.95
1. Bunche, Ralph Johnson, 1904-1971—Juvenile literature. I. Title.

JOHNSON, Ann Donegan. 341.23'3'0924 B
The value of responsibility : the story of Ralph Bunche / by Ann Donegan Johnson. 1st ed. La Jolla, Calif. : Value Communications, c1978. p. cm. (ValueTales) [E748.B885J63] 78-13960 ISBN 0-916392-29-5 : 5.95
1. Bunche, Ralph Johnson, 1904-1971—Juvenile literature. 2. Statesmen—United States—Biography—Juvenile literature. 3. Responsibility—Juvenile literature. I. Title. 5distributed by Oak Tree Pubns., 11175 Flintkote Ave., Suit e C, San Diego, CA 92121 BIP

Bunin, Ivan Alekseevich, 1870-1953.

BUNIN, Ivan Alekseevich, 1870- 928.917
Memories and portraits; translated by Vera Traill and Robin Chancellor. [1st ed.] Garden City, N. Y., Doubleday, 1951. 217 p. illus. 20 cm. [PG3453.B9Z52 1951a] 51-11520
I. Title.

KATAEV, Valentin Pertrovich, 1897- 891.78'42'03
The grass of oblivion [by] Valentin Katayev. Translated from the Russian and with an introd. by Robert Daglish. New York, McGraw-Hill Book Co. [1970, c1969] 222 p. 21 cm. Translation of Trava zabven'ia (romanized form) [PG3476.K4Z513 1970] 70-101381 5.95
1. Bunin, Ivan Alekseevich, 1870-1953. 2. Maiakovskii, Vladimir Vladimirovich, 1894-1930. 3. Authors, Russian—Correspondence, reminiscences, etc. I. Title.

Bunke, Tamara, 1937-1967.

ROJAS Rodriguez, Marta. 322.4'2'0924 B
Tania, the unforgettable guerrilla. Edited by Marta Rojas and Mirta Rodriguez Calderon. New York, Vintage Books [1971] 212 p. illus. 28 cm. Translation of Tania, la guerrillera inolvidable. [F2849.22.B8R613 1971] 72-181414 ISBN 0-394-71175-0 3.95
1. Bunke, Tamara, 1937-1967. I. Rodriguez Calderon, Mirta, joint author. II. Title.

Bunker, Chang, 1811-1874.

WALLACE, Irving, 1916- 616'.043
The two : a biography / by Irving Wallace and Amy Wallace. New York : Simon and Schuster, c1978. 352 p., [8] leaves of plates : ill. ; 24 cm. Includes index. Bibliography: p. [339]-343. [QM691.W25] 77-13890 ISBN 0-671-22627-4 : 9.95
1. Bunker, Chang, 1811-1874. 2. Bunker, Eng, 1811-1874. 3. Siamese twins—Biography. I. Wallace, Amy, joint author. II. Title. BIP

Bunker, Dennis Miller, 1861-1890.

GAMMELL, Robert Hale Ives, 1893- 759.13
Dennis Miller Bunker. New York, Coward-McCann [1953] xii, 81p. illus., ports. 22cm. [ND237.B885G3] [ND237.B885G3] 927.5 53-7057 53-7057
1. Bunker, Dennis Miller, 1861-1890. I. Title.

Bunn, Matthew, b. 1772?

BUNN, Matthew, b.1772? 973'.04'97 S
Journal of the adventures of Matthew Bunn / Matthew Bunn. New York : Garland Pub., 1977. p. cm. (The Garland library of narratives of North American Indian captivities ; v. 21) Reprint of the 1796 ed. printed by T. Collier, Litchfield. Issued with the reprint of the 1792 ed. of Rogers, John. Letter to Henry Lee. New York. 1977. [E85.G2 vol. 21] [E83.79] 970'.004'97 B 77-6472 ISBN 0-8240-1645-9 lib.bdg. : 25.00
1. Bunn, Matthew, b. 1772? 2. St. Clair's Campaign, 1791. 3. Indians of North America—Captivities. 4. Soldiers—United States—Biography. I. Title. II. Series. BIP

Bunning, James Paul David,

BUNNING, James Paul David, 1931- 927.96357
The story of Jim Bunning, by Jim Bunning as told to Ralph Bernstein. [1st ed.] Philadelphia, Lippincott [1965] 180 p. facsims., ports. 21 cm. [GV865.B83A3] 65-17475
I. Bernstein, Ralph, 1921- II. Title.

Bunny, Rupert Charles Wulsten, 1864-1947.

THOMAS, David Emlyn Liddon. 759.9'94
Rupert Bunny, 1864-1947 [by David Thomas] [Melbourne] Lansdowne [1970] 113, [14] p. illus. (part col.) 32 cm. (Australian art library) Bibliography: p. [13]-[14] (2d group) [ND1105.B85T5] 71-862592 ISBN 0-7018-0380-0 10.00
1. Bunny, Rupert Charles Wulsten, 1864-1947.

Buntain, Mark.

HEMBREE, Ron. 266'.9'9 B
Mark, an intimate portrait of the man behind the ministry in The compassionate touch / by Ron Hembree. Plainfield, N.J. : Logos International, c1979. 241 p., [4] leaves of plates : ill. ; 18 cm. [BV3269.B84H45] 79-53495 ISBN 0-88270-403-6 pbk. : 2.50
1. Buntain, Mark. 2. Missionaries—India—Calcutta—Biography. 3. Missionaries—United States—Biography. 4. Calcutta—Biography. I. Title.

Bunting, Edward, 1773-1843.

FOX, Charlotte Milligan, 1864-1916. 781.7'415
Annals of the Irish harpers. New York, Lemma Pub. Corp. [1974, c1911] p. Reprint of the ed. published by Smith, Elder, London. [ML3654.F69 1974] 72-87976 ISBN 0-87696-044-1 17.50
1. Bunting, Edward, 1773-1843. 2. O'Neill, Arthur, 1737-1816. 3. Harp. 4. Music—Ireland—History and criticism. I. Title: Irish harpers. BIP

Bunuel, Luis, 1900—

ARANDA, J. Francisco, 1926- 791.43'0233'0924 B
Luis Bunuel : a critical biography / by Francisco Aranda ; translated and edited by David Robinson. 1st American ed. New York : Da Capo Press, 1976, c1975. p. cm. Includes index. Filmography: p. [PN1998.A3B7513 1976] 75-31793 ISBN 0-306-70754-3. ISBN 0-306-80028-4 pbk.
1. Bunuel, Luis, 1900- BIP

DURGNAT, Raymond. 791.43'023'0924
Luis Bunuel. [1st American ed. Berkeley] University of California Press [1968, c1967] 152 p. illus. 18 cm. (Movie paperbacks) Bibliography: p. 147-152. [PN1998.A3B77 1968] 68-17758
1. Bunuel, Luis, 1900- BIP

Bunyan, John, 1628-1688.

BRITTAIN, Vera Mary. 928.2
In the steps of John Bunyan; an excursion into Puritan England, with 56 illus. by Cyril Hargreaves and others. London, New York, Rich and Cowan [1950] 440 p. illus., ports., maps, facsims. 19 cm. Bibliography: p. 419-428. [PR3331.B69 1950] 50-13298
1. Bunyan, John, 1628-1688. I. Title.

BRITTAIN, Vera Mary. 928.2
Valiant pilgrim; the story of John Bunyan and Puritan England. With 55 illus. by Cyril Hargreaves and others. New York, Macmillan, 1950. 440 p. illus., ports., maps. 19 cm. London ed. (Rich and Cowan) has title: In the steps of John Bunyan. Bibliography: p. 419-428. [PR3331.B69 1950a] 50-9620
1. Bunyan, John, 1628-1688. I. Title. BIP

BROWN, John, 1830-1922. 823'.4 B
John Bunyan, 1628-1688, his life, times, and work. The tercentenary ed., rev. by Frank Mott Harrison. [Hamden, Conn.] Archon Books, 1969. xxiv, 515 p. illus., facsims., geneal. table, maps, ports. 23 cm. Reprint of the 1928 ed. Includes bibliographical references. [PR3331.B7 1969] 69-13625
1. Bunyan, John, 1628-1688.

BROWN, John, 1830-1922. 828'.4'07 B
John Bunyan: his life, times and work. With illus. by Whymper. [3d ed.] London, W. Isbister. St. Clair Shores, Mich., Scholarly Press, 1972. xvi, 504 p. illus. 22 cm. Reprint of the 1887 ed. "Chronological list of Bunyan's works": p. [483]-488. [PR3331.B7 1972] 70-144906 ISBN 0-403-00844-1
1. Bunyan, John, 1628-1688.

BUCKLAND, Augustus Robert, 1857- 828'.4'07 B
John Bunyan : the man and his work / by A. R. Buckland. Folcroft, Pa. : Folcroft Library Editions, 1976. p. cm. Reprint of the 1928 ed. published by the Religious Tract Society, London. [PR3331.B8 1976] 76-16025 ISBN 0-8414-3319-4 lib. bdg. : 27.50
1. Bunyan, John, 1628-1688. BIP

COATS, Robert Hay, 1873-1956. 828'.4'07
John Bunyan / by R. H. Coats. Folcroft, Pa. : Folcroft Library Editions, 1977. 127 p. ; 23 cm. Reprint of the 1927 ed. published by Student Christian Movement, London. Includes index. [PR3331.C6 1977] 77-9277 ISBN 0-8414-1804-7 lib. bdg. : 15.00
1. Bunyan, John, 1628 1688. 2. Authors, English—Early modern, 1500-1700—Biography. BIP

DAY, Richard Ellsworth, 1884- 928.2
So Pilgrim rang the bells; the life story of John Bunyan. Grand Rapids, Zondervan Pub. House [1955] 151p. illus. 20cm. (His The broad brim books) [PR3331.D3] 55-3498
1. Bunyan, John, 1628-1688. I. Title.

FROUDE, James Anthony, 1818-1894. 823'.4 B
Bunyan. New York, AMS Press [1968] vi, 181 p. 22 cm. (English men of letters) [PR3331.F7 1968] 68-58379
1. Bunyan, John, 1628-1688.

FROUDE, James Anthony, 1818-1894. 828'.4'08 B
Bunyan. [Folcroft, Pa.] Folcroft Library Editions, 1973. p. Reprint of the 1880 ed. published by Macmillan, London, in series: English men of letters. [PR3331.F7 1973] 73-11369 12.00
1. Bunyan, John, 1628-1688. BIP

HARDING, William Henry. 828'.4'07 B
John Bunyan, pilgrim and dreamer / by William Henry Harding. Folcroft, Pa. : Folcroft Library Editions, 1977. 221 p., [3] leaves of plates : ill. ; 23 cm. Reprint of the 1928 ed. published by Revell, New York. [PR3331.H23 1977] 77-9369 ISBN 0-8414-4782-9 lib. bdg. : 25.00
1. Bunyan, John, 1628-1688. 2. Authors, English—Early modern, 1500-1700—Biography. I. Title. BIP

HARRISON, George Bagshawe, 1894- 286'.0924
John Bunyan; a study in personality, by G. B. Harrison. [Hamden, Conn.] Archon, 1967. 191p. 19cm. Reprint of the 1928 London ed. [PR3331.H3 1967] 67-14501 5.00
1. Bunyan, John, 1628-1688. I. Title.

HUTTON, William Holden, 1860-1930. 828'.4'07 B
John Bunyan / by W. H. Hutton. Folcroft, Pa. : Folcroft Library Editions, 1977. 287 p. ; 23 cm. Reprint of the 1928 ed. published by Hodder and Stoughton, London, in series: Hodder and Stoughton's people's library. Includes bibliographical references and index. [PR3331.H8 1977] 77-24947 ISBN 0-8414-4861-2 lib. bdg. : 20.00
1. Bunyan, John, 1628-1688. 2. Authors, English—Early modern, 1500-1700—Biography.

MCCREARY, William Burgess, 1894- 823'.4
John Bunyan, the immortal dreamer, by W. Burgess McCreary. Swengel, Pa., Reiner, 1970. 128 p. illus., port. 19 cm. [PR3331.M3 1970] 70-119507 1.95
1. Bunyan, John, 1628-1688. I. Title.

SHARROCK, Roger. 823'.4
John Bunvan. [New ed.; with rev. bibl.]. London, Melbourne, Macmillan; New York, St. Martin's. 1968. 163p. 21cm. Bibl. [PR3331.S47 1968] (B) 68-22423 5.95
1. Bunyan, John, 1628-1688. I. Title.

TALON, Henri Antoine, 1909- 828'.4'09 B
John Bunyan, the man and his works / by Henri Talon. Folcroft, Pa. : Folcroft Library Editions, 1976, c1951. xii, 340 p., [8] leaves of plates : ill. ; 26 cm. Reprint of the ed. published by Rockliff, London. Translation of John Bunyan, l'homme et l'oeuvre. Includes index. Bibliography: p. 321-332. [PR3331.T32 1976] 76-8161 ISBN 0-8414-8611-5 : 27.50
1. Bunyan, John, 1628-1688. I. Title. BIP

TINDALL, William York, 1903- 828.4
John Bunyan, mechanick preacher [Reissue] New York, Russell & Russell, 1964[c.1934] xii, 309p. 23cm. (Columbia Univ. studies in Eng. and comparative lit.) Bibl. 64-23462 7.50
1. Bunyan, John, 1628-1688. I. Title. II. Series.

WILLCOCKS, Mary Patricia, 1869- 828'.4'07 B
Bunyan calling : a voice from the seventeenth century / M. P. Willcocks. Folcroft, Pa. : Folcroft Library Editions, 1979. p. cm. Reprint of the 1943 ed. published by Allen & Unwin, London. Bibliography: p. [PR3331.W57 1979] 79-18313 ISBN 0-8414-9718-4 (lib. bdg.) : 25.00
1. Bunyan, John, 1628-1688. 2. Authors, English—Early modern, 1500-1700—Biography. I. Title. BIP

WINSLOW, Ola Elizabeth. 928.2
John Bunyan. New York, Macmillan, 1961. 242 p. illus. 22 cm. Includes bibliography. [PR3331.W62] 61-6890
1. Bunyan, John, 1628-1688. BIP

Bunyan, John, 1628-1688—Biography.

HARDING, Richard Winboult. 828'.4'07 B
John Bunyan, his life and times / by R. Winboult Harding. Folcroft, Pa : Folcroft Library Editions, 1976. p. cm. Reprint of the 1928 ed. published by the Epworth Press, London. Includes bibliographical references and index. [PR3331.H22 1976] 76-27749 ISBN 0-8414-4933-3 lib. bdg. : 20.00
1. Bunyan, John, 1628-1688—Biography. 2. Authors, English—Early modern, 1500-1700—Biography. I. Title. BIP

VENABLES, Edmund, 1819-1895. 828'.4'07 B
Life of John Bunyan / by Edmund Venables. Folcroft, Pa. : Folcroft Library Editions, 1977. p. cm. Reprint of the 1888 ed. published by W. Scott, London, in series: Great writers. "Bibliography, by John P. Anderson": p. [PR3331.V4 1977] 77-20805 ISBN 0-8414-9157-7 lib. bdg. : 20.00
1. Bunyan, John, 1628-1688—Biography. 2. Authors, English—Early modern, 1500-1700—Biography.

WILLIAMS, Charles. 828'.4'07 B
A bi-centenary memorial of John Bunyan, who died A.D. 1688 / by Charles Williams. Folcroft, Pa. : Folcroft Library Editions, 1976. p. cm. Reprint of the 1888 ed. published by the Baptist Tract and Book Society, London. Includes index.

[PR3331.W59 1976] 76-27709 ISBN 0-8414-9510-6 lib. bdg. : 17.50
1. Bunyan, John, 1628-1688—Biography. 2. Authors, English—Early modern, 1500-1700—Biography. I. Title. BIP

Bunyan, John—Juvenile literature.

BARR, Gladys H 92
The tinker's armor; the story of John Bunyan. Illustrated by William Hutchinson. Nashville, Broadman Press [1961] 168p. illus. 21cm. [PR3331.B35] 61-7551
1. Bunyan, John—Juvenile literature. I. Title.

BARR, Gladys (Hutchison) j92
1905-
The tinker's armor; the story of John Bunyan. Illustrated by William Hutchinson. Nashville, Broadman Press [1961] 168 p. illus. 21 cm. [PR3331.B35] 61-7551
1. Bunyan, John — Juvenile literature. I. Title.

Buonarroti, Michel Angelo, 1475-1564.

ABELES, Elivn, 1909- 927
Mike and the giant; the story of Michelangelo, told by Kerwin Bowles [pseud.] Illustrated by Mitchell Foster [pseud.] New York, Stravon Publishers [1951] 31 p. illus. 23 x 28 cm. (A Child's book of great artists) Stravon great artist series, 2. [N6923.B9A62] 51-13178
1. Buonarroti, Michel Angelo, 1475-1564. 2. Art—Juvenile literature. I. Title.

ACKER, Helen. 920.045
Five sons of Italy. New York, Nelson [1950] 191 p. 21 cm. Bibliography: p. 190-191. [DG463.A28] 50-8995
1. Leonardo da Vinci, 1452-1519. 2. Buonarroti, Michel Angelo, 1475-1564. 3. Galilei, Galileo, 1564-1642. 4. Paganini, Nicolo, 1782-1840. 5. Verdi, Giuseppe, 1813-1901. I. Title.

ALLEN, Agnes. 927
The story of Michelangelo. New York, Roy [1957?] 198p. illus. 21cm. [N6923] 57-5068
1. Buonarroti, Michel Angelo, 1475-1564. I. Title.

BRANDES, Georg Morris Cohen, 927
1842-1927.
Michelangelo: his life, his times, his era. Translated and with a foreword by Heinz Norden. With 24 [i.e. 23] half-tone plates. New York, Ungar [1963] vii, 428 p. plates. 25 cm. Includes bibliographical references. [N6923.B9B713] 63-8848
1. Buonarroti, Michel Angelo, 1475-1564. I. Title. BIP

BUONARROTI, Michel 730.945
Angelo, 1475-1564.
I, Michelangelo, sculptor; an autobiography through letters. edited by Irving and Jean Stone. From the translation by Charles Speroni. [1st ed.] Garden City, N. Y., Doubleday, 1962. 283 p. plates, facsim. 24 cm. [NB623.B9A253] 62-11312
I. Stone, Irving, 1903- ed. II. Stone, Jean, ed. III. Title.

BUONARROTI, Michel Angelo, 927
1475-1564
Letters; 2v. Tr. from the orig. Tuscan, ed., annotated by E. H. Ramsden [Stanford, Calif.] Stanford [c.]1963. 2v. illus., ports., facsims., geneal. tables. 29cm. Contents.v.1. 1496-1534.--v.2. 1537-1563. Bibl. 63-23707 45.00, set, bxd.
1. Artists—Correspondence, reminiscences, etc. I. Ramsden, E. H., ed. II. Title.

BUONARROTI, Michel Angelo, 927.5
1475-1564.
Michelangelo: a self-portrait. Edited with commentaries and new translations by Robert J. Clements. Englewood Cliffs, N. J., Prentice-Hall [1963] vii, 183 p. 21 cm. (A Spectrum book) [N6923.B9A413] 63-18807
I. Clements, Robert John, 1912- ed.

BUONARROTI, Michel 730'.924 B
Angelo, 1475-1564.
Michelangelo: a self-portrait; texts and sources. Edited with commentaries and new translations by Robert J. Clements. New York, New York University Press, 1968. xi, 193 p. illus. 24 cm. Includes bibliographical references. [N6923.B9A413 1968] 68-31495 8.50
I. Clements, Robert John, 1912- ed.

CONDIVI, Ascanio, 700'.92'4 B
b.ca.1520.
The life of Michelangelo / by Ascanio Condivi ; translated by Alice Sedgwick Wohl ; edited by Hellmut Wohl. Baton Rouge : Louisiana State University Press, c1976. xxii, 156 p. : ill. ; 26 cm. Translation of Vita di Michelagnolo Buonarroti. Includes index. Bibliography: p. 149-151. [N6923.B9C613 1976] 74-27197 15.00
1. Buonarroti, Michel Angelo, 1475-1564. I. Title. BIP

COUGHLAN, Robert, 1914- 709.24
The world of Michelangelo, 1475-1564, by Robert Coughlan and the editors of Time-Life Books New York, Time, inc. [1966] 202 p. illus. (part fold., part col.), coats of arms, geneal. tables, maps, plans, ports. (part col.) 31 cm. (Time-Life library of art) Bibliography: p. 198-199. [NB623.B9C6] 66-16540
1. Buonarroti, Michel Angelo, 1475-1564. 2. Italy—History—1492-1559. I. Time-Life Books. II. Title. BIP

DE TOLNAY, Charles, 1899 759.5
Michelangelo; sculptor, painter, architect. [Princeton, N.J.] Princeton University Press [1975] 283 p. illus. 26 cm. Translation of Michel-Ange. Bibliography: p. 235-248. [ND623.B9D4313] 75-21038 ISBN 0-691-03876-7 19.50
1. Buonarroti, Michel Angelo, 1475-1564. I. Title.

EINEM, Herbert von, 700'.92'4 B
1905-
Michelangelo [by] Herbert von Einem. Translated by Ronald Taylor. London, Methuen [1973] xix, 329, [96] p. illus. 24 cm. Rev. translation of German ed. first published in 1959. Bibliography: p. 266-270. [N6923.B9E413 1973] 73-181074 ISBN 0-416-15140-X
1. Buonarroti, Michel Angelo, 1475-1564. Distributed by Barnes and Noble, 26.50. BIP

HIBBARD, Howard, 700'.92'4 B
1928-
Michelangelo : painter, sculptor, architect / Howard Hibbard. New York : Vendome Press : distributed by Viking Press, [1978] 213 p. : ill. (some col.) ; 32 cm. "An Alexis Gregory book." Includes index. Bibliography: p. 209-212. [N6923.B9H493 1978] 78-7748 ISBN 0-670-47397-9 : 40.00
1. Buonarroti, Michel Angelo, 1475-1564. 2. Artists—Italy—Biography. BIP

PAPINI, Giovanni, 1881- 927
Michelangelo, his life and his era; translated from the Italian by Loretta Murnane. [1st ed.] New York, Dutton, 1952. 542 p. illus. 24 cm. [N6923.B9P313] 52-10425
1. Buonarroti, Michel Angelo, 1475-1564. I. Title.

RIPLEY, Elizabeth, 1906- 927
Michelangelo, a biography. With drawings, paintings, and sculpture by Michelangelo. New York, Oxford University Press, 1953. 68 p. illus. 26 cm. (Oxford books for boys and girls) [N6923.B9R53] 53-3955
1. Buonarroti, Michel Angelo, 1475-1564.

ROLLAND, Romain, 1866-1944 927
Michelangelo. New pref. by Robert J. Clements. Tr. by Frederick Street. New York, Collier [c.1915, 1962] 160p. 18cm. (AS356BBibl. 62-17571 .95 pap.,
1. Buonarroti, Michel Angelo, 1475-1564. I. Title.

SAPANARO, Michele, 1885- 927
Michelangelo. Translated from the Italian by C. J. Richards. New York, Pellegrini & Cudahy [1950] vii, 201 p. plates, ports. 25 cm. [N6923.B9S254 1950] 50-14841
1. Buonarroti, Michel Angelo, 1475-1564. I. Title.

*STONE, Irving, ed. 927
Michelangelo, sculptor; an autobiography through letters. Ed. by Irving and Jean Stone. New York, New Amer. Lib. [1964, c.1962] 256p. ports. 18cm. (Signet T2462) .75. pap.,
I. Title.

SYMONDS, John Addington, v. 12
1840-1893.
The life of Michelangelo Buonarroti. New York, Capricorn Books [1962] 544 p. 28 plates. 19 cm. (Cap 58) 68-72116
1. Buonarroti, Michel Angelo, 1475-1564. I. Title.

Buonarroti, Michel Angelo, 1475-1564—Biography.

GRIMM, Herman 709'.24 B
Friedrich, 1828-1901.
Life of Michael Angelo. Translated with the author's sanction by Fanny Elizabeth Bunnett. Boston, Little, Brown, 1865. St. Clair, Mich., Scholarly Press, 1970- v. 22 cm. Translation of Leben Michelangelos. [ND623.B9G7213] 70-115244 ISBN 0-403-00399-7
1. Buonarroti, Michel Angelo, 1475-1564—Biography. I. Title. BIP

Buonarroti, Michel Angelo, 1475-1564—Juvenile literature.

ABELES, Elvin, 1909- 927
Mike and the giant; the story of Michelangelo, told by Kerwin Bowles. Illustrated by Mitchell Foster. New York, Stravon Publishers [1951] 31 p. illus. 23 x 28 cm. (A Child's book of great artists) Stravon great artist series, 2. [N6923.B9.A62] 51-13178
1. Buonarroti, Michel Angelo, 1475-1564 — Juvenile literature. I. Title.

PECK, Anne Merriman, 1884- 92
Wings of an eagle; the story of Michelangelo, by Anne Merriman Peck, Frank and Dorothy Getlein. Illus. by Lili Pethi. New York, Guild [1965, c.1963] 190p. illus. 19cm. (Turret bks., 31500) .50 pap.,
1. Buonarroti, Michel Angelo, 1475-1564—Juvenile literature. I. Title.

PECK, Anne Merriman, 1884- 920
Wings of an eagle; the story of Michelangelo, by Anne Merriman Peck with Frank and Dorothy Getlein. Illus. by Lili Rethi. New York, Hawthorn [c.1963] 186p. illus. 22cm. (Credo bks.) 63-8785 2.95
1. Buonarroti, Michel Angelo, 1475-1564—Juvenile literature. I. Title.

RABOFF, Ernest Lloyd. 709'.24
Michelangelo Buonarroti, by Ernest Raboff. Garden City, N.Y., Doubleday [1971] [31] p. illus. (part col.), ports. 29 cm. (Art for children) (A Gemini Smith book) Discusses the life and art of the Renaissance sculptor, poet, and painter. Includes color and black and white reproductions of many of his works. [ND623.B9R3] 71-139055 3.95
1. Buonarroti, Michel Angelo, 1475-1564—Juvenile literature. I. Title.

STEARNS, Monroe. 730'.924 B
Michelangelo. New York, F. Watts [1970] x, 246 p. illus., port. 25 cm. (Immortals of art) Bibliography: p. [237]-239. The life of the Renaissance sculptor, painter, architect, and poet. [ND623.B9S7] 92 78-95640 5.95
1. Buonarroti, Michel Angelo, 1475-1564—Juvenile literature. I. Title. BIP

Burbank, Luther, 1849-1926.

BRAGDON, Lillian J. 926.3
Luther Burbank, nature's helper. Illustrated by Frederick T. Chapman. New York, Abingdon Press [1959] 124 p. illus. 21 cm. (Makers of America) [SB63.B9B73] 59-10297
1. Burbank, Luther, 1849-1926.

BURT, Olive (Woolley) 635'.0924 B
1894-
Luther Burbank, boy wizard. Illustrated by James Ponter. Indianapolis, Bobbs-Merrill [1962] 200 p. illus. 20 cm. (Childhood of famous Americans) Emphasizes the boyhood of the botanist who developed or improved many species of fruit, flower, and vegetable, including the potato which bears his name. [SB63.B9B9 1962] 92 AC 68
1. Burbank, Luther, 1849-1926. I. Porter, James, illus. II. Title.

CLAMPETT, Frederick 211'.6'0924
William.
Luther Burbank, "our beloved infidel"; his religion of humanity, by Frederick W. Clampett. Westport, Conn., Greenwood Press [1970] 144 p. facsim., port. 23 cm. Reprint of the 1926 ed. [BL2790.B8C5 1970] 73-109720
1. Burbank, Luther, 1849-1926.

DREYER, Peter, 1939- 635'.092'4 B
A gardener touched with genius : the life of Luther Burbank / by Peter Dreyer. New York : Coward, McCann & Geoghegan, c1975. 322 p., [4] leaves of plates : ill. ; 24 cm. Includes bibliographical references and index. [SB63.B9D73 1975] 75-10477 ISBN 0-698-10691-1 : 10.00
1. Burbank, Luther, 1849-1926. I. Title. BIP

KRAFT, Ken. 635'.0924 B
Luther Burbank; the wizard and the man [by] Ken and Pat Kraft. [1st ed.] New York, Meredith Press [1967] xvi, 270 p. plates (incl. ports.) 21 cm. Bibliography: p. 263-264. [SB63.B9K7] 67-12638
1. Burbank, Luther, 1849-1926. I. Kraft, Pat, joint author.

Burchard, Florence, 1914-

BURCHARD, Florence, 266'.73 B
1914-
Someone had to hold the lantern / by Florence Burchard with Sharon Boucher ; [edited by Don Short ; designed by Dean Tucher]. Nashville : Southern Pub. Association, c1979. p. cm. [BV2843.H7B873] 79-17836 ISBN 0-8127-0238-7 pbk. : 3.95
1. Burchard, Florence, 1914- 2. Missionaries—Honduras—Biography. 3. Missionaries—United States—Biography. I. Boucher, Sharon. II. Short, Dan, 1936- III. Title. BIP

Burchett, Wilfred G.,

BURCHETT, Wilfred G., 070.9'24 B
1911-
Passport; an autobiography [by] Wilfred Burchett. [Melbourne, Thomas Nelson (Australia) 1969] viii, 304 p. illus., ports. 23 cm. Includes bibliographical references. [PN5510.B8] 79-489923 4.95
1. Title.

Burchfield, Charles Ephraim, 1893-1967.

BAIGELL, Matthew. 759.13
Charles Burchfield / by Matthew Baigell. New York : Watson-Guptill Publications, 1976. p. cm. Includes index. [ND237.B89B24] 76-15169 ISBN 0-8230-0533-X : 35.00
1. Burchfield, Charles Ephraim, 1893-1967. BIP

BAUR, John Ireland Howe, 927.5
1909-
Charles Burchfield. [Research by Rosalind Irvine] New York, Published for the Whitney Museum of American Art by Macmillan, 1956. 86 p. 75 illus. (part col.) port. 27 cm. "This book grew out of a retrospective exhibition of Charles Burchfield's paintings and drawings, held at the Whitney Museum of American Art in January and February, 1956." Bibliography: p. [82]-85. [ND237.B89B3] 759.13 56-322
1. Burchfield, Charles Ephraim, 1893-1967. I. Whitney Museum of American Art, New York.

Burckhardt, Jakob Christoph,

BURCKHARDT, Jakob 928.3
Christoph, 1818-1897.
Letters. Selected, edited and translated by Alexander Dru. New York, Pantheon Books [1955] xi, 242p. illus., ports. 23cm. 'Principal editions of Burckhardt's letters': p. 240. [D15] 55-2791
1. Title.

Burdett-Coutts, Angela Georgina Burdett-Coutts, Baroness, 1814-1906.

HEALY, Edna. 942.081'092'4 B
Lady unknown : the life of Angela Burdett-Coutts / Edna Healey. 1st American ed. New York : Coward, McCann & Geoghegan, 1978. 253 p. : ill. ; 24 cm. Includes index. Bibliography: p. 231-233. [HV28.B7H4 1978] 78-5470 ISBN 0-698-10939-2 : 12.50
1. Burdett-Coutts, Angela Georgina

Burdett-Coutts, Baroness, 1814-1906. 2. Philanthropists—Biography. I. Title. **BIP**

Burdette, Selva Lewis, 1926-

SCHOOR, Gene. 927.96357
Lew Burdette of the Braves. New York, Putnam [1960] 186 p. 21 cm. [GV865.B85S3] 60-6907
1. Burdette, Selva Lewis, 1926-

Burgess, Charles Frederick, 1873-1945.

MCQUEEN, Alexander, 1886- 926.6
A romance in research; the life of Charles F. Burgess, student, teacher, researcher, industrialist. With a foreword by George W. Heise and a technical appendix by Oliver W. Storey. Pittsburgh, Instruments Pub. Co., 1951. viii, 429 p. illus., ports., map. 24 cm. Bibliography: p. 413-420. [TP140.B8M3] 51-3074
1. Burgess, Charles Frederick, 1873-1945. I. Title.

Burgess, Thornton Waldo,

BURGESS, Thornton Waldo, 925.7
1874-1965.
Now I remember; autobiography of an amateur naturalist. [1st ed.] Boston, Little, Brown [1960] 338 p. illus. 22 cm. [PS3503.U6075Z52] 60-11637
I. Title.

Burgess, Thornton Waldo, 1874-1965—Homes and haunts—Sandwich, Mass.

LOVELL, Russell A. 813'.5'2 B
The Cape Cod story of Thornton W. Burgess, by Russell A. Lovell, Jr. With an extensive bibliography of Burgess' books, prepared by Ralph M. Titcomb. [Sandwich, Mass.] Town of Sandwich [1974] 111 p. illus. 27 cm. Bibliography: p. 92-93. [PS3503.U6075Z75] 74-77478 ISBN 0-88492-001-1
1. Burgess, Thornton Waldo, 1874-1965—Homes and haunts—Sandwich, Mass. 2. Burgess, Thornton Waldo, 1874-1965—Bibliography. I. Title.

Burghley, William Cecil, baron, 1520-1598.

BARNETT, Richard C., 942.05'0922
1932-
Place, profit, and power; a study of the servants of William Cecil, Elizabethan statesman, by Richard C. Barnett. Chapel Hill, University of North Carolina Press, 1969. 180 p. 23 cm. (The James Sprunt studies in history and political science, v. 51) Includes bibliographical references. [F251.J28 vol. 51] 77-97023
1. Burghley, William Cecil, Baron, 1520-1598. 2. Gt. Brit.—Politics and government—1558-1603. 3. Gt. Brit.—Officials and employees. I. Title. II. Series. **BIP**

BECKINGSALE, B. W. 942.05/0924
Burghley: Tudor statesman, 1520-1598 [by] B. W. Beckingsale. London, Melbourne, Macmillan; New York, St. Martins Pr., 1967. x, 340p. front., 16 plates (incl. ports., facsims.). 23cm. Bibl. [DA358.B9B4] (B) 67-19278 10.00
1. Burghley, William Cecil, Baron, 1520-1598. I. Title.

BECKINGSALE, B W 942.05'0924 (B)
Burghley: Tudor statesman, 1520-1598 [by] B. W. Beckingsale London, Melbourne[etc.] Macmillan; New York, St. Martin's P., 1967. x. 340 p. front., 16 plates (incl. ports., facsims.). 22 1/3 cm. (B67-22709) Bibliography: p. 824-825. [DA358.B9B4] 67-19278 63/-
1. Burghley, William Cecil, Baron, 1520-1598. I. Title.

READ, Conyers 923.242
Lord Burghley and Queen Elizabeth. New York, Knopf, 1960[ ] 603p. (bibl. notes: p. 549-590) ports., facsim. 26cm. 60-1682 10.00
1. Burghley, William Cecil, 1520-1598. 2. Elizabeth, Queen of England, 1533-1603. I. Title.

READ, Conyers, 1881- 923.242
Mr. Secretary Cecil and Queen Elizabeth. New York, Knopf, 1955. 510p. illus., ports. 26cm. Erratum slip inserted. Bibliographical references included in 'Notes' (p. 469-495) [DA358] 54-7211
1. Burghley, William Cecil, baron, 1520-1598. 2. Elizabeth, Queen of England, 1533-1603. I. Title.

SMITH, Alan Gordon. 942.05'5'0924
William Cecil; the power behind Elizabeth. New York, Haskell House, 1971. xi, 275 p. illus. 23 cm. "First published 1934." Bibliography: p. 263. [DA358.B9S5 1971] 73-155113 ISBN 0-8383-1286-1
1. Burghley, William Cecil, Baron, 1520-1598. 2. Gt. Brit.—History—Elizabeth, 1558-1603.

Burgoyne, John, 1722-1792.

GERSON, Noel 973.3'41'0924 B
Bertram, 1914-
The man who lost America: a biography of Gentleman Johnny Burgoyne, by Paul Lewis. New York, Dial Press, 1973. 282 p. 24 cm. Bibliography: p. 275-276. [DA67.1.B8G47] 72-10285 7.95
1. Burgoyne, John, 1722-1792. I. Title.

HOWSON, Gerald. 973.3'41'0924 B
Burgoyne of Saratoga : a biography / Gerald Howson. New York : Times Books, c1978. p. cm. Includes index. Bibliography: p. [DA67.1.B8H68] 78-53303 ISBN 0-8129-0770-1 : 12.50
1. Burgoyne, John, 1722-1792. 2. Great Britain. Army—Biography. 3. United States—History—Revolution, 1775-1783—British forces. 4. United States—History—Revolution—Campaigns and battles. 5. Generals—Great Britain—Biography. I. Title. **BIP**

LUNT, James D., 973.3'41'0924 B
1917-
John Burgoyne of Saratoga / James Lunt. New York : Harcourt Brace Jovanovich, [1975] xiv, 369 p., [1] leaf of plates : ill. ; 22 cm. Includes index. Bibliography: p. 339-343. [DA67.1.B8L86] 75-15699 ISBN 0-15-146402-2 : 14.98
1. Burgoyne, John, 1722-1792. I. Title. **BIP**

LUNT, James D., 973.3'41'0924 B
1917-
John Burgoyne of Saratoga / James Lunt. London : Macdonald and Jane's, 1976. xiv, 369 p., plate : plans, port. ; 22 cm. Includes index. Bibliography: p. 339-343. [DA67.1.B8L86 1976] 76-376568 ISBN 0-356-08359-4 : £5.50
1. Burgoyne, John, 1722-1792. 2. Burgoyne's Invasion, 1777. 3. Generals—Great Britain—Biography. I. Title.

Burgoyne, John, 1722-1792—Juvenile literature.

O'CONNOR, Richard, 973.341'0924 B
1915-
John Burgoyne; gentlemen (i.e. gentleman) and general. New York, McGraw Hill [1969] 127 p. illus., maps, ports. 24 cm. (Saratoga cluster) Bibliography: p. [124]-[125] A biography of the English officer, member of Parliament, and playwright who was known as "Gentleman Johnny" and participated in several important campaigns of the Revolutionary War. [DA67.1.B8O26] 92 72-88329
1. Burgoyne, John, 1722-1792—Juvenile literature. I. Title.

Buri, Aaron, 1716-1757.

REED, V. B. ed. 923.273
The case of Aaron Burr, edited by v. B. Reed and J. D. Williams. Boston, Houghton Mifflin [1960] 204p. illus. 25cm. (Houghton Mifflin research series, no. 2) [E302.6.B9R4] 60-51331
1. Buri, Aaron, 1716-1757. I. Williams, James David, 1929- joint ed. II. Title.

Burk, Wayne.

BURK, Wayne. 364.15'5'0924 B
The thief; the autobiography of Wayne Burk as told to Ted Thackrey, Jr. Los Angeles, Nash Pub. [1971] 441 p. 23 cm. [HV6248.B775A3] 73-127488 ISBN 0-8402-1156-2 6.95
I. Thackrey, Ted. II. Title.

Burke, Arleigh Albert, 1901-

JONES, John Kenneth, 923.573
1903-
Admiral Arleigh (31-knot) Burke; the story of a fighting sailor, by Ken Jones and Hubert Kelley, Jr. [1st ed.] Philadelphia, Chilton Books [1962] 203 p. illus. 25 cm. [E182.B96J6] 62-18614
1. Burke, Arleigh Albert, 1901- I. Kelley, Hubert, joint author. II. Title.

JONES, Ken. 923.573
Admiral Arleigh (31-knot) Burke; the story of a fighting sailor, by Ken Jones and Hubert Kelley. Jr. 1st ed. Philadelphia, Chilton Books [1962] 203p. illus. 25cm. [E182.B96J6] 62-18614
1. Burke, Arleigh Albert, 1901- I. Kelley, Hubert, joint author. II. Title.

Burke Co., N.D.—Biography.

BURKE County 917.84'72'030922 B
and White Earth Valley Historical Society, 1971. [Bismarck? N.D., Printed by Quality Print. Co., 1972] 1288 p. illus. 29 cm. A history of the county covering the years 1896 to 1972. [F642.B85B87] 73-159342
1. Burke Co., N.D.—Biography. I. Burke County and White Earth Valley Historical Society.

Burke, Edmund, 1729?-1797.

BURKE, Edmund 923.242
The correspondence of Edmund Burke, v.2, July 1768-June 1774. Edited by Lucy S. Sutherland. Chicago, University of Chicago Press, 1960[ ]. xxiii, 566p. (bibl. footnotes) port. 24cm. 58-5615 12.00
I. Title.

BURKE, Edmund, 1729?- 923.242
1797.
The correspondence of Edmund Burke. v. 3. Ed. by Thomas W. Copeland. Chicago, Univ. of Chicago 0)press, 1961[ ] xxv, 478p. front. port. Bibl. 58-5615 12.00
I. Title.

BURKE, Edmund, 1729-1797 923.242
The correspondence of Edmund Burke. Ed. by Alfred Cobban, Robert A. Smith [London] Cambridge Univ. Pr.; Chicago, Univ. of Chicago Pr., 1967. v. port. 24cm. Contents.v.6. July 1789-December 1791 Bibl. [DA506.B9A18] 58-5616 13.50
I. Cobban, Alfied, ed. II. Smith, Robert A., joint ed. III. Title.

CHAPMAN, Gerald 942.07'3'0924
Wester
Edmund Burke, the practical imagination [by] Gerald W. Chapman. Cambridge, Harvard, 1967. x, 350p. port. 2icm. Bibl. [DA506B9C5] 67-17305 5.95
1. Burke, Edmund, 1729?-1797. I. Title.

CHAPMAN, Gerald 942.07'3'0924
Wester.
Edmund Burke, the practical imagination [by] Gerald W. Chapman. Cambridge, Harvard University Press, 1967. x, 350 p. port. 22 cm. Bibliography: p. [287]-203. [DA506.B9C5] 67-17305
*1. Burke, Edmund, 1720?-1707. I. Title.***BIP**

CONE, Carl B. 923.242
Burke and the nature of politics [v.2. Lexington] Univ. of Ky. Pr. [c.1964] 527p. 25cm. Contents.[2] The age of the French Revoluion. Bibl. 57-11380 9.00
1. Burket, Edmund, 1720?-1797. 2. Gt. Brit.—Pol. & govt.—1760-1820. I. Title.

CONE, Carl B 923.242
Burke and the nature of politics. [Lexington] University of Kentucky Press [1957- v. illus., port. 25cm. Contents.[1] The age of the American Revolution. Bibliographical footnotes. [DA506.B9C54] 57-11380
1. Burke, Edmund, 17297-1797. 2. Gt. Brit.—Pol. & govt.—1760-1820. I. Title.

COPELAND, Thomas 942.07'3'0924 B
Wellsted, 1907-
Our eminent friend Edmund Burke; six essays, by Thomas W. Copeland. Westport, Conn., Greenwood Press [1970, c1949] ix, 251 p. illus., port. 23 cm. Includes bibliographical references. [DA506.B9C6 1970] 76-104217 ISBN 0-8371-3334-3
1. Burke, Edmund, 1729?-1797. I. Title.

COURTNEY, Cecil 320'.092'2
Patrick.
Montesquieu and Burke / by C. P. Courtney. Westport, Conn. : Greenwood Press, 1975, c1963. xv, 204 p. ; 22 cm. Reprint of the ed. published by Blackwell, Oxford, in series: Modern language studies. Includes index. Bibliography: p. 185-194. [DA506.B9C65 1975] 74-2586 ISBN 0-8371-7406-6
1. Burke, Edmund, 1729?-1797. 2. Montesquieu, Charles Louis de Secondat, baron de La Brede et de, 1689-1755. 3. Political science—History—Great Britain. 4. Great Britain—Politics and government—1760-1820. I. Title. **BIP**

KRAMNICK, Isaac, 942.07'3'0924 B
comp.
Edmund Burke. Englewood Cliffs, N.J., Prentice-Hall [1974] vii, 180 p. 21 cm. (Great lives observed) (A Spectrum book, S-746) Bibliography: p. 177-178. [DA506.B9K65 1974] 74-12324 ISBN 0-13-090597-6 6.95; 2.45 (pbk.)
1. Burke, Edmund, 1729?-1797.

MAGNUS, Philip 942.07'3'0924 B
Montefiore, Sir, bart., 1906-
Edmund Burke: a life, by Sir Philip Magnus. New York, Russell & Russell [1973] xiii, 367 p. illus. 23 cm. Reprint of the 1939 ed. published by J. Murray, London. Bibliography: p. 351-355. [DA506.B9M3 1973] 72-94982 ISBN 0-8462-1723-6 20.00
1. Burke, Edmund, 1729?-1797. **BIP**

MILLER, Alice P. 941.07'3'0924 B
Edmund Burke and his world / Alice P. Miller ; introd. by Russell Kirk. Old Greenwich, Conn. : Devin-Adair Co., c1979. xiv, 232 p., [8] leaves of plates : ill. ; 23 cm. Includes index. Bibliography: p. [221]-226. [DA506.B9M55] 78-62647 ISBN 0-8159-5404-2 : 12.95
1. Burke, Edmund, 1729?-1797. 2. Statesmen—Great Britain—Biography. I. Title. **BIP**

MORLEY, John 942.073'0924 B
Morley, Viscount, 1838-1923.
Burke. New York, AMS Press [1968] viii, 216 p. 22 cm. (English men of letters) Reprint of the 1887 ed. [DA506.B9M8 1968] 68-58388
1. Burke, Edmund, 1729?-1797. **BIP**

MORLEY, John 941.07'3'0924 B
Morley, Viscount, 1838-1923.
Edmund Burke / John Morley. New York : Arno Press, 1979. p. cm. (European political thought) Reprint of the 1867 ed. published by Macmillan, London. [DA506.B9M82 1979] 78-67372 ISBN 0-405-11722-1 : 20.00
1. Burke, Edmund, 1729?-1797. 2. Statesmen—Great Britain—Biography. I. Title. II Series.

OLIVER, Robert 942.07'3'0922
Tarbell, 1909-
Four who spoke out: Burke, Fox, Sheridan, Pitt, by Robert T. Oliver. Freeport, N.Y., Books for Libraries Press [1969, c1946] x, 196 p. 23 cm. (Biography index reprint series) Bibliography: p. 184-196. [DA522.A1O55 1969] 75-101831
1. Burke, Edmund, 1729?-1797. 2. Fox, Charles James, 1749-1806. 3. Sheridan, Richard Brinsley Butler, 1751-1816. 4. Pitt, William, 1759-1806. 5. Orators, English. I. Title.

PRIOR, James, Sir 942.07'3'0924
1790?-1864
Memoir of the life and character of the Right Hon. Edmund Burke, with specimens of his poetry and letters, and an estimate of his genius and talents, compared with those of his great contemporaries. New York, Burt Franklin [1968] 2v. 19cm. (Burt Franklin res. & source works, 243) Reprint of 1854 ed. "List of the chief writings of the Right Hon. Edmund Burke"; v.1, p. [21]-27. [DA506] (B) 68-56758 25.00
1. Burke, Edmund, 1729?-1797. I. Title.

Burke, Edmund, 1729?-1797—Political science.

KRAMNICK, Isaac. 320.5'2'0924 B
The rage of Edmund Burke : portrait of an ambivalent conservative / Isaac Kramnick. New York : Basic Books, c1977. xiii, 225 p. ; 24 cm. Includes bibliographical references and index. [JC176.B83K7] 76-43466 ISBN 0-465-06829-4 : 15.95
1. Burke, Edmund, 1729?-1797—Political science. 2. Burke, Edmund, 1729?-1797. 3. Political scientists—Great Britain—Biography. I. Title. BIP

Burke, John Joseph, 1875-1936.

SHEERIN, John B. 282'.092'4 B
Never look back : the career and concerns of John J. Burke / John B. Sheerin. New York : Paulist Press, c1975. 254 p. ; 24 cm. Bibliography: p. 253-254. [BX4705.B898S5] 75-19689 ISBN 0-8091-0200-5 : 7.95
1. Burke, John Joseph, 1875-1936. I. Title.

Burke, Margaret Knudsen.

SPRINGER, John A., 1911-1961. 920.7
Innocent in Alaska; the story of Margaret Knudsen Burke. New York, Coward-McCann [1963] 319 p. 22 cm. [CT275.B78523S6] 62-21255
1. Burke, Margaret Knudsen. I. Title.

Burke, Thomas, 1849-1925.

NESBIT, Robert Carrington, 1917- 979.777
"He built Seattle"; a biography of Judge Thomas Burke. Seattle, University of Washington Press, 1961. 455 p. illus. 24 cm. (University of Washington publications in history [2]) Includes bibliography. [CT275.B78525N4] 61-5800
1. Burke, Thomas, 1849-1925. 2. Seattle—History. 3. Railroads—Northwest, Pacific. I. Title.

Burkitt, Denis Parsons.

GLEMSER, Bernard, 1908- 610'.924 B
Mr. Burkitt and Africa. New York, World Pub. Co. [1970] xii, 236 p. illus., ports. 21 cm. [R493.B8G57] 70-112435 6.95
1. Burkitt, Denis Parsons. 2. Burkitt's lymphoma. I. Title.

Burma—Social life and customs.

BIXLER, Norma. 915.91'03'50922
Burmese journey. [Yellow Springs, Ohio] Antioch Press, 1967. 238 p. 24 cm. Autobiographical. [DS485.B84B59] 67-11440
1. Burma—Social life and customs. I. Title. BIP

Burmester, Willy, 1869-1933.

BURMESTER, Willy, 1869-1933. 787'.1'0924 B
Fifty years as a concert violinist / by Willy Burmester ; translated from the German by Roberta Franke, in collaboration with Samuel Wolf. Linthicum Heights, Md. : Swand Publications, c1975. 168 p. ; 22 cm. Translation of Funfzig Jahre Kunstlerleben. [ML418.B96A33] 75-21393
1. Burmester, Willy, 1869-1933. 2. Musicians—Correspondence, reminiscences, etc. I. Franke, Roberta. II. Wolf, Samuel. III. Title.

Burn, June.

BURN, June. 920.7
Living high; an unconventional autobiography. 1st Wellington Books ed. Belmont, Mass, Wellington Books [1958] 292p. illus. 21cm. [PS3503.U6248Z5 1958] 58-37375
I. Title.

Burnaby, Frederick Gustavus, 1842-1885.

ALEXANDER, Michael. 923.542
The true blue; the life and adventures of Colonel Fred Burnaby. 1842-85. New York, St. Martin's Press, 1958[c1957] 215p. illus. 23cm. [DA68.32.B85A7 1958] 58-14916
1. Burnaby, Frederick Gustavus, 1842-1885. I. Title.

Burne-Jones, Edward Coley, Sir, bart., 1833-1898.

BAYLISS, Wyke, Sir, 1835-1906. 759.2
Five great painters of the Victorian era: Leighton, Millais, Burne-Jones, Watts, Holman Hunt. New York, AMS Press [1971] vii, 159 p. illus., ports. 19 cm. Reprint of the 1902 ed. [ND467.B4 1971] 72-129384 ISBN 0-404-00696-5
1. Leighton, Frederic Leighton, Baron, 1830-1896. 2. Millais, John Everett, Sir, bart., 1829-1896. 3. Burne-Jones, Edward Coley, Sir, bart., 1833-1898. 4. Watts, George Frederick, 1817-1904. 5. Hunt, William Holman, 1827-1910.

Burnes, Alexander, Sir, 1805-1841.

LUNT, James D., 1917- 915 B
Bokhara Burnes. New York, Barnes & Noble [1969] 220 p. illus., maps, ports. 21 cm. (Great travellers) Bibliography: p. 214-215. [DS475.2.B78L85 1969b] 74-8545 4.75
1. Burnes, Alexander, Sir, 1805-1841. I. Title. BIP

Burnet, David Staats, 1808-1867.

KEITH, Noel Leonard. 922.673
The story of D. S. Burnet: undeserved obscurity. St. Louis, Bethany Press [1954] 272p. illus. 23cm. [Bethany history series] [BX7343.B8K4] 55-17416
1. Burnet, David Staats, 1808-1867. I. Title.

Burnet, Frank Macfarlane, Sir, 1899-

BURNET, Frank Macfarlane, Sir, 1899- 610'.924 B
Changing patterns; an atypical autobiography [by] Sir Macfarlane Burnet. [Melbourne] Heinemann [1968] 282 p. illus., ports. 23 cm. Bibliography: p. [268]-270. [QR31.B8A3] 78-396375 5.95
I. Title.

BURNET, Frank Macfarlane, Sir, 1899- 610'.924 B
Changing patterns; an atypical autobiography [by] Sir Macfarlane Burnet. New York, American Elsevier Pub. Co., 1969 [c1968] 282 p. illus., ports. 22 cm. Bibliography: p. [268]-270. [QR31.B8A3 1969] 72-99091
I. Title.

NORRY, Roy. 610'.924 B
Virus hunter in Australia; the story of Sir Macfarlane Burnet. Illustrated by Don Angus. [Melbourne, Nelson (Australia) 1966. 27 p. col. illus. 18 x 20 cm. (Lyrebird books) [QR31.B8N6] 67-91663
1. Burnet, Frank Macfarlane, Sir, 1899- I. Title.

Burnett, Carol.

CARPOZI, George. 790.2'092'4 B
The Carol Burnett story / by George Carpozi, Jr. New York : Warner Paperback Library, 1975. 206 p. : ill. ; 18 cm. [PN2287.B85C3] 75-319621 ISBN 0-446-78639-X pbk. : 1.50
1. Burnett, Carol. I. Title.

Burnett, Carol—Juvenile literature.

PAIGE, David. 790.2'092'4 B
Carol Burnett / written by David Paige ; designed by Gene Kohler. [Mankato, Minn.] : Creative Education, [c1977] 30 p. : ill. ; 25 cm. (Stars of stage and screen) A biography of a famous comedian, star of her own long-running TV variety show, who sings, dances, and acts in dramatic films as well. [PN2287.B85P3] 92 76-40615 ISBN 0-87191-555-3 lib.bdg. : 4.95
1. Burnett, Carol—Juvenile literature. 2. Entertainers—United States—Biography—Juvenile literature. I. Title. BIP

Burnett, Frances Hodgson, 1849-1924—Biography.

BURNETT, Constance (Buel) 928.1
Happily ever after; a portrait of Frances, Hodgson Burnett by Constance Buel Burnett. New York, Vanguard Press [1965] 160 p. port 21 cm. [PS1216.B76] 65-17370
1. Burnett, Frances (Hodgson) 1849-1924 — Juvenile literature. I. Title. BIP

THWAITE, Ann. 813'.4 B
Waiting for the party; the life of Frances Hodgson Burnett, 1849-1924. New York, Scribner [1974] xii, 274 p. illus. 25 cm. Bibliography: p. [250]-[255] [PS1216.T5] 74-7794 ISBN 0-684-13989-8 10.00
1. Burnett, Frances Hodgson, 1849-1924—Biography. I. Title.

Burney, Charles, 1726-1814.

ARBLAY, Frances Burney d', 1752-1840. 780'.92'4 B
Memoirs of Doctor Burney : arranged from his own manuscripts, from family papers, and from personal recollections / by Madame d'Arblay. New York : AMS Press, [1975] p. cm. Reprint of the 1832 ed. published by E. Moxon, London. [ML423.B9A6 1975] 78-37680 ISBN 0-404-56704-5 : 74.50(3vol. set)
1. Burney, Charles, 1726-1814. I. Title.

LONSDALE, Roger H 927.8
Dr. Charles Burney; a literary biography, by Roger Lonsdale. Oxford, Clarendon press, 1965. xvi, 527 p. facsim., ports. 23 cm. Bibliography: p. [495]-507. [ML423.B9L6] 65-2503
1. Burney, Charles, 1726-1814. 2. London — Intellectual life. I. Title.

SCHOLES, Percy Alfred, 1877-1958. 780'.924 B
The great Dr. Burney; his life, his travels, his works, his family, and his friends. Westport, Conn., Greenwood Press [1971] 2 v. illus. 23 cm. Reprint of the 1948 ed. [ML423.B9S3 1971] 74-104254 ISBN 0-8371-4017-X (set)
1. Burney, Charles, 1726-1814. 2. Burney family. 3. London—Intellectual life. I. Title. BIP

Burney family.

JOHNSON, Reginald Brimley, 1867-1932, comp. 823'.6' B
Fanny Burney and the Burneys. Edited, with introd., by R. Brimley Johnson. Freeport, N.Y., Books for Libraries Press [1971] 407 p. illus. 23 cm. Selections from the writings of members of the Burney family. Reprint of the 1926 ed. [PR3316.A4A6 1971] 71-37350 ISBN 0-8369-6697-X
1. Burney family. 2. English literature. I. Title. BIP

Burney, Henry, 1792-1845.

HALL, Daniel George Edward, 1891- 327'.2'0924 B
Henry Burney : a political biography / D. G. E. Hall. London ; New York : Oxford University Press, 1974. xiii, 330 p., [3] leaves of plates : ill. ; 22 cm. Includes index. Bibliography: p. [320]-322. [DS529.7.B87H34] 75-300683 ISBN 0-19-713583-8 : 16.00
1. Burney, Henry, 1792-1845. 2. Burma—History—1824-1948. 3. Thailand—History. BIP

Burnham, Daniel Hudson, 1846-1912.

HINES, Thomas S. 720'.92'4 B
Burnham of Chicago, architect and planner / Thomas S. Hines. New York : Oxford University Press, 1974. xxiii, 445 p. : ill. ; 24 cm. Includes index. Bibliography: p. 387-400. [NA737.B85H56] 74-79625 ISBN 0-19-501836-2 : 19.50
1. Burnham, Daniel Hudson, 1846-1912. I. Title.

MOORE, Charles, 1855-1942. 720'.924 B
Daniel H. Burnham; architect, planner of cities. New York, Da Capo Press, 1968. 2 v. in 1. illus. 26 cm. (Da Capo Press series in architecture and decorative art, v. 17) (A Da Capo Press reprint edition.) Reprint of the 1921 ed. Each vol. has also special t.p. Bibliographical footnotes. [NA737.B85M6 1968] 68-27726
1. Burnham, Daniel Hudson, 1846-1912.

Burns, Anthony, 1834-1862.

STEVENS, Charles Emery, 1815-1893. 301.45'22'0924 B
Anthony Burns, a history. New York, Arno Press, 1969. 295 p. illus. 23 cm. (The Anti-slavery crusade in America) Reprint of the 1856 ed. Includes bibliographical references. [E450.B96 1969b] 74-82225
1. Burns, Anthony, 1834-1862. I. Title. II. Series. BIP

Burns, George, 1896-

BURNS, George, 1896- 791'.092'4 B
Living it up : or, They still love me in Altoona! / By George Burns. New York : Putnam, c1976. 251 p., [8] leaves of plates : ill. ; 22 cm. [PN2287.B87A34] 76-16059 8.95
1. Burns, George, 1896- 2. Comedians—United States—Biography. I. Title.

BURNS, George 1896- 791'.092'4
Living it up : or, They still love me in Altoona! / George Burns. New York : Berkley Pub. Corp., 1978,c1976. 247 p. : photos ; 18 cm. (A Berkley Book.) [PN2287B87A34] ISBN 0-425-03613-8 pbk. : 1.95
1. Burns, George,1896- 2. Comedians — United States — Biography. I. Title.
L.C. card no. for 1976 G. P. Putnam ed.: 76-16059.

BURNS, George, 1896- 791'.092'4 B
The third time around : confessions of a happy hoofer / by George Burns. New York : Putnam, c1980. p. cc. [PN2287.B87A37] 79-15370 ISBN 0-399-12169-2 : 9.95
1. Burns, George, 1896- 2. Comedians—United States—Biography. I. Title.

Burns, Harrison, 1836-1925.

BURNS, Harrison, 1836-1925. 977.2'008 S
Personal recollections of Harrison Burns, as written in 1907. Indianapolis : Indiana Historical Society, 1975. 83 p., [1] leaf of plates : port. ; 23 cm. (Publications - Indiana Historical Society ; v. 25, no. 2) [F521.I41 vol. 25, no. 2] [F532.J5] 977.2'13'0924[B 76-358072 pbk. : 1.50
1. Burns, Harrison, 1836-1925. 2. Jefferson Co., Ind.—Biography. 3. Jennings Co., Ind.—Biography. I. Series: Indiana Historical Society. Publications ; v. 25, no. 2.

Burns, John Anthony, 1909-

AMALU, Sammy. 996.9'04'0924 B
Jack Burns: a portrait in transition, by Samuel Crowningburg-Amalu. [Honolulu, Hawaii] Mamalahoa Foundation, 1974. 477 p. illus. 27 cm. [DU627.82.B87A75] 74-180341
1. Burns, John Anthony, 1909- 2. Hawaii—Politics and government—1959-

Burns, John Horne, 1916-1953.

MITZEL, John, 1948- 813'.5'4
John Horne Burns : an appreciative biography / John Mitzel. Dorchester, Mass. : Manifest Destiny Books, 1974. 135 p. : ports. ; 22 cm. Bibliography: p. 135. [PS3503.U639Z78] 74-82388 ISBN 0-914852-01-9 pbk. : 2.00
1. Burns, John Horne, 1916-1953. I. Title.

Burns, Robert, 1759-1796.

BURNS, Robert, 1759-1796. 928.2
Selected letters. Edited and with an introd. by De Lancey Ferguson. London, New York, Oxford University Press [1953] xxvii, 371p. 16cm. (The World's classics, 529) [PR4331.A3F42] 53-13068
I. Ferguson, John De Lancey, 1888- ed. II. Title.

CARSWELL, Catherine 821'.6 B
MacFarlane, 1879-1946.
The life of Robert Burns. New York, Harcourt, Brace. Ann Arbor, Mich., Gryphon Books, 1971 [c1931] x, 411 p. illus. 22 cm. Includes bibliographical references. [PR4331.C43 1971] 78-164157
1. Burns, Robert, 1759-1796. I. Title.

CUNNINGHAM, Allan, 1784- 821'.6 B
1842.
The life and land of Burns / by Allan Cunningham ; with contributions by Thomas Campbell ; to which is prefixed an essay on the genius and writings of Burns, by Thomas Carlyle. New York : AMS Press, 1975. vii, 363 p. ; 19 cm. Reprint of the 1841 ed. published by J. and H. G. Langley, New York. [PR4331.C82 1975] 76-144554 ISBN 0-404-08512-1 : 17.00
1. Burns, Robert, 1759-1796. 2. Burns, Robert, 1759-1796—Homes and haunts. 3. Burns, Robert, 1759-1796—Correspondence. I. Title.

DAICHES, David, 1912- 821.6
Robert Burns. [Rev. ed.] New York, Macmillan [1967, c1966] 334 p. 23 cm. Bibliographical references included in "Notes" (p. [321]-323) [PR4331.D25 1967] 66-26244
1. Burns, Robert, 1759-1796. BIP

DAICHES, David, 1912- 821'.6 B
Robert Burns and his world. New York, Viking Press [1972, c1971] 127 p. illus. 24 cm. (A Studio book) Bibliography: p. [117] [PR4331.D28 1972] 74-163873 ISBN 0-670-60093-8 8.95
1. Burns, Robert, 1759-1796. I. Title. BIP

DAKERS, Andrew Herbert, 821'.6 B
1887-
Robert Burns, his life and genius, by Andrew Dakers. New York, Haskell House Publishers, 1972. 229 p. port. 23 cm. Reprint of the 1923 ed. [PR4331.D3 1972] 72-3378 ISBN 0-8383-1507-0 10.95
1. Burns, Robert, 1759-1796. I. Title.

FERGUSON, John DeLancey, 928.2
1888-
Pride and passion: Robert Burns, 1759-1796 [Reissue] New York, Russell & Russell, 1964[c.1939] xix, 321p. 22cm. 64-18599 7.50
1. Burns, Robert, 1759-1796. I. Title.

FITZHUGH, Robert Tyson, 821'.6 B
1906-
Robert Burns: the man and the poet; a round, unvarnished account [by] Robert T. Fitzhugh. Boston, Houghton Mifflin, 1970. xviii, 508 p. illus., ports. (1 col) 24 cm. Bibliography: p. [443]-482. [PR4331.F57] 76-96066 10.00
1. Burns, Robert, 1759-1796. I. Title.

[GIBSON, James] 1819- 821'.6 B
1886.
The Burns calendar : a manual of Burnsiana, relating events in the poet's history, names associated with his life and writings, a concise bibliography, and a record of Burns relics. New York : AMS Press, [1975] [79] p. ; 24 cm. Compiled by James Gibson. Cf. his Bibliography of Robert Burns. Reprint of the 1874 ed. published by J. M'Kie, Kilmarnock. [PR4331.G5 1975] 70-144555 ISBN 0-404-08513-X : 11.50
1. Burns, Robert, 1759-1796. I. Title.

HENLEY, William Ernest, 821'.6 B
1849-1903.
Burns: life, genius, achievement. New York, Haskell House [1974] p. cm. "Reprinted from 'The Centenary Burns'." First published in 1897 under title: Robert Burns, his life, genius, achievement. Reprint of the 1898 ed. published by T. C. and E. C. Jack, Edinburgh. [PR4331.H4 1974] 74-6451 ISBN 0-8383-1891-6 10.95 (lib. bdg.)
1. Burns, Robert, 1759-1796. I. Title.

HEPBURN, Thomas Nicoll, 821'.6 B
1861-
Robert Burns, by Gabriel Setoun. Edinburgh, Oliphant Anderson & Ferrier [1896] Folcroft, Pa., Folcroft Library Editions, 1972. p. Original ed. issued in series: Famous Scots series. [PR4331.H44 1972] 72-12781 ISBN 0-8414-0950-1 (lib. bdg.)
1. Burns, Robert, 1759-1796.

JAMIESON, Robert. 821'.6 B
Burns in his youth, and how he grew to be a poet ; Burns in his maturity, and how he spent it : papers read before the Belfast Burns' Club, by Robert Jamieson, 1876-7. Folcroft, Pa. : Folcroft Library Editions, 1976. p. cm. Reprint of the 1878 ed. published for The Club by W. Brown, Belfast. [PR4331.J3 1976] 76-15603 ISBN 0-8414-5344-6 lib. bdg. : 10.00
1. Burns, Robert, 1759-1796. I. Jamieson, Robert. Burns in his maturity and how he spent it. 1976. II. Title: Burns in his youth, and how he grew to be a poet. BIP

KELLOW, Henry Arthur. 821'.6
Burns & his poetry [by] H. A. Kellow. London, G. G. Harrap, 1912. [New York, AMS Press, 1972] 127 p. 19 cm. (Poetry & life series) Includes selections from the poems. [PR4331.K4 1972] 70-120983 ISBN 0-404-52525-3 8.00
1. Burns, Robert, 1759-1796. I. Title. II. Series. BIP

KELLOW, Henry Arthur. 821'.6
Burns & his poetry / by H. A. Kellow. Norwood, Pa. : Norwood Editions, 1975. 127 p. : port. ; 24 cm. Reprint of the 1911 ed. published by G. C. Harrap, London, which was issued as no. 8 of Poetry and life series. Bibliography: p. 10. [PR4331.K4 1975] 75-33140 ISBN 0-88305-363-2 : 7.50
1. Burns, Robert, 1759-1796. I. Title. II. Series: Poetry and life series ; 8.

LIFE of Robert Burns; v. 12 introduction by James Kinsley. London, Dent; New York, Dutton [1959] xiii, 322p. 19cm. (Everyman's library, no. 156) Includes select letters and journals. This ed. first published 1907. Includes bibliography.
1. Burns, Robert, 1759-1796. I. Lockhart, John Gibson, 1794-1854.

LINDSAY, John Maurice, 928.2
1918-
Robert Burns, the man, his work, the legend. London, MacGibbon & Kee [dist. Chester Springs, Pa., Dufour, 1963] 291p. illus. 22cm. 55-19961 3.95 bds.,
1. Burns, Robert, 1759-1796. I. Title.

ROSS, John Dawson, 1853- 821'.6
1939.
The Burns almanac; a record of dates, events, etc., connected with the poet. New York, The Raeburn Book Co. [New York, AMS Press, 1973] 147 p. port. 17 cm. Reprint of the 1898 ed. [PR4331.R62 1973] 72-144474 ISBN 0-404-08534-2
1. Burns, Robert, 1759-1796. I. Title.

SHAIRP, John Campbell, 821'.6
1819-1885.
Burns. Freeport, N.Y., Books for Libraries Press [1971] vi, 212 p. 23 cm. "First published 1879 [under title: Robert Burns]" [PR4331.S4 1971] 73-164626 ISBN 0-8369-5909-4
1. Burns, Robert, 1759-1796. BIP

SNYDER, Franklyn Bliss, 821'.6 B
1884-1958.
The life of Robert Burns. [Hamden, Conn.] Archon Books, 1968 [c1932] xiii, 524 p. facsims., maps, port. 24 cm. Includes bibliographical references. [PR4331.S6 1968] 68-16336
1. Burns, Robert, 1759-1796. I. Title. BIP

STEWART, William, 1856- 821'.6
1947.
Robert Burns and the common people. [Folcroft, Pa.] Folcroft Library Editions, 1973. p. Reprint of the 1925 ed. published by the Independent Labour Party, London. [PR4331.S8 1973] 73-12517 ISBN 0-8414-7624-1 (lib. bdg.)
1. Burns, Robert, 1759-1796. I. Title. BIP

WATT, Lauchlan MacLean, 821'.6 B
1867-1957.
Burns. New York, Haskell House Publishers, 1974. 262 p. port. 20 cm. Reprint of the 1914 ed. published by Collins' Clear Type Press, London. Bibliography: p. [257]-258. [PR4331.W43 1974] 73-21618 ISBN 0-8383-1803-7 13.95
1. Burns, Robert, 1759-1796. BIP

Burns, Robert, 1759-1796—Biography.

BLACKIE, John Stuart, 821'.6 B
1809-1895.
Life of Robert Burns / by John Stuart Blackie. New York : Haskell House, [1976] p. cm. Reprint of the 1888 ed. published by W. Scott, London, in series: Great writers. Includes index. Bibliography: p. [PR4331.B5 1976] 75-30844 ISBN 0-8383-2102-X lib.bdg. : 12.95
1. Burns, Robert, 1759-1796—Biography. BIP

EWING, William Hollis, 821'.6 B
1902-
This I'm gaun to tell : first-person story of the life of Robert Burns / by William H. Ewing. 1st ed. Hicksville, N.Y. : Exposition Press, [1975] xvii, 178 p. ; 22 cm. (An Exposition-university book) Bibliography: p. 177-178. [PR4331.E9] 74-21440 ISBN 0-682-48193-9 : 7.50
1. Burns, Robert, 1759-1796—Biography. I. Burns, Robert, 1759-1796. II. Title.

FINDLAY, Jessie Patrick. 821'.6
Footprints of Robert Burns / by Jessie Patrick Findlay. Folcroft, Pa. : Folcroft Library Editions, 1977. 174 p. ; 22 cm. Reprint of the 1923 ed. published by A. Gardner, Paisley. [PR4331.F5 1977] 77-9341 ISBN 0-8414-4303-3 lib. bdg. : 22.50
1. Burns, Robert, 1759-1796—Biography. 2. Poets, Scottish—18th century—Biography. I. Title. BIP

HENDERSON, Thomas 821'.6 B
Finlayson, 1844-1923.
Robert Burns / by T. F. Henderson. New York : AMS Press, 1975. ix, 202 p., [12] leaves of plates : ill. ; 19 cm. Reprint of the 1904 ed. published by Methuen, London. Includes index. Bibliography: p. 191-195. [PR4331.H36 1975] 73-144556 ISBN 0-404-08514-8 : 9.50
1. Burns, Robert, 1759-1796—Biography.

HIGGINS, James Craig, 821'.6 B
1856-
Life of Robert Burns. With illus., notes, appendices, itineraries, and map. Kilmarnock, Standard Press, 1928. [New York, AMS Press, 1974] 260 p. illus. 23 cm. Originally published in 1893. [PR4331.H5 1974] 73-144513 ISBN 0-404-08515-6
1. Burns, Robert, 1759-1796—Biography.

LOCKHART, John Gibson, 821'.6 B
1794-1854.
The life of Robert Burns, by J. G. Lockhart. Enl. ed. Rev. and corr. from the latest text of the author, with new annotations and appendices, by William Scott Douglas. London, New York, G. Bell, 1892. [New York, AMS Press, 1974] xvi, 349 p. port. 19 cm. Originally issued in series: Bohn's standard library. Bibliography: p. 346-349. [PR4331.L6 1974] 70-144515 ISBN 0-404-08517-2 16.00
1. Burns, Robert, 1759-1796—Biography. I. Douglas, William Scott, 1815-1883, ed. II. Title.

MACINTOSH, John, 1853- 821'.6 B
Life of Robert Burns / by John Macintosh. New York : AMS Press, [1975] p. cm. Reprint of the 1906 ed. published by A. Gardner, Paisley, Scot. Includes index. [PR4331.M3 1975] 78-144517 ISBN 0-404-08519-9 : 18.50
1. Burns, Robert, 1759-1796—Biography. I. Title. BIP

Burns, Robert, 1759-1796—Biography—Last years and death.

M'DOWALL, William, 1815- 821'.6 B
1888.
Burns in Dumfriesshire : a sketch of the last eight years of the poet's life / by William M'Dowall. New York : AMS Press, [1976] p. cm. Reprint of the 3d ed. published in 1896 by J. Maxwell, Dumfries. [PR4332.M3 1976] 74-144516 ISBN 0-404-08518-0 : 14.50
1. Burns, Robert, 1759-1796—Biography—Last years and death. 2. Burns family. 3. Poets, Scottish—18th century—Biography. I. Title.

Burns, Robert, 1759-1796—Biography—Marriage.

ROSS, John Dawson, 1853- 821'.6 B
1939, comp.
Bonnie Jean, a collection of papers and poems relating to the wife of Robert Burns. With a pref. by Peter Ross. New York, Raeburn Book Co., 1898. [New York, AMS Press, 1974] p. cm. [PR4332.R7 1974] 71-144471 ISBN 0-404-08526-1 8.50
1. Burns, Robert, 1759-1796—Biography—Marriage. 2. Burns, Jean (Armour) 1767-1834. I. Title.

Burns, Robert, 1759-1796—Biography—Political career.

SINTON, John. 821'.6
A vindication : Burns, excise officer and poet / by John Sinton. 4th (Jubilee) ed. Folcroft, Pa. : Folcroft Library Editions, 1975. p. cm. Reprint of the 1897 ed. published by J. Menzies, Glasgow. [PR4332.S4 1975] 75-20341 ISBN 0-8414-7700-0 lib. bdg. : 10.00
1. Burns, Robert, 1759-1796—Biography—Political career. 2. Burns, Robert, 1759-1796—Biography—Last years and death. 3. Tax collection—Scotland. I. Title.

Burns, Robert, 1759-1796—Correspondence.

BURNS, Robert, 1759- 821'.6 B
1796.
The letters of Robert Burns, selected with an introd. by R. Brimley Johnson. [Folcroft, Pa.] Folcroft Library Editions, 1974. p. cm. Reprint of the 1928 ed. published by J. Lane, London; Dodd, Mead, New York. [PR4331.A3J6 1974] 74-5061 20.00
1. Burns, Robert, 1759-1796—Correspondence. I. Johnson, Reginald Brimley, 1867-1932, ed. BIP

Burns, Robert, 1759-1796—Dictionaries, indexes, etc.

ROSS, John Dawson, 1853- 821'.6
1939.
Who's who in Burns. Stirling, E. Mackay, 1927. [New York, AMS Press, 1973] 335 p. map. 19 cm. [PR4330.R6 1973] 75 144480 ISBN 0-404-08547-4 15.00
1. Burns, Robert, 1759-1796—Dictionaries, indexes, etc. 2. Burns, Robert, 1759-1796—Friends and associates. I. Title. BIP

Burns, Robert, 1759-1796—Friends and associates.

WOOD, John Maxwell. 821'.6 B
Robert Burns and the Riddell family, by J. Maxwell Wood. New York, Haskell House, 1974. 172, vii p. illus. 23 cm. Reprint of the 1922 ed. published by R. Dinwiddie, Dumfries, Scot. Includes bibliographical references. [PR4333.W6 1974] 73-21743 ISBN 0-8383-1802-9 14.95
1. Burns, Robert, 1759-1796—Friends and associates. 2. Riddell family. I. Title. BIP

Burns, Robert, 1759-1796—Homes and haunts.

CUNNINGHAM, Allan, 1784- 821'.6 B
1842.
The life and land of Burns / by Allan Cunningham ; with contributions by Thomas Campbell ; to which is prefixed an essay on the genius and writings of Burns, by Thomas Carlyle. New York : AMS Press, 1975. vii, 363 p. ; 19 cm. Reprint of the 1841 ed. published by J. and H. G. Langley, New York. [PR4331.C82 1975] 76-144554 ISBN 0-404-08512-1 : 17.00
1. Burns, Robert, 1759-1796. 2. Burns, Robert, 1759-1796—Homes and haunts. 3. Burns, Robert, 1759-1796—Correspondence. I. Title.

Burns, Robert, 1759-1796—Homes and haunts—Stirlingshire, Scot.

BURNS, Robert, 1759- 1796. 821'.6 B
Robert Burns's tours of the Highlands and Stirlingshire 1787. [Edited by] Raymond Lamont Brown. Ipswich [Eng.] Boydell Press, 1973. xii, 82 p. illus. 23 cm. "Consists of journal notes for the Highland tour with William Nicol, and letters and anecdotes for the tours in the West Highlands and Stirlingshire. These are explained by Mr Lamont Brown in his annotation and introductions."—dust jacket. Bibliography: p. 75-77. [PR4334.B8 1973] 74-163571 ISBN 0-85115-019-5
1. Burns, Robert, 1759-1796—Homes and haunts—Stirlingshire, Scot. I. Brown, Raymond Lamont, ed. II. Title.
Distributed by Rowman and Littlefield, Totowa, New Jersey for 7.50.

Burns, Robert, 1759-1796—Museums, relics, etc.

DUNCAN, Robert. 821'.6 B
The story of the Edinburgh Burns relics, with fresh facts about Burns and his family / by Robert Duncan. Folcroft, Pa. : Folcroft Library Editions, 1975. p. cm. Reprint of the 1910 ed. published by A. Elliot, Edinburgh. [PR4335.D85 1975] 75-42242 ISBN 0-8414-3722-X lib. bdg. : 20.00
1. Burns, Robert, 1759-1796—Museums, relics, etc. I. Title. BIP

Burns, William Chalmers, 1815-1868.

BURNS, Islay, 1817-1872. 266'.5'20924 B
Memoir of the Rev. Wm. C. Burns, M.A., missionary to China from the English Presbyterian Church / by Islay Burns. San Francisco : Chinese Materials Center, 1975. viii, 595 p., [1] leaf of plates : port. ; 20 cm. Reprint of the 1870 ed. published by R. Carter, New York, and J. Nisbet, London. [BV3427.B83B87 1975] 76-351598
1. Burns, William Chalmers, 1815-1868. I. Title: Memoir of the Rev. Wm. C. Burns, M.A., missionary to China ...

Burns, William John, 1861-1932.

CAESAR, Gene, 1927- 364.12'0924
Incredible detective; the biography of William J. Burns. Englewood Cliffs, N.J., Prentice-Hall [1968] 224 p. illus. 22 cm. Bibliography: p. 9-11. [HV8083.B8C33] 68-12816
1. Burns, William John, 1861-1932. I. Title.

HYND, Alan, 1908- 364.12'0924
In pursuit; the cases of William J. Burns. [Camden, N.J] Nelson [1968] 178 p. 21 cm. A biography. [HV8083.B8H9] 68-20152
1. Burns, William John, 1861-1932. I. Title. II. Title: The cases of William J. Burns.

Burr, Aaron, 1756-1836.

AARON Burr, v. 12
a biography. New York, A. S. Barnes [1961, c1937] xii, 563p. plates, ports., facsims. 21cm. (A Perpetua book) Bibliography: p. 547-553.
1. Burr, Aaron, 1756-1836. I. Schachner, Nathan, 1895-1955.

ALEXANDER, Holmes Moss, 1906- 973.4'6'0924 B
Aaron Burr: the proud pretender, by Holmes Alexander. Westport, Conn., Greenwood Press [1973, c1937] xii, 390 p. illus. 22 cm. Reprint of the ed. published by Harper, New York. Bibliography: p. 375-382. [E302.6.B9A7 1973] 73-13412 ISBN 0-8371-7128-8 16.00
1. Burr, Aaron, 1756-1836.

BURR, Aaron, 1756- 1836. 973.4'6'0924 B
Memoirs of Aaron Burr. With miscellaneous selections from his correspondence, by Matthew L. Davis. Freeport, N.Y., Books for Libraries Press [1970] 2 v. ports. 23 cm. Reprint of the 1836-37 ed. [E302.6.B9A34] 71-107798 ISBN 0-8369-5213-8
1. United States—History—Revolution, 1775-1783—Personal narratives. 2. United States—Politics and government—Constitutional period—1789-1809. 3. New York (State)—Politics and government—1775-1865. I. Davis, Matthew Livingston, 1773-1850.

BURR, Aaron, 1756- 1836. 973.4'6'0924
Memoirs of Aaron Burr, with miscellaneous selections from his correspondence, by Matthew L. Davis. New York, Da Capo Press, 1971. 2 v. ports. 23 cm. (The Era of the American Revolution) Reprint of the 1836-37 ed. [E302.6.B9A34 1971] 73-152836 ISBN 0-306-70139-1
1. United States—History—Revolution, 1775-1789—Personal narratives. 2. United States—Politics and government—Constitutional period, 1789-1809. 3. New York (State)—Politics and government—1775-1865. I. Davis, Matthew Livingston, 1773-1850.

BURR, Aaron, 1756- 1836. 914.2'04'73
Private journal [of Aaron Burr, during his residence of four years in Europe; with selections from his correspondence. Edited by Matthew L. Davis.] Upper Saddle River, N.J., Literature House [1970, c1838] 2 v. 23 cm. Covers period 1808-1812. [E302.6.B9A25 1970] 72-104425 ISBN 0-8398-0182-3
1. Europe—Description and travel—1800-1918. I. Title.

BURR, Samuel Engle, 1807- 923.273
Colonel Aaron Burr, the American Phoenix: a study of his life and career. [2d rev. ed.] New York, Exposition Press [1964] 114 p. 21 cm. (An exposition-Lochinvar book) Includes bibliographies. [E302.6.B9B95] 64-1882
1. Burr, Aaron, 1756-1836. I. Title.

BURR, Samuel Engle, Jr., 1897- 923.273
Colonel Aaron Burr: the American phoenix; a study of his life and career. [2nd rev. ed.] New York, Exposition [c.1961, 1964] 114p. 22cm. (Lochinvar bk.) Bibl. 63-5279 4.00
1. Burr, Aaron, 1756-1836. I. Title.

BURY, Samuel Engle, 1897- 320.50924
Colonel Aaron Burr: the American phoenix; a study of the life and career of a prominent American. Washington, 1963. 96 al. 28 cm. Includes bibliography. [E302.6.B8B95] 63-5279
1. Burr, Aaron, 1756-1836. I. Title.

CHIDSEY, Donald Barr, 1902- 973.4'8'0924
The great conspiracy; Aaron Burr and his strange doings in the West. New York, Crown Publishers [1967] 166 p. illus., ports. 22 cm. Bibliography: p. 156-161. [E334.C5] 67-27042
1. Burr, Aaron, 1756-1836. 2. Burr Conspiracy, 1805-1807. I. Title.

KUNSTLER, Laurence S. 973.4'6'0924
The unpredictable Mr. Aaron Burr / Laurence S. Kunstler. 1st ed. New York : Vantage Press, [1974] 140 p. ; 21 cm. Bibliography: p. 140. [E302.6.B9K83] 75-307032 ISBN 0-533-01319-4 : 5.95
1. Burr, Aaron, 1756-1836 I. Title.

LOMASK, Milton. 973.4'6'0924 B
Aaron Burr, the years from Princeton to Vice President, 1756-1805 / Milton Lomask. New York : Farrar, Straus & Giroux, c1979. xiii, 443 p., [6] leaves of plates : ill. ; 24 cm. Includes index. Bibliography: p. 411-427. [E302.6.B9L7 1979] 78-31142 ISBN 0-374-10016-0. : 10.00
1. Burr, Aaron, 1756-1836. 2. United States—Politics and government—1783-1809. 3. Vice-Presidents—United States—Biography. I. Title.

ORLOB, Helen. 973.4'6'0924 B
The wide world of Aaron Burr. Philadelphia, Westminster Press [1968] 127 p. 21 cm. Bibliography: p. [121]-122. A biography of the controversial man who, though a Revolutionary War officer and Vice-President of the United States, killed Alexander Hamilton, was charged with murder and treason, and died a ruined man. [E302.6.B9O7] 92 AC 68
1. Burr, Aaron, 1756-1836. I. Title. BIP

PARMET, Herbert S. 973.4'6'0924 B
Aaron Burr; portrait of an ambitious man, by Herbert S. Parmet & Marie B. Hecht. New York, Macmillan [1967] xii, 399 p. illus., ports. 24 cm. Bibliography: p. 377-388. [E302.6.B9P25] 67-21421
1. Burr, Aaron, 1756-1836. I. Hecht, Marie B., joint author.

PARTON, James, 1822-1891 973.4'6'0924 (B)
The life and times of Aaron Burr, lieutenant-colonel in the army of the revolution, United States senator, vice-president of the United States, etc. By J. Parton . . . New York, Mason bros.; [etc., etc.] New York, Johnson Reprint, 1967. xxiii, [25]-696p. plates. 2 port. (incl. front.) facsim. 20cm. [E302.6.B9P27] 7-14130 22.00
1. Burr, Aaron, 1756-1836. 2. U.S.—Hist.—Revolution— Personal narratives. 3. U. S.—Pol. & govt.—Constitutional period, 1789-1809. 4. New York (State)—Pol. & govt.—1775-1865. I. Title.

PARTON, James, 1822-1891. v. 12
The life and times of Aaron Burr ... New York, Mason Brothers, 1858; New York, Johnson Reprint Corp. [1967] 696 p. illus. 68-63482
1. Burr, Aaron, 1756-1836. I. Title. BIP

VAIL, Philip, pseud. 973.4'6'0924 B
The great American rascal; the turbulent life of Aaron Burr. New York, Hawthorn Books [1973] 243 p. 25 cm. Bibliography: p. 231-233. [E302.6.B9V34 1973] 72-1406 7.95
1. Burr, Aaron, 1756-1836. I. Title.

WANDELL, Samuel Henry, 1860-1943. 973.4'6'0924 B
Aaron Burr; a biography written, in large part, from original and hitherto unused material, by Samuel H. Wandell and Meade Minnigerode. New York, Putnam, 1927. St. Clair Shores, Mich., Scholarly Press [1971, c1925] 2 v. illus. 21 cm. Bibliography: v. 1, p. xxxi-xxxviii. [E302.6.B9W2 1971] 78-145356 ISBN 0-403-01263-5
1. Burr, Aaron, 1756-1836. I. Minnigerode, Meade, 1887-1967, joint author.

WISS, William. 973.4'6'0924 B
Aaron Burr. New York, Putnam [1968] 191 p. illus. 21 cm. (Lives to remember) Bibliography: p. 187-188. A biography of the controversial American who became Vice President, killed Alexander Hamilton in a duel, and was indicted for murder and treason. [E302.6.B9W5 1968] 92 AC 68
1. Burr, Aaron, 1756-1836. I. Title. BIP

Burr, Aaron, 1756-1836—Addresses, essays, lectures.

BURR, Samuel Engle, 1897- 973.4'6'0924 B
The influence of his wife and his daughter on the life and career of Col. Aaron Burr (with some remarks on related matters) : an address / by Samuel Engle Burr, Jr. 1st ed. Linden, Va. : Burr Publications, 1975. 32 p. : ill. ; 22 cm. "Delivered ... at the annual guest night and ladies' night dinner meeting of the New York Schoolmaster's Club ... May 10, 1975." Bibliography: p. 8-12. [E302.6.B9B97] 75-24506 1.15
1. Burr, Aaron, 1756-1836—Addresses, essays, lectures. 2. Jumel, Eliza Bowen, 1775?-1865—Addresses, essays, lectures. I. Title: The influence of his wife and his daughter ...

Burr, Aaron, 1756-1836—Juvenile literature.

BURR, Samuel Engle, 1897- 973.4'8'0924 B
Colonel Aaron Burr, the misunderstood man. San Antonio, Naylor Co. [1967] vii, 155 p. illus. 22 cm. [E302.6.B9B962] 67-12278
1. Burr, Aaron, 1756-1836—Juvenile literature. I. Title.

NOLAN, Jeannette (Covert) 1876- 973.4'6'0924 B
Soldier, statesman, and defendant: Aaron Burr. New York, J. Messner [1972] 191 p. 22 cm. Bibliography: p. 185-186. A biography of Aaron Burr whose political fortunes changed drastically after he fatally wounded Alexander Hamilton in a duel. [E302.6.B9N6] 92 72-1827 ISBN 0-671-32554-X 4.50
1. Burr, Aaron, 1756-1836—Juvenile literature. I. Title.
PLB 4.29 ISBN 0-671-32555-8

WISE, William. 92
Aaron Burr. New York, Putnam [1968] 191 p. illus. 21 cm. (Lives to remember) Bibliography: p. 187-188. A biography of the controversial American who became Vice President, killed Alexander Hamilton in a duel, and was indicted for murder and treason. [E302.6.B9W5 1968] 68-15086
1. Burr, Aaron, 1756-1836—Juvenile literature. I. Title.

Burr, George Elbert, 1859-1939.

SEEBER, Louise Combes. 760'.0924 B
George Elbert Burr, 1859-1939; catalogue raisonne and guide to the etched works with biographical and critical notes. Flagstaff, Ariz., Northland Press, 1971. xii, 179 p. illus. (part col.) 32 cm. Bibliography: p. 177-179. [NE2012.B8S4] 78-150685 ISBN 0-87358-067-2 15.00
1. Burr, George Elbert, 1859-1939. BIP

Burr, Samuel Engle, 1836-1917.

BURR, Samuel Engle, 1897- 923.873
Small- town merchant. [1st ed.] New York, Vantage Press [1957] 354p. 21cm. [CT275.B787A3] 56-12926
1. Burr, Samuel Engle, 1836-1917. 2. Bordentown, N. J.—Hist. I. Title.

Burr, Samuel Engle, 1897-

BURR, Samuel Engle, 1897- 973.9'092'4 B
Disaster, death, and destruction : an address / by Samuel Engle Burr, Jr., with supplementary statements .... 1st ed. Linden, Va. : Burr Publications, 1979. 56 p. : ill. ; 22 cm. Bibliography: p. 53-54. [CT275.B787A29] 79-64770 ISBN 0-911994-00-9 pbk. : 1.70
1. Burr, Samuel Engle, 1897- 2. Burr, Alice Elizabeth. 3. United States—Biography. I. Title.

Burrell, Mary (Banks) d. 1898.

WAGNER, Richard, 1813-1883. 927.8
Letters; the Burrel collection, edited with notes py John N. Burk. New York, Macmillan, 1950. x, 665 p. illus., ports. 24 cm. The letters and documents were collected by Mary Burrell. [ML410.W1A3125] 51-241
1. Burrell, Mary (Banks) d. 1898. I. Title.

Burri, Alberto, 1915-

BURRI, Alberto, 1915- 709'.2'4
Alberto Burri [by] Maurizio Calvesi. Translated from the Italian by Robert Erich Wolf. New York, Abrams [1974, i.e.1975] p. cm. Bibliography: p. [N6923.B92C313] 74-5412 ISBN 0-8109-0232-X 37.50
1. Burri, Alberto, 1915- I. Calvesi, Maurizio.

Burritt, Elihu, 1810-1879.

BURRITT, Elihu, 1810- 1879. 327'.172 B
The learned blacksmith; the letters and journals of Elihu Burritt, by Merle Curti. New York, Wilson-Erickson, 1937. [New York, J. S. Ozer, 1972] ix, 241 p. port. 22 cm. (The Peace movement in America) Includes bibliographical references. [PS1219.B7Z53 1937a] 70-137536 10.95
1. Burritt, Elihu, 1810-1879. I. Curti, Merle Eugene, 1897- ed. II. Title. III. Series. BIP

BURRITT, Elihu, 1810- 1879. 327'.172
The Learned Blacksmith; the letters and journals of Elihu Burritt, edited by Merle Eugene Curti; and A congress of nations, by Elihu Burritt. With a new introd. for the Garland ed. by Merle Eugene Curti. New York, Garland Pub., 1971 [i.e. 1972] 10, ix, 241, 24 p. port. 23 cm. (The Garland library of war and peace) Reprints of two works originally published in 1937 and 1904, respectively. Original ed. of A congress of nations issued in series: Old South leaflets. General series, v. 6, no. 146. [PS1219.B7Z53 1972] 72-147721 ISBN 0-8240-0248-2
1. Burritt, Elihu, 1810-1879. 2. Peace. 3. Arbitration, International. I. Curti, Merle Eugene, 1897- ed. II. Burritt, Elihu, 1810-1879. A congress of nations. 1972. III. Title. IV. Title: A congress of nations. V. Series. VI. Series: Old South leaflets. General series, v. 6, no. 146.

TOLIS, Peter. 341.1 B
Elihu Burritt: crusader for brotherhood. Hamden, Conn., Archon Books, 1968. ix, 309 p. port. 22 cm. Bibliography: p. 293-301. [CT275.B789T6] 68-31609
1. Burritt, Elihu, 1810-1879.

Burroughs, Edgar Rice, 1875-1950.

FARMER, Philip Jose. 813'.5'2
Tarzan alive; a definitive biography of Lord Greystoke. [1st ed.] Garden City, N.Y., Doubleday, 1972. xx, 312 p. 22 cm. [PS3503.U687Z65] 70-175371 5.95
1. Burroughs, Edgar Rice, 1875-1950. 2. Tarzan in literature. I. Title.

FENTON, Robert W. 813'.5'2 B
The big swingers [by] Robert W. Fenton. Englewood Cliffs, N.J., Prentice-Hall [1967] xvi, 258 p. illus., ports. 24 cm. [PS3503.U687Z66] 66-24975
1. Burroughs, Edgar Rice, 1875 1950. I. Title.

PORGES, Irwin. 813'.5'2 B
Edgar Rice Burroughs : the man who created Tarzan / Irwin Porgas ; Hulbert Burroughs, pictorial editor ; introduction by Ray Bradbury. 1st ed. Provo, Utah. : Brigham Young University Press, [1975] xix, 819 p. : ill. ; 29 cm. Includes bibliographical references and index. [PS3503.U687Z84] 75-15980 ISBN 0-8425-0079-0 : 14.95
1. Burroughs, Edgar Rice, 1875-1950. **BIP**

Burroughs, John Rolfe.

BURROUGHS, John Rolfe. 818.54
Headfirst in the pickle barrel. Drawings by Leo Summers. New York, Morrow, 1963. 223 p. illus. 22 cm. Autobiographical. [PS3503.U68713Z52] 63-17685
I. Title.

Burroughs, John, 1837-1921.

BARRUS, Clara, 1864- 1931. 814'.4 B
The life and letters of John Burroughs. New York, Russell & Russell [1968] 2 v. illus., facsims., ports. 23 cm. First published in 1925. [PS1226.B27 1968] 68-15094
1. Burroughs, John, 1837-1921. I. Title. **BIP**

BARRUS, Clara, 1864- 1931. 814'.4 B
Our friend John Burroughs. Incl. autobiographical sketches by Mr. Burroughs. With illus. from photos. New York, Haskell House, 1971. vii, 286 p. illus., ports. 23 cm. Reprint of the 1914 ed. [PS1226.B3 1971] 76-130262 ISBN 0-8383-1169-5
1. Burroughs, John, 1837-1921. I. Title.

BARRUS, Clara, 1864- 1931. 814'.4 B
Our friend John Burroughs. Incl. autobiographical sketches by Mr. Burroughs, with illus. from photos. Boston, Houghton Mifflin. Detroit, Gale Research Co., 1975. p. cm. Reprint of the 1914 ed. [PS1226.B3 1975] 74-19234 ISBN 0-8103-4124-7
1. Burroughs, John, 1837-1921. I. Title. **BIP**

KELLEY, Elizabeth (Burroughs) 928.1
John Burroughs: naturalist; the story of his work and family by his granddaughter. [1st ed.] New York, Exposition Press [1959] 263p. illus. 21cm. (An Exposition-banner book) Includes bibliography. [PS1226.K37] 59-13138
1. Burroughs, John, 1837-1921. I. Title.

SWIFT, Hildegarde Hoyt. 928.1
The edge of April; a biography of John Burroughs. Illustrated by Lynd Ward. New York, W. Morrow, 1957. 316 p. illus. 22 cm. [PS1226.S9] 57-8563
1. Burroughs, John, 1837-1921. I. Title.

Burroughs, John, 1837-1921—Juvenile literature.

SHATRAW, Harriet B. 500.9'2'4 B
John Burroughs; famous naturalist, by Harriet B. Shatraw. Charlotteville, N.Y., SamHar Press, 1972. 32 p. 22 cm. (Outstanding personalities, no. 47) Bibliography: p. 31-32. Biography of a naturalist famous for his vivid writings on outdoor life. [QH31.B93S5] 92 73-166140
1. Burroughs, John, 1837-1921—Juvenile literature. I. Title. **BIP**

SWIFT, Hildegarde (Hoyt) 928.1
The edge of April; a biography of John Burroughs. Illustrated by Lynd Ward. New York, W. Morrow, 1957. 316 p. illus. 22 cm. [PS1226.S9] 57-8563
1. Burroughs, John, 1837-1924. I. Title.

Burroughs, Raleigh.

BURROUGHS, Raleigh. 798'.4'00924 B
Horses, Burroughs, and other animals (mostly human) / by Raleigh Burroughs. Cranbury, N.J. : A. S. Barnes, c1976. p. cm. Autobiographical. Includes index. [SF336.B85A35 1976] 75-22568 ISBN 0-498-01833-4 : 9.95
1. Burroughs, Raleigh. 2. Horse-racing—Personal narratives. I. Title.

Burrow, Brunettie.

BURROW, Brunettie. 926.1
Angels in white. San Antonio, Naylor Co. [1959] 132p. illus. 22cm. Autobiographical. [RT37.B8A3] 59-15329
I. Title.

Burrows, Abram S.

BURROWS, Abram S. 782.81'092'4 B
Honest, Abe : is there really no business like show business? / Abe Burrows. 1st ed. Boston : Little, Brown, c1980. p. cm. "An Atlantic-Monthly Press book." Includes index. [ML429.B95A3] 79-25358 ISBN 0-316-1171-4 : 12.95
1. Burrows, Abram S. 2. Musicians—United States—Biography. 3. Theatrical producers and directors—United States—Biography. I. Title.

Burrows, Carl

BURROWS, Carl 920
Cast off the fetters; the autobiography of a dream. Illustrated by the author. Chicago, Regent House [c.1959] 196p. illus. 23cm. 59-14840 2.95
I. Title.

BURROWS, Carl, 1907- 920
Cast off the fetters; the autobiography of a dream. Illustrated by the author. Chicago, Reent House [1959] 186p. illus. 23cm. [CT275.B8115A3] 59-14840
I. Title.

Burrows, Silas Enoch, 1794-1870.

STEERS, B. MacDonald, comp. 917.3'03 B
Silas Enoch Burrow, 1794-1870: his life and letters; a compilation of material, gathered from many sources, concerning a rather unusual man ... [by] Don Steers, with collaboration of R. Earl Burrows. Chester, Conn., Pequot Press, 1971. xviii, 432 p. illus. 27 cm. 100 copies printed. [E302.6.B95S8] 77-158309
1. Burrows, Silas Enoch, 1794-1870. I. Title.

Burt, Alfred LeRoy, 1888-1971.

THOMAS, Lewis Herbert, 1917- 971.06'07'2024 B
The renaissance of Canadian history : a biography of A. L. Burt / Lewis H. Thomas. Toronto ; Buffalo : University of Toronto Press, [1975] xiv, 189 p. : port. ; 24 cm. Includes index. "A. L. Burt: a bibliography": p. [163]-167. [F1024.6.B8T47] 74-79988 ISBN 0-8020-5304-1 : 15.00
1. Burt, Alfred LeRoy, 1888-1971. I. Title. **BIP**

Burton, Annamae.

CRISS, Lillian M. 286'.73 B
That tent by the sawdust pile / Lillian Criss. Mountain View, Calif. : Pacific Press Pub. Association, 1976c1977 144 p. ; 22 cm. (A Destiny book ; D-155) [BX6193.B87C74] 76-41462 pbk. : 3.50
1. Burton, Annamae. 2. Seventh-Day Adventists—United States—Biography. I. Title. **BIP**

Burton, Clarence Monroe, 1853-1932.

BURTON, Patricia Owens. 920
Clarence Monroe Burton, Detroit's historian; a biographical sketch. Detroit, Burton Abstract & Title Co. [1953] 77p. illus. 24cm. [CT275.B812B8] 54-22958
1. Burton, Clarence Monroe, 1853-1932. I. Title.

Burton, Jack Robert.

BURTON, Jack Robert. 248
Transport of delight / [by] Jack Burton. London : S.C.M. Press, 1976. viii, 200 p. : ill. ; 23 cm. [BX8495.B89A37] 77-353519 ISBN 0-334-01682-7 : £2.50
1. Burton, Jack Robert. 2. Methodist Church—Clergy—Biography. 3. Clergy—England—Biography. I. Title.

Burton, Naomi.

BURTON, Naomi. 248
More than sentinels. [1st ed.] Garden City, N. Y., Doubleday, 1964. 346 p. 22 cm. Autobiographical. [BX4705.B945A3] 64-19288
I. Title.

Burton, Philip,

BURTON, Philip, 1904- 792'.0924
Early doors; my life and the theatre. With a pref. by Agnes de Mille. New York, Dial Press, 1969. xiv, 238 p. illus. 22 cm. [PN2598.B792A3] 78-76961 5.95
I. Title. **BIP**

Burton, Richard, 1925-

COTTRELL, John. 791.43'028'0924 B
Richard Burton, very close up, by John Cottrell and Fergus Cashin. [1st American ed.] Englewood Cliffs, N.J., Prentice-Hall [1972, c1971] 385 p. illus. 24 cm. First published in London in 1971 under title: Richard Burton; a biography. [PN2598.B795C6 1972] 70-38619 ISBN 0-13-780908-5
1. Burton, Richard, 1925- I. Title.

DAVID, Lester. 791.43'028'0922 B
Richard & Elizabeth / Lester David & Jhan Robbins. New York : Funk & Wagnalls, c1977. 242 p. : ill. ; 24 cm. Includes index. [PN2598.B795D3] 76-52382 ISBN 0-308-10294-0 : 8.95
1. Burton, Richard, 1925- 2. Taylor, Elizabeth Rosemond, 1932- 3. Actors—Great Britain—Biography. 4. Moving-picture actors and actresses—United States—Biography. I. Robbins, Jhan, joint author. II. Title. **BIP**

WATERBURY, Ruth. v. 12
Richard Burton. New York, Pyramid Books [1965] 171 p. illus., ports. 18 cm.
1. Burton, Richard, 1925- I. Title.

Burton, Richard Francis, Sir, 1821-1890.

ABDULLAH, Achmed, 1881-1945. 909'.09'712420810922
Dreamers of empire, by Achmed Abdullah [and] T. Compton Pakenham. Illustrated by B. K. Morris. Freeport, N.Y. Books for Libraries Press [1968] xiv, 368 p. ports. 23 cm. (Essay index reprint series) Reprint of the 1929 ed. Contents.Contents.—Cecil John Rhodes.—Richard Francis Burton.—John Nicholson.—Henry Montgomery Lawrence.—William Walker.—Charles George Gordon. [DA531.1.A2 1968] 68-57300
1. Rhodes, Cecil John, 1853-1902. 2. Burton, Richard Francis, Sir, 1821-1890. 3. Nicholson, John, 1822-1857. 4. Lawrence, Henry Montgomery, Sir, 1806-1857. 5. Walker, William, 1824-1860. 6. Gordon, Charles George, 1833-1885. I. Pakenham, Thomas Compton, joint author. II. Title. **BIP**

ASSAD, Thomas J. 928.2
Three Victorian travellers: Burton, Blunt, Doughty, London, Routledge & K. Paul [dist. New York, Hillary, 1965, c.1964] x, 154p. ports. 23cm. Bibl. [G245.A8] 65-2934 5.00 bds.,
1. Burton, Sir Richard Francis, 1821-1890. 2. Blunt, Wilfrid Scawen, 1840-1922. 3. Doughty, Charles Montagu, 1843-1926. I. Title.

BERCOVICI, Alfred 923.942
That blackguard Burton! Indianapolis, Bobbs [c.1962] 284p. 24cm. 61-7944 5.00
1. Burton, Richard Francis, Sir 1821-1890. I. Title.

BRODIE, Fawn McKay, 1915- 910.0942
The devil drives; a life of Sir Richard Burton, by Fawn M. Brodie. [1st ed.] New York, W. W Norton [1967] 390 p. illus., ports. 25 cm. Bibliography: p. [370]-377. [G246.B8B7] 66-18069
1. Burton, Richard Francis, Sir, 1821-1890. I. Title. **BIP**

BURTON, Isabel Arundel, Lady, 1831-1896. 910'.92'4 B
The life of Captain Sir Richard F. Burton / by Isabel Burton. Boston : Longwood Press, 1977. 2 v. : ill. ; 22 cm. Reprint of the 1893 ed. published by Chapman & Hall, London. Includes index. [G246.B8B8 1977] 77-91525 ISBN 0-89341-468-9 lib.bdg. : 60.00
1. Burton, Richard Francis, Sir, 1821-1890. 2. Explorers—Great Britain Biography. I. Title.

BURTON, Isabel (Arundell) Lady, 1831-1896. 910'.92'4 B
The life of Captain Sir Richard F. Burton. Boston, Milford House [1973] 2 v. illus. 22 cm. Reprint of the 1893 ed., published by Chapman & Hall, London. [G246.B8B8 1973] 67-31252 ISBN 0-87821-104-7 60.00
1. Burton, Richard Francis, Sir, 1821-1890. I. Title.

DEARDEN, Seton, 1905- 910'.92'4 B
Burton of Arabia : the life story of Sir Richard Francis Burton / Seton Dearden. Folcroft, Pa. : Folcroft Library Editions, 1977 [c1937] 334 p., [8] leaves of plates : ill. ; 24 cm. Published in 1936 and 1953 under title: The Arabian knight. Reprint of the ed. published by R. M. McBride, New York. Includes index. [G246.B8D4 1977] 77-18851 ISBN 0-8414-3796-3 lib. bdg. : 30.00
1. Burton, Richard Francis, Sir, 1821-1890. 2. Explorers—Great Britain—Biography. I. Title.

EDWARDES, Allen 923.942
Death rides a camel; a biography of Sir Richard Burton. New York, Julian [c.] 1963. 422p. illus. 22cm. 63-13187 6.50
1. Burton, Richard Francis, Sir 1821-1890. I. Title.

FARWELL, Byron 923.942
Burton; a biography of Sir Richard Francis Burton [New York] Avon [1965, c.1963] x, 495p. maps. 18cm. (N125) Bibl. .95 pap.,
1. Burton, Richard Francis Sir 1821-1890. I. Title. **BIP**

FARWELL, Byron. 923.942
Burton; a biography of Sir Richard Francis Burton. New York, Holt, Rinehart and Winston [1963] xi, 431 p. illus., ports., maps. 22 cm. Bibliography: p. 410-417. [G246.B8F3] 63-18422
1. Burton, Sir Richard Francis 1821-1890. I. Title.

FARWELL, Byron. 910'.92'4 B
Burton : a biography of Sir Richard Francis Burton / Byron Farwell. Westport, Conn. : Greenwood Press, 1975, c1963. xi, 431 p., [6] leaves of plates : ill. ; 22 cm. Reprint of the ed. published by Holt, Rinehart and Winston, New York. Includes index. Bibliography: p. 410-417. [G246.B8F3 1975] 75-5778 ISBN 0-8371-8056-2
1. Burton, Richard Francis, Sir, 1821-1890.

FARWELL, Byron. 910'.92'4 B
Burton : a biography of Sir Richard Francis Burton / Byron Farwell. Westport, Conn. : Greenwood Press, 1975, c1963. xi, 431 p., [6] leaves of plates : ill. ; 22 cm. Reprint of the ed. published by Holt, Rinehart and Winston, New York. Includes index. Bibliography: p. 410-417. [G246.B8F3 1975] 75-5778 ISBN 0-8371-8056-2 : 21.25
1. Burton, Richard Francis, Sir, 1821-1890.

HASTINGS, Michael, 1937- 910'.92'4 B
Sir Richard Burton : the erotic search / by Michael Hastings. New York : Stein and Day, [1976] p. cm. Includes index. Bibliography: p. [G246.B8H37] 75-34200 ISBN 0-8128-1915-2
1. Burton, Richard Francis, Sir, 1821-1890. I. Title.

HASTINGS, Michael, 1937- 910'.92'4 B
Sir Richard Burton : a biography / Michael Hastings. 1st American ed. New York : Coward, McCann & Geoghegan, 1978. 288 p., [8] leaves of plates : ill. ; 24 cm. Includes index. Bibliography: p. 273-281. [G246.B8H37 1978] 78-5486 ISBN 0-698-10936-8 : 12.50
1. Burton, Richard Francis, Sir, 1821-1890. 2. Adventure and adventurers—Biography. I. Title.

KINSLEY, D A 923.942
Death rides a camel; a biography of Sir Richard Burton, by Allen Edwardes. New York, Julian Press, 1963. 422 p. illus. 22 cm. [G246.B8K5] 63-13187
1. Burton, Sir Richard Francis, 1821-1890. I. Title.

STISTED, Georgiana M. 942.081'0924 B
The true life of Capt. Sir Richard F. Burton, K.C.M.G., F.R.G.S., etc. Written by his niece Georgiana M. Stisted, with the authority and approval of the Burton family. New York, Negro Universities Press [1969] xv, 419 p. port. 23 cm. Reprint of the 1886 ed. Includes bibliographical references. [G246.B8S7 1969] 69-18663
1. Burton, Richard Francis, Sir, 1821-1890. I. Title.

WRIGHT, Thomas, 1859-1936. 942.081'0924 B
The life of Sir Richard Burton. New York, B. Franklin [1968] 2 v. in 1. illus., maps, ports. 23 cm. (Burt Franklin research & source works series, 304) (Selected essays in literature & criticism, 17.) Reprint of the 1906 ed. Bibliographical footnotes. [G246.B8W7 1968] 68-56581
1. Burton, Richard Francis, Sir, 1821-1890. I. Title. **BIP**

Burton, Richard Francis, Sir, 1821-1890—Juvenile literature.

ORRMONT, Arthur. 910'.924 B
Fearless adventurer, Sir Richard Burton. New York, Messner [1969] 188 p. 22 cm. Bibliography: p. [181]-182. A biography of Sir Richard Burton, explorer, writer, scholar of Islamic customs, discoverer of Lake Tanganyika, and translator of "Arabian Nights." [G246.B8O7] 92 69-12102 ISBN 6-7132-0734- 3.50
1. Burton, Richard Francis, Sir, 1821-1890—Juvenile literature. I. Title.

Burton, Robert, 1577-1640—Influence—Lamb.

LAKE, Bernard, 1877- 824'.7
A general introduction to Charles Lamb : together with a special study of his relation to Robert Burton, the author of the "Anatomy of melancholy" / by Bernard Lake. Folcroft, Pa. : Folcroft Library Editions, 1977. 91 p. ; 23 cm. Reprint of the 1903 ed. published by Dr. Seele, Leipzig. Originally presented as the author's thesis, Universitat Leipzig. Includes bibliographical references and index. [PR4864.L3 1977] 77-7515 ISBN 0-8414-5815-4 lib. bdg. : 20.00
1. Lamb, Charles, 1775-1834. 2. Burton, Robert, 1577-1640—Influence—Lamb. 3. Burton, Robert, 1577-1640. The anatomy of melancholy. 4. Authors, English—18th century—Biography. I. Title.

Burton, Theodore Elljah. 1851-1929.

CRISSEY, Forrest, 1864-1943. 923.273
Theodore E. Burton, American statesman. [1st ed.] Cleveland, World Pub. Co. [1956] 352 p. illus. 25 cm. [E748.B887C7] 56-10430
1. Burton, Theodore Elljah. 1851-1929. I. Title.

Burton, William Evans, 1802-1860.

KEESE, William Linn, 1835-1904. 792'.028'0924 B
William E. Burton; a sketch of his career other than that of actor, with glimpses of his home life, and extracts from his theatrical journal. New York, B. Franklin [1970] 56 p. illus., port. 19 cm. (Burt Franklin research & source works series, 573. Theatre & drama series, 12) Originally published in 1891 as Publications of the Dunlap Society, no. 14. [PN2598.B8K39 1970] 74-130090 ISBN 0-8337-1904-1
1. Burton, William Evans, 1802-1860.

Burtsell, Richard Lalor, 1840-1912.

BURTSELL, Richard Lalor, 1840-1912. 282'.092'4 B
The diary of Richard L. Burtsell, priest of New York : the early years, 1865-1868 / edited by Nelson J. Callahan. New York : Arno Press, 1978. xxvii, 422 p. ; 24 cm. (The American Catholic tradition) [BX4705.B946A33 1978] 77-89146 ISBN 0-405-10813-3 : 28.00
1. Burtsell, Richard Lalor, 1840-1912. 2. Catholic Church—Clergy—Biography. 3. Catholic Church in New York (State)—History—Sources. 4. Clergy—New York (State)—Biography. 5. New York (State)—Biography. I. Callahan, Nelson J. II. Title. III. Series: American Catholic tradition.

Bushnell, Horace, 1802-1876.

CHENEY, Mary A. (Bushnell) ed. 285'.8'0924 B
Life and letters of Horace Bushnell [by] Mary Bushnell Cheney. New York, Arno Press, 1969. x, 579 p. ports. 23 cm. (Religion in America) Reprint of the 1880 ed. [BX7260.B9C5 1969] 74-83415
1. Bushnell, Horace, 1802-1876. **BIP**

Businessmen.

BARNARD, Alan 926.5
Visions and profits; studies in the business career of Thomas Sutcliffe Mort. [Dist. New York, Cambridge, 1961] 234p. illus. 61-59533 8.50
I. Mort, Thomas Sutcliffe, 1816-1878. II. Title. **BIP**

LEIPOLD, L. Edmond, 1902- 920
Founders of fortunes, by L. Edmond Leipold. Minneapolis, T. S. Denison [1967] 2 v. 25 cm. (Famous American heroes and leaders series) Brief biographies of twenty American businessmen who rose to success through initiative and hard work: v. 1. John Wanamaker, John D. Rockefeller, Joseph Pulitzer, George Peabody, James J. Hill, Henry Ford, George Eastman, John Jacob Astor, Andrew Carnegie, and Irenee Du Pont; v. 2. Thomas A. Edison, Charles M. Hall, Conrad Hilton, Herbert Hoover, Cyrus H. McCormick, Edward J. Noble, J. C. Penney, Spyros Skouras, Lowell Thomas, and Walt Disney. [HC102.5.A2L4] AC 68
1. Businessmen. 2. United States—Biography. I. Title.

Businessmen—Biog.

INTERNATIONAL businessmen's who's who. 650'.0922
1st ed. 1967- London, Burke's Peerage. v. 26cm. Ed.: v. 1- W. J. Potterton [HF5500.I614] 68-2468 23.00
1. Businessmen—Biog. I. Potterton, W. J. ed.
Distributed by Intl. Pubns. Serv., New York.

Businessmen—Tyne Valley.

SHURLOCK, Barry. 338'.092'2 B
Industrial pioneers of Tyneside. Newcastle upon Tyne, Graham, 1972. 31 p. illus., ports. 22 cm. (Northern history booklets, no. 23) [HC252.5.A2S58] 73-153122 ISBN 0-902833-23-5 £0.35
1. Businessmen—Tyne Valley. I. Title. II. Series.

Businessmen—U.S.

FANNING, Leonard M. 923.373
Titans of business. [1st ed.] Philadelphia, Lippincott [1964] 240 p. illus., ports. 22 cm. [HC102.5.A2F2] 63-18499
1. Businessmen—U.S. 2. U.S.—Biography. I. Title.

KELLY, Philip J 658.800924
The making of a salesman [by] Philip J. Kelly. London, New York, Abelard-Schuman [1965] 241 p. 22 cm. [HC102.5.K45A4] 65-15794
1. Businessmen — U.S. — Correspondence, reminiscences, etc. I. Title.

KELLY. PHILIP J. 658.800924
The making of a salesman. New York. Abelard [c.1965] 241p. 22cm. [HC102.5.K45A3] 65-15794 5.00
1. Businessmen—U. S.—Correspondence, reminiscences. etc. I. Title.

LAVINE, Sigmund A. 926
Famous industrialists. Illustrated by Gerald McCann. New York, Dodd, Mead, 1961. 157 p. illus. 22 cm. (Famous biographies for young people) [HC102.5.A2L3] 61-7035
1. Businessmen—U.S. I. Title.

LEIPOLD, L Edmond, 1902- 920
Founders of fortunes, by L. Edmond Leipold. Minneapolis, T. S. Denison [1967] 2 v. 25 cm. (Famous American heroes and leaders series) Contents.--v. 1. John Wanamaker. John D. Rockefeller. Joseph Pulitzer. George Peabody. James J. Hill. Henry Ford. George Eastman. John Jacob Astor. Andrew Carnegie. Irene Du Pont.--v. 2. Thomas A. Edison. Charles M. Hall. Conrad Hilton. Herbert Hoover. Cyrus H. McCormick. Edward J. Noble. J. C. Penney. Spyros Skouras. Lowell Thomas. Walt Disney. [HC102.5.A2L4] 67-22257
1. Businessmen—U. S.—Juvenile literature. 2. U. S.—Biog.—Juvenile literature. I. Title.

LEIPOLD, L. Edmond, 1902- 920 (J)
Founders of fortunes, by L. Edmond Leipold. Minneapolis, T. S. Denison [1967] 2 v. 25 cm. (His Famous American heroes and leaders series) Contents.Contents.—v. 1. John Wanamaker. John D. Rockefeller. Joseph Pulitzer. George Peabody. James J. Hill. Henry Ford. George Eastman. John Jacob Astor. Andrew Carnegie. Irenee Du Pont.—v. 2. Thomas A. Edison. Charles M. Hall. Conrad Hilton. Herbert Hoover. Cyrus H. McCormick. Edward J. Noble. J. C. Penney. Spyros Skouras. Lowell Thomas. Walt Disney. [HC102.5.A2L4] 67-22257
1. Businessmen—United States—Juvenile literature. 2. United States—Biography—Juvenile literature. I. Title.

Businessmen—United States—Biography.

BROOKS, John, 1920- comp. 338'.0092'2 B
The autobiography of American business, edited by John Brooks. [1st ed.] Garden City, N.Y., Doubleday, 1974. xx, 380 p. 24 cm. Includes bibliographical references. [HC102.5.A2B76] 74-5524 ISBN 0-385-06493-4
1. Businessmen—United States—Biography. 2. Businessmen—United States—Correspondence, reminiscences, etc. I. Title.

BROOKS, John Nixon, 1920- comp. 338'.00922 B
The autobiography of American business: the story told by those who made it, edited by John Brooks. Garden City, N.Y.: Anchor Books, 1975 [c1974] xxi, 369 p.; 18 cm. Includes bibliographical references. [HC102.5.A2B76] ISBN 0-385-06972-3 : 3.95 (pbk.)
1. Businessmen—United States—Biography. 2. Businessmen—United States—Correspondence, reminiscences, etc. I. Title.
L.C. card no. for original ed.: 74-5524. **BIP**

SOBEL, Robert, 1931(Feb.19)- 338'.0092'2 B
The entrepreneurs : explorations within the American business tradition / by Robert Sobel. New York : Weybright and Talley, [1974] xv, 413 p. : 24 cm. Includes index. Bibliography: p. [385]-399. [HC102.5.A2S56] 74-76157 ISBN 0-679-40064-8 : 12.50
1. Businessmen—United States—Biography. 2. Entrepreneur—Biography. I. Title. **BIP**

STODDARD, William Osborn, 1835-1925. 338'.0092'2 B
Men of business. Freeport, N.Y., Books for Libraries Press [1972] 317 p. illus. 22 cm. (Essay index reprint series) Reprint of the 1893 ed. issued in series: Men of achievement series. Contents.Contents.—John Jacob Astor.—Cornelius Vanderbilt.—Charles Louis Tiffany.—John Roach.—Levi Parsons Morton.—Edwin Denison Morgan.—Cyrus West Field.—Chauncey Mitchell Depew.—Alexander Turner Stewart.—Philip Danforth Armour.—Horace Brigham Claflin.—Marshall Owen Roberts.—George Mortimer Pullman.—Peter Cooper.—Marshall Field.—Leland Stanford. [HC102.5.A2S7 1972] 72-3490 ISBN 0-8369-2927-6
1. Businessmen—United States—Biography. I. Title. **BIP**

WRIGHT, Edward T. 658'.00922 B
Free enterprise is not dead, by Edward T. Wright. [1st ed.] St. Louis [Mo.], Practical Seminar Institute [1970] 137 p. 22 cm. [HC102.5.A2W75] 71-117496 4.95
1. Businessmen—U.S.—Biography. 2. Success. I. Title.

Busoni, Ferruccio Benvenuto, 1866-1924.

STUCKENSCHMIDT, Hans Heinz, 1901- 780'.924 B
Ferruccio Busoni; chronicle of a European [by] H. H. Stuckenschmidt. Translated by Sandra Morris. New York, St. Martin's Press [1972, c1970] 223 p. illus. 21 cm. Bibliography: p. 215-216. [ML410.B98S83 1972] 71-166511 7.95
1. Busoni, Ferruccio Benvenuto, 1866-1924.

Bustamante, William Alexander, Sir, 1884.

HILL, Frank, 1910- 972.92'05'0924 B
Bustamante and his letters / by Frank Hill. 1st ed. Kingston, Jamaica : Kingston Publishers, 1976. 126 p. : ports. ; 22 cm. "Bustamante, his letters" : p. 51-126. [F1887.B872H54] 77-352352
1. Bustamante, William Alexander, Sir,

1884. 2. Jamaica—Politics and government—Sources. 3. Prime ministers—Jamaica—Biography. I. Bustamante, William Alexander, Sir, 1884- II. Title.

Butler, Benjamin Franklin, 1818-1893.

HOLZMAN, Robert S. 923.273
Stormy Ben Butler. New York, Collier Bks. [1962, c.1954] 280p. (AS102) Bibl. .95 pap.,
1. Butler, Benjamin Franklin, 1818-1893. I. Title. **BIP**

HOLZMAN, Robert S 923.273
Stormy Ben Butler. New York, Macmillan, 1954. 297p. illus. 22cm. Includes bibliography. [E467.1.B87H6] 54-12163
1. Butler, Benjamin Franklin, 1818-1893. I. Title.

HOLZMAN, Robert S. 328.73'092'4 B
Stormy Ben Butler / by Robert S. Holzman. New York : Octagon Books, 1978, c1954. p. cm. Reprint of the ed. published by Macmillan, New York. Includes index. Bibliography: p. [E467.1.B87H6 1978] 78-16391 ISBN 0-374-93935-7 lib.bdg. : 14.00
1. Butler, Benjamin Franklin, 1818-1893. 2. United States. Congress. House—Biography. 3. Generals—United States—Biography. 4. Legislators—United States—Biography. 5. United States—History—Civil War, 1861-1865—Campaigns and battles. 6. United States—Politics and government—1865-1877. I. Title.

NASH, Howard 328.730924 B
Pervear, 1900-
Stormy petrel; the life and times of General Benjamin F. Butler, 1818-1893, by Howard P. Nash, Jr. Rutherford [N.J.] Fairleigh Dickinson University Press [1969] 335 p. 22 cm. Bibliography: p. 301-319. [E467.1.B87N3] 70-80085 10.00
1. Butler, Benjamin Franklin, 1818-1893. I. Title. **BIP**

TREFOUSSE, Hans 328.73'092'4 B
Louis.
Ben Butler; the South called him Beast! By Hans L. Trefousse. New York, Octagon Books, 1974 [c1957] p. cm. Reprint of the ed. published by Twayne Publishers, New York. Bibliography: p. [E467.1.B87T7 1974] 74-13716 ISBN 0-374-97977-4
1. Butler, Benjamin Franklin, 1818-1893. **BIP**

TREFOUSSE, Hans Louis. 923.273
Ben Butler, the South called him Beast! New York, Twayne Publishers [1957] 365 p. illus. 23 cm. Includes bibliography. [E467.1.B87T7] 57-2077
1. Butler, Benjamin Franklin, 1818-1893.

WERLICH, Robert 923.273
'Beast' Butler; the incredible career of Major General Benjamin Franklin Butler. Washington, D.C., Quaker Pr., 3218 'O' St., N.W. [c.1962] 166p. illus. 23cm. Bibl. 62-3147 3.95
1. Butler, Benjamin Franklin, 1818-1893. I. Title.

Butler, Bill, 1914-

BUTLER, Bill, 1914- 266'.3'0924 B
Hill ablaze / by Bill Butler. London : Hodder and Stoughton, 1976. 127 p. ; 18 cm. (Hodder Christian paperbacks) [BV3625.U4B97] 76-372933 ISBN 0-340-20436-2 : £0.70
1. Butler, Bill, 1914- 2. Missionaries—England—Biography. 3. Missionaries—Uganda—Biography. I. Title.

Butler family.

GARNETT, Martha 828'.8'09 B
Roscoe, 1869-1946.
Samuel Butler and his family relations / by Mrs. R. S. Garnett. Folcroft, Pa. : Folcroft Library Editions, 1976. vii, 228 p., [8] leaves of plates : ill. ; 23 cm. Reprint of the 1926 ed. published by J. M. Dent, London and E. P. Dutton, New York. [PR4349.B7Z73 1976] 76-53551 ISBN 0-8414-4586-9 : 25.00
1. Butler, Samuel, 1835-1902—Biography—Character. 2. Butler family. 3. Butler, Samuel, 1835-1902. The way of all flesh. 4. Authors, English—19th century—Biography. I. Title. **BIP**

Butler, George Ide, 1834-1918.

VANDE Vere, Emmett K. 286'.73 B
Rugged heart / by E. K. Vande Vere. Nashville : Southern Pub. Association, [1979] p. cm. Includes bibliographical references. [BX6193.B88V36] 79-9291 ISBN 0-8127-0241-7 pbk. : 85
1. Butler, George Ide, 1834-1918. 2. Seventh-Day Adventists—United States—Biography. I. Title. **BIP**

Butler, Hugh Alfred, 1878-1954.

PAUL, Justus F., 328.73'092'4 B
1938-
Senator Hugh Butler and Nebraska Republicanism / by Justus F. Paul. [Lincoln] : Nebraska State Historical Society ; Ann Arbor, Mich. : produced and distributed on demand by University Microfilms International, 1976. ix, 144 p. : maps ; 27 cm. (Miscellaneous series - Nebraska State Historical Society) (Monograph publishing on demand, imprint series) Includes index. Bibliography: p. [131]-133. [E748.B889P38] 76-42167 ISBN 0-8357-0185-9 : 11.25
1. Butler, Hugh Alfred, 1878-1954. 2. Legislators—United States—Biography. 3. Nebraska—Politics and government. I. Title. II. Series: Nebraska State Historical Society. Miscellaneous series — Nebraska State Historical Society ; no. 1. **BIP**

Butler, Joyce.

BUTLER, Joyce. 974.1'95 B
Pages from a journal / by Joyce Butler ; illustrated by Steve Hrehovcik ; foreword by Alexander B. Brook. Kennebunkport, Me. : Mercer House Press, c1976. 171 p. : ill. ; 24 cm. [F29.K3B94] 76-685 ISBN 0-89080-006-5 : 7.95
1. Butler, Joyce. 2. Kennebunk, Me.—Biography. 3. Maine—Social life and customs. I. Title. **BIP**

Butler, Mike.

BUTLER, Mike. 917.8
92 days in the saddle / by Mike Butler illustrated by Dale Crawford Fort Collins, Colo. : Old Army Press, c1975. 135 p. : ill. ; 23 cm. [F640.B84] 76-358647 8.95
1. Butler, Mike. 2. North Dakota—Description and travel—1951- 3. South Dakota—Description and travel—1951- 4. Wyoming—Description and travel—1951- I. Title.

Butler, Ron.

BUTLER, 362.1'9'6994420924 B
Marie.
Ron's story : a legacy of love / by Marie Butler. Westchester, Ill. : Good News Publishers, c1978. 143 p. ; 21 cm. [RC280.L9B87] 78-52686 ISBN 0-89107-155-5 : 3.50
1. Butler, Ron. 2. Lymphatics—Cancer—Biography. 3. Christian life—1960- I. Title. **BIP**

Butler, Samuel, Bp. of Lichfield and Coventry, 1774-1839.

BUTLER, Samuel, 1835- 828'.8'09 S
1902.
The life and letters of Dr. Samuel Butler. [1st AMS ed.] New York, AMS Press [1968] 2 v. illus. 24 cm. (The Shrewsbury edition of the works of Samuel Butler, v. 10-11) Reprint of the 1924 ed. [BX5199.B93] Contents.Contents.—v. 1. 30th January 1774-1st March 1831.—v. 2. 7th March 1831-4th December 1839. [PR4349.B7 1968 vol. 10-11] [BX5199.B93] 283'.092'4 B 72-186949
1. Butler, Samuel, Bp. of Lichfield and Coventry, 1774-1839. I. Title.

Butler, Samuel, 1835-1902.

BUTLER, Samuel, 1835-1902. 928.2
The correspondence of Samuel Butler with his sister May. Edited with an introd. by Daniel F. Howard. Berkeley, University of California Press, 1962. xx, 265 p. 22 cm. Includes bibliographical references. [PR4349.B7Z535] 62-13075
1. Butler, May. 1841-1916. II. Howard, Daniel Francis, ed.

BUTLER, Samuel, 1835- 828'.8'09 S
1902.
The note-books of Samuel Butler. [1st AMS ed.] New York, AMS Press [1968] lv, 493 p. port. 24 cm. (The Shrewsbury edition of the works of Samuel Butler, v. 20) Reprint of the 1926 ed. Includes bibliographical references. [PR4349.B7 1968 vol. 20] 828'.8'03 B 72-186941
I. Title.

COLE, George Douglas v. 12
Howard, 1889-
Samuel Butler. London, New York, Published for the British Council and the National Book League by Longmans, Green [1952] 52 p. port. 22 cm. (Bibliographical series of supplements to British book news, no. 30) Bibliography: p. 45-52. A 52
1. Butler, Samuel. 1835-1902. I. Title. II. Series.

FURBANK, Philip 828'.8'09
Nicholas.
Samuel Butler, 1835-1902, by P. N. Furbank. [2nd ed.] Hamden, Conn.] Archon Books, 1971. 124 p. 21 cm. Includes bibliographical references. [PR4349.B7Z726 1971] 76-131373
1. Butler, Samuel, 1835-1902.

HARRIS, John Frederick. 828'.8'09
Samuel Butler, author of Erewhon; the man and his work, by John F. Harris. London, G. Richards Ltd., 1916. [Folcroft, Pa.] Folcroft Library Editions, 1972. p. [PR4349.B7Z75 1972] 72-12738 ISBN 0-8414-0962-5 (lib. bdg.)
1. Butler, Samuel, 1835-1902. **BIP**

HENDERSON, Philip, 1906- 928.2
Samuel Butler, the incarnate bachelor. Bloomington, Indiana University Press, 1954. 241p. illus. 22cm. [PR4349] 54-8185
1. Butler, Samuel, 1835-1902. I. Title.

HENDERSON, Philip, 1906- 823'.8 B
Samuel Butler, the incarnate bachelor. New York, Barnes & Noble [1968] xiii, 249 p. ports. 23 cm. [PR4349.B7Z76 1968] 68-1521
1. Butler, Samuel, 1835-1902.

HOLT, Lee Elbert. v. 12
Samuel Butler, by Lee E. Holt. New York, Grosset & Dunlap [1964] 183 p. 21 cm. (Twayne's English authors series, 2) Bibliography: p. 167-176. 65-56957
1. Butler, Samuel, 1835-1902. I. Title.

JONES, Henry Festing, 828'.8'09 B
1851-1928.
Samuel Butler: a sketch. [Folcroft, Pa.] Folcroft Library Editions, 1973. p. Reprint of the 1921 ed. published by J. Cape, London. [PR4349.B7Z795 1973] 73-11370 7.50
1. Butler, Samuel, 1835-1902. **BIP**

JONES, Henry Festing, 828'.8'09 B
1851-1928.
Samuel Butler: a sketch. [Folcroft, Pa.] Folcroft Library Editions, 1973. 59 p. 24 cm. Reprint of the 1921 ed. published by J. Cape, London. [PR4349.B7Z795 1973] 73-11370 ISBN 0-8414-2195-1 (lib. bdg.)
1. Butler, Samuel, 1835-1902.

JONES, Joseph Jay 928.2
The cradle of Erewhon; Samuel Butler in New Zealand. Austin, University of Texas Press [c.1959] xii, 224p. illus., ports., map. 24cm. Bibliographical references included in 'Documentary notes' (p. 179-187) 59-8125 4.00
1. Butler, Samuel, 1835-1902. I. Title.

JONES, Joseph Jay, 1908- 928.2
The cradle of Erewhon; Samuel Butler in New Zealand. Austin, University of Texas Press [1959] xii, 224p. illus., ports., map. 24cm. Bibliographical references included in 'Documentary notes' (p. 179-187) [PR4349.B7Z82] 59-8125
1. Butler, Samuel, 1835-1902. I. Title.

RATTRAY, Robert 828'.8'09 B
Fleming, 1886-
Samuel Butler: a chronicle and an introduction, by R. F. Rattray. New York, Haskell House Publishers, 1974. 216 p. 20 cm. Reprint of the 1935 ed. published by Duckworth, London. Includes bibliographical references. [PR4349.B7Z9 1974] 73-21671 ISBN 0-8383-1782-0
1. Butler, Samuel, 1835-1902.

STILLMAN, Clara 828'.8'09 B
(Gruening)
Samuel Butler, a mid-Victorian modern [by] Clara G. Stillman. Port Washington, N.Y., Kennikat Press [1972] xi, 319 p. illus. 22 cm. Reprint of the 1932 ed. Bibliography: p. 307-314. [PR4349.B7Z94 1972] 74-160784 ISBN 0-8046-1616-7
1. Butler, Samuel, 1835-1902.

Butler, Samuel, 1835-1902—Biography—Character.

GARNETT, Martha 828'.8'09 B
Roscoe, 1869-1946.
Samuel Butler and his family relations / by Mrs. R. S. Garnett. Folcroft, Pa. : Folcroft Library Editions, 1976. vii, 228 p., [8] leaves of plates : ill. ; 23 cm. Reprint of the 1926 ed. published by J. M. Dent, London and E. P. Dutton, New York. [PR4349.B7Z73 1976] 76-53551 ISBN 0-8414-4586-9 : 25.00
1. Butler, Samuel, 1835-1902—Biography—Character. 2. Butler family. 3. Butler, Samuel, 1835-1902. The way of all flesh. 4. Authors, English—19th century—Biography. I. Title. **BIP**

Butler, Samuel, 1835-1902—Correspondence.

BUTLER, Samuel, 1835- 828'.8'09 B
1902.
Samuel Butler and Miss E. M. A. Savage, further correspondence / edited by Kenneth Hopkins. North Walsham : Warren House Press, 1976. 32 p. ; 22 cm. These letters "had come into my hands with doubtful provenance from the papers of Llwd ffrench-Jons, and I was uncertain of their authenticity." Cf. The Editor. Limited ed. of 250 copies of which 200 are signed and numbered; this copy is no. 60. [PR4349.B7Z54 1976] 77-360847 ISBN 0-902107-11-9 : £3.00
1. Butler, Samuel, 1835-1902—Correspondence. 2. Savage, Eliza Mary Ann, 1836-1885. 3. Authors, English—19th century—Correspondence. I. Savage, Eliza Mary Ann, 1836-1885. II. Hopkins, Kenneth. III. Title.

Butler University, Indianapolis—Hist.

BROWN, Hilton Ultimus, 920.5
1859-
A book of memories. Indianapolis, Butler University, 1951. 339 p. illus. 24 cm. [PN4874.B77A3] 51-6837
1. Butler University, Indianapolis—Hist. 2. Indianapolis news. I. Title.

Butler, William Francis, Sir, 1838-1910.

LESLIE, Shane, Sir, 920.042
bart., 1885-
Salutation to five. Freeport, N.Y., Books for Libraries Press [1970] v, 156 p. 23 cm. (Biography index reprint series) Reprint of the 1951 ed. Includes bibliographical references. [CT106.L4 1970] 75-126321 ISBN 8-369-80271-
1. Fitzherbert, Maria Anne (Smythe) 1756-1837. 2. Warre, Edmond, 1837-1920. 3. Butler, William Francis, Sir, 1838-1910. 4. Tolstoi, Lev Nikolaevich, graf, 1828-1910. 5. Sykes, Mark, Sir, bart., 1879-1919. I. Title.

Butt, Clara, Dame, 1873-1936.

PONDER, Winifred. 784'.092'4 B
Clara Butt, her life-story / by Winifred Ponder ; with a foreword by Dame Clara Butt. New York : Da Capo Press, 1978. 261 p., [23] leaves of plates : ill. ; 23 cm. (Da Capo Press music reprint series) Reprint of the 1928 ed. published by G. G.

Harrap, London. [ML420.B9P7 1978] 77-16530 ISBN 0-306-77529-8 : 22.50
1. Butt, Clara, Dame, 1873-1936. 2. Singers—England—Biography.

Butterfield, David C.

BUTTERFIELD, David C. 973'.04'97 S
Life and adventures / David C. Butterfield. New York : Garland Pub., 1978. 64 p. : ill. ; 24 cm. (The Garland library of narratives of North American Indian captivities ; v. 63) Issued with the reprint of the 1848 ed. of Barker, J. Interesting narrative of the sufferings of Joseph Barker and his wife. New York, 1978. Reprint of the 1851 ed. published by Congress Print. House, Boston under title: The life and adventures of David C. Butterfield, Northwestern pioneer for the last twenty years. [E85.G2 vol. 63] [E87.B96] 978'.02'0924 B 75-7087 ISBN 0-8240-1687-4 (set) : 25.00 (set)
1. Butterfield, David C. 2. Indians of North America—Northwest, Old—Captivities. 3. Frontier and pioneer life—Northwest, Old. 4. Northwest, Old—Biography. I. Title. II. Series. **BIP**

Buttrey, Anna Laura (Jordan)

BUTTREY, Anna Laura (Jordan) 1898or9- 001.2
Six decades to a degree, by Anna Jordan Buttrey. Craigmont, Idaho, 1964. 180 p. illus., map, ports. 24 cm. Autobiography. [CT275.B8379A3] 65-2524
I. Title.

Butzer, Martin, 1491-1551.

EELLS, Hastings, 1895- 284'.1'0924 B
Martin Bucer. New York, Russell & Russell [1971] 539 p. port. 23 cm. "First published in 1931." Bibliography: p. [424]-432. [BR350.B93E4 1971] 79-151547
1. Butzer, Martin, 1491-1551. 2. Reformation—Germany. **BIP**

Buxtehude, Dietrich. 1637-1707.

HUTCHINS, Farley Kennan, 1920- 784'.092'4
Dietrich Buxtehude, the man, his music, his era Paterson, N. J., Music Textbook Co. [1955] 68p. music. 23cm. Bibliography: p. 60-68. [ML410.B99H8] 55-58541
1. Buxtehude, Dietrich. 1637-1707. I. Title.

Byer, Etta,

BYER, Etta, 1884or5- 920.7
Transplanted people, by Yecheved (Etta Byer) Reproductions of oil paintings, by Samuel Byer. [Chicago] M. J. Aron and other members of the Lider Organization of Chicago [1955] 231p. illus. 26cm. Autobiography. [CT275.B839A3] 56-16530
I. Byer, Samuel, 1886- II. Title.

Byles, Mather, 1707-1788.

EATON, Arthur Wentworth Hamilton, 1849-1937. 285'.832'0924 B
The famous Mather Byles; the noted Boston Tory preacher, poet, and wit, 1707-1788. Freeport, N.Y., Books for Libraries Press [1971] x, 258 p. illus. 23 cm. Reprint of the 1914 ed. Includes bibliographical references. [BX7260.B95E3 1971] 74-165626 ISBN 0-8369-5933-7
1. Byles, Mather, 1707-1788. I. Title. **BIP**

EATON, Arthur Wentworth Hamilton, 1849-1937. 285'.8'0924 B
The famous Mather Byles; the noted Boston Tory preacher, poet, and wit, 1707-1788. With a new introd. and a pref. by George Athan Billias. Boston, Gregg Press, 1972 [c1914] x, x, 258 p. illus. 23 cm. (The American Revolutionary series. The Loyalist library) Reprint of the ed. published by W. A. Butterfield, Boston. "Doctor Byles's chief published writings": p. 240-246. [BX7260.B95E3 1972] 72-8697 ISBN 0-8398-0458-X 13.00 (Lib. ed.)
1. Byles, Mather, 1707-1788. I. Series: The Loyalist library.

Byrd, David Harold, 1900-

BYRD, David Harold, 1900- 338'.092'4 B
I'm an endangered species : the autobiography of a free enterpriser / David Harold "Dry Hole" Byrd. Houston : Pacesetter Press, c1978. vii, 108 p. : ill. ; 24 cm. [HG183.T4B95] 78-62614 ISBN 0-88415-258-8 : 6.95
1. Byrd, David Harold, 1900- 2. Capitalists and financiers—Texas—Biography. I. Title. **BIP**

Byrd family.

HATCH, Alden, 1898- 929.2'0973
The Byrds of Virginia. [1st ed.] New York, Holt, Rinehart and Winston [1969] xvi, 535 p. illus., ports. 24 cm. Bibliographical footnotes. [CS71.B9993 1969] 69-11808 10.00
1. Byrd family. I. Title.

Byrd, Richard Evelyn, 1888-1957.

GLADYCH, Michael. 923.973
Admiral Byrd of Antarctica. New York, Messner [1960] 192 p. 22 cm. Includes bibliographies. [G585.B8G5] 60-7053
1. Byrd, Richard Evelyn, 1888-1957. I. Title.

HOYT, Edwin Palmer. 910.0973'0924 B
The last explorer; the adventures of Admiral Byrd [by] Edwin P. Hoyt. New York, John Day Co. [1968] 380 p. illus., maps, ports. 23 cm. Bibliographical references included in "Acknowledgements" (p. [9]-10) [G585.B8H6] 68-23440 7.95
1. Byrd, Richard Evelyn, 1888-1957. I. Title.

Byrd, Richard Evelyn, 1888-1957—Juvenile literature.

DE LEEUW, Adele Louise, 1899- 92
Richard E. Byrd, Adventurer to the poles. Illustrated by Al Fiorentino. Champaign, Ill., Garrard Pub. Co. [1963] 80 p. illus. 23 cm. (A Discovery book) [G585.B8D4] 63-9218
1. Byrd, Richard Evelyn, 1888-1957 — Juvenile literature. I. Title.

DE LEEUW, Adele Louise, 1899- 92 (J)
Richard E. Byrd, adventurer to the poles. Illustrated by Al Fiorentino. Champaign, Ill., Garrard Pub. Co. [1963] 80 p. illus. 23 cm. (A Discovery book) [G585.B8D4] 63-9218
1. Byrd, Richard Evelyn, 1888-1957—Juvenile literature.

EDUCATIONAL Research Council of America. Social Science Staff. 919.8 B
Explorers and discoverers, Admiral Byrd / prepared by the Social Science Staff of the Educational Research Council of America ; [Kenneth L. Shipley, Paula Rondeau, design and illustration]. Learner-verified ed. 2. Boston : Allyn and Bacon, [1974] 49 p. : col. ill. ; 21 cm. (Concepts and inquiry, the ERC social science program) A simple account of Richard Byrd's journeys to the North and South Poles. [G585.B8E3 1974] 92 73-78344 pbk. : 1.76
1. Byrd, Richard Evelyn, 1888-1957—Juvenile literature. I. Shipley, Kenneth L., ill. II. Rondeau, Paula, ill. III. Title. IV. Series: Concepts and inquiry, the Educational Research Council social science program.

OLDS, Helen (Diehl) 1895- 910'.924 B
Richard E. Byrd, by Helen D. Olds. Illustrated by Frank Aloise. New York, Putnam [1969] 62 p. col. illus. 23 cm. (A See and read beginning to read biography) A simple biography of the explorer who was the first to fly over the North and South Poles on separate expeditions. [G585.B8O4 1969] 92 68-24540 2.68
1. Byrd, Richard Evelyn, 1888-1957—Juvenile literature. I. Aloise, Frank E., illus. II. Title. **BIP**

STEINBERG, Alfred, 1917- 923.973
Admiral Richard E., Byrd. Illustrated by Charles Beck. New York, Putnam [1960] 128 p. illus. 21 cm. (Lives to remember) [G585.B8S8] 60-6914
1. Byrd, Richard Evelyn. 1888-1957 — Juvenile literature. II. Title.

Byrd, William, 1542 or 3-1623.

HOLST, Imogen, 1907- 780'.92'4 B
Byrd. New York, Praeger Publishers [1972] 79 p. illus. 26 cm. (The Great composers) [ML410.B996H6] 75-188019 6.95
1. Byrd, William, 1542 or 3-1623. **BIP**

HOWES, Frank Stewart, 1891- 780'.92'4 B
William Byrd / by Frank Howes. Westport, Conn. : Greenwood Press, 1978. xii, 267 p., [2] leaves of plates : ill. ; 23 cm. Reprint of the 1928 ed. published by K. Paul, Trench, Trubner, London, issued in series: Masters of music. Includes bibliographical references and index. [ML410.B996H7 1978] 77-27081 ISBN 0-313-20182-X lib.bdg. : 19.00
1. Byrd, William, 1542 or 3-1623. 2. Composers—England—Biography. **BIP**

Byrd, William, 1652-1704.

THE Correspondence of the three William Byrds of Westover, Virginia, 1684-1776 / edited by Marion Tinling ; with a foreword by Louis B. Wright. Charlottesville : Published for the Virginia Historical Society [by] the University Press of Virginia, 1977. 2 v. (li, 859 p.) : ill. ; 26 cm. (Virginia Historical Society documents ; v. 12-13) Includes bibliographical references and index. [F229.C8] 77-1900 ISBN 0-8139-0669-5 : 32.50 975.5'02'0922
1. Byrd, William, 1652-1704. 2. Byrd, William, 1674-1744. 3. Byrd, William, 1728-1777. 4. Statesmen—Virginia—Correspondence. 5. Virginia—History—Colonial period, ca. 1600-1775—Sources. I. Byrd, William, 1652-1704. II. Byrd, William, 1674-1744. III. Byrd, William, 1728-1777. IV. Tinling, Marion Rose Goble, 1904- V. Series: Virginia Historical Society, Richmond. Documents ; v. 12-13.

Byrd, William, 1674-1744.

BEATTY, Richmond Croom, 1905-1961. 975.5'02'0924
William Byrd of Westover. With a new pref. and bibliography by M. Thomas Inge. [Hamden, Conn.] Archon Books, 1970 [c1932] xxxix, 243 p. illus., ports. 21 cm. Bibliography: p. [225]-240. [F229.B972 1970] 70-122393
1. Byrd, William, 1674-1744. I. Title.

BYRD, William, 1674-1744. 923.273
The London diary, 1717-1721, and other writings. Edited by Louis B. Wright and Marion Tinling. New York, Oxford University Press, 1958. vi, 647 p. illus., port. 24 cm. "The diary ... is transcribed from a shorthand notebook (Mss 5:1B 9964:1) in the library of the Virginia Historical Society." Contents.Contents.—The life of William Byrd of Virginia, 1674-1744.—The secret diary of William Byrd of Westover from December 13, 1717 to May 19, 1721.—History of the dividing line.—A journey to the land of Eden.—A progress to the mines. Bibliographical footnotes. [F229.B9685] 57-10389
1. London—Social life and customs. 2. Virginia—Social life and customs. I. Wright, Louis Booker, 1899- ed. II. Tinling, Marion Rose Goble, 1904- ed. III. Title.

BYRD, William, 1674-1744. 975.5'02'0924
The London diary (1717-1721) and other writings / William Byrd of Virginia ; edited by Louis B. Wright and Marion Tinling. New York : Arno Press, 1972, c1958. vi, 647 p. ; 24 cm. (Research library of colonial Americana) Reprint of the ed. published by Oxford University Press, New York. Includes index. [F229.B95 1972] 77-141208 ISBN 0-405-03305-2 : 24.00
1. Byrd, William, 1674-1744. 2. Virginia—Social life and customs—Colonial period, ca. 1600-1775. 3. London—Social life and customs. I. Title. II. Series. **BIP**

BYRD, William, 1674-1744. 975.5'02'0924
The secret diary of William Byrd of Westover, 1709-1712 / edited by Louis B. Wright and Marion Tinling. New York : Arno Press, 1972, c1941. xxviii, 622 p. ; 23 cm. (Research library of colonial Americana) Reprint of the ed. published by the Dietz Press, Richmond. Includes index. [F229.B9715 1972] 72-141097 ISBN 0-405-03304-4 : 24.00
1. Byrd, William, 1674-1744. 2. Virginia—Social life and customs—Colonial period, ca. 1600-1775. I. Title. II. Series. **BIP**

THE Correspondence of the three William Byrds of Westover, Virginia, 1684-1776 / edited by Marion Tinling ; with a foreword by Louis B. Wright. Charlottesville : Published for the Virginia Historical Society [by] the University Press of Virginia, 1977. 2 v. (li, 859 p.) : ill. ; 26 cm. (Virginia Historical Society documents ; v. 12-13) Includes bibliographical references and index. [F229.C8] 77-1900 ISBN 0-8139-0669-5 : 32.50 975.5'02'0922
1. Byrd, William, 1652-1704. 2. Byrd, William, 1674-1744. 3. Byrd, William, 1728-1777. 4. Statesmen—Virginia—Correspondence. 5. Virginia—History—Colonial period, ca. 1600-1775—Sources. I. Byrd, William, 1652-1704. II. Byrd, William, 1674-1744. III. Byrd, William, 1728-1777. IV. Tinling, Marion Rose Goble, 1904- V. Series: Virginia Historical Society, Richmond. Documents ; v. 12-13.

MARAMBAUD, Pierre. 975.5'02'0924
William Byrd of Westover 1674-1744 Charlottesville, University Press of Virginia [1971] ix, 297 p. illus., col. map (on lining papers), port. 24 cm. Bibliography: p. [280]-289. [F229.B98] 70-151251 ISBN 0-8139-0346-7
1. Byrd, William, 1674-1744. I. Title. **BIP**

Byrne, John Francis, 1880-

BYRNE, John Francis, 1880- 973.91'092'4 B
Silent years : an autobiography with memoirs of James Joyce and our Ireland / by J. F. Byrne. New York : Octagon Books, 1975, c1953. p. cm. [CT808.B9A3 1975] 75-11682 ISBN 0-374-91144-4 : 13.00
1. Byrne, John Francis, 1880- 2. Joyce, James, 1882-1941—Biography. I. Title. **BIP**

Byrne, Patrick James, Bp., 1888-1950.

LANE, Raymond A Bp. 922.2519
Ambassador in chains; the life of Bishop Patrick James Byrne (1888-1950) apostolic delegate to the Republic of Korea. New York, P. J. Kenedy [1955] 249p. illus. 21cm. [BV3462.B9L3] 55-6639
1. Byrne, Patrick James, Bp., 1888-1950. I. Title.

Byrom family.

MCELROY, John McConnell, 1830-1908 973'.04'97 S
Abby Byram and her father / John M. McElroy. New York : Garland Pub., 1976. p. cm. (The Garland library of narratives of North American Indian captivities ; v. 99) Issued with the reprint of the 1894 ed. of Mrs. J. E. De Camp Sweet's narrative of her captivity ... New York, 1976. Reprint of the 1898 ed. printed by Cook & Algire, Ottumwa, Iowa. [E85.G2 vol. 99] [E99.I7] 970'.004'97 75-34322 ISBN 0-8240-1723-4 lib.bdg. : 21.00
1. Byrom family. 2. Iroquois Indians—Captivities. 3. Indians of North America—Capivities. 4. United States—History—Revolution, 1775-1783—Prisoners and prisons. I. Title.

Byrom, John, 1692-1763.

HOBHOUSE, Stephen Henry, 1881-1961. 283'.092'4
William Law and eighteenth century Quakerism; including some unpublished letters and fragments of William Law and John Byrom. New York, B. Blom, 1972. 342 p. illus. 21 cm. Reprint of the 1927 ed. published by G. Allen & Unwin, London.

Includes bibliographical references. [BX5199.L3H62 1972] 77-175870 14.50
1. Law, William, 1686-1761. 2. Byrom, John, 1692-1763. 3. Dodshon, Frances (Henshaw) Paxton, 1714-1793. 4. Friends, Society of. I. Title.

Byron, Anne Isabella (Milbanke) Byron, baroness, 1792-1860.

ELWIN, Malcolm, 1902- 920.7
Lord Byron's wife. New York, Harcourt [1963, c.1962] 556p. front. port. 25cm. Bibl. 63-8083 8.75
1. Byron, Anne Isabella (Milbanke) Byron, baroness, 1792-1860. 2. Byron, George Gordon Noel Byron, baron, 1788-1824. I. Title. **BIP**

GRAHAM, William. 821'.7'09
Last links with Byron, Shelley, and Keats / by William Graham. Norwood, Pa. : Norwood Editions, 1975. p. cm. Reprint of the 1898 ed. published by L. Smithers, London. [PR590.G7 1975] 75-29340 ISBN 0-88305-234-2 : 15.00
1. Byron, Anne Isabella Milbanke Byron, Baroness, 1792-1860. 2. Clairmont, Clara Mary Jane, 1798-1879. 3. Poets, English—19th century—Biography. I. Title.

MACKAY, Charles, 1814-1889. 821'.7 B
Medora Leigh; a history and an autobiography. Edited by Charles Mackay. With an introd., and a commentary on the charges brought against Lord Byron by Mrs. Beecher Stowe. London, R. Bentley, 1869. [New York, AMS Press, 1973] 280 p. 19 cm. On spine: WOL. [PR4382.M3 1973] 78-37700 ISBN 0-404-56759-2 14.00
1. Byron, George Gordon Noel Byron, Baron, 1788-1824. 2. Stowe, Harriet Elizabeth (Beecher) 1811-1896. 3. Byron, Anne Isabella (Milbanke) Byron, Baroness, 1792-1860. 4. Leigh, Elizabeth Medora, 1814-1849. I. Leigh, Elizabeth Medora, 1814-1849. II. Title. **BIP**

STOWE, Harriet Elizabeth (Beecher) 1811-1896. 821'.7 B
Lady Byron vindicated; a history of the Byron controversy, from its beginning in 1816 to the present time. New York, Haskell House, 1970. 482 p. 23 cm. Reprint of the 1870 ed. Includes bibliographical references. [PR4382.S7 1970] 72-130245 ISBN 0-8383-1135-0
1. Byron, Anne Isabella (Milbanke) Byron, Baroness, 1792-1860. 2. Byron, George Gordon Noel Byron, Baron, 1788-1824. I. Title.

Byron, George Gordon Noel Byron, Baron, 1788-1824.

BIGLAND, Eileen. 928.2
Passion for excitement; the life and personality of the incredible Lord Byron. New York, Coward-McCann [1956] 317 p. illus. 23 cm. [PR4381.B48] 56-11474
1. Byron, George Gordon Noel Byron, Baron, 1788-1824. I. Title.

BRISCOE, Walter Alwyn, 1878-1934, comp. 821'.7
Byron, the poet; a collection of addresses and essays, by Viscount Haldane [and others] Edited by Walter A. Briscoe. New York, Haskell House Publishers, 1967. xvi, 287 p. illus., facsims., ports. 23 cm. Reprint of the 1924 ed. [PR4381.B65 1967] 67-30803
1. Byron, George Gordon Noel Byron, Baron, 1788-1824. I. Haldane, Richard Burdon Haldane, 1st Viscount, 1856-1928. II. Title.

BYRON; v. 12
translated from the French by Hamish Miles. New York, Grosset & Dunlap [1956, c1930] xiv, 596p. 22cm. (Biographies of distinction) Translation of Don Juan; ou, La vie de Byron.
1. Byron, George Gordon Noel Byron, 6th baron, 1788-1824. I. Maurois, Andre, 1885-

BYRON, George Gordon Noel Byron, 6th baron, 1788-1824. 928.2
Byron, a self-portrait; letters and diaries, 1798 to 1824, with hitherto unpublished letters. Edited by Peter Quennell. New York, Scribner [1950] 2 v. (xv, 803 p.) fronts. 22 cm. Errata slip inserted in v. 2. "Bibliographical note": v. 1, p. xiv-xv. [PR4381.A3Q4 1950a] 50-6875
I. Quennell, Peter, 1905- ed. II. Title.

BYRON, George Gordon Noel Byron, Baron, 1788-1824. 821'.7
The confessions of Lord Byron; a collection of his private opinions of men and of matters, taken from the new and enlarged edition of his Letters and journals. Arr. by W. A. Lewis Bettany. New York, Haskell House Publishers, 1973. xxviii, 402 p. ports. 23 cm. Reprint of the 1905 ed. [PR4381.A3B4 1973] 72-3739 ISBN 0-8383-1578-X 14.95 (lib. binding)
I. Bettany, Lewis, 1869- II. Title.

BYRON, George Gordon Noel Byron, Baron, 1788-1824. 821'.7
Lord Byron in his letters; selections from his letters and journals. Edited by V. H. Collins. New York, Haskell House Publishers, 1973. xvi, 301 p. port. 23 cm. Reprint of the 1927 ed. [PR4381.A3C6 1973] 72-3626 ISBN 0-8383-1582-8 11.95 (lib. bdg.)
I. Collins, Vere Henry, ed. II. Title.

BYRON, George Gordon Noel Byron, 6th baron, 1788-1824. 928.2
Selected letters; edited with an introd. by Jacques Barzun New York, Farrar, Straus and Young [1953] xliv, 276p. 22cm. (Great letters series) [PR4381.A3B3] 53-7803
I. Title.

BYRON in Italy. v. 12
[Compass books ed.] New York, Viking Press [1957] 274p. 20cm. (Compass books, C 16)
1. Byron, George Gordon Noel Byron, 6th baron, 1788-1824. I. Quennell, Peter, 1905-

CALVERT, William Jonathan, 1901- 928.2
Byron: romantic paradox. New York, Russell & Russell, 1962 [c1935] 235 p. 22 cm. Includes bibliography. [PR4381.C3 1962] 62-12442
1. Byron, George Gordon Noel Byron, 6th baron, 1788-1824.

CLINTON, George. 821'.7 B
Memoirs of the life and writings of Lord Byron / by George Clinton. Folcroft, Pa. : Folcroft Library Editions, 1975. p. cm. Reprint of the 1827 ed. published by J. Robins, London. [PR4381.C6 1975] 75-28482 ISBN 0-8414-3379-8 lib. bdg. : 100.00
1. Byron, George Gordon Noel Byron, Baron, 1788-1824. I. Title. **BIP**

DALLAS, Robert Charles, 1754-1824. 821'.7 B
Recollections of the life of Lord Byron, from the year 1808 to the end of 1814 : ... taken from authentic documents in the possession of the author / by R. C. Dallas. Folcroft, Pa. : Folcroft Library Editions, 1976. p. cm. Reprint of the 1824 ed. published by C. Knight, London. [PR4381.D3 1976] 75-29173 ISBN 0-8414-3728-9 lib. bdg. : 65.00
1. Byron, George Gordon Noel Byron, Baron, 1788-1824. I. Title.

DALLAS, Robert Charles, 1754-1824. 821'.7 B
Recollections of the life of Lord Byron, from the year 1808 to the end of 1814 : ... taken from authentic documents in the possession of the author / by R. C. Dallas. Folcroft, Pa. : Folcroft Library Editions, 1976. p. cm. Reprint of the 1824 ed. published by C. Knight, London. [PR4381.D3 1976] 75-29173 ISBN 0-8414-3728-9 lib. bdg. : 65.00
1. Byron, George Gordon Noel Byron, Baron, 1788-1824. I. Title.

DICK, William. 821'.7
Byron & his poetry. London, Harrap, 1913. [New York, AMS Press, 1972] 188, [1] p. port. 19 cm. (Poetry and life series) Bibliography: p. [189] [PR4381.D5 1972] 73-120968 ISBN 0-404-52508-3 8.00
1. Byron, George Gordon Noel Byron, Baron, 1788-1824. I. Title. II. Series. **BIP**

DU BOS, Charles, 1882-1939. 821'.7 B
Byron and the need of fatality. Translated by Ethel Colburn Mayne. New York, Haskell House, 1970. 287 p. 23 cm. Translation of Byron et le besoin de la fatalite. Reprint of the 1932 ed. [PR4381.D82 1970] 78-95423 ISBN 0-8383-0971-2
1. Byron, George Gordon Noel Byron, Baron, 1788-1824. I. Title. **BIP**

GORDON, Armistead Churchill, 1855-1931. 821'.7 B
Allegra; the story of Byron and Miss Clairmont. New York, Haskell House Publishers, 1973. vi, 266 p. 23 cm. [PR4382.G6 1973] 72-2103 ISBN 0-8383-1474-0 10.95 (lib. bdg.)
1. Byron, George Gordon Noel Byron, Baron, 1788-1824. 2. Clairmont, Clara Mary Jane, 1798-1879. I. Title.

GORDON, Cosmo, Sir, 1777-1867. 821'.7 B
Life and genius of Lord Byron. [Folcroft, Pa.] Folcroft Library Editions, 1974. p. cm. Reprint of the 1824 ed. published by Knight and Lacey, London. [PR4381.G6 1974] 74-16130 9.45 (lib. bdg.).
1. Byron, George Gordon Noel Byron, Baron, 1788-1824. I. Title. **BIP**

GRAHAM, William. 821'.7'09 B
Last links with Byron, Shelley, and Keats. Folcroft, Pa., Folcroft Press [1969] xx, 121 p. 23 cm. Reprint of the 1898 ed. [PR457.G7 1969] 72-196918
1. Byron, George Gordon Noel Byron, Baron, 1788-1824. 2. Shelley, Percy Bysshe, 1792-1822. 3. Keats, John, 1795-1821. I. Title. **BIP**

†GRAY, Duncan, 1892-1958. 082 S
The life and work of Lord Byron / by Duncan Gray. Folcroft, Pa. : Folcroft Library Editions, 1976. 122 p., [3] leaves of plates : ports. ; 23 cm. Reprint of the 1946 ed. published by Corporation of Nottingham, Nottingham, Eng., which was issued as no. 4 of Newstead Abbey publications. Includes index. [PR4381.G65 1976] 821'.7 B 76 41017 ISBN 0-8414-4447-1 lib. bdg. : 20.00
1. Byron, George Gordon Noel Byron, Baron, 1788-1824. 2. Poets, English—19th century—Biography. I. Title. II. Series: Newstead Abbey (Nottinghamshire) Publications ; no. 4. **BIP**

HUNT, Leigh, 1784-1859. v. 12
Lord Byron and some of his contemporaries, with recollections of the author's life, and of his visit to Italy. New York, AMS Press, 1966. viii, 513 p. illus., ports. 24 cm. Includes sketches of Moore, Shelley, Keats, and others. First published by H. Colburn, London, 1828. 67-100815
1. Byron, George Gordon Noel Byron, 6th baron, 1788-1824. 2. Shelley, Percy Bysshe, 1792-1822. 3. Authors — Correspondence, reminiscences, etc. 4. Italy — Descr. & trav. I. Title.

MACKAY, Charles, 1814-1889. 821'.7 B
Medora Leigh; a history and an autobiography. Edited by Charles Mackay. With an introd., and a commentary on the charges brought against Lord Byron by Mrs. Beecher Stowe. London, R. Bentley, 1869. [New York, AMS Press, 1973] 280 p. 19 cm. On spine: WOL. [PR4382.M3 1973] 78-37700 ISBN 0-404-56759-2 14.00
1. Byron, George Gordon Noel Byron, Baron, 1788-1824. 2. Stowe, Harriet Elizabeth (Beecher) 1811-1896. 3. Byron, Anne Isabella (Milbanke) Byron, Baroness, 1792-1860. 4. Leigh, Elizabeth Medora, 1814-1849. I. Leigh, Elizabeth Medora, 1814-1849. II. Title. **BIP**

MARCHAND, Leslie Alexis, 1900- 821'.7 B
Byron: a portrait [by] Leslie A. Marchand. [1st ed.] New York, Knopf, 1970. xvii, 518, xxxiv p. illus., coat of arms, facsims., geneal. tables, maps, ports. 25 cm. Bibliography: p. [514]-518. [PR4381.M3317] 76-111252 13.95
1. Byron, George Gordon Noel Byron, Baron, 1788-1824.

MAUROIS, Andre, 1885- 928.2
Byron [Tr. from French by Hamish Miles] New York, Ungar [1964, c.1930] xv, 596p. facsims., plates, ports. 24cm. Bibl. 64-15691 6.50; 2.75 pap.,
1. Byron, George Gordon Noel Byron, baron, 1788-1824. I. Title.

MAYNE, Ethel Colburn, d.1941. 821'.7 B
Byron. New York, Barnes & Noble [1969] xvi, 474 p. illus., port. 23 cm. Reprint of the 2d ed., rev., 1924. [PR4381.M4 1969] 78-9385
1. Byron, George Gordon Noel Byron, baron, 1788-1824. **BIP**

MAYNE, Ethel Colburn, d.1941. 821'.7 B
Byron. New ed. Freeport, N.Y., Books for Libraries Press [1970] xiv, 474 p. port. 23 cm. Reprint of the 1924 ed. Includes bibliographical references. [PR4381.M4 1970] 76-117883
1. Byron, George Gordon Noel Byron, Baron, 1788-1824.

MAYNE, Ethel Colburn, d.1941. 821'.7 B
Byron. New York, Scribner, 1924. St. Clair Shores, Mich., Scholarly Press, 1972. xvi, 474 p. illus. 22 cm. Includes bibliographical references. [PR4381.M4 1972] 74-145170 ISBN 0-403-01097-7
1. Byron, George Gordon Noel Byron, Baron, 1788-1824.

MEDWIN, Thomas, 1788-1869. 821.7
Conversations of Lord Byron. Rev. with a new pref. by the author for a new ed., and annotated by Lady Byron ... and others who knew the poet personally. Edited by Ernest J. Lovell, Jr. Princeton, N.J., Princeton University Press, 1966. xx, 287 p. 25 cm. "This edition is based on Medwin's copy ... of his 'new edition' of 1824 (the third London edition), heavily annotated by the author, with a new preface, and intended for another new and last edition, which was never published." Bibliography: p. 277-278. [PR4382.M4 1966] 65-17145
1. Byron, George Gordon Noel Byron, baron, 1788-1824. I. Lovell, Ernest James, 1918- ed. II. Title.

MOORE, Doris Elizabeth (Langley-Levy) 1903- 928.2
The Late Lord Byron; posthumous dramas. Philadelphia, Lippincott [c.1961] viii, 542p. plates, ports. Bibl. 61-8670 8.50
1. Byron, George Gordon Noel Byron, 6th baron, 1788-1824. I. Title.

MOORE, Doris (Langley-Levy) 1903- 928.2
The late Lord Byron; posthumous dramas. [1st ed.] Philadelphia, Lippincott [1961] viii, 542p. plates, ports, 24cm. [PR4381.M67 1961a] 61-8670
1. Byron, George Gordon Noel Byron, 6th baron, 1788-1824. I. Title.

MURRAY, John G. 821'.7 B
A poet and his publisher / John Murray. London : English Association, 1976. 16 p. ; 22 cm. (Presidential address ; 1976) Cover title. [PR4383.M87] 77-356343
1. Byron, George Gordon Noel Byron, 1788-1824—Addresses, essays, lectures. 2. Murray, John, 1778-1843. 3. Authors and publishers—England. 4. Poets, English—19th century—Biography. I. Title. II. Series: English Association. Presidential address ; 1976.

NICHOL, John, 1833-1894. 821.7 B
Byron. New York, AMS Press [1968] viii, 216 p. geneal. table. 22 cm. (English men of letters) Reprint of the 1888 ed. [PR4381.N4 1968] 68-58390
1. Byron, George Gordon Noel Byron, Baron, 1788-1824. 2. Byron family.

NICOLSON, Harold George, Sir, 1886-1968. 821'.7
Byron, the last journey, April 1823-April 1824. [Hamden, Conn.] Archon Books, 1969. xiii, 288 p. 22 cm. "Reprinted ... from the second edition of 1948 ... without abridgement or alteration." Bibliography: p. 283-286. [PR4382.N5 1969] 69-19229
1. Byron, George Gordon Noel Byron, Baron, 1788-1824.

NOEL, Roden Berkeley Wriothesley, 1834-1894. 821'.7 B
Life of Lord Byron. [Folcroft, Pa.] Folcroft Library Editions, 1973. p. Reprint of the 1890 ed. published by Walter Scott, London, issued in series: Great writers. Bibliography: p. [PR4381.N7 1973b] 73-12358 9.95
1. Byron, George Gordon Noel Byron, Baron, 1788-1824. I. Title. **BIP**

PARKER, Derek. 821'.7
Byron and his world. New York, Viking Press [1969, c1968] 143 p. illus., ports. 24 cm. (A Studio book) Bibliography: p. 141. [PR4381.P3 1969] 69-10355 6.95
1. Byron, George Gordon Noel Byron, Baron, 1788-1824. I. Title.

PRATT, Willis Winslow, 821'.7
1908-
Byron at Southwell: the making of a poet; with new poems and letters from the rare books collections of the University of Texas, by Willis W. Pratt. New York, Haskell House Publishers, 1973 [c1948] 145 p. illus. 23 cm. Original ed. issued as no. 1 of University of Texas Byron monographs. Includes bibliographical references. [PR4381.P7 1973] 72-6745 ISBN 0-8383-1646-8 8.95
1. Byron, George Gordon Noel Byron, Baron, 1788-1824. I. Title. II. Series: Texas. University. University of Texas Byron monographs, no. 1.

QUENNELL, Peter, 1905- 821'.7 B
Byron. New York, Haskell House Publishers, 1974. 143 p. 20 cm. Reprint of the 1934 ed. published by Duckworth, London, which was issued as no. 28 of Great lives. Includes bibliographical references. [PR4381.Q4 1974] 73-21772 ISBN 0-8383-1784-7 10.95
1. Byron, George Gordon Noel Byron, Baron, 1788-1824.

QUENNELL, Peter, 1905- 828'.7'09
Byron: the years of fame. [Rev. ed.] Hamden, Conn., Archon Books, 1967. 255 p. port. 22 cm. [PR4382.Q4 1967a] 67-3375
1. Byron, George Gordon Noel Byron, Baron, 1788-1824. I. Title.

RAYMOND, Dora (Neill) 821'.7 B
1889-1961.
The political career of Lord Byron. New York, Russell & Russell [1972, c1924] 363 p. 23 cm. Bibliography: p. 345-347. [PR4381.R3 1972] 72-180615
1. Byron, George Gordon Noel Byron, Baron, 1788-1824. I. Title. **BIP**

TRELAWNY, Edward John, 928.2
1792-1881
The last days of Shelley and Byron; being the complete text of Trelawny's 'Recollections' edited, with additions from contemporary sources, by J. E. Morpurgo. New York, Doubleday, 1960. xxvi, 246p. Bibl. notes. 18cm. (Anchor A225) .95 pap.,
1. Byron, George Gordon Noel Byron, 6th baron, 1788-1824. 2. Shelley, Percy Bysshe, 1792-1822. 3. Greece, Modern—Hist.—War of Independence, 1821-1829. I. Title.

TRELAWNY, Edward John, 709'.24
1792-1881.
The last days of Shelley and Byron; being the complete text of Trelawny's 'Recollections' edited, with additions from contemporary sources, by J. E. Morpurgo. New York, Philosophical Library, 1952. xvii, 208p. plates. 23cm. [PR5671.T] A53
1. Byron, George Gordon Noel Byron, 6th baron, 1788-1824. 2. Shelley, Percy Bysshe, 1792-1822. 3. Greece, Modern—Hist.—War of Independence, 1821-1829. I. Title.

TRUEBLOOD, Paul Graham. 821'.7
Lord Byron / Paul G. Trueblood. 2d ed. Boston : Twayne Publishers, c1977. p. cm. (Twayne's English authors series ; TEAS 77) Includes index. Bibliography: p. [PR4381.T7 1977] 77-10564 ISBN 0-8057-6694-4 lib.bdg. : 7.95
1. Byron, George Gordon Noel Byron, Baron, 1788-1824. 2. Poets, English—19th century—Biography. I. Title. **BIP**

WATKINS, John, fl.1792- 821'.7 B
1831.
Memoirs of the life and writings of the Right Honourable Lord Byron : with anecdotes of some of his contemporaries. Folcroft, Pa. : Folcroft Library Editions, 1975. xvi, 428 p. ; 24 cm. Reprint of the 1822 ed. published for H. Colburn, London. [PR4381.W36 1975] 75-30617 ISBN 0-8414-9443-6 lib. bdg. : 65.00
1. Byron, George Gordon Noel, Baron Byron, 1788-1824. I. Title.

Byron, George Gordon Noel Byron, Baron, 1788-1824—Biography.

BARBARY, James 92
The young Lord Byron. Illus. by Denise Brown. New York, Roy [1966, c.1965] 142p. illus. 21cm. [PR4381.B25] 66-14500 3.25 bds.,
1. Byron, George Gordon Noel Byron, baron, 1788-1824—Juvenile literature. I. Title.

BARBER, Thomas Gerrard, 821'.7 B
1875-1952.
Byron—and where he is buried. [Folcroft, Pa.] Folcroft Library Editions, 1974. p. Reprint of the 1939 ed. published by H. Morley, Hucknall. [PR4381.B3 1974] 74-8562 20.00 (lib. bdg.).
1. Byron, George Gordon Noel Byron, Baron, 1788-1824—Biography. I. Title. **BIP**

BELLAMY, Robert Lowe. 821'.7 B
Byron the man / by R. L. Bellamy. Folcroft, Pa. : Folcroft Library Editions, 1975. p. cm. Reprint of the 1924 ed. published by K. Paul, Trench, Trubner, London. [PR4381.B4 1975] 75-29104 ISBN 0-8414-3326-7 lib. bdg. : 40.00
1. Byron, George Gordon Noel Byron Baron, 1788-1824 Biography. I. Title. **BIP**

BYRON, George Gordon 821'.7 B
Noel Byron, Baron, 1788-1824.
The Ravenna journal : mainly compiled at Ravenna in 1821 and now for the first time issued in book form / by George Gordon Byron, 6th Lord Byron ; with an introd. by Lord Ernle. Norwood, Pa. : Norwood Editions, 1975. 100 p. ; 23 cm. Reprint of the 1928 ed. published by the First Edition Club, London. [PR4381.A38 1975] 75-43998 ISBN 0-88305-716-6 lib. bdg. : 17.50
1. Byron, George Gordon Noel Byron, Baron, 1788-1824—Biography. I. Title.

DREYER, Wolfgang, 1920- 821'.7 B
Byron's daughter; a biography of Elizabeth Medora Leigh. New York, Scribner [1972] xvi, 320 p. illus. 24 cm. Bibliography: p. 313-314. [PR4382.T85] 79-37206 ISBN 0-684-12753-9 8.95
1. Byron, George Gordon Noel Byron, Baron, 1788-1824—Biography. 2. Leigh, Elizabeth Medora, 1814-1849. I. Title.

GALT, John, 1779-1839. 821'.7 B
The life of Lord Byron / by John Galt. Folcroft, Pa. : Folcroft Library Editions, 1975. Reprint of the 1830 ed. published by H. Colburn and R. Bentley, London. [PR4381.G26 1975] 75-29079 ISBN 0-8414-4540-0 lib. bdg. : 50.00
1. Byron, George Gordon Noel Byron, baron, 1788-1824—Biography. I. Title.

GALT, John, 1779-1839. 821'.7 B
The life of Lord Byron / by John Galt. Folcroft, Pa. : Folcroft Library Editions, 1975. Reprint of the 1830 ed. published by H. Colburn and R. Bentley, London. [PR4381.G26 1975] 75-29079 ISBN 0-8414-4540-0 lib. bdg. : 50.00
1. Byron, George Gordon Noel Byron, baron, 1788-1824—Biography. I. Title. **BIP**

GLECKNER, Robert F. 821'.7
Byron and the ruins of paradise, by Robert F. Gleckner. Baltimore, Johns Hopkins Press [1967] xxiv, 365 p. illus., port. 24 cm. Bibliographical footnotes. [PR4388.G57] 67-25071
1. Byron, George Gordon Noel Byron, 1788-1824 Criticism and interpretation. I. Title. **BIP**

JEAFFRESON, John Cordy, 821'.7 B
1831-1901.
The real Lord Byron : the story of the poet's life / by John Cordy Jeaffreson. Standard ed. Folcroft, Pa. : Folcroft Library Editions, 1975. p. cm. Reprint of the 1884 ed. published by Hurst and Blackett, London. [PR4381.J4 1975] 75-29200 ISBN 0-8414-5332-2 lib. bdg. : 75.00
1. Byron, George Gordon Noel Byron, Baron, 1788-1824—Biography. I. Title.

LONGFORD, Elizabeth 821'.7 B
Harman Pakenham, Countess of, 1906-
The life of Byron / by Elizabeth Longford. 1st ed. Boston : Little, Brown, c1976. p. cm. (The Library of world biography) Includes index. Bibliography: p. [PR4381.L6] 76-22714 ISBN 0-316-53192-8 : 8.95
1. Byron, George Gordon Noel, Baron, 1788-1824—Biography. I. Title.

MARCHAND, Leslie Alexis, 928.2
1900-
Byron; a biography. [1st ed.] New York, Knopf, 1957. 3 v. illus., ports., fold. map. 24 cm. Issued in a case. Includes bibliographical references. [PR4381.M33] 57-7547
1. Byron, George Gordon Noel Byron, Baron, 1788-1824—Biography.

MARCHAND, Leslie Alexis, 821'.7 B
1900-
Byron, a portrait / Leslie A. Marchand. Chicago : University of Chicago Press, 1979, c1970. p. cm. Reprint of the ed. published by Knopf, New York. Includes index. Bibliography: p. [PR4381.M3317 1979] 79-13248 ISBN 0-226-50436-0 pbk. : 7.95
1. Byron, George Gordon Noel Byron, Baron, 1788-1824—Biography. 2. Poets, English—19th century—Biography. I. Title.

MOORE, Doris Langley- 821'.7 B
Levy, 1903-
The late Lord Byron : posthumous dramas / by Doris Langley Moore. New York : Harper & Row, 1977, c1961. viii, 542 p. ; 24 cm. Includes index. Bibliography: p. [525]-533. [PR4381.M67 1977] 76-22934 ISBN 0-06-013013-X : 25.00
1. Byron, George Gordon Noel Byron, Baron, 1788-1824—Biography. 2. Poets, English—19th century—Biography. I. Title.

MOORE, Doris Langley- 821'.7 B
Levy, 1903-
Lord Byron; accounts rendered [by] Doris Langley Moore. [1st U.S. ed.] New York, Harper & Row [1974] x, 511 p. illus. 24 cm. Bibliography: p. [499]-501. [PR4381.M69 1974b] 73-18668 ISBN 0-06-013009-1 17.50
1. Byron, George Gordon Noel Byron, Baron, 1788-1824—Biography. I. Title.

NOEL, Roden Berkeley 821'.7 B
Wriothesley, Hon., 1834-1894.
Life of Lord Byron. Port Washington, N.Y., Kennikat Press [1972] 215, xxxviii p. 21 cm. Reprint of the 1890 ed. issued in the series: Great writers. "Bibliography, by John P. Anderson": p. [i]-xxxviii. [PR4381.N7 1972] 73-160773 ISBN 0-8046-1605-1
1. Byron, George Gordon Noel Byron, Baron, 1788-1824—Biography. I. Anderson, John Parker, 1841- II. Title.

QUENNELL, Peter, 1905- 821'.7 B
Byron. [Folcroft, Pa.] Folcroft Library Editions, 1974. p. cm. Reprint of the 1934 ed. published by Duckworth, London, which was issued as no. [28] of Great lives. Bibliography: p. [PR4381.Q4 1974b] 74-8358 ISBN 0-8414-6904-0 (lib. bdg.)
1. Byron, George Gordon Noel Byron, baron, 1788-1824—Biography. **BIP**

Byron, George Gordon Noel Byron, Baron, 1788-1824—Biography—Last years and death.

EDGCUMBE, Richard, 1843- 821'.7 B
1937.
Byron; the last phase. New York, Haskell House Publishers, 1972. vi, 423 p. 23 cm. Reprint of the 1910 ed. [PR4382.E3 1972] 72-1332 ISBN 0-8383-1441-4
1. Byron, George Gordon Noel Byron, Baron, 1788-1824—Biography—Last years and death. I. Title. **BIP**

GAMBA, Pietro, conte, 821'.7 B
1801-1826.
A narrative of Lord Byron's last journey to Greece : extracted from the journal of Count Peter Gamba, who attended his lordship on that expedition. Folcroft, Pa. : Folcroft Library Editions, 1975. p. cm. Reprint of the 1825 ed. published by A. and W. Galignani, Paris. [PR4382.G3 1975] 75-30618 ISBN 0-8414-4441-2 lib. bdg. : 45.00
1. Byron, George Gordon Noel Byron, Baron, 1788-1824—Biography—Last years and death. 2. Byron, George Gordon Noel Byron, Baron, 1788-1824—Journeys—Greece. 3. Gamba, Pietro, conte, 1801-1826. 4. Greece, Modern—History—War of Independence, 1821-1829—Personal narratives. I. Title.

NICOLSON, Harold George, 821'.7 B
Sir, 1886-1968.
Byron, the last journey, April 1823-April 1824. Boston, Houghton Mifflin, 1924. St. Clair Shores, Mich., Scholarly Press, 1972. xiii, 288 p. 21 cm. Bibliography: p. 283-286. [PR4382.N5 1972] 79-145210 ISBN 0-403-00805-0
1. Byron, George Gordon Noel, Baron, 1788-1824—Biography—Last years and death.

Byron, George Gordon Noel Byron, Baron, 1788-1824—Biography—Marriage.

STOWE, Harriet Elizabeth 821'.7 B
Beecher, 1811-1896.
Lady Byron vindicated : a history of the Byron controversy, from its beginning in 1816 to the present time / by Harriet Beecher Stowe. Folcroft, Pa. : Folcroft Library Editions, 1975. p. cm. Reprint of the 1870 ed. published by S. Low, Son, and Marston, London. Includes bibliographical references. [PR4382.S7 1975] 75-29038 ISBN 0-8414-7746-9 lib. bdg. : 50.00
1. Byron, George Gordon Noel Byron, Baron, 1788-1824—Biography—Marriage. 2. Byron, Anne Isabella Milbanke Byron, Baroness, 1792-1860. I. Title.

Byron, George Gordon Noel Byron, Baron, 1788-1824—Correspondence.

BYRON, George Gordon 821'.7 B
Noel Byron, Baron, 1788-1824.
"Famous in my time": 1810-1812. Edited by Leslie A. Marchand. Cambridge, Mass., Belknap Press of Harvard University Press, 1973. viii, 298 p. port 23 cm. (His Letters and journals, v. 2) [PR4381.A3M35 1973 vol. 2] 74-160825 ISBN 0-674-08941-3 11.50
1. Byron, George Gordon Noel Byron, Baron, 1788-1824—Correspondence. I. Marchand, Leslie Alexis, 1900- ed. II. Title. III. Series.

BYRON, George Gordon 821'.7 S
Noel Byron, Baron, 1788-1824.
The flesh is frail / edited by Leslie A. Marchand. London : J. Murray, c1976. xiii, 289 p., [1] leaf of plates : port. ; 23 cm. (His Letters and journals ; v. 6) Includes index. Bibliography: p. 274. [PR4381.A3M35 1973b vol. 6] 821'.7 B 77-352132 ISBN 0-7195-3276-0 : £5.95
1. Byron, George Gordon Noel Byron, Baron, 1788-1824—Correspondence. 2. Poets, English—19th century—Correspondence. I. Title. II. Series.

BYRON, George Gordon 821'.7 B
Noel Byron, Bron, 1788-1824.
"In my hot youth": 1798-1810. Edited by Leslie A. Marchand. Cambridge, Mass., Belknap Press of Harvard University Press, 1973. v, 288 p. port. 23 cm. (His Letters and journals, v. 1) Bibliography: p. 271. [PR4381.A3M35 1973 vol. 1] 74-159795 ISBN 0-674-08940-5 11.50
1. Byron, George Gordon Noel Byron, Baron, 1788-1824—Correspondence. I. Marchand, Leslie Alexis, 1900- ed. II. Title. III. Series.

BYRON, George Gordon 821'.7 B
Noel Byron, Baron, 1788-1824.
Letters and journals. Edited by Leslie A. Marchand. Cambridge, Mass., Belknap Press of Harvard University Press, 1973- v. ports. 23 cm. Includes bibliographical references. [PR4381.A3M35 1973] 73-81853 ISBN 0-674-08940-5 (v. 1) 11.50 (v. 1)
1. Byron, George Gordon Noel Byron, Baron, 1788-1824—Correspondence. 2. Byron, George Gordon Noel, Baron, 1788-1824. I. Marchand, Leslie Alexis, 1900- ed.

BYRON, George Gordon 821'.7 B
Noel Byron, Baron, 1788-1824.
The life, letters, and journals of Lord Byron, by Thomas Moore. Collected and arranged with notes by Sir Walter Scott [and others] New and complete ed. London, J. Murray, 1920. St. Clair Shores, Mich., Scholarly Press, 1972. xix, 735 p.

front. 21 cm. [PR4381.A3M6 1972] 72-107163
1. Byron, George Gordon Noel Byron, Baron, 1788-1824—Correspondence. 2. Byron, George Gordon Noel Byron, Baron, 1788-1824. I. Moore, Thomas, 1779-1852, ed. II. Title. **BIP**

BYRON, George Gordon Noel 821'.7
Byron, Baron, 1788-1824.
Seventeen letters of George Noel Gordon, Lord Byron, to an unknown lady, 1811-1817 / edited, with an introd. and notes, by Walter Edwin Peck. Folcroft, Pa. : Folcroft Library Editions, 1976. p. cm. Reprint of the 1930 ed. published by Covici, Friede, New York. [PR4381.A49 1976] 76-41751 ISBN 0-8414-6765-X lib. bdg. : 12.50
1. Byron, George Gordon Noel Byron, Baron, 1788-1824—Correspondence. 2. Poets, English—19th century—Correspondence. I. Title. **BIP**

BYRON, George Gordon Noel 821'.7
Byron, Baron, 1788-1824.
"Wedlock's the devil" : 1814-1815 / edited by Leslie A. Marchand. Cambridge, Mass. : Belknap Press of Harvard University Press, 1975. 369 p. : port. ; 22 cm. (His Letters and journals ; v. 4) Includes index. [PR4381.A3M35 1973 vol. 4] 75-328032 ISBN 0-674-08944-8 : 13.50
1. Byron, George Gordon Noel Byron, Baron, 1788-1824—Correspondence. 2. Authors, English—19th century—Correspondence, reminiscences, etc. I. Title. II. Series.

Byron, George Gordon Noel Byron, Baron, 1788-1824—Friends and associates.

POLIDORI, John William, 828'.7'03
1795-1821.
The diary of Dr. John William Polidori, 1816, relating to Byron, Shelley, etc. / edited and elucidated by William Michael Rossetti. Folcroft, Pa. : Folcroft Library Editions, 1975. p. cm. Reprint of the 1911 ed. published by E. Mathews, London. [PR5187.P5A8 1975] 75-29345 ISBN 0-8414-7320-X lib. bdg. : 30.00
1. Polidori, John William, 1795-1821—Diaries. 2. Byron, George Gordon Noel Byron, Baron, 1788-1824—Friends and associates. 3. Shelley, Percy Bysshe, 1792-1822—Friends and associates. 4. Authors, English—19th century—Correspondence, reminiscences, etc. I. Rossetti, William Michael, 1829-1919. II. Title.

Byron, George Gordon Noel Byron, Baron, 1788-1824—Friends and associates—Addresses, essays, lectures.

JAMES, David Gwilym, 1905- 821'.7
1968.
Byron and Shelley / D. G. James. Folcroft, Pa. : Folcroft Library Editions, 1974. p. cm. Reprint of the 1951 ed. published by the University of Nottingham, Nottingham, which was issued as the 1951 Byron Foundation lecture. [PR4383.J3 1974] 74-30074 ISBN 0-8414-5347-0 : 4.50
1. Byron, George Gordon Noel Byron, Baron, 1788-1824—Friends and associates—Addresses, essays, lectures. 2. Shelley, Percy Bysshe, 1792-1822—Friends and Associates—Addresses, essays, lectures. I. Title. II. Series: Byron Foundation lecture ; 1951. **BIP**

Byron, George Gordon Noel Byron, Baron, 1788-1824—Journeys—Greece.

GAMBA, Pietro, conte, 821'.7 B
1801-1826.
A narrative of Lord Byron's last journey to Greece : extracted from the journal of Count Peter Gamba, who attended his lordship on that expedition. Folcroft, Pa. : Folcroft Library Editions, 1975. p. cm. Reprint of the 1825 ed. published by A. and W. Galignani, Paris. [PR4382.G3 1975] 75-30618 ISBN 0-8414-4441-2 lib. bdg. : 45.00
1. Byron, George Gordon Noel Byron, Baron, 1788-1824—Biography—Last years and death. 2. Byron, George Gordon Noel Byron, Baron, 1788-1824—Journeys—Greece. 3. Gamba, Pietro, conte, 1801-1826. 4. Greece, Modern—History—War of Independence, 1821-1829—Personal narratives. I. Title.

Byron, George Gordon Noel Byron, Baron, 1788-1824—Relationship with women.

CHAPMAN, John Stewart. 821'.7
Byron and the Honourable Augusta Leigh / John S. Chapman. New Haven : Yale University Press, 1975. xxiv, 282 p., [2] leaves of plates : ports. ; 22 cm. Includes index. Bibliography: p. 269-273. [PR4382.C45] 74-29714 ISBN 0-300-01876-2 : 10.00
1. Byron, George Gordon Noel Byron, Baron, 1788-1824—Relationship with women. 2. Leigh, Augusta, 1784-1851. 3. England—Social life and customs. I. Title. **BIP**

GREBANIER, Bernard D. N., 821'.7
1903-
The uninhibited Byron; an account of his sexual confusion [by] Bernard Grebanier. New York, Crown [1970] 354 p. illus., ports. 24 cm. Bibliography: p. 304-306. [PR4382.G68] 70-127498 7.50
1. Byron, George Gordon Noel Byron, Baron, 1788-1824—Relationship with women. I. Title.

STRICKLAND, Margot. 821'.7 B
The Byron women / Margot Strickland. New York : St. Martin's Press, 1975, c1974. 224 p., [4] leaves of plates : ill. ; 23 cm. Includes index. Bibliography: p. 217-220. [PR4382.S85 1975] 74-33912 10.00
1. Byron, George Gordon Noel Byron, Baron, 1788-1824—Relationship with women. I. Title.

SYMONDS, Emily Morse, 821'.7
d.1936.
"To Lord Byron" : feminine profiles based upon unpublished letters, 1807-1824 / by George Paston [i.e. E. M. Symonds] and Peter Quennell. Folcroft, Pa. : Folcroft Library Editions, 1975. p. cm. Reprint of the 1939 ed. published by J. Murray, London. [PR4382.S9 1975] 75-29105 ISBN 0-8414-6745-5 lib. bdg. : 50.00
1. Byron, George Gordon Noel Byron, Baron, 1788-1824—Relationship with women. I. Quennell, Peter, 1905- II. Title.

Byron, John, 1723-1786.

SHANKLAND, Peter. 910'.09'1641
Byron of the Wager / Peter Shankland. 1st American ed. New York : Coward, McCann & Geoghegan, 1975. 288 p. : ill. ; 22 cm. Includes index. Bibliography: p. 281-282. [F3146.S48 1975b] 74-25237 ISBN 0-698-10669-5 : 8.95
1. Byron, John, 1723-1786. 2. Wager (Ship) 3. Shipwrecks—Chile. I. Title.

Byzantine Empire—Queens.

DIEHL, Charles 1859-1944 923.1495
Byzantine empresses. Tr. from French by Harold Bell, Theresa de Kerpely. New York, Knopf, 1963 [c.1927, 1963] 308p. 22cm. 62-15576 5.95
1. Byzantine Empire—Queens. I. Title.

C

PEARE, Catherine Owens. 928.1
Mark Twain, his life; illustrated by Margaret Ayer. [1st ed.] New York, Holt [1954] 116 p. illus. 21 cm. [PS1331.P45] 54-10389
1. C 2. Clemens, Samuel Langhorne, 1835-1910.

Camara, Helder, 1908—

BROUCKER, Jose de. 282'.0924 B
Dom Helder Camara; the violence of a peacemaker. Translated from the French by Herma Briffault. Maryknoll, N.Y., Orbis Books [1970] xiii, 154 p. illus., ports. 24 cm. Includes bibliographical references. [BX4705.C2625B7613] 78-135536 4.95
1. Camara, Helder, 1908- **BIP**

Cao, Diogo, 15th cent.

AXELSON, Eric Victor. 916.7
Congo to Cape; early Portuguese explorers, by Eric Axelson. Edited by George Woodcock. New York, Barnes & Noble [1973] 224 p. illus. 21 cm. Bibliography: p. 207-211. [DT731.A76] 74-157787 ISBN 0-06-490252-8 11.00
1. Cao, Diogo, 15th cent. 2. Dias, Bartolomeu. 3. Africa, Southern—Discovery and exploration. 4. Discoveries in geography—Portuguese. I. Title.

Cardenas, Lazaro, Pres. Mexico, 1895—

TOWNSEND, William 923.172
Cameron, 1896-
Lazaro Cardenas, Mexican democrat, with a foreword by Frank Tannenbaum. Ann Arbor, G. Wahr Pub. Co., 1952. 379 p. illus. 22 cm. [F1234.C2385] 52-7122
1. Cardenas, Lazaro, Pres. Mexico, 1895-

Cesaire, Aime.

FRUTKIN, Susan. 841 B
Aime Cesaire; Black between worlds. [Coral Gables, Fla.] Center for Advanced International Studies, University of Miami, 1973. xi, 66 p. 23 cm. (Monographs in international affairs) "Outgrowth of a master's thesis ... University of Miami in 1968." Bibliography: p. 61-64. [PQ3949.C44Z67 1973] 73-85305 3.95
1. Cesaire, Aime. I. Title. II. Series.

Cabell, James Branch, 1879-1958—Bibl.

BREWER, Frances Joan. v. 12
James Branch Cabell. With a foreword by James Branch Cabell. Charlottesville, University of Virginia Press, 1957. 2v. 24cm. Contents.v. 1. A bibliography of his writings, biography and criticism, by Frances Joan Brewer.--v. 2. Notes on the Cabell collections at the University of Virginia, by Matthew J. Bruccoll. A58
1. Cabell, James Branch, 1879-1958—Bibl. I. Bruccoll, Matthew J. II. Title.

Cabell, James Branch, 1879-1958—Correspondence.

CABELL, James Branch, 813'.5'2 B
1879-1958.
The letters of James Branch Cabell. Edited by Edward Wagenknecht. [1st ed.] Norman, University of Oklahoma Press [1975] xvii, 277 p. illus. 24 cm. [PS3505.A153Z53 1975] 74-5963
1. Cabell, James Branch, 1879-1958—Correspondence. 2. Authors, American—Correspondence, reminiscences, etc. **BIP**

Cabell, William Lewis, 1827-1911.

HARVEY, Paul, 973.7'42'0924 B
1944-
Old Tige: General William L. Cabell, CSA. [Hillsboro, Tex., Hill Junior College Press] 1970. ix, 89 p. illus. 24 cm. (Hill Junior College monographs in Texas and Confederate history, no. 4) Bibliography: p. 82-86. [E467.1.C25H3] 79-140100
1. Cabell, William Lewis, 1827-1911. I. Title. II. Series: Hill Junior College, Hillsboro, Tex. Monographs in Texas and Confederate history, no. 4.

Cabet, Etienne, 1788-1856.

PRUDHOMMEAUX, Jules 335'.9'773'43
Jean, 1869-
Icarie et son fondateur, Etienne Cabet; contribution a l'etude du socialisme experimental. Philadelphia, Porcupine Press, 1972. xl, 688 p. illus. 22 cm. (The American utopian adventure) Reprint of the 1907 ed. Bibliography: p. [xiii]-xl. [HX656.I2P8 1972] 72-187458 ISBN 0-87991-005-4
1. Cabet, Etienne, 1788-1856. 2. Icarian Community. I. Title. **BIP**

Cable, George Washington, 1844-1925.

BIKLE, Lucy Lethingwell 818'.4'08
(Cable).
George W. Cable; his life and letters. New York, Russell & Russell [1967] xvi, 306p. illus., facsims., ports. 22cm. Reprint of the 1928 ed. Bibl. [PS1246.B5 1967] 66-27039 8.50
1. Cable, George Washington, I. Title.
Originally published by Scribners.

BUTCHER, Charles Philip. 928.1
George W. Cable: the Northampton years. New York, Columbia University Press, 1959. 286p. illus. 21cm. Includes bibliography. [PS1246.B8] 59-6213
1. Cable, George Washington, 1844-1925. I. Title.

EKSTROM, Kjell. 928.1
George Washington Cable, a study of his early life and work. Upsala, Lundequistska bokhandeln; Cambridge, Harvard University Press [1950] vii, 197 p. 24 cm. (Essays and studies on American language and literature, 10) Inaug.-diss.--Uppsala. Extra t. p. with thesis statement, inserted, has imprint: Lund, C. Bloms, boktr., 1950. Bibliography: p. [185]-193. [PS1246.E4] 51-6309
1. Cable, George Washington, 1844-1925. I. Title. II. Series: Uppsala. Universitet. Amerikanska seminariet. Essays and studies on Americanlanguage and literature, 10

RUBIN, Louis Decimus, 813'.4 B
1923-
George W. Cable: the life and times of a Southern heretic [by] Louis D. Rubin, Jr. New York, Pegasus [1969] viii, 304 p. port. 21 cm. (Pegasus American authors) Bibliography. p. 294-297. [PS1246.R8] 76-77135 6.95
1. Cable, George Washington, 1844-1925.

TURNER, Arlin. v. 12
George W. Cable, a biography. Baton Rouge, Louisiana State University Press, 1966. v, 391 p. 24 cm. 68-27390
1. Cable, George Washington, 1844-1925. I. Title. **BIP**

TURNER, ARLIN 928.1
George W. Cable, a biography. Baton Rouge, La. State Univ. Pr., 1966[c.1956] v. 391p. 23cm. (La. paperbacks, L6) Bibl. [PS1246.T8] 2.95 pap.,
1. Cable, George Washington, 1844-1925. I. Title.

TURNER, Arlin. 928.1
George W. Cable, a biography [Magnolia, Mass., Peter Smith, 1968, c. 1956] 391p. illus. 24cm. (La. State Univ. Pr. bk. rebound) [PS1246.T8] price unreported
1. Cable, George Washington, 1844-1925. I. Title.

Cable, George Washington, 1844-1925—Juvenile literature.

STILLER, Richard. 323.42'3'0922
The white minority : pioneers for racial equality / Richard Stiller. 1st ed. New York : Harcourt Brace Jovanovich, c1977. 120 p. : ill. ; 22 cm. Includes index. Bibliography: p. [114]. Biographical sketches of three early fighters for racial equality. [E185.98.A1S73] 77-76442 ISBN 0-15-295877-0 : 6.95
1. Cable, George Washington, 1844-1925—Juvenile literature. 2. Harlan, John Marshall, 1833-1911—Juvenile literature. 3. Tourgee, Albion Winegar, 1838-1905—Juvenile literature. 4. Social reformers—United States—Biography—Juvenile literature. 5. Reconstruction—Juvenile literature. 6. Afro-Americans—Civil rights—History—Juvenile literature. **BIP**

TURNER, Arlin. 928.1
George W. Cable, a biography. New York, Scribner [1956, c1955] 391 p. illus. 24 cm. [S1246.t8] 56-9165
1. Cable, George Washington, 1844-1925.

TURNER, Arlin. 928.1
George W. Cable, a biography. Durham, N. D., Duke University Press, 1956. 391 p. illus. 24 cm. [PS1246.T8] 56-9165
1. Cable, George Waxhington, 1844-1925. I. Title.

Cabot family.

CABOT, Ellsworth Sebastian, 1921- 929'.2'0973
Mostly about the Cabots [by] Ellsworth S. Cabot. St. Louis, 1966. 184 p. illus., coats of arms, facsims., geneal. tables, ports. 25 cm. Bibliography: p. 131-133. [CS71.C116 1966] 67-917
1. Cabot family. I. Title.

Cabot, George, 1751-1823.

LODGE, Henry Cabot, 1850-1924. 973.4'092'4 B
Life and letters of George Cabot. New York, Da Capo Press, 1974 [c1877] xi, 617 p. 23 cm. Reprint of the 1st ed. published by Little, Brown, Boston. Includes bibliographical references. [E302.6.C11L8 1974] 71-124902 ISBN 0-306-71001-3
1. Cabot, George, 1751-1823. **BIP**

Cabot, Godfrey Lowell, 1861-1962.

HARRIS, Leon A., 1926- 917.3'03'90924 B
Only to God; the extraordinary life of Godfrey Lowell Cabot [by] Leon Harris. [1st ed.] New York, Atheneum, 1967. xiv, 361 p. ports. 25 cm. Bibliography: p. 344-348. [CT275.C13H3] 67-25482
1. Cabot, Godfrey Lowell, 1861-1962. I. Title.

Cabot, John, d. 1490?—Juv. lit.

THE great mistake; v. 12
a story of John Cabot. Illustrations by Carolyn Lee Jagodits. Notre Dame, Ind., Dujarie Press [1961] 94p. illus. 24cm.
1. Cabot, John, d. 1490?—Juv. lit. I. Roberto, Brother, 1927-

Cabot, John, d. 1498?—Juvenile literature.

KURTZ, Henry Ira. 973.1'7'0922 B
John and Sebastian Cabot. Illustrated with authentic prints and maps. New York, F. Watts, 1973. 58 p. illus. 26 cm. (A Visual biography) A biography of the Venetian explorer who laid the first English claim to the North American continent and of his son, Sebastian, who himself made several voyages of discovery. [E129.C1K87] 920 72-12796 ISBN 0-531-00970-X 4.50 (lib. bdg.)
1. Cabot, John, d. 1498?—Juvenile literature. 2. Cabot, Sebastian, 1474 (ca.)-1557—Juvenile literature. I. Title. **BIP**

SYME, Ronald, 1910- 973.1'6'0922 B
John Cabot and his son Sebastian. Illustrated by William Stobbs. New York, Morrow, 1972. 96 p. illus. 22 cm. A biography of the Venetian explorer and his son both of whom made several voyages of discovery for England including the discovery of the North American continent in 1497. [E129.C1S9] 920 70-168477 3.75
1. Cabot, John, d. 1498?—Juvenile literature. 2. Cabot, Sebastian, ca. 1474-1557—Juvenile literature. I. Stobbs, William, illus. II. Title. **BIP**

Cabot, Sebastian, 1474 (ca.)-1557.

BIDDLE, Richard, 1796-1847. 973.1'6'0924
A memoir of Sebastian Cabot. With a review [of] the history of maritime discovery. Freeport, N.Y., Books for Libraries Press [1970] xiv, 327 p. ports. 23 cm. Reprint of the 1915 ed. Includes bibliographical references. [E129.C1B45 1970] 73-107793
1. Cabot, Sebastian, 1474 (ca.)-1557. 2. Cabot, John, d. 1498. 3. America—Discovery and exploration. I. Title.

Cabot, Thomas Dudley, 1897-

CABOT, Thomas Dudley, 1897- 338'.092'4 B
Beggar on horseback : the autobiography of Thomas D. Cabot. Boston : D. R. Godine, 1979. xi, 191 p., [31] leaves of plates : ill. ; 25 cm. [HC102.5.C32A32] 78-70524 ISBN 0-87923-268-4 : 12.50
1. Cabot, Thomas Dudley, 1897- 2. Businessmen—United States—Biography. I. Title. **BIP**

Cabrini, Frances Xavier, Saint, 1850-1917.

DAUGHTERS of St. Paul. 282'.092'4 B
Mother Cabrini / by Daughters of St. Paul. Boston : St. Paul Editions, c1977. p. cm. [BX4700.C13D35 1977] 77-10878 3.25 pbk. : 2.25
1. Cabrini, Frances Xavier, Saint, 1850-1917. 2. Christian saints—United States—Biography. I. Title.

DAUGHTERS of St. Paul. 282'.092'4 B
Mother Cabrini / by Daughters of St. Paul. Boston : St. Paul Editions, c1977. p. cm. [BX4700.C13D35 1977] 77-10878 3.25 pbk. : 2.25
1. Cabrini, Frances Xavier, Saint, 1850-1917. 2. Christian saints—United States—Biography. I. Title.

DI DONATO, Pietro, 1911- 922.273
Immigrant saint; the life of Mother Cabrini. New York, McGraw-Hill [c.1960] 246p. 21cm. 60-15756 4.95 half cloth,
1. Cabrini, Frances Xavier, Saint, 1850-1917. I. Title.

DI DONATO, Pietro, 1911- 922.273
Immigrant saint; the life of Mother Cabrini. [New York, Dell, 1962, c.1960] 224p. 17cm. (Chapel bk., F179) .50 pap.,
1. Cabrini, Frances Xavier, Saint, 1850-1917. I. Title.

GREENE, Genard, Brother, 1921- 922.273
To the ends of the earth; a story of St. Frances Xavier Cabrini. Illus. by Carolyn Lee Jagodits. Notre Dame, Ind., Dujarie Press [1955] 96p. illus. 24cm. [BX4700.C13G7] 55-33454
1. Cabrini, Frances Xavier, Saint, 1850-1917. I. Title.

JOAN MARY, Sister. 922.273
Mother Cabrini, by a Daughter of St. Paul. [Derby, N. Y.] Daughters of St. Paul, Apostolate of the Press [1955] 219p. illus. 19cm. [BX4700.C13J6] 59-23944
1. Cabrini, Frances Xavier, Saint, 1850-1917. I. Title.

Cabrini, Frances Xavier, Saint, 1850-1917—Juvenile literature.

KEYES, Frances Parkinson (Wheeler) 1885- 922.273
Mother Cabrini, missionary to the world. Illustrated by Frank Nicholas. New York, Vision Books [1959] 190p. illus. 22cm. (Vision books, 43) [BX4700.C13K4] 59 7840
1. Cabrini, Frances Xavier, Saint, 1850-1917—Juvenile literature. I. Title.

Cacchione, Peter V.

GERSON, Simon W. 335.43'092'4 B
Pete : the story of Peter V. Cacchione, New York's first Communist councilman / by Simon W. Gerson. 1st ed. New York : International Publishers, 1976. 215 p. ; 21 cm. (New World paperbacks ; 0473) Includes index. [HX84.C3G47] 76-29039 ISBN 0-7178-0482-8 : 10.00. ISBN 0-7178-0473-9 pbk. : 3.50
1. Cacchione, Peter V. 2. Communists—New York (City)—Biography. 3. New York (City)—Politics and government—1898-1951. **BIP**

Cacopardo, J. Jerry

CACOPARDO, J. Jerry 922.573
Show me a miracle; the true story of a man who went from prison to pulpit [by] J. J. Cacopardo. Don Weldon. New York, Dutton [c.]1961. 220p. 61-6017 3.95 bds.,
I. Weldon, Don, joint author. II. Title.

Cadell, Francis Campbell Bolleau, 1883-1937.

HONEYMAN, Tom John, 1891- 927.5
Three Scottish colourists: S. J. Peploe, F. C. B. Cadell, Leslie Hunter. London, New York, Nelson [1950] xi, 132 p. plates (part col.) ports. 24 cm. "As I remember them, by Ion R. Harrison": p. [117]-126. [ND496.H6 1950] 52-30535
1. Peploe. Samuel John, 1871-1935. 2. Cadell, Francis Campbell Bolleau, 1883-1937. 3. Hunter, Leslie, 1879-1931. I. Title.

Cadogan, Edward Cecil George,

CADOGAN, Edward Cecil George, Sir 1880- 923.242
Before the deluge, memories and rel0)flections, 1880-1914. [Dist. Hollywood-by-the--Sea, Fla., Transatlantic, 1962, c.1961] 232p. illus. 62-1798 6.25
I. Title.

Caesar, C. Julius.

BALSDON, John Percy Vyvian Dacre, 1901- 937'.05'0924
Julius Caesar; a political biography [by] J. P. V. D. Balsdom. [1st American ed.] New York, Atheneum, 1967. 184 p. maps. 22 cm. [DG261.B34] 67-16062
1. Caesar, C. Julius. I. Title.

CONWAY, Robert Seymour, 1864-1933. 913.3'7'0350922
Makers of Europe. Freeport, N.Y., Books for Libraries Press [1967] 89 p. 24 cm. (The James Henry Morgan lectures in Dickinson College, 1930) Essay index reprint series. Reprint of the 1931 ed. Bibliographical footnotes. [DB203.C6] 67-28748
1. Caesar, C Julius. 2. Cicero, Marcus Tullius. 3. Horatius Fiaccus, Quintus. 4. Vergilius Maro. Publius. I. Title. II. Series.

CONWAY, Robert Seymour, 1864-1933. 913.3'7'0350922
Makers of Europe. Freeport, N.Y., Books for Libraries Press [1967] 89 p. 24 cm. (Essay index reprint series.) (The James Henry Morgan lectures in Dickinson College 1930) Reprint of the 1931 ed. Bibliographical footnotes. [DG203.C6 1967] 67-28748
1. Caesar, C. Julius. 2. Cicero, Marcus Tullius. 3. Horatius Fiaccus, Quintus. 4. Vergilius Maro, Publius. I. Title. II. Series.

DODGE, Theodore Ayrault, 1842-1909. 355.3'32'0922
Great captains; showing the influence on the art of war of the campaigns of Alexander, Hannibal, Caesar, Gustavus Adolphus, Frederick, and Napoleon. Port Washington, N.Y., Kennikat Press [1968, c1889] xiii, 219 p. illus., maps. 21 cm. [U51.D6 1968] 67-27591
1. Alexander the Great—Campaigns. 2. Hannibal. 3. Caesar, C. Julius. 4. Gustaf II Adolf, King of Sweden, 1594-1632. 5. Friedrich II, der Grosse, King of Prussia, 1712-1821. 6. Napoleon I, Emperor of the French, 1769-1821. 7. Military biography. I. Title.

DUPUY, Trevor Nevitt, 1916- 355.3'31'0924
The military life of Julius Caesar, imperator. New York, F. Watts [1969] xvi, 195 p. illus., maps. 23 cm. A biography of the Roman emperor Julius Caesar, stressing the military career which he did not begin in earnest until he was forty years old. [DG262.D85] 92 78-75258 3.95
1. Caesar, C. Julius. I. Title.

FERRERO, Guglielmo 923.137
The life of Caesar. Tr. by A. E. Zimmern. New York, Norton [1962] 245p. 20cm. (Norton lib., N111) 1.95 pap.,
1. Caesar, C. Julius. 2. Rome—Hist.—Republic, 265-30 B.C. I. Zimmern, Alfred Eckhard, Sir 1879- tr. II. Title.

FERRERO, Guglielmo, 1871-1942. 923.137
The life of Caesar. Translated by A. E. Zimmern. New York, Norton [1962] [13]-515 p. 21 cm. Reprint of 1933 ed. without pref. [DG261.F37 1962] 65-3183
1. Caesar, C. Julius. 2. Rome—Hist.—Republic, 265-30 B.C. I. Zimmern, Sir Alfred Eckhard, 1870- tr. II. Title. **BIP**

FERRERO, Guglielmo, 1871-1942. 937'.05'0924 B
The life of Caesar / Guglielmo Ferrero ; translated by A. E. Zimmern. Westport, Conn. : Greenwood Press, 1977. p. cm. Translation of Grandezza e decadenza di Roma. "First published as volumes I and II of 'The greatness and decline of Rome' (5 vols.) in 1907. New abridged edition (reset) published 1933." Reprint of the 1933 ed. published by Allen & Unwin, London. [DG261.F37 1977] 77-9520 ISBN 0-8371-9090-8 lib.bdg. : 27.50
1. Caesar, C. Julius. 2. Rome—History—Republic, 265-30 B.C. 3. Heads of state—Rome—Biography. 4. Generals—Rome—Biography. I. Title.

FOWLER, William Warde, 1847-1921. 937'.05'0924 B
Julius Caesar and the foundation of the Roman imperial system / by W. Warde Fowler. New York : AMS Press, 1978. xix, 389 p., [36] leaves of plates (2 fold.) : ill. ; 19 cm. Reprint of the 1892 ed. published by Putnam, New York, in series: Heroes of the nations. Includes index. [DG261.F7 1978] 73-14443 ISBN 0-404-58261-3 : 30.00
1. Caesar, C. Julius. 2. Heads of state—Rome—Biography. 3. Generals—Rome—Biography. 4. Rome—History—Republic, 265-30 B.C. I. Title. II. Series: Heroes of the nations. **BIP**

FULLER, John Frederick Charles, 1878- 937.050924
Julius Caesar: man, soldier, and tyrant. New Brunswick, N.J., Rutgers [c.1965] 336p. maps, port. 22cm. Bibl. [DG261.F94] 65-19400 7.50
1. Caesar, C. Julius. I. Title.

FULLER, John Frederick Charles, 1878- 937.050924
Julius Caesar: man, soldier, and tyrant [by] J. F. C. Fuller. New Brunswick, N.J., Rutgers University Press [1965] 336 p. maps, port. 22 cm. Bibliographical footnotes. [DG261.F94] 65-19400
1. Caesar, C. Julius. I. Title.

FULLER, John Frederick Charles, 1878- 937.05'0924
Julius Caesar: man, soldier, and tyrant [by] J. F. C. Fuller. [New York] Minerva Press [1969, c1965] 336 p. illus., maps. 21 cm. Bibliographical footnotes. [DG261.F94 1969] 77-4221 2.95
1. Caesar, C. Julius. I. Title.

GELZER, Matthias, 1886- 937'.05'0924 B
Caesar: politician and statesman. Translated by Peter Needham. Cambridge, Harvard University Press, 1968. viii, 359 p. map, ports. 23 cm. Bibliographical footnotes. [DG261.G414 1968] 68-4657
1. Caesar, C. Julius. 2. Rome—History—Republic, 265-30 B.C.

GRANT, Michael, 1914- 937'.05'0924 B
Caesar / Michael Grant ; introd. by Elizabeth Longford. Chicago : Follett Pub. Co., 1975, c1974. 232 p. : ill. (some col.) ; 26 cm. Bibliography: p. 224-225. [DG261.G66 1975] 74-21374 ISBN 0-695-80542-8 : 10.00
1. Caesar, C. Julius. 2. Rome—History—Republic, 265-30 B.C.

GRANT, Michael, 1914- 937'.05'0924 B
Julius Caesar. New York, McGraw-Hill [1969] 271 p. illus. (part col.), geneal. table, maps. 26 cm. Includes bibliographical references. [DG261.G68 1969] 69-15490 12.95
1. Caesar, C. Julius.

GUNTHER, John, 1901- 987'.05'0924 B
Julius Caesar. Illustrated by Joseph Cellini.

New York, Random House [1959] 182 p. illus. 22 cm. (World landmark books, W-43) A biography of Caesar, scholar and leader, whom historians described as the first modern man. [DG262.5.G8] 92 AC 68
1. Caesar, C. Julius. I. Cellini, Joseph, illus. II. Title.

KOMROFF, Manuel, 1890- 923.137
Julius Caesar. New York, Messner [1955] 190 p. illus. 22 cm. [DG261.K6] 55-9859
1. Caesar, C. Julius.

KOMROFF, Manuel, 1890- 937'.05'0924 B
Julius Caesar. New York, Messner [1955] 190 p. illus. 22 cm. A biography of Julius Caesar, remembered for his eloquence, just rule, and martyr's death at the hands of deceitful friends. [DG261.K6] 92 AC 68
1. Caesar, C. Julius. I. Title.
BIP

STEARNS, Monroe. 937'.05'0924 B
Julius Caesar; master of men. New York, F. Watts [1971] 249 p. illus. 23 cm. (Immortals of history) Bibliography: p. [237]-240. A biography of Julius Caesar, from his Roman youth through his conquests and years as consul to his assassination in 44 B.C. [DG261.S7] 92 72-152738 ISBN 0-531-00965-3
1. Caesar, C. Julius. I. Title.

WALTER, Gerard, 1896- 923.137
Caesar, a biography; translated from the French by Emma Craufurd, edited by Therese Pol. New York, Scribner, 1952. ix, 637 p. illus., maps 24 cm. "Notes and references": p. 549-606. [DG261.W314] 52-8179
1. Caesar, C. Julius.

WEIGALL, Arthur Edward Pearse Brome, 1880-1934 923.132
The life and times of Cleopatra, Queen of Egypt [2d ed., abridged] Philadelphia, Mercury Bks. [c.1962] 250p. map. 18cm. (Mod. biog. ser., MB104) .75 pap.,
1. Cleopatra, Queen of Egypt, d., B.C.30. 2. Caesar, C. Julius. 3. Antonius, Marcus, B.C. 83-30. 4. Egypt—Hist.—B.C. 332-B.C.30. I. Title.

WEIGALL, Arthur Edward Pearse Brome, 1880-1934. 923.132
The life and times of Cleopatra, queen of Egypt. [2d ed.] Philadelphia, Mercury Books, [1962] 250 p. illus. 18 cm. (Modern biography series, MB104) [DT92.7.W4 1962] 62-52860
1. Cleopatra, queen of Egypt, d. 30 B.C. 2. Caesar, C. Julius. 3. Antonius, Marcus, 83?-30 B.C. 4. Egypt — Hist. — 332 B.C.-30 B.C. I. Title.

WEIGALL, Arthur Edward Pearse Brome, 1880-1934. 932'.02'0924 B
The life and times of Cleopatra, Queen of Egypt; a study in the origin of the Roman Empire. New York, Greenwood Press, 1968 [c1924] xii, 445 p. illus., geneal. table, fold. maps, plan, ports. 24 cm. Reprint of the new and rev. ed., 1924. Contents.Contents. Cleopatra and Caesar.—Cleopatra and Antony. [DT92.7.W4 1968] 69-10168
1. Cleopatra, Queen of Egypt, d. 30 B.C. 2. Caesar, C. Julius. 3. Antonius, Marcus, 83? B.C.-30 B.C. 4. Egypt—History—332 B.C.-30 B.C. I. Title.
BIP

Caesar, C. Julius—Cult.

WEINSTOCK, Stefan. 292'.2'11
Divus Julius. Oxford, Clarendon Press, 1971. xix, 469 p., [28] leaves. illus., plan. 25 cm. Bibliography: p. xix. [DG262.W4] 72-177850 ISBN 0-19-814287-0 £9.00
1. Caesar, C. Julius—Cult. 2. Emperor worship, Roman. 3. Cultus, Roman. I. Title.
BIP

Caesar, C. Julius—Juvenile literature.

FRY, Peter George Robin Somerset, 1931- 937'.05'0924 B
Great Caesar / Plantagenet Somerset Fry [i.e. P.G.R.S. Fry]. 1st U.S. ed. Cleveland, Ohio : Collins World, 1975, c1974. p. cm. Includes index. Bibliography: p. [DG262.5.F78 1975] 74-24972 ISBN 0-529-05256-3 : 6.95
1. Caesar, C. Julius—Juvenile literature. 2. Rome—History—Republic—265-30 B.C.—Juvenile literature. I. Title.

GUNTHER, John, 1901- 923.137
Julis Caesar Illustrated by Joseph Cellini. New York, Random House [1959] 182p. illus. 22cm. (World landmark books, W-43) [DG262.5.G8] 59-10971
1. Caesar. C. Julius— Juvenile literature. I. Title.

LOWE, Edith May (Kovar) 1905- 92 (J)
Julius Caesar, by Peter David. Illustrated by W. T. Mars. New York, Crowell-Collier Press [1968] 129 p. illus. 21 cm. [DG262.5.L67] 68-10817
1. Caesar, C. Julius—Juvenile literature.

Cagliostro, Alessandro, conte di, assumed name of Giuseppe Balsamo, 1743-1795.

TROWBRIDGE, William Rutherford Hayes, 1866-1938. 920.9
Cagliostro; savant or scoundrel? The true role of this splendid, tragic figure. New Hyde Park, N.Y., University Books [1961] 311 p. illus. 24 cm. Includes bibliography. [BF1598.C2T8] 60-53063
1. Cagliostro, Alessandro, conte di, assumed name of Giuseppe Balsamo, 1743-1795. I. Title.

TROWBRIDGE, William Rutherford Hayes, 1866-1938. 920.9
Cagliostro; savant or scoundrel? The true role of this splendid, tragic figure. New Hyde Park, N. Y., University Books [1961] 311 p. illus. 24 cm. Includes bibliography. [BF1598.C2T8 1961] 60-53063
1. Cagliostro, Alessandro, conte di, assumed name of Giuseppe Balsamo, 1743-1795.

TROWBRIDGE, William Rutherford Hayes, 1866-1938. 133'.092'4 B
Cagliostro : savant or scoundrel? : The true role of this splendid, tragic figure / by W. R. H. Trowbridge. New York : Gordon Press, 1975. xxiii, 311 p. : ill. ; 24 cm. Includes index. Bibliography: p. xxi-xxiii. [BF1598.C2T8 1975] 74-180 ISBN 0-87968-106-3 : 34.95
1. Cagliostro, Alessandro, conte di, assumed name of Giuseppe Balsamo, 1743-1795. I. Title.

Cagney, James, 1899-

CAGNEY, James, 1899 791.43'028'0924 B
Cagney by Cagney / James Cagney. 1st ed. Garden City, N.Y. : Doubleday, 1976. 202 p., [12] leaves of plates : ill. ; 22 cm. [PN2287.C23A33] 74-18784 ISBN 0-385-04587-5 : 8.95
1. Cagney, James, 1899- I. Title.
BIP

FREEDLAND, Michael, 1934- 791.43'028'0924 B
Cagney : a biography / by Michael Freedland. New York : Stein and Day, 1975, c1974. 255 p. : ill. ; 23 cm. British ed. published in 1974 under title: James Cagney. [PN2287.C23F7 1975] 74-79434 ISBN 0-8128-1715-X : 8.95
1. Cagney, James, 1899-

MCGILLIGAN, Patrick. 791.43'028'0924 B
Cagney : the actor as auteur / Patrick McGilligan. South Brunswick : A. S. Barnes, [1975] p. cm. Filmography: p. [PN2287.C23M3] 73-14028 ISBN 0-498-01462-2 : 12.00
1. Cagney, James, 1899-
BIP

MCGILLIGAN, Patrick. 791.43'028'0924 B
Cagney : the actor as auteur / Patrick McGilligan. South Brunswick : A. S. Barnes, [1975] 240 p. : ill. ; 26 cm. Includes index. Filmography: p. 214-234. [PN2287.C23M3] 73-14028 ISBN 0-498-01462-2 : 12.00
1. Cagney, James, 1899-

OFFEN, Ron. 791.43'028'0924
Cagney. Boston, G. K. Hall, 1972. p. Large print ed. [PN2287.C23O4] 72-8829 ISBN 0-8161-6056-2 6.95
1. Cagney, James.

OFFEN, Ron. 791.43'028'0924 B
Cagney. Chicago, Regnery [1973, c1972] xiii, 217 p. illus. 22 cm. "Complete James Cagney filmography": p. 183-217. [PN2287.C23O4 1973] 72-80934 6.95
1. Cagney, James, 1899-

Cahan, Abraham,

CAHAN, Abraham, 1860-1951. 892.49'8'303 B
The education of Abraham Cahan. Translated by Leon Stein, Abraham P. Conan, and Lynn Davison from the Yiddish autobiography Bleter fun mein leben. Introd. by Leon Stein. [1st ed.] Philadelphia, Jewish Publication Society of America, 1969. xviii, 450 p. illus., ports. 22 cm. Translation of Bleter fun mayn leben (romanized form) v. 1-2. Bibliographical footnotes. [PJ5129.C27Z513] 69-19041 7.50
I. Title.
BIP

Cahill, Tom, 1919-

WHITE, Gordon S. 796.332'0924
Coach Tom Cahill, a man for the corps, by Gordon S. White, Jr., and Mervin D. Hyman. [New York] Macmillan [1969] viii, 181 p. ports. 22 cm. [GV939.C3W45] 72-84433
1. Cahill, Tom, 1919- 2. U.S. Military Academy, West Point—Football. I. Hyman, Mervin D., joint author. II. Title.

Cahn, Sammy.

CAHN, Sammy. 784'.092'4 B
I should care : the Sammy Cahn story / by Sammy Cahn. New York : Arbor House, [1974] 318 p. : ill. ; 24 cm. Includes index. [ML423.C125A3] 74-80708 ISBN 0-87795-090-3 : 8.95
1. Cahn, Sammy. 2. Musicians—Correspondence, reminiscences, etc. I. Title.
BIP

Caine, Lynn.

CAINE, Lynn. 155.9'37
Lifelines / by Lynn Caine. New York : Dell Publishing Co., 1979, c1978. 224p. ; 18 cm. (A Dell Book) [BF575.G7C32] ISBN 0-440-15463-4 pbk. : 2.25
1. Caine, Lynn. 2. Bereavement — Psychological aspects. 3. Widows — United States — Biography. I. Title.
L.C. card no. for 1978 Doubleday ed.: 76-56274
BIP

Cairns, Robert John, 1884-1941.

REID, Richard, 1896- 922.251
Three days to eternity; being the story of Father Sandy Cairns, Maryknoll missioner and modern apostle, by Richard Reid and Edward J. Moffett. Westminster, Md., Newman Press, 1956. 179p. 21cm. [BV3427.C2R4] 56-13467
1. Cairns, Robert John, 1884-1941. I. Moffett, Edward J., 1922- joint author. II. Title.

Cajetanus, Saint, 1480-1547.

HALLETT, Paul H. 922.245
Catholic reformer; a life of St. Cajetan of Thiene. Westminster Md., Newman Press, [c.] 1959. ix, 222p. 23cm. 59-14756 3.75
1. Cajetanus, Saint, 1480-1547. I. Title.

Caldecott, Randolph, 1846-1886.

BLACKBURN, Henry, 1830-1897. 709'.24
Randolph Caldecott; a personal memoir of his early art career. London, S. Low, Marston, Searle, & Rivington, 1886. Detroit, Singing Tree Press, 1969. xvi, 216 p. illus., port. 21 cm. [NC242.C3B6 1969] 68-21757
1. Caldecott, Randolph, 1846-1886.

CALDECOTT, Randolph, 1846-1886. 709'.2'4
Randolph Caldecott, lord of the nursery / [edited by] Rodney K. Engen. New York : Two Continents Pub. Group, c1976. p. cm. (Oresko art book series) Includes index. Bibliography: p. [N6797.C28E53 1976] 77-70918 ISBN 0-8467-0244-4 : 13.95. ISBN 0-8467-0243-6 pbk. : 7.95
1. Caldecott, Randolph, 1846-1886. I. Engen, Rodney K. II. Title. III. Series.

Calder, Alexander Milne, 1846-1923.

HAYES, Margaret Calder, 1896- 709'.2'2 B
Three Alexander Calders : a family memoir / by Margaret Calder Hayes ; introd. by Malcolm Cowley. Middlebury, Vt. : P. S. Eriksson, c1977. xix, 300 p. : ill. ; 24 cm. Includes index. [NB237.C29H39 1977] 77-79244 ISBN 0-8397-8017-6 : 15.00
1. Calder, Alexander Milne, 1846-1923. 2. Calder, Alexander Stirling, 1870-1945. 3. Calder, Alexander, 1898-1976. 4. Hayes, Margaret Calder, 1896- 5. Sculptors—United States—Biography. 6. United States—Biography. I. Title.
BIP

Calder, Alexander Stirling, 1870-1945.

HAYES, Margaret Calder, 1896- 709'.2'2 B
Three Alexander Calders : a family memoir / by Margaret Calder Hayes ; introd. by Malcolm Cowley. Middlebury, Vt. : P. S. Eriksson, c1977. xix, 300 p. : ill. ; 24 cm. Includes index. [NB237.C29H39 1977] 77-79244 ISBN 0-8397-8017-6 : 15.00
1. Calder, Alexander Milne, 1846-1923. 2. Calder, Alexander Stirling, 1870-1945. 3. Calder, Alexander, 1898-1976. 4. Hayes, Margaret Calder, 1896- 5. Sculptors—United States—Biography. 6. United States—Biography. I. Title.
BIP

Calder, Alexander, 1898-1976.

BOURDON, David. 709'.2'4 B
Calder : mobilist, ringmaster, innovator / by David Bourdon. New York : Macmillan, c1979. p. cm. Includes index. Bibliography: p. Presents the life and representative works of artist and sculptor Alexander Calder against the world of contemporary art. [NB237.C28B68] 92 72-92447 ISBN 0-02-711780-4 : 9.95
1. Calder, Alexander, 1898-1976. 2. Sculpture—United States—Biography. I. Title.
BIP

CALDER, Alexander, 1898- 730.924
Calder; an autobiography with pictures. New York, Pantheon Books [1966] 285 p. illus. (part col.) ports. 28 cm. [NB237.C28A2] 66-23203
1. Calder, Alexander, 1898- 2. Sculptors—United States—Correspondence, reminiscences, etc. I. Title.

CALDER, Alexander, 1898- 709'.2'4 B
Calder's universe / Jean Lipman ; Ruth Wolfe, editorial director. New York : Viking Press in cooperation with the Whitney Museum of American Art, [1976] p. cm. (A Studio book) An exhibition based on this book is scheduled to be held at the Whitney Museum of American Art, Oct. 14, 1976 to May 1, 1977, and at other museums at later dates. Includes index. Bibliography: p. [N6537.C33L56] 76-28232 ISBN 0-670-19966-4 : 28.50
1. Calder, Alexander, 1898- I. Lipman, Jean Herzberg, 1909- II. Whitney Museum of American Art, New York. III. Title.

CALDER, Alexander, 1898-1976. 709'.2'4 B
Calder : an autobiography with pictures / with a new introd. by Jean Davidson. New York : Pantheon Books, 1977,c1966 288 p., [6] leaves of plates : ill. ; 27 cm. [NB237.C28A2 1966b] 77-5300 ISBN 0-394-42142-6 : 15.95. ISBN 0-394-73408-4 pbk. : 7.95
1. Calder, Alexander, 1898-1976. 2. Sculptors—United States—Biography. I. Title.
BIP

CALDER, Alexander, 1898-1976. 709'.2'4
Calder / text by Maurice Bruzeau ; photos. by Jacques Masson ; translated from the French by I. Mark Paris. New York : H. N. Abrams, 1979, c1975. 171 p. : chiefly

ill. (some col.) ; 29 cm. Translation of Calder a Sache. [N6853.C26A4 1979] 78-74984 ISBN 0-8109-2198-7 : 14.95
1. Calder, Alexander, 1898-1976. 2. Sache, France. I. Bruzeau, Maurice. **BIP**

HAYES, Margaret 709'.2'2 B Calder, 1896-
Three Alexander Calders : a family memoir / by Margaret Calder Hayes ; introd. by Malcolm Cowley. Middlebury, Vt. : P. S. Eriksson, c1977. xix, 300 p. : ill. ; 24 cm. Includes index. [NB237.C29H39 1977] 77-79244 ISBN 0-8397-8017-6 : 15.00
1. Calder, Alexander Milne, 1846-1923. 2. Calder, Alexander Stirling, 1870-1945. 3. Calder, Alexander, 1898-1976. 4. Hayes, Margaret Calder, 1896- 5. Sculptors—United States—Biography. 6. United States—Biography. I. Title. **BIP**

Calderon, Miguel G., 1885—

CALDERON, Miguel 917.2'03'810924 G., 1885-
Aventuras : version abreviada de las memorias del Lic. Miguel G. Calderon / editadas por Y. C. de Carter ; ilus. del autor. Austin, Tex. : Amistad Press, c1975. 85 p., [1] leaf of plates : ill. ; 23 cm. First ed. published in 1974 under title: Aventuras de la vida real. "Estan reproducidos diecinueve de los cuarenta capitulos de la obra completa ... y fue agregado un capitulo nuevo, El primer circo aereo (20), escrito por el autor en enero de 1975." [F1234.C143 1975] 75-31491
1. Calderon, Miguel G., 1885- 2. Spanish language—Readers—Autobiography. I. Carter, Yolanda C. de.

Caldera, Miguel, 1548-1597.

POWELL, Philip 972'.02'0924 Wayne.
Mexico's Miguel Caldera : the taming of America's first frontier, 1548-1597 / Philip Wayne Powell. Tucson : University of Arizona Press, c1977. xi, 322 p. : maps ; 24 cm. Includes index. Bibliography: p. 301-306. [F1219.C27P68] 76-62551 ISBN 0-8165-0638-8 : 14.95 ISBN 0-8165-0569-1 pbk. : 7.95
1. Caldera, Miguel, 1548-1597. 2. Chichimecs—Wars, 1550-1591. 3. Soldiers—Mexico—Biography. I. Title. **BIP**

Calderon de la Barca, Pedro, 1600-1681.

LUND, Harry, 1911- 862'.3
Pedro Calderon de la Barca, a biography. [Edinburg, Tex.] Andres Noriega Press [1963] 128 p. illus. 23 cm. "300 ejemplares ... no.228." Bibliographical references included in "Notes" (p. 120-122) [PQ6300.L8] 65-4585
1. Calderon de la Barca, Pedro, 1600-1681. I. Title.

Caldwell, Charles, 1772-1853.

CALDWELL, Charles, 610'.924(B) 1772-1853.
Autobiography of Charles Caldwell, M. D. with a pref., notes, appendix by Harriot W. Warner. New introd. by Lloyd G. Stevenson. New York, Da Capo Press, 1968. xxvi, viii, [17]-454 p. port 24 cm. (A Da Capo Press reprint edition) Reprint of the 1855 ed. "Catalogue of the published writings and translations of Charles Caldwell": p. 429-436. [R154.C2A5 1968] 67-27450
I. Title. **BIP**

HORINE, Emmet Field, 1885- 016.61
Biographical sketch and guide to the writings of Charles Caldwell, M.D. (1772-1853) with sections on phrenology and on hypnotism. Brooks, Ky., High Acres Press, 1960. viii, 155p. illus., ports, facsim. 26cm. 'Limited to three hundred copies ... This is copy no. 14.' Bibliographical footnotes. [Z8140.55.H6] 60-8195
1. Caldwell, Charles, 1772-1853. 2. Caldwell, Charles, 1772-1853—Bibl. I. Title.

Caldwell Co., Tex.—Biography.

EARTH has no 976.4'33'060922 B *sorrow* / edited & photographed by Dee Azadian. 1st ed. [Lockhart, Tex. : Voluntary Action Center of Caldwell County], c1977. 96 p., [12] leaves of plates : ill. ; 26 cm. [F392.C2E27] 77-88435
1. Caldwell Co., Tex.—Biography. 2. Caldwell Co., Tex.—History—Sources. 3. Interviews. I. Azadian, Dee. II. Voluntary Action Center of Caldwell County.

Caldwell, Erskine, 1903-

CALDWELL, Erskine, 1903- 928.1
Call it experience; the years of learning how to write. New York, Duell, Sloan and Pearce [1951] 239 p. 23 cm. [PS3505.A322Z53] 51-10412
I. Title.

KORGES, James. 813'.5'2
Erskine Caldwell. Minneapolis, University of Minnesota Press [1969] 48 p. 21 cm. (University of Minnesota. Pamphlets on American writers, no. 78) Bibliography: p. 47-48. [PS3505.A322Z7] 71-625289 0.95
1. Caldwell, Erskine, 1903- I. Title. II. Series: Minnesota. University. Pamphlets on American writers, no. 78 **BIP**

Caldwell, Erskine, 1903- —Journeys—Middle West.

CALDWELL, Erskine, 917.8'04'3 1903-
Afternoons in Mid-America : observations and impressions / Erskine Caldwell ; drawings by Virginia M. Caldwell. New York : Dodd, Mead, c1976. 276 p. : ill. ; 22 cm. [F355.C33] 76-25181 ISBN 0-396-07348-4 : 8.95
1. Caldwell, Erskine, 1903- —Journeys—Middle West. 2. Middle West—Description and travel. I. Title.

Calendar reform.

ACHELIS, Elisabeth, 1880- 925.295
'Be not silent.' [1st ed.] New York, Pageant Press [1961] 172p. illus. 21cm. Autobiography. [CE73.A28] 60-53293
1. Calendar reform. I. Title.

Calhoun family.

DUNDAS, Francis de 929'.2'0973 Sales, 1873-
The Calhoun settlement, district of Abbeville, South Carolina. 2d ed. [Staunton, Va., 1950] 60 p. illus., ports. 23 cm. Cover title. [CS71.C15 1950] 50-33991
1. Calhoun family. 2. Abbeville, S. C.—Hist. I. Title.

MCPHERSON, Lewin 929'.2'0973 Dwinell, 1876-
Calhoun, Hamilton, Baskin, and related families. [n.p.] c1957. 447p. illus. 29cm. [CS71.C15 1957] 57-43347
1. Calhoun family. I. Title.

Calhoun, Jack, 1923-1945.

CALHOUN, Jack, 940.54'81'73 B 1923-1945.
Somewhere the sun is shining / by Jack Calhoun and Beryl Calhoun. 1st ed. San Diego : Grossmont Press, c1976. ix, 70 p. : ill. ; 23 cm. [D811.C235 1976] 76-56901 ISBN 0-913182-85-0 pbk. : 2.95
1. Calhoun, Jack, 1923-1945. 2. World War, 1939-1945—Personal narratives, American. 3. Fighter pilots—United States—Biography. I. Calhoun, Beryl, 1896- joint author. II. Title.

Calhoun, John Caldwell, 1782-1850.

CAPERS, Gerald Mortimer. 923.273
John C. Calhoun, opportunist; a reappraisal. Gainesville, University of Florida Press, 1960. 275 p. illus. 24 cm. Includes bibliography. [E340.C15C25] 60-15788
1. Calhoun, John Caldwell, 1782-1850. **BIP**

COIT, Margaret L. 923.273
John C. Calhoun, American portrait. Boston, Houghton [1961, c.1950] ix, 593p. illus. (Sentry ed. 5) Bibl. 2.45 pap.,
1. Calhoun, John Caldwell, 1782-1850. I. Title.

COIT, Margaret L., 973.6'0924 comp.
John C. Calhoun, edited by Margaret L. Coit. Englewood Cliffs, N.J., Prentice-Hall [1970] x, 174 p. 22 cm. (Great lives observed) (A Spectrum book.) Includes bibliographical references. [E340.C15C62] 72-104843 4.95
1. Calhoun, John Caldwell, 1782-1850. **BIP**

COIT, Margaret L. 923.273
John C. Calhoun, American portrait. Boston, Houghton Mifflin, 1950. ix, 593 p. illus., ports. 23 cm. Bibliography: p. [573]-581. [E340.C15C63] 50-5234
1. Calhoun, John Caldwell, 1782-1850.

HOLST, Hermann 973.5'0924 B Eduard von, 1841-1904.
John C. Calhoun. Boston, Houghton, Mifflin. [New York, AMS Press, 1972] vi, 374 p. illus. 19 cm. (American statesmen, v. 22) Reprint of the 1899 ed. [E340.C15H72] 75-128961 ISBN 0-404-50872-3
1. Calhoun, John Caldwell, 1782-1850. I. Title. II. Series.

MEIGS, William 973.6'0924 B Montgomery, 1852-1929.
The life of John Caldwell Calhoun. New York, Da Capo Press, 1970 [c1917] 2 v. illus., ports. 24 cm. (The American scene) Includes bibliographical references. [E340.C15M52 1970] 75-127195
1. Calhoun, John Caldwell, 1782-1850. I. Title. **BIP**

THOMAS, John L., 973.6'0924 B comp.
John C. Calhoun; a profile, edited by John L. Thomas. [1st ed.] New York, Hill and Wang [1968] xxiv, 228 p. 21 cm. (American profiles) Bibliography: p. 225-226. [E340.C15T38] 68-14785
1. Calhoun, John Caldwell, 1782-1850.

WILTSE, Charles 973.6'0924 B Maurice, 1907-
John C. Calhoun, by Charles M. Wiltse. New York, Russell & Russell [1968, c1944-51] 3 v. illus., facsims., maps, ports. 24 cm. Contents.Contents.—[v. 1] Nationalist, 1782-1828.—[v. 2] Nullifier, 1829-1839.—[v. 3] Sectionalist, 1840-1850. Includes bibliographies. [E340.C15] 68-11329
1. Calhoun, John Caldwell, 1782-1850. **BIP**

Calhoun, John Caldwell, 1782-1850—Juvenile literature.

CRANE, William 973.6'0924 B Dwight.
Patriotic rebel: John C. Calhoun, by William D. Crane. New York, J. Messner [1971, c1972] 189 p. 22 cm. Bibliography: p. 183-184. A biography of the controversial Southern statesman who defended the doctrine of States' rights for the South while trying to prevent a division of the Union. [E340.C15C7] 92 72-176377 ISBN 0-671-32494-2 4.95
1. Calhoun, John Caldwell, 1782-1850—Juvenile literature. I. Title.

California

IDE, William Brown, 979.4/03/0924 1796-1852
Who conquered California? Read the following pages, and then you will know, for they contain the most particular, the most authentic, and the most reliable history of the conquest of California, in June, 1846, by the "Bear Flag Party," ever before published. Claremont, N. H., S. Ide [1880] Photo reprodn. Glorieta, N.M., Rio Grande Pr., 1967. 132p. 23cm. Bound with: Ide, Simeon. A biographical sketch of the life of William B. Ide. [F864.I23 1967] 67-9473 10.00
1. California—Hist.—1846-1850. 2. Bear Flag Battalion. I. Ide, Simeon, 1794,-1889. ed. II. Title.

IDE. WILLIAM BROWN, 979.4'03'0924 1796-1852
Who conquered California? Read the following pages, and then you will know for they contain the most particular, the most authentic, and the most reliable history of the conquest of California, in June, 1846, by the 'Bear Flag Party,' ever before published. Claremont, N. H., S. Ide [1880] Bound with: Ide, Simeon. A biographical sketch of the life of William B. Ide. Glorieta, N. M., Rio Grande Pr., 1967. 137p. 23cm. Photoreproduction. Glorieta. N.M., Rio Grande Press, 1967. [F864.I23 1967] 67-9473 price unreported
1. California—Hist.—1846-1850. 2. Bear Flag Battalion. I. Ide, Simeon, 1794-1889, ed. II. Title.

MELENDY, Howard 353.9794030922 Brett.
The Governors of California: Peter H. Burnett to Edmund G. Brown, by H. Brett Melendy and Benjamin F. Gilbert. Georgetown. Calif., Talisman Press, 1965. 482 p. illus. 24 cm. Includes bibliographies. [F860.M5] 65-28086
1. California — Governors — Biog. 2. California — Pol. & govt. I. Gilbert, Benjamin Franklin joint author. II. Title.

California—Biography.

ARMSTRONG, Alice (Catt) 920.074 ed.
Who's who executives in California. [Los Angeles] A. C. Armstrong. 1963 v. ports. 28 cm. Editor: 1963- A. C. Armstrong. [F860.W624] 63-49837
1. California — Biog. I. Title.

ARMSTRONG, Alice (Catt) 920.074 ed.
Who's who in California, 1955/56 -- [Los Angeles] v. ports. 28 cm. Editor: 1955/56- [F860.W628] 56-1715
1. California — Biog. I. Title.

BANCROFT, Hubert Howe, 920.0794 1832-1918
California pioneer register and index, 1542-1848. Including Inhabitants of California, 1769-1800, and List of pioneers. Baltimore, Regional Pub. [dist. Genealogical, c.]1964. 392p. 23cm. 64-17723 10.00
1. California—Biog. I. Title.

BANCROFT, Hubert Howe, 920.0794 1832-1918.
California pioneer register and index, 1542-1848. Including Inhabitants of California, 1769-1800, and List of pioneers Baltimore, Regional Pub. Co., 1964. 392 p. 23 cm. Extracted from the author's History of California. [F860.B27] 64 -17723
1. California — Biog. I. Title.

BIXLER, W. K. 920.07944
A dozen Sierra success stories; twelve individualists of our time: Eva Adams, Norman Biltz, Paul Claiborne, Clel Georgtta, Harvey Gross, Raymond Knisley, Wayne Poulsen, George Probasco, Archie D. Stevenot, Lester D. Summerfield, Harvey West, Jim A. E. Wilson [Tahoe Valley, Calif., Sierra Pubns., 1964] 200p. illus., facsims., map, ports. 29cm. 64-16464 price unreported
1. California—Biog. I. Title.

CRANDALL, Roland 979.4/04/0924 D., 1892- comp.
Love and nuggets. Ed. by Roland D. Crandall. [1st ed.] Old Greenwich, Conn., Stable Bks. [1967] 208p. illus., facsims., map., ports. 23cm. Chiefly journals and letters of Henry Sargent Crandall and Mary Caroline Mills. [CT275.C866A43] 67-28578 5.75
I. Crandall, Henry Sargent, 1826-1909. II. Crandall, Mary Caroline Mills. III. Title.
Publisher's address: 183 Sound Beach Ave., Old Greenwich, Conn. 06870.

DILLON, Richard H. 920.0794 B
Humbugs and heroes; a gallery of California pioneers, by Richard Dillon. [1st ed.] Garden City, N.Y., Doubleday 1970. xvi, 362 p. illus., ports. 22 cm. [F860.D5] 70-89100 7.95
1. California—Biography. I. Title.

EMINENT Californians, 920.074
1953 Palo Alto, Calif., C. W. Taylor. v. ports. 28 cm. [F860.E53] 53-27367
1. California—Biog. I. Taylor, Charles Williams, 1896-

HUNT, Rockwell Dennis, 920.074
1868-
Personal sketches of California pioneers I have known. Stockton, Calif., University of the Pacific, 1962. 109p. ports. 26cm. 500 copies printed. 'Sponsored by California History Foundation and Conference of California Historical Societies. [F860.H82] 62-6897
1. California—Biog. 2. Pioneers—California. I. Title.

HYNDING, Alan, 1938- 920'.0794
California historymakers / by Alan A. Hynding. Dubuque, Ia. : Kendall/Hunt Pub. Co., c1976. x, 154 p. : ports. ; 24 cm. Biographical sketches of twenty-three Californians who represent the diversity of the state's population. [CT225.H96] 76-1103 ISBN 0-8403-1416-7 pbk. : 4.95
1. California—Biography. I. Title. BIP

WHO'S who in California. v. 12
1955/56- [Los Angeles] v. ports. 28cm. Editor: 1855/56- A. C. Armstrong. [FS60.W28] 56-1715
1. California—Biog. I. Armstrong, Alice (Catt) ed.

California—Gold discoveries.

BOOTH, Edmund, 1810-1905. 923.973
Edmund Booth (1810-1905) forty-niner; the life story of a deaf pioneer, including portions of his autobiographican notes and gold rush diary, and selections from family letters and reminiscenses. Stockton, Calif., San Joaquin Pioneer and Historical Society. 1953. iii, 72p. mounted illus., ports. 25cm. [F865.B68] 53-3517
1. California—Gold discoveries. I. San Joaquin Pioneer and Historical Society, Stockton, Calif. II. Title.

DECKER, Peter, 1822-1888. 917.94
The diaries of Peter Decker: overland to California in 1849 and life in the mines, 1850-1851. Edited by Helen S. Giffen. Georgetown, Calif., Talisman Press, 1966. 338 p. illus., 2 fold. maps (1 col.) port. 24 cm. "Original manuscript diaries in the collection of Society of California Pioneers, San Francisco." [F865.D285A] 66-27366
1. California—Gold discoveries. 2. Frontier and pioneer life—California. 3. Overland journeys to the Pacific. I. Giffen, Helen Smith, 1893- ed. II. Title.

JOHNSTON, William 979.4'04'0924 B
Graham, 1828-1913.
Experiences of a forty-niner. New York, Arno Press, 1973. 390 p. illus. 23 cm. (The Far Western frontier) Reprint of the 1892 ed. [F865.J73 1973] 72-9454 ISBN 0-405-04982-X 12.00
1. California—Gold discoveries. 2. Overland journeys to the Pacific. I. Title. II. Series. BIP

OSBUN, Albert Gallatin, 917.94
1807-1862.
To California and the South Seas; the diary of Albert G. Osbun, 1849-1851. Edited by John Haskell Kemble. San Marino, Calif., Huntington Library, 1966. xiii, 233 p. maps. (part fold.) port. 24 cm. (Huntington Library publications) [F865.O77] 66-15695
1. California—Gold discoveries. 2. Voyages to the Pacific coast. 3. Oceanica—Description and travel. 4. Mexico—Description and travel. I. Kemble, John Haskell, 1912- ed. II. Title. III. Series: Henry E. Huntington Library and Art Gallery, San Marino, Calif. Huntington Library publications.

WINDELER, Adolphus. 917.94
The California Gold Rush diary of a German sailor. Illustrated with pencil sketches by his inseparable partner Carl (Charley) Friederich Christendorff. Edited and with an introd. by W. Turrentine Jackson. [Berkeley, Calif., Howell-North Books, 1969] 236 p. illus. 25 cm. Bibliographical references included in "Notes" (p. 199-226) [F865.W8] 70-95165 7.50
1. California—Gold discoveries. I. Jackson, William Turrentine, 1915- ed. II. Title. BIP

California—History—Chronology.

CHRONOLOGY and documentary 979.4
handbook of the State of California. Ellen Lloyd Trover, State editor. Dobbs Ferry, N.Y., Oceana Publications, 1972. vi, 118 p. illus. 23 cm. (Chronologies and documentary handbooks of the States, v. 5) Bibliography: p. 115. Contains a chronology of historical events from 1540 to 1970, a directory of political figures, an outline of the state constitution, and copies of three historical documents. [F861.C5] 72-5265 ISBN 0-379-16130-3
1. California—History—Chronology. 2. California—Biography—Dictionaries. 3. California—History—Sources. I. Trover, Ellen Lloyd, ed. II. Title. III. Series. BIP

California—Politics and government—1850-1950.

SAMISH, Arthur 328.794'07'80924 B
H., 1897-
The secret boss of California; the life and high times of Art Samish, by Arthur H. Samish and Bob Thomas. New York, Crown Publishers [1971] 192 p. 22 cm. [F866.S17 1971] 75-151022 5.95
1. California—Politics and government—1850-1950. I. Thomas, Bob, 1922- joint author. II. Title.

California. State College, San Francisco—History.

SUMMERSKILL, John, 378.1'98'1 B
1925-
President seven. New York, World Pub. Co. [1971] ix, 230 p. 22 cm. Autobiographical. [LB1837.S5S9] 70-124284 7.95
1. California. State College, San Francisco—History. I. Title.

California Theater.

RATHER, Lois, 1905- 792'.09
Bonanza theater / Lois Rather. Oakland, Calif. : Rather Press, 1977. 115 p. : ill. ; 27 cm. "Of an edition of 150 this is no. 13." Includes bibliographical references and index. [PN2277.S42C38] 77-152061 20.00
1. California Theater. 2. Ralston, Wiliam Chapman, 1826-1875. 3. Bankers—California—San Francisco—Biography. I. Title. BIP

California. University—Biog.

CALIFORNIA. University. 378.794
In memoriam. [Berkeley? 1957?] 195p. 22cm. Cover title. Short biographical essays. [LD750.A54] 57-63101
1. California. University—Biog. I. Title.

Caligula, Emperor of Rome, 12-41.

BALSDON, John 937'.07'0924 B
Percy Vyvian Dacre, 1901-
The Emperor Gaius (Caligula) / by J. P. V. D. Balsdon. New York : AMS Press, [1976] p. cm. Reprint of the 1934 ed. published by Clarendon Press, Oxford. Bibliography: p. [DG283.B3 1976] 75-41014 ISBN 0-404-14503-5 : 16.50
1. Caligula, Emperor of Rome, 12-41. I. Title. BIP

BALSDON, John 937'.07'0924 B
Percy Vyvian Dacre, 1901-
The Emperor Gaius (Caligula) / by J. P. V. D. Balsdon. Westport, Conn. : Greenwood Press, 1977. p. cm. Reprint of the 1964 ed. published by the Clarendon Press, Oxford, Eng.; first published 1934. Includes index. Bibliography: p. [DG283.B3 1977] 77-7328 ISBN 0-8371-9074-6 lib.bdg. : 18.50
1. Caligula, Emperor of Rome, 12-41. 2. Roman emperors—Biography. I. Title.

Calisher, Hortense.

CALISHER, Hortense. 813'.5'4
Herself. New York, Arbor House [1972] 401 p. 24 cm. [PS3553.A4Z5] 72-82174 ISBN 0-87795-042-3 10.00
I. Title. BIP

Calkins, Earnest Elmo,

CALKINS, Earnest 362.4'2'0924 B
Elmo, 1868-1964.
"Louder please!" The autobiography of a deaf man. Boston, Atlantic Monthly Press. Ann Arbor, Gryphon Books, 1971 [c1924] 260 p. illus. 22 cm. [HV2534.C3A3 1971] 74-164148
I. Title.

Calkins, Matthew.

PRIEST, Josiah, 973'.04'97 S
1788-1851.
The feats, adventures, and sufferings of Matthew Calkins / Josiah Priest. New York : Garland Pub., 1975. p. cm. (The Garland library of narratives of North American Indian captivities ; v. 56) Includes original t.p.: A true story of the extraordinary feats, adventures and sufferings of Matthew Calkins, Chenango Co., N.Y., in the War of the Revolution-never before published. Also, the deeply interesting story of the captivity of General Patchin, of Schoharie Co., N.Y., when a lad by Brant and his Indians in the same war, written from the lips of the respective heroes above named. The spirit of evil and the spirit of good, a Saginaw tale, from Schoolcraft's researches. And the story of Conrad Mayer, the hunter ... Lansingburgh, Printed by W. Harkness, 1840. [E85.G2 vol. 56] [E275.A2] 974.74'73'020924 75-33259 ISBN 0-8240-1680-7 lib.bdg. : 21.00
1. Calkins, Matthew. 2. United States—History—Revolution, 1775-1783—Personal narratives. 3. Iroquois Indians—Captivities. 4. Indians of North America—Captivities. I. Patchin, Freegift, d. 1831. II. Title. III. Series.

Callaghan, Daniel Judson, 1890-1942.

MURPHY, Francis Xavier, 923.573
1914-
Fighting admiral; the story of Dan Callaghan. New York, Vantage Press [1952] 214 p. illus. 23 cm. Includes bibliography. [E746.C27M87] 52-3458
1. Callaghan, Daniel Judson, 1890-1942. I. Title.

Callaghan, James, 1912-

KELLNER, Peter. 941.085'7'0924 B
Callaghan, the road to Number Ten / [by] Peter Kellner and Christopher Hitchens. London : Cassell, 1976. viii, 187 p. ; 23 cm. Includes index. Bibliography: p. 181-182. [DA591.C34K44] 77-356803 ISBN 0-304-29768-2 : £3.95
1. Callaghan, James, 1912- 2. Prime ministers—Great Britain—Biography. 3. Great Britain—Politics and government—1945- I. Hitchens, Christopher, joint author. II. Title.

Callaghan, Morley, 1903-

CALLAGHAN, Morley, 917.1'04'64
1903-
Winter / text by Morley Callaghan ; photos. by John de Visser. Boston : New York Graphic Society, c1974. [128] p. : ill. (some col.) ; 33 cm. [F1016.C2 1974b] 74-14744 ISBN 0-8212-0642-7 : 25.00
1. Callaghan, Morley, 1903- 2. Canada—Description and travel—1951- 3. Winter—Canada. I. De Visser, John. II. Title.

Callaghan, Morley, 1903- —Friends and associates.

CALLAGHAN, Morley, 818'.5'203 B
1903-
That summer in Paris : memories of tangled friendships with Hemingway, Fitzgerald, and some others / Morley Callaghan. Harmondsworth ; New York : Penguin Books, 1979. 255 p. ; 18 cm. Reprint of the 1963 ed. published by By Coward-McCann, New York. [PR9199.3.C27Z52 1978] 79-193 ISBN 0-14-005074-4 pbk. : 3.95
1. Callaghan, Morley, 1903- —Friends and associates. 2. Hemingway, Ernest, 1899-1961—Friends and associates. 3. Fitzgerald, Francis Scott Key, 1896-1940—Friends and associates. 4. Novelists Canadian—20th century—Biography. 5. Novelists American—20th century—Biography. I. Title. BIP

Callahan, Harry M.

CALLAHAN, Harry M. 779'.092'4
Callahan / edited with an introduction by John Szarkowski. Millerton, N.Y. : Aperture, c1976. 201 p. : chiefly ill. ; 32 cm. Exhibition of photos. held at the Museum of Modern Art, New York, Dec. 2, 1976-Feb. 8, 1977. Bibliography: p. 197-199. [TR654.C3 1976] 76-42104 ISBN 0-912334-75-4 : 30.00
1. Callahan, Harry M. 2. Photography, Artistic. 3. Photographers—United States—Biography. I. Szarkowski, John. II. New York (City). Museum of Modern Art. BIP

Callas, Maria, 1923-1977.

ARDOIN, John. 782.1'092'4 B
The Callas legacy / John Ardoin. New York : Scribner, c1977. xi, 224 p., [1] leaf of plates : port. ; 23 cm. Includes indexes. Bibliography: p. [212]-213. [ML420.C18A85 1977b] 77-77316 ISBN 0-684-15297-5 : 12.50
1. Callas, Maria, 1923- Performances. 2. Callas, Maria, 1923- —Discography. I. Title. BIP

CALLAS : 782.1'092'4 B
The art and the life / by John Ardoin. The great years / by Gerald Fitzgerald ; designed by Howard Sperber. 1st ed. New York : Holt, Rinehart and Winston, [1974] 282 p. : ill. ; 32 cm. "Chronology": p. [265] -275. Includes index. [ML420.C18C33] 74-4410 ISBN 0-03-011486-1 : 27.50
1. Callas, Maria, 1923- I. Ardoin, John. II. Fitzgerald, Gerald.

CALLAS, Evangelia 927.8
My daughter Maria Callas, by Evangelia Callas in collaboration with Lawrence G. Blochman. New York, Fleet Pub. Corp. [c.1960] 186p. illus. 21cm. 60-7512 4.50
1. Callas, Maria, 1923- I. Title.

CALLAS, Evangelia. 782.1'092'4 B
My daughter Maria Callas / Evangelia Callas, in collaboration with Lawrence G. Blochman. New York : Arno Press, 1977, c1960. 186 p., [9] leaves of plates : ill., ; 23 cm. (Opera biographies) Reprint of the ed. published by Fleet Pub. Corp., New York. [ML420.C18C3 1977] 76-29928 ISBN 0-405-09671-2 : 15.00
1. Callas, Maria, 1923- 2. Singers—United States—Biography. I. Blochman, Lawrence Goldtree, 1900- joint author. II. Title. BIP

GALATOPOULOS, 782.1'092'4 B
Stelios.
Callas : prima donna assoluta / Stelios Galatopoulos. London : Allen, 1976. xviii, 353 p., [21] leaves of plates : ports. ; 24 cm. Includes index. [ML420.C18G26] 76-489321 ISBN 0-491-01518-6 : £7.50
1. Callas, Maria, 1923- 2. Singers—Biography. I. Title.

GALATOPOULOS, 782.1'0924 B
Stelios.
Callas: la Divina; art that conceals art. Elmsford, N.Y., London House & Maxwell [1970] xii, 218 p. illus. 23 cm. [ML420.C18G24 1970] 79-101607 6.50
1. Callas, Maria, 1923- I. Title.

GALATOPOULOS, Stelios 782.0924
Callas: la Divina; art that conceals art. Rev., enlarged [ed.] London, Dent, 1966. xii, 218p. front., 24 plates (incl. ports.) 23cm. [ML420.C18G24] 66-78766 8.75
1. Callas, Maria, 1923- I. Title. American distributon: Intl. Pubns. Serv., New York

JELLINEK, George, 1919- 927.8
Callas; portrait of a prima donna. New York, Ziff-Davis Pub. Co. [1960] 354p. illus. 22cm. [ML420.C18J4] 60-10526
1. Callas, Maria, 1923- I. Title. BIP

JELLINEK, George, 782.1'0924 B
1919-
Callas; portrait of a prima donna. Freeport, N.Y., Books for Libraries Press [1971, c1960] xii, 354 p. illus. 23 cm. (Biography index reprint series) [ML420.C18J4 1971] 75-179728 ISBN 0-8369-8096-4
1. Callas, Maria, 1923-

REMY, Pierre Jean. 782.1'092'4 B
Maria Callas / by Pierre-Jean Remy. New York : St. Martin's Press, 1980. p. cm. [ML420.C18R45] 79-28301 ISBN 0-312-51448-4 : 12.95
1. Callas, Maria, 1923-1977. 2. Singers—Biography. BIP

WISNESKI, Henry. 782.1'092'4 B
Maria Callas : the art behind the legend / by Henry Wisneski ; with performance annals, 1947-1974, by Arthur Germond. New York : Doubleday, 1975. x, 422 p. : ill. ; 29 cm. Includes indexes. Bibliography: p. 397-399. [ML420.C18W6] 74-18837 ISBN 0-385-07837-4 : 17.50
1. Callas, Maria, 1923- I. Germond, Arthur.

Calley, William Laws, 1943-

EVERETT, Arthur. 959.7'04'34
Calley, by Arthur Everett, Kathryn Johnson [and] Harry F. Rosenthal. [New York, Dell Pub. Co., 1971] 306 p. illus., maps, ports. 18 cm. "An Associated Press book." [DS557.A67E9] 70-25628 1.25
1. Calley, William Laws, 1943- 2. My Lai (4), Vietnam—Massacre, 1968. I. Johnson, Kathryn, joint author. II. Rosenthal, Harry F., joint author.

TIEDE, Tom. 959.7'04'34
Calley, soldier or killer? New York, Pinnacle Books [1971] 158 p. illus., ports. 18 cm. [DS557.A67T5] 75-25013 0.95
1. Calley, William Laws, 1943- 2. My lai (4), Vietnam—Massacre, 1968. I. Title.

Calloway, Cab, 1908—

CALLOWAY, Cab, 1908- 780'.92'4 B
Of Minnie the Moocher & me / Cab Calloway and Bryant Rollins ; with ill. selected and edited by John Shearer. New York : Crowell, c1976. 282 p. : ill. ; 24 cm. [ML410.C265A3] 75-45160 ISBN 0-690-01032-X : 8.95
1. Calloway, Cab, 1908- 2. Jazz musicians—Correspondence, reminiscences, etc. I. Rollins, Bryant, joint author. II. Title.

Calve, Emma, 1858-1942.

CALVE, Emma, 1858-1942. 782.1'092'4 B
My life / Emma Calve ; translated by Rosamond Gilder ; with a discography by W. R. Moran. New York : Arno Press, 1977, c1922. xiii, viii, 279 p., [18] leaves of plates : ill. ; 23 cm. (Opera biographies) Reprint of the ed. published by D. Appleton, New York. Includes index. Discography: pt. 2, p. i-vii. [ML420.C2A35 1977] 76-29929 ISBN 0-405-09672-0 : 22.00
1. Calve, Emma, 1858-1942. 2. Singers—France—Biography.

Calvert, Edward, 1799-1883.

LISTER, Raymond George 759.42
Edward Calvert. London, G. Bell [Chester Springs, Pa., Dufour, 1965, c.1962] 116p. illus. 23cm. Bibl. [N6797.C3L5] 62-53442 6.95
1. Calvert, Edward, 1799-1883. I. Title.

Calvin, Jean, 1509-1564.

ALAND, Kurt. 280'.4 B
Four reformers : Luther, Melanchthon, Calvin, Zwingli / Kurt Aland ; translated by James L. Schaff. Minneapolis : Augsburg Pub. House, c1979. 174 p. ; 20 cm. Translation of Die Reformatoren. Bibliography: p. 159-174. [BR315.A4513] 79-50091 ISBN 0-8066-1709-8 pbk. : 4.95
1. Luther, Martin, 1483-1546. 2. Melanchthon, Philipp, 1497-1560. 3. Calvin, Jean, 1509-1564. 4. Zwingli, Ulrich, 1484-1531. 5. Reformation—Biography. 6. Reformation. I. Title.

CADIER, Jean, 1898- 922.444
The man God mastered; a brief biography of John Calvin. Translated from the French by O. R. Johnston. [1st ed. in English] Grand Rapids, Eerdmans [1960] 187 p. illus. 20 cm. Translation of Calvin, l'homme que Dieu a dompte. Includes bibliography. [BX9418.C313] 61-19850
1. Calvin, Jean, 1509-1564. I. Title.

JOHN Calvin; v. 12
the man and his ethics... New York, Abingdon press [c1958] 266p. 21cm. Bibliographical footnotes.
1. Calvin, Jean, 1509-1564. 2. Calvin, Jean, 1509-1564—Ethics. I. Harkness, Georgia Elma, 1891- BIP

PARKER, Thomas Henry Louis. 230'.4'20924 B
John Calvin : a biography / by T. H. L. Parker. Philadelphia : Westminster Press, c1975. xviii, 190 p., [5] leaves of plates : ill. ; 24 cm. Includes indexes. Bibliography: p. 175-180. [BX9418.P344] 75-33302 ISBN 0-664-20810-X : 10.95
1. Calvin, Jean, 1509-1564.

PARKER, Thomas Henry Louis. 922.444
Portrait of Calvin. Philadelphia, Westminster Press [1955?] 124p. illus. 20cm. [BX9418] 55-6001
1. Calvin, Jean, 1509-1564. I. Title.

PENNING, Louwrens, 1854-1927. 922.444
Genius of Geneva; a popular account of the life and times of John Calvin. [Translated from the Dutch by B. S. Berrington] Grand Rapids, Eerdmans, 1954. 392p. illus. 23cm. [BX9418.P4313] 54-11476
1. Calvin, Jean, 1509-1564. I. Title.

RICHARD, Lucien Joseph. 230'.4'20924
The spirituality of John Calvin / Lucien Joseph Richard. Atlanta : John Knox Press, [1974] 207 p.; 23 cm. Includes index. Bibliography: p. 195-203. [BV4490.R5] 73-16920 pbk. : 5.00 ISBN 0-8042-0711-9
1. Calvin, Jean, 1509-1564. 2. Spiritual life—History of doctrines. I. Title. BIP

STICKELBERGER, Emanuel, 1884- 922.444
Calvin: a life. Translated by David Georg Gelzer. Richmond, John Knox Press [1954] 174 p. illus. 22 cm. Includes bibliography. [BX9418.S73] 54-8505
1. Calvin, Jean, 1509-1564.

VAN HALSEMA, Thea (Bouma) 922.444
This was John Calvin. Grand Rapids, Zondervan Pub. House [c.1959] 180p. illus. 21cm. 59-11834 2.95
1. Calvin, Jean, 1509-1564. I. Title.

WALKER, Williston, 1860-1922. 230'.4'20924 B
John Calvin, the organiser of reformed Protestantism, 1509-1564. New York, Schocken Books [1969] lxxvii, 456 p. 21 cm. Reprint of the 1906 ed., with a bibliographical essay by J. T. McNeill. Bibliographical footnotes. [BX9418.W3 1969] 69-20336
1. Calvin, Jean, 1509-1564.

WALKER, Williston, 1860-1922. 230'.4'20924 B
John Calvin, the organiser of reformed Protestantism, 1509-1564. New York, Putnam, 1906. [New York, AMS Press, 1972] xvi, 456 p. 19 cm. Original ed. issued in series: Heroes of the Reformation. Includes bibliographical references. [BX9418.W3 1972] 78-177878 ISBN 0-404-06807-3 8.50
1. Calvin, Jean, 1509-1564. I. Title.

Calvin, Jean, 1509-1564—Sociology.

GRAHAM, W. Fred, 1930- 261.8
The constructive revolutionary; John Calvin & his socio-economic impact, by W. Fred Graham. Richmond, John Knox Press [1971] 251 p. port. 21 cm. Bibliography: p. [243]-251. [BX9418.G7] 72-107321 ISBN 0-8042-0880-8 7.95
1. Calvin, Jean, 1509-1564—Sociology. I. Title. BIP

Calvocoressi, Michel D., 1877-1944.

CALVOCORESSI, Michel D., 1877-1944. 780'.9
Music and ballet : recollections of M. D. Calvocoressi. New York : AMS Press, 1978. 320 p., [15] leaves of plates : ill. ; 23 cm. "First published ... with the title Musicians gallery." Reprint of the 1934 ed. published by Faber and Faber, London. Includes index. [ML423.C22A3 1978] 74-24053 ISBN 0-404-12877-7 : 19.00
1. Calvocoressi, Michel D., 1877-1944. 2. Music critics—Biography. 3. Music—France—Paris. 4. Music—England—London. 5. Ballet. I. Title.

Cama, Kharshedji Rustomji, 1831-1909.

EDWARDES, Stephen Meredyth, 1873-1927. v. 12
Kharshedji Rustamji Cama, 1831-1909; a memoir, by S. M. Edwardes. [n. p.] Printed at the Oxford University Press, 1923. viii, 156 p. port. 23 cm. Bibliography: p. [149]-150. [BL1560.C3E3] 65-59525
1. Cama, Kharshedji Rustomji, 1831-1909. I. Title.

Cambaceres, Jean Jacques Regis de, 1753-1824.

BOULIND, Richard, 1938- 944.05'092'4 B
Cambaceres and the Bonapartes : unpublished papers of Jean-Jacques-Regis Cambaceres, second consul and later arch-chancellor, relating to the Emperor Napoleon and his circle : a calendar / by Richard Boulind. New York : H. P. Kraus, 1976. 157 p. : port. ; 23 cm. Contents.Contents.—Cambaceres' letters to Napoleon, 1805-1814.—Papers on the personal and dynastic interests of Napoleon. [DC198.C2B68] 76-3775 ISBN 0-916568-07-5 pbk. : 9.00
1. Cambaceres, Jean Jacques Regis de, 1753-1824. 2. Napoleon I, Emperor of the French, 1769-1821. 3. France—History—Consulate and Empire, 1799-1815—Sources. I. Cambaceres, Jean Jacques Regis de, 1753-1824. II. Title.

Cambon, Paul, 1843-1924.

EUBANK, Keith 923.244
Paul Cambon; master diplomatist . Norman, University of Oklahoma Press [c.1960] xiii, 221p. illus., ports., maps. Bibl. 60-13479 4.00
1. Cambon, Paul, 1843-1924. 2. France—For. rel.—1870- I. Title.

Cambridge, Eng.—Soc. life & cust.

RAVERAT, Gwendolen Mary (Darwin) 1885- 927.6
Period piece. New York, Norton [1953, c1952] 281p. illus. 22cm. Autobiographical. [NE1217.R3A2 1953] 53-10830
1. Cambridge, Eng.—Soc. life & cust. I. Title.

RAVERAT, Gwendolen Mary (Darwin) 1885- 927.6
Period piece. Garden City, N. Y., Doubleday [1961, c.1952] 240p. illus. (Dolphin bk., C273) .95 pap.,
1. Cambridge, Eng.—Soc. life & cust. I. Title. BIP

Cambridge, N.Z.—Biography.

WILKINSON, Ruth Webb. 919.312'2
"First families of Cambridge" 1864-1899. Cambridge - inside 1971. The industrial development of Carter's Flat compiled and written by Ruth Wilkinson [Cambridge] Cambridge Historical Society, 1972. 167 p. illus., ports. 26 cm. [DU430.C27W5] 74-153156
1. Cambridge, N.Z.—Biography. I. Cambridge Historical Society, Cambridge, N.Z. II. Title.

Cambridge Platonists.

DE PAULEY, William Cecil, 1893- 230.3'0922
The candle of the Lord; studies in the Cambridge Platonists. Freeport, N.Y., Books for Libraries Press [1970] vii, 248 p. 23 cm. (Essay index reprint series) Reprint of the 1937 ed. Contents.Contents.—Benjamin Whichcote.—Benjamin Whichcote and Jeremy Taylor.—John Smith.—Ralph Cudworth.—Henry More.—Richard Cumberland.—Nathanael Culverwel.—George Rust.—Edward Stillingfleet.—Additional notes: John Calvin.—Lancelot Andrewes: Excerpt on the candle of the Lord.—William Laud: Excerpt on Scripture. Includes bibliographical references. [B1133.C2D46 1970] 75-107693
1. Cambridge Platonists. 2. Philosophy and religion. I. Title.

Cambridge. University—Biog.

EMDEN, Alfred Brotherston, 1888- 378.42
A biographical register of the University of Cambridge to 1500. [New York] Cambridge [c.]1963. xi, 695p. facsim. 25cm. 63-24688 25.00
1. Cambridge. University—Biog. I. Title. BIP

EMDEN, Alfred Brotherston, 1888- 378.42
A biographical register of the University of Cambridge to 1500. Cambridge [Eng.] University Press, 1963. xi, 695 p. facsim. 25 cm. [LF113.E4] 63-24688
1. Cambridge. University — Biog. I. Title.

Cambridge. University. Cavendish Laboratory.

THOMSON, Joseph John, Sir, 1856-1940. 530'.092'4 B
Recollections and reflections / by J. J. Thomson. New York : Arno Press, 1975, c1936. viii, 451 p., [9] leaves of plates : ill. ; 23 cm. (History, philosophy, and sociology of science) Reprint of the ed. published by G. Bell, London. Includes indexes. [QC16.T45A3 1975] 74-26297 ISBN 0-405-06622-8
1. Cambridge. University. Cavendish Laboratory. 2. Physicists—Correspondence, reminiscences, etc. 3. Physics—History. I. Title. II. Series. BIP

Cambridge. University—Literary associations.

INCE, Richard Basil, 1881- 821'.8'09
Calverley and some Cambridge wits of the nineteenth century, by Richard B. Ince. [Folcroft, Pa.] Folcroft Library Editions, 1971. 258 p. ports. 24 cm. Reprints of the 1929 ed. [PR583.I6 1971] 72-191802
1. Cambridge. University—Literary associations. 2. Poets, English—19th century—Biography. I. Title. BIP

INCE, Richard Basil, 1881- 821'.8'09
Calverley and some Cambridge wits of the nineteenth century / by Richard B. Ince. Folcroft, Pa. : Folcroft Library Editions, 1974. 258 p. : port. ; 23 cm. Reprint of the 1929 ed. published by G. Richards and H. Toulmin at the Cayne Press, London. Includes index. Bibliography: p. 5. [PR583.I6 1974] 74-28333 ISBN 0-8414-0887-4 lib. bdg. : 17.50
1. Cambridge. University—Literary associations. 2. Poets, English—19th century—Biography. I. Title.

Camelin, Emelie Eugenie (Tavernier) 1800-1851.

BURTON, Katherine (Kurz) 1890- 922.271
The table of the King; the story of Mother Gamelin, foundress of the Sisters of Charity of Providence. New York, McMullen Books [1952] 244p. illus. 21cm. [BX4705.G22B8] 53-1399
1. Camelin, Emelie Eugenie (Tavernier) 1800-1851. 2. Sisters of Charity of Providence. I. Title.

Camelot (Yacht)

MCCAIN, Laura E. 910'.45 B
Waterspout / by Laura E. McCain. Los Angeles : Crescent, c1976. 223 p. : map ; 22 cm. Autobiographical. [G477.M32] 76-27138 ISBN 0-89144-021-6 pbk. : 3.95
1. Camelot (Yacht) 2. McCain, Laura E. I. Title. BIP

Cameron, Donald, Sir, 1872-1948.

GAILEY, Harry A. 325'.342'09669 B
Sir Donald Cameron, colonial governor [by] Harry A. Gailey. Stanford, Calif., Hoover Institution Press [1974] p. cm. (Hoover Institution publications, 139) (Hoover colonial studies) Bibliography: p. [JV1009.C35G3] 74-7301 ISBN 0-8179-1391-2 9.00
1. Cameron, Donald, Sir, 1872-1948. I. Title. II. Series. III. Series: Stanford University. Hoover Institution on War, Revolution, and Peace. Publications, 139.

Cameron family.

ROSE, Louise Frances 929'.2'0973
Cameron, 1868-1954.
The Cameron family: a history of the descendants of John and Mary (Fraser) Cameron of Inverness, Scotland (to about 1784 and after that) of Princetown, Schenectady County, New York, U.S.A. Compiled to 1903 by Louise Frances (Cameron) Rose and Alexander G. Rose, Jr., and continued to 1973 by Alexander G. Rose III. [Baltimore? 1973] xix, 98 l. mounted ports. 28 cm. "Copy 88 of 90." [CS71.C177 1973] 73-159480
1. Cameron family. I. Rose, Alexander Grant, 1876-1949, joint author. II. Rose, Alexander Grant, 1913-

WHITE, Andrea 929'.2'0973 S
Hickman, 1942-
The Camerons / compiled by Andrea Hickman White. [Maitland? Fla.] : White, c1976. 40 p. : ill. ; 22 cm. (Her A sense of past ; v. 1) Includes bibliographical references and index. [CS71.C177a vol. 1] 929'.2'0973 76-379433
1. Cameron family. 2. United States—Genealogy. I. Title.

Cameron, James, 1911-

CAMERON, James, 915.4'04'40924 B
1911-
An Indian summer. New York, McGraw-Hill [1974] 223 p. 23 cm. Autobiographical. [DS414.C33 1974] 74-6396 ISBN 0-07-009673-2 7.95
1. Cameron, James, 1911- 2. India—Description and travel—1947- I. Title.

CAMERON, James, 1911- 070'.924
Point of departure; an attempt at autobiography. [1st ed.] New York, McGraw-Hill [1967] 318 p. 22 cm. [PN5123.C2A32 1967b] 67-30051
I. Title.

Cameron, Julia Margaret Pattle, 1815-1879.

CAMERON, Julia 779'.2'0924
Margaret Pattle, 1815-1879.
The Cameron collection / Julia Margaret Cameron ; with an introd. by Colin Ford. New York : Van Nostrand Reinhold, 1975. p. cm. Includes bibliographical references. [TR681.F3C35 1975] 75-26000 ISBN 0-442-20312-8 : 30.00
1. Cameron, Julia Margaret Pattle, 1815-1879. 2. Photography—Portraits. 3. Great Britain—Biography—Portraits. I. Title.

GERNSHEIM, Helmut, 779'.092'4 B
1913-
Julia Margaret Cameron : her life and photographic work / Helmut Gernsheim. [2d ed.]. Millerton, N.Y. : Aperture, [1975] 200 p. : ill. ; 28 cm. Includes index. Bibliography: p. 195-196. [TR140.C27G47 1975] 73-85258 ISBN 0-912334-50-9 : 20.00. ISBN 0-912334-51-7 pbk. : 12.50
1. Cameron, Julia Margaret Pattle, 1815-1879. 2. Photography, Artistic. 3. Photography—Portraits. **BIP**

HILL, Brian, 1896- 929'.2'0942
Julia Margaret Cameron; a Victorian family portrait. New York, St. Martin's Press [1973] 203 p. illus. 23 cm. Bibliography: p. 197-200. [TR140.C27H54 1973b] 73-79603 8.95
1. Cameron, Julia Margaret (Pattle) 1815-1879. I. Title.

A Victorian album : 779'.2'0942
Julia Margaret Cameron and her circle / edited by Graham Ovenden ; introductory essay by David Cecil. 1st American ed. New York : Da Capo Press, 1975. vii, 252 p. : chiefly ill. ; 34 cm. Includes index. [TR681.F3V52 1975b] 75-18728 ISBN 0-306-70749-7 : 60.00
1. Cameron, Julia Margaret Pattle, 1815-1879. 2. Photography—Portraits. 3. Great Britain—Biography—Portraits. I. Ovenden, Graham. **BIP**

Cameron, Simon, 1799-1889.

BRADLEY, Erwin Stanley. 973.0924
Simon Cameron, Lincoln's Secretary of War; a political biography. Philadelphia, University of Pennsylvania Press [1966] 451 p. illus., ports. 22 cm. Bibliography: p. [425]-438. [E415.9.C18B7] 65-20756
1. Cameron, Simon, 1799-1889. I. Title.

Cameroons—Description and travel.

MACKENZIE, Jean 916.7'11'032
Kenyon, 1874-1936.
Black sheep; adventures in West Africa. New York, Negro Universities Press [1969] vii, 313 p. illus. 22 cm. Reprint of the 1916 ed. [DT567.M2 1969] 70-89008
1. Cameroons—Description and travel. 2. Missions—Cameroons. I. Title. **BIP**

Camillus de Lellis, Saint, 1550-1614.

CURLEY, Edmund F. 922.245
St. Camillus. Milwaukee, Bruce [c.1962] 168p. 22cm. 62-18225 3.25
1. Camillus de Lellis, Saint, 1550-1614. I. Title.

ERNEST, Brother, 1897- 922.245
The Red Cross saint; a story of St. Camillus de Lellis. Illus. by Mary Jean Zalesak. Notre Dame, Ind., Dujarie Press [1950] 87 p. illus. 24 cm. [BX4700.C18E7] 50-945
1. Camillus de Lellis, Saint, 1550-1614. I. Title.

Camp family.

MANN, Robert Neville, 1904- 929.2
Camp-Kemp family history, by Robert Neville Mann and Cathrine Cleek Mann. Cedar Bluff, Ala., 1967- v. 29 cm. Includes bibliographical references. [CS71.C178 1967] 67-19366
1. Camp family. I. Mann, Cathrine (Cleek) 1921- joint author. II. Title.

Camp, Walter Chauncery, 1859-1925.

POWEL, Harford 796.332'0924 B
Willing Hare, 1887-1956.
Walter Camp, the father of American football; an authorized biography. With an introd. by E. K. Hall. Freeport, N.Y., Books for Libraries Press [1970] ix, 238 p. ports. 23 cm. Reprint of the 1926 ed. [GV939.C34P6 1970] 70-126246
1. Camp, Walter Chauncery, 1859-1925.

Campanella, Joe, 1930-1967.

SWEET, Ben C. 796.33'2'0924 B
Man he was, by Ben C. Sweet. [Cockeysville, Md., Printed by Universal Lithographers, c1972] 119 p. ports. 22 cm. [GV939.C35S93] 72-96487
1. Campanella, Joe, 1930-1967. I. Title.

Campanella, Roy, 1921-

CAMPANELLA, Roy 927.96357
It's good to be alive. [New York] Dell Pub. Co. [1960, c.1959] 288p. illus. 17cm. (F108) .50 pap.,
I. Title. **BIP**

CAMPANELLA, Roy, 1921- 927.96357
It's good to be alive. [1st ed.] Boston, Little, Brown [1959] 306 p. illus. 21 cm. [GV865.C3A3] 59-11889
I. Title.

CAMPANELLA, Roy, 796.357'0924 [B]
1921-
It's good to be alive. [New York] New American Library [1974, c.1959] 288 p. illus. 18 cm. (Signet Book, Y5952) [GV865.C3A3] 1.25 (pbk.)
I. Title.
L.C. card no. for the hardbound edition: 59-11889.

SCHOOR, Gene. 927.96357
Roy Campanella, man of courage. New York, Putnam [1959] 190 p. 21 cm. [GV865.C3S37] 59-8173
1. Campanella, Roy, 1921-

SHAPIRO, Milton J. 796.3570924
The Roy Campanella story. New York, Messner [1958] 192 p. illus. 22 cm. [GV865.C3S45] 927 58-10932
1. Campanella, Roy, 1921- I. Title.

YOUNG, Dick. 927.96357
Roy Campanella. New York, A. S. Barnes [1952] 184 p. illus. 21 cm. (Most valuable player series) [GV865.C3Y6] 52-6333
1. Campanella, Roy, 1921-

Campanella, Tommaso, 1568-1639.

BONANSEA, Bernardino M. 195
Tommaso Campanella; Renaissance pioneer of modern thought, by Bernardino M. Bonansea. Washington, Catholic University of America Press [1969] xi, 421 p. port. 25 cm. Bibliography: p. 403-416. [B785.C24B6] 78-76125 14.50
1. Campanella, Tommaso, 1568-1639.

GRILLO, Francesco. 921.5
Tommasco Campanella in America; a critical bibliography and a profile. New York, S. F. Vanni [1954] 110p. port. 21cm. [B785.C24G7] 55-18142
1. Campanella, Tommaso, 1568-1639. I. Title.

GRILLO, Francesco, 1898- 921.5
Tommaso Campanella in America; a critical bibliography and a profile. New York, S. F. Vanni [1954] New York, S. F. Vanni [1957] 110p. port. 21cm. 48p. 22cm. [B785.C24G7] 55-18142
1. Campanella, Tommaso, 1568-1639. I. Title. II. Title: —A supplement to the critical bibliography.

Campbell, Alastair Guy Spens, 1919-1944.

BUCHAN, Alastair. 923.542
Twenty-five years, 1919-44, Major Alastair Guy Spens Campbell, M.C. F. R. S., by Alistair Buchan and Oliver Villiers. [Welwyn Garden City? Herts., 1951] 87 p. illus. 23 cm. [CT788.C197B8] 52-22810
1. Campbell, Alastair Guy Spens, 1919-1944. I. Title.

Campbell, Alexander, 1788-1866.

FITCH, Alger 286'.6'0924 B
Morton.
Alexander Campbell, preacher of reform and reformer of preaching [by] Alger Morton Fitch, Jr. Austin, Tex., Sweet Pub. Co. [1970] 134 p. illus., facsims., port. 21 cm. Bibliography: p. 119-134. [BX7343.C2F5] 70-113160 ISBN 0-8344-0060-X
1. Campbell, Alexander, 1788-1866. I. Title.

GRESHAM, Perry Epler, 922.673
comp.
The sage of Bethany; a pioneer in broadcloth. St. Louis, Bethany Press [c.1960] 189p. (Bibl. footnotes 22cm. 60-14651 1.95 pap.,
1. Campbell, Alexander, 1788-1866. 2. Bethany College, Bethany, W.Va. I. Title.

LINDLEY, Denton Ray. 922.673
Apostle of freedom. St. Louis, Bethany Press [1957] 264p. 23cm. Includes bibliography. [BX7343.C2L5] 57-11967
1. Campbell, Alexander 1788-1866. I. Title.

Campbell-Bannerman, Henry, Sir, 1836-1908.

WILSON, John, 942.082'092'4 B
1924-
CB: a life of Sir Henry Campbell-Bannerman. New York, St. Martin's Press [1974, c1973] 717 p. illus. 25 cm. Bibliography: p. 643-653. [DA565.C15W54 1974] 73-85379 15.00
1. Campbell-Bannerman, Henry, Sir, 1836-1908. I. Title.

Campbell, Beatrice Stella (Tanner) 1865-1940.

CAMPBELL, Beatrice 790.2'0924
Stella (Tanner) 1865-1940.
My life and some letters, by Mrs. Patrick Campbell (Beatrice Stella Cornwallis-West) ... New York, Dodd, Mead and company, 1922. 5 p. l., 451 p. front., illus., plates, ports. 25 cm. [PN2598,C23A3] 22-22417
1. Actors—Correspondence, reminiscences, etc. I. Title.

CAMPBELL, 792'.028'0924 B
Beatrice Stella (Tanner) 1865-1940.
My life and some letters, by Mrs. Patrick Campbell (Beatrice Stella Cornwallis-West) New York, B. Blom [1969] 451 p. ports. 24 cm. Reprint of the 1922 ed. [PN2598.C23A3 1969] 71-83102
1. Actresses—Correspondence, reminiscences, etc. I. Title. **BIP**

DENT, Alan. 792'.028'0924
Mrs. Patrick Campbell. Westport, Conn., Greenwood Press [1973, c1961] 333 p. illus. 22 cm. Bibliography: p. 321-324. [PN2598.C23D4 1973] 72-9046 ISBN 0-8371-6560-1
1. Campbell, Beatrice Stella (Tanner) 1865-1940. **BIP**

Campbell, Donald, 1921-1967.

KNOWLES, Arthur. 797.1'4'0924
Donald Campbell C.B.E., by Arthur Knowles and Dorothy, Lady Campbell. [1st American ed.] South Brunswick [N.J.] A. S. Barnes [1970, c1969] 134 p. illus., ports. 22 cm. [GV835.K56 1970] 71-86321 4.95
1. Campbell, Donald, 1921-1967. I. Campbell, Dorothy (Whittall) Lady, joint author.

PEARSON, John, 1930- 796.720924
The last hero; the gallant story of Donald Campbell and the land speed record, 1964, by John Pearson. New York, D. McKay Co. [1966] 218 p. 21 cm. [GV1032.C25P4] 66-10675
1. Campbell, Donald, 1921- I. Title.

PEARSON, John George, 796.720924
1930-
The last hero; the gallant story of Donald Campbell and the land speed record, 1964. New York, McKay [c.1966] 218p. 21cm. [GV1032.C25P4] 66-10675 4.50
1. Campbell, Donald, 1921- I. Title.

Campbell, Duncan, 1680?-1730.

DEFOE, Daniel, 133.3'2'0924 B
1661?-1731.
The history of the life and adventures of Mr. Duncan Campbell. Edited by George A. Aitken, with illus. by J. B. Yeats. London, Dent, 1895. [New York, AMS Press, 1974] xxxii, 267 p. illus. 19 cm. Original ed. issued as v. 4 of the author's Romances and narratives. [BF1815.C2D4 1974] 74-13463 ISBN 0-404-07914-8
1. Campbell, Duncan, 1680?-1730. I. Title. **BIP**

Campbell family.

CAMPBELL, Arthur 929'.2'0973
Price, 1897-
Campbell family history, 1715-1973; descendants of Thomas Campbell, Sr., compiled by Arthur Price Campbell. [Verona? Va., 1973] 109 p. illus. 24 cm. [CS71.C19 1973b] 74-156283
1. Campbell family. I. Title.

CAMPBELL, Harlan 929.2'0973
Rogers, 1899-
The Campbell family; some of the descendants of William Campbell of Bergen County, 1718 to 1969. [Pleasant Valley, N.Y.] 1969. 1 v. (various pagings) map, port. 29 cm. [CS71.C19 1969] 78-18689
1. Campbell family.

CAMPBELL, Horace 929.2'0973
Gibson, 1896-
The Campbell story; a history of Thomas

Brown Campbell and his descendants. [Mesa? Ariz., 1970] 1 v. (loose-leaf) illus., coat of arms, facsims., geneal. tables, ports. 28 cm. [CS71.C19 1970b] 73-19989
1. Campbell family. I. Title.

Campbell, Glen.

KRAMER, Freda. 784'.0924 B
The Glen Campbell story. New York [Pyramid Publications, 1970] 125 p. ports. 18 cm. [ML420.C22K7] 73-9637 0.75
1. Campbell, Glen. I. Title.

Campbell, James Duncan, 1833-1907.

CAMPBELL, Robert Ronald, d.1961. 951'.03'0924 B
James Duncan Campbell; a memoir by his son. Cambridge, Mass., East Asian Research Center, Harvard University; distributed by Harvard University Press, 1970. xix, 125 p. 26 cm. (Harvard East Asian monographs, 38) [DS763.C25C3 1970] 72-123565 ISBN 0-674-47131-8
1. Campbell, James Duncan, 1833-1907. I. Title. II. Series.

Campbell, John Charles, 1867-1919.

CAMPBELL, Olive Arnold (Dame) 1882-1954. 285'.1'0924 B
The life and work of John Charles Campbell, September 15, 1868-May 2, 1919. [Madison, Wis., Printed by College Printing & Typing Co., 1968] viii, 657 p. map. 28 cm. [BX9225.C28C3] 68-6039
1. Campbell, John Charles, 1867-1919. I. Title.

Campbell, Malcolm, Sir, 1885-1948.

VILLA, Leo, 1899- 796.7'2'0922
The record breakers: Sir Malcolm and Donald Campbell, land and water speed kings of the 20th century [by] Leo Villa & Tony Gray. London, New York, Hamlyn, 1969. 160 p. illus., ports. 29 cm. Bibliography: p. 146. [GV1032.C27V5] 79-487937 42/-
1. Campbell, Malcolm, Sir, 1885-1948. 2. Campbell, Donald, 1921-1967. I. Gray, Tony, joint author. II. Title.

Campbell, Robert, 1769-1846.

STEVEN, Margaret. 380.10924 B
Merchant Campbell, 1769-1846; a study of colonial trade. Melbourne, New York, Oxford University Press, 1965. xii, 360 p. illus., map, ports. 23 cm. Bibliography: p. 338-347. [HC602.5.C3S75] 66-4917
1. Campbell, Robert, 1769-1846. I. Title.

Campbell, Robert, 1769-1846—Juvenile literature.

PARK, Ruth. 380'.1'0924 B
Merchant Campbell / by Ruth Park ; illustrated by Edwina Bell. Sydney : Collins, 1976. 62 p. : ill. ; 26 cm. (Australians in history series) [HF3944.5.C35P37] 77-365482 ISBN 0-00-195029-0
1. Campbell, Robert, 1769-1846—Juvenile literature. 2. Merchants—Australia—New South Wales—Biography—Juvenile literature. I. Title.

Campbell, Robin, 1959-—Juvenile literature.

JACOBS, Linda. 796.4'26 B
Robin Campbell : joy in the morning / by Linda Jacobs. St. Paul, Minn. : EMC Corp., 1976. 40 p. : ill. ; 23 cm. (Women who win ; 4) A biography of a Washington, D.C., girl whose ability to run has opened up new worlds for her. [GV697.C34J32] 92 76-8446 ISBN 0-88436-238-8 lib.bdg. : 4.95 pbk. : 2.95
1. Campbell, Robin, 1959- —Juvenile literature. 2. Track-athletics for women—Juvenile literature. I. Title. BIP

Campbell, Roy, 1901-1957—Biography.

CAMPBELL, Roy, 1901- 928.2
Light on a dark horse; an autobiography (1901-1935) Chicago, H. Regnery Co., 1952. 312 p. illus. 22 cm. [PR6005.A418Z52 1952] 52-12844
I. Title.

CAMPBELL, Roy, 1901-1957. 821 B
Broken record : reminiscences / by Roy Campbell. St. Clair Shores, Mich. : Scholarly Press, 1978. 208 p. ; 21 cm. Reprint of the 1934 ed. published by Boriswood, London. [PR9369.3.C35Z465 1978] 70-131657 ISBN 0-403-00544-2 : 22.00
1. Campbell, Roy, 1901-1957—Biography. 2. Poets, South African—20th century—Biography. I. Title.

Campbell, Sir Malcolm, 1885-1949.

CAMPBELL, Dorothy (Whittall) Lady. 926.292
Malcolm Campbell, the man as I knew him. London, New York, Hutchinson [1951] 232 p. illus. 24 cm. [GV1029.C3C3] 52-17010
1. Campbell, Sir Malcolm, 1885-1949. 2. Automobile racing. I. Title.

Campbell, Thomas, 1763-1854.

MCALLISTER, Lester G 922.673
Thomas Campbell: man of the Book. St. Louis, Bethany Press [1954] 294p. illus. 23cm. [Bethany history series] [BX7343.C2M3] 54-14506
1. Campbell, Thomas, 1763-1854. I. Title.

Campbell, Thomas, 1777-1844.

BEATTIE, William, 1793-1875. 821'.7 B
Life and letters of Thomas Campbell. Edited by William Beattie. London, E. Moxon, 1849. [New York, AMS Press, 1973] 3 v. illus. 23 cm. [PR4413.B3 1973] 70-161729 ISBN 0-404-07630-0 55.00
1. Campbell, Thomas, 1777-1844. I. Title. BIP

Campbell, Thomas, 1777-1844—Biography.

†STODDARD, Richard Henry, 1825-1903, ed. 828'.7'09 B
Personal recollections of Lamb, Hazlitt, and others / edited by Richard Henry Stoddard. Folcroft, Pa. : Folcroft Library Editions, 1976 [c1875] xxii, 322 p. [4] leaves of plates : ill. ; 24 cm. Selections from My friends and acquaintance, by P. G. Patmore. Reprint of the ed. published by Scribner, Armstrong, New York, which was issued as no. 9 of the Bric-a-brac series. Includes index. [PR105.S74 1976] 76-17557 ISBN 0-8414-7623-3 lib. bdg. : 27.50
1. Lamb, Charles, 1775-1834—Biography. 2. Haylett, William, 1778-1830—Biography. 3. Campbell, Thomas, 1777-1844—Biography. 4. Blessington, Marguerite Power Farmer Gardiner, Countess of, 1789-1849—Biography. 5. Authors, English—19th century—Correspondence, reminiscences, etc. I. Patmore, Peter George, 1786-1855. My friends and acquaintance. Selections. 1976. II. Title. III. Series: Bric-a-brac series ; no. 9. BIP

Campbell, Will D.

CAMPBELL, Will D. 323.4'092'4 B
Brother to a dragonfly / Will D. Campbell. New York : Seabury Press, 1977. p. cm. (A Continuum book) [BX6495.C28A33] 77-8339 ISBN 0-8164-9321-9 : 8.95
1. Campbell, Will D. 2. Campbell, Joseph Lee. 3. Baptists—Clergy—Biography. 4. Clergy—Mississippi—Biography. 5. Pharmacists—Mississippi—Meridian—Biography. 6. Meridian, Miss.—Biography. 7. Afro-Americans—Civil rights. 8. Civil rights workers—Mississippi—Biography. I. Title. BIP

Campion, Edmund, 1540-1581.

GARDINER, Harold Charles, 1904- 922.242
Edmund Campion, hero of God's underground. Illustrated by Rose Goudket. New York, Vision Books [1957] 189 p. illus. 22 cm. (Visions books, 17) [BX4705.C27G3] 57-5123
1. Campion, Edmund, 1540-1581.

HAGEMANN, Gerard, 1922- 922.242
Hero of the gallows, a story of blessed Edmund Campion, Illus. by Brother Bernard Howard. Notre Dame, Ind., Dujarie Press [1953] 87p. illus. 24cm. [BX4705.C27H3] 53-2390
1. Campion, Edmund, 1540-1581. I. Title.

WAUGH, Evelyn, 1903- 922.242
Edmund Campion. Garden City, N.Y., Image Books [1956, c1946] 196 p. 18 cm. (A Doubleday image book D34) [[BX4705]] 56-13671
1. Campion, Edmund, 1540-1581. I. Title.

Campion, Thomas, 1567-1620.

KASTENDIECK, Miles Merwin 927.8
England's musical poet. Thomas Campion. New York, Russell, 1963[c.1938] 203p. illus. 23cm. Bibl. 6.00
1. Campion, Thomas, 1567-1620. 2. Music and literature. 3. Lyric poetry—Hist. & crit. 4. English poetry—Early modern (to1700)—Hist. & crit. I. Title.

LOWBURY, Edward Joseph Lister. 784'.0924
Thomas Campion: poet, composer, physician, by Edward Lowbury, Timothy Salter, and Alison Young. New York, Barnes & Noble [1970] viii, 195 p. illus., facsims., music, 2 plates. 23 cm. Bibliography: p. 185-186. [PR2229.L6 1970b] 78-20216 ISBN 0-389-03999-3 7.50
1. Campion, Thomas, 1567-1620. 2. Music and literature. I. Salter, Timothy, joint author. II. Young, Alison, joint author. III. Title.

Campistron, Jean Galbert de, 1656-1723.

JONES, Dorothy F., 1927- 842'.4 B
Jean de Campistron, a study of his life and work / by Dorothy F. Jones. University, Miss. : Romance Monographs, 1979. 235 p., [1] leaf of plates : port. ; 23 cm. (Romance monographs ; no. 32) Includes index. Bibliography: p. [224]-231. [PQ1735.C2J6] 78-12575 14.50
1. Campistron, Jean Galbert de, 1656-1723. 2. Dramatists, French—17th century—Biography.

Camus, Albert, 1913-1960.

BREE, Germaine. 843'.9'14 [B]
Albert Camus. New York, Columbia University Press, 1964. 48 p. 21 cm. (Columbia essays on modern writers, no. 1) Bibliography: p. 47-48. [PQ2605.A3734Z55] 64-22637
1. Camus, Albert, 1913-1960. I. Title. II. Series.

BREE, Germaine. 840.81
Camus. New Brunswick, N. J., Rutgers University Press, 1959. 275 p. 22 cm. [PQ2605.A3734Z555] 58-10829
1. Camus, Albert, 1913-1960.

BREE, Germaine. 848.914
Camus. New Brunswick, N. J., Rutgers University Press, 1961. 281 p. 22 cm. [PQ2605.A3734Z555 1961] 61-3575
1. Camus, Albert, 1913-1960.

BREE, Germaine. v. 12
Camus. [Rev. ed.] New Brunswick, N. J., Rutgers University Press, 1961. xii, 281 p. 22 cm. Bibliography: p. 257-268. 68-33775
1. Camus, Albert, I. Title.

BREE, Germaine. 848.912
Camus. Rev. ed. New York, Harcourt, Brace & World [1964] viii, 280 p. 21 cm. Bibliography: p. 256-267. [PQ2605.A3734Z62] 64-57305
1. Camus, Albert, 1913-1960. I. Title.

BREE, Germaine. 848'.9'1409
Camus. Rev. ed. New Brunswick, N.J., Rutgers University Press [1972] viii, 281 p. 22 cm. Bibliography: p. 256-268. [PQ2605.A3734Z555 1972] 72-178591 ISBN 0-8135-0359-0 7.50
1. Camus, Albert, 1913-1960. I. Title.

LEBESQUE, Morvan, 1911- 848.9'1409 B
Portrait of Camus; an illustrated biography. Translated by T. C. Sharman. [New York] Herder and Herder [1971] 174 p. illus. 21 cm. Translation of Camus par lui-meme, which was first published under title: Albert Camus par lui-meme. Bibliography: p. 173-174. [PQ2605.A3734Z6813] 70-167863 6.95
1. Camus, Albert, 1913-1960. I. Title.

LUPPE, Robert de. 848'.9'1408
Albert Camus. Translated from the French by John Cumming and J. Hargreaves. [1st American ed.] New York, Funk & Wagnalls [1968, c1966] 101 p. 21 cm. Bibliography: p. 91-101. [PQ2605.A3734Z703 1968] 68-22177
1. Camus, Albert, 1913-1960.

O'BRIEN, Conor Cruise, 1917- 843'.9'14
Albert Camus of Europe and Africa. New York, Viking Press [1970] 116 p. 20 cm. (Modern masters) [PQ2605.A3734Z7225] 78-104141 ISBN 0-670-11177-5 4.95
1. Camus, Albert, 1913-1960. I. Title.

PETERSEN, Carol. 843'.9'12 B
Albert Camus. Translated by Alexander Gode. New York, F. Ungar Pub. Co. [1969] vii, 122 p. 21 cm. (Modern literature monographs) Bibliographical references included in "Notes" (p. 119-122) [PQ2605.A3734Z7273] 68-31455 4.50
1. Camus, Albert, 1913-1960.

THODY, Philip. 928.4
Albert Camus 1913-1960. New York, Macmillan [1962, c1961] 242 p. illus. 23 cm. [[PQ2605.A3734Z737 1962]] 62-960
1. Camus, Albert, 1913-1960. I. Title.

Camus, Albert, 1913-1960—Biography.

LOTTMAN, Herbert R. 848'.9'1409 B
Albert Camus : a biography / Herbert R. Lottman. 1st ed. Garden City, N.Y. : Doubleday, 1979. xii, 753 p., [8] leaves of plates : ill. ; 24 cm. Includes bibliographical references and index. [PQ2605.A3734Z698] 78-8199 ISBN 0-385-11664-0 : 16.95
1. Camus, Albert, 1913-1960—Biography. 2. Authors, French—20th century—Biography.

Canada—Biography.

BISSELL, Claude T. ed. 920.071
Our living tradition: seven Canadians. [Toronto] Pub. in association with Carleton Univ. by Univ. of Toronto Pr. [1962, c.1957] x, 149p. 22cm. (Canadian Univ. paperbk., 5) 1.75 pap.,
1. Canada—Biog. I. Title.

BISSELL, Claude Thomas, 1916- ed. 920.071
Our living tradition; seven Canadians. [Toronto] Published in association with Carleton University by University of Toronto Press [c1957] x., 149 p. 22 cm. "Given as public lectures at Carleton University." [F1005.B586] A58
1. Canada—Biog. I. Title.
Contents Omitted

KARR, William John. 920.02
Explorers, soldiers, and statesmen; a history of Canada through biography. Freeport, N.Y., Books for Libraries Press [1970] xii, 332 p. illus., maps, ports. 23 cm. (Essay index reprint series) Reprint of the 1938 ed. [F1026.K27 1970] 79-108640
1. Canada—Biography. 2. Canada—History. I. Title.

LOCKE, George Herbert, 1870-1937. 920.071
Builders of the Canadian Commonwealth. with an introd. by A. H. U. Colquhoun. Freeport, N.Y., Books for Libraries Press [1967] xiii, 317 p. 22 cm. (Essay index reprint series) [F1005.L81 1967] 67-28755
1. Canada—Biography. I. Title. BIP

MCDOUGALL, Robert L., ed. 920.071
Canada's past and present: a dialogue [Toronto] Pub. with Carleton Univ. by Univ. of Toronto Pr. [c.1965] xii, 179p. 23cm. (Our living tradition, ser. 5) [F1005.M18] 65-5414 5.95
1. Canada—Biog. I. Title. II. Title: Our living tradition, fifth series. BIP

MACMILLAN dictionary of 920.071
Canadian biography. (The) by W. Stewart Wallace. 3d ed., rev. and enl. London, Macmillan; New York, St. Martin's [c.] 1963. 820p. 25cm. Previous eds. pub. under title: The Dictionary of Canadian biography. Bibl. 64-10158 15.00
1. Canada—Biog. I. Wallace, William Stewart, 1884- ed.

VINING, Charles A. M., 920.071
1897-
Bigwigs; Canadians wise and otherwise, by Charles Vining (R.T.L.) With 37 illus. by Ivan Glassco. Freeport, N.Y., Books for Libraries Press [1968] 149 p. illus. 27 cm. (Essay index reprint series) "First published 1935." [F1005.V56 1968] 68-16984
1. Canada—Biography. 2. Caricatures and cartoons—Canada. I. Title.

WHO'S who in Canada; 920.071
1966-68. An illustrated biographical record of men and women of the time 54th year of issue. Toronto, Intl. Pr. [1967] v. ports. 19cm. Assos. eds.: 1964- H. Fraser, H. E. Barnett (with 1966-68 E. R. White):7158c0y [F1033.W62] 17-10282
1. Canada—Biog. I. Fraser, Hugh, ed. II. Barnet, Herbert E., joint ed. III. White, Edward R. joint ed.
American distributor: McKay, New York.

WHO'S who in Canada, 920.0971
1960-61; an illustrated biographical record of men and women of the time. Ed. by B.M. Greene; assoc. ed. G.W. Stratton [dist. New York, McKay, 1961, c.1960] 1502p. ports. Annual. 17-16282 25.00
1. Canada—Biog. I. Greene, Barnet M., ed. II. Stratton, G. W., joint ed.

WHO'S who in Canada, 1964- 920.071
65; an illustrated biographical record of men and women of the time. Assoc. eds.: Hugh Fraser, Herbert E. Barnett. 52d year of issue Toronto, Intl. Pr. [New York, McKay, 1965, c.1964] 1631p. ports. 20cm. [F1033.W62] 17-16282 35.00
1. Canada—Biog. I. Fraser, Hugh, ed. II. Barnett, Herbert E., joint ed.

Canada—Biography—Dictionaries.

DICTIONARY of Canadian 920'.071
biography, preliminary name list. Toronto, University of Toronto Press, [1974] v. 25 cm. Cover title. English and French. Title also in French: Dictionnaire biographique du Canada; liste provisoire des personnages. Contents.Contents.— — v. 3. 1741-1770. [F1005.D5 1970] 74-158242 20.00
1. Canada—Biography—Dictionaries. I. Title: Dictionnaire biographique du Canada; liste provisoire des personnages.

Canada—Biography—Juvenile literature.

CANADIAN portraits. 920'.071
Edited by Norman Sheffe. Toronto, New York, McGraw-Hill Ryerson [1972] 183 p. illus. 19 cm. Selections reprinted from a series of booklets issued under the general title: Canadian history readers. [F1005.C22] 74-156404 ISBN 0-07-077379-3
1. Canada—Biography—Juvenile literature. I. Sheffe, Norman, ed.

Canada—Description and travel—1763-1867.

CAMPBELL, Patrick. 917'.04'4
Travels in North America. [Edited, with an introd., by H. H. Langton, and with notes by H. H. Langton and W. F. Ganong] New York, Greenwood Press, 1968. xxi, 326 p. illus., ports. 24 cm. (Champlain Society publication 23) Facsimile of the 1937 ed. of the author's Travels in the interior inhabited parts of North America in the years 1791 and 1792, originally published in 1792. [F1013.C182 1937a] 68-28611
1. Canada—Description and travel—1763-1867. 2. U.S.—Description and travel—1783-1848. I. Langton, Hugh Hornby, 1862- ed. II. Title. III. Series: Champlain Society, Toronto. Publications, 23

HENRY, Alexander, 917.1'04'2
1739-1824.
Travels & adventures in Canada and the Indian territories; between the years 1760 and 1776. New ed. edited with notes, illustrative and biographical, by James Bain. New York, B. Franklin [1969] xxxiii, 347 p. illus., facsim., maps, ports. 23 cm. (American classics in history and social science, 74) (Burt Franklin research and source works series, 342.) Reprint of the 1901 ed. Bibliographical footnotes. [F1013.H52 1969] 76-80226
1. Canada—Description and travel—1763-1867. 2. Indians of North America—Canada. I. Title. BIP

HENRY, Alexander, 917.1'04'188
1739-1824.
Travels & adventures in Canada and the Indian territories, between the years 1760 and 1776. New ed; edited with notes, illustrative and bibliographical, by James Bain. Toronto, G. N. Morang, 1901. St. Clair Shores, Mich., Scholarly Press, 1972. xxxv, 347 p. illus. 22 cm. [F1013.H52 1972] 72-108491 ISBN 0-403-00393-8
1. Canada—Description and travel—1763-1867. 2. Indians of North America—Canada. I. Bain, James, 1842-1908, ed. II. Title. BIP

Canada—Dictionaries and encyclopedias.

COLOMBO, John Robert, 971'.003
1936-
Colombo's Canadian references / John Robert Colombo. Toronto ; New York : Oxford University Press, 1976. viii, 576 p. ; 25 cm. [F1006.C6] 77-356904 ISBN 0-19-540253-7 : 17.50
1. Canada—Dictionaries and encyclopedias. 2. Canada—Biography. I. Title. II. Title: Canadian references. BIP

Canada—Emigration and immigration—Bibliography.

SWANICK, Eric L. 016.3092 S
Canadian immigration in the late 1960's and in the 1970's : an introductory bibliography / Eric L. Swanick. Monticello, Ill. : Council of Planning Librarians, 1976. 10 p. ; 29 cm. (Exchange bibliography - Council of Planning Librarians ; 1179) Cover title. [Z5942.C68 no. 1179] [Z7164.I3] [JV7225] 016.32571 77-373391 1.50
1. Canada—Emigration and immigration—Bibliography. I. Title. II. Series: Council of Planning Librarians. Exchange bibliography ; 1179.

Canada, John William,

CANADA, John William, 1871- 926.3
Life at eighty; memories and comments by a tarheel in Texas. [La Porte, Tex., 1952] 198 p. 23 cm. [CT275.C27453A3] 52-25618
I. Title.

Canada—Politics and government—20th century.

PEARSON, Lester 971.06'43'0924 B
B.
Mike; the memoirs of the Right Honourable Lester B. Pearson. New York, Quadrangle Books [1972- v. illus. 24 cm. Half title and on spine: Memoirs. Contents.Contents.—v. 1. 1897-1948. [F1034.3.P4A35] 72-90360 12.50 (v. 1)
1. Canada—Politics and government—20th century. 2. Canada—Foreign relations. I. Title. BIP

Canada. Royal Canadian Mounted Police.

RIVETT-CARNAC, Charles. 363.20971
Pursuit in the wilderness. [1st ed.] Boston, Little, Brown [1965] vi, 343 p. map (on lining paper) 22 cm. Autobiography. [HV8157.R5A3] 65-20741
1. Canada. Royal Canadian Mounted Police. I. Title. BIP

Canaday, Molly Morpeth, 1903-1971.

CANADAY, Frank H., 1896- 759.9931
1976.
Triumph in color : the life and art of Molly Morpeth Canaday / Frank H. Canaday ; with art commentary by Janet Paul. Canaan, N.H. : Phoenix Pub., c1977. vii, 152 p. : ill. (some col.) ; 29 cm. Includes index. [ND1108.C36C36] 76-30866 ISBN 0-914016-38-5 : 20.00
1. Canaday, Molly Morpeth, 1903-1971. 2. Canaday, Molly Morpeth, 1903-1971. 3. Painters—New Zealand—Biography. I. Title. BIP

Canadian diaries—bibl.

MATTHEWS, William, 016.920071
1905-
Canadian diaries and autobiographies. Berkeley, University of California Press, 1950. 130 p. 24 cm. [Z5305.C3M3] 50-62732
1. Canadian diaries—bibl. 2. Canada—Biog.—Bibl. I. Title.

Canadian fiction—20th century—Bio-bibliography.

THOMAS, Clara. 813'.03 B
Canadian novelists, 1920-1945. [Folcroft, Pa.] Folcroft Library Editions, 1970 [c1946] 129 p. 23 cm. Based on the author's thesis (M.A.), University of Western Ontario. [PR9203.T5 1970] 72-194072
1. Canadian fiction—20th century—Bio-bibliography. I. Title.

Canal, Antonio,

CANAL, Antonio, called 760'.0924
Canaletto, 1697-1768.
Canaletto: paintings, drawings, and etchings selected and introduced by Gregory Martin. Boston, Newbury Books, 1970. [14] p., 62 plates (part col.) port. 22 x 30 cm. [ND623.C2M3 1970] 72-125858
I. Martin, Gregory.

Canals—New York (State)—History.

WHITFORD, Noble 386'.48'09747
Earl.
History of the canal system of the State of New York, together with brief histories of the canals of the United States and Canada, by Noble E. Whitford. Under authority of Henry A. Van Alstyne State Engineer and Surveyor. New York, B. Franklin [1973] p. Reprint of the 1906 ed., originally published as a supplement to the annual report of the State Engineer and Surveyor of the State of New York for the fiscal year ending Sept. 30, 1905. Bibliography: p [TC624.N7W62 1973] 77-144829 ISBN 0-8337-3792-9 85.00
1. Canals—New York (State)—History. 2. Canals—United States. 3. Canals—Canada. 4. Engineers—New York (State) I. New York (State). State Engineer and Surveyor. Annual report, 1904/05. Supplement. II. Title.

Canaris, Wilhelm, 1887-1945.

BRISSAUD, Andre. 940.54'87'43 B
Canaris; the biography of Admiral Canaris, chief of German Military Intelligence in the Second World War. Translated and edited by Ian Colvin. New York, Grosset & Dunlap [1974, c1973] xvii, 347 p. 22 cm. Bibliography: p. 333-334. [DD247.C35B7513 1974] 73-15133 ISBN 0-448-11621-9 8.95
1. Canaris, Wilhelm, 1887-1945. I. Title.

COLVIN, Ian Goodhope, 923.543
1912-
Master spy, the incredible story of Admiral Wilhelm Canaris, who, while Hitler's Chief of Intelligence, was a secret ally of the British. New York, McGraw-Hill [1952, c1951] 286 p. illus. 21 cm. "Published in Great Britain under the title: Chief of Intelligence." Includes bibliography. [DD247.C35C6 1952] 51-12555
1. Canaris, Wilhelm, 1887-1945. 2. World War, 1939-1945—Secret service—Germany. 3. Anti-Nazi movement. I. Title.

HOHNE, Heinz, 355.3'43'0924 B
1926-
Canaris / by Heinz Hohne ; translated from the German by J. Maxwell Brownjohn. 1st ed. Garden City, N.Y. : Doubleday, 1979. xv, 703 p., [12] leaves of plates : ill. ; 24 cm. Includes index. Bibliography: p. [672]-684. [DD247.C35H6313] 76-56303 ISBN 0-385-08777-2 : 15.95
1. Canaris, Wilhelm, 1887-1945. 2. Admirals—Germany—Biography. 3. Anti-Nazi movement—Biography.

*WHITING, Charles. 914.3
Canaris. New York, Ballantine Books [1973] 265 p. illus., 18 cm. (War book) Bibliography: p. 265 [DD247] ISBN 0-345-23552-5 1.50 (pbk.)
1. Canaris, Wilhelm, 2. Germany—History—1933-1945. I. Title.

Canary, Martha, 1852-1903.

CLAIRMONTE, Glenn. 920.7
Calamity was the name for Jane. Denver, Sage Books [dist. Alan Swallow] [c. 1959] 215p. illus. 23cm. 59-14667 3.75
1. Canary, Martha, 1852-1903. I. Title.

JENNEWEIN, John 978'.02'0924 B
Leonard, 1910-
Calamity Jane of the western trails, by J. Leonard Jennewein. [3d ed.] Mitchell, S.D., D. Grigg Enterprise Co. [1965] 72 p. illus., ports. 18 cm. Bibliography: p. 57-69. [F594.C2J4 1965] 68-2665
1. Canary, Martha, 1852-1903. I. Title.

MUMEY, Nolie, 1891- 920.7
Calamity Jane. 1852-1903; a history of her life and adventures in the West. Denver, Range Press, 1950. xix, 146 p. illus., ports., fold. map (inserted) 26 cm. Facsimile reproductions of two issues of "Life and adventures of Calamity Jane, by herself" (7 p. and 8 p. respectively) in pocket. Bibliographical footnotes. [F594.C2M8] 50-11981
1. Canary, Martha, 1850 (ca.)-1903. I. Title.

Canby, Edward Richard Sprigg, 1817-1873.

HEYMAN, Max L 923.573
Prudent soldier; a biography of Major General E. R. S. Canby, 1817-1873: his military service in the Indian campaigns, in the Mexican n War, in California, New Mexico, Utah, and Oregon; in the Civil War in the trans-Mississippi West, and as millitary governor in the post-war South. Glendale, Calif., A. H. Clark Co., 1959. 418p. illus. 25cm. (Frontier military series, 3) Includes bibliography. [E181.C26H4] 59-8004
1. Canby, Edward Richard Sprigg, 1817-1873. 2. U. S.—History, Military—To 1900. I. Title.

Canby, Henry Seidel, 1878-1961.

HENRY Seidel Canby; v. 12
in memoriam. [New York, 1961] unpaged. ports, 26cm. Includes tributes by Harry Scherman and Allan Nevins; also, 'The Book-of-the Month Club,' by Henry Seidel Canby.
1. Canby, Henry Seidel, 1878-1961. I. Book-of-the-Month Club, New York.

Cancer patients—Personal narratives.

PELGRIN, 362.1'9'699400924 B
Mark, 1908or9-1956.
And a time to die / by Mark Pelgrin ; edited by Sheila Moon and Elizabeth B. Howes. Wheaton, Ill. : Theosophical Pub. House, c1976 xiv, 159 p. ; 21 cm. (A Re-quest book) [RC262.P4 1976] 75-26836 ISBN 0-8356-0305-9 pbk. : 2.95
1. Cancer patients—Personal narratives. I. Title.

Cancer—Personal narratives.

FRICK, Marlena. 362.1'9'699400924 B
All the days of his dying. New York, Stein and Day [1972] 180 p. 22 cm. [RC263.F7 1972] 72-82854 ISBN 0-8128-1502-5 5.95
1. Cancer—Personal narratives. I. Title.

PELGRIN, Mark, 1908or9-1956. 920
And a time to die. Edited by Sheila Moon and Elizabeth B. Howes. Sausalito, Calif., Contact Editions [1962] 159p. 23cm. Autobiographical. [RC262.P4 1962] 62-15384
1. Cancer—Personal narratives. I. Title.

Candler, Asa Griggs, 1851-1929.

CANDLER, Charles Howard, 1878- 923.673
Asa Griggs Candler. Emory University, Ga., Emory University, 1950. xv, 502 p. illus., ports., geneal. table. 24 cm. Bibliography: p. [483]--487. [HD9348.U54C63] 50-12163
1. Candler, Asa Griggs, 1851-1929. 2. Coca-Cola Company, Wilmington, Del. 3. Emory University, Atlanta. I. Title.

Cane, Melville,

CANE, Melville, 1879- 818'.5'203
All and sundry; an oblique autobiography. [1st ed.] New York, Harcourt, Brace & World [1968] xiii, 253 p. 22 cm. [PS3505.A557A8] 68-18182
I. Title. BIP

Canetti, Elias, 1905- —Biography—Youth.

CANETTI, Elias, 1905- 833'.9'12 B
The tongue set free : remembrance of a European childhood / Elias Canetti ; translated from the German by Joachim Neugroschel. New York : Seabury Press, 1979. p. cm. (A Continuum book) Translation of Die gerettete Zunge. [PT2605.A58Z51513] 79-18234 ISBN 0-8164-9103-8 : 12.95
1. Canetti, Elias, 1905- —Biography—Youth. 2. Authors, Austrian—20th century—Biography. I. Title. BIP

Canfield, Cass,

CANFIELD, Cass, 1897- 070.5'0924
Up and down and around; a publisher recollects the time of his life. [1st ed.] New York, Harper's Magazine Press [1971] xiii, 272 p. illus. 25 cm. [Z473.C215A3] 73-156512 ISBN 0-06-121540-6 8.95
I. Title. BIP

Canisius, Petrus, Saint, 1521-1597.

BRODRICK, James, 1891- v. 12
Saint Peter Canisius, Chicago, Loyola University Press, 1962. xv, 859 p. illus. 24 cm. "Bibliographical note": p. xv. 63-7058
1. Canisius, Petrus, Saint, 1521-1597. I. Title. BIP

Canizio, Frank,

CANIZIO, Frank, 1913- 923.4173
A man against fate, by Frank Canizio as told to Robert Markel. New York, F. Fell [1958] 252 p. 22 cm. Autobiographical. [HV6248.C145A3] 58-13407
I. Markel, Robert. II. Title.

Cannata, Sam.

CANNATA, Sam. 266'.0092'2 B
Truth on trial / Sam and Ginny Cannata, with Jack R. Taylor. Nashville : Broadman Press, c1978. 189 p. : ill. ; 21 cm. [BV3562.A2C36] 78-104707 ISBN 0-8054-6310-0 pbk. : 3.95
1. Cannata, Sam. 2. Cannata, Ginny. 3. Missionaries—Ethiopia—Biography. 4. Missionaries—United States—Biography. 5. Baptists—Missions. I. Cannata, Ginny, joint author. II. Taylor, Jack R., joint author. III. Title. BIP

Canning, Charles John Canning, earl, 1812-1862.

MACLAGAN, Michael 923.242
'Clemency' Canning; Charles John, 1st earl Canning Governor-General and Viceroy of India, 1856-1862. New York, St. Martin's [1963, c.1962. xvi, 419p. illus., ports., maps (pt. fold.) 23cm. Bibl. 62-17719 10.00
1. Canning, Charles John Canning, earl, 1812-1862. I. Title.

Canning, George, 1770-1827.

DIXON, Peter, 1932- 320'.01
Canning, politician and statesman / Peter Dixon. London : Weidenfeld and Nicolson, c1976. 355 p. ; 22 cm. Includes index. Bibliography: p. [337]-343. [DA522.C2D59 1976b] 76-361444 ISBN 0-297-77061-6 : £7.50
1. Canning, George, 1770-1827. 2. Great Britain—Politics and government—1789-1820.

HINDE, Wendy. 942.07'4'0924 B
George Canning. New York, St. Martin's Press [1974, c1973] 519 p. illus. 24 cm. Bibliography: p. 501-505. [DA522.C2H64 1974] 73-84342 16.95
1. Canning, George, 1770-1827.

ROLO, P. J. V., 1917- 942.0740924
George Canning; three biographical studies. London, Macmillan [New York, St. Martins, c.]1965. ix, 276p. port. 23cm. Bibl. [DA522.C2R6] 65-4518 7.50
1. Canning, George, 1770-1827. I. Title.

TEMPERLEY, Harold William Vazeille, 1879-1939. 942.7'4'0924 B
Life of Canning. Westport, Conn., Greenwood Press [1970] 293 p. illus., fold. map, ports. 23 cm. Reprint of the 1905 ed. Includes bibliographical references. [DA522.C2T3 1970] 69-14110
1. Canning, George, 1770-1827. I. Title. BIP

Cannon, Elaine.

CANNON, Elaine. 979.2'25 B
The summer of my content / Elaine Cannon. Salt Lake City : Deseret Book Co., 1976. 82 p. ; 24 cm. [CT275.C2763A34] 76-292 ISBN 0-87747-585-7 : 3.95
1. Cannon, Elaine. I. Title. BIP

Cannon family.

CANNON, Clarence, 1879- 929'.2'0973
The Cannon book. [n. p.] 1958. 393p. 30cm. [CS71.C226 1958] 58-4012
1. Cannon family. I. Title.

EVANS, Beatrice Cannon. 929.2
Cannon family historical treasury. Edited by Beatrice Cannon Evans and Janath Russell Cannon. [Salt Lake City] George Cannon Family Association [c1967] 390 p. illus., geneal. tables, map (on lining papers) ports. 24 cm. [CS71.C226 1967] 68-2865
1. Cannon family. I. Cannon, Janath Russell. II. Title.

Cannon, Gaine.

BLYTHE, LeGette, 1900- 926.1
Mountain doctor. Photos. by Bruce Roberts. New York, Morrow, 1964. 221 p. illus., ports. 22 cm. [R154.C253B6] 64-10733
1. Cannon, Gaine. I. Title.

Cannon, James, Bp., 1864-1944.

DABNEY, Virginius, 1901- 287'.6'0924 B
Dry messiah; the life of Bishop Cannon. Westport, Conn., Greenwood Press [1970, c1949] vii, 353, ix p. illus., ports. 23 cm. Bibliography: p. 349-353. [BX8495.C245D2 1970] 73-110825 ISBN 0-8371-3225-8
1. Cannon, James, Bp., 1864-1944. I. Title. BIP

Cannon, James J.

CANNON, James J. 920.5
Nobody asked me. New York, Dial Press, 1951. 339 p. 21 cm. [PN4874.C24A3] 51-10245
1. Journalists—Correspondence, reminiscences, etc. 2. Sports—U. S. I. Title.

CANNON, James J. 796'.0973
Nobody asked me, but ... : the world of Jimmy Cannon / edited by Jack Cannon & T. Cannon. 1st ed. New York : Holt, Rinehart and Winston, c1978. 309 p. : ill. ; 24 cm. [GV583.C36] 77-13832 ISBN 0-03-015381-6. : 19.95
1. Cannon, James J. 2. Sports—United States—Addresses, essays, lectures. 3. Sportswriters—United States—Biography. I. Title.

CANNON, James J. 796.'.0973
Nobody asked me, but... : the world of Jimmy Cannon / edited by Jack Cannon & T. Cannon. New York : Berkley Pub. Co., 1979. 369p. : ill. ; 18 cm. [GV583.C36] ISBN 0-425-04100-X pbk. : 2.95
1. Cannon, James J. 2. Sports — United States — Addresses, essays, lectures. 3. Sportswriters — United States — Biography. I. Title.
L.C. card no. for c1978 Holt, Rinehart and Winston ed. : 77-13832 BIP

Cannon, James Patrick, 1890-1974 Addresses, essays, lectures.

CANNON, James Patrick, 1890- 335'.0092'4 B
Letters from prison [by] James P. Cannon. [2d ed.] New York, Pathfinder Press [1973] xx, 362 p. illus. 22 cm. Letters addressed to Rose Karsner. [HX86.C159 1973] 73-79781 3.45 (pbk.)
1. Socialism in the United States. 2. Socialists—Correspondence, reminiscences, etc. I. Karsner, Rose. II. Title.

JAMES P. Cannon as we knew him / by thirty-three comrades, friends, and relatives ; introduction by Jack Barnes. 1st ed. New York : Pathfinder Press, 1976. 288 p. : ill. ; 22 cm. Includes index. [HX84.C36J35] 76-25382 ISBN 0-87348-474-6 : 13.00. ISBN 0-87348-500-9 pbk. : 3.95 335'.0092'4 B
1. Cannon, James Patrick, 1890-1974—Addresses, essays, lectures. 2. Socialists—United States—Biography—Addresses, essays, lectures. BIP

Cannon, Joseph Gurney, 1836-1926.

BOLLES, Blair, 1911- 328.73'092'4 B
Tyrant from Illinois; Uncle Joe Cannon's experiment with personal power. Westport, Conn., Greenwood Press [1974, c1951] 248 p. port. 22 cm. Reprint of the ed. published by Norton, New York. Bibliography: p. 234-238. [E664.C22B6 1974] 73-16641 ISBN 0-8371-7205-5
1. Cannon, Joseph Gurney, 1836-1926. I. Title.

CANNON, Joseph Gurney, 1836-1926. 973.8'0924 B
Uncle Joe Cannon; the story of a pioneer American, as told to L. White Busbey. New York, H. Holt. St. Clair Shores, Mich., Scholarly Press, 1970 [c1927] xliv, 362 p. illus., ports. 22 cm. [E664.C22A3 1971] 77-144924 ISBN 0-403-00887-5
1. Cannon, Joseph Gurney, 1836-1926. 2. U.S.—Politics and government—1865-1933. I. Busbey, L. White, 1852-1925. II. Title. BIP

GWINN, William Rea, 1922- 923.273
Uncle Joe Cannon, archfoe of insurgency; a history of the rise and fall of Cannonism. [New York] Bookman Associates [c1957] 314p. 28cm. (Bookman monograph) Issued also in 1955 in microfilm form, as thesis, University of Notre Dame. Bibliography:p. 278-306. [E664.C22G8 1957] 58-2828
1. Cannon, Joseph Gurney, 1836-1926. I. Title.

Canter, Louis, 1797-1865.

CANLER, Louis, 1797-1865. 363.2'092'4 B
Autobiography of a French detective, from 1818 to 1858 / Louis Canler. New York : Arno Press, 1976. iv, 315 p. ; 21 cm. (Literature of mystery and detection) Translation of Memoires de Canler. Reprint of the 1862 ed. published by Ward and Lock, London. [HV7911.C35A3313 1976] 75-32738 ISBN 0-405-07866-8 : 18.00
1. Canter, Louis, 1797-1865. 2. Police—France—Correspondence, reminiscences, etc. I. Title. II. Series.

Cantine family.

HUNTINGTON, Alice (Cantine) 1867- 929'.2'0973
The Cantine family, descendants of Moses Cantine. West Hartford, Conn., Indexed and published by Chedwato Service, 1957. 82p. 27cm. [CS71.C23 1957] 58-19121
1. Cantine family. I. Title.

Canton, Ohio. National Pro Football Hall of Fame.

SULLIVAN, George Edward, 1927- 796.332'64
Pro football's all-time greats; the immortals in pro football's Hall of Fame, by George Sullivan. New York, Putnam [1968] 251 p. 22 cm. [GV939.A1S9] 68-25458 5.95
1. Canton, Ohio. National Pro Football Hall of Fame. 2. Football—Biography. I. Canton, Ohio. National Pro Football Hall of Fame. II. Title.

(Cantoni, Louise

(CANTONI, Louise 922.22
St. Germaine and her guardian angel [Boston] St. Paul Eds. [dist. Daughters of St. Paul, c.1964] 24p. illus. (pt. col.) 21cm. .35; .25 pap.,
I. Title.

Canute, the Great, King of England and Denmark, 995?-1035.

LARSON, Laurence Marcellus, 1868-1938. 948'.901'0924
Canute the Great, 995 (circ)-1035, and the rise of Danish imperialism during the Viking Age. New York, AMS Press [1970] xviii, 375 p. illus., facsim., maps. 23 cm. (Heroes of the nations) Reprint of the 1912 ed. Bibliography: p. 349-355. [DL165.L3 1970] 71-111764
1. Canute, the Great, King of England and Denmark, 995?-1035. I. Title. II. Series.

Canzoneri, Robert - Biography.

CANZONERI, Robert. 818'.5'409 B
A highly ramified tree / by Robert Canzoneri. New York : Viking Press, [1976] p. cm. [PS3553.A58Z52] 76-28363 ISBN 0-670-37205-6 : 7.95
1. Canzoneri, Robert—Biography. 2. Authors, American—20th century—Biography. I. Title. BIP

Capa, Robert, 1913-1954.

ROBERT Capa. 779'.9'9047
Text by John Hersey [and others] New York, Paragraphic Books [1969] 106 p. illus., ports. 18 cm. [TR140.C28R6] 67-21240 2.95
1. Capa, Robert, 1913-1954. I. Hersey, John Richard, 1914-

Caparn, Rhys, 1909-

CAPARN, Rhys, 1909- 730'.92'4
Rhys Caparn, by Robert Beverly Hale. Danbury, Conn., Retrospective Press [1972] [25] p., 87 [i.e. 88] plates. port. 30 cm. [NB237.C37H34] 73-152063 15.00
1. Caparn, Rhys, 1909- I. Hale, Robert Beverly, 1901-

Cape Cod—Biography.

BARNARD, Charles N. 917.44'92'0340922
The winter people; a return to Cape Cod [by] Charles N. Barnard. New York, Dodd, Mead [1973] 173 p. illus. 22 cm. [F72.C3B23] 72-12435 ISBN 0-396-06780-8 4.95
1. Cape Cod—Biography. I. Title.

Cape of Good Hope — Hist.

BELL, May, M. A. 916.8'7'0430924
They came from a far land, by May Bell, and published posthumously by Josie E. Wood. Cape Town, M. Miller, 1963. xv, 182 p. ports. 22 cm. Bibliography: p. 181-182. [DT844.2.A2B4] 67-57207
1. Cape of Good Hope — Hist. 2. Pioneers — Cape of Good Hope. I. Title.

*PICARD, Hymen W. J. 968.7 [B]
Masters of the castle; a portrait gallery of the Dutch commanders and governors of the Cape of Good Hope, 1652-1795; 1803-1806. Cape Town, C. Struik, 1972. 231 p. ports. 22 cm. Bibliography: p. 221-223. [DT843] ISBN 0-86977-019-5
1. Cape of Good Hope—History. 2. Cape of Good Hope—Governors—History. 3. South Africa—History. I. Title.
Available from Verry, Mystic, Conn., for 7.35

Caper, Samuel Paul, 1878-1956.

PARK, Julian, 1888- 923.773
Samuel P. Capen, 1878-1956. [Buffalo] University of Buffalo, 1957. 58p. illus. 23cm. (The University of Buffalo studies, v. 24, no. 1) [AS36.B95 vol. 24, no. 1] 57-44208
1. Capen, Samuel Paul, 1878-1956. I. Title.

Caperton Family.

CAPERTON, Bernard M., 1926- 929'.2'0973
The Caperton family [by] Bernard M. Caperton. Charlottesville, Va., 1973. 239 p. illus. 24 cm. Bibliography: p. 223-231. [CS71.C239 1973] 73-88728
1. Caperton family.
Publisher's address: 611 Preston Pl., Charlottesville, Va. 22903.

Capitalists and financiers—Biography.

FLYNN, John Thomas, 1883-1964. 920.02
Men of wealth; the story of twelve significant fortunes from the Renaissance to the present day. Freeport, N.Y., Books for Libraries Press [1971] xi, 531 p. ports. 23 cm. (Essay index reprint series) Reprint of the 1941 ed. Contents.Contents.—Fugger the Rich: organizer of capitalism.—John Law: money magician.—The Rothschilds: imperialist bankers.—Interlogue one: Cosimo de' Medici, Sir Thomas Gresham, Jacques Coeur, The art and industry of make-up, Writers as money-makers.—Robert Owen: the reformer. Cornelius Vanderbilt: the rail king.—Hetty Green: the miser.—Interlogue two: Misers, Poverty.—Mitsui: the dynast.—Cecil Rhodes: empire builder.—Basil Zaharoff: the warmaker.—Interlogue three: Hugo Stinnes, Land fortunes, Dynastic fortunes.—Mark Hanna: the politico.—John D. Rockefeller: the builder.—J. Pierpont Morgan: the promoter. [CT105.F55 1971] 79-142629 ISBN 0-8369-2047-3
1. Capitalists and financiers—Biography. I. Title.

Capitalists and financiers—New York (City)

BEACH, Moses Yale, 1800-1868. 920'.0747'1
The wealthy citizens of New York. New York, Arno Press, 1973. 32, 83 p. 23 cm. (Big business: economic power in a free society) Reprint of the 1845 ed. published by the Sun Office, New York under title: Wealth and biography of the wealthy citizens of New York City, and of the 1855 ed. published by the Sun Office under title: The wealth and biography of the wealthy citizens of the city of New York. [HC108.N7B34 1973] 73-1992 ISBN 0-405-05117-4 8.00
1. Capitalists and financiers—New York (City) 2. New York (City)—Biography. I. Title. II. Series.

Capitalists and financiers—U.S.

FAMOUS fortunes; 338'.0922
intimate stories of financial success. Freeport, N.Y., Books for Libraries Press [1968] 256 p. illus., ports. 22 cm. (Essay index reprint series) Reprint of the 1931 ed. Contents.Contents.—John Jacob Astor.—George Eastman.—Henry Ford.—John D. Rockefeller.—Cornelius Vanderbilt.—DuPont family.—Andrew Carnegie.—Cyrus H. McCormick.—J. Pierpont Morgan.—Leland Stanford.—Frank W. Woolworth.—Guggenheim family.—Harvey S. Firestone. [HG181.F3 1968] 68-8460
1. Capitalists and financiers—U.S.

TEBBEL, John William, 1912- 923.373
The inheritors: a study of America's great fortunes and what happened to them. New York, Putnam [1962] 310 p. illus. 22 cm. [HG181.T4] 61-15081
1. Capitalists and financiers — U.S. 2. Millionaires. I. Title.

TEBBEL, John William, 1912- 923.373
The inheritors; a study of America's great fortunes and what happened to them. New York, Popular Lib. [1963, c.1962] 237p. 18cm. (M2025) .60 pap.,
1. Capitalists and financiers.—U.S. 2. Millionaires. I. Title.

TEBBEL, John William, 1912- 923.373
The inheritors; a study of America's great fortunes and what happened to them. New York, Putnam [1962] 310 p. illus. 22 cm. [HG181.T4] 61-15081
1. Capitalists and financiers—U.S. 2. Millionaires. I. Title.

Capitalists and financiers—United States—Biography.

MILLER, William, 1912- ed. 338'.092'2 B
Men in business : essays on the historical role of the entrepreneur / with 2 additional essays on American business leaders by William Miller, not included in the original ed. Westport, Conn. : Greenwood Press, 1979, c1952. p. cm. Reprint of the 1962 ed. published by Harper & Row, New York. Bibliography: p. [HF3023.A2M5 1979] 78 21159 ISBN 0-313-20867-0 : 25.00
1. Capitalists and financiers—United States—Biography. 2. Entrepreneur—Biography. I. Title. BIP

TRAIN, John. 332.6'092'2 B
The money masters / by John Train. 1st ed. New York : Harper & Row, c1979. p. cm. Includes index [HG172.A2T7 1979] 78-20192 ISBN 0-06-014373-8 : 9.95
1. Capitalists and financiers—United States—Biography. 2. Investments—United States. I. Title.

Caples, John.

WHITE, Gordon E. 659.1'092'4
John Caples, adman / by Gordon White. Chicago : Crain Books, 1978, c1977. xv, 159 p. : ill. ; 24 cm. [HF5810.C33W48] 77-80157 ISBN 0-87251-030-1 : 11.95
1. Caples, John. 2. Advertising—United States—Biography. 3. Advertising—United States—History. I. Title. BIP

Capone, Alphonse, 1899-1947.

KOBLER, John. 364.1'0924 B
Capone; the life and world of Al Capone. New York, Putnam [1971] 409 p. illus., ports. 24 cm. Bibliography: p. [387]-393. [HV6248.C17K6] 78-150267 8.95
1. Capone, Alphonse, 1899-1947. I. Title.

MURRAY, Jesse George, 1909- 364.1'092'2 B
The legacy of Al Capone : portraits and annals of Chicago's public enemies / by George Murray. New York : Putnam, [1975] 366 p., [8] leaves of plates : ill. ; 25 cm. Includes index. [HV6248.C17M87 1975] 74-30571 ISBN 0-399-11502-1 : 10.95
1. Capone, Alphonse, 1899-1947. 2. Crime and criminals—Chicago—History. I. Title.

PASLEY, Fred D. 364.1'0924 B
Al Capone; the biography of a self-made man, by Fred D. Pasley. Freeport, N.Y., Books for Libraries Press [1971] 355 p. illus., ports. 23 cm. Reprint of the 1930 ed. [HV6248.C17P3 1971] 78-150196 ISBN 0-8369-5709-1
1. Capone, Alphonse, 1899-1947. 2. Crime and criminals—Chicago. BIP

ROEBURT, John 923.4173
Al Capone. New York, Pyramid [1963, c.1959] 144p. 18cm. Based on the screen play 'Al Capone' written by Malvin Wald, Henry F. Greenberg. (F-885) 63-4975 .40 pap.,
1. Capone, Alphonse, 1899-1947. I. Title.

SPIERING, Frank. 364.1'092'4 B
The man who got Capone / by Frank Spiering. Indianapolis . Bobbs-Merrill, c1976. 231 p., [8] leaves of plates : ill. ; 24 cm. Includes index. Bibliography: p. 224-226. [HV6248.C17S64] 76-11626 ISBN 0-672-52231-4 : 10.00
1. Capone, Alphonse, 1899-1947. 2. Wilson, Frank John, 1888- 3. United States. Office of Internal Revenue.—Officials and employees—Biography. 4. Crime and criminals—United States—Biography. I. Title.

Capone, Alphonse, 1899-1947 - Juvenile literature.

LETTS, Mary. 364.1'092'4 B
Al Capone / Mary Letts. New York : St. Martin's Press, 1975, c1974. 95 p. : ill. ; 23 cm. Includes index. A biography of the gangster who organized and ran the Chicago underground throughout the Prohibition Era. [HV6248.C17L47 1975] 92 75-7633 6.95
1. Capone, Alphonse, 1899-1947—Juvenile literature. I. Title.

Capote, Truman,

CAPOTE, Truman, 1924- 818'.5'403
The Thanksgiving visitor. New York, Random House [1968, c1967] 63 p. 24 cm. Originally appeared in McCall's. Autobiographical. [PS3505.A59Z5] 68-54587 4.95
I. Title. BIP

Cappen, Arthur, 1865-1951.

SOCOLOFSKY, Homer Edward, 1922- 923.273
Arthur Capper, publisher politician, and philanthropist. Lawrence, Univ. of Kansas Pr. [c.]1962. 283p. illus., 24cm. Bibl. 62-13869 6.00
1. Capper, Arthur, 1865-1951. I. Title.

Captain and Tennille - Juvenile literature.

SPADA, James. 784'.092'2 B
Captain and Tennille / by James Spada ; designed by Mark Landkamer. Mankato, Minn. : Creative Education, c1978. 31 p. : ill. ; 25 cm. (Rock 'n pop stars) Describes the marriage and career of a popular singing duo. [ML3930.C25S7] 92 77-24625 ISBN 0-87191-615-0 : 4.95
1. Captain and Tennille—Juvenile literature. 2. Rock musicians—United States—Biography—Juvenile literature. I. Title. BIP

Capuana, Luigi, 1839-1917.

SCALIA, Samuel Eugene, 1903- 928.5
Luigi Capuana and his times. New York, S. F. Vanni [1952] xv, 251 p. 23 cm. (Paterno Library collection of Italian studies, v, 4) Bibliography: p. xiii-xv. [PQ4684.C8Z8] 52-18935
1. Capuana, Luigi, 1839-1917. I. Title. II. Series. BIP

Caputo, Philip.

CAPUTO, Philip. 959.704'38
A rumor of war / Philip Caputo. New York : Ballantine Books, 1978,c1977. 328p. ; 18 cm. Autobiographical. [DS559.5C36] ISBN 0-345-27298-6 pbk. : 2.25
1. Caputo, Philip. 2. United States — Marine corps — Biography. 3. Vietnamese Conflict, 1961-1975 — Personal narratives, American. 4. Soldiers — United States — Biography. I. Title.
L.C. card no. for 1977 Holt, Rinehart and Winston ed.: 76-29900.

Caravaggio, Michelangelo Merisi de, 1573-1610.

BOTTARI, Stefano. 759.5
Caravaggio. [Translated from the Italian by Diane Goldrei. 1st American ed.] New York, Grossett & Dunlap [1971] 38 p. illus., 79 col. plates. 18 cm. (The New Grosset art library, 34) Bibliography: p. 11. [ND623.C26B613 1971] 77-110101
1. Caravaggio, Michelangelo Merisi da, 1573-1610.

CARAVAGGIO, 759.5
his incongruity and his fame. New York, Macmillan, 1953. 122p. 88plates. 22cm. [ND623.C26B45] [ND623.C26B45] 927.5 54-812 54-812
1. Caravaggio, Michelangelo Merisl da, 1569?-1609. I. Berenson, Bernhard, 1865-

HINKS, Roger Packman. 927.5
Michelangelo Merisi da Caravaggio: his life, his legend, his works. London, Faber and Faber [1953] 126p. 97plates (1 col.) 26cm. 'Bibliographical note':p. 121-122. [ND623.C26H5 1953] A54
1. Caravaggio, Michelangelo Merisi da, 1569?-1609. I. Title.

Cardano, Girolamo, 1501-1576.

CARDANO, Girolamo, 1501-1576. 925
The book of my life (De vita propria liber) Translated from the Latin by Jean Stoner. New York, Dover Publications [1962] xviii, 331 p. port. 22 cm. Bibliography: p. 329-331. [Q143.C3A3] 63-2615
1. "Unabridged and corrected republication of the work first published ... in 1930." I. Title.

ORE, Oystein, 1899- 925
Cardano, the gambling scholar. With a tr. from Latin of Cardano's Book on games of chance, by Sydney Henry C)0gould [Gloucester, Mass., P. Smith, 1965, c.1953] xiv, 249p. illus., ports. 22cm. (Dover bk. rebound) Bibl. [Q143.C307] 3.75
1. Cardano, Girolamo, 1501-1576. 2. Gambling. 3. Book on games of chance. I. Cardano, Girolamo, 1501-1576. II. Title.

Cardew, Michael, 1901-

CLARK, Garth. 738.3'092'4 B
Michael Cardew : a portrait / by Garth Clark. 1st ed. Tokyo ; New York : Kodansha International ; New York : distributed by Harper & Row, 1976. 228 p. : ill. (some col.) ; 26 cm. Includes index. Bibliography: p. 225-226. [NK4210.C29C55] 76-9358 ISBN 0-87011-277-5 : 25.00
1. Cardew, Michael, 1901- 2. Potters—Great Britain—Biography.

Cardew, Michael, 1901- —Addresses, essays, lectures.

MICHAEL Cardew : 738.3'092'4 B
a collection of essays / with an introd. by Bernard Leach ; and contributions by Michael Cardew ... [et al.]. London : Crafts Advisory Council ; New York : distributed in the United States of America and Canada by Watson-Guptill, c1976. 80 p. : ill. ; 21 x 22 cm. Includes index. Contents.Contents.—Leach, B. Introduction.—Houston, J. The early years.—Finch, R. Working at Winchcombe in 1936.—Bouverie, K. P. A personal account.—Houston, J. Africa and Cornwall.—Cardew, M. Slipware and stoneware.—Chronology.—Pottery marks. Bibliography: p. 77-79. [NK4210.C29M5] 76-381211 ISBN 0-903798-07-7 : 9.95.
1. Cardew, Michael, 1901- —Addresses,

essays, lectures. 2. Potters—Great Britain—Biography—Addresses, essays, lectures. I. Cardew, Michael, 1901-

Cardigan, James Thomas Brudenell, 7th earl of, 1797-1868.

THOMAS, Donald Serrell. 942.081'092'4 B
Cardigan [by] Donald Thomas. New York, Viking Press [1975, c1974] xi, 369 p. illus. 24 cm. London ed. (Routledge & K. Paul) has title: Charge! Hurrah! Hurrah! Bibliography: p. 351-356. [DA68.22.C35T46 1975] 74-3791 ISBN 0-670-20388-2
1. Cardigan, James Thomas Brudenell, 7th Earl of, 1797-1868. I. Title.

WOODHAM SMITH, cecil Blanche (Fitzgerald) 1896- 923.542
The reason why. New York, McGraw-Hill [1954, c1953] 287p. illus. 21cm. [DA536.C3W6 1954] 54-6228
1. Cardigan, James Thomas Brudenell, 7th earl of, 1797-1868. 2. Lucan, George Charles Bingham, 3d earl of, 1800-1888. 3. Balaklava, Battle of, 1854. I. Title.

WOODHAM Smith, Cecil Blanche (FitzGerald) 1896- 942.081'0924
The reason why, by Cecil Woodham-Smith. [2d ed.] New York, McGraw-Hill [1971, c1953] 287 p. illus., maps, ports. 24 cm. Bibliography: p. 273-278. [DA536.C3W6 1971] 72-155886 ISBN 0-07-071670-6 7.95
1. Cardigan, James Thomas Brudenell, 7th Earl of, 1797-1868. 2. Lucan, George Charles Bingham, 3d Earl of, 1800-1888. 3. Balaklava, Battle of, 1854. I. Title.

Cardinals.

MORGAN, Thomas Brynmor, 1886- 262'.135
Speaking of cardinals, by Thomas B. Morgan. Freeport, N.Y., Books for Libraries Press [1971, c1946] 264 p. 23 cm. (Essay index reprint series) [BX4664.M6 1971] 70-134119 ISBN 0-8369-2002-3
1. Cardinals. I. Title. BIP

Cardinals—Biography.

MACEOIN, Gary, 1909- 262'.135'0922 B
The inner elite : dossiers of papal candidates / by Gary MacEloin and the Committee for the Responsible Election of the Pope. Kansas City, Kan. : S. Andrews and McMeel, c1978. xxx, 300 p., [8] leaves of plates : ill. ; 24 cm. Includes index. Bibliography: p. 297-298. [BX4664.2.M32] 78-17845 ISBN 0-8362-3105-8 : 9.95
1. Cardinals—Biography. 2. Popes—Election. I. Committee for the Responsible Election of the Pope. II. Title.

Cardinals—U.S.

THORNTON, Francis Beauchesne, 1898- 922.273
Our American princes; the story of the seventeen American cardinals. New York, Putnam [1963] 319 p. illus. 22 cm. [BX4665.U5T5] 63-9674
1. Cardinals—U.S. I. Title.

WALSH, James Joseph, 1865-1942. 262'.135'0922
Our American cardinals; life stories of the seven American cardinals: McCloskey, Gibbons, Farley, O'Connell, Dougherty, Mundelein, Hayes. Freeport, N.Y., Books for Libraries Press [1969, c1926] xvii, 352 p. ports. 23 cm. (Essay index reprint series) [BX4665.U5W3 1969] 68-58815
1. Cardinals—U.S. I. Title.

Cardiovascular research.

WIGGERS, Carl John, 1883- 926.1
Reminiscences and adventures in circulation research. New York, Grune & Stratton, 1958 [i.e. 1959] 404 p. illus. 24 cm. Includes bibliography. [R154.W515A3] 58-11745
1. Cardiovascular research. I. Title.

Cardozo, Benjamin Nathan, 1870-1938.

HELLMAN, George Sidney, 1878-1958. 347.99'24 B
Benjamin N. Cardozo, American judge. New York, Russell & Russell [1969, c1940] 339 p. facsims., ports. 23 cm. [KF8745.C3H4 1969] 78-77670
1. Cardozo, Benjamin Nathan, 1870-1938. BIP

POLLARD, Joseph Percival, 1898- 347.99'24 B
Mr. Justice Cardozo; a liberal mind in action [by] Joseph P. Pollard. With a foreword by Roscoe Pound. Westport, Conn., Greenwood Press [1970] 327 p. 23 cm. Reprint of the 1935 ed. [KF8745.C3P6 1970] 75-98790
1. Cardozo, Benjamin Nathan, 1870-1938.

Carducci, Vincenzio, 1578-1638.

VOLK, Mary Crawford. 759.6 B
Vicencio Carducho and seventeenth century Castilian painting / Mary Crawford Volk. New York : Garland Pub., 1977, i.e.1978 428 p., [76] leaves of plates : ill. ; 22 cm. (Outstanding dissertations in the fine arts) Reprint of the author's thesis, Yale, 1973. Bibliography: p. 415-428. [ND813.C287V64 1977] 76-23650 ISBN 0-8240-2734-5 lib.bdg. : 45.00
1. Carducci, Vincenzio, 1578-1638. 2. Painters—Spain—Castile—Biography. I. Title. II. Series.

Cardus, Neville, Sir, 1889-1975.

CARDUS, Neville, Sir, 1889-1975. 070.4'49'780924 B
Autobiography / Neville Cardus. Westport, Conn. : Greenwood Press, 1975. 288 p., [8] leaves of plates : ill. ; 23 cm. Reprint of the 1947 ed. published by Collins, London. Includes index. [PN5123.C28A3 1975] 75-37825 ISBN 0-8371-8577-7 lib.bdg. : 16.00
1. Cardus, Neville, Sir, 1889-1975.

Cardyn, Leon Joseph Marie, 1882-

DE LA BEDOYERE, Michael Anthony Maurice, 1900- 922.173
The Cardijn story; a study of the life of Mgr. Joseph Cardijn and the Young Christian Workers' movement which he founded. London, Longmans, Green [Mystic, Conn., Verry, 1965, c.1958] xi, 196p. illus., ports. 21cm. Bibl. A62 3.50 bds.,
1. Cardyn, Leon Joseph Marie, 1882- 2. Young Christian Workers. I. Title.

Care, inc. Medical International Cooperation Organization.

DOOLEY, Thomas Anthony, 1927-1961. 926.1
Dr. Tom Dooley's three great books: Deliver us from evil, The edge of tomorrow [and] The night they burned the mountain. New York, Farrar, Straus & Cudahy [1960] 383 p. illus., ports., map. 22 cm. [RA390.U5D583] 60-51236
1. Care, inc. Medical International Cooperation Organization. 2. Missions, Medical—Laos. 3. Laos—Description and travel. 4. Refugees, Vietnamese. I. Dooley, Thomas Anthony, 1927-1961. Deliver us from evil. II. Dooley, Thomas Anthony, 1927-1961. The edge of tomorrow. III. Dooley, Thomas Anthony, 1927-1961. The night they burned the mountain. IV. Title: Deliver us from evil. V. Title: The edge of tomorrow. VI. Title: The night they burned the mountain.

Carew, Rod, 1945-

CAREW, Rod, 1945- 796.357'092'4 B
Carew / by Rod Carew, with Ira Berkow. New York : Simon and Schuster, c1979. 251 p., [8] leaves of plates : ill. ; 23 cm. Includes index. [GV865.C315A32] 78-23278 ISBN 0-671-24236-9 : 9.95
1. Carew, Rod, 1945- 2. Minnesota Twins (Baseball club) 3. Baseball players—United States—Biography. I. Berkow, Ira, joint author. BIP

Carew, Rod, 1945- —Juvenile literature.

BATSON, Larry, 1930- 796.357'092'4 B
An interview with Rod Carew / by Larry Batson ; photos. by John Croft. Mankato, Minn. : Creative Education, c1977. 31 p. : col. ill. ; 25 cm. (Creative Education "interviews") A biography of Rod Carew, an outstanding hitter who has prefected the hard-to-hit bunt. [GV865.C315B36] 92 76-42994 ISBN 0-87191-568-5 lib.bdg. : 5.95
1. Carew, Rod, 1945- —Juvenile literature. 2. Baseball players—United States—Biography—Juvenile literature. I. Croft, John. II. Title. BIP

BATSON, Larry, 1930- 796.357'092'4 B
Rod Carew / by Larry Batson ; photos. by John Croft. Mankato, Minn. : Creative Education, c1977. 31 p. : col. ill. ; 25 cm. (Creative Education sports superstars) A biography of Rod Carew, a strong hitter and a versatile infielder. [GV865.C315B37] 92 76-42992 ISBN 0-87191-537-5 lib.bdg. 4.95
1. Carew, Rod, 1945- —Juvenile literature. 2. Baseball players—United States—Biography—Juvenile literature. I. Croft, John. II. Title.

BURCHARD, Marshall. 796.357'092'4 B
Sports hero, Rod Carew / by Marshall Burchard. New York : Putnam, c1978. 93 p. : ill. ; 22 cm. (The Putnam sport heroes) A biography of an outstanding hitter in the major leagues, the Minnesota Twins' Rod Carew. [GV865.C315B87 1978] 92 78-738 ISBN 0-399-61120-7 lib. bdg. : 5.29
1. Carew, Rod, 1945- —Juvenile literature. 2. Baseball players—United States—Biography—Juvenile literature. I. Title. BIP

HAHN, James. 796.357'092'4 B
Rod Carew : a promise and a dream / by James and Lynn Hahn. St. Paul : EMC Corp., 1978. p. cm. (Their Champions and challengers I) A biography of the Panamanian who realized his childhood dream of coming to the United States and playing big league ball and who has become one of baseball's best hitters of all time. [GV865.C315H34] 92 78-9721 ISBN 0-88436-441-0 : 5.95
1. Carew, Rod, 1945- —Juvenile literature. 2. Baseball players—United States—Biography—Juvenile literature. I. Hahn, Lynn, joint author. II. Title. III. Series. BIP

LIBBY, Bill. 796'.357'0924 B
Rod Carew : master hitter / by Bill Libby. New York : Putnam, c1976. 127 p. : port. ; 21 cm. Includes index. A brief biography of the baseball player considered to be one of the best hitters in the history of the game. [GV865.C315L52 1976] 92 76-933 ISBN 0-399-60996-2 lib. bdg. : 5.29
1. Carew, Rod, 1945- —Juvenile literature. 2. Baseball—Juvenile literature I. Title. BIP

Carey, Henry Charles, 1793-1879.

GREEN, Arnold Wilfred, 1914- 923.373
Henry Charles Carey, nineteenth-century sociologist. Philadelphia, University of Pennsylvania Press, 1951. 218 p. 23 cm. Bibliography: p. 205-213. [HM22.U6C34] 51-6931
1. Carey, Henry Charles, 1793-1879. I. Title.

SMITH, George Winston. 923.373
Henry C. Carey and American sectional conflict. Albuquerque, University of New Mexico Press, 1951. 127 p. 23 cm. (University of New Mexico publications in history, no. 3) Bibliographical footnotes. [HB119.C3S6] 51-62438
1. Carey, Henry Charles, 1703-1879. 2. U.S.—Pol. & govt.—=1815-1861. I. Title. II. Series: New Mexico. University. University of New Mexico publications in history, no. 3

Carey, Lott.

FITTS, Leroy. 266'.6'1330924 B
Lott Carey : first Black missionary to Africa / Leroy Fitts. Valley Forge, PA : Judson Press, c1978. 159 p. ; 22 cm. Bibliography: p. 157-159. [BV3625.L6C374] 78-17254 ISBN 0-8170-0820-9 : pbk. : 5.95
1. Carey, Lott. 2. Lott Carey Baptist Foreign Mission Convention. 3. Missionaries—Liberia—Biography. 4. Missionaries—United States—Biography. BIP

Carey, Mathew, 1760-1839—Juvenile literature.

HINDMAN, Jane F 923.373
Mathew Carey, pamphleteer for freedom. Illustrated by W. N. Wilson. New York, P. J. Kenedy [1960] 190p. illus. 22cm. (American background books, 13) [Z473.C22H5] 60-7789
1. Carey, Mathew, 1760-1839—Juvenile literature. I. Title.

Carey, William, 1761-1834.

DAVIS, Walter Bruce 922.642
William Carey, father of modern missions. Chicago, Moody [c.1963] 160p. map. 19cm. (Moody pocket bks., 83) Bibl. 63-5774 .59 pap.,
1. Carey, William, 1761-1834. I. Title.

DAVIS, Walter Bruce. 922.642
William Carey, father of modern missions. Chicago, Moody Press [1963] 160 p. illus. 19 cm. (Moody pocket books, 83) Includes bibliography. [BV3269.C3D35] 63-5774
1. Carey, William, 1761-1834. I. Title.

DREWERY, Mary, 1918- 266'.6'10924 B
William Carey : a biography / by Mary Drewery. American ed. Grand Rapids : Zondervan Pub. House, 1979, c1978. p. cm. Includes bibliographical references and index. [BV3269.C3D7 1979] 79-14886 ISBN 0-310-38850-3 : 7.95
1. Carey, William, 1761-1834. 2. Missionaries—India—Biography. 3. Missionaries—England—Biography.

MILLER, Basil William, 1897- 922.642
William Carey, cobbler to missionary. Grand Rapids, Zondervan Pub. House [1952] 152 p. 20 cm. [BV3269.C3M5] 52-31844
1. Carey, William 1761-1834. I. Title.

WALKER, Frank Deaville, 1878- 922.342
William Carey, missionary, pioneer, and statesman. Chicago, Moody Press, 1951. 256p. 21cm. (The Tyndale series of great biographies) [BV3269.C3W] A 53
1. Carey, William, 1761-1834. I. Title. II. Series.

WOODALL, William L 922.642
William Carey of India. [1st ed.] New York, Pageant Press [1951] 101 p. 21 cm. [BV3269.C3W6] 51-14990
1. Carey, William, 1761-1834. I. Title.

WOODALL, William Love, 1908- 922.642
William Carey of India. [1st ed.] New York, Pageant Press [1951] 101p. 21cm. [BV3269.C3W6] 51-14990
1. Carey, William, 1761-1834. I. Title.

Carey, William, 1761-1834 — Juvenile literature.

CARVER, Saxon Rowe. 92
The shoe-leather globe; a life of William Carey. Illustrated by Paul Granger. Nashville, Broadman Press [1965] 181 p. illus. 21 cm. [BV3269.C3C36] 65-19545
1. Carey, William, 1761-1834 — Juvenile literature. I. Title.

KIEFER, James S. 922.342
The shoemaker who gave India the Bible; the story of William Carey, by James S. And Velma B. Kiefer. Illustrated by Adrian Beerhorst. Grand Rapids, Mich., Baker Book House, 1964. 63 p. illus. 29 cm. ([The Valor series] 10) [BV3269.C3K5] 64-8350

1. Carey, William, 1761-1834 — Juvenile literature. I. Kiefer, Velma B., joint author. II. Title.

Cargill, David, 1809?-1843.

CARGILL, David, 266'.7'10924 B
1809?-1843.
The diaries and correspondence of David Cargill, 1832-1843 / edited, with an introd. and annotations by Albert J. Schutz. Canberra : Australian National University Press, 1978. xvi, 255 p. : ill. ; 22 cm. (Pacific history series ; no. 10) Includes index. Bibliography: p. 247-250. [BV3680.F6C332 1977] 78-312990 ISBN 0-7081-0719-2 : 23.95
1. Cargill, David, 1809?-1843. 2. Missionaries—Scotland—Biography. 3. Missionaries—Fiji Islands—Biography. 4. Missionaries—Tonga—Biography. I. Schutz, Albert J., 1936- II. Title. III. Series.
Distributed by Books Australia, 21 Brookhedge Rd., Trumbulle, CT 06611

Cargill, Morris.

CARGILL, Morris. 972.92'05'0924 B
Jamaica farewell / by Morris Cargill. 1st ed. Secaucus, N.J. : L. Stuart, c1978. 224 p. ; 24 cm. [F1874.C37 1978] 78-5522 ISBN 0-8184-0269-5 : 8.95
1. Cargill, Morris. 2. Jamaica—Social life and customs. 3. Plantation life—Jamaica. 4. Journalists—Biography. I. Title. BIP

Caribbean area—Biography.

PERSONALITIES 920.0729
Caribbean the international guide to who's who in the West Indies, Bahamas-Bermuda, 1972-73 5th ed. Kingston, Jamaica, Personalities Ltd [1974] 1061 p 27 cm. [F2175.P4]
1. Caribbean area—Biography.
LC card no for original edition 72-626464
Distributed by International Publications Service, for 35.00

Caribbean area—History.

HART, Francis 910.09'16'365
Russell, 1868-1938.
Admirals of the Caribbean. Freeport, N.Y., Books for Libraries Press [1971] x, 203 p. illus. 23 cm. Reprint of the 1922 ed. Bibliography: p. [191]-196. [F2161.H35 1971] 77-165640 ISBN 0-8369-5949-3
1. Caribbean area—History. 2. Buccaneers. I. Title. BIP

Caribbean area—Social life and customs—1975-

BAILEY, Joyce. 972.9'05
Picture the people of the Caribbean / Joyce Bailey & Michael I. N. Dash. New York : Friendship Press, c1977. 80 p. : ill. ; 22 cm. Interviews with 16 persons. [F2183.B34] 77-2912 ISBN 0-377-00065-5 : 2.95
1. Caribbean area—Social life and customs—1975- 2. Caribbean area—Biography. I. Dash, Michael I. N., joint author. II. Title.
Publisher's address : 475 Riverside Dr., Rm.772, New York, NY 10027

Cario da Sezze, Saint, 1613-1670.

BROWN, Beverly Holladay, 922.245
1912-
Saint Charles of Sezze, by Raphael Brown [pseud.] Chicago, Franciscan Herald Press [1959] 56p. 16cm. (Troubadour series) Includes bibliography. [BX4700.C252B7] 59-34197
1. Cario da Sezze, Saint, 1613-1670. I. Title.

Carle Clinic Association—History.

ROGERS, James 362.1'09773'66
Creighton Thomas.
Carle : concept and growth : a personal history / J. C. Thomas Rogers. Urbana, Ill. : Carle Foundation, c1978. xix, 228 p. : ill. ; 24 cm. Includes index. [RA982.U72C377] 78-5654 price unreported
1. Carle Clinic Association—History. 2. Carle Foundation—History. 3. Rogers, James Creighton Thomas. 4. Surgeons—Illinois—Urbana—Biography. I. Title.

Carle family.

CARL, Skip. 929'.2'0973
A Carl family history : the story of an old Long Island family / by Skip Carl. [Baldwin, N.Y.] : Carl, [1974] 23, [14] p. ; 28 cm. [CS71.C276 1974] 75-323396
1. Carle family. I. Title.

Carle Foundation—History.

ROGERS, James 362.1'09773'66
Creighton Thomas.
Carle : concept and growth : a personal history / J. C. Thomas Rogers. Urbana, Ill. : Carle Foundation, c1978. xix, 228 p. : ill. ; 24 cm. Includes index. [RA982.U72C377] 78-5654 price unreported
1. Carle Clinic Association—History. 2. Carle Foundation—History. 3. Rogers, James Creighton Thomas. 4. Surgeons—Illinois—Urbana—Biography. I. Title.

Carlebach, Joseph, 1883-1942.

CARLEBACH, Naphtali. 922.96
Joseph Carlebach and his generation; biography of the late Chief Rabbi of Altona and Hamburg. New York, Joseph Carlebach Memorial Foundation, 1959. 316p. illus. 24cm. [BM755.C274C3] 60-32796
1. Carlebach, Joseph, 1883-1942. I. Title.

Carles, Arthur B., 1882-1952.

GARDINER, Henry G. 708'.148'11 S
Arthur B. Carles: a critical and biographical study [by Henry G. Gardiner] Philadelphia, Philadelphia Museum of Art, 1970. 139-185, [7] p. illus. (part col.) 24 cm. (Philadelphia Museum of Art. Bulletin v. 64, no. 302-303) "Catalogue of works by Arthur B. Carles in the Philadelphia Museum of Art": p. [186]-[189] Includes bibliographical references. [N685.A45 vol. 64, no. 302-303] [ND237.C27] 759.13 72-186965
1. Carles, Arthur B., 1882-1952. I. Title. II. Series.

Carleton family.

HARGRAVE, Helena M. 929'.2'0973
Goodale.
Carleton-Carlton forebears: a genealogy of some descendants of Edward Carleton, proprietor of Rowley, Mass., 1639-1648/9; with some biographical notes, compiled by Helena M. Goodale Hargrave. [Walnut Creek, Calif.] 1970. 74, [3] p. coat of arms. 28 cm. With, as issued, the author's Kinsley forebears. [Walnut Creek, Calif.] 1970. Bibliography: p. [75] and [77] [CS71.K5597 1970] 72-192073
1. Carleton family. 2. Carlton family. I. Title.

Carleton, James Henry, 1814-1873.

HUNT, Aurora. 923.573
Major General James Henry Carleton, 1814-1873, western frontier dragoon. Glendale, Calif., A. H. Clark Co., 1958. 390p. illus., ports., maps (part fold.) coats of arms, facsims. 25cm. (Frontier military series, 2) Bibliography: p.[357]-375. [E181.C3H8] 58-2255
1. Carleton, James Henry, 1814-1873. I. Title. II. Series.

Carlisle, John Griffin, 1835-1910.

BARNES, James 973.8'0924 B
Anderson.
John G. Carlisle, financial statesman, by James A. Barnes. Gloucester, Mass., P. Smith, 1967 [c1931] xiii, 552 p. illus., ports. 21 cm. (American political leaders) Bibliography: p. 523-533. [E664.C27B2 1967] 67-8821
1. Carlisle, John Griffin, 1835-1910. 2. Silver question. 3. United States—Politics and government—1865-1900. I. Title. II. Series.

Carlisle, Rosalind Frances (Stanley) Howard, Countess of, 1845-1921.

ROBERTS, Charles, 1865- 942.3'74
1959.
The radical countess; the history of the life of Rosalind, Countess of Carlisle. [1st ed.] Carlisle, Steel Bros. [1962] xii, 198 p. illus., geneal. table, plates (part col.), ports. 22 cm. [CT788.C257R6 1962] 68-52350
1. Carlisle, Rosalind Frances (Stanley) Howard, Countess of, 1845-1921. I. Title.

Carlo Borromeo, Saint, 1538-1584—Juvenile literature.

ROBERTO, Brother, 1927- 922.245
A prince on a galloping horse; a story of St. Charles Borromeo. Illus. by Carolyn Lee Jagodits. Notre Dame, Ind., Dujarie Press [1961] 94p. illus. 24cm. [BX4700.C25R6] 61-4823
1. Carlo Borromeo, Saint, 1538-1584—Juvenile literature. I. Title.

Carlo da Sezze, Saint, 1613-1670.

BROWN, Beverly Holladay, 922.245
1912-
The wounded heart: St. Charles of Sezze, Franciscan Brother, by Raphael Brown [pseud.] Chicago, Franciscan Herald Press [1960] 180p. illus. 21cm. [BX4700.C252B72] 60-8642
1. Carlo da Sezze, Saint, 1613-1670. I. Title.

BROWN, Beverly Holladay, 922.245
1912-
The wounded heart: St. Charles of Sezze, Franciscan Brother, by Raphael Brown [pseud.] Chicago, Franciscan Herald Press [c.1960] 180p. Endpaper illus., map, Bibl.: p.177-180. 60-8642 3.50 bds.,
1. Carlo da Sezze, Saint, 1613-1670. I. Title.

CARLO DA SEZZE, Saint, 922.245
1613-1670.
Autobiography. Translated and edited by Leonard Perotti. With an introd. and postscript by Severino Gori. Chicago, Franciscan Herald Press [1963] 220 p. 23 cm. Secular name: Giovanni Carlo Melchiori. [BX4700.C252A33] 63-3707
I. Perotti, Leonard David, ed. II. Title.

CARLO DA SEZZE, Saint 922.245
[Secular name: Giovanni Carlo Melchiori] 1613-1670
Autobiography. Tr. [from Italian], ed. by Leonard Perotti. Introd., postscript by Severino Gori. Chicago, Franciscan Herald [c.1963] 220p. 23cm. 63-3707 4.50
I. Perotti, Leonard David, ed. II. Title.

Carlos II, King of Spain, 1661-1700.

LANGDON-DAVIES, John, 923.146
1897-
Carlos, the king who would not die. [1st American ed.] Englewood Cliffs, N. J., Prentice-Hall [1963, c1962] 272 p. illus. 22 cm. Includes bibliography. [DP186.L3 1963] 63-16580
1. Carlos II, King of Spain, 1661-1700. I. Title.

Carlos III, King of Spain, 1716-1788.

PETRIE, Charles 946'.057'0924
Alexander, Sir, bart., 1895-
King Charles III of Spain; an enlightened despot [by] Sir Charles Petrie New York, J. Day Co. [1971] xxi, 241 p. illus., ports. 23 cm. Includes bibliographical references. [DP199.P48 1971b] 71-141792 7.95
1. Carlos III, King of Spain, 1716-1788. 2. Spain—History—Charles III, 1759-1788. I. Title.

Carlos, 1949-

DOBSON, 364.1'092'4 B
Christopher.
The Carlos complex : a study in terror / Christopher Dobson and Ronald Payne. 1st American ed. New York : Putnam, 1977. 254 p. ; 23 cm. Includes index. [HV6431.C37D6 1977] 76-57878 ISBN 0-399-11903-5 : 8.95
1. Carlos, 1949- 2. Terrorists—Biography. I. Payne, Ronald, joint author. II. Title. BIP

SMITH, Colin. 322.4'2'0924 B
Carlos : portrait of a terrorist / [by] Colin Smith. London : Deutsch, 1976. 304 p., [8] p. of plates : ill., map, ports. ; 23 cm. Includes index. [HV6431.C37S57 1976] 77-350405 ISBN 0-233-96843-1 : £4.95
1. Carlos, 1949- 2. Terrorists—Biography.

SMITH, Colin. 364.1'31'0924 B
Carlos : portrait of a terrorist / Colin Smith. New York : Holt, Rinehart and Winston, 1977, c1976. 312 p., [4] leaves of plates : ill. ; 22 cm. Includes index. [HV6431.C37S57 1977] 76-29916 ISBN 0-03-019481-4 : 8.95
1. Carlos, 1949- 2. Terrorists—Biography.

Carlota Joaquina, consort of Joao VI, King of Portugal, 1775-1830.

CHEKE, Marcus, 946'.903'0924 B
Sir.
Carlota Joaquina, queen of Portugal. Freeport, N.Y., Books for Libraries Press [1969] 212 p. ports. 23 cm. (Select bibliographies reprint series) Reprint of the 1947 ed. Bibliography: p. 205. [DP650.C42 1969] 70-94266
1. Carlota Joaquina, consort of Joao VI, King of Portugal, 1775-1830. BIP

Carlsen, Niels Christian, 1884-1950.

NIELSEN, H Skov, ed. 922.473
A guardian of the faith; notes on the life and work of Dr. N. C. Carlsen, with relevant portions of the history of his church. [Blair, Neb.] United Evangelical Lutheran Church [1951] 162 p. illus., ports. 21 cm. "Compiled and edited ... under the direction of the Literature Committee of the Board of Directors for the Lutheran Publishing House." [BX8080.C35N5] 51-5036
1. Carlsen, Niels Christian, 1884-1950. I. Title.

Carlson, Leland Henry, 1908-

THE Dissenting tradition : 273
essays for Leland H. Carlson / edited by C. Robert Cole and Michael E. Moody. Athens : Ohio University Press, c1975. xxiii, 272 p. : port. ; 25 cm. Includes bibliographical references. [BX5203.2.D57] 74-27706 ISBN 0-8214-0176-9 lib.bdg. : 13.50
1. Carlson, Leland Henry, 1908- 2. Carlson, Leland Henry, 1908- —Bibliography. 3. Dissenters, Religious—England—Addresses, essays, lectures. I. Carlson, Leland Henry, 1908- II. Cole, Charles Robert, 1939- III. Moody, Michael E.
Contents omitted

Carlson, Paul Earle, 1928-1964.

ANDERSON, Carl Philip, 922.473
comp.
There was a man, his name: Paul Carlson. Drawings by L. Birger Sponberg. Westwood, N. J., Revell [c.1965] 107p. illus., ports. 21cm. [BV3625.C63C35] 65-3558 2.50
1. Carlson, Paul Earle, 1928-1964. 2. Missions—Congo (Leopoldville) I. Title.

ANDERSON, Carl Philip, 922.473
comp.
There was a man, his name: Paul Carlson. Drawings by L. Birger Sponberg. Westwood, N. J., Revell [1965] 107 p. illus., ports. 21 cm. Essays of appreciation by friends, colleagues, and members of Dr. Carison's family. [BV3625.C63C35] 65-3558
1. Carlson, Paul Earle, 1928-1964. 2. Missions—Congo (Leopoldville) I. Title.

Carlsson, Erland, 1822-1893.

LINDQUIST, Emory 973'.04'395 S
Kempton, 1908-
Shepherd of an immigrant people : the story of Erland Carlsson / by Emory Lindquist. Rock Island, Ill. : Augustana Historical Society, 1978. xi, 236 p. : ill. ; 25 cm. (Publication - Augustana Historical Society ; no. 26) Running title: The story of Erland Carlsson. Includes index. Bibliography: p. 218-232. [F536.A96 no. 26] [BX808.C38] 284'.1'0924 B 78-108120 ISBN 0-910184-26-7 : 7.50
1. Carlsson, Erland, 1822-1893. 2. Lutheran Church—Clergy—Biography. 3. Clergy—United States—Biography. I. Title. II. Title: The story of Erland Carlsson. BIP

Carlton family.

PRESCOTT, Worrall Dumont, 929.2
1900-
A record concerning Lt. John Carlton of Rowley and Haverhill, Massachusetts, and his descent from King Edward the Third who ruled England from 1327 to 1377 and about John Carlton and Jane Gilmore Carlton of Woolwich, Maine, married December 18, 1760. [New Rochelle, N.Y., Printed by Westchester Lithographers, 1967] 39 l. illus., coat of arms, ports. 28 cm. Cover title: A Carlton genealogy and history. [CS71.C2778 1967] 67-5538
1. Carlton family. I. Title. II. Title: A Carlton genealogy and history.

Carlton, Steve, 1944- —Juvenile literature.

WARD, Martha 796.357'092'4 B
Eads.
Steve Carlton, star southpaw / Martha Eads Ward. New York : Putnam, [1975] 126 p. ; 21 cm. (Putnam sports shelf) Includes index. A biography of the left-handed pitcher who in one game in 1969 struck out nineteen batters. [GV865.C317W37 1975] 92 74-21079 ISBN 0-399-60934-2 lib. bdg. : 5.29
1. Carlton, Steve, 1944- —Juvenile literature. 2. Baseball—Juvenile literature. I. Title.

Carlyle, Aelred, 1874-1955.

ANSON, Peter Frederick, 922.271
1889-
About extraordinary; a memoir of Aelred Carlyle, monk and missionary, 1874-1955. Foreword by Maisie Ward. New York, Sheed and Ward [1959, c1958] 310p. illus. 23cm. [BX4705.C314A7 1959] 59-16263
1. Carlyle, Aelred, 1874-1955. I. Title.

Carlyle, Jane Baillie (Welsh) 1801-1866.

CARLYLE, Jane Baillie 824'.8 B
(Welsh) 1801-1866.
Letters and memorials of Jane Welsh Carlyle. Prepared for publication by Thomas Carlyle. Edited by James Anthony Froude. New York, Haskell House [1972] p. [PR4419.C5A8 1972] 72-2131 ISBN 0-8383-1492-9
I. Carlyle, Thomas, 1795-1881. II. Froude, James Anthony, 1818-1894, ed. III. Title. BIP

DREW, Elizabeth A., 824'.8 B
1887-1965.
Jane Welsh and Jane Carlyle. New York, Haskell House, 1973, c1928] 282 p. ports. 23 cm. Reprint of the 1928 ed. published by Harcourt, Brace, New York. [PR4419.C5D7 1973] 72-3641 ISBN 0-8383-1555-0 11.95
1. Carlyle, Jane Baillie (Welsh) 1801-1866. I. Title. BIP

HANSON, Lawrence. 928.2
Necessary evil; the life of Jane Welsh Carlyle, by Lawrence and Elisabeth Hanson. New York, Macmillan, 1952. 618 p. ports. 22 cm. Bibliography: p. 551-561. [PR4419.C5H3 1952a] 52-10222
1. Carlyle, Jane Baillie (Welsh) 1801-1866. 2. Carlyle, Thomas, 1795-1881. I. Hanson, Elisabeth M. joint author. II. Title.

Carlyle, Jane Baillie (Welsh) 1801-1866—Biography.

HANSON, Lawrence. 824'.8 B
Necessary evil : the life of Jane Welsh Carlyle / by Lawrence and Elisabeth Hanson. New York : Octagon Books, 1975, c1952. p. cm. Reprint of the ed. published by Macmillan, New York. Includes index. Bibliography: p. [PR4419.C5H3 1975] 75-30521 ISBN 0-374-93652-8 : 19.50
1. Carlyle, Jane Baillie (Welsh) 1801-1866—Biography. 2. Carlyle, Thomas, 1795-1881—Biography. I. Hanson, Elisabeth M., joint author. II. Title. BIP

Carlyle, Thomas, 1795-1881.

BURDETT, Osbert, 1885- 824'.8 B
1936.
The two Carlyles. Freeport, N.Y., Books for Libraries Press [1971] 319 p. 23 cm. Reprint of the 1930 ed. Bibliography: p. 313-314. [PR4433.B8 1971b] 78-164591 ISBN 0-8369-5875-6
1. Carlyle, Thomas, 1795-1881. 2. Carlyle, Jane Baillie (Welsh) 1801-1866. I. Title. BIP

CAMPBELL, Ian McIntyre, 824'.8 B
1915-
Thomas Carlyle / by Ian Campbell. New York : Scribner, [1975], c1974. xiv, 210 p., [6] leaves of plates : ill. ; 23 cm. Includes index. Bibliography: p. [194]-206. [PR4433.C19 1975] 74-24689 ISBN 0-684-14137-X : 10.00
1. Carlyle, Thomas, 1795-1881.

CARLYLE, Thomas, 1795- 824'.8 B
1881.
Letters of Thomas Carlyle, 1826-1836. Edited by Charles Eliot Norton. Freeport, N.Y., Books for Libraries Press [1972] 2 v. illus. 23 cm. Reprint of the 1888 ed. Includes bibliographical references. [PK4433.A4 1972] 70-39194 201 A0006437CARLYLE, Thomas, 1795-

CARLYLE, Thomas, 1795- 826'.8
1881.
The letters of Thomas Carlyle to his brother Alexander, with related family letters. Edited by Edwin W. Marrs, Jr. Cambridge, Belknap Press of Harvard University Press, 1968. xiii, 830 p. illus., geneal. tables, map, ports. 25 cm. Bibliography: p. [797]-799. [PR4433.A5C23] 68-21978 15.00
I. Carlyle, Alexander, 1797-1876. II. Marrs, Edwin W., ed. III. Title.

CARLYLE, Thomas, 1795- 826'.8
1881.
The letters of Thomas Carlyle to his brother Alexander, with related family letters. Edited by Edwin W. Marrs, Jr. Cambridge, Belknap Press of Harvard University Press, 1968. xiii, 830 p. illus., geneal. tables, map, ports. 25 cm. Bibliography: p. [797]-799. [PR4433.A5C23] 68-21978 15.00
I. Carlyle, Alexander, 1797-1876. II. Marrs, Edwin W., ed. III. Title.

CARLYLE, Thomas, 1795-1881. 928.2
Letters of Thomas Carlyle to William Graham, edited by John Graham, Jr. Princeton, Princeton University Press, 1950. xx, 86 p. illus. 22 cm. [PR4433.A5G7] 50-5233
I. Graham, William, b. 1770. II. Graham, John, 1888- ed. III. Title.

CARLYLE, Thomas, 828'.8'03 B
1795-1881.
Reminiscences. Edited by James Anthony Froude. London, Longmans, Green, 1881. St. Clair Shores, Mich., Scholarly Press, 1971. 2 v. 21 cm. Contents.Contents.—v. 1. James Carlyle of Ecclefechan.—Edward Irving.—v. 2. Lord Jeffrey.—Jane Welsh Carlyle.—Appendix: Southey. Wordsworth. [PR4433.R4 1971] 71-144936 ISBN 0-403-00898-0
I. Title. BIP

CARLYLE, Thomas, 1795- 824'.8 S
1881.
Sartor resartus; the life and opinions of Herr Teufelsdrockh, in three books. New York, AMS Press [1974] xxii, 250 p. port. 23 cm. (The works of Thomas Carlyle, v. 1) (Series: Carlyle, Thomas, 1795-1881. Works. 1974. vol. 1.) Reprint of the 1896 ed. published by Chapman and Hall, London. [PR4420.F74 vol. 1] [PR4429] 824'.8 B 74-808 ISBN 0-404-01411-9 17.50
I. Title. II. Series.

CAZAMIAN, Louis Francois, 828.808
1877-1965
Carlyle. Tr. by E. K. Brown. [Hamden, Conn.] Archon, 1966. ix, 289p. 22cm. Reprint of the tr. first pub. in 1932. [PR4433.C32 1966] 66-25186 8.00
1. Carlyle, Thomas, 1795-1881. I. Title.

CHESTERTON, Gilbert 824'.8 B
Keith, 1874-1936.
Thomas Carlyle, by G. K. Chesterton and J. E. Hodder Williams. London, Hodder and Stoughton, 1902. [Folcroft, Pa.] Folcroft Library Editions, 1972. p. [PR4433.C5 1972] 72-12737 ISBN 0-8414-0981-1 (lib. bdg.)
1. Carlyle, Thomas, 1795-1881. I. Hodder-Williams, John Ernest, Sir, 1876-1927, joint author.

CHESTERTON, Gilbert 824'.8 B
Keith, 1874-1936.
Thomas Carlyle, by G. K. Chesterton and J. E. Hodder Williams. New York, Haskell House, 1973. 40 p. illus. 29 cm. Reprint of the 1902 ed. published by Hodder and Stoughton, London, in series: The Bookman biographies. [PR4433.C5 1973] 73-9601 ISBN 0-8383-1705-7 9.95
1. Carlyle, Thomas, 1795-1881. I. Hodder-Williams, John Ernest, Sir, 1876-1927, joint author. II. Series: The Bookman biographies.

COLLIS, John Stewart, 824'.8 B
1900-
The Carlyles; a biography of Thomas and Jane Carlyle. New York, Dodd, Mead [1973, c1971] 186 p. illus. 23 cm. Bibliography: p. 183. [PR4433.C57 1973] 72-2555 ISBN 0-396-06637-2 6.95
1. Carlyle, Thomas, 1795-1881. 2. Carlyle, Jane Baille (Welsh), 1801-1866. I. Title.

FROUDE, James Anthony, 824'.8
1818-1894.
My relations with Carlyle. Together with a letter from the late Sir James Stephen, bart., dated December 9, 1886. Freeport, N.Y., Books for Libraries Press [1971] vi, 80 p. 23 cm. Reprint of the 1903 ed. [PR4433.F7 1971] 70-154150 ISBN 0-8369-5766-0
1. Carlyle, Thomas, 1795-1881. I. Stephen, James Fitzjames, Sir, bart., 1829-1894. II. Title. BIP

HALLIDAY, James Lorimer, 928.2
1897-
Mr. Carlyle, my patient; a psychosomatic biography. [1st American ed.] New York, Grune & Stratton, 1950. xiii, 227 p. map (on lining papers) 22 cm. "Sources": p. 225-226. [PR4433.H27 1950] 50-4358
1. Carlyle, Thomas, 1795-1881. I. Title.

HALLIDAY, James Lorimer, 824'.7 B
1897-
Mr. Carlyle, my patient; a psychosomatic biography, by James L. Halliday. New York, Haskell House Publishers, 1974. xiii, 227 p. illus. 23 cm. Reprint of the 1949 ed. published by W. Heinemann, London. Bibliography: p. 225-226. [PR4433.H27 1974] 73-18125 ISBN 0-8383-1737-5 11.95
1. Carlyle, Thomas, 1795-1881. I. Title. BIP

HOOD, Edwin Paxton, 824'.8 B
1820-1885.
Thomas Carlyle, philosophic thinker, theologian, historian, and poet. New York, Haskell House Publishers, 1970. 502 p. 23 cm. "First published 1875." [PR4433.H6 1970] 71-116795 ISBN 8-383-10370-
1. Carlyle, Thomas, 1795-1881.

LAMMOND, D. 824'.7 B
Carlyle, by D. Lammond. New York, Haskell House Publishers, 1974. 144 p. 23 cm. Reprint of the 1934 ed. published by Duckworth, London, which was issued as no. 38 of Great lives. Bibliography: p. 143-144. [PR4433.L16 1974] 73-18127 ISBN 0-8383-1740-5 9.95
1. Carlyle, Thomas, 1795-1881. I. Title. BIP

MASSON, David, 1822-1907. 824'.8
Carlyle, personally and in his writings; two Edinburgh lectures. [Folcroft, Pa.] Folcroft Library Editions, 1973. 119 p. 24 cm. Reprint of the 1885 ed. published by Macmillan, London. Contents.—Carlyle personally.—Carlyle's literary life and his creed. [PR4433.M3 1973] 73-5979 ISBN 0-8414-5921-5
1. Carlyle, Thomas, 1795-1881. I. Masson, David, 1822-1907. Carlyle's literary life and his creed. 1973. II. Title. III. Title: Carlyle personally. IV. Title: Carlyle's literary life and his creed.

NEFF, Emery Edward, 828'.8'08
1892-
Carlyle, by Emery Neff. New York, Russell & Russell [1968, c1932] 282 p. port. 23 cm. Bibliography: p. 271-276. [PR4433.N38 1968] 68-10935
1. Carlyle, Thomas, 1795-1881. BIP

NICHOL, John, 1833- 828'.8'08
1894.
Thomas Carlyle. New York, AMS Press [1968] viii, 248 p. 22 cm. (English men of letters) "Reprinted from the edition of 1892, London." Bibliographical footnotes. [PR4433.N5 1968] 68-58391
1. Carlyle, Thomas, 1795-1881.

NICOLL, Henry James. 824'.8 B
Thomas Carlyle. Rev. ed., with additional chapter. Edinburgh, MacNiven & Wallace, 1881. [Folcroft, Pa.] Folcroft Library Editions, 1972. 255 p. port. 24 cm. [PR4433.N54 1972] 72-6161 ISBN 0-8414-0058-X
1. Carlyle, Thomas, 1795-1881.

NICOLL, Henry James. 824'.8 B
Thomas Carlyle / by Henry J. Nicoll. Rev. ed., with additional chapter. Norwood, Pa. : Norwood Editions, 1976. 255 p. : port. ; 23 cm. Reprint of the 1881 ed. published by MacNiven & Wallace, Edinburgh. Includes bibliographical references. [PR4433.N54 1976] 76-10191 ISBN 0-8482-1912-0 : 17.50
1. Carlyle, Thomas, 1795-1881.

SYMONS, Julian, 1912- 824'.8
Thomas Carlyle: the life and ideas of a prophet. Freeport, N.Y., Books for Libraries Press [1970, c1952] 308 p. 23 cm. Bibliography: p. [297]-299. [PR4433.S83 1970] 76-126261
1. Carlyle, Thomas, 1795-1881.

SYMONS, Julian, 1912- 928.2
Thomas Carlyle; the life and ideas of a prophet. New York, Oxford University Press, 1952. 308 p. 23 cm. Full name: Julian Gustave Symons. Includes bibliography. [PR4433.S83 1952a] 52-11589
1. Carlyle, Thomas, 1795-1881. I. Title.

WATT, Lauchlan MacLean, 824'.8
1867-
Thomas Carlyle. [Folcroft, Pa.] Folcroft Library Editions, 1973. p. Reprint of the 1912 ed. published by T. C. & E. C. Jack, London, in series: The People's books. Bibliography: p. [PR4433.W3 1973] 73-16291 8.50
1. Carlyle, Thomas, 1795-1881. BIP

†WATT, Lauchlan MacLean, 824'.8 B
1867-1957.
Thomas Carlyle / by Lauchlan MacLean Watt. Folcroft, Pa. : Folcroft Library Editions, 1977. 94 p., [1] leaf of plates : port. ; 26 cm. Reprint of the 1912 ed. published by T. C. & E. C. Jack, London, and Dodge Pub. Co., New York, in series: The People's books. Includes index. Bibliography: p. 92. [PR4433.W3 1977] 77-28456 ISBN 0-8414-9634-X lib. bdg. : 10.00
1. Carlyle, Thomas, 1795-1881. 2. Authors, Scottish—19th century—Biography.

WILSON, John, Rev., M.A. 824'.8
Thomas Carlyle: the iconoclast of modern shams; a short study of his life and writings. [Folcroft, Pa.] Folcroft Library Editions, 1972. vi, 151 p. illus. 24 cm. Reprint of the 1881 ed., published by A. Gardner, Paisley, Scot. [PR4433.W57 1972] 72-7263 ISBN 0-8414-0300-7 (lib. bdg)
1. Carlyle, Thomas, 1795-1881.

YOUNG, Louise Merwin, 907'.2'024
1903-
Thomas Carlyle and the art of history / by Louise Merwin Young. Folcroft, Pa. : Folcroft Library Editions, 1974, c1939. p. cm. Reprint of the thesis ed., Philadelphia. Originally presented as the author's thesis,

University of Pennsylvania. Includes index. Bibliography: p. [D16.8.C32Y6 1974] 74-23128 ISBN 0-8414-9768-0 lib. bdg. : 20.00
1. Carlyle, Thomas, 1795-1881. 2. Historiography. I. Title. **BIP**

Carlyle, Thomas, 1795-1881—Biography.

CLUBBE, John, comp. 824'.8 B
Two reminiscences of Thomas Carlyle. Durham, N.C., Duke University Press, 1974. xiv, 145 p. illus. 25 cm. Contents.Contents.—Althaus, F. Thomas Carlyle: a biographical and literary portrait, with Thomas Carlyle's notes.—Reminiscence of Adam and Archibald Skirving. Includes bibliographical references. [PR4433.C54] 73-81497 ISBN 0-8223-0307-8 6.75
1. Carlyle, Thomas, 1795-1881—Biography. 2. Carlyle, Thomas, 1795-1881—Friends and associates. 3. Skirving, Adam, 1719-1803. 4. Skirving, Archibald, 1749-1819. I. Althaus, Friedrich, 1829-1897. Thomas Carlyle: a biographical and literary portrait, with Thomas Carlyle's notes. 1974. II. Carlyle, Thomas, 1795-1881. Reminiscence of Adam and Archibald Skirving. 1974. III. Title. **BIP**

CONWAY, Moncure Daniel, 824'.8 B
1832-1907.
Thomas Carlyle / by Moncure D. Conway. Folcroft, Pa. : Folcroft Library Editions, 1977. 255 p., [8] leaves of plates : ill. ; 23 cm. Reprint of the 1881 ed. published by Harper, New York. [PR4433.C6 1977] 77-648 ISBN 0-8414-3411-5 lib. bdg. : 25.00
1. Carlyle, Thomas, 1795-1881—Biography. 2. Authors, English—19th century—Biography. I. Title.

CONWAY, Moncure Daniel, 824'.8 B
1832-1907.
Thomas Carlyle / by Moncure D. Conway. Folcroft, Pa. : Folcroft Library Editions, 1977. 255 p., [8] leaves of plates : ill. ; 23 cm. Reprint of the 1881 ed. published by Harper, New York. [PR4433.C6 1977] 77-648 ISBN 0-8414-3411-5 lib. bdg. : 25.00
1. Carlyle, Thomas, 1795-1881—Biography. 2. Authors, English—19th century—Biography. I. Title.

FROUDE, James Anthony, 824'.8 B
1818-1894.
Froude's Life of Carlyle / abridged and edited by John Clubbe. Columbus : Ohio State University Press, [1978] p. cm. Abridgement of the author's Thomas Carlyle, a history of the first forty years of his life, 1795-1835 and Thomas Carlyle, a history of his life in London, 1834-1881. Includes bibliographical references and index. [PR4433.F742 1978] 78-19158 ISBN 0-8142-0274-8 : 30.00
1. Carlyle, Thomas, 1795-1881—Biography. 2. Authors, English—19th century—Biography. I. Clubbe, John. II. Title. III. Title: Life of Carlyle. **BIP**

FROUDE, James Anthony, 824'.8 B
1818-1894.
Thomas Carlyle; a history of the first forty years of his life, 1795-1835. New York, Scribner, 1882; St. Clair Shores, Mich., Scholarly Press, 1970. 2 v. 22 cm. [PR4433.F73 1970] 79-121334 ISBN 0-403-00210-9
1. Carlyle, Thomas, 1795-1881—Biography.

GARNETT, Richard, 1835- 824'.8 B
1906.
Life of Thomas Carlyle / by Richard Garnett. New York : AMS Press, [1979] p. cm. Reprint of the 1887 ed. published by W. Scott, London, in series: Great writers. Bibliography J. P. Anderson: [PR4433.G2 1979] 75-30023 ISBN 0-404-14028-9 : 21.50
1. Carlyle, Thomas, 1795-1881—Biography. 2. Carlyle, Thomas, 1795-1881—Bibliography. 3. Authors, English—19th century—Biography. **BIP**

LARKIN, Henry, 1820-1899. 824'.8
Carlyle and the open secret of his life. New York, Haskell House, 1970. ix, 371 p. 23 cm. Reprint of the 1886 ed. Includes bibliographical references. [PR4433.L2 1970] 76-122621 ISBN 0-8383-0905-4
1. Carlyle, Thomas, 1795-1881—Biography. I. Title. **BIP**

WILSON, David Alec, 824'.8 S B
1864-1933.
Carlyle at his zenith (1848-53). London, K. Paul, Trench, Trubner, 1927. St. Clair Shores, Mich., Scholarly Press, 1974. p. cm. (Series: Wilson, David Alec, 1864-1933. Life of Carlyle, v. 4.) Original ed. issued as v. 4 of the author's Life of Carlyle. [PR4433.W52 vol. 4] 824'.8 B 76-145377 ISBN 0-403-00790-9
1. Carlyle, Thomas, 1795-1881—Biography. I. Title. II. Series. **BIP**

WILSON, David Alec, 824'.8 B
1864-1933.
Life of Carlyle. London, K. Paul, Trench, Trubner, 1923- St. Clair Shores, Mich., Scholarly Press, 1974- p. cm. [PR4433.W52] 73-22094
1. Carlyle, Thomas, 1795-1881—Biography. I. Title.

Carlyle, Thomas, 1795-1881—Biography—London life.

FROUDE, James Anthony, 824'.8 B
1818-1894.
Thomas Carlyle; a history of his life in London, 1834-1881. New ed. London, Longmans, Green, 1897. St. Clair Shores, Mich., Scholarly Press [1970?] 2 v. port. 22 cm. [PR4433.F74 1970] 72-108483 ISBN 0-403-00191-9
1. Carlyle, Thomas, 1795-1881—Biography—London life. **BIP**

Carlyle, Thomas, 1795-1881—Biography—Youth.

WILSON, David Alec, 824'.8 B
1864-1933.
Carlyle till marriage (1795-1826) New York, Haskell House Publishers, 1973. xvi, 442 p. illus. 23 cm. Reprint of the 1923 ed. which was vol. 1 of the author's Life of Carlyle. Includes bibliographical references. [PR4433.W43 1973] 72-3680 ISBN 0-8383-1557-7 16.95
1. Carlyle, Thomas, 1795-1881—Biography—Youth. I. Title. **BIP**

Carlyle, Thomas, 1795-1881—Correspondence.

CARLYLE, Thomas, 1795- 821'.8 B
1881.
Early letters of Thomas Carlyle / edited by Charles Eliot Norton. Boston : Longwood Press, 1977. p. cm. Reprint of the 1886 ed. published by Macmillan, London, New York. Includes bibliographical references. [PR4433.A4 1977] 77-88563 ISBN 0-89341-460-3 lib.bdg. : 65.00
1. Carlyle, Thomas, 1795-1881—Correspondence. 2. Authors, English—19th century—Correspondence. I. Norton, Charles Eliot, 1827-1908. II. Title.

CARLYLE, Thomas, 1795- 824'.8
1881.
The love letters of Thomas Carlyle and Jane Welsh / edited by Alexander Carlyle. New York : AMS Press, 1976. 2 v. : ill. ; 23 cm. Reprint of the 1909 ed. published by J. Lane, London, New York. Includes bibliographical references and index. [PR4433.A5W4 1976] 75-30016 ISBN 0-404-14050-5 : 60.00
1. Carlyle, Thomas, 1795-1881—Correspondence. 2. Carlyle, Jane Baillie Welsh, 1801-1866—Correspondence. 3. Authors, Scottish—19th century—Correspondence. I. Carlyle, Jane Baillie Welsh, 1801-1866. **BIP**

SANDERS, Charles 824'.8 B
Richard, 1904-
Carlyle's letters to Ruskin: a finding list with some unpublished letters and comments. [Folcroft, Pa.] Folcroft Library Editions, 1974. 31 p. 26 cm. Reprint of the 1958 ed. published by the Librarian, the John Rylands Library, and Manchester University Press, Manchester. Includes bibliographical references. [Z8147.S25 1974] 74-1107 5.00
1. Carlyle, Thomas, 1795-1881—Manuscripts—Catalogs. 2. Carlyle, Thomas, 1795-1881—Correspondence. 3. Ruskin, John, 1819-1900—Correspondence. I. Carlyle, Thomas, 1795-1881. II. Ruskin, John, 1819-1900. III. Title.

Carlyle, Thomas, 1795-1881—Friends and associates.

CLUBBE, John, comp. 824'.8 B
Two reminiscences of Thomas Carlyle. Durham, N.C., Duke University Press, 1974. xiv, 145 p. illus. 25 cm. Contents.Contents.—Althaus, F. Thomas Carlyle: a biographical and literary portrait, with Thomas Carlyle's notes.—Reminiscence of Adam and Archibald Skirving. Includes bibliographical references. [PR4433.C54] 73-81497 ISBN 0-8223-0307-8 6.75
1. Carlyle, Thomas, 1795-1881—Biography. 2. Carlyle, Thomas, 1795-1881—Friends and associates. 3. Skirving, Adam, 1719-1803. 4. Skirving, Archibald, 1749-1819. I. Althaus, Friedrich, 1829-1897. Thomas Carlyle: a biographical and literary portrait, with Thomas Carlyle's notes. 1974. II. Carlyle, Thomas, 1795-1881. Reminiscence of Adam and Archibald Skirving. 1974. III. Title. **BIP**

Carlyle, Thomas, 1795-1881—Friends and associates—Addresses, essays, lectures.

SANDERS, Charles 820'.9'008
Richard, 1904
Carlyle's friendships and other studies / Charles Richard Sanders. Durham, N.C. : Duke University Press, 1977. viii, 342 p. ; 25 cm. Includes bibliographical references and index. [PR4433.S35] 77-80676 ISBN 0-8223-0389-2 : 14.75
1. Carlyle, Thomas, 1795-1881—Friends and associates—Addresses, essays, lectures. 2. Authors, English—19th century—Biography—Addresses, essays, lectures. 3. English poetry—19th century—History and criticism—Addresses, essays, lectures. I. Title.
Contents omitted

Carlyle, Thomas, 1795-1881—Homes and haunts.

HOLME, Thea (Johnston) 928.2
1907-
The Carlyles at home. Illus. by Lynton Lamb. New York, Oxford [c.]1965. 204p. illus. 23cm. Bibl. [PR4433.H57] 65-3132 5.60
1. Carlyle, Thomas, 1795-1881—Homes and haunts. 2. Carlyle, Jane Baillie (Welsh) 1801-1866. I. Title.

SLOAN, John MacGavin, 824'.8 B
1880-
The Carlyle country, with a study of Carlyle's life, by J. M. Sloan. New York, Haskell House Publishers, 1973. 283 p. ill. 24 cm. Includes bibliographical references. [PR4433.S6 1973] 72-2132 ISBN 0-8383-1490-2
1. Carlyle, Thomas, 1795-1881—Homes and haunts. 2. Literary landmarks—Scotland. I. Title.

Carlyle, Thomas, 1795-1881—Homes and haunts—Chelsea, Eng.

BLUNT, Reginald, 1857- 824'.8 B
1944.
The Carlyles' Chelsea home : being some account of No. 5, Cheyne Row / by Reginald Blunt. New York : Haskell House, [1976] p. cm. Reprint of the 1895 ed. published by G. Bell, London. Includes index. [PR4433.B5 1976] 75-30875 ISBN 0-8383-2079-1 lib.bdg. : 10.95
1. Carlyle, Thomas, 1795-1881—Homes and haunts—Chelsea, Eng. 2. Carlyle, Jane Baillie Welsh, 1801-1866. 3. Chelsea, Eng.—Description. I. Title.

Carlyle, Thomas, 1795-1881—Influence—Dickens.

GOLDBERG, Michael, 1930- 823'.8
Carlyle and Dickens. Athens, University of Georgia Press, 1972. 248 p. front. 26 cm. Bibliography: p. 239-244. [PR4583.G6] 70-184773 ISBN 0-8203-0282-1 10.00
1. Carlyle, Thomas, 1795-1881—Influence—Dickens. 2. Dickens, Charles, 1812-1870. I. Title.

Carlyle, Thomas, 1795-1881—Manuscripts—Catalogs.

SANDERS, Charles 824'.8 B
Richard, 1904-
Carlyle's letters to Ruskin: a finding list with some unpublished letters and comments. [Folcroft, Pa.] Folcroft Library Editions, 1974. 31 p. 26 cm. Reprint of the 1958 ed. published by the Librarian, the John Rylands Library, and Manchester University Press, Manchester. Includes bibliographical references. [Z8147.S25 1974] 74-1107 5.00
1. Carlyle, Thomas, 1795-1881—Manuscripts—Catalogs. 2. Carlyle, Thomas, 1795-1881—Correspondence. 3. Ruskin, John, 1819-1900—Correspondence. I. Carlyle, Thomas, 1795-1881. II. Ruskin, John, 1819-1900. III. Title.

Carmean, Harry, 1922-

CARMEAN, Harry, 1922- 759.13
Carmean, by June Harwood. [Los Angeles, Calif., 1974] 143 p. (chiefly col. illus.) 29 cm. [ND237.C28H37] 74-77101
1. Carmean, Harry, 1922- I. Harwood, June.

Carmelite Sisters of the Divine Heart of Jesus.

MARY Teresa, of St. Joseph, 922.2
Mother, 1855-1938.
Mother Mary Teresa of St. Joseph (Anna Maria Tauscher van den Bosch) the servant of God, foundress of Carmel of the Divine Heart of Jesus; an autobiography, translated by Berchmans Bittle. Wauwatosa, Wis., Carmelite Convent [1953] 267p. illus. 22cm. [BX4705.M4238A32] 54-24794
1. Carmelite Sisters of the Divine Heart of Jesus. I. Title.

Carmichael, Hoagy, 1899-

CARMICHAEL, Hoagy, 780'.92'4 B
1899-
Sometimes I wonder : the story of Hoagy Carmichael / by Hoagy Carmichael ; with Stephen Longstreet. New York : Da Capo Press, 1976. 313 p., [10] leaves of plates : ill. ; 22 cm. (The Roots of jazz) Reprint of the 1965 ed. published by Farrar, Straus and Giroux, New York. [ML410.C327A27 1976] 76-7577 ISBN 0-306-70809-4 : 17.50
1. Carmichael, Hoagy, 1899- 2. Musicians—Correspondence, reminiscences, etc. I. Longstreet, Stephen, 1907- II. Title.

Carnegie, Amos Hubert,

CARNEGIE, Amos Hubert, 1885- 922
Faith moves mountains, an autobiography. [1st ed.] Washington [1950- v. port. 21 cm. [BX8473.C3A3] 50-3933
I. Title.

Carnegie, Andrew, 1835-1919.

HACKER, Louis Morton, 330.973
1899-
The world of Andrew Carnegie: 1865-1901 [by] Louis M. Hacker. [1st ed. Philadelphia, Lippincott [1968] xxxvii, 473 p. 24 cm. Includes bibliographies. [HC105.H13] 67-24007
1. Carnegie, Andrew, 1835-1919. 2. United States—Economic conditions. 3. Industry and state—United States—History. I. Title.

HARLOW, Alvin Fay, 1875- 923.673
Andrew Carnegie. New York, J. Messner [1953] 182p. 22cm. [CT275.C3H23] 53-10503
1. Carnegie, Andrew, 1835-1919. I. Title.

HENDRICK, Burton 338.7'67'20924 B
Jesse, 1870-1949.
The life of Andrew Carnegie. Introd. to the J. & J. Harper ed. by Louis Hacker. New York, Harper & Row [1969, c1932] 2 v. illus., facsims, ports. 22 cm. (The Allan Nevins reprints in American economic history) J. & J. Harper editions. Bibliography: p. 389-400. [CT275.C3H27 1969] 70-80806

1. Carnegie, Andrew, 1835-1919. I. Title.

JUDSON, Clara 917.3'03'80924 B
(Ingram) 1879-1960.
Andrew Carnegie. With a foreword by Mary Jane Judson Rice. Illustrated by Steele Savage. Chicago, Follett Pub. Co. [1964] 157 p. illus. 25 cm. A biography of the Scottish immigrant who made a great fortune in the steel industry, and who used much of it for philanthropic causes, including libraries, foundations, and education. [CT275.C3J8] 92 AC 68
1. Carnegie, Andrew, 1835-1919. I. Savage, Steele, illus. II. Title.

MCATEE, John. 338.7'67'20924 B
Carnegie! [1st ed.] New York, Vantage Press [1968] 89 p. port. 21 cm. [CT275.C3M28] 76-1401 3.50
1. Carnegie, Andrew, 1835-1919.

MALONE, Mary. 338.4'7'6720924 B
Andrew Carnegie: giant of industry. Illustrated by Marvin Besunder. Champaign, Ill., Garrard Pub. Co. [1969] 96 p. illus. (part col.), ports. 24 cm. (Americans all) A biography of a self-made millionaire who rose from bobbin boy to tycoon and philanthropist. [HD9520.C3M3] 92 69-17611 2.49
1. Carnegie, Andrew, 1835-1919. I. Besunder, Marvin, illus. II. Title.

SHIPPEN, Katherine 923.673
Binney, 1892-
Andrew Carnegie and the age of steel. Illustrated with photos., and with drawings by Ernest Kurt Barth. New York, Random House [1958] 183 p. illus. 22 cm. (Landmark books, 80) [CT275.C3S5] 58-6179
1. Carnegie, Andrew, 1835-1919. I. Title.

SIMON, Charlie May 923.673
(Hogue) 1897-
The Andrew Carnegie story. New York, Dutton [c.1965] 224p. illus., ports. 21cm. [CT275.C3S55] 64-17342 3.25
1. Carnegie, Andrew, 1835-1919. I. Title.

WALL, Joseph 917.3'03'80924 B
Frazier.
Andrew Carnegie. New York, Oxford University Press [1970] xii, 1137 p. illus., ports. 24 cm. Includes bibliographical references. [CT275.C3W33] 74-83056 15.00
1. Carnegie, Andrew, 1835-1919. **BIP**

Carnegie, Andrew, 1835-1919—Juvenile literature.

HENRY, Joanne Landers. j92
Andrew Carnegie, young steelmaker. Illustrated by George Armstrong. Indianapolis, Bobbs-Merrill [1966] 200 p. col. illus. 20 cm. (Childhood of famous Americans) Bibliography: p. 108. [CT275.C3H28] 66-18415
1. Carnegie, Andrew, 1835-1919 — Juvenile literature. I. Title.

JUDSON, Clara 917.3'03'0924 [B]
(Ingram) 1879-1960.
Andrew Carnegie. With a foreword by Mary Jane Judson Rice. Illustrated by Steele Savage. Chicago, Follett Pub. Co. [1964] 157 p. illus. 25 cm. [CT275.C3J8] 64-19839
1. Carnegie, Andrew, 1835-1919—Juvenile literature.

KURLAND, Gerald, 917.3'03'80924 B
1942-
Andrew Carnegie, philanthropist and early tycoon. Charlotteville, N.Y., SamHar Press, 1973. 31 p. 23 cm. (Outstanding personalities, no. 50) Includes bibliographical references. A biography of the Scottish immigrant who made a fortune in the steel industry and used much of it for philanthropic causes. [CT275.C3K87] 92 72-81901 1.98 (lib. bdg.)
1. Carnegie, Andrew, 1835-1919—Juvenile literature. I. Title.
Pbk. 0.98; ISBN 0-87157-053-X

Carnegie, Mary Crowninshield (Endicott) 1864-1957.

LAING, Diana 942.080924 (B)
(Whitehill)
Mistress of herself. Barre, Mass., Barre Publishers, 1965. 246 p. illus., ports. 24 cm. Bibliography: p. 236-237. [DA565.C323L35] 65-24404
1. Carnegie, Mary Crowninshield (Endicott) 1864-1957. 2. Gt. Brit. — Pol. & govt. — 1837-1901. 3. Gt. Brit. — Pol. & govt. — 20th cent. 4. London — Soc. life & cust. I. Title.

MISTRESS of 942.080924 (B)
herself. Barre, Mass., Barre Publishers, 1965. 246 p. illus., ports. 24 cm. Bibliography: p. 236-237. [DA565.C323L35] 65-24404
1. Carnegie, Mary Crowninshield (Endicott) 1864-1957. 2. Gt. Brit. — Pol. & govt. — 1837-1901. 3. Gt. Brit. — Pol. & govt. — 20th cent. 4. London — Soc. life & cust.

Carnevali, Emanuel.

CARNEVALI, Emanuel. 818'.5'203 B
The autobiography of Emanuel Carnevali. Compiled & prefaced by Kay Boyle. New York, Horizon Press [1967] 264 p. ports. 24 cm. [PS3505.A72752Z5] 67-27908
I. Boyle, Kay, 1903- ed.

Carnot, Sadi Nicolas Leonard, 1796-1832.

SADI Carnot et l'essor de 536'.7
la thermodynamique / Table ronde du Centre national de la recherche scientifique, Paris, Ecole Polytechnique, 11-13 juin 1974. Paris : Editions du Centre national de la recherche scientifique, 1976. 435 p., [4] leaves of plates : ill. ; 24 cm. English or French. Includes bibliographical references and index. [QC310.15.S2] 77-451310 ISBN 2-222-01818-8 : 128F
1. Carnot, Sadi Nicolas Leonard, 1796-1832. 2. Thermodynamics—Congresses. 3. Physicists—France—Biography. I. France. Centre national de la recherche scientifique. II. Paris. Ecole polytechnique.

Caro, Anthony, 1924-

WHELAN, Richard. 730'.92'4
Anthony Caro / [by] Richard Whelan ; with additional texts by Clement Greenberg ... [et al.]. Harmondsworth ; New York : Penguin, 1974. 134 p. : ill. ; 20 cm. Bibliography: p. 83-84. [NB497.C35W46] 74-193694 ISBN 0-14-021797-5 : £1.10
1. Caro, Anthony, 1924-

WHELAN, Richard 730'.92'4
Anthony Caro [by] Richard Whelan; with additional texts by Clement Greenberg...[et al.] New York, E. P. Dutton, [1975 c1974] 131 [3] p. 63 ill. 21 cm. Bibliography: p. 83-84 [NB497.C35W46] ISBN 0-525-47400-5 3.50 (pbk.)
1. Caro, Anthony, 1924- I. Title.
L.C. no. for original edition: 74-193694

Caro, Joseph, 1488-1575.

WERBLOWSKY, Raphael 296.16
Jehudah Zwi, 1924-
Joseph Karo, lawyer and mystic. [London] Oxford University Press, 1962. xii, 315 p. 6 plates (incl. facsims.) 23 cm. (Scripta judaica, 4) "Manuscripts of the Maggid Mesharim": p. [297]-299. "Editions of the Maggid Mesharim": p. [304] "The works of R. Joseph Karo and the dates of their first editions": p. [305]-306. Bibliographical footnotes. [BM755.C28W4] 62-5933
1. Caro, Joseph, 1488-1575. I. Series.

Carolina Maria, consort of Ferdinand I, King of the Two Sicilies, 1752-1814.

BOTT, Ethlyn 945.7'3'060924 B
Wisegarver.
In the web of the pink spider; the story of Maria Caroline, Queen of the Two Sicilies. [1st ed.] New York, Pageant Press [1967] 206 p. illus. 21 cm. [DG848.37.C3B6] 66-30702
1. Carolina Maria, consort of Ferdinand I, King of the Two Sicilies, 1752-1814. I. Title.

Caroline Amelia Elizabeth, consort of George IV, 1768-1821.

HOLME, Thea 941.07'4'0924 B
Johnston, 1907-
Caroline, a biography of Caroline of Brunswick / Thea Holme. New York : Atheneum, 1980, c1979. p. cm. Includes index. Bibliography: p. [DA538.A2H58 1980] 79-51398 ISBN 0-689-10999-7 : 12.95
1. Caroline Amelia Elizabeth, consort of George IV, 1768-1821. 2. Great Britain—Queens—Biography. I. Title.

RUSSELL, Edward 942.07'4'0924
Frederick Langley Russell, Baron, 1895-
Caroline, the unhappy queen [by] Lord Russell of Liverpool. [1st American ed.] South Brunswick, A. S. Barnes Co. [1968, c1967] 172 p. illus., ports. 22 cm. [DA538.A2R8 1968] 68-29864 5.00
1. Caroline Amelia Elizabeth, consort of George IV, 1768-1821. I. Title.

Caroline, consort of George II, 1683-1737.

QUENNELL, Peter, 942.07'2'0924 B
1905-
Caroline of England; an Augustan portrait. Freeport, N.Y., Books for Libraries Press, 1973. p. Reprint of the 1940 ed. [DA501.A33Q4 1973] 72-12771 ISBN 0-8369-7148-5
1. Caroline, consort of George II, 1683-1737. 2. Great Britain—History—George II, 1727-1760. 3. Great Britain—Court and courtiers. I. Title.

Caroline Mathilde, consort of Christian VII, King of Denmark, 1751-1775.

CHAPMAN, Hester 948.9'03'0924 B
W., 1899-
Caroline Matilda, Queen of Denmark [by] Hester W. Chapman. [1st American ed.] New York, Coward, McCann & Geoghegan [1972, c1971] 221 p. illus. 22 cm. Bibliography: p. [212]-213. [DL199.8.C3C5 1972] 73-183530 6.95
1. Caroline Mathilde, consort of Christian VII, King of Denmark, 1751-1775.

Caroline, Mother, 1824-1892.

ZIMMERMANN, Mary Theola. 271'.979
As a magnet; life of Mother Caroline, S.S.N.D. illustrated by Jo Polseno. New York, Regina Press [1967] xi, 129 p. illus. 21 cm. [BX4705.C315Z5] 67-28216
1. Caroline, Mother, 1824-1892. I. Title.

Caron, Roger, 1938-

CARON, Roger, 1938- 365'.6'0924 B
Go-boy! : memoirs of a life behind bars / by Roger Caron. Toronto ; New York : McGraw-Hill Ryerson, c1978. xiii, 264 p. ; 23 cm. [HV9507.C373] 78-322434 ISBN 0-07-082535-1 : 10.95
1. Caron, Roger, 1938- 2. Prisoners—Canada—Biography. I. Title.

Carothers, Merlin R.

CAROTHERS, Merlin R. 289'.9 B
Victory on Praise Mountain / Merlin Carothers. Plainfield, N.J. : Logos International, c1979. viii, 177 p. ; 21 cm. [BX8762.Z8C373] 79-88266 ISBN 0-88270-378-1 pbk. : 2.95
1. Carothers, Merlin R. 2. Pentecostals—Clergy—Biography. 3. Clergy—United States—Biography. I. Title. **BIP**

Carpaccio, Vittore, 1455?-1525?

CARPACCIO: 759.5
biographical and critical study. Translated from the Italian by James Emmons. [New York] Skira [1958] 119p. mounted col. illus. 18cm. (The Taste of our time, 24) Bibliography: p.[111] [ND623.C3P53] 927.5 58-12919
1. Carpaccio, Vittore, 1455?-1525? I. Pignatti, Terisio, 1920-

Carpenter, Edward, 1844-1929—Biography.

CROSBY, Ernest 828'.8'09 B
Howard, 1856-1907.
Edward Carpenter: poet and prophet. [Folcroft, Pa.] Folcroft Library Editions, 1974. 51 p. 24 cm. Reprint of the 2d ed. published in 1905 by A. C. Fifield, London. Includes bibliographical references. [PR4451.Z5C7 1974] 74-8994 ISBN 0-8414-3358-5 (lib. bdg.)
1. Carpenter, Edward, 1844-1929—Biography. I. Title.

Carpenter, Mary, 1807-1877.

CARPENTER, Joseph 361'.92'4 B
Estlin, 1844-1927.
The life and work of Mary Carpenter. Reprinted with index added. 2d ed. Montclair, N.J., Patterson Smith, 1973. p. (Patterson Smith series in criminology, law enforcement & social problems. Publication no. 145) Reprint of the 2d ed., 1881, published by Macmillan, London. [HV28.C3C3 1973] 77-172564 ISBN 0-87585-145-2 12.50
1. Carpenter, Mary, 1807-1877. I. Title.

MANTON, Jo, 1919- 362.7'092'4 B
Mary Carpenter and the children of the streets / [by] Jo Manton. London : Heinemann Educational, 1976. xii, 268 p., [12] p. of plates : ill., ports. ; 24 cm. Includes index. Bibliography: p. 257-261. [HV28.C3M36 1976] 76-379612 ISBN 0-435-32569-8 : 33.25
1. Carpenter, Mary, 1807-1877. 2. Social work with children—Great Britain—Biography. 3. Social workers—Great Britain—Biography. I. Title.
Distributed by Heinemann Educ., Salem, New Hampshire **BIP**

Carpenter, Matthew Hale, 1824-1881.

THOMPSON, Edwin Bruce. 923.273
Matthew Hale Carpenter, Webster of the West. Madison, State Historical Society of Wisconsin, 1954. 335p. illus. 24cm. Includes bibliography. [E664.C29T5] 54-13478
1. Carpenter, Matthew Hale, 1824-1881. I. Title.

Carre, Mathilde Belard, called La Chatte, 1908—

PAINE, Lauran. 940.54'86'440924 B
Mathilde Carre, double agent / [by] Lauran Paine. London : Hale, 1976. 192 p., [4] p. of plates : ports. ; 22 cm. Includes index. Bibliography: p. [187] [D810.S8C296 1976] 76-378954 ISBN 0-7091-5511-5 : £4.25
1. Carre, Mathilde Belard, called La Chatte, 1908- 2. Spies—France—Biography. I. Title.

Carr, Emily, 1871-1945.

HEMBROFF-SCHLEICHER, 759.11 B
Edythe.
Emily Carr : the untold story / by Edythe Hembroff-Schleicher. Saanichton, B.C. : Hancock House, 1978. 408 p. : ill. ; 23 cm. Includes index. Bibliography: p. 405. [ND249.C3H39] 79-319074 ISBN 0-88839-003-3 : 14.95
1. Carr, Emily, 1871-1945. 2. Painters—Canada—Biography.
Distributed by Hancock House, 12008 First Ave. So., Seattle, WA 98168 **BIP**

SHADBOLT, Doris. 759.11
The art of Emily Carr / Doris Shadbolt. Seattle : University of Washington Press, [1979] p. cm. Bibliography: p. [ND249.C3S5] 79-4918 ISBN 0-295-95687-9 : 39.95
1. Carr, Emily, 1871-1945. 2. Painters—Canada—Biography. I. Carr, Emily, 1871-1945. II. Title. **BIP**

Carr, Eugene Asa, 1830-1910.

KING, James T. 923.573
War Eagle; a life of General Eugene A. Carr. Lincoln, Univ. of Neb. Pr. [1964, c.1963] 323p. ports., maps (on lining papers) 23cm. Bibl. 63-14694 6.00

1. Carr, Eugene Asa, 1830-1910. 2. Indians of North America—Wars. I. Title. BIP

Carr, Jess.

*CARR, Jess. 920
Birth of a book: a diary of the day-to-day writing of the Saint of the wilderness. Radford, Va., Commonwealth Press [1974] 151 p. 23 cm. [CT275] 74-84706 6.95
1. Carr, Jess. I. Title.
Publisher's address: First & Berkley, Radford, Virginia 24141.

CARR, Jess. 813'.5'4
Birth of a book : a diary of the day-to-day writing of The saint of the wilderness / by Jess Carr. Radford, Va. : Commonwealth Press, c1974 ix, 151 p. ; 23 cm. Autobiographical [PS3553.A763S233] 74-84706 6.95
1. Carr, Jess. The saint of the wilderness. 2. Authorship. 3. Carr, Jess—Biography. I. Title.

Carr, Mrs. Ezra S.

*MUIR, John, 1838-1914. 816'.4
Letters to a friend, written to Mrs. Ezra S. Carr, 1866-1879, by John Muir. Dunwood, Ga., Norman S. Berg, 1973 [c.1915] 193 p. 22 cm. ISBN 0-910220-48-4 10.00
1. Carr, Mrs. Ezra S. I. Title.
Publisher's address: "Sellanra," 2690 Mt. Vernon H'way, Dunwoody, GA 30338.

Carr, Robert Frederick, 1943-

CARR, Robert Frederick, 1943- 364.1'523'0924
Carr, five years of rape and murder : from the personal account of Robert Frederick Carr III / Edna Buchanan ; introd. by Daniel W. Schwartz. 1st ed. New York : E. P. Dutton, c1979. xvi, 261 p. ; 22 cm. "Thomas Congdon books." [HV6248.C23A33 1979] 78-25992 ISBN 0-525-07657-3 : 10.95
1. Carr, Robert Frederick, 1943- 2. Crime and criminals—Biography. 3. Rape—United States. 4. Murder—United States. I. Buchanan, Edna. II. Title.

Carr, Roland T.

CARR, Roland T. 940.54'81'73
To sea in Haste / Roland T. Carr ; ill. by Frederick Schuler Briggs. Washington : Acropolis Books, c1975. 260 p. : ill. ; 24 cm. (The Acropolis Americana bicentennial series) [D783.5.H34C37] 75-13944 ISBN 0-87491-204-0 12.50. ISBN 0-87491-020-X pbk. : 5.95
1. Carr, Roland T. 2. Haste (Ship) 3. World War, 1939-1945—Naval operations, American. 4. World War, 1939-1945—Naval operations—Submarine. 5. World War, 1939-1945—Personal narratives, American. I. Title. BIP

Carr, Wilbur John, 1870-1942.

CRANE, Katharine Elizabeth 923.273
Mr. Carr of State; forty-seven years in the Department of State. New York, St. Martin's Press [c.1960] xv, 365p. Bibliographical footnotes. illus., ports. 25cm. 60-8981 6.00 half cloth,
1. Carr, Wilbur John, 1870-1942. I. Title.

Carrasco, Fred Gomez.

MCKINNEY, Wilson. 364.1'57'0924 B
Fred Carrasco, the heroin merchant / by Wilson McKinney. Austin, Tex. : Heidelberg, 1975. xii, 310 p., [6] leaves of plates : ill. ; 24 cm. [HV5805.C37M3] 75-16126 ISBN 0-913206-06-7 : 9.95
1. Carrasco, Fred Gomez. 2. Narcotics, Control of—Mexico. 3. Narcotics, Control of—Texas.

Carreno, Teresa, 1853-1917.

MILINOWSKI, Marta, 1885- 786.1'092'4 B
Teresa Carreno : "by the grace of God" / Marta Milinowski. New York : Da Capo Press, 1977, [c1940]. xvi, 410 p., [26] leaves of plates : ill. ; 24 cm. (Da Capo Press music reprint series) Reprint of the ed. published by Yale University Press, New Haven. Includes index. Bibliography: p. [399]-403. [ML417.C4M6 1977] 76-58931 ISBN 0-306-70870-1 : 19.50
1. Carreno, Teresa, 1853-1917. 2. Pianists—Venezuela—Biography.

Carrel, Alexis, 1873-1944.

EDWARDS, William Sterling, 1920- 617'.41'0924 B
Alexis Carrel: visionary surgeon, by W. Sterling Edwards and Peter D. Edwards. With a foreword by Charles A. Lindbergh. Springfield, Ill., Thomas [1974] xi, 143 p. illus. 24 cm. Bibliography: p. 125-127. [R507.C34E36] 74-717 ISBN 0-398-03130-4 5.00
1. Carrel, Alexis, 1873-1944. 2. Heart—Surgery. 3. Blood-vessels—Surgery. I. Edwards, Peter D., joint author. BIP

Carrier-Belleuse, Albert Ernest, 1824-1887.

HARGROVE, June Ellen. 730'.92'4 B
The life and work of Albert Ernest Carrier-Belleuse / June Ellen Hargrove. New York : Garland Pub., 1977. p. cm. (Outstanding dissertations in the fine arts) Thesis—New York University, 1975. Bibliography: p. [N6853.C278H37] 76-23625 ISBN 0-8240-2695-0 lib.bdg. : 50.00
1. Carrier-Belleuse, Albert Ernest, 1824-1887. 2. Artists—France—Biography. I. Carrier-Belleuse, Albert Ernest, 1824-1887. II. Title. III. Series.

Carril, Pete.

WHITE, Dan, 1943- 796.32'3'0924 B
Play to win : a profile of Princeton Basketball coach Pete Carril / by Dan White. Englewood Cliffs, N.J. : Prentice-Hall, c1978. 204 p., [4] leaves of plates : ill. ; 22 cm. [GV884.C37W47] 77-20143 ISBN 0-13-683904-5 : 8.95
1. Carril, Pete. 2. Princeton University—Basketball. 3. Basketball coaches—United States—Biography. 4. Basketball coaching. I. Title. BIP

Carrington, Dora de Houghton,

CARRINGTON, Dora de Houghton, 1893-1932. 759.2
Carrington: letters and extracts from her diaries. Chosen and with an introd. by David Garnett. With a bibliographical note by Noel Carrington. New York, Ballantine Books [1974, c1970] xvii, 650 p. illus., geneal. tables, ports. 18 cm. Bibliography: p. 640. [ND497.C375G3 1974] ISBN 0-345-24262-9 2.25 (pbk.)
I. Title.
L.C. card no. for original ed.: 79-137332.

CARRINGTON, Dora de Houghton, 1893-1932. 759.2
Carrington: letters and extracts from her diaries. Chosen and with an introd. by David Garnett. With a bibliographical note by Noel Carrington. [1st ed.] New York, Holt, Rinehart and Winston [1971, c1970] 514 p. illus., geneal. tables (on lining papers), ports. 24 cm. Bibliography: p. [506] [ND497.C375G3 1971] 79-137332 ISBN 0-03-085659-0 12.50
I. Title.

Carrington, Margaret Irvin Sullivant, 1831-1870.

CARRINGTON, Margaret Irvin Sullivant, 1831-1870. 917.87'03'1
Ab-sa-ra-ka, land of massacre, being the experience of an officer's wife on the Plains / [by Margaret Irvin Carrington] ; with an outline of Indian operations and conferences from 1865 to 1878 by Henry B. Carrington. Rev., enl. Millwood, N.Y. : Kraus Reprint Co., 1975, c1878. xx, 383 p., [10] leaves of plates : ill. ; 19 cm. "Fifth edition of Mrs. Carrington's narrative." Reprint of the ed. published by Lippincott, Philadelphia. [F761.C37 1975] 74-20844 ISBN 0-527-15125-4
1. Carrington, Margaret Irvin Sullivant, 1831-1870. 2. Frontier and pioneer life—Wyoming. 3. Indians of North America—Wars—1866-1895. 4. Wyoming—History. 5. Indians of North America—Wyoming. 6. Crow Indians. I. Title. II. Title: Ab-sa-ra-ka, land of massacre ...

Carroll, Anna Ella, 1815-1893.

GREENBIE, Marjorie Latta Barstow, 1891- 973.7'092'4
My dear lady; the story of Anna Ella Carroll, the "great unrecognized member of Lincoln's Cabinet" [by] Marjorie Barstow Greenbie. New York, Arno Press, 1974 [c1940] xx, 316 p. illus. 24 cm. (Women in America: from colonial times to the 20th century) Reprint of the ed. published by Whittlesey House, New York. Bibliography: p. 300-305. [E472.9.C333 1974] 74-3953 ISBN 0-405-06101-3
1. Carroll, Anna Ella, 1815-1893. 2. United States—History—Civil War, 1861-1865. I. Title. II. Series. BIP

GREENBIE, Sydney, 1889-1960. 920.7
Anna Ella Carroll and Abraham Lincoln, a biography, by Sydney Greenbie and Marjorie Barstow Greenbie. [1st ed.] Manchester, Me., University of Tampa Press in cooperation with Falmouth Pub. House [1952] xvi, 539 p. illus., map, ports. 22 cm. Bibliography: p. 516-525. [E472.9.C334] 52-7050
1. Carroll, Anna Ella, 1815-1893. 2. Lincoln, Abraham, Pres. U.S., 1809-1865. 3. United States—History—Civil War, 1861-1865. I. Greenbie, Marjorie Latta (Barstow) 1891- joint author. II. Title.

Carroll, Charles, 1737-1832.

HANLEY, Thomas O'Brien. 973.3'0924 B
Charles Carroll of Carrollton: the making of a revolutionary gentleman. Washington, Catholic University of America Press, 1970. x, 293 p. geneal. table, port. 24 cm. Includes bibliographical references. [E302.6.C3H3] 74-114397 12.95
1. Carroll, Charles, 1737-1832. I. Title.

SMITH, Ellen Hart. 973.3'0924 B
Charles Carroll of Carrollton. New York, Russell & Russell [1971, c1942] x, 340 p. illus., ports. 23 cm. Bibliography: p. [315]-324. [E302.6.C3S56 1971] 75-139939
1. Carroll, Charles, 1737-1832. BIP

Carroll, Charles, 1737-1832—Juvenile literature.

LOMASK, Milton. 923.273
Charles Carroll and the American Revolution. Illustrated by Jo Polseno. Ew York, P. J. Kenedy [1959] 188p. illus. 22cm. (American background books) [E302.6.C3L65] 59-7040
1. Carroll, Charles, 1737-u832—Juvenile literature. I. Title.

Carroll, Earl.

MURRAY, Ken, 1903- 790.2'092'4 B
The body merchant : the story of Earl Carroll / by Ken Murray. 1st ed. Pasadena, Calif. : W. Ritchie Press, c1976. xiii, 243 p., [12] leaves of plates : ill. ; 24 cm. Includes index. [PN2287.C286M8] 75-41820 ISBN 0-378-05685-9 : 9.95
1. Carroll, Earl. 2. Theatrical producers and directors—United States—Biography. I. Title.

Carroll, Gladys (Hasty)

CARROLL, Gladys (Hasty) 1904- 813'.5'2 B
Years away from home. [1st ed.] Boston, Little, Brown [1972] 373 p. 22 cm. Autobiographical. [PS3505.A77533Z522] 72-5328 ISBN 0-316-13004-4
I. Title.

Carroll, John, Abp., 1735-1815.

GUILDAY, Peter Keenan, 1884-1947. 922.273
The life and times of John Carroll, Archbishop of Baltimore, 1735-1815. Westminster, Md., Newman Press, 1954. x, 864p. illus., ports., maps, geneal. table. 22cm. Includes bibliographical references. [BX4705.C33G8 1954] 54-11374
1. Carrolle, Jonn, Abp., 1735-1815. I. Title.

LAMASK, Milton. 922.273
John Carroll, bishop and patriot. Illustrated by Joshua Tolford. New York, Vision Books [1956] 183p. illus. 22cm. (Vision books, 10) [BX4705.C33L6] 56-7279
1. Carroll, John, Abp., 1735-1815. I. Title.

LOMASK, Milton 922.273
John Carroll, bishop and patriot. Illustrated by Joshua Tolford. New York, Vision Books [1956] 183p. illus. 22cm. (Vision books, 10) [BX4705.C33L6] 56-7279
1. Carroll, John. Abp., 1785-1815. I. Title.

MELVILLE, Annabelle McConnell, 1910- 922.273
John Carroll of Baltimore, founder of the American Catholic hierarchy. New York, Scribner [1955] 338 p. illus. 22 cm. [BX4705.C33M4] 55-7195
1. Carroll, John, Abp., 1735-1815.

SHEA, John Dawson Gilmary, 1824-1892. 282'.73
History of the Catholic Church within the limits of the United States/ John Gilmary Shea. New York : Arno Press, 1978, [c1886-1892] 4 v. : ill. ; 23 cm. (The American Catholic tradition) Reprint of the ed. published by the author, New York. Includes bibliographical references and indexes. [BX1406.S5 1978] 77-11310 ISBN 0-405-10852-4 : 165.00
1. Catholic Church in the United States—History. 2. Carroll, John, Abp., 1735-1815. 3. Catholic Church—Bishops—Biography. 4. Bishops—Maryland—Baltimore—Biography. 5. Baltimore—Biography. I. Title. II. Series.

Carroll, John, Abp., 1735-1815—Juvenile literature.

BETZ, Eva K. 922.273
Priest, patriot, and leader; the story of Archbishop Carroll. Illus. by Charles L. Dougherty. New York, Benziger Bros. [c.1960] 181p. (Banner book [12] 60-15495
1. Carroll, John, Abp., 1735-1815—Juvenile literature. I. Title.

BETZ, Eva (Kelly) 1897- 922.273
Priest, patriot, and leader; the story of Archbishop Carroll. Illustrated by Charles L. Dougherty. New York, Benziger Bros. [1960] 181p. illus. 22cm. (A Banner book [12]) [BX4705.C33B4] 60-15495
1. Carroll, John, Abp., 1735-1815—Juvenile literature. I. Title.

Carroll, Julian Morton, 1931-

CONN, Charles Paul. 976.9'04'0924 B
Julian Carroll of Kentucky : the inside story of a Christian in public life / by Charles Paul Conn. Old Tappan, N.J. : Revell, c1977. 126 p. : ill. ; 21 cm. [F456.26.C37C66] 76-58338 ISBN 0-8007-0838-5 : 5.95
1. Carroll, Julian Morton, 1931- 2. Kentucky—Governors—Biography. I. Title.

Carroll, Mitchell Benedict, 1898-

CARROLL, Mitchell Benedict, 1898- 341.48'4 B
Global perspectives of an interntional tax lawyer / Michtell B. Carroll. 1st ed. Hicksville, N.Y. : Exposition Press, c1978. 151 p. ; 21 cm. Includes bibliographical references. [KF373.C376A33] 78-59458 ISBN 0-682-49133-0 : 8.00
1. Carroll, Mitchell Benedict, 1898- 2. Lawyers—United States—Biography. 3. Taxation—Law. I. Title.

Carson, Christopher, 1809-1868.

BLACKWELDER, Bernice. 923.973
Great Westerner; the story of Kit Carson. Caldwell, Idaho, Caxton Printers, 1962. 373 p. illus. 22 cm. Includes bibliography. [F592.C336] 62-8186
1. Carson, Christopher, 1809-1868. I. Title.

BOESCH, Mark. 923.973
Kit Carson of the Old West. Illustrated by

Joshua Tolford. N[ew] Y[ork] Vision Books [1959] 189p. illus. 22cm. (Vision books, 40) [F592.C338] 59-5131
1. Carson, Christopher, 1809-1868. I. Title.

CARSON, Christopher, 1809-1868 923.973
Kit Carson's autobiography, ed. by Milo Milton Quaife. Lincoln. Univ. of Neb. Pr. [1966] xxxii, 192p. port. 21cm. (Bison bk., BB325) Orig. pub. by R. R. Donelley in 1935. [F592.C31] 1.50 pap.,
1. Frontier and pioneer life—The West. I. Quaife, Milo Milton, 1880- ed. II. Title.

CARSON, Christopher, 1809-1868. 978.020924 (B)
Kit Carson's autobiography, edited by Milo Milton Quaife. Lincoln, University of Nebraska Press [1966] xxxii, 192 p. facsim., port. 21 cm. (A Bison book BB325) Includes bibliographical references. [F592.C314] 66-4130
1. Frontier and pioneer life — The West. I. Quaife, Milo Milton, 1880-1959, ed. II. Title. BIP

CARSON, Christopher, 1809-1868 923.973
Kit Carson's autobiography, ed. by Milo Milton Quaife [Gloucester, Mass., P. Smith, 1966] xxxii, 192p. port. 21cm. (Bison bk., BB325 rebound.) First pub. in 1935 by R. R. Donnelley by arrangement with Lakeside Pr. First pub. in 1935 by R. R. Donnelley by arrangement with Lakeside Pr. [F592.C31] 3.50
1. Frontier and pioneer life—The West. I. Quaife, Milo Milton, 1880- ed. II. Title.

CARTER, Harvey Lewis, 1904- 978'.02'0924 B
Dear old Kit; the historical Christopher Carson, with a new ed. of the Carson memoirs, by Harvey Lewis Carter. [1st ed. Norman, University of Oklahoma Press, 1968] xix, 250 p. illus., facsim., maps, plan, ports. 26 cm. "The Kit Carson memoirs, 1809-1856" (p. 38-149) were first published in 1926 under title Kit Carson's own story of his life. Includes bibliographical references. [F592.C346] 68-15681
1. Carson, Christopher, 1809-1868. 2. Frontier and pioneer life—The West. I. Carson, Christopher, 1809-1868. Kit Carson's own story of his life. 1968. II. Title.

ESTERGREEN, M. Morgan. 923.973
Kit Carson, a portrait in courage. [1st ed.] Norman, University of Oklahoma Press [1962] 320 p. illus. 24 cm. Includes bibliography. [F592.C365] 62-11274
1. Carson, Christopher, 1809-1868. BIP

GERSON, Noel Bertram, 1914- 923.973
Kit Carson: folk hero and man, by Noel B. Gerson. [1st ed.] Garden City, N. Y., Doubleday, 1964. 255 p. 22 cm. Bibliography: p. [243]-244. [F592.C368] 64-19276
1. Carson, Christopher, 1809-1868.

GERSON, Noel Bertram, 1914- 923.973
Kit Carson, folk hero and man [New York, Avon, 1967. c. 1964] 225p. 18cm. (Camelot bk., ZS113) Bibl. .60 pap.,
1. Carson, Christopher, 1809-1868. I. Title.

MOODY, Ralph, 1898- 923.973
Kit Carson and the wild frontier; illustrated by Stanley W. Galli. New York, Random House [1955] 184 p. illus. 22 cm. (Landmark books, 53) [F592.C38] 55-5818
1. Carson, Christopher, 1809-1868.

PETERS, De Witt Clinton, d.1876. 978'.02'0924 B
The life and adventures of Kit Carson, the Nestor of the Rocky Mountains, from facts narrated by himself. With original illus. drawn by Lumley. Freeport, N.Y., Books for Libraries Press [1970] 534 p. illus., ports. 23 cm. Reprint of the 1858 ed. [F592.C395 1970] 76-109631
1. Carson, Christopher, 1809-1868. 2. Frontier and pioneer life—The West. I. Title.

STEVENSON, Augusta. 978'.02'0924 B
Kit Carson, boy trapper. Illustrated by Robert Doremus. Indianapolis, Bobbs-Merrill [1962] 200 p. illus. 20 cm. (Childhood of famous Americans) The boyhood of the frontier trapper, hunter, Indian fighter, scout, and soldier. [PZ7.S8467Ki5] 92 AC 68
1. Carson, Christopher, 1809-1868. I. Doremus, Robert, illus. II. Title.

Carson, Christopher, 1809-1868—Juvenile literature.

BOESCH, Mark J 1917- 923.973
Kit Carson of the Old West. Illustrated by Joshua Tolford. N[ew] Y[ork] Vision Books [1959] 189 p. illus. 22 cm (Vision books.40) [F592.C338] 59-5131
1. Carson, Christopher, 1809-1868—Juvenile literature. I. Title.

BRYANT, Will. 923.973
Kit Carson and the mountain men; [true tales of the trapper brigades, the great explorers of the West] Story and pictures by Will Bryant. New York, Grosset & Dunlap [1960] 60p. illus. 29cm. [F592.C339] 60-51576
1. Carson, Christopher, 1809-1868—Juvenile literature. I. Title.

BRYANT, William Harrison 923.973
Kit Carson and the mountain men. Story and pictures by Will Bryant. New York, Grosset & Dunlap [c.1960] 60p. illus. (part col.) 29cm. 60-51576 1.00 bds.,
1. Carson, Christopher, 1809-1868—Juvenile literature. I. Title.

CAMPION, Nardi (Reeder) 92
Kit Carson, pathfinder of the West. Illus. by Shannon Stirnweis. Champaign, Ill., Garrard [c.1963] 80p. col. illus. 23cm. (Discovery bk.) 63-9219 2.50 1.87 lib net,
1. Carson, Christopher, 1809-1868—Juvenile literature. I. Title.

CAMPION, Nardi (Reeder) 92
Kit Carson, pathfinder of the West. Illustrated by Shannon Stirnweis. Champaign, Ill., Garrard Pub. Co. [1963] 80 p. illus. 23 cm. (A discovery book) [F592.C345] 63-9219
1. Carson, Christopher, 1809-1868—Juvenile literature. I. Title.

GRANT, Matthew G. 978'.02'0924 B
Kit Carson, trailblazer of the West [by] Matthew G. Grant. Illustrated by John Keely and Dick Brude. [Mankato, Minn., Creative Education; distributed by Children's Press, Chicago, 1973, c1974] 29 p. illus. (part col.) 25 cm. (His Gallery of great Americans series. Frontiermen of America) An easy-to-read biography of Kit Carson, who ran away from home at the age of fifteen to begin a career as a hunter, explorer, and mountain man. [F592.C37] 92 73-10063 ISBN 0-87191-253-8 3.95
1. Carson, Christopher, 1809-1868—Juvenile literature. I. Keely, John, illus. II. Brude, Dick, illus. III. Title.

Carson, Edward Henry Carson, Baron, 1854-1935.

HYDE, Harford Montgomery, 1907- 340'.092'4 B
Carson : the life of Sir Edward Carson, Lord Carson of Duncairn / H. Montgomery Hyde. New York : Octagon Books, 1974. xviii, 515 p., [13] leaves of plates : ill. ; 23 cm. Reprint of the 1953 ed. published by Heinemann, London. Includes index. Bibliography: p. 498-501. [DA965.C25H9 1974] 73-8425 ISBN 0-374-94078-9 : 16.00
1. Carson, Edward Henry Carson, Baron, 1854-1935. I. Title.

Carson family.

GRENIER, Judson. 929'.2'0973
Reminiscences of the Dominguez Ranch and the Carson family : an oral history / by John Victor Carson ; interview by Judson Grenier. Dominguez Hills : Dominguez Archives Committee, California State College, 1976. 38 p. : ill. ; 22 cm. [CS71.C321 1976] 76-365709
1. Carson family. 2. Dominguez family. 3. Carson, John Victor, 1893-1976. 4. Rancho San Pedro, Calif. 5. Los Angeles Co., Calif.—Genealogy. I. Carson, John Victor, 1893-1976. II. Title.

Carson, Johnny, 1925-

LORENCE, Douglas. 791.45'092'4 B
Johnny Carson : a biography / by Douglas Lorence. New York : Drake Publishers, 1975. 193 p., [4] leaves of plates : ill. ; 24 cm. [PN1992.4.C28L6] 74-22593 ISBN 0-87749-815-6 : 9.95
1. Carson, Johnny, 1925-

Carson, Johnny, 1925- —Juvenile literature.

PAIGE, David. 791.45'092'4 B
Johnny Carson / written by David Paige ; designed by Gene Kohler. [Mankato, Minn.] : Creative EDucation, [c1977] 31 p. : ill. ; 25 cm. (Stars of stage and screen) A biography of Johnny Carson, the host of one of the most popular late night television programs. [PN1992.4.C28P3] 92 76-45087 ISBN 0-87191-560-X lib.bdg. : 4.95
1. Carson, Johnny, 1925- —Juvenile literature. 2. Television personalities—United States—Biography—Juvenile literature. I. Title. BIP

Carson, Rachel Louise.

STERLING, Philip. 574'.0924 B
Sea and earth; the life of Rachel Carson. New York, Crowell [1970] viii, 213 p. illus., facsim., ports. 21 cm. (Women of America) Bibliography: p. 198-207. A biography of the marine biologist, author, and conservationist whose book, Silent Spring, alerted the public to the possibility of dangerous long-range effects of pesticides. [QH91.3.C3S74] 92 70-87157 4.50
1. Carson, Rachel Louise. I. Title. II. Title: The life of Rachel Carson. BIP

STERLING, Philip. 574'.0924 [B]
Sea and earth; the life of Rachel Carson. [New York, Dell, 1974, c1970] 189 p. 18 cm. (Woman of America) Includes bibliographies. A biography of the marine biologist, author & conservationist whose book Silent Spring, alerted the public to the possibility of dangerous long range effects of pesticides. [QH91.3.C3S74] [92] 0.95 (pbk.)
1. Carson, Rachel Louise. I. Title. II. Title: The life of Rachel Carson.
L.C. card no. for hardcover: 70-87157

Carson, Rachel Louise—Juvenile literature.

LATHAM, Jean Lee. 574'.092'4 B
Rachel Carson: who loved the sea. Illustrated by Victor Mays. Champaign, Ill., Garrard Pub. Co. [1973] 80 p. illus. 23 cm. (A Discovery book) A biography of the marine biologist and nature writer well-known for her campaign against the careless use of chemicals. [QH91.3.C3L37] 92 72-11475 ISBN 0-8116-6312-4 2.59
1. Carson, Rachel Louise—Juvenile literature. I. Mays, Victor, 1927- illus. II. Title.

Carson, Virginia.

CARSON, Mary. 362.4 B
Ginny; a true story. Garden City, N.Y., Doubleday [1971] 215 p. 22 cm. [HV889.5.N4C35] 70-169920 5.95
1. Carson, Virginia. 2. Rehabilitation—New York (City) I. Title.

Carter, Amon Giles, 1879-1955.

FLEMMONS, Jerry. 070.5'092'4 B
Amon, the life of Amon Carter, Sr., of Texas / by Jerry Flemmons. Austin, Tex. : Jenkins Pub. Co., 1978. 520 p. : ill. ; 23 cm. Includes index. [PN4874.C26F55] 78-2973 ISBN 0-8363-0155-2 : 12.95
1. Carter, Amon Giles, 1879-1955. 2. Journalists—Texas—Biography. 3. Texas—Biography. I. Title.

Carter, Amy—Juvenile literature.

GILLEO, Alma, 1920- 973.926'0924 B
Amy Carter : growing up in the White House / by Alma Gilleo ; designed and illustrated by Helen Endres. Elgin, Ill. : Child's World ; Chicago : distributed by Childrens Press, c1978. p. cm. Describes President Carter's daughter's life in the White House. [E874.C26G54] 78-7812 ISBN 0-89565-028-2 : 7.35
1. Carter, Amy—Juvenile literature. 2. Carter, Jimmy, 1924- —Juvenile literature. 3. Presidents—United States—Children—Biography—Juvenile literature. I. Endres, Helen. II. Title.

Carter, Billy.

STAPLETON, Ruth Carter. 975.8'913 B
Brother Billy / Ruth Carter Stapleton. 1st ed. New York : Harper & Row, c1978. viii, 179 p., [4] leaves of plates : ill. ; 22 cm. Includes index. [E874.C29S72 1978] 78-2173 ISBN 0-06-014063-1 : 8.95
1. Carter, Billy. 2. Carter, Jimmy, 1924- 3. Presidents—United States—Brothers and sisters—Biography. I. Title. BIP

Carter, Eliot Avery,

CARTER, Eliot Avery, 1886- . 926.5
Lanes of memory, an autobiography. Edited by Emory S. Basford. [Nashua ? N. H.] 1963 [i.e 1964] 344 p. illus., ports. 24 cm. [CT275.C332A3] 64-55377
I. Title.

Carter, Elizabeth, 1717-1806.

CARTER, Elizabeth, 1717-1806. 821'.6 B
Memoirs of the life of Mrs. Elizabeth Carter; with a new edition of her poems, to which are added some miscellaneous essays in prose, together with her notes on the Bible, and answers to objections concerning the Christian religion, by Montagu Pennington. 4th ed. London, Printed for J. Cawthorn, 1825. [New York, AMS Press, 1974] 2 v. port. 19 cm. (Women of letters) Includes bibliographical references. [PR3339.C4 1974] 75-37674 ISBN 0-404-56727-4 55.00
I. Pennington, Montagu, 1762-1849, ed. II. Title.

CARTER, Elizabeth, 1717-1806. 821'.6 B
A series of letters between Mrs. Elizabeth Carter and Miss Catherine Talbot. New York, AMS Press [1974] p. cm. Reprint of the 1809 ed. published by F. C. and J. Rivington, London, under title: A series of letters between Mrs. Elizabeth Carter and Miss Catherine Talbot, from the year 1741 to 1770, to which are added Letters from Mrs. Elizabeth Carter to Mrs. Vesey, between the years 1763 and 1787; published from the original manuscripts in the possession of the Rev. Montagu Pennington. [PR3339.C4A83 1974] 73-20330 20.50
1. Carter, Elizabeth, 1717-1806. 2. Talbot, Catherine, 1721-1770. 3. Vesey, Elizabeth (Vesey) 1715?-1791. I. Talbot, Catherine, 1721-1770. II. Vesey, Elizabeth (Vesey) 1715?-1791.
Four volume set 80.00. BIP

Carter, Elizabeth, 1717-1806—Correspondence.

CARTER, Elizabeth, 1717-1806. 821'.6 B
Letters from Mrs. Elizabeth Carter to Mrs. Montagu between the years 1755 and 1800. London, Printed for F. C. and J. Rivington, 1817. [New York, AMS Press, 1973] 3 v. 19 cm. On spine: WOL [PR3339.C4A82 1973] 73-178402 ISBN 0-404-56720-7
1. Carter, Elizabeth, 1717-1806—Correspondence. 2. Montagu, Elizabeth (Robinson) 1720-1800. I. Montagu, Elizabeth (Robinson) 1720-1800. BIP

Carter Family.

CARTER, Hugh Alton, 1920- 973.926'092'2
Cousin Beedie and Cousin Hot : my life with the Carter family of Plains, Georgia / by Hugh Carter, as told to Frances Spatz Leighton. Englewood Cliffs, N.J. :

Prentice-Hall, c1978. 366 p., [12] leaves of plates : ill. ; 24 cm. Includes index. [E874.C34] 78-4975 ISBN 0-13-185470-4 : 12.50
1. Carter family. 2. Carter, Hugh Alton, 1920- 3. Carter, Jimmy, 1924- 4. Legislators—Georgia—Biography. 5. Plains, Ga.—Biography. I. Leighton, Frances Spatz. II. Title. **BIP**

CARTER, Lillian, 1898- 975.8'913
Miss Lillian and friends : the Plains, Georgia, family philosophy and recipe book, as told to Beth Tartan and Rudy Hayes. 1st ed. New York : A & W Publishers, c1977. 254 p. : ill. ; 24 cm. Includes bibliographical references. [E874.C375] 76-55941 ISBN 0-89104-074-9 : 8.95
1. Carter family. 2. Carter, Lillian, 1898- 3. Presidents—United States—Mothers—Biography. 4. Plains, Ga.—Social life and customs. 5. Cookery, American—Georgia. I. Sparks, Elizabeth Hedgecock, 1919- II. Hayes, Rudy. III. Title. **BIP**

CARTER, Lillian, 1898- 975.8'913
Miss Lillian and friends : the Plains Georgia family philosophy and recipe book / as told to Beth Tartan and Rudy Hayes 1st. ed. New York : New American Library, c1977. 244p. : ill. ; 18 cm. (A Signet Book) Includes bibliographical references. [E874.c375] ISBN 0-451-07852-7 pbk. : 1.75
1. Carter family. 2. carter, Lillian. 3. Presidents-United States-Mothers-Biography. 4. Plains, ga.-social life and customs. 5. Cookery, American-Georgia. I. Sparks, Elizabeth Hedgecock, 1919- II. Hayes, Rudy. III. Title.
L.C. card no. for 1977 A & W Pub. ed.:76-1.

HYATT, Richard, 1944- 973.926'092'2 B
The Carters of Plains / by Richard Hyatt. Huntsville, Ala. : Strode Publishers, c1977. 320 p. : ill. ; 27 cm. [E874.H9] 76 58240 ISBN 0-87397-117-5 : 8.95
1. Carter family. 2. Carter, Jimmy, 1924- 3. Presidents—United States—Biography. I. Title. **BIP**

KRISHEF, Robert K. 784'.092'2 B
The Carter Family : country music's first family / Robert K. Krishef and Stacy Harris. Minneapolis : Lerner Publications Co., c1978. p. cm. (Country music library) Includes index. Discography: p. A biography of the "Original Carter Family," A. P., Sara, and Maybelle, who were among the first performers of "hillbilly" music and who influenced the music of today's folk and bluegrass stars. [ML3930.A2K738] 920 77-90154 ISBN 0-8225-1403-6 : 4.95
1. Carter Family. 2. Country musicians—United States—Biography—Juvenile literature. I. Harris, Stacy, joint author. II. Title.

ORGILL, Michael. 784'.092'2 B
Anchored in love : the Carter Family story / Michael Orgill. Old Tappan, N.J. : Revell, [1975] 192 p. : ill. ; 21 cm. [ML421.C33O7] 75-12659 ISBN 0-8007-0735-4 : 5.95
1. Carter Family. 2. Country music—United States—History and criticism. I. Title. **BIP**

Carter, Forrest—Biography—Youth.

CARTER, Forrest. 813'.5'4
The education of Little Tree / Forrest Carter. [New York] : Delacorte Press/E. Friede, c1976. x, 216 p. ; 21 cm. [PS3553.A777Z513] 76-14782 ISBN 0-440-02319-X ; 7.95
1. Carter, Forrest—Biography—Youth. I. Title. **BIP**

Carter, Hodding, 1907-1972.

CARTER, Hodding. 920.5
Where Main Street meets the river. New York, Rinehart [1953] 339p. 22cm. Autobiographical. [PN4874.C27A3 1953] 53-6133
1. Journalists—Correspondence, reminiscences, etc. I. Title.

CARTER, Hodding, 1907- 920.5
Where Main Street meets the river. New York, Rinehart [1953] 339p. 22cm. Autobiographical. [PN4874.C27A3 1953] 53-6133
1. Journalists—Correspondence, reminiscences, etc. I. Title.

CARTER, Hodding, 1907-1972. 070'.92'4 B
First person rural / Hodding Carter. Westport, Conn. : Greenwood Press, 1977, c1963. p. cm. Autobiographical. Reprint of the ed. published by Doubleday, Garden City, N.Y. [RN4874.C27A32 1977] 77-10014 ISBN 0-8371-9727-9 lib.bdg. : 17.00
1. Carter, Hodding, 1907-1972. 2. Journalists—United States—Biography. I. Title.

Carter, Hugh Alton, 1920-

CARTER, Hugh Alton, 1920- 973.926'092'2
Cousin Beedie and Cousin Hot : my life with the Carter family of Plains, Georgia / by Hugh Carter, as told to Frances Spatz Leighton. Englewood Cliffs, N.J. : Prentice-Hall, c1978. 366 p., [12] leaves of plates : ill. ; 24 cm. Includes index. [E874.C34] 78-4975 ISBN 0 13-185470-4 : 12.50
1. Carter family. 2. Carter, Hugh Alton, 1920- 3. Carter, Jimmy, 1924- 4. Legislators—Georgia—Biography. 5. Plains, Ga.—Biography. I. Leighton, Frances Spatz. II. Title. **BIP**

Carter, Jimmy, 1924-

ALLEN, Frederick. 779'.9'9739260924 B
Jimmy Carter, a photobiography / written by Frederick Allen. Houston, Tex. : EFP Pub. Co., c1976. [80] p. : ill. ; 28 cm. [F291.3.C37A76] 76-150399 2.95
1. Carter, Jimmy, 1924- 2. Georgia—Governors—Biography. I. Title.

ALLEN, Gary. 973.925'092'4 B
Jimmy Carter, Jimmy Carter / by Gary Allen. Seal Beach, Calif. : '76 Press, [1976] 88 p. ; 18 cm. [F291.3.C37A78] 76-27187 ISBN 0-89245-006-1 pbk. : 1.00
1. Carter, Jimmy, 1924- 2. Georgia—Governors—Biography. **BIP**

BORNS, Steven. 975.8'913 B
People of Plains, Ga. / photographed & edited by Steven Borns. 1st ed. New York : McGraw-Hill, 1978. 115 p., [4] leaves of plates : ill. ; 26 cm. (McGraw-Hill paperbacks) [F294.P52B67] 78-1727 ISBN 0-07-006535-7 pbk. : 6.95
1. Carter, Jimmy, 1924- 2. Plains, Ga.—Social life and customs. 3. Plains, Ga.—Description. I. Title. **BIP**

CARTER, Jimmy, 1924- 975.8'04'0924 B
Why not the best? / Jimmy Carter. Nashville : Broadman Press, c1975. 154 p. : ill. ; 18 cm. [F291.3.C37A38] 75-22730 ISBN 0-8054-5561-2 : 4.95 ISBN 0-8054-5564-7 pbk. : 1.95
1. Carter, Jimmy, 1924- I. Title. **BIP**

CARTER, Jimmy, 1924- 975.8'04'0924 B
Why not the best? / Jimmy Carter. Presidential ed. Nashville : Broadman Press, c1977. 208 p. : ill. (some col.) ; 24 cm. [E873.A38 1977] 76-51917 ISBN 0-8054-5582-5 : 8.95
1. Carter, Jimmy, 1924- 2. Georgia—Governors—Biography. I. Title.

COLLINS, Tom. 973.925'092'4 B
The search for Jimmy Carter / Tom Collins ; director of photography, Charles M. Rafshoon with Algimantas Kezys. Waco, Tex. : Word Books, c1976. 192 p. : ill. ; 28 cm. [F291.3.C37C64] 76-27221 ISBN 0-87680-820-8 pbk. : 5.95
1. Carter, Jimmy, 1924- 2. Georgia—Governors—Biography. I. Rafshoon, Charles M. II. Kezys, Algimantas. III. Title.

CONGRESSIONAL Quarterly, inc. 329'.023'730925
President Carter. Washington : Congressional Quarterly, inc., c1977. 92 p. : ports. ; 28 cm. Includes index. [E868.C66 1977] 77-4222 ISBN 0-87187-109-2 pbk. : 5.25
1. Carter, Jimmy, 1924- 2. Mondale, Walter F., 1928- 3. Presidents—United States—Election—1976. 4. United States—Politics and government—1977. 5. Presidents—United States—Biography. 6. Vice-presidents—United States—Biography. I. Title.

KLENBORT, Marcia. 917.58'913
The road to Plains : a guide to Plains and nearby places of interest in southwest Georgia / [text, Marcia Kleinbort & Daniel Klenbort ; drawings and map, Jack Smith ; photos, Daniel Klenbort]. [Atlanta : Avery Press, c1977] 32 p. : ill. ; 22 cm. Cover title. [F294.P52K53] 77-151266
1. Carter, Jimmy, 1924- 2. Plains, Ga.—Description—Guide-books. 3. Presidents—United States—Biography. 4. Stewart Co., Ga.—Description and travel—Guide-books. 5. Sumter Co., Ga.—Description and travel—Guide-books. I. Klenbort, Daniel, joint author. II. Title.

KUCHARSKY, David. 973.925'092'4 B
The man from Plains : the mind and spirit of Jimmy Carter / by David Kucharsky. 1st ed. New York : Harper & Row, c1976. ix, 150 p. : port. ; 22 cm. Includes index. Bibliography: p. 145-146. [F291.3.C37K8 1976] 76-24970 ISBN 0-06-064891-0 : 4.95
1. Carter, Jimmy, 1924- 2. Georgia—Governors—Biography. I. Title. **BIP**

KUCHARSKY, David. 973.926'092'4
The man from Plains : the mind and spirit of Jimmy Carter / David Kucharsky. Boston : G. K. Hall, 1977, c1976. viii, 266 p. ; 25 cm. "Published in large print." Includes index. Bibliography: p. 257-258. [E873.K82 1977] 77-1858 ISBN 0-8161-6470-3 lib.bdg. : 10.95
1. Carter, Jimmy, 1924- 2. Presidents—United States—Biography. 3. Large print books. I. Title.

LASK, Victor. 973.926'092'4 B
Jimmy Carter, the man & the myth / Victgor Lasky. New York : R. Marek, c1979. 419 p. ; 24 cm. Includes index. Bibliography: p. [393]-407. [E873.L37] 79-625 ISBN 0-399-90042-X : 12.50
1. Carter, Jimmy, 1924- 2. Presidents—United States—Biography. 3. Presidents—United States—Election—1976. I. Title.

MILLER, William Lee. 973.926'092'4
Yankee from Georgia : The emergence of Jimmy Carter / William Lee Miller. New York : Time Books, c1978. 247 p. ; 22 cm. [E873.M54 1978] 77-87832 ISBN 0-8129-0753-1 : 10.95
1. Carter, Jimmy, 1924- 2. Presidents—United States Biography. 3. United States—Politics and government—1977- 4. Southern States—Politics and government 1951- 5. United States—Politics and government—1974-1977. I. Title. **BIP**

NORTON, Howard Melvin. 973.925'092'4 B
The miracle of Jimmy Carter / by Howard Norton & Bob Slosser. 1st ed. Plainfield, N.J. : Logos International, 1976. xii, 134 p., [4] leaves of plates : ill. ; 21 cm. [F291.3.C37N67] 76-20393 ISBN 0-88270-202-5 : 6.95
1. Carter, Jimmy, 1924- 2. Georgia—Governors—Biography. I. Slosser, Bob, joint author. II. Title.

STROUD,, Kandy. 973.926'092'4 B
How Jimmy won : the victory campaign from Plains to the White House / by Kandy Stroud. New York : Morrow, 1977. 442 p. ; 24 cm. Includes index. [E868.S86 1977] 77-1344 ISBN 0-688-03153-6 : 8.95
1. Carter, Jimmy, 1924- 2. Carter family. 3. Presidents—United States—Election—1976. 4. Presidents—United States—Biography. I. Title. **BIP**

WHEELER, Leslie, 1945- 975.8'04'0924 B
Jimmy who? : An examination of Presidential candidate Jimmy Carter : the man, his career, his stands on the issues / by Leslie Wheeler ; with a foreword by James W. Davis. Woodbury, N.Y. : Barron's Educational Series, c1976. xvi, 270 p., [16] leaves of plates : ill. ; 20 cm. Includes index. Bibliography: p. 257-262. [F291.3.C37W47] 76-21680 ISBN 0-8120-0748-4 pbk. : 2.95
1. Carter, Jimmy, 1924- 2. Georgia—Governors—Biography. I. Title.

WOOTEN, James. 973.926'092'.4
Dasher : the roots and the rising of Jimmy Carter / James Wooten. New York : Warner Books, 1979, c1978. 375p. ; 18 cm. [E872.W66] ISBN 0-446-91040-6 pbk. : 2.50
1. Carter, Jimmy, 1924- 2. Presidents — United States — Biography. 3. Presidents — United States — Election-1976. 4. Southern States — Politics and government — 1951- I. Title.
L.C. card no. for 1978 Summit Books ed.: 77-25272. **BIP**

Carter, Jimmy, 1924- —Addresses, essays, lectures.

JIMMY Carter and American fantasy 973.926'092'4 B
: psychohistorical essays / edited by Lloyd deMause and Henry Ebel. New York : Two Continents, c1977. p. cm. Includes index. [E873.J55] 77-9146 ISBN 0-8467-0363-7 : 8.95
1. Carter, Jimmy, 1924- —Addresses, essays, lectures. 2. Carter, Jimmy, 1924- —Personality—Addresses, essays, lectures. 3. Presidents—United States—Biography—Addresses, essays, lectures. I. DeMause, Lloyd. II. Ebel, Henry, 1938-

Carter, Jimmy, 1924- —Juvenile literature.

BEHRENS, June. 973.926'092'4 B
My name is Jimmy Carter / by June Behrens ; pictures by Marjorie Burgeson. Chicago : Childrens Press, c1978. [32] p. : col. ill. ; 25 cm. "A Golden Gate junior book." A brief biography of the Georgia peanut farmer who became the thirty-ninth President. [E873.B44] 77-16648 ISBN 0-516-08754-1 lib.bdg. : 7.35
1. Carter, Jimmy, 1924-—Juvenile literature. 2. Presidents—United States—Biography—Juvenile literature. I. Burgeson, Marjorie. II. Title. **BIP**

CALLAHAN, Dorothy M. 973.926'092'4 B
Jimmy, the story of the young Jimmy Carter / Dorothy Callahan. 1st ed. Garden City, N.Y. : Doubleday, c1979. 182 p., [6] leaves of plates : ill. ; 22 cm. A biography of the 39th President stressing the events of his childhood and Naval career. [E873.C34] 92 77-27766 ISBN 0-385-13558-0 : 5.95 ISBN 0-385-13559-9 lib.bdg. : 6.90
1. Carter, Jimmy, 1924- —Juvenile literature. 2. Presidents—United States—Biography—Juvenile literature. I. Title.

MERCER, Charles E. 973.926'092'4
Jimmy Carter / by Charles Mercer ; illustrations by Ruth Sanderson. New York : Putnam, c1977. 62 p. : ill. ; 23 cm. (A See and read biography) A biography of the thirty-ninth President, who arrived at the White House via a peanut farm, the Naval Academy, and the governorship of Georgia. [E873.M47 1977] 92 77-1861 ISBN 0-399-61094-4 lib.bdg. : 4.29
1. Carter, Jimmy, 1924- —Juvenile literature. 2. Presidents—United States—Biography—Juvenile literature. I. Sanderson, Ruth. II. Title. **BIP**

SMITH, Beatrice S. 973.926'092'4 B
From peanuts to President / Beatrice S. Smith. Milwaukee : Raintree Editions ; Chicago : distributed by Childrens Press, c1977. 47 p. : ill. ; 25 cm. A biography of Jimmy Carter, the farm boy from Georgia, who became the thirty-ninth President of the United States. [E873.S63] 92 76-51267 ISBN 0-8172-0428-8 lib. bdg. : 3.95
1. Carter, Jimmy, 1924- —Juvenile literature. 2. Presidents—United States—Biography—Juvenile literature. I. Title. **BIP**

WALKER, Barbara J. 973.926'092'4 B
The picture life of Jimmy Carter / by Barbara J. Walker. New York : Watts, 1977. [46] p. : ill. ; 22 cm. Text and photographs examine the life and political career of the thirty-ninth President of the United States. [E873.W34] 92 77-368 ISBN 0-531-01284-0 lib.bdg. : 4.47
1. Carter, Jimmy, 1924- —Juvenile

literature. 2. Presidents—United States—Biography—Juvenile literature. I. Title.

Carter, Jimmy, 1924- —Religion.

BAKER, James Thomas. 973.926'092'4 B
A Southern Baptist in the White House / by James T. Baker. Philadelphia : Westminster Press, c1977. p. cm. [E873.B34] 77-8926 ISBN 0-664-24144-1 pbk. : 3.95
1. Carter, Jimmy, 1924- —Religion. 2. Presidents—United States—Biography. I. Title. BIP

NIELSEN, Niels Christian, 1921- 973.926'092'4 B
The religion of President Carter / by Niels C. Nielson, Jr. Nashville : T. Nelson, c1977. 162 p. ; 21 cm. Includes bibliographical references. [E873.N53] 77-1438 ISBN 0-8407-5621-6 pbk. : 2.95
1. Carter, Jimmy, 1924- —Religion. I. Title.

Carter, John, d. 1669.

JONES, Christine. 975.5'22'020924 B
John Carter I of "Corotoman" Lancaster County, Virginia / compiled by Christine Jones. Irvington, Va. : Foundation for Historic Christ Church, c1977. [4], 92 leaves ; 29 cm. Includes index. Bibliography: 4th prelim leaf. [CT275.C3343J66] 77-74863
1. Carter, John, d. 1669. 2. Lancaster County, Va.—History—Sources. 3. Lancaster County, Va.—Biography. I. Title.

Carter, Lydia, Osage Indian, d. 1821.

CORNELIUS, Elias, 1794-1832. 973'.04'97 S
The little Osage captive / Elias Cornelius. New York : Garland Pub., 1977. 108 p., [2] leaves of plates : ill. ; 23 cm. (The Garland Library of narratives of North American Indian captivities ; v. 37) Issued with the reprint of the 1855 ed. of the Escape of Alexander M'Connel, New York, 1977. Reprint of the 1822 ed. published by S. T. Armstrong and Crocker & Brewster, Boston. [E85.G2 vol. 37] [E99.08] 970'.004'97 77-575 ISBN 0-8240-1661-0 : 25.00
1. Carter, Lydia, Osage Indian, d. 1821. 2. Cherokee Indians—Captivities. 3. Indians of North America—Captivities. 4. Osage Indians—Biography. I. Title. II. Series.

Carter, Robert Goldthwaite, 1845-1936.

CARTER, Robert Goldthwaite, 1845-1936. 973.7'41'0922
Four brothers in blue : or, Sunshine and shadows of the War of the Rebellion : a story of the great Civil War from Bull Run to Appomattox / by Robert Goldthwaite Carter ; foreword by Frank Vandiver ; introd. and index by John M. Carroll. Austin : University of Texas Press, c1978. xxiv, 537 p. ; 24 cm. Based on the letters and diaries of the author and his three brothers. Part of the work was first published serially in the Maine bugle, July 1896-Oct. 1898. Includes index. [E601.C33 1978] 78-56909 ISBN 0-292-72426-8: 15.00
1. Carter, Robert Goldthwaite, 1845-1936. 2. United States. Army. Army of the Potomac—Biography. 3. United States—Civil War, 1861-1865—Personal narratives—Army of the Potomac. 4. United States—History—Civil War, 1861-1865—Campaigns and battles. I. Title.

Carter, Robert, 1663-1732.

DOWDEY, Clifford, 1904- 975.5'02
The Virginia dynasties; the emergence of "King" Carter and the golden age. [1st ed.] Boston, Little, Brown [1969] 438 p. illus., map (on lining papers), ports. 25 cm. Bibliography: p. [413]-420. [F229.D7] 69-12637
1. Carter, Robert, 1663-1732. 2. Virginia—History—Colonial period, ca. 1600-1775. 3. Upper classes—Virginia. I. Title.

Carter, Robert, 1728-1804.

MORTON, Louis 926.3
Robert Carter of Nomini Hall, a Virginia tobacco planter of the eighteenth century. Charlottesville, Univ. Pr. of Va. [1964, c.1941, 1945] 332p. illus. 22cm. Orig. pub. by Colonial Williamsburg, Inc. (Dominion bks.) Bibl. 2.75 pap.,
1. Carter, Robert, 1728-1804. I. Title.

Carter, Rosalynn.

NORTON, Howard Melvin. 973.926'092'4 B
Rosalynn / by Howard Norton. Plainfield, N.J. : Logos International, c1977. x, 220 p., [4] leaves of plates : ill. ; 21 cm. [E874.C44N67] 77-85346 ISBN 0-88270-260-2 : 2.95
1. Carter, Rosalynn. 2. Carter, Jimmy, 1924- 3. Presidents—United States—Wives—Biography. I. Title. BIP

SIMMONS, Dawn Langley. 973.926'092'4 B
Rosalynn Carter, her life story / Dawn Langley Simmons. New York : F. Fell Publishers, c1979. 194 p. : ill. ; 22 cm. Bibliography: p. 194. [E874.C44S55 1979] 79-122803 ISBN 0-8119-0301-X : 9.95
1. Carter, Rosalynn. 2. Carter, Jimmy, 1924- 3. Presidents—United States—Wives—Biography. I. Title.

Carter, Rosalynn—Juvenile literature.

ROGERS, Jan Faulk. 973.926'092'4 B
First lady : Rosalynn Carter / by Jan Faulk Rogers. Chicago : Childrens Press, [1978] p. cm. Silhouettes the life of First Lady Rosalynn Carter. [E874.C44R6] 92 77-20861 ISBN 0-516-03459-6 lib.bdg. : 7.35
1. Carter, Rosalynn—Juvenile literature. 2. Presidents—United States—Wives—Biography—Juvenile literature. I. Title. BIP

Carter, Rubin, 1937-

CARTER, Rubin, 1937- 364.1'523'0924 B
The sixteenth round : from number 1 contender to #45472 / by Rubin "Hurricane" Carter. New York : Viking Press, 1974. viii, 339 p., [4] leaves of plates : ill. ; 25 cm. Autobiography. [HV6248.C353A33 1974] 73-17689 ISBN 0-670-64750-0 : 11.95
1. Carter, Rubin, 1937- I. Title.

Cartier, George Etienne, Sir, bart., 1814-1873.

BOYD, John, 1864-1933. 971.04'0924 B
Sir George Etienne Cartier, bart.: his life and times; a political history of Canada from 1814 until 1873. Freeport, N.Y., Books for Libraries Press [1971] xxi, 439 p. illus., facsims., ports. 24 cm. Reprint of the 1914 ed. Bibliography: p. 424-427. [F1033.C32 1971] 74-164590 ISBN 0-8369-5874-8
1. Cartier, George Etienne, Sir, bart., 1814-1873. 2. Cartier family. 3. Canada—Politics and government—19th century.

SWEENY, Alastair. 971.04'092'4 B
George-Etienne Cartier : a biography / Alastair Sweeny. Toronto : McClelland and Stewart, c1976. 352 p. : ill. ; 24 cm. Includes index. Bibliography: p. [331]-340. [F1033.C375] 77-353052 ISBN 0-7710-8363-7 : 16.95
1. Cartier, George Etienne, Sir, bart., 1814-1873. 2. Legislators—Canada—Biography. 3. Canada—Politics and government—19th century.
Distributed by Lippincott,N.Y.

Cartier, Jacques, 1491-1557—Juvenile literature.

TOYE, William. juv
Cartier discovers the St. Lawrence; illustrated by Laszlo Gal. London, Oxford University Press, 1971. 32 p. col. illus., 2 col. maps. 29 cm. Based on the author's The St. Lawrence. Includes translations from Jacques Cartier's Voyages. [E133.C3T68 1971] 75-857631 ISBN 0-19-273127-0 £1.10
1. Cartier, Jacques, 1491-1557—Juvenile literature. I. Gal, Laszlo, illus. II. Title.

Cartland, Barbara, 1902- —Religion and ethics.

CARTLAND, Barbara, 1902- 823'.9'12 B
I seek the miraculous / Barbara Cartland. 1st ed. New York : Dutton, c1978. 248 p. ; 22 cm. [PR6005.A765Z525] 77-15786 17.95
1. Cartland, Barbara, 1902- —Religion and ethics. 2. Cartland, Barbara, 1902- —Biography. 3. Novelists, English—20th century—Biography. I. Title. BIP

Cartland family.

WHITTIER, John Greenleaf, 1807-1892. 928.1
Whittier and the Cartlands, letters and comments; edited by Martha Hale Shackford. Wakefield, Mass., Montrose Press, 1950. vii, 91 p. illus., ports. 24 cm. [PS3281.A34] 51-378
1. Cartland family. I. Shackford, Martha Hale, 1875- ed. II. Title.

Cartographers—Biography.

TOOLEY, Ronald Vere, 1898- 526'.092'2 B
Tooley's Dictionary of mapmakers / compiled by Ronald Vere Tooley ; with a pref. by Helen Wallis. New York : A. R. Liss, 1979. p. cm. First half of work originally appeared in parts in the Map collectors' series published by the Map Collectors' Circle. Bibliography: p. [GA198.T66] 79-1936 ISBN 0-8451-1701-7 : 120.00
1. Cartographers—Biography. I. Title. II. Title: Dictionary of maps. BIP

Cartwright, Alexander Joy, 1820-1892.

PETERSON, Harold, 1939- 796.357'092'4 B
The man who invented baseball. New York, Scribner [1973] viii, 197 p. illus. 25 cm. [GV865.C32P47] 72-1183 ISBN 0-684-13185-4 7.95
1. Cartwright, Alexander Joy, 1820-1892. 2. Baseball—History. I. Title.

Cartwright, Edmund, 1743-1823.

[STRICKLAND, Mary] 677'.00924 B
A memoir of Edmund Cartwright. With an introd. by Kenneth G. Ponting. New York, A. M. Kelly [sic] 1971. 11, 372 p. 20 cm. (Documents of social history) Preface signed M. S., i.e., Mary Strickland. Cf. Halkett & Laing; Dict. nat. biog. Attributed in introd. to Margaret Strickland. Reprint of the 1843 ed. published under title: A memoir of the life, writings, and mechanical inventions, of Edmund Cartwright. [TS1440.C3M4 1971] 70-149329 ISBN 0-678-07769-X
1. Cartwright, Edmund, 1743-1823. I. M. S. II. S., M. III. Strickland, Jane Margaret, 1800-1888. IV. Title.

Cartwright, John, 1740-1824.

CARTWRIGHT, John, 1740-1824. 320.5'1 B
The life and correspondence of Major Cartwright. Edited by his niece F. D. Cartwright. New York, A. M. Kelley, 1969. 2 v. illus., map, port. 22 cm. (Reprints of economic classics) Reprint of the 1826 ed. [DA522.C27A2 1969] 68-57728
I. Cartwright, Frances Dorothy, 1780-1863. II. Title. BIP

CARTWRIGHT, John, 1740-1824. 355.3'31'0924 B
The life and correspondence of Major Cartwright. Edited by F. D. Cartwright. New York, B. Franklin [1972?] 2 v. illus. 25 cm. (Burt Franklin research and source works series, no. 192) "List of Major Cartwright's writings": v. 2, p. 299-301. [DA522.C27A2 1972] 72-187498 ISBN 0-8337-0489-3 22.50
I. Cartwright, Frances Dorothy, 1780-1863, ed.

OSBORNE, John Walter, 1927- 942.07'3'0924 B
John Cartwright [by] John W. Osborne. Cambridge [Eng.] University Press, 1972. ix, 174 p. 23 cm. (Conference on British Studies. Biographical series) Bibliography: p. 166-168. [DA522.C27O8] 74-190422 ISBN 0-521-08537-3
1. Cartwright, John, 1740-1824. I. Title. II. Series. BIP

Cartwright, Peter, 1785-1872.

CARTWRIGHT, Peter, 1785-1872. 922.773
Autobiography. With an introd., bibliography, and index by Charles L. Wallis. Nashville, Abingdon Press [c1956] 349p. 24cm. 'Centennial edition.'--Dust jacket. Includes bibliography. [F545.C3192] 56-5127
I. Title.

CARTWRIGHT, Peter, 1785-1872. 287'.632'0924 B
Autobiography of Peter Cartwright, the backwoods preacher. Edited by W. P. Strickland. Freeport, N.Y., Books for Libraries Press [1972] 525 p. port. 23 cm. Reprint of the 1856 ed. [BX8495.C36A3 1972] 70-38344 ISBN 0-8369-6761-5
201 A0006639GREEBIE, Sydney, 1889-

GREEBIE, Sydney, 1889-1960. 922.773
A true chronicle of the life and wild times of Peter Cartwright, circuit rider, by Sydney Greenbie and Marjorie Barstow Greenbie. [1st ed.] Penobscot, Me., Traversity Press [1955- v. illus., ports., map (on lining papers) 22 cm. "Bibliographical note": v. 2, p. 501-502. [BX8495.C36G73] 62-20778
1. Cartwright, Peter, 1785-1872. I. Greenbie, Marjorie Latta (Barstow) 1891- joint author. II. Title. III. Title: Hoof beats to heaven. IV. Title: Hoof beats in the canebrake.
Contents omitted

GREENBIE, Sydney, 1889- 922.773
Hoof beats to heaven; a true chronicle of the life and wild times of Peter Cartwright, circuit rider, by Sydney Greenbie and Marjorie Barstow Greenbie. [1st ed.] Penobscot, Me., Traversity Press [1955- v. illus., ports., map (on lining papers) 22 cm. [BX8495.C36G73] 55-8650
1. Cartwright, Peter, 1785-1872. I. Greenbie, Marjorie Latta Barstow, 1891- joint author. II. Title.

Caruso, Enrico, 1873-1921.

CARUSO, Dorothy Park (Benjamin). 920.7
Dorothy Caruso, a personal history. [1st ed.] New York, Hermitage House [1952] 191 p. illus. 21 cm. [ML420.C259C17] 52-8191
1. Caruso, Enrico, 1873-1921. 2. Gurdjieff, Georges Ivanovitch,1872-1949. I. Title.

CARUSO, Dorothy Park (Benjamin) 927.8
Enrico Caruso. his life and death. New York, S. & S. [1963, c.1945] 305p. illus. 21cm. (Essandess paperback) 1.75 pap.,
1. Caruso, Enrico, 1873-1921. 2. Caruso, Enrico, 1873-1821—discography. I. Title.

JACKSON, Stanley, 1910- 782.1'092'4 B
Caruso. New York, Stein and Day [1972] xiii, 302 p. illus. 25 cm. Bibliography: p. 294-296. [ML420.C259J2] 77-187313 ISBN 0-8128-1473-8 7.95
1. Caruso, Enrico, 1873-1921.

JACKSON, Stanley, 1910- 782.1'092'4 B
Caruso. London, New York, W. H. Allen, 1972. x, 302, [17] p. illus., ports. 23 cm. Bibliography: p. 294-296. [ML420.C259J2 1972b] 72-172561 ISBN 0-491-00664-0 £3.50
1. Caruso, Enrico, 1873-1921.

KEY, Pierre Van 782.1'092'4 B
Rensselaer, 1872-1945.
Enrico Caruso; a biography, by Pierre V. R. Key. In collaboration with Bruno Zirato. New York, Vienna House, [1973, c1922] xv, 455 p. illus. 23 cm. [ML420.C259K3 1972] 72-81091 ISBN 0-8443-0074-8 12.50
1. Caruso, Enrico, 1873-1921. I. Zirato, Bruno, joint author. BIP

YBARRA, Thomas Russell, 927.8
1880-
Caruso; the man of Naples and the voice of gold. [1st ed.] New York, Harcourt, Brace [1953] 315 p. illus. 22 cm. [ML420.C259Y25] 53-11458
1. Caruso, Enrico, 1873-1921.

Caruso, Enrico, 1873-1921—Iconography.

ROBINSON, Francis. 927.8
Caruso: his life in pictures. With Caruso discography by John Secrist. New York, Studio Publication [1957] 160 p. illus. 29 cm. [ML88.C3R6] 57-9252
1. Caruso, Enrico, 1873-1921—Iconography. 2. Caruso, Enrico, 1873-1921—Discography.

Caruthers, Jimmy.

HIGDON, Hal. 796.7'2'0924 B
Summer of triumph / Hal Higdon. New York : Putnam, c1977. 254 p. ; 23 cm. [GV1032.C33H53 1977] 77-2217 ISBN 0-399-11911-6 : 6.95
1. Caruthers, Jimmy. 2. Automobile racing drivers—United States—Biography. I. Title. BIP

Caruthers, William Alexander, 1800 (ca.)-1846.

DAVIS, Curtis Carroll, 928.1
1916-
Chronicler of the cavaliers; a life of the Virginia novelist, Dr. William A. Caruthers. Richmond, Dietz Press, 1953. xxi, 570p. illus., facsims. 24cm. Bibliography: p. [521]-547. [PS1262.C8Z67] 54-294
1. Caruthers, William Alexander, 1800 (ca.)-1846. I. Title.

Carvajal, Luis de, 1567?-1596.

COHEN, Martin A. 272'.2'0924 B
The martyr; the story of a secret Jew and the Mexican Inquisition in the sixteenth century [by] Martin A. Cohen. [1st ed.] Philadelphia, Jewish Publication Society of America, 1973. xv, 373 p. illus. 25 cm. Bibliography: p. [335]-357. [F1231.C32C63] 72-14055 ISBN 0-8276-0011-9 7.95
1. Carvajal, Luis de, 1567?-1596. 2. Inquisition. Mexico. 3. Jews in Mexico. I. Title. BIP

Carvalho, Solomon Nunes, 1815-1897.

STURHAHN, Joan, 1930- 770'.92'4 B
Carvalho, artist-photographer-adventurer-patriot : portrait of a forgotten American / by Joan Sturhahn. [Merrick, N.Y. : Richwood Pub. Co., 1975] p. cm. Bibliography: p. [TR140.C29S88] 75-22386 ISBN 0-915172-01-1 : 18.50
1. Carvalho, Solomon Nunes, 1815-1897. I. Title.

Carvalho, Solomon Nunes, 1815-1897—Juvenile literature.

GREENSPAN, Sophie. 917.8'04'2
Westward with Fremont; the story of Solomon Carvalho. Philadelphia, Jewish Publication Society of America, 1969. 164 p. illus., map (on lining papers) 21 cm. (Covenant 22) Relates the fifth expedition of Charles Fremont concentrating on the activities of Solomon Carvalho who travelled with the party as an artist and daguerreotypist. [F593.G817] 69-13551 2.95
1. Carvalho, Solomon Nunes, 1815-1897—Juvenile literature. 2. Fremont, John Charles, 1813-1890—Juvenile literature. 3. The West—Description and travel—1848-1860—Juvenile literature. I. Title.

Carver, George Washington, 1864?-1943.

BONTEMPS, Arna Wendell, 1902- 925
1973.
The story of George Washington Carver; illustrated by Harper Johnson. New York, Grosset & Dunlap [1954] 181 p. illus. 22 cm. (Signature books, 17) [S417.C3B6] 52-13746
1. Carver, George Washington, 1864?-1943.

COY, Harold. 925
The real book about George Washington Carver; illustrated by Elinore Blaisdell. Garden City, N. Y., Garden City Book, by arrangement with F. Watts [New York, 1951] 191 p. illus. 21 cm. (Real books) [S417.C3C69] 51-12206
1. Carver, George Washington, 1864?-1943. I. Title.

COY, Harold. 925
The real book about George Washington Carver; illustrated by Elinore Blaisdell. Garden City, N. Y., Garden City Book, by arrangement with F. Watts [New York, 1951] 191 p. illus. 21 cm. (Real books) [S417.C3C69] 51-12206
1. Carver, George Washington, 1864?-1943. I. Title.

ELLIOTT, Lawrence. 630.924 B
George Washington Carver: the man who overcame. Englewood Cliffs, N.J., Prentice-Hall [1966] x, 256 p. port. 22 cm. Bibliography: p. 255-256. [S417.C3E4] 66-23368
1. Carver, George Washington, 1864?-1943.

GRAHAM, Shirley. v. 12
Dr. George Washington Carver, scientist, by Shirley Graham and George D. Lipscomb, illustrated by Elton C. Fax. New York, J. Messner, inc. [1966, 1944] viii, 248 p. incl. front. (port.) illus. 22 cm. Bibliography: p. 242-243. 67-98440
1. Carver, George Washington, 1864?-1943. I. Lipscomb, George Dewey, 1898- joint author. II. Title. BIP

HOLT, Rackham. v. 12
George Washington Carver, an American biography. Rev. ed. Nashville, Abingdon Press [c1963] 360 p. ports. 21 cm. (Apex books, Y-3) 68-487
1. Carver, George Washington, 1864?-1943. I. Title. BIP

HOLT, Rackham 925
George Washington Carver: an American biography. Rev. ed. Nashville. Abingdon [1966. c.1943] 360p. illus. 22cm. (Apex bk., Y3) Bibl. 2.75 pap.,
1. Carver, George Washington, 1864?-1943. I. Title.

HOLT, Rackham. 925
George Washington Carver, an American biography. Rev. ed. Garden City, N.Y., Doubleday [1963] 360 p. illus. 22 cm. [S417.C3H6 1963] 62-11430
1. Carver, George Washington, 1864?-1943.

MANBER, David. 630'.924 B
Wizard of Tuskegee; the life of George Washington Carver. New York, Crowell-Collier Press [1967] vi, 168 p. illus., ports. 21 cm. (America in the making) Bibliography: p. [165] [S417.C3M27] 67-1676
1. Carver, George Washington, 1864?-1943. 2. Tuskegee Institute. I. Title.

MEANS, Florence (Crannell) 925
1891-
Carvers' George, a biography of George Washington Carver; illustrated by Harve Stein. Boston, Houghton Mifflin, 1952. 176 p. illus. 22 cm. [S417.C3M33] 52-5905
1. Carver, George Washington, 1864?-1943. I. Title.

SMITH, Alvin D 925
George Washington Carver, man of God. [1st ed.] New York, Exposition Press [1954] 76p. 21cm. [S417.C3S5] 54-6185
1. Carver, George, Washington, 1864?-1943. I. Title.

STEVENSON, Augusta. 581'.0924 B
George Carver, boy scientist. Illustrated by Wallace Wood. Indianapolis, Bobbs-Merrill [1959] 192 p. illus. 20 cm. (Childhood of famous Americans) The boyhood of the Negro botanist who developed products from such southern crops as sweet potatoes, pecans, and especially peanuts. [PZ7.S8467Gc2] 92 AC 68
1. Carver, George Washington, 1864?-1943. I. Wood, Wallace, illus. II. Title.

THOMAS, Henry, 1886- 925
George Washington Carver. Illustrated by Andre Le Blanc. New York, Putnam [1958] 126 p. illus. 21 cm. (Lives to remember) [S417.C3T48] 58-13316
1. Carver, George Washington, 1864?-1943. I. Title.

WHITE, Anne Terry. 925
George Washington Carver, the story of a great American; illustrated by Douglas Gorsline. New York, Random House [1953] 182 p. illus. 22 cm. (Landmark books, 38) [S417.C3W46] 53-6262
1. Carver, George Washington, 1864?-1943.

Carver, George Washington, 1864?-1943—Juvenile literature.

†DAVY, Yvonne. 630'.92'4 B
Mr. Creator's borrowed brown hands / Yvonne Davy; illustrated by Tom Dunbedin. Mountain View, Calif. : Pacific Press Pub. Association, c1977. 96 p. : ill. ; 22 cm. (Panda book) A biography of the black scientist famed for his revolutionary agricultural research. [S417.C3D38] 92 75-46424 pbk. : 3.50
1. Carver, George Washington, 1864?-1943—Juvenile literature. 2. Agriculturists—United States—Biography—Juvenile literature. I. Dunbedin, Thomas. II. Title. BIP

EPSTEIN, Samuel, 1909- 925
George Washington Carver, Negro scientist, by Samuel and Beryl Epstein. Illus. by William Moyers. New York, Grosset [1963, c.]1960. 79p. col. illus. 23cm. (Garrard Discovery bk., 4164) 1.00 bds.,
1. Carver, George Washington, 1864?-1943—Juvenile literature. I. Epstein, Beryl (Williams) 1910- joint author. II. Title.

*EPSTEIN, Samuel, 1909- 925
George Washington Carver; negro scientist. By Samuel & Beryl Epstein. Illus. by William Moyers. New York, Dell 79p. illus. 19cm. (Yearling Bk. 2848, Discovery Bk.) .50 pap.,
1. Carver, George Washington, 1864?-1943—Juvenile literature. I. Epstein, Beryl (Williams), 1910- joint author. II. Title.

NABOKOV, Peter. 630'.92'4 B
George Washington Carver / by Peter Towne [i.e. P. Nabokov] ; illustrated by Elzia Moon. New York : Crowell, [1975] 32 p. : ill. (some col.) ; 24 cm. (A Crowell biography) A simple biography of the Negro scientist famed for his revolutionary agricultural research. [S417.C3N32 1975] 92 74-34296 ISBN 0-690-00776-0 : 4.50 ISBN 0-690-00777-9 lib.bdg. : 5.25
1. Carver, George Washington, 1864?-1943—Juvenile literature. I. Moon, Elzia, ill. II. Title.

Carver, Humphrey.

CARVER, Humphrey. 712'.092'4 B
Compassionate landscape / Humphrey Carver. Toronto ; Buffalo : University of Toronto Press, [1975] viii, 251 p. : ill. ; 24 cm. Includes index. [HT166.C32A33] 75-22280 ISBN 0-8020-2186-7 : 15.00. ISBN 0-8020-6269-5 pbk. : 6.00
1. Carver, Humphrey. I. Title. BIP

Carver, Will.

EATON, John. 917.64'03'60924 B
Will Carver, outlaw. San Angelo, Tex., Anchor Pub. Co. [1972] 141 p. illus. 23 cm. Includes bibliographical references. [F595.C322E18] 73-153600
1. Carver, Will. 2. Outlaws. I. Title.

Carver, William F., 1840-1927.

CARVER, William 799.3'1'0924 B
F., 1840-1927.
Life of William F. Carver of California / William F. Carver. New York : Garland Pub., 1977. iv, 177 p. ; 19 cm. (The Garland library of narratives of North American Indian captivities ; v. 92) Reprint of the 1878 ed. published by Rockwell and Churchill, Boston. [E85.G2 vol. 92] [GV1157.C37] 75-7527 ISBN 0-8240-1716-1 lib.bdg. : 25.00
1. Carver, William F., 1840-1927. 2. Shooters—United States—Biography. 3. Indians of North America—Captivities. I. Title. II. Series.

Cary, Diana Serra, 1918-

CARY, Diana 791.43'028'0922 B
Serra, 1918-
Hollywood's children : an inside account of the child star era / Diana Serra Cary. Boston : Houghton Mifflin, 1978. xii, 290 p., [8] leaves of plates : ill. ; 24 cm. Includes index. Bibliography: p. [277]-280. [PN2287.C32A34] 78-12585 ISBN 0-395-27095-2 : 10.95
1. Cary, Diana Serra, 1918- 2. Moving-picture actors and actresses—United States—Biography. 3. Children as actors. I. Title. BIP

Cary, Freeman Grant,

LANGSTROTH, Theodore v. 12
Ashmead, comp.
"Ruin awaits the idle." Biographical sketch [of] Freeman Grant Cary. Advice to a daughter. [Cincinnati, 1966] Cincinnati, 1965?] 1 v. (unpaged) illus. port. 37 cm. 1 v. plates. 31 cm. Scrapbook containing newspaper clippings; a photostat of a biographical sketch of Cary from "History of Hamilton County, Ohio" by H. A. Ford, 1881; holograph letter of Cary to his daughter and Cary's wife to their daughter; holograph lesson pages written by Cary at the age of ten. 67-98937 65-101032
1. Cary, Freeman Grant, 1810- 2. Bewick, Thomas, I. Langstroth, Theodore Ashmead, comp. II. Bewick, Thomas, 1753-1828. III. Title. IV. Title: Thomas Bewick;

Cary, William S.

CARY, William S. 919.6'11'04
Wrecked on the Feejees [by] William S. Cary. Fairfield, Wash., Ye Galleon Press, 1972. 73 p. illus. 26 cm. Three hundred copies printed. [DU600.C23] 73-154493 ISBN 0-87770-085-0
1. Cary, William S. 2. Fiji Islands—Description and travel. I. Title. BIP

Casal, Mary.

CASAL, Mary. 301.41'57'0924 B
The stone wall : an autobiography / by Mary Casal. New York : Arno Press, 1975. 227 p. ; 23 cm. (Homosexuality) Reprint of the 1930 ed. published by Eyncourt Press, Chicago. [HQ76.3.U5C37 1975] 75-12307 ISBN 0-405-07404-2 : 12.00
1. Casal, Mary. 2. Lesbianism—United States—Personal narratives. I. Title. II. Series.

Casaldaliga, Pedro.

CASALDALIGA, Pedro. 282'.092'4 B
I believe in justice and hope / Pedro Casaldaliga. Notre Dame, Ind. : Fides/Claretian, c1978. v, 232 p. ; 20 cm. Translation of Yo creo en la justicia y en la esperanza! [BX4705.C33547A3813] 78-21694 ISBN 0-8190-0628-9 pbk. : 5.95
1. Casaldaliga, Pedro. 2. Catholic Church—Bishops—Biography. 3. Bishops—Brazil—Biography. 4. Church and social problems—Brazil. 5. Church and social problems—Catholic Church. 6. Christianity and justice. I. Title. BIP

Casals, Pablo, 1876-1973.

CASALS, Pablo, 1876- 927.8
Conversations with Casals [by] J. Ma. Corredor, translated from the French by Andre Mangeot. With an introd. by Pablo Casals and an an appreciation by Thomas Mann. [1st. ed.] New York, Dutton, 1957 [c1956] 240p. illus., ports. 22cm. [ML418.C4A333 1957] 57-5322
I. Corredor, Jose Maria. II. Title.

CASALS, Pablo, 1876- 787'.3'0924 B
Joys and sorrows; reflections, by Pablo Casals as told to Albert E. Kahn. New York, Simon and Schuster [1970] 314 p. illus., facsims., ports. 24 cm. [ML418.C4A35] 73-101879 7.95
1. Musicians—Correspondence, reminiscences, etc. I. Kahn, Albert Eugene, 1912- II. Title.

CASALS, Pablo, 1876- 787'.3'0924 1974.
Joys and sorrows [by] Pablo Casals as told to Albert E. Kahn. [New York] Simon and Schuster [1974, c1970] 314 p. illus. 23 cm. (A Touchstone book) [ML418.C4A35] [[B]] 0-671-21774-7 3.95 (pbk.)
1. Musicians-Correspondence, reminiscences, etc. I. Kahn, Albert Eugene, 1912- II. Title.
L.C. card number for original ed.: 73-101879

FORSEE, Aylesa. 927.8
Pablo Casals; cellist for freedom. New York, T. Y. Crowell [1965] 229 p. illus., ports. 21 cm. Bibliography: p. [224] [ML418.C4F7] 65-14900
1. Casals, Pablo, 1876- I. Title.

KIRK, H. L. 787'.3'0924 B
Pablo Casals; a biography, by H. L. Kirk. [1st ed.] New York, Holt, Rinehart and Winston [1974] xi, 692 p. illus. 25 cm. Bibliography: p. 657-666. [ML418.C4K6] 72-91569 ISBN 0-03-007616-1 15.00
1. Casals, Pablo, 1876-1973.

LITTLEHALES, Lillian. 787'.3'0924 B
Pablo Casals. Westport, Conn., Greenwood Press [1970, c1929] 232 p. illus., music, ports. 23 cm. Reprint of the 2d ed., 1948. [ML418.C4L5 1970] 72-97385
1. Casals, Pablo, 1876- **BIP**

TAPER, Bernard. 927.8
Cellist in exile, a portrait of Pablo Casals. New York, McGraw-Hill [1962] 120 p. illus. 21 cm. [ML418.C4T4] 62-18530
1. Casals, Pablo, 1876- I. Title.

Casals, Pablo, 1876- —Iconography.

HENLE, Fritz, 1909- 787'.3'0924
Casals / [photos. by Fritz Henle]. Garden City, N.Y. : American Photographic Book Pub. Co., c1975. ca. 150 p. : chiefly ill. ; 21 cm. [ML88.C32H4] 75-13882 ISBN 0-8174-0593-3 : 7.95
1. Casals, Pablo, 1876-1973—Iconography.

VALAITIS, Vytas. 780.924
Casals. Photographed by Vytas Valaitis. Text selected and arranged by Theodore Strongin. [New York, Paragraphic Books, c1966] 1 v. (unpaged) 28 cm. [ML88.C32V3] 66-26545
1. Casals, Pablo, 1876- —Iconography.

Casals, Rosemary, 1948- —Juvenile literature.

JACOBS, Linda. 796.34'2'0924 B
Rosemary Casals : the rebel Rosebud / by Linda Jacobs. St. Paul : EMC Corp., [1975] p. cm. (Women who win 3) A biography of the tennis star who is one of the driving forces behind the growing success of women's tennis. [GV994.C37J32] 92 75-4646 ISBN 0-88436-166-7 lib.bdg. : 4.95 ISBN 0-88436-167-5 pbk. : 2.95
1. Casals, Rosemary, 1948- —Juvenile literature. 2. Tennis—Juvenile literature. I. Title. **BIP**

Casanova, Danielle (Perini) 1909-1943.

TERY, Simone. 923.344
Danielle; the wonderful story of Danielle Casanova. [Adapted and translated from the French by Helen Simon Travis] New York, International Publishers [1953] 126p. 21cm. Translation of Du solell plein le coeur. [HX263.C36T42] 53-11701
1. Casanova, Danielle (Perini) 1909-1943. I. Title.

Casanova de Seingalt, Giacomo Girolamo, 1725-1798.

BUCK, Mitchell Starrett, 1887- 940.2'53'0924 B
The life of Casanova from 1774 to 1798 : a supplement to the Memoirs / drawn from the work of J. F. H. Adnesse and other sources by Mitchell S. Buck. Brooklyn : Haskell House, 1977. 130 p. ; 21 cm. Reprint of the 1924 ed. published by N. L. Brown, New York. "Bibliographical index": p. 129-130. [D285.8.C4B8 1977] 76-51406 ISBN lib.bdg. : 10.95
1. Casanova de Seingalt, Giacomo Girolamo, 1725-1798. 2. Europe—Biography. I. Adnesse, J. F. H. II. Title.

CASANOVA de Seingalt, Giacomo Girolamo, 1725-1798. 848'.5'09 B
The memoirs of Jacques Casanova; an autobiography. Translated into English by Arthur Machen. With an appreciation by Havelock Ellis. London, New York, Issued for subscribers only by the Venetian Society, 1928. St. Clair Shores, Mich., Scholarly Press, 1974. p. cm. The unabridged London ed. of 1894 to which has been added the chapters discovered by Arthur Symons, a suppl., and bibliography. [D285.8.C32 1974] 74-4431 ISBN 0-403-03093-5 (v. 1)
1. Casanova de Seingalt, Giacomo Girolamo, 1725-1798. I. Machen, Arthur, 1863-1947, tr.

CASANOVA DE SEIGALT, Giacomo Girolamo, 1725-1798. 920
Memoirs; the first complete and unabridged English translation by Arthur Machen. Illustrated with old engravings. New York, Putnam [1959-61] 6v. illus. 22cm. Contents.[1] Venetian years.--2. To Paris and prison.--3. The eternal quest.--4. Adventures in the South--5. In London and Moscow.--6. Spanish passions. [D285.8.C32 1959] 59-16015
I. Title.

CASANOVA DE SEINGALT, Giacomo, 1725-1798 920
Memoirs. 3.v. Tr. [from French] by Arthur Machen. Introd. by Arthur Symons. Illus. by Rockwell Kent. New York, Dover [1961] 2216p. (T338; T339; T340) 2.00 pap., ea.,
I. Title.

CASANOVA DE SEINGALT, Giacomo Giarolamo, 1725-1798 920
Memoirs; the first complete and unabridged English translation by Arthur Machem. Illus. with old engravings. New York, Putnam [1960,1961] vol. 4. Adventures in the South. Vol. 5. In London and Moscow, Vol. 6. Spanish passions. 59-16015 v.4, v.5, v.6, ea., 5.00
I. Title.

CASANOVA DE SEINGALT, Giacomo Girolamo, 1725-1798. 920
Memoirs; being an autobiographical account of the loves and adventures of Jacques Casanova, chevalier de Seingalt, written down by himself at the Castle of Dux, in the year of grace 1798, and now fully done into the English language. New York, Universal, 1953- v. in 18cm. (A Universal giant, no. G-10) 'Many passages have been . . . revised to suit the modern reader and certain portions . . . have been compressed.' [D285.8.C327] 53-34140
I. Title.

CASANOVA DE SEINGALT, Giacomo Girolamo, 1725-1798. 920
The memoirs of Jacques Casanova de Seigalt, as translated into English by Arthur Machen. With an introd. by Arthur Symons; illustrated by Rockwell Kent. New York, Dover Publications [1961] 3v. fronts., plates. 21cm. The twelve-volume Aventuros edition (New York, 1925) has been used as a basis for the present edition; the eight-volume French edition (Paris, Garnier) has also been employed. Cf. Editor's note. [D285.8] CD62
I. Title.

CASANOVA DE SEINGATT, Giacomo Givolamo 1725-1798. 848'.5'03 B
The memoirs of Casanova. A modern translation and abridgement by Lowell Bair. With an introd. by F. W. Dupee. New York, Bantam Books [1968] xv, 429 p. 18 cm. [D285.8.C322 1968] 68-19246
1. Casanova de Seingalt, Giacomo Girolamo, 1725-1798. I. Bair, Lowell, ed.

KESTEN, Hermann 828.5
Casanova. Tr. from German by James Stern, Robert Pick. New York, Collier, [1962,c.1955] 413p. (AS163V) Bibl. 0.95pap.
1. Casanova de Seinigall, Giacomo Girolamo, 1725-1798. I. Title.

KESTEN, Hermann, 1900- 920
Casanova. Translated by James Stern and Robert Pick from the German original. [1st ed.] New York, Harper [c1955] 396p. illus. 22cm. [D285.8.C4K42] 54-6285
1. Casanova de Seingalt, Giacomo Girolamo, 1725-1796. I. Title.

MASTERS, John, 1914- 914'.03'2530924 B
Casanova. New York, Bernard Geis Associates [1969] 302 p. illus. (part col.), facsims., ports. (part col.) 26 cm. Bibliography: p. 296. [D285.8.C4M28] 74-84183 15.00
1. Casanova de Seingalt, Giacomo Girolamo, 1725-1798. I. Title.

MONTGOMERY, James Stuart. 920
The incredible Casanova, the magnificent follies of a peerless adventurer, amorist and charlatan; a biography. [1st ed.] Garden City, N.Y., Doubleday, 1950. 437 p. 22 cm. [D285.8C4M63] 50-6313
1. Casanova de Seingalt, Giacomo Girolamo, 1725-1798. I. Title.

Casas, Bartolome de las, Bp. of Chiapa, 1474-1566.

BARTOLOME de las 972.02'0924 B
Casas in history: toward an understanding of the man and his work. Edited by Juan Friede and Benjamin Keen. DeKalb, Northern Illinois University Press [1971] xiii, 632 p. illus. 25 cm. "Las Casas: a selective bibliography [by] Raymond Marcus": p. [603]-616. [E125.C4B26] 76-157648 ISBN 0-87580-025-4 20.00
1. Casas, Bartolome de las, Bp. of Chiapa, 1474-1566. I. Friede, Juan, ed. II. Keen, Benjamin, 1913- ed. **BIP**

HANKE, Lewis. 922.272
Bartolome de las Casas, bookman, scholar & propagandist. Philadelphia, University of Pennsylvania Press, 1952. xii, 119 p. facsims. 23 cm. "The Rosenbach Fellowship in Bibliography." Bibliographical references included in "Notes" (p. 98-116) [E125.C4H33] 52-7741
1. Casas, Bartolome de las, Bp. of Chiapa, 1474-1566. I. Pennsylvania. University. Rosenbach Fellowship in Bibliography Fund. II. Title.

JONES, Evan, 1927- 922.272
Protector of the Indians. Illustrated by George Fulton. New York, Nelson [1958] 154p. illus. 21cm. [E125.C4J6] 58-10588
1. Casas, Bartolome de las, Bp. of Chiapa, 1474-1566. I. Title.

MACNUTT, Francis Augustus, 1863-1927. 972'.02'0924 B
Bartholomew de las Casas; his life, his apostolate, and his writings. New York, G. P. Putnam's Sons, 1909. [New York, AMS Press, 1972] xxxviii, 472 p. illus. 19 cm. Bibliography: p. xxxi. [E125.C4M2 1972] 70-172712 ISBN 0-404-07146-5 17.50
1. Casas, Bartolome de las, Bp. of Chiapa, 1474-1566. **BIP**

MILLER, Hubert J. 972'.02'0924 B
Bartolome de las Casas: protector of the Indians [by] Hubert J. Miller. [Edinburg, Tex., Printed by the New Santander Press, 1972] vii, 61 p. illus. 22 cm. (The Tinker pamphlet series for the teaching of Mexican American heritage) Bibliography: p. 59-61. [E125.C4M45] 73-181309
1. Casas, Bartolome de las, Bp. of Chiapa, 1474-1556. I. Title. II. Series.

PARISH, Helen Rand. 972'.02'0924 B
Las Casas as a bishop : a new interpretation based on his holograph petition in the Hans P. Kraus Collection of Hispanic American manuscripts = Las Casas, obispo : una nueva interpretacion basada en su peticion autografa conservada en la Coleccion Hans P. Kraus de manuscritos hispanoamericanos / by Helen Rand Parish. [Washington : Library of Congress, 1977] p. cm. Spanish and English. Includes index. Bibliography: p. [E125.C4P35] 76-608204 ISBN 0-8444-0195-1
1. Casas, Bartolome de las, Bp. of Chiapa, 1474-1566. 2. Bishops—Mexico—Biography. I. Title. II. Title: Las Casas, obispo.

WAGNER, Henry Raup, 1862-1957. 973.1'6 B
The life and writings of Bartolome de las Casas, by Henry Raup Wagner, with the collaboration of Helen Rand Parish. [1st ed.] Albuquerque, University of New Mexico Press [1967] xxv, 310 p. 26 cm. "Narrative and critical catalogue of Casas' writings": p. [253]-298. [E125.C4W3] 66-29983
1. Casas, Bartolome de las, Bp. Chiapa, 1474-1566. I. Parish, Helen Rand. **BIP**

Case, John Francis,

CASE, John Francis, 1876- 920.5
Stepping stones and memories. [Wright City?Mo., 1955] 95p. illus. 22cm. [CT275.C3425A3] 56-16532
I. Title.

Casement, Roger, Sir 1864-1916.

THE accusing ghost of Roger v. 12
Casement. New York, Citadel Press, 1957. 191p. port. 23cm.
1. Casement, Sir Roger, 1864-1916. I. Noyes, Alfred, 1880-

INGLIS, Brian, 1916- 941.59'092'4 B
Roger Casement. [1st American ed.] New York, Harcourt Jovanovich [1974, c1973] 448 p. illus. 24 cm. Bibliography: p. [417]-426. [DA965.C3I53 1974] 73-17115 ISBN 0-15-178327-6 8.95
1. Casement, Roger, Sir, 1864-1916. **BIP**

MACKEY, Herbert O v. 12
The life and times of Roger Casement. Dublin, C. J. Fallon, 1954. 144p. plates, ports., facsims. 22cm. Bibliography: p. 144. A56
1. Casement, Roger, Sir 1864-1916. I. Title.

MCCOLL, Rene, 1905- 923.2415
Roger Casement; a new judgment. New York, Norton [1957] 328p. illus. 22cm. [DA965.C3M28 1957] 57-6557
1. Casement, Roger, Sir 1864-1916. I. Title.

REID, Benjamin Lawrence. 941.5082'1'0924 B
The lives of Roger Casement / B. L. Reid. New Haven : Yale University Press, 1976. xix, 532 p. : ill. ; 24 cm. Includes index. Bibliography: p. 517-520. [DA965.C3R44] 75-18184 ISBN 0-300-01801-0 : 25.00
1. Casement, Roger, Sir, 1864-1916. I. Title. **BIP**

SINGLETON GATES, Peter. 923.2415
The black diaries; an account of Roger Casement's life and times, with a collection of his diaries and public writings [by] Peter Singleton-Gates and Maurice Girodias.

New York, Grove Press [1959] 536 p. illus., ports., maps, facsims. 26 cm. Bibliographical footnotes. [DA965.C3S53] 59-9807
1. Casement, Roger, Sir, 1864-1916. I. Girodias, Maurice, joint author. II. Title.

SINGLETON-GATES, Peter. 923.2415
The black diaries; an account of Roger Casement's life and times with a collection of his diaries and public writings [by] Peter Singleton-Gates and Maurice Girodias. [Special ed. n.p.] Olympia Press, 1959. 626 p. illus., ports., maps (2 col. on lining papers) facsims. 26 cm. Bibliographical footnotes. [DA965.C3S53 1959a] 59-52948
1. Casement, Sir Roger, 1864-1916. I. Girodias, Maurice. II. Title.

Casey, Solanus, 1870-1957.

DERUM, James Patrick. 271'.36'0924 B
The porter of Saint Bonaventure's; the life of Father Solanus Casey, Capuchin. Detroit, Fidelity Press [1968] 279 p. illus., ports. 23 cm. [BX4705.C33573D4] 78-1230 4.95
1. Casey, Solanus, 1870-1957. I. Title.

Cash, Johnny.

CARPOZI, George. 784'.0924 B
The Johnny Cash story. New York [Pyramid Publications, 1970] 128 p. illus., ports. 18 cm. [ML420.C265C4] 76-14877 0.75
1. Cash, Johnny. I. Title.

CASH, Johnny. 784'.092'4 B
Man in black / Johnny Cash. Grand Rapids : Zondervan Pub. House, c1975. 244 p., [12] leaves of plates : ill. ; 23 cm. [ML420.C265A3] 75-6178 6.95
1. Cash, Johnny. I. Title.

CASH, Johnny. 784.0924
Man in black / Johnny Cash. New York : Warner Books, 1976 c1975 222 p. : ill. ; 18 cm. [ML420.C265A3] ISBN 0-446-89086-3 pbk. : 1.95
1. Cash, Johnny. I. Title.
L.C. card no. for 1975 Zondervan edition: 75-6178. BIP

CONN, Charles Paul. 248'.2 B
The new Johnny Cash. Old Tappan, N.J., F. H. Revell Co. [1973] 94 p. illus. 20 cm. [BV4935.C28C66] 73-2381 ISBN 0-8007-0607-2 2.95
1. Cash, Johnny. 2. Conversion. I. Title. BIP

GOVONI, Albert. 784'.0924 B
A boy named Cash. New York, Lancer Books [1970] 190 p. port. 18 cm. "Johnny Cash song catalogue": p. 179-185. [ML420.C265G7] 79-14343 0.75
1. Cash, Johnny. I. Title.

WREN, Christopher S., 1936- 784'.0924 B
Winners got scars too; the life and legends of Johnny Cash, by Christopher S. Wren. New York, Dial Press, 1971. 229 p. 22 cm. [ML420.C265W7] 75-150399 6.95
1. Cash, Johnny. I. Title.

WREN, Christopher S., 1936- 784'.0924 [B]
Winners got scars too; the life and legends of Johnny Cash. New York, A Country Music/Ballantine Book [1974, c.1971] 252 p. ports. 18 cm. [ML420.C265W7] 1.25 (pbk.)
1. Cash, Johnny. I. Title.
L.C. card no. for the hardbound edition: 75-150399.

Cash, Johnny—Juvenile literature.

TAYLOR, Paula. 784'.092'4 B
Johnny Cash. Illus.: John Keely. Mankato, Minn., Creative Education; [distributed by Childrens Press, Chicago, 1974, c1975] 31 p. illus. (part col.) 25 cm. (Rock 'n pop stars) A brief biography emphasizing the career of the singer whose songs often express his concern for "poor and forgotten people." [ML3930.C27T4] 92 74-14549 ISBN 0-87191-391-7
1. Cash, Johnny—Juvenile literature. I. Keely, John, illus. II. Title. BIP

Cash, June Carter, 1929-

CASH, June Carter, 1929- 784'.092'4 B
Among my klediments / June Carter Cash. Grand Rapids : Zondervan Pub. House, c1979. 152 p., [2] leaves of plates : ill. ; 22 cm. [ML420.C2653A3] 79-10959 ISBN 0-310-38170-3 : 6.95
1. Cash, June Carter, 1929- 2. Country musicians—United States—Biography. 3. Christian biography—United States. I. Title. BIP

Cash, Wilbur Joseph, 1900-1941.

MORRISON, Joseph L. 975'.04'0924 B
W. J. Cash, Southern prophet; a biography and reader, by Joseph L. Morrison. [1st ed.] New York, Knopf, 1967. xiii, 309, vii p. port. 22 cm. [E175.5.C27M6] 67-18611
1. Cash, Wilbur Joseph, 1900-1941. I. Cash, Wilbur Joseph, 1900-1941. II. Title.

Caskey, Jessie Jane (Hussey)

CASKEY, Jessie Jane (Hussey) 920.5
Journalizing Jane, the autobiography of Jessie Jane Caskey. New York, Exposition Press [c.1960] 143p. 21cm. 60-2138 3.00
I. Title.

CASKEY, Jessie Jane (Hussey) 1875- 920.5
Journalizing Jane, the autobiography of Jessie Jane Caskey. [1st ed.] New York, Exposition Press [1960] 143p. 21cm. [CT275.C344A3] 60-2138
I. Title.

Caspary, Vera, 1904- —Biography.

CASPARY, Vera, 1904- 813'.5'2 B
The secrets of grown-ups / Vera Caspary. New York : McGraw-Hill, c1979. 287 p., [4] leaves of plates : ill. ; 25 cm. Includes index. [PS3505.A842Z474] 79-1333 ISBN 0-07-010223-6 : 14.95
1. Caspary, Vera, 1904- —Biography. 2. Authors, American—20th century—Biography. I. Title. BIP

Casper, Billy, 1931-

MILLER, Hack. 248.2'46
The new Billy Casper; more important things in life than golf. Salt Lake City, Deseret Book Co., 1968. 144 p. illus., ports. 24 cm. [GV964.C3A3] 68-59516 3.95
1. Casper, Billy, 1931- 2. Converts, Mormon. I. Title.

PEERY, Paul Denver, 1906- 796.352'0924 B
Billy Casper, winner [by] Paul D. Peery. Englewood Cliffs, N.J., Prentice-Hall [1969] ix, 207 p. illus. 24 cm. [GV964.C3P4] 77-82905 5.95
1. Casper, Billy, 1931- 2. Golf—Biography. I. Title.

Casse, Clifford.

CASSE, Clifford. 620'.0092'4 B
Power in nature : a narrative in report form of a twentieth-century engineer / by Clifford Casse. [Rockcliffe] : [The author], [1976] [8], 271 [i.e. 284] p., [18] leaves of plates : ill., ports. ; 31 cm. [TA140.C37A37] 76-373201 ISBN 0-9504940-0-3
1. Casse, Clifford. 2. Engineers—Biography. I. Title.

Cass, Lewis, 1782-1866.

DUNBAR, Willis Frederick, 1902- 973.5'0924 B
Lewis Cass. [Grand Rapids] Eerdmans [1970] 96 p. port. 22 cm. (Great men of Michigan) Includes bibliographical references. [E340.C3D8] 68-56121 1.95
1. Cass, Lewis, 1782-1866.

MCLAUGHLIN, Andrew Cunningham, 1861-1947. 973.5'0924 B
Lewis Cass. Boston, Houghton, Mifflin. [New York, AMS Press, 1972] ix, 390 p. illus. 19 cm. (American statesmen, v. 24) Reprint of the 1899 ed. [E340.C3M15 1972] 70-128957 ISBN 0-404-50874-X
1. Cass, Lewis, 1782-1866. I. Title. II. Series. BIP

WOODFORD, Frank Bury, 1903- 923.273
Lewis Cass, the last Jeffersonian. New Brunswick, Rutgers University Press, 1950. ix, 380 p. port. 22 cm. Bibliography: p. 357-369. [E340.C3W66] 50-9741
1. Cass, Lewis, 1782-1866. I. Title. BIP

WOODFORD, Frank Bury, 1903-1967. 973.5'092'4 B
Lewis Cass, the last Jeffersonian. New York, Octagon Books, 1973 [c1950] ix, 380 p. port. 23 cm. Reprint of the ed. published by Rutgers University Press. Bibliography: p. 357-369. [E340.C3W66 1973] 73-2014 ISBN 0-374-98718-1 14.00 (lib. ed.)
1. Cass, Lewis, 1782-1866.

Cassady, Carolyn.

CASSADY, Carolyn. 813'.5'4 B
Heart beat : my life with Jack & Neal / by Carolyn Cassady. Berkeley, CA : Creative Arts Book Co. : distributed by Book People, 1976. 93 p. : ill. ; 23 cm. [PS3521.E735Z59] 76-12732 ISBN 0-916870-03-0 pbk. : 4.00
1. Kerouac, John, 1922-1969—Relationship with women—Carolyn Cassady. 2. Cassady, Carolyn. 3. Cassady, Neal. 4. Authors, American—20th century—Biography. 5. Wives—United States—Biography. I. Title. BIP

Cassady, Neal.

GINSBERG, Allen, 1926- 810'.9'0054 B
The visions of the great rememberer / by Allen Ginsberg ; with letters by Neal Cassady ; & drawings by Basil King. Amherst, Mass. : Mulch Press, c1974. 71 p., [3] leaves of plates : ill. ; 22 cm. (A Haystack book) [PS3521.E735Z65] 74-77758 ISBN 0-913142-03-4 : 2.50
1. Kerouac, John, 1922-1969—Biography. 2. Cassady, Neal. 3. Ginsberg, Allen, 1926- —Correspondence. 4. Authors—Correspondence, reminiscences, etc. I. Title. BIP

Cassatt, Alexander Johnston, 1839-1906.

DAVIS, Patricia Talbot. 385'.092'4 B
End of the line : Alexander J. Cassatt and the Pennsylvania railroad / Patricia T. Davis. New York : Neale Watson Academic Publications, c1978. 208 p., [8] leaves of plates : ill. ; 24 cm. Includes index. Bibliography: p. [199]-203. [HE2754.C3D38] 78-977 ISBN 0-88202-181-8 : 15.00
1. Cassatt, Alexander Johnston, 1839-1906. 2. Pennsylvania Railroad. 3. Businessmen—United States—Biography. I. Title. BIP

Cassatt, Mary, 1844-1926.

MCKOWN, Robin. 759.13 B
The world of Mary Cassatt. Illustrated with photos. New York, Crowell [1972] xiii, 253 p. illus. 21 cm. (Women of America) Bibliography: p. 239-241. [ND237.C3M3] 77-139106 ISBN 0-690-90274-3 4.50
1. Cassatt, Mary, 1844-1926. I. Title. BIP

ROUDEBUSH, Jay. 759.13 B
Mary Cassatt / by Jay Roudebush ; [translated from the French by Alice Sachs]. New York : Crown Publishers, c1979. p. cm. [ND237.C3R6813] 78-21706 ISBN 0-517-53740-0 : 5.95
1. Cassatt, Mary, 1844-1926. 2. Painters—United States—Biography. I. Title. BIP

Cassatt, Mary, 1844-1926—Juvenile literature.

CARSON, Julia Margaret (Hicks) 1899- 759.1 B
Mary Cassatt, by Julia M. H. Carson. Illustrated with photos. from paintings and color prints by Mary Cassatt. New York, D. McKay Co., 1966. xi, 193 p. illus. 21 cm. Bibliography: p. 177-178. [ND237.C3C3] 66-9532
1. Cassatt, Mary, 1844-1926—Juvenile literature.

MYERS, Elisabeth P. 759.13 B
Mary Cassatt: a portrait, by Elisabeth P. Myers. Chicago, Reilly & Lee Books [1971] 138 p. illus., port. 24 cm. Bibliography: p. [137]-138. A biography of the American artist who spent most of her life in Europe because she felt her homeland restricted women in certain areas of artistic study. [ND237.C3M9] 92 75-143869 5.95
1. Cassatt, Mary, 1844-1926—Juvenile literature. I. Title.

SCHEADER, Catherine. 759.13 B
Mary Cassatt / by Catherine Scheader. Chicago : Childrens Press, [1977] p. cm. (They found a way) A biography of an American artist whose many paintings of women and children reveal the influence of French Impressionism. [ND237.C3S3] 92 77-7359 ISBN 0-516-01852-3 lib.bdg. : 6.60
1. Cassatt, Mary, 1844-1926—Juvenile literature. 2. Painters—United States—Biography—Juvenile literature. I. Title. II. Series. BIP

SWEET, Frederick Arnold, 1903- 759.1
Miss Mary Cassatt, impressionist from Pennsylvania, by Frederick A. Sweet. Norman, Univ. of Okla. Pr. [1966] xx, 242p. illus. (pt. col.) 23cm. Bibl. [ND237.C3S9] 66-13423 7.95
1. Cassatt, Mary, 1845-1926. I. Title.

WILSON, Ellen Janet (Cameron) 759.13 B
American painter in Paris; a life of Mary Cassatt, by Ellen Wilson. New York, Farrar, Straus & Giroux [1971] xii, 205 p. illus., ports. (part col.) 24 cm. (An Ariel book) Bibliography: p. 198-201. The biography of the nineteenth-century Pennsylvania woman who became one of America's best known artists. [ND237.C3W53 1971] 92 70-149223 ISBN 0-374-30270-7 4.95
1. Cassatt, Mary, 1844-1926—Juvenile literature. I. Title. BIP

Cassel, Abraham H.

KLINEFELTER, Walter, 1899- 917.48'06'31
The ABC books of the Pennsylvania Germans [by] Walter Klinefelter. Abraham Harley Cassel, nineteenth century Pennsylvania German American book collector [by] Marlin L. Heckman. Marriages performed at the Evangelical Lutheran Church of the Holy Trinity, 1748-1767 [by] Fritz Braun and Frederick S. Weiser. Breinigsville, Pennsylvania German Society, 1973. viii, 299 p. illus. 24 cm. (Publications of the Pennsylvania German Society, v. 7) Includes bibliographical references. [GR110.P4A372 vol. 7] [Z1033.H8] 74-158463
1. Cassel, Abraham H. 2. Primers, German—History and criticism. 3. Pennsylvania Germans—Education. 4. Registers of births, etc.—Lancaster, Pa. 5. Lancaster, Pa.—Genealogy. I. Heckman, Marlin L. Abraham Harley Cassel, nineteenth century Pennsylvania German American book collector. 1973. II. Braun, Fritz. Marriages performed at the Evangelical Lutheran Church of the Holy Trinity, 1748-1767. 1973. III. Title. IV. Title: Abraham Harley Cassel, nineteenth century Pennsylvania German American book collector. V. Title: Marriages performed at the Evangelical Lutheran Church of the Holy Trinity, 1748-1767. VI. Series: Pennsylvania-German Society. Publications, v. 7.

Cassels, Louis.

CASSELS, Louis. 917.57'75 B
Coontail Lagoon; a celebration of life. Boston, G. K. Hall, 1974. 196 p. 25 cm. Large print ed. [F279.A2C37 1974b] 74-14928 ISBN 0-8161-6240-9
1. Cassels, Louis. 2. Aiken, S.C.—Description. 3. Sight-saving books. I. Title.

CASSELS, Louis. 917.5775 B
Coontail Lagoon: a celebration of life. Philadelphia, Westminster Press [1974] 126 p. 21 cm. [F279.A2C37] 73-21770 5.00
1. Cassels, Louis. 2. Aiken, S.C.—Description. I. Title.

Cassidy, Butch, b. 1866 or 7.

BETENSON, Lula 364.1550924
Parker, 1884-
Butch Cassidy, my brother / Lula Parker Betenson, as told to Dora Flack. New York : Penguin Books, [1976], c1975. p. cm. Includes index. Bibliography: p. [F595.C362B47 1976] 76-18720 ISBN 0-14-004187-7 pbk. : 2.95
1. Cassidy, Butch, b. 1866 or 7. 2. Betenson, Lula Parker, 1884- I. Flack, Dora. II. Title. BIP

BETENSON, Lula 364.1550924
Parker, 1884-
Butch Cassidy, my brother / Lula Parker Betenson, as told to Dora Flack. New York : Penguin Books, [1976], c1975. p. cm. Includes index. Bibliography: p. [F595.C362B47 1976] 76-18720 ISBN 0-14-004187-7 pbk. : 2.95
1. Cassidy, Butch, b. 1866 or 7. 2. Betenson, Lula Parker, 1884- I. Flack, Dora. II. Title. BIP

BETENSON, Lula 364.1'55'0924 B
Parker, 1884-
Butch Cassidy, my brother / by Lula Parker Betenson, as told to Dora Flack. Provo, Utah : Brigham Young University Press, [1975] xiii, 265 p. : ill. ; 24 cm. Includes index. Bibliography: p. 259-260. [F595.C362B47] 75-2332 ISBN 0-8425-1222-5 : 7.95
1. Cassidy, Butch, b. 1866 or 7. 2. Betenson, Lula Parker, 1884- I. Flack, Dora. II. Title.

BETENSON, Lula 364.1'55'0924 B
Parker, 1884-
Butch Cassidy, my brother / by Lula Parker Betenson, as told to Dora Flack. Provo, Utah : Brigham Young University Press, [1975] xiii, 265 p. : ill. ; 24 cm. Includes index. Bibliography: p. 259-260. [F595.C362B47] 75-2332 ISBN 0-8425-1222-5 : 7.95
1. Cassidy, Butch, b. 1866 or 7. 2. Betenson, Lula Parker, 1884- I. Flack, Dora. II. Title.

POINTER, Larry, 364.1'55'0924 B
1940-
In search of Butch Cassidy / by Larry Pointer. Norman : University of Oklahoma Press, c1977. xvii, 294 p. : ill. ; 22 cm. Includes index. Bibliography: p. 277-284. [F595.C362P64] 77-14066 ISBN 0-8061-1455-X : 9.95
1. Cassidy, Butch, b. 1866 or 7. 2. The West—History—1848-1950. 3. Outlaws—The West—Biography. I. Title. BIP

Cassidy, Shaun, 1958-

BERMAN, Connie. 784'.092'4 B
The Shaun Cassidy scrapbook : an illustrated biography / by Connie Berman. New York : Sunridge Press, c1978. 123 p. : ill. ; 28 cm. [ML420.C28B5] 78-52381 ISBN 0-441-76087-2 : 4.95
1. Cassidy, Shaun, 1958- 2. Singers—United States—Biography. 3. Actors—United States—Biography. I. Title.

Cassidy, Shaun, 1958- —Juvenile literature.

SCHUMACHER, Craig. 784'.092'4 B
Shaun Cassidy / by Craig Schumacher. Mankato, MN : Creative Education, [1979] p. cm. A biography of a young entertainer whose interest in music and acting stems from his famous brother and parents. [ML3930.C275S4] 92 79-11154 ISBN 0-87191-672-X : 5.95 ISBN 0-89812-097-7 pbk. : 2.75
1. Cassidy, Shaun, 1958- —Juvenile literature. 2. Singers, American—Biography—Juvenile literature. I. Title.
Publisher's Address : 123 South Broad St., Mankato, MN 56001 BIP

TURNER, Mark. 791.45'72
Hardy boys / by Mark Turner. Mankato, Minn. : Creative Education, c1979. 32 p. : ill. ; 23 cm. (TV and movie tie-ins) [PN1992.77.H346T8] 79-53040 ISBN 0-87191-703-3 : 5.95 ISBN 0-89812-035-7 pbk. : 2.95
1. Cassidy, Shaun, 1958- —Juvenile literature. 2. Stevenson, Parker, 1952- —Juvenile literature. 3. Hardy boys (Television program)—Juvenile literature. 4. Television personalities—United States—Biography—Juvenile literature. I. Title. II. Series.
Publisher's Address : 123 S. Broad St., Mankato, MN 56001

Cassidy, Sheila, 1937-

CASSIDY, Sheila, 1937- 364.1'34
Audacity to believe / Sheila Cassidy. Cleveland : Collins World, 1978, c1977. xiv, 333 p., [6] leaves of plates : ill. ; 23 cm. Autobiographical. [HV9598.C37A32 1978] 77-18195 ISBN 0-529-05464-7 : 8.95
1. Cassidy, Sheila, 1937- 2. Political prisoners—Chile—Biography. 3. Surgeons—England—Biography. 4. Catholics—Chile—Biography. I. Title. BIP

Cassini, Igor, 1915-

CASSINI, Igor, 791.43'092'4 B
1915-
I'd do it all over again : the life and times of Igor Cassini / by Igor Cassini with Jeanne Molli. New York : Putnam, c1976. p. cm. Includes index. [PN4874.C315A3 1976] 75-44160 8.95
1. Cassini, Igor, 1915- I. Molli, Jeanne, joint author. II. Title.

Cassini, Marguerite,

CASSINI, Marguerite, 1882- 920.7
Never a dull moment; the memoirs of Countess Marguerite Cassini. [1st ed.] New York, Harper [1956] 366 p. illus. 22 cm. [D413.C3A35] 55-6571
I. Title.

Cassiodorus Senator, Flavius Magnus Aurelius, ca. 487-ca. 580.

O'DONNELL, James 271'.0092'4 B
Joseph, 1950-
Cassiodorus / James J. O'Donnell. Berkeley : University of California Press, c1979. xvi, 303 p. ; 23 cm. Includes index. Bibliography: p. 273-296. [BR1720.C4O36] 77-93470 ISBN 0-520-03646-8 : 17.50
1. Cassiodorus Senator, Flavius Magnus Aurelius, ca. 487-ca. 580. 2. Christian biography—Italy. BIP

Cassirer, Ernst, 1874-1945.

LIPTON, David R., 1947- 193
Ernst Cassirer : the dilemma of a liberal intellectual in Germany, 1914-1933 / David R. Lipton. Toronto ; Buffalo : University of Toronto Press, 1978. p. cm. Includes index. Bibliography: p. [B3216.C34L56] 78-6945 ISBN 0-8020-5408-0 : 15.00
1. Cassirer, Ernst, 1874-1945. 2. Philosophers—Germany—Biography. 3. Germany—Intellectual life—20th century.

Castaneda, Carlos.

CASTANEDA, Carlos. 299'.7
The second ring of power / by Carlos Castaneda. New York : Simon and Schuster, c1977. 316 p. ; 22 cm. [E99.Y3C288] 77-22107 ISBN 0-671-22942-7 : 8.95
1. Castaneda, Carlos. 2. Yaqui Indians—Religion and mythology. 3. Hallucinogenic drugs and religious experience. 4. Indians of Mexico—Religion and mythology. 5. Anthropologists—Mexico—Biography. I. Title. BIP

CASTANEDA, Carlos. 299'.7
The second ring of power / by Carlos Castaneda. 1st Touchstone ed. New York : Simon and Schuster, 1979, c1977. 316 p. ; 21 cm. (A Touchstone book) [E99.Y3C288 1979] 78-26557 ISBN 0-671-24851-0 pbk. : 3.95
1. Castaneda, Carlos. 2. Yaqui Indians—Religion and mythology. 3. Hallucinogenic drugs and religious experience. 4. Indians of Mexico—Religion and mythology. 5. Anthropologists—Mexico—Biography. I. Title.

DE MILLE, Richard, 301.2'092'4 B
1922-
Castaneda's journey : the power and the allegory / by Richard de Mille ; graphics by Frederick A. Usher. Santa Barbara, CA. : Capra Press, 1976. 205 p. : ill. ; 24 cm. Includes index. Bibliography: p. 197-201. [F1221.Y3C374] 76-26030 ISBN 0-88496-067-6 : 10.00. ISBN 0-88496-068-4 pbk. : 4.95
1. Castaneda, Carlos. 2. Anthropologists—United States—Biography. I. Title. BIP

Castellani, Aldo

CASTELLANI, Aldo Sir 926.1
A doctor in many Lands; the autobiography of Aldo Castellani. Garden City, N.Y., Doubleday, [c.]1960. 359p. 22cm. 60-9469 4.95
I. Title.

CASTELLANI, Aldo, Sir 1875- 926.1
A doctor in many lands; the autobiography of Aldo Castellani. [1st ed.] Garden City, N. Y., Doubleday, 1960. 359p. 22cm. [R520.C33A3] 60-9469
I. Title.

Castello Branco, Humberto de Alencar.

DULLES, John W. F. 981'.06'0924 B
Castello Branco : the making of a Brazilian president / by John W. F. Dulles ; foreword by Roberto de Oliveira Campos. 1st ed. College Station : Texas A&M University Press, c1978. xxi, 487 p., [17] leaves of plates : ill. ; 24 cm. Includes index. Bibliography: p.[447]-462. [F2538.22.C37D84] 77-99279 ISBN 0-89096-043-7 : 17.50
1. Castello Branco, Humberto de Alencar. 2. Brazil—Presidents—Biography. 3. Brazil—History—1954- 4. Brazil—History—1930-1954. BIP

Castiglione, Baldassare, conte, 1478-1529.

ADY, Julia Mary 327'.2'0924 B
(Cartwright) d.1924.
Baldassare Castiglione, the perfect courtier; his life and letters, 1478-1529. New York, E. P. Dutton, 1908. [New York, AMS Press, 1973] 2 v. illus. 19 cm. Bibliography: v. 1, p. xiii-xx. [DG540.8.C3A3 1973] 75-154138 ISBN 0-404-09206-3 42.50
1. Castiglione, Baldassare, conte, 1478-1529. 2. Italy—History—1492-1559. I. Title.

ROEDER, Ralph, 1890- 920.045
The man of the Renaissance; four lawgivers: Savonarola, Machiavelli, Castiglione, Aretino. New York, Meridian Books [1958] 504 p. illus. 21 cm. (Meridian books, MG17) [DG533.R6 1958] 58-11929
1. Savonarola, Girolamo Maria Francesco Matteo, 1452-1498. 2. Machiavelli, Niccolo, 1469-1527. 3. Castiglione, Baldassare, conte, 1478-1529. 4. Aretino, Pietro, 1492-1556. 5. Renaissance—Italy. I. Title.

Castillo Armas, Carlos, Pres. Guatemala, 1914-1957—Juvenile literature.

[STEFFAN, Alice Jacqueline 920
(Kennedy)] 1907-
Fire of freedom; the story of Col. Carlos Castillo Armas, by Jack Steffan [pseud.] Illus. by Carolyn Cather. New York, Hawthorn [c.1963] 185p. illus. (pt. col.) 22cm. (Credo bks. [10]) 63-8783 2.95
1. Castillo Armas, Carlos, Pres. Guatemala, 1914-1957—Juvenile literature. I. Title.

Castle, Mabel (Wing)

CASTLE, Mabel (Wing) 920.7
My mother's reminiscences: a memorial to Mabel Wing Castle, born in Providence, Rhode Island, June 19, 1864, died in Chicago, April 22, 1950. By Elinor Castle Nef. Chicago, 1954. 75p. illus. 24cm. [CT275.C348A3] 55-20353
I. Nef, Elinor (Castle) 1894 or 5-1953. II. Title.

Castle, Samuel Northrup, 1808-1894.

LIFE of Samuel Northrup v. 12
Castle, written by his grandson. Honolulu, Published by the Samuel N. and Mary Castle Foundation in cooperation with the Hawaiian Historical Society, 1960. 210p. port.
1. Castle, Samuel Northrup, 1808-1894. 2. Hawaiian Islands—Hist. 3. Missions—Hawaiian Islands. I. Castle, William Richards, 1878-

Castle, Vernon, 1887-1918.

CASTLE, Irene (Foote) 927.933
1893-
Castles in the air, by Irene Castle as told to Bob and Wanda Duncan. [1st ed.] Garden City, N. Y., Doubleday, 1958. 264p. illus. 22cm. [PN2287.C35C27] 58-13273
1. Castle, Vernon, 1887-1918. I. Duncan, Bob, 1927- II. Duncan, Wanda. III. Title.

CASTLE, Irene 793.3'092'4 B
Foote, 1893-1963.
My husband / by Mrs. Vernon Castle (Irene Castle) ; new introd. by Iris M. Fanger. New York : Da Capo Press, 1978, c1919. p. cm. (Da Capo series in dance) Reprint of the ed. published by Scribner, New York; with minor changes and additions and a new introd. [GV1785.C37C37 1978] 78-12730 ISBN 0-306-79505-1 : 19.50
1. Castle, Vernon, 1887-1918. 2. Castle, Irene Foote, 1893-1963. 3. Dancers—Biography. I. Title. BIP

Castle, William.

CASTLE, 791.43'0232'0924 B
William.
Step right up! : ... I'm gonna scare the pants off America / by William Castle. New York : Putnam, c1976. 256 p., [4] leaves of plates : ill. ; 22 cm. [PN1998.A3C335] 75-43519 ISBN 0-399-11470-X : 7.95
1. Castle, William. I. Title.

Castle, William Bosworth, 1897-

WILLIAM B. Castle number. v. 12
[Chicago] American Medical Association, 1958. over-title. 173-514p. illus., port. (Archives of internal medicine, v. 101, no. 2, Feb. 1958) Bio-bibliography: p. 175-183.
1. Castle, William Bosworth, 1897- I. A. M. A. archives of internal medicine.

Castle, William Richards, 1849-1935.

REMINISCENSES. v. 12
Honolulu, Privately printed, 1960. iii, 108p. group port.
1. Castle, William Richards, 1849-1935. I. Castle, William Richards, 1849-1935.

Castle, William Richards, 1878-1963—Manuscripts.

HERBERT Hoover 016.97391'6'0924
Presidential Library.
William R. Castle papers. [West Branch, Iowa, 1971?] 67 l. 28 cm. Caption title. [Z6616.C38H47] 72-171250
1. Castle, William Richards, 1878-1963—Manuscripts. I. Title.

Castleden, George Frederick, 1861-1945.

CASTELDEN, Louise Decatur. 927.5
George Frederick Castleden, etcher-painter; a brief biography, Wth a foreword by Elihu Root, Jr. [1st ed.] New York, Exposition Press [1954, c1953] 72p. illus. 21cm. [ND497.C38C3] 53-12070
1. Castleden, George Frederick, 1861-1945. I. Title.

Caston, Leonard, 1917-

CASTON, Leonard, 784'.092'4 B
1917-
From blues to pop : the autobiography of Leonard "Baby Doo" Caston / edited by Jeff Titon. Los Angeles : John Edwards Memorial Foundation, [1974] 29 p. : ill. ; 23 cm. (JEMF special series ; no. 4) [ML417.C425A3] 74-195691
1. Caston, Leonard, 1917- 2. Jazz musicians—Correspondence, reminiscences, etc. I. Titon, Jeff, ed. II. Title. III. Series: John Edwards Memorial Foundation. JEMF special series ; no. 4.

Castro, Fidel, 1927-

BONSAL, Philip 327.7291'073
Wilson, 1903-
Cuba, Castro, and the United States [by] Philip W. Bonsal. [Pittsburgh] University of Pittsburgh Press [1971] xii, 318 p. illus. 24 cm. Bibliography: p. 303-309. [E183.8.C9B6] 72-151505 ISBN 0-8229-3225-3 9.95
1. Castro, Fidel, 1927- 2. U.S.—Foreign relations—Cuba. 3. Cuba—Foreign relations—U.S. I. Title. BIP

DUBOIS, Jules, 1910- 923.27291
Fidel Castro: rebel—liberator or dictator? [1st ed.] Indianapolis, Bobbs-Merrill [1959] 391 p. illus. 23 cm. [F1788.C3D8] 59-10236
1. Castro, Fidel, 1927- 2. Cuba—Politics and government—1933-1959.

GARCIA- 972.91'064'0924 B
CALZADILLA, Miguel A., 1915-
The Fidel Castro I knew; biographical fragments on the Cuban revolution [by] Miguel A. G.-Calzadilla. [1st ed.] New York, Vantage Press [1971] 80 p. illus., map, port. 21 cm. [F1788.22.A2G2] 72-27793 3.75
1. Castro, Fidel, 1927- 2. Cuba—Politics and government—1959- 3. Cuba—Biography. I. Title.

HALPERIN, 972.91'064'0924
Maurice, 1906-
The rise and decline of Fidel Castro; an essay in contemporary history. Berkeley, University of California Press [1972] x, 380 p. illus. 24 cm. Includes bibliographical references. [F1788.H27] 77-182794 ISBN 0-520-02182-7 12.95
1. Castro, Fidel, 1927- 2. Cuba—Foreign relations. 3. Cuba—History—1959- I. Title. BIP

MARTIN, Lionel. 972.91'064'0924 B
The early Fidel : roots of Castro's communism / by Lionel Martin. Secaucus, N.J. : L. Stuart, [1977] p. cm. Includes index. [F1788.22.C3M27] 77-12245 ISBN 0-8184-0254-7 : 8.95
1. Castro, Fidel, 1927- 2. Heads of state—Cuba—Biography. I. Title.

MORTON, Ward M. 972.91'064'0924 B
Castro as charismatic hero [by] Ward M. Morton. [Lawrence] University of Kansas, Center of Latin American Studies, 1965. 30 p. 23 cm. ([Kansas. University. Center of Latin American Studies] Occasional publications, no. 4) Includes bibliographical references. [F1401.K3 no. 4] 66-65127
1. Castro, Fidel, 1927- I. Title. II. Series.

STEIN, Edwin C. 923.27291
Cuba, Castro, and communism. [New York, Macfadden, c.1962] 175p. 18cm. (50-144) 62-6713 .50 pap.,
1. Castro, Fidel, 1927- 2. Communism—Cuba. I. Title.

Castro, Fidel, 1927—Juvenile literature.

GERASSI, John. 972.91'064'0924 B
Fidel Castro, a biography. [1st ed.] Garden City, N.Y., Doubleday, 1973. 137 p. map. 21 cm. A biography of the man who became dictator of Cuba in 1959 after a successful revolution against Batista's military dictatorship and reorganized the country into a Communist state. [F1788.22.C3G47 1973] 92 70-180076 ISBN 0-385-02791-5 3.95
1. Castro, Fidel, 1927—Juvenile literature. I. Title.

KURLAND, 972.91'064'0924 B
Gerald, 1942-
Fidel Castro, communist dictator of Cuba. Charlotteville, N.Y., SamHar Press, 1972. 32 p. 22 cm. (Outstanding personalities, no. 36) Bibliography: p. 32. A brief biography of the man who has been the military dictator of Cuba since 1959. [F1788.22.C3K87] 92 72-75370 ISBN 0-87157-536-1 1.98
1. Castro, Fidel, 1927—Juvenile literature. I. Title.
Pap. $0.98 ISBN 0-87157-036-X

Castro, Raul Hector, 1916- —Juvenile literature.

WHEELOCK, Warren H. 973'.04'68 S
Raul H. Castro, la adversidad es mi angel. Tommy Nunez, arbitro del NBA. !Presentando a Vikki Carr! / Warren H. Wheelock ; adaptacion, J. O. "Rocky" Maynes ; consultantes, Jorge Valdivieso, Amalia Perez, Ruben A. Soruco B. St. Paul, Minn. : EMC, 1976. p. cm. (His Ilustres hispanos de EE. UU. ; 1) Translation of Raul H. Castro, adversity is my angel. Brief biographies of three Spanish Americans: the Arizona governor, a professional basketball referee, and a popular female singer. [E184.S75W517 vol. 1] 920'.0092'6873 920 76-2420 ISBN 0-88436-248-5. ISBN 0-88436-249-3 pbk.
1. Castro, Raul Hector, 1916- —Juvenile literature. 2. Nunez, Tommy, 1938- —Juvenile literature. 3. Carr, Vikki—Juvenile literature. I. Maynes, J. O. II. Title. III. Title: Tommy Nunez, arbitro del NBA. IV. Title: !Presentando a Vikki Carr!

Catalans in Puerto Rico—Biography.

CIFRE de 301.45'19'607295
Loubriel, Estela.
La formacion del pueblo puertorriqueno : la contribucion de los catalanes, balearicos y valencianos / Estela Cifre de Loubriel. San Juan, Puerto Rico : Instituto de Cultura Puertorriquena, 1975. 485 p. : ill. ; 25 cm. [F1983.C38C57] 76-460878
1. Catalans in Puerto Rico—Biography. I. Title.

Catarina de San Juan, d. 1688.

STINETORF, Louise A. 920.7
La China Poblana. [1st ed.] Indianapolis, Bobbs-Merrill [1960] 256 p. 24 cm. Includes bibliography. [CT558.C3S78] 60-12625
1. Catarina de San Juan, d. 1688. I. Title.

Catchers (Baseball)—Biography—Juvenile literature.

ZANGER, Jack. 796.357'0922
Great catchers of the major leagues. New York, Random House [1970] xi, 173 p. illus., ports. 22 cm. (Little League library 12) Profiles of ten men who made baseball history as major league catchers: Berra, Campanella, Cochrane, Dickey, Freehan, Hartnett, Howard, Lombardi, McCarver, and Torre. [GV865.A1Z3] 920 70-109230
1. Catchers (Baseball)—Biography—Juvenile literature. I. Title.

Catchers (Baseball)—United States—Biography—Juvenile literature.

TUTTLE, Anthony. 796.357'092'2 B
Meet the catchers / by Anthony Tuttle. [Mankato, MN] : Creative Education, [c1977] 30 p. : ill. (some col.) ; 20 cm. (Creative Education early sports books) Brief profiles of five big-league catchers: Johnny Bench, Ted Simmons, Carlton Fisk, Manny Sanguillen, and Jerry Grote. [GV865.A1T89] 920 76-28358 ISBN 0-87191-575-8 lib.bdg. 4.95
1. Catchers (Baseball)—United States—Biography—Juvenile literature. I. Title. II. Series. BIP

Catching (Baseball)—Juvenile literature.

SHAPIRO, Milton J. 796.357'0922
Heroes behind the mask; America's greatest catchers, by Milton J. Shapiro. New York, J. Messner [1968] 191 p. ports. 22 cm. Contents.Contents.—Yogi Berra.—Roy Campanella.—Mickey Cochrane.—Bill Dickey.—Gabby Hartnett.—Joe Torre.—Elston Howard.—Duke Bresnahan.—Johnny Kling.—"Schnoz" Lombardi. [GV873.S47] 920 68-25106 3.95
1. Catching (Baseball)—Juvenile literature. I. Title.

SULLIVAN, George, 796.357'23
1927-
The catcher, baseball's man in charge / George Sullivan. New York : Dodd, Mead, c1976. 124 p. : ill. ; 19 x 24 cm. Includes index. Discusses the qualities and skills catchers need, spotlighting exemplary players throughout baseball history. [GV872.S78] 920 75-37650 ISBN 0-396-07278-X : 4.95
1. Catching (Baseball)—Juvenile literature. 2. Catchers (Baseball)—Biography—Juvenile literature. I. Title.

Caterina da Genova, Saint, 1447-1510.

CATERINA DAGENOVA, Saint 922.22
1447-1510.
The life and sayings of Saint Catherine of Genoa. Translated and edited by Paul Garvin. Staten Island, New York Alba House [1964] 139 p. 21 cm. Selections translated from Libro de la vita mirabile e dottrina santa de la beta Caterinetta de Genoa. [BX4700.C36A33] 64-20113
1. Caterina da Genova, Saint, 1447-1510. I. Garvin, Paul, ed. and tr. II. Title.

CATERINA DA GENOVA, Saint, 922.22
1747-1510
The life and sayings of Saint Catherine of Genoa. Tr. from Italian and ed. by Paul Garvin. Staten, Island, N.Y., Alba [c.1964] 139p. 21cm. 64-20113 2.95
I. Garvin, Paul, editor and trans. II. Garvin, Paul, editor and trans. III. Title.

KAYE-SMITH, Sheila, 1887- 922.2
Quartet in heaven. [1st ed.] New York, Harper [1952] viii, 279 p. 22 cm. [BX4667.K3] 52-5455
1. Caterina da Genova, Saint, 1447-1510. 2. Connelly, Cornelia Augusta (Peacock) 1809-1879. 3. Rosa of Lima, Saint, 1586-1617. 4. Therese, Saint, 1873-1897. I. Title.
Contents Omitted.

KAYE-SMITH, Sheila, 282'.0922 B
1887-1956.
Quartet in heaven. Freeport, N.Y., Books for Libraries Press [1970, c1952] viii, 244 p. 23 cm. (Biography index reprint series) Contents.Contents.—The matrons: Caterina Fiesca Adorna. Cornelia Connelly.—The maidens: Isabella Rosa de Santa Maria de Flores. Therese Martin.—Some notes on the nature of sanctity. [BX4667.K3 1970] 75-136649
1. Caterina da Genova, Saint, 1447-1510. 2. Connelly, Cornelia Augusta (Peacock) 1809-1879. 3. Rosa, of Lima, Saint, 1586-1617. 4. Therese, Saint, 1873-1897. I. Title. BIP

REGGIO, Edwin, 1933- 922.245
Heart afire; a story of St. Catherine of Genoa. Illus. by Mary Kandzor. Notre Dame, Ind., Dujarie Press [1955] 95p. illus. 24cm. [BX4700.C36R4] 55-33457
1. Caterina da Genova, Saint, 1447-1510. I. Title.

Caterina da Siena, Saint, 1347-1380.

GILLET, Martin Stanislas, 922.245
Abp., 1875-1951.
The mission of St. Catherine. Translated by Sister M. Thomas Lopez. St. Louis, Herder [1955] 222p. 21cm. (Cross and crown series of spirituality, no. 4) Translation of La mission de sainte Catherine de Sienne. [BX4700.C4G513] 55-6451
1. Caterina da Siena, Saint, 1347-1380. I. Title.

GIORDANI, Igino, 271'.972'024 B
1894-
Saint Catherine of Siena, doctor of the Church / by Igino Giordani ; translated from the Italian by Thomas J. Tobin. Boston : St. Paul Editions, [1975] 258 p., [12] leaves of plates : ill. ; 24 cm. Translation of Vita di santa Caterina da Siena. Includes bibliographical references. [BX4700.C4G5613] 75-1624 5.95
1. Caterina da Siena, Saint, 1347-1380. I. Title.

GREENE, Genard, 1921- 922.245
Behind shuttered windows; a story of St. Catherine of Siena. Illus. by Dorothy Lahey. Notre Dame, Ind., Dujarie Press [1954] 95p. illus. 24cm. [BX4700.C4G7] 54-3700
1. Caterina da Siena, Saint, 1347-1380. I. Title.

LEVASTI, Arrigo, 1886- 922.245
My servant, Catherine. Translated by Dorothy M. White. Westminster, Md., Newman Press [1954] 406p. illus. 23cm. Translation of Santa Caterina da Siena. [BX4700.C4L4513] 54-4862
1. Caterina da Siena, Saint, 1347-1380. I. Title.

PERRIN, Joseph Marie, 922.22
1905-
Catherine of Siena. Tr. [from French] by Paul Barrett. Westminster, Md., Newman [c.1961, 1965] xxxii, 233p. 23cm. Bibl. [BX4700.C4P43] 64-66333 4.95
1. Caterina da Siena, Saint, 1347-1380. I. Title.

RAYMUNDUS DE VINEIS, 922.245
1330-1399.
The life of St. Catherine of Siena by Blessed Raymond of Capua. Tr. [from Italian and Latin] by George Lamb. New York, P. J. Kenedy [1960]c.1934,1960] 384p. illus. Bibl. 60-14110 4.95
1. Caterina da Siena, Saint, 1347-1380. I. Title.

UNDSET, Sigrid, 1882- 922.245
1949.
Catherine of Siena; translated by Kate Austin-Lund. New York, Sheed and Ward, 1954. 293p. 22cm. [BX4700.C4U52] 54-6143
1. Caterina da siena, Saint, 1347-1380. I. Title.

Caterina da Siena, Saint, 1347-1380—Juvenile literature

NEWLAND, Mary (Reed) 922.245
The adventures of Catherine of Siena; story and pictures by Mary Reed Newland. New York, Kenedy [c.1960] 32p. illus. (part col.) 27cm. 60-7791 2.50
1. Caterina da Siena, Saint, 1347-1380—Juvenile literature I. Title.

Catharina, Saint, of Alexandria.

FLAVIUS, Brother, 1927- 922.262
A star in the East, a story of St. Catherine of Alexandria. Illus. by Rosemary Donatino. Notre Dame, Ind., Dujarie Press [1952] 94 p. illus. 24 cm. [BX4700.C3F6] 52-40062
1. Catharina, Saint, of Alexandria. I. Title.

Catharine

SCHERMAN, Katharine. 923.147
Catherine the Great. Illustrated by Pranas Lape. New York, Random House [1957] 184p. illus. 22cm. (World landmark books, W-29) [DK171.6.S36] 57-7513
1. Catharine 2. Empress of Russia, 1729-1796. I. Title.

Catharine Howard, consort of Henry VIII, King of England, d. 1542.

SMITH, Lacey Baldwin, 923.142
1922-
A Tudor tragedy; the life and times of Catherine Howard. [New York] Pantheon Books [1961] 222 p. illus. 23 cm. [DA333.H7S6] 61-14770
1. Catharine Howard, consort of Henry VIII, King of England, d. 1542. I. Title.

Catharine I, Empress of Russia, d. 1727.

LONGWORTH, Philip, 947'.06'0922 B
1933-
The three empresses: Catherine I, Anne, and Elizabeth of Russia. New York, Holt, Rinehart and Winston [1973, c1972] x,

242 p. illus. 22 cm. Bibliography: p. 231-234. [DK151.L65 1973] 72-78124 ISBN 0-03-001411-5 7.95
1. Catharine I, Empress of Russia, d. 1727. 2. Anne, Empress of Russia, 1693-1740. 3. Elizabeth, Empress of Russia, 1709-1762. I. Title.

Catharine II, Empress of Russia, 1729-1796.

ALMEDINGEN, Martha Edith, 1898-1971. 923.147
Catherine, Empress of Russia, by E. M. Almedingen. New York, Dodd, Mead, 1961. 312 p. 22 cm. [DK170.A59] 61-12400
1. Catharine II, Empress of Russia, 1729-1796.

ANTHONY, Katharine Susan, 1877-1965. 947'.06'0924 B
Catherine the Great. Westport, Conn., Greenwood Press [1973, c1925] 331 p. ports. 22 cm. [DK170.A6 1973] 70-136512 ISBN 0-8371-5430-8 15.00
1. Catharine II, Empress of Russia, 1729-1796.

CATHARINE II, Empress of Russia, 1729-1796. 923.147
The memoirs of Catherine the Great. With the pref. to the 1st ed. (1859) by Alexander Herzen. Translated, with foreword and epilogue, by Lowell Bair. New York, Bantam Books [1957] 305p. 18cm. (A Bantam biography, FB410, 0) [DK170.A262 1957] 57-5192
I. Title.

CATHARINE II, Empress of Russia, 1729-1796. 923.147
The memoris of Catherine the Great. Edited by Dominique Maroger, with an introd. by G. P. Gooch; translated from the French by Moura Budberg. New York, Macmillan [1955] 400p. ports. 23cm. [DK170.A262] 55-1967
I. Maroger, Dominique, ed. II. Title.

CATHERINE the Great; a profile. Edited by Marc Raeff. [1st ed.] New York, Hill and Wang [1972] xiii, 331 p. 21 cm. (World profiles) Includes bibliographical references. [DK170.C35 1972] 77-163575 ISBN 0-8090-3367-4 2.45 947'.06'0924 B
1. Catharine II, Empress of Russia, 1729-1796. I. Raeff, Marc, ed. BIP

CRONIN, Vincent. 947'.06'0924 B
Catherine, Empress of all the Russias / Vincent Cronin. 1st ed. New York : Morrow, 1978. 349 p., [12] leaves of plates : ill. ; 24 cm. Includes bibliographical references and index. [DK170.C76 1978] 77-28809 ISBN 0-688-03305-9 : 12.95
1. Catharine II, Empress of Russia, 1729-1796. 2. Russia—Kings and rulers—Biography. 3. Russia—History—Catharine II, 1762-1796. I. Title.

GOOCH, George Peabody, 1873- 920.02
Catherine the Great, and other studies [by] G. P. Gooch. Hamden, Conn. [dist. Shoe String] 1966. xi, 292p. ports. 22cm. First pub. in 1954. [DK170.G65] 66-18227 7.50
1. Catharine II, Empress of Russia. 1729-1796. 2. Voltaire, Francois Marie Arouet de, 1694-1778. 3. Bismarck, Otto, Furst von, 1815-1898. 4. France—Intellectual life. I. Title.

GREY, Ian, 1918- 947'.06'0924 B
Catherine the Great, autocrat and Empress of all Russia / by Ian Grey. Westport, Conn. : Greenwood Press, 1975, c1961. 254 p., [4] leaves of plates : ill. ; 22 cm. Reprint of the ed. published by Hodder and Stoughton, London. Includes index. Bibliography: p. 246-247. [DK170.G68 1975] 75-14598 ISBN 0-8371-8219-0 lib.bdg. : 15.00
1. Catharine II, Empress of Russia, 1729-1796. I. Title.

HASLIP, Joan, 1911- 947'.06'0924 B
Catherine the Great / by Joan Haslip. 1st American ed. New York : Putnam, 1977c1976 p. cm. Includes index. [DK170.H37 1976] 76-20630 10.95
1. Catherine II, Empress of Russia, 1729-1796. I. Title.

KAUS, Gina, 1894- 947'.06'0924 B
Catherine, the portrait of an empress. Translated from the German by June Head. Freeport, N.Y., Books for Libraries Press [1971] 384 p. illus. 23 cm. Translation of Katharina die Grosse. Reprint of the 1935 ed. [DK170.K35 1971] 75-37351 ISBN 0-8369-6698-8
1. Catharine II, Empress of Russia, 1729-1796.

MASSON, Charles Francois Philibert, 1762-1807. 947'.06
Secret memoirs of the court of Petersburg. New York, Arno Press, 1970. vii, 321 p. 23 cm. (Russia observed) Reprint of the 1802 ed. Translation of Memoires secrets sur la Russie. [DK171.M413] 75-115563 ISBN 0-405-03049-5
1. Catharine II, Empress of Russia, 1729-1796. 2. Paul I, Emperor of Russia, 1754-1801. I. Title.

NOBLE, Iris. 947.060924 (B)
Empress of all Russia: Catherine the Great. New York, J. Messner [1966] 191 p. 22 cm. [DK170.N6] 66-14003
1. Catherine II, Empress of Russia, 1729-1796. I. Title.

OLDENBOURG, Zoe, 1916- 923.147
Catherine the Great. Tr. from French by Anne Carter. New York, Pantheon [c.1965] xvii, 378p. 32 plates (incl. ports.) 22cm. Bibl. [DK170.O373] 64-18348 5.95
1. Catharine II, Empress of Russia, 1762-1796. I. Title.

OLDENBOURG, Zoe, 1916- 923.147
Catherine the Great. Translated from the French by Anne Carter. New York, Pantheon Books [c1965] xvii, 378 p. 32 plates (incl. ports.) 22 cm. Bibliography: p. [370]-371. [DK170.O373] 64-18348
1. 1. Catherine II, Empress of Russia, 1762-1796. I. Title.

OLIVA, Lawrence Jay, 1933- comp. 947'.06'0924 B
Catherine the Great. Edited by L. Jay Oliva. Englewood Cliffs, N.J., Prentice-Hall [1971] viii, 184 p. 21 cm. (Great lives observed) (A Spectrum book) Bibliography: p. 177-179. [DK170.O38] 72-153439 ISBN 0-13-121160-9 5.95
1. Catharine II, Empress of Russia, 1729-1796. BIP

Catharine II, Empress of Russia, 1729-1796—Juvenile literature.

ALMEDINGEN, Martha Edith, 1898- 947.060924
The young Catherine the Great. Illus. by Denise Brown. New York, Roy [1966, c.1965] 141p. illus. 21cm. [DK170.A598] 65-22986 3.25 bds.,
1. Catharine II, Empress of Russia, 1762-1796—Juvenile literature. I. Title.

KOCHAN, Miriam. 947'.06'0924 B
Catherine the Great / Miriam Kochan. New York : St. Martin's Press, 1977. p. cm. Includes index. Bibliography: p. A biography of the German princess who became the absolute ruler of the Russian empire and won for herself the reputation of a great enlightened monarch. [DK170.K54 1977] 92 77-293 ISBN 0-312-12442-2 : 6.95
1. Catharine II, Empress of Russia, 1729-1796—Juvenile literature. 2. Russia—History—Catharine II, 1762-1796—Juvenile literature. 3. Russian empresses—Biography—Juvenile literature. I. Title.

Catharine of Aragon, consort of Henry VIII, King of England, 1485-1536.

DU BOYS, Albert, 1804-1889. 942.05'2'0924 B
Catharine of Aragon and the sources of the English Reformation. Edited from the French, with notes by Charlotte M. Yonge. New York, B. Franklin [1968] 2 v. in 1. 19 cm. (Burt Franklin research & source works series, 319) (Selected essays in history, economics, & social science, 55.) Reprint of the 1881 ed. Bibliographical footnotes. [DA333.A6D9 1968] 68-58232
1. Catharine of Aragon, consort of Henry VIII, King of England, 1485-1536. 2. Henry VIII, King of England, 1491-1547. I. Yonge, Charlotte Mary, 1823-1901.

LUKE, Mary M. 942.05'2'0924 B
Catherine, the queen, by Mary M. Luke. New York, Coward-McCann [1967] 510 p. illus., ports. 22 cm. Sequel: A crown for Elizabeth. Bibliography: p. 493-494. [DA333.A6L8] 67-21514
1. Catharine of Aragon, consort of Henry VIII, King of England, 1485-1536. I. Title.

MATTINGLY, Garrett 923.142
Catherine of Aragon. New York, Vintage Books 1960 [c.1941] viii, 415, xiip. 19cm. (K-92) 1.45 pap.,
1. Catharine of Aragon, consort of Henry VIII, 1485-1536. I. Title.

PAUL, John E. 942.0520924
Catherine of Aragon and her friends, by John E. Paul. New York, Fordham [1966] xii. 263p. illus., facsim., ports. 23cm. Bibl. [DA333.A6P3 1966a] 66-15774 6.00
1. Catharine of Aragon, consort of Henry VIII, King of England, 1485-1536. 2. Gt. Brit.—Court and courtiers. I. Title.

ROLL, Winifred, Lady. 942.05'2'0924 B
The pomegranate and the rose: the story of Katharine of Aragon. Englewood Cliffs, N.J., Prentice-Hall [1970] vi, 288 p. illus., facsim., geneal. table, maps, ports. 22 cm. Bibliography: p. 270-273. [DA333.A6R64 1970] 70-105861 ISBN 0-13-686238-1 4.95
1. Catharine of Aragon, consort of Henry VIII, King of England, 1485-1536. I. Title.

Catharine Parr, consort of Henry VIII, King of England, 1512-1548.

MARTIENSSEN, Anthony K. 942.05'2'0924 B
Queen Katherine Parr [by] Anthony Martienssen. New York, McGraw-Hill [1974, c1973] x, 249 p. 24 cm. [DA333.P3M37 1974] 73-14768 ISBN 0-07-040610-3 8.95
1. Catharine Parr, consort of Henry VIII, King of England, 1512-1548. I. Title.

Cather, Willa Sibert, 1873-1947.

BENNETT, Mildred R. 928.1
The world of Willa Cather; illustrated with photos. and drawings. New York, Dodd, Mead [1951] xviii, 226 p. illus., ports. 21 cm. [PS3505.A87Z58] 51-9633
1. Cather, Willa Sibert, 1875-1947. I. Title.

BENNETT, Mildred R. 928.1
The world of Willa Cather. New ed. with notes and index. Lincoln, University of Nebraska Press, 1961. 285 p. illus. 21 cm. (A Bison book, BB112) [PS3505.A87Z58 1961] 61-7235
1. Cather, Willa Sibert, 1873-1947. I. Title. BIP

BROWN, Edward Killoran, 1905-1951. 928.1
Willa Cather, a critical biography [by] E. K. Brown; completed by Leon Edel. [1st ed.] New York, Knopf, 1953. xxiv, 351 p. port. 22 cm. "Bibliographical note": p. [346]-351. [PS3505.A87Z584] 52-12204
1. Cather, Willa Sibert, 1873-1947. BIP

CATHER, Willa Sibert, 1873-1947. 928.1
Willa Cather in Europe; her own story of the first journey. With an introd. and incidental notes by George N. Kates. [1st ed.] New York, Knopf, 1956. xii, 178p. 22cm. [PS3505.A87Z53] 56-10906
1. Europe—Descr. & trav.—1800-1918. I. Title.

DAICHES, David, 1912- v. 12
Willa Cather, a critical introduction. [1st Collier Books ed.] New York, Collier Books [1962, c1961] 126 p. 18 cm. 64-43165
1. Cather, Willa Sibert, 1875-1947. I. Title. BIP

RAPIN, Rene. 813'.5'2
Willa Cather. [Folcroft, Pa.] Folcroft Library Editions, 1973. 115 p. front. 24 cm. Reprint of the 1930 ed. published by McBride & Co., New York, which was issued as v. 8 of Modern American writers. Bibliography: p. 99-104. [PS3505.A87Z8 1973] 73-482 ISBN 0-8414-1598-6 (lib. bdg.)
1. Cather, Willa Sibert, 1873-1947. BIP

SERGEANT, Elizabeth Shepley, 1881- 928.1
Willa Cather, a memoir. [1st ed.] Philadelphia, Lippincott [1953] 288p. illus. 21cm. [PS3505.A87Z83] 52-13732
1. Cather, Willa Sibert, 1873-1947. I. Title.

SERGEANT, Elizabeth Shepley, 1881- 928.1
Willa Cather, a memoir. [n.p.] University of Nebraska Press [1963] 303 p. illus. 21 cm. (A Bison book) Includes bibliography. 63-3155
1. Cather, Willa Sibert, 1873-1947. I. Title. BIP

VAN GHENT, Dorothy (Bendon) 1907- 813'.5'2
Willa Cather. Minneapolis, University of Minnesota Press [1964] 46 p. 21 cm. (University of Minnesota pamphlets on American writers, no. 36) Bibliography: p. 45-46. [PS3505.A87Z93] 64-63341
1. Cather, Willa Sibert, 1873-1947. I. Series: Minnesota. University. Pamphlets on American writers, no. 36

VERMORCKEN, Elizabeth (Moorhead) 927.8
These too were here: Louise Homer and Willa Cather. [Pittsburgh] University of Pittsburgh Press [1950] 62 p. 21 cm. Homer, Louise Dilworth (Beatty) 1871-1947. [ML420.H6V4] 50-14813
1. Cather, Willa Sibert, 1875-1947. I. Title.

WOODRESS, James Leslie. 813'.5'2 B
Willa Cather : her life and art / James Woodress. Lincoln : University of Nebraska Press, 1975, c1970. 288 p. ; 20 cm. "A Bison book." Includes index. Bibliography: p. 270-271. [PS3505.A87Z95 1975] 75-301308 ISBN 0-8032-5815-1 pbk. : 3.50
1. Cather, Willa Sibert, 1873-1947. BIP

WOODRESS, James Leslie. 813'.5'2 B
Willa Cather; her life and art [by] James Woodress. New York, Pegasus [1970] 288 p. port. 22 cm. (Pegasus American authors) Bibliography: p. 270-271. [PS3505.A87Z95] 71-124673 6.95
1. Cather, Willa Sibert, 1873-1947.

Cather, Willa Sibert, 1873-1947—Addresses, essays, lectures.

KNOPF (Alfred A.) inc., New York. 813'.5'2 B
Willa Cather : a biographical sketch, an English opinion, reviews and articles concerning her later books, and an abridged bibliography. Folcroft, Pa. : Folcroft Library Editions, 1975. p. cm. Reprint of the 1927 ed. published by Knopf, New York. "An abridged bibliography of Willa Cather's books": p. 26-28. [PS3505.A87Z69 1975] 75-4036 ISBN 0-8414-2937-5 lib. bdg. : 4.50
1. Cather, Willa Sibert, 1873-1947—Addresses, essays, lectures.

KNOPF (Alfred A.) inc., New York. 813'.5'2 B
Willa Cather : a biographical sketch, an English opinion, reviews and articles concerning her later books, and an abridged bibliography. Folcroft, Pa. : Folcroft Library Editions, 1975. 28 p. ; 24 cm. Reprint of the 1927 ed. published by Knopf, New York. "An abridged bibliography of Willa Cather's books": p. 26-28. [PS3505.A87Z69 1975] 75-40365 ISBN 0-8414-2937-5 lib. bdg. : 10.00
1. Cather, Willa Sibert, 1873-1947—Addresses, essays, lectures.

Cather, Willa Sibert, 1873-1947—Biography.

LEWIS, Edith. 813'.5'2
Willa Cather living : a personal record /

by Edith Lewis. New York : Octagon Books, 1976, c1953. xviii, 197 p. ; 21 cm. Reprint of the ed. published by Knopf, New York. [PS3505.A87Z72 1976b] 76-22556 ISBN 0-374-94980-8 : 10.50
1. Cather, Willa Sibert, 1873-1947—Biography. I. Title. BIP

Cather, Willa Sibert, 1873-1947—Juvenile literature.

BONHAM, Barbara. 813'.5'2 B
Willa Cather. [1st ed.] Philadelphia, Chilton Book Co. [1970] 120 p. illus., ports. 21 cm. Bibliography: p. 115. A biography of the Pulitzer Prize winner whose works frequently drew from the author's knowledge of the Great Plains. [PS3505.A87Z5833] 92 76-111603 4.13
1. Cather, Willa Sibert, 1873-1947—Juvenile literature. I. Title.

BROWN, Marion (Marsh) 813'.5'2 B
Willa Cather, the woman and her works [by] Marion Marsh Brown and Ruth Crone. New York, Scribner [1970] 160 p. 22 cm. Bibliography: p. 157-158. A biography of the teacher, editor, and author whose works reflect the Nebraska countryside where she grew up. [PS3505.A87Z585] 92 76-123838 4.50
1. Cather, Willa Sibert, 1873-1947—Juvenile literature. I. Crone, Ruth, joint author. II. Title.

Catherine de Medici, consort of Henry II, King of France, 1519-1589—Juvenile literature.

VANCE, Marguerite 920
Dark eminence; Catherine de Medici and her children. Illus. by J. Luis Pellicer. New York, Dutton [c.1961] 159p. 61-12459 3.25
1. Catherine de Medici, consort of Henry II, King of France, 1519- 1589—Juvenile literature. I. Title.

Catherine de Medicis, consort of Henry II, King of France, 1519-1589.

HERITIER, Jean, 1892- 923.144
Catherine de Medici. Translated by Charlotte Haldane. New York, St. Martin's press [1963] 480 p. illus. 23 cm. Full name: Jean Marie Heritier. [DC119.8.H443] 62-19708
1. Catherine de Medicis, consort of Henry II, King of France, 1519-1589. I. Title.

HERITIER, Jean Marie, 1892- 923.144
Catherine de Medici. Tr. [from French] by Charlotte Haldane. New York, St. Martin's [c.1963] 480p. illus. 23cm. Bibl. 62-19708 7.50 bds.,
1. Catherine de Medicis, consort of Henry II King of France, 1519-1589. I. Title.

MAHONEY, Irene. 944'.028'0924 B
Madame Catherine / Irene Mahoney. New York : Coward, McCann & Geoghegan, [1975] 381 p., [8] leaves of plates : ill. ; 24 cm. Includes index. Bibliography: p. [355]-365. [DC119.8.M27] 74-79688 ISBN 0-698-10617-2 : 12.95
1. Catherine de Medicis, Consort of Henry II, King of France, 1519-1589. I. Title.

Catherine II, Empress of Russia, 1729-1796.

GREY, Ian, 1918- 923.147
Catherine the Great; autocrat and Empress of all Russia. Philadelphia, Lippincott, 1962 [c.1961] 254p. illus. Bibl. 62-7180 6.00
1. Catherine II, Empress of Russia, 1729-1796. I. Title. BIP

HASLIP, Joan, 1911- 947'.06'0924 B
Catherine the Great / by Joan Haslip. 1st American ed. New York : Putnam, 1977c1976 p. cm. Includes index. [DK170.H37 1976] 76-20630 10.95
1. Catherine II, Empress of Russia, 1729-1796. I. Title.

NOBLE, Iris. 947.060924 (B)
Empress of all Russia: Catherine the Great. New York, J. Messner [1966] 191 p. 22 cm. [DK170.N6] 66-14003
1. Catherine II, Empress of Russia, 1729-1796. I. Title.

Catherine of Aragon, queen consort of Henry VIII, 1485-1536.

MATTINGLY, Garrett 923.142
Catherine of Aragon [Gloucester, Mass., P. Smith, 1965, c.1941] 415, xiip. incl. geneal tables. (Vintage bk. rebound) Bibl. [DA333.A6M3] 3.50
1. Catherine of Aragon, queen consort of Henry VIII, 1485-1536. I. Title.

Catherine, Thomas of Divine Providence,

CATHERINE, Thomas of Divine Providence, Mother. 922.273
My beloved; the story of a Carmelite nun. New York, McGraw-Hill [1955] 252 p. illus. 21 cm. [BX4705.C346A3] 55-6175
I. Title.

Catherwood, Frederick.

VON HAGEN, Victor Wolfgang, 1908- 720.9'24
F. Catherwood, architect-explorer of two worlds. Introd. by Aldous Huxley. Barre, Mass., Barre, 1968 [c1967] xv, 60p. illus. 24cm. Bibl. [NA997.C33V57] 67-25571 6.95
I. Catherwood, Frederick. II. Title.

VON HAGEN, Victor Wolfgang, 1908- 927.2
Frederick Catherwood, arch. Introd. by Aldous Huxley. New York, Oxford University Press, 1950. xix, 177 p. illus., maps. 24 cm. Bibliography: p. 165-169. [NA997.C33V6] 49-50430
1. Catherwood, Frederick.

Catholic authors—Biography.

THE Book of 810'.9'9222 B
Catholic authors (Fourth series) Informal self-portraits of famous modern Catholic writers, edited with pref. and notes by Walter Romig. Freeport, N.Y., Books for Libraries Press [1971, c1948] 330 p. illus. 23 cm. (Biography index reprint series) Includes bibliographical references. [PS153.C3B62 1971] 70-179740 ISBN 0-8369-8108-1
1. Catholic authors—Biography. 2. Authors, American—Biography. 3. Catholic authors—Portraits. I. Romig, Walter, 1905- ed.

Catholic Church—Biog.

ALLAN, Alfred K. 282.0922
Catholics courageous. Foreword by Richard Cardinal Cushing. Garden City, N.Y., Doubleday [1966, c.1965] 196p. 18cm. (Echo bk., E31) .75 pap.,
1. Catholic Church—Biog. I. Title.

ALLAN, Alfred K. 282.0922
Catholics courageous. Foreword by Richard Cardinal Cushing. New York, Citadel [c.1965] xi, 240p. illus., ports. 21cm. [BX4651.2.A4] 65-27091 4.95
1. Catholic Church—Biog. I. Title.

BAIRD, Mary Julian. 922.2
The court of the Queen. St. Meinrad, Ind., Grail Publications [1956] 73p. 22cm. [BX4652.B27] 55-11578
1. Catholic Church—Biog. 2. Mary, Virgin—Apparitions and miracles (Modern) I. Title.

BOLAND, Peg, ed. 922.2
Valiant woman. Foreword by Loretta Young. St. Meinrad, Ind., Grail Publications [1956] 195p. 19cm. [BX4667.B6] 57-174
1. Catholic Church—Biog. 2. Woman—Biog. I. Title.

BURTON, Doris. 922.2
Daring to live; great Christians of our day. Chicago, H. Regnery Co., 1955 c176p. 19cm. [BX4669] 55-13659
1. Catholic Church—Biog. I. Title.

BURTON, Doris. 922.2
Valiant achievements; great Christians of our day. Chicago, H. Regnery Co., 1956 [i.e. 1957] 184p. 19cm. [BX4652] 57-13601
1. Catholic Church—Biog. I. Title.

BURTON, Doris. 922.2
Pioneers for Christ; ten great founders. Fresno, Calif, Academy Library Guild [c1958] 171p. 19cm. [BX4669.B8] 59-12592
1. Catholic Church—Biog. I. Title.

CUNNINGHAM, Thomas W 922.22
Saints off pedestals. Newark, N. J., Washington Irving Pub. Co. [c1953] 208p. illus. 22cm. [BX4652.C8] 55-15753
1. Catholic Church—Biog. I. Title.

ENGLEBERT, Omer, 1893- 922.22
Adventurer saints: Joan of Arc, Martin of Tours, Peter Chanel, Junipero [and] Giles of Assisi. Translated by Donal O'Kelly. New York, Kenedy [1956] 276 p. 22 cm. [BX4652.E3] 56-8936
1. Catholic Church—Biog. 2. Saints. I. Title.

KANE, George Louis, 1911- ed. 922.2
Lay workers for Christ. With an introd. by Valerian Cardinal Gracias. Westminster, Md., Newman Press, 1957. 171p. 22cm. [BX4669.K3] 57-11817
1. Catholic Church —Biog. I. Title.

KANE, George Louis, 1911- ed. 922.2
Lay workers for Christ. With an introd. by Valerian Cardinal Gracias. Westminster, Md., Newman Press, 1957. 171p. 22cm. [BX4669.K3] 57-11817
1. Catholic Church—Biog. I. Title.

KITTLER, Glenn D. 282.0922 B
The wings of eagles [by] Glenn D. Kittler. [1st ed.] Garden City, N.Y., Doubleday [1966] 215 p. 22 cm. [BX4651.2.K5] 66-12246
1. Catholic Church—Biography. I. Title.

NEILL, Thomas Patrick, 1915- 922.2
They lived the faith; great lay leaders of modern times. Milwaukee, Bruce [1951] x, 388 p. ports. 23 cm. (Science and culture series) Contents.Daniel O'Connell. -- Count Charles Montalembert -- Ludwig Windthorst. -- Garcia Moreno. -- Pauline Marie Jaricot. -- Frederic Ozanam. -- Albert de Mun. -- Joseph de Maistre. -- Joseph Gorres. -- Donoso Cortes. -- Orestes Brownson. -- Louis Veuillot. -- Wilfrid Ward. Bibliography (p. 363-379) [BX4651.N4] 51-2741
1. Catholic Church — Biog. I. Title.

RAYMOND, Father, 1903- 922.273
Your hour. Milwaukee, Bruce Pub. Co. [1962] 204p. 24cm. [BX4652.R3] 62-202
1. Catholic Church— Biog. I. Title.

RAYMOND, Father 1903- 922.273
Your hour. Milwaukee, Bruce [c.1962] 204p. 24cm. 62-20237 4.50
1. Catholic Church—Biog. I. Title.

SULLIVAN, John J ed. and tr. 922.2
Divine masterpieces; sketches of some heroic lovers of God. Paterson, N.J., St. Anthony Guild Press [1960] 211 p. 19 cm. [BX4652.S8] 60-16429
1. Catholic Church—Biog. 2. Saints. I. Title.

SULLIVAN, John L., ed. and tr. 922.2
Divine masterpieces; sketches fo some heroic lovers of God. Paterson, N. J., St. Anthony Guild Press [c.1960] 211p. 60-16429 2.50
1. Catholic Church—Biog. 2. Saints. I. Title.

WILLIAMSON, Claude Charles H 1892- ed. 922.2
Great Catholics. New York, Collier Books [1963] 447 p. 18 cm. (Catholic readers series) "BS178." Includes bibliography. [BX4651.W5] 63-10206
1. Catholic Church — Biog. 2. Saints. I. Title.

Catholic Church—Biog.—Dictionaries.

DELANEY, John J. 922.2
Dictionary of Catholic biography [by] John J. Delaney, James Edward Tobin. Garden City, N. Y., Doubleday [c.1961] xi, 1245p. 27cm. 62-7620 18.50;
1. Catholic Church—Biog.—Dictionaries. I. Tobin, James Edward, 1905- joint author II. Title.

Catholic Church—Clergy—Correspondence, reminiscences, etc.

BASSET, Bernard 282.0924
Priest in paradise; with God to Illinois. [New York] Herder & Herder [1966] 107p. illus. 21cm. [BX4705.B2518A3] 66-22599 3.50 3.50
1. Catholic Church—Clergy—Correspondence, reminiscences, etc. I. Title.

CUNNINGHAM, James F. 253.0924
American pastor in Rome [by] James F. Cunningham.[1st ed.] Garden City, N.Y., Doubleday, 1966. 285p. illus., ports. 22cm. Autobiographical. [BX4705.C792A3] 66-20921 4.95
1. Catholic Church—Clergy—Correspondence, reminiscences, etc. I. Title.

GIESE, Vincent J. 282.0924
Journal of a late vocation [by] Vincent J. Giese. Notre Dame, Ind. Fides [1966] 159p. 18cm. (Fides dome bk., D-53) Autobiographical. [BX4705.G513 A3] 66-28038 .95 pap.,
1. Catholic Church—Clergy—Correspondence, reminiscences, etc. I. Title.

GREMILLION, Joseph B 922.273
The journal of a southern pastor. Chicago, Fides Publishers Association [1957] 305p. illus. 23cm. [BX4705.G6217A3] 56-11630
1. Catholic Church—Clergy—Correspondence,reminiscences, etc. I. Title.

LA FARGE, John, 1880- 922.273
The manner is ordinary. [1st ed.] New York, Harcourt, Brace [1954] 408 p. illus. 22 cm. Autobiography. [BX4705.L237A3] 54-5250
1. Catholic Church—Clergy—Correspondence, reminiscences, etc. I. Title.

LA FARGE, John, 1880- 922.273
The manner is ordinary. Garden City, N. Y., Image Books [1957] 352p. 19cm. (A Doubleday image book, D52) Autobiography. [BX4705.L237A3 1957] 57-3403
1. Catholic Church—Clergy—Correspondence, reminiscences, etc. I. Title.

LORD, Daniel Aloysius, 1888-1955. 922.273
Played by ear. With an introd. by R. Bakewell Morrison. Chicago, Loyol University Press, 1956. 383p. illus. 24cm. Autobiography. [BX4705.L742A4] 56-7099
1. Catholic Church—Clergy—Correspondence, reminiscences, etc. I. Title.

LORD, Daniel Aloysius, 1888-1955. 922.273
Played by ear; the autobiography of Daniel A. Lord, S.J. Introd. by R. Bakewell Morrison. Chicago, Loyola University Press; Hanover House, distributor, Garden City, N.Y., [1956] 398p. 22cm. [BX4705.L742A4 1956a] 56-7800
1. Catholic Church—Clergy—Correspondence, reminiscences, etc. I. Title.

MCWILLIAMS, Le Roy E. 922.273
Parish priest [by] Father Le Roy E. McWilliams with Jim Bishop. New York, McGraw-Hill [1953] 250 p. illus., 23 cm. [BX4705.M2565A3] 53-5189
1. Catholic Church—Clergy—Correspondence, reminiscences, etc. I. Title.

NEWMAN, John Henry, Cardinal, 1801-1890. 922.242
Autobiographical writings; edited with introductions by Henry Tristram. Enw York, Sheed and Ward [1957] 338p. 22cm. [BX4705.N5A15] 57-6045
1. Catholic Church—Clergy—Correspondence, reminiscences, etc. I. Title.

NEWMAN, John Henry, Cardinal, 1801-1890. 922.242
Letters; a selection, edited and introduced, by Derek Stanford and Muriel Spark. Westminster, Md., Newman Press, 1957. i51p. port. 22cm. Bibliographical footnotes. [BX4705.N5A43] 57-11825
1. Catholic Church—Clergy—Correspondence, reminiscences, etc. I. Title.

NEWMAN, John Henry, Cardinal 1801-1890 922.242
Letters and diaries; v.12, Ed. at the Birmingham Oratory with notes, introd. by Charles Stephen Dessain. New York, Nelson [1962] 441p. 25cm. Contents.v.12, Rome to Birmingham: Jan. 1847 to Dec. 1848. 61-65738 15.00
1. Catholic Church—Clergy—Correspondence, reminiscences, etc. I. Dessain, Charles Stephen, ed. II. Title.

NEWMAN, John Henry, 1801-1890 922.342
Letters and diaries. Ed. at the Birmingham Oratory, with notes, introd. by Charles Stephen Dessain London. New York. Nelson [1967] v. 25cm. Contents.v. 17. Opposition in Dublin and London. October 1855- to March 1857 [BX4705.N5A4] 61-65738 6.00
1. Catholic Church—Clergy Correspondence. reminiscences, etc. I. Dessain, Charles Stephen. Cardinal, ed. II. Title.

Catholic Church—Doctrinal and controversial works—Catholic authors.

NEWMAN, John Henry, Cardinal, 1801-1890. 922.242
Apologia pro vita sua. Edited with an introd. and note by A. Dwight Culler. Boston, Houghton Mifflin [1956] 384p. 21cm. (Riverside editions, B10) [BX4705.N5A3 1956] 56-2548
1. Catholic Church—Doctrinal and controversial works—Catholl authors. I. Title.

NEWMAN, John Henry, 230.2'0924
Apologia pro vita sua: being a history of his religious opinions; ed. introd. notes, by Martin J. Svaglic. Oxford, Clarendon. Pr., 1967. ardinal, 1801-1890 1x, 604p. 23cm. Bibl. [BX4705.N5A3 1967] 68-75872 bds., price unreported
1. Catholic Church—Doctrinal and controversial works—Catholic authors. I. Svaglic, Martin J. ed. II. Title.
Available from Oxford Univ. Pr., New York. **BIP**

NEWMAN, John Henry, Cardinal, 1801-1890. 922.242
Apologia pro vita sua. With an introd. by Philip Hughes. Garden City, N. Y., Image Books [1956] 440p. 19cm. (A Doubleday image book, D37) 'Newman's list of his writings': p. 434-435. [BX4765.N5A3 1956a] 56-8735
1. Catholic Church—Doctrinal and controversial works—Catholic authors. I. Title.

NEWMAN, John Henry, Cardinal, 1801-1890. 230.2'0924
Apologia pro vita sua: being a history of his religious opinions; edited, with an introduction and notes, by Martin J. Svaglic. Oxford, Clarendon P., 1967. ix, 604 p. 22 1/2 cm. (B67-17788) Bibliographical references. [BX4705.N5A3] 68-75872
1. Catholic Church—Doctrinal and controversial works—Catholic authors. I. Svaglic, Martin J., ed. II. Title.

NEWMAN, John Henry, Cardinal, 1801-1890. 922.242
Apologia pro vta sua, Edited with an introd. and notes by A. Dwight Culler. Boston, Houghton Mifflin [1956] 384p. 21cm. (Riverside editions, B10) [BX4705.N5A3 1956] 56-2548
1. Catholic Church—Doctrinal and controversial works—Catholic authors. I. Title.

NEWMAN, John Henry, Cardinal, 1801-1890. 922.242
Apologia pro vita sua [by] John Henry Cardinal Newman, being a history of his religious opinions. With an introd. by Basil Willey. London, Oxford University Press, 1964. xxxiv, 405 p. 16 cm. (The World's classics, 601) [BX4705.N5A3] 64-4741
1. Catholic Church — Doctrinal and controversial works — Catholic authors. I. Title. **BIP**

Catholic Church—Doctrinal and controversial works—Miscellaneous authors.

MCLOUGHLIN, Emmett, 1907- 923.673
People's padre [an autobiography. New York] Macfadden [1965, c.1964] 191p. 18cm. (60-211) [BX1765.M244] .60 pap.,
1. Catholic Church—Doctrinal and controversial works—Miscellaneous authors. I. Title.

Catholic Church—Apologetic works.

HECKER, Isaac Thomas, 1819-1888. 230'.2
Questions of the soul / Isaac Thomas Hecker ; with an introd. by Joseph F. Gower. New York : Arno Press, 1978. 294 p. ; 21 cm. (The American Catholic tradition) Reprint of the 1855 ed. published by D. Appleton, New York. [BX1752.H35 1978] 77-11290 ISBN 0-405-10834-6 : 18.00
1. Catholic Church—Apologetic works. 2. Hecker, Isaac Thomas, 1819-1888. 3. Paulist Fathers—United States—Biography. I. Title. II. Series.

Catholic Church—Biography.

BLUNT, Hugh Francis, 1877- 282'.0922
The great Magdalens. Freeport, N.Y., Books for Libraries Press [1969] ix, 335 p. 23 cm. (Essay index reprint series) Reprint of the 1928 ed. Contents.Contents.—Penitents of the stage.—Voices from the desert.—Magdalens of the ages of penance.—The woman Augustine loved.—Rosamond Clifford.—Saint Margaret of Cortona.—Blessed Angela of Foligno.—Blessed Clare of Rimini.—Saint Hyacintha of Mariscotti.—Cataline de Cardona, "the sinner."—Beatrice Cenci.—The Princess Palatine.—Madame de Longueville.—Louise de la Valliere.—Madame de Montespan.—Madame de la Sabliere.—Madame Pompadour.—Madame Tiquet. [BX4667.B5 1969] 71-86731
1. Catholic Church—Biography. 2. Woman—Biography. I. Title.

BONEY, William Jerry. 230.2'0922
The new day; Catholic theologians of the renewal. Edited by Wm. Jerry Boney and Lawrence E. Molumby. Richmond, John Knox Press [1968] 142 p. 21 cm. Includes bibliographical references. [BT28.B62] 68-13664
1. Catholic Church—Biography. 2. Theologians. 3. Theology, Doctrinal—History—20th century. I. Molumby, Lawrence E., joint author. II. Title.

DELANY, Selden Peabody, 1874-1935. 282'.0922
Married saints. Freeport, N.Y., Books for Libraries Press [1969] x, 338 p. 23 cm. (Essay index reprint series) Reprint of the 1935 ed. Bibliographical footnotes. [BX4661D38 1969] 69-17573
1. Catholic Church—Biography. 2. Christian saints. I. Title. **BIP**

GREGORY, Isabella Augusta (Persse) Lady, 1852-1932. 398.2'2
A book of saints and wonders put down here by Lady Gregory according to the old writings and the memory of the people of Ireland. With illus. by Margaret Gregory and a foreword by Edward Malins. [3d ed.] New York, Oxford University Press, 1971. 116 p. illus. 24 cm. (The Coole edition of Lady Gregory's works, v. 12) Bibliography: p. [115] [BX4659.I7G7 1971b] 72-190667 8.50
1. Catholic Church—Biography. 2. Christian saints—Ireland. I. Title. **BIP**

HOGAN, John Gerard, 1896- 282'.0922
Heralds of the king, by John G. Hogan. Freeport, N.Y., Books for Libraries Press [1970] ii, 190 p. 23 cm. (Essay index reprint series) "First published 1934." Contents.Contents.—St. Francis of Assisi.—St. Dominic.—St. Ignatius Loyola.—St. Teresa of Avila.—St. Jane Frances de Chantal.—Mother Elizabeth Ann Seton. [BX4655.H55 1970] 79-107714 ISBN 0-8369-1516-X
1. Catholic Church—Biography. 2. Christian saints. I. Title. **BIP**

MAYNARD, Theodore, 1890-1956. 270 B
Pillars of the church. Freeport, N.Y., Books for Libraries Press [1970, c1945] xi, 308 p. 23 cm. (Essay index reprint series) Bibliography: p. 301-308. [BX4651.M38 1970] 76-136763
1. Catholic Church—Biography. I. Title. **BIP**

STEUART, Robert Henry Joseph, 1874-1948. 282'.0922
Diversity in holiness. Freeport, N.Y., Books for Libraries Press [1967] vii, 221 p. 22 cm. (Essay index reprint series) Reprint of the 1937 ed. Contents.Contents.—Mother Julian of Norwich.—St. Francis de Sales.—Brother Lawrence.—St. Benedict Joseph Labre.—The holy man of Tours.—St. Catherine of Genoa.—Marie-Eustelle Harpain.—St. Teresa of Lisieux.—The Abbe Huvelin.—St. Bernadette Soubirous.—St. John-Baptist Vianney, cure d'Ars.—St. Ignatius Loyola. [BX4651.S7 1967] 67-28770
1. Catholic Church—Biography. I. Title. **BIP**

STEVENS, Clifford J. 282'.092'2 B
Portraits of faith / Clifford Stevens. Huntington, Ind. : Our Sunday Visitor, c1975. 176 p. ; 18 cm. [BX4651.2.S8] 74-21891 ISBN 0-87973-764-6 pbk. : 2.25
1. Catholic Church—Biography. I. Title. **BIP**

UNDSET, Sigrid, 1882-1949. 282'.0922 B
Stages on the road. Translated from the Norwegian for the first time by Arthur G. Chater. Freeport, N.Y., Books for Libraries Press [1969, c1934] ix, 266 p. 23 cm. (Essay index reprint series) Translation of Etapper. Ny rakke. [BX4651.U52 1969] 74-80405
1. Catholic Church—Biography. 2. Catholic Church—Doctrinal and controversial works—Catholic authors. I. Title. **BIP**

VIDLER, Alexander Roper, 1899- 282'.0922
A variety of Catholic modernists, by Alex R. Vidler. [London] Cambridge University Press, 1970. viii, 232 p. illus., ports. 22 cm. (The Sarum lectures, 1968-69) Bibliography: p. 221-226. [BX1396.V52 1970] 70-93712 50/- ($8.50)
1. Catholic Church—Biography. 2. Modernism—Catholic Church. I. Title. II. Series. **BIP**

Catholic Church—Bishops—Biography.

BLANCHET, Augustine Magloire Alexander, 1797-1887. 282'.092'4 B
Journal of a Catholic bishop on the Oregon trail : the overland crossing of the Rt. Rev. A. M. A. Blanchet, Bishop of Walla Walla, from Montreal to Oregon Territory, March 23, 1847 to January 23, 1851. Blackrobe buries Whitmans / J. B. A. Brouillet ; [edited by] Edward J. Kowrach. Fairfield, Wash. : Ye Galleon Press, 1978. 190 p. : ill. ; 29 cm. Translated by E. J. Kowrach from the French mss. Includes index. Bibliography: p. 172-182. [BX4705.B529A33] 78-27768 ISBN 0-87770-166-0 : 14.95
1. Blanchet Augustine Magloire Alexander, 1797-1887. 2. Catholic Church—Bishops—Biography. 3. Whitman, Marcus, 1802-1847. 4. Bishops—United States—Biography. 5. Oregon Trail. 6. Whitman Massacre, 1847. I. Kowrach, Edward J. II. Brouillet, Jean Baptiste Abraham, 1813-1884. Blackrobe buries Whitmans. 1978. III. Title.

CURRAN, Robert Emmett. 282'.092'4 B
Michael Augustine Corrigan and the shaping of conservative Catholicism in America, 1878-1902 / Robert Emmett Curran. New York : Arno Press, 1978. xiii, 547 p. : ports. ; 24 cm. (The American Catholic tradition) Rev. and enl. from the author's thesis. Includes index. Bibliography: p. 516-529. [BX4705.C778C87 1978] 77-11277 ISBN 0-405-10814-1 : 34.00
1. Corrigan, Michael Augustine, Abp., 1839-1902. 2. Catholic Church—Bishops—Biography. 3. Catholic Church in the United States—History. 4. McGlynn, Edward, 1837-1900. 5. Bishops—New York (City)—Biography. 6. New York (City)—Biography. I. Title. II. Series.

GARCIA Diego y Moreno, Francisco, Bp., 1785-1846. 282'.092'4 B
The writings of Francisco Garcia Diego y Moreno, Obispo de Ambas Californias / translated and edited by Francis J. Weber. Los Angeles : Weber, 1976. xiii, 192 p. : group port. ; 27 cm. Includes bibliographical references. [BX4705.G244.G37] 76-21434
1. Garcia Diego y Moreno, Francisco, Bp., 1785-1846. 2. Catholic Church—Bishops—Biography. 3. Catholic Church in California—History—Sources. 4. Bishops—California—Biography.

Catholic Church—Clergy.

CODE, Joseph Bernard, 1899- 262'.12
American bishops, 1964-1970. St. Louis, Wexford Press [1970?] 25 p. 28 cm. [BX4666.C6] 79-289632 3.00
1. Catholic Church—Clergy. 2. Bishops—U.S. I. Title.

LIEDERBACH, Clarence A., 1910- 282'.092'2 B
America's thousand bishops: from 1513 to 1974 ... from Abramowicz to Zuroweste [by] Clarence A. Liederbach. Cleveland, Dillon/Liederbach, 1974. 67 p. 22 cm. (Saint Mary's College historical series) [BX4670.L5] 73-94081 ISBN 0-913228-09-5 2.95 (pbk.)
1. Catholic Church—Clergy. 2. Bishops—United States. I. Title. **BIP**

MERWICK, Donna. 282'.744'61
Boston priests, 1848-1910; a study of social and intellectual change. Cambridge, Mass., Harvard University Press, 1973. xiii, 276 p. 22 cm. Bibliography: p. 249-259. [BX1418.B7M43] 72-79309 ISBN 0-674-07975-2 12.00
1. Catholic Church—Clergy. 2. Catholic Church in Boston. 3. Clergy—Massachusetts—Boston. I. Title.

Catholic Church—Clergy—Biography.

BISSONNETTE, Georges. 282'.092'4
Moscow was my parish / Georges Bissonnette. Westport, Conn. : Greenwood Press, 1978, c1956. p. cm. Reprint of the ed. published by McGraw-Hill, New York. [BX4705.B5235A34 1978] 78-16489 ISBN 0-313-20594-9 lib.bdg. : 19.50
1. Bissonnette, Georges. 2. Catholic Church—Clergy—Biography. 3. Catholic Church in Russia. 4. Clergy—United States—Biography. I. Title. **BIP**

BURTSELL, Richard Lalor, 1840-1912. 282'.092'4 B
The diary of Richard L. Burtsell, priest of New York : the early years, 1865-1868 / edited by Nelson J. Callahan. New York : Arno Press, 1978. xxvii, 422 p. ; 24 cm. (The American Catholic tradition) [BX4705.B946A33 1978] 77-89146 ISBN 0-405-10813-3 : 28.00
1. Burtsell, Richard Lalor, 1840-1912. 2. Catholic Church—Clergy—Biography. 3. Catholic Church in New York (State)—History—Sources. 4. Clergy—New York (State)—Biography. 5. New York (State)—Biography. I. Callahan, Nelson J. II. Title. III. Series: American Catholic tradition.

DE ARAGON, Ray John. 282'.092'3 B
Padre Martinez and Bishop Lamy / by Ray John de Aragon. Las Vegas, N.M. : Pan-American Pub. Co., c1978. vi, 141 p. : ill. ; 22 cm. Includes bibliographies. [BX4705.M412553D4] 78-70565 ISBN 0-932906-00-1 pbk. : 6.95
1. Martinez, Antonio Jose, 1793-1867. 2. Catholic Church—Clergy—Biography. 3. Lamy, John Baptist, Abp., 1814-1888. 4. Clergy—New Mexico—Biography. I. Title. **BIP**

KOTRE, John N. 282'.092'4 B
The best of times, the worst of times :

Andrew Greeley and America Catholicism, 1950-1975 / John N. Kotre. Chicago : Nelson-Hall Co., [1978] p. cm. "Books by Andrew M. Greeley": p. Includes index. Bibliography: p. [BX4705.G6185K67] 78-14224 ISBN 0-88229-380-X. ISBN 0-88229-597-7 pbk. : 11.95
1. Greeley, Andrew M., 1928- 2. Catholic Church—Clergy—Biography. 3. Catholic Church in the United States—History. 4. Clergy—United States—Biography. I. Title.

RATIU, Alexander. 272'.9
Stolen church, martyrdom in Communist Romania / Alexander Ratiu & William Virtue. Huntington, Ind. : Our Sunday Visitor, c1979. 192 p. ; 21 cm. [BX4711.495.R37A37] 79-87926 ISBN 0-87973-730-1 pbk. : 4.95
1. Ratiu, Alexander. 2. Catholic Church—Clergy—Biography. 3. Catholic Church in Romania—Clergy. 4. Clergy—Romania—Biography. 5. Prisoners—Romania—Biography. 6. Persecution—Romania. I. Virtue, William, joint author. II. Title.

TACKETT, Timothy, 282'.44'97
1945-
Priest & parish in eighteenth-century France : a social and political study of the cures in a diocese of Dauphine, 1750-1791 / by Timothy Tackett. Princeton, N.J. : Princeton University Press, c1977. xiii, 350 p. : ill. ; 23 cm. Includes index. Bibliography: p. 307-331. [BX1532.G3T3] 76-29801 ISBN 0-691-05243-3 : 19.50
1. Catholic Church—Clergy—Biography. 2. Clergy—France—Gap (Diocese)—Biography. 3. Parishes—France—Gap (Diocese) I. Title.

WALSH, James Joseph, 282'.0922
1865-1942, comp.
These splendid priests. Freeport, N.Y., Books for Libraries Press [1968] 248 p. 22 cm. (Essay index reprint series) Reprint of the 1926 ed. Contents.Contents.—St. Benedict, founder of the Rule of St. Benedict, by C. F. de Tryon, Comte de Montalembert.—Friar William de Rubruquis, explorer and traveler in the Orient; his journal, translated by J. Mandeville.—Friar Odoric, missionary traveler in the East; his journal, translated by J. Mandeville.—St. Ignatius Loyola, founder of the Society of Jesus; from the Life by Father Bouhours, translated by J. Dryden. Life work of Ignatius Loyola.—St. Francis Xavier, apostle to the Indies; from the Life by Father Bouhours, translated by J. Dryden. Missionary labors of St. Francis Xavier, by J. Schurhammer.—Father James Marquette, explorer of the Mississippi and missionary to the Indians of North America, by J. G. Shea.—St. Vincent de Paul, founder of charitable orders, by F. Goldie.—Father Isaac Jogues, missionary to the Iroquois, by C.OThese splendid priests. Freeport, N.Y., Books for Libraries Press [1968] 248 p. 22 cm. (Essay index reprint series) Reprint of the 1926 ed. Contents.Contents.—St. Benedict, founder of the Rule of St. Benedict, by C. F. de Tryon, Comte de Montalembert.—Friar William de Rubruquis, explorer and traveler in the Orient; his journal, translated by J. Mandeville.—Friar Odoric, m
1. Catholic Church—Clergy—Biography. 2. Priests. I. Title. BIP

Catholic Church—Clergy—Correspondence, reminiscences, etc.

NEWMAN, John Henry, 922.242
Cardinal, 1801-1890
Letters and diaries; v. 13. Ed. at the Birmingham Oratory with notes, introd. by Charles Stephen Dessain. New York, Nelson [c.1963] 520p. 25cm. Contents.v.13. Birmingham and London, Jan., 1849-June, 1850. Bibl. 61-65738 15.00
1. Catholic Church—Clergy—Correspondence, reminiscences, etc. I. Dessain, Charles Stephen, ed. II. Title.

RUSSELL, Stephen. 253'.0924
A man in the middle; the journal of a young priest in conflict with himself. Dayton, Ohio, Pflaum Press, 1969. viii, 130 p. 22 cm. [BX1912.R83] 69-20167 3.95
1. Catholic Church—Clergy—Correspondence, reminiscences, etc. I. Title.

Catholic Church—Collected works.

BONAVENTURA, Saint, 230'.2
Cardinal, 1221-1274.
Bonaventure / translation and introd. by Ewert Cousins ; pref. by Ignatius Brady. New York : Paulist Press, c1978. xx, 353 p. ; 23 cm. (The Classics of Western spirituality) Translated from the Latin. Includes indexes. Contents.Contents.—The soul's journey into God.—The tree of life.—The life of St. Francis. Bibliography: p. 329-333. [BX890.B6731313 1978] 78-60723 ISBN 0-8091-0240-4 : 9.95 ISBN 0-8091-2121-2 pbk. : 6.95
1. Catholic Church—Collected works. 2. Theology—Collected works—Middle Ages, 600-1500. I. Cousins, Ewert H. II. Title. III. Series.

Catholic Church—Doctrinal and controversial works.

GIRANDOLA, Anthony, 282'.0924
1924-
The most defiant priest; the story of the priest who married. New York, Crown Publishers [1968] 277 p. 24 cm. [BX1765.2.G57 1968] 68-31204 5.95
1. Catholic Church—Doctrinal and controversial works. I. Title.

Catholic Church—Doctrinal and controversial works—Catholic authors.

FOX, Robert Joseph, 1927- 270 B
Saints & heroes speak / by Robert J. Fox. Huntington, Ind. : Our Sunday Visitor, c1977. 512 p. : ports. ; 21 cm. [BX1751.2.F68] 77-70206 ISBN 0-87973-640-2 pbk. : 7.50
1. Catholic Church—Doctrinal and controversial works—Catholic authors. 2. Christian saints—Biography. 3. Catholics—Biography. I. Title. BIP

Catholic Church—Doctrinal and controversial works, Popular.

WHY Catholic? / 282'.092'1 B
John J. Delaney, editor. 1st ed. Garden City, N.Y. : Doubleday, 1979. 186 p. ; 22 cm. [BX4670.W47] 78-14653 ISBN 0-385-14184-X : 7.95
1. Catholic Church—Doctrinal and controversial works, Popular. 2. Catholics—United States—Biography. I. Delaney, John J. BIP

Catholic Church—History—1965-

MARTIN, Malachi. 282
Three Popes and the Cardinal. New York, Farrar, Straus and Giroux [1972] xiv, 300 p. 23 cm. [BX1389.M37 1972] 74-181756 ISBN 0-374-27675-7 7.95
1. Catholic Church—History—1965- 2. Papacy—History—20th century. 3. Civilization, Modern—1950- I. Title. BIP

Catholic Church in America—Biog.

ATTWATER, Donald, 1892- 922.273
Saints westward; some colorful and heroic men and women who planted and watered the seed of the faith in the Western Hemisphere. With drawings by Sister Mary of the Compassion. New York, P. J. Kenedy [1953] 130p. illus. 21cm. [BX4669.8.A8] 53-9153
1. Catholic Church in America—Biog. I. Title.

Catholic Church in Avila, Spain (Province)—Biography.

KEYES, Frances Parkinson 922.246
(Wheeler) 1885-
The land of stones and saints. [1st ed.] Graden City, N. Y., Doubleday, 1957. 357p. illus. 22cm. Includes bibliography. [BX4688.K4] 57-11427
1. Catholic Church in Avila, Spain (Province)—Biog. 2. Avila, Spain (Province)—Biog. I. Title.

KEYES, Frances Parkinson 922.246
Wheeler, 1885-1970.
The land of stones and saints. [1st ed.] Garden City, N.Y., Doubleday, 1957. 357 p. illus. 22 cm. Includes bibliography. [BX4688.K4] 57-11427
1. Catholic Church in Avila, Spain (Province)—Biography. 2. Avila, Spain (Province)—Biography. I. Title.

Catholic Church in Canada.

LIEDERBACH, Clarence 262'.12'0971
A., 1910-
Canada's bishops from 1120 to 1975 ... from Allen to Yelle / Clarence A. Liederbach ; pref. by Philip Pocock. Cleveland : Dillon/Liederbach, [1975] 64 p. : ill. ; 21 cm. (Saint Mary's College historical series) [BX4671.L53] 73-94082 ISBN 0-913228-10-9 pbk. : 3.50
1. Catholic Church in Canada. 2. Bishops—Canada. I. Title.

Catholic Church in Indiana—History.

MCAVOY, Thomas Timothy, 282.772
1903-1969.
The Catholic Church in Indiana, 1789-1834. New York, AMS Press, 1967 [c1940] 226 p. 23 cm. (Studies in history, economics, and public law, no. 471) Originally presented as the author's thesis, Columbia University. Bibliography: p. 209-219. [BX1415.I6M2 1967] 75-29193
1. Catholic Church in Indiana—History. 2. Catholics in Indiana. 3. French in Indiana. I. Title. II. Series: Columbia studies in the social sciences, no. 471.

Catholic Church in Kentucky.

SPALDING, Martin John, 282.769
Abp., 1810-1872.
Sketches of the early Catholic missions of Kentucky; from their commencement in 1787 to the jubilee of 1826-7. New York, Arno Press, 1972. xvi, 308 p. 22 cm. (Religion in America, series II) Reprint of the 1844 ed. [BX1415.K4S6 1972] 70-38548 ISBN 0-405-04087-3
1. Catholic Church in Kentucky. 2. Catholic Church in Kentucky—Biography. 3. Kentucky—Church history. I. Title.

Catholic Church in Oregon—History.

LYONS, Letitia 266'.2'0924 B
Mary, Sister, 1903-
Francis Norbert Blanchet and the founding of the Oregon missions (1838-1848). Washington, Catholic University of America Press, 1940. [New York, AMS Press, 1974] p. Reprint of the author's thesis, Catholic University of America, 1940, which was issued as v. 30 [i.e. 31] of the Catholic University of America. Studies in American church history. Bibliography: p. [BX1415.O7L9 1974] 73-3585 ISBN 0-404-57781-4 9.50
1. Catholic Church in Oregon—History. 2. Blanchet, Francis Norbert, Abp., 1795-1883. 3. Portland, Or. (Ecclesiastical province) I. Title. II. Series: Catholic University of America. Studies in American church history, v. 31.

Catholic Church in the United States—Biography.

MCNAMARA, Robert 282'.092'2 B
Francis, 1910-
Catholic Bicentennial profiles / by Robert F. McNamara. [Rochester, N.Y. : Christopher Press], c1975. 31 p. ; 18 cm. [BX4670.M25] 76-359391
1. Catholic Church in the United States—Biography. 2. United States—Biography. I. Title.

Catholic Church in the United States—Biography—Study and teaching.

CLARK, Mary Ann. 282'.092'2 B
Great American Catholics / by Mary Ann Clark, Jerri Pogue, Diane Rickard ; ill. by Robert L. Mutchler. Notre Dame, Ind. : Ave Maria Press, c1976. 191 p. : ill. ; 23 cm. Includes bibliographical references. [BX4670.C48] 76-7278 ISBN 0-87793-111-9 pbk. : 3.50
1. Catholic Church in the United States—Biography—Study and teaching. 2. Catholic Church in the United States—Biography. 3. United States—Biography—Study and teaching. I. Pogue, Jerri, joint author. II. Rickard, Diane, joint author. III. Title. BIP

Catholic Church in the United States—History.

CURRAN, Robert 282'.092'4 B
Emmett.
Michael Augustine Corrigan and the shaping of conservative Catholicism in America, 1878-1902 / Robert Emmett Curran. New York : Arno Press, 1978. xiii, 547 p. : ports. ; 24 cm. (The American Catholic tradition) Rev. and enl. from the author's thesis. Includes index. Bibliography: p. 516-529. [BX4705.C778C87 1978] 77-11277 ISBN 0-405-10814-1 : 34.00
1. Corrigan, Michael Augustine, Abp., 1839-1902. 2. Catholic Church—Bishops—Biography. 3. Catholic Church in the United States—History. 4. McGlynn, Edward, 1837-1900. 5. Bishops—New York (City)—Biography. 6. New York (City)—Biography. I. Title. II. Series.

SHEA, John Dawson 282'.73
Gilmary, 1824-1892.
History of the Catholic Church within the limits of the United States/ John Gilmary Shea. New York : Arno Press, 1978, [c1886-1892] 4 v. : ill. ; 23 cm. (The American Catholic tradition) Reprint of the ed. published by the author, New York. Includes bibliographical references and indexes. [BX1406.S5 1978] 77-11310 ISBN 0-405-10852-4 : 165.00
1. Catholic Church in the United States—History. 2. Carroll, John, Abp., 1735-1815. 3. Catholic Church—Bishops—Biography. 4. Bishops—Maryland—Baltimore—Biography. 5. Baltimore—Biography. I. Title. II. Series.

Catholic Church. Pope, 1073-1085 (Gregorius VII)

CATHOLIC Church. 262'.13'0924
Pope, 1073-1085 (Gregorius VII)
The correspondence of Pope Gregory VII; selected letters from the Registrum. Translated with an introd. by Ephraim Emerton New York, Norton [1969, c1932] xxxi, 212 p. 21 cm. (Records of civilization: sources and studies [14]) Bibliography: p. [196]-197. [BX1187.A4 1969] 70-8470
1. Emerton, Ephraim, 1851-1935, ed. & tr. II. Title. III. Series.

Catholic Foreign Mission Society of America—Biography.

KELLER, James Gregory, 266.2
1900-
Men of Maryknoll, by James Keller and Meyer Berger. Freeport, N.Y., Books for Libraries Press [1972, c1943] 191 p. 23 cm. (Essay index reprint series) [BV2300.C35K4 1972] 78-142650 ISBN 0-8369-2775-3
1. Catholic Foreign Mission Society of America—Biography. I. Berger, Meyer, 1898-1959, joint author. II. Title. BIP

Catholic Interracial Council.

HUNTON, George K., 301.451'96'073
1888-
All of which I saw, part of which I was; the autobiography of George K. Hunton as told to Gary MacEoin. Introd. by Roy Wilkins. [1st ed.] Garden City, N.Y., Doubleday, 1967. 283 p. 22 cm. [E185.61.H96] 67-12841
1. Catholic Interracial Council. 2. Negroes—Civil rights. 3. Church and race problems—Catholic Church. I. MacEoin, Gary, 1909- II. Title.

Catholic literature—Bio-bibliography.

GILLOW, Joseph, 914.2'03'0922 B
1850-1921.
A literary and biographical history; or, Bibliographical dictionary of the English Catholics, from the breach with Rome, in

1534, to the present time. New York, B. Franklin [1968] 5 v. 24 cm. (Burt Franklin bibliography and reference series, 25) Reprint of the 1885-1902 ed. Contents.Contents.—v. 1. A-C—v. 2. D-Grad—v. 3. Gran-Kem—v. 4. Kem-Met—v. 5. Mey-Zoo. [Z2010.G483 1968] 74-6323
1. Catholic literature—Bio-bibliography. 2. English literature—Catholic authors—Bibliography. 3. Catholic Church in England—Bibliography. 4. English literature—Bio-bibliography. I. Title. II. Title: Bibliographical dictionary of the English Catholics.

Catholic Worker Movement.

MILLER, William D., 1916- 261.8'3
A harsh and dreadful love; Dorothy Day and the Catholic Worker Movement [by] William D. Miller. New York, Liveright [1973] xvi, 370 p. illus. 23 cm. Bibliography: p. [351]-357. [BX810.M5] 72-87098 ISBN 0-87140-558-X 9.95
1. Catholic Worker Movement. 2. Day, Dorothy, 1897- 3. The Catholic worker. I. Title. BIP

Catholics.

SHEED, Francis Joseph, 1897- comp. 922.2
Born Catholics. New York, Sheed & Ward, 1954. 279p. 22cm. [BX4669.S47] 54-11144
1. Catholics. I. Title.

Catholics—Biography.

KNOWLES, Leo. 282'.092'2 B
Candidates for sainthood / by Leo Knowles. St. Paul : Carillon Books, 1978. ix, 138 p. ; 22 cm. Bibliography: p. 137-138. [BX4651.2.K56] 78-55247 ISBN 0-89310-035-8 : 8.95. ISBN 0-89310-036-6 pbk. : 3.95
1. Catholics—Biography. 2. Christian biography. I. Title.
Contents omitted. BIP

Catholics in England.

GERARD, John, 1564-1637. 922.242
The autobiography of a hunted priest. Translated from the Latin by Philip Caraman. With an introd. by Graham Greene. Garden City, N. Y., Image Books [1955, c1952] 318p. 19cm. (Image books, D24) Translated from me.; published in London in 1951 under title: The autobiography of an Elizabethan. [BX4705] 55-14904
1. Catholics in England. 2. Catholic Church in England—Clergy—Correspondence, reminiscences, etc. I. Title.

GERARD, John, 1564-1637. 922.242
The autobiography of an Elizabethan, translated from the Latin by Philip Caraman. With an introd. by Graham Greene. London, New York, Longmans, Green [1951] xxiv, 287 p. illus., ports. 22 cm. [BX4705.G418A33 1951] A52
1. Catholics in England. 2. Catholic Church in England—Clergy—Correspondence, reminiscences, etc. I. Title.

Catholics in the U.S.

MAYNARD, Theodore, 1890- 922.273
Great Catholics in American history. [New York, All Saints, 1962, c.1957] 209p. (AS221) .50 pap.,
1. Catholics in the U.S. I. Title.

Catholics, Negro.

FOLEY, Albert Sidney, 1912- 922.273
God's men of color; the colored Catholic priests of the United States, 1854-1954. With a foreword by Richard J. Cushing, Archbishop of Boston. New York, Farrar, Straus [1955] 322p. 22cm. [BX4670.F6] 55-6683
1. Catholics, Negro. 2. Catholic Church in the U.S.—Biog. I. Title.

FOLEY, Albert Sidney, 1912- 282'.0922
God's men of color [by] Albert S. Foley. New York, Arno Press, 1969. x, 322 p. 23 cm. (The American Negro: his history and literature) Reprint of the 1955 ed. [BX4670.F6 1969] 69-18569
1. Catholics, Negro. 2. Catholic Church in the United States—Biography. I. Title. II. Series.

Catilina, Lucius Sergius, 108 (ca.)-62 B.C.

CATILINE; 937'.05'0924
the man and his role in the Roman Revolution. [1st ed.] New York, Exposition [1968] xi, 192p. 21cm. (Exposition-univ. bk.) Bibl. [DG259.K37] (B) 67-25395 7.50
1. Catilina, Lucius Sergius, 108 (ca.)-62 B.C. I. Kaplan, Arthur, 1908-

KAPLAN, Arthur, 1908- 937'.05'0924 (B)
Catiline; the man and his role in the Roman Revolution. [1st ed.] New York, Exposition Press [1968] xi, 192 p. 21 cm. (An Exposition-university book) Bibliography: [189]-192. [DG259.K37] 67-26395
1. Catilina, Lucius Sergius, 108 (ca.)-62 B. C. I. Title.

Catlin, George, 1796-1872.

HAVERSTOCK, Mary Sayre. 759.13 B
Indian gallery; the story of George Catlin. New York, Four Winds Press [1973] xx, 229 p. illus. 26 cm. Bibliography: p. 221-222. [ND237.C35H38] 72-87075 7.88 (reinforced bdg.)
1. Catlin, George, 1796-1872. 2. Indians of North America—The West. I. Catlin, George, 1796-1872. II. Title. BIP

PLATE, Robert. 927.5
Palette and tomahawk; the story of George Catlin, July 27, 1796--December 23, 1872. Illus. from drawings by George Catlin. New York, D. McKay Co., 1962. 248p. illus. 22cm. Includes bibliography. [ND237.C35P6] 62-18967
1. Catlin, George, 1796-1872. I. Title.

TRUETTNER, William H. 759.13 B
The natural man observed : a study of Catlin's Indian gallery / William H. Truettner. 1st ed. Washington : Smithsonian Institution Press, [1978] p. cm. Includes indexes. Bibliography: p. [ND237.C35T78] 78-15152 ISBN 0-87474-918-2 : 35.00
1. Catlin, George, 1796-1872. 2. Painters—United States—Biography. 3. Indians of North America—Pictorial works. 4. The West in art. I. Title. BIP

Catnach, James, 1792-1841.

HINDLEY, Charles, d.1893. 784.4'924 B
The life and times of James Catnach, (late of Seven Dials), ballad monger. London, Reeves and Turner, 1878. Detroit, Singing Tree Press, 1968. 432 p. illus. 20 cm. [Z232.C36H2 1968] 68-20122
1. Catnach, James, 1792-1841. 2. English ballads and songs. 3. Chap-books. I. Title.

Cato, Marcus Porcius, Censorius.

ASTIN, A. E. 937.04'0924 B
Cato the censor / by Alan E. Astin. Oxford [Eng]. : Clarendon Press ; New York : Oxford University Press, 1978. x, 371 p. ; 24 cm. Includes indexes. Bibliography: p. [351]-362. [DG253.C3A87] 77-30281 ISBN 0-19-814809-7 : 39.00
1. Cato, Marcus Porcius, Censorius. 2. Statesmen—Rome—Biography. 3. Orators—Rome—Biography. I. Title. BIP

FORDE, Nels W. 937'.04'0924 B
Cato the censor / by Nels W. Forde. New York : Twayne, [1975] 292 p. ; 22 cm. (Twayne's world leaders series ; TWLS 49) Includes index. Bibliography: p. 277-280. [DG253.C3F67] 74-28128 ISBN 0-8057-3017-6 lib.bdg. : 8.50
1. Cato, Marcus Porcius, Censorius. 2. Rome—History—Republic, 265-30 B.C. I. Title. BIP

Cato, Marcus Porcius, Uticensis.

JAEGER, Muriel. 920.02
Adventures in living, from Cato to George Sand. Freeport, N.Y., Books for Libraries Press [1970] viii, 216 p. 23 cm. (Essay index reprint series) Reprint of the 1932 American ed. Published in London in 1932 under title: Experimental lives. Includes bibliographical references. [CT105.J3 1970] 79-121480 ISBN 8-369-17588-
1. Cato, Marcus Porcius, Uticensis. 2. Francesco d'Assisi, Saint, 1182-1226. 3. Chesterfield, Philip Dormer Stanhope, 4th Earl of, 1694-1773. 4. Day, Thomas, 1748-1789. 5. Sand, George, pseud. of Mme. Dudevant, 1804-1876. I. Title. BIP

Cato, 1911-1959.

DELMER, Sefton, 1904- 940.548'6'42
The counterfeit spy. [1st U.S. ed.] New York, Harper & Row [1971] 256 p. 23 cm. Includes bibliographical references. [D810.S8C3584 1971] 71-95948 ISBN 0-06-011019-8 6.95
1. Cato, 1911-1959. 2. World War, 1939-1945—Secret service—Gt. Brit. I. Title. BIP

Caton, John Dean, 1812-1895.

PRATT, Harry Edward, 1901-1956. v. 12
The life of John Dean Caton. Urbana, Ill. [19--] 150 l. illus. 29cm. 62-4921
1. Caton, John Dean, 1812-1895. I. Title.

Catron, Thomas Benton, 1840-1921.

WESTPHALL, Victor. 978.9'04'0924 B
Thomas Benton Catron and his era. Tucson, University of Arizona Press [1973] x, 462 p. ports. 23 cm. Bibliography: p. 423-437. [F801.C332W47] 73-75304 ISBN 0-8165-0341-9 12.00
1. Catron, Thomas Benton, 1840-1921. 2. New Mexico—History—1848- I. Title.
Pbk. 6.95; ISBN 0-8165-0454-7. BIP

Catt, Carrie Lane Chapman, 1859-1947.

PECK, Mary Gray. 324'.3'0924 B
Carrie Chapman Catt : a biography / by Mary Gray Peck. New York : Octagon Books, 1975, c1944. p. cm. Reprint of the ed. published by H. W. Wilson Co., New York. Includes index. [HQ1413.C3P4 1975] 75-1350 ISBN 0-374-96336-3 : 17.50
1. Catt, Carrie Lane Chapman, 1859-1947.

PECK, Mary Gray. 324'.3'0924 B
Carrie Chapman Catt : a biography / by Mary Gray Peck. Westport, Conn. : Hyperion Press, 1976, c1944. 495 p., [8] leaves of plates : ill. ; 22 cm. (Pioneers of the woman's movement) Reprint of the ed. published by H. W. Wilson Co., New York. Includes index. [HQ1413.C3P4 1976] 75-23159 ISBN 0-88355-279-5 : 29.00
1. Catt, Carrie Lane Chapman, 1859-1947.

Cattell, James McKeen, 1860-1944—Bibliography.

CATTELL, James McKeen, 1860-1944. 150'.8
James McKeen Cattell, 1860-1944; man of science. A. T. Poffenberger, editor. New York, Arno Press, 1973 [c1947] viii, 582 p. illus. 24 cm. (Classics in psychology) Reprint of v. 1, Psychological research, of the ed. published by Science Press, Lancaster, Pa. "Bibliography of the writings of James McKeen Cattell": p. 577-582. [BF121.C37] 73-2984 ISBN 0-405-05155-7 27.00
1. Cattell, James McKeen, 1860-1944—Bibliography. 2. Psychology. I. Title. II. Series.

Cattle trade — U.s.

PONTING, Tom Candy, 1824-1916. 926.36
Life of Tom Candy Onting, an autobiography. Introd. & notes by Herbert O. Brayer; illus. by David T. Vernon. Evanston, Ill., Branding Iron Press, 1952. x, 132 p. illus., ports., map. 20 cm. "The second in the series of 'vignettes' of the cattle industry prepared by the Western Range Cattle Industry Study." 500 copies printed. "Copyright copy *" [HD9433.U4P58] 52-1745
1. Cattle trade — U.s. I. Brayer, Herbert Oliver, ed. II. Title.

Cattle trade—Texas.

DOUGLAS, Claude Leroy, 1901- 976.4
Cattle kings of Texas, by C. L. Douglas. Fort Worth, Tex., Branch-Smith [1968, c1939] 376 p. illus., map, ports. 23 cm. [F391.D714 1968] 68-58541 5.95
1. Cattle trade—Texas. 2. Frontier and pioneer life—Texas. 3. Texas—Biography. I. Title. BIP

Cattle trade—The West.

ATHERTON, Lewis Eldon. 917.8
The cattle kings. Bloomington, Indiana University Press [1961] 308 p. illus. 25 cm. Includes bibliography. [F596.A8] 61-13722
1. Cattle trade—The West. 2. Ranch life—The West. 3. The West—Biography. I. Title. BIP

Catts, Sidney Johnston, 1863-1936.

FLYNT, Wayne, 1940- 975.9'06'0924 B
Cracker messiah, Governor Sidney J. Catts of Florida / Wayne Flynt. Baton Rouge : Louisiana State University Press, c1977. xiv, 359 p., [3] leaves of plates : ill. ; 24 cm. (Southern biography series) Includes index. [F316.C27F59] 76-57664 ISBN 0-8071-0263-6 : 20.00
1. Catts, Sidney Johnston, 1863-1936. 2. Florida—Politics and government—1865-1950. 3. Florida—Governors—Biography. I. Title. II. Series.

Caulaincourt, Armand Augustin Louis, marquis de, duc de Vicence, 1773-1827.

CAULAINCOURT, Armand Augustin Louis, marquis de, duc de Vicence, 1773-1827. 940.2'7'0924 B
With Napoleon in Russia : the memoirs of General de Caulaincourt, Duke of Vicenza : from the original memoirs / as edited by Jean Hanoteau ; abridged, edited, and with an introd. by George Libaire. Westport, Conn. : Greenwood Press, 1976, c1935. p. cm. Translation of Memoires du general de Caulaincourt. Reprint of the ed. published by W. Morrow, New York. Includes index. Bibliography: p. [DC198.C35A33 1976] 75-40914 ISBN 0-8371-8689-7 lib.bdg. : 25.00
1. Caulaincourt, Armand Augustin Louis, marquis de, duc de Vicence, 1773-1827. 2. Napoleon I, Emperor of the French, 1769-1821—Invasion of Russia, 1812. 3. France. Armee—Biography. 4. France—History—Consulate and Empire, 1799-1815. 5. Generals—France—Biography. I. Libaire, George. II. Title.

Caulfield, Genevieve.

CAULFIELD, Genevieve. 923.773
The kinbdam within. Edited by Ed Fitzgerald. New York, Harper [c.1960] 278p. 22cm. 59-13279 4.00 bds.,
I. Title.

CAULFIELD, Genevieve. 923.773
The kingdom within. Edited by Ed Fitzgerald. [1st ed.] New York, Harper [1960] 278p. 22cm. Autobiographical. [HV1624.C3A3] 59-13279
I. Title.

RAU, Margaret 923.773
Dawn from the West; the story of Genevieve Caulfield. Illus. by Dan Dickas. New York, Hawthorn [c.1964] 188p. illus.

(pt. col.) map. 22cm. (Credo bks., 17) 64-11242 2.95
1. Caulfield, Genevieve. I. Title.

RAU, Margaret. 923.773
Dawn from the West; the story of Genevieve Caulfield. Illustrated by Dan Dickas. New York, Hawthorn Books [1964] 188 p. illus. (part col.) map. 22 cm. (Credo books [17]) [HV1624.C3R3] 64011242
1. Caulfield, Genevieve. I. Title.

Causer, H. Phillip.

CAUSER, H. Phillip. 940.53'44'0924
M.I.A., missing in action / written & illustrated by H. Phillip Causer. 1st ed. Norwell, Mass. : Phipps Pub. Co., c1977. 169 p. : ill. ; 24 cm. [D802.C8C38] 77-88747 ISBN 0-918442-00-1 : 7.95
1. Causer, H. Phillip. 2. World War, 1939-1945—Underground movements—France—Biography. 3. World War, 1939-1945—Personal narratives, English. 4. Guerrillas—France—Biography. 5. Fighter pilots—Great Britain—Biography. I. Title. **BIP**

Cauthen, Baker James.

FLETCHER, Jesse C. 266'.6'1320924 B
Baker James Cauthen : a man for all nations / Jesse C. Fletcher. Nashville, Tenn. : Broadman Press, c1977. 272 p. : ill. ; 21 cm. [BX6495.C38F55] 77-80941 ISBN 0-8054-7219-3 : 6.95
1. Cauthen, Baker James. 2. Baptists—Clergy—Biography. 3. Clergy—United States—Biography. 4. Missionaries—United States—Biography. **BIP**

Cauthen, Steve, 1960-

AXTHELM, Peter M. 798'.43'0924 B
The kid / Pete Axthelm. New York : Viking Press, c1978. x, 265 p., [6] leaves of plates : ill. ; 21 cm. [SF336.C38A97 1978] 78-15267 ISBN 0-670-41296-1 : 2.50
1. Cauthen, Steve, 1960- 2. Jockeys—United States—Biography. I. Title. **BIP**

Cauthen, Steve, 1960- —Juvenile literature.

KEELY, Scott. 798.4'3'0924 B
Steve Cauthen / by Scott Keely. Mankato, Minn. : Creative Education, c1979 32 p. : ill. ; 23 cm. (Creative Education sports superstars) A brief biography of the young jockey who was the first to win six million dollars in one year. [SF336.C38K43] 92 79-52896 ISBN 0-87191-693-2 : 5.95 ISBN 0-89812-163-9 pbk. : 2.75
1. Cauthen, Steve, 1960- —Juvenile literature. 2. Jockeys—United States—Biography—Juvenile literature. I. Title.
Publisher's Address : 123 South Broad St., Mankato, MN 56001

MCMILLAN, Constance Van Brunt. 798'.43'0924 B
Steve Cauthen : million dollar baby / by Constance Van Brunt McMillan. St. Paul : EMC Corp., 1977. p. cm. (So young, so far) A biography of the jockey who earned more than a million dollars in purse money by the time he was sixteen years old. [SF336.C38M3] 92 77-24072 ISBN 0-88436-406-2 lib.bdg. : 4.95 ISBN 0-88436-407-0 pbk. : 2.95
1. Cauthen, Steven, 1960- —Juvenile literature. 2. Jockeys—United States—Biography—Juvenile literature. I. Title. **BIP**

MUESER, Anne Marie. 798'.43'0924 B
The picture story of jockey Steve Cauthen / by Anne Marie Mueser. New York : J. Messner, c1979. 64 p. : ill. ; 22 cm. A biography emphasizing the career of the 18-year-old jockey who led Affirmed to a Triple Crown victory in 1978. [SF336.C38M83] 92 78-27884 ISBN 0-671-32990-1 : 6.97
1. Cauthen, Steve, 1960- —Juvenile literature. 2. Jockeys—United States—Biography—Juvenile literature. I. Title. **BIP**

TUTTLE, Anthony. 798'.43'0924 B
Steve Cauthen, boy jockey / by Anthony Tuttle ; photos. by Bruce Curtis. New York : Putnam, c1978. 47 p. : ill. ; 20 x 28 cm. A biography of the jockey who began his record-breaking professional career at the age of sixteen. [SF336.C38T87 1978] 92 77-16770 ISBN 0-399-20631-0 : 7.95
1. Cauthen, Steve, 1960- —Juvenile literature. 2. Jockeys—United States—Biography—Juvenile literature. I. Curtis, Bruce. II. Title. **BIP**

Cavalli, Pier Francesco, 1602-1676.

GLOVER, Jane. 782.1'092'4 B
Cavalli / Jane Glover. New York : St. Martin's Press, 1978. 191 p., [2] leaves of plates : ill. ; 24 cm. Includes index. Bibliography: p. 171-181. [ML410.C3913G6 1978b] 77-23638 ISBN 0-312-12546-1 : 16.50.
1. Cavalli, Pier Francesco, 1602-1676. 2. Composers—Italy—Biography. **BIP**

Cavanaugh, Arthur

CAVANAUGH, Arthur 928.1
My own back yard. Garden City, N.Y., Doubleday, 1962[c.1961] 240p. 62-7610 3.95 bds.,
I. Title.

CAVANAUGH, Arthur. 928.1
My own back yard. [1st ed.] Garden. City, N. Y., Doubleday, 1962 c1961] 240p. 22cm. [PS3505.A899Z5] 62-7610
I. Title.

Cavanugh, Arthur

CAVANUGH, Arthur 928.1
My own back yard. New York, Guild [1966, c.1961] 246p. 17cm. (All Saints, AS250) [PS3505.A899Z5] .50 pap.,
I. Title.

Cavell, Edith Louisa, 1865-1915.

CLARK-KENNEDY, Archibald Edmund, 1893- 926.1
Edith Cavell, pioneer and patriot. London. Faber & Faber [New York. Hillary House. c.1965] 248p. illus., facsims., maps, plans, ports. 23cm. Bibl. [D630.C3C55] 65-66486 6.00
1. Cavell, Edith Louisa. 1865-1915. I. Title.

DE LEEUW, Adele Louise, 1899- 940.4'86'42 B
Edith Cavell; nurse, spy, heroine, by Adele De Leeuw. Illustrated by Charles Brey. New York, Putnam [1968] 95 p. illus. 22 cm. (Spies of the world) A biography of the English nurse who used her directorship of a nursing school and clinic in Belgium during World War I as a front to aid the escape of Allied soldiers from German occupied territory, an act for which the Germans executed her as a spy. [RT37.C3D4] 92 AC 68
1. Cavell, Edith Lois, 1865-1915. I. Brey, Charles, illus. II. Title.

ELKON, Juliette. 926.1
Edith Cavell, heroic nurse. New York, J. Messner [1956] 192 p. 22 cm. Includes bibliography. [D630.C3E4] 56-10448
1. Cavell, Edith Louisa, 1865-1915.

[HOGG, Beth Tootill] 1917- 926.1
Friend within the gates; the story of nurse Edith Cavell, by Elizabeth Grey [pseud.] Boston, Houghton Mifflin, 1961 [c.1960] 194p. 61-7727 3.00
1. Cavell, Edith Louisa, 1865-1915. I. Title.

HOGG, Beth Tootill, 1917- 926.1
Friend within the gates; the story of nurse Edith Cavell, by Elizabeth Grey. New York, Dell [1968, c.1960] 194p. 19cm. (Yearling bk. 2734) .75 pap.,
1. Cavell, Edith Louisa, 1865-1915. I. Title.

RYDER, Rowland. 940.4'86'41 B
Edith Cavell / Rowland Ryder. New York : Stein and Day, [1975] p. cm. Includes index. Bibliography: p. [D630.C3R94 1975] 75-15751 ISBN 0-8128-1868-7 : 8.95
1. Cavell, Edith Louisa, 1865-1915. I. Title.

VINTON, Iris. 926.1
The story of Edith Cavell. Illustrated by Gerald McCann. New York, Grosset & Dunlap [1959] 178 p. illus. 22 cm. (Signature books, 47) [D630.C3V35] 59-5673
1. Cavell, Edith Louisa, 1865-1915.

Cavell, Edith Louisa, 1865-1915—Juvenile literature.

DE LEEUW, Adele Louise, 1899- 92 (J)
Edith Cavell; nurse, spy, heroine, by Adele De Leeuw. Illustrated by Charles Brey. New York, Putnam [1968] 95 p. illus. 22 cm. (Spies of the world) [RT37.C3D4] 67-24147
1. Cavell, Edith Louisa, 1865-1915—Juvenile literature.

Cavendish, Henry, 1731-1810.

WILSON, George, 1818-1859. 540'.92'4 B
The life of the Honorable Henry Cavendish / George Wilson. New York : Arno Press, 1975. xiv, 478 p. : port. ; 23 cm. (History, philosophy, and sociology of science) Reprint of the 1851 ed. printed for the Cavendish Society, London, in series : Works of the Cavendish Society. Includes bibliographical references. [QD22.C4W7 1975] 74-26308 ISBN 0-405-06631-7 : 28.00
1. Cavendish, Henry, 1731-1810. 2. Water—Composition. I. Title. II. Series. III. Series: Cavendish Society, London. Works. **BIP**

Cavendish, Thomas, 1560-1592.

CAVENDISH, Thomas, 1560-1592. 910'.41 B
The last voyage of Thomas Cavendish, 1591-1592 : the autograph manuscript of his own account of the voyage, written shortly before his death : from the collection of Paul Mellon / with an introd., transcription, and notes by David Beers Quinn. Chicago : Published for the Newberry Library by the University of Chicago Press, [1975] p. cm. (Studies in the history of discoveries) Includes index. [G246.C38A34 1975] 74-11619 ISBN 0-226-09819-2 : 22.50 7.95
1. Cavendish, Thomas, 1560-1592. 2. America—Discovery and exploration—English. I. Quinn, David Beers, ed. II. Newberry Library, Chicago. III. Title. IV. Series.

Cavett, Dick.

CAVETT, Dick 791.450924 B
Cavett [by] Dick Cavett and Christopher Porterfield. New York, Bantam Books [1975] 374 p. illus. 18 cm. [PN1992.4C33A32] 1.95 (pbk.)
1. Cavett, Dick. I. Porterfield, Christopher, joint author. II. Title.
L.C. card no. for original edition: 74-8492

CAVETT, Dick. 791.45'092'4 B
Cavett [by] Dick Cavett and Christopher Porterfield. [1st ed.] New York, Harcourt Brace Jovanovich [1974] 373 p. illus. 22 cm. [PN1992.4.C33A32] 74-8492 8.95
1. Cavett, Dick. I. Porterfield, Christopher, joint author. II. Title.

Cavour, Camillo Benso, conte di, 1810-1861.

CADOGAN, Edward Cecil George, Sir, 1880- 940.2'8'0922
Makers of modern history; three types: Louis Napoleon-Cavour-Bismarck, by Edward Cadogan. Port Washington, N.Y., Kennikat Press [1970] ix, 216 p. 22 cm. Reprint of the 1905 ed. [D352.5.C16 1970] 75-112797
1. Napoleon III, Emperor of the French, 1808-1873. 2. Cavour, Camillo Benso, conte di, 1810-1861. 3. Bismarck, Otto, Furst von, 1815-1898. I. Title.

MACK Smith, Denis, 1920- 945'.08'0922
Victor Emanuel, Cavour and the Risorgimento. London, New York, Oxford University Press, 1971. xviii, 381 p. 1 illus., maps, ports. 25 cm. Bibliography: p. [xiii]-xv. [DG552.5.M3] 74-31860 ISBN 0-19-212550-8 £7.00
1. Cavour, Camillo Benso, conte di, 1810-1861. 2. Vittorio Emanuele II, King of Italy, 1820-1878. 3. Italy—History—1849-1870. I. Title.

MARTINENGO-CESARESCO, Evelyn Lilian Hazeldine (Carrington) contessa, 1852-1931. 945'.08'0924 B
Cavour. Port Washington, N.Y., Kennikat Press [1970] viii, 222 p. 21 cm. Reprint of the 1898 ed. Bibliography: p. [221]-222. [DG552.8.C3M3 1970] 79-112798
1. Cavour, Camillo Benso, conte di, 1810-1861. **BIP**

MARTINENGO-CESARESCO, Evelyn Lilian Hazeldine (Carrington) contessa, 1852-1931. 945'.08'0924 B
Cavour. Freeport, N.Y., Books for Libraries Press [1971] viii, 222 p. 23 cm. "First published 1898." Bibliography: p. [221]-222. [DG552.8.C3M3 1971] 76-150174 ISBN 0-8369-5687-7
1. Cavour, Camillo Benso, conte di, 1819-1861.

PALEOLOGUE, Georges Maurice, 1859-1944. 945'.08'0924 B
Cavour, by Maurice Paleologue. Translated by Ian F. D. Morrow and Muriel M. Morrow. Freeport, N.Y., Books for Libraries Press [1970] 307 p. ports. 23 cm. Translation of Un grand realiste, Cavour. Reprint of the 1927 ed. [DG552.8.C3P4 1970] 77-130561
1. Cavour, Camillo Benso, conte di, 1810-1861. **BIP**

THAYER, William Roscoe, 1859-1923. 945'.08'0924 B
The life and times of Cavour. New York, H. Fertig, 1971 [c1911] 2 v. geneal. tables, maps, ports. 23 cm. Bibliography: v. 2, p. [510]-515. [DG552.8.C3T5 1971] 68-9634
1. Cavour, Camillo Benso, conte di, 1810-1861. 2. Italy—History—1849-1870. I. Title. **BIP**

WHYTE, Arthur James Beresford. 945'.08'0924 B
The early life and letters of Cavour, 1810-1848 / by A. J. Whyte. Westport, Conn. : Greenwood Press, 1976. p. cm. Continued by the political life and letters of Cavour, 1858-1861. Reprint of the 1925 ed. published by Oxford University Press, H. Milford, London. [DG552.8.C3W5 1976] 75-31428 ISBN 0-8371-8504-1 lib.bdg. : 24.00
1. Cavour, Camillo Benso, conte di, 1810-1861. 2. Statesmen—Italy—Biography. I. Title. **BIP**

WHYTE, Arthur James Beresford. 945'.08'0924 B
The political life and letters of Cavour, 1848-1861 / by A. J. Whyte. Westport, Conn. : Greenwood Press, 1975. xv, 478 p. : port. ; 22 cm. Sequel to The early life and letters of Cavour, 1810-1848. Reprint of the 1930 ed. published by Oxford University Press, London. Includes index. Bibliography: p. [468]-470. [DG552.8.C3W52 1975] 74-30983 ISBN 0-8371-7939-4 lib.bdg. : 21.50
1. Cavour, Camillo Benso, conte di, 1810-1861. I. Title. **BIP**

Cawein, Madison Julius, 1865-1914.

ROTHERT, Otto Arthur, 1871- 811'.4 B
The story of a poet: Madison Cawein; his intimate life as revealed by his letters and other hitherto unpublished material, including reminiscences by his closest associates; also articles from newspapers and magazines and a list of his poems, by Otto A. Rothert. Freeport, N.Y., Books for Libraries Press [1971] x, 545 p. illus., ports. 23 cm. Reprint of the 1921 ed. Includes bibliographical references. [PS1278.R6 1971] 76-146871 ISBN 0-8369-5640-0
1. Cawein, Madison Julius, 1865-1914. I. Title.

Cawthon, Pete, 1898-1961.

LYNCH, Etta. 796.33'2'0924 B
Tender tyrant : the legend of Pete Cawthon / by Etta Lynch. Canyon, Tex. : Staked Plains Press, c1976. vii, 285 p. : ill. ; 24 cm. [GV939.C38L94] 77-359178 12.50
1. Cawthon, Pete, 1898-1961. 2. Football coaches—United States—Biography. I. Title. BIP

Caxton, William, 1422 (ca.)-1491.

AURNER, Nellie (Slayton) 926.55 1873-
Caxton, mirrour of fifteenth-century letters; a study of the literature of the first English press [Reissue] New York, Russell & Russell, 1965. 304p. illus., facsims., plan, port. 23cm. First pub. in 1926. Bibl. [Z232.C38A9] 65-13948 7.50
1. Caxton, William, 1422 (ca.)-1491. 2. English literature—Middle English (1100-1500)—Hist. & crit. I. Title.

BLADES, William, 686'.20924 B 1824-1890.
The biography and typography of William Caxton, England's first printer. With an introd. by James Moran. Totowa, N.J., Rowman and Littlefield, 1971. xxii, 383 p. illus. 23 cm. Reprint of the 1877 ed., with a new introd. [Z232.C38B6 1971] 77-29487
1. Caxton, William, ca. 1422-1491. I. Title.

BLADES, William, 686.2'092'4 1824-1890.
The biography and typography of William Caxton, England's first printer. [1st ed., reprinted]; with an introduction by James Moran. London, Muller, 1971. xxii, 383 p. [1], xviii leaves. illus., facsims. 23 cm. Reprint of 1st ed., London, Trubner, 1877. [Z232.C38B6 1971b] 72-193238 ISBN 0-584-10916-4
1. Caxton, William, ca. 1422-1491. I. Title. Available from Rowman and Littlefield, 13.50, ISBN 0-87471-036-7.

BLADES, William, 1824- 655.1 B 1890.
The life and typography of William Caxton, England's first printer, with evidence of his typographical connection with Colard Mansion, the printer at Bruges. New York, B. Franklin [1965] 2 v. facsims., port. 27 cm. (Burt Franklin bibliography and reference series, #74) Reprint of the 1861-1863 ed. published in London. Bibliography: v. 1, p. [287]-288; v. 2, p. 294-[295] [Z232.C38B5 1965] 76-6310
1. Caxton, William, 1422 (ca.)-1491. I. Title. BIP

BLAKE, Norman 070.5'092'4 B Francis.
Caxton : England's first publisher / N. F. Blake. New York : Barnes & Noble Books, 1976, c1975. 220 p. : ill. ; 25 cm. "Caxton's editions": p. [192]-196. Includes index. Bibliography: p. [211]-212. [Z232.C38B635 1976] 76-2874 ISBN 0-06-490450-4 : 22.50
1. Caxton, William, 1422(ca.)-1491. 2. Printers—England—Biography. BIP

BLAKE, Norman 070.5'092'4 Francis.
Caxton : England's first publisher / [by] N. F. Blake. London : Osprey Publishing, 1976. xi, 220 p. : ill., facsims., ports. ; 25 cm. Includes index. "Caxton's editions": p. [192]-196. [Z232.C38B635 1976b] 77-355083 ISBN 0-85045-106-X : £7.00
1. Caxton, William, 1422(ca.)-1491. 2. Printers—England—Biography. 3. Publishers and publishing—England—Biography.

CHILDS, Edmund 686.2'092'4 Lunness.
William Caxton : a portrait in a background / Edmund Childs. New York : St. Martin's Press, [1979] c1976. 190 p., [2] leaves of plates (1 fold.) : ill. ; 21 cm. Includes index. Bibliography: p. 181-183. [Z232.C38C5 1978] 77-25770 ISBN 0-312-88031-6 : 10.00
1. Caxton, William, 1422 (ca)-1491. 2. Printers—England—Biography. BIP

CHILDS, Edmund 686.2'092'4 B Lunness.
William Caxton : a portrait in a background / [by] Edmund Childs. London : Northwood Publications Ltd, 1976. 190 p., [4] p. of plates (2 fold.) : ill., facsims., map, ports. ; 21 cm. Includes index. Bibliography: p. 181-183. [Z232.C38C5] 76-380633 ISBN 0-7198-2579-2 : £3.50. ISBN 0-7198-2569-5 pbk.
1. Caxton, William, 1422 (ca.)-1491. 2. Printers—England—Biography.

DEACON, Richard. 686.2'092'4 B
A biography of William Caxton : the first English editor, printer, merchant, and translator / [by] Richard Deacon. London : Muller, 1976. viii, 198 p. : ill., facsims., plans, ports. ; 24 cm. Includes index. Bibliography: p. [188]-190. [Z232.C38D42] 76-358702 ISBN 0-584-10022-1 : £6.50
1. Caxton, William, 1422 (ca.)-1491. I. Title.

DUFF, Edward Gordon, 655.1'42 B 1863-1924.
William Caxton. New York, B. Franklin [1970] 118 p. illus., facsims. 24 cm. (Burt Franklin bibliography & reference series, 359) Reprint of the 1905 ed. Bibliography: p. 91-98. [Z232.C38D7 1970] 79-128840
1. Caxton, William, ca. 1422-1491.

PAINTER, George 686.2'092'4 B Duncan, 1914-
William Caxton : a biography / by George D. Painter. 1st American ed. New York : Putnam, 1977, c1976. xi, 227 p., [4] leaves of plates : ill. ; 25 cm. Includes index. Bibliography: p. 196-202. [Z232.C38P33 1976] 76-41134 ISBN 0-399-11888-8 : 14.95
1. Caxton, William, 1422 (ca.)-1491. 2. Printers—England—Biography. 3. Printing—History—England. BIP

PLOMER, Henry Robert, 655.1'4'2 B 1856-1928.
William Caxton(1424-1491). New York, B. Franklin [1968] 195 p. 23 cm. (Burt Franklin: Bibliography & reference series, 137) Reprint of the 1925 ed. Bibliography: p. 187-189. [Z232.C38P7 1968] 70-6441
1. Caxton, William, 1422 (ca.)-1491. BIP

Caxton, William, 1422 (ca.)-1491—Addresses, essays, lectures.

CAXTON : 686.2'092'4 B
an American contribution to the quincentenary celebration / edited by Susan Otis Thompson. New York : The Typophiles, 1976. xvi, 54 p., [3] leaves of plates : ill. ; 19 cm. (Typophile chap book ; 52) Contents.Contents.—Blumenthal, J. Introduction.—Dunlap, J. R. From Westminster to Hammersmith vis Chiswick.—Lawton, J. Caxton's autograph?—Griffith, R. R. The early years of William Caxton. Includes bibliographical references. [Z232.C38C37] 76-29112
1. Caxton, William, 1422 (ca.)-1491—Addresses, essays, lectures. 2. Printing—History—England—Addresses, essay, lectures. I. Thompson, Susan Otis. II. The Typophiles, New York. III. Series: The Typophiles, New York. Typophile chap books ; 52.

DREYFUS, John. 070.5'092'4 B
William Caxton and his quincentenary / by John Dreyfus. New York : Typophiles, 1976. 54 p. : ill. ; 19 cm. (Typophile chap book ; 51) [Z232.C38D66] 77-351420
1. Caxton, William, 1422 (ca.)-1491—Addresses, essays, lectures. I. Title. II. Series: The Typophiles, New York. Typophile chap books ; 51.

Caxton, William, 1422 (ca.)-1491—Bibliography.

ST. Bride Printing 686.2'092'4 Library.
Caxtoniana : or, The progress of Caxton studies from the earliest times to 1976 : [catalogue of] an exhibition at the St Bride Printing Library ... 20 September-29 October 1976 .... London : The Library, 1976. 16 p. : ill. ; 25 cm. Selected and with an introd. by Robin Myers. [Z232.C38S24 1976] 77-361465 ISBN 0-9504161-2-6 : £0.75
1. Caxton, William, 1422 (ca.)-1491—Bibliography. 2. Printing—England—History—Bibliography. 3. Bibliographical exhibitions. I. Myers, Robin, fl. 1967- II. Title. III. Title: The progress of Caxton studies from the earliest times to 1976.

Cayce, Edgar, 1877-1945.

BRO, Harmon Hartzell, 131.3'2 1919-
Begin a new life; the approach of Edgar Cayce. [1st ed.] New York, Harper & Row [1971] 216 p. 22 cm. [BF1027.C3B695 1971] 72-124712 5.95
1. Cayce, Edgar, 1877-1945. 2. Conduct of life. I. Title.

EDGAR Cayce, mystery man of v. 12
miracles. New York, Fawcett Publications [1956] 207p. 18cm. (Gold medal book)
1. Cayce, Edgar, 1877-1945. I. Millard, Joseph.

KAHN, David E. 133.80924
My life with Edgar Cayce, by David E. Kahn, as told to Will Oursler. [1st ed.] Garden City, N.Y., Doubleday, 1970. 214 p. 22 cm. [BF1027.C3K3] 76-89071 5.95
1. Cayce, Edgar, 1877-1945. I. Oursler, William Charles, 1913- II. Title.

MILLARD, Joseph. 133.3'2'0924
Edgar Cayce; mystery man of miracles. Rev. ed. Greenwich, Conn., Fawcett Publications [1967] 223 p. 19 cm. (A Fawcett gold medal book) [BF1027.C3M5 1967] 68-2087
1. Cayce, Edgar, 1877-1945.

STEARN, Jess. 133.320924
Edgar Cayce, the sleeping prophet. [1st ed.] Garden City, N.Y., Doubleday, 1967. 280 p. 22 cm. [BF1027.C3S7] 66-24335
1. Cayce, Edgar, 1877-1945.

STEARN, Jess. 133.8'092'4 B
A prophet in his own country: the story of the young Edgar Cayce. New York, Morrow, 1974. 301 p. illus. 24 cm. [BF1027.C3S72] 74-700 ISBN 0-688-00258-7 7.95
1. Cayce, Edgar, 1877-1945. I. Title. BIP

STEARN, Jess. 133.8'092'4 B
A prophet in his own country; the story of the young Edgar Cayce. Boston, G. K. Hall, 1974. 575 p. 25 cm. Large print ed. [BF1027.C3S72 1974b] 74-14982 ISBN 0-8161-6239-5
1. Cayce, Edgar, 1877-1945. 2. Sight-saving books. I. Title.

STEARN, Jess 133.8'092'4 B
A prophet in his own country; the story of the young Edgar Cayce. With an epilque by Hugh Lynn Cayce. New York, Ballantine Books [1975, c1974] 309 p. illus. 18 cm. [BF1027.C3S72] 74-700 ISBN 0-345-24464-8 1.75 (pbk.)
1. Cayce, Edgar, 1877-1945. I. Title.

SUGRUE, Thomas, 1907-1953. v. 12
There is a river; the story of Edgar Cayce. Rev. ed. New York, Holt [1956, c1945] 453 p. front. (port.)
1. Cayce, Edgar, 1877-1945. 2. Clairvoyance. I. Title.

THERE is a river; v. 12
the story of Edgar Cayce. Rev. ed. New York, Holt [1956, c1945] 453p. front. (port.)
1. Cayoe, Edgar, 1877-1945. 2. Clairvoyance. I. Sugrue, Thomas, 1907-1953.

Cayce, Edgar, 1877-1945—Juvenile literature.

NEIMARK, Anne E. 133.8'092'4
With this gift : the story of Edgar Cayce / by Anne E. Neimark. 1st ed. New York : Morrow, 1978. 192 p. ; 22 cm. Includes index. Bibliography: p. 188. A biography of the psychic whose powers included long-distance diagnoses of illnesses and prescriptions for their cure. [BF1027.C3N44] 92 B 78-4159 ISBN 0-688-22147-5 : 6.95 ISBN 0-688-32147-X lib.bdg. : 6.43
1. Cayce, Edgar, 1877-1945—Juvenile literature. 2. Psychical research—Biography—Juvenile literature. I. Title. BIP

Cayley, George, bart, Sir 1773-1857.

PRITCHARD, John 926.2913 Laurence, 1885-
Sir George Cayley, the inventor of the aeroplane. New York, Horizon [1962, c.1961] 277p. illus. Bibl. 62-7958 6.50 bds.,
1. Cayley, George, bart, Sir 1773-1857. 2. Flying-machines. 3. Aeronautics—Hist. I. Title.

Cazalet, Victor Alexander, 1896-1943.

JAMES, Robert 941.082'092'4 Rhodes, 1933-
Victor Cazalet : a portrait / [by] Robert Rhodes James. London : Hamilton, 1976. xiv, 306 p., [8] p. of plates : 1 ill., ports. ; 23 cm. Includes bibliographical references and index. [DA574.C39J34 1976] 76-376022 ISBN 0-241-89405-0 : £5.95
1. Cazalet, Victor Alexander, 1896-1943. 2. Statesmen—Great Britain—Biography.

Cecchetti, Enrico, 1850-1928.

RACSTER, Olga. 792.8'092'4 B
The master of the Russian ballet : (the memoirs of Cav. Enrico Cecchetti) / by Olga Racster ; with an introd. by Anna Pavlova. New York : Da Capo Press, 1978. p. cm. (The Da Capo series in dance) Reprint of the 1922 ed. published by Hutchinson, London. [GV1785.C4R3 1978] 78-18777 ISBN 0-306-77589-1 lib.bdg. : 19.50
1. Cecchetti, Enrico, 1850-1928. 2. Dancers—Biography. I. Title. BIP

Cecil family.

BUTLER, Ewan 929.7
The Cecils. London, F. Muller [New York, Hillary. 1966, c.1964] 288p. illus., geneal. table (on lining papers) ports. 23cm. [DA306.C4B8] 65-50245 6.00
1. Cecil family. 2. Gt. Brit.—Hist.—Modern period, 1485- I. Title.

CECIL, David, Lord, 1902- 929.7'2
The Cecils of Hatfield House, an English ruling family. [1st U.S. ed.] Boston, Houghton Mifflin, 1973. 320 p. illus. 26 cm. Bibliography: p. 312. [DA306.C4C4] 73-175464 ISBN 0-395-17120-2 15.00
1. Cecil family. 2. Great Britain—History—Modern period, 1485- I. Title.

ROSE, Kenneth, 1924- 929'.2'0942
The later Cecils / Kenneth Rose. 1st U.S. ed. New York : Harper & Row, c1975. 406 p., [8] leaves of plates : ill. ; 25 cm. (A Cass Canfield book) Includes index. Bibliography: p. 333-338. [DA306.C4R67 1975b] 75-6355 ISBN 0-06-013599-9 : 12.95
1. Cecil family. I. Title.

Cecilia, Saint.

GREENE, Genard, Brother, 922.1 1921-
A song in her heart; a story of St. Cecilia. Illus. by Thomas Daugherty. Notre Dame, Ind., Dujarie Press [1951] 79 p. illus. 24 cm. [BX4700.C5G7] 52-18158
1. Cecilia, Saint. I. Title.

Cecilia, Sister,

CECILIA, Sister, 1911- 922.2437
The deliverance of Sister Cecilia, as told to William Brinkley. London, New York, Longmans, Green [1955] 344p. 19cm. [BX4705.C347A3 1955] 56-33592
I. Brinkley, William, 1917- II. Title.

CECILIA, Sister, 1911- 922.2437
The deliverance of Sister Cecilia, as told to William Brinkley. New York, Farrar, Straus and Young [1954] 360p. 22cm. [BX4705.C347A3] 54-11973
I. Brinkley, William W., 1913- II. Title.

Cela, Camilo Jose, 1916-

HISPANIC Institute in the v. 12 United States.
Camilo Jose Cela: vida y obra, bibliografia, antologia. New York, 1962. 177 p. illus.,

ports. (Hispanic Institute in the United States. Autores modernos) Includes bibliography. 64-20549
1. Cela, Camilo Jose, 1916- I. Title. II. Series.

Cellini, Benvenuto,

CELLINI, Benvenuto, 1500-1571 927.3
The autobiography. Tr. [from Italian] by John Addington Symonds. Introd. by John Charles Nelson. New York, Washington Sq. [c.1963] 427p. 18cm. (W590) .60 pap.,
I. Title.

CELLINI, Benvenuto, 1500-1571. 927.3
Autobiography; translated by John Addington Symonds, with an introd. by David B. Guralnik. Cleveland, Fine Editions Press [1952] 435 p. 21 cm. [NB623.C3S45 1952] 52-4477
I. Title.

CELLINI, Benvenuto, 1500-1571. 927.3
Autobiography. Tr. [from Italian] by Robert Hobart Cust, with 8 full-page illus., introd. by Raimondo Legame. New York, Dodd [c.1961] xvi, 547p. illus. (Great illustrated classics: Titan eds.) 61-15988 4.50
I. Cust, Robert Henry Hobart, 1861- tr. II. Title.

CELLINE, Benvenuto, 1500-1571 927.3
Autobiography of Benvenuto Cellum Tr. by John Addington Symonds. Garden City, N.Y., Doubleday [1960] 518p. (Dolphin bk. C 129) .95 pap.,
I. Symonds, John Addington, 1840-1893, tr. II. Title.

Celtes, Conradus, 1459-1508.

SPITZ, Lewis William, 1895- 928.79
Conrad Celtis, the German arch-humanist. Cambridge, Harvard University Press, 1957. x. 142 p. 22 cm. Bibliographical references included in "Notes" (p. 121-132) [PA8485.C48Z9] 57-9080
1. Celtes, Conradus, 1459-1508. I. Title.

Cendrars, Blaise, 1887-1961.

BOCHNER, Jay, 1940- 841'.9'12 B
Blaise Cendrars : discovery and re-creation / Jay Bochner. Toronto ; Buffalo : University of Toronto Press, c1977. p. cm. Includes index. Bibliography: p. [PQ2605.E55Z563] 77-2580 ISBN 0-8020-5352-1 : 22.50
1. Cendrars, Blaise, 1887-1961. 2. Authors, Swiss—20th century—Biography. BIP

Centers (Basketball)—United States—Biography—Juvenile literature.

ARMSTRONG, Robert, 1938- 796.32'3'0922 B
The centers / by Robert Armstrong. Mankato, MN : Creative Education, c1977. 47 p. : col. ill. ; 28 cm. (Stars of the NBA) Biographical sketches of five basketball centers: Kareem Abdul-Jabbar, Bob McAdoo, Dave Cowens, Wes Unseld, and Bill Walton. [GV884.A1A73] 920 76-44443 ISBN 0-87191-565-0 lib. bdg. 5.95
1. Centers (Basketball)—United States—Biography—Juvenile literature. I. Title. BIP

Centlivre, Susanna, 1667?-1723.

BOWYER, John Wilson, 1901- 822'.5 B
The celebrated Mrs. Centlivre. New York, Greenwood Press, 1968 [c1952] vii, 267 p. illus., port. 22 cm. "A bibliography of Mrs. Centlivre's writings": p. [253]-256. [PR3339.C6B6 1968] 68-9539
1. Centlivre, Susanna, 1667?-1723. I. Title. BIP

Central America—Biography.

TAPLIN, Glen W. 972'.00099 B
Middle American governors. Compiled by Glen W. Taplin. Metuchen, N.J., Scarecrow Press, 1972. viii, 196 p. 22 cm. Bibliography: p. 170-171. [F1426.T3] 73-185184 ISBN 0-8108-0465-4
1. Central America—Biography. 2. Mexico—Biography. I. Title.

Cepeda, Orlando.

CEPEDA, Orlando. 796.357'0924
My ups and downs in baseball, by Orlando Cepeda with Charles Einstein. New York, Putnam [1968] 191 p. 21 cm. ([Putnam sports shelf]) [GV865.C4A3] 68-15042
I. Einstein, Charles. II. Title.

CEPEDA, Orlando. 796.357
My ups and downs in baseball, by Orlando Cepeda with Charles Einstein. New York, Putnam [1968] 191 p. 21 cm. ([Putnam sports shelf]) The National League's most valuable player of the 1967 season relates the ups and downs of his career in baseball and his struggle to overcome the handicap of a crippled leg. [GV865.C4A3] AC 68
I. Einstein, Charles, joint author. II. Title.

Cerebral palsy—Biography.

SCHULTZE, Russell S. 362.1'9683600924 B
How many mountains? / Russell S. Schultze, with Willetta J. Balla. Nashville, Tenn. : Broadman Press, c1980. 141 p. : ill. ; 20 cm. [RC388.S38] 79-54921 ISBN 0-8054-5272-9 : 4.95
1. Cerebral palsy—Biography. 2. Schultze, Russell S. I. Balla, Willetta J., joint author. II. Title. BIP

Cerebral palsy—Personal narratives.

AYRAULT, Evelyn West, 1922- 920.9616836
Take one step. [1st ed.] Garden City, N. Y., Doubleday, 1963. 310 p. 22 cm. Autobiographical. [RC388.A9] 62-7599
1. Cerebral palsy—Personal narratives. I. Title.

MIERS, Earl Schenck, 1910- 616.8360924
The trouble bush. Chicago, Rand McNally [1966] 342 p. port. 22 cm. Autobiography. [RC388.M5] 66-22132
1. Cerebral palsy—Personal narratives. I. Title.

Cerf, Bennett Alfred, 1898-1971.

CERF, Bennett Alfred, 1898-1971. 070.5'092'4 B
At Random : the reminiscences of Bennett Cerf. 1st ed. New York : Random House, c1977. ix, 306 p. : ill. ; 25 cm. Includes index. [Z473.C45A36 1977] 77-1867 ISBN 0-394-47877-0 : 12.50
1. Cerf, Bennett Alfred, 1898-1971. 2. Publishers and publishing—United States—Biography. I. Title. BIP

Cermak, Anton Joseph, 1873-1933.

GOTTFRIED, Alex 923.273
Boss Cermak of Chicago: a study of political leadership. Seattle. Univ. of Wash. Pr. [c.]1962. 459p. illus. 24cm. Bibl. 61-15063 6.50
1. Cermak, Anton Joseph, 1873-1933. 2. Chicago—Pol. & govt. I. Title.

Cerutty, Percy Wells.

KELLY, Graeme 927.96
Mr. Controversial; the story of Percy Wells Cerutty. London, S. Paul [New Yochelle, N.Y., SportShelf, c.1964] 168p. illus., ports. 22cm. 64-7416 5.00 bds.,
1. Cerutty, Percy Wells. I. Title.

Cervantes, Alfonso J.

CERVANTES, Alfonso J. 309.2'62'0977866
Mr. Mayor / by A. J. Cervantes, with Lawrence G. Blochman; foreword by Hubert H. Humphrey Los Angeles : Nash Pub., c1974. 193 p., [1] leaf of plates : port. ; 22 cm. [F474.S2C47] 74-83035 ISBN 0-8402-1350-6 : 7.95
1. Cervantes, Alfonso J. 2. St. Louis—Politics and government. 3. Urban renewal—St. Louis. I. Blochman, Lawrence Goldtree, 1900- joint author. II. Title.

Cervantes Saavedra, Miguel de, 1547-1616.

ARBO, Sebastian Juan, 1902- 928.6
Cervantes: adventurer, idealist, and destiny's fool. [Rendered from the Spanish by Ilsa Barea] London. New York, Thames and Hudson [1955] x, 261p. 22cm. [PQ6337.A612] 56-2935
1. Cervantes Saavedra, Miguel de, 1547-1616. I. Title.

BELL, Aubrey Fitz Gerald, 1882- v. 12
Cervantes. New York, Collier Books [1961] 247 p. Includes bibliography. NUC66
1. Cervantes Saavedra, Miguel de, 1547-1616. I. Title.

BUSONI, Rafaello, 1900- 928.6
The man who was Don Quixote; the story of Miguel Cervantes. Written, illus. by Rafaello, editorially assisted by Johanna Johnston [New York, Avon, 1968,c.1958] 238p. illus 18cm. (Camelot bk., ZS133) [PQ6337.B8] .60 pap.,
1. Cervantes Saavedra, Miguel de, 1547-1616. I. Title.

BUSONI, Rafaello, 1900- 928.6
The man who was Don Quixote; the story of Miguel Cervantes. Written and illustrated by Rafaello Busoni, editorially assisted by Johanna Johnston. Englewood Cliffs, N. J., Prentice-Hall [1958] 209 p. illus. 25 cm. [PQ6337.B8] 58-13746
1. Cervantes Saavedra, Miguel de, 1547-1616. I. Title.

DIAZ-PLAJA, Fernando. 863'.3 B
Cervantes; the life of a genius. Translated from the Spanish by Sue Matz Soterakos. New York, Scribner [1970] xv, 144 p. 22 cm. Bibliography: p. 138-140. [PQ6337.D54] 79-121744 4.50
1. Cervantes, Saavedra Miguel, 1547-1616.

ENTWISTLE, William James, 1895- v. 12
Cervantes. Oxford, Clarendon Press [1965] 192 p. 66-47899
1. Cervantes Saavedra, Miguel de. I. Title. BIP

MACEOIN, Gary, 1909- 928.6
Cervantes. Milwaukee, Bruce [1950] v. 223 p. 22 cm. Bibliography: p. 215-219. [PQ6337.M13] 50-11175
1. Cervantes Saavedra, Miguel de, 1547-1616. I. Title.

MONDADORI (Arnoldo) editore. 863'.3 B
Cervantes; his life, his times, his works. Created by Arnoldo Mondadori editore. Translated from the Italian by Salvator Attanasio. Anthology by Thomas G. Bergin. New York, American Heritage Press [1970, c1968] 167 p. illus. (part col.), coat arms, facsim., col. ports. 22 cm. (Giants of world literature) Translation of Miguel de Cervantes. Includes bibliographical references. [PQ6337.M613 1970] 79-85204 ISBN 0-07-004854-1
1. Cervantes Saavedra, Miguel de, 1547-1616. I. Bergin, Thomas Goddard, 1904- comp.

OLIPHANT, Margaret Oliphant Wilson, 1828-1897. 863'.3 B
Cervantes. [Folcroft, Pa.] Folcroft Library Editions, 1974. p. cm. Reprint of the 1880 ed. published by W. Blackwood, Edinburgh, in series: Foreign classics for English readers. [PQ6337.O5 1974] 74-16137 17.50 (lib. bdg.).
1. Cervantes Saavedra, Miguel de, 1547-1616.

PREDMORE, Richard Lionel. 863'.3 B
Cervantes [by] Richard L. Predmore. New York, Dodd, Mead [1973] 224 p. illus. 27 cm. Bibliography: p. 214-215. [PQ6337.P7] 72-13587 ISBN 0-396-06797-2 15.00
1. Cervantes Saavedra, Miguel de, 1547-1616.

SCHEVILL, Rudolph, 1874-1946. 868.309
Cervantes. New York, F. Ungar Pub. Co. [1966] iv, 388 p. 21 cm. "Reprinted from the edition of 1919." Bibliography: p. 373-376. [PQ6337.S35 1966] 66-19467
1. Cervantes Saavedra, Miguel de, 1547-1616. BIP

WATTS, Henry Edward, 1826-1904. 863'.3 B
Life of Miguel de Cervantes. Ann Arbor, Mich., Plutarch Press, 1971. 185, xxiii p. 22 cm. Reprint of the 1891 ed. Bibliography: p. [i]-xxiii. [PQ6337.W2 1971] 79-141743
1. Cervantes Saavedra, Miguel de, 1547-1616. I. Title. BIP

Cervantes Saavedra, Miguel de, 1547-1616—Appreciation—Russia.

TURKEVICH, Ludmilla Buketoff. 863'.3 B
Cervantes in Russia / by Ludmilla Buketoff Turkevich. New York : Gordian Press, 1975, c1950. xv, 255 p. ; 22 cm. Reprint of the ed. published by Princeton University Press, Princeton, N.J., which was issued as no. 8 of Princeton publications in modern languages. Includes index. "A bibliography of the Russian translations of Cervantes' works": p. 227-249. [PQ6349.R9T8 1975] 75-31685 ISBN 0-87752-175-1
1. Cervantes Saavedra, Miguel de, 1547-1616—Appreciation—Russia. 2. Literature, Comparative—Spanish and Russian. 3. Literature, Comparative—Russian and Spanish. I. Title. II. Series: Princeton University. Princeton publications in modern languages ; no. 8. BIP

Cervantes Saavedra, Miguel de, 1547-1616—Bibliography.

FORD, Jeremiah Denis Matthias, 1873-1958, comp. 016.863'3
Cervantes : a tentative bibliography of his works and of the biographical and critical material concerning him / prepared by Jeremiah D. M. Ford and Ruth Lansing. Boston : Longwood Press, 1977. xii, 239 p. ; 22 cm. Reprint of the 1931 ed. published by Harvard University Press, Cambridge. Includes bibliographical references. [Z8158.F69 1977] [PQ6337] 77-13539 ISBN 0-89341-454-9 lib.bdg. : 20.00
1. Cervantes Saavedra, Miguel de, 1547-1616—Bibliography. I. Lansing, Ruth, joint author.

Cervantes Saavedra, Miguel de, 1547-1616—Biography.

BYRON, William. 863'.3 B
Cervantes, a biography / William Byron. 1st ed. Garden City, N.Y. : Doubleday, 1978. xiv, 583 p., [10] leaves of plates : ill. ; 24 cm. Includes index. Bibliography: p. [549]-560. [PQ6337.B9] 74-33633 ISBN 0-385-00279-3 : 14.50
1. Cervantes Saavedra, Miguel de, 1547-1616—Biography. 2. Authors, Spanish—17th century—Biography. I. Title.

CALVERT, Albert Frederick, 1872-1946. 863'.3 B
The life of Cervantes : with numerous portraits and reproductions from early editions of Don Quixote / by Albert F. Calvert. Tercentenary ed. Folcroft, Pa. : Folcroft Library Editions, 1976. p. cm. Reprint of the 1905 ed. published by the Bodley Head, London. Bibliography: p. [PQ6337.C2 1976] 76-10970 ISBN 0-8414-3637-1 lib. bdg. : 20.00
1. Cervantes Saavedra, Miguel de, 1547-1616—Biography. I. Title.

SMITH, Robinson, 1876- 863'.3 B
The life of Cervantes. [Folcroft, Pa.] Folcroft Library Editions, 1974. 121 p. front. 24 cm. Reprint of the 1914 ed. published by G. Routledge, London. Includes bibliographical references. [PQ6337.S6 1974b] 74-1099 ISBN 0-8414-7734-5 (lib. bdg.)
1. Cervantes Saavedra, Miguel de, 1547-1616—Biography. I. Title. BIP

Cerwin, Herbert,

CERWIN, Herbert, 1908- 659.20924
In search of something; the memoirs of a public relations man. With an introd. by Frank H. Bartholomew. Los Angeles, Sherbourne Press [1966] 318 p. ports. 22 cm. [CT275.C384A3] 66-26076
I. Title.

Cesnola, Luigi Palma di, 1832-1904.

MCFADDEN, Elizabeth. 708'.00924 B
The glitter & the gold; a spirited account of the Metropolitan Museum of Art's first director, the audacious and high-handed Luigi Palma di Cesnola. New York, Dial Press, 1971. ix, 277 p. illus. 22 cm. Bibliography: p. [263]-267. [N406.C46M3] 78-131178 7.95
1. Cesnola, Luigi Palma di, 1832-1904. I. Title.

Cettiwayo, King of Zululand, ca. 1826-1884.

CETTIWAYO, King of Zululand, ca.1826-1884. 968'.4 B
A Zulu king speaks : statements made by Cetshwayo kaMpande on the history and customs of his people / edited by C. de B. Webb and J. B. Wright. Pietermaritzburg : University of Natal, 1978. xxiv, 126 p., [16] leaves of plates : ill. ; 21 cm. (Reprint series - Killie Campbell Africana Library ; no. 3) Includes bibliographical references and index. [DT878.Z9C524] 79-314629 ISBN 0-86980-153-8 : 17.00
1. Cettiwayo, King of Zululand, ca. 1826-1884. 2. Zulu War, 1879—Sources. 3. Zulus—History—Sources. 4. Zululand—History—Sources. 5. Zulus—Kings and rulers—Biography. I. Webb, Colin de B. II. Wright, John B. III. Title. IV. Series: Pietermaritzburg. University of Natal. Killie Campbell Africana Library, Durban. Reprint series — Killie Campbell Africana Library ; no. 3.
Distributed by Verry, Mystic, CT

Cezanne, Paul, 1839-1906.

BEUCKEN, Jean de, 1905- 927.5
Cezanne, a pictorial biography. Translated and adapted by Lothian Small. New York, Viking Press [1962] 143p. illus. (part col.) ports. 24cm. (A Studio book) Translation of Cezanne, eine Bildblographie. The original french ed. has title: Un portrait de Cezanne. [ND553.C33B453] 61-8824
1. Cezanne, Paul, 1839-1906. I. Title.

CEZANNE, Paul, 1839-1906. 759.4
Cezanne. Text and notes by Keith Roberts. New York, Tudor Pub. Co. [1967] 36 p., 92 col. plates. 18 cm. Bibliography: p. 15. [ND553.C33R59] 67-19840
I. Roberts, Keith, 1937- II. Title.

CEZANNE, Paul, 1839-1906. 759.4 B
Paul Cezanne, letters / edited by John Rewald ; [translated from the French by Marguerite Kay]. 4th ed. rev. and enl. Oxford [Eng.] : B. Cassirer, 1976. 374 p. ; 22 cm. "The letters of Zola represent nearly one-third of the whole correspondence." Includes index. [ND553.C33A212 1976] 77-359768 ISBN 0-85181-061-6 : £6.50
1. Cezanne, Paul, 1839-1906. 2. Painters—France—Correspondence. I. Rewald, John, 1912- ed. II. Zola, Emile, 1840-1902. III. Kay, Marguerite, tr.

DOWNER, Marion. 927.5
Paul Cezanne. Illustrated with half-tones. New York, Lothrop, Lee & Shepard [1951] 117 p. illus. 21 cm. [ND553.C33D63] 51-8762
1. Cezanne, Paul, 1839-1906. I. Title.

ELGAR, Frank. 759.4 B
Cezanne. New York, N.N. Abrams [196-] 287 p. illus. (part col.) 22 cm. Bibliography: p. 273-274. [ND553.C33E483 1960z] 75-76013
1. Cezanne, Paul, 1839-1906. I. Title.

ELGAR, Frank. 759.4 B
Cezanne / Frank Elgar. New York : Praeger Publishers, 1975. 287 p. : ill. (some col.) ; 21 cm. (Praeger world of art paperbacks) (A Praeger world of art profile) Translated from the French. Includes index. Bibliography: p. 273-274. [ND553.C33E483 1975] 75-24042 ISBN 0-275-71700-3 pbk. : 5.95
1. Cezanne, Paul, 1839-1906. I. Title.

FRY, Roger Eliot, 1866-1934. v. 12
Cezanne, a study of his development. Introd. by Alfred Werner. [2d Noonday paper-bound ed.] 88 p. illus., 51 plates. 21 cm. "Reprinted from the second edition by arrangement with the Macmillan Company." 65-30929
1. Cezanne, Paul, 1839-1906. I. Title.

HANSON, Lawrence. 759.4
Mortal victory; a biography of Paul Cezanne. [1st ed.] New York, Holt, Rinehart and Winston [1960] 245 p. illus. 22 cm. Includes bibliographies. [ND553.C33H3] 60-9054
1. cezanne, Paul, 1839-1906. I. Title.

HUYGHE, Rene 759.4
Cezanne. [Tr. from French by Kenneth Martin Leake] New York, Abrams [1963] 87p. illus. 19cm. 62-15678 1.95
1. Cezanne, Paul, 1839-1906. I. Title.

LINDSAY, Jack, 1900- 759.4 B
Cezanne; his life and art. [Greenwich, Conn.] New York Graphic Society [1969] viii, 360 p. illus. (part col.), ports. 25 cm. Title on spine: Cezanne; life and art. Bibliography: p. 354-358. [ND553.C33L5 1969b] 76-77230 12.50
1. Cezanne, Paul, 1839-1906.

MACK, Gerstle, 1894- 759.4 B
Paul Cezanne / Gerstle Mack. New York : Octagon Books, 1976, c1935. xiv, 437, xxiv p., [24] leaves of plates : ill. ; 24 cm. Reprint of the ed. published by Knopf, New York. Includes index. Bibliography: p. 435-437. [ND553.C33M3 1976] 76-7909 ISBN 0-374-95241-8 : 20.00
1. Cezanne, Paul, 1839-1906.

MCLEAVE, Hugh. 759.4 B
A man and his mountain : a biography of Paul Cezanne / by Hugh McLeave. New York : Macmillan, 1977. p. cm. [ND553.C33M33] 77-9511 ISBN 0-02-583670-6 : 9.95
1. Cezanne, Paul, 1839-1906. 2. Painters—France—Biography. I. Title. **BIP**

MICHELI, Mario de. 759.4
Cezanne. [1st American ed. Translated from the Italian by Pearl Sanders] New York, Grosset & Dunlap [1967, c1968] 39, [80] p. col. illus. 18 cm. (The New Grosset art library, 10) On cover: Cezanne; the life and work of the artist. Bibliography: p. 29-31. [ND553.C33M513 1968] 68-12744
1. Cezanne, Paul, 1839-1906.

PERRUCHOT, Henri, 1917- 927.5
Cezanne. Tr. [from French] by Humphrey Hare. New York, Grosset [1963, c.1958, 1961] 346p. illus. 21cm. (Universal lib. UL149) Bibl. 2.25 pap.,
1. Cezanne, Paul, 1839-1906. I. Title.

TAYLOR, Basil. 759.4
Cezanne. Revised ed. Feltham, Hamlyn, 1968. 39 p. 48 plates. 54 illus. (48 col.). 28 cm. (The Colour library of art) Bibliography: p. 30. [ND553.C33T38 1968] 79-499550 17/6
1. Cezanne, Paul, 1839-1906.

Ch'i, Pai-shih, 1861-1957.

CH'I, Pai-shih, 1861-1957. 759.951
Ch'i Pai-shih, the versatile genius = I yuan ch'i ying / introd. by C. C. Wang. 1st ed. Fort Thomas, Ky. : Pine Studios, 1976. [16] p., 50 leaves of plates : col. ill. ; 31 cm. Introd. in English and Chinese. [ND2070.C45A43] 75-17069 40.00
1. Ch'i, Pai-shih, 1861-1957. I. Title. II. Title: I yuan ch'i ying.

Ch'in Shih-huang-ti, Emperor of China, 259-210 B.C.

THE First Emperor of China / edited by Li Yu-ning. 931'.00994 B White Plains, N.Y. : International Arts and Sciences Press, [1975] lxxiii, 357 p. : ill. ; 24 cm. (The Politics of historiography) Includes bibliographical references. [DS747.5.F57] 74-15390 ISBN 0-87332-067-0 : 15.00
1. Ch'in Shih-huang-ti, Emperor of China, 259-210 B.C. I. Li, Yu-ning.

Ch'ing Hsuan-t'ung, Emperor of China, 1906-1967.

BRACKMAN, Arnold C. 951'.03'0924 B
The last emperor / by Arnold C. Brackman. New York : Scribner, [1975] xii, 360 p. ; 24 cm. Includes index. Bibliography: p. 341-352. [DS773.C518B7] 75-1427 ISBN 0-684-14233-3 : 12.50
1. Ch'ing Hsuan-t'ung, Emperor of China, 1906-1967. I. Title.

Ch'ing Hsuan-tsung, Emperor of China, 1782-1850.

GUTZLAFF, Karl Friedrich August, 1803-1851. 951'.03'0924 B
The life of Taou-Kwang, late Emperor of China: with memoirs of the court of Peking; including a sketch of the principal events in the history of the Chinese empire during the last fifty years, by the late Charles Gutzlaff. Wilmington, Del., Scholarly Resources [1972] xvi, 279 p. 23 cm. Reprint of the 1852 ed. published by Smith, Elder, London. [DS757.G83 1972] 72-79825 ISBN 0-8420-1351-2
1. Ch'ing Hsuan-tsung, Emperor of China, 1782-1850. I. Title.

Ch'ing Sheng-tsu, Emperor of China, 1654-1722.

CH'ING Sheng-tsu, Emperor of China, 1654-1722. 951'.03'0924 B
Emperor of China; self portrait of K'ang Hsi, by Jonathan D. Spence. New York, Vintage Books [1975, c1974] xxv, 217, viii p. illus. 21 cm. Bibliography: p. [208]-[218] [DS754.4.C53A33 1975] 74-17106 ISBN 0-394-71411-3
1. Ch'ing Sheng-tsu, Emperor of China, 1654-1722. I. Spence, Jonathan D. II. Title.

CH'ING Sheng-tsu, Emperor of China, 1654-1722. 951'.03'0924 B
Emperor of China; self portrait of K'ang Hsi, 1654-1722, by Jonathan D. Spence. [1st ed.] New York, Knopf, 1974. p. cm. Bibliography: p. [DS754.4.C53A33 1974] 73-20743 ISBN 0-394-48835-0 7.95
1. Ch'ing Sheng-tsu, Emperor of China, 1654-1722. I. Spence, Jonathan D. II. Title.
Distributed by Longman, New York, 8.85.

KESSLER, Lawrence D. 951'.03'0924 B
Kang-hsi and the consolidation of Ching rule, 1661-1684 Lawrence D. Kessler. Chicago : University of Chicago Press, 1976. xi, 251 p. ; 23 cm. Includes index. Bibliography: p. 229-241. [DS754.4.C53K47] 75-20897 ISBN 0-226-43203-3 : 13.50
1. Ch'ing Sheng-tsu, Emperor of China, 1654-1722. 2. China—History—K'ang-hsi, 1662-1722. I. Title. **BIP**

WU, Silas H. L., 1929- 951'.03'0924 B
Passage to power : K'ang-hsi and his heir apparent, 1661-1722 / Silas H. L. Wu. Cambridge : Harvard University Press, 1979. xv, 252 p. : maps ; 24 cm. (Harvard East Asian series ; 91) Includes index. Bibliography: p. 227-240. [DS754.4.C53W8] 79-4191 ISBN 0-674-65625-3 : 22.50
1. Ch'ing Sheng-tsu, Emperor of China, 1654-1722. 2. China—History—K'ang-hsi, 1662-1722. I. Title. II. Series. **BIP**

Chogyam Trungpa, Trungpa Tulku, 1939—

†CHOGYAM Trungpa, Trungpa Tulku, 1939- 294.3'6'10924 B
Born in Tibet / by Chogyam Trungpa, the eleventh Trungpa Tulku, as told to Esme Cramer Roberts ; with a foreword by Marco Pallis. 3d ed. Boulder, Colo. : Shambhala ; [New York] : distributed by Random House, 1977, c1966. 280 p., [8] leaves of plates : ill. ; 22 cm. (The Clear light series) Includes index. [BQ946.O347A32 1977] 76-53358 ISBN 0-87773-106-3 : 4.95
1. Chogyam Trungpa, Trungpa Tulku, 1939- 2. Lamas—Tibet—Biography. I. Roberts, Esme Cramer, joint author. II. Title.

Ch'ung Hsuan-t'ung, Emperor of China, 1906-1967.

JOHNSTON, Reginald Fleming, Sir, 1874-1938. 951.04'1
Twilight in the Forbidden City. With a pref. by the Emperor. Wilmington, Del., Scholarly Resources [1973] 486 p. illus. 23 cm. Reprint of the 1934 ed. published by V. Gollancz, London. Includes bibliographical references. [DS774.J6 1973] 72-79826 ISBN 0-8420-1378-4 31.00
1. Ch'ung Hsuan-t'ung, Emperor of China, 1906-1967. 2. China—History—1912-1937. I. Title.

Chaikovskii, Petr Il'ich, 1840-1893.

ABRAHAM, Gerald Ernest Heal, 1904- 780'.92'4 B
Tchaikovsky : a short biography / by Gerald Abraham. Westport, Conn. : Hyperion Press, 1979. p. cm. (Core collection reprints) Reprint of the 1945 ed. published by Duckworth, London. "Tchaikovsky's compositions": p. [ML410.C4A53 1979] 78-58996 ISBN 0-88355-672-3 : lib.bdg. : 13.50
1. Chaikovski, Petr, Ilich, 1840-1893. 2. Composers—Russia—Biography.

BOWEN, Catherine Drinker, 1897- 780'.92'4 B
Beloved friend : the story of Tchaikowsky and Nadejda von Meck / by Catherine Drinker Bowen and Barbara von Meck. Westport, Conn. : Greenwood Press, 1976. p. cm. Includes index. "Chronological list of Tchaikowsky's compositions": p. [ML410.C4A35 1976] 73-3923 ISBN 0-8371-6861-9 lib.bdg. : 20.50
1. Chaikovskii, Petr Il'ich, 1840-1893. 2. Meck, Nadezhda Filaretovna Frolovskaia von, 1831-1894. I. Meck, Barbara Karpoff von, 1889- joint author. II. Title. **BIP**

BOWEN, Catherine Drinker, 1897- 927.8
"Beloved friend": the story of Tchaikowsky and Nadejda von Meck, by Catherine Drinker Bowen and Barbara Von Meck. Boston, Little, Brown [1961, c1937] 484 p. ports., music. 22 cm. Largely excerpts from the correspondence between Tchaikowsky and Nadejda von Meck, translated by Barbara von Meck from the original Russian edition (Moscow, 1934-6) and given by her, with notes and recollections of persons and places involved, to Mrs. Bowen, who wrote the connecting narrative. "Chronological list of Tchaikowsky's compositions": p. 465-475. [ML410.C4B67 1961] 61-14926
1. Chaikovskii, Petr Il'ich, 1840-1893. 2. Meck, Nadezhda Filaretovna Froloviskaia von, 1831-1894. I. Meck, Barbara Karpoff von, 1889- joint author. II. Title.

CHAIKOVSKII, Modest Il'ich, 1850-1916 780'.92'4 B
The life & letters of Peter Ilich Tchaikovsky, by Modeste Tchaikovsky. Edited from the Russian, with an introd. by Rosa Newmarch. New York, Vienna House [1973] 2 v. (xi, 782 p.) illus. 21 cm. Reprint of the 1906 ed. published by J. Lane, London. An abridged translation. Cf. pref. Appendices (p. 726-772): A. Chronological list of Tchaikovsky's compositions from 1866-1893.—B. The plots of Tchaikovsky's chief operas.—C. Extracts from German press notices during Tchaikovsky's tours abroad in 1888 and 1889. [ML410.C4C3 1973] 73-86365 ISBN 0-8443-0034-9 4.45 per vol.
1. Chaikovskii, Petr Il'ich, 1840-1899. I. Newmarch, Rosa Harriet (Jeaffreson) 1857-1940, tr. II. Title. **BIP**

CHAIKOVSKII, Modest Il'ich, 1850-1916. 780'.924 B
The life and letters of Peter Ilich Tchailkovsky, by Modeste Tchaikovsky. Edited from the Russian with an introd. by Rosa Newmarch. New York, Haskell House Publishers, 1970. 2 v. (xi, 782 p.) illus., music, ports. 22 cm. Reprint of the 1905 ed. [ML410.C4C3 1970] 72-95443

1. Chaikovskii, Petr Il'ich, 1840-1893.

CHAIKOVSKII, Petr Il'ich, 1840-1893. 780'.92'4 B
The diaries of Tchaikovsky. Translated from the Russian, with notes by Wladimir Lakond. Westport, Conn., Greenwood Press [1973] 385 p. illus. 22 cm. Reprinted from the ed. of 1945. [ML410.C4A22 1973] 79-138104 ISBN 0-8371-5680-7 19.50
1. Chaikovskii, Petr Il'ich, 1840-1893. I. Lake, Walter, tr. II. Title. **BIP**

EVANS, Edwin, 1874-1945. 927.8
Tchaikovsky: complete & unabridged. New York, Avon, [1935, c.1960] 191p. music, catalog of works. (Bard 10: Avon G-10) Bibl. .50 pap.,
1. Chaikovskii, Petr Il ich, 1840-1893. I. Title.

EVANS, Edwin, 1874-1945 927.8
Tchaikovsky. Rev. by Gerald Abraham. New York, Collier [c.1963] 192p. illus. 18cm. (Collier bks., BS171V. Great composers ser.) Bibl. 62-20835 1.50 pap.,
1. Chaikovskii, Petr Il'ich, 1840-1893. I. Title.

EVANS, Edwin, 1874-1945. 927.8
Tchaikovsky, Rev. by Gerald Abraham. [First Collier Books ed.] New York, Collier Books [1963] 192 p. illus. 18 cm. (Collier books, BS171V. Great composers series) Includes list of compositions and bibliography. [ML410.C4E8] 62-20835 MN
1. Chalkovskll, Petr Il'ich, 1840-1893. I. Title.

EVANS, Edwin, 1874-1945. 780.924 (B)
Tchaikovsky. Revised ed. London, Dent; New York, Farrar, Straus & Giroux, 1966. ix, 226 p. front. (port.) illus. (music) 7 plates (incl. ports., facsims.) tables. 19 1/2 cm. (The Master musicians series) "Catalogue of works": p. 203-212. Bibliography: p. 220. [Ml410.C4E8] 66-70309
1. Chalkovskll, Petr Il'ich, 1840-1893. I. Title. II. Series. III. Series: The Master musicians

HANSON, Lawrence. 780.924 B
Tchaikovsky: the man behind the music, by Lawrence and Elisabeth Hanson. New York, Dodd, Mead [1966] xiv, 385 p. illus., facsims. (music), ports. 24 cm. Bibliography: p. 369-373. [ML410.C4H35 1966] 66-13606
1. Chaikovskii, Petr Il'ich, 1840-1893. I. Hanson, Elisabeth M., joint author. II. Title.

HOFMANN, Rostislav, 1915- 780.8
Tchaikovsky [by] Michel R. Hofmann. Tr. [from French] by Angus Heriot. London, J. Calder [New York, Hillary House, 1966] 192p. illus., facsims., music, ports. 21cm. (Illus. Calderbk., CB. 59) Orig. pub. in French in 1959. Bibl. [ML410.C4H623] 65-53191 4.00 bds.,
1. Chaikovskii, Petr Il'ich, 1840-1893. I. Title.

NEWMARCH, Rosa Harriet (Jeaffreson) 1857-1940. 780'.924 B
Tchaikovsky; his life and works, with extracts from his writings, and the diary of his tour abroad in 1888, by Rosa Newmarch. New York, Greenwood Press [1969] ix, 232 p. facsim., port. 18 cm. "Originally published in 1900." [ML410.C4N3 1969] 69-14011
1. Chaikovskii, Petr Il'ich, 1840-1893. I. Chaikovskii, Petr Il'ich, 1840-1893.

NEWMARCH, Rosa Harriet (Jeaffreson) 1857-1940. 780'.924
Tchaikovsky; his life and works, with extracts from his writings, and the diary of his tour abroad in 1888, by Rosa Newmarch. Edited with a complete classific account of works, copious analyses of important works, analytical and other indices; also, supplement dealing with The relation of Tchaikovsky to art-questions of the day, by Edwin Evans. New York, Haskell House Publishers, 1969. xvi, 418 p. music, port. 23 cm. "First published 1900." [ML410.C4N3 1969b] 68-25298
1. Chaikovskii, Petr Il'ich, 1840-1893. I. Chaikovskii, Petr Il'ich, 1840-1893. II. Evans, Edwin, 1844-1923.

RUSSIAN symphony; 780'.924
thoughts about Tchaikovsky, by Dmitri Shostakovich and others. Freeport, N.Y., Books for Libraries Press [1969, c1947] 271 p. port. 23 cm. (Essay index reprint series) First published in 1947. Contents.Contents.—Thoughts about Tchaikovsky, by D. Shostakovich.—The great Russian composer, by B. Assafyev (I. Glebov).—Tchaikovsky, the man and his outlook, by Y. Keldysh.—Operas, by B. Yarustovsky.—Symphonies, by D. Zhitomirsky.—The ballets of Tchaikovsky, by V. Yakovlev.—Chamber music, by A. Alshvang.—The archives of the Tchaikovsky museum, by K. Davidova.—List of Tchaikovsky's works for the stage (p. 213-263)—Literary works (p. 265-267) [ML410.C4R8 1969] 78-86781
1. Chaikovskii, Petr Il'ich, 1840-1893. I. Shostakovich, Dmitrii Dmitrievich, 1906-

VOLKOFF, Vladimir. 780'.92'4 B
Tchaikovsky : a self-portrait / Vladimir Volkoff. Boston : Crescendo Pub. Co., c1975. 348 p. [6] leaves of plates : ill. ; 23 cm. Includes index. Bibliography: p. 337-338. [ML410.C4V57] 73-84133 ISBN 0-87597-088-5 : 15.00
1. Chaikovskii, Petr Il'ich, 1840-1893. **BIP**

WARRACK, John Hamilton, 1928- 780'.92'4 B
Tchaikovsky [by] John Warrack. New York, C. Scribner's Sons [1973] 287 p. illus. 26 cm. "Comprehensive list of works": p. 271-279. [ML410.C4W36] 73-7216 ISBN 0-684-13558-2 14.95
1. Chaikovskii, Petr Il'ich, 1840-1893.

Chaikovskii, Petr Il'ich, 1840-1893.

WHEELER, Opal. 927.8
The story of Peter Tschaikowsky; illustrated by Christine Price. [1st ed.] New York, Dutton, 1953- For children, with excerpts from his music arr. for the piano. [ML3930.C4W5] 53-10875
1. Chaikovskii, Petr Il'ich, 1840-1893. 2. Music—Juvenile literature. I. Title.

Chaadaev, Petr IAkovlevich, 1794-1856.

MCNALLY, Raymond T., 1931- 197'.2 B
Chaadayev and his friends; an intellectual history of Peter Chaadayev and his Russian contemporaries [by] Raymond T. McNally. Tallahassee, Fla., Diplomatic Press [1971] 315 p. port. 23 cm. Bibliography: p. [233]-303. [B4238.C5M33] 70-150297 ISBN 0-910512-11-6
1. Chaadaev, Petr IAkovlevich, 1794-1856. I. Title. **BIP**

Chabrol, Claude, 1930-

WOOD, Robin. 791.43'0233'0924
Claude Chabrol [by] Robin Wood [and] Michael Walker. [New York] Praeger [1970] 144 p. illus., ports. 18 cm. (Praeger film library) "Filmography": p. 140-143. [PN1998.A3C347 1970] 73-129352 4.95
1. Chabrol, Claude, 1930- I. Walker, Michael, joint author.

Chadwick, Edwin, Sir, 1800-1890.

FINER, Samuel Edward. 354.42'008'4'0924 B
The life and times of Sir Edwin Chadwick, by S. E. Finer. New York, Barnes & Noble [1970] x, 555 p. illus., ports. 23 cm. Reprint of the 1952 ed. Bibliography: p. 516-540. [RA424.5.C5F55 1970] 71-13048 ISBN 0-389-03963-2
1. Chadwick, Edwin, Sir, 1800-1890. 2. Public health—Great Britain—History. 3. Great Britain—Social conditions—19th century. I. Title.

Chadwick, Elizabeth Bigley, 1857-1907.

CROSBIE, John S., 1920- 364.1'63 B
The incredible Mrs. Chadwick : the most notorious woman of her age / by John S. Crosbie. Toronto ; New York : McGraw-Hill Ryerson, c1975. 240 p., [4] leaves of plates : ill. ; 23 cm. [HV6695.C88] 75-327150 ISBN 0-07-082194-1 : 7.95
1. Chadwick, Elizabeth Bigley, 1857-1907. I. Title.

Chadwick, Margaret Lee.

CHADWICK, Margaret Lee. 370'.92'4 B
Looking at the sunset upside down : the autobiography of Margaret Lee Chadwick. Corte Madera, Calif. : Omega Books, c1976. 173 p. : ill. ; 23 cm. [LA2317.C45A34] 76-18615 ISBN 0-89353-006-9 : 6.50
1. Chadwick, Margaret Lee. 2. Educators—United States—Biography. I. Title.

Chaffee, Allane.

CHAFFEE, Allane. 973'.0994
Tomorrow's echo / by Allane Chaffee. Huntsville, Ala. : Strode Publishers, c1979. 143 p. : ill. ; 24 cm. [CT275.C43A35] 78-73691 ISBN 0-87397-144-2 : 7.95
1. Chaffee, Allane. 2. United States—Biography. 3. Farm life—United States. I. Title.

Chaffee, Burns,

CHAFFEE, Burns, 1880- 926.1
My first eighty years; the life story of a California surgeon. With a foreword by Merton E. Hill. Los Angeles. Westernlore Press, 1960. 264p. illus. 21cm. [R154.C317A3] 60-53399
I. Title.

Chaffin family.

ABNER Chaffin of Jackson County, Tennessee, and sons, Bailaam, Elias, Joseph, William: 9292
an account of their migrations to Missouri, Illinois, and Montana. Related families: Albert, Fox, Van Oss, Vaughn, Wilkerson, Young. Compilers: Carl Bert Albert [and others] [Provo? Utah] 1966. v, 190 p. maps. 30 cm. Preface signed: Olive Chaffin Peterson. [CS71.C436 1966] 66-9132
1. Chaffin family. I. Albert, Carl Bert, 1908- II. Peterson, Olive May (Chaffin) 1923-

Chagall, Marc, 1887-

ALEXANDER, Sidney, 1912- 759.7 B
Marc Chagall : the artist with seven fingers / by Sidney Alexander. New York : Putnam, c1978. p. cm. Includes index. [ND699.C5A67 1978] 77-16526 15.00
1. Chagall, Marc, 1887- 2. Painters—Russian Republic—Biography.

BIDERMANAS, Izis. 709'.24
The world of Marc Chagall. Photographed by Izis Bidermanas. Text by Roy McMullen. Garden City, N.Y., Doubleday [1968] 267 p. illus. (part col.) 34 cm. At head of title: Izis. Bibliography: p. 264. [ND699.C5B5] 68-20454 25.00
1. Chagall, Marc, 1887- I. McMullen, Roy.

CHAGALL, Marc 927.5
My life. Translated from the French by Elisabeth Abbott. New York, Orion Press [c.1960] 173p. illus. 22cm. 60-8361 6.00
I. Title.

CHAGALL, Marc, 1887- 927.5
My life. Translated from the French by Elisabeth Abbott. New York, Orion Press [1960] 173p. illus. 22cm. [ND699.C5A233] 60-8361
I. Title.

COGNIAT, Raymond, 1896- 759.7
Chagall, by Raymond Cogniat. [Translated from the French by Anne Ross] New York, Crown Publisher [1965] 95 p. illus. (part col.) plates (part mounted col.) 29 cm. Bibliography: p. 95. [ND699.C5C63] 65-8841
1. Chagall, Marc, 1887-

CRESPELLE, Jean Paul. 759.7
Chagall. Translated from the French by Benita Eisler. [1st American ed.] New York, Coward-McCann [1970] 287 p. illus., ports. 22 cm. Translation of Chagall, l'amour, le reve, et la vie. Bibliography: p. 275-276. [ND699.C5C713 1970] 76-104686 7.95
1. Chagall, Marc, 1887-

ERBEN, Walter 759.7
Marc Chagall [Tr. by Michael Bullock] Rev. ed. New York, Praeger [1966] 166p. illus. (pt. mounted col.) ports. 26cm. [ND699.C5E713 1966] 66-21776 10.00
1. Chagall, Marc, 1887- I. Title.

GREENFELD, Howard. 92
Marc Chagall. With reproductions of the artist's work in color and black and white. Chicago, Follett Pub. Co. [1967] 192 p. illus. (part col.), ports. 25 cm. Bibliography: p. 189. A biography of the Russian-born painter famous for his dream-like paintings, use of brilliant colors, and his creation of the stained glass Jerusalem Windows for a synagogue. [ND699.C5G7] AC 67
1. Chagall, Marc, 1887-

MARC Chagall. 759.7
[Translated by Michael Bullock from the German ed.] New York, Praeger [1957] 158 p. illus. (part mounted col.) port. 26 cm. [ND699.C5E7] [ND699.C5E7] 927.5 57-12449 57-12449
1. Chagall, Marc, 1887- I. Erben, Walter.

NEGRI, Renata. 709'.2'4
Chagall / by Renata Negri. 1st U.S. ed. New York : Avenel Books ; distributed by Crown Publishers, 1979. p. cm. [N6999.C46N4313 1979] 78-71515 ISBN 0-517-27788-3 pbk. : 4.98
1. Chagall, Marc, 1887- 2. Artists—Russian Republic—Biography.

RABOFF, Ernest Lloyd. 760
Marc Chagall, by Ernest Raboff. Garden City, N.Y., Doubleday, 1968. [31] p. illus. (part col.) 29 cm. (Art for children) A Gemini-Smith book. A brief biography of this twentieth-century artist and an explanation of his philosophy of art are followed by analyses of twelve of his paintings. Includes color reproductions of the paintings. [ND699.C5R3] AC 68
1. Chagall, Marc, 1887- I. Title. **BIP**

VENTURI, Lionello, 1885- [759.7] 927.5
Chagall: [biographical and critical study. Translated by S. J. C. Harrison and James Emmons. New York] Skira [1956] 122 p. mounted col. illus. 19 cm. (The Taste of our time, v. 18) Bibliography: p. 108-[113] [ND699.C5V42] 56-10713
1. Chagall, Marc, 1887- I. Title.

VENTURI, Lionello, 1885-1961. 927.5
Chagall: [biographical and critical study. Translated by S. J. C. Harrison and James Emmons. New York] Skira [1956] 122 p. mounted col. illus. 19 cm. (The Taste of our time, v. 18) Bibliography: p. 108-[113] [ND699.C5V42] 759.7 56-10713
1. Chagall, Marc, 1887-

Chagall, Marc, 1887- —Juvenile literature.

GREENFELD, Howard. 759.7 B
Marc Chagall. With reproductions of the artist's work in color and black and white. Chicago, Follett Pub. Co. [1967] 192 p. illus. (part col.), ports. 25 cm. Bibliography: p. 189. [ND699.C5G7] 68-10479
1. Chagall, Marc, 1887- —Juvenile literature.

RABOFF, Ernest Lloyd. 760'.0924 (J)
Marc Chagall, by Ernest Raboff. Garden City, N.Y., Doubleday, 1968. 1 v. (unpaged) illus. (part col.) 29 cm. (Art for children) (A Gemini-Smith book.) [ND699.C5R3] 68-26549 3.95
1. Chagall, Marc, 1887- —Juvenile literature.

Chaitanya, 1486-1534.

KRSHNADASA Kaviraja, b.1518or19. 294.5'6'3 B
Sri Caitanya-caritamrta of Krsnadasa Kaviraja Gosvami : with the original Bengali text, Roman transliterations, synonyms, translation and elaborate

purports / [by] A. C. Bhaktivedanta Swami. New York : Bhaktivedanta Book Trust, c1973- v. : col. ill., map ; 27 cm. Includes index. [BL1245.V36K7713 1973] 74-193363 ISBN 0-912776-51-X (v. 2)
1. Chaitanya, 1486-1534. I. Bhaktivedanta Swami, A. C., 1896- ed. II. Title.

Chaitanya, 1486-1534—Juvenile literature.

GREENE, Joshua. 294.5'6'30924 B
Readings in Vedic literature for children / edited by Joshua Greene ; illustrated by Jan Steward, Theresa Gorman, and Patrick Wire. 1st ed. New York : Bala Books, 1977. p. cm. A retelling of stories from the ancient scriptures of India, the Shrimad-Bhagavatam and the Chaitanya-charitamrita, the former describing the pastimes of Krishna and the latter relating the life of Chaitanya Mahaprabhu. [BL1245.V36G73] 92 77-17485 5.95
1. Chaitanya, 1486-1534—Juvenile literature. 2. Hindus in India—Biography—Juvenile literature. 3. Krishna—Juvenile literature. I. Steward, Jan. II. Gorman, Theresa. III. Wire, Patrick. IV. Title. BIP

Chaka, Zulu chief, 1787?-1828.

KEATING, Bern. 968'.03'0924 B
Chaka, King of the Zulus. New York, Putnam [1968] 126 p. 21 cm. (Lives to remember) A biography of the South African shepherd boy whose cunning and intelligence made him a powerful Zulu chief in the early nineteenth century, but whose extreme cruelty brought his ruin. [DT878.Z9K4 1968] 92 AC 68
1. Chaka, Zulu chief, 1787-1828. I. Title.

RITTER, E. A., 1890- 923.1683
Shaka Zulu; the rise of the Zulu Empire. [1st American ed.] New York, Putnam [1957, c1955] 383 p. illus. 22 cm. [DT878.Z9R68 1957] 57-6735
1. Chaka, Zulu chief, 1787?-1828. 2. Zulus—History.

RITTER, E. A., 1890- 968.4 [B]
Shaka Zulu; the rise of the Zulu Empire. New York, New American Lib. [1973, c.1955] xx, 21-407 p. illus. 18 cm. (Mentor Book, MJ1231) [DT878.Z9R68] 1.95 (pbk.)
1. Chaka, Zulu Chief, 1787?-1828. 2. Zulus—History. I. Title.
L.C. card no. for the hardbound ed.: 57-6735.

RITTER, E A 1890- 923.1683
Shaka Zulu; the rise of the Zulu Empire. London, New York, Longmans, Green [1955] 383p. illus. 23cm. [DT878.Z9R68] 55-3983
1. Chaka, Zulu chief, 1787?-1828. 2. Zulus—Hist. I. Title.

Chaka, Zulu chief, 1787?-1828—Juvenile literature.

COHEN, Daniel. 968.03'092'4 B
Shaka, king of the Zulus; a biography. [1st ed.] Garden City, N.Y., Doubleday, 1973. xii, 171 p. illus. 22 cm. Bibliography: p. [165]-166. A biography of the outcast who, through his military abilities, eventually became a controversial Zulu chief known as both a genius and madman, hero and devil incarnate. [DT878.Z9C56] 92 73-180066 ISBN 0-385-06316-4 4.50
1. Chaka, Zulu chief, 1787?-1828—Juvenile literature. 2. Zulus—Juvenile literature. I. Title.

KEATING, Bern. 92 (J)
Chaka, King of the Zulus. New York, Putnam [1968] 126 p. 21 cm. (Lives to remember) Bibliography: p. 121. [DT878.Z9K4 1968] 68-15060
1. Chaka, Zulu chief, 1787-1828—Juvenile literature. I. Title.

Chakravarti, Sashi Bhushan.

*TAPASYANANDA, Swami. 294.5'6'2
Swami Ramakrishnananda; the apostle of Sri Ramakrishna to the South, by Swami Tapasyananda. Madras, India, Shri Ramakrishna math, 1972. 270 p., 18 cm. [BL1175.]
1. Chakravarti, Sashi Bhushan. I. Title.
Distributed by Vedanta Press, Hollywood, Calif. 90068

Chakravarti, Surath Chandra, 1914-

RAMAKRISHNA Ananda. 294.5'6'10924
The real guru / by Ramakrishna Ananda. Costa Mesa, Calif. : Life-Realization Books, c1978. vii, 352 p., [2] leaves of plates : ill. ; 22 cm. Includes index. [BL1175.C523R35] 78-107948 12.95
1. Chakravarti, Surath Chandra, 1914- 2. Ramakrishna Ananda. 3. Gurus—India—Biography. I. Title.

Chalmers, James, 1841-1901.

LANGMORE, Diane. 266'.023'0924 B
Tamate, a king : James Chalmers in New Guinea, 1877-1901 / [by] Diane Langmore. Carlton, Vic. : Melbourne University Press, 1974. xv, 169 p., [4] leaves of plates : ill. ; 23 cm. Includes index. Bibliography: p. 159-164. [DU740.72.C48L36] 75-308804 ISBN 0-522-84079-5 : 17.80
1. Chalmers, James, 1841-1901. I. Title.
Distributed by International Scholarly Book Services, Beaverton, Or. BIP

Chamberlain family.

AVELING, James Hobson, 1828-1892. 618.2'0092'2 B
The Chamberlens and the midwifery forceps, memorials of the family, and an essay on the invention of the instrument / by J. H. Aveling. New York : AMS Press, [1977] p. cm. Reprint of the 1882 ed. published by J. & A. Churchill, London. Includes index. [RG509.A93 1977] 75-23677 ISBN 0-404-13230-8 : 19.00
1. Chamberlain family. 2. Obstetricians—England—Biography. 3. Forceps, Obstetric—History. I. Title.

Chamberlain, John, 1554?-1628.

CHAMBERLAIN, John, 1554?-1628. 942.05'5'0924
The letters of John Chamberlain / edited, with an introd., by Norman Egbert McClure. Westport, Conn. : Greenwood Press, 1979. 2 v. : ports. ; 24 cm. Reprint of the 1939 ed. published by the American Philosophical Society, Philadelphia, and issued as its Memoirs, v. 12, pts. 1 and 2. Includes index. [DA391.1.C4A4 1979] 78-23784 ISBN 0-313-20710-0 lib. bdg. : 72.50
1. Chamberlain, John, 1554?-1628. 2. Great Britain—History—Elizabeth, 1558-1603—Sources. 3. Great Britain—History—James I, 1603-1625—Sources. 4. Great Britain—Social life and customs—16th century. 5. Great Britain—Social life and customs—17th century. 6. Intellectuals—Great Britain—Biography. I McClure, Norman Egbert, 1893- II. Title. III. Series: American Philosophical Society, Philadelphia. Memoirs ; v. 12, pts. 1-2. BIP

NOTESTEIN, Wallace, 1878- 920.042
Four worthies: John Chamberlain, Anne Clifford, John Taylor, Oliver Heywood. New Haven, Yale University Press, 1957. 248p. illus. 21cm. [DA377.N6] 57-1426
1. Chamberlain, John, 1554?-1628. 2. Pembroke, Anne (Clifford) Herbert, countess of, 1590-1676. 3. Taylor, John, 1580-1653. 4. Heywood, Oliver, 1629-1702. I. Title.

Chamberlain, Joseph, 1836-1914.

BROWNE, Harry, 1918- 941.081'092'4 B
Joseph Chamberlain, radical and imperialist / [by] Harry Browne. London : Longman, 1974. vi, 107 p. ; 20 cm. (Seminar studies in history) Includes index. Bibliography: p. 99-103. [DA565.C4B76] 75-308382 ISBN 0-582-35214-2 pbk. : 2.75
1. Chamberlain, Joseph, 1836-1914. 2. Great Britain—Politics and government—1837-1901. I. Title.
Distributed by Longman New York.

CHAMBERLAIN, Joseph, 1836-1914. 941.081'092'4 B
A political memoir, 1880-92 / by Joseph Chamberlain ; edited from the original ms. by C. H. D. Howard. Westport, Conn. : Greenwood Press, 1975. xx, 340 p., [6] leaves of plates : ill. ; 22 cm. Reprint of the 1953 ed. published by Batchworth Press, London. Includes bibliographical references and index. [DA565.C4A32 1975] 75-7235 ISBN 0-8371-8101-1 lib.bdg. : 19.00
1. Chamberlain, Joseph, 1836-1914. 2. Great Britain—Politics and government—1837-1901. I. Title. BIP

FRASER, Peter 942.081'0924 (B)
Joseph Chamberlain; radicalism and empire, 1868-1914. [1st Amer. ed.] South Brunswick [N.J.] A. S. Barnes [1967, c.1966] xv, 349p. illus., ports. 24cm. Bibl. [DA565.C4 F7 1967] 67-13131 7.50
1. Chamberlain, Joseph, 1836-1914. I. Title.

GULLEY, Elsie Elizabeth, 1889- 942.081'092'4 B
Joseph Chamberlain and English social politics, by Elsie E. Gulley. New York, Octagon Books, 1974 [c1926] 340 p. 23 cm. Reprint of the ed. published by Columbia University Press, New York, which was issued as no. 270 of Studies in history, economics, and public law. Thesis—Columbia University, 1926. Bibliography: p. 331-333. [DA565.C4G7 1974] 74-11087 ISBN 0-374-93322-7
1. Chamberlain, Joseph, 1836-1914. 2. Great Britain—Politics and government—1837-1901. I. Title. II. Series: Columbia studies in the social sciences, no. 270. BIP

HURST, Michael 942.081'0924
Joseph Chamberlain and Liberal reunion: the Round Table Conference of 1887. London, Routledge & K. Paul; Toronto, Univ. of Toronto Pr., 1967 xv, 407p. front., 8 plates (ports.) 23cm. (Studies in political hist.) [DA565.C4H8] 67-85739 10.50
1. Chamberlain, Joseph, 1836-1914. 2. Liberal Party (gt.Brit.) 3. Gt. Brit.—Pol. & govt.—1837-1901. I. Title. BIP

KUBICEK, Robert V. 320.9'42
The administration of imperialism: Joseph Chamberlain at the Colonial Office [by] Robert V. Kubicek. Durham, N.C., Duke University Press, 1969. xiv, 192 p. 24 cm. (Duke University Commonwealth Studies Center. Publication no. 37) Bibliography: p. [177]-187. [DA565.C4K8] 72-89874
1. Chamberlain, Joseph, 1836-1914. 2. Gt. Brit. Colonial Office. 3. Gt. Brit.—Politics and government—1837-1901. I. Title. II. Series: Duke University, Durham, N.C. Commonwealth-Studies Center. Publication no. 37

Chamberlain, Joshua Lawrence, 1828-1914.

WALLACE, Willard Mosher 923.573
Soul of the lion; a biography of General Joshua L. Chamberlain. New York, T. Nelson [c.1960] 357p.Bibl. notes p.317-340; Bibl. p.341-345 illus. 22cm. 60-11484 5.00
1. Chamberlain, Joshua Lawrence, 1828-1914. I. Title.

WALLACE, Willard Mosher, 1911- 923.573
Soul of the lion; a biography of General Joshua L. Chamberlain. New York, T. Nelson [1960] 357 p. illus. 22 cm. Includes bibliography. [E467.1.C47W3] 60-11484
1. Chamberlain, Joshua Lawrence, 1828-1914. I. Title.

Chamberlain, Neville, 1869-1940.

FEILING, Keith Grahame, Sir, 1884- 942.084'0924 B
The life of Neville Chamberlain, by Keith Feiling. Hamden, Conn., Archon Books, 1970. xi, 477 p. facsim., ports. 23 cm. Reprint of the 1946 ed. with a new pref. and bibliography (p. 467-468) [DA585.C5F4 1970] 75-95598 13.50
1. Chamberlain, Neville, 1869-1940. I. Title. BIP

HYDE, Harford Montgomery, 1907- 941.084'092'4 B
Neville Chamberlain / H. Montgomery Hyde. London : Weidenfeld & Nicolson, 1976. xii, 188 p., [4] leaves of plates : ill. ; 23 cm. Includes index. Bibliography: p. 181-182. [DA585.C5H9] 76-382851 ISBN 0-297-77229-5 : £4.95
1. Chamberlain, Neville, 1869-1940. 2. Prime ministers—Great Britain—Biography. 3. Great Britain—Politics and government—1936-1945.

MACLEOD, Iain. 923.242
Neville Chamberlain. [1st American ed.] New York, Atheneum, 1962 [c1961] 319 p. illus. 20 cm. [DA585.C5M3 1962] 62-13222
1. Chamberlain, Neville, 1869-1940.

ROCK, William R. 942.084'0924 B
Neville Chamberlain, by William R. Rock. New York, Twayne Publishers [1969] 242 p. 22 cm. (Twayne's rulers and statesmen of the world series, 11) "Bibliographical essay": p. 231-235. [DA585.C5R6] 74-77034
1. Chamberlain, Neville, 1869-1940.

Chamberlain, Wilton Norman, 1936-

CHAMBERLAIN, Wilton Norman, 1936- 796.32'3'0924 B
Wilt; just like any other 7-foot Black millionaire who lives next door [by] Wilt Chamberlain and David Shaw. New York, Macmillan [1973] vi, 310 p. illus. 24 cm. [GV884.C5A38] 73-2124 6.95
1. Chamberlain, Wilton Norman, 1936- 2. Basketball. I. Shaw, David, 1943- joint author. II. Title.

LIBBY, Bill. 796.32'3'0924 B
Goliath : the Wilt Chamberlain story / by Bill Libby. New York : Dodd, Mead, c1977. vii, 248 p., [15] leaves of plates : ill. ; 21 cm. [GV884.C5L5] 76-50104 ISBN 0-396-07392-1 : 7.95
1. Chamberlain, Wilton Norman, 1936- 2. Basketball players—United States—Biography. I. Title. BIP

SULLIVAN, George, 1927- 796.323640924
Wilt Chamberlain, by George Sullivan. New York, Grosset & Dunlap [1966] 183 p. illus. 20 cm. (Grosset sports library) [GV884.A2C48 1966] 66-18953
1. Chamberlain, Wilton Norman, 1936-

SULLIVAN, George, 1927- 796.32'3'0924 B
Wilt Chamberlain. [Rev. ed.] New York, Grosset & Dunlap [1971, c1970] 184 p. illus. 20 cm. (Grosset sports library) [GV884.C5S8 1971] 72-24113 2.50
1. Chamberlain, Wilton Norman, 1936-

Chamberlain, Wilton Norman, 1936—Juvenile literature.

ETTER, Les. 796.32'3'0922
Basketball superstars: three great pros. Champaign, Ill., Garrard Pub. Co. [1974] 96 p. illus. 24 cm. Brief biographies stressing the careers of basketball stars Wilt Chamberlain, Jerry West, and Oscar Robertson. [GV884.A1E87] 920 73-9659 ISBN 0-8116-6667-0 2.98 (lib. bdg.)
1. Chamberlain, Wilton Norman, 1936- —Juvenile literature. 2. West, Jerry, 1938- —Juvenile literature. 3. Robertson, Oscar, 1938- —Juvenile literature. I. Title.

HEASLIP, George. 796.32'3'0924 B
Wilt Chamberlain; a winner. Illustrated by Jack Norman. [Mankato, Minn., Creative Education; distributed by Childrens Press, Chicago, 1973, 1974] 31 p. illus. (part col.) 25 cm. (Creative's superstars) Biography of a seven-foot tall basketball player who set

unbelievable records. [GV884.C5H42] 92 73-13894 4.95
1. Chamberlain, Wilton Norman, 1936- — Juvenile literature. I. Norman, Jack, illus. II. Title.

KLEIN, Dave. 796.32'3'0922 B
Pro basketball's big men. Illustrated with photos. New York, Random House [1973] 151 p. illus. 22 cm. (Pro basketball library) Brief biographies of three prominent basketball stars renowned for their skill and height. [GV884.A1K56 1973] 920 73-6743 ISBN 0-394-82627-2 1.95
1. Russell, William Felton, 1934- — Juvenile literature. 2. Chamberlain, Wilton Norman, 1936- —Juvenile literature. 3. Abdul-Jabbar, Kareem, 1947- —Juvenile literature. 4. Basketball—Biography—Juvenile literature. I. Title.

RUDEEN, Kenneth. 796.32'3'0924 B
Wilt Chamberlain. Illustrated by Frank Mullins. New York, Crowell [1970] 32 p. illus. 24 cm. (Crowell biographies) An easy-to-read biography of the seven feet one inch basketball player who once scored 100 points in a game. [GV884.C5R8] 92 74-94800 3.75
1. Chamberlain, Wilton Norman, 1936-— Juvenile literature. I. Mullins, Frank, illus. II. Title.

Chambers, Andrew Jackson, 1825-

CHAMBERS, Andrew Jackson, 1825- 978'.02'0924 B
Recollections / Andrew Jackson Chambers. Fairfield, Wash. : Ye Galleon Press, 1975. p. cm. "Reminiscences [by] Margaret White Chambers": p. [F593.C47 1975] 75-45379 ISBN 0-87770-156-3
1. Chambers, Andrew Jackson, 1825- 2. Chambers, Margaret White. 3. Overland journeys to the Pacific. I. Chambers, Margaret White. Reminiscences. 1975. II. Title.

Chambers, Jessie.

CORKE, Helen, 1882- 823'.9'12 B
D. H. Lawrence's "Princess"; a memory of Jessie Chambers. [Folcroft, Pa.] Folcroft Library Editions, 1973. 47 p. ports. 24 cm. Reprint of the 1951 ed. published by the Merle Press, Thames Ditton, Surrey, Eng. [PR6023.A93Z622 1973] 73-18344 ISBN 0-8414-3528-6 (lib. bdg.)
1. Lawrence, David Herbert, 1885-1930. 2. Chambers, Jessie. 3. Corke, Helen, 1882- I. Title.

Chambers, Mary Jane.

CHAMBERS, Mary Jane. 248'.2 B
Here am I! Send me. Atlanta, Forum House [1973] 169 p. 23 cm. Autobiographical. [BX9225.C48A34] 72-97824 ISBN 0-913618-08-X 4.95
1. Chambers, Mary Jane. I. Title.

Chambers, Stanley Warren, 1915-

CHAMBERS, Catherine, 1920- 289.9 B
The measure of a man : the biography of Stanley Warren Chambers / by Catherine Chambers. Hazelwood, Mo. : Word Aflame Press, c1978. 191 p., [16] leaves of plates : ill. ; 22 cm. [BX8780.Z8C463] 78-111263 7.94
1. Chambers, Stanley Warren, 1915- 2. Pentecostals—Clergy—Biography. 3. Clergy—United States—Biography. I. Title.
Pub. Address: 8855 Dunn Rd., Hazelwood MO 63042

Chambord, Henri Charles Ferdinand Marie Dieudonne d'Artois, duc de Bordeaux, comte de, 1820-1883.

BROWN, Marvin Luther. 944.07'0924 B
The Comte de Chambord; the Third Republic's uncompromising king [by Marvin L. Brown. Jr. Durham, N.C., Duke University Press, 1967. vii, 225 p. illus., ports. 24 cm. Bibliography: p. 203-209. [DC280.5.C38B7] 67-23300
1. Chambord, Henri Charles Ferdinand Marie Dieudonne d'Artois, duc de Bordeaux, comte de, 1820-1883. I. Title.
BIP

Chaminade, Cecile Louise Stephanie, 1861-1944.

KERR, Laura (Nowak) 1904- 927.8
Scarf dance; the story of Cecile Chaminade. New York, Abelard Press [1953] 172p. 22cm. [ML410.C416K4] 53-6807
1. Chaminade, Cecile Louise Stephanie, 1861-1944. I. Title.

Chaminade, Guillaume Joseph, 1761-1850.

CHAMINADE, Marie. 922.244
Our Lady's tinker, William Joseph Chaminade; illustrated by Gedge Harmon. St. Meinrad, Ind. [1950] 57 p. illus. 23 cm. "Grail publication." [BX4705.C44C5] 50-12988
1. Chaminade, Guillaume Joseph, 1761-1850. I. Title.

Champion, Jackson R.

CHAMPION, Jackson R. 329.6'0092'4 B
Blacks in the Republican Party? : One man's experiences, a revolutionary, conservative Black Republican / Jackson R. Champion. Washington : LenChamps Publishers, 1975. 256 p., [4] leaves of plates : ill. ; 23 cm. Includes index. Bibliography: p. [205]-234. [F200.C45] 75-322329 5.95
1. Champion, Jackson R. 2. Republican Party. 3. Washington, D.C.—Politics and government. 4. Afro-Americans—Politics and suffrage. I. Title.

Champlain, Samuel de, 1567-1635.

BERRY, Gerald L., 1915- 971.01'1'0924 B
Samuel de Champlain, Father of New France [by Gerald L. Berry] Richmond, Ont., Simon & Schuster of Canada [1967] 128 p. 18 cm. [F1030.1.B4] 68-100339 75c. Can.
1. Champlain, Samuel de, 1567-1635.

BISHOP, Morris, 1893-1973. 971.01'13'0924 B
Champlain, the life of fortitude / Morris Bishop. New York : Octagon Books, 1978,c1948 p. cm. Reprint of the ed. published by Knopf, New York. Includes index. [F1030.1.B6 1979] 78-27239 ISBN 0-374-90642-4 lib.bdg. : 19.00
1. Champlain, Samuel de, 1567-1635. 2. Canada—History—To 1763 (New France) 3. Explorers—France—Biography. 4. Explorers—Canada—Biography. I. Title.

DIONNE, Narcisse Eutrope, 1848-1917. 923.971
Champlain. [Toronto] University of Toronto Press, 1963. 299 p. 21 cm. (Canadian University paperbooks 13) [F1030.1.D6 1963] 64-2614
1. Champlain, Samuel de, 1567-1635. 2. Canada—History—To 1763 (New France) I. Title.

MORISON, Samuel Eliot, 1887- 971.01'13'0924
Samuel de Champlain, Father of New France. [1st ed.] Boston, Little, Brown [1972] xix, 299 p. illus. 25 cm. "An Atlantic Monthly Press book." Bibliography: p. 269-273. [F1030.1.M6] 71-186963 10.00
1. Champlain, Samuel de, 1567-1635. 2. New France—Discovery and exploration. 3. America—Discovery and exploration—French. 4. Indians of North America—Canada.

NEW Brunswick Historical Society. 922.271
Champlain and the St. John, 1604-1954, edited by George MacBeath: assistant editors: Jessie I. Lawson, Wm. D. F. Smith, William F. Ryan. With an introd. by A. G. Bailey. [St. John] 1954. 80p. illus. 31cm. [F1030.1.N4] 59-37505
1. Champlain, Samuel de, 1567-1635. 2. St. John River. 3. New Brunswick—Hist. I. MacBeath, George B., ed. II. Title.

SYME, Ronald, 1910- 923.971
Champlain of the St. Lawrence; illustrated by William Stobbs. New York, Morrow, 1952. 189 p. illus. 21 cm. [F1030.1.S97] 52-5070
1. Champlain, Samuel de, 1567-1635. 2. Canada—History—To 1763 (New France) I. Title.

Champlain, Samuel de, 1567-1635—Juvenile literature.

GRANT, Matthew G. 971.01'13'0924 B
Champlain; explorer of New France, by Matthew G. Grant. [Mankato, Minn., Creative Educational Society, 1973] p. cm. (Explorers in America) (Gallery of great American[s] series) A biography of the French explorer who founded Quebec, discovered Lake Champlain, and was called the Father of New France. [F1030.1.G74] 92 73-13714 ISBN 0-87191-287-2 3.95
1. Champlain, Samuel de, 1567-1635—Juvenile literature. 2. New France—Discovery and exploration—Juvenile literature. I. Henriksen, Harold, illus. II. Title: Explorer of New France.

GRANT, Matthew G. 971.01'13'0924 B
Champlain; explorer of New France [by] Matthew G. Grant. Illustrated by Harold Henriksen. [Mankato, Minn., Creative Education; distributed by Childrens Press, Chicago, 1974] 30 p. illus. (part col.) 25 cm. (His Gallery of great Americans series. Explorers of America) A biography of the French explorer who founded Quebec, discovered Lake Champlain, and was called the Father of New France. [F1030.1.G74] 92 73-13714 ISBN 0-87191-287-2
1. Champlain, Samuel de, 1567-1635—Juvenile literature. 2. New France—Discovery and exploration—Juvenile literature. I. Henriksen, Harold, illus. II. Title.

JACOBS, William Jay. 973.1'8'0924 B
Samuel de Champlain [by] W. J. Jacobs New York, Watts, 1974. 58 p. illus. 26 cm (A Visual biography) Bibliography: p. 55. A biography of the French explorer who was the founder of Quebec and the "Father of New France." [F1030.1.J32] 92 73-14554 ISBN 0-531-01275-1 4.50
1. Champlain, Samuel de, 1567-1635—Juvenile literature. 2. New France—Discovery and exploration—Juvenile literature. I. Title.
BIP

RITCHIE, Cicero T. 1914- v. 12
The first Canadian; the story of Champlain. Illustrated by William Wheeler. Toronot, Macmillan, 1961. 155 p. illus. 22 cm. (Great stories of Canada, 24) Includes bibliography. 66-110402
1. Champlain, Samuel de, 1567-1635 — Juvenile literature. I. Title.

RITCHIE, Cicero T., 1914- 920
The first Canadian; the story of Champlain. Illus. by William Wheeler. New York, St. Martin's, 1962 [c.1961] 155p. illus. (pt. col.) 22cm. (Great stories of Canada, 24) Bibl. 62-4360 2.95
1. Champlain, Samuel de, 1567-1635—Juvenile literature. I. Title.

SYME, Ronald, 1910- 923.971
Champlain of the St. Lawrence. Illustrated by William Stobbs. New York, Morrow, 1952. 189 p. illus. 21 cm. [F1030.1.S97] 52-5070
1. Champlain, Samuel de, 1567-1635 — Juvenile literature. Full name: Neville Ronald Syme. I. Title.

WILSON, Charles Morrow, 1905- 923.971
Wilderness explorer; the story of Samuel de Champlain. Illustrated by Richard Lewis. New York,Hawthorn Books [c1963] 188 p. illus. (part col.) 22 cm. (Credo books) [F1030.1.W5] 63-17465
1. Champlain, Samuel de, 1567-1653 — Juvenile literature. I. Title.

Champmesle, Charles Chevillet, sieur de, 1642-1701.

PRIVITERA, Joseph Frederic, 1914- 842'.4
Charles Chevillet de Champmesle, actor and dramatist, 1642-1701, with a critical edition of his hitherto unpublished play, La veuve. Baltimore, Johns Hopkins Press, 1938. [New York, Johnson Reprint Corp., 1973] 179 p. 22 cm. English and French. Originally presented as the author's thesis, New York University. Original ed. issued as v. 32 of the Johns Hopkins studies in Romance literatures and languages, v. 32. Bibliography: p. 171-173. [PQ1735.C68Z88 1973] 72-12565 ISBN 0-384-47973-1
1. Champmesle, Charles Chevillet, sieur de, 1642-1701. I. Champmesle, Charles Chevillet, sieur de, 1642-1701. La veuve. II. Series: The Johns Hopkins studies in Romance literatures and languages, v. 32.
BIP

Champness, W.

CHAMPNESS, W. 917.11'04'2
To Cariboo and back in 1862. Fairfield, Wash., Ye Galleon Press, 1972. p. cm. Originally published serially in the Leisure hour, April 1865, under title: To Cariboo and back. [F1089.C3C52 1972] 73-22291 ISBN 0-87770-109-1
1. Champness, W. 2. Cariboo District. 3. British Columbia—Description and travel. I. Title.

Champney, Benjamin, 1817-1907.

CHAMPNEY, Benjamin, 1817-1907. 704'.7 B
Sixty years' memories of act and artists / by Benjamin Champney ; [edited with an introduction by H. Barbara Weinberg]. [New York : Garland Pub., 1977] c1899. 178 p., [13] leaves of plates : ill. ; 19 cm. (The Art experience in late nineteenth-century America) Title page preceded by introd. (13 p.). Reprint of the 1900 ed. published by The News Print., Wallace & Andrews, Woburn, Mass. [N6537.C46A25 1977] 75-28887 ISBN 0-8240-2244-0 lib.bdg. : 25.00
1. Champney, Benjamin, 1817-1907. 2. Artists—United States—Biography. 3. Art, American—History. 4. Art, Modern—19th century—United States—History. I. Title. II. Series.

Champolion. Jean Francois, 1790 1832—Juvenile literature.

HONOUR, Alan 410.924
The man who could read stones; Champollion and the Rosetta Stone. Illus. by Anthony Aviles. New York, Hawthorn [c.1966] 190p. illus. 22cm. Bibl. [PJ1064.C6H6] 66-15250 3.25
1. Champolion. Jean Francois, 1790-1832—Juvenile literature. 2. Egyptology—Juvenile literature. I. Title.

Chandler, Greene Callier,

CHANDLER, Greene Callier, 1829-1905. 923.273
Journal and speeches. With foreword by Walter Chandler. [Memphis? Tenn., 1954, c1953] 244p. illus. 22cm. [F341.C45] 54-39134
I. Title.

Chandler, Julian Alvin Carroll, 1872-1934.

BUTLER, Solomon R. 370'.92'4 B
The life of Dr. Julian Alvin Carroll Chandler and his influence on education in Virginia [by] Solomon R. Butler [and] Charles D. Walters. [Hampton, Hampton Institute Press, 1973] 55 p. 24 cm. Includes bibliographical references. [LA2317.C47B87] 72-78020
1. Chandler, Julian Alvin Carroll, 1872-1934. 2. Education—Virginia—History. I. Walters, Charles D., joint author. II. Title.

Chandler, Raymond, 1888-1959.

MACSHANE, Frank. 813'.5'2 B
The life of Raymond Chandler / Frank MacShane. 1st ed. New York : E. P. Dutton, c1976. xii, 306 p., [8] leaves of plates : ill. ; 25 cm. Includes bibliographical references and index. [PS3505.H3224Z7] 75-38791 10.95
1. Chandler, Raymond, 1888-1959. **BIP**

Chandler, Zachariah, 1813-1879.

GEORGE, Mary Karl. 973.8'0924 B
Zachariah Chandler; a political biography. East Lansing, Michigan State University Press, 1969. x, 301 p. 22 cm. Includes bibliographical references. [E664.C4G4] 70-84443 8.50
1. Chandler, Zachariah, 1813-1879. 2. U.S.—Politics and government—1849-1877. **BIP**

Chandrasekharendra Saraswati, Jagatguru Sankaracharya of Kamakoti, 1893- —Addresses, essays, lectures.

THE Sage of Kanchi 294.5'6'1 B
/ edited by T. M. P. Mahadevan. New Delhi : Arnold-Heinemann Publishers (India), 1975. 93 p., [2] leaves of plates : ill. ; 22 cm. [BL1175.C56S24] 75-904253 ISBN 0-89253-018-9 lib.bdg. : 6.25
1. Chandrasekharendra Saraswati, Jagatguru Sankaracharya of Kamakoti, 1893- —Addresses, essays, lectures. I. Mahadevan, Telliyavaram Mahadevan Ponnambalam, 1911-
Distributed by Interculture **BIP**

Chanel, Coco, 1883-1971.

BAILLEN, Claude. 746.9'2'0924 B
Chanel solitaire / by Claude Baillen ; translated from the French by Barbara Bray. New York : Quadrangle/New York Times Book Co., 1974, c1973. 192 p. : ill. ; 25 cm. [TT505.C45B313 1974] 74-78651 ISBN 0-8129-0474-5 : 7.95
1. Chanel, Coco, 1883-1971. I. Title.

CHARLES-ROUX, 746.9'2'0924 B
Edmonde.
Chanel : her life, her world, and the woman behind the legend she herself created / by Edmonde Charles-Houx. 1st ed. New York : Knopf, 1975. p. cm. Translation of L'irreguliere. Includes index. [TT505.C45C4613] 75-8254 ISBN 0-394-47613-1 : 15.00
1. Chanel, Coco, 1883-1971. **BIP**

GALANTE, Pierre. 746.9'2'0924 B
Mademoiselle Chanel. Translated by Eileen Geist and Jessie Wood. Chicago, H. Regnery Co. [1973] 298 p. 23 cm. [TT505.C45G35] 72-11173 8.95
1. Chanel, Coco, 1883-1971. I. Title.

HAEDRICH, Marcel, 746.9'2'0924 B
pseud.
Coco Chanel; her life, her secrets. Translated from the French by Charles Lam Markmann. [1st English language ed.] Boston, Little, Brown [1972] 277 p. illus. 25 cm. Translation of Coco Chanel secrete. [TT505.C45H313] 79-187788 8.95
1. Chanel, Coco, 1883-1971.

Chanel, 1803-1841.

CLOUPEAU, J 922.299
In the land of taboos; life of St. Peter Chanel, Marist, the first martyr of Oceania. Translated from the French by James M. Darby. Paterson, N. J., St. Anthony Guild Press, 1957. 129p. illus. 20cm. [BX4700.C55C6] 57-35730
1. Chanel, 1803-1841. I. Title.

Chang, Ch'ien, 1853-1926.

CHU, Ch'ang-ling, 951.030924
1929-
Reformer in modern China, Chang Chien, 1853-1926 [by] Samuel C. Chu. New York, Columbia 1965 [c.1958, 1965] xiii, 256p. maps. 25cm. *Columbia Univ. Studies of the East Asian Inst.) Bibl. [DS763.C38C53] 65-10541 6.00
1. Chang, Ch'ien, 1853-1926. I. Title.

Chang, Hsueh-ch'eng, 1738-1801.

NIVISON, David S. 951.0072
The life and thought of Chang Hsueh-ch'eng (1738-1801) Stanford, Calif., Stanford Univ. Pr., [c.]1966. ix, 336p. map. 23cm. (Stanford studies in the civilization of eastern Asia) Bibl. [DS734.9.C4N5] 65-13112 8.50
1. Chang, Hsueh-ch'eng, 1738-1801. I. Title. II. Series.

NIVISON, David S 951.0072 (B)
The life and thought of Chang Hsueh-ch'eng (1738-1801) [by] David S. Nivison. Stanford, Calif., Stanford University Press, 1966. ix, 336 p. map. 23 cm. (Stanford studies in the civilization[s] of eastern Asia) "Bibliographical note": p. [319]-322. [DS734.9.C4N5] 65-13112
1. Chang, Hsueh-ch'eng, 1738-1801. I. Title. II. Series.

Chang, Nai-ying, 1911-1942.

GOLDBLATT, Howard, 895.1'3'5 B
1939-
Hsiao Hung / by Howard Goldblatt. Boston : Twayne Publishers, c1976. 161 p. : port. ; 21 cm. (Twayne's world authors series ; TWAS 386 : China) Includes index. Bibliography: p. 153-158. [PL2740.N3Z64] 75-30650 ISBN 0-8057-6228-0 lib. bdg. : 8.95
1. Chang, Nai-ying, 1911-1942. **BIP**

Chang, Tso-lin, 1875?-1928.

MCCORMACK, Gavan. 951.04'1'0924
Chang Tso-lin in northeast China, 1911-1928 : China, Japan, and the Manchurian idea / Gavan McCormack. Stanford, Calif. : Stanford University Press, 1977. vi, 334 p. : ill. ; 24 cm. Includes index. Bibliography: p. [311]-322. [DS778.C5M3] 76-48028 ISBN 0-8047-0945-9 : 18.50
1. Chang, Tso-lin, 1875?-1928. 2. Generals—China—Biography. 3. Manchuria—History. 4. Japanese in Manchuria. I. Title. **BIP**

Change of sex—Personal narratives.

CONN, Canary. 362.1'9'66 B
Canary : the story of a transsexual / by Canary Conn. Los Angeles : Nash Pub., [1974] 335 p. : ill. ; 22 cm. [RC560.C4C66] 73-92975 ISBN 0-8402-1345-X : 8.95
1. Change of sex—Personal narratives.

Chanler, Winthrop,

CHANLER, Winthrop, 1863- 923.573
1926.
Letters; collected by Margaret Terry Chanler. New York, 1951. 237 p. illus. 24 cm. [CT275.C465A39] 51-39737
I. Title.

Channing, William Ellery, 1780-1842.

BROWN, Arthur W 1917- 922.8173
Always young for liberty, a biography of William Ellery Channing. [Suracuse, N. Y.] Syracuse University Press [1956] xi, 268p. 24cm. 'Literature and sources': p. 245-261. [BX9869.C4B84] 56-9464
1. Channing, William Ellery, 1780- 1842. I. Title. **BIP**

BROWN, Arthur W., 1917- 922.8173
William Ellery Channing. New York, Twayne Publishers [1962, c1961] 172 p. 21 cm. (Twayne's United States authors series, 7) Includes bibliography. [BX9869.C4B86 1962] 61-13051
1. Channing, William Ellery, 1780-1842. **BIP**

EDGELL, David P 922.8173
William Ellery Channing; an intellectual portrait. Boston, Beacon Press [1955] 264p. illus. 22cm. [BX9869.C4E3] 54-10687
1. Channing, William Ellery, 1780-1842. I. Title.

ELIOT, Charles 973'.0992 B
William, 1834-1926.
Four American leaders. [Folcroft, Pa.] Folcroft Library Editions, 1973. p. Reprint of the 1907 ed. published by P. Green, London. Contents.Contents.—Franklin.—Washington.—Channing.—Emerson. [E176.E42 1973] 73-14550 ISBN 0-8414-3916-8 (lib. bdg.)
1. Franklin, Benjamin, 1706-1790. 2. Washington, George, Pres. U.S., 1732-1799. 3. Channing, William Ellery, 1780-1842. 4. Emerson, Ralph Waldo, 1803-1882. I. Title. **BIP**

MENDELSOHN, Jack, 288'.0924 B
1918-
Channing, the reluctant radical; a biography. [1st ed.] Boston, Little, Brown [1971] 308 p. illus. 22 cm. Includes bibliographical references. [BX9869.C4M45 1971] 75-161863 8.95
1. Channing, William Ellery, 1780-1842.

MENDELSOHN, Jack, 288'.092'4 B
1918-
Channing, the reluctant radical : a biography / Jack Mendelsohn. Westport, Conn. : Greenwood Press, 1980, c1971. p. cm. Reprint of the ed. published by Little, Brown, Boston. Includes bibliographical references and index. [BX9869.C4M45 1980] 79-17863 ISBN 0-313-22101-4 lib. bdg. : 26.00
1. Channing, William Ellery, 1780-1842. 2. Unitarians—Clergy—Biography. 3. Clergy—United States—Biography. I. Title.

RICE, Madeleine (Hooke) 922.8173
1903-
Federal Street pastor; the life of William Ellery Channing. New York, Bookman Associates [1961] 360p. illus. 22cm. Includes bibliography. [BX9869.C4R5] 61-15676
1. Channing, William Ellery, 1780-1842. I. Title. **BIP**

Channing, William Ellery, 1818-1901.

MCGILL, Frederick T. 818'.2'09 B
Channing of Concord: a life of William Ellery Channing II [by] Frederick T. McGill, Jr. New Brunswick, N.J., Rutgers University Press [1967] xiii, 219 p. illus., ports. 22 cm. Bibliography: p. 209-214. [PS1291.M3] 67-20389
1. Channing, William Ellery, 1818-1901. I. Title.

Chantal, Jeanne Francoise (Fremiot) de Rabutin, baronne de, Saint, 1572-1641.

HEAGNEY, Harold Jerome, 922.244
1890-
Madame de Chantal. New York, P. J. Kenedy [1950] 285 p. 22 cm. [BX4700.C56H4] 50-58302
1. Chantal, Jeanne Francoise (Fremiot) de Rabutin, baronne de, Saint, 1572-1641. I. Title.

STOPP, Elisabeth 922.244
Madame de Chantal; portrait of a saint. Westminster, Md., Newman, 1963[c.1962] 272p. illus. 23cm. Bibl. 63-12260 4.50
1. Chantal, Jeanne Francoise (Fremiot) de Rabutin, baronne de, Saint, 1572-1641. I. Title.

Chantal, Jeanne Francoise (Fremlot) de Rabutin, baronne de, Saint, 1572-1641—Juvenile literature.

ROBERTO, Brother, 1927- 922.244
No jewels for Jane; a story of St. Jane Frances de Chantal. Illus. by Carolyn Lee Jagodits. Notre Dame, Ind., Dujarie Press [1959] 94p. illus. 24cm. [BX4700.C56R6] 59-65512
1. Chantal, Jeanne Francoise (Fremlot) de Rabutin, baronne de, Saint, 1572-1641—Juvenile literature. I. Title.

Chao, Yuen Ren, 1892-

CHAO, Yuen Ren, 495.1'092'4 B
1892-
Autobiography of Yuen Ren Chao : the first 30 years from 1892 until 1921. Ithaca, N.Y. : Spoken Language Services, c1975. p. cm. (Life with Chaos ; v. 2) Includes bibliographical references. [CT1828.C518A32] 75-15931 ISBN 0-87950-405-6 : 15.00. ISBN 0-87950-404-8 lim. autographed ed. : 50.00
1. Chao, Yuen Ren, 1892- I. Title. II. Series.

Chapin, Charles E., 1858-1930.

CHAPIN, Charles E., 070'.92'4 B
1858-1930.
Charles E. Chapin's story. New York, Beekman Publishers, 1974. xxv, 334 p. port. 23 cm. (American newspapermen, 1790-1933) Reprint of the 1920 ed. published by Putnam, New York. [PN4874.C45A4 1974] 74-544 ISBN 0-8464-0028-6 16.00
1. Chapin, Charles E., 1858-1930.

Chapin, Henry—Biography.

CHAPIN, Henry. 818'.5'209 B
A countdown at eighty / by Henry Chapin. Dublin, N.H. : W. L. Bauhan, 1977. ix, 188 p., [5] leaves of plates : ill. ; 22 cm. [PS3505.H3514Z515] 77-4360 ISBN 0-87233-045-1 pbk. : 5.95
1. Chapin, Henry—Biography. 2. Authors, American—20th century—Biography. I. Title.

Chapin, Schuyler.

CHAPIN, Schuyler. 780'.92'4 B
Musical chairs : a life in the arts / by Schuyler Chapin. New York : Putnam, c1977. p. cm. Includes index. [ML429.C497A3] 77-5814 12.50
1. Chapin, Schuyler. 2. Impresarios—United States—Biography. I. Title. **BIP**

Chaplains, Prison—Correspondence, reminiscences, etc.

ESHELMAN, Byron E. 365.66
Death row chaplain, by Byron E. Eshelman with Frank Riley. Englewood Cliffs, N.J., Prentice-Hall [1962] 252 p. illus. 22 cm. [BV4340.E75] 62-13619
1. Chaplains, Prison—Correspondence, reminiscences, etc. 2. Capital punishment. I. Title.

Chaplin, Annabel.

CHAPLIN, 133.9'013'0926 B
Annabel.
The bright light of death / by Annabel Chaplin. Marina del Rey, Calif. : DeVorss, c1977. xii, 133 p. ; 22 cm. [BF1283.C485A33] 77-75169 ISBN 0-87516-230-4 pbk. : 3.00
1. Chaplin, Annabel. 2. Spiritualists—United States—Biography. I. Title. **BIP**

Chaplin, Charles, 1889-

BOWMAN, William 791.43'028'0924 B
Dodgson.
Charlie Chaplin; his life and art. New York, Haskell House, 1974. 142 p. illus. 23 cm. Reprint of the 1931 ed. published by G. Routledge, London. [PN2287.C5B6 1974] 74-1090 ISBN 0-8383-1841-X 13.95
1. Chaplin, Charles, 1889- I. Title.

CHAPLIN, Charles 927.92
My father, Charlie Chaplin, by Charles Chaplin, Jr., with N. and M. Rau. New York, Random House [c.1960] 369p. illus. 24cm. 60-5537 4.95
1. Chaplin, Charles, 1889- I. Title.

CHAPLIN, Charles, 1889- 927.92
My autobiography. New York, Simon and Schuster [1964] 512 p. illus., ports. 25 cm. [PN2287.C5A32] 64-19937
1. Actors—Correspondence, reminiscences, etc.

CHAPLIN, 791.430280924 (B)
Charles, 1889-
My autobiography. Harmondsworth, Penguin, 1966. 494 p. 64 plates (113 illus.) 18 1/2 cm. 10/6 [PN2287.C5A32 1966] 67-71441
1. Actors — Correspondence, reminiscences, etc. I. Title.

CHAPLIN, Charles, 1889- 927.92
My autobiography. New York, Pocket Bks. [1966, c.1964] 560p. illus., ports. 18cm. (Cardinal ed., 95026) [PN2287.C5A32] .95 pap.,

1. Actors—Correspondence, reminiscences, etc. I. Title. **BIP**

*CHAPLIN, Charles, 791.430280 B 1889-
My life in pictures, designed by David King. Introduction by Francis Wyndham. New York, Grosset & Dunlap [1975 c1974] 1v. illus. (part col.) 29 cm. [PN2287] 75-18583 ISBN 0-448-12037-2 19.95
1. Chaplin, Charles, 1889- I. Title.

CHAPLIN, Charles, Jr., 927.92 1925-
My father, Charlie Chaplin [by] Charles Chaplin, Jr., with N. and M. Rau. New York, Popular Lib. [1961, c.1960] 287p. (Popular Special SP98) .50 pap.,
I. Title.

CHAPLIN, Charles, 1925- 927.92
My father, Charlie Chaplin, by Charles Chaplin, Jr., with N. and M. Rau. New York, Random House [1960] 369p. illus. 24cm. [PN2287.C5C5] 60-5537
1. Chaplin, Charles, 1889- I. Title.

CHAPLIN, Charles, 1925- v. 12
My father, Charlie Chaplin [by] Charles Chaplin, jr. with N. and M. Rau. New York, Popular Library [1960] 286 p. 17 cm. (Popular Library Sp. 98) 67-40663
1. Chaplin, Charles, 1889- I. Title.

CHAPLIN, Lita Grey, 791.430924 1908-
My life with Chaplin; an intimate memoir, by Lita Grey Chaplin with Morton Cooper. [New York] B. Geis Assocs., dist. by Grove [1966] 325p. illus., ports. 22cm. [PN2287.C5C52] 66-13707 5.95
1. Chaplin, Charles, 1895- I. Cooper, Morton, 1925- II. Title.

COTES, Peter, 1912- 927.92
The little fellow; the life and work of Charles Spencer Chaplin [by] Peter Cotes and Thelma Niklaus. With a foreword by W. Somerset Maugham. New York, Philosophical Library [1951] 160 p. illus. 22 cm. [PN2287.C5C6 1951a] 51-13515
1. Chaplin, Charles, 1889- I. Title.

COTES, Peter, 1912- 927.92
The little fellow; the life and work of Charles Spencer Chaplin, by Peter Cotes, Thelma Niklaus. Foreword by W. Somerset Maugham. New York, Citadel [c.1965] 181p. illus., ports. 21cm. Bibl. [PN2287.C5C6] 65-15482 4.00
1. Chaplin, Charles, 1889- I. Niklaus, Thelma, joint author. II. Title.

GIFFORD, Denis. 791.43'092'4
Chaplin / Denis Gifford. 1st ed. Garden City, N.Y. : Doubleday, 1974, 128 p. : ill. (some col.) : 26 cm. (The Movie makers) Includes index. Bibliography: p. 126-127. [PN2287.C5G5 1974] 73-11632 ISBN 0-385-01123-7 : 7.50
1. Chaplin, Charles, 1889-

HUFF, Theodore. v. 12
Charlie Chaplin. New York, Pyramid Books [1964] 272 p. illus. 19 cm. 68-54702
1. Chaplin, Charles, 1889- I. Title. **BIP**

HUFF, Theodore. 927.92
Charlie Chaplin. New York, Schuman [1951] 354 p. illus., ports. 24 cm. [PN2287.C5H8] 51-10104
1. Chaplin, Charles, 1889-

HUFF, Theodore. 791.43'028'0924
Charlie Chaplin. New York, Arno Press, 1972 [c1951] 354 p. illus. 24 cm. (The Literature of cinema) Reprint of the ed. published by H. Schuman, New York. [PN2287.C5H8 1972] 72-169358 ISBN 0-405-03920-4
1. Chaplin, Charles, 1889- I. Title. II. Series.

MCCABE, John, 791.43'028'0924 B 1920-
Charlie Chaplin / John McCabe. 1st ed. Garden City, N.Y. : Doubleday, 1978. xii, 297 p., [8] leaves of plates : ill. ; 22 cm. Includes index. Bibliography: p. [245]-257. [PN2287.C5M2] 77-11771 ISBN 0-385-11445-1 : 10.00
1. Chaplin, Charles, 1889-1977. 2. Moving-picture actors and actresses—United States—Biography. 3. Comedians—United States—Biography.

MANVELL, Roger, 791.43'028'0924 B 1909-
Chaplin. [1st ed.] Boston, Little Brown [1974] ix, 240 p. illus. 21 cm. (The Library of world biography) Bibliography: p. [227]-230. [PN2287.C5M28] 74-13119 ISBN 0-316-54550-3 6.95
1. Chaplin, Charles, 1889- **BIP**

*MOSS, Robert 791.43'028'0922 B F.
Charlie Chaplin, by Robert F. Moss New York, Pyramid [1975] 158 p. illus. 20 cm. (Pyramid illustrated history of the movies) Bibliography: p. 149 [PN2287] ISBN 0-515-03640-4 1.75 (pbk.)
1. Chaplin, Charlie I. Title. **BIP**

*PAYNE, Pierre Stephen 927.92 Robert, 1911-
Charlie Chaplin (Orig. title: The great god Pan) New York, Ace [1964, c.1962] 253p. 18cm. (K204) .50 pap.,
1. Chaplin, Charles, 1889- I. Title.

PAYNE, Pierre Stephen 927.92 Robert, 1911-
The great god Pan; a biography of the tramp played by Charles Chaplin. New York, Hermitage House [1952] 301 p. illus. 22 cm. [PN2287.C5P3] 52-9130
1. Chaplin, Charles, 1889- I. Title.

TYLER, Parker. 791.43'028'0924
Chaplin: last of the clowns. [New York] Horizon Press [1972] 249 p. illus. 22 cm. [PN2287.C5T8 1972] 72-88993 7.50
1. Chaplin, Charles, 1889-

Chaplin, Charles, 1889- —Juvenile literature.

FINKE, Blythe 791.43'028'0924 B Foote.
Charlie Chaplin; famous silent movie actor and comic. Charlotteville, N.Y.; SamHar Press, 1972. 31 p. 22 cm. (Outstanding personalities, no. 43) Bibliography: p. 27-31. A biography of one of the most famous actors in motion picture history who was rocketed to stardom by his comic portrayal of "the Tramp." [PN2287.C5F53] 92 72-89207
1. Chaplin, Charles, 1889-—Juvenile literature. I. Title. **BIP**

JACOBS, David, 791.43'028'0924 B 1939-
Chaplin, the movies, & Charlie / by David Jacobs. 1st ed. New York : Harper & Row, c1975. xii, 143 p., [16] leaves of plates : ill. ; 25 cm. Includes bibliographical references and index. A biography of one of the most famous film comedians of the twentieth century who contributed greatly to the art of filmmaking both as a performer and as a director. [PN2287.C5J28] 92 75-6291 ISBN 0-06-022782-6 : 6.95. ISBN 0-06-022783 4 lib.bdg.
1. Chaplin, Charles, 1889- —Juvenile literature. I. Title. **BIP**

OLEKSY, Walter 791.43'028'0924 B G., 1930-
Laugh clown, cry : the story of Charlie Chaplin / by Walter Oleksy. Milwaukee : Raintree Editions ; Chicago : distributed by Childrens Press, c1976. 62 p. : ill. ; 23 cm. A biography of Charlie Chaplin which reveals his attitudes, successes, and failures. Illustrated with black and white photographs. [PN2287.C5O4] 92 76-15001 ISBN 0-8172-0427-X : 4.95. ISBN 0-8172-0426-1 lib. bdg. : 4.95
1. Chaplin, Charles, 1889- —Juvenile literature. I. Title. **BIP**

Chapman, Caroline Randolph.

WELDON, Warren. 133.9'1'0924 B
A happy medium: the life of Caroline Randolph Chapman. Foreword by Hugh Lynn Cayce. Englewood Cliffs, N.J., Prentice-Hall [1970] xiii, 174 p. 22 cm. [BF1283.C49W4 1970] 75-110488 ISBN 0-13-383703-3 5.95
1. Chapman, Caroline Randolph. I. Title.

Chapman, Charles C.

CHAPMAN, Charles C. 338'.092'4 B 1853-
The career of a creative Californian, 1853-1944 / edited by Donald H. Pflueger ; foreword by C. Stanley Chapman. Los Angeles : Anderson, Ritchie & Simon, 1976. ix, 241 p. : ill. ; 24 cm. Autobiography. [HC102.5.C4A33] 76-361523
1. Chapman, Charles C. I. Title.

Chapman, Guy—Biography.

CHAPMAN, Guy. 941'.082'0924 B
A kind of survivor : the autobiography of Guy Chapman / [edited by Storm Jameson]. London : Gollancz, 1975. 288 p., plate : port. ; 23 cm. [PR6005.H3164Z5] 75-322601 ISBN 0-575-01951-4 : 17.50
1. Chapman, Guy—Biography. I. Title. Distributed by Verry.

Chapman, James Allen, 1881-1966.

TYSON, Carl N. 338.7'66'550922 B
The McMan : the lives of Robert M. McFarlin and James A. Chapman / by Carl N. Tyson, James H. Thomas, Odie B. Faulk. 1st ed. [Norman] : Published for the Oklahoma Heritage Association by the University of Oklahoma Press, c1977. xiii, 224 p. : ill. ; 22 cm. (Oklahoma trackmaker series) Includes index. Bibliography: p. 213-217. [HD9570.M22T97] 77-9113 ISBN 0-8061-1446-0 : 7.75
1. McFarlin, Robert Martin, 1866-1942. 2. Chapman, James Allen, 1881-1966. 3. McMann Oil Company—History. 4. McMan Oil and Gas Company—History. 5. Petroleum industry and trade—Oklahoma—History. 6. Businessmen—Oklahoma—Biography. I. Thomas, James Harold, 1943- joint author. II. Faulk, Odie B., joint author. III. Oklahoma Heritage Association. IV. Title. V. Series. **BIP**

Chapman, John Jay, 1862-1933.

HOVEY, Richard Bennett, 928.1 1917-
John Jay Chapman, an American mind. New York, Columbia University Press, 1959. 391p. 24cm. Includes bibliography. [PS1292.C3Z65] 59-11725
1. Chapman, John Jay, 1862-1933. I. Title.

Chapman, John Wilbur, 1859-1918.

RAMSAY, John Cummins 922.573
John Wilbur Chapman, the man, his methods and his message. Boston, Christopher [c.1962] 230p. illus. 21cm. Bibl. 62-20694 3.95
1. Chapman, John Wilbur, 1859-1918. I. Title.

Chapman, John, 1774-1845.

ALIKI. 635'.092'4 B
The story of Johnny Appleseed. Written and illustrated by Aliki. [Library ed.] Englewood Cliffs, N.J., Prentice-Hall [1963] [32] p. illus. (part col.) 24 cm. Retells the wandering of John Chapman whose devotion to planting apple trees made him a legendary figure in American history. [S417.C45A57] 63-8507
1. Chapman, John, 1774-1845—Juvenile literature. I. Title.

ANDERSON, LaVere. 635'.092'4 B
The story of Johnny Appleseed. Illustrated by Kelly Oechsli. Champaign, Ill., Garrard Pub. Co. [1974] 47 p. col. illus. 22 cm. A brief biography of John Chapman who wandered across the new frontier planting apple trees and helping pioneers. [S417.C45A65] 92 73-17255 ISBN 0-8116-4040-X (lib. bdg.)
1. Chapman, John, 1774-1845—Juvenile literature. I. Oechsli, Kelly, illus. II. Title. III. Title: Johnny Appleseed. **BIP**

HOLBERG, Ruth (Langland), 926.3 1891-
Restless Johnny, the story of Johnny Appleseed; illustrated by Lloyd Coe. New York, Crowell [1950] 210 p. illus. 21 cm. [S417.C45H6] 50-5868
1. Chapman, John, 1774-1845. I. Title.

HUNT, Mabel Leigh, 1892- 926.3
Better known as Johnny Appleseed. Decorations by James Daugherty. [1st ed.] Philadelphia, Lippincott [1950] xii, 212 p. illus., map. 21 cm. [S417.C45H8] 50-14382
1. Chapman, John, 1774-1845. I. Title. **BIP**

JOHNSON, Ann 635'.092'4 B Donegan.
The value of love : the story of Johnny Appleseed / by Ann Donegan Johnson ; illustrated by Pileggi. 1st ed. La Jolla, Calif. : Value Communications, c1979. 63 p. : col. ill. ; 28 cm. (ValueTales series) A biography of John Chapman whose distribution of appleseeds and trees across the Midwest made him a legend and left us a legacy we can still enjoy today. [SB63.C46J63] 92 78-31873 ISBN 0-916392-35-X : 5.95
1. Chapman, John, 1774-1845—Juvenile literature. 2. Apple growers—United States—Biography—Juvenile literature. 3. Frontier and pioneer life—Middle West—Juvenile literature. I. Pileggi, Steve. II. Title. **BIP**

MOORE, Eva 920
Johnny Appleseed. Pictures by Judith Ann Lawrence. New York, Scholastic [c.1964] 63p. illus. (pt. col.) 21cm. (TW637) .45 pap.,
1. Chapman, John, 1775-1845— Juvenile literature. I. Title.

NORMAN, Gertrude 926.3
Johnny Appleseed. Illustrated by James Caraway. New York, Putnam [c.1960] 44p. illus. 23cm. (See and read biography) 60-12531 2.00; 2.19 lib. ed.,
1. Chapman, John. 1774-1845—Juvenile literature. I. Title.

PRICE, Robert, 1900- 926.3
Johnny Appleseed; man and myth. Bloomington, Indiana University Press, 1954. xv, 320p. illus., maps (part fod.) facsims. 22cm. Bibliography: p.299-303. [S417.C45P7] 54-7972
1. Chapman, John, 1774-1845. I. Title. **BIP**

PRICE, Robert, 1900- 635'.0924
Johnny Appleseed: man and myth. Gloucester, Mass., P. Smith, 1967 [c1954] xv, 320 p. illus., maps. 21 cm. Bibliography: p. 299-303. [S417.C45P7 1967] 67-4052
1. Chapman, John, 1774-1845. I. Title.

Chapman, Nathaniel, 1780-1853.

RICHMAN, Irwin. v. 12
The brightest ornament; a biography of Nathaniel Chapman. Bellefonte, Pa., Pennsylvania Heritage [c1967] vii, 213, p. 24 cm. 68-71292
1. Chapman, Nathaniel, 1780-1853. I. Title.

Chappell, Clovis Gillham, 1882-1972.

CHAPPELL, Wallace 287'.6'0924 B D.
Clovis Chappell : preacher of the word / Wallace D. Chappell. Nashville, Tenn. : Broadman Press, 1979, c1978. 96 p. : ill. ; 20 cm. [BX8495.C48C48] 78-59305 ISBN 0-8054-7223-1 : 3.95
1. Chappell, Clovis Gillham, 1882-1972. 2. Methodist Church—Clergy—Biography. 3. Clergy—United States—Biography. I. Title. **BIP**

Characters and characteristics.

WALLACE, Irving, 1916- 920.02
The square pegs; some Americans who dared to be different. [1st ed.] New York, Knopf, 1957. 315 p. 22 cm. [CT9990.W3] 57-7552
1. Characters and characteristics. 2. Biography. I. Title.

Charcoal, 1856-1896.

DEMPSEY, Hugh Aylmer, 1929- 970'.004'97 B
Charcoal's world / Hugh A. Dempsey. Lincoln : University of Nebraska Press, 1979, c1978. p. cm. Reprint of the ed. published by Western Producer Prairie Books, Saskatoon. Includes index. Bibliography: p. [E99.K15C452 1979] 79-14920 ISBN 0-8032-1651-3 : 11.95 ISBN 0-8032-6552-2 pbk. : 3.95
1. Charcoal, 1856-1896. 2. Kainah Indians—Biography. 3. Crime and criminals—Alberta—Biography. I. Title. BIP

Charcot, Jean Martin, 1825-1893.

GUILLAIN, Georges, 1876- 926.1
J.-M. Charcot, 1825-1893; his life—his work. Edited and translated by Pearce Bailey. [New York] Hoeber [1959] 202 p. illus. 22 cm. Includes bibliography. [R507.C45G8] 59-11089
1. Charcot, Jean Martin, 1825-1893.

Chardenon, Ludo.

*DURRELL, Lawrence. 615'.321 [B]
The plant magic man. Santa Barbara [Calif.] Capra Press, 1973. 25 p. illus. (some col.) ports. 18 cm. (Yes! Capra chapbook series, no. 5) [RS164] ISBN 0-912264-51-9 2.50 (pbk.)
1. Chardenon, Ludo. 2. Herbs. 3. Botany, Medical. I. Title. II. Series. BIP

Chardin, Jean Baptiste Simeon, 1699-1779.

ROSENBERG, Pierre. 759.4
Chardin. [Biographical and critical study; translated from the French by Helga Harrison. Lausanne] Skira [distributed in the U.S. by World Pub. Co., Cleveland, 1963] 126 p. mounted col. illus. 19 cm. (The Taste of our time, v. 40) Bibliography: p. 113-[118] [ND553.C4R583] 63-20241
1. Chardin, Jean Baptiste Simeon, 1699-1779. I. Title.

Chargaff, Erwin.

CHARGAFF, Erwin. 574.1'92'0924 B
Heraclitean fire : sketches from a life before nature / Erwin Chargaff. New York : Rockefeller University Press, 1978. 252 p. ; 23 cm. Includes index. Bibliography: p. 229-252. [QP511.8.C45A33] 77-95216 ISBN 0-87470-029-9 : 13.00
1. Chargaff, Erwin. 2. Biochemists—United States—Biography. I. Title. BIP

Charke, Charlotte (Cibber)

CHARKE, Charlotte (Cibber) d.1760? 792'.028'0924 B
A narrative of the life of Mrs. Charlotte Charke (youngest daughter of Colley Cibbler [sic], Esq.) Written by herself. Introd. by Leonard R. N. Ashley. Gainsville, Fla., Scholars' Facsimiles & Reprints, 1969. xxiv, x, 281 p. illus., ports. 23 cm. Facsimile reproduction of the 2d ed., 1755. [PN2598.C28A3 1755a] 70-81365
I. Title.

Charlemagne, 742-814.

CABANISS, James Allen, 1911- 944'.01'0924 B
Charlemagne, by Allen Cabaniss. New York, Twayne Publishers [1972] 176 p. 21 cm. (Twayne's rulers and statesmen of the world series, TROW 15) Includes bibliographical references. [DC73.C15] 79-181717 4.95
1. Charlemagne, 742-814.

CHARLEMAGNE, v. 12
the legend and the man. New York, Bantam books [1958] 247p. 18cm. (A Bantam biography)
1. Charlemagne, 742-814. I. Lamb, Harold, 1892- BIP

DAVIS, Henry William Carless, 1874-1928. 944'.01'0924 B
Charlemagne (Charles the Great) the hero of two nations. Freeport, N.Y., Books for Libraries Press [1972] xvi, 338 p. illus. 23 cm. Original ed. issued as vol. 26 of Heroes of the nations series. Reprint of the 1899 ed. [DC73.D26 1972] 72-24 ISBN 0-8369-9957-6
1. Charlemagne, 742-814. I. Series: Heroes of the nations, v. 26. BIP

EINHARD, 770(ca.)-840. 944'.01 B
Early lives of Charlemagne, by Eginhard & the Monk of St. Gall. Translated and edited by A. J. Grant. New York, Cooper Square Publishers, 1966. xxv, 179 p. front. 17 cm. (The Medieval library) Translation of Einhard's Vita Karoli Magni imperatoris and of Notker's Gesta Karoli Magni as published in 1867 in v. 4 of Bibliotheca rerum germanicarum. [DC73.32.G7 1966] 66-27656
1. Charlemagne, 742-814. I. Grant, Arthur James, 1862-1948, ed. and tr. II. Notker Balbulus, 840 (ca.)-912. Gesta Karoli Magni. English. 1966. III. Title.

EINHARD, 770(ca.)--840. 923.14
The life of Charlemagne. With a foreword by Sidney Painter. [Translated by Samuel Epes Turner. Ann Arbor] University of Michigan Press [c.1960] 74p. fold. map, geneal. table. 21cm. (Ann Arbor paperbacks, AA35) 60-16107 1.25 pap.,
1. Charlemagne, 742-814. I. Title.

EINHARD, 770(ca)-840. 944.01'092'4 B
Vita Karoli Magni. The life of Charlemagne. The Latin text with a new English translation, introd. and notes by Evelyn Scherabon Firchow and Edwin H. Zeydel. Coral Gables, Fla., University of Miami Press, [1972] 144 p. illus. 22 cm. Bibliography: p. 141-144. [DC73.3 1972] 71-163840 ISBN 0-87024-212-1 7.95
1. Charlemagne, 742-814. I. Firchow, Evelyn Scherabon, ed. II. Zeydel, Edwin H., ed. III. Title. BIP

FOLZ, Robert. 944'.01'0924 B
The coronation of Charlemagne, 25 December 800 / Robert Folz translated by J. E. Anderson London : Routledge & K. Paul, 1974. xii, 266 p., [12] leaves of plates : ill. ; 22 cm. Translation of Le couronnement imperial de Charlemagne, 25 decembre 800. Includes index. Bibliography: p. 250-257. [DC73.F613] 75-300794 ISBN 0-7100-7847-1 : 18.00
1. Charlemagne, 742-814. I. Title.
Distributed by Routledge & Kegan Paul, Boston.

HEER, Friedrich, 1916- 943'.01'0924 B
Charlemagne and his world / Frederich Heer. 1st American ed. New York : Macmillan, 1975. p. cm. Includes index. [DC73.H35 1975] 74-22219 ISBN 0-02-550450-9 : 15.00
1. Charlemagne, 742-814. I. Title.

HODGKIN, Thomas, 1831-1913. 944'.01'0924
Charles the Great. Port Washington, N.Y., Kennikat Press [1970] x, 251 p. geneal. tables. 21 cm. Reprint of the 1897 ed. [DC73.H68 1970] 71-112808
1. Charlemagne, 742-814. BIP

KARL der Grosse; 923.14
Werk und Wirkung [New York, N.Y. 10019. 250 W. 57th St., World Wide Bks. . 1966] x1, 567p. 158 plates (pt. col.) maps (3 fold.) 22cm. price unreported pap.,
1. Charlegmagne, 742-814.

KOMROFF, Manuel, 1890- 944'.01'0924 B
Charlemagne. New York, Messner [1964] 191 p. map. 22 cm. Bibliography: p. 183-184. A biography of the medieval ruler of Europe who established Christianity in the lands he conquered, set up many schools, codified laws, and gave a unity to his Roman Empire that endured subsequent years of disorder. [DC73.K65] 92 AC 68
1. Charlemagne, 742-814. I. Title.

LAMB, Harold, 1892-1962. 923.14
Charlemagne: the legend and the man. [1st ed.] Garden City, N.Y., Doubleday, 1954. 320 p. 22 cm. [DC73.L24] 54-5368
1. Charlemagne, 742-814.

LAMB, Harold Albert, 1892- 923.14
Charlemagne: the legend and the man. New York, Bantam [1963, c.1954] 247p. 18cm. (Pathfinder ed., FP24) .50 pap.,
1. Charlemagne, 742-814. I. Title.

MOHAMMED and Charlemagne. v. 12
[Translated by Bernard Miall] New York, Barnes & Noble [1958] 293p. 19cm. Bibliographical footnotes.
1. Europe—Hist.—476-1492. 2. Gaul—Hist. 3. Mohammedan countries—Hist. I. Pirenne, Henri, 1862-1935.

POETA Saxo, 9th cent. 923.14
The Saxon Poet's life of Charles the Great. Translated by Mary E. McKinney. [1st ed.] New York, Pageant Press [1956] vii, 118p. 21cm. Translation based on P. Jaffe's text of the Annales de gestis Caroll Magni imperatoris in the Bibliotheca rerum Germanicarum. [DC73.6.P613] 56-13127
1. Charlemagne, 742-814. I. McKinney, Mary Emma, 1887- tr. II. Title.

WINSTON, Richard 923.14
Charlemagne: from the hammer to the cross. [Gloucester, Mass., P. Smith, 1965, c.1954] xix, 418p. map. 19cm. (Vintage bk. V106 rebound) [DC73.W5] 3.50
1. Charlemagne, 742-814. I. Title.

WINSTON, Richard 923.14
Charlemagne: from the hammer to the cross. New York, Random House, 1960[c.1954] viii, 418p. xiv, Bibl.: p.[415]-418. 19cm. (Vintage book, V-106) 1.45 pap.,
1. Charlemagne, 742-814. I. Title.

WINSTON, Richard. 923.14
Charlemagne: from the hammer to the cross. [1st ed.] Indianapolis, Bobbs-Merrill [1954] 346p. map (on lining papers) 23cm. Bibliography: p. [329]-334. [DC73.W5] 54-10850
1. Charlemagne, 742-814. I. Title.

WINSTON, Richard. v. 12
Charlemagne; from the hammer to the cross. New York, Random house [1960, c1954] viii, 418, xivp. map. 18 cm. (Vintage books, V-106) "Originally published by the Bobbs-Merrill co., inc., in 1954" Bibliography: p. [415]-418. 65-97227
1. Charlemagne, 742-814 I. Title.

Charlemagne, 742-814 — Juvenile literature.

KOMROFF, Manuel, 1890- 920
Charlemagne. New York, Messner [c.1964] 191p. map. 22cm. Bibl. 64-20149 3.25; 3.19 lib. ed.,
1. Charlemagne, 742-814—Juvenile literature. I. Title.

KOMROFF, Manuel, 1890- j92
Charlemagne. New York, Messner, [1964] 191 p. map. 22 cm. Bibliography: p. 183-184. [DC73.K65] 64-20149
1. Charlemagne, 742-814 — Juvenile literature. I. Title.

STEARNS, Monroe. 944'.01'0924 B
Charlemagne, monarch of the Middle Ages [map by Walter Hortens] London, New York, F. Watts, 1971. ix, 182 p. illus., facsims., map. 22 cm. Bibliography: p. 173-175. [DC73.S77 1971b] 73-154623 ISBN 0-85166-327-3 £1.25
1. Charlemagne, 742-814—Juvenile literature. I. Title.

Charles d'Orleans, 1394-1465.

GOODRICH, Norma Lorre. 923.244
Charles, duke of Orleans; a literary biography. New York, Macmillan [1963] 340 p. 22 cm. Includes bibliography. [PQ1553.C5G6] 63-15681
1. Charles d'Orleans, 1394-1465.

MCLEOD, Enid. 841'.2 B
Charles of Orleans, prince and poet. New York, Viking Press [1970, c1969] xvi, 407 p. illus., facsims., geneal. tables, ports. 23 cm. Bibliography: p. 391-398. [PQ1553.C5M3 1970] 77-101687 ISBN 0-670-21250-4 8.50
1. Charles d'Orleans, 1394-1465. I. Title.

Charles Edward, the Young Pretender, 1720-1788.

DAICHES, David, 1912- 941.07'092'4 B
The last Stuart; the life and times of Bonnie Prince Charlie. New York, Putnam [1973] 335 p. illus. 25 cm. Bibliography: p. 326-[329] [DA814.A5D33 1973] 72-94434 ISBN 0-399-11109-3 10.00
1. Charles Edward, the Young Pretender, 1720-1788. 2. Jacobite Rebellion, 1745-1746. I. Title. BIP

DUKE, Winifred. 923.242
In the steps of Bonnie Prince Charlie. London, New York, Rich and Cowan [1953] 280p. illus., ports., maps (on lining papers) 19cm. [DA814.A5D76] 54-350
1. Charles Edward, the Young Pretender, 1720-1788. I. Title.

FORSTER, Margaret, 1938- 941.07'092'4 B
The rash adventurer; the rise and fall of Charles Edward Stuart. New York, Stein and Day [1974, c1973] 331 p. 25 cm. Bibliography: p. [311]-324. [DA814.A5F63 1974] 73-80842 ISBN 0-8128-1607-2 12.50
1. Charles Edward, the Young Pretender, 1720-1788. I. Title.

MCLAREN, Moray. 941.07'092'4 B
Bonnie Prince Charlie. [1st American ed.] New York, Saturday Review Press [1972] 223 p. 22 cm. Bibliography: p. 215-218. [DA814.A5M36 1972b] 72-79058 ISBN 0-8415-0195-5 6.95
1. Charles Edward, the Young Pretender, 1720-1788. I. Title.

SORLEY, Herbert Tower, 1892- 928
Exile, a study in three books. Ilfracombe, Eng., A.H. Stockwell [Port Washington, N.Y., Clark McCutcheon, 176 Main, 1965] x, 203p. 29cm. Bibl. [CT105.S724] 65-7394 2.75
1. Ovidius Naso, Publius. 2. Charles Edward, the Young Pretender, 1720-1788. 3. Hugo, Victor Marie, comte, 1802-1885. 4. Exiles. I. Title.
Contents omitted.

Charles Edward, the Young Pretender, 1720-1788—Juvenile literature.

CARRUTH, James Aloysius. 942.07'2'0924 B
The Bonnie Prince Charlie country and the 1745 Jacobite rising; text by J. A. Carruth. Norwich, Jarrold and Sons, 1971. [34] p. illus. (chiefly col.), col. coats of arms, geneal. table, col. map, ports. (some col.). 25 cm. [DA814.5.C33] 72-190411 ISBN 0-85306-294-3 £0.30
1. Charles Edward, the Young Pretender, 1720-1788—Juvenile literature. 2. Jacobite Rebellion, 1745-1746—Juvenile literature. I. Title.

Charles I, King of Great Britain, 1600-1649.

BOWLE, John. 941.06'2'0924 B
Charles I : a biography / John Bowle 1st American ed. Boston : Little, Brown, 1976 c1975 xiv, 362 p., [8] leaves of plates : ill. ; 24 cm. Includes bibliographical references and index. [DA396.A2B65 1975b] 75-45483 ISBN 0-316-10404-3 : 12.50
1. Charles I, King of Great Britain, 1600-1649. BIP

HIBBERT, Christopher, 1924- 942.06'2'0924 B
Charles I. [1st U. S. ed.] New York, Harper & Row [1968] 295 p. illus. (part col.), facsims., ports. 26 cm. Bibliography: p. 282-286. [DA396.A2H5] 68-28202 11.95
1. Charles I, King of Great Britain, 1600-1649.

HIGHAM, Florence May Greir Evans, 1896- 941.06'2'0924 B
Charles I : a study / by F. M. G. Higham. Westport, Conn. : Greenwood Press, 1979. 315 p., [3] leaves of plates : ill. ; 22 cm. Reprint of the 1932 ed. published by H. Hamilton, London. Includes index. [DA396.A2H53 1979] 78-27522 ISBN 0-8371-6188-6 lib. bdg. : 22.50
1. Charles I, King of Great Britain, 1600-1649. 2. Great Britain—Kings and rulers—

Biography. 3. Great Britain—Politics and government—1603-1649. I. Title.

HIGHAM, Florence 941.06'2'0924 B
May Greir Evans, 1896-
Charles I : a study / by F. M. G. Higham. Folcroft, Pa. : Folcroft Library Editions, 1977. p. cm. Reprint of the 1932 ed. published by H. Hamilton, London. Includes index. Bibliography: p. [DA396.A2H53 1977] 77-22385 ISBN 0-8414-4951-1 : 30.00
1. Charles I, King of Great Britain, 1600-1649. 2. Great Britain—Kings and rulers—Biography. 3. Great Britain—Politics and government—1603-1649. **BIP**

OLLARD, Richard 941.06'2
Lawrence.
The image of the king : a biography of Charles I and Charles II / Richard Ollard. 1st American ed. New York : Atheneum, 1979. p. cm. Includes index. Bibliography: p. [DA396.A2O38 1979] 79-50965 ISBN 0-689-11006-5 : 12.95
1. Charles I, King of Great Britain, 1600-1649. 2. Charles II, King of Great Britain, 1630-1685. 3. Great Britain—History—Charles I, 1625-1649. 4. Great Britain—History—Charles II, 1660-1685. 5. Great Britain—Kings and rulers—Biography. I. Title. **BIP**

PETRIE, Charles 941.06'2'0922
Alexander, Sir, bart., 1895-
King Charles, Prince Rupert, and the Civil War : from original letters / edited by Sir Charles Petrie. London : Routledge & K. Paul, 1974 [i.e., 1975] viii, 136 p. : map (on lining papers) ; 23 cm. Includes letters of King Charles I, and others. Includes index. [DA415.P47] 74-196158 ISBN 0-7100-7969-9 : 9.25
1. Charles I, King of Great Britain, 1600-1649. 2. Rupert, Prince, Count Palatine, 1619-1682. 3. Great Britain—History—Civil War, 1642-1649. I. Charles I, King of Great Britain, 1600-1649. II. Title.

SIMPSON, Evan John, 1901- 923.142
King Charles I, by Evan John [pseud.] New York, Roy [1952] 314 p. illus. 23 cm. [DA396.A2S5 1952] 52-3605
1. Charles I, King of Great Britain, 1600-1649. I. Title.

WEDGWOOD, Cicely 942.062
Veronica, Dame, 1910-
A coffin for King Charles; the trial and execution of Charles I [by] C. V. Wedgwood. New York, Macmillan [1964] 307 p. illus., facsims., ports. 21 cm. London ed. (Collins) has title: The trial of Charles I. "Bibliographical note": p. 263-264. [DA396.A22W4] 64-15454
1. Charles I, King of Great Britain, 1600-1649. I. Title.

WINGFIELD- 941.06'2'0924 B
STRATFORD, Esme Cecil, 1882-
Charles, King of England, 1600-1637 / by Esme Wingfield-Stratford. Westport, Conn. : Greenwood Press, 1975. xii, 361 p., [7] leaves of plates : ill. ; 22 cm. Reprint of the 1949 ed. published by Hollis & Carter, London. Includes index. Bibliography: p. [349]-358. [DA396.A2W48 1975] 74-31871 ISBN 0-8371-7949-1
1. Charles I, King of Great Britain, 1600-1649. **BIP**

WINGFIELD- 941.06'2'0924 B
STRATFORD, Esme Cecil, 1882-
Charles, King of England, 1600-1637 / by Esme Wingfield-Stratford Westport, Conn. : Greenwood Press, 1975. xii, 361 p., [7] leaves of plates : ill. ; 22 cm. Reprint of the 1949 ed. published by Hollis & Carter, London. Includes index. Bibliography: p. [349]-358. [DA396.A2W48 1975] 74-31871 ISBN 0-8371-7949-1 lib.bdg. : 19.00
1. Charles I, King of Great Britain, 1600-1649.

WINGFIELD- 941.06'2'0924 B
STRATFORD, Esme Cecil, 1882-
King Charles the martyr, 1643-1649 / by Esme Wingfield-Stratford Westport, Conn. : Greenwood Press, 1975. xi, 385 p., [4] leaves of plates : ill. ; 22 cm. Reprint of the 1950 ed. published by Hollis & Carter, London. Includes index. [DA396.A2W52 1975] 74-28760 ISBN 0-8371-7922-X : 20.00
1. Charles I, King of Great Britain, 1600-1649. 2. Great Britain—History—Civil War, 1642-1649. I. Title. **BIP**

Charles II, King of Great Britain, 1630-1685.

ASHLEY, Maurice 942.06'6'0924 B
Percy.
Charles II, the man and the statesman [by] Maurice Ashley. New York, Praeger [1971] 358 p. illus. 23 cm. Bibliography: p. 327-345. [DA445.A85 1971b] 79-100906 10.00
1. Charles II, King of Great Britain, 1630-1685. I. Title.

CHAPMAN, Hester W. 1899- 923.142
The tragedy of Charles II in the years 1630-1660 [by] Hester W. Chapman. 1st American ed. Boston, Little, Brown [1964] 415 p. geneal. table, map, ports. 22 cm. Bibliography: p. 402-407. [DA445.C45 1964a] 64-15054
1. Charles II, King of Great Britain, 1630-1685. I. Title.

FALKUS, 942.06'6'0924 B
Christopher.
The life and times of Charles II. Introd. by Antonia Fraser. Garden City, N.Y., Doubleday, 1972. 223 p. illus. (part col.) 26 cm. Bibliography: p. 217-218. [DA445.F3 1972b] 74-189537 10.00
1. Charles II, King of Great Britain, 1630-1685. I. Title.

FRASER, Antonia 941.06'6'0924 B
Pakenham, Lady, 1932-
Royal Charles : Charles II and the Restoration / Antonia Fraser. 1st American ed. New York : Knopf, 1979. p. cm. Includes index. Bibliography: p. [DA445.F68 1979] 79-2208 ISBN 0-394-49721-X : 15.95
1. Charles II, King of Great Britain, 1630-1685. 2. Great Britain—History—Charles II, 1660-1685. 3. Great Britain—Kings and rulers—Biography. I. Title. **BIP**

NORMAN, Charles, 1904- 923.142
The flight and adventures of Charles II. Illustrated by C. Walter Hodges. New York, Random House [1958] 182 p. illus. 22 cm. (World landmark books, W-38) [DA446.N6] 58-6190
1. Charles II, King of Great Britain, 1630-1685. I. Title.

OLLARD, Richard 942.06'3'0924
Lawrence.
The escape of Charles II after the battle of Worcester, by Richard Ollard New York, Scribner [1966] xiv, 160 p. illus., map (on lining paper), ports. 22 cm. [DA446.O55 1966b] 67-24063
1. Charles II, King of Great Britain, 1630-1685. I. Title.

PEARSON, Hesketh 923.142
Merry monarch; the life and likeness of Charles II. New York, Harper [c.1960] 274p. Bibl. illus. London ed. has title: Charles II: his life and likeness. 60-7535 5.00
1. Charles II, King of Great Britain, 1630-1685. I. Title.

PEARSON, Hesketh, 1887- 923.142
Merry monarch; the life and likeness of Charles II. New York, Harper [1960] 274p. illus. 22cm. London ed. (Heinemann) has title: Charles II: his life and likeness. [DA445.P35 1960a] 60-7535
1. Charles II, King of Great Britain, 1630-1685. I. Title.

PEPYS, Samuel, 1633- 942.06'3
1703, ed.
Charles II's escape from Worcester; a collection of narratives assembled by Samuel Pepys. Edited by William Matthews. Berkeley, University of California Press, 1966. 178 p. illus., facsims., map, ports. 23 cm. Contents.Contents.—Introduction, by W. Matthews.—A synopsis of events.—Relation from the Queen Mother.—Order of the Council of State.—The King's account of his escape.—An exact narrative and relation (1660)—A letter from the Lady Tuke.—Father Huddleston's original account.—Thomas Whitgreave, an account of Charles the Second's preservation.—The Alford depositions.—Original notes from Colonel Phillips.—Colonel Gounter's report. [DA446.P4 1966] 66-26143
1. Charles II, King of Great Britain, 1630-1685. I. Matthews, William, 1905- ed. II. Title.

Charles le Temeraire, Duke of Burgundy, 1433-1477.

VAUGHAN, Richard, 944'.025'0924 B
1927-
Charles the Bold; the last Valois Duke of Burgundy. New York, Barnes & Noble Books [1974, c1973] xvi, 491 p. illus. 23 cm. Bibliography: p. 433-467. [DC611.B781V38 1974] 74-166215 ISBN 0-06-497171-6 28.00
1. Charles le Temeraire, Duke of Burgundy, 1433-1477. 2. Burgundy—History. 3. Europe—History—476-1492. I. Title.

Charles Martel, mayor of the palace, 688 (ca.)-741—Juvenile literature.

MILLER, Shane 92
Charles the Hammer, the story of Charles Martel. (Title orig.: The Hammer of Gaul) Written, illus. by Shane Miller. New York, Guild [1965, c.1964] 192p. illus. maps. 18cm. (Turret bks., 31501) [DC71.M5] .50 pap.,
1. Charles Martel, mayor of the palace, 688 (ca.)-741—Juvenile literature. I. Title.

MILLER, Shane 92
The Hammer of Gaul; the story of Charles Martel, written, illus. by Shane Miller. New York, Hawthorn [c.1964] 188p. illus. (pt. col.) maps (pt. col.) 22cm. (Credo bks) 64-11244 2.95
1. Charles Martel, mayor of the palace, 688 (ca.)-741—Juvenile literature. I. Title.

MILLER, Shane 920
The Hammer of Gaul; the story of Charles Martel, written, illus. by Shane Miller. New York, Hawthorn [c.1964] 188p. illus. (pt. col.) maps (pt. col.) 22cm. (Credo bks) 64-11244 2.95
1. Charles Martel, mayor of the palace, 688 (ca.)-741—Juvenile literature. I. Title.

MILLER, Shane. 92
The Hammer of Gaul; the story of Charles Martel, written and illustrated by Shane Miller. New York, Hawthorn Books [1964] 188 p. illus. (part col.) maps (part col.) 22 cm. (Credo books) [DC71.M5] 64-11244
1. Charles Martel, mayor of the palace, 688 (ca.) 741 Juvenile literature. I Title.

Charles, Prince of Wales, 1948-

CATHCART, Helen. 941'.085'0924 B
Prince Charles : the biography / by Helen Cathcart. London : W. H. Allen, 1976. 184 p., [8] leaves of plates : ill. ; 23 cm. Bibliography: p. 183-184. [DA591.A33C37] 77-364719 ISBN 0-491-01907-6 : £3.50
1. Charles, Prince of Wales, 1948- 2. Great Britain—Princes and princesses—Biography. I. Title.

FISHER, Graham. 942.085'0924 B
Prince Charles: the future king [by] Graham & Heather Fisher. [1st American ed.] New York, Hawthorn Books [1967] 221 p. ports. 23 cm. [DA591.A33F5 1967] 67-24655
1. Charles, Prince of Wales, 1948- I. Fisher, Heather, joint author. II. Title.

FISHER, Graham. 942.085'0924 (B)
Prince Charles: the future king [by] Graham & Heather Fisher. [1st American ed.] New York, Hawthorn Books [1967] 221 p. ports. 23 cm. [DA591.A33F5] 67-24655
1. Charles, Prince of Wales, 1948- I. Fisher, Heather, joint author. II. Title.

HEALD, Tim. 941.085'092'4 B
H. R. H., the man who will be king / by Tim Heald and Mayo Mohs. New York : Arbor House, c1979. 229 p., [24] leaves of plates : ill. ; 24 cm. [DA591.A33H4 1979] 78-73860 ISBN 0-87795-212-4 : 11.95
1. Charles, Prince of Wales, 1948- 2. Great Britain—Princes and princesses—Biography. I. Mohs, Mayo, joint author. II. Title.

WAKEFORD, 942.085'0924 B
Geoffrey.
The heir apparent; an authentic study of the life and training of H. R. H. Charles Prince of Wales. [1st American ed.] South Brunswick [N.J.] A. S. Barnes Co. [1968, c1967] 240 p. 22 cm. Bibliography: p. [8] [DA591.A33W3 1968] 68-29861 6.00
1. Charles, Prince of Wales, 1948- I. Title.

Charles, Prince of Wales, 1948- Juvenile literature.

GILLEO, Alma, 941.085'092'4 B
1920-
Prince Charles, growing up in Buckingham Palace / by Alma Gilleo ; designed and illustrated by Helen Endres. Elgin, Ill. : Child's World ; Chicago : distributed by Childrens Press, c1978. p. cm. Briefly describes the childhood of the heir to the British crown. [DA591.A33G54] 92 78-18938 ISBN 0-89565-029-0 : 7.35
1. Charles, Prince of Wales, 1948- Juvenile literature. 2. Great Britain—Princes and princesses—Biography—Juvenile literature. 3. Great Britain—History—Elizabeth II, 1952- —Juvenile literature. 4. Buckingham Palace—Juvenile literature. I. Endres, Helen. II. Title. **BIP**

Charles, Ray, 1930-

CHARLES, Ray 784'.092'4 B
Brother Ray : Ray Charles' own story / Ray Charles and Davit Ritz. New York : Warner Books, inc., 1979, c1978 366p. ; 18 cm. [ML420.aC459A3] ISBN 0-446-95094-7 pbk. : 2.75
1. Charles, Ray, 1930- 2. Jazz musicians - United States -Biography. I. Rity, David. II. Title.
L.C. card no. for 1978 Dial Press ed: 78-8472

CHARLES, Ray, 1930- 784'.092'4 B
Brother Ray : Ray Charles' own story / Ray Charles and David Ritz. New York : Dial Press, c1978. xii, 340 p. ; 24 cm. [ML420.C459A3] 78-8472 ISBN 0-8037-0828-9 : 8.95
1. Charles, Ray, 1930- 2. Jazz musicians—United States—Biography. I. Ritz, David, joint author. II. Title.

Charles, Ray, 1932-—Juvenile literature.

MATHIS, Sharon Bell. 784'.092'4 B
Ray Charles. Illustrated by George Ford. New York, Crowell [1973] 31 p. illus. (part col.) 24 cm. (A Crowell biography) A biography of the Black musician who became famous despite his blindness. [ML3930.C443M4] 92 72-7552 ISBN 0-690-67065-6
*1. Charles, Ray, 1932-—Juvenile literature. I. Ford, George, fl. 1969- illus. II. Title.***BIP**

Charles VII, King of France, 1403-1461.

VALE, Malcolm 944'.026'0924 B
Graham Allan.
Charles VII / M.G.A. Vale. Berkeley : University of California Press, 1974. xiii, 267 p., [7] leaves of plates : ill. ; 25 cm. Includes index. Bibliography: p. [248]-255. [DC102.V34] 74-79775 ISBN 0-520-02787-6 : 18.00
1. Charles VII, King of France, 1403-1461. 2. France—History—Charles VII, 1422-1461.

Charles X, King of France, 1757-1836.

BEACH, Vincent Woodrow, 944.06'2
1917-
1825: the decisive year of Charles X's reign, by Vincent W. Beach. Boulder, University of Colorado Press, 1967. 30 p. 26 cm. (University of Colorado studies. Series in history, no. 4) Cover title. Bibliographical footnotes. [D6.C58 no. 4] 67-64371
1. Charles X, King of France, 1757-1836. I. Title. II. Series: Colorado. University. University of Colorado studies. Series in history, no. 4.

Charless, Joseph, 1772-1834.

KASER, David, 1924- 655.092
Joseph Charless; printer in the western country. Philadelphia, Univ. of Pa. Pr.

[c.1963] 160p. illus., facsims. 22cm. Bibl. 63-15011 4.50
1. Charless, Joseph, 1772-1834. I. Title.

Charlotte Augusta, of Wales, consort of Prince Leopold of Saxe-Coburg-Saalfeld, 1796-1817.

HOLME, Thea 941.07'3'0924 B
Johnston, 1907-
Prinny's daughter : a life of Princess Charlotte of Wales / [by] Thea Holme. London : Hamilton, 1976. [10], 261 p., 16 p. of plates : ill., geneal. table, ports. ; 24 cm. Bibliography: p. 253-254. [DA538.A4H64 1976] 76-365038 ISBN 0-241-89298-8 : £6.50
1. Charlotte Augusta, of Wales, consort of Prince Leopold of Saxe-Coburg-Saalfeld, 1796-1817. I. Title.

Charlotte, consort of Maximilian, Emperor of Mexico, 1840-1927.

O'CONNOR, Richard, 972'.07'0924 B
1915-
The cactus throne; the tragedy of Maximilian and Carlotta. New York, Putnam [1971] 375 p. illus., ports. 22 cm. Bibliography: p. [361]-362. [F1233.O36 1971] 72-136797 7.95
1. Charlotte, consort of Maximilian, Emperor of Mexico, 1840-1927. 2. Maximilian, Emperor of Mexico, 1832-1867. 3. Mexico—History—European intervention, 1861-1867. I. Title.

Charnin, Martin.

CHARNIN, Martin. 782.8'1
Annie : a theatre memoir / by Martin Charnin. 1st ed. New York : Dutton, c1977. ca. 150 p. : ill. ; 28 cm. [ML423.C49A3] 77-92357 ISBN 0-525-05550-9. ISBN 0-525-03010-7 pbk. : 7.95
1. Charnin, Martin. Annie. 2. Strouse, Charles. Annie. I. Title.
BIP

Charriere, Henri, 1906-1973.

CHARRIERE, Henri, 365'.6'0924 B
1906-1973.
Banco: the further adventures of Papillon. Translated from the French by Patrick O'Brian. New York, Morrow, 1973. xi, 270 p. 24 cm. [HV8956.G8C4813] 73-13897 ISBN 0-688-00218-8 8.95
1. Charriere, Henri, 1906-1973. Papillon. I. Title.

CHARRIERE, Henri, 365'.6'0924 B
1906-1973.
Banco: the further adventures of Papillon. Translated from the French by Patrick O'Brian. New York, Pocket Books [1974, c1973] xi, 306 p. 18 cm. [HV8956.G8C4813] ISBN 0-671-78688-1. 1.95 (pbk.)
1. Charriere, Henri, 1906-1973. Papillon. I. Title.
L.C. card number for original ed.: 73-13897.

Charriere, Isabella Agneta (van Tuyll) de, d. 1805.

SCOTT, Geoffrey, 1885-1929. 928.4
The portrait of Zelide. [Introd. by George Dangerfield] New York, Scribner [1959] 226p. 21cm. [PQ1963.C55Z93 1959] 59-6075
1. Charriere, Isabella Agneta (van Tuyll) de, d. 1805. 2. Constant de Rebecque, Henri Benjamin, 1767-1830. I. Title.

WEST, Anthony, 1914- 840'.9' B
Mortal wounds. New York, McGraw Hill [1973] x, 371 p. 24 cm. Bibliography: p. [365]-371. [PQ149.W4] 72-10469 ISBN 0-07-069475-3 10.00
1. Stael-Holstein, Anne Louise Germaine (Necker) baronnede, 1766-1817. 2. Charriere, Isabella Agneta (van Tuyll) de, d. 1805. 3. Sand, George, pseud. of Mme. Dudevant, 1804-1876. I. Title.

Chartwell.

FEDDEN, Henry 942.084'0924
Romilly, 1908-
Churchill at Chartwell [by] Robin Fedden. [1st ed.] Oxford, New York, Pergamon Press [1969] xiii, 50 p. illus. (part col.), geneal. table, ports. 26 cm. 1968 ed. published under title: Churchill and Chartwell. [DA566.9.C5F35 1969] 75-89777 ISBN 0-08-006439-6
1. Chartwell. I. Title.

Chase, Harry Woodburn, 1883-1955.

WILSON, Louis Round 923.773
Harry Woodburn Chase . . . Chapel Hill, University of North Carolina Press [c.] 1960. vi, 55p. 21cm. 60-2985 2.00 bds.,
1. Chase, Harry Woodburn, 1883-1955. I. Title.
BIP

WILSON, Louis Round, 923.773
1876-
Harry Woodburn Chase ... Chapel Hill, University of North Carolina Press, 1960. 55 p. 21 cm. [LD3875 1933.W5] 60-2985
1. Chase, Harry Woodburn, 1883-1955. I. Title.

Chase, Heman.

CHASE, Heman. 974.3'04'0924
More than land : stories of New England country life and surveying / Heman Chase ; foreword by Lael Wertenbaker ; wood engravings by Randy Miller. Dublin, N.H. : W. L. Bauhan, 1978. xiii, 159 p. : ill. ; 21 cm. [TA533.C47A33 1978] 78-604 ISBN 0-87233-045-1 pbk. : 4.95
1. Chase, Heman. 2. Surveying—New England. 3. Surveyors—New England—Biography. 4. Country life—New England. I. Title.
BIP

Chase, Kate, 1840-1899.

SOKOLOFF, Alice 917.53'03'0924 B
Hunt.
Kate Chase for the defense. Illustrated with photos. New York, Dodd, Mead [1971] 315 p. illus., ports. 24 cm. Includes bibliographical references. [E415.9.S76S6] 71-147134 ISBN 0-396-06330-6 8.50
1. Chase, Kate, 1840-1899. 2. Chase, Salmon Portland, 1808-1873. 3. Sprague, William, 1830-1915. I. Title.

Chase, Salmon Portland, 1808-1873.

CHASE, Salmon 973.7'0924
Portland, 1808-1873.
Diary and correspondence of Salmon P. Chase. New York, Da Capo Press, 1971. 527 p. 23 cm. "Sixth report of the Historical Manuscripts Commission." Reprint of the 1903 ed., published as v. 2 of the Annual report of the American Historical Association for the year 1902. Contents.Contents.—Calendar of Chase letters heretofore printed, and list of letters now printed, compiled by S. H. Dodson.—Diary of S. P. Chase, July 21 to October 12, 1862.—Selected letters of Chase, 1846-1861.—Letters from George S. Denison to Chase, 1862-1865.—Miscellaneous letters to Chase, 1842-1870. [E415.9.C4A4 1971] 74-75301 ISBN 0-306-71264-4
I. Dodson, Samuel H., comp. II. Denison, George Stanton, 1833-1866. III. Title. BIP

HART, Albert 973.7'0924 B
Bushnell, 1854-1943.
Salmon Portland Chase. Boston, Houghton Mifflin. [New York, AMS Press, 1972] ix, 465 p. illus. 19 cm. (American statesmen, v. 28) Reprint of the 1899 ed. [E415.9.C4H28] 79-128954 ISBN 0-404-50878-2
1. Chase, Salmon Portland, 1808-1873. I. Title. II. Series.

SCHUCKERS, Jacob W. 973.7'0924 B
The life and public services of Salmon Portland Chase, by J. W. Schuckers. New York, Da Capo Press, 1970. xv, 669 p. illus., port. 24 cm. (Da Capo Press reprints in American constitutional and legal history) Reprint of the 1874 ed. Includes bibliographical references. [E415.9.C4S3 1970] 76-118202
1. Chase, Salmon Portland, 1808-1873. I. Title.
BIP

SCHUCKERS, Jacob W. 473.7'0924 B
The life and public services of Salmon Portland Chase, United States Senator and Governor of Ohio; Secretary of the Treasury, and Chief-Justice of the United States. To which is added the eulogy on Mr. Chase, delivered by William M. Evarts, before the alumni of Dartmouth College, June 24, 1874. New York, D. Appleton, 1874. Miami, Fla., Mnemosyne Pub. Co. [1969] xv, 669 p. illus., port. 23 cm. Running title: Life of Salmon Portland Chase. [E415.9.C4S3 1969] 73-89432
1. Chase, Salmon Portland, 1808-1873. I. Title.

SOKOLOFF, Alice 917.53'03'0924 B
Hunt.
Kate Chase for the defense. Illustrated with photos. New York, Dodd, Mead [1971] 315 p. illus., ports. 24 cm. Includes bibliographical references. [E415.9.S76S6] 71-147134 ISBN 0-396-06330-6 8.50
1. Chase, Kate, 1840-1899. 2. Chase, Salmon Portland, 1808-1873. 3. Sprague, William, 1830-1915. I. Title.

Chase, Warren, 1813-1891.

CHASE, Warren, 133.9'092'4 B
1813-1891.
The life-line of the Lone One : or, Autobiography of the world's child / by the author, Warren Chase. 3d ed. New York : AMS Press, 1975. 310 p., [2] leaves of plates : ports. ; 19 cm. (Communal societies in America) Reprint of the 1865 ed. published by B. Marsh, Boston. [BF1283.C5A3 1975] 72-2950 ISBN 0-404-10715-X : 16.00
1. Chase, Warren, 1813-1891. I. Title.

Chase, William Curtis, 1895-

CHASE, William 940.54'26'0924 B
Curtis, 1895-
Front line general : the commands of Maj. Gen. Wm. C. Chase : an autobiography. Houston, Tex. : Pacesetter Press, c1975. xi, 228 p., [8] leaves of plates : ill. ; 24 cm. Includes index. Bibliography: p. [220] [E745.C3A33] 74-30802 ISBN 0-88415-020-8 : 8.95
1. Chase, William Curtis, 1895- I. Title.

Chase, William Merritt, 1849-1916.

PISANO, Ronald G. 759.13 B
William Merritt Chase / Ronald G. Pisano. New York : Watson-Guptill, [1979] p. cm. Bibliography: p. [ND237.C48P57] 79-13532 ISBN 0-8230-5739-9 : 20.00
1. Chase, William Merritt, 1849-1916. 2. Painters—United States—Biography.

ROOF, Katharine Metcalf. 759.13
The life and art of William Merritt Chase / Katherine [i.e. Katharine] Metcalf Roof. New York : Hacker Art Books, 1975. xii, 352 p., [32] leaves of plates : ill. ; 24 cm. Reprint of the 1917 ed. published by Scribner, New York. Includes index. [ND237.C48R7 1975] 74-78545 ISBN 0-87817-080-4 : 25.00
1. Chase, William Merritt, 1849-1916. I. Title.
BIP

Chateaubriand, Francois Auguste Rene, vicomte de, 1768-1848.

BEALL, Chandler Baker, 848'.6'09
1901-
Chateaubriand et le Tasse, par Chandler B. Beall. Baltimore, Johns Hopkins Press, 1934. [New York, Johnson Reprint Corp., 1973] p. Original ed. issued as v. 24 of the Johns Hopkins studies in Romance literatures and languages. Bibliography: p. [PQ2205.Z5B37 1973] 72-11845 ISBN 0-384-03675-9
1. Chateaubriand, Francois Auguste Rene, vicomte de, 1768-1848. 2. Tasso, Torquato, 1544-1595. 3. Literature, Comparative—French and Italian. 4. Literature, Comparative—Italian and French. I. Title. II. Series: The Johns Hopkins studies in Romance literatures and languages, v. 24.
BIP

CHATEAUBRIAND, 917.4'04'3
Francois Auguste Rene, vicomte de, 1768-1848.
Travels in America. Translated by Richard Switzer. Lexington, University of Kentucky Press, 1969. xxi, 224 p. illus., ports. 25 cm. Translation of Voyages en Amerique. Bibliography: p. [209]-210. [E164.C4983] 68-55043 7.95
1. U.S.—Description and travel—1783-1848. 2. Indians of North America. I. Title.

MAUROIS, Andre, 1885- 928.4
Chateaubriand. Translated from the French by Vera Fraser. New York, Harper [1958?] 360p. illus. 22cm. [PQ2205.Z5M32 1958] 59-16017
1. Chateaubriand, Francois Auguste Rene, viscomte de, 1768-1848. I. Title.

MAUROIS, Andre, 848'.6'09 B
1885-1967.
Chateaubriand; poet, statesman, lover. Translated from the French by Vera Fraser. New York, Greenwood Press [1969] x, 352 p. ports. 23 cm. "Originally published in 1938." [PQ2205.Z5M32 1969] 72-88905
1. Chateaubriand, Francois Auguste Rene, viscomte de, 1768-1848.

Chateaubriand, Francois Auguste Rene, vicomte de, 1768-1848—Anniversaries, etc.

CHATEAUBRIAND, 917.3'04'4108
Francois Auguste Rene, vicomte de, 1768-1848.
Chateaubriand's America; excerpts from the works of Chateaubriand. Compiled by Richard Switzer. With illus. from contemporary maps and engravings and modern photos. Madison, French Dept., University of Wisconsin, 1968. iii, 96 p., 97-109 l. illus., map, ports. 28 cm. "Souvenir programme of the International Commemoration of the Bicentenary of the Birth of Chateaubriand, the University of Wisconsin, October 16-19, 1968." In French; pref., program and abstracts of conference papers in French or English. [E164.C485] 70-625645
1. Chateaubriand, Francois Auguste Rene, vicomte de, 1768-1848—Anniversaries, etc. 2. U.S.—Description and travel—1783-1848. 3. Indians of North America. I. Switzer, Richard, ed. II. International Commemoration of the Bicentenary of the Birth of Chateaubriand, University of Wisconsin, University of Wisconsin, 1968. III. Title.

Chateaubriand, Francois Auguste Rene, vicomte de, 1768-1848—Biography.

PAINTER, George 848'.6'09 S
Duncan, 1914-
Chateaubriand : a biography/ George D. Painter. 1st American ed. New York : Knopf : distributed by Random House, 1978, c1977- v. : ill. ; 25 cm. Includes index. Contents.Contents.—v. 1. The longed-for tempests. Bibliography: v. 1, p. [285]-296. [PQ2205.Z5P34 1978] 77-27522 ISBN 0-394-42658-4 (v. 1) : 12.95 (v. 1)
1. Chateaubriand, Francois Auguste Rene, vicomte de, 1768-1848—Biography. 2. Authors, French—19th century—Biography.

Chateaubriand, Francois Auguste Rene, vicomte de, 1768-1848—Biography—Youth.

PAINTER, George 848'.6'09 S
Duncan, 1914-
The longed-for tempests : (1768-93) / George D. Painter. 1st American ed. New York : Knopf : distributed by Random House, 1978, c1977. x, 327 p., [11] leaves of plates : ill. ; 25 cm. (His Chateaubriand ; v. 1) Includes index. Bibliography: p. [285]-296. [PQ2205.Z5P34 1978 vol. 1] 848'.6'09 B 78-7933 ISBN 0-394-42658-4 : 12.95
1. Chateaubriand, Francois Auguste Rene, vicomte de, 1768-1848—Biography—Youth. 2. Authors, French—19th century—Biography. I. Title.

Chateaubriand, Francois Auguste Rene, vicomte de, 1768-1848—Technique.

PORTER, Charles Allan. 848'.6'09
Chateaubriand : composition, imagination, and poetry / Charles A. Porter. Saratoga, Calif. : Anma Libri, 1978. 145 p. ; 24 cm. (Stanford French and Italian studies ; v. 9) Bibliography: p. 141-145. [PQ2205.Z5P65] 79-100364 ISBN 0-915838-37-0 pbk. : 20.00
1. Chateaubriand, Francois Auguste Rene, vicomte de, 1768-1848—Technique. I. Title. II. Series.

Chatterton, Fenimore,

CHATTERTON, Fenimore, 923.273
1860-1958.
Yesterday's Wyoming; the intimate memoirs of Fenimore Chatterton, Territorial citizen, governor, and statesman, an autobiography. [Aurora, Colo.] Powder River Publishers, 1957. 133p. illus. 24cm. [F761.C48A3] 58-34733
I. Title.

Chatterton, Thomas, 1752-1770.

DIX, John, 1800?-1865. 821'.6 B
The life of Thomas Chatterton, including his unpublished poems and correspondence. [Folcroft, Pa.] Folcroft Library Editions, 1973. p. Reprint of the 1836 ed. published by Hamilton, Adams, London. [PR3343.D5 1973] 73-12368 30.00
1. Chatterton, Thomas, 1752-1770.

NEVILL, John Cranstoun, 928.2
1893-
Thomas Chatterton. London, F. Muller [dist. Chester Springs, Pa., Dufour, 1964] 261p. 20cm. Bibl. 49-4077 3.50
1. Chatterton, Thomas, 1752-1770. I. Title.

NEVILL, John Cranstoun, 821'.6 B
1893-
Thomas Chatterton. Port Washington, N.Y., Kennikat Press [1970] 261 p. 21 cm. Bibliography: p. 254. [PR3343.N4 1970] 71-103208
1. Chatterton, Thomas, 1752-1770.

NEVILL, John Cranstoun, 821'.6 B
1893-
Thomas Chatterton. [Folcroft, Pa.] Folcroft Library Editions, 1973. p. Reprint of the 1948 ed. published by F. Muller, London. Bibliography: p. [PR3343.N4 1973] 73-12962 ISBN 0-8414-6252-6 (lib. bdg.)
1. Chatterton, Thomas, 1752-1770.

Chatterton, Thomas, 1752-1770—Biography.

ELLINGER, Esther Parker. 821'.6 B
Thomas Chatterton, the marvelous boy; to which is added The exhibition, a personal satire. [Folcroft, Pa.] Folcroft Library Editions, 1974. p. cm. Reprint of the 1930 ed. published by University of Pennsylvania Press, Philadelphia. Bibliography: p. [PR3343.E6 1974] 74-13489 ISBN 0-8414-3974-5 (lib. bdg.)
1. Chatterton, Thomas, 1752-1770—Biography. I. Chatterton, Thomas, 1752-1770. The exhibition. 1974. II. Title.

MEYERSTEIN, Edward Harry 821'.6 B
William, 1889-1952.
A life of Thomas Chatterton. New York, Russell & Russell [1972] xix, 584 p. illus. 23 cm. Reprint of the 1930 ed. "List of mss.": p. 547-550. [PR3343.M4 1972] 70-173551
1. Chatterton, Thomas, 1752-1770—Biography. **BIP**

RUSSELL, Charles Edward, 821'.6 B
1860-1941.
Thomas Chatterton: the marvelous boy; the story of a strange life, 1752-1770. New York, Haskell House, 1970. xvii, 289 p. illus., port. 23 cm. Reprint of the 1908 ed. [PR3343.R8 1970] 70-130258 ISBN 0-8383-1162-8
1. Chatterton, Thomas, 1752-1770—Biography.

Chattopadhyaya, Kamaladevi, 1903-

BRIJ Bhushan, 301.24'2'0924 B
Jamila.
Kamaladevi Chattopadhyaya : portrait of a rebel / Jamila Brijbhushan. 1st ed. New Delhi : Abhinav Publications, 1976. vi, 187 p., [9] leaves of plates : ill. ; 23 cm. Includes index. Bibliography: p. 173-175. [HN683.B65] 76-900583 11.00
1. Chattopadhyaya, Kamaladevi, 1903- 2. Social reformers—India. I. Title.
Distributed by South Asia Books. **BIP**

Chaucer, Geoffrey, d. 1400.

BREWER, Derek Stanley. 821'.1 B
Chaucer [by] D. S. Brewer. 3rd ed., extensively rev. and with additional material. London, Longmans [1973] 230 p. illus. 22 cm. Bibliography: p. 221-224. [PR1924.B73 1973] 73-179613 ISBN 0-582-48512-6 6.00 (pbk.)
1. Chaucer, Geoffrey, d. 1400.
Distributed by Longman, New York, 12.50, ISBN 0-582-48516-9.

CHESTERTON, Gilbert Keith, v. 12
1874-1936.
Chaucer. New York, Pellegrini & Cudahy [1956?] 286 p. 21 cm. 65-76328
1. Chaucer, Geoffrey, d. 1400. I. Title. **BIP**

CHESTERTON, Gilbert Keith, 928.2
1874-1936.
Chaucer. New York, Sheed and Ward, 1956. 285 p. 20 cm. (New World Chesterton) [PR1905.C4 1956] 56-6129
1. Chaucer, Geoffrey, d. 1400.

COGHILL, Nevill, 1899- v. 12
Geoffrey Chaucer. London, New York, Published for the British Council and the National Book League by Longmans, Green [1956] 77p. port. 22cm. (Bibliographical series of supplements to British book news, no. 79) Bibliography: p. 64-67. A57
1. Chaucer, Geoffrey, d. 1400. I. Title. II. Series. **BIP**

COGHILL, Nevill, 1899- v. 12
Geoffrey Chaucer by Nevill Coghill. Sir Thomas Malory by M. C. Bradbrook. Lincoln, University of Nebraska Press [c1963] 110 p. 21 cm. (British writers and their work, no. 1) Includes bibliography. 65-44636
1. Chaucer, Geoffrey, d. 1400. 2. Malory, Sir Thomas, 15th cent. I. Bradbrook, Muriel Clara. II. Title.

COGHILL, Nevill, 1899- v. 12
Geoffrey Chaucer. [London, New York] Published for the British Council and the National Book League by Longmans, Green (1959] 67 p. port. 22 cm. (Bibliographical series of supplements to British book news on writers and their work, no. 79) "First published in 1956." Reprinted with additions. Bibliography: p. 64-67. 63-4029
1. Chaucer, Geoffrey, D. 1400. I. Title.

COWLING, George Herbert, 821'.1
1881-1946.
Chaucer. Freeport, N.Y., Books for Libraries Press [1971] viii, 223 p. illus., facsims., ports. 23 cm. Reprint of the 1927 ed. Bibliography: p. 215-218. [PR1905.C6 1971] 74-150179 ISBN 0-8369-5692-3
1. Chaucer, Geoffrey, d. 1400.

EDMUNDS, Edward William. 821'.1
Chaucer & his poetry, by E. W. Edmunds. London, G. G. Harrap, 1914. [New York, AMS Press, 1972] 218 p. port. 19 cm. (Poetry and life series) Bibliography: p. [219] [PR1924.E4 1972] 79-120972 ISBN 0-404-52509-1 8.00
1. Chaucer, Geoffrey, d. 1400. I. Title. II. Series. **BIP**

JEFFERSON, Bernard Levi, 821'.1
1887-1939.
Chaucer and the Consolation of philosophy of Boethius, by Bernard L. Jefferson. New York, Gordian Press, 1968. v, 168 p. 24 cm. Reprint of the author's thesis, Princeton University, 1914. Bibliography: p. 167-168. [PR1912.B65J4 1968] 67-30878
1. Chaucer, Geoffrey, d. 1400. 2. Boethius, d. 524. De consolatione philosophiae. I. Title. **BIP**

POLLARD, Alfred William, 821'.1
1859-1944.
Chaucer. New York, Greenwood Press [1969] 136 p. 23 cm. Reprint of the 1931 ed. [PR1905.P6 1969] 69-14038 ISBN 8-371-18565-
1. Chaucer, Geoffrey, d. 1400.

PRESTON, Raymond. 811'.1
Chaucer. New York, Greenwood Press [1969, c1952] xvi, 325 p. illus. 24 cm. Bibliographical footnotes. [PR1905.P7 1969] 69-14041
1. Chaucer, Geoffrey, d. 1400.

PRESTON, Raymond. 821.17
Chaucer. London, New York, Sheed and Ward [1952] 325 p. illus. 23 cm. Includes bibliography. [PR1905.P7 1952] 52-14472
1. Chaucer, Geoffrey, d. 1400. **BIP**

RANDS, William Brighty, 821'.1
1823-1882.
Chaucer's England, by Matthew Browne. London, Hurst and Blackett, 1869. [New York, AMS Press, 1970] 2 v. illus., port. 23 cm. [DA185.R18 1970] 74-113566 ISBN 0-404-01139-X
1. Chaucer, Geoffrey, d. 1400. 2. England—Social life and customs—Medieval period, 1066-1485. I. Title.

STANLEY-WRENCH, Margaret 92
Teller of tales, the story of Geoffrey Chaucer. Illus. by Erwin Schachner. New York, Hawthorn [c.1965] 192p. illus., map. 22cm. (Credo bks., 24) Bibl. [PR1905.S7] 65-12733 2.95
1. Chaucer, Geoffrey, d. 1400—Juvenile literature. I. Title.

THREE Chaucer studies: I 821'.1
Chaucerian problems: especially the Petherton forestership and the question of Thomas Chaucer, by Russell Krauss. II. The parlement of foules in its relation to contemporary events, by Haldeen Braddy III. Observations on the shifting positions of groups G and DE in the manuscripts of the Canterbury tales, by C. Robert Kase. [Folcroft, Pa.] Folcroft Library Editions, 1973 [c1932] vii, 182, 101, 89 p. illus. 23 cm. Reprint of the ed. published by Oxford University Press, New York. The 2d work was published separately under title: Chaucer's Parlement of foules in its relation to contemporary events. Originally presented as the author's theses, New York University, 1934, 1934, and 1935, respectively. Includes bibliographies. [PR1901.T5 1973] 73-12732 7.95
1. Chaucer, Geoffrey, d., 1400—Biography. 2. Chaucer, Geoffrey, d., 1400. Parlament of foules. 3. Chaucer, Geoffrey, d., 1400 Canterbury tales—Manuscripts. 4. Chaucer, Thomas, 1367?-1434. I. Krauss, Russell. Chaucerian problems: especially the Petherton forestership and the question of Thomas Chaucer. 1973. II. Braddy, Haldeen, 1908- Chaucer's Parlement of foules in its relation to contemporary events. 1973. III. Kase, Charles Robert. Observations on the shifting positions of groups G and DE in the manuscripts of the Canterbury tales 1973.

TUCKWELL, William, 1829- 821'.1
1919.
Chaucer. [Folcroft, Pa.] Folcroft Library Editions, 1973. 96 p. illus. 24 cm. Original ed. issued in series: Bell's miniature series of great writers. Reprint of the 1904 ed. [PR1905.T8 1973] 72-10253 7.50
1. Chaucer, Geoffrey, d. 1400. I. Series: Bell's miniature series of great writers. **BIP**

WAGENKNECHT, Edward 821'.1
Charles, 1900-
The personality of Chaucer [by] Edward Wagenknecht. [1st ed.] Norman, University of Oklahoma Press [1968] xiii, 155 p. 23 cm. Bibliographical footnotes. [PR1905.W27] 67-24621
1. Chaucer, Geoffrey, d. 1400. I. Title. **BIP**

Chaucer, Geoffrey, d. 1400—Biography.

CHESTERTON, Gilbert Keith, 821'.1
1874-1936.
Chaucer. New York, Greenwood Press [1969] 286 p. 23 cm. Reprint of the 1956 ed.; originally published in 1932. [PR1905.C4 1969] 69-13856 ISBN 0-8371-2237-6
1. Chaucer, Geoffrey, d. 1400—Biography.

COGHILL, Nevill, 1899- 821'.1
The poet Chaucer. 2nd ed. London, New York [etc.] Oxford U.P., 1967. xi, 145 p. 21 cm. (Oxford paperbacks, university series, opus 23) Bibliography: p. 137-139. [PR1905.C55 1967] 68-97162 7/6
1. Chaucer, Geoffrey, d. 1400—Biography. I. Title. **BIP**

GARDNER, John Champlin, 821'.1 B
1933-
The life & times of Chaucer / by John Gardner ; ornaments by J. Wolf. New York : Vintage Books, 1978, c1977. ix, 328, x p. ; 21 cm. Includes bibliographical references and index. [PR1905.G3 1978] 77-12801 ISBN 0-394-72500-X pbk. : 3.95
1. Chaucer, Geoffrey, d. 1400—Biography. 2. Poets, English—Middle English, 1100-1500—Biography. I. Title. **BIP**

GARDNER, John Champlin, 821'.1 B
1933-
The life & times of Chaucer / by John Gardner. 1st ed. New York : Knopf : distributed by Random House, 1977. ix, 328, x p. ; 25 cm. Includes bibliographical references and index. [PR1905.G3] 76-1915 ISBN 0-394-49317-6 : 12.50
1. Chaucer, Geoffrey, d. 1400—Biography. 2. Poets, English—Middle English, 1100-1500—Biography. I. Title.

GODWIN, William, 1756- 821'.1 B
1836.
Life of Geoffrey Chaucer, the early English poet: including memoirs of his near friend and kinsman, John of Gaunt, Duke of Lancaster: with sketches of the manners, opinions, arts, and literature of England in the fourteenth century. London, R. Phillips, 1804. [New York, AMS Press, 1974] p. cm. [PR1905.G6 1974] 71-168173 ISBN 0-404-02850-0 36.50
1. Chaucer, Geoffrey, d. 1400—Biography. 2. John of Gaunt, duke of Lancaster, 1340-1399. 3. England—Civilization—Medieval period, 1066-1485. I. Title.

JENKS, Tudor, 1857-1922. 821'.1 B
In the days of Chaucer. With an introd. by Hamilton Wright Mabie. [Folcroft, Pa.] Folcroft Library Editions, 1974 [c1904] p. cm. Reprint of the ed. published by A. S. Barnes, New York, in series: Lives of great writers. Bibliography: p. [PR1905.J4 1974] 74-18407 ISBN 0-8414-5316-0 (lib. bdg.)
1. Chaucer, Geoffrey, d. 1400—Biography. I. Title. **BIP**

NICOLAS, Nicholas 821'.1 B
Harris, Sir, 1799-1848.
Life of Chaucer. [Folcroft, Pa.] Folcroft Library Editions, 1973. p. Reprint of the memoir of Chaucer contained in v. 1 of The poetical works of Geoffrey Chaucer (London, W. Pickering, 1845) and first published separately in 1843 under title: Life of Geoffrey Chaucer. Includes bibliographical references. [PR1905.N5 1973] 73-13594 ISBN 0-8414-2361-X (lib. bdg.)
1. Chaucer, Geoffrey, d. 1400.—Biography. I. Title.

POLLARD, Alfred William, 821'.1
1859-1944.
Chaucer. 2d ed. Freeport, N.Y., Books for Libraries Press [1970] 136 p. 23 cm. (Library of Old English and medieval literature) Reprint of the 1931 ed. [PR1905.P6 1970] 73-114911 ISBN 0-8369-5316-9
1. Chaucer, Geoffrey, d. 1400—Biography.

RYE, Walter, 1843-1929. 821'.1
Chaucer, a Norfolk man / by Walter Rye. Norwood, Pa. : Norwood Editions, 1975. 104 p. ; 24 cm. Reprint of the 1915 ed. published by Roberts, Norwich. Includes bibliographical references and index. [PR1905.1.R9 1975] 75-34181 ISBN 0-88305-563-5 lib. bdg. : 20.00
1. Chaucer, Geoffrey, d. 1400—Biography. 2. Chaucer family. I. Title.

SEDGWICK, Henry Dwight, 821'.1
1861-1957.
Dan Chaucer: an introduction to the poet, his poetry, and his times. New York, AMS Press [1971, c1934] 391 p. port. 18 cm.

Bibliography: p. 378-379. [PR1905.S4 1971] 73-155610 ISBN 0-404-05669-5
1. Chaucer, Geoffrey, d. 1400—Biography. I. Title.

Chaucer, Geoffrey, d. 1400. Canterbury tales.

BARTHOLOMEW, Barbara 821.1
Fortuna and Natura; a reading of three Chaucer narratives. The Hague, Mouton, [New York, Humanities, c.] 1966. 112p. 22cm. (Studies in Eng. lit., v. 16) Essays on The psysician's tale, The clerk's tale, and The knight's tale. Bibl. [PR1874.B35] 65-27398 5.50
1. Chaucer, Geoffrey, d. 1400. Canterbury tales. I. Title.

Chaucer, Geoffrey, d. 1400—Contemporary England.

BREWER, Derek Stanley. 821'.1 B
Chaucer and his world / Derek Brewer. New York : Dodd, Mead, 1978. 224 p., [8] leaves of plates : ill. ; 26 cm. Includes index. Bibliography: p. [216]-218. [PR1906.5.B68] 77-10790 ISBN 0-396-07519-3 : 20.00
1. Chaucer, Geoffrey, d. 1400—Contemporary England. 2. England—Social life and customs—Medieval period, 1066-1485. 3. Poets, English—Middle English, 1100-1500—Biography. I. Title.

SERRAILLIER, Ian. 914.2
Chaucer and his world. [1st American ed.] New York, H. Z. Walck, 1968 [c1967] 45 p. illus. 26 cm. Describes home life, food, dress, "open field" agriculture, illness and medical knowledge, education, recreation, industry and trade, military life, the church, and art and architecture during the medieval period that inspired poet Geoffrey Chaucer. [PR1906.5.S4 1968] AC 68
1. Chaucer, Geoffrey, d. 1400—Contemporary England. 2. England—Social life and customs—Medieval period, 1066-1485. I. Title.

THOMPSON, W. H. 821'.1
Chaucer and his times, by W. H. Thompson. With foreword by W. L. Andrews. [Folcroft, Pa.] Folcroft Press [1970] xii, 135 p. illus. 26 cm. "First published 1936." [PR1906.5.T5 1970] 72-191962
1. Chaucer, Geoffrey, d. 1400—Contemporary England. I. Title. BIP

Chaucer, Geoffrey, d. 1400—Friends and associates.

COOK, Albert Stanburrough, 1853-1927. 821'.1 B
The last months of Chaucer's earliest patron. New Haven, 1916. [New York, AMS Press, 1973] 144 p. illus. 23 cm. Reprint of the ed. published by Tuttle, Morehouse & Taylor Co., which was issued as v. 21, p. 1-144 of Transactions of the Connecticut Academy of Arts and Sciences. Includes bibliographical references. [PR1906.C6 1973] 72-1000 ISBN 0-404-01698-7 6.50
1. Chaucer, Geoffrey, d. 1400—Friends and associates. 2. Lionel of Antwerp, Duke of Clarence, 1338-1368. 3. Visconti family. 4. Alan (Hound) I. Title. II. Series: Connecticut Academy of Arts and Sciences, New Haven. Transactions, v. 21, p. 1-144. BIP

HULBERT, James Root, 1884- 821'.1
Chaucer's official life. New York, Phaeton Press, 1970. 96 p. 23 cm. Reprint of the 1912 ed., the author's thesis, University of Chicago. Includes bibliographical references. [PR1906.H8 1970] 75-93246
1. Chaucer, Geoffrey, d. 1400—Friends and associates. 2. John of Gaunt, duke of Lancaster, 1340-1399. I. Title. BIP

Chaucer, Geoffrey, d. 1400—Friends and associates—Addresses, essays, lectures.

†KITTREDGE, George Lyman, 1860-1941. 821'.1
Chaucer and some of his friends / by G. L. Kittredge. Folcroft, Pa. : Folcroft Library Editions, 1977. 18 p. ; 26 cm. Reprinted from Modern philology, v. 1, no. 1, June 1903. Includes bibliographical references. [PR1906.K5 1977] 77-27260 ISBN 0-8414-2201-X lib. bdg. : 6.00
1. Chaucer, Geoffrey, d. 1400—Friends and associates—Addresses, essays, lectures. 2. Poets, English—Middle English 1100-1500—Biography—Addresses, essays, lectures. I. Title. BIP

Chaucer, Geoffrey, d. 1400—Knowledge—Folk-lore, mythology.

MCCALL, John P. 821'.1
Chaucer among the gods : the poetics of classical myth / John P. McCall. University Park : Pennsylvania State University Press, 1979. 189 p. ; 23 cm. Includes bibliographical references and index. [PR1933.M96M3] 78-50003 ISBN 0-271-00201-8 : 10.95
1. Chaucer, Geoffrey, d. 1400—Knowledge—Folk-lore, mythology. 2. Mythology in literature. 3. Mythology, Classical. I. Title. BIP

Chaucer, Thomas, 1367?-1434.

RUUD, Martin Bronn, 1885-1941. 821'.1 B
Thomas Chaucer. Minneapolis, University of Minnesota, 1926. [New York, AMS Press, 1972] 131 p. 24 cm. Reprint of the 1926 ed. which was issued as no. 9 of Studies in language and literature, Research publications of the University of Minnesota. Bibliography: p. [129]-131. [PR1905.1.R8 1972] 78-174797 ISBN 0-404-05469-2 7.50
1. Chaucer, Thomas, 1367?-1434. I. Series: Minnesota. University. Studies in language and literature, no. 9. II. Series: Minnesota. University. Research publications. BIP

Chaudri, Nazir Ahmad Khan.

CHAUDRI, Nazir Ahmad Khan. 340'.092'4 B
The making of a lawyer : my experiences in court / by Chaudri Nazir Ahmad Khan ; with a foreword by Hamoodur Rehman. Lahore : Law Pub. Co., 1976. x, 202 p. ; 23 cm. [LAW] 76-930140 Rs20.00
1. Chaudri, Nazir Ahmad Khan. 2. Lawyers—Pakistan—Biography. I. Title.

Chauncy, Charles, 1705-1787.

GRIFFIN, Edward M., 1937- 285.8'32'0924 B
Old Brick, Charles Chauncy of Boston, 1705-1787 / by Edward M. Griffin. Minneapolis : University of Minnesota Press, 1980. p. cm. (Minnesota monographs in the humanities ; v. 11) Includes index. Bibliography: p. [BX7260.C527G74] 79-27203 ISBN 0-8166-0907-1 : 20.00
1. Chauncy, Charles, 1705-1787. 2. Congregational churches—Clergy—Biography. 3. Clergy—Massachusetts—Boston—Biography. 4. Boston—Biography. I. Title. II. Series.

Chausson, Ernest, 1855-1899.

BARRICELLI, Jean Pierre. 927.8
Ernest Chausson; the composer's life and works, by Jean Pierre Barricelli & Leo Weinstein. [1st ed.] Norman, University of Oklahoma Press [1955] xiii, 241p. illus., ports., facsim., music. 21cm. Bibliography: p. 209-212. 'List of Ernest Chausson's compositions': p. 213-226. [ML410.C455B3] 55-9627
1. Chausson, Ernest, 1855-1899. I. Weinstein, Leo, joint author. II. Title.

BARRICELLI, Jean Pierre. 780'.92'4 B
Ernest Chausson; the composer's life and works, by Jean-Pierre Barricelli & Leo Weinstein. Westport, Conn., Greenwood Press [1973, c1955] xiii, 241 p. illus. 22 cm. Reprint of the ed. published by University of Oklahoma Press, Norman. "List of Ernest Chausson's compositions": p. 213-226. [ML410.C455B3 1973] 73-7192 ISBN 0-8371-6915-1 11.75
1. Chausson, Ernest, 1855-1899. I. Weinstein, Leo, joint author. BIP

GROVER, Ralph Scott, 1917- 780'.92'4 B
Ernest Chausson, the man and his music / Ralph Scott Grover. Lewisburg : Bucknell University Press, c1979. p. cm. Includes index. Bibliography: p. [ML410.C455G76] 77-74404 12.00
1. Chausson, Ernest, 1855-1899. 2. Composers—France—Biography.

Chauvel, Henry George, Sir, 1865-1945.

HILL, Alec Jeffrey, 1916- 355.03'31'0924 B
Chauvel of the Light Horse : a biography of General Sir Harry Chauvel, G.C.M.G., K.C.B. / [by] A. J. Hill. Carlton, Vic. : Melbourne University Press, 1978. xx, 265 p., [13] leaves : ill. (some col.) ; 25 cm. Includes index. Bibliography: p. 248-255. [DU116.2.C47H54] 79-309006 ISBN 0-522-84146-5 : 35.00
1. Chauvel, Henry George, Sir, 1865-1945. 2. Australia. Army—Biography. 3. Generals—Australia—Biography. 4. European War, 1914-1918—Biography. 5. European War, 1914-1918—Campaigns—Turkey and the Near East. I. Title.
Distributed by ISBS, Forest Grove, OR

Chaves, Manuel Antonio, 1818-1889.

SIMMONS, Marc. 917.89'03'40924 B
The Little Lion of the Southwest; a life of Manuel Antonio Chaves. [1st ed.] Chicago, Sage Books [1973] xii, 263 p. illus. 23 cm. Bibliography: p. 249-255. [F801.C46S55] 73-1500 ISBN 0-8040-0632-6 8.95
1. Chaves, Manuel Antonio, 1818-1889. 2. New Mexico—History. I. Title. BIP

Chavez, Cesar Estrada.

LEVY, Jacques E. 331.88'13'0924 B
Cesar Chavez : autobiography of La Causa / Jacques E. Levy. 1st ed. New York : Norton, [1975] xxiii, 546 p., [16] leaves of plates : ill. ; 24 cm. Includes index. [HD6509.C48L48 1975] 75-15747 ISBN 0-393-07494-3 : 12.95
1. Chavez, Cesar Estrada. 2. United Farm Workers. 3. Migrant agricultural laborers—United States. I. Chavez, Cesar Estrada. BIP

YINGER, Winthrop. 331.88'13'0924 B
Cesar Chavez : the rhetoric of nonviolence / Winthrop Yinger. 1st ed. Hicksville, N.Y. : Exposition Press, c1975. 143 p. ; 21 cm. (An Exposition-university book) Includes index. Bibliography: p. 117-140. [HD6509.C48Y55] 75-10624 ISBN 0-682-48274-9 : 6.50
1. Chavez, Cesar Estrada. BIP

Chavez, Cesar Estrada—Juvenile literature.

FRANCHERE, Ruth. 331.881'3'48850924 [B]
Cesar Chavez. Illus. by Earl Thollander. New York, T. Y. Crowell [1973, c.1970] 42 p. illus. (pt. col.) 23 cm. (Crowell crocodile) (Crowell biographies) An easy-to-read biography of the Mexican-American who led the nation-wide boycott of grapes as part of his movement to organize and help farm laborers in the United States. [HD5325.A29F7] 78-101927 ISBN 0-690-18385-2 0.95 (pbk.)
1. Chavez, Cesar Estrada—Juvenile literature. 2. Strikes and lockouts—Vineyard laborers—California—Juvenile literature. I. Thollander, Earl, illus. II. Title. BIP

TERZIAN, James P. 331.881'34'8850924
Mighty hard road; the story of Cesar Chavez [by] James P. Terzian and Kathryn Cramer. [1st ed.] Garden City, N.Y., Doubleday, 1970. 136 p. illus., ports. 22 cm. (Doubleday signal books) A biography of vineyard worker Cesar Chavez, who orgainzed the California grape pickers so they could bargain more effectively for better wages and working conditions. [HD5325.A29T47] 92 71-103780 3.50
1. Chavez, Cesar Estrada—Juvenile literature. 2. Strikes and lockouts—Vineyard laborers—California—Juvenile literature. I. Cramer, Kathryn, joint author. II. Title.

WHITE, Florence Meiman, 1910- 331.88'13'0924 B
Cesar Chavez, man of courage, by Florence M. White. Illustrated by Victor Mays. Champaign, Ill., Garrard Pub. Co. [1973] 96 p. illus. 24 cm. (Americans all) An easy-to-read biography of the Mexican American who organized the agricultural laborers' struggles for better pay and working conditions. [HD5325.A29W45] 92 72-6803 ISBN 0-8116-4579-7 2.79
1. Chavez, Cesar Estrada—Juvenile literature. 2. Strikes and lockouts—Vineyard laborers—California—Juvenile literature. I. Mays, Victor, 1927- illus. II. Title.

Chavis, Ben, 1948-

MYERSON, Michael, 1940- 323.4'09756
Nothing could be finer / by Michael Myerson. 1st ed. New York : International Publishers, 1978. 245 p. ; 21 cm. (New World paperbacks) Includes bibliographical references. [E185.93.N6M93] 78-17407 ISBN 0-7178-0553-0 : 12.00. ISBN 0-7178-0498-4 pbk. : 3.95
1. Chavis, Ben, 1948- 2. Afro-Americans—Civil rights—North Carolina. 3. Civil rights—North Carolina. 4. North Carolina—Politics and government—1951- 5. Clergy—North Carolina—Biography. I. Title. BIP

Chea Aim.

LAWRENCE, Carl. 325'.21'0924 B
The Prince still smiled : amazing love breaks through a Cambodian family's night of terror : a true story / by Carl Lawrence. Wheaton, Ill. : Tyndale House Publishers, c1979. 132 p. ; 21 cm. [DS554.83.C46L38] 78-73216 ISBN 0-8423-4879-4 (pbk.) : 2.95
1. Chea Aim. 2. Cambodia—History—1975- 3. Refugees, Political—Cambodia—Biography. I. Title.

Cheke, John, Sir, 1514-1557.

STRYPE, John, 1643-1737. 942.05'3'0924 B
The life of the learned Sir John Cheke, kt., first instructor, afterwards Secretary of State, to King Edward VI ... To which is added, A treatise of superstition, writ by the said learned knight. New York, B. Franklin [1974] xiv, 218 p. port. 23 cm. (Burt Franklin research and source works series. Philosophy and religious history monographs, 143) "A treatise of superstition": p. [183]-187. Reprint of the "new edition," 1821, published at the Clarendon Press, Oxford. [DA345.1.C5S9 1974] 78-183699 ISBN 0-8337-3446-6 17.50
1. Cheke, John, Sir, 1514-1557. I. Cheke, John, Sir, 1514-1557. A treatise of superstition. 1974. II. Title. III. Title: A treatise of superstition.

Chekhov, Anton Pavlovich, 1860-1904.

AVILOVA, Lidiia Alekseevna, 1865-1942. 891.7'2'3 B
Chekhov in my life [by] Lydia Avilov. Translated with an introd. by David Magarshack. With drawings by Lynton Lamb. Westport, Conn., Greenwood Press [1971, c1950] 159 p. illus. 23 cm. [PG3458.A9 1971] 79-138198 ISBN 0-8371-5551-7
1. Chekhov, Anton Pavlovich, 1860-1904. I. Title. BIP

CHEKHOV, Anton Pavlovich, 1860-1904. 891.7'2'3 B
Letters of Anton Chekhov. Selected and edited by Avrahm Yarmolinsky. New York, Viking Press [1973] xvii, 490 p. 25 cm. [PG3458.A3Y3 1973] 72-9585 ISBN 0-670-42596-6 12.50
1. Chekhov, Anton Pavlovich, 1860-1904. I. Title. BIP

CHUKOVSKII, Kornei Ivanovich, 1882-1969. 891.7'2'3 B
Chekhov the man, by Kornei Chukovsky. Translated from the Russian by Pauline

Rose. New York, Haskell House, 1974. 64 p. port. 20 cm. Reprint of the 1945 ed. published by Hutchinson, London. [PG3458.C52 1974] 74-6384 ISBN 0-8383-1867-3 8.95 (lib. bdg.)
1. Chekhov, Anton Pavlovich, 1860-1904. I. Title.

GILLES, Daniel. 891.7'2'3 B
Chekhov: observer without illusion. Translated by Charles Lam Markmann. New York, Funk & Wagnalls [1968] 436 p. 24 cm. Translation of Tchekhov; ou, Le spectateur desenchante. Bibliography: p. [425]-428. [PG3458.G4913] 68-27514 10.00
1. Chekhov, Anton Pavlovich, 1860-1904.

HINGLEY, Ronald. 891.78309
Chekhov; a biographical and critical study. New York, Barnes & Noble [1966] 256 p. 19 cm. "First published in 1950." Bibliography: p. [248]-250. [PG3458.H47 1966] 66-1681
1. Chekhov, Anton Pavlovich, 1860-1904.

MAGARSHACK, David. 928.917
Chekhov. a life. New York, Grove Press [1953, c1952] 431p ports. 24cm. 'Bibliographical index of the complete works of Anton Chekhov': p.393-423. [PG3458] 53-11901
1. Chekhov, Anton Pavlovich, 1860-1904. I. Title.

SAUNDERS, Beatrice 928.917
Tchekhov: the man. Chester Springs, Pa., Dufour Editions, 1961 [c.1960] 195p. illus. (front port.) Bibl. 61-10598 4.50
1. Chekhov, Anton Pavlovich, 1860-1904. I. Title.

SIMMONS, Ernest Joseph, 1903- 928.917
Chekhov; a biography Boston, Atlantic-Little. [1964, c1962] 669p. illus. 20cm. (45) 2.95 pap.,
1. Chekhov, Anton Pavlovich, 1860-1904. I. Title. **BIP**

SIMMONS, Ernest Joseph, 1903-1972. 928.917
Chekhov; a biography. [1st ed.] Boston, Little, Brown [1962] 609 p. illus. 22 cm. [PG3458.S5] 62-16958
1. Chekhov, Anton Pavlovich, 1860-1904.

Chekhov, Anton Pavlovich, 1860-1904—Biography.

HINGLEY, Ronald. 891.7'2'3 B
A new life of Anton Chekhov / Ronald Hingley. 1st American ed. New York : Knopf, 1976. xx, 352, vi p., [9] leaves of plates : ill. ; 25 cm. Includes indexes. Bibliography: p. [345]-348. [PG3458.H475 1976] 75-36818 ISBN 0-394-49058-4 : 12.50
1. Chekhov, Anton Pavlovich, 1860-1904—Biography. I. Title.

MAGARSHACK, David. 891.7'2'3 B
Chekhov; a life. Westport, Conn., Greenwood Press [1970, c1952] 433 p. ports. 24 cm. "Bibliographical index of the complete works of Anton Chekhov": p. 393-423. [PG3458.M29 1970] 69-13983 ISBN 0-8371-4095-1
1. Chekhov, Anton Pavlovich, 1860-1904—Biography. **BIP**

NEMIROVSKY, Irene, 1903-1942. 891.7'2'3 B
A life of Chekhov. Translated by Erik de Mauny. New York, Haskell House, 1974. 181 p. 22 cm. Translation of La vie de Tchekov. Reprint of the 1950 ed. published by Grey Walls Press, London. [PG3458.N413 1974] 74-7101 ISBN 0-8383-1865-7
1. Chekhov, Anton Pavlovich, 1860-1904—Biography. I. Title. **BIP**

Chekhov, Anton Pavlovich, 1860-1904—Correspondence.

CHEKHOV, Anton Pavlovich, 1860-1904. 891.7'2'3 B
Anton Chekhov's life and thought : selected letters and commentary / translated from the Russian by Michael Henry Heim, in collaboration with Simon Karlinsky ; selection, commentary and introd. by Simon Karlinsky. Berkeley : University of California Press, 1975, c1973. xiv, 494 p. ; 23 cm. Published in 1973 under title: Letters of Anton Chekhov. Includes index. Bibliography: p. 479-481. [PG3458.A3K3 1975] 76-357949 ISBN 0-520-02684-5 : 6.95
1. Chekhov, Anton Pavlovich, 1860-1904—Correspondence. I. Karlinsky, Simon. II. Title.

CHEKHOV, Anton Pavlovich, 1860-1904. 928.917
Selected letters. Edited by Lillian Hellman; translated by Sidonie Lederer. New York, Farrar, Straus [1955] xxxv, 331 p. 22 cm. (Great letters series) [PG3458.A3H4 1955] 55-5563

Chemists.

FARBER, Eduard, 1892- ed. 925.4
Great chemists. New York, Interscience [dist Wiley, 1962, c.1961] 1642p. illus. 25cm. Bibl. 60-16809 29.50 bds.,
I. Title.

FARBER, Eduard, 1892- 925.4
Nobel prize winners in chemistry, 1901-1961. Rev. ed. London, New York, Abelard [c.1956 1963] 341p. illus. 23cm. (Life of sci. lib., no. 41) Bibl. 62-17263 6.50
1. Chemists. 2. Novel prizes. I. Title.

FARBER, Edward, 1892- 925.4
Nobel prize winners in chemistry, 1901-1961. Rev. ed. London, New York, Abelard-Schuman [1963] 341 p. illus. 23 cm. (The Life of science library, no. 41) [QD21.F37 1963] 62-17263
1. Chemists. 2. Nobel prizes. I. Title.

HAYNES, Williams, 1886-1960. 338.4'7'6600922
Chemical pioneers; the founders of the American chemical industry. Freeport, N.Y., Books for Libraries Press [1970] 288 p. illus., plan, ports. 23 cm. (Essay index reprint series) Reprint of the 1939 ed. "Originally the chapters ... were published serially in Chemical industries." [TP139.H38 1970] 74-99701 ISBN 0-8369-1442-2
1. Chemists. 2. Chemical engineers—United States—Biography. 3. Chemicals—Manufacture and industry—United States. I. Title.

KENDALL, James, 1889- 925.4
Great discoveries by young chemists. London, New York, Nelson [1953] 231 p. illus. 21 cm. [QD21.K29] 54-2480
1. Chemists. 2. Chemistry—History. I. Title.

KENDALL, James, 1889- 540'.922 B
Young chemists and great discoveries. Freeport, N.Y., Books for Libraries Press [1969] xvi, 272 p. illus., ports. 23 cm. (Essay index reprint series) Reprint of the 1939 ed. Contents.Contents.—Humphry Davy.—Michael Faraday.—Some young organic chemists.—The chemistry of space and of solutions.—Elements, old and new.—Some young American chemists. Includes bibliographies. [QD21.K3 1969] 76-76907
1. Chemists. 2. Chemistry—History. I. Title. **BIP**

NOBEL prize winners in chemistry, 1901-1950. New York, H. Schuman [1953] 219p. illus. 22cm. (The Life of science library, no. 31) [QD21.F37] [QD21.F37] 925.4 53-10371 53-10371 378.32
1. Chemists. 2. Nobel prizes. I. Farber, Eduard, 1892-

RUBEN, Samuel. 541'.37'0922 B
The founders of electrochemistry / Samuel Ruben. Philadelphia : Dorrance, [1975] 107 p. : ill. ; 22 cm. Includes index. Bibliography: p. 101-102. [QD21.R82] 75-312668 ISBN 0-8059-2107-9 : 5.95
1. Chemists. 2. Electrochemistry—History. I. Title. **BIP**

TILDEN, William Augustus, Sir, 1842-1926. 540'.922
Famous chemists; the men and their work. Freeport, N.Y., Books for Libraries Press [1968] xvi, 296 p. illus., ports. 22 cm. (Essay index reprint series) Reprint of the 1921 ed. "Principal authorities": p. xi-xii. [QD21.T6 1968] 68-20344
1. Chemists. 2. Chemistry—History. I. Title.

TYNDALL, John, 1820-1893 925.3
Faraday as a discoverer. New York, Apollo Eds. [c.1961] 213p. illus. (A-20) 1.75 pap.,
I. Title.

Chemists—Biography.

LEONARD, Jonathan Norton, 1903- 540'.92'2 B
Crusaders of chemistry: six makers of the modern world. Freeport, N.Y., Books for Libraries Press [1972, c1930] 307 p. illus. 23 cm. (Essay index reprint series) [QD21.L4 1972] 72-8533 ISBN 0-8369-7320-8
1. Chemists—Biography. 2. Chemistry—History. I. Title.

Chemists—Germany—Biography.

NACHMANSOHN, David, 1899- 509'.2'2 B
German-Jewish pioneers in science, 1900-1933 : highlights in atom physics, chemistry, biochemistry : destruction by Hitler and world wide repercussions / by David Nachmansohn. New York : Springer-Verlag, [1979] p. cm. Bibliography: p. [QD21.N33] 79-10550 ISBN 0-387-90402-6 : 29.80
1. Chemists—Germany—Biography. 2. Biochemists—Germany—Biography. 3. Physicists—Germany—Biography. 4. Jews in Germany—Biography. I. Title.

Chemists—United States—Biography.

AMERICAN chemists and chemical engineers / Wyndham D. Miles, editor. Washington : American Chemical Society, 1976. x, 544 p. ; 25 cm. Includes bibliographical references and index. [QD21.A43] 76-192 ISBN 0-8412-0278-8 : 28.50 540'.92'2 B
1. Chemists—United States—Biography. 2. Chemical engineers—United States—Biography. I. Miles, Wyndham D., 1916- **BIP**

Chen, Norbu, 1926-

CHEN, Norbu, 1926- 615'.53 B
Norbu Chen, the Tibetan way / Norbu Chen and Tom Valentine. New York : Simon and Schuster, c1977. p. cm. [RZ408.C47A34] 77-24447 ISBN 0-671-22569-3 : 8.95
1. Chen, Norbu, 1926- 2. Healers—Texas—Biography. 3. Lamas—Texas—Biography. I. Valentine, Tom, joint author. II. Title.

Chenier, Andre Marie, 1762-1794.

LOGGINS, Vernon, 1893- 841.5
Andre Chenier: his life, death, and glory. Athens, Ohio, Ohio University Press [1965] xii, 292 p. port. 22 cm. Bibliography: p. [275]-281. [PQ1965.L6] 65-13701
1. Chenier, Andre Marie, 1762-1794. I. Title. **BIP**

SCARFE, Francis, 1911- 928.4
Andre Chenier, his life and work. 1762-1794 [New York] Oxford, [c.]1965. xv, 391p. facsims., ports. 22cm. Bibl. [PQ1965.S3] 65-4246 8.50
1. Chenier, Andre Marie, 1762-1794. I. Title.

Chennault, Claire Lee, 1890-1958.

ARCHIBALD, Joseph, 1898- 358.41332 B
Commander of the Flying Tigers: Claire Lee Chennault, by Joe Archibald. New York, J. Messner [1966] 191 p. 22 cm. Bibliography: p. 186. [E745.C35A8] 66-14002
1. Chennault, Claire Lee, 1890-1958. I. Title.

CHENNAULT, Anna. 923.573
Chennault and the Flying Tigers. Introd. by Thomas G. Corcoran. New York, P. S. Eriksson [1963] xx, 298 p. illus., ports., map (on lining papers) 21 cm. [E745.C35C44] 63-19390
1. Chennault, Claire Lee, 1890-1958. II. Title.

CHENNAULT, Anna 923.573
A thousand springs; the biography of a marriage. Introd. by Lin Yutang. New York, Popular Lib. [1963, c.1962] 190p. 18cm. (M2032) .60 pap.,
1. Chennault, Claire Lee, 1890-1958. I. Title.

CHENNAULT, Anna. 923.573
A thousand springs; the biography of a marriage. Introd. by Lin Yutang. New York, P. S. Eriksson [1962] 318 p. illus. 22 cm. [E745.C35C45] 62-13655
1. Chennault, Claire Lee, 1890-1958. I. Title.

SCOTT, Robert Lee, Jr. 923.573
Flying Tiger: Chennault of China. [New York] Berkley Pub. Corp. [1960, c.1959] 220p. 19cm. (Berkley medallion bk. G408) .50 pap.,
1. Chennault, Claire Lee, 1890- 2. China Air Force: American Volunteer Group. 3. World War, 1939-1945—Aerial operations, Chinese. I. Title. **BIP**

SCOTT, Robert Lee, 1908- 358.4'13'320924 B
Flying Tiger: Chennault of China [by] Robert Lee Scott Jr. Westport, Conn., Greenwood Press [1973, c1959] 285 p. 22 cm. [DS777.53.S38 1973] 73-439 ISBN 0-8371-6774-4 12.00
1. Chennault, Claire Lee, 1890-1958. 2. China. K'ung chun. American Volunteer Group. 3. World War, 1939-1945—Aerial operations, Chinese. I. Title.

Cher, 1947-

*CARPOZI, George. 784'092'4 B
Cher. [New York], Berkley Publishing Corp. [1975] 178 p., illus. 18 cm. (A Berkley Medallion Book) [ML3930.B593] ISBN 0-425-02973-5 1.50 (pbk.)
1. Cher, 1947- I. Title.

Cher, 1947- —Juvenile literature.

JACOBS, Linda. 784'.092'4 B
Cher : simply Cher / by Linda Jacobs. St. Paul : EMC Corp., [1975] p. cm. (Behind the bright lights) A biography of the singing star who has remained as popular on her own as she was as just the other half of "Sonny and ...." [ML3930.B593J2] 92 75-15552 ISBN 0-88436-186-1 lib.bdg. : 4.95 ISBN 0-88436-187-X pbk. : 2.95 pbk.
1. Cher, 1947- —Juvenile literature. I. Title. **BIP**

Cherniaev, Mikhail Grigor'evich, 1828-1898.

MACKENZIE, David. 947.08'092'4 B
The Lion of Tashkent; the career of General M. G. Cherniaev. [Athens] University of Georgia Press [1974] xx, 267 p. illus. 25 cm. Bibliography: p. 248-258. [DK219.6.C425M3] 73-81625 ISBN 0-8203-0322-4 11.00
1. Cherniaev, Mikhail Grigor'evich, 1828-1898. 2. Russia—History—Alexander II, 1855-1881. I. Title.

Chernyshevskii, Nikolai Gavrilovich, 1828-1889.

WOEHRLIN, William F., 1928- 320.5'3'0924 B
Chernyshevskii: the man and the journalist [by] William F. Woehrlin. Cambridge, Harvard University Press, 1971. 404 p. ports. 25 cm. (Russian Research Center studies, 67) Bibliography: p. 343-358. [B4238.C64W6] 73-156137 ISBN 0-674-11385-3 12.50
1. Chernyshevskii, Nikolai Gavrilovich, 1828-1889. I. Title. II. Series: Harvard University. Russian Research Center. Studies, 67.

Cherokee Indians.

TIMBERLAKE, Henry, d.1765. 973.2'6'0924 B
The memoirs of Lieut. Henry Timberlake. [New York] Arno Press [1971, c1927] 197 p. illus. 23 cm. (The First American frontier) First published in 1765 as The memoirs of Lieut. Henry Timberlake; reprinted in 1927 with title: Lieut Henry

Timberlake's Memoirs. Bibliography: p. [177]-184. [E99.C5T62 1971] 74-146423 ISBN 0-405-02903-9
1. Cherokee Indians. 2. U.S.—History—French and Indian War, 1755-1763. I. Title. II. Series. BIP

Cherokee Indians—Biography.

CANTRELL, Roy. 970.3
My friends, the Cherokees. Cherokee, N.C., Howineetah Publications [1973] 32 p. illus. 24 cm. [E99.C5C2] 73-81157
1. Cherokee Indians—Biography. I. Title.

Cherokee language—Alphabet.

FOREMAN, Grant, 1869-1953. v. 12
Sequoyah. Norman, Univ. of Oklahoma Press [1959] 94 p. illus., facsims. 24 cm. (The Civilization of the American Indian, v. 16) "First edition...1938. Second printing, entirely reset...1959." "For further study of Sequoyah": p. 83. 64-32044
1. Cherokee language—Alphabet. 2. Sequoya, Cherokee Indian 1770?-1843. 3. Cherokee Indians. I. Title. II. Series. BIP

Cherubini, Luigi, 1760-1842.

BELLASIS, Edward, 784'.0924 B 1852-1922.
Cherubini; memorials illustrative of his life and work. New York, Da Capo Press, 1971. xv, 356 p. illus., music, ports. 23 cm. (Da Capo Press music reprint series) Reprint of the 1912 ed. "A chronological catalogue of Cherubini's works": p. [312]-344. [ML410.C5B4 1971] 70-138497 ISBN 0-306-70071-9
1. Cherubini, Luigi, 1760-1842. BIP

Cheshire, Geoffrey Leonard, 1917-

HUGHES, Cledwyn [John Cledwyn Hughes] 1920- 922.242
Leonard Cheshire, V. C. [dist. New York, Roy, c.1961] 106p. illus. (Living biographies series) 60-14483 2.50 bds.,
1. Cheshire, Geoffrey Leonard, 1917- I. Title.

Cheshire, Leonard.

BRADDON, Russell. 922.242
New wings for a warrior; the story of Group-Captain Leonard Cheshire, v. c., D. S. O., D. F. C. New York, Rinehart [1955, c1954] 240p. illus. 22cm. First published in London in 1954 under title: Cheshire, v. c.; a story of war and peace. [BX4705.C4636B7 1955] 55-7553
1. Cheshire, Leonard. 2. World War, 1939-1945—Aerial operations. 3. Institutional missions—Gt. Brit. I. Title.

Cheshire, Maxine, 1930-

CHESHIRE, Maxine, 1930- 070'92'4
Maxine Cheshire : reporter / by Maxine Cheshire with John Greenya. New York : Dell Pub. Co., 1979. 333p. ; 18 cm. Includes index. [PN4874.C48A36] ISBN 0-440-15788-9 pbk. : 2.25
1. Cheshire, Maxine, 1930- 2. Journalists — United States — Biography. I. Greenya, John. II. Title.
L. C. card no. for 1978 Houghton Mifflin ed.: 78-5198

CHESHIRE, Maxine, 070'.92'4 B 1930-
Maxine Cheshire, reporter / Maxine Cheshire, with John Greenya. Boston : Houghton Mifflin, 1978. 307 p., [4] leaves of plates : ill. ; 22 cm. Includes index. [PN4874.C48A36] 78-5198 ISBN 0-395-26303-4 : 10.00
1. Cheshire, Maxine, 1930- 2. Journalists—United States—Biography. I. Greenya, John, joint author. II. Title. BIP

Cheshire, Thomas.

SCOTT, Elizabeth, 1901- 973.7'469'0924 B
More fox than lion. [1st ed.] New York, Vantage Press [1972] 124 p. 22 cm. Chapters 9 and 10 (p. 89-118) by T. Cheshire. [E612.A5S3] 72-178667 ISBN 0-533-00142-0 3.95
1. Cheshire, Thomas. 2. Andersonville, Ga. Military Prison. I. Cheshire, Thomas. II. Title.

Chesler, Phyllis.

CHESLER, Phyllis. 301.41'2'0924 B
With child, a diary of motherhood / Phyllis Chesler. 1st ed. New York : Crowell, c1979. 288 p. ; 24 cm. Bibliography: p. [283]-288. [RG560.C47 1979] 79-7081 ISBN 0-690-01835-5 : 9.95
1. Chesler, Phyllis. 2. Pregnancy—Psychological aspects. 3. Childbirth—Psychological aspects. 4. Mother and child. 5. Mothers—United States—Biography. 6. Feminists—United States—Biography. I. Title.

Chesnut, Mary Boykin (Miller) 1823-1886.

CHESNUT, Mary Boykin 973.782
Diary from Dixie. Ed. by Ben Ames Williams Boston, Houghton [1961, c.1905, 1949] 572p. (Sentry ed., SE2) 2.45 pap.,
I. Title.

WILEY, Bell Irvin, 1906- 973.7'13'0922 B
Confederate women. Westport, Conn., Greenwood Press [1975] xiv, 204 p. illus. 22 cm. (Contributions in American history, no. 38) Bibliography: p. 195-198. [E467.W48] 74-5995 ISBN 0-8371-7534-8 10.95 (lib. bdg.)
1. Chesnut, Mary Boykin (Miller) 1823-1886. 2. Clay-Clopton, Virginia, 1825-1915. 3. Davis, Varina (Howell) 1826-1906. 4. Women—Confederate States of America. I. Title. BIP

Chesnutt, Charles Waddell, 1858-1932.

HEERMANCE, J. Noel. 813'.4 B
Charles W. Chesnutt; America's first great Black novelist, by J. Noel Heermance. [Hamden, Conn.] Archon Books, 1974. xiii, 258 p. 22 cm. Bibliography: p. [247]-253. [PS1292.C6Z7] 73-14595 ISBN 0-208-01380-6 8.50
1. Chesnutt, Charles Waddell, 1858-1932. BIP

Chesnutt, Charles Waddell, 1858-1932—Biography.

KELLER, Frances Richardson, 1917- 813'.4 B
An American crusade : the life of Charles Waddell Chestnutt / Frances Richardson Keller. Provo, Utah : Brigham Young University Press, c1978. xvi, 304 p. : ill. ; 24 cm. Includes index. Bibliography: p. 286-290. [PS1292.C6Z75] 77-14608 11.95
1. Chesnutt, Charles Waddell, 1858-1932—Biography. 2. Novelists, American—19th century—Biography. I. Title.

Chess—Biography.

EUWE, Machgielis, 1901- 794.1'0922
Meet the masters; the modern chess champions and their most characteristic games, with annotations and biographies, by Max Euwe. Translated from the Dutch by L. Prins and B. H. Wood. Freeport, N.Y., Books for Libraries Press [1969] viii, 279 p. illus., ports. 23 cm. (Essay index reprint series) Translation of Zoo schaken zij. Reprint of the 1940 ed. [GV1438.E813 1969] 78-90636
1. Chess—Biography. I. Title.

EUWE, Machgielis, 1901- 794.1'092'2 B
Meet the masters : eight great chess players and their most characteristic games / by Max Euwe ; translated from the Dutch by L. Prins and B. H. Wood. 2d ed. New York : Dover Publications, 1975, c1945. viii, 279 p., [1] leaf of plates : ill. ; 21 cm. Translation of Zoo schaken zij. Reprint of the ed. published by Pitman, London. [GV1438.E813 1975] 75-12063 ISBN 0-486-23207-7 : 3.50
1. Chess—Biography. I. Title. BIP

GAIGE, Jeremy. 794.1'0922
A catalog of chessplayers & problemists. Philadelphia, 1969. iii, 82 p. 24 cm. Bibliography: p. 81-82. [GV1438.G3] 70-7949
1. Chess—Biography. I. Title. II. Title: Chessplayers & problemists.

GAIGE, Jeremy. 794.1'0922
A catalog of chessplayers & problemists. Rev. ed. Philadelphia, 1971. ii, 107, [7] p. 23 cm. Bibliography: p. [113]-[114] [GV1438.G3 1971] 70-24107
1. Chess—Biography. I. Title. II. Title: Chessplayers & problemists.

KOTOV, Aleksandr Aleksandrovich, 1913- 794.1'092'2 B
Soviet chess kings / by A. Kotov and M. Yudovich ; translated by Peter Evan Zimmermann. New York : Macmillan, 1976. p. cm. Includes index. [GV1438.K67 1976] 75-45024 ISBN 0-02-566580-4 : 8.95
1. Chess—Biography. 2. Chess—Collections of games. I. IUdovich, Mikhail Mikhailovich, 1911- joint author. II. Title.

KOTOV, Aleksandr Aleksandrovich, 1913- 794.1'092'2 B
Soviet chess kings / by A. Kotov and M. Yudovich ; translated by Peter Evan Zimmermann. New York : Collier Books, 1976. p. cm. Includes index. [GV1438.K67 1976b] 75-45021 ISBN 0-02-029910-9 pbk. : 4.95
1. Chess—Biography. 2. Chess—Collections of games. I. IUdovich, Mikhail Mikhailovich, 1911- joint author. II. Title.

LOMBARDY, William. 794.1'57'0922
Chess panorama / William Lombardy and David Daniels. 1st ed. Radnor, Pa. : Chilton Book Co., [1975] v, 196 p. : ill. ; 22 cm. Includes indexes. [GV1438.L65 1975] 75-19333 ISBN 0-8019-6078-9 : 6.95
1. Chess—Biography. 2. Chess—Collections of games. I. Daniels, David, 1942- joint author. II. Title. BIP

Chess—Biography—Juvenile literature.

LERNER, Peter Morris. 794.1'092'2
Famous chess players. Minneapolis, Lerner Publications Co. [1973] 87 p. illus. 22 cm. (A Pull ahead book) Contents.Contents.—Harry N. Pillsbury.—Emanuel Lasker.—Jose R. Capablanca.—Alexander A. Alekhine.—Frank J. Marshall.—Vera Menchik. Mikhail M. Botvinnik.—Samuel Reshevsky.—Paul Keres.—Mikhail Tal.—Boris Spassky.—Bobby Fischer. [GV1438.L47] 920 72-3593 ISBN 0-8225-0466-9 3.95
1. Chess—Biography—Juvenile literature. I. Title. BIP

Chess-Collections of games.

REINFELD, Fred, 1910-1964. 794.1590922
Great games by chess prodigies. New York, Macmillan [c1967] x, 246 p. illus. 22 cm. [GV1452.R352] 67-10155
1. Chess — Collections of games. 2. Chess — Biog. I. Title.

REINFELD, Fred, 1910-1964 794.1590922
Great games by chess prodigies. New York, Macmillan [c.1967] x. 246p. illus. 22cm. [GV1452.R352] 67-10155 5.95
1. Chess—Collections of games. 2. Chess—Biog. I. Title. BIP

WADE, Robert Graham, comp. 794.1'0922
Soviet chess / compiled by R. G. Wade. No. Hollywood, Calif. : Wilshire Book Company, 1976c1968. 288p. : ill ; 21 cm. [GV1330.R9W3] ISBN 0-87980-311-8 pbk. : 3.00
1. Chess-Collections of games. 2. Chess-Biography. I. Title.

Chess—History.

SCHONBERG, Harold C. 794.1'09
Grandmasters of chess, by Harold C. Schonberg. [1st ed.] Philadelphia, Lippincott [1973] 317 p. illus. 25 cm. Bibliography: p. 303-307. [GV1317.S33] 73-10391 ISBN 0-397-01004-4 10.00
1. Chess—History. 2. Chess—Biography. I. Title. BIP

Chess players—Biography.

CHERNEV, Irving, 1900- 794.1'092'2 B
The golden dozen : the twelve greatest chess players of all time / Irving Chernev. New York : Oxford University Press, 1976. 331 p. : ill. ; 21 x 22 cm. (Oxford chess books) Includes indexes. Bibliography: p. [326]-328. [GV1438.C46 1976b] 75-39504 ISBN 0-19-217536-X : 12.95
1. Chess players—Biography. 2. Chess—Collections of games. I. Title.
Contents omitted

Chess—Psychology.

COCKBURN, Alexander. 794.1'01'9
Idle passion; chess and the dance of death. New York, Village Voice [1974] 248 p. 22 cm. Includes bibliographical references. [GV1448.C62] 74-10751 ISBN 0-671-21817-4
1. Chess—Psychology. 2. Chess—Biography. I. Title. BIP

Chess—Tournaments.

SOLTIS, Andrew. 794.1'57
The great chess tournaments and their stories / Andy Soltis. 1st ed. Radnor, Pa. : Chilton Book Co., [1975] viii, 257 p. : ill. ; 22 cm. Includes indexes. [GV1455.S67 1975] 75-1218 ISBN 0-8019-6138-6 : 8.95
1. Chess—Tournaments. 2. Chess—Biography. I. Title.

Chessman, Caryl,

CHESSMAN, Caryl, 1921- 923.4173
Trial by ordeal. Englewood Cliffs [N. J.] Prentice-Hall [1955] 309p. 22cm. Autobiographical. [HV6248.C44A32] 55-10671
I. Title.

Chesterfield, Philip Dormer Stanhope, 4th Earl of, 1694-1773.

CHESTERFIELD, Philip Dormer Stanhope, 4th Earl of, 1694-1773. 942.07'092'4
The letters of Philip Dormer Stanhope, 4th Earl of Chesterfield. Edited, with an introd. by Bonamy Dobree. [1st AMS ed.] New York, AMS Press [1968] 6 v. illus. 24 cm. Reprint of the 1932 ed. "Explanation of references to sources": v. 1, p. xv-xvi. [DA501.C5A32 1968] 68-59007
I. Dobree, Bonamy, 1891- ed.

COXON, Roger. 941.07'092'4 B
Chesterfield and his critics / by Roger Coxon. Folcroft, Pa. : Folcroft Library Editions, 1976. xii, 328 p. ; 26 cm. Reprint of the 1925 ed. published by G. Routledge, London. Includes bibliographical references and index. [DA501.C5C6 1976] 76-48055 ISBN 0-8414-3461-1 lib. bdg. : 40.00
1. Chesterfield, Philip Dormer Stanhope, 4th Earl of, 1694-1773. 2. Statesmen—Great Britain—Biography. 3. Authors, English—18th century—Biography. I. Title. BIP

JAEGER, Muriel. 920.02
Adventures in living, from Cato to George Sand. Freeport, N.Y., Books for Libraries Press [1970] viii, 216 p. 23 cm. (Essay index reprint series) Reprint of the 1932 American ed. Published in London in 1932 under title: Experimental lives. Includes bibliographical references. [CT105.J3 1970] 79-121480 ISBN 8-369-17588-
1. Cato, Marcus Porcius, Uticensis. 2. Francesco d'Assisi, Saint, 1182-1226. 3. Chesterfield, Philip Dormer Stanhope, 4th Earl of, 1694-1773. 4. Day, Thomas, 1748-1789. 5. Sand, George, pseud. of Mme. Dudevant, 1804-1876. I. Title. BIP

SCOTT, Temple, 1864-1939. 941.07'092'4 B
Lord Chesterfield and his letters to his sons / by Temple Scott. Folcroft, Pa. : Folcroft Library Editions, 1976 [c1929] p. cm. Reprint of the ed. imprinted for A. Zinkin, Meridian Bookshop, Indianapolis.

[DA501.C5S36 1976] 76-29703 ISBN 0-8414-7551-2 lib. bdg. : 12.50
1. Chesterfield, Philip Dormer Stanhope, 4th Earl of, 1694-1773. 2. Statesmen—England—Biography. I. Title. **BIP**

SHELLABARGER, Samuel, 1888- 923.242
Lord Chesterfield and his world. Boston, Little, Brown, 1951. 456 p. port. 23 cm. Bibliography: p. [423]-435. [DA501.C5S52] 51-14196
1. Chesterfield, Philip Dormer Stanhope, 4th earl of, 1604-1773. I. Title. **BIP**

SHELLABARGER, Samuel, 1888-1954. 942.07'1'0924
Lord Chesterfield and his world. New York, Biblo and Tannen, 1971 [c1951] 456 p. port. 23 cm. Bibliography: p. [423]-435. [DA501.C5S52 1971] 72-156737 ISBN 0-8196-0272-8
1. Chesterfield, Philip Dormer Stanhope, 4th Earl of, 1694-1773. I. Title.

Chesterton, Gilbert Keith, 1874-1936.

ATTWATER, Donald, 1892- ed. 270.8'1'0922
Modern Christian revolutionaries; an introduction to the lives and thought of: Kierkegaard, Eric Gill, G. K. Chesterton, C. F. Andrews [and] Berdyaev. Edited by Donald Attwater. Freeport, N.Y., Books for Libraries Press [1971, c1947] xiii, 390 p. illus., ports. 23 cm. (Essay index reprint series) Contents.Contents.—Soren Kierkegaard, by M. Chaning-Pearce.—G. K. Chesterton, by F. A. Lea.—Eric Gill, by D. Attwater.—C. F. Andrews, by N. MacNichol.—Nicolas Berdyaev, by E. Lampert.—Bibliography (p. [383]-390) [BR1700.A8 1971] 76-156608 ISBN 0-8369-2304-9
1. Kierkegaard, Soren Aabye, 1813-1855. 2. Chesterton, Gilbert Keith, 1874-1936. 3. Gill, Eric, 1882-1940. 4. Andrews, Charles Freer, 1871-1940. 5. Berdiaev, Nikolai Aleksandrovich, 1874-1948. I. Title.

BARKER, Dudley. 828'.9'1209 B
G. K. Chesterton; a biography. New York, Stein and Day [1973] 304 p. illus. 25 cm. Bibliography: p. 289-295. [PR4453.C4Z529] 72-95988 ISBN 0-8128-1544-0 8.95
1. Chesterton, Gilbert Keith, 1874-1936.

CLEMENS, Cyril, 1902- 828'.9'1209 B
Chesterton, as seen by his contemporaries. With introd. by E. C. Bentley. New York, Haskell House Publishers, 1969. iv, 180 p. illus. 23 cm. Reprint of the 1939 ed. [PR4453.C4Z585 1969] 76-92958 7.95
1. Chesterton, Gilbert Keith, 1874-1936. I. Title. **BIP**

HOLLIS, Christopher, 1902- v. 12
G. K. Chesterton. London, New York, Published for the British Council and the National Book League by Longmans, Green [1950] 32 p. port. 23 cm. (Bibliographical series of supplements to British book news) "G. K. Chesterton, a select bibliography": p. 20-32. A52
1. Chesterton, Gilbert Keith, 1874-1936. I. Title. II. Series. **BIP**

SULLIVAN, John, 1904- v. 12
G. K. Chesterton; a bibliography. With an essay, On books, by G. K. Chesterton; and an epitaph by Walter de la Mare. New York, Barnes and Noble [1958] 208 p. port., facsims. 23 cm.
1. Chesteron, Gilbert Keith, 1874-1936—Bibl. I. Title. **BIP**

TITTERTON, William Richard. 828'.9'1209 B
G. K. Chesterton: a portrait, by W. R. Titterton. [Folcroft, Pa.] Folcroft Library Editions, 1973. p. Reprint of the 1947 ed. published by D. Organ, London. [PR4453.C4Z77 1973b] 73-14569 10.75
1. Chesterton, Gilbert Keith, 1874-1936. **BIP**

WARD, Maisie, 1889- 928.2
Return to Chesterton. New York, Sheed and Ward, 1952. 336p. illus. 22cm. 'Made up chiefly of unpublished letters, verses and jeux d'esprit of Chesterton's ... of the memories of many who knew him, of fresh stories, and other material.' [PR4453.C4Z842 1952] 52-7518
1. Chesterton, Gilbert Keith, 1874-1936. I. Title.

WARD, Maisie, 1899- 928.2
Return to Chesterton. New York, Sheed and Ward, 1952. 336 p. illus. 22 cm. "Made up chiefly of unpublished letters, verses and jeux d'esprit of Chesterton's...of the memories of many who knew him, of fresh stories, and other material." [PR4453.C4Z842] 52-7518
1. Chesterton, Gilbert Keith, 1874-1936. I. Title.

WILLS, Garry, 1934- 928.2
Chesterton, man and mask. New York, Sheed & Ward [c.1961] 243p. Bibl. 61-7283 4.50
1. Chesterton, Gilbert Keith, 1874-1936. I. Title.

Chesterton, Gilbert Keith, 1874-1936—Biography.

TITTERTON, William Richard. 828'.9'1209 B
G. K. Chesterton; a portrait, by W. R. Titterton. New York, Haskell House Publishers, 1973. 235 p. front. 23 cm. "First published 1936." [PR4453.C4Z77 1973] 72-8980 ISBN 0-8383-1679-4 7.95
1. Chesterton, Gilbert Keith, 1874-1936—Biography. I. Title.

Chestnut, Wilhelmine,

CHESTNUT, Wilhelmine, 1891- 920.7
I made my dreams come true. [1st ed.] New York, Pageant Press [1952] 313p. 24cm. [CT1098.C45A3] 53-504
I. Title.

Chevalier, Maurice, 1888-1972.

CHEVALIER, Maurice, 1888- 784'.0924
I remember it well. Pref. by Marcel Pagnol. Translated from the French by Cornelia Higginson. [New York] Macmillan [1970] 221 p. illus., ports. 22 cm. Translation of Mome a cheveux blancs. [ML420.C473A383] 79-126515
1. Musicians—Correspondence, reminiscences, etc. I. Title.

CHEVALIER, Maurice, 1888- 784'.0924 B
I remember it well. Pref. by Marcel Pagnol. Translated from the French by Cornelia Higginson. Boston, G. K. Hall, 1972 [c1970] 315 p. 25 cm. "Large print" ed. Translation of Mome a cheveux blancs. [ML420.C473A383 1972] 73-38980 ISBN 0-8161-6022-8 (l. print)
1. Musicians—Correspondence, reminiscences, etc. I. Title.

CHEVALIER, Maurice, 1888-1972. 927.8
With love, by Maurice Chevalier, as told to Eileen and Robert Mason Pollock. [1st ed.] Boston, Little, Brown [1960] 424 p. illus. 23 cm. Autobiographical. [ML420.C473A39] 60-11641
1. Musicians—Correspondence, reminiscences, etc. I. Pollock, Eileen. II. Title.

RINGGOLD, Gene. 782.8'1'0924
Chevalier; the films and career of Maurice Chevalier, by Gene Ringgold and Dewitt Bodeen. Foreword by Rouben Mamoulian. [1st ed.] Secaucus, N.J., Citadel Press [1973] 242 p. illus. 29 cm. [ML420.C473R5] 72-95413 ISBN 0-8065-0354-8 12.00
1. Chevalier, Maurice, 1888-1972. 2. Moving-pictures, Musical. I. Bodeen, DeWitt, joint author. **BIP**

Cheverus, Jean Louis Aime Madeleine Lefebvre de, Abp., 1768-1836.

MELVILLE, Annabelle (McConnell) 1910- 922.273
Jean Lefebvre de Cheverus, 1768-1836. Milwaukee, Bruce Pub. Co. [1958] 527p. illus. 23cm. Includes bibliography. [BX4705.C465M4] 58-13623
1. Cheverus, Jean Louis Aime Madeleine Lefebvre de, Abp., 1768-1836. I. Title.

Cheyenne Indians—Biography.

HOIG, Stan. 970'.004'97
The peace chiefs of the Cheyennes / by Stan Hoig ; foreword by Boyce D. Timmons. 1st ed. Norman : University of Oklahoma Press, c1979. p. cm. Includes index. Bibliography: p. [E99.C53H63] 79-4739 ISBN 0-8061-1573-4 : 14.95
1. Cheyenne Indians—Biography. 2. Cheyenne Indians—History. I. Title. **BIP**

Chezard de Matel, Jeanne, 1596-1670.

BURTON, Katherine (Kurz) 1890- 922.244
My Beloved to me; the life of Jeanne de Matel, foundress of the Sisters of the Incarnate Word and Blessed Sacrament. Milwaukee, Bruce Press [1957] 185p. illus. 23cm. (Catholic life publications) [BX4705.C47B8] 57-2152
1. Chezard de Matel, Jeanne, 1596-1670. I. Title.

Chiang, Ch'ing.

TAI, Dwan L., 1941- 951.05'092'4 B
Chiang Ch'ing; the emergence of a revolutionary political leader [by] Dwan L. Tai. [1st ed.] Hicksville, N.Y., Exposition Press [1974] xxviii, 222 p. 22 cm. (An Exposition-university book) Bibliography: p. 199-213. [DS778.C5374T34] 74-10618 ISBN 0-682-48060-6
1. Chiang, Ch'ing. 2. China—Politics and government—1949-

WITKE, Roxane. 951.05'092'4 B
Comrade Chiang Ch'ing / Roxane Witke. 1st ed. Boston : Little, Brown, c1977. xxvi, 549 p., [17] leaves of plates : ill. ; 24 cm. Includes bibliographical references and index. [DS778.C5374W57] 77-935 ISBN 0-316-94900-0 : 15.00
1. Chiang, Ch'ing. 2. Statesmen—China—Biography. 3. Women—China—Biography. 4. China—Biography. 5. China—History—1900- I. Title.

Chiang, I, 1903-

CHIANG, I, 1903- v. 12
A Chinese childhood by Chiang Yee. New York, Norton [1963] 304 p. geneal. table. (Norton library. N185) 63-50417
1. Chiang, I, 1903- 2. China — Soc. life & cust. I. Title.

Chiang, Kai-shek, 1887-1975.

BERKOV, Robert. 951.04'2'0924
Strong man of China; the story of Chiang Kai-shek. Freeport, N.Y., Books for Libraries Press [1970] xv, 288 p. ports. 22 cm. Reprint of the 1938 ed. Bibliography: p. [287]-288. [DS778.C55B4 1970] 70-124225 ISBN 0-8369-5413-0
1. Chiang, Kai-shek, 1887-1975. 2. China—Politics and government—1912-1949. I. Title.

CROZIER, Brian. 951.04'2'0924 B
The man who lost China : the first full biography of Chiang Kai-shek / by Brian Crozier, with the collaboration of Eric Chou. New York : Scribner, c1976. xv, 430 p., [8] leaves of plates : ill. ; 25 cm. Includes bibliographical references and index. [DS778.C55C7] 76-10246 ISBN 0-684-14686-X : 12.50
1. Chiang, Kai-shek, 1887-1975. I. Chou, Eric, 1915- joint author. II. Title.

CURTIS, Richard. 951.04'2'0924 B
Chiang Kai-shek. [1st ed.] New York, Hawthorn Books [1969] 272 p. illus., ports. 22 cm. Bibliography: p. 259-262. [DS778.C55C8] 69-10919 5.95
1. Chiang, Kai-shek, 1887-1975.

HAHN, Emily, 1905- 923.551
Chiang Kai-shek, an unauthorized biography. [1st ed.] Garden City, N. Y., Doubleday, 1955. 382 p. 22 cm. [DS778.C55H3] 55-5582
1. Chiang, Kai-shek, 1886-1975.

HEDIN, Sven Anders, 1865-1952. 951.04'2'0924 B
Chiang Kai-shek, marshal of China / by Sven Hedin ; translated from the Swedish by Bernard Norbelie. New York : DaCapo Press, 1975, c1940. xiv, 290 p., [8] leaves of plates : ill. ; 23 cm. (China in the 20th century) Reprint of the ed. published by John Day Co., New York. Includes index. [DS778.C55H42 1975] 74-31277 ISBN 0-306-70690-3 : 17.50
1. Chiang, Kai-shek, 1886- 2. China—History—Republic, 1912-1949.

LOH, Pichon Pei Yung, 1928- 951.04'2'0924 B
The early Chiang Kai-shek: a study of his personality and politics, 1887-1924 [by] Pichon P. Y. Loh. New York, Columbia University Press, 1971. vi, 216 p. 21 cm. (Occasional papers of the East Asian Institute, Columbia University) Bibliography: p. 180-204. [DS778.C55L63] 70-158461 ISBN 0-231-03596-9 7.50
1. Chiang, Kai-shek, 1886- I. Title. II. Series: Columbia University. East Asian Institute. Occasional papers.

PAYNE, Pierre Stephen Robert, 1911- 951.04'2'0924 B
Chiang Kai-shek [by] Robert Payne. New York, Weybright and Talley [1969] viii, 338 p. illus., map, ports. 25 cm. Bibliography: p. 327-328. [DS778.C55P38] 68-17754 10.00
1. Chiang, Kai-shek, 1887-1975.

WELCH, Robert Henry Winborne, 1899- 327
Again, may God forgive us! by Robert Welch. [Belmont, Mass.] Belmont Pub. Co. [1971] ix, 204 p. 21 cm. Reprint of May God forgive us, first published in 1952, together with a biographical sketch of Chiang Kai-shek, first published in the May 1957 issue of One man's opinion. [D843.W43 1971] 76-31176
1. Chiang, Kai-shek, 1887-1975. 2. World politics—1945-1955. 3. Communism—1945- 4. United States—Foreign relations—1945-1953. I. Welch, Robert Henry Winborne, 1899- Chiang Kai-shek. 1971. II. Title.

YAUKEY, Grace (Sydenstricker) 1899- 951.04'2'0924 B
Chiang Kai-shek, generalissimo of Nationalist China [by] Cornelia Spencer. New York, John Day Co. [1968] 253 p. illus., map, ports. 21 cm. Bibliography: p. 245-246. [DS778.C55Y38] 68-11308
1. Chiang, Kai-shek, 1886-

Chicago

WADE, Louise C 923.673
Graham Taylor, pioneer for social justice, 1851-1938 [by] Louise C. Wade. Chicago, University of Chicago Press [1964] 268 p. illus, ports. 25 cm. "Graham Taylor's writings": p. [235]-255. [Taylor, Graham, 1851-1968.] [HN80.C5W3] 64-24976
1. Chicago—Soc. condit. I. Title. **BIP**

Chicago. Foot-ball club (National League)

VASS, George. 796.332'0924 B
George Halas and the Chicago Bears. Chicago, Regnery [1971] v, 343 p. illus. 22 cm. [GV956.C5V3] 70-163261 6.95
1. Chicago. Foot-ball club (National League) 2. Halas, George Stanley, 1895- I. Title.

Chicago. Graceland Cemetery.

LANCTOT, Barbara. 977.3'11
A walk through Graceland Cemetery / by Barbara Lanctot ; photos. by Rosemary Kluke. [Chicago : Chicago School of Architecture Foundation], c1977. 61 p. : ill. ; 22 cm. Bibliography: p. 60-61. [F548.612.G72L36] 77-153147
1. Chicago. Graceland Cemetery. 2. Chicago—Biography. I. Chicago School of Architecture Foundation. II. Title.

Chicago—Haymarket square riot, 1886.

FONER, Philip Sheldon, 1910- comp. 977.3'11'030922 B
The autobiographies of the Haymarket martyrs, edited and with an introd. by Philip S. Foner. New York, Published for

A.I.M.S. by Humanities Press, 1969. 198 p. 24 cm. (AIMS historical series, no. 5) Contents.Contents.—Introduction, by W. P. Black.—Autobiography of Albert R. Parsons.—Autobiography of August Spies.—Autobiography of Adolph Fischer.—Autobiography of George Engel.—Autobiography of Michael Schwab.—Autobiography of Samuel Fielden.—Autobiography of Oscar Neebe.—Autobiography of Louis Lingg.—Bibliography (p. [191]) [HX846.C4F6] 74-7887 6.00
1. Chicago—Haymarket square riot, 1886. 2. Anarchism and Anarchists—U.S. I. Title. II. Series: American Institute for Marxist Studies. AIMS historical series, no. 5 BIP

Chicago (Musical septet)—Juvenile literature.

O'SHEA, Mary Jo. 784'.092'2
Chicago / text, Mary Jo O'Shea ; ill., John Keely. Mankato, Minn. : Creative Education, [1975]. p. cm. [ML3930.C45O8] 75-23074 ISBN 0-87191-458-1 lib.bdg. : 4.95
1. Chicago (Musical septet)—Juvenile literature. I. Keely, John. II. Title. BIP

Chichester, Francis Charles, Sir, 1901- —Juvenile literature.

ROWLAND, John, 1907- 910'.924 B
Lone adventurer; the story of Sir Francis Chichester. New York, Roy Publishers [1968] 140 p. 21 cm. A biography of Sir Francis Chichester, seeker of adventure, who at the age of sixty-six was knighted for a solo voyage around the world. [G530.C475R6] 92 69-12123 3.75
1. Chichester, Francis Charles, Sir, 1901- —Juvenile literature. I. Title.

Chifley, Joseph Benedict, 1885-1951—Juvenile literature.

BENNETT, Scott Cecil. 994.04'092'4 B
J. B. Chifley [by] Scott Bennett. Melbourne, New York, Oxford University Press, 1973. 30 p. ill. 19 cm. (Great Australians) Bibliography: p. 30. Brief biography of the Australian who became Labor party leader in 1945 and served as prime minister from that date until 1949. [DU116.2.C48B46] 92 75-310129 ISBN 0-19-550419-4 0.70
1. Chifley, Joseph Benedict, 1885-1951—Juvenile literature. 2. Labor Party (Australia)—Juvenile literature. 3. Australia—Politics and government—Juvenile literature. I. Title.

Child, Francis James, 1825-1896—Correspondence.

CHILD, Francis James, 1825-1896. 928.1
The scholar-friends; letters of Francis James Child and James Russell Lowell, edited by M. A. De Wolfe Howe and G. W. Cottrell, Jr. Cambridge, Harvard University Press, 1952. 84 p. illus., ports. 25 cm. "Reprinted from the ... Harvard Library bulletin, vol. v, nos. 2, 3 ... vol. vi, nos. 1, 2." [PS1292.C85Z53] 52-9390
I. Lowell, James Russell, 1819-1891. II. Howe, Mark Antony De Wolfe, 1864- ed. III. Cottrell, George William. ed. IV. Title. BIP

CHILD, Frnacis James, 1825-1896. 821'.04
Letters on Scottish ballads from Professor Francis J. Child to W. W., Aberdeen. Darby, Pa. : Arden Library, 1978. 37 p., [1] leaf of plates : port. ; 23 cm. The recipient of the letters was William Walker of Aberdeen. Cf. Brit. Mus. Reprint of the 1930 ed. privately printed at the Bon Accord Press, Aberdeen, Scot. [PR8580.C5 1978] 78-7613 ISBN 0-8495-0723-5 : 8.50
1. Child, Francis James, 1825-1896—Correspondence. 2. Walker, William, of Aberdeen. 3. Ballads, Scottish—History and criticism. 4. Authors, American—19th century—Correspondence. I. Walker, William, of Aberdeen. II. Title. BIP

Child. Lydia Maria (Francis) 1802-1880.

BAER, Helena (Gilbert) 1908-1964. 920.7
The heart is like heaven; the life of Lydia Maria Child. Philadelphia, University of Pennsylvania Press, [1964] 339 p. illus., facsims., ports. 22 cm. Bibliography: p. 317-333. [E449.C5383] 64-10895
1. Child. Lydia Maria (Francis) 1802-1880. I. Title.

Child, Lydia Maria (Francis) 1802-1880.

BAER, Helene (Gilbert) 1908-1964 920.7
The heart is like heaven; the life of Lydia Maria Child. Philadelphia, Univ. of Pa. Pr. [c.1964] 339p. illus., facsims., ports. 22cm. Bibl. 64-10895 6.50
1. Child, Lydia Maria (Francis) 1802-1880. I. Title. BIP

CHILD, Lydia Maria (Francis) 1802-1880. 973'.0974'96
The freedmen's book. New York, Arno Press, 1968. vi, 277 p. 21 cm. (The American Negro, his history and literature) Reprint of the 1865 ed. [E185.86.C46 1968] 68-28989
1. Negroes. 2. Negroes—Biography. 3. Freedman. I. Title. II. Series. BIP

CHILD, Lydia Maria (Francis) 1802-1880. 816'.2
Letters of Lydia Maria Child. New York, Arno Press, 1969. xxv, 280 p. port. 23 cm. (The Anti-slavery crusade in America) Reprint of the 1883 ed. "List of Mrs. Child's works": p. 272-274. [PS1293.Z8 1969] 72-82183
I. Title. II. Series. BIP

CHILD, Lydia Maria (Francis) 1802-1880. 818'.2'09 B
Letters of Lydia Maria Child, with a biographical introd. by John G. Whittier and an appendix by Wendell Phillips. New York, Negro Universities Press [1969] xxv, 280 p. port. 23 cm. Reprint of the 1883 ed. Bibliography: p. 272-274. [PS1293.A83 1969] 73-92740 ISBN 0-8371-2189-2

CHILD, Lydia Maria (Francis) 1802-1880. 818'.2'09 B
Letters of Lydia Maria Child. With a biographical introduction by John G. Whittier and an appendix by Wendell Phillips. Boston, Houghton, Mifflin, 1883. [New York, AMS Press, 1971] xxv, 280 p. port. 18 cm. Bibliography: p. 272-274. [PS1293.Z5A4 1971] 73-165169 ISBN 0-404-00141-6
I. Whittier, John Greenleaf, 1807-1892. II. Title.

MELTZER, Milton, 1915- 920.7
Tongue of flame; the life of Lydia Maria Child. New York, Crowell [c.1965] 210p. 21cm. Bibl. [E449.C5393] 65-14903 3.95
1. Child, Lydia Maria (Francis) 1802-1880. I. Title. BIP

MELTZER, Milton, 1915- 920.7
Tongue of flame; the life of Lydia Maria Child. [New York, Dell, 1975, c1965] 191 p. 18 cm. (Laurel-Leaf library) (Women of America) Bibliography: [p. 178]-179 [E449.C5393] 0.95 (pbk.)
1. Child, Lydia Maria (Francis) 1802-1880. I. Title.
L.C. card number for original ed.: 65-14903.

Childers, Erskine, 1870-1922.

BOYLE, Andrew, 1919- 941.5082'1'0924 B
The riddle of Erskine Childers / Andrew Boyle. London : Hutchinson, 1977, i.e.1978 351 p., [2] leaves of plates ; 23 cm. Includes index. Bibliography: p. [333]-336. [DA965.C45B69 1977] 77-369573 ISBN 0-09-128490-2 : 15.95
1. Childers, Erskine, 1870-1922. 2. Ireland—Politics and government—1910-1921. 3. Revolutionists—Ireland—Biography. 4. Authors, Irish—20th century—Biography. I. Title.
Distributed by Hutchinson, Salem, NH BIP

COX, Tom, 1906- 941.5082'1'0924 B
Damned Englishman : a study of Erskine Childers (1870-1922) / by Tom Cox. 1st ed. Hicksville, N.Y. : Exposition Press, [1975] vii, 374 p., [1] leaf of plates : port. ; 24 cm. (An Exposition-university book) Includes index. Bibliography: p. 357-364. [DA965.C45C69] 73-86542 ISBN 0-682-47821-0 : 10.00
1. Childers, Erskine, 1870-1922. 2. Ireland—Politics and government—1910-1921. 3. Ireland—Politics and government—1922-1949. I. Title. BIP

Children as musicians.

FISHER, Renee B. 780'.92'2 B
Musical prodigies: masters at an early age [by] Renee B. Fisher. New York, Association Press [1973] 240 p. illus. 23 cm. Bibliography: p. 232-236. [ML81.F58] 72-13970 ISBN 0-8096-1854-0 7.95
1. Children as musicians. 2. Gifted children. 3. Musicians—Biography. I. Title.

HISTORY of Music Project. 780'.9794'61 S
Fifty local prodigies, 1906-1940. New York, AMS Press [1972] xii, 203 p. ports. 27 cm. (History of music in San Francisco series, v. 5) Reprint of the 1940 ed. Bibliography: p. 197-203. [ML200.8.S2H4 v. 5 1972] 70-38301 ISBN 0-404-07245-3
1. Children as musicians. 2. Musicians—San Francisco. I. Title. II. Series.

Children, Blind.

ULRICH, Sharon. 362.7'8'410924 B
Elizabeth, by Sharon Ulrich (with Anna W. M. Wolf). With an introd. and commentary by Selma Fraiberg and Edna Adelson. Ann Arbor, University of Michigan Press [1972] 122 p. illus. 22 cm. [HV1792.U57U57] 72-163626 ISBN 0-472-93000-1 4.95
1. Children, Blind. I. Title. BIP

WALSTON, Marie. 362.7'8'41
To see the wind. Valley Forge [Pa.] Judson Press [1974] 127 p. 23 cm. [HV1792.C58W3] 74-3231 ISBN 0-8170-0622-2 4.95
1. Children, Blind. I. Title. BIP

Children in the Bible.

JENKINS, Sara Lucile, 1905- 220.92
The young people of the Bible. New York, Appleton Century-Crofts [1958] 210p. 21cm. [BS576.J4] 58-6919
1. Children in the Bible. 2. Bible—Biog. I. Title.

Children in the U. S.—Biog.

CARMER, Carl Lamson, 1893- ed. 920.073
A canvalcade of young Americans. Illustrated in color by Howard Simon. New York, Lothrop, Lee & Shepard [1958] 256p. illus. 26cm. [E176.8.C3] 58-11823
1. Children in the U. S.—Biog. I. Title.

Children in Wisconsin.

WE were children then : stories from the Yarns of Yesteryear Project / general editors, Robert E. Gard, Fred Lengfeld ; literary editor, Mark E. Lefebvre ; illustrations by Marian Lefebvre. 1st ed. [Madison] : Wisconsin House Book Publishers, c1976. xvii, 187 p. ; 22 x 27 cm. [HQ781.W38] 76-22961 ISBN 0-88361-041-8 : 5.95 301.43'14'09775
1. Children in Wisconsin. 2. Wisconsin—Social life and customs. 3. Wisconsin—Biography. 4. Aged—Wisconsin. I. Gard, Robert Edward. II. Lengfeld, Fred. III. Lefebvre, Mark E.

Children—Management—Personal narratives.

WRIGHT, Anna Maria Rose, 1890- 649.1
The gentle house [by] Anna Perrott Rose. Boston, Houghton Mifflin, 1954. 177 p. 22 cm. Autobiographical. "Parts of this book appeared in the Ladies' home journal under the title 'Frightened boy.'" [HQ770.W7] 54-6819
1. Children—Management—Personal narratives. I. Title.

Children of entertainers—United States—Biography.

STRAIT, Raymond. 791.43'028'0922 B
Star babies / by Raymond Strait. New York : St. Martin's Press, [1980] p. cm. [PN2285.S743] 79-22784 ISBN 0-312-75575-9 : 10.95
1. Children of entertainers—United States—Biography. 2. Moving-picture industry—California—Hollywood. I. Title. BIP

Children of the rich—United States.

COLES, Robert. 309.1'73'092 S
Privileged ones : the well-off and the rich in America / Robert Coles. 1st ed. Boston : Little, Brown, c1977. xviii, 583 p., [16] leaves of plates : ill. ; 22 cm. (His Children of crisis ; v. 5) "An Atlantic Monthly Press book." Includes index. Bibliography: p. [560]-570. [HC110.P6C56 vol. 5] [HQ792.U5] 301.43'14'0973 77-10825 ISBN 0-316-15149-1 : 15.00
1. Children of the rich—United States. I. Title. BIP

Children's literature—Addresses, essays, lectures.

HOFFMAN, Miriam, comp. 809'.89282
Authors and illustrators of children's books: writings on their lives and works [by] Miriam Hoffman and Eva Samuels. New York, Bowker, 1972. xi, 471 p. 24 cm. Appendix (p. 437-471) includes the English-language works of each author and author-illustrator. [PN1009.A1H58] 76-38607 ISBN 0-8352-0523-1
1. Children's literature—Addresses, essays, lectures. 2. Authors—Biography. I. Samuels, Eva, joint comp. II. Title.

Children's literature, American—Pennsylvania—Bio-Bibliography.

PENNSYLVANIA Council of Teachers of English. 810'.9'9748 B
Biographical companion to the Literary map of Pennsylvania, juvenile edition. Rev. [s.l.] : Pennsylvania Council of Teachers of English, 1975, c1965. 39 p. ; 23 cm. Bibliography: p. [4] [PS253.P4P4 1975] 76-353464
1. Children's literature, American—Pennsylvania—Bio-Bibliography. I. Title.

Children's literature—Bio-bibliography.

BENET, Laura. 028.52
Famous storytellers for young people. New York, Dodd, Mead [1968] 159 p. ports. 22 cm. (Famous biographies for young people) Contents.Contents.—Jacob (Ludwig Carl) Grimm and Wilhelm (Carl) Grimm.—Hans Christian Andersen.—William Makepeace Thackeray.—Frances Browne.—John Ruskin.—Lucretia Peabody Hale.—Charlotte Mary Yonge.—George Macdonald.—Dinah Maria Mulock Craik.—Mary Elizabeth Mapes Dodge.—Frank R. Stockton.—Mary Louisa Stewart Molesworth.—Juliana Horatia (Gatty) Ewing.—Margaret Sidney.—Frances Hodgson Burnett.—Howard Pyle.—Lyman Frank Baum.—Kate Douglas Wiggin.—E. Nesbit.—Kenneth Grahame.—Rudyard Kipling.—Padraic Colum. [PN452.B38] 68-13595
1. Children's literature—Bio-bibliography. I. Title.

BENET, Laura. 920
Famous storytellers for young people. New York, Dodd, Mead [1968] 159 p. ports. 22 cm. (Famous biographies for young people) Profiles of Jacob (Ludwig Carl) Grimm and Wilhelm (Carl) Grimm, Hans Christian Andersen, William Makepeace Thackeray, Frances Browne, John Ruskin, Lucretia Peabody Hale, Charlotte Mary Yonge, George Macdonald, Dinah Maria Mulock Craik, Mary Elizabeth Mapes Dodge, Frank R. Stockton, Mary Louisa Stewart Molesworth, Juliana Horatia (Gatty) Ewing, Margaret Sidney, Frances Hodgson Burnett, Howard Pyle, Lyman

Frank Baum, Kate Douglas Wiggin, E. Nesbit, Kenneth Grahame, Rudyard Kipling, and Padraic Colum. [PN452.B38] AC 68
1. Children's literature—Bio-bibliography. 2. Authors. I. Title.

HOPKINS, Lee Bennett. 810'.9 B
More books by more people; interviews with sixty-five authors of books for children. New York, Citation Press, 1974. xx, 410 p. ports. 20 cm. [PN452.H66] 73-87223 ISBN 0-590-07357-5 8.95
1. Children's literature—Bio-bibliography. 2. Illustrators. I. Title.
Pbk. 4.95; ISBN 0-590-09401-7.

SOMETHING about 028.52'0922 [B]
the author. Detroit, Gale Research [1971- v. illus., ports. 29 cm. "Facts and pictures about contemporary authors and illustrators of books for young people." [PN451.S6] [920] 72-27107 15.00 (per vol.)
1. Children's literature—Bio-bibliography. I. Gale Research Company.
4 volumes are now in print

WARD, Martha Eads. 809.8'9282 B
Authors of books for young people, by Martha E. Ward and Dorothy A. Marquardt. 2d ed. Metuchen, N.J., Scarecrow Press, 1971. 579 p. 22 cm. [PN452.W35 1971] 70-157057 ISBN 0-8108-0404-2
1. Children's literature—Bio-bibliography. I. Marquardt, Dorothy A., joint author. II. Title. **BIP**

WARD, Martha Eads. 809'.89282 B
Authors of books for young people : supplement to the second edition / by Martha E. Ward and Dorothy A. Marquardt. Metuchen, N.J. : Scarecrow Press, 1979. v, 302 p. ; 22 cm. [PN497.W3 1979] 78-16011 ISBN 0-8108-1159-6 : 12.00
1. Children's literature—Bio-bibliography. I. Marquardt, Dorothy A., joint author. II. Title.

Children's literature—History and criticism.

SMARIDGE, Norah. 809 B
Famous literary teams for young people / Norah Smaridge ; illustrated with photographs. New York : Dodd, Mead, c1977. 152 p., [4] leaves of plates : ill. ; 22 cm. Includes index. A collection of biographical sketches of literary teams known for their contributions to children's literature. [PN1009.A1S47] 920 76-53636 ISBN 0-396-07407-3 : 5.50
1. Children's literature—History and criticism. 2. Authors—Biography. I. Title. **BIP**

Children's poetry, American.

I sing the song of 811'.5'408
myself : an anthology of autobiographical poems / edited by David Kherdian. New York : Greenwillow Books, [1978] p. cm. Includes indexes. A collection of autobiographical poems by modern American poets. [PN6110.C4I24] 78-5807 ISBN 0-688-80172-2 : 6.95. ISBN 0-688-84172-4 lib. bdg. : 6.43
1. Children's poetry, American. 2. American poetry—20th century. I. Kherdian, David. **BIP**

Children's writings, American.

LISLE, Ruth Johns. 818'.5'403
Chickens don't turn to dust. Philadelphia, Dorrance [1968] [132] p. illus. 22 cm. The author's childhood diary. [PS3562.I78Z5] 68-26696 3.50
1. Children's writings, American. I. Title.

Childs, William Macbride, 1869-1939.

CHILDS, Hubert, 378.1'1'0924 B
1905-
W. M. Childs : an account of his life and work / by Hubert Childs. Reading : The author, 1976. [9], 204 p., [1], 7 leaves of plates : ill., geneal. table, ports. ; 25 cm. Includes index. [LF750.C48] 76-381577 ISBN 0-9505142-0-9 : £3.60
1. Childs, William Macbride, 1869-1939. 2. Reading, Eng. University—Faculty. 3. Teachers—Great Britain—Biography.

Chiles, Joseph Ballinger, 1810-1885.

GIFFEN, Helen 978.1'02'0924
Smith, 1893-
Trail-blazing pioneer, Colonel Joseph Ballinger Chiles, by Helen S. Giffen. [San Francisco] J. Howell, 1969. 100 p. illus., ports. 26 cm. Bibliography: p. 97-100. [F593.C52G5] 75-15106
1. Chiles, Joseph Ballinger, 1810-1885. 2. Overland journeys to the Pacific. I. Title.

Chillingworth, William, 1602-1644.

ORR, Robert R. 283'.0924
Reason and authority: the thought of William Chillingworth, by Robert R. Orr. London, Oxford U.P., 1967. xi, 217 p. 22 1/2 cm. Rewritten and shortened verson of author's thesis, University of London. Bibliography: p. [206]-213. [BX5199.C47O7] 67-99857
1. Chillingworth, William, 1602-1644. 2. Authority (Religion) I. Title.

China.

TAYLOR, Charles, 1935- 915.1045
Reporter in Red China. New York, Random House [1966] xi, 208 p. illus. 22 cm. Autobiographical account of the author's 18 months spent in China as resident correspondent for the Toronto Globe and mail, May 1964 to Oct. 1965. [DS777.55.T33] 66-23497
1. China. I. Title.

China—Biography.

BIOGRAPHICAL 951'.00922
dictionary of Republican China. Howard L. Boorman, editor; Richard C. Howard, associate editor. New York, Columbia University Press, 1967- v. 28 cm. Includes bibliographies. [DS778.A1B5] 67-12006
1. China—Biography. I. Boorman, Howard L., ed. II. Howard, Richard C., ed.

BOORMAN, Howard L ed. 920.051
Men and politics in modern China: preliminary... biographies. New York, Columbia University, 1960- v. 28cm. [DS778.A1B6] 60-1816
1. China—Biog. I. Title.

BOORMAN, Howard L., 951'.00922
ed.
Biographical dictionary of Republican China. Howard L. Boorman, editor, Richard C. Howard, associate editor. New York, Columbia University Press, 1967- v 28 cm. Includes bibliographies. [DS778.A1B5] 67-12006
1. China—Biog. I. Howard, Richard C., ed. II. Title. **BIP**

HAN, Suyin, pseud. 951.040922
The crippled tree: China, biography, history, autobiography. [1st American ed.] New York, Putnam [1965] 461 p. map, ports. 22 cm. [PR6015.A4674C7 1965a] 65-20715
1. China—Biography. 2. China—History—1900- I. Title.

HAN, Suyin, pseud. 951.040922
The crippled tree: China, biography, history, autobiography.[1st Amer. ed.] New York, Putnam [c.1965] 461p. map, ports. 23cm. [DS763.A2H3] 65-20715 5.95
1. China—Biog. 2. China.—Hist.—1900- I. Title.

KLEIN, Donald W. 951.04'922 B
Biographic dictionary of Chinese communism, 1921-1965 [by] Donald W. Klein [and] Anne B. Clark. Cambridge, Mass., Harvard University Press, 1971. 2 v. (1194 p.) maps. 27 cm. (Harvard East Asian series, 57) Bibliography: p. [1031]-1038. [DS778.A1K55 1971] 69-12725 ISBN 0-674-07410-6 30.00
1. China—Biography. 2. Communists—China. I. Clark, Anne B., joint author. II. Title. III. Series.

LIPPA, Ernest M 926.1
Captive surgeon; adventures and misadventures of a doctor in Red China New York, Morrow, 1953. 280p. 22cm. 'Based in part on, and considerably expanded from, three articles by Dr. Lippa which appeared in the Saturday evening post for April 28 ... May 5 and 12, 1951.' [R502.L5A3] 52-13827
1. China—Soc. condit. 2. Communism—China. I. Title.

MARTIN, Bernard, 915.1'03'0922 B
1897-
Makers of China, Confucius to Mao [by] Bernard Martin and Shui Chien-Tung. New York, Halsted Press Division, Wiley [1972] p. [DS734.M29] 72-3114 ISBN 0-470-57359-7
1. China—Biography. 2. China—Civilization. I. Shui, Chien-Tung, 1921- joint author. II. Title.

WU, Eugene Wen-chin, 016.920051
1922-
Leaders of twentieth-century China; an annotated bibliography of selected Chinese biographical works in the Hoover Library. Stanford, Calif., Stanford University Press, 1956. vii, 106 p. 26 cm. (Hoover Institute and Library. Bibliographical series, 4) [Z3106.W8] 56-13811
1. China — Biog. — Bibl. I. Title. II. Series: Stanford University. Hoover Institution on War, Revolution, and Peace. Bibliographical series, 4

WU, Wen-chin. 016.920051
Leaders of twentieth-century China; an annotated bibliography of selected Chinese biographical works in the Hoover Library, by Eugene Wu. Stanford, Calif., Stanford University Press, 1956. vii, 106p. 26cm. (Hoover Institute and Library Bibliographical series. 4) [Z3106.W8] 56-13811
1. China—Biog.—Bibl. I. Title. II. Series: Stanford University. Hoover Institute and Library on War. Revolution, and Peace. Bibliographical series. 4

YAUKEY, Grace 920.051
(Sydenstricker) 1899-
China's leaders in ideas and action [by] Cornelia Spencer. Philadelphia, Macrae Smith [1966] 190 p. maps. 22 cm. Bibliography: p. [189]-190. [DS734.Y35] 66-16518
1. China — Biog. I. Title.

China—Diplomatic and consular service—Registers.

BARTKE, Wolfgang. 950 S
The diplomatic service of the People's Republic of China as of January 1976, (including biographies) / Wolfgang Bartke. Hamburg : Institut fur Asienkunde, 1976. 178, xiv p. ; 21 cm. (Mitteilungen des Instituts fur Asienkunde Hamburg ; nr. 77) "Biographies translated into English by Mrs. Waltraut Jarke, Hamburg." [DS1.I55 nr. 77] [JX1837.A2] 354'.51'00892 77-364555 ISBN 3-921469-24-4
1. China—Diplomatic and consular service—Registers. 2. Diplomats—China—Biography. I. Title. II. Series: Institut fur Asienkunde. Mitteilungen ; nr. 77.

China—History—Han dynasty, 202 B.C.-220 A.D.

PAN, Ku, 32-92. 931
Courtier and commoner in ancient China; selections from the History of the former Han. Translated by Burton Watson. New York, Columbia University Press, 1974. 282 p. 23 cm. "Translations from the Oriental classics." Translation of selections from Han shu. Includes bibliographical references. [DS748.P3 1974] 73-18003 ISBN 0-231-03765-1 12.50
1. China—History—Han dynasty, 202 B.C.-220 A.D. I. Title.

China—History—Ming dynasty, 1368-1644—Biography.

ASSOCIATION for 951'.026'0922 B
Asian Studies. Ming Biographical History Project Committee.
Dictionary of Ming biography, 1368-1644 / the Ming Biographical History Project of the Association for Asian Studies ; L. Carrington Goodrich, editor, Chaoying Fang, associate editor. New York : Columbia University Press, 1975 [i.e.,1976] p. cm. Added title: Ming tai ming jen chuan. Includes index. Bibliography: p. [DS753.5.A84 1975] 75-26938 ISBN 0-231-03801-1 (v. 1). ISBN 0-231-03833-X (v. 2) : 75.00(set)
1. China—History—Ming dynasty, 1368-1644—Biography. 2. China—Biography. I. Goodrich, Luther Carrington, 1894- II. Fang, Chao-ying, 1908- III. Title.

China—History—Sung dynasty, 960-1279—Biography.

SUNG biographies / 915.1'03'2
ed. by Herbert Franke. 1. Aufl. Wiesbaden : Steiner, 1976. 3 v. (1271 p.) ; 24 cm. (Munchener ostasiatische Studien ; Bd. 16) English, French, or German. [DS751.5.S96] 77-462858 ISBN 3-515-02412-3 : DM96.00
1. China—History—Sung dynasty, 960-1279—Biography. 2. China—Biography. I. Franke, Herbert, 1914- II. Title. III. Series.

China—History—1900-

HAN, Suyin, pseud. 730'.92'4
Birdless summer; China: autobiography, history. [1st American ed.] New York, Putnam [1968] 347 p. illus., map, ports. 22 cm. [PR6015.A4674B5 1968] 68-25435 6.95
1. China—History—1900- I. Title.

STUART, John Leighton, 951.04
1876-
Fifty years in China; the memoirs of John Leighton Stuart, missionary and ambassador. New York, Random House [1954] 346 p. illus. 22 cm. [DS775.S84] 54-7808
1. China—History—1900- I. Title.

China—History—1912-1937.

SUN, Yat-sen, 1866- 951.04'1'0924
1925.
Memoirs of a Chinese revolutionary; a programme of national reconstruction for China. New York, AMS Press [1970] 254 p port. 23 cm. Reprint of the 1927 ed. [DS777.A32 1970] 73-111786
1. China—History—1912-1937. I. Title.

China (People's Republic of China, 1949- -Biog.

CLARK, Anne B v. 12
Selected biographies of Chinese Communist military leaders. Cambridge, Mass., East Asian Research Center, Harvard University, 1964. 60 p. 28 cm. 65-98692
1. China (People's Republic of China, 1949- -Biog. 2. China (People's Republic of China, 1949-) Army-Biog. I. Harvard University. East Asian Research Center. II. Title.

WHO'S who in Communist 951.050922
China. [Kowloon] Hong Kong, Union Res. Inst. [S. Pasadena, Calif., Hutchins Oriental] c. 1966 v, 754p. 24cm. [DS778.A1W45] 66-4063 25.00
1. China (People's Republic of China, 1949-)—Biog. I. Yu lien yen chiu so, Kowloon.

China—Politics and government—1912-1949.

HOLCOMBE, Arthur 320.9'51'04
Norman, 1884-
The spirit of the Chinese revolution, by Arthur N. Holcombe. Westport, Conn., Hyperion Press [1973, c1930] 185, vi p. 23 cm. Reprint of the ed. published by Knopf, New York, issued as the 1930 Lowell Institute lectures. [DS774.H6 1973] 73-876 ISBN 0-88355-070-9

1. China—Politics and government—1912-1949. 2. China—Biography. I. Title. II. Series: Lowell Institute lectures, 1930. BIP

China—Registers.

BIOGRAPHIC briefs on 354.51'002 *selected Chinese Communist personalities.* [Washington? 1968] v. 327 p. 27 cm. (Reference aid) Cover title. [JQ1507.B54] 70-6642
1. China—Registers.

China—Social life and customs.

NING, Lao T'ai-t'ai, 1867- 915.1'03'30924 B
A daughter of Han; the autobiography of a Chinese working woman [by] Ida Pruitt, from the story told her by Ning Lao T'ai-t'ai. Stanford, Calif., Stanford University Press [1967, c1945] vi, 254 p. map, plan, ports. 23 cm. [CT1828.N5A3 1967] 68-10633
1. China—Social life and customs. I. Pruitt, Ida. II. Title.

NING, Lao T'ai-t'ai, 1867- 915.1'03'30924 (B)
A daughter of Han; the autobiography of a Chinese working woman [by] Ida Pruitt, from the story told her by Ning Lao T'ai-t'ai. Stanford, Calif., Stanford University Press [1967, c1945] vi, 254 p. map, plan, ports. 23 cm. [CT1828.N5A3 1967] 68-10633
1. China—Soc. life & cust. I. Pruitt, Ida. II. Title.

RASMUSSEN, Albert Henry. 915.1
China trader. New York, Crowell [1954] 274 p. illus. 21 cm. Autobiographical. [DS721.R29] 54-5530
1. China—Social life and customs. 2. China—Commerce. I. Title.

Chiniquy, Charles Paschal Telesphore,

CHINIQUY, Charles Paschal Telesphore, 1809-1899. 922.571
Fifty years in the Church of Rome; the life story of Pastor Chiniquy who was for twenty-five years a priest in the Roman Catholic Church. Grand Rapids, Baker Book House, 1958. 597 p. illus. 23 cm. [BX1765.C47 1958] 58-11377
I. Title.

Chinn family.

CHINN, Walter Neal, 1905- 929'.2'0973
An autobiography of Walter Neal Chinn, Jr., his relatives, and friends / by Walter Neal Chinn, Jr. Fredericksburg, Va. : Fredericksburg Press, 1976. 167 p., [6] leaves of plates : ill. ; 23 cm. Includes index. [CS71.C5406 1976] 76-42962
1. Chinn family. 2. Chinn, Walter Neal, 1905- 3. Virginia—Biography. I. Title.

Chinov, Sultan

CHINOV, Sultan Sir 1885 926.5
Pioneering in Indian business. Foreword by R. P. Massani. [2d ed.] New York, Asia Pub. House [1962] 124p. illus. 20cm. Autobiographical. [HF3784.5.C47A3 1962] 62-6820
I. Title.

Chinoy, Sultan Meherally,

CHINOY, Sultan Meherally, Sir 1885- 926.5
Pioneering in Indian business. Foreword by R. P. Masani. [2d ed.] New York, Asia [dist.] Taplinger [c.1962] 124p. illus. 20cm. 62-6820 5.75
I. Title.

Chipperfield, Jimmy.

CHIPPERFIELD, Jimmy. 791.3'092'4 B
My wild life / by Jimmy Chipperfield. New York : Putnam, [1975, i.e.1976] p. cm. Includes index. [GV1811.C49A34] 75-23497 8.95
1. Chipperfield, Jimmy. 2. Circus. I. Title. BIP

Chirico, Giorgio de, 1888-

CHIRICO, Giorgio de, 1888- 759.5
The memoirs of Giorgio de Chirico. Translated from the Italian and with an introd. by Margaret Crosland. Coral Gables, Fla., University of Miami Press [1971] 262 p. illus. 23 cm. Translation of Memorie della mia vita, di Giorgio de Chirico. Bibliography: p. 253-258. [ND623.C56A2713 1971b] 74-102694 ISBN 0-87024-125-7 12.50
1. Chirico, Giorgio de, 1888- 2. Painters—Italy—Correspondence, reminiscences, etc. I. Title. BIP

Chirinos, Lito.

CHIRINOS, Lito. 301.44'1
Lito the shoeshine boy / by Lito Chirinos as told to and translated by David Mangurian ; photos. by David Mangurian. New York : Four Winds Press, [1975] [64] p. : ill. ; 19 x 28 cm. An eleven-year-old shoeshine boy in Honduras tells about his daily life. [HV747.H6C5] 74-26826 ISBN 0-590-07382-6 : 5.95
1. Chirinos, Lito. 2. Children, Vagrant—Tegucigalpa—Personal narratives—Juvenile literature. I. Mangurian, David. II. Title. BIP

Chisholm, Shirley, 1924-

BLACK Americans in government. 973.92'0922 [Text and exercises by Sheila Hobson and Harvey D. Goldenberg. General editor: Saunders Redding]. Produced by Buckingham Learning Corporation. [Jamaica, N.Y., Buckingham Learning Corp., 1969] 5 v. illus., ports. 28 cm. Cover title. Contents.Contents.—[1] The three wars of Edward Brooke; the story of the first black U.S. Senator since Reconstruction.—[2] Fighting Shirley Chisholm; the story of the first black U.S. Congresswoman.—[3] Ambassador for progress; the story of Patricia Harris, former U.S. Ambassador to Luxembourg.—[4] Equal under the law; the story of Supreme Court Justice Thurgood Marshall.—[5] Robert Weaver sees a new city; the story of the first Secretary of Housing and Urban Development. [E185.96.B53] 79-20085
1. Brooke, Edward William, 1919- 2. Chisholm, Shirley, 1924- 3. Harris, Patricia Roberts, 1924- 4. Marshall, Thurgood, 1908- 5. Weaver, Robert Clifton, 1907- I. Hobson, Sheila. II. Goldenberg, Harvey D.

Chisholm, Shirley, 1924- —Juvenile literature.

BROWNMILLER, Susan. 328.73'0924 B
Shirley Chisholm; a biography. [1st ed.] Garden City, N.Y., Doubleday [1970] 139 p. illus. 22 cm. (Doubleday signal books) A biography of the New York politician who was the first black woman to be elected to the United States Congress. [E840.8.C48B7] 92 77-103736 3.50
1. Chisholm, Shirley, 1924- —Juvenile literature. I. Title. BIP

BROWNMILLER, Susan. 328.73'0924
Shirley Chisholm; a biography. Garden City, N.Y., Doubleday [1971] 141 p. ports. 22 cm. (Doubleday signal books) A biography of the outspoken New York politician who became the first black person to the elected to Congress from Brooklyn and the first black Congresswoman in history. [E840.8.C48B7 1971] 92 79-28347 3.50
1. Chisholm, Shirley, 1924- —Juvenile literature. I. Title.

HASKINS, James, 1941- 328.73'092'4 B
Fighting Shirley Chisholm / James Haskins. New York : Dial Press, [1975] 211 p., [1] leaf of plates : ill. ; 22 cm. Includes index. Bibliography: p. 201-205. A biography of the first black congresswoman and the first black woman to run for the presidential nomination. [E840.8.C48H37] 92 74-20384 ISBN 0-8037-4835-3 : 5.95
1. Chisholm, Shirley, 1924- —Juvenile literature. I. Title.

HICKS, Nancy. 328.73'0924 B
The Honorable Shirley Chisholm, Congresswoman from Brooklyn. New York, Lion Books, 1971. 118 p. 22 cm. A biography of the schoolteacher who became the first black woman elected to the United States Congress. [E840.8.C48H5 1971] 92 78-127394 ISBN 0-87460-236-X 4.59
1. Chisholm, Shirley, 1924-—Juvenile literature. I. Title.

ITZKOWITZ, Leonore K., 1933- 328.73'092'4 B
Shirley Chisholm for President—the story of Shirley Chisholm [by] Leonore K. Itzkowitz. [New York] Random House [1974] p. cm. A brief biography of the first black woman ever to run for President. [E840.8.C48I89] 92 74-1243 ISBN 0-394-12312-3
1. Chisholm, Shirley, 1924- —Juvenile literature. I. Title.

Chissin, Chaim, 1865-1932.

CHISSIN, Chaim, 1865-1932. 956.94'001'0924 B
A Palestine diary : memoirs of a Bilu pioneer, 1882-1887 / by Chaim Chissin : translated from the Russian by Frances Miller. New York : Herzl Press, 1976. 281 p., [3] leaves of plates : ill. ; 23 cm. Hebrew translation has title: Mi-yoman ahad ha-Biluyim. [DS151.C5A313] 76-6041 10.00
1. Chissin, Chaim, 1865-1932. 2. Zionists—Biography. 3. Bilu. 4. Jews in Palestine—Biography. 5. Palestine—Biography. I. Title.

Chittenden, Hiram Martin, 1858-1917.

DODDS, Gordon Barlow, 1932- 363.5'092'4 B
Hiram Martin Chittenden; his public career [by] Gordon B. Dodds. [Lexington] University Press of Kentucky [1973] xi, 220 p. illus., map (on lining papers) 25 cm. Bibliography: p. [211]-216. [TC140.C45D63] 72-91664 ISBN 0-8131-1283-4 11.50
1. Chittenden, Hiram Martin, 1858-1917. BIP

Chivalry—Dictionaries.

UDEN, Grant. 394'.7'03
A dictionary of chivalry. Illustrated by Pauline Baynes. New York, Crowell [1969, c1968] 352 p. illus., coats of arms, ports. 25 cm. Part of the illustrative matter is colored. This illustrated dictionary includes customs, events, items of clothing and armor, historical figures, and places of the Middle Ages. [CR13.U3 1969] 70-10564
1. Chivalry—Dictionaries. 2. Knights and knighthood—Biography. I. Baynes, Pauline, illus. II. Title. BIP

Chivington, John Milton, 1821-1894.

CRAIG, Reginald S. 923.973
The fighting parson; the biography of Colonel John M. Chivington. Los Angeles, Westernlore Press, 1959. 284 p. illus. 22 cm. (Great West and Indian series, 17) Includes bibliography. [F780.C48C7] 59-14854
1. Chivington, John Milton, 1821-1894. 2. Colorado—History—Civil War. 3. Cheyenne Indians—Wars, 1864. 4. Sand Creek, Battle of, 1864. I. Title.

Chiwatenws, Joseph, d. 1640—Juvenile literature.

BOSCO, Antoinette, 1928- j 92
Joseph the Huron. Illustrated by Norman Pomerantz. New York, P. J. Kenedy [1961] 190p. illus. 22cm. (American background books, 19) [E99.H9C52] 61-15564
1. Chiwatenws, Joseph, d. 1640—Juvenile literature. I. Title.

Choate, Rufus, 1799-1859.

FUESS, Claude Moore, 1885-1963. 340'.0924 B
Rufus Choate, the wizard of the law. [Hamden, Conn.] Archon Books, 1970 [c1928] 278 p. illus., ports. 22 cm. [KF368.C4F8 1970] 70-114421
1. Choate, Rufus, 1799-1859. I. Title: The wizard of the law. BIP

Chodorov, Frank,

CHODOROV, Frank, 1887- 920
Out of step; the autobiography of an individualist. Introd. by E. Victor Milione. New York, Devin [c.]1962. 261p. 21cm. 62-13461 4.50
I. Title.

CHODOROV, Frank, 1887- 920
Out of step the Autobiography of an individualist With introd. by E. Victor Milione. New York, Devin-Adair Co., 1962. 261p. 21cm. [H59.C43A3] 62-13461
I. Title.

Chomsky, Noam.

LEIBER, Justin. 410'.92'4
Noam Chomsky; a philosophic overview. Boston, Twayne Publishers [1975] 192 p. port. 22 cm. (Twayne's world leaders series) Based on lectures given at Lehman College of the City University of New York in the 1973 spring term. Bibliography: p. 187-190. [P85.C47L4] 74-10583 ISBN 0-8057-3661-1 7.50
1. Chomsky, Noam. BIP

LYONS, John. 410'.924
Noam Chomsky. New York, Viking Press [1970] xii, 143 p. illus. 20 cm. (Modern masters) Bibliography: p. [135]-137. [P85.C47L9 1970b] 73-104148 5.75
1. Chomsky, Noam. BIP

LYONS, John. 410.92'4 B
Noam Chomsky / John Lyons. Rev. ed. [New York] : Penguin Books, [1978,i.e.1977] p. cm. (Penguin modern masters) Includes index. Bibliography: p. [P85.C47L9 1978] 77-21346 ISBN 0-14-004370-5 pbk. : 2.50
1. Chomsky, Noam. 2. Linguists—United States—Biography.

Chopin, Fryderyk Franciszek, 1810-1849.

BOUCOURECHLIEV, Andre 927.8
Chopin; a pictorial biography. [Tr. from French by Edward Hyams] New York, Viking [c.1963] 144p. illus. 24cm. (Studio bk.) 63-8850 6.95
1. Chopin, Eryderyk Franciszek, 1810-1849—Homes and haunts. 2. Chopin, Fryderyk Franciszek, 1810-1849—Iconography. I. Title.

BOURNIQUEL, Camille 927.8
Chopin. Translated [from the French] by Sinclair Road. New York, Grove Press [1960] 192p. (bibl.) illus. 18cm. (Evergreen profile book, 8) 59-6399 1.35 pap.,
1. Chopin, Fryderyk Franciszek, 1810-1849. I. Title.

CHISSELL, Joan. 786.0924
Chopin. New York, T. Y. Crowell Co. [1965] 94 p. illus., facsims., music, ports. 26 cm. (The Great composers) [ML410.C54C432] 65-20724
1. Chopin, Fryderyk Franciszek, 1810-1849. I. Title.

CHISSELL, Joan 786.0924
Chopin. London, Faber & Faber [dist. New York, Crowell, c.1965] 94p. illus., facsim., music. ports. 26cm. (Great composers) [ML410.C54C43] 65-6278 3.95 bds.,
1. Chopin, Fryderyk Franciszek, 1810-1849. I. Title.

CHOPIN, Fryderyk Franciszek, 1810-1849. 786.1'092'4 B
Letters; collected by Henryk Opienski. Translated from the original Polish and French, with a pref. and editorial notes by E. L. Voynich. New York, Vienna House [1971] x, 420, iv p. music. 24 cm. Reprint of the 1931 ed. [ML410.C54A26 1971] 79-163798 ISBN 0-8443-0020-9

I. Voynich, Ethel Lillian (Boole) 1864-1960, ed. and tr. II. Opienski, Henryk, 1870-1942.

FERRA, Bartolome, 1893-1946. 786.1'092'4 B
Chopin and George Sand in Majorca. Translated from the Spanish by James Webb. Preceded by an extract from "The memoirs of Aurore Sand." New York, Haskell House, 1974. 82, [4] p. illus. 23 cm. Reprint of the 1936 ed. published by Ediciones La Cartuja, Palma de Mallorca. Translation of Chopin i George Sand a la Cartoixa de Valldemosa. Bibliography: p. [85] [ML410.C54F513] 73-21620 ISBN 0-8383-1807-X 11.95
1. Chopin, Fryderyk Franciszek, 1810-1849. 2. Sand, George, pseud. of Mme. Dudevant, 1804-1876. I. Title. BIP

GAVOTY, Bernard. 786.1'092'4 B
Frederic Chopin / by Bernard Gavoty ; translated from the French by Martin Sokolinsky. New York : Scribner, c1977. xii, 452 p. ; 25 cm. Includes bibliographical references and index. [ML410.C54G2753] 77-3966 ISBN 0-684-14930-3 : 12.50
1. Chopin, Fryderyk Franciszek, 1810-1849. 2. Composers—Biography.

GIDE, Andre Paul Guillaume, 1869-1951. 786.1'092'4 B
Notes on Chopin / Andre Gide ; translated from the French by Bernard Frechtman. Westport, Conn. : Greenwood Press, [1978] c1949. vii p., p. 20-126. : music ; 23 cm. Reprint of the ed. published by Philosophical Library, New York. [ML410.C54G53 1978] 78-3640 ISBN 0-313-20371-7 lib.bdg. : 13.00
1. Chopin, Fryderyk Franciszek, 1810-1849. 2. Composers—Biography. I. Title. BIP

HADDEN, James Cuthbert, 1861-1914. 786.1'092'4 B
Chopin / by J. Cuthbert Hadden. New York : AMS Press, 1977. xii, 243 p., [8] leaves of plates : ill. ; 19 cm. Reprint of the 1934 ed. published by Dent, London, in series: The Master musicians. Includes index. Bibliography: p. 229-231. [ML410.C54H2 1977] 74-24094 ISBN 0-404-12939-0 : 18.00
1. Chopin, Fryderyk Franciszek, 1810-1849. 2. Composers- Poland Biography. I. Series: The Master musicians.

HEDLEY, Arthur 927.8
Chopin. New York, Collier [1962] 222p. 18cm. (BS139V) Bibl. 1.50 pap.,
1. Chopin, Fryderyk Franciszek, 1810-1849. I. Title. BIP

HOLCMAN, Jan, 1922- 927.8
The legacy of Chopin. New York, Philosophical Library [1954] 113p. illus. 21cm. [ML410.C54H68] 54-7902
1. Chopin, Fryderyk Franciszek, 1810-1849. I. Title.

HUNEKER, James Gibbons, 1857-1921. 786.1'092'4 B
Chopin; the man and his music. New York, Scribner, 1926. St. Clair Shores, Mich., Scholarly Press, 1972 [c1900] vii, 414 p. port., music. 22 cm. Bibliography: p. 391-396. [ML410.C54H9 1972] 72-181182 ISBN 0-403-01587-1 24.50
1. Chopin, Fryderyk Franciszek, 1810-1849.

HUNEKER, James Gibbons, 1857-1921 786.1'0924 B
Chopin; the man and his music, by James Huneker. New. introd. footnotes, index by Herbert Weinstock. New York, Dover [c.1966] xi, 239p. music, port. 22cm. This Dover ed. is an unabridged repubn. of the work first pub. by Charles Scribner's Sons in 1960. Bibl. [ML410.C54H1966] 65-25713 1.75 pap.,
1. Chopin, Fryderyk Franciszek, 1810-1849. I. Title.

HUNEKER, James Gibbons, 1857-1921. 784'.092'4
Chopin; the man and his music, by James Huneker. With new. introd. footnotes and index by Herbert Weinstock. New York, Dover Publications [c1966] xi, 239 p. music port. 22 cm. "This Dover edition is an unabridged repulication of the work first published by Charles Scribner's Sons in 1960." Bibliography: p. 221-224. [ML410.C54H9] [786'1.0924 (B)] 65-25713
1. Chopin, Fryderyk Francisnek, 1810-1849. I. Title. BIP

JORDAN, Ruth. 786.1'092'4 B
Nocturne : a life of Chopin / Ruth Jordan. New York : Taplinger Pub. Co., 1978. 286 p., [7] leaves of plates : ill. ; 23 cm. Includes index. Bibliography: p. [277]-280. [ML410.C54J85 1978b] 78-53797 ISBN 0-8008-5593-0 : 12.50
1. Chopin, Fryderyk Franciszek, 1810-1849. 2. Composers—Biography. I. Title. BIP

KARASOWSKI, Maurycy, 1823-1892. 780'.924 B
Frederic Chopin; his life and letters, by Moritz Karasowski. Translated by Emily Hill. Westport, Conn., Greenwood Press [1970] xiii, 479 p. illus., facsims., ports. 23 cm. Reprint of the 3d ed., 1938. [ML410.C54K3 1970] 70-104285
1. Chopin, Fryderyk Franciszek, 1810-1849.

KELLEY, Edgar Stillman, 1857-1944. 786.1'0924
Chopin the composer; his structural art and its influence on contemporaneous music. New York, Cooper Square Publishers, 1969 [c1913] vii, 190 p. music, port. 23cm. [ML410.C54K4 1969] 69-18885 6.00
1. Chopin, Fryderyk Franciszek, 1810-1849. I. Title. BIP

LENZ, Wilhelm von, 1808-1883. 786.1'092'2 B
The great piano virtuosos of our time, by W. von Lenz; this revised translation [from the German] edited by Philip Reder. London, New York, Regency Press, 1971. [7], 91 p. ports. 20 cm. Revised translation of Die grossen piano-virtuosen unserer zeit aus persönlicher bekanntschaft. [ML397.L57 1971] 72-190224 ISBN 0-7212-0138-5 £1.20
1. Liszt, Franz, 1811-1886. 2. Chopin, Fryderyk Franciszek, 1810-1849. 3. Tausig, Karl, 1841-1871. 4. Henselt, Adolf von, 1814-1889. I. Title. BIP

LISZT, Franz. 927.8B
Frederic Chopin. translated with an introduction, by Edward N. Waters. New York, Vienna House [1973, c1963] vii, 184 p. 21 cm. Translation of F. Chopin. [ML410.C54] 72-81575 ISBN 0-8443-0066-7 2.45 (pbk.)
1. Chopin, Fryderyk Franciszek, 1810-1849. I. Waters, Edward Neighbor. 1960- tr. II. Title. BIP

LISZT, Franz, 1811-1886 927.8
Frederic Chopin. Tr. [from French] introd. by Edward N. Waters. [New York] Free Pr. [c.1963] vii, 184p. 22cm. Bibl. 63-10651 4.95 bds.,
1. Chopin, Fryderyk Franciszek, 1810-1849. I. Waters, Edward Neighbor, 1906- tr. II. Title.

LISZT, Franz, 1811-1886. 927.8
Frederic Chopin. Translated, with an introd. by Edward N. Waters. London [New York] Free Press of Glencoe, Collier-Macmillan [1963] vii, 184 p. 22 cm. [ML410.C54L37] 63-106511
1. Choppin, Fryderyk Franciszek, 1810-1849. 2. Translation of F. Chopin. I. Waters, Edward Neighbor, 1906- tr. II. Title.

MAREK, George Richard, 1902- 786.1'092'4 B
Chopin / George R. Marek with Maria Gordon-Smith. New York : Harper & Row, 1978. p. cm. Includes index. Bibliography: [ML410.C54M37] 76-57880 ISBN 0-06-012843-7 : 12.95
1. Chopin, Fryderyk Franciszek, 1810-1849. 2. Composers—Biography. I. Gordon-Smith, Maria, joint author.

MELVILLE, Derek. 786.1'092'4 B
Chopin : a biography, with a survey of books, editions and recordings / by Derek Melville. London : C. Bingley ; bLinnet Books, 1977. 108 p. ; 23 cm. (The Concertgoer's companions) Includes index. Discography: p. 92-99. [ML410.C54M47] 76-53009 ISBN 0-208-01542-6 : 6.50
1. Chopin, Fryderyk Franciszek, 1810-1849. 2. Chopin, Fryderyk Franciszek, 1810-1849—Bibliography. 3. Composers—Biography. BIP

MURDOCH, William David, 1888-1942. 786.1'0924 B
Chopin: his life. Westport, Conn., Greenwood Press [1971, c1962] xvi, 410 p. illus. 23 cm. Reprint of the 1935 ed. Bibliography: p. 395-397. [ML410.C54M97 1971] 70-136077 ISBN 0-8371-5227-5
1. Chopin, Fryderyk Franciszek, 1810-1849.

NIECKS, Frederick, 1845-1924. 786.1'092'4 B
Frederick Chopin as a man and musician. New York, Cooper Square Publishers, 1973. 2 v. port. 23 cm. Reprint of the 1902 ed. published by Novello, London. Includes bibliographical references. [ML410.C54N4 1973] 73-75023 ISBN 0-8154-0478-6 22.50 (Lib. ed.)
1. Chopin, Fryderyk Franciszek, 1810-1849. I. Title.

ORGA, Ates. 786.1'092'4 B
Chopin : his life and times / Ates Orga. London : Midas Books, 1976. 144 p. : ill., ports. ; 26 cm. Errata slip inserted. Includes index. Bibliography: p. [7] [ML410.C54O73] 76-378024 ISBN 0-85936-057-1 : £5.95
1. Chopin, Fryderyk Franciszek, 1810-1849. 2. Composers—Poland—Biography. BIP

TARNOWSKI, Stanislaw, hrabia, 1837-1917. 786.1'092'4 B
Chopin: as revealed by extracts from his diary, by Count Stanislas Tarnowski. [Translated from the Polish by Natalie Janotha. 2d ed. New York, Musical Scope Publishers, 1972] 55 p. illus. 22 cm. Cover title. [ML410.C54T2 1972] 72-76896 ISBN 0-913000-01-9
1. Chopin, Fryderyk Franciszek, 1810-1849.

WALKER, Alan ed. 786.1'0924
Frederic Chopin: profiles of the man and the musician [by] Paul Badura-Skoda [et al.] Ed. by Alan Walker. [1st Amer. ed.] New York, Taplinger [1967] 334p. facsims., music, port. 24cm. Bibl. [ML410.C54W16 1967] 67-16594 10.00
1. Chopin, Fryderyk Franciszek, 1810-1849. I. Title.

WALKER, Alan, writer on music, ed. 786.1'0924
Frederic Chopin: profiles of the man and the musician [by] Paul Badura-Skoda [et al.] Edited by Alan Walker. [1st Amer. ed.] New York, Taplinger Pub. Co. [1967] 334 p. facsims., music, port. 24 cm. Dibliography: p. [323]-324; discography: p. [301]-321. [ML410.C54W16 1967] 67-16594
1. Chopin, Fryderyk Franciszek, 1810-1849. I. Title.

Chopin, Fryderyk Franciszek, 1810-1849 — Iconography.

BOUCOURECHLIEV, Andre. 927.8
Chopin; a pictorial biography. [Translated from the French by Edward Hyams] New York, Viking Press [1963] 144 p. illus. 24 cm. (A Studio book) [ML88.C46B7] 63-8850
1. Chopin, Fryderyk Franciszek, 1810-1849 — Iconography. 2. Chopin, Fryderyk Franciszek, 1810-1849 — Homes and haunts. I. Title.

Choquette, Buck, 1829-1898.

CLARK, Henry W 917.90946
Buck Choquette, stampeder. [Washington? 1960] 152p. 29cm. Includes bibliography. [F851.C57C55] 61-43186
1. Choquette, Buck, 1829-1898. 2. Frontier and pioneer life-Pacific coast. 3. Frontier and pioneer life-Canada. I. Title.

Chotzinoff, Samuel, 1889-1964.

CHOTZINOFF, Samuel, 1889-1964. 786.1'092'4 B
A lost paradise : early reminiscences / Samuel Chotzinoff. New York : Arno Press, 1975, c1955. viii, 373 p. ; 23 cm. (The Modern Jewish experience) Continued by Day's at the morn. Reprint of the ed. published by Knopf, New York. [ML423.C564A3 1975] 74-27970 ISBN 0-405-06700-3 : 23.00
1. Chotzinoff, Samuel, 1889-1964. 2. Musicians—Correspondence, reminiscences, etc. I. Title. II. Series.

Chou, Cynthia L.,

CHOU, Cynthia L., 1926- 917.3'03'920924 B
My life in the United States, by Cynthia L. Chou. North Quincy, Mass., Christopher Pub. House [1970] 274 p. 25 cm. [CT275.C573A3] 70-125923 ISBN 0-8158-0244-7 9.75
I. Title. BIP

Chou, En-lai, 1898-1976.

ARCHER, Jules. 951.05'092'4 B
Chou En-lai. New York, Hawthorn Books [1973] 198 p. 22 cm. Bibliography: p. 187-188. A biography of the Chinese leader stressing his role in events in Communist China which culminated in its recognition as a member of the United Nations in 1972. [DS778.C593A8] 92 72-11217 5.95
1. Chou, En-lai, 1898- —Juvenile literature. I. Title.

HSU, Kai-yu, 1922- 951.04'0924 B
Chou En-lai: China's gray eminence. [1st ed.] Garden City, N.Y., Doubleday, 1968. xviii, 294 p. illus., maps (part col.), ports. 22 cm. Bibliography: p. [271]-283. [DS778.C593H8] 68-10566
1. Chou, En-lai, 1898-

ROOTS, John McCook. 951.05'092'4 B
Chou : an informal biography of China's legendary Chou En-lai / John McCook Roots. 1st ed. Garden City, N.Y. : Doubleday, 1977. p. cm. Includes index. Bibliography: p. [DS778.C593R66] 74-2758 ISBN 0-385-03804-6 : 7.95
1. Chou, En-lai, 1898-1976. 2. Prime ministers—China—Biography.

Chouart, Medard, sieur des Groseilliers, 17th century.

NUTE, Grace Lee, 1895- 971.01'6'0922
Caesars of the wilderness : Medard Chouart, Sieur des Groseilliers and Pierre Esprit Radisson, 1618-1710 / by Grace Lee Nute. Reprint ed. St. Paul : Minnesota Historical Society Press, 1978, c1943. xx, 386 p., [7] leaves of plates : ill. ; 24 cm. (Publications of the Minnesota Historical Society) Reprint of the ed. published by Appleton-Century, New York. Includes index. Bibliography: p. 359-370. [F1060.7.C483N87 1978] 78-811 ISBN 0-87351-127-1 : 12.50 ISBN 0-87351-128-X pbk. : 5.95
1. Chouart, Medard, sieur des Groseilliers, 17th century. 2. Radisson, Pierre Esprit, 1620?-1710. 3. Hudson's Bay Company. 4. New France—Discovery and exploration. 5. Explorers—France—Biography. 6. Fur trade—New France. I. Title. II. Series: Minnesota Historical Society. Publications. BIP

Chow, Ching Lie, 1936-

CHOW, Ching Lie, 1936- 951.05'092'4 B
Journey in tears : memory of a girlhood in China / Chow Ching-li ; [translated by Abby Israel]. New York : McGraw-Hill, c1978. p. cm. Translation of Le palanquin des larmes. [CT1828.C544A3413] 78-18171 ISBN 0-07-010818-8 : 10.95
1. Chow, Ching Lie, 1936- 2. China—Social life and customs. 3. China—Biography. I. Title.

Choy, Jun Ke, 1892-

CHOY, Jun Ke, 1892- 320.9'51'04 B
My China years, 1911-1945; practical politics in China after the 1911 revolution. San Francisco, East/West Pub. Co. [1973] xix, 260 p. 29 cm. Autobiography. [DS778.C5964A34] 73-168167
1. Choy, Jun Ke, 1892- 2. China—Politics and government—1912-1949. I. Title.

Christian biography.

ADAIR, James R, 1923- 922
Saints alive; introd, by A. W. Tozer. Wheaton, Ill., Van Kampen Press [1951] 159 p. illus. 20 cm. [BR1700.A37] 51-8316
1. Christian biography. I. Title.

ADAIR, James R., 280'.4'0922
1923-
Saints alive, by James R. Adair. Introd. by A. W. Tozer. Freeport, N.Y., Books for Libraries Press [1970, c1951] 159 p. illus. 23 cm. (Biography index reprint series) [BR1700.2.A3 1970] 76-117319
1. Christian biography. I. Title. **BIP**

ALAND, Kurt. 270.1'0922 B
Saints and sinners; men and ideas in the early church. Translated by Wilhelm C. Linss. Philadelphia, Fortress Press [1970] vi, 250 p. 19 cm. Translation of Kirchengeschichte in Lebensbildern dargestellt, v. 1, Die Fruhzeit. [BR1706.A413] 76-123507 3.95
1. Christian biography. 2. Fathers of the church. I. Title.

&BARSTAD, Glenna. 209.22
They dared for God. Illustrated by Dick Cole. Mountain View, Calif., Pacific Press Pub. Association [1958] 128p. illus. 21cm. [BR1704.B3] 58-10579
1. Christian biography. I. Title.

ANDERSON, Courtney 922.654
To the golden shore; the life of Adoniram Judson. Garden City, N.Y., Doubleday [1961, c.1956] 520p. (Dolphin bk. C. 192) Bibl. 1.45 pap.,
I. Title. **BIP**

BACH, Marcus, 1906- 922
Adventures in faith; stories about people who have found a guiding light within their hearts and minds. Minneapolis, T. S. Denison [1959] 240p. 22cm. [BR1702.B28] 59-13856
1. Christian biography. I. Title.

BARKER, William Pierson. 209'.22
Who's who in church history [by] William P. Barker. Old Tappan, N.J., F. H. Revell Co. [1969] 319 p. 24 cm. [BR1700.2.B37] 74-85306 6.95
1. Christian biography. I. Title. **BIP**

BOWIE, Walter Russell, 1882- 922
Men of fire; torchbearers of the gospel. [1st ed.] New York, Harper [1961] 244p. 22cm. Includes bibliography. [BR1703.B65] 61-13282
1. Christian biography. I. Title.

BROWN, LeRoy C 922
Christian go-givers; [stories] Illus. by Siegfried E. Bohlmann. Washington, Review and Herald Pub. Association [1961] 128p. illus. 22cm. [BR1702.B73] 61-11983
1. Christian biography. I. Title.

BRUSH, John W. 922
Who's who in church history. [1st ed.] Boston, Whittemore Associates [1962] 64 p. illus. 19 cm. [BR1703.B7] 62-51555
1. Christian biography. I. Title. **BIP**

CHANDLER, Russell. 209'.2'2
The overcomers / Russell Chandler. Old Tappan, N.J. : Revell, c1978. p. cm. [BR1700.2.C46] 78-16621 ISBN 0-8007-0944-6 : 6.95
1. Christian biography. 2. Christian life—1960- I. Title.
Contents omitted **BIP**

CUMMING, James Elder 922
Holy men of God, dating back to St. Augustine. [Rev. ed.] Chicago, Moody [c.1961] 254p. 61-4894 .89 pap.,
1. Christian biography. I. Title.

DAUGHTERS of St. Paul. 209'.2'2 B
Every man's challenge; profiles of great men and women. [Boston] St. Paul Editions [1974] 345 p. illus. 22 cm. [BR1700.2.D345 1974] 73-89938 5.00
1. Christian biography. I. Title.

DAVEY, Cyril James. 209'.22 B
Fifty lives for God [by] Cyril Davey. Valley Forge [Pa.] Judson Press [1974, c1973] 167 p. 23 cm. Bibliography: p. 166-167. [BR1700.2.D35 1974] 73-13450 ISBN 0-8170-0629-X 4.95
1. Christian biography. I. Title. **BIP**

DAY, Richard Ellsworth, 209'.22 B
1884-
Beacon lights of grace. Freeport, N.Y., Books for Libraries Press [1971, c1947] 169 p. illus., ports. 23 cm. (Biography index reprint series) "Twelve biographical vignettes: Amos of Tekoa [and others]" [BR1700.D4 1971] 71-148210 ISBN 0-8369-8057-3
1. Christian biography. I. Title.

DILLARD, Pauline (Hargis) 232.92
1916-
My book about Jesus [by] Polly Hargis Dillard. Pictures by Anne R. Kasey. Nashville, Broadman Press [1968] 32 p. col. illus. 21 cm. An easy to read story of Christ's birth, his early years, and his teachings. [BT302.D55] AC 68
I. Kasey, Anne R., illus. II. Title.

FLOOD, Robert. 920.71'0973
Men who shaped America / by Robert Flood. Chicago : Moody Press, c1976. 96 p. ; 18 cm. Contents.Contents.—Christopher Columbus.—William Bradford.—John Eliot.—William Penn.—Samuel Adams.—John Witherspoon.—Jonathan Edwards.—Francis Asbury.—Noah Webster.—Francis Scott Key.—Abraham Lincoln.—Dwight L. Moody. Includes bibliographical references. [BR1700.2.F52] 75-34339 ISBN 0-8024-5242-6 : 0.95
1. Christian biography. 2. United States—Biography. I. Title.

GIBBARD, Mark. 209'.2'2 B
Twelve who prayed : 20th century models of prayer / Mark Gibbard. 1st U.S. ed. Minneapolis : Augsburg Pub. House, 1977, c1974. vii, 120 p. ; 20 cm. Originally published under title: Twentieth-century men of prayer. Includes index. Bibliography: p. 115-119. [BR1702.G44 1977] 77-72459 ISBN 0-8066-1595-8 pbk. : 3.50
1. Christian biography. 2. Prayer—Case studies. I. Title.

GOULOOZE, William, 1903-1955. 922
These also suffer. [1st ed.] Grand Rapids, Baker Book House, 1955. 86p. 21cm. [BR1702.G6] 55-12152
1. Christian biography. 2. Suffering. I. Title.

GREEN, Vivian Hubert 270 B
Howard.
From St. Augustine to William Temple; eight studies in Christian leadership, by Vivian H. H. Green. Freeport, N.Y., Books for Libraries Press [1971] 172 p. 23 cm. (Biography index reprint series) Reprint of the 1948 ed. Includes bibliographies. [BR1700.G7 1971] 72-148213 ISBN 0-8369-8060-3
1. Christian biography. I. Title.

HARCOURT, Melville, ed. 922
Thirteen for Christ. New York, Sheed and Ward [1963] xv, 271 p. 22 cm. Contents.Contents.—Preface, by M. Harcourt.—T. S. Eliot, by P. Kirk.—Martin Luther King, by J. H. Griffin.—Pope Pius XII, by Daniel-Rops.—Paul Tillich, by J. E. Smith.—Trevor Huddleston, by A. Paton.—Albert Schweitzer, by G. Seaver.—Tubby Clayton, by M. Harcourt.—Ronald Knox, by A. Lunn.—Boris Pasternak, by R. Payne.—William Temple, by A. Baker.—John LaFarge, by G. N. Shuster.—Billy Graham, by J. S. Bonnell.—Dorothy Day, by D. Macdonald. [BR1700.H26] 63-8544
1. Christian biography. I. Title.

HARRELL, Irene Burk, comp. 248.2
God ventures; true accounts of God in the lives of men. Waco, Tex., Word Books, [1970] 131 p. 23 cm. Contents.Contents.—Cannibal talk, by J. L. Sherrill.—Something made me go, by M. Aussant.—Gang war, by D. Wilkerson.—Race to save a traitor, by E. Lundby as told to H. Cronsioe.—Facing death on the Atlantic, by D. L. Moody.—Am I my brother's keeper? By C. Coffey.—The ice-pan adventure, by W. Grenfell.—Out of the dungeon, by C. Marshall.—Four-footed angel, by O. Broadway as told to E. L. Vogt.—My grave was number 12, by J. Lee as told to E. Erny.—Blizzard, by O. A. Hunter.—A gentleman in prison, by T. Ishii.—Christmas Eve miracle, by A. Lake.—Birth on death row, by A. Sanford.—Return from tomorrow, by G. C. Ritchie, Jr.—Fire! By C. Marshall.—We thought we heard the angels sing, by J. C. Whittaker. [BR1700.2.H32 1970] 76-119888 3.95
1. Christian biography. I. Title.

HASKIN, Dorothy (Clark) 1905- 922
Christians you would like to know. Grand Rapids, Zondervan Pub. House [1954] 89p. illus. 20cm. [BR1700.H28] 55-226
1. Christian biography. I. Title.

HERRICK, Samuel Edward, 270 B
1841-1904.
Some heretics of yesterday. Freeport, N.Y., Books for Libraries Press [1973] p. (Essay index reprint series) Reprint of the 1884 ed. Contents.Contents.—Tauler and the mystics.—Wiclif.—Hus.—Savonarola.—Latimer.—Cranmer.—Melancthon.—Knox.—Calvin.—Coligny.—William Brewster.—Wesley. [BR1700.H47 1973] 72-14160 ISBN 0-518-10013-8
1. Christian biography. I. Title.

HILL, David C. 280'.4'0922 B
Messengers of the King, by David C. Hill. Illustrated by Paul Konsterlie. Minneapolis, Augsburg Pub. House [1968] 167 p. illus. 21 cm. Contents.Contents.—Francis of Assisi, God's laughing beggar.—John Wycliffe, battling scholar.—John Huss, flame of truth from Bohemia.—John Calvin, master of Geneva.—John Knox, stern saint of the Scots.—John Milton, Puritan prophet.—Roger Williams, disciple of liberty.—George Fox, apostle of peace.—David Brainerd, aflame for God.—Johann Sebastian Bach: "Sing to the Lord."—John Wesley, minister to millions.—Isaac Watts, the father of hymns.—George Whitefield, evangelist extraordinary.—Dorothea Dix, angel of mercy.—William Booth, general for God.—Fanny Crosby, sweet blind singer.—Billy Sunday, battlin' Billy.—Wilfred Grenfell, the man who did things.—Dietrich Bonhoeffer, witness for today.—C. S. Lewis, unwilling apostle. [BR1700.2.H5] 68-25802 3.95
1. Christian biography. I. Title.

HILLERBRAND, Hans 209'.22
Joachim.
A fellowship of discontent, [by] Hans J. Hillerbrand. [1st ed.] New York., Harper & Row [1967] xiv, 176 p. 22 cm. [BR1702.H5] 67-11509
1. Christian biography. I. Title.

HODGES, George, 1856- 209'.22 B
1919.
Saints and heroes since the Middle Ages. Freeport, N.Y., Books for Libraries Press [1970] 318 p. illus., ports. 23 cm. (Essay index reprint series) Reprint of the 1912 ed. Contents.Contents.—Luther, 1483-1546.—More, 1478-1535.—Loyola, 1491-1556.—Cranmer, 1489-1556.—Calvin, 1509-1564.—Knox, 1505-1572.—Coligny, 1519-1572.—William the Silent, 1533-1584.—Brewster, 1560-1644.—Laud, 1573-1645.—Cromwell, 1599-1658.—Bunyan, 1628-1688.—Fox, 1624-1691.—Wesley, 1703-1791. [BR1700.H58 1970] 75-107713
1. Christian biography. I. Title. **BIP**

HODGES, George, 1856- 282'.0922
1919.
Saints and heroes to the end of the Middle Ages. Freeport, N. Y., Books for Libraries Press [1967] 268 p. ports. 22 cm. (Essay index reprint series) Reprint of the 1911 ed. Contents.--Cyprian, 200-258.--Athanasius, 296-373.--Ambrose, 340-397.--Chrysostom, 347-407.--Jerome, 340-420.--Augustine, 354-430.--Benedict, 480-543.--Gregory the Great, 540-604.--Columba, 521-597.--Charlemagne, 742-814.--Hildebrand, 1020-1085.--Anselm, 1033-1109.--Bernard, 1091-1153.--Becket, 1118-1170.--Langton, 1170-1228.--Dominic, 1170-1221.--Francis, 1182-1226.--Wycliffe, 1320-1384.--Hus, 1373-1415.--Savonarola, 1452-1498. [BR1703.H6 1967] 67-26749
1. Christian biography. I. Title. **BIP**

HOSIER, Helen Kooiman. 209'.2'2 B
Profiles : people who are helping to change the world / Helen Kooiman Hosier. New York : Hawthorn Books, c1977. viii, 184 p. : ports ; 22 cm. [BR1700.2.H67 1977] 75-2566 ISBN 0-8015-6082-9 : 6.95
1. Christian biography. I. Title.

HUNT, Gladys M. 209'.22
Does anyone here know God? Stories of women who do [by] Gladys M. Hunt. Grand Rapids, Zondervan Pub. House [1967] 224 p. ports. 23 cm. Bibliographical footnotes. [BR1713.H78] 67-11622
1. Christian biography. 2. Woman—Biography. I. Title.

JARRETT-KERR, 266'.0092'2 B
Martin, 1912-
Patterns of Christian acceptance: individual response to the missionary impact, 1550-1950. London, New York, Oxford University Press, 1972. xviii, 342 p. 23 cm. Bibliography: p. [325]-336. [BR1702.J37 1972] 72-178732 ISBN 0-19-213946-0 £4.50
1. Christian biography. 2. Missions. I. Title.

JOHNSON, Paul Emanuel, 209.2'2 B
1898-
Healer of the mind; a psychiatrist's search for faith. Paul E. Johnson, editor. Nashville, Abingdon Press [1972] 270 p. 23 cm. Includes bibliographical references. [BR1702.J58] 78-186824 ISBN 0-687-16738-8 6.95
1. Christian biography. I. Title.

JOHNSON, Ruth I 922
Christians you should know. Chicago, Moody Press [1960] 127p. 18cm. (Moody Colportage library, 394) [BR1703.J6] 60-1760
1. Christian biography. I. Title.

KENNETH, Brother, C. 209'.2'2 B
G. A.
Saints of the twentieth century / by Brother Kenneth. London : Mowbrays, 1976. xvii, 206 p. ; 21 cm. Includes index. Bibliography: p. 190-195. [BR1700.2.K38] 76-383579 ISBN 0-264-66285-7 : £3.75
1. Christian biography. I. Title.

KEPLER, Thomas Samuel, 1897- 922
A journey with the saints. [1st ed.] Cleveland, World Pub. Co. [1951] 150 p. 21 cm. [BR1700.K4] 51-11265
1. Christian biography. I. Title.

KEPLER, Thomas Samuel, 209'.22 B
1897-
A journey with the saints, by Thomas S. Kepler. Freeport, N.Y., Books for Libraries Press [1971, c1951] 150 p. 23 cm. (Biography index reprint series) Includes bibliographical references. [BR1700.2.K4 1971] 70-148223 ISBN 0-8369-8070-0
1. Christian biography. I. Title. **BIP**

KITTLER, Glenn D 922
Profiles in faith. Introd. by Catherine Marshall. New York, Coward-McCann [1962] 318p. 22cm. [BR569.K5] 62-10948
1. Christian biography. 2. U. S.—Biog. I. Title.

KNOWLES, Leo. 282'.092'2 B
Candidates for sainthood / by Leo Knowles. St. Paul : Carillon Books, 1978. ix, 138 p. ; 22 cm. Bibliography: p. 137-138. [BX4651.2.K56] 78-55247 ISBN 0-89310-035-8 : 8.95. ISBN 0-89310-036-6 pbk. : 3.95
1. Catholics—Biography. 2. Christian biography. I. Title.
Contents omitted. **BIP**

LIND, Marie. 209'.22 B
Dramatic stories for missionary programs; accounts of witnessing Christians in West Africa. Photos. by Marilyn Birch. Grand Rapids, Mich., Baker Book House [1972] 175 p. illus. 22 cm. [BR1700.2.L54] 72-93075 ISBN 0-8010-5525-3 2.95
1. Christian biography. 2. Sierra Leone—Biography.

LOCKYEAR, Herbert 209'.22
The man who changed the world; or, conquests of Christ through the centuries. Grand Rapids. Zondervan [1966] 2v. 24cm. Bibl. [BR1700.2.L6] 66-13696 9.95
1. Christian biography. I. Title.

LOCKYER, Herbert. 209'.22
The man who changed the world; or, Conquests of Christ, through the centuries. Grand Rapids, Zondervan Publ. House [1966] 2 v. 24 cm. Bibliography: v. 2, p. 427-428. [BR1700.2.L6] 66-13696
1. Christian biography. I. Title.

LOTZ, Philip Henry, 1889- 270 B ed.
Founders of Christian movements. Freeport, N.Y., Books for Libraries Press [1970, c1941] x, 160 p. 23 cm. (Essay index reprint series) "Originally published as v. 3 of the [author's] Creative personality series." Contents.Contents.—Robert Raikes, founder of the Sunday School, by A. J. W. Myers.—William Booth, founder of the Salvation Army, by F. G. Lankard.—Walter Rauschenbusch, prophet of social justice, by G. W. Fiske.—John Calvin, man of iron will who lived for God's glory, by G. Harkness.—St. Paul, the man who dared, by L. R. Robison.—Nicolaus Ludwig von Zinzendorf, founder of the Moravian Church, by H. H. Meyer.—St. Benedict, founder of western monasticism, by L. B. Hazzard.—St. Francis of Assisi, saint of the Middle Ages, by W. D. Schermerhorn.—Horace Bushnell, pioneer in religious education, by A. J. W. Myers.—Martin Luther, saint or devil, by J. V. Thompson.—Alexander Campbell, adventurer in freedom, by E. J. Wrather.—Ignatius Loyola, author of "A spiritual manual OFounders of Christian movements. Freeport, N.Y., Books for Libraries Press [1970, c1941] x, 160 p. 23 cm. (Essay index reprint series) "Originally published as v. 3 of the [author's] Creative personality series." Contents.Contents.—Robert Raikes, founder of the Sunday School, by
1. Christian biography. 2. Reformers—Biography. I. Title. BIP

LUDWIG, Charles, 1918- 209'.2'2 B
Their finest hour / Charles Ludwig Elgin, Ill. : D. C. Cook Pub. Co., c1974. 108 p., [8] leaves of plates : ill. ; 18 cm. [BR1600.2.L8] 74-82112 ISBN 0-912692-45-6 : 1.95
1. Christian biography. I. Title. BIP

MACGREGOR, William Malcolm, 1861-1944. 209'.2'4 B
Persons and ideals; addresses to my students and others. Freeport, N.Y., Books for Libraries Press [1973] p. (Essay index reprint series) Reprint of the 1939 ed. published by T. & T. Clark, Edinburgh. [BR1700.M254 1973] 73-5626 ISBN 0-518-10116-9
1. Christian biography. 2. Theology—Addresses, essays, lectures. I. Title.

MCPHERSON, Anna Talbott. 922
Forgotten saints. Grand Rapids; Zondervan Pub. House [1961] 113p. illus. 21cm. Includes bibliography. [BR1703.M25] 61-66598
1. Christian biography. I. Title.

MCPHERSON, Anna Talbott 922
Spiritual secrets of famous Christians. Grand Rapids, Mich., Zondervan [c.1964] 152p. illus. 22cm. Bibl. 64-11963 2.50 bds.,
1. Christian biography. I. Title.

MCPHERSON, Anna Talbott. 209'.22
They dared to be different. Chicago, Moody Press [1967] 192 p. 18 cm. (Moody pocket books, 99) Contents.--Fire kindled in his soul: D. L. Moody.--Through portals of song: Ira D. Sankey. Prince among preachers: Charles Haddon Spurgeon.--Born to suffer: Henry Martyn.--Because they knew she loved them: Capt. Catherine Booth.--Out of a gypsy camp: Gypsy Smith.--A desperate Scotsman in a desperate day: John Knox.--Neither persecution nor peril: Hester Ann (Roe) Rogers.--Sweet singer of Methodism: Charles Wesley.--In prison and she visited them: Elizabeth Gurney Fry.--To the heart: William Bramwell.--Great things for God: William Carey.--The shepherd-heart: Andrew Murray.--So valuable a life: Richard Watson.--She walked in white: Mary Bosanquet.--Beloved friend of little waifs: George Mueller.--The seeing heart: Fanny Crosby. [BR1700.2.M3] 68-3068
1. Christian biography. I. Title.

THE man who changed the world; or, Conquests of Christ, through the centuries. 209'.22 Grand Rapids, Zondervan Publ. House [1966] 2 v. 24 cm. Bibliography: v. 2, p. 427-428. [BR1700.2.L6] 66-13696
1. Christian biography.

MEAD, Frank Spencer, 1898- 922
Rebels with a cause [by] Frank S. Mead. New York, Abingdon Press [1964] 160 p. 21 cm. Bibliography: p. 154-160. [BR1702.M4] 64-20520
1. Christian biography. I. Title.

MOLNAR, Enrico S., 1913- 741.9'437'1
Five Bohemian windows; historical vignettes in pen and ink, by Enrico S. Molnar. Los Angeles, 1965. [16] p. illus. 22 cm. Cover title. [BR1700.2.M63] 75-284599
1. Christian biography. 2. Bohemia—Biography. I. Title.

MOYER, Elgin Sylvester, 1890- v. 12
Great leaders of the Christian church. Chicago, Moody Press [1951] xiii, 490p. 21cm. Includes bibliographical references. A53
1. Christian biography. 2. Church history. I. Title.

MOYER, Elgin Sylvester, 1890- ed. 922
Who was who in church history. Chicago, Moody Press, 1962. vi, 452 p. 25 cm. [BR1700.M64] 62-20221
1. Christian biography. I. Title. BIP

MOYER, Elgin Sylvester, 1890- ed. 200'.922
Who was who in church history, by Elgin S. Moyer. Rev. ed. Chicago, Moody Press [1968] vi, 466 p. 24 cm. [BR1700.M64 1968] 67-14391
1. Christian biography. I. Title.

MUNRO, William Fraser, 1894- 922
Men like mountains; studies in dynamic discipleship. Nashville, Tidings [1960] 72p. 19cm. [BR1703.M78] 60-15984
1. Christian biography. I. Title.

NEWTON, Joseph Fort, 1876-1950. 251'.0922 B
Some living masters of the pulpit; studies in religious personality. Freeport, N.Y., Books for Libraries Press [1971, c1923] 261 p. 23 cm. (Essay index reprint series) Contents.Contents.—George A. Gordon.—John A. Hutton.—Dean Inge, of St. Paul's.—Charles E. Jefferson.—W. E. Orchard.—Charles D. Williams.—A. Maude Royden.—Samuel McChord Crothers.—T. Reaveley Glover.—S. Parkes Cadman.—Reginald J. Campbell.—William E. Quayle.—George W. Truett.—Edward L. Powell.—Frank W. Gunsaulus: In memoriam. [BR1700.N4 1971] 71-152203 ISBN 0-8369-2287-5
1. Christian biography. 2. Preaching. I. Title. BIP

OUR struggle to serve : the stories of 15 evangelical women / Virginia Hearn, editor. 280'.4'0922 B Waco, Tex. : Word Books, c1979. 191 p. ; 23 cm. Includes bibliographical references. [BR1713.O97] 78-59434 ISBN 0-8499-0089-1 : 7.95
1. Christian biography. 2. Women—Biography. I. Hearn, Virginia.

PAYNE, Pierre Stephen Robert, 1911- 922
The Fathers of the Western Church. New York, Viking Press, 1951. 312 p. illus. 22 cm. [BR1700.P3] 51-13882
1. Christian biography. I. Title.

PEABODY, Francis Greenwood, 1847-1936. 209'.22
Reminiscences of present-day saints. Freeport, N.Y., Books for Libraries Press [1972] vii, 307 p. illus. 23 cm. (Essay index reprint series) Reprint of the 1927 ed. Contents.Contents.—Ephraim Peabody.—Andrew Preston Peabody.—James Freeman Clarke.—Friedrich August Gottreu Tholuck.—Edward Everett Hale.—Charles Carroll Everett.—Alfred Tredway White.—Phillips Brooks.—Samuel Chapman Armstrong.—Henry Drummond.—Carl Hilty.—Louisa and Georgina Schuyler.—Frederic Illsley Phillips.—Charles William Eliot. [BR1700.P4 1972] 74-37525 ISBN 0-8369-2576-9
1. Christian biography. I. Title. BIP

POLLOCK, John Charles. 209'.22 B
Victims of the long march, and other stories [by] John Pollock. Waco, Tex., Word Books [1970] 115 p. 21 cm. "These sketches first appeared either in World vision or Crusade magazines." Contents.Contents.—All my friends are but one.—Judson's darkest hour.—Friend of the slaves.—Young man with a pigtail.—He tamed the tribes.—Lord Apostol.—Stroke oar.—Cannibal Easter.—Left in Lagos.—Santa Claus of the north.—Victims of the long march.—Tuan change. [BR1700.2.P64] 79-125270 2.95
1. Christian biography. I. Title.

THE Power of one : men and women of faith who make a difference / edited by James L. Merrell. 248'.2'0922 B St. Louis : Bethany Press, c1976. 124 p. ; 22 cm. [BR1700.2.P68] 76-16064 ISBN 0-8272-2925-9 pbk. : 3.95
1. Christian biography. I. Merrell, James L.

PROPHETS in the church. 209'.22 Edited by Roger Aubert. New York, Paulist Press [1968] viii, 152 p. 24 cm. (Concilium: theology in the age of renewal. Church history, v. 37) Includes articles translated from several languages by various persons. Bibliographical footnotes. [BR1702.P7] 68-57877 4.50
1. Christian biography. 2. Reformers—Biography. I. Aubert, Roger, ed. II. Series: Concilium: theology in the age of renewal, v. 37 BIP

REDDING, David A. 209'.22 B
What is the man? [By] David A. Redding. Waco, Tex., Word Books [1970] 169 p. 23 cm. Includes bibliographical references. [BS571.R37] 71-128447 4.50
1. Bible—Biography. 2. Christian biography. I. Title.

ROBERTSON, Edwin Hanton. 209'.2'2 B
Breakthrough / by Edwin Robertson. Belfast : Christian Journals Ltd, 1976. 141 p. ; 18 cm. Bibliography: p. 139-141. [BR1700.2.R56] 76-380407 ISBN 0-904302-20-2 : £0.90
1. Christian biography. I. Title.

ROCHE, Aloysius, 1886- 922
Christians courageous; tales of Christian adventure. Illustrated by Anthony Lake. New York, Sheed and Ward [1955] 143p. illus. 22 cm. [BR1703.R6 1955a] 55-9457
1. Christian biography. I. Title.

ROWE, Henry Kalloch, 1869-1941. 209'.22
Modern pathfinders of Christianity; the lives and deeds of seven centuries of Christian leaders. Freeport, N.Y., Books for Libraries Press [1968] 253 p. 23 cm. (Essay index reprint series) Reprint of the 1928 ed. [BR1700.R65 1968] 68-16973
1. Christian biography. I. Title. BIP

ROWLAND, Benjamin Jr. 209.22
Men for others. New York, Friendship [c.1965] 175p. 21cm. [BR1700.2R6] 65-11439 1.95 pap.,
1. Christian biography. I. Title.

RUSSELL, Arthur James. 209'.22 B
Their religion, by Arthur J. Russell. Freeport, N.Y., Books for Libraries Press [1971, c1935] ix, 352 p. 23 cm. (Essay index reprint series) The religious belief of Abraham Lincoln, Robert Burns, Marshal Foch, Gladstone, Napoleon, Disraeli, Nelson, Dickens, Washington, Livingstone, Cromwell, Darwin, Shakespeare and Jesus of Nazareth. [BR1700.R8 1971] 78-128308 ISBN 0-8369-2131-3
1. Christian biography. I. Title. BIP

SEAMANDS, John T. 266'.022'0922
Pioneers of the younger churches [by] John T. Seamands. Nashville, Abingdon Press [1967] 221 p. 23 cm. Bibliography: p. 215-218. [BR1702.S4] 67-22166
1. Christian biography. I. Title.

SHORT, Ruth Gordon 922
Evenings with famous Christians. Washington, D.C., Review & Herald [c.1964] 192p. 22cm. [BR1703.S48] 64-17662 3.95
1. Christian biography. I. Title.

SMART, William James, 1895- 209.22
Profiles in Christian commitment, by W. J. Smart. Cleveland, World Pub. Co. [1965, c1961] 196 p. 21 cm. First published in London in 1961 under title: Miracles of achievement. [BR1702.S6 1965] 65-5072
1. Christian biography. I. Title.

SPEER, Robert Elliott, 1867-1947. 209'.22
Some great leaders in the world movement. Freeport, N.Y., Books for Libraries Press [1967] 295 p. 22 cm. (The Cole lectures, 1911) (Essay index reprint series) "First published 1911." Contents.Contents.—Raymond Lull, the Christian crusader and his conquest.—William Carey, the Christian pioneer and his problems.—Alexander Duff, the Christian student and the world's education. —George Bowen, the Christian mystic and the ascetic ideal.—John Lawrence, the Christian statesman and the problem of religion and politics.—Charles George Gordon, the Christian knight errant and the power of pure devotion. [BR1703.S7 1967] 67-26786
1. Christian biography. I. Title. II. Series: The Cole lectures. Vanderbilt University, 1911. BIP

STEPHEN, James, Sir, 1789-1859. 280'.092'2 B
Essays in ecclesiastical biography. New ed. Freeport, N.Y., Books for Libraries Press [1973] p. (Essay index reprint series) Reprint of the 1875 ed. published by Longmans, Green, Reader, and Dyer, London. Contents.Contents.—Hildebrand.—Saint Francis of Assisi.—The founders of Jesuitism.—Martin Luther.—The French Benedictines.—The Port-Royalists.—Richard Baxter.—The "evangelical" succession.—William Wilberforce.—The Clapham sect.—The historian of enthusiasm.—The epilogue. [BR1700.S8 1973] 73-5593 ISBN 0-518-10134-7
1. Christian biography. I. Title.

THOMAS, Reuen, 1840-1907. 209'.2'2 B
Leaders of thought in the modern church. Freeport, N.Y., Books for Libraries Press [1972] 191 p. 23 cm. (Essay index reprint series) Reprint of the 1892 ed. Contents.Contents.—Jonathan Edwards.—William Ellery Channing.—John Henry Newman.—Thomas Chalmers.—Frederick W. Robertson.—Emanuel Swedenborg.—Horace Bushnell.—Frederick Denison Maurice. [BR1700.T5 1972] 72-8559 ISBN 0-8369-7333-X
1. Christian biography. I. Title. BIP

TILTMAN, Marjorie (Hand) Hessell. 209'.22
God's adventures, by Marjorie H. Tiltman. Freeport, N.Y., Books for Libraries Press [1968] 317 p. illus., ports. 23 cm. (Essay index reprint series) Reprint of the 1933 ed. [BV3700.T53 1968] 68-16979
1. Christian biography. 2. Missionaries. I. Title.

TOWNS, Elmer L. 270 B
The Christian Hall of Fame [by] Elmer L. Towns. Grand Rapids, Baker Book House [1971] 223 p. ports. 22 cm. [BR1700.2.T68] 72-159668 ISBN 0-8010-8770-8 2.95
1. Christian biography. I. Title.

TOWNS, Elmer L. 209'.2'2 B
The Christian Hall of Fame / Elmer L. Towns ; [introd. by Harold Henniger]. Rev. ed. Grand Rapids : Baker Book House, c1975. 247 p. : ports. ; 22 cm. [BR1700.2.T68 1975] 76-353728 pbk. : 3.95
1. Christian biography. I. Title.

WALKER, Williston, 1860-1922. 209'.22
Great men of the Christian church. Freeport, N.Y., Books for Libraries Press [1968] 378 p. 23 cm. (Essay index reprint series) Reprint of the 1908 ed. Contents.Contents.—Justin Martyr.—Tertullian.—Athanasius.—Augustine.—Patrick.—Benedict.—Hildebrand.—Godfrey.—Francis.— Thomas Aquinas.—John Wiclif.—Martin Luther.—John Calvin.—John Knox.—Ignatius Loyola.—George Fox.—Nicolaus Ludwig von Zinzendorf.—John Wesley.—Jonathan Edwards.—Horace Bushnell. Includes bibliographies. [BR1700.W3 1968] 68-8502
1. Christian biography. I. Title. BIP

WALLACE, Archer, 1884- 209'.22
The religious faith of great men. Freeport, N.Y., Books for Libraries Press [1967] 217 p. 22 cm. (Essay index reprint series)

Reprint of the 1934 ed. Bibliography: p. [v]-[vii] [BR1702.W3 1967] 67-26792
1. Christian biography. I. Title. **BIP**

WARNER, Gary. 209'.22
The home team wears white; unsung All-Americans on the number one team. Grand Rapids, Mich., Zondervan Pub. House [1969] 152 p. ports. 21 cm. (A Zondervan paperback) [BR1702.W34] 70-82800 0.95 (pbk)
1. Christian biography. 2. Athletes, American—Biography. I. Title.

WASHBURN, Henry Bradford, 1869-1962. 270 B
Men of conviction. Freeport, N.Y., Books for Libraries Press [1971, c1931] viii, 250 p. illus. 22 cm. (Essay index reprint series) Originally published as The Bohlen lectures, 1931. Contents.Contents.—Autobiographic.—Athanasius.—Benedict of Nursia.—Hildebrand.—Francis of Assisi.—Ignatius Loyola.—Pius IX. "A list of recommended books": p. 243-244. [BR1700.W33 1971] 74-134152 ISBN 0-8369-2081-3
1. Christian biography. I. Title. **BIP**

WATERBURY, Jared Bell, 1799-1876. 280'.092'2 B
Sketches eloquent preachers. Freeport, N.Y., Books for Libraries Press [1973] p. (Essay index reprint series) Reprint of the 1864 ed. published by American Tract Society, New York. Contents.Contents.—Dr. John M. Mason.—Dr. Archibald Alexander.—Rev. John Summerfield.—Rev. Sylvester Larned.—Dr. Asahel Nettleton.—Dr. Lyman Beecher.—Dr. Henry B. Bascom.—Dr. Edward Payson.—Dr. Edward Dorr Griffin.—Dr. Robert Hall.—Dr. Thomas Chalmers.—Rev. Henry Melvill.—Rev. Rowland Hill.—Rev. Legh Richmond.—Dr. Timothy Dwight.—Rev. Jonathan Edwards.—Rev. George Whitefield—Rev. Richard Baxter.—Rev. John Bunyan.—Rev. James Saurin.—John Baptist Massillon.—Martin Luther.—The Apostle Paul. [BR1700.W35 1973] 73-5594 ISBN 0-518-10138-X
1. Christian biography. 2. Clergy. I. Title.

Christian biography—Juvenile literature.

BROWN, LeRoy C. 209.22
Champions all, by LeRoy Brown. Cover painting by Thomas Dunbebin. Washington, Review and Herald Pub. Association [1966] 96 p. ports. 22 cm. [BR1704.B7] 66-19421
1. Christian biography—Juvenile literature. I. Title.

HASKIN, Dorothy (Clark) 1905- 922
Brave boys and girls of long ago. Grand Rapids, BakerBook House, 1958. 61p. illus. 20cm. [BR1704.H2] 58-59821
1. Christian biography—Juvenile literature. I. Title.

TOWER, Grace Storms. 920
Pioneers of the church. Illustrated by Roger Martin. Boston, United Church Press [1964] 91 p. illus. (part col.) 23 cm. "Part of the United Church curriculum, prepared and published by the Division of the Christian Education and the Division of Publication of the United Church Board for Homeland Ministries." [BR1704.T6] 64-19471
1. Christian biography — Juvenile literature. I. United Church Board of Homeland Ministries. Division of Christian Education. II. United Church Board for Homeland Ministries. Division of Publication. III. Title.

Christian biography—United States.

STRAHAN, Thomas W. 209'.2'2 B
Retainer from the Lord / by Thomas W. Strahan. Lake Mills, Iowa : Graphic Pub. Co., c1976. viii, 126 p. : ports. ; 21 cm. Bibliography: p. 123-126. [BR569.S87] 76-42134 ISBN 0-89279-003-2 pbk. : 2.95
1. Christian biography—United States. 2. Lawyers—United States—Biography. I. Title. **BIP**

UNITED Lutheran Church in America. Board of Publication. 922.473
Mr. Protestant: an informal biography of Franklin Clark Fry. [Philadelphia? 1960] 76 p. ports. 21 cm. [BX8080.F74U5] 60-38562
I. Fry, Franklin Clark, 1900- II. Title.

Christian, Fletcher, 1764-1793.

HOUGH, Richard Alexander, 1922- 359.1'334
Captain Bligh & Mr. Christian; the men and the mutiny [by] Richard Hough. [1st ed.] New York, E. P. Dutton, 1973 [c1972] 320 p. illus. 25 cm. Bibliography: p. 309-314. [DA87.1.B6H68 1973] 72-82713 ISBN 0-525-07310-8 10.00
1. Bligh, William, 1754-1817. 2. Christian, Fletcher, 1764-1793. 3. Bounty (Ship) 4. Pitcairn Island. I. Title.

Christian life—Stories.

BROWN, LeRoy C. 922
They stood tall for God. Illus. by Thomas Dunbebin. Washington, D.C. Review and Herald Pub. Assn. [c.1963] 128p. illus. 22cm. 63-17756 3.50
1. Christian life—Stories. I. Title.

*HICKERSON, Vivian 922.673
Thy kingdom come. New York, Vantage [c.1964] 102p. 21cm. 2.5 bds.,
I. Title.

Christian life—Early church.

DAVIES, John Gordon, 1919- 270.1'0922 B
Daily life of early Christians, by J. G. Davies. New York, Greenwood Press [1969, c1953] xvi, 268 p. 23 cm. First published in London in 1952 under title: Daily life in the early church. Bibliographical footnotes. [BR195.C5D3 1969] 75-91757
1. Christian life—Early church. 2. Christian biography. I. Title. **BIP**

Christian life—Methodist authors.

JOHNSON, Pierce. 280'.092'2 B
Dying into life; a study in Christian life styles. Nashville, Abingdon Press [1972] 176 p. 22 cm. Includes bibliographical references. [BV4501.2.J57] 72-186828 ISBN 0-687-11279-6 4.95
1. Christian life—Methodist authors. 2. Christian biography. I. Title.

Christian life—1960-

ANTHONY, Ole. 209'.2'2
Cross fire / Ole Anthony. Plainfield, N.J. : Logos International, c1976. ix, 210 p. ; 20 cm. Selections from interviews originally broadcast on radio program One Trinity Place, KDTX, Dallas, Tex. [BV4501.2.A57] 75-38198 ISBN 0-88270-157-6 pbk. : 2.95
1. Christian life—1960- 2. Christian biography. 3. Conversion. I. Title. **BIP**

BARRETT, Ethel. 221.9'22 B
I'm no hero. Glendale, Calif., G/L Regal Books [1974] 150 p. illus. 20 cm. (A Regal venture book) [BS571.B37] 73-85395 ISBN 0-8307-0254-7 0.95 (pbk.).
1. Bible. O.T.—Biography. 2. Christian life—1960- I. Title. **BIP**

GOD lives! : 209'.2'2 B
True stories of God's work in the lives of famous people such as Helen Hayes, Pat O'Brien, Anita Bryant, Pat Boone, and many others / edited by Shifra Stein ; illustrated by James Hamil. [Kansas City, Mo. : Hallmark Cards, 1975] 45 p. : ill. ; 20 cm. (Hallmark editions) [BV4510.2.G63] 74-76162 ISBN 0-87529-391-3 : 3.50
1. Christian life—1960- 2. Christian biography. I. Stein, Shifra.

HAVNER, Vance, 1901- 248'.4
Moments of decision / Vance Havner. Old Tappan, N.J. : Revell, c1979. p. cm. [BV4501.2.H3683] 79-20786 ISBN 0-8007-1091-6 : 5.95
1. Bible—Biography. 2. Christian life—1960- 3. Decision-making (Ethics) I. Title. **BIP**

KEIPER, Ralph L. 248'.4
The power of Biblical thinking / Ralph L. Keiper. Old Tappan, N.J. : F. H. Revell Co., c1977. 159 p. ; 21 cm. [BV4501.2.K417] 77-2956 ISBN 0-8007-0862-8 : 5.95
1. Bible—Biography. 2. Christian life—1960- I. Title.

KEIPER, Ralph L. 248'.4
The power of Biblical thinking / Ralph L. Keiper. Old Tappan, N.J. : F. H. Revell Co., c1977. 159 p. ; 21 cm. [BV4501.2.K417] 77-2956 ISBN 0-8007-0862-8 : 5.95
1. Bible—Biography. 2. Christian life—1960- I. Title. **BIP**

KIRBAN, Salem. 248'.4
How to live above & beyond your circumstances / by Salem Kirban. Huntingdon Valley, Pa. : Kirban, c1974. 218 p. : ill. ; 18 cm. [BV4501.2.K498] 74-19641 ISBN 0-912582-20-0 : 3.95
1. Bible—Biography. 2. Christian life—1960- I. Title. **BIP**

POWELL, Terry. 248'.4
Nobody's perfect / by Terry Powell. Wheaton, Ill. : Victor Books, c1979. 116 p. : ill. ; 18 cm. (SonPower youth publication) [BS2430.P68] 78-65556 ISBN 0-88207-577-2 pbk. : 1.75
1. Bible. N.T.—Biography. 2. Christian life—1960- I. Title. **BIP**

SMITH, Charles Merrill. 248'.4
The case of a middle class Christian. Waco, Tex., Word Books [1973] 149 p. 23 cm. [BV4501.2.S527] 73-84579 4.95
1. Christian life—1960- 2. Christianity—20th century. 3. Smith, Charles Merrill. I. Title.

Christian martyrs—Biography.

HEFLEY, James C. 272'.092'2 B
By their blood / by James and Marti Hefley. Milford, MI : Mott Media, c1978. p. cm. Includes index. Bibliography: p. [BR1601.2.H43] 78-6187 ISBN 0-915134-28-4. ISBN 0-915134-16-0 pbk. : 9.95
1. Christian martyrs—Biography. I. Hefley, Marti, joint author. II. Title.

Christian martyrs—Egypt.

REYMOND, Eve A. E., comp. 272'.1
Four martyrdoms from the Pierpont Morgan Coptic codices, edited by E. A. E. Reymond and J. W. B. Barns. Oxford, Clarendon Press, 1973. xii, 278 p. 24 cm. Coptic and/or English. Bibliography: p. [ix]-xii. [BR1608.E3R49] 74-159108 ISBN 0-19-815448-8 £7.50
1. Christian martyrs—Egypt. I. Barns, John Wintour Baldwin, joint comp. II. Pierpont Morgan Library, New York. III. Title. **BIP**

Christian poetry, English—History and criticism.

HATFIELD, Edwin Francis, 1807-1883. 264'.2'0922 B
The poets of the church : a series of biographical sketches of hymn-writers with notes on their hymns / by Edwin F. Hatfield. Boston : Longwood Press, 1977. vii, 719 p. ; 22 cm. First published in 1884 by A. D. F. Randolph, New York. Includes indexes. [PR508.C65H3 1977] 77-91533 ISBN 0-89341-195-7 : 45.00
1. Christian poetry, English—History and criticism. 2. Christian poetry, American—History and criticism. 3. Hymns, English—History and criticism. 4. Hymn writers—Biography. I. Title.

Christian saints.

DAUGHTERS of St. Paul. 282'.092'2 B
Moments of decision / by the Daughters of St. Paul. Boston : St. Paul Editions, c1975. p. cm. [BX4655.2.D3 1975] 75-25893
1. Christian saints. I. Title. **BIP**

GOODIER, Alban, Abp., 1869-1939. 282'.0922 B
Saints for sinners. Freeport, N.Y., Books for Libraries Press [1970] vi, 200 p. 23 cm. (Essay index reprint series) Reprint of the 1943 ed. [BX4655.G6 1970] 70-99637 ISBN 0-8369-1504-6
1. Christian saints. I. Title. **BIP**

GUMBLEY, Walter, 1887- 282'.0922 B
Parish priests among the saints; canonized or beatified parish priests. Foreword by Vincent McNabb. Freeport, N.Y., Books for Libraries Press [1971] 105 p. 23 cm. (Biography index reprint series) Originally published in 1947. Includes bibliographical references. [BX4655.G84 1971] 76-148214 ISBN 0-8369-8061-1
1. Christian saints. 2. Clergy—Religious life. I. Title.

JACOBUS de Varagine. 270 B
The golden legend of Jacobus de Voragine. Translated and adapted from the Latin by Granger Ryan and Helmut Ripperger. New York, Arno Press, 1969 [c1941] xxiv, 800 p. illus. 23 cm. [BX4654.J334 1969] 72-88826
1. Christian saints. I. Title.

KALBERER, Augustine. 282'.092'2 B
Lives of the saints; daily readings. Chicago, Franciscan Herald Press [1975] p. cm. [BX4655.2.K34] 74-10761 ISBN 0-8199-0539-9 10.95
1. Christian saints. 2. Devotional calendars—Catholic Church. I. Title.

MARTINDALE, Cyril Charlie, 1879-1963. 282'.0922
What are saints? Fifteen chapters in sanctity, broadcast by C. C. Martindale. Freeport, N.Y., Books for Libraries Press [1968] 157 p. 22 cm. (Essay index reprint series) Biographical sketches. "First published 1932." [BX4655.M35 1968] 68-16954
1. Christian saints. I. Title. **BIP**

MONRO, Margaret Theodora, 1896- 282'.0922 B
A book of unlikely saints, by Margaret T. Monro. Freeport, N.Y., Books for Libraries Press [1970, c1943] vii, 220 p. 23 cm. (Essay index reprint series) "Note on sources": p. 9-12. [BX4655.2.M6 1970] 77-107727 ISBN 0-8369-1528-3
1. Christian saints. I. Title. **BIP**

SCHAMONI, Wilhelm, 1905- 282'.092'2 B
The face of the saints. Translation by Anne Fremantle. Freeport, N.Y., Books for Libraries Press [1972, c1947] 278 p. illus., ports. 24 cm. (Biography index reprint series) Translation of Das wahre Gesicht der Heiligen. [BX4655.S342 1972] 70-38328 ISBN 0-8369-8128-6
1. Christian saints. 2. Christian saints in art. I. Title. **BIP**

Christian saints—Algeria—Hippo—Biography.

AUGUSTINUS, Aurelius, Saint, Bp. of Hippo. 242'.1
The confessions of Augustine in modern English / translated and abridged by Sherwood E. Wirt. Grand Rapids : Zondervan Pub. House, 1977, c1971. xvi, 143 p. ; 21 cm. Translation of selections from Confessiones. Reprint of the ed. published by Harper & Row, New York, under title: Love song. Includes bibliographical references and index. [BR65.A6E53 1977] 77-13398 ISBN 0-310-34641-X pbk. : 3.95
1. Christian saints—Algeria—Hippo—Biography. 2. Hippo, Algeria—Biography. I. Wirt, Sherwood Eliot. II. Title.

Christian saints—America.

HABIG, Marion Alphonse, 1901- 282'.092'2 B
Saints of the Americas / M. A. Habig. Huntington, Ind. : Our Sunday Visitor, 1974. 384 p. : ill. ; 24 cm. Includes index. Bibliography: p. 378-380. [BX4659.A45H3] 74-15269 ISBN 0-87973-880-4 : 9.95
1. Christian saints—America. I. Title. **BIP**

Christian saints—Biography.

FREMANTLE, Anne Jackson, 1909- 209'.2'2 B
Saints alive : the lives of thirteen heroic saints / Anne Fremantle. Garden City, N.Y. : Doubleday, 1978. p. cm.

[BX4655.2.F66] 78-4789 ISBN 0-385-12441-4 : 7.95
1. Christian saints—Biography. I. Title. **BIP**

GARVEY, John. 270 B
Saints for confused times / by John Garvey. Chicago : Thomas More Press, c1976. 176 p. ; 21 cm. [BX4655.2.G35] 76-370967 ISBN 0-88347-066-7 : 8.50
1. Christian saints—Biography. I. Title.

HANLEY, Boniface. 282'.092'2 B
Ten Christians : by their deeds you shall know them / Boniface Hanley. Notre Dame, Ind. : Ave Maria Press, c1979. 269 p. : ill. ; 22 cm. [BX4655.2.H27] 79-53836 ISBN 0-87793-183-6 pbk. : 5.95
1. Christian saints—Biography. 2. Catholics—Biography. I. Title. **BIP**

KNOWLES, Leo. 281'.092'2 B
Saints who changed things / by Leo Knowles. St. Paul : Carillon Books, 1977. iv, 246 p. ; 22 cm. Bibliography: p. 244-246. [BX4655.2.K595] 77-87154 ISBN 0-89310-022-6 : 6.95.
1. Christian saints—Biography. I. Title. **BIP**

LIPTAK, David Q. 270 B
Saints for our time / David Q. Liptak. New York : Arena Lettres, 1977,c1976 xiii, 169 p. ; 18 cm. Bibliography: p. 169. [BX4655.2.L55] 76-45725 ISBN 0-88479-002-9 : 1.75
1. Christian saints—Biography. I. Title. **BIP**

NEWLAND, Mary Reed. 282'.092'2 B
The saint book : for parents, teachers, homilists, storytellers, and children / Mary Reed Newland ; illustrated by the author. New York : Seabury Press, c1979. p. cm. "A Crossroad book." Brief sketches of more than 55 saints, arranged by the dates of their feast days, focusing on personal details and factual incidents of their lives. [BX4655.2.N48] 920 79-16457 ISBN 0-8164-0210-8 : 8.95
1. Christian saints Biography. I. Title.

SAINTS for all seasons / 270 B
John J. Delaney, editor. 1st ed. New York : Doubleday, 1978. x, 205 p. ; 22 cm. [BX4655.2.S24] 77-81438 ISBN 0-385-12908-4 : 7.95
1. Christian saints—Biography. 2. Christian life—Catholic authors. I. Delaney, John J. **BIP**

SHERIDAN, John V. 270 B
Saints in times of turmoil / by John V. Sheridan ; foreword by Timothy Manning. New York : Paulist Press, c1977. v, 130 p. ; 19 cm. (A Deus book) [BX4655.2.S49] 76-39774 ISBN 0-8091-2005-4 pbk. : 2.45
1. Christian saints—Biography. 2. Catholics—Biography. I. Title. **BIP**

WIDDOWSON, Gregory 282'.092'2 B
An outline of lay sanctity / Gregory Widdowson. Huntington, Ind. : Our Sunday Visitor, c1979. 160 p. ; 21 cm. [BX4661.W47] 79-84532 ISBN 0-87973-737-9 pbk. : 2.95
1. Christian saints—Biography. 2. Laity. I. Title. **BIP**

Christian saints—Biography—Juvenile literature.

MARBACH, Ethel. 282'.092'2 B
Once-upon-a-time saints : faith-tales for children / by Ethel Marbach ; with ill. by Victoria Brzustowicz. [Cincinnati, OH] : St. Anthony Messenger Press, c1977. vii, 72 p. : ill. ; 21 cm. Relates briefly the lives and deeds of nineteen saints including Germaine, Swithin, Clement, and Bridgid. [BX4658.M415] 920 77-153145 ISBN 0-912228-37-7 pbk. : 1.95
1. Christian saints—Biography—Juvenile literature. I. Brzustowicz, Victoria. II. Title. **BIP**

Christian saints—Byzantine Empire—Biography.

TOPPING, Eva C. 281'.5'0922 B
Sacred stories from Byzantium / by Eva C. Topping ; with ill. by Antonia Mellen. Brookline, Mass. : Holy Cross Orthodox Press, c1977. xiii, 77 p : ill. ; 22 cm. [BX393.T66] 77-16696 ISBN 0-916586-15-4 : 5.95 ISBN 0-916586-16-2 pbk. : 3.95
1. Christian saints—Byzantine Empire—Biography. I. Title.
Contents omitted **BIP**

Christian saints—Calendar.

COLLEDGE, Edmund. 270 B
Following the saints, by Edmund Colledge and James Walsh. Gastonia, N.C., Good Will Publishers [1970] 3 v. (xvii, 959, xiii p.) col. illus., col. ports. 25 cm. (The Catholic layman's library, v. 4-6) Contents.Contents.—[1] January 1st through April 30th.—[2] May 1st through August 31st.—[3] September 1st through December 31. Includes bibliographies. [BX4655.2.C6] 74-92778
1. Christian saints—Calendar. I. Walsh, James, 1920- joint author. II. Title. III. Series.

Christian saints—Dictionaries.

HOLWECK, Frederick 282'.0922
George, 1856-1927.
A biographical dictionary of the saints, with a general introduction on hagiology. St. Louis, Herder, 1924. Detroit, Gale Research Co., 1969. xxix, 1053 p. 23 cm. [BX4655.H6 1969] 68-30625
1. Christian saints—Dictionaries. I. Title.

Christian saints—England.

GIBBS, Margaret. 274.2 B
Saints beyond the White Cliffs; stories of English saints. Illustrated by T. H. Robinson. Freeport, N.Y., Books for Libraries Press [1971] vii, 213 p. illus. 23 cm. (Biography index reprint series) Reprint of the 1947 ed. [BX4659.G7G5 1971] 75-148211 ISBN 0-8369-8058-1
1. Christian saints—England. I. Robinson, Thomas Heath, 1869-1950, illus. II. Title. **BIP**

Christian saints—Great Britain—Biography.

FARMER, David Hugh. 270 B
The Oxford dictionary of saints / David Hugh Farmer. Oxford : Clarendon Press, 1978. xxiv, 435 p. ; 23 cm. Includes bibliographical references and index. [BX4659.G7F37] 78-326714 ISBN 0-19-869120-3 : 17.50
1. Christian saints—Great Britain—Biography. 2. Christian saints—Ireland—Biography. I. Title.
Distributed by Oxford University Press, New York, NY **BIP**

Christian saints—Great Britain—Biography—Addresses, essays, lectures.

KNOWLES, Leo. 282'.092'2 B
Saints who spoke English / by Leo Knowles. St. Paul, Minn. : Carillon Books, 1979. vii, 187 p. ; 22 cm. Bibliography: p. 185-187. [DX4676.K56] 78-74329 ISBN 0-89310-045-5 : 8.95 ISBN 0-89310-046-3 pbk. : 4.95
1. Christian saints—Great Britain—Biography—Addresses, essays, lectures. 2. Christian saints—Ireland—Biography—Addresses, essays, lectures. 3. Christian saints—United States—Biography—Addresses, essays, lectures. I. Title. **BIP**

Christian saints—Ireland.

D'ARCY, Mary Ryan. 270
The saints of Ireland : a chronological account of the lives and works of Ireland's saints and missionaries at home and abroad / by Mary Ryan D'Arcy. St. Paul : Irish American Cultural Institute, c1974. xi, 241 p. ; 25 cm. Includes index. Bibliography: p. 230-233. [BX4659.I7D37] 74-83242 7.50
1. Christian saints—Ireland. 2. Christian martyrs—Ireland. 3. Missionaries, Irish. I. Title.

FLOOD, Joseph Mary, 1882- 270 B
Ireland; its saints and scholars, by J. M. Flood. Port Washington, N.Y., Kennikat Press [1970] x, 118 p. illus. 19 cm. (Series in Irish history and culture) (Kennikat Press scholarly reprints.) Reprint of the 1918 ed. [BX4659.I7F6 1970] 79-102604 ISBN 0-8046-0781-8
1. Christian saints—Ireland. I. Title.

Christian saints—Italy.

JACOBI, Andrea. 282'.092'2 B
The saints of the Benedictine Order of Montefano, by Andrew Jacobi. Clifton, N.J., Holy Face Monastery [1972] 268 p. illus. 21 cm. Translations of Latin mss. by Francis Fattorini. Contents.Contents.—Guzzolini, Sylvester, Saint. The life of Blessed Bonfil, bishop and confessor of Christ.—Jacobi, A. The life of Saint Sylvester Guzzolini, founder of the Benedictine Order of Montefano.—Jacobi, A. The life of Saint John of the Staff, O. S. B. Syl.—The Life of Blessed Hugo, O. S. B. Syl., by an anonymous Sylvestrine monk, O. S. B. Syl. Includes bibliographical references. [BX4659.I8J3] 72-171246
1. Christian saints—Italy. I. Guzzolini, Silvestro, Saint, 1177-1267. The life of Blessed Bonfil, bishop and confessor of Christ. 1972. II. The Life of Blessed Hugo, O. S. B. Syl. 1972. III. Title.

Christian saints—Juvenile literature.

PETRY, Ann (Lane) 1911- 270 B
Legends of the saints, by Ann Petry. Illustrated by Anne Rockwell. New York, Crowell [1970] 47 p. illus. (part col.) 24 cm. Retells the legends of ten saints: Christopher, Genesius, George, Blaise, Catherine of Alexandria, Nicholas, Francis of Assisi, Joan of Arc, Thomas More, and Martin de Porres. [BX4658.P44 1970] 920 72-106576 4.50
1. Christian saints—Juvenile literature. I. Rockwell, Anne F., illus. II. Title.

SPICER, Dorothy Gladys. 398.2
13 jolly saints. Illustrated by Sofia. New York, Coward-McCann [1970] 127 p. illus. 27 cm. Thirteen tales from eight countries about the deeds of saints, people the author calls the "Happy Ones." [BR1711.S68 1970] 79-88876 3.86
1. Christian saints—Juvenile literature. I. Sofia, illus. II. Title.

Christian Science.

POWELL, Lyman Pierson, 922.8573
1866-1946.
Mary Baker Eddy, a life size portrait. Boston, Christian Science Pub. Society [1950] 350 p. illus., ports. 22 cm. Bibliographical references included in "Notes" (p. 273-310) [BX6995.P75 1950] 51-544
1. Christian Science. I. Eddy, Mary (Baker) 1821-1910. II. Title.

Christian Science—Biography.

BABBITT, Marcy. 289.5'092'2 B
Living Christian Science : fourteen lives / by Marcy Babbitt. Englewood Cliffs, N.J. : Prentice-Hall, [1975] x, 255 p. : ports. ; 22 cm. Includes bibliographical references. [BX6990.B3] 74-20673 ISBN 0-13-538884-8 : 7.95
1. Christian Science—Biography. I. Title. **BIP**

Christiansen, Frederik Melius, 1871-1955.

BERGMANN, Leola Marjorie 780'.924
(Nelson), 1912-
Music master of the Middle West; the story of F. Melius Christiansen and the St. Olaf Choir, by Leola Nelson Bergmann. New foreword by Frederick Freedman. New York, Da Capo 1968. v, 230p. illus., port. 23cm. (Da Capo music reprint ser.) This Da Capo Press ed. is an unabridged repubn. of the first ed. pub. in 1944. Bibl. [ML410.C543B4 1968] 68-16222 12.50
1. Christiansen, Frederik Melius, 1871-1955. 2. St. Olaf College, Northfield, Minn. Choir. I. Title. **BIP**

Christie, Agatha Miller, Dame, 1891-1976.

CHRISTIE, Agatha 956.91'04
Miller, Dame, 1891-1976.
Come, tell me how you live / Agatha Christie Mallowan. New York : Dodd, Mead, [1976] c1946. 192 p., [4] leaves of plates : ill. ; 22 cm. [DS94.5.C5 1976] 76-359189 8.95
1. Christie, Agatha Miller, 1891-1976—Journeys—Syria. 2. Excavations (Archaeology)—Syria. 3. Syria—Social life and customs. 4. Authors, English—Biography. I. Title. **BIP**

FEINMAN, Jeffrey. 823'.9'12
The mysterious world of Agatha Christie / Jeffrey Feinman. New York : Award Books, 1975. 190 p. : ill. ; 18 cm. (An Award biography) Bibliography: p. 177-190. [PR6005.H66Z64] 76-350500 1.75
1. Christie, Agatha Miller, Dame, 1891- I. Title. **BIP**

†MURDOCH, Derrick. 823'.9'12 B
The Agatha Christie mystery / Derrick Murdoch. Toronto : Pagurian Press ; New York : distributed by Publishers Marketing Group, c1976. 192 p. : ill. ; 24 cm. Includes index. Bibliography: p. 186-187. [PR6005.H66Z76] 77-358644 ISBN 0-88932-034-9 : 8.95
1. Christie, Agatha Miller, Dame, 1891-1976. 2. Novelists, English—20th century—Biography. I. Title.

Christie, Agatha Miller, Dame, 1891-1976—Biography.

CHRISTIE, Agatha 823'.9'12
Miller, Dame, 1891-1976.
An autobiography / Agatha Christie. New York : Dodd, Mead, c1977. xiii, 529 p., [8] leaves of plates : ill. ; 25 cm. Includes index. [PR6005.H66Z512 1977] 77-11689 ISBN 0-396-07516-9 : 15.00
1. Christie, Agatha Miller, Dame, 1891-1976—Biography. 2. Authors, English—20th century—Biography.

ROBYNS, Gwen. 823'.9'12 B
The mystery of Agatha Christie / Gwen Robyns. 1st ed. Garden City, N.Y. : Doubleday, 1978. xii, 247 p., [16] leaves of plates : ill. ; 22 cm. Includes index. [PR6005.H66Z83] 77-76259 ISBN 0-385-12623-9 : 8.95
1. Christie, Agatha Miller, Dame, 1891-1976—Biography. 2. Authors, English—20th century—Biography. I. Title.

ROBYNS, Gwen. 823'.9'12 B
The mystery of Agatha Christie / Gwen Robyns. [New York] : Penguin Books, [1979] p. cm. Reprint of the 1978 ed. published by Doubleday, New York. Includes index. [PS6005.H66Z83 1979] 79-9781 ISBN 0-14-005228-3 pbk. : 2.95
1. Christie, Agatha Miller, Dame, 1891-1976—Biography. 2. Authors, English—20th century—Biography. I. Title. **BIP**

Christie, John Reginald Halliday, 1899-1953.

FURNEAUX, Rupert. v. 12
The two stranglers of Rillington Place. [New York, Panther Books, c1961] 188 p. 18 cm. (A Panther book) 65-60161
1. Christie, John Reginald Halliday, 1899-1953. 2. Evans, Timothy John, 1924-1950. I. Title.

Christie, William, 1870-1955.

VAN DYCK, Howard. 922
William Christie, apostle to Tibet. Harrisburg, Pa., Christian Publications [1956] 176 p. illus. 20 cm. [BV3420.T5V33] 56-34616
1. Christie, William, 1870-1955. I. Title.

Christina, of Markyate, Saint, 1096 (cs.)-1160.

THE life of Christina of 922.242
Markyate, a twelfth century recluse. Edited and translated by C. H. Talbot. Oxford, Clarendon Press, 1959. ix, 193p. map, facsim. 22cm. 'One of several lives of saintly persons which have been added at the end of what is now the second volume

of [the British Museum's] MS. Cotton Tiberius E. 1.' Text in Latin and English. [BX4700.C567L53] 59-65443
1. Christina, of Markyate, Saint, 1096 (ca.)-1160. I. Talbot, C. H., ed. and tr. II. British Museum. Mas. (Cottonian Tiberius E. 1)

TALBOT, Charles H., ed. 922.242
and tr.
The life of Christina of Markyate, a twelfth century recluse. Edited and translated by C. H. Talbot. Oxford, Clarendon Press, 1959. ix, 193 p. map, facsim. 22 cm. "One of several lives of saintly persons which have been added at the end of what is now the second volume of [the British Museum's] MS. Cotton Tiberius E. I." Text in Latin and English. [BX4700.C56753] 59-65443
1. Christina, of Markyate, Saint, 1096 (cs.)-1160. I. British Museum. Mss. (Cottonian Tiberius E. I) II. Title.

Christine, consort of Francis I, Duke of Lorraine, 1522-1590.

ADY, Julia Mary 944'.38'0280924 B
(Cartwright) d.1924.
Christina of Denmark, Duchess of Milan and Lorraine, 1522-1590. New York, E. P. Dutton, 1913. [New York, AMS Press, 1973] xii, 562 p. illus. 23 cm. Bibliography: p. 528-532. [D226.8.C5A63 1973] 73-154140 ISBN 0-404-09205-5 25.00
1. Christine, consort of Francis I, Duke of Lorraine, 1522-1590. BIP

Christophe, Henri, King of Haiti, 1767-1820.

CHRISTOPHE, Henri, 923.17294
King of Haiti, 1767-1820.
Henry Christophe & Thomas Clarkson, a correspondence edited by Earl Leslie Griggs and Clifford H. Prator. Berkeley, University of California Press, 1952. 287 p. illus., ports., maps, facsim. 24 cm. Bibliography: p. 281-282. [F1924.C46] 52-901
1. Haiti—Hist. I. Clarkson, Thomas, 1760-1846. II. Griggs, Earl Leslie, 1899- ed. III. Title.

CHRISTOPHE, Henri, 972'.94'040924
King of Haiti, 1767-1820.
Henry Christophe & Thomas Clarkson; a correspondence, edited by Earl Leslie Griggs and Clifford H. Prator. New York, Greenwood Press, 1968 [c1952] 287 p. illus., facsim., maps, ports. 24 cm. Bibliography: p. 281-282. [F1924.C46 1968] 68-23281
1. Haiti—History. I. Clarkson, Thomas, 1760-1846. II. Griggs, Earl Leslie, 1899- ed. III. Prator, Clifford Holmes, ed. IV. Title.

COLE, Hubert. 972.94040924
Christophe, King of Haiti. New York, Viking Press [1967] 307 p. illus. 22 cm. Bibliography: p. [292]-296. [F1924.C47 1967b] 67-13501
1. Christophe, Henri, King of Haiti, 1767-1820. 2. Haiti — Hist. I. Title.

VANDERCOOK, John 923.17294
Womack, 1902-
Black majesty; the life of Christophe, King of Haiti. Garden City, N.Y., Doubleday [1961, c. 1928, 1956] 160p. (Dolphin bk., C219) .95 pap.,
1. Christophe, Henri, King of Haiti, 1767-1820. 2. Haiti—Hist.—Revolution, 1791-1804. 3. Haiti—Hist.—1804-1844. I. Title.

Christophe, Henri, king of Haiti, 1767-1820—Fiction.

NEWCOMB, Covelle, 1908- v. 12
Black fire, a story of Henri Christophe, by Covelle Newcomb, illustrated by Avery Johnson. New York, Toronto, Longmans, Green and co. [1966, c1940] xii, 275, [1] p. illus. 22 cm. Illustrated t.-p. Bibliography: p. [276] 68-65503
1. Christophe, Henri, king of Haiti, 1767-1820—Fiction. 2. Haiti—Hist.—Revolution, 1791-1804—Fiction. I. Title.

Christophe, Henri, King of Haiti, 1767-1820—Juvenile literature.

HEATTER, Basil, 972.94'04'0924 B
1918-
A king in Haiti; the story of Henri Christophe. Illustrated by Toni Evins. New York, Farrar, Straus & Giroux [1972] 106 p. illus. 22 cm. A biography of the black man who was born a slave and died King Henri I of Haiti. [F1924.H4] 92 72-184125 ISBN 0-374-34140-0 4.50
1. Christophe, Henri, King of Haiti, 1767-1820—Juvenile literature. I. Evins, Toni, illus. II. Title. III. Title: The story of Henri Christophe. BIP

Christopher,

CHRISTOPHER, Sir George 942.3'74
Perrin, 1890-
Roots and branches, by Sir George P. Christopher. Liverpool, C. Birchall [1963] viii, 158 p. 23 cm. Autobiographical. [CT788.C43A3] 65-68654
I. Title.

Christopher, Saint.

BEEBE, Catherine, 1898- 922.1
Saint Christopher for boys and girls; story by Catherine Beebe, pictures by Robb Beebe. Milwaukee, Bruce Pub. Co. [1955] 54p. illus. 23cm. [BX4700.C57B35] 55-7859
1. Christopher, Saint. I. Title.

BISHOP, Claire (Huchet). 922.1
Christopher the giant. Illustrated by Berkeley Williams, Jr. Boston, Houghton Mifflin, 1950. 54 p. illus. (part col.) 22 cm. [BX4700.C57B5] 50-8841
1. Christopher, Saint. I. Title.

Christowe, Stoyan, 1898- — Biography.

CHRISTOWE, Stoyan, 1898- 813'.5'2
The eagle and the stork / Stoyan Christowe. 1st ed. New York : Harper's Magazine Press, c1976. 332 p. ; 24 cm. [PS3505.H93Z47] 75-9359 ISBN 0-06-121545-7 : 10.95
1. Christowe, Stoyan, 1898- —Biography. I. Title.

Christy, Howard Chandler, 1873-1952—Exhibitions.

CHRISTY, Howard 760'.092'4
Chandler, 1873-1952.
Howard Chandler Christy, artist/illustrator of style : September 25 through November 6, 1977, Allentown Art Museum. [Allentown, Pa.] : The Museum, c1977. [56] p. : ill. (some col.) ; 28 cm. Catalogue of the exhibition. [N6537.C4973A4 1977] 77-74176
1. Christy, Howard Chandler, 1873-1952—Exhibitions. I. Allentown, Pa. Art Museum. II. Title.

Chronology, Historical.

LAUNAY, Andre Joseph. 920'.003
Dictionary of contemporaries, compiled by A. J. Launay. [New York] Philosophical Library [1967] 368 p. 23 cm. [D11.5.L3 1967b] 67-31998
1. Chronology, Historical. 2. Biography—Dictionaries. I. Title. BIP

Chrysler, Walter Percy,

CHRYSLER, Walter Percy, 923.373
1875-1940.
Life of an American workman, by Walter P. Chrysler in collaboration with Boyden Sparkes. New York, Dodd, Mead [1950] 219 p. port. 22 cm. [CT275.C578A3 1950] 50-10162
I. Title.

Chrysostomus, Joannes, Saint, patriarch of Constantinople, d. 407.

BAUR, Chrysostomus, 1876- 922.1
John Chrysostom and his time. Translated by Sr. M. Gonzaga. Westminster, Md., Newman Press [c1959-60] 2v. 23cm. Translation of Der heilige Johannes Chrusostomus und seine Zelt. Includes bibliography. [BR1720.C5B34] 60-3807
1. Chrysostomus, Joannes, Saint, Patriarch of Constantinople, d. 407. I. Title.

VANDENBERGHE, Bruno H. 922.1
1909-
John of the Golden Mouth. Translated by the author. Westminster, Md., Newman Press, 1958. 91 p. 19 cm. [BR1720.C5V2] 58-8752
1. Chrysostomus, Joannes, Saint, patriarch of Constantinople. I. Title.

Chu, Te, 1886-

SMEDLEY, Agnes, 1890- 923.551
1950.
The great road; the life and times of Chu Teh. New York Monthly Review Press, 1956. 461 p. illus. 22 cm. [DS778.C6S5] 56-11272
1. Chu, Te, 1886- 2. Communism — China. I. Title. BIP

Chubb, Thomas, 1679-1747.

BUSHELL, Thomas L. 211'.6'0924
The sage of Salisbury: Thomas Chubb, 1679-1747, by T. L. Bushell. New York, Philosophical Lib. [1967] 159p. port. 22cm. Bibl. [BL2790.C5B8] 50211 67-17633 5.00
1. Chubb, Thomas, 1679-1747. I. Title.

Chudleigh, Elizabeth, countess of Bristol, calling herself Duchess of Kingston, 1720-1788.

MAVOR, Elizabeth, 1927- 920.7
The virgin mistress, a study in survival. [1st ed. in the U.S.A.] Garden City, N. Y., Doubleday, 1964. 206 p. 22 cm. Bibliography: p. [205]-206. [DA483.C6M3 1964a] 64-19320
1. Chudleigh, Elizabeth, countess of Bristol, calling herself Duchess of Kingston, 1720-1788. I. Title.

Chulalong Korn, King of Thailand, 1853-1910.

BRISTOWE, William 959.3'03'0922
Syer.
Louis and the King of Siam / by W. S. Bristowe. London : Chatto & Windus, 1976. 156 p., [2] leaves of plates : ill. ; 23 cm. [DS578.32.L46B74 1976b] 77-358245 ISBN 0-7011-2164-5 : £4.50
1. Leonowens, Louis, ca. 1855-1919. 2. Chulalong Korn, King of Thailand, 1853-1910. 3. Mongkut, King of Thailand, 1804-1868. 4. Thailand—Biography. 5. Thailand—History. I. Title. BIP

BRISTOWE, William 959.3'03'0924 B
Syer.
Louis and the King of Siam / by W. S. Bristowe. New York : Thai-American Publishers, c1976. 156 p., [2] leaves of plates : ill. ; 23 cm. Includes bibliographical references. [DS578.32.L46B74] 76-24045 ISBN 0-915806-03-7 : 8.95
1. Leonowens, Louis, ca. 1855-1919. 2. Chulalong Korn, King of Thailand, 1853-1910. 3. Mongkut, King of Thailand, 1804-1868. 4. Thailand—Biography. 5. Thailand—History. I. Title.

Church history.

CASE, Shirley Jackson, 270 B
1872-1947.
Makers of Christianity; from Jesus to Charlemagne. Port Washington, N.Y., Kennikat Press [1971, c1934] xii, 256 p. 22 cm. (Essay and general literature index reprint series) Originally issued as the first volume of Makers of Christianity. Bibliography: p. 241-249. [BR145.C35 1971] 79-118460
1. Church history. 2. Christian biography. I. Title. BIP

DAVIDSON, Henry Martin 209'.22 B
Perkins, 1901-
Good Christian men [by] Henry Martin P. Davidson. Freeport, N.Y., Books for Libraries Press [1971, c1940] x, 260 p. 23 cm. (Essay index reprint series) Bibliography: p. 251-256. [BR150.D3 1971] 70-142616 ISBN 0-8369-2390-1
1. Church history. 2. Christian biography. I. Title. BIP

Church history—Primitive and early church, ca. 30-600.

BARCLAY, William, lecturer 270.1
in the University of Glasgow.
God's young church. Philadelphia, Westminster Press [1970] 120 p. 19 cm. [BR165.B277] 70-110082 ISBN 0-664-24884-5 1.85
1. Bible. N.T.—Biography. 2. Church history—Primitive and early church, ca. 30-600. 3. Christian life—1960- I. Title. BIP

Church of England—Biog.

CRANAGE, David Herbert 283'.092'4
Somerset, 1866-
Not only a dean, being the reminiscences of the Very Reverend D. H. S. Cranage. London, Faith Press; New York, Morehouse-Gorham [1952] 234p. illus. 23cm. [BX5199.C73A3] 55-18133
1. Church of England—Clergy—Correspondence, reminiscences, etc. I. Title.

EDWARDS, David 283'.0922 B
Lawrence.
Leaders of the Church of England, 1828-1944, [by] David L. Edwards. London, New York, Oxford University Press, 1971. viii, 358 p. 8 plates, illus., ports. 23 cm. Includes bibliographical references. [BX5197.E3] 71-883686 ISBN 0-19-213110-9 £3.90
1. Church of England—Biography. I. Title. BIP

MACKAY, Henry Falconar 270 B
Barclay, 1864-1936.
Followers in the way. Freeport, N.Y., Books for Libraries Press [1969] 207 p. 23 cm. (Essay index reprint series) Reprint of the 1934 ed. Contents.Contents.—Gaius.—Demas.—Diotrephes.—Antipas.—The martyrdoms at Lyons and Vienne.—Phocas.—Constantine.—The life and death of St. John Chrysostom.—St. Edward the Confessor.—St. Thomas of Canterbury.—The life and death of Blessed Thomas More.—St. Francis de Sales.—Hurrell Froude.—The martyrdom of Bishop John Coleridge Patteson.—A hundred years in Margaret Street. [BR1700.M265 1969] 71-93359
1. Church of England—Biography. 2. Christian biography. 3. Fathers of the church. I. Title. BIP

MORSE-BOYCOTT, 283'.0922 B
Desmond Lionel, 1892-
Lead, kindly light; studies of the saints and heros of the Oxford movement. Freeport, N.Y., Books for Libraries Press [1970] 240 p. 23 cm. (Essay index reprint series) Reprint of the 1933 ed. Contents.Contents.—Introduction. The romance of the century.—John Henry Newman.—Hugh James Rose.—Richard Hurrell Froude.—Isaac Williams.—John Keble.—Edward Bouverie Pusey.—Charles Marriott.—Frederick William Faber.—Henry Edward Manning.—Christina Rossetti.—Charles Fuge Lowder.—Robert Radclyffe Dolling.—Henry Parry Liddon.—Father Ignatius.—Arthur Henry Stanton.—Mary Scharlieb.—Frank Weston.—Arthur Tooth.—Thomas Alexander Lacey.—Mother Kate. [BX5100.M6 1970] 70-107728 ISBN 8-369-15291-
1. Church of England—Biography. 2. Oxford movement. 3. Anglo-Catholicism. I. Title.

RICE, Hugh Ashton 922.342
Lawrence.
The bridge builders; biographical studies in the history of Anglicanism. London,

Darton, Longman & Todd; New York, Longmans, Green [1961] 193p. 23cm. Includes bibliography. [BX5197.R5 1961] 61-19956
1. Church of England—Biog. I. Title.

ROGERS, Guy. 922.342
A rebel at heart; the autobiography of a nonconforming churchman. London, New York, Longmans, Green [1956] 322p. 19cm. [BX5199.R728A3] 56-3963
1. Church of England—Clergy—Correspondence, reminiscences, etc. I. Title.

Church of England—Clergy—Biography.

COLLOMS, Brenda. 283'.092'2 B
Victorian country parsons / Brenda Colloms. Lincoln : University of Nebraska Press, 1978,c1977. 288 p., [6] leaves of plates : ill. ; 23 cm. Includes index. Bibliography: p. [275]-276. [BX5197.C723 1977] 77-82027 ISBN 0-8032-0981-9 : 11.95
1. Church of England—Clergy—Biography. 2. Clergy—England—Biography. I. Title. BIP

LE QUESNE, A. Laurence. 941.08
After Kilvert / A. L. Le Quesne. Oxford [Eng.] ; New York : Oxford University Press, 1978. ix, 233 p. : ill. ; 23 cm. Includes index. [BX5199.K49A32] 78-40173 ISBN 0-19-211748-3 : 15.95
1. Kilvert, Robert Francis, 1840-1879. Kilvert's diary. 2. Kilvert, Robert Francis, 1840-1879. 3. Church of England—Clergy—Biography. 4. Le Quesne, A. Laurence. 5. Clergy—England—Biography. 6. Clyro, Wales—Description. I. Title. BIP

Church of God (Anderson, Ind.)—Biog.

SMITH, John W V 1914- 922.89
Heralds of a brighter day; biographical sketches of early leaders in the Church of God reformation movement. Anderson, Ind., Gospel Trumpet Co. [1955] 144p. 19cm. [BX7094.C678A4] 55-42349
1. Church of God (Anderson, Ind.)—Biog. I. Title.

Church of God of Prophecy.

TOMLINSON, Ambrose Jessup, Bp., 1865-1943. 922.89
Diary of A. J. Tomlinson, editorial notes by his son, Homer A. Tomlinson. Queens Village, N.Y. Church of God, World Headquarters [1949-55] 3 v. port. 20 cm. [BX7060.Z8T6] 49-4269
1. Church of God of Prophecy. I. Tomlinson, Homer Aubrey, Bp., 1892- ed. II. Title.

Church of Jesus Christ (Cutlerites)

FLETCHER, Rupert J. 289.3'092'4 B
Alphcus Cutler and the Church of Jesus Christ, by Rupert J. Fletcher and Daisy Whiting Fletcher. [Independence, Mo., Church of Jesus Christ, 1973] 350 p. 21 cm. [BX8680.C84F55] 73-92999
1. Church of Jesus Christ (Cutlerites) 2. Cutler, Alpheus, 1784-1864. I. Fletcher, Daisy Whiting, joint author. II. Title.

Church of Jesus Christ of Latter-Day Saints—Biography.

ANDERSON, Joseph, 1889- 289.3'092'2 B
Prophets I have known; Joseph Anderson shares life's experiences. [Salt Lake City] Deseret Book Co., 1973. xii, 248 p. illus. 24 cm. [BX8693.A5] 73-88327 ISBN 0-87747-508-3 4.95
1. Church of Jesus Christ of Latter-Day Saints—Biography. I. Title.

FLAKE, Lawrence R. 289.3'3 B
Mighty men of Zion : General Authorities of the last dispensation / Lawrence R. Flake. Salt Lake City : K. D. Butler, 1974. xx, 536 p. : ports. ; 24 cm. Includes indexes. Bibliography: p. [521]-[525] [BX8693.F57] 75-308408 7.95
1. Church of Jesus Christ of Latter-Day Saints—Biography. I. Title.

HARTSHORN, Leon R., comp. 289.3'092'2 B
Exceptional stories from the lives of our apostles. Compiled by Leon R. Hartshorn. Salt Lake City, Deseret Book Co., 1972. x, 307 p. ports. 24 cm. Includes bibliographical references. [BX8693.H293] 72-90346 ISBN 0-87747-486-9 4.95
1. Church of Jesus Christ of Latter-Day Saints—Biography. I. Title. BIP

HARTSHORN, Leon R., comp. 289.3'3 B
Outstanding stories by general authorities. Compiled by Leon R. Hartshorn. Salt Lake City, Deseret Book Co., 1970-73. 3 v. ports. 24 cm. [BX8693.H3] 73-136241 ISBN 0-87747-369-2 (v. 1) 4.95 per vol.
1. Church of Jesus Christ of Latter-Day Saints—Biography. I. Title. BIP

HARTSHORN, Leon R., comp. 289.3'092'2 B
Powerful stories from the lives of Latter-day Saint men, compiled by Leon R. Hartshorn. Salt Lake City, Deseret Book Co., 1974. ix, 298 p. ports. 24 cm. [BX8693.H32] 74-75033 ISBN 0-87747-504-0 4.95
1. Church of Jesus Christ of Latter-Day Saints—Biography. I. Title. BIP

HARTSHORN, Leon R., comp. 289.3'092'2 B
Remarkable stories from the lives of Latter-Day Saint women. Compiled by Leon R. Hartshorn. Salt Lake City, Utah, Deseret Book Co., 1973. xi, 274 p. illus. 24 cm. Includes bibliographical references. [BX8693.H33] 73-87239 ISBN 0-87747-504-0 4.95
1. Church of Jesus Christ of Latter-Day Saints—Biography. 2. Woman—Biography. I. Title. BIP

WEST, Emerson Roy. 289.3'092'2 B
Profiles of the presidents. Salt Lake City, Desert Book Co., 1974. viii, 418 p. illus. 24 cm. Bibliography: p. [403]-405. [BX8693.W47 1974] 74-167281 ISBN 0-87747-489-3 5.95
1. Church of Jesus Christ of Latter-Day Saints—Biography. 2. Church of Jesus Christ of Latter-Day Saints—Government. I. Title.

WEST, Emerson Roy. 289.3'3'0922 B
Profiles of the Presidents. Salt Lake City, Deseret Book Co., 1972. 375 p. illus. 24 cm. Bibliography: p. [361]-363. [BX8693.W47] 72-90347 ISBN 0-87747-489-3 5.95
1. Church of Jesus Christ of Latter-Day Saints—Biography. 2. Church of Jesus Christ of Latter-Day Saints—Government. I. Title.

Church of Jesus Christ of Latter-Day Saints—Collections.

HARTSHORN, Leon R., comp. 289.3'0922 B
Classic stories from the lives of our prophets. Compiled by Leon R. Hartshorn. Salt Lake City, Utah, Deseret Book Co., 1971. ix, 334 p. ports. 24 cm. Contents.Contents.—Joseph Smith.—Brigham Young.—John Taylor.—Wilford Woodruff.—Lorenzo Snow.—Joseph F. Smith.—Heber J. Grant.—George Albert Smith.—David O. McKay.—Joseph Fielding Smith. Includes bibliographical references. [BX8693.H29] 73-155235 ISBN 0-87747-438-9 4.95
1. Church of Jesus Christ of Latter-Day Saints—Collections. I. Title. BIP

Church of Jesus Christ of Latter-Day Saints—Doctrinal and controversial works.

PETERSEN, Mark E. 230'.8'933
Adam, who is he? / Mark E. Petersen. Salt Lake City : Deseret Book Co., 1976. 96 p. ; 24 cm. Includes index. [BS580.A4P47] 76-7299 ISBN 0-87747-592-X : 4.95
1. Church of Jesus Christ of Latter-Day Saints—Doctrinal and controversial works. 2. Adam (Biblical character) I. Title.

Church of Jesus Christ of Latter-Day Saints—Missions.

INSPIRATIONAL missionary stories / compiled by Leon R. Hartshorn. Salt Lake City : Deseret Book Co., 1976. ix, 206 p. ; 24 cm. Includes index. [BX8661.I57] 76-7300 ISBN 0-87747-588-1 : 5.95 266'.8'33
1. Church of Jesus Christ of Latter-Day Saints—Missions. 2. Missionaries—Correspondence, reminiscences, etc. I. Hartshorn, Leon R. BIP

Church of Scotland — Biog.

WRIGHT, Ronald Selby, 1908- ed. 922.541
Fathers of the kirk; some leaders of the church in Scotland from the Reformation to the reunion. London, New York, Oxford University Press, 1960. 287 p. 21 cm. [BX9099.W7] 60-50024
1. Church of Scotland — Biog. I. Title.

Church of the Brethern-Biog.

CHURCH of the Brethren. 922.673
Brethren builders in our century. Elgin, Ill., Brethren Pub. House [1952] 192 p. illus. 20 cm. [BX7841.C45] 52-64992
1. Church of the Brethren—Blog. I. Title.

GARBER, Mary Crumpacker 922.6
Brethren trail blazers [by] Mary Garber and others. Illustrated by Harry Durkee. Elgin, Ill., Brethren Press [c.1960] 192p. illus. (col.) 21cm. 60-2896 2.50
1. Church of the Brethren—Biog. I. Title.

LONG, Inez (Goughnour) 922.6
Faces among the faithful. Elgin, Ill., Brethren [c.1962] 194p. 22cm. 62-5029 2.75
1. Church of the Brethren—Biog. I. Title. BIP

Church of the Brethren—Clergy—Biography.

BOWMAN, Earl McKinley, 1896- 286'.5 B
An unknown parson / Earl McKinley Bowman. [s.l. : s.n., c1976] ([Verona, Va. : McClure Print. Co.]) viii, 240 p., [2] leaves of plates : ill. ; 23 cm. [BX7843.B67A36] 76-19707
1. Bowman, Earl McKinley, 1896- 2. Church of the Brethren—Clergy—Biography. 3. Church of the Brethren—Sermons. 4. Clergy—United States—Biography. 5. Sermons, American. I. Title.

Church of the Province of New Zealand—History.

MORRELL, William Parker, 1899- 283'.931
The Anglican Church in New Zealand; a history [by] W. P. Morrell. Dunedin, Anglican Church of the Province of New Zealand; [distributed by J. McIndoe] 1973. 277 p. illus. 22 cm. Bibliography: p. [254]-265. [BX5720.5.A4M67] 73-177145
1. Church of the Province of New Zealand—History. I. Title. BIP

Church of Uganda, Rwanda, Burundi, and Boga—Zaire—Bishops—Biography.

KIVENGERE, Festo. 283'.092'4 B
I love Idi Amin : the story of triumph under fire in the midst of suffering and persecution in Uganda / Festo Kivengere, with Dorothy Smoker. Old Tappan, N.J. : F. H. Revell Co., c1977. 63 p. : ill. ; 18 cm. (New Life ventures) [BX5700.8.Z8K58] 77-79929 ISBN 0-8007-9004-9 : 0.95
1. Kivengere, Festo. 2. Church of Uganda, Rwanda, Burundi, and Boga—Zaire—Bishops—Biography. 3. Amin, Idi, 1925- 4. Bishops—Uganda—Biography. I. Smoker, Dorothy, joint author. II. Title.

Church, Richard,

CHURCH, Richard, 1893- 824.91
Over the bridge; an autobiography. [1st American ed.] New York, Dutton, 1956 [c1955] 231 p. 22 cm. [PR6005.H8Z5 1956] 56-10537

CHURCH, Richard, 1893- 828.91203
The voyage home. [1st American ed.] New York, John Day Co. [1966, c1964] 223 p. 26 cm. Autobiographical. [PR6005.H8Z528 1966] 65-20731
I. Title.

Church, William Conant, 1836-1917.

BIGELOW, Donald Nevius. 355'.005
William Conant Church & the Army and Navy journal. New York, AMS Press [1968] viii, 266 p. 23 cm. (Studies in history, economics and public law, no. 576) Series statement also appears as: Columbia University studies in the social sciences, 576. Reprint of the 1952 ed. Bibliography: p. [249]-257. [U1.B5 1968] 68-59264
1. Church, William Conant, 1836-1917. 2. The Journal of the Armed Forces. I. Title. II. Series: Columbia studies in the social sciences, 576. BIP

Church work with criminals.

ASMUTH, Robert C. 361.7'5'0924 B
Preacher with a billy club, by Robert C. Asmuth. Plainfield, N.J., Logos International [1971] 176 p. illus. 21 cm. [BV4464.7.A8] 76-154969 ISBN 0-912106-18-2 3.95
1. Church work with criminals. 2. Chaplains, Police—Correspondence, reminiscences, etc. I. Title.

Church work with loggers—United States.

REED, Frank A., 1895- 209'.2'2 B
Lumberjack sky pilot / by Frank A. Reed. Rev. ed. Lakemont, N.Y. : North Country Books, c1976. ix, 221 p., [24] leaves of plates : ill. ; 24 cm. [BV4470.R43 1976] 77-357002 7.95
1. Church work with loggers—United States. 2. Lumbering—United States. 3. Clergy—United States—Biography. I. Title. BIP

Churches of Christ—Clergy.

BAXTER, Batsell Barrett, 1916- ed. 922.89
Preachers of today; a book of brief biographical sketches and pictures of living gospel preachers, edited by Batsell Barrett Baxter and M. Norvel Young. Nashville, Christian Press [1952]- v. ports. (part col.) 24cm. Vol. 2- have imprint: Nashville, Gospel Advocate Co. [BX7077.Z8A2] 53-1367
1. Churches of Christ—Clergy. I. Young, Matt Norvel, joint ed. II. Title.

Churchill, Charles, 1731-1764.

BROWN, Wallace Cable. 928.2
Charles Churchill: poet, rake, and rebel. Lawrence, University of Kansas Press, 1953. 240p. illus., port. 22cm Bibliographical references included in 'Notes' (p. [217]-233) [PR3346.C8B7] 53-7064
1. Churchill, Charles, 1731-1764. I. Title. BIP

BROWN, Wallace Cable. 821'.6 B
Charles Churchill; poet, rake, and rebel. New York, Greenwood Press [1968, c1953] 240 p. illus., port. 23 cm. Bibliographical references included in "Notes" (p. [217]-233) [PR3346.C8B7 1968] 69-13842
1. Churchill, Charles, 1731-1764.

Churchill, Clementine Ogilvy Hozier, Lady, 1885-

FISHMAN, Jack. 920.7
My darling Clementine; the story of Lady Churchill. With an introd. by Eleanor Roosevelt. New York, D. McKay Co. [1963] 384 p. illus. 22 cm. Includes bibliography. [DA566.9.C5F5] 63-17288
1. Churchill, Clementine Ogilvy Hozier, Lady, 1885- 2. Churchill, Winston Leonard Spencer, Sir, 1874-1965. I. Title.

SOAMES, Mary. 941.08'092'4 B
Clementine Churchill : the biography of a marriage / Mary Soames. Boston : Houghton Mifflin, 1979. p. cm. Includes bibliographical references and index. [DA566.9.C48S66] 79-16207 ISBN 0-395-27597-0 : 16.95
1. Churchill, Clementine Ogilvy Hozier, Lady, 1885- 2. Churchill, Winston Leonard Spencer, Sir, 1874-1965. 3. Great Britain—Politics and government—20th century. 4. Prime ministers' wives—Great Britain—Biography. 5. Prime ministers—Great Britain—Biography. BIP

Churchill, Edward D.,

CHURCHILL, Edward D., 1895- 355.3'45'0924 B
Surgeon to soldiers; diary and records of the Surgical Consultant, Allied Force Headquarters, World War II [by] Edward D. Churchill. Philadelphia, Lippincott [1972] xiii, 490 p. illus. 24 cm. Bibliography: p. 483-490. [UH347.C45A3] 72-157864 ISBN 0-397-59053-9 12.00
I. Title. BIP

Churchill family.

FLEMING, Kate, 1946- 941'.00992 B
The Churchills / Kate Fleming. New York : Viking Press, 1975. 224 p. : ill. ; 26 cm. (A Studio book) Includes index. Bibliography: p. 218-219. [DA28.35.C45F55] 75-4314 ISBN 0-670-22222-4 : 12.95
1. Churchill family. I. Title.

ROUSE, Alfred Leslie, 1903- 929.2
The Churchills; the story of a family [by] A. L. Rowse. Abridged ed. London, Melbourne [etc.] Macmillan, 1966. xiii, 577 p. diagr. 18 1/2 cm. (Papermac P152) (B66-21408) Previous ed. in 2 vols.: The early Churchills. The later Churchills. [DA28.35.C45R596] 67-78507
1. Churchill family. I. Title.

ROWSE, Alfred Leslie, 1903- 929.7203
The Churchills: from the death of Marlborough to the present. [1st ed.] New York, Harper [1958] 430 p. illus. 25 cm. [DA28.35.C45R59] 58-1688
1. Churchill family. I. Title.

ROWSE, Alfred Leslie, 1903- 929.2
The Churchills; the story of a family [by] A. L. Rowse [1st U. S. ed.] New York, Harper [c.1966, i.e. 1967] xi, 577p. illus., geneal. table, ports. 25cm. Orig. pub. in 2 vs.: The early Churchills, 1956, and The Churchills, 1968. Bibl. [DA28.35.C45R596 1966] 67-15970 8.95
1. Churchill family. I. Title.

ROWSE, Alfred Leslie, 1903- 929.2
The Churchills: the story of a family [by] Al. L. Rowse, 1st U.S. ed. New York, Harper & Row [c1966] xi, 577 p. illus., geneal, table, ports, 22 cm. Originally published in 2 vols: The early Churchills, 1956, and The Churchills, 1958. Bibliographical footnotes. [DA28.35.C45R596] 67-15970
1. Churchill family. I. Title.

ROWSE, Alfred Leslie, 1903- 929.7'2
The Churchills: from the death of Marlborough to the present [by] A. L. Rowse. Westport, Conn., Greenwood Press [1974, c1958] xiii, 430 p. illus. 23 cm. A continuation of the author's The early Churchills, an English family. Reprint of the ed. published by Harper, New York. Includes bibliographical references. [DA28.35.C45R59 1974] 73-21491 ISBN 0-8371-6396-X 20.00
1. Churchill family. I. Title.

ROWSE, Alfred Leslie, 1903- 942.06'0922 B
The early Churchills [by] A. L. Rowse. Harmondsworth, Penguin, 1969. 445 p. geneal. table. 19 cm. [DA28.35.C45R6 1969] 76-538720 ISBN 0-14-003047-6 10/-
1. Churchill family. I. Title.

WATNEY, John Basil, 1915- 929'.2'0942
The Churchills : portrait of a great family / by John Watney. London ; New York : Gordon Cremonesi, c1977. 168 p., [8] leaves of plates : ill. ; 27 cm. Includes index. [CS439.C6283 1977] 78-305188 ISBN 0-86033-043-5 : 12.95
1. Churchill family. 2. Churchill, Winston Leonard Spencer, Sir, 1874-1965. 3. England—Genealogy. 4. Prime ministers—Great Britain—Biography. I. Title.
Available from Atheneum

Churchill, Jennie (Jerome) Randolph Churchill, Lady, 1854-1921.

CHURCHILL, Peregrine. 942.081'092'4 B
Jennie, Lady Randolph Churchill : a portrait with letters / Peregrine Churchill and Julian Mitchell. New York : St. Martins's Press, [1975] c1974. 285 p., [16] leaves of plates : ill. ; 22 cm. Includes bibliographical references and index. [DA565.C6C57 1975] 74-14403 8.95
1. Churchill, Jennie Jerome, Lady Randolph Churchill, 1854-1921. I. Mitchell, Julian, joint author. II. Churchill, Jennie Jerome, Lady Randolph Churchill, 1854-1921.

CHURCHILL, Peregrine. 942.081'092'4 B
Jennie, Lady Randolph Churchill; a portrait with letters [by] Peregrine Churchill and Julian Mitchell. New York, Ballantine Books [1976 c1974] 318 p., 16 leaves of plates illus. 18 cm. Includes bibliographic references and index. [DA565.C6C57] ISBN 0-345-25019-2
1. Churchill, Jennie Jerome, Lady Randolph Churchill, 1854-1921. I. Mitchell, Julian, joint author. II. Churchill, Jennie Jerome, Lady Randolph Churchill, 1854-1921. III. Title.
L.C. card no. of 1975 St. Martin's Press edition: 74-14403.

CURTIS, Rosemary A. (Stevens) 920.7
Jennie, the young Lady Churchill. Foreword by Shane Leslie. Philadelphia, Chilton [c.1963] 127p. 20cm. 63-19646 3.50
1. Churchill, Jennie (Jerome) Lady Randolph Churchill, 1854-1921. 2. Churchill, Lord Randolph Henry Spencer, 1849-1895. I. Title.

CURTIS, Rosemary A (Stevens) 920.7
Jennie, the young lady Churchill. With a foreword by Shane Leslie. [1st ed.] Philadelphia, Chilton Books [1963] 127 p. 20 cm. [DA565.C6C8] 63-19646
1. Churchill, Jennie (Jerome) Lady Randolph Churchill, 1854-1921. 2. Churchill, Lord Randolph Henry Spencer, 1849-1895. I. Title.

MARTIN, Ralph G., 1920- 942.081'0924 B
Jennie: the life of Lady Randolph Churchill, by Ralph G. Martin. Englewood Cliffs, N.J., Prentice-Hall [1969-71] 2 v. illus., facsims., ports. 24 cm. Contents.—v. 1. The romantic years, 1854-1895.—v. 2. The dramatic years, 1895-1921. Includes bibliographical references. [DA565.C6M3] 68-54197
1. Churchill, Jennie (Jerome) Randolph Churchill, Lady, 1854-1921. I. Title.

Churchill, Lord Randolph Henry Spencer, 1849-1895.

JAMES, Robert Rhodes 923.242
Lord Randolph Churchill; Winston Churchill's father, New York, Barnes [c.1959, 1960] 384p. Bibl.: p.375-378 illus. 24cm. 60-13082 7.50
1. Churchill, Lord Randolph Henry Spencer, 1849-1895. I. Title.

JAMES, Robert Rhodes, 1933- 923.242
Lord Randolph Churchill; Winston Churchill's father. New York, Barnes [1960] 384p. illus. 24cm. [DA565.C6J3 1960] 60-13082
1. Churchill, Lord Randolph Henry Spencer, 1849-1895. I. Title.

LESLIE, Shane, Sir bart., 1885- 920.042
Men were different; five studies in late Victorian biography. Freeport, N. Y., Books for Libraries Press [1967] 288 p. 22 cm. (Essay index reprint series) Reprint of the 1937 ed. Contents.CONTENTS.--Randolph Churchill, 1849-1895.--Augustus Hare, 1834-1903.--Arthur Dunn, 1860-1902.--George Wyndham, 1863-1913.--Wilfrid Blunt, 1840-1922. Includes bibliographies. [DA562.L46] 67-26754
1. Churchill, Lord Randolph Henry Spencer, 1849-1895. 2. Hare, Augustus John Cuthbert, 1834-1903. 3. Dunn, Arthur Tempest Blakiston, 1860-1902. 4. Wyndham, George, 1863-1913. 5. Blunt, Wilfrid Scawen, 1840-1922. I. Title. BIP

Churchill, Odette Marie Celine Brailly 1912—

CHURCHILL, Peter. 940.547243
The spirit in the cage. [1st American ed.] New York, Putnam [1955, c1954] 312 p. illus. 21 cm. Autobiographical. [D805.G3C525 1955] 55-10099
1. Churchill, Odette Marie Celine Brailly 1912- 2. World War, 1939-1945—Prisoners and prisons, German.

Churchill, Randolph Henry Spencer, Lord, 1849-1895.

LESLIE, Shane, Sir, bart., 1885-1971. 920.042
Men were different; five studies in late Victorian biography. Freeport, N.Y., Books for Libraries Press [1967] 288 p. 22 cm. (Essay index reprint series) Reprint of the 1937 ed. Contents.Contents.—Randolph Churchill, 1849-1895.—Augustus Hare, 1834-1903.—Arthur Dunn, 1860-1902.—George Wyndham, 1863-1913.—Wilfrid Blunt, 1840-1922. Includes bibliographies. [DA562.L46 1967] 67-26754
1. Churchill, Randolph Henry Spencer, Lord, 1849-1895. 2. Hare, Augustus John Cuthbert, 1834-1903. 3. Dunn, Arthur Tempest Blakiston, 1860-1902. 4. Wyndham, George, 1863-1913. 5. Blunt, Wilfrid Scawen, 1840-1922. I. Title.

Churchill, Samuel, 1911-

CHURCHILL, Samuel, 1911- 634.9'82'0924 B
Don't call me Ma / Sam Churchill. 1st ed. Garden City, N.Y. : Doubleday, 1977. 201 p., [6] leaves of plates : ill. ; 22 cm. [SD537.52.C49A3] 77-70895 ISBN 0-385-08481-1 : 7.95
1. Churchill, Samuel, 1911- 2. Western Cooperage Company. 3. Lumbermen—Oregon—Biography. 4. Clatsop Co., Or.—Biography. I. Title. BIP

Churchill, Victor Alexander Spencer,

CHURCHILL, Victor Alexander Spencer, 2d viscount, 1890- 920.5
Be all my sins remembered [by] Viscount Churchill. [1st American ed.] New York, Coward-McCann [1965, c1964] 201 p. 22 cm. [CT788.C47A3 1965] 65-13273
I. Title.

CHURCHILL, Victor Alexander Spencer, 2dviscount, 1890- 942.3'74
All my sins remembered [by] Viscount Churchill. London, Heinemann [1964] 201 p. port. 23 cm. Imprint covered by label: New York, Coward-McCann. Autobiographical. [CT788.C47A3 1964] 65-68900
I. Title.

Churchill, Winston Leonard Spencer, Sir, 1874-1965.

ALBJERG, Victor Lincoln, 1892- 942.082'092'4 B
Winston Churchill, by Victor L. Albjerg. New York, Twayne Publishers [1973] 259 p. 21 cm. (Twayne's rulers and statesmen of the world series, TROW 22) Bibliography: p. 243-254. [DA566.9.C5A399] 71-161811 5.95
1. Churchill, Winston Leonard Spencer, Sir, 1874-1965.

BERLIN, Isaiah Sir 923.242
Mr. Churchill in 1940. Boston, Houghton [1964] 38p. port. 21cm. Orig. appeared in 1949 as a review of the first volume of Sir Winston Churchill's War memoirs. 64-8813 3.00
1. Churchill, Winston Leonard Spencer, Sir 1874- I. Title.

BIBESCO, Marthe Lucie Lahovary, "Princesse G. V. Bibesco," 1887- 923.242
Sir Winston Churchill, master of courage. [Translated from the French by Vladimir Kean] [1st American ed.] New York, J. Day Co. [1959, c1957] 181 p. illus. 21 cm. Translation of Churchill; ou, Le courage. [DA566.9.C5B53 1959] 59-7122
1. Churchill, Winston Leonard Spencer, Sir, 1874-1965.

BLACK, Edgar. 923.242
Sir Winston Churchill; the com pelling life story of one of the towering figures of the 20th century. Derby, Conn., Monarch Books [1961] 297p. 18cm. (Monarch giants K56) [DA566.9C5B56] 62-34137
1. Churchill, Winston Leonard Spencer, Sir 1874- I. Title.

BOCCA, Geoffrey 923.242
The adventurous life of Winston Churchill [New York] Avon [1964, c.1958] 160p. illus. 18cm. (G1234) .50 pap.,
1. Churchill, Winston Leonard Spencer, Sir 1874- I. Title.

BOCCA, Geoffrey. 923.242
The adventurous life of Winston Churchill. New York, J. Messner [1958] 256 p. illus. 24 cm. [DA566.9.C5B58] 58-11843
1. Churchill, Winston Leonard Spencer, Sir, 1874-1965. I. Title.

BONHAM-CARTER, Lady Violet (Asquith) 1887- 923.242
Winston Churchill: an intimate portrait. New York, Harcourt [c.1965] x, 413p. illus., ports. 24cm. Pub. in Great Britain under title: Winston Churchill as I knew him. Bibl. [DA566.9.C5B63] 65-183161 8.50
1. Churchill, Winston Leonard Spencer, Sir 1874-1965. I. Title.

BONHAM-CARTER, Violet (Asquith) Lady, 1887- 923.242
Winston Churchill: an intimate portrait [by] Violet Bonham Carter. [1st American ed.] New York, Harcourt, Brace & World [1965] x, 413 p. illus., ports. 24 cm. Published in Great Britain under title: Winston Churchill as I knew him. Bibliography: p. 387-388. [DA566.9.C5B63 1965] 65-18316
1. Churchill, Winston Leonard Spencer, Sir, 1874-1965.

BOOTH, Arthur Harold. 923.273
The true book about Sir Winston Churchill, Illustrated by F. Stocks May. iLondon, Muller stamped: distributed by Sportshelf. New Rochelle, N. Y., [1958] 144p. illus. 20cm. [DA566.9.C5B64] 58-4989
1. Churchill, Winston Leonard Spencer, Sir I. Title.

BROAD, Lewis, 1900- 923.242
Winston Churchill, a biography. [1st ed.] New York, Hawthorn Books [1958- v. illus. 24 cm. Contents.Contents.—1. The years of preparation. [DA566.9.C5B69] 58-11830
1. Churchill, Winston Leonard Spencer, 1874-1965. BIP

BROAD, Lewis, 1900- 923.242
Winston Churchill, 1874-1951. [Rev. and further extended] London, New York, Hutchinson [1951] xx, 611 p. port. 24 cm. "Books [by Churchill]": p. 589-590. [DA566.9.C5B68 1951] 52-6736
1. Churchill, Winston Leonard Spencer, 1874- I. Title.

BROAD, Lewis, 1900- 923.242
Winston Churchill, 1874-1951 New York, Philosophical Library [1952] 611 p. illus. 24 cm. [DA566.9.C5B68 1952] 52-6986
1. Churchill, Winston Leonard Spencer, 1874- I. Title.

BROAD, Lewis, 1900- 923.242
Winston Churchill, 1874-1952. [Rev. and further extended] London, New York, Hutchinson [1952] xx, 627p. port. 24cm. 'Books [by Churchill] :p. 605-606. [DA566.9.C5B68 1952a] 53-29786

1. Churchill, Winston Leonard Spencer, 1874- I. Title.

BROAD, Lewis, 942.082'0924 B
1900-
Winston Churchill, a biography. Westport, Conn., Greenwood Press [1972, c1958- v. 22 cm. Contents.Contents.—[1] The years of preparation.—[2] The years of achievement. [DA566.9.C5B6923] 74-138206 ISBN 0-8371-5559-2 (v. 1)
1. Churchill, Winston Leonard Spencer, Sir, 1874-1965.

CHURCHILL, Randolph 942.080924
Spencer, 1911-
Winston S. Churchill. Boston, Houghton, 1967. v. illus. general. tables. maps. ports. 23 cm Contents.V.2Young statesman, 1901-1914. [DA566.9C5C47] 66-12065
1. Churchill, Sir Winston Leonard Spencer, 1874-1965. I. Title.

CHURCHILL, 942.08'092'4 B
Randolph Spencer, 1911-1968.
Winston S. Churchill [by] Randolph S. Churchill. Boston, Houghton Mifflin, 1966- v. illus., geneal. tables, maps, ports. 24 cm. Vols. 3- by Martin Gilbert. Contents.Contents.—v. 1. Youth, 1874-1900.—v. 2. Young statesman, 1901-1914. Companion. pt. 1. 1901-1907. pt. 2. 1907-1911. pt. 3. 1911-1914—v. 3. 1914-1916, the challenge of war. Companion. pt. 1. July 1914-April 1915. pt. 2. May 1915-December 1916. [DA566.9.C5C47] 66-12065 ISBN 0-395-13153-7 (v. 3) 15.00 (v. 3)
1. Churchill, Winston Leonard Spencer, Sir, 1874-1965. I. Gilbert, Martin, 1936-

CHURCHILL revised; 942.082'0924
a critical assessment [by] A. J. P. Taylor [and others] New York, Dial Press, 1969. 274 p. 24 cm. Contents.Contents.—The statesman, by A. J. P. Taylor.—The politician, by R. R. James.—The historian, by J. H. Plumb.—The military strategist, by B. L. Hart.—The man, by A. Storr. Includes bibliographical references. [DA566.9.C5C48 1969] 69-11621 5.95
1. Churchill, Winston Leonard Spencer, Sir, 1874-1965. I. Taylor, Alan John Percivale, 1906-

CHURCHILL, Winston 942.080924
Leonard Spencer, Sir 1874-1965
Churchill. Ed. by Martin Gilbert. Englewood Cliffs, N. J., Prentice [1967] ix, 180p. 21cm. (Great lives observed) Bibl. [DA566.9.C5A3593] 67-28397 4.95; 1.95 pap.,
1. Gt. Brit.—Pol. & govt.—20th cent. I. Gilbert, Martin, 1936- ed. II. Title.

CHURCHILL, Winston 942.08'0924
Leonard Spencer, Sir 1874-1965.
Churchill. Edited by Martin Gilbert. Englewood Cliffs, N.J., Prentice-Hall [1967] ix, 180 p. 21 cm. (Great lives observed) "Bibliographical note": p. 173-175. [DA566.9.C5A3593] 67-28397
1. Gt. Brit.—Pol. & govt.—20th cent. I. Gilbert, Martin, 1936- ed. II. Title.

*CHURCHILL, Winston 923.424
Leonard Spencer, Sir 1874-1965
Churchill. Memorial ed. [New York, Dell, c.1965] unpaged (chiefly illus.) 29cm. (1263) 1.00 pap.,
I. Title.

CHURCHILL, Winston 942.0820924
Leonard Spencer Sir 1874-1965
A man of destiny: Winston S. Churchill, by the eds. of Country beautiful. Waukesha, Wis. 53186, 24198 W. Bluemound Rd. Country Beautiful Found., [1966] 96p. illus. (pt. col.) facsim., ports. 32cm. [DA566.9.C5A373] 65-21475 5.95
1. Gt. Brit.—Hist.—20th cent. 2. Painting. I. Country beautiful. II. Title.

CHURCHILL, Winston 942.082'0924 B
Leonard Spencer, Sir, 1874-1965.
The roar of the lion [by] Winston S. Churchill. London, New York, A. Wingate
Content omitted

CHURCHILL, Winston Leonard 940.53
Spencer, Sir, 1874-1965.
Memoirs of the Second World War : an abridgement of the six volumes of The Second World War / Winston S. Churchill ; with an epilogue by the author on the postwar years written for this volume ; abridgement by Denis Kelly. New York : Bonanza Books, 1978, c1959. xiv, 1065 p. : maps ; 24 cm. Includes index. [D743.C484 1978] 78-25660 ISBN 0-517-27032-3 : 6.98
1. Churchill, Winston Leonard Spencer, Sir, 1874-1965. 2. World War, 1939-1945—Sources. 3. World War, 1939-1945—Great Britain—Sources. 4. Prime ministers—Great Britain—Biography. I. Kelly, Denis. II. Title.
Available from Outlet Book Co., one Park Ave., New York, NY 10016

COOLIDGE, Olivia E. 923.242
Winston Churchill and the story of two World Wars. Boston, Houghton Mifflin, 1960. 278 p. illus. 23 cm. [DA566.9.C5C57] 60-9098
1. Churchill, Winston Leonard Spencer, Sir, 1874-1965.

COWLES, Virginia Spencer 923.242
Winston Churchill: the era and the man. New York, Grosset [1960, c.1953, 1956] 384p. (Universal lib., UL81) 1.65 pap.,
1. Churchill, Winston Leonard Spencer, Sir 1874- I. Title.

COWLES, Virginia Spencer. 923.242
Winston Churchill; the era and the man. New York, Harper [1953] 378 p. illus. 22 cm. [DA566.9.C5C64 1953a] 53-5363
1. Churchill, Winston Leonard Spencer, Sir, 1874-1965.

COWLES, Virginia Spencer. 923.242
Winston Churchill: the era and the man. New York, Grosset & Dunlap [1956] 384 p. illus. 22 cm. (Biographies of distinction) [DA566.9.C5C64 1956] 56-58106
1. Churchill, Winston Leonard Spencer, Sir, 1874-1965

DAVIS, Richard Harding, v. 12
1864-1916.
The young Winston Churchill; a biography of the statesman written in 1906. Austin Tex., Pemberton Press, 1964. 1 v. (unpaged) ports. 21 cm. 65-56042
1. Churchill, Winston Leonard Spencer, 1874-1965. I. Title.

DE MENDELSSOHN, Peter, 923.242
1908-
The age of Churchill. New York, Knopf [c.]1961. xix, 661, xiiip. illus. 25cm. Bibl. 61-13952 8.95
1. Churchill, Winston Leonard Spencer, Sir 1874- I. Title.

EADE, Charles, 1903- ed. 923.242
Churchill, by his contemporaries. New York, Simon and Schuster, 1954 [c1953] 461 p. illus. 22 cm. [DA566.9.C5E3 1954] 54-5894
1. Churchill, Winston Leonard Spencer, Sir, 1874-1965.

GILBERT, Martin, 942.08'0924
1936- comp.
Churchill. Englewood Cliffs, N.J., Prentice-Hall [1967] ix, 180 p. 21 cm. (Great lives observed) "Bibliographical note": p. 173-175. [DA566.9.C5G44] 67-28397
1. Churchill, Winston Leonard Spencer, Sir, 1874-1965. 2. Gt. Brit.—Politics and government—20th century.

GILBERT, Martin, 942.08'0924
1936-
Winston Churchill. New York, Dial Press [1967] 112 p. ports. 21 cm. Bibliography: p. 108-110. [DA566.9.C5G43 1967] 67-22253
1. Churchill, Winston Leonard Spencer, Sir, 1874-1965.

GRAEBNER, Walter, 1909- 923.242
My dear Mr. Churchill. Boston, Houghton Mifflin, 1965. vi, 118 p. port. 23 cm. [DA566.9.C5G67] 64-21982
1. Churchill, Winston Leonard Spencer, Sir, 1874-1965. I. Title.

GRAENNER, Walter 923.242
My dear Mr. Churchill. Boston, Houghton [c.]1965. vi, 118p. port. 23cm. [DA566.9.C5G67] 64-21982 4.00
1. Churchill, Winston Leonard Spencer, Sir 1874-1965. I. Title.

GREENE, Jay Elihu, 1914- 920.02
ed.
Four complete biographies. New York, Globe Book Co. [1962] 750p. illus. 22cm. [CT106.G652] 62-5357
1. Churchill, Winston Leonard Spencer, Sir 1874- 2. Keller, Helen Adams, 1880- 3. Schweitzer, Albert, 1875- 4. Barnum, Phineas Taylor, 1810-1891. I. Title.
Contents omitted.

HOWELLS, Roy. 942.080924 B
Churchill's last years. [1st American ed.] New York, D. McKay Co. [1966] ix, 214 p. 21 cm. First published in 1965 under title: Simply Churchill. [DA566.9.C5H6 1966] 66-13503
1. Churchill, Winston Leonard Spencer, Sir, 1874-1965. I. Title.

HUGHES, Emrys. 923.242
Winston Churchill: British bulldog; his career in war and peace. [1st American ed.] New York, Exposition Press [1955] 346p. illus. 21cm. (A Banner book) 'Some of the material in this book was published in Great Britian Britain in 1950 under the title Winston Churchill in war and peace." [DA566.9.C5H8 1955] 54-7041
1. Churchill, Winston Leonard Spencer, Sir I. Title.

HUMES, James C. 941.082'092'4 B
Winston Churchill : titan of eloquence / by James C. Humes. 1st ed. New York : Harper & Row, c1979. p. cm. Includes indexes. Bibliography: p. [DA566.9.C5H85 1979] 78-2144 ISBN 0-06-012015-0 : 12.00
1. Churchill, Winston Leonard Spencer, Sir, 1874-1965. 2. Churchill, Winston Leonard Spencer, Sir, 1874-1965—Quotations. 3. Great Britain—Politics and government—20th century. 4. Prime ministers—Great Britain—Biography. 5. Orators, English—Biography.

JACOBS, William 941.082'092'4 B
Jay.
Churchill / William Jay Jacobs. Beverly Hills : Benziger, c1976. 95 p. : ill. ; 24 cm. (Twentieth-century biographies) Bibliography: p. 95. [DA566.9.C5J25] 74-82863
1. Churchill, Winston Leonard Spencer, Sir, 1874-1965.

KAVANAGH, Dennis. 301.15'53
Crisis, charisma and British political leadership : Winston Churchill as the outsider / Dennis Kavanagh. London ; Beverly Hills : Sage Publications, 1974. 42 p. : ill. ; 22 cm. (Sage professional papers in contemporary political sociology ; 06-001) Bibliography: p. 39-42. [DA566.9.C5K37] 74-81020 ISBN 0-8039-9904-6 : £1.00
1. Churchill, Winston Leonard Spencer, Sir, 1874-1965. 2. Leadership. I. Title. BIP

LE VIEN, Jack 923.242
Winston Churchill: the valiant years, by Jack Le Vien, John Lord. Maps by Liam Dunne. New York, Scholastic [1963, c.1962] 424p. 17cm. (T391) .50 pap.,
1. Churchill, Winston Leonard Spencer, Sir 1874- 2. World War, 1839-1945—Gt. Brit. I. Lord, John, 1924- joint author. II. Title.

LE VIEN, Jack 923.242
Winston Churchill: The valiant years, by Jack Le Vien, John Lord. Maps by Liam Dunne. New York, Avon [1963, c.1962] 320p. 18cm. (V-2065) .75 pap.,
1. Churchill, Winston Leonard Spencer, Sir 1874- 2. World War, 1939-1945—Gt. Brit. I. Lord, John, 1924- joint author. II. Title.

LE VIEN, Jack. 923.242
Winston Churchill: the valiant years, by Jack Le Vien and John Lord. Maps by Liam Dunne. [New York] Bernard Geis Associates; distributed by Random House [1962] 411 p. illus. 24 cm. [DA566.9.C5L45] 62-9157
1. Churchill, Winston Leonard Spencer, Sir, 1874-1965. 2. World War, 1939-1945—Gt. Brit. I. Lord, John, 1924- joint author.

LEWIN, Ronald. 942.084'092'4 B
Churchill as warlord. New York, Stein and Day [1973] 283 p. illus. 23 cm. Bibliography: p. [268]-272. [DA566.9.C5L46 1973] 72-96544 ISBN 0-8128-1560-2 10.00
1. Churchill, Winston Leonard Spencer, Sir, 1874-1965. 2. World War, 1939-1945—Great Britain. I. Title. BIP

LONGFORD, 942.082'092'4 B
Elizabeth Harman Pakenham, Countess of, 1906-
Winston Churchill; a pictorial life story, authorized by the Winston Churchill Foundation, by Elizabeth Longford. Chicago, Rand McNally [1974] 224 p. illus. 29 cm. [DA566.9.C5L66] 74-13104 ISBN 0-528-81822-8 14.95
1. Churchill, Winston Leonard Spencer, Sir, 1874-1965.

MCGOWAN, Norman 923.242
My years with Churchill. Greenwich, Conn., Fawcett [1965, c.1958] 143p. illus. 18cm. (Gold medal bk., R1550) [DA566.9.C5M2] .60 pap.,
1. Churchill, Winston Leonard Spencer, Sir 1874- I. Title.

MALKUS, Alida Sims, 1895- 923.242
The story of Winston Churchill. Illustrated by Herman B. Vestal. Enid Lamonte Meadowcroft, supervising editor. New York, Grosset & Dunlap [1957] 181p. illus. 22cm. (Signature books, 40) [DA566.9.C5M25] 57-5038
1. Churchill, Winston Leonard Spencer, Sir 1874- I. Title.

MASON, David, 942.084'092'4 B
1938-
Churchill. [New York, Ballantine Books, 1972] 159, [1] p. illus. 21 cm. (Ballantine's illustrated history of the violent century. War leader book no. 16) Bibliography: p. [160] [DA566.9.C5M34] 73-152750 ISBN 0-345-02998-4 1.00 (pbk.)
1. Churchill, Winston Leonard Spencer, Sir, 1874-1965.

MOOREHEAD, Alan, 1910- 923.242
Winston Churchill in trial and triumph. Boston, Houghton Mifflin, 1955. 117 p. 23 cm. [DA566.9.C5M65 1955] 55-8878
1. Churchill, Winston Leonard Spencer, Sir, 1874-1965.

MORIN, Relman, 1907- 923.242
Churchill: portrait of greatness. Englewood Cliffs, N.J., Prentice-Hall [1965] 127 p. illus., ports. 32 cm. [DA566.9.C5M68] 65-17844
1. Churchill, Sir Winston Leonard Spencer. 1874-1965. I. Title.

MORIN, Relman, 1907- 923.242
Churchill: portrait of greatness. Englewood Cliffs, N.J., Prentice c.1965. 127p. illus., ports. 32cm. [DA566.9.C5M68] 65-17844 3.95
1. Churchill, Winston Leonard Spencer, Sir 1874-1965. I. Title.

MY years with Churchill. v. 12
New York, British Book Centre, 1958. 167p. plates, ports.
1. Churchill, Winston Spencer, Sir 1874- I. McGowan, Norman.

NEILSON, Francis, 1867- 923.242
The Churchill legend. Appleton, Wis., C. C. Nelson Pub. Co., 1954. 470p. 23cm. [DA566.9.C5N4] 54-3847
1. Churchill, Winston Leonard Spencer, Sir 1874- I. Title.

NEL, Elizabeth (Layton) 923.242
Mr. Churchill's secretary. New York, Coward-McCann [1958] 185p. illus. 21cm. [DA566.9.C5N43] 58-12117
1. Churchill, Sir Winston Leonard Spencer, 1874- I. Title.

NEW York Times 942.0820924
Churchill. Written, ed. by the Staff of the New York Times. New York, Bantam [c.1965] 160p. ports. 19cm. (Bantam extra) [DA566.9.C5N48] 65-17780 .75 pap.,
1. Churchill, Winston Leonard Spencer, Sir 1874-1965. I. Title.

NORRIS, Albert George 923.242
Samuel.
A very great soul; a biographical character study of the Rt. Hon. Sir Winston S. Churchill, K.G., P. C., O. M., C.H., M.P. Edinburgh, International Pub. Co. [1957] 336p. illus. 22cm. [DA566.9.C5N62] 57-59070
1. Churchill, Winston Leonard Spencer, Sir I. Title.

PAYNE, Pierre 942.082'092'4 B
Stephen Robert, 1911-
The great man; a portrait of Winston Churchill [by] Robert Payne. New York, Coward, McCann & Geoghegan [1974] 416 p. illus., geneal. tables (on lining papers) 24 cm. Bibliography: p. 391-396. [DA566.9.C5P363 1974] 73-78766 10.95
1. Churchill, Winston Leonard Spencer, Sir, 1874-1965. I. Title.

PELLING, Henry. 942.082'092'4 B
Winston Churchill / Henry Pelling. 1st ed. New York : Dutton, [1974] 724 p., [8] leaves of plates : ill. ; 23 cm. Includes index. Bibliography: p. 646-660. [DA566.9.C5P38 1974b] 73-21276 ISBN 0-525-23510-8 : 12.95
1. Churchill, Winston Leonard Spencer, Sir, 1874-1965.

PILPEL, Robert. 941.082'092'4 B
Churchill in America, 1895-1961 : an affectionate portrait / Robert H. Pilpel. 1st ed. New York : Harcourt Brace Jovanovich, c1976. p. cm. Includes index. Bibliography: p. [DA566.9.C5P54] 76-21239 ISBN 0-15-117880-1 : 10.00
1. Churchill, Winston Leonard Spencer, Sir, 1874-1965. I. Title. BIP

THE Reader's digest. 942.0820924
Man of the century; a Churchill cavalcade, compiled by editors of the Reader's digest. [1st ed.] Boston, Little, Brown [1965] viii, 335 p. ports. 24 cm. [DA566.9.C5R36] 65-24441
1. Churchill, Sir Winston Leonard Spencer, 1874-1965 — Anecdotes. I. Title.

READER'S digest (The) 942.0820924
Man of the century; a Churchill cavalcade. comp. by eds. of the Reader's digest. Boston, Little [c.1965] viii.335p. ports. 24cm. [DA566.9.C5R36] 65-24441 6.95
1. Churchill, Sir Winston Leonard Spencer, 1874-1965—Anecdotes.

SCHNEIDER, Robert W. 813'.5'2
Novelist to a generation : the life and thought of Winston Churchill / by Robert W. Schneider. Bowling Green, Ohio : Bowling Green University Popular Press, c1976. xvi, 333 p. : port. ; 24 cm. Includes index. Bibliography: p. 324-328. [PS1298.S3] 76-4643 ISBN 0-87972-116-2 : 12.95 ISBN 0-87972-117-0 pbk. :
1. Churchill, Winston, 1871-1947. 2. Novelists, American—20th century—Biography. I. Title. BIP

SCHOENFELD, 942.082'092'4 B
Maxwell Philip, 1936-
Sir Winston Churchill: his life and times [by] Maxwell P. Schoenfeld. Hinsdale, Ill., Dryden Press [1973] viii, 192 p. 21 cm. (Berkshire studies in history) Bibliography: p. [178]-181. [DA566.9.C5S35] 72-93889 ISBN 0-03-086722-3 3.00 (pbk.)
1. Churchill, Winston Leonard Spencer, Sir, 1874-1965.

SCHOENFELD, Maxwell 942.084
Philip, 1936-
The war ministry of Winston Churchill. [1st ed.] Ames, Iowa State University Press [1972] xix, 283 p. illus. 23 cm. Bibliography: p. 257-260. [DA566.9.C5S36] 72-153159 ISBN 0-8138-0260-1
1. Churchill, Winston Leonard Spencer, Sir, 1874-1965. 2. World War, 1939-1945—Great Britain. 3. Great Britain—Foreign relations—1936-1945. I. Title. BIP

SILVERMAN, Al, ed. 923.242
Churchill; a memorial album [Al Silverman, ed. New York, Macfadden 1965] 79p. illus., ports. 28cm. Cover title. [DA566.9C5S45] 65-4026 .50 pap.,
1. Churchill, Winston Leonard Spencer, Sir 1874-1965. I. Title.

SMITH, N. D. 923.242
Winston Churchill. New York, Roy [1964] 108p. illus. ports. 22cm. (Informative ref. ser) Bibl. 64-10855 3.95
1. Churchill, Winston Leonard Spencer, Sir 1874- I. Title.

SMITH, Norman David. 923.242
Winston Churchill [by] N. D. Smith. New York, Roy Publishers [1964] 108 p. illus., ports. 22 cm. "A select book list": p. 104-105. [DA566.9.C5S58] 64-10855
1. Churchill, Sir Winston Leonard Spencer, 1874- I. Title.

SPARROW, Gerald, 820'.9'0091
1903-
Churchill, man of the century, 1874-1965. London, Odhams Books [1 965] 152 p. ports. 18 cm. [DA566.9.C5S6] 67-2351
1. Churchill, Sir Winston Leonard Spencer, I. Title.

STANSKY, Peter, 942.082'092'4 B
comp.
Churchill; a profile. [1st ed.] New York, Hill and Wang [1973] xviii, 270 p. 21 cm. (World profiles) Bibliography: p. 263-266. [DA566.9.C5S68 1973] 70-163576 ISBN 0-8090-3447-6 7.95
1. Churchill, Winston Leonard Spencer, Sir, 1874-1965. BIP

STEWART, Herbert Leslie, 923.242
1882-
Winged words: Sir Winston Churchill as writer and speaker. New York, Bouregy & Curl [1954] 114p. 21cm. [DA566.9.C5S8 1954] 54-7188
1. Churchill, Sir Winston Leonard Spencer, 1874- I. Title.

TAYLOR, Robert Lewis 923.242
The amazing Mister Churchill; an informal study of greatness. New York, McGraw [1962, c.1952] 433p. 22cm. First pub. in 1952 under title: Winston Churchill. 62-21120 6.50
1. Churchill, Winston Leonard Spencer, Sir 1874- I. Title.

TAYLOR, Robert Lewis. 923.242
The amazing Mister Churchill; an informal study of greatness. New York, McGraw-Hill [1962, c1952] 433 p. 22 cm. First published in 1952 under title: Winston Churchill. [DA566.9.C5T3 1962] 62-21120
1. Churchill, Sir Winston Leonard Spencer, 1874- I. Title.

TAYLOR, Robert Lewis. 923.242
Winston Churchill; an informal study of greatness. [1st ed.] Garden City, N.Y., Doubleday, 1952. 433 p. illus. 22 cm. [DA566.9.C5T3] 52-7606
1. Churchill, Winston Leonard Spencer, Sir, 1874-1965.

THOMPSON, 942.084'092'4 B
Reginald William.
Generalissimo Churchill [by] R. W. Thompson. New York, Scribner [1974, c1973] 252 p. illus. 24 cm. Bibliography: p. 237-239. [DA566.9.C5T425 1973b] 73-19553 ISBN 0-684-13557-4 8.95
1. Churchill, Winston Leonard Spencer, Sir, 1874-1965. 2. World War, 1939-1945—Great Britain. I. Title.

THOMPSON, Reginald 923.242
William.
Winston Churchill, the Yankee Marlborough. [1st ed. in the U.S.A.] Garden City, N.Y., Doubleday, 1963. ix, 342 p. 22 cm. Bibliography: p. [331]-334. [DA566.9.C5T43] 63-17456
1. Churchill, Winston Leonard Spencer, 1874- I. Title.

THE Times, London. 942.080924
The Churchill years, 1874-1965. [Edited, designed, and produced] by the editors of the Viking Press. Text by the Times of London. With a foreword by Lord Butler of Saffron Walden. New York, Viking Press [1965] 264 p. (chiefly illus. (part col.) coat of arms, geneal. table) 33 cm. Bibliography: p. 261-262. [DA566.9.CtT55] 65-23956
1. Churchill, Sir Winston Leonard Spencer, 1874-1965. I. Viking Press, inc. New York. II. Title.

WIBBERLEY, Leonard. 923.273
The life of Winston Churchill. New York, Ariel Books [1956] 214p. illus. 21cm. [DA566.9.C4W45] 56-6165
1. Churchill, Sir winston Le Spencer, 1874- I. Title.

WIBBERLEY, Leonard 923.273
Patrick O'Connor, 1915-
The life of Winston Churchill. New York, Ariel Books [1956] 214 p. illus. 21 cm. [DA566.9.C5W45] 56-6165
1. Churchill, Sir Winston Leonard Spencer, 1874- I. Title.

WIBBERLY, Leonard Patrick 923.242
O'Connor, 1915-
The life of Winston Churchill. Complete rev. New York, Farrar [1965] vii, 248p. illus., ports. 21cm. (Ariel bks.) Bibl. [DA566.9C5W45] 65-3640 3.50
1. Churchill, Winston Leonard Spencer, Sir 1874-1965. I. Title.

YOUNG, Kenneth, 320.9'42'0922
1916-
Churchill and Beaverbrook; a study in friendship and politics. New York, J. H. Heineman [1967, c.1966] 349p. illus., ports. 23cm. Bibl. [DA566.9.C5Y6 1967a] 67-17619 6.50
1. Churchill, Winston Leonard Spencer, Sir 2. Beaverbrook, William Maxwell Aitken, Baron, 1879-1964. I. Title. BIP

Churchill, Winston Leonard Spencer, Sir, 1874-1965—Juvenile literature.

BOOTH, Arthur Harold 92
The true story of Sir Winston Churchill, British statesman. Chicago, Childrens [c.1958,1964] 143p. col. illus., col. ports. 23cm. On spine: Sir Winston Churchill. First pub. in England in 1958 under title: The true book about Sir Winston Churchill. 64-19879 3.50 2.63 lib. ed.,
1. Churchill, Sir Winston Leonard, Spencer, 1874- —Juvenile literature. I. Title.

BOOTH, Arthur Harold. j 92
The true story of Sir Winston Churchill, British statesman, by Arthur H. Booth. Chicago, Childrens Press [1964] 143 p. col. illus., col. ports. 23 cm. On spine: Sir Winston Churchill. First published in 1958 under title: The true book about Sir Winston Churchill. [DA566.9.C5B64] 64-19879
1. Churchill, Sir Winston Leonard, Spencer, 1874- — Juvenile literature. I. Title.

CLARK, Ronald William. 92
Sir Winston Churchill. New York, Roy Publishers [1962] 128p. illus. 19cm. (The Living biographies series) [DA566.9.C5C55] 62-10724
1. Churchill, Winston Leonard Spencer, Sir 1874—Juvenile literature. I. Title.

DOLAN, Ellen M. 942.082'0924 B
Churchill. Adapted by Ellen M. Dolan from the text by Anthony Th. Mertens. Pictures by Raymond Renard. St. Louis, Webster Division, McGraw-Hill, c1968. [28] p. illus. (part col.), coats of arms, facsim., ports. 20 cm. (Around the world library) (Men of genius books.) Part of illustrative matter on lining paper. A brief biography of the British soldier, statesman, and historian. [DA566.9.C5D6] 92 75-13231
1. Churchill, Winston Leonard Spencer, Sir, 1874-1965—Juvenilie literature. I. Mertens, Antonius Theodorus Leonardus Maria. II. Renard, Raymond, fl. 1967- illus. III. Title.

DUPUY, Trevor 942.082'0924
Nevitt, 1916-
The military life of Winston Churchill of Britain. New York, F. Watts [1970] xviii, 207 p. illus., maps, ports. 23 cm. A biography of the British soldier, historian, and politician with emphasis on his military experiences and accomplishments. [DA566.9.C5D84] 92 69-17459
1. Churchill, Winston Leonard Spencer, Sir, 1874-1965—Juvenile literature. I. Title. BIP

EPSTEIN, Samuel, 942.082'0924 B
1909-
Winston Churchill: Lion of Britain, by Sam and Beryl Epstein. Champaign, Ill., Garrard Pub. Co. [1971] 175 p. illus. 22 cm. (A Century book) A biography of the British statesman, author, and military strategist who was one of the world leaders of the twentieth century. [DA566.9.C5E77] 92 78-146704 ISBN 0-8116-4752-8
1. Churchill, Winston Leonard Spencer, Sir, 1874-1965—Juvenile literature. I. Epstein, Beryl (Williams) 1910- joint author. II. Title.

FARRELL, Alan. 923.242
Sir Winston Churchill. [1st American ed.] New York, Putnam [1964, c1962] 158 p. ports. 21 cm. [DA566.9.C5F3 1964] 64-25761
1. Churchill, Winston Leonard Spencer, Sir, 1874-1965—Juvenile literature.

MIERS, Earl Schenk, 1910- 923.242
The story of Winston Churchill. Edit. prod.: Donald D. Wolf. Design, layout by Margot L. Wolf. New York, Grosset [c.1965] 48p. illus. (pt. col.) ports. (pt. col.) 28cm. (Spotlight Wonder bk.) [DA566.9.C5M5] 65-18289 1.95; .69 pap.,
1. Churchill, Winston Leonard Spencer, Sir 1874-1965—Juvenile literature. I. Title.

NATHAN, Adele (Gutman) 920
Churchill's England. New York, Grosset [c.1963] 92p. illus., ports. 26cm. 63-18971 2.50 bds.,
1. Churchill, Sir Winston Leonard Spencer, 1874—Juvenile literature. I. Title.

REYNOLDS, Quentin James, 920
1902-
Winston Churchill. New York, Random [c.1963] x, 183p. illus., ports. 22cm. (World landmark bks., W-56) Bibl. 63-7831 1.95 bds.,
1. Churchill, Winston, Leonard Spencer, Sir 1874- Juvenile literature. I. Title.

REYNOLDS, Quentin James, 1902- 92
Winston Churchill. New York, Random House [1963] x, 183 p. illus., ports. 22 cm. (World landmark books, W-56) Includes bibliography. [DA566.9.C5R4] 63-7831
1. Churchill, Sir Winston Leonard Spencer, 1874- — Juvenile literature. I. Title.

WEBB, Robert N. 942.082'0924 B
Winston Churchill, man of the century, by Robert N. Webb. New York, F. Watts [1968, c1969] viii, 120 p. maps, ports. 22 cm. (Immortals of history) A biography of Winston Churchill, the "Renaissance man," outlining the main events in his long and varied career. [DA566.9.C5W36] 92 69-11258
1. Churchill, Winston Leonard Spencer, Sir, 1874-1965—Juvenile literature. I. Title.

Churchill, Winston Leonard Spencer, Sir, 1874-1965—Portraits, caricatures, etc.

BRUCE, George, writer on 923.242
Churchill.
Churchill; a life in pictures] A memorial ed. [New York, Dell Pub. Co., 1965] 1 v. (unpaged) illus., ports. 29 cm. Cover title. [DA566.9.C5B78] 65-20265
1. Churchill, Sir Winston Leonard Spencer, 1874-1965 — Portraits, Caricatur I. Title.

CHURCHILL, Randolph 923.242
Spencer, 1911-1968, ed.
Churchill, his life in photographs, edited by Randolph S. Churchill and Helmut Gernsheim. New York, Rinehart [1955] unpaged. illus. 29 cm. [DA566.9.C5C45] 55-14646
1. Churchill, Winston Leonard Spencer, Sir, 1874-1965—Portraits, caricatures, etc. I. Gernsheim, Helmut, 1913- joint ed. II. Title.

FERRIER, Neil, ed. 923.242
Churchill, the man of the century; a pictorial biography. Garden City, N.Y., Doubleday, 1965. 60p. illus., facsims., ports. 28cm. [DA566.9.C5F43] 65-3144 2.95 bds.,
1. Churchill, Winston Leonard Spencer, Sir 1874-1965—Portraits, carictures, etc. I. Title.

GILBERT, Martin, 942.082'092'4
1936- comp.
Churchill; a photographic portrait. [1st American ed.] Boston, Houghton Mifflin, 1974. 1 v. (unpaged) illus. 25 cm. [DA566.9.C5G444 1974] 74-4204 ISBN 0-395-19405-9 12.50
1. Churchill, Winston Leonard Spencer, Sir, 1874-1965—Portraits, caricatures, etc. I. Title.

HARRITY, Richard. 923.242
Man of the century: Churchill [by] Richard Harrity and Ralph G. Martin. [1st ed.] New York, Duell, Sloan and Pearce [1962] 247p. illus. 26cm. [DA566.9.C5H25] 62-8521
1. Churchill, Winston Leonard Spencer, Sir 1874- —Portraits, caricatures, etc. I. Martin, Ralph G., 1920- joint author. II. Title.

MILLER, Harry Tatlock, 923.242
comp.
Churchill: the walk with destiny, compiled and designed by H. Tatlock Miller [and] Loudon Sainthill. New York, Macmillan [1959] 253p. (chiefly illus., plates (part col.) ports. (part col.) coats of arms (part col.)) 33cm. [DA566.9.C5M55] 59-65213
1. Churchill, Sir Winston Leonard Spencer, 1874- —Portraits, caricatures, etc. I. Sainthill, Loudon, joint comp. II. Title.

MOOREHEAD, Alan [McCrae] 923.242
Churchill: a pictorial biography. New York, Viking Press [1960] 143p. illus., ports., facsims. 24cm. (A Studio book) 60-50912 6.50
1. Churchill, Sir Winston Leonard Spencer, 1874—Portraits, caricatures, etc. I. Title.

Chyatte, Samuel B.

CHYATTE, Samuel B. 616.6'1
On borrowed time : living with hemodialysis / Samuel B. Chyatte. Oradell, NJ : Medical Economics Co., Book Division, c1979. x, 133 p. ; 24 cm. [RC918.R4C62] 79-109938 ISBN 0-87489-213-9 pbk. : 10.95
1. Chyatte, Samuel B. 2. Renal insufficiency—Biography. 3. Hemodialysis. I. Title.

Chynoweth, Bradford Grethen, 1890-

CHYNOWETH, 355.3'31'0924 B
Bradford Grethen, 1890-
Bellamy Park : memoirs / by Bradford Grethen Chynoweth. 1st ed. Hicksville, N.Y. : Exposition Press, [1975] 301 p. : maps ; 22 cm. [U53.C48A33] 75-300646 ISBN 0-682-48065-7 : 10.00
1. Chynoweth, Bradford Grethen, 1890- I. Title.

Ciano, Caleazzo, Conte, 1903-1944.

CIANO, Edda 945.091'092'4 B
Mussolini, Contessa.
My truth / by Edda Mussolini Ciano as told to Albert Zarca ; translated from the French by Eileen Finletter. New York : Morrow, 1977, c1976. p. cm. Translation of Temoignage pour un homme. Includes index. [DG575.C516A3513 1977] 76-26503 ISBN 0-688-03099-8 : 8.95
1. Ciano, Edda Mussolini, Contessa. 2. Ciano, Caleazzo, Conte, 1903-1944. 3. Mussolini, Benito, 1883-1945. 4. Statesmen's wives—Italy—Biography. 5. Statesmen—Italy—Biography. 6. Italy—Politics and government—1922-1945. I. Zarca, Albert. II. Title. **BIP**

Ciano, Edda Mussolini, Contessa.

CIANO, Edda 945.091'092'4 B
Mussolini, Contessa.
My truth / by Edda Mussolini Ciano as told to Albert Zarca ; translated from the French by Eileen Finletter. New York : Morrow, 1977, c1976. p. cm. Translation of Temoignage pour un homme. Includes index. [DG575.C516A3513 1977] 76-26503 ISBN 0-688-03099-8 : 8.95
1. Ciano, Edda Mussolini, Contessa. 2. Ciano, Caleazzo, Conte, 1903-1944. 3. Mussolini, Benito, 1883-1945. 4. Statesmen's wives—Italy—Biography. 5. Statesmen—Italy—Biography. 6. Italy—Politics and government—1922-1945. I. Zarca, Albert. II. Title. **BIP**

Cibber, Susannah Maria Arne, 1714-1766.

NASH, Mary, 1925- 792'.028'0924 B
The provoked wife : the life and times of Susannah Cibber / Mary Nash. 1st ed. Boston : Little, Brown, c1977. xii, 369 p. : ill. ; 24 cm. Includes index. Bibliography: p. 353-358. [PN2598.C4N3] 76-30336 ISBN 0-316-59831-3 : 12.50
1. Cibber, Susannah Maria Arne, 1714-1766. 2. Actors—Great Britain—Biography. I. Title. **BIP**

Cibulka, Alois,

CIBULKA, Alois, 1890- 926.2
All this could happen only to an engineer. [Highlands? Tex., 1950] 237 p. port. 22 cm. Autobiography. [TA140.C52A3] 50-26182
I. Title.

Cicero, Marcus Tullius.

BADILLO Gerena, 937'.05'0924 B
Pedro.
Ciceron y el Imperio / Pedro Badillo Gerena. [Rio Piedras] : Editorial Universitaria, Universidad de Puerto Rico, 1976. p. cm. (Serie Humanidades) (Coleccion Uprex) [DG260.C53B3] 76-10131 ISBN 0-8477-0050-X : 2.00
*1. Cicero, Marcus Tulius. 2. Rome—History—Republic, 265-30 B.C. I. Title.***BIP**

BAILEY, David Roy 937'.05'0924 B
Shackleton.
Cicero [by] D. R. Shackleton Bailey. New York, Scribner [1972, c1971] xii, 290 p. front. 23 cm. (Classical life and letters) [DG260.C5B27 1972] 78-176156 ISBN 0-684-12683-4 10.00
1. Cicero, Marcus Tullius.
Pbk. 3.50; ISBN 0-684-13216-8.

BAILEY, David Roy 937'.05'0924 B
Shackleton.
Cicero [by] D. R. Shackleton Bailey. New York, Scribner [1973, c1971] xii, 290 p. illus. 21 cm. (Classical life and letters) (The Scribner library. Lyceum editions: history) Includes bibliographical references. [DG260.C5B27 1973] 74-161825 ISBN 0-684-12683-4 3.50
1. Cicero, Marcus Tullius.

CARCOPINO, Jerome, 937.05'0924
1881-1970.
Cicero, the secrets of his correspondence. New York, Greenwood Press [1969] 2 v. (vii, 596 p.) 23 cm. "Originally published in 1951." Translation of Les secrets de la correspondance de Ciceron. Includes bibliographical references. [PA6298.C313 1969] 70-90702
1. Cicero, Marcus Tullius. Epistolae. I. Title. **BIP**

CONWAY, Robert 913.3'7'0350922
Seymour, 1864-1933.
Makers of Europe. Freeport, N.Y., Books for Libraries Press [1967] 89 p. 24 cm. (The James Henry Morgan lectures in Dickinson College, 1930) Essay index reprint series. Reprint of the 1931 ed. Bibliographical footnotes. [DB203.C6] 67-28748
1. Caesar, C Julius. 2. Cicero, Marcus Tullius. 3. Horatius Fiaccus, Quintus. 4. Vergilius Maro. Publius. I. Title. II. Series.

CONWAY, Robert 913.3'7'0350922
Seymour, 1864-1933.
Makers of Europe. Freeport, N.Y., Books for Libraries Press [1967] 89 p. 24 cm. (Essay index reprint series.) (The James Henry Morgan lectures in Dickinson College 1930) Reprint of the 1931 ed. Bibliographical footnotes. [DG203.C6 1967] 67-28748
1. Caesar, C. Julius. 2. Cicero, Marcus Tullius. 3. Horatius Flaccus, Quintus. 4. Vergilius Maro, Publius. I. Title. II. Series.

DOREY, T A ed. 928.7
Cicero. Chapters by H. H. Scullard [and others] Edited by T. A. Dorey. New York, Basic Books [1965] xiii, 218 p. 22 cm. (Studies in Latin literature and its influence) Includes bibliographical references. [DG260.C5D6] 65-10506
1. Cicero, Marcus Tullius. I. Title.

HASKELL, Henry Joseph, v. 12
1874-
This was Cicero. Greenwich, Fawcett [1964, c1942] 320 p. map. 18 cm. (A premier book, t236) 67-34573
1. Cicero, Marcus Tullius. I. Title.

LACEY, Walter 937'.05'0924 B
Kirkpatrick.
Cicero and the end of the Roman Republic / W. K. Lacey. New York : Barnes & Noble, 1978. vi, 184 p. : maps ; 22 cm. Includes index. Bibliography: p. [177]-179. [DG260.C5L25] 78-1101 ISBN 0-06-494013-6 : 16.50
1. Cicero, Marcus Tullius. 2. Rome—History—Republic, 265-30 B.C. 3. Statesmen—Rome—Biography. 4. Orators—Rome—Biography. I. Title. **BIP**

PETERSSON, Torsten, 1878- 928.7
Cicero, a biography. New York, Biblo & Tannen, 1963. 699p. 21cm. Bibl. 63-10768 7.50
1. Cicero, Marcus Tullius. I. Title. **BIP**

PLUTARCHUS. [888.8] 920.03
Life stories of men who shaped history, from Plutarch's Lives. Translated by John and William Langhorne, selected and edited by Eduard C. Lindeman. [New York] New American Library [1950] 222 p. 18 cm. (A Mentor book, 55) [DE7.P7L5] 50-38593
1. Alcibiades. 2. Cicero, Marcus Tuillus. 3. Alexander the Great, 356-323 B.C. 4. Lycurgus, orator, 6 BC. 338-326. 5. Solon. 6. Pericles, 499-429 BC. I. Title.

RICHARDS, George 937'.05'0924 B
Chatterton, 1867-
Cicero; a study. Westport, Conn., Greenwood Press [1970] x, 298 p. port. 23 cm. [DG260.C5R5 1970] 79-109830 ISBN 0-8371-4321-7
1. Cicero, Marcus Tullius.

SIHLER, Ernest 937'.05'0924 B
Gottlieb, 1853-1942.
Cicero of Arpinum; a political and literary biography being a contribution to the history of ancient civilization and a guide to the study of Cicero's writings. New York, Cooper Square Publishers, 1969. xi, 487 p. 23 cm. Reprint of the 1914 ed. Bibliography: p. [470]-477. [DG260.C5S5 1969] 70-79204 15.00
1. Cicero, Marcus Tullius. 2. Rome—Politics and government—265-30 B.C. I. Title.

SMITH, Richard 937.050924 (B)
Edwin
Cicero the statesman, by R. E. Smith. London, Cambridge Univ. Pr., 1966. vii, 269p. 23cm. Bibl. [DG260.C5S6] 66-17061 8.50
1. Cicero, Marcus Tullius. I. Title.
Available from the publisher's New York office.

STOCKTON, David. 937'.05'0924 B
Cicero: a political biography. London, Oxford University Press, 1971. xvi, 359 p., plate. maps, port. 21 cm. Includes bibliographical references. [DG260.C5S77] 70-565489 ISBN 0-19-872032-7 £3.50
1. Cicero, Marcus Tullius.

STRACHAN-DAVIDSON, 937'.05'0924 B
James Leigh, 1843-1916.
Cicero and the fall of the Roman Republic. Freeport, N.Y., Books for Libraries Press [1972] vii, 446 p. illus. 22 cm. Reprint of the 1894 ed. issued in series: Heroes of the nations. Includes bibliographical references. [DG260.C5S8 1972] 72-2510 ISBN 0-8369-6866-2
1. Cicero, Marcus Tillius. 2. Rome—History—Republic, 265-30 B.C. I. Title. II. Series: Heroes of the nations. **BIP**

STRACHAN-DAVIDSON, 937'.05'0924 B
James Leigh, 1843-1916
Cicero and the fall of the Roman Republic. Freeport, N.Y., Books for Libraries Press [1972] vii, 446 p. illus. 22 cm. Reprint of the 1894 ed. issued in series: Heroes of the nations. Includes bibliographical references. [DG260.C5S8 1972] 72-2510 ISBN 0-8369-6866-2 19.75
1. Cicero, Marcus Tillius. 2. Rome—History—Republic, 265-30 B.C. I. Title. II. Series: Heroes of the nations.

Cicero, Marcus Tullius—Contemporary Rome.

BOISSIER, Gaston, 937.05'0924
1823-1908.
Cicero and his friends; a study of Roman society in the time of Caesar. Translated, with an index and table of contents, by Adnah David Jones. New York, Cooper Square Publishers, 1970. vii, 399 p. 23 cm. "A Marandell book." Reprint of the 1897 ed. Translation of Ciceron et ses amis. Includes bibliographical references. [DG260.A1B62 1970] 75-114085
1. Cicero, Marcus Tullius—Contemporary Rome. 2. Rome—History—Republic, 265-30 B.C. I. Title. **BIP**

Cicero, Marcus Tullius—Correspondence.

CICERO, Marcus Tullius. 876'.01
Cicero's Letters to Atticus / translated with an introd. by D. R. Shackleton Bailey. Harmondsworth, Eng. , New York : Penguin Books, 1978. 735 p. : maps ; 18 cm. (Penguin classics) Originally published in parallel Latin and English texts under title: Letters to Atticus. Bibliography: p. 25-26. [PA6308.E6B3] 79-304440 ISBN 0-14-044309-6 pbk. : 5.95
1. Cicero, Marcus Tullius—Correspondence. 2. Atticus, Titus Pomponius. 3. Authors, Latin—Correspondence. I. Atticus, Titus Pomponius. II. Bailey, David Roy Shackleton. III. Title. IV. Title: Letters to Atticus. **BIP**

CICERO, Marcus Tullius. 876'.01
Cicero's letters to his friends / Cicero ; translated by D. R. Shackleton Bailey. Harmondsworth, Eng. ; New York : Penguin Books, 1978. 2 v. : maps ; 19 cm. (The Penguin classics) Includes bibliographical references. [PA6308.E5B34] 79-310701 ISBN 0-14-044340-1 (v. 1) pbk. : 5.95 ISBN 0-14-044341-X (v. 2) pbk. : 5.95
1. Cicero, Marcus Tullius—Correspondence. 2. Authors, Latin—Correspondence. I. Bailey, David Roy Shackleton. II. Title.

Cincinnati. Baseball club (National League)

COLLETT, 796.357'64'0977178
Ritter.
Men of the (Reds) Machine : an inside look at baseball's team of the '70's / by Ritter Collett. Dayton, Ohio : Landfall Press, c1977. 254 p. : ill. ; 22 cm. [GV875.C65C65] 77-376973 ISBN 0-913428-28-0 : 7.95.
1. Cincinnati. Baseball club (National League) 2. Baseball players—United States—Biography. I. Title.

MCCOY, Hal. 796.357'64'0977178
The relentless Reds / Hal McCoy, text ; Earl Lawson, foreword ; Dennis Gruelle, photos. Shelbyville, Ky. : PressCo, c1976. 240 p. : ill. ; 28 cm. [GV875.C65M32] 76-359780 ISBN 0-916794-01-6
1. Cincinnati. Baseball club (National League) 2. Baseball—Biography. I. Title.

Cinematographers—Correspondence, reminiscences, etc.

HIGHAM, Charles, 1931- 791.43'025
Hollywood cameramen: sources of light. Bloomington, Indiana University Press [1970] 176 p. illus., ports. 20 cm. (Cinema one series, 14) [TR849.A1H53 1970] 74-115457 5.95
1. Cinematographers—Correspondence, reminiscences, etc. I. Title.

Cintron, Conchita, 1924-

CINTRON, Conchita, 791.8'2'0924
1924-
Memoirs of a bullfighter. With an introd. by Orson Wells. [1st ed.] New York, Holt, Rinehart and Winston [1968] xvi, 272 p. illus., ports. 22 cm. Translation of Recuerdos. [GV1108.C5A33] 68-12203

I. Title.

CINTRON, Lola (Verrill) 927.9182
Goddess of the bullring; the story of Conchita Cintron, the world's greatest matadors. [1st ed.] Indianapolis, Bobbs-Merrill [1960] 349p. illus. 24cm. [GV1108.C5C52] 60-7165
1. Cintron, Conchita, 1924- I. Title.

Circus.

REYNOLDS, Butch. 927.913
Broken hearted clown; [an autobiography] Illustrated by the author. New York, Roy Publishers, 1955. 200p. illus. 23cm. [GV1811] 55-9765
1. Circus. I. Title.

Circus—Biography.

DRIMMER, Frederick. 791.3'5 B
Very special people; the struggles, loves, and triumphs of human oddities. New York, Bantam [1976 c1973] 357 p. illus. 18 cm. Bibliography: p. 353-357. [GV1835.D74] 1.95 (pbk.)
1. Circus—Biography. 2. Deformities. I. Title.
L.C. card no. of 1973 Amjon Publishers edition: 73-87451.

DRIMMER, Frederick. 791.3'5 B
Very special people; the struggles, loves, and triumphs of human oddities. New York, Amjon Publishers [1973] 411 p. illus. 22 cm. Bibliography: p. 407-411. [GV1835.D74] 73-87451 6.95
1. Circus—Biography. 2. Deformities. I. Title.
Publisher's address: 245 West 19th Street, New York N.Y. 10011 Publisher's address: 245 West 19th Street, New York N.Y. 10011

Circus—Biography—Juvenile literature.

KIRK, Rhina. 791.3'092'2
Circus heroes and heroines. [Maplewood, N.J.] Hammond Inc. [1972] 91 p. illus. (part col.) 27 cm. Bibliography: p. 71. Brief profiles of famous circus personalities such as P. T. Barnum, Tom Thumb, Clyde Beatty, and Annie Oakley plus a short history of the origins of the circus. [GV1811.A1K5] 74-189632 ISBN 0-8437-3879-0 4.50
1. Circus—Biography—Juvenile literature. I. Title.

Cirile, Marie.

CIRILE, Marie. 363.2'092'4 B
Detective Marie Cirile : memoirs of a police officer. 1st ed. Garden City, N.Y. : Doubleday, 1975. 222 p., [4] leaves of plates : ill. ; 22 cm. [HV7911.C57A34] 74-18787 ISBN 0-385-07621-5 : 6.95
1. Cirile, Marie. 2. Policewomen—New York (City)—Correspondence, reminiscences, etc. 3. Detectives—New York (City)—Correspondence, reminiscences, etc. I. Title.

Cirtercian nuns—Biog.

RAYMOND, Father, 1903- 922.2
These women walked with God. Milwaukee, Bruce Pub. Co. [1956] 255p. 22cm. (His The saga of Citeaux. 3d epoch) [BX4330.C5R3] 56-13337
1. Cirtercian nuns—Biog. 2. Saints, Women I. Title.

Cisler, Walker Lee, 1897-

CISLER, Walker Lee, 1897- 621.3'092'4 B
A measurable difference : the reminiscences of Walker Lee Cisler, in collaboration with James P. McCormick. Ann Arbor : Graduate School of Business Administration, University of Michigan, c1976. x, 161 p., [4] leaves of plates : ill. ; 22 cm. (The Entrepreneurial autobiographical series) Includes index. [TK140.C48A36] 76-383096 ISBN 0-89117-054-5
1. Cisler, Walker Lee, 1897- 2. Electric engineers—United States—Biography. 3. Executives—United States—Biography. I. McCormick, James Patton, 1911- joint author. II. Title. III. Series.

Cist, Jacob, 1782-1825.

POWELL, Howard Benjamin, 1937- 338.2'7'2509748
Philadelphia's first fuel crisis : Jacob Cist and the developing market for Pennsylvania anthracite / H. Benjamin Powell. University Park : Pennsylvania State University Press, c1978. p. cm. Includes bibliographical references and index. [HD9547.P4P63] 78-5777 ISBN 0-271-00533-5 : 10.00
1. Cist, Jacob, 1782-1825. 2. Anthracite coal—Pennsylvania—History. 3. Businessmen—United States—Biography. I. Title. **BIP**

Cistercians—Bibliography.

MICHIGAN. Western Michigan University, Kalamazoo. Institute of Cistercian Studies. 016.255'12
A guide to Cistercian scholarship / edited by E. Rozanne Elder. Kalamazoo : Institute of Cistercian Studies, Western Michigan University, 1974. 32 p. ; 22 cm. Cover title. Includes index. [Z7840.C5M53 1974] [BX3402.2] 76-620534
1. Cistercians—Bibliography. 2. Cistercians—Biography. I. Elder, Ellen Rozanne. II. Title.

Cities and towns—Planning.

GEDDES, Patrick, Sir, 1854-1932. 309.2'62
Patrick Geddes: spokesman for man and the environment; a selection. Edited and with an introd. by Marshall Stalley. New Brunswick, N.J., Rutgers University Press [1972] xiv, 476 p. illus. 24 cm. Contents.Contents.—Biography of Patrick Geddes, by A. Ziffren.—Cities in evolution.—Talks from the outlook tower.—Town planning in Lahore: a report to the municipal council. Includes bibliographical references. [HT166.G43 1972] 75-163963 ISBN 0-8135-0697-2 15.00
1. Cities and towns—Planning. I. Title.

Citizen (Ship)

BILL, Erastus, 1826-1905. 910'.41 B
Citizen : an American boy's early manhood aboard a Sag Harbor whale-ship chasing delirium and death around the world, 1843-1849 : being the story of Erastus Bill who lived to tell it : with notes on Erastus Bill by Robert Wesley Bills. Anchorage, Alaska : O. W. Frost, 1978. 136 p. : ill. ; 24 cm. (World discovery books ; 2) Includes index. [SH383.2.B54 1978] 78-50525 ISBN 0-930766-01-6 : 10.00. ISBN 0-930766-02-4 pbk. : 4.95
1. Citizen (Ship) 2. Whaling. 3. Whalemen—New Yorks (State)—Sag Harbor—Biography. I. Title. II. Series. **BIP**

Citrine, Walter McLennan Citrine, Baron, 1887-

CITRINE, Walter McLennan Citrine, Baron, 1887- 941.084'092'4 B
Men and work : an autobiography / Lord Citrine. Westport, Conn. : Greenwood Press, 1976, c1964. 384 p., [1] leaf of plates : port. ; 24 cm. Reprint of the ed. published by Hutchinson, London. Includes index. [HD8393.C54A33 1976] 75-36094 ISBN 0-8371-8613-7 lib. bdg. : 22.00
1. Citrine, Walter McLennan Citrine, Baron, 1887- 2. Trade-unions—Great Britain—Political activity—History. 3. Great Britain—Politics and government—20th-century. I. Title.

City churches—Bibliography.

WHITE, Anthony G. 016.3092'08 S
Religion as an urban institution: a selected bibliography [by] Anthony G. White. Monticello, Ill., Council of Planning Librarians, 1973. 11 p. 29 cm. (Council of Planning Librarians. Exchange bibliography 450) Cover title. [Z5942.C68 no. 450] [Z7164.S685] 016.3015'8 73-177608 1.50
1. City churches—Bibliography. 2. Sociology, Urban—Bibliography. I. Title. II. Series.

Civil engineers, American—Biography.

AMERICAN Society of Civil Engineers. Committee on History and Heritage of American Civil Engineering. 624'.092'2 B
A biographical dictionary of American civil engineers. New York, 1972. x, 163 p. illus. 23 cm. (ASCE historical publication no. 2) [TA139.A53] 72-194203 5.00
1. Civil engineers, American—Biography. I. Title. II. Series: American Society of Civil Engineers. ASCE historical publication no. 2. **BIP**

Civil rights—U. S.

MURPHY, Frank, 1893-1949 323.40924
Mr. Justice Murphy and the Bill of rights. Dobbs Ferry, N. Y., Oceana [c.]1965. xxiii, 568p. 24cm. Bibl. 65-22168 7.50
1. Civil rights—U. S. I. Norris, Harold, ed. II. Title.

Civil service—United States—Biography.

LASSON, Kenneth. 353'.00092'2
Private lives of public servants / Kenneth Lasson. Bloomington : Indiana University Press, c1978. xii, 203 p. ; 22 cm. [JK693.A2L37 1978] 77-15758 ISBN 0-253-34606-1 : 10.95
1. Civil service—United States—Biography. 2. United States—Officials and employees—Biography. I. Title. **BIP**

Cour, Jacques, d. 1456.

KERR, Albert Boardman, 1875- 380.1'0924 B
Jacques Cour, merchant prince of the Middle Ages. Freeport, N.Y., Books for Libraries Press [1971] xiii, 327 p. illus., facsims., ports. 23 cm. Reprint of the 1927 ed. Includes bibliographical references. [HJ1077.C6K4 1971] 72-146862 ISBN 0-8369-5629-X
1. Cour, Jacques, d. 1456. I. Title.

Claassen, Johann, 1820-1876.

KLASSEN, Elizabeth Suderman, 1933- 289.7'3 B
Traveler for the Brethren / Elizabeth Suderman Klassen. Scottdale, Pa. : Herald Press, 1978. p. cm. Bibliography: p. [BX8143.C55K57] 78-11994 ISBN 0-8361-1214-8 : 6.95
1. Claassen, Johann, 1820-1876. 2. Mennonite Brethren Church—Biography. I. Title.

Claiborne, William Charles Cole, 1775-1817.

HATFIELD, Joseph T. 973.4'092'4 B
William Claiborne : Jeffersonian centurion in the American Southwest / Joseph T. Hatfield. Lafayette : University of Southwestern Louisiana, 1976. xiv, 393 p., [7] leaves of plates : ill. ; 24 cm. (The USL history series ; no. 9) Originally presented as the author's thesis, Emory University. Includes index. Bibliography: p. 374-380. [E353.1.C6H37 1976] 76-19654 10.00
1. Claiborne, William Charles Cole, 1775-1817. 2. Legislators—United States—Biography. 3. Louisiana—Governors—Biography. 4. Southwest, Old—Politics and government. I. Series: Louisiana. University of Southwestern Louisiana, Lafayette. The U.S.L. history series ; no. 9.

Claiborne, William. 1600-1677?

HALE, Nathaniel Claiborne, 1903- 923.273
Virginia venturer, a historical biography of William Claiborne, 1600-1677; the story of the merchant venturers who founded Virginia, and the war in the Chesapeake. Richmond, Dietz Press ['1951] xvi, 340 p. map (on lining papers) 24 cm. Bibliography: p. 317-322. [F229.C589H3] 52-902
1. Claiborne, William. 1600-1677? 2. Virginia—Hist.—Colonial period. 3. Maryland—Hist.—Colonial period. 4. Chesapeake Bay. I. Title.

Clancy, Francis Michael,

CLANCY, Francis Michael, 1903- 796.9'62'0924 B
Clancy; the King's story, as told to Brian McFarlane. Toronto, New York [etc.] McGraw-Hill [1968] 157 p. illus., ports. 23 cm. [GV848.5.C55A3] 68-55597
I. McFarlane, Brian. II. Title.

Clancy, Frank J.

CLANCY, Frank J. 926.1
Doctor come quickly. [1st ed.] Seattle, Superior Pub. Co. [1950] xii, 248 p. 22 cm. Autobiographical. [R154.C337A3] 50-9675
I. Title.

Clap, Thomas, 1703-1767.

TUCKER, Louis Leonard, 1927- 923.773
Puritan protagonist: President Thomas Clap of Yale College. Chapel Hill, Published for the Institute of Early American History and Culture, Williamsburg, Va., by University of North Carolina Press [1962] 283 p. illus. 24 cm. [LC6330 1740.T8] 62-16069
1. Clap, Thomas, 1703-1767. I. Title. **BIP**

Clapp, Theodore,

CLAPP, Theodore, 1792-1866. 922.8173
Parson Clapp of the Strangers'Church of New Orleans, edited by John Duffy. Baton Rouge, Louisiana State University Press [1957] ix, 191p. illus., port., facsim. 24cm. (Louisiana State University studies. Social science series, no. 7) Selections from the author's Autobiographical sketches and recollections, during a thirty-five years' residence in New Orleans, with an account of his life by the editor. Bibliographical references included in 'Notes'(p. 175-188) New Orleans--Hist. [F379.N5C584] 57-9481
I. Duffy, John, 1915- ed. II. Title. III. Series.

Clapper, Raymond, 1892-1944.

CLAPPER, Olive (Ewing) 1896- 920.5
One lucky woman. [1st ed.] Garden City, N.Y., Doubleday, 1961. 503p. 22cm. Autobiographical. [PN4874.C52A3] 61-9490
1. Clapper, Raymond, 1892-1944. I. Title.

Clapton, Eric.

TURNER, Steve. 787'.61'0924 B
Conversations with Eric Clapton / [by] Steve Turner. London : Abacus, 1976. 116 p., [24] p. of plates : ports. ; 20 cm. Discography: p. 112-116. [ML419.C58T9] 77-372592 ISBN 0-349-13402-2 : £1.25
1. Clapton, Eric. 2. Rock musicians—England—Interviews. I. Title.

Clara, of Assisi, Saint, d. 1253.

BOYLE, John, 1922- 922.245
Princess of poverty; a story of St. Clare of Assisi. Illus. by Judith E. Quinn. Notre Dame, Ind., Dujarie Press [1955] 91p. illus. 24cm. [BX4700.C6B6] 55-38175
1. Clara of Assisi, Saint, d. 1253. I. Title.

DANIEL-ROPS, Henry, 1901- 922.245
The call of St. Clare. Translated from the French by Salvator Attanasio. [1st ed.] New York, Hawthorn Books [1963] 144 p. illus. 24 cm. Translation of Claire dans la clarte. "Selected bibliography": p. 141. [BX4700.C6D314] 63-8020
1. Clara, of Assisi, Saint, d. 1253. I. Title.

DANIEL-ROPS, Henry [Henry Jules Charles Petiot] 1901- 922.245
The call of St. Clare. Tr. from French by Salvator Attanasio. New York, Hawthorn [c.1963] 144p. illus. 24cm. Bibl. 63-8020 4.95
1. Clara, of Assisi, Saint, d. 1253. I. Title.

DE ROBECK, Nesta. 922.245
St. Clare of Assisi. Milwaukee, Bruce [1951] vii, 242 p. illus., ports. 22 cm. Bibliography: p. 238-240. [BX4700.C6D4] 51-6954
1. Clara of Assisi, Saint, d. 1253. I. Title.

ERNEST, Brother, 1897- 922.245
A story of Saint Clare. Pictures by Carolyn Lee Jagodits. Notre Dame, Ind., Dujarie Press [1957] unpaged. illus. 21cm. [BX4700.C6E7] 57-4991
1. Clara, of Assisi, Saint, d. 1253. I. Title.

FARNUM, Mabel Adelaide, 1887- v. 12
Saint Clare, patroness of television. Pulaski, Wis., Franciscan Publishers [c1961] 96 p. 19 cm. 63-15249
1. Clara, of Assisi, Saint, d. 1253. I. Title.

ROGGEN, Heribert. 271'.973'0924 B
The spirit of St. Clare. Translated by Paul Joseph Oligny. [Chicago] Franciscan Herald Press [1971] xiii, 93 p. 21 cm. Translation from German ed. (1970) of the work first published in Dutch under title: Franciscaans evangelische levensstijl volgens de II. Clara van Assisi. Includes bibliographical references. [BX4700.C6R6413] 74-123595 ISBN 0-8199-0410-4 3.95
1. Clara, of Assisi, Saint, d. 1253. I. Title.
BIP

Clara, of Assisi, Saint, d. 1253—Juvenile literature.

PETERS, Caroline 92
The story of Saint Clare. Pictures by Carol Young, Paterson [N.J.] St. Anthony Guild Pr. [c.1965] 35p. col. illus. 23cm. [BX4700.C6P4] 65-19593 1.39 bds.,
1. Clara, of Assisi, Saint, d. 1253—Juvenile literature. I. Young, Carol, illus. II. Title. III. Title: Saint Clare.

Clare, Dollie.

CLARE, Dollie. 942.9085'092'4 B
The tantalizing disclosures of a Welsh girl / by Dollie Clare. New York : Philosophical Library, c1978. xi, 142 p. : ill. ; 22 cm. [CT848.C56A37] 77-87938 ISBN 0-8022-2218-8 : 8.50
1. Clare, Dollie. 2. Wales—Biography. I. Title.
BIP

Clare, John Fitzgibbon, 1st Earl of, 1749-1802.

MOLONY, John Chartres, 1877- 920.415
Ireland's tragic comedians. Freeport, N.Y., Books for Libraries Press [1970] ix, 313, [1] p. port. 23 cm. (Essay index reprint series) Reprint of the 1934 ed. "Bibliographical note": p. 313-[314] [DA948.6.A1M6 1970] 73-134117
1. Clare, John Fitzgibbon, 1st Earl of, 1749-1802. 2. Tone, Theobald Wolfe, 1763-1798. 3. Fitzgerald, Edward, Lord, 1763-1798. 4. Emmet, Robert, 1778-1803. I. Title.
BIP

Clare, John, 1793-1864.

CLARE, John, 1793-1864. 821'.7 B
Sketches in the life of John Clare, written by himself. Now first published, with an introd., notes, and additions by Edmund Blunden. [Folcroft, Pa.] Folcroft Library Editions, 1974. p. "Clare on the Londoners": The introd. includes letters of Clare to John Taylor, to whom the sketches are also addressed. Reprint of the 1931 ed. published by Cobden-Sanderson, London. [PR4453.C6Z5 1974] 74-3125 ISBN 0-8414-9932-2 20.00 (lib. bdg.)
1. Clare, John, 1793-1864. I. Blunden, Edmund Charles, 1896-1974, ed. II. Taylor, John, 1781-1864. III. Title.

MARTIN, Frederick, 1830-1883 928.2
The life of John Clare. Introd., notes by Eric Robinson, Geoffrey Summerfield. 2d ed. New York, Barnes & Noble [1964] xxxii, 319p. illus., ports. 22cm. Bibl. 64-55543 6.50
1. Clare, John, 1793-1864. I. Title.

TIBBLE, John William, 1901- 821'.7 B
John Clare, a life [by] J. W. & Anne Tibble. [New ed. completely rev.] Totowa, N.J., Rowman and Littlefield [1972] xxi, 441 p. illus. 23 cm. Bibliography: p. 409-416. [PR4453.C6Z94 1972] 73-150722 ISBN 0-87471-150-9 17.50
1. Clare, John, 1793-1864. I. Tibble, Anne (Northgrave), joint author. II. Title.

Clarendon, Edward Hyde, 1st earl of, 1609-1674.

CLARENDON, Edward Hyde, 1st earl of, 1609-1674. 941.06'2
Selections from the History of the rebellion and the Life by himself / Clarendon ; edited by G. Huehns ; with a new introd. by Hugh Trevor-Roper. Oxford ; New York : Oxford University Press, 1979 xxx, 492 p. ; 21 cm. Includes bibliographical references and index. [DA415.C48 1978] 78-40717 ISBN 0-19-215852-X : 12.95
1. Clarendon, Edward Hyde, 1st earl of, 1609-1674. 2. Great Britain—History—Civil War, 1642-1649. 3. Statesmen—England—Biography. I. Huehns, Gertrude. II. Clarendon, Edward Hyde, 1st earl of, 1609-1674. The history of the rebellion. Selections. 1978. III. Title.
BIP

Claret y Clara, Antonio Maria, Saint, Abp., 1807-1870.

ROYER, Fanchon, 1902- 922.246
Saint Anthony Claret, modern prophet and healer. New York, Farrar, Straus and Cudahy [1957] 302p. 22cm. [BX4700.C62R7] 57-11297
1. Claret y Clara, Antonio Maria, Saint, Abp., 1807-1870. I. Title.

ROYER, Fanchon, 1902- 922.246
Saint Anthony Claret, modern prophet and healer. New York, Farrar, Straus and Cudahy [1957] 302p. 22cm. [BX4700.C62R7] 57-11297
1. Claret y Clara, Antonio Maria, Saint, Abp., 1807-1870. I. Title.

Clark, Ava Milam,

CLARK, Ava Milam, 1884- 640'.924 B
Adventures of a home economist [by] Ava Milam Clark & J. Kenneth Munford. Introd. by Betty E. Hawthorne. Corvallis, Oregon State University Press [1969] xii, 432 p. illus., ports. 26 cm. Autobiography. [TX140.C5A3] 69-12558 8.00
I. Munford, James Kenneth, joint author. II. Title.

Clark, Charles Badger, 1883-1957.

MORGANTI, Helen F 928.1
The Badger Clark story. [1st ed. n. p.] c1960. 89p. illus. bIncludes bibliography. [PS3505.L245Z7] 60-44633
1. Clark, Charles Badger, 1883-1957. I. Title.

Clark, Chris, 1962-1973.

CLARK, Robert Ernest, 1925- 976'.04'0924 B
Someone glanced on me / written and compiled by Robert E. Clark, Jr. [Oklahoma City] : Clark, [1974] 29 p. ; 23 cm. [CT275.C62156C54 1974] 74-22848
1. Clark, Chris, 1962-1973. I. Title.

Clark, Clare A.

CLARK, Clare A. 133
Psychic adventures and the unseen world / [by Clare A. Clark]. St. Petersburg, Fla. : Valkyrie Press, c1977. 122 p. ; 22 cm. [BF1283.C548A36] 76-42918 ISBN 0-912760-33-8 pbk. : 3.50
1. Clark, Clare A. 2. Spiritualists—Florida—Biography. I. Title.

Clark, Columbus Andrew,

CLARK, Myrtice (Neal) 922.773
Pioneering for Christ; biography of C. A Clark. San Antonio, Naylor [c.1963] xiv, 307p. illus., ports. 22cm. 63-21192 6.95
1. Clark, Columbus Andrew, I. Title.

Clark, Edith (Martz)

CLARK, Edith (Martz) 388.3
Confessions of a girl cab driver. New York, Vantage Press [1954] 197p. 23cm. Autobiographical. [CT275.C6216A3] 54-10450
I. Title.

Clark, Edith McGill, 1882-

CLARK, Edith McGill, 1882- 266'.023'0924 B
My friends, the Chinese : a missionary in old China / Edith McGill Clark. 1st ed. New York : Vantage Press, [1974] 121 p. : ill. ; 21 cm. Autobiographical. [BV3427.C549A35] 75-316992 ISBN 0-533-01328-3 : 7.95
1. Clark, Edith McGill, 1882- 2. Missionaries—Correspondence, reminiscences, etc. 3. Missions—China. I. Title.

Clark, Edward Hardy,

CLARK, Edward Hardy, 1896- 923.373
Something doing every minute; memoirs of the professional life of Edward Clark. 1st ed.] New York, Exposition Press [1964] 291 p. 22 cm. [HG2463.C55A3] 64-56211
I. Title.

Clark, Eleanor, 1913- —Biography.

CLARK, Eleanor, 1913- 813'.5'4 B
Eyes, etc. : a memoir / by Eleanor Clark. 1st ed. New York : Pantheon Books, c1977. x, 175 p. ; 22 cm. [PS3505.L254Z52 1977] 77-76505 ISBN 0-394-41550-7 : 7.95
1. Clark, Eleanor, 1913- —Biography. 2. Authors, American—20th century—Biography. I. Title.
BIP

Clark, Eugene Lincoln, 1925-

PALMER, Bernard Alvin, 1914- 786.5'092'4 B
Nothing is impossible / Bernard Palmer. Chicago : Moody Press, c1979. 152 p., [4] leaves of plates : ill. ; 22 cm. [ML410.C608P3] 79-126810 ISBN 0-8024-5963-3 pbk. : 5.95.
1. Clark, Eugene Lincoln, 1925- 2. Composers—United States—Biography. I. Title.
BIP

Clark, Eugenie.

CLARK, Eugenie. 925.97
Lady with a spear. [1st ed.] New York, Harper, [1953] 243 p. illus. 22 cm. Autobiographical. [QL31.C56A3] 53-5362
1. Clark, Eugenie. 2. Spear fishing. 3. Fishes. I. Title.

CLARK, Eugenie. 597'.0092'4 B
Lady with a spear. [Expanded ed.] New York, Ballantine Books [1974] x, 246 p. illus. 21 cm. Autobiographical. [QL31.C56A3 1974] 74-158419 ISBN 0-345-23733-1 2.00 (pbk)
1. Clark, Eugenie. 2. Spear fishing. 3. Marine fishes. I. Title.

Clark, Ezra Thompson, 1823-1901.

TANNER, Annie Clark, 1864-1941. 289.3'3 B
A biography of Ezra Thompson Clark / by Annie Clark Tanner ; introd. by Obert C. Tanner. Salt Lake City : Tanner Trust Fund, University of Utah Library, c1975. xi, 82 p. : ill. ; 23 cm. (Utah, the Mormons, and the West ; no. 5) Includes index. [BX8695.C286T36 1975] 74-82361 8.50
1. Clark, Ezra Thompson, 1823-1901. I. Title. II. Series.

Clark family.

CLARK, Lawrence A., 1908- 929'.2'0973
The William David Clark genealogy, 1814 1972, compiled by Lawrence A. Clark Modesto, Calif. [1972?] 64 p. illus. 28 cm. [CS71.C6 1972b] 74-153554
1. Clark family. I. Title.

Clark, Galen, 1814-1910.

SARGENT, Shirley. 925.7
Galen Clark, Yosemite guardian. Foreword by Carl P. Russell. San Francisco, Sierra Club [1964] 176 p. illus., ports.22 cm. Bibliography: p. 171-173. [F868.Y6S2] 64-21730
1. Clark, Galen, 1814-1910. I. Title.

Clark, George Rogers, 1752-1818.

ALBERTS, Robert C. 973.3'3'0924
George Rogers Clark and the winning of the old Northwest / by Robert C. Alberts. Washington : National Park Service, [1976] p. cm. Bibliography: p. [E263.N84A42] 76-2594
1. Clark, George Rogers, 1752-1818. 2. Northwest, Old—History—Revolution, 1775-1783. I. Title.

BAKELESS, John Edwin, 1894- 923.973
Background to glory; the life of George Rogers Clark. [1st ed.] Philadelphia, Lippincott, 1957. 386 p. illus. 22 cm. [E207.C5B15] 56-11684
1. Clark, George Rogers, 1752-1818. 2. Northwest, Old—History—Revolution. I. Title.

DE LEEUW, Adele Louise, 1899- 92
George Rogers Clark; frontier fighter, by Adele deLeeuw. Illustrated by Russ Hoover. Champaign, Ill., Garrard Pub. Co. [1967] 80 p. col. illus. 23 cm. (A Discovery book) A biography of an Indian fighter whose foresight and leadership during the Revolutionary War saved the Northwest Territory for the United States. [E207.C5D4] AC 67
1. Clark, George Rogers, 1752-1818.

HARRISON, Lowell Hayes, 1922- 973.3'3'0924 B
George Rogers Clark and the war in the West / Lowell H. Harrison. Lexington : University Press of Kentucky, c1976. x, 119 p. : port. ; 22 cm. (The Kentucky bicentennial bookshelf) Includes bibliographical references. [E263.N84H37] 76-4431 ISBN 0-8131-0224-3 : 3.95
1. Clark, George Rogers, 1752-1818. 2. United States. Army. Continental Army—Biography. 3. Northwest, Old—History—Revolution, 1775-1783. 4. Generals—United States—Biography. I. Title. II. Series.
BIP

JAMES, James Alton, 1864-1962. 973.33'0924 B
The life of George Rogers Clark. New York, AMS Press [1970] xiii, 534 p. illus., facsim., maps, ports. 23 cm. Reprint of the 1928 ed. Bibliography: p. 516-526. [E207.C5J3 1970] 74-108769
1. Clark, George Rogers, 1752-1818. I. Title.

JAMES, James Alton, 1864-1962. 973.33'0924 B
The life of George Rogers Clark, by James Alton James. New York, Greenwood Press [1969, c1928] xiii, 534 p. illus., port. 23 cm. Bibliography: p. 516-526. [E207.C5J3 1969] 69-13950
1. Clark, George Rogers, 1752-1818. **BIP**

JAMES, James Alton, 1864-1962. 973.33'0924 B
The life of George Rogers Clark. Chicago, University of Chicago Press. St. Clair Shores, Mich., Scholarly Press, 1970 [c1928] xiii, 534 p. illus., maps, ports. 21 cm. Bibliography: p. 516-526. [E207.C5J3 1970b] 79-145107 ISBN 0-403-01044-6
1. Clark, George Rogers, 1752-1818. I. Title.

Clark, George Rogers, 1752-1818—Juvenile literature.

DE LEEUW, Adele Louise, 1899- 92 (J)
George Rogers Clark; frontier fighter, by Adele deLeeuw. Illustrated by Russ Hoover. Champaign, Ill., Garrard Pub. Co. [1967] 80 p. col. illus. 23 cm. (A Discovery book) [E207.C5D4] 67-10098
1. Clark, George Rogers, 1752-1818—Juvenile literature.

LEE, Susan. 973.3'3'0924 B
George Rogers Clark : war in the West / by Susan and John Lee ; illustrated by Richard Wahl. Chicago : Childrens Press, [1975] 47 p. : ill. (some col.) ; 24 cm. (Events of the Revolution) Follows the campaigns of Major George Rogers Clark whose small army of Virginians captured several frontier forts for the colonists during the Revolution. [E207.C5L4] 75-9798 ISBN 0-516-04676-4 lib.bdg. : 6.60
1. Clark, George Rogers, 1752-1818—Juvenile literature. 2. Northwest, Old—History—Revolution, 1775-1783—Juvenile literature. I. Lee, John, joint author. II. Wahl, Richard, 1939- III. Title.

MILLER, Helen Markley. 92 (J)
George Rogers Clark, frontier fighter. Illustrated by Albert Orbaan. New York, Putnam [1968] 95 p. col. illus., col. map. 24 cm. (American pioneer biographies) [E207.C5M5] 68-15068
1. Clark, George Rogers, 1752-1818—Juvenile literature.

Clark, Georgie White.

CLARK, Georgie White. 917.8'04'30924 B
Riverwoman : the adventures of Georgie Clark / by Georgie White Clark and Duane Newcomb. San Francisco : Chronicle Books, 1977. p. cm. Bibliography: p. [CT275.C6265A34] 77-25448 7.95
1. Clark, Georgie White. 2. The West—Biography. 3. Rafting (Sports)—The West. I. Newcomb, Duane G., joint author. II. Title.

Clark, Grenville, 1882-1967.

MEMOIRS of a man, 340'.092'4 B
Grenville Clark / collected by Mary Clark Dimond ; edited by Norman Cousins and J. Garry Clifford. 1st ed. New York : Norton, [1975] xiv, 319 p. ; 21 cm. Includes index. [KF373.C53M4] 74-20778 ISBN 0-393-08716-6 : 10.00
1. Clark, Grenville, 1882-1967. I. Clark, Grenville, 1882-1967. II. Dimond, Mary Clark. III. Cousins, Norman, ed. IV. Clifford, John Garry, ed.

Clark, Harold Willard,

CLARK, Harold Willard, 1891- 920
Skylines and detours. Washington, Review and Herald [c1959] 320p. illus. 22cm. Autobiography. [CT275.C627A3] 60-1336
I. Title.

Clark, James, 1936-1968.

GAULD, Graham. 796.7'2'0924
Jim Clark: portrait of a great driver [by] Graham Gauld in collaboration with Ian Scott Watson [and others] Foreword by Stirling Moss. New York, Arco Pub. Co. [1968] 204 p. illus. (part col.) 21 cm. [GV1032.C6G28] 68-55305 ISBN 6-680-18429- 3.95
1. Clark, James, 1936-1968. I. Watson, Ian Scott, joint author.

Clark, John Kenneth.

CLARK, John Kenneth. 286'.1'0924 B
Telling it like it was : a country preacher tells his story / by J. Kenneth Clark. Halifax, Va. : Clark, 1974. ix, 200 p. ; 24 cm. [BX6495.C552A37] 74-194714 4.95
1. Clark, John Kenneth. I. Title.

Clark, John McLane, 1910-1950.

BRADLEY, David, 1915- 920.5
Journey of a Johnny-come-lately. Hanover, N. H., Dartmouth Publications, 1957. 213p. illus. 25cm. [PN4874.C535B7] 58-307
1. Clark, John McLane, 1910-1950. I. Title.

Clark, Joshua Reuben, 1871-1961.

YARN, David H. 327'.2'0924 B
Young Reuben; the early life of J. Reuben Clark, Jr. [by] David H. Yarn, Jr. [Provo, Utah, Brigham Young University Press, 1973] x, 166 p. port. 23 cm. Bibliography: p. 161-164. [KF373.C55Y37] 73-180410 ISBN 0-8425-0356-0
1. Clark, Joshua Reuben, 1871-1961. I. Title.

Clark, Joshua Reuben, 1871-1961—Addresses, essays, lectures.

J. Reuben Clark, Jr., diplomat and statesman. 327'.2'0924 B
Ray C. Hillam, editor. Charles D. Tate, Jr., associate editor. Laura Wadley, assistant editor. Provo, Utah, Brigham Young University Press [1973] v, 236 p. group ports. 23 cm. Papers presented at a symposium held at Brigham Young University, Nov. 21-23, 1972, sponsored by the Dept. of Political Science and the Student Office of Academics of the university. "Originally published as vol. 13, no. 3, spring 1973 issue of BYU studies." Includes bibliographical references. [E748.C55J12 1973] 73-8060 ISBN 0-8425-0171-1
1. Clark, Joshua Reuben, 1871-1961—Addresses, essays, lectures. I. Hillam, Ray C., ed. II. Tate, Charles D., ed. III. Wadley, Laura, ed. IV. Brigham Young University, Provo, Utah. Dept. of Political Science. V. Brigham Young University, Provo, Utah. Student Office of Academics.

J. Reuben Clark, Jr., diplomat and statesman. 327'.2'0924 B
Ray C. Hillam, editor. Charles D. Tate, Jr., associate editor. Laura Wadley, assistant editor. Provo, Utah, Brigham Young University Press [1973] v, 236 p. group ports. 23 cm. Papers presented at a symposium held at Brigham Young University, Nov. 21-23, 1972, sponsored by the Dept. of Political Science and the Student Office of Academics of the university. "Originally published as vol. 13, no. 3, spring 1973 issue of BYU studies." Includes bibliographical references. [E748.C55J12 1973] 73-8060 ISBN 0-8425-0171-1 2.25 (pbk.)
1. Clark, Joshua Reuben, 1871-1961—Addresses, essays, lectures. I. Hillam, Ray C., ed. II. Tate, Charles D., ed. III. Wadley, Laura, ed. IV. Brigham Young University, Provo, Utah. Dept. of Political Science. V. Brigham Young University, Provo, Utah. Student Office of Academics.

Clark, Kenneth Bancroft, 1914- —Bibliography.

JENKINS, Betty. 016.301'0924
Kenneth B. Clark; a bibliography. [Compilers: Betty Jenkins, Lorna Kent and Jeanne Perry. 1st ed. New York, Metropolitan Applied Research Center, 1970] v, 69 p. 28 cm. [Z8173.9.J4] 73-267490
1. Clark, Kenneth Bancroft, 1914- —Bibliography. I. Kent, Lorna, joint author. II. Perry, Jeanne, joint uthor. III. Metropolitan Applied Research Center.

Clark, Kenneth McKenzie, Baron Clark, 1903-

CLARK, Kenneth McKenzie, Baron Clark, 1903- 709'.2'4
Another part of the wood : a self portrait / Kenneth Clark. 1st U.S. ed. New York : Harper & Row, [1975] c1974. xi, 287 p., [12] leaves of plates : ill. ; 22 cm. Autobiographical. Includes index. [N7483.C55A32 1975] 74-15816 ISBN 0-06-010783-9 : 11.00
1. Clark, Kenneth McKenzie, Baron Clark, 1903- I. Title.

CLARK, Kenneth McKenzie, Baron Clark, 1903- 709'.2'4 B
The other half : a self portrait / Kenneth Clark. 1st U.S. ed. New York : Harper & Row, c1977. xii, 259 p., [8] leaves of plates : ill. ; 22 cm. Continues the author's Another part of the wood. Includes index. [N7483.C55A33 1977b] 77-82356 ISBN 0-06-010774-X : 12.95
1. Clark, Kenneth McKenzie, Baron Clark, 1903- 2. Art historians—Great Britain—Biography. I. Title. **BIP**

CLARK, Kenneth McKenzie, Baron Clark, 1903- 709'.2'4
Another part of the wood: a self portrait [by] Kenneth Clark. New York, Ballantine Books [1976 c1974] 336 p. ill. 18 cm. Autobiographical. Includes index. [N7483.C55A32] 2.25 (pbk.)
1. Clark, Kenneth McKenzie, Baron Clark, 1903- I. Title.
L.C. card no. of 1975 Harper & Row edition: 74-15816. **BIP**

Clark, Leonard.

CLARK, Leonard. 379'.15'0924 B
The inspector remembers : diary of one of Her Majesty's Inspectors of Schools, 1936-1970 / [by] Leonard Clark. London : Dobson, 1976. 192 p. ; 23 cm. [LA2375.G72C544 1976] 77-367056 ISBN 0-234-77948-9 : £4.75
1. Clark, Leonard. 2. Educators—Great Britain—Biography. I. Title.

Clark, Randolph-Lee, 1906-

MACON, N. Don. 362.1'9'699400924 B
Clark and the Anderson : a personal profile / by N. Don Macon. Houston : Texas Medical Center, c1976. 272 p. : ill. ; 20 cm. (Texas Medical Center history series) [R154.C343M3] 76-150408
1. Clark, Randolph Lee, 1906- 2. Anderson Hospital and Tumor Institute, Houston, Tex.—History. 3. Surgeons—Texas—Biography. I. Title. II. Series: Texas Medical Center, Houston. Texas Medical Center history series.

Clark, Ransom.

CLARK, Ransom. 973'.04'97 S
Narrative of Ransom Clark. New York : Garland Pub., 1977. 16 p. : ill. ; 23 cm. (The Garland library of narratives of North American Indian captivities ; 54) Reprint of the 1839 ed. published by J. R. Orton, Binghamton, N.Y., under title: The surprising adventures of Ransom Clark. Issued with the reprint of the 1838 ed. of Plummer, C. Narrative of the captivity of Clarissa Plummer. New York, 1977. [E85.G2 vol. 54] [E83.835] 973.5'7 76-30528 lib.bdg. : 25.00
1. Clark, Ransom. 2. United States. Army—Biography. 3. Seminole War, 2d 1835-1842—Personal narratives. 4. Dade's Battle, 1835—Personal narratives. 5. Soldiers—United States—Biography. I. Title. II. Series.

Clark, Roger, 1939-

CLARK, Roger, 1939- 796.7'2'0924 B
Sideways, to victory! / [by] Roger Clark ; in collaboration with Graham Robson. Croydon : Motor Racing Publications, 1976. 256 p. : ill., ports. ; 23 cm. [GV1032.C63A37] 77-356284 ISBN 0-900549-29-7 : £4.50
1. Clark, Roger, 1939- 2. Automobile racing drivers—Great Britain—Biography. 3. Automobile rallies. I. Robson, Graham, joint author. II. Title.

Clark, William, 1770-1838.

STEFFEN, Jerome O., 1942- 917.8'04'20924 B
William Clark : Jeffersonian man on the frontier / by Jerome O. Steffen. 1st ed. Norman : University of Oklahoma Press, c1977. xii, 196 p. : ill. ; 22 cm. Includes index. Bibliography: p. 179-191. [F592.C56S74] 76-15355 ISBN 0-8061-1373-1 : 8.95
1. Clark, William, 1770-1838. 2. Indians of North America—Government relations—1789-1869. **BIP**

Clarke, Adam, 1760?-1832—Addresses, essays, lectures.

SELLERS, Ian. 230'.7'10924 B
Adam Clarke, controversialist : Wesleyanism and the historic faith in the age of Bunting / [by] Ian Sellers. [St Columb Major] : [Wesley Historical Society], [1976] [9], 21, a-h p. ; 30 cm. (Lecture - Wesley Historical Society ; 1975) Bibliography: p. [9] (1st group) [BX8495.C57S44] 77-351857 ISBN 0-900798-08-4
1. Clarke, Adam, 1760?-1832—Addresses, essays, lectures. 2. Methodists in England—Biography—Addresses, essays, lectures. I. Title. II. Series: Wesley Historical Society. The Wesley Historical Society lectures ; 1975.

Clarke, Arthur Charles, 1917-

RABKIN, Eric S. 823'.9'14
Arthur C. Clarke / Eric S. Rabkin. West Linn, Or. : Starmont House, c1979. 80 p. : port. ; 21 cm. (Starmont reader's guides to contemporary science fiction and fantasy authors ; 1) Includes index. Bibliography: p. 61-75 [PR6005.L36Z86] 79-84709 ISBN 0-916732-03-7 : 3.95
1. Clarke, Arthur Charles, 1917- 2. Authors, English—20th century—Biography. I. Title. II. Series.

Clarke, Arthur Charles, 1917- —Biography.

CLARKE, Arthur Charles, 1917- 823'.9'14
The view from Serendip / Arthur C. Clarke. 1st ed. New York : Random House, c1977. 273 p. ; 22 cm. Includes bibliographical references. [PR6005.L36Z52 1977] 77-5989 ISBN 0-394-41796-8 : 8.95
1. Clarke, Arthur Charles, 1917- —Biography. 2. Authors, English—20th century—Biography. I. Title. **BIP**

CLARKE, Arthur Charles, 1917- 823'.9'14
The view from Serendip : speculations on space, science, and the sea, together with fragments of an equatorial autobiography / Arthur C. Clarke. 1st ed. New York : Random House, c1977. p. cm. [PR6005.L36Z52 1977] 77-5740 ISBN 0-394-41796-8 : 8.95
1. Clarke, Arthur Charles, 1917- —Biography. 2. Authors, English—20th century—Biography. I. Title.

Clarke, Bobby, 1949- —Juvenile literature.

DOLAN, Edward F., 1924- 796.9'62'0924 B
Bobby Clarke / Edward F. Dolan, Jr. and Richard B. Lyttle. 1st ed. Garden City, N.Y. : Doubleday, c1977. 94 p., [12] leaves of plates : ill. ; 22 cm. A biography of the hockey player who was three times voted Most Valuable Player in the National Hockey League. [GV848.5.C58D64] 92 76-56280 ISBN 0-385-12523-2 5.95
1. Clarke, Bobby, 1949- —Juvenile literature. 2. Philadelphia Flyers (Hockey club)—Juvenile literature. 3. Hockey players—Canada—Biography—Juvenile

literature. I. Lyttle, Richard B., joint author. II. Title. **BIP**

GILBERT, John, 1942- 796.9'62'0924 B
An interview with Bobby Clarke / by John Gilbert ; photos. by Peter S. Mecca and Jack Mecca. Mankato, Minn. : Creative Education, c1977. 31 p. : col. ill. : 25 cm. (Interviews) A brief biography of the hockey player who overcame many setbacks, including diabetes, to become the star of the Philadelphia Flyers. [GV848.5.C58G54] 92 76-42272 ISBN 0-87191-573-1 lib.bdg. 5.95
1. Clarke, Bobby, 1949- —Juvenile literature. 2. Hockey players—Canada—Biography—Juvenile literature. I. Mecca, Peter S. II. Title. **BIP**

WRIGHT, James, 1950- 796.9'62'0924 B
Bobby Clarke : pride of the team / by Jim Wright. New York : Putnam, c1977. 127 p. : ill. ; 21 cm. (Putnam sports shelf) Includes index. A biography of the determined young Canadian who overcame diabetes in order to play hockey. [GV848.5.C58W74 1977] 92 76-48956 ISBN 0-399-61067-7 lib. bdg. : 5.29
1. Clarke, Bobby, 1949- —Juvenile literature. 2. Hockey players—United States—Biography—Juvenile literature. I. Title. **BIP**

Clarke, Bruce C.

ELLIS, William Donohue. 355.3'31'0924
Clarke of St. Vith; the sergeants' general [by] William Donohue Ellis and Thomas J. Cunningham, Jr. Introd. by Hal C. Pattison. Cleveland, Dillon/Liederbach [1974] xiii, 344 p. illus. 23 cm. Bibliography: p. 344. [U53.C54E38] 73-94080 ISBN 0-913228-08-7 10.00
1. Clarke, Bruce C. I. Cunningham, Thomas J., joint author. II. Title. **BIP**

Clarke, Charles Cowden, 1787-1877.

ALTICK, Richard Daniel, 1915- 822.3'3 B
The Cowden Clarkes, by Richard D. Altick. Westport, Conn., Greenwood Press [1973] xiii, 268 p. illus. 22 cm. Reprint of the 1948 ed. Includes bibliographical references. [PR4453.C7Z6 1973] 73-136895 ISBN 0-8371-5338-7 12.25
1. Clarke, Charles Cowden, 1787-1877. 2. Clarke, Mary Cowden, 1809-1898. **BIP**

Clarke, George, 1806-1835.

BOYCE, Dean. 994'.4'01
Clarke of the Kindur; convict, bushranger, explorer. [Melbourne] Melbourne University Press [1970] 100 p. illus., maps, plates. 23 cm. Stamped on t.p.: Distributed in the Western Hemisphere by International Scholarly Book Services, Zion, Ill. Bibliography: p. 95-97. [DU172.C55B6] 77-478985 4.80
1. Clarke, George, 1806-1835. 2. New South Wales—Discovery and exploration. I. Title. **BIP**

Clarke, James Freeman,

CLARKE, James Freeman, 1810-1888. 288'.0924 B
Autobiography, diary, and correspondence. Edited by Edward Everett Hale. New York, Negro Universities Press [1968, c1891] 430 p. port. 23 cm. "Writings of James Freeman Clarke": p. [416]-419. [BX9869.C6A3 1968] 68-55876
I. Title.

Clarke, John Hessin, 1857-1945.

WARNER, Hoyt Landon. 923.473
The life of Mr. Justice Clarke; a testament to the power of liberal dissent in America. Cleveland, Western Reserve University Press, 1959. ix, 232 p. port. 24 cm. Bibliography: p. 210-218. 58-13341
1. Clarke, John Hessin, 1857-1945. I. Title.

Clarke, Marcus Andrew Hislop, 1846-1881.

ELLIOTT, Brian Robinson, 1910- 823
Marcus Clarke [by] Brian Elliott. MElbourne, New York, Oxford University Press [1969] 30 p. illus. 19 cm. (Great Australians) [PR4453.C75Z67] 76-446085 0.60
1. Clarke, Marcus Andrew Hislop, 1846-1881.

Clarkson family.

CLARKSON, Francis O. 929'.2'0973
Thomas Boston Clarkson of South Carolina, his forebears and his descendants through his son William, including brief genealogies of Simons, Heriot, and Marion families of South Carolina. Compiled by Francis O. Clarkson. Charlotte, N.C., 1973. 1 v. (various pagings) 29 cm. [CS71.C612 1973] 74-151366
1. Clarkson family. I. Title.

Clarkson, Thomas, 1760-1846.

CHRISTOPHE, Henri, King of Haiti, 1767-1820. 923.17294
Henry Christophe & Thomas Clarkson, a correspondence edited by Earl Leslie Griggs and Clifford H. Prator. Berkeley, University of California Press, 1952. 287 p. illus., ports., maps, facsim. 24 cm. Bibliography: p. 281-282. [F1924.C46] 52-901
1. Haiti—Hist. I. Clarkson, Thomas, 1760-1846. II. Griggs, Earl Leslie, 1899- ed. III. Title.

CHRISTOPHE, Henri, King of Haiti, 1767-1820. 972'.94'040924
Henry Christophe & Thomas Clarkson; a correspondence, edited by Earl Leslie Griggs and Clifford H. Prator. New York, Greenwood Press, 1968 [c1952] 287 p. illus., facsim., maps, ports. 24 cm. Bibliography: p. 281-282. [F1924.C46 1968] 68-23281
1. Haiti—History. I. Clarkson, Thomas, 1760-1846. II. Griggs, Earl Leslie, 1899- ed. III. Prator, Clifford Holmes, ed. IV. Title.

GRIGGS, Earl Leslie, 1899- 322'.4'0924 B
Thomas Clarkson; the friend of slaves. Westport, Conn., Negro Universities Press [1970] 210 p. illus., ports. 23 cm. Reprint of the 1936 ed. "Bibliographies": p. [199]-204. [HT1029.C5G7 1970] 75-107476
1. Clarkson, Thomas, 1760-1846. 2. Slavery. 3. Slave-trade. **BIP**

Classical biography.

RADICE, Betty. 913'.03'0122 B
Who's who in the ancient world: a handbook to the survivors of the Greek and Roman classics; selected with an introduction by Betty Radice. London, Blond, 1971. xlvi, 225 p. illus., col. map (on lining papers). 25 cm. Bibliography: p. xlvi. [DE7.R33 1971b] 72-176196 ISBN 0-218-51263-5 12.50
1. Classical biography. I. Title.
Available from Stein & Day

RADICE, Betty. 920'.038
Who's who in the ancient world; a handbook to the survivors of the Greek and Roman classics, selected with an introduction by Betty Radice. Revised [ed.] Harmondsworth, Penguin, 1973. 336, [32] p. illus., geneal. tables, maps. 20 cm. (Penguin reference books) Includes index. Bibliography: p. 45-[46] [DE7.R33 1973] 74-161490 ISBN 0-14-051055-9
1. Classical biography. I. Title.
Distributed by Penguin, Baltimore, Md., 2.85 (pbk.).

Classical biography—Dictionaries.

RADICE, Betty. 913'.03'0922 B
Who's who in the ancient world. New York, Stein and Day [1971] xlvi, 225 p. illus., maps (on lining papers) 27 cm. Bibliography: p. xlvi. [DE7.R33 1971] 73-127027 ISBN 0-8128-1338-3 12.50
1. Classical biography—Dictionaries. I. Title. **BIP**

Claudel, Paul, 1868-1955.

CHAIGNE, Louis, 1899- 928.4
Paul Claudel: the man and the mystic. Translated from the French by Pierre de Fontnouvelle. New York, Appleton-Century-Crofts [1961] 280p. 21cm. Includes bibliography. [PQ2605.L2Z6123] 61-14364
1. Claudel, Paul, 1868-1955. I. Title.

CHAIGNE, Louis Joseph Felix, 1899- 928.4
Paul Claudel: the man and the mystic. Tr. from French by Pierre de Fontnouvelle. New York, Appleton [c.1961] 280p. Bibl. 61-14364 4.95
1. Claudel, Paul, 1868-1955. I. Title.

CLAUDEL, Paul Louis Charles Marie 1868-1955. 928.4
The correspondence, 1899-1926, between Paul Claudel and Andre Gide. Introd., notes by Robert Mallet, prefaced [from French] by John Russell. Boston, Beacon [1964, c.1962] 299p. 21cm. (BP 175) Bibl. 1.95 pap.,
I. Gide, Andre Paul Guillaume, 1869-1951. II. Title.

Claudel, Paul, 1868-1955—Biography.

CHAIGNE, Louis, 1899-1973. 848'.9'1209
Paul Claudel : the man and the mystic / by Louis Chaigne ; translated from the French by Pierre de Fontnouvelle. Westport, Conn. : Greenwood Press, 1978, c1961. 280 p. ; 23 cm. Translation of Vie de Paul Claudel. Reprint of the ed. published by Appleton-Century-Crofts, New York. Includes bibliographical references. [PQ2605.L226123 1978] 78-5951 ISBN 0-313-20465-9 lib.bdg : 19.75
1. Claudel, Paul, 1868-1955—Biography. 2. Authors, French—20th century—Biography. I. Title. **BIP**

Claudius, Emperor of Rome.10B.C.-54A.D.

MOMIGLIANO, Arnaldo 923.137
Claudius the Emperor and his achievement. Tr. by W. D. Hogarth. New bibliography, 1942-59. [New ed.] New York, Barnes & Noble [1962] 143p. 19cm. 62-53113 3.25
1. Claudius, Emperor of Rome.10B.C.-54A.D. I. Title.

Claus, Tom, 1929-

CLAUS, Tom, 1929- 269'.2'0924 B
On eagles' wings / by Tom Claus. [Orange?, CA] : Thunderbird Indian Co., c1976. 162 p. : ill. ; 22 cm. [E99.M8C53] 77-354780 3.95
1. Claus, Tom, 1929- 2. Claus family. 3. Mohawk Indians—Biography. 4. Evangelists—United States—Biography. 5. Indians of North America—Missions. I. Title.

Clausewitz, Karl von, 1780-1831.

PARET, Peter. 355'.0092'4 B
Clausewitz and the state / Peter Paret. New York : Oxford University Press, 1976. viii, 467 p. : ill. ; 24 cm. Includes indexes. Bibliography: p. [445]-459. [DD422.C5P33] 75-16901 ISBN 0-19-501988-1 : 18.95
1. Clausewitz, Karl von, 1780-1831. 2. State, The. 3. War. I. Title. **BIP**

PARKINSON, Roger. 355'.00924 B
Clausewitz, a biography. New York, Stein and Day [1971, c1970] 352 p. illus., facsim., plans, ports. 24 cm. Bibliography: p. [345]-348. [DD422.C5P34 1971] 79-150602 ISBN 0-8128-1369-3 10.00
1. Clausewitz, Karl von, 1780-1831.

Clauson, Elizabeth, 1630 or 31-1714.

MARCUS, Ronald. 345'.746'0288
"Elizabeth Clawson ... thou deseruest to dye" : an account of the trial in 1692 of a woman from Stamford, Connecticut who was accused of being a witch / by Ronald Marcus. Stamford, Conn. : Stamford Historical Society, 1976. 20 p. ; 23 cm. Includes bibliographical references. [BF1576.M35] 76-367157
1. Clauson, Elizabeth, 1630 or 31-1714. 2. Witchcraft—Stamford, Conn. I. Title.

Claver, Pedro, Saint, 1580 (ca.)-1654—Juvenile literature.

GREENE, Genard, 1921- 922.2729
Saint of the slaves forever; a story of Saint Peter Claver, S. J. Notre Dame, Ind., Dujarie Press [1959] 143p. illus. 22cm. [BX4700.C65G7] 59-65326
1. Claver, Pedro, Saint, 1580 (ca.)-1654—Juvenile literature. I. Title.

Clawson, Bertha Fidelia,

CLAWSON, Bertha Fidelia, 1868-1957. 922.652
Bertha Fidelia, her story as told to Jessie M. Trout. Illustrated by Louis LeVier. St. Louis, Bethany Press [1957] 128p. illus. 21cm. [BV3457.C5A3] 57-9777
I. Trout, Jessie M. II. Title.

Clay, Cassius Marcellus, 1810-1903.

CLAY, Cassius Marcellus, 1810-1903. 973.6'0924 B
The life of Cassius Marcellus Clay; memoirs, writings, and speeches, showing his conduct in the overthrow of American slavery, the salvation of the Union, and the restoration of the autonomy of the States. [Vol. 1] New York, Negro Universities Press [1969] xiii, 600 p. illus., ports. 23 cm. Reprint of the 1886 ed. No more published. [E415.9.C55A3 1969] 75-89028
1. U.S.—Politics and government—1849-1877. I. Title.

SMILEY, David L., 1921- 923.273
Lion of White Hall; the life of Cassius M. Clay. Madison, Univ. of Wisc. Pr. [c.]1962. 294p. illus. Bibl. 62-7215 6.00
1. Clay, Cassius Marcellus, 1810-1903. I. Title. **BIP**

SMILEY, David L 1921- 923.273
Lion of White Hall; the life of Cassius M Clay. Madison, University of Wisconsin Press, 1962. 294 p. illus.22 cm. Includes bibliography. [E415.9.C55S47] 62-7215
1. Clay, Cassius Marcellus, 1810-1903. I. Title.

SMILEY, David L., 1921- 973.6'0924 B
Lion of White Hall; the life of Cassius M. Clay [by] David L. Smiley. Gloucester, Mass., P. Smith, 1969 [c1962] ix, 294 p. illus., ports. 21 cm. Includes bibliographical references. [E415.9.C55S47 1969] 73-12393
1. Clay, Cassius Marcellus, 1810-1903. I. Title.

TOWNSEND, William Henry, 1890- 973.6'0924
The Lion of Whitehall, by William H. Townsend. Illustrated by Thornton Utz. [1st ed.] Dunwoody, Ga., N. S. Berg, 1967. 48 p. illus., ports. 20 cm. Originally delivered as an address before the Chicago Civil War Round Table, Oct. 17, 1952. [E415.9.C55T6] 67-7028
1. Clay, Cassius Marcellus, 1810-1903. I. Title.

Clay, Cassius Marcellus, 1810-1903—Addresses, essays, lectures.

TOWNSEND, William Henry, 1890-1964. 322.4'4'0924 B
The Lion of White Hall / by William H. Townsend ; illustrated by Thornton Utz. Marietta, Ga. : Larlin Corp., 1978, c1967. p. cm. Originally delivered as an address before the Chicago Civil War Round Table, Oct. 17, 1952. Reprint of the ed.

published by N. S. Berg, Dunwoody, Ga. [E415.9.C55T6 1978] 78-12420 ISBN 0-89783-004-0 : 6.00
1. Clay, Cassius Marcellus, 1810-1903—Addresses, essays, lectures. 2. Abolitionists—United States—Biography—Addresses, essays, lectures. 3. Diplomats—United States—Biography—Addresses, essays, lectures. I. Title.

Clay-Clopton, Virginia, 1825-1915.

WILEY, Bell 973.7'13'0922 B
Irvin, 1906-
Confederate women. Westport, Conn., Greenwood Press [1975] xiv, 204 p. illus. 22 cm. (Contributions in American history, no. 38) Bibliography: p. 195-198. [E467.W48] 74-5995 ISBN 0-8371-7534-8 10.95 (lib. bdg.)
1. Chesnut, Mary Boykin (Miller) 1823-1886. 2. Clay-Clopton, Virginia, 1825-1915. 3. Davis, Varina (Howell) 1826-1906. 4. Women—Confederate States of America. I. Title. BIP

Clay, Henry, 1777-1852.

CLAY, Henry, 1777- 973.6'3'0924 B
1852.
The life and speeches of the Hon. Henry Clay. Compiled and edited by Daniel Mallory. Freeport, N.Y., Books for Libraries Press [1972] p. Reprint of the 1843 ed. [E337.8.C594] 72-8481 ISBN 0-8369-6983-9
1. United States—Politics and government—1815-1861. I. Mallory, Daniel, ed.

CLAY, Henry, 1777-1852 923.273
Papers; v.3 James F. Hopkins, ed.; Mary W. M. Hargreaves, assoc. ed. [Lexington, Univ. of Ky. Pr. [c.1963] 933p. illus., ports. 25cm. Contents.v.3. Presidential Candidate, 1821-1824. 59-13605 15.00
I. Title.

CLAY, Henry, 1777-1852. 923.273
Papers, v.2. James F. Hopkins, ed.; Mary W. M. Hargreaves, assoc. ed. [Lexington] Univ. of Ky. Pr. [c.1961] 939p. col. front port. 25cm. Contents.v.2: The rising statesman, 1815-1820. 59-13605 15.00
I. Title.

CLAY, Henry, 1777- 973.6'3'0924 B
1852.
The private correspondence of Henry Clay. Edited by Calvin Colton. Freeport, N.Y., Books for Libraries Press [1971] viii, 642 p. 24 cm. Reprint of the 1855 ed. [E337.8.C598 1971] 78-169756 ISBN 0-8369-5976-0
I. Colton, Calvin, 1789-1857, ed. II. Title. BIP

COLTON, Calvin, 973.5'092'4 B
1789-1857.
The life and times of Henry Clay. With an introd. for the Garland ed. by Michael Hudson. New York, Garland Pub., 1974. 2 v. 22 cm. (The Neglected American economists, no. 9) Reprint of the 1846 ed. published by A. S. Barnes, New York. [E340.C6C74 1974] 74-10883 ISBN 0-8240-1008-6
1. Clay, Henry, 1777-1852. 2. United States—Politics and government—1815-1861. I. Title. II. Series. BIP

EATON, Clement, 1898- 923.273
Henry Clay and the art of American politics. [1st ed.] Boston, Little, Brown [1957] 209 p. 22 cm. (The Library of American biography) Includes bibliography. [E340.C6E2] 57-5825
1. Clay, Henry, 1777-1852. BIP

MAYO. BERNARD. 1902- 973.40924
Henry Cay, spokesman of the new West. [Unaltered unabridged ed. Hamden. Conn.] Archon 1966 [c.1937] 570p. illus., ports. 23cm. Bibl. [E340.C6M2 1966] 66-2518 13.00
1. Clay, Henry, 1777-1852. I. Title.

SCHURZ, Carl, 973.6'3'0924 B
1829-1906.
Henry Clay. New York, F. Ungar Pub. Co. [1968] 2 v. 21 cm. (American classics) Reprint of the 1915 ed. First published under title: Life of Henry Clay. [E340.C6S42 1968] 68-26170
1. Clay, Henry, 1777-1852. BIP

SCHURZ, Carl, 973.6'3'0924 B
1829-1906.
Henry Clay. Boston, Houghton, Mifflin. [New York, AMS Press, 1972] 2 v. illus. 19 cm. (American statesmen, v. 19-20) First published under title: Life of Henry Clay. Reprint of the 1899 ed. [E340.C6S425] 70-128965 ISBN 0-404-50891-X
1. Clay, Henry, 1777-1852. I. Title. II. Title: Life of Henry Clay. III. Series.

VAN DEUSEN, Glyndon 973.4'0924
Garlock, 1897-
Henry Clay, by Glyndon G. Van Deusen and the editors of Silver Burdett. Morristown, N. J., Silver Burdett Co. [1967] 240 p. illus. (part col.), facsims., maps, ports. (part col.) 27 cm. (Illustrious Americans) Bibliography: p. 232-234. [E340.C6V29] 66-24454
1. Clay, Henry, 1777-1852. I. Title.

VAN DEUSEN, 973.6'3'0924 B
Glyndon Garlock, 1897-
Henry Clay, by Glyndon G. Van Deusen and the editors of Silver Burdett. Morristown, N.J., Silver Burdett Co. [1967] 240 p. illus. (part col.), facsims., maps, ports. (part col.) 27 cm. (Illustrious Americans) Bibliography: p. 232-234. A three part study of the famous American statesman of the nineteenth century: a biography accompanied by brief anecdotes; a section of pictures portraying life of the period in general, and Clay's life in particular; and a compilation of excerpts from Clay's own writings. [E340.C6V29] 92 AC 68
1. Clay, Henry. 1777-1852. I. Title.

VAN DEUSEN, Glyndon 923.273
Garlock, 1897-
The life of Henry Clay, by Glyndon G. Van Deusen. Boston, Little [1963, c.1937] 448p. 20cm. (25) Bibl. 2.45 pap.,
1. Clay, Henry, 1777-1852. I. Title.

VAN DEUSEN, Glyndon 923.273
Garlock, 1897-
The life of Henry Clay [Gloucester, Mass., P. Smith, 1965, c.1937] viii, 448p. 20cm. (Little, Brown bk. rebound) [E340.C6V3] 4.50
1. Clay, Henry, 1777-1852. I. Title. BIP

VAN DEUSEN, Glyndon 973.5'092'4 B
Garlock, 1897-
The life of Henry Clay / by Glyndon G. Van Deusen. Westport, Conn. : Greenwood Press, 1979, c1937. viii, 448 p., [15] leaves of plates : ill. ; 24 cm. Reprint of the ed. published by Little Brown, Boston. Includes index. Bibliography: p. [427]-437. [E340.C6V3 1979] 78-23688 ISBN 0-313-20717-8. : 31.25
1. Clay, Henry, 1777-1852. 2. United States. Congress—Biography. 3. United States—Politics and government—1783-1865. 4. Legislators—United States—Biography. I. Title.

Clay, Henry, 1777-1852— Juvenile literature.

MOONEY, Booth, 1912- 92 (J)
Henry Clay. Illustrated by Jo Polseno. Chicago, Follett Pub. Co. [1966] 144 p. col. illus. 22 cm. (Library of American heroes) [E340.C6M817] 67-1281
1. Clay, Henry, 1777-1852—Juvenile literature.

PETERSON, Helen Stone. 92 (J)
Henry Clay; leader in Congress. Illustrated by Vic Dowd. Champaign, Ill., Garrard Pub. Co. [1964] 80 p. col. illus. 23 cm. (A Discovery book) [E340.C6P4] 64-10210
1. Clay, Henry, 1777-1852—Juvenile literature. BIP

WILKIE, Katharine 923.273
Elliott, 1904-
The man who wouldn't give up: Henry Clay. New York, J. Messner [1961] 192 p. 22 cm. Includes bibliography. [E340.C6W5] 61-6370
1. Clay, Henry, 1777-1852 — Juvenile literature. I. Title.

Clay, John Randolph, 1808-1885.

OESTE, George Irvin, 327.20924
1906-
John Randolph Clay; America's first career diplomat. Philadelphia, Univ. of Pa. Pr. [c.1966] 602p. ports. 22cm. Bibl. [E415.9.C5703] 66-10220 10.00
1. Clay, John Randolph, 1808-1885. 2. U.S.—For. rel.—1815-1861. I. Title.

Clayton, Geoffrey Hare, Abp., 1884-1957.

PATON, Alan. 283'.092'4 B
Apartheid and the archbishop: the life and times of Geoffrey Clayton, Archbishop of Cape Town. New York, Scribner [1974, c1973] xiii, 311 p. ports. 23 cm. Bibliography: p. xi-xii. [BX5700.6.Z8C556 1974] 73-17998 ISBN 0-684-13713-5 10.00
1. Clayton, Geoffrey Hare, Abp., 1884-1957. I. Title.

Clayton, Gilbert Falkingham,

CLAYTON, Gilbert 327'.2'0924
Falkingham, Sir, 1875-1929.
An Arabian diary. Introduced and edited by Robert O. Collins. Berkeley, University of California Press, 1969. xiv, 379 p. maps, ports. 24 cm. Bibliography: p. [361]-363. [DS228.G7C5] 73-83211 8.50
I. Collins, Robert O., ed. II. Title. BIP

Clayton, John, 1686-1773.

BERKELEY, Edmund 925.8
Hohn Clauton, pioneer of American botany, by Edmund Berkeley, Dorothy Smith Berkeley. Chapel Hill, Univ. of N. C. [c.1963] 236p. illus. 24cm. Bibl. 63-4274 6.00
1. Clayton, John, 1686-1773. I. Berkeley, Dorothy Smith, joint author. II. Title. III. Title: Pioneer of American botany.

BERKELEY, Edmund. 925.8
John Clayton, pioneer of American botany, by Edmund Berkeley and Dorothy Smith Berkeley. Chapel Hill, University of North Carolina [1963] 236 p. illus 24 cm. Includes bibliography. [QK31.C55B4] 63-4274
1. Clayton, John, 1686-1773. I. Berkeley, Dorothy Smith, joint author. II. Title. III. Title: Pioneer of American botany.

Clayton, Philip Thomas Byard, 1885-

HARCOURT, Melville. 922.342
The impudent dreamer; the story of Tubby Clayton... New York, Oxford University Press, 1953. 259p. illus. 23cm. [BX5199.C55H3] 53-965
1. Clayton, Philip Thomas Byard, 1885- 2. Toc H. I. Title.

Clayton, William, 1814-1879.

DAHL, Paul E v. 12
William Clayton, missionary, pioneer, and public servant. 2d ed. Boise, Idaho, 1964. 275 p. illus. 24 cm. Bibliography: p. 261-264. 67-13535
1. Clayton, William, 1814-1879. I. Title.

DAHL, Paul E 920
William Clayton, missionary, pioneer, and public servant, by Paul E. Dahl. 2d ed. Provo, Utah, Printed by J. G. Stevenson c1964. viii, 275 p. illus., facsims, ports. 25 cm. Includes 2 hymns with music. Bibliography: p. 261-264. [CT275.C6414D3 1964] 65-4853
1. Clayton, William, 1814-1879. I. Title.

Cleage, Albert B.

WARD, Hiley H. 289.9 B
Prophet of the black nation [by] Hiley H. Ward. Philadelphia, Pilgrim Press [1969] xviii, 222 p. 22 cm. Bibliographical references included in "Notes" (p. 213-222) [BX9886.Z8C57] 71-94451 5.95
1. Cleage, Albert B. I. Title.

Cleaveland, Agnes Morley, 1874-

CLEAVELAND, Agnes 978.9'04'0924 B
Morley, 1874-
No life for a lady / by Agnes Morley Cleaveland ; ill. by Edward Borein. Santa Fe : W. Gannon, 1976, c1941. ix, 356 p. : ill. ; 24 cm. Reprint of the ed. published by Houghton, Mifflin, Boston, in the Life in America series. [F801.C62 1976] 75-25302 ISBN 0-88307-519-9 : 15.00
1. Cleaveland, Agnes Morley, 1874- 2. Frontier and pioneer life—New Mexico. 3. Ranch life—New Mexico. 4. New Mexico—History. I. Title. II. Series: Life in America series.

Cleaver, Eldridge, 1935—

CLEAVER, Eldridge, 301.451'96'073
1935-
Eldridge Cleaver: post-prison writings and speeches. Edited and with an appraisal by Robert Scheer. New York, Random House [1969] xxxiii, 211 p. 22 cm. [E185.615.C63] 77-76279 5.95
1. Negroes—Addresses, essays, lectures. I. Scheer, Robert, ed.

CLEAVER, Eldridge, 1935- 248'.2 B
Soul on fire / Eldridge Cleaver. Waco, Tex. : Word Books, c1978. 240 p. : ill. ; 23 cm. [BV4935.C54A34] 77-83335 ISBN 0-8499-0046-8 : 8.95
1. Cleaver, Eldridge, 1935- 2. Converts—United States—Biography. I. Title. BIP

LOCKWOOD, Lee. 323'.2'0924 B
Conversation with Eldridge Cleaver; Algiers. [1st ed.] New York, McGraw-Hill [1970] 131 p. 21 cm. [E185.97.C6L6] 70-118010 4.95
1. Cleaver, Eldridge, 1935- I. Title.

†OLIVER, John A. 248'.2 B
Eldridge Cleaver reborn / by John A. Oliver. Plainfield, N.J. : Logos International, c1977. xiv, 284 p., [3] leaves of plates : ill. ; 28 cm. [BV4935.C54O44] 77-74797 ISBN 0-88270-233-5 pbk. : 1.95
1. Cleaver, Eldridge, 1935- 2. Converts—United States—Biography. I. Title.

Cleburne, Patrick Ronayne, 1828-1864.

MAGUIRE, John Francis, 1815- 973
1872.
The Irish in America. New York, Arno Press, 1969. xvii, 653 p. 21 cm. (The American immigration collection) Reprint of the 1868 London ed. "Biographical sketch of Major General P. R. Cleburne, by General W. T. Hardee": p. 642-653. [E184.I6M2 1969] 69-18784
1. Cleburne, Patrick Ronayne, 1828-1864. 2. Irish in the United States. 3. Irish in Canada. I. Hardee, William Joseph, 1815-1873. II. Title.

NASH, Charles 973.7'42'0924 B
Edward.
Biographical sketches of Gen. Pat Cleburne and Gen. T. C. Hindman, together with humorous anecdotes and reminiscences of the late Civil War / by Charles Edward Nash. Dayton, Ohio : Press of Morningside Bookshop, 1977. 300 p., [4] leaves of plates : ill., ports. ; 21 cm. "Facsimile 39." "Malthus theory": p. [289]-300. Reprint of the 1898 ed. printed by Tunnah & Pittard, Little Rock, Ark.; with new introd. [E496.4.C55N37 1977] 77-153871 15.00
1. Cleburne, Patrick Ronayne, 1828-1864. 2. Hindman, Thomas Carmichael, 1818-1868. 3. Confederate States of America. Army—Biography. 4. Arkansas—History—Civil War, 1861-1865. 5. Generals—Confederate States of America—Biography. I. Title: Biographical sketches of Gen. Pat Cleburne and Gen. T. C. Hindman ...

PURDUE, Howell. 973.7'42'0924 B
Pat Cleburne, Confederate general; a definitive biography, by Howell and Elizabeth Purdue. Hillsboro, Tex., Hill Jr. College Press, 1973. xv, 498 p. illus. 24

cm. Bibliography: p. 462-480. [E467.1.C58P87] 73-76245 ISBN 0-912172-18-5 10.50
1. Cleburne, Patrick Ronayne, 1828-1864. I. Purdue, Elizabeth, joint author.

Cleland family.

OLIVER, Glenn 929'.2'0973
William, 1895-
Cleland cousins; a genealogy and biographical album of Cleland and the allied families of Baker, Blair, Collins, Fisher, Gowdey, Haylett, Hume, Moody, Oliver, Richards, Ross, Wells, etc. Being the story of Samuel and Jane (Martin) Cleland and their descendants in America, with the lineage of Samuel Cleland through 200 years in County Down, Ireland, and a review of his ancestors of Lanarkshire, Scotland, to the 13th centure. Compiled by Glenn and Rebekah (Deal) Oliver. Dallas, Lithography by Lamb-Wilkerson, 1962. 143 p. illus., ports., map, col. coats of arms. 29 cm. [CS71.C623] 62-22232
1. Cleland family. 2. Baker family. I. Oliver, Rebekah (Deal) 1901- joint author II. Title.

Cleland, John, 1709-1789.

EPSTEIN, William H. 828'.6'09 B
John Cleland: images of a life, by William H. Epstein. New York, Columbia University Press, 1974. viii, 284 p. illus. 23 cm. Bibliography: p. [243]-259. [PR3348.C65Z62] 74-9798 ISBN 0-231-03725 2 9.95
1. Cleland, John, 1709-1789. I. Title.

Cleland, Thomas Maitland, 1880-1964.

ECKMAN, James Russell, 681'.62 B
1908-
Week ends with Tom Cleland [by] James Eckman. Rochester, Minn., Doomsday Press, 1971. 12 p. ports. 21 cm. 150 copies printed. First presented as the 2d lecture of the 13th series of lectures delivered at Gallery 303, New York City under the title: "Heritage of the graphic arts." [N6537.C5E3] 79-179674
1. Cleland, Thomas Maitland, 1880-1964. I. Title. II. Title: Heritage of the graphic arts.

Clem, James R,

CLEM, James R, 1872- 923.873
He bragged on their cotton, an autobiography. Illus. by Jack Patton. Dallas, B. Upshaw [1952] 152 p. illus. 21 cm. [CT275.C6422A3] 52-29348
I. Title.

Clemenceau, Georges Eugene Benjamin, 1841-1929.

BRUUN, Geoffrey 1898- 923.244
Clemenceau. Hamden, Conn., Archon [Dist. Shoe String] 1962 [c.1943] 225p. illus. 22cm. (Makers of modern Europe) Bibl. 62-4985 6.50
1. Clemenceau, Georges Eugene Benjamin, 1841-1929. 2. France—Hist.—Third Republic, 1870-1940. I. Title. **BIP**

Clemens, Jane (Lampton) 1803-1890.

VARBLE, Rachel (McBrayer) 920.7
Jane Clemens; the story of Mark Twain' mother. Garden City, N. Y., Doubleday [c.]1964. 374p. illus., facsim., ports. 25cm. Bibl. 64-19286 5.95
1. Clemens, Jane (Lampton) 1803-1890. I. Title. II. Title: The story of Mark Twain's mother.

VARBLE, Rachel (McBrayer) 920.7
Jane Clemens; the story of Mark Twain's mother, by Rachel M. Varble. [1st ed.] Garden City, N.Y., Doubleday, 1964. 374 p. illus., facsim., ports. 25 cm. Illustrative matter on lining papers. Bibliography: p. 358-362. [PS1332.V3] 64-19286
1. Clemens, Jane (Lampton) 1803-1890. I. Title. II. Title: The story of Mark Twain's mother.

Clemens, Marie Louise,

CLEMENS, Marie Louise, 920.7
1863-
Autobiography. Boston, Bruce Humphries [c1953] 316p. illus. 22cm. [CT275.C6426A3] 53-13082
I. Title.

Clemens, Olivia (Langdon) 1845-1904 — Juvenile literature.

STOUTENBURG, Adrien. 920.7
Dear, dear Livy; the story of Mark Twain's wife, by Adrien Stoutenburg and Laura Nelson Baker. New York, Scribner [1963] 192 p. 21 cm. Includes bibliography. [PS1332.S8] 63-8618
1. Clemens, Olivia (Langdon) 1845-1904 — Juvenile literature. 2. Clemens, Samuel Langhorne, 1835-1910 — Juvenile literature. I. Baker, Laura Nelson, 1911- joint author. II. Title.

STOUTENBURG, Adrien. 920.7
Dear, dear Livy; the story of Mark Twain's wife, by Adrien Stoutenburg and Laura Nelson Baker. New York, Scribner [1963] 192 p. 21 cm. Includes bibliography. [PS1332.S8] 63-8618
1. Clemens, Olivia Langdon, 1845-1904—Juvenile literature. 2. Clemens, Samuel Langhorne, 1835-1910—Juvenile literature. I. Baker, Laura Nelson, 1911- joint author. II. Title.

Clemens, Samuel Langhorne, 1835-1910.

ALLEN, Jerry, 1911- 928.1
The adventures of Mark Twain. [1st ed.] Boston, Little, Brown [1954] 359 p. illus. 21 cm. [PS1331.A7 1954] 54-6873
1. Clemens, Samuel Langhorne, 1835-1910. I. Title. **BIP**

ANDREWS, Kenneth Richmond, 928.1
1916-
Nook Farm, Mark Twain's Hartford circle. Cambridge, Harvard University Press, 1950. xii, 288 p. illus., ports. 25 cm. Bibliography: p. [271]-280. [PS1334.A6] 50-9751
1. Clemens, Samuel Langhorne, 1835-1910. 2. Hartford. **BIP**

BENSON, Ivan, 1896- 817.4
Mark Twain's western years, together with hitherto unreprinted Clemens western items. New York, Russell & Russell, 1966 [c1965] x, 218 p. illus., ports. 23 cm. Bibliography: p. 161-164. "Periodical bibliography: bibliography of the writings of Mark Twain in the newspapers and magazines of Nevada and California, 1861-1866": p. 165-174. [PS1332.B4 1966] 66-24668
1. Clemens, Samuel Langhorne, 1835-1910. 2. Clemens, Samuel Langhorne, 1835-1910—Bibliography. I. Title.

BRASHEAR, Millie May 928.1
Mark Twain, son of Missouri. New York, Russell & Russell, 1964[c.1934] xvi,294p. illus., maps, facsims. 23cm. Bibl. 64-10708 7.50
1. Clemens, Samuel Langhorne, 1835-1910. I. Title. **BIP**

BRASHEAR, Minnie May. 928.1
Mark Twain, son of Missouri. New York, Russell & Russell, 1964 [c1934] xvi, 294 p. illus., maps, facsims. 23 cm. Bibliography: p. 264-284. [PS1331.B67] 64-10708
1. Clemens, Samuel Langhorne, 1835-1910. I. Title.

BROOKS, Van Wyck, 1886- 928.1
The ordeal of Mark Twain. Introd. by Malcolm Cowley. New York, Meridian Books, 1955 [c1948] 256p. 18cm. (Meridian books, M14) [PS1331] 55-9699
1. Clemens, Samuel Langhorne, I. Title.

CANBY, Henry Seidel, 1878- 928.1
1961.
Turn west, turn east: Mark Twain and Henry James. Boston, Houghton Mifflin, 1951. xii, 318 p. ports. (on lining papers) 22 cm. Bibliography: p. 301-303. [PS1331.C25] 51-14000
1. Clemens, Samuel Langhorne, 1835-1910. 2. James, Henry, 1843-1916. I. Title.

CARDWELL, Guy Adams, 1905- 928.1
Twins of genius. [East Lansing] Michigan State College Press, 1953. iii, 134 p. groupt port. 23 cm. "Letters [of Mark Twain, George W. Cable, and others]": p. [79]-112. Bibliographical references included in "Footnotes" (p. [113]-128) [PS1333.C3] 53-12009
1. Clemens, Samuel Langhorne, 1835-1910. 2. Cable, George Washington, 1844-1925. I. Title.

CLEMENS, Cyril, 1902- 928.1
Mark Twain for young people. With an introd. by James Hilton. New York, Whittier Books [1953] 159p. 22cm. [PS1331.C454] 53-11923
1. Clemens, Samuel Langhorne, 1835-1910. I. Title.

[CLEMENS, Samuel Langhorne] 928.1
1835-1910
The autobiography of Mark Twain [pseud.] Introd., notes, special essay by Charles Neider. New York, Washington Sq. Pr. [1961,c.1917-1960] xxv, 446p. illus. (W-1075) .90 pap.,
I. Title.

CLEMENS, Samuel Langhorne, 928.1
1835-1910.
The autobiography of Mark Twain [pseud.] including chapters now published for the first time, as arr. and edited, with an introd. and notes, by Charles Neider. New York, Harper [1959] 388 p. illus. 25 cm. [PS1331.A2 1959] 59-6005

CLEMENS, Samuel 818'.4'03
Langhorne, 1835-1910.
Mark Twain's notebook Prepared for publication with comments by Albert Bigelow Paine. New York, Cooper Square Publishers, 1972 [c1935] xi, 413 p. illus. 24 cm. [PS1331.A4 1972] 72-77127 ISBN 0-8154-0418-2 12.00
1. Clemens, Samuel Langhorne, 1835-1910. I. Title. **BIP**

CLEMENS, William 818'.4'09 B
Montgomery, 1860-1931.
Mark Twain : his life and work : a biographical sketch / by Will M. Clemens. Folcroft, Pa. : Folcroft Library Editions, 1975. 213 p. : port. ; 23 cm. Reprint of the 1894 ed. published by F. T. Neely, Chicago. [PS1331.C5 1975] 75-11841 ISBN 0-8414-3643-6 lib. bdg. : 20.00
1. Clemens, Samuel Langhorne, 1835-1910. I. Title.

CLEMENS, William 818'.4'09 B
Montgomery, 1860-1931.
Mark Twain, his life and work; a biographical sketch. [Folcroft, Pa.] Folcroft Press [1969, c1894] 213 p. port. 19 cm. [PS1331.C5 1969] 72-195252
1. Clemens, Samuel Langhorne, 1835-1910.

DE VOTO, Bernard 818'.4'09
Augustine, 1897-1955.
Mark Twain's America / by Bernard DeVoto. Westport, Conn. : Greenwood Press, 1979, c1932. xviii, 351 p. : ill. ; 23 cm. Reprinted from the 1967 ed. published by Houghton Mifflin, Boston, under title: Mark Twain's America, and Mark Twain at work. Includes index. Bibliography: p. [323]-334. [PS1331.D4 1978] 78-4109 ISBN 0-313-20368-7 lib. bdg. : 21.00
1. Clemens, Samuel Langhorne, 1835-1910. 2. Clemens, Samuel Langhorne, 1835-1910—Contemporary United States. 3. Authors, American—19th century—Biography. I. Title. **BIP**

EATON, Jeanette. 928.1
America's own Mark Twain. Illustrated by Leonard Everett Fisher. New York, Morrow, 1958. 251 p. illus. 22 cm. [Morrow junior books] [PS1331.E2] 58-9098
1. Clemens, Samuel Langhorne, 1835-1910. I. Title.

FERGUSON, John De Lancey, 928.1
1888-
Mark Twain: man and le gend. bobbs [dist. New York, Macfadden, 1963, c.1943] 352p. 21cm. (Charter bk. 129) 1.95 pap.,
1. Clemens, Samuel Langhorne, 1835-1910. I. Title.

FERGUSON, John De Lancey, v. 12
1888-
Mark Twain, man and legend. [New york] Charter Books [c1943, 1963] 352 p. 21 cm. Bibliography: p. 333-337. 64-30363
1. Clemens, Samuel Langhorne, 1835-1910. I. Title.

FERGUSON, John De 817.4(B)
Lancey, 1888-
Mark Twain, man and legend, by De Lancey Ferguson. New York, Russell & Russell, 1965 [i.e.1966, c1943] 352p. ports. 23cm. [PS1331.F4 1966] 66-15430 8.00
1. Clemens, Samuel Langhorne, 1835-1910. I. Title.

FERGUSON, John DeLancey, v. 12
1888-
Mark Twain: man and legend [by] DeLancey Ferguson. [Charter ed. Indianapolis, Bobbs-Merrill, 1963] 352 p. 21 cm. (Charter books) Reprint, without the illus., of the 1943 Bobbs-Merrill hardcover ed. Bibliography: p. 333-337. 67-81680
1. Clemens, Samuel Langhorne, 1835-1910. I. Title.

FONER, Philip Sheldon, 928.1
1910-
Mark Twain: social critic. New York, Intl. Pubs. 335p. 21cm. (New World bks., NW-9) Bibl. 1.85 pap.,
1. Clemens, Samuel Langhorne, 1835-1910. I. Title. **BIP**

FULLER, Edmund Maybank, 920.073
1914- ed.
4 American biographies [by] Edmund Fuller, O. B. Davis. New York, Harcourt, [c.1961] 779p. illus. (Adventures in good bks.) 61-19640 3.75
1. Lincoln, Abraham, Pres. U. S., 1809-1865. 2. Holmes, Oliver Wendell, 1841-1935. 3. Clemens, Samuel Langhorne, 1835-1910. 4. Keller, Helen Adams, 1880- I. Davis, O. B., joint ed. II. Title.
Content omitted.

GEISMAR, Maxwell David, 817'.4
1909-
Mark Twain: an American prophet [by] Maxwell Geismar. Boston, Houghton Mifflin, 1970. 564 p. 24 cm. [PS1331.G4] 71-108681 10.00
1. Clemens, Samuel Langhorne, 1835-1910. I. Title.

GRANT, Douglas 818.4
Mark Twain. New York, Grove [1963, c.1962] 120p. 19cm. (Evergreen pilot bks.) Bibl. 62-12936 .95 pap.,
1. Clemens, Samuel Langhorne, 1835-1910. I. Title.

GRANT, Douglas 818.4
Mark Twain [Gloucester, Mass., P. Smith, 1963, c.1962] 117p. 18cm. (Evergreen pilot bk. rebound) Bibl. 3.00
1. Clemens, Samuel Langhorne, 1835-1910. I. Title.

HARNSBERGER, Caroline 928.1
Thomas, 1902-
Mark Twain, family man. [1st ed.] New York, Citadel Press [1960] 296 p. illus. 22 cm. Includes bibliography. [PS1331.H3] 60-9379
1. Clemens, Samuel Langhorne, 1835-1910.

HENDERSON, Archibald, 818'.4'09
1877-1963.
Mark Twain. With photos. by Alvin Langdon Coburn. Folcroft, Pa., Folcroft Press [1969] xiii, 230 p. illus. 23 cm. Reprint of the 1912 ed. Bibliography: p. 215-230. [PS1331.H4 1969] 72-190934
1. Clemens, Samuel Langhorne, 1835-1910.

HILL, Hamlin Lewis, 818'.4'09 B
1931-
Mark Twain; God's fool, by Hamlin Hill. New York, Harper & Row [1975 c1973] xxviii, 308 p. illus. 21 cm. (Colophon books) Includes bibliographical references [PS1332.H5] ISBN 0-06-090391-0 3.95 (pbk.)
1. Clemens, Samuel Langhorne, 1835-1910 I. Title.
L.C. card no. for original ed.: 72-9754 **BIP**

HILL, Hamlin Lewis, 818'.4'09 B
1931-
Mark Twain; God's fool, by Hamlin Hill. New York, Harper & Row [1975 c1973] xxviii, 308 p. illus. 21 cm. (Colophon books) Includes bibliographical references [PS1332.H5] ISBN 0-06-090391-0 3.95 (pbk.)

1. Clemens, Samuel Langhorne, 1835-1910 I. Title.
L.C. card no. for original ed.: 72-9754 BIP

HILL, Hamlin Lewis, 1931- 928.1
Mark Twain and Elisha Bliss. Columbia, Univ. of Mo. Pr. [c.1964] xi, 214p. mounted port. 23cm. Bibl. 64-17646 5.95
1. Clemens, Samuel Langshorne, 1835-1910. 2. Bliss, Elisha, 1822-1880. 3. American Publishing Company, Hartford. I. Title.

HILL, Hamlin Lewis, 1931- 928.1
Mark Twain and Elisha Bliss, by Hamilin Hill. Columbia, University of Missouri Press [1964] xi, 214 p. mounted port. 23 cm. "A bibliography of American Publishing Company books": p. 183-186. Bibliographical references included in "Notes" (p. 187-206) [PS1334.H5] 64-17646
1. "An earlier version of this study was submitted as a doctoral dissertation at the University of Chicago in 1959." 2. Clemens, Samuel Langhorne, 1835-1910. 3. Bliss, Elisha, 1822-1880. 4. American Publishing Company, Hartford. I. Title.

HILL, Hamlin Lewis, 818'.4'09 B 1931-
Mark Twain. God's fool, by Hamlin Hill. [1st ed.] New York, Harper & Row [1973] xxviii, 308 p. illus. 25 cm. Includes bibliographical references. [PS1332.H5] 72-9754 ISBN 0-06-011893-8 10.00
1. Clemens, Samuel Langhorne, 1835-1910. I. Title.

HOWELLS, William 818'.4'09 B Dean, 1837-1920.
My Mark Twain : reminiscences and criticisms / by W. D. Howells. Brooklyn : Haskell House, 1977. 186 p. ; 21 cm. Reprint of the 1910 ed. published by Harper, New York. [PS1331.H6 1977] 76-53025 ISBN 0-8383-2176-3 lib. bdg. : 11.95
1. Clemens, Samuel Langhorne, 1835-1910. 2. Authors, American—19th century—Biography. I. Title. BIP

KAPLAN, Justin. 818'.4'09
Mark Twain and his world / Justin Kaplan. New York : Simon and Schuster, [1974] 224 p., [16] leaves of plates : ill. ; 26 cm. Includes bibliographical references and index. [PS1331.K325 1974] 72-87659 ISBN 0-671-21462-4 : 19.95
1. Clemens, Samuel Langhorne, 1835-1910. 2. United States—Civilization—19th century. I. Title.

KAPLAN, Justin. 817'.4
Mr. Clemens and Mark Twain, a biography. New York, Pocket Bks. [1968,c.1967] 512p. illus., ports. 18cm. (12507) Bibl. [PS1331.K33] 1.25 pap.,
1. Clemens, Samuel Langhorne, 1835-1910. I. Title.

KAPLAN, Justin. 817.4 B
Mr. Clemens and Mark Twain, a biography. New York, Simon and Schuster [1966] 424 p. illus., ports. 24 cm. Bibliographical references included in "Notes" (p. 389-410) [PS1331.K33] 66-17603
1. Clemens, Samuel Langhorne, 1835-1910. I. Title.

LEACOCK, Stephen 818'.4'09 B Butler, 1869-1944.
Mark Twain. New York, Haskell House, 1974. 167 p. port. 20 cm. Reprint of the 1932 ed. published by P. Davies, London. Bibliography: p. 161. [PS1331.L4 1974] 73-21633 ISBN 0-8383-1789-8 11.95
1. Clemens, Samuel Langhorne, 1835-1910. I. Title.

LEARY, Katy. 818'.4'09 B
A lifetime with Mark Twain; the memories of Katy Leary, for thirty years his faithful and devoted servant. Written by Mary Lawton. New York, Haskell House Publishers, 1972 [i.e. 1973] xviii, 352 p. illus. 23 cm. Reprint of the 1925 ed. published by Harcourt, Brace, New York. [PS1331.L415 1972] 72-3627 ISBN 0-8383-1562-3 15.95
1. Clemens, Samuel Langhorne, 1835-1910. I. Lawton, Mary. II. Title.

MACNAUGHTON, William 818'.4'09 B R., 1939-
Mark Twain's last years as a writer / William R. Macnaughton. Columbia : University of Missouri Press, 1979. x, 254 p. ; 23 cm. Includes index. Bibliography: p. 243-247. [PS1332.M34] 78-19846 ISBN 0-8262-0264-0 : 16.50
1. Clemens, Samuel Langhorne, 1835-1910. 2. Clemens, Samuel Langhorne, 1835-1910—Biography—Last years and death. 3. Authors, American—19th century—Biography. I. Title. BIP

MASTERS, Edgar Lee, 817.4 (B) 1869-1950
Mark Twain; a portrait. New York, Biblo & Tannen. 1966[c.1938] 259p. port. 22cm. [PS1331.M3 1966] 66-15216 price unreported.
1. Clemens, Samuel Langhorne, 1835-1910. I. Title. BIP

PEARE, Catherine 818'.4'09 B Owens.
Mark Twain, his life; illustrated by Margaret Ayer. [1st ed.] New York, Holt [1954] 116 p. illus. 21 cm. A biography of Samuel Clemens which traces not only the childhood which so greatly influenced his writing, but also his marriage and family life, his travels, and his career as a famous author. [PS1331.P45] 92 AC 68
1. Clemens, Samuel Langhorne, 1835-1910. I. Ayer, Margaret, illus. II. Title.

RAMSAY, Robert Lee, 1880- 817.4 1953
A Mark Twain lexicon, by Robert L. Ramsay, Frances G. Emberson. New York, Russell, 1963. xix, 278p. 27cm. Bibl. 63-9325 10.00
1. Clemens, Samuel Langhorne, 1835-1910—Dictionaries, indexes, etc. 2. Americanisms. I. Emberson, Frances Guthrie, 1912- joint author. II. Title.

SANDERLIN, George 818'.4'09 B William, 1915-
Mark Twain : as others saw him / by George Sanderlin. New York : Coward, McCann & Geoghegan, c1978. 173 p. : ill. ; 21 cm. Includes index. Bibliography: 169-170. A portrait of Mark Twain, including an examination of his opinions on a wide variety of topics and a compilation of comments about Twain by people from his time to the present. [PS1331.S18] 92 77-18273 ISBN 0-698-30686-4 lib.bdg. : 5.89
1. Clemens, Samuel Langhorne, 1835-1910. 2. Authors, American—19th century—Biography. I. Title. BIP

SEELYE, John D. 818'.4'09 B
Mark Twain in the movies : a meditation with pictures / by John Seelye. New York : Viking Press, [1977] p. cm. [PS1331.S37] 77-21472 ISBN 0-670-45830-9 : 10.00
1. Clemens, Samuel Langhorne, 1835-1910. 2. Clemens, Samuel Langhorne, 1835-1910—Portraits, etc. 3. Authors, American—19th century—Biography. 4. Authors, American—19th century—Portraits. I. Title. BIP

SELBY, Paul Owen, 1890- 817'.4 B
A chronology of the life of Mark Twain, by P. O. Selby. Kirksville, Missouriana Library, Northeast Missouri State College, 1969. 67 l. 28 cm. Cover title. Bibliography: leaf 67. [PS1331.S4] 71-10831
1. Clemens, Samuel Langhorne, 1835-1910. I. Title.

STEARNS, Monroe. 928.1
Mark Twain. New York, F. Watts [1965] 186 p. port. 22 cm. (Immortals of literature) Bibliography: p. 181-182. [PS1331.S74] 65-13679
1. Clemens, Samuel Langhorne, 1835-1910. I. Title.

WAGENKNECHT, Edward 928.1 Charles, 1900-
Mark Twain, the man and his work. New and rev. ed. Norman, University of Oklahoma Press [1961] xiii, 272 p. port. 24 cm. Bibliography: p. 247-264. [PS1331.W3 1961] 61-6501
1. Clemens, Samuel Langhorne, 1835-1910. BIP

WECTER, Dixon, 1906-1950. 928.1
Sam Clemens of Hannibal. Boston, Houghton Mifflin, 1952. ix, 335 p. port. 22 cm. Bibliography: p. 317-322. [PS1332.W4] 52-5258
1. Clemens, Samuel Langhorne, 1835-1910. BIP

WOOD, James Playsted, 818'.4'09 B 1905-
Spunkwater, spunkwater! A life of Mark Twain. [New York] Pantheon Books [1968] 182 p. illus., ports. 22 cm. ([A Pantheon portrait]) Bibliography: p. 181-182. Chronicles the adventurous life of one of America's greatest humorists as he lived on the gold fields, the river, and the West Coast and as he travelled, lectured, and wrote in his middle and late years. [PS1331.W6] 92 AC 68
1. Clemens, Samuel Langhorne, 1835-1910. I. Title.

Clemens, Samuel Langhorne, 1835-1910—Appreciation—England.

WELLAND, Dennis Sydney 818'.4'09 Reginald.
Mark Twain in England / by Dennis Welland. Atlantic Highlands, N.J. : Humanities Press, c1978. 267 p., [1] leaf of plates : ports. ; 23 cm. Errata slip inserted. Includes bibliographical references and index. [PS1333.W4 1978] 77-17348 ISBN 0-391-00553-7 : 10.00
1. Clemens, Samuel Langhorne, 1835-1910—Appreciation—England. 2. Authors and publishers—England. 3. Authors, American—19th century—Biography. I. Title. BIP

Clemens, Samuel Langhorne, 1835-1910—Biography.

CLEMENS, Clara. 818'.4'09 B
My father, Mark Twain / by Clara Clemens ; illustrated from family photos. with hitherto unpublished letters of Mark Twain. New York : AMS Press, [1976] p. cm. Reprint of the 1931 ed. published by Harper, New York. [PS1331.C4 1976] 74-6024 ISBN 0-404-11544-6 : 15.00
1. Clemens, Samuel Langhorne, 1835-1910—Biography. I. Title. BIP

CLEMENS, Cyril, 1902- 810'.9
My cousin Mark Twain. With an introd. by Booth Tarkington. [Folcroft, Pa.] Folcroft Press [1969, c1939] 215 p. illus. 23 cm. [PS1331.C47 1969] 74-170391
1. Clemens, Samuel Langhorne, 1835-1910—Biography. I. Title. BIP

CLEMENS, Cyril, 1902- 818'.4'09 B
My cousin Mark Twain. With an introd. by Booth Tarkington. New York, Haskell House Publishers, 1974. xi, 219 p. ; 22 cm. Reprint of the 1939 ed. published by Rodale Press, Emmaus, Pa. "Principal books of Mark Twain with date of publication:" p. 216. [PS1331.C47 1974b] 74-16297 ISBN 0-8383-1744-8
1. Clemens, Samuel Langhorne, 1835-1910—Biography. I. Title.

CLEMENS, Cyril, 1902- 818'.4'09 B
My cousin Mark Twain. With an introd. by Booth Tarkington. [Folcroft, Pa.] Folcroft Library Editions, 1974 [c1939] p. cm. Reprint of the ed. published by Rodale Press, Emmaus, Pa. "Principal books of Mark Twain with date of publication": p. [PS1331.C47 1974] 74-10995 ISBN 0-8414-3601-0 (lib. bdg.)
1. Clemens, Samuel Langhorne, 1835-1910—Biography. I. Title.

HASSLER, Kenneth 818'.4'03 B Wayne.
Mark Twain, dean of American humorists / by Kenneth Hassler ; compiled with the assistance of the research staff of the SamHar Press. Charlotteville, N.Y. : SamHar Press, 1975. p. cm. (Outstanding personalities ; no. 82) Bibliography: p. [PS1331.H38] 75-16279 lib.bdg. : 2.29 pbk. : 0.98
1. Clemens, Samuel Langhorne, 1835-1910—Biography. BIP

MELTZER, Milton, 1915- 928.1
Mark Twain himself; a pictorial biography produced by Milton Meltzer. New York, Bonanza [1960] xii, 303 p. illus., ports., maps, facsims. 29 cm. "Picture sources": p. 295-297. [PS1331.M38] 60-11545
1. Clemens, Samuel Langhorne, 1835-1910—Biography. I. Title.

Clemens, Samuel Langhorne, 1835-1910—Biography—Character.

PELLOWE, William 818'.4'09 B Charles Smithson, 1890-
Mark Twain, pilgrim from Hannibal / by William C. S. Pellowe. Folcroft, Pa. : Folcroft Library Editions, 1975, c1945. p. cm. Reprint of the ed. published by Hobson Book Press, New York. Includes index. Bibliography: p. [PS1331.P5 1975] 75-28485 ISBN 0-8414-6743-9 lib. bdg. : 30.00
1. Clemens, Samuel Langhorne, 1835-1910—Biography—Character. 2. Clemens, Samuel Langhorne, 1835-1910—Religion and ethics. I. Title. BIP

Clemens, Samuel Langhorne, 1835-1910—Biography—Juvenile literature.

BENSON, Ginny, 1923- 818'.4'09 B
Mark Twain; in his footsteps. Illustrated by Harold Henriksen. Mankato, Minn., Creative Education; [distributed by Childrens Press, Chicago, 1974] 36 p. col. illus. 25 cm. (Creative Education close-ups) A brief biography of the well-known nineteenth-century author of "Tom Sawyer" and "Huckleberry Finn." [PS1331.B4] 92 74-2105 ISBN 0-87191-325-9 4.95 (lib. bdg.).
1. Clemens, Samuel Langhorne, 1835-1910—Biography—Juvenile literature. I. Henriksen, Harold, illus. II. Title.

MCKOWN, Robin. 818'.4'03 B
Mark Twain: novelist, humorist, satirist, grassroots historian, and America's unpaid goodwill ambassador at large. New York, McGraw-Hill [1974] 160 p. port. 21 cm. Bibliography: p. 155-156. A biography stressing the wide range of literary achievements of the author considered by many to be America's greatest writer. [PS1331.M24] 92 74-9583 4.72 (lib. bdg.).
1. Clemens, Samuel Langhorne, 1835-1910—Biography—Juvenile literature. I. Title.

MCNEER, May Yonge, 1902- 92
America's Mark Twain. With illus. by Lynd Ward. Boston, Houghton Mifflin, 1962. 159p. 25cm. [PS1331.M25] 60-9097
1. Clemens, Samuel Langhorne, 1835-1910—Juvenile literature. I. Title.

NORTH, Sterling, 1906- 928.1
Mark Twain and the river. Illustrated by Victor Mays. Boston. Houghton Mifflin, 1961. 184p. illus. 22cm. (North star books [24]) [PS1331.N6] 61-5138
1. Clemens, Samuel Langhorne, 1835-1910—Juvenile literature. I. Title.

Clemens, Samuel Langhorne, 1835-1910—Biography—Youth.

CLEMENS, Cyril, 1902- 818'.4'09 B
Young Sam Clemens / by Cyril Clemens ; foreword by Hendrik Willem Van Loon and introd. by Grant Wood. Folcroft, Pa. : Folcroft Library Editions, 1977, c1942 282 p., 5 leaves of plates : ill. ; 23 cm. Reprint of the 1st ed. published by L. Tebbetts Editions, Portland, Me. Includes index. [PS1332.C5 1976] 76-49929 ISBN 0-8414-3473-5 lib. bdg. : 30.00
1. Clemens, Samuel Langhorne, 1835-1910—Biography—Youth. 2. Authors, American—19th century—Biography. I. Title. BIP

WECTER, Dixon, 1906- 818'.4'09 B 1950.
Sam Clemens of Hannibal / by Dixon Wecter. New York : AMS Press, 1979. ix, 335 p. : port. ; 22 cm. Reprint of the 1952 ed. published by Riverside Press, Cambridge, and by Houghton Mifflin, Boston. Includes index. Bibliography: p. 317-322. [PS1332.W4 1979] 76-6595 ISBN 0-404-15328-3 : 27.00
1. Clemens, Samuel Langhorne, 1835-1910—Biography—Youth. 2. Authors, American—19th century—Biography. I. Title.

Clemens, Samuel Langhorne, 1835-1910—Biography—Youth—Juvenile literature.

CLEMENS, Samuel Langhorne, 1835-1910. 818'.4'09 B
The boys' ambition : [from] Life on the Mississippi / by Mark Twain [i.e. S. L. Clemens] ; pictures by George Overlie. Minneapolis : Lerner Publications Co., 1975. [32] p. : ill. (some col.) ; 20 cm. (A Seedling book) Mark Twain relates the boyhood experiences on the Mississippi that led to his ambition to be a river-boat pilot. [PS1314.A35 1975] 92 72-12489 ISBN 0-8225-0283-6 lib.bdg. : 3.95
1. Clemens, Samuel Langhorne, 1835-1910—Biography—Youth—Juvenile literature. 2. Mississippi River—Description and travel. I. Overlie, George. II. Title.

Clemens, Samuel Langhorne, 1835-1910—Correspondence.

CLEMENS, Samuel Langhorne, 1835-1910. 818'.4'09 B
The love letters of Mark Twain / edited and with an introd. by Dixon Wecter. Westport, Conn. : Greenwood Press, 1976 [c1949] p. cm. Letters to Olivia Langdon Clemens written between 1868 and 1904. Reprint of the 1st ed. published by Harper, New York. [PS1331.A44 1976] 76-20557 ISBN 0-8371-8995-0 lib.bdg. : 19.75
1. Clemens, Samuel Langhorne, 1835-1910—Correspondence. 2. Clemens, Olivia Langdon, 1845-1904. I. Clemens, Olivia Langdon, 1845-1904. II. Title. BIP

†CLEMENS, Samuel Langhorne, 1835-1910. 818'.4'09
Mark Twain's letters to Will Bowen : "my first, & oldest & dearest friend". Folcroft, Pa. : Folcroft Library Editions, 1976. 34 p., [1] leaf of plates : ill. ; 26 cm. Reprint of the 1941 ed. published by the University of Texas, Austin. Includes bibliographical references. [PS1331.A43 1976] 76-28963 ISBN 0-8414-8618-2 lib. bdg. : 8.50
1. Clemens, Samuel Langhorne, 1835-1910—Correspondence. 2. Bowen, William, 1836-1893. 3. Authors, American—19th century—Correspondence. I. Bowen, William, 1836-1893. II. Title.

Clemens, Samuel Langhorne, 1835-1910—Friends and Associates.

DUCKETT, Margaret. 928.1
Mark Twain and Bret Harte. Norman, University of Oklahoma Press [1964] xiii, 365 p. illus., ports. 23 cm. Bibliography: p. 345-353. [PS1333.D8] 64-21709
1. Clemens, Samuel Langhorne, 1835-1910—Friends and Associates. 2. Harte, Bret, 1836-1902. I. Title. BIP

SELBY, Paul Owen, 1890- 817'.4
116 short biographies of persons associated with Mark Twain; condensed biographical sketches of the close relatives and other persons associated with Samual L. Clemens (Mark Twain), women are mostly alphabetized by their maiden names [by P. O Selby. Kirksville, Missouriana Library, 1970. 18 l. 28 cm. [PS1333.S4] 79-630719
1. Clemens, Samuel Langhorn, 1835-1910—Friends and associates. I. Pickler Memorial Library. II. Title.

Clemens, Samuel Langhorne, 1835-1910—Juvenile literature.

DAUGHERTY, Charles Michael. 817'.4 B
Samuel Clemens. Illustrated by Kurt Werth. New York, Crowell [1970] 41 p. illus. (part col.) 24 cm. (A Crowell biography) An easy-to-read biography of the American author whose writings greatly reflected the events in his life. [PS1331.D3] 92 70-113853 3.75
1. Clemens, Samuel Langhorne, 1835-1910—Juvenile literature. I. Werth, Kurt, illus. II. Title.

GORDON, Edwin, 1925- 817.4 (B)
Mark Twain. New York, Crowell-Collier [1966] 149p. illus., ports. 22cm. (America in the making) [PS1331.G6] 66-7515 2.95;3.24 lib ed.,
1. Clemens, Samuel Langhorne, 1835-1910—Juvenile literature. I. Title.

GRAVES, Charles Parlin, 1911- 818'.4'09 B
Mark Twain, by Charles Graves. Illustrated by Fermin Rocker. New York, Putnam [1972] 64 p. illus. (part col.) 23 cm. (A See and read beginning to read biography) An easy-to-read biography of the well-known American author emphasizing the personal experiences that he incorporated into his books. [PS1331.G75] 92 76-161535 2.97
1. Clemens, Samuel Langhorne, 1835-1910—Juvenile literature. I. Rocker, Fermin, illus. II. Title.

NORTH, Sterling, 1906- 928.1
Mark Twain and the river. Illus. by Victor Mays. Boston, Houghton Micfin [c.] 1961. 184p. col. illus. (North star books [24]) 61-5138 1.95;2.80 lib. ed.,
1. Clemens, Samuel Langhorne, 1835-1910—Juvenile literature. I. Title.

RIKHOFF, Jean. 928.1
Mark Twain; writing about the frontier. Illustrated by Richard Mlodock. Chicago, Kingston House [1961] 191p. illus. 22cm. (Bookshelf for young Americans) [PS1331.R55] 61-9811
1. Clemens, Samuel Langhorne, 1835-1910—Juvenile literature. I. Title.

WOOD, James Playsted, 1905- 817'.4 B
Spunkwater, spunkwater! A life of Mark Twain. [New York] Pantheon Books [1968] 182 p. illus., ports. 22 cm. ([A Pantheon portrait]) Bibliography: p. 181-182. [PS1331.W6] 68-12659
1. Clemens, Samuel Langhorne, 1835-1910—Juvenile literature. I. Title.

Clemens, Titus Flavius, Alexandrinus.

LILLA, Salvatore R. C. 281'.3'0924 B
Clement of Alexandria: a study in Christian Platonism and Gnosticism, by Salvatore R. C. Lilla. [London] Oxford University Press, 1971. xiv, 266 p. 23 cm. (Oxford theological monographs) Revision of thesis, Oxford. Bibliography: p. [235]-245. [B666.Z7L54 1971] 77-881314 ISBN 0-19-826706-1 £3.50
1. Clemens, Titus Flavius, Alexandrinus. I. Title. II. Series. BIP

Clemens VII, Pope, 1478-1534.

VANASCO, Rocco R. 262'.13'0924 B
The role of Clement VII in Guicciardini's works [by] Rocco R. Vanasco. Strasburg, Mo., E. B. Greene [1969] 24 p. 23 cm. Bibliography: p. 21-24. [BX1317.V3] 73-625749
1. Clemens VII, Pope, 1478-1534. 2. Guicciardini, Francesco, 1483-1540. I. Title.

VAUGHAN, Herbert Millingchamp, 1870-1948. 945'.05
The Medici Popes (Leo X and Clement VII). Port Washington, N.Y., Kennikat Press [1971] xxii, 359 p. illus., geneal. table, ports. 22 cm. Reprint of the 1908 ed. Bibliography: p. xxi-xxii. [DG540.V3 1971] 74-118554 ISBN 0-8046-1179-3
1. Leo X, Pope, 1475-1521. 2. Clemens VII, Pope, 1478-1534. 3. Medici, House of. 4. Italy—History—1492-1559. I. Title.

Clemente, Roberto, 1934-1972.

CHRISTINE, Bill. 796.357'092'4 B
Roberto! [New York] Stadia Sports Pub. [1973] 159 p. illus. 20 cm. (Sport-spectrum classic) On cover: Numero uno: Roberto! [GV865.C45C48] 73-77299 1.50 (pbk.)
1. Clemente, Roberto, 1934-1972. I. Title. II. Title: Numero uno: Roberto!
Distributed by Dell.

HANO, Arnold, 1922- 796.357'0924 B
Roberto Clemente; batting king. Rev. ed. [New York] [Dell] [1973 c.1968] 188 p. 18 cm. (Laurel Leaf Library) [GV865.C45H3] 0.95 (pbk)
1. Clemente, Roberto Walker, 1935-1973. I. Title.
L.C. card no. for orig. ed.: 68-15049. BIP

HANO, Arnold, 1922- 796.357'0924 B
Roberto Clemente, batting king. New York, Putnam [1968] 192 p. 22 cm. (Putnam sports shelf) [GV865.C45H3] 68-15049
1. Clemente, Roberto, 1934-

MUSICK, Phil. 796.357'092'4 B
Who was Roberto? A biography of Roberto Clemente. [1st ed.] Garden City, N.Y., Doubleday, 1974. 306 p. illus. 22 cm. "An Associated Features book." [GV865.C45M87] 73-15358 ISBN 0-385-08421-8 7.95
1. Clemente, Roberto, 1934-1972. I. Title. BIP

WAGENHEIM, Kal. 796.357'092'4 B
Clemente! Foreword by Wilfrid Sheed. New York, Praeger Publishers [1973] xiii, 274 p. illus. 22 cm. [GV865.C45W33] 73-6893 6.95
1. Clemente, Roberto, 1934-1972. I. Title. BIP

Clemente, Roberto, 1934-1972—Juvenile literature.

BRONDFIELD, Jerry, 1913- 796.357'092'4 B
Roberto Clemente, pride of the Pirates / by Jerry Brondfield ; illustrated by Victor Mays. Champaign, Ill. : Garrard Pub. Co., [1976] p. cm. A biography of the baseball superstar from Puerto Rico killed in a 1972 airplane crash. [GV865.C45B76] 75-22145 ISBN 0-8116-6675-1 : 3.58
1. Clemente, Roberto, 1934-1972—Juvenile literature. 2. Baseball—Juvenile literature. I. Mays, Victor, 1927- II. Title.

HANO, Arnold, 1922- 796.357'092'4 B
Roberto Clemente, batting king. [Rev.] New York, Putnam [1973] 190 p. 22 cm. (Putnam sports shelf) Traces the baseball career of the Puerto Rican who, though plagued by numerous physical ailments from the beginning of his career, won the National League's Most Valuable Player Award in 1966. [GV865.C45H3 1973] 92 73-82028 ISBN 0-399-20375-3 4.89
1. Clemente, Roberto, 1937-1972—Juvenile literature. I. Title.

MAY, Julian. 796.357'092'4 B
Roberto Clemente and the world series upset. Mankato, Minn., Crestwood House [1973] 46 p. illus. 24 cm. (Sports close-up books) A biography of the first Latin player to be elected to Baseball's Hall of Fame. [GV865.C45M38 1973] 92 73-80421 ISBN 0-913940-01-1
1. Clemente, Roberto, 1934-1972—Juvenile literature. I. Title.

MERCER, Charles E. 796.357'092'4
Roberto Clemente / by Charles Mercer ; illustrated by George Loh. New York : Putnam, c1974. 57 p. : ill. ; 23 cm. (A See and read biography) An easy-to-read biography of the Pittsburgh Pirate, famous for his hitting and his utimely death at an early age. [GV865.C45M47 1974] 92 73-93753 ISBN 0-399-20397-4. ISBN 0-399-60887-7 lib. bdg. : 3.96
1. Clemente, Roberto, 1934-1972—Juvenile literature. 2. Baseball—Juvenile literature. I. Loh, George. II. Title.

OLSEN, James T. 796.357'092'4 B
Roberto Clemente: the great one, by James T. Olsen. Illustrated by Harold Henriksen. Mankato, Minn., Creative Education; distributed by Childrens Press, Chicago, [1974] 31 p. illus. (part col.) 25 cm. (Creative's superstars) Emphasizes the career and the kind deeds of a Puerto Rican baseball star. [GV865.C45O47] 92 73-13645 ISBN 0-87191-279-1 4.95
1. Clemente, Roberto, 1934-1972—Juvenile literature. I. Henriksen, Harold, illus. II. Title.

RUDEEN, Kenneth. 796.357'092'4 B
Roberto Clemente. Illustrated by Frank Mullins. New York, Crowell [1973] (A Crowell biography) A biography of Puerto Rico's baseball hero, Roberto Clemente, the Pittsburgh Pirate who lost his life performing a final act of generosity. [GV865.C45R82 1973] 92 73-12794 ISBN 0-690-00315-3 3.75
1. Clemente, Roberto, 1934-1972—Juvenile literature. I. Mullins, Frank, illus. II. Title.
Library edition 4.50; ISBN 0-690-00322-6. BIP

TAYLOR, Paula. 796.357'092'4 B
Roberto Clemente / written by Paula Taylor ; illustrated by Harold Henriksen. Mankato, Minn. : Creative Education, [1976] p. cm. A biography of the Puerto Rican who became legendary for his baseball playing and his generosity. [GV865.C45T39] 92 76-5813 ISBN 0-87191-279-1
1. Clemente, Roberto, 1934-1972—Juvenile literature. 2. Baseball—Juvenile literature. I. Henriksen, Harold. II. Title.

WHEELOCK, Warren. 973'.04'68 S
Carmen Rosa Maymi, to serve American women ; Roberto Clemente, death of a proud man ; Jose Feliciano, one voice, one guitar / written by Warren H. Wheelock and J. O. "Rocky" Maynes, Jr. ; consultants, Jorge Vadivieso, Amalia Perez, Ruben A. Soruco B. St. Paul : EMC Corp., [1976] p. cm. (Their Hispanic heroes of the U.S.A. ; 3) Brief biographies of three Spanish Americans: the director of the Women's Bureau in the Department of Labor, a popular singer, and a major league baseball star. [E184.S75W5 vol. 3] 920'.0092'6873 75-40230 ISBN 0-88436-244-2. ISBN 0-88436-245-0 pbk.
1. Maymi, Carmen R.—Juvenile literature. 2. Clemente, Roberto, 1934-1972—Juvenile literature. 3. Feliciano, Jose—Juvenile literature. I. Maynes, J. O., joint author. II. Title. III. Title: Roberto Clemente, death of a proud man. IV. Title: Jose Feliciano, one voice, one guitar.

WHEELOCK, Warren H. 973'.04'68
Carmen Rosa Maymi, para servir a las mujeres americanas. Roberto Clementes, la muerte de un hombre orgulloso. Jose Feliciano, una voz, una guitarra / Warren H. Wheelock ; adaptacion, J. O. "Rocky" Maynes ; consultantes, Jorge Valdivieso, Amalia Perez, Fabiola Franco. St. Paul, Minn. : EMC, 1976. p. cm. (His Ilustres hispanos de los EE. UU. : 3) Translation of Carmen Rosa Maymi, to serve American women. Brief biographies of three Spanish Americans: the director of the Women's Bureau in the Department of Labor, a major league baseball star, and a popular singer. [E184.S75W517 vol. 3] 920'.0092'6873 920 76-2421 ISBN 0-88436-252-3. ISBN 0-88436-253-1 pbk.
1. Maymi, Carmen R.—Juvenile literature. 2. Clemente, Roberto, 1934-1972—Juvenile literature. 3. Feliciano, Jose—Juvenile literature. I. Maynes, J. O. II. Title. III. Title: Roberto Clemente, la muerte de un hombre orgulloso. IV. Title: Jose Feliciano, una voz, una guitarra.

Clementi, Muzio, 1752-1832.

PLANTINGA, Leon B. 786.1'092'4 B
Clementi : his life and music / Leon Plantinga. London ; New York : Oxford University Press, 1977. xiii, 346 p., [4] leaves of plates : ill. ; 24 cm. Includes index. Bibliography: p. [328]-335. [ML410.C64P5] 77-359247 ISBN 0-19-315227-4 : 33.00
1. Clementi, Muzio, 1752-1832. BIP

Cleobury, F. H.

CLEOBURY, F. H. 283'.092'4 B
From clerk to cleric / [by] F. H. Cleobury ; with a foreword by Edward Carpenter. Cambridge : J. Clarke, 1976. [4], 44 p. ; 20 cm. [BX5199.C564A34] 77-359492 ISBN 0-227-67825-7 : £1.50
1. Cleobury, F. H. 2. Church of England—Clergy—Biography. 3. Clergy—England—Biography. I. Title. BIP

Cleopatra, queen of Egypt, d. 30 B.C.

BRADFORD, Ernle Dusgate Selby. 932'.02'0924 B
Cleopatra [by] Ernle Bradford. New York, Harcourt Brace Jovanovich, 1972. 279 p. illus. 27 cm. Bibliography: p. 272. [DT92.7.B7 1972] 73-153683 ISBN 0-15-118140-3 13.75
1. Cleopatra, Queen of Egypt, d. 30 B.C.

BRADFORD, Ernle Dusgate Selby. 932.02'092'4 B
Cleopatra [by] Ernle Bradford. London, Hodder and Stoughton, 1971. 279 p. illus. (some col.), maps, ports. (some col.). 26 cm. Illus on lining papers. Bibliography: p. 272. [DT92.7.B7 1971] 72-176454 ISBN 0-340-14864-0
1. Cleopatra, Queen of Egypt, d. B.C. 30. Available from Harcourt Brace Jovanovich, Inc. 13.75 ISBN 0-15-118140-3

CLEOPATRA, the story of a queen. v. 12
Tr. by Bernard Miall. New York, Bantam Books [1959, c1937] 245p. 18cm.
1. Cleopatra, Queen of Gypt, d. B. C. 30. I. Ludwig, Emil, 1881-1948.

DESMOND, Alice (Curtis) 1897- 937'.07'0922
Cleopatra's children. New York, Dodd, Mead [1971] xix, 295 p. illus., geneal. tables, maps. 22 cm. Bibliography: p. 279-286. [DT92.7.D47] 79-160859 ISBN 0-396-06376-4 5.00
1. Cleopatra, Queen of Egypt, d. 30 B.C. 2. Cleopatra, wife of Juba II, King of Mauretania, b. 40 B.C. 3. Juba II, King of Mauretania, d. ca. 23. I. Title. BIP

FRANZERO, Charles Marie, 1892- 923.132
The life and times of Cleopatra. New York, New Amer. Lib. [1963, c.1962] 223p. 18cm. (Signet bk. P2163) .60 pap.,
1. Cleopatra, Queen of Egypt, d.30 B.C. I. Title.

FRANZERO, Charles Marie, 1892- 923.132
The life and times of Cleopatra. [New York] Philosophical Library [1957] 299 p. illus. 22 cm. [DT92.7.F7 1957a] 57-14228
1. Cleopatra, Queen of Egypt, d. 30 B.C.

GRANT, Michael, 1914- 932'.02'0924 B
Cleopatra. New York, Simon and Schuster [1973, c1972] xvi, 301 p. illus. 25 cm. Bibliography: p. 239-247. [DT92.7.G7 1973] 72-12428 ISBN 0-671-21521-3 10.00
1. Cleopatra, Queen of Egypt, d. 30 B.C.

LINDSAY, Jack, 1900- 932'.02'0924 B
Cleopatra. [1st American ed.] New York, Coward McCann & Geoghegan [1971, c1970] xvi, 560 p. illus., maps, port. 22 cm. Includes bibliographical references. [DT92.7.L55 1971b] 74-136445 8.95
1. Cleopatra, Queen of Egypt, d. 30 B.C.

LUDWIG, Emil, 1881-1948 923.132
Cleopatra, the story of a queen. Tr. [from German] by Bernard Miall. New York, Bantam [1963, c.1937] 245p. 18cm. (FC27) .50 pap.,
1. Cleopatra, queen of Egypt, d. 30 B. C. I. Miall, Bernard, 1876- tr. II. Title.

MEADOWCROFT, Enid (La Monte) 1898- 932'.02'0924 B
Cleopatra's Egypt, by Jean Davis [pseud.] New York, Grosset & Dunlap [1963] 91 p. illus., map. 25 cm. A biography of the Queen of Egypt and wife of Julius Caesar and Mark Antony, who never achieved her ambition of ruling the Roman world. [DT92.7.M4] 92 AC 68
1. Cleopatra, queen of Egypt, d. 30 B.C. I. Davis, Jean, pseud. II. Title.

SVENDSEN, Ruth G v. 12
Cleopatra speaks; tells own story. Santa Clara, Calif. Williams pub. co. [1962] 208 p. illus. 22 cm. 63-78016
1. Spiritualism — Communications. I. Cleopatra, Queen of Egypt, d. 30 B.C. II. Title.

WEIGALL, Arthur Edward Pearse Brome, 1880-1934 923.132
The life and times of Cleopatra, Queen of Egypt [2d ed., abridged] Philadelphia, Mercury Bks. [c.1962] 250p. map. 18cm. (Mod. biog. ser., MB104) .75 pap.,
1. Cleopatra, Queen of Egypt, d., B.C.30. 2. Caesar, C. Julius. 3. Antonius, Marcus, B.C. 83-30. 4. Egypt—Hist.—B.C. 332-B.C.30. I. Title.

WEIGALL, Arthur Edward Pearse Brome, 1880-1934. 923.132
The life and times of Cleopatra, queen of Egypt. [2d ed.] Philadelphia, Mercury Books, [1962] 250 p. illus. 18 cm. (Modern biography series, MB104) [DT92.7.W4 1962] 62-52860
1. Cleopatra, queen of Egypt, d. 30 B.C. 2. Caesar, C. Julius. 3. Antonius, Marcus, 83?-30 B.C. 4. Egypt — Hist. — 332 B.C.-30 B.C. I. Title.

WEIGALL, Arthur Edward Pearse Brome, 1880-1934. 932'.02'0924 B
The life and times of Cleopatra, Queen of Egypt; a study in the origin of the Roman Empire. New York, Greenwood Press, 1968 [c1924] xii, 445 p. illus., geneal. table, fold. maps, plan, ports. 24 cm. Reprint of the new and rev. ed., 1924. Contents.Contents.—Cleopatra and Caesar.—Cleopatra and Antony. [DT92.7.W4 1968] 69-10168
1. Cleopatra, Queen of Egypt, d. 30 B.C. 2. Caesar, C. Julius. 3. Antonius, Marcus, 83? B.C.-30 B.C. 4. Egypt—History—332 B.C.-30 B.C. I. Title. BIP

Cleopatra, Queen of Egypt, d. 30 B.C.—Juvenile literature.

CRAYDER, Teresa, pseud. 932'.02'0924 B
Cleopatra. New York, Coward-McCann [1969] vii, 119 p. 22 cm. [DT92.7.C7] 68-23870 3.95
1. Cleopatra, Queen of Egypt, d. 30 B.C.—Juvenile literature.

HORNBLOW, Leonora, 1920- 923'.1'32
Cleopatra of Egypt. Illustrated by W. T. Mars. N[ew] Y[ork] Random House [1961] 184 p. illus. 22 cm. (World landmark books. W-50) Includes bibliography. [DT92.7.H67] 61-7784
1. Cleopatra, Queen of Egypt, d. 30 B.C.—Juvenile literature. I. Title. BIP

LEIGHTON, Margaret (Carver) 932'.02'0924 B
Cleopatra, sister of the moon, by Margaret Leighton. New York, Farrar, Straus & Giroux [1969] 215 p. 21 cm. Bibliography: p. 214-215. The life of the Egyptian queen who gained and maintained power over her kingdom through her alliance with Julius Caesar and later Marc Antony. [DT92.7.L4] 92 75-85368 3.95
1. Cleopatra, Queen of Egypt, d. 30 B.C.—Juvenile literature. I. Title.

NOBLE, Iris. 92
Egypt's Queen Cleopatra. New York, Messner [1963] 191 p. 22 cm. [DT92.7.N6] 63-8641
1. Cleopatra, Queen of Egypt, d. 30 B.C. — Juvenile literature. I. Title.

Cleopatra, wife of Juba II, King of Mauretania, b. 40 B.C.

DESMOND, Alice (Curtis) 1897- 937'.07'0922
Cleopatra's children. New York, Dodd, Mead [1971] xix, 295 p. illus., geneal. tables, maps. 22 cm. Bibliography: p. 279-286. [DT92.7.D47] 79-160859 ISBN 0-396-06376-4 5.00
1. Cleopatra, Queen of Egypt, d. 30 B.C. 2. Cleopatra, wife of Juba II, King of Mauretania, b. 40 B.C. 3. Juba II, King of Mauretania, d. ca. 23. I. Title. BIP

Clergue, Francois Auguste Leon, 1825-1907.

BEALIEU, Ernest marie de Father 922.244
Teeth in the Devil's hide; the life of Pere MarieAntoine, O.F.M. CAP., 1825- 1907. Translated [from the French] and adapted by Gregory Vand der Becken. Chicago, Franciscan Herald Press [c.1959] 184p. 22cm. 59-14709 3.75 bds.,
1. Clergue, Francois Auguste Leon, 1825-1907. I. Title.

Clergy—U. S.—Biog.

BLASSINGAME, Wyatt. 922
They rode the frontier. New York, Watts [1959] 182p. 22cm. [BR569.B5] 59-9798
1. Clergy—U. S.—Biog. 2. Frontier and pioneer life—U. S. I. Title.

GRAY, Joseph M. M., 1877- 230'.0922
Prophets of the soul [by] Joseph M. M. Gray. Freeport, N.Y., Books for Libraries Press [1971] 267 p. 23 cm. (Essay index reprint series) Reprint of the 1936 ed. Contents.Contents.—Those Mathers and the Puritan Commonwealth.—Jonathan Edwards, his God.—George Whitefield and his Master's voice.—Methodist itinerants: creators of climate.—William Ellery Channing: a theological hamlet.—Horace Bushnell: the beloved heretic.—Phillips Brooks: a prophetic goodness.—George A. Gordon: the magnificent rebel.—Washington Gladden and applied Christianity.—What of the light? Includes bibliographies. [BR569.G7 1971] 71-156655 ISBN 0-8369-2277-8
1. Clergy—United States—Biography. I. Title. BIP

HANZSCHE, William Thomson, 1891- 922
Forgotten Founding Fathers of the American church and state. Boston, Christopher Pub. House [1954] 209p. illus. 21cm. [BR569.H3] 54-763
1. Clergy—U. S.—Biog. I. Title.

*MILLER, Basil 285.00924 (B)
Charles G. Finney; official biography for the Finney Sesquicentennial Conference Chicago 1942. Minneapolis, Bethany Fellowship [1966, c.1941] 137p. 19cm. (BF 150) 1.50 pap.,
I. Title.

WHO'S who in the Protestant clergy. 922
Encino, Calif., Nygaard Associates [1957] 264 p. 24 cm. [BR569.W5] 57-59372
1. Clergy — U.S. — Biog. 2. Protestants in the U.S.

Clergy—Virginia.

HUGHES, William Dudley Foulke. 922.373
Prudently with power; William Thomas Manning, tenth Bishop of New York [by] W. D. F. Hughes. With a foreword by the Bishop of New York. West Park, N.Y., Holy Cross Publications [196-?] x, 255 p. illus., ports. 24 cm. [BX5995.M34H8]
I. Manning, William Thomas, Bp., 1806-1949. II. Title.

WEIS, Frederick Lewis, 1895- 922
The colonial clergy of Virginia. North Carolina, and South Carolina. Boston 1955. vii, 100p. front. 24cm. (Publications of the Society of the Descendants of the Colonial Clergy, 7) [BR569.W42] 55-8812
1. Clergy—Virginia. 2. Clergy—North Carolina. 3. Clergy—South Carolina. I. Title. II. Series: Society of the Descendants of the Colonial Clergy. Publications, 7 BIP

Clergy—Biography.

DAUGHERTY, Edgar Fay. 922.673
A Hoosier parson; his boosts and bumps (an apologia promea vita) Boston, Meador [1951] 224 p. illus. 21 cm. [BX7343.D27A3] 51-7594
I. Title.

WIERSBE, Warren W. 280'.092'2 B
Walking with the giants : a minister's guide to good reading and great preaching / Warren Wiersbe. Grand Rapids : Baker Book House, c1976. 289 p. : ports. ; 24 cm. Includes bibliographies and index. [BR1700.2.W49] 76-22989 ISBN 0-8010-9578-6 : 7.95
1. Clergy—Biography. 2. Preaching—History—Bibliography. 3. Pastoral theology—Bibliography. I. Title. BIP

Clergy—Correspondence, reminiscences, etc.

THE Hills beyond the hills; 253'.2'0922 B
"400 years in the ministry" [by] Paul F. Swarthout [and others] Lakemont, N.Y., North Country Books [1971] 327 p. illus. 24 cm. Autobiographical accounts by eight Christian ministers. [BR1700.2.H53] 79-32293 6.75
1. Clergy—Correspondence, reminiscences, etc. I. Swarthout, Paul Franklin.

NIEBUHR, Reinhold. 1892- 922.473
Leaves from the notebook of a tamed cynic. Hamden, Conn., Shoe, String Press. 1956 [c1929] 198p. 22cm. [BX4827.N5A4 1956] 56-6353
1. Clergy—Correspondence, reminiscences, etc. I. Title. BIP

NIEBUHR, Reinhold, 1892- 922.473
Leaves from the notebook of a tamed cynic. New York, Meridian Books, 1957 [c1929] 225p. 18cm. (Living age books, LA13) [BX4827.N5A4 1957] 57-10846
1. Clergy— Correspondence, reminiscences, etc. I. Title.

Clergy—England.

BEGBIE, Harold, 1871-1929. 274.2'0922 B
Painted windows; a study in religious personality, by Harold Begbie (a gentleman with a duster) Port Washington, N.Y., Kennikat Press [1970] 204 p. 21 cm. (Essay and general literature index reprint series) Reprint of the 1922 ed. Contents.Contents.—Bishop Gore.—Dean Inge.—Father Knox.—Dr. L. P. Jacks.—Bishop Hensley Henson.—Miss Maude Royden.—Canon E. W. Barnes.—General Bramwell Booth.—Dr. W. E. Orchard.—Bishop Temple.—Dr. W. B. Selbie.—Archbishop Randall Davidson. [BR767.B4 1970] 77-108696
1. Clergy—England. I. Title.

Clergy—France—Gap (Diocese)—Biography.

TACKETT, Timothy, 1945- 282'.44'97
Priest & parish in eighteenth-century France : a social and political study of the cures in a diocese of Dauphine, 1750-1791 / by Timothy Tackett. Princeton, N.J. : Princeton University Press, c1977. xiii, 350 p. : ill. ; 23 cm. Includes index. Bibliography: p. 307-331. [BX1532.G3T3] 76-29801 ISBN 0-691-05243-3 : 19.50
1. Catholic Church—Clergy—Biography. 2. Clergy—France—Gap (Diocese)—Biography. 3. Parishes—France—Gap (Diocese) I. Title.

Clergy—Great Britain—Biography.

RYLE, John Charles, Bp. of Liverpool, 1816-1900. 280'.4'0922 B
Christian leaders of the eighteenth century / J. C. Ryle. Edinburgh ; Carlisle, Pennsylvania : Banner of Truth Trust, 1978. ix, 432 p. ; 18 cm. First published in 1869 under title: The Christian leaders of the last century. "A series of biographical papers, contributed to [the Family treasury] ... during the years 1866 and 1867." Includes bibliographical references. [BR758.R9 1978] 79-322530 ISBN 0-85151-268-2 pbk. : 3.95
1. Clergy—Great Britain—Biography. 2. Preaching—Great Britain—History. I. Title.

Clergy—Northwestern States—Biography.

FOSTER, John W. 280'.4'0922 B
Four Northwest fundamentalists / by John W. Foster. Portland, Or. : Foster, [1975] 128 p. : ill. ; 21 cm. Contents.Contents.—The great Northwest country.—Fundamentalism.—Dr. John James Staub.—Dr. Mark Allison Matthews.—Dr. Walter Benwell Hinson.—Dr. Albert Garfield Johnson.—Neo-fundamentalism? Appendix. [BR550.F67] 75-309309 2.95
1. Clergy—Northwestern States—Biography. 2. Fundamentalism. I. Title.

Cleveland, Barbara (Villiers) Palmer, Duchess of, 1641-1709.

ANDREWS, Allen. 942.06'6'0924 B
The royal whore, Barbara Villiers,

Countess of Castlemaine. [1st ed.] Philadelphia, Chilton Book Co. [1970] xix, 314 p. illus., ports. 21 cm. Includes bibliographical references. [DA447.C63A66 1970] 77-133031 7.50
1. Cleveland, Barbara (Villiers) Palmer, Duchess of, 1641-1709. I. Title.

Cleveland. Football club (National League, Browns)

BROWN, Paul E., 1908- 796.33'2'0924 B
PB, the Paul Brown story / Paul Brown with Jack Clary. 1st ed. New York : Atheneum, 1979. 338 p. : ill. ; 24 cm. [GV939.B77A35 1979] 79-7314 ISBN 0-689-10985-7 : 12.95
1. Brown, Paul E., 1908- 2. Cleveland. Football club (National League, Browns) 3. Cincinnati Bengals (Football club) 4. Football coaches—United States—Biography. I. Clary, Jack T., joint author. II. Title.

HEATON, Chuck. 796.33'264'0977132
The Cleveland Browns : power and glory / by Chuck Heaton ; [photography by Timothy Culek ... et al.]. Englewood Cliffs, N.J. : Prentice-Hall, [1974] 123 p. : ill. ; 28 cm. (Reward books) "A Stuart L. Daniels book." [GV956.C6H42] 74-9242 ISBN 0-13-136754-4 : 3.95
1. Cleveland. Football club (National League, Browns) 2. Football. 3. Football—Biography. I. Title.

Cleveland, Grover, Pres. U.S., 1837-1908.

CLEVELAND, Grover, Pres. U.S., 1837-1908. 973.8'5'0924
Letters of Grover Cleveland, 1850-1908. Selected and edited by Allan Nevins. New York, Da Capo Press, 1970. xix, 640 p. port. 24 cm. Reprint of the 1933 ed. [E697.C63 1970] 70-123752
I. Nevins, Allan, 1890- ed. II. Title. BIP

NEVINS, Allan, 1890-1971. 973.8'5'0924 B
Grover Cleveland; a study in courage. Freeport, N.Y., Books for Libraries Press [1973, c1932] p. Reprint of the 1966 ed. published by Dodd, Mead, New York. Bibliography: p. [E697.N46 1973] 73-6512 ISBN 0-518-19064-1
1. Cleveland, Grover, Pres. U.S., 1837-1908. I. Title.

PARKER, George Frederick, 1847-1928. 973.8'5'0924 B
Recollections of Grover Cleveland. Freeport, N.Y., Books for Libraries Press [1971] xv, 427 p. illus. 23 cm. Reprint of the 1909 ed. Bibliography: p. 409. [E697.P25 1971] 70-165649 ISBN 0-8369-5958-2
1. Cleveland, Grover, Pres. U.S., 1837-1908. I. Title. BIP

TUGWELL, Rexford Guy, 1891- 973.8'5'0924 B
Grover Cleveland [by] Rexford G. Tugwell. New York, Macmillan [1968] xviii, 298 p. illus., ports. 22 cm. [E697.T8] 68-12399
1. Cleveland, Grover, Pres. U.S., 1837-1908. BIP

Cleveland, Grover, Pres. U. S., 1837-1908—Juvenile literature.

HOYT, Edwin Palmer 92
Grover Cleveland. Chicago, Reilly [c.] 1962. 170p. illus. Bibl. 62-7506 3.95
1. Cleveland, Grover, Pres. U. S., 1837-1908—Juvenile literature. I. Title.

Cleveland Twist Drill Company.

COX, Jacob Dolson, 1852-1930. 926.219
Building an American industry; the story of the Cleveland Twist Drill Company and its founder, an autobiography. Cleveland, Cleveland Twist Drill Co. [1951] 179 p. illus., ports. 22 cm. [HD9703.U62C53] 51-4207
1. Cleveland Twist Drill Company. I. Title.

Cliburn, Van, 1934-

CAHN, William, 1912- 927.8
The amazing story of a new American hero, Van Cliburn. NewYork, Published for Scholastic Book Services by the Ridge Press [c1959] 64p. illus. 21cm. (A Rutledge book, RP11) [ML417.C67C3] 60-1088
1. Cliburn, Van, 1934- I. Title.

CHASINS, Abram, 1903- 786.1'092'4
The Van Cliburn legend, by Abram Chasins, with Villa Stiles. [1st ed.] Garden City, N.Y., Doubleday, 1959. 238 p. illus. 22 cm. [ML417.C67C5] 59-8260
1. Cliburn, Van, 1934-

Clifford, Richard L.

CLIFFORD, Richard L. 266'.2'0924
A human touch / by Richard L. Clifford ; [edited by Carol Mulvehill ; ill. by Robert Handville]. Maryknoll, N.Y. : Maryknoll Fathers, c1979. 93 p., [1] leaf of plates : ill. ; 26 cm. [BV2853.P7C543] 79-50933 8.95
1. Clifford, Richard L. 2. Missionaries—Peru—Biography. 3. Missionaries—United States—Biography. I. Mulvehill, Carol. II. Title.

Clift, Jeannette.

CLIFT, Jeannette. 248'.4
Some run with feet of clay / Jeannette Clift. Old Tappan, N.J. : F. H. Revell Co., c1978. 126 p. ; 21 cm. [BR1725.C524A37] 77-20907 ISBN 0-8007-0901-2 : 5.95
1. Clift, Jeannette. 2. Christian biography—Texas—Houston. 3. Actors—Texas—Houston—Biography. 4. Houston, Texas—Biography. 5. Christian life—1960- I. Title. BIP

Clift, Montgomery.

BOSWORTH, Patricia. 791.43'028'0924 B
Montgomery Clift : a biography / Patricia Bosworth. 1st ed. New York : Harcourt Brace Jovanovich, c1978. ix, 438 p., [12] leaves of plates : ill.; 25 cm. Includes index. [PN2287.C545B6] 77-84385 ISBN 0-15-162123-3 : 12.95
1. Clift, Montgomery. 2. Moving-picture actors and actresses—United States—Biography. I. Title.

KASS, Judith M. 791.43'028'0924 B
The films of Montgomery Clift / by Judith M. Kass ; foreword by Brooks Cliff. 1st ed. Secaucus, N.J. : Citadel Press, c1979. 223 p. : ill. ; 29 cm. [PN2287.C545K3] 79-16345 ISBN 0-8065-0717-9 : 14.95
1. Clift, Montgomery. 2. Moving-picture actors and actresses—United States—Biography. I. Title.

LAGUARDIA, Robert. 791.43'028'0924 B
Monty : a biography of Montgomery Clift / by Robert LaGuardia. New York : Arbor House, c1977. ix, 304 p. : ill. ; 25 cm. Includes index. [PN2287.C545L3 1977] 77-78968 ISBN 0-87795-155-1 : 12.95
1. Clift, Montgomery. 2. Moving-picture actors and actresses—United States Biography. I. Title. BIP

Clifton, Bernice.

CLIFTON, Bernice. 920.936241
None so blind. With drawings by David Cunningham. Chicago, Rand McNally [1963, c1962] 253 p. illus. 21 cm. Autobiographical. [HV1792.C55A3] 62-19546
I. Title.

Clinton Co., N. Y. — Hist.

KELLOGG, David Sherwood, 1874-1910. 309.2
Recollections of Clinton County and the Battle of Plattsburgh, 1800-1840; memoirs of early residents from the notebooks of D. S. Kellogg. Edited by Allan S. Everest. Plattsburgh, N. Y., Clinton County Historical Association, 1964. 75 p. maps. 24 cm. "Sesquicentennial memorial edition." [F127.C77K4] 64-55114
1. Clinton Co., N. Y. — Hist. 2. Plattsburg, Battle of, 1814. I. Everest, Allan Seymour, ed. II. Title.

Clinton, De Witt, 1769-1828.

BOBBE, Dorothie (De Bear) 923.273
De Witt Clinton. New ed., introd. by Henry Steele Commager Port Washington, N.Y., I. J. Friedman, 1962. xiv, 308p. ports., map. 23cm. (Empire State historical pubn. 11) Bibl. 62-19668 7.50
1. Clinton, De Witt, 1769-1828 I. Title. II. Series.

BOBBE, Dorothie (De Bear) 974.7'03'0924 B
De Witt Clinton, by Dorothie Bobbe. New York, Putnam [1968] 159 p. port. 21 cm. (Lives to remember) Bibliography: p. 154-155. A biography of the man who promoted the building of the Erie Canal, served in the Senate, and ran for President on the Federalist ticket. [E340.C65B7 1968] 92 AC 68
1. Clinton, De Witt, 1769-1828. I. Title.

Clinton, De Witt, 1769-1828—Juvenile fiction.

WIDDEMAR, Mabel (Cleland) 920
De Witt Clinton, boy builder. Illus. by Robert Doremus. Indianapolis, Bobbs [c.1961] 200p. col. illus. (Childhood of famous Americans) 61-11886 2.25
1. Clinton, De Witt, 1769-1828—Juvenile fiction. I. Title.

Clinton, De Witt, 1769-1828—Juvenile literature.

BOBBE, Dorothie (De Bear) 92 (J)
De Witt Clinton, by Dorothie Bobbe. New York, Putnam [1968] 159 p. port. 21 cm. (Lives to remember) Bibliography: p. 154-155. [E340.C65B7 1968] 68-15039
1. Clinton, De Witt, 1769-1828—Juvenile literature.

Clinton, George, 1739-1812.

SPAULDING, Ernest Wilder, 1899- 923.273
His Excellency George Clinton, critic of the Constitution. 2d ed. New introd. by Ralph Adams Brown. Port Washington, N.Y., Friedman [c.1938, 1964] 325p. illus., ports., map. 22cm. (Empire State hist. pubn., 28) Bibl. 64-11842 7.50, avail on direct order only
1. Clinton, George, 1739-1812. I. Title. II. Series.

Clitherow, Margaret (Middleton) 1556(ca.)-1586.

CLARIDGE, Mary 282.0924
Margaret Clitherow. 1556?-1586. Foreword by Philip Caraman. New York, Frrdham [1966] x, 196p. port. 23cm. Bibl. [BX4705.C64C5 1966a] 66-19228 5.00
1. Clitherow, Margaret (Middleton) 1556(ca.)-1586. I. Title.

ROBERTO, Brother, 1927- 922.242
A crown for the butcher's wife; a story of Blessed Margaret Clitherow. Illus. by Anthony Joyce. Notre Dame, Ind., Dujarie Press [1955] 96p. illus. 24cm. [BX4705.C64R6] 55-38169
1. ClitherowMargaret (Middleton) 1556 (ca.)—1586. I. Title.

Clive, Catherine (Raftor) 1711-1785.

FITZGERALD, Percy Hetherington, 1834-1925. 792'.028'0924 B
The life of Mrs. Catherine Clive, with an account of her adventures on and off the stage, a round of her characters, together with her correspondence. New York, B. Blom, 1971. viii, 112 p. port. 22 cm. Reprint of the 1888 ed. [PN2598.C5F5 1971] 76-91496
1. Clive, Catherine (Raftor) 1711-1785. I. Title.

Clive, Robert Clive, Baron, 1725-1774.

BENCE-JONES, Mark. 954.02'9'0924 B
Clive of India / Mark Bence-Jones. New York : St. Martin's Press, 1975, c1974. xvi, 377 p., [14] leaves of plates (1 fold.) : ill. ; 24 cm. Includes index. Bibliography: p. 361-362. [DS471.B46 1975] 74-83570 8.95
1. Clive, Robert Clive, Baron, 1725-1774. 2. India—History—British occupation, 1765-1947. I. Title.

EDWARDES, Allen 954.02909224(B)
The rape of India; a biography of Robert Clive and a sexual history of the conquest of Hindustan. New York, Julian [1966] xi, 350p. 24cm. Bibl. [DS471.E3] 66-18110 8.50
1. Clive, Robert Clive, Baron, 1725-1774. I. Title.

GARRETT, Richard. 954.02'9'0924 B
Robert Clive / Richard Garrett. London : A. Barker, c1976. 224 p., [4] leaves of plates : ill. ; 23 cm. Includes index. Bibliography: p. [217] [DS471.G27] 77-352259 ISBN 0-213-16610-0 : £4.95
1. Clive, Robert Clive, Baron, 1725-1774. 2. India—History, Military. 3. Statesmen—India—Biography.

KINSLEY, D A 954.02909224 (B)
The rape of India; a biography of Robert Clive and a sexual history of the conquest of Hindustan [by] Allen Edwardes. New York, Julian Press [1966] xi, 350 p. 24 cm. Bibliography: p. [335]-338. [DS471.K5] 66-18110
1. Clive, Robert Clive, baron, 1725-1774. I. Title.

LAWFORD, James Philip. 954.02'9'0924 B
Clive, Proconsul of India : a biography / by James P. Lawford. London : Allen & Unwin, 1976. 432 p. : ill. ; 23 cm. Includes index. Bibliography: p. [417]-418. [DS471.L38] 76-363995 ISBN 0-04-923067-0 : 19.50
1. Clive, Robert Clive, Baron, 1725-1774. 2. India—Politics and government—997-1765. I. Title.
Distributed by Allen & Unwin 198 Ash St. Reading, Mass. 01867

WATNEY, John Basil, 1915- 954.02'9'0924 B
Clive of India / [by] John Watney. Farnborough, Hants. : Saxon House, 1974. [6], 226 p., 24 p. of plates. : ill., map, plans, ports. ; 24 cm. Includes index. [DS471.W37] 74-189505 ISBN 0-347-00008-8 : 9.50
1. Clive, Robert Clive, Baron, 1725-1774. 2. India—History—18th century. I. Title.
Distributed by Atheneum Pub.

Clock and watch makers—Connecticut.

HOOPES, Penrose Robinson, 1892- 681'.133'0922 B
Connecticut clockmakers of the eighteenth century [by] Penrose R. Hoopes. 2d ed. New York, Dover Publications [1974] 182 p. illus. 24 cm. Bibliography: p. 169-171. [TS543.U6H6 1974] 72-93610 ISBN 0-486-22922-X 3.00 (pbk.).
1. Clock and watch makers—Connecticut. 2. Clock and watch making—Connecticut. I. Title.

HOOPES, Penrose Robinson, 1892- 681'.113'0922
Connecticut clockmakers of the eighteenth century / Penrose R. Hoopes. Rutland, Vt. : C. E. Tuttle Co., 1975. 178 p., [1] leaf of plates : ill. ; 23 cm. First published in 1930. Includes index. Bibliography: p. 171-173. [TS543.U6H6 1975] 75-328515 ISBN 0-8048-1152-0 : 12.50
1. Clock and watch makers—Connecticut. 2. Clock and watch making—Connecticut. I. Title. BIP

Clock and watch makers—Lancaster Co., Pa.

WOOD, Stacy B. C. 681'.113'0922 B
Clockmakers of Lancaster County and their clocks, 1750-1850 / Stacy B. C. Wood, Jr., Stephen E. Kramer, III ; with a study of Lancaster County clock cases by John J. Snyder, Jr. New York : Van Nostrand Reinhold, 1977. 224 p. : ill. ; 29

cm. Includes bibliographical references and indexes. [TS543.U6W66 1977] 76-30279 ISBN 0-442-29531-6 : 16.50
1. Clock and watch makers—Lancaster Co., Pa. 2. Clock and watchmaking—Lancaster Co., Pa.—History. 3. Lancaster Co., Pa.—Biography. I. Kramer, Stephen E., joint author. II. Snyder, John J., 1946- III. Title. BIP

Cloete, Stuart,

CLOETE, Stuart, 1897- 823 B
A Victorian son: an autobiography, 1897-1922. [1st American ed.] New York, J. Day Co. [1973, c1972] 319 p. port. 22 cm. [PR6005.L8Z5 1973] 72-10774 ISBN 0-381-98234-3 7.95
I. Title.

Clooney, Rosemary.

CLOONEY, Rosemary. 784'.92'4
This for rememberance / by Rosemary Clooney, with Raymond Strait ; foreword by Bing Crosby. Chicago : Playboy Press, 1979, c1977. 256p. : ill. ; 18 cm. [ML420.C58A3] ISBN 0-872-16542-6 pbk. : 1.95
1. Clooney, Rosemary. 2. Singers—United States—Biography. I. Strait, Raymond, joint author. II. Title.
L.C. card no. for 1977 hardcover ed.: 77-13490.

CLOONEY, Rosemary. 784'.092'4 B
This for remembrance / by Rosemary Clooney, with Raymond Strait. New York : Playboy Press, 1977. p. cm. [ML420.C58A3] 77-13490 ISBN 0-671-16976-9 : 8.95
1. Clooney, Rosemary. 2. Singers—United States—Biography. I. Strait, Raymond, joint author. II. Title. BIP

CLOONEY, Rosemary. 784'.092'4 B
This for remembrance : the autobiography of Rosemary Clooney, an Irish-American singer / by Rosemary Clooney, with Raymond Strait. 1st ed. New York : Playboy Press ; trade distribution by Simon and Schuster, c1977. xii, 250 p., [4] leaves of plates : ill. ; 22 cm. [ML420.C58A3] 77-13766 ISBN 0-671-16976-9 : 10.00
1. Clooney, Rosemary. 2. Singers—United States—Biography. I. Strait, Raymond, joint author. II. Title.

Cloud, Kevin—Juvenile literature.

CLOUD, Kevin. 917.73'11'0697
Kevin Cloud; Chippewa boy in the city, by Carol Ann Bales. Chicago, Reilly & Lee Books [1972] [34] p. illus. 29 cm. Text and photographs introduce the home, family, and daily life of a young Chippewa boy living in Chicago. [E99.C6C553] 79-183833
1. Cloud, Kevin—Juvenile literature. I. Bales, Carol Ann, 1940- II. Title.

Clough, Arthur Hugh, 1819-1861.

ARNOLD, Matthew, 1822-1888. 826'.8
The letters of Matthew Arnold to Arthur Hugh Clough. Edited with an introductory study by Howard Foster Lowry. New York, Russell & Russell [1968] xi, 191 p. 23 cm. Reprint of the 1932 ed. Bibliographical footnotes. [PR4023.A47C6 1968] 68-15092
1. Clough, Arthur Hugh, 1819-1861. I. Lowry, Howard Foster, 1901-1967, ed. II. Title. BIP

CLOUGH, Arthur Hugh, 1819-1861. 928.2
Correspondence. Edited by Frederick L. Mulhauser. Oxford, Clarendon Press, 1957. 2v. (xxiii, 655p.) 23cm. [PR4458.A4 1957] 57-59593
1. Authors—Correspondence, reminiscences, etc. I. Title.

WADDINGTON, Samuel, 1844-1923. 821'.8 B
Arthur Hugh Clough : a monograph / by Samuel Waddington. New York : AMS Press, 1975. x, 333 p. ; 19 cm. Reprint of the 1883 ed. published by G. Bell, London. [PR4458.W3 1975] 70-148321 ISBN 0-404-08921-6 : 21.50
1. Clough, Arthur Hugh, 1819-1861. BIP

Clough, Arthur Hugh, 1819-1861—Bibliography.

GOLLIN, Richard M. 016.828'8'09
Arthur Hugh Clough; a descriptive catalogue; poetry, prose, biography, and criticism, by Richard M. Gollin, Walter E. Houghton, and Michael Timko. [New York] New York Public Library [1967] 117 p. port. 26 cm. "Reprinted, with additions and revisions, from the Bulletin of the New York Public Library, July 1960, November 1966, January-March 1967." [Z8176.7.G6] 67-25798
1. Clough, Arthur Hugh, 1819-1861—Bibliography. I. Houghton, Walter Edwards, 1904- joint author. II. Timko, Michael, 1925- joint author. BIP

Clough, Carman G.

BLOUGH, Carman G. 657
Carman G. Blough, his professional career and accounting thought / edited by William G. Shenkir ; with a pref. New York : Arno Press, 1978. ca. 350 p. in various pagings : ill. ; 24 cm. (The Development of contemporary accounting thought) Reprint of papers published 1937-1974. [HF5616.U5B48 1978] 77-87319 ISBN 0-405-10931-8 : 25.00
1. Clough, Carman G. 2. Accounting—United States—History. 3. Accountants—United States—Biography. I. Shenkir, William G. II. Title. III. Series.

Clouser, John William.

CLOUSER, John William. 364.3 B
The most wanted man in America / by John William Clouser, with David Fisher. New York : Stein and Day, 1975. 191 p. : ill. ; 25 cm. [HV6248.C48A34] 74-26961 ISBN 0-8128-1771-0 : 7.95
1. Clouser, John William. 2. Crime and criminals—Correspondence, reminiscences, etc. I. Fisher, David, 1946- II. Title. BIP

Clower, Jerry, 1926-

CLOWER, Jerry, 1926- 791'.092'4 B
Let the hammer down! / Jerry Clower, with Gerry Wood. Waco, Tex. : Word Books, c1978. 189 p. : ill. ; 23 cm. Discography: p. 185-189. [PN2287.C547A35] 77-92448 ISBN 0-8499-0062-X : 6.95
1. Clower, Jerry, 1926- 2. Comedians—United States—Biography. I. Wood, Gerry, joint author. II. Title. BIP

Clowns.

WETTACH, Adrien, 1880-1959. 791.3'3'0924 B
Grock; life's a lark, by Grock. [Translated from the German by Madge Pemberton. Edited by Eduard Behrens] New York, B. Blom [1969] viii, 276 p. illus., ports. 21 cm. Reprint of the 1931 ed. Translation of Grock; ich lebe gern! [GV1811.W4A32 1969] 73-84515
1. Clowns. I. Behrens, Eduard, 1884-1944, ed. II. Title. III. Title: Life's a lark.

Clowns—Biography.

SWORTZELL, Lowell S. 791.3'3'0922 B
Here come the clowns : a cavalcade of comedy from antiquity to the present / Lowell Swortzell ; illustrated by C. Walter Hodges. 1st ed. New York : Viking Press, 1978. 245 p. : ill. ; 24 cm. Includes index. Bibliography: p. [233]-236. Discusses comedians and the use of comedy throughout history from ancient Greek drama through traveling shows to present day radio and television. [GV1811.A1S95 1978] 920 77-10115 ISBN 0-670-36874-1 : 10.00
1. Clowns—Biography. 2. Comedians—Biography. 3. Comedy. I. Hodges, Cyril Walter, 1909- II. Title. BIP

Club Eighteen.

BRYAN, Joseph, 1904- 647'.957471
The merry madmen of 52nd Street [by]J. Bryan, III [Richmond, Va., Printed by Whittet & Shepperson] 1968. 31 p. 17 cm. "Fifty printed copies." [TX945.5.C58B78] 79-12306
1. Club Eighteen. I. Title.

Clubb, Oliver Edmund, 1901-

CLUBB, Oliver Edmund, 1901- 353.001'3242'0924 B
The witness and I [by] O. Edmund Clubb. New York, Columbia University Press, 1974 [c1975] xiv, 314 p. illus. 21 cm. Autobiographical. Bibliography: p. [307] [E748.C59A38] 74-11385 ISBN 0-231-03859-3 9.95
1. Clubb, Oliver Edmund, 1901- 2. Internal security—United States. 3. Loyalty-security program, 1947- I. Title. BIP

Clum, John Philip, 1851-1932.

CLUM, Woodworth. 970'.004'97
Apache agent : the story of John P. Clum / by Woodworth Clum. Lincoln : University of Nebraska Press, 1978, c1936. xiv, 296 p., [8] leaves o fplates : ports. ; 21 cm. "A Bison book." Reprint of the ed. published by Houghton Mifflin, New York. Includes index. [E99.A6C52 1978] 77-14135 ISBN 0-8032-0967-3 : 13.95 ISBN 0-8032-5886-0 pbk. : 4.95
1. Clum, John Philip, 1851-1932. 2. Geronimo, Apache chief, 1829-1909. 3. United States. Bureau of Indian Affairs—Officials and employees—Biography. 4. Apache Indians. 5. Apache Indians—Government relations. 6. San Carlos Indian Reservation, Arizona. I. Title. BIP

Clurman, Harold, 1901-

CLURMAN, Harold, 1901- 792'.0233'0924 B
All people are famous (instead of an autobiography). [1st ed.] New York, Harcourt Brace Jovanovich [1974] 327 p. 22 cm. [PN2287.C548A33] 74-13820 ISBN 0-15-104775-8 8.95
1. Clurman, Harold, 1901- I. Title.

Clyman, James, 1792-1881 — Juvenile literature.

EVARTS, Hal George, 1915-1958. 923.973
Jim Clyman. New York, Putnam [1959] 191 p. 21 cm. (A Westerners book) [F592.C65E8] 59-11430
1. Clyman, James, 1792-1881 — Juvenile literature. I. Title.

Coaches (Athletics)—Biography.

HEUMAN, William. 796'.077'0922
Famous coaches. New York, Dodd, Mead [1968] 151 p. ports. 22 cm. (Famous biographies for young people) [GV697.A1H42] 68-21897
1. Coaches (Athletics)—Biography. I. Title.

HEUMAN, William. 920
Famous coaches. New York, Dodd, Mead [1968] 151 p. ports. 22 cm. (Famous biographies for young people) Biographies of fifteen coaches of college and professional athletic teams: Connie Mack, Amos Stagg, Pop Warner, John McGraw, Dean Cromwell, Les Patrick, Knute Rockne, Joe McCarthy, Casey Stengel, Rusty Callow, Bob Kiphuth, Joe Lapchick, Adolph Rupp, Vince Lombardi, and Red Auerbach. [GV697.A1H42] AC 68
1. Coaches (Athletics)—Biography. I. Title. BIP

LIBBY, Bill. 796.33'2077'0922 B
The coaches. Chicago, Regnery [1972] 247 p. illus. 24 cm. [GV697.A1L52] 72-80929 7.95
1. Coaches (Athletics)—Biography. I. Title.

Coaching (Athletics)

ROMNEY, Ernest Lowell, 1895- 796.0770924
The "Dick" Romney story, by E. L. "Dick" Romney. Salt Lake City, Deseret Book Co., 1965. xxi, 248 p. illus., ports. 24 cm. [GV697.R6A3] 65-19184
1. Coaching (Athletics) I. Title.

Coal miners' strike, Colorado, 1913-1914.

O'NEAL, Mary T., 1887- 331.89'2822'330924 B
Those damn foreigners [by] Mary T. O'Neal. [Hollywood, Calif.] Minerva Book [1971] 220 p. port. 22 cm. Autobiography. [HD5325.M63 1913.C855] 73-184491 5.98
1. Coal miners' strike, Colorado, 1913-1914. I. Title.

Coal mines and mining—United States.

WITT, Matt. 338.2'7'20973
In our blood : four coal mining families / by Matt Witt ; photos. by Earl Dotter. 1st ed. Washington : Highlander Research and Education Center, c1979. 90 p. : ill. ; 29 cm. [TN805.A5W67] 78-71518 ISBN 0-9602226-1-8 : 6.95
1. Coal mines and mining—United States. 2. Coal-miners—United States—Biography. I. Dotter, Earl. II. Title. BIP

Coats, Peter.

COATS, Peter. 941.082'092'4 B
Of generals and gardens : the autobiography of Peter Coats. London : Weidenfeld and Nicolson, 1976. 326 p., [8] p. of plates : ill., ports. ; 23 cm. Includes index. [SB470.C6A33] 76-382729 ISBN 0-297-77145-0 : £6.95
1. Coats, Peter. 2. Garden historians—Great Britain—Biography. I. Title.

Coatsworth, Elizabeth Jane, 1893- — Biography.

COATSWORTH, Elizabeth Jane, 1893- 811'.5'2 B
Personal geography : almost an autobiography / by Elizabeth Coatsworth. Brattleboro, Vt. : S. Greene Press, c1976. xv, 192 p. ; 22 cm. "A Janet Greene book." Includes index. [PS3505.O136Z52] 76-13807 ISBN 0-8289-0282-8 : 10.00
1. Coatsworth, Elizabeth Jane, 1893- — Biography. 2. Authors, American—20th century—Biography. I. Title.

Cobb, Howell, 1815-1868.

SIMPSON, John Eddins. 973.6'8'0924 B
Howell Cobb: the politics of ambition. [Chicago, Adams Press, c1973] v, 198 p. 22 cm. Bibliography: p. 193-198. [E415.9.C655S55] 74-155460 4.95
1. Cobb, Howell, 1815-1868. I. Title.

Cobb, Irving Shrewsbury, 1876-1944.

COBB, Irvin Shrewsbury, 1876-1944. 818'.5'209 B
Exit laughing. Ann Arbor, Mich., Gryphon Books, 1971. 572 p. 22 cm. Autobiography. "Facsimile reprint of the 1941 edition." [PS3505.O14Z5 1941a] 78-145707
I. Title. BIP

COBB, Irvin Shrewsbury, 1876-1944. 818'.5'209 B
Exit laughing. Indianapolis, Bobbs-Merrill. Detroit, Gale Research Co., 1974. 572 p. 22 cm. Autobiography. Reprint of the 1941 ed. [PS3505.O14Z5 1974] 73-19798 18.50
1. Cobb, Irving Shrewsbury, 1876-1944. I. Title.

Cobb, Irving Shrewsbury, 1876-1944—Biography.

CHAPMAN, Elisabeth (Cobb) 818'.5'209 B
My wayward parent; a book about Irvin S. Cobb, by Elisabeth Cobb (Elisabeth Chapman). Illustrated by F. Strobel. Westport, Conn., Greenwood Press [1971, c1945] 255 p. illus. 23 cm. [PS3505.O14Z58 1971] 71-156182 ISBN 0-8371-6125-8

1. Cobb, Irvin Shrewsbury, 1876-1944—Biography. I. Title. **BIP**

NEUMAN, Fred Gus, 1893- 818'.5'209 B
Irvin S. Cobb: his life and achievements. New York, Beekman Publishers, 1974. 275 p. illus. 23 cm. (American newspapermen, 1790-1933) Reprint of the 1934 ed. published by Young Pub. Co., Paducah, Ky. [PS3505.O14Z83 1974] 74-2057 ISBN 0-8464-0011-1 12.50
1. Cobb, Irving Shrewsbury, 1876-1944—Biography.

Cobb, Jerrie,

COBB, Jerrie, 1931- 926.2913
Woman into space, the Jerrie Cobb story. By Jerrie Cobb with Jane Rieker. Englewood Cliffs, N.J., Prentice-Hall [1963] 223 p. illus. 22 cm. [TL540.C59A3] 63-12304
I. Rieker, Jane. II. Title.

Cobb, Kirkpatrick.

COBB, Kirkpatrick. 818.54
Whoa! Nellie, whoa! Artworks by R. H. Scott. Dallas, Royal Pub. Co. [1964] 184 p. illus. 21 cm. Autobiographical. [CT275.C653A3] 64-54969
I. Title.

Cobb, Lorie Lynn, 1974-

COBB, Mary Ann. 362.7'8'30926
Lorie : a story of hope / Mary Ann Cobb. Nashville : T. Nelson, c1979. 181 p. ; 21 cm. Bibliography: p. 179-181. [RJ506.D68C6] 78-20951 ISBN 0-8407-5677-1 pbk.: 3.95
1. Cobb, Lorie Lynn, 1974- 2. Down's syndrome—Biography. 3. Christian life—1960- **BIP**

Cobb, Richard Charles, 1917-

COBB, Richard Charles, 1917- 907'.2'024 B
A sense of place / Richard Cobb. New York : Holmes & Meier Publishers, [1978] c1975. p. cm. Includes index. [DC36.98.C6A33 1978] 78-13527 ISBN 0-8419-7100-5 : 13.50
1. Cobb, Richard Charles, 1917- 2. Perken, Cornelis, 1789-1810. 3. Historians—England—Biography. 4. Unmarried mothers—France—Lyons. I. Title. **BIP**

Cobb, Tyrus Raymond, 1886-1961.

MCCALLUM, John Dennis, 1924- 927.96357
The Tiger wore spikes; an informal biography of Ty Cobb. New York, Barnes [1956] 240p. illus. 22cm. [GV865.C6M3] 56-5563
1. Cobb, Tyrus Raymond, 1886- I. Title.

MCCALLUM, John Dennis, 1924- 796.357'092'4 B
Ty Cobb / John D. McCallum. New York : Praeger, 1975. xiii, 225 p., [8] leaves of plates : ill. ; 23 cm. [GV865.C6M32] 75-51 ISBN 0-275-22520-8 : 8.95
1. Cobb, Tyrus Raymond, 1886-1961. 2. Baseball.

SCHOOR, Gene. 927.96357
The story of Ty Cobb, baseball's greatest player, by Gene Schoor, with Henry Gilfond. New York, Messner [1952] 181 p. illus. 22 cm. [GV865.C6S4] 52-8230
1. Cobb, Tyrus Raymond, 1886-1961. I. Title.

Cobbett, William, 1763-1835.

BOOTH, Simon. 941.07'3'0924 B
William Cobbett : an introduction to his life and writings / by Simon Booth. 2d ed. Farnham [Eng.] : Farnham Museum Society, 1976. 15 p. : port. ; 30 cm. Bibliography: p. 15. [DA522.C5B56 1976] 76-371451 ISBN 0-901638-05-6
1. Cobbett, William, 1763-1835.

BOWEN, Marjorie, pseud. 942.07'3'0924 B
Peter Porcupine; a study of William Cobbett, 1762-1835. Ann Arbor, Mich., Plutarch Press, 1971. xii, 312 p. port. 22 cm. "Facsimile reprint of the 1935 edition." "Bibliography of works on Cobbett and his times": p. [299]-303. [DA522.C5B6 1935a] 78-145715
1. Cobbett, William, 1763-1835. I. Title.

CLARK, Mary Elizabeth, 1901- 941.07'3'0924 B
Peter Porcupine in America: the career of William Cobbett. New York, Beekman Publishers, 1974. v, 193 p. 23 cm. (American newspapermen, 1790-1933) Originally presented as the author's thesis, University of Pennsylvania, 1937. Bibliography: p. 186-193. [DA522.C5C5 1974] 74-501
1. Cobbett, William, 1763-1835. I. Title.

CLARK, Mary Elizabeth, 1901- 942.07'3'0924 B
Peter Porcupine in America: the career of William Cobbett, 1792-1800. [Folcroft, Pa.] Folcroft Library Editions, 1973 [c1939] p. Reprint of the 1939 ed. published in Philadelphia. Originally presented as the author's thesis, University of Pennsylvania, 1937. Bibliography: p. [DA522.C5C5 1973] 73-16217 25.00
1. Cobbett, William, 1763-1835. I. Title. **BIP**

CLARK, Mary Elizabeth, 1901- 941.07'3'0924 B
Peter Porcupine in America: the career of William Cobbett, 1792-1800. [Folcroft, Pa.] Folcroft Library Editions, 1973 [c1939] v, 193 p. 26 cm. Reprint of the ed. published in Philadelphia. Originally presented as the author's thesis, University of Pennsylvania, 1937. Bibliography: p. 186-193. [DA522.C5C5 1973] 73-16217 ISBN 0-8414-3512-X (lib. bdg.)
1. Cobbett, William, 1763-1835. I. Title.

CLARK, Mary Elizabeth, 1901- 941.07'3'0924 B
Peter Porcupine in America : the career of William Cobbett, 1792-1800 / Mary Elizabeth Clark. Norwood, Pa. : Norwood Editions, 1975, [c1939] v, 193 p. ; 26 cm. Reprint of the ed. published in Philadelphia. Originally presented as the author's thesis, University of Pennsylvania, 1937. Bibliography: p. 187-193. [DA522.C5C5 1975] 75-43683 ISBN 0-88305-807-3 lib. bdg.
1. Cobbett, William, 1763-1835. I. Title.

COBBETT, William, 1763-1835. 942.07'3'0924 B
Life and adventures of Peter Porcupine, with other records of his early career in England & America. [Folcroft, Pa.] Folcroft Library Editions, 1973. p. Reprint of the 1927 ed. published by Nonesuch Press, London. Contents.Contents.—Life & adventures.—The scarecrow.—Remarks of the pamphlets.—Talleyrand: a spy.—Farewell to America.—A court martial.—A retrospect. Includes bibliographical references. [DA522.C5A2 1973] 73-16319 ISBN 0-8414-3510-3 (lib. bdg.)
I. Title.

COLE, George Douglas Howard, 1889-1959. 942.07'3'0924 B
The life of William Cobbett. With a chapter on Rural rides by F. E. Green. New York, Russell & Russell [1971] xi, 455 p. 22 cm. Reprint of the 3d. rev. ed., 1947. Bibliography: p. 438-445. [DA522.C5C6 1971b] 71-152534
1. Cobbett, William, 1763-1835. I. Title. **BIP**

COLE, George Douglas Howard, 1889-1959. 942.07'3'0924
The life of William Cobbett. With a chapter on Rural rides, by F. E. Green. Westport, Conn., Greenwood Press [1971] xii, 455 p. 23 cm. Reprint of the 1947 ed. "A brief bibliography of Cobbett's writings": p. 438-445. [DA522.C5C6 1971] 77-114502 ISBN 0-8371-4781-6
1. Cobbett, William, 1763-1835. I. Green, Frederick Ernest, 1867-1922.

COLE, George Douglas Howard, 1889-1959. 300'.8 S
William Cobbett. [Folcroft, Pa.] Folcroft Library Editions, 1973. 19 p. 24 cm. Original ed. issued as Biographical series no. 9 of Fabian tract no. 215. [HX11.F25 no. 215] [DA522.C5] 942.07'3'0924 B 72-13697 4.00
1. Cobbett, William, 1763-1835. I. Series: Fabian Society, London. Tract, no. 215. II. Series: Fabian biographical series, no. 9.

COLE, George Douglas Howard, 1889-1959. 941.07'3'0924 B
William Cobbett / by G. D. H. Cole. Norwood, Pa. : Norwood Editions, 1976. 19 p. ; 23 cm. Reprint of the 1925 ed. published by the Fabian Society, London which was issued as Fabian tract no. 215 and no. 9 of Fabian biographical series. "A note on Cobbett's writings": p. 19. [DA522.C5C63 1976] 76-2414 ISBN 0-88305-337-3 lib. bdg. : 4.50
1. Cobbett, William, 1763-1835. I. Series: Fabian Society, London. Tract ; no. 215. II. Series: Fabian biographical sereis ; no. 9.

OSBORNE, John W. 070.0924
William Cobbett; his thought and his times by John W. Osborne. New Brunswick, N. J., Rutgers [1966] x, 272p. port. 22cm. Bibl. [DA522.C508] 66-18874 10.00
1. Cobbett. William 1763-1835. I. Title.

OSBORNE, John W. 070.0924
William Cobbett; his thought and his times, by John W. Osborne. New Brunswick, N. J., Rutgers University Press [1966] x, 272 p. port. 22 cm. Bibliography: p. [259]-263. [DA522.C5O8] 66-18874
1. Cobbett, William, 1763-1835.

SAMBROOK, James 942.07'3'0924 B
William Cobbett. London, Boston, Routledge & Kegan Paul [1973] xi, 224 p. 22 cm. (Routledge author guides) Includes bibliographical references. [DA522.C5S25 1973] 73-79113 ISBN 0-7100-7560-X 9.95
1. Cobbett, William, 1763-1835. Pbk; 4.95, ISBN 0-7100-7561-8. **BIP**

WILLIAM Cobbett. 942.07'0924
London, Oxford Univ. Pr., 1967. 63p. 8 plates (incl. ports.). 21cm. (Clarendon biographies, 17) Bibl. [DA522.C5B7 1967] (B) 68-92843 1.55 bds.,
1. Cobbett, William, 1763-1835. I. Briggs, Asa, 1921-
Available from the publisher's New York office.

Cobbett, William, 1763-1835—Bibliography.

GAINES, Pierce Welch. 016.94207'3'0924
William Cobbett and the United States, 1792-1835; a bibliography with notes and extracts by Pierce W. Gaines Worcester, Mass., American Antiquarian Society, 1971. xxi, 249 p. illus. 25 cm. [Z8177.G34] 79-168901 ISBN 0-912296-00-3 17.50
1. Cobbett, William, 1763-1835—Bibliography. I. Title.

Cobden-Sanderson, Thomas James, 1840-1922.

A Letter from Stella; 686.3'0092'4
an epilogue to the publication of C-S the master craftsman. [Harper Woods, Mich.] Adagio Press, 1971. [19] p. 26 cm. "Copy 292." Contents.Contents.—Strouse, N. H. Introduction.—Cobden-Sanderson, T. J. Last letter, to his daughter, Stella, Dated Sept. 6, 1922.—Russell, Countess E. A tribute to C-S, originally published in London Times, Sept. 13, 1922.—Cobden-Sanderson, S. A letter from Stella, to N. H. Strouse, dated Dec. 15, 1969.—Dreyfus, J. Corrigenda/C-S the master craftsman. [Z232.C65L46] 73-165363
1. Cobden-Sanderson, Thomas James, 1840-1922. I. Strouse, Norman H. C-S the mater craftsman.

Cobe, Albert.

COBE, Albert. 796.352'64'023
Great spirit, by Albert Cobe, with George Elrick and R. E. Simon, Jr. [Chicago, Childrens Press, 1970] 64 p. illus., ports. 19 cm. (An Open door book) Autobiographical. A Chippewa Indian recounts his early life on a reservation and how he became a professional golfer. [E90.C58A3] 92 71-101735
I. Elrick, George, joint author. II. Simon, Richard Edward, 1945- joint author. III. Title.

Cobham, Richard Temple, 1st Viscount, 1669?-1749.

TEMPLE, Albert R. 929'.2 S
Lord Cobham : the life of Sir Richard Temple, Viscount, 1675-1749 / by Albert R. Temple ; with a foreword by the tenth viscount. 1st ed. Cincinnati : Temple Family Association, 1976. 133 p., [5] leaves of plates : ill. ; 23 cm. (His The rise of the Temples ; book 2) Includes bibliographical references. [CS71.T285 1973 bk. 2] [DA437.C62] 355.3'31'0924 B 76-151142
1. Cobham, Richard Temple, 1st Viscount, 1669?-1749. 2. Great Britain. Army—Biography. 3. Generals—Great Britain—Biography. I. Title.

Coblentz, William Weber,

COBLENTZ, William Weber, 1873- 925.3
From the life of a researcher. New York, Philosophical Library [1951] xi, 238 p. illus., ports. 22 cm. [QC16.C63A3] 51-9947
I. Title.

Cobos y Molina, Francisco de los, d. 1547.

KENISTON, Hayward, 1883- 923.246
Francisco de los Cobos, secretary of the Emperor Charles v. [Pittsburgh] University of Pittsburgh Press [1960] xvi, 463 p. maps, ports., plates, facsims., geneal. tables. 24 cm. Bibliography: p. 427-448. [DD180.K4] 59-15245
1. Cobos y Molina, Francisco de los, d. 1547. 2. Karl V, Emperor of Germany, 1500-1558. I. Title.

Coburn, Alvin Frederick, 1899-

COBURN, Alvin Frederick, 1899- 610'.92'4 B
Commitment total / Alvin F. Coburn. New York : Walker, 1974. xv, 231 p. ; 22 cm. [R154.C418A33 1974] 73-93939 ISBN 0-8027-0449-2 : 7.95
1. Coburn, Alvin Frederick, 1899- 2. Physicians—Correspondence, reminiscences, etc. 3. Rheumatic fever. I. Title. **BIP**

Coburn, Vic.

ROBERTS, Cecil A. 269'.2'0924 B
Vic Coburn : man with the healing touch / by C. A. Roberts. Nashville : T. Nelson, [1975] 204 p., [4] leaves of plates : ill. ; 21 cm. "Sermons by Vic Coburn": p. 163-204. [BV3785.C554R6] 75-12931 ISBN 0-8407-5597-X pbk. : 3.50
1. Coburn, Vic. 2. Faith-cure. 3. Sermons, American. I. Coburn, Vic.

Cochise, Apache chief, d. 1874.

COCHISE, Ciye, 1874- 970.3 B
The first hundred years of Nino Cochise; the untold story of an Apache Indian chief, as told by Ciye "Nino" Cochise to A. Kinney Griffith. London, New York, Abelard-Schuman [1971] 346 p. illus. 24 cm. [E99.A6C57] 70-157980 ISBN 0-200-71830-4 9.95 (U.S.)
1. Apache Indians. I. Griffith, A. Kinney. II. Title.

JOHNSON, Enid, 1892- 970.3 B
Cochise, great Apache chief. Illus. by Lorence F. Bjorklund. New York, J. Messner [1953] 180 p. illus. 22 cm. A biography of Cochise, Chief of the Chiricahua nation, whose fierceness in battle was matched only by the quiet courage of Jeffords, "the white eye," who sought a peaceful union between the United States and the Apaches. [PZ7.J63176Co] 92 AC 68
1. Cochise, Apache chief, d. 1874. I. Bjorklund, Lorence F., illus. II. Title.

Cochise, Apache chief, d. 1874—Fiction.

WYATT, Edgar. 920
Cochise, Apache warrior and statesman; illustrated by Allan Houser. New York, Whittlesey House [1953] 192 p. illus. 21 cm. Includes bibliography. [PZ7.W966Co] 53-5193
1. Cochise, Apache chief, d. 1874—Fiction.

Cochise, Apache chief, d. 1874—Juvenile literature.

CARLSON, Vada F. 970.3 B
Cochise, chief of the Chiricahaus [i.e. Chiricahuas] by Vada F. Carlson. Illustrated by William A. Orr. Irvington-on-Hudson, N.Y., Harvey House [1973] 174, [1] p. illus. 23 cm. The life of the Apache chief who, after many betrayals by the white man, distinguished himself in savage warfare against his enemy. Bibliography: p. [175] [E99.A6C37] 71-148107 ISBN 0-8178-4951-3 3.95
1. Cochise, Apache chief, d. 1874—Juvenile literature. I. Orr, William A., illus. II. Title.

JOHNSON, Ann Donegan. 970'.004'97 B
The value of truth and trust : the story of Cochise / by Ann Donegan Johnson ; illustrated by Pileggi. 1st ed. La Jolla, Calif. : Value Communications, inc., c1977. 62 p. : col. ill. ; 28 cm. A biography of Cochise, the Apache chief, whose life illustrates the values of trust and truth. [E99.A6C574] 92 77-3294 ISBN 0-916392-09-0 : 4.95
1. Cochise, Apache chief, d. 1874—Juvenile literature. 2. Apache Indians—Biography—Juvenile literature. I. Pileggi, Steve. II. Title. BIP

Cochran, Jacqueline.

COCHRAN, Jacqueline. 926.2913
The stars at noon, by Jacqueline Cochrane, with Floyd Odlum as wingman. [1st ed.] Boston, Little, Brown [1954] 274 p. illus. 21 cm. Autobiography. [TL540.C63A3] 54-8316
I. Odlum, Floyd B. II. Title. BIP

Cochran, Jacqueline—Juvenile literature.

FISHER, Marquita O. 629.13'092'4 B
Jacqueline Cochran: first lady of flight, by Marquita O. Fisher. Illustrated by Victor Mays. Champaign, Ill., Garrard Pub. Co. [1973] 96 p. illus. (part col.) 24 cm. (Americans all) A biography of the woman pilot who organized and commanded the Women's Airforce Service Pilots during World War II and became the first civilian woman to receive the Distinguished Service Medal. [TL540.C63F57] 92 72-14368 2.98
1. Cochran, Jacqueline—Juvenile literature. I. Mays, Victor, 1927- illus. II. Title.

WAYNE, Bennett. 920.72
Four women of courage, edited with commentary by Bennett Wayne. Champaign, Ill., Garrard Pub. Co. [1975] 167 p. illus. 22 cm. (A Target book) Brief biographies of four women who achieved their ambitions against great odds. [HQ1412.W39] 920 74-13482 ISBN 0-8116-4911-3 3.98 (lib. bdg.)
1. Cochran, Jacqueline—Juvenile literature. 2. Dix, Dorothea Lynde, 1802-1887—Juvenile literature. 3. Keller, Helen Adams, 1880-1968—Juvenile literature. 4. Richards, Linda Ann Judson, 1841-1930—Juvenile literature. I. Title. BIP

Cochran, John, 1730-1807.

SAFFRON, Morris Harold. 616.9'8023'0924 B
Surgeon to Washington, Dr. John Cochran, 1730-1807 / Morris H. Saffron. New York : Columbia University Press, 1977. x, 302 p. : port. ; 24 cm. Includes index. Bibliography: p. [275]-288. [R154.C43S23] 77-2675 ISBN 0-231-04186-1 : 12.50
1. Cochran, John, 1730-1807. 2. Physicians—United States—Biography. 3. Physicians—United States—Correspondence. 4. United States—History—Revolution, 1775-1783—Medical and sanitary affairs. I. Title.

Cochrane, Elizabeth, 1867-1922.

AMERICAN Flange and Manufacturing Company, inc. 920.5
The story of Nellie Bly. [New York, 1951] 61 p. illus. 26 cm. [PN2287.C55A7] 52-1529
1. Cochrane, Elizabeth, 1867-1922. I. Title.

BAKER, Nina (Brown) 1888- 920.5
Nellie Bly: illustrated by George Fulton. [1st ed.] New York, Holt 531956] 124p. illus. 21cm. [PN4874.C59B3] 56-10037
1. Cochrane. Elizabeth. 1867-1922. I. Title.

NOBLE, Iris. 920.5
Nellie Bly, first woman reporter (1867-1922) New York, Messner [1956] 192p. 22cm. [PN4874.C59N6] 56-6792
1. Cochrane, Elizabeth, 1867-1922. I. Title.

NOBLE, Iris. 920.5
Nellie Bly, first woman reporter (1867-1922) New York, Messner [1956] 192 p. 22 cm. [PN4874.C59N6] 56-6792
1. Cochrane, Elizabeth, 1867-1922.

RITTENHOUSE, Mignon. 920.5
The amazing Nelie Bly. [1st ed.] New York, Dutton, 1956. 254p. illus. 22cm. [PN4874.C59R5] 56-8324
1. Cochrane, Elizabeth, 1867-1922. I. Title.

RITTENHOUSE, Mignon. 070'.924 B
The amazing Nellie Bly. Freeport, N.Y., Books for Libraries Press [1971, c1956] 254 p. illus., ports. 23 cm. (Biography index reprint series) [PN4874.C59R5 1971] 74-148227 ISBN 0-8369-8074-3
1. Cochrane, Elizabeth, 1867-1922. I. Title. BIP

Cochrane, Elizabeth, 1867-1922—Juvenile literature.

DUNNAHOO, Terry. 070'.924 B
Nellie Bly: a portrait. Chicago, Reilly & Lee Books [1970] 168 p. port. 24 cm. A biography of the woman who became a newspaper reporter over objections that it was not a suitable career for proper young ladies in the 1880's. [PN4874.C59D8] 92 70-105128 4.95
1. Cochrane, Elizabeth, 1867-1922—Juvenile literature. I. Title.

GRAVES, Charles Parlin, 1911- 070'.924 B
Nellie Bly, reporter for the world, by Charles P. Graves. Illustrated by Victor Mays. Champaign, Ill., Garrard Pub. Co. [1971] 95 p. illus. (part col.), ports. 24 cm. (Americans all) A biography of one of the first women reporters, whose trip around the world in less than eighty days made her an international celebrity. [PN4874.C59G7] 92 70-133619 ISBN 0-8116-4567-3 2.49
1. Cochrane, Elizabeth, 1867-1922—Juvenile literature. I. Mays, Victor, 1927- illus. II. Title.

JOHNSON, Ann Donegan. 070'.92'4 B
The value of fairness : the story of Nellie Bly / by Ann Donegan Johnson ; illustrated by Pileggi. 1st ed. San Diego : Value Communications, inc., c1977. p. cm. (ValueTales) [PN4874.C59J6] 77-13275 ISBN 0-916392-16-3 : 4.95
1. Cochrane, Elizabeth, 1867-1922—Juvenile literature. 2. Journalists—United States—Biography—Juvenile literature. I. Title. BIP

Cochrane, Gordon Stanley—Juvenile literature.

VAN RIPER, Guernsey, 1909- 796.357'092'2
Behind the plate: three great catchers, by Guernsey Van Riper, Jr. Illustrated by Jack Hearne. Champaign, Ill., Garrard Pub. Co. [1973] 95 p. illus. 24 cm. Brief biographies of three well-known catchers emphasizing their development of the skills that made them valuable ball players. [GV865.A1V29] 920 73-2952 ISBN 0-8116-6665-4 2.95
1. Cochrane, Gordon Stanley—Juvenile literature. 2. Dickey, Bill, 1907- —Juvenile literature. 3. Campanella, Roy, 1921- —Juvenile literature. 4. Catching (Baseball)—Juvenile literature. I. Hearne, Jack, illus. II. Title.

Cock, Hieronymus, 1510 (ca.)-1570.

RIGGS, Timothy A., 1942- 769'.92'4 B
Hieronymus Cock, printmaker and publisher / Timothy A. Riggs. New York : Garland Pub., 1977, i.e.1978 xxxii, 416 p., [68] leaves of plates : ill. ; 21 cm. (Outstanding dissertations in the fine arts) Originally presented as the author's thesis, Yale, 1971. Bibliography: p. 395-416. [NE674.C6R43 1977] 76-23706 ISBN 0-8240-2724-8 lib.bdg. : 52.50
1. Cock, Hieronymus, 1510 (ca.)-1570. 2. Printmakers—Belgium—Biography. I. Title. II. Series.

Cockburn, Claud,

COCKBURN, Claud, 1904- 920.5
A discord of trumpets, an autobiography. New York, Simon and Schuster, 1956. 314p. 22cm. London ed. (Hart-Davis) has title: In time of trouble. [PN5123.C45A3 1956a] 56-7491
I. Title.

COCKBURN, Claud, 1904- 920.5
A discord of trumpets, an autobiography. New York, Simon and Schuster, 1956. 314p. 22cm. London ed. (Hart-Davis) has title: In time of trouble. [PN5123.C45A3 1956a] 56-7491
I. Title.

COCKBURN, Claud, 1904- 070.9'24 B
I, Claud ... : the autobiography of Claud Cockburn. Harmondsworth, Penguin, 1967. 454 p. 18 cm. First published in 3 v.: In time of trouble, Crossing the line, and View from the west. [PN5123.C45A34] 70-351297 7/6
I. Title.

Cockburn, Claud [Francis Claud Cockburn]

COCKBURN, Claud [Francis Claud Cockburn] 920.5
Crossing the line, being the second volume of autobiography. New York, Monthly Review Press, 1960 210p. 23cm. 60-6305 3.50 bds.,
I. Title.

COCKBURN, Claud [Francis Claud Cockburn] 1904- 920.5
View from the West, being the third volume of autobiography. New York, Monthly Review, 1962 [c.1961] 208p. 23cm. 62-175588 3.75
I. Title.

Cockcroft, John Douglas, Sir 1897-

CLARK, Ronald William. 925.3
Sir John Cockcroft, O. M., F. R. S. New York, Roy Publishers [1960, c1959] 100p. illus. 19cm. (The Living biographies series) [QC774.C6C53 1960] 60-7678
1. Cockcroft, John Douglas, Sir 1897- I. Title.

Cockerell, Sir Sydney Carlyle, 1867-1962.

BLUNT, Wilfrid, 1901- 927
Cockerell; Sydney Carlyle Cockerell, friend of Ruskin and William Morris and director of the Fitzwilliam Museum, Cambridge. [1st Amer. ed.] New York, Knopf, 1965[c.1964] xviii, 385p. illus., facsim., ports. 22cm. [N8375.C6B55] 65-11117 7.50
1. Cockerell, Sir Sydney Carlyle, 1867-1962. I. Title.

Cockerell, Theodore Dru Alison, 1866-1948.

COCKERELL, Theodore Dru Alison, 1866-1948. 978.8'52
Theodore D. A. Cockerell : letters from West Cliff, Colorado, 1887-1889 / edited by William A. Weber. Boulder : Colorado Associated University Press, c1976. xxvii, 222 p. : ill. ; 24 cm. Includes bibliographical references. [QH31.C56A4 1976] 76-15775 ISBN 0-87081-070-7 : 8.95
1. Cockerell, Theodore Dru Alison, 1866-1948. 2. Naturalists—Colorado—Correspondence.

Cockerill, John Albert, 1845-1896.

KING, Homer W. 920.5
Pulitzer's prize editor; a biography of John A. Cockerill, 1845-1896, by Homer W. King. Durham, N. C., Duke University Press, 1965. xx, 336 p. illus., ports. 23 cm. Bibliography: p. [324]-329. [PN4874.C6Z7] 64-7798
1. Cockerill, John Albert, 1845-1896. I. Title. BIP

cocking, George,

COCKING, George, 1862- 922.773
From the mines to the pulpit; or, Success hammered out of the rock. Cincinnati, Printed for the author by Jennings & Pye [c1901] 177 p. port. 19 cm. [BX495.C58A3] 3-8352
I. Title.

Cockram (T.R. & L.) Pty. Ltd.

SHAW, Mary Turner. 338.4'7'69009945
Builders of Melbourne: the Cockrams and their contemporaries, 1853-1972. Melbourne, Cypress Books, 1972. 116 p. illus., plans. 25 cm. Bibliography: p. 111. [TA217.C58S47] 73-163185 ISBN 0-909807-07-8 6.75
1. Cockram (T.R. & L.) Pty. Ltd. 2. Melbourne—History. I. Title.

Cockran, William Bourke, 1854-1923.

MCGURRIN, James. 328.73'092'4 B
Bourke Cockran: a free lance in American politics. New York, Arno Press, 1972 [c1948] xv, 361 p. ports. 23 cm. (The Right wing individualist tradition in America) Bibliography: p. 337-339. [E664.C543M3 1972] 74-172219 ISBN 0-405-00428-1
1. Cockran, William Bourke, 1854-1923. 2. United States—Politics and government—1865-1933. I. Title. II. Series. BIP

Cockrell, Francis Marion, 1834-1915.

COCKRELL, Francis Marion. 923.273
The Senator from Missouri; the life and times of Francis Marion Cockrell. Foreword by Stuart Symington. [1st ed.] New York, Exposition Press [1962] 114p. illus. 22cm. [E664.C545C57] 62-13678
1. Cockrell, Francis Marion, 1834-1915. I. Title.

Cocteau, Jean, 1889-1963.

COCTEAU, Jean, 1889-1963. 920.044
My contemporaries. [Translated from the French]; edited and introduced by Margaret Crosland. [1st ed.] Philadelphia, Chilton Book Co. [1968] xii, 146 p. illus., ports. 21 cm. [PQ2605.O15M89 1968] 68-31695
1. France—Biography. 2. France—Civilization—1901- I. Crosland, Margaret, 1920- ed. II. Title.

COCTEAU, Jean, 1889-1963. 838'.9'1209 B
Professional secrets; an autobiography of Jean Cocteau, drawn from his lifetime writings by Robert Phelps. Translated from the French by Richard Howard. New York, Farrar, Straus & Giroux, 1970. xiii, 331 p. illus., facsim., ports. 22 cm. Includes bibliographical references. [PQ2605.O15Z5] 70-82626 8.50
I. Phelps, Robert, 1922- ed. II. Title.

CROSLAND, Margaret, 1920- 928.4
Jean Cocteau; a biography. [1st American ed.] New York, Knopf, 1956. x, 238 p. illus., ports. 22 cm. 'Bibliography of works by Jean Cocteau': p. [223]-236. Bibliography: p. [237]-238. [PQ2605.O15Z66 1956] 56-5293

1. Cocteau, Jean, 1889- I. Title.

PETERS, Arthur King, 1919- 848'.9'1209 B
Jean Cocteau and Andre Gide: an abrasive friendship. New Brunswick, N.J., Rutgers University Press [1973] xv, 426 p. illus. 23 cm. "The entire known correspondence between the two men is contained in this book, in both French and English." Bibliography: p. [399]-405. [PQ2605.O15Z77] 73-10002 ISBN 0-8135-0709-X
1. Cocteau, Jean, 1889-1963. 2. Gide, Andre Paul Guillaume, 1869-1951. I. Cocteau, Jean, 1889-1963. II. Gide, Andre Paul Guillaume, 1869-1951. III. Title.

SPRIGGE, Elizabeth, 1900- 848'.9'1209 B
Jean Cocteau: the man and the mirror, by Elizabeth Sprigge and Jean-Jacques Kihm. [1st American ed.] New York, Coward-McCann [1968] 286 p. illus., ports. 23 cm. Includes bibliographies. [PQ2605.O15Z85 1968b] 68-14306
1. Cocteau, Jean, 1889-1963. I. Kihm, Jean Jacques, joint author.

Cocteau, Jean, 1889-1963—Biography.

STEEGMULLER, Francis, 1906- 848'.9'1209 B
Cocteau, a biography. [1st ed.] Boston, Little, Brown [1970] xiv, 583 p. illus., ports. 25 cm. "An Atlantic Monthly Press book." Bibliography: p. [533]-539. [PQ2605.O15Z86] 76-117039 12.50
1. Cocteau, Jean, 1889-1963—Biography.

Cocteau, Jean, 1889-1963—Journeys—Levant.

COCTEAU, Jean, 1889-1963. 848'.9'1203
Maalesh : a theatrical tour in the Middle-East / Jean Cocteau ; translated by Mary C. Hoeck. Westport, Conn. : Greenwood Press, 1978. 136 p., [4] leaves of plates : ill. ; 23 cm. Reprint of the 1956 ed. published by P. Owen, London. Includes index. [PQ2605.O15Z543 1978] 77-26022 ISBN 0-313-20054-8 lib.bdg. : 12.75
1. Cocteau, Jean, 1889-1963—Journeys—Levant. 2. Authors, French—20th century—Biography. 3. Theater—Levant. 4. Levant—Description and travel. I. Title. BIP

Codorus Church of the Brethren, Loganville, Pa.

GOULD, William L., 1917- 286'.5
A light in the valley : a history of the Codorus Church of the Brethren / by William L. Gould. Loganville, Pa. : The Church, 1976. 189 p., [20] leaves of plates : ill., map (on lining papers) ; 24 cm. Includes bibliographical references. [BX7831.L633G68] 77-153075
1. Codorus Church of the Brethren, Loganville, Pa. 2. Codorus Church of the Brethren, Loganville, Pa.—Biography. 3. Loganville, Pa.—Biography. I. Title.

GOULD, William L., 1917- 286'.5
A light in the valley : a history of the Codorus Church of the Brethren / by William L. Gould. Loganville, Pa. : The Church, 1976. 189 p., [20] leaves of plates : ill., map (on lining papers) ; 24 cm. Includes bibliographical references. [BX7831.L633G68] 77-153075
1. Codorus Church of the Brethren, Loganville, Pa. 2. Codorus Church of the Brethren, Loganville, Pa.—Biography. 3. Loganville, Pa.—Biography. I. Title.

Codreanu, Cornelinu Zelea, 1899-1938.

CODREANU, Corneliu Zelea, 1899-1938. 320.5'33'0924 B
For my legionaries : the Iron Guard / Corneliu Zelea Codreanu. Madrid : Editura "Libertatea", 1976. xvi, 353 p. : port. ; 21 cm. Translation of Pentru legionari. Label mounted on inside back cover: Available from Liberty Bell Publications, Reedy, W. Va. [DR262.C6A324] 77-565552 6.00 (U.S.)
1. Codreanu, Cornelinu Zelea, 1899-1938. 2. Garda de Fier. 3. Politicians—Romania—Biography. I. Title.

Codrescu, Andrei, 1946- —Biography.

CODRESCU, Andrei, 1946- 811'.5'4 B
The life and times of an involuntary genius / Andrei Codrescu. New York : G. Braziller, [1975] 192 p. ; 22 cm. (A Venture book) [PS3553.O3Z52] 74-24906 ISBN 0-8076-0773-8 : 7.95
1. Codrescu, Andrei, 1946- —Biography. I. Title. BIP

Cody, William Frederick, 1846-1917.

CODY, William Frederick, 1846-1917. 978'.02'0924 B
The life of Hon. William F. Cody, known as Buffalo Bill, the famous hunter, scout, and guide : an autobiography / foreword by Don Russell. Lincoln : University of Nebraska Press, 1978. p. cm. "A Bison book." [F594.C6745 1978] 78-18732 ISBN 0-8032-1406-5 : 15.00 ISBN 0-8032-6303-1 pbk. : 4.95
1. Cody, William Frederick, 1846-1917. 2. Pioneers—The West—Biography. 3. Scouts and scouting—The West—Biography. 4. Frontier and pioneer life—The West. I. Title.

GARST, Doris Shannon, 1899- v. 12
Buffalo Bill. Illus. by Elton C. Fax. New York, J. Messner [1965] 214 p. illus., port. 23 cm. Bibliography: p. 205-207. 68-48028
1. Cody, William Frederick, 1846-1917. I. Title.

LEONARD, Elizabeth Jane. 923.973
Buffalo Bill, King of the Old West; biography of William F. Cody, pony express rider, buffalo hunter, plains scout & guide, master showman, by Elizabeth Jane Leonard and Julia Cody Goodman. Edited by James Williams Hoffman. New York, Library Publishers [1955] 320 p. illus., ports., map (on lining papers) 21 cm. Bibliography: p. 311-314. [F594.C6827] 55-10309
1. Cody, William Frederick, 1846-1917. I. Goodman, Julia Cody, 1843-1928, joint author.

O'CONNOR, Richard, 1915- 978'.02'0924 B
Buffalo Bill: the noblest whiteskin, by John Burke. New York, Putnam [1972, c1973] 320 p. illus. 23 cm. Bibliography: p. [305]-306. [F594.C684 1973] 72-87607 ISBN 0-399-11060-7 7.95
1. Cody, William Frederick, 1846-1917.

POMPEY, Sherman Lee. 978'.02'0924
The truth about Buffalo Bill Cody's government service / Sherman Lee Pompey. Independence, Calif. : Historical and Genealogical Pub. Co., c1966. [2] leaves ; 28 cm. Cover title. [F594.C6864] 75-303962
1. Cody, William Frederick, 1846-1917. I. Title.

REGLI, Adolph Casper, 1896- 923.973
The real book about Buffalo Bill; illustrated by Robert J. Lee. [1st ed.] Garden City, N. Y., Garden City Books, by arrangement with F. Watts [New York] [1952] 191 p. illus. 21 cm. (Real books [R32]) [F594.C6866] 52-12507
1. Cody, William Frederick, 1846-1917. I. Title.

REGLI, Adolph Casper, 1896- 923.973
The real book about Buffalo Bill; illustrated by Robert J. Lee. [1st ed.] Garden City, N. Y., Garden City Books, by arrangement with F. Watts [New York] [1952] 191 p. illus. 21 cm. (Real books [R32]) [F594.C6866] 52-12507
1. Cody, William Frederick, 1846-1917. I. Title.

RUSSELL, Don, 1899- 923.973
The lives and legends of Buffalo Bill. [1st ed.] Norman, University of Oklahoma Press [1960] 514 p. illus. 24 cm. Includes bibliography. [F594.C6867] 60-13470
1. Cody, William Frederick, 1846 1917. I. Title. BIP

RUSSELL, Donald Bert, 1899- 923.973
The lives and legends of Buffalo Bill. Norman, University of Oklahoma Press [c.1960] 514p. Bibl. p.482-493 and bibl. notes illus. 24cm. 60-13470 5.95
1. Cody, William Frederick, 1846-1917. I. Title.

SELL, Henry Blackman. 923.973
Buffalo Bill and the Wild West, by Henry Blackman Sell and Victor Weybright. New York, Oxford University Press, 1955. 278 p. illus. 26 cm. Includes bibliography. [F594.C6869] 55-10932
1. Cody, William Frederick, 1846-1917. I. Weybright, Victor, joint author. II. Title.

WETMORE, Helen (Cody) 923.973
Last of the great scouts; the life story of Col. William F. Cody, 'Buffalo Bill,'as told by his sister [Gloucester, Mass., P. Smith, 1965] xvi, 296p. illus., ports. 21cm. Reproduced from the 1899 ed. (Bison bk., BB315 rebound) [F594.C692] 3.50
1. Cody, William Frederick, 1846-1917. I. Title.

WETMORE, Helen (Cody) 923.973
Last of the great scouts; the life story of Col. William F. Cody, 'Buffalo Bill,' as told by his sister. Lincoln, Univ. of Neb. Pr. [1965] xvi, 296p. illus., ports. 21cm. (Bison bk. BB315) Reproduced from the 1899 ed. [F594.C692] 65-13258 1.50 pap.,
1. Cody, William Frederick, I. Title.

Cody, William Frederick, 1846-1917—Juvenile literature.

AULAIRE, Ingri Mortenson d', 1904- juv
Buffalo Bill, by Ingri & Edgar Parin d'Aulaire. Garden City, N.Y., Doubleday, c1952. 44 p. illus. (part col.) 29 cm. [PZ7.A914Bu] 52-10232
1. Cody, William Frederick, 1846-1917—Juvenile literature.

GRANT, Matthew G. 978'.02'0924 B
Buffalo Bill of the Wild West [by] Matthew G. Grant. Illustrated by John Keely and Dick Brude. [Mankato, Minn., Creative Education; distributed by Childrens Press, Chicago, [1973, c1974] 29 p. illus. (part col.) 25 cm. (His Gallery of great Americans series. Frontiersmen of America) A brief biography of the frontiersman whose many careers during a lifetime of ups and downs included Pony Express rider, Indian fighter, scout, and star of the Wild West Show [F594.C6817] 73-10073 ISBN 0-87191-255-4 4.95
1. Cody, William Frederick, 1846 1917 Juvenile literature. I. Keely, John, illus. II. Brude, Dick, illus. III. Title.

KOLARS, Frank. 923.973
The long trail; the story of Buffalo Bill. Illustrated by Albert Micale. New York, Benziger Bros. [1960] 181p. illus. 22cm. (Banner books [11]) Includes bibliography. [F594.C6825] 60-15494
1. Cody, William Frederick, 1846-1917—Juvenile literature. I. Title.

STEVENS, Eden Vale. 978'.02'0924 B
Buffalo Bill / by Eden Vale Stevens : illustrated by Joseph Ciardiello. New York : Putnam, [1976] p. cm. (See and read biography) Easy-to-read biography of the frontiersman whose many careers included Pony Express rider, Indian fighter, scout, and star of his own Wild West Show. [F594.C6875 1976] lib.bdg. : 3.96
1. Cody, William Frederick, 1846-1917—Juvenile literature. I. Ciardiello, Joseph. II. Title. BIP

Coe family.

COE, Wilbur, 1894- 630.11'789'64
Ranch on the Ruidoso; the story of a pioneer family in New Mexico, 1871-1968. With an introd. by Peter Hurd. [1st ed.] New York, Knopf, 1968. xviii, 279 p. illus. (part col.) 24 cm. [CT275.C66A3] 68-26490 8.95
1. Coe family. 2. Ranch life—Lincoln Co., N.M. I. Title.

Coe, Jack,

COE, Jack, 1918- 922
The story of Jack Coe; from pup tent to world's largest gospel tent, prepared and edited by Gordon Lindsay [in collaborationwith Jack Coe. Shreveport? La.] '1951. 110 p. illus. 19 cm. [BV3785.C556A3] 52-403
I. Lindsay. Gordon. ed. II. Title.

Coffin, Robert Peter Tristram, 1892-1955.

SANBORN, Annie (Coffin) 811'.009
The life of Robert Peter Tristram Coffin and family. Alton, N. H., 1963. 111 p. illus., ports. 22 cm. [PS3505.O234Z87] 64-3436
1. Coffin, Robert Peter Tristram, 1892-1955. I. Title.

Coffin, Robert Peter Tristram, 1892-1955—Homes and haunts—Maine.

COFFIN, Robert Peter Tristram, 1892-1955. 818'.5'209 B
Lost paradise; a boyhood on a Maine coast farm. New York, Macmillan, 1947. St. Clair Shores, Mich., Scholarly Press, 1971 [c1934] 284 p. 22 cm. [PS3505.O234Z5 1971] 78-144951 ISBN 0-403-00904-9
I. Title. BIP

COFFIN, Robert Peter Tristram, 1892-1955. 974.1
Maine doings / by Robert P. Tristram Coffin ; with decorations by the author. Thorndike, Me. : Thorndike Press, [1979?] c1950. 266 p. : ill. ; 20 cm. Reprint of the 1st ed. published by Bobbs-Merrill, Indianapolis, with a new introd. [F25.C66 1979] 78-26413 ISBN 0-89621-025-1 lib. bdg. : 11.50 ISBN 0-89621-024-3 pbk. : 4.95
1. Coffin, Robert Peter Tristram, 1892-1955—Homes and haunts—Maine. 2. Maine—Social life and customs. 3. Authors, American—20th century—Biography. I. Title. BIP

Coffman, Edward

COFFMAN, Edward 922.673
Happy years, an autobiography. Nashville, Parthenon Pr. [1964] 127p. illus., ports. 23cm. 64-7900 price unreported
I. Title.

Coffman, John Samuel, 1848-1899.

COFFMAN, Barbara Frances. 922.8773
His name was John; the life story of an early Mennonite leader. by Barbara F. Coffman. Scottdale, Pa., Herald Press [1964] 352 p. illus., ports. 23 cm. [BX8143.C6] 64-18732
1. Coffman, John Samuel, 1848-1899. I. Title.

Coffman, William Milo,

COFFMAN, William Milo, 1883- 920
American in the rough; the autobiography of W. M. (Bill) Coffman. New York, Simon and Schuster, 1955. 309p. illus. 24cm. [RD701.C58] 55-10058
I. Title.

Cofresi y Ramirez de Arellano, Roberto, 1791-1825—Juvenile literature.

COOPER, Lee. 364.135 B
The pirate of Puerto Rico. Illustrated by David Stone. New York, Putnam [1972] 78 p. illus. 21 cm. In an attempt to buy the freedom of two slave friends, Roberto Cofresi turns to piracy and becomes one of the most famous buccaneers of the nineteenth century. [F1973.C632C6 1972] 92 74-165484 3.75
1. Cofresi y Ramirez de Arellano, Roberto, 1791-1825—Juvenile literature. I. Stone, David K., illus. II. Title.

Coggan, Frederick Donald, 1909-

COGGAN, Frederick Donald, 1909- 230'.3
Convictions / by Donald Coggan. Grand Rapids : Eerdmans, c1975. 320 p. ; 23 cm. [BX5199.C567A33] 75-42458 ISBN 0-8028-3481-7 : 9.95
1. Coggan, Frederick Donald, 1909- 2. Theology—Addresses, essays, lectures. 3. England—Biography. I. Title.

Coggan, Jean, 1908-

ARNOTT, Anne. 283'.092'4 B
Wife to the archbishop / by Anne Arnott. London : Mowbrays, 1976. x, 161 p., [12] p. of plates : ill., ports. ; 23 cm. [BX5199.C5673A8] 77-355087 ISBN 0-264-66266-0 : £3.60
1. Coggan, Jean, 1908- 2. Clergymen's wives—England—Biography. I. Title.

Cogswell, Arthur Edward, 1858-1934.

NASH, Andy. 720'.92'4
A. E. Cogswell, architect within a Victorian city / [by] Andy Nash. Portsmouth : School of Architecture, Portsmouth Polytechnic, 1975. [3], 115, viii, iii leaves : ill., map, plans ; 30 cm. Cover title. Bibliography: leaves i-iii. [NA997.C64N37] 76-359799 ISBN 0-905320-00-X : £3.50
1. Cogswell, Arthur Edward, 1858-1934. 2. Architecture, Victorian—Portsmouth, Eng. I. Title.

Cohan, George Michael, 1878-1942.

COHAN, George Michael, 1878-1942. 792.0924
Twenty years on Broadway, and the years it took to get there; the true story of a trouper's life from the cradle to the "closed shop". Westport, Conn., Greenwood Press [1971, c1925] 264 p. illus. 23 cm. [PN2287.C56A3 1971] 76-138106 ISBN 0-8371-5682-3
1. Actors—United States—Correspondence, reminiscences, etc. I. Title. BIP

MCCABE, John, 1920 792'.092'4 B
George M. Cohan: the man who owned Broadway. [1st ed.] Garden City, N.Y., Doubleday, 1973. xii, 296 p. illus. 22 cm. [PN2287.C56M3] 72-89328 ISBN 0-385-01578-X 7.95
1. Cohan, George Michael, 1878-1942. I. Title: The man who owned Broadway. BIP

MOREHOUSE, Ward, 1898-1966. 792'.092'4 B
George M. Cohan, prince of the American theater. Westport, Conn., Greenwood Press [1972, c1943] 240 p. illus. 22 cm. [PN2287.C56M6 1972] 79-165445 ISBN 0-8371-6225-4
1. Cohan, George Michael, 1878-1942. BIP

WINDERS, Gertrude (Hecker) 792'.0924 B
George M. Cohan; boy theater genius. Illustrated by James Cummins. Indianapolis, Bobbs-Merrill Co. [1968] 200 p. col. illus. 20 cm. (Childhood of famous Americans) A biography stressing the childhood theater experiences of the boy who became a leading vaudeville director and performer, a successful musical play writer, and a composer of patriotic songs for which he was awarded a special Congressional Medal of Honor. [PN2287.C56W5] 92 AC 68
1. Cohan, George Michael, 1878-1942. I. Cummins, James, illus. II. Title. BIP

Cohan, George Michael, 1878-1942—Juvenile literature.

WINDERS, Gertrude (Hecker) 92 (J)
George M. Cohan; boy theater genius. Illustrated by James Cummings. Indianapolis, Bobbs-Merrill Co. [1968] 200 p. col. illus. 20 cm. (Childhood of famous Americans) [PN2287.C56W5] 68-17022 2.05
1. Cohan, George Michael, 1878-1942—Juvenile literature.

Cohen, Eliahou Ben Shaul, 1924-1965.

ALDOUBY, Zwy. 956'.04'0924
The shattered silence; the Eli Cohen affair, by Zwy Aldouby and Jerrold Ballinger. New York, Coward, McCann & Geoghegan [1971] x, 453 p. illus., ports. 22 cm. Bibliography: p. 429-433. [DS126.5.A685] 73-81016 7.95
1. Cohen, Eliahou Ben Shaul, 1924-1965. 2. Espionage, Israeli—Syria. I. Ballinger, Jerrold, joint author. II. Title.

BEN-HANAN, Eli. 327'.12'0924 B
Our man in Damascus: Elie Cohn. New York, Crown Publishers [1969] 192 p. illus., facsim., ports. 22 cm. [DS126.5.B45 1969] 76-75078 4.95
1. Cohen, Eliahou Ben Shaul, 1924-1965. 2. Espionage, Israeli—Syria. I. Title.

Cohen, Ephraim Leo, 1941 or 2-1956.

COHEN, Ruth Kolko. 920
A boy's quiet vioce. New York, Greenberg [1957] 115p. 21cm. [CT275.C667C6] 57-12499
1. Cohen, Ephraim Leo, 1941 or 2-1956. I. Title.

Cohen, Henry, 1863-1952.

GALVESTON. Congregation B'nai Israel. 922.96
Henry Cohen, messenger of the Lord; a tribute to the memory of its beloved rabbi on the one hundredth anniversary of his birth by Congregation B'naiIsrael of Galvestan Comp. by A. Stanley Dreyfus. New York, Bloch [c.]1963. 175p. illus. 24cm. 63-14151 4.00
1. Cohen, Henry, 1863-1952. I. Dreyfus, A. Stanley, comp. II. Title.

Cohen, Jacob Xenab, 1889-1955.

COHEN, Sadie Alta, 1891- 922.96
Engineer of the soul; a biography of Rabbi J. X. Cohen, 1889-1955. New York, Bloch Pub. Co. [1961] 222p. illus. 22cm. Includes bibliography. [BM755.C64C6] 60-16527
1. Cohen, Jacob Xenab, 1889-1955. I. Title.

Cohen, Michael Mickey.

COHEN, Michael Mickey. 364.1'092'4 B
Mickey Cohen, in my own words : the underworld autobiography of Michael Mickey Cohen, as told to John Peer Nugent. Englewood Cliffs, N.J. : Prentice-Hall, [1975] 264 p., [8] leaves of plates : ill. ; 24 cm. Includes index. [HV6248.C58A34] 75-20119 ISBN 0-13-580852-9 : 8.95
1. Cohen, Michael Mickey. I. Nugent, John Peer. II. Title.

Cohen, Morris Abraham, 1889-

DRAGE, Charles, 1897- 923.9
The life and times of General Two-Gun Cohen. New York, Funk & Wagnalls, 1954. 312p. illus. 22cm. 'Published in England under the title Two-Gun Cohen.' [G539.C6 1954a] 54-7761
1. Cohen, Morris Abraham, 1889- I. Title.

Cohen, Morris Raphael, 1880-1947.

COHEN, Morris Raphael, 1880-1947. 191 B
A dreamer's journey : the autobiography of Morris Raphael Cohen. New York : Arno Press, 1975, c1949. xiii, 318 p., [7] leaves of plates : ports. ; 24 cm. (The Modern Jewish experience) Reprint of the ed. published by Beacon Press, Boston. Includes index. "Bibliography of the published writings of Morris R. Cohen": p. 291-303. [B945.C54A3 1975] 74-27972 ISBN 0-405-06702-X : 22.00
1. Cohen, Morris Raphael, 1880-1947. 2. Cohen, Morris Raphael, 1880-1947—Bibliography. 3. Jews in the United States—Addresses, essays, lectures. I. Title. II. Series. BIP

ROSENFIELD, Leonora Davidson (Cohen) 1909- 921.1
Portrait of a philosopher: Morris R. Cohen in life and letters. New York, Harcourt [c.1948, 1962] 461p. 24cm. Bibl. 62-19591 10.00
1. Cohen, Morris Raphael, 1880-1947. I. Title.

ROSENFIELD, Leonora Davidson (Cohen) 1909- 921.1
Portrait of a philosopher: Morris R. Cohen in life and letters. [1st ed.] New York, Harcourt, Brace & World [1962] 461p. 24cm. [B945.C54R6] 62-19591
1. Cohen, Morris Raphael, 1880-1947. I. Title.

Cohen, Wilbur Joseph, 1913-

SHEARON, Marjorie O'Connell, 1890- 353.84'0924
Wilbur J. Cohen: the pursuit of power; a bureaucratic biography [by] Marjorie Shearon. [2d rev. ed. Chevy Chase, Md., Shearon Legislative Service, 1967] vii, 269 p. illus. 24 cm. Bibliography: p. 241-248. [HD7102.U5S5 1967b] 67-31614
1. Cohen, Wilbur Joseph, 1913- 2. Insurance, Health—United States. 3. Insurance, Social—United States. I. Title.

SHEARON, Marjorie O'Connell, 1890- 353.84'0924
Wilbur J. Cohen: the pursuit of power: a bureaucratic biography [by] Marjorie Shearon. [Chevy Chase, Md., Shearon Legislative Service] 1967. vii, 240 p. 23 cm. Bibliography: p. 215-220. [HD7102.U5S5] 67-27538
1. Cohen, Wilbur Joseph, 1913- 2. Insurance, Health—United States. 3. Insurance, Social—United States. I. Title.

Cohn, Harry, 1891-1958.

THOMAS, Bob, 1922- 791.43'0232'0924
King Cohn; the life and times of Harry Cohn. New York, Putnam [1967] 381 p. illus., ports. 22 cm. [PN1998.A3C78] 66-20298
1. Cohn, Harry, 1891-1958. I. Title.

Cohnstaedt, Wilhelm, 1880-1937.

COHNSTAEDT, Wilhelm, 1880-1937. 917.12'04'2
Western Canada 1909 : travel letters / by Wilhelm Cohnstaedt; translated by Herta Holle-Scherer ; editor, Klaus H. Burmeister. Regina, Sask. : Canadian Plains Research Center, University of Regina, 1976. 76 p. : ill. ; 23 cm. (Canadian plains studies ; 7) ISSN 03176290) Translation of Aus Westkanada. [F1060.9.C6313] 77-375204 ISBN 0-88977-003-4 : 4.00
1. Cohnstaedt, Wilhelm, 1880-1937. 2. Prairie Provinces—Description and travel. 3. Northwest, Canadian—Description and travel. I. Burmeister, Klaus H. II. Title. III. Series.

Coit, Joshua, 1758-1798.

DESTLER, Chester McArthur, 1904- 923.273
Joshua Coit, American Federalist, 1758-1798. Middletown, Conn. Wesleyan Univ. Pr. c.1962 xiii, 191p. illus. Bibl. 62-10571 5.75
1. Coit, Joshua, 1758-1798. 2. U. S.—Pol. & govt.—1789-1797. 3. Connecticut—Pol. govt.—1775-1865. I. Title. BIP

Coke, Edward, Sir, 1552-1634.

BOWEN, Catherine (Drinker) 1897- 923.442
The lion and the throne; the life and times of Sir Edward Coke (1552-1634) Boston, Atlantic-Little [1963, c.1956, 1957] xiii, 652p. 20cm. (29) 2.65 pap.,
1. Coke, Edward, Sir 1552-1634. I. Title.

BOWEN, Catherine (Drinker) 1897- 923.442
The lion and the throne; the life and times of Sir Edward Coke (1552-1634). 1st ed. Boston, Little, Brown [1957] xiii, 652 p. port., map (on lining papers) 22 cm. Bibliography: p. [565]-608. "Source references": p. [609]-637. [LAW] 56-10656
1. Coke, Edward, Sir, 1552-1634. I. Title.

WOOLRYCH, Humphry William, 1795-1871. 328.42'0924 B
The life of the Right Honourable Sir Edward Coke, knt., lord chief justice of the king's bench, &c. South Hackensack, N.J., Rothman Reprints, 1972. 243 p. 23 cm. Reprint of the 1826 ed. Includes bibliographical references. [DA390.1.C7W6 1972] 76-181857
1. Coke, Edward, Sir, 1552-1634. I. Title.

Coke, Thomas, Bp., 1747-1814.

VICKERS, John Ashley. 287'.6'0924 B
Thomas Coke: apostle of Methodism [by] John Vickers. Nashville, Abingdon Press [1969] xiv, 394 p. illus., maps (on lining papers), port. 26 cm. (The Wesley Historical Society lecture, no. 30) "A list of Coke's publications": p. 375-382. Bibliography: p. 383-387. [BX8495.C6V5 1969b] 70-14555 14.50
1. Coke, Thomas, Bp., 1747-1814. I. Title. II. Series: Wesley Historical Society. The Wesley Historical Society lectures, no. 30

Coke, Thomas, Bp., 1747-1814—Addresses, essays, lectures.

VICKERS, John Ashley. 287'.092'4 B
Thomas Coke and World Methodism / [by] John A. Vickers. Bognor Regis : World Methodist Historical Society (British Section), 1976. 20 p. ; 21 cm. A Wesley Historical Society lecture delivered at the Methodist Conference in Sheffield, 1964. [BX8495.C6V49] 77-366326 ISBN 0-9505559-0-8 : £0.40
1. Coke, Thomas, Bp., 1747-1814—Addresses, essays, lectures. 2. Methodist Church—Bishops—Biography—Addresses, essays, lectures. 3. Bishops—England—Biography—Addresses, essays, lectures. 4. Bishops—United States—Biography—Addresses, essays, lectures. I. Title.

Coker family.

SIMPSON, George Lee. 929.2
The Cokers of Carolina; a social biography of a family. Chapel Hill, Published for the Institute for Research in Social Science by the University of North Carolina Press [1956] xvi, 327 p. illus., ports., map, geneal, table. 24 cm. Bibliography: p. [309]-321. [CS71.C683 1956] 56-63273
1. Coker family. I. Title.

Coker, George W,

COKER, George W, 1896- 920
Son of the farmlands. [Crosbyton? Tex., 1951] 301 p. port. 24 cm. [CT275.C672A3] 51-22663
I. Title.

Colbert, Claudette, 1905-

*EVERSON, William K. 791.43'028'0924
Claudette Colbert / by William K. Everson. New York : Pyramid Publications, 1976. 159p. : ill., ports. : 20 cm. (A Pyramid illustrated history of the movies.) Includes index. Bibliography: p. 146. [PN2287] [B.] 76-3341 ISBN 0-515-03960-8 pbk. : 1.75
1. Colbert, Claudette, 1905- I. Title.

Colbert, Jean Baptiste, 1618-1683.

TROUT, Andrew. 944'.033'0924
Jean-Baptiste Colbert / by Andrew Trout. Boston : Twayne Publishers, c1978. 244 p. ; 22 cm. (Twayne's world leaders series ; TWLS 64) Includes index. Bibliography: p. 237-238. [DC130.C6T76] 77-5621 ISBN 0-8057-7715-6 : 12.50
1. Colbert, Jean Baptiste, 1618-1683. 2. Statesmen—France—Biography. BIP

Colby, Constance Taber, 1927-

COLBY, Constance Taber, 1927- 974.7'1'0922
The view from Morningside : one family's New York / Constance Taber Colby. 1st ed. Philadelphia : Lippincott, c1978. 216 p. ; 24 cm. [F128.5.C75] 78-4052 ISBN 0-397-01257-8 : 8.95
1. Colby, Constance Taber, 1927- 2. New York (City)—Biography. I. Title. **BIP**

Colden, Cadwallader, 1688-1776.

COLDEN, Cadwallader, 1688-1776. 973.2'092'4 B
The letters and papers of Cadwallader Colden. New York, AMS Press [1973] 9 v. illus. 22 cm. Reprint of the 1918-1937 ed. (in 9 v.) originally printed for the New York Historical Society in its series: Collections of the New York Historical Society for the year 1917-1935, and as v. 50-56, 67-68 in its series: The John Watts De Peyster publication fund series. Contents.Contents.—v. 1. 1711-1729.—v. 2. 1730-1742.—v. 3. 1743-1747.—v. 4. 1748-1754.—v. 5. 1755-1760.—v. 6. 1761-1764.—v. 7. 1765-1775.—v. 8. Additional letters and papers, 1715-1748.—v. 9. Additional letters and papers, 1749-1775, and some of Colden's writings. [F122.C67 1973] 72-996 ISBN 0-404-01690-1 225.00 (9 vols.)
1. Colden, Cadwallader, 1688-1776. I. Series: New York Historical Society. Collections, 1917-1935. II. Series: The John Watts De Peyster publication fund series, v. 50-56 [etc.] **BIP**

Colditz, Germany. Castle.

REID, Patrick R., 1910- 940.54'72'43094321
The Colditz story / P. R. Reid. Westport, Conn. : Greenwood Press, 1978, c1952. 288 p. : maps ; 22 cm. Sequel: Men of Colditz. Reprint of the 1953 ed. published by Lippincott, Philadelphia. [D805.G3R35 1978] 77-28513 ISBN 0-313-20245-1 lib.bdg. : 19.75
1. Colditz, Germany. Castle. 2. Reid, Patrick R., 1910- 3. World War, 1939-1945—Prisoners and prisons, German. 4. World War, 1939-1945—Personal narratives, English. 5. Prisoners of war—Germany—Biography. I. Title. **BIP**

Coldwater, Barry Morris, 1909-

SHADEGG, Stephen C. 923.273
Barry Goldwater: freedom is his flight plan Foreword by Clarence Budington Kelland. [New York] Macfadden [1963, c.1962] 192p. 18cm. (MB60-123) .60 pap.,
1. Coldwater, Barry Morris, 1909- I. Title.

Cole, Duane.

COLE, Duane. 797.5'4'0924 B
The flying Coles : an autobiography / by Duane Cole. Milwaukee : Ken Cook Transnational, [1974] iv, 108 p. : ill. , 29 cm. [TL540.C644A33] 74-20037
1. Cole, Duane. 2. Stunt flying. I. Title.

Cole, George Douglas Howard, 1889-1959.

CARPENTER, Luther P. 330'.092'4 B
G. D. H. Cole; an intellectual biography [by] L. P. Carpenter. Cambridge [Eng.] University Press, 1973. 271 p. 22 cm. (Conference on British Studies. Biographical series) Bibliography: p. 257-268. [HD8393.C57C37] 72-88614 ISBN 0-521-08702-3
1. Cole, George Douglas Howard, 1889-1959. 2. Gild socialism. I. Title.
Distributed by Cambridge University Press N.Y., 11.50. **BIP**

Cole, Margaret Rice.

COLE, Margaret Rice. 266'.0092'4 B
Never too old for God / Margaret Rice Cole, as told to Don Tanner and Bruce Anderson. Old Tappan, N.J. : Revell, c1979. 127 p. ; 18 cm. (Spire books) [BV3705.C585A35] 78-21953 ISBN 0-8007-8348-4 pbk. : 1.50
1. Cole, Margaret Rice. 2. Missionaries—United States—Biography. I. Tanner, Don, joint author. II. Anderson, Bruce, 1946- joint author. III. Title. **BIP**

Cole, Natalie, 1950-

JACOBS, Linda. 784'.092'4 B
Natalie Cole : star child / by Linda Jacobs. St. Paul, Minn. : EMC Corp., 1977. p. cm. A biography of a young grammy-award winning singer whose style is often compared to her late father's. [ML420.C62J3] 92 77-23114 ISBN 0-88436-410-0 lib.bdg. : 4.95 ISBN 0-88436-411-9 pbk. : 2.95
1. Cole, Natalie, 1950- 2. Singers—United States—Biography. I. Title.

JACOBS, Linda. 784'.092'4 B
Natalie Cole : star child / by Linda Jacobs. St. Paul, Minn. : EMC Corp., 1977. p. cm. A biography of a young grammy-award winning singer whose style is often compared to her late father's. [ML420.C62J3] 92 77-23114 ISBN 0-88436-410-0 lib.bdg : 4.95 ISBN 0 88436-411-9 pbk. : 2.95
1. Cole, Natalie, 1950- 2. Singers—United States—Biography. I. Title. **BIP**

Cole, Nathaniel, 1919-1965.

COLE, Maria. 784'.0924 B
Nat King Cole; an intimate biography, by Maria Cole, with Louie Robinson. New York, W. Morrow, 1971. 184 p. illus. 22 cm. Discography: p. [163]-184. [ML420.C63C6] 75-151921 5.95
1. Cole, Nathaniel, 1919-1965. I. Robinson, Louie, joint author.

Cole, Thomas, 1801-1848.

NOBLE, Louis Legrand, 1813-1882 927.5
The life and works of Thomas Cole. Ed. by Elliot S. Vesell. Cambridge, Mass., Belknap Pr. of Harvard [c.]1964. xxxix, 333p. illus. 25cm. (John Harvard lib.) Bibl. 64-22725 7.50
1. Cole, Thomas, 1801-1848. I. Title. II. Series.

Coleman, Ann Raney Thomas, 1810-1897.

COLEMAN, Ann Raney Thomas, 1810-1897. 917.64'03
Victorian lady on the Texas frontier; the journal of Ann Raney Coleman. Edited by C. Richard King. Norman, University of Oklahoma Press [1971] xxi, 206 p. port. 19 cm. Bibliography: p. 190-198. [CT275.C684A3] 69-16721 ISBN 0-8061-0906-8
1. Coleman, Ann Raney Thomas, 1810-1897. I. Title.

COLEMAN, Ann Raney Thomas, 1810-1897. 917.64'03
Victorian lady on the Texas frontier: the journal of Anne Raney Coleman; edited by C. Richard King. London, New York, Foulsham, [1972]. 190 p. facsim. 23 cm. Bibliography: p. 182-187. [CT275.C684A3 1972] 73-163532 ISBN 0-572-00803-1 £2.50
1. Coleman, Ann Raney Thomas, 1810-1897. I. King, Clyde Richard, ed. II. Title.

Coleman, Elizabeth Tyler.

COLEMAN, Elizabeth Tyler. 920.7
Priscilla Cooper Tyler and the American scene, 1816-1889. [University] University of Alabama Press, 1955. xiii, 203p. illus., ports., facsim. 24cm. [E340.T94C6] 55-5625
I. Title.

Coleman family.

PEAKE, Richard Brinsley, 1792-1847. 822'.6'09 B
Memoirs of the Colman family, including their correspondence with the most distinguished personages of their time. New York, B. Blom, 1972. 2 v. ports. 21 cm. [PN2598.C7P4 1972] 68-20242
1. Coleman family. 2. Colman, George, 1732-1794. 3. Colman, George, 1762-1836.

Coleman, George Sander, 1880-

COLEMAN, George Sanger, 1880- 791.3'092'4 B
The Sanger story : the story of his life with his grandfather "Lord" George Sanger / George Sanger Coleman ; as told to John Lukens. London ; New York : White Lion Publishers, 1974. 256 p. : geneal. tables, port. ; 21 cm. First published in 1956. Includes index. [GV1811.C57A37 1974] 75-314388 ISBN 0-85617-737-7 : £2.75
1. Coleman, George Sander, 1880- 2. Sanger, George, 1827-1911. 3. Circus. I. Lukens, John. II. Title.

Coleman, James.

COLEMAN, James. 658.3'00924
Whatever you can't have, by James Coleman, with Gene Klinger. [Chicago, Childrens Press, 1970] 64 p. illus., ports. 19 cm. (An Open door book) Autobiographical. A well-known basketball player relates briefly his career in the sport and his new career in personnel administration. [HF5549.C563] 92 79-101737
I. Klinger, Gene, joint author. II. Title.

Coleman, John Royston, 1921-

COLEMAN, John Royston, 1921- 378.1'1'0924 B
Blue-collar journal: a college president's sabbatical [by] John R. Coleman. [1st ed.] Philadelphia, Lippincott, [1974] 252 p. 21 cm. [HB119.C57A3] 73-21902 ISBN 0-397-01030-3 6.95
1. Coleman, John Royston, 1921- 2. Labor and laboring classes—United States—1970- —Case studies. 3. College teachers—Leaves of absence—Case studies. I. Title.

Coleman, Thomas, 1945-

NANCE, John, 1935- 738'.092'4 B
The mud-pie dilemma : a master potter's struggle to make art and ends meet / John Nance. Forest Grove, Or. : Timber Press, c1978. vi, 116 p., [24] leaves of plates : ill. (some col.) ; 29 cm. (Timber Press series in arts and crafts) [NK4210.C63N37] 78-13888 ISBN 0-917304-18-7 : 14.95
1. Coleman, Thomas, 1945- 2. Potters—United States—Biography. I. Title. II. Series. **BIP**

Coleridge, Arthur Duke, 1830-1913.

COLERIDGE, Arthur Duke, 1830-1913. 941.081'092'4 B
Reminiscences / Arthur Coleridge ; edited by J. A. Fuller-Maitland ; with additions by F. Warre Cornish, W. Ryland Adkins, and L. Spencer Holland. Boston : Longwood Press, 1978. xv, 204 p. ; 22 cm. Reprint of the 1921 ed. published by Constable, London. Includes index. [CT788.C695A37 1977] 77-75179 ISBN 0-89341-055-1 lib.bdg. : 25.00
1. Coleridge, Arthur Duke, 1830-1913. 2. England—Biography. I. Fuller-Maitland, John Alexander, 1856-1936.

Coleridge, Hartley, 1796-1849.

GRIGGS, EarlLeslie, 1899- 821'.7 B
Hartley Coleridge; his life and work. [Folcroft, Pa.] Folcroft Library Editions, 1971. xi, 255 p. 23 cm. Reprint of the 1929 ed. Originally presented as the author's thesis, University of London, 1927. "Limited to 150 copies." Bibliography: p. 228-245. [PR4468.G7 1971] 72-194098 15.00
1. Coleridge, Hartley, 1796-1849.

GRIGGS, Earl Leslie, 1899- 821'.7 B
Hartley Coleridge; his life and work. [Folcroft, Pa.] Folcroft Library Editions, 1971. xi, 255 p. 23 cm. Reprint of the 1929 ed. Originally presented as the author's thesis, University of London, 1927. "Limited to 150 copies." Bibliography: p. 228-245. [PR4468.G7 1971] 72-194098
1. Coleridge, Hartley, 1796-1849.

Coleridge, Hartley, 1796-1849—Correspondence.

COLERIDGE, Hartley, 1796-1849. 821'.7
Letters of Hartley Coleridge / edited by Grace Evelyn Griggs and Earl Leslie Griggs. New York : AMS Press, [1976] p. cm. Reprint of the 1936 ed. published by Oxford University Press, London. Includes index. Bibliography: p. [PR4468.A4 1976] 75-41063 ISBN 0-404-14524-8 : 15.50
1. Coleridge, Hartley, 1796-1849—Correspondence. 2. Poets, English—19th century—Correspondence. **BIP**

Coleridge, Hartley, 1796-1849—Correspondence—Catalogs.

STEPHENS, Fran Carlock. 821'.7 B
The Hartley Coleridge letters : a calendar and index / by Fran Carlock Stephens. [Austin] : Humanities Research Center, University of Texas at Austin, c1978. 217 p., [1] leaf of plates : ill. ; 24 cm. (Tower bibliographical series ; no. 15) Based primarily on the holdings of the Humanities Research Center of the University of Texas at Austin. [Z6616.C7S73] [PR4468.A4] 76-620064 ISBN 0-87959-078-5 : 18.50
1. Coleridge, Hartley, 1796-1849—Correspondence—Catalogs. 2. Texas. University of Austin. Humanities Research Center. 3. Authors, English—19th century—Correspondence—Catalogs. I. Texas. University at Austin. Humanities Research Center. II. Title. III. Series. **BIP**

Coleridge, Mary Elizabeth,

COLERIDGE, Mary Elizabeth, 1861-1907. 828'.8'09
Gathered leaves from the prose of Mary E. Coleridge, with a memoir by Edith Sichel. Freeport, N.Y., Books for Libraries Press [1971] x, 338 p. front. 21 cm. (Short story index reprint series) Reprint of the 1910 ed. [PR6005.O3G3 1971] 70-169545 ISBN 0-8369-4006-7
I. Sichel, Edith Helen, 1862-1914. II. Title.

Coleridge, Samuel Taylor, 1772-1834.

BENET, Laura. 928.2
Coleridge, poet of wild enchantment. New York, Dodd, Mead, 1952. 216 p. illus. 22 cm. [PR4483.B4] 52-9956
1. Coleridge, Samuel Taylor, 1772-1834. I. Title.

BYRON, May Clarissa Gillington, d.1936. 821'.7 B
A day with Samuel Taylor Coleridge / by May Byron. Folcroft, Pa. : Folcroft Library Editions, 1978. p. cm. Reprint of the 1912 ed. published by Hodder & Stoughton, London. [PR4483.B76 1978] 78-14436 ISBN 0-8414-1745-8 : 8.50
1. Coleridge, Samuel Taylor, 1772-1834. 2. Authors, English—19th century—Biography. I. Title. **BIP**

CAMPBELL, James Dykes, 1838-1895. 821'.7 B
Samuel Taylor Coleridge: a narrative of the events of his life. With a memoir of the author by Leslie Stephen. 2d ed. [Folcroft, Pa.] Folcroft Library Editions, 1970. xlviii, 319 p. port. 23 cm. "Limited to 150 copies." Reprint of the 1896 ed. Includes bibliographical references. [PR4483.C35 1970b] 72-195931
1. Coleridge, Samuel Taylor, 1772-1834.

CAMPBELL, James Dykes, 1838-1895. 821'.7 B
Samuel Taylor Coleridge; a narrative of the events of his life. With a memoir of the author by Leslie Stephen. 2d. ed. [Folcroft, Pa.] Folcroft Library Editions, 1973. xlviii, 319 p. port. 24 cm. Reprint of the 1896 ed. published by Macmillan, London and New York. Includes bibliographical references. [PR4483.C35 1973] 73-4598 ISBN 0-8414-1846-2 (lib. bdg.)
1. Coleridge, Samuel Taylor, 1772-1834.

CHAMBERS, Edmund Kerchever, Sir 1866- v. 12
Samuel Taylor Coleridge; a biographical study. [Reprinted from corrected sheets of the first edition] Oxford, Clarendon Press [1963] xvi, 373 p. Bibliography: p. [xii]-xvi. 64-61497
1. Coleridge, Samuel Taylor, 1772-1834. I. Title.

CHARPENTIER, John, 1880- 821'.8
Coleridge, the sublime somnambulist. Translated by M. V. Nugent. New York, Haskell House, 1970. x, 332 p. port. 23 cm. Reprint of the 1929 ed. Includes bibliographical references. [PR4483.C52 1970] 74-130259
1. Coleridge, Samuel Taylor, 1772-1834. I. Title.

COLERIDGE, Samuel Taylor, 1772-1834. 928.2
Collected letters, edited by Earl Leslie Griggs. Oxford, Clearendon Press, 1956- v. ports. 23cm. Contents.v.1. 1785-1800.--v. 2. 1801-1806. Includes bibliographical references. [PR4483.A428] 56-2923
I. Title.

COLERIDGE, Samuel Taylor, 1772-1834. 821'.7
Unpublished letters from Samuel Taylor Coleridge to the Rev. John Prior Estlin. [Edited] by Henry A. Bright. [Folcroft, Pa.] Folcroft Press, 1970. 117 p. 22 cm. Reprint of the 1884 ed. [PR4483.A43 1970] 72-190701
I. Estlin, John Prior, 1747-1817.

FAUSSET, Hugh I'Anson, 1895- 821'.7 B
Samuel Taylor Coleridge. London, J. Cape. St. Clair Shores, Mich., Scholarly Press, 1970. 350 p. ports. 21 cm. Reprint of the 1926 ed. [PR4483.F3 1970] 77-145006 ISBN 0-403-00792-5
1. Coleridge, Samuel Taylor, 1722-1834. BIP

FRUMAN, Norman. 821'.7 B
Coleridge, the damaged archangel. New York, G. Braziller [1971] xxiii, 607 p. 24 cm. Includes bibliographical references. [PR4484.F7] 71-148734 ISBN 0-8076-0607-3 12.50
1. Coleridge, Samuel Taylor, 1772-1834. I. Title. BIP

GARNETT, Richard, 1835-1906. 821'.7
Coleridge. [Folcroft, Pa.] Folcroft Library Editions, 1972. 111 p. ports. 24 cm. Reprint of the 1904 ed., issued in series: Bell's miniature series of great writers. Bibliography: p. 100-111. [PR4483.G3 1972] 72-6637 ISBN 0-8414-0174-8 (lib. bdg.)
1. Coleridge, Samuel Taylor, 1772-1834. I. Series: Bell's miniature series of great writers.

GILLMAN, James, 1782-1839. 821'.7
The life of Samuel Taylor Coleridge. [Folcroft, Pa.] Folcroft Library Editions, 1972. x, 362 p. 24 cm. "Limited to 150 copies." Reprint of the 1838 ed. Includes bibliographical references. [PR4483.G5 1972] 72-187489
1. Coleridge, Samuel Taylor, 1772-1834.

GILLMAN, James, 1782-1839. 821'.7 B
The life of Samuel Taylor Coleridge / by James Gillman. Norwood, Pa. : Norwood Editions, 1975. x, 362 p. ; 23 cm. Reprint of the 1838 ed. published by W. Pickering, London. Includes bibliographical references. [PR4483.G5 1975] 75-29122 ISBN 0-88305-225-3 lib. bdg. : 35.00
1. Coleridge, Samuel Taylor, 1772-1834. I. Title.

GILLMAN, James, 1782-1839. 821'.7 B
The life of Samuel Taylor Coleridge / by James Gillman. Norwood, Pa. : Norwood Editions, 1975. p. cm. Reprint of the 1838 ed. published by W. Pickering, London. Includes bibliographical references. [PR4483.G5 1975] 75-29122 ISBN 0-88305-225-3 lib. bdg. : 35.00
1. Coleridge, Samuel Taylor, 1772-1834. I. Title.

HANSON, Lawrence. 928.2
The life of S. T. Coleridge, the early years. New York, Russell & Russell, 1962. 575 p. illus. 22 cm. Includes bibliography. [PR4483.H3 1962] 61-13766
1. Coleridge, Samuel Taylor, 1772-1834. BIP

SAYERS, William Charles Berwick, 1881-1960. 780'.924 B
Samuel Coleridge-Taylor, musician; his life and letters, by W. C. Berwick Sayers. Foreword by Blyden Jackson. Chicago, Afro-Am Press, 1969. xiv, 328 p. music, ports. 22 cm. "The original edition was published in London in 1915." "Compositions of Samuel Coleridge-Taylor, by J. H. Smither Jackson": p. 312-322. [ML410.C74S4 1969] 75-99345
1. Coleridge-Taylor, Samuel, 1875-1912. I. Jackson, J. H. Smither.

TORTOLANO, William. 780'.92'4 B
Samuel Coleridge-Taylor : Anglo-Black composer, 1875-1912 / by William Tortolano. Metuchen, N.J. : Scarecrow Press, 1977. 223 p. : ill. ; 23 cm. Includes index. "Catalog of music by Coleridge-Taylor": p. 163-205. [ML410.C74T7] 76-57172 ISBN 0-8108-1010-7 : 8.50
1. Coleridge-Taylor, Samuel, 1875-1912. 2. Composers—England—Biography. BIP

TRAILL, Henry Duff, 1842-1900. 821'.7 B
Coleridge. London, Macmillan [1884] Detroit, Gale Research Co., 1968. xi, 218 p. 22 cm. (The Gale library of lives and letters: British writers series) [PR4483.T7 1968] 67-23874
1. Coleridge, Samuel Taylor, 1772-1834.

WATSON, Lucy Eleanor (Gillman) 1838- 821'.7 B
Coleridge at Highgate. [Folcroft, Pa.] Folcroft Library Editions, 1970. ix, 196 p. illus. 24 cm. 150 copies printed. Reprint of the 1925 ed. [PR4483.W3 1970] 72-187872
1. Coleridge, Samuel Taylor, 1772-1834. I. Title. BIP

Coleridge, Samuel Taylor, 1772-1834—Addresses, essays, lectures.

BLUNDEN, Edmund Charles, 1896- ed. 821'.7 B
Coleridge; studies by several hands on the hundredth anniversary of his death, edited by Edmund Blunden and Earl Leslie Griggs. [Folcroft, Pa.] Folcroft Library Editions, 1973. viii, 243 p. port. 24 cm. Reprint of the 1934 ed. published by Constable, London. Contents.Contents.—Coleridge, G. H. B. Biographical notes; being chapters of Ernest Hartley Coleridge's unpublished Life of Coleridge.—Blunden, E. Coleridge and Christ's Hospital.—Eagleston, A. J. Wordsworth, Coleridge, and the spy.—Morley, E. J. Some contemporary allusions to Coleridge's death.—Wilkinson, C. H. A note on some early editions of Coleridge.—Haney, J. L. Coleridge the commentator.—Harper, G. M. Gems of purest ray.—Beeley, H. The political thought of Coleridge.—Muirhead, J. H. Metaphysician or mystic?—Snyder, A. D. American comments on Coleridge a century ago.—Griggs, E. L. The death of Coleridge: an unpublished letter from Mrs. Henry Nelson Coleridge to her brother. Includes bibliographical references. [POColeridge; studies by several hands on the hundredth an
1. Coleridge, Samuel Taylor, 1772-1834—Addresses, essays, lectures. I. Coleridge, Samuel Taylor, 1772-1834. II. Griggs, Earl Leslie, 1899- joint ed.

BLUNDEN, Edmund Charles, 1896-1974, ed. 821'.7 B
Coleridge : studies by several hands on the hundredth anniversary of his death / edited by Edmund Blunden and Earl Leslie Griggs. Norwood, Pa. : Norwood Editions, 1975. viii, 243 p. : port. ; 24 cm. Reprint of the 1934 ed. published by Constable, London. Contents.Contents.—Bibliographical notes; being chapters of Ernest Hartley Coleridge's unpublished Life of Coleridge, contributed by G. H. B. Coleridge.—Blunden, E. Coleridge and Christ's Hospital.—Eagleston, A. J. Wordsworth, Coleridge, and the spy.—Morley, E. J. Some contemporary allusions to Coleridge's death.—Wilkinson, C. H. A note on some early editions of Coleridge.—Haney, J. L. Coleridge the commentator.—Harper, G. M. Gems of purest ray.—Beeley, H. The political thought of Coleridge.—Muirhead, J. H. Metaphysician or mystic?—Snyder, A. D. American comments on Coleridge a century ago.—The death of Coleridge: an unpublished letter from Mrs. Henry Nelson Coleridge to her brother, contributed by Earl Leslie Griggs. InclOColeridge : studies by several hands on the hundredth anniversary of his death / edited by Edmund Blunden
1. Coleridge, Samuel Taylor, 1772-1834—Addresses, essays, lectures. I. Griggs, Earl Leslie, 1899- joint ed. II. Coleridge, Samuel Taylor, 1772-1834. BIP

Coleridge, Samuel Taylor, 1772-1834—Biography.

CAINE, Hall, Sir, 1853-1931. 821'.7 B
Life of Samuel Taylor Coleridge. Port Washington, Kennikat Press [1972] 154, xxi p. 20 cm. Reprint of the 1887 ed. "Bibliography, by John P. Anderson": p. [i]-xxi. [PR4483.C3 1972] 79-160745 ISBN 0-8046-1558-6
1. Coleridge, Samuel Taylor, 1772-1834—Biography. I. Title.

CARPENTER, Maurice. 821'.7
The indifferent horseman : the divine comedy of Samuel Taylor Coleridge / by Maurice Carpenter. Folcroft, Pa. : Folcroft Library Editions, 1978. p. cm. Reprint of the 1954 ed. published by Elek Books, London. Includes index. Bibliography: p. [PR4483.C4 1978] 78-27464 ISBN 0-8414-9981-0 lib. bdg. : 30.00
1. Coleridge, Samuel Taylor, 1772-1834—Biography. 2. Poets, English—19th century—Biography. I. Title.

CHAMBERS, Edmund Kerchever, Sir, 1866-1954. 821'.7 B
Samuel Taylor Coleridge : a biographical study / by E. K. Chambers. Westport, Conn. : Greenwood Press, [1978] c1938. p. cm. Reprint of the 1967 ed. first published in 1938 by The Clarendon Press, Oxford, Eng. "Letters from Coleridge": p. Includes bibliographical references and index. [PR4483.C48 1978] 78-19152 ISBN 0-313-20457-8 lib.bdg. : 20.50
1. Coleridge, Samuel Taylor, 1772-1834—Biography. 2. Authors, English—19th century—Biography. BIP

LEFEBURE, Molly. 821'.7 B
Samuel Taylor Coleridge : a bondage of opium / by Molly Lefebure. New York : Stein and Day, 1974. 534 p., [4] leaves of plates : ill. ; 25 cm. Includes index. Bibliography: p. 516-518. [PR4483.L4 1974] 74-80899 ISBN 0-8128-1711-7 : 15.00
1. Coleridge, Samuel Taylor, 1772-1834—Biography. 2. Narcotic habit. BIP

Coleridge, Samuel Taylor, 1772-1834—Criticism and interpretation.

COOKE, Katharine. 821'.7
Coleridge / Katharine Cooke. London ; Boston : Routledge & Kegan Paul, 1979. 266 p. ; 23 cm. Incudes index. Bibliography: p. 255-259. [PR4484.C65] 78-41237 ISBN 0-7100-0141-X : 16.75
1. Coleridge, Samuel Taylor, 1772-1834—Criticism and interpretation.

Coleridge, Samuel Taylor, 1772-1834—Editors.

COBURN, Kathleen. 821'.7
In pursuit of Coleridge / Kathleen Coburn. London : Bodley Head, 1978. 202 p. : ill. ; 23 cm. Includes index. [PR4485.C6] 78-307705 ISBN 0-370-30002-5 : 11.00
1. Coleridge, Samuel Taylor, 1772-1834—Editors. 2. Coleridge, Samuel Taylor, 1772-1834—Manuscripts. 3. Coburn, Kathleen. 4. Editors—Biography. I. Title.
Dist. by Rowman & Littlefield, Totowa, NJ BIP

Coleridge, Samuel Taylor, 1772-1834—Friends and associates.

KNIGHT, William Angus, 1836-1916. 821'.7'09 B
Coleridge and Wordsworth in the West Country : their friendship, work, and surroundings / by Professor Knight. Norwood, Pa. : Norwood Editions, 1975. xvi, 237 p. : ill. ; 24 cm. Reprint of the 1913 ed. published by E. Mathews, London. Includes index. [PR4483.K5 1975] 75-33022 ISBN 0-88305-355-1 : 30.00
1. Coleridge, Samuel Taylor, 1772-1834—Friends and associates. 2. Wordsworth, William, 1770-1850—Friends and associates. 3. Literary landmarks—West Country, Eng. 4. West Country, Eng.—Description and travel. I. Title.

Coleridge, Samuel Taylor, 1772-1834—Homes and haunts—Highgate, Eng. (Middlesex)

WATSON, Lucy Eleanor Gillman, 1838- 821'.7 B
Coleridge at Highgate / by Lucy E. Watson (nee Gillman). Norwood, Pa. : Norwood Editions, 1975. ix, 196 p., [4] leaves of plates : ill. ; 23 cm. Reprint of the 1925 ed. published by Longmans, Green, London. Includes index. [PR4483.W3 1975] 75-37677 ISBN 0-88305-772-7 : 22.00
1. Coleridge, Samuel Taylor, 1772-1834—Homes and haunts—Highgate, Eng. (Middlesex) 2. Coleridge, Samuel Taylor, 1772-1834—Biography. I. Title.

Coleridge, Samuel Taylor, 1772-1834—Influence.

MARSH, James, 1794-1842. 191 B
Coleridge's American disciples: the selected correspondence of James Marsh. Edited by John J. Duffy. Amherst, University of Massachusetts Press, 1973. xv, 272 p. 24 cm. Includes bibliographical references. [B931.M34A4 1973] 72-90497 15.00
1. Coleridge, Samuel Taylor, 1772-1834—Influence. 2. Philosophers—United States—Correspondence, reminiscences, etc. 3. Transcendentalism (New England) I. Duffy, John J., ed. II. Title. BIP

Coleridge, Samuel Taylor, 1772-1834—Manuscripts.

COBURN, Kathleen. 821'.7
In pursuit of Coleridge / Kathleen Coburn. London : Bodley Head, 1978. 202 p. : ill. ; 23 cm. Includes index. [PR4485.C6] 78-307705 ISBN 0-370-30002-5 : 11.00
1. Coleridge, Samuel Taylor, 1772-1834—Editors. 2. Coleridge, Samuel Taylor, 1772-1834—Manuscripts. 3. Coburn, Kathleen. 4. Editors—Biography. I. Title.
Dist. by Rowman & Littlefield, Totowa, NJ BIP

Coleridge, Samuel Taylor, 1772-1834—Religion and ethics.

BARTH, J. Robert. 230'.0924
Coleridge and Christian doctrine [by] J. Robert Barth. Cambridge, Mass., Harvard University Press, 1969. xi, 215 p. 25 cm. Bibliography: p. 201-206. [PR4487.R4B3] 75-75426 7.50
1. Coleridge, Samuel Taylor, 1772-1834—Religion and ethics. I. Title. BIP

Coleridge, Sara (Coleridge) 1802-1852.

COLERIDGE, Sara Coleridge, 1802-1852. 821'.7 B
Memoir and letters of Sara Coleridge. Edited by her daughter. New York, Harper, 1874. [New York, AMS Press, 1973] 528 p. port. 23 cm. On spine: WOL. Includes bibliographical references. [PR4489.C2A8 1973] 76-37677 ISBN 0-404-56736-3
1. Coleridge, Sara Coleridge, 1802-1852. I. Title. BIP

GRIGGS, Earl Leslie, 1899- 821'.7 B
Coleridge fille; a biography of Sara Coleridge. London, New York, Oxford

University Press, 1940. [Folcroft, Pa.] Folcroft Library Editions, 1973. p. Bibliography: p. [PR4489.C2G7 1973] 73-3457 ISBN 0-8414-2015-7 20.00
1. Coleridge, Sara (Coleridge) 1802-1852. I. Title. BIP

Coleson, Ann.

†COLESON, Ann. 973'.04'97 S
Miss Coleson's narrative / Ann Coleson. New York : Garland Pub., 1977. xii, 769 p.,[8] leaves of plates : ill. ; 25 cm. (The Garland library of narratives of North American Indian captivities ; v. 79) Reprint of the 1864 ed. published by Barclay, Philadelphia, under title: Miss Coleson's narrative of her captivity among the Sioux Indians! Issued with the reprint of the 2d ed., 1864, of Wakefield, S. F. Six weeks in the Sioux tepees. New York, 1977. [E85.G2 vol. 79] [E83.86] 970'.004'97 77-1422 ISBN 0-8240-1703-X : 25.00
1. Coleson, Ann. 2. Dakota Indians—Captivities. 3. Dakota Indians—Wars, 1862-1865. 4. Indians of North America—Captivities. 5. Minnesota—Biography. I. Title. II. Series.

Colet, John, 1467?-1519.

DARK, Sidney, 1874-1947. 283'.0922
Five Deans: John Colet, John Donne, Jonathan Swift, Arthur Penrhyn Stanley, William Ralph Inge. Freeport, N.Y., Books for Libraries Press [1969] 255 p. 23 cm. (Essay index reprint series) Reprint of the 1928 ed. [BX5197.D25 1969b] 71-93332
1. Colet, John, 1467?-1519. 2. Donne, John, 1573-1631. 3. Swift, Jonathan, 1667-1745. 4. Stanley, Arthur Penrhyn, 1815-1881. 5. Inge, William Ralph, 1860-1954. I. Title.

DARK, Sidney, 1874-1947. 283'.0922
Five Deans: John Colet, John Donne, Jonathan Swift, Arthur Penrhyn Stanley, William Ralph Inge. Port Washington, N.Y., Kennikat Press [1969] 255 p. 21 cm. (Essay and general literature index reprint series) Reprint of the 1928 ed. [BX5197.D25 1969] 70-86011
1. Colet, John, 1467?-1519. 2. Donne, John, 1573-1631. 3. Swift, Jonathan, 1667-1745. 4. Stanley, Arthur Penrhyn, 1815-1881. 5. Inge, William Ralph, 1860-1954. I. Title.

LUPTON, Joseph Hirst, 1836-1905. 922
A life of John Colet, D. D., dean of St. Paul's and founder of St. Paul's School. With an appendix of some of his English writings. [2d ed.] Hamden, Conn., Shoe String Press, 1961. xiv, 323p. port., geneal. table 23cm Bibliographical footnotes. [BR754.C6L8 1961] 61-4942
1. Colet, John, 1467?-1519. I. Title.

LUPTON, Joseph Hirst, 1836-1905. 230'.2'0924 B
A life of John Colet, D.D., dean of St. Paul's, and founder of St. Paul's school. With an appendix of some of his English writings. New York, B. Franklin [1974] xiv, 323 p. port. 23 cm. (Burt Franklin research and source works series. Studies in the history of education 12) Reprint of the 1887 ed. published by G. Bell, London. Includes bibliographical references. [BR754.C6L8 1974] 74-18291 ISBN 0-8337-4243-4 16.50
1. Colet, John, 1467?-1519. I. Title.

Colette, Sidonie Gabrielle, 1873-1954.

COLETTE, Sidonie Gabrielle, 1873-1954 928.4
The blue lantern. Tr. [from French] by Roger Senhouse. New York, Farrar [c.1963] 161p. 21cm. 63-19563 3.95 bds.,
I. Title.

COLETTE, Sidonie Gabrielle, 1873-1954. 848.91203
Earthly paradise; an autobiography, drawn from her lifetime writings by Robert Phelps. Translated by Herma Briffault, Derek Coltman, and others. New York, Farrar, Straus & Giroux, 1966. xxxiv, 505 p. 22 cm. [PQ2605.O28Z5] 65-23837
I. Phelps, Robert, 1922- ed. II. Title.

COLETTE, Sidonie Gabrielle, 1873-1954. 848'.9'1203 B
My mother's house, and Sido [by] Colette. Westport, Conn., Greenwood Press [1972, c1953] xviii, 217 p. 22 cm. Translations of La maison de Claudine and Sido. [PQ2605.O28M32 1972] 76-178782 ISBN 0-8371-6294-7 10.00
I. Colette, Sidonie Gabrielle, 1873-1954. Sido. English. 1972. II. Title. III. Title: Sido.

COLETTE, Sidonie Gabrielle, 1873-1954. 848'.9'1203 B
Places. Translated from the French by David Le Vay, and with a foreword by Margaret Crosland. Indianapolis, Bobbs-Merrill [1971] 157 p. illus. 23 cm. "Selected from Trois-six-neuf, En pays connu, Prisons et paradis, Paysages et portraits, Journal intermittent." [PQ2605.O28A254 1971] 70-163017 6.95
I. Title.

COTTRELL, Robert D. 848'.9'1209
Colette [by] Robert D. Cottrell. New York, F. Ungar Pub. Co. [1974] ix, 150 p. 21 cm. (Modern literature monographs) Bibliography: p. 135-141. [PQ2605.O28Z638] 73-84598 ISBN 0-8044-2130-7 6.00
1. Colette, Sidonie Gabrielle, 1873-1954.

CROSLAND, Margaret, 1920- 928.4
Colette, a provincial in Paris. [1st American ed.] New York, British Book Centre [1954] 282 p. illus. 22 cm. Published in England in 1953 under title: Madame Colette, a provincial in Paris. Includes bibliography. [PQ2605.O28Z65 1954] 54-4607
1. Colette, Sidonie Gabrielle, 1873-1954.

CROSLAND, Margaret, 1920- 848'.9'1209
Colette the difficulty of loving a biography. New York, Dell 1975, c1973 203 p. illus. facism., ports. 18 cm. (Laurel edition) Bibliography. p. 194-198. [PQ2605.0282647] 73-161800 1.25 (pbk.)
1. Colette, Sidonie Gabrielle, 1873-1954 I. Title.

GOUDEKET, Maurice, 1889- 928.4
Close to Colette; an intimate portrait of a woman of genius. With an introd. by Harold Nicolson. New York, Farrar, Straus and Cudahy, 1957. 245 p. illus. 21 cm. [PQ2605.O28Z673] 57-6766
1. Colette, Sidonie Gabrielle, 1873-1954. I. Title.

GOUDEKET, Maurice, 1889- 848'.9'1209 B
Close to Colette; an intimate portrait of a woman of genius With an introd. by Harold Nicolson. Westport, Conn., Greenwood Press [1972, c1957] vii, 245 p. illus. 22 cm. Translation of Pres de Colette. Uniform title: Pres de Colette. English [PQ2605.O28Z673 1972] 70-178786 ISBN 0-8371-6290-4 11.25
1. Colette, Sidonie Gabrielle, 1873-1954. I. Title.

MARKS, Elaine. 843.912
Colette. New Brunswick, N. J., Rutgers University Press [1960] 265p. 22cm. Includes bibliography. [PQ2605.O28Z73] 60-9694
1. Colette, Sidonie Gabrielle, 1873-1954. I. Title.

Colette, Sidonie Gabrielle, 1873-1954—Biography.

COLETTE, Sidonie Gabrielle, 1873-1954. 848'.9'1209 B
Looking backwards / Colette ; translated from the French by David Le Vay ; with an introd. by Maurice Goudeket. Bloomington : Indiana University Press, 1975. 214 p. ; 24 cm. Translation of Journal a rebours and De ma fenetre. [PQ2605.O28J613 1975] 74-29051 ISBN 0-253-14900-2 : 10.00
1. Colette, Sidonie Gabrielle, 1873-1954—Biography. I. Colette, Sidonie Gabrielle, 1873-1954. De ma fenetre. English. 1975. II. Title. BIP

CROSLAND, Margaret, 1920- 848'.9'1209 B
Colette—the difficulty of loving : a biography / by Margaret Crosland. Indianapolis : Bobbs-Merrill, [1974?] c1973. xxx, 284 p., [8] leaves of plates : ill. ; 22 cm. Includes index. Bibliography: p. 275-284. [PQ2605.O28Z647 1974] 73-1741 ISBN 0-672-51760-4 : 8.95
1. Colette, Sidonie Gabrielle, 1873-1954—Biography.

MITCHELL, Yvonne. 848'.9'1209 B
Colette : a taste for life / Yvonne Mitchell. 1st American ed. New York : Harcourt Brace Jovanovich, c1975. 240 p. : ill. ; 26 cm. Includes index. Bibliography: p. 234-235. [PQ2605.O28Z74 1975b] 76-351179 ISBN 0-15-118513-1 : 14.95
1. Colette, Sidonie Gabrielle, 1873-1954—Biography. I. Title. BIP

MITCHELL, Yvonne. 848'.9'1209 B
Colette : a taste for life / Yvonne Mitchell. New York : Harcourt Brace Jovanovich, [1977] c1975. p. cm. (A Harvest/HBJ book) Includes index. Bibliography: p. [PQ2605.O28Z74 1977] 77-3517 ISBN 0-15-618550-4 pbk. : 5.95
1. Colette, Sidonie Gabrielle, 1873-1954—Biography. 2. Authors, French—20th century—Biography. I. Title.

SARDE, Michele. 848'.9'1209 B
Colette / by Michele Sarde ; translated from the French by Richard Miller. New York : Morrow, 1980. p. cm. Translation of Colette, libre et entravee. Includes index. Bibliography: p. [PQ2605.O28Z8313] 79-24978 ISBN 0-688-03601-5 : 12.95
1. Colette, Sidonie Gabrielle, 1873-1954—Biography. 2. Authors, French—20th century—Biography. I. Title. BIP

Colfax, Schuyler, 1823-1885.

SMITH, Willard H 1900- 923.273
Schuyler Colfax; the changing fortunes of a political idol. Indianapolis, Indiana Historical Bureau, 1952. 475 p. illus., port. 24 cm. (Indiana historical collections, v. 33) Based on the author's thesis, Indiana University. Bibliography: p. 449-455. [E415.9.C68S5] 52-4586
1. Colfax, Schuyler, 1823-1885. I. Title. II. Series.

Colin, Jean Claude Marie, 1790-1875.

ANONYMOUS apostle; 271(B)
the life of Jean Claude Colin, Marist, by Stanley W. Hosie. New York, Morrow, 1967. xi, 302p. maps. 22cm. Bibl. [BX4705.C687H6] 67-29842 1922- 6.50
1. Colin, Jean Claude Marie, 1790-1875.

College prose, American.

ROSENBAUM, Robert A., 1926- comp. 917.3'03'92092?
Growing up in America. Edited by Robert A. Rosenbaum. Introd. by Harvey Swados. [1st ed.] Garden City, N.Y., Doubleday, 1969. xxi, 380 p. 22 cm. An anthology of 23 autobiographical essays. [PS647.C6R6] 74-78685 5.95
1. College prose, American. I. Title.

College readers.

COMPREHENSION and 808'.0427
composition : an introduction to the essay / [compiled] by Ann B. Dobie, Andrew J. Hirt. New York : Macmillan, c1980. p. cm. Includes index. [PE1417.C638] 78-26598 ISBN 0-02-329920-7 pbk. : 7.95
1. College readers. 2. English language—Rhetoric. I. Dobie, Ann B. II. Hirt, Andrew J. BIP

COURSEN, Herbert R., comp. 808.04'275
As up they grew; autobiographical essays [by] Herbert R. Coursen, Jr. [Glenview, Ill.] Scott, Foresman [1970] 419 p. illus. 23 cm. [PE1122.C64] 70-97828
1. College readers. 2. Readers—Autobiography. I. Title. BIP

Collier family.

COLLIER, Thomas Cleaton, 1913- 929'.2'0973
Presidents of Virginia ancestry. [Silver Spring? Md., 1964?] 148-149 p. (geneal. table) 26 cm. Caption title. Photocopy of holograph, with additions in red ink. Refers to S. P. Hardy: Colonial families of the Southern States of America. [CS71.C7 1964] 73-165466
1. Collier family. 2. Presidents—United States—Genealogy. I. Hardy, Stella Pickett, 1887- Colonial families of the Southern States of America. II. Title.

Collier, John,

COLLIER, John, 1884- 923.273
From every zenith: a memoir; and some essays on life and thought. Denver, Sage Books [1963] 477 p. illus. 23 cm. Autobiographical. [PS3505.O32Z5] 62-19348
1. Title.

Collier, John Payne, 1789-1883—Biography.

COLLIER, John Payne, 1789-1883. 828'.8'03 B
An old man's diary, forty years ago ... 1832 [-1833] London, Printed by T. Richards, 1871. [New York, AMS Press, 1974 [i.e.1975] 4 v. in 1. 19 cm. Originally issued in 4 parts, 1871-72. [PR4489.C23O4 1975] 72-979 ISBN 0-404-07289-5 : 24.50
1. Collier, John Payne, 1789-1883—Biography. 2. Literature—Miscellanea. I. Title.

Collier, Sophia, 1956-

COLLIER, Sophia, 1956- 299 B
Soul rush : the odyssey of a young woman of the '70s / by Sophia Collier. 1st ed. New York : Morrow, 1978. 240 p. ; 22 cm. [BP605.D58C64] 77-13901 ISBN 0-688-03276-1 : 8.95
1. Collier, Sophia, 1956- 2. Divine Light Mission—Biography. 3. Divine Light Mission. 4. Guru Maharaj Ji, 1957- I. Title. BIP

Collingwood, Cuthbert Collingwood, Baron, 1748-1810.

KLUKVIN, Boris. 359.3'31'0924 B
Vice-Admiral Lord Collingwood. Newcastle upon Tyne, Oriel Press, 1972. 39 p. illus., ports. 22 cm. [DA87.1.C7K58] 72-169422 ISBN 0-85362-136-5 £0.50
1. Collingwood, Cuthbert Collingwood, Baron, 1748-1810.

WARNER, Oliver, 1903- 940.27'0924 (B)
The life and letters of Vice-Admiral Lord Collingwood. London, New York[etc] Oxford U.P., 1968. xix, 276 p. 13 plates, illus., 2 maps, ports. 25 cm. 42/- (B 68-13548) Bliblography: p. [265]-267. [DA87.1.C7W3 -1968] 68-115715
1. Collingwood, Cuthbert Collingwood, Horton, 1748-1810. I. Title.

Collingwood, Robin George, 1889-1943.

COLLINGWOOD, Robin George, 1889-1943. 192
An autobiography / by R. G. Collingwood. [1st ed.] reprinted ; with a new introduction by Stephen Toulmin. Oxford [etc.] : Oxford University Press, 1978. xix, 172 p. ; 20 cm. Includes index. [B1618.C74A3 1978] 79-310127 ISBN 0-19-281247-5 pbk. : 5.95
1. Collingwood, Robin George, 1889-1943. 2. Philosophers—England—Biography. Distributed by Oxford University Press, New York, NY

TOMLIN, Eric Walter Frederick, 1913- v. 12
R. G. Collingwood. London, New York, Published for the British Council by Longmans, Green [1953] 42p. port. 22cm. (Bibliographical series of supplements to British book news, no. 42) Bibliography: p. 41-42. A54

1. Collingwood, Robin George, 1889-1943. I. Title. II. Series. BIP

Collins, Carr Pritchett, 1892-

NEVILLE, Dorothy. v. 12
Carr P. Collins, man on the move. [Dallas, Tex., Park Press, c 1963] 185 p. illus., ports. 67-26216
1. Collins, Carr Pritchett, 1892- I. Title.

Collins, Caspar Wever, 1844-1865.

SPRING, Agnes (Wright) 978.7'93 B
1894-
Caspar Collins; the life and exploits of an Indian fighter of the sixties. Lincoln, University of Nebraska Press [1969, c1927] 187 p. illus., facsims, map, plan, ports. 21 cm. "A Bison book." Part 2, "The Casper Collins papers": p. 105-181. Bibliography: p. 100-101. [E83.86.S6 1969] 71-5947
1. Collins, Caspar Wever, 1844-1865. 2. Indians of North America—Wars—1862-1865.

Collins, Dan.

MOORE, Lettie Wheeler. 286'.73 B
My son Dan / by Lettie Wheeler Moore. Mountain View, Calif. : Pacific Press Pub. Association, c1978. 128 p. ; 22 cm. (A Destiny book) [BV4935.C62M66] 77-94241 pbk. : 3.50
1. Collins, Dan. 2. Converts, Seventh-Day Adventist—United States—Biography. I. Title. BIP

Collins, Floyd, 1890-1925.

MURRAY, Robert K. 796.5'25'0924 B
Trapped! : The story of the struggle to rescue Floyd Collins from a Kentucky cave in 1925 ... / by Robert K. Murray and Roger W. Brucker. New York : Putnam, c1979. 335 p., [4] leaves of plates : ill. ; 24 cm. Includes bibliographical references and index. [GB601.6.C64M87 1979] 79-10840 ISBN 0399-12320-2 : 12.50
1. Collins, Floyd, 1890-1925. 2. Speleologists—United States—Biography. 3. Mammoth Cave, Ky. I. Brucker, Roger W., joint author. II. Title.

Collins, John W.

COLLINS, John W. 794.1'092'2
My seven chess prodigies : Bobby Fischer, Robert E. Byrne, William J. Lombardy, Donald Byrne, Raymond A. Weinstein, Salvatore J. Matera, Lewis H. Cohen / by John W. Collins ; with a foreword by William J. Lombardy. New York : Simon and Schuster, [1975] c1974. 313 p. : ill. ; 22 cm. Includes indexes. [GV1439.C64A35 1975] 74-26547 ISBN 0-671-21941-3
1. Collins, John W. 2. Chess. 3. Chess—Biography. 4. Chess—Collections of games. I. Title.

Collins, Joseph Lawton, 1896-

COLLINS, Joseph 355.3'31'0924 B
Lawton, 1896-
Lightning Joe : an autobiography / by J. Lawton Collins. Baton Rouge : Louisiana State University Press, c1979. p. cm. Includes index. Bibliography: p. [E745.C64A34] 78-27375 ISBN 0-8071-0499-X : 20.00
1. Collins, Joseph Lawton, 1896- 2. United States. Army—Biography. 3. Generals—United States—Biography. 4. United States—History, Military—20th century. I. Title. BIP

Collins, Judy.

CLAIRE, Vivian. 784'.092'4 B
Judy Collins / by Vivian Claire. New York : Flash Books, c1977. 78 p. : ill. ; 26 cm. Discography: p. [72]-77. [ML420.C65C6] 77-78538 ISBN 0-8256-3914-X : 3.95
1. Collins, Judy. 2. Singers—United States—Biography. BIP

Collins, Lee, 1901-1960.

COLLINS, Lee, 1901- 788'.1'0924 B
1960.
Oh, didn't he ramble; the life story of Lee Collins, as told to Mary Collins. Edited by Frank J. Gillis and John W. Miner. [Urbana, University of Illinois Press, 1974] xv, 159 p. illus. 27 cm. (Music in American life) Discography: p. 141-147; bibliography: p. 149-150. [ML419.C64A3] 73-85485 ISBN 0-252-00234-2 10.00
1. Collins, Lee, 1901-1960. 2. Musicians—Correspondence, reminiscences, etc. I. Collins, Mary Spriggs. II. Title.

Collins, Mary, 1973-

COLLINS, Patricia. 362.7'8'30926
Your daughter is brain damaged : a mother's story / by Patricia Collins. New York : Paddington Press, [1980] p. cm. [RJ496.B7C64] 79-21423 ISBN 0-448-22126-8 : 10.00
1. Collins, Mary, 1973- 2. Collins, Patricia. 3. Brain-damaged children—New York (State)—Biography. 4. Mothers—New York (State)—Biography. I. Title. BIP

Collins, Michael, 1930- —Juvenile literature.

COLLINS, Michael, 629.4'092'4 B
1930-
Flying to the Moon and other strange places / Michael Collins. 1st ed. New York : Farrar, Straus and Giroux, 1976. 159 p., [10] leaves of plates : ill. ; 21 cm. The author, an astronaut, discusses his early career, his training for space flight, his trips into space including the first lunar landing, and the possibilities for life and flight in space in the future. [TL789.85.C65A34 1976] 92 76-25496 ISBN 0-374-32412-3 : 5.95
1. Collins, Michael, 1930- —Juvenile literature. 2. Space flight to the moon—Juvenile literature. I. Title. BIP

Collins, Wilkie, 1824-1889.

ASHLEY, Robert Paul, 823'.8 B
1915-
Wilkie Collins, by Robert Ashley. [Folcroft, Pa.] Folcroft Library Editions, 1974. p. Reprint of the 1952 ed. published by A. Barker, London, issued in series: The English novelists. Includes bibliographical references. [PR4496.A7 1974] 74-6031 ISBN 0-8414-2975-8 (lib. bdg.)
1. Collins, Wilkie, 1824-1889. I. Series: The English novelists (London)

ASHLEY, Robert Paul, 823'.8 B
1915-
Wilkie Collins, by Robert Ashley. [Folcroft, Pa.] Folcroft Library Editions, 1974. p. Reprint of the 1952 ed. published by A. Barker, London, issued in series: The English novelists. Includes bibliographical references. [PR4496.A7 1974] 74-6031 12.50 (lib. bdg.).
1. Collins, Wilkie, 1824-1889. I. Series: The English novelists (London) BIP

DAVIS, Nuel Pharr, 1915- 928.2
The life of Wilkie Collins. Introd. by Gordon N. Ray. Urbana, University of Illinois Press, 1956. 360 p. illus. 24 cm. Includes bibliography. [PR4496.D3] 56-8418
1. Collins, Wilkie, 1824-1889.

ROBINSON, Kenneth, 1911- 928.2
Wilkie Collins, a biography. New York, Macmillan, 1952 [c1951] 348 p. illus., ports. 22 cm. Bibliography: p. 335-339. [PR4496.R6 1952] 52-7833
1. Collins, Wilkie, 1824-1889.

ROBINSON, Kenneth, 1911- 823'.8 B
Wilkie Collins, a biography. Westport, Conn., Greenwood Press [1972] 348 p. illus. 22 cm. Reprint of the 1951 ed. Bibliography: p. 335-339. [PR4496.R6 1972] 72-5653 ISBN 0-8371-6447-8 14.50
1. Collins, Wilkie, 1824-1889.

SAYERS, Dorothy Leigh, 823'.8 B
1893-1957.
Wilkie Collins : a critical and biographical study / Dorothy L. Sayers ; edited from the manuscript, Humanities Research Center, Austin, Texas, by E. R. Gregory. [Toledo, Ohio] : The Friends of the University of Toledo Libraries, 1977. 120 p., [1] leaf of plates : ill. ; 23 cm. Includes bibliographical references. [PR4497.S28 1977] 76-53108 ISBN 0-918160-01-4 : 12.50
1. Collins, Wilkie, 1824-1889. 2. Novelists, English—19th century—Biography. I. Title.

Collins, William, 1721-1759.

CARVER, P. L. 821'.5 B
The life of a poet; a biography of William Collins, by P. L. Carver. With a foreword by Edmund Blunden. New York, Horizon Press [1967] xiv, 210 p. 22 cm. Includes bibliographies. [PR3353.C3 1967b] 67-27910
1. Collins, William, 1721-1759. I. Title.

GARROD, Heathcote William, 821'.5
1878-1960.
Collins. [Folcroft, Pa.] Folcroft Press [1969] 123 p. 23 cm. Reprint of the 1928 ed. [PR3353.G3 1969] 72-190598
1. Collins, William, 1721-1759. BIP

GARROD, Heathcote William, 821'.5
1878-1960.
Collins. New York, Octagon Books, 1973. 123 p. 20 cm. Reprint of the 1928 ed. published by Clarendon Press, Oxford. [PR3353.G3 1973b] 73-6734 ISBN 0-374-93011-2 7.50 (lib. bdg.)
1. Collins, William, 1721-1759.

GARROD, Heathcote William, 821'.5
1878-1960.
Collins. [Folcroft, Pa.] Folcroft Library Editions, 1973. 123 p. 23 cm. Reprint of the 1928 ed. published by Clarendon Press, Oxford. Includes bibliographical references. [PR3353.G3 1973] 73-3458 ISBN 0-8414-2018-1
1. Collins, William, 1721-1759.

Collura, Steven Allie, 1946-

DAVIDSON, Bill. 363.2'092'4 B
Collova : actor with a gun / Bill Davison. New York : Pocket Books 1979, c1977. 223p. ; 18 cm. [HV7911.C64D38] ISBN 0-671-81539-3 pbk. : 1.95
1. Collova, Steven Allie, 1946- 2. Police — New York (city)-Biography. 3. Undercover operations. 4. Narcotics, Control of-New York (City) I. Title.
L.C. card no. for 1977 Simon and Schuster ed.: 77-2007.

DAVIDSON, William, 363.2'092'4 B
1918-
Collura : actor with a gun / Bill Davidson. New York : Simon and Schuster, c1977. 221 p. ; 23 cm. [HV7911.C64D38] 77-2007 ISBN 0-671-22780-7 : 8.95
1. Collura, Steven Allie, 1946- 2. Police—New York (City)—Biography. 3. Undercover operations. 4. Narcotics, Control of—New York (City) BIP

Collyer, Langley.

GERSCH, Charles E. 363.2'33
The search for the Collyer brothers / Charles E. Gersch and Frances Spatz Leighton. New York : Stein and Day, [1976] p. cm. [CT9991.C64G47] 76-9743
1. Collyer, Langley. 2. Collyer, Homer. 3. Recluses—Biography. I. Leighton, Frances Spatz, joint author. II. Title.

Colman, Benjamin, 1673-1747.

TURELL, Ebenezer, 285'.2'0924 B
1702-1778.
The life and character of the Reverend Benjamin Colman, D.D. A facsim. reproduction with an introd. by Christopher R. Reaske. Delmar, N.Y., Scholars' Facsimiles & Reprints, 1972. xxiii, 18, 238 p. port. 23 cm. Original ed. has imprint: Boston, New-England, Printed and sold by Rogers and Fowle in Queen-street, and by J. Edwards in Cornhill, MDCCXLIX. "A catalogue of Dr. Colman's works": p. 233-236. [BX7260.C683T8 1749ab] 72-4539 ISBN 0-8201-1104-X
1. Colman, Benjamin, 1673-1747. BIP

Colman, George, 1732-1794.

PEAKE, Richard 822'.6'09 B
Brinsley, 1792-1847.
Memoirs of the Colman family, including their correspondence with the most distinguished personages of their time. New York, B. Blom, 1972. 2 v. ports. 21 cm. [PN2598.C7P4 1972] 68-20242
1. Coleman family. 2. Colman, George, 1732-1794. 3. Colman, George, 1762-1836.

Colman, Ronald.

COLMAN, Juliet 791.43'028'0924 B
Benita.
Ronald Colman, a very private person : a biography / by Juliet Benita Colman. New York : Morrow, 1975. vii, 294 p. : ill. ; 21 cm. Includes index. Bibliography: p. 287-288. [PN2287.C57C6] 74-23224 ISBN 0-688-00274-9 : 7.95
1. Colman, Ronald. I. Title.

Colombiere, Claude de la, 1641-1682.

GUITTON, Georges, 1877- 922.244
Perfect friend; the life of Blessed Claude La Colombiere, s. j., 1641-1682. Translated by William J. Young. St. Louis, B. Herder Book Co. [1956] 440p. illus. 22cm. Translation of Le bienheureux Claude la Colombiere. [BX4705.C689G83] 56-7079
1. Colombiere, Claude de la, 1641-1682. I. Title.

LAVIGNE, Ruth H. 271'.53'024 B
Special messenger : Claude de la Colombiere / by Ruth H. LaVigne. Boston : St. Paul Editions, 1978. p. cm. Bibliography: p. [BX4705.C689L38] 77-28071 3.50 pbk. : 2.50
1. Colombiere, Claude de la, 1641-1682. 2. Catholic Church—Clergy—Biography. 3. Clergy—France—Biography. I. Title.
Publisher's address: St. Paul Catholic Film and Book Center, Tremont St., Boston, MA

Colombia—Politics and government—1946- —Addresses, essays, lectures.

TORRES Restrepo, 986.1'063'0924 B
Camilo.
Camilo Torres: his life and his message. The text of his original platform and all his messages to the Colombian people, edited by John Alvarez Garcia and Christian Restrepo Calle. Translated by Virginia M. O'Grady. Springfield, Ill., Templegate Publishers [1968] 128 p. port. 19 cm. [F2278.T613] 68-28866
1. Colombia—Politics and government—1946- —Addresses, essays, lectures. I. Alvarez Garcia, John, ed. II. Restrepo Calle, Christian, ed.

Colombo, Cristoforo.

ADAMS, Herbert Baxter, 973'.08 S
1850-1901.
Columbus and his discovery of America, by Herbert B. Adams and Henry Wood. Baltimore, Johns Hopkins Press, 1892. [New York, Johnson Reprint Corp., 1973] 88 p. 22 cm. Pages also numbered 472-552. Original ed. issued as no. 10-11 of Church and state—Columbus and America, which forms the 10th series of Johns Hopkins University studies in historical and political science. Contents.Contents.—Adams, H. B. Oration.—Wood, H. Oration.—Kayserling, M. The first Jew in America.—Adler, C. Columbus in Oriental literature.—Bump, C. W. Bibliographies of the discovery of America (p. 55-68).—Bump, C. W. Public memorials of Columbus. [E18.C54 no. 10-11] [E111] 973.1'5'0924 B 72-14274 ISBN 0-384-00326-5 pap 4.50
1. Colombo, Cristoforo. 2. America—Discovery and exploration—Bibliography. I. Wood, Henry, 1849-1925. II. Title. III. Series: Johns Hopkins University. Studies in historical and political science, 10th ser., 10-11. IV. Series: Church and state—Columbus and America, no. 10-11. BIP

AULAIRE, Ingri (Mortenson) 923.9
d', 1904-
Columbus [by] Ingri & Edgar Parin d'Aulaire. 1st ed. Garden City, N. Y.,

Doubleday, c1955. 56p. illus. 32cm. [E111.A85] 55-9011
1. Colombo, Cristoforo. I. Aulaire, Edgare Parin d', 1898- joint author. II. Title.

AULAIRE, Ingri 973.15'0924 B
(Mortenson) d', 1904-
Columbus [by] Ingri & Edgar Parin d'Aulaire. 1st ed. Garden City, N.Y., Doubleday, c1955. 56 p. illus. 32 cm. A life of the Genoese weaver's son who sought to prove the world is round, telling how he studied map-making in Portugal, waited long years for financial and material support from Isabella of Spain, and finally made four voyages to the New World. [E111.A85] 92 AC 68
1. Colombo, Cristoforo. I. Aulaire, Edgar Parin d', 1898- joint author. II. Title.

CARRISON, Daniel J. 92
Christopher Columbus; navigator to the New World, by Daniel J. Carrison. New York, F. Watts [1967] xi, 178 p. illus., ports. 22 cm. (Immortals of history) Bibliography: p. 170-171. A biography of the courageous seaman who made the first significant and enduring contact with the New World. [E111.C3] AC 67
1. Columbus, Christopher. I. Title.

COLLIS, John 970'.01'50924 B
Stewart, 1900-
Christopher Columbus / John Stewart Collis. New York : Stein and Day, 1977. ix, 208 p. : maps ; 24 cm. Includes index. Bibliography: p. 201-203. [E111C63 1977] 76-48986 10.00
1. Colombo, Cristoforo. 2. Explorers—Italy—Biography. 3. America—Discovery and exploration—Spanish. I. Title.

COLLIS, John 970.01'5'0924 B
Stewart, 1900
Christopher Columbus / [by] John Stewart Collis. London : Macdonald and Jane's, 1976. 208 p. : maps, ports. ; 23 cm. Includes index. Bibliography: p. 201-203. [E111.C63 1976] 76-381984 ISBN 0-356-08441-8 : £5.50
1. Colombo, Cristoforo. 2. Explorers—Italy—Biography. 3. America—Discovery and exploration—Spanish. I. Title.

COLON, Fernando, 970'.01'50924 B
1488-1539.
The life of the Admiral Christopher Columbus / by his son Ferdinand ; translated and annotated by Benjamin Keen. Westport, Conn. : Greenwood Press, 1978, c1959. xxxii, 316 p. : ill. ; 24 cm. Translation of Historie del S. D. Fernando Colombo; nelle quali s'ha particolare, & vera relatione della vita, & de' fatti dell' Ammiraglio D. Cristoforo Colombo, suo padre ... Reprint of the ed. published by Rutgers University Press, New Brunswick, N.J. Includes bibliographical references and index. [E111.C713 1978] 77-27400 ISBN 0-313-20175-7 lib.bdg. : 21.75
1. Colombo, Cristoforo. 2. Indians of the West Indies—History. 3. Explorers—Spain—Biography. I. Keen, Benjamin, 1913-

DALGLIESH, Alice, 1893- 923.9
The Columbus story. Pictures by Leo Politi. New York, Scribner [1955] unpaged. illus. 27 cm. [E111.D14] 55-14976
1. Colombo, Cristoforo. I. Title.

DALGLIESH, Alice, 973.15'0924 B
1893-
The Columbus story. Pictures by Leo Politi. New York, Scribner [1955] [32] p. illus. 27 cm. Events in the life of Columbus, the Admiral, including his efforts to obtain ships and money to sail to the West, his first voyage, and his discovery of the New World. [E111.D14] 92 AC 68
1. Colombo, Cristoforo. I. Politi, Leo, 1908- illus. II. Title. **BIP**

FERNANDEZ-ARNESTO,973.1'5'0924 B
Felipe.
Columbus and the conquest of the impossible / Felipe Fernandez-Armesto. New York : Saturday Review Press, [1974] 224 p. : ill. (some col.) ; 26 cm. (The Great explorers) Includes index. Bibliography: p. 217. [E111.F36] 74-3630 ISBN 0-8415-0330-3 : 14.95
1. Colombo, Cristoforo. I. Title.

GRAHAM, Alberta (Powell). 923.9
Christopher Columbus, discoverer; illustrated by Janice Holland. New York, Abingdon-Cokesbury Press [1950] 127 p. illus. 22 cm. [E111.G77] 50-8693
1. Colombo, Cristoforo. I. Title.

IRVING, 970'.01'50924 B
Washington, 1783-1859.
The life and voyages of Christopher Columbus / Washington Irving ; edited by John Harmon McElroy. Boston : Twayne Publishers, 1979. p. cm. (The Complete works of Washington Irving ; v. 11) [E111.I816 1979] 78-32075 ISBN 0-8057-8516-7 : 35.00
1. Colombo, Cristoforo. 2. America—Discovery and exploration—Spanish. 3. Explorers—Spain—Biography. 4. Explorers—America—Biography. I. McElroy, John Harmon. II. Title. **BIP**

IRVING, 973.1'5'0924 B
Washington, 1783-1859.
The life and voyages of Christopher Columbus, to which are added those of his companions. New York, Putnam. [New York, AMS Press, 1973] 3 v. illus. 19 cm. (The works of Washington Irving, v. 5-7) At head of title: Hudson edition. "The author's revised edition." Reprint of the 1889 ed. [E111.I816 1973] 73-8739 20.00 ea.
1. Colombo, Cristoforo. I. Title.

IRVING, Washington, 1783- 923.9
1859.
The voyages of Columbus. Edited by Winifred Hulbert. Illustrated by Henry Pitz. New York, Ungar [1960] 254 p. illus. 20 cm. Shorter version of the author's The life and voyages of Christopher Columbus. [E111.I805 1960] 60-13984
1. Colombo, Cristoforo.

JUDSON, Clara 973.15'0924 B
(Ingram) 1879-1960.
The picture story and biography of Admiral Christopher Columbus. Illustrated by W. T. Mars. Chicago, Follett Pub. Co. [1965] 141 p. col. illus., 4 fold. maps, col. port. 22 cm. (The Library of American heroes) A biography of the son of a Genoan weaver who wanted to be a sailor, under the flag of Spain discovered the new world in 1492, and returned on three subsequent voyages. [E111.J95] 92 AC 68
1. Colombo, Cristoforo. I. Mars, Witold T., illus. II. Title.

KONINGSBERGER, 970'.015'0924 B
Hans.
Columbus : his enterprise / by Hans Koning. New York : Monthly Review Press, c1976. 128 p. : ill. ; 21 cm. Includes index. Bibliography: p. 125-126. A biography of the fifteenth-century Italian seaman and navigator who unknowingly discovered a new continent while looking for a western route to India. [E111.K85] 92 75-15346 ISBN 0-85345-379-9 : 7.95
1. Colombo, Cristoforo.

LANDSTROM, Bjorn. 973.1'5'0924
Columbus; the story of Don Cristobal Colon, Admiral of the Ocean, and his four voyages westward to the Indies, according to contemporary sources, retold and illustrated by Bjorn Landstrom. [Translated from the Swedish by Michael Phillips and Hugh W. Stubbs] New York, Macmillan [1967] 207 p. illus. (part col.), facsims. (on lining papers), maps, ports. 29 cm. Bibliography: p. 199-201. [E111.L2643] 67-19550
1. Colombo, Cristoforo. I. Title.

LOWITZ, Sadyebeth. 973.1'5'0924 B
The cruise of Mr. Christopher Columbus; a really truly story; by Sadyebeth & Anson Lowitz. With illus. by the latter. [Rev. ed.] Minneapolis, Lerner Publications Co. [1967, c1932] [79] p. illus. 19 x 22 cm. A brief biography of Columbus that relates how he developed an interest in sailing and describes the journey that resulted in the discovery of America and proof that the world was round. [E111] 92 AC 68
1. Colombo, Cristoforo. I. Lowitz, Anson, joint author. II. Title.

MADARIAGA, 970.015'092'4 B
Salvador de, 1886-
Christopher Columbus : being the life of the very magnificent lord, Don Cristobal Colon / Salvador de Madariaga. Westport, Conn. : Greenwood Press, [1979] c1940. p. cm. Reprint of the 1967 ed. published by Christopher Colubmus Pub., New York. Includes index. Bibliography: p. [E111.M17 1979] 79-16973 ISBN 0-313-22031-X : 33.50
1. Colombo, Cristoforo. 2. America—Discovery and exploration—Spanish. 3. Explorers—Spain—Biography. 4. Explorers—America—Biography.

MADARIAGA, 973.1'5'0924 (B)
Salvador de, 1886-
Christopher Columbus; being the life of the very magnificent lord, Don Cristobal Colon. [1st ed.] New York, F. Ungar Pub. Co. [1967] xviii, 524 p. port., maps (part fold.) 25 cm. Bibliographical references included in "Notes to the chapters" (p. 417-503) Bibliography: p. 412-416 [E111.M172] 67-25588
1. Colombo, Cristoforo. I. Title. **BIP**

MAHN-LOT, Marianne. 923.9
Columbus. Translated by Helen R. Lane. New York, Grove Press [1961] 192 p. illus., ports., maps. 18 cm. (Evergreen profile book, 33) Includes bibliography. [E111.M1873] 61-5531
1. Colombo, Cristoforo.

MORISON, Samuel Eliot, 923.9
1887-
Christopher Columbus, mariner. Maps by Erwin Raisz. [1st ed.] Boston, Little, Brown [1955] 224 p. illus. 22 cm. [E111.M863] 55-8096
1. Colombo, Cristoforo.

MORISON, Samuel Eliot, v. 12
1887-
Christopher Columbus, mariner. Maps by Erwin Raisz. [New York] New American Library [1956, c1955] 160 p. illus. (A Mentor book) 65-74454
1. Colombo, Cristoforo. I. Title. **BIP**

NECTARIO Maria,, 973.1'5'0924 B
Brother.
Colon (alias Cristobal Colon, alias Christopher Columbus) the Spaniard; lecture given in the city hall of Cadiz on December 10, 1966, by Brother Nectario M. Edited by Emanuel M. Josephson. New York, Chedney Press [1971] 31 p. illus. 22 cm. Cover title: Juan Colon, alias Cristobal Colon, alias Christopher Columbus, was a Spanish Jew. Includes bibliographical references. [E112.N413] 72-166573
1. Colombo, Cristoforo. I. Title.

PARMELEY, June. 92
Christopher Columbus. Pictures by Raymond Renard. Adapted by June Parmeley from the original text. St. Louis, Webster Division, McGraw-Hill [1967] [28 p.] col. illus., port. 19 x 21 cm. (Men of genius books) (Around the world library.) A short biography of the explorer who set out to prove the world is round and, in his desire to reach the Indies, discovered the islands of Cuba and Haiti and the continent of South America. [E111.P246] AC 67
1. Columbus, Christopher. I. Renard, Raymond, illus. II. Title.

Colombo, Cristoforo—Juvenile literature.

DE KAY, James T. 973.1'5'0924 B
Meet Christopher Columbus, by James T. de Kay. Illustrated by Victor Mays. New York, Random House [1968] 84 p. col. illus., col. maps (on lining papers) 22 cm. (Step-up books) An easy-to-read biography of the sailor who never fully recognized the importance of his discovery which changed history. [E111.D28] 92 68-23104
1. Colombo, Cristoforo—Juvenile literature. I. Mays, Victor, 1927- illus. II. Title. **BIP**

EDUCATIONAL 973.1'5'0924 B
Research Council of America. Social Science Staff.
Explorers and discoverers : Columbus / prepared by the Social Science Staff of the Educational Research Council of America. Learner-verified ed. 2. Boston : Allyn and Bacon, [1974] 43 p. : col. ill. ; 21 cm. (Concepts and inquiry, the ERC social science program) An account of Columbus' attempt to reach India by sailing west. [E111.E3 1974] 92 73-78340 pbk. : 1.75
1. Colombo, Cristoforo—Juvenile literature. I. Title. II. Series: Concepts and inquiry, the Educational Research Council social science program.

GRANT, Matthew G. 973.1'5'0924 B
Columbus; discoverer of the New World [by] Matthew G. Grant. Illustrated by John Keely and Dick Brude. [Mankato, Minn., Creative Education; distributed by Childrens Press, Chicago, 1974] 29 p. illus. (part col.) 25 cm. (His Gallery of great Americans series. Explorers of America) A brief biography of the Italian weaver's son who never achieved his dream of finding a trade route to India but in pursuing it opened the door to the New World. [E111.G78] 92 73-13959 ISBN 0-87191-286-4 3.95
1. Colombo, Cristoforo—Juvenile literature. 2. Columbus, Christopher. I. Keely, John, illus. II. Brude, Dick, illus. III. Title: Discoverer of the New World.

HEIMANN, Susan F. 973.1'5'0924 B
Christopher Columbus, by Susan Heimann. Illustrated with authentic prints, documents, and maps. New York, F. Watts, 1973. 57 p. illus. 26 cm. (A Visual biography) A biography stressing the navigational skills and voyages of discovery of the Italian seaman who discovered a new continent while trying to find a route to the Indies. [E111.H44] 92 72-10402 ISBN 0-531-00971-8 4.50
1. Colombo, Cristoforo—Juvenile literature. I. Title.

JOHNSON, Spencer. 970.01'5'0924 B
The value of curiosity : the story of Christopher Columbus / by Spencer Johnson. 1st ed. La Jolla, Calif. : Value Communications, c1977. 63 p. : col. ill. ; 29 cm. (ValueTales) Demonstrates the value of curiosity in the life of Christopher Columbus. [E111.J68] 92 77-11032 ISBN 0-916392-13-9 : 4.95
1. Colombo, Cristoforo—Juvenile literature. 2. America—Discovery and exploration—Spanish—Juvenile literature. 3. Explorers—Spain—Biography Juvenile literature. 4. Curiosity—Juvenile literature. I. Title. **BIP**

JUDSON, Clara (Ingram) 1879- j92
1960.
The picture story and biography of Admiral Christopher Columbus. Illustrated by W. T. Mars. Chicago, Follett Pub. Co. [1965] 141 p. col. illus., 4 fold. maps, col. port. 22 cm. (The Library of American heroes) [E111.J95] 65-14470
1. Colombo, Christoforo — Juvenile literature. I. Mars, Witold T., illus. II. Title.

KAUFMAN, Mervyn D. 920
A world explorer: Christopher Columbus. Illus. by Nathan Goldstein. Champaign, Ill., Garrard [c.1963] 96p. col. illus. 24cm. (World explorer bks.) 63-7875 2.75
1. Colombo, Cristoforo Juvenile literature. I. Title.

KNIGHT, Frank 923.9
The young Columbus. Illus. by Azpelicueta. New York, Roy [1964, c.1963] 144p. illus. 21cm. 64-16354 3.25 bds.,
1. Colombo, Cristoforo—Juvenile literature. I. Title.

MCGOVERN, Ann. 92 (J)
The story of Christopher Columbus. Illus. by Joe Lasker. New York, Random House, [1963, c1962] 53 p. col. illus., map (on lining papers) 24 cm. (The Random House easy to read library, R-31) [E111.M13 1963] 63-18613
1. Colombo, Cristoforo—Juvenile literature. I. Title.

NEWCOMB, pcovelle, 1908- j92
Christopher Columbus, the sea lord. Illustrated by Addison Burbank. New York, Dodd, Mead [1963] 271 p. illus. 21 cm. Bibliography: p. 263-267. [E111.N53] 61-7031
1. Colombo, Cristoforo — Juvenile literature. I. Title.

OLDS, Helen (Diehl) 1895- 92 (J)
Christopher Columbus. Illustrated by Al Davidson. New York, Putnam, c1964. 64 p. col. illus. 23 cm. (A See and read beginning to read biography) [E111.O5] 64-12600
1. Colombo, Cristoforo—Juvenile

literature. I. Title.

RICHARDS, Dorothy Fay, 1915- 970'.1'50924
Christopher Columbus, who sailed on! / By Dorothy Fay Richards ; illustrated by John Nelson. Elgin, Ill. : Child's World ; Chicago : distributed by Childrens Press, [1978] p. cm. Relates the attempts of Christopher Columbus to find a short sea route to the Indies. [E111.R5] 92 78-7664 ISBN 0-89565-032-0 : 7.35
1. Columbus, Cristoforo—Juvenile literature. 2. Explorers—Spain—Biography—Juvenile literature. I. Nelson, John, 1928- II. Title. BIP

ROBERTO, Brother, 1927- 923.9
Follow the setting sun; a story of Christopher Columbus. Illus. by Carolyn Lee Jagodits. Notre Dame, Ind., Dujarie Press [1959] 95p. illus. 24cm. [E111.R665] 59-3361
1. Colombo, Cristoforo—Juvenile literature. I. Title.

SELFRIDGE, Barbara 973.10924
Christopher Columbus. Illus. by Pablo Ramirez, Cleveland, World [c.1965] 1v. (unpaged) col. illus. 24cm. (Holly Story bk. lib.) [E111.546] 65-24742 1.50
1. Colombo, Cristoforo—Juvenile literature. I. Ramirez, Pablo, illus. II. Title.

VENTURA, Piero. 970.01'5'0924 B
Christopher Columbus / Piero Ventura ; based on the text by Gian Paolo Ceserani. New York : Random House, c1978. [32] p. : col. ill. ; 21 cm. Based on Il viaggio Colombo. A brief biography of Christopher Columbus highlighting his ocean voyages and discovery of new lands. [E111.V47] 92 77-86146 ISBN 0-394-83907-2 : 3.95 ISBN 0-394-83908-0 pbk. : 0.95. ISBN 0-394-93907-7 lib. bdg. : 4.99
1. Colombo, Cristoforo—Juvenile literature. 2. America—Discovery and exploration—Spanish—Juvenile literature. 3. Explorers—Spain—Biography—Juvenile literature. I. Ceserani, Gian Paolo, 1939- Il viaggio di Colombo. II. Title.

VERLEYEN, Cyriel. 973.1'5
The egg of Christopher Columbus. Illustrated by Henry Branton. New York, Crowell, [1971] c1970. [23] p. col. illus. 19 x 21 cm. (His Tales from history) "Also published as L'ouf de Christophe Colomb." A brief account of Columbus's first voyage and his parable of the egg. [E111.V513 1971] 70-94798 2.95
1. Colombo, Cristoforo—Juvenile literature. I. Branton, Henry, illus. II. Title.

Colombo, Cristoforo—Relations with Jews.

KAYSERLING, Meyer, 1829-1905. 970'.01'504924
Christopher Columbus and the participation of the Jews in the Spanish and Portuguese discoveries / by M. Kayserling ; translated from the author's manuscript with his sanction and revision by Charles Gross. Folcroft, Pa. : Folcroft Library Editions, 1978, c1894. xv, 189 p. ; 24 cm. Reprint of the ed. published by Longmans, Green, New York. English, Spanish, and Latin. Includes bibliographical references and index. [E111.K23 1978] 78-26172 ISBN 0-8414-5478-7 lib. bdg. : 25.00
1. Colombo, Cristoforo—Relations with Jews. 2. Maranos. 3. Santangel, Luis de, d. 1505. 4. Santangel family. 5. America—Discovery and exploration—Spanish. 6. Jews in Spain—History. 7. Spain—History—Ferdinand Isabella, 1479-1516. I. Title. BIP

Colombo, Cristoforo—Tomb.

MURATORE, Joseph R. 973.1'5'0924
The remains of Christopher Columbus; a revealing, documented narrative about Columbus' remains [by] Joseph R. Muratore. Los restos de Cristobal Colon; una narracion reveladora y documentada sobre los restos de Colon. [Warwick, R.I., Muratore Agency, 1973, c1972] 90 p. illus. 22 cm. Cover title. English and Spanish. Bibliography: p. 9. [E112.M87 1973] 72-91984
1. Colombo, Cristoforo—Tomb. 2. Santo Domingo. Catedral. I. Title. II. Title: Los restos de Cristobal Colon.

Colonna, Maria (Mancini) principessa di Paliano, 1639-1715.

MALLET, Francoise 944.0330924
The uncompromising heart; a life of Marie Mancini, LouisXIV's first love [by] Francoise Mallet-Joris. Tr. from French by Patrick O'Brian. New York, Parrar [c.1964,1966] viii,274p. port. 22cm. [DC130.M3M353] 66-12327 5.50 bds.,
1. Colonna, Maria (Mancini) principessa di Paliano, 1639-1715. 2. Louis XVI, King of France, 1638-1715. I. Title.

Colonna, Vittoria, Marchesa di Pescara, 1492-1547.

JERROLD, Maud F. 841'.3 B
Vittoria Colonna, with some account of her friends and her times, by Maud F. Jerrold. Freeport, N.Y., Books for Libraries Press [1969] 336 p. geneal. tables, ports. 23 cm. (Select bibliographies reprint series) Reprint of the 1906 ed. Bibliography: p. 322-326. [DG540.8.C8J5 1969] 72-103653
1. Colonna, Vittoria, Marchesa di Pescara, 1492-1547.

Colorado—Pol. & govt.

KEATING, Edward, 1875- 923.273
The gentleman from Colorado, a memoir. Denver, Sage Bks. [dist. Swallow, 1965, c.1964] 522p. illus., ports. 23cm. [E748.K28A3] 64-25345 6.75
1. Colorado—Pol. & govt. 2. U. S.—Pol. &govt.—1913-1921. I. Title.

Colorado—Biography.

BUELER, Gladys R. 978.8'02'0922
Colorado's colorful characters / Gladys R. Bueler. 1st ed. Golden, Colo. : Smoking Stack Press, [1975] 114, [1] p. : ill. ; 22 cm. Bibliography: p. 113-[115] [F775.B83] 74-25452 3.50
1. Colorado—Biography. 2. Frontier and pioneer life—Colorado. 3. Colorado—Gold discoveries. I. Title.

HUNT, Inez. 917.88'03'30922 B
Crazy quilt, by Inez Hunt and Wanetta Draper. [Sketches by Kathy Goff] Colorado Springs, Colo., HAH Publications [1971] 94 p. illus. 23 cm. Half title: Colorado crazy quilt. Includes bibliographies. [F775.H85] 72-181060
1. Colorado—Biography. 2. Colorado—History. I. Draper, Wanetta W., joint author. II. Title. III. Title: Colorado crazy quilt.

HUNT, Inez 920.0788
To Colorado's restless ghosts [by] Inez Hunt and Wanetta W. Draper. [Denver, Alan Swallow c.1960] 330p. Bibls., illus. (Sage Books) 60-14584 5.00
1. Colorado—Biog. I. Draper, Wanetta W., joint author. II. Title.

VALDES, Daniel T., 1916- ed. 920.0788
Who's who in Colorado. [Editor: Daniel T. Valdes] Centennial anniversary ed. [Denver, Who's Who in Colorado, inc.; distributed by Sage Books, 1958. 607 p. 25 cm. [F775.W57] 58-1659
1. Colorado — Biog. I. Title.

VALDES, Daniel T., 1916- ed. v. 12
Who's who in Colorado: a biographical record of Colorado's outstanding civic business, professional, religious, labor and government leaders. Editor: Daniel T. Valdes. Assistant editor: Tom Pino [1966/67 ed. Denver? Who's Who in Colorado, inc., c1967] 441 p. port. 19 cm. 68-86181
1. Colorado—Biog. 2. Colorado—Hist. I. Pino, Tom Eugene, 1937- joint ed. II. Title.

Colorado. University — Hist.

SEWALL, Jane. 378.788
Jane, dear child. With a foreword by Robert L. Stearns. Boulder, University of Colorado Press, 1957. 198 p. illus. 24 cm. Autobiographical. [LD1178.3.S4] 58-17290
1. Colorado. University — Hist. I. Title.

Colorow, ca. 1810-1888.

URQUHART, Lena M. 970.3'0924
Colorow, the angry chieftain, by Lena M. Urquhart. [1st ed.] Denver, Golden Bell Press [1968] 51 p. illus., map, ports. 22 cm. Bibliography: p. 51. [E99.U8U8] 68-5479
1. Colorow, ca. 1810-1888. 2. Ute Indians—Wars.

Colquhoun, Janet (Sinclair) Lady, 1781-1846.

HAMILTON, James, 1814-1867. 285'.2'0924 B
Life of Lady Colquhoun. Inverness, Free Presbyterian Church of Scotland, 1969. [8], 210 p. 19 cm. [BX9225.C637H34] 71-529178 ISBN 0-902506-02-1 7/6
1. Colquhoun, Janet (Sinclair) Lady, 1781-1846. I. Title.

Colson, Charles W.

COLSON, Charles W. 248'.2'0924 B
Born again / Charles W. Colson. Boston : G. K. Hall, 1976. p. cm. Large print ed. [BV4935.C63A33 1976b] 76-41314 ISBN 0-8161-6428-2 : 18.95
1. Colson, Charles W. 2. Converts—United States—Biography. 3. Watergate Affair, 1972- 4. Sight-saving books. I. Title. BIP

COLSON, Charles W. 248'.2'0924 B
Born again / Charles W. Colson. Old Tappan, N.J. : Chosen Books :distributed by F. H. Revell Co., c1976. 351 p., [8] leaves of plates : ill. ; 24 cm. Includes index. [BV4935.C63A33] 75-40462 ISBN 0-912376-13-9 : 8.95
1. Colson, Charles W. 2. Converts—United States—Biography. 3. Watergate Affair, 1972- I. Title. BIP

COLSON, Charles W. 248'.2'0924 B
Life sentence / by Charles W. Colson. Lincoln, Va. : Chosen Books Pub. Co., [1979] p. cm. [BX6495.C5687.A34] 79-18715 ISBN 0-912376-41-4 : 9.95
1. Colson, Charles W. 2. Prison Fellowship. 3. Fellowship House. 4. Baptists—United States—Biography. I. Title. BIP

Colt revolver.

WINDERS, Gertrude (Hecker) 926.7
Sam Colt and his gun; the life of the inventory of the revolver. With sketches by the author. New York, J. Day Co. [1959] 159 p. illus. 21 cm. [TS535.C6W5] 59-6723
1. Colt revolver. I. Colt, Samuel, 1814-1862. II. Title.

Colt, Samuel, 1814-1862.

EDWARDS, William B. 926.7
The story of Colt's revolver; the biography of Col. Samuel Colt. Harrisburg, Pa., Stackpole Co. [1953] 470 p. illus., ports., coat of arms, facsims. 28 cm. Bibliography: p. 381-382. [TS535.E3] 53-5351
1. Colt, Samuel, 1814-1862. 2. Revolvers. I. Title: Colt's revolver.

EDWARDS, William Bennett. 926.7
The story of Colt's revolver; the biography of Col. Samuel Colt. Harrisburg, Pa., Stackpole Co. [1953] 470 p. illus., ports., coat of arms, facsims. 28 cm. Bibliography: p. 381-382. [TS535.E3] 53-5351
1. Colt, Samuel, 1814-1862. 2. Revolvers. I. Title. II. Title: Colt's revolver.

RYWELL, Martin, 1905- 926.7
Samuel Colt, a man and an epoch. Harriman, Tenn., Pioneer Press [1952] 200 p. illus. 23 cm. [TS535.C649] 52-8549
1. Colt, Samuel, 1814-1862. 2. Revolvers. I. Title.

WINDERS, Gertrude (Hecker) 926.7
Sam Colt and his gun; the life of the inventory of the revolver. With sketches by the author. New York, J. Day Co. [1959] 159 p. illus. 21 cm. [TS535.C6W5] 59-6723
1. Colt revolver. I. Colt, Samuel, 1814-1862. II. Title.

Colter, John, 1775 (ca.)-1813—Juvenile literature.

BOESCH, Mark. 923.973
John Colter, man who found Yellowstone. New York, Putnam [1959] 189p. 22cm. [F592.C713] 59-11416
1. Colter, John 1775 (ca.)-1813—Juvenile literature. I. Title.

BOESCH, Mark J 1917- 923.973
John Colter, man who found Yellowstone. New York Putnam [1959] 189 p. 22 cm. [F592.C713] 59-11416
1. Colter, John, 1775 (ca.)-1813—Juvenile literature. I. Title.

Colton, Ann Ree.

COLTON, Ann Ree. 920.9133
Prophet for the archangels, by Ann Ree Colton and Jonathan Murro. [1st ed.] Glendale, Calif., ARC Pub. Co. [1964] x, 289 p. illus., ports. 22 cm. Autobiographical. [BF1815.C58A3] 64-6257
I. Murro, Jonathan. II. Title.

Colton, Walter, 1797-1851.

COLTON, Walter, 1797-1851. 979.4'03
Three years in California / by Walter Colton. New York : Arno Press, 1976. p. cm. (The Chicano heritage) Reprint of the 1850 ed. published by A. S. Barnes, New York. [F865.C7 1976] 76-1221 ISBN 0-405-09496-5 : 26.00
1. Colton, Walter, 1797-1851. 2. California—History—1846-1850—Sources. 3. California—Description and travel—1848-1869. I. Title. II. Series. BIP

Coltrane, John, 1926-1967.

COLE, Bill, 1937- 788'.66'0924 B
John Coltrane / by Bill Cole. New York : Schirmer Books, c1976. vi, 264 p. : ill. ; 24 cm. Includes indexes. Bibliography: p. 241-250. [ML419.C645C6] 76-14289 12.95
1. Coltrane, John, 1926-1967. 2. Jazz musicians—United States—Biography. BIP

SIMPKINS, Cuthbert Ormond, 1947- 788'.66'0924 B
Coltrane : a biography / by Cuthbert Ormond Simpkins. New York : Herdon House Publishers, [1975] 287 p., [10] leaves of plates : ill. ; 24 cm. Includes bibliographical references. [ML419.C645S5] 75-7459 ISBN 0-915542-82-X
1. Coltrane, John, 1926-1967. BIP

THOMAS, J. C. 788'.66'0924
Chasin' the Trane : the music and mystique of John Coltrane / J. C. Thomas. New York : Da Capo Press, 1976. 252 p., [8] leaves of plates : ill. ; 22 cm. (A Da Capo paperback) Reprint of the 1975 ed. published by Doubleday, Garden City, N.Y. Discography: p. [233]-252. [ML419.C645T5 1976] 76-6560 ISBN 0-306-80043-8 pbk. : 4.95
1. Coltrane, John, 1926-1967. I. Title.

Columba, Saint, 521-597.

ADAMNAN, Saint, 625?-704. 922.2415
Adomnan's Life of Columbia. Edited with translation and notes by Alan Orr Anderson and by Marjorie Ogilvie Anderson. London, New York, T. Nelson [1961] xxiv, 590p. facsims. 23cm. Bibliography: p. [xv,54-xxiii. [BX4700.C7A2 1961] 62-3911
1. Columba. Saint. 521-597. I. Anderson, Alan Orr, 1879-1958, ed. and tr. II. Anderson, Marjorie Ogilvie, ed. and tr. III. Title.

SIMPSON, William Douglas. 922.241 1896-
The historical Saint Columba [rev. 3d ed.] Edinburgh, Oliver & Boyd [Mystic. Conn., Verry, 1965, c.1963] vi, 127p. facsim. 19cm. Bibl. [BX4700.C7S5] 65-29573 3.50
1. Columba, Saint, 521-597. 2. Christian antiquities—Scotland. I. Title.

Columba, Saint, 521-597—Juvenile literature.

BETZ, Eva (Kelly) 1897- 922.2415
Saint Colum and the the crane. Illus. by Charles B. Vukovich. Paterson, N. J., St. Anthony Guild Press [c.1961] 47p. (Her Easy reading books of saints and friendly beasts) 61-10680 1.75 bds.,
1. Columba, Saint, 521-597—Juvenile literature. I. Title.

Columban, Saint, 543-615.

MACMANUS, Francis, 1909- 922.2415
Saint Columban. New York, Sheed and Ward [1962] 240p. 21cm. Includes bibliography. [BX4700.C75M25] 62-9108
1. Columban, Saint, 543-615. I. Title.

Colville, Lady Cynthia (Crewe-Milnes)

COLVILLE, Lady Cynthia 920.7 (Crewe-Milnes) 1884-
Crowded life; the autobiography of Lady Cynthia Colville. London, Evans Bros. [New York, Hillary House. 1966, c.1963] 215p. illus., ports. 23cm. [DA566.9.C57A3] 64-1532 5.00
I. Title.

Colwell, Annie Wallace Andrew, 1885-

ALLEN, Lorna 266'.025'0924 B Margaret, 1915- comp.
Thursday's daughter / Lorna Margaret Allen. 1st ed. New York : Vantage Press, [1974] 306 p. ; 21 cm. Consists of letters of Annie and Harry Colwell. [R722.C58A44] 74-194711 ISBN 0-533-01040-3 : 5.95
1. Colwell, Annie Wallace Andrew, 1885- 2. Colwell, Harry. 3. Missionaries, Medical—India—Correspondence, reminiscences, etc. I. Colwell, Annie Wallace Andrew, 1885- II. Colwell, Harry. III. Title.

Comaneci, Nadia, 1961-

CONNOCK, Marion. 796.4'10924
Nadia of Romania / Marion Connock. London : Duckworth, 1977. 132 p. : ill. ; 23 cm. [GV460.2C65C66] 78-310268 ISBN 0-7156-1249-2 pbk. : 2.95
1. Comaneci, Nadia, 1961- 2. Gymnasts—Romania—Biography. I. Title. BIP

GRUMEZA, Ion. 796.4'2'0924 B
Nadia : the success secrets of the amazing Romanian gymnast / by Ion Grumeza ; edited by Fred Kerner ; drawings by Lisa Craig Wesson ; photos. by Bruce Curtis, Bob Greene, Joe DiMaggio, and others. New York : K. S. Giniger Co. : distributed by Hawthorn Books, c1977. 127 p. : ill. ; 24 cm. [GV460.2.C65G78 1977] 76-151622 3.95
1. Comaneci, Nadia, 1961- 2. Gymnast—Romania—Biography.

GRUMEZA, Ion. 796.4'2'0924 B
Nadia : the success secrets of the amazing Romanian gymnast / by Ion Grumeza ; edited by Fred Kerner ; drawings by Lisa Craig Wesson ; photos. by Bruce Curtis, Bob Greene, Joe DiMaggio, and others. New York : K. S. Giniger Co. : distributed by Hawthorn Books, c1977. 127 p. : ill. ; 24 cm. [GV460.2.C65G78 1977] 76-151622 3.95
1. Comaneci, Nadia, 1961- 2. Gymnast—Romania—Biography. BIP

Comaneci, Nadia, 1961- —Juvenile literature.

MCMILLAN, 796.4'1'0924 B Constance Van Brunt.
Nadia Comaneci : enchanted sparrow / by Constance Van Brunt McMillan. St. Paul : EMC Corp., c1977. p. cm. (So young, so far) A biography of the young Romanian gymnast who received seven perfect scores during the 1976 Olympics. [GV460.2.C65M3] 92 77-24082 ISBN 0-88436-402-X lib.bdg. : 4.95 ISBN 0-88436-403-8 pbk. : 2.95
1. Comaneci, Nadia, 1961- —Juvenile literature. 2. Gymnasts—Romania—Biography—Juvenile literature. I. Title. BIP

MIKLOWITZ, Gloria D. 794.4'1'0924
Nadia Comaneci / by Gloria D. Miklowitz. New York : Grosset & Dunlap, c1977. 90 p. : ill. ; 21 cm. A brief biography emphasizing the training and gymnastic achievements of the fourteen-year-old Romanian who earned a perfect score seven times in the 1976 Olympic Games. [GV460.2.C65M54 1977] 76-47128 ISBN 0-448-12973-6 pbk. : 1.50
1. Comaneci, Nadia, 1961- —Juvenile literature. 2. Gymnasts—Romania—Biography—Juvenile literature. I. Title. BIP

SULLIVAN, George, 796.4'1'0924 B 1927-
The picture story of Nadia Comaneci / by George Sullivan. New York : Messner, [1977] p. cm. A biography of the Romanian who in 1976 became the youngest gymnastics champion in the history of the Olympic Games. [GV460.2.C65S84] 92 77-21345 ISBN 0-671-32925-1 lib.bdg. : 6.64
1. Comaneci, Nadia, 1961- —Juvenile literature. 2. Gymnasts—Romania—Biography—Juvenile literature. I. Title. BIP

Comber, Thomas J., 1852-1887.

MYERS, John Brown, 266.6'1'0924 B 1844or45-1915.
Thomas J. Comber: missionary pioneer to the Congo. New York, Negro Universities Press [1969] 160 p. illus., map, ports. 23 cm. Reprint of the 1888 ed. [BV3625.C63C64 1969] 74-98739
1. Comber, Thomas J., 1852-1887. BIP

Comboni, Daniele, Bp., 1831-1881.

COMBONI, Daniele, 282'.092'4 Bp., 1831-1881.
The power of an ideal / [edited] by Luis Butera ; translated by Amanda C. Serrato. Chicago : Franciscan Herald Press, [1978] p. cm. Bibliography: p. [BV3532.C6A34] 78-16122 ISBN 0-8199-0743-X : 8.95
1. Comboni, Daniele, Bp., 1831-1881. 2. Catholic Church—Bishops—Biography. 3. Missionaries—Italy—Biography. 4. Missionaries—Africa, East—Biography. 5. Bishops—Biography. I. Butera, Luis. II. Title.

MONDINI, A. G. 922.245
Africa or death; a biography of Bishop Daniel Comboni, founder of the missionary societies of the Verona Fathers (Sons S. H.) and the Verona Sisters [Boston] St. Paul [1964] 318 [13]p. illus., ports. 22cm. Bibl. [BV3532.C6M6] 64-22431 4.00; 3.00 pap.,
1. Comboni, Danieke, Bp., 1831-1881. 2. Missions—Africa, East. I. Title.

Combs, Ann, 1935-

COMBS, Ann, 1935- 979.7'76 B
Helter shelter / Ann Combs. 1st ed. Philadelphia : Lippincott, 1979. 281 p. ; 22 cm. [CT275.C73A36] 78-26921 ISBN 0-397-01334-5 : 8.95
1. Combs, Ann, 1935- 2. Bainbridge Island, Wash.—Biography. I. Title. BIP

Comedians, American.

*FEIN, Irving A. 791.4'092'4 1977-
Jack Benny / Irving A. Fein New York : Pocket Books, 1977c1976 306p. ; 18 cm. (A Kangaroo Book) Includes index. [PN2287.B4325F4] ISBN 0-671-80917-2 pbk. : 1.95
I. Title.
L.C. card no. of 1976 Putnam ed.:75-30975

*FEIN, Irving A. 791.4'092'4 1977-
Jack Benny / Irving A. Fein New York : Pocket Books, 1977c1976 306p. ; 18 cm. (A Kangaroo Book) Includes index. [PN2287.B4325F4] ISBN 0-671-80917-2 pbk. : 1.95
I. Title.
L.C. card no. of 1976 Putnam ed.:75-30975 BIP

TREADWELL, Bill. 927.91
50 years of American comedy. New York, Exposition Press [1951] 241 p. 23 cm. [PN2285.T67] 51-11874
1. Comedians, American. I. Title.

Comedians, American—Biography.

MANCHEL, Frank. 792.2'028'0922
Yesterday's clowns; the rise of film comedy. New York, F. Watts, 1973. 154 p. illus. 24 cm. Bibliography: p. 148-151. [PN1998.A2M28] 72-7302 ISBN 0-531-02624-8 5.95 (Lib. ed.)
1. Comedians, American—Biography. 2. Comedy films. I. Title.

Comedians—Great Britain—Biography.

MIDWINTER, Eric C. 791'.092'2
Make 'em laugh : famous comedians and their worlds / Eric Midwinter. London ; Boston : Allen & Unwin, 1979. 209 p. : ill. ; 26 cm. Includes index. [PN2597.M5] 79-314974 ISBN 0-04-792011-4 : 16.50
1. Comedians—Great Britain—Biography. I. Title. BIP

Comedians—United States.

*ADLER, Bill v. 12 B
Woody Allen clown prince of American humor, by Bill Adler & Jeffrey Feinman. New York, Pinnacle Books [1975] 178 p. illus. 18 cm. [PN2287] 791.43'028'0924 ISBN 0-523-00786-8 1.75 (pbk.)
I. Feinman, Jeffrey, joint author. II. Title. BIP

BERGER, Phil. 791'.092'2
The last laugh : the world of the stand-up comics / by Phil Berger. New York : Morrow, 1975. 377 p. : ill. ; 21 cm. [PN2285.B47] 74-20690 ISBN 0-688-02888-8 8.95
1. Comedians—United States. I. Title. BIP

WILDE, Larry. 791'.0922
The great comedians talk about comedy. [1st ed.] New York, Citadel Press [1968] 382 p. ports. 22 cm. Interviews between the author and 16 comedians. Contents.Contents.—Woody Allen.—Jack Benny.—Milton Berle.—Shelley Berman.—Joey Bishop.—George Burns.—Johnny Carson.—Maurice Chevalier.—Phyllis Diller.—Jimmy Durante.—Dick Gregory. Bob Hope.—George Jessel.—Jerry Lewis.—Danny Thomas.—Ed Wynn. [PN2285.W47] 68-28452 6.95
1. Comedians—United States. I. Title.

Comedians—United States—Biography.

KEESE, William 792'.028'0922 B Linn, 1835-1904.
A group of comedians. New York, B. Franklin [1970] 91 p. illus., ports. 19 cm. (Burt Franklin research and source works series, 573. Theatre and drama series, 12) Reprint of the 1901 ed. Contents.Contents.—Henry Placide.—William Rufus Blake.—John Brougham.—George Holland.—Charles Fisher. [PN2285.K4 1970] 71-130104 ISBN 0-8337-1903-3
1. Comedians—United States—Biography. I. Title. BIP

THOMEY, Tedd. 791'.0922
The comedians, by Ted Thomey and Norman Wilner. New York, Pyramid Books [1970] 208 p. 18 cm. Contents.Contents.—Red Skeleton: laughing outside, crying inside.—Hungry comic.—Hollywood's twisted genius.—Up from reform school.—Suffering comic.—The frenzied world of Jack Carter.—Milton "the miserable" Berle.—Hollywood's biggest losers.—Jackie Mason's war with Frank Sinatra's "pals."—Scarred comic.—Martha Raye-unfunny girl.—The great glutton. [PN2285.T5] 79-15383 ISBN 0-515-22647-5 0.75
1. Comedians—United States—Biography. I. Wilner, Norman, joint author. II. Title.

Comedians—United States—Biography—Dictionaries.

FRANKLIN, Joe. 791'.092'2 B
Joe Franklin's Encyclopedia of comedians. Secaucus, N.J. : Citadel Press, 1979. p. cm. [PN2285.F7] 79-13952 ISBN 0-8065-0566-4 : 14.95
1. Comedians—United States—Biography—Dictionaries. I. Title. II. Title: Encyclopedia of comedians.

Comedy.

*FRY, William F. 792.2092.
Make 'em laugh, life studies of comedy writers by William F. Fry and Melanie Allen Palo Alto, Ca. Science and Behavior Books [1975] xviii, 203p. ill. 23 cm. Bibliography: p.201-202. [PS336.] 75-23593 ISBN 0-8314-0041-2. 8.95.
1. Comedy. I. Allen, Melanie, joint author II. Title. BIP

Comedy films—History and criticism.

LAHUE, Kalton C. 791.43'028'0922
Clown princes and court jesters, by Kalton C. Lahue and Samuel Gill. South Brunswick, A. S. Barnes [1970] 406 p. illus. 27 cm. [PN1995.9.C55L28] 70-88276 ISBN 0-498-06949-4 8.50
1. Comedy films—History and criticism. 2. Comedians—United States. I. Gill, Samuel, 1946- joint author. II. Title.

Comenius, Johann Amos, 1592-1670.

JAKUBEC, Jan, 1862- 370'.924 B 1936.
Johannes Amos Comenius. New York, Arno Press, 1971. 59 p. port. 23 cm. (The Eastern Europe collection) Reprint of the 1928 ed. [LB475.C6J3 1971] 70-135811 ISBN 0-405-02753-2
1. Comenius, Johann Amos, 1592-1670. BIP

LAURIE, Simon 370'.92'4 B Somerville, 1829-1909.
John Amos Comenius, bishop of the Moravians: his life and educational works. New York, B. Franklin [1973] 272 p. illus. 22 cm. "Reading-circle edition." Reprint of the 1892 ed., published by C. W. Bardeen, Syracuse, N.Y. "Bibliography of the educational works of Comenius [by] C. W. Bardeen": p. 227-260. [LB475.C6L3 1973] 72-10020 ISBN 0-8337-2028-7 15.00
1. Comenius, Johann Amos, 1592-1670. BIP

SPINKA, Matthew, 1890 370'.924 B 1972.
John Amos Comenius, that incomparable Moravian. New York, Russell & Russell [1967] 177 p. 22 cm. First published in 1943. Bibliography: p. 156-[171] [LB475.C6S7 1967] 66-27150
1. Comenius, Johann Amos, 1592-1670.

YOUNG, Robert 370'.924 B Fitzgibbon, 1879- ed.
Comenius in England. New York, Arno Press, 1971. 99 p. illus., facsim., ports. 24 cm. (The Eastern Europe collection) Reprint of the 1932 ed. Includes bibliographical references. [LB475.C6Y63 1971] 70-135838 ISBN 0-405-02730-3
1. Comenius, Johann Amos, 1592-1670. 2. Royal Society of London. 3. Learned institutions and societies. 4. Indians of North America—Education. I. Title.

Comenius, Johann Amos, 1592-1670—Congresses.

CZECHOSLOVAK Society 370'.92'4 B of Arts and Sciences in America.
Comenius / edited by Vratislav Busek ; translations from Czech by Kaca Polackova ; cover design by Ladislav Sutnar. New York : Czechoslovak Society of Arts and Sciences in America, c1972. 184 p. : port. ; 25 cm. "A symposium held at the 5th Congress of the Czechoslovak Society of Arts and Sciences in America at New York University School of Law, New York City, November 13-15, 1970 to commemorate the 300th anniversary of the death of Jan Amos Comenius [Komensky]

on November 15, 1670." Contents.Contents.—Busek, V. Introduction.—Odlozilik, O. Jan Amos Komensky.—Bradbrook, B. R. Comenius in England.—Capek, M. Comenius and the moral problem of exile.—Hujer, K. Comenius and his astronomical world view.—Krempl, R. K. The Thrinitary System in the works of Comenius.—Pollak, O. J. John Amos Comenius "Letters to Heaven."—Sebor, M. M. Comenian Pansophia: Geographic comments.—Spinka, M. Comenius' ideal of World Church.—Starkova, V. The Return of the first great exile.—StrOComenius / edited by Vratislav Busek ; translations from Czech by Kaca Polackova ; cover design by Ladislav Sutnar. New York : Czechoslovak Society of Arts and Sciences in America, c1972. 184 p. : port. ; 25 cm. "A symposium held at the 5th Congress of the Czechoslovak Society of Arts and Sciences in America at New York University School of Law, New York City, November 13-15, 1970 t
1. Comenius, Johann Amos, 1592-1670—Congresses. I. Comenius, Johann Amos, 1592-1670. II. Busek, Vratislav, ed.

Comic books, strips, etc.—American—Biography.

BAILS, Jerry G. 741'.092'2 B
The who's who of American comic books. Editors: Jerry Bails and Hames Ware. 1st ed. [Detroit, 1973- v. illus. 28 cm. [PN6725.B3] 73-174050
1. Comic books, strips, etc.—American—Biography. I. Ware, Hames, joint author. II. Title.

Comic books, strips, etc.—American—History and criticism.

SHERIDAN, Martin, 1914- 741.5'973
Comics and their creators; life stories of American cartoonists. New York, Luna Press [1971, c1944] 304 p. illus. 23 cm. [PN6725.S5 1971] 78-176227 4.00
1. Comic books, strips, etc.—American—History and criticism. 2. Cartoonists—United States—Biography. I. Title.

Commerce—Biography.

BRIDGES, Thomas Charles, 1868- 338'.0922
Kings of commerce, by T. C. Bridges and H. Hessell Tiltman. Freeport, N.Y., Books for Libraries Press [1968] 288 p. illus. 23 cm. (Essay index reprint series) Reprint of the 1928 ed. [HF3023.A2B7 1968] 68-8442
1. Commerce—Biography. 2. United States—Biography. 3. Great Britain—Biography. I. Tiltman, Hubert Hessell, 1897- joint author. II. Title. BIP

Commercial art—Europe.

GRAPHIC designers in Europe. 741.6'094 [Edited by Henri Hillebrand] New York, Universe Books [1971-73] 4 v. illus. (part col.) 27 cm. Text in English, French, and German. Contents.Contents.—1. Jan Lenica. Jean-Michel Folon. Josef Muller-Brockmann. Dick Elffers.—2. Giovanni Pintori. Edward Bawden. Hans Hillmann. Herbert Leupin.—3. Karl Gerstner. Crosby/ Fletcher/ Forbes. Andre Francois. Bob Gill.—v. 4. Franco Grignani. Heinz Edelmann. Jacques Richez. Celestino Piatti. [NC998.6.E87G72] 72-147894 ISBN 0-87663-143-X (v. 1) varies 7.95 per vol.
1. Commercial art—Europe. 2. Commercial artists—Europe. I. Hillebrand, Henri, ed.

Commins, Saxe.

COMMINS, Dorothy Berliner. 070.5'092'4 B
What is an editor? : Saxe Commins at work / Dorothy Commins. Chicago : University of Chicago Press, 1978. xv, 243 p. : ill. ; 23 cm. Includes index. [PN149.9.C6C6] 77-81716 ISBN 0-226-11427-9 : 10.00
1. Commins, Saxe. 2. Editors—United States—Biography. 3. American literature—20th century—History and criticism. I. Title. BIP

Commons, John Rogers,

COMMONS, John Rogers, 1892-1945 923.373
Myself, the autobiography of John R. Commons. Madison, Univ. of Wis. Pr., 1963. 201p. illus. 21cm. 63-15619 5.00
I. Title. BIP

Communication—Biography.

FONZI, Gaeton. 070.9'24 B
Annenberg; a biography of power. New York, Weybright and Talley [1970] 246 p. ports. 24 cm. [PN4874.A56F6 1970] 72-106028 7.95
I. Annenberg, Walter H., 1908-

STEIN, Meyer L. 070'.92'2
Blacks in communications: journalism, public relations, and advertising, by M. L. Stein. New York, J. Messner [1972] 191 p. illus. 22 cm. Bibliography: p. 175-176. [P92.5.A1S74] 78-182947 ISBN 0-671-32511-6 4.95
1. Communication—Biography. 2. Negro journalists—Biography. I. Title.

Communication in personnel management.

KEEFE, William Ford, 1921- 658.3'14'0926
Open minds : the forgotten side of communication / William F. Keefe. New York : AMACOM, [1975] 228 p. ; 22 cm. Includes bibliographical references. [HF5549.5.C6K373] 75-2412 ISBN 0-8144-5372-4 : 12.95
1. Communication in personnel management. 2. Psychology, Industrial. I. Title.

Communication—United States—Biography.

FOREMOST women in communications; 001.5'0922 a biographical reference work on accomplished women in broadcasting, publishing, advertising, public relations, and allied professions. [New York] Foremost Americans Pub. Corp. [1970] xvii, 788 p. ports. 25 cm. [P92.5.A1F6] 79-125936 ISBN 0-8352-0414-6
1. Communication—United States—Biography. 2. Women—United States—Biography.

Communism—History.

BALABANOFF, Angelica, 1878-1965. 335.43'0924 B
My life as a rebel. [3d ed.] New York, Greenwood Press, 1968 [c1938] ix, 324 p. 22 cm. [HX312.B3 1968] 68-23270
1. Communism—History. 2. Socialism—History. I. Title. BIP

Communism—Hungary.

PALOCZI Horvath, Gyorgy. 920.5
The undefeated. [1st American ed.] Boston, Little, Brown [1959] 305 p. 22 cm. Autobiographical. [PN5166.P3A3 1959a] 59-11104
1. Communism—Hungary. I. Title.

Communism—South America.

RAVINES, Eudocio. 335.43'098
The Yenan way. Westport, Conn., Greenwood Press [1972, c1951] 319 p. 22 cm. Issued also in Spanish under title: La gran estafa. [HX177.R38 1972] 71-142860 ISBN 0-8371-5959-8
1. Communism—South America. 2. Communism. I. Title. BIP

Communism—United States—1917-

DENNIS, Eugene, 1905?- 923.273
Letters from prison. Selected by Peggy Dennis. New York, International Publishers [1956] 157p. illus. 21cm. [HX84.D53A44] 56-2531
1. Communism—U. S.—1917- I. Title.

GITLOW, Benjamin, 1891-1965. 335.43'0973
The whole of their lives; communism in America—a personal history and intimate portrayal of its leaders. With a foreword by Max Eastman. Freeport, N.Y., Books for Libraries Press [1971, c1948] xvi, 387 p. 23 cm. (Biography index reprint series) [HX89.G54 1971] 78-179726 ISBN 0-8369-8094-8
1. Communism—United States—1917- 2. Communists—United States. I. Title. BIP

HICKS, Granville, 1901- 335.43'0973
Where we came out. Westport, Conn., Greenwood Press [1973, c1954] v, 250 p. 22 cm. Reprint of the ed. published by Viking Press, New York. [HX84.H48A3 1973] 73-8559 ISBN 0-8371-6970-4
1. Communism—United States—1917- I. Title. BIP

Communist International—Biography.

LAZIC, Branko M. 329'.072'0922 B
Biographical dictionary of the Comintern, by Branko Lazitch in collaboration with Milorad M. Drachkovitch. Stanford, Calif., Hoover Institution Press, 1973. xxxxii, 458 p. 24 cm. (Hoover Institution publications, 121) [HX11.I5L3378] 72-187265 ISBN 0-8179-1211-8 15.00
1. Communist International—Biography. I. Drachkovitch, Milorad M., joint author. II. Title. III. Series: Stanford University. Hoover Institution on War, Revolution, and Peace. Publications, 121.

Communist Party of Australia.

MCEWAN, Keith. 335.430924
Once a jolly comrade. Brisbane, Sydney [etc.] Jacaranda [1966] 119 p. 22 cm. [JQ4098.C6M3] 67-76633
1. Communist Party of Australia. 2. Communists—Correspondence, reminiscences, etc. I. Title.

Communists.

LEADERS of the communist world. 335.43'0922 B Edited by Rodger Swearingen. New York, Free Press [1971] xv, 632 p. illus. 24 cm. Includes bibliographical references. [HX23.L4] 74-84751
1. Communists. I. Swearingen, Arthur Rodger, 1923- ed. BIP

Communists—Biography.

TROTSKII, Lev, 1879-1940. 335.43'092'2 B
Portraits, political & personal / by Leon Trotsky ; [edited by George Breitman and George Saunders]. 1st ed. New York : Pathfinder Press, 1977. 237, [1] p. : ill. ; 23 cm. Includes index. Bibliography: p. [238] [HX23.T74 1977] 77-50342 ISBN 0-87348-503-3 : 11.00. ISBN 0-87348-504-1 pbk. : 2.95
1. Communists—Biography. 2. Communists—Russia—Biography. 3. Socialists—Biography. I. Breitman, George. II. Saunders, George, 1936- III. Title.

Communists—China.

ELEGANT, Robert S. 951.04'2'0922
China's Red masters; political biographies of the Chinese Communist leaders [by] Robert S. Elegant. Westport, Conn., Greenwood Press [1971, c1951] 264 p. illus. 23 cm. London ed. (The Bodley Head) has title: China's Red leaders. Bibliography: p. 256-259. [DS778.A1E4 1971] 76-136065 ISBN 0-8371-5215-1
1. Communists—China. 2. China—Biography. I. Title. BIP

SNOW, Helen (Foster) 1907- 335.43'4 B
The Chinese Communists: sketches and autobiographies of the Old Guard. Book 1: Red dust. Book 2: Autobiographical profiles and biographical sketches. Introd. to book 1 by Robert Carver North. Westport, Conn., Greenwood Pub. Co. [1972] xxi, 398 p. illus. 24 cm. First published in 1952 under title: Red Dust. [DS778.A1S499] 77-104236 ISBN 0-8371-6321-8
1. Communists—China. 2. China—Biography. I. Snow, Helen (Foster) 1907- Red dust. 1972. II. Title.

Communists—Correspondence.

MARX, Karl, 1818-1883. 335.4'092'4
The letters of Karl Marx / selected and translated with explanatory notes and an introd. by Saul K. Padover. Englewood Cliffs, N.J. : Prentice-Hall, c1979. xxvii, 576 p. ; 24 cm. Includes indexes. Bibliography: p. 532-534. [HX39.5.A4 1979] 79-10894 ISBN 0-13-531533-6 : 19.95
1. Communists—Correspondence. 2. Communists—Biography. I. Padover, Saul Kussiel, 1905- BIP

Communists—Correspondence, reminiscences, etc.

GRAMSCI, Antonio, 1891-1937 v. 12 B
Letters from prison. Selected, translated from the Italian, and introduced by Lynne Lowner. New York, Harper and Row [1975 c1973] 292 p. illus. 21 cm. (A Harper Colophon Book) Translated from lettere dal carcere. Bibliography: p. 283-284 [HX288.G7A4213] 335.43'092'4 B ISBN 0-06-090452-6 3.95 (pbk.)
1. Communists—Correspondence, reminiscences, etc. I. Title.
L.C. card no. for original edition: 74-156531 BIP

KOLLONTAI, Aleksandra Mikhailovna, 1872-1952. 335.43'0924 B
The autobiography of a sexually emancipated Communist woman [by] Alexandra Kollontai. Edited with an afterword by Iring Fetscher. Translated by Salvator Attanasio. [New York] Herder and Herder [1971] xvi, 137, [1] p. 22 cm. Bibliography: p. 137-[138] [DK268.K56A313] 77-165502 5.95
1. Communists—Correspondence, reminiscences, etc. I. Title.

Communists—Russia.

HAUPT, Georges, comp. 947.084'092'2 B
Makers of the Russian revolution : biographies of Bolshevik leaders / Georges Haupt and Jean-Jacques Marie ; translated from the Russian by C. I. P. Ferdinand ; commentaries translated from the French by D. M. Bellos. Ithaca, N.Y. : Cornell University Press, 1974. 452 p. ; 23 cm. Translation of Les Bolcheviks par eux-memes. Includes bibliographical references and index. [HX313.H3613] 73-20814 ISBN 0-8014-0809-1 : 15.00
1. Communists—Russia. I. Marie, Jean Jacques, joint comp. II. Title. BIP

Community health nursing—United States.

INNOVATIONS in community health nursing : 610.73'43'0973 health care delivery in shortage areas / edited by Anne R. Warner. Saint Louis : C. V. Mosby Co., 1978. xii, 235 p. : ill. ; 24 cm. Includes bibliographies. [RT98.I56] 77-20114 ISBN 0-8016-53509 pbk. : 7.95
1. Community health nursing—United States. 2. Nurses—United States—Biography. I. Warner, Anne R., 1928- BIP

Comnena, Anna, b. 1083.

DELVEN, Rae. 949.5'03'072024 B
Anna Comnena. New York, Twayne Publishers [1972] 186 p. 21 cm. (Twayne's world authors series, TWAS 213: Greece) Bibliography: p. 173-177. [DF605.3.D35] 78-169634 5.95
1. Comnena, Anna, b. 1083. 2. Byzantine Empire—History—Alexius I Comnenus, 1081-1118.

Composers.

BACHARACH, Alfred Louis, 927.8
1891- ed.
The music masters. [Lives of the great composers. Harmondsworth, Middlesex] Penguin Books [1957-- v. 19cm. (Pelican books A388- Contents.v. 1. From the sixteenth century to the time of Beethoven, by W. H. Anderson [and others]--v. 2. After Beethoven to Wagner, by G. Abraham [and others]--v. 3. The romantic age, by G. Abraham [and others] [ML390.B139] 58-3117
1. Composers. I. Bacharach, Alfred Louis, 1891-ed. Lives of the great composers. II. Title.

BAKELESS, Katherine Little, 927.8
1895-
Story-lives of great composers. [Rev. ed.] Philadelphia, Lippincott [1953] 265 p. illus. 21 cm. [ML390.B22 1953] 53-5424
1. Composers. I. Title. BIP

BECKETT, Walter, 1914- 927.8
Liszt. London, J. M. Dent; New York, Farrar, Straus, and Cudahy [1956] 185p. illus. 19cm. (The Master musicians) [ML410.L7B295] 56-13950
I. Title.

BIANCOLLI, Louis Leopold. 927.8
Masters of the orchestra from Bach to Prokofieff. by Louis Biancolli and Herbert F. Peyser, with contributions by Robert Bagar and Pitts Sanborn; introd. by Dimitri Mitropoulos. New York, Putnam [1954] 481p. 22cm. [ML390.B566] 54-7704
1. Composers. I. Peyser, Herbert Francis. 1886-1953. II. Title.

BUTTERWORTH, 780'.92'2 B
Hezekiah, 1839-1905.
The great composers. Plainview, N.Y., Books for Libraries Press [1974] p. cm. (Essay index reprint series) Reprint of the 1884 ed. published by D. Lothrop, Boston, in series: Little biographies. 2d ser. [ML60.B98 1974] 74-4176 ISBN 0-518-10175-4 12.50
1. Composers. I. Title. II. Series: Little biographies. Boston, 1884- 2d ser.
Contents omitted.

CLARKE, Cyril. ed. 927.8
The composer in love. London, New York, P. Nevill [1951] 177 p. ports. 22 cm. Principally letters. [ML390.C6] 51-2930
1. Composers. I. Title.

CROSS, Milton John, 1897- 927.8
Encyclopedia of the great composers and their music [by] Milton Cross and David Ewen. Garden City, N. Y., Doubleday [1953] 2 v. (viii, 1009 p.) 22 cm. "One hundred basic works for the record library": p. [917] 926. Bibliography: p. [965]-977. [ML385.C7] 53-9139
1. Composers. 2. Music—Discography. I. Ewen, David, 1907- joint author. II. Title.

ELSON, Louis Charles, 780'.922
1848-1920.
Great composers and their work. Freeport, N.Y., Books for Libraries Press [1972] 302 p. illus. 23 cm. (Essay index reprint series) Reprint of the 1898 ed. Contents.Contents.—The old Flemish school.—The old Italian composers, Palestrina.—Opera and oratorio, Gluck, Bach, Handel.—Haydn and Mozart.—Ludwig van Beethoven.—Franz Peter Schubert.—Chopin and the modern piano composers.—Mendelssohn and Schumann.—A batch of operatic composers.—Wagner, his life and theories.—Johannes Brahms.—Giuseppe Verdi.—Other influences in modern music. [ML390.E49 1972] 71-37472 ISBN 0-8369-2545-9
1. Composers. I. Title.

EWEN, David, 1907- ed. 927.8
The book of modern composers. 2d ed., rev. and enl. New York, Knopf, 1950 ['1942] x, 586, xv p. 25 cm. "Principal works, selected recordings, bibliography": p. 523-579. "General bibliography": p. 580-581. [ML390.E83 1950] 50-7043
1. Composers. 2. Music—Hist. & crit.—Modern. I. Title. II. Title: Modern composers.

FREEMAN, Warren Samuel, 927.8
1911-
Great composers; 18 makers of music, by Warren S. Freeman and Ruth W. Whittaker. Illustrated by Virginia E. Grilley. New York, Abelard Press [1952] 160 p. illus. 24 cm. [ML390.F87] 52-2566
1. Composers. 2. Music—Juvenile literature. I. Title.

HORTON, John. 927.8
Some nineteenth century composers. London, New York, Oxford University Press, 1950. xi, 106 p. 19 cm. [ML390.H78] 51-5962
1. Composers. I. Title.
Contents Omitted.

HUGHES, Gervase. 780'.922
Composers of operetta. New York, St. Martin's Press, 1962. 283p. illus. 23cm. Includes bibliography. [ML390.H887C6] 62-4876
1. Composers. I. Title. BIP

HUSSEY, Dyneley, 1893- 927.8
Some composers of opera. London, New York, Oxford University Press, 1952. 102 p. 19 cm. [ML390.H967] 52-8680
1. Composers. I. Title. BIP

KAUFMANN, Helen Babette 927.8
(Loeb)
The story of one hundred great composers. Ed. under the supervision of Thomas K. Scherman. New York, Grosset & Dunlap [1960, c.1943, 1960] 308p. 15cm. (The Listener's music library) 60-51519 1.50 bds.,
1. Composers. I. Title.

KAUFMANN, Helen (Loeb) 927.8
History's 100 greatest composers. Biographies by Helen L. Kalfmann. Portraits by Samuel Nisenson. New York, Grosset & Dunlap [1957] 145p. illus. 29cm. (Illustrated true books) [ML390.K2] 57-10568
1. Composers. I. Title.

LEONARD, Richard Anthony 927.8
The stream of music. New rev. ed. [Gloucester, Mass., P. Smith, 1963, c.1943, 1962] 550p. illus. 19cm. (Dolphin bk., C358 rebound) 3.50
1. Composers. I. Title.

LEONARD, Richard Anthony 927.8
The stream of music. New and rev. ed. Garden City, N. Y., Doubleday [c.1943, 1962] 550p. illus. 19cm. (Dolphin bks., C358) 62-14692 1.45 pap.,
1. Composers. I. Title.

LEONARD, Richard Anthony. 927.8
The stream of music. New and rev. ed. Garden City, N. Y., Doubleday [1962] 550p. illus. 19cm. (Dolphin books, C358) 'Bibliography and acknowledgments': p. [535]-538. [ML390.L54 1962] 62-14692
1. Composers. I. Title.

MASON, Daniel Gregory, 780'.924
1873-1953.
The romantic composers. Westport, Conn., Greenwood Press [1970] xi, 353 p. music, ports. 23 cm. Reprint of the 1906 ed. Contents.Contents.—Romanticism in music.—Franz Schubert.—Robert Schumann.—Felix Mendelssohn.—Frederic Chopin.—Hector Berlioz.—Franz Liszt. [ML390.M415 1970b] 69-13990
1. Composers. 2. Romanticism in music. I. Title. BIP

PRESTON, Novella D 927.8
Makers of music. Illustrated by Sandor Bodo. Teacher's ed. Nashville, Tenn., Convention Press [1960] 95p. illus. 19cm. 'Church study course for teaching and training [of the Sunday School Board of the Southern Baptist Convention] This book is number 1991 in category 19, section D. [ML3930.P74] 61-11463
1. Composers. 2. Music—Juvenile literature. I. southern Baptist Convention. Sunday School Board. II. Title.

ROSENFELD, Paul, 1890- 780'.922
1946.
Musical portraits: interpretations of twenty modern composers. Freeport, N.Y., Books for Libraries Press [1968] 314 p. 22 cm. (Essay index reprint series) "First published 1920; reprinted 1968." [ML390.R78 1968] 68-29243
1. Composers. 2. Music—History and criticism—19th century. 3. Music—History and criticism—20th century. I. Title.

SMITH, Delos. 927.8
Music in your life; the lives of the great composers. [1st ed.] New York, Harper [1957] 272 p. 22 cm. [[ML390]] 57-10253
1. Composers. I. Title.

THOMAS, Henry, 1886- 780'.922
Living biographies of great composers, by Henry Thomas and Dana Lee Thomas. Garden City, N.Y., Garden City Books [1959] 327 p. illus. 22 cm. [ML390.T385 1959] 59-2998
1. Composers. I. Thomas, Dana Lee, 1918- joint author. II. Title.

YOUNG composers. 927.8
[Translated by Leo Black] Bryn Mawr, Pa., Theodore Presser Co. in association with Universal Edition, London [1960] 135 p. illus., diagrs., music. 21 cm. (Die Reibe; a periodical devoted to developments in contemporary music, 4) [ML390.J953] 62-1478
1. Composers. 2. Music — Hist. & crit. — 20th cent. I. Series.

Composers, American.

BAKELESS, Katherine Little, 927.8
1895-
Story-lives of American composers. [2d] rev. ed. Philadelphia, Lippincott, 1953. 291 p. illus. 21 cm. [ML390.B2 1953] 53-5425
1. Composers, American. I. Title.

BERNSTEIN, Shirley 927.8
Making music: Leonard Bernstein. Chicago, Encyclopaedia Britannica [c.1963] 192p. illus. 22cm. (Britanica bookshelf--Great lives) 63-13513 2.95; 2.36 lib. ed.,qBernstein, Leonard, 1918-
I. Title.

GOSS, Madeleine Binkley, 927.8
1892-
Modern music-makers, contemporary American composers. [1st ed.] New York, Dutton, 1952. 499 p. ports., music. 25 cm. Includes musical autographs and lists of works. [ML390.G69] 52-5304
1. Composers, American. I. Title.

PANZERI, Louis. 780'.92'2 B
Louisiana composers. [New Orleans, La., Printed by Dinstuhl Print. and Pub., 1972] 102 p. illus. 23 cm. [ML390.P196] 72-188152
1. Composers, American. I. Title.

PARIS, Leonard Allen, 1912- 927.8
Men and melodies. New York, Crowell [1954] 197 p. 21 cm. [ML390.P24] 54-9151
1. Composers, American. I. Title.

PARIS, Leonard Allen, 1912- 927.8
Men and melodies. Rev. ed. New York, Crowell [c1959] 213p. 21cm. [ML390.P24 1959] 59-15522
1. Composers, American. I. Title.

POSELL, Elsa Z. 927.8
American composers. Boston, Houghton Mifflin, 1963. 183 p. illus. 22 cm. [ML390.P758A4] 63-7329
1. Composers, American

WIGGIN, Frances (Turgeon) 927.8
1891-
Maine composers and their music; a biographical dictionary by Frances Turgeon Wiggin. [Rockland? Me.] Maine Federation of Music Clubs, 1959. xvii, 121 p. 23 cm. [ML390.W5] 60-26410
1. Composers, American. I. Title.

Composers, American—Biography.

ANDERSON, Ruth. 780'.92'2 B
Contemporary American composers : a biographical dictionary / compiled by E. Ruth Anderson. Boston : G. K. Hall, c1976. v, 513 p. ; 29 cm. [ML390.A54] 76-2395 ISBN 0-8161-1117-0 lib.bdg. : 50.00
1. Composers, American—Biography. I. Title. BIP

EWEN, David, 1907- 927.8
Popular American composers from Revolutionary times to the present; a biographical and critical guide. New York, H. W. Wilson Co., 1962. 217 p. ports. 26 cm. [ML390.E845] 62-9024
1. Composers, American—Biography. I. Title.

GOSS, Madeleine 780'.922 B
(Binkley) 1892-
Modern music-makers; contemporary American composers, by Madeleine Goss. Westport, Conn., Greenwood Press [1970, c1952] 499 p. facsims., ports. 23 cm. [ML390.G69 1970] 73-97345 ISBN 0-8371-2957-5
1. Composers, American—Biography. I. Title. BIP

HOWARD, John Tasker, 780'.92'2 B
1890-1964.
Our contemporary composers : American music in the twentieth century / John Tasker Howard ; with the assistance of Arthur Mendel. Plainview, N.Y. : Books for Libraries Press, 1975, c1941. p. cm. (Essay index reprint series) Reprint of the ed. published by Crowell, New York. Includes index. Bibliography: p. [ML390.H8 1975] 75-14233 ISBN 0-518-10201-7 : 24.75
1. Composers, American—Biography. 2. Music, American—History and criticism. 3. Music—History and criticism—20th century. I. Mendel, Arthur, 1905- II. Title.

Composers, Australian.

MURDOCH, James. 780'.92'2 B
Australia's contemporary composers. [Melbourne] Macmillan [1972] xiii, 223 p. ports. 25 cm. Includes discographies. [ML106.A93M9] 73-181398 ISBN 0-333-13913-5
1. Composers, Australian. 2. Music—Australia—Bio-bibliography. I. Title.

MURDOCH, James. 780'.92'2 B
Australia's contemporary composers / [by] James Murdoch. Melbourne : Sun Books, 1975, c1972. xiii, 223 p., [18] leaves of plates : ill. ; 24 cm. Bibliography: p. 210. [ML106.A93M9 1975] 76-355543 ISBN 0-7251-0199-7 : 8.50
1. Composers, Australian. 2. Music—Australia—Bio-bibliography. I. Title.

Composers Biography.

ANDERSON, Arvid C. 780'.922
Masters of music, by Arvid C. Anderson. Freeport, N.Y., Books for Libraries Press [1970, c1948] 192 p. ports. 23 cm. (Biography index reprint series) [ML390.A53 1970] 70-117320
1. Composers—Biography. I. Title. BIP

ANGOFF, Charles, 1902- 780'.922
Fathers of classical music. Illus. by La Verne Reiss. Freeport, N.Y., Books for Libraries Press [1969, c1947] viii, 164 p. ports. 23 cm. (Essay index reprint series) Discography: p. 153-161. [ML390.A57 1969] 73-84294
1. Composers—Biography. 2. Music—Discography. I. Title. BIP

BACHARACH, Alfred 780'.92'2 B
Louis, 1891-1966, ed.
Lives of great composers, by W. R. Anderson [and others] With an introd. by H. C. Colles. Freeport, N.Y., Books for Libraries Press [1972] 658 p. 23 cm. (Essay index reprint series) Reprint of the 1935 ed. Includes bibliographies. [ML390.B13 1972] 72-276 ISBN 0-8369-2783-4
1. Composers—Biography. I. Title. BIP

BELLAIGUE, Camille, 780'.92'2 B
1858-1930.
Portraits and silhouettes of musicians / translated from the French of Camille Bellaigue by Ellen Orr. Boston : Longwood Press, 1978. 302 p., [14] leaves of plates : ill. ; 22 cm. Reprint of the 1898 ed. published by Dodd, Mead, New York. [ML390.B43 1978] 77-90807 ISBN 0-89341-424-7 lib.bdg. : 35.00
1. Composers—Biography. I. Orr, Ellen. II. Title.

BIANCOLLI, Louis 780'.922 B
Leopold.
Masters of the orchestra from Bach to Prokofieff, by Louis Biancolli and Herbert F. Peyser, with contributions by Robert Bagar and Pitts Sanborn. Introd. by Dimitri Mitropoulos. New York,

Greenwood Press [1969, c1954] xv, 481 p. 23 cm. [ML390.B566 1969] 70-94578
1. Composers—Biography. I. Peyser, Herbert Francis, 1886-1953. II. Title. **BIP**

BROOK, Donald. 780'.922 B
Composers' gallery; biographical sketches of contemporary composers. Freeport, Books for Libraries Press [1970, c1946] 218 p. ports. 23 cm. (Biography index reprint series) [ML390.B857 1970] 76-136641
1. Composers—Biography. I. Title. **BIP**

BROWER, Harriette 780'.922 B
Moore, 1869-1928.
Story-lives of master musicians. Freeport, N.Y., Books for Libraries Press [1971, c1922] 371 p. ports. 23 cm. (Essay index reprint series) [ML390.B86 1971] 74-167316 ISBN 0-8369-2338-3
1. Composers—Biography. I. Title. **BIP**

CARDUS, Neville, Sir, 780'.922
1889-
Composers eleven. With drawings by Milein Cosman. Freeport, N.Y., Books for Libraries Press [1970, c1958] 255 p. illus., ports. 23 cm. (Essay index reprint series) Rev. and enl. ed. of the author's Ten composers. Contents.Contents.—Franz Shubert.—Wagner.—Brahms.—Anton Bruckner.—Gustav Mahler.—Strauss, the tragic-comedian.—Cesar Franck.—Debussy.—Edward Elgar.—Delius.—Sibelius. [ML390.C3 1970] 75-105002 ISBN 0-8369-1554-2
1. Composers—Biography. I. Title. **BIP**

CROSS, Milton John, 1897- 927.8
Encyclopedia of the great composers and their music [by] Milton Cross and David Ewen. New rev. ed. Garden City, N.Y., Doubleday, 1962. 2 v. (viii, 1009 p.) 22 cm. "One hundred basic works for the record library": p. [917]-926. Bibliography: p. [965]-978. [ML385.C7 1962] 62-8097
1. Composers—Biography. 2. Music—Discography. I. Ewen, David, 1907- joint author. II. Title.

CROSS, Milton John, 780'.922 B
1897-
The Milton Cross new encyclopedia of the great composers and their music [by] Milton Cross and David Ewen. Rev. and expanded. Garden City, N.Y., Doubleday, 1969. 2 v. (xi, 1284 p.) 22 cm. "Basic works for the record library": p. [1185]-1192. Bibliography: p. [1235]-1250. [ML385.C7 1969] 70-87097
1. Composers—Biography. 2. Music—Discography. I. Ewen, David, 1907- joint author. II. Title: New encyclopedia of the great composers and their music. **BIP**

CROWEST, Frederick 780'.922 B
James, 1850-1927.
The great tone-poets; being short memoirs of the greater musical composers. Freeport, N.Y., Books for Libraries Press [1972] xvi, 373 p. 23 cm. (Essay index reprint series) Reprint of the 1874 ed. Contents.Contents.—Bach.—Handel.—Gluck.—Haydn.—Mozart.—Beethoven.—Spohr.—Weber.—Rossini.—Schubert.—Mendelssohn.—Schumann. [ML390.C95 1972] 70-38711 ISBN 0-8369-2641-2
1. Composers—Biography. I. Title. **BIP**

THE Dictionary of 780'.92'2 B
composers / edited by Charles Osborne. New York : Taplinger Pub. Co., 1978, c1977. 380 p. : ill. ; 24 cm. "A Crescendo book." [ML105.D53 1978] 78-58291 ISBN 0-8008-2194-7 : 14.95
1. Composers—Biography. 2. Music—Bio-bibliography. I. Osborne, Charles, 1927- **BIP**

DOLE, Nathan Haskell, 780.92'2
1852-1935.
Famous composers. 4th ed., with appendix by David Ewen. Freeport, N.Y., Books for Libraries Press [1968, c1964] xi, 866 p. ports. 22 cm. (Essay index reprint series) "Reprinted 1968." First published 1891 under title A score of famous composers. [ML390.D66 1968] 68-24848
1. Composers—Biography. I. Ewen, David, 1907- II. Title.

ELSON, Louis Charles, 780'.92'2
1848-1920.
Great composers and their work / by Louis C. Elson. Boston : Longwood Press, 1978. ix, 302 p., [15] leaves of plates : ill. ; 22 cm. Reprint of the 1898 ed. published by L. C. Page, Boston. Includes index. Contents.Contents.—The old Flemish school.—The old Italian composers, Palestrina.—Opera and oratorio, Gluck, Bach, Handel.—Haydn and Mozart.—Ludwig van Beethoven.—Franz Peter Schubert.—Chopin and the modern piano composers.—Mendelssohn and Schumann.—A batch of operatic composers.—Wagner, his life and theories.—Johannes Brahms.—Giuseppe Verdi.—Other influences in modern music. [ML390.E49 1978] 77-90806 ISBN 0-89341-423-9 lib.bdg. : 30.00
1. Composers—Biography. I. Title.
Contents omitted **BIP**

EWEN, David, 1907- ed. 780'.922
Composers since 1900; a biographical and critical guide. New York, H. W. Wilson Co., 1969. 639 p. ports. 27 cm. This vol. replaces: Composers of today, American composers today, and European composers today, originally published in 1934, 1949, and 1954, respectively. Bibliography: p. 639. [ML390.E833] 72-102368
1. Composers—Biography. 2. Music—Bio-bibliography. I. Title.

EWEN, David, 1907- 927.8
The new book of modern composers. 3d ed., rev. and enl. New York, Knopf, 1961. 491 p. 25 cm. Previously published under the title The book of modern composers. Includes lists of works for each composer and bibliography. [ML390.E83 1961] 61-15040
1. Composers—Biography. 2. Music—History and criticism—20th century. I. Title.

EWEN, David, 1907- ed. 927.8
The world of great composers. Englewood Cliffs, N.J., Prentice-Hall [1962] 576 p. 25 cm. Includes bibliographies and lists of compositions. [ML390.E86] 62-8731
1. Composers—Biography. I. Title. **BIP**

GOUGH-YATES, 782.8'5'0922 B
Kevin.
The film music book : a guide to film composers / written & compiled by Kevin Gough Yates & Margaret Tarratt ; edited by David Cumming. New Rochelle, N.Y. : Arlington House Publishers, 1978. p. cm. Includes index. [ML390.G7] 77-27625 ISBN 0-87000-411-5 : 20.00
1. Composers—Biography. I. Tarratt, Margaret, joint author. II. Title.

HOOVER, Kathleen 782.1'0922
O'Donnell.
Makers of opera. Introd. by Carleton Sprague Smith. Port Washington, N.Y., Kennikat Press [1971, c1948] xiii, 209 p. 50 plates (incl. facsims., ports.) 23 cm. (Essay and general literature index reprint series) Includes bibliographical references. [ML390.H77 1971] 73-132084 ISBN 0-8046-1412-1
1. Composers—Biography. 2. Opera—History and criticism. I. Title. **BIP**

HORTON, John. 780'.922 B
Some nineteenth century composers. Freeport, N.Y., Books for Libraries Press [1971, c1950] xi, 105 p. 23 cm. (Biography index reprint series) Contents.Contents.—Mendelssohn.—Liszt.—Smetana.—Borodin.—Rimsky-Korsakov.—Grieg.—Franck.—Saint-Saens.—Faure.—Debussy.—Elgar.—Mahler. [ML390.H78 1971] 72-148221 ISBN 0-8369-8068-9
1. Composers—Biography. I. Title.

HUGHES, Gervase. 782.8'1'0922 B
Composers of operetta. Westport, Conn., Greenwood Press [1974, c1962] xi, 283 p. illus. 23 cm. Reprint of the ed. published by Macmillan, London; St. Martin's Press, New York. Bibliography: p. 257-258. [ML390.H887C6 1974] 74-9604 ISBN 0-8371-7612-3 14.00
1. Composers—Biography. I. Title.

HUSSEY, Dyneley, 782.1'0922 B
1893-
Some composers of opera. Freeport, N.Y., Books for Libraries Press [1972, c1952] 102 p. 23 cm. (Essay index reprint series) Contents.Contents.—Claudio Monteverdi.—Christoph Willibald Gluck.—Carl Maria von Weber.—Terzetto all'italiana (Rossini, Donizetti; and Bellini)—Charles Gounod and Georges Bizet.—Modeste Mussorgsky.—Giacomo Puccini. [ML390.H967 1972] 79-167360 ISBN 0-8369-2654-4
1. Composers—Biography. 2. Opera—Addresses, essays, lectures. I. Title.

JELL, George 782.1'0922 B
Clarence.
Master builders of opera, by George C. Jell. Illustrated by Frank R. Southard. Freeport, N.Y., Books for Libraries Press [1970, c1933] x, 257 p. ports. 23 cm. (Essay index reprint series) [ML390.J29 1970] 78-134102
1. Composers—Biography. 2. Opera—History and criticism. I. Title. **BIP**

LEONARD, Richard 780'.922
Anthony.
The stream of music. New and rev. ed. with sixteen illus. Gloucester, Mass., P. Smith, 1968. vi, 550 p. ports. 21 cm. "Originally published in 1943. Dolphin Books edition, 1962. Reprinted [from Dolphin Books edition], 1968." [ML390.L54 1968] 68-4885
1. Composers—Biography. I. Title. **BIP**

MASON, Daniel Gregory, 780'.922
1873-1953.
The romantic composers. New York, AMS Press [1970] xi, 353 p. music, ports. 23 cm. "This book completes the series of studies ... which was begun with From Grieg to Brahms (1902) and continued in Beethoven and his forerunners (1904)" Reprint of the 1906 ed. Contents.Contents.—Romanticism in music.—Franz Schubert.—Robert Schumann.—Felix Mendelssohn.—Frederic Chopin.—Hector Berlioz.—Franz Liszt. [ML390.M415 1970] 73-119654
1. Composers—Biography. 2. Romanticism in music. I. Title.

MATHEWS, William 780'.922 B
Smythe Babcock, 1837-1912.
The masters and their music; [a series of illustrative programs, with biographical, esthetical, and critical annotations, designed as an introduction to music as literature, for the use of clubs, classes, and private study] New York, AMS Press [1971] xi, 248 p. ports. 19 cm. Reprint of the 1898 ed. [ML390.M464 1971] 78-153364 ISBN 0-404-07209-7
1. Composers—Biography. 2. Music—Analysis, appreciation. I. Title.

PANNAIN, Guido, 1891- 780'.922
Modern composers. Translated with a note by Michael R. Bonavia. Freeport, N.Y., Books for Libraries Press [1970] ix, 258 p. music, ports. 23 cm. (Essay index reprint series) Translation of Musicisti dei tempi nuovi. Reprint of the 1932 ed. Contents.Contents.—Changing values in modern music.—Richard Strauss.—Igor Stravinsky.—Manuel de Falla.—Paul Hindemith.—Zoltan Kodaly.—Arnold Schonberg.—Karol Szymanowski.—Maurice Ravel.—Ralph Vaughan Williams.—Ferruccio Busoni.—Ernest Bloch.—Arthur Honegger.—A survey of American music. [ML390.P192 1970] 76-99644 ISBN 0-8369-1715-4
1. Composers—Biography. 2. Music—History and criticism—20th century. I. Title. **BIP**

ROLLAND, Romain, 1866- 780'.922
1944.
Musicians of to-day, by Romain Rolland. Translated by Mary Blaiklock, with an introd. by Claude Landi. Freeport, N.Y., Books for Libraries Press [1969] xii, 324 p. 23 cm. (Essay index reprint series) "First published 1915." Translation of Musiciens d'aujourd'hui. Contents.Contents.—Berlioz.—Wagner: Siegfried, Tristan.—Camille Saint-Saens.—Vincent d'Indy.—Richard Strauss.—Hugo Wolf.—Don Lorenzo Perosi.—French and German music.—Claude Debussy: Pelleas et Melisande.—The awakening: a sketch of the musical movement in Paris since 1870. [ML390.R653 1969] 72-86777 ISBN 0-8369-1188-1
1. Composers—Biography. 2. Music, French—History and criticism. 3. Music, German—History and criticism. 4. Music—France—Paris. I. Blaiklock, Mary, tr. II. Title. **BIP**

ROWLAND-ENTWISTLE, 780'.92'2 B
Theodore.
Famous composers [by] Theodore Rowland-Entwistle and Jean Cooke. Newton Abbot, David & Charles [1974, i.e.1975] 128 p. 22 cm. (Brief biographies) [ML390.R875F3] 74-163207 ISBN 0-7153-6375-1 7.95
1. Composers—Biography. I. Cooke, Jean, fl. 1974- joint author. II. Title.
Distributed by David and Charles, North Pomfret, Vermont.

SAMACHSON, Dorothy. 780'.0922
Masters of music: their works, their lives, their times [by] Dorothy and Joseph Samachson. [1st ed.] Garden City, N.Y., Doubleday, 1967. ix, 272 p. illus., facsims. (incl. music), ports. 24 cm. [ML390.S184M4] 67-10705
1. Composers Biography. I. Samachson, Joseph, joint author. II. Title.

SCHONBERG, Harold C. 780'.922
The lives of the great composers [by] Harold C. Schonberg. [1st ed.] New York, W. W. Norton [1970] 599 p. illus., ports. 25 cm. Bibliography: p. 581-592. [ML390.S393L6] 73-116112 10.00
1. Composers—Biography. I. Title. **BIP**

SHARP, Robert 780'.92'2 B
Farquharson, 1864-1945.
Makers of music; biographical sketches of the great composers, with chronological summaries of their works, portraits, facsimiles of their compositions, and a general chronological table. Freeport, N.Y., Books for Libraries Press [1972] 212 p. illus. 22 cm. (Essay index reprint series) Reprint of the 1898 ed. [ML390.S53 1972] 72-5562 ISBN 0-8369-7278-3
1. Composers—Biography. I. Title.

SMITH, Jane Stewart. 780'.92'2 B
A gift of music : great composers and their influence / Jane Stuart Smith and Betty Carlson ; with pref. by Francis A. Schaeffer. Westchester, Ill. : Good News Publishers, c1978. 255 p. ; 22 cm. Includes index. Bibliography: p. 248-249. [ML390.S642] 78-68420 ISBN 0-89107-159-8 : 8.95
1. Composers—Biography. I. Carlson, Betty, joint author. II. Title.

WARREN, Clarence Henry, 780'.922
1895- comp.
The men behind the music. Edited by C. Henry Warren. Port Washington, N.Y., Kennikat Press [1970] iv, 156 p. 19 cm. "First published in 1931." "These sixteen biographical interpretations of famous composers originally appeared in the Radio Times." Contents.Contents.—J. S. Bach, by F. Young.—Beethoven, by H. N. Brailsford.—Hector Berlioz, by W. Rooke-Ley.—Brahms, by R. Church.—Chopin, by W. Holtby.—Handel, by C. H. Warren.—Haydn, by W. Rooke-Ley.—Liszt, by F. Brettargh.—Mozart, by J. C. Squire.—Mendelssohn, by S. Sitwell.—Mussorgsky, by C. H. Warren.—Schubert, by J. W. N. Sullivan.—Tchaikovsky, by J. Mann.—Verdi, by H. Ould.—Wagner, by R. Church.—Weber, by F. Brettargh. [ML390.W2 1970] 74-102844 ISBN 0-8046-0766-4
1. Composers—Biography. I. Title. **BIP**

Composers, Canadian—Biography.

CANADIAN Broadcasting 780'.92'2 B
Corporation. International Service.
Thirty-four biographies of Canadian composers. Trente-quatre biographies de compositeurs canadiens. St. Clair Shores, Mich., Scholarly Press, 1972. 110 p. ports. 27 cm. Reprint of the 1964 ed. Includes lists of compositions. [ML390.C26 1972] 75-166224 ISBN 0-403-01351-8 7.50
1. Composers, Canadian—Biography. 2. Music—Canada—Bio-bibliography. I. Title. II. Title: Trente-quatre biographies de compositeurs canadiens.

CONTEMPORARY Canadian 780'.92'2 B
composers / edited by Keith MacMillan and John Beckwith. Toronto ; New York : Oxford University Press, 1975. xxiv, 248 p., [4] leaves of plates : ill. ; 25 cm. Includes bibliographies. [ML106.C3C66] 76-351189 ISBN 0-19-540244-8 : 14.95
1. Composers, Canadian—Biography. 2. Music—Canada—Bio-bibliography. I. MacMillan, Keith Campbell, 1920- II. Beckwith, John. **BIP**

Composers—Correspondence.

LISZT, Franz, 1811-1886. 780'.92'4 B
The letters of Franz Liszt to Olga von Meyendorff, 1871-1886, in the Mildred Bliss Collection at Dumbarton Oaks / translated by William R. Tyler ; introd. and notes by Edward N. Waters. Washington : Dumbarton Oaks, Trustees for Harvard University ; Cambridge, Mass. : distributed by Harvard University Press, 1979. xxi, 532 p. ; 25 cm. Includes bibliographical references and index. [ML410.L7A363] 77-82381 ISBN 0-88402-078-9 : 30.00
1. Composers—Correspondence. I. Meyendorff, Olga von, Baroness, 1838-1926. II. Title. BIP

NORMAN, Gertrude, ed. 780'.92'2 B
Letters of composers : an anthology, 1603-1945 / compiled and edited by Gertrude Norman and Miriam Lubell Shrifte. Westport, Conn. : Greenwood Press, 1979, c1946. xviii, 422, xx p. ; 24 cm. Reprint of the ed. published by Knopf, New York. Includes index. Bibliography: p. 418-422. [ML90.N67 1979] 78-11483 ISBN 0-313-20664-3 lib. bdg. : 27.75
1. Composers—Correspondence. I. Shrifte, Miriam Lubell, joint author. II. Title. BIP

Composers—Correspondence, reminiscences, etc.

PUCCINI, Giacomo, 1858-1924. 782.1'0924 B
Letters of Giacomo Puccini, mainly connected with the composition and production of his operas. Edited by Giuseppe Adami. Translated from the Italian and edited for the English ed. by Ena Makin. New York, AMS Press [1971] 335 p. facsims., port. 23 cm. Reprint of Lippincott ed., 1931. [ML410.P89A23 1971] 71-140038 ISBN 0-404-05149-9
1. Composers—Correspondence, reminiscences, etc. I. Adami, Giuseppe, 1878-1946, ed.

Composers, Dutch—Biography.

SOLLITT, Edna Richolson. 780'.922 B
Dufay to Sweelinck; Netherlands masters of music. Westport, Conn., Greenwood Press [1970] 168 p. 23 cm. Reprint of the 1933 ed. [ML390.S66 1970] 79-100843 ISBN 0-8371-4028-5
1. Composers, Dutch—Biography. 2. Music—Netherlands—History and criticism. I. Title.

Composers—England—Biography.

BRIDGE, Frederick, Sir, 1844-1924. 780'.92'2 B
Twelve good musicians, from John Bull to Henry Purcell / by Frederick Bridge. Boston : Longwood Press, 1977. p. cm. Reprint of the 1920 ed. published by K. Paul, Trench, Trubner, London. Includes index. [ML390.B84 1977] 77-75210 ISBN 0-89341-110-8 : 17.50
1. Composers—England—Biography. I. Title.

WILLEBY, Charles, 1865- 780'.92'2
Masters of English music / by Charles Willeby. Boston : Longwood Press, 1977. p. cm. Reprint of the 1893 ed. published by J. R. Osgood, McIlvaine, London, in series: Masters of contemporary music. [ML390.W69 1977] 77-23963 ISBN 0-89341-132-9 lib.bdg. : 30.00
1. Composers—England—Biography. I. Title. II. Series: Masters of contemporary music.

Composers—England—Correspondence.

ELGAR, Edward William, Sir, 1857-1934. 780'.92'4 B
Letters of Edward Elgar and other writings / selected, edited, and annotated by Percy M. Young. Westport, Conn. : Hyperion Press, 1979. p. cm. (Encore music editions) Reprint of the 1956 ed. published by G. Bles, London. Includes index. Bibliography: p. [ML410.E41A4 1979] 78-66901 ISBN 0-88355-738-X : 31.50
1. Composers—England—Correspondence. I. Young, Percy Marshall, 1912- II. Title. III. Series.

Composers, English.

PULVER, Jeffrey, 1884- 780'.922
A biographical dictionary of old English music. [New York] B. Franklin [1969] xii, 537 p. port. 23 cm. (Burt Franklin bibliography and reference series, 295) Reprinted from the 1927 ed. Bibliography: p. [vii]-viii. [ML106.G7P9 1969] 73-80260
1. Composers, English. I. Title.

PULVER, Jeffrey, 1884- 780'.92'2 B
A biographical dictionary of old English music. With a new introd. and a bibliography of the writings of Jeffrey Pulver by Gilbert Blount. New York, Da Capo Press, 1973. xii, 537 p. 23 cm. (Da Capo Press music reprint series) Reprint of the 1927 ed. Includes bibliographies. [ML106.G7P9 1973] 69-16666 ISBN 0-306-71103-6 19.50
1. Composers, English. I. Title.

WILLEBY, Charles, 1865- 780'.92'2 B
Masters of English music. Boston, Milford House [1973] p. Reprint of the 1893 ed. published by J. R. Osgood, McIlvaine, London, in series: Masters of contemporary music. Contents.Contents.—Arthur Seymour Sullivan.—Alexander Campbell Mackenzie.—Frederic Hymen Cowen.—Charles Hubert Hastings Parry.—Charles Villiers Stanford. [ML390.W69 1973] 73-12692 ISBN 0-87821-174-8 20.00
1. Composers, English. I. Title. II. Series: Masters of contemporary music. BIP

WILLEBY, Charles, 1865- 780'.92'2 B
Masters of English music. Freeport, N.Y., Books for Libraries Press [1972] 301 p. illus. 22 cm. (Essay index reprint series) Reprint of the 1893 ed., issued in series: Masters of contemporary music. Contents.Contents.—Arthur Seymour Sullivan.—Alexander Campbell Mackenzie.—Frederic Hymen Cowen.—Charles Hubert Hastings Parry.—Charles Villiers Stanford. [ML390.W69 1972] 72-5561 ISBN 0-8369-7280-5
1. Composers, English. I. Title. II. Series: Masters of contemporary music.

Composers, English—Biography.

BARRETT, William Alexander, 1836-1891. 783'.0922
English church composers. Freeport, N.Y., Books for Libraries Press [1969] vii, 179 p. 23 cm. (Select bibliographies reprint series) (The great musicians.) "First published 1882." [ML390.B27 1969] 70-102224 ISBN 0-8369-5109-3
1. Composers, English—Biography. 2. Church music—England. I. Title.

FLOOD, William Henry Grattan, 1859-1928. 780'.922
Early Tudor composers; biographical sketches of thirty-two musicians and composers of the period 1485-1555, by William H. Grattan Flood. With a pref. by Sir W. Henry Hadow. Freeport, N.Y., Books for Libraries Press [1968] 121 p. music. 22 cm. (Essay index reprint series.) (Oxford musical essays) "First published 1925." [ML390.F65 1968] 68-25603
1. Composers, English—Biography. I. Title. II. Series. BIP

Composers—Europe—Biography.

ELSON, Arthur, 1873-1940. 780'.92'2 B
Modern composers of Europe / by Arthur Elson. Boston : Longwood Press, 1978. viii, 291 p., [32] leaves of plates : ports. ; 22 cm. Reprint of the 1905 ed. published by L. C. Page, Boston. [ML390.E472 1978] 77-90802 ISBN 0-89341-419-0 lib.bdg. : 35.00
1. Composers—Europe—Biography. I. Title. BIP

Composers, European.

EWEN, David, 1907- ed. 927.8
European composers today, a biographical and critical guide. New York, Wilson, 1954. 200 p. ports. 26 cm. "A companion volume to the previously-published American composers today; together, these two volumes replace...Composers of today, originally issued in 1934." Includes lists of works. "A select bibliography": p. [199]-200. [ML390.E834] 53-9024
1. Composers, European. I. Title.

Composers—France—Correspondence.

BERLIOZ, Hector, 1803-1869. 780'.92'4 B
Hector Berlioz : selections from his letters, and aesthetic, humorous, and satirical writings / translated, and preceded by a biographical sketch of the author, by William F. Apthorp. Portland, Me. : Longwood Press, 1976. p. cm. Reprint of the 1879 ed. published by H. Holt, New York, in series: Amateur series. [ML410.B5A33 1976] 76-22325 ISBN 0-89341-018-7 lib.bdg. : 40.00 40.00 lib. bdg.
1. Composers—France—Correspondence. 2. Music—Addresses, essays, lectures. 3. Music—Anecdotes, facetiae, satire, etc. I. Apthorp, William Foster, 1848-1913.

Composers, French.

BROOK, Donald. 780'.922 B
Five great French composers: Berlioz, Cesar Franck, Saint-Saens, Debussy, Ravel; their lives and works. Freeport, N.Y., Books for Libraries Press [1971, c1946] xi, 216 p. illus., ports. 23 cm. (Biography index reprint series) [ML390.B858 1971] 77-160916 ISBN 0-8369-8079-4
1. Composers, French. I. Title.

MICHOTTE, Edmond. 780'.922
Richard Wagner's visit to Rossini (Paris 1860); and, An evening at Rossini's in Beau-Sejour (Passy) 1858. Translated from the French and annotated, with an introd. and appendix, by Herbert Weinstock. Chicago, University of Chicago Press [1968] xi, 144 p. illus., facsims., music, ports. 23 cm. Translation of Souvenirs personnels. La visite de R. Wagner a Rossini (Paris 1860) and Souvenirs: Une soiree chez Rossini a Beau-Sejour (Passy) 1858. [ML410.W11M42] 68-16706
I. Wagner, Richard, 1813-1883. II. Rossini, Gioacchino Antonio, 1792-1868. III. Weinstock, Herbert, 1905- IV. Michotte, Edmond. Souvenirs: Une soiree chez Rossini a Beau-Sejour (Passy) 1858. V. Title. VI. Title: An evening at Rossini's in Beau-Sejour (Passy) 1858.

Composers, French—Biography.

HERVEY, Arthur, 1855-1922. 780'.92'2 B
Masters of French music. Boston, Milford House [1973] xii, 289 p. illus. 22 cm. Reprint of the 1894 ed. published by Scribner, New York, in series Masters of contemporary music. [ML390.H57 1973b] 73-9964 ISBN 0-87821-060-1 20.00 (lib. bdg.)
1. Composers, French—Biography. I. Title. II. Series: Masters of contemporary music. BIP

Composers, German.

STUCKENSCHMIDT, Hans Heinz, 1901- 780'.922 B
Germany and Central Europe [by] H. H. Stuckenschmidt. [1st ed.] New York, Holt, Rinehart, and Winston [1971] 256 p. illus., facsims., ports. 23 cm. (Twentieth-century composers, v. 2) [ML390.S946] 73-80366 ISBN 0-03-076460-2 10.95
1. Composers, German. 2. Composers, European. 3. Music—History and criticism—20th century. I. Title. II. Series.

Composers, German—Biography.

FULLER-MAITLAND, John Alexander, 1856-1936. 780'.92'2 B
Masters of German music. Boston, Milford House [1973] 288 p. illus. 22 cm. Reprint of the 1894 ed. published by Scribner, New York, in series: Masters of contemporary music. Contents.Contents.—Johannes Brahms.—Max Bruch.—Karl Goldmark.—Josef Rheinberger.—Theodor Kirchner, Carl Reinecke, Woldemar Bargiel.—Joseph Joachim, Clara Schumann.—Heinrich von Herzogenberg, Heinrich Hoffmann, Anton Bruckner, Felix Draeseke.—Jean Louis Nicode, Richard Strauss, Hans Sommer, Cyrill Kistler. [ML390.F95 1973] 73-9962 ISBN 0-87821-059-8 20.00 (lib. bdg.)
1. Composers, German—Biography. I. Title. II. Series: Masters of contemporary music.
Contents omitted.

Composers—Germany—Biography.

FULLER-MAITLAND, John Alexander, 1856-1936. 780'.92'2 B
Masters of German music / by J. A. Fuller-Maitland. Boston : Longwood Press, 1977. p. cm. Reprint of the 1894 ed. published by Scribner, New York, in series: Masters of contemporary music. Contents.Contents.—Johannes Brahms.—Max Bruch.—Karl Goldmark.—Josef Rheinberger.—Theodor Kirchner, Carl Reinecke, Woldemar Bargeil.—Joseph Joachim, Clara Schumann.—Heinrich von Herzogenberg, Heinrich Hoffmann, Anton Bruckner, Felix Draeseke.—Jean Louis Nicode, Richard Strauss, Hans Sommer, Cyrill Kistler. [ML390.F95 1977] 77-20818 ISBN 0-89341-133-7 lib.bdg. : 30.00
1. Composers—Germany—Biography. I. Title. II. Series: Masters of contemporary music. BIP

Composers, Italian.

STREATFEILD, Richard Alexander, 1866-1919. 780'.92'2 B
Masters of Italian music. Freeport, N.Y., Books for Libraries Press [1972] p. (Essay index reprint series.) Reprint of the 1895 ed., issued in series: Masters of contemporary music. Contents.Contents.—Giuseppe Verdi.—Arrigo Boito.—Pietro Mascagni.—Giacomo Puccini.—Ruggiero Leoncavallo.—Some other Italian composers. [ML390.S91 1972] 72-3381 ISBN 0-8369-2929-2
1. Composers, Italian. 2. Opera, Italian—History and criticism. I. Title. II. Series: Masters of contemporary music. BIP

Composers, Italian—Biography.

FERRIS, George Titus, b.1840. 780'.92'2 B
Great Italian and French composers. Freeport, N.Y., Books for Libraries Press [1972] p. (Essay index reprint series) Reprinted from the ed. of 1879, New York. [ML390.F394 1972] 72-6820 ISBN 0-8369-7260-0
1. Composers, Italian—Biography. 2. Composers, French—Biography. I. Title. BIP

Composers—Juvenile literature.

BERGER, Melvin. 780'.922 B
Masters of modern music. New York, Lothrop, Lee & Shepard Co. [1970] 256 p. ports. 22 cm. Bibliography: p. 245-246; discography: p. 247-251. Brief biographies of fourteen twentieth-century composers, some known for carrying on the romantic traditions of the nineteenth-century and others for promoting popular and modern experimental music. [ML3930.A2B498] 920 76-120162 4.95
1. Composers—Juvenile literature. I. Title.

GOUGH, Catherine 927.8
Boyhoods of great composers. Illustrated by Edward Ardizzone. New York, H. Z. Walck [c.]1960. 53p. illus. 22cm. (The Young reader's guide to music, 1) 60-50271 2.50
1. Composers—Juvenile literature. I. Title.

GOUGH, Catherine 920
Boyhoods of great composers; bk. 2. Illus. by Edward Ardizzone. New York, Walck, 1965 [c.1963] 58p. illus. 22cm. (Young reader's guide to music, 2) [ML3930.A2G68] 60-50271 3.00
1. Composers—Juvenile literature. I. Title.

GOUGH, Catherine. 780'.922
Boyhoods of great composers; illustrated by Edward Ardizzonne. [New ed.] London, Melbourne [etc.] Oxford U.P., 1968. 120 p. illus. 22 cm. [ML3930.A2G68 1968] 78-436898 16/6
1. Composers—Juvenile literature. I. Title. BIP

NEEDHAM, Irene Bennett 920
Biographies of great composers. Music arrangements by Irene Harrington Young. Columbus, Ohio, Highlights for Children [c.1964] 96p. illus. 29cm. (Highlights jumbo handbk.) Music principally for piano. 64-25252 2.95 bds.,
1. Composers—Juvenile literature. I. Title.

WICKER, Ireene (Seaton) j920
1905-
Young music makers; boyhoods of famous composers. Illustrated by Jules Gotlieb. Indianapolis, Bobbs-Merrill [1961] 238 p. illus. 22 cm. [ML3930.A2W5] 61-14410
1. Composers — Juvenile literature. I. Title.

Composers—Michigan—Bio-bibliography.

FINK, Robert R., 785'.092'2 B
comp.
Annotated directory of Michigan orchestral composers. Robert R. Fink: editor. Julie Ann Johnson: associate editor. [Detroit] Michigan State Council for the Arts, in cooperation with Michigan Orchestra Association, 1967. 38 p. 23 cm. [ML125.M5F5] 74-153449
1. Composers—Michigan—Bio-bibliography. 2. Orchestral music—Bibliography. 3. Music—Michigan—Bio-bibliography. I. Johnson, Julie Ann, joint comp. II. Michigan State Council for the Arts. III. Title.

Composers, Russian.

POSELL, Elsa Z. 780'.922
Russian composers [by] Elsa Z. Posell. Boston, Houghton, 1967. 181p. ports. 22cm. [ML390.P758R9] 67-22172 3.50
1. Composers, Russian. I. Title.

POSELL, Elsa Z. 920
Russian composers [by] Elsa Z. Posell. Boston, Houghton Mifflin Co., 1967. 181 p. ports. 22 cm. Bibliography: p. [182] Gives a short history of music in Russia and briefly describes the lives and music of seventeen Russian composers, from Glinka to Shostakovich. [ML390.P758R9] AC 68
1. Composers, Russian. I. Title. BIP

Composers, Russian—Biography.

ABRAHAM, Gerald Ernest 780'.922 B
Heal, 1904-
Eight Soviet composers [by] Gerald Abraham. Westport, Conn., Greenwood Press [1970] 102 p. music. 23 cm. Reprint of the 1943 ed. Contents.Contents.—Dmitry Shostakovich.—Sergey Prokofiev.—Aram Khachaturyan.—Lev Knipper.—Vissarion Shebalin.—Dmitry Kabalevsky.—Ivan Dzerzhinsky.—Yury Shaporin. [ML390.A13 1970] 71-106679 ISBN 0-8371-3350-5
1. Composers, Russian—Biography. 2. Music—Russia—1917- BIP

BELZA, Igor' 780'.922 B
Fedorovich, 1904-
Handbook of Soviet musicians, by Igor Boelza. Edited by Alan Bush. Westport, Conn., Greenwood Press [1971] xiv, 101 p. ports. 23 cm. Reprint of the 1943 ed. Bibliography (list of composers' works): p. 62-101. [ML390.B467H3 1971] 74-114468 ISBN 0-8371-4764-6
1. Composers, Russian—Biography. I. Bush, Alan Dudley, 1900- ed. II. Title.

BELZA, Igor' 780'.92'2 B
Fedorovich, 1904-
Handbook of Soviet musicians, by Igor Boelza. Edited by Alan Bush. London, Pilot Press [1944] St. Clair Shores, Mich., Scholarly Press, 1972. xiv, 101 p. illus. 21 cm. Reprint of the 1943 ed. Bibliography (list of composers' works): p. 62-101. [ML390.B467H3 1972] 74-166221 ISBN 0-403-01348-8
1. Composers, Russian—Biography. I. Bush, Alan Dudley, 1900- ed. II. Title. BIP

CALVOCORESSI, Michel 780'.922 B
D., 1877-1944.
Masters of Russian music, by M. D. Calvocoressi and Gerald Abraham. New York, Johnson Reprint Corp., 1971. 511 p. 23 cm. Reprint of the 1936 ed. Contents.Contents.—Glinka.—Dargomyjsky.—Serof.—Cui.—Borodin.—Mussorgsky.—Tchaikovsky.—Rimsky-Korsakof.—Liadof.—Glazunof.—Liapunof.—Taneief.—Scriabin. Bibliography: p. 501-502. [ML390.C17 1971] 76-143983
1. Composers, Russian—Biography. I. Abraham, Gerald Ernest Heal, 1904- joint author. II. Title. BIP

MONTAGU-NATHAN, 780'.92'2
Montagu.
Contemporary Russian composers, by M. Montagu-Nathan. Westport, Conn., Greenwood Press [1970] xv, 329 p. ports. 22 cm. Reprinted from the ed. of 1917, London. [ML390.M68 1970] 72-109795 ISBN 0-8371-4285-7
1. Composers, Russian—Biography. I. Title. BIP

SABANEEV, Leonid 780'.92'2 B
Leonidovich, 1881-
Modern Russian composers / by Leonid Sabaneyeff ; translated from the Russian by Judah A. Joffe. New York : Da Capo Press, 1975, c1927. 253 p. ; 22 cm. (Da Capo Press music reprint series) Reprint of the ed. published by International Publishers, New York. [ML390.S123M6 1975] 75-14232 ISBN 0-306-70673-3 lib.bdg. : 15.00
1. Composers, Russian—Biography. I. Title. BIP

Composers—United States—Biography.

†REIS, Claire 780'.92'2 B
Raphael.
Composers in America : biographical sketches of contemporary composers with a record of their works / by Claire R. Reis ; with a new introd. by William Schuman. Rev. and enl. ed. New York : Da Capo Press, 1977, c1947. xvi, 399 p. ; 24 cm. (Da Capo Press music reprint series) Reprint of the ed. published by Macmillan, New York. [ML390.R38 1977] 77-4158 ISBN 0-306-70893-0 : 19.50
1. Composers—United States—Biography. 2. Music, American—Bio-bibliography. I. Title.

Compton-Burnett, Ivy, Dame, 1892-1969.

SPRIGGE, Elizabeth, 823'.9'12 B
1900-
The life of Ivy Compton-Burnett. New York, G. Braziller [1973] 191 p. illus. 23 cm. "The novels of I. Compton-Burnett": p. [181] [PR6005.O3895Z9 1973] 72-96072 ISBN 0-8076-0685-5 7.95
1. Compton-Burnett, Ivy, Dame, 1892-1969. I. Title. BIP

Compton, Henry, Bp. of London 1632-1713.

CARPENTER, Edward 922.342
Frederick, 1910-
The Protestant bishop, being the life of Henry Compton, 1632-1713, Bishop of London. London, New York, Longmans, Green [1956] 398p. illus. 23cm. [BX5199.C62C3] 56-58166
1. Compton, Henry, Bp. of London 1632-1713. I. Title.

Comstock, Anthony, 1844-1915.

BENNETT, De 364.17'4'0924 B
Robigne Mortimer, 1818-1882.
Anthony Comstock; his career of cruelty and crime [A chapter from "The champions of the church," by D. M. Bennett] New York, Da Capo Press, 1971. 1009-1119 p. 23 cm. (Civil liberties in American history) Reprint of the 1878 ed. Reprinted from the author's Champions of the church, New York, 1878, p. 1009-1091; with the addition of a Recapitulation, p. 1092-1105, and Concluding remarks, p. 1106-1119. [HV6705.B5 1971] 73-121102 ISBN 0-306-71968-1
1. Comstock, Anthony, 1844-1915. I. Title. II. Series.

Comstock, John Henry, 1849-1931.

COMSTOCK, Anna (Botsford) 925.9
1854-1930.
The Comstocks of Cornell: John Henry Comstock and Anna Botsford Comstock, an autobiography by Anna Botsford Comstock. Edited by Glenn W. Herrick and Ruby Green Smith. New York, Comstock Publishing Associates [1953] 286p. illus. 24cm. [QL31.C65C6] 53-13083
1. Comstock, John Henry, 1849-1931. I. Title.

Comte, Auguste, 1798-1857.

MARVIN, Francis Sydney, 301.0924
1863-1943
Comte, the founder of sociology. New York, Russell & Russell, 1965. 216p. port. 23cm. First pub. 1936. Bibl. [HM22.F8C65] 65-17911 6.50
1. Comte, Auguste, 1798-1857. I. Title. BIP

THOMPSON, Kenneth, 301'.092'4
1923-
Auguste Comte : the foundation of sociology / Kenneth Thompson. New York : Wiley, c1975. xiv, 220 p. ; 23 cm. (The making of sociology series) "A Halsted Press book." Includes index. Bibliography: p. 213-214. [HM22.F8C75 1975] 75-12566 ISBN 0-470-85988-1
1. Comte, Auguste, 1798-1857. BIP

Conant, James Bryant,

CONANT, James Bryant, 370'.924 B
1893-
My several lives; memoirs of a social inventor, by James B. Conant. [1st ed.] New York, Harper & Row [1970] xvi, 701 p. ports. 25 cm. Bibliography: p. 304. [CT275.C757A3] 72-83590 12.50
I. Title.

Conaty, Thomas James, Bp., 1847-1915.

WEBER, Francis J. 271'.75'0924 B
Thomas James Conaty, pastor-educator-bishop, by Francis J. Weber. Los Angeles, Westernlore Press [1969] xiv, 81 p. illus., port. 22 cm. 250 copies printed. Bibliographical references included in "Notes" (p. 73-81) [BX4705.C737W4] 70-77980
1. Conaty, Thomas James, Bp., 1847-1915.

Conchita, 1862-1937.

CONCHITA, 1862-1937. 282'.092'4 B
A mother's spiritual diary / Conchita ; edited by M. M. Philipon ; translated by Aloysius J. Owen. New York : Alba House, c1978. xx, 256 p. ; 21 cm. Translation of Journal spirituel d'une mere de famille. [BX4705.C742A3313] 78-1929 ISBN 0-8189-0368-6 : 5.95
1. Conchita, 1862-1937. 2. Catholics—Mexico—Biography. 3. Spiritual life—Catholic authors. I. Philipon, Marie Michel, 1898- II. Title.

Concord, Mass.—Biography.

BROWN, Mary Hosmer. 920'.0744'4
Memories of Concord. Illustrated from photos. and from paintings by J. Randolph Brown. [Folcroft, Pa.] Folcroft Library Editions, 1973 [c1926] 111 p. illus. 24 cm. Reprint of the 1926 ed. Contents.Contents.—Edmund Hosmer and his ancestry.—Concord neighbors.—Ralph Waldo Emerson.—Emerson as a lecturer.—Ellen Emerson.—Nathaniel Hawthorne.—The Alcotts.—Henry D. Thoreau. [F74.C8B8 1973] 72-10118 17.50
1. Concord, Mass.—Biography. I. Title. BIP

GREELEY, Dana McLean, 974.4'4 B
1908-
Know these Concordians : 24 minute biographies / by Dana McLean Greeley. [Concord, Mass.] : Greeley : [may be purchased from Publications Office, First Parish], 1975. viii, 88 p. : ill. ; 23 cm. [F74.C8G74] 75-324543 2.95
1. Concord, Mass.—Biography. I. Title.

SOCIAL Circle in 367'.9744'4 B
Concord, Concord, Mass.
Memoirs of members of the Social Circle in Concord : sixth series, from 1939-1974 / [edited by Harold C. Smith ... et al.]. [Concord] : The Circle, 1975. xix, 297 p. : ports. ; 24 cm. On spine: Social Circle memoirs. [F74.C8S58 1975] 76-353350
1. Concord, Mass.—Biography. I. Smith, Harold C. II. Title.

Concord, Mass.—Biography—Juvenile literature.

WOOD, James Playsted, 810.9 B
1905-
The people of Concord. Drawings by Richard Cuffari. New York, Seabury Press [1970] 152 p. illus. 22 cm. Bibliography: p. [147]-148. Describes the role of Concord, Massachusetts, in the history of the nation through portraits of her famous citizens and early settlers. [F74.C8W84] 920 71-97035 4.95
1. Concord, Mass.—Biography—Juvenile literature. I. Cuffari, Richard, 1925- illus. II. Title.

Condottieri.

DEISS, Joseph Jay. 945'.05'0922
Captains of fortune; profiles of six Italian condottieri. New York, Crowell [1967, c1966] 304 p. illus., map, ports. 23 cm. Contents.Contents.—Foreword: The flavour of history.—Son of the devil, Ezzelino da Romano.—Prince of the wolfhounds, Castruccio Castracani.—Giovanni the sharp, Sir John Hawkwood.—Serpent and lion, the Count of Carmagnola.—The abominable pagan, Sigismondo Pandolfo Malatesta.—Giovanni of the black bands, Giovanni de' Medici. Bibliography: p. 291-294. [DG530.D4 1967] 67-11786
1. Condottieri. I. Title.

Conductors (Music)—Biography.

EWEN, David, 1907- 785'.092'2 B
Dictators of the baton / by David Ewen. Great Neck, N.Y. : Core Collection Books, 1978. x, 305 p., [7] leaves of plates : ports. ; 23 cm. Reprint of the 1943 ed. published by Alliance Book Corp., Chicago. Includes index. Bibliography: p. 301-[304] [ML402.E9 1978] 77-92507 ISBN 0-8486-3002-5 : 28.50
1. Conductors (Music)—Biography. 2. Conducting. 3. Orchestra. I. Title. BIP

SCHONBERG, Harold C. 780.922
The great conductors [by] Harold C. Schonberg. New York, Simon and Schuster [1967] 384 p. illus., facsims., music, ports. 24 cm. [ML402.S387G7] 67-19821
1. Conductors (Music)—Biography. I. Title. BIP

Conductors (Music)—Juvenile literature.

EWEN, David, 1907- 781.635092
Famous conductors. New York, Dodd. [c.1966] 152p. ports. 22cm. (Famous biog. for young people) [ML3930.A2E9] 66-17847 3.25
1. Conductors (Music)—Juvenile literature. I. Title.

EWEN, David, 1907- 780.922
Famous modern conductors. New York, Dodd, Mead [1967] 159 p. ports. 22 cm. (Famous biographies for young people) [ML3930.A2E93] 66-12812
1. Conductors (Music)—Juvenile literature. I. Title.

Cone, Claribel.

POLLACK, Barbara. 706.992
The collectors: Dr. Claribel and Miss Etta Cone. With a portrait by Gertrude Stein. [1st ed.] Indianapolis, Bobbs-Merrill [1962] 320 p. illus., ports. 22 cm. "Two women, by Gertrude Stein": p. [273]-300. [N8384.C6P6] 61-9937

1. Cone, Claribel. 2. Cone, Etta. 3. Art—Collectors and collecting. I. Stein, Gertrude, 1874-1946. Two women. II. Title.

Confederate States of America. Army—Biography—Addresses, essays, lectures.

RANK and file : 973.7'092'2 B
Civil War essays in honor of Bell Irvin Wiley / edited by James I. Robertson, Jr. and Richard M. McMurry. San Rafael, Calif. : Presidio Press, c1976. 164 p. ; 24 cm. "Bibliography of Bell Irvin Wiley," by J. P. Bloom: p. 157-164. [E467.R37] 76-48787 ISBN 0-89141-011-2 : 8.95
1. United States. Army—Biography—Addresses, essays, lectures. 2. Confederate States of America. Army—Biography—Addresses, essays, lectures. 3. Wiley, Bell Irvin, 1906- —Addresses, essays, lectures. 4. United States—History—Civil War, 1861-1865—Biography—Addresses, essays, lectures. 5. United States—Biography—Addresses, essays, lectures. 6. Historians—United States—Biography—Addresses, essays, lectures. I. Wiley, Bell Irvin, 1906- II. Robertson, James I. III. McMurry, Richard M.
Contents omitted

Confederate States of America. Army. Cavalry.

KNAPP, David. 973.742
The Confederate horsemen. [1st ed.] New York, Vantage Press [1966] 302 p. illus. 21 cm. Bibliography: p. 289-293. [E546.5.K6] 66-3828
1. Confederate States of America. Army. Cavalry. 2. U.S.—Hist.—Civil War—Cavalry operations. 3. Confederate States of America—Blog. I. Title.

Confederate States of America. Army. Stonewall Brigade—Biography.

EDMONDSON, James K., 1832-1898. 973.7'82'0924
My dear Emma : war letters of Col. James K. Edmondson, 1861-1865 / edited by Charles W. Turner. Verona, Va. : McClure Press, c1978. 151 p., [3] leaves of plates : ill. ; 24 cm. Letters to Emma Edmondson. Includes index. [E581.4.S8E353] 78-113096 8.00
1. Edmondson, James K., 1832-1898. 2. Confederate States of America. Army. Stonewall Brigade—Biography. 3. Edmondson, Emma. 4. United States—History—Civil War, 1861-1865—Personal narratives—Confederate side. 5. United States—History—Civil War, 1861-1865—Regimental histories—Stonewall Brigade. 6. Soldiers—Virginia—Correspondence. I. Edmondson, Emma. II. Turner, Charles Wilson. III. Title.

Confederate States of America—Biography.

ANDERS, Curtis, 1927- 973.7'42'0922
Fighting Confederates. New York, Putnam [1968] 315 p. maps. 22 cm. Contents.Contents.—Introduction—Brief chronology of the Civil War.—Jefferson Davis; the splendid failure.—Joseph E. Johnston; a professional's professional.—Nathan Bedford Forrest; nature's soldier.—James Ewell Brown Stuart; the knight of the golden spurs.—Thomas Jonathan Jackson; the bellicose deacon.—Robert E. Lee; last leader of the lost cause.—Bibliography (p. 303-304) [E467.A5] 68-15496
1. Confederate States of America—Biography. I. Title.

BRADFORD, Gamaliel, 1863-1932. 973.7'42'0922
Confederate portraits. Freeport, N.Y., Books for Libraries Press [1968, c1914] xviii, 291 p. ports. 22 cm. (Essay index reprint series) Contents.Contents.—Joseph E. Johnston.—J. E. B. Stuart.—James Longstreet.—P. G. T. Beauregard.—Judah P. Benjamin.—Alexander H. Stephens.—Robert Toombs.—Raphael Semmes.—The Battle of Gettysburg. Includes bibliographical references. [E467.B78 1968] 68-29193
1. Confederate States of America—Biography. 2. Gettysburg, Battle of, 1863. I. Title. BIP

DOTSON, Susan Merle, comp. 973.7420922
Who's who of the Confederacy; a symposium by the members of the Albert Sidney Johnston Chapter, no. 2060, United Daughters of the Confederacy. Compiled by Susan Merle Dotson. [San Antonio, Tex.] Printed by Naylor Co. [1966] xvi, 368 p. illus., ports. 22 cm. [E467.D68] 67-138
1. Confederate States of America—Biography. 2. United States—History—Civil War—Biography. I. United Daughters of the Confederacy. Texas Division. Albert Sidney Johnston Chapter, No. 2060, San Antonio. II. Title.

DUFOUR, Charles L. 923.573
Nine men in gray. Garden City, N.Y., Doubleday [c.]1963. 364p. illus. 24cm. Bibl. 63-8762 4.95
1. Confederate States of America—Biog. 2. U.S.—Hist— Civil War—Biog. I. Title.

DUFOUR, Charles L 923.573
Nine men in gray. [1st ed.] Garden City, N.Y., Doubleday, 1963. 364 p. illus. 24 cm. Includes bibliography. [E467.D88] 63-8762
1. Confederate State of Amercia — Biog. 2. U.S. — Hist. — Civil War — Biog. I. Title.

HESSELTINE, William Best, 1902-1963. 973.71'3
Confederate leaders in the New South. Westport, Conn., Greenwood Press [1970, c1950] xi, 146 p. 23 cm. [E467.H58 1970] 71-100230 ISBN 0-8371-3686-5
1. Confederate States of America—Biography. 2. Southern States—History—1865- I. Title. BIP

MAPP, Alf Johnson 920.073
Frock coats and epaulets. New York, Yoseloff [c. 1963] 501p. illus. 22cm. Bibl. 62-14961 10.00
1. Confederate States of America—Biog. 2. Confederate States of America—Hist. I. Title.

REAL Daughters of the Confederacy Club, San Antonio. 973.794
Father wore gray, by Lela Whitton Hegarty [President,54 San Antonio, Naylor [c.1963] xii, 205p. illus., ports., facsim. 22cm. 63-20163 5.95 bds.,
1. Fonfederate States of America—Biog. 2. U. S.—Hist.—Biog. I. Hegarty, Lela (Whitton) II. Title.

REAL Daughters of the Confederacy Club, San Antonio. 923.273
Father wore gray, by Lela Whitton Hegarty [president] San Antonio, Naylor Co. [1963] xii, 205 p. illus., ports. facsim 22 cm. Biographies of 22 Confederate veterans written by their daughters. [E467.R4] 63-20163
1. Confederate States of America — Biog. 2. U.S. — Hist. Civil War — Biog. I. Hegarty, Lela (Whitton) II. Title.

WAKELYN, Jon L. 973.7'13'03
Biographical dictionary of the Confederacy / Jon L. Wakelyn. Westport, Conn. : Greenwood Press, c1976. p. cm. Includes index. Bibliography: p. [E467.W2] 72-13870 ISBN 0-8371-6124-X lib.bdg. : 29.95
1. Confederate States of America—Biography. 2. United States—History—Civil War, 1861-1865—Biography. I. Title. BIP

Confederate States of America. Congress—Biography.

WARNER, Ezra J. 328.75'092'2 B
Biographical register of the Confederate Congress / Ezra J. Warner and W. Buck Yearns. Baton Rouge : Louisiana State University Press, c1975. xxii, 319 p., [5] leaves of plates : ill. ; 25 cm. Bibliography: p. 307-319. [JK9663.W3] 74-77329 ISBN 0-8071-0092-7 : 15.00
1. Confederate States of America. Congress—Biography. 2. Confederate States of America. Congress—Registers. I. Yearns, Wilfred Buck, 1918- joint author. II. Title. BIP

Confederate States of America. Marine Corps—Biography.

DONNELLY, Ralph W. 973.7'42'0922 B
Biographical sketches of the commissioned officers of the Confederate States Marine Corps, by Ralph W. Donnelly. [Alexandria, Va., 1973] vi, 68 l. ports. 28 cm. Bibliography: leaves 61-68. [E467.D66] 74-156780
1. Confederate States of America. Marine Corps—Biography. 2. United States—History—Civil War, 1861-1865—Biography. I. Title.

Confucius.

CHOW, Shu-kai, 1913- 181'.09'512
Confucius; the ideal teacher. [Jamaica, N.Y., Center of Asian Studies, St. John's University, 196-] 4 l. 28 cm. (St. John's papers in Asian studies, no. 13) Address delivered on the occasion of presenting a collection of Chinese cultural objects to St. John's University, Oct. 29, 1966. [B128.C8C53] 74-154155
1. Confucius. I. Title. II. Series.

CREEL, Herrlee Glessner, 1905- 299'.5126'4
Confucius, the man and the myth [by] H. G. Creel. Westport, Conn., Greenwood Press [1972, c1949] xi, 363 p. map. 22 cm. Bibliography: p. 341-354. [B128.C8C65 1972] 72-7816 ISBN 0-8371-6531-8 14.75
1. Confucius. I. Title. BIP

KELEN, Betty. 299'.512'64 B
Confucius: in life and legend. [1st ed.] New York, T. Nelson [1971] 160 p. port. 21 cm. Bibliography: p. 155-156. [B128.C8K43] 72-164970 ISBN 0-8407-6152-X
1. Confucius. I. Title. BIP

LIU, Wu-chi, 1907- 299'.5126'4 B
Confucius, his life and time. Westport, Conn., Greenwood Press [1972, c1955] xv, 189 p. 22 cm. Bibliography: p. 180-183. [B128.C8L56 1972] 73-138159 ISBN 0-8371-5616-5
1. Confucius.

SIMS, Bennett B. 181'.11
Confucius, by Bennett B. Sims. New York, F. Watts [1968] 139 p. illus., map. 22 cm. (Immortals of philosophy and religion) Bibliography: p. 136. [B128.C8S53] 68-11128
1. Confucius.

SMITH, David Howard. 181'.095'12
Confucius, by D. Howard Smith. New York, Scribner [1973] 240 p. map. 25 cm. (Makers of new worlds) Bibliography: p. [219]-223. [B128.C8S58 1973b] 72-9821 ISBN 0-684-13257-5 10.00
1. Confucius. BIP

Confucius and Confucianism.

LIU, Wu-chi, 1907- 921.9
Confucius, his life and time. New York, Philosophical Library [c1955] 189p. 23cm. [B128.C8L56] 56-1686
1. Confucius and Confucianism. I. Title.

LIU, Wu-chi, 1907- 921.9
Confucius, his life and time. New York, Philosophical Library [c1955] 189p. 23cm. [B128.C8L56] 56-1686
1. Confucius and Confucianism. I. Title.

Confucius—Juvenile literature.

JOHNSON, Spencer. 299'.5126'3 B
The value of honesty : the story of Confucius / by Spencer Johnson ; illustrated by Pileggi. 1st ed. La Jolla, Calif. : Value Communications, c1979. 63 p. : col. ill. ; 29 cm. (ValueTales) A biography of the Chinese philosopher and teacher emphasizing his ideas about the value of honesty. [B128.C8J63] 92 79-4351 ISBN 0-916392-36-8 : 5.95
1. Confucius—Juvenile literature. 2. Philosophers—China—Biography—Juvenile literature. 3. Honesty—Juvenile literature. I. Pileggi, Steve. II. Title. BIP

Conger, Arthur Latham, 1872-1951.

SHURLOCK, Aileen Brittain. 920
Biographical sketch of Colonel Arthur Latham Conger, fifth leader of the Theosophical Society, Point Loma-Covina, philosopher. scholar, soldier, author, musician, i[Oakland? Calif, 1955] 65p. 22cm. ovina, Calif. [BP585.C6S5] 56-16956
1. Conger, Arthur Latham, 1872-1951. 2. Theosophical Society. I. Title.

Congregational churches — Biog.

BOYLSTON, Ruth Harrington. 285'.8'0924 (B)
Before many witnesses; the life of Howard James Chidley. [Winchester, Mass., University Press, 1967] [BX7260.C56B6] 67-9765
I. Chidley, Howard James, 1878-1966. II. vii, 155 p. illus. ports. 23 cm. III. Title.

LOBINGIER, John Leslie, 1884- 285.8330922 (B)
Pilgrims and pioneers in the Congregational Christian tradition. Philadelphia, United Church Press [1965] 191 p. 21 cm. Includes bibliographical references. [BX7259.L6] 65-17465
1. Congregational churches — Biog. I. Title.

WALKER, Williston, 1860-1922. 285'.8'0922
Ten New England leaders. New York, Arno Press, 1969. v, 471 p. 23 cm. (Religion in America) "Lectures ... delivered on the 'Southworth Foundation' in Andover Theological Seminary in 1898-1899." Reprint of the 1901 ed. Contents.Contents.—William Bradford.—John Cotton.—Richard Mather.—John Eliot.—Increase Mather.—Jonathan Edwards.—Charles Chauncy.—Samuel Hopkins.—Leonard Woods.—Leonard Bacon. Includes bibliographical references. [BX7259.W3 1969] 76-83445
1. Congregational churches—Biography. 2. New England—Church history. I. Title. BIP

Congreve, William, 1670-1729.

CONGREVE, William, 1670-1729. 928.2
Letters & documents. Collected & edited by John C. Hodges. [1st ed.] New York, Harcourt, Brace and World [1964] xxii, 295 p. ports., facsim. 24 cm. Bibliography: p. 281-282. [PR3366.A55] 64-11528
1. Authors—Correspondence, reminiscences, etc. I. Hodges, John Cunyus, 1892- ed.

GOSSE, Edmund William, Sir, 1849-1928. 822'.4 B
Life of William Congreve. London, W. Heinemann, 1924. [Folcroft, Pa.] Folcroft Library Editions, 1973. p. [PR3366.G6 1973] 73-270 ISBN 0-8414-1428-9 15.00
1. Congreve, William, 1670-1729. I. Title.

GOSSE, Edmund William, Sir, 1849-1928. 822'.4 B
Life of William Congreve. London, W. Heinemann, 1924. [Folcroft, Pa.] Folcroft Library Editions, 1973. p. [PR3366.G6 1973] 73-270 ISBN 0-8414-1428-9
1. Congreve, William, 1670-1729. I. Title. BIP

HODGES, John Cunyus, 1892- v. 12
William Congreve, the man; a biography from new sources. New York, Kraus Reprint Corp., 1966. xvii, 151 p. illus., ports., facsim., geneal. tables. 25 cm. (Modern Language Association of America. General series, 11) First published in 1941 by Modern Language Association of America. 67-93584
1. Congreve, William, 1670-1729. I. Title. II. Series.

LYNCH, Kathleen Martha. 928.2
A Congreve gallery. Cambridge, Harvard University Press, 1951. xiv, 196 p. ports., facsim. 22 cm. Bibilography: p. 175-183. [PR3366.L9] 51-11748
1. Congreve, William, 1670-1729. I. Title. BIP

TAYLOR, Daniel Crane, 1897- 822'.4
William Congreve, by D. Crane Taylor. Folcroft, Pa., Folcroft Press [1969] x, 252 p. port. 24 cm. Reprint of the 1931 ed. Bibliography: p. [231]-240. [PR3366.T3 1969] 72-193756
1. Congreve, William, 1670-1729. **BIP**

Congreve, William, 1670-1729—Biography.

GOSSE, Edmund William, Sir, 1849-1928. 822'.4 B
Life of William Congreve. Port Washington, N.Y., Kennikat Press [1972] 192, ix p. 19 cm. Reprint of the 1888 ed. Bibliography: p. [i]-ix. [PR3366.G6 1972] 77-153215 ISBN 0-8046-1525-X
1. Congreve, William, 1670-1729—Biography. I. Title.

GOSSE, Edmund William, Sir, 1849-1928. 822'.4 B
Life of William Congreve. St. Clair Shores, Mich., Scholarly Press [1974] p. cm. Reprint of the 1888 ed. published by W. Scott, London and T. Whittaker, New York, in series: Great writers. Bibliography: p. [PR3366.G6 1974] 74-3129 ISBN 0-403-03070-6
1. Congreve, William, 1670-1729—Biography. I. Title.

Conigliaro, Tony, 1945- —Juvenile literature.

CONIGLIARO, Tony, 1945- 796.357'0924 B
Seeing it through, by Tony Conigliaro with Jack Zanger. [New York, Macmillan [1970] 238 p. illus. 21 cm. [GV865.C66A3] 72-124869
1. Baseball—Biography. I. Zanger, Jack. II. Title.

RUBIN, Robert, 1941- 796.357'0924 B
Tony Conigliaro: up from despair. New York, Putnam [1971] 157 p. front. 22 cm. (Putnam sports shelf) A biography of the Red Sox's home run hitter who defied the doctors' reports that he would never play ball again after being hit in the head with a fastball. [GV865.C66R8 1971] 92 73-140573 3.86
1. Conigliaro, Tony, 1945- —Juvenile literature. I. Title. **BIP**

Conjuring.

RAPP, Augustus, 1871- 793.8'092'2
The life and times of Augustus Rapp, the small town showman, written by himself, and with an introd. by Robert Parrish. [Chicago, J. Marshall for the Ireland Magic Co., c1959] 136p. illus. 29cm. [GV1545.R35A3] 60-20349
1. Conjuring. I. Title.

Conjuring—Biography.

GOLDSTON, Will, 1877-1948. 793.8
Secrets of famous illusionists. With a foreword by J. C. Cannell. London, J. Long, 1933. Ann Arbor, Mich., Gryphon Books, 1971. 285 p. illus. 22 cm. [GV1545.A2G6 1971] 75-157495
1. Conjuring—Biography. I. Title.

Conjuring—History—Juvenile literature.

EDMONDS, I. G. 793.8'092'2 B
The magic makers : magic and the men who made it / by I. G. Edmonds. 1st ed. Nashville : T. Nelson, c1976. 188 p. : ill. ; 21 cm. Includes indexes. Introduces famous magicians throughout history and describes some of their best-known tricks. [GV1543.E35] 920 76-145 ISBN 0-8407-6476-6 : 6.95
1. Conjuring—History—Juvenile literature. 2. Conjuring—Biography—Juvenile literature. I. Title. **BIP**

Conklin, Henry, 1832-1915—Juvenile literature.

CONKLIN, Henry, 1832-1915. 917.47'03'40924 B
Through "Poverty's Vale": a hardscrabble boyhood in upstate New York, 1832-1862. Edited with an introd. by Wendell Tripp. [1st ed.] [Syracuse] Syracuse University Press, 1974. xxiii, 262 p. illus. 23 cm. (A York State book) Includes bibliographical references. An autobiographical account of a frontier family's struggles in a backwoods environment a century ago. [F123.C6917 1974] 92 73-19980 ISBN 0-8156-0098-4 8.50
1. Conklin, Henry, 1832-1915—Juvenile literature. 2. Frontier and pioneer life—New York (State)—Juvenile literature. 3. United States—History—Civil War, 1861-1865—Personal narratives—Juvenile literature. I. Title. **BIP**

Conkling, Roscoe, 1829-1888.

JORDAN, David M., 1935- 328.73'0924 B
Roscoe Conkling of New York: voice in the Senate, by David M. Jordan. Ithaca [N.Y.] Cornell University Press [1971] xiii, 464 p. ports. 24 cm. Bibliography: p. 441-452. [E664.C75J6] 76-148021 ISBN 0-8014-0625-0 15.00
1. Conkling, Roscoe, 1829-1888. 2. U.S.—Politics and government—1865-1900. I. Title.

Conlan, Jocko,

CONLAN, Jocko, 1899- 796.3573'0924
Jocko, by Jocko Conlan and Robert Creamer. [1st ed.] Philadelphia, Lippincott [1967] 240 p. 21 cm. [GV876.C6] 67-20285
I. Creamer, Robert. II. Title.

Conley, Lawrence Alden, 1908-1947.

COSGROVE, Joseph G 922.251
Accent on laughter; a life sketch of Father Lawrence A. Conley, M. M., Maryknoll missioner in South China. New York, McMullen Books [c1952] 102p. 20cm. [BV3427.C55C6] 52-12840
1. Conley, Lawrence Alden, 1908-1947. I. Title.

Connally, John Bowden, 1917-

CRAWFORD, Ann Fears. 353.2'092'4 B
John B. Connally, portrait in power / Ann Fears Crawford and Jack Keever. Austin, Tex. : Jenkins Pub. Co., c1973. x, 460 p. : ill. ; 24 cm. Includes index. Bibliography: p. [435]-443. [E840.8.C66C72] 75-316888 9.50
1. Connally, John Bowden, 1917- I. Keever, Jack, joint author. II. Title.

Connally, Thomas Terry,

CONNALLY, Thomas Terry, 1877- 923.273
My name is Tom Connally, by Tom Connally, as told to Alfred Steinberg. New York, Crowell [1954] 376 p. illus. 22 cm. [E748.C76A3] 54-9157
I. Title.

Connaughton, Charles A .

MAUNDER, Elwood R. 634.9'092'4 B
Forty-three years in the field with the U.S. Forest Service : an interview with Charles A. Connaughton / conducted by Elwood R. Maunder. Santa Cruz, Calif. : Forest History Society, 1976. vi, 153 leaves, [6] leaves of plates : ill. ; 28 cm. Includes index. [SD129.C65M38] 76-362211 38.10
1. Connaughton, Charles A . 2. United States Forest Service. 3. Foresters—Correspondence, reminiscences, etc. 4. Forests and forestry—United States. I. Connaughton, Charles A. II. Title.

Connecticut—Biography.

PERRY, Charles Edward, ed. 974.6'0922
Founders and leaders of Connecticut, 1633-1783. Freeport, N.Y., Books for Libraries Press [1971] ix, 319 p. illus. 23 cm. (Essay index reprint series) Reprint of the 1934 ed. Bibliography: p. 311-312. [F93.P38 1971] 78-177965 ISBN 0-8369-2518-1
1. Connecticut—Biography. 2. Connecticut—History—Colonial period, ca. 1600-1775. I. Title.

Connelly, Cornelia Augusta (Peacock) 1809-1879.

BISGOOD, Marie Therese, 1891- 922.273
Cornelia Connelly; a study in fidelity. With an introd. by James Walsh. Westminster, Md., Newman Press [1963] xiii, 326 p. illus., ports. 22 cm. "Sources": p. 318-319. Bibliographical footnotes. [BX4705.C77B58] 63-25041
1. Connelly, Cornelia Augusta (Peacock) 1809-1879. 2. Society of the Holy Child Jesus. I. Title.

KAYE-SMITH, Sheila, 1887- 922.2
Quartet in heaven. [1st ed.] New York, Harper [1952] viii, 279 p. 22 cm. [BX4667.K3] 52-5455
1. Caterina da Genova, Saint, 1447-1510. 2. Connelly, Cornelia Augusta (Peacock) 1809-1879. 3. Rosa of Lima, Saint, 1586-1617. 4. Therese, Saint, 1873-1897. I. Title.
Contents Omitted.

KAYE-SMITH, Sheila, 1887-1956. 282'.0922 B
Quartet in heaven. Freeport, N.Y., Books for Libraries Press [1970, c1952] viii, 244 p. 23 cm. (Biography index reprint series) Contents.Contents.—The matrons: Caterina Fiesca Adorna. Cornelia Connelly.—The maidens: Isabella Rosa de Santa Maria de Flores. Therese Martin.—Some notes on the nature of sanctity. [BX4667.K3 1970] 75-136649
1. Caterina da Genova, Saint, 1447-1510. 2. Connelly, Cornelia Augusta (Peacock) 1809-1879. 3. Rosa, of Lima, Saint, 1586-1617. 4. Therese, Saint, 1873-1897. I. Title. **BIP**

MARIE Therese, Mother, 1891- 922.273
Cornelia Connelly; a study in fidelity. Introd. by James Walsh. Westminster, Md., Newman [c.1963] xii, 326p. illus., ports. 22cm. Bibl. 63-25041 5.75
1. Connelly, Cornelia Augusta (Peacock) 1809-1879. 2. Society of the Holy Child Jesus. I. Title.

MARY Eleanor, Mother. 922.273
The triumph of trust; the story of Mother Connelly. With illus. by Victoria Donohoe. Philadelphia, P. Reilly Co. [1950] vii, 171 p. illus. 21 cm. Secular name: Eleanor Sister. [BX4705.C77M3] 51-9533
1. Connelly, Cornelia Augusta (Peacock) I. Title.

MARY Eleanor, Mother, 1903- 922.273
The triumph of trust; the story of Mother Connelly. With illus. by Victoria Donohoe. Philadelphia, P. Reilly Co., [1950] vii, 171p. illus. 21cm. [BX4705.C77M3] 51-9533
1. Connelly, Cornelia Augusta (Peacock) 1809-1879. I. Title.

SLATER, Eleanor Chapin, 1903- 922.273
The triumph of trust: the story of Mother Connelly. With illus. by Victoria Donohoe. Philadelphia. p. Reilly Co. [1950] vii, 171p. illus. 21cm. [BX4705.C77S6] 51-9533
1. Connelly, Cornelia Augusta (Peacock) 1809-1879. I. Title.

WADHAM, Juliana, 1926- 922.273
The case of Cornelia Connelly. [New York] Pantheon [1957] 276 p. illus. 22 cm. Includes bibliography. [BX4705.C77W3 1957] 57-5619
1. Connelly, Cornelia Augusta (Peacock) 1809-1879. I. Title.

WADHAM, Juliana, 1926- 922.273
The case of Cornelia Connelly. [New York] Pantheon [1957] 276 p. illus. 22 cm. Includes bibliography. [BX4705.C77W3 1957] 57-5619
1. Connelly, Cornelia Augusta Peacock, 1809-1879. I. Title.

Connelly, John F. I. Pie. Anna D.

CONNELLY, Josephine C. (O'Nell) 920
Cardboard, Crowns, and children, too; a biography of John F. Connelly, by Josephine C. Connelly as told to Anna D. Pie. Philadelphia, Dorrance [c.1963] c221p. illus. 25cm. 63-17560 4.95
1. Connelly, John F. I. Pie. Anna D. I. Title.

Connelly, Marcus Cook, 1890-

NOLAN, Paul T. 812'.5'2 B
Marc Connelly, by Paul T. Nolan. New York, Twayne Publishers [1969] 175 p. 21 cm. (Twayne's United States authors series, 149) Includes bibliographical references. [PS3505.O4814Z78] 69-18500
1. Connelly, Marcus Cook, 1890- **BIP**

Conner, Dennis.

CONNER, Dennis. 623.88'092'4 B
No excuse to lose : winning yacht races with Dennis Connor / as told to John Rousmaniere. 1st ed. New York : Norton, c1978. p. cm. [GV812.5.C66A36 1978] 78-8110 ISBN 0-393-03212-4 : 9.95
1. Conner, Dennis. 2. Sailors—United States—Biography. 3. Yacht racing. I. Rousmaniere, John. II. Title.

Conner, Walter Thomas, 1877-1952.

NEWMAN, Stewart A. 922.673
W. T. Conner, theologian of the Southwest. Nashville, Broadman [c.1964] 148p. 22cm. Bibl. 64-12412 3.95 bds.,
1. Conner, Walter Thomas, 1877-1952. I. Title.

Connolly, Billy.

CONNOLLY, Billy. 827'.9'14
Billy Connolly : the authorized version / compiled and with an introduction by Duncan Campbell. London : Pan Books, 1976. 203 p., [8] p. of plates : map, ports. ; 18 cm. [ML420.C663A3] 77-354389 ISBN 0-330-24767-0 : £0.75
1. Connolly, Billy. 2. Entertainers—Scotland—Biography. I. Campbell, Duncan, 1944-

Connolly, Cyril Vernon,

CONNOLLY, Cyril Vernon, 1903- 820.904
Enemies of promise, ; a and other essays: an autobiography [Gloucester, Mass., Peter Smith, 1961, c.1938-1960] 421p. (Doubleday Anchor bk. A194 rebound) 3.50
I. Title.

Connolly, Harold.

CONNOLLY, Olga. 796.4'8'0922
The rings of destiny. New York, D. McKay Co. [1968] 311 p. illus., ports. 21 cm. Autobiography. [GV697.C65C6] 68-20777
1. Connolly, Harold. I. Title.

Connolly, James, 1868-1916.

EDWARDS, Owen Dudley. 335.4'092'4 B
The mind of an activist — James Connolly: the centenary lecture delivered on 10 May 1968 under the auspices of the Irish Congress of Trade Unions, in Liberty Hall. Dublin, Gill and Macmillan, 1971. xiii, 132 p. 19 cm. Includes bibliographical references. [DA965.C7E35] 72-176403 ISBN 0-7171-0533-4 £1.00
1. Connolly, James, 1868-1916. I. Title.

GREAVES, C. Desmond. 335.4'092'4 B
The life and times of James Connolly, by

C. Desmond Greaves. New York, International Publishers [1971, c1961] 448 p. 20 cm. (New World paperbacks, NW-S-14) Includes bibliographical references. [DA965.C7G7 1971] 78-188758 1.65
1. Connolly, James, 1868-1916. I. Title. BIP

REEVE, Carl. 941.5082'1
James Connolly and the United States : the road to the 1916 Irish rebellion / by Carl Reeve and Ann Barton Reeve. Atlantic Highlands, N.J. : Humanities Press, c1978. xvi, 307 p. : port. ; 24 cm. (AIMS historical series ; no. 10) Includes index. Bibliography: p. 293-300. [DA965.C7R44] 78-17273 ISBN 0-391-00879-X : 16.00
1. Connolly, James, 1868-1916. 2. Irish question. 3. Ireland—History—Sinn Fein Rebellion, 1916. 4. Labor and laboring classes—United States. 5. Socialists—United States—Biography. 6. Revolutionists—Ireland—Biography. 7. Socialists—Ireland—Biography. I. Reeve, Ann Barton. II. Title. III. Series: American Institute for Marxist Studies. AIMS historical series ; no. 10 BIP

Connor, Robert, 1950-

CONNER, Robert, 1950- 282'.092'4 B
Walled in / Robert Connor. New York : New American Library, c1979. 308 p. ; 18 cm. (A Signet book) [BX4795.S52C663] 79-110500 ISBN 0-451-08662-7 : 2.25
1. Connor, Robert, 1950- 2. Slaves of the Immaculate Heart of Mary—Biography. I. Title.

Connors, Jimmy, 1952-

*BURKE, Jim. 796.34'2'0924 B
The world of Jimmy Connors. New York, Leisure Books [1976] 217 p. illus. 18 cm. [GV994] 1.50 (pbk.)
1. Connors, Jimmy, 1952- 2. Tennis—Biography. I. Title. BIP

Connors, Jimmy, 1952- —Juvenile literature.

BURCHARD, Marshall. 796.34'2'0924 B
Sports hero, Jimmy Connors / by Marshall Burchard. New York : Putnam, c1976. 93 p. : ill. ; 22 cm. A biography of the feisty young man who has played tennis since the age of three and was the world's number one tennis player in 1975. [GV994.C66B87 1976] 92 76-6148 ISBN 0-399-60993-8 lib. bdg.
1. Connors, Jimmy, 1952- —Juvenile literature. 2. Tennis Juvenile literature. I. Title

SABIN, Francene. 796.34'2'0924 B
Jimmy Connors, king of the courts / by Francene Sabin. New York : Putnam, c1978. 159 p. : ill. ; 21 cm. (Putnam sports shelf) Includes index. Highlights the life of champion Jimmy Connors on and off the tennis courts. [GV994.C66S22 1978] 92 77-11688 ISBN 0-399-61115-0 lib. bdg. : 5.69
1. Connors, Jimmy, 1952- —Juvenile literature. 2. Tennis players—United States—Biography—Juvenile literature. I. Title.

SMITH, Jay H. 796.34'2'0924 B
Fiery tennis star : Jimmy Connors / by Jay H. Smith. [Mankato, Minn.] : Creative Education, [c1977] 30 p. : ill. (some col.) ; 19 cm. A brief biography of the controversial tennis star. [GV994.C66S54] 92 76-44497 ISBN 0-87191-587-1 lib.bdg. : 4.95
1. Connors, Jimmy, 1952- —Juvenile literature. 2. Tennis players—United States—Biography—Juvenile literature. I. Title. BIP

Conolly, Lady Louisa Augusta (Lennox) 1748-1821.

FITZGERALD, Brian. 920.7
Lady Louisa Conolly, 1743-1821; an Anglo-Irish biography. London, New York, Staples Press [1950] 196 p. plate, ports. 22 cm. Bibliography: p. 189-190. [DA483.C68F5] 50-11633
1. Conolly, Lady Louisa Augusta (Lennox) 1748-1821. I. Title.

Conover, Harry, 1912-

CONOVER, Carole. 659.1'52 B
Cover girls : the story of Harry Conover / by Carole Conover. Englewood Cliffs, N.J. : Prentice-Hall, c1978. p. cm. [HD6073.M772U543] 78-15686 ISBN 0-13-188300-3 : 10.95
1. Conover, Harry, 1912- 2. Models, Fashion—United States. 3. Businessmen—United States—Biography. I. Title.

Conrad, Barnaby,

CONRAD, Barnaby, 1922- 813'.5'4
Fun while it lasted. Illus. by the author. New York, Random House [1969] 392 p. illus. 22 cm. Autobiographical [PS3553.O515Z5] 68-28554 7.95
I. Title.

Conrad, Joseph, 1857-1924.

ADAMS, Elbridge L., 1866- 823'.9'12 B
Joseph Conrad: the man, by Elbridge L. Adams. A burial in Kent, by John Sheridan Zelie. Together with some bibliographical notes. [Folcroft, Pa.] Folcroft Library Editions, 1973 [c1925] 71 p. port. 26 cm. Reprint of the ed. published by W. E. Rudge, New York. Includes bibliographical references. [PR6005.O4Z544 1973] 73-11239 8.50
1. Conrad, Joseph, 1857-1924. I. Zelie, John Sheridan, 1866-1942. A burial in Kent. 1973. II. Title. III. Title: A burial in Kent.

ALLEN, Jerry, 1911- 928.2
The thunder and the sunshine; a biography of Joseph Conrad. New York, Putnam [1958] 256p. illus. 22cm. Includes bibliography. [PR6005.O4Z546] 58-7441
1. Conrad, Joseph, 1857-1924. I. Title.

AUBRY, Georges Jean, 1882- 928.2
The sea dreamer; a definitive biography of Joseph Conrad. Translated by Helen Sebba. [1st ed.] Garden City, N. Y., Doubleday, 1957. 321 p. 21 cm. Translation of Vie de Conrad. [PR6005.O4Z5523] 57-5528
1. Conrad, Joseph, 1857-1924. I. Title.

BAINES, Jocelyn. 928.2
Joseph Conrad, a critical biography. New York, McGraw-Hill [1960] 523 p. illus. 22 cm. [PR6005.O4Z554] 59-15429
1. Conrad, Joseph, 1857-1924. I. Title. BIP

BRADBROOK, Muriel Clara 823.912
Joseph Conrad: Jozef Teodor Konrad Nalecz Korzeniowski, Poland's English genius. New York, Russell & Russell, 1965. 79p. 23cm. First pub. in 1941 Bibl. [PR6005.O4Z565] 65-18792 5.00
1. Conrad, Joseph, 1857-1924. I. Title.

CONRAD, Borys, 1898- 823'.9'12
My father Joseph Conrad. [1st American ed.] New York, Coward-McCann [1970] 182 p. plates (incl. facsims., ports.) 22 cm. [PR6005.O4Z575 1970b] 74-132517 5.95
1. Conrad, Joseph, 1857-1924. I. Title.

CONRAD, Jessie (George) 928.2
Joseph Conrad and his circle. 2d ed. Port Washington, N. Y., Kennikat, 1964 [c.1935-1964] 283, 23p. illus., ports. 23cm. Bibl. 64-24449 7.50
1. Conrad, Joseph, 1857-1924. I. Curle, Richard, 1883- A handlist of the various books . . . about Joseph Conrad. II. Title.

CONRAD, Jessie (George) 823'.9'12 B
Joseph Conrad as I knew him, by Jessie Conrad. Garden City, N.Y., Doubleday, Page, 1926. St. Clair Shores, Mich., Scholarly Press, 1972. xxi, 162 p. ports. 21 cm. [PR6005.O4Z58 1972] 70-131673 ISBN 0-403-00560-4
1. Conrad, Joseph, 1857-1924. I. Title. BIP

CONRAD, Joseph, 1857-1924. 823'.9'12
Letters: Joseph Conrad to Richard Curle. Edited with an introd. and notes by R. C. [Folcroft, Pa.] Folcroft Library Editions, 1973 [c1928] p. Reprint of the ed. published by C. Gaige, New York. [PR6005.O4Z534 1973] 73-14720 20.00
1. Conrad, Joseph, 1857-1924. 2. Curle, Richard, 1883- I. Curle, Richard, 1883- II. Title. BIP

CONRAD, Joseph, 1857-1924. 823'.9'12 B
Letters of Joseph Conrad to Marguerite Poradowska, 1890-1920. Translated from the French and edited with an introd., notes, and appendices by John A. Gee and Paul J. Sturm. Port Washington, N.Y., Kennikat Press [1973, c1940] xxiv, 147 p. illus. 22 cm. Bibliography: p. [141]-143. [PR6005.O4Z538 1973] 72-86272 ISBN 0-8046-1747-3 9.50
I. Poradowska, Marguerite (Gachet) II. Gee, John Archer, ed. III. Sturm, Paul Jones, ed. BIP

CONRAD, Joseph [Joseph Conrad Theodore Korezeniowski] 1857-1924. 928.2
Letters from Joseph Conrad, 1895-1924. Ed., introd., notes, by Edward Garnett. [Bobbs, Dist. New York, Macfadden, c.1928-1962] 312p. 21cm. (Charter bks. 117) 1.85 pap.,
I. Garnett, Edward, 1868-1937, ed. II. Title.

COOLIDGE, Olivia E. 823'.9'12 B
The three lives of Joseph Conrad [by] Olivia Coolidge. Boston, Houghton Mifflin, 1972. vii, 230 p. illus. 23 cm. Bibliography: p. [224] [PR6005.O4Z582] 72-75603 ISBN 0-395-13890-6 5.95
1. Conrad, Joseph, 1857-1924. I. Title. BIP

FORD, Ford Madox, 1873-1939. 928.2
Joseph Conrad: a personal remembrance, by Ford Madox Ford (Ford Madox Hueffer) New York, Octagon Books, 1965 [c1924] vii, 276 p. port. 21 cm. [PR6005.O4Z72 1965] 65-16772
1. Conrad, Joseph, 1837-1924. I. Title.

FORD, Ford Madox (Ford Madox Hueffer) 1873-1939 928.2
Joseph Conrad: a personal remembrance. New York, Octagon 1965[c.1924] vii, 276p. port. 21cm. [PR6005.O4Z72] 65-16772 7.00
1. Conrad, Joseph, 1857-1924. I. Title.

GURKO, Leo, 1914- 823'.9'12
Joseph Conrad, giant in exile / by Leo Gurko ; with a new introd. New York : Macmillan, [1979] p. cm. First published in 1962. [PR6005.O4Z7417 1979b] 79-9871 ISBN 0-02-546700-X : 10.00
1. Conrad, Joseph, 1857-1924. 2. Novelists, English—20th century—Biography. I. Title.

JEAN-AUBREY, Georges, 1882-1950. 823'.9'12 B
Joseph Conrad in the Congo. [Folcroft, Pa.] Folcroft Library Editions, 1973. p. Reprint of the 1926 ed. published by Little, Brown, Boston. [PR6005.O4Z7483 1973b] 73-12137 ISBN 0-8414-2197-8 (lib. bdg.)
1. Conrad, Joseph, 1857-1924. 2. Congo—Description and travel. I. Title. BIP

JEAN-AUBRY, Georges, 1882-1950. 823'.9'12 B
Joseph Conrad in the Congo, by G. Jean-Aubry. New York, Haskell House Publishers, 1973. 75 p. port. 23 cm. Reprint of the 1926 ed. Includes bibliographical references. [PR6005.O4Z7483 1973] 72-6769 ISBN 0-8383-1638-7 7.95
1. Conrad, Joseph, 1857-1924. 2. Congo—Description and travel. I. Title. BIP

JEAN-AUBRY, Georges, 1882-1950. 823'.9'12 B
The sea dreamer: a definitive biography of Joseph Conrad [by] Gerard Jean-Aubry. Translated by Helen Sebba. [Hamden, Conn.] Archon Books, 1967 [c1957] 321 p. 22 cm. Translation of Vie de Conrad. Bibliography: p. 295-312. [PR6005.O4Z48513 1967] 67-28553
1. Conrad, Joseph, 1857-1924. I. Title.

JOSEPH Conrad : 823'.9'12
a sketch with a bibliography / illustrated with many drawings by Edw. A. Wilson. Norwood, Pa. : Norwood Editions, 1975, c1924. p. cm. Reprint of the ed. published by Doubleday Page, Garden City, N.Y. Bibliography: p. [PR6005.O4Z75 1975] 75-38822 ISBN 0-88305-043-9 lib. bdg. : 6.00
1. Conrad, Joseph, 1857-1924.

JOSEPH Conrad; 823'.9'12
a sketch with a bibliography. Illustrated with many drawings by Edw. A. Wilson. [Folcroft, Pa.] Folcroft Library Editions, 1973 [c1924] 45 p. illus. 23 cm. Reprint of the ed. published by Doubleday Page & Co., Garden City, N.Y. Bibliography: p. 40-45. [PR6005.O4Z75 1973] 73-9746 ISBN 0-8414-2868-9 (lib. bdg.)
1. Conrad, Joseph, 1857-1924.

MEYER, Bernard C. 823'.9'12
Joseph Conrad; a psychoanalytic biography, by Bernard C. Meyer. Princeton, N.J., Princeton University Press, 1967. viii, 396 p. illus., port. 24 cm. "Bibliographical notes": p. 363-384. [PR6005.O4Z777] 66-14312
1. Conrad, Joseph, 1857-1924. BIP

RETINGER, Joseph Hieronim, 1888-1960. 823'.9'12 B
Conrad and his contemporaries; souvenirs. London, Minerva Pub. Co. [Folcroft, Pa.] Folcroft Library Editions, 1973. p. Reprint of the 1941 ed. [PR6005.O4Z787 1973] 73-1491 ISBN 0-8414-2550-7
1. Conrad, Joseph, 1857-1924. I. Title.

THE sea dreamer: 823/.9/12
a definitive biography of Joseph Conrad [by] Gerard Jean-Aubry. Tr. by Helen Sebba. [Hamden, Conn.] Archon 1967[c.1957] 321p. 22cm. Tr. of Vie de Conrad. Bibl. [PR6005.O4Z5523 1967] (B) 67-28553 9.00
1. Conrad, Joseph, 1857-1924. I. Aubry, Georges Jean, 1882-
Originally published by Doubleday.

STEWART, John Innes MacKintosh, 1906- 823'.9'12 B
Joseph Conrad, by J. I. M. Stewart. New York, Dodd, Mead [1968] 272 p. port. 21 cm. "Conrad's works": p. 263-265. Bibliography: p. 267-268. [PR6005.O4Z82] 68-15412
1. Conrad, Joseph, 1857-1924. BIP

WARNER, Oliver, 1903- 928.2
Joseph Conrad. London, New York, Longmans, Green [1951] 196p. illus. 19cm. (Men and books) [PR6005.O4Z92 1951] 53-2049
1. Conrad, Joseph, 1857-1924. I. Title. BIP

Conrad, Joseph, 1857-1924—Addresses, essays, lectures.

JOSEPH Conrad. 823'.9'12 B
Folcroft, Pa. : Folcroft Library Editions, 1977. p. cm. Reprint of the 1913? ed. published by Double Day Page, Garden City, N.Y. Contents.Contents.—Huneker, J. A pen portrait.—Knopf, A. A. The romance of his life and of his books. Bibliography: p. [PR6005.O4Z7495 1977] 76-58515 ISBN 0-8414-4715-2 : 10.00
1. Conrad, Joseph, 1857-1924—Addresses, essays, lectures. 2. Novelists, English—20th century—Biography—Addresses, essays, lectures. I. Huneker, James Gibbons, 1857-1921. A pen portrait. 1977. II. Knopf, Alfred A., 1892- The romance of his life and of his books. 1977.

Conrad, Joseph, 1857-1924—Biography.

ADAMS, Elbridge L., 1866- 823'.9'12 B
Joseph Conrad : the man / by Elbridge L. Adams. A burial in Kent / by John Sheridan Zelie ; together with some bibliographical notes. Norwood, Pa. : Norwood Editions, 1975 [c1925] 71 p., [1] leaf of plates : port. ; 26 cm. Reprint of the ed. published by W. E. Rudge, New York. [PR6005.O4Z544 1975] 75-37951 ISBN 0-88305-018-8 lib. bdg. : 10.00
1. Conrad, Joseph, 1857-1924—Biography. I. Zelie, John Sheridan, 1868-1942. A burial in Kent. 1975. II. Title. III. Title: A burial in Kent. BIP

BAINES, Jocelyn. 823'.9'12 B
Joseph Conrad : a critical biography / Jocelyn Baines. Westport, Conn : Greenwood Press, 1975, c1960. 507 p., [4] leaves of plates : ill. ; 22 cm. Reprint of the 1961 ed. published by Readers Union-

Contemporary Fiction, London. Includes bibliographies and index. [PR6005.O4Z554 1975] 75-17476 ISBN 0-8371-8304-9 : 23.25
1. Conrad, Joseph, 1857-1924—Biography.

CONRAD, Jessie (George) 823'.9'12
Joseph Conrad as I knew him, by Jessie Conrad. Freeport, N.Y., Books for Libraries Press [1970, c1925] xxi, 162 p. 23 cm. [PR6005.O4Z58 1970] 76-128877 ISBN 0-8369-5497-1
1. Conrad, Joseph, 1857-1924—Biography. I. Title.

CURLE, Richard, 1883- 823'.9'12
The last twelve years of Joseph Conrad. New York, Russell & Russell [1968, c1928] 212 p. illus., facsim., ports. 23 cm. [PR6005.O4Z62 1968] 68-10914
1. Conrad, Joseph, 1857-1924—Biography. I. Title. BIP

KARL, Frederick Robert, 1927- 823'.9'12 B
Joseph Conrad : the three lives / a biography by Frederick R. Karl. 1st ed. New York : Farrar, Straus, and Giroux, 1979. xvi, 1008 p., [32] leaves of plates : ill. ; 24 cm. Includes index. Bibliography: p. 971-976. [PR6005.O4Z759] 78-13515 ISBN 0-374-18014-8 : 25.00
1. Conrad, Joseph, 1857-1924—Biography. 2. Novelists, English—20th century—Biography. BIP

Conrad, Joseph, 1857-1924—Homes and haunts—Poland.

†MORF, Gustav. 823'.9'12 B
The Polish shades and ghosts of Joseph Conrad / by Gustav Morf. New York : Astra Books ; Boston : distributed by Twayne Publishers, c1976. 334 p. : ill. ; 23 cm. Includes index. Bibliography: p. 327-330. [PR6005.O4Z7815] 75-18281 ISBN 0-913994-20-0 : 12.95
1. Conrad, Joseph, 1857-1924—Homes and haunts—Poland. 2. Conrad, Joseph, 1857-1924—Political and social views. 3. Novelists, English—20th century—Biography. I. Title. BIP

Conrad, Joseph, 1857-1924—Journeys—United States—New York (City)

†MORLEY, Christopher Darlington, 1890-1957. 823'.9'12 B
Conrad and the reporters / by Christopher Morley. Folcroft, Pa. : Folcroft Library Editions, 1977. 63 p. : ill. ; 22 cm. Reprint of the 1923 ed. published by Doubleday, Page, Garden City, N.Y. [PR6005.O4Z783 1977] 77-8439 ISBN 0-8414-6094-9 lib. bdg. : 12.50
1. Conrad, Joseph, 1857-1924—Journeys—United States—New York (City) 2. Novelists, English—20th century—Biography. 3. New York (City)—Harbor. I. Title. BIP

Conrad, Joseph, 1857-1924—Journeys—Zaire.

JEAN-AUBRY, Georges, 1882-1950. 823'.9'13 B
Joseph Conrad in the Congo / by G. Jean-Aubry. Norwood, Pa. : Norwood Editions, 1976. 75 p. : ill. ; 26 cm. Reprint of the 1926 ed. published by Little, Brown, Boston. Includes bibliographical refrences. [PR6005.O4Z7483 1976] 76-11839 ISBN 0-8482-1260-6 lib bdg. : 10.00
1. Conrad, Joseph, 1857-1924—Journeys—Zaire. 2. Zaire—Description and travel—1881-1950. I. Title.

Conrad, Joseph, 1857-1924—Philosophy.

GEKOSKI, R. A. 823'.9'12
Conrad : the moral of world of the novelist / R. A. Gekoski. New York : Barnes & Noble Books, 1978. p. cm. (Novelists and their world) A revision of the author's thesis, University of Oxford, 1972. Includes index. Bibliography: p. [PR6005.O4Z7255 1978] 78-2118 ISBN 0-06-492348-7 : 19.50
1. Conrad, Joseph, 1857-1924—Philosophy. I. Title. BIP

Conrad, Joseph, 1857-1924. The secret sharer.

WINKLER, Miriam. v. 12
The secret sharer. Heart of darkness, Critical biography by David Mason Greene. Text by Miriam Winkler. New York, American R.D.M. Corp. [1965] 84 p. 21 cm. (Study-master publication, 199) Bibliography: p. 83-84. 67-73960
1. Conrad, Joseph, 1857-1924. The secret sharer. 2. Conrad, Joseph, 1857-1924. Heart of darkness. I. Greene, David Mason. II. Title. III. Title: Heart of darkness.

Conrad, Max, 1903-

BUEGELEISEN, Sally. 629.13'092'4 B
Into the wind; the story of Max Conrad. [1st ed.] New York, Random House [1973] xv, 261 p. illus. 22 cm. [TL540.C72B8] 70-37032 ISBN 0-394-46306-4 6.95
1. Conrad, Max, 1903- I. Title.

Conried, Heinrich, 1855-1909.

MOSES, Montrose Jonas, 1878-1934. 782.1'092'4 B
The life of Heinrich Confried / Montrose J. Moses. New York : Arno Press, 1977. p. cm. Reprint of the 1916 ed. published by T. Y. Crowell, New York. [ML429.C6M6 1977] 76-29959 ISBN 0-405-09699-2 : 25.00
1. Conried, Heinrich, 1855-1909. 2. Impresarios—Biography. I. Title.

Conroy, Frank, 1936- —Biography.

CONROY, Frank, 1936- 973 B
Stop-time / Frank Conroy. New York : Penguin Books, 1977, c1967. 283 p. ; 18 cm. [CT275.C7643A3 1976] 76-53807 ISBN 0-14-004446-9 pbk. : 2.50
1. Conroy, Frank, 1936- —Biography. 2. Authors, American—20th century—Biography. I. Title. BIP

Conservationists—Biography—Juvenile literature.

SQUIRE, C. B. 333.7'2'0922
Heroes of conservation, by C. B. Squire. New York, Fleet Press Corp. [1974] 107 p. illus. 24 cm. Bibliography: p. 101-102. Seventeen brief biographies include Henry Thoreau, John Muir, Rachel Carson, the Duke of Edinburgh, Jacques-Yves Cousteau, and other champions of conservation for earth's resources. [S926.A2S66] 920 B 70-179015 ISBN 0-8303-0103-8 5.95
1. Conservationists—Biography—Juvenile literature. 2. Conservation of natural resources—History—Juvenile literature. BIP

Conservationists—U.S.

CLEPPER, Henry Edward, 1901- comp. 333.7'2'0922 B
Leaders of American conservation, edited by Henry Clepper. New York, Ronald Press Co. [1971] vii, 353 p. 24 cm. Includes bibliographical references. [S926.A2C54] 75-155206
1. Conservationists—U.S. I. Title. BIP

STRONG, Douglas Hillman. 333.7'2'0922 B
The conservationists [by] Douglas H. Strong. Menlo Park, Calif., Addison-Wesley Pub. Co. [1971] 196 p. illus. 21 cm. (Specialized studies in American history series) Bibliography: p. 183-185. [S926.A2S7] 79-31087
1. Conservationists—U.S. I. Title. BIP

Considerant, Victor Prosper, 1808-1893.

COLLARD, Pierre. 335'.2'0924 B
Victor Considerant (1808-1893); sa vieses idees. New York, B. Franklin [1973] p. Reprint of the 1910 ed. These—Dijon. Bibliography: p. [HX704.C58 1973] 73-168921 ISBN 0-8337-0625-X 14.50
1. Considerant, Victor Prosper, 1808-1893. 2. Fourier, Francois Marie Charles, 1772-1837. 3. Socialism. BIP

Considine, Robert Bernard, 1960-

DEMPSEY, Jack [Williams Harrison Dempsey] 1895- 927.9683
Dempsey, by the man himself, as told to Bob Considine, Bill Slocum. New York, Avon [1961,c.1959,1960] 176p. illus. (G1068) .50 pap.,
1. Considine, Robert Bernard, 1960- I. Title.

Constable, John, 1776-1837.

FRASER, John Lloyd. 759.2 B
John Constable, 1776-1837 : the man and his mistress / John Lloyd Fraser. London : Hutchinson, 1976. 253 p., [9] leaves of plates : ill. ; 24 cm. Includes index. Bibliography: p. [239]-241. [ND497.C7F72] 76-362067 ISBN 0-09-125540-6 : £6.95
1. Constable, John, 1776-1837.

GADNEY, Reg, 1941- 759.2 B
Constable and his world / Reg Gadney. London : Thames and Hudson, c1976. 128 p. : ill. ; 24 cm. Includes index. Bibliography: p. 116. [ND497.C7G23] 76-357781 ISBN 0-500-13056-6 : £3.50
1. Constable, John, 1776-1837. I. Title.

GADNEY, Reg, 1971- 759.2 B
Constable and his world / Reg Gadney. 1st American ed. New York : Norton, 1976. 128 p. : ill. ; 24 cm. Includes index. Bibliography: p. 116. [ND497.C7G23 1976b] 76-365643 ISBN 0-393-04440-8 : 10.00
1. Constable, John, 1776-1837. I. Title.

Constant, Alphonse Louis, 1810-1875.

WILLIAMS, Thomas Andrew, 1931- 133.4'092'4 B
Eliphas Levi, master of occultism / Thomas A. Williams. University : University of Alabama Press, [1975] x, 174 p., [5] leaves of plates : ill. ; 22 cm. Errata slip inserted. Includes index. Bibliography: p. 167-169. [BF1598.C6W54] 74-493 ISBN 0-8173-7061-7 : 9.00
1. Constant, Alphonse Louis, 1810-1875. I. Title.

Constant de Rebecque, Charlotte, 1769-1845.

CONSTANT DE REBECQUE, Henri Benjamin, 1767-1830. 843.63
Cecile; edited and annotated by Alfred Roulin; translated by Norman Cameron. [Norfolk, Conn., James Laughlin, 1953] xx, 125p. 21cm. (A New Directions book) 'An autobiographical narrative.' [PQ2211.C24A8414] 53-10423
1. Constant de Rebecque, Charlotte, 1769-1845. I. Title.

Constant de Rebecque, Henri Benjamin, 1767-1830.

SCHERMERHORN, Elizabeth Wheeler. 320'.0924 B
Benjamin Constant; his private life and his contribution to the cause of liberal government in France, 1767-1830, by Elizabeth W. Schermerhorn. With a pref. by Fernand Baldensperger. New York, Haskell House, 1970. xxiii, 424 p. illus., ports. 23 cm. Reprint of the 1924 ed. "Letters, journals, and works of Benjamin Constant consulted": p. 407-409. [DC255.C7S2 1970] 70-132445 ISBN 0-8383-1199-7
1. Constant de Rebecque, Henri Benjamin, 1767-1830. BIP

Constantinus I, the Great, Emperor of Rome, d. 337.

BAYNES, Norman Hepburn, 1877-1961. 270.1'092'4 B
Constantine the Great and the Christian church / by Norman H. Baynes. New York : Haskell House, 1975. 102 p. ; 21 cm. Reprint of the 1930 ed. published by H. Milford, London, which was issued as the Raleigh lecture on history, 1930. Includes bibliographical references. [BR180.B3 1975] 74-34500 ISBN 0-8383-0131-2 : 7.95
1. Constantinus I, the Great, Emperor of Rome, d. 337. 2. Church history—Primitive and early church, ca. 30-600. I. Title. II. Series: British Academy, London (Founded 1901) Annual Raleigh lecture ; 1930. BIP

BAYNES, Norman Hepburn, 1877-1961. 270.1
Constantine the Great and the Christian Church. 2nd ed. (i.e. 1st ed. reprinted) with a preface by Henry Chadwick. London, Oxford University Press for the British Academy, 1972. viii, 107 p. 23 cm. Reprint of the 1930 ed., issued in series: The Raleigh lecture on history, 1929. Includes bibliographical references. [BR180.B3 1972] 72-188266 ISBN 0-19-725672-4 £1.00
1. Constantinus I, the Great, Emperor of Rome, d. 337. 2. Church history—Primitive and early church, ca. 30-600. I. Title. II. Series: British Academy, London (Founded 1901) Annual Raleigh lecture, 1929.

DORRIES, Hermann, 1895- 270.1'0924
Constantine the Great. Translated by Roland H. Bainton. New York, Harper & Row [1972] xi, 250 p. 21 cm. (Harper torchbooks, HR 1567) Bibliography: p. [235]-245. [DG315.D613 1972] 72-179281
1. Constantinus I, the Great, Emperor of Rome, d. 337. 2. Church history—Primitive and early church, ca. 30-600.

JONES, Arnold Hugh Martin, 1904- 923.137
Constantine and the conversion of Europe. New, rev. ed. New York, Collier Books [1962] 223p. illus. 18cm. (Men and history) [BR180.J6 1962] 62-19201
1. Constantinus I, the Great, Emperor of Rome, d. 337. 2. Church history—Primitive and early church. 3. Missions—Europe. I. Title.

MACMULLEN, Ramsay, 1928- 937'.08'0924 B
Constantine. New York, Dial Press, 1969. vi, 263 p. illus., map, ports. 22 cm. (Crosscurrents in world history) "Bibliographical note": p. [341]-345. [DG315.M3] 77-91117 7.95
1. Constantinus I, the Great, Emperor of Rome, d. 337. BIP

SMITH, John Holland. 937.08'0924 [B]
Constantine the Great. New York, Scribners [1973? c.1971] 359 p. illus., ports., geneal. tables, maps. 21 cm. (Lyceum Editions, SL415) Bibliography: p. 327-329. [DG315.S6 1971b] 77-143935 pap., 3.50
1. Constantine I, the Great, Emperor of Rome, d. 397. I. Title.

Constantinus I, the Great, Emperor of Rome, d. 337—Addresses, essays, lectures.

EADIE, John William, comp. 937'.08'0924 B
The conversion of Constantine. Edited by John W. Eadie. New York, Holt, Rinehart and Winston [1971] 111 p. illus. 24 cm. (European problem studies) Includes bibliographical references. [BR180.E2] 73-113827 ISBN 0-03-083645-X
1. Constantinus I, the Great, Emperor of Rome, d. 337—Addresses, essays, lectures. 2. Church history—Primitive and early church, ca. 30-600—Addresses, essays, lectures. I. Title.

EADIE, John William, comp. 937'.08'0924 B
The conversion of Constantine / edited by John W. Eadic. Huntington, N.Y. : R. E. Krieger Pub. Co., 1976, c1971. p. cm. Reprint of the ed. published by Holt, Rinehart and Winston, New York, in series: European problem studies. Includes bibliographical references. Explores two areas of Constantine's religious affiliation: his conversion to Christianity and the specific details connected to his actions. [BR180.E2 1976] 76-25480 ISBN 0-88275-453-X pbk. : 3.95
1. Constantinus I, the Great, Emperor of Rome, d. 337—Addresses, essays, lectures. 2. Church history—Primitive and early church, ca. 30-600—Addresses, essays, lectures. I. Title. BIP

Contarini, Gasparo, Cardinal, 1484-1542.

MATHESON, Peter. 270.6'092'4 B
Cardinal Contarini at Regensburg. Oxford, Clarendon Press, 1972. x, 193 p. 23 cm. Bibliography: p. [183]-190. [BX4705.C774M38] 72-180270 ISBN 0-19-826431-3 £3.25
1. Contarini, Gasparo, Cardinal, 1484-1542. 2. Ratisbon, Colloquy of, 1941. I. Title.

Continental Air Lines, inc.

SERLING, Robert J. 387.7'4
Maverick: the story of Robert Six and Continental Airlines [by] Robert J. Serling. [1st ed.] Garden City, N.Y., Doubleday, 1974. viii, 351 p. illus. 22 cm. [HE9803.C65S47] 73-18910 ISBN 0-385-04057-1 7.95
1. Continental Air Lines, inc. 2. Six, Robert F. I. Title.

Contract bridge.

REESE, Terence. 795.4'15'0924 B
Bridge at the top / Terence Reese ; with an introd. by Victor Mollo. London : Faber, 1977. xiii, 143 p. : ill. ; 21 cm. Includes index. [GV1282.3.R33826] 77-368926 ISBN 0-571-11123-8 : 9.95
1. Contract bridge. I. Title.
Distributed by Faber & Faber Salem, N. H. BIP

Contract bridge—Biography.

MOLLO, Victor. 795.4'15'0922
The bridge immortals. New York, Hart Pub. Co. [1968, c1967] 256 p. illus., ports. 24 cm. [GV1282.3.M59 1968] 68-29525 5.95
1. Contract bridge—Biography. I. Title.

Converse, Frederick Shepherd, 1871-1940.

GAROFALO, Robert Joseph. 780'.924 B
The life and works of Frederick Shepherd Converse (1871-1940). Washington, 1969. viii, 280 l. illus., facsims., music, 8 plates (ports.) 29 cm. (Catholic University of America. Studies in music, no. 38) Thesis—Catholic University of America. Bibliography: leaves 269-280. [ML410.C754G4] 78-12275
1. Converse, Frederick Shepherd, 1871-1940. I. Title. II. Series.

Conversion.

LEESTMA, Harold F. 248'.24
God at my elbow; the meaning of conversion [by] Harold F. Leestma. Waco, Tex., Word Books [1973, c1972] 84 p. 23 cm. [BV4916.L43] 72-84165 2.95
1. Bible—Biography. 2. Conversion. I. Title.

RUUD, Brian, 1946- 248'.24
The trip beyond, by Brian Ruud with Walter Wagner. Englewood Cliffs, N.J., Prentice-Hall [1972] 211 p. 21 cm. Autobiography. [BV4935.R76A3] 72-3720 ISBN 0-13-930958-6
1. Conversion. I. Wagner, Walter, 1927- II. Title. BIP

SULLIVAN, J. C., 1907- 248'.2
They couldn't kill Sullivan: ... formerly "From crime to Christ." A true story, by J. C. Sullivan. Fort Worth, Nu-Way Foundation, Publications Dept., [1972] 127 p. illus. 18 cm. [BV4935.S83A3] 71-188610
1. Conversion. I. Title.

Converts.

ANTHONY, Susan Brownell, 1916- 248.2'4'0924 B
The ghost in my life [by] Susan B. Anthony. Special before and after chapters by Catherine Marshall. New York, Chosen Books [1971] 221 p. 22 cm. [BV4935.A65A3] 70-159836 ISBN 0-912376-00-7 5.95
1. Converts. I. Title. BIP

BEHANNA, Gertrude Florence (Ingram) 248.2'4
The late Liz; the autobiography of an ex-pagan, by Elizabeth Burns. With an introd. by the author, Gertrude Behanna. [Rev. ed.] New York, Meredith Press [1968] x, 342 p. 21 cm. [BV4935.B4A3 1968] 68-3342
1. Converts. I. Title.

BURNS, Elizabeth. 248
The late Liz; the autobiography of an ex-pagan. New York, Appleton-Century-Crofts [1957] 342 p. 22 cm. [BV4935.B8A3] 57-7207
1. Converts. I. Title.

EDMAN, Victor Raymond 922
They found the secret; twenty transformed lives that reveal a touch of eternity. Grand Rapids, Mich., Zondervan Pub House [c.1960] 159p. (3p. bibl.) 21 cm. 60-10239 2.50
1. Converts. 2. Christian biography. I. Title.

ZAMPERINI, Louis, 1917- 922
Devil at my heels; the story of Louis Zamperini, by Louis Zamperini with Helen Itria. Foreword by Billy Graham. With line illus. and 16 pages of photos. [1st ed.] New York, Dutton, 1956. 251p. illus. 21cm. [BV4935.Z3A3] 56-5259
1. Converts. I. Title.

Converts, Baptist—Bangladesh—Biography.

WALSH, Jay, 1932- 248'.246
Ripe mangoes : miracle missionary stories from Bangladesh / by Jay Walsh with Patricia C. Oviatt ; foreword by Viggo B. Olsen. Schaumburg, Ill. : Regular Baptist Press, c1978. 124 p. : ill. ; 23 cm. [BX6493.W34] 78-8671 ISBN 0-87227-060-2 pbk. : 2.95
1. Converts, Baptist—Bangladesh—Biography. 2. Missions—Bangladesh. 3. Bangladesh—Biography. 4. Bangladesh—Church history. I. Oviatt, Patricia C., 1928- joint author. II. Title. BIP

Converts, Catholic.

ARMSTRONG, April (Oursler) 928.1
House with a hundred gates. [1st ed.] New York, McGraw-Hill [1965] 286 p. 22 cm. Autobiographical. [BX4668.A7] 64-8408
1. Converts, Catholic. I. Title.

ARMSTRONG, April (Oursler). 928.1
House with a hundred gates, a memoir. Garden City, New York, Doubleday [1968, c.1965] 278p. 18cm. (Echo bks., E54) .95 pap.,
1. Converts, Catholic. I. Title.

BURTON, Katherine (Kurz) 1890- 248.2'42
In no strange land; some American Catholic converts. Freeport, N.Y., Books for Libraries Press [1970, c1942] xix, 254 p. 23 cm. (Essay index reprint series) Bibliography: p. 253-254. [BX4668.A1B87 1970] 72-99619
1. Converts, Catholic. 2. Catholic Church in the United States—Biography. I. Title. BIP

CORCAO, Gustavo. 922.281
My neighbour as myself. Translated by Clotilde Wilson. London, New York, Longmans, Green [1957] 213p. 21cm. 'Originally published in Portuguese as A descoberta do outro.' [BX4668.C592] 57-4956
1. Converts, Catholic. 2. Love. I. Title.

DAY, Dorothy, 1899- 922.273
The long loneliness; the autobiography of Dorothy Day, illustrated by Fritz Eichenberg. [1st ed.] New York, Harper [1952] 288 p. illus. 22 cm. [BX4668.D32] 51-11898
1. Converts, Catholic. I. Title.

DAY, Dorothy, 1899- 922.273
The Long Loneliness the autobiography of Dorothy Day. New York, Curtis Books [1972] 320 p. 18 cm. [BX4668.D32] 51-11898 Pap. 125 (502-01034-125)
1. Converts, Catholic. I. Title.

HSUEH, Kuang-ch'ien, 1909- 923.251
From Confucius to Christ, by Paul K. T. Sih. New York, Sheed & Ward, 1952. 231 p. illus. 22 cm. Autobiographical. [BX4668.H8] 52-10612
1. Converts. Catholic. I. Title.

KANE, George Louis, 1911- ed. 922.2
Twice called; the autobiographies of seventeen convert sisters. Milwaukee, Bruce Pub. Co. [1959] 174p. 22cm. [BX4668.A1K3] 59-14653
1. Converts. Catholic. 2. Monasticism and religious orders for women. I. Title.

KERNAN, William Charles, 1900- 922.273
My road to certainty. New York, D. McKay Co. [1953] 212p. 21cm. [BX4668.K37] 53-7544
1. Converts, Catholic. I. Title.

LEIGH, Margaret Mary, 1894- 922.242
The fruit in the seed, chapters of autobiography New York, Sheed & Ward, 1952. 128 p. 21 cm. [BX4668.L38 1952a] 52-10611
1. Converts, Catholic. I. Title.

MURDICK, Olin John, 1917- 922.273
Journey into truth; the autobiography of a Catholic convert. Foreword by George N. Shuster. [1st ed.] New York, Exposition Press [1958] 177p. 21cm. [BX4668.M77A3] 58-2573
1. Converts, Catholic. I. Title.

O'BRIEN, John Anthony, 1893- ed. 922.2
The way to Emmaus; the intimate personal stories of converts to the Catholic faith. New York, McGraw-Hill [1953] 368p. 21cm. [BX4668.O255] 52-13019
1. Converts. Catholic. I. Title.

O'BRIEN, John Anthony, 1893- ed. 922.273
Where I found Christ; the intimate personal stories of fourteen converts to the Catholic faith [1st ed.] Garden City, N.Y., Doubleday, 1950. 271 p. 20 cm. [BX4668.O26] 50-9175
1. Converts. Catholic. I. Title.

O'HARA, Constance Marie. 282
Heaven was not enough. [1st ed.] Philadelphia, Lippincott [1955] 381 p. 21 cm. Autobiography. [BX4668.O5] 55-6308
1. Converts, Catholic. I. Title.

ROSS WILLIAMSON, Hugh, 1901- 922.242
The walled garden; an autobiography. New York, Macmillan, 1957 [c1956] 231p. illus. 22cm. [BX4668.R57 1957] 57-8269
1. Converts, Catholic. I. Title.

SARGENT, Daniel, 1890- 248.2'4
Four independents. Freeport, N.Y., Books for Libraries Press [1968, c1935] 243 p. 23 cm. (Essay index reprint series) Contents.Contents.—Charles Peguy.—Paul Claudel.—Gerard Manley Hopkins.—Orestes Augustus Brownson. [BX4668.A1S26 1968] 68-55856
1. Converts, Catholic. I. Title. BIP

SIH, Paul Kwang Tsien, 1909- 922.251
From Confucius to Christ, by Paul K. T. Sih. New York, Sheed & Ward, 1952. 231 p. illus. 22 cm. Autobiographical. [BX4668.S48A3] 52-10612
1. Converts, Catholic. 2. Converts from Confucianism. I. Title.

STERN, Gladys Bronwyn, 1890- 928.2
All in good time. New York, Sheed and Ward [1954] 154 p. 21 cm. Autobiographical. [BX4668.S75] 54-6146
1. Converts, Catholic. I. Title.

VANDON, Elizabeth. 922.273
Late dawn. New York, Sheed & Ward [1958] 184 p. 21 cm. Autobiographical. [BX4668.V3] 58-10557
1. Converts, Catholic. I. Title.

Converts from Islam.

ABOUADAOU, Said, 1890-1964. 248.2'46 B
I was an Algerian preacher. Autobiography and parables translated and edited with a prologue, an epilogue, and a survey article by W. N. Heggoy. [1st ed.] New York, Vantage Press [1971] xiii, 92 p. illus., maps, port. 21 cm. [BV2626.4.A25A3] 76-27987 3.50
1. Converts from Islam. I. Heggoy, W. N., 1912- ed. II. Title.

Converts from Judaism.

EVANS, Mike, 1947- 248'.246
Young Lions of Judah [by] Mike Evans with Bob Summers. Plainfield, N.J., Logos International [1974] xii, 116 p. 18 cm. [BV2623.A1E9] 73-84781 1.25 (pbk.)
1. Converts from Judaism. I. Summers, Bob, 1942- joint author. II. Title. BIP

TORRES, Tereska. 843'.9'14 B
The converts. [1st ed.] New York, Knopf, 1970. 308 p. 22 cm. Autobiographical. [BV2623.T66A3] 79-98653 6.95
1. Converts from Judaism. I. Title.

Converts from Judaism—Biography.

GARTENHAUS, Jacob, 1896- 280'.4'0922 B
Famous Hebrew Christians / Jacob Gartenhaus ; [ill. by Allen Wallace]. Grand Rapids, Mich. : Baker Book House, c1979. 206 p. : ports. ; 22 cm. [BV2623.A1G37] 80-105567 ISBN 0-8010-3733-6 : 5.95
1. Converts from Judaism—Biography. I. Title. BIP

LEVITT, Zola. 248'.246
Meshumed! / By Zola Levitt. Chicago : Moody Press, c1979. 147 p. ; 22 cm. [BV2623.A1L48] 78-21111 ISBN 0-8024-5253-1 pbk. : 3.50
1. Converts from Judaism—Biography. I. Title.
Contents omitted. BIP

Converts, Mormon.

BERNHARD, John T 922.8373
Journey into light. Salt Lake City, Deseret Book Co., 1960. 68p. 20cm. Autobiographical. [BX8695.B4A3] 60-44464
1. Converts, Mormon. I. Title.

Converts—United States—Biography.

PROCTOR, William. 248.2'0924 B
On the trail of God / by William Proctor. 1st ed. Garden City, N.Y. : Doubleday, 1977. xiii, 151 p. ; 22 cm. [BV4930.P73] 76-42385 ISBN 0-385-11680-2 : 6.95
1. Converts—United States—Biography. I. Title.

Conway, Moncure Daniel, 1832-1907.

BURTIS, Mary Elizabeth. 922.8173
Moncure Conway,1839-1907. New Brunswick, Rutgers University Press, 1952. xii, 230 p. port. 21 cm. Bibliography: p. 242-254. [BX9869.C8B8] 52-12091
1. Conway, Moncure daniel, 1882-1907. I. Title.

CONWAY, Moncure Daniel, 1832-1907. 288'.0924 B
Autobiography; memories and experiences of Moncure Daniel Conway. New York, Da Capo Press, 1970 [c1904] 2 v. illus., facsims., ports. 24 cm. [BX9869.C8A3 1970] 76-87495
1. Slavery in the United States—Anti-slavery movements.

CONWAY, Moncure Daniel, 1832-1907. 288'.0924 B
Autobiography: memories and experiences of Moncure Daniel Conway. New York, Negro Universities Press [1969] 2 v. illus., facsims., ports. 22 cm. Reprint of the 1904 ed. [BX9869.C8A3 1969] 71-88405
1. Slavery in the United States—Anti-slavery movements.

WALKER, Peter, 1931- 322.4'4'0922 B
Moral choices : memory, desire, and imagination in nineteenth-century American abolition / Peter Walker. Baton Rouge : Louisiana State University Press, c1978. p. cm. Includes index. Bibliography: p. [E449.W185] 78-5922 24.95
1. Conway, Moncure Daniel, 1832-1907. 2. Swisshelm, Jane Grey Cannon, 1815-1884. 3. Douglass, Frederick, 1817(?)-1895. 4. Abolitionists—United States—Biography. 5. Slavery in the United States—Anti-slavery movements. I. Title. BIP

Cook, Ebenezer, fl. 1708-1732.

COHEN, Edward H. 811'.1
Ebenezer Cooke : the sot-weed canon / by Edward H. Cohen. Athens : University of Georgia Press, [1975] x, 125 p. ; 25 cm. Includes bibliographical references and index. [PS732.C6] 73-89716 ISBN 0-8203-0346-1 : 9.00
1. Cook, Ebenezer, fl. 1708-1732. BIP

Cook, Everett R.

COOK, Everett R. 973.91'092'4 B
The life and times of Everett R. Cook / Everett R. Cook. Glen Rock, N.J. : Microfilming Corp. of America, 1976. p. cm. (New York times oral history program) (Tennessee regional oral history collection of the Memphis Public Library ; pt. 1, no. 3) [U53.C58A28] 76-13465 ISBN 0-667-00039-9
1. Cook, Everett R. I. Title. II. Series.

COOK, Everett R. 917.3'03'910924 B
A memoir [by] Everett R. Cook. Edited by Joseph Riggs and Margaret Lawrence. Designer: Lynda Ireland. Printing adviser: Jesse O'Dell. [Memphis] Memphis Public Library [1971] xv, 198 p. illus. (part col.), ports. 23 cm. A taped interview, edited and transcribed into manuscript form. [U53.C58A3] 78-22324 7.50
I. Riggs, Joseph Howard, 1928- ed. II. Lawrence, Margaret, 1922- ed.

Cook, George Hammell, 1818-1889.

SIDAR, Jean Wilson. 630'.92'4 B
George Hammell Cook : a life in agriculture and geology / Jean Wilson Sidar. New Brunswick, N.J. : Rutgers University Press, c1976. xvi, 282 p., [8] leaves of plates : ill. ; 24 cm. Includes bibliographical references and index. [S417.C636S5] 76-15950 11.95
1. Cook, George Hammell, 1818-1889. 2. Rutgers University, New Brunswick, N.J.—Biography. 3. Agriculturists—New Jersey—Biography. 4. Geologists—New Jersey—Biography. 5. New Brunswick, N.J.—Biography.

Cook, Henrietta Barrett, d. 1860.

BROWNING, Elizabeth Barrett, 1806-1961. 821'.8 B
Twenty-two unpublished letters of Elizabeth Barrett Browning and Robert Browning addressed to Henrietta and Arabella Moulton-Barrett. Folcroft, Pa. : Folcroft Library Editions, 1975. x, 89 p. ; 23 cm. Reprint of the 1935 ed. published by the United Feature Syndicate, New York. [PR4193.A353 1975] 75-44045 ISBN 0-8414-3236-8 lib. bdg. : 9.00
1. Browning, Elizabeth Barrett, 1806-1861—Correspondence. 2. Browning, Robert, 1812-1889—Correspondence. 3. Cook, Henrietta Barrett, d. 1860. 4. Barrett, Arabella, d. 1868. I. Browning, Robert, 1812-1889. II. Cook, Henrietta Barrett, d. 1860. III. Barrett, Arabella, d. 1868. IV. Title: Twenty-two unpublished letters of Elizabeth Barrett Browning and Robert Browning ...

Cook, James, 1728-1779.

BEAGLEHOLE, John Cawte. 910'.92'4 B
The life of Captain James Cook. Stanford, Calif., Stanford University Press [1974] xi, 760 p. illus. 25 cm. Bibliography: p. 715-734. [G246.C7B38] 73-87124 ISBN 0-8047-0848-7 18.50
1. Cook, James, 1728-1779. I. Title. BIP

CARRISON, Daniel J. 910.09'42
Captain James Cook: genius afloat, by Daniel J. Carrison. New York, F. Watts [1967] vii, 194 p. maps. 22 cm. (Immortals of history) Bibliography: p. 181. [G246.C7C38] 67-1142
1. Cook, James, 1728-1779. I. Title.

CARRISON, Daniel J. 910.924
Captain James Cook: genius afloat, by Daniel J. Carrison. New York, F. Watts [1967] vii, 194 p. maps. 22 cm. (Immortals of history) Bibliography: p. 181. [G246.C7C38] 67-11425
1. Cook, James, 1728-1779. I. Title.

CARRISON, Daniel J. 910'.92'4 B
Captain James Cook - genius afloat, by Daniel J. Carrison. London, New York, Franklin Watts Ltd, [1972]. vii, 194 p. 23 cm. Bibliography: p. 181. [G246.C7C38 1972] 72-169549 ISBN 0-85166-201-3
1. Cook, James, 1728-1779. I. Title. 4.50

CARRISON, Daniel J. 92
Captain James Cook: genius afloat, by Daniel J. Carrison. New York, F. Watts [1967] vii, 194 p. maps. 22 cm. (Immortals of history) Bibliography: p. 181. A biography of a common British seaman who becomes a navigator, scientist, and explorer; accurately charts and sails the Pacific; and discovers the islands of Hawaii. [G246.C7C38] AC 67
1. Cook, James, 1728-1779. I. Title.

CHICKERING, William Henry, 1916-1945. 919.69'03
Within the sound of these waves; the story of the kings of Hawaii Island, containing a full account of the death of Captain Cook, together with the Hawaiian adventures of George Vancouver and sundry other mariners. Illus. by John Kelly. Westport, Conn., Greenwood Press [1971, c1941] xiv, 327 p. illus. 23 cm. [DU625.C5 1971] 70-138584 ISBN 0-8371-5783-8
1. Cook, James, 1728-1779. 2. Vancouver, George, 1757-1798. 3. Hawaii—Kings and rulers. I. Title. BIP

CONNER, Daniel. 910'.92'4 [B]
Master mariner, Capt. James Cook and the peoples of the Pacific / Daniel Conner and Lorraine Miller. Seattle : University of Washington Press, 1978. p. cm. [G420.C65C66] 78-2989 ISBN 0-295-95621-6 : 16.95
1. Cook, James, 1728-1779. 2. Explorers—Great Britain—Biography. I. Miller, Lorraine, joint author. II. Title.

DE LEEUW, Adele Louise, 1899- 910'.924 B
A world explorer: James Cook. Illustrated by Nathan Goldstein. Champaign, Ill., Garrard Pub. Co. [1963] 96 p. illus. 24 cm. (World explorer books) A brief survey of the explorer who made the original "Cook's tour" discovering and accurately mapping many islands and coastal areas throughout the world. [G246.C7D4] 92 AC 68
1. Cook, James, 1728-1779. I. Goldstein, Nathan, illus. II. Title.

GREENHILL, Basil. 910'.92'4' B
James Cook, the opening of the Pacific / Basil Greenhill. North American ed. [Palo Alto, Calif.] : Pendragon House, [1978] 32 p. : ill. ; 22 x 28 cm. Originally published in 1970 by H. M. Stationery Off., London, for the Trustees of the National Maritime Museum. [G246.C7G7 1978] 78-17844 ISBN 0-916988-14-7 pbk. : 2.50
1. Cook, James, 1728-1779. 2. Explorers—England—Biography. 3. Pacific Ocean. I. Greenwich, Eng. National Maritime Museum. II. Title.

KENNEDY, Gavin. 910'.92'4 B
The death of Captain Cook / Gavin Kennedy. London : Duckworth, 1978. 103 p., [4] leaves of plates : ill. ; 24 cm. Includes index. Bibliography: p. 95-99. [G246.C7K4] 79-300664 ISBN 0-7156-0956-4 : 11.95
1. Cook, James, 1728-1779. 2. Explorers—Great Britain—Biography. I. Title. Distributed by Biblio Distribution Centre, Totowa, NJ 07511 BIP

LLOYD, Christopher, 1906- 923.942
Captain Cook. New York, Roy Publishers [1955?] 172p. illus. 21cm. [G246] 55-9185
1. Cook, James, 1728-1779. I. Title.

LLOYD, Christopher [Charles Christopher Lloyd] 1906- 923.942
Captain Cook. London. Faber & Faber [Mystic. Conn., Verry. 1966] 172p. illus. 21cm. [G246.C7L75] 53-15760 3.50
1. Cook, James, 1728-1779. I. Title.

MACLEAN, Alistair, 1922or3- 910'.92'4 B
Captain Cook. [1st ed. in U.S.] Garden City, N.Y., Doubleday [1972] 192 p. illus. 24 cm. [G246.C7M3 1972] 70-180092 9.95
1. Cook, James, 1728-1779.

THE Magnificent mariner, Captain James Cook R.N. 910.924
[Melbourne, Australian Paper Manufacturers, 1970] 11 pieces. 20-36 cm. Includes 3 col. illus., 3 facsims., 4 col. maps, 2 col. ports., and a booklet ([32] p. illus., ports. 20 cm.); title from booklet cover. "Part of a direct mail campaign undertaken by Australian Paper Manufacturers Limited in honour of the 200th anniversary of the discovery of Australia by Captain James Cook R.N." [G420.C62M3] 79-593545 ISBN 0-9500998-0-5
1. Cook, James, 1728-1779. 2. Voyages around the world. I. Australian Paper Manufacturers, ltd.

MERRETT, John. 923.942
Captain James Cook. Illustrated by H. Lawrence Hoffman. New York, Criterion Books [1957] 192p. illus. 22cm. (A Criterion book for young people) [G246.C7M4] 57-6247
1. Cook, James, 1728-1779. I. Title.

MURRAY-OLIVER, Anthony Audrey St. Clair Murray, 1915- 910'.92'4 B
Captain Cook's Hawaii as seen by his artists / by Anthony Murray-Oliver. Wellington, N.Z. : Millwood Press, 1975[i.e.1976] 215 p. : ill. (some col.) ; 23 x 26 cm. Label mounted on t.p.: Available from International Publications Service, New York. Includes index. Bibliography: p. 214-215. [G420.C73M87] 76-381660 29.00
1. Cook, James, 1728-1779. 2. Explorers—Great Britain—Biography. 3. Hawaii in art. I. Title.

RIENITS, Rex. 910'.924 B
James Cook. Melbourne, New York, Oxford University Press [1969] 32 p. illus. 19 cm. (Australian explorers) Bibliography: p. 32. [G246.C7R49] 79-861589 ISBN 0-19-550319-8 0.60
1. Cook, James, 1728-1779. 2. Voyages and travels.

SAMWELL, David, d.1799. 923.942
Captain Cook and Hawaii, a narrative, with an introd. by Maurice Holmes. San Francisco, D. Magee, 1957. x, 42 p. illus., ports., facsim. 23 cm. First published in 1786 under title: A narrative of the death of Captain James Cook. [G246.C7S3 1957] 58-17173
1. Cook, James, 1728-1779. I. Title.

SPERRY, Armstrong, 1897- 910'.924 B
Captain Cook explores the South Seas, written and illustrated by Armstrong Sperry. New York, Random House [1955] 184 p. illus. 22 cm. (World landmark books, W-19) A biography of James Cook, self-taught sailor and navigator, whose charting and exploratory voyages took him around the world. [G246.C7S7] 92 AC 68
1. Cook, James, 1728-1779. I. Title.

SYME, Ronald, 1910- 910.09
The travels of Captain Cook. [Photographs by] Werner Forman. New York, McGraw-Hill [1971] 179 p. illus., 102 plates (part col.) 29 cm. Includes selections from The journals of Captain James Cook on his voyages of discovery and A voyage to the Pacific Ocean, by J. Cook, published in 1955-67 and 1784, respectively. Bibliography: p. [6] [G420.S9] 70-150463 ISBN 0-07-062650-2 12.95
1. Cook, James, 1728-1779. 2. Voyages and travels. I. Forman, Werner, illus. II. Title.

THROWER, Norman Joseph William. 994'.4'01
Captain James Cook & his voyages of discovery in the Pacific; an essay by Norman J. W. Thrower to accompany a Captain Cook exhibition, November 6, 1970, to January 4, 1971, in the University Research Library at UCLA, commemorating the bicentenary year of the European discovery of New South Wales. Los Angeles, University of California Library, 1970. [12] p. illus., facsims., maps, ports. 19 x 27 cm. Cover title. [G246.C7T45] 70-634300
1. Cook, James, 1728-1779. 2. Voyages around the world. I. California. University. University at Los Angeles. Library. II. Title.

VANDERCOOK, John Womack, 1902-1963. 923.942
Great sailor, a life of the discoverer, Captain James Cook. New York, Dial Press, 1951. viii, 339 p. port., map (on lining-papers) 21 cm. [G246.C7V35] 51-9943
1. Cook, James, 1728-1779. I. Title.

VILLIERS, Alan John, 1903- 910'.942
Captain James Cook [by] Alan Villiers. New York, Scribner [1967] xii, 307 p. illus., maps, ports. 24 cm. Bibliography: p. 299-302. [G246.C7V53] 67-21345
1. Cook, James, 1728-1779. I. Title. BIP

Cook, James, 1728-1779—Bibliography.

HOLMES, Maurice, Sir, 1885- 016.91'0924
Captain James Cook; a bibliographical excursion. New York, B. Franklin [1968] 103 p. facsims. 23 cm. (Literature of discovery, exploration, and geography, 4) (Burt Franklin bibliography and reference series, 262.) Title on spine: Bibliography of Captain Cook. Reprint of the 1952 ed., a revised and expanded ed. of An introduction to the bibliography of Captain James Cook, R.N. [Z8191.H74 1968] 73-75857
1. Cook, James, 1728-1779—Bibliography. I. Title: Bibliography of Captain Cook.

Cook, James, 1728-1779—Congresses.

CAPTAIN James Cook and his times / edited by Robin Fisher & Hugh Johnston. 910'.92'4 B
Seattle : University of Washington Press, 1979. 278 p. : ill. ; 24 cm. Twelve papers from a conference on Captain Cook's explorations held at Simon Fraser University in 1978. Includes bibliographical references and index. [G246.C7C33] 78-73989 ISBN 0-295-95654-2 : 14.95
1. Cook, James, 1728-1779—Congresses. 2. Explorers—England—Biography—Congresses. I. Fisher, Robin, 1946- II. Johnston, Hugh J. M., 1939-

Cook, James, 1728-1779—Juvenile literature.

BELLIS, Hannah. 910'.924 B
Captain Cook [by] H. Bellis. London, New York, McGraw-Hill [1968] 60 p. illus., map, port. 21 cm. (Historical characters) Bibliography: p. 60. A biography of the British navigator and explorer who accurately mapped much of the South Pacific region on his three famous voyages. [G246.C7B45] 92 78-466536 unpriced
1. Cook, James, 1728-1779—Juvenile literature. I. Title.

EDUCATIONAL Research Council of America. Social Science Staff. 910'.924 B
Explorers and discoverers: Captain Cook, and people Captain Cook met. Boston, Allyn and Bacon [1970] 52 p. col. illus. 21 cm. (Concepts and inquiry: the ERC social science program) An account of the voyages of Captain Cook, the discoveries he made, and the people he met. [G246.C7E3] 92 77-97102
1. Cook, James, 1728-1779—Juvenile literature. I. Title. II. Title: Captain Cook, and people Captain Cook met. III. Series: Concepts and inquiry: the Educational Research Council social science program

LATHAM, Jean Lee. 910'.924
Far voyager; the story of James Cook. Maps by Karl W. Stuecklen. New York, Harper & Row [1970] xii, 242 p. maps. 22 cm. The life of a laborer's son who attained his dream of becoming a British Navy Captain in a day when officers came only from the upper class. [G246.C7L33] 92 74-104751 4.50
1. Cook, James, 1728-1779—Juvenile literature. I. Title.

QUEENSLAND. Dept. of Education. 910'.4
Captain James Cook; bi-centenary celebrations, Queensland schools; souvenir 1970 [compiled by the Dept. of Education and authorised by the Captain Cook Bi-Centenary Celebrations Committee. Brisbane, Campbell Advertising, 1970] 32 p. illus. (part col.) diagrs., maps, music, ports. 19 x 25 cm. Cover title. [G246.C7Q4] 73-150501
1. Cook, James, 1728-1779—Juvenile literature. 2. Endeavour (Ship)—Juvenile literature. I. Captain Cook Bi-Centenary Celebrations Committee (Queensland) II. Title.

Cook, James, 1728-1779—Juvenile literature.

SYME, Ronald, 1910- 923.942
Captain Cook, Pacific explorer. Illustrated by William Stobbs. New York, Morrow, 1960. 96 p. illus. 22 cm. [Morrow junior books] [G246.C7S9] 60-5007
1. Cook, James, 1728-1779—Juvenile literature.

SYME, Ronald, 1910- 923.942
Captain Cook, Pacific explorer. Illustrated by William Stobbs. New York, Morrow, 1960. 96 p. illus. 22 cm. [Morrow junior books] [G246.C7S9] 60-5007
1. -Cook, James, 1728-1779 — Juvenile literature. I. Title.

Cook, James, 1728-1779. Voyages. 1st.

GWYTHER, John Michael. 923.947
Captain Cook and the South Pacific; the voyage of the "Endeavour," 1768-1771. Boston, Houghton Mifflin, 1955 [c1954] 269 p. illus. 22 cm. First ed. published in 1954 under title: First voyage. [G420.C68G9 1955] 55-6551
1. Cook, James, 1728-1779. Voyages. 1st. I. Title.

SPERRY, Armstrong, 1897- 923.942
Captain Cook explores the South Seas, written and illustrated by Armstrong Sperry. New York, Random House [1955] 184 p. illus. 22 cm. (World landmark books, W-19) [G246.C7S7] 55-5827
I. Title.

Cook, Robert Cecil, 1903-

COOK, Robert Cecil, 1903- 917.62
McGowah Place, and other memoirs. Hattiesburg, Miss., Educators' Biographical Press [1973] 388 p. 27 cm. "First edition of 325 copies. This being no. 248." Autobiographical. [Z473.C75A3] 73-84304 15.00
1. Cook, Robert Cecil, 1903- I. Title.
Publisher's address: Box 509, Hattiesburg, Mississippi, 39401.

Cooke, George Frederick, 1756-1812.

DUNLAP, William, 1766-1839. 792'.028'0924 B
The life of George Fred. Cooke ... Comprising original anecdotes of his theatrical contemporaries. 2d ed. rev. and improved. London, Printed for H. Coburn, 1815. [New York] B. Blom, 1972. 2 v. 2 fronts. 22 cm. First published in 1813 under title: Memoirs of George Fred. Cooke. [PN2598.C78D8 1972] 68-20222
1. Cooke, George Frederick, 1756-1812.

WILMETH, Don B. 792'.028'0924 B
George Frederick Cooke, Machiavel of the stage / Don Burton Wilmeth. Westport, Conn. : Greenwood Press, c1980. p. cm. (Contributions in drama and theatre studies ; no. 2) ISSN 0163-3821) Includes index. Bibliography: p. [PN2598.C78W5] 79-7589 ISBN 0-313-21487-5 lib. bdg. : 29.95
1. Cooke, George Frederick, 1756-1812. 2. Actors—Great Britain—Biography. I. Title. II. Series.

Cooke, Harry, 1894-

COOKE, Harry, 1894- 919.4'03'40924 B
Legends of Harry Cooke: including poems and sketches and autobiography 1894 to 1968, by Harry Cooke. Auburn, N.S.W., Paragon Publications, 1973. x, 373 p. ill. 22 cm. [CT2808.C66A34] 74-186623 ISBN 0-9599208-0-3
1. Cooke, Harry, 1894- I. Title.

Cooke, Jay, 1821-1905.

LARSON, Henrietta Melia. 332.1'0924 B
Jay Cooke, private banker, by Henrietta M. Larson. New York, Greenwood Press, 1968 [c1936] xvii, 512 p. illus., facsim., map, ports. 22 cm. "References and notes": p. [435]-498. [HG2463] 69-10116
1. Cooke, Jay, 1821-1905. 2. Banks and banking—U.S.—History. BIP

MINNIGERODE, Meade, 1887-1967. 650'.0922 B
Certain rich men; Stephen Girard, John Jacob Astor, Jay Cooke, Daniel Drew, Cornelius Vanderbilt, Jay Gould, Jim Fisk. Freeport, N.Y., Books for Libraries Press [1970] xi, 210 p. illus., facsim., ports. 23 cm. (Essay index reprint series) Reprint of the 1927 ed. Bibliography: p. ix-xi. [CT219.M55 1970] 71-121489
1. Girard, Stephen, 1750-1831. 2. Astor, John Jacob, 1763-1848. 3. Cooke, Jay, 1821-1905. 4. Drew, Daniel, 1797-1879. 5. Vanderbilt, Cornelius, 1794-1877. 6. Gould, Jay, 1836-1892. 7. Fisk, James, 1835-1872. I. Title.

OBERHOLTZER, Ellis Paxson, 1868-1936. 332.1'0924 B
Jay Cooke, financier of the Civil War. [1st ed.] New York, A. M. Kelley, 1968. 2 v. illus., facsims., map, ports. 23 cm. (Library of money and banking history) (Reprints of economic classics.) Reprint of the 1907 ed. [HJ251.O2 1968] 68-18222
1. Cooke, Jay, 1821-1905. 2. United States—History—Civil War, 1861-1865—Finance, commerce, confiscations, etc. BIP

OBERHOLTZER, Ellis Paxson, 1868-1936. 332.1'0924 B
Jay Cooke, financier of the Civil War. New York, B. Franklin [1970] 2 v. illus., facsims., map, ports. 23 cm. (American Classics in history and social science, 95) (Burt Franklin research & source works series, 419.) Reprint of the 1907 ed. [HJ251.O2 1970] 68-58212
1. Cooke, Jay, 1821-1905. 2. United States—History—Civil War, 1861-1865—Finance, commerce, confiscations, etc.

Cooke, Morris Llewellyn, 1872-

TROMBLEY, Kenneth E. 926.2
The life and times of a happy liberal; a biography of Morris Llewellyn Cooke. [1st ed.] New York, Harper [1954] 270 p. illus. 22 cm. [TA140.C62T7] 54-8998
1. Cooke, Morris Llewellyn, 1872- I. Title.

Cooke, Philip St. George, 1809-1895.

COOKE, Philip St. George, 1809-1895. 978.9'03
The conquest of New Mexico and California / Philip St. George Cooke. New York : Arno Press, 1976, c1878. p. cm. (The Chicano heritage) Reprint of the ed. published by Putnam, New York. [E411.C74 1976] 76-1244 ISBN 0-405-09497-3 : 18.00
1. Cooke, Philip St. George, 1809-1895. 2. New Mexico—History—War with Mexico, 1845-1848—Personal narratives. 3. United States—History—War with Mexico, 1845-1848—Personal narratives. 4. California—History—1846-1850—Sources. I. Title. II. Series. BIP

Cookery, American.

JONES, Robert, 1920- 641.5
The Presidents' own White House cookbook. Melanie H. De Proft, editor in chief. Chicago, Culinary Arts Institute, 1972. 110 p. illus. 24 cm. [TX715.J82 1972] 73-157151
1. Cookery, American. 2. Presidents—United States—Biography. I. De Proft, Melanie H., ed. II. Title. III. Title: White House cookbook.

Cookson, Catherine—Biography.

COOKSON, Catherine. 823'.9'14 B
Our Kate; an autobiography. Indianapolis, Bobbs-Merrill [1971] 238 p. 22 cm. [PR6053.O525Z5 1971] 74-161241 5.95
1. Cookson, Catherine—Biography. I. Title.

*COOKSON, Catherine 823'.9'14 [B]
Our Kate. New York, Bantam Books [1974, c.1971] 248 p. 18 cm. [PR6053.O525Z5] 1.25 (pbk.)
I. Title.
L.C. card no. for the hardbound edition: 74-161241. BIP

Coolbrith, Ina Donna, 1842-1928.

RHODEHAMEL, Josephine DeWitt. 811'.4 B
Ina Coolbrith, librarian and laureate of California [by] Josephine DeWitt Rhodehamel [and] Raymund Francis Wood. [Provo, Utah] Brigham Young University Press [1973] xxiv, 531 p. illus. 24 cm. Bibliography: p. 461-489. [PS1397.C5Z9] 72-84093 ISBN 0-8425-1445-7 11.95
1. Coolbrith, Ina Donna, 1842-1928. I. Wood, Raymund Francis, 1911- joint author. II. Title.

Coole, Arthur Braddan, 1900-

COOLE, Arthur Braddan, 1900- 266'.7'6320924 B
A troubleshooter for God in China / Arthur Braddan Coole. [Denver] : Coole, 1977,c1976. 440 p. : ill. ; 24 cm. [BV3427.C58A37] 76-380750 ISBN 0-912706-05-8 : 14.00
1. Coole, Arthur Braddan, 1900- 2. Missionaries—China—Biography. 3. Missionaries—United States—Biography. I. Title. BIP

Cooley, Charles Horton, 1864-1929.

JANDY, Edward Clarence, 1899- 301'.0924 B
Charles Horton Cooley, his life and his social theory, by Edward C. Jandy. With an introd. by Willard Waller. New York, Octagon Books, 1969 [c1942] viii, 319 p. 23 cm. Originally presented as the author's thesis, University of Michigan, 1938. Bibliography: p. 270-281. [HM22.U6C65 1969] 79-86279
1. Cooley, Charles Horton, 1864-1929. I. Title.

Cooley, Corydon Eliphalet, 1836-1917.

WHARFIELD, H. B. 917.91034 (B)
Cooley: Army scout, Arizona pioneer, wayside host, Apache friend, by H. B. Warfield. El Cajon? Calif., 1966] vii, 102p. illus., ports. 22cm. [F811.C77W5] 66-20413 1.50 pap.,
1. Cooley, Corydon Eliphalet, 1836-1917. 2. Frontier and pioneer life—Arzona. I. Title.

Cooley, Denton A., 1920-

MINETREE, Harry. 617'.09'24 B
Cooley: the career of a great heart surgeon. [1st ed.] New York, Harper's Magazine Press [1973] x, 298 p. illus. 22 cm. [R154.C566M56 1973] 72-79716 ISBN 0-06-126382-6 8.95
1. Cooley, Denton A., 1920- 2. Heart—Surgery. I. Title.

Cooley, Mortimer Elwyn,

COOLEY, Mortimer Elwyn, 1855-1944. 624'.092'4 B
Scientific blacksmith, by Mortimer E. Cooley, with the assistance of Vivien B. Keatley. New York, Arno Press, 1972 [c1947] 290 p. illus. 23 cm. (Technology and society) [TA140.C63A3 1972] 72-5041 ISBN 0-405-04693-6
I. Title. II. Series. BIP

Coolidge, Archibald Cary, 1866-1928.

COOLIDGE, Harold Jefferson, 1870-1934. 907'.2'024 B
Archibald Cary Coolidge: life and letters, by Harold Jefferson Coolidge and Robert Howard Lord. Freeport, N.Y., Books for Libraries Press [1971] xiv, 368 p. illus. 24 cm. Reprint of the 1932 ed. "Bibliography of the more important works of Archibald Cary Coolidge": p. [354]-355. [E175.5.C74C6 1971] 70-179512 ISBN 0-8369-6641-4
1. Coolidge, Archibald Cary, 1866-1928. I. Lord, Robert Howard, 1885-1954.

Coolidge, Calvin, Pres. U.S., 1872-1933.

BRYANT, Blanche (Brown) 1877- 973.91'5'0924 B
Calvin Coolidge as I knew him. Edited by Beatrice S. Crooker. DeLeon Springs, Fla., E. O. Painter Print. Co. [1971] 27 p. illus. 23 cm. [E792.B8] 76-165865
1. Coolidge, Calvin, Pres. U.S., 1872-1933. I. Title.

FUESS, Claude Moore, 1885-1963. 973.91'5'0924 B
Calvin Coolidge, the man from Vermont / by Claude M. Fuess. Westport, Conn. : Greenwood Press, [1976], c1940. xii, 522 p., [23] leaves of plates : ill. ; 23 cm. Reprint of the 1965 ed. published by Archon Books, Hamden, Conn. Bibliography: p. [501]-504. [E792.F85 1976] 76-48974 ISBN 0-8371-9320-6 lib. bdg. : 32.50
1. Coolidge, Calvin, Pres. U.S., 1872-1933. 2. Presidents—United States—Biography. I. Title.

LATHEM, Edward Connery, 923.173
Meet Calvin Coolidge: the man behind the myth. Brattleboro, Vt., Stephen Greene Press, 1960. 223 p. 23 cm. [E792.L3] 60-10051
1. Coolidge, Calvin, Pres. U.S., 1872-1933. I. Title.

MCCOY, Donald R. 973.9150924 B
Calvin Coolidge; the quiet President [by] Donald R. McCoy. New York, Macmillan [1967] viii, 472 p. 21 cm. Bibliography: p. 437-460. [E792.M117] 67-11629
1. Coolidge, Calvin, Pres. U.S., 1872-1933.

MORAN, Philip R., comp. 973.91'5'0924
Calvin Coolidge, 1872-1933; chronology, documents, bibliographical aids. Edited by Philip R. Moran. Dobbs Ferry, N.Y., Oceana Publications, 1970. 144 p. 24 cm. (Oceana presidential chronology series) Bibliography: p. 137-142. [E791.M6] 74-116060 ISBN 0-379-12079-8
1. U.S.—History—1919-1933—Sources. I. Coolidge, Calvin, Pres. U.S., 1872-1933. II. U.S. President, 1923-1929 (Coolidge)

WEYANDT, Dorothy E. 799.1'2
I was a guide for three U.S. Presidents : as taken from the log of a famous Brule guide, Steve Weyandt I / by Dorothy E. Weyandt. [Brule, Wis.] : Weyandt, c1976. 298 p., [4] leaves of plates : ill. ; 24 cm. [SH415.W47] 75-25219
1. Weyandt, Steve, 1905- 2. Coolidge, Calvin, Pres. U.S., 1872-1933. 3. Hoover, Herbert Clark, Pres. U.S., 1874-1964. 4. Eisenhower, Dwight David, Pres. U.S., 1890-1969. 5. Trout fishing—Wisconsin—Brule River. 6. Guides for hunters, fishermen, etc.—Biography. I. Weyandt, Steve, 1905- II. Title.

WHITE, William Allen, 1868-1944. v. 12
A Puritan in Babylon; the story of Calvin Coolidge. New York, Capricorn Books [1965] xvi, 460 p. 67-1200
1. Coolidge, Calvin, Pres. U.S., 1872-1933. I. Title. BIP

WHITE, William Allen, 1868-1944 923.173
A Puritan in Babylon, the story of Calvin Coolidge. [Gloucester, Mass., P. Smith, 1965, c.1938] xvi p., 460p. 21cm. (Capricorn bks. rebound) Bibl. [E792.W577] 4.50
1. Coolidge, Calvin, pres. U.S., 1872-1933. I. Title.

WHITE, William Allen, 1868-1944. 973.91'5'0924 B
A Puritan in Babylon; the story of Calvin Coolidge. Gloucester, Mass., Peter Smith 1973 [c1938] xvi, 460 p. 22 cm. Reprint of the ed. published by Macmillan, New York. Includes bibliographical references. [E792.W577 1973] 73-166256 ISBN 0-8446-3173-6 7.50
1. Coolidge, Calvin, Pres. U.S., 1872-1918. I. Title.

Coolidge family.

WINSLOW, Grace Davenport, 1877- 929.2
My first day and my last day with Grandma Coolidge. [1st ed.] Cleveland, Priv. print. by the Lezius-Hiles Co., 1967. 54 p. illus. (part col.), ports. 26 cm. [CS71.C773 1967] 67-31629
1. Coolidge family. 2. Coolidge, Martha Sturtevant, 1822-1904. I. Title.

Coolidge, Grace Goodhue, 1879-1957.

ROSS, Ishbel, 1897- 920.7
Grace Coolidge and her era; the story of a President's wife. New York, Dodd, Mead, 1962. 370 p. illus. 22 cm. Includes bibliography. [E792.1.C6R6] 62-8017
1. Coolidge, Grace Goodhue, 1879-1957.

Coolidge, William David, 1873-

LIEBHAFSKY, H. A. 541'.3'0924 B
William David Coolidge: a centenarian and his work [by] Herman A. Liebhafsky. New York, Wiley [1974] xiv, 96 p. illus. 23 cm. "A Wiley-Interscience publication." Includes bibliographical references. [TK140.C65L53] 74-11233 ISBN 0-471-53430-7 6.95
1. Coolidge, William David, 1873- 2. Tungsten.

MILLER, John Anderson, 1895- 925
Yankee scientist: William David Coolidge. Schenectady, N.Y. Mohawk Development Serv., 611 State St. [c.1963] vii, 216p. illus., ports., facsims. (on lining papers) 21cm. Bibl. 63-21209 3.95
1. Coolidge, William David, 1873- I. Title.

Coon, Carleton Stevens, 1904-

COON, Carleton Stevens, 1904- 940.54'86'73
A north Africa story : the anthropologist as OSS agent, 1941-43 / by Carleton S. Coon, with historical settings from the editors of Gambit. Ipswich, Mass. : Gambit, c1980. p. cm. [D810.S8C618] 80-11997 ISBN 0-87645-108-3 : 11.95
1. Coon, Carleton Stevens, 1904- 2. United States. Office of Strategic Services—Biography. 3. World War, 1939-1945—Secret service—United States. 4. World War, 1939-1945—Personal narratives, American. 5. World War, 1939-1945—Africa, North. 6. Spies—United States—Biography. 7. Spies—Africa, North—Biography. I. Gambit (Firm) II. Title. BIP

Coon, Helen L.

COON, Helen L. 331.4'092'4 B
Trial and triumph; or, I never gave up, never! [By] Helen L. Coon. Clearwater, Fla., Eldnar Press [1973] iii, 95 p. illus. 20 cm. [HF5500.3.U54C66] 73-87105 4.75
1. Coon, Helen L. 2. Women in business. I. Title.

Cooper, Duff, 1st viscount Norwich, 1890-1954.

COOPER, Diana (Manners) viscountess Norwich, 1892- 920.7
Trumpets from the steep. Boston, HoughtonMifflin, [c.]1960. 268p. illus. (geneal. trees) 22cm. 60-13173 5.00
1. Cooper, Duff, 1st viscount Norwich, 1890-1954. 2. World War, 1939-1945—Gt. Brit. I. Title.

COOPER, Duff, 1st viscount Norwich, 1890-1954. 923.242
Old men forget; the autobiography of Duff Cooper (Viscount Norwich) [1st American ed.] New York, Dutton, 1954. 399p. illus. 22cm. [DA566.9.C64A3 1954] 54-11701
1. Gt. Brit.—Pol. & govt.—20th cent. I. Title.

Cooper, Gary, 1901-1961.

ARCE, Hector. 791.43'028'0924 B
Gary Cooper, an intimate biography / by Hector Arce. 1st ed. New York : Morrow, 1979. 288 p. : ill. ; 24 cm. Bibliography: p. 284-288. [PN2287.C59A9] 79-91040 ISBN 0-688-03604-X : 10.95
1. Cooper, Gry, 1901-1961. 2. Moving-picture actors and actresses—United States—Biography. I. Title.

CARPOZI, George. 791.43'028'0924 B
The Gary Cooper story, by George Carpozi Jr. New Rochelle, N.Y., Arlington House [1970] xi, 263 p. illus., ports. 22 cm. [PN2287.C59C3] 79-101954 ISBN 8-7000-0756- 6.95
1. Cooper, Gary, 1901-1961. I. Title.

KAMINSKY, Stuart M. 791.43'028'0924 B
Coop / by Stuart Kaminsky. New York : St. Martin's Press, 1980. p. cm. [PN2287.C59K3] 79-22534 ISBN 0-312-16955-8 : 10.95
1. Cooper, Gary, 1901-1961. 2. Moving-picture actors and actresses—United States—Biography. I. Title. BIP

Cooper, Gary, 1901-1961—Juvenile literature.

GEHMAN, Richard 92
The tall American; the story of Gary Cooper. Illus. by Albert Micale. Title page illus. by Maria Cooper. New York, Hawthorn [c.1963] 187p. illus. 22cm. (Credo bks. 7) 63-8788 2.95
1. Cooper, Gary, 1901-1961—Juvenile literature. I. Title.

Cooper, Gladys, 1888-

MORLEY, Sheridan, 1941- 791'.092'4 B
Gladys Cooper : a biography / by Sheridan Morley. New York : McGraw-Hill, c1979. xxii, 313 p. : ill. ; 24 cm. Includes index. Bibliography: p. 301-303. [PN2598.C785M67] 78-27824 ISBN 0-07-043148-5 : 10.95
1. Cooper, Gladys, 1888- 2. Actors—Great Britain—Biography.

Cooper, Helen Marie (Lyon).

COOPER, Helen Marie (Lyon). 920.7
The wealth she gathered. Edited by Gertrude Helen Cooper. Boston, Chapman & Grimes [1950] 260 p. illus. 21 cm. Autobiography. [CT275.C77514A3] 50-12451
I. Title.

Cooper, James Fenimore, 1789-1851.

BOYNTON, Henry Walcott, 1869-1947 813.2
James Fenimore Cooper. New York, Ungar [1966] 408p. illus., facsim., ports. 23cm. (Amer. classics) Reprinted from the 1931 ed. [PS1431.B6 1966] 66-19952 7.50
1. Cooper, James Fenimore, 1789-1851. I. Title.

CLYMER, William Branford Shubrick. 813'.2 B
James Fenimore Cooper. Boston, Small, Maynard, 1900. St. Clair Shores, Mich., Scholarly Press [1969] xviii, 149 p. port. 19 cm. (The Beacon biographies of eminent Americans) Bibliography: p. [146]-149. [PS1431.C5 1969] 79-8802
1. Cooper, James Fenimore, 1789-1851. I. Series: The Beacon biographies of eminent Americans. [Boston]

COOPER, James Fenimore 928.1
Letters and journals. Edited by James Franklin Beard. [2 vols.] Cambridge, Mass., Belknap Press of Harvard University Press [c.]1960. xliv, 444p.: vii, 420p. illus., ports., facsims. (col. front.) 25cm. Contents.v. 1, 1800-1830. --v. 2. 1830-1833. 60-5388 20.00
I. Title.

COOPER, James Fenimore, 1789-1851. 813'.2 B
Correspondence of James Fenimore-Cooper. Edited by his grandson, James Fenimore Cooper. Freeport, N.Y., Books for Libraries Press [1971] 2 v. (776 p.) illus., port. 23 cm. Reprint of the 1922 ed. [PS1431.A3 1971b] 70-164597 ISBN 0-8369-5881-0 201

COOPER, James Fenimore, 1789-1851 928.1
Letters and journals; v.3&4. Ed. by James Franklin Beard. Cambridge, Mass., Belknap Pr. of Harvard [c.]1964. 2v. (466;508p.) illus., ports., facsims. 25cm. Contents.v.3. 1833-1839.--v.4. 1840-1844. 60-5388 25.00 set.,
I. Title.

DEKKER, George. 813'.2
James Fenimore Cooper: the American Scott. New York, Barnes & Noble [1967] xvii, 265 p. 23 cm. London ed. (Routledge & K. Paul) has title: James Fenimore Cooper: the novelist. Bibliographical footnotes. [PS1438.D4 1967b] 67-8598
1. Cooper, James Fenimore, 1789-1851. I. Title.

GROSSMAN, James 813'.2
James Fenimore Cooper. Stanford, Calif., Stanford Univ. Pr. [1967, c.1949] viii, 292p. port. 23cm. Bibl. [PS1431.G77 1967] 67-13190 6.50
1. Cooper, James Fenimore, 1789-1851. I. Title. BIP

LOUNSBURY, Thomas Raynesford, 1838-1915. 813'.2 B
James Fenimore Cooper. Boston, Houghton, Mifflin [c1882] Detroit, Gale Research Co., 1968. 306 p. port. 23 cm. (The Gale library of lives and letters: American writers series) "Partial bibliography of Cooper's writing": p. [290]-299. [PS1431.L6 1968] 67-23882
1. Cooper, James Fenimore, 1789-1851.

RAILTON, Stephen, 1948- 813'.2
Fenimore Cooper : a study of his life and imagination / by Stephen Railton. Princeton, N.J. : Princeton University Press, c1978. p. cm. Includes index. [PS1431.R3] 77-85560 ISBN 0-691-06358-3 : 16.00
1. Cooper, James Fenimore, 1789-1851. 2. Novelists, American—19th century—Biography. BIP

Cooper, James Fenimore, 1789-1851—Biography.

PHILLIPS, Mary Elizabeth, 1857- 813'.2 B
James Fenimore Cooper. [Folcroft, Pa.] Folcroft Library Editions, 1974. p. cm. Reprint of the 1913 ed. published by J. Lane Co., New York. [PS1431.P5 1974] 74-9802 35.00 (lib. bdg.).
1. Cooper, James Fenimore, 1789-1851—Biography. BIP

Cooper, John Sherman, 1901-

SCHULMAN, Robert. 328.73'092'4 B
John Sherman Cooper : the global Kentuckian / Robert Schulman. Lexington : University Press of Kentucky, c1976. 112 p., [2] leaves of plates : ill. ; 22 cm. (The Kentucky bicentennial bookshelf) [E840.8.C68S38] 76-9514 ISBN 0-8131-0220-0 : 3.95
1. Cooper, John Sherman, 1901- 2. Legislators—United States—Biography. I. Title. II. Series. BIP

Cooper, John, 1923-

COOPER, John, 1923- 796.7'2'0924 B
The Grand Prix carpetbaggers : the autobiography of John Cooper / with John Bentley ; foreword by Ken Tyrrell. 1st ed. Garden City, N.Y. : Doubleday, 1977. p. cm. Includes index. [GV1032.C68A35] 76-2763 ISBN 0-385-03081-9 : 8.95
1. Cooper, John, 1923- 2. Automobile racing drivers—Great Britain—Biography. 3. Grand Prix racing. I. Bentley, John, 1908- joint author. II. Title.

Cooper, Madison A.

TRAVIS, Marion. 813'.5'4 B
Madison Cooper. Waco, Tex., Word Books [1971] 128 p. illus., ports. 23 cm. Includes bibliographical references. [PS3553.O597Z9] 70-161063 4.95
1. Cooper, Madison A.

Cooper, Miriam, 1891-

COOPER, Miriam, 1891- 791.43'028'0924 B
Dark lady of the silents; my life in early Hollywood, by Miriam Cooper, with Bonnie Herndon. Indianapolis, Bobbs-Merrill [1973] 256 p. illus. 24 cm. [PN2287.C593A33] 73-3907 ISBN 0-672-51725-6 8.95
1. Cooper, Miriam, 1891- I. Herndon, Bonnie. II. Title.

Cooper, Peter, 1791-1883.

NEVINS, Allan, 1890- 920.073
Abram S. Hewitt, with some account of Peter Cooper. New York, Octagon Books, 1967 [1935] xiii, 623 p. illus., facsims., map, ports. 24 cm. "A note upon sources": p. 603. [E664.H523N4] 67-18777
1. Hewitt, Abram Stevens, 1822-1903. 2. Cooper, Peter, 1791-1883. 3. New York (City)—Pol. & govt.—To 1898. I. Title.

RAYMOND, Rossiter Worthington, 1840-1918. 361.7'4'0924 B
Peter Cooper. Freeport, N.Y., Books for Libraries Press [1972] xiii, 109 p. port. 22 cm. Reprint of the 1901 ed., which was issued as no. 4 of The Riverside biographical series. [HV28.C7R3 1972] 72-1252 ISBN 0-8369-6835-2
1. Cooper, Peter, 1791-1883. I. Series: The Riverside biographical series, no. 4 BIP

Cooper, Peter, 1791-1883—Juvenile literature.

GURKO, Miriam. 923.673
The lives and times of Peter Cooper. Illustrated by Jerome Snyder. Diagrs. by Ava Morgan. New York, Crowell [1959] 277p. illus. 21cm. [HV28.C7G8] 59-11393
1. Cooper, Peter, 1791-1883—Juvenile literature. I. Title.

Cooper, Thomas,

COOPER, Thomas, 1805-1892. 322.4'4'0924 B
The life of Thomas Cooper. With an introd. by John Saville. New York, Humanities Press, 1971 [i.e. 1972] 400 p. port. 19 cm. (The Victorian library) Reprint of the 1872 ed. Includes bibliographical references. [PR4503.C2Z5 1972] 72-180070 ISBN 0-391-00159-0 11.00
I. Title. BIP

Cooper, Thomas Sidney, 1803-1902.

SARTIN, Stephen. 759.2 B
Thomas Sidney Cooper, C.V.O., R.A., 1803-1902 / [compiled] by Stephen Sartin. Leigh-on-Sea : F. Lewis, 1976. 79 p., [40] p. of plates : ill. (incl. 1 tipped in) ; 30 cm. Limited ed. of 500 copies. Bibliography: p. 79. [ND497.C73S27] 77-354191 ISBN 0-85317-037-1 : £15.50
1. Cooper, Thomas Sidney, 1803-1902. 2. Painters—Great Britain—Biography.

Cooper, Thomas, 1759-1839.

MALONE, Dumas, 973.5'092'4 B
1892-
The public life of Thomas Cooper, 1783-1839 / by Dumas Malone. 1st AMS ed. New York : AMS Press, 1979. xv, 432 p. : port. ; 23 cm. Reprint of the 1926 ed. published by Yale University Press, New Haven. Includes index. Bibliography: p. [402]-416. [E302.6.C7M2 1979] 75-3122 ISBN 0-404-59117-5 : 37.50
1. Cooper, Thomas, 1759-1839. 2. United States—Politics and government—1783-1865. 3. Statesmen—United States—Biography. I. Title. BIP

Cooperation—United States—Biography.

KNAPP, Joseph Grant, 334'.0922
1900- comp.
Great American cooperators: biographical sketches of 101 major pioneers in cooperative development, by Joseph G. Knapp and associates. Washington, American Institute of Cooperation [1967] xvi. 607 p. 24 cm. [HD3444.5.A2K56] 67-5366
1. Cooperation—United States—Biography. I. Title.

Cooperstown, N.Y. National Baseball Hall of Fame and Museum.

ALLEN, Lee, 1915- 927.96357
Kings of the diamond; the immortals in baseball's Hall of Fame, by Lee Allen, Tom Meany. New York, Putnam [c.1965] 252p. i22m. [GV865.A1A4] 65-13968 4.95
1. Cooperstown, N. Y. National Baseball Hall of Fame and Museum 2. Baseball—Biog. I. Meany, Thomas. II. Title.

ALLEN, Lee, 1915- 927.96357
Kings of the diamond; the immortals in baseball's Hall of Fame, by Lee Allen and Tom Meany. New York, Putnam [1965] 252 p. 22 cm. [GV865.A1A4] 65-13968
1. Cooperstown, N.Y. National Baseball Hall of Fame and Museum. 2. Baseball — Biog. I. Title.

APPEL, Martin. 796.357'092'2 B
Baseball's best : the Hall of Fame Gallery / Martin Appel and Burt Goldblatt. New York : McGraw-Hill, 1976,c1977 p. cm. [GV865.A1A66] 77-6721 ISBN 0-07-002144-9 : 19.95
1. Cooperstown, N.Y. National Baseball Hall of Fame and Museum. 2. Baseball players—United States—Biography. I. Goldblatt, Burt, joint author. II. Title. BIP

COOPERSTOWN, 796.357'074'014774
N.Y. National Baseball Hall of Fame and Museum.
National Baseball Hall of Fame and Museum, Cooperstown, New York. Cooperstown : The Museum, c1976. 68 p. : ill. ; 22 x 28 cm. Cover title. [GV863.A1C63 1976] 76-377108
1. Cooperstown, N.Y. National Baseball Hall of Fame and Museum. 2. Baseball players—Biography. I. Title.

Cooperstown, N.Y. National Baseball Hall of Fame and Museum—Juvenile literature.

DAVIS, Mac, 1905- 796.357'092'2
Hall of Fame baseball / Mac Davis. Cleveland : Collins, World, [1975] xii, 146 p. : ill. ; 24 cm. On cover: Hall of Fame greats: baseball. Brief biographies of thirty-three baseball players and managers whose skill in the game earned them a place in the Hall of Fame. [GV865.A1D362 1975] 920 72-9966 ISBN 0-529-05062-5 : 3.95. ISBN 0-529-05063-3 lib. bdg. : 3.91
1. Cooperstown, N.Y. National Baseball Hall of Fame and Museum—Juvenile literature. 2. Baseball—Biography—Juvenile literature. I. Title.

Cope, Edward Drinker, 1840-1897.

OSBORN, Henry 500.9'2'4 B
Fairfield, 1857-1935.
Cope, master naturalist : [the life and letters of Edward Drinker Cope, with a bibliography of his writings classified by subject] / Henry Fairfield Osborn. New York : Arno Press, 1978. p. cm. (Biologists and their world) Reprint of the 1931 ed. published by Princeton University Press, Princeton, N.J. [QE707.C63O33 1978] 77-81135 ISBN 0-405-10735-8 lib bdg. : 45.00
1. Cope, Edward Drinker, 1840-1897. 2. Cope, Edward Drinker, 1840-1897—Bibliography. 3. Paleontologists—United States—Biography. I. Title. II. Series. BIP

Cope, Thomas Pym, 1768-1854.

COPE, Thomas Pym, 974.8'11'03
1768-1854.
Philadelphia merchant : the diary of Thomas P. Cope, 1800-1851 / edited and with an introd. and appendices by Eliza Cope Harrison. South Bend, Ind. : Gateway Editions, c1978. xii, 628 p., [8] leaves of plates : ill. ; 25 cm. Includes index. Bibliography: p. [609]-615. [F158.44.C66] 78-60231 ISBN 0-89526-689-X : 19.95
1. Cope, Thomas Pym, 1768-1854. 2. Philadelphia—History. 3. Philadelphia—Social conditions. 4. Philadelphia—Biography. 5. Merchants—Pennsylvania—Philadelphia—Biography. I. Harrison, Eliza Cope. II. Title. BIP

Copeland, Charles Townsend, 1860-1952.

ADAMS, James Donald 923.773
Copey of Harvard; a biography of Charles Townsend Copeland. Boston, Houghton Mifflin [c.]1960. 306p. illus. 22cm. 59-8852 5.00
1. Copeland, Charles Townsend, 1860-1952. I. Title. BIP

ADAMS, James Donald, 923.773
1891-
Copey of Harvard; a biography of Charles Townsend Copeland. Boston, Houghton Mifflin, 1960. 306p. illus. 22cm. [PR29.C6A6] 59-8852
1. Copeland, Charles Townsend, 1860-1952. I. Title.

ADAMS, James 808'.0092'4 B
Donald, 1891-1968.
Copey of Harvard; a biography of Charles Townsend Copeland. Westport, Conn., Greenwood Press [1972, c1960] 306 p. illus. 22 cm. [PR29.C6A6 1972] 72-6191 ISBN 0-8371-6465-6 13.50
1. Copeland, Charles Townsend, 1860-1952. I. Title.

Copernicus, Nicolaus, 1473-1543.

*ADAMCZCWSKI, Jan 520.924
Nicolaus Copernicus and his epoch Philadelphia, Pa., Copernicus Society of America, [1974] [161 p] illus., (part col.) 27 cm. [QB36.C8]
1. Copernicus, Nicolaus, 1473-1543 I. Title.
Distributed by Charles Scribner at 7.95

ADAMCZEWSKI, Jan. 520'.92'4 B
Nicolaus Copernicus and his epoch [by] Jan Adamczewski, in cooperation with Edward J. Piszek. Philadelphia, Copernicus Society of America [197-] 160 p. illus. (part col.) 27 cm. Translation of Mikolaj Kopernik i jego epoka. [QB36.C8A62613] 74-174362 7.95
1. Copernicus, Nicolaus, 1473-1543. I. Title.

ARMITAGE, Angus, 1902- 925.2
Copernicus, the founder of modern astronomy. New York, T. Yoseloff [1957] 236 p. illus. 23 cm. [QB36.C8A7 1957] 57-6897
1. Copernicus, Nicolaus, 1473-1543. 2. Astronomy—History.

ARMITAGE, Angus, 1902- 925.2
The world of Copernicus (Sun, stand thou still) [New York] New American Library [1951, c1947] 165 p. illus. 19 cm. (A Mentor book, M65) Bibliography: p. [161]-[162] [QB36.C8A72 1951] 51-6144
1. Copernicus, Nicolaus, 1473-1543. I. Title.

ARMITAGE, Angus, 1962- v. 12
The world of Copernicus (Original title: Sun, stand thous still) [New York] New American Library [1963 c 1947] 160 p. illus. 18 cm. (A Signet Science Library book, P2370) NUC65
1. Copernicus, Nicolaus, 1473-1543. I. Title.

HOYLE, Fred. 520'.92'4 B
Nicolaus Copernicus: an essay on his life and work. [1st U.S. ed.] New York, Harper & Row [1973] xi, 94 p. illus. 21 cm. Bibliography: p. 89. [QB36.C8H75 1973] 73-4092 ISBN 0-06-011971-3 5.95
1. Copernicus, Nicolaus, 1473-1543.

KNIGHT, David C. 520.0924 (B)
Copernicus; titan of modern astronomy [by] David D. Knight. New York, F. Watts [1965] 232 p. illus., facsims., map. ports. 22 cm. (Immortals of science) [QB36.C8K5] 63-7154
1. Copernicus, Nicolaus, 1473-1543. I. Title.

MIZWA, Stephen Paul, 520'.924 B
1892-
Nicholas Copernicus, 1543-1943, by Stephen Mizwa. Port Washington, N.Y., Kennikat Press [1969, c1943] 85 p. illus., facsims, map, ports. 23 cm. Includes music. "Bibliographical suggestions and comments": p. 60-64. [QB36.C8M58 1969] 68-8205
1. Copernicus, Nicolaus, 1473-1543.

STACHIEWICZ, Wanda M. 520'.92'4 B
Copernicus and the changing world; a biographical sketch, by Wanda M. Stachiewicz. [2d. rev. ed.] Montreal, New York, sponsored by the Polish Institute of Arts and Sciences in America, Canadian Branch, 1973 [c1972] 64 p. illus. 23 cm. Bibliography: p. 58-64. [QB36.C8S66 1973] 75-300618
1. Copernicus, Nicolaus, 1473-1543. I. Polish Institute of Arts and Sciences in America. Canadian Branch. II. Title.

THOMAS, Henry 925.2
Copernicus New York, Messner [c.1960] 192p. Bibl.: p.185-186. 22cm. (Julian Messner shelf of biographies) 60-13265 2.95
1. Copernicus, Nicolaus, 1473-1543. I. Title.

THOMAS, Henry, 1886- 925.2
Copernicus. New York, Messner [1960] 192 p. 22 cm. Includes bibliography. [QB36.C8T5] 60-13265
1. Copernicus, Nicolaus, 1473-1543. I. Title.

THE world of Copernicus. v. 12
(Original title: Sun, stand thou still) [New York] New American Library [1956] 165p. illus. (A Mentor book, M65) Bibliography: p. [161]-[162]
1. Copernicus, Nicolaus, 1473-1543. I. Armitage, Angus, 1902-

Copher, Glover Hancock, 1893 —

GIBBANY, Etta May. 926.1
The career of Glover Hancock Copher, master surgeon; a biography. Philadelphia, Dorrance [1964] 146 p. illus., map. ports. 20 cm. "Publications of Dr. Glover Hancock Copher": p. 135-139. [R154.C575G5] 64-20011
1. Copher, Glover Hancock, 1893 — I. Title.

Copland, Aaron, 1900-

BERGER, Arthur 785'.0924 B
Victor, 1912-
Aaron Copland [by] Arthur Berger. Westport, Conn., Greenwood Press [1971, c1953] vii, 120 p. illus. 23 cm. Bibliography: p. 107-116. [ML410.C756B4 1971] 79-136055 ISBN 0-8371-5205-4
1. Copland, Aaron, 1900- BIP

DOBRIN, Arnold. 780'.924 B
Aaron Copland, his life and times. New York, Thomas Y. Crowell Co. [1967] 211 p. illus., music, ports. 21 cm. "Musical works by Aaron Copland": p. 197-201. "Books by Aaron Copland": p. 205. [ML410.C756D6] 67-15398
1. Copland, Aaron, 1900-

SMITH, Julia Frances, 1911- 927.8
Aaron Copland, his work and contribution to American music. [1st ed.] New York, Dutton, 1955. 336 p. port., music. 22 cm. "List of musical works": p. [299]-311. "List of recordings": p. [312]-313. "Critical works": [319]-322. Bibliographical citations included in "Notes" (p. [323]-328) [ML410.C756S5] 55-9659
1. Copland, Aaron, 1900- 2. Copland, Aaron, 1900- Discography.

Copland, Aaron, 1900-—Juvenile literature.

PEARE, Catherine 780'.924 B
Owens.
Aaron Copland, his life. Illustrated by Mircea Vasiliu. [1st ed.] New York, Holt, Rinehart and Winston [1969] 148 p. illus., port. 22 cm. Bibliography: p. 143-144. A biography of one of the prominent twentieth-century American composers whose music encompasses many forms including opera, ballet, symphony, and concerto. [ML3930.C66P4] 92 69-10245 3.95
1. Copland, Aaron, 1900-—Juvenile literature. I. Vasiliu, Mircea, illus. II. Title.

Copley, John Singleton, 1737-1815.

AMORY, Martha Babcock 759.13
(Greene) 1812-1880.
The domestic and artistic life of John Singleton Copley. New York, Kennedy Galleries, 1969 [c1882] xii, 478 p. port. 24 cm. (Library of American art) "With notices of his works, and reminiscences of his son, Lord Lyndhurst, Lord High Chancellor of Great Britain." Includes bibliographical references. [ND237.C7A5 1969] 71-77698
1. Copley, John Singleton, 1737-1815. 2. Lyndhurst, John Singleton Copley, Baron, 1772-1863. I. Title.

AMORY, Martha Babcock 759.13 B
(Greene) 1812-1880.
The domestic and artistic life of John Singleton Copley, R.A. With notices of his works, and reminiscences of his son, Lord Lyndhurst, High Chancellor of Great Britain. Freeport, N.Y., Books for Libraries Press [1970] xii, 478 p. port. 23 cm. Reprint of the 1882 ed. [ND237.C7A5 1970] 70-119925
1. Copley, John Singleton, 1737-1815. 2. Lyndhurst, John Singleton Copley, Baron, 1772-1863. I. Title. BIP

COPLEY, John Singleton, 759.13 B
1738-1815.
Letters & papers of John Singleton Copley and Henry Pelham, 1739-1776. New York, Kennedy Graphics, 1970 [c1914] xxii, 384 p. illus., facsims., ports. 24 cm. (Library of American art) Includes bibliographical references. [ND237.C7A3 1970] 78-100615 ISBN 0-306-71406-X
1. Painters—United States—Correspondence, reminiscences, etc. I. Pelham, Henry, 1749-1806. II. Title. BIP

COPLEY, John Singleton, 759.13 B
1738-1815.
Letters & papers of John Singleton Copley and Henry Pelham, 1739-1776. [Boston] Massachusetts Historical Society, 1914. [New York, AMS Press, 1972] xxii, 384 p. illus. 23 cm. Original ed. issued as v. 71 of Massachusetts Historical Society collections. [ND237.C7A3 1972] 72-456 ISBN 0-404-01719-3 15.00
1. Painters—United States—Correspondence, reminiscences, etc. I. Pelham, Henry, 1749-1806. II. Title. III. Series: Massachusetts Historical Society, Boston. Collections, v. 71.

RIPLEY, Elizabeth. 759.13 B
Copley; a biography. [1st ed.] Philadelphia, Lippincott [1967] 72 p. illus., ports. 26 cm. Bibliography: p. 70. A biography of the New England portrait painter who gained fame in both the colonies and England. Illustrated with reproductions of his works, and includes information on the subjects of his paintings. [ND497.C738R5] 92 AC 68
1. Copley, John Singleton, 1737-1815. I. Title.

Copley, John Singleton, 1737-1815—Juvenile literature.

FLEXNER, James Thomas, 1908- 759.13 B
The double adventure of John Singleton Copley, first major painter of the new world. [1st ed.] Boston, Little, Brown [1969] 169 p. illus., ports. 22 cm. "This book is a reworking of material previously published in the author's books America's old masters and John Singleton Copley." Bibliography: p. [157]-158. A biography of the eighteenth-century painter who was America's first major artist. [ND237.C7F58] 92 69-10659 4.95
1. Copley, John Singleton, 1737-1815—Juvenile literature. I. Title.

Copper, Arnold.

COPPER, Arnold. 133.9'092'6
Psychic summer / Arnold Copper and Coralee Leon. New York : Dial Press, 1976. 184 p. ; 24 cm. [BF1283.C823A36] 76-40420 ISBN 0-8037-7182-7 : 7.95
1. Copper, Arnold. 2. Spiritualism—Biography. I. Leon, Coralee, joint author. II. Title.

COPPER, Arnold. 133.9'092'6
Psychic summer / Arnold Copper and Coralee Leon. New York : Dell Pub. Co., 1977c1976. 250p. ; 18 cm. (A Dell Book) [BF1283.C823A36] ISBN 0-440-17166-0 pbk. : 1.95
1. Copper, Arnold. 2. Spiritualism-Biography. I. Leon, Coralee, joint author. II. Title.
L.C. card no. for 1976 Dial Press ed.:76-40420.

Coppin, George Selth, 1819-1906.

BAGOT, Edward Daniel Alexander 792.0924
Coppin the great, father of the Australian theatre [by] Alec Bagot. [Melbourne] Melbourne Univ. Pr.; New York, Cambridge [1965] xiv, 356p. illus., geneal. table, ports. 26cm. Bibl. [PN3018.C6B3] 65-8993 12.00
1. Coppin, George Selth, 1819-1906. I. Title.

BAGOT, Edward Daniel Alexander. 792.0924(B)
Coppin the great, father of the Australian theatre [by] Alec Bagot. [Melbourne] Melbourne University Press; New York, Cambridge University Press [1965] xiv, 356 p. illus., geneal. table, ports. 26 cm. Bibliography: p. 345-346. [PN3018.C6B3] 65-8993
1. 1. Coppin, George Seith, 1819-1906. I. Title. BIP

Coppola, Ann Drahmann, 1921-1962.

MESSICK, Hank. 364.1'0924 B
Syndicate wife; the story of Ann Drahmann Coppola. Pref. by Sheldon S. Cohen. New York, Macmillan [1968] 214 p. 22 cm. [HV6248.C662M4] 68-19823
1. Coppola, Ann Drahmann, 1921-1962. 2. Racketeering—United States. I. Title.

Corbett, Pearson H.

CORBETT, Pearson H. 920.961672
Arthritis and I a clinical history and an autobiography. New York, Vantage [c.1963] 218p. 21cm. 3.75
I. Title.

Corbit, Julia.

CORBIT, Julia. 770'.92'4 B
Julia's book : photography / by Julia Corbit ; [text editor, Iver Sonnack ; halftone photography, Christopher Sonnack ; picture editors, Mike Hatchimonji and Iver Sonnack]. Gardena, Calif. : Xenos Books, 1979. 93 p. : chiefly ill. ; 31 cm. [TR654.C673] 79-66049 ISBN 0-934724-00-8 : 11.95
1. Corbit, Julia. 2. Photography, Artistic. 3. Women photographers—United States—Biography. I. Sonnack, Iver. II. Sonnack, Christopher. III. Hatchimonji, Mike. IV. Title.

Corbitt, Theodore.

CHODES, John J. 796.4'26 B
Corbitt : the story of Ted Corbitt, long distance runner / John Chodes. Los Altos, Calif. : Tafnews Press, 1974. v, 154 p. : ill. ; 21 cm. [GV697.C67C45 1974] 73-76246 ISBN 0-911520-45-7 pbk. : 3.95
1. Corbitt, Theodore. 2. Marathon running. BIP

Corbly family.

FORDYCE, Nannie L. 929.2'0973
The life and times of Reverend John Corbly and the John Corbly family genealogy. 2d ed., rev. and published by Leola Wright Murphy. Pendleton, Ind.; Reprinted by Mayhill Publications, Knightstown, Ind., 1970. xii, 315 p. illus., coat of arms, facsims., maps, ports. 27 cm. Title on spine: Reverend John Corbly. Corrections in ms. [CS71.C792 1970] 73-15080
1. Corbly family. 2. Corbly, John. I. Murphy, Leola Wright.

Corbly, John.

FORDYCE, Nannie L 929'.2'0973
The life and times of Reverend John Corbly and the John Corbly family genealogy. Washington, Pa. [195] 215p. illus. 27cm. [CS71.C792] 56-46027
1. Corbly, John. 2. Corbly family. I. Title.

Corcoran, William Wilson, 1798-1888.

COHEN, Henry, 1933- 332'.0924 B
Business and politics in America from the age of Jackson to the Civil War; the career biography of W. W. Corcoran. Westport, Conn., Greenwood Pub. Corp. [1971] xvii, 409 p. illus., ports. 22 cm. (Contributions in economics and economic history, no. 4) Bibliography: p. 371-392. [HG2463.C65C6] 79-98708 ISBN 0-8371-3300-9
1. Corcoran, William Wilson, 1798-1888. 2. Riggs National Bank of Washington, D.C. 3. Business and politics—U.S. 4. Finance—U.S.—History. I. Title. BIP

Corday D'Armont, Marie Anne Charlotte de, 1768-1793.

DOBSON, Austin, 1840-1921. 944.04'092'2 B
Four Frenchwomen. Freeport, N.Y., Books for Libraries Press [1972] p. (Essay index reprint series) Reprint of the 1923 ed., which was issued as no. 248 of The World's classics. Contents.Contents.—Mademoiselle de Corday.—Madame Roland.—The Princess de Lamballe.—Madame de Genlis. [DC145.D7 1972] 72-6853 ISBN 0-8369-7269-4
1. Corday d'Armont, Marie Anne Charlotte de, 1768-1793. 2. Roland de la Platiere, Marie Jeanne (Phlipon) 1754-1793. 3. Lamballe, Marie Therese Louise de Savoie-Carignan, princesse de, 1749-1792. 4. Genlis, Stephanie Felicite Ducrest de Saint-Aubin, comtesse de, afterwards marquise de Sillery, 1746-1830. I. Title. BIP

SCHERR, Marie. 944.04'0924
Charlotte Corday and certain men of the revolutionary torment. New York, AMS Press [1970] 237 p. port. 22 cm. Reprint of the 1929 ed. [DC146.C8S3 1970] 79-100512 ISBN 0-404-05588-5
1. Corday D'Armont, Marie Anne Charlotte de, 1768-1793. 2. Danton, Georges Jacques, 1759-1794. 3. Marat, Jean Paul, 1743-1793. 4. Robespierre, Maximilien Marie Isidore de, 1758-1794. 5. France—History—Revolution, 1789-1799. 6. Girondists. I. Title. BIP

Cordelier, Jeanne.

CORDELIER, Jeanne. 301.41'54'0924
"The life" : memoirs of a French hooker / Jeanne Cordelier ; translated from the French by Harry Mathews. New York : Viking Press, 1978. 368 p. ; 24 cm. Translation of La derobade. "A Seaver book." [HQ194.C6713] 77-28565 ISBN 0-670-42814-0 : 10.00
1. Cordelier, Jeanne. 2. Prostitutes—Biography. I. Title.

CORDELIER, Jeanne. 301.41'54'924
"The life" : memoirs of a French hooker / Jeanne Cordelier; translated from the French by Harry Mathews. New York : Avon Books, 1980, c1978 376 p. ; 18 cm. Translation of La derobade. [HQ194.C6713] ISBN 0-380-45609-5 pbk. : 2.75
1. Cordelier, Jeanne 2. Prostitutes — Biography I. Title.
L.C. card no. for 1978 Viking Press ed: 77-28565

Corelli, Arcangelo, 1653-1713.

PINCHERLE, Marc, 1888- 927.8
Corelli: his life, his work. Translated from the French by Hubert E. M. Russell. [1st ed.] New York, Norton [1956] 236p. illus., ports., facsims., music. 22cm. Translation of Corelli et son temps. Bibliographical references included in 'Notes' (p. 188-205) 'Musical bibliography': p. 206-225. Bibliograpgy: p. 226-230. [ML410.C78P52] 56-10096
1. Corelli, Arcangelo, 1653-1713. I. Title.

PINCHERLE, Marc, 1888- 927.8
Corelli: his life, his work. Translated from the French by Hubert E.M. Russell. [1st ed.] New York, Norton [1956] 236p. illus., ports., facsims., music. 22cm. Translation of Corelli et son temps. Bibliographical references included in Notes (p.188-205) Musical bibliography. p. 206-225. Bibliography: p. 226-230. [ML410.C78P52] 56-10096
1. Corelli, Arcangelo, 1658-1713. I. Title.

PINCHERLE, Marc, 1888-1974. 787'.1'0924 B
Corelli : his life, his work / Marc Pincherle ; translated from the French by Hubert E. M. Russell. New York : Da Capo Press, 1979. p. cm. (Da Capo Press music reprint series) Reprint of the 1956 ed. published by W. W. Norton, New York. Includes bibliographies and index. [ML410.C78P52 1979] 79-9155 ISBN 0-306-79576-0 : 19.50
1. Corelli, Arcangelo, 1653-1713. 2. Composers—Italy—Biography.

Corelli, Marie, 1885-1924.

BIGLAND, Eileen. 928.2
Marie Corelli, the woman and the legend; a biography. London, New York, Jarrolds [1953] 274 p. illus. 22 cm. [PR4505.B5] 53-29476
1. Corelli, Marie, 1885-1924.

Corey, Vickie Hyde, 1954-

COREY, Vickie Hyde, 1954- 266'.6'73 B
The glad game / Vickie Hyde Corey. Washington : Review and Herald Pub. Association, c1979. 156 p. ; 19 cm. [BV3625.S5C67] 78-10259 pbk. : 3.95
1. Corey, Vickie Hyde, 1954- 2. Seventh-Day Adventists—United States—Biography. 3. Missionaries—Sierra Leone—Biography. 4. Missionaries—United States—Biography. 5. Students—Religious life. I. Title.

Corke, Helen, 1882- —Biography.

CORKE, Helen, 1882- 823'.9'12 B
In our infancy : an autobiography / Helen Corke. Cambridge [Eng.] ; New York : Cambridge University Press, 1975- v. : ports. ; 23 cm. Contents.Contents.—pt. 1. 1882-1912. [PR6005.O64Z52] 74-31799 ISBN 0-521-20797-5(pt.1) : 15.95
1. Corke, Helen, 1882- —Biography. 2. Lawrence, David Herbert, 1885-1930—Biography. I. Title.

Corlett, Charles H.

CORLETT, Charles H. 355.3'32'0924 B
Cowboy Pete; the autobiography of Major General Charles H. Corlett. Edited by Wm. Farrington. [1st ed.] Santa Fe, N.M., Sleeping Fox [1974] 127 p. illus. 23 cm. [E745.C67A33] 74-78849 3.95
1. Corlett, Charles H. I. Title.

Cornaro, Luigi, 1475-1566.

CORNARO, Luigi, 1475-1566. 613'.04'38
The art of living long / Luigi Cornaro. New York : Arno Press, 1979. p. cm. (Aging and old age) Translation of Discorsi della vita sobria. Reprint of the 1917 ed. published by W. F. Butler, Milwaukee. [RA775.C82 1979] 78-22195 ISBN 0-405-11812-0 : 14.00
1. Cornaro, Luigi, 1475-1566. 2. Health—Early works to 1800. 3. Longevity—Early works to 1800. 4. Centenarians—Italy—Biography. I. Title. II. Series. BIP

Corneille, Pierre, 1606-1684.

TURNELL, Martin. 842'.4'09
The classical moment; studies of Corneille, Moliere, and Racine. Westport, Conn., Greenwood Press [1971] xv, 261 p. ports. 23 cm. "Originally published in 1948." Bibliography: p. 251-257. [PQ527.T8 1971] 79-138601 ISBN 0-8371-5803-6
1. Corneille, Pierre, 1606-1684. 2. Moliere, Jean Baptiste Poquelin, 1622-1673. 3. Racine, Jean Baptiste, 1639-1699. I. Title. BIP

YARROW, Philip John 842.4
Corneille. New York, St. Martin's [c.]1963. ix, 325p. 23cm. Bibl. 63-11342 12.00 [corrected entry]
1. Corneille, Pierre, 1606-1684. I. Title.

YARROW, Philip John. 842'.051
Corneille. London, Macmillan; New York, St. Martin's Press, 1963. ix. 325 p. 23 cm. Bibliography: p. 320-321. [PQ1772.Y3] 63-11342
1. Corneille, Pierre, 1606-1684. I. Title.

Cornell, Ezra, 1807-1874.

DORF, Philip. 923.773
The builder; a biography of Ezra Cornell. New York, Macmillan, 1952. x, 459 p. illus., ports. 22 cm. Bibliographical references included in "Note" (p. [vii]-viii) [LD1364.5.C7D67] 52-14325
1. Cornell, Ezra, 1807-1874. I. Title.

Cornell, Julien D.,

CORNELL, Julien D., 1910- ed. 343.31
The trial of Ezra Pound; a documented account of the treason case, by the defendant's lawyer, Julien Cornell. New York, J. Day Co. [1966] 215 p. facsims. 22 cm. "Appendix IV. Transcript of trial; transcript of hearing in the United States District Court for the District of Columbia, February 13, 1946": p. 154-215. 66-19537
I. Pound, Ezra Loomis, 1885- defendant. II. Title.

Cornell, Katharine, 1898-

MCCLINTIC, Guthrie. 927.92
Me and Kit. [1st ed.] Boston, Little, Brown [1955] 341 p. illus. 23 cm. [PN2287.M14A3] 55-5847
1. Cornell, Katharine, 1898- 2. Theater—U.S. I. Title.

Cornfeld, Bernie, 1927-

CANTOR, Bert, 1922- 332.6'0924 B
The Bernie Cornfeld story. New York, L. Stuart [1970] 320 p., illus., ports. 22 cm. [HG4530.C27] 77-118615 8.95
1. Cornfeld, Bernie, 1927- 2. Investors Overseas Services.

Corning, Erastus, 1794-1872.

NEU, Irene D. 923.373
Erastus Corning, merchand and financier, 1794-1872. Ithaca, N.Y., Cornell University Press [c.1960] xi, 212p. Bibl.: p.195-205. illus. 24cm. 60-4824 4.00
1. Corning, Erastus, 1794-1872. I. Title.

NEU, Irene D 923.373
Erastus Corning, merchant and financier, 1791-1872. Ithaca, N. Y., Cornell University Press [1960] 212p. illus. 24cm. Includes bibliography. [HC102.5.C58N4] 60-4824

1. Corning, Erastus, 1794-1872. I. Title. **BIP**

NEU, Irene D. 338'.092'4 B
Erastus Corning, merchant and financier, 1794-1872 / Irene D. Neu. Westport, Conn. : Greenwood Press, 1977. p. cm. Reprint of the 1960 ed. published by Cornell University Press, Ithaca, N.Y. Includes index. Bibliography: p. [HC102.5.C58N4 1977] 77-22015 ISBN 0-8371-9791-0 lib.bdg. : 16.50
1. Corning, Erastus, 1794-1872. 2. Businessmen—United States—Biography. I. Title.

Cornish, Louis Craig, 1870-

CORNISH, Frances Eliot(Foote) 922.8173
Louis Craig Cornish, interpreter of life. Boston, Beacon Press [1953] 149p. illus. 22cm. [BX9869.C82C6] 53-6620
1. Cornish, Louis Craig, 1870- I. Title.

Cornwallis, Charles Cornwallis, 1st marquis, 1738-1805.

WICKWIRE, Franklin B. 973.3'41'0924 B
Cornwallis: the American adventure [by] Franklin and Mary Wickwire. Boston, Houghton Mifflin, 1970. xvi, 486 p. maps, plates, ports. (part col.) 23 cm. Bibliography: p. [463]-468. [E267.W48] 75-91059 10.00
1. Cornwallis, Charles Cornwallis, 1st marquis, 1738-1805. 2. United States—History—Revolution, 1775-1783—British forces. 3. United States—History—Revolution, 1775-1783—Campaigns and battles. I. Wickwire, Mary, joint author. II. Title.

Cornwell, Dean, 1892-1960.

CORNWELL, Dean, 1892-1960. 759.13 B
Dean Cornwell : dean of illustrators / Patricia Janis Broder ; pref. By Norman Rockwell. New York : Balance House : distrubuted by Watson-Guptill Publications, 1978. 239 p. : chiefly ill. (some col.) ; 28 x 30 cm. Includes index. Bibliography: p. 235-236. [NC975.5.C65A4 1978] 78-4621 ISBN 0-8230-1269-7 : 35.00
1. Cornwell, Dean, 1892-1960. I. Broder, Patricia Janis.

Corona, Juan Vallejo.

TALBITZER, Bill. 364.1'523'0924 B
Too much blood / Bill Talbitzer. 1st ed. New York : Vantage Press, c1978. 228 p. : ill. ; 21 cm. [HV6248.C668T34] 78-57825 ISBN 0-533-03801-4 : 8.95
1. Corona, Juan Vallejo. 2. Crime and criminals—California—Biography. 3. Trials (Murder)—California. I. Title. **BIP**

Corpulence—Personal narratives.

GREENE, Herbert, orchestral conductor. 362.1'9'6398080924 B
Diary of a food addict [by] Herbert Greene [and] Carolyn Jones. New York, Grosset & Dunlap [1974] 209 p. 22 cm. [RC628.G74] 73-15130 ISBN 0-448-11656-1 6.95
1. Corpulence—Personal narratives. I. Jones, Carolyn, 1933- joint author. II. Title.

Correia de Sa e Benavides, Salvador, 1594-1688.

BOXER, Charles Ralph, 1904- 981'.03'0924
Salvador de Sa and the struggle for Brazil and Angola, 1602-1686 / by C. R. Boxer Westport, Conn. : Greenwood Press, [1975] p. cm. Reprint of the ed. published in 1952 by University of London, Athlone Press, London. Bibliography: p. [F2528.C67B6 1975] 74-2583 ISBN 0-8371-7411-2
1. Correia de Sa e Benavides, Salvador, 1594-1688. 2. Brazil—History—1549-1762. 3. Angola—History. I. Title. **BIP**

Corrigan, Mairead.

DEUTSCH, Richard. 941.6082'4'0922
Mairead Corrigan, Betty Williams : two women who ignored danger in campaigning for peace in Northern Ireland / by Richard Deutsch ; with a foreword by Joan Baez. Woodbury, N.Y. : Barron's, c1977. p. cm . Translation of La paix par les femmes. [DA990.U46D4413] 77-17696 ISBN 0-8120-5268-4 : 8.95
1. Corrigan, Mairead. 2. Williams, Betty. 3. Northern Ireland—History—1969- 4. Women in politics—Northern Ireland.

DEUTSCH, Richard. 941.6082'4'0922
Mairead Corrigan, Betty Williams : two women who ignored danger in campaigning for peace in Northern Ireland / by Richard Deutsch ; with a foreword by Joan Baez. Woodbury, N.Y. : Barron's, c1977. p. cm . Translation of La paix par les femmes. [DA990.U46D4413] 77-17696 ISBN 0-8120-5268-4 : 8.95
1. Corrigan, Mairead. 2. Williams, Betty. 3. Northern Ireland—History—1969- 4. Women in politics—Northern Ireland.

Corrigan, Michael Augustine, Abp., 1839-1902.

CURRAN, Robert Emmett. 282'.092'4 B
Michael Augustine Corrigan and the shaping of conservative Catholicism in America, 1878-1902 / Robert Emmett Curran. New York : Arno Press, 1978. xiii, 547 p. : ports. ; 24 cm. (The American Catholic tradition) Rev. and enl. from the author's thesis. Includes index. Bibliography: p. 516-529. [BX4705.C778C87 1978] 77-11277 ISBN 0-405-10814-1 : 34.00
1. Corrigan, Michael Augustine, Abp., 1839-1902. 2. Catholic Church—Bishops—Biography. 3. Catholic Church in the United States—History. 4. McGlynn, Edward, 1837-1900. 5. Bishops—New York (City)—Biography. 6. New York (City)—Biography. I. Title. II. Series.

Corrothers, James David,

CORROTHERS, James David, 1869-1917. 301.45'19'6073024
In spite of the handicap; an autobiography. With an introd. by Ray Stannard Baker. Westport, Conn., Negro Universities Press [1970] 238 p. ports. 23 cm. Reprint of the 1916 ed. [E185.97.C82 1970] 71-111571 ISBN 0-8371-4596-1
I. Title. **BIP**

CORROTHERS, James David, 1869-1917. 301.45'19'6073024 B
In spite of the handicap; an autobiography. Freeport, N.Y., Books for Libraries Press, 1971. 238 p. illus. 23 cm. (The Black heritage library collection) Reprint of the 1916 ed. [E185.97.C82 1971] 75-170694 ISBN 0-8369-8884-1
I. Title.

Corruption (in politics)—United States—History.

COOK, Fred J. 320.9'73'09
American political bosses and machines [by] Fred J. Cook. New York, F. Watts, 1973. 153 p. illus. 24 cm. Bibliography: p. [147] [JS401.C66] 73-6777 ISBN 0-531-02646-9 5.95
1. Corruption (in politics)—United States—History. 2. Municipal government—United States—History. I. Title. **BIP**

Cortes, Hernando, 1485-1547.

CORTES, Hernando, 1485-1547. 972'.02'0924
Fernando Cortes, his five letters of relation to the Emperor Charles V [1519-1526] / Translated and edited, with a biographical introd. and notes compiled from original sources, by Francis Augustus MacNutt. Glorieta, N.M. : Rio Grande Press, 1977,[c1908]. 2 v. : ill. ; 24 cm. (A Rio Grande classic) On spine: Letters of Corte's to Emperor Charles V. Reprint of the ed. published by A. H. Clark Co., Cleveland. "An introduction to an age of conquest, by John Greenway": v. 1, p. Bibliography: p. 94-104. [F1230.C856 1977] 77-1155 ISBN 0-87380-125-3 lib.bdg. : 40.00
1. Cortes, Hernando, 1485-1547. 2. Mexico—History—Conquest, 1519-1540. 3. Aztecs. 4. Mexico—Governors—Biography. 5. Explorers—Mexico—Biography. I. Karl V, Emperor of Germany, 1500-1558. II. MacNutt, Francis Augustus, 1863-1927. III. Greenway, John. An introduction to an age of conquest. 1977. IV. Title.

CORTES, Hernando, 1485-1547. 972'.02
Five letters, 1519-1526. Translated by J. Bayard Morris, with an introd. New York, Norton [196-] xlvii, 388 p. 20 cm. On cover: 5 letters of Cortes to the Emperor. [F1230.C8524] 76-7405 1.95
1. Mexico—History—Conquest, 1519-1540. I. Morris, John Bayard, ed. II. Title: 5 letters of Cortes to the Emperor. **BIP**

GOMARA, Francisco Lopez de, 1510-1560? 923.572
Cortes: the life of the conqueror by his secretary. Translated and edited by Lesley Byrd Simpson. Berkeley, University of California Press, 1964. xxvi, 425 p. illus., map (on lining papers) 24 cm. Translation of Istoria de la conquista de Mexico, the 2d part of the author's Historia general de las Indias. Bibliography: p. 415-417. [F1230.C9216] 64-13474
1. Cortes, Hernando, 1485-1547. 2. Mexico—History—Conquest, 1519-1540. I. Simpson, Lesley Byrd, 1891- ed. and tr.

JOHNSON, William Weber, 1909- 972'.02'0924 B
Cortes / William Weber Johnson. 1st ed. Boston : Little, Brown, [1975] xviii, 238 p. : port. ; 21 cm. (The Library of world biography) Includes index. Bibliography: p. [227]-229. [F1230.C9257] 75-19345 ISBN 0-316-46754-5 : 8.95
1. Cortes, Hernando, 1485-1547. 2. Mexico—History—Conquest, 1519-1540. **BIP**

MADARIAGA, Salvador de, 1886- 972'.02'0924 (B)
Hernan Cortes, conqueror of Mexico. Coral Gables, Fla., University of Miami Press [1967, c1942] ix, 554 p. port., maps. 24 cm. [F1230.C927] 67-28274
1. Cortes, Hernando, 1485-1547. 2. Mexico—Hist.—Conquest, 1519-1540. I. Title.

MADARIAGA, Salvador de, 1886- 972'.02'0924 B
Hernan Cortes, conqueror of Mexico / Salvador de Madariaga. Westport, Conn. : Greenwood Press, 1979, c1942. p. cm. Reprint of the ed. published by University of Miami Press, Coral Gables, Fla. Includes indexes. Bibliography: p. [F1230.C927 1979] 79-2370 ISBN 0-313-22030-1 : 34.75
1. Cortes, Hernando, 1485-1547. 2. Mexico—History—Conquest, 1519-1540. 3. Mexico—Governors—Biography. 4. Explorers—Mexico—Biography. I. Title.

MATHES, W. Michael, comp. 972'.02'0924
The conquistador in California: 1535; the voyage of Fernando Cortes to Baja California in chronicles and documents. Translated and edited by W. Michael Mathes Los Angeles, Dawson's Book Shop, 1973. 123 p. illus. 23 cm. (Baja California travels series, 31) Contents.Contents.—Mathes, W. M. Introduction to the documents.—Gomara, F. Lopez de. History of the conquest of Mexico.—Diaz del Castillo, B. The true history of the conquest of New Spain.—Herrera y Tordesillas, A. de. A general history of the actions of the Castillians on the islands and mainland of the ocean sea.—Lorenzana, F. A. Voyage of Hernan Cortes to the peninsula of the Californias.—A royal order amplifying the appointment of Fernando Cortes as Captain General of New Spain and the South Sea, 1 April 1529.—The contract made by Queen Juana.—The act of possession and discovery.—A royal order, 1535.—Letter from Fernando Cortes at Santa Cruz to Cristobol de Onate at Compostela, 14, May 1535.—Bibliography (p. OThe conquistador in California: 1535; the voyage
1. Cortes, Hernando, 1485-1547. 2. Baja California—Discovery and exploration. 3. Mexico—History—Conquest, 1519-1540. I. Title. II. Series.

SEDGWICK, Henry Dwight, 1861-1957. 972'.02'0924 B
Cortes the conqueror; the exploits of the earliest and greatest of the gentlemen adventurers in the New World. [Boston] Milford House [1974, c1926] p. cm. Reprint of the ed. published by Bobbs-Merrill, Indianapolis. Bibliography: p. [F1230.C937 1974] 74-871 ISBN 0-87821-263-9
1. Cortes, Hernando, 1485-1547. 2. Mexico—History—Conquest, 1519-1540. I. Title. **BIP**

Cortes, Hernando, 1485-1547—Juvenile literature.

GRAFF, Stewart. 972'.02'0924
A world explorer: Hernando Cortes. Illustrated by Raymond Burns. Champaign, Ill., Garrard Pub. Co. [1970] 96 p. col. illus., col. maps (on lining papers) 24 cm. (World explorer books) A biography of the sixteenth-century Spanish explorer who discovered the Aztec empire. [F1230.G73] 92 71-93123 ISBN 0-8116-6466-X 2.59
1. Cortes, Hernando, 1485-1547—Juvenile literature. I. Burns, Raymond, 1924- illus. II. Title.

JACOBS, William Jay. 972'.02'0924 B
Hernando Cortes [by] W. J. Jacobs. New York, Watts, 1974. 58 p. illus. 26 cm. (A Visual biography) A biography of Spanish adventurer, Cortes, who conquered Mexico in the early 1500's thus ending the Aztec nation. [F1230.C925] 92 73-9509 ISBN 0-531-00974-2 4.95 (lib. bdg.)
1. Cortes, Hernando, 1485-1547—Juvenile literature. I. Title. **BIP**

WILKES, John, 1937- 972'.02'0924 B
Hernan Cortes : conquistador in Mexico / John Wilkes. Minneapolis : Lerner Publications Co., 1977, c1974. 51 p. : ill. ; 21 x 23 cm. (A Cambridge topic book) Includes index. A brief biography of the sixteenth-century Spanish conquistador, focusing on his role in the invasion and destruction of the Aztec civilization in Mexico. [F1230.C9397W54 1977] 92 76-22436 lib.bdg. : 4.95
1. Cortes, Hernando, 1485-1547—Juvenile literature. 2. Mexico—Governors—Biography—Juvenile literature. 3. Explorers—Mexico—Biography—Juvenile literature. 4. Mexico—History—Conquest, 1519-1540—Juvenile literature. I. Title. **BIP**

Cortes, Manuel, 1905-

FRASER, Ronald, 1930- 946.08'0924 [B]
In hiding; the life of Manuel Cortes [by] Ronald Fraser. New York, New American Library [1973] xvii, 258 p., 18 cm. [DP257.F73 1973b] 1.50 (pbk)
1. Cortes, Manuel, 1905- 2. Cortes, Juliana, 1913- 3. Spain—Politics and government—1931-1939. I. Title.

FRASER, Ronald, 1930- 946.08'0924 B
In hiding; the life of Manuel Cortes. [1st American ed.] New York, Pantheon Books [1972] xiv, 238 p. map. 22 cm. Includes bibliographical references. [DP257.F73 1972] 75-39628 ISBN 0-394-47941-6 6.95
1. Cortes, Manuel, 1905- 2. Cortes, Juliana, 1913- 3. Spain—Politics and government—1931-1939. I. Title.

Cortina, Juan Nepomuceno, 1824-1892.

WOODMAN, Lyman L 923.572
Cortina, rogue of the Rio Grande. San Antonio, Naylor [1950] ix, 111 p. illus., ports., map (on lining papers) 22 cm. [F391.C77W6] 50-11535
1. Cortina, Juan Nepomuceno, 1824-1892. I. Title.

Cortisone.

KENDALL, Edward Calvin, 1886- 612'.405'0924 B
Cortisone [by] Edward C. Kendall. New York, Scribner [1971] 175 p. illus., ports. 25 cm. (Scribners scientific memoirs) Autobiography. [R154.K275A3] 72-123853 7.95
1. Cortisone. BIP

Coryate, Thomas, 1577?-1617.

STRACHAN, Michael 923.9
The life and adventures of Thomas Coryate. New York, Oxford [c.]1962. x, 317p. illus., maps (1 fold.) 23cm. Bibl. 62-52512 6.75
1. Coryate, Thomas, 1577?-1617. I. Title.

Coryell, Don.

STEIN, Joe. 796.33'2'0924 B
Don Coryell "Win with honor" / by Joe Stein & Diane Clark. San Diego, Calif. : Joyce Press, 1976. 224 p. : ill. ; 23 cm. Spine title: Coryell "Win with honor." [GV939.C65S76] 76-28011 ISBN 0-89325-003-1 : 8.95
1. Coryell, Don. 2. Football coaches—United States—Biography. I. Clark, Diane, joint author. II. Title. BIP

Cosby, William H.—Juvenile literature.

ITZKOWITZ, Leonore K., 1933- 790.2'092'4 B
A funny things happened ... the Bill Cosby story [by] Leonore K. Itzkowitz. [New York] Random House [1974] p. cm. A biography of a popular black comedian, famous for his stories about growing up. [PN2287.C632I8] 92 74-1254 ISBN 0-394-12313-1
1. Cosby, William H.—Juvenile literature. I. Title.

OLSEN, James T. 790.2'092'4 B
Bill Cosby: look back in laughter, by James T. Olsen. Illustrated by Harold Henriksen. Mankato, Minn., Creative Education; [distributed by Childrens Press, Chicago, 1974] 29 p. col. illus. 25 cm. (Close-ups) A biography of the black comedian famous for anecdotes about his childhood. [PN2287.C632O4] 74-6454 ISBN 0-87191-356-9
1. Cosby, William H.—Juvenile literature. I. Henriksen, Harold, illus. II. Title.

ZIEGLER, Sandra, 1938- 790.2'092'4 B
Bill Cosby, coming at you / by Sandra Ziegler ; illustrated by Diana Magnuson. Elgin, Ill. : Child's World ; Chicago : distributed by Childrens Press, c1978. 32 p. : ill. (some col.) ; 25 cm. A biographical sketch of the black comedian famous for anecdotes about his childhood. [PN2287.C632Z5] 92 78-9577 ISBN 0-89565-031-2 : 7.35
1. Cosby, William H.—Juvenile literature. 2. Comedians—United States—Biography—Juvenile literature. I. Magnuson, Diana. II. Title. BIP

Cosell, Howard, 1920-

COSELL, Howard, 1920- 070.4'49'7960924 B
Cosell, by Howard Cosell, with the editorial assistance of Mickey Herskowitz. [1st ed. Chicago, Playboy Press, 1973] ix, 390 p. illus. 25 cm. [GV719.C67A32 1973] 73-84918 8.95
1. Cosell, Howard, 1920- 2. Television broadcasting of sports. I. Title. BIP

Cosimo III, de'Medici, Grand Duke of Tuscany, 1642-1723.

ACTON, Harold Mario Mitchell, 1904- 923.1455
The last Medici. [Rev. ed.] New York, St. Martin's Press [1959, c1958] 327 p. illus. 23 cm. [DG737.42.A3 1959] 59-5479
1. Cosimo III, de'Medici, Grand Duke of Tuscany, 1642-1723. 2. Giovanni Gastone, de'Medici, Grand Duke of Tuscany, 1671-1737. 3. Medici, House of. I. Title.

Coslow, Sam, 1902-

COSLOW, Sam, 1902- 780'.92'4 B
Cocktails for two / Sam Coslow. New Rochelle, N.Y. : Arlington House, c1977. p. cm. Autobiographical. Discography: p. [ML410.C825A3] 77-6822 ISBN 0-87000-392-5 : 12.95
1. Coslow, Sam, 1902- 2. Composers—United States—Biography. I. Title.

Coss, Richard David, 1944-

COSS, Richard David, 1944- 248'.246 B
Wanted / Richard David Coss, with Jo An Summers; introduction by Chaplain Ray. San Diego : Beta Books, c1977. p. cm. A convicted criminal relates how he found God and how his conversion affected his life. [BV4935.C634A38] 92 77-23275 ISBN 0-89293-016-0 : 2.95
1. Coss, Richard David, 1944- 2. Converts—United States—Biography. I. Summers, Jo An, joint author. II. Title. BIP

Costello, Frank.

BRENNAN, Bill 364.14
The Frank Costello story; the true story of the underworld's prime minister. Derby, Conn., Monarch [c.1962] 142p. 18cm. (Monarch Americana ser., MA326) 62-6318 .35 pap.,
1. Costello, Frank. I. Title.

*HANNA, David. 364.106
Frank Costello: the gangster with a thousand faces. New York, Belmont Tower Books, [1974] 199 p. illus. 18 cm. (The Godfather series) [HV6446] 1.25 (pbk.)
1. Costello, Frank 2. Mafia. I. Title.

KATZ, Leonard, 1926- 364.1'092'4 B
Uncle Frank; the biography of Frank Costello. With a foreword by Anthony Quinn. New York, Drake Publishers [1973] 272 p. illus. 24 cm. [HV6248.C67K38] 73-5943 ISBN 0-87749-549-1 7.95
1. Costello, Frank. I. Title. BIP

KATZ, Leonard, 1926- 364.1'092'4 B
Uncle Frank : the biography of Frank Costello / by Leonard Katz ; with a foreword by Anthony Quinn. London ; New York : W. H. Allen, 1974. 272 p., [8] p. of plates : ill., facsim., ports. ; 23 cm. Includes index. [HV6248.C67K38 1974] 75-319013 ISBN 0-491-01540-2 : £3.25
1. Costello, Frank. I. Title.

WOLF, George. 364.1'092'4 B
Frank Costello: prime minister of the underworld, by George Wolf with Joseph DiMona. New York, Morrow, 1974. 266 p. illus. 25 cm. [HV6248.C67W6] 74-1128 ISBN 0-688-00256-0 7.95
1. Costello, Frank. 2. Crime and criminals—Biography. 3. Mafia. I. DiMona, Joseph, joint author. II. Title.

WOLF, George. 364.1'092'4 B
Frank Costello: prime minister of the underworld, by George Wolf with Joseph DiMona. New York, Bantam Books [1975, c1974] xv, 270 p. illus. 18 cm. [HV6248C67W6] 1.75 (pbk.)
1. Costello, Frank. 2. Crime and criminals—Biography. 3. Mafia. I. DiMona, Joseph, joint author. II. Title.
L.C. card number for original ed.: 74-1128.

Costigan, Edward Prentiss, 1874-1939.

GREENBAUM, Fred, 1930- 328.73'0924 B
Fighting progressive; a biography of Edward P. Costigan. Washington, Public Affairs Press [1971] 192 p. 24 cm. Bibliography: p. 181-187. [E748.C865G7] 70-168553 7.00
1. Costigan, Edward Prentiss, 1874-1939. I. Title.

Costume designers—Biography.

AMERICAN fashion 746.9'2'0922 B
: the life and lines of Adrian, Mainbocher, McCardell, Norell, and Trigere / edited by Sarah Tomerlin Lee for the Fashion Institute of Technology. New York : Quadrangle/New York Times Book Co., [1975] p. cm. Bibliography: p. [TT505.A1A44] 75-8295 ISBN 0-8129-0524-5 : 25.00
1. Costume designers—Biography. I. Lee, Sarah. II. New York. Fashion Institute of Technology.

EPSTEIN, Beryl (Williams) 1910- 746.9'2
Fashion is our business. Freeport, N.Y., Books for Libraries Press [1970, c1945] 204 p. illus., ports. 23 cm. (Essay index reprint series) Contents.Contents.—You are interested in clothes.—Clare Potter.—Emily Wilkens.—Hattie Carnegie.—Claire McCardell.—Norman Norell.—Jo Copeland.—Philip Mangone.—Edith Head.—Louella Ballerino.—Mariska Karasz.—Mabs and Voris. [TT505.A1E6 1970] 72-117787 ISBN 0-8369-1920-3
1. Costume designers—Biography. 2. Fashion. I. Title. BIP

WATKINS, Josephine Jay. 746.9'2'0922 B
Who's who in fashion. [New York] Office of Community Resources, Fashion Institute of Technology [1972] 150 l. 28 cm. [TT505.A1W37] 72-190664
1. Costume designers—Biography. I. Title.

Cottington, Francis Cottington, Baron, 1578?-1652.

HAVRAN, Martin J. 942.06'2'0924 B
Caroline courtier: the life of Lord Cottington [by] Martin J. Havran. With an introd. by A. L. Rowse. Columbia, University of South Carolina Press [1973] xviii, 232 p. illus. 22 cm. Includes bibliographical references. [DA396.C65H38 1973] 73-4510 ISBN 0-87249-284-2 9.95
1. Cottington, Francis Cottington, Baron, 1578?-1652. I. Title. BIP

Cotton, Ella Earls.

COTTON, Ella Earls. 923.773
A spark for my people; the sociological autobiography of a Negro teacher. [1st ed.] New York, Exposition Press [1954] 288p. 21cm. [LA2317.C64A3] 54-7034
I. Title.

Cotton, John, 1585-1652.

NORTON, John, 1606-1663. 285'.8'0924 B
Abel being dead, yet speaketh / by John Norton ; a facsimile reproduction with an introd. by Edward J. Gallagher. Delmar, N.Y. : Scholars' Facsimiles & Reprints, 1978. p. cm. Reprint of the 1658 ed. printed by T. Newcomb for L. Lloyd, London. Includes bibliographical references. [BX7260.C79N6 1978] 78-8184 ISBN 0-8201-1310-7 : 15.00
1. Cotton, John, 1585-1652. 2. Congregational churches—Clergy—Biography. 3. Clergy—Massachusetts—Boston—Biography. 4. Boston—Biography. I. Title. BIP

ZIFF, Larzer, 1927- 922.89
The career of John Cotton: Puritanism and the American experience. Princeton, N.J., Princeton [c.]1962. 280p. 23cm. Bibl. 62-7415 6.00
1. Cotton, John, 1584-1652. I. Title.

Cotton, Mary Ann, 1832-1873.

APPLETON, Arthur. 364.1'523'0924 B
Mary Ann Cotton; her story and trial. London, Joseph [1973] 154 p. illus. 23 cm. Bibliography: p. 147-149. [HV6248.C676A6] 74-174886 ISBN 0-7181-1184-2
1. Cotton, Mary Ann, 1832-1873. 2. Poisoning—Durham, Eng. (County)—Case studies.
Distributed by Transatlantic Arts; 9.50. BIP

Cotton, Norris.

COTTON, Norris. 328.73'092'4 B
In the Senate : amidst the conflict and the turmoil / by Norris Cotton. New York : c1978. 1978. vii, 239 p., [1] leaf of plates : port. ; 23 cm. Includes index. [E748.C867A34] 78-1934 ISBN 0-396-07571-1 : 12.95
1. Cotton, Norris. 2. United States. Congress. Senate—Biography. 3. Legislators—United States—Biography. 4. United States—Politics and government—20th century. I. Title. BIP

Cotton, Robert Bruce, Sir, Bart., 1571-1631.

SHARPE, Kevin. 941.06'1'0924 B
Sir Robert Cotton, 1586-1631 : history and politics in early modern England / by Kevin Sharpe. Oxford ; New York : Oxford University Press, c1979. p. cm. (Oxford historical monographs) Includes index. Bibliography: p. [DA391.1.C67S48] 79-40265 ISBN 0-19-821877-X : 36.00
1. Cotton, Robert Bruce, Sir, Bart., 1571-1631. 2. Great Britain—Politics and government—1558-1603. 3. Great Britain—Politics and government—1603-1649. 4. Great Britain—Intellectual life—17th century. 5. Politicians—Great Britain—Biography. 6. Intellectuals—England—Biography.

Cottrell, Frederick Gardner, 1877-1948.

CAMERON, Frank Thomas, 1909- 925.4
Cottrell, Samaritan of science. Foreword by Ernest O. Lawrence. [1st ed.] Garden City, N. Y., Doubleday, 1952. 414 p. 22 cm. [QD22.C63C3] 52-5532
1. Cottrell, Frederick Gardner, 1877-1948. I. Title.

Cottrell, Roy Franklin, 1878-

EDWARDS, Josephine Cunnington. 266.6'7'30922
Pioneers together; a biography of the Roy F. Cottrells. Nashville, Southern Pub. Association [1967] 238 p. port. 21 cm. [BX6193.C6E3] 67-6137
1. Cottrell, Roy Franklin, 1878- 2. Cottrell, Myrtie Ball. 3. Missions—China. I. Title.

Couch, Darius Nash.

KENNEDY, Edward F. 973.6'2
Lt. Darius Nash Couch in the Mexican War / Edward F. Kennedy, Jr. Taunton, Mass. : Old Colony Historical Society, c1977. 34 p. : ill. ; 23 cm. [E403.1.C74K46] 78-300385
1. Couch, Darius Nash. 2. United States. Army—Biography. 3. United States—History—War with Mexico, 1845-1848. 4. Soldiers—United States—Biography. I. Title.

Coucy, Enguerrand de, 1340-1397.

TUCHMAN, Barbara Wertheim. 944'.025
A distant mirror : the calamitous 14th century / Barbara W. Tuchman. 1st trade ed. New York : Knopf, 1978. xx, 677 p., [20] leaves of plates : ill. ; 25 cm. Includes index. Bibliography: p. [599]-617. [DC97.5.T82 1978] 78-5985 ISBN 0-394-40026-7 : 15.00
1. Coucy, Enguerrand de, 1340-1397. 2. France—History—14th century. 3. France—Nobility—Biography. I. Title.

Couderc, Therese, 1805-1885.

I. Title.

MULLER, Gerald Francis, 1927- 271'.979 B
Diamond in the dust; a story of blessed

Therese Couderc, by Brother Roberto. With front. by Carolyn Lee Jagodits. Notre Dame [Ind.] Dujarie Press [1968] 94 p. port. 22 cm. The life of the nineteenth-century French nun who founded the order called the Religious of the Cenacle which provides places of retreat for women. [BX4705.C7794M8] 92 68-23380
1. Couderc, Therese, 1805-1885—Juvenile literature. I. Title.

ROBERTO, Brother, 1927- 271'.979
Diamond in the dust; a story of blessed Therese Couderc. Frontispiece by Carolyn Lee Jagodits. Notre Dame, Dujarie [1968] 94p. port. 22cm. [BX4705.C7794R6] (B) 68-23380 2.75
1. Couderc, Therese, 1805-1885. I. Title.

SURLES, Eileen. 922.244
Surrender to the Spirit; the life of Mother Therese Couderc, foundress of the Society of Our Lady of the Retreat in the Cenacle, 1805-1885. New York, P. J. Kenedy [1951] xxi, 243 p. port. 21 cm. Bibliography: p. 243. [BX4705.C7794S8] 51-3428
1. Couderc, Therese, Mother, 1805-1885. 2. Religious of Our Lady of the Cenacle. I. Title.

Couffer, Jack.

BEARDWOOD, Valerie. 778.930924
The still hunt; the story of naturalist-wildlife photographer, Jack Couffer. With photos. by Jack Couffer. New York, McKay, 1965. x. 148 p. illus. ports. 21 cm. Bibliography: p. 144. [QH31.C84B4] 65-18876
1. Couffer, Jack. I. Title.

Coulomb, Charles Augustin de, 1736-1806.

GILLMOR, C. Stewart, 1938- 530'.0924 B
Coulomb and the evolution of physics and engineering in eighteenth-century France [by] C. Stewart Gillmor. Princeton, N.J., Princeton University Press, 1971 [i.e. 1972, c1971] xvii, 328 p. illus. 25 cm. Bibliography: p. 297-315. [Q143.C65G55] 79-155006 ISBN 0-691-08095-X 13.50
1. Coulomb, Charles Augustin de, 1736-1806. 2. Physics—History—France. 3. Engineering—History—France. I. Title. BIP

Coulter, Bonna.

WRENN, Marie-Claude Palmieri. 617'.092'4 B
"You're the only one here who doesn't look like a doctor" : portrait of a woman surgeon / Marie-Claude Wrenn. New York : Crowell, c1977. p. cm. Includes index. [R154.C617W7] 77-7871 ISBN 0-690-01420-1 : 8.95
1. Coulter, Bonna. 2. Surgeons—Maryland—Biography. 3. Women surgeons—United States—Biography. I. Title.

Country life—Arizona.

ERNO, Richard B. 917.91'51'03
An ultimate retreat; a family's journey back to nature and self-renewal [by] Richard B. Erno. New York, Crown Publishers [1971] 191 p. illus. 22 cm. Autobiographical. [S521.E75 1971] 71-147343 4.95
1. Country life—Arizona. I. Title.

Country life—Connecticut.

HARWOOD, Michael. 917.46'1'034 B
A country journal [by] Michael Harwood & Mary Durant. Drawings by Marcia Erickson. New York, Dodd, Mead [1974] ix, 245 p. illus. 22 cm. [S521.5.C8H37] 73-11547 ISBN 0-396-06872-3 7.95
1. Country life—Connecticut. I. Durant, Mary B., joint author. II. Title. BIP

Country life—England.

BELL, Adrian, 1901- 942.6'4'082 B
A countryman's notebook / [by] Adrian Bell. Ipswich : Boydell Press, 1975. [5], 122 p. ; 22 cm. (The Suffolk library) [PR6003.E423C6] 76-355667 ISBN 0-85115-050-0 : £2.95. ISBN 0-85115-054-3 pbk.
1. Country life—England. I. Title.

Country life—Maine.

GOULD, Ralph Ernest, 1870- 923.873
Yankee boyhood: my adventures on a Maine farm seventy years ago. Illustrated by Arthur Conrad. [1st ed.] New York, Norton [1950] 251 p. illus. 22 cm. [S521.G68] 50-7255
1. Country life—Maine. I. Title.

Country music—Dictionaries.

SHESTACK, Melvin. 784'.092'2 B
The country music encyclopedia. New York, T. Y. Crowell Co. [1974] xii, 410 p. ports. 26 cm. Discography: p. 325-375. [ML102.C7S5] 74-9644 ISBN 0-690-00442-7 13.95
1. Country music—Dictionaries. 2. Musicians, American. 3. Folk music—United States. I. Title. BIP

Country music—History and criticism.

GRAY, Andy. 784'.092'2
Great country music stars / [by] Andy Gray. London ; New York : Hamlyn, 1975. 176 p. : facsim., ports. (some col.) ; 31 cm. Includes index. Bibliography: p. 174. [ML3545.G645G68] 75-327625 ISBN 0-600-33979-3 : £2.95
1. Country music—History and criticism. 2. Country musicians. I. Title.

Country musicians—Juvenile literature.

KRISHEF, Robert K. 784'.092'2 B
More new breed stars / Robert K. Krishef. Minneapolis : Lerner Publications Co., c1979. p. cm. (Country music library) Includes index. Presents biographies of 10 contemporary country music stars: Mac Davis, Freddy Fender, Crystal Gayle, Kris Kristofferson, Anne Murray, Willie Nelson, Olivia Newton-John, Charley Pride, Linda Ronstadt, and Hank Williams, Jr. [ML3930.A2K7396] 920 79-16937 ISBN 0-8225-1410-9 : 5.95
1. Country musicians—Juvenile literature. I. Title. BIP

Country musicians—United States—Biography.

CHALKER, Bryan. 784'.092'2 B
Country music / [written by Bryan Chalker ; with additional material by others]. London : Phoebus, 1976. 95 p. : ill. (some col.), ports. (some col.) ; 31 cm. Ill. on lining papers. [ML385.C427] 77-353969 ISBN 0-7026-0015-6 : £2.50
1. Country musicians—United States—Biography. I. Title.

DAVIS, Paul. 784'.092'2 B
New life in country music / by Paul Davis ; with foreword by Cliff Richard and introduction by George Hamilton IV ; illustrations by Richard Deverell. Worthing : Walter, 1976. 111 p. : ports. ; 18 cm. [ML394.D38] 77-353970 ISBN 0-85479-591-X : £1.00
1. Country musicians—United States—Biography. 2. Christian biography. I. Title.

DEW, Joan. 784'.092'2 B
Singers & sweethearts : the women of country music / by Joan Dew. 1st ed. Garden City, N.Y. : Dolphin Books, 1977. 148 p., [1] leaf of plates : ill. ; 28 cm. (A Country music magazine press book) [ML394.O495S5] 76-54009 ISBN 0-385-12595-X pbk. : 4.95
1. Country musicians—United States—Biography. 2. Women musicians—Biography. I. Title. II. Series.

HOLLARAN, Carolyn. 784'.092'2 B
Meet the stars of country music / Carolyn Rada Hollaran. Nashville, Tenn. : Aurora Publishers, 1977- v. : ill. ; 28 cm. Biographical sketches of forty-two popular country and western musicans. [ML394.H63] 920 77-22602 pbk. : 3.95
1. Country musicians—United States—Biography. I. Title. BIP

HOLLARAN, Carolyn. 784'.092'2 B
Your favorite country music stars / by Carolyn Hollaran. New York : Popular Library, c1975. 283 p. : ports. ; 18 cm. [ML394.H64] 75-328021 pbk. : 1.50
1. Country musicians—United States—Biography. I. Title. BIP

MALONE, Bill C., comp. 784.0922
The stars of country music : Uncle Dave Macon to Johnny Rodriguez / edited by Bill C. Malone and Judith McCulloh New York : Avon ,1976 c1975 x, 532 p. : ill. ; 18 cm. Includes index Bibliography - Discography: pp. 486-488 [ML385.S73] ISBN 0-380-00867-X pbk. : 2.50
1. Country musicians—United States—Biography. I. McCulloh, Judith, 1935- , joint comp. II. Title.
L.C. card no. for 1975 University of Illinois Press edition: 75-15848.

STARS of country music : Uncle Dave Macon to Johnny Rodriguez / edited by Bill C. Malone and Judith McCulloh. Urbana : University of Illinois Press, [1975] xii, 476 p., [8] leaves of plates : ill. ; 24 cm. (Music in American life) Includes discographies and index. [ML385.S73] 75-15848 ISBN 0-252-00527-9 : 10.00 784'.092'2 B
1. Country musicians—United States—Biography. I. Malone, Bill C. II. McCulloh, Judith, 1935-

Country musicians—United States—Biography—Juvenile literature.

HARRIS, Stacy. 792.7'092'2 B
Comedians of country music / Stacy Harris. Minneapolis : Lerner Publications Co., 1977,c1978. p. cm. (Country music library) Includes index. Biographical sketches of 12 country music comedians including Minnie Pearl, Homer and Jethro, and George Gobel. [ML3930.A2H285] 920 77-90149 ISBN 0-8225-1409-5 lib.bdg. : 4.95
1. Country musicians—United States—Biography—Juvenile literature. 2. Comedians—United States—Biography—Juvenile literature. I. Title. BIP

KRISHEF, Robert K. 784'.092'2 B
The new breed / Robert K. Krishef. Minneapolis : Lerner Publications, Co., c1978. p. cm. (Country music library) Includes index. Biographies of nine contemporary country music stars, including Glen Campbell, John Denver, Emmylou Harris, and Dolly Parton. [ML3930.A2K74] 920 77-90153 ISBN 0-8225-1406-0 : 5.95
1. Country musicians—United States—Biography—Juvenile literature. I. Title. BIP

County life—Maine.

*NEARING, Helen. 917.41
The good life album of Helen & Scott Nearing by Helen Nearing. New York, Dutton 1974 127 p. illus. 26 cm. (A Chatham Book) [CT31] 74-81421 ISBN 0-87690-144-5 5.95 (pbk.)
1. County life—Maine. 2. Maine—Description and travel. I. Title.

Courant, Richard, 1888-1972.

REID, Constance. 510'.92'4 B
Courant in Gottingen and New York : the story of an improbable mathematician / Constance Reid. New York : Springer-Verlag, c1976. 314 p. : ports. ; 25 cm. Includes index. [QA29.C68R44] 76-17062 ISBN 0-387-90194-9 : 12.80
1. Courant, Richard, 1888-1972. 2. Mathematicians—Biography. I. Title.

Courbet, Gustave, 1819-1877.

MACK, Gerstle, 1894- 927.5
Gustave Courbet. [1st ed.] New York, Knopf, 1951. xv, 406, xix p. illus, ports., fold. map. 25 cm. Bibliography: p. 397-406. [ND553.C9M3] 51-11099
1. Courbet, Gustave, I. Title. BIP

MACK, Gerstle, 1894- 927.5
Gustave Courbet. [1st ed.] New York, Knopf, 1951. xv, 406, xix p. illus, ports., fold. map. 25 cm. Bibliography: p. 397-406. [ND553.C9M3] 51-11099
1. Courbet, Gustave, I. Title. BIP

MACK, Gerstle, 1894- 759.4 B
Gustave Courbet. Westport, Conn., Greenwood Press [1970, c1951] xv, 406, xix p. illus., map, ports. 23 cm. Bibliography: p. 397-406. [ND553.C9M3 1970] 73-110833 ISBN 0-8371-2588-X
1. Courbet, Gustave, 1819-1877.

Court, Margaret Smith, 1942-

COURT, Margaret Smith, 1942- 796.34'2'0924 B
Court on Court, a life in tennis / by Margaret Smith Court, with George McGann. New York : Dodd, Mead, [1975] xii, 211 p., [4] leaves of plates : ill. ; 22 cm. [GV994.C68A33] 75-17650 ISBN 0-396-07210-0 : 8.95
1. Court, Margaret Smith, 1942- 2. Tennis. I. McGann, George. II. Title.

Courtenay, William, Abp. of Canterbury, 1342?-1396.

DAHMUS, Joseph Henry, 1909- 262.120924
William Courtenay: Archbishop of Canterbury, 1381-1396, by Joseph Dahmus. University Park, Pennsylvania State University Press, 1966. 341 p. 24 cm. Bibliography: p. [327]-334. [BR754.C66D33] 66-18194
1. Courtenay, William, Abp. of Canterbury, 1342?-1396.

Courts and courtiers.

GOOCH, George Peabody, 1873-1968. 940
Courts and cabinets. Freeport, N.Y., Books for Libraries Press [1972, c1946] p. (Essay index reprint series) Studies of the memoirs of thirteen English, French and German writers, with quotations from their works. Seven of the studies are reprinted from Contemporary review. Includes bibliographical references. [D107.G6 1972] 72-3304 ISBN 0-8369-2901-2
1. Courts and courtiers. 2. Europe—Kings and rulers. I. Title. BIP

Courvoisie, Thomas Nugent, 1916-

CONROY, Pat. 355'.0071'1757915 B
The Boo. Verona, Va., McClure Press [1970] 174 p. illus., ports. 24 cm. [U430.C5C65] 78-142965 4.50
1. Courvoisie, Thomas Nugent, 1916- 2. The Citadel, the Military College of South Carolina, Charleston.

Cousin, Victor, 1792-1867.

BREWER, Walter Vance. 370.19'5'0924
Victor Cousin as a comparative educator. [New York] Teachers College Press [1971] xiv, 167 p. 19 cm. (Columbia University. Teachers College. Comparative education studies) A revision of the author's thesis, Columbia University. Bibliography: p. 139-149. [LA128.B73 1971] 75-148593
1. Cousin, Victor, 1792-1867. 2. Comparative education. I. Title. II. Series. BIP

Cousins, Norman.

COUSINS, Norman. 362.1'9'67709 B
Anatomy of an illness as perceived by the patient : reflections on healing and regeneration / by Norman Cousins ; introd. by Rene Dubos. New York : Norton, [1979] p. cm. [RC924.C65] 79-10597 ISBN 0-393-01252-2 : 9.95
1. Cousins, Norman. 2. Collagen diseases—Biography. 3. Mind and body. 4. Will. 5. Medicine—Philosophy. 6. Authors, American—Biography. I. Title.

Cousteau, Jacques Yves—Juvenile literature.

EDUCATIONAL Research 551.4'6'0924 Council of America. Social Science Staff. *Explorers and discoverers: Cousteau.* Boston, Allyn and Bacon [1970] 48 p. illus. (part col.), ports. 21 cm. (Concepts and inquiry: the ERC social science program) A simple account of the life and work of the French pioneer in underwater exploration. [PZ10.E25Ex] 92 71-97106 1.32
1. Cousteau, Jacques Yves—Juvenile literature. 2. Underwater exploration—Juvenile literature. I. Title. II. Series: Concepts and inquiry: the Educational Research Council social science program

EDUCATIONAL Research 551.4'6'0924 Council of America. Social Science Staff. *Explorers and discoverers, Cousteau* / prepared by the Social Science Staff of the Educational Research Council of America. Learner-verified ed. 2. Boston : Allyn and Bacon, [1974] 51 p. : ill. ; 20 x 21 cm. (Concepts and inquiry, the ERC social science program) A simple account of the work of the French pioneer in underwater exploration. [GC380.C68E38 1974] 92 73-78337 pbk. : 1.75
1. Cousteau, Jacques Yves—Juvenile literature. 2. Underwater exploration—Juvenile literature. I. Title. II. Series: Concepts and inquiry: the Educational Research Council social science program.

IVERSON, Genie. 551.4'6'00924 B *Jacques Cousteau* / by Genie Iverson ; ill. by Hal Ashmead. New York : Putnam, c1976. 62 p. : ill. ; 23 cm. A biography of Jacques-Yves Cousteau, French oceanographer, author, and motion-picture producer, emphasizing the development of the aqualung and his achievements in exploring the world under the sea. [GC30.C68I83 1976] 92 75-25822 ISBN 0-399-60987-3 lib.bdg. : 3.96
1. Cousteau, Jacques Yves—Juvenile literature. I. Ashmead, Hal. **BIP**

Cousy, Robert, 1928-

COUSY, Robert, 1928- 927.96357 *Basketball is my life,* as told to Al Hirshberg. Rev. ed. New York, J.L. Pratt [c.1957-1963] 186p. 18cm. (Amer. lib., 109) 63-21861 .50 pap.,
1. Basketball—Hist. I. Hirshberg, Albert. 1909- II. Title.

DEVANEY, John. 796.323 *Bob Cousy.* New York, Putnam [1965] 191 p. port. 22 cm. [GV885.D49] 65-10866
1. Cousy, Robert, 1928- **BIP**

Coute, Manny.

CORCORAN, Janet. 362.1'9'699436 *Conversation with a dying friend* : a tape-script interview with Manny Coute / by Janet Corcoran ; with introd. and closing remarks by Lucille M. Coute. Downey, Calif. : L. M. Coute, c1977. 38 p. ; 22 cm. [RC280.L5C67] 76-51119 ISBN 0-914664-03-4 : 1.95
1. Coute, Manny. 2. Liver—Cancer—Biography. I. Coute, Manny. II. Title.

Couturier, Paul, 1881-1953.

CURTIS, Geoffrey William 922.244 Seymour. *Paul Couturier and unity in Christ* [by] Geoffrey Curtis. Westminster, Md., J. W. Eckenrode [1964] 366 p. illus., port. 23 cm. Bibliographical footnotes. [BX6.8.C6C8] 64-56991
1. Couturier, Paul, 1881-1953. 2. Christian union — Catholic Church. 3. Week of Prayer for Christian Unity. I. Title.

Couzens, James, 1872-1936.

BARNARD, Harry, 1906- 923.273 *Independent man;* the life of Senator James Couzens. New York, Scribner [1958] 376p. illus. 24cm. Includes bibliography. [E748.C87B3] 58-7518
1. Couzens, James, 1872-1936. I. Title.

Covelli, Pat.

COVELLI, Pat. 362.1'9'646209 B *Borrowing time* : growing up with juvenile diabetes / Pat Covelli. 1st ed. New York : Crowell, c1979. 160 p. ; 22 cm. [RJ420.D5C69 1979] 79-7083 ISBN 0-690-01841-X : 8.95
1. Covelli, Pat. 2. Diabetes in children—Biography. 3. Diabetes—Biography. I. Title. **BIP**

Covello, Leonard.

PEEBLES, Robert 373.1'2'0120924 B Whitney. *Leonard Covello* : a study of an immigrant's contribution to New York City / Robert Whitney Peebles. New York : Arno Press, 1978, c1968. p. cm. (Bilingual-bicultural education in the United States) Thesis—New York University, 1967. Bibliography: p. [LA2317.C66P43] 77-90551 ISBN 0-405-11090-1 : 28.00
1. Covello, Leonard. 2. Teachers—New York (City)—Biography. I. Title. II. Series. **BIP**

Coventry, Eng.—Biography.

COVENTRY Information 920'.0424'98 Centre. *Coventry's famous people* / Coventry Information Centre. Coventry : C.I., [1975] [2], 24 p. ; 30 cm. [DA690.C75C595 1975] 76-351585 ISBN 0-904529-04-5 : £0.30
1. Coventry, Eng.—Biography. I. Title.

Coverts, Catholic.

GRAEF, Hilda C 922.242 *From fashions to the Fathers;* the story of my life. Westminster, Md., Newman Press, 1957. 329p. illus. 23cm. [BX4668.G64] 57-10749
1. Coverts, Catholic. I. Title.

Covey, Earl William, 1876-1952.

COVEY, Frances Alden 926 *The Earl Covey story,* a biography. New York, Expostiion [c.1964] 164p. illus., ports. 22cm. 64-6595 5.00
1. Covey, Earl William, 1876-1952. I. Title.

Covington, Ga.—Historic houses, etc.

WILLIFORD, William 917.58'593 Bailey. *The glory of Covington.* Atlanta, Cherokee Pub. Co., 1973. xiii, 320 p. illus. 24 cm. Bibliography: p. 295-299. [F294.C76W54] 72-96820 ISBN 0-87797-024-6 10.00
1. Covington, Ga.—Historic houses, etc. 2. Covington, Ga.—Biography. I. Title.

Coward, Noel Pierce, Sir, 1899-1973.

BRAYBROOKE, Patrick, 792'.092'4 B 1894- *The amazing Mr. Noel Coward.* [Folcroft, Pa.] Folcroft Library Editions, 1974. xv, 168 p. ports. 24 cm. Reprint of the 1933 ed. published by D. Archer, London. [PR6005.O85Z6 1974] 73-13664 ISBN 0-8414-3250-3 (lib. bdg.)
1. Coward, Noel Pierce, Sir, 1899-1973. I. Title.

BRAYBROOKE, 792'.028'0924 B Patrick, 1894- *The amazing Mr. Noel Coward* / by Patrick Braybrooke. Norwood, Pa. : Norwood Editions, 1975. xv, 168 p., [8] leaves of plates : ill. ; 23 cm. Reprint of the 1933 ed. published by D. Archer, London. Includes index. [PR6005.O85Z6 1975] 75-41478 ISBN 0-88305-964-9 lib. bdg. : 20.00
1. Coward, Noel Pierce, 1899-1973—Biography. I. Title.

COWARD, Noel Pierce, Sir, 928.2 1899-1973. *Future indefinite.* [1st American ed.] Garden City, N.Y. Doubleday, 1954. 352 p. illus. 22 cm. Autobiographical. [PR6005.O85Z52 1954a] 54-7666
I. Title.

COWARD, Noel Pierce, 792'.092'4 Sir, 1899-1973. *A last encore.* Words by Noel Coward. Pictures from his life and times. Edited by John Hadfield. [1st American ed.] Boston, Little, Brown [1973] 144 p. illus. 29 cm. [PR6005.O85L3 1973] 73-10352 12.95
I. Title.

MARCHANT, 792'.028'0924 B William, 1923- *The privilege of his company* : Noel Coward remembered / by William Marchant. Indianapolis : Bobbs-Merrill, c1975. 276 p., [4] leaves of plates : ill. ; 21 cm. [PR6005.O85Z72] 73-22683 ISBN 0-672-51973-9 : 10.00
1. Coward, Noel Pierce, Sir, 1899-1973. 2. Marchant, William, 1923- —Friends and associates. I. Title.

MORLEY, Sheridan, 792'.028'0924 B 1941- *A talent to amuse;* a biography of Noel Coward. [1st ed. in the U.S.] Garden City, N.Y., Doubleday, 1969. 453 p. illus., ports. 25 cm. Bibliography: p. [434]-437. [PR6005.O85Z74 1969] 70-78736 8.95
1. Coward, Noel Pierce, 1899-1973—Biography. I. Title.

Coward, Noel Pierce, Sir, 1899-1973—Biography.

BRAYBROOKE, 792'.028'0924 B Patrick, 1894- *The amazing Mr. Noel Coward* / by Patrick Braybrooke. Norwood, Pa. : Norwood Editions, 1975. xv, 168 p., [8] leaves of plates : ill. ; 23 cm. Reprint of the 1933 ed. published by D. Archer, London. Includes index. [PR6005.O85Z6 1975] 75-41478 ISBN 0-88305-964-9 lib. bdg. : 20.00
1. Coward, Noel Pierce, 1899-1973—Biography. I. Title.

CASTLE, Charles, 792'.092'4 B 1939- *Noel.* [1st ed. in the U.S.A.] Garden City, N.Y., Doubleday, 1973 [c1972] 272 p. illus. 27 cm. [PR6005.O85Z62 1973] 72-89296 ISBN 0-385-00422-2 12.95
1. Coward, Noel Pierce, Sir, 1899-1973—Biography. I. Title.

LESLEY, Cole. 792'.028'0924 B *The life of Noel Coward* / Cole Lesley. London : J. Cape, 1976. xx, 499 p., [24] leaves of plates : ill. ; 24 cm. Includes index. Bibliography: p. [483]-485. [PR6005.O85Z67] 76-383447 ISBN 0-224-01288-6 : £7.50
1. Coward, Noel Pierce, Sir, 1899-1973—Biography. 2. Dramatists, English—20th century—Biography. I. Title. **BIP**

LESLEY, Cole. 792'.028'0924 B *Noel Coward and his friends* / Cole Lesley, Graham Payn & Sheridan Morley ; designed by Craig Dodd. New York : Morrow, 1979. 216 p. : ill. ; 29 cm. [PR6005.O85Z673 1979] 79-88008 ISBN 0-688-03510-8 : 20.00
1. Coward, Noel Pierce, Sir, 1899-1973—Biography. 2. Coward, Noel Pierce, Sir, 1899-1973—Archives. 3. Dramatists, English—20th century—Biography. 4. Entertainers—Great Britain—Biography. I. Payn, Graham, joint author. II. Morley, Sheridan, 1941- joint author. III. Title. **BIP**

MORLEY, Sheridan, 792'.028'0924 B 1941- *A talent to amuse;* a biography of Noel Coward. [1st ed. in the U.S.] Garden City, N.Y., Doubleday, 1969. 453 p. illus., ports. 25 cm. Bibliography: p. [434]-437. [PR6005.O85Z74 1969] 70-78736 8.95
1. Coward, Noel Pierce, 1899-1973—Biography. I. Title.

Coward, Noel Pierce, Sir, 1899-1973—Criticism and interpretation.

MORSE, Clarence Ralph. 792'.092'4 *Mad dogs and Englishmen:* a study of Noel Coward. Emporia, School of Graduate and Professional Studies, Kansas State Teachers College, 1973. 52 p. 23 cm. (The Emporia State research studies, v. 21, no. 4) A revision of the author's thesis (M.S.), Kansas State Teachers College, 1954. Bibliography: p. 48-50. [PR6005.O85Z76 1973] 73-622977
1. Coward, Noel Pierce, Sir, 1899-1973—Criticism and interpretation. I. Title. II. Series.

Cowboys.

*ADAMS, Andy. 923.873 *The log of a cowboy.* [New York] Leisure Books [1976] 238 p. 18 cm. [F596] 1.25 (pbk.)
1. Cowboys. 2. West—Biography. I. Title. **BIP**

JONES, Mat 338.17620924 (B) Ennis, 1875-1957. *Fiddlefooted.* With the assistance of Morice E. Jones. Denver, Sage Books [1966] 304 p. illus., maps, ports. 23 cm. Autobiography. [F596.J59] 65-16516
1. Cowboys. 2. Ranch life—The West. I. Title.

KENNON, Bob, 1876- 917.8 *From the Pecos to the Powder;* a cowboy's autobiography, as told to Ramon F. Adams by Bob Kennon. With drawings by Joe Beeler. [1st ed.] Norman, University of Oklahoma Press [1965] xi, 251 p. illus., map. 23 cm. [F596.K4] 65-10113
1. Cowboys. 2. Ranch life—Montana. I. Adams, Ramon Frederick, 1889- II. Title.

LEMMON, Ed, 1857- 917.8'03'20924 1946 *Boss Cowman* the recollections of Ed Lemmon, 1857-1946. Edited by Nellie Snyder Yost. Lincoln University of Nebraska Press [1974, c1969] xii, 321 p. illus. 21 cm. (Pioneer Heritage Series, Vol. 6) Includes bibliographic references. [F596.L5] [[B]] ISBN 0-8032-5810-0 3.50 (pbk.)
1. Cowboys. 2. Cattle trade—The West. I. Yost, Nellie (Snyder) ed. II. Title. III. Series.
L.C. card number for original ed.: 69-10313. **BIP**

SCHMEDDING, Joseph, 1887- 917.89 *Cowboy and Indian trader.* Caldwell, Idaho, Caxton Printers, 1951. 364 p. illus., ports., map (on lining papers) 24 cm. Autobiographical. [F595.S33] 51-9436
1. Cowboys. 2. The West—History. I. Title. **BIP**

Cowboys in art.

PHIPPEN, George. 709'.24 *The life of a cowboy,* told through the drawings, paintings, and bronzes of George Phippen, as selected by Louise Phippen. Tucson, University of Arizona Press [1969] 104 p. illus. (part col.), port. 24 x 32 cm. [N6537.P45A49] 70-101102 ISBN 8-16-502056- 15.00
1. Cowboys in art. I. Phippen, Louise, comp. II. Title. **BIP**

Cowboys—Nebraska—Biography.

WADDILL, Olin, 978.2'00992 B 1897- *Saddle strings* / by Olin Waddill ; [edited by Wyonia Wagner]. [Gordon? Neb.] : Tri State Old Time Cowboys Memorial Museum, 1976, c1975. x, 156 p. : ill. ; 29 cm. [F665.W32 1976] 76-378084
1. Cowboys—Nebraska—Biography. 2. Nebraska—Biography. I. Tri State Old Time Cowboys Memorial Museum. II. Title.

Cowboys—The West.

LEMMON, Ed, 917.8'03'20924 B 1857-1946. *Boss cowman;* the recollections of Ed Lemmon, 1857-1946. Edited by Nellie Snyder Yost. Lincoln, University of Nebraska Press, 1969. xii, 321 p. illus., maps. 25 cm. (The Pioneer heritage series, v. 6) Bibliographical footnotes. [F596.L5] 69-10313 6.95
1. Cowboys—The West. 2. Cattle trade—The West. I. Yost, Nellie Irene (Snyder), ed. II. Title. III. Series.

Cowboys—The West—Biography—Juvenile literature.

KEATING, Bern. 978'.02'0922 B
Famous American cowboys / by Bern Keating ; line drawings by Lorence Bjorklund. Chicago : Rand McNally, c1977. 92 p. : ill. (some col.) ; 29 cm. Includes index. Biographical sketches of nine cowboys including the cowboy showman, Will Rogers, Richard King, the cattle baron, and Fredric Remington, an artist whose drawings portrayed cowboy life. [F596.K37] 920 77-5329 ISBN 0-528-82250-0 : 5.95 ISBN 0-528-80250-X lib.bdg. : 5.97
1. Cowboys—The West—Biography—Juvenile literature. 2. The West—Biography—Juvenile literature. I. Bjorklund, Lorence F. II. Title. BIP

Cowdery, Oliver.

GUNN, Stanley R. 922.8373
Oliver Cowdery, second elder and scribe. Salt Lake City, Bookcraft [1962] 281p. illus. 24cm. 62-4975 3.50
1. Cowdery, Oliver. I. Title.

Cowdray, Weetman Dickinson Pearson, 1st viscount, 1856-1927.

MIDDLEMAS, Robert Keith, 926.2
1935-
The master builders: Thomas Brassey, Sir John Aird, Lord Cowdray, London, Hutchinson [dist. Chester Springs, Pa., Dufour, 1964, c.1963] 328p. illus., maps, ports. 22cm. Bibl. [TA139.M5] 65-439 6.95
1. Brassey, Thomas, 1805-1870. 2. Aird, Sir John, bart., 1833-1911. 3. Cowdray, Weetman Dickinson Pearson, 1st viscount, 1856-1927. 4. Norton-Griffiths, Sir John, bart., 1871-1930. I. Title.

SPENDER, John 624'.092'4 B
Alfred, 1862-1942.
Weetman Pearson, First Viscount Cowdray, 1856-1927 / J. A. Spender. New York : Arno Press, 1977. p. cm. (European business) Reprint of the 1930 ed. published by Cassell, London. [TA140.C67S6 1977] 76-40616 ISBN 0-405-09801-4 lib. bdg. : 21.00
1. Cowdray, Weetman Dickinson Pearson, 1st viscount, 1856-1927. 2. Engineers—Biography. I. Title. II. Series. BIP

Cowen, Evelyn—Biography—Youth.

COWAN, Evelyn. 823'.9'14 B
Spring remembered : a Scottish Jewish childhood / Evelyn Cowan. New York : Taplinger Pub. Co., 1978, c1974. 160 p. ; 21 cm. [PR6053.O943Z473 1978] 78-66450 ISBN 0-8008-7367-X : 8.50
1. Cowen, Evelyn—Biography—Youth. 2. Jews in Glasgow—Biography. 3. Authors, Scottish—20th century—Biography. 4. Glasgow—Biography. I. Title. BIP

Cowens, Dave, 1948- —Juvenile literature.

ARMSTRONG, 796.32'3'0924 B
Robert, 1938-
Dave Cowens / by Robert Armstrong ; photos. by Bruce Curtis. Mankato, Minn. : Creative Education ; Chicago : distributed by Children Press, c1978. 31 p. : ill. ; 25 cm. (Creative Education sports superstars) A biography of the star center of the Boston Celtics who earned the Rookie of the Year award for the 1970-71 season. [GV884.C7A75] 92 77-25147 ISBN 0-87191-668-1 lib.bdg. : 4.95
1. Cowens, Dave, 1948- —Juvenile literature. 2. Boston Celtics (Basketball team)—Juvenile literature. 3. Basketball players—United States—Biography—Juvenile literature. I. Curtis, Bruce. II. Title. BIP

SULLIVAN, George, 796.32'3'0924 B
1927-
Dave Cowens : a biography / by George Sullivan. 1st ed. Garden City, N.Y. : Doubleday, c1977. vi, 152 p. : ill. ; 22 cm. Includes index. A biography of the basketball center whose speed has helped place his team in several play-off games. [GV884.C7S93] 92 76-50795 ISBN 0-385-11523-7 : 5.95.
1. Cowens, Dave, 1948- —Juvenile literature. 2. Basketball players—United States—Biography—Juvenile literature. I. Title. BIP

Cowherd, Barney, 1922-1972.

COWHERD, Barney, 1922- 779'.092'4
1972.
Barney Cowherd, photographer. By Bill Strode. [Louisville, Ky.] The Courier-Journal [1973] 152 p. illus. 23 x 27 cm. Bibliography: p. 151. [TR654.C68] 73-89551 4.95
1. Cowherd, Barney, 1922-1972. 2. Photography, Artistic. I. Strode, Bill.
Publisher's address: 525 W Broadway, Louisville, Kentucky 40202.

Cowles, Anna (Roosevelt) 1855-1931.

RIXEY, Lilian 920.7
Bamie; Theodore Roosevelt's remarkable sister. New York, McKay [c.1963] xi, 308p. ports. 21cm. Bibl. 63-19339 5.95
1. Cowles, Anna (Roosevelt) 1855-1931. 2. Roosevelt Theodore, Pres. U. S., 1858-1919. I. Title.

RIXEY, Lillian. 920.7
Bamie; Theodore Roosevelt's remarkable sister. New York, D. McKay Co. [1963] xi, 308 p. ports. 21 cm. Bibliography: p. 295-300. [E757.3.R56] 63-19339
1. Cowles, Anna (Roosevelt) 1855-1961. 2. Roosevelt, Theodore, Pres. U.S., 1858-1919. I. Title.

Cowles, Fleur.

COWLES, Fleur. 909.82 B
Friends & memories / Fleur Cowles. New York : Reynal, 1978, c1975. 311 p. : ill. ; 24 cm. Includes index. [CT275.C8553A34 1978] 77-83826 ISBN 0-688-61200-8 : 10.00
1. Cowles, Fleur. 2. United States—Biography. 3. England—Biography. I. Title. BIP

Cowles, Raymond Bridgman, 1896-1975.

COWLES, Raymond 574.5'265
Bridgman, 1896-1975.
Desert journal : a naturalist reflects on arid California / by Raymond B. Cowles, in collaboration with Elna S. Bakker ; foreword by Robert C. Stebbins ; ill. by Gerhard Bakker ; photos. by Raymond B. Cowles and Roy Pence. Berkeley : University of California Press, c1977. xv, 263 p. : ill. ; 23 cm. Includes index [QH105.C2C67 1977] 74-22959 ISBN 0-520-02879-1 : 10.95
1. Cowles, Raymond Bridgman, 1896-1975. 2. Desert biology—California. 3. Biologists—California—Biography. I. Bakker, Elna S., joint author. II. Title. BIP

Cowley, Abraham, 1618-1667.

NETHERCOT, Arthur Hobart, 821'.4
1895-
Abraham Cowley, the muse's Hannibal, by Arthur H. Nethercot. New York, Russell & Russell [1967] vii, 367 p. illus., ports. 22 cm. "First published in 1931, reissued, 1967, with additional notes." Bibliography: p. [332]-345. [PR3373.N4 1967] 66-24739
1. Cowley, Abraham, 1618-1667. BIP

Cowley, Malcolm, 1898- —Biography—Youth.

COWLEY, Malcolm, 1898- 810'.9'005
And I worked at the writer's trade : chapters of literary history, 1918-1978 / Malcolm Cowley. New York : Viking Press, c1978. xi, 276 p. ; 23 cm. Includes index. [PS221.C646] 77-28713 ISBN 0-670-12291-2 : 12.50
1. American literature—20th century—History and criticism—Addresses, essays, lectures. 2. Authors, American—20th century—Biography—Addresses, essays, lectures. I. Title. BIP

COWLEY, Malcolm, 1898- 810'.9'005
And I worked at the writer's trade : chapters of literary history, 1918-1978 / Malcolm Cowley. New York : Penguin Books, 1979, c1978. xi, 276 p. ; 20 cm. Includes index. [PS221.C646 1979] 78-24122 ISBN 0-14-005075-2 pbk. : 2.95
1. American literature—20th century—History and criticism—Addresses, essays, lectures. 2. Authors, American—20th century—Biography—Addresses, essays, lectures. I. Title.

COWLEY, Malcolm, 1898- 811'.5'2 B
Exile's return : a literary odyssey of the 1920s / by Malcolm Cowley. New York : Penguin Books, [1976] p. cm. Reprint of the 1969 ed. published by the Viking Press, New York, which was issued as no. C4 of A Viking compass book. Includes index. [PS129.C6 1976] 76-26484 ISBN 0-670-30125-6 : 4.00 ISBN 0-670-00004-3 pbk. : 2.75
1. Cowley, Malcolm, 1898- —Biography—Youth. 2. Authors, American—20th century—Biography. 3. American literature—20th century—History and criticism. I. Title. BIP

Cowley, Matthew,

SMITH, Henry Allen, 922.8373
1907-
Matthew Cowley, man of faith. Salt Lake City, Bookcraft [1956, c1954] 302 p. illus. 23 cm. [BX8695.C6S57] 58-48851
1. Cowley, Matthew, I. Title.

Cowling, Donald John, 1880-1965.

GREENLEAF, Robert 378.1'12'0924 B
K.
Life style of greatness, by Robert K. Greenleaf. Northfield, Minn., Carleton College, 1966. 32 p. port. 23 cm. [LD791.C817 1909] 73-155894
1. Cowling, Donald John, 1880-1965. I. Title.

Cowman, Lettle (Burd) 1870-1900.

PEARSON, Benjamin Harold, 922
1893-
The vision lives; a profile of Mrs. Charles E. Cowman. Los Angeles, Cowman Publications [1961] 341p. 22cm. [BV3705.C63P4] 61-17434
1. Cowman, Lettle (Burd) 1870-1900. I. Title.

Cowper, Charles, Sir, 1807-1875.

POWELL, Alan Walter, 994.03'0924
1936-
Patrician democrat : the political life of Charles Cowper, 1843-1870 / [by] Alan Powell. Carlton, Vic. : Melbourne University Press, 1977. viii, 192 p., [1] leaf of plates : port. ; 22 cm. Includes index. Bibliography: p. 178-187. [DU272.C66P68] 78-305228 ISBN 0-522-84132-5 : 17.00
1. Cowper, Charles, Sir, 1807-1875. 2. New South Wales—Politics and government. 3. Statesmen—New South Wales—Biography. I. Title.
Distributed by ISBS, Forest Groove, Or. BIP

Cowper, Spencer,

COWPER, Spencer, 1713- 922.342
1774.
Letters. Edited by Edward Hughes. Durham, Published for the Society by Andrews, 1956. xv, 224p. port. 23cm. (The Publications of the Surtees Society, v.165) [DA20.S9 vol.165] 56-14492
I. Title. II. Series: Surtees Society, Durham, Eng. Publications, v. 165

Cowper, William, 1731-1800.

COWPER, William, 1731- 821'.6
1800.
The correspondence of William Cowper, arranged in chronological order, with annotations by Thomas Wright. London, Hodder and Stoughton, 1904. St. Clair Shores, Mich., Scholarly Press [1969?] 4 v. maps. 22 cm. [PR3383.A3W7 1969b] 79-107170
I. Wright, Thomas, 1859-1936, ed. II. Title.

COWPER, William, 1731- 821'.6 B
1800.
The correspondence of William Cowper, arranged in chronological order, with annotations, by Thomas Wright. New York, AMS Press [1968] 4 v. illus. 23 cm. Reprint of the 1904 ed. [PR3383.A3W7 1968] 68-58329
I. Title.

COWPER, William, 1731- 826'.6
1800.
The correspondence of William Cowper arranged in chronological order, with annotations by Thomas Wright. New York, Haskell House Publishers, 1969. 4 v. maps. 23 cm. Reprint of the 1904 ed. Bibliographical footnotes. [PR3383.A3W7 1969] 68-24904
I. Wright, Thomas, 1859-1936, ed. II. Title.

COWPER, William, 1731- 821'.6
1800.
Letters of William Cowper, chosen and edited with a memoir and a few notes by J. G. Frazer. Freeport, N.Y., Books for Libraries Press [1969] 2 v. 23 cm. (Select bibliographies reprint series) Reprint of the 1912 ed. [PR3383.A3F7 1969] 70-103647
I. Frazer, James George, Sir, 1854-1941, ed. BIP

COWPER, William, 1731-1800. 928.2
Selected letters; edited, with an introd., by Mark Van Doren. New York, Farrar, Straus and Young [1951] xiv, 306 p. 22 cm. (Great letter series) Bibliography: p. xiii-xiv. [PR3383.A3V3] 51-12906

FAUSSET, Hugh I'Anson, 821'.6 B
1895-
William Cowper. New York, Russell & Russell [1968] 319 p. illus., ports. 21 cm. Reprint of the 1928 ed. [PR3383.F3 1968] 68-11325
1. Cowper, William, 1731-1800.

FREE, William N., 1933- 821'.6 B
William Cowper, by William N. Free. New York, Twayne Publishers [1970] 216 p. 21 cm. (Twayne's English authors series 101) Bibliography: p. 203-209. [PR3383.F7] 70-99531
1. Cowper, William, 1731-1800.

HUANG, Ts'ui-en. 821.65
William Cowper; nature poet, by Roderick Huang. London, Published on behalf of the University of Malaya by the Oxford University Press, 1957. 150p. illus. 19cm. [PR3384.H8] 57-59300
1. Cowper, William, 1731-1800. I. Title.

NICHOLSON, Norman, 1914- 821'.6
William Cowper / Norman Nicholson. St. Clair Shores, Mich. : Scholarly Press 1976. p. cm. Reprint of the 1951 ed. published by J. Lehman, London. Bibliography: p. [PR3383.N5 1976] 75-45165 ISBN 0-403-03152-4
1. Cowper, William, 1731-1800.

QUINLAN, Maurice James, 928.2
1904-
William Cowper, a critical life. Minneapolis, University of Minnesota Press [c1953] xiii, 251p. illus.,port. 23cm. Bibliographical references included in 'Notes' (p. 235-241) [PR3383.Q5] 52-12061
1. Cowper, William, 1731-1800. I. Title. BIP

QUINLAN, Maurice James, 821'.6 B
1904-
William Cowper; a critical life, by Maurice J. Quinlan. Westport, Conn., Greenwood Press [1970, c1953] xiii, 251 p. illus., port. 23 cm. Includes bibliographical references. [PR3383.Q5 1970] 79-106670 ISBN 8-371-34250-
1. Cowper, William, 1731-1800.

ROY, James Alexander, 821'.6
1884-
Cowper & his poetry, by James A. Roy. London, G. G. Harrap, 1914. [New York, AMS Press, 1972] 181, [1] p. port. 19 cm. (Poetry and life series) Bibliography: p. 181-[182] [PR3383.R7 1972] 76-120982 ISBN 0-404-52530-X
1. Cowper, William, 1731-1800. I. Title. II. Series. BIP

ROY, James Alexander, 1884- 821'.6
Cowper & his poetry / by James A. Roy. Folcroft, Pa. : Folcroft Library Editions, 1976. p. cm. Reprint of the 1914 ed. published by Harrap, which was issued as no. 24 of Poetry & life series. Bibliography: p. [PR3383.R7 1976] 76-40146 ISBN 0-8414-7340-4 lib. bdg. : 7.50
1. Cowper, William, 1731-1800. 2. Poets, English—18th century—Biography. I. Cowper, William, 1731-1800. Poems. 1976. II. Title. III. Series: Poetry and life series ; 24.

SMITH, Goldwin, 1823-1910. 821'.6 B
Cowper. New York, AMS Press [1968] 131 p. 22 cm. (English men of letters) [PR3383.S5 1968] 68-58396
1. Cowper, William, 1731-1800. BIP

WRIGHT, Thomas, 1859-1936. 821'.6 B
The life of William Cowper. New York, Haskell House [1971?] 681 p. illus., geneal. table, map, ports. 23 cm. Reprint of the 1892 ed. [PR3383.W7 1971] 77-153641 ISBN 0-8383-1251-9
1. Cowper, William, 1731-1800.

WRIGHT, Thomas, 1859-1936. 821'.6 B
The life of William Cowper. [Folcroft, Pa.] Folcroft Library Editions, 1973. 681 p. illus. 22 cm. Reprint of the 1892 ed. published by T. F. Unwin, London. [PR3383.W7 1973] 73-18309
1. Cowper, William, 1731-1800. I. Title. BIP

WRIGHT, Thomas, 1859-1936. 821'.6 B
The life of William Cowper. [Folcroft, Pa.] Folcroft Library Editions, 1973. 681 p. illus. 22 cm. Reprint of the 1892 ed. published by T. F. Unwin, London. [PR3383.W7 1973] 73-18309 ISBN 0-8414-9505-X (lib. bdg.)
1. Cowper, William, 1731-1800. I. Title.

Cowper, William, 1731-1800—Biography.

CECIL, David, Lord, 1902- 821'.6 B
The stricken deer; or, The life of Cowper. St. Clair Shores, Mich., Scholarly Press [1974, c1930] p. cm. Reprint of the ed. published by Bobbs-Merrill, Indianapolis. [PR3383.C35 1974] 74-3128 ISBN 0-403-03063-3
1. Cowper, William, 1731-1800—Biography. I. Title.

MEMES, John Smythe. 821'.6 B
The life of William Cowper. Port Washington, N.Y., Kennikat Press [1972] 269 p. illus. 21 cm. Reprint of the 1837 ed. Includes bibliographical references. [PR3383.M4 1972] 76-160771 ISBN 0-8046-1602-7
1. Cowper, William, 1731-1800—Biography. I. Title. BIP

Cox family.

MORELL, Louise Cox. 929'.2'0973
Jamestown to Washington; little biographies of twelve generations from Beheathland to Cox, 1607-1950. Baltimore, Gateway Press, 1974. v, 76 p. 22 cm. Bibliography: p. 75-76. [CS71.C877 1974] 73-93853 6.50 (pbk.)
1. Cox family. I. Title.

MORELL, Louise Cox. 929.2'0973
Jamestown to Washington: some biographies in a family line, 1607-1950 (Cox and related families) [n.p., 1970] 1 v. (various pagings) 28 cm. Includes bibliographical references. [CS71.C877 1970] 70-278731
1. Cox family. I. Title.

Cox, Lynne—Juvenile literature.

LIBMAN, Gary. 797.2'1'0924 B
An interview with Lynne Cox / by Gary Libman ; photographs by Dave Cox. Mankato, Minn. : Creative Education, c1977. 31 p. : col. ill. ; 25 cm. ("Interviews") A biography of a young American who is a record-breaking long distance and channel swimmer. [GV838.C69L5] 92 76-42270 ISBN 0-87191-571-5 lib.bdg. 5.95
1. Cox, Lynne—Juvenile literature. 2. Swimmers—United States—Biography—Juvenile literature. I. Cox, Dave. II. Title. BIP

Cox, Samuel Sullivan, 1824-1889.

LINDSEY, David. 923.273
'Sunset' Cox, irrepressible Democrat. Detroit, Wayne State University Press, 1959. xx, 323p. port. 21cm. Bibliography: p. 302-313. [F664.C8L5] 59-9324
1. Cox, Samuel Sullivan, 1824-1889. I. Title.

Coxe, Tench, 1755-1824.

COOKE, Jacob Ernest, 1924- 973.4'092'4 B
Tench Coxe and the early Republic / Jacob E. Cooke. Chapel Hill : Published for the Institute of Early American History and Culture, Williamsburg, Va., by the University of North Carolina Press, c1978. xiv, 573 p. : port. ; 24 cm. Includes index. Bibliography: p. 525-543. [E302.6.C74C66] 77-28832 ISBN 0-8078-1308-7 : 24.95
1. Coxe, Tench, 1755-1824. 2. Politicians—United States—Biography. 3. Merchants—United States—Biography. 4. American loyalists—Biography. 5. United States—Politics and government—1783-1865. I. Institute of Early American History and Culture, Williamsburg, Va. II. Title. BIP

Cozine, John C.

COZINE, John C. 974
The day-book account of John C. Cozine : a journey from Harrodsburg, Kentucky, to New York, and return, September 10th through November 27th, 1828. Lexington : King Library Press, University of Kentucky Libraries, 1976. viii, a-d, 56 p., [6] leaves of plates : ill. ; 21 cm. "One hundred numbered copies." No. 80. "Illustrations from Basil Hall, Forty etchings from sketches made ... in 1827 and 1828, Edinburgh, 1830; Alcide Orbigny, Voyage pittoresque ... Paris, Tenre, 1836." Includes index. [F455.C68] 77-362992
1. Cozine, John C. 2. Kentucky—Description and travel. 3. Ohio—Description and travel. 4. Pennsylvania—Description and travel. 5. New York (State)—Description and travel. I. Title.

Crabbe, George, 1754-1832.

AINGER, Alfred, 1837-1904 821'.7
Crabbe. Detroit, Gale Research Co., 1970. viii, 210 p. 22 cm. Reprint of the 1903 ed. [PR4513.A5 1970] 72-78107
1. Crabbe, George, 1754-1832. BIP

CRABBE, George, 1785-1857 928.2
The life of George Crabbe, by his son; introd. by Edmund Blunden. London, Cresset Press [Chester Springs, Pa., Dufour, 1966] xxx, 286p. 20cm. (Cresset lib.) [PR4513.C7] 3.95
1. Crabbe, George, 1754-1832. I. Title.

HUCHON, Rene Louis, 1872- 821'.7
George Crabbe and his times, 1754-1832; a critical and biographical study, by Rene Huchon. Translated from the French by Frederick Clarke. New York, Barnes & Noble [1968] xvi, 561 p. facsims., ports. 23 cm. 1st ed., 1907; new impression, 1968. Bibliography: p. 518-530. [PR4513.H8 1968b] 68-5584
1. Crabbe, George, 1754-1832. I. Title.

Crabtree, Lotta, 1847-1924.

DEMPSEY, David K. 792'.0924
The triumphs and trials of Lotta Crabtree, by David Dempsey with Raymond P. Baldwin. New York, Morrow, 1968. viii, 341 p. illus., ports. 22 cm. Bibliography: p. 318-321. [PN2287.C645D4] 68-22434
1. Crabtree, Lotta, 1847-1924. I. Baldwin, Raymond P., joint author. II. Title.

Cradock, Walter, 1606;-1659.

NUTTALL, Geoffrey Fillingham, 1911- v. 12
The Welsh saints, 1640-1660: Walter Cradock, Vavasor Powell, Morgan Llwyd. iCardiff, University of Wales Press, 1957. x, 93p. 22cm. 'Delivered as a course of lectures (under the title 'The Welsh saints, 1640-1660') at the University College of North Wales during March 1957.' Bibliographical references included in 'Notes' (p.79-90) A59
1. Cradock, Walter, 1606;-1659. 2. Powell, Vavasor, 1617-1670. 3. Lloyd(Morgan, 1619-1639. I. Title.

Craft, Ellen.

STERLING, Dorothy, 1913- 973'.0992
Black foremothers : three lives / Dorothy Sterling ; introd. by Margaret Walker ; ill. by Judith Eloise Hooper. Old Westbury, N.Y. : Feminist Press, c1979. xxiii, 167 p. : ill.; 23 cm. (Women's lives/women's work) Includes index. Bibliography: p. 160-162. [E185.96.S75] 78-8094 ISBN 0-07-020434-9 teacher's ed. : 3.69 ISBN 0-07-020433-0 pbk. : 4.25
1. Craft, Ellen. 2. Wells, Ida B., 1862-1931. 3. Terrell, Mary Church, 1863-1954. 4. Afro-American women—Biography. I. Title. II. Series. BIP

Craft, William—Juvenile literature.

FREEDMAN, Florence B. 301.44'93'0922
Two tickets to freedom; the true story of Ellen and William Craft, fugitive slaves [by] Florence B. Freedman. Illustrated by Ezra Jack Keats. New York, Simon and Schuster [1971] 96 p. illus. 22 cm. Traces the search for freedom by a black man and wife who traveled to Boston and eventually to England after their escape from slavery in Georgia. [HT869.C7F7] 920 71-162713 ISBN 0-671-65169-2 4.50
1. Craft, William—Juvenile literature. 2. Craft, Ellen—Juvenile literature. I. Keats, Ezra Jack, illus. II. Title. BIP

Cragg, Timothy Michael.

CRAGG, Sheila, 1938- 362.2'092'6 B
Tantrums, toads, and Teddy bears / Sheila Cragg ; introd. by James Dobson. Scottdale, Pa. : Herald Press, 1979. 221 p. ; 20 cm. [RJ506.H9C7] 79-13771 ISBN 0-8361-1891-X : 8.95
1. Cragg, Timothy Michael. 2. Hyperactive children—United States—Biography. 3. Epileptics—United States—Biography. I. Title. BIP

Craig, Edward Gordon, 1872-1966.

BABLET, Denis. 792.0250924
Edward Gordon Craig. Translated by Daphne Woodward. [New York] Theatre Arts Books [1966] ix, 207 p. illus., ports. 23 cm. Includes bibliographical references. [PN2091.S8B223 1966a] 66-23134
1. Craig, Edward Gordon, 1872-1966. 2. Theaters—Stage-setting and scenery. BIP

CARRICK, Edward, 1905- 792'.0924 B
Gordon Craig; the story of his life, by Edward Craig. [1st American ed.] New York, Knopf, 1968. 398 p. illus. 25 cm. Includes bibliographical references. [PN2598.C85C3 1968] 68-23948 10.00
1. Craig, Edward Gordon, 1872-1966.

CRAIG, Edward Gordon, 1872-1966. 927.92
Index to the story of my days; some memoirs of Edward Gordon Craig, 1872-1907. New York, Viking Press, 1957. 308 p. illus. 23 cm. [PN2598.C85A3] 57-12227
I. Title.

NASH, George. 792'.0924
Edward Gordon Craig, 1872-1966. London, H. M. S. O., 1967. [2], 30 p. front., 36 plates (incl. ports., facsims.) 25cm. (Large picture bk. no. 35) At head of title: Victoria & Albert Mus. [N1150.A752 no. 35] 68-30057 2.50 pap.,
1. Craig, Edward Gordon, 1872-1966. I. Title. II. Series: Victoria and Albert Museum, South Kensington. Large picture books, no. 35
Available from British Info., New York.

Craig, Robert W.

†CRAIG, Robert W. 796.5'22'09586
Storm & sorrow in the high Pamirs / Robert W. Craig. Seattle : Mountaineers, c1977. xi, 171 p., [8] leaves of plates : ill. ; 21 cm. [GV199.44.P3C7 1977] 77-93359 6.95
1. Craig, Robert W. 2. Mountaineering—Pamir. 3. Pamir—Description. 4. Mountaineers—United States—Biography. 5. Mountaineering—Russia. I. Title. BIP

Craighill, Lloyd Rutherford, 1886-1971.

CRAIGHILL, Marian G. 226'.3'0922 B
The Craighills of China [by] Marian G. Craighill. Ambler, Pa., Trinity Press [1972] xii, 285 p. illus. 21 cm. [BV3427.C68C7] 72-92010 ISBN 0-912046-08-2 3.95
1. Craighill, Lloyd Rutherford, 1886-1971. I. Title.

Crain, Clara (Moore)

CRAIN, Clara (Moore) 1905- 922
We shall rise. New York, Pageant Press [1955] 68p. 21cm. Autobiography. [BR1725.C69A3] 55-12391
I. Title.

Crain, J. Dean, 1881-1955.

WESTMORELAND, Lillie B. v. 12
J. Dean Crain; a biography by Lillie B. Westmoreland, assisted by Alfred S. Reid. Foreword by A.E. Tibbs. Greenville, S.C., 1959. xiv, 160 p. plates. ports. Bibliography: p. 149-152.
1. Crain, J. Dean, 1881-1955. I. Title.

Cram, Ralph Adams, 1863-1942.

TUCCI, Douglass Shand. 720'.92'4
Ralph Adams Cram, American medievalist / by Douglass Shand Tucci. [Boston] : Boston Public Library, 1975. 49 p., [2] fold. leaves of plates : ill. ; 27 cm. Catalogue of an exhibition held at the Boston Public Library. Bibliography: p. 45-49. [NA737.C7T82] 76-358972
1. Cram, Ralph Adams, 1863-1942. 2. Romanesque revival (Architecture)—United States. 3. Gothic revival (Architecture)—United States. I. Boston. Public Library. II. Title. BIP

Cranch, Christopher Pearse,

CRANCH, Christopher Pearse, 1813-1892. 759.13 B
The life and letters of Christopher Pearse Cranch, by his daughter Leonora Cranch Scott. New York, AMS Press [1969] xii, 395 p. illus., ports. 23 cm. Reprint of the 1917 ed. [PS1449.C8Z5] 72-90096
I. Scott, Leonora (Cranch) 1848- II. Title. BIP

MILLER, Frederick De Wolfe. 928.1
Christopher Pearse Cranch and his caricatures of New England transcendentalism. Cambridge, Harvard University Press, 1951. xi, 81 p. illus. 22 cm. Bibliography [and] notes": p. [67]-77. [PS1449.C8Z8] 51-10752
1. Cranch, Christopher Pearse, 1813-1892. 2. Transcendentalism (New England) I. Title.

Crane, Hart, 1899-1932.

HORTON, Philip. 811'.009
Hart Crane; the life of an American poet. New York, Viking Press [1957] 352p. 20cm. (Compass books, C15) [PS3505.R272Z] A 57
1. Crane, Hart, 1899-1932. I. Title. II. Series: Compass book C15 BIP

PAUL, Sherman. 811'.5'2
Hart's Bridge. Urbana, University of Illinois Press [1972] viii, 315 p. 24 cm. Includes bibliographical references.

[PS3505.R272Z76] 76-188133 ISBN 0-252-00257-1 10.00
1. Crane, Hart, 1899-1932. I. Title. **BIP**

WEBER, Brom, 1917- 811'.5'2 B
Hart Crane; a biographical and critical study. Corr. ed. New York, Russell & Russell [1970, c1948] 452 p. facsims., ports. 23 cm. Includes an appendix of Hart Crane's uncollected poetry and prose and the worksheets of Atlantis. Bibliography: p. 441-443. [PS3505.R272Z8 1970] 74-110678
1. Crane, Hart, 1899-1932. I. Crane, Hart, 1899-1932. **BIP**

Crane, Hart, 1899-1932—Biography.

BROWN, Susan Jenkins. 811'.5'2
Robber rocks; letters and memories of Hart Crane, 1923-1932. [1st ed.] Middletown, Conn., Wesleyan University Press [1969] 176 p. illus., ports. 22 cm. [PS3505.R272Z57] 73-82537 5.95
1. Crane, Hart, 1899-1932—Biography. 2. Crane, Hart, 1899-1932—Friends and associates. I. Crane, Hart, 1899-1932. II. Title. **BIP**

CRANE, Hart, 1899-1932. 811'.5'2 B
Letters of Hart Crane and his family. Edited by Thomas S. W. Lewis. New York, Columbia University Press, 1974. xxiv, 675 p. 23 cm. Includes bibliographical references. [PS3505.R272Z54 1974] 73-21675 ISBN 0-231-03740-6 20.00
1. Crane, Hart, 1899-1932—Biography. 2. Crane family. I. Title. **BIP**

HORTON, Philip. 811'.5'2 B
Hart Crane : the life of an American poet / by Philip Horton. New York : Octagon Books, 1976, c1937. 352 p. ; 22 cm. Reprint of the ed. published by Viking Press, New York, which was issued as no. C15 of Compass books. Includes index. [PS3505.R272Z7 1976] 76-18798 ISBN 0-374-93958-6 : 14.00
1. Crane, Hart, 1899-1932—Biography. I. Title.

UNTERECKER, John Eugene, 1922- 811'.5'2 B
Voyager; a life of Hart Crane, by John Unterecker. New York, Farrar, Straus and Giroux [1969] xii, 787 p. illus. 25 cm. [PS3505.R272Z797] 69-11575 15.00
1. Crane, Hart, 1899-1932—Biography. I. Title. **BIP**

Crane, Hart, 1899-1932—Correspondence.

CRANE, Hart, 1899-1932. 928.1
Letters, 1916-1932; edited by Brom Weber. [1st ed.] New York, Hermitage House [1952] xvi, 426 p. port. 22 cm. [PS3505.R272Z54] 52-12760
I. Title.

CRANE, Hart [Harold Hart Crane] 1899-1932 928.1
Letters, 1916-1932; ed. by Brom Weber. Berkeley, Univ. of Calif. Pr., 1965 [c.1952] xvi, 426p. port. 22cm. [PS3505.R272Z54] 5.00; 2.25 pap.,
I. Title.

PARKINSON, Thomas Francis, 1920- 811'.5'209 B
Hart Crane and Yvor Winters : their literary correspondence / Thomas Parkinson. Berkeley : University of California Press, c1978. xxiii, 174 p. ; 24 cm. Includes index. Bibliography: p. [167]-168. [PS3505.R272Z547] 77-80475 ISBN 0-520-03538-0 : 11.95
1. Crane, Hart, 1899-1932—Correspondence. 2. Winters, Yvor, 1900-1968—Correspondence. 3. Poets, American—20th century—Correspondence. I. Title. **BIP**

Crane, Stephen, 1871-1900.

BERRYMAN, John, 1914- 928.1
Stephen Crane. Cleveland, World [1962,c.1950] 347p. 18cm. (Meridian bks., M131) Bibl. 62-10788 1.65 pap.,
1. Crane, Stephen, 1871-1900. I. Title.

BERRYMAN, John, 1914- 928.1
Stephen Crane [Magnolia, Mass., P. Smith, 1967, c.1950] xvii, 347p. 18cm. (Meridian bks., M131 rebound) Bibl. [PS1449.C85Z261962] 62-107889 3.75
1. Crane, Stephen, 1871-1900. I. Title.

BERRYMAN, John, 1914-1972. 928.1
Stephen Crane. [New York] Sloane [1950] xv, 347 p. port. 22 cm. (The American men of letters series) Bibliography: p. 326-331. [PS1499.C85Z56] 50-10964
1. Crane, Stephen, 1871-1900. I. Series.

BERRYMAN, John, 1914-1972. 818'.4'09 B
Stephen Crane / John Berryman. New York : Octagon Books, 1975, c1950. xvii, 347 p. : port. ; 22 cm. Reprint of the ed. published by World Pub. Co., Cleveland, Ohio, in series: Meridian books. Includes index. Bibliography: p. 326-332. [PS1449.C85Z56 1975] 74-22232 ISBN 0-374-90618-1 : 13.00
1. Crane, Stephen, 1871-1900.

CRANE, Stephen 928.1
Stephen Crane: letters. Edited by R. W. Stallman and Lillian Gilkes. With an introd. by R. W. Stallman. [New York] New York University Press, [c.] 1960. xxx, 366p. port. 25cm. 59-15192 6.50 bds.,
1. Authors—Correspondence, reminiscences, etc. I. Title.

CRANE, Stephen, 1871-1900. 928.1
Love letters to Nellie Crouse, with six other letters, new materials on Crane at Syracuse University, and a number of unusual photographs. Edited with notes and introductionsby Edwin H. Cady and Lester G. Wells. [Syracuse, N. Y.] Syracuse University Press, 1954. xi, 87p. ports., facsims. 23cm. 'The George Arents Stephen Crae collection at Syracuse University': p. 75-87. [PS1449.C85Z53] 54-9916
I. Carpenter, Nellie Janes (Crous 1872-1943. II. Cady, Edwin Harrison, ed. III. Title.

FRANCHERE, Ruth. 928.1
Stephen Crane, the story of an American writer. New York, Crowell [1961] 216 p. 21 cm. [PS1449.C85Z58] 61-7166
1. Crane, Stephen, 1871-1900.

LINSON, Corwin Knapp, 1864- 928.1
My Stephen Crane. Edited with an introd. by Edwin H. Cady. [Syracuse, N. Y.] Syracuse University Press, 1958. xiv, 115 p. ports. 24 cm. [PS1449.C85Z73] 58-9279
1. Crane, Stephen, 1871-1900. I. Title. **BIP**

RAYMOND, Thomas Lynch, 1875-1928. 818'.4'09
Stephen Crane. Newark, N.J., The Carteret Book Club [1923. Folcroft, Pa.] Folcroft Library Editions, 1973. ix, 42 p. port. 24 cm. "Notes on Stephen Crane in Books & journals": p. [39]-42. [PS1449.C85Z8 1973] 73-495 ISBN 0-8414-1484-X (lib. bdg.)
1. Crane, Stephen, 1871-1900. **BIP**

SOLOMON, Eric 813.4
Stephen Crane, from parody to realism. Cambridge, Harvard University Press, 1966. 301 p. 22 cm. Bibliographical reference included in "Notes" (p. 285-294) [PS1449.C85Z848] 66-21347
1. Crane, Stephen, 1871-1900.

STALLMAN, Robert Wooster, 1911- 813'.8
Stephen Crane; a biography, by R. W. Stallman. New York, G. Braziller [1968] xvi, 664 p. illus., facsims., ports. 24 cm. Bibliographical references included in "Notes" (p. 563-624). "Checklist" [of works by and about Stephen Crane] p. 625-641. [PS1449.C85Z9] 68-16110
1. Crane, Stephen, 1871-1900.

Crane, Stephen, 1871-1900—Biography.

CRANE, Stephen, 1871-1900. 818'.4'08
The war dispatches of Stephen Crane / edited by R. W. Stallman and E. R. Hagemann. Westport, Conn. : Greenwood Press, 1977, c1964. xv, 343 p. : ill. ; 23 cm. Reprint of the ed. published by New York University Press, New York. Includes bibliographical references and index. [PS1449.C85Z5 1977] 77-2994 ISBN 0-8371-9549-7 lib.bdg. : 20.00
1. Crane, Stephen, 1871-1900—Biography. 2. Greco-Turkish War, 1897—Personal narratives. 3. United States—History—War of 1898—Personal narratives. 4. South African War, 1899-1902—Personal narratives. 5. Authors, American—19th century—Biography. I. Title.

DAVIS, Richard Harding, 1864-1916. 818'.4'09 B
How Stephen Crane took Juana Dias [i.e. Diaz] / by Richard Harding Davis, with a prefatory note by John T. Winterich. La Crosse, [Wis.] : Sumac Press, 1976. [15] p. : map ; 24 cm. First published in In many wars, by many war-correspondents, edited by G. Lynch and F. Palmer. Tokyo, 1904, p. 43-45. "300 copies." [PS1522.H68] 77-362852
1. Crane, Stephen, 1871-1900—Biography. 2. Juana Diaz, P.R.—History. 3. Authors, American—19th century—Biography. I. Title.

Crane, Walter, 1845-1915.

CRANE, Walter, 1845-1915. 760'.0924
An artist's reminiscences. With 12 illus. by the author, and others from photos. London, Methuen, 1907. Detroit, Singing Tree Press, 1968. xvi, 520 p. illus., ports. 22 cm. [ND497.C86A5 1968] 68-21763
I. Title. **BIP**

SPENCER, Isobel. 760'.092'4 B
Walter Crane / Isobel Spencer. 1st American ed. New York : Macmillan, 1975. 208 p. : ill. ; 28 cm. Includes index. Bibliography: p. 200-205. [ND497.C86S63 1975] 75-18567 25.00
1. Crane, Walter, 1845-1915.

Crane, Winthrop Murray, 1853-1920.

JOHNSON, Carolyn W. 329.6'00924
Winthrop Murray Crane: a study in Republican leadership, 1892-1920, by Carolyn W. Johnson. Northampton, Mass., Smith College, 1967. ix, 100 p. 24 cm. (The Edwin H. Land prize essays) Bibliography: p. 96-100. [E664.C88J6] 66-30523
1. Crane, Winthrop Murray, 1853-1920. I. Title. II. Series.

Cranmer, Thomas, Abp. of Canterbury, 1489-1556.

BELLOC, Hilaire, 1870-1953. 283'.092'4 B
Cranmer, Archbishop of Canterbury 1533-1556 New York, Haskell House Publishers, 1973 [c1931] 333 p. illus. 23 cm. [DA317.8.C8B4 1973] 72-4495 ISBN 0-8383-1610-7 13.95 (lib. bdg.)
1. Cranmer, Thomas, Abp. of Canterbury, 1489-1556.

BROMILEY, G. W. 922.342
Thomas Cranmer, theologian. New York, Oxford University Press, 1956. 108 p. 22 cm. [DA317.8.C8B7] 56-13716
1. Cranmer, Thomas, Abp., 1489-1556. **BIP**

BROMILEY, Geoffrey William. 922.342
Thomas Cranmer, theologian. New York, Oxford University Press, 1956. 108p. 22cm. [DA317.8.C8B7] 56-13716
1. Cranmer, Thomas, Abp. of Canterbury, 1489-1556. I. Title.

THE life of Thomas v. 12
Cranmer, the first Protestant Archbishop of Canterbury. Philadelphia, American Sunday-School Union [n.d.] vi, 192 p. 16 cm. 65-78021
1. Cranmer, Thomas, Abp. of Canterbury, 1489-1556.

MAYNARD, Theodore, 1890- 922.342
The life of Thomas Cranmer. Chicago, H. Regnery Co., 1956. 242p. 22cm. [DA317.8.C8M45] 56-7646
1. Cranmer, Thomas, Abp. of Canterbury, 1489-1556. I. Title.

RIDLEY, Jasper 922.342
Thomas Cranmer. [New York] Oxford [c.] 1962[ ] 450p. illus. Bibl. 62-2124 5.60
1. Cranmer, Thomas, Abp. of Canterbury, 1489-1556. I. Title.

RIDLEY, Jasper 922.342
Thomas Cranmer. Oxford, Clarendon Pr. [1966, c.1962] 450p. illus. 20cm. Bibl. [DA317.8.C8R5] 2.95 pap.,
1. Cranmer, Thomas, Abp. of Canterbury, 1489-1556. I. Title.
Available from Oxford Univ. Pr., New York

SMYTH, Charles Hugh Egerton, 1903- 274.2
Cranmer & the Reformation under Edward VI, by C. H. Smyth Westport, Conn., Greenwood Press [1970] x, 315 p. 23 cm. Reprint of the 1926 ed. Bibliography: p. [303]-306. [BR375.S6 1970] 75-100842 ISBN 0-8371-4025-0
1. Cranmer, Thomas, Abp. of Canterbury, 1489-1556. 2. Reformation—England. I. Title.

Crapo, Henry Howland, 1804-1869.

LEWIS, Martin Deming, 1924- 923.273
Lumberman from Flint; the Michigan career of Henry H. Crapo, 1855-1869. Detroit, Wayne State University Press, 1958. 289p. illus. 24cm. Includes bibliography. [F566.C93L4 1958] 57-13065
1. Crapo, Henry Howland, 1804-1869. I. Title.

Crapper, Thomas, 1837-1910.

REYBURN, Wallace. 696'.182'0924 B
Flushed with pride; the story of Thomas Crapper. Englewood Cliffs, N.J., Prentice-Hall [1971, c1969] 95 p. illus. 18 cm. [TH140.C7R4 1971] 73-129143 ISBN 0-13-322560-7
1. Crapper, Thomas, 1837-1910. 2. Water-closets. I. Title. **BIP**

Crapsey, Adelaide, 1878-1914.

BUTSCHER, Edward. 811'.5'2 B
Adelaide Crapsey / by Edward Butscher ; [editor of this vol., David Nordloh]. Boston : Twayne Publishers, 1979. 129 p. : port. ; 21 cm. (Twayne's United States authors series ; TUSAS 337) Includes index. Bibliography: p. 120-125. [PS3505.R277Z6 1979] 78-26595 ISBN 0-8057-7273-1 : 10.50
1. Crapsey, Adelaide, 1878-1914. 2. Authors, American—20th century—Biography. I. Nordloh, David.

Crashaw, Richard, 1613?-1649.

WILLY, Margaret. v. 12
Richard Crashaw, Henry Vaughan, Thomas Traherne. Lincoln, University of Nebraska Press [c1964] [87]-143 p. 21 cm. (British writers and their work, no. 4) A Bison book. 67-34369
1. Crashaw, Richard, 1613?-1649. 2. Vaughan, Henry, 1622-1695. 3. Traherne, Thomas, d. 1674. I. Title. II. Series.

Crashaw, Richard, 1613?-1649—Addresses, essays, lectures.

†WILLEY, Basil, 1897- 821'.4
Richard Crashaw (1612/13-1649) : a memorial lecture delivered at Peterhouse, Cambridge, on 11 July 1949 / by Basil Willey. Folcroft, Pa. : Folcroft Library Editions, 1976. 25 p. ; 23 cm. Reprint of the 1949 ed. published by University Press, Cambridge. [PR3386.W5 1976] 76-26647 ISBN 0-8414-9386-3 lib. bdg. : 8.50
1. Crashaw, Richard, 1613?-1649—Addresses, essays, lectures. 2. Poets, English—Early modern, 1500-1700—Biography—Addresses, essays, lectures.

Crassus, Marcus Licinius.

MARSHALL, B. A. 937'.05'0924 B
Crassus : a political biography / B. A. Marshall. Amsterdam : A. M. Hakkert, 1976. 205 p., [2] leaves of plates : ill., geneal. table ; 22 cm. A revision of the author's thesis, University of Sydney. Includes index. Bibliography: p. 191-198. [DG260.C73M37 1976] 76-488909

1. Crassus, Marcus Licinius. 2. Rome—Politics and government—265-30 B.C. 3. Consuls, Roman—Biography. I. Title.

WARD, Allen M., 1942- 937'.05'0924 B
Marcus Crassus and the late Roman Republic / Allen M. Ward. Columbia : University of Missouri Press, c1977. p. cm. Includes index. Bibliography: p. [DG260.C73W37] 76-56794 ISBN 0-8262-0216-0 : 15.00
1. Crassus, Marcus Licinius. 2. Statesmen—Rome—Biography. 3. Businessmen—Rome—Biography. I. Title. BIP

Craster, John,

CRASTER, John, Sir, 1901- 914.28'2'03820924 B
North country squire: the reminiscences of a Northumbrian. Newcastle upon Tyne, Oriel, 1971. [10], 165, [12] p. ports. 23 cm. [CT788.C783A3 1971] 73-166001 ISBN 0-85362-134-9 £3.50
I. Title.

Crater, Joseph Force, 1889-

CRATER, Stella (Wheeler) 1887- 923.473
The empty robe [by] Stella Crater with Oscar Fraley. Garden City, N. Y., Doubleday [c.]1961. 210p. illus. 61-8880 4.50
1. Crater, Joseph Force, 1889- I. Title.

CRATER, Stella (Wheeler 1888- 923.473
The empty robe [by] Stella Crater with Oscar Fraley [New York] Dell [1964, c.1961] 159p. 17cm. (2346) .50 pap.,
1. Crater, Joseph Force, 1889- I. Title.

Craven, Margaret—Biography.

CRAVEN, Margaret. 813'.5'4 B
Again calls the owl / by Margaret Craven ; illustrated by Joan Miller. New York : Putnam, 1980. p. cm. [PS3553.R277Z463] 79-22388 ISBN 0-399-12453-5 : 7.95
1. Craven, Margaret—Biography. 2. Novelists, American—20th century—Biography. I. Title. BIP

Crawford, Cheryl.

CRAWFORD, Cheryl. 792'.0232'0924 B
One naked individual : my fifty years in the theatre / Cheryl Crawford. Indianapolis : Bobbs-Merrill, c1977. x, 275 p., [8] leaves of plates : ill. ; 24 cm. [PN2287.C665A35] 76-44666 ISBN 0-672-52185-7 : 10.95
1. Crawford, Cheryl. 2. Theatrical producers and directors—United States—Biography. I. Title.

Crawford Co., Kan.—Biography.

A Twentieth century history and biographical record of Crawford County, Kansas / by home authors. [Clinton, Mo. : The Printery, 1976] 683 p., [3] leaves of plates : ill. ; 25 cm. "Index and acknowledgment listing added by the Crawford County Genealogical Society of Pittsburg, Kansas." Reprint of the 1905 ed. published by Lewis Pub. Co., Chicago. [F687.C9T9 1976] 76-24553 978.1'98'0922 B
1. Crawford Co., Kan.—Biography. 2. Crawford Co., Kan.—History.

Crawford, Jesse.

LANDON, John W., 1937- 786.5'092'4 B
Jesse Crawford, poet of the organ, wizard of the mighty Wurlitzer [by] John W. Landon. Vestal, N.Y., Vestal Press [1974] xi, 372 p. illus. 24 cm. Bibliography: p. 244-251. [ML416.C8L3] 74-13654 ISBN 0-911572-11-2 12.00
1. Crawford, Jesse. I. Title. BIP

Crawford, Jim, 1924-

CRAWFORD, Jim, 1924- 797.1'24'0924 B
Count the cats in Zanzibar / Jim Crawford. Cambridge, Md. : Distributed by Tidewater Publishers, 1975. ix, 113 p. : ill. ; 23 cm. [GV812.5.C72A33] 75-38934 ISBN 0-87033-216-3
1. Crawford, Jim, 1924- 2. Sailing. 3. Sailboat racing. I. Title. BIP

Crawford, Joan, 1908-1977.

CARR, Larry. 791.43'028'0922
Four fabulous faces : Swanson, Garbo, Crawford, Dietrich / Larry Carr. New York : Penguin Books, 1978. 492 p. : ill. ; 28 cm. Reprint of the 1970 ed. published by Arlington House, New Rochelle, N.Y. [PN1998.A2C34 1978] 78-18862 ISBN 0-14-004988-6 : 12.95
1. Garbo, Greta, 1905- 2. Swanson, Gloria. 3. Crawford, Joan, 1908-1977. 4. Dietrich, Marlene, 1905- 5. Moving-picture actors and actresses—United States—Biography. I. Title. BIP

CRAWFORD, Joan, 1908- 131.3
My way of life. New York, Simon and Schuster [1971] 224 p. illus. 24 cm. [PN2287.C67A32] 70-154098 ISBN 0-671-20970-1 7.50
I. Title. BIP

CRAWFORD, Joan, 1908- 927.92
A portait of Joan, with Jane Kesner Ardmore. New York, Paperback [1964, c.1962] 176p. 18cm. (Silver sd., 52-271) .50 pap.,
I. Title.

NEWQUIST, Roy. 791.43'028'0924 B
Conversations with Joan Crawford / by Roy Newquist ; foreword by John Springer. Secaucus, N.J. : Citadel Press, [1980] p. cm. [PN2287.C67N4] 80-227 ISBN 0-8065-0720-9 : 9.95
1. Crawford, Joan, 1908-1977. 2. Moving-picture actors and actresses—United States—Interviews. I. Crawford, Joan, 1908-1977. II. Title. BIP

THOMAS, Bob, 1922- 791.43'028'0924 B
Joan Crawford, a biography / by Bob Thomas. New York : Simon and Schuster, c1978. p. cm. Includes index. [PN2287.C67T5] 78-14250 ISBN 0-671-24033-1 : 10.95
1. Crawford, Joan, 1908-1977. 2. Moving-picture actors and actresses—United States—Biography. I. Title.

Crawford, Raymond Robert, 1891-1965.

APOSTOLIC Faith Mission. v. 12
Saved to serve; a sketch of the life and theology of Raymond Robert Crawford, late leader and general overseer of the Apostolic Faith Church with headquarters in Portland, Oregon. Portland, Or., Apostolic Faith Pub. House [1967] 96 p. illus., ports. 23 cm. 68-89081
1. Crawford, Raymond Robert, 1891-1965. I. Title.

Crawford, Samuel Johnson, 1835-1913.

PLUMMER, Mark A., 1929- 978.1'03'0924 B
Frontier Governor: Samuel J. Crawford of Kansas, by Mark A. Plummer. Lawrence, University Press of Kansas [1971] xiii, 210 p. illus. 23 cm. Bibliography: p. [199]-204. [F686.C9P55] 72-161656 ISBN 0-7006-0080-9
1. Crawford, Samuel Johnson, 1835-1913. I. Title.

Crawford, William Harris, 1772-1834.

GREEN, Philip Jackson, 1891- 973.50924
The life of William Harris Crawford [Charlotte, Univ. of N. C. at Charlotte, 1965] ix, 258p. 24cm. Bibl. [E340.C89G68] 65-5557 5.00
1. Crawford, William Harris, 1772-1834. I. Title.

MOONEY, Chase Curran, 1913- 973.5'092'4 B
William H. Crawford, 1772-1834 [by Chase C. Mooney] [Lexington] University Press of Kentucky [1974] xi, 364 p. port. 24 cm. Bibliography: p. [347]-353. [E340.C89M66] 70-147853 ISBN 0-8131-1270-2 15.00
1. Crawford, William Harris, 1772-1834. BIP

Crawhall, Joseph, 1821-1896.

FELVER, Charles Stanley, 1916- 769'.92'4 B
Joseph Crawhall: the Newcastle wood engraver (1821-1896), by Charles S. Felver. Newcastle upon Tyne, Graham, [1973]. viii, 144 p. illus., facsims. 22 cm. Bibliography: p. 137-141. [NE1147.6.C7F44] 73-161709 ISBN 0-902833-07-3 £3.00
1. Crawhall, Joseph, 1821-1896.

Crawley-Boevey, Mateo, 1875-1960—Juvenile literature.

†BALSKUS, Pat. 271'.7 B
Trailblazer for the Sacred Heart / by Pat Balskus. Boston : St. Paul Editions, c1976. 120 p., [8] leaves of plates : ill. ; 22 cm. The life of the founder of the Enthronment of the Sacred Heart of Jesus. [BX4705.C7817B34] 92 75-37947 pbk. : 3.00
1. Crawley-Boevey, Mateo, 1875-1960—Juvenile literature. I. Title.

Crazy Horse, Oglala Indian, 1842 (ca.)-1877.

AMBROSE, Stephen E. 973.8'2'0922
Crazy Horse and Custer : the parallel lives of two American warriors / by Stephen E. Ambrose ; illustrated by Kenneth Francis Dewey. 1st ed. Garden City, N.Y. : Doubleday, 1975. x, 486 p., [8] leaves of plates : ill. ; 24 cm. Includes index. Bibliography: p. [473]-476. [E99.O3A46] 75-2852 ISBN 0-385-09666-6 : 12.50
1. Crazy Horse, Oglala Indian, 1842 (ca.)-1877. 2. Custer, George Armstrong, 1839-1876. 3. Indians of North America—Wars—1866-1895. I. Title.

BROWN, Vinson, 1912- 970.3 B
Great upon the mountain; the story of Crazy Horse, legendary mystic and warrior. New York, Macmillan [1975, c1971] xxii, 169 p. map. 22 cm. [E99.O3C722 1975] 74-13458 ISBN 0-02-517350-2 4.95
1. Crazy Horse, Oglala Indian, 1842 (ca.)-1877. I. Title. BIP

CRAZY Horse, the strange man of the Oglalas, a biography [Lincoln] University of Nebraska Press, 1961. x, 428p. illus., map. 21cm. (A Bison book) v. 12
1. Crazy House, Oglala Indian, 1842 (ca.)-1877. 2. Oglala Indians. I. Sandoz, Mari, 1907- BIP

GARST, Doris Shannon, 1899- 970.3 B
Crazy Horse, a great warrior of the Sioux; illustrated by William Moyers. Boston, Houghton Mifflin, 1950. 260 p. illus. 24 cm. Bibliography: p. 258-260. A biography of the Oglala Sioux Indian first called Has-ka, the light-skinned one, who won the name Crazy Horse and grew up to lead his people in unified and relentless warfare against the whites. [E90.C94G3] 92 AC 68
1. Crazy Horse, Oglala Indian, 1842 (ca.)-1877. I. Moyers, William, illus. II. Title.

THE Killing of Chief Crazy Horse : three eyewitness views by the Indian Chief He Dog, the Indian-white William Garnett, the white doctor Valentine McGillycuddy / edited, with introd. by Robert A. Clark ; with commentary by Carroll Friswold. Glendale, Calif. : A. H. Clark Co., 1976. 152 p. : ill. ; 26 cm. (Hidden springs of Custeriana ; 4) Includes index. Bibliography: p. 147-148. [E99.O3K54] 76-17961 ISBN 0-87062-112-2 : 27.50 973.8'3'0924 B
1. Crazy Horse, Oglala Indian, 1842 (ca.)-1877. 2. Oglala Indians—Biography. 3. Indians of North America—Wars—1866-1895. I. He Dog, 1837-1936. II. Garnett, William, 1855-1929. III. McGillycuddy, Valentine, 1849-1939. IV. Clark, Robert A., 1948- V. Friswold, Carroll. VI. Series.

MEADOWCROFT, Enid (La Monte) 1898- 970.3 B
Crazy Horse, Sioux warrior. Illustrated by Cary. Champaign, Ill., Garrard Pub. Co. [1965] 80 p. col. illus. 23 cm. A biography of the Sioux Indian called Curly who grew up to win the name Crazy Horse and to lead his tribe against Custer at the Little Bighorn. [E90.C94M4] 92 AC 68
1. Crazy Horse, Oglala Indian, 1842 (ca.)-1877. I. Cary, illus. II. Title.

SANDOZ, Mari, 1907- 970.2
Crazy Horse, the strange man of the Oglalas, a biography New York, Hastings House [1955, c1942] 428p. illus. 21cm. [E90] 55-4571
1. Crazy Horse, Oglala Indian, 1842 (ca.)-1877. 2. Oglala Indians. I. Title.

SANDOZ, Mari, 1907-n3 v. 12
Crazy horse, the strange man of the Oglalas; a biography. New York, Hastings House [1961] x, 428 p. fold. map. 23 cm. Bibliography: p. 417-422. 64-11407
1. Crazy Horse, Oglala Indian, 1842 (ca.)-1877. 2. Oglala Indians. I. Sandoz, Mari, 1907- II. Title.

SANDOZ, Mari [Susette] 1907- 970.2
Crazy horse the strange man of the Oglalas; a biography. Lincoln, Univ. of Nebraska Press, 1961 [c.1942] 428p. map. (Bison bk. BB110) Bibl. 1.65 pap.,
1. Crazy Horse, Oglala Indian, 1842 (ca.)-1877. 2. Oglala Indians. I. Title.

WHITTAKER, Jane. 970.3 B
Patriots of the plains: Sitting Bull, Crazy Horse, Chief Joseph. New York, Scholastic Book Services [1973] 128 p. illus. 21 cm. (Firebird books) [E99.D1W85] 72-90573 1.24 (pbk.)
1. Sitting Bull, Dakota chief, 1831-1890. 2. Crazy Horse, Oglala Indian, 1842 (ca.)-1877. 3. Joseph, Nez Perce chief, 1840-1904. I. Title.
Library binding; 2.79.

Crazy Horse, Oglala Indian, 1842 (ca.)-1877—Juvenile literature.

GRANT, Matthew G. 970.3 B
Crazy Horse, war chief of the Oglala [by] Matthew G. Grant. Illustrated by John Keely and Dick Brude. [Mankato, Minn., Creative Education; distributed by Childrens Press, Chicago, 1973, c1974] 30 p. illus. (part col.) 25 cm. (His Gallery of great Americans series. Indians of America) A brief biography of the Oglala Sioux leader whose resistance to the Army's attempt to move his people to a reservation resulted in Custer's defeat at Little Bighorn and his own premature death. [E99.O3C723] 92 73-12403 ISBN 0-87191-269-4 3.95
1. Crazy Horse, Oglala Indian, 1842 (ca.)-1877—Juvenile literature. I. Keely, John, illus. II. Brude, Dick, illus. III. Title.

MILTON, John R. 970.3 B
Crazy Horse, by John R. Milton. Minneapolis, Dillon Press [1974] 58 p. illus. 23 cm. (Story of an American Indian) A biography of the Oglala Sioux who helped defeat Custer at the Battle of the Little Bighorn. [E99.O3M54] 92 74-13056 ISBN 0-87518-063-9
1. Crazy Horse, Oglala Indian, 1842 (ca.)-1877—Juvenile literature. I. Title. BIP

Creaton, David.

CREATON, David. 636'.0092'4 B
Beasts go west / by David Creaton. New York : St. Martin's Press, 1980. p. cm. [SF33.C73A325] 79-5327 ISBN 0-312-07049-7 : 9.95
1. Creaton, David. 2. Farmers—England—Cornwall—Biography. 3. Farm life—England—Cornwall. I. Title. BIP

CREATON, David. 636'.0092'4 B
The beasts of my field / by David Creaton. New York : St. Martin's Press, c1977. 254 p. : ill. ; 22 cm. [SF33.C73A33] 76-62757 ISBN 0-312-07052-7 : 8.95
1. Creaton, David. 2. Farmers—England—

Kent—Biography. 3. Farm life—England—Kent. I. Title. BIP

Creeley, Robert, 1926- —Bibliography.

NOVIK, Mary. 016.818'5'409
Robert Creeley; an inventory, 1945-1970. With a foreword by Robert Creeley. Montreal, McGill-Queen's University Press, 1973. xvii, 210 p. 23 cm. [Z8198.9.N68 1973b] 74-156902 ISBN 0-7735-0191-6 6.00
1. Creeley, Robert, 1926- —Bibliography. Available from 136 S. Broadway, Irvington, N.Y. 10533. BIP

Crehan, Fern M.

CREHAN, Fern M. 920.7
The days before yesterday. Illustrated by Charles Walker. New York, Dodd, Mead [1958] 206 p. illus. 21 cm. [CT275.C8855A3] 58-6832
I. Title.

CREHAN, Fern M. 920.7
The days before yesterday. Illustrated by Charles Walker. New York, Dodd, Mead [1958] 206 p. illus. 21 cm. [CT275.C8855A3] 58-6832
I. Title.

Creighton, Helen.

CREIGHTON, Helen. 398'.092'4 B
Helen Creighton : a life in folklore / by Helen Creighton. Toronto ; New York : McGraw-Hill Ryerson, c1975. 244 p., [4] leaves of plates : ill. ; 24 cm. Includes bibliographical references. [GR55.C74A33] 76-352397 ISBN 0-07-082241-7 : 8.95
1. Creighton, Helen 2. Folk-songs, Canadian—Maritime Provinces—History and criticism. 3. Folk-lore—Field work. I. Title: A life in folklore.

Creighton, Mandell, Bp. of London, 1843-1901.

FALLOWS, W G 922.342
Mandell Creighton and the English Church, by W. G. Fallows. London, New York, Oxford University Press, 1964. vi, 127 p. port. 22 cm. Bibliography: p. [117] [BX5199.C75F3] 64-4562
1. Creighton, Mandell, Bp. of London, 1843-1901. I. Title.

Cremer, Jacoous Jan, 1827-1880.

CREMER, Jan 920.71
I, Jan Cremer. Introd. by Seymour Krim [New York] New Amer. Lib. [1966, c.1965] 285p. 18cm. (Signet bk., T2910) .75 pap.,
I. Title.

CREMER, Jan FIC
I, Jan Cremer [1st Amer. ed.] Introd by Seymour Krim. New York, Shorecrest [dist. Shorewood, c.1965] xiv, 312p. 22cm. [PZ4.C917I] 920.71 65-23716 4.95 pap.,
I. Title.

SANDERS, Hugo. v. 12
Jacob Cremer. Haarlem, J. H. Gottmer [1952] 120p. plates, port. 27cm. 'Bibliographie': p. 108-117. A53
1. Cremer, Jacoous Jan, 1827-1880. I. Title.

Cremer, William Randal, Sir, 1828-1908.

EVANS, Howard, 327'.172'0924 B
1839-1915.
Sir Randal Cremer; his life and work. With a new introd. for the Garland ed. by Naomi Churgin Miller. New York, Garland Pub., 1973. 18, 356 p. illus. 22 cm. (The Garland library of war and peace) Reprint of the 1909 ed. published by T. F. Unwin, London. [JX1962.C8E85 1973] 74-147455 ISBN 0-8240-0250-4
1. Cremer, William Randal, Sir, 1828-1908. 2. Peace. I. Title. II. Series. BIP

Cresap, Michael, 1742-1775.

JACOB, John 977'.01'0924 B
Jeremiah, 1758?-1839.
A biographical sketch of the life of the late Captain Michael Cresap. With an introd. by Otis K. Rice. Parsons, W. Va., McClain Print. Co., 1971. 48, 158 p. 23 cm. Reprint of the 1866 ed. with a new introd. Includes bibliographical references. [F517.C87J3 1971] 76-128684 ISBN 0-87012-077-8
1. Cresap, Michael, 1742-1775. 2. Jefferson, Thomas, Pres. U.S., 1743-1826. Notes on the State of Virginia. I. Title. BIP

JACOB, John 973.2'7'0924 B
Jeremiah, 1758?-1839.
A biographical sketch of the life of the late Captain Michael Cresap. [New York] Arno Press [1971] 158, 4-23 p. 24 cm. (The First American frontier) Reprint of the 1866 ed. A defense of Capt. Cresap, contradicting the statements made by T. Jefferson in his Notes on the State of Virginia and J. Doddridge in his Notes on the settlement and Indian wars of the western parts of Virginia and Pennsylvania from 1763 to 1783. "A journal of Wayne's campaign ... by Lieutenant Boyer": p. [1]-23 (2d group) [F517.C87J3 1971b] 73-146404 ISBN 0-405-02863-6
1. Cresap, Michael, 1742-1775. 2. Jefferson, Thomas, Pres. U.S., 1743-1826. Notes on the State of Virginia. 3. Doddridge, Joseph, 1769-1826. Notes on the settlement and Indian wars of the western parts of Virginia and Pennsylvania from 1763 to 1783. 4. Wayne's Campaign, 1794. I. Boyer, Lieutenant. A journal of Wayne's campaign. 1972. II. Title. III. Series.

Cresson, Warder, 1798-1860.

CRESSON, Warder, 1798- 296.7'1
1860.
The key of David / Warder Cresson. New York : Arno Press, 1977. 344 p. : ill. ; 21 cm. (America and the Holy Land) Reprint of the 1852 ed. published in Philadelphia. Includes bibliographical references. [BM590.C7 1977] 77-70671 ISBN 0-405-10239-9 : 20.00
1. Cresson, Warder, 1798-1860. 2. Christianity—Controversial literature. 3. Messiah. 4. Proselytes and proselyting, Jewish—Biography. I. Title. II. Series.

Crews, Harry, 1935- —Biography—Youth.

CREWS, Harry, 1935- 813'.5'4 B
A childhood, the biography of a place / Harry Crews. 1st ed. New York : Harper & Row, c1978. 171 p. ; 22 cm. [PS3553.R46Z463 1978] 78-54677 ISBN 0-06-010932-7 : 8.95
1. Crews, Harry, 1935- —Biography—Youth. 2. Novelists, American—20th century—Biography. 3. Bacon Co., Ga.—Biography. I. Title. BIP

CREWS, Harry, 1935- 813'.5'4 B
A childhood, the biography of a place / Harry Crews. Boston : G K Hall, 1979, c1978. p. cm. "Published in large print." [PS3553.R46Z463 1979] 79-16426 ISBN 0-8161-6752-4 : 12.95
1. Crews, Harry, 1935- —Biography—Youth. 2. Novelists, American—20th century—Biography. 3. Bacon Co., Ga.—Biography. 4. Large type books.

Crichton-Miller, Hugh, 1877-1959.

CRICHTON-MILLER, Hugh, 1877- v. 12
1959.
Hugh Crichton-Miller, 1877-1959, a personal memoir by his friends and family, 1961. Dorchester, Longmans, 1961. 79 p. ports. 67-53184
1. Crichton-Miller, Hugh, 1877-1959. I. Title.

Cricket.

INGLEBY-MACKENZIE, 927.96358
Colin, 1933-
Many a slip. London, Oldbourne distributed by Sportshelf, New Rochelle, N. Y., [1962] 190p. illus. 23cm. Autobiography. [GV915.I4A3] 62-51027
1. Cricket. I. Title.

Cricket—Biography.

GIANTS of the 796.358'092'2 B
game : being reminiscences of the stars of cricket from Daft down to 1900 / by R. H. Lyttelton ... [et al.] ; illustrated from photographs. [1st ed. reprinted] / with a new introduction by John Arlott. Wakefield : EP Publishing, 1973. viii, 5-192 p., [8] leaves of plates : ports. ; 20 cm. Reprint of the 1899 ed. published by Ward Lock, London. [GV915.A1G54 1973] 74-188118 £2.50
1. Cricket—Biography. I. Lyttelton, Robert Henry, Hon., 1854-1939.

Criddle, Russell,

CRIDDLE, Russell, 1916- 920.96177
Love is not blind. [1st ed.] New York, Norton [1953] 272 p. 22 cm. Autobiographical. [HV1792.C7A3] 53-6968
I. Title.

Crillon, Louis Balbis de Berton de, 1543-1615.

LUSSAN, Marguerite de, 823'.6 S
1682-1758.
The life and heroic actions of Balbe Berton (1760) by Marguerite de Lussan. Rev. by Samuel Richardson. New York, Garland Pub., 1974. 2 v. 18 cm. (The Life & times of seven major British writers. Richardsoniana, 20-21) Rev. translation of Vie de Louis Balbe-Berton de Crillon, printed in 1757. Reprint of the ed. printed for H. Woodgate and S. Brooks, London. [PR3667.R5 vol. 20-21] [DC112.C7] 843'.5 74-16010 ISBN 0-8240-1319-0
1. Crillon, Louis Balbis de Berton de, 1543-1615. I. Richardson, Samuel, 1689-1761. II. Title. III. Series: Richardsoniana, 20-21.

Crimaldi, Charles.

KIDNER, John, 364.1'523'0924 B
1923-
Crimaldi, contract killer : a true story / by John Kidner. Washington : Acropolis Books, c1976. 301 p. ; 24 cm. [HV6248.C685K53] 76-43221 ISBN 0-87491-206-7 : 8.95
1. Crimaldi, Charles. 2. Crime and criminals—United States—Biography. I. Title.

Crime and criminals.

GILMORE, John. 364.15'23 B
The Tucson murders. New York, Dial Press, 1970. 274 p. illus., facsim., ports. 22 cm. [HV6534.T8G5 1970] 71-76970 5.95
I. Schmid, Charles Howard. II. Title.

LEBRUN, George P. 923.473
Call me if it's murder [by] George P. LeBrun as told to Edward D. Radin. (Orig. title: It's time to tell.) New York, Bantam [1965, c.1962] 182p. 18cm. (F2996) .50 pap.,
1. Crime and criminals—New York (City) 2. Coroners—New York (City)—Correspondence, reminiscences, etc. I. Radin, Edward D. II. Title.

LEBRUN, George Petit, 923.473
1862-
It's time to tell; as told to Edward D. Radin. New York, Morrow, 1962. 255 p. 22 cm. [HV6795.N5L46] 62-15753
1. Crime and criminals—New York (City) 2. Coroners—New York (City)—Correspondence, reminiscences, etc. I. Radin, Edward D. II. Title.

MARTIN, William, 1895- 923.573
1950.
Bill Martin, American, by Bill Martin and Molly Radford Martin. Cover, jacket design, and end sheets by Frances Owen. Caldwell, Idaho, Caxton Printers, 1959. 263p. illus. 22cm. 'All of his own story was told by Bill, and much it was recorded on wire ... [Molly Radford Martin has]tried to transcribe his words as characteristically as possible.' [HV7914.M37] 59-5481
1. Crime and criminals—New Mexico. I. Martin, Molly (Radford) II. Title.

SILLITOE, Percy, Sir 923.542
1888-
Cloak without dagger. New York, Abelard-Schuman [1955] 206p. illus. 21cm. Autobiography. [HV914] 55-13570
1. Crime and criminals—Gt. Brit. 2. Crime and criminals—Africa, South. I. Title.

WHIBLEY, Charles, 364.15'5 B
1859-1930.
A book of scoundrels. New ed. New York, B. Blom, 1971. viii, 287 p. 21 cm. Reprint of the 1912 ed. [HV6245.W6 1971] 70-174393
1. Crime and criminals. I. Title. BIP

Crime and criminals—Biography.

GRIBBLE, Leonard 364.15'23'0922 B
Reginald, 1908-
Such women are deadly [by] Leonard Gribble. New York, Arco [1969, c1965] 176 p. 23 cm. [HV6245.G76 1969] 69-17875 4.95
1. Crime and criminals—Biography. 2. Murder. I. Title.

IRVING, Henry 364.3'092'2 B
Brodribb, 1870-1919.
A book of remarkable criminals / by H. B. Irving. Westport, Conn. : Hyperion Press, 1974, c1918. p. cm. Reprint of the ed. published by G. H. Doran, New York. Contents.Contents.—The life of Charles Peace.—The career of Robert Butler.—M. Derues.—Dr. Castaing.—Professor Webster.—The mysterious Mr. Holmes.—Partnership in crime: The widow Gras. Vitalis and Marie Boyer. The Fenayrou case. Eyraud and Bompard. [HV6245.I82 1974] 74-10427 ISBN 0-88355-194-2 : 11.95
1. Crime and criminals—Biography. I. Title. BIP

LIPTON, Dean, 1919 364.2'4
The faces of crime and genius; the historical impact of the genius-criminal. South Brunswick, A. S. Barnes [1970] 252 p. ports. 22 cm. [HV6245.L44] 74-107126 6.95
1. Crime and criminals—Biography. 2. Genius—Case studies. I. Title.

Crime and criminals—Biography—Addresses, essays, lectures.

WILLIAMS, Roger M., 364.1'092'2 B
1934- comp.
The super crooks; a Rogues' gallery of famous hustlers, swindlers, and thieves. Edited by Roger M. Williams. [1st ed. Chicago, Playboy Press, 1973] xv, 284 p. 22 cm. [HV6245.W748] 73-84920 8.95
1. Crime and criminals—Biography—Addresses, essays, lectures. I. Title. Contents omitted.

Crime and criminals—California.

CHESSMAN, Caryl, 1921- 923.4173
Cell 2455, Death Row. New York, Prentice-Hall [1954] 361p. 22cm. Autobiography. [HV6248.C44A3] 54-8475
1. Crime and criminals—California. I. Title.

CHESSMAN, Caryl, 365'.6'0924 B
1921-1960.
Cell 2455; death row. Westport, Conn., Greenwood Press [1969, c1954] 361 p. 23 cm. Autobiography. [HV6248.C44A3 1969] 69-10074 ISBN 0-8371-1631-7
1. Crime and criminals—California. 2. Prisoners—California—Personal narratives. I. Title.

CHESSMAN, Caryl 923.4173
[Whittier]
Cell 2455, Death Row. New expanded ed. Englewood Cliffs, N.J., Prentice-Hall [c.1954, 1960] 402p. 22cm. 4.95
1. Crime and criminals—California. I. Title.

Crime and criminals—Canada—Biography.

ROBIN, Martin. 364.1'55'0922 B
The bad and the lonely : seven stories of the best—and worst—Canadian outlaws / Martin Robin. Toronto : J. Lorimer, 1976. 221 p., [8] leaves of plates : ill. ; 24 cm. Includes bibliographies. [F1031.5.R58] 77-353728 ISBN 0-88862-121-3. ISBN 0-88862-122-1 pbk.
1. Crime and criminals—Canada—Biography. 2. Frontier and pioneer life—Canada. 3. Canada—Biography. I. Title.

Crime and criminals—Correspondence, reminiscences, etc.

*JOEY. 364.1'523'0924 B
Joey Kills by Joey, with Dave Fisher. New York, Pocket Books [1975] 221 p. 18 cm. [HV6248] 0-671-80193-7 1.75 (pbk.)
1. Crime and criminals—Correspondence, reminiscences, etc. 2. Mafia. I. Title. BIP

JOEY. 364.1'523'0924 B
Killer; autobiography of a hit man for the Mafia, by Joey, with Dave Fisher. [1st ed. Chicago, Playboy Press, 1973] 318 p. 22 cm. [HV6248.J57A3] 73-76279 8.95
1. Crime and criminals—Correspondence, reminiscences, etc. 2. Mafia. I. Fisher, David, 1946- joint author. II. Title.

Crime and criminals—Ontario.

LAMB, Marjorie. 364.1'6'0922 B
The Boyd gang / Marjorie Lamb and Barry Pearson. Toronto : P. Martin Associates, [1976?] x, 256 p. : ill. ; 24 cm. [HV6809.O6L35] 77-360057 ISBN 0-88778-145-4 : 12.00
1. Crime and criminals—Ontario. 2. Gangs—Ontario. 3. Crime and criminals—Ontario—Biography. I. Pearson, Barry, joint author. II. Title.

Crime and criminals—Southwest, New.

CALHOUN, Samuel H., 1839-1862. 923.4173
A desperado in Arizona, 1858-1860; or, The life, trial, death, and confession of Samuel H. Calhoun, the soldier-murderer. By Jonathan H. Greene. Santa Fe, Stagecoach Press, 1964. xvi, 89 p. illus., port. 18 cm. Calhoun told his life story to J. H. Greene. First published in 1862 under title: The life, death, and confession of Samuel H. Calhoun. [F786.C18 1964] 64-17593
1. Crime and criminals—Southwest, New. I. Greene, Jonathan Harrington, b. 1812. II. Title.

Crime and criminals—Texas—Biography.

MADDOX, Web. 364.1'092'2 B
The black sheep / by Web Maddox. [Quanah, Tex.] : Nortex Press, c1975. ix, 158 p. : ill. ; 22 cm. Bibliography: p. 155-157. [HV6785.M29] 76-358983 ISBN 0-89015-079-6 : 5.95
1. Crime and criminals—Texas—Biography. I. Title.

Crime and criminals—The West.

COOK, David J., 1840-1907. 923.573
Hands up; or, Twenty years of detective life in the mountains and on the plains; reminiscences, a condensed criminal history of the Far West. With an introd. by Everett L. DeGolyer, Jr. [New ed.] Norman, University of Oklahoma Press [1958] 319 p. illus. 20 cm. (The Western frontier library, 11) [HV7914.C78 1958] 58-11605
1. Crime and criminals—The West. I. Title.

HORAN, James David, 1914- 978
Pictorial history of the wild West; a true account of the bad men, desperadoes, rustlers, and outlaws of the old West—and the men who fought them to establish law and order, by James H. Horan and Paul Sann. New York, Crown Publishers [1954] 254 p. illus., ports. facsims. 31 cm. Bibliography: p. 248-250. [F591.H76] 54-11180
1. Crime and criminals—The West. 2. Frontier and pioneer life—The West. 3. Outlaws. 4. The West—Biography. I. Sann, Paul, joint author. II. Title.

MACDONALD, Craig. 364'.978
Leather 'n lead : an anthology of desperadoes in the Far West, 1820-1920 / by Craig MacDonald. Boston : Branden Press, c1976. 144 p., [20] leaves of plates : ill. ; 23 cm. Bibliography: p. 142-144. [F591.M125] 75-21412 ISBN 0-8283-1639-2 : 7.95
1. Crime and criminals—The West. 2. Crime and criminals—The West—Biography. 3. The West—Biography. I. Title.

METZ, Leon Claire. 364.1'5'0922
The shooters : this unique chronicle depicts rare, historical & true stories of notorious gunmen : authentic, factual, uncommon / by Leon Claire Metz. 1st ed. El Paso, Tex. : Mangan Books, 1976. 300 p. : ill. ; 24 cm. At head of title: Genuine & authoritative. "Most of the material ... appeared first in the El Paso times during 1973-74." Bibliography: p. 293-298. [F594.M53] 76-21578 14.95
1. Crime and criminals—The West. 2. Crime and criminals—The West—Biography. 3. The West—History—1860-1880. 4. The West—Biography. I. Title.

Crime and criminals—The West—Biography.

GARRETT, Richard. 364.1'5'0922 B
Famous characters of the Wild West / Richard Garrett. New York : St. Martin's Press, 1977, c1975. 156 p. : map ; 23 cm. [F594.G37 1977] 76-45855 7.95
1. Crime and criminals—The West—Biography. 2. The West—Biography. 3. The West—History—1848-1950. BIP

Crime and criminals—The West—Juvenile literature.

JOHNSON, Dorothy M. 364.15'0922 B
Western badmen [by] Dorothy M. Johnson. New York, Dodd, Mead [1970] xii, 276 p. ports. 21 cm. Bibliography: p. [265]-269. Twenty-two biographical sketches of the frontier's most notorious badmen. Includes Billy the Kid, Butch Cassidy, Cole Younger, Doc Holliday, and others. [F591.J615] 920 73-121981
1. Crime and criminals—The West—Juvenile literature. 2. Outlaws—Juvenile literature. I. Title.

WILLIAMS, Brad. 364.1'523'0922 B
Legendary outlaws of the West / Brad Williams ; ill. by Paul Blaine Henrie. New York : H. Z. Walck, c1976. ix, 168 p. : ill. ; 26 cm. Biographical sketches of eleven less notorious but notable western outlaws who plundered everything from stagecoaches to airplanes. [F591.W717] 920 75-43036 ISBN 0-8098-5006-0 : 10.95
1. Crime and criminals—The West—Juvenile literature. 2. The West—Biography—Juvenile literature. 3. The West—Biography. I. Henrie, Paul Blain, 1932- II. Title. BIP

Crime and criminals—U.S.—Case studies.

BYRNES, Thomas, 1842-1910. 364'.922
1886 professional criminals of America. Introductions by Arthur M. Schlesinger, Jr. [and] S. J. Perelman. New York, Chelsea House Publishers [1969] xxxi, 433 p. facsim., ports. 29 cm. Reprint of the 1886 ed. published under title: Professional criminals of America. [HV6785.B93 1969] 77-97780 10.00
1. Crime and criminals—U.S.—Case studies. I. Title. II. Title: Professional criminals of America.

Crime and criminals—United States.

MAC ISAAC, John. 364.1'0924
Half the fun was getting there. Englewood Cliffs, N.J., Prentice-Hall [1968] 246 p. 22 cm. Autobiographical. [HV6248.M175A3] 68-25877 5.95
1. Crime and criminals—United States. I. Title.

MY life in crime; 923.4173
the autobiography of a professional criminal, reported by John Bartlow Martin. [1st ed.] New York, Harper [1952] 279 p. 22 cm. [HV6248.A2M9] 51-11937
1. Crime and criminals—U.S. I. Martin, John Bartlow, 1915- BIP

PINKERTON, Allan, 1819-1884. 364'.973
Thirty years a detective. Reprinted with the addition of an introductory essay "The Pinkerton Detective Agency" by James D. Horan. Montclair, N.J., Patterson Smith, 1975. 621 p. illus. 22 cm. (Patterson Smith series in criminology, law enforcement & social problems, publication no. 154) Reprint of the 1884 ed. published by G. W. Carleton, New York. [HV7914.P7 1975] 77-172572 ISBN 0-87585-154-1
1. Crime and criminals—United States. 2. Detectives—United States—Correspondence, reminiscenses, etc. I. Title.

SICILIANO, Vincent. 362.1'0924 B
Unless they kill me first, by Vincent ("The Cat") Siciliano. New York, Hawthorn Books [1970] 174 p. 24 cm. Autobiographical. [HV6248.S56185A3] 73-107899 5.95
1. Crime and criminals—United States. I. Title. BIP

WARREN, Paul, 1916- 364.15
Next time is for life. [New York, Dell Pub. Co., 1953] 223p. 17cm. (A Dell first edition, 6) Autobiography. [HV6248.W44A3] 364 53-10784
1. Crime and criminals—U. S. I. Title.

Crime and criminals—United States—Biography.

MY life in crime; 364.1 B
the autobiography of a professional criminal, reported by John Bartlow Martin. Westport, Conn., Greenwood Press [1970, c1952] 279 p. 23 cm. [HV6248.A2M9 1970] 78-97349 ISBN 8-371-31316-
1. Crime and criminals—U.S.—Biography. I. Martin, John Bartlow, 1915-

NASH, Jay Robert. 364'.092'2 B
Bloodletters and badmen; a narrative encyclopedia of American criminals from the Pilgrims to the present. New York, M. Evans; distributed in association with Lippincott, Philadelphia [1973] 640 p. illus. 29 cm. Bibliography: p. 627-632. [HV6785.N37] 72-95977 ISBN 0-87131-113-5 16.95
1. Crime and criminals—United States—Biography. I. Title. BIP

RICE, Robert. 364.3'092'2 B
The business of crime. Westport, Conn., Greenwood Press [1974, c1956] xix, 268 p. 22 cm. Reprint of the ed. published by Farrar, Straus & Cudahy, New York. [HV6785.R52 1974] 73-19297 ISBN 0-8371-7317-5 12.75
1. Crime and criminals—United States—Biography. I. Title. BIP

Crime and criminals United States Biography.

GETTINGER, Stephen H. 364.6'6'0922 B
Sentenced to die : the people, the crimes, and the controversy / by Stephen H. Gettinger. New York : Macmillan, c1979. xxi, 284 p. ; 22 cm. Includes index. Bibliography: p. 270-274. [HV6785.G4 1979] 79-4552 ISBN 0-02-543070-X pbk. : 9.95
1. Crime and ciminals—United States—Biography. 2. Capital punishment—United States. 3. Criminal justice, Administration of—United States. I. Title. BIP

THURMAN, Steve 923.4173
'Baby Face' Nelson. Derby, Conn., Monarch Bks. [c.1961] 139p. (MA 313) .35 pap.,
I. Title.

Crime passionel.

SPARROW, Gerald, 1903- 364.1'0922
The great deceivers. New York, Roy Publishers [1967 or 8] 170 p. 22 cm. [HV6053.S6 1967b] 68-14354
1. Crime passionel. 2. Crime passionel—Gt. Brit. I. Title.

SPARROW, Gerald, 1903- 364.1'0922
The great deceivers. New York, Roy Publishers [1967 or 8] 170 p. 22 cm. [HV6053.S6 1967b] 68-14354
1. Crime passionel. 2. Crime passionel—Great Britain. I. Title.

Criminal investigation—Juvenile literature.

LARRANAGA, Robert D. 364.12'0922 B
Famous crimefighters [by] Robert D. Larranaga. Minneapolis, Lerner Publications Co. [1970] 78 p. illus., facsim., ports. 21 cm. (A Pull ahead book) Describes pioneers in such criminology techniques as fingerprinting, forensic medicine, and handwriting analysis. [HV8073.8.L35] 78-84413
1. Criminal investigation—Juvenile literature. I. Title. BIP

Criminologists.

MANNHEIM, Hermann, 1889- ed. 923.6
Pioneers in criminology. Edited and introduced by Hermann Mannheim. Chicago, Quadrangle Books, 1960. xi, 402p. 25cm. (The Library of criminology, no. 1) Bibl. 60-14892 7.50
1. Criminologists. I. Title. II. Series.

MANNHEIM, Hermann, 1889- ed. 364'.092'2 B
Pioneers in criminology. Edited and introduced by Hermann Mannheim. 2d ed., enl. Montclair, N.J., Patterson Smith, 1972. xv, 505 p. 23 cm. (Patterson Smith reprint series in criminology, law enforcement, and social problems. Publication no. 121) Includes bibliographical references. [HV6025.M322 1972] 78-108238 ISBN 0-87585-121-5 14.00
1. Criminologists. I. Title.
pap. 4.75. BIP

Crippen, Hawley Harvey, 1862-1910.

CULLEN, Tom A. 364.1'523'0924
The mild murderer : the true story of the Dr. Crippen case / Tom Cullen ; illustrated with photos. Boston : Houghton Mifflin, 1977. p. cm. [HV6248.C687C84] 77-24440 ISBN 0-395-25776-X : 7.95
1. Crippen, Hawley Harvey, 1862-1910. 2. Crime and criminals—England—London—Biography. 3. Murder—England—London—Case studies. I. Title. BIP

Cripple Creek, Colo.—Social life and customs.

LEE, Mabel (Barbee) 917.88'58'0330924
Back in Cripple Creek. [1st ed.] Garden City, N.Y., Doubleday, 1968. 192 p. map (on lining papers) 22 cm. Autobiographical. [F784.C8L39] 68-10679
1. Cripple Creek, Colo.—Social life and customs. I. Title.

Crippoles.

THOMASSEN, Rolf, 1902- 616.83
Beyond today; translated by Torgrim and Linda Hannaas. Minneapolis, Augsburg Pub. House [1953] 163p. illus. 21cm. Autobiography. Translation of Over de hoye fjeelle. [CT9983.T5A33] 53-13114
1. Crippoles. 2. Disabled—Rehabilitation, etc. I. Title.

Crisp, Quentin.

CRISP, Quentin. 301.41'57'0924 B
The naked civil servant / Quentin Crisp ; pref. by Michael Holroyd. New York : Holt, Rinehart and Winston, [1977] c1968.

x, 212 p. ; 22 cm. [HQ75.8.C74A35 1977] 77-73866 ISBN 0-03-022451-9 : 7.95
1. Crisp, Quentin. 2. Homosexuals, Male—Great Britain—Biography. I. Title. **BIP**

Crist, Evamae Barton.

CRIST, Evamae Barton. 248 B
Take this house / Evamae Barton Crist ; introd. by Frances Hunter. Scottdale, Pa. : Herald Press, c1977. 141 p. : ill. ; 18 cm. [BV4470.C7] 77-151776 ISBN 0-8361-1817-0 pbk. : 1.95
1. Crist, Evamae Barton. 2. Church work with refugees. 3. Christian biography—Pennsylvania. 4. Refugees—Pennsylvania. 5. Refugees—Vietnam. 6. Vietnamese Conflict, 1961-1975—Refugees. I. Title. **BIP**

Cristiani, Armando—Juvenile literature.

POWLEDGE, Fred. 791.3'092'4 B
Born on the circus / by Fred Powledge ; illustrated with photos. by the author. 1st ed. New York : Harcourt Brace Jovanovich, c1976. 94 p. : ill. ; 26 cm. Describes the hard work and excitement of circus life as seen through the eyes of an eleven-year-old who performs as juggler, trampoline artist, and horseback rider. [GV1811.C74P68] 92 76-2449 ISBN 0-15-209970-0 : 7.95
1. Cristiani, Armando—Juvenile literature. 2. Circus—Juvenile literature. I. Title. **BIP**

Cristofano Ceffini.

CIPOLLA, Carlo M. 614'.0945'51
Cristofano and the plague; a study in the history of public health in the age of Galileo [by] Carlo M. Cipolla. Berkeley, University of California Press [1973] 188 p. illus. 22 cm. Bibliography: p. 171-177. [RA424.C56] 72-89797 ISBN 0-520-02341-2 7.50
1. Cristofano Ceffini. 2. Hygiene, Public—Prato—History. 3. Plague—Prato—History. I. Title. **BIP**

Criswell, Wallie A.

KEITH, Billy. 286'.1'0924 B
W. A. Criswell: the authorized biography; the story of a courageous and uncompromising Christian leader. Old Tappan, N.J., Revell [1973] 224 p. illus. 21 cm. [BX6495.C74K4] 73-14830 ISBN 0-8007-0615-3 5.95
1. Criswell, Wallie A.

Criticism.

TYNAN, Kenneth, 1927- 801'.95
Tynan right & left; plays, films, people, places and events. [1st American ed.] New York, Atheneum, 1967. ix, 479 p. 25 cm. [PN94.T9 1967] 67-25489
1. Criticism. I. Title.

Crittenden, John Jordan, 1787-1863.

COLEMAN, Ann Mary 976.9'03'0924 Butler (Crittenden) 1813-1891.
The life of John J. Crittenden, with selections from his correspondence and speeches. Edited by Mrs. Chapman Coleman. New York, Da Capo Press, 1970. 2 v. ports. 24 cm. Reprint of the 1871 ed. [E340.C9C6 1970] 72-99469
1. Crittenden, John Jordan, 1787-1863. I. Title.

Croats in the United States—Directories.

BIOGRAPHICAL directory of 920.07 *scholars, artists, and professionals of Croation descent in the United States and Canada,* v.2. 1964-1965. Ed. by Francis H. Eterovich. Chicago, F. H. Eterovich, 1125 E. 50th St. [c.1965] xii, 139, 5p. 28cm. Began pubn. in 1963. [E184.C93B5] 65-5564 3.00 pap.,
1. Croats in the U. S.—Direct. 2. Croats in Canada—Direct. I. Eterovich, Francis H., ed. **BIP**

ETEROVICH, Francis H. 920.073
Biographical directory of scholars, artists, and professionals of Croatian descent in the United States and Canada. Compiled and edited by Francis H. Eterovich. [3d enl. ed.] Cleveland Heights, Ohio, 1970. xxiv, 203 p. 28 cm. Sponsored and published by Institute for Soviet and East European Studies, John Carroll University. The 1st ed. was published in Croatian in 1963 under title: Hrvati profesori na americkim i kanadskim visokim skolama. [E184.C93E85 1970] 70-13452
1. Croats in the United States—Directories. 2. Croats in Canada—Directories. I. John Carroll University, Cleveland. Institute for Soviet and East European Studies. II. Title.

Croce, Benedetto, 1866-

CROCE, Benedetto, 1866-1952. 195
An autobiography. Translated from the Italian by R. G. Collingwood. With a pref. by J. A. Smith. Freeport, N.Y., Books for Libraries Press [1970] 116 p. 23 cm. Translation of Contributo alla critica di me stesso. Reprint of the 1927 ed. Includes bibliographical references. [B3614.C74A33 1970] 79-114871

SPRIGGE, Cecil Jackson 921.5 Squire, 1896-
Benedetto Croce, man and thinker. New Haven, Yale University Press, 1952. 64 p. 23 cm. (Studies in modern European literature and thought) [B3614.C74S6 1952a] 52-10461
1. Croce, Benedetto, 1866- I. Title.

Croce, Jim—Juvenile literature.

JACOBS, Linda. 784'.092'4 B
Jim Croce : the feeling lives on / by Linda Jacobs. St. Paul : EMC Corp., c1975. p. cm. (Men behind the bright lights) A brief biography of the popular singer and musician who died in a plane crash just as his career began to develop. [ML3930.C925J3] 92 75-26984 ISBN 0-88436-215-9 lib.bdg. : 4.95 ISBN 0-88436-216-7 pbk. : 2.95
1. Croce, Jim—Juvenile literature. I. Title. **BIP**

Crocker, William Henry, 1861-1937.

RYDER, David 979.4050924 (B) Warren, 1892-
"Great citizen"; a biography of William H.Crocker. With decorations by Dan Adair. San Francisco, Historical Publications, 1962. xviii, 271 p. illus., ports. 24 cm. [CT275.C88744R9] 62-18007
1. Crocker, William Henry, 1861-1937. I. Title.

Crockett Co., Tex.—History.

A History of Crockett 976.4'876 *County :* the Crockett County Historical Society American Revolution Bicentennial project. San Angelo, Tex. : Anchor Pub. Co., c1976. 592 p. : ill. ; 29 cm. Includes index. [F392.C84H57] 77-371956
1. Crockett Co., Tex.—History. 2. Crockett Co., Tex.—Genealogy. 3. Crockett Co., Tex.—Biography. I. Crockett County Historical Society.

A History of 976.4'247'00496073 *Crockett County :* the Crockett County Historical Society American Revolution Bicentennial project. San Angelo, Tex. : Anchor Pub. Co., c1976. 592 p. : ill. ; 29 cm. Includes index. [F392.C84H57] 77-371956
1. Crockett Co., Tex.—History. 2. Crockett Co., Tex.—Genealogy. 3. Crockett Co., Tex.—Biography. I. Crockett County Historical Society.

Crockett, David, 1786-1836.

BAUGH, Virgil E 923.973
Rendezvous at the Alamo; highlights in the lives of Bowie, Crockett and Travis. [1st ed.] New York, Pageant Press [1960] 251p. illus. 24cm. Includes bibliography. [F390.B38] 60-12286
1. Bowie, James, d. 1836. 2. Crockett, David, 1786-1836. 3. Travis, William Barret, 1809-1836. 4. Alamo—Siege, 1836. I. Title.

BLAIR, Walter, 1900- 923.973
Davy Crockett, frontier hero; the truth as he told it, the legend as friends built it. Illustrated by Richard Powers. New York, Coward-McCann, c1955. 215 p. illus. 21 cm. [F436.C9454] 55-10792
1. Crockett, David, 1786-1836.

CROCKETT, David, 1786- 923.973 1836.
The adventures of Davy Crockett, told mostly by himself. With illus. by John W. Thomason, Jr. New York, Scribner [1955] 246 p. illus. 24 cm. Includes "Col. Crockett's exploits and adventures in Texas," a pseudo-autobiography generally ascribed to Richard Penn Smith. [F436.C87 1955] 55-12944
1. Tennessee—History. 2. Creek War, 1813-1814. 3. U.S.—Description and travel—1783-1848. 4. Texas—History—Revolution, 1835-1836. I. Smith, Richard Penn, 1799-1854, supposed author. Col. Crockett's exploits and adventures in Texas. II. Title.

CROCKETT, David, 1786- 923.973 1836.
Davy Crockett's own story, as written by himself the autobiography of America's great folk hero Illustrated by Milton Glaser New York, Citadel Press [1955] 377 p. illus. 22 cm. 'Consists of . . . A narrative of the life of David Crockett . . . written by himself, published in 1834; An account of Col. Crockett's tour to the North and down East, published in 1834, and Col. Crockett's exploits and adventures in Texas, published posthumously in 1836.' 'Col. Crockett's exploits and adventures in Texas' is a pseudo-autobiography generally ascribed to Richard Penn Smith. [F436.C9 55-10010
1. Tennessee-Hist. 2. Creek War, 1813-1814. 3. U. S.— Descr. & trav.—1783-1848. 4. Texas—Hist.—Revolution, 1835-1836. I. Smith, Richard Penn, 1799-1854. Col. Crockett s explots and adventures in Texas. II. Title.

CROCKETT, David, 1786- 923.973 1836.
The life of Davy Crockett, by himself. To which is added an account of his glorious death at the Alamo while fighting in defense of Texan independence. [New York] New American Library [1955] 263 p. 18 cm. (A Signet book, S1214) 'Reprinted from the Keystone Publishing Company edition, published in Philadelphia in 1889. [F436.C939] 55-2913
1. Tennessee—Hist. 2. Creek War: 1813-1814. 3. U. S.—Descr. & trav.— 1783-1848. 4. Texas—Hist.—Revolution, 1835-1836. I Title.

CROCKETT, David, 976.8'04'0924 B 1786-1836.
A narrative of the life of David Crockett / by David Crockett. St. Clair Shores, Mich. : Scholarly Press, 1978. xxiv, 415 p. ; 21 cm. [F436.C9395 1978] 78-19230 ISBN 0-403-07781-8 : 15.00
1. Crockett, David, 1786-1836. 2. Pioneers—Tennessee—Biography. 3. Tennessee—Biography. 4. Legislators—United States—Biography. I. Title. **BIP**

CROCKETT, David, 976.8'04'0924 B 1786-1836.
A narrative of the life of David Crockett of the State of Tennessee. A facsim. ed. with annotations and an introd. by James A. Shackford and Stanley J. Folmsbee. Knoxville, University of Tennessee Press, [1973, c1834] xx, 211 p. illus. 20 x 22 cm. (Tennesseana editions) Original ed. published by E. L. Carey and A. Hart, Philadelphia. Includes bibliographical references. [F436.C9395 1834aa] 72-177358 ISBN 0-87049-119-9 7.95
1. Crockett, David, 1786-1836. 2. Tennessee—History. 3. Creek War, 1813-1814. I. Shackford, James Atkins, ed. II. Folmsbee, Stanley John, 1899- ed. III. Title. IV. Series. **BIP**

HOLBROOK, Stewart Hall, 923.973 1893-1964.
Davy Crockett; illustrated by Ernest Richardson. New York, Random House [1955] 179 p. illus. 22 cm. (Landmark books, 57) [F436.C952] 55-9514
1. Crockett, David, 1786-1836.

MEADOWCROFT, Enid 976.4'02'0924 B (La Monte) 1898-
The story of Davy Crockett; illustrated by Charles B. Falls. New York, Grosset & Dunlap [1952] 178 p. illus. 22 cm. (Signature books) A biography of the famous woodsman and hunter who could snuff a candle with a bullet, was hated by every bear in the county, and was known by politicians as "the gamecock of the wilderness." [PZ7.M506Su] 92 AC 68
1. Crockett, David, 1786-1836. I. Falls, Charles Buckles, 1874- illus. II. Title.

NULL, Marion Michael 923.973
The forgotten pioneer; the life of Davy Crockett. New York, Vantage Press [1954] 183p. illus. 23cm. [F436.C955] 53-12146
1. Crockett, David, 1786-1836. I. Title.

ROURKE, Constance 923.973 Mayfield, 1885-1941.
Davy Crockett; illustrated by Walter Seaton. Garden City, N. Y., Junior Deluxe Editions [1956] 256p. illus. 22cm. Includes bibliography. [F436.C958 1956] 56-1155
1. Crockett, David, 1786-1836. I. Title.

ROURKE, Constance 923.973 Mayfield, 1885-1941.
Davy Crockett; illustrated by James MacDonald. Introd. and study guides by Geraldine Murphy. [School ed.] New York, Harcourt, Brace [1955] 262p. illus. 21cm. [F436.C958 1955] 55-4803
1. Crockett, David, 1786-1836. I. Title.

ROURKE, Constance Mayfield, v. 12 1885-1941.
Davy Crockett, by Constance Rourke; illustrated by James MacDonald. [New York] Harcourt, Brace and World [c1962] xiii, 276 p. incl. front., illus., plates. 22 cm. Maps on lining-papers. "Behind this book": p. 247-276. 68-10878
1. Crockett, David, 1786-1836. I. Title. **BIP**

SHACKFORD, James Atkins. 923.973
David Crockett, the man and the legend. Edited by John B. Shackford. Chapel Hill, University of North Carolina Press [1956] xiv, 338 p. port., map (on lining papers) 24 cm. Bibliography: p. 317-324. [F436.C9594] 56-13913
1. Crockett, David, 1786-1836.

TAYLOR, Vincent Frank, 923.973 1915-
David Crockett, the bravest of them all, who died in the Alamo San Antonio, Naylor Co. [1955] 79p. illus. 20cm. [F436.C9615] 55-14485
1. Crockett, David, 1786-1836. I. Title.

Crockett, David, 1786-1836—Juvenile literature.

FORD, Anne. 92 (J)
Davy Crockett. Illustrated by Leonard Vosburgh. New York, Putnam, c1961. 45 p. illus. 23 cm. [F436.C949] 61-13592
1. Crockett, David, 1786-1836—Juvenile literature. I. Title.

GRANT, Matthew G. 976.8'04'0924 B
Davy Crockett, frontier adventurer [by] Matthew G. Grant. Illustrated by Jack Norman. [Mankato, Minn., Creative Education; distributed by Childrens Press, Chicago, 1973, c1974] 29 p. illus. (part col.) 25 cm. (His Gallery of great Americans series. Frontiersmen of America) A brief biography of the Tennessee woodsman renowned as a hunter, scout, politician, and soldier. [F436.C9515] 92 73-10072 ISBN 0-87191-258-9 3.95
1. Crockett, David, 1786-1836—Juvenile literature. I. Norman, Jack, illus. II. Title.

MOSELEY, Elizabeth 92 (J) Robards.
Davy Crockett, hero of the wild frontier, by Elizabeth R. Moseley. Illustrated by Thomas Beecham. Champaign, Ill., Garrard Pub. Co. [1967] 80 p. col. illus. 23 cm. (A Discovery book) [F436.C9544] 67-11949
1. Crockett, David, 1786-1836—Juvenile literature.

TAYLOR, Vincent Frank, 1915- 92
David Crockett, by V. F. Taylor. [Enl. and rev. ed.] San Antonio, Naylor [1967] xiii, 93p. illus. 20cm. Bibl. [F436.C9615 1967] 67-13398 2.95
1. Crockett, David, 1786-1836—Juvenile literature. I. Title.

WAYNE, Bennett. 973.5'092'2 B
Men of the wild frontier. Edited, with commentary, by Bennett Wayne. Champaign, Ill., Garrard Pub. Co. [1974] 167 p. illus. (part col.) 22 cm. (A Target book) Brief biographies of four men instrumental in opening up new American frontiers. [F454.B844] 920 73-13615 ISBN 0-8116-4905-9
1. Boone, Daniel, 1734-1820—Juvenile literature. 2. Jackson, Andrew, Pres. U.S., 1767-1845—Juvenile literature. 3. Crockett, David, 1786-1836—Juvenile literature. 4. Houston, Samuel, 1793-1863—Juvenile literature. I. Title. BIP

Crockett family.

SIMMONS, June Pitts. 929'.2'0973
Nathan Crockett, the eldest brother of "Davy" : genealogy of his son, John / June Pitts Simmons (Mrs. Robert W. Simmons). Sharon, Tenn. : Simmons, [1975] 40 leaves ; 28 cm. [CS71.C938 1975] 75-310582
1. Crockett family. I. Title.

Crockford, William, 1775-1844.

BLYTH, Henry. 364.17'2'0924 B
Hell and hazard; or, William Crockford versus the gentlemen of England. Chicago, H. Regnery Co. [1970, c1969] 214 p. illus., ports. 22 cm. Bibliography: p. 205-208. [HV6722.G86L63 1970] 70-126045 5.95
1. Crockford, William, 1775-1844. 2. Gambling—London—History. I. Title.

Croft-Cooke, Rupert, 1903- — Biography.

CROFT-COOKE, Rupert, 1903- 828'.9'1209 B
The caves of Hercules / Rupert Croft-Cooke. London ; New York : W. H. Allen, 1974. 173 p. ; 23 cm. [PR6005.R673Z499] 75-306185 ISBN 0-491-01322-1 : £2.75
1. Croft-Cooke, Rupert, 1903- — Biography. 2. Tangier—Description. I. Title.

CROFT-COOKE, Rupert, 1903- 828'.9'1209 B
The dogs of peace. London, New York, W. H. Allen, 1973. 190 p. 22 cm. [PR6005.R673D6] 73-164087 ISBN 0-491-00864-3 £2.75
1. Croft-Cooke, Rupert, 1903- — Biography. I. Title.

Croft, Herbert, Sir, 1564?-1629.

†HAM, R. E. 354'.42'083 B
The county and the kingdom : Sir Herbert Croft and the Elizabethan state / R. E. Ham. Washington : University Press of America, c1977. x, 301 p. ; 22 cm. A revision of the author's thesis, University of California, 1974, which was published under title: The career of Sir Herbert Croft. Includes bibliographical references. [JS3137.H27 1977] 78-303830 ISBN 0-8191-0260-1 pbk. : 10.75
1. Croft, Herbert, Sir, 1564?-1629. 2. Decentralization in government—Great Britain—History. 3. Local officials and employees—Great Britain—Biography. 4. Great Britain—Politics and government—1485-1603. 5. Great Britain—Politics and government—1603-1625. I. Title.

Croghan, George d. 1782.

WAINWRIGHT, Nicholas B 923.273
George Croghan, wilderness diplomat. Chapel Hill, Published for the Institute of Early American History and Calture, at Williamsburg by the University of North Carolina Press [1959] 334 p. illus. 24 cm. Includes bibliography. [F483.C76W3] 59-2353
1. Croghan, George d. 1782. I. Title. BIP

Croiset, Gerard, 1909-

POLLACK, Jack Harrison. 133.8
Croiset, the clairvoyant. [1st ed.] Garden City, N. Y., Doubleday, 1964. 318 p. illus., ports. 22 cm. [BF1283.C87P6 1964] 63-12958
1. Croiset, Gerard, 1909- I. Title.

Croke, Thomas William, 1823-1902.

TIERNEY, Mark. 282'.092'4 B
Croke of Cashel : the life of Archbishop Thomas William Croke, 1823-1902 / Mark Tierney. Dublin : Gill and Macmillan, 1976. xvi, 293 p. : ill. ; 23 cm. Includes bibliographical references and index. [BX4705.C7829T54 1976] 77-359491 ISBN 0-7171-0804-X : £8.50
1. Croke, Thomas William, 1823-1902. 2. Catholic Church—Bishops—Biography. 3. Bishops—Ireland—Cashel—Biography. 4. Cashel, Ire.—Biography. I. Title.

Crombrugghe, Constant William van, 1789-1865.

MARY Ignatius, Mother. 922.2493
. . . as the stars they shall shine . . . The story of Canon Van Crombrugghe, priest-educator. New York, Vantage Press [c1952] 192p. illus. 23cm. [BX4705.C783M3] 59-12889
1. Crombrugghe, Constant William van, 1789-1865. I. Title.

Crompton, Samuel, 1753-1827.

FRENCH, Gilbert James, 1804-1866. 677'.00924 B
Life and times of Samuel Crompton. New York, A. M. Kelley, 1970. xv, xiv, 299 p. illus., port. 23 cm. (Documents of social history) Reprint of the 1860 ed., with an introd. by Stanley D. Chapman. Includes bibliographical references. [TS1440.C9F8 1970] 70-107527
1. Crompton, Samuel, 1753-1827. 2. Spinning. I. Title. BIP

Cromwell, Helen (Worley)

CROMWELL, Helen (Worley) 301.4150924
Dirty Helen; an autobiography, by Helen Cromwell with Robert Dougherty. Los Angeles. Sherbourne [1966] 286p. 22cm. [HQ146.M45C7] 66-22232 4.95 bds.,
I. Dougherty, Robert. II. Title.

Cromwell, Jarvis.

CROMWELL, Jarvis. 380.1'45'67700924 B
With a great deal of luck : business adventures of Jarvis Cromwell / by Jarvis Cromwell. [s.l. : s.n.], c1976 (Dalton, Mass. : Studley Press) xxii, 149 p. ; 23 cm. [HF5421.C76A33] 76-375129
1. Cromwell, Jarvis. 2. Commission merchants—United States—Biography. 3. Textile industry—United States. I. Title.

Cromwell, Oliver, 1599-1658.

ASHLEY, Maurice Percy, comp. 942.06'4'0924 B
Cromwell, edited by Maurice Ashley. Englewood Cliffs, N.J., Prentice-Hall [1969] x, 177 p. 22 cm. (Great lives observed) (A Spectrum book) "Bibliographical note": p. 171-173. [DA428.1.A77] 69-17373 4.95
1. Cromwell, Oliver, 1599-1658.

ASHLEY, Maurice Percy. v. 12
The greatness of Oliver Cromwell. New York, Collier Books [1966 c1957] 383 p. maps. 18 cm. Bibliography: p. 371-373. NUC67
1. Cromwell, Oliver, 1599-1658. I. Title.

ASHLEY, Maurice Percy. 942.06'4'0924 B
Oliver Cromwell and his world [by] Maurice Ashley. New York, Putnam [1972] 128 p. illus. 24 cm. Bibliography: p. 117. A biography of the Puritan country gentleman who led the rebellion against Charles I in the English Civil War and ruled England as Lord Protector for ten years. [DA428.A8 1972b] 92 72-189783 6.95
1. Cromwell, Oliver, 1599-1658. 2. Great Britain—History—Puritan Revolution, 1642-1660. I. Title.

BARKER, Ernest, Sir, 1874-1960. 942.06'4'0924 B
Oliver Cromwell and the English people. Freeport, N.Y., Books for Libraries Press [1971] 105 p. 23 cm. An address delivered before the Friedrich Sthamer-Gesellschaft in Hamburg, a branch of the Deutsch-Englische Gesellschaft in Berlin, on 17 Dec. 1936. Reprint of the 1937 ed. Includes bibliographical references. [DA428.1.B37 1971] 72-37329 ISBN 0-8369-6674-0
1. Cromwell, Oliver, 1599-1658. I. Title. BIP

BOYER, Richard E., ed. 942.0640924
Oliver Cromwell and the Puritan revolt; failure of a man or a father? Edited with an introd. by Richard E. Boyer. Boston, Heath [1966] xvi, 90 p. 24 cm. (Problems in European civilization) Bibliography: p. 87-90. [DA426.B63] 66-26809
1. Cromwell, Oliver, 1599-1658. 2. Puritans—England. I. Title. II. Series.

FIRTH, Charles Harding, Sir, 1857-1936. 923.142
Oliver Cromwell and the rule of the Puritans in England. With an introd. by G. M. Young. London, New York, Oxford University Press [1953] xx, 488 p. 16 cm. (The World's classics, 536) [DA426.F52 1953] 53-4098
1. Cromwell, Oliver, 1599-1658. 2. Gt. Brit.—History—Commonwealth and Protectorate, 1649-1660. 3. Gt. Brit.—History—Civil War, 1642-1649. BIP

FRASER, Antonia (Pakenham) Lady, 1932- 942.06'4'0924 B
Cromwell, the Lord Protector [by] Antonia Fraser. [1st American ed.] New York, Knopf, 1973. xx, 774 p. illus. 25 cm. Bibliography: p. [728]-744. [DA426.F7 1973] 73-7270 ISBN 0-394-47034-6 12.50
1. Cromwell, Oliver, 1599-1658. I. Title.

FRASER, Antonia (Pakerham) Lady, 1932- 942.06'4'0924 B
Cromwell, the Lord Protector [by] Antonia Fraser. [New York, Dell, 1975, c1973] 878 p. 18 cm. Bibliography: [p. 829]-843. [DA426.F7 1975] 1.95 (pbk.)
1. Cromwell, Oliver, 1599-1658. I. Title.
L.C. card number for original ed.: 73-7270

GARDINER, Samuel Rawson, 1829-1902. 923.142
Oliver Cromwell. With a new introd. by Maurice Ashley. New York, Collier Books [1962] 220 p. 18 cm. (Collier books, AS210) [DA426.G24] 62-12074
1. Cromwell, Oliver, 1599-1658. 2. Gt. Brit.—History—Commonwealth and Protectorate, 1649-1660.

GILLINGHAM, John Bennett. 942.06'0924 B
Cromwell : portrait of a soldier / John Gillingham. London : Weidenfeld and Nicolson, c1976. 149 p., [8] leaves of plates : ill. ; 23 cm. Includes index. Bibliography: p. 143-144. [DA426.G54] 76-383790 ISBN 0-297-77148-5 : £5.25
1. Cromwell, Oliver, 1599-1658. 2. Great Britain. Army—Biography. 3. Generals—Great Britain—Biography. 4. Statesmen—Great Britain—Biography.

HARRISON, Frederic, 1831-1923. 942.06'4'0924 B
Oliver Cromwell. Freeport, N.Y., Books for Libraries Press [1972] vi, 228 p. 23 cm. Reprint of the 1888 ed., issued in series: Twelve English statesmen. [DA428.H37 1972] 78-39196 ISBN 0-8369-6798-4
1. Cromwell, Oliver, 1599-1658. 2. Great Britain—History—Commonwealth and Protectorate, 1649-1660. I. Series: Twelve English statesmen.

HILL, John Edward Christopher, 1912- 942.06'4'0924 B
God's Englishman; Oliver Cromwell and the English Revolution [by] Christopher Hill. New York, Dial Press, 1970. 324 p. illus., ports. 22 cm. (Crosscurrents in world history) Bibliography: p. [301]-304. [DA426.H49 1970b] 75-111450 7.95
1. Cromwell, Oliver, 1599-1658. 2. Gt. Brit.—History—Puritan Revolution, 1642-1660. I. Title. BIP

HILLARY, A. A. 942.06'4'0924
Oliver Cromwell and the challenge to the monarchy, by A. A. Hillary. [1st ed.] Oxford, New York, Pergamon Press [1969] viii, 134 p. port. 20 cm. (The Commonwealth and international library. History division) Bibliography: p. 131. [DA426.H53 1969] 72-76799
1. Cromwell, Oliver, 1599-1658. 2. Gt. Brit.—History—Commonwealth and Protectorate, 1649-1660. I. Title.

HOWELL, Roger. 942.06'4'0924 B
Cromwell / by Roger Howell, Jr. 1st ed. Boston : Little, Brown, c1977. xii, 269 p. ; 21 cm. (The Library of world biography) Includes index. Bibliography: p. [257]-261. [DA426.H68] 76-52498 ISBN 0-316-37581-0 : 8.95
1. Cromwell, Oliver, 1599-1658. 2. Statesmen—Great Britain—Biography. 3. Generals—Great Britain—Biography. 4. Great Britain—Politics and government—1642-1660.

KORR, Charles P. 327.41'044
Cromwell and the new model foreign policy : England's policy toward France, 1649-1658 / Charles P. Korr. Berkeley : University of California Press, c1975. x, 268 p. ; 24 cm. Includes index. Bibliography: p. 253-261. [DA47.1.K67] 72-82231 ISBN 0-520-02281-5 : 12.50
1. Cromwell, Oliver, 1599-1658. 2. Great Britain—Foreign relations—France. 3. France—Foreign relations—Great Britain. 4. Great Britain—Foreign relations—1649-1660. I. Title.

LARNED, Josephus Nelson, 1836-1913. 153.9'8'0922 B
A study of greatness in men. Freeport, N.Y., Books for Libraries Press [1972] 303 p. 23 cm. (Essay index reprint series) Reprint of the 1911 ed. Contents.Contents.—What goes into the making of a great man?—Napoleon: a prodigy, without greatness.—Cromwell: imperfect in greatness.—Washington: impressive in greatness.—Lincoln: simplest in greatness. [BF412.L4 1972] 73-156677 ISBN 0-8369-2557-2
1. Napoleon I, Emperor of the French, 1769-1821. 2. Cromwell, Oliver, 1599-1658. 3. Washington, George, Pres. U.S., 1732-1799. 4. Lincoln, Abraham, Pres. U.S., 1809-1865—Addresses, essays, lectures. 5. Genius. I. Title. BIP

LEVINE, Israel E. 942.0640924
Oliver Cromwell. New York, Messner [c.1966] 191p. 22cm. [DA426.L46] 66-14006 3.19 lib. ed.,
1. Cromwell, Oliver, 1599-1658—Juvenile literature. I. Title.

MARTIN, Bernard 923.142
Our chief of men; the story of Oliver Cromwell. Introd. by Maurice Ashley. Illustrated by Hans Schwarz. [New York] Longmans [1960] 166p. illus. 21cm. 60-50709 2.00 bds.,
1. Cromwell, Oliver, 1599-1658. I. Title.

NEW, John F. H., comp. 942.06'4'0924 B
Oliver Cromwell: pretender, Puritan, statesman, paradox? Edited by John F. H. New. New York, Holt, Rinehart and Winston [1971, c1972] 124 p. port. 24 cm. (European problem studies) Contents.Contents.—Cromwell, the usurper, by J. Heath.—Festering ambition, by E. Ludlow.—Self-justification, by O. Cromwell.—The Christian in politics, by R. S. Paul.—Defender of Protestantism, by M. D'Aubigne.—The hero cometh, by T. Carlyle.—The ordinary Englishman, by J. Buchan.—Hitler illuminates Cromwell, by W. C. Abbott.—Against an analogy between Cromwell and Napoleon, by Lord Macaulay.—A high assessment, by C. Firth.—Political ends miscarry, by J. Morley.—Cromwell's failure with parliaments, by H. R. Trevor-Roper.—Paradoxes of personality and revolution, by C. Hill.—Cromwell and the paradoxes of Puritanism, by J. F. H. New.—Cromwell's place in history, by S. R. Gardiner.—Bibliography (p. 121-124) [DA428.1.N49] 74-167813 ISBN 0-03-085178-5
1. Cromwell, Oliver, 1599-1658. I. Title.

SMITH, Goldwin, 1823- 1910. 942.06 B
Three English statesmen: a course of lectures on the political history of England. Freeport, N.Y., Books for Libraries Press [1972] 328 p. 22 cm. (Essay index reprint series) Reprint of the 1867 ed. [DA307.S5 1972] 72-4587 ISBN 0-8369-2979-9 12.50
1. Pym, John, 1584-1643. 2. Cromwell, Oliver, 1599-1658. 3. Pitt, William, 1759-1806. I. Title. BIP

TANGYE, Richard, Sir, 1833-1906. 942.06'3
The two protectors: Oliver and Richard Cromwell. Port Washington, N.Y., Kennikat Press [1971] 302 p. illus., facsims., map, ports. 22 cm. Reprint of the 1899 ed. Bibliography: p. [17] [DA425.T16 1971] 78-118504 ISBN 0-8046-1252-8
1. Cromwell, Oliver, 1599-1658. 2. Cromwell, Richard, 1626-1712. 3. Gt. Brit.—History—Commonwealth and Protectorate, 1649-1660. I. Title.

WEDGWOOD, Cicely Veronica, Dame 1910- 942.0640924 B
The life of Cromwell [by] C. V. Wedgwood. [1st ed.] New York, Collier Books [1966] 127 p. 18 cm. First published in 1939 under title: Oliver Cromwell. Bibliography: p. 125-127. [DA426.W4 1966] 62-16978
1. Cromwell, Oliver, 1599-1658. 2. Great Britain—History—Puritan Revolution, 1642-1660. I. Title.

WOOLRYCH, Austin H. 923.142
Oliver Cromwell [New York] Oxford [1965, c.1964] 64p. illus., facsims., ports. 21cm. (Clarendon biogs., 2) Bibl. [DA426.W6] 65-2226 1.40 bds.,
1. Cromwell, Oliver, 1599-1658. I. Title.

Cromwell, Oliver, 1599-1658—Addresses, essays, lectures.

NEW, John F. H., comp. 941.06'4'0924 B
Oliver Cromwell : pretender, Puritan, statesman, paradox? / Edited by John F. H. New. Huntington, N.Y. : R. E. Krieger Pub. Co., 1976 [c1972] p. cm. Reprint of the ed. published by Holt, Rinehart and Winston, New York, in series: European problem studies. [DA428.1.N49 1976] 76-23190 ISBN 0-88275-457-2 pbk. : 3.95
1. Cromwell, Oliver, 1599-1658—Addresses, essays, lectures. BIP

Cromwell, Thomas, Earl of Essex, 1485?-1540.

BECKINGSALE, B. W. 942.05'2'0924 B
Thomas Cromwell, Tudor minister / by B. W. Beckingsale. Totowa, N.J. : Rowman and Littlefield, 1978. p. cm. Includes index. Bibliography: p. [DA334.C9B42 1978] 77-29057 ISBN 0-8476-6053-2 : 15.00
1. Cromwell, Thomas, Earl of Essex, 1485?-1540. 2. Great Britain—History—Henry VIII, 1509-1547. 3. Statesmen—Great Britain—Biography. I. Title.

ELTON, Geoffrey Rudolph. 942.05'2'0924 B
Reform and renewal; Thomas Cromwell and the common weal [by] G. R. Elton. Cambridge [Eng.] University Press, 1973. x, 175 p. 23 cm. (The Wiles lectures, 1972) Includes bibliographical references. [DA334.C9E47] 72-87180 ISBN 0-521-20054-7 8.75
1. Cromwell, Thomas, Earl of Essex, 1485?-1540. I. Title. II. Series.
Distributed by Cambridge U. Press, N.Y. 8.75, pap. 3.75.

Cronin, Patrick, 1913-

FISCHER, Edward. 266'.009599'7
Mindanao mission : Archbishop Patrick Cronin's forty years in the Philippines / Edward Fischer. New York : Seabury Press, 1978. viii, 177 p. : ill. ; 24 cm. "A Crossroad book." [BX4705.C7834F57] 78-12802 ISBN 0-8164-0412-7 : 8.95
1. Cronin, Patrick, 1913- 2. Catholic Church—Bishops—Biography. 3. Bishops—Philippine Islands—Biography. I. Title. BIP

Crook, George, 1828-1890.

CROOK, George, 1828-1890. 923.573
General George Crook, his autobiography. Edited and annotated by Martin F. Schmitt. [new ed.] Norman, University of Oklahoma Press [1960] xx, 326 p. illus., ports., maps. 22 cm. Bibliography: p. 310-317. [E83.866.C93 1960] 60-8386
1. Indians of North America—Wars—1866-1895. 2. Pacific coast Indians, Wars with, 1847-1865.

KING, Charles, 1844-1933. 970.5
Campaigning with Crook, and stories of army life. Ann Arbor [Mich.] University Microfilms [1966] v, 295 p. illus., port. 20 cm. (March of America facsimile series no. 98) Original t.p. has imprint: New York, Harper, 1890. Contents.Contents.—Campaigning with Crook.—Captain Santa Claus.—The mystery of 'Mahbin Mill.—Plodder's promotion. [E83.866.K552] 66-26366
1. Crook, George, 1828-1890. 2. United States. Army. 5th Cavalry. 3. Indians of North America—Wars—1866-1895. I. Title. II. Series.

Cropley, Ruve.

CROPLEY, Ruve. 253'.2'0924 B
Forty "odd" years in a manse. [Granville, Australia, Printed by Ambassador Press, 1962] 100 p. illus. 23 cm. [BX9225.C763A3] 73-172017
1. Cropley, Ruve. I. Title.

Cropsey, Jasper Francis, 1823-1900.

TALBOT, William S. 759.13 B
Jasper F. Cropsey, 1823-1900 / William S. Talbot. New York : Garland Pub., 1977. xviii, 578 p., [56] leaves of plates : ill. ; 21 cm. (Outstanding dissertations in the fine arts) Originally presented as the author's thesis, New York University, 1972. Bibliography: p. 570-578. [ND237.C819T342 1977] 76-23652 ISBN 0-8240-2731-0 lib.bdg. : 60.00
1. Cropsey, Jasper Francis, 1823-1900. 2. Landscape painters—United States—Biography. I. Title. II. Series.

Crosby, Bing, 1904-1977.

BAUER, Barbara. 790.2'092'4 B
Bing Crosby / by Barbara Bauer. New York : Pyramid Publications, 1977. 159 p. : ill. ; 20 cm. (A Pyramid illustrated history of the movies) Includes index. Bibliography: p. 146. [ML420.C93B4] 77-5264 ISBN 0-515-04331-1 pbk. : 1.95
1. Crosby, Bing, 1904-1977. 2. Singers—United States—Biography. 3. Moving-picture actors and actresses—United States—Biography. BIP

CROSBY, Bing, 1901- 927.92
Call me lucky, by Bing Crosby as told to Pete Martin. New York, Simon and Schuster, 1953. 344p. illus. 23cm. [ML420.C93A3] 53-10768
1. Musicians—Correspondence, reminiscences, etc. I. Title.

CROSBY, Kathryn, 1933- 791.43'0924
Bing and other things. [1st ed.] New York, Meredith Press [1967] viii, 214 p. illus., ports. 21 cm. [PN2287.C683A3] 67-28779
1. Crosby, Bing, 1904- I. Title.

THOMAS, Bob, 1922- 790.2'092'4 B
The one and only Bing / Bob Thomas. New York : Grosset & Dunlap, c1977. 150 p. : ill. ; 28 cm. "With a special tribute by Bob Hope." Filmography: p. [93]-130. [ML420.C93T48] 77-92310 ISBN 0-448-14669-X. ISBN 0-448-14670-3 pbk. : 5.95
1. Crosby, Bing, 1904-1977. 2. Singers—United States—Biography. I. Title. BIP

THOMPSON, Charles. 790.2'092'4 B
Bing : the authorized biography / by Charles Thompson. 1st American ed. New York : McKay, 1976, c1975. vi, 249 p., [16] leaves of plates : ill. ; 22 cm. Includes index. [ML420.C93T5 1976] 75-37320 ISBN 0-679-50590-3 : 8.95
1. Crosby, Bing, 1904-

ZWISOHN, Laurence J. 784'.092'4 B
Bing Crosby : a lifetime of music / Laurence J. Zwisohn. Los Angeles : Palm Tree Library, c1978. 147 p. : ill. ; 28 cm. Discography: p. 65-142. [ML420.C93Z9] 78-71333 pbk. : 7.95
1. Crosby, Bing, 1904-1977. 2. Crosby, Bing, 1904-1977—Discography. 3. Singers—United States—Biography. I. Title. BIP

Crosby, Bob.

CORSBY, Thelma. v. 12
Bob Crosby, world champion cowboy, by Thelma Crosby and Eve Ball. Illus. by Olive Vandruff Bugbee. Clarendon, Tex., Clarendon Press, 1966. xii, 244 p. illus. 27 cm. "The Trophy edition." 68-41998
1. Crosby, Bob. 2. Cowboys. I. Ball, Eve, joint author. II. Title. III. Title: World champion cowboy. BIP

Crosby, Caresse, 1892- —Biography.

CROSBY, Caresse, 1892- 928.1
The passionate years. New York, Dial Press, 1953. 342 p. illus. 22 cm. Autobiography. [PS3505.R865Z52] 52-10093
I. Title. BIP

CROSBY, Caresse, 1892- 818'.5'203 B
The passionate years. Carbondale, Southern Illinois University Press [1968, c1953] 370 p. illus. 21 cm. (Arcturus book, AB45) Autobiography. [PS3505.R865Z52 1968] 68-25561 2.85
I. Title.

CROSBY, Caresse, 1892- 818'.5'203
The passionate years / Caresse Crosby. New York : Ecco Press, 1979, c1953. 370 p., [12] leaves of plates : ill. ; 22 cm. (Neglected books of the 20th century) Reprint of the ed. published by Dial Press, New York. Includes index. [PS3505.R865 1979] 78-31388 ISBN 0-912946-66-0 pbk. : 5.95
1. Crosby, Caresse, 1892- —Biography. 2. Poets, American—20th century—Biography. 3. Publishers and publishing—France—Biography. 4. Americans in Paris. I. Title. II. Series.

Crosby, Enoch, 1750-1835.

BARNUM, H. L. 973.3'85'0924 B
The spy unmasked : or, Memoirs of Enoch Crosby, alias Harvey Birch, the hero of James Fenimore Cooper's The spy / by H. L. Barnum. A facsim. of the 1st ed. (1828) / with a new introd. by James H. Pickering ; and an appendix, Enoch Crosby, secret agent of the neutral ground, his own story. Harrison, N.Y. : Harbor Hill Books, 1975. p. cm. Photoreprint of the 1828 ed. published by J. & J. Harper, New York. Appendix reprinted from the New York history, vol. 47, no. 1, January 1966. Includes bibliographical references. [E280.C95B6 1975] 75-29452 11.50
1. Crosby, Enoch, 1750-1835. 2. Cooper, James Fenimore, 1789-1851. The spy. 3. United States—History—Revolution, 1775-1783—Secret service. I. Title. BIP

Crosby, Harry, 1898-1929—Biography.

WOLFF, Geoffrey, 1937- 811'.5'2 B
Black Sun : the brief transit and violent eclipse of Harry Crosby / Geoffrey Wolff. 1st ed. New York : Random House, c1976. xiii, 367 p., [4] leaves of plates : ill. ; 25 cm. Includes index. Bibliography: p. 351-359. [PS3505.R883Z95] 76-8162 ISBN 0-394-47450-3 : 12.95
1. Crosby, Harry, 1898-1929—Biography. I. Title. BIP

WOLFF, Geoffrey, 1937- 811'.5'2 B
Black Sun : the brief transit and violent eclipse of Harry Crosby / Geoffrey Wolff. New York : Vintage Books, 1977, c1976. xiii, 367 p., [8] leaves of plates : ill. ; 24 cm. Includes index. Bibliography: p. 351-359. [PS3505.R883Z95 1977] 77-5019 ISBN 0-394-72472-0 pbk. : 4.95
1. Crosby, Harry, 1898-1929—Biography. 2. Poets, American—20th century—Biography. I. Title.

Crosby, Harry, 1898-1929—Diaries.

CROSBY, Harry, 1898-1929. 811'.5'2 B
Shadows of the sun : the diaries of Harry Crosby / edited by Edward B. Germain. Santa Barbara, CA : Black Sparrow Press, 1977. 304 p. ; 23 cm. Includes index. Bibliography: p. 18. [PS3505.R883Z52 1977] 77-2869 ISBN 0-87685-304-1 : 14.00. ISBN 0-87685-303-3 pbk. : 4.00
1. Crosby, Harry, 1898-1929—Diaries. 2. Poets, American—20th century—Biography. I. Title. BIP

Crosby, Percy Leo, 1891-1964.

ROBINSON, Jerry. 741.5'973 B
Skippy and Percy Crosby / Jerry Robinson ; with the art of Percy Crosby. 1st ed. New York : Holt, Rinehart and Winston, c1978. x, 155 p. : ill. (some col.) ; 29 cm. [NC1429.C76R62] 78-53777 ISBN 0-03-018491-6 : 16.95
1. Crosby, Percy Leo, 1891-1964. 2. Cartoonists—United States—Biography. I. Crosby, Percy Leo, 1891-1964. II. Title. BIP

Crosby, Robert Anderson, 1897-1947.

CROSBY, Thelma (Jones) 791.8 B
Bob Crosby, world champion cowboy, by Thelma Crosby and Eve Ball. Illus. by Olive Vandruff Bugbee. [The Trophy ed.] Clarendon, Tex., Clarendon Press, 1966. xii, 244 p. illus., ports. 27 cm. "One hundred and seventy-five copies — copy number 115." [GV1834.C7] 71-4398
1. Crosby, Robert Anderson, 1897-1947. 2. Rodeos. I. Ball, Eve, joint author. II. Title: World champion cowboy.

Crosby, William Otis, 1850-1925.

SHROCK, Robert Rakes, 1904- 550'.92'4 B
The geologists Crosby of Boston; William Otis Crosby (1850-1925) and Irving Ballard Crosby (1891-1959), by Robert R. Shrock. Cambridge, Massachusetts Institute of Technology, 1972. xii, 96, 79 p. illus. 24 cm. Includes bibliographies. [QE22.C83S48] 72-9383
1. Crosby, William Otis, 1850-1925. 2. Crosby, Irving Ballard. I. Title.

Cross, Henry, 1821-1864.

HARTLEY, W Douglas, 1921- 736'.5'0924
The search for Henry Cross; an adventure in biography and Americana, by W. Douglas Hartley. Indianapolis, Indiana Historical Society, 1966. 91-168 p. illus., map. 23 cm. (Indiana Historical Society. Publications, v. 23, no. 3) Bibliography: p. 164-166. [NB1528.C7H3] 67-1090
1. Cross, Henry, 1821-1864. I. Title.

Crossman, Richard Howard Stafford, 1907-1974.

CROSSMAN, Richard Howard Stafford, 1907-1974. 354'.41'050924 B
The diaries of a Cabinet minister / Richard Crossman. New York : Holt, Rinehart and Winston, 1977 c1976- p. cm. Includes index. Contents.Contents.— —v. 2. Lord President of the Council and Leader of the House of Commons, 1966-1968. [DA591.C76A34 1977] 76-30680 ISBN 0-03-020616-2(v. 2) : 16.95
1. Crossman, Richard Howard Stafford, 1907-1974. 2. Statesmen—Great Britain—Biography. 3. Great Britain—Politics and government—1945- I. Title.

Crothers, George Edward, 1870-1957.

CLAUSEN, Henry C. 340'.0924 [B]
Stanford's Judge Crothers; the life story of George E. Crothers, faithful son, loyal citizen and political leader, successful

lawyer, jurist and businessman, wise counselor and kindly benefactor, by Henry C. Clausen. San Francisco, George E. Crothers Trust [1967] xiii, 161 p. illus., ports. 23 cm. [KF373.C7C55] 67-17964
1. Crothers, George Edward, 1870-1957. 2. Stanford University — Hist. I. Title.

Crouch, Andrae.

CROUCH, Andrae. 783.7 B
Through it all / Andrae Crouch, with Nina Ball. Waco, Tex. : Word Books, [1974] 148 p. : ill. ; 23 cm. [ML420.C945A3] 74-82311 5.95
1. Crouch, Andrae. 2. Musicians—Correspondence, reminiscences, etc. I. Ball, Nina. II. Title.

Crouch, John Russell, 1916-

PATTERSON, Becky 976.4'65 B
Crouch, 1945-
Hondo, my father / by Becky Crouch Patterson. 1st ed. Austin, Tex. : Shoal Creek Publishers, c1979. xx, 268 p. : ill. ; 22 cm. Includes index. Bibliography: p. 263-264. [F394.L92C766] 79-10229 ISBN 0-88319-044-3 : 12.50
1. Crouch, John Russell, 1916- 2. Luckenbach, Tex.—Biography. 3. German Americans—Texas—Luckenbach—Biography. I. Title.

Crouter, Natalie, 1898-

CROUTER, 940.54'72'5209599
Natalie, 1898-
Forbidden diary : a record of wartime internment, 1941-1945 / Natalie Crouter ; edited with an introd. by Lynn Z. Bloom. New York : B. Franklin, [1979] p. cm. (American women's diary series ; 2) [D805.J3C76] 79-27116 ISBN 0-89102-105-1 : 18.95
1. Crouter, Natalie, 1898- 2. World War, 1939-1945—Prisoners and prisons, Japanese. 3. World War, 1939-1945—Personal narratives, American. 4. Prisoners of war—United States—Biography. 5. Prisoners of war—Philippine Islands—Baguio—Biography. 6. Baguio, Philippines—Biography. I. Bloom, Lynn Z., 1934- II. Title. III. Series.

Crow Indians.

PLENTY-COUPS, Crow chief, 970.3 B
1848-1932.
Plenty-Coups, chief of the Crows [by] Frank B. Linderman. Illustrated by H. M. Stoops. New York, John Day Co. [1972, c1930] ix, 312 p. illus. 23 cm. First published in 1930 under title: American: the life story of a great Indian, Plenty-Coups, chief of the Crows. Reprint of the 1962 ed. [E99.C92P55 1972] 72-3272 8.95
1. Crow Indians. I. Linderman, Frank Bird, 1868-1938.

PLENTY-COUPS, Crow chief. 970.2
1848-1932.
American: the life story of a great Indian. Plenty-Coups, chief of the Crows, by Frank B. Linderman. Illustrated by H. M. Stoops. New York, John Day Co. [1930] xi,313 p. illus. 21 cm. [E90.P56A3 1930] 30-11369
1. Crow Indians. I. Lindermann, Frank Bird. 1868-1938. II. Title.

Crowell, Grace (Noll) 1877-

GRACE Noll Crowell, v. 12
the poet and the woman,by Beatrice Plumb; containing a foreword and nine new poems by Grace Noll Crowell. New York and London, Harper & brothers, 1938 [Ann Arbor, 1958] 56p., 1 l. 2 port. (incl. front.) 18cm. Photocopy (postive) made by University Microfilms. Printed on double leaves.
1. Crowell, Grace (Noll) 1877- I. Plumb, Beatrice, 1886-

Crowell, Thomas Young, 1836-1915.

CROWELL, Thomas 655.40924 (B)
Irving, 1866-1942.
Thomas Young Crowell, 1836-1915; a biographical sketch, with events since 1915. New York, Crowell [1965] 77 p. illus., ports. 20 cm. "Events since 1915" (p. 55-77) includes yearly lists of titles published by the T. Y. Crowell Co. [Z473.C95C9 1965] 66-6475
1. Crowell, Thomas Young, 1836-1915. I. Title.

Crowfoot, 1830-1890.

DEMPSEY, Hugh Aylmer, 970.3 B
1929-
Crowfoot, chief of the Blackfeet, by Hugh A. Dempsey. Foreword by Paul F. Sharp. [1st ed.] Norman, University of Oklahoma Press [1972] xix, 226 p. 22 cm. (The Civilization of the American Indian series, v. 122) Bibliography: p. 217-220. [E99.S54C73] 72-865 ISBN 0-8061-1025-2 7.95
1. Crowfoot, 1830-1890. 2. Siksika Indians. 3. Kainah Indians. I. Title. II. Series.

Crowley, Aleister, 1875-1947.

CAMMELL, Charles Richard. 928.2
Aleister Crowley: the man, the mage, the poet. New Hyde Park, N. Y., University Books [1962] 229p. illus. 25cm. Includes bibliography. [PR6005.R7Z7 1962] 62-12565
1. Crowley, Aleister, 1875-1947. I. Title.

CAMMELL, Charles Riehard 928.2
Alesiter Croweley; the man, the mage, the poet. New Hyde Park, N. Y., University Bks. [c.1962] 229p. illus. 25cm. Bibl. 62-12565 6.00
1. Crowley, Aleister, 1875-1947. I. Title.

CROWLEY, Aleister, 828'.9'1209 B
1875-1947.
The confessions of Aleister Crowley; an autohagiography. Edited by John Symonds and Kenneth Grant. [1st American ed.] New York, Hill and Wang [1970, c1969] 960 p. ports. 24 cm. Bibliographical references included in "Editors' notes" (p. 925-937) [PR6005.R7Z5 1970] 79-88013 14.95
I. Title.

CROWLEY, Aleister, 133'.092'4 B
1875-1947.
The confessions of Aleister Crowley : an autohagiography / edited by John Symonds and Kenneth Grant. Corrected ed. London ; Boston : Routledge & Kegan Paul, 1979. 960 p., [12] leaves of plates : ill. ; 25 cm. — Includes bibliographical references and index. [BF1598.C7A29 1979] 78-41175 ISBN 0-7100-0175-4 : 45.00
1. Crowley, Aleister, 1875-1947. 2. Occult sciences—Biography. I. Symonds, John. II. Grant, Kenneth, 1924- III. Title.

KING, Francis. 133'.092'4 B
The magical world of Aleister Crowley / Francis King. 1st American ed. New York : Coward, McCann & Geoghegan, 1978, c1977. 210 p., [4] leaves of plates : ill. ; 22 cm. Includes index. Bibliograpy: p. [199]-201. [BF1598.C7K56 1978] 77-13610 ISBN 0-698-10884-1 : 8.95
1. Crowley, Aleister, 1875-1947. 2. Occult sciences—Biography. 3. Authors, English—20th century—Biography. I. Title. **BIP**

MANNIX, Daniel Pratt, 1911- 928.2
The beast. New York, Ballantine Books [1959] 139p. 18cm. (Ballantine books, 302K) [PR6005.R7Z8] 59-9210
1. Crowley, Aleister, 1875-1947. I. Title.

SYMONDS, John. 928.2
The great beast; the life of Aleister Crowley. New York, Roy [c1952] 316p. illus. 24cm. Includes bibliography. [PR6005.R7Z9 1952] 53-2302
1. Crowley, Aleister, 1875-1947. I. Title.

SYMONDS, John. 928.2
The great beast; the life of Aleister Crowley. London, New York, Rider [1951] 316 p. illus., ports. 24 cm. "Bibliography of the works of Aleister Crowley, compiled by Gerald Yorke": p. 301-310. [PR6005.R7Z9] 52-28519
1. Crowley, Aleister, 1875-1947. I. Title.

Crowley, Aleister, 1875-1947—Biography.

ROBERTS, Susan. 133'.092'4 B
The magician of the golden dawn : the story of Aleister Crowley / Susan Roberts. Chicago : Contemporary Books, c1978. xv, 337 p. ; 24 cm. Includes index. Bibliography:325-326. [PR6005.R7Z86] 77-91167 ISBN 0-8092-7802-2 : 10.00
1. Crowley, Aleister, 1875-1947—Biography. 2. Authors, English—20th century—Biography. 3. Occult sciences—Biography. I. Title. **BIP**

Crowley, Dale.

CROWLEY, Dale. 286'.1'0924 B
My life, a miracle. Washington, National Bible Knowledge Association [1971] xi, 211 p. illus., facsims., ports. 23 cm. [BV3785.C86A3] 73-155933 5.00
I. Title.

Crowne, John —

WHITE, Arthur Franklin, v. 12
1890-1959.
John Crowne; his life and dramatic works. Cleveland, Western Reserve University Press, 1922. 211 p. 24 cm. Issued also as Western Reserve University bulletin, new ser., v. 23 [i.e. 25] no. 7. Bibliography: p. 197-208. [PR3388.C2Z7 1922a] 23-12604
1. Crowne, John — 1640?-1712. I. Title.

Crowther, Samuel Adjai, Bp., 1806?-1891.

MCKENZIE, Peter 291'.0966
Rutherford.
Inter-religious encounters in West Africa : Samuel Ajayi Crowther's attitude to African traditional religion and Islam / by P. R. McKenzie. [Leicester] : Study of Religion Sub-department, University of Leicester, 1976. 115 p., 4 p. of plates : ill., maps, ports. ; 24 cm. (Leicester studies in religion ; 1) Distributed by Leicester University Bookshop. Includes index. Bibliography: p. 107-110. [BV3625.N6C68] 77-367628 ISBN 0-905510-00-3 : £3.00
1. Crowther, Samuel Adjai, Bp., 1806?-1891. 2. Missionaries—Nigeria—Biography. 3. Missions—Nigeria. 4. Africa, West—Religion. I. Title. II. Series.

PAGE, Jesse. 283'.092'4 B
The Black bishop, Samuel Adjai Crowther / by Jesse Page ; with pref. by Eugene Stock. Westport, Conn. : Greenwood Press, 1979. xv, 440 p., [17] leaves of plates (1 fold.) : ill. ; 23 cm. Reprint of the 1908 ed. published by Hodder and Stoughton, London. Includes index. [BV3625.N6C7 1979] 79-100 ISBN 0-8371-4610-0 : 29.00
1. Crowther, Samuel Adjai, Bp., 1806?-1891. 2. Missionaries—Nigeria—Biography. 3. Missionaries—England—Biography. 4. Bishops—Nigeria—Biography. I. Title.

Crozier, Roger.

COHEN, Tom. 796.9'62'0924
Roger Crozier, daredevil goalie. London, New York, T. Nelson [1967] 128 p. ports. 22 cm. (Champion books) (A Rutledge book) [GV847.C56] 67-3025
1. Crozier, Roger.

Cruikshank, George, 1792-1878.

EVANS, Hilary, 1929- 760'.092'4 B
The life & art of George Cruikshank, 1792-1878 : the man who drew The Drunkard's daughter / Hilary and Mary Evans. New York : S. G. Phillips, 1978. p. cm. [NC1479.C9E82] 77-19166 ISBN 0-87599-227-7 : 35.00
1. Cruikshank, George, 1792-1878. 2. Cartoonists—England—Biography. I. Evans, Mary, 1890- joint autor. II. Title.

Cruise, Boyd.

CRUISE, Boyd. 759.13
Boyd Cruise. 1st ed. New Orleans : Kemper and Leila Williams Foundation, c1976. 72 p. : ill. (some col.) ; 29 cm. Published in conjunction with the artist's exhibition held at the Historic New Orleans Collection, December 1976-February 1977. "Biography of the artist [by] Mary Louise Christovich": p. 2-13. [ND237.C843C48] 76-24712 ISBN 0-917860-01-2
1. Cruise, Boyd. 2. Painters—Louisiana—New Orleans—Biography. I. Christovich, Mary Louise. II. Historic New Orleans Collection.

Crummell, Alexander, 1819-1898—Addresses, essays, lectures.

FERRIS, William 973'.04'96073 S
Henry, 1893-1941.
Alexander Crummell, an apostle of Negro culture / by William H. Ferris. [New York : Arno Press, 1969] 16 p. ; 24 cm. (The American Negro, his history and literature) Issued in a vol. with the other 21 papers in the series. Reprint of the 1920 ed. published by the American Negro Academy as its Occasional papers, no. 20. [E185.5.A51 1969 no. 20] [E185.97.C87] 301.45'19'6073024 B 76-358967
1. Crummell, Alexander, 1819-1898—Addresses, essays, lectures. 2. American Negro Academy, Washington, D.C.—Addresses, essays, lectures. I. Title. II. Series. III. Series: American Negro Academy, Washington, D.C. Occasional papers ; no. 20.

Crump, Edward Hull, 1874-1954.

MILLER, William D. 923.273
Mr. Crump of Memphis [by] William D. Miller. Baton Rouge, Louisiana State University Press, 1964. xiii, 373 p. illus., ports. 24 cm. (Southern biography series) "Critical essay on authorities": p. 353-359. [F444.M5M66] 64-21594
1. Crump, Edward Hull, 1874-1954. 2. Memphis—Politics and government. I. Title. II. Series.

Crumpton, Howard Ulmer, 1878-1960.

CRUMPTON, Ethel (Howard) v. 12
1883-
Than silver and gold. (n.p. 1964?] 92 p. illus., ports. 23 cm. 67-88203
1. Crumpton, Howard Ulmer, 1878-1960. 2. Pleasant Hill, Ala. I. Title.

Cruttenden, Joseph.

CRUTTENDEN, 382'.45'615094212
Joseph.
Atlantic merchant-apothecary : letters of Joseph Cruttenden, 1710-1717 / edited by I. K. Steele. Toronto ; Buffalo : University of Toronto Press, c1977. p. cm. Includes bibliographical references and index. [KS73.C7A4 1977] 77-2832 ISBN 0-8020-5364-5 : 12.50
1. Cruttenden, Joseph. 2. Pharmacists—England—London—Correspondence. 3. Drug trade—England—History. I. Steele, Ian Kenneth. II. Title. **BIP**

Cruz, Nicky.

CRUZ, Nicky. 248.2'4
Run, baby, run [by] Nicky Cruz with Jamie Buckingham. Plainfield, N.J., Logos International [1968] xv, 240 p. 21 cm. Autobiography of Nicky Cruz. [BV4935.C73A3] 68-23446 4.95
I. Buckingham, Jamie, joint author. II. Title. **BIP**

Cruz, Pablo.

CRUZ, Pablo. 331.6'2'720794 B
Pablo Cruz and the American dream; the experiences of an undocumented immigrant from Mexico. Compiled by Eugene Nelson. Introd. by Julian Samora. Illus. by Carlos Cortez. [Salt Lake City] Peregrine Smith, 1975. 171 p. illus. 23 cm. [HD8081.M6C78] 74-19157 ISBN 0-87905-021-7 8.95
1. Cruz, Pablo. 2. Alien labor, Mexican—United States. I. Nelson, Eugene, 1929- ed. II. Title.

Crying Wind.

CRYING Wind. 970'.004'97 B
Crying Wind / by Crying Wind. Chicago : Moody Press, c1977. 189 p. : ill. ; 22 cm. Continued by My searching heart. [E90.C85A33] 77-154272 ISBN 0-8024-1676-4 : 6.95
1. Crying Wind. 2. Indians of North America—Biography. 3. Converts—United States—Biography. BIP

CRYING Wind. 970'.004'97 B
My searching heart / by Crying Wind. Chicago : Moody Press, c1979. 238 p. : ill. ; 22 cm. Continues the author's Crying Wind. [E99.K4C78] 78-14244 ISBN 0-8024-5691-X : 7.95
1. Crying Wind. 2. Kickapoo Indians—Biography. 3. Indians of North America—Biography. 4. Converts—United States—Biography. I. Title. BIP

Csonka, Larry.

CSONKA, Larry. 796.33'2'0922
Always on the run, by Larry Csonka and Jim Kiick, with Dave Anderson. [1st ed.] New York, Random House [1973] xi, 223 p. 22 cm. Two stars of the Miami Dolphins exchange their thoughts about their lives, football, Coach Shula, and other topics. [GV939.A1C78] 73-5052 6.95
1. Csonka, Larry. 2. Kiick, Jim. 3. Miami Dolphins (Football club) 4. Backfield play (Football) I. Kiick, Jim. II. Anderson, Dave. III. Title.

Csonka, Larry—Juvenile literature.

BATSON, Larry, 1930- 796.33'2'0924 B
Larry Csonka. Illustrated by Harold Henriksen. Mankato, Minn., Amecus Street; [distributed by Childrens Press, Chicago, 1974] 31 p. col. illus. 25 cm. (Superstars) Profile of the professional career and attainments of Larry Csonka, fullback for the Miami Dolphins. [GV939.C75B37] 92 74-16419 ISBN 0-87191-382-8 4.95
1. Csonka, Larry—Juvenile literature. 2. Football—Juvenile literature. I. Henriksen, Harold, illus. II. Title. BIP

BURCHARD, Marshall. 796.33'2'0924 B
Sports hero, Larry Csonka / by Marshall and Sue Burchard. New York : Putnam, [1975] 95 p. : ill. ; 22 cm. (The Sports hero biographies) A biography concentrating on the career of the star running back of the Miami Dolphins. [GV939.C75B87 1975] 92 74-21063 ISBN 0-399-60938-5 lib. bdg. : 4.69
1. Csonka, Larry—Juvenile literature. 2. Football—Juvenile literature. I. Burchard, S. H., joint author. II. Title.

GUTMAN, Bill. 796.33'2'0924 B
Csonka / by Bill Gutman. New York : Grosset & Dunlap, c1974. 89 p., [2] leaves of plates : ill., ports ; 21 cm. (Tempo books) A brief easy-to read biography of the star running back who left the Miami Dolphins to join the World Football League for the 1975 season. [GV939.C75G87] 92 74-7688 ISBN 0-448-07438-9 : 1.50
1. Csonka, Larry—Juvenile literature. 2. Football—Juvenile literature.

SULLIVAN, George, 1927- 796.33'2'0924 B
Larry Csonka, power and pride / George Sullivan. New York : Putnam, c1975. 158 p. ; 22 cm. Includes index. A biography of the football superstar whose record performance in the Super Bowl game of 1974 made football history. [GV939.C75S84] 92 75-4424 ISBN 0-399-60953-9 lib. bdg. : 5.29
1. Csonka, Larry—Juvenile literature. 2. Football—Juvenile literature. I. Title.

Cuba—Description and travel.

HOWE, Julia (Ward) 1819-1910. 917.291'03'5
A trip to Cuba. New York, Negro Universities Press [1969] iv, 251 p. 23 cm. First published in 1860. [F1763.H85 1969b] 79-92747
1. Cuba—Description and travel. I. Title. BIP

HOWE, Julia (Ward) 1819-1910. 917.291'04'5
A trip to Cuba. New York, Praeger [1969] x, iv, 251 p. 22 cm. (Source books and studies on Latin America) (Praeger scholarly reprints.) Reprint of the 1860 ed. [F1763.H85 1969] 77-75405
1. Cuba—Description and travel. I. Title.

TURNBULL, David. 917.291
Travels in the West; Cuba, with notices of Porto Rico, and the slave trade. New York, Negro Universities Press [1969] xvi, 574 p. map. 23 cm. Reprint of the 1840 ed. [F1763.T94 1969] 74-91667 ISBN 0-8371-2075-6
1. Cuba—Description and travel. 2. Slavery in Cuba. 3. Slave-trade. I. Title.

Cuba—Description and travel—1951-

MARTINEZ, Elizabeth Sutherland, 1925- 309.1'7291
The youngest revolution; a personal report on Cuba. With photos. by Leroy Lucas. New York, Dial Press, 1969. 277 p. illus. 22 cm. [F1765.2.M36] 68-9462 5.95
1. Cuba—Description and travel—1951- 2. Cuba—Social life and customs. I. Title.

Cuba—History—1933-1959.

MACAULAY, Neill. 972.91'063'0924 B
A rebel in Cuba: an American's memoir. Chicago, Quadrangle Books, 1970. 199 p. map (on lining papers) 22 cm. [F1787.5.M3 1970] 72-101072 5.95
1. Cuba—History—1933-1959. 2. Cuba—History, Military. I. Title.

Cubberley, Ellwood Patterson, 1868-1941.

SEARS, Jesse Brundage, 1876- 923.773
Cubberley of Stanford and his contribution to American education, by Jesse B. Sears and Adin D. Henderson. Stanford, Calif., Stanford University Press, 1957. xii, 301 p. illus., ports., facsim. 24 cm. "A chronological list of Cubberley's writings": p. 283-289. Bibliography: p. 290-296. [LB875.C782S4] 57-7382
1. Cubberley, Ellwood Patterson, 1868-1941. I. Henderson, Adin D., joint author.

Cubitt, Thomas, 1788-1855.

HOBHOUSE, Hermione. 711'.4'0924 B
Thomas Cubitt; master builder. New York, Universe Books [1971] xx, 568 p. illus. 25 cm. Bibliography: p. 551-552. [NA997.C8H6] 79-122323 ISBN 0-87663-706-3 32.50
1. Cubitt, Thomas, 1788-1855. I. Title.

Cudjoe.

MCFARLANE, Milton C. 322.4'2'0924 B
Cudjoe of Jamaica : pioneer for Black freedom in the New World. Short Hills, N.J. : R. Enslow, [1977] p. cm. Includes index. [F1884.C8M3] 77-7583 ISBN 0-89490-001-3 : 7.95
1. Cudjoe. 2. Maroons—Jamaica—Biography. 3. Jamaica—History. I. Title. BIP

Cuesta, Juan de la, fl. 1605.

SCHNEER, Richard James. 070.5'0946'41
Juan de la Cuesta, first printer of Don Quixote de la Mancha; a bibliographic record of his works, 1604-1625. University, University of Alabama Press [1973] xii, 89 p. 22 cm. [Z232.C963S35] 72-11809 ISBN 0-8173-9513-X 6.00
1. Cuesta, Juan de la, fl. 1605.

Cuffe, Paul, 1759-1817.

THE History of Prince 910.4'53
Lee Boo, to which is added, The life of Paul Cuffee, a man of colour, also, Some account of John Sackhouse, the Esquimaux. Dublin, Printed by C. Crooks, 1820. Miami, Fla., Mnemosyne Pub. Co. [1969] 180 p. illus. 23 cm. [G525.H58 1969] 72-89405
1. Lee Boo, d. 1784. 2. Cuffe, Paul, 1759-1817. 3. Sackhouse, John, 1797-1819.

SALVADOR, George Arnold. 973.4'0924 B
Paul Cuffe, the black yankee, 1759-1817. [New Bedford, Mass., Reynolds-DeWalt Printing, 1969] 76 p. illus. 24 cm. Bibliography: p. 74-76. [E185.97.C96S3] 79-95268 3.95
1. Cuffe, Paul, 1759-1817. 2. Sierra Leone—History.

Cuffe, Paul, 1759-1817—Juvenile literature.

ATKIN, Mary Gage. 973.4'092'4 B
Paul Cuffe and the African promised land / by Mary Gage Atkin. 1st ed. Nashville : T. Nelson, c1976. p. cm. Includes index. A biography of the Afro-American sea captain who sought to attract freed blacks from America to the colony of Sierra Leone. [E185.97.C96A84] 92 76-26607 ISBN 0-8407-6521-5 : 6.95
1. Cuffe, Paul, 1759-1817—Juvenile literature. 2. Afro-Americans—Biography—Juvenile literature. 3. Sierra Leone—History—Juvenile literature. I. Title. BIP

HARBISON, David. 920'.073
Reaching for freedom: Paul Cuffe, Norbert Rillieux, Ira Aldridge, James McCune Smith. [New York] Scholastic Book Services [1972] 128 p. illus. 22 cm. (Firebird biographies) (Firebird books) Short biographies of four men who overcame racial obstacles to become famous as a sea captain, an inventor, an actor, and a doctor. [E185.96.H33] 920 70-187886
1. Cuffe, Paul, 1759-1817—Juvenile literature. 2. Rillieux, Norbert, 1806-1894—Juvenile literature. 3. Aldridge, Ira Frederick, d. 1867—Juvenile literature. 4. Smith, James McCune—Juvenile literature. I. Title.

JOHNSTON, Johanna. 973.4'0924
Paul Cuffee: America's first black captain. Illustrated by Elton C. Fax. New York, Dodd, Mead [1970] 95 p. illus., map. 24 cm. Bibliography: p. 95. The life of the eighteenth-century black sailing captain who, among other firsts, was the first to petition Massachusetts for the right of Negroes to vote. [E185.97.C96J6] 92 75-117620 3.50
1. Cuffe, Paul, 1759-1817—Juvenile literature. I. Fax, Elton C., illus. II. Title.

Cukor, George Dewey, 1899-

LAMBERT, Gavin. 791.43'0233'0924
On Cukor [Interviews by] Gavin Lambert. New York, Putnam [1972] viii, 276 p. illus. 25 cm. "A Cukor filmography": p. 259-270. [PN1998.A3C85] 74-189884 ISBN 0-399-10925-0 8.95
1. Cukor, George Dewey, 1899- I. Cukor, George Dewey, 1899- II. Title.

Culbertson, William.

WIERSBE, Warren W. 207'.773'11 B
William Culbertson: a man of God, by Warren W. Wiersbe. Chicago, Moody Press [1974] 176 p. illus. 22 cm. [BX6093.C77W53] 74-162937 ISBN 0-8024-9559-1 4.95
1. Culbertson, William.

Culbreath, Agnes (Morgan)

CULBREATH, Agnes (Morgan) 920.7
My mother told me, by Lucille Culbreath Byrd. [1st ed.] New York, Pageant Press [1956] 189p. 21cm. [CT275.C926A3] 56-12500
I. Byrd, Lucille (Culbreath) II. Title.

Cullen, Countee, 1903-1946.

FERGUSON, Blanche E. 811.52
Countee Cullen and the Negro renaissance, by Blanche E. Ferguson. New York, Dodd, Mead [1966] ix, 213 p. illus., ports. 22 cm. Bibliography: p. 205-206. [PS3505.U287Z6] 66-24265
1. Cullen, Countee, 1903-1946. I. Title.

PERRY, Margaret, 1933- 811'.5'2
A bio-bibliography of Countee P. Cullen, 1903-1946. Foreword by Don M. Wolfe. Westport, Conn., Greenwood Pub. Co. [1971] xix, 134 p. port. 22 cm. (Contributions in Afro-American and African studies, no. 8) "A Negro Universities Press Publication." Bibliography: p. 121-122. [PS3505.U287Z83] 75-105995 ISBN 0-8371-3325-4
1. Cullen, Countee, 1903-1946. 2. Cullen, Countee, 1903-1946—Bibliography. I. Title. II. Series. BIP

Cullen, Hugh Roy, 1881-

KILMAN, Edward W., 1896- 923.373
Hugh Roy Cullen: a story of American opportunity, by Ed Kilman and Theon Wright. Illustrated by Nick Eggenhoffer. New York, Prentice-Hall [1954] 376 p. illus. 23 cm. [HD9570.C8K5] 54-8482
1. Cullen, Hugh Roy, 1881- I. Wright, Theon, joint author.

Cullen, Mike, 1941-

CULLEN, Mike, 1941- 364.1'31 B
A time to dance: the Mike Cullen story, as told to Don Ranly. [Celina, Ohio, Messenger Press, c1972] 196 p. 23 cm. [HV28.C84A3] 73-84682 3.50
1. Cullen, Mike, 1941- I. Ranly, Don. II. Title.

Cullinan, Joseph Stephen, 1860-1937.

KING, John O. 338.2'7'28209764
Joseph Stephen Cullinan; a study of leadership in the Texas petroleum industry, 1897-1937 [by] John O. King. Nashville, Published for the Texas Gulf Coast Historical Association by Vanderbilt University Press, 1970. ix, 229 p. illus., ports. 24 cm. Bibliography: p. 217-224. [HD9570.C83K54] 70-112935 10.95
1. Cullinan, Joseph Stephen, 1860-1937. 2. Petroleum industry and trade—Texas—History. I. Texas Gulf Coast Historical Association. BIP

Cullinan, Thomas Major, Sir, 1862-1936.

HELME, Nigel. 968'.204'0924 B
Thomas Major Cullinan : a biography / by Nigel Helme. Johannesburg ; New York : McGraw-Hill, [1974] 271 p. : ill. ; 24 cm. Includes index. Bibliography: p. 260-263. [DT940.3.C84H44] 75-313434 ISBN 0-07-091286-6. ISBN 0-07-091295-5 (lim. ed.)
1. Cullinan, Thomas Major, Sir, 1862-1936.

Culpepper. Burke.

CULPEPPER, James. 922.773
Burke Culpepper, prince of evangelists. Louisville, Ky., Herald Press [1952] 191p. illus. 20cm. [BV3785.C89C85] 53-18792
1. Culpepper. Burke. I. Title.

Cumberland Co., N.S. — Biog.

NORTH Cumberland Historical Society. 971.6'33'030924
Some North Cumberlandians at home and abroad, past and present. [Pugwash, N.S.] 1965. 61 p. ports. 23 cm. (Its Publication no. 2) $2.50 Can. (C 66-434) [F1039.C8N6] 67-80061
1. Cumberland Co., N.S. — Biog. I. Title. II. Series.

Cumberland, Richard,

CUMBERLAND, Richard, 1732-1811. 822'.6 B
Memoirs of Richard Cumberland, London, 1806. Edited by Henry Flanders, 1856. New York, B. Blom, 1969. 397 p. 23 cm. Reprint of the 1856 ed. [PR3393.A4 1969] 72-91487
I. Flanders, Henry, 1826-1911, ed.

Cuming, Alexander, Sir, bart., 1690?-1775.

STEELE, William O., 1917- 970'.004'97 B
The Cherokee crown of Tannassy / William O. Steele. Winston-Salem, N.C. : J. F. Blair Publisher, c1977. p. cm. Bibliography: p. While attempting to charm the Cherokees into loyalty to England, Sir Alexander Cuming is offered by them the crown of the Cherokee kingdom. [E99.C5S85] 77-19997 ISBN 0-910244-99-5 : 7.95
1. Cuming, Alexander, Sir, bart., 1690?-1775. 2. Cherokee Indians—History. 3. Cherokee Indians—Government relations. 4. Statesmen—Great Britain—Biography. I. Title. BIP

Cumming, Katherine H., 1836-1921.

CUMMING, Katharine H., 1836-1921. 973.7'82'0924
A northern daughter and a southern wife : the Civil War reminiscences and letters of Katharine H. Cumming, 1860-1865 / edited by W. Kirk Wood ; with a foreword by Joseph B. Cumming. Augusta, Ga. : Richmond County Historical Society, 1976. xvii, 126 p. : ill. ; 24 cm. Includes bibliographical references. [E487.C97145] 76-23934
1. Cumming, Katherine H., 1836-1921. 2. United States—History—Civil War, 1861-1865—Personal narratives—Confederate side. 3. Augusta, Ga.—Biography. I. Title. BIP

Cummings, Bruce Frederick, 1889-1919—Biography.

CUMMINGS, Bruce Frederick, 1889-1919. 574'.092'4 B
The journal of a disappointed man, by W. N. P. Barbellion. With an introd. by H. G. Wells. New York, Gordon Press, 1974. viii, 312 p. 24 cm. Reprint of the 1919 ed. published by G. H. Doran Co., New York. [PR6005.U5Z52 1974] 73-15413 ISBN 0-87968-150-0 34.95 (lib. bdg.)
1. Cummings, Bruce Frederick, 1889-1919—Biography. I. Title.

Cummings, Edward Estlin, 1894-1962.

FRIEDMAN, Norman. 811.52
E. E. Cummings; the growth of a writer With a pref. by Harry T. Moore. Carbondale, Southern Illinois University Press [1964] x, 193 p. 22 cm. (Crosscurrents; modern critiques) Bibliography: p. [187]-188. [PS3505.U334Z66] 64-11165
1. Cummings, Edward Estlin, 1894-1962. I. Title. BIP

KENNEDY, Richard S. 811'.5'2 B
Dreams in the mirror : a biography of E. E. Cummings / by Richard S. Kennedy. 1st ed. New York : Liveright Pub. Corp., c1979. p. cm. Includes bibliographical references and index. [PS3505.U334Z7] 79-18301 ISBN 0-87140-638-1 : 18.50
1. Cummings, Edward Estlin, 1894-1962. 2. Poets, American—20th century—Biography. I. Title.

NORMAN, Charles, 1904- 811'.5'2
E. E. Cummings, a biography. New York, Dutton, 1967. viii, 246 p. 19 cm. First published in 1958 under title: The magic-maker, E. E. Cummings. Bibliographical footnotes. [PS3505.U334Z8 1967] 67-9503
1. Cummings, Edward Estlin, 1894-1962.

NORMAN, Charles, 1904- 811'.5'2 B
E. E. Cummings, the magic-maker. Indianapolis, Bobbs-Merrill [1972] xv, 365 p. illus. 22 cm. First published in 1958 under title: The magic-maker, E. E. Cummings. [PS3505.U334Z8 1972] 75-173219 10.00
1. Cummings, Edward Estlin, 1894-1962.

NORMAN, Charles, 1904- 928.1
E. E. Cummings, the magic-maker. [Rev. ed.] New York, Duell, Sloan and Pearce [1964] ix, 246 p. 22 cm. "A revised version of The magic maker: E. E. Cummings, published in 1958." Bibliographical footnotes. [PS3505.U334Z8] 64-12438
1. Cummings, Edward Estlin, 1894-1962. I. Title. BIP

NORMAN, Charles, 1904- 928.1
E. E. Cummings, the magic-maker [Rev. ed.] New York, Duell [dist. Meredith, c.1958, 1964] ix, 246p. 22cm. Rev. version of The magic maker: E. E. Cummings, pub. in 1958. Bibl. 64-124381 4.95 bds.,
1. Cummings, Edward Estlin, 1894-1962. I. Title.

NORMAN, Charles, 1904- 811'.5'2 [B]
E. E. Cummings, the magic-maker. Boston, Little, Brown [1973, c.1972] xv, 365 p. illus., ports. 20 cm. First published in 1958 under the title: The magic-maker, E. E. Cummings. [PS3505.U334Z8] 75-173219 3.45 (pbk.)
1. Cummings, Edward Estlin, 1894-1962. I. Title.

NORMAN, Charles, 1904- 928.1
The magic- maker, E. E. Cummings. New York, Macmillan, 1958. 400p. illus. 22cm. Includes bibliography. [PS3505.U334Z8] 58-12439
1. Cummings, Edward Estlin, 1894- I. Title.

Cummings, Edward Estlin, 1894-1962—Biography.

CUMMINGS, Edward Estlin, 1894-1962. 940.4'81'73 B
The enormous room / E. E. Cummings ; a typescript edition with drawings by the author ; edited, with an afterword by George James Firmago ; foreword by Richard S. Kennedy. New York : Liveright, c1978. xxvi, 275 p. : ill. ; 22 cm. [D570.9.C82 1978] 77-28827 ISBN 0-87140-630-6 : 12.95 ISBN 0-87140-119-3 pbk. : 3.95
1. Cummings, Edward Estlin, 1894-1962—Biography. 2. European War, 1914-1918—Personal narratives, American. 3. European War, 1914-1918—Prisoners and prisons, French. 4. Soldiers—United States—Biography. I. Firmage, George James. II. Title. BIP

Cummins Engine Company, inc., Columbus, Ind.

CUMMINS, Clessie L. 629.22
My days with the diesel; the memoirs of Clessie L. Cummins, father of the highway diesel. [1st ed.] Philadelphia, Chilton Books [1967] x, 190 p. 23 cm. [TL140.C8A3] 67-11846
1. Cummins Engine Company, inc., Columbus, Ind. 2. Automobiles—Motors (Diesel) I. Title.

Cunard, Maude Alice (Burke) Lady, 1872-1948.

FIELDING, Daphne (Vivian) 1904- 914.2'03'820922
Those remarkable Cunards: Emerald and Nancy [by] Daphne Fielding. [1st American ed.] New York, Atheneum, 1968. 205 p. illus., ports. 23 cm. London ed. (Eyre & Spottiswoode) has title: Emerald and Nancy: Lady Cunard and her daughter. Bibliographical footnotes. [CT788.C8755F5 1968b] 68-27442 6.50
1. Cunard, Maude Alice (Burke) Lady, 1872-1948. 2. Cunard, Nancy, 1896-1965. I. Title.

Cunard, Nancy, 1896-1965.

FORD, Hugh D., 1925- comp. 821'.9'14
Nancy Cunard: brave poet, indomitable rebel, 1896-1965. Edited by Hugh Ford. [1st ed.] Philadelphia, Chilton Book Co. [1968] xiv, 383 p. illus., ports. 24 cm. English, French, or Spanish. "Bibliography of Nancy Cunard's writings": p. 373-375. [PR6005.U6Z6] 68-23514
1. Cunard, Nancy, 1896-1965.

Cunard, Nancy, 1896-1965—Biography.

CHISHOLM, Anne. 828'.9'1407 B
Nancy Cunard : a biography / by Anne Chisholm. 1st ed. New York : Knopf, 1979. xiii, 366 p., [16] leaves of plates : ill. ; 25 cm. "Bibliography of Hours Press publications": p. [340]-342. [PR6053.U447Z6] 78-20385 ISBN 0-394-49200-5 : 15.00
1. Cunard, Nancy, 1896-1965—Biography. 2. Authors, English—20th century—Biography.

Cunard, Samuel, Sir, bart., 1787-1865—Juvenile literature.

BASSETT, John M., 1914- 387.5'092'4 B
Samuel Cunard / John M. Bassett. Don Mills, Ont. : Fitzhenry & Whiteside, c1976. 60, [1] p. : ill. ; 22 cm. (The Canadians) Bibliography: p. [61] [HE569.C8B37] 77-358434 ISBN 0-88902-206-2
1. Cunard, Samuel, Sir, bart., 1787-1865—Juvenile literature. 2. Merchant marine—Canada—Biography—Juvenile literature. I. Title. II. Series.

Cundall, Joseph, 1818-1895.

MCLEAN, Ruari. 070.5'092'4 B
Joseph Cundall, a Victorian publisher : notes on his life and a check-list of his books / by Ruari McLean. Pinner : Private Libraries Association, 1976. viii, 96 p. : ill. (some col.), facsims., geneal. table, ports. ; 28 cm. Includes index. [Z325.C85M3] 77-362190 ISBN 0-900002-13-1 : £8.00
1. Cundall, Joseph, 1818-1895. 2. Publishers and publishing—England—London—Biography. 3. London—Biography.

Cuney, Norris Wright, 1846-1899.

HARE, Maud (Cuney), 1874-1936 976.4'06'0924
Norris Wright Cuney: a tribune of the Black people. Introd. by Robert C. Cotner. Austin, Tex., Steck-Vaughn [c.1968] xv, 230p. illus., ports. 20cm. (Steck-Vaughns Life & adventure ser.) Facsim. reprodn. of the 1913 ed. with new introd. [E185.97.C97H3 1913a] (B) 68-29063 5.95
1. Cuney, Norris Wright, 1846-1899. 2. Texas—Pol. & govt.—1865-1950. I. Title.

Cunningham, Andrew Browne Cunningham, 1st Viscount, 1883-1963.

CUNNINGHAM, Andrew Browne 923.542
Cunningham, 1st viscount, 1883-
A sailor's odyssey; the autobiography of Admiral of the Fleet, Viscount Cunningham of Hyndhope. [1st ed.] New York, Dutton, 1951. 715 p. illus. 24 cm. [DA89.1.C8A3 1951a] 51-14146
1. World War, 1939-1945—Naval operations, British. 2. World War, 1939-1945—Mediterranean Sea. I. Title.

WARNER, Oliver, 1903- 359.3'31'0924 B
Admiral of the fleet: Cunningham of Hyndhope; the battle for the Mediterranean; a memoir. Athens, Ohio University Press [1967] 301 p. illus., fold. map, ports. 22 cm. London ed. (Murray) has title: Cunningham of Hyndhope, Admiral of the Fleet; a memoir. [DA89.1.C8W3 1967b] 67-26124
1. Cunningham, Andrew Browne Cunningham, 1st Viscount, 1883-1963. 2. Great Britain—History, Naval—20th century. I. Title.

Cunningham, Imogen, 1883-1976.

IMOGEN Cunningham : 770'.92'4 B
a portrait / by Judy Dater, in association with the Imogen Cunningham Trust. 1st ed. Boston : New York Graphic Society, c1979. 126 p., [30] leaves of plates : ill. ; 29 cm. [TR140.C78I47] 79-2375 ISBN 0-8212-0751-2 : 19.95
1. Cunningham, Imogen, 1883-1976. 2. Photography, Artistic. 3. Photographers—United States—Biography. I. Cunningham, Imogen, 1883-1976. II. Dater, Judy. III. Imogen Cunningham Trust.

Curie, Irene, 1897-1956.

MCKOWN, Robin. 925.3
She lived for science: Irene Joliot-Curie. New York, J. Messner [1961] 192 p. 22 cm. [QC16.C78M3] 61-7996
1. Curie, Irene, 1897-1956. I. Title.

Curie, Marie Sklodowska, 1867-1934.

BIGLAND, Eileen. 925.4
Madam Curie. Illustrated by Lili Cassel. New York, Criterion Books [1957] 191 p. illus. 22 cm. (A Criterion book for young people) [QD22.C8B49] 57-5540
1. Curie, Marie Sklodowska, 1867-1934.

BIGLAND, Eileen. 925.4
Madame Curie. Illustrated by Lili Cassel. New York, Criterion Books [1957] 191p. illus. 22cm. (A Criterion book for young people) [QD22.C8B49] 57-5540
1. Curie, Marie (Sklodowska) 1867-1934. I. Title.

CUEIE, Eve, 1904- 925.
Madame Curie. Tr. [from French] by Vincent Sheean. Introd. Introd. by John La0)ear; suggestions for reading and discussions by Olive B. ,macPherson. Sch. ed. Boston, Houghton [c.1937, 1963] 400p. 21cm. (RLS, Riverside lit. ser., R24) 2.68; 1.52 pap.,
1. Curie, Marie (Skodowaska) 1867-1934. I. Sheean, Vincent, 1899- tr. II. Title.

DE LEEUW, Adele Louise, 1899- 530'.0924 B
Marie Curie, woman of genius. Illustrated by Cary. Champaign, Ill., Garrard Pub. Co. [1970] 144 p. illus., ports. 22 cm. A biography of the woman scientist whose dedication and hard work resulted in the discovery of radium and two awards of the Nobel Prize. [QD22.C8D4] 92 70-90816 2.59
1. Curie, Marie (Sklodowska) 1867-1934—Juvenile literature. I. Cary, illus. II. Title.

DOORLY, Eleanor. 925.4
The radium woman, a life of Marie Curie; woodcuts by Robert Gibbings New York, Roy Publishers [1954?] 181 p. illus. 21 cm. [QD22.C8D6 1954] 54-10466
1. Curie, Marie Sklodowska, 1867-1934. I. Title.

*FEUERLICHT, Roberta 925.4
Madame Curie, a concise biography. New York, Amer. R.D.M. [c.1965] 77p. illus. 21cm. (Study master pubn., 901) Bibl. 1.00 pap.,
1. Curie, Marie (Sklodovska) 1867-1934. I. Title.

FEUERLICHT, Roberta Strauss. v. 12
Madame Curie; a concise biography. New York, American R.D.M. Corp. [1965] 77 p. (A Study master publication) Includes bibliography. 67-19732
1. Curie, Marie (Sklodowska) I. Title.

HENRIOD, Lorraine. 530'.0924 B
Marie Curie. Illustrated by Fermin Rocker. New York, Putnam [1970] 60 p. illus. (part col.) 23 cm. (A See and read beginning to read biography) An easy-to-read biography of the scientist who, with her husband, was awarded the 1903 Nobel Prize for discovering radium. [QD22.C8H4 1970] 92 79-99283 2.68
1. Curie, Marie (Sklodowska) 1867-1934—Juvenile literature. I. Rocker, Fermin, illus. II. Title.

HENRY, Joanne Landers 92
Marie Curie, discoverer of radium. Illus. by John Martinez. New York, Macmillan [1966] 44p. col. illus. 24cm. (Sci. story lib.) [QC16.C79H4] 66-18767 2.95; 3.24 lib. ed.,
1. Curie, Marie (Sklodowska) 1867-1934—Juvenile literature. I. Title.

IVIMEY, Alan. 530'.0924 B
Marie Curie; pioneer of the Atomic Age. New York, Praeger [1969, c1964] vi, 122 p. illus., ports. 23 cm. (Praeger pathfinder biographies) Bibliography: p. 119. A biography of the Polish-born scientist who, with her husband's help, isolated radium receiving the Nobel Prize for the achievement in 1903. [QD22.C8I9 1969] 92 71-86514 4.25
1. Curie, Marie (Sklodowska) 1867-1934—Juvenile literature. I. Title.

MCKOWN, Robin. 925.4
Marie Curie. Illustrated by Lili Rethi. New

York, Putnam [1959] 128p. illus. 21cm. [QD22.C8M3] 59-9864
1. Curie, Marie (Skiodowaka) 1867-1934. I. Title.

MCKOWN, Robin. 530'.0924 B
Marie Curie. Illustrated by Karl W. Swanson. New York, Putnam [1971] 95 p. illus. 24 cm. (A World pioneer biography) Bibliography: p. 92. A biography of the chemist whose research with radium made her the first woman to receive a Nobel Prize and the first person to receive the award twice. [QD22.C8M32] 92 74-137990 3.86
1. Curie, Marie (Sklodowska) 1867-1934—Juvenile literature. I. Swanson, Karl W., illus. II. Title. **BIP**

REID, Robert William. 530'.092'4 B
Marie Curie [by] Robert Reid. New York, Saturday Review Press [1974] 349 p. illus. 22 cm. Bibliography: p. 337-338. [QD22.C8R4 1974] 74-3469 ISBN 0-8415-0317-6 8.95
1. Curie, Marie Sklodowska, 1867-1934. **BIP**

RUBIN, Elizabeth. 925.4
The Curies and radium. Pictures by Alan Moyler. New York, F. Watts [1961] 112 p. illus. 22 cm. (A First biography) [QD22C8R8] 60-5579
1. Curie, Marie Sklodowska, 1867-1934. 2. Curie, Pierre, 1859-1906. I. Title.

VEGLAHN, Nancy. 530'.092'4 B
The mysterious rays : Marie Curie's world / by Nancy Veglahn ; illustrated by Victor Juhasz. New York : Coward, McCann & Geoghegan, c1977. 63 p. : ill. ; 21 cm. Bibliography: p. 63. A brief biography of Marie Curie concentrating on her search and discovery of the then new element, radium. [QD22.C8V43 1977] 92 77-8361 ISBN 0-698-30681-3 lib. bdg. : 4.99
1. Curie, Marie Sklodowska, 1867-1934—Juvenile literature. 2. Chemists—Biography—Juvenile literature. I. Juhasz, Victor. II. Title. **BIP**

Curie, Marie (Sklodowska) 1867-1934—Juvenile literature.

ABRAHALL, Clare Constance (Drury) Hoskyns. 92
The young Marie Curie. Illustrated by Denise Brown. New York, Roy Publishers [1961] 128p. illus. 21cm. [QD22.C8A5] 61-11042
1. Curie, Marie (Sklodowska) 1867-1934—Juvenile literature. I. Title.

ABRAHALL, Clare Constance (Dury) Hoskyns 92
The young Marie Curie. Illus. by Denise Brown. New York, Roy [c.1961] 128p. 61-11042 3.00 bds.,
1. Curie, Marie (Sklodowska) 1867-1934—Juvenile literature. I. Title.

Curie, Pierre, 1859-1906.

CURIE, Marie (Sklodowaska) 1867-1934 925.4
Pierrie Curie. Autobiographical of Marie Curie Tr. by Charlotte and Vernon Kellogg. Introd. by Mrs William Brown Meloney [Gloucester, Mass., P. Smith, 1963] 118p. illus. 22cm. (Dover bk., T199 revound) 3.00
1. Curie, Pierre, 1859-1906. I. Kellogg, Charlotte (Hoffman) tr. II.)Kellogg, Vernon Lyman, 1867-1937, tr. III. Title.

CURIE, Marie (Sklodowska) 1867-1934 925.4
Pierre Curie. Autobiographical notes of Marie Curie. Tr. by Charlotte and Vernon Kellogg introd. by Mrs. William Brown Meloney. New York, Dover [1963] 118p. illus. 22cm. (T199) 63-3594 1.00 pap.,
1. Curie, Pierre, 1859-1906. I. Kellogg, Charlotte (Hoffman tr. II. Kellogg, Vernon Lyman,- 1867-1937, tr. III. Title.

Curley, James Michael, 1874-1958.

CURLEY, James Michael, 1874-- 923.273
I'd do it again, a record of all my uproarious years. Englewood Cliffs, N. J., Prentice-Hall [1957] 372p. illus. 23cm. [F70.C83] 57-8558
I. Title. **BIP**

CURLEY, James Michael, 1874-1958. 320.9'744'6104 B
I'd do it again / James Michael Curley. New York : Arno Press, 1976, c1957. x, 372 p., [16] leaves of plates : ill. ; 23 cm. (The Irish Americans) Reprint of the ed. published by Prentice-Hall, Englewood Cliffs, N.J. [F70.C83 1976] 76-6333 ISBN 0-405-09329-2 : 24.00
1. Curley, James Michael, 1874-1958. I. Title. II. Series.

Curry, George, 1861-1947.

CURRY, George, 1861-1947. 923.273
George Curry, 1861-1947; an autobiography. Edited by H. B. Hening. Illustrated with photos. and a portrait and sketches by Sam Smith. [1st ed.] [Albuquerque] University of New Mexico Press [1958] xv, 336 p. illus., ports. (1 mounted col.) 25 cm. [F801.C95A3] 58-13147
I. Title.

DYKES, Jefferson Chenowth, 1900- 978.9'64'040922 B
Law on a wild frontier: four sheriffs of Lincoln County, by Jeff C. Dykes. Washington, Potomac Corral, The Westerners 1969. iv, 25 p. illus., map, ports. 23 cm. (The Great Western series, no. 5) Bibliography: p. 23. [F802.L7D9] 70-86594
1. Brady, William, 1825-1878. 2. Curry, George, 1861-1947. 3. Garrett, Patrick Floyd, 1850-1908. 4. Poe, John William, 1850-1923. I. Title.

Curry, John.

MONEY, Keith. 796.9'1'0924 B
John Curry / by Keith Money. 1st American ed. New York : Knopf, 1978, c1977. p. cm. [GV850.C87M65 1978] 77-90928 ISBN 0-394-50134-9 : 17.50
1. Curry, John. 2. Skaters—Great Britian—Biography. **BIP**

Curtias, Glenn Hammond, 1878-1930 — Juvenile literature.

TERZIAN, Kathryn. 92
Glenn Curtiss, pioneer pilot, by Kathryn and James P. Terzian. New York, Grosset & Dunlap [1966] 176 p. illus. (part col.) 22 cm. (Pioneer books) A Rutledge book. [TL540.C9T4] 67-3372
1. Curtias, Glenn Hammond, 1878-1930 — Juvenile literature. I. Terzian James P. II. Title.

Curtis, Benjamin Robbins, 1809-1874.

CURTIS, Benjamin Robbins, 1855-1891, ed. 347.99'24
A memoir of Benjamin Robbins Curtis; with some of his professional and miscellaneous writings, edited by Benjamin R. Curtis, Jr. New York, Da Capo Press, 1970. 2 v. ports. 24 cm. Reprint of the 1879 ed. Contents.Contents.—v. 1. Memoir, by G. T. Curtis.—v. 2. Professional and miscellaneous writings. [E415.9.C96C9 1970] 77-75298
1. Curtis, Benjamin Robbins, 1809-1874. I. Curtis, George Ticknor, 1812-1894. II. Title.

Curtis, Edward S., 1868-1952—Juvenile literature.

BOESEN, Victor. 779'.9'970004970924 B
Edward S. Curtis, photographer of the North American Indian / Victor Boesen and Florence Curtis Graybill. New York : Dodd, Mead & Co., [1977] p. cm. Includes index. A biography of Edward Curtis who spent many years photographing, writing about, and recording the songs of the North American Indians. [TR140.C82B63] 92 76-53435 ISBN 0-396-07430-8 : 6.95
1. Curtis, Edward S., 1868-1952—Juvenile literature. 2. Photographers—United States—Biography—Juvenile literature. 3. Indians of North America—Juvenile literature. I. Graybill, Florence Curtis, joint author.

Curtis, George William, 1824-1892.

CURTIS, George William, 1824-1892. 816'.3
Early letters of George Wm. Curtis to John S. Dwight. New York, AMS Press [1971] 293 p. 22 cm. Reprint of the 1898 ed. [PS1493.A33 1971b] 75-134372 ISBN 0-404-08420-6 12.00
I. Title.

MILNE, Gordon. 928.1
George William Curtis & the genteel tradition. Bloomington, Indiana University Press, 1956. 294p. illus. 24cm. [PS1493.M5] 56-6705
1. Curtis, George William, 1824-1892. I. Title.

Curtis, John, 1791-1862.

ORDISH, George. 632'.7'0924 B
John Curtis and the pioneering of pest control. Reading, Osprey, 1974. vii, 121 p., [16] p. of plates. illus., ports. 23 cm. (The Great innovators) Includes index. Bibliography: p. [113]-116. [SB63.C87O7] 74-174687 ISBN 0-85045-159-0 £2.45
1. Curtis, John, 1791-1862. 2. Insect control—History. 3. Entomology—History. 4. Insects—Great Britain. I. Title.

Curtiss, Glenn Hammond, 1878-1930.

ROSEBERRY, Cecil R. 629.13'00924 B
Glenn Curtiss: pioneer of flight [by] C. R. Roseberry. [1st ed.] Garden City, N.Y., Doubleday, 1972. x, 514 p. illus. 24 cm. Bibliography: p. [489]-491. [TL540.C9R67] 70-171316 12.50
1. Curtiss, Glenn Hammond, 1878-1930. I. Title.

TERZIAN, Kathryn. 92
Glenn Curtiss, pioneer pilot, by Kathryn and James P. Terzian. New York, Grosset & Dunlap [1966] 176 p. illus. (part col.) 22 cm. (Pioneer books) (A Rutledge book) A biography of a contemporary of the Wright brothers whose interest in bicycle racing led to contributions in the development of aviation, notably the seaplane and aircraft carrier. [TL540.C9T4] AC 66
1. Curtiss, Glenn Hammond, 1878-1930. I. Terzian, James P. II. Title.

Curtiss, Glenn Hammond, 1878-1930—Juvenile literature.

SCHARFF, Robert. 629.13'00924
Over land and sea; a biography of Glenn Hammond Curtiss, by Robert Scharff and Walter S. Taylor. New York, D. McKay Co. [1968] vii, 310 p. illus., ports. 21 cm. [TL540.C9S34] 68-20776
1. Curtiss, Glenn Hammond, 1878-1930—Juvenile literature. I. Taylor, Walter S., joint author. II. Title.

Curtiss, Mina Stein Kirstein, 1896- —Biography.

CURTISS, Mina Stein Kirstein, 1896- 816'.5'2
Other people's letters : a memoir / by Mina Curtiss. Boston : Houghton Mifflin, 1978. xii, 243 p., [8] leaves of plates : ill. ; 22 cm. Includes bibliographical references and index.. [PS3505.U912Z47] 77-27846 ISBN 0-395-26291-7 : 9.95
1. Curtiss, Mina Stein Kirstein, 1896- —Biography. 2. Authors, American—20th century—Biography. I. Title. **BIP**

Curwen, Samuel, 1715-1802.

CURWEN, Samuel, 1715-1802. 973.3'0924
The journal and letters of Samuel Curwen, 1775-1783. Edited by George Atkinson Ward. New York, Da Capo Press, 1970. xxiv, 678 p. port. 23 cm. (The Era of the American Revolution) (A Da Capo Press reprint series.) Reprint of the 4th ed., 1864. [E278.C98C94] 70-114720 ISBN 0-306-71923-1
1. Curwen, Samuel, 1715-1802. 2. American loyalists. 3. United States—History—Revolution, 1775-1783—Biography. 4. England—Description and travel—1701-1800.

CURWEN, Samuel, 1715-1802. 973.3'14'0924
The journal of Samuel Curwen, loyalist. Edited by Andrew Oliver. Cambridge, Mass., Harvard University Press, for the Essex Institute, Salem, Mass., 1972. 2 v. (xxxiv, 1083 p.) illus. 25 cm. (The Loyalist papers) Includes bibliographical references. [E278.C9A34 1972] 72-180150 ISBN 0-674-48380-4
1. Curwen, Samuel, 1715-1802. 2. American loyalists. 3. United States—History—Revolution, 1775-1783—Biography. 4. England—Description and travel—1701-1800. I. Oliver, Andrew, 1906- ed. II. Title. III. Series. **BIP**

Curzon, George Nathaniel Curzon, 1st marquis, 1859-1925.

CURZON, Garce Elvina Trillia (Hinds) Curzon, marchioness, 1879-- 920.7
Reminiscences. New York, Coward-McCann [1957,c1955] 256p. illus. 24cm. [DA565] 57-13677
1. Curzon, George Nathaniel Curzon, 1st marquis, 1859-1925. I. Title.

DILKS, David, 1938- 954.03'5'0924 B
Curzon in India. New York, Taplinger Pub. Co. [1970, c1969] 2 v. illus., maps, ports. 23 cm. Contents.Contents.—1. Achievement.—2. Frustration. Bibliography: v. 2, p. 290-303. [DS480.D52] 70-88619 ISBN 8-00-821068- (v. 1) 10.00 per vol.
1. Curzon, George Nathaniel Curzon, 1st Marquis, 1859-1925. I. Title. **BIP**

MOSLEY, Leonard Oswald, 1911- 923.242
The glorious fault; the life of Lord Curzon. [1st ed.] New York, Harcourt, Brace [1960] 334 p. illus. 22 cm. [DA565.C95M6] 60-9396
1. Curzon, George Nathaniel Curzon, 1st marquis, 1859-1925. I. Title.

ROSE, Kenneth, 1924- 942.081'092'4 B
Superior person; a portrait of Curzon and his circle in late Victorian England. New York, Weybright and Talley [1970, c1969] xv, 475 p. illus. 24 cm. Bibliography: p. 397-404. [DA565.C95R6 1970] 76-93553 10.00
1. Curzon, George Nathaniel Curzon, 1st Marquis, 1859-1925. I. Title.

ZETLAND, Lawrence John Lumley Dundas, 2d Marquis of, 1876-1961. 954.03'5'0924 B
The life of Lord Curzon, being the authorized biography of George Nathaniel, Marquess Curzon of Kedleston, by the Rt. Hon. the Earl of Ronaldshay. Freeport, N.Y., Books for Libraries Press [1972] p. Reprint of the 1928 ed. [DA565.C95Z4 1972] 72-8474 ISBN 0-8369-6988-X
1. Curzon, George Nathaniel Curzon, 1st Marquis, 1859-1925. 2. India—Politics and government—1765-1947. 3. Great Britain—Politics and government—1910-1936.

Curzon, Mary, 1870-1906.

†NICOLSON, Nigel. 954.03'5'0924 B
Mary Curzon / Nigel Nicolson. 1st U.S. ed. New York : Harper & Row, c1977. xii, 227 p., [8] leaves of plates : 29 ill. ; 24 cm. Includes index. [CT788.C879N5 1977b] 77-3765 ISBN 0-06-013197-7 : 10.00
1. Curzon, Mary, 1870-1906. 2. Curzon, George Nathaniel Curzon, 1st Marquis,

1859-1925. 3. Great Britain—Nobility—Biography. I. Title.

Cusack, Mary Francis, 1829 or 30-1899.

VIDULICH, Dorothy. 271'.976 B
Peace pays a price : a study of Margaret Anna Cusack, the nun of Kenmare, foundress of the Sisters of St. Joseph of Peace / by Sister Dorothy Vidulich ; photos. by Ray Gora. Englewood Cliffs, N.J. : Center for Peace and Justice, 1975. 80, [3] p. : ill. ; 23 cm. Bibliography: p. [82] [BX4490.5.Z8C878] 75-32628 pbk. : 4.95
1. Cusack, Mary Francis, 1829 or 30-1899. 2. Sisters of St. Joseph of Newark. I. Title.

Cushing, Caleb, 1800-1879.

FUESS, Claude Moore, 1885-1963 923.273
The life of Caleb Cushing [2v.] Hamden, Conn., Archon [dist. Shoe String] 1965 [c.1923, 1951] 2v. (442; 454p.) illus., ports. 22cm. [E415.9.C98F9] 65-14189 20.00 set,
1. Cushing, Caleb, 1800-1879. I. Title.

Cushing, Harvey Williams, 1869-1939.

THOMSON, Elizabeth Harriet, 1907- 926.1
Harvey Cushing: surgeon, author, artist. Foreword by John F. Fulton. New York, Schuman, 1950. xviii, 347 p. illus., ports. 22 cm. (Historical Library, Yale University School of Medicine. Publication no. 24) The Life of science library [13] Bibliography: p. 325-328. [R154.C96T5] 50-3130
1. Cushing, Harvey Williams, 1869-1939. I. Series: Yale University. School of Medicine. Yale Medical Library. Historical Library Publication no. 24)

THOMSON, Elizabeth Harriet, 1907- v. 12
Harvey Cushing, surgeon, author, artist. Foreword by John F. Fulton. New York, Collier Books, [1961] 318 p. (Historical Library, Yale University School of Medicine. Publication no. 24) 63-79099
1. Cushing, Harvey Williams, 1869-1939. I. Title.

Cushing, Harvey Williams, 1869-1939—Juvenile literature.

DENZEL, Justin F. 617'.0924 B
Genius with a scalpel, Harvey Cushing [by] Justin F. Denzel. New York, Messner [1971] 189 p. 22 cm. Bibliography: p. 179-183. A biography of the pioneer brain surgeon whose perfection of many surgical techniques made him foremost in his field. [R154.C96D4] 92 72-139082 ISBN 0-671-32367-9 3.95
1. Cushing, Harvey Williams, 1869-1939—Juvenile literature. I. Title.

Cushing, Richard James, Cardinal, 1895-1970.

CUTLER, John Henry, 1910- 262'.135'0924 B
Cardinal Cushing of Boston. New York, Hawthorn Books [1970] xi, 404 p. illus., ports. 24 cm. Includes bibliographical references. [BX4705.C8C9 1970] 70-107898 8.95
1. Cushing, Richard James, Cardinal, 1895- I. Title.

DEVER, Joseph, 1919- 262.1350924 (B)
Cushing of Boston, a candid-portrait. Boston, Bruce Humphries [1965] 287 p. 24 cm. [BX4705.C8D37] 65-20920
1. Cushing, Richard James, Cardinal, 1895- I. Title.

DEVER, Joseph, 1919- 262.1350924
Cushing of Boston, a candid portrait. Boston, BruceHumphries [c.1965] 287p. 24cm. [BX4705.C8D37] 65-20920 5.95
1. Cushing, Richard James, Cardinal, 1895- I. Title. BIP

DEVINE, M. C. 922.273
The world's Cardinal [Boston] St. Paul Eds. [dist. Daughters of St. Paul, c.1964] 356p. illus., ports. (pt. col.) facsim. 22cm. 64-24360 5.75; 4.75 pap.,
1. Cushing, Richard James, Cardinal, 1895- I. Title.

FENTON, John H. 922.273
Salt of the earth; an informal profile of Richard Cardinal Cushing, by John H. Fenton. New York, Coward-McCann [1965] xi, 242 p. ports. 22 cm. [BX4705.C8F4] 65-13275
1. Cushing, Richard James, Cardinal, 1895-1970. I. Title.

Cushing, William Barker, 1842-1874.

ROSKE, Ralph Joseph, 1921- 923.573
Lincoln's commando; the biography of Commander W. B. Cushing, U. S. N., by Ralph J. Roske and Charles Van Doren. [1st ed.] New York, Harper [1957] 310p. illus. 22cm. [E467.1.C98R6] 56-11083
1. Cushing, William Barker, 1842-1874. I. Van Doren. Charles, joint author. II. Title.

ROSKE, Ralph Joseph, 1921- 359.3'3'20924 B
Lincoln's commando; the biography of Commander W. B. Cushing, U.S.N., by Ralph J. Roske and Charles Van Doren. Westport, Conn., Greenwood Press [1973, c1957] x, 310 p. illus. 22 cm. Reprint of the 1st ed., published by Harper, New York. [E467.1.C98R6 1973] 73-7311 ISBN 0-8371-6923-2 13.50
1. Cushing, William Barker, 1842-1874. I. Van Doren, Charles Lincoln, 1926- joint author. II. Title.

Cushman, Charlotte Saunders, 1816-1876.

LEACH, Joseph. 792'.028'0924 B
Bright particular star; the life & times of Charlotte Cushman. New Haven, Yale University Press, 1970. xvi, 453 p. illus., facsim., ports. 24 cm. Includes bibliographical references. [PN2287.C8L4] 76-99829 12.50
1. Cushman, Charlotte Saunders, 1816-1876. I. Title. BIP

WATERS, Clara Erskine Clement, 1834-1916. 792'.028'0924
Charlotte Cushman, by Clara Erskine Clement. Freeport, N.Y., Books for Libraries Press [1973] p. Reprint of the 1882 ed., issued in series: American actor series, v. 4. [PN2287.C8W4 1973] 72-12702 ISBN 0-8369-7143-4
1. Cushman, Charlotte Saunders, 1816-1876.

Custer, Elizabeth Bacon, 1842-1933.

FROST, Lawrence A. 973.8'092'4
General Custers' "Libbie" / by Lawrence A. Frost. Seattle : Superior Pub. Co., [1976] p. cm. Includes index. Bibliography: p. [E467.1.C99F76] 76-2682 ISBN 0-87564-806-1 : 19.95
1. Custer, Elizabeth Bacon, 1842-1933. I. Title. BIP

FROST, Lawrence A. 973.8'092'4
General Custer's Libbie / Lawrence A. Frost ; ill., E. Lisle Reedstrom. 1st ed. Seattle : Superior Pub. Co., c1976. 336 p. : ill. ; 28 cm. Includes bibliographical references and index. [E467.1.C99F76] 76-2682 ISBN 0-87564-806-1 : 19.95
1. Custer, Elizabeth Bacon, 1842-1933. 2. Custer, George Armstrong, 1839-1876. 3. United States. Army—Biography. 4. Wives—United States—Biography. 5. Generals—United States—Biography. I. Title.

Custer, Elizabeth (Bacon) 1842-1933—Juvenile literature.

RANDALL, Ruth (Painter) 917.3038 B
I, Elizabeth; a biography of the girl who married General George Armstrong Custer of "Custer's last stand." [1st ed.] Boston, Little, Brown [1966] xii, 260 p. illus., ports. 21 cm. Bibliography: p. [ix]-x. [E467.1.C99R3] 66-11008
1. Custer, Elizabeth (Bacon) 1842-1933—Juvenile literature. I. Title.

Custer, George Armstrong, 1839-1876.

CUSTER, Elizabeth (Bacon) 1842-1933. 923.573
Boots and saddles; or, Life in Dakota with General Custer. Introd. by Jane R. Stewart. [New ed.] Norman, University of Oklahoma Press [c.1961] 280p. (Western frontier library, 17) 61-8999 2.00 bds.,
1. Custer, George Armstrong, 1839-1876. 2. U. S. Army—Military life. 3. Frontier and pioneer life—Dakota. I. Title.

CUSTER, George Armstrong. 973.820924
My life on the plains George Armstrong Custer. New York : Leisure Books [1976] 280 p. ; 18 cm. (Golden West Series) [E467.1.C99] ISBN 0-8439-00377 pbk. : 1.25
1. Custer, George Armstrong, 1839-1876. I. Title.

CUSTER, George Armstrong, 1839-1876. 923.573
The Custer story; the life and intimate letters of General George A, Custer and his wife Elizabeth. Edited by Marguerite Merington. New York, Devin-Adair, 1950. xii, 339 p. illus., ports, maps. 24 cm. [E467.1.C99A3] 50-5474
1. Custer, Elizabeth (Bacon), d. 1933. II. Merington, Marguerite. ed. III. Title.

CUSTER, George Armstrong, 1839-1876. 923.573
My life on the Plains. [Edited by Milo Milton Quaife] New York, Citadel Press [1962] 625 p. illus. 17 cm. (A Citadel pioneer book) 62-9215
1. Indians of North America — Wars — 1866-1895. 2. Great Plains — Descr. & trav. I. Title.

CUSTER, George Armstrong, 1839--1876. 923.573
My life on the plains. Edited by Milo Milton Quaife. Chicago, Lakeside Press, 1952. xiix, 626p. illus., ports., map. facsim. 17cm. (The Lakeside classics. no. 50) [F594.C97 1952] 53-1763
1. Indians of North America—Wars—1866-1895. 2. Great Plains—Descr. & trav. I. Title.

CUSTER, George Armstrong, 1893-1876. v. 12
My life on the Plains. Edited by Milo Milton Quaife. Lincoln, University of Nebraska Press [1966?] xli, 626 p. illus. (Bison books. BB328) 67-2618
1. Indians of North America — Wars — 1866-1895. 2. Great Plains — Descr. & trav. I. Title. BIP

FROST, Lawrence A. 973.8'092'4
General Custer's Libbie / Lawrence A. Frost ; ill., E. Lisle Reedstrom. 1st ed. Seattle : Superior Pub. Co., c1976. 336 p. : ill. ; 28 cm. Includes bibliographical references and index. [E467.1.C99F76] 76-2682 ISBN 0-87564-806-1 : 19.95
1. Custer, Elizabeth Bacon, 1842-1933. 2. Custer, George Armstrong, 1839-1876. 3. United States. Army—Biography. 4. Wives—United States—Biography. 5. Generals—United States—Biography. I. Title.

HEUMAN, William. 928'.02'0924 B
Custer, man and legend. Illustrated with photos., old prints, and maps. New York, Dodd, Mead [1968] xvi, 203 p. illus., maps. 21 cm. Bibliography: p. 199-200. The life of the Civil War general whose controversial fame rests chiefly on the disaster at the Little Big Horn in 1876. [E467.1.C99H4] 92 AC 68
1. Custer, George Armstrong, 1839-1876. I. Title.

KAUFMAN, Fred S., 1902- 978.3'02
Custer passed our way, by Fred S. Kaufman. [Aberdeen, S.D., North Plains Press, 1971] 365 p. illus., facsims., maps, ports. 24 cm. Includes bibliographical references. [F655.K3] 73-149213 7.95
1. Custer, George Armstrong, 1839-1876. 2. South Dakota—History. I. Title.

KINSLEY, D A 973.7'0924
Favor the bold; Custer: the Civil War years [by] D. A. Kinsley. [1st ed.] New York, Holt, Rinehart and Winston [1967]- v. map, ports. 22 cm. Bibliography: v. 1. p. 301-302. [E467.1.C99K5] 67-13482
1. Custer, George Armstrong, 1839-1876. I. Title.

KINSLEY, D. A. 973.8'1'0924 B
Favor the bold / D. A. Kinsley. [New York] : Promontory Press, [1974] c1967-1968. 2 v. : ill. ; 22 cm. Reprint of the ed. published by Holt, Rinehart and Winston, New York. Contents.Contents.—v. 1. Custer, the Civil War years.—v. 2. Custer, the Indian fighter. Includes bibliographies and indexes. [E467.1.C99K52] 73-92084 ISBN 0-88394-029-9(v.1) 2.98ea.
1. Custer, George Armstrong, 1839-1876. I. Title.

MONAGHAN, James, 1891- 923.573
Custer; the life of General Armstrong Custer, by Jay Monaghan. [1st ed.] Boston, Little, Brown [1959] 469 p. illus. 22 cm. [E467.1.C99M65] 59-5937
1. Custer, George Armstrong, 1839-1876.

REYNOLDS, Quentin James, 1902-1965. 973.8'1'0924 B
Custer's last stand, by Quentin Reynolds. Illustrated by Frederick T. Chapman. New York, Random House [1951] 185 p. illus. 22 cm. (Landmark books, 20) A biography of the boy who not only saw his dream to be a general come true, but also became the famous Indian fighter who led the attack against Crazy Horse and Sitting Bull at the Battle of the Little Big Horn. [E467.1.C99R4] 92 AC 68
1. Custer, George Armstrong, 1839-1876. 2. Little Big Horn, Battle of the, 1876. I. Chapman, Frederick T., illus. II. Title.

STEVENSON, Augusta. 973.8'1'0924 B
George Custer, boy of action. Illustrated by Al Fiorentino. Indianapolis, Bobbs-Merrill [1963] 200 p. illus. 20 cm. (Childhood of famous Americans) The boyhood of the great Indian fighter who died in the controversial Battle of Little Big Horn. [PZ7.S8467Gd] 92 AC 68
1. Custer, George Armstrong, 1839-1876. I. Fiorentino, Al, illus. II. Title.

VAN DE WATER, Frederic Franklyn, 1890- 923.573
Glory-hunter; a life of General Custer. New York, Argosy-Antiquarian, 1963 [c1934] 394 p. illus., ports., maps. 24 cm. Bibliography: p. 373-376. [E467.1.C99V3 1963] 63-20840
1. Custer, George Armstrong, 1839-1876. I. Title.

VAN DE WATER, Frederic Franklyn, 1890- 923.573
Glory-hunter; a life of General Custer. New York, Argosy-Antiquarian, 1963 [c1934] 394 p. illus., ports, maps. 24 cm. Bibliography: p. 373-376. [E467.1.C99V3] 63-20840
1. Custer, George Armstrong, 1839-1876. I. Title.

Custer, George Armstrong, 1839-1876—Portraits, caricatures, etc.

FROST, Lawrence A. 923.573
The Custer album; a pictorial biography of General George A. Custer, by Lawrence A. Frost. [1st ed.] Seattle, Superior Pub. Co. [1964] 192 p. illus., facsims., maps, ports. 28 cm. "Garry Owen; regimental battle song of Seventh U.S. Calvary" (for piano): p. 183. Bibliography: p. 186-189. [E83.876.F7] 64-21319
1. Custer, George Armstrong, 1839-1876—Portraits, caricatures, etc. I. Title.

Cut Bank, Mont.

WHETSTONE, Daniel W. 920.5
Frontier editor. New York, Hastings House [1956] 217 p. illus. 21 cm. [PN4874.W47A3] 56-8125
1. Cut Bank, Mont. I. Title.

WHETSTONE, Daniel W. 920.5
Frontier editor. New York, Hastings House [1956] 287 p. illus. 21 cm. [PN4874.W47A3] 56-8125
1. Cut Bank, Mont. I. Title.

Cutler, Carl C., 1878-1966.

DICKERMAN, Marion. 917.46'5 B
The three founders: Dr. Charles Kirtland Stillman, Carl C. Cutler [and] Edward Eugene Bradley. With a foreword by Philip R. Mallory. [Mystic, Conn.] Marine Historical Association, 1965. 42 p. illus., ports. 23 cm. Cover title: The three founders of Mystic Seaport. [F104.M99D5] 71-17343
1. Mystic Seaport, Mystic, Conn. 2. Stillman, Charles Kirtland, 1879-1938. 3. Cutler, Carl C., 1878-1966. 4. Bradley, Edward Eugene, 1857-1938. I. Marine Historical Association. II. Title.

Cutler, Ephraim, 1767-1853.

CUTLER, Julia Perkins, 1814-1904. 328.771'0924 B
Life and times of Ephraim Cutler. [New York] Arno Press [1971, c1890] vi, 353 p. illus. 23 cm. (The First American frontier) [F495.C92 1971] 71-146389 ISBN 0-405-02840-7
1. Cutler, Ephraim, 1767-1853. 2. Cutler, William Parker, 1812-1889. 3. Cutler, Jervis, 1768-1844. 4. Ohio—History—1787-1865. I. Title. II. Series.

Cutler, G. Ripley.

CUTLER, G. Ripley. 940.4'753
Of battles long ago : memoirs of an American ambulance driver in World War I / G. Ripley Cutler ; edited and with an introd. by Charles H. Knickerbocker. 1st ed. Hicksville, N.Y. : Exposition Press, c1979. 280 p. : ill. ; 21 cm. [D630.C8A36] 79-50656 ISBN 0-682-49396-1 : 15.00
1. Cutler, G. Ripley. 2. European War, 1914-1918—Medical and sanitary affairs. 3. European War, 1914-1918—France. 4. European War, 1914-1918—Personal narratives, American. 5. Ambulance drivers—United States—Biography. 6. Ambulance drivers—France—Biography. I. Knickerbocker, Charles H. II. Title.

Cutler, Henry Franklin, 1862-1945.

DAY, Richard Ward. 923.773
A New England schoolmaster; the life of Henry Franklin Cutler. Bristol, Conn., Hildreth Press, 1950. 274 p. illus., ports., geneal. table. 24 cm. Bibliography: p. 260-269. [LD7501.M92817 1890] 50-2261
1. Cutler, Henry Franklin, 1862-1945. 2. Mt. Hermon School for Boys, Mount Hermon, Mass. I. Title.

Cutler, Julian Stearns, b. 1854.

DIXON, Madeline Cutler. 288.0924
With halo atilt [by] Madeline C. Dixon. Boston, Beacon Press [1965] 236 p. 21 cm. [BX9869.C94D5] 65-23470
1. Cutler, Julian Stearns, b. 1854. I. Title.

Cutler, William Parker, 1812-1889.

CUTLER, Julia Perkins, 1814-1904. 328.771'0924 B
Life and times of Ephraim Cutler. [New York] Arno Press [1971, c1890] vi, 353 p. illus. 23 cm. (The First American frontier) [F495.C92 1971] 71-146389 ISBN 0-405-02840-7
1. Cutler, Ephraim, 1767-1853. 2. Cutler, William Parker, 1812-1889. 3. Cutler, Jervis, 1768-1844. 4. Ohio—History—1787-1865. I. Title. II. Series.

Cutter, Charles Ammi, 1837-1903.

CUTTER, William Parker, 1867-1935. 020'.924
Charles Ammi Cutter. Boston, Gregg Press, 1972 [c1931] 66 p. illus. 23 cm. (The Library reference series. Library history and biography) Reprint of the ed. published by American Library Association, Chicago, which was issued as no. 3 of American library pioneers. [Z720.C99C9 1972] 72-8801 ISBN 0-8398-0284-6 6.25
1. Cutter, Charles Ammi, 1837-1903. I. Series: Library history and biography. II. Series: American library pioneers, no. 3.

Cutter, James Bird,

CUTTER, James Bird, 1868-- 926.1
The voyage of the Vega, and other tales; or, The birth of self-reliance. New York, Comet Press Books [1953] 120p. illus. 23cm. Autobiographical. [R154.C98A3] 53-31629
I. Title. II. Title: The birth of self-reliance.

Cuyp, Aelbert, 1620-1691.

REISS, Stephen. 759.9492
Aelbert Cuyp / Stephen Reiss. Boston : New York Graphic Society, c1975. 223 p. : ill. (some col.) ; 27 cm. Includes index. Bibliography: p. 215. [ND653.C8R45 1975] 73-91130 ISBN 0-8212-0578-1 : 37.50
1. Cuyp, Aelbert, 1620-1691.

Cycling.

TAYLOR, Marshall William, 1878- 796.6 B
The fastest bicycle rider in the world; the autobiography of Major Taylor. Abridged ed. Brattleboro, Vt., S. Greene Press [1972] x, 214 p. illus. 23 cm. [GV1051.T3A29] 70-189332 ISBN 0-8289-0159-7 3.95
1. Cycling. I. Title.

Cynewulf.

SISAM, Kenneth. 829'.4
Cynewulf and his poetry / by Kenneth Sisam. Folcroft, Pa. : Folcroft Library Editions, 1975. 29 p. ; 23 cm. Reprint of the 1933 ed. published by H. Milford, London, which was reprinted from the Proceedings of the British Academy, v. 18. Original ed. issued as the 1932 Sir Israel Gollancz lecture. Includes bibliographical references. [PR1663.S5 1975] 75-1103 ISBN 0-8414-7838-4 lib. bdg. : 5.00
1. Cynewulf. I. Title. II. Series: British Academy, London (Founded 1901) Sir Israel Gollancz memorial lecture ; 1932.
BIP

Cyprianus, Saint, Bp. of Carthage.

SAGE, Michael M. 270.1'092'4 B
Cyprian / by Michael M. Sage. Cambridge, Mass. : Philadelphia Patristic Foundation : [sole distributors, Greeno, Hadden], 1975. v, 439 p. ; 24 cm. (Patristic monograph series ; no. 1) Includes index. Bibliography: p. 411-429. [BR1720.C8S23] 75-11008 ISBN 0-915646-00-5
1. Cyprianus, Saint, Bp. of Carthage. I. Title. II. Series.
BIP

Cyrano (Yacht)

BUCKLEY, William Frank, 1925- 910'.45
Airborne : a sentimental journey / William F. Buckley, Jr. New York : Macmillan, c1976. xviii, 252 p., [4] leaves of plates : ill. ; 24 cm. [G530.B88 1976] 76-25512 ISBN 0-02-518040-1 : 12.95
1. Cyrano (Yacht) 2. Buckley, William Frank, 1925- 3. Atlantic Ocean. I. Title.
BIP

Cyrillus, Saint, of Thessalonica, 827 (ca-869.

FENSIK, Eugene A 1844-1903. 922.1495
Saints Cyril and Methodius; a translation of an historical narrative about the apostles to the Slavs, written in the Carpatho-Ruthenian literary language. Translated by Michael Roman. Munhall, Pa., Printed by Greek Catholic Union Messenger, c1954. 142p. illus. 23cm. [BX4700.C9F4] 54-27099
1. Cyrillus, Saint, of Thessalonica, 827 (ca-869. 2. Methodius, Saint, Abp. of Moravia, d.885. I. Title.

Cyrus, the Great, King of Persia, d. 529 B.C.

LAMB, Harold, 1892- 923.135
Cyrus the Great. [1st ed.] Garden City, N. Y., Doubleday, 1960. 309p. illus. 22cm. [DS282.L3] 60-12436
1. Cyrus, the Great, King of Persia, d. 529 B. C. I. Title.

LAMB, Harold [Albert] 923.135
Cyrus the Great. Garden City, N.Y., Doubleday [c.]1960. 309p. illus., endpaper map. 22cm. 60-12436 4.50
1. Cyrus, the Great, King of Persia, d. 529 B.C. I. Title.

LAMB, Harold Albert, 1892- 923.135
Cyrus the Great. New York, Bantam [1963, c.1960] 278p. 18cm. (F2535) .50 pap.,
1. Cyrus, the Great, king of Persia, d.529 B.C. I. Title.
BIP

Cystic fibrosis—Biography.

WOODSON, Meg. 618.9'23'7 B
Following Joey home / Meg Woodson. Grand Rapids : Zondervan Pub. House, c1978. 158 p. : port. ; 22 cm. [RJ456.C9W65] 77-29009 ISBN 0-310-34860-9 : 6.95
1. Cystic fibrosis—Biography. 2. Terminally ill children—Biography. 3. Woodson, Joey. 4. Consolation. I. Title.
BIP

Czartoryski, Adam Jerzy, Kaiaze, 1770-1861.

CZARTORYSKI, Adam Jerzy, ksiaze, 1770-1861. 947'.07'0924 B
Memoirs of Prince Adam Czartoryski. Edited by Adam Gielgud. New York, Arno Press, 1971. viii, 336, viii, 367 p. ports. 24 cm. (The Eastern Europe collection) Reprint of the 1888 ed. Translation of Memoires, first published in 1865 under title: Alexandre I et le prince Czartoryski. [DK435.5.C83A313 1971] 78-135808 ISBN 0-405-02750-8
1. Europe—Politics and government—1789-1815. 2. Russia—Foreign relations—1801-1825. 3. Polish question. I. Alexander I, Emperor of Russia, 1777-1825.

KUKIEL, Marian, 1885- 923.2438
Czartoryski and European unity, 1770-1861. Princeton, Princeton University Press, 1955. 354p. illus. 23cm. (Poland's millennium series of the Kosciuszko Foundation) [DK435.5.C83K8] 54-6076
1. Czartoryski, Adam Jerzy, Kaiaze, 1770-1861. 2. Poland—Pol. & govt.—1796-1918. 3. Europe—Politics—1789-1900. I. Title.

Czechoslovak Society of Arts and Sciences in America—Directories.

CZECHOSLOVAK Society of Arts and Sciences in America. 917.3'06'91860922
Biographical directory of the members of the Czechoslovak Society of Arts and Sciences in America, inc. Compiled and edited by Eva Rechcigl and Miloslav Rechcigl, Jr. New York, 1972. viii, 134 p. 25 cm. [E184.B67C9817] 72-91907 8.00
1. Czechoslovak Society of Arts and Sciences in America—Directories. 2. Czechs in the United States—Directories. I. Rechcigl, Eva Edwards, 1932- ed. II. Rechcigl, Miloslav, ed. III. Title.

Czechs in the United States—History.

PANORAMA; 301.451'918'073
a historical review of Czechs and Slovaks in the United States of America. Cicero, Ill., Czechoslovak National Council of America [1970] 328 p. illus. 27 cm. [E184.B67P35] 75-294518
1. Czechs in the United States—History. 2. Czechs in the United States—Biography. 3. Slovak Americans—History. 4. Slovaks in the United States—Biography. I. Czechoslovak National Council of America.

Czerniakow, Adam, 1880-1942.

CZERNIAKOW, Adam, 1880-1942. 943.8'4
The Warsaw diary of Adam Czerniakow : prelude to doom / edited by Raul Hilberg, Stanislaw Staron, and Josef Kermisz ; translated by Staron and the staff of Yad Vashem. New York : Stein and Day, 1978. p. cm. Translation of Dziennik getta warszawskiego. Includes index. [DS135.P62W2613] 78-9272 ISBN 0-8128-2523-3 : 16.96
1. Czerniakow, Adam, 1880-1942. 2. Jews in Warsaw—Persecutions. 3. Holocaust, Jewish (1939-1945)—Poland—Warsaw. 4. Jews in Warsaw—Biography. 5. Warsaw—History. I. Hilberg, Raul, 1926- II. Staron, Stanislaw. III. Kermish, Joseph.

Czernin, Manfred, 1913-1962.

FRANKS, Norman L. R. 940.54'49'410924 B
Double mission : RAF fighter ace and SOE agent, Manfred Czernin, DSO, MC, DFC / [by] Norman L. R. Franks. London : Kimber, 1976. 192 p., [12] p. of plates : ill., maps, ports. ; 24 cm. Includes index. [D786.F67] 76-383432 ISBN 0-7183-0254-0 : £4.95
1. Czernin, Manfred, 1913-1962. 2. Great Britain. Royal Air Force—Biography. 3. World War, 1939-1945—Aerial operations, British. 4. World War, 1939-1945—Biography. 5. Air-pilots—Great Britain—Biography. I. Title.

Czolgosz, Leon Franz, 1873?-1901.

JOHNS, A. Wesley. 973.8'8'0924 B
The man who shot McKinley, by A. Wesley Johns. South Brunswick [N.J.] A. S. Barnes [1970] 293 p. illus., map, ports. 25 cm. Bibliography: p. 277-281. [E711.9.J6] 75-88272 9.50
1. Czolgosz, Leon Franz, 1873?-1901. 2. McKinley, William, Pres. U.S., 1843-1901—Assassination. I. Title.

Da Ponte, Lorenzo, 1749-1838.

DA PONTE, Lorenzo, 1749- 709'.24 B
1838.
Memoirs of Lorenzo Da Ponte. Translated from the Italian by Elisabeth Abbott. Edited and annotated by Arthur Livingston. With a new pref. by Thomas G. Bergin. New York, Dover Publications [1967] x, 512 p. illus., facsims., ports. 22 cm. (Dover books on music, T1706) "This Dover edition is an unabridged and unaltered republication of the work first published in 1929." [ML423.D15A22 1967] 66-29054
I. Title. BIP

FITZLYON, April. 927.8
The libertine librettist; a biography of Mozart's librettist Lorenzo da Ponte. New York, Abelard-Schuman [1957] 292p. illus. 22cm. [ML423] 57-5134
1. Da Ponte, Lorenzo, 1749-1838. I. Title.

Dabney, Robert Lewis, 1820-1898.

JOHNSON, Thomas Cary, 230.51'0924
1859-1936.
The life and letters of Robert Lewis Dabney / Thomas Cary Johnson. Edinburgh ; Carlisle, Pa. : Banner of Truth Trust, 1977. 1 xvi, 585p., 10 leaves of plates (2 fold.) : ill., 2 geneal. tabls, 2 ports. ; 23 cm. Includes bibliographical references and index. [BX9225.D2J6 1977] 78-312202 ISBN 0-85151-253-4 11.95
1. Dabney, Robert Lewis, 1820-1898. 2. Presbyterian Church — Clergy — Biography. 3. Clergy — United States — Biography. I. Title.

Dabney, Virginius, 1901-

DABNEY, Virginius, 070.4'092'4 B
1901-
Across the years : memories of a Virginian / Virginius Dabney. 1st ed. Garden City, N.Y. : Doubleday, 1978. xii, 420 p., [8] leaves of plates : ill. ; 22 cm. Includes index. [CT275.D165A3] 77-15147 ISBN 0-385-12247-0 : 10.00
1. Dabney, Virginius, 1901- 2. Journalists—Virginia—Biography. 3. Historians—Virginia—Biography. 4. Virginia—Biography. I. Title.

Dabul, John, 1903-

DABUL, John, 956.92'04'0924 B
1903-
A man of Lebanon / by John Dabul. Virginia Beach, Va. : Donning, [1975] p. cm. [CT1919.L4D3] 75-25676 ISBN 0-915442-07-8 : 3.95
1. Dabul, John, 1903- I. Title.

Dacier, Anne Lefevre, 1654-1720.

FARNHAM, Fern. 880'.09
Madame Dacier : scholar and humanist / by Fern Farnham. Monterey, CA. : Angel Press, 1976. 221 p., [3] leaves of plates : ill. ; 22 cm. Includes bibliographical references and index. [PA85.D27F3] 76-15515 ISBN 0-912216-12-3
1. Dacier, Anne Lefevre, 1654-1720. 2. Classicists—France—Biography. I. Title.

FARNHAM, Fern. 880'.09
Madame Dacier : scholar and humanist / by Fern Farnham. Monterey, CA. : Angel Press, 1976. 221 p., [3] leaves of plates : ill. ; 22 cm. Includes bibliographical references and index. [PA85.D27F3] 76-15515 ISBN 0-912216-12-3
1. Dacier, Anne Lefevre, 1654-1720. 2. Classicists—France—Biography. I. Title.

Daggett, Mike, ca. 1845-1911.

HYDE, Dayton O., 1925- 979.6'37
The last free man; the true story behind the massacre of Shoshone Mike and his band of Indians in 1911 [by] Dayton O. Hyde. New York, Dial Press, 1973. 264 p. illus. 24 cm008/1(C [E99.B33D34] 73-7784 7.95
1. Daggett, Mike, ca. 1845-1911. 2. Bannock Indians. I. Title. II. Title: Shoshone Mike and his band of Indians in 1911.

Daguerre, Louis Jacques Mande, 1787-1851.

GERNSHEIM, Helmut, 770'.924 B
1913-
L. J. M. Daguerre; the history of the diorama and the daguerreotype, by Helmut and Alison Gernsheim. New York, Dover Publications [1968] xxii, 226 p. illus., facsims., ports. 24 cm. "An unabridged and revised republication of the work originally published ... in 1956 [under title: L. J. M. Daguerre (1787-1851), the world's first photographer] A new preface has been written by the authors for this edition." Includes bibliographical references. [TR140.D3G47 1968] 68-8044 2.95
1. Daguerre, Louis Jacques Mande, 1787-1851. I. Gernsheim, Alison, joint author. II. Title. BIP

GERNSHEIM, Helmut, 1913- 927.7
L. J. M. Daguerre (1787-1851) the world's first photographer, by Helmut and Alison Gernsheim, Cleveland, World Pub. Co. [1956] xx, 216p. illus., plates, ports. 26cm. Includes bibliographies. [TR140.D3G47] 56-11832
1. Daguerre, Louis Jacques Mande, 1787-1831. I. Gernsheim, Alison, joint author. II. Title.

Dahlberg, Charles Clay.

DAHLBERG, Charles 616.8'1'09 B
Clay.
Stroke : a doctor's personal story of his recovery / by Charles Clay Dahlberg and Joseph Jaffe. 1st ed. New York : Norton, c1977. 200 p. : ill. ; 22 cm. [RC388.5.D33 1977] 77-414 ISBN 0-393-08720-4 : 8.95
1. Dahlberg, Charles Clay. 2. Cerebrovascular disease—Biography. I. Jaffe, Joseph, 1924- joint author. II. Title.

DAHLBERG, Charles 616.8'1'09 B
Clay.
Stroke : a doctor's personal story of his recovery / by Charles Clay Dahlberg and Joseph Jaffe. 1st ed. New York : Norton, c1977. 200 p. : ill. ; 22 cm. [RC388.5.D33 1977] 77-414 ISBN 0-393-08720-4 : 8.95
1. Dahlberg, Charles Clay. 2. Cerebrovascular disease—Biography. I. Jaffe, Joseph, 1924- joint author. II. Title. BIP

Dahlberg, Edward,

DAHLBERG, Edward, 1900- 928.1
Because I was flesh: the autobiography of Edward Dahlberg [New York] New Directions [1967, c.1963] 234p. 21cm. (NDP227) 2.35 pap.,
I. Title.

DAHLBERG, Edward, 1900- 928.1
Because I was flesh; the autobiography of Edward Dahlberg. [New York] New Direction [1964, c1963] 234 p. 21 cm. [PS3507.A33Z52] 64-10079
I. Title.

DAHLBERG, Edward, 818'.5'203
1900-
The confessions of Edward Dahlberg. New York, G. Braziller [1971] 312 p. 22 cm. [PS3507.A33Z52 1971] 74-132367 ISBN 0-8076-0589-1 6.50
I. Title. BIP

Dahlberg, Edwin Theodore, 1892-

DAHLBERG, Edwin 286'.131 B
Theodore, 1892-
I pick up hitchhikers / Edwin T. Dahlberg. Valley Forge, PA : Judson Press, c1978. 112 p. ; 22 cm. Includes bibliographical references. [BX6495.D25A34] 77-25498 ISBN 0-8170-0774-1 pbk. : 3.95
1. Dahlberg, Edwin Theodore, 1892- 2. Baptists—Clergy—Biography. 3. Clergy—United States—Biography. 4. Hitchhiking—United States. I. Title. BIP

Dai, Hsiao-ai.

BENNETT, Gordon A. 951.05'0924
Red Guard; the political biography of Dai Hsiao-ai, by Gordon A. Bennett and Ronald N. Montaperto. [1st ed.] Garden City, N.Y., Doubleday, 1971. xx, 267 p. 22 cm. Bibliography: p. 255-256. [DS778.D34B45] 70-116236 5.95
1. Dai, Hsiao-ai. 2. Hung wei ping. I. Montaperto, Ronald N., joint author. II. Title. BIP

Dakota Indians—Biography.

FIELDER, Mildred. 978'.004'97 B
Sioux Indian leaders / by Mildred Fielder. Seattle : Superior Pub. Co., [1975] p. cm. Includes index. Bibliography: p. [E99.D1F5] 75-2687 ISBN 0-87564-335-3 : 13.95
1. Dakota Indians—Biography. 2. Dakota Indians—History. I. Title.

HUGHES, Thomas, 1854- 970.4'76 B
1934.
Indian chiefs of southern Minnesota. [2d ed.] Illustrated by A. Anderson. Minneapolis, Ross & Haines, 1969. 121 p. illus. 23 cm. [E99.D1H83] 70-98191 8.75
1. Dakota Indians—Biography. 2. Winnebago Indians—Biography. 3. Indians of North America—Minnesota—Biography. I. Title. BIP

SNEVE, Virginia 983'.04'97 B
Driving Hawk.
They led a nation : [biographical & pictorial essays of 20 Dakota leaders] / by Virginia Driving Hawk Sneve ; edited by N. Jane Hunt ; ports. by Loren Zephier. Sioux Falls, S.D. : Brevet Press, 1975. 46 p. : ports. ; 30 cm. Includes index. Bibliography: p. 44. [E99.D1S63] 75-254 ISBN 0-88498-027-8 pbk. : 2.95
1. Dakota Indians—Biography. I. Title.

Dakota Indians—Captivities.

CAPTIVITIES of Mrs. 973'.04'97 S
J. E. De Camp Sweet, Nancy McClure, and Mary Schwandt. New York : Garland Pub., 1976. p. cm. (The Garland library of narratives of North American Indian captivities ; v. 99) Originally appeared in Minnesota Historical Society collections, v. 6, 1894, under title: Mrs. J. E. De Camp Sweet's narrative of her captivity in the Sioux outbreak of 1862. Issued with McElroy, J. M. Abby Byram and her father. New York, 1976. Dabney, O. P. True story of the lost shackle. New York, 1976. [E85.G2 vol. 99, 1976b] [E83.86] 970'.004'97 75-38555 ISBN 0-8240-1723-4 lib.bdg. : 21.00
1. Dakota Indians—Captivities. 2. Dakota Indians—Wars, 1862-1865. 3. Indians of North America—Captivities. I. Sweet, Jannette E. De Camp, b. 1833. II. McClure, Nancy, b. 1836. III. Schwandt, Mary, b. 1848. IV. Minnesota Historical Society. Collections. V. Series.

Dakota Indians—Wars.

WHITE Bull, Dakota 970.3'0924
chief, b.1849.
The warrior who killed Custer; the personal narrative of Chief Joseph White Bull. Translated and edited by James H. Howard. Lincoln, University of Nebraska Press [1969, c1968] xix, 84 p. illus. (part col.) 24 cm. Bibliography: p. 83-84. [E99.D1W66] 68-25321 6.95
1. Dakota Indians—Wars. I. Howard, James Henri, 1925- ed. II. Title.

Dale, Edward Everett, 1879-1972—Addresses, essays, lectures.

DALE, Edward 978'.007'2024 B
Everett, 1879-1972.
Frontier historian : the life and work of Edward Everett Dale / edited by Arrell M. Gibson ; with introductory essays by Arrell M. Gibson, Angie Debo, John S. Ezell. 1st ed. Norman : University of Oklahoma Press, [1975] v, 367 p. : port. ; 22 cm. Includes bibliographical references. [E175.5.D22A25 1975] 75-11774 ISBN 0-8061-1305-7 : 9.95
1. Dale, Edward Everett, 1879-1972—Addresses, essays, lectures. 2. Frontier and pioneer life—The West—Addresses, essays, lectures. I. Title.

Dale, Samuel, 1772-1841.

CLAIBORNE, John 977'.02'0924 B
Francis Hamtramck, 1809-1884.
Life and times of Gen. Sam Dale, the Mississippi partisan / by J. F. H. Claiborne ; illustrated by John M'Lenan. Spartanburg, S.C. : Reprint Co., 1976 [c1860] 233 p. : ill. ; 22 cm. Reprint of the ed. published by Harper, New York. [F396.D13 1976] 75-46532 ISBN 0-87152-214-4 : 12.00
1. Dale, Samuel, 1772-1841. 2. Creek War, 1813-1814. I. Title.

FOSTER, John T. 92
Southern frontiersman; the story of General Sam Dale, by John Foster. Illustrated by Leslie Gray. New York, Morrow, 1967. 191 p. illus., maps. 22 cm. Bibliography: p. [184]-186. Describes Dale's youth on the frontier, his years as guide, trader and Indian fighter, and his exploits in the Battle of New Orleans. [F396.D18] AC 67
1. Dale, Samuel, 1772-1841. I. Gray, Leslie, illus. II. Title.

Dale, Samuel, 1772-1841—Juvenile literature.

FOSTER, John T. 976 B
Southern frontiersman; the story of General Sam Dale, by Leslie Gray. New York, Morrow, 1967. 191 p. illus., maps 22 cm. Bibliography: p. [184]-186. [F396.D18] 67-20748
1. Dale, Samuel, 1772-1841—Juvenile literature. I. Title.

Daley, Elliot A.

DALEY, Eliot A. 301.42'7'0924 B
Father feelings / Eliot A. Daley. New York : Morrow, 1978, c1977. 192 p. ; 22

cm. [HQ756.D34A33 1978] 77-22820 ISBN 0-688-03251-6 : 7.95
1. Daley, Eliot A. 2. Fathers—Biography. 3. Father and child. I. Title.

DALEY, Elliot A. 301.42'1'024
Father feelings / Elliot A. Daley New York : Pocket Books, 1979,c.1977. 192p. ; 18 cm. [HQ756.D34A33 1978]
1. Daley, Elliot A. 2. Fathers — Biography. 3. Father and Child I. Title.
L.C. card no. for 1978 Morrow edition:77-22820 BIP

Daley, Richard J., 1902—Juvenile literature.

KURLAND, Gerald, 1942- 977.3'11'040924 B
Richard Daley, the strong willed Mayor of Chicago. Charlotteville, N.Y., SamHar Press, 1972. 32 p. 22 cm. (Outstanding personalities, no. 18) Bibliography: p. 32. A biography of the Chicago Mayor reelected to a fifth consecutive term in 1971. [F548.52.D35K87] 92 70-190236 1.98
1. Daley, Richard J., 1902—Juvenile literature. I. Title.
Pap. 0.98

Daley, Richard J., 1902-1976.

THE Daley record. 352.0773'11
[Chicago? 1970?] [24] p. 22 cm. [JS708.D34] 73-170322
1. Daley, Richard J., 1902- 2. Chicago—Politics and government—1951- 3. Municipal services—Chicago.

GLEASON, William Francis, 1922- 352.000924
Daley of Chicago; the man, the Mayor, and the limits of conventional politics [by] Bill Gleason. New York, Simon and Schuster [1970] 384 p. 22 cm. Bibliography: p. 369-370. [F548.52.G55] 77-130474 7.50
1. Daley, Richard J., 1902- I. Title.

KENNEDY, Eugene C. 977.3'11'040924 B
Himself! : The life and times of Mayor Richard J. Daley / Eugene Kennedy. New York : Viking Press, 1978. xv, 288 p., [8] leaves of plates : ill. ; 22 cm. Includes index. [F548.52.D35K46 1978] 77-28792 ISBN 0-670-37258-7 : 10.00
1. Daley, Richard J., 1902-1976. 2. Chicago—Mayors—Biography. 3. Chicago—Politics and government—1950- I. Title.

KURLAND, Gerald, 1942- 977.3'11'040924 B
Richard Daley, the strong willed Mayor of Chicago. Charlotteville, N.Y., SamHar Press, 1972. 32 p. 22 cm. (Outstanding personalities, no. 18) Bibliography: p. 32. A biography of the Chicago Mayor reelected to a fifth consecutive term in 1971. [F548.52.D35K87] 92 70-190236 1.98
1. Daley, Richard J., 1902—Juvenile literature. I. Title.
Pap. 0.98

O'CONNOR, Len. 977.3'11'040924
Clout—Mayor Daley and his city / Len O'Connor. Chicago : H. Regnery Co., [1975] ix, 272 p. ; 24 cm. Includes index. [F548.52.D35O25 1975] 74-27824 ISBN 0-8092-8291-7 : 10.00
1. Daley, Richard J., 1902- 2. Chicago—Politics and government—1951- I. Title.

O'CONNOR, Len. 977.3'11'040924
Requiem : the decline and demise of Mayor Daley and his era / Len O'Connor. Chicago : Contemporary Books, c1977. 203 p. ; 24 cm. Includes index. [F548.52.D35O27 1977] 77-75845 ISBN 0-8092-7920-7 : 8.95
1. Daley, Richard J., 1902-1976. 2. Chicago—Mayors—Biography. 3. Chicago—Politics and government—1950- I. Title. BIP

RAKOVE, Milton L. 320.9'773'1104
Don't make no waves—don't back no losers : an insider's analysis of the Daley machine / Milton L. Rakove. Bloomington : Indiana University Press, [1975] xii, 296 p., [4] leaves of plates : ill. ; 25 cm. Includes index. Bibliography: p. 285-289. [F548.52.R34 1975] 75-1939 ISBN 0-253-11725-9
1. Daley, Richard J., 1902- 2. Chicago—Politics and government—1951- I. Title. BIP

Dali, Salvador, 1904-

DALI, Salvador, 1904- 759.6
Diary of a genius. Foreword and notes by Michel Deon. Translated from the French by Richard Howard. [1st ed. in the U.S.A.] New York, Doubleday, 1965. ix, 280 p. illus., ports. 22 cm. [ND813.D3A353] 65-25448
I. Title.

DALI, Salvador, 1904- 927.5
The secret life of Salvador Dali. Tr. by Haakon M. Chevalier. New enl. ed. New York. Dial. 1961c.1942, 1961] 417p. illus. (part col.) 26cm. 61-11999 12.50
I. Title.

DESCHARNES, Robert. 927.5
The world of Salvador Dali [Translation by Albert Field. 1st ed.] New York, Harper & Row [1962] 228 p. illus. (part mounted; part col.), ports. 31 cm. Captions of the illustrations by Dali; translated by Haakon Chevalier. Translation of Dali de Gala. [ND813.D3D43] 62-15741
1. Dali, Salvador, 1904- I. Title.

MADDOX, Conroy. 759.6 B
Dali / Conroy Maddox. New York : Harmony Books, [1979] p. cm. [N7113.D3M32] 78-9924 ISBN 0-517-53675-7 : 9.95
1. Dali, Salvador, 1904- 2. Artists—Spain—Biography. I. Title. BIP

MORSE, Albert Reynolds, 1914- 759.6
Dali: a study of his life and work. Text by A. Reynolds Morse and a special appreciation by Michel Tapie. Descriptive captions for the color plates written especially for this volume by Salvador Dali. [1st American ed.] Greenwich, Conn., New York Graphic Society [1958] 96p. illus. (17 mounted col.) ports. 35 x 37cm. [ND813.D3M58] 927.5 58-6725
1. Dalf, Salvador, I. Title.

SALVADOR Dali. 759.6
[Cleveland 1954] 64 p. illus., port., map. 14 cm. 'The paintings reproduced in this catalog are from the collection of Mr. and Mrs. A. Reynolds Morse Clevdrland, Ohio.' [ND813.D3M6] [ND813.DM6] 927.5 55-18275 55-18275
1. Dali Salvador, 1904- II. Morse, Albert Reynolds, 1914-

Dall, William Healey, 1845-1927.

HERRON, Edward Albert, 1912- 925.7
First scientist of Alaska: William Healey Dall, born August 21, 1845—died March 27, 1927. New York, J. Messner [1958] 192 p. 22 cm. Includes bibliography. [QH31.D15H4] 58-10927
1. Dall, William Healey, 1845-1927. I. Title.

Dallas, Alexander James, 1759-1817.

WALTERS, Raymond, 1912- 973.5'1'0924 B
Alexander James Dallas, lawyer, politician, financier 1759-1817. New York, Da Capo Press, 1969 [c1943] vi, 251 p. port. 24 cm. (The American scene: comments and commentators) Reprint of the ed. published by University of Pennsylvania Press, Philadelphia, in series: Pennsylvania lives. Originally presented as the author's thesis, Columbia University. Bibliography: p. 239-243. [E302.6.D14W3 1969] 75-86582
1. Dallas, Alexander James, 1759-1817. 2. Pennsylvania—Politics and government—1775-1865. 3. United States—Politics and government—Constitutional period, 1789-1809. 4. United States—Politics and government—1809-1817. I. Series: Pennsylvania lives. BIP

Dallas Cowboys.

MEYERS, Jeff. 796.33'264'097642812
Dallas Cowboys / by Jeff Meyers. New York : Macmillan, 1974. 192 p. : ill. ; 26 cm. (Great teams' great years) Discusses the football history of the Dallas Cowboys, winners of Super Bowl VI in 1971, presents interviews with some of the outstanding players, and details some of their notable games. [GV956.D3M49] 73-21299 8.95
1. Dallas Cowboys. 2. Football. 3. Football—Biography. I. Title. BIP

Dallas, George Mifflin, 1792-1864.

BELOHLAVEK, John M. 973.6'1'0924 B
George Mifflin Dallas : Jacksonian patrician / John M. Belohlavek. University Park : Pennsylvania State University Press, [1977] p. cm. Includes index. Bibliography: p. [E340.D14B44] 77-1415 ISBN 0-271-00510-6 : 12.50
1. Dallas, George Mifflin, 1792-1864. 2. Vice-Presidents—United States—Biography. 3. United States—Politics and government—1815-1861. BIP

Dallin, Cyrus Edwin, 1861-1944.

FRANCIS, Rell G., 1928- 730'.92'4 B
Cyrus E. Dallin : let justice be done / by Rell G. Francis. [Springfield? Utah : Francis], 1976. p. cm. Includes index. Bibliography: p. [NB237.D25F72] 76-12352 15.95
1. Dallin, Cyrus Edwin, 1861-1944.

FRANCIS, Rell G., 1928- 730'.92'4 B
Cyrus E. Dallin : let justice be done / Rell G. Francis. Springville, Utah : Francis, c1976. xv, 262 p. : ill. ; 29 cm. "Published for Springville Museum of Art ... in cooperation with Utah American Revolution Bicentennial Commission." Includes index. Bibliography: p. 255-258. [NB237.D25F72] 76-12352 15.95
1. Dallin, Cyrus Edwin, 1861-1944. I. Springville Museum of Art.

Dalou, Jules, 1838-1902.

HUNISAK, John M., 1944- 730'.92'4
The sculptor Jules Dalou : studies in his style and imagery / John M. Hunisak. New York : Garland Pub., 1977. p. cm. (Outstanding dissertations in the fine arts) Reprint of the author's thesis, New York University, 1975. Bibliography: p. [NB553.D25H86 1977] 76-23629 ISBN 0-8240-2699-3 : 42.50
1. Dalou, Jules, 1838-1902. I. Title. II. Series. BIP

Dalrymple, George Elphinstone, 1826-1876.

FARNFIELD, Jean. 994'.3'030924 B
Frontiersman; a biography of George Elphinstone Dalrymple. Melbourne, New York [etc.] Oxford University Press, 1968. xi, 171 p. illus., maps, ports. 23 cm. Bibliography: 162-166. [DU272.D32F3 1968] 70-365503 5.75
1. Dalrymple, George Elphinstone, 1826-1876. I. Title. BIP

Dalton family.

LATTA, Frank Forrest, 1892- 364.1'55'0922
Dalton gang days / by Frank F. Latta. Bicentennial ed. Santa Cruz, Calif. : Bear State Books, c1976. xviii, 293 p. : ill. ; 27 cm. Includes index. [F595.D15L37] 76-3295
1. Dalton family. 2. Dalton, Littleton, 1857-1942. 3. Outlaws—The West—Biography. 4. The West—History—1848-1950. I. Title. BIP

[VALCOURT-VERMONT, Edgar de] 364.1'55'0922 B
The Dalton brothers and their astounding career of crime / by an eye witness ; with an introd. by James D. Horan. New York : Jingle Bob/Crown Publishers, c1977. p. cm. [F595.D15V34 1977] 77-4435 ISBN 0-517-53108-9 : 6.95
1. Dalton family. 2. Outlaws—The West. 3. Outlaws—The West—Biography. 4. The West—Biography. I. An eye witness. II. Title.

Dalton, Henry, 1803-1884.

JACKSON, Sheldon Glenn, 1918- 979.4'04'0924 B
A British ranchero in old California : the life and times of Henry Dalton and the Rancho Azusa / by Sheldon G. Jackson. Glendale, Calif. : A. H. Clark Co., 1977. 265 p. : ill. ; 25 cm. (Western frontiersman series ; 17) Includes index. Bibliography: p. [251]-256. [F864.D22J3] 77-79745 ISBN 0-87062-122-X 16.50
1. Dalton, Henry, 1803-1884. 2. Ranchers—California—Biography. 3. California—History. 4. Land titles—California—Los Angeles Co. 5. Ranch life—California—History. I. Title. BIP

Dalton, John, 1766-1844.

GREENAWAY, Frank. 540.924 (B)
John Dalton and the atom. Ithaca, N.Y., Cornell University Press [1966] vii, 244 p. port. 22 cm. Bibliographical references included in "Notes and references" (p. 228-238) [QD22.D2G7 1966a] 66-27470
1. Dalton, John, 1766-1844. I. Title. BIP

JOHN DALTON and the progress of science; papers presented to a conference of historians of science held in Manchester, September 19-24, 1966 to mark the bicentenary of Dalton's birth. Ed. by D. S. L. Cardwell. Manchester, Manchester Univ. Pr.; New York, Barnes & Noble [1968] xxii, 352p. illus., port. 23cm. Convened by the Manchester Lit. & Philosophical Soc., the Royal Soc., the Chem. Soc. & the Soc. of Chem. Industry. [QD22.D2A5] 68-132637 9.50 540'.924
1. Dalton, John, 1766-1844. I. Cardwell, David Stephen Lowell. ed.

MILLINGTON, John Price. 540'.924 B
John Dalton. [1st AMS ed.] London, J. M. Dent; New York, Dutton, 1906. [New York, AMS Press, 1971] xii, 225 p. port. 19 cm. (English men of science, v. 6) Bibliography: p. 217-221. [QD22.D2M6 1971] 73-149666 ISBN 0-404-07896-6
1. Dalton, John, 1766-1844. I. Title. II. Series. BIP

PATTERSON, Elizabeth C. 540'.924 B
John Dalton and the atomic theory; the biography of a natural philosopher [by] Elizabeth C. Patterson. [1st ed.] Garden City, N.Y., Doubleday, 1970. x, 348 p. illus., facsims., geneal. table, ports. 22 cm. (The Science study series) Bibliography: p. [325]-335. [QD22.D2P3] 77-97677 6.95
1. Dalton, John, 1766-1844. I. Title. II. Series.

THACKRAY, Arnold, 1939- 540'.92'4 B
John Dalton; critical assessments of his life and science. Cambridge, Harvard University Press, 1972. xiv, 190 p. illus. 24 cm. (Harvard monographs in the history of Science) Bibliography: p. 175-184. [QD22.D2T47] 72-75403 ISBN 0-674-47525-9
1. Dalton, John, 1766-1844. I. Title. II. Series.

Dalton, John, 1766-1844 — Bibl.

SMYTH, Albert Leslie. 016.540924
John Dalton, 1766-1844: a bibliography of works by and about him, by A.L. Smyth. Manchester, Manchester U.P. [1966] xvi, 114 p. 11 plates. (inc. ports., facisms.) 25 1/2 cm. (B 66-7768) [Z8212.7.S5] 66-70775
1. Dalton, John, 1776-1844 — Bibl. I. Title.

SMYTH, Albert Leslie 016.540924
John Dalton, 1766-1844: a bibliography of works by and about him. Manchester [Eng.] Manchester Univ. Pr. [New York, Barnes & Noble, c.1966] cxvi, 114p. 11 plates. (incl. ports., facsims.) 26cm. [Z8212.7.S5] 66-707750 7.50
1. Dalton, John, 1766-1844 — Bibl. I. Title.

Daly, Augustin, 1838-1899.

RANOUS, Dora Knowlton (Thompson) 1859-1916. 792'.028'0922
Diary of a Daly debutant, being passages from the journal of a member of Augustin Daly's famous company of players [by] Dora (Ranous) Knowlton [sic] New York, B. Blom, 1972. 249 p. illus. 21 cm. Reprint of the 1910 ed. [PS3535.A63Z52 1972] 72-79946
1. Daly, Augustin, 1838-1899. 2. Actresses—Correspondence, reminiscences, etc. I. Title.

Daly, James Jeremiah, 1872-

THOMPSON, Francis, 1859-1907. v. 12
The hound of heaven. [Introd. by James J. Daly. With illustrations by Stella Langdale] New York, Dodd, Mead, 1965 [c1922] 60 p. illus. 20 cm. NUC68
1. Daly, James Jeremiah, 1872- I. Title. BIP

Daly, Marcus, 1841-1900.

SCHOEBOTHAM, H Minar. v. 12
Anaconda; life of Marcus Daly, the copper king. [1st ed.] Harrisburg, Pa., Stackpole Co. [1956] 220p. illus. 23cm. Bibliography, p.219-220.
1. Daly, Marcus, 1841-1900. 2. Anaconda copper mining company. I. Title.

SHOEBOTHAM, H. Minar. 926.22
Anaconda; life of Marcus Daly, the copper king. [1st ed.] Harrisburg, Pa., Stackpole Co. [1956] 220 p. illus. 23 cm. [HD9539.C72A657] 56-11275
1. Daly, Marcus, 1841-1900. 2. Anaconda Copper Mining Company. I. Title.

Damien, Father, 1840-1889.

BEEVERS, John. 266'.2'0924 B
A man for now; the life of Damien de Veuster, friend of lepers. [1st ed.] Garden City, N.Y., Doubleday, 1973. 192 p. 22 cm. [BX4705.D25B36] 73-83584 ISBN 0-385-05574-9 5.95
1. Damien, Father, 1840-1889. I. Title.

BETTZ, Eva (Kelly) 1897- 922.2493
Knight of Molokai. Illus. by June Driscoll. Paterson, N. J., St. Anthony Guild Press, 1956. 154p. illus. 20cm. [BX4705.D25B4] 56-14071
1. Damlen, Father, 1840-1889. I. Title.

BETZ, Eva K 922.2493
Knight of Molokai. Illus. by June Driscoll. Paterson, N. J., St. Anthony Guild Press, 1956. 154p. illus. 20cm. [BX4705.D25B4] 56-14071
1. Damien, Father, 1840-1889. I. Title.

DAWS, Gavan. 282'.092'4 B
Holy man: Father Damien of Molokai. [1st ed.] New York, Harper & Row [1973] xi, 293 p. illus. 22 cm. Bibliography: p. 281-288. [BX4705.D25D38] 73-4075 8.95
1. Damien, Father, 1840-1889. I. Title.

DEBROEY, Steven. v. 12
Father Damien: the priest of the lepers; with a preface by His Eminence Amleto Cardinal Cicognani; translated from the Flemish by Staf Gebruers. Dublin, Clonmore, Reynolds, 1966. j melaatsen. 175 p. table. Translation of 68-42654
1. Damien, Father, 1840-1889. I. Title.

DUTTON, Charles Judson, 1888- 266.2'0922 B
The samaritans of Molokai; the lives of Father Damien and Brother Dutton among the lepers, by Charles J. Dutton. Freeport, N.Y., Books for Libraries Press [1971] xiv, 286 p. illus., facsim., ports. 23 cm. Reprint of the 1932 ed. Bibliography: p. 281-286. [BX4705.D25D8 1971] 70-152981 ISBN 0-8369-5733-4
1. Damien, Father, 1840-1889. 2. Dutton, Joseph, 1843-1931. 3. Missions to lepers—Hawaii. I. Title.

FARROW, John, 1904- 922.2493
Damien, the leper. Garden City, N. Y., Image Books [1954, c1937] 234p. 19cm. (A Doubleday image book, D3) [RC154.9] 54-13005
1. Damien, Father, 1840-1889. 2. Molokal. 3. Leprosy—Hawaiian Islands. 4. Missions—Lepers. I. Title. BIP

FARROW, John, 1904-1963. 922.2493
Damien, the leper. Edited by Malcolm A. Duffy. [Unabridged school ed.] New York, Macmillan [1963] 194 p. 23 cm. (Literary heritage; a Macmillan paperback series) [(RC154.9)] 63-6790
1. Damien, Father, 1840-1889. 2. Molokal. 3. Leprosy — Hawaiian Islands. 4. Missions — Lepers. I. Title.

FLECK, Raymond, 1927- 922.2493
Christ comes to Molokai; a story of Father Damien. Illus. by Brother Harold Ruplinger. Notre Dame, Ind., Dujarie Press [1953] 102p. illus. 24cm. [BX4705.D25F5] 53-38205
1. Damlen, Father,1840-1889. I. Title.

JOURDAN, Vital, [Secular name: Joseph Jourdan] 1897- 922.2493
The heart of Father Damien, 1840-1889. Tr. from French by Francis Larkin, Charles Davenport. Rev. ed. [St. Paul] Guild Press; dist. by Golden Press, New York [1961,c.1955,1960] 500p. 17cm. (Angelus book 31160) 61-1027 1.25 bds.,
1. Damien, Father, 1840-1889. I. Title.

Damien, Father, 1840-1889—Drama.

MORRIS, Aldyth, 1901- 812'.5'4
Damien / Aldyth Morris. Honolulu : University Press of Hawaii, c1980. p. cm. Bibliography: p. [PS3563.O87397D3] 79-22915 ISBN 0-8248-0693-X : 3.50
1. Damien, Father, 1840-1889—Drama. I. Title. BIP

Damon, Samuel Chenery, 1815-1885.

DAMON, Ethel Moseley, 1883-1965. 266'.023'099
Samuel Chenery Damon: chaplain and friend of seamen, historian, traveler,diplomat, doctor of divinity, journalist, genial companion, genealogist. Honolulu, Published under the sponsorship of the Hawaiian Mission Children's Society, 1966 141 p. illus., coat-of-arms, fold. geneal, table, ports. 24 cm. [BV3680.H4D34] 67-2589
1. Damon, Samuel Chenery, 1815-1885. I. Title.

Dampier, William, 1652-1715.

LLOYD, Christopher, 1906- 910.453
William Dampier. [1st ed.] Hamden, Conn., Archon Books [1966] 164 p. illus., maps, port. 21 cm. Bibliography: p. 161. [G246.D17L5] 67-799
1. Dampler, William, 1652-1715. I. Title.

LLOYD, Christopher, 1906- 910.453
William Dampier. [1st ed.] Hamden, Conn., Archon Books [1966] 164 p. illus., maps, port. 21 cm. Bibliography: p. 161. [G246.D17L5] 67-799
1. Dampier, William, 1652-1715. BIP

SHIPMAN, Joseph C. 923.942
William Dampier, seaman-scientist. Lawrence, Univ. of Kansas Lib. [c.]1962. 63p. illus. 23cm. (Univ. of Kansas pubns. Library ser. no 15) Bibl. 62-63442 1.50 pap.,
1. Dampier, William, 1652-1715. I. Title.

SHIPMAN, Joseph C 923.942
William Dampier, seaman-scientist. Lawrence, University of Kansas Libraries, 1962. 63 p. illus. 23 cm. (University of Kansas publications. Library series no. 15) [G246.D17S5] 62-63442
1. Dampier, William, 1652-1715. I. Title.

Dan Fodio, Usuman, 1744-1817.

HISKETT, M. 966.9'01'0924 B
The sword of truth; the life and times of the Shehu Usuman dan Fodio [by] Mervyn Hiskett. New York, Oxford University Press, 1973. xxii, 194 p. illus. 21 cm. Bibliography: p. 171-183. [DT515.9.F8H57] 72-91010 ISBN 0-19-501648-3 7.50
1. Dan Fodio, Usuman, 1744-1817. 2. Fulah Empire. I. Title.

Dana, James Dwight, 1813-1895.

GILMAN, Daniel Coit, 1831-1908. 550'.92'4 B
The life of James Dwight Dana, scientific explorer, mineralogist, geologist, zoologist, professor in Yale University. Freeport, N.Y., Books for Libraries Press [1973] p. Reprint of the 1899 ed. [QE22.D26G4 1973] 72-12700 ISBN 0-8369-7138-8
1. Dana, James Dwight, 1813-1895. I. Title.

Dana, John Cotton, 1856-1929.

HADLEY, Chalmers, 1872-1958. 020'.92'4 B
John Cotton Dana, a sketch. Boston, Gregg Press, 1972 [c1943] 105 p. port. 23 cm. (The Library reference series. Library history and biography) Reprint of the ed. published by the American Library Association, Chicago, which was issued as no. 5 of American library pioneers. [Z720.D2H2 1972] 72-8774 ISBN 0-8398-0806-2
1. Dana, John Cotton, 1856-1929. I. Series: Library history and biography. II. Series: American library pioneers, no. 5.

Dana, Richard Henry, 1815-1882.

ADAMS, Charles Francis, 1835-1915. 973.7'0924 (B)
Richard Henry Dana; a biography. Boston, Houghton, Mifflin, 1890. Detroit, Gale Research Co., 1968. 2 v. ports. 23 cm. (The Gale library of lives and letters: American writers series) [E415.9.D15A2 1968] 67-23883
1. Dana, Richard Henry, 1815-1882. 2. U. S.—Pol. & govt.—1849-1961. 3. Slavery in the U. S.—Anti-slavery movements. I. Title.

DANA, Richard Henry, 1815-1882. 928.1
An autobiographical sketch (1815-1842) Edited by Robert F. Metzdorf. With an introd. by Norman Holmes Pearson. Hamden, Conn., Shoe String Press, 1953. x, 119 p. 23 cm. 'In 1842 Dana wrote the autobiographical sketch which is here printed in its entirety for the first time.' [E415.9.D15A15] 53-13472
I. Title.

SHAPIRO, Samuel. v. 12
Richard Henry Dana, Jr., 1815-1882. [East lansing] Michigan State University Press, 1961. xi, 251 p. 24 cm. Bibliography, p. 241-244. Bibliographical references included in "Notes" (p. 199-240) 66-53631
1. Dana, Richard Henry, 1815-1882. I. Title.

SHAPIRO, Samuel 928.1
Richard Henry Dana, Jr., 1815-1882. [East Lansing] Mich. State Univ. Pr. [c.]1961. vi, 251p. Bibl. 61-13704 5.00
1. Dana, Richard Henry, 1815-1888. I. Title. BIP

Danby, Ken, 1940-

DUVAL, Paul. 760'.092'4 B
Ken Danby / by Paul Duval. Toronto : Clarke, Irwin, c1976. 192 p. : ill. (some col.) ; 28 cm. Includes index. [N6549.D36D83] 77-354056 ISBN 0-7720-1093-5

1. Danby, Ken, 1940- I. Danby, Ken, 1940-

Dancers.

ATKINSON, Margaret Fleming. 927.933
Dancers of the ballet; biographies by Margaret F. Atkinson New York, Knopf [1955] 174 p. illus. 26 cm. [GV1785.A1A8] 53-7624
1. Dancers. I. Hipshman, May B., 1919- joint author.

DE MILLE, Agnes 792.8'2'0924
Speak to me, dance with me. [1st ed.] Boston, Little, Brown [1973] x, 404 p. illus. 22 cm. "An Atlantic Monthly Press book." [GV1785.D36A37] 72-10732 ISBN 0-316-18038-6 8.95
I. Title. **BIP**

GOODMAN, Saul 927.933
Dancers you should know; twenty magazine biographies. Text by Saul Goodman photos by zachary Freyman. Pref. by Alicia Markova. Dance Magazine; dist. New Rochelle, N.Y., SportShelf, 1965, c.1964 59p. illus., ports. 28cm. Previously published in Dance mag. during the last ten years. [GV1785.A1G6] 65-1741 3.50 pap.,
1. Dancers. I. Freyman, Zachary, illus. II. Title.

MCCONNELL, Jane (Tompkins) 1898- 927.933
Famous ballet dancers. New York, Crowell [1955] 176p. illus. 21cm. [GV1785.A1T6] 55-5978
1. Dancers. I. Title.

MOORE, Lillian. 792.8'0922
Artists of the dance. [Brooklyn, Dance Horizons, inc., 1969] 320 p. illus. 21 cm. (A Dance horizon republication, 18) "Unabridged republication of the ... edition ... published in 1938." Bibliographical footnotes. [GV1781.M64 1969] 79-77176 4.95
1. Dancers. 2. Ballet. 3. Dancing. I. Title.

MUIR, Jane. 927.933
Famous dancers. New York, Dodd, Mead, 1956. 159 p. illus. 22 cm. (Famous biographies for young people) [GV1785.A1M8] 56-10920
1. Dancers.

TERRY, Walter. 927.933
Star performance; the story of the world's great ballerinas. Illustrated by Marta Becket. [1st ed.] Garden City, N.Y., Doubleday, 1954. 224 p. illus. 22 cm. [GV1785.A1T4] 54-5179
1. Dancers. 2. Ballet. I. Title.

Dancers—Biography.

HOLLINSHED, Marjorie. v. 12
Some professional dancers of, or from, Queensland, and some teachers of the past and present. Also results of the first R.A.D. (1935 and 1937) and Cecchetti (1959) examinations held in Brisbane. Brisbane, W. R. Smith & Paterson Pty., 1963. 92 p. plate, ports. 22 cm. On cover: Dancers of Queensland. Pages 90-92 blank for "Autographs." [GV1721.H6] 75-228708
1. Dancers—Biography. 2. Dancing—Queensland. I. Title. II. Title: Dancers of Queensland.

MIGEL, Parmenia. 792.8'2'0922
The ballerinas, from the court of Louis XIV to Pavlova. New York, Macmillan [1972] xv, 304 p. illus. 24 cm. Bibliography: p. [283]-291. [GV1785.A1M47] 74-158169 10.95
1. Dancers—Biography. 2. Ballet—History. I. Title.

PHILIP, Richard, 1943- 792.8'092'2 B
Danseur : the male in ballet / by Richard Philip and Mary Whitney ; special photography by Herbert Migdoll. New York : McGraw-Hill, [1977] p. cm. "A Rutledge book." Includes index. [GV1785.A1P47] 77-5844 ISBN 0-07-049811-3 : 19.95
1. Dancers—Biography. I. Whitney, Mary, 1947- joint author. II. Title. **BIP**

Dancing.

DE MILLE, Agnes 927.933
Dance to the piper. New York, Bantam [1964, c.1951, 1952] 326p. illus. 18cm. (Pathfinder ed., HP61) .60 pap.,
1. Dancing. 2. Ballet. I. Title. **BIP**

DE MILLE, Agnes. 927.933
Dance to the piper. [1st American ed.] Boston, Little, Brown, 1952. 342 p. illus. 22 cm. "An Atlantic Monthly Press book." [GV1785.D36A3 1952] 52-119
1. Dancing. 2. Ballet. I. Title.

*DUNCAN, Isadora, 1878-1927 793.320924(B)
My life. New York [Universal Pub. &Dist., 1966, c.1955] 319p. 18cm. (Award bks., A179S) .75 pap.,
1. Dancing. I. Title.

Dancing—United States—History.

KENDALL, Elizabeth. 793.3'1973
Where she danced / Elizabeth Kendall. 1st ed. New York : Knopf, 1979. xiv, 238 p. : ill. ; 25 cm. Includes index. Bibliography: p. [219]-221. [GV1623.K46 1979] 78-20544 ISBN 0-394-40029-1. :
1. Dancing—United States—History. 2. Dancers—United States—Biography. I. Title.

Dandridge, Dorothy,

DANDRIDGE, Dorothy, 1924-1965. 791.43'028'0924 B
Everything and nothing; the Dorothy Dandridge tragedy [by Dorothy Dandridge and Earl Conrad. New York, Abelard-Schuman [1970] viii, 215 p. ports. 22 cm. [PN2287.D256A3 1970] 79-123209 6.95
I. Conrad, Earl, joint author. II. Title.

Danforth, William Henry, 1870-1955.

PHILPOTT, Gordon M 926.5
Daring venture; the life story of William H. Danforth. New York, Random House [1960] 174p. illus. 21cm. [HD9052.U54R35] 60-6378
1. Danforth, William Henry, 1870-1955. 2. Ralston Purina Company. I. Title.

D'Angelo, Pascal, 1894-

D'ANGELO, Pascal, 1894- 331.6'2'45073 B
Son of Italy, Pascal D'Angelo. New York : Arno Press, 1975, [c1974] p. cm. (The Italian American experience) Reprint of the ed. published by Macmillan, New York, under title: Pascal D'Angelo, son of Italy. [E184.I8D163 1975] 74-17925 ISBN 0-405-06398-9
1. D'Angelo, Pascal, 1894- 2. Italian Americans—Personal narratives. 3. Padrone systems. I. Title. II. Series.

Daniel, Peter Vivian, 1784-1860.

FRANK, John Paul, 1917- 923.4
Justice Daniel dissenting; a biography of Peter V. Daniel, 1784-1860: Cambridge, Mass., Harvard [c.] 1964. xvii, 336p. port. 22cm. Bibl. 64-16062 7.95
1. Daniel, Peter Vivian, 1784-1860. I. Title.

Daniel, the prophet.

CAMPBELL, Donald K. 224'.5'077
Daniel, decoder of dreams / Donald K. Campbell. Wheaton, Ill. : Victor Books, c1977. 143 p. ; 21 cm. [BS1555.3.C35] 77-154330 ISBN 0-88207-747-3 pbk. : 1.95
1. Daniel, the prophet. 2. Bible. O.T. Daniel—Commentaries. 3. Bible. O.T.—Biography. 4. Bible. O.T. Daniel—Prophecies. 5. Prophets—Iraq—Babylon—Biography. 6. Babylon—Biography. I. Title.

Daniel, the prophet—Juvenile literature.

CHRISTIAN, Mary Blount. 224'.5'09505
Daniel, who dared : Daniel in the lions' den for beginning readers : Daniel 1:1-8, 6 for children / by Mary Blount Christian ; illustrated by Aline Cunningham. St. Louis : Concordia Pub. House, c1977. [48] p. : col. ill. ; 23 cm. (I can read a Bible story) Tells the story of Daniel in the lions' den. [BS580.D2C47] 77-6412 ISBN 0-570-07325-1 : 3.95. ISBN 0-570-07319-7 pbk. : 1.95
1. Daniel, the prophet—Juvenile literature. 2. Bible. O.T.—Biography—Juvenile literature. I. Cunningham, Aline. II. Title.

Daniels, Anna (Kleegman)

SINGER, Joy Daniels. 610'.924 B
My mother, the doctor. [1st ed.] New York, Dutton, 1970. 224 p. 22 cm. [R154.D236S5 1970] 71-95475 5.95
1. Daniels, Anna (Kleegman) I. Title.

Daniels, Jonathan, 1902-

DANIELS, Jonathan, 1902- 320.9'73'0917
White House witness, 1942-1945 / Jonathan Daniels. 1st ed. Garden City, N.Y. : Doubleday, 1975. xii, 299 p., [8] leaves of plates : ill. ; 22 cm. Includes index. [E806.D34] 74-9482 ISBN 0-385-00762-0 : 8.95
1. Daniels, Jonathan, 1902- 2. United States—Politics and government—1933-1945. I. Title.

Daniels, Josephus, 1862-1948.

DANIELS, Jonathan, 1902- 973.91
The end of innocence. New York, Da Capo Press, 1972 [c1954] 351 p. front. 22 cm. (Franklin D. Roosevelt and the era of the New Deal) [E766.D26 1972] 73-37285 ISBN 0-306-70423-4
1. Daniels, Josephus, 1862-1948. 2. Roosevelt, Franklin Delano, Pres. U.S., 1882-1945. 3. United States—Politics and government—1913-1921. I. Title. II. Series. **BIP**

DANIELS, Josephus, 1862-1948. 070.4'092'4
Editor in politics. Westport, Conn., Greenwood Press [1974, c1941] xix, 644 p. illus. 24 cm. The 2d vol. of the author's memoirs, covering the period between 1893 and 1912. The 1st vol. has title: Tar Heel editor. Reprint of the ed. published by University of North Carolina Press, Chapel Hill. [PN4874.D33A35 1974] 74-2839 ISBN 0-8371-7439-2
1. Daniels, Josephus, 1862-1948. 2. Journalists—Correspondence, reminiscences, etc. 3. Journalism—North Carolina. I. Daniels, Josephus, 1862-1948. Tar Heel editor. II. Title. **BIP**

DANIELS, Josephus, 1862-1948. 973.91'092'4 B
Shirt-sleeve diplomat. Westport, Conn., Greenwood Press [1973, c1947] xix, 547 p. illus. 22 cm. Reprint of the ed. published by the University of North Carolina Press, Chapel Hill. [E183.8.M6D3 1973] 73-11621 ISBN 0-8371-7082-6 23.50
1. Daniels, Josephus, 1862-1948. 2. United States—Foreign relations—Mexico. 3. Mexico—Foreign relations—United States. 4. Mexico—Politics and government—1910-1946. I. Title. **BIP**

DANIELS, Josephus, 1862-1948. 070.4'092'4 B
Tar Heel editor. Westport, Conn., Greenwood Press [1974, c1939] xix, 544 p. illus. 23 cm. The 1st vol. of the author's memoirs, covering the period between 1885 to 1893. The 2d vol. has title: Editor in politics. Reprint of the ed. published by University of North Carolina Press, Chapel Hill. [PN4874.D33A3 1974] 74-2840 ISBN 0-8371-7440-6 29.00
1. Daniels, Josephus, 1862-1948. 2. Journalists—Correspondence, reminiscences, etc. 3. Journalism—North Carolina. I. Daniels, Josephus, 1862-1948. Editor in politics. II. Title. **BIP**

MORRISON, Joseph L. 973.90924
Josephus Daniels; the small-d Democrat, by Joseph L. Morrison. Chapel Hill, Univ. of N.C. Pr. [1966] ix, 316p. ports. 24cm. Bibl. [E748.D19M6] 66-25358 7.50
1. Daniels, Josephus, 1862-1948. I. Title.

MORRISON, Joseph L. 923.273
Josephus Daniels says . . . An editor's political odyssey from Bryan to Wilson and F. D. R., 1894-1913. Chapel Hill, Univ. of N. C. Pr. [c.1962] x, 339p. port. 24cm. Bibl. 62-53249 7.50
1. Daniels, Josephus, 1862-1948. 2. North Carolina—Pol. & govt.—1865-1950. I. Title.

MORRISON, Joseph pl 923.273
Josephus Daniels says ... An editor's political odyssey from Bryan to Wilson and F. D. R., 1894-1913. Chapel Hill, University of North Carolina Press [1962] x, 339 p. port. 24 cm. Bibliography: p. [320]-332. [PN4874.D33M6] 62-53249
1. Daniels, Josephus, 1862-1948. 2. North Carolina — Pol. & govt. — 1865-1950. I. Title.

Daniels, Josephus, 1862-1948—Manuscripts—Catalogs.

UNITED States. Library of Congress. Manuscript Division. 973.9'092'4
Josephus Daniels : a register of his papers in the Library of Congress / Manuscript Division, Reference Department. Washington : Library of Congress, 1975. p. cm. (Registers of papers in the Manuscript Division of the Library of Congress ; no. 47) [Z6616.D17U54 1975] [E748.D17] 75-619045 ISBN 0-8444-0157-9
1. Daniels, Josephus, 1862-1948—Manuscripts—Catalogs. 2. United States. Library of Congress. Maunscript Division. I. Series: United States. Library of Congress. Manuscript Division. Registers of papers in the Manuscript Division of the Library of Congress ; no. 47.

Danielson, Elmer R.

DANIELSON, Elmer R. 266'.4'10924 B
Forty years with Christ in Tanzania, 1928-1968 / Elmer R. Danielson. New York : World Mission Interpretation, Lutheran Church in America, c1977. xii, 236 p. ; 21 cm. Bibliography: p. 236. [BV3625.T42D36] 77-78401 ISBN 0-87808-953-5
1. Danielson, Elmer R. 2. Lutheran Church—Missions. 3. Missionaries—Tanzania—Biography. 4. Missionaries—United States—Biography. 5. Missions—Tanzania. I. Title.

Danilevskii, Nicolai IAkovlevich, 1822-1885.

MACMASTER, Robert E. 320.5'0924(B)
Danilevsky, a Russian totalitarian philosopher, by Robert E. MacMaster. Cambridge, Harvard 1967. ix, 368p. port. 22cm. (Russian Res. Ctr. studies. 53) Danielevsky's writings: p. [313]-319. Bibl. [DK219.6.D2M3] 66-21340 7.95
1. Danilevskii, Nicolai IAkovlevich, 1822-1885. I. Title. II. Series: Harvard University. Russian Research Center. Studies, 53

Dante Alighieri, 1265-1321.

BARBI, Michele. 1867-1941 851.1
Life of Dante. Tr. [from Italian] and ed. by Paul G. Ruggiers [Gloucester, Mass., Peter Smith, 1961, c.1954] 132p. (Univ. of California bk. rebound) Bibl. 3.25
1. Dante Alighieri, 1265-1321. 2. Dante Alighieri. Divina Commedia. I. Title.

BARBI, Michele, 1867-1941. 851.15
Life of Dante; translated and edited by Paul Ruggiers. Berkeley, University of California Press, 1954. 132 p. illus. 23 cm. Translation of Dante: vita, opere e fortuna. [PQ4339.B453] 54-6466
1. Dante Alighieri, 1265-1321. 2. Dante Alighieri, 1265-1321. Divina commedia.

BERGIN, Thomas Goddard, 1904- 851'.1
Dante / Thomas G. Bergin. Westport, Conn. : Greenwood Press, 1976, c1965. 326 p. : ill. ; 23 cm. Reprint of the ed. published by Houghton Mifflin, Boston, in series: Riverside studies in literature. Includes bibliographical references and index. [PQ4335.B4 1976] 76-10974 ISBN 0-8371-7973-4 lib.bdg. : 17.50
1. Dante Alighieri, 1265-1321.

BOCCACCIO, Giovanni. The life of Dante. 928.5
The Earliest lives of Dante. [Translated from the Italian by James Robinson Smith] Introd. by Francesco Basetti-Sani. New York, F. Ungar Pub. Co. [c1963] 103 p. 21 cm. (Milestones of thought in the history of ideas) Contents.--The life of Dante, by G. Boccaccio,--The life of Dante, by L.B. Aretino.--A passage from the life of Dante, by F. Villani. [PQ4338.B6E45 1963] 63-18510
1. Dante—Biog. I. Bruni, Leonardo Aretino, 1369-1444. The life of Dante. II. Villani, Flippo, d. 1405? III. Smith, Robinson, 1876- tr. IV. Title. V. Series.

BROPHY, Liam. 928.5
Brother Dante. Chicago, Franciscan Herald Press [1965] 140 p. 22 cm. [PQ4335.B58] 64-14254
1. Dante, Alighieri, 1265-1321. I. Title. **BIP**

BROWNING, Oscar, 1837-1923. 851'.1
Dante; his life and writings. London, S. Sonnenschein; New York, Macmillan, 1891. New York, Haskell House Publishers, 1972. vii, 104 p. front. 23 cm. Based on an article in the 9th ed. of the Encyclopaedia britannica. Original ed. issued in series: The Dilettante library. Bibliography: p. 93-104. [PQ4335.B6 1972] 72-3093 ISBN 0-8383-1520-8
1. Dante Alighieri, 1265-1321. I. Series: The Dilettante library.

BUTLER, Arthur John, 1844-1910. 851'.1
Dante, his times and his work. Freeport, N.Y., Books for Libraries Press [1973] p. "First published in 1901." [PQ4335.B8 1973] 73-2722 ISBN 0-8369-7156-6
1. Dante Alighieri, 1265-1321. 2. Dante Alighieri, 1265-1321—Contemporary Italy. I. Title.

CHUBB, Thomas Caldecot, 1899- 851.1
Dante and his world. [1st ed.] Boston, Little, Brown [1967, c1966] xxviii, 831 p. illus., ports. 25 cm. Bibliography: p. [801]-805. [PQ4335.C53] 66-22038
1. Dante Alighieri, 1265-1321. I. Title.

DANTE: his life, his times, his works. 851'.1
Created by the editors of Arnoldo Mondadori editore. Translated from the Italian by Giuseppina T. Salvadori and Bernice L. Lewis. Anthology by Thomas G. Bergin. New York, American Heritage Press [1970, c1968] 168 p. illus. (part col.) 21 cm. (Giants of world literature) [PQ4335.D3] 76-83804
1. Dante Alighieri, 1265-1321. I. Dante Alighieri, 1265-1321. II. Mondadori (Arnoldo) editore. III. Bergin, Thomas Goddard, 1904- ed.

EARLIEST lives of Dante (The) 928.5
[Tr. from Italian by James Robinson Smith] Introd. by Francesco Basetti-Sani. New York, Ungar [c.1963] 103p. 21cm. (Milestones of thought in the hist. of ideas) 63-18510 2.75; 1.25 pap.,
1. Dante—Biog. I. Boccaccio, Giovanni. The life of Dante. II. Bruni, Leonardo Aretino, 1369-1444. The life of Dante. III. Villani, Filippo, d. 1405? IV. Smith, Robinson, 1876- tr. V. Series.
Contents omitted.

FEDERN, Karl, 1868-1942. 851'.1 B
Dante & his time. With an introd. by A. J. Butler. New York, Haskell House Publishers, 1970. xx, 306 p. 5 ports. 23 cm. Reprint of the 1902 ed. Translation of Dante. [PQ4337.F5 1970] 78-132439
1. Dante Alighieri, 1265-1321. 2. Dante Alighieri, 1265-1321—Contemporary Italy. 3. Civilization, Medieval. I. Title.

FEDERN, Karl, 1868-1942. 851'.1 B
Dante & his time. With an introd. by A. J. Butler. Port Washington, N.Y., Kennikat Press [1969] xx, 306 p. illus., ports. 22 cm. Reprint of the 1902 ed. Translation of Dante. [PQ4337.F5 1969] 70-101026
1. Dante Alighieri, 1265-1321. 2. Dante Alighieri, 1265-1321—Contemporary Italy. 3. Civilization, Medieval. I. Title. **BIP**

FERGUSSON, Francis. 851.1
Dante. New York, Macmillan [1966] x, 214 p. 21 cm. (Masters of world literature) "Bibliographical notes": p. [201]-208. [PQ4335.F4 1966] 66-14202
1. Dante, Alighieri, 1265-1321.

FERGUSSON, Francis. 851'.1
Dante / by Francis Fergusson. New York : Collier Books, [1975] c1966. p. cm. (Masters of world literature series) Includes bibliographical references and index. [PQ4355.F4 1975] 75-14006 4.95 pbk. : 2.95
1. Dante Alighieri, 1265-1321. I. Title. **BIP**

FLETCHER, Jefferson Butler, 1865-1946 851.1
Dante. Introd. by Mark Musa. [Notre Dame, Ind.] Univ. of Notre Dame Pr. [c.] 1965. 181p. 21cm. (NDP43) First pub. in 1916. Bibl. [QP4335.F5] 65-22369 4.50; 2.25 pap.,
1. Dante Alighieri, 1265-1321. I. Title.

GRANDGENT, Charles Hall, 1862-1939 851.1
Dante Alighieri. New York, Ungar [1966] 397p. 20cm. First pub. in 1916 under title: Dante. Bibl. [PQ4335.G65 1966] 65-29154 7.50
1. Dante Alighieri, 1265-1321. I. Title. **BIP**

LIFE of Dante. v. 12
Translated and edited by Paul G. Ruggiers. Berkeley, University of California Press, 1960. x, 132p. 19cm. Bibliography: p. [125]-132.
1. Dante—Biog. I. Barbi, Michele, 1867-1941.

MAZZOTTA, Giuseppe, 1942- 851'.1
Dante, poet of the desert : history and allegory in the Divine comedy / Giuseppe Mazzotta. Princeton, N.J. : Princeton University Press, c1979. x, 343 p. ; 23 cm. Includes bibliographical references and index. [PQ4390.M54] 78-27468 ISBN 0-691-06399-0 : 20.00
1. Dante Alighieri, 1265-1321. Divina commedia. 2. Dante Alighieri, 1265-1321—Allegory. I. Title. **BIP**

PAPINI, Giovanni, 1881-1956. 851'.1
Dante vivo. Translated from the Italian by Eleanor Hammond Broadus and Anna Benedetti. Port Washington, N.Y., Kennikat Press [1969] xiii, 340 p. illus., ports. 22 cm. Reprint of the 1934 ed. Bibliographical footnotes. [PQ4339.P252 1969] 76-101030
1. Dante Alighieri, 1265-1321. I. Title. **BIP**

TOYNBEE, Paget Jackson, 1855-1932 851.9001
Dante Alighieri, his life and works [rev., enl. ed.] Ed. [new] introd., notes. Bibl. by Charles S. Singleton. New York, Harper [c.1965] xxviii, 316p 21cm. (Harper torchbk., Acad. lib., TB12061) Bibl. [PQ4335.T1] 1.95 pap.,
1. Dante Alighieri, 1265-1321. I. Title.

TOYNBEE, Paget Jackson, 1855-1932 851.1
Dante Alighieri, his life and works. Ed., introd., notes, bibl., by Charles S. Singleton. [4th ed.] New York, Harper [1965] xxiii, 316p. illus., geneal, table, ports. 21cm. (Harper Torchbks., TB1206L. Acad. lib.) Reprint of the 1910 ed. Bibl. [PQ4335.T7 1965] 66-539 2.25 pap.,
1. Dante Alighieri, 1265-1321. I. Title.

TOYNBEE, Paget Jackson, 1885-1932 851.9001
Dante Alighieri, his life and works. Ed., introd., notes, Bibl. by Charles S. Singleton [Gloucester, Mass., P. Smith, c.1965] xxviii, 316p. 21cm. (Harper torchbk., Acad. lib., TB12061 rebound) Bibl. [PQ4335.T1] 4.00
1. Dante Alighieri, 1265-1321. I. Title.

Dante, Alighieri, 1265-1321—Biog.

BOCCACCIO, Giovanni. 851'.1
Earliest lives of Dante (The) Tr. from Italian of Giovani Boccaccio, Lionardo Bruni Aretino, by James Robinson Smith. New York, Russell & Russell [1968] 103p. 22cm. (Yale studies in English, 10) Reprint of the 1901 ed. [PQ4338.B6E45 1968] (B) 68-15161 5.00
1. Dante Alighieri, 1265-1321—Biog. I. Bruni, Leonarao Aretino, 1369-1444. II. Villani, Filippo, 1405? III. Smith, Robinson, 1876- tr. IV. Title. V. Title: The life of Dante. VI. Title: The life of Dante. VII. Series.
Contents Omitted.

BOCCACCIO, Giovanni. The life of Dante. v. 12
The Earliest lives of Dante, Translated from the Italian of Giovanni Boccaccio and Lionardo Bruni Aretino, by James Robinson Smith. New York, Holt, 1901. 103 p. 23 cm. (Yale studies in English, 10) Contents.--The life of Dante, by G. Boccaccio.--The life of Dante, by L.B. Aretino.--A passage from the life of Dante, by F. Villani.
1. Dante, Alighieri, 1265-1321—Biog. I. Bruni, Leonardo Aretino, 1369-1444. The life of Dante. II. Villani, Flippo, d. 1405? III. Smith, Robinson, 1876- tr. IV. Title. V. Series.

BOCCACCIO, Giovanni. The life of Dante. 928.5
The Earliest lives of Dante, Translated from the Italian of Giovanni Boccaccio and Lionardo Bruni Aretino, by James Robinson Smith. New York, Holt, 1901. 103 p. 23 cm. (Yale studies in English, 10) Contents.--The life of Dante, by G. Boccaccio.--The life of Dante, by L.B. Aretino.--A passage from the life of Dante, by F. Villani. [PQ4338.B6E45 1901] 3-23694
1. Dante, Alighieri, 1265-1321—Biog. I. Bruni, Leonardo Aretino, 1369-1444. The life of Dante. II. Villani, Flippo, d. 1405? III. Smith, Robinson, 1876- tr. IV. Title. V. Series.

DANTE Alighieri, 1265-1321. 851'.1
Dante and Giovanni del Virgilio, including a critical edition of the text of Dante's "Eclogae Latinae" and of the poetic remains of Giovanni del Virgilio, by Philip H. Wicksteed and Edmund G. Gardner. Freeport, N.Y., Books for Libraries Press [1971] x, 340 p. geneal. tables. 22 cm. Reprint of the 1902 ed. Includes bibliographical references. [PQ4311.E2 1971] 70-148908 ISBN 0-8369-5671-0
1. Dante Alighieri, 1265-1321—Biography. 2. Dante Alighieri, 1265-1321—Contemporaries. 3. Mussato, Albertino, 1261-1329. I. Giovanni del Virgilio, fl. 1319. II. Wicksteed, Philip Henry, 1844-1927. III. Gardner, Edmund Garratt, 1869-1935. IV. Title.

DANTE Alighieri, 1265-1321. 851'.1
Dante and Giovanni del Virgilio, including a critical edition of the text of Dante's Eclogae Latinae, and of the poetic remains of Giovanni del Virgilio. By Philip H. Wicksteed and Edmund G. Gardner. New York, Haskell House Publishers, 1970 [c1902] x, 340 p. geneal. tables. 23 cm. Contents.Contents.—Prolegomena: Albertino Mussato, Dante Alighieri.—Introduction.—Critical text and translation.—Commentary.—Editions and manuscripts.—Texts and scholia from the MSS.—Appendices (p. 314-336):—I. Del Virgilio's treatise on Ovid's Metamorphoses. II. Lovato. III. The letter of Frate Ilario. IV. The houses of Polenta and Malatesta. Includes bibliographical references. [PQ4311.E2 1970] 74-132446 ISBN 0-8383-1223-3
1. Dante Alighieri, 1265-1321—Biography. 2. Dante Alighieri, 1265-1321—Contemporaries. 3. Mussato, Albertino, 1261-1329. I. Giovanni del Virgilio, fl. 1319. II. Wicksteed, Philip Henry, 1844-1927, ed. III. Gardner, Edmund Garratt, 1869-1935, ed.

THE Earliest lives of Dante / 851'.1 B
translated from the Italian of Giovanni Boccaccio and Lionardo Bruni Aretino by James Robinson Smith. Folcroft, Pa. : Folcroft Library Editions, 1975. 103 p. ; 23 cm. Reprint of the 1901 ed. published by Holt, New York, which was issued as no. 10 of Yale studies in English. Includes index. Contents.Contents.—Boccaccio, G. The life of Dante (p. [7]-78).—Bruni, L. A. The life of Dante.—Villani, F. A passage from the life of Dante. [PQ4338.A2E3 1975] 75-28483 ISBN 0-8414-7848-1 lib. bdg. : 12.50
1. Dante Alighieri, 1265-1321—Biography. I. Boccaccio, Giovanni. La vita di Dante. English. 1975. II. Bruni, Leonardo Aretino, 1369-1444. La vita di Dante. English. 1975. III. Series: Yale studies in English ; 10.
Contents omitted

MOORE, Edward, 1835-1916. 851'.1
Dante and his early biographers. New York, Haskell House Publishers, 1970. viii, 181 p. 22 cm. "First published 1889." Based on three lectures delivered in 1889, as Barlow lecturer on Dante in University College, London. Contents.Contents.—The lives attributed to Boccaccio.—The life by Filippo Villani.—The life by Lionardo Bruni.—The life by Giannozzo Manetti.—The life by Giovanni Mario Filelfo.—Some minor biographical notices.—Personal traits and characteristics of Dante as gathered from the early biographers, and illustrated by passages in his own writings. [PQ4346.M7 1970] 70-122459 ISBN 8-383-10028-
1. Dante Alighieri, 1265-1321—Biography. I. Title. **BIP**

Dante Alighieri, 1265-1321—Biography—Youth.

LEIGH, Gertrude. 851'.1
New light on the youth of Dante; the course of Dante's life prior to 1290 traced in the Inferno, cantos 3-13. Port Washington, N.Y., Kennikat Press [1969] viii, 278 p. 22 cm. Reprint of the 1929 ed. Bibliography: p. 266-271. [PQ4349.L4 1969] 78-101028
1. Dante Alighieri, 1265-1321—Biography—Youth. 2. Dante Alighieri, 1265-1321. Divina commedia. Inferno. I. Title.

Dante Alighieri, 1265-1321—Contemporaries.

DANTE Alighieri, 1265-1321. 851'.1
Dante and Giovanni del Virgilio, including a critical edition of the text of Dante's "Eclogae Latinae" and of the poetic remains of Giovanni del Virgilio, by Philip H. Wicksteed and Edmund G. Gardner. Freeport, N.Y., Books for Libraries Press [1971] x, 340 p. geneal. tables. 22 cm. Reprint of the 1902 ed. Includes bibliographical references. [PQ4311.E2 1971] 70-148908 ISBN 0-8369-5671-0
1. Dante Alighieri, 1265-1321—Biography. 2. Dante Alighieri, 1265-1321—Contemporaries. 3. Mussato, Albertino, 1261-1329. I. Giovanni del Virgilio, fl. 1319. II. Wicksteed, Philip Henry, 1844-1927. III. Gardner, Edmund Garratt, 1869-1935. IV. Title.

DANTE Alighieri, 1265-1321. 851'.1
Dante and Giovanni del Virgilio, including a critical edition of the text of Dante's Eclogae Latinae, and of the poetic remains of Giovanni del Virgilio. By Philip H. Wicksteed and Edmund G. Gardner. New York, Haskell House Publishers, 1970 [c1902] x, 340 p. geneal. tables. 23 cm. Contents.Contents.—Prolegomena: Albertino Mussato, Dante Alighieri.—Introduction.—Critical text and translation.—Commentary.—Editions and manuscripts.—Texts and scholia from the MSS.—Appendices (p. 314-336):—I. Del Virgilio's treatise on Ovid's Metamorphoses. II. Lovato. III. The letter of Frate Ilario. IV. The houses of Polenta and Malatesta. Includes bibliographical references. [PQ4311.E2 1970] 74-132446 ISBN 0-8383-1223-3
1. Dante Alighieri, 1265-1321—Biography. 2. Dante Alighieri, 1265-1321—Contemporaries. 3. Mussato, Albertino, 1261-1329. I. Giovanni del Virgilio, fl. 1319. II. Wicksteed, Philip Henry, 1844-1927, ed. III. Gardner, Edmund Garratt, 1869-1935, ed.

Dante Alighieri, 1265-1321—Criticism and interpretation.

ANDERSON, William. 851'.1
Dante the maker / William Anderson. London ; Boston : Routledge & Kegan Paul, 1979. p. cm. Includes index. Bibliography: p. [PQ4390.A62] 79-41311 ISBN 0-7100-0322-6 : 45.00
1. Dante Alighieri, 1265-1321—Criticism and interpretation. I. Title. **BIP**

Dante Alighieri, 1265-1321—Religion and ethics.

MASSERON, Alexandre, 1880- 851'.1
1959.
Dante Alighieri, the poet who loved St. Francis so much / by Alexandre Masseron ; translated by Richard Arnandez. Chicago : Franciscan Herald Press, [1979] p. cm. (Tau series) Translation of Dante Alighieri, le grand poete qui tant aima saint Francois. [PQ4417.M37E5 1979] 78-14835 ISBN 0-8199-0757-X : 5.95
1. Dante Alighieri, 1265-1321—Religion and ethics. 2. Francesco d'Assisi, Saint, 1182-1226. I. Title.

Danton, Georges Jacques, 1759-1794.

BELLOC, Hilaire, 944.04'3'0924 B
1870-1953.
Danton; a study. 1st American ed., with new pref. and 17 illus. New York, AMS Press [1969] xxiv, 448 p. illus., facsims., ports. 23 cm. Reprint of the 1928 ed. "Report of the first Committee of public safety, treating of the general condition of the republic, and read by Barrere to the Convention on Wednesday, May 29, 1793": p. 399-438. [DC146.D2B7 1969] 70-100534
1. Danton, Georges Jacques, 1759-1794. I. France. Convention nationale, 1792-1795. Comite de salut public. **BIP**

CHRISTOPHE, Robert. 944.04'0924 B
Danton; a biography. Translated from the French by Peter Green. [1st ed. in the U.S.A.] Garden City, N.Y., Doubleday, 1967. 449 p. illus., ports. 22 cm. [DC146.D2C54 1967] 67-12861
1. Danton, Georges Jacques, 1759-1794.

HAMPSON, Norman. 944.04'3'0924 B
Danton / Norman Hampson. New York : Holmes & Meier Publishers, 1978. x, 182 p. : port. ; 23 cm. Includes index. Bibliography: p. 175-177. [DC146.D2H35 1978] 78-9817 ISBN 0-8419-0408-1 : 18.00
1. Danton, Georges Jacques, 1759-1794. 2. France—History—Revolution, 1789-1794. 3. Revolutionists—France—Biography. **BIP**

SCHERR, Marie. 944.04'0924
Charlotte Corday and certain men of the revolutionary torment. New York, AMS Press [1970] 237 p. port. 22 cm. Reprint of the 1929 ed. [DC146.C8S3 1970] 79-100512 ISBN 0-404-05588-5
1. Corday D'Armont, Marie Anne Charlotte de, 1768-1793. 2. Danton, Georges Jacques, 1759 1794. 3. Marat, Jean Paul, 1743-1793. 4. Robespierre, Maximilien Marie Isidore de, 1758-1794. 5. France—History—Revolution, 1789-1799. 6. Girondists. I. Title. **BIP**

Darbee, Harry.

DARBEE, Harry. 688.7'9
Catskill flytier : my life, times, and techniques / Harry Darbee, with Mac Francis ; illustrated by Francis W. Davis ; introd. by Sparse Grey Hackle. 1st ed. Philadelphia : Lippincott, c1977. 174 p. : ill. ; 24 cm. Includes index. Bibliography: p. 160-169. [SH451.D36] 77-22503 ISBN 0-397-01214-4 : 8.95
1. Darbee, Harry. 2. Fly tying. 3. Fishermen—New York (State)—Catskill—Biography. 4. Catskill, N.Y.—Biography. I. Francis, Mac, joint author. II. Title. **BIP**

Darby, Jemima, 1794-1884.

CAWTHON, John Ardis 973.08
The inevitable guest; life and letters of Jemima Darby. San Antonio, Naylor [c.1965] xix, 412p. illus., ports. 22cm. Based on letters addressed to Jemima Darby and others. Bibl. [F277.D2C3] 64-8903 10.00
1. Darby, Jemima, 1794-1884. 2. Darlington Co., S.C.—Soc. life & cust. I. Title.

CAWTHON, John Ardis. 973.08
The inevitable guest: life and letters of Jemima Darby San Antonio, Naylor Co. [1965] xix, 412 p. illus., ports. 22 cm. Based on letters addressed to Jemima Darby and others. Bibliography: p. [367]-384. [F277.D2C3] 64-8903
1. Darby, Jemima, 1794-1884. 2. Darlington Co., S. C. — Soc. life & cust. I. Title.

Darby, John Fletcher, 1803-1882.

DARBY, John 977.8'66'030924
Fletcher, 1803-1882.
Personal recollections / John Fletcher Darby. New York : Arno Press, 1975. p. cm. (The Mid-American frontier) Reprint of the 1880 ed. published by G. I. Jones, St. Louis, under title: Personal recollections of many prominent people whom I have known. [F474.S2D2 1975] 75-94 ISBN 0-405-06860-3 : 27.00
1. Darby, John Fletcher, 1803-1882. 2. St. Louis—History. 3. St. Louis—Biography. I. Title. II. Series.

Darcy, James Leslie. 1895-1917.

SWANWICK, Raymond 796.830924
Les Darcy. Australia's golden boy of boxing. Sidney, U. Smith. San Francisco, Tri-Ocean [c.1965] 238p. illus., facsims., ports. 21cm. [GV1132.D3S9] 65-23903 4.75 bds.,
1. Darcy, James Leslie. 1895-1917. I. Title.

SWANWICK, Raymond. 796.830924 (B)
Les Darcy, Australia's golden boy of boxing. [1st ed.] Sidney, U. Smith; San Francisco, Tri-Ocean Books [1965] 238 p. illus., facsims., ports. 21 cm. [GV1132.D3S9] 65-23903
1. Darcy, James Leslie, 1895-1917. I. Title.

Dardan, Francois, 1733-1792.

MOREAU, Roland, 282'.092'4 B
abbe.
Francois Dardan d'Isturitz, martyr des Carmes (1733-1792) [Bayonne, Impr. des Cordeliers, 1966] 30 p. illus. 24 cm. Cover and half title: Un Basque martyr de la Revolution: Francois Dardan, 1733-1792. [BX4705.D2735M67] 74-156638
1. Dardan, Francois, 1733-1792. I. Title: Un Basque martyr de la Revolution: Francois Dardan

Darden, Colgate Whitehead, 1897-

FRIDDELL, Guy. 975.5'04'0924
Colgate Darden : conversations with Guy Friddell. Charlottesville : University Press of Virginia, 1978. p. cm. Includes index. [F231.D27F74] 78-7026 ISBN 0-8139-0744-6 . 12.95
1. Darden, Colgate Whitehead, 1897- 2. Virginia. University—Presidents—Biography. 3. Virginia—Governors—Biography. 4. College presidents—Virginia—Biography. I. Darden, Colgate Whitehead, 1897- joint author. **BIP**

Darden family.

DARDEN, Norma. 64.5'973
Spoonbread and strawberrywine : recipes and reminiscences of a family / Norma Jean Darden, Carol Darden, with line drawings by Doug Jamieson ; wood engravings throughout text by Thomas Bewick. 1st ed. New York : Fawcett Crest Books, 1980, c1978. 288 p. : ill. ; 18 cm. Includes index. [TX715.D222] ISBN 0-449-24264-1 pbk. : 2.50
1. Darden family. 2. Cookery, American — Biography. I. Darden, Carole, joint author. II. Title.
L.C. card no. for 1978 Anchor Press/Doubleday ed.: 77 20 **BIP**

DARDEN, Norma Jean. 641.5'973
Spoonbread and strawberry wine : recipes and reminiscences of a family / Norma Jean Darden, Carole Darden ; with line drawings by Doug Jamieson ; wood engravings throughout text by Thomas Bewick. 1st ed. New York : Anchor Press, 1978. p. cm. Includes index. [TX715.D222] 77-82620 ISBN 0-385-12468-6 : 9.95
1. Darden family. 2. Cookery, American. 3. United States—Biography. I. Darden, Carole, joint author. II. Title.

Dario, Ruben, 1867-1916.

WATLAND, Charles Dunton, 861 (B)
1913-
Poet-errant: a biography of Ruben Dario, by Charles D. Watland. New York, Philosophical Library [1965] 266 p. 22 cm. Includes bibliographical references. [PQ7519.D3Z955] 64-21467
1. Dario, Ruben, 1867-1916. I. Title. **BIP**

Darley, Felix Octavius Carr, 1822-1888.

KING, Ethel M. 927.4
Darley, the most popular illustrator of his time. Brooklyn, N.Y., Gaus [c.1964] 156p. plates, port. 23cm. Bibl. [NC139.D37K5] 64-8864 3.00
1. Darley, Felix Octavius Carr, 1822-1888. I. Title.

KING, Ethel M. 927.4
Darley, the most popular illustrator of his time, by Ethel King. Brooklyn, N.Y., T. Gaus' Sons [c1964] 156 p. plates, port. 23 cm. Bibliography: p. 151-152. [NC139.D37K5] 64-8864
1. Darley, Felix Octavius Carr, 1822-1888. I. Title.

Darley, George, 1795-1846.

ABBOTT, Claude Colleer, 821'.7
1889-
The life and letters of George Darley, poet and critic. [1st ed.] reprinted lithographically. Oxford, Clarendon P., [1967] xv, 285 p. front., 3 plates (ports.). 22 1/2 cm. "First published 1928." Bibliography: p. 271-277. [PR4525.D2Z6 1967] 67-87299
1. Darley, George, 1795-1846. I. Title. **BIP**

Darling, Jay Norwood, 1876-1962.

LENDT, David L. 741'.092'4 B
Ding : the life of Jay Norwood Darling / David L. Lendt. 1st ed. Ames : Iowa State University Press, 1979. ix, 202 p., [30] leaves of plates : ill. ; 24 cm. Includes index. Bibliography: p. 191-197. [NC1429.D237L46] 78-10321 ISBN 0-8138-0010-2 : 7.95
1. Darling, Jay Norwood, 1876-1962. 2. Cartoonists—United States—Biography. I. Title. **BIP**

Darling, Ralph, Sir, 1775-1858.

SHAW, Alan George 994.02'0924 B
Lewers, 1916-
Ralph Darling [by] A. G. L. Shaw. Melbourne, New York, Oxford University Press [1971] 30 p. illus., ports. 19 cm. (Great Australians) Includes bibliographical references. [DU172.D3S54 1971] 75-869393 ISBN 0-19-550351-1
1. Darling, Ralph, Sir, 1775-1858. 2. New South Wales—History.

Darlington, Charles Joseph,

DARLINGTON, Charles 540.924
Joseph, 1894-1966.
Memoirs by Charles J. Darlington. [Philadelphia?] 1966-67] 2 v. illus., facsims, ports. 23 cm. Contents.Farm and school: 1894-1911, [aud] Swarthmore College: 1911-1916.--v. Wilmington: 1916-1925, [and] Woodstown: 1925-1965. [BX7795.D33A3] 66-29411
I. Title.

DARLINGTON, Charles 540.0924
Joseph, 1894-1966.
Memoirs of Charles J. Darlington. [Philadelphia?] 1966-67] 2 v. illus., facsims., ports. 23 cm. Contents.Contents.—v. 1. Farm and school: 1894-911, [and] Swarthmore College: 1911-1916.—v. 2. Wilmington: 1916-1925, [and] Woodstown: 1925-1965. [BX7795.D33A3] 66-29411
I. Title.

Darnley, Henry Stewart, Lord, 1545-1567.

THOMSON, George 941'.05'0924
Malcolm, 1899-
The crime of Mary Stuart, [1st ed.] New York, Dutton, 1967. 175 p. geneal, table, col, map (on lining papers), ports. 22 cm. Bibliography: p. 167-169. [DA787.A1T5] 67-26602
1. Mary Stuart, Queen of the Scots, 1542-1587. 2. Darnley, Henry Stewart, Lord, 1545-1567. 3. Bothwell, James Hepburn, 4th Earl of, 1536?-1578. I. Title.

THOMSON, George 941'.05'0924
Malcolm, 1899-
The crime of Mary Stuart. [1st ed.] New York, Dutton, 1967. 175 p. geneal. table, col. map (on lining papers), ports. 22 cm. Bibliography: p. 167-169. [DA787.A1T5 1967b] 67-26602
1. Mary Stuart, Queen of the Scots, 1542-1587. 2. Darnley, Henry Stewart, Lord, 1545-1567. 3. Bothwell, James Hepburn, 4th Earl of, 1536?-1578. I. Title.

Darrow, Clarence Seward, 1857-1938.

DARROW, Clarence Seward, 923.473
1857-1938.
The story of my life. New York, Scribners [1965, c.1932, 1960] viii, 495p. illus. 21cm. (SL109) [CT275.D2374A3] 1.95 pap.,
1. Lawyers—Correspondence, reminiscences, etc. I. Title.

DARROW, Clarence 345'.73'00924 B
Seward, 1857-1938.
The story of my life. Illustrated from photos. Clifton [N.J.] A. M. Kelley, 1973 [c1932] p. (Scribner reprint editions) Reprint of the ed. published by Scribner, New York. [KF373.D35A3 1973] 73-12218 ISBN 0-678-02766-8
1. Darrow, Clarence Seward, 1857-1938. 2. Lawyers—United States—Correspondence, reminiscences, etc. I. Title.

HYND, Alan, 1908- 923.473
Defenders of the damned. New York, A.S. Barnes [1960] 182 p. 22cm. [KF372.H9] 60-12187
1. Rogers, Earl, 1870-1922. 2. Darrow, Clarence Seward, 1857-1938. 3. Fallon, William Joseph, 1886-1927. I. Title.

KURLAND, Gerald, 345'.73'00924 B
1942-
Clarence Darrow, "attorney for the damned." Charlotteville, N.Y., SamHar Press, 1972. 32 p. 22 cm. (Outstanding personalities, no. 22) Bibliography: p. 32. A biography of the lawyer who devoted himself to unpopular causes and was involved in some of the most famous and important cases of the early twentieth century. [KF373.D35K87] 92 75-190240 1.98
1. Darrow, Clarence Seward, 1857-1938. I. Title.
Pap. 0.98

NOBLE, Iris. 923.473
Clarence Darrow, defense attorney. New York, Messner [1958] 192p. 22cm. Includes bibliography. 58-7261
1. Darrow, Clarence Seward, 1857-1938. I. Title.

TIERNEY, Kevin. 345'.73'00924 B
Darrow, a biography / Kevin Tierney. 1st ed. New York : Crowell, c1979. vi, 490 p., [8] leaves of plates : ill. ; 24 cm. Includes index. Bibliography: p. 467-475. [KF373.D35T53] 78-3319 ISBN 0-690-01408-2 : 16.95
1. Darrow, Clarence Seward, 1857-1938. 2. Lawyers—United States—Biography. I. Title.

Darrow, Clarence Seward, 1857-1938—Juvenile literature.

FABER, Doris 1924- 92
Clarence Darrow: defender of the people. Illus. by Paul Frame. Englewood Cliffs, N.J., Prentice [c.1965] 72p. illus. 22cm. 3.50

1. Darrow, Clarence Seward, 1857-1938—Juvenile literature. I. Title.

FABER, Doris, 1924- 92 (J)
Clarence Darrow: defender of the people. Illustrated by Paul Frame. Englewood Cliffs, N.J., Prentice-Hall [1965] 72 p. illus. 22cm. [KF373.D35F3] 65-11774
1. Darrow, Clarence Seward, 1857-1938—Juvenile literature.

D'Arusmont, Frances (Wright) Mme., 1795-1852.

PERKINS, Alice J. G. 301.24'2'0924 B
Frances Wright, free enquirer. The study of a temperament, by A. J. G. Perkins and Theresa Wolfson. Philadelphia, Porcupine Press, [1972 i.e.1973] 393 p. illus. 22 cm. (The American utopian adventure) Bibliography: p. 385-388. [HQ1413.D2P4 1972] 79-187457 ISBN 0-87991-008-9 14.95
1. D'Arusmont, Frances (Wright) Mme., 1795-1852. I. Wolfson, Theresa, 1897- joint author. **BIP**

D'Arusmont, Frances (Wright) 1795-1852—Juvenile literature.

STILLER, Richard. 301.24'2'0924 B
Commune on the frontier; the story of Frances Wright. New York, Crowell [1972] xii, 259 p. illus. 21 cm. (Women of America) Bibliography: p. [248]-253. A biography of the woman who founded a commune, published a radical newspaper, spoke out against slavery and for women's rights 140 years ago. [HQ1413.D2S74] 92 79-187946 ISBN 0-690-20401-9 4.50
1. D'Arusmont, Frances (Wright) 1795-1852—Juvenile literature. I. Title. **BIP**

Darwin, Charles Robert, 1809-1882.

ALLAN, Mea. 575'.009'24 B
Darwin and his flowers : the key to natural selection / Mea Allan. New York : Taplinger Pub. Co., 1977. 318 p. : ill. ; 24 cm. Includes index. Bibliography: p. [305]-308. [QH31.D2A78 1977] 77-155104 ISBN 0-8008-2113-0 : 14.50
1. Darwin, Charles Robert, 1809-1882. 2. Natural selection. 3. Plant genetics. 4. Naturalists—England—Biography. 5. Botanists—England—Biography. I. Title. **BIP**

APPLEMAN, Philip, 1926- comp. 575'.0092'4
Darwin / edited by Philip Appleman. 2d ed. New York : Norton, c1979. p. cm. (A Norton critical edition) Includes index. Bibliography: p. [QH365.Z9A7 1979] 79-13599 ISBN 0-393-01192-5 : 24.95 ISBN 0-393-95009-3 pbk. : 4.95
1. Darwin, Charles Robert, 1809-1882. 2. Evolution—History. 3. Naturalists—Great Britain—Biography. **BIP**

AUTOBIOGRAPHIES / 575'.0092'4 B
Charles Darwin, Thomas Henry Huxley ; edited with an introd. by Gavin de Beer. London ; New York : Oxford University Press, 1974. xxvi, 123 p., [6] leaves of plates : ill. ; 25 cm. (Oxford English memoirs and travels) Includes index. [QH31.D2A93] 75-321823 ISBN 0-19-255410-7 : £3.30 ($10.75)
1. Darwin, Charles Robert, 1809-1882. 2. Huxley, Thomas Henry, 1825-1895. 3. Naturalists—Correspondence, reminiscences, etc. I. Darwin, Charles Robert, 1809-1882. II. Huxley, Thomas Henry, 1825-1895. III. DeBeer, Gavin Rylands, Sir, 1899- IV. Title. V. Series. **BIP**

BARNETT, Samuel Anthony, ed. 575.01'62
A century of Darwin. Freeport, N.Y., Books for Libraries Press [1969, c1958] xv, 376 p. illus., maps, ports. 23 cm. (Essay index reprint series) [QH311.B33 1969] 71-76891
1. Darwin, Charles Robert, 1809-1882. 2. Biology—Addresses, essays, lectures. I. Title. **BIP**

CHEESMAN, Evelyn, 1881- 925.9
Charles Darwin and his problems. Illustrated by Geoffrey Whittam. New York, Abelard-Schuman [1955] 192p. illus. 21cm. [QH31.D2C53] 55-5154
1. Darwin, Charles Robert, 1809-1882. I. Title.

CLARK, Robert Edward David. 575.01'62
Darwin, before and after : the story of evolution / by Robert E. D. Clark. Folcroft, Pa. : Folcroft Library Editions, 1977. 192 p. ; 23 cm. Reprint of the 1948 ed. published by Paternoster Press, London, which as issued as no. 1 in The Second thoughts library. Includes bibliographical references and index. [QH361.C53 1977] 77-7227 ISBN 0-8414-1802-0 lib. bdg. : 20.00
1. Darwin, Charles Robert, 1809-1882. 2. Evolution—History. 3. Naturalists—England—Biography. I. Title.

COLP, Ralph. 575'.0092'4 B
To be an invalid : the illness of Charles Darwin / Ralph Colp, Jr. Chicago : University of Chicago Press, 1977. xiii, 285 p., [8] leaves of plates : ill. ; 24 cm. Includes bibliographical references and index. [QH31.D2C6] 76-17698 ISBN 0-226-11401-5 : 15.00
1. Darwin, Charles Robert, 1809-1882. 2. Naturalists—United States—Biography. 3. Chronic diseases—Cases, clinical reports, statistics. I. Title.

DARWIN, Charles Robert 925.9
The autobiography of Charles Darwin and selected letters, edited by Francis Darwin. [Gloucester, Mass., Peter Smith, 1960, c.1958] vi, 365p. 'An unabridged and unaltered republication of the work first published in 1892 . . . under the title, Charles Darwin, his life told in an autobiographical chapter.' illus. facsim. 21cm. (Dover paperback rebound in cloth) 3.75
I. Title.

DARWIN, Charles Robert, 1809-1882. 925.9
Autobiography and selected letters; edited by Francis Darwin. New York, Dover Publications [1958] vi, 365 p. illus., facsim. 21 cm. "An unabridged and unaltered republication of the work first published in 1892 ... under the title, Charles Darwin, his life told in an autobiographical chapter." Includes bibliography. [QH31.D2A18 1958] 58-13934 201 A0010030DARWIN, Charles Robert,

DARWIN, Charles Robert, 1809-1882. 925.9
Charles Darwin's Autobiography, with his notes and letters depicting the growth of the Origin of species; edited by Sir Francis Darwin. And an introductory essay, The meaning of Darwin, by George Gaylord Simpson. New York, Schuman [1950] 266 p. port. 22 cm. [The Life of science library] [QH31.D2A18 1950] 50-10428
I. Darwin, Francis, Sir 1848-1925. II. Title.

DARWIN, Charles Robert, 1809-1882. 925.9
The life and letters of Charles Darwin, including an autobiographical chapter, edited by his son, Francis Darwin. Foreword by George Gaylord Simpson. New York, Basic Books, 1959. 2 v. illus., ports., facsim. 22 cm. [QH31.D2A2 1959] 59-16177
I. Darwin, Francis, Sir, 1848-1925, ed.

DARWIN, Charles Robert, 1809-1882. 575'.00924 B
The life and letters of Charles Darwin, including an autobiographical chapter. Edited by his son, Francis Darwin. London, J. Murray, 1888. New York, Johnson Reprint Corp. [1969] 3 v. ports. 23 cm. (The Sources of science, no. 102) [QH31.D2A2 1969] 77-12465
I. Darwin, Francis, Sir, 1848-1925, ed. II. Title.

DARWIN, Charles Robert, 1809-1882. 575'.00924 B
The life and letters of Charles Darwin; including an autobiographical chapter. Edited by his son, Francis Darwin. New York, D. Appleton, 1896. [New York, AMS Press, 1972] 2 v. illus. 23 cm. (The Works of Charles Darwin, v. 17-18) [QH31.D2A2 1972] 72-3904 ISBN 0-404-08417-6 (v. 1)
I. Darwin, Francis, Sir, 1848-1925, ed. II. Title.

DARWIN, Charles Robert, 1809-1882. 575.01'62
More letters of Charles Darwin; a record of his work in a series of hitherto unpublished letters. Edited by Francis Darwin and A. C. Seward. New York, Appleton, 1903. [New York, Johnson Reprint Corp., 1972] 2 v. illus. 22 cm. (The Sources of science, no. 137) [QH31.D2A4 1972] 72-2492
1. Evolution. I. Darwin, Francis, Sir, 1848-1925, ed. II. Seward, Albert Charles, Sir, 1863-1941, ed. III. Title.

DARWIN, Charles Robert, 1809-1882. 575'.0092'4 B
The voyage of Charles Darwin / [selected] by Christopher Ralling. New York : Mayflower Books, [1979] p. cm. Includes index. [QH31.D2A25 1979] 79-916 ISBN 0-8317-9212-4 : 12.50
1. Darwin, Charles Robert, 1809-1882. 2. Naturalists—England—Biography. I. Ralling, Christopher. II. Title. **BIP**

DE Beer, Gavin Rylands, Sir 1899- v. 12
Charles Darwin: a scientific biography. Garden City, N.Y., Doubleday, 1965. 295 p. illus., ports, maps, facsims. 18 cm. (The Natural history library, N41) Published in cooperation with the American Museum of Natural History. Earlier edition has title: Charles Darwin; evolution by natural selection. 67-3960
1. Darwin, Charles Robert, 1809-1882. I. Title.

DE BEER, Gavin Rylands, Sir. 1899- 925.7
Charles Darwin; evolution by natural selection. London, New York, T. Nelson [1963] xi, 290 p. illus., ports., maps, facsims. 21 cm. (British men of science) Bibliography: p. 281-282. [QH31.D2D4] 63-23628
1. Darwin, Charles Robert, 1809-1892. I. Title.

DE BEER, Gavin Rylands, Sir, 1899- 925.9
Charles Darwin; evolution by natural selection. [1st ed.] Garden City, N.Y., Doubleday, 1964 [c1963] xi, 290 p. illus., ports. maps, facsims. 21 cm. (British men of science) Bibliography: p. 281-282. [QH31.D2D4 1964] 64-10233
1. Darwin, Charles Robert, 1809-1882. I. Title.

DE BEER, Gavin Rylands, Sir, 1899- 575'.00924 B
Charles Darwin; evolution by natural selection [by] Sir Gavin de Beer. [Melbourne] Nelson [(Australia) 1968] x, 290 p. illus., diagrs., ports. 19 cm. (Nelson's Australasian paperbacks) (British men of science.) Bibliography: p. 281-282. [QH31.D2D4 1969] 77-560903
1. Darwin, Charles Robert, 1809-1882. I. Title.

DE BEER, Gavin Rylands, Sir 1899- 925.9
Charles Darwin; a scientific biography. Garden City, N.Y., Pub. in coop. with The Amer. Mus. of Natural Hist. [by] Doubleday, 1965[c.1963] xx, 295p. illus. maps. 18cm. (Natural hist. lib., Anchor bk. N41) 1.45 pap.,
1. Darwin, Charles Robert, 1809-1882. I. Title.

DICKINSON, Alice. 925.9
Charles Darwin & natural selection. New York, Watts [1964] xi, 212 p. 22 cm. (Immortals of science) Bibliography: p. ix-xi. [QH31.D2D52] 64-11921
1. Darwin, Charles Robert, 1809-1882. 2. Natural selection. I. Title. **BIP**

GILLESPIE, Neal C., 1932- 575'.0092'4
Charles Darwin and the problem of creation / Neal C. Gillespie. Chicago : University of Chicago Press, c1979. p. cm. Includes index. Bibliography: p. [QH31.D2G55] 79-11231 ISBN 0-226-29374-2 : 16.50
1. Darwin, Charles Robert, 1809-1882. 2. Life—Origin. 3. Naturalists—England—Biography. I. Title.

HIMMELFARB, Gertrude 925.9
Darwin and the Darwinian revolution [Gloucester, Mass., P. Smith, 1963, c.1959] 1962. 510p. 19cm. (Anchor bk. A325 rebound) Bibl. 3.50
1. Darwin, Charles Robert, 1809-1882. 2. Origin of species. I. Title.

HIMMELFARB, Gertrude. 575.01'62
Darwin and the Darwinian revolution. Gloucester, Mass., P. Smith, 1967 [c1962] x, 510 p. 21 cm. Bibliography: p. [496]-504. [QH31.D2H57 1967] 67-4641
1. Darwin, Charles Robert, 1809-1882. 2. Evolution. I. Title. **BIP**

HIMMELFARB, Gertrude. 925.9
Darwin and the Darwinian revolution. [1st ed.] Garden City, N. Y., Doubleday, 1959. 480 p. 22 cm. (Doubleday anchor books) Includes bibliography. [QH31.D2H57] 59-7908
1. Darwin, Charles Robert, 1809-1882. 2. Origin of species.

HUXLEY, Julian Sorell, Sir, 1887- 575.0924 B
Charles Darwin and his world, by Julian Huxley and H. B. D. Kettlewell. New York, Viking Press [1965] 144 p. illus., facsims., ports. 24 cm. (A Studio book) [QH31.D2H78] 65-10184
1. Darwin, Charles Robert, 1809-1882. I. Kettlewell, H. B. D., joint author. II. Title.

IRVINE, William, 1906- 575.0162
Apes, angels, and Victorians; the story of Darwin, Huxley, and evolution. New York, McGraw-Hill [1955] 399 p. illus. 21 cm. [QH31.D2I7] 54-11269
1. Darwin, Charles Robert, 1809-1882. 2. Huxley, Thomas Henry, 1825-1895. 3. Evolution. I. Title.

IRVINE, William, 1906- 575.01'62
Apes, angels, and Victorians; the story of Darwin, Huxley, and evolution. New York, McGraw-Hill [1972, c1955] 399 p. 21 cm. Includes bibliographical references. [QH31.D2I7 1972] 72-181814 ISBN 0-07-032048-9
1. Darwin, Charles Robert, 1809-1882. 2. Huxley, Thomas Henry, 1825-1895. 3. Evolution. I. Title.

MONTAGU, Ashley, 1905- 595.01'62
Darwin: competition & cooperation. Westport, Conn., Greenwood Press [1973, c1952] 148 p. 22 cm. Bibliography: p. 117-137. [QH365.D8M6 1973] 72-11332 ISBN 0-8371-6657-8 8.50
1. Darwin, Charles Robert, 1809-1882. 2. Natural selection. I. Title.

MOORE, Ruth E. 925.9
Charles Darwin, a great life in brief. [1st ed.] New York, Knopf, 1955 [c1954] 206 p. 19 cm. (Great lives in brief, a new series of biographies) [QH31.D2M6] 54-7221
1. Darwin, Charles Robert, 1809-1882. I. Title.

MOORE, Ruth E v. 12
Charles Drawin; a great life in brief. New York, Alfred A. Knopf, 1962. 206 p. 65-37607
1. Darwin, Charles Robert, 1809-1882. I. Title.

OLBY, Robert Cecil. 575/.00924
Charles Darwin, by Robert Olby. London, Oxford Univ. Pr., 1967. 64p. 8 plates (incl. ports., facsims.) map, tables, diagrs. 21cm. (Clarendon biographies 16) Maps on end-papers. Bibl. [QH31.D2] (B) 67-69438 1.55 bds.,
1. Darwin, Charles Robert, 1809-1882. I. Title.
Order from publisher's New York office.

OLBY, Robert Cecil. 575'.00924 (B)
Charles Darwin, by Robert Olby. London, Oxford U. P., 1967. 64 p. 8 plates (incl. ports., facsims.) map, tables, diagrs. 20 1/2 cm. (The Clarendon biographies 16) 9/6 (5/-lp.) (B 67-21504) Maps on endpapers. Bibliography: p. [62]. [QH31.D2] 67-69438
1. Darwin, Charles Robert, 1809-1882. [NLM: Darwin, Charles Robert, 1809-1882. 2. Evolution—hist. WZ 100 D2280 1967] I. Title.

REINFELD, Fred, 1910- 925.9
Young Charles Darwin. Illustrated with drawings from the 1st ed. of 'The voyage of the Beagle.' New York, Sterling Pub. Co. [1956] 184p. illus. 21cm. [QH31.D2R4] 56-7711
1. Darwin, Charles Robert, 1809-1882. I. Title.

SEARS, Paul Bigelow, 1891- 925.9
Charles Darwin, the naturalist as a cultural force. New York, Scribner, 1950. ix, 124 p. 24 cm. (Twentieth century library) "A brief bibliography": p. 120. [GH31.D2S4] 50-5297

1. Darwin, Charles Robert, 1809-1882. I. Title.

STEVENS, Lewell Robert. 575'.0092'4 B
Charles Darwin / L. Robert Stevens. Boston : Twayne Publishers, 1978. p. cm. (Twayne's English authors series ; TEAS 240) Includes index. Bibliography: p. [QH31.D2S83] 78-8289 ISBN 0-8057-6718-5 lib. bdg. : 8.95
1. Darwin, Charles Robert, 1809-1882. 2. Naturalists—Great Britain—Biography. I. Title. BIP

WICHLER, Gerhard 925.9
Charles Darwin, the founder of the theory of evolution and natural selection. New York, Pergamon Press [c.]1961[1961[ ] xvii, 228p. illus. 60-53465 6.50
1. Darwin, Charles Robert, 1809-1882. I. Title.

Darwin, Charles Robert, 1809-1882—Addresses, essays, lectures.

VANDERPOOL, Harold Y., comp. 301'.0424
Darwin and Darwinism; revolutionary insights concerning man, nature, religion, and society. Edited and with an introd. by Harold Y. Vanderpool. Lexington, Mass., Heath [1973] xxxi, 220 p. illus. 21 cm. (Problems in European civilization) [HM108.V36] 73-7052 ISBN 0-669-85407-7 2.50 (pbk.)
1. Darwin, Charles Robert, 1809-1882—Addresses, essays, lectures. 2. Evolution—Addresses, essays, lectures. 3. Social evolution—Addresses, essays, lectures. I. Title. II. Series.
Contents omitted.

Darwin, Charles Robert, 1809-1882—Dictionaries, Indexes, etc.

FREEMAN, Richard Broke. 575'.0092'4
Charles Darwin, a companion / by R. B. Freeman. Folkestone, Eng. : W. Dawson ; Hamden, Conn. : Archon Books, 1978. 309 p., [1] leaf of plates : port. ; 23 cm. [QH31.D2F73] 78-40928 ISBN 0-208-01739-9 (Archon Books) : 27.50
1. Darwin, Charles Robert, 1809-1882—Dictionaries, Indexes, etc. 2. Naturalists—England—Biography. I. Title.

Darwin, Charles Robert, 1809-1882—Juvenile literature.

COOPER, George Allen 92
Charles Darwin, voyager-naturalist, written, illus. by George Allen Cooper. New York, Macmillan [c.1966] 38p. col. illus. 23cm. (Sci. story lib.) [QH31.D2C65] 66-10358 2.95; 3.24 lib. ed.,
1. Darwin, Charles Robert, 1809-1882—Juvenile literature. I. Title.

DE CAMP, Lyon Sprague, 1907- 575'.0092'4 B
Darwin and his great discovery, by L. Sprague de Camp and Catherine Crook de Camp. New York, Macmillan [1972] 248 p. illus. 21 cm. Bibliography: p. [241]-243. A biography of the English naturalist whose theories of man's evolution aroused world controversy. Includes discussions of other conflicting and supporting theories of the time concerning evolution and natural selection. [QH31.D2D42] 92 71-185146 5.95
1. Darwin, Charles Robert, 1809-1882—Juvenile literature. 2. Evolution—Juvenile literature—History. I. De Camp, Catherine Crook, joint author. II. Title. BIP

GALLANT, Roy A. 575'.00924 B
Charles Darwin: the making of a scientist [by] Roy A. Gallant. [1st ed.] Garden City, N.Y., Doubleday [1972] xi, 172 p. illus. 24 cm. A biography of the nineteenth-century English scientist whose publication The Origin of the Species greatly influenced scientific thinking. [QH31.D2G3] 92 74-171289 4.95
1. Darwin, Charles Robert, 1809-1882—Juvenile literature. I. Title.

GREENE, Carla, 1906- 575'.00924 B
Charles Darwin. Illustrated by David Hodges. New York, Dial Press [1969, c1968] 64 p. illus. 23 cm. Bibliography: p. 62. A summary of the life and contributions of Charles Darwin, who was the first to set forth the theory of evolution through natural selection. [PZ10.G7Ch] 92 68-28735 3.50
1. Darwin, Charles Robert, 1809-1882—Juvenile literature. I. Hodges, David, illus. II. Title.

GREGOR, Arthur S. 575.0924 (B)
Charles Darwin [by] Arthur S. Gregor. [1st ed.] New York, Dutton [1966] 189p. illus., map, ports. 22cm. Bibl [QH31.D2G72] 66-11382 4.75
1. Darwin, Charles Robert, 1809-1882—Juvenile literature. I. Title.

HOPE, Charlotte 92
The young Charles Darwin. Illus. by A. Walter Atkinson. New York, Roy [1966, c. 1965] 127p. illus. 21cm. [QH31.D2H76] 65-22981 3.25 bds.,
1. Darwin, Charles Robert, 1809-1882—Juvenile literature. I. Title.

MELLERSH, H. E. L. 575'.00924 B
Charles Darwin, pioneer in the theory of evolution [by] H. E. L. Mellersh. New York, Praeger [1969, c1964] vii, 120 p. illus., map, ports. 22 cm. (Praeger pathfinder biographies) Bibliography: p. 117. A biography of scientist Charles Darwin, whose theory of natural selection in evolution was greatly influenced by the unique wildlife he encountered in the Galapagos Islands. [QH31.D2M4 1969] 92 68-55015 3.95
1. Darwin, Charles Robert, 1809-1882—Juvenile literature. 2. Beagle Expedition, 1831-1836—Juvenile literature. I. Title.

RIEDMAN, Sarah Regal, 1902- 925.9
Charles Darwin. Introd. by Bert James Loewenberg. [1st ed.] New York, Holt [1959] 192p. 21cm. [QH31.D2R48] 59-7570
1. Darwin, Charles Robert, 1809-1882—Juvenile literature. I. Title.

SHAPIRO, Irwin, 1911- 575'.0092'4 B
Darwin and the enchanted isles / by Irwin Shapiro ; illustrated by Christopher Spollen. New York : Coward, McCann & Geoghegan, [1977] p. cm. (A Science discovery book) Bibliography: p. Describes the events leading to Darwin's voyage on the Beagle and the subsequent theories on evolution he posed based mainly on observations made on the Galapagos Islands. [QH31.D2S5] 92 77-7544 ISBN 0-698-30679-1 lib. bdg. : 4.99
1. Darwin, Charles Robert, 1809-1882—Juvenile literature. 2. Evolution—History—Juvenile literature. 3. Naturalists—England—Biography—Juvenile literature. I. Spollen, Christopher J. II. Title. BIP

Darwin, Erasmus, 1731-1802.

KING-HELE, Desmond, 1927- 925.9
Erasmus Darwin. New York, Scribners [1964, c.1963] vii, 183p. ports. map. 22cm. Bibl. 64-10622 3.95
1. Darwein, Erasmus, 1731-1802 I. Title.

KING-HELE, Desmond, 1927- 500.9'2'4 B
Doctor of revolution : the life and genius of Erasmus Darwin / by Desmond King-Hele. London : Faber & Faber, 1977. 361 p., [6] leaves of plates : ill., map, ports. ; 23 cm. Includes index. Bibliography: p. [342]-343. [QH31.D3K49] 77-379522 ISBN 0-571-10781-8 : 11.95+
1. Darwin, Erasmus, 1731-1802. 2. Naturalists—England—Biography. 3. Physicians—England—Biography. I. Title.
Distributed by Faber & Faber, Salem, NH BIP

PEARSON, Hesketh, 1887- 925.9
Doctor Darwin. New York, Walker [1964] ix, 235p. port. 21cm. Bibl. 93-19203 5.00
1. Darwin, Erasmus, 1731-1802. I. Title. BIP

Dasburg, Andrew, 1887-

AMERICAN Federation of Arts. 759.13
Andrew Dasburg, by Jerry Bywaters. New York, Author, 1083 Fifth Ave. c.1959. 28p. (Bibl.: p.21-23) illus. (part col.) port. 18cm. 60-2726 2.00; .50 pap.,
1. Dasburg, Andrew. I. Bywaters, Jerry. II. Title.

DASBURG, Andrew, 1887- 759.13 B
Andrew Dasburg / Van Deren Coke, Andrew Dasburg. 1st ed. Albuquerque : University of New Mexico Press, c1979. p. cm. Includes bibliographical references and index. [ND237.D25A4 1979] 79-4931 ISBN 0-8263-0516-4 : 24.95
1. Dasburg, Andrew, 1887- 2. Painters—United States—Biography. I. Coke, Van Deren, 1921- joint author. BIP

Dashkova, Ekaterina Romanovna (Vorontsova) kniaginia, 1743-1810.

BRADFORD, Martha (Wilmot) 1775-1873. 914.7'03'7
The Russian journals of Martha and Catherine Wilmot [being an account by two Irish ladies of their adventures in Russia as guests of the celebrated Princess Daschkaw, containing vivid descriptions of contemporary court life and society, and lively anecdotes of many interesting historical characters, 1803-1808] Edited by the Marchioness of Londonderry & H. Montgomery Hyde. New York, Arno Press, 1971. xxvi, 423 p. illus., ports. 23 cm. (Russia observed) Reprint of the 1934 ed. [DK172.B7 1971] 71-115597 ISBN 0-405-03139-4
1. Dashkova, Ekaterina Romanovna (Vorontsova) kniaginia, 1743-1810. 2. Russia—Court and courtiers. 3. Russia—Social life and customs. 4. Russia—Description and travel. I. Wilmot, Catherine, 1773 (ca.)-1824. II. Londonderry, Edith Helen (Chaplin) Vane-Tempest-Stewart, marchioness of, 1878- joint ed. III. Hyde, Harford Montgomery, 1907- joint ed. IV. Title.

Datini, Francesco di Marco, 1335 (ca.)-1410.

ORIGO, Iris(Cutting) 1902- 923.845
The merchant of Prato, Francesco di Marco Datini, 1335-1410. [1st American ed.] New York, Knopf, 1957. xxii, 415, vii p. illus. (part col.) facsims. 24cm. Bibliography: p. 394-400. [HF3584.5.D3O7 1957] 56-8927
1. Datini, Francesco di Marco, 1335 (ca.)-1410. I. Title.

ORIGO, Iris Cutting, marchesa, 1902- 380.1'092'4 B
The merchant of Prato, Francesco di Marco Datini / Iris Origo. New York : Octagon Books, 1979, c1963. 389 p. ; 21 cm. Reprint of the rev. ed. published by Penguin Books, New York. Includes index. Bibliography: p. 347-354. [HF3584.5.D3O7 1979] 78-21174 ISBN 0-374-96149-2 lib.bdg. : 20.00
1. Datini, Francesco di Marco, 1335 (ca.)-1410. 2. Merchants—Italy—Biography. I. Title.

ORIGO, Iris(Cutting) marchesa, 1902- 923.845
The merchant of Prato, Francesco di Marco Datini, 1335-1410. [1st American ed.] New York, Knopf, 1957. xxii, 415, viip. illus. (part col.) facsims. 24cm. Bibliography: p. 394-400. [HF3584.5.D3O7 1957a] 56-8927
1. Datini, Francesco di Marco, 1335 (ca.)-1410. I. Title.

Daudet, Alphonse, 1840-1897.

DOBIE, G. Vera. 843'.8 B
Alphonse Daudet, by G. V. Dobie. [Folcroft, Pa.] Folcroft Library Editions, 1974. p. cm. Reprint of the 1949 ed. published by T. Nelson, London, New York. Bibliography: p. [PQ2216.Z5D6 1974] 74-19263 25.00
1. Daudet, Alphonse, 1840-1897. BIP

Daugherty, Harry Micajah, 1860-1941.

GIGLIO, James N., 1939- 973.91'092'4 B
H. M. Daugherty and the politics of expediency / James N. Giglio. Kent, Ohio : Kent State University Press, c1978. xii, 256 p. : port. ; 24 cm. Based on the author's thesis, Ohio State University. Includes index. Bibliography: p. [234]-246. [E664.D23G53] 78-17106 ISBN 0-87338-215-3 : 15.00
1. Daugherty, Harry Micajah, 1860-1941. 2. Politicians—United States—Biography. 3. Lawyers—United States—Biography. 4. United States—Politics and government—1865-1933. I. Title. BIP

Daugherty, Hugh.

DAUGHERTY, Hugh. 796.33'2'0924 B
Duffy: an autobiography [by] Duffy Daugherty with Dave Diles. Garden City, N.Y., Doubleday, 1974. 168 p. illus. 22 cm. [GV939.D34A32] 73-14044 ISBN 0-385-05821-7 6.95
1. Daugherty, Hugh. 2. Football. 3. Football coaching. I. Diles, Dave. II. Title.

Daughters of the American Revolution. Georgia. Nancy Hart Chapter, Milledgeville—History.

COOK, Anna Maria Green, 1844-1936. 975.8'573'03
History of Baldwin County, Georgia / by Anna Maria Green Cook ; with new index compiled by Mrs. Fred H. Hodges, Sr. Spartanburg, S.C. : Reprint Co., 1978. 521 p., [7] leaves of plates : ill. ; 24 cm. Reprint of the 1925 ed. published by Keys-Hearn, Anderson, S.C. Includes bibliographical references and index. [F292.B15C7 1978] 78-13226 ISBN 0-87152-279-9 : 22.50
1. Daughters of the American Revolution. Georgia. Nancy Hart Chapter, Milledgeville—History. 2. Baldwin Co., Ga.—History. 3. Baldwin Co., Ga.—Biography. 4. Baldwin Co., Ga.—Genealogy. I. Title. BIP

Daumier, Honore Victorin, 1808-1879.

DAUMIER, Honore Victorin, 1808-1879. v. 12
Honore Daumier, 1808-1879; text by Robert Rey. New York, H. N. Abrams [1959] 1 v. 39 col. plates (part fold.) 17 cm. (The Pocket library of great art) Includes bibliography. 67-89597
1. Daumier, Honore Victorin, 1808-1879. I. Rey, Robert, 1888- II. Title.

LARKIN, Oliver W. 709.24
Daumier, man of his time. New York. McGraw [c.1966] x, 245p. illus., facsim., col. plates, ports. 24cm. Bibl. [ND553.D24L37] 65-28729 9.95
1. Daumier, Honore Victorin, 1808-1879. I. Title.

LARKIN, Oliver W 709.24
Daumier, man of his time, by Oliver W. Larkin. New York, McGraw-Hill [1966] x, 245 p. illus., facsim., col. plates, ports. 24 cm. Bibliographical references included in "Notes" (p. 222-236) [ND553.D24L37] 65-28729
1. Daumier, Honore Victorin, 1808-1879. I. Title.

VINCENT, Howard Paton, 1904- 760'.0924
Daumier and his world [by] Howard P. Vincent. Evanston [Ill.] Northwestern University Press, 1968. xvii, 267 p. illus., facsims., ports. 28 cm. Bibliographical references included in "Notes" (p. 239-261) [ND553.D24V5] 66-12961
1. Daumier, Honore Victorin, 1808-1879. I. Title. BIP

Davaine, Casimir Joseph, 1812-1882.

THEODORIDES, Jean. 610'.9 S
Un grand medecin et biologiste, Casimir-Joseph Davaine (1812-1882) / par Jean Theodorides ; pref. de Jean Rostand. 1. ed. Oxford ; New York : Pergamon Press, 1968. 238 p., 12 leaves of plates : ill. ; 25 cm. (Analecta medico-historica ; 4) Includes index. Bibliography: p. 223-230.

[R131.A1A5 vol. 4] [R507.D38] 610'.92'4 B 75-20852 ISBN 0-08-003258-3
1. Davaine, Casimir Joseph, 1812-1882. I. Title. II. Series.

Daveko, ca. 1818-1897 or 8.

MCALLISTER, J. Gilbert, 1904- 917.64'0308 S
Daveko; Kiowa-Apache medicine man, by J. Gilbert McAllister. With a summary of Kiowa-Apache history and culture by W. W. Newcomb, Jr. Austin, Texas Memorial Museum, 1970. 61 p. illus., ports. 26 cm. (Bulletin of the Texas Memorial Museum, 17) Includes bibliographical references. [GN37.A8T4 no. 17] [E99.K52] 970.3 B 79-634489
1. Daveko, ca. 1818-1897 or 8. 2. Kiowa Apache Indians. I. Newcomb, William Wilmon, 1921- II. Title. III. Series: Texas. Memorial Museum, Austin. Bulletin 17

D'Avenant, William, Sir, 1606-1668.

HARBAGE, Alfred, 1901- 821'.4 B
Sir William Devenant, poet venturer, 1606-1668. New York, Octagon Books, 1971 [c1935] 317 p. port. 24 cm. Bibliography: p. 288-303. [PR2476.H3 1971] 75-120624 ISBN 0-374-93659-5
1. D'Avenant, William, Sir, 1606-1668. I. Title.

Davenport, Abraham, 1715-1789.

BROMLEY, J. Robert. 974.6'03'0924 B
Abraham Davenport, 1715 to 1789 : a study of the man / by J. Robert Bromley. Westport, Conn. : Technomic Pub. Co., c1976. 66 p. : ill. ; 19 cm. Includes bibliographical references. [F97.D26B76] 75-45773 ISBN 0-87762-187-X
1. Davenport, Abraham, 1715-1789.

Davenport, Edward Loomis, 1814-1877.

EDGETT, Edwin Francis, 1867-1946, ed. 792'.028'0924 B
Edward Loomis Davenport; a biography. New York, B. Franklin [1970] x, 145 p. illus., ports. 19 cm. (Burt Franklin research & source works series, 573. Theatre drama series, 12) Reprint of the 1901 ed. [PN2287.D3E3 1970] 78-130103 ISBN 0-8337-0996-8
1. Davenport, Edward Loomis, 1814-1877.

Davenport, Harold, 1907—

DAVENPORT, Harold, 1907- 512'.7'08
The collected works of Harold Davenport / edited by B. J. Birch, H. Halberstam, C. A. Rogers. London ; New York : Academic Press, 1977. 4 v. : ports. ; 24 cm. Includes bibliographical references. [QA241.D29] 76-1098 ISBN 0-12-099301-5 : 32.00 (vol. 1)
1. Davenport, Harold, 1907- 2. Numbers, Theory of—Collected works. I. Birch, Bryan John. II. Halberstam, Heini. III. Rogers, Claude Ambrose, 1920- IV. Title.

Davenport, Homer Calvin, 1867-1912.

HUOT, Leland. 741.5'973 B
Homer Davenport of Silverton; life of a great cartoonist, by Leland Huot and Alfred Powers. Bingen, Wash., West Shore Press [1973] 260, [189] p. illus. 26 cm. [NC1429.D3H86] 73-156268
1. Davenport, Homer Calvin, 1867-1912. I. Powers, Alfred, joint author.

Davenport, Ira Erastus, 1839-1911.

NICHOLS, Thomas Low, 1815-1901. 133.9'092'2
A biography of the brothers Davenport / T. L. Nichols. New York : Arno Press, 1976. p. cm. (The Occult) Reprint of the 1864 ed. published by Saunders, Otley, London. [BF1283.D3N6 1976] 75-36912 ISBN 0-405-07969-9 : 20.00
1. Davenport, Ira Erastus, 1839-1911. 2. Davenport, William Henry, 1841-1877. 3. Spiritualism. I. Title. II. Series: The Occult (New York, 1976-) BIP

David ben Samuel, ha-Levi, 1536 (ca.)-1667.

SCHOCHET, Elijah Judah. 296'.092'4
"TaZ", Rabbi David Halevi / by Elijah J. Schochet. New York : Ktav Pub. House, 1979. 79 p. ; 24 cm. Includes bibliographical references. [BM755.D33S36] 78-31657 7.50
1. David ben Samuel, ha-Levi, 1536 (ca.)-1667. 2. Rabbis—Poland—Biography. 3. Scholars, Jewish—Poland—Biography. I. Title.

David, Charles Weldell, 1885-

DAVID, Charles Wendell, 1885- Riggs, John Beverley, 1918- ed. 920.2
Charles Weldell David; scholar, teacher, librarian. [Edited by John Beverley Riggs] Philadelphia, 1965. 68 p. col. port. 23 cm. Contents.Introduction, by J. F. Lewis, Jr. -- The first half century, by C. Robbins. -- The Union Library Catalogue, by E. E. Campion. -- The peaceful revolution, by R. Hirsch and M. C. Nolan. -- Bibliographical vision, by V. W. Clapp. -- The library builder, by D. F. Cameron. -- The Longwood achievement, by R. D. Williams. -- The academic advisor, by H. C. Symons. -- Mentor at Mystic, by R. G. Albion. [Z720.D23C5] 65-19257
1. David, Charles Weldell, 1885- I. Title.

David, Connie.

WOLF, Bernard. 362.4'1'0926
Connie's new eyes / written and photographed by Bernard Wolf. 1st ed. Philadelphia : Lippincott, c1976. p. cm. [HV1792.D37W64] 76-17014 ISBN 0-397-31697-6 : 8.95
1. David, Connie. 2. Blind—Biography. 3. Guide dogs. I. Title. BIP

WOLF, Bernard. 362.4'1'0926
Connie's new eyes / written and photographed by Bernard Wolf 1st ed. New York : Pocket Books, 1978,c1976. 122p. : ill. ; 18 cm. (An Archway Paperback) [HV1792.D37W64] ISBN 0-671-29897-6 pbk. : 1.25
1. David, Connie. 2. Blind — Biography. 3. Guide dogs. I. Title.
L.C. card no. for 1976 Lippincott ed.: 76-17014

David, King of Israel.

BOSCH, Juan, Pres. Dominican Republic, 1909- 221.924
David, the biography of a king. Translated by John Marks. [1st American ed.] New York, Hawthorn Books [1966] 224 p. 21 cm. [BS580.D3B633 1966] 66-23401
1. David, King of Israel. I. Title.

CORVIN, R O. 221.92
David and his mighty men. Grand Rapids, Eerdmans, 1950. 175 p. 21 cm. [BS580.D3C65] 50-9186
1. David, King of Israel. 2. Bible. O. T.—Biog. I. Title. BIP

CORVIN, R. O. 221.92'2 B
David and his mighty men, by R. O. Corvin. Freeport, N.Y., Books for Libraries Press [1970, c1950] 175 p. 23 cm. (Biography index reprint series) [BS580.D3C65 1970] 74-136646
1. David, King of Israel. 2. Bible. O.T.—Biography. I. Title.

GIBBS, Paul T. 221.92'4 B
David and his mighty men [by] Paul T. Gibbs. Washington, Review and Herald Pub. Association [1970] 205 p. 22 cm. [BS580.D3G5] 79-102115
1. David, King of Israel. 2. Bible. O.T.—Biography. I. Title.

HAZEN, Barbara Shook. 221.95
David and Goliath. Pictures by Robert J. Lee. New York, Golden Press [1968] [26] p. col. illus. 33 cm. (A Big golden book) A retelling of the Bible story about a young boy whose faith in God helped him overcome the Philistine giant. [BS580.D3H3] AC 68
1. David, King of Israel. 2. Bible stories—Old Testament. I. Lee, Robert J., 1921- illus. II. Title.

HERCUS, John. 221.92'4
David. [Rev. ed.] Chicago, Inter-varsity Press [1968] ix, 136 p. 20 cm. At head of title: Another "casebook." [BS580.D3H44 1968] 68-28327 4.50
1. David, King of Israel. I. Title.

LANDAY, Jerry M. 222'.4'09
The House of David [by] Jerry M. Landay. [1st ed.] New York, Saturday Review Press; [distributed by] E. P. Dutton [1973, i.e.1974] 272 p. illus. 26 cm. Bibliography: p. 268. [BS580.D3L34] 73-87729 ISBN 0-8415-0290-0 14.95
1. David, King of Israel. I. Title.

MEYER, Frederick Brotherton, 1847-1929. 221.92
David: shepherd, psalmist, king Grand Rapids, Zondervan Pub. House [1953] 160p. 21cm. [BS580.D3M4 1953] 53-13074
1. David, King of Irsrel. I. Title.

PARMITER, Geoffrey de Clinton. 221.92
King David. [1st American ed.] New York, Nelson [1961, c1960] 195p. illus. 23cm. Bibliographical footnotes. [BS580.D3P3 1961] 61-2156
1. David, King of Israel. I. Title.

PARMITER, Geoffrey Vincent de Clinton 221.92
King David. New York, T. Nelson [1961, c.1960] 195p. front. Bibl. 3.95
1. David, King of Israel. I. Title.

PETERSHAM, Maud Fuller, 1890-1971. 221.92
David, from the story told in the First book of Samuel and the First book of Kings [by] Maud and Miska Petersham. New York, Macmillan, 1958. unpaged. illus. 24 cm. [BS580.D3P47 1958] 58-8035
1. David, King of Israel. I. Petersham, Miska, 1888-1960, joint author.

SCHMID, Evan, 1920- 221.92
David; the story of the King of Israel. Illus. by Brother Bernard Howard. Notre Dame, Ind., Dujarie Press [1953] 95p. illus. 24cm. [BS580.D3S35] 53-2903
1. David, King of Israel. I. Title.

SLAUGHTER, Frank G. 221.92
David: warrior and king. New York, Pocket Bks. [1963, c.1962] 389p. 17cm. (Permabk. ed. M5066) .50 pap.,
1. David, King of Israel. I. Title.

SLAUGHTER, Frank Gill, 1908- 221.92
David, warrior and king, a Biblical biography. [1st ed.] Cleveland, World Pub. Co. [1962] 411 p. 22 cm. [BS580.D3S48] 62-9050
1. David, King of Israel. I. Title.

WILSON, Clifford A. 221.92'4
A greater than David is here, by Clifford Wilson. [Melbourne, Australian Institute of Archaeology in association with Word of Truth Productions, 1968?] 32 p. 23 cm. (A Word of Truth production) [BS580.D3W53] 73-426936 unpriced
1. David, King of Israel. I. Australian Institute of Archaeology. II. Title.

David, King of Israel—Juvenile literature.

BEARMAN, Jane. 92
David. Author and illustrator: Jane Bearman. New York, Jonathan David [1965] 1 v. (unpaged) illus. 23 cm. (A Bible heroes library book) [BS580.D3B38] 65-21753
1. David, King of Israel—Juvenile literature. I. Title.

GROOM, Arthur William, 1898- 920
The young David. Illus. by Azpelicueta. New York, Roy [1963, c.1962] 127p. 21cm. 62-18558 3.00 bds.,
1. David, Kind of Israel—Juvenile literature. I. Title.

David, Mihaly, 1894-

KOVACH, Desider. 920
David Mihaly eletrajza. Aurora, Ill., 1959. 103p. illus. 20cm. [CT275.D23743K6] 61-28834
1. David, Mihaly, 1894- I. Title.

David (Name)—Juvenile literature.

GLAZER, Tom. 929.4
All about your name, David (Davies, Dave, Davis, Davidson, Davy) / by Tom Glazer ; illustrated by Demi. 1st ed. Garden City, N.Y. : Doubleday, c1978. 45 p. : ill. ; 22 cm. Discusses the name David and people of historical, literary, and theatrical significance who have held that name. [CS2391.D38G46] 77-82443 ISBN 0-385-06388-1 : 4.95. ISBN 0-385-06397-0 lib.bdg. : 5.90
1. David (Name)—Juvenile literature. 2. Biography—Miscellanea—Juvenile literature. I. Hitz, Demi. II. Title.

David, Saint, 6th cent.

RHYGYFARCH, 1056-1099 282'.0924
Life of St. David: the basic mid twelfthcentury Latin text with introduction, critical apparatus and translation by J. W. James. Cardiff, pub. on behalf of the Bd. of Celtic Studies by Wales Univ. Pr., 1967 xliv, 49p. plate (diagr.) 26cm. Tr. of Vita Davidis. [BX4700.D3R5 1967] 67-88094 6.00
1. David, Saint, 6th cent. I. James, John Williams. ed. II. Wales. University. Board of Celtic Studies. III. Title.
Distributor: Verry, Mystic, Conn.

David, Saint, 6th cent.—Juvenile literature

BETZ, Eva K. 922.1429
David. Drawings by R. M. Sax. New York, Sheed & Ward [c.1960] unpaged. illus. (part col.,) map 21cm. (A Patron saint book) 60-6288 2.00 half cloth,
1. David, Saint, 6th cent.—Juvenile literature I. Title.

BETZ, Eva (Kelly) 1897- 922.1429
David. Drawings by R. M. Sax. New York, Sheed & Ward [1960] unpaged. illus. 21cm. (A Patron saint book) [BX4700.D3B4] 60-6288
1. David, Saint, 6th cent.—Juvenile literature. I. Title.

Davidson, George, 1825-1911.

LEWIS, Oscar, 1893- 923.9
George Davidson, pioneer west coast scientist. Berkeley, University of California Press, 1954. viii, 146 p. illus., ports. (1 col.) maps (1 fold.) 24 cm. "Published writings of George Davidson": p. 135-140. [QB298.D3L4] 54-7628
1. Davidson, George, 1825-1911.

Davidson, John W., 1825-1881.

DAVIDSON, Homer K. 357'.1'0924 B
Black Jack Davidson, a cavalry commander on the Western frontier : the life of General John W. Davidson / by Homer K. Davidson. Glendale, Calif. : A. H. Clark Co., 1974. 273 p. : ill. ; 25 cm. (Frontier military series ; 10) Includes index. Bibliography: p. [260]-264. [E181.D252D38] 74-80944 ISBN 0-87062-109-2 : 15.50
1. Davidson, John W., 1825-1881. 2. United States—History, Military. I. Title. II. Series.

Davidson, John, 1857-1909—Biography.

MACLEOD, Roderick Donald, 1886- 821'.8 B
John Davidson : a study in personality / by R. D. Macleod. [Folcroft, Pa.] : Folcroft Library Editions, 1974. p. cm. Reprint of the 1957 ed. published by W. & R. Holmes (Books), Glasgow. Includes bibliographical references. [PR4525.D5Z73 1974] 74-20619 ISBN 0-8414-5944-4 lib.bdg.: 6.50
1. Davidson, John, 1857-1909—Biography.

Davidson. Randall Thomas, Abp. of Canterbury. 1848-1930.

BELL, George Kennedy Allen, Bp. of Chichester, 1883- 922.342
Randall Davidson. Archbishop of Canterbury. 3d ed. London. New York, Oxford University Press, 1952. xxxiii, 1441p. illus., ports. 23cm. [BX5199.D25B4 1952] 53-609
1. Davidson. Randall Thomas, Abp. of Canterbury. 1848-1930. I. Title.

Davidson, William,

DAVIDSON, William, 1918- 813'.5'4
Cut off; behind enemy lines in the Battle of the Bulge with two small children, Ernest Hemingway, and other assorted misanthropes [by] Bill Davidson. New York, Stein and Day [1972] 202 p. 22 cm. Autobiographical. [PS3554.A926Z5] 70-186495 ISBN 0-8128-1452-5 6.95
I. Title.

Davidson, William Lee, 1746-1781.

DAVIDSON, Chalmers Gaston, 1907- 923.573
Piedmont partisan; the life and times of Brigadier-General William Lee Davidson. Davidson, N. C., Davidson College, 1951. 190 p. 24 cm. Bibliography: p. 172-188. [E207.D3D3] 51-146824
1. Davidson, William Lee, 1746-1781. 2. U. S.—Hist.—Revolution—Campaigns and battles. I. Title.

DAVIDSON, Chalmers Gaston, 1907- 973.3'0924 B
Piedmont partisan; the life and times of Brigadier-General William Lee Davidson. [2d ed.] Davidson, N.C., Davidson College [1968] 190 p. 19 cm. Bibliography: p. 176-183. [E207.D3D3 1968] 71-514
1. Davidson, William Lee, 1746-1781. 2. United States—History—Revolution, 1775-1783—Campaigns and battles. I. Title.

Davie, William Richardson, 1756-1820.

ROBINSON, Blackwell P 923.273
William R. Davie. Chapel Hill, University of North Carolina Press [1957] 495p. illus. 24cm. Includes bibliography. [E302.6.D2R6] 57-4640
1. Davie, William Richardson, 1756-1820. I. Title.

ROBINSON, Blackwell Pierce. 923.273
William R. Davie. Chapel Hill, University of North Carolina Press [1957] 496 p. illus. 24 cm. Includes bibliography. [E302.6D2R6] 57-4640
1. Davie, William Richardson, 1756-1820. I. Title.

Davies, Celia, 1902-

DAVIES, Celia, 1902- 942.082'092'4 B
Far to go / by Celia Davies. Lavenham [Eng.] : Dalton, 1976. 171 p., [12] leaves of plates : ill., ports. ; 23 cm. Continues Clean clothes on Sunday. [CT788.D284A34] 77-351691 ISBN 0-900963-71-9 : £3.80
1. Davies, Celia, 1902- 2. England—Biography. I. Title.

Davies, David Richard,

DAVIES, David Richard, 1889-1958. 922.342
In search of myself; the autobiography of D. R. Davies. New York, Macmillan [c.] 1961. 223p. 61-15180 3.50
I. Title.

Davies, Emlyn, 1896-

DAVIES, Emlyn, 1896- 940.4'81'41
Taffy went to war / [by] Emlyn Davies. [Knutsford] : [The author], [1976] [3], 87 leaves ; 30 cm. Bibliography: leaf 87. [D640.D3227] 77-359739 ISBN 0-9505221-0-4 : £1.50
1. Davies, Emlyn, 1896- 2. Great Britain. Army. Royal Welsh Fusiliers—Biography. 3. European War, 1914-1918—Personal narratives, English. 4. European War, 1914-1918—Campaigns—Western. 5. Soldiers—Great Britain—Biography. I. Title.

Davies, Marion, 1897-1961.

DAVIES, Marion, 1897-1961 791.43'0280924 B
The times we had, life with William Randolph Hearst. Edited by Pamela Pfau and Kenneth S. Marx with a foreword by Orson Welles. New York, Bobbs-Merrill, [1975] 276 p., 27 cm. [PN2287.D315.A35] 75-7015 ISBN 0-672-52112-1 12.50
1. Davies, Marion, 1897-1961 2. Hearst, William Randolph, 1863-1951 I. Title.

GUILES, Fred Lawrence. 791.43'028'0924 B
Marion Davies; a biography. New York, McGraw-Hill [1972] xii, 419 p. illus. 24 cm. [PN2287.D315G8] 79-38936 ISBN 0-07-025114-2 8.95
1. Davies, Marion, 1897-1961.

Davies, Samuel, 1723-1761.

DAVIES, Samuel, 1723-1761. 253'.0924
The Reverend Samuel Davies abroad; the diary of a journey to England and Scotland, 1753-55. Edited, with an introd., by George William Pilcher. Urbana, University of Illinois Press, 1967. xv, 176 p. 24 cm. Bibliographical footnotes. [BX9225.D33A3] 67-12991
1. Great Britain—Description and travel—1701-1800. I. Pilcher, George William, ed. II. Title.

PILCHER, George William. 285'.1'0924 B
Samuel Davies; apostle of dissent in colonial Virginia. [1st ed.] Knoxville, University of Tennessee Press [1971] xi, 229 p. map, port. 24 cm. Bibliography: p. 196-214. [BX9225.D33P55] 77-134737 ISBN 0-87049-121-0 9.75
1. Davies, Samuel, 1723-1761.

Davies, Samuel Watts, 1776-1843.

STEVENS, Harry Robert, 1914- v. 12
Samuel Watts Davies and the Industrial Revolution in Cincinnati. [Cincinnati? 1961?] [95]-127 p. 24 cm. "Reprinted from the Ohio historical quarterly, volume 70, number 2, April 1961." Bibliographical footnotes. 67-95909
1. Davies, Samuel Watts, 1776-1843. 2. Cincinnati — Economic conditions. I. Title.

Davies, William Henry, 1871-1940.

STONESIFER, Richard James, 1922- 821.912
W. H. Davies, a critical biography. [1st Amer. ed] Middletown, Conn., Wesleyan Univ. Pr. [1965, c.1963] 256p. 23cm. Bibl. [PR6007.A8Z77] 65-21078 6.50
1. Davies, William Henry, 1871-1940. I. Title.

Davis, Angela Yvonne, 1944-

DAVIS, Angela Yvonne, 1944- 322.4'20924 B
Angela Davis - an autobiography [by] Angela Davis. New York, Bantam Books [1975, c1974] 399 p. 18 cm. [E185.97.D23A32] 1.95 (pbk.)
1. Davis, Angela Yvonne, 1944- I. Title.
L.C. card number for original ed.: 73-20580.

DAVIS, Angela Yvonne, 1944- 322.4'2'0924 B
Angela Davis—an autobiography [by] Angela Davis. [1st ed.] New York, Random House [1974] x, 400 p. 22 cm. "A Bernard Geis Associates book." [E185.97.D23A32] 73-20580 ISBN 0-394-48978-0 8.95
1. Davis, Angela Yvonne, 1944- I. Title.

NADELSON, Regina. 322.4'2'0924 B
Who is Angela Davis? The biography of a revolutionary. New York, P. H. Wyden [1972] xvi, 208 p. 22 cm. [E185.97.D23N32] 72-85993 5.95
1. Davis, Angela Yvonne, 1944- I. Title.

PARKER, J. A., 1936- 322.4'2'0924
Angela Davis: the making of a revolutionary [by] J. A. Parker. New Rochelle, N.Y., Arlington House [1973] 272 p. 24 cm. [E185.97.D23P37] 72-77642 ISBN 0-87000-175-2 9.95
1. Davis, Angela Yvonne, 1944- I. Title.

PEACE, friendship, 322.4'2'0924 B
solidarity: Angela Davis in the GDR. Dresden, Verlag Zeit im Bild [1969] 14 p. illus., ports. 20 cm. [E185.97.D23P42] 73-162721
1. Davis, Angela Yvonne, 1944-

Davis, Angela Yvonne, 1944- — Juvenile literature.

FINKE, Blythe Foote. 322.4'2'0924
Angela Davis: traitor or martyr of the freedom of expression. Charlotteville, N.Y., SamHar Press, 1972. 28 p. 22 cm. (Outstanding personalities, no. 28) Bibliography: p. 27-28. A biography of Angela Davis emphasizing the events leading to her trial on, and acquittal of, charges of murder, kidnapping, and criminal conspiracy. [E185.97.D23F56] 92 77-190246 ISBN 0-87157-528-0 1.98
1. Davis, Angela Yvonne, 1944- —Juvenile literature. I. Title.
Pap. .98, ISBN 0-87157-028-9.

Davis, Arthur Hoey, 1899-1935—Biography.

DAVIS, Eric Drayton, 1908- 823 B
The life and times of Steele Rudd : creator of On our selection, Dad and Dave / by his son Eric Drayton Davis. Melbourne : Lansdowne Press, 1976. 223 p. : ill. ; 23 cm. Bibliography: p. 223. [PR9619.3.D3Z6] 76-375041 ISBN 0-7018-0329-0
1. Davis, Arthur Hoey, 1899-1935—Biography. 2. Authors, Australian—20th century—Biography. I. Title.

Davis, Benjamin Jefferson,

DAVIS, Benjamin Jefferson, 1903-1964. 335.43'0924 B
Communist councilman from Harlem; autobiographical notes written in a Federal penitentiary. [1st ed.] New York, International Publishers [1969] 218 p. illus., ports. 21 cm. [HX84.D28A3] 69-17615 6.95
I. Title.

Davis, Bette, 1908-

DAVIS, Bette, 1908- 927.92
The lonely life; an autobiography. New York, Lancer [1963, c.1962] 224p. 18cm. (73-419) .60 pap.,
I. Title.

DAVIS, Bette, 1908- 927.92
The lonely life; an autobiography. New York, Putnam [1962] 315 p. illus. 22 cm. [PN2287.D32A3] 62-7344
I. Title.

STINE, Whitney, 1930- 791.43'028'0924
Mother Goddam : the story of the career of Bette Davis / by Whitney Stine ; with a running commentary by Bette Davis. New York : Hawthorn Books, [1974] 374 p. : ill. ; 25 cm. Includes index. Filmography: p. 343-360. [PN2287.D32S7 1974] 73-10265 12.95
1. Davis, Bette, 1908- I. Davis, Bette, 1908- II. Title.

VERMILYE, Jerry 791.43'028'0924
Bette Davis / by Jerry Vermilye ; general editor: Ted Sennett. New York : Galahad Books, [1974] c1973. 158 p. : ill. ; 22 cm. (The Pictorial treasury of film stars) Includes index. Bibliography: p. 134. [PN2287.D32V4 1974] 73-90220 ISBN 0-88365-167-X : 4.95
1. Davis, Bette, 1908- BIP

Davis, Clarence Augustus, 1886-1935.

DAVIS, Claude William, 1886- 920
'Gone are the days'; the true story of twin boys, Claude W. Davis and Clarence A. Davis, who were born and reared on a cotton plantation in Crittenden County, Arkansas, in the Delta county. Little Rock, Ark., Printed by Democrat Print. and Litho Co., 1954. 90p. 23cm. [CT275.D273D3] 55-24194
1. Davis, Clarence Agustus, 1886-1935. I. Title.

Davis, Clive.

DAVIS, Clive. 338.4'7'7899120924 B
Clive: inside the record business, by Clive Davis with James K. Willwerth. New York, W. Morrow, 1975 [c1974] 300 p. illus. 24 cm. [ML429.D36A3] 74-12246 ISBN 0-688-02872-1
1. Davis, Clive. 2. Phonorecords—Industry and trade—United States. 3. Music, Popular (Songs, etc.)—United States. I. Willwerth, James, joint author. II. Title.

Davis, Colin, 1927-

BLYTH, Alan. 785'.092'4 B
Colin Davis. New York, Drake Publishers [1973] 64 p. illus. 25 cm. Discography: p. 60-64. [ML422.D29B6] 72-6428 ISBN 0-87749-365-0 5.95
1. Davis, Colin, 1927-

Davis, David, 1815-1886.

KING, Willard Leroy, 1893- 923.473
Lincoln's manager, David Davis. Cambridge, Harvard University Press, 1960. 383p. illus. 24cm. Includes bibliography. [E415.9.D25K5] 60-13290
1. Davis, David, 1815-1886. 2. Lincoln, Abraham, Pres. U. S., 1809-1865. 3. U. S.— Pol. & govt.—1849-1877. 4. Illinois—Soc. life & cust. I. Title.

Davis, Drew, 1951-

DAVIS, Drew, 1951- 917.5'03'40924 B
On the other side of anger / Drew Davis. Atlanta : John Knox Press, [1974] 123 p. ; 21 cm. [CT275.D2735A35] 74-7618 ISBN 0-8042-1046-2 4.95
1. Davis, Drew, 1951- I. Title.
Pbk. 2.50; ISBN 0-8042-1047-0. **BIP**

Davis, Elmer Holmes, 1890-1958.

BURLINGAME, Roger, 1889- 928.1
Don t let them scare you the life and times of Elmer Davis. [1st ed.] Philadelphia, Lippincott [1961] 352p. illus. 22cm. [PN4874.D36B8] 61-8669
1. Davis, Elmer Holmes, 1890-1958. I. Title.

BURLINGAME, Roger [William Roger Burlingame] 1889- 928.1
Don't let them scare you; the life and times of Elmer Davis. Philadelphia, Lippincott [c.1961] 352p. front. port. 61-8669 5.95
1. Davis, Elmer Holmes, 1890-1958. I. Title.

Davis, Frances Elliott—Juvenile literature.

PITRONE, Jean Maddern. 610.73'0924 B
Trailblazer; Negro nurse in the American Red Cross. [1st ed.] New York, Harcourt, Brace & World [1969] 191 p. port. 21 cm. A biography of the woman whose determination to help relieve the physical pains of her people led her to become the first Negro nurse enrolled by the American Red Cross. [RT37.D3P5] 92 69 11600 1.25
1. Davis, Frances Elliott—Juvenile literature. 2. Negro nurses—Juvenile literature. I. Title.

Davis, Francis W., 1887-

BRANCH, Houston, 1903- 629.2'0924 B
The unreasonable American: Francis W. Davis, inventor of power steering, by Houston Branch & Wendell Smith. Washington, Acropolis Books [1968] 215 p. illus. 24 cm. (The Academy of Applied Science series) Bibliography: p. 207-208. [TL140.D35B7] 68-9034 6.95
1. Davis, Francis W., 1887- I. Smith, Wendell, joint author. II. Title. III. Series: Academy of Applied Science. The Academy of Applied Science series

Davis, James Wagner, 1886-1955.

BLYTHE, Le Gette, 1900- 926.1
James W. Davis, North Carolina surgeon. With a foreword by Johnson J. Hayes. Charlotte, W. Loftin, 1956. 227p. illus. 23cm. [R154.D288B5] 57-1474
1. Davis, James Wagner, 1886-1955. I. Title.

BLYTHE, Le Gette, 1900- 926.1
James W. Davis, North Carolina surgeon. With a foreword by Johnson J. Hayes. Charlotte, W. Loftin, 1956. 227p. illus. 23cm. [R154.D288B5] 57-1474

1. Davis, James Wagner, 1886-1955. I. Title.

Davis, Jeff, 1883-

DAVIS, Jeff, 1883- v. 12
Devil on wheels. Cincinnati, J. Davis, c1962- v. illus. 63-8043
1. Davis, Jeff, 1883- I. Title.

Davis, Jefferson, 1808-1889.

CANFIELD, Cass, 973.7'13'0924 B
1897-
The iron will of Jefferson Davis / Cass Canfield. 1st ed. New York : Harcourt Brace Jovanovich, c1978. xiv, 146 p. : ill. ; 21 cm. Includes index. Bibliography: p. 137-139. [E467.1.D26C3] 78-53908 ISBN 0-15-145642-9 : 7.95
1. Davis, Jefferson, 1808-1889. 2. Statesmen—United States—Biography. 3. Confederate States of America—Presidents—Biography. I. Title. **BIP**

DAVIS, Jefferson, 973.7'13'0924 B
1808-1889.
Jefferson Davis, constitutionalist; his letters, papers, and speeches, collected and edited by Dunbar Rowland. Jackson, Printed for the Mississippi Dept. of Archives and History, 1923. [New York, AMS Press, 1973] 10 v. illus. 23 cm. Bibliography: v. 10, p. 283-289. [E467.1.D2594 1973] 71-163682 ISBN 0-404-02000-3 275.00
1. Davis, Jefferson, 1808-1889. 2. Confederate States of America—History—Sources. I. Rowland, Dunbar, 1864-1937, ed.
Ten volume set 27.50 ea. **BIP**

DAVIS, Jefferson, 1808- 973.80924
1889.
Private letters, 1823-1889. Selected and edited by Hudson Strode. [1st ed.] New York, Harcourt, Brace & World [1966] xxi, 580 p. port. 24 cm. [E664.D28A4] 66-22288
I. Strode, Hudson, 1893- ed.

DAVIS, Varina 973.71'3'0924 B
(Howell) 1826-1906.
Jefferson Davis: ex-President of the Confederate States of America; a memoir by his wife. Freeport, N.Y., Books for Libraries Press [1971] 2 v. illus. 23 cm. Reprint of the 1890 ed. [E467.1.D26D3 1971] 77-175696 ISBN 0-8369-6611-2
1. Davis, Jefferson, 1808-1889.

DODD, William Edward, 973.7130924
1869-1940
Jefferson Davis. New York, Russell & Russell, 1966. 396p. port. 23cm. First pub. in 1907. Bibl. [E467.1.D26D8] 65-17888 8.50
1. Davis, Jefferson, 1808-1889. I. Title.

ECKENRODE, 973.71'3'0924 B
Hamilton James, 1881-
Jefferson Davis, president of the South, by Hamilton J. Eckenrode. Freeport, N.Y., Books for Libraries Press [1971] 371 p. 23 cm. Reprint of the 1923 ed. Includes bibliographical references. [E487.E2 1971] 78-165627 ISBN 0-8369-5934-5
1. Davis, Jefferson, 1808-1889. 2. Confederate States of America—History. 3. United States—History—Civil War, 1861-1865. 4. United States—History—Civil War, 1861-1865—Causes. I. Title. **BIP**

LANGHEIN, Eric. 923.273
Jefferson Davis, patriot; a biography, 1808-1865. [1st ed.] New York, Vantage Press [1962] 101p. 21cm. Includes bibliography. [E467.1.D26L3] 62-1264
1. Davis, Jefferson, 1808-1889. I. Title.

LOUISIANA Historical 973.8'0924
Association.
Calendar of the Jefferson Davis postwar manuscripts. New York, B. Franklin [1970] ii l., 325 p. 29 cm. (American classics in history & social science, 121) (Burt Franklin bibliography & reference series, 329.) Reprint of the 1943 ed. Includes bibliographical references. [CD3047.L6 1970] 70-114342
1. United States—History—Civil War, 1861-1865—Sources. 2. Confederate States of America—History—Sources. 3. Manuscripts—United States—Catalogs. I. Davis, Jefferson, 1808-1889. II. Title.

POLLARD, Edward 973.71'3'0924 B
Alfred, 1831-1872.
Life of Jefferson Davis, with a secret history of the Southern Confederacy, gathered "behind the scenes in Richmond." Containing curious and extraordinary information of the principal southern characters in the late war, in connection with President Davis, and in relation to the various intrigues of his administration. Freeport, N.Y., Books for Libraries Press [1969] viii, 536 p. port. 23 cm. (Select bibliographies reprint series) Reprint of the 1869 ed. [E467.1.D26P5 1969] 75-95074
1. Davis, Jefferson, 1808-1889. 2. Confederate States of America—History. I. Title.

STRODE, Hudson, 973.7130924 B
1892-
Jefferson Davis. [1st ed.] New York, Harcourt, Brace [1955-64] 3 v. ports. 25 cm. Contents.Contents.—[1] American patriot, 1808-1861.—[2] Confederate President.—[3] Tragic hero, the last twenty-five years, 1864-1889. Includes bibliographies. [E467.1.D26S73] 64-18295
1. Davis, Jefferson, 1808-1889.

STRODE, Hudson, 1893- 923.273
Jefferson Davis. [1st ed.] New York, Harcourt, Brace [1955- v. ports. 25cm. 'Sources and notes on sources': v. 1. p.436-452. Contents.[1] American patriot, 1808-1861. [E467.1.D26S73] 55-5322
1. Davis, Jefferson, 1808-1889. I. Title.

STRODE, Hudson, 1893- 923.273
Jefferson Davis [1st ed.] New York, Harcourt, Brace [1955-64] 3 v. ports. 25 cm. Contents.Contents. -- [1] American patriot. 1806-1861. -- [2] Confederate President. -- [3] Tragic hero, the last twenty-five years, 1864-1889. Includes bibliographies. [E467.1.D26S73] 64-18295
1. Davis, Jefferson, 1808-1889. I. Title.

Davis, Jefferson, 1808-1889—Juvenile literature.

GREEN, Margaret. 92
President of the Confederacy: Jefferson Davis. New York, J. Messner [1963] 191 p. 22 cm. Includes bibliography. [E467.1.D26G73] 63-8650
1. Davis, Jefferson, 1808-1889—Juvenile literature. I. Title.

LEE, Susan. 973.7'13'0924 B
Jefferson Davis / by Susan Dye Lee ; illustrated by Len W. Meents. Chicago : Childrens Press, c1978. 44 p. : col. ill. ; 24 cm. (Heroes of the Civil War) A brief biography of the statesman who served as President of the Confederate States of America during the Civil War. [E467.1.D26L4] 77-20054 ISBN 0-516-04702-7 lib.bdg. : 6.60
1. Davis, Jefferson, 1808-1889—Juvenile literature. 2. Statesmen—United States—Biography—Juvenile literature. 3. Confederate States of America—History—Juvenile literature. I. Meents, Len W. II. Title. III. Series.

MARTIN, Patricia Miles 92
Jefferson Davis. Illus. by Salem Tamer. New York, Putnam [c.1966] 63p. col. illus. 23cm. (See and read beginning to read biog.) [E467.1.D26M34] 66-14331 2.29 lib. ed.,
1. Davis, Jefferson, 1808-1889—Juvenile literature. I. Title.

TATE, Allen, 973.71'3'0924 B
1899-
Jefferson Davis. New York, Putnam [1969] 189 p. 22 cm. (Lives to remember) A biography of the man who was a hero to the Confederacy and a traitor to the Union because of his leadership of the Southern States during the Civil War. [E467.1.D26T2] 92 69-11607 3.49
1. Davis, Jefferson, 1808-1889—Juvenile literature. I. Title. **BIP**

Davis, Jerome,

DAVIS, Jerome, 285'.80924 (B)
1891-
A life adventure for peace; an autobiography. Foreword by James A. Pike. [1st ed.] New York, Citadel Press [1967] xiii, 208 p. 21 cm. 67-18083
I. Title.

DAVIS, Jerome, 285'.80924(B)
1891-
A life adventure for peace: an autobiography: Foreword by Mames A. Pike. [1st ed.] New York, Citadel [1967] xiii, 208p. 21cm. [BX7260.D34A3] 67-18083 2.45 pap.,
I. Title.

DAVIS, Jerome, 1891- 920.02
World leaders I have known. New York, Citadel Press [1963] 191 p. 21 cm. Biography -- 20th cent. [D412.D3] 63-16726
I. Title. **BIP**

Davis, Jimmie, 1900-

WEILL, Gus. 784'.092'4 B
You are my sunshine : the Jimmie Davis story : an affectionate biography / by Gus Weill. Waco, Tex. : Word Books, c1977. 187 p. : ill. ; 23 cm. [ML420.D315W4] 76-48546 ISBN 0-87680-497-0 : 7.95
1. Davis, Jimmie, 1900- 2. Country musicians—United States—Biography. I. Title.

Davis, Joe.

DAVIS, Joe. 794.7'3'0924 B
The breaks came my way / Joe Davis. London : W. H. Allen, 1976. xv, 240 p., [12] leaves of plates : ill. ; 23 cm. [GV900.S6D27] 76-373676 ISBN 0-491-01686-7 : £3.95
1. Davis, Joe. 2. Snooker. 3. Billiard players—England—Biography. I. Title.

Davis, John William, 1873-1955.

HARBAUGH, William 340'.092'4 B
Henry, 1920-
Lawyer's lawyer : the life of John W. Davis / William H. Harbaugh. Oxford ; New York : Oxford University Press, 1978, c1973. xviii, 648 p. ; 21 cm. (A Galaxy book ; GB 526) "The text of this edition is identical in substance to the original; only misprints and factual errors have been corrected." Includes bibliographical references and index. [KF373.D387H37 1978] 77-13267 ISBN 0-19-502354-4 pbk. : 5.95
1. Davis, John William, 1873-1955. 2. Lawyers—United States—Biography. I. Title. **BIP**

HARBAUGH, William 340'.092'4 B
Henry, 1920-
Lawyer's lawyer; the life of John W. Davis [by] William H. Harbaugh. New York, Oxford University Press, 1973. xvi, 648 p. illus. 24 cm. Includes bibliographical references. [KF373.D387H37] 73-83938 ISBN 0-19-501699-8 15.00
1. Davis, John William, 1873-1955. I. Title.

Davis, Loyal Edward, 1896-

DAVIS, Loyal Edward, 617'.092'4 B
1896-
A surgeon's odyssey [by] Loyal Davis. [1st ed.] Garden City, N.Y., Doubleday, 1973. 336 p. 22 cm. Autobiography. [R154.D294A33] 73-79659 ISBN 0-385-02230-1 8.95
1. Davis, Loyal Edward, 1896- 2. Surgeons—Correspondence, reminiscences, etc. I. Title.

Davis, Mabel Lancaster

DAVIS, Mabel Lancaster 920.7
Me and Jim and our folks. New York, Pageant [c.1963] 105p. 21cm. 3.00
I. Title.

Davis, Miles, 1926-

COLE, Bill, 1937- 788'.1'0924 B
Miles Davis: a musical biography. New York, W. Morrow, 1974. 256 p. music. 22 cm. A revision of the author's thesis (M.A.), University of Pittsburgh. "Recording sessions": p. 169-198. Bibliography: p. 201-218. [ML419.D39C6] 74-2405 ISBN 0-688-00203-X 7.95
1. Davis, Miles. 2. Jazz music. **BIP**

MILES Davis. v. 12
New York, A. S. Barnes [1961] 89, [1]p. ports. 21cm. (Kings of jazz) (Series. Perpetua book, P-4054) Perpetua book, P-4054. Discography: p.81-[90]
1. Davis, Miles, 1926- I. James, Michael. II. Series. **BIP**

Davis, Noah, 1803 or 4-

DAVIS, Noah, 286'.1'0924 B
1803or4-
A narrative of the life of Rev. Noah Davis, a colored man, written by himself. [Philadelphia, Rhistoric Publications, 1969] 86 p. illus., port. 21 cm. (Afro-American history series) (Rhistoric publications, no. 213.) Cover title. Reprint of the 1859 ed., with "Noah Davis and the Narrative of restraint; a bibliographical note, by Maxwell Whiteman" added. [E444.D37 1969] 74-77050
1. Davis, Noah, 1803 or 4- 2. Slavery in the United States—Personal narratives. 3. Freedmen in Maryland. I. Title.

Davis, Ossie—Juvenile literature.

FUNKE, Lewis, 1912- 812'.5'4 B
The curtain rises; the story of Ossie Davis. Illustrated by H. B. Vestal. New York, Grosset & Dunlap [1971] 64 p. col. illus. 18 x 24 cm. "A New York times book." A biography of the black playwright and actor whose works and performances promoted pride in being black. [PS3507.A7444Z7] 92 75-145733 ISBN 0-448-02465-9 2.95
1. Davis, Ossie—Juvenile literature. I. Vestal, Herman B., illus. II. Title.

Davis, Philip,

DAVIS, Philip, 1876- 920
And crown thy good. New York, Philosophical Library [1952] 239 p. 21 cm. Autobiography. [CT275.D284A3] 52-7363
I. Title.

Davis, Richard Harding, 1864-1916.

LANGFORD, Gerald, 1911- 928.1
The Richard Harding Davis years: a biography of a mother and son. [1st ed.] New York, Holt, Rinehart and Winston [1961] 336p. illus. 22cm. [PS1523.L3] 61-5801
1. Davis. Richard Harding, 1864-1916. 2. Davis, Rebecca (Harding) 1831-1910. I. Title.

MINER, Lewis S 928.1
Front lines and hedlines; the story of Richard Hardiing Davis. New York, J. Messner [1959] 192p. 22cm. Based on the author's Mightier than the sword. [PS1523.M48] 59-7137
1. Davis, Richard Harding, 1864-1916. I. Title.

Davis, Richard Harding, 1864-1916—Correspondence.

DAVIS, Richard 070'.92'4 B
Harding, 1864-1916.
The adventures and letters of Richard Harding Davis. Charles Belmont Davis, editor. New York, Beekman Publishers, 1974 [c1917] viii, 417 p. illus. 23 cm. (American newspapermen, 1790-1933) Reprint of the ed. published by Scribner, New York. [PS1523.A43 1974] 74-769 ISBN 0-8464-0024-3 18.50
1. Davis, Richard Harding, 1864-1916—Correspondence. 2. Davis, Richard Harding, 1864-1916—Biography. I. Davis, Charles Belmont, 1866-1926, ed. **BIP**

Davis, Samuel, 1842-1863.

WHITLEY, Edythe 973.78'6'0924 B
Johns (Rucker) 1900-
Sam Davis, hero of the Confederacy, 1842-1863. Coleman's Scouts. [1st ed.] Nashville [Blue and Gray Press] 1971. ix, 251 p.

illus. 24 cm. Bibliography: p. 235-238. [E608.D25] 73-30852
1. Davis, Samuel, 1842-1863.

Davis, Stephen Chapin, 1833-1856.

DAVIS, Stephen Chapin, 1833-1856. 979.4'04'0924
California gold rush merchant; the journal of Stephen Chapin Davis. Edited by Benjamin B. Richards. Westport, Conn., Greenwood Press [1974, c1956] xvii, 124 p. map. 23 cm. Reprint of the ed. published by Huntington Library, San Marino, Calif., in series: Huntington Library publications. Includes bibliographical references. [F865.D27 1974] 73-21490 ISBN 0-8371-6408-7 9.25
1. Davis, Stephen Chapin, 1833-1856. 2. California—Gold discoveries. 3. Voyages to the Pacific Coast. I. Title. II. Series: Henry E. Huntington Library and Art Gallery, San Marino, Calif. Huntington Library publications. BIP

Davis, Stuart, 1894-

STUART Davis. v. 12
New York, Grove Press [1960] 64p. illus. (part col.) port. 21cm.
1. Davis, Stuart, 1894- I. Blesh, Rudi, 1899-

Davis, Tommy, 1939- —Juvenile literature.

RUSSELL, Patrick. 796.357'0924
The Tommy Davis story. [1st ed.] Garden City, N.Y., Doubleday [1969] 143 p. illus. 22 cm. (Doubleday signal books) A biography of the boy from a Brooklyn slum whose major league baseball career opened up a new world for him. [GV865.D3R8] 92 69-11007 3.50
1. Davis, Tommy, 1939- —Juvenile literature. I. Title.

Davis, Varina (Howell) 1826-1906.

ROSS, Ishbel, 1897- 920.7
First lady of the South; the life of Mrs. Jefferson Davis. [1st ed.] New York, Harper [1958] 475 p. illus. 22 cm. Includes bibliography. [E467.1.D27R6] 57-8180
1. Davis, Varina Howell, 1826-1906. 2. Davis, Jefferson, 1808-1889. I. Title. BIP

ROSS, Ishbel, 1897- 973.7'13'0924 B
First lady of the South; the life of Mrs. Jefferson Davis. Westport, Conn., Greenwood Press [1973, c1958] xii, 475 p. illus. 22 cm. Reprint of the 1st ed. published by Harper, New York. Bibliography: p. 452-458. [E467.1.D27R6 1973] 73-7381 ISBN 0-8371-6927-5 17.50
1. Davis, Varina (Howell) 1826-1906. 2. Davis, Jefferson, 1808-1889. I. Title.

Davis, Westmoreland.

KIRBY, Jack Temple. 975.5'04'0924 B
Westmoreland Davis: Virginia planter-politician, 1859-1942 Charlottesville, University Press of Virginia [1968] viii, 215 p. ports. 24 cm. "Essay on sources": p. [200]-210. [F231.D3K5] 68-22730
1. Davis, Westmoreland.

Davis, William Hardy.

†DAVIS, William, Hardy. 320.9'763'3506 B
Aiming for the jugular in New Orleans / by William Hardy Davis. 1st ed. Port Washington, N.Y. : Ashley Books, c1976. p. 11-232 ; 23 cm. [F379.N557D38 1976] 75-16561 ISBN 0-87949-035-7 : 8.95
1. Davis, William Hardy. 2. Garrison, Jim, 1921- 3. New Orleans—Politics and government. 4. Bail bondsmen—Louisiana—New Orleans—Biography. 5. New Orleans—Biography. I. Title. BIP

Davis, William Heath, 1822-1909.

ROLLE, Andrew F. 923.973
An American in California; the biography of William Heath Davis, 1822-1909. San Marino, Calif., Huntington Library, 1956. 155p. illus. 25cm. (Huntington Library publications) [F864.D27R6] 56-10064
1. Davis, William Heath, 1822-1909. I. Title.

Davison, Frank Dalby, 1893-1970—Biography.

WEBSTER, Owen. 823 B
The outward journey / Owen Webster. Canberra ; Norwalk, Conn. : Australian National University Press, 1978. xiii, 258 p. : ill. ; 25 cm. Includes bibliographical references. [PR9619.3.D35Z94] 78-54743 ISBN 0-7081-0830-X : 23.95
1. Davison, Frank Dalby, 1893-1970—Biography. 2. Authors, Australian—20th century—Biography. I. Title.
Publisher's address: 25 Van Zant St., Norwalk, CT 06855 BIP

Davison, Frank Elon,

DAVISON, Frank Elon, 1887- 922.673
Thru the rear-view mirror. St. Louis, Bethany Press [1955] 160p. illus. 23cm. [BX7343.D29A3] 55-9479
I. Title.

Davison, Henry Pomeroy, 1867-1922.

LAMONT, Thomas William, 1870-1948. 332.1'092'4 B
Henry P. Davison : the record of a useful life / Thomas W. Lamont. New York : Arno Press, 1975, c1933. xxii, 373 p., [16] leaves of plates : ill. ; 23 cm. (Wall Street and the security markets) Reprint of the ed. published by Harper, New York. [HG2463.D3L3 1975] 75-2644 ISBN 0-405-06969-3 : 26.00
1. Davison, Henry Pomeroy, 1867-1922. 2. Bankers—United States—Biography. I. Title. II. Series. BIP

Davison, Jaquie, 1938-

DAVISON, Jaquie, 1938- 616.9'94'00926 B
Cancer winner : how I purged myself of melanoma / by Jaquie Davison. Pierce City, MO : Pacific Press, c1977. vii, 195 p. ; 23 cm. [RC262.D43] 77-81564 pbk. : 4.95
1. Davison, Jaquie, 1938- 2. Melanoma—Biography. I. Title.

Davison, William, 1781-1858.

ISAAC, Peter C. G. 655.1'428'2
William Davison of Alnwick: pharmacist and printer 1781-1858 [by] Peter C. G. Isaac. Oxford, Clarendon P., 1968. ix, 40 p. 2 plates, illus., facsims. 22 cm. Bibliography: p. 40. [Z232.D25I8] 68-114665 45/-
1. Davison, William, 1781-1858. 2. Printing—History—Alnwick, Eng.

Davout, Louis Nicolas, duc d'Auerstadt et prince d'Eckmuhl, 1770-1823.

GALLAHER, John G. 355.3'31'0924 B
The iron marshal : a biography of Louis N. Davout / John G. Gallaher. Carbondale : Southern Illinois University Press, c1976. xi, 420 p. : ill. ; 24 cm. Includes index. Bibliography: p. 397-406. [DC198.D2G34] 75-37956 ISBN 0-8093-0691-3 : 15.00
1. Davout, Louis Nicolas, duc d'Auerstadt et prince d'Eckmuhl, 1770-1823. I. Title. BIP

Davy, Humphry, Sir, bart., 1778-1829.

JONES, Henry Bence, 1814-1873. 506'.241
The Royal Institution, its founder and its first professors / by Bence Jones. New York : Arno Press, 1975. x, 431 p. ; 21 cm. (History, philosophy, and sociology of science) Reprint of the 1871 ed. published by Longmans, Green, London. Includes index. [Q41.R88J7 1975] 74-26270 ISBN 0-405-06598-1 : 25.00
1. Royal Institution of Great Britain, London. 2. Rumford, Benjamin Thompson, Sir, count, 1753-1814. 3. Davy, Humphry, Sir, bart., 1778-1829. 4. Young, Thomas, 1773-1829. I. Title. II. Series.

WILLIAMS-ELLIS, Amabel, 1894- 925.4
Laughing gas and safety lamp; the story of Sir Humphry Davy, by Amabel Williams-Ellis and Euan Cooper Willis. Illustrated by Serena Chance. New York, Abelard-Schuman [1954] 182p. illus. 22cm. [QD22.D3W5] 54-10216
1. Davy, Sir Humphry, bart, 1778-1829. I. Cooper-Willis, Euan Stewart, joint author. II. Title.

Dawes, Charles Gates, 1865-1951.

TIMMONS, Bascom Nolly, 1890- 923.273
Portrait of an American: Charles G. Dawes. [1st ed.] New York, Holt [1953] 344p. illus. 24cm. [E748.D22T55] 53-5274
1. Dawes, Charles Gates, 1865-1951. I. Title.

Dawson, John William, Sir, 1820-1899.

O'BRIEN, Charles F. 550'.924 B
Sir William Dawson, a life in science and religion [by] Charles F. O'Brien. Philadelphia, American Philosophical Society, 1971. vii, 207 p. 24 cm. (Memoirs of the American Philosophical Society, v. 84) Bibliography: p. 198-204. [Q11.P612 vol. 84] [QE22.D3] 71-153381
1. Dawson, John William, Sir, 1820-1899. I. Title. II. Series: American Philosophical Society, Philadelphia. Memoirs, v. 84

Dawson, Joseph Martin,

DAWSON, Joseph Martin, 1879- 922.673
A thousand months to remember, an autobiography. Waco, Tex., Baylor Univ. Pr. [c.1964] Pr. [c.1964] xi, 280p. illus., ports. 24cm. 64-57109 4.95
I. Title.

DAWSON, Joseph Martin, 1879- 922.673
A thousand months to remember, an autobiography. Waco, Tex., Baylor University Press [1964] xi, 280 p. illus., ports. 24 cm. 64-57109
I. Title.

Dawson, Len.

BORTSTEIN, Larry. 796.332'0924
Len Dawson: superbowl quarterback. New York, Grosset & Dunlap [1970] 180 p. 18 cm. (Tempo books, 5352) [GV939.D35B6] 70-123461 0.95
1. Dawson, Len. I. Title.

DAWSON, Len. 796.332'0924 B
Len Dawson; pressure quarterback [by] Len Dawson with Lou Sahadi. [1st ed.] New York, Cowles Book Co. [1970] 245 p. ports. 22 cm. [GV939.D35A3 1970] 74-124411 5.95
I. Sahadi, Lou.

Dawson, William L., 1886-

UNITED States. Congress. House. Committee on Government Operations. Special Studies Subcommittee. 362
William L. Dawson's programs to help the disadvantaged; a staff study. Washington, U.S. Govt. Print. Off., 1970. iii, 15 p. 24 cm. At head of title: 91st Congress, 2d session. House of Representatives. Committee print. [HV1553.A518] 70-610195
1. Dawson, William L., 1886- 2. Socially handicapped—Rehabilitation—United States. I. Title.

Day, Doris, 1924-

DAY, Doris, 1924- 791.43'028'0924 B
Doris Day : her own story / A. E. Hotchner. Boston : G. K. Hall, 1976, c1975. 2 v. (687 p.) ; 25 cm. "Published in Large print." [PN2287.D324A34 1976b] 76-18794 18.95
1. Day, Doris, 1924- 2. Sight-saving books. I. Hotchner, A. E.

DAY, Doris, 1924- 791.43'028'0924 B
Doris Day : her own story / [as told to] A. E. Hotchner. New York : Morrow, 1976, c1975. p. cm. Includes index. Filmography: p. [PN2287.D324A34 1976] 75-22354 ISBN 0-688-02968-X : 8.95
1. Day, Doris, 1924- I. Hotchner, A. E.

GELB, Alan. 791.43'028'0924
The Doris Day scrapbook / by Alan Gelb. New York : Grosset & Dunlap, c1977. 159 p. : ill. ; 28 cm. [PN2287.D324G4] 76-48024 ISBN 0-448-12868-3 : 14.95 ISBN 0-448-12862-4 pbk. : 5.95
1. Day, Doris, 1924- 2. Moving-picture actors and actresses—United States—Biography. I. Title. BIP

MORRIS, George, 1943- 791.43'028'0924
Doris Day / by George Morris. New York : Pyramid Publications, 1976. 159 p. : ill. ; 20 cm. (A Pyramid illustrated history of the movies) Includes index. Filmography: p. 149-153. [PN2287.D324M6] 75-42514 ISBN 0-515-03959-4 : 1.75
1. Day, Doris, 1924- 2. Moving-picture actors and actresses—United States—Biography. BIP

THOMEY, Tedd. 927.92
Doris Day; the dramatic story of America's number one box office star. Derby, Conn., Monarch Books [1962] 139 p. 19 cm. (Monarch books) [PN2287.D324T5] 63-1251
1. Day, Doris, 1924- . I. Title.

Day, Frank, 1862-

DAY, Owen T. 286'.1'0924 B
The hallelujah hole : the story of a frontier preacher / Owen T. Day with Nancy C. Thomas. Valley Forge, Pa. : Judson Press, c1976. 174 p. : map ; 23 cm. [BX6495.D42D39] 76-18149 ISBN 0-8170-0709-1 : 6.95
1. Day, Frank, 1862- I. Thomas, Nancy C., joint author. II. Title. BIP

Day, Thomas, 1748-1789.

JAEGER, Muriel. 920.02
Adventures in living, from Cato to George Sand. Freeport, N.Y., Books for Libraries Press [1970] viii, 216 p. 23 cm. (Essay index reprint series) Reprint of the 1932 American ed. Published in London in 1932 under title: Experimental lives. Includes bibliographical references. [CT105.J3 1970] 79-121480 ISBN 8-369-17588-
1. Cato, Marcus Porcius, Uticensis. 2. Francesco d'Assisi, Saint, 1182-1226. 3. Chesterfield, Philip Dormer Stanhope, 4th Earl of, 1694-1773. 4. Day, Thomas, 1748-1789. 5. Sand, George, pseud. of Mme. Dudevant, 1804-1876. I. Title. BIP

KEIR, James, 1735-1820. 823'.6 B
Account of the life and writing of Thomas Day. New York, Garland Pub., 1970. iii, 144 p. 22 cm. Facsim. of the Yale University Library copy, with original imprint: London, Printed for J. Stockdale, 1791. "A list of Mr. Day's publications": p. [143]-144. [PR3398.D3K4 1791a] 74-112167
1. Day, Thomas, 1748-1789. I. Title.

Dayal, Har, 1884-1939.

BROWN, Emily Clara. 954.03'5'0924 B
Har Dayal, Hindu revolutionary and rationalist / Emily C. Brown. Tucson : University of Arizona Press, [1975] xiv, 321 p. ; 23 cm. Includes index. Bibliography: p. 293-303. [DS481.D365B76] 74-16895 ISBN 0-8165-0422-9 : 14.50. ISBN 0-8165-0512-8 pbk. : 7.95
1. Dayal, Har, 1884-1939. I. Title.

Dayan, Moshe, 1915-

DAYAN, Moshe, 1915- 956'.044
The diary of the Sinai Campaign / Moshe

Dayan. Westport, Conn. : Greenwood Press, [1979] p. cm. Translation of Yoman ma'arekhet Sinai. Reprint of the 1st ed. (1966) published by Harper & Row, New York. Includes index. [DS110.5.D313 1979] 78-27859 20.75
1. Dayan, Moshe, 1915- 2. Sinai Campaign, 1956—Personal narratives, Israeli. 3. Israel—Armed Forces—Biography. I. Title. BIP

DAYAN, Moshe, 1915- 221.9'5
Living with the Bible / Moshe Dayan. New York : W. Morrow, 1978. 232 p. : ill. ; 26 cm. Includes index. [BS1197.D35] 78-52478 ISBN 0-688-03361-X : 14.95
1. Dayan, Moshe, 1915- 2. Bible. O.T.—History of Biblical events. 3. Statesmen—Israel—Biography. 4. Palestine—Antiquities. I. Title. BIP

DAYAN, Moshe, 1915- 956.94'05'0924 B
Moshe Dayan : story of my life / by Moshe Dayan. New York : Morrow, c1976. p. cm. Includes index. [DS126.6.D3A35] 76-18144 ISBN 0-688-03076-9 : 15.00
1. Dayan, Moshe, 1915- 2. Israel—History, Military. BIP

DAYAN, Moshe, 1915- 956.94'05
Moshe Dayan : story of life / by Moshe Dayan. New York : Warner Books, 1977,c1976. 796[16]p. : ill. ; 18 cm. Includes index. [DS126.6D3A35] ISBN 0-446-83425-4 pbk. : 2.95
1. Dayan, Moshe, 1915- 2. Israel-History,Military. I. Title.
L.C. card no. for 1976 Morrow ed.:76-18144.

DAYAN, Moshe, 1915- 956.94'05'0924 B
Story of my life / [by] Moshe Dayan. London : Weidenfeld and Nicolson, 1976. [9], 530 p., [16] p. of plates : ill., maps, ports. ; 25 cm. Includes index. [DS126.6.D3A35 1976b] 77-350984 ISBN 0-297-77182-5 : £6.95
1. Dayan, Moshe, 1915- 2. Statesmen—Israel—Biography. 3. Israel—History, Military. I. Title.

JURMAN, Pinchas. 956.94'05'0924 B
Moshe Dayan; a portrait, edited by Pinchas Jurman. New York, Dodd, Mead [1969, c1968] [135] p. (chiefly illus., ports.) 32 cm. [DS126.6.D3J8 1969] 70-78377
1. Dayan, Moshe, 1915-

LAU-LAVIE, Naftali, 1926- 956.94'05'0924 B
Moshe Dayan; a biography, by Naphtali Lau-Lavie. Hartford, Hartmore House [1969, c1968] 223 p. ports., map (on lining papers) 23 cm. [DS126.6.D3L3 1969] 71-1893 ISBN 0-85303-004-9 4.95
1. Dayan, Moshe, 1915-

TEVETH, Shabtai, 1925- 956.94'05'0924 B
Moshe Dayan, the soldier, the man, the legend. Translated from the Hebrew by Leah and David Zinder. [1st American ed.] Illustrated with photos. Boston, Houghton Mifflin, 1973 [c1972] 372 p. illus. 24 cm. [DS126.6.D3T4213 1973] 72-5221 ISBN 0-395-15475-8 8.95
1. Dayan, Moshe, 1915-

TEVETH, Shabtai, 1925- 956.94'05'0924 B
Moshe Dayan, the soldier, the man, the legend. Translated from the Hebrew by Leah and David Zindler. [New York Dell, 1974, c1973] 478 p. 18 cm. [DS126.6.D3T4213 1974] 1.95 (pbk.)
1. Dayan, Moshe, 1915- I. Title.
L.C. card number for original ed.: 72-5221.

Dayan, Moshe, 1915- —Juvenile literature.

TASLITT, Israel Isaac. 956.9405'0924 B
Soldier of Israel; the story of General Moshe Dayan, by Israel I. Taslitt. New York, Funk and Wagnalls [1969] 190 p. ports. 23 cm. (A Sabra book) A biography of the man who became one of modern Israel's most prominent generals and its Minister of Defense. [DS126.6.D3T3 1969] 92 69-13465 4.50
1. Dayan, Moshe, 1915- —Juvenile literature. I. Title.

Dayan, Ruth.

DAYAN, Ruth. 956.94'05'0924 B
And perhaps ... The story of Ruth Dayan, by Ruth Dayan and Helga Dudman. [1st American ed.] New York, Harcourt Brace Jovanovich [1973] xvi, 236 p. illus. 22 cm. [CT1919.P38D39 1973] 72-79920 ISBN 0-15-106845-3 6.95
1. Dayan, Ruth. 2. Dayan, Moshe, 1915- I. Dudman, Helga, 1925- joint author. II. Title. III. Title: The story of Ruth Dayan. BIP

Daye, Stephen, 1611-1668.

DERRY, William C v. 12
Stephen Daye, America's first printer. Cincinnati, The Stratford Press, private press of Elmer Gleason, 1963. viii, 35, [1] p. illus. (part fold.) 19 cm. 65598
1. Daye, Stephen, 1611-1668. I. Title.

Daytona International Speedway Race—Juvenile literature.

HIGDON, Hal. 796.7'2'0680975921
Showdown at Daytona / by Hal Higdon. New York : Putnam, c1976. 159 p. : ill. ; 21 cm. Includes index. Dramatizes the 1975 Daytona 500 and the lives of a half dozen drivers who made that race such an exciting and surprising event. [GV1033.5.D39H53 1976] 920 75-43731 ISBN 0-399-20507-1 : 5.95.
1. Daytona International Speedway Race—Juvenile literature. 2. Automobile racing—Biography—Juvenile literature. I. Title. BIP

De Benneville, George, 1703-1793.

BELL, Albert Dehner, 1911- 922.89
The life and times of Dr. George de Benneville, 1703-1793. [1st ed.] Boston, Dept. of Publications of the Universalist Church of America, 1953. 67p. illus. 23cm. [BX9969.D4B4] 53-11812
1. De Benneville, George, 1703-1793. I. Title.

De Bottazzi, Ana Maria Trenchi.

DE BOTTAZZI, Ana Maria Trenchi. 786.1'092'4 B
To live again / Ana Maria Trenchi de Bottazzi. New York : Dodd, Mead, c1978. 209 p. ; 22 cm. [ML417.D3A3] 78-5029 ISBN 0-396-07570-3 : 8.95
1. De Bottazzi, Ana Maria Trenchi. 2. Pianists—Biography. I. Title.

De Bow, James Dunwoody Brownson, 1820-1867.

SKIPPER, Ottis Clark, 1898- 928.1
J. D.B. De Bow, magazinist of the Old South. Athens, University of Georgia Press [1958] 269 p. illus. 25 cm. Includes bibliographies. [PN4874.D395S53] 58-9172
1. De Bow, James Dunwoody Brownson, 1820-1867. 2. De Bow's review. I. Title.

De Cleyre, Voltairine, 1866-1912.

AVRICH, Paul. 335'.83'0924 B
An American anarchist : the life of Voltairine de Cleyre / by Paul Avrich. Princeton, N.J. : Princeton University Press, c1978. xxii, 266 p., [12] leaves of plates : ill. ; 23 cm. Includes index. Bibliography: p. [241]-256. [HX843.A97] 78-51153 ISBN 0-691-04657-3 : 16.50
1. De Cleyre, Voltairine, 1866-1912. 2. Anarchism and anarchists—United States—Biography. 3. Feminists—United States—Biography. I. Title. BIP

De Cordova, Jacob, 1808-1868.

DAY, James M v. 12
Jacob de Cordova, land merchant of Texas. Foreword by Roger N. Conger. Waco, Texian Press, 1962. xv, 189 p. port. 24 cm. Bibliography: p. 174-180. 64-38472
1. De Cordova, Jacob, 1808-1868. I. Title.

De Forest, David Curtis, 1774-1825.

KEEN, Benjamin, 1913- 982'.03
David Curtis DeForest and the revolution of Buenos Aires. Westport, Conn., Greenwood Press [1970, c1947] 186 p. ports. 23 cm. Includes bibliographical references. [E340.D4K4 1970] 75-104249 ISBN 0-8371-3970-8
1. De Forest, David Curtis, 1774-1825. 2. Argentine Republic—History—War of Independence, 1810-1817. I. Title. BIP

De Forest, John William, 1826-1906.

LIGHT, James F. 928.1
John William De Forest. New York, Twayne [c.1965] 192p. 22cm. (Twayne's U. S. authors ser., 82) Bibl. [PS1525.D5Z75] 65-13002 3.50 bds.,
1. De Forest, John William, 1826-1906. I. Title. BIP

De Forest, Lee, 1873-1961.

LEVINE, Irving Englander. 926.2
Electronics pioneer, Lee De Forest. New York, Messner [1964] 191 p. 22 cm. Bibliography: p. 185. [TK5739.D4L3] 64-11370
1. De Forest, Lee, 1873-1961. I. Title.

LEVINE,ISRAEL E 926.2
Electronics pioneer; Les De Forest. New York, Messner [1964] 191 p. 22 cm. Bibliography: p. 185. [TK5739.D4L3] 64-11370
1. De Forest, Lee, 1873-1961. I. Title.

De Forest, Lee, 1873-1961—Juvenile literature.

WOLLHEIM, Donald A. 920
Lee de Forest; advancing the electronic age. Illus. by Robert Boehmer. Chicago, Ency. Britannica [1963, c.1962] 191p. col. illus. 22cm. (Britannica bkshelf. Great lives for young Amers.) 62-10421 2.36 lib. ed.,
1. De Forest, Lee, 1873-1961—Juvenile literature. I. Title.

De Gast, Robert, 1936-

DE GAST, Robert, 1936- 917.52'1'044
Western wind, eastern shore : a sailing cruise around the Eastern Shore of Maryland, Delaware, and Virginia / written and photographed by Robert de Gast ; foreword by John Barth. Baltimore : Johns Hopkins University Press, [1975] xiv, 176 p. : ill. ; 21 x 22 cm. Bibliography: p. 176. [F187.E2D43] 75-10924 ISBN 0-8018-1767-6 : 14.95
1. De Gast, Robert, 1936- 2. Delmarva Peninsula—Description and travel. 3. Sailing. I. Title. BIP

De la Itamee, Louise, 1839-1908.

BIGLAND, Eileen. 928.2
Ouida, the passionate Victorian. New York, Duell, Sloan and Pearce [1951] 272 p. plates, ports, facsims. 22 cm. Bibliography: p. 265-266. [PR4528.B5 1951] 51-10422
1. De la Itamee, Louise, 1839-1908. I. Title.

De La Mare, Walter John, 1873-1956.

ATKINS, John Alfred, 1916- 821'.9'12 B
Walter De La Mare : an exploration / New York : Haskell House, [1976 i.e.1975] p. cm. Reprint of the 1947 ed. published by C. & J. Temple, London. [PR6007.E3Z6 1976] 75-22359 ISBN 0-8383-2105-4 lib.bdg. : 9.95
1. De La Mare, Walter John, 1873-1956. BIP

CLARK, Leonard. 928.2
Walter De La Mare. [1st American ed.] New York, H. Z. Walck [1961, c1960] 81 p. illus. 19 cm. Includes bibliography. [PR6007.E3Z63 1961] 61-8579
1. De La Mare, Walter John, 1873-1956.

De La Roche, Harry, 1958-

ROESCH, Roberta Fleming. 364.1'523'0924 B
Anyone's son / Roberta Roesch, with Harry De La Roche, Jr. Kansas City, [Ks.] : Andrews and McMeel, c1979. ix, 294 p. : ill. ; 24 cm. [HV6248.D36R63] 79-11355 ISBN 0-8362-6608-0 : 9.95
1. De La Roche, Harry, 1958- 2. Crime and criminals—New Jersey—Biography. 3. Murder—New Jersey—Case studies. 4. Parricide—New Jersey—Case studies. I. De La Roche, Harry, 1958- joint author. II. Title.

De La Roche, Mazo, 1885-1961.

HAMBLETON, Ronald, 1917- 813.52 B
Mazo De La Roche of Jalna. [1st ed.] New York, Hawthorn Books [1966] 239 p. illus., map, ports. 24 cm. "Check list of the writings of Mazo de la Roche": p. 223-229. Bibliography: p. 230-231. [PR6007.E34Z64] 66-22660
1. De La Roche, Mazo, 1885-1961. I. Title.

De Laguna, Frederica, 1906-

DE LAGUNA, Frederica, 1906- 998'.2'00497
Voyage to Greenland : a personal initiation into anthropology / Frederica de Laguna. 1st ed. New York : Norton, c1977. 285 p., [8] leaves of plates : ill. ; 24 cm. [E99.E7D385 1977] 76-51808 ISBN 0-393-06413-1 : 9.95
1. De Laguna, Frederica, 1906- 2. Eskimos—Greenland. 3. Ethnology—Field work. 4. Greenland—Antiquities. 5. Anthropologists—United States—Biography. I. Title. BIP

De Leon, Daniel, 1852-1914.

PETERSEN, Arnold, 1885- v. 12
Daniel De Leon: social architect. Brooklyn, N.Y., New York Labor News, 1966. 59 p. illus. 19 cm. 68-62772
1. De Leon, Daniel, 1852-1914. I. Title. BIP

REEVE, Carl. 335'.0092'4 B
The life and times of Daniel De Leon. Foreword by Oakley C. Johnson. New York, Published for AIMS by Humanities Press [1972] 193 p. front. 22 cm. (AIMS historical series, no. 8) Imprint covered by label: Distributed in the U.S.A. by Humanities Press, New York. Includes bibliographies. [HX84.D5R44] 75-174555 ISBN 0-391-00208-2 6.50
1. De Leon, Daniel, 1852-1914. I. Title. II. Series: American Institute for Marxist Studies. AIMS historical series, no. 8. BIP

De Lorenzo, Giovanni, 1907-1973.

COLLIN, Richard. 945.092'092'4 B
The de Lorenzo gambit : the Italian coup manque of 1964 / Richard Collin. Beverly Hills, Calif. : Sage Publications, c1976. 65 p. ; 22 cm. (Sage research papers in the social sciences ; v. 5, ser. no. 90-034 : Contemporary European studies) Includes bibliographical references. [DG579.D44C64] 75-6104 pbk. : 3.00
1. De Lorenzo, Giovanni, 1907-1973. 2. Italy. Servizio informazione forze armate. 3. Italy. Servizio informazione forze armate—Officials and employees—Biography. 4. Italy—Politics and government—1945- 5. Coups d'etat. 6. Generals—Italy—Biography. 7. Fascists—Italy—Biography. I. Title. II. Series: Sage research papers in the social sciences : Contemporary European studies.

De Mille, Agnes.

DE MILLE, Agnes. 792.8'2'0924
Where the wings grow / Agnes de Mille. 1st ed. Garden City, N.Y. : Doubleday, 1978. 286 p., [8] leaves of plates : ill. ; 22 cm. [GV1785.D36A39] 76-18339 ISBN 0-385-12106-7 : 8.95
1. De Mille, Agnes. 2. Choreographers—United States—Biography. I. Title. BIP

De Mille, Cecil Blount, 1881-1959.

DE MILLE, Cecil Blount, 1881-1959. 927.914
Autobiography. Edited by Donald Hayne. Englewood Cliffs, N. J., Prentice-Hall [1959] 465 p. illus. 24 cm. [PN1998.A3D37] 59-15367

HIGHAM, Charles, 1931- 791.43'0233'0924 B
Cecil B. DeMille. New York, Scribner [1973] xii, 335 p. illus. 24 cm. Cecil B. DeMille pictures": p. 315-322. [PN1998.A3D39] 73-1119 ISBN 0-684-13379-2 9.95
1. De Mille, Cecil Blount, 1881-1959.

KOURY, Phil A 927.914
Yes, Mr. De Mille. New York, Putnam [1959] 319p. 22cm. [PN1998.A3D4] 59-12004
1. De Mille, Cecil Blount, 1881-1959. I. Title.

De Onis, Harriet, tr.

LAZARILLO DE TORMES 863.3
The life of Lazarillo de Tormes, his fortunes and adversities. Translated from the Spanish, with notes and introduction by Harriet de Onis. Great Neck, N.Y., Barron's Educational Series. [c.1959] xviii, 74p. 19cm. 59-2360 .75 pap.,
1. De Onis, Harriet, tr. I. Title.

De Palma, Ralph—Juvenile literature.

OLNEY, Ross Robert, 1929- 796.7'2'0922 B
Great auto racing champions, by Ross Olney. Illustrated by Victor Mays. Champaign, Ill. Garrard Pub. Co. [1973] 95 p. illus. (part col.) 24 cm. Biographies of three winners of the Indy 500: Ralph De Palma, Johnnie Parsons, and A. J. Foyt. [GV1032.A1O42] 920 73-5696 ISBN 0-8116-6666-2 2.98
1. De Palma, Ralph—Juvenile literature. 2. Parsons, Johnnie, 1918- —Juvenile literature. 3. Foyt, A. J., 1935- —Juvenile literature. I. Mays, Victor, 1927- illus. II. Title. BIP

De Quincey, Thomas, 1785-1859.

BONNER, Willard Hallam, 1899- ed. 828'.8'09 B
De Quincey at work. [Folcroft, Pa.] Folcroft Library Editions, 1973 [c1936] 111 p. illus. 26 cm. Reprint of the ed. published by Airport Publishers, Buffalo. Contents.Contents.—James T. Fields and the first American edition.—James Hogg and the first British edition. [PR4536.B6 1973] 73-9715 10.00
1. De Quincey, Thomas, 1785-1859. 2. Fields, James Thomas, 1816-1881. 3. Hogg, James, 1806-1888. 4. Hogg, James, 1830-1910. I. De Quincey, Thomas, 1785-1859. II. Title. BIP

EATON, Horace Ainsworth, 1871- 828'.8'09 B
Thomas De Quincey; a biography. New York, Octagon Books, 1972 [c1936] xiii, 542 p. illus. 23 cm. Bibliography: p. 525-529. [PR4536.E3 1972] 74-159182 ISBN 0-374-92459-7
1. De Quincey, Thomas, 1785-1859.

JAPP, Alexander Hay, 1839-1905. 828'.8'09 B
Thomas De Quincey: his life and writings. With unpublished correspondence. A new ed., thoroughly rev. and rearranced with additional matter. London, J. Hogg, 1840-St. Clair Shores, Mich., Scholarly Press, 1971. xiv, 520 p. illus. 22 cm. [PR4536.J4 1971] 76-145109 ISBN 0-403-01046-2
1. De Quincey, Thomas, 1785-1859.

JAPP, Alexander Hay, 1839-1905. 828'.8'09 B
Thomas de Quincey: his life and writings with unpublished correspondence, by H. A. Page. New York, Haskell House Publishers [1972] p. Reprint of the 1877 ed. [PR4536.J4 1972] 72-1973 ISBN 0-8383-1451-1
1. De Quincey, Thomas, 1785-1859.

JORDAN, John Emory, 1919- v. 12
Thomas De Quincey, literary critic; his method and achievement. Berkeley, University of California Press, 1952. ix, 301p. 24cm. (University of California publications. English studies, 4) Bibliography: p. 273- 277. 'Notes' (bibliographical): p. 281-226. A52
1. De Quincey, Thomas, 1785-1859. I. Title. II. Series: California. University. University of California publications. English studies, 4

SACKVILLE-WEST, Edward, Hon., 1901-1965. 828'.8'09 B
A flame in sunlight : the life and work of Thomas de Quincey / Edward Sackville-West. New ed. / with preface and notes by John E. Jordan. London : Bodley Head, 1974. xviii, 362 p., [4] leaves of plates : 2 ill., facsim., ports. ; 23 cm. American ed. published in 1936 under title: Thomas de Quincey, his life and work. Includes index. Bibliography: p. 349-353. [PR4536.S25 1974] 75-300185 ISBN 0-370-10494-3 : 13.50
1. De Quincey, Thomas, 1785-1859. I. Jordan, John Emory, 1919- II. Title.
Distributed by Rowman and Littlefield. BIP

SALT, Henry Stephens, 1851-1939. 828'.8'09 B
De Quincey / by Henry S. Salt Folcroft, Pa. : Folcroft Library Editions, 1977. p. cm Reprint of the 1904 ed. published by G. Bell, London, in series: Bell's miniature series of great writers. Includes index. Bibliography: p. [PR4536.S3 1977] 77-23085 ISBN 0-8414-7771-X lib. bdg. : 15.00
1. De Quincey, Thomas, 1785-1859. 2. Authors, English—19th century—Biography. I. Series: Bell's miniature series of great writers.

De Quincey, Thomas, 1785-1859—Correspondence.

DE QUINCEY, Thomas, 1785-1859 828'.2'09 B
Unpublished letters of Thomas De Quincey and Elizabeth Barrett Browning / edited from the originals in the Grey collection, Auckland Public Library by S. Musgrove. Folcroft, Pa. : Folcroft Library Editions, 1975. 37 p. ; 22 cm. Reprint of the 1954 ed. published by Auckland University College, Auckland, which was issued as no. 44 of its Bulletin and as no. 7 of its English series. Includes bibliographical references. [PR4536.A63 1975] 75-19429 ISBN 0-8414-6037-X lib. bdg. : 6.50
1. De Quincey, Thomas, 1785-1859—Correspondence. 2. Browning, Elizabeth Barrett, 1806-1861—Correspondence. 3. Authors, English—19th century—Correspondence. I. Browning, Elizabeth Barrett, 1806-1861. II. Title. III. Series: Auckland, N.Z. University. English series ; no. 7.

De Ropp, Robert S.

DE ROPP, Robert S. 973.91'092'4 B
Warrior's way : the challenging life games / Robert S. deRopp. New York : Delacorte Press/S. Lawrence, c1979. x, 405 p., [1] leaf of plates : port. ; 21 cm. "A Merloyd Lawrence book." Includes index. [CT275.D366A38] 78-26917 ISBN 0-440-09438-0 : 10.00
1. De Ropp, Robert S. 2. United States—Biography. I. Title.

De Sapio, Carmine, 1908-

MOSCOW, Warren. 329.3'0924 B
The last of the big-time bosses; the life and times of Carmine De Sapio and the rise and fall of Tammany Hall. New York, Stein and Day [1971] 227 p. 25 cm. [JK2319.N56M66] 79-160351 ISBN 0-8128-1400-2 7.95
1. De Sapio, Carmine, 1908- 2. Tammany Hall. 3. New York (City)—Politics and government. I. Title.

De Soto, Hernando, 1500?-1542.

CURCIO, Louis Leroy. v. 12
...Hernando de Soto, by Louis L. Curcio and Carlos M. Teran. New York, American Book Co., 1961. vi, 58 p. illus. 19 cm. (Cultural Graded Readers, Spanish Series: 2) 64-38061
1. De Soto, Hernando, 1500?-1542. 2. Spanish language-Readers. I. Teran, Carlos M., joint author. II. Title.

De Valera, Eamonn, 1882-1975.

EAMON de Valera, 1882-1975 941.7082'3'0924 B
: the controversial giant of modern Ireland, a survey in text and pictures of the life and influence of a famous leader / [editor, Peter Tynan O'Mahony]. Dublin : Irish Times, c1976. 144 p. : ill. ; 25 cm. [DA965.D4E15] 77-352277 ISBN 0-9503418-1-9 : £6.00
1. De Valera, Eamonn, 1882-1975. 2. Ireland—Presidents—Biography. 3. Ireland—Politics and government—20th century. I. The Irish Times, Dublin.

FITZ Gibbon, Constantine. 941.59'092'4 B
The life and times of Eamon de Valera. Text: Constantine FitzGibbon. Illustrative material: George Morrison. New York, Macmillan [1974, c1973] 150 p. illus. 29 cm. [DA965.D4F57 1974] 73-7353 8.95
1. De Valera, Eamonn, 1882- 2. Ireland—Politics and government—20th century. I. Morrison, George, illus. II. Title. BIP

LONGFORD, Frank Pakenham, 7th Earl of, 1905- 941.5'9'0924 B
Eamon de Valera [by] the Earl of Longford & Thomas P. O'Neill. [1st American ed.] Boston, Houghton Mifflin, 1971, [c1970] xix, 499 p. illus., maps, ports. 24 cm. Includes bibliographical references. [DA965.D4L6 1971] 77-144076 ISBN 0-395-12101-9 12.50
1. De Valera, Eamonn, 1882- I. O'Neill, Thomas P., joint author.

SEVERN, William. 941.5'9'0924 B
Irish statesman and rebel: the two lives of Eamon De Valera, by Bill Severn. New York, Washburn [1970] viii, 184 p. 21 cm. A biography of the revolutionary who became President of the Irish Republic he helped establish. [DA965.D4S48] 92 78-120953 4.95
1. De Valera, Eamonn, 1882- —Juvenile literature. I. Title.

STEFFAN, Alice Jacqueline (Kennedy) 941.590924
The Long Fellow; the story of the great Irish patriot, Eamon de Valera, by Jack Steffan. New York, Macmillan [c.1966] xxv, 197p. ports. 21cm. [DA965.D4S7] 66-10164 3.95; 3.94 lib. ed.,
1. De Valera, Eamonn, 1882- —Juvenile literature. I. Title.

De Voto, Bernard Augustine, 1897-1955.

FOUR portraits and one subject: 818.52
Bernard DeVoto. Boston, Houghton, 1963. ix, 206p. port. 22cm. Bibl. 63-7524 4.00
1. De Voto, Bernard Augustine, 1897-1955.
Contents ommitted.

SAWEY, Orlan, 1920- 813'.5'2 B
Bernard DeVoto. New York, Twayne Publishers [1969] 147 p. 21 cm. (Twayne's United States authors series, 151) "Notes and references": p. 132-138. Bibliography: p. 139-141. [PS3507.E867Z87] 69-18502
1. De Voto, Bernard Augustine, 1897-1955. BIP

De Voto, Bernard Augustine, 1897-1955—Biography.

STEGNER, Wallace Earle, 1909- 818'.5'209 B
The uneasy chair; a biography of Bernard DeVoto [by] Wallace Stegner. [1st ed.] Garden City, N.Y., Doubleday, 1974. xi, 464 p. illus. 24 cm. Includes bibliographical references. [PS3507.E867Z9] 73-81985 ISBN 0-385-07884-6 12.50
1. De Voto, Bernard Augustine, 1897-1955—Biography. I. Title.

De Voto, Bernard Augustine, 1897-1955—Correspondence.

DE VOTO, Bernard Augustine, 1897-1955 818'.5'209 B
The letters of Bernard DeVoto / [edited by] Wallace Stegner. 1st ed. Garden City, N.Y. : Doubleday, 1975. xiv, 393 p. ; 25 cm. Includes bibliographical references and index. [PS3507.E867Z53 1975] 74-12715 ISBN 0-385-03706-6 : 10.00
1. De Voto, Bernard Augustine, 1897-1955—Correspondence. 2. Authors, American—Correspondence, reminiscences, etc. I. Stegner, Wallace Earle, 1909- ed.

De Vries, Lini.

DE VRIES, Lini. 362.1'092'4 B
Up from the cellar / Lini de Vries. Minneapolis : Vanilla Press, [1978] p. cm. [CT558.D48A38] 78-66429 ISBN 0-917266-17-X : 9.95. ISBN 0-917266-18-8 pbk. : 3.95
1. De Vries, Lini. 2. Mexico—Biography. 3. United States—Biography. I. Title. BIP

De Wolfe, Elsie, 1865-1950.

BEMELMANS, Ludwig, 1898-1962. 927.47
To the one I love the best. New York, Viking Press, 1955. 255 p. illus. 22 cm. [CT275.D382B4] 54-9596
1. De Wolfe, Elsie, 1865-1950. I. Title.

DE WOLFE, Elsie, 1865-1950. 910'.03 B
After all. New York, Arno Press, 1974 [c1935] x, 278 p. illus. 23 cm. (Women in America: from colonial times to the 20th century) Autobiography. Reprint of the 1st ed. published by Harper, New York. [CT275.D382A3 1974] 74-3938 ISBN 0-405-06085-8
1. De Wolfe, Elsie, 1865-1950. I. Title. II. Series.

Deady, Matthew Paul, 1824-1893.

DEADY, Matthew Paul, 1824-1893. 347'.73'22034 B
Pharisee among Philistines : the diary of Judge Matthew P. Deady, 1871-1892 / edited and with introd. by Malcolm Clark, Jr. Portland : Oregon Historical Society, c1975. 2 v. (xxxvii, 662 p., [31] leaves of plates) : ill. ; 27 cm. Includes bibliographical references and index. [KF368.D37A36] 74-75363 ISBN 0-87595-046-9 : 27.50 deluxe ed. : 30.00
1. Deady, Matthew Paul, 1824-1893. 2. Judges—Oregon—Correspondence, reminiscences, etc. 3. Oregon—Biography. I. Title. BIP

Deaf—Personal narratives.

ISRAELSEN, Orson Winso, 1887-1968. 627'.5'0924 B
Forty years of sound and forty years of silence; an autobiography, by Orson W. Israelsen. [Salt Lake City? Printed by Utah Print. Co., 1968] ix, 130 p. illus., ports. (part col.) 24 cm. [HV2534.I8A3] 68-5715
1. Deaf—Personal narratives. I. Title.

Deak, Ferencz, 1803-1876.

KIRALY, Bela K., 1912- 943.9'04'0924 B
Ferenc Deak / Bela K. Kiraly. Boston : Twayne Publishers, [1975] 243 p. : ill. ; 21 cm. (Twayne's world leaders series) Includes index. Bibliography: p. 221-235. [DB933.3.D2K57] 74-20558 ISBN 0-8057-3030-3 : 8.50
1. Deak, Ferencz, 1803-1876. 2. Hungary—Politics and government—19th century. BIP

Deakin, Alfred, 1856-1919.

LA NAUZE, John Andrew, 1911- 994.040924 (B)
Alfred Deakin; a biography [by] J. A. La Nauze. [Melbourne] Melbourne University Press; New York, Cambridge University Press [1965] 2 v. (xiv, 695 p.) ports. 25 cm. Bibliography: p. 673-682. [DU114.D35L29] 65-25718
1. Deakin, Alfred, 1856-1919. I. Title. BIP

Dealey, George Bannerman, 1859-1946.

SHARPE, Ernest. 920.5
G. B. Dealey of the Dallas news. [1st ed.] New York, Holt [1955] 304p. illus. 22cm. [PN4874.D39S5] 55-7907
1. Dealey, George Bannerman, 1859-1946. 2. The Dallas morning news. I. Title.

Dean, Dizzy, 1911-

ALLEN, Lee, 1915- 92
Dizzy Dean; his story in baseball. New York, Putnam [1967] 159 p. front. 21 cm. A biography of a colorful, confident, and competent baseball pitcher who was voted the National League's Most Valuable Player in 1934 and led the National League in strike-outs from 1932-1935. [GV865.D4A65] AC 67
1. Dean, Dizzy, 1911- 2. Baseball—Biography.

SMITH, Curt. 796.357'092'4 B
America's Dizzy Dean / by Curt Smith. St. Louis : Bethany Press, c1978. 191 p. : ill. ; 24 cm. Includes index. [GV865.D4S59] 77-29060 ISBN 0-8272-0014-5 : 9.95
1. Dean, Dizzy, 1911- 2. Baseball players—United States—Biography. I. Title. BIP

Dean, James, 1931-1955.

BAST, William, 1931- 927.92
James Dean; a biography. New York, Ballantine Books [c1956] 153p. illus. 21cm. [PN2287.D33B3] 56-12808
1. Dean, James, 1961-1955. I. Title.

DALTON, David. 791'.092'4 B
James Dean, the mutant King: a biography. [New York, Dell, 1975, c1974] 396 p. illus. 18 cm. Bibliography: [p. 381-389] [PN2287.D33D3] 1.75 (pbk.)
1. Dean, James, 1931-1955. I. Title.
L.C. card number for original ed.: 74-76600.

DALTON, David. 791'.092'4 B
James Dean, the mutant king; a biography. [San Francisco, Straight Arrow Books, 1974] 356 p. illus. 25 cm. Bibliography: p. 344-350. [PN2287.D33D3] 74-76600 ISBN 0-87932-076-1 9.95
1. Dean, James, 1931-1955.

GILMORE, John. 791'.0924 B
The real James Dean / John Gilmore. New York : Pyramid Books, 1975. 160 p., [4] leaves of plates : ill., ports ; 18 cm. [PN2287.D33G5] 75-13624 ISBN 0-515-03814-8 pbk. : 1.50
1. Dean, James, 1931-1955. I. Title.

HERNDON, Venable. 791.43'028'0924 B
James Dean: a short life. [1st ed.] Garden City, N.Y., Doubleday, 1974. 288 p. illus. 22 cm. Bibliography: p. 277-278. [PN2287.D33H4] 73-9162 ISBN 0-385-02155-0 8.95
1. Dean, James, 1931-1955. I. Title. BIP

HOWLETT, John, 1940- 791.43'028'0924 B
James Dean : a biography / John Howlett. New York : Simon and Schuster, c1975. 191 p. : ill. ; 28 cm. (A Fireside book) Bibliography: p. 191. [PN2287.D33H6] 75-40036 ISBN 0-671-22281-3 : 5.95
1. Dean, James, 1931-1955. BIP

I, James Dean; v. 12
the real story behind America's most popular idol. New York, Popular library [1957] 128p. ports. 18cm. (Popular library. W400)
1. Dean, James, 1931-1955. 2. Actors and acting—U. S. I. Thomas, T T

*MARTINETTI, Ronald 791.43'028'0924 B
The James Dean story New York, Pinnacle Books [1975] 185 p. illus. 18 cm. Bibliography: p. 180-181 [PN2287] ISBN 0-523-00633-0 1.50 (pbk.)
1. Dean, James, 1931-1955 I. Title.

Dean, James, 1931-1955—Portraits, etc.

STOCK, Dennis. 791.43'028'0924 B
James Dean revisited / text and photos. by Dennis Stock. New York : Viking Press, 1978. 127 p. : ill. ; 26 cm. (A Studio book) [PN2287.D33S7 1978b] 78-9846 ISBN 0-670-40481-0 : 15.95
1. Dean, James, 1931-1955—Portraits, etc. 2. Moving-picture actors and actresses—United States—Portraits. I. Title. BIP

Dean, Jerome Herman.

SHAPIRO, Milton J. 927.96357
The Dizzy Dean story. New York, Messner [c.1963] 190p. ports. 22cm. 63-8640 3.25
1. Dean, Jerome Herman. I. Title.

Deane, Frederic Liewellyn, Bp. of Aberdeen and Orkney, 1868-1952.

SNOW, William George Sinclair. v. 12
Frederic Llewellyn Deane. Bishop of Aberdeen and Orkney. Edinburgh, Blackwood [1952] 116p. illus. 19cm. A54
1. Deane, Frederic Liewellyn, Bp. of Aberdeen and Orkney, 1868-1952. I. Title.

Deane, Silas, 1737-1789.

JAMES, Coy Hilton. 973.3'092'4 B
Silas Deane, patriot or traitor? / Coy Hilton James. [East Lansing] : Michigan State University Press, 1975. viii, 152 p. : port. ; 24 cm. Includes bibliographical references and index. [E302.6.D25J35] 75-16636 ISBN 0-87013-194-X : 8.50
1. Deane, Silas, 1737-1789. I. Title. BIP

Deans (in schools)—Correspondence, reminiscences, etc.

LEE, Mabel (Barbee) 923.773
And suddenly it's evening; a fragment of life [1st ed.] Garden City, N.Y., Doubleday, 1963. xii. 201 p. 22 cm. [LA2317.L46A3] 63-17888
1. Deans (in schools) — Correspondence, reminiscences, etc. I. Title.

Dearing, Trevor, 1933-

DEARING, Trevor, 1933- 615'.852 B
Exit the Devil / by Tervor Dearing ; with Dan Wooding. Ongar : Logos Publishing International Ltd., 1976. [7], 117 p. ; 18 cm. [BX5199.D365A33] 77-368363 ISBN 0-905156-03-X
1. Dearing, Trevor, 1933- 2. Church of England—Clergy—Biography. 3. Clergy—England—Biography. 4. Pentecostalism. 5. Faith-cure. 6. Exorcism. 7. Christianity and occult sciences. I. Wooding, Dan, joint author. II. Title.

DEARING, Trevor, 1933- 615'.852
Supernatural superpowers / Trevor Dearing ; edited by Howard Earl. Plainfield, N.J. : Logos International, c1977. ix, 131 p. ; 21 cm. [BX5199.D365A37] 77-86524 ISBN 0-88270-244-0 pbk. : 2.95
1. Dearing, Trevor, 1933- 2. Church of England—Clergy—Biography. 3. Clergy—England—Biography. 4. Exorcism. I. Earl, Howard G. II. Title. BIP

Death—Psychological aspects—Case studies.

LIFTON, Robert Jay, 1926- 155.9'37'0926
Six lives, six deaths : portraits from modern Japan / Robert Jay Lifton, Shuichi Kato, and Michael R. Reich. New Haven, Conn. : Yale University Press, 1979. xiii, 305 p. : ports. ; 24 cm. Includes index. Bibliography: p. 291-296. [BF789.D4L54] 78-11926 ISBN 0-300-02266-2 : 16.95
1. Death—Psychological aspects—Case studies. 2. National characteristics, Japanese. 3. Japan—Biography. I. Kato, Shuichi, 1919- joint author. II. Reich, Michael, 1950- joint author. III. Title. BIP

DeAutremont, Hugh.

†CHIPMAN, Art. 364.1'55 B
"Tunnel 13" : the story of the DeAutremont brothers and the West's last great train hold up / by Art Chipman Medford, Or. : Pine Cone Publishers, c1977. 159 p. : ill. ; 24 cm. Includes index. [HV6661.O72 1923.C46] 77-75859 ISBN 0-912720-05-0 : 12.50
1. DeAutremont, Hugh. 2. DeAutremont, Ray. 3. DeAutremont, Roy. 4. Train robberies—Oregon. 5. Brigands and robbers—Biography. I. Title.

DeAutremont, Ray.

†CHIPMAN, Art. 364.1'55 B
"Tunnel 13" : the story of the DeAutremont brothers and the West's last great train hold up / by Art Chipman Medford, Or. : Pine Cone Publishers, c1977. 159 p. : ill. ; 24 cm. Includes index. [HV6661.O72 1923.C46] 77-75859 ISBN 0-912720-05-0 : 12.50
1. DeAutremont, Hugh. 2. DeAutremont, Ray. 3. DeAutremont, Roy. 4. Train robberies—Oregon. 5. Brigands and robbers—Biography. I. Title.

DeBakey, Michael Ellis, 1908-

KESTEN, Yehuda, 1926- 616.1'0924
Diary of a heart patient; twice operated on by Dr. DeBakey, a patient tells of his experience. [1st ed.] New York, McGraw [1968] 272p. 22cm. [RC682.K42] 68-9554 7.95
1. DeBakey, Michael Ellis, 1908- 2. Heart—Diseases—Personal narratives. I. Title.

Deborah, judge of Israel.

JONES, Juanita Nuttall, 1912- 221.92
Deborah, the woman who saved Israel [by] Juanita Nuttall Jones and James Banford McKendry New York, Association Press [1956] 127p. 20cm. (Heroes of God series) [BS580.D4J6] 56-9186
1. Deborah, judge of Israel. I. McKendry, James Banford, joint author. II. Title.

Debs, Eugene Victor, 1855-1926.

COLEMAN, McAlister, 1889- 335'.3'0924 B
Eugene V. Debs, a man unafraid / by McAlister Coleman. Westport, Conn. : Hyperion Press, 1975, c1930. p. cm. (The Radical tradition in America) Reprint of the ed. published by Greenberg, New York. Includes index. Bibliography: p. [HX84.D3C6 1975] 75-310 ISBN 0-88355-214-0 : 22.50
1. Debs, Eugene Victor, 1855-1926. I. Title.

CURRIE, Harold W. 335'.3'0924 B
Eugene V. Debs / [by] Harold W. Currie. Boston : Twayne Publishers, c1976. 157 p. : port. ; 21 cm. (Twayne's United States authors series ; TUAS 267) Includes index. Bibliography: p. 151-154. [HX84.D3C87] 76-3780 ISBN 0-8057-7167-0 lib.bdg. : 7.95
1. Debs, Eugene Victor, 1855-1926. BIP

GINGER, Ray. 335'.3'0924 B
The bending cross; a biography of Eugene Victor Debs. New York, Russell & Russell [1969, c1949] x, 516 p. port. 23 cm. Bibliography: p. 489-501. [HX84.D3G5 1969] 70-83848
1. Debs, Eugene Victor, 1855-1926. I. Title. BIP

GINGER, Ray 923.373
Eugene V. Debs: a biography [Orig. title: The bending cross] New York, Collier [1962, c.1949] 543p. 18cm. (BS21) Bibl. 1.50 pap.,
1. Debs, Eugene Victor, 1855-1926. I. Title.

MORGAN, Howard Wayne. 335'.3'0924 B
Eugene V. Debs; socialist for President [by] H. Wayne Morgan. Westport, Conn., Greenwood Press [1973, c1962] x, 257 p. illus. 21 cm. Reprint of the ed. published by Syracuse University Press, Syracuse, N.Y., which was issued in Men and movements series. Bibliography: p. 207-209. [HX84.D3M63 1973] 73-5270 ISBN 0-8371-6885-6 12.00
1. Debs, Eugene Victor, 1855-1926. I. Series: Men and movements (Syracuse) BIP

NOBLE, Iris. 335.30924 (B)
Labor's advocate, Eugene V. Debs. New York, Messner [1966] 191 p. 22 cm. [HX84.D3N6] 66-8729
1. Debs, Eugene Victor, 1855-1926. I. Title.

NOBLE, Iris 335.30924
Labor's advocate, Eugene V. Debs. New York, Messner [1966] 191p. 22cm. [HX84.D3N6] 66-8729 3.25; 3.19 lib. ed.,
1. Debs, Eugene Victor, 1855-1926. I. Title.

SELVIN, David F. 335.30924
Eugene Debs: rebel, labor leader. prophet: a biography. New York, Lothrop [c.1966] 192p. illus. 22cm. Bibl. [HX84.D3S4] 66-13213 3.75
1. Debs, Eugene Victor, 1855-1926. I. Title.

SOCIALIST Society, U.S.A. Debs Centennial Committee. v. 12
Eugene Victor Debs (1855-1955): the centennial year. [New York] 1956. 53 p.
1. Debs, Eugene Victor, 1855-1926. I. Title.

Debs, Eugene Victor, 1855-1926—Juvenile literature.

WHITE, Anne Terry. 335'.3'0924 B
Eugene Debs: American Socialist. [1st ed.] New York, L. Hill [1974] 137 p. illus. 22 cm. A biography of the trade union leader, political activist, and pacifist who ran five times as the socialist candidate for president. [HX84.D3W48] 92 74-9350 ISBN 0-88208-045-8 5.95
1. Debs, Eugene Victor, 1855-1926—Juvenile literature. I. Title.

Debussy, Claude, 1862-1918.

DUMESNIL, Maurice, 1886- 780'.92'4 B
Claude Debussy, master of dreams / Maurice Dumesnil. Westport, Conn. : Greenwood Press, 1979, c1940. 326 p. : port. ; 23 cm. Reprint of the ed. published by I. Washburn, New York. [ML410.D28D8 1979] 78-23438 ISBN 0-313-20775-5 : 20.25
1. Debussy, Claude, 1862-1918. 2. Composers—France—Biography.

LOCKSPEISER, Edward, 1905- 927.8
Debussy. New York, Collier [1962] 286p. 18cm. (Gt. composers ser., BS143V) Bibl. 1.50 pap.,
1. Debussy, Claude, 1862-1918. I. Title. BIP

LOCKSPEISER, Edward, 1905- 927.8
Debussy: his life and mind. New York, Macmillan [c.]1965. 337p. illus., ports., music. 22cm. Bibl. [ML410] 62-52835 8.00
1. Debussy, Claude, 1862-1918. I. Title. BIP

LOCKSPEISER, Edward, 1905- 780'.92'4 B
Debussy. New York, McGraw-Hill [1972, c1963] xv, 303 p. music, port. 21 cm.

Bibliography: p. 277-282. [ML410.D28L8 1972] 72-187096 ISBN 0-07-038275-1
1. Debussy, Claude, 1862-1918.

LOCKSPEISER, Edward, 1905- v. 12
Debussy, [3d ed.] New York, Collier Books [1962], 1951] 286 p. illus. 18 cm. (The Great composers series, BS 143V) "First published in 1936. Revised in 1951. First Collier Books edition, 1962." 65-1046001
1. Debussy, Claude, 1862-1918. I. Title.

LOCKSPEISER, Edward, 1905- v. 12
Debussy. [3d ed.] New York, Pellegrini and Cudahy, 1949 [i.e. 1951] xv, 304p. ports., music. 18cm. (The Master musicians) Preface to third edition, p.v-vii, dated 1951. A53
1. Debussy, Claude. 1862-1918. I. Title. II. Series: The Master musicians. New series

LOCKSPEISER, Edward, 780'.92'4 B
1905-1973.
Debussy, his life and mind / Edward Lockspeiser. Cambridge ; New York : Cambridge University Press, 1978. 2 v. : ill. ; 23 cm. Reprint of the 1962 ed. published by Cassell, London. Includes indexes. Contents.—v. 1. 1862-1902.—v. 2. 1902-1918. Bibliography: v. 1, p. 245-255 ; v. 2, p. 301-311. [ML410.D28L85 1978] 78-6795 ISBN 0-521-22054-8 : 29.50 ISBN 0-521-29342-1 pbk. : 7.95
1. Debussy, Claude, 1862-1918. 2. Composers—France—Biography.

LOCKSPERISER, Edward, 1905- 927.8
Debussy: his life and mind; v.1. 1862-1902. New York, Macmillan [c.]1962. 275p. illus., music 22cm. Bibl. 62-52835 8.00
1. Debussy, Claude, 1862-1918. I. Title.

MASON, Daniel 780'.92'2 B
Gregory, 1873-1953.
Contemporary composers. New York, Macmillan Co., 1918. [New York, AMS Press, 1973] xi, 290 p. illus. 19 cm. Contents.Contents.—Introduction: Democracy and music.—Richard Strauss.—Sir Edward Elgar.—Claude Debussy.—Vincent d'Indy.—Music in America. [ML390.M383 1973] 72-1726 ISBN 0-404-08327-7 13.00
1. Strauss, Richard, 1864-1949. 2. Elgar, Edward William, Sir, 1857-1934. 3. Debussy, Claude, 1862-1918. 4. Indy, Vincent d', 1851-1931. 5. Music—History and criticism—19th century. I. Title. BIP

MYERS, Rollo H. 780'.92'4 B
Debussy / by Rollo H. Myers. Westport, Conn. : Hyperion Press, 1979. p. cm. (Encore music editions) Reprint of the 1949 ed. published by A. A. Wyn, New York. Bibliography: p. [ML410.D28M9 1979] 78-66912 ISBN 0-88355-752-5 : 14.50
1. Debussy, Claude, 1862-1918. 2. Composers—France—Biography. I. Title. II. Series. BIP

NICHOLS, Roger. 780'.92'4
Debussy. London, Oxford University Press, 1973. 86 p. music. 22 cm. (Oxford studies of composers, 10) Bibliography: p. 85-86. [ML410.D28N5] 73-176514 ISBN 0-19-315426-9 £1.20
1. Debussy, Claude, 1862-1918. Works. I. Title. II. Series. BIP

NICHOLS, Roger. 780'.92'4
Debussy. London, Oxford University Press, 1973. 86 p. music. 22 cm. (Oxford studies of composers, 10) Bibliography: p. 85-86. [ML410.D28N5] 73-176514 ISBN 0-19-315426-9 3.00 (pbk.)
1. Debussy, Claude, 1862-1918. Works. I. Title. II. Series.
Distributed by Oxford University Press, New York.

SEROFF, Victor Ilyitch, 927.8
1902-
Debussy; musician of France. New York, Putnam [1956] 367p. illus. 21cm. [ML410.D28S28] 56-6626
*1. Debussy, Claude, 1862-1918. I. Title.*BIP

SEROFF, Victor 780'.924 B
Ilyitch, 1902-
Debussy; musician of France [by] Victor I. Seroff. Freeport, N.Y., Books for Libraries Press [1970, c1958] 367 p. illus., ports. 23 cm. (Biography index reprint series) [ML410.D28S28 1970] 73-126326
1. Debussy, Claude, 1862-1918.

THOMPSON, Oscar, 1887- 780/.924
1945
Debussy; man and artist. New York, Dover [1967,c1965] xi, 393p. illus., facsims. (music), ports. 22cm. (Dover bks on music, T1783) This Dover ed. is an unabridged and slightly corrected repubn. of the work orig. pub. in 1937. Bibl. [ML410.D28T47 1967] (B) 67-16875 2.25 pap.,
*1. Debussy, Claude, 1862-1918. I. Title.*BIP

THOMPSON, Oscar, 1887- 784'.092'4
1945.
Debussy; man and artist. New York, Dover Publications [1967, c1965] xi, 393 p. illus., facsims. (music), ports. 22 cm. (Dover books on music, T1783) "This Dover edition is an unabridged and slightly corrected republication of the work originally published in 1937." Bibliography: p. 364-378. [ML410.D28T47] 67-16875
1. Debussy, Claude, 1862-1918. I. Title.

VALLAS, Leon, 1879- 780'.92'4 B
1956.
Claude Debussy, his life and works; translated from the French by Marie and Grace O'Brien. New York, Dover Publications [1973] 275, lxxxiii p. illus. 22 cm. Translation of Claude Debussy et son temps.; reprint of the 1933 ed. published by Oxford University Press, London. Thematic catalog and bibliography: lxxxiii p. at end. [ML410.D28V1673 1973] 72-93606 ISBN 0-486-22916-5 3.50 (pbk.)
1. Debussy, Achille Claude, 1862-1918. I. O'Brien, Marie, tr. II. O'Brien, Grace, joint tr. BIP

Debussy, Claude, 1862-1918—Knowledge—Literature.

WENK, Arthur B. 780'.92'4
Claude Debussy and the poets / Arthur B. Wenk. Berkeley : University of California Press, c1976. x, 345 p. : music ; 25 cm. Includes index. Bibliography: p. [319]-340. [ML410.D28W4] 74-82854 ISBN 0-520-02827-9 : 22.50
1. Debussy, Claude, 1862-1918—Knowledge—Literature. 2. Music and literature. I. Title. BIP

Decamps, Alexandre Gabriel, 1803-1860.

MOSBY, Dewey F., 1942- 759.4 B
Alexandre-Gabriel Decamps, 1803-1860 / Dewey F. Mosby. New York : Garland Pub., 1977. 2 v. (xli, 699 p., 232 leaves of plates) ; ill. ; 21 cm. (Outstanding dissertations in the fine arts) Thesis—Harvard, 1973. Bibliography: v. 2, p. [665]-699. [ND553.D29M83 1977] 76-23651 ISBN 0-8240-2714-0 : 95.00
1. Decamps, Alexandre Gabriel, 1803-1860. 2. Painters—France—Biography. I. Title. II. Series.

Decatur, Stephen, 1779-1820.

LEWIS, Charles 973.4'7'0924 B
Lee, 1886-
The romantic Decatur. Freeport, N.Y., Books for Libraries Press [1971] 296 p. illus., ports. 23 cm. Reprint of the 1937 ed. Bibliography: p. [258]-270. [E353.1.D29L5 1971] 79-164614 ISBN 0-8369-5898-5
1. Decatur, Stephen, 1779-1820. I. Title. BIP

Decatur, Stephen, 1779-1820—Juvenile literature.

BLASSINGAME, Wyatt. 92 (J)
Stephen Decatur; fighting sailor. Illustrated by Paul Frame. Champaign, Ill., Garrard Pub. Co. [1964] 80 p. col. illus. 23 cm. (A Discovery book) [E353.1.D29B55] 64-11622
1. Decatur, Stephen, 1779-1820—Juvenile literature. BIP

Decembrists—Personal narratives.

VOICES in exile : 322.4'4'0922
the Decembrist memoirs / [compiled by] G. R. V. Barratt. Montreal : McGill-Queen's University Press, 1974. xxi, 381 p. : ill. ; 25 cm. Includes bibliographical references and index. [DK212.V56] 75-310670 ISBN 0-7735-0183-5 : 17.00
1. Decembrists—Personal narratives. I. Barratt, G. R. V.
Distributed by McGill Queens University Irvington, New York. BIP

DeCenzo, John.

DECENZO, John. 286'.73 B
The seekers : a young couple's desperate search for God / by John DeCenzo, with Jeanise M. DeCenzo. Mountain View, Calif. : Pacific Press Pub. Association, c1977. 112 p. ; 22 cm. (A Destiny book ; D159) [BX6189.D425A37] 76-20904 pbk. 3.50
1. DeCenzo, John. 2. DeCenzo, Jeanise M. 3. Converts, Seventh-Day Adventist—United States—Biography. I. DeCenzo, Jeanise M., joint author. II. Title.

Decker, Benton Weaver, 1899-

DECKER, Benton 940.53'144'0952 B
Weaver, 1899-
Return of the black ships / by Benton Weaver Decker and Edwina Naylor Decker. 1st ed. New York : Vantage Press, c1978. x, 420 p. : ill. ; 21 cm. [DS889.15.D42] 79-106940 ISBN 0-533-03368-3 : 11.95
1. Decker, Benton Weaver, 1899- 2. United States. Navy—Biography. 3. United States. Navy—Foreign service—Japan—Biography. 4. Decker, Edwina Naylor. 5. Japan—History—Allied occupation, 1945-1952. 6. Admirals—United States—Biography. 7. Japan—Description and travel—1945- 8. Yokosuka, Japan—Description. I. Decker, Edwina Naylor, joint author. II. Title. BIP

Decker, Mary, 1958- —Juvenile literature.

JACOBS, Linda. 796.4'2'0924 B
Mary Decker : speed records and spaghetti / by Linda Jacobs. St. Paul : EMC Corp., [1975] p. cm. (Her Women who win ; 3) A biography of a California schoolgirl who by the age of fifteen had already broken world speed records in running. [GV697.D37J32] 92 75-2225 ISBN 0-88436-162-4 lib.bdg. : 4.95 ISBN 0-88436-163-2 pbk. : 2.95
1. Decker, Mary, 1958- —Juvenile literature. 2. Running—Juvenile literature. I. Title. BIP

Deckert, Josef, 1843-1901.

BLOCH, Josef 301.45'19'24024 B
Samuel, 1850-1923.
My reminiscences [by] Joseph S. Bloch New York, Arno Press, 1973 [c1922] 576 p. illus. 23 cm. (The Jewish people: history, religion, literature) Translation of Erinnerungen aus meinem Leben. Reprint of the ed. published by R. Lowit, Vienna. "Lawsuit against Dr. Joseph Deckert and Paulus Meyer": p. [357]-570. [DS135.A93B63 1973] 73-2188 ISBN 0-405-05254-5 30.00
1. Bloch, Josef Samuel, 1850-1923. 2. Deckert, Josef, 1843-1901. 3. Meyer, Paulus. 4. Antisemitism—Austria. 5. Blood accusation. I. Title. II. Series.

Decoys (Hunting)—Massachusetts—Martha's Vineyard.

MURPHY, Stanley. 745.59'3
Martha's Vineyard decoys / Stanley Murphy ; photos. by George Moffett. Boston : D. R. Godine, c1978. viii, 165 p. : ill. (some col.) ; 25 x 26 cm. [SK335.M88] 78-58592 ISBN 0-87923-260-9 : 25.00
1. Decoys (Hunting)—Massachusetts—Martha's Vineyard. 2. Wood-carvers—Massachusetts—Martha's Vineyard—Biography. 3. Martha's Vineyard, Mass.—Biography. I. Moffett, George. II. Title. BIP

Deere, John, 1804-1886.

BARE, Margaret Ann. 672'.0924 B
John Deere, blacksmith boy. Illustrated by Robert Doremus. Indianapolis, Bobbs-Merrill [1964] 200 p. col. illus. 20 cm. (Childhood of famous Americans) Bibliography: p. 198. Describes the boyhood and youth of John Deere, who loved hard work, became a blacksmith's apprentice, invented the steel plow, and built a farm implements factory. [PZ7.B25028Jo] 92 AC 68
1. Deere, John, 1804-1886. I. Doremus, Robert, illus. II. Title.

Defoe, Daniel, 1661?-1731.

CHADWICK, William. 823'.5
The life and times of Daniel De Foe: with remarks digressive and discursive. London, J. R. Smith, 1859. [Folcroft, Pa.] Folcroft Library Editions, 1972. p. [PR3406.C4 1972] 72-7274 ISBN 0-8414-0312-0 (lib. bdg.)
1. Defoe, Daniel, 1661?-1731. I. Title.

CHADWICK, William. 828'.5'09 B
The life and times of Daniel DeFoe with remarks digressive and discursive. New York, B. Franklin [1968] viii, 464 p. port. 23 cm. (Essays in literature and criticism, 19) (Burt Franklin research and source works series, 328) Reprint of the 1859 ed. [PR3406.C4 1968] 68-58464
1. Defoe, Daniel, 1661?-1731. I. Title.

CHALMERS, George, 1742- 823'.5 B
1825.
The life of Daniel De Foe. Oxford, Printed by D. A. Talboys for T. Tegg, 1841. [Folcroft, Pa.] Folcroft Library Editions, 1972. 157 p. 24 cm. Reprint of the 1841 ed. Bibliography: p. [PR3406.C5 1972] 72-10191 ISBN 0-8414-0670-7 20.00
1. Defoe, Daniel, 1661?-1731.

DOTTIN, Paul, 1895-1965. 823'.5 B
The life and strange and surprising adventures of Daniel De Foe. Translated from the French by Louise Ragan. New York, Octagon Books, 1971 [c1929] vii, 322 p. illus., facsim., ports. 24 cm. Translation of pt. 1 of Daniel De Foe et ses romans. "List of Daniel De Foe's works:" p. 267-304: Bibliography: p. 305-311. [PR3406.D613 1971] 70-154663 ISBN 0-374-92257-8
1. Defoe, Daniel, 1661?-1731. 2. Defoe, Daniel, 1661?-1731—Bibliography. I. Title. BIP

FITZGERALD, Brian. 823'.5
Daniel Defoe : a study in conflict / Brian Fitzgerald. Norwood, Pa. : Norwood Editions, 1976. 248 p. : ill. ; 23 cm. Reprint of the 1954 ed. published by Secker & Warburg, London. Includes index. Bibliography: p. 241-243. [PR3406.F5 1976] 76-29033 ISBN 0-8402-0778-5 lib. bdg. : 25.00
1. Defoe, Daniel, 1661?-1731. 2. Novelists, English—18th century—Biography.

FITZGERALD, Edward, 1809- 821'.8
1883.
Letters & literary remains of Edward FitzGerald. New York, AMS Press, 1966. 7 v. illus. 23 cm. On spine: The works of Edward FitzGerald. Reprint of the 1902-1903 ed. Includes bibliographical references. [PR4700.A2 1966] 72-183517
I. Title. BIP

FORSTER, John, 1812- 823'.5 B
1876.
Daniel De Foe. [Folcroft, Pa.] Folcroft Library Editions, 1973. p. Reprint of the 1855 ed. published by Longman, Brown, Green & Longmans, London. [PR3406.F6 1973] 73-12454 20.00
1. Defoe, Daniel, 1661?-1731. BIP

MINTO, William, 1845- 823.5 B
1893.
Daniel Defoe. New York, AMS Press [1968] viii, 171 p. 22 cm. (English men of letters) Reprint of the 1887 ed. [PR3406.M5 1968] 68-58386
1. Defoe, Daniel, 1661?-1731.

MOORE, John Robert, 1890- 928.2
Daniel Defoe, citizen of the world [Chicago] University of Chicago Press [1958] xv, 408p. illus., maps. 25cm.

Bibliographical references included in 'Notes' (p. 356-385) [PR3406.M58] 58-11950
1. Defoe, Daniel, 1661?-1731. I. Title.

SUTHERLAND, James Runcieman, 1900- 823'.5 B
Defoe, by James Sutherland. New York, Barnes & Noble [1971] xiii, 300 p. illus. 23 cm. Reprint of the 1937 ed. Includes bibliographical references. [PR3406.S8 1971] 75-28137 ISBN 0-389-04143-2
1. Defoe, Daniel, 1661?-1731. BIP

WATSON, Francis, 1907- v. 12
Daniel Defoe. London, New York, Longmans, Green [1952] vii, 240p. illus. 19cm. (Men and books) 'Reading note': p. 228-229. A 53
1. Defoe, Daniel, 1661?-1731. I. Title. II. Series. BIP

WATSON, Francis, 1907- 823'.5
Daniel Defoe. Port Washington, N.Y., Kennikat Press [1969] vii, 240 p. illus., facsim. 21 cm. Reprint of the 1952 ed. Includes bibliographical references. [PR3406.W3 1969] 70-86578
1. Defoe, Daniel, 1661?-1731.

WHERRY, Albinia Lucy (Cust) 1857- 823'.5
Daniel Defoe. [Folcroft, Pa.] Folcroft Library Editions, 1973. 128 p. illus. 24 cm. Reprint of the 1905 ed. published by G. Bell, London, in series: Bell's miniature series of great writers. "Abbreviated list of Defoe's works": p. 125-128. [PR3406.W35 1973] 73-70 10.00
1. Defoe, Daniel, 1661-1731. I. Series: Bell's miniature series of great writers.

WHERRY, Albinia Lucy (Cust) 1857- 823'.5
Daniel Defoe. [Folcroft, Pa.] Folcroft Library Editions, 1973. 128 p. illus. 24 cm. Reprint of the 1905 ed. published by G. Bell, London, in series: Bell's miniature series of great writers. "Abbreviated list of Defoe's works": p. 125-128. [PR3406.W35 1973] 73-70 10.00
1. Defoe, Daniel, 1661-1731. I. Series: Bell's miniature series of great writers.

WILSON, Walter, 1781-1847. 823'.5 B
Memoirs of the life and times of Daniel De Foe: containing a review of his writings, and his opinions upon a variety of important matters, civil and ecclesiastical. London, Hurst, Chance, 1830. [New York, AMS Press, 1973] 3 v. port. 23 cm. Includes bibliographical references. [PR3406.W5 1973] 71-153602 ISBN 0-404-09790-1 67.50
1. Defoe, Daniel, 1661-1731. I. Title.

WILSON, Walter, 1781-1847. 823'.5 B
Memoirs of the life and times of Daniel De Foe: containing a review of his writings, and his opinions upon a variety of important matters, civil and ecclesiastical. London, Hurst, Chance, 1830. [New York, AMS Press, 1973] 3 v. port. 23 cm. Includes bibliographical references. [PR3406.W5 1973] 71-153602 ISBN 0-404-09790-1 67.50
1. Defoe, Daniel, 1661-1731. I. Title.

Defoe, Daniel, 1661?-1731—Biography.

CHALMERS, George, 1742-1825. 823'.5 B
The life of Daniel Defoe. New York, Garland Pub., 1970. 86 p. 22 cm. Facsim. of the Yale University Library copy, with imprint: London, J. Stockdale, 1790. "A list of writings, which are considered as undoubtedly De Foe's": p. 71-86. [PR3406.C5 1790a] 73-112093
1. Defoe, Daniel, 1661?-1731—Biography. BIP

DEFOE, Daniel, 1661?-1731. 828'.5'08 B
Daniel Defoe: his life and recently discovered writings, extending from 1716 to 1729, by William Lee. New York, B. Franklin [1969] 3 v. illus., facsims., ports. 24 cm. (Burt Franklin research and source works series, 369.) (Selected papers in literature and criticism, no. 28) Reprint of the 1869 ed. Contents.Contents.—v. 1. The life of Daniel Defoe.—v. 2. The first volume of his writings.—v. 3. The second volume of his writings. "A chronological catalogue of Daniel Defoe's works": v. 1, p. [xxvii]-lv. [PR3401.L4 1969] 78-82017
I. Lee, William, inspector, General Board of Health. II. Title. III. Series.

WHITTEN, Wilfred, 1864-1942. 823'.5 B
Daniel Defoe. New York, Haskell House, 1974. xix, 117 p. 20 cm. Reprint of the 1900 ed. published by K. Paul, Trench, Trubner, London, in series: The Westminster biographies. Bibliography: p. [113]-117. [PR3406.W4 1974] 73-21562 ISBN 0-8383-1806-1 9.95
1. Defoe, Daniel, 1661?-1731—Biography. I. Series: Westminster biographies. BIP

Defoe, Daniel, 1661?-1731—Contemporary England.

EARLE, Peter, 1937- 823'.5 B
The world of Defoe / Peter Earle. 1st American ed. New York : 1977, c1976. 1977. xii, 353 p. : maps (on lining papers) ; 22 cm. Includes bibliographical references and index. [PR3408.E46E2 1977] 76-40310 ISBN 0-689-10772-2 : 12.50
1. Defoe, Daniel, 1661?-1731—Contemporary England. 2. England—Civilization—17th century. 3. England—Civilization—18th century. I. Title. BIP

DeForest, Lockwood, 1850-1932.

LEWIS, Anne Suydam. 709'.2'4 B
Lockwood de Forest, painter, importer, decorator / foreword by Eva Ingersoll Gatling ; essay by Anne Suydam Lewis. Huntington, N.Y. : Heckscher Museum, 1976. 52 p. : ill. ; 28 cm. & catalog in pocket. Errata sheet inserted. Bibliography: p. 42-43. [N6537.D36L48] 76-53309
1. DeForest, Lockwood, 1850-1932. 2. Artists—United States—Biography. I. DeForest, Lockwood, 1850-1932. II. Heckscher Museum. III. Title.

Degas, Hilaire Germain Edgar, 1834-1917.

BOURET, Jean 759.4
Degas. [Tr. from French by Daphne Woodward] New York, Tudor [1966, c.1965] 272p. illus. (pt. col.) ports. (pt. col.) 22cm. [ND553.D3B683] 66-4672 5.95
1. Degas, Hilaire Germain Edgar, 1834-1917. I. Title.

CABANNE, Pierre. 759.4
Edgar Degas. [Translated by Michel Lee Landa] Paris, P. Tisne New York, Universe Books [1958] 138p. illus., 160 plates (incl. ports.; part col.) 29cm. Bibliography: p. 127-131. [ND553.D3C313] [ND553.D3C313] 927.5 58-8338 58-8338
1. Degas, Hilaire Germain Edgar, 1834-1917. I. Title.

CHARENSOL, Georges, 1899- 759.4
Degas. [Translated from the French by James Oliver] New York, H. N. Abrams [1959] 87p. col. illus. 19cm. [ND553.D3C453] 59-11866
1. Degas, Hilaire Germain Edgar, 1834-1917. I. Title.

DEGAS, Hilaire Germain Edgar, 1834-1917. 759.4
Degas / by Giovanni Carandente ; [translated by Stephen Sartarelli]. 1st U.S. ed. New York : Avenel Books : distributed by Crown Publishers, 1979. p. cm. [ND553.D3A4 1979] 78-71507 ISBN 0-517-27790-5 pbk. : 4.98
1. Degas, Hilaire Germain Edgar, 1834-1917. I. Carandente, Giovanni.

DEGAS, Hilaire Germain Edgar, 1834-1917. 927.5
My friend Degas [by] Daniel Halevy. Translated and edited with notes by Mina Curtiss. [1st American ed.] Middletown, Conn., Wesleyan University Press [1964] 127 p. illus., ports. 22 cm. Translation of Degas parie. 64-22375
I. Halevy, Daniel, 1872- II. Title.

DEGAS, Hilaire Germain Edgar, 1834-1917. 927.5
My friend Degas [by] Daniel Halevy. Translated and edited with notes by Mina Curtiss. [1st American ed.] Middletown, Conn., Wesleyan University Press [1964] 127 p. illus., ports. 22 cm. Translation of Degas parle. [ND553.D3H273] 64-22375
I. Halevy, Daniel, 1872- II. Title.

HUTTINGER, Eduard. 759.4
Degas. [Translated by Ellen Healy] New York, Crown Publishers. 1960 92 [3] p. illus. (part mounted, part col.) 29 cm. Bibliography: p. [89]-[93] [ND553.D3H83] [ND553.D3H83] 759.4 60-51440 60-51440
1. Degas, Hilaire Germain Edgar, 1834-1917. I. Title. BIP

HUTTINGER, Edward 759.4
Degas. [Translated by Ellen Healy] New York, Crown Publishers, 1960[ ] 92, [3]p. Bibliography: p.[89]-[93] illus. (part mounted, part col.) 29cm. 60-51440 2.95 bds.,
1. Degas, Hilaire Germain Edgar, 1834-1917. I. Title.

ISAAC Delgado Museum of Art, New Orleans. v. 12
Edgar Degas, his family and friends in New Orleans. On the occasion of an exhibition of Degas' New Orleans work, May 2-June 16, 1965. New Orleans [1965] 96 p. illus. (part col.) 28 cm. Includes bibliographical references. 66-81634
1. Degas, Hilaire Germain Edgar, 1834-1917. I. Title.

DeGautier, Felisa Rincon

GRUBER, Ruth. v. 12 B
Felisa Rincon de Gautier; the mayor of San Juan. New York, Dell 1975 190 p. 18 cm. (Women of America) Bibliography, p. 176-177 [F1971] 320.97295 0.95 (pbk.)
1. DeGautier, Felisa Rincon I. Title.
L.C. card no. for original edition: 72-83789. BIP

GRUBER, Ruth. v. 12 B
Felisa Rincon de Gautier; the mayor of San Juan. New York, Dell 1975 190 p. 18 cm. (Women of America) Bibliography, p. 176-177 [F1971] 320.97295 0.95 (pbk.)
1. DeGautier, Felisa Rincon I. Title.
L.C. card no. for original edition: 72-83789. BIP

DeGolyer, Everette Lee, 1886-1956.

TINKLE, Lon. 338.2'7'20924 B
Mr. De; a biography of Everette Lee DeGolyer. With a foreword by Norman Cousins. [1st ed.] Boston, Little, Brown [1970] xix, 393 p. illus., ports. 22 cm. [HD9570.D4T53] 75-121439 7.95
1. DeGolyer, Everette Lee, 1886-1956. I. Title.

DeGrazia, Ted Ettore, 1909-

REED, William, 1929- 709'.24
De Grazia, the irreverent angel. San Diego, Calif., Frontier Heritage Press, 1971. ix, 191 p. illus. (part col.) 24 x 32 cm. Bibliography: p. [186]-191. [N6537.D4R4] 72-157994 14.95
1. DeGrazia, Ted Ettore, 1909- I. Title.

ROSENFELD, Dorcas. 759.13
DeGrazia as I know him. [Phoenix, Ariz., O'Sullivan Woodside, 1974] p. cm. [ND237.D3337R67] 74-17066 ISBN 0-89019-042-9 7.95
1. DeGrazia, Ted Ettore, 1909- I. Title.

DeHaven, Jean, 1928—

WAKEFIELD, Bob. 917.3'04'923
Jean DeHaven's "Trial of the jackasses." [1st ed. Aberdeen, S.D., North Plains Press, 1968] 431 p. illus. (part col.), maps (on lining papers), ports. 24 cm. [E169.O2.W27] 68-58725 5.50
1. DeHaven, Jean, 1928- 2. U.S.—Description and travel—1960- 3. Muleteers—U.S. I. Title. II. Title: "Trial of the jackasses."

Deism—Biography.

PIKE, Edgar Royston, 1896- 211'.5'0922
Slayers of superstition; a popular account of some of the leading personalities of the deist movement, by E. Royston Pike. Port Washington, N.Y., Kennikat Press [1970] vi, 106 p. ports. 19 cm. Reprint of the 1931 ed. Contents.Contents.—The origins of European scepticism.—The pioneers of deism.—Toland and Collins.—Wollaston and Tindal.—Woolston and Chubb.—Hume.—Gibbon.—French scepticism, from Descartes to the Revolution. [BL2785.P5 1970] 78-102581
1. Deism—Biography. I. Title.

Dekker, Thomas, 1570?-1641?

HUNT, Mary Leland. 822'.3 B
Thomas Dekker; a study. [Folcroft, Pa.] Folcroft Library Editions, 1973 [c1911] p. Reprint of the ed. published by the Columbia University Press, New York, in series: Columbia University studies in English. Bibliography: [PR2493.H8 1973] 73-8949 25.00
1. Dekker, Thomas, 1570?-1641? I. Title. II. Series: Columbia University studies in English. BIP

HUNT, Mary Leland. 822'.3 B
Thomas Dekker; a study. [Folcroft, Pa.] Folcroft Library Editions, 1973 [c1911] p. Reprint of the ed. published by the Columbia University Press, New York, in series: Columbia University studies in English. Bibliography: [PR2493.H8 1973] 73-8949 ISBN 0-8414-4706-3 (lib. bdg.)
1. Dekker, Thomas, 1570?-1641? I. Title. II. Series: Columbia University studies in English.

Delcev, Goce, 1872-1903.

MACDERMOTT, Mercia, 1927- 322.4'2'0924 B
Freedom or death, the life of Gotse Delchev / by Mercia MacDermott. London ; West Nyack, N.Y. : Journeyman Press, 1978. vi, 405 p., [8] leaves of plates : ill., maps (on lining papers) ; 23 cm. Includes index. Bibliography: p. [388]-396. [DR701.M42D4263] 79-307187 ISBN 0-904526-32-1 : 17.50
1. Delcev, Goce, 1872-1903. 2. Revolutionists—Macedonia—Biography. 3. Macedonia—History—1453- I. Title.

Delacroix, Eugene, 1798-1863.

BAUDELAIRE, Charles Pierre, 1821-1867. 759.4
Eugene Delacroix, his life and work / Charles Baudelaire. New York : Garland Pub., 1979. p. cm. (Connoisseurship, criticism, and art history in the nineteenth century ; 2) Reprint of the 1947 ed. published by Lear Publshers, New York. Translation of La vie et l'oeuvre d'Eugene Delacroix. [ND553.D33B3 1979] 77-18676 ISBN 0-8240-3258-6 : 22.00
1. Delacroix, Eugene, 1798-1863. 2. Painters—France—Biography. I. Title. II. Series.

DELACROIX, Engene. 927.5
[Ferdinand Victor Eugene Delacroix] 1798-1863.
Journal. Tr. from French by Walter Pach. Illus. with reproductions of the drawings of the artist. New York, Grove Press [1961, c.1937, 1948] 750p. illus. 26cm. (Evergreen encyclopedia, v. 9, E-265) 61-1184 4.95 pap.,
I. Title.

DELACROIX, Eugene, 1798-1863. 759.4 B
The journal of Eugene Delacroix. Translated from the French by Walter Pach. Illustrated with reproductions of drawings by the artist. New York, Viking Press [1972] 762 p. illus. 20 cm. (A Viking compass book, C335) Bibliography: p. 737-740. [ND553.D33A32 1972] 70-182804 ISBN 0-670-00335-2 4.95

DELACROIX, Eugene, 1798-1863. 927.5
The Journal of Eugene Delacroix; a selection edited with an introd. by Hubert Wellington, translated from the French by Lucy Norton. New York, Phaidon Publishers; distributed by Oxford University Press [1951] xxxiv, [1]. 504 p. plates, ports., facsim. 20 cm. (Phaidon

pocket series] Bibliography: p. [xxxv] [ND553.D33A318 1951] 52-11273
I. Title.

DESLANDRES, Yvonne. 759.4
Delacroix, a pictorial biography. [Translated from the French by Jonathan Griffin] New York, Viking Press [1963] 144 p. illus. 24 cm. (A Studio book) [ND553.D33D43] 63-9301
1. Delacroix, Eugene, 1798-1863. I. Title.

Delany, Martin Robison, 1812-1885.

GRIFFITH, Cyril E. 973.7'092'4 B
The African dream : Martin R. Delany and the emergence of pan-African thought / Cyril E. Griffith. University Park : Pennsylvania State University Press, [1975] p. cm. Includes index. Bibliography: p. [E185.97.D4G74] 74-20559 ISBN 0-271-01181-5 : 10.00
1. Delany, Martin Robison, 1812-1885. 2. Negroes—Colonization—Africa. I. Title. BIP

ROLLIN, Frank A. 973.7'0924
Life and public services of Martin R. Delany [by] Frank A. Rollin. New York, Arno Press, 1969. vii, 367 p. 21 cm. (The American Negro, his history and literature) Reprint of the 1883 ed. [E185.97.D33 1969] 77-92236
1. Delany, Martin Robison, 1812-1885. 2. United States. Bureau of Refugees, Freedmen and Abandoned Lands. 3. United States—History—Civil War, 1861-1865—Negro troops. I. Title. II. Series. BIP

STERLING, Dorothy, 1913- 973.7'0924
The making of an Afro-American: Martin Robison Delany, 1812-1885. [1st ed.] Garden City, N.Y., Doubleday [1971] 352 p. port. 22 cm. "A Perspective book." Bibliography: p. 333-345. [E185.97.D34] 79-141542 4.95
1. Delany, Martin Robison, 1812-1885. I. Title.

Delany, Mary Granville Pendarves, 1700-1788.

DELANY, Mary Granville Pendarves, 1700-1788. 942.07'3'0924 B
The autobiography and correspondence of Mary Granville, Mrs. Delany: with interesting reminiscences of King George the Third and Queen Charlotte. Edited by Lady Llanover. [1st-2d series] London, R. Bentley, 1861-62. [New York, AMS Press, 1974] 6 v. illus. 23 cm. [DA483.D3A2 1974] 75-163683 ISBN 0-404-02080-1 180.00 (6 vols.)
1. Delany, Mary Granville Pendarves, 1700-1788. 2. George III, King of Great Britain, 1738-1820. 3. Charlotte, Queen consort of George III, 1744-1818. I. Llanover, Augusta Waddington Hall, Lady, d. 1896, ed. II. Title. BIP

Delany, Samuel R. - Addresses, essays, lectures.

DELANY, Samuel R. 808.387'6
The jewel-hinged jaw : notes on the language of science fiction / Samuel R. Delany. 1st ed. Elizabethtown, N.Y. : Dragon Press, 1977. 326 p. ; 23 cm. [PS3554.E437J4] 78-105248 12.95 signed ed. : 25.00
1. Delany, Samuel R.—Addresses, essays, lectures. 2. Science fiction—Technique—Addresses, essays, lectures. 3. Authors, American—20th century—Biography—Addresses, essays, lectures. I. Title.
Publisher's address: Box 445 Elizabethtown, NY 12932 BIP

DELANY, Samuel R. 808.387'6
The jewel-hinged jaw : notes of the language of science fiction / Samuel R. Delany. New York : Berkley Pub. Corp., 1978, c1977. 303p. ; 20 cm. (A Berkley Windhover Book) [PS3554.E437J4] ISBN 0-425-03852-1 pbk. : 4.95
1. Delany, Samuel R. — Addresses, essays, lectures. 2. Science fiction — Technique — Addresses, essays, lectures. 3. Authors, American — 20th century — Biography — Addresses, essays, lectures. I. Title.
L.C. card no. for 1977 Dragon Press ed.: 78-105248.

Delaroche, Hippolyte, called Paul, 1797-1856.

ZIFF, Norman D. 759.4 B
Paul Delaroche : a study in nineteenth-century French history painting / Norman D. Ziff. New York : Garland Pub., 1977. xv, 410 p. : ill. ; 21 cm. (Outstanding dissertations in the fine arts) Originally presented as the author's thesis, New York University, 1974. Bibliography: p. 308-328. [ND553.D3553 1977] 76-23663 ISBN 0-8240-2741-8 lib.bdg. 40.00
1. Delaroche, Hippolyte, called Paul, 1797-1856. 2. Painters—France—Biography. 3. History in art. I. Delaroche, Hippolyte, called Paul, 1797-1856. II. Title. III. Series.

Delaunay, Robert, 1885-1941.

DELAUNAY, Robert, 1885-1941. 759.4
R. Delaunay / by Michel Hoog ; [translated from the French by Alice Sachs]. New York : Crown Publishers, 1977,c1976 96 p. : ill. (some col.) ; 29 cm. Bibliography: p. 95. [ND553.D357H6613] 76-41382 ISBN 0-517-52875-4 : 4.95
1. Delaunay, Robert, 1885-1941. I. Hoog, Michel.

Delaunay, Sonia.

COHEN, Arthur Allen, 1928- 760'.092'4
Sonia Delaunay / Arthur A. Cohen. New York : H. N. Abrams, [1975] p. cm. Includes index. Bibliography: p. [N6853.D34C63] 75-8738 ISBN 0-8109-0292-3 : 37.50
1. Delaunay, Sonia. BIP

Delavan, James.

DELAVAN, James. 917.94'04'40924
The gold rush : letters of Dr. James Delavan from California to the Adrian, Michigan, Expositor, 1850-1856. Mount Pleasant, Mich. : Cumming Press, c1976. xxvi, 97 p. ; 24 cm. Edition limited to 487 copies. [F865.D35] 77-366948
1. Delavan, James. 2. California—Gold discoveries. 3. California—History—1850-1950. 4. Voyages to the Pacific coast. 5. Journalists—United States—Biography. I. Title.

Delaware—Biography.

WILSON, W. Emerson. 975.1 B
Forgotten heroes of Delaware [by] Emerson Wilson. Cambridge, Mass., Deltos Pub. Co. [1970, c1969] iv, 188 p. illus., ports. 24 cm. [F163.W53 1969] 72-78013
1. Delaware—Biography. I. Title.

Delbo, Charlotte.

DELBO, Charlotte. 940.54'72'48094385
None of us will return / Charlotte Delbo ; translated by John Githens. Boston : Beacon Press, [1978] p. cm. Translation of Aucun de nous ne reviendra. Reprint of the 1968 ed. published by Grove Press, New York. [D805.P7D413 1978] 77-88586 ISBN 0-8070-6371-1 pbk. : 3.95
1. Delbo, Charlotte. 2. Oswiecim (Concentration camp) 3. World War, 1939-1945—Personal narratives, French. 4. Prisoners of war—Germany—Biography. I. Title.

Delderfield, Ronald Frederick,

DELDERFIELD, Ronald Frederick, 1912- 828'.9'1203 B
For my own amusement [by] R. F. Delderfield. New York, Simon and Schuster [1972] 381 p. 22 cm. Autobiographical stories assembled from the author's For my own amusement (1968) and Overture for beginners (1970) [PR6007.E36Z5252 1972] 77-165474 ISBN 0-671-21125-0 8.95
I. Delderfield, Ronald Frederick, 1912- Overture for beginners. Selections. 1972. II. Title.

Deledda, Grazia, 1871-1936—Biography—Juvenile literature.

BALDUCCI, Carolyn. 853'.9'12 B
A self-made woman : biography of Nobel-prize-winner Grazia Deledda / by Carolyn Balducci. Boston : Houghton Mifflin, 1975. p. cm. A biography of a Sardinian woman who determinedly rose above the restrictions of her environment to win the Novel Prize for literature in 1926. [PQ4811.E6Z58] 92 75-17032 ISBN 0-395-21914-0 : 6.95
1. Deledda, Grazia, 1871-1936—Biography—Juvenile literature. I. Title. BIP

Delius, Frederick, 1862-1934.

BEECHAM, Thomas, Sir, bart., 1879- 927.8
Frederick Delius. New York, Knopf, 1960 [c1959] 227 p. illus. 24 cm. [ML410.D35B4 1960] 60-16206
1. Delius, Frederick, 1862-1934. BIP

BEECHAM, Thomas, Sir, bart., 1879-1961. 780'.92'4 B
Frederick Delius [by] Thomas Beecham. New York, Vienna House [1973, c1959] 227 p. illus. 21 cm. [ML410.D35B4 1973] 73-89930 ISBN 0-8443-0082-9 2.95 (pbk.)
1. Delius, Frederick, 1862-1934.

CARLEY, L. 780'.92'4 B
Delius : a life in pictures / Lionel Carley and Robert Threlfall. Oxford : Oxford University Press, 1977. iv, 99 p. : ill., music, ports. ; 31 cm. Includes bibliographical references. [ML410.D35C28] 78-301800 ISBN 0-19-315437-4 : 16.00
1. Delius, Frederick, 1862-1934. 2. Composers—Biography. 3. Composers—Iconography. I. Threlfall, Robert, joint author.
Distributed by Oxford University Press, New York BIP

A Delius companion 780'.92'4 B
/ edited, with a pref. by Christopher Redwood. New York : Da Capo Press, 1977. 270 p., [10] leaves of plates : ill. ; 23 cm. (Da Capo Press music reprint series) [ML410.D35D44 1977] 76-57756 ISBN 0-306-70858-2
1. Delius, Frederick, 1862-1934. 2. Composers—England—Biography. I. Redwood, Christopher, 1939-

FENBY, Eric, 1906- 780'.92'4 B
Delius. New York, T. Y. Crowell Co. [1972, c1971] 100 p. illus. 26 cm. (The Great composers) Bibliography: p. 94. Biography of a composer whose music was influenced by his stays in England, the United States, France, and Norway. [ML410.D35F38 1972] 92 75-157645 ISBN 0-690-23495-3 4.95
1. Delius, Frederick, 1862-1934. I. Title.

FENBY, Eric, 1906- 780'.92'4 B
Delius as I knew him / Eric Fenby. Westport, Conn. : Greenwood Press, 1975. p. cm. Reprint of the 1948 ed. published by Quality Press, London. Includes index. [ML410.D35F4 1975] 75-25255 ISBN 0-8371-8394-4 lib.bdg. : 14.25
1. Delius, Frederick, 1862-1934. BIP

FENBY, Eric, 1906- 780.924
Deluis as I knew him; with an introduction by Sir Malcolm Sargent. [New ed.] rev. ed. by the author. London, Icon Bks., 1966. xiv, 250p. front. (port.) illus. (music) 20cm. [ML410.D35F41966] 66-74680 6.95; 1.95 pap.,
1. Delius, Frederick, 1862-1934. I. Title.
American distributor: Dufour, Chester Springs, Pa.

HESELTINE, Philip, 1894-1930. 927.8
Frederick Delius, by Peter Warlock (Philip Heseltine) Reprinted with additions, annotations, and comments by Hubert Foss. [Rev. ed.] New York, Oxford University Press, 1952. 224 p. port., music. 21 cm. "A list of Frederick Delius' compositions ... published and unpublished": p. 197-215. [ML410.D35H36 1952] 52-9915
1. Delius, Frederick, 1862-1934. I. Title.

HUTCHINGS, Arthur, 1906- 780'.924 B
Delius. Westport, Conn., Greenwood Press [1970] ix, 193 p. illus., music, ports. 23 cm. Reprint of the 1948 ed. Bibliography: p. 191. [ML410.D35H85 1970] 74-104289 ISBN 0-8371-3958-9
1. Delius, Frederick, 1862-1934. BIP

JAHODA, Gloria. 780'.924 B
The road to Samarkand: Frederick Delius and his music. New York, C. Scribner's Sons [1969] xi, 248 p. illus., music, ports. 22 cm. [ML410.D35J3] 69-17063 4.50
1. Delius, Frederick, 1862-1934. I. Title.

PALMER, Christopher. 780'.92'4 B
Delius : portrait of a cosmopolitan / Christopher Palmer ; with a foreword by Eric Fenby. New York : Holmes & Meier Publishers, 1976. xi, 199 p., [9] leaves of plates : ill. ; 24 cm. Includes index. Bibliography: p. 195-196. [ML410.D35P3] 76-8893 ISBN 0-8419-0274-7 : 19.00
1. Delius, Frederick, 1862-1934. BIP

Dell, William, d. 1664.

WALKER, Eric Charles, 1903- 285'.9'0924 B
William Dell: master Puritan, by Eric C. Walker. Cambridge, Heffer, 1970. x, 238 p., 2 plates. illus., map, ports. 22 cm. Bibliography: p. 228-231. [BX9339.D37W3] 79-552862 ISBN 0-85270-018-0 £3.00
1. Dell, William, d. 1664. I. Title.

Della Femina, Jerry.

DELLA Femina, Jerry. 974.7'1'040924 B
An Italian grows in Brooklyn / Jerry Della Femina, Charles Sopkin. 1st ed. Boston : Little, Brown, c1978. 215 p. ; 22 cm. [F129.B7D444] 78-11562 ISBN 0-316-17991-4 : 8.95
1. Della Femina, Jerry. 2. Italian Americans—New York (City)—Biography. 3. Italian Americans—New York (City)—Social life and customs. 4. Brooklyn—Biography. 5. Brooklyn—Social life and customs. I. Sopkin, Charles, joint author. II. Title. BIP

Deller, Alfred.

HARDWICK, John Michael Drinkrow, 1924- 784'.0924 B
Alfred Deller; a singularity of voice, by Michael and Mollie Hardwick. With a foreword by Sir Michael Tippett. Illustrated by John Ward. New York, F. A. Praeger [1969, c1968] xi, 204 p. illus., ports. 22 cm. Discography: p. 181-190. [ML420.D44H4 1969] 69-16086 6.50
1. Deller, Alfred. I. Hardwick, Mollie, joint author.

Delsarte, Francois Alexandre Nicolas Cheri, 1811-1871.

SHAWN, Ted, 1891- 793.3'0924
Every little movement; a book about Francois Delsarte, the man and his philosophy, his science and applied aesthetics, the application of this science to the art of the dance, the influence of Delsarte on American dance. [Brooklyn, Dance Horizons, 1968?] 127 p. illus. 21 cm. (Series of republications by Dance Horizons, 15) "Unabridged republication of the second revised and enlarged edition published in 1963." Bibliography: p. 91-126. [GV463.S46 1968] 68-28049 2.95
1. Delsarte, Francois Alexandre Nicolas Cheri, 1811-1871. 2. Delsarte system. 3. Dancing. I. Title.

Demara, Ferdinand Waldo.

CRICHTON, Robert [Collier] 920.8
The great imposter. New York, Permabooks [dist. Pocket Books 1960, c.1959] vi, 245p. 17cm. (Permabooks M5027) .50 pap.,
1. Demara, Ferdinand Waldo. I. Title.

Demarest, Charles Howell, 1880-

DEMAREST, David Franklin, 1919- 923.273
One of the few; the story of Charles Howell Demarest. New York, Canyon

Press of New York, 1950. viii, 212 p. illus., ports. 21 cm. [CT275.D3425D4] 50-9947
1. Demarest, Charles Howell, 1880- I. Title.

Demarest, Victoria Booth-Clibborn.

DEMAREST, Victoria Booth-Clibborn. 262'.14
God, woman & ministry / by Victoria Booth Demarest ; photos. by Sacred Arts International, inc. Rev. ed. St. Petersburg, Fla. : Sacred Arts International, c1978. 182 p. : ports. ; 23 cm. First ed. published in 1977 under title: Sex & spirit. Bibliography: p. 180-182. [BV639.W7D45 1978] 78-103638 ISBN 0-912760-61-3: 6.95
1. Demarest, Victoria Booth-Clibborn. 2. United Church of Christ—Clergy—Biography. 3. Women in Christianity. 4. Women clergy. 5. Clergy—United States—Biography. I. Title. BIP

DEMAREST, Victoria Booth-Clibborn. 262'.14
Sex & spirit : God, woman, & ministry / by Victoria Booth Demarest. 1st ed. [St. Petersburg, Fla. : Published by Sacred Arts International, in cooperation with Valkyrie Press, c1977] 182 p. : ill., ports. ; 22 cm. Bibliography: p. 181-182. [BV639.W7D4] 76-42915 ISBN 0-912760-29-X pbk. : 4.95 ISBN 0-912760-38-9 : 6.95
1. Demarest, Victoria Booth-Clibborn. 2. United Church of Christ—Clergy—Biography. 3. Women in Christianity. 4. Women as ministers. 5. Clergy—United States—Biography. I. Title.

DEMAREST, Victoria Booth-Clibborn. 262'.14
Sex & spirit : God, woman, & ministry / by Victoria Booth Demarest. 1st ed. [St. Petersburg, Fla. : Published by Sacred Arts International, in cooperation with Valkyrie Press, c1977] 182 p. : ill., ports. ; 22 cm. Bibliography: p. 181-182. [BV639.W7D4] 76-42915 ISBN 0-912760-29-X pbk. : 4.95 ISBN 0-912760-38-9 : 6.95
1. Demarest, Victoria Booth-Clibborn. 2. United Church of Christ—Clergy—Biography. 3. Women in Christianity. 4. Women as ministers. 5. Clergy—United States—Biography. I. Title. BIP

Dembskis, Vladislovas, 1831-1913.

KUNINGAS Vladislavas 891.78900303
Dembskis; jo gyvenimas, rastai ir darbai. [New York, Spauda 'Tevynes,' c1916] 165p. illus. 23cm. Edited by Jonas Sllupas. [CT1218.D4K8] 56-53874
1. Dembskis, Vladislovas, 1831-1913. I. Szlupas, John, 1861-1944, ed.

Demetrias, Mother, 1859-1940.

MURRETT, John C. 922.273
The Mary of Saint Martin's; the life of Mother Demetrias, foundress of the Mission Helpers of the Sacred Heart. Westminster, Md., Newman Press [1961, c] 1960. 187p. illus. 61-823 3.50
1. Demetrias, Mother, 1859-1940. 2. Mission Helpers of the Sacred Heart. I. Title.

Demetrius (Pseudo-Demetrius) I, Czar of Russia, 1581-1606.

BARBOUR, Philip L. 947.040924
Dimitry, called the Pretender, Tsar and Great Prince of all Russia, 1605-1606 [by] Philip L. Barbour. Illus. with photos. maps and tables by Samuel H. Bryant. Boston, Houghton, 1966. xxvii, 387p. illus. geneal. tables, maps, ports. 23cm. Bibl. [DK112.B3] 66-12062 6.95
1. Demetrius (Pseudo-Demetrius) I, Czar of Russia, 1581-1606. I. Title.

BAUMANN, Hans, 1914- 947'.04'0924 B
Dimitri and the false Tsars. Translated by Anthea Bell. New York, H. Z. Walck [1972] 188 p. map. 22 cm. A biography of the supposed son of Ivan the Terrible whose reign in the 17th century was brief but impressive. [DK112.B3813] 92 78-182529 ISBN 0-8098-3106-6 5.50
1. Demetrius (Pseudo-Demetrius) I, Czar of Russia, d. 1606—Juvenile literature. I. Title.

DeMeyer, Adolf, 1868-1949.

DE MEYER, Adolf, 1868-1949. 770'.92'4 B
DeMeyer / edited by Robert Brandau ; with a biographical essay by Philippe Jullian. 1st ed. New York : Knopf : distributed by Random House, 1976. 50 p., [51] leaves of plates : ill. ; 33 cm. [TR679.D45 1976] 75-36796 ISBN 0-394-49744-9 : 25.00
1. DeMeyer, Adolf, 1868-1949. 2. Fashion photography. 3. Photography—Portraits. I. Brandau, Robert. II. Jullian, Philippe.

Demin, Mikhail.

DEMIN, Mikhail. 364'.092'4 B
The day is born of darkness / by Mikhail Dyomin ; translated from the Russian by Tony Kahn. 1st American ed. New York : Knopf : distributed by Random House, 1976. 368 p. ; 22 cm. "Originally published in Germany as Die Tatowierten by S. Fischer Verlag, Frankfurt." [HV6248.D42A33 1976] 75-36783 ISBN 0-394-49166-1 : 10.95
1. Demin, Mikhail. 2. Crime and criminals—Russia—Correspondence, reminiscences, etc. I. Title. BIP

Deming, Edwin Willard, 1860-1942.

LAMB, Thomas G. 709'.2'4 B
Eight Bears : a biography of E. W. Deming, 1860-1942 / by Thomas G. Lamb. Oklahoma City : Griffin Books, c1978. xiv, 145 p. : ill. (some col.) ; 28 cm. Includes index. Bibliography: p. 133-138. [N6537.D44L35] 78-59986 15.95
1. Deming, Edwin Willard, 1860-1942. 2. Artists—United States—Biography. 3. Indians of North America—Pictorial works. I. Title.

Democracy.

BROWN, Alfred Barratt, 1887-1947, ed. 300'.922 B
Great democrats. Freeport, N.Y., Books for Libraries Press [1970] 704 p. 23 cm. (Essay index reprint series) Forty studies by various writers, including individual biographies of the pioneers of democracy during the past 150 years and essays on the Chartists, Christian Socialists, and early Fabians. Reprint of the 1934 ed. [H57.B7 1970] 70-128216 ISBN 0-8369-1942-4
1. Democracy. 2. Political science—History. 3. Biography. I. Title. BIP

Demorest, William Jennings, 1822-1895

ROSS, Ishbel, 1897- 917.471
Crusades and crinolines, the life and times of Ellen Curtis Demorest and William Jennings Demorest. New York, Harper [c.1963] x, 290p. illus., ports. 22cm. Bibl. 62-20116 6.00
1. Demorest, William Jennings, 1822-1895 2. Demorest, Ellen Louise(Curtis) 1825-1898 3. Demorest, Ellen Louise (Curtis) 1825-1898. 4. Demorest, William Jennings, 1822-1895. 5. New York (City)—Soc. life & cust. I. Title.

Dempsey, Jack, 1895-

DEMPSEY, Jack, 1895- 796.8'3'0924 B
Dempsey / Jack Dempsey with Barbara Piattelli Dempsey. South Yarmouth, Ma. : J. Curley, 1978. p. cm. Large print ed. [GV1132.D4A27 1978] 78-2533 ISBN 0-89340-125-0 (v. 1) pbk. : 8.95
1. Dempsey, Jack, 1895- 2. Boxers (Sports)—United States—Biography. I. Dempsey, Barbara Piattelli, joint author. BIP

DEMPSEY, Jack, 1895- 796.8'3'0924 B
Dempsey / by Jack Dempsey with Barbara Piattelli Dempsey ; introd. by Joseph Durso. 1st ed. New York : Harper & Row, c1977. xiii, 320 p., [12] leaves of plates : ill. ; 24 cm. Includes index. [GV1132.D4A27 1977] 76-26220 ISBN 0-06-011054-6 : 12.50
1. Dempsey, Jack, 1895- 2. Boxers (Sports)—United States—Biography. I. Dempsey, Barbara Piattelli, joint author. II. Title.

DEMPSEY, Jack, 1895- 796.8'3'0924 B
Dempsey / by Jack Dempsey with Barbara Piattelli Dempsey ; introd. by Joseph Durso. 1st ed. New York : Harper & Row, c1977. xiii, 320 p., [12] leaves of plates : ill. ; 24 cm. Includes index. [GV1132.D4A27 1977] 76-26220 ISBN 0-06-011054-6 : 12.50
1. Dempsey, Jack, 1895- 2. Boxers (Sports)—United States—Biography. I. Dempsey, Barbara Piattelli, joint author. II. Title.

DEMPSEY, Jack [William Harrison Dempsey] 927.9683
Dempsey, by the man himself, as told to Bob Considine and Bill Slocum. New York, Simon and Schuster, 1960 [c.1959,1960] 249p. illus. 22cm. 60-6719 3.95
I. Considine, Robert Bernard II. Title.

FLEISCHER, Nathaniel S. 796.8'3'0924 B
Jack Dempsey, by Nat Fleischer. New Rochelle, N.Y., Arlington House [1972] 256 p. illus. 24 cm. [GV1132.D4F59] 72-78480 ISBN 0-87000-151-5 8.95
1. Dempsey, Jack, 1895-

GREEN, Bill. 796.8'3'0924 B
Jack Dempsey, champion heavyweight boxer. Compiled with the assistance of the research staff of SamHar Press. Charlotteville, N.Y., SamHar Press, 1974. p. cm. (Outstanding personalities, no. 76) Bibliography: p. [GV1132.D4G73] 74-14588 2.29; 0.98 (pbk.)
1. Dempsey, Jack, 1895- 2. Boxing. BIP

ROBERTS, Randy, 1951- 796.8'3'0924 B
Jack Dempsey, the Manassa mauler / Randy Roberts. Baton Rouge : Louisiana State University Press, c1979. p. cm. Includes index. Bibliography: p. [GV1132.D4R62] 79-15145 ISBN 0-8071-0588-0 : 14.95
1. Dempsey, Jack, 1895- 2. Boxers (Sports)—United States—Biography. I. Title.

SCHOOR, Gene. 927.9683
The Jack Dempsey story, by Gene Schoor, with Henry Gilfond. New York, J. Messner [1954] 186 p. illus. 22 cm. [GV1132.D4S2] 54-6775
1. Dempsey, Jack, 1895- I. Title.

Dempsey, Lotta.

DEMPSEY, Lotta. 070.4'092'4 B
No life for a lady / by Lotta Dempsey. Don Mills, Ont. : Musson Book Co., 1976. 207 p., [9] leaves of plates : ill. ; 22 cm. [PN4913.D37A36] 76-375335 ISBN 0-7737-0029-3
1. Dempsey, Lotta. 2. Journalists—Canada—Biography. I. Title.

Dempsey, Michael Ryan.

BURKE, Ann Dempsey. 282'.092'4 B
The bishop who dared : a biography of Bishop Michael Ryan Dempsey / by Ann Dempsey Burke. 1st ed. St. Petersburg, Fla. : Valkyrie Press, c1978. 157 p. : ill. ; 23 cm. [BX4705.D4228B86] 78-55556 ISBN 0-912760-72-9 pbk. : 5.95
1. Dempsey, Michael Ryan. 2. Catholic Church—Bishops—Biography. 3. Bishops—Illinois—Chicago—Biography. 4. Chicago—Biography. I. Title.

Demuth, Charles, 1883-1935.

FARNHAM, Emily, 1912- 759.13 B
Charles Demuth; behind a laughing mask. [1st ed.] Norman, University of Oklahoma Press [1971] xvii, 238 p. illus., col. plates, ports. 23 cm. Bibliography: p. 212-220. [ND237.D36F3] 70-108804 ISBN 0-8061-0913-0
1. Demuth, Charles, 1883-1935. BIP

Dengler, Dieter.

DENGLER, Dieter. 959.704'37 B
Escape from Laos : Dieter Dengler. San Rafael, Calif. : Presidio Press, c1979. 211 p. ; 24 cm. [DS559.4.D44] 78-32056 ISBN 0-89141-076-7 : 9.95
1. Dengler, Dieter. 2. Vietnamese Conflict, 1961-1975—Prisoners and prisons, Lao. 3. Prisoners of war—United States—Biography. 4. Prisoners of war—Laos—Biography. I. Title.

Denham, John, Sir, 1615-1669.

O HEHIR, Brendan. 821'.4 B
Harmony from discords; a life of Sir John Denham. Berkeley, University of California Press, 1968. xvi, 288 p. front. 24 cm. Bibliographical footnotes. [PR3409.D2Z8] 68-27162 7.50
1. Denham, John, Sir, 1615-1669. I. Title. BIP

Denham, Reginald,

DENHAM, Reginald, 1894- 927.92
Stars in my hair, being certain indiscreet memoirs. New York, Crown Publishers [1958] 256 p. illus. 23 cm. [PN2598.D45A3] 58-12891
I. Title.

Deniehy, Daniel Henry, 1828-1865.

PEARL, Cyril. 328.94'092'4 B
Brilliant Dan Deniehy: a forgotten genius. Melbourne, Thomas Nelson (Australia), 1972. 174 p. plates. 24 cm. Bibliography: p. 163-164. [DU114.D4P4] 73-157656 ISBN 0-17-001971-3 7.95
1. Deniehy, Daniel Henry, 1828-1865. 2. Australia—Politics and government—To 1900. I. Title.

Denikin, Anton Ivanovich, 1872-1947.

DENIKIN, Anton Ivanovich, 1872-1947. 947.08'092'4 B
The career of a Tsarist officer : memoirs, 1872-1916 / By Anton I. Denikin ; an annotated translation from the Russian by Margaret Patoski. Minneapolis : University of Minneapolis Press, c1975. xxii, 333 p., [4] leaves of plates : maps ; 24 cm. Translation of Put' russkogo ofitsera. Includes index. Bibliography: p. 319-322. [DK254.D45A313] 75-14625 ISBN 0-8166-0698-6 : 17.95
1. Denikin, Anton Ivanovich, 1872-1947. 2. Russia. Armiia—Military life. 3. Russia—History—Nicholas II, 1894-1917. I. Title. BIP

Denious, Jess C., 1879-1953.

LANE, Larry N. 978.1'03'0924 B
J. C. Denious: public servant and State promoter of Southwestern Kansas [by] Larry N. Lane. [Hays, Fort Hays Kansas State College] 1968. vii, 58, [1] p. ports. 23 cm. (Fort Hays studies. New series. History series, no. 5) Bibliography: p. [59] [D6.F6 no. 5] 68-65510
1. Denious, Jess C., 1879-1953. I. Title. II. Series.

Denison, Edward, 1840-1870.

DENISON, Edward, 1840-1870. 328.42'092'4 B
Letters and other writings of the late Edward Denison, M.P. for Newark. Edited by Sir Baldwyn Leighton, bart. Boston, Milford House [1974] p. cm. Reprint of the 1875 ed. published by R. Bentley, London. [HV28.D4A4 1974] 74-12259 ISBN 0-87821-276-0 30.00 (lib. bdg.).
1. Denison, Edward, 1840-1870.

Denison family.

GAGAN, David Paul, 1940- 929'.2'0971
The Denison family of Toronto, 1792-1925 [by] David Gagan. [Toronto] University of Toronto Press [1973] 113 p. port. 21 cm. (Canadian biographical studies, 5) Bibliography: p. 103-110. [CS90.D43 1973] 72-90741 ISBN 0-8020-3296-6 2.95

1. Denison family. I. Title. BIP

Denison, John.

IGLAUER, Edith. 917.19'04
Denison's ice road. [1st ed.] New York, Dutton, 1975 [c1974] xi, 237 p. 22 cm. [F1060.92.I35] 74-8810 ISBN 0-525-09006-1 8.95
1. Denison, John. 2. Northwest Territories, Can.—Description and travel. 3. Roads, Ice. I. Title. BIP

Denman, Harry, 1893-1976.

ROGERS, Harold, 1907- 287'.6'0924 B
Harry Denman : a biography / Harold Rogers. Nashville : The Upper Room, c1977. 142 p., [4] leaves of plates : ill. ; 23 cm. [BX8495.D44R63] 77-93277 ISBN 0-8358-0370-8 : 5.50 ISBN 0-8358-0369-4 pbk. : 3.25
1. Denman, Harry, 1893-1976. 2. Methodist Church—Clergy—Biography. 3. Clergy—United States—Biography. 4. Evangelists—United States—Biography.

SMITH, Asbury 287.60924
Love abounds; a profile of Harry Denman, a modern disciple, by Asbury Smith, J. Manning Potts. Nashville, Upper Room [1965] 112p. port. 20cm. [BX8495.D44S5] 65-26133 price unreported
1. Denman, Harry, 1893- I. Potts, James Manning, 1895- joint author. II. Title.

Dennie, Joseph, 1768-1812.

ELLIS, Harold Milton, 1885-1947. 814'.2 B
Joseph Dennie and his circle; a study in American literature from 1792-1812. Austin, University of Texas. [New York, AMS Press, 1971] 285 p. 23 cm. Originally published as Studies in English no. 3, in the Bulletin of the University of Texas, 1915: no. 40, July 15, 1915. Bibliography: p. [223]-227. [PS1534.D6Z63 1971] 73-131489 ISBN 0-404-02308-8
1. Dennie, Joseph, 1768-1812. 2. American literature—1783-1850—History and criticism. I. Title. BIP

Dennis, Clarence James, 1876-1938.

HUTTON, Geoffrey William, 1909- 821 B
C. J. Dennis : the sentimental bloke : an appraisal after 100 years of his birth / by Geoffrey Hutton. Melbourne : Premier's Dept., 1976. 51 p. : ill. ; 22 cm. [PR9619.3.D43Z65] 77-375291
1. Dennis, Clarence James, 1876-1938. 2. Poets, Australian—20th century—Biography.

Dennis, Clyde H.

DENNIS, Muriel. 070.5'092'4 B
Apprentice to the King; the biography of Clyde H. Dennis, founder of Good News Publishers. By Muriel Dennis with B. H. Pearson. Westchester, Ill., Good News Publishers [1972] 81 p. illus. 19 cm. [BV2372.D46D46] 72-170088
1. Dennis, Clyde H. 2. Good News Publishers. I. Pearson, Benjamin Harold, 1893- joint author. II. Title.

Dennis, John, 1657-1734.

PAUL, Harry Gilbert, 1874- v. 12
John Dennis: his life and criticism, by H.G. Paul. New York, AMS Press, 1966. 229 p. port. Reprint of 1911 ed. "List of Dennis's writings": p. 213-218. 68-56940
1. Dennis, John, 1657-1734. I. Title.

PAUL, Harry Gilbert, 1874-1945. 809 B
John Dennis; his life and criticism. New York, AMS Press, 1966 [c1911] viii, 229 p. 23 cm. Original ed. issued in series: Columbia University studies in English. "List of Dennis's writings": p. 213-218. [PR3409.D3P3 1966] 75-181968
1. Dennis, John, 1657-1734. I. Series: Columbia University studies in English.

Dennis, Peggy.

DENNIS, Peggy. 335.43'092'4 B
The autobiography of an American communist / by Peggy Dennis. Westport, [Conn.] : L. Hill, 1977. p. cm. Includes index. [HX84.D56A32] 77-23607 ISBN 0-88208-081-4 : 12.95. ISBN 0-88208-080-3 pbk. : 5.95
1. Dennis, Peggy. 2. Communists—United States—Biography. 3. Communism—United States—1917- I. Title.

Denny, David Thomas.

NEWELL, Gordon R. 979.7'77 B
Westward to Alki : the story of David and Louisa Denny / by Gordon Newell. 1st ed. Seattle : Superior Pub. Co., c1977. 122 p. : ill. ; 27 cm. Includes index. [F899.S453D466] 76-56785 ISBN 0-87564-807-X : 9.95
1. Denny, David Thomas. 2. Denny, Louisa Boren. 3. Seattle—Biography. 4. Frontier and pioneer life—Washington (State)—Seattle. I. Title.

Denon, Dominique Vivant, Baron, 1747-1825.

NOWINSKI, Judith. 709'.24
Baron Dominique Vivant Denon (1747-1825); hedonist and scholar in a period of transition. Rutherford, Fairleigh Dickinson University Press [1970] 280 p. plates (incl. ports) 23 cm. Bibliography: p. 263-272. [PQ1977.D33N6] 78-86651 ISBN 0-8386-7470-4 8.50
1. Denon, Dominique Vivant, Baron, 1747-1825. BIP

Densen-Gerber, Judianne, 1934-

DENSEN-GERBER, Judianne, 1934- 301.41'2'0973
Walk in my shoes : an odyssey into womanlife / Judianne Densen-Gerber. 1st ed. New York : Saturday Review Press, c1976. xxiv, 289 p. : ill. ; 22 cm. [HQ1413.D4A36] 75-40326 ISBN 0-8415-0435-0 : 8.95
1. Densen-Gerber, Judianne, 1934- 2. Women—United States—Social conditions. 3. Women—Psychology. I. Title.

Denslow, William Wallace, 1856-1915.

GREENE, Douglas G. 741'.092'4 B
W. W. Denslow / by Douglas G. Greene and Michael Patrick Hearn ; with an introd by Patricia Denslow Eykyn. [Mount Pleasant] : Clarke Historical Library, Central Michigan University, c1976. vii, 225 p. : ill. ; 24 cm. (Juvenile series ; no. 2) "A bibliography of the work of W. W. Denslow": p. 168-211. [NC975.5.D46G73] 77-353964
1. Denslow, William Wallace, 1856-1915. 2. Illustrators—United States—Biography. I. Hearn, Michael Patrick, joint author. II. Series: Juvenile series (Mount Pleasant, Mich.) ; no. 2.

Dent, Abraham, 1729-1803.

WILLAN, Thomas Stuart. 338.7'61'6588700942
An eighteenth-century shopkeeper, Abraham Dent of Kirkby Stephen, by T. S. Willan. New York, A. M. Kelley, 1970. vii, 208 p. illus., facsim., geneal. table, map. 23 cm. Includes bibliographical references. [HC252.5.D4W5 1970b] 70-99783
1. Dent, Abraham, 1729-1803. I. Title. BIP

Dent, Edward Joseph, 1876-1957.

RADCLIFFE, Philip. 780'.01'0924 B
E. J. Dent : a centenary memoir / [by] Philip Radcliffe. Rickmansworth : Triad Press [for] the E. J. Dent Centenary Committee, 1976. 3-32 p., plate : port. ; 23 cm. Limited ed. of 400 numbered copies, no. 148. [ML423.D37R3] 76-376625 ISBN 0-902070-18-5 : £1.50
1. Dent, Edward Joseph, 1876-1957. 2. Musicians—England—Biography.

Dent, John Horry, d. 1892—Manuscripts—Indexes.

DENT, John Horry, d.1892. 630'.92'4 B
Introduction and index to the John Horry Dent farm journals and account books, 1840-1892 / Ray Mathis and Mary Mathis. University : University of Alabama Press, c1977. xxii, 174 p. ; 24 cm. [Z6611.A33D46] [S417.D43] 77-22355 ISBN 0-8173-5251-1 : 10.00
1. Dent, John Horry, d. 1892—Manuscripts—Indexes. 2. Dent, John Horry, d. 1892. 3. Farmers—Alabama—Barbour Co.—Manuscripts—Indexes. 4. Farmers—Georgia—Floyd Co.—Manuscripts—Indexes. 5. Farmers—Alabama—Barbour Co.—Biography. 6. Farmers—Georgia—Floyd Co.—Biography. 7. Barbour Co., Ala.—Biography. 8. Floyd Co., Ga.—Biography. I. Mathis, Gerald Ray, 1937- II. Mathis, Mary. III. Title.

Dent, Marmaduke, 1801-1880.

REID, John Phillip. 347.99'24 B
An American judge; Marmaduke Dent of West Virginia. New York, New York University Press, 1968. xii, 230 p. ports. 24 cm. Bibliographical references included in "Notes" (p. 213-225) [KF368.D4R4] 68-28004 8.50
1. Dent, Marmaduke, 1801-1880. I. Title. BIP

Dentists — U.S. — Biog.

DE BRE, Alvin Jack, 1922- ed. 927.6
Who's who in American dentistry. Edited by Alvin J. De Bre. Los Angeles, Dale Dental Pub. Co.,1963. xi, 198 p. 27 cm. [RK41.W6] 62-13884
1. Dentists — U.S. — Biog. I. Title.

Denton, Jeremiah A.

DENTON, Jeremiah A. 959.704'37
When hell was in session / by Jeremiah A. Denton, Jr., with Ed. Brandt. New York : Readers Digest Press : distributed by Crowell, 1976. x, 246 p. ; 24 cm. Includes index. [DS559.4.D46 1976] 76-18981 ISBN 0-88349-112-5 : 8.95
1. Denton, Jeremiah A. 2. Vietnamese Conflict, 1961-1975—Prisoners and prisons, North Vietnamese. 3. Vietnamese Conflict, 1961-1975—Personal narratives, American. I. Brandt, Ed, joint author. II. Title.

Denver and Salt Lake Railroad—History.

BOLLINGER, Edward Taylor, 1907- 385'.09788
Rails that climb : a narrative history of the Moffat Road / by Edward T. Bollinger ; edited by William C. Jones ; indexes by A. D. Mastrogiuseppe. Golden : Colorado Railroad Museum, c1979. vii, 323 p. : ill. (3 fold. inpocket) ; 29 cm. Reprint of the 1950 ed. published by Rydal Press, Santa Fe. Includes index. Bibliography: p. [324] [HE2791.D4432 1979] 79-14634 ISBN 0-918654-29-7 : 24.95
1. Denver and Salt Lake Railroad—History. 2. Moffat, David Halliday, 1839-1911. 3. Capitalists and financiers—United States—Biography. I. Jones, William C. 1937- II. Title. BIP

Denver—Biography.

PARKHILL, Forbes, 1892- 978.883
The wildest of the West. [1st ed.] New York, Holt [1951] x, 310 p. illus., ports. 21 cm. Bibliography: p. 289-293. [F784.D4P3] 51-10777
1. Denver—Biography. I. Title.

Denver Broncos (Football team)

GORDON, Larry. 796.33'264'0978883
Barely audible : a history of the Denver Broncos / by Larry Gordon and Dick Burnell. Denver : Graphic Impressions, 1975. 224 p. : ill. ; 30 cm. [GV956.D37G67] 74-84775 ISBN 0-914628-01-1 : 15.95
1. Denver Broncos (Football team) 2. Football—Biography. I. Burnell, Dick, joint author. II. Title. BIP

Denver, John.

FLEISCHER, Leonore. 784'.092'4 B
John Denver / by Leonore Fleischer. New York : Flash, c1976. 80 p. : ill. ; 26 cm. Discography: p. 76-79. A brief biography concentrating on the career of singer and songwriter John Denver. [ML410.D3634F6] 92 76-8065 ISBN 0-8256-3909-3 : 3.95
1. Denver, John. 2. Country musicians—United States—Biography. I. Title. BIP

Denver, John—Juvenile literature.

JACOBS, Linda. 784.4'92'4 B
John Denver : a natural high / by Linda Jacobs. St. Paul : EMC Corp., c1975. p. cm. (Men behind the bright lights) A biography of the architecture student turned singer who uses his songs to share with others his feelings about life. [ML3930.D42J3] 92 75-26649 ISBN 0-88436-211-6 lib.bdg. : 4.95 ISBN 0-88436-212-4 pbk. : 2.95
1. Denver, John—Juvenile literature. I. Title. BIP

†MCGREANE, Meagan. 784.4'092'4 B
On stage, John Denver / text Meagan McGreane ; design concept Larry Soule. Mankato, Minn. : Creative Education ; Chicago : distributed by Childrens Press, c1976. 47 p. : ill. (some col.) ; 23 cm. (The Entertainers) A biography of John Denver who uses his music to illustrate contemporary issues and the land he loves. [ML3930.D42M2] 92 75-42504 ISBN 0-87191-483-2 lib.bdg. : 6.60
1. Denver, John—Juvenile literature. I. Title. BIP

MORSE, Charles. 784.4'92'4 B
John Denver. Text: Charles and Ann Morse. Illus.: John Keely. Mankato, Minn., Creative Education; [distributed by Childrens Press, Chicago, 1974, c1975] 31 p. illus. (part col.) 25 cm. (Rock 'n pop stars) A brief biography stressing the professional career of singer and songwriter, John Denver. [ML3930.D42M7] [93] 74-14551 ISBN 0-87191-392-5
1. Denver, John,—Juvenile literature. I. Morse, Ann, joint author. II. Keely, John, illus. III. Title. BIP

Denver. Juvenile Court of the City and County of Denver.

LINDSEY, Benjamin Barr, 1869-1943. 345'.78883'08 B
The dangerous life [by] Ben B. Lindsey and Rube Borough. New York, Arno Press, 1974 [c1931] xiv, 450 p. 23 cm. (Metropolitan America) Autobiography of Judge Lindsey. Reprint of the ed. published by H. Liveright, New York. [HV9094.D4L48 1974] 73-11938 ISBN 0-405-05400-9 22.00
1. Denver. Juvenile Court of the City and County of Denver. I. Borough, Rube, 1883- joint author. II. Title. III. Series. BIP

Denvir, Bernard.

CHARDIN, Jean Baptiste Simeon, 1699-1779. [927.5]
Chardin, by Bernard Denvir. [1st American ed.] New York, Harper [1950] 16, [1] p. 39 plates (part col.) 28 cm. (Masters of painting) Harper's art library. Bibliography: p. [17] [ND553.C4D43] 759.4 50-7873
1. Denvir, Bernard. I. Title. II. Series: Masters of painting (New York)

Denvir, John, 1843-1916.

DENVIR, John, 1843-1916. 914.27'2'069162 B
The life story of an old rebel. Introd. by Leon Broin. Shannon, Irish University Press [1973, c1972] x, viii, 288 p. port. 23 cm. Reprint of the 1910 ed. published by Sealy, Bryers & Walker, Dublin; with new introd. and bibliography added.

Bibliography: p. x. [DA125.I7D46 1972] 74-160881 ISBN 0-7165-0012-4
1. Denvir, John, 1843-1916. 2. Irish in England—Personal narratives. 3. Ireland—Politics and government—1837-1901. I. Title.
Distributed by Irish University Press, New York, 9.75. **BIP**

Deoxyribonucleic acid.

WATSON, James D., 1928- 547'.596
The double helix; a personal account of the discovery of the structure of DNA, by James D. Watson. [1st ed.] New York, Atheneum, 1968. xvi, 226 p. illus., facsims., ports. 22 cm. Autobiographical. [QD341.A2W315] 68-16217
1. Deoxyribonucleic acid. I. Title.

DePree, Gladis, 1933-

DEPREE, Gladis, 1933- 266'.5'70924 B
The self-anointed / Gladis Lenore DePree. 1st ed. New York : Harper & Row, c1978. 282 p. ; 22 cm. Autobiographical. [BX9543.D43A37 1978] 77-3746 ISBN 0-06-011058-9 : 8.95
1. DePree, Gladis, 1933- 2. Reformed Church in America—Biography. 3. Kentucky—Biography. I. Title.

Depressions—1929- —United States.

HASTINGS, Robert J. 917.3'03'916
A nickel's worth of skim milk; a boy's view of the Great Depression [by] Robert J. Hastings. [Carbondale] University Graphics and Publications, Southern Illinois University at Carbondale, 1972. x, 149 p. illus. 21 cm. Issued in case. [BX6495.H272A33] 72-619595 4.95
1. Depressions—1929- —United States. I. Title. **BIP**

DeQuincey, Thomas, 1785-1859—Biography—Last years and death.

FINDLAY, John Ritchie, 1824-1898. 828'.8'09 B
Personal recollections of Thomas De Quincey / by John Ritchie Findlay. Folcroft, Pa. : Folcroft Library Editions, 1976. x, 74 p., [2] leaves of plates : ill. ; 21 cm. Reprint of the 1886 ed. published by A. & C. Black, Edinburgh. Includes bibliographical references. [PR4536.F5 1976] 76-15258 ISBN 0-8414-4155-3 lib. bdg. : 12.50
1. DeQuincey, Thomas, 1785-1859—Biography—Last years and death. 2. Authors, English—19th century—Biography. I. Title. **BIP**

Der, Lillian—Juvenile literature.

BALES, Carol Ann, 1940- 917.3'06'951
Chinatown Sunday: the story of Lilliann Der. Chicago, Reilly & Lee Books [1973] [32] p. illus. 29 cm. A ten-year-old Chinese-American girl describes her family and their life in a Chicago suburb. [E184.C5B185] 73-6481 5.95 (lib. bdg.)
1. Der, Lillian—Juvenile literature. 2. Chinese in the United States—Juvenile literature. I. Title.

Der Megerditchian, Ervant,

DER MEGERDITCHIAN, Ervant, 1888- 917.3'06'91992
The life of an Armenian emigrant. North Quincy, Mass., Christopher Pub. House [1970] 186 p. illus., ports. 21 cm. [Z232.D38A3] 76-112339 ISBN 0-8158-0234-X 4.95
I. Title.

Derain, Andre, 1880-1954.

DIEHL, Gaston. 759.4
Derain. [Translated from the French by A. P. H. Hamilton] New York, Crown Publishers [1964] 92, [2] p. illus. (part col, part mounted col.) 29 cm. Bibliography: p. 92-[93] [ND553.D37D54] 64-3284
1. Derain, Andre, 1880-1954. **BIP**

Derby, Edward George Geoffrey Smith Stanley, 14th earl of, 1799-1869.

LORD Derby and Victorian conservatism. v. 12 Athens, University of Georgia Press, 1956. xi, 367p. 23cm.
1. Derby, Edward George Geoffrey Smith Stanley, 14th earl of, 1799-1869. I. Jones, Wilbur Devereux. **BIP**

Derby, Edward George Villiers Stanley, 17th earl of, 1865-1948.

CHURCHILL, Randolph Spencer 1911- 923.242
Lord Derby, King of Lancashire; the official life of Edward, seventeenth earl of Derby, 1865-1948. New York, Putnam [1961, c.1959] 641p. illus. 60-8467 7.50
1. Derby, Edward George Villiers Stanley, 17th earl of, 1865-1948. I. Title.

Derby, George Horatio, 1823-1861.

STEWART, George Rippey, 1895- 818'.3'07 B
John Phoenix, Esq., the veritable Squibob; a life of Captain George H. Derby, U.S.A., by George R. Stewart. New York, Da Capo Press, 1969 [c1937] xiv, 242 p. illus., ports. 24 cm. (The American scene) (A Da Capo Press reprint series.) Bibliography: p. 205-208. "Bibliography of Derby's writings": p. 209-217. [PS1535.Z5S8 1969] 75-87721
1. Derby, George Horatio, 1823-1861. I. Title. II. Title: The veritable Squibob.

Derby, Pat.

DERBY, Pat. 791.3'2'0924 B
The lady and her tiger / Pat Derby, with Peter Beagle. 1st ed. New York : Dutton, c1976. 284 p. : ill. ; 22 cm. "Thomas Congdon books." [GV1829.D37 1976] 75-43856 8.95
1. Derby, Pat. 2. Animals, Training of. I. Beagle, Peter S., joint author. II. Title. **BIP**

DERBY, Pat. 791.3'2'0924
The lady and her tiger / Pat Derby, with Peter Beagle. New York : Ballantine Books, 1977,c1976. 263, [32]p. : ill. ; 18 cm. [GV1829.D37 1976] ISBN 0-345-25711-1 pbk. : 1.95
1. Derby, Pat. 2. Animals, Training of. I. Beagle, Peter S., joint author. II. Title.
L.C. card no. for 1976 Dutton ed.:75-43856.

Derleth, August William, 1909-1971—Friends and associates.

DERLETH, August William, 1909-1971. 810'.9'0052
Three literary men : a memoir of Sinclair Lewis, Sherwood Anderson, Edgar Lee Masters / by August Derleth. Folcroft, Pa. : Folcroft Library Editions, 1978 [c1963] p. cm. Reprint of the ed. published by Candlelight Press, New York. [PS3507.E69Z475 1978] 78-11518 ISBN 0-8414-3686-X lib. bdg. : 10.00
1. Derleth, August William, 1909-1971—Friends and associates. 2. Lewis, Sinclair, 1885-1951—Interviews. 3. Anderson, Sherwood, 1876-1941—Interviews. 4. Masters, Edgar Lee, 1869-1950—Interviews. 5. Authors, American—20th century—Biography. I. Title.

Derricotte, Juliette Aline, 1897-1931—Juvenile literature.

BURT, Olive Wooley, 1894- 920.72'0973 B
Black women of valor, by Olive W. Burt. Illustrated by Paul Frame. New York, J. Messner [1974] 96 p. illus. 22 cm. Contents.Contents.—Juliette Derricotte.—Maggie Mitchell Walker.—Ida Wells Barnett.—Septima Poinsette Clark.—Other Black women of valor. [E185.96.B95] 920 74-7595 ISBN 0-671-32699-6 6.25
1. Derricotte, Juliette Aline, 1897-1931—Juvenile literature. 2. Walker, Maggie Lena—Juvenile literature. 3. Barnett, Ida B. Wells, 1862-1931—Juvenile literature. 4. Clark, Septima (Poinsette) 1898- Juvenile literature. I. Frame, Paul, illus. II. Title.
Library binding; 5.79, ISBN 0-671-32700-3. Contents omitted. **BIP**

Derwentwater, James Radcliffe, 3d Earl of, 1689-1716.

ARNOLD, Ralph [Crispian Marshall] 923.242
Northern lights; the story of Lord Derwentwater. London, Constable [dist. Chester Springs, Pa., Dufour Editions, 1959, i.e., 1960] 268p. illus. 23cm. 59-2004 5.50
1. Derwentwater, James Radcliffe, 3d earl of, 1689-1716. I. Title.

DICKINSON, Frankie. 942.8'2
The castle on Devil's Water: the legends and history of Dilston Castle, Northumberland, and the tragedy of James Radcliffe, Third Earl of Derwentwater. Newcastle upon Tyne, Oriel, 1969. 32 p. illus., plan. 22 cm. Bibliography: p. 32. [DA483.D35D5] 78-95249 5/-
1. Derwentwater, James Radcliffe, 3d Earl of, 1689-1716. I. Title.

Des Barres, Joseph Frederick Wallet, 1722-1824.

EVANS, Geraint Nantglyn Davies, 1935- 971.7'02'0924 B
North American soldier, hydrographer, governor: the public careers of J. F. W. DesBarres, 1721-1824, by Geraint N. D. Evans. New Haven, 1965 [c1966] v, 305 l. fold. map, port. 23 cm. Thesis—Yale. Photocopy of typescript. Ann Arbor, Mich., University Micro-films, 1967. 23 cm. "Bibliographical notes": leaves [278]-305. [F1032.D47E85 1966a] 77-48
1. Des Barres, Joseph Frederick Wallet, 1722-1824. I. Title.

Des Jarlait, Patrick, 1921-1972—Juvenile literature.

DES JARLAIT, Patrick, 1921-1972 977.6'82'00497 B
Patrick Des Jarlait : the story of an American Indian artist / as told to Neva Williams. Minneapolis : Lerner Publications Co., [1975] 57 p. : ill. (some col.) ; 23 cm. ([Voices of the American Indian]) An autobiography of an American Indian artist concentrating on his early years growing up on the Red Lake Indian Reservation in Minnesota and highlighting his development as an artist. [E99.C6D477 1975] 92 74-33523 ISBN 0-8225-0642-4 lib.bdg. : 5.95
1. Des Jarlait, Patrick, 1921-1972—Juvenile literature. 2. Chippewa Indians—Biography. 3. Indians of North America—Biography. I. Williams, Neva. II. Title. III. Series.

Desai, Morarji Ranchodji, 1896-

DESAI, Morarji Ranchodji, 1896- 954.04'092'4 B
The story of my life / by Morarji Desai. Oxford ; New York : Pergamon Press, c1978. p. cm. (Leaders of the world : biographical series) [DS481.D385A33 1978] 78-40613 ISBN 0-08-023566-2 : 40.00
1. Desai, Morarji Ranchodji, 1896- 2. India—Politics and government—20th century. 3. Prime ministers—India—Biography. I. Title. II. Series: Leaders of the world.

Descartes, Rene, 1596-1650.

DESCARTES, Rene, 1596-1650. 194
Descartes' conversation with Burman / translated with introd. and commentary by John Cottingham. Oxford : Clarendon Press, 1976. xl, 133 p. ; 23 cm. Translation from the Latin ms.; known under the title: Entretien avec Burman. Spine title: Conversation with Burman. Includes index. Bibliography: p. 127-128. [B1868.E52E5 1976] 76-363862 ISBN 0-19-824528-9 : 17.00
1. Descartes, Rene, 1596-1650. 2. Burman, Frans, 1628-1679. 3. Philosophy. I. Burman, Frans, 1628-1679. II. Title. III. Title: Conversation with Burman.
Distributed by Oxford University Press N.Y. N.Y.

HALDANE, Elizabeth Sanderson, 1862-1937. v. 12
Descartes, his life and times, by Elizabeth S. Haldane. New York, American Scholar Publications, 1966. xxviii, 398 p. port. 23 cm. 67-94233
1. Descartes, Rene', 1596-1650. I. Title.

KEELING, Stanley Victor. 194
Descartes, by S. V. Keeling. Westport, Conn., Greenwood Press [1970] xi, 282 p. 23 cm. (Leaders of philosophy) Reprint of the 1934 ed. Bibliography: p. 273-275. [B1875.K4 1970] 78-109759 ISBN 0-8371-4249-0
1. Descartes, Rene, 1596-1650. **BIP**

MAHAFFY, John Pentland, Sir, 1839-1919. 194 B
Descartes. Freeport, N.Y., Books for Libraries Press [1969] vi, 211 p. 23 cm. (Select bibliographies reprint series.) (Philosophical classics for English readers [v. 1]) Reprint of the 1880 ed. [B1873.M3 1969] 71-94277
1. Descartes, Rene, 1596-1650. I. Title. II. Series.

REE, Jonathan, 1948- 194
Descartes / Jonathan Ree. New York : Pica Press : distributed by Universe Books, 1975, c1974. 203 p. ; 22 cm. Includes index. Bibliography: p. 197-200. [B1875.R43 1975] 74-27243 ISBN 0-87663-717-9 : 8.50
1. Descartes, Rene, 1596-1650. **BIP**

VROOMAN, Jack Rochford. 194 B
Rene Descartes; a biography. New York, Putnam [1970] 308 p. illus., ports. 23 cm. Bibliography: p. 296-300. [B1873.V7 1970] 68-25463 7.95
1. Descartes, Rene, 1596-1650.

Descartes, Rene, 1596-1650—Juvenile literature.

HOYT, Edwin Palmer. 194 B
He freed the minds of men: Rene Descartes [by] Edwin P. Hoyt. New York, Messner [1969] 187 p. 22 cm. Bibliography: p. [179]-180. A biography of the seventeenth-century French mathematician and philosopher whose revolutionary methods of reasoning greatly influenced future scientific thinking. [B1875.H63] 92 69-17428 3.50
1. Descartes, Rene, 1596-1650—Juvenile literature. I. Title.

Desjardins, Gerry, 1944-

LIBBY, Bill. 796.9'62'0924
Rookie goalie, Gerry Desjardins. New York, J. Messner [1970] 192 p. illus., ports. 22 cm. [GV848.5.D4L5] 75-100570 ISBN 6-7132-2273- 3.95
1. Desjardins, Gerry, 1944- I. Title.

Desmond, J. Patrick.

CORSON, Ace L., 1867or8-1960 923.873
Ace Corson, railroader, 1878-1960 [as told to] J. Patrick Desmond. New York, Fell [c.1964] 250p. 22cm. 64-17299 4.95 bds.,
1. Desmond, J. Patrick. I. Title.

Desmond, Shaw,

DESMOND, Shaw, 1877- 928.2
Pilgrim to paradise; an autobiography. London, New York, Rider [1951] 272 p. illus. 24 cm. [PR6007.E645Z53 1951] 51-14663
I. Title.

Dessler, Julia (Shapiro)

DESSLER, Julia (Shapiro) 920.7
Eyes on the goal. New York, Vantage Press [1954] 54p. 23cm. Autobiography. [CT275.D368A3] 54-8346
I. Title.

Destouches, Louis Ferdinand, 1894-1961.

OSTROVSKY, Erika. 843'.9'12 B
Voyeur voyant; a portrait of Louis-Ferdinand Celine. [1st ed.] New York, Random House [1971, i.e. 1972] 398 p. illus. 25 cm. Bibliography: p. [375]-392. [PQ2607.E834Z814 1972] 76-159362 ISBN 0-394-46524-5 10.00
1. Destouches, Louis Ferdinand, 1894-1961. I. Title.

THOMAS, Merlin. 843'.9'12 B
Louis-Ferdinand Celine / Merlin Thomas. New York : New Directions, 1980, c1979. p. cm. Includes index. Bibliography: p. [PQ2607.E834Z933 1980] 79-20591 ISBN 0-8112-0754-4 : 16.50
1. Destouches, Louis Ferdinand, 1894-1961. 2. Authors, French—20th century—Biography. BIP

Destouches, Louis Ferdinand, 1894-1961—Biography.

MCCARTHY, Patrick, 1941- 843'.9'12 B
Celine / Patrick McCarthy. New York : Penguin Books, 1977, c1975. 352 p. ; 20 cm. Includes index. Bibliography: p. 341-344. [PQ2607.E834Z77 1977] 77-5323 ISBN 0-14-004534-1 pbk. : 3.50
1. Destouches, Louis Ferdinand, 1894-1961—Biography. 2. Authors, French—20th century—Biography. I. Title.

Detectives.

BLOCK, Eugene B. 364.12'0922
Famous detectives; true stories of great crime detection [by] Eugene B. Block. [1st ed.] Garden City, N.Y., Doubleday, 1967. 264 p. 22 cm. Contents.—America's pioneer detective: Allan Pinkerton.—A great detective: Raymond C. Schindler.—Chief of the FBI: J. Edgar Hoover.—A prophecy come true: Frederick R. Cherrill.—Pandora's box: George W. Cornish.—Dope traffickers' nemesis: George Hunter White.—Great Teigin mystery: Tamegoro Ikii.—War on the Mafia: Joseph Petrosino.—Trapping dynamiters: William J. Burns.—A game of cat and mouse: Charles Chenevier.—Ohio's ace investigator: Ora E. Slater.—Crime scientist: Edward Oscar Heinrich.—Chasing train bandits: Daniel J. O'Connell. [HV7914.B54] 67-18238
1. Detectives. I. Title.

Detectives—Case studies.

DEELEY, Peter. 364.12'092'6
The manhunters. [1st American ed.] New York, McCall Pub. Co. [1970] 192 p. illus., ports. 22 cm. Contents.Contents.—Mathias Eynck: Germany; the Dusseldorf doubles' killer.—Romolo Imundi: America; the missing women mystery.—Guy Denis: France; the Peugeot kidnapping.—Gijs Toorenaar: Holland; the smugglers' trail.—Richard Chitty: England; the London police murders. [HV7914.D38] 75-122121 5.95
1. Detectives—Case studies. I. Title.

HENDERSON, Bruce. 363.2'092'2 B
The super sleuths / Bruce Henderson and Sam Summerlin. New York : Macmillan, c1976. xii, 291 p. : ill. ; 22 cm. [HV7914.H38] 76-7445 ISBN 0-02-550950-0 : 8.95
1. Detectives—Case studies. 2. Criminal investigation—Case studies. I. Summerlin, Sam, joint author. II. Title.

Detectives—Correspondence, reminiscences, etc.

SODERMAN, Harry, 1902- 923.5485
Policeman's lot; a criminologist's gallery of friends and felons. New York, Funk & Wagnalls [1956] 388 p. illus. 22 cm. [HV7914.S66] 56-10604
1. Detectives — Correspondence, reminiscences, etc. I. Title.

SODERMAN, Harry, 1902-1956. 923.5485
Policeman's lot; a criminologist's gallery of friends and felons. New York, Funk & Wagnalls [1956] 388 p. illus. 22 cm. [HV7914.S66] 56-10604
1. Detectives—Correspondence, reminiscences, etc. I. Title.

Detectives—Juvenile literature.

LISTON, Robert A. 364.120922
Great detectives; famous real-life sleuths and their most baffling cases. New York, Platt & Munk [c.1966] 270p. 22cm. [HV7911.A1L5] 66-5043 2.95 bds.,
1. Detectives—Juvenile literature. I. Title.

LISTON, Robert A 364.120922
Great detectives; famous real-life sleuths and their most baffling cases [by] Robert Liston. New York, Platt & Munk [1966] 270 p. 22 cm. [HV7911.A1L5] 66-5043
1. Detectives — Juvenile literature. I. Title.

Detectives—London—Correspondence, reminiscences, etc.

GODDARD, Henry, 1800-1883. 364.942
Memoirs of a Bow Street runner. With an introd. by Patrick Pringle. New York, Morrow [1957] 253 p. illus. 23 cm. [HV7914.G57] 56-14718
1. Detectives—London—Correspondence, reminiscences, etc. 2. London—Police. 3. Crime and criminals—England—London. I. Title.

Deterding, Henri, Sir, 1866-1939.

DETERDING, Henri, Sir, 1866-1939. 338.2'7'2820924 B
An international oilman / Henri Deterding, as told to Stanley Naylor. New York : Arno Press, 1977. p. cm. (European business) Reprint of the 1934 ed. published by Harper, London, New York. [HD9560.5.D55 1977] 76-29771 ISBN 0-405-09784-0 . 10.00
1. Deterding, Henri, Sir, 1866-1939. 2. Petroleum industry and trade—History. 3. Capitalists and financiers—Biography. I. Naylor, Stanley, joint author. II. Title. III. Series.

ROBERTS, Glyn. 338.7'62'233820924 B
The most powerful man in the world : the life of Sir Henri Deterding / by Glyn Roberts. Westport, Conn. : Hyperion Press, 1975, c1938. p. cm. Reprint of the ed. published by Covici Friede, New York. Bibliography: p. [D413.D38R6 1975] 75-6484 ISBN 0-88355-301-5 : 22.00
1. Deterding, Henri, Sir, 1866-1939. 2. Petroleum industry and trade. 3. World politics—20th century. I. Title. BIP

Dett, Robert Nathaniel, 1882-1943.

MCBRIER, Vivian Flagg. 780'.92'4 B
R. Nathaniel Dett, his life and works, 1882-1943 / Vivian Flagg McBrier. Washington : Associated Publishers, c1977. 152 p. : ill. ; 24 cm. (The Sigma Pi Phi series) Includes bibliographical references. [ML410.D375M2] 77-368036 7.95
1. Dett, Robert Nathaniel, 1882-1943. 2. Composers—United States—Biography. I. Title. II. Series: Sigma Pi Phi. The Sigma Pi Phi series.

Detzer, Karl William,

DETZER, Karl William, 1891- 818'.5'203
Myself when young [by] Karl Detzer. New York, Funk & Wagnalls [1968] 248 p. 22 cm. [PS3507.E78Z5] 68-12005
I. Title.

Deuchar, Seafield, 1886-1971.

DEUCHAR, Seafield, 1886-1971. 919.46
We were the first, by Seafield Deuchar. Melbourne, Hawthorn Press, 1973. 53 p. col. plates. 25 cm. Aus [DU480.T76D48] 73-169086 ISBN 0-7256-0094-2 4.95
1. Deuchar, Seafield, 1886-1971. 2. Trowutta, Australia—History. I. Title.

Deutsch, Helene, 1884-

DEUTSCH, Helene, 1884- 616.8'9'00924 B
Confrontations with myself: an epilogue. [1st ed.] New York, Norton [1973] 217 p. illus. 22 cm. Includes bibliographical references. [RC339.52.D48A33 1973] 73-4380 ISBN 0-393-07472-2 6.95
1. Deutsch, Helene, 1884- 2. Psychiatrists—Correspondence, reminiscences, etc. I. Title.

Devas, Nicolette.

DEVAS, Nicolette. 828'.9'1403
Two flamboyant fathers. New York, Morrow, 1967 [c1966] 287 p. illus., ports. 22 cm. Autobiographical. [PR6007.E77T9 1967] 67-19242
I. Title.

Devereaux, Franklin, 1830-1883.

SHARKEY, Reginald F., 1913- 917.74'03'30924 B
Sign of the bear; the life and death of Franklin Devereaux, by Reginald F. Sharkey. Detroit, Harlo Press [1969] 111 p. illus., map (on lining papers), ports. 23 cm. Bibliography: p. 111. [CT275.D376S5] 71-13502 4.95
1. Devereaux, Franklin, 1830-1883. I. Title.

Devereux, Julien Sidney, 1805-1856.

WINFREY, Dorman H. 976.4
Julien Sidney Devereux and his Monte Verdi Plantation, by Dorman H. Winfrey. Foreword by H. Bailey Carroll. Introd. by O. Douglas Weeks. Waco, Texian Press [1964, c1962] xii, 162 p. illus., facsims., geneal. table, maps, plans, ports. 24 cm. Thesis—University of Texas. Bibliography: p. 154-157. [F392.R8W53] 70-211410
1. Devereux, Julien Sidney, 1805-1856. 2. Monte Verdi, Tex. I. Title.

DeVito, Anthony.

BLUM, Howard, 1948- 364.1'38'0924 B
Wanted! : The search for Nazis in America / Howard Blum. New York : Quadrangle/New York Times Book Co., c1977. 256 p. ; 24 cm. [D804.G4B57 1977] 76-9689 ISBN 0-8129-0607-1 : 8.95
1. DeVito, Anthony. 2. United States. Immigration and Naturalization Service—Officials and employees—Biography. 3. War criminals—Germany. I. Title. BIP

BLUM, Howard, 1948- 364.1'38'0924 [B]
Wanted : The search for Nazis in America / Howard Blum. Greenwich, CT : Fawcett Books, 1978,c1977. 285p. ; 18 cm. (A Fawcett Crest Book) [D804.G4B57 1977] ISBN 0-449-23409-6 pbk. : 1.95
1. DeVito, Anthony. 2. United States.Immigration and Naturalization Service — Officials and employees — Biography. 3. War criminals — Germany. I. Title.
L. C. card no. for 1977 Quadrangle / New York Times Book Co. 76-9689.

Devonshire, Andrew Robert Buxton Cavendish, 11th Duke of, 1920-

DEVONSHIRE, Andrew Robert Buxton Cavendish, 11th Duke of, 1920- 798'.43
Park Top : a romance of the turf / by Andrew Devonshire. London : London Magazine Editions, 1976. 170 p., [6] leaves of plates : ill. ; 24 cm. [SF355.P37D48] 76-380914 ISBN 0-904388-17-4 : £5.00
1. Devonshire, Andrew Robert Buxton Cavendish, 11th Duke of, 1920- 2. Park Top (Race horse) 3. Horsemen—England—Biography. 4. Horse-racing—England. I. Title.

Devonshire, Elizabeth Hervey Cavendish, Duchess of, 1757-1824.

CALDER-MARSHALL, Arthur, 1908- 941.07'092'2 B
The two duchesses / Arthur Calder-Marshall. 1st U.S. ed. New York : Harper & Row, c1978. 208 p., [6] leaves of plates : ill. ; 24 cm. Includes index. Bibliography: p. 195-[197] [DA522.D5C34 1978] 76-26215 ISBN 0-06-010617-4 : 9.95
1. Devonshire, Elizabeth Hervey Cavendish, Duchess of, 1757-1824. 2. Devonshire, Georgiana Spencer Cavendish, Duchess of, 1757-1806. 3. Mistresses—Great Britain—Biography. 4. Wires—Great Britain—Biography. I. Title. BIP

Devotional calendars—Catholic Church.

SAINT and thought for every day / profiles of saints by a Daughter of St. Paul ; thoughts by J. Alberione. Boston, Mass. : Daughters of St. Paul, c1976. p. cm. [BV4811.S18] 76 54162 3.95 242'.2
1. Devotional calendars—Catholic Church. 2. Christian saints—Calendar. 3. Christian saints—Biography. I. Alberione, Giacomo Giuseppe, 1884-1971. II. Daughters of St. Paul. BIP

†SAINT and thought for every day / profiles of saints by the Daughters of St. Paul ; thoughts by James Alberione. Boston, Mass. : St. Paul Editions, c1976. 315 p. : ill. ; 19 cm. [BV4811.S18] 76-53946 3.95 pbk. : 2.95 242'.2
1. Devotional calendars—Catholic Church. 2. Christian saints—Calendar. 3. Christian saints—Biography. I. Alberione, Giacomo Giuseppe, 1884-1971. II. Daughters of St. Paul.

Dewey, George, 1837-1917.

DEWEY, George, 1837-1917. 973.8'95'0924 B
Autobiography of George Dewey, admiral of the Navy. New York, Scribner, 1913. St. Clair Shores, Mich., Scholarly Press, 1971. x, 337 p. 21 cm. [E714.6.D51A3 1971] 73-144974 ISBN 0-403-00942-1
1. United States—History—War of 1898—Naval operations. 2. Manila Bay, Battle of, 1898. 3. United States—History—Civil War, 1861-1865—Naval operations. BIP

SPECTOR, Ronald. 359.3'31'0924 B
Admiral of the new empire : the life and career of George Dewey / Ronald Spector. Baton Rouge : Louisiana State University Press, [1974] xvi, 220 p., [4] leaves of plates : ill. ; 24 cm. Includes index. Bibliography: p. 205-214. [V63.D48S64] 73-90870 ISBN 0-8071-0078-1 : 10.00
1. Dewey, George, 1837-1917. I. Title. BIP

WEST, Richard Sedgewick, 1902- 359'.00922 B
Admirals of American empire; the combined story of George Dewey, Alfred Thayer Mahan, Winfield Scott Schley, and William Thomas Sampson, by Richard S. West, Jr. Westport, Conn., Greenwood Press [1971, c1948] 354 p. illus. 23 cm. Includes bibliographical references. [E182.W45 1971] 73-156216 ISBN 0-8371-6167-3
1. Dewey, George, 1837-1917. 2. Mahan, Alfred Thayer, 1840-1914. 3. Schley, Winfield Scott, 1839-1911. 4. Sampson, William Thomas, 1840-1902. 5. U.S.—History, Naval—To 1900. I. Title. BIP

Dewey, George, 1837-1917 — Juvenile fiction.

LONG, Laura. JUV
George Dewey, Vermont boy. Illustrated by Robert Doremus. Indianapolis, Bobbs-Merrill [1963] 200 p. illus. 20 cm. (Childhood of famous Americans) [PZ7.L855Ge10] fic 62-16622
1. Dewey, George, 1837-1917 — Juvenile fiction. I. Title.

Dewey, George. 1837-1917 — Juvenile literature.

SMITH, Fredrika Shumway. j92
George Dewey, admiral of the Navy. Illustrated by Albert Orbann Chicago, Rand McNally [1963] 240 p. illus. 21 cm. [E714.6.D51S6] 63-18775
1. Dewey, George. 1837-1917 — Juvenile literature. I. Title.

Dewey, John, 1859-1952.

BERNSTEIN, Richard J. 191
John Dewey [by] Richard J. Bernstein. New York, Washington Square Press, 1966. ix, 213 p. 22 cm. (The Great American thinkers series) "Bibliographical note": p. 187-190. [B945.D44B43] 66-16176
1. Dewey, John, 1859-1952.

BRICKMAN, William W. ed. v. 12
John Dewey: master educator, edited by William W. Brickman and Stanley Lehrer. New York, Atherton press, 1966 [c1965] 172 p. port. 22 cm. (An Atheling book, EP-102) Includes bibliography. 66-52805
1. Dewey, John, 1859-1952. I. Lehrer, Stanley, ed. II. Title.

DYKHUIZEN, George, 1899- 191 B
The life and mind of John Dewey. Introd. by Harold Taylor. Edited by Jo Ann Boydston. Carbondale, Southern Illinois University Press [1973] xxv, 429 p. illus. 25 cm. Includes bibliographical references. [B945.D44D94] 73-4602 ISBN 0-8093-0616-6 15.00
1. Dewey, John, 1859-1952. I. Title. BIP

HOOK, Sidney, 1902- 191
John Dewey, an intellectual portrait. Westport, Conn., Greenwood Press [1971] ix, 242 p. 22 cm. Reprint of the 1939 ed. Bibliography: p. 240-242. [B945.D44H47 1971] 78-104239 ISBN 0-8371-3951-1
1. Dewey, John, 1859-1952. I. Dewey, John, 1859-1952.

HOWLETT, Charles F. 327'.172'0924
Troubled philosopher : John Dewey and the struggle for world peace / Charles F. Howlett. Port Washington, N.Y. : Kennikat Press, 1977. p. cm. (National university publications) (Series in American studies) Includes index. Bibliography: p. [JX1962.D48H68] 76-22784 ISBN 0-8046-9153-3 : 12.50
1. Dewey, John, 1859-1952. 2. Peace. I. Title. BIP

LAMONT, Corliss, 1902- ed. 921.1
Dialogue on John Dewey [by] James T. Farrell [and others] Edited by Corliss Lamont, with the assistance of Mary Redmer. New York, Horizon Press, 1959. 155p. 21cm. [B945.D44L3] 59-14697
I. Dewey, John, 1859-1952. II. Farrell, James Thomas, 1904- III. Title.

NATHANSON, Jerome. 191
John Dewey; the reconstruction of the democratic life. New York, F. Ungar Pub. Co. [1967, c1951] ix, 129 p. 21 cm. (Ethical culture publications) Bibliography: p. 123-125. [B945.D44N3 1967] 66-26511
1. Dewey, John, 1859-1952. BIP

THOMAS, Milton Halsey, 1903- 012
John Dewey, a centennial biography. Chicago, Univ. of Chic. Pr. [c.1962] xiii, 370p. 22cm. First pub. [in 1929] as A bibliography of John Dewey, by Milton Halsey Thomas and Herbert Wallace Schneider. 62-12638 6.50
1. Dewey, John, 1859-1952—Bibl. I. Title.

Dewey, John, 1859-1952—Bibliography.

BOYDSTON, Jo Ann, 016.37'01'0924 1924-
Checklist of writings about John Dewey, 1887-1973 [by] Jo Ann Boydston [and] Kathleen Poulos. Carbondale, Southern Illinois University Press [1974] ix, 396 p. 24 cm. [Z8228.B59] 74-5236 ISBN 0-8093-0670-0 12.50
1. Dewey, John, 1859-1952—Bibliography. I. Poulos, Kathleen, 1944- joint author. II. Title. BIP

Dewey, Maybelle (Jones),

DEWEY, Maybelle (Jones), 920.7 1888-
Push the button; the chronicle of a professor's wife. Atlanta, Tupper and Love [1951] 180 p. 22 cm. Autobiography. [LA2317.D4A3] 51-14750
I. Title.

Dewey, Melvil, 1851-1931.

DEWEY, Melvil, 1851- 020'.92'4 B 1931.
Melvil Dewey, his enduring presence in librarianship / edited by Sarah K. Vann. Littleton, Colo. : Libraries Unlimited, inc., 1977. p. cm. (The Heritage of librarianship series ; no. 4) Includes index. Bibliography: p. [Z720.D5A3] 77-21852 ISBN 0-87287-134-7 lib.bdg. : 17.50
1. Dewey, Melvil, 1851-1931. 2. Dewey, Melvil, 1851-1931—Bibliography. 3. Librarians—United States—Biography. 4. Libraries—United States—Collected works. 5. Library science—Collected works. I. Vann, Sarah K., 1916- II. Title. III. Series.

Dewey, Richard Smith, 1845-1933.

DEWEY, Richard 616.8'9'00924 B Smith, 1845-1933.
Recollections of Richard Dewey, pioneer in American psychiatry. [Edited by Ethel L. Dewey] New York, Arno Press, 1973 [c1936] xii, 173 p. illus. 22 cm. (Mental illness and social policy: the American experience) Reprint of the ed. published by The University of Chicago Press, Chicago. Bibliography: p. 166-168. [RC339.52.D49A33 1973] 73-2395 ISBN 0-405-05203-0 10.00
1. Dewey, Richard Smith, 1845-1933. I. Title. II. Series. BIP

Dewey, Thomas Edmund, 1902-1971.

BEYER, Barry K., 973.91'092'4 B 1931-
Thomas E. Dewey, 1937-1947 : a study in political leadership / Barry K. Beyer. New York : Garland Pub., 1979. p. cm. (Modern American history) Based on the author's thesis, University of Rochester. Includes index. Bibliography: p. [E748.D48B49] 78-62375 ISBN 0-8240-3626-3 : 35.00
1. Dewey, Thomas Edmund, 1902-1971. 2. United States—Politics and government—1945-1953. 3. New York (State)—Politics and government—1865-1950. 4. New York (State)—Governors—Biography. I. Title. II. Series.

KURLAND, Gerald, 1942- 92
Thomas Dewey, the upset presidential candidate of 1948. Charlotteville, N.Y., SamHar Press, 1971. 32 p. 22 cm. (Outstanding personalities, no. 3) Bibliography: p. 32. A biography of the Governor of New York who was the unsuccessful Republican candidate for the Presidency two consecutive times. [E748.D48K8] 70-185659
1. Dewey, Thomas Edmund, 1902- I. Title.

DeWitt, John Lesesne, 1880-

BOSIA, Remo. 940.54'81'73
The general and I. [1st ed.] New York, Phaedra [1971] 163 p. 21 cm. [CT275.B58463A3] 79-156220 4.95
1. DeWitt, John Lesesne, 1880- 2. World War, 1939-1945—Personal narratives, American. I. Title.

DeWitt, Simeon, 1756-1834.

HEIDT, William. 974.7'71'030924 B
Simeon DeWitt; founder of Ithaca Carol K. Kammen, editor. Ithaca, N.Y., DeWitt Historical Society of Tompkins County [1968] viii, 75 p. port. 23 cm. Bibliography: p. 41-43. [F123.D53H4] 76-1243
1. DeWitt, Simeon, 1756-1834. 2. Ithaca, N.Y.—History.

Dewlish, Eng.—History.

MARSH, Bernard W. 942.3'31
Memories of Dewlish / by Bernard W. Marsh ; drawings by Mrs. R. J. Tennent. [Dorchester] : Dorset County Council Education Committee, [1977] [1], 20 p. : ill., ports. ; 21 cm. (Booklet - Dorchester County Council Education Committee ; no. 623) [DA690.D52M37] 77-369101 ISBN 0-85216-145-X
1. Dewlish, Eng.—History. 2. Marsh, Bernard W. 3. Dewlish, Eng.—Biography. I. Title. II. Series: Dorchester, Eng. County Council. Education Committee. Booklet — Dorchester County Council Education Committee ; no. 623.

Dexter, Juliane Nick, 1902-

DEXTER, Juliane Nick, 979.4'95 B 1902-
Gold! ... no gold / by Juliane Nick Dexter. Escondido, CA : Omni Publishers, 1977,c1976 xiv, 151 p. : ill. ; 24 cm. Includes the text of the diary by the author's father, Peter Nick. [F869.S18D48] 76-44259 ISBN 0-89127-021-3 pbk. : 4.95
1. Dexter, Juliane Nick, 1902- 2. Nick, Peter. 3. San Bernardino, Calif.—Biography. I. Nick, Peter. II. Title. BIP

Dexter, Timothy, 1747-1806.

MARQUAND, John Phillips, 920.8 1893-1960.
Timothy Dexter revisited. Illustrated by Philip Kappel. [1st ed.] Boston, Little, Brown [1960] 306 p. illus. 22 cm. [F74.N55D4843] 60-9335
1. Dexter, Timothy, 1747-1806. I. Title.

Deyneka, Peter.

ROHRER, Norman B. 266'.023'0924 B
Peter Dynamite, "twice-born" Russian : the story of Peter Deyneka, missionary to the Russian world / Norman B. Rohrer and Peter Deyneka, Jr. Grand Rapids : Baker Book House, c1975. 192 p. : ill. ; 21 cm. [B3785.D45R64] 76-354201 ISBN 0-8010-7639-0 pbk. : 3.95
1. Deyneka, Peter. I. Deyneka, Peter, 1931- joint author. II. Title.

Di Maggio, Joseph Paul, 1914-

ALLEN, Maury, 1932- 796.357'092'4
Where have you gone, Joe DiMaggio? : The story of America's last hero / by Maury Allen. 1st ed. New York : Dutton, 1975. 222 p., [8] leaves of plates : ill. ; 22 cm. [GV865.D5A79] 75-6523 7.95
1. Di Maggio, Joseph Paul, 1914- 2. Baseball. I. Title. BIP

SCHOOR, Gene. 927.96357
Joe Di Maggio, the Yankee Clipper. New York, J. Messner [1956] 192 p. illus. 22 cm. [GV865.D5S28] 56-10455
1. Di Maggio, Joseph Paul, 1914-

SILVERMAN, Al. 796.357'0922
Joe Di Maggio: the golden year, 1941. Englewood Cliffs, N.J., Prentice-Hall [1969] xiii, 234 p. illus., ports. 22 cm. [GV865.D5S5] 70-80775 5.95
1. Di Maggio, Joseph Paul, 1914- I. Title: The golden year, 1941.

Di Maggio, Joseph Paul, 1914- — Juvenile literature.

FINLAYSON, Ann. 796.357'092'2
Champions at bat; three power hitters. Illustrated by Paul Frame. Champaign, Ill., Garrard Pub. Co. [1970] 96 p. illus., ports. 24 cm. (Garrard sports library) Biographical sketches of three baseball players renowned for their batting skill: Rogers Hornsby, Joe DiMaggio, Ted Williams. [GV865.A1F5] 74-113838 ISBN 0-8116-6661-1 2.59
1. Hornsby, Rogers, 1896- —Juvenile literature. 2. Di Maggio, Joseph Paul, 1914- —Juvenile literature. 3. Williams, Theodore Samuel, 1918- —Juvenile literature. I. Frame, Paul, 1913- illus. II. Title. BIP

Diabetes—Personal narratives.

REDMOND, 362.1'9'646200924 B Ruth.
Hole in my head. New York, Carlton Press [1973] 192 p. illus. 21 cm. (A Hearthstone book) [RC660.R39] 73-179157 3.50
1. Diabetes—Personal narratives. I. Title.

Diagilev, Sergei Pavlovich, 1872-1929.

BUCKLE, Richard. 792.8'092'4
Diaghilev / Richard Buckle. 1st American ed. New York : Atheneum, 1979. xxiv, 616 p., [12] leaves of plates : ill. ; 25 cm. Includes index. Bibliography: p. 587-592. [GV1785.D5B79 1979b] 78-73084 ISBN 0-689-10952-0 : 19.95
1. Diagilev, Sergei Pavlovich, 1872-1929. 2. Impresarios—Russia—Biography.

LIFAR, Serge, 1905- 792.8'092'4 B
Serge Diaghilev, his life, his work, his legend : an intimate biography / by Serge Lifar. New York : Da Capo Press, 1976, c1940. xiv, 399 p., [33] leaves of plates : ill. ; 24 cm. (The Lyric stage.) Translation of Diagilev i s Diagilevym. Reprint of the ed. published by Putnam, New York. Includes index. [GV1785.D5L48 1976] 76-25041 ISBN 0-306-70839-6 : 22.50
1. Diagilev, Sergei Pavlovich, 1872-1929. 2. Ballet. I. Title.

PERCIVAL, John. 792.8'092'4 B
The world of Diaghilev / by John Percival ; designed by Gillian Greenwood. Rev. ed. New York : Harmony Books, c1979. p. cm. Includes index. Bibliography: p. [GV1785.D5P4 1979] 79-12971 ISBN 0-517-53902-0 : 10.00 ISBN 0-517-53903-9 pbk. : 5.95
1. Diagilev, Sergei Pavlovich, 1872-1929. 2. Impresarios—Russia—Biography. I. Title. BIP

SOKOLOVA, Lydia, 1896- 927.928
Dancing for Diaghilev; the memoirs of Lydia Sokolova. Edited by Richard Buckle. New York, Macmillan, 1961 [c.1960] 287p. illus. 61-1563 5.00
1. Diagilev, Sergei Pavlovich, 1872-1929. I. Title.

Dial, Nathaniel Barksdale, 1862-1940.

DIAL, Rebecca. 328.73'092'4 B
True to his colors : a story of South Carolina's Senator Nathaniel Barksdale Dial / by his daughter Rebecca Dial. 1st ed. New York : Vantage Press, [1974] 200 p. : ill. ; 21 cm. Bibliography: p. 199-200. [E748.D53D52] 75-302463 ISBN 0-533-01226-0 : 6.95
1. Dial, Nathaniel Barksdale, 1862-1940. I. Title.

Diamond, John, 1895 or 6-1931.

CURZON, Sam 923.4173
Legs Diamond Derby, Conn., Monarch [c.1962] 143p. (Monarch Americana bk., MA318) 62-1469 .35 pap.,
1. Diamond, John, 1895 or 6-1931. I. Title.

LEVINE, Gary, 1938- 364.1'092'4 B
Anatomy of a gangster : Jack "Legs" Diamond / Gary Levine. South Brunswick, [N.J.] : A. S. Barnes, c1979. 200 p. : ill. ; 24 cm. Includes indexes. [HV6248.D48L48 1979] 78-55448 ISBN 0-498-02246-3 : 12.00
1. Diamond, John, 1895 or 6-1931. 2. Crime and criminals—United States—Biography. I. Title.

Diamond, Neil.

O'REGAN, Suzanne K. 784'.092'4 B
Neil Diamond / text, Suzanne K. O'Regan ; ill., John Keely. Mankato, Minn. : Creative Education, [1975] p. cm. Bibliography: p. [ML3930.D45O7] 75-22462 ISBN 0-87191-464-6 lib.bdg. : 4.95
1. Diamond, Neil. I. Keely, John. II. Title. BIP

Diaries.

DUNAWAY, Philip, ed. 920
A treasury of the world's great diaries. Edited by Philip Dunaway and Mel Evans. With an introd. by Louis Untermeyer. Garden City, N. Y., Doubleday [1957] 586 p. 22 cm. [CT105.D8] 57-9502
1. Diaries. I. Evans, Philip, Aug. 21, 1911- II. Title.

Diaz del Castillo, Bernal, 1496-1584.

CERWIN, Herbert, 1908- 923.972
Bernal Diaz, historian of the conquest. Norman, Univ. of Oklahoma Pr. [c.1963] 239p. illus. 23cm. Bibl. 63-8985 4.95
1. Diaz del Castillo, Bernal, 1496-1584. I. Title.

CERWIN, Herbert, 1908- 923.972
Bernal Dinz, historian of the conquest. [1st ed] Norman, University of Oklahoma Press [1963] 239 p. illus. 23 cm. Includes bibliography. [F1230.D5712] 63-8985
1. Diaz del Castillo, Bernal, 1496-1584. I. Title.

Diaz, Porfirio, Pres. Mexico, 1830-1915.

BEALS, Carleton, 1893- 972.08'1'0924 B
Porfirio Diaz, dictator of Mexico. Westport, Conn., Greenwood Press [1971, c1959] 463 p. illus., map, ports. 24 cm. [F1233.5.D53B4 1971] 72-135241 ISBN 0-8371-5159-7
1. Diaz, Porfirio, Pres. Mexico, 1830-1915. BIP

HANNAY, David, 1853-1934. 972.08'1'0924
Diaz. Port Washington, N.Y., Kennikat Press [1970] vi, 319 p. port. 22 cm. Reprint of the 1917 ed. Bibliography: p. [307]-308. [F1233.5.D53H3 1970] 77-112804 ISBN 0-8046-1071-1
1. Diaz, Porfirio, Pres. Mexico, 1830-1915. BIP

Diaz, Tony.

DIAZ, Tony. 248'.246 B
Ride the hot wind / by Tony Diaz, with Mark Fackler. Carol Stream, Ill. : Creation House, c1978. 135 p. ; 22 cm. [BV4935.D5A35] 77-78850 ISBN 0-88419-126-5 pbk. : 2.95
1. Diaz, Tony. 2. Converts—Biography. 3. Narcotic addicts—Biography. I. Fackler, Mark, joint author. II. Title.

Dibelius, Otto, Bp., 1880-

DAY is dawning; 922.443
the story of Bishop Otto Dibelius, based on his proclamations andauthentic documents. Philadelphia, Christian Education Press [c1956] 222p. illus. 21cm. Editor's pref. signed: Fred D. Wentzel. [BX8080.D47D3] 56-12720
1. Dibelius, Otto, Bp., 1880- I. Wentzel, Fred De Hart, 1895- ed.

DIBELIUS, Otto, Bp., 1880- 284.143
In the service of the Lord: the autobiography of Otto Dibelius. Translated from the German by Mary Ilford. [1st ed.] New York, Holt, Rinehart and Winston [1964] 280 p. illus., ports. 22 cm. Translation of Ein Christ ist immer im Dienst. [BX8080.D47A323] 63-22051
I. Title.

Dick, John Henry, 1919-

DICK, John Henry, 1919- 574'.092'4
Other Edens : the sketchbook of an artist naturalist / John Henry Dick ; foreword by S. Dillon Ripley. Old Greenwich, Conn. : Devin-Adair Co., c1979. xi, 272 p. : ill. ; 24 cm. [QH31.D48A3] 79-67270 ISBN 0-8159-6412-9 : 19.95
1. Dick, John Henry, 1919- 2. Naturalists—United States—Biography. 3. Artists—United States—Biography. I. Title. BIP

Dickens, Catherine Thomson Hogarth, 1815-1879.

DICKENS, Charles, 1812-1870. 823'.8 B
Mr. & Mrs. Charles Dickens; his letters to her. With a foreword by their daughter Kate Perugini, and notes, appendices, etc. by Walter Dexter. New York, Haskell House Publishers, 1972. xvii, 298 p. ports. 23 cm. Includes bibliographical references. [PR4581.A4D5 1972] 72-1331 ISBN 0-8383-1429-5 11.95
1. Dickens, Catherine Thomson Hogarth, 1815-1879. I. Dexter, Walter, 1877-1944, ed. II. Title. BIP

Dickens, Charles, 1812-1870.

BROWN, Ivor John Carnegie, 1891- 914.2'03'81
Dickens and his world [by] Ivor Brown. New York, H. Z. Walck [1970] 47 p. illus., facsims., ports. 26 cm. [PR4581.B75] 71-109122 4.50
1. Dickens, Charles, 1812-1870. 2. Gt. Brit.—Social conditions—19th century. I. Title.

BROWN, Ivor John Carnegie, 1891- 914.2
Dickens in his time. [New York] Nelson [1964, c.1963] 248p. illus., ports. 23cm. 64-719 5.00
1. Dickens, Charles, 1812-1870. 2. Gt. Brit.—Soc. condit. I. Title.

CHARLES Dickens, 1812-1870; 823'.8
a centennial volume, edited by E. W. F. Tomlin. New York, Simon and Schuster [1969] 288 p. illus., facsims., ports. 26 cm. Part of illustrative matter colored. Bibliographical references included in "Notes" (p. 274-277) [PR4581.C48 1969] 70-87141 12.50
1. Dickens, Charles, 1812-1870. I. Tomlin, Eric Walter Frederick, 1913- ed.

CHESTERTON, Gilbert Keith, 1874-1936. 823.8
Charles Dickens. Introd. by Steven Marcus. New York, Schocken Books [1965] xviii, 302 p. 21 cm. (Schocken paperbacks, SB91) [PR4588.C5 1965] 65-14824
1. Dickens, Charles, 1812-1870. I. Title.

CLARK, Cumberland, 1862- 823'.8
Charles Dickens and the begging letter writer. With publication of Dickens' original letter. New York, Haskell House, 1972. 31 p. 23 cm. Reprint of the 1923 ed. [PR4583.C55 1972] 72-3492 ISBN 0-8383-1532-1
1. Dickens, Charles, 1812-1870. I. Title. BIP

DARK, Sidney, 1874-1947. 823'.8
Charles Dickens. [Folcroft, Pa.] Folcroft Library Editions, 1973. 123 p. port. 24 cm. Reprint of the 1919 ed. published by T. C. & E. C. Jack, London. [PR4581.D3 1973] 72-13466 ISBN 0-8414-1200-6 (lib. bdg.)
1. Dickens, Charles, 1812-1870.

DICKENS, Charles, 1812-1870. 917.3'04'58
American notes for general circulation / Charles Dickens ; with an introd. by Angus Wilson ; [notes by John S. Whitley and Arnold Goldman] ; ill. by Raymond F. Houlihan. Avon, Conn. : Limited Editions Club, 1975. xv, 272 p., [10] leaves of plates : ill. (some col.) ; 26 cm. Includes bibliographical references. [E165.D53 1974] 75-323537
1. Dickens, Charles, 1812-1870. 2. United States—Description and travel—1783-1848. 3. United States—Social life and customs—1783-1865. I. Houlihan, Ray. II. Title.

DICKENS, Charles, 1812-1870. 823'.8 B
Dickens to his oldest friend; the letters of a lifetime from Charles Dickens to Thomas Beard. Edited by Walter Dexter. New York, Haskell House Publishers, 1973. xxiii, 295 p. facsims. 23 cm. Reprint of the 1932 ed. [PR4581.A4B4 1973] 72-6506 ISBN 0-8383-1620-4 12.95
I. Beard, Thomas, d. 1891. II. Title.

DICKENS, Charles, 1812-1870. 823'.8 B
The letters of Charles Dickens, edited by his sister-in-law and his eldest daughter. Freeport, N.Y., Books for Libraries Press [1972- p. Reprint of the 1879 ed. Contents.Contents.—v. 1. 1833-1856.—v. 2. 1857-1870. [PR4581.A3D6 1972] 72-8556 ISBN 0-8369-7100-0
I. Hogarth, Georgina, 1827-1917, ed. II. Dickens, Mary, 1838-1896, ed. III. Title.

DICKENS, Charles, 1812-1870. 823'.8 B
Letters of Charles Dickens to Wilkie Collins, 1851-1870. Selected by Georgina Hogarth; edited by Laurence Hutton. New York, Haskell House, 1974. 191 p. 22 cm. Reprint of the 1892 ed. published by J. R. Osgood, McIlvaine, London. [PR4581.A4C6 1974] 73-20382 ISBN 0-8383-1823-1
1. Dickens, Charles, 1812-1870. 2. Collins, Wilkie, 1824-1889. I. Collins, Wilkie, 1824-1889. BIP

DICKENS, Charles, 1812-1870. 823'.8 B
The unpublished letters of Charles Dickens to Mark Lemon. Edited by Walter Dexter. New York, Haskell House, 1971. vii, 164 p. facsims. 23 cm. Reprint of the 1927 ed. [PR4581.A4L4 1971] 76-155146 ISBN 0-8383-1281-0
1. Dickens, Charles, 1812-1870. 2. Lemon, Mark, 1809-1870. I. Lemon, Mark, 1809-1870. II. Dexter, Walter, 1877-1944, ed. III. Title.

DICKENS, Charles, 1812-1870. 823'.8 B
The unpublished letters of Charles Dickens to Mark Lemon. Edited by Walter Dexter. [Folcroft, Pa.] Folcroft Library Editions, 1973. p. Reprint of the 1927 ed. published by H. & T. Smith, London. [PR4581.A4L4 1973] 73-16260 25.00
1. Dickens, Charles, 1812-1870. 2. Lemon, Mark, 1809-1870. I. Lemon, Mark, 1809-1870. II. Dexter, Walter, 1877-1944, ed. III. Title.

DUNLOP, Agnes Mary Robertson. 823'.8 B
Great ambitions; a story of the early years of Charles Dickens, by Elisabeth Kyle. [1st ed.] New York, Holt, Rinehart and Winston [1968, c1966] 217 p. 22 cm. Bibliography: p. 217. A biography of Charles Dickens which focuses upon the unusual characters that throng the pages of his books, revealing them as real and influential people whom he adapted to his needs in fiction. [PR4582.D84 1968] 92 AC 68
1. Dickens, Charles, 1812-1870. I. Kyle, Elizabeth, pseud. II. Title.

FIDO, Martin. 823'.8
Charles Dickens. New York, Humanities Press [1968] viii, 119 p. 19 cm. (The Profiles in literature series) Bibliography: p. 118-119. [PR4581.F38 1968b] 68-29355 1.35
1. Dickens, Charles, 1812-1870 BIP

FITZGERALD, Percy Hetherington, 1834-1925. 823'.8
The life of Charles Dickens as revealed in his writings. New York, Haskell House Publishers, 1973. 2 v. illus. 23 cm. Reprint of the 1905 ed. [PR4581.F59 1973] 72-4115 ISBN 0-8383-1607-7 28.95
1. Dickens, Charles, 1812-1870. I. Title.

FITZGERALD, Percy Hetherington, 1834-1925. 823'.8 B
Memories of Charles Dickens, with an account of Household words, and All the year round, and of the contributors thereto. New York, B. Blom, 1971. xiv, 383 p. illus. 21 cm. Reprint of the 1913 ed. [PR4581.F6 1971] 77-176090
1. Dickens, Charles, 1812-1870. 2. Household words. 3. All the year round. I. Title.

FORSTER, John, 1812-1876. 823'.8 B
Charles Dickens / by John Forster. Folcroft, Pa. : Folcroft Library Editions, 1977. p. cm. Reprint of a pamphlet published by Chapman and Hall, London. [PR4581.F68 1977] 77-1326 ISBN 0-8414-4192-8 lib. bdg. : 10.00
1. Dickens, Charles, 1812-1870. 2. Novelists, English—19th century—Biography.

GISSING, George Robert, 1857-1903 823.8
Charles Dicken. Port Washington, N.Y., Kennikat [1966] 293p. 22cm. First pub. in 1898. This printing based on the 1924 ed. [PR4588.G5] 66-21384 7.50
1. Dickens, Charles, 1812-1870. I. Title.

GRAHAM, Eleanor, 1896- 928.2
The story of Charles Dickens. Illustrated with plates from the original editions of his works, and with additional drawings by Norman Meredith. New York, Abelard-Schuman [1954] 219p. illus. 22cm. [PR4581.G68] 54-10217
1. Dickens, Charles, 1812-1870. I. Title.

HAMMOND, R. A. 823'.8
The life and writings of Charles Dickens: A memorial volume. Containing personaa recollections, amusing anecdotes, letters, and uncollected papers by "BOZ" never before published. With and introd. by Elihu Burritt. New York, Haskell House Publishers, 1972. 426 p. illus. 23 cm. Reprint of the 1870 ed. [PR4581.H27 1972] 72-3998 ISBN 0-8383-1606-9 15.95
1. Dickens, Charles, 1812-1870. I. Title.

HIBBERT, Christopher, 1924- 823'.8
The making of Charles Dickens. [1st U.S. ed.] New York, Harper & Row [1967] xiv, 321 p. illus., ports. 22 cm. Bibliography: p. 303-307. [PR4581.H5 1967] 66-20738
1. Dickens, Charles, 1812-1870. I. Title.

HOTTEN, John Camden, 1832-1873. 823'.8 B
Charles Dickens, the story of his life / by J. C. Hotten. Folcroft, Pa. : Folcroft Library Editions, 1978. 110 p. : ill. ; 33 cm. Reprint of the 1870 ed. published by Harper, New York. [PR4581.H8 1978] 78-12611 ISBN 0-8414-4873-6 lib. bdg. : 25.00
1. Dickens, Charles, 1812-1870. 2. Novelists, English—19th century—Biography. I. Title.

JOHNSON, Edgar 928.2
Charles Dickens, his tragedy and triumph. v. 1 & 2. Boston, Little [1965, c.1952] 2v. illus.,. facsim., geneal. tables, ports. 22cm. Bibl. [PR4581.J6] 65-328 15.00 set.,
1. Dickens, Charles, 1812-1870. I. Title.

JOHNSON, Edgar. 928.2
Charles Dickens, his tragedy and triumph. [New York] Simon and Schuster, 1952. 2 v. illus., ports., geneal. tables. 22 cm. Bibliography: v. 2, p. xcix-xcv. [PR4581.J6] 52-4460
1. Dickens, Charles, 1812-1870.

KENT, Charles, 1823-1902. 823'.8
Charles Dickens as a reader. London, Chapman & Hall, 1872. New York, Haskell House Publishers, 1973. vii, 271 p. 23 cm. [PR4581.K4 1973] 72-4156 ISBN 0-8383-1608-5 10.95
1. Dickens, Charles, 1812-1870. I. Title. BIP

LUPTON, Edward Basil. 823'.8
Dickens, the immortal / by Edward Basil Lupton. Folcroft, Pa. : Folcroft Library Editions, 1976. p. cm. Reprint of the 1923 ed. published by A. Fowler, Kansas City. [PR4581.L8 1976] 76-16834 ISBN 0-8414-5723-9 lib. bdg. : 10.00
1. Dickens, Charles, 1812-1870. I. Title. BIP

MARCUS, Steven 823.8
Dickens: from Pickwick to Dombey. New York, Basic [c.1965] 389p. 23cm. Bibl. [PR4588.M3] 64-21189 5.95
1. Dickens, Charles, 1812-1870. I. Title.

MAUROIS, Andre, 1885-1967. 823.8
Dickens. [Translated from the French by Hamish Miles] New York, Ungar Pub. Co. [1967] 183 p. 20 cm. First published in 1934. Translation of Un essai sur Dickens. [PR4581.M46 1967] 66-26514
1. Dickens, Charles, 1812-1870. I. Miles, Hamish, 1894-1937, tr.

MILLER, Joseph Hillis. 823'.8
Charles Dickens and George Cruikshank; papers read at a Clark Library Seminar on May 9, 1970, by J. Hillis Miller and David Borowitz. With an introd. by Ada B. Nisbet. [Los Angeles] William Andrews Clark Memorial Library, University of

California, 1971. vi, 99 p. illus., facsims. 23 cm. [PR4588.M53] 78-26985
1. Dickens, Charles, 1812-1870. 2. Cruikshank, George, 1792-1878. I. Borowitz, David, 1906- II. Title.

MONOD, Sylvere, 1921- 823'.8
Dickens, the novelist. With an introd. by Edward Wagenknecht. [1st ed.] Norman, University of Oklahoma Press [1968] xvi, 512 p. port. 24 cm. Rev. translation by the author, of Dickens, romancier. Bibliographical footnotes. [PR4581.M5913] 67-15589
1. Dickens, Charles, 1812-1870. I. Title.
BIP

PERKINS, Frederic Beecher, 823'.8
1828-1899.
Charles Dickens: a sketch of his life and works. [Folcroft, Pa.] Folcroft Library Editions, 1973 [i.e. 1974] p. Reprint of the 1870 ed. published by Putnam, New York. [PR4581.P4 1974] 73-21778 27.50
1. Dickens, Charles, 1812-1870. BIP

PRIESTLEY, John Boynton, 928.2
1894-
Charles Dickens, a pictorial biography. New York, Viking Press [1962, c1961] 144 p. illus., ports., facsims. 24 cm. (A Studio book) [PR4581.P67 1962] 61-15437
1. Dickens, Charles, 1812-1870.

PRIESTLEY, John Boynton, 823'.8
1894-
Charles Dickens and his world, by J. B. Priestley. New York, Viking Press [1969, c1961] 144 p. illus., facsims., ports. 24 cm. (A Studio book) [PR4581.P67 1969] 74-7209 6.95
1. Dickens, Charles, 1812-1870. BIP

PRIESTLEY, John Boynton, 823'.8 B
1894-
Charles Dickens and his world / J. B. Priestley. New York : Scribner, [1978] c1961. 144 p. : ill. ; 24 cm. Reprint of the 1969 ed. published by Viking Press, New York. Includes index. [PR4581.P67 1978] 77-90490 ISBN 0-684-15574-5 : 10.95
1. Dickens, Charles, 1812-1870. 2. Novelists, English—19th century—Biography. I. Title.

PUGH, Edwin William, 1874- 823'.8
1930.
The Charles Dickens originals / by Edwin Pugh. New York : AMS Press, [1975] p. cm. Reprint of the 1912 ed. published by Scribner, New York. Includes index. [PR4581.P8 1975] 71-148288 ISBN 0-404-08895-3 : 18.00
1. Dickens, Charles, 1812-1870. I. Title.
BIP

PUGH, Edwin William, 1874- 823'.8
1930.
Charles Dickens, the apostle of the people / by Edwin Pugh. New York : AMS Press, 1975. vi, 316 p. ; 19 cm. Reprint of the 1908 ed. published by New Age Press, London. [PR4581.P83 1975] 78-148287 ISBN 0-404-08894-5 : 10.50
1. Dickens, Charles, 1812-1870. I. Title.

ROOKE, Patrick J. 914.2'03'81
The age of Dickens, by Patrick Rooke. New York, Putnam [1970] 128 p. illus., ports. 24 cm. (Putnam documentary history series) Bibliography: p. 123-124. [PR4583.R6 1970b] 79-116151 4.95
1. Dickens, Charles, 1812-1870. 2. Gt. Brit.—History—Victoria, 1837-1901. I. Title.

†SHORE, William 823'.8
Teignmouth, 1865-1932.
Dickens / by W. Teignmouth Shore. Folcroft, Pa. : Folcroft Library Editions, 1977. 83 p., [7] leaves of plates : ill. ; 24 cm. Reprint of the 1904 ed. published by G. Bell, London, issued in series: Bell's miniature series of great writers. Bibliography: p. 83. [PR4581.S5 1977] 77-24525 ISBN 0-8414-7863-5 lib. bdg. : 10.00
1. Dickens, Charles, 1812-1870. 2. Novelists, English—19th century—Biography. I. Series: Bell's miniature series of great writers.

SITWELL, Osbert, Sir, 823'.8
bart., 1892-1969.
Dickens. [Folcroft, Pa.] Folcroft Library Editions, 1973. p. Reprint of the 1932 ed. published by Chatto & Windus, London, in series: The Dolphin books. [PR4588.S5 1973b] 73-11381 6.50
1. Dickens, Charles, 1812-1870. BIP

STONEHOUSE, John Harrison, 823'.8
1865?-1937.
Green leaves; new chapters in the life of Charles Dickens. Rev. and enl. ed. New York, Haskell House Publishers 1973. 123 p. illus. 23 cm. Reprint of the 1931 ed. Bibliography: p. [114] [PR4581.S66 1973] 72-6782 ISBN 0-8383-1643-3 8.95
1. Dickens, Charles, 1812-1870. 2. Hogarth family. I. Title.

STOREY, Gladys. 823'.8 B
Dickens and daughter. New York, Haskell House Publishers, 1971. 236 p. illus. 23 cm. Reprint of the 1939 ed. [PR4581.S67 1971] 79-164657 ISBN 0-8383-1321-3
1. Dickens, Charles, 1812-1870. 2. Perugini, Kate (Dickens) Mrs., 1839-1929. I. Title. BIP

WAGENKNECHT, Edward 823.8 B
Charles, 1900-
The man Charles Dickens; a Victorian portrait, by Edward Wagenknecht. Rev. ed. Norman, University of Oklahoma Press [1966] xiv, 269 p. illus., ports. 24 cm. Bibliography: p. 249-258. [PR4581.W2 1966] 66-10294
1. Dickens, Charles, 1812-1870. I. Title.
BIP

WILSON, Angus. 823'.8 B
The world of Charles Dickens. New York, Viking Press [1970] 302 p. illus. (part col.), facsims., col. plates, ports. (part col.) 26 cm. (A Studio book) [PR4581.W52] 70-101775 12.95
1. Dickens, Charles, 1812-1870. I. Title.

WILSON, Angus, 1913- 823'.8
The world of Charles Dickens. Harmondsworth, Penguin, 1972. [2], 302 p. illus. (some col.) facsims., music, ports (incl. 1 col.) 25 cm. [PR4581.W52 1972] 73-330817 ISBN 0-14-003488-9 £1.50
1. Dickens, Charles, 1812-1870. I. Title.

Dickens, Charles, 1812-1870— Addresses, essays, lectures.

THE Bookman, February 1912 823'.8
: Dickens centenary number, with presentation plate portrait. Folcroft, Pa. : Folcroft Library Editions, 1977. x, p., 226-274 : ill. ; 37 cm. Reprint of an issue of the serial published in London by Hodder and Stoughton. [PR4585.Z9B6] 77-20085 ISBN 0-8414-2944-8 : lib.bdg. : 10.00
1. Dickens, Charles, 1812-1870—Addresses, essays, lectures. 2. Novelists, English—19th century—Biography—Addresses, essays, lectures.

Dickens, Charles, 1812-1870— Appreciation—U.S.

WILKINS, William Glyde, 823'.8
1854-1921, ed.
Charles Dickens in America. New York, Haskell House, 1970. xii, 318 p. illus., ports. 23 cm. Reprint of the 1911 ed. [PR4582.W5 1970] 70-120131
1. Dickens, Charles, 1812-1870—Appreciation—U.S. I. Title. BIP

Dickens, Charles, 1812-1870— Bibliography—Catalogs.

DICKENS memento / 745.1
with introd. by Francis Phillimore and "Hints to Dickens collectors" by John F. Dexter. Catalogue with purchasers' names & prices realised of the pictures, drawings, and objects of art of the late Charles Dickens sold by auction in London by Messrs. Christie, Manson & Woods on July 9th, 1870. Folcroft, Pa. : Folcroft Library Editions, 1978. 11 p. ; 33 cm. The Catalogue has special t.p. Reprint of the 1884 ed. published by Field & Tuer, London, and Scribner & Welford, New York. [Z8230.D54 1978] [PR4585] 78-16479 ISBN 0-8414-6817-6 lib. bdg. : 17.50
1. Dickens, Charles, 1812-1870—Bibliography—Catalogs. 2. Dickens, Charles, 1812-1870—Art collections. I. Phillimore, Francis. II. Dexter, John Furber, 1847-1927. III. Christie, Manson, and Woods, ltd., London.

Dickens, Charles, 1812-1870— Biography.

CHESTERTON, Gilbert 823'.8 B
Keith, 1874-1936.
Charles Dickens, by G. K. Chesterton and F. G. Kitton. London, Hodder and Stoughton, 1903. [Folcroft, Pa.] Folcroft Library Editions, 1972. p. [PR4581.C6 1972] 72-12735 ISBN 0-8414-0978-1 (lib. bdg.)
1. Dickens, Charles, 1812-1870—Biography. I. Kitton, Frederic George, 1856-1904, joint author.

DARWIN, Bernard Richard 823'.8 B
Meirion, 1876-
Dickens, by Bernard Darwin. New York, Haskell House, 1973. 134 p. 23 cm. (Great lives) Reprint of the 1933 ed. published by Duckworth, London. [PR4581.D34 1973] 73-8958 ISBN 0-8383-1710-3 8.95
1. Dickens, Charles, 1812-1870—Biography.

DARWIN, Bernard Richard 823'.8 B
Meirion, 1876-
Dickens. [Folcroft, Pa.] Folcroft Library Editions, 1973. p. Reprint of the 1933 ed. published by Duckworth, London, which was issued as no. 11 in series: Great lives. [PR4581.D34 1973b] 73-11304 ISBN 0-8414-1891-8 (lib. bdg.)
1. Dickens, Charles, 1812-1870—Biography. BIP

DEXTER, Walter, 1877-1944. 823'.8
Dickens : the story of the life of the world's favourite author / by Walter Dexter. Folcroft, Pa. : Folcroft Library Editions, 1977. 85 p. : ill. ; 26 cm. Reprint of the 1937 ed. published by Dickens Fellowship, London. Includes bibliographical references. [PR4581.D39 1977] 77-17827 ISBN 0-8414-3653-3 lib. bdg. : 12.50
1. Dickens, Charles, 1812-1870—Biography. 2. Novelists, English—19th century—Biography. BIP

DICKENS, Charles, 1812- 928.2
1870.
Selected letters. Edited, with an introd., by F. W. Dupee. New York, Farrar, Straus and Cudahy [1960] xxiv, 293 p. 22 cm. (Great letters series) [PR4581.A3D8] 60-8013
1. Authors—Correspondence, reminiscences, etc. I. Dupee, Frederick Wilcox, 1904- ed. II. Title.

DICKENS, Henry Fielding, 823'.8 B
Sir, 1849-1933.
Memories of my father. New York, Haskell House, 1972. 30 p. illus. 23 cm. [PR4581.D45 1972] 72-3169 ISBN 0-8383-1509-7
1. Dickens, Charles, 1812-1870—Biography. I. Title.

DICKENS, Mary, 1838- 823'.8 B
1896.
My father as I recall him, by Mamie Dickens. New York, Haskell House, 1974. 128 p. illus. 23 cm. Reprint of the 1896 ed. published by Roxburghe Press, London. [PR4581.D5 1974] 73-21523 ISBN 0-8383-1814-2 11.95
1. Dickens, Charles, 1812-1870—Biography. I. Title.

DOLBY, George, d.1900. 823'.8 B
Charles Dickens as I knew him; the story of the reading tours in Great Britain and America (1866-1870) New York, Haskell House, 1970. xiii, 466 p. 23 cm. Reprint of the 1885 ed. [PR4581.D8 1970] 79-130252 ISBN 0-8383-1142-3
1. Dickens, Charles, 1812-1870—Biography. I. Title.

DOLBY, George, d.1900. 823'.8
Charles Dickens as I knew him; the story of the reading tours in Great Britain and America (1866-1870). [Folcroft, Pa.] Folcroft Library Editions, 1973. p. Reprint of the 1912 ed. published by Everett, London. [PR4581.D8 1973] 73-16389 20.00
1. Dickens, Charles, 1812-1870—Biography. I. Title.

FIDO, Martin. 823'.8 B
Charles Dickens: an authentic account of his life & times. Feltham, New York, Hamlyn, 1973 [c1970] 5-140 p. illus. (some col.), facsims., geneal. table, ports. (some col.). 29 cm. [PR4581.F39 1973] 73-165645 ISBN 0-600-36922-6 £1.75
1. Dickens, Charles, 1812-1870—Biography.

FIELDS, James Thomas, 823'.8 B
1816-1881.
In and out of doors with Charles Dickens / by James T. Fields. New York : AMS Press, [1976] p. cm. First published in 1872 as pt. 4 of the author's Yesterdays with authors under title: Dickens. Reprint of the 1876 ed. published by J. R. Osgood, Boston, in Vest-pocket series of standard and popular authors. [PR4581.F5 1976] 74-148775 ISBN 0-404-08749-3
1. Dickens, Charles, 1812-1870—Biography. I. Title. BIP

FITZGERALD, Percy 823'.8 B
Hetherington, 1834-1925.
Memories of Charles Dickens. With an account of Household words and All the year round and of the contributors thereto. Bristol, J. W. Arrowsmith, 1913. [New York, AMS Press, 1973] xiv, 383 p. illus. 23 cm. [PR4581.F6 1973] 75-148778 ISBN 0-404-08779-5 13.75
1. Dickens, Charles, 1812-1870—Biography. 2. Household words. 3. All the year round. I. Title.

HARRISON, Michael. 823'.8 B
Charles Dickens : a sentimental journey in search of an unvarnished portrait / by Michael Harrison. New York : Haskell House, [1975] p. cm. Reprint of the 1953 ed. published by Cassell, London. [PR4581.H35 1975] 74-34403 ISBN 0-8383-2113-5 : 15.95
1. Dickens, Charles, 1812-1870—Biography.

JOHNSON, Edgar. 823'.8 B
Charles Dickens, his tragedy and triumph / Edgar Johnson. Rev. and abridged. Harmondsworth, Eng. : New York : Penguin Books, 1979, c1977. 601 p. ; 20 cm. Includes index. [PR4581.J6 1979] 78-20982 ISBN 0-14-004895-2 pbk. : 3.95
1. Dickens, Charles, 1812-1870—Biography. 2. Novelists, English—19th century—Biography. I. Title.

JOHNSON, Edgar. 823'.8 B
Charles Dickens, his tragedy and triumph / Edgar Johnson. New York : Viking Press, 1977. p. cm. "A Richard Seaver book." Includes index. Bibliography: p. [PR4581.J6 1977] 77-22196 ISBN 0-670-21227-X : 15.00
1. Dickens, Charles, 1812-1870—Biography. 2. Novelists, English—19th century—Biography. I. Title.

LINDSAY, Jack, 1900- 928.2
Charles Dickens; a biographical and critical study. New York, Philosophical Library [1950] 459 p. 23 cm. [PR4581.L5 1950a] 50-9420
1. Dickens. Charles—Biog. I. Title. BIP

LUNN, Hugh Kingsmill, 823'.8 B
1889-1949.
The sentimental journey; a life of Charles Dickens, by Hugh Kingsmill. New York, Morrow, 1935. [Folcroft, Pa.] Folcroft Library Editions, 1972 [i.e. 1973] p. [PR4581.L76 1973] 72-13516 ISBN 0-8414-1228-6
1. Dickens, Charles, 1812-1870—Biography. I. Title.

MACKENZIE, Norman Ian. 823'.8 B
Dickens, a life / Norman and Jeanne MacKenzie. Oxford ; New York : Oxford University Press, 1979. x, 434 p., [8] leaves of plates : ill. ; 24 cm. Includes bibliographical references and index. [PR4581.M18] 78-40833 ISBN 0-19-211741-6 : 16.95
1. Dickens, Charles, 1812-1870—Biography. 2. Novelists, English—19th century—Biography. I. MacKenzie, Jeanne Daisy, 1922- II. Title.

MANKOWITZ, Wolf. 823'.8 B
Dickens of London / Wolf Mankowitz. 1st American ed. New York : Macmillan, 1977, c1976. 252 p. : ill. ; 26 cm. Includes index. Bibliography: p. [247] [PR4581.M3 1977] 76-19156 ISBN 0-02-579410-8 : 14.95

1. Dickens, Charles, 1812-1870—Biography. 2. Novelists, English—19th century—Biography. I. Title. **BIP**

MARZIALS, Frank Thomas, Sir, 1840-1912. 823'.8 B
Life of Charles Dickens. [Folcroft, Pa.] Folcroft Library Editions, 1973. p. Reprint of the 1887 ed. published by W. Scott, London, in the series: Great writers. [PR4581.M4 1973] 73-11357 ISBN 0-8414-5966-5 (lib. bdg.)
1. Dickens, Charles, 1812-1870—Biography. I. Title. **BIP**

NICOLL, William Robertson, Sir, 1851-1923. 823'.8 B
Dickens's own story : side-lights on his life and personality / by Sir William Robertson Nicoll. Folcroft, Pa. : Folcroft Library Editions, 1976. p. cm. Reprint of the 1923 ed. published by Chapman and Hall, London. [PR4581.N5 1976] 76-18190 ISBN 0-8414-6290-9 lib bdg. : 20.00
1. Dickens, Charles, 1812-1870—Biography. I. Title.

PAYNE, Edward F. 823'.8 B
Dickens days in Boston; a record of daily events, by Edward F. Payne. Boston, Milford House [1973] p. Reprint of the 1927 ed. published by Houghton Mifflin, Boston. [PR4582.P3 1973] 73-9955 ISBN 0-87821-157-8
1. Dickens, Charles, 1812-1870—Biography. 2. Boston—Intellectual life. I. Title.

STODDARD, Richard Henry, 1825-1903, ed. 823'.8 B
Anecodte biographies of Thackeray and Dickens / edited by Richard Henry Stoddard. Folcroft, Pa. : Folcroft Library Editions, 1979. p. cm. Reprint of the 1875 ed. published by Scribner, Armstrong, New York, which was issued as no. 2 of the Bric-a-brac series. Includes index. [PR5631.S75 1979] 79-20240 ISBN 0-8414-8022-2 (lib. bdg.) : 30.00
1. Thackeray, William Makepeace, 1811-1863—Biography. 2. Dickens, Charles, 1812-1870—Biography. 3. Thackeray, William Makepeace, 1811-1863—Anecdotes. 4. Dickens, Charles, 1812-1870—Anecdotes. 5. Novelists, English—19th century—Biography. I. Title. II. Series: Bric-a-brac series ; 2.

STONEHOUSE, John Harrison, 1865?-1937. 823'.8 B
Green leaves; new chapters in the life of Charles Dickens. Rev. and enl. ed. [Folcroft, Pa.] Folcroft Library Editions, 1973. 123 p. illus. 26 cm. Reprint of the 1931 ed. published by the Piccadilly Fountain Press, London. Bibliography: p. [115] [PR4581.S66 1973] 73-12135 ISBN 0-8414-7604-7 8.75
1. Dickens, Charles, 1812-1870—Biography. 2. Hogarth family. I. Title.

WRIGHT, Thomas, 1859-1936. 823'.8 B
The life of Charles Dickens. [Folcroft, Pa.] Folcroft Library Editions, 1973. p. Reprint of the 1935 ed. published by H. Jenkins, London. [PR4581.W7 1973] 73-15773 ISBN 0-8414-9475-4 (lib. bdg.)
1. Dickens, Charles, 1812-1870—Biography. I. Title.

Dickens, Charles, 1812-1870—Biography—Juvenile literature.

COOPER, Lettice Ulpha, 1897- 823'.8 B
A hand upon the time; a life of Charles Dickens, by Lettice Cooper. [New York] Pantheon Books [1968] 182 p. illus., ports. 22 cm. A biography of the English novelist whose stories and essays captured the social and economic flavor of the nineteenth century. [PR4581.C67] 92 68-24565
1. Dickens, Charles, 1812-1870—Biography—Juvenile literature. I. Title. **BIP**

JOHNSON, Spencer. 823'.8 B
The value of imagination : the story of Charles Dickens / by Spencer Johnson ; illustrated by Pileggi. 1st ed. La Jolla, Calif. : Value Communications, c1977. p. cm. (ValueTales) A biography of the nineteenth-century English novelist, Charles Dickens, emphasizing the value of an imaginative mind. [PR4581.J66] 92 77-13947 ISBN 0-916392-15-5 : 4.95
1. Dickens, Charles, 1812-1870—Biography—Juvenile literature. 2. Novelists, English—19th century—Biography—Juvenile literature. 3. Imagination—Juvenile literature. I. Pileggi, Steve. II. Title. **BIP**

Dickens, Charles, 1812-1870—Biography—Marriage.

PHILIP, Alexander John, 1879- 823'.8 B
Dickens's honeymoon and where he spent it. [Folcroft, Pa.] Folcroft Library Editions, 1973. 47 p. illus. 24 cm. Reprint of the 1912 ed. published by Chapman & Hall, London. [PR4582.P5 1973] 73-471 ISBN 0-8414-1493-9
1. Dickens, Charles, 1812-1870—Biography—Marriage. I. Title.

PHILIP, Alexander John, 1879- 823'.8 B
Dickens's honeymoon and where he spent it, by Alex J. Philip. London, Chapman & Hall, 1912. New York, Haskell House Publishers 1973. 47 p. illus. 23 cm. [PR4582.P5 1973b] 72-6507 ISBN 0-8383-1619-0 6.95
1. Dickens, Charles, 1812-1870—Biography—Marriage. I. Title.

PHILIP, Alexander John, 1879- 823'.8
Dickens'shoneymoon and where he spent it / by Alex. J. Philip. Norwood, Pa. : Norwood Editions, 1976. p. cm. Reprint of the 1912 ed. published by Chapman & Hall, London. [PR4582.P5 1976] 76-11844 ISBN 0-8482-2060-9 : 7.50
1. Dickens, Charles, 1812-1870—Biography—Marriage. 2. Dickens, Charles, 1812-1870—Homes and haunts—England—Chalk. 3. Chalk, Eng.—Description. I. Title.

Dickens, Charles, 1812-1870—Biography—Youth.

LANGTON, Robert, 1825-1900. 823'.8 B
The childhood and youth of Charles Dickens : with retrospective notes, and elucidations, from his books and letters / by Robert Langton. New York : AMS Press, 1975. 260 p. : ill. ; 19 cm. Reprint of the 1891 ed. published by Hutchinson, London. Includes bibliographical references and index. [PR4582.L3 1975] 76-148809 ISBN 0-404-08875-9 : 16.00.
1. Dickens, Charles, 1812-1870—Biography—Youth. I. Title.

Dickens, Charles, 1812-1870—Correspondence.

DICKENS, Charles, 1812-1870. 823'.8 B
Charles Dickens and Maria Beadnell: private correspondence. Edited by George Pierce Baker. [Folcroft, Pa.] Folcroft Library Editions, 1974. p. cm. Reprint of the 1908 ed. published by the Bibliophile Society, Boston. [PR4581.A4W6 1974] 74-14754 35.00
1. Dickens, Charles, 1812-1870—Correspondence. 2. Dickens, Charles, 1812-1870—Relationship with women—Maria Beadnell Winter. 3. Winter, Maria Sarah Beadnell, 1811 or 12-1886. I. Winter, Maria Sarah Beadnell, 1811- or 12-1886. II. Baker, George Pierce, 1866-1935, ed. III. Title.

DICKENS, Charles, 1812-1870. 823'.8
Charles Dickens as editor, being letters written by him to William Henry Wills, his sub-editor. Selected and edited by R. C. Lehmann. New York, Haskell House, 1972. xvi, 404 p. ports. 23 cm. Reprint of the 1912 ed. [PR4581.A4W5 1972] 73-38842 ISBN 0-8383-1393-0
1. Dickens, Charles, 1812-1870—Correspondence. 2. Wills, William Henry, 1810-1880. I. Wills, William Henry, 1810-1880. II. Lehmann, Rudolph Chambers, 1856-1929, ed.

DICKENS, Charles, 1812-1870. 823'.8 B
The earliest letters of Charles Dickens (written to his friend Henry Kolle) / edited by Harry B. Smith. Folcroft, Pa. : Folcroft Library Editions, 1976, [c1910] xi, 90 p., [4] leaves of plates : ill. ; 23 cm. Reprint of the ed. printed by University Press, Cambridge, Mass. [PR4581.A4K6 1976] 76-58366 ISBN 0-8414-7555-5 lib. bdg. : 20.00
1. Dickens, Charles, 1812-1870—Correspondence. 2. Kolle, William Henry, d. 1881. 3. Novelists, English—19th century—Correspondence. I. Kolle, William Henry, d. 1881. II. Smith, Harry Bache, 1860-1936. III. Title.

DICKENS, Charles, 1812-1870. 823'.8 B
The love romance of Charles Dickens; told in his letters to Maria Beadnell (Mrs. Winter) with introd. and notes by Walter Dexter. [Folcroft, Pa.] Folcroft Library Editions, 1974. p. cm. Reprint of the 1936 ed. published by Argonaut Press, London. [PR4581.A4W6 1974b] 74-18404 ISBN 0-8414-3807-2 (lib. bdg.)
1. Dickens, Charles, 1812-1870—Correspondence. 2. Dickens, Charles, 1812-1870—Relationship with women—Maria Beadnell Winter. 3. Winter, Maria Sarah (Beadnell) Mrs., 1811 or 12-1886. I. Winter, Maria Sarah Beadnell, 1811 or 12-1886. II. Title.

Dickens, Charles, 1812-1870—Criticism and interpretation.

SHORE, William Teignmouth, 1865-1932. 823'.8
Charles Dickens / by W. Teignmouth Shore ; with six ill. by Fred Barnard. Folcroft, Pa. : Folcroft Library Editions, 1979. p. cm. Reprint of the 1910 ed. published by Cassell, London, New York. [PR4588.S4 1979] 79-10465 ISBN 0-8414-7901-1 lib. bdg. : 12.50
1. Dickens, Charles, 1812-1870—Criticism and interpretation. 2. Dickens, Charles, 1812-1870—Characters.

Dickens, Charles, 1812-1870—Dictionaries, indexes, etc.

HARDWICK, John Michael Drinkrow, 1924- 823'.8
The Charles Dickens encyclopedia, compiled by Michael and Mollie Hardwick. New York, Scribner [1973] xi, 531 p. 27 cm. [PR4595.H28 1973] 73-7212 ISBN 0-684-13562-0 15.00
1. Dickens, Charles, 1812-1870—Dictionaries, indexes, etc. 2. Dickens, Charles, 1812-1870—Quotations. I. Hardwick, Mollie, joint author. II. Title. **BIP**

Dickens, Charles, 1812-1870—Friends and associates.

PATTEN, Robert L. 823'.8 B
Charles Dickens and his publishers / by Robert L. Patten. Oxford [Eng.] : Clarendon Press ; New York : Oxford University Press, 1978. xiv, 502 p., [4] leaves of plates : ill. ; 22 cm. Includes index. Bibliography: p. [465]-483. [PR4583.P29 1978] 77-30164 ISBN 0-19-812076-1 : 39.00
1. Dickens, Charles, 1812-1870—Friends and associates. 2. Authors and publishers. 3. Serial publication of books. 4. Novelists, English—19th century—Biography. I. Title. **BIP**

STEIG, Michael, 1936- 823'.8
Dickens and "Phiz" / Michael Steig. Bloomington : Indiana University Press, c1978. p. cm. Includes bibliographical references and index. [PR4583.S8] 77-23645 ISBN 0-253-31705-3 : 12.50
1. Dickens, Charles, 1812-1870—Friends and associates. 2. Dickens, Charles, 1812-1870—Illustrations. 3. Browne, Hablot Knight, 1815-1882. I. Title. **BIP**

Dickens, Charles, 1812-1870—Homes and haunts.

HALL, Hammond, 1857- 823'.8 B
Mr. Pickwick's Kent : a photographic record of the tour of the Corresponding Society of the Pickwick Club in Rochester, Chatham, Muggleton, Dingley Dell, Cobham, and Gravesend / with descriptive letterpress by Hammond Hall. Folcroft, Pa. : Folcroft Library Editions, 1974. 92 p., [1] leaf of plates : ill. ; 23 cm. Reprint of the 1899 ed . published by W. & J. Mackay, Rochester, Eng. [PR4584.H24 1974] 74-28420 lib. bdg. : 17.50
1. Dickens, Charles, 1812-1870—Homes and haunts. 2. Literary landmarks—Kent, Eng. 3. Kent, Eng.—Description and travel. I. Title.

HARDWICK, John Michael Drinkrow, 1924- 823'.8
Dickens's England, by Michael & Mollie Hardwick. South Brunswick, A. S. Barnes [1970] ix, 172 p. illus. 22 cm. Bibliography: p. 162-163. [PR4584.H26] 77-107116 8.00
1. Dickens, Charles, 1812-1870—Homes and haunts. 2. Literary landmarks—Gt. Brit. I. Hardwick, Mollie, joint author. II. Title.

KITTON, Frederic George, 1856-1904. 823'.8 B
The Dickens country / by Frederick G. Kitton. Folcroft, Pa. : Folcroft Library Editions, 1979. xiv, 235 p., 32 leaves of plates : ill. ; 23 cm. Reprint of the 2d ed. published in 1911 by A. and C. Black, London, in The pilgrimage series. Includes bibliographical references and index. [PR4584.K6 1979] 79-14586 ISBN 0-8414-5488-4 lib. bdg. : 25.00
1. Dickens, Charles, 1812-1870—Homes and haunts. 2. Novelists, English—19th century—Biography. I. Title. II. Series: The Pilgrimage series. **BIP**

MORELAND, Arthur. 823'.8
Dickens landmarks in London, written and illustrated by Arthur Moreland. With a foreword by Sir Henry F. Dickens. New York, Haskell House Publishers, 1973. xiv, 82 p. illus. 29 cm. Reprint of the 1931 ed. [PR4584.M63 1973] 72-6291 ISBN 0-8383-1625-5 13.95
1. Dickens, Charles, 1812-1870—Homes and haunts. 2. Literary landmarks—London. I. Title. **BIP**

Dickens, Charles, 1812-1870—Homes and haunts—England—London.

SCHWARZBACH, F. S. 823'.8 B
Dickens and the city / F. S. Schwarzbach. London : Athlone Press ; [Atlantic Highlands, N.J.] : distributed by Humanities Press, 1979. xii, 258 p., [4] leaves of plates : ill. ; 23 cm. Includes index. Bibliography: p. [225]-234. [PR4584.S3] 79-306781 ISBN 0-485-11174-8 : 22.50
1. Dickens, Charles, 1812-1870—Homes and haunts—England—London. 2. London in literature. 3. Cities and towns in literature. 4. Novelists, English 19th century—Biography. I. Title.

Dickens, Charles, 1812-1870—Illustrations.

STEIG, Michael, 1936- 823'.8
Dickens and "Phiz" / Michael Steig. Bloomington : Indiana University Press, c1978. p. cm. Includes bibliographical references and index. [PR4583.S8] 77-23645 ISBN 0-253-31705-3 : 12.50
1. Dickens, Charles, 1812-1870 Friends and associates. 2. Dickens, Charles, 1812-1870—Illustrations. 3. Browne, Hablot Knight, 1815-1882. I. Title. **BIP**

Dickens, Charles, 1812-1870—Juvenile literature.

HAINES, Charles. 823'.8 B
Charles, Dickens. New York, F. Watts [1969] x, 181 p. illus., ports. 22 cm. (Immortals of literature) Bibliography: p. 176-177. A biography of the English writer whose numerous novels recorded the social conditions and way of life of the poor in nineteenth-century London. [PR4581.H25] 92 77-79672 3.95
1. Dickens, Charles, 1812-1870—Juvenile literature. I. Title.

PEARE, Catherine Owens. 928.2
Charles Dickens; his life. Illustrated by Douglas Gorsline. [1st ed.] New York, Holt [1959] 125 p. illus. 21 cm. [PR4581.P33] 59-7573
1. Dickens, Charles—Juvenile literature. **BIP**

PRINGLE, Patrick. 928.2
The young Dickens. Illustrated by Denise Brown. New York, Roy Publishers [c1959] 159p. illus: 21cm. [PR4581.P7] 60-6622
1. Dickens, Charles—Juvenile literature. I. Title.

Dickens, Charles, 1812-1870—Knowledge—Folk-lore, mythology.

STONE, Harry, 1926- 823'.8
Dickens and the invisible world : fairy tales, fantasy, and novel-making / Harry Stone. Bloomington : Indiana University Press, c1979. p. cm. Includes index. Bibliography: p. [PR4592.F6S75] 78-20281 ISBN 0-253-18366-9 : 17.50
1. Dickens, Charles, 1812-1870—Knowledge—Folk-lore, mythology. 2. Fairy tales—History and criticism. 3. Fantasy in literature. I. Title. BIP

Dickens, Charles, 1812-1870—Relationship with women.

DU CANN, Charles Garfield Lott, 1889- 823'.8 B
The love-lives of Charles Dickens, by C. G. L. Du Cann. Westport, Conn., Greenwood Press [1972, c1961] 288 p. illus. 22 cm. [PR4582.D8 1972] 72-6192 ISBN 0-8371-6464-8 12.75
1. Dickens, Charles, 1812-1870—Relationship with women. I. Title. BIP

Dickens, Charles, 1812-1870—Relationship with women—Maria Beadnell Winter.

DICKENS, Charles, 1812-1870. 823'.8 B
Charles Dickens and Maria Beadnell: private correspondence. Edited by George Pierce Baker. [Folcroft, Pa.] Folcroft Library Editions, 1974. p. cm. Reprint of the 1908 ed. published by the Bibliophile Society, Boston. [PR4581.A4W6 1974] 74-14754 35.00
1. Dickens, Charles, 1812-1870—Correspondence. 2. Dickens, Charles, 1812-1870—Relationship with women—Maria Beadnell Winter. 3. Winter, Maria Sarah Beadnell, 1811 or 12-1886. I. Winter, Maria Sarah Beadnell, 1811- or 12-1886. II. Baker, George Pierce, 1866-1935, ed. III. Title.

DICKENS, Charles, 1812-1870. 823'.8 B
The love romance of Charles Dickens; told in his letters to Maria Beadnell (Mrs. Winter) with introd. and notes by Walter Dexter. [Folcroft, Pa.] Folcroft Library Editions, 1974. p. cm. Reprint of the 1936 ed. published by Argonaut Press, London. [PR4581.A4W6 1974b] 74-18404 ISBN 0-8414-3807-2 (lib. bdg.)
1. Dickens, Charles, 1812-1870—Correspondence. 2. Dickens, Charles, 1812-1870—Relationship with women—Maria Beadnell Winter. 3. Winter, Maria Sarah (Beadnell) Mrs., 1811 or 12-1886. I. Winter, Maria Sarah Beadnell, 1811 or 12-1886. II. Title.

Dickens, Charles, 1812-1870—Religion and ethics.

POPE, Norris, 1945- 823'.8
Dickens and charity / by Norris Pope. New York : Columbia University Press, 1978. p. cm. Includes index. Bibliography: p. [PR4592.R4P65] 78-3867 ISBN 0-231-04478-X : 15.00
1. Dickens, Charles, 1812-1870—Religion and ethics. 2. Dickens, Charles, 1812-1870—Political and social views. 3. Evangelicalism—Church of England. 4. Great Britain—Social conditions—19th century. I. Title. BIP

Dickenson, Susanna.

KING, Clyde Richard. 976.4'03'0924 B
Susanna Dickinson : messenger of the Alamo / by C. Richard King. 1st ed. Austin, Tex. : Shoal Creek Publishers, c1976. xviii, 166 p. : ill. ; 22 cm. Includes index. Bibliography: p. 123-130. [F390.D52K56] 76-14814 ISBN 0-88319-023-0 : 7.95
1. Dickenson, Susanna. 2. Alamo—Siege, 1836.

Dickey, Bill, 1907- —Juvenile literature.

VAN RIPER, Guernsey, 1909- 796.357'092'2
Behind the plate: three great catchers, by Guernsey Van Riper, Jr. Illustrated by Jack Hearne. Champaign, Ill., Garrard Pub. Co. [1973] 95 p. illus. 24 cm. Brief biographies of three well-known catchers emphasizing their development of the skills that made them valuable ball players. [GV865.A1V29] 920 73-2952 ISBN 0-8116-6665-4 2.95
1. Cochrane, Gordon Stanley—Juvenile literature. 2. Dickey, Bill, 1907- —Juvenile literature. 3. Campanella, Roy, 1921- —Juvenile literature. 4. Catching (Baseball)—Juvenile literature. I. Hearne, Jack, illus. II. Title.

Dickey, Sarah A., 1838-1904.

GRIFFITH, Helen. 370'.92'4 B
Dauntless in Mississippi : the life of Sarah A. Dickey, 1838-1904 / by Helen Griffith. 2d ed. Washington : Zenger Pub. Co., 1975, c1966. p. cm. Reprint of the ed. published by Dinosaur Press, South Hadley, Mass. Includes index. [LA2317.D47G7 1975] 75-35885 ISBN 0-89201-006-1 : 10.95
1. Dickey, Sarah A., 1838-1904. I. Title. BIP

Dickinson, Anna Elizabeth, 1842-1932.

CHESTER, Giraud, 1922- 920.7
Embattled maiden; the life of Anna Dickinson. New York, Putnam [1951] xi, 307 p. illus., ports. 23 cm. Bibliography: p. 294-296. [E415.9.D48C5] 51-13934
1. Dickinson, Anna Elizabeth, 1842-1932. I. Title.

Dickinson, Emily, 1830-1886.

BIANCHI, Martha Gilbert (Dickinson) 1866-1943. 811'.4
Emily Dickinson face to face; unpublished letters with notes and reminiscences. With a foreword by Alfred Leete Hampson. [Hamden, Conn.] Archon Books, 1970 [c1932] xxii, 290 p. illus., coat of arms, facsims., group port. 19 cm. Includes bibliographical references. [PS1541.Z5B5 1970] 76-103993
1. Dickinson, Emily, 1830-1886. I. Title. BIP

BINGHAM, Millicent (Todd) 1880- 928.1
Emily Dickinson, a revelation. [1st ed.] New York, Harper [1954] 109 p. ports. facsims. 22cm. Includes some unpublished letters, and some late poems by Emily Dickinson. [PS1541.Z5B54] 54-12227
1. Dickinson, Emily, 1830-1886. I. Title.

CHASE, Richard Volney, 1914-1962. 811'.4 B
Emily Dickinson. Westport, Conn., Greenwood Press [1971, c1951] xii, 328 p. 23 cm. Includes bibliographical references. [PS1541.Z5C5 1971] 70-136058 ISBN 0-8371-5208-9
1. Dickinson, Emily, 1830-1886.

CHASE, Richard Volney, 1914-1962. v. 12
Emily Dickinson. [New York, Sloane] 1965, [c1951] viii, 328 p. port. 20 cm. (The American men of letters series) "Bibliographical note": p. 313-317. "A Delta Book 2304." 66-83469
1. Dickinson, Emily, 1830-1886. I. Title. II. Series. BIP

CODY, John, 1925- 811'.4 B
After great pain; the inner life of Emily Dickinson. Cambridge, Mass., Belknap Press of Harvard University Press, 1971. ix, 538 p. 25 cm. Includes bibliographical references. [PS1541.Z5C6] 79-148937 ISBN 0-674-00878-2 14.95
1. Dickinson, Emily, 1830-1886. I. Title. BIP

DICKINSON, Emily, 1830-1886. 928.1
Letters. Edited by Thomas H. Johnson. Associate editor: Theodora Ward. Cambridge, Belknap Press of Harvard University Press, 1958. 3 v. (xxvii, 999 p.) illus., ports., facsims. 25 cm. [PS1541.Z5A3 1958] 58-5594

DICKINSON, Emily, 1830-1886 928.1
Letters of Emily Dickinson; ed. by Mabel Loomis Todd, introd. by Mark Van Doren. New York, Grosset [1962, c.1961] 389p. 21cm. (Universal lib., 0144) 1.95 pap.,
I. Title.

DICKINSON, Emily, 1830-1886. 928.1
Letters of Emily Dickinson; edited by Mabel Loomis Todd, with an introd. by Mark Van Doren. Cleveland, World Pub. Co. [1951] xxiv, 389 p. port., facsims. 22 cm. [PS1541.Z5A3 1951] 51-9898
I. Title.

DICKINSON, Emily, 1830-1886. 811'.4 B
The life and letters of Emily Dickinson. By Martha Dickinson Bianchi. New York, Biblo and Tannen, 1971 [c1924] 386 p. illus. 22 cm. [PS1541.Z5A3 1971] 70-162296 ISBN 0-8196-0276-0
I. Bianchi, Martha Gilbert (Dickinson) 1866-1943. II. Title. BIP

DONOGHUE, Denis. 811'.4
Emily Dickinson. Minneapolis, University of Minnesota Press [1969] 47 p. 21 cm. (University of Minnesota pamphlets on American writers, no. 81) Bibliography: p. 45-47. [PS1541.Z5D6] 76-628284 0.95
1. Dickinson, Emily, 1830-1886. I. Series: Minnesota. University. Pamphlets on American writers, no. 81

FERLAZZO, Paul J. 811'.4 B
Emily Dickinson / by Paul J. Ferlazzo. Boston : Twayne, c1976. 168 p. : port. : 21 cm. (Twayne's United States authors series ; TUSAS 280) Includes index. Bibliography: p. 157-163. [PS1541.Z5F4] 76-48304 ISBN 0-8057-7180-8 : 7.95
1. Dickinson, Emily, 1830-1886. 2. Poets, American—19th century—Biography.

GELPI, Albert J. 928.1
Emily Dickinson: the mind of the poet. Cambridge, Mass., Harvard [c.] 1965. xiii, 201p. 22cm. Bibl. [PS1541.Z5G4] 65-13844 4.75 bds.,
1. Dickinson, Emily, 1830-1886. I. Title. BIP

GILBERT, Sandra M. 820'.9'9287
The madwoman in the attic : the woman writer and the nineteenth-century literary imagination / Sandra M. Gilbert and Susan Gubar. New Haven : Yale University Press, 1979. p cm. Includes bibliographical references and index. [PR115.G5] 78-20792 ISBN 0-300-02286-7 : 25.00
1. Dickinson, Emily, 1830-1886. 2. Milton, John, 1608-1674—Influence. 3. English literature—Women authors—History and criticism. 4. English literature—19th century—History and criticism. 5. Fall of man in literature. 6. Women in literature. 7. Women authors—Biography. I. Gubar, Susan, 1944- joint author. II. Title.

LEYDA, Jay, 1910- 928.1
The years and hours of Emily Dickinson. New Haven, Conn., Yale University Press [c.]1960. 2 v. 'The sources': p. 485-488. 'Locations of manuscripts, illustrations, memorabilia'. p.489-503. illus., ports., facsims. 24cm. 'Variety of juxtaposed documents(transcribed and extracted from manuscript and printed sources, ordered and dominated by a single chronology. 60-11132 25.00, back., bxd.
I. Title.

LEYDA, Jay, 1910- 811'.4 B
The years and hours of Emily Dickinson. [Hamden, Conn.] Archon Books, 1970 [c1960] 2 v. illus., facsims., ports. 23 cm. "Variety of juxtaposed documents, transcribed and extracted from manuscript and printed sources, ordered and dominated by a single chronology." "The sources": v. 2, p. 485-488. "Locations of manuscripts, illustrations, memorabilia": v. 2, p. 489-503. [PS1541.Z5L4 1970] 72-95025
1. Dickinson, Emily, 1830-1886. I. Title.

PATTERSON, Rebecca. 928.1
The riddle of Emily Dickinson. Boston, Houghton Mifflin, 1951. xiii, 434 p. 22 cm. Bibliography: p. 417-420. [PS1541.Z5P3] 51-7408
1. Dickinson, Emily, 1830-1886. I. Title. BIP

TAGGARD, Genevieve, 1894-1948. 811'.4 B
The life and mind of Emily Dickinson. New York, Cooper Square Publishers, 1967 [c1930] xxi, 378, vi p. illus., facsims., ports. 21 cm. Bibliography: p. 341-344. [PS1541.Z5T3 1967] 66-30447
1. Dickinson, Emily, 1830-1886. I. Title. BIP

WARD, Theodora (van Wagenen) 1890- 928.1
The capsule of the mind; chapters in the life of Emily Dickinson. Cambridge, Mass., Belknap Pr., Harvard, 1961 [c.1951-1961] 205p. 61-13746 4.50
1. Dickinson, Emily, I. Title.

WARD, Theodora (Van Wagenen) 1890- 928.1
The capsule of the mind; chapters in the life of Emily Dickinson. Cambridge, Mass., Belknap Press, 1961. 205 p. 22 cm. [PS1541.Z5W3] 61-137469
1. Dickinson, Emily, 1830-1886. I. Title.

WHICHER, George Frisbie, 1889-1954. 928.1
This was a poet; a critical biography of Emily Dickinson. [1st ed. as an Ann Arbor paperback. Ann Arbor] University of Michigan Press [1957, c1938] 337 p. 21 cm. (Ann Arbor paperbacks, AA 12) [PS1541.Z5W5 1957] 57-4676
1. Dickinson, Emily, 1830-1886. I. Title.

Dickinson, Emily, 1830-1886.

BINGHAM, Millicent Todd, 1880-1968. 928.1
Emily Dickinson's home; letters of Edward Dickinson and his family. With documentation and comment by Millicent Todd Bingham. [1st ed.] New York, Harper [1955] xvii, 600 p. illus., ports., maps (part fold.) facsims. 22 cm. Includes bibliographies. [PS1541.Z5B543] 55-6573
1. Dickinson, Emily, 1830-1886. 2. Dickinson, Edward, 1803-1874.

Dickinson, Emily, 1830-1886—Biography.

BENET, Laura. 811'.4 B
The mystery of Emily Dickinson. New York, Dodd, Mead [1974] xii, 112 p. illus. 22 cm. Bibliography: p. 107-108. A biography of the American poet whose great love and life as a recluse have remained a mystery to scholars. [PS1541.Z5B4] 92 73-19087 ISBN 0-396-06934-7 4.25
1. Dickinson, Emily, 1830-1886—Biography. I. Title.

JOHNSON, Thomas Herbert. 811.49
Emily Dickinson: an interpretive biography. Cambridge, Mass., Belknap Press, 1955. 276 p. illus. 24 cm. [PS1541.Z5J6] 55-9439
1. Dickinson, Emily, 1830-1886—Biography. BIP

SEWALL, Richard Benson. 811'.4 B
The life of Emily Dickinson, by Richard B. Sewall. New York, Farrar, Straus and Giroux [1974] p. Bibliography: p. [PS1541.Z5S42] 74-8764 ISBN 0-374-18696-0 30.00 (2 vol.).
1. Dickinson, Emily, 1830-1886—Biography. I. Title. BIP

WALSH, John Evangelist, 1927- 811'.4 B
The hidden life of Emily Dickinson. New York, Simon and Schuster [1971] 286 p. ports. 22 cm. Includes bibliographical references. [PS1541.Z5W26] 73-133101 ISBN 0-671-20815-2 7.95
1. Dickinson, Emily, 1830-1886—Biography. I. Title.

Dickinson, Emily, 1830-1886—Juvenile literature.

BARTH, Edna. 811'.4 B
I'm nobody! Who are you? The story of Emily Dickinson. Drawings by Richard Cuffari. New York, Seabury Press [1971] 128 p. illus. 24 cm. Bibliography: p. 121-124. A biography of the woman whose posthumously published poetry brought her the public attention she had carefully avoided during her lifetime. Includes many of her poems. [PS1541.Z5B3] 92 72-129211 4.95
1. Dickinson, Emily, 1830-1886—Juvenile literature. I. Cuffari, Richard, 1925- illus. II. Title. BIP

WOOD, James Playsted, 1905- 811'.4 B
Emily Elizabeth Dickinson. [1st ed.] Nashville, T. Nelson [1972] 190 p. 22 cm. Bibliography: p. 181-183. A biography of the enigmatic Amherst poet who during a life of seclusion produced some of America's most famous poetry. [PS1541.Z5W65] 92 72-5903 ISBN 0-8407-6232-1 4.95
1. Dickinson, Emily, 1830-1886—Juvenile literature. I. Title.

Dickinson, Emily, 1830-1886—Knowledge—Manners and customs.

EMILY Dickinson : 811'.4 B
profile of the poet as cook : with selected recipes / by guides at the Dickinson homestead, Nancy Harris Brose ... [et al.]. Amherst, Mass. : [s.n.], 1976. 28 p. : ill. ; 22 cm. Bibliography: p. 27-28. [PS1541.Z5E4] 76-382081
1. Dickinson, Emily, 1830-1886—Knowledge—Manners and customs. 2. Cookery, American—Massachusetts. 3. Poets, American—19th century—Biography. I. Brose, Nancy Harris.

Dickinson, John, 1732-1808.

FREDMAN, Lionel E. 973.3'0924 B
John Dickinson, American Revolutionary statesman, by Lionel E. Fredman. Compiled with the assistance of the research staff of SamHar Press. Charlotteville, N.Y., SamHar Press, 1974. p. cm. (Outstanding personalities of the American Revolution, no. 7) (Outstanding personalities, no. 75) Bibliography: [E302.6.D5F73] 74-14599 2.29; 0.98 (pbk.)
1. Dickinson, John, 1732-1808. BIP

STILLE, Charles Janeway, 1819-1899. 973.3'0924 B
The life and times of John Dickinson, 1732-1808. New York, B. Franklin [1969] xi, 437 p. facsim., port. 22 cm. (American classics in history and social science, 89) (Burt Franklin research and source work series, 388.) Reprint of the 1891 ed. issued as Memoirs of the Historical Society of Pennsylvania, v. 13. [E302.6.D5S85 1969] 74-99594
1. Dickinson, John, 1732-1808. I. Title.

Dickinson, Jonathan, 1663-1722.

DICKINSON, Jonathan, 1663-1722. 973'.04'97 S
Gods protecting providence / Jonathan Dickinson. New York : Garland Pub., 1977. 95 p. ; 23 cm. (The Garland library of narratives of North American Indian captivities ; v. 4) Reprint of the 1699 ed. printed by R. Jansen, Philadelphia. Issued with the reprint of the 1706 ed. of Mather, C. Good fetch'd out of evil. New York, 1977, and with the reprint of the 1707 ed. of Mather, C. A memorial of the present deplorable state of New-England. New York, 1977. [E85.G2 vol. 4] [E78.F6] 917.59'04'10924 B 75-7023 ISBN 0-8240-1628-9 lib.bdg. : 25.00
1. Dickinson, Jonathan, 1663-1722. 2. Barrow, Robert, d. 1697. 3. Indians of North America—Florida—Captivities. 4. Shipwrecks—Florida. 5. United States—Biography. I. Title. II. Series.

Dickson, Harry Ellis.

DICKSON, Harry Ellis. 785'.06'274461
Gentlemen, more dolce, please! (Second movement) An irreverent memoir of thirty-five years in the Boston Symphony Orchestra. Boston, Beacon Press [1974] xi, 176 p. illus. 24 cm. [ML418.D42A3 1974] 74-207 ISBN 0-8070-5178-0
1. Dickson, Harry Ellis. 2. Boston Symphony Orchestra. 3. Musicians—Correspondence, reminiscences, etc. I. Title.

Dickson, Murray.

PALMER, Jim, 1929- 266.76'0924 B
Red poncho and big boots; the life of Murray Dickson. Nashville, Abingdon Press [1969] 224 p. port. 21 cm. [BV2853.B5D5] 70-84715 4.50
1. Dickson, Murray. 2. Missions—Bolivia. 3. Methodist Church—Missions. I. Title.

Dictators.

ARCHER, Jules. 920
The dictators. [1st ed.] New York, Hawthorn Books [1967] viii, 179 p. ports. 24 cm. Bibliography: p. 167-170. Describes the nature and prototype of the modern dictator and presents biographical sketches of eighteen twentieth century absolute rulers. [D412.7.A7] AC 68
1. Dictators. I. Title.

CARR, Albert H. Z. 909'.00922
Juggernaut; the path of dictatorship, by Albert Carr. Drawings by Vivian Springford. Freeport, N.Y., Books for Libraries Press [1969] xvii, 531 p. ports. 23 cm. (Essay index reprint series) Reprint of the 1939 ed. Contents.—Dynasts: Richelieu. Louis XIV. Frederick the Great. Bismarck. Primo de Rivera. Alexander, Metaxas, Carol.—Revolutionaries: Cromwell. Robespierre. Bolivar. Lenin. Stalin.—Crisis-men: Napoleon. Napoleon III. Gomez. Mussolini. Ataturk, Salazar. Hitler.—Conclusion: The path of dictatorship. The trend in America. [D108.C3 1969] 75-93325
1. Dictators. I. Title. BIP

CARR, Albert H. Z. 923.2
Men of power; a book of dictators. Illus. by Marc Simont. Rev. ed. New York, Viking Press, 1956. 298 p. illus. 22 cm. [D107.C28 1956] 56-1185
1. Dictators. I. Title.

KING-HALL, Stephen, Sir 1893- 321.90922
Three dictators: Mussolini, Hitler, Stalin. London, Faber & Faber [Levittown, N.Y., Transatlantic, 1966,c.1964] 132p. ports. 19cm. (Men & events) Bibl. [D412.6.K5] 66-1802 2.50 bds.,
1. Dictators—Juvenile literature. I. Title.

Dictators—Biography.

ARCHER, Jules. 321.9'0922
The dictators. [1st ed.] New York, Hawthorn Books [1967] viii, 179 p. ports. 24 cm. Bibliography: p. 167-170. [D412.7.A7] 67-24002
1. Dictators—Biography.

CARR, Albert H. Z. 920'.02
Juggernaut: the path of dictatorship, by Albert Carr. With 17 portrait drawings by Vivian Springford. New York, Viking Press, 1939. [New York, AMS Press, 1973] xxi, 531 p. ports. 23 cm. Contents.—Dynasts: Richelieu: the technique of dictatorship. Louis XIV: the perversion of power. Frederick the Great: the nation militant. Bismarck: the diplomacy of empire. Primo de Rivera: the forlorn hope. Alexander, Metaxas, Carol: ferment in the Balkans.—Revolutionaries: Cromwell: the revolutionary process. Robespierre: terrorism and conscience. Bolivar: liberator into dictator. Lenin: the science of revolution. Stalin: toward a classless society?—Crisis-men: Napoleon: the empire of the middle class. Napoleon III: the "idea." Gomez: crisis in Latin America. Mussolini: the "idea" up to date. Ataturk, Salazar: variations on a theme. Hitler: toward the servile state?—Conclusion: The path of dictatorship. The trend in America. [D108.C3 1973] 79-180393 ISBN 0-404-56109-8
1. Dictators—Biography. I. Title. BIP

Dictators—Biography—Juvenile literature.

APPEL, Benjamin, 1907- 909.82'0922
The age of dictators. New York, Crown Publishers [1968] 224 p. 22 cm. (Young adult books from Crown) Bibliography: p. 221. A history of the world's dictators since World War I—particularly Stalin, Hitler, Mao Tse-tung—and the events preceding and surrounding their rise and rule. [D412.6.A75 1968] 68-9059 4.95
1. Dictators—Biography—Juvenile literature. I. Title.

BOARDMAN, Fon Wyman, 1911- 909'.2'2 B
Tyrants and conquerors / Fon W. Boardman, Jr. ; [illustrated by Zenko Onyshkewych]. New York : H. Z. Walck, c1977. p. cm. Includes biographies of such notorious tyrants as Nero, Tamerlane, Attila, and Hitler and discusses the characteristics that constitute a tyrant or a conqueror. [D107.B6] 920 77-10899 ISBN 0-8098-0010-1 : 8.95
1. Dictators—Biography—Juvenile literature. 2. Biography—Juvenile literature. I. Onyshkewych, Zenkowij. II. Title.

Didelot, Charles Louis, 1767-1838.

SWIFT, Mary Grace. 792.8'2'0924 B
A loftier flight; the life and accomplishments of Charles-Louis Didelot, balletmaster. [1st ed.] Middletown, Conn., Wesleyan University Press [1974] x, 230 p. illus. 23 cm. Includes bibliographical references. [GV1785.D54S94] 73-15007 ISBN 0-8195-4070-6 15.00
1. Didelot, Charles Louis, 1767-1838. I. Title. BIP

Diderot, Denis, 1713-1784.

BLUM, Carol, 1934- 194 B
Diderot: the virtue of a philosopher. New York, Viking Press [1974] viii, 182 p. 23 cm. Bibliography: p. [171]-176. [B2016.B54 1974] 74-490 ISBN 0-670-27227-2 7.95
1. Diderot, Denis, 1713 1784. I. Title.

CROCKER, Lester G 921.4
The embattled philosopher; a biography of Denis Diderot. [East Lansing] Michigan State College Press, 1954. 442 p. 22 cm. [B2016.C68] 54-11829
1. Diderot, Denis, 1713-1784. I. Title.

DIDEROT, Denis, 1713-1784. 194
Diderot's letters to Sophie Volland: a selection, translated [from the French] by Peter France. London, Oxford University Press, 1972. [5], 218 p., leaf. port. 23 cm. A selection from the original French ed. published in 1938: Lettres a Sophie Volland. Includes bibliographical references. [PQ1979.A82V613 1972] 73-151601 ISBN 0-19-212551-6 11.75
I. Volland, Louise Henriette, known as Sophie, 1716-1784. II. Title.
Distributed by Oxford University Press N.Y. BIP

FREDMAN, Alice Green, 1924- 848'.5'09
Diderot and Sterne. New York, Octagon Books, 1973 [c1954] 264 p. 23 cm. Reprint of the author's thesis published in 1955 by Columbia University Press. Bibliography: p. [239]-252. [PQ1979.F75 1973] 72-13743 ISBN 0-374-92884-3 10.25 (Lib. ed.)
1. Diderot, Denis, 1713-1784. 2. Sterne, Laurence, 1713-1768. I. Title. BIP

WILSON, Arthur McCandless, 1902- 921.4
Diderot: the testing years, 1713-1759. New York, Oxford University Press, 1957. xii, 417 p. illus., port. 24 cm. Bibliography: p. 399-403. [PQ1979.W5] 57-8485
1. Diderot, Denis, 1713-1784.

WILSON, Arthur McCandless, 1902- 194 B
Diderot, by Arthur M. Wilson. New York, Oxford University Press, 1972. xviii, 917 p. illus. 24 cm. "Part I of this book was published in 1957 under title of Diderot: the testing years, 1713-1759." Contents.—The testing years, 1713-1759.—The appeal to posterity, 1759-1784. Includes bibliographical references. [PQ1979.W52] 73-151716 25.00
1. Diderot, Denis, 1713-1784. BIP

WILSON, Arthur McCandless, 1902- 921.4
Diderot: the testing years, 1713-1759. New York, Oxford University Press, 1957. xii, 417 p. illus., port. 24 cm. Bibliography: p. 399-403. [PQ1979.W5] 57-8485
1. Diderof, Denis, 1713-1784. I. Title.

Diebold, John, 1926-

CROSS, Wilbur. 658.500924
John Diebold; breaking the confines of the possible. Introd. by Karl A. Hill. New York, J. H. Heineman [1965] xiv, 303 p. illus., ports. 24 cm. (The Future makers) "Selected writings of John Diebold": p. 285-290. Bibliography: p. 283-284. [HD45.C69] 64-236238
1. Diebold, John, 1926-

Diefenbaker, John George.

VAN DUSEN, Thomas. 971.06'4'0924
The Chief. New York, McGraw-Hill [1968] ix, 278 p. 23 cm. [F1034.3.D5V3] 68-55594
1. Diefenbaker, John George. 2. Canada—Politics and government—1945- I. Title.

Diego, Jose de, 1866-1918.

STERLING, Philip. 920
The quiet rebels; four Puerto Rican leaders Jose Celso Barbosa, Luis Munoz Rivera, Jose de Diego, Luis Munoz Marin by Philip Sterling and Maria Brau. Illus. by Tracy Sugarman [1st ed.] Garden City, N.Y., Doubleday, 1968. 118 p. col. illus., col. map, col. ports. 21 cm. (Zenith books) Profiles of four Puerto Ricans who fought for independence and equal rights for their island people. [F1955.S7] AC 68
1. Barbosa, Jose Celso, 1857-1921. 2. Munoz Rivera, Luis, 1859-1916. 3. Diego, Jose de, 1866-1918. 4. Munoz Marin, Luis, 1898- I. Brau, Maria, joint author. II. Sugarman, Tracy, 1921- illus. III. Title.

Diego, Jose de, 1866-1918—Juvenile literature.

STERLING, Philip. 920(J)
The quiet rebels; four Puerto Rican leaders: Jose Celso Barbosa, Luis Munoz Rivera, Jose de Diego, Luiz Munoz Marin, by Philip Sterling and Maria Brau. Illustrated by Tracy Sugerman. [1st ed.] Garden City, N.Y., Doubleday, 1968. 118 p. col. illus., col. map, col. ports. 21 cm. (Zenith books) [F1955.S7] 67-11153 2.95
1. Barbosa, Jose Celso, 1851-1921—Juvenile literature. 2. Munoz Rivera, Luis, 1859-1916—Juvenile literature. 3. Diego, Jose de, 1866-1918—Juvenile literature. 4. Munoz Marin, Luis, 1898- —Juvenile literature. I. Brau, Maria M., 1932- joint author. II. Title.

Diego, Juan, fl. 1531—Juvenile literature.

WAHL, Jan. 248.2 B
Juan Diego and the lady. La dama y Juan Diego. Spanish translation by Dolores Janes Garcia. Illustrated by Leonard Everett Fisher. New York, Putnam [1974] 48 p. col. illus. 24 cm. A bilingual edition of the story of the miraculous appearance of Our Lady of Guadalupe to a humble Mexican Indian in 1531. [BX4705.D513W33] 72-97317 ISBN 0-399-20356-7 4.97
1. Diego, Juan, fl. 1531—Juvenile literature. 2. Guadalupe, Nuestra Senora de—Juvenile literature. I. Fisher, Leonard Everett, illus. II. Title. III. Title: La dama y Juan Diego.

Diekema, Gerrit John, 1859-1960.

SCHRIER, William. 923.273
Gerrit J. Diekema, orator; a rhetorical study of the political and occasional addresses of Gerrit J. Diekema. Grand Rapids, Eerdmans, 1950. xix, 269 p. ports. 23 cm. Thesis -- University of Michigan. Bibliography: p. 259-269. [E748.D55S3] 51-308
1. Diekema, Gerrit John, 1859-1960. I. Title.

VANDER Hill, C. Warren, 1937- 328.73'0924
Gerrit J. Diekema, by C. Warren Vander Hill. [Grand Rapids, Mich.] W. B. Eerdmans [1970] 95 p. port. 22 cm. (A Great men of Michigan book) Includes bibliographical references. [E748.D55V3] 72-120843 1.95
1. Diekema, Gerrit John, 1859-1930. 2. Michigan—Politics and government—1837-1950.

Dienstag, Eleanor.

DIENSTAG, Eleanor. 973.92'092'4 B
Whither thou goest : the story of an uprooted wife / by Eleanor Dienstag. 1st ed. New York : Dutton, 1976. 187 p. ; 22 cm. [CT275.D463A34 1976] 75-25751 7.95
1. Dienstag, Eleanor. I. Title.

Dies, Martin, 1901-

GELLERMANN, William, 1897- 328.73'0924 B
Martin Dies. New York, Da Capo Press, 1972 [c1944] 310 p. 22 cm. (Civil liberties in American history) Includes bibliographical references. [E743.5.D55G4 1972] 77-151620 ISBN 0-306-70200-2
1. Dies, Martin, 1901- 2. United States. Congress. House. Special Committee on Un-American Activities (1938-1944) I. Title. II. Series. BIP

Diesel, Rudolf, 1858-1913.

GROSSER, Morton. 621.43'6'09
Diesel, the man & the engine / by Morton Grosser. 1st ed. New York : Atheneum, 1978. xvi, 166 p., [20] leaves of plates : ill. ; 25 cm. Includes index. Bibliography: p. 152-153. An introduction to the invention, historical development, and operation of the diesel engine, with a biography of Dr. Rudolf Diesel. [TJ795.G75 1978] 78-6196 ISBN 0-689-30652-0 : 8.95 8.95
1. Diesel, Rudolf, 1858-1913. 2. Diesel motor. 3. Mechanical engineers—Germany—Biography. I. Title. BIP

NITSKE, W. Robert 926.2
Rudolf Diesel, pioneer of the age of power, by W. Robert Nitske, Charles Morrow Wilson. Norman, Univ. of Okla. Pr. [c.1965] ix, 318p. illus., ports. 23cm. Bibl. [TJ140.D5N5] 65-10110 5.95
1. Diesel, Rudolf, 1858-1913. I. Wilson, Charles Morrow, 1905- joint author. II. Title.

Diesel, Rudolf, 1858-1913—Juvenile literature.

WILSON, Charles Morrow, 1905- 621.4360924
Diesel; his engine changed the world. Drawings by Denny McMains. Princeton, N.J., Van Nostrand [c.1966] v, 181p. illus., port, 22cm. [TJ140.D5W5] 66-16910 4.75; 4.53 bds., lib. ed.,
1. Diesel, Rudolf, 1858-1913—Juvenile literature. I. Title.

Dietrich, Marlene, 1904-

FREWIN, Leslie, 1916- 927.92
Blond Venus; a life of Marlene Dietrich. New York, Roy Publishers [1956?] 159p. illus. 23cm. [PN2658] 56-8725
1. Dietrich, Marlene, 1904- 2. Moving-pictures— Hist. I. Title.

FREWIN, Leslie Ronald 1916- v. 12
Blond Venus; a life of Marlene Dietrich. New York, Roy Publishers [1956?] 159 p. illus. 23 cm. [927.92] 56-8725
1. Dietrich, Marlene, 1904- 2. Moving-pictures — Hist. Title. I. Title.

FREWIN, Leslie Ronald, 1916- 791'.092'4
Dietrich; the story of a star [by] Leslie Frewin. New York, Stein and Day [1967] 191 p. ports. 22 cm. First ed. published in 1955 under title: Blond Venus. [PN2658.D5F7 1967b] 67-24485
1. Dietrich, Marlene, 1904- 2. Moving-pictures—History. I. Title.

HIGHAM, Charles, 1931- 791.43'028'0924 B
Marlene : the life of Marlene Dietrich / by Charles Higham. 1st ed. New York : Norton, c1977. p. cm. [PN2658.D5H5 1977] 77-24940 ISBN 0-393-07515-X : 9.95
1. Dietrich, Marlene, 1904- 2. Entertainers—Germany—Biography. I. Title. BIP

HIGHAM, Charles, 1931- 791.43'028'0924 [B]
Marlene / Charles Higham. New York : Pocket Books, 1979. 261p. ; ill ; 18 cm. Includes index. [PN2658.D5H5] ISBN 0-671-82182-2 pbk. : 2.50
1. Dietrich, Marlene, 1904- 2. Entertainers — Germany — Biography. I. Title.
.C. card no. for 1977 Norton ed.:77-24940. BIP

MORLEY, Sheridan, 1941- 791.43'028'0924 B
Marlene Dietrich / by Sheridan Morley. New York : McGraw-Hill, 1977, c1976. 128 p. : ill. ; 24 cm. Includes index. Filmography: p. 119-123. [PN2658.D5M6 1977] 76-43087 ISBN 0-07-043147-7 : 6.95
1. Dietrich, Marlene, 1904- 2. Entertainers—Germany—Biography. BIP

Dietz, Howard, 1896-

DIETZ, Howard, 1896- 782.8'1'0924 B
Dancing in the dark. Words by Howard Dietz. [New York] Quadrangle [1974] xii, 370 p. illus. 25 cm. [ML423.D557A3] 73-79909 ISBN 0-8129-0439-7 10.00
1. Dietz, Howard, 1896- I. Title.

DIETZ, Howard, 1896- 782.8'1'0924 B
Dancing in the dark. Words by Howard Dietz. New York, Bantam Books [1976 c1974] xii, 370 p. illus. 18 cm. [ML423.D557A3] 1.95 (pbk.)
1. Dietz, Howard, 1896 I. Title.
L.C. card no. for original edition: 73-79909.

Dilas, Milovan.

CILAS, Milovan. 940.53'497'0924 B
Wartime / Milovan Djilas ; translated by Michael B. Petrovich. 1st ed. New York : Harcourt Brace Jovanovich, c1977. x, 470 p., [8] leaves of plates : ill. ; 25 cm. Autobiographical. Includes index. [D802.Y8D548] 76-55148 ISBN 0-15-194609-4 : 16.95
1. Dilas, Milovan. 2. World War, 1939-1945—Underground movements—Yugoslavia—Biography. 3. Statesmen—Yugoslavia—Biography. 4. World War, 1939-1945—Personal narratives, Serbian. I. Title.

Dilke, Charles Wentworth, Sir, bart., 1843-1911.

JENKINS, Roy 320.924
Victorian scandal; a biography of the right honorable gentleman Sir Charles Dilke. [Rev. ed.] New York, Chilmark [dist. Random, c.1965] 447p. ports. 22cm. First ed. pub. under title: Sir Charles Dilke; a Victorian tragedy. Bibl. [DA565.D6J4] 65-17840 7.95
1. Dilke, Sir Charles Wentworth, bart., 1843-1911. I. Title.

JENKINS, Roy. 320.924
Victorian scandal: a biography of The Right Honorable Gentleman Sir Charles Dilke. [Rev. ed.] New York, Chilmark Press [1965] 447 p. ports. 22 cm. First ed. published under title: Sir Charles Dilke; a Victorian tragedy. "References": p. 425-431. [DA565.D6J4 1965] 65-17840
1. Dilke, Charles Wentworth, Sir, bart., 1843-1911. I. Title.

Dillinger, John, 1903-1934.

CROMIE, Robert Allen, 1909- 364.15
Dillinger, a short and violent life, by Robert Cromie and Joseph Pinkston. [1st ed.] New York, McGraw-Hill [1962] 266 p. illus. 22 cm. [HV6248.D5C7] 62-21112
1. Dillinger, John, 1903-1934. I. Pinkston, Joseph, joint author.

DEMARIS, Ovid 364.15
The Dillinger story . . . the dramatic story of John Dillinger--gangster, bank robber, killer, and public enemy. Derby, Conn., Monarch Bks. [c.1961] 139p. (Monarch American bk., MA311) 61-4518 .35 pap.,
1. Dillinger, John, 1902-1934. I. Title.

FREDERICKS, Dean 923.4173
John Dillinger. New York, Pyramid [c.1963] 143p. 19cm. (F-844) 63-4388 .40 pap.,
1. Dillinger, John, 1903-1934. I. Title.

LOUDERBACK, Lew, 1930- 364.1'523'0924 B
He only robbed banks; the life and times of John Dillinger. New Rochelle, N.Y., Arlington House [1974] p. cm. [HV6248.D5L68] 74-11384 ISBN 0-87000-192-2
1. Dillinger, John, 1903-1934. I. Title.

TOLAND, John. v. 12
The Dillinger days. [New York, Avon Books, c1963] 351 p. illus. 18 cm. (An Avon book) 68-18711
1. Dillinger, John, 1903-1934. 2. Crime and criminals—Middle West. I. Title. BIP

TOLAND, John. 364.10977
The Dillinger days. New York, Random House [1963] 371 p. illus. 22 cm. [HV6248.D5T6] 62-17171
1. Dillinger, John, 1903-1934. 2. Crime and criminals—Middle West. I. Title.

Dillingham, Richard, b. 1811.

FORSTER, Harley W., ed. 364.6'8
The Dillingham convict letters, edited by Harley W. Forster. Melbourne, Cypress Books in association with the Victorian Historical Association [1970] 27 p. 22 cm. (Cypress historical backgrounds, no. 4) Cover title: The Dillingham convict letters from the hulks, Woolwich, the transport ship Catherine Stewart Forbes and from Sandy Bay and Hobart Town, Van Diemen's Land. Includes bibliographical references. [HV8950.T3F65] 72-177972 ISBN 0-909807-00-0 0.60
1. Dillingham, Richard, b. 1811. 2. Penal colonies, British. 3. Tasmania—Exiles. I. Title.

Dilworth, Richard McLean, 1885-

RECK, Franklin Mering, 1896- 926.2
The Dilworth story; the biography of Richard Dilworth, pioneer developer of the diesel locomotive. New York, McGraw-Hill [1954] 105 p. illus. 22 cm. [TJ140.D53R4] 54-12259
1. Dilworth, Richard McLean, 1885-

Dilworth, Richardson, 1899-

MORRIS, Joe Alex, 1904- v. 12
The Richardson Dilworth story. Philadelphia, Mercury Books [c1962] 128 p. (Modern biography series) 65-45512
1. Dilworth, Richardson, 1899- I. Title.

Diment, Eunice.

DIMENT, Eunice. 364.1'54'0924 B
Kidnapped! : Eunice Diment's story. Exeter : Paternoster Press, 1976. 79 p. : ill., maps, ports. ; 18 cm. [HV6604.P52D53] 77-364627 ISBN 0-85364-199-4 : £0.75
1. Diment, Eunice. 2. Kidnapping—Philippine Islands—Case studies. 3. Victims of crimes—Biography. I. Title.

Dimitt, Philip, 1801-ca. 1841.

HUSON, Hobart, 1893- 976.4'123'030924
Captain Phillip Dimmitt's commandancy of Goliad, 1835-1836 : an episode of the Mexican Federalist war in Texas, usually referred to as the Texian Revolution / by Hobart Huson. Austin : Von Boeckmann-Jones Co., 1974. xxix, 299 p., [3] leaves of plates : ill., facsims. ; 24 cm. Bibliography: p. [279]-295. [F390.H955] 74-196034
1. Dimitt, Philip, 1801-ca. 1841. 2. Goliad, Tex.—Massacre, 1836. 3. Texas—History—Revolution, 1835-1836. I. Title.

Dingle, John,

DINGLE, John, 1889- 926.4794
International chef: Paris, New York, London, Monte Carlo, Lisbon, Frankfurt. [1st American ed.] New York, Dutton, 1955 [c1954] 253p. 21cm. Autobiography. First published in London in 1954 under title: A pinch of pound notes. [TX140.D5A3 1955] 55-7521
I. Title.

Dinwiddie, Robert, 1693-1770.

ALDEN, John Richard, 1908- 975.5'02'08 S
Robert Dinwiddie: servant of the Crown. Williamsburg, Va., Colonial Williamsburg Foundation; distributed by University Press of Virginia, Charlottesville [1973] x, 126 p. illus. 24 cm. (Williamsburg in America series, 9) [F234.W7W7 vol. 9] [F229] 975.5'02'0924 b 72-86731 ISBN 0-87935-002-4 5.95
1. Dinwiddie, Robert, 1693-1770. I. Title. II. Series.

Diogenes, of Oenoanda.

CHILTON, C. W. 187
Diogenes of Oenoanda: the fragments; a translation and commentary by C. W. Chilton. London, New York, Published for the University of Hull by Oxford University Press, 1971. xlviii, 141 p., 8 plates. illus., maps. 23 cm. (University of Hull. Publications) "Diogenes of Oenoanda. The fragments: translation": p. [3]-22. Bibliography: p. xlviii. [B557.D653D53] 70-885582 ISBN 0-19-713416-5 £3.00
1. Diogenes, of Oenoanda. Diogensis Oenoandensis Fragmenta. I. Diogenes, of Oenoanda. II. Title.

Diogenes, the Cynic—Juvenile literature.

ALIKI. 183'.4 B
Diogenes: the story of the Greek philosopher. Told and illustrated by Aliki. Englewood Cliffs, N.J., Prentice-Hall [1968] [32] p. illus. (part col.) 23 x 24 cm. Briefly describes the life of the man who chose to live as a beggar and yet became one of the most famous and respected men of ancient Greece. [B305.D44A54] 92 68-28512
1. Diogenes, the Cynic—Juvenile literature. I. Title.

Dionne quintuplets.

BARKER, Lillian. 920
The Dionne legend; quintuplets in captivity. [1st ed.] Garden City, N. Y., Doubleday, 1951. 269 p. illus., ports. 22 cm. [CT9998.Q5B32] 51-9919
1. Dionne quintuplets. I. Title.

BARKER, Lillian. 920
The truth about the Dionne quins. London, New York, Hutchinson [1951] 192 p. illus. 22 cm. [CT9998.Q5B36] 52-2136
1. Dionne quintuplets. I. Title.

BERTON, Pierre, 1920- 971.3'03'0922 B
The Dionne years : a Thirties melodrama / by Pierre Berton. 1st American ed. New York : Norton, 1978. 232 p., [8] leaves of plates : ill. ; 25 cm. Includes index. Bibliography: p. 221-224. [CT9998.D5B4

1978] 78-7306 ISBN 0-393-07529-X : 10.95
1. Dionne quintuplets. I. Title. **BIP**

BROUGH, James, 1918- 920
"We were five;" the Dionne quintuplets story from birth through girlhood to womanhood, by James Brough, with Annette, Cecile, Marie, and Yvonne Dionne. New York, Simon and Schuster, 1965. 256 p. ports. 22 cm. [CT9998.D5B7] 65-11160
1. Dionne quintuplets. I. Title.

BROUGH, James, 1918- 920
'we were five': the Dionne quintuplets' story from birth through girlhood to womanhood, by James Brough, with Annette, Cecile, Marie, and Yvonne Dionne. [New York] New Amer. Lib. [1966, c.1963, 1964] 256p. ports. 22cm. (Signet bk., T2880) [CT9998.D5B7] .75 pap.,
1. Dionne quintuplets. I. Title.

Dior, Christian.

DIOR, Christian 926.46
Christian Dior and I. Translated from the French by Antonia Fraser. [1st ed.] New York, Dutton, 1957. 251 p. illus., ports. 22 cm. London ed. (Weidenfeld and Nicolson) has title: Dior. [TT505.D5A353 1957a] 57-8971

Diplomats—Correspondence, reminiscences, etc.

ABRIKOSOV, Dmitrii Ivancvich, 1876-1951 923.247
Revelations of a Russian diplomat; the memoirs of Dmitri I. Abrikossow. Ed. by George Alexander Lensen. Seattle, Univ. of Wash. Pr., [c.]1964. xxii, 329p. illus., ports. 24cm. 64-18426 6.95
1. Diplomats Correspondence. reminiscences, etc. 2. Russia—For. rel.—1894-1917. I. Lensen, George Alexander, 1923- ed. II. Title.

ABRIKOSOV, Dmitrii Ivanovich, 1876-1951. 923.247
Revelations of a Russian diplomat; the memoirs of Dmitrii I. Abrikossow. Edited by George Alexander Lensen. [1st ed.] Seattle, University of Washington Press, 1964. xxii, 329 p. illus. ports. 24 cm. [D413.A2A3] 64-18426
1. Diplomats — Correspondence, reminiscences, etc. 2. Russia — For. rel. — 1804-1917. I. Lensen, George Alexander, 1923- ed. II. Title. **BIP**

ANDERSON, Richard Clough, Jr., 1788-1826. 923.273
Diary and journal, 1814-1826. Ed. by Alfred Tischendorf. E. Taylor Parks. Durham, N. C., Duke [c.]1964. xxvii, 342p. facsims., maps, port. 22cm. Bibl. 64-19178 7.50
1. Diplomats—Correspondence, reminiscences, etc. 2. Kentucky—Soc. life & cust. I. Tischendorf, Alfred Paul, 1929- ed. II. Parks, E. Taylor, ed. III. Title.

ANDERSON, Richard Clough, 1788-1826. 923.273
Diary and journal, 1814-1826. Edited by Alfred Tischendorf and E. Taylor Parks. Durham, N. C., Duke University Press, 1964. xxvii. 342 p. facsims., maps, port. 22 cm. Bibliography: p. [325]-331. [E340.A6A3] 64-19178
1. Diplomats — Correspondence, reminiscences, etc. 2. Kentucky — Soc. life and cust. I. Tischendorf, Alfred Paul, 1929- ed. II. Parks, E. Taylor, ed. III. Title.

BEAULAC, Willard Leon, 1899- 923.273
Career ambassador. New York, Macmillan, 1951. 262 p. 21 cm. Autobiographical. [E744.B434] 51-11377
1. Diplomats—Correspondence. reminiscences, etc. 2. U. S.—For. rel.—20th cent. I. Title.

CORREA DA SERRA, Jose Francesco, 1750-1823. 923.2469
The Abbe Correa in America, 1812-1820: The contributions of the diplomat and natural philosopher to the foundations of our national life. Correspondence with Jefferson and other members of the American Philosophical Society and with other prominent Americans. [Edited by] Richard Beale Davis. Philadelphia, American Philosophical Society, 1955. 87-197p. ports., facsim. 30cm. (Transactions of the American Philosophical Society, new ser., v. 45, pt. 2) Bibliographical footnotes. [Q11.P6 n. s., vol. 45, pt. 2] 55-5432
1. Diplomats—Correspondence, reminiscences, etc. I. Davis, Richard Beale. II. Title. III. Series: American Philosophical Society. Philadelphia. Transactions, new ser., v. 45, pt. 2

GREW, Joseph Clark, 1880-1965. 923.273
Turbulent era; a diplomatic record of forty years, 1904-1945. Edited by Walter Johnson, assisted by Nancy Harvison Hooker. Boston, Houghton Mifflin, 1952. 2 v. (xxvi, 1560 p.) illus., ports. 23 cm. [E748.G835A3] 52-5262
1. Diplomats—Correspondence, reminiscences, etc. 2. U.S.—Foreign relations—20th century. I. Title.

KELEN, Emery, 1896- 923.2
Peace in their time; men who led us in and out of war, 1914-1945. Drawings by Derso & Kelen. [1st ed.] New York, Knopf, 1963. 444, ix p. illus. 22 cm. [D413.K37A3] 63-9152
1. Diplomats—Correspondence, reminiscences, etc. 2. World politics—20th century. I. Title.

KIRKPATRICK, Ivone. Sir 923.242
Inner circle memoirs London, Macmillan; New York, St. Martin's Press, 1959. x, 275p. illus., ports. 23cm. [DA585.K5A3] A60
1. Diplomats—Correspondence, reminiscences, etc. 2. Gt. Brit.—For. Rel. 20th cent. I. Title.

LIPSKI, Jozef. 327.43'0438
Diplomat in Berlin, 1933-1939; papers and memoirs of Jozef Lipski, Ambassador of Poland. Edited by Waclaw Jedrzejewicz. New York, Columbia University Press, 1968. xxxvi, 679 p. facsims., group ports. 24 cm. Bibliography: p. [653]-660. [DK418.5.G3L5] 67-25871
1. Diplomats—Correspondence, reminiscences, etc. 2. Poland—Foreign relations—Germany. 3. Germany—Foreign relations—Poland. I. Jedrzejewicz, Waclaw, 1893- ed. II. Title.

LUKASIEWICZ, Juliusz, 1892-1951. 940.532'2'438
Diplomat in Paris, 1936-1939; papers and memoirs of Juliusz Lukasiewicz, Ambassador of Poland. Edited by Waclaw Jedrzejewicz. New York, Columbia University Press, 1970. xxvi, 408 p. illus., ports. 24 cm. Bibliography: p. [385]-397. [DK418.L83] 79-83530 12.50
1. Diplomats—Correspondence, reminiscences, etc. 2. Poland—Foreign relations. 3. Poland—Foreign relations—France. 4. France—Foreign relations—Poland. I. Jedrzejewicz, Waclaw, 1893- ed. II. Title.

PHILLIPS, William, 1878- 923.273
Ventures in diplomacy. Boston, Beacon Press [1953, c1952] 477p. illus. 24cm. [E744] 53-12714
1. Diplomats—Correspondence, reminiscences, etc. 2. U. S.—For. rel.—20th cent. I. Title.

PHILLIPS, William, 1878- 923.273
Ventures in diplomacy. [North Beverly? Mass.] Priv. print. 1952. 464 p. illus. 24 cm. [E744.P47] 52-39722
1. Diplomats — Correspondence, reminiscences, etc. 2. U.S. — For. rel. — 20th cent. I. Title.

QUARONI, Pietro 341.70924
Diplomatic bags: an ambassador's memoirs. Tr. from Italian, ed. by Anthony Rhodes. New York, D. White [1966] xiii, 158p. 23cm. Consists of selections from the author's Valigia diplomatica and his Ricordi di un ambasciatore [D413.Q4A353 1966a] 66-21352 5.95
1. Diplomats—Correspondence, reminiscences, etc. I. Rhodes, Anthony Richard Ewart, ed. and tr. II. Title.

THAYER, Charles Wheeler, 1910- 923.273
Bears in the caviar. [1st ed.] Philadelphia, Lippincott [1951] 303 p. 21 cm. [E744.T47] 51-10087
1. Diplomats—Correspondence, reminiscences, etc. I. Title.

Diplomats' wives.

MICHAL, Mira, 1914- 920.7
Nobody told me how; a diplomatic entertainment. [1st ed.] Philadelphia, Lippincott [1962] 184p. illus. 21cm. [D839.7.M5A3] 62-16858
1. Diplomats' wives. 2. London—Soc. life & cust. 3. New York (City)—Soc. life & cust. I. Title.

Dirksen, Everett McKinley.

DIRKSEN, Everett McKinley. 973.91'0924
Ev: the man and his words. Edited by Fred Bauer. Old Tappan, N.J., Hewitt House [1969] 187 p. 22 cm. [E840.8.D5A3] 74-85314 4.95
I. Bauer, Fred, ed. II. Title.

DIRKSEN, Louella, 1899- 973.91'092'4 B
The Honorable Mr. Marigold; my life with Everett Dirksen. By Louella Dirksen, with Norma Lee Browning. [1st ed.] Garden City, N.Y., Doubleday, 1972. xii, 297 p. illus. 22 cm. Autobiographical. [E748.D557A3] 72-180071 7.95
1. Dirksen, Everett McKinley. I. Browning, Norma Lee, joint author. II. Title.

MACNEIL, Neil, 1923- 973.91'0924 B
Dirksen: portrait of a public man. New York, World Pub. Co. [1970] xii, 402 p. ports. 24 cm. [E840.8.D5M3 1970] 79-112432 12.50
1. Dirksen, Everett McKinley. I. Title.

PENNEY, Annette Culler. 328.73'0924
The golden voice of the Senate. Foreword by Mike Mansfield. Washington, Acropolis Books [1968] 143 p. ports. 23 cm. (Americana by Acropolis.) (Congressional leadership series, vol. no. 3) [E840.8.D5P4] 68-56200 4.95
1. Dirksen, Everett McKinley. I. Title. II. Series.

Disabled — Biog.

MILLER, Basil William, 1897- 920.02
Ten handicapped people who became famous. Grand Rapids, Zondervan Pub. House [1951] 73 p. illus. 20 cm. [CT9983.A1M5] 51-14996
1. Disabled — Biog. I. Title.

Disciples of Christ.

STONE, Barton Warren, 1772-1844. 286'.6'0924 B
The biography of Eld. Barton Warren Stone, written by himself; with additions and reflections, by John Rogers. New York, Arno Press, 1972. ix, 404, 4 p. port. 23 cm. (Religion in America, series II) Reprint of the 1847 ed. [BX7343.S8A3 1972] 79-38463 ISBN 0-405-04089-X
1. Disciples of Christ. I. Rogers, John, 1800-1867, ed. II. Title. **BIP**

Disciples of Christ—Clergy—Correspondence, reminiscences, etc.

LAPPIN, Samuel Strahl, 1870- 922.673
Run, Sammy, run; sixty-five years a preacher man. St. Louis, Bethany Press [1958] 224p. 23cm. Autobiographical. [BX7343.L27A3] 58-6595
1. Disciples of Christ—Clergy—Correspondence, reminiscences, etc. I. Title.

Disney, Walt, 1901-1966.

COMFORT, Mildren Houghton, 1886- 791'.0924 B
Walt Disney; master of fantasy. Minneapolis, Denison [1968] 168 p. 23 cm. (Men of achievement series) A biography of Walt Disney, whose creations of fantasy and technical advances in cartoon production made his name and those of his characters household items. [PN1998.A3D5] 92 AC 68
1. Disney, Walt, 1901-1966. I. Title. II. Title: Master of fantasy.

FINCH, Christopher. 791'.092'4 B
Walt Disney's America / Christopher Finch. New York : Abbeville Press, [1978] p. cm. [PN1998.A3D522] 78-16863 ISBN 0-89659-000-3 : 25.00
1. Disney, Walt, 1901-1966. 2. Moving-picture producers and directors—United States—Biography. 3. Animators—United States—Biography. I. Title. **BIP**

KURLAND, Gerald, 1942- 791.43'3'0924
Walt Disney, the master of animation. Charlotteville, N.Y., SamHar Press, 1971. 31 p. 22 cm. (Outstanding personalities, no. 8) On spine: R. Lichello [sic] Bibliography: p. 31. [PN1998.A3D527] 70-185664
1. Disney, Walt, 1901-1966.

MILLER, Diane (Disney) 927.914
The story of Walt Disney [by] Diane Disney Miller as told to Pete Martin. [1st ed.] New York, Holt [1957] 247p. illus. 22cm. [PN1998.A3D53] 57-10423
1. Disney, Walt, 1901- I. Martin, Thornton, 1901- II. Title.

SCHICKEL, Richard. 790.2'0924
The Disney version; the life, times, art, and commerce of Walt Disney. New York, S. & S. [1968] 384p. 22cm. Bibl. [PN1998.A3D56] 68-12174 6.50
1. Disney, Walt, 1901-1966. I. Title.

SCHICKEL, Richard. 791'.0924 B
The Disney version; the life, times, art, and commerce of Walt Disney. New York, Simon and Schuster [1968] 384 p. 22 cm. Bibliography. p. 367-374. [PN1998.A3D56] 68-12174
1. Disney, Walt, 1901-1966. I. Title.

THOMAS, Bob, 1929- 92
Walt Disney, magician of the movies. New York, Grosset & Dunlap [1966] 176 p. illus. (part col.) 22 cm. (Pioneer books) (A Rutledge book) A biography of the internationally beloved cartoonist-creator of Mickey Mouse, Donald Duck, Snow White and the Seven Dwarfs, and Disneyland. [PN1998.A3D57] AC 66
1. Disney, Walt, 1901-1966. I. Vosburgh, Leonard, illus. II. Title.

Disney, Walt, 1901-1966—Juvenile literature.

COMFORT, Mildred Houghton, 1886- 790.2'0924 B
Walt Disney; master of fantasy. Minneapolis, Denison [1968] 168 p. 23 cm. (Men of achievement series) [PN1998.A3D5] 68-29772
1. Disney, Walt, 1901-1966—Juvenile literature. I. Title: Master of fantasy.

HAMMONTREE, Marie. 791'.0924 B
Walt Disney, young movie maker. Illustrated by Fred Irvin. Indianapolis, Bobbs-Merrill [1969] 200 p. col. illus. 20 cm. (Childhood of famous Americans) A biography concentrating on the boyhood of the cartoonist and film maker who created Mickey Mouse, Donald Duck, and Porky Pig. [PN1998.A3D524] 92 78-77820
1. Disney, Walt, 1901-1966—Juvenile literature. I. Irvin, Fred M., illus. II. Title.

LARSON, Norita. 791'.092'4 B
Walt Disney. Illustrated by Harold Henriksen. Mankato, Minn., Creative Education [1974] p. cm. A brief biography of the well-known producer of animated cartoons who became world-famous as creator of Mickey Mouse and Disneyland. [PN1998.A3D528] 92 74-14925 ISBN 0-87191-407-7 4.95
1. Disney, Walt, 1901-1966—Juvenile literature. I. Henriksen, Harold, illus. II. Title.

LARSON, Norita. 791'.092'4 B
Walt Disney, an American original. Illustrated by Harold Henriksen. Mankato, Minn., Creative Education [1974] 31 p. col. illus. 25 cm. (Creative Education close-ups) A brief biography of the well-

known producer of animated cartoons who became world-famous as creator of Mickey Mouse and Disneyland. [PN1998.A3D528] 92 74-14925 ISBN 0-87191-407-7
1. Disney, Walt, 1901-1966—Juvenile literature. I. Henriksen, Harold, illus. II. Title.

MONTGOMERY, Elizabeth Rider. 791.43'0232'0924 B
Walt Disney; master of make-believe. Illustrated by Vic Mays. Champaign, Ill., Garrard Pub. Co. [1971] 96 p. illus. (part col.) 24 cm. (Americans all) A biography of cartoonist Walt Disney stressing his professional contribution to the film industry and influence on American life. [PN1998.A3D535] 92 71-146705 ISBN 0-8116-4568-1 2.79
1. Disney, Walt, 1901-1966—Juvenile literature. I. Mays, Victor, 1927- illus. II. Title.

WALKER, Greta. 791'.092'4 B
Walt Disney / by Greta Walker ; illustrated by Ruth Sanderson. New York : Putnam, c1977. p. cm. A biography of the animator whose character Mickey Mouse helped launch the animated cartoon industry. [NC1766.U52D59 1977] lib.bdg. : 4.29
1. Disney, Walt, 1901-1966—Juvenile literature. 2. Animators—United States—Biography—Juvenile literature. I. Sanderson, Ruth. II. Title. BIP

Dissenters.

THOMAS, Norman Mattoon, 1884- 920.02
Great dissenters. [1st ed.] New York, Norton [1961] 220 p. 22 cm. [CT105.T56] 61-11350
1. Dissenters. I. Title. BIP

Dissenters, Religious.

OZMENT, Steven E. 273'.6
Mysticism and dissent; religious ideology and social protest in the sixteenth century, by Steven E. Ozment. New Haven, Yale University Press, 1973. xii, 270 p. 25 cm. Bibliography: p. 248-263. [BX4817.O96 1973] 72-91316 ISBN 0-300-01576-3 10.00
1. Dissenters, Religious. 2. Mysticism—Middle Ages. I. Title. BIP

Dissident art—Russia.

GOLOMSHTOK, I. N. 709'.47
Soviet art in exile / by Igor Golomshtok and Alexander Glezer ; introd. by Sir Roland Penrose ; edited by Michael Scammell. 1st American ed. New York : Random House, c1977. p. cm. Bibliography: p. [N6988.G58 1977] 77-3344 ISBN 0-394-41644-9 : 17.50
1. Dissident art—Russia. 2. Art, Modern—20th century—Russia. 3. Dissenters, Artistic—Russia—Biography. I. Glezer, Aleksandr, joint author. II. Title.

GOLOMSHTOK, I. N. 709'.47
Soviet art in exile / by Igor Golomshtok and Alexander Glezer ; introd. by Sir Roland Penrose ; edited by Michael Scammell. 1st American ed. New York : Random House, c1977. p. cm. Bibliography: p. [N6988.G58 1977] 77-3344 ISBN 0-394-41644-9 : 17.50
1. Dissident art—Russia. 2. Art, Modern—20th century—Russia. 3. Dissenters, Artistic—Russia—Biography. I. Glezer, Aleksandr, joint author. II. Title. BIP

Distilling, Illicit.

KEARINS, Jack J. 364.13'3
Yankee revenooer [by] Jack J. Kearins. Durham, N.C., Moore Pub. Co. [1969] 271 p. 24 cm. Autobiographical. [HJ5021.K4] 70-79094 5.95
1. Distilling, Illicit. I. Title. BIP

Ditzen, Lowell Russell.

SYMON, Benjamin Goodall, 1935-1957. 285'.7'0924
Benjamin Goodall Symon, Jr., his biography and letters, by Lowell Russell Ditzen in collaboration with Elizabeth Carter Symon. Amherst, Mass., Amherst College Press, 1963. xiii, 91 p. port. 24 cm. [BX9593.S9A4] 63-23346
1. Ditzen, Lowell Russell. I. Title.

Divine Light Mission.

COLLIER, Sophia, 1956- 299 B
Soul rush : the odyssey of a young woman of the '70s / by Sophia Collier. 1st ed. New York : Morrow, 1978. 240 p. ; 22 cm. [BP605.D58C64] 77-13901 ISBN 0-688-03276-1 : 8.95
1. Collier, Sophia, 1956- 2. Divine Light Mission—Biography. 3. Divine Light Mission. 4. Guru Maharaj Ji, 1957- I. Title. BIP

Divine Light Mission—Biography.

COLLIER, Sophia, 1956- 299 B
Soul rush : the odyssey of a young woman of the '70s / by Sophia Collier. 1st ed. New York : Morrow, 1978. 240 p. ; 22 cm. [BP605.D58C64] 77-13901 ISBN 0-688-03276-1 : 8.95
1. Collier, Sophia, 1956- 2. Divine Light Mission—Biography. 3. Divine Light Mission. 4. Guru Maharaj Ji, 1957- I. Title. BIP

Diving, Submarine.

JOHNSTONE, John Edward. 926.27
Johnno, the deep-sea diver: the life-story of diver John Johnstone as told to Peter Dawlish [pseud.] New York, Watts [1960] 160 p. illus. 21 cm. [G530.J63] 60-50815
1. Diving, Submarine. I. Kerr, James Lennox, 1899- II. Title.

Divins, Ralph B, 1889-

*CARLSON, Alexander S. 670.92
Factory hand to executives: the story of Ralph Divins, [by] Alexander S. Carlson [1st ed.] New York, Vantage Press [1973] 116 p. illus., 21 cm. [HD9730] ISBN 0-533-00727-5 4.50
1. Divins, Ralph B, 1889- I. Title.

Divizich, Peter John, 1897-

FOLEY, Henry Arthur, 1913- 338.7'63'480924 B
They called him King of the Grapes : memoirs of Peter J. Divizich / recorded by Henry A. Foley. [Porterville? Calif.] : Foley, c1976. 436 p. : ill. ; 24 cm. Includes index. [HD9377.C2F64] 76-358123 12.00
1. Divizich, Peter John, 1897- 2. Viticulture—California—History. I. Divizich, Peter John, 1897- II. Title.

FOLEY, Henry Arthur, 1913- 338.7'63'480924 B
They called him King of the Grapes : memoirs of Peter J. Divizich / recorded by Henry A. Foley. [Porterville? Calif.] : Foley, c1976. 436 p. : ill. ; 24 cm. Includes index. [HD9377.C2F64] 76-358123 12.00
1. Divizich, Peter John, 1897- 2. Viticulture—California—History. I. Divizich, Peter John, 1897- II. Title.

FOLEY, Henry Arthur, 1913- 338.7'63'480924 B
They called him King of the Grapes : memoirs of Peter J. Divizich / recorded by Henry A. Foley. [Porterville? Calif.] : Foley, c1976. 436 p. : ill. ; 24 cm. Includes index. [HD9377.C2F64] 76-358123 12.00
1. Divizich, Peter John, 1897- 2. Viticulture—California—History. I. Divizich, Peter John, 1897- II. Title.

Dix, Dorothea Lynde, 1802-1887.

BAKER, Rachel (Mininberg) 1903- 923.673
Angel of mercy; the story of Dorothea Lynde Dix. New York, Messner [1955] 191p. illus. 22cm. [HV28.D6B3] 55-9849
1. Dix. Dorothea Lynde, 1802-1887. I. Title.

BROOKS, Gladys. 920.7
Three wise virgins. [1st ed.] New York, Dutton, 1957. 244 p. illus. 21 cm. [HV28.D6B7] 57-12754
1. Dix, Dorothea Lynde, 1802-1887. 2. Peabody, Elizabeth Palmer, 1804-1894. 3. Sedgwick, Catharine Maria, 1789-1867. I. Title.

MARSHALL, Helen E. 360'.924(B)
Dorothea Dix, forgotten Samaritan, by Helen E. Marshall. New York, Russell & Russell [1967, c.1937] x, 298p. port. 22cm. Bibl. [HV28.D6M3 1967] 66-24729 8.00
1. Dix, Dorothea Lynde, 1802-1887. I. Title.
Originally published by the Univ. of N.C. Pr.

NORMAN, Gertrude. 923.673
Dorothea Lynde Dix. Illustrated by Lili Rethi. New York, Putnam [1959] 122 p. illus. 22 cm. (Lives to remember) [HV28.D6N6] 59-6504
1. Dix, Dorothea Lynde, 1802-1887.

TIFFANY, Francis, 1827-1908. 360'.924 B
Life of Dorothea Lynde Dix. Ann Arbor, Mich., Plutarch Press, 1971. xiii, 392 p. port. 22 cm. "A facsimile reprint of the 1918 ed." Includes bibliographical references. [HV28.D6T6 1918a] 70-145702
1. Dix, Dorothea Lynde, 1802-1887. I. Title.

WILSON, Dorothy Clarke. 361'.92'4 B
Stranger and traveler : the story of Dorothy Dix, American reformer / by Dorothy Clarke Wilson. 1st ed. Boston : Little, Brown, [1975] xxiii, 360 p. : ill. ; 22 cm. Includes index. Bibliography: p. 343-347. [HV28.D6W54] 75-15711 ISBN 0-316-94496-3 : 8.95
1. Dix, Dorothea Lynde, 1802-1887. 2. Reformers—Biography. I. Title.

Dix, Dorothea Lynde, 1802-1887—Juvenile literature.

MALONE, Mary. 92 (J)
Dorothea L. Dix: hospital founder. Illustrated by Katharine Sampson. Champaign, Ill., Garrard Pub. Co. [1968] 80 p. col. illus. 23 cm. (A Discovery book) [HV28.D6M27] 68-14776
1. Dix, Dorothea Lynde, 1802-1887—Juvenile literature. I. Title.

WAYNE, Bennett. 920.72
Four women of courage, edited with commentary by Bennett Wayne. Champaign, Ill., Garrard Pub. Co. [1975] 167 p. illus. 22 cm. (A Target book) Brief biographies of four women who achieved their ambitions against great odds. [HQ1412.W39] 920 74-13482 ISBN 0-8116-4911-3 3.98 (lib. bdg.)
1. Cochran, Jacqueline—Juvenile literature. 2. Dix, Dorothea Lynde, 1802-1887—Juvenile literature. 3. Keller, Helen Adams, 1880-1968—Juvenile literature. 4. Richards, Linda Ann Judson, 1841-1930—Juvenile literature. I. Title. BIP

Dixon, Billy, 1850-1913.

MCCARTY, John Lawton, 1901- 923.973
Adobe walls bride; the story of Billy and Olive King Dixon. San Antonio, Naylor Co. [1955] 281p. illus. 22cm. [F594.D62M3] 55-4804
1. Dixon, Billy, 1850-1913. 2. Dixon, Olive (King) 3. Frontier and pioneer life—The West. I. Title.

Dixon, Jeane.

DIXON, Jeane. 133.3'0924
Jeane Dixon: my life and prophecies; her own story as told to Rene Noorbergen. New York, W. Morrow, 1969. 219 p. 22 cm. [BF1283.D48A3] 70-94472 5.95
1. Prophecies (Occult sciences) I. Noorbergen, Rene. II. Title.

DIXON, Jeane. 133.3'0924 B
Jeane Dixon: my life and prophecies; her own story as told to Rene Noorbergen. Boston, G. K. Hall, 1971 [c1969] 373 p. 25 cm. Large print ed. [BF1283.D48A3 1971] 70-38008 ISBN 0-8161-6004-X 7.95
1. Prophecies (Occult sciences) I. Noorbergen, Rene. II. Title.

MONTGOMERY, Ruth (Schick) 1912- 133.30924
A gift of prophecy: the phenomenal Jeane Dixon. New York, Morrow [c.]1965. ix, 182p. 22cm. [BF1283.D48M6] 65-21204 4.50 bds.,
1. Dixon, Jeane. I. Title.

MONTGOMERY, Ruth (Shick) 1912- 133.30924
A gift of prophecy: the phenomenal Jeane Dixon [by] Ruth Montgomery. New York, Morrow, 1965. ix, 182 p. 22 cm. [BF1283.D48M6] 65-21204
1. Dixon, Jeane. I. Title.

SMITH, Noel, 1900- 133.3'0924
Jeane Dixon: the Washington prophetess. Springfield, Mo., Baptist Bible tribune [1969] 36 p. port. 22 cm. [BF1283.D48S6] 78-19966
1. Dixon, Jeane.

Dixon, Joseph Moore, 1867-1934.

KARLIN, Jules A. 328.73'092'4 B
Joseph M. Dixon of Montana / Jules A. Karlin. [Missoula : University of Montana], c1974- v. : ill. ; 24 cm. (University of Montana publications in history) Includes index. Contents.Contents.—pt. 1. Senator and Bull Moose manager. Bibliography: p. [234]-245. [E748.D58K37] 75-310320
1. Dixon, Joseph Moore, 1867-1934. I. Title. II. Series: Montana. University, Missoula. Publications in history. BIP

Dixon, Paul.

DIXON, Paul. 791.45'0924 B
Paul Baby; confessions of the Mayor of Kneesville. Introd. by Bob Hope. Cleveland, World Pub. Co. [1968] 250 p. illus., ports. 22 cm. [PN1992.4.D5A3] 68-29836 4.95
I. Title.

Dixon, Richard Watson, 1833-1900—Biography.

BRIDGES, Robert Seymour, 1844-1930. 821'.8'09 B
Three friends : memoirs of Digby Mackworth Dolben, Richard Watson Dixon, Henry Bradley / by Robert Bridges. Westport, Conn. : Greenwood Press, 1975. 243 p. : ports. ; 20 cm. The memoirs of Dolben and Dixon appeared originally in editions of these authors' poems edited by Bridges in 1911 and 1909; the memoir of Bradley, privately printed in 1926, appeared in his Collected papers in 1928. Reprint of the 1932 ed. published by Oxford University Press, London. Includes bibliographical references. [PR107.B68 1975] 75-3863 ISBN 0-8371-8094-5 lib.bdg. : 13.50
1. Dolben, Digby Mackworth, 1848-1867—Biography. 2. Dixon, Richard Watson, 1833-1900—Biography. 3. Bradley, Henry, 1845-1925. 4. Authors—Correspondence, reminiscences, etc. I. Title.

Dixon, Thomas, 1864-1946.

COOK, Raymond Allen. 818'.5'209 B
Thomas Dixon, by Raymond A. Cook. New York, Twayne Publishers [1974] 165 p. 22 cm. (Twayne's United States authors series, TUSAS 235) Bibliography: p. 151-158. [PS3507.I93Z63] 73-15765 ISBN 0-8057-0206-7 5.95
1. Dixon, Thomas, 1864-1946.

Doane, Gustavus Cheyney, 1840-1892.

BONNEY, Orrin H. 917.8
Battle drums and geysers; the life and journals of Lt. Gustavus Cheyney Doane, soldier and explorer of the Yellowstone and Snake River regions [by] Orrin H. and Lorraine Bonney. [1st ed.] Chicago, Sage Books [1970] xxv, 622 p. illus., facsims., maps (4 fold.), ports. 24 cm. Includes Doane's journals of the Yellowstone exploration of 1870 and the Snake River exploration of 1876-1877. Bibliography: p. [591]-604. [F594.D627B6] 70-91169
1. Doane, Gustavus Cheyney, 1840-1892. 2. Yellowstone River. 3. Snake River. I. Bonney, Lorraine G., joint author. II.

Doane, Gustavus Cheyney, 1840-1892. III. Title. BIP

Dobbs, Arthur, 1689- 1765.

CLARKE, Desmond. 923.2415
Arthur Dobbs, esquire, 1689-1765; surveyor-general of Ireland, prospector and Governor of North Carolina. Chapel Hill, University of North Carolina Press [1957] 232p. port. 23cm. Includes bibliographies. [F257.C55] 58-14501
1. Dobbs, Arthur, 1689- 1765. I. Title.

Dobie, James Frank, 1888-1964.

OWENS, William A., 1905- 081
Three friends: Roy Bedichek, J. Frank Dobie, Walter Prescott Webb, by William A. Owens. [1st ed.] Garden City, N.Y., Doubleday, 1969. 335 p. 22 cm. "Acknowledgments, bibliographies, notes": p. [323]-335. [LD5332.2.O95] 70-82957 6.95
1. Bedichek, Roy, 1878-1959. 2. Dobie, James Frank, 1888-1964. 3. Webb, Walter Prescott, 1888-1963. 4. Folk-lore—Texas. I. Title.

Dobin, Abraham, 1907-

DOBIN, Abraham, 1907- 974.9'41 B
Fertile fields : recollections and reflections of a busy life / Abraham Dobin. South Brunswick : A. S. Barnes, [1975] 519 p. ; 21 cm. [CT275.D6A34 1975] 74-290 ISBN 0-498-01545-9 : 8.95
1. Dobin, Abraham, 1907- I. Title. BIP

Doctors—Correspondence, reminiscences, etc.

*LOWERY, John Robert. 926.1
Memoirs of a country doctor. New York, Carlton [1968] 128p. 21cm. (Hearthstone bk.) 3.50
1. Doctors—Correspondence, reminiscences, etc. I. Title.

Doctors of the church.

SIMMONS, Ernest. 922.22
The Fathers and Doctors of the church. Milwaukee, Bruce Pub. Co. [1959] 188 p. 23 cm. [BX4669.S55] 59-14256
1. Doctors of the church. I. Title.

Dodd, Charles Harold, 1884-1973.

DILLISTONE, Frederick William, 1903 225.6'092'4 B
C. H. Dodd, interpreter of the New Testament / by F. W. Dillistone. Grand Rapids : Eerdmans, c1977. 255 p. ; 25 cm. Includes index. Bibliography: p. 249-251. [BS2351.D6D54 1977] 76-54324 ISBN 0-8028-3496-5 : 11.95
1. Dodd, Charles Harold, 1884-1973. 2. New Testament scholars—England—Biography. I. Title.

Dodd, Thomas J., 1907-

BOYD, James, 1929- 328.73'0924
Above the law. [New York] New American Library [1968] viii, 337 p. 22 cm. [E840.8.D6B6] 68-17056
1. Dodd, Thomas J., 1907- I. Title.

Dodd, William Edward, 1869-1940.

DALLEK, Robert. 973.917'0924 B
Democrat and diplomat; the life of William E. Dodd. New York, Oxford University Press, 1968. ix, 415 p. port. 22 cm. Includes bibliographical references. [E748.D6D3] 68-29717 8.50
1. Dodd, William Edward, 1869-1940. 2. United States—Foreign relations—Germany. 3. Germany—Foreign relations—United States. I. Title.

Dodds, Eric Robertson, 1893-

DODDS, Eric Robertson, 1893- 880'.09 B
Missing persons : an autobiography / E. R. Dodds. Oxford [Eng.] : Clarendon Press, 1977. 202 p., [4] leaves of plates : ports. ; 23 cm. Includes index. [PA85.D6A35] 77-30116 ISBN 0-19-812086-9 : 13.50
1. Dodds, Eric Robertson, 1893- 2. Classicists—Great Britain—Biography. I. Title.
Distributed by Oxford University Press, NY BIP

Dodds, Thomas Carter, 1919-

DODDS, Thomas Carter, 1919- 796.358'092'4 B
Hit hard and enjoy it / by T. C. "Dickie" Dodds ; with a preface by Sir Neville Cardus. Tunbridge Wells : The Cricketer Ltd, 1976. 120 p., [8] p. of plates : ill., chiefly ports. ; 22 cm. [GV915.D58A34] 77-365278 ISBN 0-902211-04-8 : £4.00. ISBN 0-902211-05-6 pbk.
1. Dodds, Thomas Carter, 1919- 2. Cricket players—England—Biography. I. Title.

Dodge, D. Witherspoon

DODGE, D. Witherspoon 920.9
Southern rebel in reverse; the autobiography of an idol-shaker by D. Witherspoon Dodge in cooperation with Clair M. Cook. New York, American [1962, c.1961] 178p. 3.00
I. Title.

Dodge family.

BARNES, Valerie. 974.9'74
Behind the scenes at Giralda Farms : [Geraldine Rockefeller Dodge's fabled estate] / Valerie Barnes. Bernardsville, N.J. : Bernardsville Book Co., 1976. 119 p. ; 18 cm. [F144.M18B37] 76-9518 ISBN 0-916600-01-7 pbk. : 2.95
1. Madison, N.J. Giralda Farms. 2. Dodge, Geraldine Rockefeller, 1882-1973. 3. Dodge family. 4. Rockefeller family. I. Title.

Dodge, Geraldine Rockefeller, 1882-1973.

BARNES, Valerie. 974.9'74
Behind the scenes at Giralda Farms : [Geraldine Rockefeller Dodge's fabled estate] / Valerie Barnes. Bernardsville, N.J. : Bernardsville Book Co., 1976. 119 p. ; 18 cm. [F144.M18B37] 76-9518 ISBN 0-916600-01-7 pbk. : 2.95
1. Madison, N.J. Giralda Farms. 2. Dodge, Geraldine Rockefeller, 1882-1973. 3. Dodge family. 4. Rockefeller family. I. Title.

Dodge, Grenville Mellen, 1831-1916.

HIRSHSON, Stanley P., 1928- 973.730924 B
Grenville M. Dodge, soldier, politician, railroad pioneer [by] Stanley P. Hirshson. Bloomington, Indiana University Press [1967] xiv, 334 p. illus., ports. 25 cm. Bibliography: p. 265-276. [E467.1.D6H5] 67-10106
1. Dodge, Grenville Mellen, 1831-1916.

Dodge, Mary Abigail, 1833-1896.

DODGE, Mary Abigail, 1833-1896. 081
Wool-gathering. Freeport, N.Y., Books for Libraries Press, 1973 [c1867] p. (The Black heritage library collection) [PS1544.Z5A3 1973] 72-13861 ISBN 0-8369-9241-5
1. Dodge, Mary Abigail, 1833-1896. 2. United States—Description and travel—1865-1900. I. Title. II. Series.

Dodgson, Charles Lutwidge, 1832-1898.

COLLINGWOOD, Stuart Dodgson, 1870- 828'.8'09 (B)
The life and letters of Lewis Carroll (Rev. C. L. Dodgson) Detroit, Gale Research Co, 1967. xx, 448 p. illus., facsims., ports. 22 cm. (The Gale library of lives and letters. British writers series) Title page includes original imprint: New York, Century Co., 1899. Bibliography: p. 431-443. [PR4612.C6 1967] 67-23871
1. Dodgson, Charles Lutwidge, 1832-1808. I. Dodgson, Charles Lutwidge, 1832-1898. II. Title.

DE LA MARE, Walter John, 1873-1956. 828'.8'09
Lewis Carroll / by Walter De La Mare. Norwood, Pa. : Norwood Editions, 1976. 67 p. ; 24 cm. Reprint of the 1932 ed. published by Faber & Faber, London. [PR4612.D4 1976] 76-2429 ISBN 0-88305-172-9 lib. bdg. : 7.50
1. Dodgson, Charles Lutwidge, 1832-1898. BIP

DODGSON, Charles Lutwidge, 1832-1898. 928.2
The diaries of Lewis Carroll [pseud.] Now first edited and supplemented by Roger Lancelyn Green. New York, Oxford University Press, 1954. 2 v. (xxvi, 604p.) illus., ports. 23cm. [PR4612.A2 1954] 54-8453
I. Title.

DODGSON, Charles Lutwidge, 1832-1898. 828'.8'03
The diaries of Lewis Carroll. Now first edited and supplemented by Roger Lancelyn Green. Westport, Conn., Greenwood Press [1971, c1954] 2 v. (xxvi, 604 p.) illus., ports. 23 cm. [PR4612.A2 1971] 74-110268 201

GREEN, Roger Lancelyn. 928.2
The story of Lewis Carroll. New York, H. Schuman [1950] 179 p. illus., ports. 20 cm. "Writings by and about Lewis Carroll": p. 175-178. [PR4612.G7] 51-9791
1. Dodgson, Charles Lutwidge, 1832-1898. I. Title.

HUDSON, Derek. 828'.8'09 B
Lewis Carroll. Westport, Conn., Greenwood Press [1972] xiii, 354 p. illus. 23 cm. Reprint of the 1954 ed. Includes bibliographical references. [PR4612.H8 1972] 72-5453 ISBN 0-8371-6439-7 15.00
1. Dodgson, Charles Lutwidge, 1832-1898. BIP

HUDSON, Derek. 828'.8'09 B
Lewis Carroll / Derek Hudson. Folcroft, Pa. : Folcroft Library Editions, 1976. p. cm. Reprint of the 1954 ed. published by Constable, London. Includes bibliographical references and index. [PR4612.H8 1976] 76-25858 ISBN 0-8414-4808-6 lib. bdg. : 25.00
1. Dodgson, Charles Lutwidge, 1832-1898. 2. Authors, English—19th century—Biography.

LENNON, Florence Becker. 928.2
The life of Lewis Carroll. New, rev. ed. New York, Collier Books [1962] 448p. illus., 18cm. (Collier books, AS379) 'Originally appeared under the title: Victoria through the lookingglass.' Includes bibliography. [PR4612.L4 1962] 62-18589
1. Dodgson, Charles Lutwidge, 1832-1898. I. Title.

TAYLOR, Alexander L. 828'.8'09 B
The white knight; a study of C. L. Dodgson (Lewis Carroll) by Alexander L. Taylor. [Folcroft, Pa.] Folcroft Library Editions, 1974. viii, 209 p. 26 cm. Reprint of the 1952 ed. published by Oliver & Boyd, Edinburgh. Bibliography: p. [201]-206. [PR4612.T3 1974] 74-3131 ISBN 0-8414-8570-4 (lib. bdg.)
1. Dodgson, Charles Lutwidge, 1832-1898. I. Title.

Dodgson, Charles Lutwidge, 1832-1898—Biography.

CLARK, Anne, 1933- 828'.8'09 B
Lewis Carroll, a biography / Anne Clark. New York : Schocken Books, 1979. 284 p., [12] leaves of plates : ill. ; 24 cm. Includes index. Bibliography: p. [273]-275. [PR4612.C55 1979] 79-64116 ISBN 0-8052-3722-4 : 12.95
1. Dodgson, Charles Lutwidge, 1882-1898—Biography. 2. Authors, English—19th century—Biography. I. Title.

COLLINGWOOD, Stuart Dodgson, 1870- 828'.8'09 B
The life and letters of Lewis Carroll (Rev. C. L. Dodgson) Detroit, Gale Research Co., 1967. xx, 448 p. illus., facsims., ports. 22 cm. (The Gale library of lives and letters. British writers series) Title page includes original imprint: New York, Century Co., 1899. Bibliography: p. 431-443. [PR4612.C6 1967] 67-23871
1. Dodgson, Charles Lutwidge, 1832-1898—Biography. I. Dodgson, Charles Lutwidge, 1832-1898. II. Title. BIP

HUDSON, Derek. 828'.8'09 B
Lewis Carroll : an illustrated biography / by Derek Hudson. New illustrated ed. London : Constable, 1976. 272 p. : ill. (incl 1 col.), facsims., map, ports. ; 26 cm. Includes index. Bibliography: p. 265-266. [PR4612.H8 1976b] 77-356344 ISBN 0-09-460590-4 : £6.50
1. Dodgson, Charles Lutwidge, 1832-1898—Biography. 2. Authors, English—19th century—Biography.

HUDSON, Derek. 828'.8'09 B
Lewis Carroll : an illustrated biography / by Derek Hudson. 1st American ed. New York : C. N. Potter : distributed by Crown Publishers, 1977. 272 p. : ill. ; 27 cm. Includes index. Bibliography: p. 265-266. [PR4612.H8 1977] 77-1482 ISBN 0-517-53078-3 : 10.00
1. Dodgson, Charles Lutwidge, 1832 1898—Biography. 2. Authors, English—19th century—Biography. BIP

LENNON, Florence Becker. 828'.8'09 B
The life of Lewis Carroll (Victoria through the looking glass) [3d rev. ed.] New York, Dover Publications [1972] 448 p. illus. 22 cm. First ed. published in 1945 under title: Victoria through the looking-glass. Bibliography: p. [419]-432. [PR4612.L4 1972] 74-186594 ISBN 0-486-22838-X 3.95
1. Dodgson, Charles Lutwidge, 1832-1898—Biography. I. Title. II. Title: Victoria through the looking glass.

PUDNEY, John, 1909- 828'.8'09 B
Lewis Carroll and his world / John Pudney. London : Thames & Hudson, c1976. 127 p. : ill. ; 24 cm. Includes index. Bibliography: p. 122. [PR4612.P8] 76-380506 ISBN 0-500-13058-2 : £3.50
1. Dodgson, Charles Lutwidge, 1832-1898—Biography. 2. Authors, English—19th century—Biography. I. Title. BIP

REED, Langford, 1889- 828'.8'09 B
The life of Lewis Carroll. [Folcroft, Pa.] Folcroft Library Editions, 1974. 142 p. illus. 24 cm. Reprint of the 1932 ed. published by W. & G. Foyle, London. [PR4612.R4 1974] 74-2271 20.00
1. Dodgson, Charles Lutwidge, 1832-1898—Biography. I. Title. BIP

Dodgson, Charles Lutwidge, 1832-1898—Biography—Character.

GATTEGNO, Jean. 828'.8'09 B
Lewis Carroll, a life : fragments of a looking-glass / by Jean Gattegno ; translated by Rosemary Sheed. New York : Crowell, [1976] p. cm. Translation of Lewis Carroll, une vie d'Alice a Zenon d'Elee. Includes index. Bibliography: p. [PR4612.G3E5 1976] 75-23388 ISBN 0-690-01028-1
1. Dodgson, Charles Lutwidge, 1832-1898—Biography Character. I. Title.

Dodgson, Charles Lutwidge, 1832-1898—Juvenile literature.

BOWMAN, Isa. 828'.8'09 B
Lewis Carroll as I knew him. With a new introd. by Morton N. Cohen. New York, Dover Publications [1972] xix, 132 p. illus. 21 cm. Reprint of the 1899 ed., published under title: The story of Lewis Carroll. [PR4612.B6 1972] 78-189345 ISBN 0-486-20560-6 2.00
1. Dodgson, Charles Lutwidge, 1832-1898—Juvenile literature. I. Title. BIP

GREEN, Roger Lancelyn. 928.2
The story of Lewis Carroll. New York, H. Schuman [1951] 179 p. illus., facsims, ports 20 cm. (Story biographies [1]) Bibliography: p. 175-177. [[PR4612]] 64-7300 CD
1. Dodgson, Charles Lutwidge, 1882-1896—Juvenile literature. I. Title.

RICHARDSON, Joanna 92
The young Lewis Carroll. Illus. by Susan

E. Sims. New York, Roy [1965, c.1963] 134p. illus. 21cm. [PR4612.R5] 64-23914 3.25 bds.,
1. Dodgson, Charles Lutwidge, 1832-1898—Juvenile literature. I. Title.

Dodrill family.

DODRILL, Charles Tunis 929.2'0973
Heritage of a pioneer, being the story of William (English Bill Doddridge) Dodrill and his wife, Rebecca (Lewis) Daugherty, their family, the times in which they lived,and a genealogy of the families of their sons. A biography and a genealogy. Huntington, W. Va., 1967. 782p. illus. 23cm. [CS71.D646 1967] 67-22005 14.95
1. Dodrill family. 2. Dodrill, William I. Title.
Available from McClain Print Co., Parsons, W. Va.

Dodshon, Frances (Henshaw) Paxton, 1714-1793.

HOBHOUSE, Stephen Henry, 1881-1961. 283'.092'4
William Law and eighteenth century Quakerism; including some unpublished letters and fragments of William Law and John Byrom. New York, B. Blom, 1972. 342 p. illus. 21 cm. Reprint of the 1927 ed. published by G. Allen & Unwin, London. Includes bibliographical references. [BX5199.L3H62 1972] 77-175870 14.50
1. Law, William, 1686-1761. 2. Byrom, John, 1692-1763. 3. Dodshon, Frances (Henshaw) Paxton, 1714-1793. 4. Friends, Society of. I. Title.

Dogen, 1200-1253.

YOKOI, Yuho, 1918- 294.3'927
Zen Master Dogen : an introduction with selected writings / by Yuho Yokoi, with the assistance of Daizen Victoria ; and with a foreword by Minoru Kiyota. 1st ed. New York : Weatherhill, 1976. 217 p. ; 23 cm. [BQ9449.D652Y63] 75-33200 ISBN 0-8348-0112-4 : 10.00 pbk. : 4.50
1. Dogen, 1200-1253. 2. Sotoshu—Collected works. I. Victoria, Daizen, 1939- joint author. II. Dogen, 1200-1253. Selected works. 1976. III. Title. BIP

Doggett, Laurence Locke, 1864-1957.

HALL, Lawrence Kingsley, 1886- 923.773
Doggett of Springfield; a biography of Laurence Locke Doggett, PHD. Introd. by Charles Francis Hall. Springfield, Mass., Springfield Coll. [1964] xx, 249p. illus., ports. 22cm. Bibl. 64-22007 price unreported
1. Doggett, Laurence Locke, 1864-1957. I. Title.

Dogho, Chief of Warri, d. 1932—Juvenile literature.

IKIME, Obaro. 966.9'03'0924 B
Chief Dogho of Warri / [by] Obaro Ikime. London : Heinemann Educational, 1976, i.e.1977 48 p. : ill., maps, ports. ; 15 x 21 cm. (African historical biographies ; 10) [DT515.72.D63I38] 77-354180 ISBN 0-435-94473-8 pbk. : 1.25
1. Dogho, Chief of Warri, d. 1932—Juvenile literature. 2. Nigeria—Colonization—Juvenile literature. 3. Jekri (African people)—Kings and rulers—Biography—Juvenile literature. 4. Colonial agents—Nigeria—Biography—Juvenile literature. 5. Colonial agents—Great Britain—Biography—Juvenile literature. I. Title. II. Series.
Distributed by Heinemann Educ., Salem, New Hampshire BIP

Dogs—Training.

MEISTERFELD, C. W. 636.7'08'8
Tails of a dog psychoanalyst / by C. W. Meisterfeld ; ill. by Walt Lee. 1st ed. Petaluma, Calif. : M-R-K Publishing, 1978. 216 p. : ill. ; 24 cm. [SF431.M524] 78-58492 ISBN 0-9601292-2-7 : 10.95
1. Dogs—Training. 2. Dogs—Behavior. 3. Dogs—Legends and stories. 4. Meisterfeld, C. W. 5. Animal trainers—California—Biography. I. Title. II. Title: Dog psychoanalyst. BIP

Doherty, Catherine de Hueck, 1900-

DOHERTY, Catherine de Hueck, 1900- 248'.48'2
I live on an island / Catherine de Hueck Doherty. Notre Dame, Ind. : Ave Maria Press, c1979. 126 p. : ill. ; 21 cm. [BX2350.2.D623] 78-74433 ISBN 0-87793-171-2 pbk. : 2.75
1. Doherty, Catherine de Hueck, 1900- 2. Christian life—Catholic authors. 3. Catholics—Ontario—Biography. 4. Ontario—Biography. I. Title. BIP

Doig, Ivan.

DOIG, Ivan. 978.6'612'030924 B
This house of sky : landscapes of a Western mind / Ivan Doig. 1st ed. New York : Harcourt Brace Jovanovich, c1978. 314 p. ; 25 cm. [F737.M4D643] 78-53897 ISBN 0-15-190054-X : 9.95
1. Doig, Ivan. 2. Doig family. 3. Meagher Co., Mont.—Biography. I. Title. BIP

Dolben, Digby Mackworth, 1848-1867—Biography.

BRIDGES, Robert Seymour, 1844-1930. 821'.8'09 B
Three friends : memoirs of Digby Mackworth Dolben, Richard Watson Dixon, Henry Bradley / by Robert Bridges. Westport, Conn. : Greenwood Press, 1975. 243 p. : ports. ; 20 cm. The memoirs of Dolben and Dixon appeared originally in editions of these authors' poems edited by Bridges in 1911 and 1909; the memoir of Bradley, privately printed in 1926, appeared in his Collected papers in 1928. Reprint of the 1932 ed. published by Oxford University Press, London. Includes bibliographical references. [PR107.B68 1975] 75-3863 ISBN 0-8371-8094-5 lib.bdg. : 13.50
1. Dolben, Digby Mackworth, 1848-1867—Biography. 2. Dixon, Richard Watson, 1833-1900—Biography. 3. Bradley, Henry, 1845-1925. 4. Authors—Correspondence, reminiscences, etc. I. Title.

Dolbun, Alexander.

DOLGUN, Alexander. 365.60924
Alexander Dolgun's story : an American in the Gulag / Alexander Dolgun with Patrick Watson. New York : Ballantine Books, 1976c1975. 503p. ; 18 cm [HV8959.R9D57] ISBN 0-345-25801-0 pbk. : 1.95
1. Dolbun, Alexander. I. Watson, Patrick, 1929-, joint author. II. Title.
L.C. card no. for 1975 Knopf edition: 7-21290

Dolci, Danilo.

HARCOURT, Melville 248.0922
Portraits of destiny. Illus. by Giles Harcourt. New York, Sheed [1966] 239p. ports. 22cm. [BR1700.2.H3] 66-22014 5.50
1. Dolci, Danilo. 2. Luthuli, Albert John, 1898- 3. Munk, Kaj Harold-Leininger, 1898-1944. 4. Szabo, Violette (Bushnell) 1921-1945. I. Title.

MCNEISH, James 301.1530924
Fire under the ashes; the life of Danilo Dolci. Boston, Beacon [c.1965, 1966] xix, 324p. illus., map. ports. 21cm. Bibl. [HN488.S5M3] 66-14489 5.95 bds.,
1. Dolci, Danilo. 2. Sicily—Soc. condit. 3. Passive resistance to government. I. Title.

Dolensek, Emil.

BUCHENHOLZ, Bruce. 636.089
Doctor in the zoo / Bruce Buchenholz ; introd. by Cleveland Amory. New York : Penguin Books, 1976, c1974. 190 p. : ill. ; 26 cm. [SF996.B82 1976] 75-41424 ISBN 0-670-00620-3 pbk. : 4.50
1. Dolensek, Emil. 2. New York (City). Zoological park. 3. Zoo animals—Diseases. 4. Zoo animals—Pictorial works. I. Title. BIP

BUCHENHOLZ, Bruce. 636.08'899
Doctor in the zoo / Bruce Buchenholz ; introd. by Cleveland Amory. New York : Viking Press, 1974. 190 p. : ill. ; 26 cm. (A studio book) Follows the routine and emergency activities during one week in the life of the chief veterinarian of New York's Bronx Zoo. [SF996.B82 1974] 74-10491 ISBN 0-670-27527-1 : 10.95
1. Dolensek, Emil. 2. New York (City). Zoological Park. 3. Zoo animals—Diseases. 4. Zoo animals—Pictorial works. I. Title.

Dolet, Etienne, 1508-1546.

CHRISTIE, Richard Copley, 1830-1901. 686.2'092'4 B
Etienne Dolet, the martyr of the Renaissance, 1508-1546; a biography. New ed., rev. and corr. Freeport, N.Y., Books for Libraries Press [1972] p. Reprint of the 1899 ed. Bibliography: p. [Z232.D66C5 1972] 72-8440 ISBN 0-8369-6999-5
1. Dolet, Etienne, 1508-1546.

Dolgun, Alexander.

DOLGUN, Alexander. 365'.6'0924 B
Alexander Dolgun's story : an American in the Gulag / by Alexander Dolgun with Patrick Watson. 1st ed. New York : Knopf : distributed by Random House. 1975. 370 p. ; 25 cm. [HV8959.R9D57] 74-21290 ISBN 0-394-49497-0 : 10.00
1. Dolgun, Alexander. I. Watson, Patrick, 1929- joint author. II. Title. BIP

Dollfuss, Engelbert, 1892-1934.

BROOK-SHEPHERD, Gordon, 1918- 943.6'05'0924 B
Dollfuss / by Gordon Brook-Shepherd. Westport, Conn. : Greenwood Press, 1978, c1961. xvii, 295 p., [7] leaves of plates : ill. ; 22 cm. Reprint of the ed. published by Macmillan, London. Includes index. Bibliography: p. 291. [DB98.D6B76 1978] 78-17396 ISBN 0-313-20527-2 lib. bdg. : 20.75
1. Dollfuss, Engelbert, 1892-1934. 2. Statesmen—Austria—Biography. 3. Austria—Politics and government—1918-1938. BIP

SHEPHERD, Gordon 943.6050924(B)
Dollfuss. by Gordon Brook-Shepherd. London. Macmillan. 1961. 295p. illus. 23cm. Bibl. [DB98.D6S5 1961] 62-6303 5.00
1. Dollfuss. Englebert, 1892-1934. I. Title.
Available from Hillary House in New York.

[SHEPHERD, Gordon] 923.2436
Prelude to infamy: the story of Chancellor Dollfuss of Austria, by Gordon Brook-Shepherd. New York, Obolensky [1962, c.1961] 295p. Bibl. 62-10805 5.00
1. Dollfuss, Engelbert, 1892-1934. I. Title.

Dolliver, Jonathan Prentiss, 1858-1910.

ROSS, Thomas Richard. 923.273
Jonathan Prentiss Dolliver; a study in political integrity and independence. Iowa City, State Historical Society of Iowa, 1958. 366p. illus. 24cm. Includes bibliography. [E664.D66R6] 58-13539
1. Dolliver, Jonathan Prentiss, 1858-1910. I. Title.

Dolmetsch, Arnold, 1858-1940.

CAMPBELL, Margaret. 781.9'1'0924 B
Dolmetsch : the man and his work / by Margaret Campbell. Seattle : University of Washington Press, 1975. xv, 318 p., [9] leaves of plates : ill. ; 25 cm. Includes indexes. Bibliography: p. [301]-306. [ML424.D65C3] 75-4558 ISBN 0-295-95416-7 : 14.95
1. Dolmetsch, Arnold, 1858-1940. BIP

Dolphy, Eric.

SIMOSKO, Vladimir. 788'.0092'4
Eric Dolphy: a musical biography and discography, by Vladimir Simosko and Barry Tepperman. Washington, Smithsonian Institution Press; [distributed in the U.S. and Canada by G. Braziller, New York] 1974 [c1971] ix, 132 p. illus. 24 cm. Bibliography: p. 131-132. [ML419.D646S5] 73-16248 ISBN 0-87474-142-4 10.00
1. Dolphy, Eric. 2. Dolphy, Eric—Discography. I. Tepperman, Barry, joint author. II. Title. BIP

Domingo de Guzman, Saint, 1170-1221.

BRADY, Gerard K 1929- 922.246
Saint Dominic, pilgrim of light. With a pref. by Cardinal Lercaro, Archbishop of Bologna. New York, P. J. Kenedy [1957] 169p. illus. 23cm. Includes bibliography. [BX4700.D7B7] 57-11963
1. Domingo de Guzman, Saint, 1170-1221. I. Title.

DORCY, Mary Jean 922.246
Saint Dominic. St. Louis, B. Herder [c.1959] xi, 173p. Includes bibliography. 21cm. (Cross and crown series of spirituality, no. 15) 59-13389 3.25
1. Domingo de Guzman, Saint, 1170-1221. I. Title.

ERNEST, Brother, 1897- 922.246
The Hound of God; a story of Saint Dominic. Illus. by Nancy Langenbahn. Notre Dame, Ind., Dujarie Press [1954] 95p. illus. 24cm. [BX4700.D7E7] 54-1906
1. Domingo de Guzman, Saint, 1170-1221. I. Title.

LEHNER, Francis C ed. 922.246
Saint Dominic; biographical documents, edited with an introd. by Francis C. Lehner. Foreword by Aniceto Fernandez. Washington, Thomist Press [1964] vii, 258 p. illus. 24 cm. Bibliography p. 252-253. [BX4700.D7L4] 64-6781
1. Domingo de Guzman, Saint, 1170-1221. I. Title.

MATT, Leonard von. 922.246
St. Dominic, a pictorial biography. [Illus.] by Leonard von Matt and [text by] Marie Humbert Vicaire. Translated from the French by Gerard Meath. Chicago, H. Regnery Co. [1957] 88p. illus. 25cm. [BX4700.D7M353] 58-779
1. Domingo de Guzman, Saint, 1170-1221. 2. Dominicans—Hist. I. Vicaire, Marie Humbert, 1906- II. Title.

O'HANLON, Assumpta. 922.246
St. Dominic, servant but friend. St. Louis, Herder [1954] 182p. 21cm. [BX4700.D7O37] 54-8528
1. Domingo de Guxman, Saint, 1170-1221. I. Title.

POINSENET, Marie Dominique, 1906- 922.246
Saint Dominic. Tr. by John Chapin. New York, Macmillan [c.1961,1963] 129p. 18cm. (Your name--your saint ser.) Bibl. 63-8397 2.50
1. Domingo de Guzman, Saint, 1170-1221. I. Title.

VICAIRE, Marie Humbert, 1906- 922.22
Saint Dominic and his times. Tr. [from French] by Kathleen Pond. New York, McGraw [1965, c.1964] xi, 548p. illus., maps. 26cm. Bibl. [BX4700.D7V513] 62-8965 13.50
1. Domingo de Guzman, Saint, I. Title.

WILMS, Jerome, 1878- 922.246
As the morning star; the life of St. Dominic. Translated from the German by a Dominican Sister of the Perpetual Rosary. Milwaukee, Bruce Pub. Co. [1956] 134p. 21cm. [BX4700.D7W513] 56-13236
1. Domingo de Guzman, Saint, 1170-1221. I. Title.

Dominguez family.

GRENIER, Judson. 929'.2'0973
Reminiscences of the Dominguez Ranch and the Carson family : an oral history / by John Victor Carson ; interview by Judson Grenier. Dominguez Hills : Dominguez Archives Committee, California State College, 1976. 38 p. : ill. ; 22 cm. [CS71.C321 1976] 76-365709
1. Carson family. 2. Dominguez family. 3. Carson, John Victor, 1893-1976. 4. Rancho San Pedro, Calif. 5. Los Angeles Co., Calif.—Genealogy. I. Carson, John Victor, 1893-1976. II. Title.

Dominic of the Mother of God, Father, 1792-1849.

MEAD, Jude. 271'.62'0924 B
Shepherd of the second spring; the life of Blessed Dominic Barberi, C. P., 1792-1849. Paterson, N.J., St. Anthony Guild Press [1968] vii, 240 p. illus., port. 24 cm. Bibliography: p. 233-235. [BX4705.D583M4] 68-22313
1. Dominic of the Mother of God, Father, 1792-1849. I. Title.

Dominic, Saint, 1170-1221.

DORCY, Mary Jean, 1914- 922.2
Saint Dominic's family; lives and legends. Dubuque, Iowa, Priory Press [1964] xxiii, 632 p. 25 cm. Bibliography: p. 613-621. [BX3555.D62] 64-15580
1. Dominicans — Biog. I. Title.

JARRETT, Bede 922.246
Life of St. Dominic, 1170-1221. Garden City, N.Y., Doubleday [1964] 160p. 18cm. (Image bk., D165) Bibl. .75 pap.,
1. Dominic, Saint, 1170-1221. I. Title.

Dominic, Sister Mary

DOMINIC, Sister Mary 922.2415
Little Nellie of Holy God. Pictures by Sister M. John Vianney. Milwaukee, Bruce [c.1961] unpaged. col. illus. .50 bds.,
I. Title.

Dominicans — Biog.

DORCY, Mary Jean, 1914- 922.2
Saint Dominic's family; lives and legends. Dubuque, Iowa, Priory Press [1964] xxiii, 632 p. 25 cm. Bibliography: p. 613-621. [BX3555.D62] 64-15580
1. Dominicans — Biog. I. Title.

Domsaitis, Pranas, 1880-1965.

DOMSAITIS, Pranas, 1880- 741.973 1965.
Pranas Domsaitis / [text] by Elsa Verloren van Themaat. Cape Town : Struik (C.), 1976. 64 p. : chiefly ill. (some col., 1 fold.) ; 25 x 28 cm. (South African art library ; 6) Includes index. Bibliography: p. 63. [ND588.D65V37] 77-558243 ISBN 0-86977-070-5 : R9.75
1. Domsaitis, Pranas, 1880-1965. 2. Painters—Germany—Biography. I. Verloren van Themaat, Elsa. II. Title. III. Series.

Donahue, Joseph A.

DONAHUE, Joseph A. 940.54'59'73
Tin cans and other ships : a war diary, 1941-1945 / by Joseph A. Donahue. North Quincy, Mass. : Christopher Pub. House, c1979. 255 p. : ill. ; 22 cm. [D774.N48D66] 78-74696 ISBN 0-8158-0378-8 : 7.50
1. Niblack (Ship) 2. Donahue, Joseph A. 3. Oklahoma City (Ship) 4. United States. Navy—Biography. 5. World War, 1939-1945—Personal narratives, American. 6. World War, 1939-1945—Naval operations, American. 7. Seamen—United States—Biography. I. Title.

Donaldson, William.

DONALDSON, 301.41'54'0924 William.
Don't call me Madam : the life and hard times of a gentleman pimp / William Donaldson. New York : Mason/Charter, 1977, c1975. 199 p. ; 22 cm. [HQ186.L66D66 1977] 77-1691 ISBN 0-88405-556-6 pbk. : 7.95
1. Donaldson, William. 2. Prostitution—England—London. 3. Pimps—England—London—Biography. I. Title.

Donat, Alexander.

DONAT, 940.53'1503'924 B Alexander.
The Holocaust kingdom : a memoir / Alexander Donat. New York : Holocaust Library, c1978. 361 p. ; 22 cm. Label mounted on cover: Distributed by Schocken Book[s], New York. [D810.J4D68 1978] 77-89067 pbk. : 4.95
1. Donat, Alexander. 2. Holocaust, Jewish (1939-1945)—Personal narratives. 3. Warsaw—History—Uprising of 1943. I. Title.
Publisher's address : 216 W. 18th St., New York, NY 10011 BIP

Donato, Joe.

DONATO, Joe. 364.1'092'4 B
Tell it to the Mafia / by Joe Donato ; as told to Wyn Hope. Plainfield, N.J. : Logos International, [1975] 154 p. ; 21 cm. "A Logos book." Autobiographical. [HV6248.D59A38] 75-2801 ISBN 0-88270-107-X pbk. : 2.95
1. Donato, Joe. 2. Crime and criminals—United States—Correspondence, reminiscences, etc. I. Hope, Wyn. II. Title. BIP

Donders, Petrus, 1809-1887.

CARR, John, 1878- 922.2492
A fisher of men, the venerable Peter Donders, C. ss. e. Dublin, Clonmore & Reynolds, 1952. 144p. illus. 19cm. [BX4705.D585C3] 53-20680
1. Donders, Petrus, 1809-1887. 2. Missions —Lepers. I. Title.

Dongan, Thomas, 2d Earl of Limerick, 1634-1715.

KENNEDY, John 974.7'02'0924 Harold, 1898-
Thomas Dongan, Governor of New York (1682-1688), by John H. Kennedy. Washington, 1930. [New York, AMS Press, 1974] ix, 131 p. 23 cm. Reprint of the author's thesis, Catholic University of America, 1930, which was issued as v. 9 of the Catholic University of America. Studies in American church history. Bibliography: p. 121-128. [F122.D695 1974] 73-3564 ISBN 0-404-57759-8 6.00
1. Dongan, Thomas, 2d Earl of Limerick, 1634-1715. 2. New York (State)—History—Colonial period, ca. 1600-1775. 3. New York (State)—Politics and government—Colonial period, ca. 1600-1775. I. Title. II. Series: Catholic University of America. Studies in American church history, v. 9. BIP

Donicht, Mark.

DONICHT, Mark. 291.9
Chrysalis, "a journey into the new spiritual America" / Mark Donicht. Berkeley, Calif. : Pan Pub., [1978] p. cm. [BL2530.U6D66] 77-28335 ISBN 0-89496-011-3 pbk. : 3.95
1. Donicht, Mark. 2. United States—Religion—1945- 3. Spiritual life. 4. Religion—Biography. I. Title.

Donitz, Karl, 1891—

DONITZ, Karl, 1891- 940.54'59'43
Memoirs : ten years and twenty days / by Admiral Doenitz ; translated by R. H. Stevens, in collaboration with David Woodward. Westport, Conn. : Greenwood Press, 1976, c1959. p. cm. Translation of Zehn Zahre und zwanzig Tage. Reprint of the ed. published by Weidenfeld and Nicolson, London. Includes index. [D781.D613 1976] 74-24613 ISBN 0-8371-7867-3
1. Donitz, Karl, 1891- 2. World War, 1939-1945—Naval operations—Submarine. 3. World War, 1939-1945—Naval operations, German. 4. World War, 1939-1945—Personal narratives, German. I. Title: Ten years and twenty days. BIP

Donizetti, Gaetano, 1797-1848.

WEINSTOCK, Herbert, 782.1'092'4 B 1905-
Donizetti and the world of opera in Italy, Paris, and Vienna in the first half of the nineteenth century / by Herbert Weinstock. New York : Octagon Books, 1979, c1963. xxii, 453 p., [10] leaves of plates : ill. ; 25 cm. Reprint of the edition published by Pantheon Books, New York. Includes index. "The music: a chronological list of Donizetti's operas ... [and] a list of Donizetti's nonoperatic compositions": p. 313-404. [ML410.D7W4 1979] 79-9542 ISBN 0-374-98337-2 lib. bdg. : 24.00
1. Donizetti, Gaetano, 1797-1848. 2. Composers—Biography. 3. Opera—Italy. 4. Opera—France—Paris. 5. Opera—Austria—Vienna. I. Title. BIP

Donne, John, 1572-1631.

BALD, Robert Cecil, 821'.3 B 1901-
John Donne, a life [by] R. C. Bald. New York, Oxford University Press, 1970. x, [2], 627 p. illus., facsims., ports. 22 cm. Bibliography: p. [xi]-[xii] [PR2248.B35 1970b] 71-83007 15.00
1. Donne, John, 1572-1631. I. Title.

DARK, Sidney, 1874- 283'.0922 1947.
Five Deans: John Colet, John Donne, Jonathan Swift, Arthur Penrhyn Stanley, William Ralph Inge. Port Washington, N.Y., Kennikat Press [1969] 255 p. 21 cm. (Essay and general literature index reprint series) Reprint of the 1928 ed. [BX5197.D25 1969] 70-86011
1. Colet, John, 1467?-1519. 2. Donne, John, 1573-1631. 3. Swift, Jonathan, 1667-1745. 4. Stanley, Arthur Penrhyn, 1815-1881. 5. Inge, William Ralph, 1860-1954. I. Title.

JESSOPP, Augustus, 1823- 821'.3 B 1914.
John Donne, sometime dean of St. Paul's A.D. 1621-1631. New York, Haskell House Publishers, 1972. xi, 239 p. illus. 23 cm. [PR2248.J4 1972] 71-39284 ISBN 0-8383-1395-7
1. Donne, John, 1572-1631.

JESSOPP, Augustus, 1823- 821'.3 B 1914.
John Donne, sometime dean of St. Paul's, A.D. 1621-1631. Freeport, N.Y., Books for Libraries Press [1973] p. Reprint of the 1897 ed., issued in series: Leaders of religion. [PR2248.J4 1973] 72-10752 ISBN 0-8369-7114-0
1. Donne, John, 1572-1631. I. Series: Leaders of religion.

LE COMTE, Edward Semple, 928.2 1916-
Grace to a witty sinner: a life of Donne [by] Edward Le Comte. New York, Walker [1965] 307 p. 21 cm. Bibliography: p. [285]-294. [PR2248.L39] 64-22092
1. Donne, John, 1572-1631. I. Title.

Donne, John, 1572-1631—Biography.

PARKER, Derek. 821'.3 B
John Donne and his world / Derek Parker. London : Thames and Hudson, c1975. 127 p. : ill. ; 24 cm. Bibliography: p. 117. [PR2248.P27] 75-325698 ISBN 0-500-13049-3 : 11.25
1. Donne, John, 1572-1631—Biography. I. Title.
Distributed by Transatlantic Arts. BIP

Donne, John, 1604-1662—Correspondence.

DONNE, John, 1572-1631. 821'.3 B
Letters to severall persons of honour (1651) / John Donne ; a facsimile reproduction with an introd. by M. Thomas Hester. Delmar, N.Y. : Scholars' Facsimiles & Reprints, 1977. xxii, 318 p. : port. ; 22 cm. Reprint of the 1651 ed. printed by J. Flescher for R. Marriot, London. Includes bibliographical references. [PR2248.A4 1977] 77-10078 ISBN 0-8201-1296-8 lib.bdg. : 25.00
1. Donne, John, 1604-1662—Correspondence. 2. Poets, English—Early modern, 1500-1700—Correspondence. I. Title.

Donnelly, Dan, 1786-1820.

MYLER, Patrick. 796.8'3'0924 B
Regency rogue : Dan Donnelly, his life and legends / Patrick Myler. [Dublin] : O'Brien, [1976] 168 p. : ill. ; 22 cm. Includes index. Bibliography: p. 160-161. [GV1132.D57M94] 77-359586 ISBN 0-905140-06-0 : £4.50
1. Donnelly, Dan, 1786-1820. 2. Boxers (Sports)—Ireland—Biography. I. Title. BIP

Donnelly, Ignatius, 1831-1991.

RIDGE, Martin. 928.1
Ignatius Donnelly; the portrait of a politician. [Chicago] University of Chicago Press [1962] 427p. illus. 25cm. Includes bibliography. [E664.D68R5] 62-19937
1. Donnelly, Ignatius, 1831-1991. I. Title.

Donnelly, Joseph W.,

DONNELLY, Joseph W., 1899- 133.9
Diary of a psychic; the anecdotes and personal experiences in the development of extra sensory perception (E.S.P.), by Joseph W. Donnelly. [Hollywood, Fla., Graphic Press] c1966. 60 p. 28 cm. Caption title. [BF1027.D65A3] 75-17817 2.50
I. Title.

Doods, Johhny, 1892-1940.

LAMBERT, George Edmund. v. 12
Johnny Dodds. New York, A.S. Barnes [1961] 2 p. l., 88 p. ports. 21 cm. (Kings of jazz) A perpetua book, P-4053. "Johnny Dodds recommended records": p. 79-88. 63-31670
1. Doods, Johhny, 1892-1940. I. Title. II. Series. BIP

Dooley, Thomas Anthony, 1927-1961.

*DOLEY, Thomas Anthony, 926.1 M.D., 1927-1961
Doctor Tom Dooley, my story. New rev. ed. [New York] New Amer. Lib. [1964, c.1956-1962] 128p. illus., map. 18cm. (Signet bk. D2555) .50 pap.,
I. Title.

DOOLEY, Agnes (Wise) 926.1
Promises to keep; the life of Doctor Thomas A. Dooley. New York, Farrar [c.1961, 1962] 272p. illus. 22cm. 61-13680 4.95
1. Dooley, Thomas Anthony, 1927-1961. I. Title.

DOOLEY, Thomas A., M.D. 926.1
Doctor Tom Dooley, my story. New York, Popular Lib. [1961, c.1956-1960] 127p. (Popular giant, G555) .35 pap.,
I. Title.

DOOLEY, Thomas A. 926.1
Doctor Tom Dooley, my story. New York, Ariel Books [dist. Farrar, Straus & Cudahy] [c.1960] 151p. illus., map 22cm. 60-9734 2.95 bds.,
I. Title.

GALLAGHER, Teresa 610.924
Give joy to my youth; a memoir of Dr. Tom Dooley. New York Farrar [c.1965] xvii, 238p. illus., ports. 22cm. [R154.D634G3] 65-26571 4.95
1. Dooley, Thomas Anthony, 1927-1961. I. Title. BIP

MONAHAN, James, 1904- ed. 926.1
Before I sleep; the last days of Dr. Tom Dooley. New York, Farrar, Straus and Cudahy [1961] 275 p. 22 cm. [R154.D634M6] 62-8612
1. Dooley, Thomas Anthony, 1927-1961. I. Title.

O'BRIEN, Mary Celine 610.924
I charge each of you; the story of Dr. Thomas A. Dooley [by] Mary Celine O'Brien. Illus. by Sister Mary Irene. Valatie, N. Y., Holy Cross Pr. [1966] 103p. illus., port. 23cm. [R154.D634O2] 66-7697 2.95
1. Dooley, Thomas Anthony, 1927-1961. I. Title.

Dooley, Thomas Anthony, 1927-1961—Juvenile literature.

MORRIS, Terry, 1914- 920
Doctor America; the story of Tom Dooley. Illus. by Richard Lewis. New York, Hawthorn [c.1963] 187p. illus. (pt. col.) col. map. 22cm. (Credo bks. [11]) Bibl. 63-15101 2.95
1. Dooley, Thomas Anthony, 1927-1961—Juvenile literature. I. Title.

Dooley, Thomas Anthony, 1927-1961 — Juvenile literature.

MORRIS, Terry, 1914- j92
Doctor America; the story of Tom Dooley. Illustrated by Richard Lewis. New York, Hawthorn Books [1963] 187 p. illus. (part col.) col. map. 22 cm. (Credo books [11])

Bibliography: p. 187. [R154.D634M63] 63-15101
1. Dooley, Thomas Anthony, 1927-1961 — Juvenile literature. I. Title.

Doolin, Bill, 1858-1896.

HANES, Bailey C. 364.1'0924 B
Bill Doolin, outlaw O.T. [by] Bailey C. Hanes. With an introd. by Ramon F. Adams. [1st ed.] Norman, University of Oklahoma Press [1968] xxii, 207 p. illus. 19 cm. (The Western frontier library) Bibliography: p. 201-207. [HV6452.O5D6] 68-15673
1. Doolin, Bill, 1858-1896. 2. Outlaws.

Doolittle, James Harold, 1896-

GLINES, Carroll V., 1920- 629.13'092'4 B
Jimmy Doolittle: daredevil aviator and scientist [by] Carroll V. Glines. New York, Macmillan [1972] vii, 183 p. illus. 24 cm. (Air Force Academy series) [TL540.D62G55] 72-83761 5.95
1. Doolittle, James Harold, 1896- I. Title.

REYNOLDS, Quentin James, 1902-1965. 629.13'092'4 B
The amazing Mr. Doolittle; a biography of Lieutenant General James H. Doolittle. [New York] Arno Press [1972, c1953] 313 p. 22 cm. (Literature and history of aviation) [TL540.D62R4 1972] 71-169434 ISBN 0-405-03778-3
1. Doolittle, James Harold, 1896- I. Title. II. Series. **BIP**

THOMAS, Lowell Jackson, 1892- 629.13'092'4 B
Doolittle : a biography / Lowell Thomas and Edward Jablonski. 1st ed. Garden City, N.Y. : Doubleday, 1976. xvi, 368 p., [16] leaves of plates : ill. ; 22 cm. Includes index. Bibliography: p. [350]-351. [UG626.2.D66T46] 75-21247 ISBN 0-385-06495-0 : 8.95
1. Doolittle, James Harold, 1896- I. Jablonski, Edward, joint author.

Dorchester Abbey.

STEDMAN, Edith Gratia. 914.25'72
A Yankee in an English village, [by] Edith G. Stedman. Dorchester-on-Thames (Dorchester-on-Thames, Oxon), Dorchester Abbey Museum, 1971. [11], 84 p. 23 cm. [DA690.D63S83] 73-153714 ISBN 0-9502114-0-0 £1.00
1. Dorchester Abbey. 2. Stedman, Edith Gratia. 3. Dorchester, Eng. (Oxfordshire)—Description. I. Title.

Dorchester, Mass.—History.

CLAP, Roger, 1609-1691. 974.4'6 B
Memoirs of Roger Clap, 1630. Freeport, N.Y., Books for Libraries Press [1971] xvi, 62 p. 23 cm. (Collections of the Dorchester Antiquarian and Historical Society, no. 1) "First published 1843." [F74.D5C4815 1971] 73-150176 ISBN 0-8369-5869-3
1. Dorchester, Mass.—History. 2. New England—History—Colonial period, ca. 1600-1775. I. Title. II. Series: Dorchester Antiquarian and Historical Society, Dorchester, Mass. Collections, no. 1

Dore, Gustave, 1832-1883.

GOSLING, Nigel. 759.4
Gustave Dore. New York, Praeger [1974, c1973] 112 p. illus. 29 cm. Includes bibliographical references. [ND553.D7G67 1974] 73-13525 12.50
1. Dore, Gustave, 1832-1883.

JERROLD, Blanchard, 1826-1884. 759.4 B
Life of Gustave Dore. With one hundred and thirty-eight illus. from original drawings by Dore. London, W. H. Allen, 1891. Detroit, Singing Tree Press, 1969. vi, 415 p. illus., port. 22 cm. [NC248.D6J4 1969] 69-17492
1. Dore, Gustave, 1832-1883. I. Title. **BIP**

Dorn family.

MARTIN, Ethel Dorn, 1903- 929.2'09771
The life of Peter and Katharine Dorn. [Maryville, Tenn.] Brazos [1968] 144 p. illus., ports. 23 cm. [CS71.D712 1968] 68-3937
1. Dorn family. I. Title.

Dorr, Thomas Wilson, 1805-1854.

KING, Dan, 1791-1864. 974.5'03'0924
The life and times of Thomas Wilson Dorr, with outlines of the political history of Rhode Island. Freeport, N.Y., Books for Libraries Press [1969] 368 p. port. 23 cm. (Select bibliographies reprint series) Reprint of the 1859 ed. [F83.4.K52 1969] 74-95071
1. Dorr, Thomas Wilson, 1805-1854. 2. Dorr Rebellion, 1842. I. Title.

Dorris, Jonathan Truman,

DORRIS, Jonathan Truman, 1883- 923.773
An Illini-bluegrass schoolmaster; seventy-five years in the schoolroom, 1889-1964. Richmond, Ky., Eastern Progress, 1964. 239p. illus., ports. 24cm. 64-64352 4.75
I. Title.

Dorset, Charles Sackville, 6th Earl of, 1643-1706.

HARRIS, Brice. 821'.4 B
Charles Sackville, sixth Earl of Dorset, patron and poet of the restoration. New York, Lemma Pub. Corp., 1972. 269 p. port. 24 cm. Reprint of the 1940 ed., which was issued as no. 3-4 of Illinois studies in language and literature, v. 26. Bibliography: p. 247-251. [PR3409.D75Z6 1972] 70-180774 ISBN 0-87696-027-1 12.50
1. Dorset, Charles Sackville, 6th Earl of, 1643-1706. I. Series: Illinois. University. Illinois studies in language and literature, v. 26, no. 3-4

Dorsett, Tony.

MUSICK, Phil. 796.33'2'0924 B
The Tony Dorsett story / Phil Musick. Short Hills, N.J. : R. Enslow Publishers, [1977] p. cm. [GV939.D67M87] 77-17558 ISBN 0-89490-011-0 lib bdg. : 5.98. ISBN 0-89490-010-2 pbk. : 3.45
1. Dorsett, Tony. 2. Football players—United States—Biography. I. Title. **BIP**

Dorsett, Tony—Juvenile literature.

BURCHARD, S. H. 796.33'2'0924 B
Tony Dorsett / S. H. Burchard. 1st ed. New York : Harcourt Brace Jovanovich, c1978. p. cm. (Sports star) [GV938.D67B87] 78-52808 ISBN 0-15-278015-7 : 4.95 ISBN 0-15-684792-2 pbk. : 1.95
1. Dorsett, Tony—Juvenile literature. 2. Football players—United States—Biography—Juvenile literature. I. Title.

CONRAD, Dick. 796.33'2'0924 B
Tony Dorsett, from Heisman to Super Bowl in one year / by Dick Conrad. Chicago : Childrens Press, [1979] p. cm. (Sports stars) A biography of the Heisman Trophy winner who was named the 1977 NFL Rookie of the Year. [GV939.D67C66] 92 78-11378 ISBN 0-516-04305-6 lib.bdg. : 6.00
1. Dorsett, Tony—Juvenile literature. 2. Football players—United States—Biography. I. Title. II. Series.

Dorsey, Stephen Wallace, 1842-1916.

CAPERTON, Thomas J. 973.8'092'4 B
Rogue : being an account of the life and high times of Stephen W. Dorsey, United States Senator and New Mexico cattle baron / by Thomas J. Caperton. 1st ed. Sante Fe : Museum of New Mexico Press, c1978. 56 p. : ill. ; 28 cm. Bibliography: p. 55. [E664.D7C36] 78-72863 ISBN 0-89013-114-7 : 3.95
1. Dorsey, Stephen Wallace, 1842-1916. 2. United States. Congress. Senate—Biography. 3. Legislators—United States—Biography. 4. Ranch life—New Mexico. 5. Dorsey Mansion State Monument, N.M. I. Title.

TURNER, Don. 973.8'0924 B
The life and castle of Stephen W. Dorsey; the hard-working Vermont boy who became a Senator from Arkansas, a cattle baron in New Mexico and the key figure in a national political scandal. Amarillo, Tex., Humbug Gulch Press [1967] 32 p. illus., port. 16 cm. "500 copies." [E664.D7T8] 77-298851
1. Dorsey, Stephen Wallace, 1842-1916. I. Title.

Dorsey, Tommy, 1905-1956.

SANFORD, Herb. 785.4'1'0924 B
Tommy and Jimmy; the Dorsey years. New Rochelle, N.Y., Arlington House [1972] 305 p. illus. 24 cm. [ML422.D67S2] 72-78483 ISBN 0-87000-146-9 8.95
1. Dorsey, Tommy, 1905-1956. 2. Dorsey, Jimmy, 1904-1957. I. Title. **BIP**

Dortzbach, Debbie.

DORTZBACH, Karl. 364.1'54'0924 B
Kidnapped / Karl and Debbie Dortzbach. 1st ed. New York : Harper & Row, [1975] 177 p. : ill. ; 21 cm. [HV6604.E82D673 1975] 74-25708 ISBN 0-06-061975-9 : 5.95
1. Dortzbach, Debbie. 2. Kidnapping—Ethiopia—Case studies. I. Dortzbach, Debbie, joint author. II. Title. **BIP**

Dos Passos, John, 1896-1970.

LANDSBERG, Melvin. 813'.5'2 B
Dos Passos' path to U.S.A.; a political biography, 1912-1936. Boulder, Colorado, Associated University Press, 1972. 292 p. illus. 24 cm. [PS3507.O743Z66] 72-75880 ISBN 0-87081-018-9 10.00
1. Dos Passos, John, 1896-1970. I. Title. **BIP**

Dos Passos, John, 1896-1970—Biography—Ancestry.

ROGERS, Francis Millet. 813'.5'2 B
The Portuguese heritage of John Dos Passos / Francis M. Rogers. Boston : Portuguese Continental Union of the United States of America, 1976. 53 p. : port ; 22 cm. "List of books by John Dos Passos": p. 48-50. [PS3507.O743Z78] 76-15863
1. Dos Passos, John, 1896-1970—Biography—Ancestry. 2. Dos Passos, John, 1896-1970—Knowledge—Portugal. 3. Authors, American—20th century—Biography. I. Title.

Dos Passos, John, 1896-1970—Correspondence.

DOS Passos, John, 1896-1970. 813'.5'2 B
The fourteenth chronicle; letters and diaries of John Dos Passos. Edited and with a biographical narrative by Townsend Ludington. Boston, Gambit, 1973. xvi, 662 p. illus. 25 cm. Includes bibliographical references. [PS3507.O743Z53 1973] 72-94006 ISBN 0-87645-073-7 15.00
1. Dos Passos, John, 1896-1970—Correspondence. 2. Dos Passos, John, 1896-1970—Biography. I. Title.

Doss, Desmond Thomas, 1919-

HERNDON, Booton. 940.548'1'73
The unlikeliest hero; the story of Desmond T. Doss, conscientious objector, who won his nation's highest military honor. Mountain View, Calif., Pacific Press Pub. Association [1967] 199 p. illus., ports. 23 cm. [D811.H473] 67-26302
1. Doss, Desmond Thomas, 1919- I. Title.

Dossick, Philip.

DOSSICK, Philip. 362.1'9'7412 B
Transplant : a family chronicle / Philip Dossick. New York : Viking Press, 1978. xiv, 271 p., [8] leaves of plates : ill. ; 22 cm. [RD598.D62 1978] 77-27290 ISBN 0-670-72427-0 : 10.95
1. Dossick, Philip. 2. Heart—Transplantation—Biography. I. Title.

Dost Muhammad, Amir of Afghanistan, 1793-1863.

MOHANA Lala, Munshi, 1812-1877. 958.1'03'0924 B
Life of the Amir Dost Mohammed Khan of Kabul / by Mohan Lal ; with a new introd. by Nancy Hatch Dupree. Karachi : Oxford University Press, 1978- v. : ill. ; 23 cm. (Oxford in Asia historical reprints from Pakistan) Reprint of 1846 ed. published by Longman, Brown, Green, London. [DS363.M6 1978] 79-103709 ISBN 0-19-577237-7 : 39.95
1. Dost Muhammad, Amir of Afghanistan, 1793-1863. 2. Afghanistan—History. 3. Eastern question (Central Asia) 4. Afghanistan—Kings and rulers—Biography. I. Title. II. Series.
Available from Oxford, NYC

Doster, Frank, 1847-1933.

BRODHEAD, Michael J. 347.99'24 B
Persevering populist; the life of Frank Doster, by Michael J. Brodhead. Reno, University of Nevada Press, 1969. xi, 196 p. illus., ports. 22 cm. Includes bibliographical references. [KF373.D6B7] 69-20037 5.00
1. Doster, Frank, 1847-1933. I. Title.

Dostoevskii, Fedor Mikhailovich, 1821-1881.

CARR, Edward Hallett, 1892- 928.917
Dostoevsky, 1821-1881. New York, Barnes & Noble [1963, c.1962] 256p. 19cm. (Unwin bks., U-514) 1.50 pap.,
1. Dostoevskii, Fedor Mikhailovich, 1821-1881. I. Title.

DOSTOEVSKAIA, Anna Grigor'evna Snitkina, 1846-1918. 891.7'3'3 B
Dostoevsky : reminiscences / by Anna Dostoevsky ; translated and edited by Beatrice Stillman ; with an introd. by Helen Muchnic. New York : Liveright, [1975] xxxii, 448 p., [6] leaves of plates : ill. ; 21 cm. Translation of Vospominaniia. Includes index. Bibliography: p. [439]-440. [PG3328.D628513] 75-14197 ISBN 0-87140-592-X : 12.50
1. Dostoevskii, Fedor Mikhailovich, 1821-1881. **BIP**

DOSTOEVSKAIA, Liubov' Fedorovna, 1869- 891.7'3'3 B
Fyodor Dostoyevsky; a study, by Aimee Dostoyevsky. New York, Haskell House, 1972. x, 294 p. 23 cm. Reprint of the 1922 ed. [PG3328.D635 1972] 72-1329 ISBN 0-8383-1438-4 11.95
1. Dostoevskii, Fedor Mikhailovich, 1821-1881.

DOSTOEVSKII, Fedor Mikhailovich, 1821-1881. 891.7'3'3 B
Dostoevsky: letters and reminiscences. Translated from the Russian by S. S. Koteliansky and J. Middleton Murry. Freeport, N.Y., Books for Libraries Press [1971] 286 p. facsim., port. 23 cm. Reprint of the 1923 ed. "Reminiscences of Dostoevsky, by his wife": p. [97]-153. [PG3328.A3K6 1971] 77-160967 ISBN 0-8369-5835-7
I. Dostoevskaia, Anna Grigor'evna (Snitkina) 1846-1918. II. Title.

DOSTOEVSKII, Fedor Mikhailovich, 1821-1881. 891.7'3'3 B
The letters of Dostoevsky to his wife / translated from the Russian by Elizabeth Hill and Doris Mudie ; with an introd. by Prince D. S. Mirsky. New York : Haskell House Publishers, [1976] p. cm. Translation of Pis'ma F. M. Dostoevskogo k zhene. Reprint of the 1930 ed. published by Constable, London. Includes bibliographical references and index. [PG3328.A5D53 1976] 76-177 ISBN 0-8383-1875-4 lib.bdg. : 18.95
1. Dostoeuskii, Fedor Mikhailovich, 1821-1881—Correspondence. 2. Dostoevskaia,

Anna Grigor'evna Snitkina, 1846-1918. I. Title.

DOSTOEVSKII, Fedor 928.917
Mikhailovich, 1821-1881.
Letters of Fyodor Michailovitch Dostoevsky. Tr. by Ethel Colburn Mayne. Introd. by Avrahm Yarmolinsky. New York, McGraw [1964, c.1961] xxiv, 344p. illus., ports. 21cm. 2.95 pap.,
I. Title.

DOSTOEVSKII, Fedor 928.917
Mikhailovich, 1821-1881.
Letters of Fyodor Michailovitch Dostoevsky to his family and friends. Translated by Ethel Colburn Mayne. With an introd. by Avrahm Yarmolinsky. New York, Horizon Press [1961] xxiv, 344 p. illus., ports. 24 cm. [PG3328.A3M3 1961] 61-8505

DOSTOEVSKII, Fedor 891.7'3'3 B
Mikhailovich, 1821-1881.
New Dostoevsky letters. Translated from the Russian by S. S. Koteliansky. New York, Haskell House Publishers, 1974. 102 p. port. 19 cm. Reprint of the 1929 ed., published by Mandrake Press, London. [PG3328.A3K62 1974] 73-20335 ISBN 0-8383 1824-X 9.95 (lib. bdg.).
1. Dostoevskii, Fedor Mikhailovich, 1821-1881. I. Koteliansky, Samuel Solomonovitch, 1880- tr. II. Title.

FANGER, Donald, ed. 891.783
O Dostoevskom; stat'i [by] P. M. Bitsilli [others. Ed.,] introd., by Donald Fanger. Providence, Brown Univ. Pr., 1966. viii, 229p. 21cm. (Brown Univ. Slavic reprint ser., 4) Text in Russian [PG3328.Z6F24] 66-23779 4.00 pap.,
1. Dostoevskii, Fedor Mikhailovich, 1821-1881. I. Bitsilli, Petr Mikhailovich. II. Title. III. Series.

HINGLEY, Ronald. 891.7'3'3 B
Dostoyevsky, his life and work / Ronald Hingley. New York : Charles Scribner's Sons, c1978. 222p. : ill. ; 24 cm. Includes indexes. Bibliography: p. 213-215. [PG3328.H54 1978b] 78-7162 ISBN 0-684-15916-3 : 14.95
1. Dostoevskii, Fedor Mikhailovich, 1821-1881. 2. Novelists, Russian—19th century—Biography. I. Title.

LLOYD, John Arthur 891.7'3'3 B
Thomas, 1870-1956.
Fyodor Dostoevsky. New York, Cooper Square Publishers, 1971 [c1947] 324 p. 22 cm. Includes bibliographical references. [PG3328.L5 1971] 78-164532 ISBN 0-8154-0401-8 8.50
1. Dostoevskii, Fedor Mikhailovich, 1821-1881.

LLOYD, John Arthur 891.7'3'3
Thomas, 1870-1956.
Fyodor Dostoevsky / by J. A. T. Lloyd. New York : Haskell House Publishers, [1976] p. cm. Reprint of the 1946 ed. published by Eyre & Spottiswoode, London. Bibliography: p. [PG3328.L5 1976] 75-30857 ISBN 0-8383-2099-6 lib.bdg. : 11.95
1. Dostoevskii, Fedor Mikhailovich, 1821-1881. I. Title. BIP

MACKIEWICZ, 891.7'3'3 B
Stanislaw, 1896-1966.
Dostoyevsky. London, Orbis. New York, Haskell House Publishers, 1974. 203 p. 22 cm. Reprint of the 1948 ed. published by Orbis, London. [PG3328.M3 1974] 73-21635 ISBN 0-8383-1818-5
1. Dostoevskii, Fedor Mikhailovich, 1821-1881.

MAGARSHACK, David. 928.917
Dostoevsky. [1st American ed.] New York, Harcourt, Brace & World [1963, c1962] 399 p. illus. 24 cm. Includes bibliography. [PG3328.M35 1963] 63-8102
1. Dostoevskii, Fedor Mikhailovich, 1821-1881.

MEIER-GRAEFE, Julius, 891.7'3'3
1867-1935.
Dostoevsky, the man and his work. Translated by Herbert H. Marks. New York, Haskell House, 1972. vii, 406 p. illus. 23 cm. Reprint of the 1928 ed. Translation of Dostojewski, der Dichter. Bibliography: p. 405-406. [PG3328.M413 1972] 77-38843 ISBN 0-8383-1390-6 14.95
1. Dostoevskii, Fedor Mikhailovich, 1821-1881. I. Title. BIP

MOCHUL'SKII, 891.7'3'3
Konstantin Vasil'evich, 1892-1948.
Dostoevsky: his life and work. Translated, with an introd., by Michael A. Minihan. [Princeton, N.J.] Princeton University Press, 1967. xxii, 687 p. port. 25 cm. Translated from the Russian. (romanized: Dostoevskii; zhizn' i tvorchestvo) Bibliographical footnotes. [PG3328.M613] 65-10833
1. Dostoevskii, Fedor Mikhailovich, 1821-1881. BIP

PAYNE, Pierre Stephen 891.733
Robert, 1911-
Dostoyevsky: a human portrait, [by] Robert Payne. New York, Knopf, 1961 [c.1958, 1961] 404p. illus. Bibl. 60-53443 5.75
1. Dostoevskii, Fedor Mikhailovich, 1821-1881. I. Title.

SIMMONS, Ernest Joseph. v. 12
1903-
Dostoevsky; the making of a novelist. New York, Vintage Books [1962, c1940] 395 p. (Vintage Russian library. V-736) Includes bibliography. 63-74003
1. Dostoevskii, Fedor Mikhailovich, 1821-1881. I. Title.

SIMMONS, Ernest Joseph, 891.7'3'3
1903-
Feodor Dostoevsky, by Ernest J. Simmons. New York, Columbia University Press, 1969. 48 p. 21 cm. (Columbia essays on modern writers, no. 40) Bibliography: p. 46-48. [PG3328.S53] 77-76252 1.00
1. Dostoevskii, Fedor Mikhailovich, 1821-1881. I. Title. II. Series. BIP

SLONIM, Mark L'vovich. 928.917
Three loves of Dostoevsky. New York, Rinehart [1955] 300 p. 22 cm. [PG3328.S552] 55-10526
1. Dostoevskii, Fedor Mikhailovich, 1821-1881. I. Title.

SOLOV'EV, Evgenii 891.7'3'3 B
Andreevich, 1863-1905,
Dostoievsky, his life and literary activity; a biographical sketch by Evgenii Soloviev. Translated from the Russian by C. J. Hogarth. [Folcroft, Pa.] Folcroft Library Editions, 1973, [i.e.1975] 247 p. 24 cm. Reprint of the 1916 ed. published by G. Allen & Unwin, London; and Macmillan Co., New York. [PG3328.S653 1973] 72-13517 20.00
1. Dostoevskii, Fedor Mikhailovich, 1821-1881.

THURNEYSEN, Eduard, 1888- 891.733
Dostoevsky. Tr. by Keith R. Crim. Richmond, Va., Knox [c.1964] 84p. 21cm. Bibl. 64-12264 1.50 pap.,
1. Dostoevskii, Fedor Mikhailovich, 1821-1881. I. Title.

THURNEYSEN, Eduard, 1888- 891.733
Dostoevsky. Translated by Keith R. Crim. Richmond, John Knox Press [1964] 84 p. 21 cm. Bibliographical footnotes. [PG3328.Z6T513] 64-12264
1. Dostoevskh, Fedor Mikhalovich, I. Title.

YARMOLINSKY, Avrahm, 928.917
1890-
Dostoevsky, his life and art. [2d ed., completely rev. and enl.] New York, Criterion Books [1957] 434 p. illus. 22 cm. [PG3328.Y3 1957] 56-6213
1. Dostoevskii, Fedor Mikhailovich, 1821-1881.

YARMOLINSKY, Avrahm, 1890- v. 12
Dostoevsky, his life and art. [2d ed., completely rev. and enl.] New Jersey, S. G. Phillips [1965, c1957] 434 p. illus. 22 cm.
1. Dostoevskii, Fedor Mikhailovich, 1821-1881. I. Title.

YARMOLINSKY, Avrahm, 928.917
1890-
Dostoevsky, his life and art. [2d ed., completely rev. and enl.] New York,Criterion Books [1957] 434 p. illus. 22 cm. [PG3328.Y 1957] 56-6213
1. Dostoevskii, Fedor Mikhailovich, 1821-1881. I. Title.

Dostoevskii, Fedor Mikhailovich, 1821-1881—Biography.

ABRAHAM, Gerald 891.7'3'3 B
Ernest Heal, 1904-
Dostoevsky, by Gerald Abraham. New York, Haskell House, 1974. 139, [2] p. 20 cm. Reprint of the 1936 ed. published by Duckworth, London, which was issued as no. 69 of Great lives. Bibliography: p. [141] [PG3328.A64 1974] 74-6398 ISBN 0-8383-1869-X
1. Dostoevskii, Fedor Mikhailovich, 1821-1881—Biography.

CARR, Edward Hallett, 891.7'3'3 B
1892-
Dostoevsky (1821-1881) : a new biography / by Edward Hallett Carr; with a pref. by D.s. Mirsky. Folcroft, Pa. : Folcroft Library Editions, 1977. 331 p. ; 23 cm. Reprint of the 1931 ed. published by G. Allen & Unwin, London. Includes index. [PG3328.C27 1977] 77-25843 ISBN 0-8414-1104-2 lib. bdg. : 30.00
1. Dostoevskii, Fedor Mikhailovich, 1821-1881—Biography. 2. Novelists, Russian—19th century—Biography. I. Title. BIP

GROSSMAN, Leonid 891.7'3'3 B
Petrovich, 1888-1965.
Dostoevsky : a biography / Leonid Grossman ; translated by Mary Mackler. Indianapolis : Bobbs-Merrill Co., [1975] xxii, 647 p. ; 24 cm. Translation of Dostoevskii. Bibliography: p. [609]-621. [PG3328.G6613 1975] 75-313948 ISBN 0-672-51912-7 : 12.50
1. Dostoevskii, Fedor Mikhailovich, 1821-1881—Biography.

MAGARSHACK, David. 891.7'3'3 B
Dostoevsky / by David Magarshack. Westport, Conn. : Greenwood Press, 1975, c1962. p. cm. Reprint of the ed. published by Harcourt, Brace & World, New York. Includes index. Bibliography: p. [PG3328.M35 1975] 75-29446 ISBN 0-8371-8403-7 lib.bdg. : 21.00
1. Dostoevskii, Fedor Mikhailovich, 1821-1881—Biography.

Dostoevskii, Fedor Mikhailovich, 1821-1881—Correspondence.

COULSON, Jessie 891.7'3'3 B
Senior, 1903-
Dostoevsky : a self-portrait / by Jessie Coulson. Westport, Conn. : Greenwood Press, 1975, c1962. p. cm. Includes selections from the letters of Dostoevsky, translated by the author. Reprint of the ed. published by Oxford University Press, London, New York. Includes index. [PG3328.A3C6 1975] 75-26212 ISBN 0-8371-8405-3 lib.bdg. : 15.75
1. Dostoevskii, Fedor Mikhailovich, 1821-1881—Correspondence. I. Dostoevskii, Fedor Mikhailovich, 1821 1881.

Dostoevskii, Fedor Mikhailovich, 1821-1881—Religion and ethics.

MEREZHKOVSKII, 891.7'3'3
Dmitrii Sergeevich, 1865-1941.
Dostoievski. From the Russian of Merejkowski, by G. A. Mounsey. New York, Haskell House Publishers, 1974. 67 p. 19 cm. Reprint of the 1912? ed., published by A. Moring, London. [PG3328.Z7R426 1974] 73-21712 ISBN 0-8383-1816-9 8.95
1. Dostoevskii, Fedor Mikhailovich, 1821-1881—Religion and ethics.

Doty, James Duane, 1799-1865.

SMITH, Alice Elizabeth, 923.273
1896-
James Duane Doty, frintier promoter. Madison, State Historical Society of Wisconsin [1954] 472p. illus. 24cm. Includes bibliography. [E340.D74S5] 55-171
1. Doty, James Duane, 1799-1865. I. Title.

Doud family.

SCHAAF, James 973.921'092'4 B
Edward.
Mamie Doud Eisenhower and her chicken farmer cousin. [Whitehouse Station, N.J., Printed by Wilkie Print., 1974] 75 p. illus. 24 cm. [E837.E4S32] 74-157039
1. Eisenhower, Mamie (Doud) 1896- 2. Schaaf, James Edward. 3. Doud family. 4. Schaaf family. I. Title.

Dougherty, Blanford Barnard, 1870-1957.

LANIER, Ruby J. 370'.92'4 B
Blanford Barnard Dougherty, mountain educator [by] Ruby J. Lanier. Durham, N.C., Duke University Press, 1974. ix, 282 p. 25 cm. Bibliography: p. [261]-274. [LA2317.D6182L36] 73-89810 ISBN 0-8223-0315-9 12.00
1. Dougherty, Blanford Barnard, 1870-1957. I. Title.

Doughty, Charles Montagu, 1843-1926.

HOGARTH, David 821'.9'12 B
George, 1862-1927.
The life of Charles M. Doughty. Garden City, N.Y., Doubleday, Doran, 1929. St. Clair Shores, Mich., Scholarly Press, 1972. viii, 216 p. illus. 22 cm. Includes bibliographical references. [PR6007.O85Z7 1972] 70-131744 ISBN 0-403-00631-7
1. Doughty, Charles Montagu, 1843-1926. BIP

Douglas, Alfred Bruce,

DOUGLAS, Alfred 821'.9'12 B
Bruce, Lord, 1870-1945.
The autobiography of Lord Alfred Douglas. London, M. Secker, 1929. St. Clair Shores, Mich., Scholarly Press, 1971. 340 p. 22 cm. [PR6007.O86Z5 1971] 71-144979 ISBN 0-403-00796-8
I. Title. BIP

DOUGLAS, Alfred 821'.9'12 B
Bruce, Lord, 1870-1945.
The autobiography of Lord Alfred Douglas. Freeport, N.Y., Books for Libraries Press [1970] xiv, 340 p. port. 23 cm. Reprint of the "new edition," first published 1931. [PR6007.O86Z5 1970] 76-124232

Douglas, David, 1799-1834.

MORWOOD, William. 581'.092'4 B
Traveler in a vanished landscape; the life and times of David Douglas. [1st ed.] New York, C. N. Potter; distributed by Crown Publishers [1973] 244 p. illus. 24 cm. Bibliography: p. 223-231. [QK31.D6M67] 72-80843 ISBN 0 517 50064-7 7.95
1. Douglas, David, 1798-1834. I. Title.

STOUTENBURG, Adrien. 925.8
Wild treasure; the story of David Douglas, by Adrien Stoutenburg and Laura Nelson Baker. New York, Scribner [1958] 216 p. 21 cm. [QK31.D6S74] 58-10637
1. Douglas, David, 1799-1834. I. Baker, Laura Nelson, 1911- joint author. II. Title.

YOUNG, Bob, 1916- 581.0924 B
Plant detective: David Douglas, by Bob and Jan Young. New York, Messner [1966] 189 p. 22 cm. [QK31.D6Y6] 66-7545
1. Douglas, David, 1799-1834. I. Young, Jan, 1919- joint author. II. Title.

Douglas, Gilean.

DOUGLAS, Gilean. 500.9'711
Silence is my homeland : life on the Teal River / Gilean Douglas. ; ill. by Stephanie Scott Brown. Harrisburg, Pa. : Stackpole Books, c1978. 160 p. : ill. ; 22 cm. [QH106.2.B8D68 1978] 78-2324 ISBN 0-8117-1521-3 : 8.95
1. Douglas, Gilean. 2. Natural history—British Columbia. 3. Outdoor life—British Columbia. 4. Naturalists—British Columbia—Biography. I. Title.

Douglas, Harriet, 1790-1872.

DAVIDSON, Angus, 1898- 920.7
Miss Douglas of New York; a biography. New York, Viking Press, 1953 [c1952] 255p. illus. 22cm. [CT275.D8674D3 1953] 53-5611

1. Douglas, Harriet, 1790-1872. I. Title.

Douglas, Henry Kyd, 1838-1903.

DOUGLAS, Henry Kyd, 1838-1903. 378.748'15
The Douglas diary; student days at Franklin and Marshall College, 1856-1858. Edited by Frederic Shriver Klein and John Howard Carrill. Illustrated by Florence Starr Taylor. Lancaster, Pa., Franklin and Marshall College, 1973. xxvi, 192 p. illus. 20 cm. [LD1871.F24D68 1973] 73-89382 ISBN 0-910626-00-6 7.95
1. Douglas, Henry Kyd, 1838-1903. 2. Franklin and Marshall College, Lancaster, Pa.—History. I. Title. BIP

Douglas, James, Sir, d. 1330.

DAVIS, I. M. 941.03'092'4 B
The Black Douglas. London, Routledge and K. Paul, 1974. vi, 184 p. geneal. table, map. 23 cm. Includes index. Bibliography: p. 177-178. [DA783.45.D68D38] 74-174696 ISBN 0-7100-7753-X
1. Douglas, James, Sir, d. 1330. 2. Scotland—History—Robert I, 1306-1329. I. Title.
Distributed by Routledge and K. Paul, Boston; 9.95 BIP

Douglas, James, Sir, 1803-1877—Juvenile literature.

GARDNER, Alison F. 971.1'02'0924 B
James Douglas / Alison F. Gardner. Don Mills, Ont. : Fitzhenry & Whiteside, c1976. 61, [1] p. : ill. ; 22 cm. (The Canadians) Bibliography: p. [62] [F1088.D737] 76-362319 ISBN 0-88902-222-4
1. Douglas, James, Sir, 1803-1877—Juvenile literature. I. Title. II. Series.

Douglas, Keith Castellain, 1920-1944—Biography.

GRAHAM, Desmond. 821'.9'12
Keith Douglas, 1920-1944; London, New York, Oxford University Press, 1974. xii, 295 p. illus. 24 cm. Bibliography: p. 259-[260] [PR6054.O836Z6] 74-174164 ISBN 0-19-211716-5 17.75
1. Douglas, Keith Castellain, 1920-1944—Biography.

GRAHAM, Desmond. 821'.9'12
Keith Douglas, 1920-1944; a biography. London, New York, Oxford University Press, 1974. xii, 295 p. illus. 24 cm. Bibliography: p. 259-[260] [PR6054.O836Z6] 74-174164 ISBN 0-19-211716-5 £5.50
1. Douglas, Keith Castellain, 1920-1944—Biography.

Douglas, Kirk, 1916-

MCBRIDE, Joseph. 791.43'028'0924
Kirk Douglas / by Joseph McBride. New York : Pyramid Publications, 1976. 159 p. : ill. ; 20 cm. (A Pyramid illustrated history of the movies) Includes index. Filmography: p. 148-154. [PN2287.D54M3] 77-152768 ISBN 0-515-04084-3 : 1.75
1. Douglas, Kirk, 1916- 2. Moving-picture actors and actresses—United States—Biography. BIP

Douglas, Lloyd Cassel, 1877-1951.

DAWSON, Virginia Douglas. 928.1
The shape of Sunday; an intimate biography of Lloyd C. Douglas, by Virginia Douglas Dawson and Betty Douglas Wilson. Boston, Houghton Mifflin, 1952. 372 p. illus. 22 cm. [PS3507.O7573Z6] 52-11451
1. Douglas, Lloyd Cassel, 1877-1951. I. Title.

Douglas, Lord Alfred Bruce, 1870-1945.

CROFT-COOKE, Rupert, 1903- 928.2
Bosie, Lord Alfred Douglas, his friends and enemies. Indianapolis, Bobbs [1964, c.1963] 414p. illus., ports. 22cm. Bibl. 64-15654 7.50
1. Douglas, Lord Alfred Bruce, 1870-1945. I. Title.

Douglas, Mike.

DOUGLAS, Mike. 791.45'092'4 B
Mike Douglas, my story. New York : Putnam, c1978. 320 p., [8] leaves of plates : ill. ; 22 cm. Includes index. [PN1992.4.D58A36 1978] 78-2694 10.00
1. Douglas, Mike. 2. Television personalities—United States—Biography. 3. Singers—United States—Biography. I. Title.

*HARRIS, Harry. 791.457
Mike Douglas. New York, Award Books [1976] 187 p. 18 cm. [PN1992] [B] 1.50 (pbk.)
1. Douglas, Mike. I. Title.

Douglas, Norman, 1868-1952.

LINDEMAN, Ralph D. 828.91209 B
Norman Douglas, by Ralph D. Lindeman. New York, Twayne Publishers [1965] 208 p. 21 cm. (Twayne's English authors series, 19) Bibliography: p. 197-200. [PR6007.O88Z75] 64-8327
1. Douglas, Norman, 1868-1952.

Douglas, Norman, 1868-1952—Biography.

HOLLOWAY, Mark, 1917- 828'.9'1209 B
Norman Douglas : a biography / Mark Holloway. London : Secker & Warburg, 1976. xvii, [3], 519 p., [8] leaves of plates : ill. ; 25 cm. Includes index. Bibliography: 19th prelim. page. [PR6007.O88Z68] 77-352850 ISBN 0-436-20075-9 : £7.90
1. Douglas, Norman, 1868-1952—Biography. 2. Authors, English—20th century—Biography.

TOMLINSON, Henry Major, 1873-1958. 828'.9'1209 B
Norman Douglas. [Folcroft, Pa.] Folcroft Library Editions, 1974. p. cm. Reprint of the 1931 ed. published by Chatto & Windus, London. [PR6007.O88Z8 1974b] 74-3395 ISBN 0-8414-8572-0 8.50 (lib. bdg.)
1. Douglas, Norman, 1868-1952—Biography. BIP

Douglas, Sholto,

DOUGLAS, Sholto, baron Douglas of Kirtleside, 1893- 358.400924
Combat and command; the story of an airman in two world wars, by Lord Douglas of Kirtleside with Robert Wright. New York, Simon and Schuster [1966] 806 p. illus., ports. 22 cm. [TL540.D66A3] 66-11063
I. Wright, Robert, 1912- II. Title.

Douglas, Stephen Arnold, 1813-1861.

CAPERS, Gerald Mortimer. 923.273
Stephen A. Douglas, defender of the Union. Edited by Oscar Handlin. [1st ed.] Boston, Little, Brown [1959] 239 p. 21 cm. (The Library of American biography) Includes bibliography. [E415.9.D73C28] 59-5277
1. Douglas, Stephen Arnold, 1813-1861.

JOHANNSEN, Robert Walter, 1925- 973.6'8'0924 B
Stephen A. Douglas [by] Robert W. Johannsen. New York, Oxford University Press, 1973. xii, 993 p. illus. 24 cm. Includes bibliographical references. [E415.9.D73J55] 72-92293 ISBN 0-19-501620-3 19.95
1. Douglas, Stephen Arnold, 1813-1861. I. Title. BIP

JOHNSON, Allen, 1870-1931. 973.68'0924 B
Stephen A. Douglas; a study in American politics. New York, Da Capo Press, 1970 [c1908] x, 503 p. 24 cm. (The American scene) (A Da Capo Press reprint series.) Includes bibliographical references. [E415.9.D73J6 1970] 77-98690
1. Douglas, Stephen Arnold, 1813-1861. BIP

WELLS, Damon. 973.6'8'0924 B
Stephen Douglas; the last years, 1857-1861. Austin, University of Texas Press [1971] xvi, 342 p. illus., ports. 24 cm. Based on the author's thesis, Rice University, 1968, with title: Man in motion; the last years of Stephen Douglas, 1857-1861. Bibliography: p. [313]-329. [E415.9.D73W4 1971] 73-149020 ISBN 0-292-70118-7 10.00
1. Douglas, Stephen Arnold, 1813-1861. BIP

Douglas, Stephen Arnold, 1813-1861— Juvenile literature.

NOLAN, Jeannette (Covert) 1896- 920
The little giant, Stephen A. Douglas. New York, Messner [c.1964] 191p. 22cm. Bibl. 64-11369 3.25;3.19 lib. ed.,
1. Douglas, Stephen Arnold, 1813-1861—Juvenile literature. I. Title. BIP

Douglas, William Orville, 1898-

DOUGLAS, William Orville, 1898- 347'.73'2634
Douglas of the Supreme Court; a selection of his opinions. Edited and with a biographical sketch by Vern Countryman. Westport, Conn., Greenwood Press [1973, c1959] 401 p. 22 cm. Reprint of the ed. published by Doubleday, Garden City, N.Y. [KF213.D6C6 1973] 73-719 ISBN 0-8371-6790-6
1. Douglas, William Orville, 1898- 2. Judicial opinions—United States. I. Title. BIP

Douglass, Frederick Wingfield, 1866-1949.

FATHER Douglass of Behala, by some of his friends. London, Oxford University Press, 1952. 171 p. illus. 21 cm. [BV3269.D63F3] 52-11983 922.354
1. Douglass, Frederick Wingfield, 1866-1949.

Douglass, Frederick, 1817?-1895.

CHESNUTT, Charles Waddell, 1858-1932. 973.8'0924 B
Frederick Douglas. Boston, Small, Maynard, 1899. New York, Johnson Reprint Corp. [1970] xix, 141 p. port. 17 cm. (The Beacon biographies of eminent Americans) (Series in American studies.) Bibliography: p. [136]-141. [E449.D752 1970] 72-19028
1. Douglass, Frederick, 1817?-1895. I. Title. II. Series.

DOUGLASS, Frederick, 1817?-1895. 973.8'0924 B
From slave to statesman: the life and times of Frederick Douglass, written by himself. Specially abridged by Glenn Munson. [New York] Noble and Noble [1972] 231 p. 18 cm. (A Falcon book) Abridgement of The life and times of Frederick Douglass, which was originally published in 1892 as an enlargement of the Author's autobiography: My bondage and my freedom. [E449.D7382 1972] 70-38825
1. Slavery in the United States—Anti-slavery movements. 2. Slavery in the United States—Maryland. I. Munson, Glenn. II. Title.

DOUGLASS, Frederick, 1817?-1895. 326'.0924 B
Life and times of Frederick Douglass. Edited and abridged by Genevieve S. Gray. Illustrated by Scott Duncan. New York, Grosset & Dunlap [1970] viii, 181 p. illus. 24 cm. Abridged ed. of the author's autobiography as enlarged from his: My bondage and my freedom. [E449.D7382] 79-86689 4.50
1. Slavery in the United States—Anti-slavery movements. 2. Slavery in the United States—Maryland. I. Gray, Genevieve S., ed. II. Title.

DOUGLASS, Frederick, 1817?-1895. 326'.0924 B
Life and times of Frederick Douglass. Adapted by Barbara Ritchie. New York, Crowell [1966] viii, 210 p. 21 cm. Shortened version, adapted from the 2d rev. ed. of the authors's autobiography: Life and times, published in 1892, as enlarged from his My bondage and my freedom, 1855. [E449.D744 1966] 66-7048
1. Slavery in the United States—Anti-slavery movements. 2. Slavery in the United States—Maryland. I. Ritchie, Barbara. BIP

DOUGLASS, Frederick, 1817?-1895 923.673
The life and writings of Frederick Douglass [by] Philip S. Foner. New York, Intl. Pubs. [1967,c.1950] 4v. ports. 21cm. (New world paperbacks, NW-73-6) Contents.1. Early years, 1817-1849.--2. Pre-Civil War decade, 1850-1860.--3. The Civil War, 1861-1865.--4. Reconstruction and after. Bibl. [E449.D736] 50-7654 12.50 pap., bxd. set,
1. Slavery in the U. S.—Anti-slavery movements. I. Foner, Philip Sheldon, 1910- II. Title.

DOUGLASS, Frederick, 1817?-1895. 322.4'4'0924
The life and writings of Frederick Douglass, [ed. by] Philip S. Foner. New York: International Publishers, [1950-1975] 5 v.; 21 cm. Contents.Contents:—1. Early years, 1817-1849.—2. Pre-Civil War decade, 1850-1860.—3. The Civil War, 1861-1865.—4. Reconstruction and after.—5. Supplementary volume, 1844-1860. Includes bibliographical references and index. [E449.D736] 50-7654
1. Slavery in the United States—Anti-slavery movements—Collected works. I. Foner, Philip Sheldon, 1910- ed.
V. 5, 1975, is available for 15.00, ISBN 0-7178-0453-4; pbk. 5.95, ISBN 0-7178-0454-2. BIP

DOUGLASS, Frederick, 1817?-1895 973.71'14'0924
My bondage and my freedom. New York, Arno Pr., 1968. 464p. illus., port. 21cm. (Amer. Negro, his hist. & lit.) Reprint of the 1855 ed. [E449.D738 1968] 68-28994 14.50
1. Slavery in the U.S.—Anti-slavery movements. 2. Slavery in the U.S.—Maryland. I. Title. II. Series. BIP

DOUGLASS, Frederick, 1817?-1895. 973.71'14'0924
My bondage and my freedom. New York, Arno Press, 1968. 464 p. illus., port. 21 cm. (The American Negro, his history and literature) Reprint of the 1855 ed. [E449.D738] 68-28994
1. Slavery in the U.S.—Anti-slavery movements. 2. Slavery in the U.S.—Maryland. I. Title. II. Series. BIP

DOUGLASS, Frederick, 1817?-1895. 326.0924 B
My bondage and my freedom. Chicago, Johnson Pub. Co., 1970. xii, 370 p. illus., port. 24 cm. (Ebony classics) Reprint of the 1855 ed. [E449.D738 1970] 70-102981 7.95
1. Slavery in the United States—Anti-slavery movements. 2. Slavery in the United States—Maryland. I. Title.

DOUGLASS, Frederick, 1817?-1895. 301.45'22'0924
My bondage and my freedom. With a new introd. by Philip S. Foner. New York, Dover Publications [1969] xiii, 464 p. illus., port. 21 cm. (Black rediscovery) "Unabridged and unaltered republication of the work first published in 1855." [E449.D738 1969] 73-92688 3.50
1. Slavery in the United States—Anti-slavery movements. 2. Slavery in the United States—Maryland. I. Title.

DOUGLASS, Frederick, 1817?-1895 326.92
Narrative of the life of Frederick Douglass, an American slave, written by himself. New York, New Amer. Lib. [1968, 1960] xviii, 126p. 18cm. (Signet bk., D3434) [E449.D74905] .50 pap.,
1. Slavery in the U. S.—Maryland. I. Title.

DOUGLASS, Frederick, 1817?-1895. 326.92
Narrative of the life of Frederick Douglass, an American slave, written by himself. Edited by Benjamin Quarles. Cambridge, Mass., Belknap Press, 1960. xxvi, 163 p.

port., map. 22 cm. (The John Harvard library) [E449.D74905] 59-11516
1. Slavery in the United States—Maryland. I. Title. II. Series.

DOUGLASS, Frederick [Name 326.92 orig.: Frederick Augustus Washington Bailey] 1817?-1895
Narrative of the life of Frederick Douglass, an American slave, written by himself. Garden City, N.Y., Doubleday [1963] 124p. facsimile t.p. 18cm. (Dolphin bk., C419) .95 pap.,
1. Slavery in the U.S.—Maryland. I. Title.

DOUGLASS, Frederick, [Name 326.92 orig.: Frederick Augustus Washington Bailey] 1817?-1895
Narrative of the life of Frederick Douglass, an American slave. Written by himself. Ed. by Benjamin Quarles. Cambridge, Mass., Belknap Pr. of Harvard, 1967[c.1960] xxvi, 163p. map. 21cm. (John Harvard lib., JHL15) [E449.D74905] 59-11616 1.45 pap.,
1. Slavery in the U.S.—Maryland. I. Title. II. Series.

[DOUGLASS, Helen 973.8'0924 B (Pitts)] 1838-1903, ed.
In memoriam: Frederick Douglass. Freeport, N.Y., Books for Libraries Press, 1971. 350 p. port. 23 cm. (The Black heritage library collection) Reprint of the 1897 ed. Contents.Contents.—Obsequies at Washington, D.C.—Obsequies at Rochester, N.Y.—Tender words from loving hearts, in letters received.—Preambles and resolutions.—Poems and sonnets.—Memorial services; addresses, and sermons.—Tributes of the press.—Reminiscences.—Biographical sketch. [E449.D753 1971] 79-164385 ISBN 0-8369-8844-2
1. Douglass, Frederick, 1817?-1895. I. Title. II. Series.

GREGORY, James 322'.4'0924 B Monroe, 1849-1915.
Frederick Douglass, the orator; containing an account of his life, his eminent public services, his brilliant career as orator, selections from his speeches and writings, by James M. Gregory. With an introd. by W. S. Scarborough. Chicago, Afro-Am Press, 1969. 309 p. illus., ports. 22 cm. Reprint of the 1893 ed. [E449.D76 1969] 76-99380
1. Douglass, Frederick, 1817?-1895. I. Title.

GREGORY, James 973.8'0924 B Monroe, 1849-1915.
Frederick Douglass, the orator; containing an account of his life, his eminent public services, his brillant career as orator, selections from his speeches and writings. With an introd. by W. S. Scarborough. New York, Crowell [1971] 309 p. illus., ports. 20 cm. (Apollo editions, A-288) "Original edition ... published in 1893." [E449.D76 1971] 76-25572 2.65
1. Douglass, Frederick, 1817?-1895. I. Title.

HOLLAND, Frederic 973.8'092'4 B May, 1836-1908.
Frederick Douglass: the colored orator. Westport, Conn., Negro Universities Press [1970] 423 p. port. 23 cm. Reprint of the 1891 ed. "List of publications by Frederick Douglass": p. 402-407. [E449.D7662 1970] 75-109994 ISBN 0-8371-4118-4
1. Douglass, Frederick, 1817?-1895. **BIP**

HOLLAND, Frederic 301.45'22 B May, 1836-1908.
Frederick Douglass: the colored orator. Rev. ed. New York, Haskell House Publishers, 1969. 431 p. 23 cm. Reprint of the 1895 ed. "List of publications by Frederick Douglass": p. 411-416. [E449.D7662 1969] 77-92969
1. Douglass, Frederick, 1817?-1895.

QUARLES, Benjamin. v. 12
Frederick Douglass. With a new preface by James M. McPherson. New York, Atheneum, 1968 [c1948] xvi, 378 p. illus., ports. 21 cm. (Studies in American Negro life) "Atheneum paperback, NL4." Bibliography: p. 351-362. 68-106451
1. Douglass, Frederick, 1817?-1895. I. Title. **BIP**

QUARLES, Benjamin. 973.8'0924 B
Frederick Douglass. With a new pref. by James M. McPherson. New York, Atheneum, 1968 [c1948] xvi, 378 p. illus., ports. 21 cm. (Studies in American Negro life) (Atheneum NL4) Bibliography: p. 351-362. [E449.D774 1968] 68-16416 3.25
1. Douglass, Frederick, 1817?-1895.

STERLING, Philip. 920
Four took freedom; the lives of Harriet Tubman, Frederick Douglass, Robert Smalls, and Blanche K. Bruce [by] Philip Sterling and Rayford Logan. Illustrated by Charles White. [1st ed.] Garden City, N.Y., Doubleday, 1967. 116 p. illus., ports. 21 cm. (Zenith books, Z10) Biographical portraits of four famous Negro Americans who escaped the slavery into which they were born to further the fight for freedom and equality. [E185.96.S78] AC 67
1. Tubman, Harriet (Ross) 1815?-1913. 2. Douglass, Frederick, 1817?-1895. 3. Smalls, Robert, 1839-1915. 4. Bruce, Blanche Kelso, 1841-1898. 5. Negroes—Biography. I. Logan, Rayford Whittlingham, 1897- joint author. II. White, Charles, illus. III. Title. **BIP**

WASHINGTON, 973.71'14'0924 B Booker Taliaferro, 1859?-1915.
Frederick Douglass. New York, Greenwood Press, [1969, c1906] 365 p. 23 cm. Bibliography: p. [353] [E449.D8 1969] 69-14140
1. Douglass, Frederick, 1817?-1895. **BIP**

WASHINGTON, 973.71'14'0924 B Booker Taliaferro, 1859?-1915.
Frederick Douglass. New York, Haskell House, 1968. 365 p. port. 23 cm. Reprint of the 1907 ed. Bibliography: p. [353] [E449.D8 1968] 68-25001
1. Douglass, Frederick, 1817?-1895.

WASHINGTON, 973.71'14'0924 B Booker Taliaferro, 1859?-1915.
Frederick Douglass. Edited by Ellis Paxson Oberholtzer. [New York] Argosy-Antiquarian, 1969. 365 p. port. 22 cm. Reprint of the 1907 ed. Bibliography: p. [353] [E449.D8 1969] 69-20416
1. Douglass, Frederick, 1817?-1895. I. Oberholtzer, Ellis Paxson, 1868-1936, ed.

Douglass, Frederick, 1817?-1895—Juvenile literature.

BONTEMPS, Arna Wendell, 923.673 1902-
Frederick Douglass: slave, fighter, freeman. Illustrated by Harper Johnson. [1st ed.] New York, Knopf, 1959. 177 p. illus. 20 cm. [E449.D75] 59-6410
1. Douglass, Frederick, 1817?-1895—Juvenile literature.

DAVIDSON, Mickie. 973.8'092'4 B
Frederick Douglass fights for freedom, by Margaret Davidson. New York, Four Winds Press [1970, c1968] 92 p. illus. 24 cm. A biography of the man who, after escaping slavery, became an orator, writer, and leader in the anti-slavery movement of the early nineteenth century. [E449.D7525] 92 75-124185
1. Douglass, Frederick, 1817?-1895—Juvenile literature. I. Title. **BIP**

GRAVES, Charles 326'.0924 B Parlin, 1911-
Frederick Douglass, by Charles P. Graves. Illustrated by Joel Snyder. New York, Putnam [1970] 64 p. illus. (part col.) 23 cm. (A See and read beginning to read biography) An easy-to-read biography of the escaped slave who became a renowned lecturer and writer against slavery. [E449.D759 1970] 92 78-110321 2.68
1. Douglass, Frederick, 1817?-1895—Juvenile literature. I. Snyder, Joel, illus. II. Title.

HERSCHLER, 973.71'14'0924 B Mildred Barger.
Frederick Douglass. Illustrated with drawings by John Downs, and contemporary pictorial material. Chicago, Follett [1969] 156, [4] p. illus., ports. 23 cm. (Library of American heroes) Bibliography: p. [158] A biography of a Negro who became an influential voice against slavery in America, founded and operated a newspaper to further abolition, and became Minister to Haiti and one of Abraham Lincoln's advisers. [E449.D764] 92 73-7458 1.95
1. Douglass, Frederick, 1817?-1895—Juvenile literature. I. Downs, John, illus. II. Title.

HUMPHREVILLE, 322'.4'0924 B Frances T., 1909-
For all people; the story of Frederick Douglass [by] Frances T. Humphreville. Boston, Houghton Mifflin [1969] 136 p. illus., facsim., map, ports. 21 cm. A biography of the slave who escaped North in 1838, became a lecturer and writer for the anti-slavery movement, and subsequently held several government posts. [E449.D7663] 92 74-78354
1. Douglass, Frederick, 1817?-1895—Juvenile literature. I. Title.

MYERS, Elisabeth P. 973.8'0924 B
Frederick Douglass, boy champion of human rights, by Elisabeth P. Myers. Illustrated by Robert Doremus. Indianapolis, Bobbs-Merrill [1970] 200 p. col. illus. 20 cm. (Childhood of famous Americans) Bibliography: p. 198. A biography emphasizing the boyhood of the man who escaped from slavery to become a prominent orator and writer for the cause of abolition. [E449.D768] 92 78-127587
1. Douglass, Frederick, 1817?-1895—Juvenile literature. I. Doremus, Robert, illus. II. Title.

PATTERSON, Lillie 92
Frederick Douglass, freedom fighter. Illus. by Gray Morrow. Champaign, Ill., Garrard [c.1965] 80p. col. illus. 23cm. (Discovery bk.) [E449.D7685] 65-10154 1.98
1. Douglass, Frederick, 1817?-1895—Juvenile literature. I. Title.

PATTERSON, Lillie. 92 (J)
Frederick Douglass, freedom fighter. Illustrated by Gray Morrow. Champaign, Ill. Garrard Pub. Co. [1965] 80 p. col. illus. 23 cm. (A Discovery book) [E449.D7685] 65-10154
1. Douglass, Frederick, 1817?-1895—Juvenile literature.

Douglass State Bank.

SEWING, Henry 332.1'23'0924 B Warren, 1891-
Henry Warren Sewing, founder of the Douglass State Bank; an autobiography. [1st ed.] New York, Exposition Press [1971] 137 p. illus., ports. 21 cm. [E185.97.S48A3] 77-24779 ISBN 0-682-47213-1 5.00
1. Douglass State Bank. I. Title.

Doust, W. A., 1895-

DOUST, W. A., 387.5'5'0924 B 1895-
The ocean on a plank / W. A. Doust, with Peter Black. London : Seeley, Service, 1976. xiv, 161 p., [4] leaves of plates : ill. ; 23 cm. [VK1491.D68 1976] 76-373688 ISBN 0-85422-088-7 : £4.95
1. Doust, W. A., 1895- 2. Salvage—Great Britain—Biography. I. Black, Peter, 1913- II. Title. **BIP**

Dove, Arthur Garfield, 1880-1946.

WIGHT, Frederick [759.13] 927.5 Stallknecht, 1902-
Arthur G. Dove. Berkeley, University of California Press, 1958. 96 p. illus. 28 cm. Bibliography: p 91-94. [ND237.D67W7] 58-10625
1. Dove, Arthur Garfield, 1880-1946. I. Title.

Dove, Patrick Edward, 1815-1873.

DAVIDSON, John 330.1'0922 Morrison.
Concerning four precursors of Henry George and the single tax, as also the land gospel according to Winstanley "the Digger", by J. Morrison Davidson. Port Washington, N.Y., Kennikat Press [1971] 151 p. 21 cm. Half title: Four precursors of Henry George. Reprint of 1899 ed. [HD1313.D2 1971] 77-115317
1. Ogilvie, William, 1736-1819. 2. Spence, Thomas, 1750-1814. 3. Paine, Thomas, 1737-1809. 4. Dove, Patrick Edward, 1815-1873. 5. Winstanley, Gerrard, b. 1609. I. Title. II. Title: Four precursors of Henry George.

Dove (Sloop)—Juvenile literature.

GRAHAM, Robin Lee. 910'.41 B
The boy who sailed around the world alone, by Robin Lee Graham with Derek L. T. Gill. Editor: Vera R. Webster. Art director: Frances Giannoni. New York, Golden Press [1973] 140 p. col. illus. 29 cm. Recounts the voyage of a California sixteen-year-old who spent nearly five years sailing alone around the world. [G530.G599712] 73-85652 5.95
1. Dove (Sloop)—Juvenile literature. 2. Voyages around the world—1951- —Juvenile literature. I. Gill, Derek L. T. II. Title. **BIP**

Dover, Thomas, 1660-1742.

THE quicksilver doctor, v. 12
the life and times of Thomas Dover, physician and adventurer. Bristol, Wright, 1957. ix, 192p. illus.
1. Dover, Thomas, 1660-1742. I. Dewhurst, Kenneth.

Dow, Alden B.,

DOW, Alden B., 1904- 720'.924
Reflections [by] Alden B. Dow. [Midland, Mich., Northwood Institute, c1970] 192 p. illus. (part col.), plans. 35 x 38 cm. [NA737.D67A55] 75-109044
I. Title.

Dow, Herbert Henry, 1866-1930.

CAMPBELL, Murray, 1904- 926.6
Herbert H. Dow, pioneer in creative chemistry, by Murray Campbell and Harrison Hatton. New York, Appleton-Century-Crofts [1951] 168 p. illus. 27 cm. [TP140.D6C3] 51-12222
1. Dow, Herbert Henry, 1866-1930. I. Title.

Dow, Neal, 1804-1897.

BYRNE, Frank Loyola, 923.673 1928-
Prophet of prohibition; Neal Dow and his crusade. Madison, State Historical Society of Wisconsin for Dept. of History, Univ. of Wisconsin [c.]1961. vii, 184p. (Logmark editions) Bibl. 61-63120 4.00
1. Dow, Neal, 1804-1897. I. Title. **BIP**

Dowd. Charles Edward, 1925-

DOWD, Virginia Fritz, 1895- 927.8
Through his mother's eyes; a portrait of a boy. [Chicago; 1955] 191p. illus. 29cm. [ML410.D806D6] 55-3925
1. Dowd. Charles Edward, 1925- I. Title.

Dowd, Connor.

DOWD, Alton L. 975.6'2
Deep River : the story of a man and his family during the American Revolution / Alton L. Dowd, Sr. Durham, N.C. : Moore Pub. Co., c1977. 374 p. ; 24 cm. Includes bibliographical references. [E277.D69D68] 76-56711 7.95
1. Dowd, Connor. 2. American loyalists—North Carolina—Cape Fear River Valley—Biography. 3. Cape Fear River Valley—Biography. 4. North Carolina—History—Revolution, 1775-1783. I. Title.

Dowden, Edward, 1843-1913.

LUDWIGSON, Kathryn 820'.9'008 B R.
Edward Dowden, by Kathryn R. Ludwigson. New York, Twayne Publishers [1973] 170 p. 22 cm. (Twayne's English authors series, TEAS 148) Bibliography: p. 163-166. [PR4613.D445Z7] 72-939 5.95
1. Dowden, Edward, 1843-1913. **BIP**

Dowden, Hester.

BENTLEY, Edmund 920.9133 Clerihew, 1875-
Far horizon; a biography of Hester Dowden, medium and psychic investigator. London, New York, Rider [1951] 191p. illus. 22cm. [BF1283.D49B4] 54-16583

1. Dowden, Hester. I. Title.

Dowding, Hugh Caswall Tremenheere Dowding, Baron, 1882-1970.

WRIGHT, Robert, 1912- 940.542'1'0924 B
The man who won the Battle of Britain. New York, Scribner [1970, c1969] 291 p. 22 cm. [DA89.6.D6W73] 70-108130 6.95
1. Dowding, Hugh Caswall Tremenheere Dowding, Baron, 1882-1970. 2. Britain, Battle of, 1940. I. Title.

Dowdy, Leonard, 1927-

STENQUIST, Gertrude. 362.4'1'0924 B
The story of Leonard Dowdy : deaf-blindness acquired in infancy / by Gertrude Stenquist. Watertown, Mass. : Perkins School for the Blind, 1974. viii, 64 p. : ill. ; 23 cm. Includes bibliographical references. [HV1624.D68S73] 76-356042
1. Dowdy, Leonard, 1927- 2. Blind-deaf. 3. Blind-deaf—Means of communication. I. Title.

Dowell, Benjamin S., 1818-1880.

HAMILTON, Nancy, 1929- 976.4'96 B
Ben Dowell, El Paso's first mayor / by Nancy Hamilton. [El Paso] : Texas Western Press, c1976. 80 p. : ill. ; 23 cm. (Southwestern studies ; monograph no. 49) Includes bibliographical references. [F394.E4H35] 76-374231 3.00
1. Dowell, Benjamin S., 1818-1880. 2. El Paso, Tex.—Mayors—Biography. I. Title. II. Series: Southwestern studies (El Paso, Tex.) ; monograph no. 49. BIP

Dowland, John, 1563-1626.

POULTON, Diana. 780'.92'4 B
John Dowland; his life and works. Berkeley, University of California Press, 1972. 520 p. illus. 26 cm. Bibliography: p. 460-496. [ML410.D808P7 1972b] 76-169229 ISBN 0-520-02109-6 30.00
1. Dowland, John, 1563-1626.

Dowling, Colette.

DOWLING, Colette. 973.92'092'4 B
How to love a member of the opposite sex : a memoir / by Colette Dowling. New York : Coward, McCann & Geoghegan, c1976. 220 p. ; 22 cm. [CT275.D8683A34 1976] 76-15193 ISBN 0-698-10686-5 : 7.95
1. Dowling, Colette. I. Title.

Downer, Silas.

BRIDENBAUGH, Carl. 973.3'11'0924 B
Silas Downer, forgotten patriot : his life and writings / by Carl Bridenbaugh. Providence : Rhode Island Bicentennial Foundation, 1974. 118 p. : ill. ; 24 cm. (Publication - Rhode Island Bicentennial Commission ; no. 1) "Documents by or relating to Silas Downer": p. [40]-113. [F82.D68B74] 74-83462
1. Downer, Silas. 2. Sons of Liberty. I. Downer, Silas. Silas Downer, forgotten patriot. 1974. II. Title. III. Series: Rhode Island. Bicentennial Commission. Publication — Rhode Island Bicentennial Commission ; no. 1. BIP

Downie, Edward Blake.

PEAKER, Ora. 923.473
Meet the Judge! [1st ed.] Boston, Meador Pub. Co. [1958] 304p. 21cm. 58-14248
1. Downie, Edward Blake. I. Title.

Downing, Emanuel, 1585-1660.

SIMMONS, Frederick Johnson, 1884- 273'.6'09744
Emanuel Downing. [Montclair, N.J.] 1958. 93 p. illus. 23 cm. Includes bibliography [F67.D69D5] 60-39974
1. Downing, Emanuel, 1585-1660. I. Title.

SIMMONS, Frederick Johnson, 1884- v. 12
Emanuel Downing, A narrative outline for a biography, by Frederick Johnson Simmons. n.p., Forest city printing company, [1959?] 3 p.l., 3-93 p., 6 l. illus. 24 cm. Date on title-page given as 1958, on imprint statement as 1959 and in text as 1960. "Limited edition of 150 copies."
1. Downing, Emanuel, 1585-1660. I. Title. II. Title: A narrative outline for a biography of Emanuel Downinge.

SIMMONS, Frederick Johnson, 1884- v. 12
A narrative outline for a biography of Emanuel Downinge, 1585-1660, of the Inner Temple and defender of the charter of the Massachusetts Bay colony. [Montclair, N.J.] Simmons, 1958. 93 p. illus. 24 cm. "References": p. [95]
1. Downing, Emanuel, 1585-1660. I. Title.

Dowson, Ernest Christopher, 1867-1900.

DOWSON, Ernest Christopher, 1867-1900. 826'.8
The letters of Ernest Dowson. Collected & edited by Desmond Flower and Henry Maas. Rutherford [N.J.] Fairleigh Dickinson University Press [1968, c1967] viii, 470 p. illus., facsims., ports. 26 cm. Bibliography: p. 444-445. [PR4613.D5Z544 1968] 67-29136
I. Flower, Desmond, 1907- ed. II. Maas, Henry, ed. III. Title. BIP

LONGAKER, John Mark, 1900- 821'.8 B
Ernest Dowson, by Mark Longaker. [3d ed.] Philadelphia, University of Pennsylvania Press [1967, c1945] x, 308 p. facsims., ports. 24 cm. Bibliography: p. 299-303. [PR4613.D5Z65 1967] 68-1016
1. Dowson, Ernest Christopher, 1867-1900.

Dowson, Ernest Christopher, 1867-1900—Biography.

PLARR, Victor Gustave, 1863-1929. 821'.8 B
Ernest Dowson, 1888-1897 : reminiscences, unpublished letters, and marginalia / by Victor Plarr ; with a bibliography compiled by H. Guy Harrison. Folcroft, Pa. : Folcroft Library Editions, 1976. 147 p. ; 22 cm. Reprint of the 1914 ed. published by L. J. Gomme, New York. Includes index. Bibliography: p. 131-142. [PR4613.D5Z7 1976] 76-30643 ISBN 0-8414-6769-2 lib. bdg. : 20.00
1. Dowson, Ernest Christopher, 1867-1900—Biography. 2. Authors, English—19th century—Biography.

Doyle, Arthur Conan, Sir, 1859-1930.

CARR, John Dickson, 1905- 928.2
The life of Sir Arthur Conan Doyle. Garden City, N.Y., Doubleday [1961, c.1949] 359p. (Dolphin bk. C117) Bibl. .95 pap.,
i. Doyle, Sir Arthur Conan, 1859-1930. I. Title.

CARR, John Dickson, 1905- 823'.9'12 B
The life of Sir Arthur Conan Doyle. [Folcroft, Pa.] Folcroft Library Editions, 1973. p. Reprint of the 1949 ed. published by J. Murray, London. [PR4623.C3 1973] 73-12144 27.50
1. Doyle, Arthur Conan, Sir, 1859-1930. I. Title.

CARR, John Dickson, 1905- 823'.9'12 B
The life of Sir Arthur Conan Doyle / by John Dickson Carr. New York : Vintage Books, 1975, c1949. ix, 447 p. ; 18 cm. Reprint of the 1st ed. published by Harper, New York. "Biographical archives": p. [421]-434. Includes index. Bibliography: p. 434-436. [PR4623.C3 1975] 75-5535 ISBN 0-394-71608-6 pbk. : 2.45
1. Doyle, Arthur Conan, Sir, 1859-1930. I. Title.

HARDWICK, John Michael Drinkrow, 1924- 928.2
The man who was Sherlock Holmes [by] Michael and Mollie Hardwick. [1st ed. in the U. S. A.] Garden City, N. Y., Doubleday, 1964. 92 p. illus., facsims., ports. 22 cm. [PR4623.H3 1964a] 64-19109
1. Doyle, Arthur Conan, Sir, 1859-1930. I. Hardwick, Mollie, joint author. II. Title.

HOEHLING, Mary (Duprey) 1914- 92
The real Sherlock Holmes: Arthur Conan Doyle. New York, Messner [c.1965] 191p. 22cm. Bibl. [PR4623.H56] 65-12952 3.25; 3.19 lib. ed.,
1. Doyle, Arthur Conan, Sir I. Title.

LAMOND, John. 823'.9'12 B
Arthur Conan Doyle; a memoir. With an epilogue by Lady Conan Doyle. Port Washington, N.Y., Kennikat Press [1972] xiv, 310 p. ports. 21 cm. Reprint of the 1931 ed. [PR4623.L3 1972] 77-160766 ISBN 0-8046-1588-8
1. Doyle, Arthur Conan, Sir, 1859-1930. I. Doyle, Arthur Conan, Sir, 1859-1930.

THE life of Sir Arthur Conan Doyle, v. 12 Garden City, N.Y. Doubleday [1961?] 359p. 18cm. (Dolphin books, C117) Includes bibliographical references.
1. Doyle, Arthur Conan, Sir 1859-1930. I. Carr, John Dickson, 1905-

NORDON, Pierre, 1927- 823'.9'12 B
Conan Doyle; a biography. [Translated from the French by Frances Partridge] New York, Holt, Rinehart and Winston [1967, c1966] 370 p. illus. 24 cm. Translation of Sir Arthur Conan Doyle: l'homme et l'ouvre. Includes bibliographies. [PR4623.N613 1967] 67-10075
1. Doyle, Arthur Conan, Sir, 1859-1930. I. Title.

PEARSON, Hesketh, 1887- 928.2
Conan Doyle. New York, Walker [1961] 256 p. illus. 22 cm. [PR4623.P4 1961] 61-16983
1. Doyle, Sir Arthur Conan, 1859-1930.

WOOD, James Playsted, 1905- 823'.9'12 B
The man who hated Sherlock Holmes; a life of Sir Arthur Conan Doyle. Illustrated by Richard M. Powers. [New York, Pantheon Books, 1965] 180 p. illus. 22 cm. "Bibliographical note": p. 179-180. A biography of the Scotsman who was sportsman, sailor, soldier, physician and historian as well as creator of the modern detective story and the best known detective. [PR4623.W6] 92 AC 68
1. Doyle, Arthur Conan, Sir, 1859-1930. I. Powers, Richard M., illus. II. Title.

Doyle, Arthur Conan, Sir, 1859-1930—Biography.

HIGHAM, Charles, 1931- 823'.9'12 B
The adventures of Conan Doyle : the life of the creator of Sherlock Holmes / by Charles Higham. 1st ed. New York : Norton, c1976. 368 p., [7] leaves of plates : ill. ; 22 cm. Includes index. Bibliography: p. [347]-354. [PR4623.H5 1976] 76-20499 ISBN 0-393-07507-9 : 9.95
1. Doyle, Arthur Conan, Sir, 1859-1930—Biography. I. Title. BIP

PEARSALL, Ronald, 1927- 823'.9'12 B
Conan Doyle, a biographical solution / Ronald Pearsall. New York : St. Martin's Press, 1977. vii, 208 p., [4] leaves of plates : ill. ; 23 cm. Includes index. Bibliography: p. 196-200. [PR4623.P38] 76-58019 ISBN 0-312-15907-2 : 10.00
1. Doyle, Arthur Conan, Sir, 1859-1930—Biography. 2. Authors, English—19th century—Biography. I. Title.

Doyle, Arthur Conan, Sir, 1859-1930—Juvenile literature.

HOEHLING, Mary Duprey, 1914- 928
The real Sherlock Holmes: Arthur Conan Doyle, by Mary Hoehling. New York, J. Messner [1965] 191 p. 22 cm. Bibliography: p. 181-183. [PR4623.H56] 65-129521
1. Doyle, Arthur Conan, Sir, 1859-1930—Juvenile literature. I. Title.

WOOD, James Playsted, 1905- 928.2
The man who hated Sherlock Holmes; a life of Sir Arthur Conan Doyle. Illustrated by Richard M. Powers. [New York, Pantheon Books, 1965] 180 p. illus. 22 cm. "Bibliographical note": p. 179-180. [PR4623.W6] 65-11443
1. Doyle, Sir Arthur Conan, 1859-1930 — Juvenile literature. I. Title.

Doyle, Lawrence, 1847?-1907.

IVES, Edward D. 784'.0924 B
Lawrence Doyle: the farmer-poet of Prince Edward Island; a study in local songmaking [by] Edward D. Ives. Orono, University of Maine Press, 1971. xviii, 269 p. illus. 24 cm. (University of Maine studies, no. 92) Bibliography: p. [259]-261. [ML410.D809I9] 71-30045 7.95
1. Doyle, Lawrence, 1847?-1907. 2. Prince Edward Island—Social life and customs. I. Title. II. Series: Maine. University. University of Maine studies, 2d ser., no. 92

DOYLE, Charles Altamont. 741'.092'4 B
The Doyle diary : the last great Conan Doyle mystery : with a Holmesian investigation into the strange and curious case of Charles Altamont Doyle / by Michael Baker. New York : Paddington Press, c1978. xxix, 91 p. : ill. ; 18 x 25 cm. Facsim. of the author's diary-sketchbook, with an additional introd., and a page transcription of the words of Charles Doyle as they appear in the diary. [N6797.D68A2 1978] 78-6356 ISBN 0-448-22068-7 : 12.95
1. Doyle, Charles Altamont. 2. Artists—England—Biography. I. Baker, Michael, 1948- II. Title.

D'oyly Carte Opera Company.

GREEN, Martyn, 1899- 927.8
Here's a how-de-do; my life in Gilbert & Sullivan. [1st ed.] New York, Norton [1952] 283 p. illus. 22 cm. [ML420.G85A3] 52-12462
1. D'oyly Carte Opera Company. 2. Musicians—Correspondence, reminiscences, etc. I. Title.

Drai-Khmara, Mykhailo, 1889-1939.

ASHER, Oksana. 891.79'1'3
A Ukrainian poet in the Soviet Union [by Oksana Asher. New York, Svoboda, 1959] 49, [2] p. port. 25 cm. Bibliography: p. 48-[50] [PG3948.D73Z56] 73-215217
1. Drai-Khmara, Mykhailo, 1889-1939. I. Title.

Drag racing.

GARLITS, Don 796.7'2'0924
King of the dragsters; the story of Big Daddy 'Don' Garlits [by] Don Garlits, Brock Yates. [1st ed.] Philadelphia, Chilton [1967] viii, 217p. 21cm. [GV1029.3.G3] 67-3471 4.95
1. Drag racing. I. Yates, Brock W., joint author. II. Title.

GARLITS, Don. 796.7'2'0924
King of the dragsters; the story of Big Daddy "Don" Garlits [by] Don Garlits and Brock Yates. Enl. and updated ed. Philadelphia, Chilton Book Co. [1970] viii, 246 p. 21 cm. [GV1029.3.G3 1970] 75-115685
1. Drag racing. I. Yates, Brock W., joint author. II. Title.

Drag racing—Juvenile literature.

OLNEY, Ross Robert, 1929- 796.7'2
Kings of the drag strip [by] Ross Olney. New York, Putnam [1968] 192 p. illus., ports. 21 cm. Contents.Contents.—Don Prudhomme.—Tony Nancy.—Dick Landy.—Tommy Ivo.—Art Malone.—Mickey Thompson.—Chris Karamesines.—Gas Ronda.—Jack Williams.—Tom McEwen.—John Rhodes.—Don Garlits.—Drag racing classes.—Glossary. Bibliography: p. [184] [GV1029.3.O4] 68-24541 3.49
1. Drag racing—Juvenile literature. I. Title. BIP

STAMBLER, Irwin. 796.7'2
Top fuelers : drag racing royalty / Irwin Stambler. New York : Putnam, c1978. 125 p. : ill. ; 24 cm. Includes index. Introduces those elite cars of drag racing known as Top Fuelers and profiles some of their top drivers. [GV1029.3.S72 1978] 77-13328 ISBN 0-399-61116-9 lib. bdg. : 5.89
1. Drag racing—Juvenile literature. 2. Automobile racing drivers—Biography—Juvenile literature. I. Title. BIP

Drage, William Henry, 1901-

DRAGE, William Henry, 1901- 386'.3'0924 B
Riverboats and rivermen / [by] William Drage [and] Michael Page. Adelaide : Rigby, 1976. 221 p. : ill. ; 25 cm. [VK140.D7A37] 76-381449 ISBN 0-7270-0138-8
1. Drage, William Henry, 1901- 2. Boatmen—Australia—Biography. 3. River steamers—Australia. 4. Australia—Description and travel. I. Page, Michael F., 1922- joint author. II. Title.

Drake, Daniel, 1785-1852.

HORINE, Emmet Field, M.D., 1885- 926.1
Daniel Drake, 1785-1852; pioneer physician of the Midwest. Introd. by J. Christian Bay. Philadelphia, Univ. of Pennsylvania Press [c.1961] 425p. illus. Bibl. 61-5544 6.00
1. Drake, Daniel, 1785-1852. I. Title.

MANSFIELD, Edward Deering, 1801-1880. 610'.92'4 B
Memoirs of the life and services of Daniel Drake, M.D. / Edward Deering Mansfield. New York : Arno Press, 1975. p. cm. (The Mid-American frontier) Reprint of the 1855 ed. published by Applegate, Cincinnati. [R154.D7M3 1975] 75-108 ISBN 0-405-06875-1 : 23.00
1. Drake, Daniel, 1785-1852. 2. Cincinnati—History. I. Title. II. Series.

Drake, Francis, Sir, 1540?-1596.

BRADFORD, Ernle Dusgate Selby 359.332
The wind commands me; a life of Sir Francis Drake. New York, Harcourt [c.1965] 251p. illus., coat of arms, maps, ports. 22cm. First pub. in London in 1965 under the title: Drake. Bibl. [DA86.22.D7B66] 64-18281 4.95
1. Drake, Sir Francis, 1540?-1596. I. Title.

CORBETT, Julian Stafford, Sir, 1854-1922. 942.055'0924
Sir Francis Drake. New York, AMS Press [1969] vi, 209 p. port. 23 cm. Reprint of the 1890 ed. [DA86.22.D7C8 1969] 77-105513
1. Drake, Francis, Sir, 1540?-1596.

CORBETT, Julian Stafford, Sir, 1854-1922. 942.05'5'0924 B
Sir Francis Drake. New York, Haskell House, 1968. vi, 209 p. illus. 23 cm. Reprint of the 1890 ed. [DA86.22.D7C8 1968] 68-25228
1. Drake, Francis, Sir, 1540?-1596.

CORBETT, Julian Stafford, Sir, 1854-1922. 942.05'5'0924
Sir Francis Drake. Westport, Conn., Greenwood Press [1970] vi, 209 p. port. 23 cm. Reprint of the 1890 ed. [DA86.22.D7C8 1970] 69-13865
1. Drake, Francis, Sir, 1540?-1596.

HALWOOD, Will. 923.542
The true book about Sir Francis Drake. Illustrated by Gerald Pacey. London, Muller stamped: distributed by Sportshelf, New Rochelle, N. Y., [1958] 142p. illus. 19cm. [DA86.22.D7H6] 58-4991
1. Drake, Francis, Sir I. Title.

HAMPDEN, John, 1898- comp. 910'.41
Francis Drake, privateer; contemporary narratives and documents. University, University of Alabama Press, 1972. 286 p. illus. 25 cm. Bibliography: p. 258-266. [DA86.22.D7H26 1972] 72-2881 ISBN 0-8173-5703-3 12.75
1. Drake, Francis, Sir, 1540?-1596. I. Title. BIP

LATHAM, Jean Lee. 942.05'5'0924 B
Drake, the man they called a pirate. Illustrated by Frederick T. Chapman. New York, Harper [1960] 278 p. illus. 22 cm. Adventures of the piratical Elizabethan mariner who contributed enormously to the growth of sixteenth-century English sea power. [PZ7.L348Dr] 92 AC 68
1. Drake, Francis, Sir, 1540?-1596. I. Chapman, Frederick T., illus. II. Title.

MCKEE, Alexander, 1918- 910'.41
The queen's corsair : Drake's journey of circumnavigation, 1577-1580 / by Alexander McKee. New York : Stein and Day, 1979, c1978. p. cm. Includes index. [G420.D7M32] 78-66256 ISBN 0-8128-2595-0 : 12.95
1. Drake, Francis, Sir, 1540?-1596. 2. Voyages around the world. 3. Explorers—England—Biography.

THOMSON, George Malcolm, 1899- 359.3'3'20924
Sir Francis Drake. New York, Morrow, 1972. x, 358 p. illus. 24 cm. Bibliography: p. 343-349. [DA86.22.D7T48 1972b] 70-182961 10.00
1. Drake, Francis, Sir, 1540?-1596.

WILBUR, Marguerite Knowlton (Eyer) 1889- 923.542
Immortal pirate; the life of Sir Francis Drake. New York, Hastings House [1951] 314 p. 21 cm. [DA86.22.D7W5] 51-13884
1. Drake, Sir Francis, 1540?-1596. I. Title.

WILLIAMSON, James Alexander, 1886- 923.542
Sir Francis Drake. New York, Collier [1962] 124p. maps, 18cm. (AS242V) .95 pap.,
1. Drake, Francis, Sir 1540?-1596. 2. Gt. Brit.—History, Naval—Tudors, 1485-1603. I. Title. II. Series. BIP

WILLIAMSON, James Alexander, 1886 359.3320924
Sir Francis Drake, by James A. Williamson. Hamden, Conn., Archon Books, 1966. 160 p. illus., maps, ports. 21 cm. (Makers of history) "First published in 1951." [DA86.22.D7W53 1966] 66-21096
1. Drake, Francis, Sir, 1540?-1596. 2. Great Britain—History, Naval—Tudors, 1485-1603.

WILLIAMSON, James Alexander, 1886- 359.3'31'0924 B
Sir Francis Drake / by James A. Williamson. Westport, Conn. : Greenwood Press, 1975. 160 p., [1] leaf of plates : ill. ; 19 cm. Reprint of the 1951 ed. published by Collins, London, which was issued as no. 1 of Brief lives. [DA86.22.D7W53 1975] 74-30930 ISBN 0-8371-7886-X lib.bdg. : 10.50
1. Drake, Francis, Sir, 1540?-1596. 2. Great Britain—History, Naval—Tudors, 1485-1603. I. Series: Brief lives ; no. 1.

Drake, Francis, Sir 1540?-1596—Juvenile literature.

KNIGHT, Frank Edgar 920
The young Drake. Illus. by Azpelicueta. New York, Roy [1963, c.1962] 126p. 21cm. 62-18555 3.00 bds.,
1. Drake, Francis, Sir 1540?-1596—Juvenile literature. I. Title.

SANDERLIN, George William, 1915- comp. 942.05'5'0924
The sea-dragon; journals of Francis Drake's voyage around the world [compiled by] George Sanderlin. New York, Harper & Row [1969] xxxix, 243 p. illus. 25 cm. Bibliography: p. 219-220. Selections from sixteenth and seventeenth-century works on the exploits of Sir Francis Drake as well as excerpts from his own journals concerning his three year voyage around the world. [DA86.22.D7S2] 72-77946 5.95
1. Drake, Francis, Sir, 1540?-1596—Juvenile literature. I. Title. BIP

SYME, Ronald, 1910- 923.542
Francis Drake, sailor of the unknown seas. Illustrated by William Stobbs. New York, Morrow, 1961. 96 p. illus. 22 cm. [DA86.22.D7S9] 61-5018
1. Drake, Sir Francis, 1540?-1596 — Juvenile literature. I. Title.

WOOD, William Hollingsworth, 1914- j92
The true story of Sir Francis Drake, privateer, by Will Holwood (pseud. American ed.] Chicago, Childrens Press [1964] 139 p. col. illus 23 cm. First published in London in 1958 under title: The true book about Sir Francis Drake. [DA86.22.D7W6] 64-12905
1. Drake, Sir Francis, 1540?-1596 — Juvenile literature. I. Title.

Drake, Rodger E., 1924—

DRAKE, Rodger E., 1924- 371.9'092'4
Once a pony time / Rodger E. Drake. Philadelphia : Dorrance, c1975. vii, 201 p. ; 22 cm. [LC4019.D8] 75-328949 ISBN 0-8059-2148-6 : 5.95
1. Drake, Rodger E., 1924- 2. Handicapped children—Education. I. Title. BIP

Drama.

BENTLEY, Eric Russell, 1916- 809.2
The life of the drama [by] Eric Bentley. [1st ed.] New York, Atheneum, 1964. ix, 371 p. 22 cm. Bibliography: p. 355-359. [PN1631.B4] 64-14930
1. Drama. 2. Drama—History and criticism—Addresses, essays, lectures. 3. Theater—Addresses, essays, lectures. I. Title. BIP

Drama—19th century—Addresses, essays, lectures.

HENDERSON, Archibald, 1877-1963. 809.2'034
European dramatists. Rev. ed. Freeport, N.Y., Books for Libraries Press [1971, c1926] 479 p. ports. 23 cm. (Essay index reprint series) Contents.Contents.—August Strindberg.—Henrik Ibsen.—Maurice Maeterlinck.—Oscar Wilde.—Bernard Shaw.—Granville Barker.—Arthur Schnitzler.—John Galsworthy. [PN1851.H4 1971] 78-142642 ISBN 0-8369-2163-1
1. Drama—19th century—Addresses, essays, lectures. I. Title. BIP

Dramatists—Biography.

INGRAM, John Henry, 1842-1916. 822.3
Christopher Marlowe and his associates. New York, Cooper Square Publishers, 1970. xvi, 305 p. illus., facsims., ports. 22 cm. Reprint of the 1904 ed. Bibliography: p. 280-298. [PR2673.15 1970] 70-116374
I. Marlowe, Christopher, 1564-1593. II. Title. BIP

WAGER, Walter H. comp. 809.2
The playwrights speak. With an introd. by Harold Clurman. New York, Delacorte Press [1967] xxx, 290 p. 21 cm. A collection of interviews with 11 playwrights. Contents.Contents.—Arthur Miller.—Edward Albee.—Friedrich Durrenmatt.—John Osborne.—William Inge.—Eugene Ionesco.—Harold Pinter.—Peter Weiss.—Tennessee Williams.—John Arden.—Arnold Wesker. [PN453.W28] 67-17162
1. Dramatists—Biography. 2. Drama—20th century—Addresses, essays, lectures. I. Title.

Dramesi, John A.

DRAMESI, John A. 959.704'38
Code of honor / John A. Dramesi. 1st ed. New York : Norton, [1975] 271 p. ; 21 cm. Autobiographical. [DS559.4.D7] 75-5594 ISBN 0-393-05533-7 : 7.95
1. Dramesi, John A. 2. Vietnamese Conflict, 1961-1975—Prisoners and prisons, North Vietnamese. 3. Vietnamese Conflict, 1961-1975—Personal narratives, American. I. Title. BIP

Draper, John William, 1811-1882.

FLEMING, Donald Harnish, 1923- 925
John William Draper and the religion of science. Philadelphia, University of Pennsylvania Press, 1950. ix, 205 p. port. 23 cm. At head of title: The American Historical Association. "This book began as a doctor's dissertation at Harvard University." Bibliography: p. 183-197. [Q143.D77F6 1950] 50-4661
1. Draper, John William, 1811-1882. I. American Historical. Association. II. Title. BIP

Draper, Lyman Copeland, 1815-1891.

HESSELTINE, William Best, 1902- v. 12
Pioneer's mission; the story of Lyman Copeland Draper. Madison, State Historical Society of Wisconsin, 1964. ix 384 p. illus., port. 24 cm. 65-86732
1. 1. Draper, Lyman Copeland, 1815-1891. I. Title. BIP

HESSELTINE, William Best, 1902-1963. 973'.072'024 B
Pioneer's mission; the story of Lyman Copeland Draper. Westport, Conn., Greenwood Press [1970, c1954] ix, 384 p. illus., facsim., ports. 23 cm. Includes bibliographical references. [E175.5.D763 1970] 79-98227
1. Draper, Lyman Copeland, 1815-1891. I. Title.

Draper, Ruth, 1884-1956.

DRAPER, Ruth, 1884-1956. 792'.028'0924
The letters of Ruth Draper : 1920-1956, a self-portrait of a great actress / edited, with narrative notes by Neilla Warren ; foreword by Sir John Gielgud. New York : Scribner, c1979. xxi, 362 p. ; ill. ; 24 cm Includes index. Bibliography: p. 348-349. [PN2287.D549A4 1979] 78-10442 ISBN 0-684-15818-3 : 12.95
1. Draper, Ruth, 1884-1956. 2. Actors—United States—Correspondence. I. Warren, Neilla.

Draper, Stanley Carlyle, 1889-1976.

SMALLWOOD, James. 309.2'62'0924 B
Urban builder : life and times of Stanley Draper / by James M. Smallwood. 1st ed. Norman : Published for the Oklahoma Heritage Association by the University of Oklahoma Press, c1977. p. cm. (Oklahoma trackmaker series ; v. 5) Includes index. Bibliography: p. [HT168.O45S57] 77-9115 ISBN 0-8061-1447-9 : 7.75
1. Draper, Stanley Carlyle, 1889-1976. 2. City planners—Oklahoma—Oklahoma City—Biography. 3. Boards of trade—Oklahoma—Oklahoma City—Employees—Biography. I. Title. II. Series. BIP

Drayton, William Henry, 1742-1779.

DABNEY, William M. 975.702
William Henry Drayton & the American Revolution [by] William M. Dabney and Marion Dargan. [1st ed.] Albuquerque, University of New Mexico Press [1962] xiii, 225 p. ports., facsims. 24 cm. Bibliography: p. 209-217. [E302.6.D7D3] 62-19918

1. Drayton, William Henry, 1742-1779. 2. South Carolina—History—Revolution, 1775-1783. I. Dargan, Marion, joint author.

Dreikurs, Rudolf, 1897-1972.

TERNER, Janet R. 616.8'9'0924 B
The courage to be imperfect : the life and work of Rudolf Dreikurs / Janet Terner and W. L. Pew ; with the editorial assistance of Robert A. Aird. New York : Hawthorn Books, c1978. xv, 412 p. : ill. ; 24 cm. Includes index. "Rudolf Dreikurs bibliography": p. 377-392. [RC339.52.D73T47 1978] 75-220 ISBN 0-8015-1784-2 : 14.95
1. Dreikurs, Rudolf, 1897-1972. 2. Adler, Alfred, 1870-1937. 3. Dreikus, Rudolf, 1897-1972—Bibliography. 4. Psychiatrists—United States—Biography. 5. Group psychotherapy. I. Pew, W. L., joint author. II. Aird, Robert A. III. Title.

Dreiser, Theodore, 1871-1945.

A Book about Theodore 813'.5'2
Dreiser and his work. [Folcroft, Pa.] Folcroft Library Editions, 1973. p. Essays on Dreiser's work by Sherwood Anderson and others. Reprint of the ed. published by Boni & Liveright, New York. [PS3507.R55Z59] 73-12228 5.50
1. Dreiser, Theodore, 1871-1945. I. Anderson, Sherwood, 1876-1941.

DREISER, Helen (Patges). 928.1
My life with Dreiser. [1st ed.] Cleveland, World Pub. Co. [1951] 328 p. illus., ports., facsims. 22 cm. [PS3507.R55Z58] 51-10332
1. Dreiser. Theodore, 1871-1945. I. Title.

DREISER, Theodore, 1871- 928.1
1945.
Letters to Louise; Theodore Dreiser's letters to Louise Campbell. Edited, with commentary, by Louise Campbell. Philadelphia, University of Pennsylvania Press [1959] 123 p. 22 cm. [PS3507.R55Z55] 59-6698
I. Campbell, Louise. II. Title.

DREISER, Theodore, 070.4'092'4 B
1871-1945.
Newspaper days. New York, Beekman Publishers, 1974 [c1931] 502 p. 23 cm. (American newspapermen, 1790-1933) First published under title: A book about myself. Reprint of the ed. published by H. Liveright, New York, which was issued as v. 2 of the author's A history of myself. [PS3507.R55Z5 1974] 74-531 ISBN 0-8464-0023-5 20.00
1. Dreiser, Theodore, 1871-1945. I. Title.
BIP

DUDLEY, Dorothy, 1884- 813'.5'2
Forgotten frontiers; Dreiser and the land of the free. New York, AMS Press [1970] v, 485 p. 23 cm. Reprint of the 1932 ed. Includes bibliographical references. [PS3507.R55Z6 1970] 77-119663
1. Dreiser, Theodore, 1871-1945. I. Title.

ELIAS, Robert Henry, 813'.5'2
1914-
Theodore Dreiser, apostle of nature [by] Robert H. Elias. Emended ed. with a survey of research and criticism. Ithaca, Cornell University Press [1970] x, 435 p. port. 22 cm. Includes bibliographical references. [PS3507.R55Z63 1970] 70-129563 12.50
1. Dreiser, Theodore, 1871-1945. I. Title.

KAZIN, Alfred, 1915- ed. 813.5
The stature of Theodore Dreiser; a critical survey of the man and his work. Edited by Alfred Kazin and Charles Shapiro; with an introd. by Alfred Kazin. Bloomington, Indiana University Press [1955] 303 p. 24 cm. Bibliography: p. [271]-303. [PS3507.R55Z64] 55-8446
1. Dreiser, Theodore, 1871-1945. I. Shapiro, Charles, joint ed. II. Title. BIP

LEHAN, Richard Daniel, 813'.5'2
1930-
Theodore Dreiser: his world and his novels [by] Richard Lehan. Carbondale, Southern Illinois University Press [1969] xiv, 280 p. illus., ports. 24 cm. Includes bibliographical references. [PS3507.R55Z66] 69-19748 8.95
1. Dreiser, Theodore, 1871-1945. I. Title.

LEHAN, Richard Daniel, 813'.5'2
1930-
Theodore Dreiser: his world and novels [by] Richard Lehan. Carbondale, Southern Illinois University Press [1974, c1969] xiv, 280 p. illus. 20 cm. (Arcturus books, AB121) Includes bibliographical references. [PS3507.R55Z66 1974] 73-12637 ISBN 0-8093-0663-8 3.25 (pbk.)
1. Dreiser, Theodore, 1871-1945.

LUNDQUIST, James. 813'.5'2
Theodore Dreiser. New York, Ungar [1974] ix, 150 p. 20 cm. (Modern literature monographs) Bibliography: p. 135-141. [PS3507.R55Z668] 73-84600 ISBN 0-8044-2563-9 6.00
1. Dreiser, Theodore, 1871-1945.

MATTHIESSEN, Francis Otto, 928.1
1902-1950.
Theodore Dreiser. [New York]Sloane [1951] 267 p. port. 22 cm.d(The American men of letters series) "Bibliographical notes":p. 253-258 [PS3507.R55Z7] 51-1734
1. Dreiser, Theodore I. Title.

MATTHIESSEN, Francis 813'.5'2 B
Otto, 1902-1950.
Theodore Dreiser. Westport, Conn., Greenwood Press [1973, c1951] 267 p. port. 22 cm. Original ed. issued in series: The American men of letters. Bibliography: p. 253-258. [PS3507.R55Z7 1973] 72-7876 ISBN 0-8371-6550-4 12.00
1. Dreiser, Theodore, 1871-1945. I. Series: The American men of letters series.

MOERS, Ellen, 1928- 813'.5'2 B
Two Dreisers. New York, Viking Press [1969] xvii, 404 p. 22 cm. Bibliographical references included in "Reference notes" (p. 359-401) [PS3507.R55Z74] 69-15660 10.00
1. Dreiser, Theodore, 1871-1945. I. Title.

MOERS, Ellen, 1928- 813'.5'2 B
Two Dreisers. New York, Viking Press [1969] xvii, 404 p. 22 cm. Bibliographical references included in "Reference notes" (p. 359-401) [PS3507.R55Z74] 69-15660 10.00
1. Dreiser, Theodore, 1871-1945. I. Title.

SWANBERG, W. A., 1907- 928.1
Dreiser. New York, Scribners [c.1965] xvii, 614p. illus., ports. 25cm. Bibl. [PS3507.R55Z84] 65-13661 10.00
1. Dreiser, Theodore, 1871-1945. I. Title.

*SWANBERG, W. A., 1907- 928.1
Dreiser. New York, Bantam [1967, c.1965] xii, 722p. 18cm. (Q3345) Bibl. [PS3507.R55Z84] 1.25 pap.,
1. Dreiser, Theodore, 1871-1945 I. Title.
BIP

THEODORE Dreiser, 813'.5'2
America's foremost novelist. [Folcroft, Pa.] Folcroft Library Editions, 1973. 23 p. illus. 23 cm. Reprint of the 1917(?) ed. published by J. Lane Co., New York. Contents.—Masters, E. L. Theodore Dreiser: a portrait.—Lyon, H. M. What manner of man he is.—Ficke, A. D. To Theodore Dreiser on reading "The genius".—Powys, J. C. The writer and his writings. [PS3507.R55Z847 1973] 73-10411 5.50
1. Dreiser, Theodore, 1871-1945.

TJADER, Marguerite. 813'.5'2 B
Theodore Dreiser: a new dimension. Norwalk, Conn., Silvermine Publishers [1965] x, 244 p. 22 cm. [PS3507.R55Z85] 65-20596
1. Dreiser, Theodore, 1871-1945. I. Title.

Dreiser, Theodore, 1871-1945—Biography.

DRIESER, Vera. 813'.5'2 B
My Uncle Theodore / by Vera Dreiser, with Brett Howard. New York : Nash Pub., c1976. ix, 238 p. : ill. ; 25 cm. Includes bibliographical references. [PS3507.R55Z589] 75-30392 ISBN 0-8402-1366-2 : 9.95
1. Dreiser, Theodore, 1871-1945—Biography. 2. Dreiser, Theodore, 1871-1945—Relationship with women. I. Howard, Brett, joint author. II. Title.

Dreiser, Theodore, 1871-1945—Juvenile literature.

PALEY, Alan L. 813'.5'2 B
Theodore Dreiser: American editor and novelist, by Alan L. Paley. Charlotteville, N.Y., SamHar Press, 1973. 32 p. 22 cm. (Outstanding personalities, no. 55) Bibliography: p. 31-32. Traces the life and analyzes the works of the controversial twentieth-century American novelist, Theodore Dreiser. [PS3507.R55Z77] 92 73-77603 0.98 (pbk.)
1. Dreiser, Theodore, 1871-1945—Juvenile literature. I. Title.
Library binding; 1.98.

Drew, Charles Richard, 1904-1950.

HARDWICK, 615'.65'00924 (B)
Richard.
Charles Richard Drew, pioneer in blood research. New York, Scribner [1967] 144 p. 22 cm. [QP26.D7H3] 67-24049
1. Drew, Charles Richard, 1904-1950. 2. Blood banks. I. Title.
BIP

HARDWICK, 615'.65'00924 B
Richard.
Charles Richard Drew, pioneer in blood research. New York, Scribner [1967] 144 p. 22 cm. [QP26.D7H3] 67-24049
1. Drew, Charles Richard, 1904-1950. 2. Blood banks.

LICHELLO, Robert, 615'.65'00924 B
1926-
Pioneer in blood plasma: Dr. Charles Richard Drew. New York, J. Messner [1968] 190 p. 22 cm. Bibliography: p. 185. [R154.D75L5] 68-27032 3.50
1. Drew, Charles Richard, 1904-1950. 2. Negro physicians. I. Title.

Drew, Charles Richard, 1904-1950—Juvenile literature.

BERTOL, Roland. 615'.65'00924 B
Charles Drew. Illustrated by Jo Polseno. New York, Crowell [1970] 31 p. illus. (part col.) 24 cm. (Crowell biographies) An easy-to-read biography of the Negro physician who pioneered blood preservation and plasma transfusions in the United States and became the first director of the American Red Cross Blood Bank. [PZ10.B29522535Ch] 92 77-94789
1. Drew, Charles Richard, 1904-1950—Juvenile literature. I. Polseno, Jo, illus. II. Title. BIP

Drew, Daniel, 1797-1879.

MINNIGERODE, Meade, 650'.0922 B
1887-1967.
Certain rich men; Stephen Girard, John Jacob Astor, Jay Cooke, Daniel Drew, Cornelius Vanderbilt, Jay Gould, Jim Fisk. Freeport, N.Y., Books for Libraries Press [1970] xi, 210 p. illus., facsim., ports. 23 cm. (Essay index reprint series) Reprint of the 1927 ed. Bibliography: p. ix-xi. [CT219.M55 1970] 71-121489
1. Girard, Stephen, 1750-1831. 2. Astor, John Jacob, 1763-1848. 3. Cooke, Jay, 1821-1905. 4. Drew, Daniel, 1797-1879. 5. Vanderbilt, Cornelius, 1794-1877. 6. Gould, Jay, 1836-1892. 7. Fisk, James, 1835-1872. I. Title.

WHITE, Bouck, 1874- 332'.092'4 B
The book of Daniel Drew. New York, Arno Press, 1973 [c1910] vi, 423 p. 23 cm. (Big business: economic power in a free society) Reprint of the ed. published by G. H. Doran Co., New York. [F124.D774] 73-2539 ISBN 0-405-05118-2 20.00
1. Drew, Daniel, 1797-1879. 2. New York (State)—Politics and government—1865-1950. I. Title. II. Series. BIP

WHITE, Bouck, 1874- 923.373
The book of Daniel Drew; a glimpse of the Fisk-Gould-Tweed regime from the inside. With a new introd. by Benton W. Davis. Larchmont, N.Y., American Research Council [1965] xvi, 423 p. illus., ports. 21 cm. (The Library of stock market classics) First published in 1910. [F124.D773] 65-20320
1. Drew, Daniel, 1797-1879. 2. New York (State) — Pol. & govt. I. Title.

WHITE, Bouck, 1874- 923.373
The book of Daniel Drew; a glimpse of the Fisk-Gould-Tweed regime from the inside. [rev. ed.] New introd. by Benton W. Davis. Amer. Res. Council [dist. New York, Citadel, c.1965] xvi, 423p. illus., ports. 21cm. (Lib. of stock market classics) First pub. in 1910 by Doubleday. [F124.D773] 65-20320 5.00
1. Drew, Daniel, 1797-1879. 2. New York (State)—Pol. &govt. I. Title.

Drew, Louisa (Lane)

DREW, Louisa 792'.028'0924 B
(Lane) 1820-1897.
Autobiographical sketch of Mrs. John Drew. With an introd. by her son John Drew. With biographical notes by Douglas Taylor. New York, B. Blom, 1971. xiii, 200 p. illus., facsims., ports. 22 cm. "First published in 1899." [PN2287.D7A3 1971] 76-81207
I. Title.

Drexel, Katharine, 1858-1955.

BURTON, Katherine (Kurz) 922.273
1890-
The golden door; the life of Katharine Drexel. New York, Kenedy [1957] 329p. illus. 21cm. [BX4705.D755B8] 57-5759
1. Drexel, Katharine, 1858-1955. I. Title.

DUFFY, Consuela Marie. 271'.979
Katharine Drexel; a biography. With an introd. by Richard Cardinal Cushing. Philadelphia, P. Reilly Co. [c1966] 434 p. ports. 23 cm. Bibliographical references included in "Footnotes" (p. 400-421) [BX4705.D755D8] 66-29382
1. Drexel, Katharine, 1858-1955. I. Title.

DUFFY, Consuela Marie. v. 12
Katharine Drexel; a biography, with an introduction by His Eminence Richard Cardinal Cushing. Philadelphia, The Peter Reilly Co. [1966] xiii, 1 l, 16-434 p. 23 cm. 67-88301
1. Drexel, Katharine, Mother, 1858-1955. 2. Missions — Indians. 3. Missions — Negroes. 4. Sisters of the Blessed Sacrament for Indians and Colored People. I. Title.

TARRY, Ellen, 1906- 922.273
Katharine Drexel, friend of the neglected. Illustrated by Donald Bolognese. New York, Farrar, Straus & Cudahy [1958] 190 p. illus. 22 cm. (Vision books, 32) [BX4705.D755T3] 58-5456
1. Drexel, Katharine, 1858-1955. I. Title.

Drexel, Katharine, 1858-1955-Juvenile literature.

ROBERTO, Brother, 1927- 922.273
More than money can buy; a story of Mother Katharine Drexel. Illus. by Carolyn Lee Jagodits. Notre Dame, Ind., Dujarie Press [1959] 95p. illus. 24cm. [BX4705.D755R6] 59-65388
1. Drexel, Katharine, 1858-1955-Juvenile literature. I. Title.

Drexel, Katharine, 1858-1965 — Juvenile literature.

BURTON, Katherine (Kruz) 1890- 92
The door of hope; the story of Katharine Drexel. Illustrated by Irene Murray. New York, Hawthorn Books [1963] 187 p. illus. 22 cm. (Credo books) [BX4705.D755B79] 63-8784
1. Drexel, Katharine, 1858-1965 — Juvenile literature. I. Title.

Driberg, Tom, Baron Bradwell.

DRIBERG, Tom, 941.082'092'4 B
Baron Bradwell.
Ruling passions / by Tom Driberg. New York : Stein and Day, [1977] p. cm. Autobiography. Includes index. [CT788.D785A37] 76-49058 10.00
1. Driberg, Tom, Baron Bradwell. 2. Driberg, Tom. 3. England—Biography. I. Title. BIP

Drieu La Rochelle, Pierre, 1893-1945—Biography.

DRIEU La Rochelle, Pierre, 1893-1945. 848'.9'1203
Secret journal and other writings; translated [from the French] and with an introduction by Alastair Hamilton. Cambridge, Rivers P. Ltd., 1973. xlii, 81 p., leaf. port. 23 cm. Translation of Recit secret; suivu de journal, 1944-1945 et d'Exorde. [PQ2607.R5R3613 1973b] 74-168513 ISBN 0-903747-02-2 £3.00
1. Drieu La Rochelle, Pierre, 1893-1945—Biography. I. Hamilton, Alastair, 1941- II. Title.

DRIEU La Rochelle, Pierre, 1893-1945. 848'.9'1203 B
Secret journal and other writings. Translated and with an introd. by Alastair Hamilton. [1st American ed.] New York, H. Fertig [1973] xlii, 81 p. port. 22 cm. Translation of Recit secret, suivi du Journal, 1944-1945, et d'Exorde. Contents.Contents.—Secret journal.—Diary, 1944-45.—Final reckoning.—Notes. Includes bibliographical references. [PQ2607.R5R3613 1973] 73-14648 8.00
I. Title. **BIP**

Drinkwater, John,

DRINKWATER, John, 1882-1937. 822'.9'12 B
Discovery; being the second book of an autobiography, 1897-1913. Boston, Houghton Mifflin, 1933. St. Clair Shores, Mich., Scholarly Press, 1970. 235 p. illus., ports. 22 cm. The first book appeared under title: Inheritance. [PR6007.R5Z52 1970] 78-131691 ISBN 0-403-00578-7
I. Title. **BIP**

Driscoll, John Lynn, 1891-

BARRETT, Glen. 332.1'092'4 B
J. Lynn Driscoll; Western banker. A black diamond history. [Boise, Idaho, Syms-York, 1974] xiv, 297 p. illus. 24 cm. Bibliography: p. 269-287. [HG2463.D7B37] 74-80761 9.00
1. Driscoll, John Lynn, 1891-

Driscoll, Robert Henry.

DRISCOLL, Robert Edward 923.373
Diary of a country banker. New York, Vantage Press [c.1960] 140p. 21cm. 60-3469 2.95 bds.,
1. Driscoll, Robert Henry. I. Title.

Droge, Edward F.

DROGE, Edward F. 363.2'092'4 B
The patrolman: a cop's story, by Edward F. Droge, Jr. [New York] New American Library [1973] 240 p. 18 cm. (A Signet book) Autobiographical. [HV7911.D7A3] 73-173490 1.25 (pbk.)
1. Droge, Edward F. I. Title.

Dromgoole family.

HEATH, Dromgoole, 1907- 929'.2'0973
Canaan ; home of the Edward Dromgoole family, built 1780-84, Brunswick County, Virginia / written by Dromgoole and Lou Allie Heath. Richmond, Calif. : Heath. : Heath, 1972. 9, [5] leaves, [2] leaves of plates : ill. (some col.), geneal. table ; 30 cm. Bibliography: leaf [11] [CS71.D788 1972] 75-319465
1. Dromgoole family. 2. Heath family. I. Heath, Lou Allie, joint author. II. Title: Canaan : home of the Edward Dromgoole family ...

Dronfield, William, 1826-1894.

THORNES, Vernon. 331.88'092'4 B
William Dronfield, 1826-1894 : influences on nineteenth century Sheffield / by Vernon Thornes [Sheffield] : Sheffield City Libraries, 1976. 16 p. : ill., facsims., port. ; 30 cm. (Local studies leaflets) Cover title. [HD6665.D75T46] 76-378225 ISBN 0-900660-28-7 : £0.50
1. Dronfield, William, 1826-1894. 2. Trade-unions—England—Sheffield—Officials and employees—Biography. 3. Sheffield, Eng.—Economic conditions. I. Title. II. Series.

Droste-Hulshoff, Annette Elisabeth, Freiin von, 1797-1848.

MARE, Margaret Laura 831.7
Annette von Droste-Hulshoff. Tr. [from German] by Ursula Prideaux. Lincoln, Univ. of Neb. Pr. [c.1965] xiii, 322p. illus., ports. 23cm. Bibl. [PT1848.Z5M3] 65-13257 6.00
1. Droste-Hulshoff, Annette Elisabeth, Freiin von, 1797-1848. I. Title.

Drucker, Peter Ferdinand, 1909-

DRUCKER, Peter Ferdinand, 1909- 658.4'0092'4 B
Adventures of a bystander / Peter F. Drucker. 1st ed. New York : Harper & Row, c1979. viii, 344 p. ; 24 cm. Includes index. [H59.D75A33 1979] 78-2120 ISBN 0-06-011101-1 : 10.95
1. Drucker, Peter Ferdinand, 1909- 2. Social scientists—United States—Biography. I. Title. **BIP**

Drug abuse—Personal narratives.

LEAH. 248'.86
Leah. Old Tappan, N.J., F. H. Revell Co. [1973] 90 p. illus. 18 cm. Autobiographical. [HV5805.L4A3] 73-4042 ISBN 0-8007-0595-5 3.95
1. Drug abuse—Personal narratives. 2. Prostitutes—Correspondence, reminiscences, etc. **BIP**

QUINN, Barbara, 1942- 362.2'93'0924 B
Cookie. [New York] Bartholomew House [1971] 256 p. 22 cm. [HV5805.Q5A3] 70-155025 ISBN 0-87794-026-6 6.95
1. Drug abuse—Personal narratives. I. Title.

Drummond, William, 1585-1649.

MASSON, David, 1822-1907. 821'.3 B
Drummond of Hawthornden; the story of his life and writings. New York, Haskell House, 1969. xv, 490 p. illus., port. 23 cm. Reprint of the 1873 ed. Bibliographical footnotes. [PR2263.M3 1969b] 68-24912
1. Drummond, William, 1585-1649. I. Title. **BIP**

Dryden, John, 1631-1700.

DRYDEN, John, 1631-1700. 821'.4 B
The letters of John Dryden, with letters addressed to him. Collected and edited by Charles E. Ward. New York, AMS Press [1965, c1942] xvii, 196 p. illus. 23 cm. Original ed. issued in series: Duke University publications. Includes bibliographical references. [PR3423.A45 1965] 74-164791
I. Ward, Charles Eugene, ed.

HOLLIS, Christopher, 1902- 821'.4 B
Dryden. Folcroft, Pa., Folcroft Press [1969] 224 p. port. 24 cm. Reprint of the 1933 ed. Bibliography: p. 221. [PR3423.H6 1969] 72-195404
1. Dryden, John, 1631-1700. **BIP**

HOLLIS, Christopher, 1902- 821'.4 B
Dryden. New York, Haskell House Publishers, 1974. 224 p. 21 cm. Reprint of the 1933 ed. published by Duckworth, London. Bibliography: p. 221. [PR3423.H6 1974] 74-6383 ISBN 0-8383-1753-7
1. Dryden, John, 1631-1700.

HOLLIS, Christopher, 1902- 821'.4 B
Dryden. [Folcroft, Pa.] Folcroft Library Editions, 1974. 224 p. port. 26 cm. Reprint of the 1933 ed. published by Duckworth, London. Bibliography: p. 221. [PR3423.H6 1974b] 74-11135 ISBN 0-8414-4828-0 (lib. bdg.)
1. Dryden, John, 1631-1700.

NICOLL, Allardyce, 1894- 821'.4
Dryden & his poetry. New York, Russell & Russell [1967] 151, [1] p. port. 17 cm. "First published in 1923." Bibliography: p. 151-[152] [PR3423.N5 1967] 66-27134
1. Dryden, John, 1631-1700. I. Title. **BIP**

NICOLL, Allardyce, 1894- 821'.4
Dryden & his poetry / by Allardyce Nicoll. Norwood, Pa. : Norwood Editions, 1976. p. cm. Reprint of the 1923 ed. published by G. G. Harrap, London, which was issued as no. 32 of Poetry & life series. [PR3423.N5 1976] 76-9065 ISBN 0-8482-1901-5 : 7.00
1. Dryden, John, 1631-1700. I. Title. II. Series: Poetry and life series ; 32.

OSBORN, James Marshall 828.409
John Dryden: some biographical facts and problems. Rev. ed. Gainesville, Univ. of Fla. Pr. 1965[c.1940-1965] xvi, 316p. facsims., ports. 24cm. [PR3423.O7] 65-29104 7.50
1. Dryden, John, 1631-1700. 2. Dryden, John, 1631-1700—Bibl. I. Title.

SAINTSBURY, George Edward Bateman, 1845-1933. 828'.4'09
Dryden. Detroit, Gale Research Co., 1968. vi, 196 p. 22 cm. (The Gale library of lives and letters: British writers series) Title page includes original imprint: London, Macmillan, 1881. Reprint of the 1881 ed. [PR3423.S3 1968] 67-23875
1. Dryden, John, 1631-1700. **BIP**

SCOTT, Sir Walter, bart., 1771-1832. 821.4
The life of John Dryden. Edited with an introd. by Bernard Kreissman. Lincoln, University of Nebraska Press [1963] xix, 471 p. 21 cm. "Reproduced from volume I of the Miscellaneous prose works of Sir Walter Scott, bart., published by Robert Cadell, Edinburgh, 1834." Bibliographical references included in "Editor's notes" (p. 455-464) Bibliographical footnotes. [PR3423.S34 1963] 63-8121
1. Dryden, John, 1631-1700. I. Kreissman, Bernard, ed. II. Title. **BIP**

SCOTT, Walter, bart., Sir 1771-1832 821.4
The life of John Dryden. Ed., introd. by Bernard Kreissman. Lincoln, Univ. of Nebr. Pr. [c.1963] xix, 471p. 21cm. Reproduced from vol. I of the Miscellaneous prose works of Sir Walter Scott. bart., pub. by Robert Cadell, Edinburgh, 1834. Bibl. 63-8121 5.00;1.70 pap.,
1. Dryden, John, 1631-1700, I. Kreissman, Bernard, ed. II. Title.

WARD, Charles Eugene. 928.2
The life of John Dryden. Chapel Hill, University of North Carolina Press [1961] 380 p. illus. 24 cm. [PR3423.W3] 61-18582
1. Dryden, John, 1631-1700. I. Title. **BIP**

WYKES, David. 821'.4 B
A preface to Dryden / David Wykes. London ; New York : Longman, 1977. xix, 236 p. : ill. ; 22 cm. (Preface books) Includes index. Bibliography: p. 225-230. [PR3423.W9] 76-12598 ISBN 0-582-35101-4 : 9.00 ISBN 0-582-35102-2 pbk. : 5.50
1. Dryden, John, 1631-1700. I. Title. **BIP**

YOUNG, Kenneth, 1916- 821'.4 B
John Dryden; a critical biography. New York, Russell & Russell [1969] xvi, 240 p. 22 cm. Reprint of the 1954 ed. Includes bibliographical references. [PR3423.Y6 1969] 69-16777
1. Dryden, John, 1631-1700.

Dryden, Ken, 1947-

DRYDEN, Murray. 796.9'62'0922
Playing the shots at both ends: the story of Ken and Dave Dryden [by] Murray Dryden with Jim Hunt. Toronto, New York, McGraw-Hill Ryerson [1972] xi, 155 p. illus. 23 cm. [GV848.5.D79D79] 72-9534 ISBN 0-07-077505-2
1. Dryden, Ken, 1947- 2. Dryden, Dave, 1941- 3. Hockey. I. Hunt, James R. II. Title.

Drysdale, Don.

SHAPIRO, Milton J 796.35722
The Don Drysdale story, by Milton J. Shapiro. New York, J. Messner [1964] 191 p. ports. 22 cm. [GV865.D7S5] 64-11366
1. Drysdale, Don. I. Title.

Du Barry, Jeanne Becu, comtesse, 1743-1793.

LOOMIS, Stanley. 920.7
Du Barry, a biography. [1st ed.] Philadelphia, Lippincott [1959] 320p. illus. 22cm. Includes bibliography. [DC135.D8L6] 59-7780
1. Du Barry, Jeanne Becu, comtesse, 1743-1793. I. Title.

STOECKI, Agnes (Barron), baroness de 944.D340924(B)
Mistress of Versailles: the life of Madame Du Barry [by] Agnes de Stoeckl. London, J. Murray [1966] 183p. front., 7 plates (incl. ports.) 23cm. Bibl. [DC135.D8S8] 66-71487 6.75
1. Du Barry, Jeanne Becu, comtesse, 1743-1793. I. Title.
American distributor: Transatlantic in New York.

Du Bois, William Edward Burghardt, 1868-1963.

BRODERICK, Francis L. 928.1
W. E. B. Du Bois, Negro leader in a time of crisis. Stanford, Calif., Stanford University Press, 1959. 259 p. illus. 23 cm. Includes bibliography. [E185.97.D73B7] 59-7422
1. Du Bois, William Edward Burghardt, 1868-

DUBOIS, William Edward Burghardt, 1868-1963. 370'.924 B
The autobiography of W. E. B. DuBois; a soliloquy on viewing my life from the last decade of its first century. [1st ed. New York] International Publishers [1968] 448 p. ports. 22 cm. [E185.97.D73A3] 68-14103
I. Title. **BIP**

DU BOIS, William Edward Burghardt, 1868-1963. 301.24'2'0924 B
The correspondence of W. E. B. Du Bois. Edited by Herbert Aptheker. [Amherst] University of Massachusetts Press, 1973- v. illus. 25 cm. Contents.Contents.—v. 1. Selections, 1877-1934. Includes bibliographical references. [E185.97.D73A4 1973] 72-90496 20.00 (v. 1)
1. Du Bois, William Edward Burghardt, 1868-1963. I. Aptheker, Herbert, 1915- ed.

DU BOIS, William Edward Burghardt, 1868-1963. 370'.924 B
A W. E. B. Du Bois reader. Edited by Andrew G. Paschal. Introd. by Arna Bontemps. New York, Macmillan [1971] xxix, 376 p. 21 cm. Bibliography: p. [371]-376. [E185.97.D73A25 1971] 70-150672
1. Negroes—Addresses, essays, lectures. 2. Africa—Addresses, essays, lectures. I. Title.

LOGAN, Rayford Whittingham, 1897- 301.45'19'0073022 B
Two bronze titans: Frederick Douglass and William Edward Burghardt Du Bois. [Washington] Dept. of History, Howard University, 1972. 19 p. port. 24 cm. (Dept. of History, Howard University. Second series of historical publications) [E185.97.D73L58] 73-156264
1. Du Bois, William Edward Burghardt, 1868-1963. 2. Douglass, Frederick, 1817?-1895. I. Title. II. Series: Howard University, Washington, D.C. Dept. of History. Second series of historical publications.

LOGAN, Rayford Whittingham, 1897- comp. 370'.924
W. E. B. Du Bois: a profile, edited by Rayford W. Logan. [1st ed.] New York, Hill and Wang [1971] xxii, 324 p. 21 cm. (American profiles) (American century series) Contents.Contents.—The search for a career, by F. L. Broderick.—"Radicals and conservatives," a modern view, by A. Meier.—The paradox of W. E. B. Du Bois, by A. Meier.—The emerging leader, a contemporary view, by W. H. Ferris.—The NAACP and The crisis, by C. F. Kellogg.—An accomodationist in wartime, by E. M. Rudwick.—The continuing debate: Washington vs. Du Bois, by B. Mathews.—Pan-Africanism as "romantic

racism," by H. R. Isaacs.—The historian, by H. Aptheker.—A Black messianic visionary, by V. Harding.—Bibliographical essay (p. 294-318) [E185.97.D73L6] 75-150959 ISBN 0-8090-0213-2 2.45
1. Du Bois, William Edward Burghardt, 1868-1963. I. Title.

RUDWICK, Elliott M. 301.15'3'0924 B
W. E. B. Du Bois, propagandist of the Negro protest, by Elliott M. Rudwick. With a new pref. by Louis Harlan and an epilogue by the author. New York, Atheneum, 1968. 390 p. 21 cm. (Studies in American Negro life, NL6) (Atheneum paperbacks.) Bibliographical references included in "Notes": p. 319-376. [E185.97.D73R8 1908] 68-16418 3.25
1. Du Bois, William Edward Burghardt, 1868-1963. 2. Negroes. BIP

RUDWICK, Elliott M. 928.1
W. E. B. Du Bois; a study in minority group leadership. Philadelphia, University of Pennsylvania Press [1960] 382 p. 22 cm. Includes bibliography. [E185.97.D73R8] 60-6754
1. Du Bois, William Edward Burghardt, 1868- 2. Negroes.

RUDWICK, Elliott M 301.15'3'0924 (B)
W. E. B. Du Bois, propagandist of the Negro protest, by Elliott M. Rudwick. With a new pref. by Louis Harlan and an epilogue by the author. New York. Atheneum, 1968. 390 p. 21 cm. (Studies in American Negro life, NL6) $3.25 Atheneum paperbacks. Bibliographical references included in "Notes": p. 319-376. [W185.97.D73R8 1968] 68-16418
1. Du Bois, William Edward Burghardt, 1868-1963. 2. Negroes. I. Title.

STERNE, Emma (Gelders) 1894- 300'.924 B
His was the voice; the life of W. E. B. Du Bois. Foreword by Ronald Stevenson. New York, Crowell-Collier Press [1971] xv, 232 p. illus., ports. 21 cm. Bibliography: p. 221-225. [E185.97.D73S7] 76-138027 4.95
1. Du Bois, William Edward Burghardt, 1868-1963. I. Title. BIP

TUTTLE, William M., 1937- comp. 301.24'2'0924 B
W. E. B. Du Bois, edited by William M. Tuttle, Jr. Englewood Cliffs, N.J., Prentice-Hall [1973] vi, 186 p. 21 cm. (Great lives observed) (A Spectrum book) Bibliography: p. 180-183. [E185.D73T86 1973] 73-9544 ISBN 0-13-220905-5 6.95
1. Du Bois, William Edward Burghardt, 1868-1963. 2. United States—Race question. 3. Negroes—Race identity.
Pbk. 2.45; ISBN 0-13-220889-X. BIP

Du Bois, William Edward Burghardt, 1868-1963—Juvenile literature.

HAMILTON, Virginia. 370'.92'4 B
W. E. B. Du Bois; a biography, by Virginia Hamilton. New York, T. Y. Crowell [1972] 218 p. illus. 21 cm. Bibliography: p. [204]-208. This American Negro leader, author, and sociologist spent his life fighting for the rights of blacks everywhere. [E185.97.D73H3 1972] 92 70-175106 ISBN 0-690-87256-9 4.50
1. Du Bois, William Edward Burghardt, 1868-1963—Juvenile literature. I. Title. BIP

LACY, Leslie Alexander. 301.15'3'0924 B
Cheer the lonesome traveler; the life of W. E. B. Du Bois. Illustrated by James Barkley, and with photos. New York, Dial Press [1970] 183 p. illus., ports. 22 cm. Bibliography: p. 170-177. A biography of the black sociologist and author who devoted his life to gaining equality for the Negro. [E185.97.D73L3] 92 78-102829 4.95
1. Du Bois, William Edward Burghardt, 1868-1963—Juvenile literature. I. Title. BIP

STERLING, Dorothy, 1913- 920.073
Lift every voice; the lives of Booker T. Washington, W. E. B. Du Bois, Mary Church Terrell, and James Weldon Johnson [by] Dorothy Sterling and Benjamin Quarles. Illustrated by Ernest Crichlow. [1st ed.] Garden City, N.Y., Doubleday, 1965. 116 p. illus., ports. 22 cm. (Zenith books) [E185.96.S77] 65-17237
1. Washington, Booker Taliaferro, 1859-1915—Juvenile literature. 2. Du Bois, William Edward Burghardt, 1868-1963—Juvenile literature. 3. Terrell, Mary (Church) 1863-1954—Juvenile literature. 4. Johnson, James Weldon, 1871-1938—Juvenile literature. I. Quarles, Benjamin, joint author. II. Title.

Du Feu, Paul.

DUFEU, Paul. 301.41'2'0924 B
Let's hear it for the long-legged women. New York, Putnam [1973] 254 p. 22 cm. [CT788.D8A34 1973] 73-87183 ISBN 0-399-11243-X 6.95
1. Du Feu, Paul. I. Title.

Du Maurier, Daphne, Dame, 1907- — Biography—Youth.

DU MAURIER, Daphne, Dame, 1907- 823'.9'12
Myself when young : the shaping of a writer / Daphne du Maurier. 1st ed. in the U.S. Garden City, N.Y. : Doubleday, 1977. ix, 204 p., [12] leaves of plates : ill. ; 22 cm. Includes index. [PR6007.U47Z52 1977] 76-56283 ISBN 0-385-13016-3 : 7.95
1. Du Maurier, Daphne, Dame, 1907- — Biography—Youth. 2. Authors, English—20th century—Biography. I. Title. BIP

DU MAURIER, Daphne, Dame, 1907- 823'.9'12
Myself when young : the shaping of a writer / Daphne du Maurier. 1st ed. in the U.S. Garden City, N.Y. : Doubleday, 1977. ix, 204 p., [12] leaves of plates : ill. ; 22 cm. Includes index. [PR6007.U47Z52 1977] 76-56283 ISBN 0-385-13016-3 : 7.95
1. Du Maurier, Daphne, Dame, 1907- — Biography—Youth. 2. Authors, English—20th century—Biography. I. Title. BIP

Du Maurier, George Louis Palmella Busson, 1834-1896.

DU MAURIER, George Louis Palmella Busson, 1834-1896. 741'.0924
The young George du Maurier; a selection of his letters, 1860-67. Edited by Daphne du Maurier, with a biographical appendix by Derek Pepys Whiteley and illus. from contemporary drawings by du Maurier. Westport, Conn., Greenwood Press [1969] xxi, 307 p. illus., ports. 23 cm. Reprint of the 1951 ed. [NC242.D8A32 1969] 73-97329
I. Du Maurier, Daphne, 1907- ed. II. Title. BIP

ORMOND, Leonee. 741'.0924 B
George Du Maurier. [Pittsburgh, Pa.] University of Pittsburgh Press [1969] xv, 516 p. illus., ports. (part col.) 26 cm. Bibliography: p. [499]-501. [NC242.D8O7 1969b] 79-80031 14.95
1. Du Maurier, George Louis Palmella Busson, 1834-1896.

Du Maurier, Gerald, Sir 1873-1934.

DU MAURIER, Daphne, 1907- 927.92
Gerald: a portrait. New York, Pocket Bks. [1963, c.1934, 1935] 246p. 17cm. (Giant cardinal, GC167) .50 pap.,
1. Du Maurier, Gerald, Sir 1873-1934. I. Title.

Du Pont de Nemours (E. I.) and Company.

CARR, William H. A. 926.6
The duPonts of Delaware. New York, Dodd, Mead [1964] xi, 368 p. illus., ports., map, geneal. tables. 24 cm. Bibliography: p. 352-356. [HD9651.9.D8C3] 64-13693
1. Du Pont de Nemours (E. I.) and Company. 2. Du Pont family (Pierre Samuel du Pont de Nemours, 1739-1817) I. Title.

Du Pont family.

DUKE, Marc. 338'.092'2 B
The du Ponts : portrait of a dynasty / Marc Duke. 1st ed. New York : Saturday Review Press, c1976. 340 p., [5] leaves of plates : ill. ; 24 cm. Includes index. Bibliography: p. 311-319. [CS71.D935 1976] 75-40068 12.95
1. Du Pont family. I. Title.

Du Puiset, Hugh, Bp. of Durham, 1125?-1195.

SCAMMELL, Geoffrey Vaughn. v. 12
Hugh Du Puiset, Bishop of Durham. Cambridge [Eng.] University Press, 1956. x, 354p. 23cm. Bibliography: p. 314-328. A57
1. Du Puiset, Hugh, Bp. of Durham, 1125?-1195. I. Title.

Dubinsky, David, 1892-

DEWEY, John, 1859- 923.373
David Dubinsky; a pictorial biography. Foreword by William Green; introd. by Walter P. Reuther. New York, Inter-allied Publications ['1951] 95 p. illus. 26 cm. [HD6509.D8D45] 52-23719
1. Dubinsky, David, 1892- I. Title.

DUBINSKY, David, 1892- 331.88'18'7120924
David Dubinsky : a life with labor / David Dubinsky and A. H. Raskin. New York : Simon and Schuster, c1977. 351 p., [8] leaves of plates : ill. ; 22 cm. Includes index. [HD6509.D8A33] 76-52414 ISBN 0-671-22437-9 : 10.00
1. Dubinsky, David, 1892- 2. Trade-unions—Clothing workers—United States—History. 3. Trade-unions—United States—Officials and employees—Biography. I. Raskin, Abraham Henry, 1911- joint author. BIP

Dublin. Abbey Theatre.

FAY, William George, 1872-1947. 792'.09418'3
The Fays of the Abbey Theatre; an autobiographical record, by W. G. Fay & Catherine Carswell. With a foreword by James Bridie. New York, B. Blom, 1971. 313 p. illus. 22 cm. Reprint of the 1935 ed. [PN2601.F3 1971] 79-91494
1. Dublin. Abbey Theatre. I. Carswell, Catherine MacFarlane, 1876-1946, joint author. II. Title.

Dublin—Biography.

FAULKNER, George, 1699?-1775. 914.18'3'030924
Prince of Dublin printers; the letters of George Faulkner [by] Robert E. Ward. [Lexington] University Press of Kentucky [1972] x, 141 p. 23 cm. Bibliography: p. 137-140. [Z232.F27A4 1972] 71-160053 ISBN 0-8131-1271-0 7.25
1. Dublin—Biography. I. Ward, Robert E., ed. II. Title.

Dublin. Gate Theatre.

MACLIAMMHOIR, Micheal, 1899- 792'.0924 B
All for Hecuba; an Irish theatrical autobiography, by Micheal MacLiammoir. [1st American ed.] Boston, Branden Press [1967, c1961] 356 p. illus., ports. 23 cm. "This new and revised edition with extra material first published 1961." [PN2601.M3 1967] 67-26024
1. Dublin. Gate Theatre. 2. Actors—Correspondence, reminiscences, etc. I. Title.

Dublin. Municipal Gallery of Modern Art.

GREGORY, Isabella Augusta (Persse), Lady, 1852-1932. 704'.7 B
Sir Hugh Lane: his life and legacy. With a foreword by James White. New York, Oxford University Press, 1973. 324 p. illus. 23 cm. (Coole edition, 10) [N5247.L3G73 1973] 73-164508 19.25
1. Lane, Hugh Perry, Sir, 1875-1915. 2. Dublin. Municipal Gallery of Modern Art. 3. Dublin. National Gallery of Ireland.

Dubois de Saligny, A.

DUBOIS de Saligny, A. 917.64'03'4
Alphonse in Austin; being excerpts from the official letters written to the French Foreign Ministry by Alphonse Dubois de Saligny. Selected & translated by Katherine Hart. [Austin, Tex.] Published by the Encino Press for the Friends of the Austin Public Library [1972? c1967] vi, 56 p. 24 cm. (Waterloo book no. 4) [F390.D82] 73-160681
1. Dubois de Saligny, A. 2. Texas—History—Republic, 1836-1846—Sources. I. Friends of the Austin Public Library. II. Title. III. Series. BIP

Duccio di Buoninsegna, d. 1319.

STUBBLEBINE, James H. 759.5
Duccio di Buoninsegna and his school / James H. Stubblebine. Princeton, N.J. : Princeton University Press, c1980. p. cm. Includes index. Bibliography: p. [ND623.D8S84] 78-22016 ISBN 0-691-03944-5 : 50.00
1. Duccio di Buoninsegna, d. 1319. 2. Painting, Gothic—Italy. I. Title. BIP

Duchamp, Marcel, 1887-1968.

ALEXANDRIAN, Sarane. 759.4 B
Marcel Duchamp / by Alexandrian ; [translated from the French by]. New York : Crown Publishers, c1977. p. cm. Bibliography: p. [ND553.D774A7613] 76-56831 ISBN 0-517-53008-2 : 4.95
1. Duchamp, Marcel, 1887-1968.

CABANNE, Pierre. 709'.2'2 B
The brothers Duchamp : Jacques Villon, Raymond Duchamp-Villon, Marcel Duchamp / text by Pierre Cabanne ; [translated from the French by Helga and Dinah Harrison]. 1st U.S. ed. Boston : New York Graphic Society, c1976. 269 p. : ill. (some col.) ; 29 cm. Translation of Les 3 Duchamp. Bibliography: p. 266. [N6853.D8C2213] 75-37285 ISBN 0-8212-0666-4 : 49.50
1. Duchamp, Marcel, 1887-1968. 2. Duchamp-Villon, Raymond, 1876-1918. 3. Villon, Jacques, 1875-1963. I. Title. BIP

DUCHAMP, Marcel, 1887-1968. 759.4
Marcel Duchamp. Text by Arturo Schwarz. New York, H. N. Abrams [1975, c1970] [51] p., [159] p. of illus. (part col.) 32 cm. Bibliography: 40th-42d prelim. page. [ND553.D774S31813] 73-16230 ISBN 0-8109-0087-4 37.50
1. Duchamp, Marcel, 1887-1968. I. Schwarz, Arturo, 1924-

SCHWARZ, Arturo, 1924- 709'.24
The complete works of Marcel Duchamp. New York, H. N. Abrams [1969] xxi, 630 p. illus., plates (part col.) 32 cm. Bibliography: p. 607-617. [ND553.D774S3] 69-11987
1. Duchamp, Marcel, 1887-1968. I. Title.

TOMKINS, Calvin, 1925- 709.04
The world of Marcel Duchamp, 1887- by Calvin Tomkins and the editors of Time-Life Books New York, Time, inc. [1966] 192 p. illus. (part col.) ports. (part col.) 31 cm. (Time-Life library of art) Bibliography: p. 185. [N6853.D8T6] 66-28544
1. Duchamp, Marcel, 1887- I. Time-Life Books. II. Title. BIP

Duchamp-Villon, Raymond, 1876-1918.

CABANNE, Pierre. 709'.2'2 B
The brothers Duchamp : Jacques Villon, Raymond Duchamp-Villon, Marcel Duchamp / text by Pierre Cabanne ; [translated from the French by Helga and Dinah Harrison]. 1st U.S. ed. Boston : New York Graphic Society, c1976. 269 p. : ill. (some col.) ; 29 cm. Translation of Les 3 Duchamp. Bibliography: p. 266. [N6853.D8C2213] 75-37285 ISBN 0-8212-0666-4 : 49.50
1. Duchamp, Marcel, 1887-1968. 2. Duchamp-Villon, Raymond, 1876-1918. 3. Villon, Jacques, 1875-1963. I. Title. BIP

Duchesne, Rose Philippine, 1769-1852.

CALLAN, Louise, 1893- 922.273
Philippine Duchesne, frontier missionary of the Sacred Heart, 1769-1852. With an introd. by Joseph E. Ritter. Westminster, Md., Newman Press, 1957. 805p. illus. 24cm. [BX4705.D85C3] 57-8616
1. Duchesne, Rose Philippine, 1769-1852. I. Title.

CALLAN, Louise, 1893- 922.273
Philippine Duchesne, frontier missionary of the Sacred Heart, 1769-1852. Abridged ed. With an introd. by Joseph E. Cardinal Ritter. Westminister, Md., Newman Press, 1965. xi, 504 p. illus., geneal. tables, ports. 24 cm. [BX4705.D85C35 1965] 63-12256
1. Duchesne, Rose Philippine, 1769-1852. I. Title.

PHILIPPINE 377'.8'277866 B
Duchesne and her times. Edited by Harriet Lane Cates Hardaway [and] Dorothy Garesche Holland. Saint Louis, Maryville College, 1968. 58 p. illus., ports. 24 cm. Papers presented at a conference held at Maryville College on March 7, 1968. Contents.Contents.—St. Louis 1818, by G. R. Brooks.—Philippine Duchesne: pioneer educator, by D. G. Holland.—Sidelights and souvenirs, by H. L. C. Hardaway.—The restoration of St. Ferdinand's: the church, the convent, and rectory, by G. Kramer.—Education in St. Louis before 1818, by J. F. McDermott. Bibliographical footnotes. [LC503.S3P5] 68-58112
1. Duchesne, Rose Philippine, 1769-1852. 2. Catholic Church in St. Louis—Education—History. I. Hardaway, Harriet Lane Cates, ed. II. Holland, Dorothy (Garesche) ed. III. Maryville College, St. Louis.

Ducks.

RIPLEY, Sidney Dillon, 598.4
1913-
A paddling of ducks, by Dillon Ripley. Illustrated by Francis Lee Jaques. Washington, Smithsonian Institution Press [1969, c1957] 256 p. illus. 23 cm. Autobiographical. Bibliography: p. 253. [QL696.A5R5 1969] 69-19396 5.95
1. Ducks. 2. Geese. 3. Zoological specimens—Collection and preservation. I. Jaques, Francis Lee, illus. II. Title.

Ducrow, Andrew, 1793-1842.

SAXON, A. H. 791.3'092'4 B
The life and art of Andrew Ducrow and the romantice age of the English circus / by A. H. Saxon. Hamden, Conn. : Archon Books, 1977. p. cm. Includes index. Bibliography: p. [GV1811.D78S39] 77-13010 ISBN 0-208-01651-1 : 25.00
1. Ducrow, Andrew, 1793-1842. 2. Circus—England—History. 3. Horsemanship. 4. Performing arts—England—History. 5. Entertainers—England—Biography. I. Title.

Dudevant, Amadine Aurore Lucie Dupin, Baroness, 1804-1876.

WINWAR, Frances. 843'.8
George Sand and her times; the life of the heart. New York, Lancer [1973?] 416 p. 18 cm. (Contempora bks., 33026) First ed. published in 1945 under title: The life of the heart. [PQ2414.W5] pap. 1.25.
1. Dudevant, Amadine Aurore Lucie Dupin, Baroness, 1804-1876.

Dudley, Jane, Lady, known as Lady Jane Grey, 1537-1554.

CHAPMAN, Hester W., 1899- 920.7
Lady Jane Grey, October 1537-February 1554. [1st American ed.] Boston, Little, Brown [1963, c1962] 224 p. illus. 22 cm. Includes bibliography. [DA345.1.D9C5 1963] 62-9555
1. Dudley, Jane, Lady, known as Lady Jane Grey, 1537-1554.

Dudley, Robert, Sir 1574-1649.

LEE, Arthur Stanley Gould 942.06
The son of Leicester; the story of Sir Robert Dudley, titular Earl of Warwick, Earl of Leicester, and Duke of Northumberland, only surviving issue of Queen Elizabeth's Favourite, the Earl of Leicester. London, Gollancz [Mystic, Conn., Verry, 1965,c.1964] 256p. geneal. table, port. 23cm. Bibl. [DA390.1.D9L44] 65-29679 5.00 bds.,
1. Dudley, Robert, Sir 1574-1649. I. Title.

Duff, Douglas Valder, 1901-

DUFF, Douglas Valder, 923.542
1901-
On swallowing the anchor. London, New York, J. Long [1954] 224p. illus. 22cm. [DA89.1.D84A3] 55-21748
1. Autobiographical. I. Title.

Duffey, Joseph Daniel.

GOLDBAUM, Howard, 329'.00973
1947-
A campaign album; a case study of the new politics. Photos. by Howard Goldbaum. Text by Eric Rennie. Philadelphia, United Church Press [1973] 128 p. illus. 26 cm. "A Pilgrim Press book." Includes bibliographical references. [JK1184.C8G62] 73-1874 ISBN 0-8298-0249-5 7.95
1. Duffey, Joseph Daniel. 2. United States. Congress. Senate—Elections—Case studies. 3. Elections—Connecticut—Case studies. I. Rennie, Eric, 1947- II. Title.

Duffy, Francis Patrick, 1871-1932.

BISHOP, James Alonzo, 922.273
1907-
Fighting Father Duffy. by Jim and Virginia Lee Bishop. Illustrated by H. Lawrence Hoffman. New York, Vision Books [1956] 189p. illus. 22cm. (Vision books, 7) [BX4705.D86B5] 56-5199
1. Duffy, Francis Patrick, 1871-1932. I. Bishop, Virginia Lee. joint author. II. Title.

Dufy, Raoul, 1877-1953.

COGNIAT, Raymond, 1896- 759.4
Raoul Dufy [Tr. from French by Thomas L. Callow] New York Crown, 1962. 92p. illus. (pt. col.) 29cm. 62-11813 3.50
1. Dufy, Raoul, 1877-1953. I. Title.

DUFY, Raoul, 1877- 759.4
Raoul Dufy [texte par] Raymond Cogniat New York [1950] [63] p. 60 illus. 17 cm. (Collection des maltres) Text in French, English and German. Bibliography: p. [63] [ND553.D78C56] 52-28621
I. Cogniat, Raymond, 1896- II. Title. III. Series: Collection "Les Maltres"

DUFY, Raoul, 1877-1953. 927.5
Raoul Dufy (1877-1953) Text by Alfred Werner New York, H. N. Abrams in association with Pocket Books [1953] [74] p. 34 illus. part col.) 18 cm. (The Pocket library of great art, A5) An Abrams art book. Bibliography: p. [74] [ND553.D78W4] 759.4 53-4518
I. Werner, Alfred, 1911-

Dugan family.

GRACY, Alice Duggan. 929'.2'0973
Thomas Hinds Duggan, descendant and ancestor / by Alice Duggan Gracy ; maps and illustrations by Watt Harris, Jr. Austin, Tex. : Gracy, c1976. x, 225 p. : ill. ; 28 cm. "Privately published." Includes bibliographical references and index. [CS71.D87 1976] 77-355243
1. Dugan family. 2. Duggan, Thomas Hinds, 1815-1865. 3. United States—Genealogy. 4. United States—Biography. I. Title.

GRACY, Alice Duggan. 929'.2'0973
Thomas Hinds Duggan, descendant and ancestor / by Alice Duggan Gracy ; maps and illustrations by Watt Harris, Jr. Austin, Tex. : Gracy, c1976. x, 225 p. : ill. ; 28 cm. "Privately published." Includes bibliographical references and index. [CS71.D87 1976] 77-355243
1. Dugan family. 2. Duggan, Thomas Hinds, 1815-1865. 3. United States—Genealogy. 4. United States—Biography. I. Title.

Duhring, Louis Adolphus, 1845-1913.

PARISH, Lawrence 616.5'00924 B
Charles.
Louis A. Duhring, M. D., pathfinder for dermatology. With a foreword by Donald Marion Pillsbury. Springfield, Ill., C. C. Thomas [1967] xviii, 137 p. illus., facsims., ports. 24 cm. Includes bibliographical references. [R154.D86P3] 66-16817
1. Duhring, Louis Adolphus, 1845-1913.

Duka, Norman, 1940-

DUKA, Norman, 322.4'2'0924 B
1940-
From shantytown to forest, the story of Norman Duka : [South Africa ANC] / recorded and edited by Dennis and Ginger Mercer. Richmond, B.C. : LSM Information Center, [1974] 108 p. : ill. (some col.) ; 22 cm. (Life histories from the Revolution ; 1) [DT779.95.D84A33] 75-310664 1.75
1. Duka, Norman, 1940- 2. African National Congress. I. Mercer, Dennis. II. Mercer, Ginger. III. Title. IV. Series.

Dulac, Edmund, 1882-1953.

*DULAC, Edmund. 741.642
Dulac edited by David Larkin, introduction by Brian Sanders New York, Peacock Press/Bantam Book [1975] [90 p. (chiefly ill plates), 30 cm. [NC965] 5.95 (pbk.)
1. Dulac, Edmund I. Larkin, David comp. II. Title.

WHITE, Colin. 741'.092'4 B
Edmund Dulac / Colin White. New York : Scribner, c1976. 205 p. : ill. (some col.) ; 29 cm. Includes bibliographical references and index. [NC980.5.D84W47] 76-9562 ISBN 0-684-14791-2 : 25.00
1. Dulac, Edmund, 1882-1953. 2. Illustrators—France—Biography. **BIP**

WHITE, Colin. 741'.092'4 B
Edmund Dulac / [by] Colin White. London : Studio Vista, 1976. 208 p. : ill. (some col.), facsims., map, music, plan, ports. ; 29 cm. Includes bibliographical references and index. [NC980.5.D84W47 1976b] 77-364635 ISBN 0-289-70751-X : £10.50
1. Dulac, Edmund, 1882-1953. 2. Illustrators—France—Biography.

Dulany, Daniel, 1685-1753.

LAND, Aubrey C. 975.2'02'0922
The Dulanys of Maryland; a biographical study of Daniel Dulany, the Elder (1685-1753) and Daniel Dulany, the Younger (1722-1797) by Aubrey C. Land. Baltimore, Johns Hopkins Press [1968, c1955] xiv, 390 p. 24 cm. "Originally published by the Maryland Historical Society." Bibliographical references included in "Notes" (p. 335-370) Bibliography: p. 371-373. [F184.D8L3 1968] 68-28873
1. Dulany, Daniel, 1685-1753. 2. Dulany, Daniel, 1722-1797. I. Title.

Dulce, Sister, 1914-

HAVERSTOCK, Nathan A. 361.70924
Give us this day; the story of Sister Dulce, the angel of Bahia. New York, Appleton-Century [dist. Meredith. 1966, c.1965] 154p. illus., ports. 22cm. [HV530.H35] 65-25359 4.95 bds.,
1. Dulce, Sister, 1914- 2. Catholic Church in Salvador, Brazil—Charities. I. Title.

Dulles, Eleanor Lansing, 1895-

MOSLEY, Leonard 973.9'092'2 B
Dulles : a biography of Eleanor, Allen, and John Foster Dulles and their family network / Leonard Mosley New York : Dell Publishing Co., 1979, c1978 576p. : ill. ; 18 cm. Includes index Bibliography: p. 538-562 [E748.D87M67] ISBN 0-440-12196-5 pbk. : 2.95
1. Dulles family 2. Dulles, John Foster, 1888-1959 3. Dulles, Eleanor Lansing, 1895- 4. Dulles, Allen Welsh, 1893-1969 5. Statesmen — United States — Biography 6. Economists — United States — Biography 7. United States — Central Intelligence Agency — Official and Employees — Biography 8. United States — Foreign relations — 20th century I. Title.
L.C. card no. for 1977 Dial Press ed: 77-19042 **BIP**

MOSLEY, Leonard, 973.9'092'2 B
1913-
Dulles : a biography of Eleanor, Allen and John Foster Dulles and their family network / by Leonard Mosley. New York : Dial Press, 1978. xii, 530 p., [16] leaves of plates : ill ; 24 cm. Includes index. Bibliography: p. 499-518. [E748.D87M67] 77-19042 ISBN 0-8037-1744-X : 12.95
1. Dulles family. 2. Dulles, John Foster, 1888-1959. 3. Dulles, Eleanor Lansing, 1895- 4. Dulles, Allen Welsh, 1893-1969. 5. Statesmen—United States—Biography. 6. Economists—United States—Biography. 7. United States—Central Intelligence Agency—Officials and employees—Biography. 8. United States—Foreign relations—20th century. I. Title.

Dulles family.

MOSLEY, Leonard 973.9'092'2 B
Dulles : a biography of Eleanor, Allen, and John Foster Dulles and their family network / Leonard Mosley New York : Dell Publishing Co., 1979, c1978 576p. : ill. ; 18 cm. Includes index Bibliography: p. 538-562 [E748.D87M67] ISBN 0-440-12196-5 pbk. : 2.95
1. Dulles family 2. Dulles, John Foster, 1888-1959 3. Dulles, Eleanor Lansing, 1895- 4. Dulles, Allen Welsh, 1893-1969 5. Statesmen — United States — Biography 6. Economists — United States — Biography 7. United States — Central Intelligence Agency — Official and Employees — Biography 8. United States — Foreign relations — 20th century I. Title.
L.C. card no. for 1977 Dial Press ed: 77-19042 **BIP**

MOSLEY, Leonard, 973.9'092'2 B
1913-
Dulles : a biography of Eleanor, Allen and John Foster Dulles and their family network / by Leonard Mosley. New York : Dial Press, 1978. xii, 530 p., [16] leaves of plates : ill ; 24 cm. Includes index. Bibliography: p. 499-518. [E748.D87M67] 77-19042 ISBN 0-8037-1744-X : 12.95
1. Dulles family. 2. Dulles, John Foster, 1888-1959. 3. Dulles, Eleanor Lansing, 1895- 4. Dulles, Allen Welsh, 1893-1969. 5. Statesmen—United States—Biography. 6. Economists—United States—Biography. 7. United States—Central Intelligence Agency—Officials and employees—Biography. 8. United States—Foreign relations—20th century. I. Title.

Dulles, John Foster, 1888-1959.

BEAL, John Robinson, 923.273
1906-
John Foster Dulles, a biography. Foreword by Thomas E. Dewey. [1st ed.] New York, Harper [1957] 331 p. illus. 22 cm. [E835.D85B4] 56-8746
1. Dulles, John Foster, 1888-1959.

BEAL, John 973.921'092'4 B
Robinson, 1906-
John Foster Dulles: 1888-1959. Foreword by Thomas E. Dewey. Westport, Conn., Greenwood Press [1974, c1959] xvi, 358 p. illus. 22 cm. Originally published in 1957 under title: John Foster Dulles, a biography. Reprint of the ed. published by Harper & Row, New York. [E835.D85B4 1974] 74-12626 ISBN 0-8371-7730-8
1. Dulles, John Foster, 1888-1959. I. Title.

BEAL, John 973.921'092'4 B
Robinson, 1906-
John Foster Dulles: 1888-1959. Foreword by Thomas E. Dewey. Westport, Conn., Greenwood Press [1974, c1959] p. cm. Originally published in 1957 under title: John Foster Dulles, a biography. Reprint of the ed. published by Harper & Row, New York. [E835.D85B4 1974] 74-12626 ISBN 0-8371-7730-8 19.25
1. Dulles, John Foster, 1888-1959. I. Title.

COMFORT, Mildred Houghton 923.273
John Foster Dulles, peacemaker; a

biographical sketch of the former Secretary of State. Minneapolis T S. Denison [c.1960] 202p. 22cm. 60-9237 3.00
1. Dulles, John Foster, 1888-1959. I. Title.

GUHIN, Michael A., 1940- 973.921'092'4 B
John Foster Dulles: a statesman and his times [by] Michael A. Guhin. New York, Columbia University Press, 1972. viii, 404 p. illus. 24 cm. Bibliography: p. [375]-395. [E835.D85G8] 72-5873 ISBN 0-231-03664-7 12.95
1. Dulles, John Foster, 1888-1959. **BIP**

HELLER, Deane 923.273
John Foster Dulles; soldier for peace, by Deane and David Heller. New York, Holt, Rinehart and Winston [c.1960] 328p. (Front.) 22cm. 60-12320 4.50
1. Dulles, John Foster, 1888-1959. I. Heller, David, joint author. II. Title.

HELLER, Deane, 1924- 923.273
John Foster Dulles, solider for peace, by Deane and David Heller. [1st ed.] New York, Holt, Rinehart and Winston [1960] 328p. illus. 22cm. [E835.D85H4] 60-12320
1. Dulles, John Foster, 1888-1959. I. Heller, David, 1922- joint author. II. Title.

HOOPES, Townsend, 1922- 973.921'092'4 B
The devil and John Foster Dulles. [1st ed.] Boston, Little, Brown [1973] xiv, 562 p. illus. 25 cm. "An Atlantic Monthly Press book." Bibliography: p. [537]-540. [E835.D85H66] 73-12690 ISBN 0-316-37235-8 12.50
1. Dulles, John Foster, 1888-1959. 2. United States—Foreign relations—1945- I. Title.

JOHN Foster Dulles, 353.1
by Louis L. Gerson. New York, Cooper Sq., 1957 [ie. 1968,c.1967] xiv, 372p. port. 22cm. (Amer. Secretaries of p. 350-363. [E835.D85G4] (B) 67-24039 7.95
1. Dulles, John Foster, 1888-1959. I. Gerson, Louis L. II. Series: Bemis, Samuel Flagg, 1891- ed. The American Secretaries of State and their diplomacy, v. 17

MOSLEY, Leonard, 1913- 973.9'092'2 B
Dulles : a biography of Eleanor, Allen and John Foster Dulles and their family network / by Leonard Mosley. New York : Dial Press, 1978. xii, 530 p., [16] leaves of plates : ill ; 24 cm. Includes index. Bibliography: p. 499-518. [E748.D87M67] 77-19042 ISBN 0-8037-1744-X : 12.95
1. Dulles family. 2. Dulles, John Foster, 1888-1959. 3. Dulles, Eleanor Lansing, 1895- 4. Dulles, Allen Welsh, 1893-1969. 5. Statesmen—United States—Biography. 6. Economists—United States—Biography. 7. United States—Central Intelligence Agency—Officials and employees—Biography. 8. United States—Foreign relations—20th century. I. Title.

STANG, Alan. 973.921'0924
The actor; the true story of John Foster Dulles, Secretary of State, 1953-1959. Boston, Western Islands [1968] 346 p. 19 cm. (The Americanist classics, AC-020) [E835.D85S7] 68-7163 1.00
1. Dulles, John Foster, 1888-1959. I. Title.

Dulles, John Foster, 1888-1959—Juvenile literature.

FINKE, Blythe Foote. 973.921'092'4 B
John Foster Dulles, master of of brinksmanship [sic] and diplomacy. Charlotteville, N.Y., SamHar Press, 1971. 28 p. 22 cm. (Outstanding personalities, no. 10) Bibliography: p. 25-28. A brief biography of the man who served as Secretary of State from 1953 to 1959. [E835.D85F56] 92 77-185666
1. Dulles, John Foster, 1888-1959—Juvenile literature. I. Title.

Dumas, Alexandre, 1802-1870.

BELL, A. Craig. 843'.7
Alexandre Dumas, a biography and study / by A. Craig Bell. Folcroft, Pa. : Folcroft Library Editions, 1979. p. cm. Reprint of the 1950 ed. published by Cassell, London. "Index of authentic works": p. "Spurious works and works of doubtful authenticity": p. Includes index. Bibliography: p. [PQ2230.B29 1979] 79-1153 ISBN 0-8414-9832-6 lib. bdg. : 40.00
1. Dumas, Alexandre, 1802-1870. 2. Authors, French—19th century—Biography.

DUMAS, Alexandre, 1802-1870 928.4
My memoirs. Tr. [from French], ed. by A. Craig Bell. Philadelphia, Chilton [c.1961] 257p. illus. 61-4416 3.50 bds.,
I. Title.

DUMAS, Alexandre, 1802-1870. 928.4
The road to Monte Cristo; a condensation from The memoirs of Alexandre Dumas by Jules Eckert Goodman. New York, Scribner [1956] viii, 395 p. illus., ports. 24 cm. [PQ2230.A27] 56-10203
I. Title.

MAUROIS, Andre, 1885- 928.4
Alexandre Dumas; a great life in brief. [Translated from the French by Jack Palmer White. 1st ed.] New York, Knopf, 1955 [i. e. 1954] 198p. 19cm. (Great lives in brief; a new series of biographies) [PQ2230.M32] 54-8759
1. Dumas, Alexandre, 1802-1870. I. Title.

MAUROIS, Andre 1885- 928.4
The Tians, a three-generation biography of the Dumas. Tr. from French by Gerald Hopkins. New York, Pyramid [1967, c.1957] 528p. illus. 18cm. (V-1528) Tr. of Les trois Dumas. Bibl. [PQ2230.M3313] 1.25 pap.,
1. Dumas, Thomas Alexandre, 1762-1806 2. Dumas, Alexandre, 1802-1870. 3. Dumas, Alexandre, 1824-1895. I. Title.

MAUROIS, Andre, 1885- 928.4
The Titans, a three-generation biography of the Dumas. Translated from the French by Gerard Hopkins. New York, Harper [c1957] 508p. illus. 24cm. Translation of Les trois Dumas. Includes bibliography. [PQ2230.M3313] 57-8173
1. Dumas, Thomas Alexandre, 1762-1806. 2. Dumas, Alexandre, 1802-1870. 3. Dumas, Alexandre, 1824-1895. I. Title.

MAUROIS, Andre, 1885-1967. 840.9'007 B
The Titans; a three-generation biography of the Dumas. Translated from the French by Gerard Hopkins. Westport, Conn., Greenwood Press [1971, c1957] 508 p. illus. 24 cm. Translation of Les trois Dumas. Bibliography: p. 483-495. [PQ2230.M3313 1971] 78-156201 ISBN 0-8371-6151-7
1. Dumas, Thomas Alexandre, 1762-1806. 2. Dumas, Alexandre, 1802-1870. 3. Dumas, Alexandre, 1824-1895. I. Title.

SAUNDERS, Edith. 928.4
The prodigal father; Dumas pere et fils and the Lady of the Camellias. London, New York, Longmans, Green [1951] xii, 257 p. illus., ports. 23 cm. Full name: Edith Alice Saunders. Bibliography: p. 251-254. [PQ2230.S3] 51-12376
1. Dumas, Alexandre, 1802-1870. 2. Dumas, Alexandre, 1824-1895. 3. Duplessis, Marie, 1824-1847. I. Title.

SPURR, Harry A., d.1906. 843'.7
The life and writings of Alexandre Dumas. A new ed. with line and half-tone illus. New York, Haskell House Publishers, 1973. xiii, 321 p. illus. 23 cm. Reprint of the 1929 ed. Bibliography: p. 318-321. [PQ2230.S8 1973] 72-3515 ISBN 0-8383-1549-6 14.95
1. Dumas, Alexandre, 1802-1870. **BIP**

Dumas, Alexandre, 1802-1870—Biography.

DUMAS, Alexandre, 1802-1870. 843'.7 B
My memoirs / Alexandre Dumas ; translated and edited by A. Craig Bell. Westport, Conn. : Greenwood Press, 1975, c1961. 257 p., [5] leaves of plates : ill. ; 22 cm. Translation of Mes memoires. An abridgment limited "to events in which Dumas himself is engaged." Reprint of the ed. published by Chilton Co., Book Division, Philadelphia. Includes index. [PQ2230.A27 1975] 75-17781 ISBN 0-8371-8186-0 lib.bdg. : 13.50
1. Dumas, Alexandre, 1802-1870—Biography. I. Title.

HEMMINGS, Frederick William John. 843'.7 b
Alexandre Dumas, the king of romance / F. W. J. Hemmings. New York : Scribner, c1979. p. cm. Includes bibliographical references and index. [PQ2230.H38] 79-22689 ISBN 0-684-16391-8 : 12.50
1. Dumas, Alexandre, 1802-1870—Biography. 2. Authors, French—19th century—Biography. I. Title.

Dumas, Alexandre, 1824-1895.

SAUNDERS, Edith. 928.4
The prodigal father; Dumas pere et fils and the Lady of the Camellias. London, New York, Longmans, Green [1951] xii, 257 p. illus., ports. 23 cm. Full name: Edith Alice Saunders. Bibliography: p. 251-254. [PQ2230.S3] 51-12376
1. Dumas, Alexandre, 1802-1870. 2. Dumas, Alexandre, 1824-1895. 3. Duplessis, Marie, 1824-1847. I. Title.

SCHWARZ, Henry Stanley, 1890- 842'.8
Alexandre Dumas, fils, dramatist, by H. Stanley Schwarz. New York, B. Blom, 1971. xv, 216 p. 22 cm. Reprint of the 1927 ed. Bibliography: p. [197]-207. [PQ2231.Z5S4 1971] 75-177514
1. Dumas, Alexandre, 1824-1895.

Dumas, Thomas Alexandre, 1762-1806.

MAUROIS, Andre 1885- 928.4
The Tians, a three-generation biography of the Dumas. Tr. from French by Gerald Hopkins. New York, Pyramid [1967, c.1957] 528p. illus. 18cm. (V-1528) Tr. of Les trois Dumas. Bibl. [PQ2230.M3313] 1.25 pap.,
1. Dumas, Thomas Alexandre, 1762-1806 2. Dumas, Alexandre, 1802-1870. 3. Dumas, Alexandre, 1824-1895. I. Title.

MAUROIS, Andre, 1885- 928.4
The Titans, a three-generation biography of the Dumas. Translated from the French by Gerard Hopkins. New York, Harper [c1957] 508p. illus. 24cm. Translation of Les trois Dumas. Includes bibliography. [PQ2230.M3313] 57-8173
1. Dumas, Thomas Alexandre, 1762-1806. 2. Dumas, Alexandre, 1802-1870. 3. Dumas, Alexandre, 1824-1895. I. Title.

MAUROIS, Andre, 1885-1967. 840.9'007 B
The Titans; a three-generation biography of the Dumas. Translated from the French by Gerard Hopkins. Westport, Conn., Greenwood Press [1971, c1957] 508 p. illus. 24 cm. Translation of Les trois Dumas. Bibliography: p. 483-495. [PQ2230.M3313 1971] 78-156201 ISBN 0-8371-6151-7
1. Dumas, Thomas Alexandre, 1762-1806. 2. Dumas, Alexandre, 1802-1870. 3. Dumas, Alexandre, 1824-1895. I. Title.

Dummer, Jeremiah, 1645-1718.

CLARKE, Hermann Frederick, 1882-1947. 739.2'3'0924
Jeremiah Dummer, colonial craftsman & merchant, 1645-1718 [by] Hermann Frederick Clarke and Henry Wilder Foote. Foreward by E. Alfred Jones. New York, Da Capo Press, 1970 [c1935] xviii, 204 p. illus., facsims., ports. 26 cm. (Da Capo Press series in architecture and decorative art, v. 33) A Da Capo Press reprint edition. Reprint of the 1935 ed. [NK7198.D8C5 1970] 75-87563
1. Dummer, Jeremiah, 1645-1718. I. Foote, Henry Wilder, 1875- joint author. II. Title.

Dumont, Jean Paul, 1940-

DUMONT, Jean Paul, 1940- 301.2'07'2
The headman and I : ambiguity and ambivalence in the fieldworking experience / by Jean-Paul Dumont. Austin : University of Texas Press, c1978. p. cm. (Texas Pan American series) Includes index. Bibliography: p. [GN346.D85] 78-8091 ISBN 0-292-73007-1 : 12.95.
1. Dumont, Jean Paul, 1940- 2. Ethnology—Field work. 3. Panare Indians. 4. Anthropologists—French—Biography. I. Title. **BIP**

Dunaly, Daniel, 1685-1753.

LAND, Aubrey C 923.273
The Dulanys of Maryland; a biographical study of Daniel Dulany, the elder (1685-1753) and Daniel Dulany, the younger (1722-1797) Baltimore, Maryland Historical Society, 1955. xviii, 390p. ports. 24cm. (Studies in Maryland history, no. 3) series: Maryland Historical Society. Studies in Maryland History, no, 3) Bibliographical references included in 'Notes' (p. 335-370) 'Bibliographical note' :p. 371- 373. [F184.D8L3] 55-31927
1. Dunaly, Daniel, 1685-1753. 2. Dunalny, Daniel, 1722-1797. I. Title. II. Series.

Dunant, Jean Henry, 1828-1910.

LIBBY, Violet Kelway. 923.6494
Henry Dunant: prophet of peace. [1st ed.] New York, Pageant Press [1964] 377 p. illus., ports. 24 cm. "Sources": p. 365. [HV569.D8L5] 64-8235
1. Dunant, Jean Henry, 1828-1910. I. Title.

RICH, Josephine. 923.6494
Jean Henri Dunant, founder of the International Red Cross. Foreword by James T. Nicholson; photos. by Courtesy of the American National Red Cross. New York, Messner [1956] 190p. illus. 22cm. [HV569.D8R5] 56-6794
1. Dunant, Jean Henry, 1828-1910. I. Title.

RICH, Josephine. 923.6494
Jean Henri Dunant, founder of the International Red Cross. Foreword by James T. Nicholson; photos. by courtesy of the American National Red. Cross. New York, Messner [1956] 190p. illus. 22cm. [HV569.D8R5] 56-6794
1. Dunant, Jean Henry, 1828- 1910. I. Title.

ROTHKOPF, Carol Zeman. 361.5'0924 B
Jean Henri Dunant, father of the Red Cross, by Carol Z. Rothkopf. New York, Watts [1969] 177 p. illus., ports. 22 cm. (Immortals of history) Bibliography: p. 167-171. A biography of the Swiss founder of the International Red Cross who was one of two recipients of the first Nobel Peace Prize awarded in 1901. [HV569.D8R63] 92 70-79670
1. Dunant, Jean Henry, 1828-1910. 2. Red Cross.

Dunant, Jean Henry, 1828-1910—Juvenile literature.

STOIBER, Rudolf Maria, 1925- 920
Henri Dunant: man in white [Tr. from German] New York, Abelard [c.1963] 143p. 21cm. 63-18778 3.00
1. Dunant, Jean Henry, 1828-1910—Juvenile literature. I. Title.

Dunaway, Judson, 1890-

MAPP, Alf Johnson. 650'.0924 B
Just one man, the widening world of Judson Dunaway, by Alf J. Mapp, Jr. Richmond, Va., Dietz Press, 1968. vii, 198 p. illus., ports. 24 cm. Bibliography: p. 195-196. [CT275.D8814M34] 68-5073
1. Dunaway, Judson, 1890- I. Title. II. Title: The widening world of Judson Dunaway.

Dunbar, Paul Laurence, 1872-1906—Biography.

BRAWLEY, Benjamin Griffith, 1882-1939. 811'.4 B
Paul Laurence Dunbar, poet of his people. Port Washington, N.Y., Kennikat Press [1967, c1936] xi, 159 p. port. 21 cm. "Appendix. The praise of Dunbar": p. 127-140. Bibliography: p. 141-159. [PS1557.B7 1967] 67-27578
1. Dunbar, Paul Laurence, 1872-1906—Biography.

GAYLE, Addison, 1932- 811'.4 B
Oak and ivy; a biography of Paul Laurence

Dunbar. [1st ed.] Garden City, N.Y., Doubleday [1971] xv, 175 p. 22 cm. "A Perspective book." "Works of Paul Laurence Dunbar": p. 166-168. Bibliography: p. [169]-170. [PS1557.G3] 78-152052 4.50
1. Dunbar, Paul Laurence, 1872-1906—Biography. I. Title.

Dunbar, Paul Laurence, 1872-1906—Biography—Juvenile literature.

SCHULTZ, Pearle Henriksen. 811'.4 B
Paul Lawrence Dunbar: Black poet laureate. Illustrated by William Hutchinson. Champaign, Ill., Garrard Pub. Co. [1974] p. cm. (Creative people in the arts and sciences) Biography of a black American poet whose early dialectic works were superseded by works exposing the problems of his race. [PS1557.S3] 92 73-22071 ISBN 0-8116-4516-9 4.25
1. Dunbar, Paul Laurence, 1872-1906—Biography—Juvenile literature. I. Hutchinson, William M., illus.

Dunbar, William, 1460?-1520

BAXTER, J. W. 928.2
William Dunbar; a biographical study. Edinburgh, Oliver & Body [Mystic, Conn., Verry, 1965] viii, 254p. 23cm. Bibl. [PR2268.B3] 5.00 bds.,
1. Dunbar, William, 1460?-1520 I. Title.

Dunbar, William, 1460?-1520?

BAXTER, John Walker. 821'.2
William Dunbar; a biographical study, by J. W. Baxter. Edinburgh, Oliver and Boyd. St. Clair Shores, Mich., Scholarly Press, 1971. viii, 254 p. 22 cm. Reprint of the 1952 ed. Bibliography: p. 240-246. [PR2268.B3 1971b] 78-161967 ISBN 0-403-01327-5
1. Dunbar, William, 1460?-1520? **BIP**

BAXTER, John Walker. 821'.2 B
William Dunbar; a biographical study, by John W. Baxter. Freeport, N.Y., Books for Libraries Press [1971, c1952] 256 p. 23 cm. (Library of Old English and medieval literature) Bibliography: p. 240-246. [PR2268.B3 1971] 71-148872 ISBN 0-8369-5672-9
1. Dunbar, William, 1460?-1520?

SMEATON, William Henry Oliphant, 1856-1914. 821'.2 B
William Dunbar / by Oliphant Smeaton. New York : AMS Press, 1975. 159 p. ; 23 cm. Reprint of the 1898 ed. published by Oliphant, Anderson & Ferrier, Edinburgh, in series: Famous Scots series. Includes index. [PR2268.S5 1975] 70-144487 ISBN 0-404-08604-7 : 14.50
1. Dunbar, William, 1460?-1520? **BIP**

Duncan, Douglas Moerdyke, 1902-1968—Art patronage.

JARVIS, Alan, 1915-1972. 704'.361
Douglas Duncan, a memorial portrait. Edited by Alan Jarvis. [Toronto, Buffalo] University of Toronto Press [1974] viii, 74 p. illus. (part col.) 18 x 23 cm. [N5230.C3D864] 72-97526 ISBN 0-8020-1977-3 7.50
1. Duncan, Douglas Moerdyke, 1902-1968—Art patronage. I. Title.

Duncan, E. H.

DUNCAN, E. H. 362.7'092'6 B
Night-duty social worker / by E. H. Duncan. 1st ed. New York : Elsevier/Nelson Books, c1979. 214 p. ; 24 cm. [HV746.W56D86] 79-4382 ISBN 0-525-66630-3 : 8.95
1. Duncan, E. H. 2. Children's Aid Society of Winnipeg. 3. Social workers—Manitoba—Winnipeg—Biography. I. Title. **BIP**

Duncan, Irma.

DUNCAN, Irma. 793.320924 B
Duncan dancer; an autobiography. [1st ed.] Middletown, Conn., Wesleyan University Press [1966] x, 352 p. illus., ports. 22 cm. [GV1785.D79A3] 66-14664
I. Title.

DUNCAN, Irma. 793.3'2'0924
Follow me! The autobiography of Irma Duncan. With an introd. by Doris Hering. [New York, Johnson Reprint Corp., 1973, c1965] p. Original ed. issued as nos. 21-22 of Dance perspectives. [GV1785.D79A32 1973] 73-778 ISBN 0-384-13305-3 Pap. 6.00 ea. (2 vols.)
1. Duncan, Irma. I. Title. II. Series: Dance perspectives, 21-22.

Duncan, Isadora, 1878-1927.

DUNCAN, Isadora, 1878-1927. 793.3'2'0924
"Your Isadora": the love story of Isadora Duncan & Gordon Craig. Edited, with a connecting text, by Francis Steegmuller. [1st ed.] New York, Random House [1974] vii, 399 p. illus. 25 cm. Includes bibliographical references. [GV1785.D8A42] 74-5178 ISBN 0-394-48698-6
I. Craig, Edward Gordon, 1872-1966. II. Steegmuller, Francis, 1906- ed. III. Title.

DUNCAN, Isadora, 1878-1927. 793.3'2'0924 B
"Your Isadora" : the love story of Isadora Duncan & Gordon Craig / edited with a connecting text by Francis Steegmuller. New York : Vintage Books, 1976, c1974. vii, 399 p., [8] leaves of plates : ill. ; 20 cm. Bibliography: p. [367]-370. [GV1785.D8A42 1976] 76-9748 ISBN 0-394-72078-4 pbk. : 4.95
1. Duncan, Isadora, 1878-1927. 2. Craig, Edward Gordon, 1872-1966. I. Craig, Edward Gordon, 1872-1966. II. Steegmuller, Francis, 1906- III. Title.

MACDOUGALL, Allan Ross, 1893- 927.933
Isadora; a revolutionary in art and love. Edinburgh, New York, T. Nelson [1960] 296 p. illus. 22 cm. [GV1785.D8M26] 59-15034
1. Duncan, Isadora, 1878-1927. I. Title.

MCVAY, Gordon. 793.3'2'0924 B
Isadora and Esenin : the story of Isadora Duncan and Sergei Esenin / Gordon McVay. Ann Arbor, Mich. : Ardis, 1980. p. cm. Includes index. Bibliography: p [GV1785.D8M27] 79-55037 ISBN 0-88233-337-2 : 15.00
1. Duncan, Isadora, 1878-1927. 2. Esenin, Sergei Aleksandrovich, 1895-1925. 3. Dancers—United States—Biography. 4. Russian poets—20th century—Biography. I. Title.

SEROFF, Victor Ilyitch, 1902- 793.3'2'0924 B
The real Isadora. New York, Dial Press, 1971. 441 p. illus., ports. 24 cm. Bibliography: p. 435-436. [GV1785.D8S47] 75-144385 10.00
1. Duncan, Isadora, 1878-1927. I. Title. **BIP**

SHNEIDER, Il'ia Il'ich. 793.3'2'0924
Isadora Duncan: the Russian years. Translated by David Magarshack. [1st American ed.] New York, Harcourt, Brace & World [1969, c1968] 221 p. illus., ports. 23 cm. "A Helen and Kurt Wolff book." [GV1785.D8S53 1969] 69-14517 6.95
1. Duncan, Isadora, 1878-1927. I. Title.

TERRY, Walter. 927.933
Isadora Duncan; her life, her art, her legacy. Illustrated with photos. and drawings. [1st ed.] New York, Dodd, Mead [1964, c1963] xiv, 174 p. illus., ports., facsim. 22 cm. Bibliography: p. 169. [GV1785.D8T4] 64-10954
1. Duncan, Isadora, 1878-1927. I. Title.

Duncan, Jane—Biography.

DUNCAN, Jane. 823'.9'14
Letter from Reachfar / Jane Duncan. New York : St. Martin's Press, 1976, c1975. 150 p., [2] leaves of plates : ill. ; 23 cm. [PR6054.U46Z52 1976] 75-13787 7.95
1. Duncan, Jane—Biography. I. Title. **BIP**

DUNCAN, Jane. 823'.9'14 B
Letter from Reachfar / [by] Jane Duncan. London : Macmillan, 1975. [5], 152 p., [4] p. of plates : ports. ; 23 cm. [PR6054.U46Z52 1975] 76-360477 ISBN 0-333-18755-5 : 7.95
1. Duncan, Jane—Biography. I. Title.
Distributed by St. Martin.

Duncan, Robert Edward, 1919- — Addresses, essays, lectures.

ROBERT Duncan, scales of the marvelous / edited by Robert J. Bertholf and Ian W. Reid. New York : New Directions Pub. Corp., c1979. p. cm. (Insights, working papers in contemporary criticism) Bibliography: p. [PS3507.U629Z86] 79-19663 ISBN 0-8112-0735-8 pbk. : 4.95 811'.5'4
1. Duncan, Robert Edward, 1919- — Addresses, essays, lectures. 2. Poets, American—20th century—Biography—Addresses, essays, lectures. I. Bertholf, Robert J. II. Reid, Ian, 1943- III. Series.

Duncan, William Asa, 1891-

BRANAN, Donie Leone. 922.673
My pastor; a biography of William Asa Duncan, D.D., LL. D., Baptist executive, minister, teacher, and traveler, affectionately known by many as 'my pastor.' i[Atlanta? 1957] 125p. illus. 22cm. [BX6495.D83B7] 57-48091
1. Duncan, William Asa, 1891- I. Title.

Duncan, William, 1832-1918.

POYNTER, Margaret. 266'.023'0924 B
Miracle at Metlakatla : the inspiring story of William Duncan, a missionary / written by Margaret Poynter ; illustrated by James Padgett. St. Louis : Concordia Pub. House, c1978. 123 p. ; ill. ; 24 cm. (Greatness with faith) A biography of the Christian missionary who helped the Tsimshian Indians establish a new home in Alaska. [E99.T8D856] 92 77-29125 ISBN 0-570-07876-8 : 4.95. ISBN 0-570-07881-4 pbk. : 2.95
1. Duncan, William, 1832-1918. 2. Tsimshian Indians—Missions. 3. Metlakahtla, Alaska—History. 4. Metlakatla, B.C.—History. 5. Missionaries—British Columbia—Biography. 6. Missionaries—England—Biography. I. Padgett, James. II. Title. III. Series.

WENTWORTH, Elaine. 266'.023'0924 B
Mission to Metlakatla. Boston, Houghton Mifflin, 1968. 194 p. illus., map. 22 cm. Records the missionary work of a nineteenth-century Englishman, who was sent to civilize the Tsimshians, a savage tribe of Alaskan Indians, and who spent a lifetime protecting and helping his adopted people in their endeavor to adjust to the modern world. [E99.T8W54] 92 AC 68
1. Duncan, William, 1832-1918. 2. Tsimshian Indians—Missions. 3. Metlakahtla, Alaska. I. Title.

WILLIAM Duncan, founder and developer of Alaska's Metlakatla Christian mission. [Palo Alto, Calif., National Press, 1957] 82p. illus., ports. 22cm. v. 12
1. Duncan, William, 1832-1918. 2. Metlakahtla, Alaska. 3. Tsimshian Indians. 4. Missions— British Columbia. I. Kohlstedt, Edward Delor, 1874-

Dundonald, Thomas Cochrane, 10th Earl of, 1775-1860.

THOMAS, Donald. 359.3'31'0924 B
Cochrane / Donald Thomas. New York : Viking Press, [1978] p. cm. Includes index. Bibliography: p. [DA88.1.D9T44] 78-6940 ISBN 0-670-22644-0 : 12.95
1. Dundonald, Thomas Cochrane, 10th Earl of, 1775-1860. 2. Great Britain—History, Naval—19th cntury. 3. Admirals—Great Britain—Biography.

Dunglison, Robley,

DUNGLISON, Robley, 1798-1869. 926.1
The autobiographical ana of Robley Dunglison, M.D. Edited with notes and introd. by Samuel X. Radbill. Philadelphia, American Philosophical Society, 1963. 212 p. illus., ports., facsims. 30 cm. (Transactions of the Aemrican Philosophical Society, new ser., v. 53, pt. 8) Bibliography: p. 196-199. [Q11.P6 n.s., vol. 53, pt. 8] 63-22636
I. Radbill, Samuel X., ed. II. Title. III. Series. IV. Series: American Philosophical Society, Philadelphia. Transactions, new ser., v. 53, pt. 8

Dunham, Katherine.

BECKFORD, Ruth. 793.3'2'0924 B
Katherine Dunham, a biography / Ruth Beckford ; foreword by Arthur Mitchell. New York : M. Dekker, c1979. ix, 146 p., [11] leaves of plates : ill. ; 24 cm. (The Dance program ; v. 14) Includes index. [GV1785.D82B4] 79-4577 ISBN 0-8247-6828-0 : 17.50
1. Dunham, Katherine. 2. Dancers—United States—Biography. 3. Choreographers—United States—Biography. I. Title. II. Series.

Dunham, Katherine—Juvenile literature.

BIEMILLER, Ruth. 793.3'2'0924
Dance; the story of Katherine Dunham. [1st ed.] Garden City, N.Y., Doubleday [1969] 144 p. illus. 22 cm. (A Doubleday signal book) A biography of the American dancer and anthropologist noted for her West Indian, Polynesian, and jazz dances. [GV1785.D82B5] 92 69-11000 3.50
1. Dunham, Katherine—Juvenile literature. I. Title.

Duniway, Abigail Scott, 1834-1915.

SMITH, Helen Krebs. 324'.3'0924 B
The presumptuous dreamers : a sociological history of the life and times of Abigail Scott Duniway, 1834-1915 / by Helen Krebs Smith. 1st ed. Lake Oswego, Or. : Smith, Smith and Smith Pub. Co., [1974- v. ; 22 cm. (A Western Americana book) Includes index. Contents.—v. 1. 1834-1871. Bibliography: p. [268]-278. [JK1899.D85S6] 74-79460 ISBN 0-913626-10-4 : 7.95 (v. 1). ISBN 0-913626-12-0 pbk. 4.95 (v. 1)
1. Duniway, Abigail Scott, 1834-1915. 2. Women—Suffrage—Oregon—History. 3. Women—Suffrage—United States—History. I. Title. **BIP**

Duniway, Abigail Scott, 1834-1915—Juvenile literature.

MORRISON, Dorothy M. 324'.3'0924 B
Ladies were not expected : Abigail Scott Duniway and women's rights / by Dorothy Naftus Morrison. 1st ed. New York : Atheneum, 1977. x, 146 p. : ill. ; 22 cm. Includes index. Bibliography: p. 137-140. Summary: A biography of the leader of the women's suffrage movement in Oregon. [HQ1413.D86M67 1977] 92 77-2969 ISBN 0-689-30599-0 . 6.95
1. Duniway, Abigail Scott, 1834-1915—Juvenile literature. 2. Feminists—United States—Biography—Juvenile literature. 3. Women—Suffrage—United States—Juvenile literature. I. Title.

Dunkelman, Ben, 1913-

DUNKELMAN, Ben, 1913- 940.54'09'71 B
Dual allegiance : an autobiography / by Ben Dunkelman. New York : Crown Publishers, c1976. xi, 336 p., [16] leaves of plates : ill. ; 24 cm. Includes index. [D811.D863] 77-1908 ISBN 0-517-53011-2 : 8.95
1. Dunkelman, Ben, 1913- 2. World War, 1939-1945—Personal narratives, Canadian. 3. Israel-Arab War, 1948-1949—Personal narratives. 4. Jews in Canada—Biography. 5. Canada—Biography. I. Title.

Dunlap, Elijah Scott, 1866-1944.

HERON, Frances (Dunlap) 922.673
Here comes Elijah. Illustrated by Arthur FitzSimmons. St. Louis, Bethany Press

[1959] 281p. illus. 23cm. [BX7343.D84H4] 59-13166
1. Dunlap, Elijah Scott, 1866-1944. I. Title.

Dunlap, William, 1766-1839.

COAD, Oral Sumner, 1887- 812.2
William Dunlap, a study of his life and works and of his place in contemporary culture. New York, Russel, 1962[c.1917] 313p. front. port. 21cm. 62-10680 7.50
1. Dunlap, William, 1766-1839. I. Title. BIP

DUNLAP, William, 1766- 700'.924
1839.
Diary of William Dunlap, 1766-1839; the memoirs of a dramatist, theatrical manager, painter, critic, novelist, and historian. New York, B. Blom [1969] 3 v. in 1 (xxxv, 964 p.) illus., ports. 22 cm. (Collections of the New York Historical Society for the year 1929-31. The John Watts DePeyster publication fund series, 62-64) Reprint of the 1930 ed. "The Diary has been transcribed, edited and indexed by Dorothy C. Barck." Includes many of the portraits painted by Dunlap. [PS1561.A3 1969] 78-84204 28.50
I. Barck, Dorothy C., ed. II. Series: New York Historical Society. Collections. The John Watts De Peyster publication fund series, 62-64

Dunn, Arthur Tempest Blakiston, 1860-1902.

LESLIE, Shane, Sir 920.042
bart., 1885-
Men were different; five studies in late Victorian biography. Freeport, N. Y., Books for Libraries Press [1967] 288 p. 22 cm. (Essay index reprint series) Reprint of the 1937 ed. Contents.CONTENTS.--Randolph Churchill, 1849-1895.--Augustus Hare, 1834-1903.--Arthur Dunn, 1860-1902.--George Wyndham, 1863-1913.--Wilfrid Blunt, 1840-1922. Includes bibliographies. [DA562.L46] 67-26754
1. Churchill, Lord Randolph Henry Spencer, 1849-1895. 2. Hare, Augustus John Cuthbert, 1834-1903. 3. Dunn, Arthur Tempest Blakiston, 1860-1902. 4. Wyndham, George, 1863-1913. 5. Blunt, Wilfrid Scawen, 1840-1922. I. Title. BIP

LESLIE, Shane, Sir, 920.042
bart., 1885-1971.
Men were different; five studies in late Victorian biography. Freeport, N.Y., Books for Libraries Press [1967] 288 p. 22 cm. (Essay index reprint series) Reprint of the 1937 ed. Contents.Contents.—Randolph Churchill, 1849-1895.—Augustus Hare, 1834-1903.—Arthur Dunn, 1860-1902.—George Wyndham, 1863-1913.—Wilfrid Blunt, 1840-1922. Includes bibliographies. [DA562.L46 1967] 67-26754
1. Churchill, Randolph Henry Spencer, Lord, 1849-1895. 2. Hare, Augustus John Cuthbert, 1834-1903. 3. Dunn, Arthur Tempest Blakiston, 1860-1902. 4. Wyndham, George, 1863-1913. 5. Blunt, Wilfrid Scawen, 1840-1922. I. Title.

Dunn, Harvey, 1884-1952.

KAROLEVITZ, Robert F. 759.13 B
Where your heart is; the story of Harvey Dunn, artist, by Robert F. Karolevitz. [Aberdeen, S.D., North Plains Press, 1970] 208 p. illus. (part col.), ports. 32 cm. Expanded version of The prairie is my garden. [ND237.D79K3 1970] 78-125992 15.00
1. Dunn, Harvey, 1884-1952. I. Title. BIP

Dunn, John, 1857-1953.

EVANS, Max. 923.973
Long John Dunn of Taos. Los Angeles, Westernlore Press, 1959. 174 p. illus. 22 cm. (Great West and Indian series, 15) [F804.T2D8] 59-10903
1. Dunn, John, 1857-1953. 2. Taos, N.M. 3. Frontier and pioneer life—Southwest, New.

Dunn, Natalie, 1956- —Juvenile literature.

MIKLOWITZ, Gloria 796.2'1'0924 B
D.
Natalie Dunn, world roller skating champion / Gloria D. Miklowitz. 1st ed. New York : Harcourt Brace Jovanovich, c1979. p. cm. (A Handy book) A biography of a three-time world champion roller skater who began skating at the age of two and competing at six. [GV858.22.D86M54] 92 79-87524 ISBN 0-15-256716-X : 2.95
1. Dunn, Natalie, 1956- —Juvenile literature. 2. Roller skaters—United States—Biography—Juvenile literature. I. Title.

Dunn, Robert.

DUNN, Robert. 920.5
World alive; a personal story. New York, Crown Publishers [1956] 480p. 22cm. [CT275.D88225A35] 56-7189
I. Title.

Dunn, Sir James Hamet, bart., 1874-1956.

BEAVERBROOK, 338.4'7'67209815
William Maxwell Aitken, Baron, 1879-1964.
Courage, the story of Sir James Dunn. London, Collins [1962, c1961] 280 p. ports. (part col.) 23 cm. [HD9524.C2B4] 67-8273
1. Dunn, Sir James Hamet, bart., 1874-1956. I. Title.

Dunne, Finley Peter, 1867-1936.

ELLIS, Elmer, 1901- 817'.5'2 B
Mr. Dooley's America; a life of Finley Peter Dunne. [Unaltered and unabridged ed. Hamden, Conn.] Archon Books, 1969 [c1941] x, 310, vii p. illus., ports. 22 cm. Bibliographical footnotes. [PS3507.U6755Z6 1969] 69-18271
1. Dunne, Finley Peter, 1867-1936. I. Title.

Dunne, Mary Frederic, Father, 1874-1948.

RAYMOND, Father, 1903- 922.273
The less traveled road; a memoir of Dom Mary Frederic Dunne, first American Trappist abbot. Milwaukee, Bruce Pub. Co. [1953] 250p. illus. 22cm. [BX4705.D88R3] 53-13234
1. Dunne, Mary Frederic, Father, 1874-1948. I. Title.

Dunnigan, Alice Allison, 1906-

DUNNIGAN, Alice 070'.92'4 B
Allison, 1906-
A Black woman's experience : from schoolhouse to White House / Alice Allison Dunnigan. Philadelphia : Dorrance, [1974] 673 p. : ill. ; 23 cm. Includes index. [PN4874.D85] 73-80761 ISBN 0-8059-1882-5 : 15.00
1. Dunnigan, Alice Allison, 1906- I. Title.

Duns, Joannes, Scotus, 1265?-1308?

DUNS Scotus. v. 12
New York, Humanities Press, 1959. 2v. 23cm. Originally published in 1927 by the Oxford Univ. Press.
1. Duns, Joannes, Scotus, 1265-?-1308? I. Harris, Charles Reginald Schiller, 1896-

SAINT-MAURICE, Beraud de. 189.4
John Duns Scotus, a teacher for our times. Translated by Columban Duffy. St. Bonaventure, N. Y., Franciscan Institute, 1955. 348p. 20cm. [B765.D74S23] 56-4375
1. Duns, Joannes, Scotus, 1265?-1308? I. Title.

Dunsany, Edward John Moreton Drax Plunkett, baron,

SMITH, Hazel Littlefield. 928.2
Lord Dunsany: king of dreams; a personal portrait. Foreword by Stanton Coblentz. [1st ed.] New York, Exposition Press [1959] 147 p. illus. 21 cm. [PR6007.U6Z85] 59-4548
1. Dunsany, Edward John Moreton Drax Plunkett, baron, I. Title.

Dunstan, Saint, Abp. of Canterbury, d. 988.

DUCKETT, Eleanor Shipley. 922.242
Saint Dunstan of Canterbury; a study of monastic reform in the tenth century. [1st ed.] New York, Norton [1955] 249p. 22cm. (Books that live) [BX4700.D85D8] 55-14175
1. Dunstan, Saint, Abp. of Canterbury, d. 988. I. Title.

Dunton, John, 1659-1733.

DUNTON, John, 1659- 655.4'24 B
1733.
The life and errors of John Dunton, citizen of London, with the lives and characters of more than a thousand contemporary divines and other persons of literary eminence, to which are added Dunton's conversation in Ireland, selections from his other genuine works and a faithful portrait of the author. New York, B. Franklin [196 v. port. 23 cm. (Burt Franklin research and source works series, 402 Essays in literature & criticism, 37) Reprint of the 1818 ed. [Z325.D912] 74-108028
1. Dunton, John, 1659-1733. 2. Booksellers and bookselling—Great Britain—Correspondence, reminiscences, etc. I. Title.

Duplessis, Maurice Le Noblet, 1890-1959.

BLACK, Conrad. 971.4'03'0924
Duplessis / Conrad Black. Toronto : McClelland and Stewart, 1978. 743 p., [8] leaves of plates : ill. ; 24 cm. Includes bibliographical references and index. [F1053.D78B55] 77-357064 ISBN 0-7710-1530-5 : 16.95
1. Duplessis, Maurice LeNoblet, 1890-1959. 2. Union nationale (Canada) 3. Prime ministers—Quebec (Province)—Biography. 4. Quebec (Province)—Politics and government.
: Distributed by J. B. Lippincott, East Washington Sq., Philadelphia, PA 19105 Distributed by Harper & Row.

LAPORTE, Pierre 923.271
The true face of Duplessis [Trans. from the French] Montreal [6], Harvest House, Ltd. [Box 340, Postal Sta. Westmount] 1960[ ] 140p. 21cm. 60-15152 3.50; 1.50 pap.,
1. Duplessis, Maurice Le Noblet, 1890-1959. I. Title.

Dupont, Leon Papin, 1797-1876.

BEEVERS, John. 922.2
Shining as stars. Westminster, Md., Newman Press [1956] 184p. illus. 22cm. Bibliographies of Leon Dupont and Matt Talbot. [BX4705.D923B4] 56-4815
1. Dupont, Leon Papin. 1797-1876. 2. Talbot, Matthew, I. Title.

SCALLAN, Emeric B 923.444
God demands reparation; the life of Leo Dupont. New York, William- Frederick Press, 1952. 213p. illus. 23cm. [BX4705.D923S3] 52-8944
1. Dupont, Leon Papin, 1797-1876. I. Title.

Durand, Asher Brown, 1798-1886.

DURAND, Asher Brown, 760'.0924
1796-1886.
A. B. Durand, 1796-1886; [exhibition Montclair Art Museum, Montclair, New Jersey, October 24-November 28, 1971 [Newark, N.J., Printed by Schillat-Farrell Press, 1971] 111 p. illus., 8 col. plates. 24 cm. Critical essay and catalog by David B. Lawall. Bibliography: p. 109-111. [ND237.D8L3] 75-198395
I. Lawall, David B. II. Montclair, N.J. Art Museum.

DURAND, John, 1822- 760'.0924 B
1908.
The life and times of A. B. Durand. New York, Kennedy Graphics, 1970. ix, 232 p. illus., ports. 26 cm. (Library of American art) Reprint of the 1894 ed. [ND237.D8D8 1970] 68-8688 ISBN 3-06-711672-
1. Durand, Asher Brown, 1798-1886. I. Title.

Durand, Edward Dana,

DURAND, Edward Dana, 923.373
1871-
Memoirs. [Washington?] 1954. 438p. 24cm. [HA23.D8A35] 54-37550
I. Title.

Durant, William Crapo, 1861-1947.

GUSTIN, 338.7'62'920924 B
Lawrence R., 1937-
Billy Durant: creator of General Motors, by Lawrence R. Gustin. Grand Rapids, Eerdmans [1973] 285 p. illus. 24 cm. Bibliography: p. 274-275. [HD9710.U54G474] 73-2291 ISBN 0-8028-3435-3 7.95
1. Durant, William Crapo, 1861-1947. 2. General Motors Corporation. I. Title.

Durant, William James, 1885-

DURANT, William 973'.07'2022 B
James, 1885-
A dual autobiography / by Will and Ariel Durant. New York : Simon and Schuster, c1977. p. cm. Includes index. Bibliography: p. [D15.D87A33] 77-24590 ISBN 0-671-22925-7 : 20.00
1. Durant, William James, 1885- 2. Durant, Ariel. 3. Historians—United States—Biography. I. Durant, Ariel, joint author. II. Title. BIP

DURANT, William 973.91'092'4 B
James, 1885-
Transition : a sentimental story of one mind and one era / by Will Durant. New York : Simon and Schuster, [1978] c1927. 352 p. ; 21 cm. (A Touchstone book) [D15.D87A37 1978] 78-103140 ISBN 0-671-24203-2 : 5.95
1. Durant, William James, 1885- 2. Historians—United States—Biography. I. Title.

Durante, Jimmy.

CAHN, William, 1912- 927.92
Good night, Mrs. Calabash; the secret of Jimmy Durante. [1st ed.] New York, Duell, Sloan and Pearce [1963] 191 p. illus. 24 cm. [PN2287.D87C3] 63-8475
1. Durante, Jimmy. I. Title.

FOWLER, Gene, 1890-1960. 927.92
Schnozzola, the story of Jimmy Durante. New York, Viking Press, 1951. 261 p. illus. 22 cm. [PN2287.D87F6] 51-12878
1. Durante, Jimmy. I. Title.

Durante, Jimmy—Portraits, caricatures, etc.

HALSMAN, Philippe. 927.92
The candidate, a photographic interview with the Honorable James Durante. Photos. by Philippe Halsman [and others] New York, Simon and Schuster, 1952. 118 p. illus. 26 cm. [PN2287.D87H3] 52-2714
1. Durante, Jimmy—Portraits, caricatures, etc. I. Title.

Durbin, Joseph Walter, 1860-1916.

STEPHENS, Robert W. 363.2'0924 B
Walter Durbin; Texas Ranger and sheriff [by] Robert W. Stephens. Clarendon, Tex., Clarendon Press, 1970. xviii, 174 p. illus.,

ports. 24 cm. Bibliography: p. 167-168. [F391.D963S7] 73-119559
1. Durbin, Joseph Walter, 1860-1916.

Duren, Ryne.

DUREN, Ryne. 796.357'092'4 B
The comeback / by Ryne Duren, with Robert Drury. Dayton, Ohio : Lorenz Press, c1978. vii, 169 p., [2] leaves of plates : ill. ; 22 cm. [GV865.D82A32] 78-103549 ISBN 0-89328-014-3 : 7.95
1. Duren, Ryne. 2. Baseball players—United States—Biography. 3. Alcoholics—United States—Biography. I. Drury, Robert F., joint author. II. Title.

Durer, Albrecht, 1471-1528.

ANZELEWSKY, Fedja, 1919- 741.9'43
Durer and his time; an exhibition from the collection of the Print Room, State Museum, Berlin, Stiftung Preussischer Kulturbesitz. Catalogue and notes by Fedja Anzelewski. Washington, Smithsonian Press, 1967. 252 p. 150 illus. 26 cm. (Smithsonian publication 4647) Originally issued in 1965 when the exhibition was circulated by the Smithsonian Institution Traveling Exhibition Service to four institutions in the U.S. Bibliography: p. 31-33. [NE651.A65 1967] 66-60559
1. Durer, Albrecht, 1471-1528. 2. Engravings, German—Exhibitions. I. Berlin. Kupferstichkabinett (West Berlin) II. Title.

BRION, Marcel 759.3
Durer, his life and work. [Translated from the French by James Cleugh] New York, Tudor Pub. Co. [1960] 320p. illus. (part col.) 22cm. 60-50461 5.95
1. Durer, Albrecht, 1471-1528. I. Title.

GROTE, Ludwig, 1893- 759.3
Durer; biographical and critical study. Translated from the German by Helga Harrison. [Geneva] Skira [distributed in the U.S. by World Pub. Co., Cleveland, 1965] 140 p. mounted col. illus. 19 cm. (The Taste of our time, v. 43) Bibliography: p. 131-[132] [ND588.D9G733] 65-16669
1. Durer, Albrecht, 1471-1528. I. Title.

THE life and art of 759.3
Albrecht Durer. [4th ed.] Princeton, N. J., Princeton University Press, 1955. xxxii, 317p. illus. 27cm. Previous editions published under title: Albrecht Durer. Bibliography: p. 287-296. [ND588.D9P28 1955] [ND588.D9P28 1955] 925.5 55-6248 55-6248
1. Durer, Albrecht, 1471-1528. I. Panofsky, Erwin, 1892-

STECK, Max, 1907- 927.5
Durer and his world. [Translated from the German by J. Maxwell Brownjohn] New York, Viking Press [1964] 147 p. illus., ports., maps, coat of arms, facsims. 24 cm. (A Studio book) Translation of Durer; eine Bildbiographie. [ND588.D93843] 64-12234
1. Durer, Albrecht, 1471-1528. I. Title.

STRIEDER, Peter. 760'.092'4
The hidden Durer / Peter Strieder ; [translated from the German by Vivienne Menkes]. Chicago : Rand McNally Co., 1978. 191 p. : ill (some col.) ; 34 cm. Translation of Albrecht Durer. Includes index. Bibliography: p. 189. [N6888.D8S7313] 78-50816 ISBN 0-528-81041-3 : 19.95
1. Durer, Albrecht, 1471-1528. I. Title. **BIP**

Durer, Albrecht, 1471-1528—Juvenile literature.

RABOFF, Ernest Lloyd. 759.3
Albrecht Durer, by Ernest Raboff. Garden City, N.Y., Doubleday [1970] [31] p. illus. (part col.), ports. (part col.) 29 cm. (Art for children) (A Gemini Smith book.) Briefly discusses the influences upon Durer, the fifteenth-century German artist, and the outstanding features of some of his paintings. [ND588.D9R17] 78-121784 3.95
1. Durer, Albrecht, 1471-1528—Juvenile literature. I. Title.

Durham, Betty.

DURHAM, Betty. 248'.2'0924 [B]
I give up God / by Betty Durham with Muriel Larson. Van Nuys, Calif. : Bible Voice, c1977. 189 p. ; 21 cm. [BR1725.D77A34] 78-102309 pbk. : 2.95
1. Durham, Betty. 2. Christian biography—United States. I. Larson, Muriel,joint author. II. Title.

Durham, Robert Lee,

DURHAM, Robert Lee, 1870- 920
1949.
Since I was born; edited by Marshall William Fishwick. Richmond, Whittet & Shepperson, 1953. 217p. illus. 21cm. [CT275.D8846A3] 53-40253
I. Title.

Durkheim, Emile, 1858-1917.

BIERSTEDT, Robert, 1913- 301.0924
Emile Durkheim. [New York, Dell Pub. Co., 1966] 255 p. 19 cm. (The Laurel great lives and thought) Bibliography: p. [9]-[15] [HM22.F8D77] 66-1040
1. Durkheim, Emile, 1858-1917. I. Title. II. Series.

DURKHEIM, Emile, 301'.092'4
1858-1917.
On morality and society; selected writings. Edited and with an introd. by Robert N. Bellah. Chicago, University of Chicago Press [1973] 1 v, 244 p. 22 cm. (The Heritage of sociology) [HM22.F8D779 1973] 73-76594 ISBN 0-226-17335-6 10.50
1. Durkheim, Emile, 1858-1917. 2. Sociology. I. Title.
Contents omitted.

GIDDENS, Anthony. 301'.092'4 B
Emile Durkheim / Anthony Giddens. New York : Viking Press, 1979. 132 p. ; 19 cm. (Modern masters.) Includes index. Bibliography: p. [126]-127. [HM22.F8D82 1979] 78-26657 ISBN 0-670-29283-4 : 9.95
1. Durkheim, Emile, 1858-1917. 2. Sociologists—France—Biography. **BIP**

GIDDENS, Anthony. 301'.092'4 B
Emile Durkheim / Anthony Giddens. New York : Penguin Books, 1979. 132 p. ; 18 cm. (Penguin modern masters) Includes index. Bibliography: p. [126]-127. [HM22.F8D82 1979b] 78-26656 ISBN 0-14-005002-7 pbk. : 3.95
1. Durkheim, Emile, 1858-1917. 2. Sociologists—France—Biography.

LACAPRA, Dominick, 301'.0924 B
1939-
Emile Durkheim: sociologist and philosopher. Ithaca [N.Y.] Cornell University Press [1972] x, 315 p. 22 cm. Bibliography: p. 297-309. [HM22.F8D83] 71-37779 ISBN 0-8014-0701-X 12.50
1. Durkheim, Emile, 1858-1917. I. Title.

LUKES, Steven. 301'.092'4 B
Emile Durkheim, his life and work : a historical and critical study / Steven Lukes. Harmondsworth : Penguin, 1975[i.e.1977] xi, 676 p. ; 20 cm. (Peregrine books) Includes indexes. "Bibliography of Durkheim's publications". p. [561]-590. [HM22.F8D845 1975] 76-364613 ISBN 0-14-055093-3 pbk. : 4.00
1. Durkheim, Emile, 1858-1917. I. Title.
Distributed by Penguin,Baltimore, Md.

NISBET, Robert A. 301.01
Emile Durkheim [by] Robert A. Nisbet. With selected essays. Englewood Cliffs, N.J., Prentice-Hall [1965] x, 179 p. 21 cm. (Makers of modern social science) Spectrum book, S-118. Bibliography: p. 177-178. Bibliographical footnotes. [HM22.F8D86] 65-14994
1. Durkheim, Emile, 1858-1917. I. Title. II. Series.

NISBET, Robert A. 301'.01
Emile Durkheim / Robert A. Nisbet ; with selected essays. Westport, Conn. : Greenwood Press, 1976, c1965. x, 179 p. ; 23 cm. Reprint of the ed. published by Prentice-Hall, Englewood Cliffs, N.J., in series: Makers of modern social science. Bibliography: p. 177-178. [HM22.F8D86 1976] 75-36358 ISBN 0-8371-8626-9 : 12.00
1. Durkheim, Emile, 1858-1917. I. Series: Makers of modern social science.

Durocher, Leo Ernest, 1906-

DAY, Laraine, 1920- 796.357
Day with the Giants; edited by Kyle Crichton. Drawings by Leo Hershfield. [1st ed.] Garden City, N. Y., Doubleday, 1952. 219 p. illus. 21 cm. [GV865.D83D3] 52-5758
1. Durocher, Leo Ernest, 1906- 2. New York. Baseball club (National League) I. Title.

DUROCHER, Leo 796.357'092'4 B
Ernest, 1906-
Nice guys finish last / by Leo Durocher, with Ed Linn. New York : Simon and Schuster, [1975] 448 p., [16] leaves of plates : ill. ; 23 cm. Includes index. [GV865.D83A36] 75-1462 ISBN 0-671-22057-8 : 9.95
1. Durocher, Leo Ernest, 1906- 2. Baseball. I. Linn, Edward. II. Title.

DUROCHER, Leo 796.357'092'4 B
Ernest, 1906-
Nice guys finish last by Leo Durocher with Ed Linn. New York, Pocket Books [1976 c1975] 404 p. illus. 18 cm. Includes index. [GV865.D83A36] ISBN 0-671-80446-4 1.95 (pbk.)
1. Durocher, Leo Ernest, 1906- 2. Baseball. I. Title.
L.C. card no. of 1975 Simon and Schuster edition: 75-1462. **BIP**

MANN, Arthur William, 927.96357
1901-
Baseball journey. New York, F. J. Low Co., c1951. 199 l. 28 cm. [GV865.D83M3] 51-58127
1. Durocher, Leo Ernest, I. Title.

SCHOOR, Gene. 927.96357
The Leo Durocher story. New York, Messner [1955] 192 p. illus. 22 cm. [GV865.D83S3] 55-9866
1. Durocher, Leo Ernest, 1906-

Durrell, Gerald Malcolm, 1925-

DURRELL, Gerald 500.9'495'5
Malcolm, 1925-
Birds, beasts, and relatives / Gerald Durrell. New York : Penguin Books, [1976] c1969. p. cm. [QH151.D78 1976] 76-27842 ISBN 0-670-16775-4 : 5.95 ISBN 0-670-00315-8 pbk. : 2.25
1. Durrell, Gerald Malcolm, 1925- 2. Natural history—Corfu. 3. Corfu—Description and travel. 4. Zoologists—Great Britain—Biography. I. Title. **BIP**

DURRELL, Gerald 828'.9'1403 B
Malcolm, 1925-
Fillets of plaice / Gerald Durrell. [New York] : Penguin Books, 1976, c1971. p. cm. Reprint of the 1971 ed. published by Viking Press, New York. [PR6054.U74Z5 1976] 76-28546 ISBN 0-670-31327-0 pbk. : 1.95
I. Title. **BIP**

Durrell, Jacquie, 1929-

DURRELL, Jacquie, 1929- 599
Intimate relations / Jacquie Durrell. Boston : G. K. Hall, 1977, c1976. 211 p. ; 24 cm. Large print ed. [QL791.D877 1977] 77-3140 ISBN 0-8161-6481-9 lib.bdg. : 8.95 lib.bdg. : 8.95
1. Durrell, Jacquie, 1929- 2. Animals, Legends and stories of. 3. Wild animal collectors—Great Britain—Biography. 4. Sight-saving books. I. Title. **BIP**

Durrell, Lawrence.

DURRELL, Lawrence. 928.2
Lawrence Durrell [and] Henry Miller; a private correspondence. Edited by George Wickes. [1st ed.] New York, Dutton, 1963. 400 p. illus. 22 cm. [PR6007.U76Z53] 62-14726
I. Miller, Henry, 1891-

DURRELL, Lawrence George, 928.2
1912-
Lawrence Durrell [and] Henry Miller; a private correspondence. Ed. by George Wickes. New York, Dutton [1964, c.1962, 1963] 398p. ports. 18cm. (D149) 1.85 pap.,
I. Miller, Henry, 1891- II. Title.

PERLES, Alfred. 730'.92'4
My friend Lawrence Durrell; an intimate memoir on the author of The Alexandrian quartet. With a bibliography by Bernard Stone. [Northwood, Middlesex] Scorpion Press [1961] 62p. illus. 22cm. [PR6007.U76Z8] 62-5793
1. Durrell, Lawrence. I. Title.

WEIGEL, John A. 828.91209
Lawrence Durrell by John A. Weigel. New York, Dutton 1966 [c.1965] 174p. 19cm. (D185) Bibl. [PR6007.U76Z95 1966] 1.25 pap.,
1. Durrell, Lawrence, 1912- I. Title.

Durrell, Lawrence—Homes and haunts—Greece.

DURRELL, Lawrence. 828'.9'1209 B
Blue thirst / Lawrence Durrell. Santa Barbara, Calif. : Capra Press, 1975. 56 p. : ill. ; 24 cm. [PR6007.U76Z498 1975] 75-310914 ISBN 0-88496-018-8 : 15.00 ISBN 0-88496-017-X pbk. : 3.25
1. Durrell, Lawrence—Homes and haunts—Greece. 2. Authors—Correspondence, reminiscences, etc. 3. Greece, Modern—Description and travel—1951- I. Title. **BIP**

Duryea, Charles E., 1861-1938.

MAY, George 338.4'7'6292220924 B
W.
Charles E. Duryea—automaker, by George W. May. Ann Arbor,Mich., Lithographed by Edward Bros., 1973. 175 p. illus. 19 cm. Bibliography: p. 174-175. [HD9710.U52D875] 73-181302
1. Duryea, Charles E., 1861-1938. 2. Automobile industry and trade—United States. I. Title.

Duryea, John Ackerly,

DURYEA, Jennie Sworn. v. 12
John A. Duryea: spirit-filled evangel. Wilmore, Ky. [n. d.] 24 p. illus., ports. 20 cm. 65-44292
1. Duryea, John Ackerly, I. Title.

DuSable High School—Basketball—Juvenile literature.

BERKOW, Ira. 796.32'37
The DuSable Panthers : the greatest, blackest, saddest team from the meanest street in Chicago / by Ira Berkow. 1st ed. New York : Atheneum, 1978. x, 188 p., [3] leaves of plates : ill. ; 22 cm. An account of the 1954 Illinois High School State Championship basketball game between the DuSable Panthers, the first all-black team to make the finals, and a team from Mount Vernon High School. [GV885.43.D87B47 1978] 77-21088 ISBN 0-689-30612-1 : 7.95
1. DuSable High School—Basketball—Juvenile literature. 2. Mount Vernon High School—Basketball—Juvenile literature. 3. Basketball players—Illinois—Biography—Juvenile literature. I. Title.

Duse, Eleonora, 1858-1924.

DE BONIS, Sofia 792'.028'0924 B
(McQuaide) 1885-
Eleonora Duse: the story of her life, by Jeanne Bordeux. [New York] B. Blom [1971] ix, 308 p. illus., ports. 22 cm. Reprint of the 1924 ed. [PN2688.D8D35 1971] 79-91896
1. Duse, Eleonora, 1858-1924. I. Title.

LE GALLIENNE, Eva, 1899- 792.0924
The mystic in the theatre: Eleonora Duse. [New York,] Farrar [c.1965, 1966] 185p. 21cm. [PN2688.D8L4] 66-14417 4.50 bds.,
1. Duse, Eleonora, 1858-1924. I. Title. **BIP**

LE GALLIENNE, Eva, 792'.028'0924
1899-
The mystic in the theatre: Eleonora Duse. Carbondale, Southern Illinois University Press [1973, c1966] 185 p. 20 cm. (Arcturus books, AB108) [PN2688.D8L4 1973] 72-11975 ISBN 0-8093-0631-X 2.45
1. Duse, Eleonora, 1858-1924. I. Title.

RHEINHARDT, Emil 792'.028'0924 B Alphons, 1889-
The life of Eleonora Duse, by E. A. Rheinhardt. [English version by Willa and Edwin Muir] New York, B. Blom [1969] 292 p. ports. 20 cm. Reprint of the 1930 ed. Includes bibliographical references. [PN2688.D8R52 1969] 73-82841
1. Duse, Eleonora, 1858-1924. I. Title.

SYMONS, Arthur, 792'.028'0924 1865-1945.
Eleonora Duse. New York, B. Blom [1969] 164 p. 23 cm. Reprint of the 1927 ed. [PN2688.D8S8 1969] 78-84527
1. Duse, Eleonora, 1858-1924. BIP

Dusky, Lorraine.

DUSKY, Lorraine. 301.42'7
Birthmark / Lorraine Dusky. New York : M. Evans, c1979. 191 p. ; 22 cm. [HQ759.D865] 79-16273 ISBN 0-87131-299-9 : 8.95
1. Dusky, Lorraine. 2. Mothers—United States—Biography. 3. Adoption—United States. I. Title. BIP

Duston, Hannah Emerson, b. 1657.

MATHER, Cotton, 973'.04'97 S 1663-1728.
Decennium luctuosum / Cotton Mather. New York : Garland Pub., 1977. p. cm. (The Garland Library of narratives of North American Indian captivities ; v. 3) Reprint of the 1699 ed. printed by B. Green for S. Philips, Boston, under title: Decennium luctuosum: an history of remarkable occurrences in the long war which New England hath had with the Indian salvages, from the year 1688 to the year 1698. [E85.G2 vol. 3] [E196] 973.2'5 75-7022 ISBN 0-8240-1627-0 lib.bdg. : 25.00
1. Duston, Hannah Emerson, b. 1657. 2. United States—History—King William's War, 1689-1697. 3. Indians of North America—Captivities. I. Title. II. Series.

Dutton, Joseph, 1843-1931.

BETZ, Eva K. 922.273
Yankee at Molokai. Paterson, N.J., St. Anthony Guild Press [c.1960] vii, 150p. illus. 20cm. 60-9770 2.50
1. Dutton. Joseph, 1843-1931. I. Title.

BETZ, Eva (Kelly) 1897- 922.273
Yankee at Molokai. Paterson, N. J., St. Anthony Guild Press [1960] 150p. illus. 20cm. [BX4705.D94B4] 60-9770
1. Dutton, Joseph, 1843-1931. I. Title.

Dutton, Ninette.

DUTTON, Ninette. 738.4'092'4 B
Portrait of a year / Ninette Dutton. Melbourne : Nelson, 1976. viii, 176 p. ; 24 cm. [N7405.D87A56] 77-373787 ISBN 0-17-005089-0
1. Dutton, Ninette. 2. Artists—Australia—Biography. I. Title.

DuVal family.

NEWMAN, Harry 927'.2*09752 Wright, 1894-
Mareen Duvall of Middle Plantation; a genealogical history of Mareen Duvall, Gent., of the Province of Maryland and his descendants, with histories of the allied families of Tyler, Clarke, Poole, Hall, and Merriken. Washington, 1952. 590 p. illus., coat of arms, map, plan, ports. 24 cm. "Limited to 350 copies ... number 302." [CS71.D985 1952] 74-110
1. DuVal family. I. Title.

Duval, John Crittenden, 1816-1897.

DOBIE, James Frank, 1888- 818.4 1964.
John C. Duval, first Texas man of letters; his life and some of his unpublished writings [by] J. Frank Dobie. With sketches by Tom Lea. [2d ed.] Dallas, Southern Methodist University Press [1965, c1939] 105 p. illus. 24 cm. Includes bibliographical references. [PS1562.D67D6 1965] 65-2977
1. Duval, John Crittenden, 1816-1897. I. Duval, John Crittenden, 1816-1897. II. Title.

Duvalier, Francois, Pres. Haiti, 1907-1971.

DIEDERICH, 972'.9406'0924 Bernard.
Papa Doc; the truth about Haiti today, by Bernard Diederich & Al Burt. Foreword by Graham Greene. [1st ed.] New York, McGraw-Hill [1969] xii, 393 p. 23 cm. Bibliographical footnotes. [F1928.D86D5] 71-81605
1. Duvalier, Francois, Pres. Haiti, 1907- 2. Haiti—History—1934- I. Burt, Al, joint author.

DIEDERICH, 972.94'06'0924 Bernard.
Papa Doc—Haiti and its dictator [by] Bernard Diederich and Al Burt. Harmondsworth, Penguin, 1972. 424 p. 18 cm. [F1928.D86D5 1972] 73-162130 ISBN 0-14-003458-7 £0.50
1. Duvalier, Francois, Pres. Haiti, 1907-1971. 2. Haiti—History—1934- I. Burt, Al, joint author. II. Title.

GINGRAS, Jean Pierre 320.9'7294 O.
Duvalier, Caribbean cyclone; the history of Haiti and its present government, by Jean-Pierre O. Gingras. [1st ed.] New York, Exposition Press [1967] 136 p. 22 cm. "Selected bibliography" p. [134]-136. [F1928.G5] 67-3196
1. Duvalier, Francois, Pres. Haiti, 1907- 2. Haiti—Politics and government—1934- 3. Haiti—History. I. Title.

Duveen Brothers.

FOWLES, Edward. 706'.5 B
Memories
Edward Fowles ; introduction by Sir Ellis Waterhouse. London : Times Books, 1976 [7], 215 p., [16] p. of plates : ill., facsim., ports. ; 24 cm. "Abridged by Michael Glover." Includes index. [N8660.F67A25 1976] 77-359790 ISBN 0-7230-0155-3 : £7.95
1. Fowles, Edward. 2. Duveen Brothers. 3. Duveen, Joseph Duveen, Baron, 1869-1939. 4. Art dealers—Great Britain—Biography. I. Title.

Duveneck, Josephine Whitney, 1891-

DUVENECK, 289.6'092'4 B Josephine Whitney, 1891-
Life on two levels : an autobiography / by Josephine Whitney Duveneck. Los Altos, Ca. : W. Kaufmann, [1978] p. cm. Includes index. [BX7795.D83A34] 78-17903 ISBN 0-913232-56-4 : 10.00
1. Duveneck, Josephine Whitney, 1891- 2. Friends, Society of—United States—Biography. I. Title. BIP

Duvergier de Hauranne, Ernest, 1843-1877.

DUVERGIER de Hauranne, 917.3'04'7 Ernest, 1843-1877.
A Frenchman in Lincoln's America = Huit mois en Amerique : lettres et notes de voyage, 1864-1865 / by Ernest Duvergier de Hauranne ; translated and edited by Ralph H. Bowen ; with introd. and notes by Ralph H. Bowen and Albert Krebs. Chicago : Lakeside Press, 1974- v. : ill. ; 18 cm. (The Lakeside classics ; no. 72) Includes index. [E167.D9813] 75-307537
1. Duvergier de Hauranne, Ernest, 1843-1877. 2. United States—Description and travel—1848-1865. 3. United States—Politics and government—Civil War, 1861-1865. 4. United States—History—Civil War, 1861-1865—Personal narratives. I. Title. II. Title: Huit mois en Amerique.

Dvbwad, Johanne (Juell), 1867-1950.

WAAL, Carla Rae, 1933- 792.0924
Johanne Dvbwad, Norwegian actress. Oslo, Universitets--forlaget. 1967. viii, 353p. 4 plates. 23cm. Bibl. [PN2768.D9W3] 67-95945 7.75 pap.,
1. Dvbwad, Johanne (Juell), 1867-1950. I. Title.
American distributor: Humanities, New York.

Dvorak, Antonin, 1841-1904.

HOFFMEISTER, Karel, 780'.92'4 B 1868-
Antonin Dvorak. Edited and translated, with a foreword, by Rosa Newmarch. Westport, Conn., Greenwood Press [1970] xxi, 132 p. music, port. 23 cm. "Originally published in 1928." [ML410.D99H7 1970] 72-104275 ISBN 0-8371-3946-5
1. Dvorak, Anton, 1841-1904. I. Newmarch, Rosa Harriet (Jeaffreson) 1857-1940, ed. BIP

HUGHES, Gervase. 780'.924 B
Dvorak; his life and music. New York, Dodd, Mead [1967] viii, 247 p. port. 21 cm. "A few notes on the bibliography, with special reference to books published in English": p. 231-233. [ML410.D99H79 1967b] 67-26843
1. Dvorak, Antonin, 1841-1904.

ROBERTSON, Alec. 927.8 Collingwood Cuthbert
Dvorak. New York, Collier [1962] 253p. 18cm. (Gr. composers ser., BS117x) Bibl. 1.50 pap.,
1. Dvorak, Antomn, 1841-1904. I. Title. BIP

Dwight D. Eisenhower Library, Abilene, Kan.

MUELLER, Betty Jean. 026
The Dwight D. Eisenhower Library. Narration and decorations by Betty Jean Mueller and Edward Miller. With a foreword by John S. D. Eisenhower. [1st ed.] New York, Meredith Press [1966] 109 p. illus. (part col.) col. maps, ports. 24 cm. (A Halls of greatness book) A description of the library and museum housing the documents and and papers of our thirty-fourth President with a brief outline of the events that highlighted his term in office. [Z733.A2M8] AC 66
1. Dwight D. Eisenhower Library, Abilene, Kan. I. Miller, Edward, 1905- joint author. II. Title.

Dwight, John Sullivan, 1813-1893.

COOKE, George Willis, 780'.92'4 B 1848-1923.
John Sullivan Dwight: Brook-farmer, editor, and critic of music; a biography. [New ed.] Hartford, Transcendental Books [1973] 84 l. illus. 28 cm. [ML423.D9C7 1973] 74-151207
1. Dwight, John Sullivan, 1813-1893. 2. Brook Farm. I. Title.

Dwight, Mary Carter (Singleton) 1871-1958.

DWIGHT, Mary Carter v. 12 (Singleton) 1871-1958.
A history of my long life to leave my children and other descendants. [n.p., 1960?] 65 p. illus., ports. 21 cm. Cover title. 64-35157
1. Dwight, Mary Carter (Singleton) 1871-1958. I. Title.

Dwight, Timothy, 1752-1817.

CUNINGHAM, Charles E. 370'.92'4 B
Timothy Dwight, 1752-1817 : a biography / by Charles E. Cunningham New York : AMS Press, 1976. viii, 403 p., [7] leaves of plates : ill. ; 23 cm. Reprint of the 1942 ed. published by Macmillan, New York. Includes index. Bibliography: p. 353-362. [LD6330 1795.C8 1976] 75-41069 ISBN 0-404-14746-1 : 21.50
1. Dwight, Timothy, 1752-1817. I. Title.

Dwight, Timothy, 1828-1916.

PARSONS, Francis, 378.746'8 B 1871-1937.
Six men of Yale. Foreword by Charles Seymour. Freeport, N.Y., Books for Libraries Press [1971, c1939] xii, 145 p. ports. 23 cm. (Essay index reprint series) Contents.Contents.—Elisha Williams, 1694-1755.—Ezra Stiles, 1727-1795.—The young Silliman in Nelson's England, 1805-1806.—Edward J. Phelps, 1822-1900.—The second President Dwight, 1828-1916.—Henry Augustin Beer, 1847-1926. [LD6319.P3 1971] 72-156702 ISBN 0-8369-2329-4
1. Williams, Elisha, 1694-1775. 2. Stiles, Ezra, 1727-1795. 3. Silliman, Benjamin, 1779-1864. 4. Phelps, Edward John, 1822-1900. 5. Dwight, Timothy, 1828-1916. 6. Beers, Henry Augustin, 1847-1926. I. Title. BIP

Dwyer, Karen Anne, 1937-1961.

*DWYER, Mabel 920.961615
No tomorrow. Detroit, Mich., Harlo Pr., 16854 Hamilton Ave. [c.]1964. 128p. 21cm. 3.95
1. Dwyer, Karen Anne, 1937-1961. I. Title.

*DWYER, Mabel 920.961615
No tomorrow. Detroit, Mich., Harlo Pr., 16854 Hamilton Ave. [c.]1964. 128p. 21cm. 3.95
1. Dwyer, Karen Anne, 1937-1961. I. Title.

Dyce, Alexander,

DYCE, Alexander, 828'.7'03 B 1798-1869.
The reminiscences of Alexander Dyce. Edited, with a biography, by Richard J. Schrader. [Columbus] Ohio State University Press [1972] xiii, 267 p. illus. 23 cm. [PR29.D9A3 1972] 75-157716 ISBN 0-8142-0160-1 11.00
I. Schrader, Richard J., ed. II. Title. BIP

Dye, Jacob, 1875-1961.

DYE, Jacob, 1875- 634.9'82'0922 B 1961. *f Duveen Brothers* / [by]
Lumber camp life in Michigan : an autobiographical account / by Jacob Dye, 1880-1893, and his son Rex J. Dye, 1904-1909. 1st ed. Hicksville, N.Y. : Exposition Press, [1975] 48 p. : ill. ; 24 cm. (An Exposition-Lochinvar book) [SD538.2.M5D9] 75-309147 ISBN 0-682-48102-5 : 5.00
1. Dye, Jacob, 1875-1961. 2. Dye, Rex. 3. Lumber camps—Michigan—History. 4. Lumbermen—Correspondence, reminiscences, etc. I. Dye, Rex, joint author. II. Title. BIP

Dyer, Alfred John, 1884-1968.

COLE, Edmund Keith, 266'.3'0924 B 1919-
Oenpelli pioneer: a biography of the Reverend Alfred John Dyer; pioneer missionary among the aborigines in Arnhem Land and founder of the Oenpelli Mission. [Melbourne] Church Missionary Historical Publications, 1972. 96 p. illus. 18 cm. (Great Australian missionaries no. 4) [BV3667.D93C64] 79-184183 ISBN 0-909821-07-0
1. Dyer, Alfred John, 1884-1968. I. Title.

Dyer, Edward, Sir, 1543-1607.

SARGENT, Ralph Milland. 821'.3 B
The life and lyrics of Sir Edward Dyer (formerly entitled At the court of Queen Elizabeth), by Ralph M. Sargent. Oxford, Clarendon P., 1968. xiii, 229 p. 2 plates, 1 illus., facsim. 23 cm. [PR2270.D5S3 1968] 68-117306 ISBN 0-19-821363-8 42/-
1. Dyer, Edward, Sir, 1543-1607. 2. Great Britain—History—Elizabeth, 1558-1603. 3. Great Britain—Court and courtiers. I. Title.

Dyer, John 1700?-1758.

WILLIAMS, Ralph M 928.2
Poet, painter, and parson: the life of John Dyer. New York, Bookman Associates [c1956] 151p. illus., ports. 23cm. Includes bibliographies. [PR3431.D5Z9] A57
1. Dyer, John 1700?-1758. I. Title.

WILLIAMS, Ralph M. 928.2
Poet, painter, and parson: the life of John Dyer. New York, Bookman Associates

[c1956] 151 p. illus., ports. 23 cm. Includes bibliographies. [PR3431.D5Z9] A 57
1. Dyer, John 1700?-1758. I. Title.

Dyer, Mary, d. 1660.

CRAWFORD, Deborah. 973.2'2'0922 B
Four women in a violent time: Anne Hutchinson (1591-1643) Mary Dyer (1591?-1660) Lady Deborah Moody (1600-1659) Penelope Stout (1622-1732) New York, Crown Publishers [1970] 191 p. 22 cm. Bibliography: p. 185-186. Traces the lives of four women who struggled for civil rights and justice in seventeenth-century America. [E187.5.C7 1970] 920 74-127519 4.50
1. Hutchinson, Anne (Marbury) 1591-1643. 2. Dyer, Mary, d. 1660. 3. Moody, Deborah, Lady, 1600-1659. 4. Stout, Penelope, 1622-1732. I. Title.

Dykes, John Bacchus, 1823-1876.

ROE, Gordon. 283'.092'4 B
J. B. Dykes (1823-1876), priest & musician : essays / by Gordon Roe & Arthur Hutchings. [Durham] : [St Oswald's Parochial Church Council], [1976]. [5], 25, [3] p. : ill., port. ; 22 cm. Cover title. Bibliography: p. [2]. [BX5199.D94R63] 77-356903 ISBN 0-9505339-0-4 : £0.45
1. Dykes, John Bacchus, 1823-1876. 2. Church of England—Clergy—Biography. 3. Clergy—England—Biography. 4. Musicians—England—Biography. I. Hutchings, Arthur, 1906- joint author.

Dylan, Bob, 1941-

DYLAN, Bob, 1941- 784'.092'4 B
Bob Dylan in his own words / compiled by Miles ; edited by Pearce Marchbank ; designed by Perry Neville. New York : Quick Fox, c1978. 126 p., [1] leaf of plates : ill. ; 26 cm. [ML420.D98A3] 78-56239 ISBN 0-8256-3924-7 pbk. 4.95
1. Dylan, Bob, 1941- 2. Singers—United States—Biography. I. Miles, Barry, fl. 1963- II. Marchbank, Pearce. III. Title. BIP

GROSS, Michael 784'.092'4 B
Bob Dylan : an illustrated history / produced by Michael Gross ; with a text by Robert Alexander. New York : Grosset & Dunlap, c1978. 148 p. : ill. ; 29 cm. Bibliography: p. 148-149. [ML420.D98G76] 77-87808 ISBN 0-448-14574-X : 12.95
1. Dylan, Bob, 1941- 2. Rock musicians—United States—Biography.

**KNOCKING on* 784.4'92'4 [B]
Dylan's door: on the road in '74. [by the editors of Rolling Stone Magazine]. New York, Pocket Books [1974] 137 p. photos. 18 cm. (A Rolling Stone book) [ML420] ISBN 0-671-78682-2. 1.50 (pbk.)
1. Dylan, Bob, 1941- I. Rolling Stone Magazine.

KRAMER, Daniel. 780'.924
Bob Dylan. [1st ed.] New York, Citadel Press [1967] 150 p. ports. 28 cm. [ML420.D98K7] 66-19752 MN
1. Dylan, Bob, 1941- I. Title.

MCGREGOR, Craig, comp. 784.4'92'4 B
Bob Dylan; a retrospective. New York, Morrow, 1972. viii, 407 p. illus. 22 cm. Includes bibliographical references. [ML420.D98M2] 77-182455 10.00
1. Dylan, Bob, 1941- BIP

RINZLER, Alan. 784'.092'4
Bob Dylan : the illustrated record / by Alan Rinzler ; designed by Jon Goodchild. New York : Harmony Books, c1978. 120 p. : ill. (some col.) ; 30 cm. Bibliography: p. 120. [ML420.D98R56] 78-7006 ISBN 0-517-53354-5 : 15.00 ISBN 0-517-53355-3 pbk. : 8.95
1. Dylan, Bob, 1941- 2. Singers—United States—Biography. I. Goodchild, Jon. BIP

SCADUTO, Anthony. 784.4'92'4 B
Bob Dylan. New York, Grosset & Dunlap [1972, c1971] 280 p. ports. 22 cm. [ML420.D98S27] 72-144064 ISBN 0-448-02034-3 7.95
1. Dylan, Bob, 1941- BIP

SCADUTO, Anthony. 784.4'92'4 B
Bob Dylan / by Anthony Scaduto. Updated with a new afterword / by Steven Gaines. New York : New American Library, [1979] c1973. 366 p., [4] leaves of plates : ill. ; 18 cm. (A Signet book) Includes index. Discography: p. 252-261. [ML420.D98S27 1979] 79-316819 ISBN 0-451-08609-0 pbk. : 2.25
1. Dylan, Bob, 1941- 2. Singers—United States—Biography.

THOMPSON, Toby. 784.4'924
Positively Main Street; an unorthodox view of Bob Dylan. New York, Coward-McCann [1971] 187 p. 22 cm. [ML420.D98T5] 79-136449 5.95
1. Dylan, Bob, 1941- I. Title. II. Title: An unorthodox view of Bob Dylan. BIP

Dylan, Bob, 1941- —Juvenile literature.

BEAL, Kathleen. 784'.092'4 B
Bob Dylan. Illustrator: John Keely. Mankato, Minn., Creative Education [1974] p. cm. [ML3930.D97B4] 74-13936 ISBN 0-87191-399-2 4.95 (lib. bdg.)
1. Dylan, Bob, 1941- —Juvenile literature. I. Keely, John, illus. II. Title.

Dylan, Bob, 1941- —Religion and ethics.

PICKERING, Stephen, 1947- 784'.092'4
Bob Dylan approximately : a portrait of the Jewish poet in search of God : a Midrash / Stephen Pickering ; photography by George Gruel, Peter Vogl, and others. New York : McKay, [1975] 204 p. : ill. (some col.) ; 27 cm. Includes bibliographical references. [ML420.D98P5] 74-29325 ISBN 0-679-50493-1 : 14.95. ISBN 0-679-50529-6 pbk. : 5.95
1. Dylan, Bob, 1941- —Religion and ethics. 2. Mysticism—Judaism—Miscellanea. I. Title.

Dyott, Thomas W.

MCKEARIN, Helen. 666'.19
Bottles, flasks, and Dr. Dyott. New York, Crown Publishers [1970] 160 p. illus., facsims., map., port. 26 cm. Bibliography: p. 155. [NK5198.D95M3 1970] 74-127499 5.95
1. Dyott, Thomas W. I. Title.

Dysart, Stella.

ARMITAGE, Merle, 1893- 926.22
Stella Dysart of Ambrosia Lake. Foreword by Dennis Chavez. [1st limited ed.] New York, Duell, Sloan and Pearce [1959] 160p. illus. 23cm. [TN140.D9A7] 58-7766
1. Dysart, Stella. I. Title.

Dyson, Freeman, J.

DYSON, Freeman J. 530'.092'4 B
Disturbing the universe / Freeman Dyson. 1st ed. New York : Harper & Row, c1979. x, 283 p. ; 24 cm. Includes bibliographical references and index. [QC16.D95A33 1979] 78-20665 ISBN 0-06-011108-9 : 12.95
1. Dyson, Freeman, J. 2. Physicists—United States—Biography. 3. Science. I. Title.

Eads, James Buchanan, 1820-1887.

THE Eads Bridge 624.6'7'0977866
: an exhibition prepared by the Art Museum and the Department of Civil Engineering, Princeton University : [The Art Museum, Princeton University, October 13-November 10, 1974, The St. Louis Art Museum, November 26, 1974-January 5, 1975]. Princeton, N.J. : Art Museum, Princeton University, c1974. 84 p. : ill. ; 18 x 22 cm. [TG25.S15E23] 75-306267 pbk. : 3.50
1. Eads, James Buchanan, 1820-1887. 2. St. Louis—Bridges. I. Princeton University. Art Museum. II. St. Louis Art Museum. Contents omitted.

HOW, Louis, 1873-1947. 620'.00924 B
James B. Eads. Freeport, N.Y., Books for Libraries Press [1970] vi, 120 p. port. 23 cm. "First published 1900." [TA140.E2H7 1970] 75-117880
1. Eads, James Buchanan, 1820-1887. BIP

ORRMONT, Arthur. 620'.00924 B
James Buchanan Eads, the man who mastered the Mississippi. Illustrated by Jerry Contreras. Englewood Cliffs, N.J., Prentice-Hall [1970] 143 p. illus. 22 cm. (Hall of Fame books) "A Rutledge book." Bibliography: p. 143. A biography of the engineer who invented the diving bell and was responsible for the design of the steel-arch bridge across the Mississippi River at St. Louis. [TA140.E2O7] 92 71-92098 4.50
1. Eads, James Buchanan, 1820-1887. I. Contreras, Jerry, illus. II. Title. III. Series.

YAGER, Rosemary, 1909- 620'.00924 B
James Buchanan Eads; master of the Great River. Illustrated by John Hackmaster. Princeton, N.J., Van Nostrand [1968] 126 p. illus. 22 cm. Bibliography: p. 120-122. A biography of the self-taught engineer who designed armored gunboats for the Union Army, supervised construction of the jetties across the New Orleans harbor, and built the first bridge at St. Louis across the Mississippi River. [TA140.E2Y3] 92 AC 68
1. Eads, James Buchanan, 1820-1887. I. Hackmaster, John, illus. II. Title.

Eakins, Thomas, 1844-1916.

HENDRICKS, Gordon. 759.13 B
The life and work of Thomas Eakins / Gordon Hendricks. New York : Grossman Publishers, 1974. xxx, 367 p., [25] leaves of plates : 306 ill. (some col.) ; 31 cm. Includes index. Bibliography: p. 305-314. [ND237.E15H46 1974] 73-4174 ISBN 0-670-42795-0 : 45.00
1. Eakins, Thomas, 1844-1916. I. Eakins, Thomas, 1844-1916. II. Title.

SCHENDLER, Sylvan. 759.13
Eakins. [1st ed.] Boston, Little, Brown [1967] xix, 300 p. illus., ports. 25 cm. [ND237.E15S3] 67-18109
1. Eakins, Thomas, 1844-1916.

Eames, Emma, 1865-1952.

EAMES, Emma, 1865-1952. 782.1'092'4 B
Some memories and reflections / Emma Eames ; with a discography by W. R. Moran. New York : Arno Press, 1977. p. cm. (Opera biographies) Reprint of the 1927 ed. published by Appleton, New York. [ML420.E17A3 1977] 76-29934 ISBN 0-405-09676-3 : 24.00
1. Eames, Emma, 1865-1952. 2. Singers—Biography. I. Title. BIP

Eames, Wilberforce, 1853-1937.

LYDENBERG, Harry Miller, 1874- 920.1
Wilberforce Eames as I recall him. Worcester, Mass., American Antiquarian Society, 1956. 214-236p. 25cm. 'Reprinted from the Proceedings of the American Antiquarian Society for October 1955. [Z1004.E2L9] 56-58838
1. Eames, Wilberforce, 1853-1937. I. Title.

Eardley, Joan.

BUCHANAN, William. 759.9411 B
Joan Eardley / by William Buchanan. Edinburgh : Edinburgh University Press, c1976. 91 p. : ill. (some col.) ; 16 x 22 cm. (Modern Scottish painters ; no. 5) Bibliography: p. 88. [ND497.E25B8] 77-360043 ISBN 0-85224-301-4 : 5.00
1. Eardley, Joan. 2. Painters—Scotland—Biography. I. Eardley, Joan.
Distributed by Edinburgh Univ. Press, c/o Biblio Distribution Center, 81 Adams Dr., Totowa, NJ07512

Eareckson, Joni.

EARECKSON, Joni. 362.4'3'0926 B
Joni / by Joni Eareckson, with Joe Musser. Grand Rapids : Zondervan Pub. House, c1976. 228 p., [8] leaves of plates : ill. ; 22 cm. [RC406.T4E18] 76-10450 6.95
1. Eareckson, Joni. 2. Tetraplegia—Biography. I. Musser, Joe, joint author. II. Title. BIP

EARECKSON, Joni. 362.4'3'0926 B
A step further / Joni Eareckson & Steve Estes ; illustrated by Joni. Grand Rapids : Zondervan Pub. House, c1978. 192 p., [8] leaves of plates : ill. ; 23 cm. Bibliography: p. 191-192. [RC406.T4E19] 78-12084 ISBN 0-310-23970-2 : 6.95
1. Eareckson, Joni. 2. Tetraplegia—Biography. I. Estes, Steve, joint author. II. Title. BIP

Earhart, Amelia, 1898-1937.

BRIAND, Paul L. 926.2913
Daughter of the sky; the story of Amelia Earhart. [1st ed.] New York, Duell, Sloan and Pearce [1960] 230 p. illus. 21 cm. Includes bibliography. [TL540.E3B7] 60-5457
1. Earhart, Amelia, 1898-1937. I. Title.

BRLAND, Paul L. 926.2913
Daughter of the sky; the story of Amelia Earhart [by] Paul L. Briand, Jr. New York, Pyramid [1967, c.1960] 207p. 18cm. (X1624) [TL540.E3 B7] .60 pap.,
1. Earhart, Amelia, 1898-1937. I. Title.

EARHART, Amelia, 1898-1937. 629.13'092'4 B
The fun of it; random records of my own flying and of women in aviation. New York, Harcourt Brace. Detroit, Gale Research Co., 1975 [c1932] 218 p. illus. 22 cm. [TL540.E3A3 1975] 71-159945 ISBN 0-8103-4078-X 14.00
1. Earhart, Amelia, 1898-1937. 2. Women in aeronautics. I. Title. BIP

GOERNER, Fred G. 629.132520924 B
The search for Amelia Earhart [by] Fred Goerner. Garden City, N.Y., Doubleday, 1966. 326 p. illus., ports. 24 cm. [TL540.E3G6] 66-23412.
1. Earhart, Amelia, 1898-1937. I. Title.

O'CONNOR, Richard, 1915- 629.13'0924 B
Winged legend; the story of Amelia Earhart, by John Burke. New York, Putnam [1970] 255 p. illus., ports. 23 cm. Bibliography: p. 246. [TL540.E3O25] 75-123441 6.95
1. Earhart, Amelia, 1898-1937. I. Title.

*PARLIN, John. 92
Amelia Earhart, pioneer in the sky. Illus. by Anthony D'Amado. New York, Dell [1968, c.1962] 80p. illus. 19cm. (Yearling, Discovery bk. 0117) .50 pap.,
1. Earhart, Amelia, 1896-1937—Juvenile literature. I. Title.

PELLEGRENO, Ann Holtgren. 629.13
World flight; the Earhart trail. [1st ed.] Ames, Iowa State University Press [1971] xi, 225 p. illus. 24 cm. Bibliography: p. 223-225. [TL721.P38A3] 70-153161 ISBN 0-8138-1760-9 6.95
1. Earhart, Amelia, 1898-1937. 2. Aeronautics—Flights. 3. Flights around the world. I. Title.

STRIPPEL, Dick. 629.13'092'4 B
Amelia Earhart; the myth and the reality ... [1st ed.] New York, Exposition Press [1972] 181 p. illus. 22 cm. (An Exposition-banner book) Bibliography: p. [159]-163.

[TL540.E3S75] 76-186486 ISBN 0-682-47447-9 6.00
1. Earhart, Amelia, 1898-1937. BIP

Earhart, Amelia, 1898-1937—Juvenile fiction.

HOWE, Jane Moore 920
Amelia Earhart, Kansas girl. Illus. by Gray Morrow. Indianapolis, Bobbs [1962, c.1950, 1961] 200p. col. illus. 20cm. (Childhood of famous Americans) 2.25
1. Earhart, Amelia, 1898-1937—Juvenile fiction. I. Title.

HOWE, Jane Moore. JUV
Amelia Earhart, Kansas girl. Illustrated by Gray Morrow. Indianapolis, Bobbs-Merrill [c1961] 200p. illus. 20cm. (Childhood of famous Americans) [PZ7.H8373Am4] 920 62-9246
1. Earhart, Amelia, 1898-1937—Juvenile fiction. I. Title.

Earhart, Amelia, 1898-1937—Juvenile literature.

BLAU, Melinda, 1943- 629.13'092'4 B
What ever happened to Amelia : Earhart / by Melinda Blau. New York : Contemporary Perspectives ; Milwaukee : distributor, Raintree Publishers, c1977. 48 p. : ill. (some col.) ; 24 cm. A biography of the woman who set many records as a pilot. Discusses the mystery surrounding her disappearance while attempting to fly around the world. [TL540.E3B58] 92 77-22173 ISBN 0-8172-1057-1 lib. bdg. : 4.95
1. Earhart, Amerlia, 1898-1937—Juvenile literature. 2. Air pilots—United States—Biography—Juvenile literature. I. Title.

EDUCATIONAL Research Council of America. Social Science Staff. 629.13'092 B
Explorers and discoverers, Amelia Earhart / prepared by the Social Science Staff of the Educational Research Council of America ; [Kenneth J. Torda, illustration]. Boston : Allyn and Bacon, [1974] 44 p. : ill. (some col.) ; 21 cm. (Concepts and inquiry, the ERC social science program) A biography of the aviation pioneer who was the first woman to fly alone across the Atlantic. [TL540.E3E38 1974] 92 73-78338 pbk.: 1.76 pbk. : 1.76
1. Earhart, Amelia, 1898-1937—Juvenile literature. I. Torda, Kenneth J., ill. II. Title. III. Series: Concepts and inquiry, the Educational Research Council social science program.

HAZEN, Barbara Shook. 629.13'092'4 B
Amelia's flying machine / Barbara Shook Hazen ; illustrated by Charles Robinson. 1st ed. Garden City, N.Y. : Doubleday, c1977. [64] p. : col. ill. ; 24 cm. Relates how Amelia Earhart built and rode her own roller coaster when she was a young girl. [TL540.E3H39] 92 76-51861 ISBN 0-385-07945-1 : 6.95.
1. Earhart, Amelia, 1898-1937—Juvenile literature. 2. Air pilots—United States—Biography—Juvenile literature. 3. Women in aeronautics—Juvenile literature. I. Robinson, Charles, 1931- II. Title.

MANN, Peggy. 629.13'0924 B
Amelia Earhart; first lady of flight. Illustrated by Kiyo Komoda. New York, Coward-McCann [1970] 126 p. col. illus., facsim. 20 cm. A biography of the first woman to fly across the Atlantic alone and to solo between Hawaii and California. [TL540.E3M3] 92 71-106932 3.64
1. Earhart, Amelia, 1898-1937—Juvenile literature. I. Komoda, Kiyo, illus. II. Title. BIP

MAY, Julian. 629.13'092'4 B
Amelia Earhart: pioneer of aviation. Illustrated by Phero Thomas. Mankato, Minn., Creative Educational Society; distributed exclusively by Childrens Press, Chicago, 1973. [39 p.] illus. 24 cm. (Personal close-up books) A brief biography of "Lady Lindy"—the first woman to fly the Atlantic as well as the first female to receive the Distinguished Flying Cross. [TL540.E3M35] 92 72-14157 ISBN 0-87191-226-0 4.95 (lib. bdg.)
1. Earhart, Amelia, 1898-1937—Juvenile literature. I. Thomas, Phero, illus. II. Title.

SEIBERT, Jerry. 926.2913
Amelia Earhart; First Lady of the Air. Illustrated by Marvin Friedman. Boston, Houghton Mifflin [1960] 191p. illus. 22cm. [TL540.E3S4] 59-8405
1. Earhart, Amelia, 1898-1937—Juvenile literature. I. Title.

PARLIN, John. 92 (J)
Amelia Earhart, pioneer in the sky. Illustrated by Anthony D'Adamo. Champaign, Ill., Garrard Pub. Co. [1962] 80 p. illus. 23 cm. (A Discovery book) [TL540.E3P3] 62-8030
1. Earhart, Amelia, 1898-1937—Juvenile literature.

WAYNE, Bennett. 920.72
Women who dared to be different. Edited, with commentary by Bennett Wayne. Champaign, Ill., Garrard Pub. Co. [1973] 168 p. illus. 22 cm. (A Torch book) Brief biographies of four women who pioneered in professions traditionally reserved for men. [CT3260.W39] 920 72-6802 ISBN 0-8116-4902-4 3.48
1. Oakley, Annie, 1860-1926—Juvenile literature. 2. Mitchell, Maria, 1818-1889—Juvenile literature. 3. Earhart, Amelia, 1898-1937—Juvenile literature. 4. Cochrane, Elizabeth, 1867-1922—Juvenile literature. 5. Women in the United States—Biography—Juvenile literature. 6. Women in the United States—Biography. I. Title. BIP

ZIERAU, Lillee D. 629.13'092'4 B
Amelia Earhart, leading lady of the air age, by Lillee D. Zierau. Charlotteville, N.Y., SamHar Press, 1972. 32 p. 22 cm. (Outstanding personalities, no. 19) Bibliography: p. 32. A biography of the aviation pioneer who was the first woman to fly alone across the Atlantic. [TL540.E3Z5] 92 73-190237 1.98
1. Earhart, Amelia, 1898-1937 Juvenile literature. I. Title.
Pap. 0.98

Earl, Ralph, 1754-1801.

GOODRICH, Laurence B. 759'.13
Ralph Earl, recorded for an era, by Laurence B. Goodrich. Albany, State University of New York [1967] vii, 96 p. illus., ports. (part col.) 27 cm. Bibliographical reference included in "Notes" (p. 95-96) [ND237.E18G6] 66-64728
1. Earl, Ralph, 1754-1801. I. Title.

Earle, Pliny, 1809-1892.

SANBORN, Franklin Benjamin, 1831-1917, ed. 616.8'9'00924 B
Memoirs of Pliny Earle, M.D. Edited with a general introd. by F. B. Sanborn. New York, Arno Press, 1973 [c1898] xvi, 409 p. port. 22 cm. (Mental illness and social policy: the American experience) Reprint of the ed. published by Damrell & Upham, Boston. Includes bibliographical references. [RC339.52.E37S36 1973] 73-2396 ISBN 0-405-05204-9 19.00
1. Earle, Pliny, 1809-1892. I. Title. II. Series.

Early, Jordan W., b. 1814.

EARLY, Sarah J. W. 287'.6'0924 B
Life and labors of Rev. Jordan W. Early, one of the pioneers of African Methodism in the West and South, by Sarah J. W. Early. Freeport, N.Y., Books for Libraries Press, 1971. 161 p. port. 23 cm. (The Black heritage library collection) "First published 1894." On spine: Rev. Jordan W. Early. [BX8473.E27E27] 72-164386 ISBN 0-8369-8845-0
1. Early, Jordan W., b. 1814. I. Title. II. Series.

Early, Jubal Anderson, 1816-1894.

BUSHONG, Millard Kessler. 923.573
Old Jube, a biography of General Jubal A. Early. Illus. and maps by Timothy T. Pohmer. Boyce, Va., Carr Pub. Co. [1955] 343p. illus. 24cm. Includes bibliography. [E467.1.E3B8] 55-3898
1. Early, Jubal Anderson, 1816-1894. I. Title.

Earp, Josephine Sarah Marcus.

EARP, Josephine Sarah Marcus. 978'.02'0924 B
I married Wyatt Earp : the recollections of Josephine Sarah Marcus Earp / collected and edited by Glenn G. Boyer. Tucson, Ariz. : University of Arizona Press, c1976. ix, 277 p. : ill. ; 23 cm. Includes index. Bibliography: p. 259-266. [F786.E175] 76-4673 ISBN 0-8165-0484-9 : 10.50 ISBN 0-8165-0583-7 pbk. : 4.95
1. Earp, Josephine Sarah Marcus. 2. Earp, Wyatt Berry Stapp, 1848-1929. 3. The West—Biography. 4. United States marshals—Biography. I. Boyer, Glenn G. II. Title. BIP

Earp, Wyatt Berry Stapp, 1848-1929.

BARTHOLOMEW, Ed Ellsworth 923.573
Wyatt Earp, 1848 to 1880, the untold story. Toyahvale, Tex., Frontier Bk. Co., 1963. 328p. 23cm. Bibl. 63-25978 6.00
1. Earp, Wyatt Berry Stapp, 1848-1929. I. Title.

BARTHOLOMEW, Ed Ellsworth 923.573
Wyatt Earp, 1879 to 1882, the man & the myth, by Ed. Bartholomew. [1st ed. Toyahvale, Tex., Frontier Book Co., 1964. 335 p. ports. 23 cm. Sequel to Wyatt Earp, 1848 to 1880, the untold story. Bibliography: p. 328-333. [F786.E1115] 64-6641
1. Earp, Wyatt Berry Stapp, 1848-1929.

BOYER, Glenn G. 917.8'03'20924
Suppressed murder of Wyatt Earp, by Glenn G. Boyer. San Antonio, Naylor Co. [1967] xix, 135 p. illus., ports. 22 cm. Includes bibliographical references. [F786.E1116] 67-12279
1. Earp, Wyatt Berry Stapp, 1848-1929. I. Title.

HALL-QUEST, Olga (Wilbourne) 923.573
Wyatt Earp: marshal of the old West. New York, Ariel Books [1956] 177p. 22cm. [F786.E112] 56-6514
1. Earp, Wyatt Berry Stapp, 1848-1929. I. Title.

HALL-QUEST, Olga (Wilbourne) 923.573
Wyatt Earp: marshal of the old West. New York, Ariel Books [1956] 177p. 22cm. [F786.E112] 56-6514
1. Earp, Wyatt Berry Stapp, 1848-1929. I. Title.

LAKE, Stuart N. 923.573
The life and times of Wyatt Earp. Illustrated by John McCormack. Boston, Houghton Mifflin, 1956. 271 p. illus. 22 cm. A shortened version of the author's Wyatt Earp, frontier marshal. [F786.E12 1956] 56-8271
1. Earp, Wyatt Berry Stapp, 1848-1929. 2. Frontier and pioneer life—Southwest, New. 3. Crime and criminals—Southwest, New.

WATERS, Frank, 1902- 978'.02'0924 B
The Earp brothers of Tombstone : the story of Mrs. Virgil Earp / by Frank Waters. Lincoln : University of Nebraska Press, [1976] "A Bison book." Reprint of the 1960 ed. published by C. N. Potter, New York. Bibliography: p. [F786.E123 1976] 75-38611 ISBN 0-8032-0873-1. ISBN 0-8032-5838-0 pbk.
1. Earp, Wyatt Berry Stapp, 1848-1929. 2. Earp, Alvira Packingham Sullivan, 1847-1947. 3. Tombstone, Ariz.—History. 4. Crime and criminals—Tombstone, Ariz. I. Title. BIP

East Carroll Parish, La.—History.

†PINKSTON, Georgia Payne Durham. 976.3'82'06 B
A place to remember : East Carroll Parish, La., 1832-1976 / by Georgia Payne Durham Pinkston. Baton Rouge : Claitor's Pub. Division, c1977. xiv, 359 p. : ill. ; 24 cm. Bibliography: p. 353-355. [F377.E2P56] 76-53253 12.50
1. East Carroll Parish, La.—History. 2. East Carroll Parish, La.—Biography. I. Title.
Publisher's address 3165 S. Acadia, P. O. Box 3333 Baton, Rouge, LA

East Lake Church, Atlanta.

BARNHART, Phil. 261.8'34'5196073
Don't call me preacher; for laymen and other ministers. Atlanta, Forum House [1972, i.e. 1973] 118 p. 23 cm. [BX8495.B326A33] 72-87066 ISBN 0-8028-1517-0 3.95
1. East Lake Church, Atlanta. 2. Church and race problems—Atlanta. I. Title.

East—Religion.

EPSTEIN, Perle S. 291.6'2
Oriental mystics & magicians / Perle Epstein. 1st ed. Garden City, N.Y. : Doubleday, [1975] 151, [2] p. : ill. ; 25 cm. Bibliography: p. [153] [BL1035.E65] 74-22407 ISBN 0-385-02338-3 : 5.95 ISBN 0-385-08343-2 lib.bdg. : 6.70
1. East—Religion. 2. Magic—East. 3. Religions—Biography. I. Title.

Easter—Juvenile literature.

SOCKMAN, Ralph Washington, 1889- 232.9
The Easter story for children. Illus. by Gordon Laite. Nashville, Abingdon [c.1957,1966] 1v. (unpaged) col. illus. 23cm. [BT302.S63] 66-10566 2.25
1. Easter—Juvenile literature. 2. Jesus Christ—Biog.—Juvenile literature. I. Laite, Gordon, illus. II. Title.

Eastgate, Nigel.

EASTGATE, Nigel. 769'.563'09931
Stamp out kiwis / Nigel Eastgate. Dunedin [N.Z.] : J. McIndoe, 1976. [24] p. : ill. ; 22 cm. [CT2888.E2A37] 77-354610 ISBN 0-908565-15-1
1. Eastgate, Nigel. 2. New Zealand—Biography. 3. Postage-stamps—New Zealand—Miscellanea. I. Title.

Eastlake, Elizabeth Rigby, Lady, 1809-1893—Biography.

EASTLAKE, Elizabeth Rigby, Lady, 1809-1893. 828'.8'09 B
Journals and correspondence of Lady Eastlake / edited by her nephew, Charles Eastlake Smith ; with facsims. of her drawings and a port. New York : AMS Press, [1975] 2 v. : ill. ; 19 cm. (Women of letters) Reprint of the 1895 ed. published by J. Murray, London. Includes index. [PR4639.E25A3 1975] 79-37691 ISBN 0-404-56746-0 : 38.50 (set)
1. Eastlake, Elizabeth Rigby, Lady, 1809-1893—Biography. BIP

LOCHHEAD, Marion 928.2
Elizabeth Rigby, Lady Eastlake. [Dist. Hollywood-by-the-Sea, Fla., Transtlantic, 1962, c.1961] 162p. illus. Bibl. 61-4120 4.50
1. Eastlake, Elizabeth (Rigby) Lady, 1809-1893. I. Title.

Eastman, Charles Alexander, 1858-1939.

COPELAND, Marion W. 970'.004'97
Charles Alexander Eastman (Ohiyesa) / by Marion W. Copeland. Boise, Idaho : Boise State University, c1978. 43 p. ; 21 cm. (Boise State University Western writers series ; no. 33) Bibliography: p. 41-43. [E99.S22E182] 78-52562 ISBN 0-88430-057-9 pbk. : 2.00
1. Eastman, Charles Alexander, 1858-1939. 2. Dakota Indians—Historiography. 3. Santee Indians—Biography. I. Title. II. Series: Boise State University. Boise State University Western writers series ; no. 33. BIP

†EASTMAN, Charles Alexander, 1858-1939. 970'.004'97 B
From the deep woods to civilization : chapters in the autobiography of an Indian / by Charles A. Eastman (Ohiyesa) ; introd. by Raymond Wilson. Lincoln :

University of Nebraska Press, 1977, c1916. xxii, 206 p., [13] leaves of plates : ill. ; 21 cm. Reprint of the 1936 ed. published by Little, Brown, Boston. Includes index. [E99.S22E183 1977] 77-7226 ISBN 0-8032-0936-3 : 11.95 ISBN 0-8032-5873-9 pbk. : 3.75
1. Eastman, Charles Alexander, 1858-1939. 2. Santee Indians—Biography. I. Title. BIP

Eastman, Charles Alexander, 1858-1939—Juvenile literature.

EASTMAN, Charles Alexander, 1858-1939. 970'.004'97 B
Indian boyhood / by Ohiyesa (Charles A. Eastman) ; illustrated by E. L. Blumenschein. Glorieta, N.M. : Rio Grande Press, c1976. p. cm. Reprint of the 1929 ed. published by Little, Brown, Boston; with new introd. A full-blooded Santee Sioux Indian describes his childhood experiences and training as a warrior in the late nineteenth century until he was taken to live in the white man's world at age fifteen. [E99.S22E184 1976] 92 76-46274 ISBN 0-87380-114-8 lib.bdg. : 10.00
1. Eastman, Charles Alexander, 1858-1939—Juvenile literature. 2. Santee Indians—Biography—Juvenile literature. 3. Indians of North America—Children—Juvenile literature. I. Blumenschein, Ernest Leonard, 1874-1960. II. Title.

LEE, Betsy, 1949- 970'.004'97 B
Charles Eastman / by Betsy Lee. Minneapolis : Dillon Press, c1979. p. cm. (The Story of an American Indian ; 27) A biography of Dr. Charles Eastman, doctor, writer, lecturer, and worker for Indian rights, pride, and a maintenance of and appreciation for their culture. [E99.S22E185] 92 79-9193 ISBN 0-87518-175-9 lib. bdg. : 5.95
1. Eastman, Charles Alexander, 1858-1939—Juvenile literature. 2. Santee Indians—Biography—Juvenile literature. 3. Physicians—United States Biography Juvenile literature. 4. Dakota Indians—Juvenile literature. I. Title. BIP

Eastman, Elaine Goodale, 1863-1953.

EASTMAN, Elaine Goodale, 1863-1953. 970'.004'97
Sister to the Sioux : the memoirs of Elaine Goodale Eastman, 1885-91 / edited by Kay Graber. Lincoln : University of Nebraska Press, 1978. xiii, 175 p., [5] leaves of plates : ill. ; 25 cm. (The Pioneer heritage series ; v. 7) Includes bibliographical references. [E99.S22E23 1978] 77-25018 ISBN 0-8032-0971-1 : 10.95
1. Eastman, Elaine Goodale, 1863-1953. 2. Santee Indians. 3. Dakota Indians. 4. Teachers—South Dakota—Biography. I. Graber, Kay, 1938- II. Title. III. Series. BIP

Eastman family.

EASTMAN, Charles John, 1885- 929'.2'0973
That man Eastman. [Hollywood, Calif., 1952-54] 2v. illus. 21cm. [CS71.E137 1952] 54-28246
1. Eastman family. I. Title.

Eastman, George, 1854-1932.

ACKERMAN, Carl William, 1890- 338.7'61'77 B
George Eastman, by Carl W. Ackerman. With an introd. by Edwin R. A. Seligman. Clifton [N.J.] A. M. Kelley, 1973 [c1930] xviii, 522 p. illus. 22 cm. (Library of early American business and industry, 54) [TR140.E3A3 1973] 70-128074 ISBN 0-678-03556-3
1. Eastman, George, 1854-1932. I. Title. BIP

Eastman, Joseph Bartlett, 1882-1944.

FUESS, Claude Moore, 1885- 923.873
Joseph B. Eastman, Servant of the people. New York, Columbia University Press, 1952. 363 p. illus. 24 cm. [HE2754.E3F8] 52-8268
1. Eastman, Joseph Bartiett, 1882-1944. I. Title.

FUESS, Claude Moore, 1885-1963. 353.008'7 B
Joseph B. Eastman, servant of the people. Westport, Conn., Greenwood Press [1974, c1952] xv, 363 p. illus. 23 cm. Reprint of the ed. published by Columbia University Press, New York. [HE2754.E3F8 1974] 74-12881 ISBN 0-8371-7769-3 18.50
1. Eastman, Joseph Bartlett, 1882-1944. BIP

Eastman, Max,

EASTMAN, Max, 1883-1969. 928.1
Love and revolution; my journey through an epoch. New York, Random House [1964] xiii, 665 p. illus., ports. 25 cm. "Continuation of a previous memoir...called Enjoyment of living." [PS3509.A752Z52] 62-12729
I. Title.

Easton, Tom.

KERNAN, Michael, 1927- 942.8'8'0820924 B
The violet dots / by Michael Kernan. 1st ed. New York : G. Braziller, 1978. ix, 161 p. ; 22 cm. [CT788.E23K47] 77-94496 ISBN 0-8076-0887-4 : 7.95
1. Easton, Tom. 2. Northumberland, Eng.—Biography. I. Title.

Eastwood, Clint, 1930-

AGAN, Patrick. 791.43'028'0924 B
Clint Eastwood : the man behind the myth / Patrick Agan. New York : Pyramid Books, 1975. 188 p., [4] leaves of plates : ill. ; 18 cm. Filmography: p. [169]-188. [PN2287.E37A7] 75-29547 ISBN 0-515-03625-0 pbk. : 1.25
1. Eastwood, Clint, 1930-

DOUGLAS, Peter, 1936- 791.43'028'0924 B
Clint Eastwood: movin' on. Chicago, H. Regnery Co. [1974] viii, 147 p. illus. 22 cm. "Filmography": p. 127-142. [PN2287.E37D6] 73-20675 ISBN 0-8092-9014-6 7.95
1. Eastwood, Clint, 1930-

DOWNING, David. 791.43'028'0924 B
Clint Eastwood, all-American anti-hero : a critical appraisal of the world's top box office star and his films / by David Downing and Gary Herman. London ; New York : Omnibus Press ; New York : distributed by Quick Fox, 1977. 144 p. : ill. ; 26 cm. Filmography: p [139]-[143] [PN2287.E37D64] 79-308187 ISBN 0-86001-412-6 : 4.95
1. Eastwood, Clint, 1930- I. Herman, Gary, joint author. II. Title.

*KAMINSKY, Stuart M. 791.43028092
Clint Eastwood by Stuart M. Kaminsky. [New York] New American Library [1974] vii, 150 p. 18 cm. (A Signet book) Filmography p. 136-150. [PN2287] 1.50 (pbk.)
1. Eastwood, Clint I. Title.

KAMINSKY, Stuart M. 791.43'028'0924 B
Clint Eastwood / Stuart M. Kaminsky. New York : New American Library, 1974. vii, 150 p., [8] leaves of plates : ill. ; 18 cm. (Signet film series) (A Signet book) Filmography: p. 136-150. [PN2287.E37K35] 74-193240 pbk. : 1.50
1. Eastwood, Clint, 1930-

Eatherly, Claude.

HUIE, William Bradford, 1910- 923.573
The Hiroshima pilot. New York, Putnam [1964] 318 p. 22 cm. [CT275.E237H8] 63-7742
1. Eatherly, Claude. I. Title.

Eaton, Cyrus Stephen, 1883-

GLEISSER, Marcus 332.60924
The world of Cyrus Eaton. New York, A. S. Barnes [1965] 337p. illus., ports. 22cm. [CT275.E242G55] 65-17212 6.00
1. Eaton, Cyrus Stephen, 1883- I. Title.

Eaton, Evelyn Sybil Mary, 1902- — Religion and ethics.

EATON, Evelyn Sybil Mary, 1902- 813'.5'2 B
I send a voice / by Evelyn Eaton. 1st Quest Book ed. Wheaton, Ill. : Theosophical Pub. House, 1978. 178 p. : ill. ; 21 cm. (Quest books) (A Quest book original) [PS3509.A84Z465 1978] 78-7273 10.95 ISBN 0-8356-0511-6 pbk. : 4.95
1. Eaton, Evelyn Sybil Mary, 1902- — Religion and ethics. 2. Authors, American—20th century—Biography. 3. Indians of North America—California—Religion and mythology. I. Title. BIP

Eaton, Frank, 1860-

EATON, Frank, 1860- 978'.02'0924 B
Pistol Pete, veteran of the Old West / by Frank Eaton. Perkins, Okla. : Evans Publications, 1979, c1952. x, 278 p., [4] leaves of plates : ill. ; 22 cm. "Eva Gillhouse wrote this book ... just the way I told it to her." Reprint of the 1st ed. published by Little, Brown, Boston. [F700.E22A36 1979] 79-109054 14.95
1. Eaton, Frank, 1860- 2. Frontier and pioneer life—Oklahoma. 3. Oklahoma—History. 4. Frontier and pioneer life—Texas. 5. Texas—History—1846-1950. 6. Pioneers—Oklahoma—Biography. 7. Scouts and scouting—Oklahoma—Biography. I. Gillhouse, Eva Olenna. II. Title. BIP

Eaton, Norman, 1902-1966.

HARROP-ALLIN, Clinton, 1936- 720'.92'4
Norman Eaton, architect : a study of the work of the South African architect Norman Eaton 1902-1966 / Clinton Harrop-Allin ; foreword by Alexis Preller. Cape Town : C. Struik, 1975. 128 p. : ill. ; 28 cm. Includes index. Bibliography: p. 125-126. [NA1596.E17H37] 76-350679 ISBN 0-86977-053-5 : 23.00
1. Eaton, Norman, 1902-1966. I. Title.
Distributed by Verry

Eaton, William H., 1764-1811.

GERSON, Noel Bertram, 1914- 973.4'0924 B
Barbary General; the life of William H. Eaton [by] Samuel Edwards. Englewood Cliffs, N.J., Prentice-Hall [1968] ix, 277 p. 24 cm. [E340.E18G4] 68-11551
1. Eaton, William H., 1764-1811. I. Title.

MINNIGERODE, Meade, 1887-1967. 920.073
Lives and times; four informal American biographies. Freeport, N.Y., Books for Libraries Press [1970] viii, 215 p. illus., ports. 23 cm. (Essay index reprint series) Reprint of the 1925 ed. Contents.Contents.—Stephen Jumel, merchant.—William Eaton, hero.—Theodosia Burr, prodigy.—Edmond Charles Genet, citizen. [E302.5.M66 1970] 76-121490
1. Jumel, Stephen, 1755-1832. 2. Eaton, William, 1764-1811. 3. Alston, Theodosia (Burr) 1783-1813. 4. Genet, Edmond Charles, 1763-1834. I. Title.

Eban, Abba Solomon, 1915-

ST. John, Robert, 1902- 956.94'05'0924 B
Eban. [1st ed.] Garden City, N.Y., Doubleday, 1972. 542 p. illus. 25 cm. Bibliography: p. [527] [DS126.6.E2S24] 72-83151 ISBN 0-385-08944-9 10.00
1. Eban, Abba Solomon, 1915- 2. Israel—Foreign relations. BIP

Eberhardt, Isabelle, 1877-1904.

MACKWORTH, Cecily. 965'.03'0924 B
The destiny of Isabelle Eberhardt / Cecily Mackworth. New York : Ecco Press, [1975] p. cm. Includes index. [DT294.7.E2M3 1975] 75-12764 ISBN 0-912946-22-9 : 6.95
1. Eberhardt, Isabelle, 1877-1904. I. Title. BIP

Eberhardt, Johann Ludwig, 1758-1839.

ALBRIGHT, Frank P. 681'.113'0924 B
Johann Ludwig Eberhardt and his Salem clocks / by Frank P. Albright ; photos. by Bradford L. Rauschenberg. Chapel Hill : Published for Old Salem, inc., Winston-Salem N.C. by University of North Carolina Press, c1978. x, 160 p. : ill. ; 23 cm. (The Old Salem series) Includes index. Bibliography: p. 155-156. [TS544.8.E23A4] 77 18955 ISBN 0-8078-1324-9 : 12.95
1. Eberhardt, Johann Ludwig, 1758-1839. 2. Clock and watch makers—North Carolina—Winston-Salem—Biography. 3. Clocks and watches—North Carolina—Winston-Salem. 4. Winston-Salem, N.C.—Biography. I. Old Salem, inc., Winston-Salem, N.C. II. Title. III. Series. BIP

Eboue, Adolphe Felix Sylvestre, 1884-1944.

WEINSTEIN, Brian. 967'.4103'0924 B
Eboue. New York, Oxford University Press, 1972. xiii, 350 p. illus. 21 cm. Bibliography: p 321-337. [JV1809.E3W44] 70-173329 8.95
1. Eboue, Adolphe Felix Sylvestre, 1884-1944.

Eby, James Brian, 1896-

EBY, James Brian, 1896- 550'.92'4 B
My two roads / J. Brian Eby. 2d ed. Houston : Pacesetter Press, c1976. xi, 298 p. : ill. ; 24 cm. Includes index Bibliography: p. 285-288. [QE22.E28A33 1976] 75-30380 ISBN 0-88415-570-6 : 7.95
1. Eby, James Brian, 1896- I. Title. BIP

Eccentrics and eccentricities.

THE British eccentric / [edited by] Harriet Bridgeman and Elizabeth Drury. 1st American ed. New York : C. N. Potter : distributed by Crown Publishers, 1976, c1975. 159 p. : ill. ; 28 cm. [CT9990.B73 1976] 75-41406 ISBN 0-517-52499-6 : 12.50 920'.041
1. Eccentrics and eccentricities. 2. Great Britain—Biography. I. Bridgeman, Harriet. II. Drury, Elizabeth. BIP

SITWELL, Dame Edith, 1887- 920.042
English eccentrics. New York, Vanguard Press [1957] 376 p. 22 cm. [CT775.S55 1957] 57-14192
1. Eccentrics and eccentricities. I. Title. BIP

Eccles, David, 1849 or 50-1912.

ARRINGTON, Leonard J. 338'.092'4 B
David Eccles : pioneer western industrialist / Leonard J. Arrington. Logan : Utah State University, 1975. viii, 294 p. : ill. ; 24 cm. Includes index. Bibliography: p. 275-280. [HC102.5.E2A77] 75-2093 ISBN 0-87421-078-X : 10.00
1. Eccles, David, 1849 or 50-1912.

Eccles, Marriner Stoddard, 1890-

ECCLES, Marriner Stoddard, 1890- 923.373
Beckoning frontiers; public and personal recollections. Edited by Sidney Hyman. [1st ed.] New York, Knopf, 1951. xii, 499. viii p. ports. 22 cm. [HG2463.E35A3] 51-11280
I. Title.

HYMAN, Sidney. 332.1'1'0924 B
Marriner S. Eccles, private entrepreneur and public servant / Sidney Hyman ; with a foreword by G. L. Bach. Stanford, Calif. : Graduate School of Business, Stanford University, 1976. xviii, 456 p., [7] leaves of plates : ill. ; 24 cm. Includes bibliographical references and index. [HG2463.E35H95] 76-46152 15.00
1. Eccles, Marriner Stoddard, 1890- 2. Bankers—United States—Biography. I. Title.

Eccleston, Daniel, 1745-1816.

TYSON, Edith. 914.27'2 B
Daniel Eccleston. Lancaster, Lancaster City Museum and Art Gallery, [1971] [1], 13 p. 30 cm. "A Lancaster Museum monograph." [CT788.E25T97] 73-160360 ISBN 0-9500360-2-1 £0.04
1. Eccleston, Daniel, 1745-1816.

Echols, Timothy B

ECHOLS, Timothy B 922.773
Pioneering in religious education; four decades in the Methodist Church. [1st ed.] New York, Exposition Press [1964] 159 p. ports. 21 cm. Autobiographical. [BV1470.3.E3A3] 64-2285
I. Title.

Eckhart, Meister, d. 1327.

CLARK, James Midgley, 1888-1961. 149'.3
The great German mystics: Eckhart, Tauler, and Suso. Folcroft, Pa., Folcroft Press [1969] vii, 121 p. 25 cm. Reprint of the 1949 ed., which was issued as no. 5 of Modern language studies. Bibliography: p. 110-117. [BV5077.G3C58 1969] 72-193479
1. Eckhart, Meister, d. 1327. 2. Tauler, Johannes, 1300 (ca.)-1361. 3. Suso, Heinrich, 1300?-1366. 4. Mysticism—Germany. I. Title.

Ecologists, American.

COX, Donald William. 301.31'092'2 B
Pioneers of ecology, by Donald W. Cox. Portrait illus. by Ted Lewin. [Maplewood, N.J.] Hammond [1971] 93 p. illus. (part col.) 27 cm. Bibliography: p. 91. Brief biographies of fifteen early pioneers in the field of ecology. [QH26.C68] 920 77-158132 ISBN 0-8437-3832-4 4.39
1. Ecologists, American. 2. Ecology—United States—History. I. Lewin, Ted, illus. II. Title.

Ecology—United States—History—Juvenile literature.

HIRSCH, S. Carl. 574.5'0922 B
Guardians of tomorrow; pioneers in ecology [by] S. Carl Hirsch. Illustrated by William Steinel. [1st ed.] New York, Viking Press [1971] 192 p. illus. (part col.), ports. 24 cm. Bibliography: p. [181]-182. Brief biographies of eight American pioneers in conservation and ecology: Henry David Thoreau, George Perkins Marsh, Frederick Law Olmsted, John Muir, Gifford Pinchot, George Norris, Aldo Leopold, and Rachel Carson. [QH541.14.H57 1971] 920 76-136818 ISBN 0-670-35646-8 4.95
1. Ecology—United States—History—Juvenile literature. 2. Conservation of natural resources—United States—History—Juvenile literature. 3. Naturalists—Juvenile literature. I. Title. BIP

Economic assistance.

JORDAN, Robert S., 1929- 309.2'23
Multinational cooperation; economic, social and scientific development. Edited by Robert S. Jordan. New York, Oxford University Press, 1972. xiii, 392 p. illus. 21 cm. Bibliography: p. 367-382. [HC60.J59] 71-161889
1. Economic assistance. 2. International cooperation. I. Title.

Economic development—Biog.

CONWAY Research, inc., Atlanta. 338'.0922
Leaders in development. Atlanta, Conway Research 1968 v. ports. 23 cm. "The international guide to professional development executives." [HD82.L327] 68-6154
1. Economic development—Biog. 2. Economic development—Direct. I. Title.

Economics.

BREIT, William. 330'.0922
The academic scribblers; American economists in collision [by] William Breit [and] Roger L. Ransom. New York, Holt, Rinehart and Winston [1971] x, 275 p. illus. 24 cm. Includes bibliographical references. [HB87.B72] 70-122546 ISBN 0-03-085260-9
1. Economics. 2. Economists, American. I. Ransom, Roger L., 1938- joint author. II. Title.

TURGOT, Anne Robert Jacques, baron de l'Aulne, 1727-1781. 330'.0924 B
The life and writings of Turgot, comptroller general of France, 1774-6. Edited for English readers by W. Walker Stephens. New York, Burt Franklin [1971] xiv, 331 p. port. 23 cm. (Burt Franklin research and source works series, 760. Selected essays in history, economics, and social science, 274) Reprint of the 1895 ed. Includes bibliographical references. [HB153.T76 1971] 74-161008 ISBN 0-8337-4451-8
1. Economics. 2. Social sciences. 3. Finance, Public—France—To 1789. I. Stephens, William Walker, ed.

Economics—History.

MITCHELL, Broadus, 1892- 330.10922
Great economists in their times. Totowa, N. J., Littlefield , Adams, 1966. xix, 236 p. 21 cm. (Littlefield quality paperbacks, 56) Includes bibliographies. [HB75.M543] 66-6541
1. Economics—History. I. Title. BIP

Economists.

HARRIS, Seymour Edwin, 1897- 330'.0924
Schumpeter, social scientist. Freeport, N.Y., Books for Libraries Press [1969, c1951] x, 142 p. ports. 29 cm. (Essay index reprint series) Contents.Contents.—Introductory remarks, by S. E. Harris.—Some personal reminiscences on a great man, by R. Frisch.—Memorial: Joseph Alois Schumpeter, 1883-1950, by A. Smithies.—Joseph Alois Schumpeter, 1883-1950, by G. Haberler.—Schumpeter as a teacher and economic theorist, by P. A. Samuelson.—Schumpeter's early German work, 1906-1917, by E. Schneider.—Schumpeter and quantitative research in economics, by J. Tinbergen.—The monetary aspects of the Schumpeterian system, by A. W. Marget.—Schumpeter's theory of interest, by G. Haberler.—Schumpeter's contribution to business cycle theory, by A. H. Hansen.—The impact of recent monopoly theory on the Schumpeterian system, by E. H. Chamberlin.—Schumpeter on monopoly and the large firm, by E. S. Mason.—Schumpeter's economic methodology, by F. Machlup.—Reflections on Schumpeter's writings, by WOSchumpeter, social scientist. Freeport, N.Y., Books for Libraries Press [1969, c1951] x, 142 p. ports. 29 cm. (Essay index reprint series) Contents.Contents.—Introductory remarks, by S. E. Harris.—Some personal reminiscences on a great man, by R. Frisch.—Memorial: Joseph Alois Schumpeter, 1883-1950, by A. Smithies.—Joseph Alois Schumpeter, 1883-1950, by G. Haberler.—Schumpeter
I. Schumpeter, Joseph Alois, 1883-1950. II. Title.

HEILBRONER, Robert L. 330.1'0922
The worldly philosophers; the lives, times, and ideas of the great economic thinkers [by] Robert L. Heilbroner. [3d ed., newly rev.] New York, Simon and Schuster [1967] 320 p. 22 cm. "Guide to further reading": p. 307-312. [HB76.H4 1967] 67-25391
1. Economists. 2. Economics—History. I. Title.

HEILBRONER, Robert L. 330.1'092'2
The worldly philosophers; the lives, times, and ideas of the great economic thinkers [by] Robert L. Heilbroner. 4th ed., completely rev. for the 1970's. New York, Simon and Schuster [1972] 347 p. 22 cm. Bibliography: p. 327-333. [HB76.H4 1972] 76-190507 ISBN 0-671-21325-3 7.95
1. Economists. 2. Economics—History. I. Title.

Economists, American.

NORTON, Hugh Stanton, 1921- 330'.0973
The world of the economist [by] Hugh S. Norton. [1st ed.] Columbia, University of South Carolina Press [1973] xii, 169 p. front. 22 cm. Bibliography: p. 149-160. [HB119.A3N6] 73-7819 ISBN 0-87249-273-7 5.95
1. Economists, American. I. Title. BIP

Economists—Biography.

HEILBRONER, Robert L. 330.1'092'2
The worldly philosophers : the lives, times, and ideas of the great economic thinkers / Robert L. Heilbroner. 5th ed., completely rev. for the 1980's. New York : Simon and Schuster, c1979. p. cm. (A Touchstone book) Includes index. Bibliography: p. [HB76.H4 1979] 79-10331 ISBN 0-671-21325-3 : 12.95
1. Economists—Biography. 2. Economics—History. I. Title.

MAI, Ludwig H. 330'.092'? B
Men and ideas in economics : a dictionary of world economists, past and present / by Ludwig H. Mai. Totowa, N.J. : Littlefield, Adams, 1975. xii, 270 p. ; 22 cm. (A Littlefield, Adams quality paperback ; no. 284) Bibliography: p. 269-270. [HB76.M3] 75-20243 ISBN 0-8226-0284-9 pbk. : 3.95
1. Economists—Biography. I. Title. BIP

Economists—Correspondence, personal reminiscences, etc.

JEVONS, William Stanley, 1835-1882. 330'.08 S
Biography and personal journal. Edited by R. D. Collison Black and Rosamond Konekamp. Clifton [N.J.] A. M. Kelley, 1972. xiv, 243 p. illus. 25 cm. (Papers and correspondence of William Stanley Jevons, v. 1) (Series: Jevons, William Stanley, 1835-1882. Papers and correspondence of William Stanley Jevons, v. 1.) Includes bibliographical references. [HB103.J5A4 1972 vol. 1] 330'.092'4 B 72-171256 ISBN 0-678-07011-3 25.00
1. Economists—Correspondence, personal reminiscences, etc. I. Title. II. Series.

Economists—Correspondence, reminiscences, etc.

OVERSTONE, Samuel Jones Loyd, 1st Baron, 1796-1883. 330'.0924 B
The correspondence of Lord Overstone. Edited by D. P. O'Brien. Cambridge [Eng.] University Press, 1971- v. illus. 24 cm. Includes bibliographical references. [HB103.O95A4 1971] 77-134615 ISBN 0-521-08097-5 (v. 1)
1. Economists—Correspondence, reminiscences, etc. I. O'Brien, Denis Patrick, ed.

Economists—United States—Biography.

SILK, Leonard. 330.'.92'2
The economists / by Leonard Silk. New York : Avon Books, 1978,c1976. 276p. ; 18 cm. (A Discus Book) Includes bibliographical references and index. [HB119.A3S54] pbk. : 250
1. Economists — United States — biography. I. Title.
L.C. card no. for 1976 Basic Books ed.: 76-27741. BIP

SILK, Leonard Solomon, 1918- 330'.092'2 B
The economists / Leonard Silk. New York : Basic Books, c1976. xii, 294 p. ; 22 cm. Includes bibliographical references and index. [HB119.A3S54] 76-27741 ISBN 0-465-01810-6 : 10.95
1. Economists—United States—Biography. I. Title.

Economou, Elly.

ECONOMOU, Elly. 286'.7'0924
Beloved enemy. Mountain View, Calif., Pacific Pr. Pub. Assn. [c.1968] 136p. 22cm. (Destiny bk.) [BX61913.E25A3] 68-25796 pap., price unreported
I. Title.

Eddington, Arthur Stanley, 1882-1944.

THE life of Arthur Stanley v. 12
Eddington. London, New York, T. Nelson [1956] xi, 207p. plates, ports. 'Published works of Arthur Stanley Eddington':p. 193-198. 'Genealogical table of the Eddington family':. 200-201.
1. Eddington, Arthur Stanley, 1882-1944. I. Douglas, Allie Vibert, 1894-

Eddy, George Sherwood,

EDDY, George Sherwood, 1871- 922
Eighty adventurous years; an autobiography. [1st ed.] New York, Harper [1955] 255 p. 22 cm. [BV1085.E3A28] 54-12328
I. Title.

Eddy, Mary Baker, 1821-1910.

BEASLEY, Norman 922.8573
Mary Baker Eddy. [dist. Meredith, c.1963] vi, 371p. col. port. 22cm. Bibl. 62-15467 5.95
1. Eddy, Mary (Baker) 1821-1910. I. Title.

BEASLEY, Norman. 922.8573
Mary Baker Eddy. [1st ed.] New York, Duell, Sloan and Pearce [1963] vi. 371 p. col. port. 22 cm. Bibliographical footnotes. [BX6995.B4] 62-15467
1. Eddy, Mary (Baker) 1821-1910. I. Title.

CHRISTIAN Science Publishing Society. 922.8573
We knew Mary Baker Eddy. 2d ser. Boston, Christian Science Pub. Society [1950] 75 p. col. port. 21 cm. Contents.Contents. -- The star in my crown of rejoicing: the class of 1885, by C.L. Blackman. -- Our leader as teacher and friend, by F.W. Gale -- The call to Concord, by G.W. Adams. -- An intimate picture of our leader's final class, by S.H. Mima. -- An interview with Mary Baker Eddy, and other memories, by M. Stewart. -- "With sandals on and staff in hand." by C.K. McKee. [BX6905.W42] 50-6966
1. Eddy, Mary (Baker) 1821-1910. I. Title.

DAKIN, Edwin Franden, 1898- 289.5'0924 B
Mrs. Eddy. Gloucester, Mass., P. Smith, 1968 [c1929] 553 p. 21 cm. On spine: Mrs. Eddy: the biography of a virginal mind. Bibliography: p. [525]-537. [BX6995.D3 1968] 72-107
1. Eddy, Mary (Baker) 1821-1910. I. Title.

DAKIN, Edwin Franden, 1898- 289.5'0924 B
Mrs. Eddy; the biography of a virginal mind. New York, Scribner [1970] xx, 563 p. 21 cm. (The Scribner library. Emblem editions) First published in 1930. [BX6995.D3 1970] 79-99571 2.95
1. Eddy, Mary (Baker) 1821-1910. I. Title. BIP

D'HUMY, Fernand Emile, 1873- 922.8573
Mary Baker Eddy in a new light. New York, Library Publishers [1952] 181p. illus. 24cm. [BX6995.D43] 52-377
1. Eddy, Mary (Baker) 1821-1910. I. Title.

D'HUMY, Fernard Emile 922.8573
Mary Baker Eddy in a new light. New York, Library Publishers [1952] 181 p. illus. 24 cm. [BX6995.D43] 52-377
1. Eddy, Mary (Baker) 1821-1910. I. Title.

KING, Marian. 289.5'0924 B
Mary Baker Eddy: child of promise. Illustrated by David Hodges. Englewood Cliffs, N.J., Prentice-Hall [1968] vi, 184 p. illus. 22 cm. [BX6995.K5] 68-11942
1. Eddy, Mary (Baker) 1821-1910.

MILMINE, Georgine. 289.5'0924 B
The life of Mary Baker G. Eddy and the history of Christian Science. Grand Rapids, Baker Book House [1971, c1909]

xxxiv, 495 p. illus., facsims., ports. 22 cm. "Willa Sibert Cather, editor."—dust jacket. "It will probably never be possible to determine exactly which passages are primarily the work of Miss Cather, those which remain substantially the work of Mrs. Milmine, or even those portions which are the work of other editiorial writers in the New York Offices of McClure's." [BX6995.M5 1971] 76-155860 5.95
1. Eddy, Mary (Baker), 1821-1910. 2. Christian Science. I. Cather, Willa Sibert, 1873-1947, ed. II. Title. BIP

PEEL, Robert, 1909- 289.5'0924 B
Mary Baker Eddy; the years of discovery. New York, Holt, Rinehart and Winston [1972, c1966] xi, 370 p. 21 cm. Includes bibliographical references. [BX6995.P4 1972] 72-200871 ISBN 0-03-086648-0 3.45
1. Eddy, Mary (Baker) 1821-1910.

PEEL, Robert, 1909- 289.50924 B
Mary Baker Eddy; the years of discovery. [1st ed.] New York, Holt, Rinehart and Winston [1966] xi, 372 p. port. 25 cm. Bibliographical references included in "Notes" (p. 309-359) [BX6995.P4] 66-14855
1. Eddy, Mary (Baker) 1821-1910. BIP

PEEL, Robert, 1909- 289.5'0924 B
Mary Baker Eddy; the years of trial. [1st ed.] New York, Holt, Rinehart and Winston [1971] vii, 391 p. port. 25 cm. Includes bibliographical references. [BX6995.P42] 73-31119 ISBN 0-03-086700-2 8.95
1. Eddy, Mary (Baker) 1821-1910. BIP

PEEL, Robert, 1909- 289.5'092'4
Mary Baker Eddy : the years of discovery / Robert Peel. Boston : Christian Science Pub. Society, [1973] c1966. xi, 372 p., [1] leaf of plates : port. ; 25 cm. Originally published by Holt, Rinehart and Winston, New York. Includes bibliographical references and index. [BX6995.P4 1973] 75-322478
1. Eddy, Mary Baker, 1821-1910.

PEEL, Robert, 1909- 289.5'092'4 B
Mary Baker Eddy : the years of authority / Robert Peel. 1st ed. New York : Holt, Rinehart and Winston, c1977. p. cm. Third vol. in the author's 3-vol. biography, the 1st and 2d of which are Mary Baker Eddy: the years of discovery, and Mary Baker Eddy: the years of trial. Includes bibliographical references and index. [BX6995.P38] 77-6275 ISBN 0-03-021081-X : 14.95
1. Eddy, Mary Baker, 1821-1910. 2. Christian Scientists—United States—Biography. I. Title. BIP

POWELL, Lyman Pierson, 1866-1946. 922.8573
Mary Baker Eddy a life size portrait. Boston, Christian Science Pub. Society [1950] 350 p. illus., ports. 22 cm. Bibliographical references included in "Notes" (p. 273-318) [BX6995.P75 1950] 51-544
1. Christian Science. I. Eddy, Mary (Baker) 1821 1910. II. Title.

SMAUS, Jewel (Spangler) 289.5'0924 B
Mary Baker Eddy: the golden days. Illustrated with photos. by Gordon Noble Converse. Boston, Christian Science Pub. Society, 1966. 193 p. illus., port. 25 cm. Bibliography: p. 186-188. [BX6995.S52] 66-30537
1. Eddy, Mary (Baker) 1821-1910. I. Title.

WE knew Mary Baker 289.5'0924
Eddy. [- ser.] Boston, Christian Science Pub. Society [1967- v. col. port. 21 cm. [BX6995.W42] 68-128
1. Eddy, Mary (Baker) 1821-1910. I. Christian Science Publishing Society.

WILBUR, Sibyl, 1871-1946. 289.5'092'4 B
The life of Mary Baker Eddy / Sibyl Wilbur. Boston : Christian Science Pub. Society, 1976. xvi, 406 p., [17] leaves of plates : ill. ; 23 cm. Includes bibliographical references and index. [BX6995.W5 1976] 76-368305 ISBN 0-87510-006-6 : 7.50
1. Eddy, Mary Baker, 1821-1910. I. Title. BIP

ZWEIG, Stefan, 1881-1942. 615.851
Mental healers: Franz Anton Mesmer, Mary Baker Eddy, Sigmund Freud. [Tr. from German by Eden and Cedar Paul] New York, Unger [1962, c.1932] 363p. 22cm. 62-14082 5.50
1. Mesmer, Franz Anton, 1734—1815. 2. Eddy, Mary (Baker) 1821-1910. 3. Freud, Sigmund, 1856-1939. 4. Mental healing. I. Title. BIP

Eddy, Mary Baker, 1821-1910—Addresses, essays, lectures.

WE knew Mary Baker 289.5'092'4
Eddy / [steel engraving of Mary Baker Eddy by Jules Maurice Gaspard ; wood engravings by Charles Joslin]. Boston : Christian Science Pub. Society, c1979. x, 219 p. : ill. ; 24 cm. Includes index. [BX6995.W4 1979] 79-51759 ISBN 0-87510-115-1 : 10.50
1. Eddy, Mary Baker, 1821-1910—Addresses, essays, lectures. 2. Church of Christ, Scientist—Biography—Addresses, essays, lectures. I. Christian Science Publishing Society.

Eddy, Mary (Baker) 1821-1910. Works—Indexes.

CHRISTIAN Science sentinel. 920.02
Mary Baker Eddy mentioned them. Boston, Christian Science Pub. Society [1961] 239p. 21cm. 'Most of the biographical sketches in this book have appeared in substantially the same form in the Christian Science sentinel under the heading, 'Mrs. Eddy mentioned them." [BX6941.Z9C5] 61-18918
1. Eddy, Mary (Baker) 1821-1910. Works—Indexes. 2. Biography. I. Title.

Eddy, Thomas, 1758-1827.

KNAPP, Samuel Lorenzo, 1783-1838. 361'.92'4 B
The life of Thomas Eddy / by Samuel L. Knapp. New York : Arno Press, 1976, c1834. 394 p. ; 23 cm. (Social problems and social policy—the American experience) Reprint of the ed. published by Connor & Cooke, New York. [HV8978.E3K6 1976] 75-17229 ISBN 0-405-07499-9
1. Eddy, Thomas, 1758-1827. I. Title. II. Series.

Edelman, John W., 1893-1971.

EDELMAN, John W., 1893-1971. 331.88'092'4 B
Labor lobbyist; the autobiography of John W. Edelman. Edited by Joseph Carter. Indianapolis, Bobbs-Merrill [1974] 231 p. 24 cm. [HD8073.E33A3] 73-1729 ISBN 0-672-51677-2 9.95
1. Edelman, John W., 1893-1971. 2. Labor and laboring classes—United States—1914- I. Carter, Joseph, ed. II. Title.

Edelmann, Johann Christian, 1698-1767.

GROSSMANN, Walter, 1918- 211'.4'0924 B
Johann Christian Edelmann : from orthodoxy to enlightenment / by Walter Grossman. The Hague : Mouton, [1976] ix, 209 p. ; 24 cm. (Religion and society ; 3) Includes index. Bibliography: p. [199]-203. [BL2790.E33G76] 76-377412 ISBN 9-02-797691-0 : 14.00
1. Edelmann, Johann Christian, 1698-1767. 2. Rationalists—Germany—Biography. I. Title. II. Series: Religion and society (The Hague) ; 3.
Distributed by Humanities BIP

Eden, Anthony, Sir, 1897-

ASTER, Sidney, 1942- 941.082'092'4 B
Anthony Eden / Sidney Aster ; introduction by A. J. P. Taylor. New York : St. Martin's Press, 1976. 176 p., [4] leaves of plates : ill ; 23 cm. Includes index. Bibliography: p. 167-169. [DA566.9.E28A9 1976] 76-22932 8.95
1. Eden, Anthony, Earl of Avon, 1897- 2. Prime ministers—Great Britain—Biography. 3. Great Britain—Politics and government—20th century. BIP

BARDENS, Dennis. 923.242
Portrait of a statesman; [the personal life story of Sir Anthony Eden] New York, Philosophical Library [1956] 326p. illus. 22cm. [DA566.9] 57-2137
1. Eden, Sir Anthony, 1897- I. Title.

CAMPBELL-JOHNSON, Alan, 1913- 923.242
Eden; the making of a statesman. New York, Washburn [1955] 306p. illus. 22cm. First published in 1938 under title: Anthony Eden. [DA566.9.E28C3 1955] 55-2908
1. Gt. Brit.—Pol. & govt.—20th cent. I. Title. BIP

CAMPBELL-JOHNSON, Alan, 1913- 941.084'092'4 B
Eden : the making of a statesman / by Alan Campbell-Johnson. Westport, Conn. : Greenwood Press, 1976, c1955. x, 306 p., [8] leaves of plates : ill. ; 23 cm. First published in 1938 under title: Anthony Eden. Reprint of the ed. published by I. Washburn, New York. Includes index. [DA566.9.E28C3 1976] 76-6056 ISBN 0-8371-8813-X lib.bdg. : 17.50
1. Eden, Anthony, Sir, 1897- 2. Great Britain—Politics and government—20th century. 3. Great Britain—Foreign relations—20th century.

CHURCHILL, Randolph Spencer, 1911- 923.242
The rise and fall of Sir Anthony Eden. [1st American ed.] New York, Putnam [1959] 327p. illus. 22cm. [DA566.9.E28C5 1959] 59-11008
1. Eden, Sir Anthony, 1897- I. Title.

EDEN, Anthony Sir 923.242
Full circle; the memoirs of Anthony Eden. Boston, Houghton Mifflin, [c.]1960. 676p. illus. 22cm. 59 8856 6.75
1. Gt. Brit.—Pol. & govt.—1945- I. Title.

EDEN, Anthony, Earl of Avon, 1897- 941.082'092'4 B
Another world, 1897-1917 / Anthony Eden. London : A. Lane, 1976. 156 p., [6] leaves of plates : ill. ; 23 cm. Includes index. [DA566.9.E28A33] 76-375607 ISBN 0-7139-1003-8 : £3.95
1. Eden, Anthony, Earl of Avon, 1897- 2. Great Britain. Army—Biography. 3. European War, 1914-1918—Personal narratives, English. 4. Somme, Battle of the, 1916—Personal narratives. 5. Soldiers—Great Britain—Biography. I. Title. BIP

EDEN, Anthony, Earl of Avon, 1897- 941.082'092'4 B
Another world, 1897-1917 / Anthony Eden, Earl of Avon. 1st ed. in the U.S. Garden City, N.Y. : Doubleday, 1977, c1976. xiv, 175 p., [6] leaves of plates : ill. ; 22 cm. Autobiographical. Includes index. [DA566.9.E28A33 1977] 77-74298 ISBN 0-385-12719-7 : 7.95
1. Eden, Anthony, Earl of Avon, 1897- 2. Great Britain Army—Biography. 3. European War, 1914-1918—Personal narratives, English. 4. Somme, Battle of the 1916—Personal narratives, English. 5. Soldiers—Great Britain—Biography. I. Title.

Eden, Robert, Sir, 1741-1784.

STEINER, Bernard Christian, 1867-1926. 327.73'042 S
Life and administration of Sir Robert Eden. Baltimore, Johns Hopkins Press, 1898. [New York, Johnson Reprint Corp., 1973] 142 p. port. 22 cm. Pages also numbered 342-476. Original ed. issued as no. 7-9 of Anglo-American relations and Southern history, which forms the 16th series of Johns Hopkins University studies in historical and political science. Includes bibliographical references. [E183.8.G7A67 no. 7-9] [F184] 975.2'02'0924 B 72-14356 ISBN 0-384-57827-6 pap. 7.00
1. Eden, Robert, Sir, 1741-1784. 2. Maryland—Politics and government—Revolution. I. Title. II. Series: Johns Hopkins University. Studies in historical and political science, 16th ser., 7-9. III. Series: Anglo-American relations and Southern history, no. 7-9. BIP

Eder, Shirley.

EDER, Shirley. 791.43'092'4
Not this time, Cary Grant! and other stories about Hollywood. [1st ed.] Garden City, N.Y., Doubleday, 1973. ix, 295 p. illus. 22 cm. [PN1998.A2E3] 73-79660 ISBN 0-385-02854-7 6.95
1. Eder, Shirley. 2. Moving-picture actors and actresses—Biography. I. Title.

Edgerton, Mary Wright, 1827-1884.

EDGERTON, Mary Wright, 1827-1884. 978.6'02'0924 B
A governor's wife on the mining frontier : the letters of Mary Edgerton from Montana, 1863-1865 / edited and with an introd. by James L. Thane, Jr. Salt Lake City : Tanner Trust Fund, University of Utah Library, c1976. 148 p. : ill., map (on lining paper) ; 25 cm. (Utah, the Mormons, and the West ; no. 7) Includes index. Bibliography: p. 137-141. [F731.E33 1976] 76-27429
1. Edgerton, Mary Wright, 1827-1884. 2. Montana—Governors—Wives—Correspondence. 3. Bannack, Mont.—Gold discoveries—Sources. I. Thane, James L. II. Title. III. Series.

Edgeworth, Maria, 1767-1849.

BUTLER, Marilyn. 823'.7
Maria Edgeworth: a literary biography. Oxford, Clarendon Press, 1972. x, 531, [7] p. illus., facsim., ports. 23 cm. Bibliography: p. [501]-509. [PR4646.B85] 72-190759 £6.50
1. Edgeworth, Maria, 1767-1849. BIP

CLARKE, Isabel Constance. 823'.7 B
Maria Edgeworth, her family and friends, by Isabel C. Clarke. [Folcroft, Pa.] Folcroft Library Editions, 1972. 208 p. illus. 24 cm. Reprint of the 1949 ed. published by Hutchinson, London, New York. Bibliography: p. [PR4646.C6 1972] 72-10250 ISBN 0-8414-0691-X (lib. bdg.)
1. Edgeworth, Maria, 1767-1849.

EDGEWORTH, Maria, 1767-1849. 823'.7 B
Letters from England, 1813-1844; edited by Christina Colvin. Oxford, Clarendon Press, 1971. iii-xlii, 649 p., 5 plates. illus., facsims., ports. 23 cm. Includes bibliographical references. [PR4646.A52 1971] 73-870110 ISBN 0-19-812430-9 £7.50
I. Colvin, Christina, ed. II. Title.

EDGEWORTH, Maria, 1797-1849. 823'.7 B
The life and letters of Maria Edgeworth. Edited by Augustus J. C. Hare. Freeport, N.Y., Books for Libraries Press [1971] 2 v. (704 p.) illus., port. 23 cm. Reprint of the 1894 ed. [PR4646.A5 1971] 73-152982 ISBN 0-8369-5734-2
I. Hare, Augustus John Cuthbert, 1834-1903, ed. BIP

NEWBY, Percy Howard, 1918- 823'.7 B
Maria Edgeworth / by P. H. Newby. Norwood, Pa. : Norwood Editions, 1975. 98 p. ; 24 cm. Reprint of the 1950 ed. published by A. Barker, London, in series: The English novelists. Includes index. Bibliography: p. [95] [PR4646.N4 1975] 75-43794 ISBN 0-88305-461-2 : 12.50
1. Edgeworth, Maria, 1767-1849. I. Title. II. Series: The English novelists (London) BIP

Edgeworth, Maria, 1767-1849—Biography.

CLARKE, Isabel Constance. 823'.7 B
Maria Edgeworth : her family and friends / by Isabel C. Clarke. Norwood, Pa. : Norwood Editions, 1975. 208 p., [8] leaves of plates : ill. ; 23 cm. Reprint of the 1949 ed. published by Hutchinson, London. Includes index. Bibliography: p. 201. [PR4646.C6 1975] 75-44043 ISBN 0-88305-748-4 : 17.50
1. Edgeworth, Maria, 1767-1849—Biography. BIP

Edgren, August Hjalmar, 1840-1903.

LINDQUIST, Emory 301.45'1'395073
Kempton, 1908-
An immigrant's two worlds: a biography of Hjalmar Edgren, by Emory Lindquist. Rock Island, Ill., Augustana Historical Society [1972] x, 97 p. port. 24 cm. (Augustana Historical Society publication no. 23) Includes bibliographical references. [F536.A96 vol. 23] [P85.E34] 409'.24 B 72-80673 ISBN 0-910184-23-2
1. Edgren, August Hjalmar, 1840-1903. I. Title. II. Series: Augustana Historical Society, Rock Island, Ill. Publication, no. 23. **BIP**

Edinburgh. University—Biography.

FAMOUS Edinburgh 920'.042
students. [Folcroft, Pa.] Folcroft Library Editions, 1973. 186 p. ports. 24 cm. Reprint of the 1914 ed. published by T. N. Foulis, Edinburgh, Boston. Contents.Contents.—Webster, A. B. Drummond of Hawthornden.—Smith, G. G. James Thomson.—Seth Pringle Pattison, A. David Hume.—Brown, P. H. Principal Robertson.—Smeaton, O. Oliver Goldsmith.—Nicoll, Sir W. R. James Boswell.—Saintsbury, G. E. B. Sir Walter Scott.—Bruce, W. S. Mungo Park, explorer.—Crockett, W. S. John Leyden, poet and orientalist.—MacPherson, J. I. Henry, Lord Brougham.—Laurie, A. P. Sir David Brewster.—Whyte, A. F. Viscount Palmerston.—Crichton-Browne, Sir J. Thomas Carlyle.—Smith, W. C. Lord John Russell.—Bell, J. James Syme, surgeon.—Horsburgh, E. M. James Nasmyth, engineer.—Thomson, J. A. Charles Darwin.—Simpson, Sir A. R. Sir James Y. Simpson, bart.—Brown, A. C. Doctor John Brown.—Turner, Sir W. Professor John Goodsir.—Knott, C. G. James Clerk Maxwell.—Kelman, J. Robert Louis Stevenson. [CT774.F35 1973] 73-12975 ISBN 0-[Folcroft, Pa.] Folcroft L
1. Edinburgh. University—Biography. 2. Great Britain—Biography.

Edison, Thomas Alva, 1847-1931.

BEASLEY, Rex. 926
Edison. Foreword by Herbert Hoover. [1st ed.] Philadelphia, Chilton Books [c1964] 176 p. illus., ports., facsims. 25 cm. [TK140.E3B4] 64-13468
1. Edison, Thomas Alva, 1847-1931. I. Title.

BRADFORD, Gamaliel, 1863- 920.02
1932.
The quick and the dead. Port Washington, N.Y., Kennikat Press [1969, c1931] x, 282 p. ports. 22 cm. (Essay and general literature index reprint series) Contents.—Theodore Roosevelt.—Woodrow Wilson.—Thomas Alva Edison.—Henry Ford.—Nikolai Lenin.—Benito Mussolini.—Calvin Coolidge. Bibliographical references included in "Notes" (p. [259]-[274]) [CT120.B65 1969] 70-85991
1. Roosevelt, Theodore, Pres. U.S., 1858-1919. 2. Wilson, Woodrow, Pres. U.S., 1856-1924. 3. Edison, Thomas Alva, 1847-1931. 4. Ford, Henry, 1863-1947. 5. Lenin, Vladimir Il'ich, 1870-1924. 6. Mussolini, Benito, 1883-1945. 7. Coolidge, Calvin, Pres. U.S., 1872-1933. I. Title.

CLARK, Graves Glenwood, [925.3]
1894-
Thomas Alva Edison. Illustrated by Millard McGee. [1st ed.] New York, Aladdin Books, 1950. 165 p. illus. 21 cm. [TK140.E3C4] 926 50-7139
I. Edison. Thomas Alva, 1847-1931. II. Title.

CLARK, Ronald 621.3'092'4 B
William.
Edison : the man who made the future / Ronald W. Clark. 1st American ed. New York : Putnam, 1977. 256 p. : ill. ; 25 cm. Includes index. Bibliography: p. 244-245. [TK140.E3C43 1977] 76-56653 ISBN 0-399-11952-3 : 12.95
1. Edison, Thomas Alva, 1847-1931. 2. Electric engineers—United States—Biography. 3. Inventors—United States—Biography. **BIP**

*COMPERE, Mickie 92
The story of Thomas Alva Edison, inventor; the wizard of Menlo Park. Pictures by Jerome B. Moriarty New York, Four Winds [dist. Scholastic, 1966, c.1964] 64p. illus. (pt. col.) 22cm. 2.50
I. Title.

CONOT, Robert E. 621.3'092'4 B
A streak of luck / Robert Conot. 1st ed. New York : Seaview Books ; trade distribution by Simon and Schuster, c1979. xvii, 565 p., [12] leaves of plates : ill. ; 24 cm. Includes bibliographical references and index. [TK140.E3C56] 78-24126 ISBN 0-87223-521-1 : 15.00
1. Edison, Thomas Alva, 1847-1931. 2. Inventors—United States—Biography. 3. Electric engineers—United States—Biography. I. Title. **BIP**

EDISON, Thomas Alva, 1847- 081
1931.
The diary and sundry observations of Thomas Alva Edison. Edited by Dagobert D. Runes. New York, Greenwood Press, 1968 [c1948] 181 p. port. 23 cm. [TK140.E3A3 1968] 68-28588
I. Runes, Dagobert David, 1902- ed. II. Title. **BIP**

EDISON, Thomas Alva, 1847- 081
1931.
The diary of Thomas A. Edison. Introd. by Kathleen L. McGuirk. Old Greenwich, Conn., Chatham Press; distributed by Viking Press [New York, 1971] 72 p. illus. 24 cm. Photocopy of the diary written in 1885. Includes bibliographical references. [TK140.E3A3 1971] 71-107081 ISBN 0-85699-017-5 5.95

FREEDMAN, Russell 621.30924(B)
Thomas Alva Edison; a concise biography. New York, Amer. R. D. M. [c.1966] 72p. ports. 21cm. (Study master pubn., 907) [TK140.E3] 66-28704 1.00 pap.,
1. Edison, Thomas Alva, 1847-1931. I. Title.

FREEDMAN, Russell. 621.30924 (B)
Thomas Alva Edison; a concise biography. New York, American R. D. M. Corp. [c1966] 72 p. ports. 21 cm. (A Study master publication, 907) [[TK140.E3]] 66-28704
1. Edison, Thomas Alva, 1847-1931. I. Title.

FROST, Lawrence A. 621.3'0924 B
The Edison album; a pictorial biograpy of Thomas Alva Edison, by Lawrence A. Frost. [1st ed.] Seattle, Superior Pub. Co. [1969] 175 p. illus., facsims., ports. 28 cm. Bibliography: p. 170-171. [TK140.E3F74] 70-87807 12.95
1. Edison, Thomas Alva, 1847-1931. I. Title.

HANFORD, Barbara. 92
Thomas Edison. Pictures by Raymond Renard. Adapted by Barbara Hanford from the original text. St. Louis, Webster Division, McGraw-Hill [1967] [28 p.] col. illus., port. 19 x 21 cm. (Men of genius books) (Around the world library) A short biography of an ingenious American inventor whose creativity brought us the ticker-tape, electric light, record players, and movies. [TK140.E3H3] AC 67
1. Edison, Thomas Alva, 1847-1931. I. Renard, Raymond, illus. II. Title.

HUGHES, Thomas 621.3'092'4 B
Parke.
Thomas Edison, professional inventor. London : H.M.S.O., 1976. 48 p. : ill., ports. ; 22 cm. (A Science Museum booklet) Includes bibliographical references. [TK140.E3H83] 77-360551 ISBN 0-11-290225-1 : £1.00
1. Edison, Thomas Alva, 1847-1931. 2. Electric engineers—United States—Biography. 3. Inventors—United States—Biography. I. Title. II. Series: London. Science Museum. A Science Museum booklet.

JOSEPHSON, Matthew, 1899- 926
Edison; a biography. New York, McGraw [1963, c.1959] 1959] 511p. illus. 24cm. (33046) Bibl. 2.95 pap.,
1. Edison, Thomas Alva, 1847-1931. I. Title.

JOSEPHSON, Matthew, 1899- 926
Edison; a biography. [1st ed.] New York, McGraw-Hill [1959] 511 p. illus. 24 cm. [TK140.E3J75] 59-13204
1. Edison, Thomas Alva, 1847-1931.

KURLAND, Gerald, 621.3'092'4 B
1942-
Thomas Edison, father of electricity and master inventor of our modern age. Charlotteville, N.Y., SamHar Press, 1972. 31 p. 23 cm. (Outstanding personalities, no. 46) Bibliography: p. 31. A biography of the inventor of the light bulb, phonograph, motion picture machine, and many other items. [TK140.E3K87] 92 72-89210
1. Edison, Thomas Alva, 1847-1931. I. Title. **BIP**

LOMBARD, Rose. 621.3'092'4
Behind the biographies; a personal study of Thomas Alva Edison, by Rose Lombard (Mrs. Thomas Russell Lombard) [n.p., 1951] 1 v. illus. 29 cm. [TK140.E3L6]
1. Edison, Thomas Alva, 1847-1931. 2. Lombard, Thomas R. I. Title.

LOWITZ, Sadyebeth. 621.3'0924 B
Tom Edison finds out; a really truly story by Sadyebeth and Anson Lowitz, with illus. by the latter. [Rev. ed.] Minneapolis, Lerner Publications Co. [1967] [48] p. illus. 19 x 22 cm. A short biography of an inquisitive boy, telling the innumerable questions, escapades, and experiments that led him to trouble as a youngster, but to great inventions as a young man. [TK140.E3L63 1967] 92 AC 68
1. Edison, Thomas Alva, 1847-1931. I. Lowitz, Anson, joint author. II. Title.

MEADOWCROFT, Enid 621.3'0924 B
(La Monte) 1898-
The story of Thomas Alva Edison; illustrated by Harve Stein. New York, Grosset & Dunlap [1952] 181 p. illus. 22 cm. (Signature books) A biography of inventor Edison whose discoveries were important to entertainment because he discovered electric lights, motion pictures, and a method of recording the human voice. [PZ7.M506Sw] 92 AC 68
1. Edison, Thomas Alva, 1847-1931. I. Stein, Harve, 1904- illus. II. Title.

NORTH, Sterling, 1906- 926
Young Thomas Edison. Illustrated with photos., decorations, diagrs., and maps by William Barss. Boston, Houghton Mifflin, 1958. 182 p. illus., port., maps, facsims. 22 cm. (North Star books, 3) [TK140.E3N6] 58-9637
1. Edison, Thomas Alva, 1847-1931. **BIP**

PROBST, George E., ed. 926
The indispensable man; the story of Thomas Alva Edison's life and inventive genius seen in 130 photographs and told in th words of David Sarnoff [others] New York, Shorewood [1962] 126p. illus. 24cm. Record of the formal installation of the bust of Thomas Alva Edison into the Hall of Fame at New York Univ., June 4, 1961. 62-21408 2.95
1. Edison, Thomas Alva, 1847-1931. I. Sarnoff, David, 1891-. II. Title.

THOMAS Alva Edison; v. 12
illustrated by Millard McGee. New York, Dutton, 1958 [c1950] 165p. illus. 21cm.
1. Edison, Thomas Alva, 1847-1931. I. Clark, Graves Glenwood, 1894-

THOMAS, Henry, 1886- 926
Thomas Alva Edison. Illustrated by Andre Le Blanc. New York, Putnam [1958] 128 p. illus. 21 cm. (Lives to remember) [TK140.E3T48] 58-7457
1. Edison, Thomas Alva, 1847-1931. I. Title.

VANDERBILT, Byron 660'.0924 B
Michael, 1906-
Thomas Edison, chemist [by] Byron M. Vanderbilt. Washington, American Chemical Society, 1971. ix, 373 p. illus. 22 cm. Includes bibliographical references. [TK140.E3V35] 75-172526 ISBN 0-8412-0129-3
1. Edison, Thomas Alva, 1847-1931. I. Title. **BIP**

WEIR, Ruth Cromer, 1912- 925.3
Thomas Alva Edison, inventor. Illustrated by Albert Orbaan. New York, Abingdon-Cokesbury Press [1953] 128p. illus. 21cm. [TK140.E3W4] 926 53-7582
1. Edison, Thomas Alva, 1847-1931. I. Title.

Edison, Thomas Alva, 1847-1931—Juvenile literature.

COUSINS, Margaret, 1905- 621.3
The story of Thomas Alva Edison. Illus. with photos. and map. New York, Random [1965] 175p. illus., map, ports. 22cm. (Landmark bks.) [TK140.E3C64] 65-22652 1.95; 2.28 lib. ed. net,
1. Edison, Thomas Alva, 1847-1931—Juvenile literature. I. Title.

HIEBERT, Roselyn. 621.3'0924 B
Thomas Edison, American inventor, by Roselyn and Ray Eldon Hiebert. Illustrated with photos. New York, F. Watts [1969] 214 p. illus., ports. 22 cm. (Immortals of engineering) A biography of the American scientist whose many inventions, especially the electric light bulb, helped usher in the Age of Technology. [TK140.E3H53] 92 71-79668
1. Edison, Thomas Alva, 1847-1931—Juvenile literature. I. Hiebert, Ray Eldon, joint author. II. Title.

KAUFMAN, Mervyn D. 920
Thomas Alva Edison, miracle maker. Illus. by Cary. Champaign, Ill., Garrard [c.1962] 80p. col. illus. 23cm. (Discovery bk.) 62-7776 2.25
1. Edison, Thomas Alva, 1847-1931—Juvenile literature. I. Title.

*KAUFMAN, Mervyn D. 92
Thomas Alva Edison, miracle maker. Illus. by Cary. New York, Dell [1968, c. 1962] 80p. illus. 19cm. (Yearling BK. 8813 Discovery bk.) .50 pap.,
1. Edison, Thomas Alva, 1847-1931—Juvenile literature. I. Title.

LOWITZ, Sadyebeth. 92 (J)
Tom Edison finds out; a really truly story by Sadyebeth and Anson Lowitz, with illus. by the latter. [Rev. ed.] Minneapolis, Lerner Publications Co. [1967] 1 v. (unpaged) illus. 19 x 22 cm. [TK140.E3L63 1967] 67-29826
1. Edison, Thomas Alva, 1847-1931—Juvenile literature. I. Lowitz, Anson, joint author. II. Title. **BIP**

MARTIN, Patricia 621.3'0924 B
Miles.
Thomas Alva Edison. Illustrated by Fermin Rocker. New York, Putnam [1971] 62 p. illus. (part col.) 23 cm. (A See and read beginning to read biography) A biography of the inventor who created the lightbulb, phonograph, and motion-picture machine. [TK140.E3M29] 92 70-133923 2.97
1. Edison, Thomas Alva, 1847-1931—Juvenile literature. I. Rocker, Fermin, illus. II. Title.

PRINGLE, Patrick 920
The young Edison. Illus. by William Randell. New York, Roy [1964, c.1963] 126p. illus. 21cm. 64-10523 3.25 bds.,
1. Edison, Thomas Alva, 1847-1931—Juvenileliterature. I. Title.

SHAPP, Martha 92
Let's find out about Thomas Alva Edison, by Martha and Charles Shapp. Pictures by Marvin Friedman. New York, Watts [c.1966] 59p. col. illus. 22cm. [TK140.E3S45] 66-12549 2.50; 1.88 lib. ed.,
1. Edison Thomas Alva, 1847-1931—Juvenile literature. I. Shapp, Charles, joint author. II. Friedman, Marvin, Illus. III. Title.

Edman, Victor Raymond, 1900-1967.

CAIRNS, Earle 378.1'12'0924 B
Edwin, 1910-
V. Raymond Edman: in the presence of the king, by Earle E. Cairns. With a tribute by Billy Graham. Chicago, Moody Press [1972] 255 p. illus. 22 cm. Bibliography: p. 241-243. [BR1725.E32C3] 72-77948 ISBN 0-8024-9180-4 4.95
1. Edman, Victor Raymond, 1900-1967.

Edmonds, Francis William, 1806-1863.

MANN, Maybelle. 759.13 B
Francis William Edmonds, Mammon and

art / Maybelle Mann. New York : Garland Pub., 1977. vii, 170 p., [8] leaves of plates : ill. ; 21 cm. (Outstanding dissertations in the fine arts) Originally presented as the author's thesis, New York University, 1972. Bibliography: p. 165-170. [ND237.E394M36 1977] 76-23638 ISBN 0-8240-2708-6 lib.bdg. : 30.00
1. Edmonds, Francis William, 1806-1863. 2. Painters—United States—Biography. I. Title. II. Series.

Edmonds, Henry Morris,

EDMONDS, Henry Morris, 1878-1960 922.573
A parson's notebook. Birmingham, Ala., Elizabeth Agee's Bookshelf, 1915 11th Ave. [c.]1961. 310p. illus. 61-18303 5.00
I. Title.

Edmondson, James K., 1832-1898.

EDMONDSON, James K., 1832-1898. 973.7'82'0924
My dear Emma : war letters of Col. James K. Edmondson, 1861-1865 / edited by Charles W. Turner. Verona, Va. : McClure Press, c1978. 151 p., [3] leaves of plates : ill. ; 24 cm. Letters to Emma Edmondson. Includes index. [E581.4.S8E353] 78-113096 8.00
1. Edmondson, James K., 1832-1898. 2. Confederate States of America. Army. Stonewall Brigade—Biography. 3. Edmondson, Emma. 4. United States—History—Civil War, 1861-1865—Personal narratives—Confederate side. 5. United States—History—Civil War, 1861-1865—Regimental histories—Stonewall Brigade. 6. Soldiers—Virginia—Correspondence. I. Edmondson, Emma. II. Turner, Charles Wilson. III. Title.

Edmondson, William, 1883?-1951.

EDMONDSON, William, 1883?-1951. 730'.92'4
Visions in stone: the sculpture of William Edmondson [by] Edmund L. Fuller. With photos. by Edward Weston. [Pittsburgh] University of Pittsburgh Press [1973] xi, 123 p. illus. 27 cm. [NB237.E35F84] 72-91108 ISBN 0-8229-3259-8 14.95
1. Edmondson, William, 1883?-1951. I. Fuller, Edmund L., 1941- II. Title.

Edmonton, Alberta.

THE Edmonton story; v. 12
the life and times of Edmonton(Alberta. Edmonton(Institute of applied art, ltd., 1956. 279p. illus. 23cm.
1. Edmonton, Alberta. I. Cashman, A W 1923-

Edmund Rich, Saint, Abp. of Canterbury, d. 1240.

LAWRENCE, Clifford Hugh 922.242
St. Edmund of Abingdon; a study in hagiography and history. Oxford, Clarendon Press [New York, Oxford] 1960[ ] x, 339p. 'List of manuscripts cited': p. [326]-328. Bibliographical footnotes. 22cm. 60-969 9.60
1. Edmund Rich, Saint, Abp. of Canterbury, d. 1240. I. Title.

Edmund Rich, Saint, Abp. of Canterbury, d.1240.

LAWRENCE, Clifford Hugh. 922.242
St. Edmund of Abingdon; a study in hagiography and history. Oxford, Clarendon Press, 1960. x, 339p. 22cm. 'List of manuscripts cited': p.[326]-328. Bibliographical footnotes. [BX4700.E2L3] 60-969
1. Edmund Rich, Saint, Abp. of Canterbury, d.1240. I. Title.

Edmund, Saint, King of East Anglia, 841-870.

AELFRIC, Abbot of Eynsham. v. 12
Lives of three English saints; edited by G. I. Needham. New York, Appleton-Century-Crofts [1966] viii, 119 p. 19 cm. (Emthuen's Old English Library. Series B: Prose selections) Bibliography: p. 82-85. [NUC67-74378]
1. Oswald, Saint, King of Northumbria, 6057-642. 2. Edmund, Saint, King of East Anglia, 841-870. 3. Swithun, Saint, Bp. of Winchester, d. 862. I. Needbam, Geoffrey Ivor, ed. II. Title.
Contents Omitted.

Edmundson, Sarah Emma, 1841-1898.

DANNETT, Sylvia G. 973.781
She rode with the generals; the true and incredible story of Sarah Emma Seeyle, alias Franklin Thompson. New York, T. Nelson [c.1960] 326p. Bibl. p.308-312 and bibl. notes p. 301-307 illus. 22cm. 60-11485 5.00
1. Edmundson, Sarah Emma, 1841-1898. I. Title.

Edmundson, Sarah Emma, 1841-1898—Juvenile literature.

HOEHLING, Mary Duprey, 1914- 973.781
Girl soldier and spy, Sarah Emma Edmundson. New York, Messner [1959] 192 p. 22 cm. Includes bibliography. [E608.E26] 59-12763
1. Edmundson, Sarah Emma, 1841-1898—Juvenile literature. 2. U.S.—History—Civil War. I. Title.

TALMADGE, Marian. 973.78'5'0924 B
Emma Edmonds: nurse and spy, by Marian Talmadge and Iris Gilmore. New York, Putnam [1970] 127 p. illus., port. 22 cm. (Spies of the world) Bibliography: p. 125-126. A biography of the woman who, disguised as a man, served as a "male" nurse and spy for several years during the Civil War. [E608.E26T3 1970] 92 78-92823 3.49
1. Edmundson, Sarah Emma, 1841-1898—Juvenile literature. 2. United States—History—Civil War, 1861-1865—Secret service—Juvenile literature. I. Gilmore, Iris, joint author. II. Title.

Edmundson, William, 1627-1712.

EDMUNDSON, William, 1627-1712. 289.6'0924 B
The journal (abridged) of Wm. Edmondson, Quaker apostle to Ireland & the Americas, 1627-1712. Edited by Caroline N. Jacob. Foreword by Henry J. Cadbury. [Philadelphia] Philadelphia Yearly Meeting [of the] Religious Society of Friends; [distributed by Friends Books Store, 1968] xii, 124 p. 18 cm. Bibliography: p. 124. [BX7795.E4A32] 68-54861 1.50
1. Edmundson, William, 1627-1712. I. Jacob, Caroline Nicholson, ed. II. Cadbury, Henry Joel, 1883-

Edsall, David Linn, 1869-1945.

AUB, Joseph Charles, 1890- 610'.924 B
Pioneer in modern medicine: David Linn Edsall of Harvard, by Joseph C. Aub and Ruth K. Hapgood. Foreword by Paul Dudley White. [Cambridge, Mass.] Harvard Medical Alumni Association, 1970. xi, 384 p. illus., ports. 25 cm. Includes bibliographical references. [R154.E43A9] 78-145896 12.00
1. Edsall, David Linn, 1869-1945. I. Hapgood, Ruth K., joint author. II. Title. BIP

Education, American—Biography.

BARDWELL, Wilma. 370'.92'2
Early childhood education : personalities / Wilma Bardwell, Rose Spicola. Dallas, Tex. : Bardwell, [1975] iii, 125 p. ; 23 cm. Includes index. [LA2311.B27] 75-7531
1. Education, American—Biography. I. Spicola, Rose, joint author. II. Title.

RUSSELL E. 925.8
Belored professor life and times of William Dodge Frost. New York, Vantage qFrost, William Dodge, 1867-1957. 60-15570
I. Title.

Education—Collections.

BLACK, Hugh C., comp. 370'.92'2
The great educators; readings for leaders in education [compiled by] Hugh C. Black, Kenneth V. Lottich [and] Donald S. Seckinger. Chicago, Nelson-Hall Co. [1972] xvi, 784 p. 24 cm. (Professional-technical series) Includes bibliographical references. [LB7.B49] 72-88717 ISBN 0-911012-48-6 12.00
1. Education—Collections. I. Lottich, Kenneth V., joint comp. II. Seckinger, Donald S., joint comp. III. Title. BIP

Education — Early works to 1800.

STUDER, Gerald C 371.100924 [B]
Christopher Dock; colonial schoolmaster; the biography and writings of Christopher Dock [by] Gerald C. Studer. Scottsdale, Pa., Herald Press [1967] 445 p. illus., facsims, (part col.) maps, ports. (part col.) 21 cm. Bibliography: p. 412-419. [LB575.D66S8] 67-186482
1. Education — Early works to 1800. I. Dock, Christopher, 1608 [ca.]-1771. II. Title.

Education—History.

QUICK, Robert Hebert, 1831-1891. 370'.9
Essays on educational reformers. [1st AMS ed.] New York, D. Appleton, 1896. [New York, AMS Press, 1971] xxxiv, 568 p. 19 cm. "Only authorized edition of the work as rewritten in 1890." [LA91.Q5 1971] 72-172422 15.50
1. Education—History. 2. Educators. I. Title. BIP

Education—Louisiana—History.

CLINE, Rodney. 370'.92'2 B
Pioneer leaders and early institutions in Louisiana education. Baton Rouge, Claitor's Pub. Division, 1969. x, 354 p. illus. 23 cm. Includes bibliographies. [LA295.C56] 72-82794
1. Education—Louisiana—History. 2. Teachers—Louisiana—Biography. I. Title. BIP

Education—Michigan—History.

RIEGLE, John L., 1887- 370'.9744 B
Day before yesterday; an autobiography and history of Michigan schools, by John L. Riegle. Minneapolis, Denison [1971] 363 p. illus. 24 cm. [LA307.R5] 70-183714 7.95
1. Education—Michigan—History. I. Title.

Education—New Mexico—Finance.

WILEY, Tom, 1906- 370'.92'4 B
Forty years in politics and education: some memories, recollections, and observations. [1st ed.] Albuquerque, N.M., C. Horn Publisher [1973] 166 p. 24 cm. [LB2826.N6W48] 73-83961 ISBN 0-910750-27-0 8.50
1. Education—New Mexico—Finance. 2. School management and organization—New Mexico. I. Title.

Education—New York (City)

COVELLO, Leonard. 923.773
The heart is the teacher [by] Leonard Covello with Guido D'Agostino. [1st ed.] New York, McGraw-Hill [1958] 275 p. 21 cm. Autobiographical. [LC3733.N5C6] 58-12993
1. Education—New York (City) 2. Americanization. I. Title.

Education—Philosophy.

ARNOLD, Matthew, 1822-1888. 370.1'0924
Matthew Arnold; edited, with an introduction by James Gribble. London, Collier-Macmillan; New York, Macmillan, 1967. 182 p. 23 cm. (Educational thinkers series) Bibliography: p. 182. [LB675.A77 1967] 67-17500 unpriced
1. Education—Philosophy. I. Gribble, James, ed. II. Title.

Education—U. S.

DAVIS, Jesse Buttrick, 1871- 923.773
The saga of a schoolmaster; an autobiography. Boston, Boston University Press, 1956. 311p. illus. 23cm. [LB875.D23A3] 56-8134
1. Education—U. S. I. Title.

FLEXNER, Abraham, 1866-1959. 923.773
Abraham Flexner: an autobiography. Introd. by Allan Nevins. New York, Simon and Schuster, 1960. xvi, 302 p. port. 22 cm. "A revision, brought up to date, of the author's I remember, published in 1940." [LB875.F583A3 1960] 60-8007
1. Education—U.S. 2. Medicine—Study and teaching.

Educators.

FRIEDMAN, Rose. 370'.922
Freedom builders; great teachers from Socrates to John Dewey. [1st ed.] Boston, Little, Brown [1968] 271 p. 22 cm. "For further reading": p. [253]-257. Bibliography: p. [258]-262. [LA2303.F7] 68-15555 4.95
1. Educators. I. Title.

GRAVES, Frank Pierrepont, 1869-1943. 370'.922
Great educators of three centuries; their work and its influence on modern education. [1st AMS ed.] New York, AMS Press [1971] ix, 289 p. 23 cm. Reprint of the 1912 ed. "Largely an outgrowth of ... lectures before extension classes, teachers' institutes, and other informal gatherings in the States of Missouri and Ohio." Contents.Contents.—John Milton and his "academy."—Francis Bacon and the inductive method.—Ratich and educational claims.—Comenius and his great didactic.—John Locke and education as discipline.—Francke and his institutions.—Rousseau and naturalism in education.—Basedow and the Philanthropinum.—Pestalozzi and education as development.—Herbart and education as a science.—Froebel and the kindergarten.—Lancaster and Bell, and the monitorial system.—Horace Mann and the American educational revival.—Herbert Spencer and the relative value of studies. Includes bibliographies. [LA2301.G7 1971] 70-121285 ISBN 0-404-02891-8
1. Educators. 2. Education—History. I. Title. BIP

WHITNEY, Frank P 1875- 923.773
School and I; the autobiography of an Ohio schoolmaster. [Yellow Springs, Ohio] Antioch Press [c1957] 173 p. illus. 22 cm. [LA2317.W44A3] 57-12040
1. Educators — Correspondence, reminiscences, etc. 2. Education — Philosophy. I. Title.

Educators, American—Biography.

BEASLEY, Wallis, 1915- 923.773
The life and educational contributions of James D. Porter. Nashville, Bureau of Publications, George Peabody College for Teachers, 1950. 191 p. 24 cm. (George Peabody College for Teachers [Nashville] Contribution to education no. 405) Bibliography: p. 184-191. [LB1960.N417 1902] 50-3592
I. Porter. James Davis, 1828-1912. II. Title. III. Series.

**LEADERS in education,* edited by The Jacques Cattell Press. Fifth ed. New York, R. R. Bowker [1975, c1974] ix, 1309 p. 29 cm. [LA2311] 32-10194 ISBN 0-8352-0699-8 49.50 370'.92'2 B
1. Educators, American—Biography. I. Jacques Cattell Press BIP

Educators, American—Biography—Juvenile literature.

LEIPOLD, L. Edmond, 1902- 370'.92'2 B
Famous American teachers, by L. E. Leipold. Minneapolis, T. S. Denison [1972] 87 p. 25 cm. (His Famous American heroes and leaders series) Includes brief biographies of ten educators emphasizing their philosophy and their role in propagating educational opportunity in the United States. [LA2311.L44] 920 74-174954 ISBN 0-513-01199-4
1. Educators, American—Biography—Juvenile literature. I. Title.

Educators, Christian—Biography.

A History of religious educators / Elmer L. Towns, editor. 209'.2'2 B Grand Rapids : Baker Book House, c1975. 330 p. ; 23 cm. Includes bibliographies and index. [BV1470.2.H57] 75-16794 ISBN 0-8010-8829-1 : 8.95
1. Educators, Christian—Biography. 2. Christian biography. 3. Christian education—History. I. Towns, Elmer L. BIP

Educators—India.

HAMPTON, Henry Verner, 1890- 370'.92'2 B
Biographical studies in modern Indian education, by Henry V. Hampton. Freeport, N.Y., Books for Libraries Press [1970] viii, 256 p. ports. 23 cm. (Biography index reprint series) Reprint of the 1947 ed. Contents.Contents.—Charles Grant.—Ram Mohun Roy.—David Hare.—Alexander Duff.—Sir Thomas Munro.—Mountstuart Elphinstone.—James Thomason.—Sir Syed Ahmed Khan.—Bibliography (p. [241]-249) [LA2383.I6H3 1970] 78-136647 ISBN 0-8369-8042-5
1. Educators—India. I. Title. BIP

Educators—United States—Biography.

BARNARD, Henry, 1811-1900, ed. 370'.922 B
Memoirs of teachers and educators. Edited by Henry Barnard. New York, Arno Press, 1969. 524 p. illus., ports. 24 cm. (American education: its men, ideas, and institutions) Reprint of the 2d ed., 1861, first published under title: Educational biography, memoirs of teachers, educators, and promoters and benefactors of education, literature, and science, pt. 1. Reprinted from the American journal of education. [LA2311.B3 1969] 74-89147
1. Educators—United States—Biography. I. Title. II. Series.

BIOGRAPHICAL dictionary of American educators / edited by John F. Ohles. 370'.973 B Westport, Conn. : Greenwood Press, c1978. 3 v. (li, 1666 p.) ; 24 cm. Includes index. [LA2311.B54] 77-84750 ISBN 0-8371-9893-3 lib.bdg. : 95.00
1. Educators—United States—Biography. I. Ohles, John F. BIP

†*WHO'S who biographical record : school district officials* / compiled by the editors of Who's who in America. 370'.92'2 B 1st ed. Chicago : Marquis Who's Who, c1976. xiv, 666 p. ; 27 cm. [LA2311.W44] 76-27259 ISBN 0-8379-3801-5 : 47.50
1. Educators—United States—Biography. I. Who's who in America. II. Marquis-Who's Who, inc.

Educators—United States—Biography—Juvenile literature.

BURGESS, Mary W. 370'.92'2 B
Education / by Mary W. Burgess. Minneapolis : Dillon Press, [1975] 143 p. : ill. ; 22 cm. (Contributions of women) Bibliography: p. [142]-143. Brief biographies of six influential women in the field of education : Emma Hart Willard, Mary Lyon, Patty Smith Hill, Florence Sabin, Mary McLeod Bethune. [LA2311.B87] 920 74-32070 ISBN 0-87518-080-9
1. Educators—United States—Biography—Juvenile literature. I. Title.

Edward Augustus, Duke of Kent, 1767-1820.

GILLEN, Mollie. 942.07'3'0924 B
The prince and his lady; the love story of the Duke of Kent and Madame de St. Laurent. New York, St. Martin's Press [1971, c1970] xiii, 314 p. illus. 24 cm. [DA506.A6G5 1971] 70-162367
1. Edward Augustus, Duke of Kent, 1767-1820. 2. St. Laurent, Julie de, 1760-1830. I. Title.

Edward I, King of England, 1239-1307.

MORRIS, John Edward, 1859-1933. 942.9'03'5
The Welsh wars of Edward I; a contribution to mediaeval military history, based on original documents. New York, Haskell House Publishers, 1969. xii, 327 p. geneal. tables, map. 24 cm. Reprint of the 1901 ed. Bibliographical footnotes. [DA715.M67 1969] 68-25253
1. Edward I, King of England, 1239-1307. 2. Wales—History—To 1536. 3. Military art and science—History. I. Title.

PATMORE, Katherine Alexandra. 942
The seven Edwards of England, by K. A. Patmore. Port Washington, N.Y., Kennikat Press [1971] xi, 367 p. illus., geneal. table, ports. 22 cm. Reprint of the 1911 ed. [DA28.1.P3 1971] 71-118493 ISBN 0-8046-1241-2
1. Edward I, King of England, 1239-1307. 2. Edward II, King of England, 1284-1327. 3. Edward III, King of England, 1312-1377. 4. Edward IV, King of England, 1442-1483. 5. Edward V, King of England, 1470-1483. 6. Edward VI, King of England, 1537-1553. 7. Edward VII, King of Great Britain, 1841-1910. 8. Great Britain—Kings and rulers—Biography. I. Title. BIP

SALZMAN, Louis Francis. 942.03'5'0924
Edward I [by] L.F. Salzman. New York, Praeger [1968] 224p. illus., ports. 23cm. Bibl. [DA229.S25 1968b] (B) 68-25473 5.50
1. Edward I, King of England, 1239-1307. I. Title.

SALZMAN, Louis Francis, 1878- 942.03'5'0924 (B)
Edward I [by] L.F. Salzman. New York, Praeger [1968] 224 p. illus., ports. 23 cm. Bibliography: p. [216] [DA229.S25] 68-25473 5.50
1. Edward I, King of England, 1239-1307. I. Title.

STONES, Edward Lionel Gregory, 1914- 942.03'5'0924 (B)
Edward I, by E.L.G. Stones. London, Oxford U. P., 1968. [4], 60 p. 8 plates, illus., 2 geneal. tables (on lining papers), 2 maps (on lining papers). 21 cm. (The Clarendon biographies, 19) Bibliography: p. 57. [DA229.S7 1968] 68-115751
1. Edward I. King of England, 1239-1307. I. Title.

Edward II, King of England, 1284-1327.

HUTCHISON, Harold Frederick. 942.03'6'0924 B
Edward II [by] Howard F. Hutchinson. New York, Stein and Day [1972, c1971] 180 p. illus. 25 cm. Bibliography: p. [x]-[xi] [DA230.H88 1972] 71-184654 ISBN 0-8128-1448-7 6.95
1. Edward II, King of England, 1284-1327.

PATMORE, Katherine Alexandra. 942
The seven Edwards of England, by K. A. Patmore. Port Washington, N.Y., Kennikat Press [1971] xi, 367 p. illus., geneal. table, ports. 22 cm. Reprint of the 1911 ed. [DA28.1.P3 1971] 71-118493 ISBN 0-8046-1241-2
1. Edward I, King of England, 1239-1307. 2. Edward II, King of England, 1284-1327. 3. Edward III, King of England, 1312-1377. 4. Edward IV, King of England, 1442-1483. 5. Edward V, King of England, 1470-1483. 6. Edward VI, King of England, 1537-1553. 7. Edward VII, King of Great Britain, 1841-1910. 8. Great Britain—Kings and rulers—Biography. I. Title. BIP

Edward III, King of England, 1312-1377.

LONGMAN, William, 1813-1877. 942.03'7
The history of the life and times of Edward the Third. New York, B. Franklin [1969] 2 v. illus., maps, plans, ports. 23 cm. (Burt Franklin research and source works series, 362) (Selected essays in history, economics, and social science, 50.) Reprint of 1869 ed. Bibliographical footnotes. [DA233.L8 1969] 71-80222
1. Edward III, King of England, 1312-1377. 2. Great Britain—History—Edward III, 1327-1377. BIP

MACKINNON, James, 1860-1945. 942.03'7
The history of Edward the Third (1327-1377) Totowa, N.J., Rowman and Littlefield [1974] xx, 625 p. 23 cm. Reprint of the 1900 ed. published by Longmans, Green, London, New York. Includes bibliographical references. [DA233.M2 1974] 73-16316 ISBN 0-87471-465-6 20.00
1. Edward III, King of England, 1312-1377. 2. Great Britain—History—Edward III, 1327-1377. I. Title. BIP

PATMORE, Katherine Alexandra. 942
The seven Edwards of England, by K. A. Patmore. Port Washington, N.Y., Kennikat Press [1971] xi, 367 p. illus., geneal. table, ports. 22 cm. Reprint of the 1911 ed. [DA28.1.P3 1971] 71-118493 ISBN 0-8046-1241-2
1. Edward I, King of England, 1239-1307. 2. Edward II, King of England, 1284-1327. 3. Edward III, King of England, 1312-1377. 4. Edward IV, King of England, 1442-1483. 5. Edward V, King of England, 1470-1483. 6. Edward VI, King of England, 1537-1553. 7. Edward VII, King of Great Britain, 1841-1910. 8. Great Britain—Kings and rulers—Biography. I. Title. BIP

Edward IV, King of England, 1442-1483.

PATMORE, Katherine Alexandra. 942
The seven Edwards of England, by K. A. Patmore. Port Washington, N.Y., Kennikat Press [1971] xi, 367 p. illus., geneal. table, ports. 22 cm. Reprint of the 1911 ed. [DA28.1.P3 1971] 71-118493 ISBN 0-8046-1241-2
1. Edward I, King of England, 1239-1307. 2. Edward II, King of England, 1284-1327. 3. Edward III, King of England, 1312-1377. 4. Edward IV, King of England, 1442-1483. 5. Edward V, King of England, 1470-1483. 6. Edward VI, King of England, 1537-1553. 7. Edward VII, King of Great Britain, 1841-1910. 8. Great Britain—Kings and rulers—Biography. I. Title. BIP

ROSS, Charles Derek. 942.04'4'0924 B
Edward IV / Charles Ross. Berkeley : University of California Press, 1974. xvi, 479 p., [12] leaves of plates : ill. (1 col.) ; 25 cm. Includes index. Bibliography: p. [443]-456. [DA258.R67] 74-79771 ISBN 0-520-02781-7 : 25.00
1. Great Britain—Politics and government—1461-1483.

SCOFIELD, Cora Louise 942.04'4'0924(B)
The life and reign of Edward the Fourth, King of England and of France and Lord of Ireland [by] Cora L. Scofield. New York, Octagon, 1967. 2v. 22cm. Reprint of the 1923 ed. Bibl. [DA258.S4 1967] 67-14886 30.00 set,
1. Edward IV, King of England, 1442-1483. 2. Gt. Brit.—Hist.—Edward IV, 1461-1483. I. Title.

Edward, Prince of Wales, called the Black Prince, 1330-1376.

BARBER, Richard W. 942.03'7'0924 B
Edward, Prince of Wales and Aquitaine : a biography of the Black Prince / Richard Barber. New York : Scribner, c1978. 298 p., [8]leaves of plates : ill. ; 23 cm. Includes index. Bibliography: p. [267]-277. [DA234.B37] 78-54019 ISBN 0-684-15864-7 : 17.50
1. Edward, Prince of Wales, called the Black Prince, 1330-1376. 2. Great Britain—History—Edward III, 1327-1377. 3. Great Britain—Princes and princesses—Biography. I. Title. BIP

CHANDOS, Herald, fl.1350-1380. 942.03'7'0924 B
Life of the Black Prince, by the herald of Sir John Chandos. Edited from the manuscript in Worcester College, with linguistic and historical notes, by Mildred K. Pope and Eleanor C. Lodge. Oxford, Clarendon Press, 1910. [New York, AMS Press, 1974] lxii, 256 p. 24 cm. French text of the Worcester ms., and a corrected version, in parallel columns, followed by English translation. Includes bibliographical references. [DA234.C4 1974] 74-178519 ISBN 0-404-56532-8 18.50
1. Edward, Prince of Wales, called the Black Prince, 1330-1376. 2. Hundred Years' War, 1339-1453. I. Pope, Mildred Katherine, 1872- ed. II. Lodge, Eleanor C., ed. III. Title.

COLE, Hubert. 941.03'7'0924 B
The Black Prince / Hubert Cole. London : Hart-Davis, MacGibbon, 1976. 223 p. : ill. ; 24 cm. Includes index. Bibliography: p. 219. [DA324.C64 1976] 76-363585 ISBN 0-246-10778-2 £5.95
1. Edward, Prince of Wales, called the Black Prince, 1330-1376. 2. Great Britain—History—Edward III, 1327-1377. I. Title.

EMERSON, Barbara. 942.03'7'0924 B
The Black Prince / Barbara Emerson. London : Weidenfeld and Nicolson, c1976. 298 p., [4] leaves of plates : ill. ; 23 cm. Includes index. Bibliography: p. 275-281. [DA234.E45] 76-359945 ISBN 0-297-77055-1 : £4.95
1. Edward, Prince of Wales, called the Black Prince, 1330-1376. I. Title.

HARVEY, John Hooper. 942.3'7'0924 B
The Black Prince and his age / John Harvey. Totowa, N.J. : Rowman and Littlefield, 1976. 184 p., [4] leaves of plates : ill. ; 24 cm. Includes index. Bibliography: p. [168]-171. [DA234.H37 1976] 76-34 ISBN 0-87471-818-X : 14.50
1. Edward, Prince of Wales, called the Black Prince, 1330-1376. 2. Great Britain—History—Edward III, 1327-1377. 3. Hundred Years' War, 1339-1453. I. Title. BIP

Edward, the Confessor, King of England, Saint, d. 1066.

BARLOW, Frank. 942.02'0924
Edward the Confessor. Berkeley, University of California Press, 1970. xxviii, 375 p. fold. geneal. table, maps, plates. 25 cm. Bibliography: p. 345-357. [DA154.8.B297] 70-104107 ISBN 0-520-01671-8 10.95
1. Edward, the Confessor, King of England, Saint, d. 1066. BIP

DUGGAN, Alfred Leo, 1903-1964. v. 12
The cunning of the dove. Garden City, N.Y., Image Books [1966] 239 p. maps. 18 cm. (Image book, D208) 67-88580
1. Edward, the Confessor, King of England, Saint, d. 1066. I. Title.

LIFE of King Edward (The) who rests at Westminster. 923.142 Attributed to a monk of St. Bertin. Ed., tr. with introd. and notes by Frank Barlow. [Dist. New York, Oxford, c.1962] ixxxii, 81, 8185-145p. illus. 23cm. (Medieval texts) English and Latin an opposite pages numbered in duplicate. Bibl. 62-6101 8.00
1. Edward, the Confessor, King of England, Saint, d. 1066. I. A monk of St. Bertin. II. Barlow, Frank, ed. and tr. III. Series: Medieval classics, London

Edward, the Confessor, King of England, Saint, d. 1066—Juvenile literature.

STANLEY-WRENCH, Margaret. 942.020924
The silver king; Edward the confessor, the last great Anglo-Saxon ruler. Illustrated by

Leonard Vosburgh. [1st ed.] New York, Hawthorn Books [1966] 189 p. illus. 22 cm. Bibliography: p. 183-184. [DA154.8.S8] 66-15258
1. Edward, the Confessor, King of England, Saint, d. 1066—Juvenile literature. I. Title.

Edward V, King of England, 1470-1483.

PATMORE, Katherine Alexandra. 942
The seven Edwards of England, by K. A. Patmore. Port Washington, N.Y., Kennikat Press [1971] xi, 367 p. illus., geneal. table, ports. 22 cm. Reprint of the 1911 ed. [DA28.1.P3 1971] 71-118493 ISBN 0-8046-1241-2
1. Edward I, King of England, 1239-1307. 2. Edward II, King of England, 1284-1327. 3. Edward III, King of England, 1312-1377. 4. Edward IV, King of England, 1442-1483. 5. Edward V, King of England, 1470-1483. 6. Edward VI, King of England, 1537-1553. 7. Edward VII, King of Great Britain, 1841-1910. 8. Great Britain—Kings and rulers—Biography. I. Title. BIP

WILLIAMSON, 942.04'4'0922 B
Audrey, 1913-
The mystery of the princes : an investigation into a supposed murder / Audrey Williamson. Totowa, N.J. : Rowman and Littlefield, 1978. 215 p., [7] leaves of plates : ill. ; 22 cm. Includes index. Bibliography: p. [200]-205. [DA259.W54 1978b] 78-113647 ISBN 0-8476-6103-2 : 16.00
1. Edward V, King of England, 1470-1483. 2. Richard, Duke of York, 1473-1483. 3. Great Britain—History—Edward IV, 1461-1483. 4. Great Britain—Kings and rulers—Biography. 5. Great Britain—Princes and princesses—Biography. I. Title. BIP

Edward VI, King of England, 1537-1553.

CHAPMAN, Hester W., 1899- 923.142
The last Tudor king; a study of Edward VI, October 12th, 1537-July 6th, 1553. New York, Macmillan, 1959 [c1958] 304 p. illus. 22 cm. Includes bibliography. [DA345.C4 1959] 59-13702
1. Edward VI, King of England, 1537-1553. 2. Edward VI, King of England, 1537-1553. I. Title.

PATMORE, Katherine Alexandra. 942
The seven Edwards of England, by K. A. Patmore. Port Washington, N.Y., Kennikat Press [1971] xi, 367 p. illus., geneal. table, ports. 22 cm. Reprint of the 1911 ed. [DA28.1.P3 1971] 71-118493 ISBN 0-8046-1241-2
1. Edward I, King of England, 1239-1307. 2. Edward II, King of England, 1284-1327. 3. Edward III, King of England, 1312-1377. 4. Edward IV, King of England, 1442-1483. 5. Edward V, King of England, 1470-1483. 6. Edward VI, King of England, 1537-1553. 7. Edward VII, King of Great Britain, 1841-1910. 8. Great Britain—Kings and rulers—Biography. I. Title. BIP

Edward VII, King of Great Britain, 1841-1910.

BROOK-SHEPHERD, 941.082'092'4
Gordon, 1918-
Uncle of Europe : the social and diplomatic life of Edward VII / Gordon Brook-Shepherd. 1st American ed. New York : Harcourt Brace Jovanovich, 1976, c1975. 384 p., [12] leaves of plates : ill. ; 24 cm. Includes bibliographical references and index. [DA567.B83 1976] 75-29366 ISBN 0-15-192697-2 : 12.95
1. Edward VII, King of Great Britain, 1841-1910. I. Title.

COWLES, Virginia Spencer. 942.082
Gay monarch, the life and pleasures of Edward VII. New York, Harper [1956] 378 p. illus. 22 cm. "Published in England under the title of Edward VII and his circle." [DA567.C7 1956a] 56-8748
1. Edward VII, King of Great Britain, 1841-1910. I. Title.

HIBBERT, 941.082'3'0924 B
Christopher, 1924-
The royal Victorians : King Edward VII, his family and friends / Christopher Hibbert. Philadelphia : Lippincott, c1976. xi, 339 p., [8] leaves of plates : ill. ; 24 cm. Includes index. Bibliography: p. 315-322. [DA567.H5] 75-46507 ISBN 0-397-01111-3 : 12.95
1. Edward VII, King of Great Britain, 1841-1910. I. Title. BIP

*JUDD, Denis 941.082
The House of Windsor New York, St. Martins, [1974 c1973] [223 p.] illus. 25 cm. [DA566] 73-91378 10.95
1. Edward VII, King of Great Britain, 1841-1910 2. George V, King of Great Britain, 1865-1936 3. George VI, King of Great Britain, 1895-1952 4. Elizabeth II, Queen of Great Britain, 1926- I. Title.

JULLIAN, Philippe. 942.082'0924 B
Edward and the Edwardians. Translated from the French by Peter Dawnay. New York, Viking Press [1967] viii, 312 p. illus., geneal. tables. 22 cm. Translation of Edouard VII. Bibliography: p. 301-304. [DA567.J813] 66-15904
1. Edward VII, King of Great Britain, 1841-1910. I. Title.

MAGNUS, Philip 923.142
Montefiore, Sir, bart., 1906-
King Edward the Seventh [by] Philip Magnus. [1st ed.] New York, Dutton, 1964. xv, 528 p. illus., geneal. tables, ports. (part col.) 24 cm. [DA567.M26 1964] 64-11062
1. Edward VII, King of Great Britain, 1841-1910. BIP

MIDDLEMAS, Robert 942.082'092'4 B
Keith, 1935-
The life and times of Edward VII [by] Keith Middlemas. Introd. by Antonia Fraser. Garden City, N.Y., Doubleday, 1972. 224 p. illus. 26 cm. On spine: Edward VII. Bibliography: p. 219. [DA567.M5 1972b] 70-189536 10.00
1. Edward VII, King of Great Britain, 1841-1910. I. Title. II. Title: Edward VII.

PEARSON, John, 941.082'092'4 B
1930-
Edward the rake : an unwholesome biography of Edward VII / by John Pearson. 1st American ed. New York : Harcourt Brace Jovanovich, [1975] 181 p., [8] leaves of plates : ill. ; 23 cm. Includes index. Bibliography: p. 173-174. [DA567.P4 1975] 75-1450 ISBN 0-15-127965-9
1. Edward VII, King of Great Britain, 1841-1910. I. Title.

ST. Aubyn, 941.082'3'0924 B
Giles.
Edward VII, Prince and King / Giles St. Aubyn. New York : Atheneum, 1979. 555 p., [16] leaves of plates : ill. ; 24 cm. Includes index. Bibliography: p. [489]-506. [DA567.S24] 78-63294 ISBN 0-689-10937-7 : 19.95
1. Edward VII, King of Great Britain, 1841-1910. 2. Great Britain—History—Victoria, 1837-1901. 3. Great Britain—History—Edward VII, 1901-1910. 4. Great Britain—Kings and rulers—Biography.

Edward VII, King of Great Britain, 1841-1910—Iconography.

JUDD, Denis, 941.082'092'4 B
1938-
The royal Victorians : a pictorial biography / Denis Judd. New York : St. Martin's Press, [1975] 207 p. : chiefly ill. ; 25 cm. Bibliography: p. 207. [DA567.J78] 74-21087 11.95
1. Edward VII, King of Great Britain, 1841-1910—Iconography. 2. Great Britain—History—Edward VII, 1901-1910—Pictorial works. I. Title.

Edward VIII, King of Great Britain, 1894-1972.

BOLITHO, Hector 1898- 923.142
King Edward VIII, Duke of Windsor. [Rev. ed., with a new introd. chapter]. London, P. Owen [New York, Hillary House, 1966] 225p. illus. 23cm. [DA580.B65] 54-34183 3.00 bds.,
1. Edward VIII, King of Great Britain, 1894- I. Title.

BRODY, Iles. 923.142
Gone with the Windsors. Philadelphia, Winston [1953] vii, 328p. illus., ports. 23cm. [DA580.B75 1953a] 54-851
1. Edward VIII, King of Great Britain, 1894- 2. Windsor; Wallis Warfield duchess of, 1886- I. Title.

BRODY, Iles. 923.142
Gone with the Windsors. [1st ed.] Philadelphia, Winston [1953] 327 p. illus. 22 cm. [DA580.B75] 53-7341
1. Edward VIII, King of Great Britain, 1894-1972. 2. Windsor, Wallis Warfield, duchess of, 1896- I. Title.

BRYAN, Joseph, 941.081'092'2 B
1904-
The Windsor story / J. Bryan III. and Charles J. V. Murphy. 1st ed. New York : Morrow, 1979. 639 p., [24] leaves of plates : ill. ; 24 cm. Includes index. Bibliography: p. 617-621. [DA580B79] 79-17576 ISBN 0-688-03553-1 : 15.00
1. Edward VIII, King of Great Britain, 1894-1972. 2. Windsor, Wallis Warfield, Duchess of, 1896- 3. Great Britain—History—Edward VIII, 1936. 4. Great Britain—Kings and rulers—Biography. 5. Great Britain—Nobility—Biography. 6. United States—Biography. I. Murphy, Charles John Vincent. 1904- joint author. II. Title.

DONALDSON, Frances 941.084
Lonsdale, Lady.
Edward VIII : the road to abdication / Frances Donaldson. Abridged ed. Philadelphia : Lippincott, c1978. p. cm. [DA580.D642] 78-8233 ISBN 0-397-01319-1 : 12.95
1. Edward VIII, King of Great Britain, 1894-1972. 2. Great Britain—Kings and rulers—Biography. 3. Great Britain—History—Edward VIII, 1936. BIP

DONALDSON, 942.084'092'4 B
Frances Lonsdale, Lady.
Edward VIII / by Frances Donaldson Philadelphia : Lippincott, [1975] 477 p. [8] leaves of plates : ill. ; 25 cm. Includes bibliographical references and index. [DA580.D64 1975] 74-31274 ISBN 0-397-00765-5: 15.00
1. Edward VIII, King of Great Britain, 1894-1972.

EDWARD, VIII, King of 923.142
Great Britain,
Windsor revisited, by H. R. H. the Duke of Windsor. Boston, Houghton Miffin [c.] 1960. 216p. illus. 24cm. 60-12999 6.00
I. Title.

EDWARD VIII, King of 923.142
Great Britain, 1894-
A king's story; the memoirs of the Duke of Windsor. New York, Putnam [1951] xi, 435 p. illus., ports., map (on lining papers) facsims. 22 cm. [DA580.A2 1951] 51-10339
I. Title.

GONE with the Windsors v. 12
... Philadelphia, Winston [1956, c1953] 328p. illus. 22cm.
1. Edward VIII, King of Great Britain, 1894- 2. Windsor, Wallis (Warfield) duchess of, 1896- I. Brody, Iles.

INGLIS, Brian, 1916- 942.0840924
Abdication. New York, Macmillan [1966] xiv, 433 p. ports. 21 cm. Bibliography:p. 413-417. [DA580.I 5] 66-20212
1. Edward viii, King of Great Britain, 1894- I. Title.

KINROSS, John 942.0840924 B
Patrick Douglas Balfour, baron, 1904-
The Windsor years; the life of Edward, as Prince of Wales, King, and Duke of Windsor. Text by Lord Kinross. Photos. selected by the editors. New York, Viking Press [1967] 303 p. illus., coat of arms, facsim., ports. 34 cm. (A Studio book) [DA580.K5] 67-25917
1. Edward VIII, King of Great Britain, 1894- I. Title.

LOCKRIDGE, Norman. 923.142
Lese majesty; the private lives of the Duke & Duchess of Windsor. New York, Boar's Head Books, 1952. 190 p. ports. 22 cm. [DA580.L6] 52-3507
1. Edward VIII, King of Great Britain, 1894- I. Title.

Edwards, Anne, 1927- —Biography.

EDWARDS, Anne, 1927- 813'.5'4 B
The inn and us / Anne Edwards & Stephen Citron. 1st ed. New York : Random House, c1976. 181 p. ; 22 cm. [PS3555.D87Z52] 75-40557 ISBN 0-394-49602-7 : 7.95
1. Edwards, Anne, 1927- —Biography. 2. Citron, Stephin. I. Citron, Stephen, joint author. II. Title. BIP

Edwards, Benjamin Franklin, 1865-1959.

MEADOWS, Lorena 332.1'2'0924 B
Edwards. 1915-
A sagebrush heritage; the story of Ben Edwards and his family. Illus. by Patricia Meadows Robertson. San Jose, Calif. [Harlan-Young Press] 1972. xiv, 283 p. illus. 23 cm. Bibliography: p. 269-276. [HG2463.E38M4] 72-78398 7.50
1. Edwards, Benjamin Franklin, 1865-1959. 2. Nevada—History. 3. California—History—1850-1950. I. Title.

Edwards, George, 1950-

EDWARDS, George, 1950- 248'.2 B
Crawling out; a young man's search for life. Grand Rapids, Mich., Zondervan Pub. House [1973] 165 p. 18 cm. [BV4935.E38A33] 73-8358 0.95 (pbk.)
1. Edwards, George, 1950- I. Title.

Edwards, Jonathan, 1703-1758.

ALDRIDGE, Alfred Owen, 922.573
1915-
Jonathan Edwards. New York, Washington Square Press [1964] 181 p. 18 cm. (The Great American thinkers series, W881) Bibliography: p. 167-172. [BX7260.E3A59] 65-935
1. Edwards, Jonathan, 1703-1758.

ALLEN, Alexander 285'.8'0924 B
Viets Griswold, 1841-1908.
Jonathan Edwards. New York, B. Franklin [1974, c1889] Reprint of the ed. published by Houghton, Mifflin, Boston, in series: American religious leaders. Bibliography: p. [BX7260.E3A6 1974] 72-81931 ISBN 0-8337-3926-3
1. Edwards, Jonathan, 1703-1758.

DAVIDSON, Edward 230'.0924
Hutchins
Jonathan Edwards; the narrative of a Puritan mind [by] Edward H. Davidson. Cambridge, Harvard University Press, 1968 [c1966] xii, 161 p. 22 cm. Bibliographical references included in "Notes" (p. 149-158) [BX7260.E3] 68-7254 6.00
1. Edwards, Jonathan, 1703-1758.

DAVIDSON, Edward 230.0924
Hutchins.
Jonathan Edwards; the narrative of a Puritan mind [by] Edward H. Davidson. Boston, Houghton Mifflin Co. [1966] xii, 161 p. 21 cm. (Riverside studies in literature, L7) Bibliographical references included in "Notes" (p. 149-158) [BX7260.E3D3] 66-3058
1. Edwards, Jonathan, 1708-1758. I. Title.

DODDS, Elisabeth D. 285'.8'0922 B
Marriage to a difficult man; the "uncommon union" of Jonathan and Sarah Edwards, by Elisabeth D. Dodds. Philadelphia, Westminster Press [1971] 224 p. 21 cm. Includes bibliographical references. [BX7260.E3D6] 73-141195 ISBN 0-664-20900-9 5.95
1. Edwards, Jonathan, 1703-1758. 2. Edwards, Sarah, 1710-1758. I. Title. BIP

JONATHAN Edwards; 285'.8'0924 B
his life and influence. Papers and discussions by Conrad Cherry [and others] Edited by Charles Angoff. Rutherford [N.J.] Fairleigh Dickinson University Press [1974, c1975] 65 p. 21 cm. (The Leverton lecture series) Includes bibliographical references. [BX7260.E3J66] 74-4516 ISBN 0-8386-1571-6 4.50
1. Edwards, Jonathan, 1703-1758. I.

Cherry, C. Conrad. II. Angoff, Charles, 1902- ed. III. Title. IV. Series.

LEVIN, David, 1924- comp. 285'.8'0924 B
Jonathan Edwards; a profile. [1st ed.] New York, Hill and Wang [1969] xxi, 263 p. 21 cm. (American profiles) Bibliography: p. 257-259. [BX7260.E3L4] 68-30760 5.95
1. Edwards, Jonathan, 1703-1758.

MILLER, Perry, 1905- 922.573
Jonathan Edwards. New York, Meridian Books [1959, c1949] 340 p. 19 cm. (Meridian books, M75) Includes bibliography. [BX7260.E3M5 1959] 59-12142
1. Edwards, Jonathan, 1703-1758.

MILLER, Perry, 1905-1963. 285'.8'0924 B
Jonathan Edwards. Westport, Conn., Greenwood Press [1973, c1949] xv, 348 p. port. 22 cm. Original ed. issued in the American men of letters series. Bibliography: p. 331-333. [BX7260.E3M5 1973] 72-7877 ISBN 0-8371-6551-2 14.25
1. Edwards, Jonathan, 1703-1758. I. Series: The American men of letters series.

PARKES, Henry Bamford, 1904- 285'.8'0924 B
Jonathan Edwards, the fiery Puritan / by Henry Bamford Parkes. 1st AMS ed. New York : AMS Press, 1979, c1930. 271 p. ; 19 cm. (Philosophy in America) Reprint of the ed. published by Minton, Balch, New York. Includes index. Bibliography: p. 259-266. [BX7260.E3P3 1979] 75-3135 ISBN 0-404-59144-2 : 24.50
1. Edwards, Jonathan, 1703-1758. 2. Congregationalists—Clergy—Biography. 3. Clergy—New England—Biography. I. Title. **BIP**

SIMONSON, Harold Peter, 1926- 285'.8'0924 B
Jonathan Edwards, theologian of the heart, by Harold P. Simonson. Grand Rapids, W. B. Eerdmans Pub. Co. [1974] 174 p. 23 cm. Includes bibliographical references. [BX7260.E3S56] 74-4494 ISBN 0-8028-3448-5
1. Edwards, Jonathan, 1703-1758. I. Title.

WINSLOW, Ola Elizabeth 922.573
Jonathan Edwards, 1703-1758. New York, Collier Bks. [1962, c.1940] 375p. (BS44) Bibl. 1.50 pap.,
1. Edwards, Jonathan, 1703-1758. I. Title. **BIP**

WINSLOW, Ola Elizabeth 922.573
Jonathan Edwards, 1703-1758 [Gloucester, Mass., P. Smith, 1964, c.1940] 375p. 19cm. (Collier paperback rebound) Bibl. 3.50
1. Edwards, Jonathan, 1703-1758. I. Title.

WINSLOW, Ola Elizabeth. 285'.8'0924 B
Jonathan Edwards, 1703-1758; a biography. New York, Octagon Books, 1973 [c1940] xii, 406 p. illus. 24 cm. Reprint of the ed. published by Macmillan. Bibliography: p. 373-393. [BX7260.E3W5 1973] 73-9771 14.00
1. Edwards, Jonathan, 1703-1758.

WOOD, James Playsted, 1905- 285'.8'0924 B
Mr. Jonathan Edwards. New York, Seabury Press [1968] 166 p. 22 cm. Bibliography: p. [159]-160. A biography of the eighteenth-century Congregational minister who, as a philosopher, theologian, and scholar, affected the religious life of colonial America. [BX7260.E3W6] 92 AC 68
1. Edwards, Jonathan, 1703-1758. I. Title.

Edwards, Jonathan, 1745-1801.

FERM, Robert L. 230'.8'0924 B
Jonathan Edwards the Younger, 1745-1801 : a colonial pastor / by Robert L. Ferm. Grand Rapids, MI : Eerdmans, c1976. 214 p. ; 23 cm. Includes index. Bibliography: p. 195-210. [BX7260.E3F4] 76-12408 ISBN 0-8028-3485-X : 7.95
1. Edwards, Jonathan, 1745-1801. I. Title.

Edwards, Ralph A.

STOWE, Leland, 1899- 917.11
Crusoe of Lonesome Lake. New York, Random House [1957] 234 p. 21 cm. [F1087.E3S8] 57-5363
1. Edwards, Ralph A. 2. Frontier and pioneer life—British Columbia. I. Title. **BIP**

Edwards, Ross,

EDWARDS, Ross, 1884- 920
Fiddle dust. Denver, Big Mountain Press [1965] 102 p. illus., ports. 23 cm. Autobiographical. [CT275.E359A3] 65-25807
I. Title. **BIP**

Egede, Hans Poulsen, 1686-1758.

BOBE, Louis Theodor Alfred, 1867- 922
Hans Egede, colonizer and missionary of Greenland. Copenhagen, Rosenkilde and Bagger, 1952. 207p. illus. (part col.) ports., maps (part fold., 1 col.) 27cm. [BV3695.E4B63] 52-67018
1. Egede, Hans Poulsen, 1686-1758. I. Title.

GARNETT, Eve. 266.4'1'0924 B
To Greenland's icy mountains; the story of Hans Egede, explorer, coloniser missionary. With a foreword by Nils Egede Bloch-Hoell. Illustrated with photos. and with drawings by the author. New York, Roy Publishers [1968] xv, 189 p. illus., maps, ports. 23 cm. [G762.E35G3] 69-12999 5.50
1. Egede, Hans Poulsen, 1686-1758. I. Title.

Egestorff, Georg, 1802-1868.

TREUE, Wilhelm, 1909- 330.9431
Egestorff. [Hannover] 1956. 58 p. illus. 21 cm. (Bedeutende Niedersachsen; Lebensbilder, Heft 4) [HC287.S3T7] 59-44589
1. Egestorff, Georg, 1802-1868. 2. Egestorff, Johann, 1772-1834. I. Title.

Eggenhofer, Nicholas, 1897-

EGGENHOFER, Nicholas, 1897- 741'.092'4
Eggenhofer : the pulp years / John M. Carroll ; introd. by Jeff Dykes. 1st ed. Fort Collins, Colo : Old Army Press, c1975. 145 p. : ill. (some col.) ; 29 cm. [NC975.5.E33C37] 75-333132 15.00
1. Eggenhofer, Nicholas, 1897- 2. The West in art. I. Carroll, John M.

Eggleston, Edward, 1837-1902.

RANDEL, William Peirce, 1909- 928.1
Edward Eggleston Coll. & Univ. Pr.; dist. New York, Grosset [1964, c.1963] 190p. 21cm. (Twayne's United States authors ser., 45) Bibl. 1.95 pap.,
1. Eggleston, Edward 1837-1902. I. Title. **BIP**

RANDEL, William Peirce, 1909- 928.1
Edward Egglleston. New York, Twayne [c.1963] 190p. 21cm. (Twayne's U.S. authors ser., 45) Bibl. 63-17373 3.50 bds.,
1. Eggleston, Edward, 1837-1902. I. Title.

RANDEL, William Peirce, 1909- 928.1
Edward Eggleston, author of The Hoosier schoolmaster. [Gloucester, Mass., Petdr Smith, 1962, c.1946] xi, 319p. (King's Crown Pr. bk., rebound) Bibl. 5.01
1. Eggewleston, Edward, 1837-1902. I. Title.

Eggleston, George Teeple, 1906-

EGGLESTON, George Teeple, 1906- 070.4'092'4 B
Roosevelt, Churchill, and the World War II opposition : a revisionist autobiography / George T. Eggleston. Old Greenwich, Conn. : Devin-Adair Co., c1979. xiii, 255 p., [8] leaves of plates : ill. ; 24 cm. Includes bibliographical references and index. [PN4874.E55A37] 79-1727 ISBN 0-8159-5311-9 : 12.95
1. Eggleston, George Teeple, 1906- 2. Journalists—United States—Biography. 3. World War, 1939-1945—Neutrality of the United States. I. Title.

Eggleston, Hazel.

EGGLESTON, Hazel. 972.9'843
St. Lucia diary : a Caribbean memoir / by Hazel Eggleston. Old Greenwich, Conn. : Devin-Adair Co., c1977. vii, 168 p. : ill. ; 21 cm. Includes index. [F2100.E43] 77-90853 ISBN 0-8159-6839-6 pbk. : 5.00
1. Eggleston, Hazel. 2. St. Lucia—Social life and customs. 3. St. Lucia—Description and travel. 4. St. Lucia—Biography. I. Title.

Egypt—Kings and rulers.

BUDGE, Ernest Alfred Thompson Wallis, Sir, 1857-1934. 962'.00992
The book of the kings of Egypt : or, The Ka, Nebti, Horus, Suten Bat, and Ra names of the pharaohs with transliterations from Menes, the first dynastic king of Egypt, to the emperor Decius, with chapters on the royal names, chronology, etc. / by E. A. Wallis Budge. New York : AMS Press, [1975] p. cm. Reprint of the 1908 ed. published by K. Paul, Trench, Trubner, London, which was issued as v. 23-24 of Books on Egypt and Chaldaea. Includes index. Contents.Contents.—v. 1. Dynasties I-XIX.—v. 2. Dynasties XX-XXX. Macedonians and Ptolemies. Roman emperors. Kings of Napata and Meroe. [DT83.B9 1975] 73-18837 ISBN 0-404-11309-5 : 34.50
1. Egypt—Kings and rulers. 2. Chronology, Egyptian. I. Title. II. Series: Books on Egypt and Chaldaea ; v. 23-24.

Egypt—Queens.

COTTRELL, Leonard. 913.2'03'10922
Five queens of ancient Egypt. [1st ed.] Indianapolis, Bobbs-Merrill Co. [1969] 181 p. illus., geneal. table, ports. 24 cm. First published in 1966 under title: Queens of the Pharaohs. Bibliography: p. 173-175. Portraits of five esteemed women of ancient Egypt — Hashepsowe, Tiye, Nefertiti, Ankhesnamun, Nefertari — describing as well their husbands and servants. [DT80.C6 1969] 920 69-12439 5.00
1. Egypt—Queens. 2. Egypt—Social life and customs. I. Title.

Ehrlich, Paul, 1854-1915.

MARQUARDT, Martha. 926.1
Paul Ehrlich; with an introd. by Sir Henry Dale. New York, Schuman [1951] xx, 255 p. illus., ports. 22 cm. [The Life of science library, 19] "An extention of [the author's] 'Paul Ehrlich als Mensch und Arbeiter.'" [R512.E4M3 1951] 51-9683
1. Ehrlich, Paul, 1854-1915.

Ehrmann, Max, 1872-1945.

EHRMANN, Bertha Pratt (King). 928.1
Max Ehrmann, a poet's life. Boston, Humphries [1951] 118 p. illus. 21 cm. [PS3509.H7Z7] 51-11422
1. Ehrmann, Max, 1872-1945. I. Title.

EHRMANN, Max, 1872-1945. 928.1
Journal; edited by Bertha K. Ehrmann. Boston, Bruce Humphries [1952] 344 p. 21 cm. [PS3509.H7Z52] 52-11555
I. Title.

Eichmann, Adolf, 1906-1962.

HULL, William Lovell, 1897- 923.543
The struggle for a soul. Garden City, N.Y., Doubleday [c.]1963. 175p. 22cm. 63-8740 3.50
1. Eichmann, Adolf, 1906-1962. I. Title.

HULL, William Lovell, 1897- 923.543
The struggle for a soul. [1st ed.] Garden City, N.Y., Doubleday, 1963. 175 p. 22 cm. [DD247.E5H8] 63-8740
1. Eichmann, Adolf, 1906-1962. I. Title.

Eide, Harald, 1896-

EIDE, Harald, 1896- 979.8'04'0924
The Alaska adventures of a Norwegian cheechako : or, Greenhorn with a gold pan / by Harald Eide. Anchorage : Alaska Northwest Pub. Co., [1975] p. cm. Autobiographical. [F909.E34] 75-23014 ISBN 0-88240-063-0
1. Eide, Harald, 1896- 2. Alaska—Gold discoveries. 3. Frontier and pioneer life—Alaska. I. Title. **BIP**

Eielson, Carl Benjamin, 1897-1929.

ROLFSRUD, Erling Nicolai, 1912- 926.2913
Brother to the eagle. [The story of Carl Ben Eielson] With a pref. by Sir Hubert Wilkins. Alexandria, Minn., Lantern Books [1952] 181 p. illus. 22 cm. [TL540.E45R6] 52-37341
1. Eielson, Carl Benjamin, 1897-1929. I. Title.

Eielson, Carl Benjamin, 1897-1929—Juvenile literature.

HERRON, Edward Albert, 1912- 926.2913
Wings over Alaska, the story of Carl Ben Eielson, born: July 10, 1897; died: November 9, 1929. New York, J. Messner [1959] 192p. 22cm. [TL540.E45H4] 59-7133
1. Eielson, Carl Benjamin, 1897-1929—Juvenile literature. I. Title.

Eighteenth century.

ELWIN, Whitwell, 1816-1900. 820.9'006
Some XVIII century men of letters; biographical essays by the Rev. Whitwell Elwin...with a memoir. Edited by his son Warwick Edwin. Port Washington, N.Y., Kennikat Press [1970] 2 v. illus., facsims., ports. 22 cm. Originally published in the Quarterly review, 1853-1860. Reprint of the 1902 ed. Contents.Contents.—v. 1. Memoir [by Warwick Elwin]. Cowper.—v. 2. Sterne. Fielding. Goldsmith. Boswell and Dr. Johnson. Gray. Includes bibliographical references. [PR443.E6 1970] 75-113333
1. Eighteenth century. 2. English literature—18th century—History and criticism. 3. Authors, English. I. Elwin, Warwick, 1849- ed. II. Title.

Eikins, Stephen Benton, 1841-1911.

LAMBERT, Oscar Doane, 1888- 923.273
Stephen Benton Elkins. Pittsburgh, University of Pittsburgh, 1955. 336p. illus., ports. 22cm. Bibliography: p. 329-336. Bibliographical footnotes. [E664.E39L3] 55-12052
1. Eikins, Stephen Benton, 1841-1911. I. Title.

Eils, John.

*HAGEE, John C. 266'.52'0924
Scandalous saint, by John C. Hagee. Introductions by Merlin R. Carothers and David Coote. Monroeville, Pa. Whitaker House [1974] 178 p. 18 cm. [BV2087] ISBN 0-88368-056-4 1.25 (pbk.)
1. Eils, John. 2. Missionaries. I. Title.

Eilshemius, Louis Michel, 1864-1941.

KARLSTROM, Paul J. 759.13 B
Louis Michel Eilshemius / by Paul J. Karstrom. New York : H. N. Abrams, [1978] p. cm. (Contemporary artists series) Includes index. Bibliography: p. [ND237.E45K37] 77-26777 ISBN 0-8109-0856-5 : 45.00
1. Eilshemius, Louis Michel, 1864-1941. 2. Painters—United States—Biography. I. Title.

Einstein, Albert, 1879-1955.

ALBERT Einstein; philosopher- scientist. [1st Harper torchbook ed.] New York, Harper [1959] 2v. (xii, 781p.) ports., diagrs. facsim. 21cm. (Harper torchbooks. TB 502-503 Science library) Contents.v. 1. Einstein's autobiography, in German, and in English translation. Descriptive and critical essays on the work of Albert Einstein, 1-12.-v.2. Descriptive and critical essays on the work of Albert Einstein, 13-25. Einstein's reply. Bibliography of the writings of Albert Einstein to May 1951, compiled by Margaret C. Shields (p. [689]-758) v. 12
1. Einstein, Albert, I. Schilpp, Paul Arthur, 1897- ed. II. Einstein, Albert, 1879-1955.

ALBERT Einstein's theory of general relativity / edited by Gerald E. Tauber. New York : Crown Publishers, c1979. p. cm. Includes bibliographical references and index. [QC173.6.A4 1979] 79-1471 ISBN 0-517-53661-7 : 12.95 530.1'1
1. Einstein, Albert, 1879-1955. 2. General relativity (Physics) 3. Physicists—Biography. I. Tauber, Gerald E. **BIP**

BERNSTEIN, Jeremy, 1924- 530'.092'4 B
Einstein. New York, Viking Press [1973] xii, 242 p. 20 cm. (Modern masters) "Most of the material ... appeared originally in the New Yorker." Bibliography: p. [231]-234. [QC16.E5B45] 72-76429 ISBN 0-670-29077-7 6.95
1. Einstein, Albert, 1879-1955.
Pbk. 1.95; ISBN 0-670-01959-3.

BERNSTEIN, Jeremy, 1924- 530'.092'4 B
Einstein / Jeremy Bernstein New York : Penguin Books, 1976, c1973. p. cm. (Penguin modern masters) Reprint of the ed. published by Viking Press, New York, in series Modern masters. "Most of the material ... appeared originally in the New Yorker." Includes index. Bibliography: p. [QC16.E5B45 1976] 76-22629 ISBN 0-14-004317-9 pbk. : 2.75
1. Einstein, Albert, 1879-1955.

CAHN, William, 1912- 925.3
Einstein, a pictorial biography. [1st ed.] New York, Citadel Press [1955] 126 p. illus. 26 cm. [QC16.E5C3] 55-11867
1. Einstein, Albert, 1879-1955.

CLARK, Ronald William. 530'.0924 B
Einstein: the life and times [by] Ronald W. Clark. New York, World Pub. Co. [1971] xv, 718 p. illus., ports. 24 cm. Bibliography: p. 633-648. [QC16.E5C5] 71-149419 15.00
1. Einstein, Albert, 1879-1955. I. Title.

CUNY, Hilaire. 530.0924
Albert Einstein; the man and his theories Translated by Mervyn Savill. [1st American ed.] New York, P. S. Eriksson [1965, c1962] 175 p. illus., ports. 24 cm. (A Profile in science) Bibliography: p. 169-171. [QC16.E5C83 1965] 65-15777
1. Einstein, Albert, 1879-1955. I. Title.

EINSTEIN / 530'.092'4 B
Louis de Broglie, Louis Armand, Pierre-Henri Simon et al. New York : Peebles Press : distributed in the United States by Ferrar, Straus & Giroux, 1979. 219 p. : ill. ; 24 cm. Translation of Einstein. [QC16.E5E3613] 78-55393 ISBN 0-85690-070-2 : 12.95
1. Einstein, Albert, 1879-1955. 2. Physicists—Biography. I. Broglie, Louis, Prince de, 1892- II. Armand, Louis, 1905- III. Simon, Pierre Henri, 1903-1972.
Contents omitted

EINSTEIN, Albert, 1879-1955. 530'.092'4 B
Albert Einstein, the human side : new glimpses from his archives / selected and edited by Helen Dukas and Banesh Hoffmann. Princeton, N.J. : Princeton University Press, c1979. viii, 167 p. : port. ; 21 cm. English or German. [QC16.E5A33] 78-70289 ISBN 0-691-08231-6 : 8.95
1. Einstein, Albert, 1879-1955. 2. Physicists—Biography. 3. Physicists—Correspondence. I. Dukas, Helen. II. Hoffmann, Banesh, 1906- III. Title. **BIP**

EINSTEIN, Albert, 1879-1955. 081
Out of my later years. Rev. reprint ed. Westport, Conn., Greenwood Press [1970, c1950] 282 p. illus. 23 cm. Essays. [QC16.E5A3 1970] 70-89016 ISBN 0-8371-2086-1
1. Einstein, Albert, 1879-1955. I. Title. **BIP**

FORSEE, Aylesa. 925.3
Albert Einstein: theoretical physicist. New York, Macmillan, 1963. xiii, 202 p. illus., ports., diagrs. 21 cm. "Selected bibliography": p. 196-198. [QC16.E5F6] 63-14538
1. Einstein, Albert, 1879-1955. I. Title.

FORSEE, Aylesa 925.3
Albert Einstein; theoretical physicist. New York, Macmillan [c.]1963. xiii, 202p. illus., ports., diagrs. 21cm. Bibl. 63-14538 4.95
1. Einstein, Albert, 1879-1955. I. Title.

FRANK, Philipp, 1884- v. 12
Einstein, his life and times; translated from a German ms. by George Rosen. Edited and rev. by Shuichi Kusaka; with a new introd. New York, Knopf, 1965 [c1953] xxvii, 298 p. illus. 25 cm. 67-88476
1. Einstein, Albert, 1879-1955. I. Title.

FRANK, Philipp, 1884- 925.3
Einstein, his life and times; translated from a German ms. by George Rosen. Edited and rev. by Shuichi Kusaka; with a new introd. New York, Knopf, 1953. 298p. illus. 25cm. [QC16.E5F7 1953] 53-5471
1. Einstein, Albert, 1879- I. Title.

HAMILTON, Peter Napier. 530.1'1
Albert Einstein, by Peter N. Hamilton. Valley Forge, Pa., Judson Press [1973] 59 p. 19 cm. (Makers of modern thought) Bibliography: p. 59. [QC6.H275] 72-7722 ISBN 0-8170-0595-1 1.50 (pbk.)
1. Einstein, Albert, 1879-1955. 2. Relativity (Physics) I. Title.

HOFFMANN, Banesh, 1906- 530'.092'4 B
Albert Einstein, creator and rebel [by] Banesh Hoffmann with the collaboration of Helen Dukas. New York, Viking Press [1972] xv, 272 p. illus. 25 cm. [QC16.E5H64 1972] 70-186740 ISBN 0-670-11181-3 8.95
1. Einstein, Albert, 1879-1955. I. Dukas, Helen, joint author. **BIP**

INFELD, Leopold, 1898-1968. 925.3
Albert Einstein, his work and its influence in the world. New York, Scribner, 1950. vi, 132 p. (Twentieth century library) Bibliography: p. 127. [QC16.E515] 50-5314
1. Einstein, Albert, 1879-

KUZNETSOV, Boris Grigorievich, 1903- 530'.092'4 B
Einstein [by] B. Kuznetsov. [Translated from the Russian by V. Talmy]. New York, Phaedra [1970] 377 p. illus., ports. 22 cm. Translation of Einshtein. Bibliography: p. [371] [QC16.E5K813 1970] 79-107915 3.95
1. Einstein, Albert, 1879-1955.

MICHELMORE, Peter 925.3
Einstein, profile of the man. New York, Didd [c.1962] 269p. 22cm. Bibl. 62-17989 3.75
1. Einstein, Albert, 1879-1955. I. Title.

MICHELMORE, Peter 925.3
Einstein, profile of the man. New York [Apollo Eds., 1963, c.1962] 269p. 20cm. (A63) 1.75 pap.,
1. Einstein, Albert, 1879-1955. I. Title.

MOSZKOWSKI, Alexander, 1851-1934. 530'.0924 B
Conversations with Einstein. Translated by Henry L. Brose. Introd. by Henry LeRoy Finch. New York, Horizon Press [1971, c1970] xxiii, 246 p. 22 cm. Translation of Einstein, Einblicke in seine Gedankenwelt. [QC6.M5913] 74-132324 ISBN 0-8180-0215-8 8.50
1. Einstein, Albert, 1879-1955. 2. Relativity (Physics) I. Title. **BIP**

OLDFIELD, Ruth L. 925.3
The true story of Albert Einstein; man of science. Chicago, Childrens Pr. [1964] 143 p. illus. 23cm. Bibl. [QC16.E5O4] 64-19880 lib. ed., list, 3.50; lib. ed., net, 2.63
1. Einstein, Albert, 1879-1955. I. Title.

SCHILPP, Paul Arthur, 1897- ed. 925.3
Albert Einstein: philosopher-scientist. [2d ed.] New York, Tudor Pub. Co. [1951] xvi, 781 p. ports., diagrs., facsim. 24 cm. (The Library of living philosophers) Contents.Contents.—Einstein's autobiography, in German, and in English translation.—Descriptive and critical essays on the work of Albert Einstein.—Einstein's reply.—Bibliography of the writings of Albert Einstein to May 1951, compiled by M. C. Shields (p. [689]-758) [QC16.E5S3 1951] 52-3833
1. Einstein, Albert, 1879-1955. I. Einstein, Albert, 1879-1955. II. Series.

VALLENTIN, Antonina, 1893-1957. 925.3
The drama of Albert Einstein. Translated by Moura Budberg. [1st American ed.] Garden City, N. Y., Doubleday, 1954. 312 p. illus. 22 cm. London ed. (Weidenfeld and Nicolson) has title: Einstein, a biography. [QC16.E5V314 1954a] 54-5715
1. Einstein, Albert, 1879-1955.

Einstein, Albert, 1879-1955—Juvenile fiction.

HAMMONTREE, Marie 920
Albert Einstein, young thinker. Illus. by Robert Doremus. Indianapolis, Bibbs [c.1961] 200p. col. illus. (Childhood of famous Americans) 60-14831 2.25
1. Einstein, Albert, 1879-1955—Juvenile fiction. I. Title.

Einstein, Albert, 1879-1955—Juvenile literature.

BECKHARD, Arthur J. 925.3
Albert Einstein. New York, Avon. [c.1959] 127p. 17cm. (Avon T-09: Bard 9) .35 pap.,
1. Einstein, Albert, 1879-1955—Juvenile literature. I. Title.

BECKHARD, Arthur J 925.3
Albert Einstein. Illustrated by Charles Beck. New York, Putnam [1959] 126p. illus. 21cm. (Lives to remember) [QC16.E5B4] 59-11414
1. Einstein, Albert, 1879-1955—Juvenile literature. I. Title.

PRINGLE, Patrick 92
The young Einstein, Illus. by Cecile Curtis. New York, Roy [1966, c.1965] 128p. illus. 21cm. [QC16.E5P7] 65-22983 3.25 bds.,
1. Einstein, Albert, 1879-1955—Juvenile literature. I. Title.

WISE, William. 925.3
Albert Einstein, citizen of the world Illustrated by Simon Jeruchim. [New York] Farrar, Straus & Cudahy [1960] 181 p. illus. 22 cm. (Covenant books, 10) [QC16.E5W5] 60-9078
1. Einstein, Albert, 1879-1955 — Juvenile literature. I. Title.

Eiseley, Loren C., 1907-

EISELEY, Loren C., 1907- 500.9'2'4 B
All the strange hours : the excavation of a life / by Loren Eiseley ; ill. by Emanuel Haller. New York : Scribner, [1975] 273 p. : ill. ; 24 cm. Autobiography. [QH31.E54A33] 75-22433 ISBN 0-684-14427-1 : 9.95
1. Eiseley, Loren C., 1907- I. Title.

Eisenhower, Dwight David, Pres. U.S., 1890-1969.

AMBROSE, Stephen E. 940.54 B
The Supreme Commander; the war years of General Dwight D. Eisenhower [by] Stephen E. Ambrose. [1st ed.] Garden City, N.Y., Doubleday, 1970. ix, 732 p. col. maps, port. 24 cm. Includes bibliographical references. [E836.A83] 77-111141 10.00
1. Eisenhower, Dwight David, Pres. U.S., 1890-1969. 2. World War, 1939-1945—Campaigns. I. Title.

ARCHER, Jules. 92
Battlefield President: Dwight D. Eisenhower. New York, J. Messner [1967] 191 p. 22 cm. Bibliography: p. [183]-186. Son of a devout pacifist, Eisenhower enters West Point despite his family and later becomes Supreme Commander of the Allied Forces in World War II, and eventually the thirty-fourth president of the United States. [E836.A85] AC 67
1. Eisenhower, Dwight David, Pres. U.S., 1890- I. Title.

ARMY Times, Washington, D.C. 973.9210924
The challenge and the triumph; the story of General Dwight D. Eisenhower, by the eds. of the Army times. New York, Putnam [c.1966] 192p. illus., ports. 27cm. Bibl. [E836.A87] 66-10462 6.95
1. Eisenhower, Dwight David, Pres. U.S 1890- I. Title.

BECKHARD, Arthur J. 973.921'0924 B
The story of Dwight D. Eisenhower. Illustrated by Charles Geer. New York, Grosset & Dunlap [1956] vii, 180 p. illus., ports. 22 cm. (Signature books, 38) A biography of "Ike" Eisenhower whose flamboyant life included positions as chief of staff to General Douglas MacArthur, Supreme Commander of the Allied Forces in Europe, President of Columbia University, and President of the United States. [PZ7.B38172St] 92 AC 68
1. Eisenhower, Dwight David, Pres. U.S., 1890- I. Geer, Charles, illus. II. Title.

BLUMENSON, Martin. 940.54
Eisenhower. [New York, Ballantine Books, 1972] 159, [1] p. illus. 21 cm. (Ballantine's illustrated history of the violent century. War leader book, no. 9) Bibliography: p. [160] [E836.B55] 72-183242 ISBN 0-345-02551-2 1.00
1. Eisenhower, Dwight David, Pres. U.S., 1890-1969. 2. World War, 1939-1945—Campaigns.

DAVIS, Kenneth Sydney, 1912- 923.573
Soldier of democracy; a biography of Dwight Eisenhower. [New ed.] Garden City, N. Y., Doubleday, 1952. 577 p. maps. 22 cm. [E745.E35D3 1952] 52-1785
1. Eisenhower, Dwight David, 1890- I. Title.

EISENHOWER, Dwight David, Pres. U.S. 1890 973.91'0924
At ease: stories I tell to friends [by] Dwight D. Eisenhower. [New York] Avon [1968, c. 1967] 384p. 18cm. (N185) Partly autobiographical. [E836.A3] (B) .95 pap.,
I. Title.

EISENHOWER, Dwight David Pres. U. S., 1890 973.91'0924 (B)
At ease: stories I Tell to friends [by] Dwight D. Eisenhower. [1st ed.] Garden City, N. Y., Doubleday, 1967. 400p. illus. 24cm. Partly autobiographical. [E836.A3] 67-13781 6.95
I. Title.

EISENHOWER, Dwight David, Pres. U.S., 1890- 973.921'0924 B
In review: pictures I've kept; a concise pictorial autobiography [by] Dwight D. Eisenhower. [1st ed.] Garden City, N.Y., Doubleday, 1969. 237 p. illus., ports. 27 cm. Cover title: Pictures I've kept. Selected and condensed by E. Corbin from the author's books: Crusade in Europe, The White House years, and At ease. [E836.A33] 68-57660 7.95
I. Corbin, Edwin. II. Title. III. Title: Pictures I've kept.

EISENHOWER, Dwight David, Pres. U.S., 1890-1969. 973.921'092'4 B
Ike, a great American. With an introd. by Mamie Doud Eisenhower. Selected by Don Ramsey. [Kansas City, Mo., Hallmark, 1972] 60 p. ports. 20 cm. (Hallmark Editions) [E836.A32] 74-114188 ISBN 0-87529-096-5 2.50

1. Eisenhower, Dwight David, Pres. U.S., 1890-1969. I. Title.

EISENHOWER, Dwight 940.54 B
David, Pres. U.S., 1890-1969.
Letters to Mamie / Dwight D. Eisenhower ; edited, and with commentary, by John S. D. Eisenhower. 1st ed. Garden City, N.Y. : Doubleday, 1978. 282 p. ; 22 cm. [E836.A44] 77-11247 ISBN 0-385-12931-9 : 8.95
1. Eisenhower, Dwight David, Pres. U.S., 1890-1960. 2. Eisenhower, Mamie Doud, 1896- 3. Generals—United States—Correspondence. I. Eisenhower, Mamie Doud, 1896- II. Eisenhower, John S. D., 1922- III. Title. **BIP**

FIELD, Rudolph. 923.573
Ike, man of the hour. New York, Universal, 1952. 142 p. illus. 18 cm. (Unibook, 40) [E745.E35F5] 52-2619
1. Eisenhower, Dwight David, 1890- I. Title.

FIELD, Rudolph. 923.573
Mister American; Dwight David Eisenhower, an evaluation. New York, R. Field Co. [1952] 132 p. illus. 21 cm. [E745.E35F52] 52-10786
1. Eisenhower, Dwight David, 1890- I. Title.

GUNTHER, John, 1901-1970. 923.573
Eisenhower, the man and the symbol. [1st ed.] New York, Harper [1952] 180 p. 22 cm. [E745.E35G8] 52-5442
1. Eisenhower, Dwight David, Pres., U.S., 1890-

HATCH, Alden, 1898- 923.573
General Ike, a biography of Dwight D. Eisenhower. Rev. and enl. ed. New York, Holt [1952] 320 p. illus. 22 cm. [E745.E35H3 1952] 52-7638
1. Eisenhower, Dwight David, 1890- I. Title.

HATCH, Alden, 1898- 923.173
Young Ike; illustrated by Jules Gotieb. New York, J. Messmer [1953] 146p. illus. 22cm. [E836.H3] 53-9070
1. Eisenhower, Dwight David, Pres. U. S., 1890- I. Title.

JOHNSON, George, 1917- 923.173
Eisenhower; the life and times of a great general, President and statesman. Derby, Conn., Monarch Books [1962] 159p. 18cm. (A Monarch books original biography, K64) [E836.J6] 62-52038
1. Eisenhower, Dwight David, Pres. U. S., 1890- I. Title.

LARSON, Arthur. 973.921'0924
Eisenhower: the President nobody knew. New York, Scribner [1968] xii, 210 p. illus., ports. 22 cm. [E836.L3] 68-27778 5.95
1. Eisenhower, Dwight David, Pres. U.S., 1890- I. Title.

LOVELACE, Delos Wheeler 923.573
1891-
"Ike" Eisenhower; statesman and soldier of peace. New York, Crowell [1952] 203 p. illus. 21 cm. First published in 1944 under title: General "Ike" Eisenhower. [E745.E35L6 1952] 52-8855
1. Eisenhower, Dwight David, 1800- I. Title.

LOVELACE, Delos Wheeler, 923.173
1894-
'Ike' Eisenhower, statesman and soldier of peace. New York, Crowell [1957] 279p. illus. 21cm. First published in 1944 under title: General 'Ike' Eisenhower. [E836.L6 1957] 57-8156
1. Eisenhower, Dwight David, Pres. U. S., 1890- I. Title.

LOVELACE, Delos Wheeler, 923.173
1894-
'Ike' Eisenhower, statesman and soldier of peace. Illustrated with photos. New York, Crowell [c1953] 279p. illus. 21cm. First published in 1944 under title: General 'Ike' Elsenhower. [E836.L6 1953] 53-10185
1. Elsenhower, Dwight David, Pres. U. S., 1890- I. Title.

LYON, Peter, 973.921'092'4 B
1915-
Eisenhower: portrait of the hero. [1st ed.] Boston, Little, Brown [1974] xii, 937 p. illus. 24 cm. Bibliography: p. 911-916. [E836.L96] 74-746 ISBN 0-316-54021-8 15.00
1. Eisenhower, Dwight David, Pres. U.S., 1890-1969. I. Title.

MCCANN, Kevin. 923.573
Man from Abilene. [1st ed.] Garden City, N.Y., Doubleday, 1952. 252 p. maps (on lining paper) 22 cm. [E745.E35M2] 52-6738
1. Eisenhower, Dwight David, Pres. U.S., 1890-1969. I. Title.

MORIN, Relman, 973.921'0924 B
1907-
Dwight D. Eisenhower; a gauge of greatness. New York, Simon and Schuster [1969] 256 p. illus., facsim., ports. (part col.) 29 cm. (An Associated Press biography) Bibliography: p. 252. [E836.M63] 67-20032 4.95
1. Eisenhower, Dwight David, Pres. U.S., 1890-1969. I. Title. II. Title: A gauge of greatness.

PINKLEY, Virgil. 973.921'092'4 B
Eisenhower declassified / Virgil Pinkley, with James F. Scheer. Old Tappan, N.J. : Revell, c1979. p. cm. Includes bibliographical references. [E836.P56] 79-20763 ISBN 0-8007-1063-0 : 12.95
1. Eisenhower, Dwight David, Pres., U.S., 1890-1969. 2. United States. Army—Biography. 3. Presidents—United States—Biography. 4. Generals—United States—Biography. I. Scheer, James F., joint author. II. Title. **BIP**

REEDER, Russell 973.921'0924 B
Potter.
Dwight David Eisenhower, fighter for peace, by Red Reeder. Illustrated by Cary. Champaign, Ill., Garrard Pub. Co. [1968] 159 p. illus., plans, ports. 24 cm. (Defenders of freedom) A biography of the World War II American general who became the thirty-fourth President of the United States. [E836.R42] 92 AC 68
1. Eisenhower, Dwight David, Pres. U.S., 1890- I. Cary, illus. II. Title.

RICHARDSON, Elmo R. 973.921
The Presidency of Dwight D. Eisenhower / by Elmo Richardson. Lawrence : Regents Press of Kansas, c1979. x, 218 p. ; 24 cm. (American Presidency series) Includes index. Bibliography: p. 203-211. [E835.R53] 78-17923 12.00
1. Eisenhower, Dwight David, Pres. U.S., 1890-1969. 2. United States—Politics and government—1953-1961. 3. Presidents—United States—Biography. I. Title. II. Series. **BIP**

RUSSELL, Don, 1899- 923.573
Invincible Ike; the inspiring life story of Dwight D. Eisenhower. Chicago, Successful Living Publications [1952] 127 p. illus. 19 cm. [E836.R8] 52-3325
1. Eisenhower, Dwight David, Pres. U. S., 1890- I. Title.

RUSSELL, Don, 1899- 923.573
Invincible Ike; the inspiring life story of Dwight D. Eisenhower. Chicago, Successful Living Publications [1952] 127 p. illus. 19 cm. [E836.R8] 52-3325
1. Eisenhower, Dwight David, Pres. U. S., 1890- I. Title.

RUSSELL, Donald Bert, 923.573
1899-
Invincible Ike; the inspiring life story of Dwight D. Eisenhower. Chicago, Successful Living Publications [1952] 127 p. illus. 19 cm. [E745.E35R88] 52-3325
1. Eisenhower, Dwight David, 1890- I. Title.

SHERMAN, Diane 973.921'0924 B
Finn.
Thc boy from Abilcnc; the story of Dwight D. Eisenhower, by Diane Sherman. Philadelphia, Westminster Press [1968] 159 p. illus., ports. 22 cm. Bibliography: p. 153. A biography of the World War II general who later became thirty-fourth President of the United States. [E836.S5] 92 AC 68
I. Title.

SMITH, A. Merriman, 1913- 923.173
Meet Mister Eisenhower. New York, Harper [1955] 308 p. illus. 22 cm. [E836.S55] 54-12199
1. Eisenhower, Dwight David, Pres. U.S., 1890-1969. I. Title.

SMITH, A Merriman, 1913- 923.173
A President's odyssey. [1st ed.] New York, Harper [1961] 272 p. 22 cm. [E835.S55] 61-6198
1. Eisenhower, Dwight David, Pres. U.S., 1890- 2. Visits of state. 3. U.S. — Relations (general) with foreign countries. I. Title. **BIP**

SNYDER, Marty, 1913- 923.173
My friend Ike, by Marty Snyder with Glenn D. Kittler. New York,F. Fell, 1956. 237 p. illus. 22 cm. [E836.S58] 56-7086
1. Eisenhower, Dwight David, Pres. U.S., 1890- I. Title.

SNYDER, Marty, 1913- 923.173
My friend Ike, by Marty Snyder with Glenn D. Kittler. New York, F. Fell, 1956. 237p. illus. 22cm. [E836.S58] 56-7086
1. Elsenhower. Dwight David, Pres. U. S., 1890- I. Title.

STEINBERG, Alfred, 973.921'0924 B
1917-
Dwight David Eisenhower. New York, Putnam [1968, c1967] 223 p. 21 cm. (Lives to remember) A biography of the man, born of a Kansas pacifist family, who became the Supreme Allied Commander in World War II and thirty-fourth President of the United States. [E836.S7] 92 AC 68
1. Eisenhower, Dwight David, Pres. U.S., 1890- I. Title.

WELCH, Robert Henry 923.173
Winborne, 1899-
The politican, by Robert Welch. [Belmont, Mass., Belmont Pub. Co., 1964] cxlviii, 300 p. 24 cm. Bibliography: p. [xxxix]-lxix. [E835.W43 1964] 64-8456
1. Eisenhower, Dwight David, Pres. U.S., 1890- 2. Subversive activities—United States. 3. United States—Foreign relations—Russia. 4. Russia—Foreign relations—United States. I. Title.

WHITNEY, David C. 973.921'0924 B
The picture life of Dwight D. Eisenhower, by David C. Whitney. Illustrated with photos. New York, F. Watts [1968] 56 p. illus., ports. 22 cm. A concise biography of the famous soldier who after a successful military career, became America's thirty-fourth President at the age of 62. [E863.W48] 92 AC 68
1. Eisenhower, Dwight David, Pres. U.S., 1890- I. Title.

Eisenhower, Dwight David, Pres. U.S., 1890-1969—Juvenile literature.

ALTMAN, Frances. 973.921'.0924 B
Dwight D. Eisehower; crusader for peace. Minneapolis, T. S. Denison [1970] 223 p. ports. 22 cm. (Men of achievement series) A biography of the athlete, soldier, and thirty fourth President — Dwight D. Eisenhower. [E836.A82] 92 77-85371
1. Eisenhower, Dwight David, Pres. U.S., 1890-1969—Juvenile literature. I. Title.

ARCHER, Jules. 973.921'0924 B
Battlefield President: Dwight D. Eisenhower. New York, J. Messner [1967] 191 p. 22 cm. Bibliography: p. [183]-186. [E836.A85] 67-3004
1. Eisenhower, Dwight David, Pres. U.S., 1890- Juvenile literature. I. Title.

BECKHARD, Arthur 973.921'0924 B
J.
The story of Dwight D. Eisenhower, by Arthur J. Beckhard. Illustrated by Charles Geer. Enid Lamonte Meadowcroft, supervising editor. New York, Grosset & Dunlap [1970] vii, 182 p. illus. 22 cm. (Signature books) A biography of a man whose careers included those of soldier, college president, and United States President. [E836.B42 1970] 92 76-108188 2.50
1. Eisenhower, Dwight David, Pres. U.S., 1890-1969—Juvenile literature. I. Geer, Charles, illus. II. Title.

FABER, Doris, 973.921'092'4 B
1924-
Dwight Eisenhower / Doris Faber. New York : Abelard-Schuman, c1977. 116 p. : ill. ; 21 cm. Includes index. Bibliography: p. 113. [E836.F32 1977] 76-44001 lib.bdg. : 6.95
1. Eisenhower, Dwight David, Pres. U.S., 1890-1969—Juvenile literature. 2. Presidents—United States—Biography—Juvenile literature. I. Title. **BIP**

HENDRIX, Sue. 973.921'092'4 B
Dwight D. Eisenhower. Illustrated by Harold Henriksen. Mankato, Minn., Creative Education [1974] p. cm. A biography of the commanding general of the Allied forces in Europe in World War II who became the thirty-fourth President of the United States. [E836.H37] 92 74-19176 ISBN 0-87191-409-3 4.95
1. Eisenhower, Dwight David, Pres. U.S., 1890-1969—Juvenile literature. I. Henriksen, Harold, illus. II. Title. **BIP**

HUDSON, Wilma J. 973.8 B
Dwight D. Eisenhower; young military leader, by Wilma J. Hudson. Illustrated by Robert Doremus. Indianapolis, Bobbs-Merrill [1970] 200 p. col. illus. 20 cm. (Childhood of famous Americans) A biography which concentrates on the Kansas youth of military leader and President, Dwight David Eisenhower. [E836.H82] 92 78-105942
1. Eisenhower, Dwight David, Pres. U.S., 1890-1969—Juvenile literature. I. Doremus, Robert, illus. II. Title. **BIP**

LOVELACE, Delos 973.921'0924 B
Wheeler, 1894-1967.
"Ike" Eisenhower, statesman and soldier of peace. [New rev. ed.] New York, Crowell [1969] 294 p. 21 cm. First ed., 1944, has title: General Ike Eisenhower. A biography of the Supreme Commander of the Allied Forces in World War II who became the thirty-fourth President of the United States. [E836.L6 1969] 92 75-94783 4.50
1. Eisenhower, Dwight David, Pres. U.S., 1890-1969—Juvenile literature. I. Title.

LOVELACE, Delos Wheeler, 920
1894-
'Ike' Eisenhower, statesman New York, Crowell [1962, c.1944-1961] 294p. illus. 21cm. 'Orig. pub. [in 1944] under title: General 'Ike' Eisenhower.' 62-3258 3.50
1. Eisendhower, Dwight David, Pres. U. S., 1890-Juvenile literature. I. Title.

MOOS, Malcolm Charles, 923.173
1916-
Dwight D. eisenhower, by Malcolm Moos. New York, Random House [1964] 175 p. illus., maps, ports. 22 cm. (Landmark books, 108) [E836.M6] 64-12019
1. Eisenhower, Dwight David, Pres. U.S., 1890-1969—Juvenile literature. I. Title.

REEDER, Russell Potter. 92 (J)
Dwight David Eisenhower, fighter for peace, by Red Reeder. Illustrated by Cary. Champaign, Ill., Garrard Pub. Co. [1968] 159 p. illus., plans, ports. 24 cm. ([Defenders of freedom]) Part of the illustrative matter is colored. [E836.R42] 68-14779
1. Eisenhower, Dwight David, Pres. U.S., 1890- —Juvenile literature.

SHERMAN, Diane Finn. 92
The boy from Abilene; the story of Dwight D. Eisenhower, by Diane Sherman. Philadelphia, Westminster 1968] 159p. illus., ports. 22cm. Bibl. [E836 S5] 68-25396 3.95
1. Eisenhower, Dwight David, Pres. U.S., 1890—Juvenile literature. I. Title.

THOMAS, Henry, 973.921'0924 B
1886-
Dwight D. Eisenhower: general, President. Illustrated by Steele Savage. New York, Putnam [1969] 63 p. illus. 24 cm. (An American hero biography) A biography of the Supreme Commander of the Allied Forces during World War II, the man who became the thirty-fourth President of the United States. [E836.T45] 92 73-77764 3.29
1. Eisenhower, Dwight David, Pres. U.S., 1890-1969—Juvenile literature. I. Savage, Steele, illus. II. Title.

Eisenhower, Dwight David, Pres. U.S., 1890-1969—Portraits, caricatures, etc.

HICKS, Wilson. ed. 923.573
This is Ike; the picture story of the man. Text by Gardner Soule, picture research by Helen Fays. [1st ed.] New York, Holt [1952] unpaged. illus. 29 cm. (A Holt picture-book) [E745.E35H5] 52-9921

1. Eisenhower, Dwight David, 1890- Portraits, caricatures, etc. I. Soule, Gardner. II. Title.

IKE, a pictorial 973.921'0924 B *biography.* Text by William F. Longgood. Picture editor: Simone Daro Gossner. New York, Time-Life Books [1969] 144 p. illus., facsims, plans, ports. 28 cm. [E836.I37] 68-54473 1.50
1. Eisenhower, Dwight David, Pres. U.S., 1890-1969—Portraits, caricatures, etc. I. Longgood, William Frank, 1917- II. Time-Life Books.

NATIONAL Cartoonists 923.173 Society.
President Eisenhower's cartoon book, by 95 of America's leading cartoonists, members of the National Cartoonists Society. Foreword by George M. Humphrey. New York, Published in conjunction with United States savings bonds program by F. Fell, 1956. unpaged. illus. 24 cm. [E836.N35] 56-10366
1. Eisenhower, Dwight David, Pres. U.S., 1890-1969—Portraits, caricatures, etc. I. Title.

Eisenhower family.

KORNITZER, Bela. 929.2
The great American heritage; the story of the five Eisenhower brothers. New York, Farrar, Straus and Cudahy [1955] 331 p. illus. 23 cm. [E837.A2K6] 55-8756
1. Eisenhower family. I. Title.

NEAL, Steve, 973.921'092'2 B 1949-
The Eisenhowers : reluctant dynasty / Steve Neal. 1st ed. Garden City, N.Y. : Doubleday, 1978. x, 493 p. ; 22 cm. Includes index. Bibliography: p. [471]-474. [E837.E4N42] 77-80904 ISBN 0-385-12447-3 : 10.95
1. Eisenhower family. I. Title. BIP

Eisenhower, Mamie Doud, 1896-

BRANDON, Dorothy Barrett, 920.7 1899-
Mamie Doud Eisenhower; a portrait of a First Lady. New York, Scribner, 1954. 307 p. illus. 22 cm. [E837.B7] 54-6298
1. Eisenhower, Mamie Doud, 1896-

HATCH, Alden, 1898- 920.7
Red carpet for Mamie. Illus. by Allene Gaty. [1st ed.] New York, Holt [1954] 277p. illus. 22cm. [E837.E4H3] 54-927
1. Eisenhower, Mamie (Dou 1896- I. Title.

SCHAAF, James 973.921'092'4 B Edward.
Mamie Doud Eisenhower and her chicken farmer cousin. [Whitehouse Station, N.J., Printed by Wilkie Print., 1974] 75 p. illus. 24 cm. [E837.E4S32] 74-157039
1. Eisenhower, Mamie (Doud) 1896- 2. Schaaf, James Edward. 3. Doud family. 4. Schaaf family. I. Title.

Eisenhower, Milton Stover, 1899-

EISENHOWER, Milton 973.9'092'4 B Stover, 1899-
The President is calling [by] Milton S. Eisenhower. [1st ed.] Garden City, N.Y., Doubleday, 1974. xxiii, 598 p. 24 cm. Bibliography: p. 575-578. [E748.E3A36] 73-9154 ISBN 0-385-01584-4 12.50
1. Eisenhower, Milton Stover, 1899- 2. United States—Politics and government—20th century. 3. Presidents—United States. I. Title.

Eisenstein, Sergei Mikhailovich, 1898-1948.

BARNA, Ion. 791.43'0233'0924 B
Eisenstein, by Yon Barna. With a foreword by Jay Leyda. Bloomington, Indiana University Press [1973] 287 p. illus. 23 cm. (Cinema two) Translation of Serghei Eisenstein. Includes bibliographical references. [PN1998.A3E53413] 73-81159 ISBN 0-253-12135-3 10.00
1. Eisenstein, Sergei Mikhailovich, 1898-1948. I. Title.

BARNA, Ion. 791.43'0233'0924 B
Eisenstein / by Yon Barna ; with a foreword by Jay Leyda ; [translated by Lise Hunter]. Boston : Little, Brown, [1975] c1973. 287 p. : ill. ; 22 cm. Translation of Serghei Eisenstein. Reprint of the ed. published by Indiana University Press, Bloomington. Includes index. Bibliography: p. 279-281. [PN1998.A3E53413 1975] 75-11632 ISBN 0-316-08130-2 pbk : 3.95
1. Eisenstein, Sergei Mikhailovich, 1898-1948. BIP

MONTAGU, Ivor 791.43'0233'0924 Goldsmid Samuel, Hon., 1904-
With Eisenstein in Hollywood; a chapter of autobiography by Ivor Montagu, including the scenarios of Sutter's Gold and American tragedy. New York, International Publishers [1969, c1967] 356 p. illus., ports. 19 cm. (New world paperbacks NW-S-4) Bibliography: p. 350-352. [PN1998.A3E558 1969] 77-3547 1.95
1. Eisenstein, Sergei Mikhailovich, 1898-1948. I. Title. II. Title: Sutter's gold. III. Title: American tragedy.

MOUSSINAC, 791.43'0233'0924 Leon, 1890-1964.
Sergei Eisenstein. Translated by D. Sandy Petrey. New York, Crown Publisers [1970] 226 p. illus., ports. 17 cm. (Editions Seghers' Cinema d'aujourd'hiu in English) Translation of Serge Eisenstein. Bibliography: p. 218-223. [PN1998.A3E5613] 75-93412 2.95
1. Eisenstein, Sergei Mikhailovich, 1898-1948. BIP

SETON, Marie. 927.914
Sergei M. Eisenstein a biography. New York Grove Press [1960] 533 p. illus. 21 cm. (Evergreen E-251) [PN1998.A3E57 1960] 60-11107
1. Eisenstein, Sergei Mikhailovich, 1898-1948. II. Title.

SWALLOW, Norman. 791.43'0233'0924
Eisenstein : a documentary portrait / Norman Swallow. 1st ed. New York : Dutton, 1977, c1976. 155 p. : ill. ; 21 cm. "A Dutton paperback." Filmography: p. [146]-149. [PN1998.A3E593 1977] 76-44663 ISBN 0-525-47443-9 pbk. : 3.50
1. Eisenstein, Sergei Mikhailovich, 1898-1948. 2. Moving-picture producers and directors—Russia—Biography. BIP

Eisler, Charles

EISLER, Charles 926.213
The million-dollar bend; the autobiography of the benefactor of the radio tube and lamp industry. New York, William-Frederick Press, [c.]1960. 306p. diagrs., illus. 23cm. 60-11909 4.75
I. Title

Eland, G., ed.

WOTTON, Thomas, 1521- 923.242 1587.
Thomas Wotton's letter-book, 1574-1586. Ed. by G. Eland. New York, Oxford Univ. Press, [c.]1960[ ] xxi, 75p. illus. Bibl. 60-52119 2.60
1. Eland, G., ed. I. Title.

Elder, Lee, 1934- —Juvenile literature.

JACOBS, Linda. 796.352'092'4 B
Lee Elder : the daring dream / by Linda Jacobs ; photos. by Jeffrey Blackman. St. Paul, Minn. : EMC Corp., 1976. 39 p. : ill. ; 23 cm. (Black American athletes) A brief biography of the professional golfer who was the first black to gain an invitation to the Masters Tournament in 1975. [GV964.E42J32] 92 75-45429 ISBN 0-88436-267-1 lib.bdg. : 4.95 ISBN 0-88436-268-X pbk. :
1. Elder, Lee, 1934- —Juvenile literature. 2. Golf—Juvenile literature. I. Blackman, Jeffrey. II. Title. III. Series. BIP

Elder, Shirley

ELDER, Shirley. 791.43'092'4
Not this time Cary Grant! and other stories about Hollywood [by] Shirley Eder. New York Bantam Books. [1974, c1973] 277 p. illus. 18 cm. [PN1998.A2E3] 1.50 (pbk.)
1. Elder, Shirley 2. Moving-picture actors and actresses—Biography. I. Title.

Eldridge, Elleanor, b. 1785.

[MCDOUGALL, 917.3'06'96073 Frances Harriet (Whipple) Greene, 1805-1878]
Memoirs of Elleanor Eldridge. 2d ed. Freeport, N.Y., Books for Libraries Press, 1971. 127 p. port. 23 cm. (The Black heritage library collection) Reprint of the 1843 ed. [E185.97.E377] 70-149866 ISBN 0-8369-8748-9
1. Eldridge, Elleanor, b. 1785. I. Title. II. Series. BIP

Eldridge family.

THE Captain's 974.4'94'040922 *daughters of Martha's Vineyard* / as recalled by the Eldridge sisters—Nina, Mary, Ruth, Gratia ; edited by Eliot Eldridge Macy. Old Greenwich, Conn. : Chatham Press : distributed by the Devin-Adair Co., c1978. xii, 163 p., [6] leaves of plates : ill. ; 22 cm. [F72.M5C35] 78-62650 ISBN 0-85699-141-4 : 10.00.
1. Eldridge family. 2. Martha's Vineyard, Mass.—Biography. 3. Martha's Vineyard, Mass.—Social life and customs. I. Eldridge, Nina, 1878-1960. II. Macy, Eliot Eldridge. BIP

Eleanor of Aquitaine, consort of Henry II, 1122?-1204.

ELEANOR of Aquitaine and v. 12 *the four kings.* Cambridge, Harvard University Press, 1959 [c1950] 427p. illus. Includes bibliography.
1. Eleanor, of Aquitaine, consort of Henry II, 1122?-1204. 2. Gt. Brit.—Hist.—Plantagenets, 1154-1399. I. Kelley, Amy Ruth, 1878-

ELEANOR of 942.03'1'0924 *Aquitaine, patron or politician* / edited by William W. Kibler. Austin : University of Texas Press, [1975] p. cm. (Symposia in the arts and the humanities ; no. 3) Rev. versions of papers presented at a symposium held at the University of Texas at Austin, Apr. 23-25, 1973. Includes index. [DA209.E6E43] 75-16080 ISBN 0-292-72014-9 : 12.95
1. Eleanor, of Aquitaine, Consort of Henry II, 1122?-1204—Congresses. 2. England—Intellectual life—Medieval period, 1066-1485—Congresses. 3. France—Intellectual life—Congresses. I. Kibler, W. W. II. Title. III. Series.

KELLY, Amy Ruth, 1878- 923.142
Eleanor of Aquitaine and the four kings. [1st Vintage ed.] New York, Vintage Books, 1957 [c1950] 521p. illus. 19cm. (A Vintage book, K50) [DA209.E6] 57-4021
1. Eleanor of Aquitaine, consort of Henry II, 1122?-1204. 2. Gt. Brit.—Hist. —Plantagenets, 1154-1399. I. Title.

KELLY, Amy Ruth, 1878- 923.142
Eleanor of Aquitaine and the four kings. Cambridge, Harvard University Press, 1950. xii, 431 p. illus., map (on lining papers) 24 cm. Bibliography: p. [407]-417. [DA209.E6K45 1950] 50-6545
1. Eleanor, of Aquitaine, consort of Henry II, 1122?-1204. 2. Great Britain—History—Plantagenets, 1154-1399. BIP

MEADE, Marion, 942.03'1'0924 B 1934-
Eleanor of Aquitaine : a biography / Marion Meade. New York : Hawthorn Books, c1977. xii, 389 p., [5] leaves of plates : ill. ; 25 cm. Includes index. Bibliography: p. 375-382. [DA209.E6M4 1977] 76-15418 ISBN 0-8015-2231-5 : 12.95
1. Eleanor, of Aquitaine, consort of Henry II, 1122?-1204. 2. Great Britain—Queens—Biography. 3. France—Queens—Biography. BIP

PERNOUD, Regine, 942.03'1'0924 B 1909-
Eleanor of Aquitaine. Translated by Peter Wiles. [1st American ed.] New York, Coward-McCann [1968, c1967] 286 p. illus., maps. 22 cm. Bibliography: p. 271-273. [DA209.E6P4 1968] 68-14734
1. Eleanor of Aquitaine, consort of Henry II, 1122?-1204.

SEWARD, Desmond, 942.03'1'0924' B 1935-
Eleanor of Aquitaine / Desmond Seward. New York : Times Books, c1979. 264 p. : ill. ; 22 cm. Includes index. Bibliography: p. 257-260. [DA209.E6S45 1979] 78-19611 ISBN 0-8129-0749 3 : 10.00
1. Eleanor of Aquitaine, Consort of Henry II, 1122?-1204. 2. Great Britain—Kings and rulers—Biography.

WALKER, Curtis Howe. 923.142
Eleanor of Aquitaine; illustrated by M. S. Nowicki. [Chapel Hill] University of North Carolina Press [1950] xiv, 274 p. illus., map (on lining papers) 25 cm. "Explanatory notes and source references": p. [239]-263. [DA209.E6W3] 50-7097
1. Eleanor, of Aquitaine, consort of Henry II, 1122?-1204.

WALKER, Curtis Howe. 942.031[B]
Eleanor of Aquitaine. Illus. by M. S. Nowicki. New York, Lancer Books [1973? c.1950] 274 p. illus. 18 cm. "Explanatory notes and source references": p. 241-263. [DA209.E6W3] pap., 1.25
1. Eleanor, of Auquitaine, Consort of Henry II, 1122?-1204. I. Title.
L.C. card no. for original ed.: 50-7097.

Eleazer, James M.,

ELEAZER, James M., 630.11'24 B 1895-
50 years along the roadside, by J. M. Eleazer. Illustrated by Corrie McCallum. [1st ed.] Anderson, S.C., Independent Pub. Co. [1968] 192 p. illus. 24 cm. Autobiographical. [CT275.E38425A32] 68-28777
I. Title.

Electricians.

DUNSHEATH, Percy, 1886- 537'.0922
Giants of electricity. New York, Crowell [1967] xii, 200 p. illus., ports. 23 cm. [QC514.D8] 67-6584
1. Electricians. I. Title.

DUNSHEATH, Percy, 1886- 920
Giants of electricity. New York, Crowell [1967] xii, 200 p. illus., ports. 23 cm. Biographical portraits of eighteenth and nineteenth century scientists who pioneered in the field of electricity. [QC514.D8] AC 67
1. Electricians. 2. Electricity. I. Title.

Electricity—Biography.

APPLEYARD, Rollo, 621.382'0922 1867-1943.
Pioneers of electrical communication. Freeport, N.Y. Books for Libraries Press [1968] ix, 347 p. illus., facsims., ports. 22 cm. (Essay index reprint series) Reprint of the 1930 ed. Contents.Contents.—James Clerk Maxwell.—Andre Marie Ampere.—Alessandro Volta.—Charles Wheatstone.—Heinrich Rudolf Hertz.—Hans Christian Oersted.—Georg Simon Ohm.—Oliver Heaviside.—Claude Chappe.—Francis Ronalds. [QC514.A6 1968] 68-54322
1. Electricity—Biography. I. Title. BIP

Electronic data processing-Biog.

WHO'S who in computer 926.5 *field, 63'/64'.* a biographical dictionary of leading people who build or use computers. Newtonville, Mass., Computers and Automation, Berkeley Enterprises, 815 Washington St. [1964, c.1963] 253p. 29cm. 64-4523 24.95
1. Electronic data processing-Biog. 2. Automation—Biog. 3. Electronics—Biog.

Electronics—Biography.

MCGRAW-HILL'S 621.381'092'2 B *leaders in electronics* / Electronics magazine. New York : McGraw-Hill, c1979. xvi, 6541 p. ; 29 cm. [TK7806.M3] 79-111719 ISBN 0-07-019149-2 : 39.50

1. Electronics—Biography. 2. Electronic industries—Biography. I. McGraw-Hill Book Company. II. Electronics. III. Title: Leaders in electronics.

Elelson, Carl Benjamin, 1897-1929-Juvenile literature.

CHANDLER, Edna Walker. 926.2913
Pioneer of Alaska skies; the story of Ben Eielson [by] Edna Walker Chandler [and] Barrett Willoughby. Illustrated by Ray Quigley. [Boston] Ginn [1959] 179p. illus. 22cm. [TL540.E45C47] 59-16431
1. Elelson, Carl Benjamin, 1897-1929-Juvenile literature. I. Wiloughby, Florance (Barrett) joint author. II. Title.

Elephants.

WILLIAMS, James Howard, 636.9 1897-1958.
Elephant Bill. [1st American ed.] Garden City, N. Y., Doubleday [1950] 250 p. illus., ports., map (on lining papers) 22 cm. Autobiographical. [SF401.E3W5 1950a] 50-8421
1. Elephants.

Elgar, Edward William, Sir, 1857-1934.

MCVEAGH, Diana M., 780'.92'4 1926-
Edward Elgar, his life and music / by Diana M. McVeagh. Westport, Conn. : Hyperion Press, 1979. ix, 260 p., [8] leaves of plates : ill. ; 22 cm. (Encore music editions) Reprint of the 1955 ed. published by Dent, London. Includes index. "Catalogue of works": p. 220-245. [ML410.E41M16 1979] 78-62332 ISBN 0-88355-750-9 : 23.50
1. Elgar, Edward William, Sir, 1857-1934. 2. Composers—England—Biography. I. Title. BIP

MASON, Daniel 780'.92'2 B Gregory, 1873-1953.
Contemporary composers. New York, Macmillan Co., 1918. [New York, AMS Press, 1973] xi, 290 p. illus. 19 cm. Contents.Contents.—Introduction: Democracy and music.—Richard Strauss.—Sir Edward Elgar.—Claude Debussy.—Vincent d'Indy.—Music in America. [ML390.M383 1973] 72-1726 ISBN 0-404-08327-7 13.00
1. Strauss, Richard, 1864-1949. 2. Elgar, Edward William, Sir, 1857-1934. 3. Debussy, Claude, 1862-1918. 4. Indy, Vincent d', 1851-1931. 5. Music—History and criticism—19th century. I. Title. BIP

NEWMAN, Ernest, 1868- 780'.92'4 1959.
Elgar / by Ernest Newman. New York : AMS Press, 1976. 188 p. : ill. ; 18 cm. Reprint of the 1922 ed. published by J. Lane, London, in series: The Music of the masters. "List of Elgar's published works": p. 186-188. [MT92.E4N5 1976] 74-24163 ISBN 0-404-13058-5 : 12.50
1. Elgar, Edward William, Sir, 1857-1934. Works. I. Series: The Music of the masters. BIP

PORTE, John Fielder. 780'.924 B
Sir Edward Elgar. Freeport, N.Y., Books for Libraries Press [1970] viii, 214 p. port., music. 23 cm. "Analytical and descriptive notes on Elgar's works, from opus 1 to the last, including those without opus number." "First published 1921." [MT92.E4P6 1970b] 75-107827
1. Elgar, Edward William, Sir, 1857-1934. Works.

PORTE, John Fielder. 780.924
Sir Edward Elgar, by J. F. Porte. With a portrait of Sir Edward Elgar and musical illus. in the text. Port Washington, N.Y., Kennikat Press [1970] 214 p. music, port. 22 cm. "First published in 1921." "Contemporary books on Elgar": p. 207-208. [MT92.E4P6 1970] 70-102843
1. Elgar, Edward William, Sir, 1857-1934. Works. BIP

REED, William Henry, 780'.92'4 B 1877-1942.
Elgar. St. Clair Shores, Mich., Scholarly Press [1972] p. Reprint of the 1943 ed., issued in series: The Master musicians. Bibliography: p. [ML410.E41R3 1972] 71-181234 ISBN 0-403-01656-8
1. Elgar, Edward William, Sir, 1857-1934. I. Series: The Master musicians. BIP

YOUNG, Percy 780'.92'4 B Marshall, 1912-
Elgar, O. M.: a study of a musician, by Percy M. Young. [Revised ed.] London, New York, White Lion Publishers, 1973. 447 p., 19 p. of plates. illus., facsims., music, ports. 21 cm. Includes index. Bibliography: p. 426-428. [ML410.E41Y7 1973] 74-177430 ISBN 0-85617-333-9 £4.00
1. Elgar, Edward William, Sir, 1857-1934.

Elgar, Sir Edward William, 1857-1934.

KENNEDY, Michael. 780'.924 (B)
Portrait of Elgar. London, New York [etc.] Oxford U. P., 1968. xi, 324 p. 15 plates, illus., facsims., music, ports. 23 cm. 50/- (B 68-09532) Bibliography: p. 299-301. [ML410.E41K5] 68-101411
1. Elgar, Sir Edward William, 1857-1934. I. Title.

Elgin, James Bruce, 8th Earl of, 1811-1863.

MORISON, John Lyle, 909'.09'71242 1875-1952.
The eighth Earl of Elgin; a chapter in nineteenth-century imperial history. Westport, Conn., Greenwood Press [1970] 317 p. illus., ports. 23 cm. Reprint of the 1928 ed. [DA17.E4M6 1970] 73-109798 ISBN 0-8371-4289-X
1. Elgin, James Bruce, 8th Earl of, 1811-1863. 2. Great Britain—Colonies—Administration. 3. Canada—Politics and government—1841-1867. 4. China—History—Foreign intervention, 1857-1861. I. Title.

Elgin, Robert, 1921-

ELGIN, Robert 636.08'899'0924 1921-
The tiger is my brother / by Robert Elgin. New York : W. Morrow, 1980. p. cm. [QL31.E49A34] 79-25876 ISBN 0-688-03575-2 pbk. : 10.95
1. Elgin, Robert, 1921- 2. Des Moines Children's Zoo. 3. Zoologists—United States—Biography. I. Title. BIP

Eliade, Mircea, 1907-

ELIADE, Mircea, 291'.092'4 B 1907-
No souvenirs : journal, 1957-1969 / Mircea Eliade ; translated from the French by Fred H. Johnson, Jr. 1st ed. New York : Harper & Row, c1977. xiv, 343 p. ; 22 cm. Includes index. [BL43.E4A34 1977] 76-9969 ISBN 0-06-062141-9 : 15.00
1. Eliade, Mircea, 1907- 2. Religion historians—United States—Biography. I. Title. BIP

Elias, Esther.

ELIAS, Esther. 636.7'3
Profile of Glindy, a Welsh corgi / by Esther Elias. North Quincy, Mass. : Christopher Pub. House, c1976. 128 p. : ill. ; 27 cm. [SF429.W35E44] 76-4265 ISBN 0-8158-0337-0 : 6.95
1. Elias, Esther. 2. Welsh corgis—Legends and stories. I. Title.

Elijah Muhammad, 1897-

CUSHMEER, Bernard. 297'.87'0924 B
This is the one: Messenger Elijah Muhammad, we need not look for another. [Phoenix, Truth Publications, 1971] 160 p. col. port. 23 cm. [BP223.Z8E43] 76-24532 3.95
1. Elijah Muhammad, 1897- I. Title.

*MCNEIL, Mayo. 297.870'.92
Elijah Muhammad the false prophet. [Denver] [1973] 53 p. 14 cm. [BP223.Z8]
1. Black Mulism—Biography. 2. Black Mulism—History and criticism. I. Title. Available from author: Box 7212, Denver, Colorado 80207

Elijah, the prophet.

FRASER, Gordon Holmes. 221.92
Elijah, the pilgrim prophet; a study of the life and ministry of Elijah the Tishbite. Chicago, Moody Press [1956] 126p. 20cm. [BS580.E4F7] 56-4538
1. Elijah, the prophet. I. Title.

THE life of Elijah. v. 12
Grand Rapids, Mich., Zondervan Pub. House [1956] 314p.
1. Elijah, the prophet. I. Pink, Arthur Walkington, 1886-1952. BIP

MACDUFF, John Ross, 1818- 221.92 1895.
Elijah, the prophet of fire. Grand Rapids, Baker Book House, 1956. 351p. illus. 21cm. [BS580.E4M2 1956] 56-7579
1. Elijah, the prophet. I. Title.

MUTH, Don. 221.92
Elijah, the man who went to heaven. Illus. by author. Mountain View, Calif., Pacific Press Pub. Association, c1954. 1 v. (unpaged) illus. 29 cm. [BS580.E4M8] 55-16782
1. Elijah, the prophet.

WOOD, Leon James. 221.92'4
Elijah, prophet of God, by Leon J. Wood. Des Plaines, Ill., Regular Baptist Pr. [1968] 160p. 22cm. [BS580.E4W6] 67-25970 2.95
1. Elijah, the prophet. I. Title.

Elijah, the prophet—Juvenile literature.

ENTZ, Angeline J. 222'.5'0924 B
Elijah, brave prophet / Angeline J. Entz ; illustrated by H. Don Fields. Nashville : Broadman Press, c1978. 47 p. : col. ill. ; 24 cm. (Biblearn series) Relates the persistent efforts of the prophet Elijah to convert the people of Israel from idol worship to the worship of one true God. [BS580.E4E57] 78-105202 ISBN 0-8054-4244-8 : 3.95
1. Elijah, the prophet—Juvenile literature. 2. Bible. O.T.—Biography—Juvenile literature. I. Fields, H. Don. II. Title.

KOLBREK, Loyal. 222'.53'09505
The day God made it rain : I Kings 17-18 for children / written by Loyal Kolbrek ; illustrated by Herb Halpern Productions. St. Louis : Concordia Publishing House, c1976. p. cm. (Arch books, series 14) Relates in rhyme the story of Elijah and how his faith in God was vindicated. [BS580.E4K63] 76-26574 ISBN 0-570-06108-3 : 0.59
1. Elijah, the prophet—Juvenile literature. 2. Bible. O.T.—Biography—Juvenile literature. I. Herb Halpern Productions. II. Title.

Elington. Duke. 1899-

LAMBERT, George Edmund. 927.8
Duke Ellington. New York, Barnes [1961, c1959] 88p. illus. 2cm. (Kings of jazz) A Perpetual book, P--4029. [ML410.E44L3 1961] 60-16819
1. Elington. Duke. 1899- 2. Jazz music. I. Title. BIP

Eliot, Charles, 1859-1897.

[ELIOT, Charles 712'.0924 B William] 1834-1926.
Charles Eliot, landscape architect; a lover of nature and of his kind, who trained himself for a new profession, practised it happily and through it wrought much good. Freeport, N.Y., Books for Libraries Press [1971] xxiv, 770 p. illus., maps (part fold.), plans (part fold.), ports. 23 cm. Reprint of the 1902 ed. [SB470.E6E6 1971] 72-160971 ISBN 0-8369-5839-X
1. Eliot, Charles, 1859-1897. 2. Landscape architecture. I. Title.

Eliot, Charles William, 1834-1926.

JAMES, Henry, 378.1'12'0924 B 1879-1947.
Charles W. Eliot, president of Harvard University, 1869-1909. Boston, Houghton Mifflin, 1930. [New York, AMS Press, 1973] 2 v. illus. 23 cm. Bibliography: v. 2, p. [361]-363. [LD2148 1869.J32] 75-153331 ISBN 0-404-03545-0 18.00 (per vol.)
1. Eliot, Charles William, 1834-1926. 2. Harvard University.
Two vol. set 35.00. BIP

Eliot, George, pseud., i.e. Marian Evans afterwards Cross, 1819-1880.

BENNETT, Joan [Frankau] v. 12
George Eliot, her mind and her art. Cambridge [Eng.] University Press, 1962. 202 p. 21 cm. [NUC63-5999]
1. Eliot, George, pseud., i.e. Marian Evans afterwards Cross, 1819-1880. I. Title. BIP

BLIND, Mathilde, 1841- 823'.8 B 1896.
George Eliot. [Folcroft, Pa.] Folcroft Library Editions, 1973 [c1883] p. Reprint of the 1903 ed. published by Little, Brown, Boston, which was issued in series: Famous women. Bibliography: p. [PR4681.B5 1973] 73-10496 10.75
1. Eliot, George, pseud., i.e. Marian Evans, afterwards Cross, 1819-1880.

BULLETT, Gerald William, 823'.8 B 1894-1958.
George Eliot, her life and books. Westport, Conn., Greenwood Press [1971, c1948] 273 p. ports. 23 cm. [PR4681.B8 1971] 76-156178 ISBN 0-8371-6121-5
1. Eliot, George, pseud., i.e. Marian Evans, afterwards Cross, 1819-1880.

COOKE, George Willis, 823'.8 1848-1923.
George Eliot: a critical study of her life, writings, and philosophy. [Folcroft, Pa.] Folcroft Library Editions, 1973. p. Reprint of 1883 ed. published by J. R. Osgood, Boston. Bibliography: [PR4681.C6 1973] 73-11158 ISBN 0-8414-3376-3 (lib. bdg.)
1. Eliot, George, pseud., i.e. Marian Evans, afterwards Cross, 1819-1880.

ELIOT, George, pseud., 823'.8 i.e. Marian Evans, afterwards Cross, 1819-1880.
George Eliot's life as related in her letters and journals. Arranged and edited by her husband J. W. Cross. New ed. New York, AMS Press [1970] xi, 646 p. illus. 23 cm. Reprint of the 1885 ed. [PR4681.A3C7 1970] 78-111475 ISBN 0-404-01866-1
I. Cross, John Walter, ed. II. Title. BIP

ELIOT, George, pseud., 823'.8 B i.e. Marian Evans, afterwards Cross, 1819-1880.
George Eliot's life as related in her letters and journals. Arr. and edited by J. W. Cross. Boston, D. Estes [1901?] Grosse Pointe, Mich., Scholarly Press, 1968. 3 v. illus., ports. 21 cm. (The Works of George Eliot, v. 1-3) [PR4681.A3C7 1968] 79-3987
I. Cross, John Walter, 1840-1924, ed.

ELIOT, George, pseud., i. 928.2 e. Marian Evans, afterwards Cross, 1819-1880.
The George Eliot letters, edited by Gordon S. Haight. New Haven, Yale University Press, 1954-55. 7v. 25cm. [PR4681.A3H3] 52-12063
I. Haight, Gordon Sherman, ed. II. Title.

FREMANTLE, Anne 823'.8 B (Jackson) 1909-
George Eliot, by Anne Fremantle. London, Duckworth. New York, Haskell House Publishers, 1972. 144 p. 23 cm. Reprint of the 1933 ed., which was issued as no. 8 of Great lives. Bibliography: p. 144. [PR4681.F7 1972] 72-3177 ISBN 0-8383-1503-8
1. Eliot, George, pseud., i.e. Marian Evans, afterwards Cross, 1819-1880.

FREMANTLE, Anne 823'.8 B (Jackson) 1909-
George Eliot, by Anne Fremantle. [Folcroft, Pa.] Folcroft Library Editions, 1973. p. Reprint of the 1933 ed. published by Duckworth, London, which was issued as no. 8 of Great lives. Bibliography: p. [PR4681.F7 1973] 73-11359 8.75
1. Eliot, George, pseud., i.e. Marian Evans, afterwards Cross, 1819-1880. BIP

KENYON, Frank Wilson, 1912- 823'.8 B
The consuming flame; the story of George Eliot [by] F. W. Kenyon. New York, Dodd, Mead [1970] 223 p. 22 cm. [PR4681.K4 1970b] 75-14902 5.95
1. Eliot, George, pseud., i.e. Marian Evans, afterwards Cross, 1819-1880. I. Title.

KENYON, Frank Wilson, 1912- 823'.8 B
The consuming flame; the story of George Eliot [by] F. W. Kenyon. [Richmond, Vic.] Hutchinson of Australia [1970] 223 p. 22 cm. [PR4681.K4 1970c] 70-564047 ISBN 0-09-101440-9 4.00
1. Eliot, George, pseud., i.e. Marian Evans, afterwards Cross, 1819-1880. I. Title.

LERNER, Laurence. 823'.009
The truthtellers: Jane Austen, George Eliot, D. H. Lawrence. New York, Schocken Books [1967] 291 p. 23 cm. Bibliographical footnotes. [PR861.L4 1967] 67-12148
1. Austen, Jane, 1775-1817. 2. Eliot, George, pseud., i.e. Marian Evans, afterwards Cross, 1819-1880. 3. Lawrence, David Herbert, 1885-1930. I. Title.

LONSDALE, Margaret. 823'.8 B
George Eliot : thoughts upon her life, her books, and herself / by Margaret Lonsdale. Folcroft, Pa. : Folcroft Library Editions, 1977. 52 p. ; 23 cm. Reprint of the 1886 ed. published by K. Paul, French, London. [PR4681.A3C735 1977] 77-6414 ISBN 0-8414-5816-2 lib. bdg. : 10.00
1. Eliot, George, pseud., i.e. Marian Evans, afterwards Cross, 1819-1880. George Eliot's life as related in her letters and journals. 2. Eliot, George, pseud., i.e. Marian Evans, afterwards Cross, 1819-1880—Biography. 3. Authors, English—19th century—Biography. BIP

MORGAN, William. 823'.8 B
George Eliot. London, Hamilton, 1881. [Folcroft, Pa.] Folcroft Library Editions, 1973. p. "A paper read before the Portsmouth Literary and Scientific Society, March 29th, 1881." [PR4681.M6 1973] 73-512 ISBN 0-8414-0965-X (lib. bdg.)
1. Eliot, George, pseud., i.e. Marian Evans, afterwards Cross, 1819-1880.

PEARCE, T. S. 823'.8 B
George Eliot [by] T. S. Pearce. Totowa, N.J., Rowman and Littlefield [1973] 152 p. illus. 20 cm. (Literature in perspective) Bibliography: p. 148. [PR4681.P4 1973] 73-160762 ISBN 0-87471-138-X 4.00
1. Eliot, George, pseud., i.e. Marian Evans, afterwards Cross, 1819-1880

REDINGER, Ruby Virginia, 1915- 823'.8 B
George Eliot : the emergent self / Ruby V. Redinger. 1st ed. New York : Knopf : distributed by Random House, 1975. x, 515, xxv p. ; 25 cm. Includes bibliographical references and index. [PR4681.R4 1975] 74-21301 ISBN 0-394-49010-X : 15.00
1. Eliot, George, pseud., i.e. Marian Evans, afterwards Cross, 1819-1880. BIP

THOMSON, Clara Linklater. 823'.8 B
George Eliot, by Clara Thomson. [Folcroft, Pa.] Folcroft Library Editions, 1973. xii, 132 p. port. 24 cm. Reprint of the 1901 ed published by Kegan Paul, Trench, Trubner & Co., London, in series: The Westminster biographies. Bibliography: p. [128]-132. [PR4681.T5 1973] 73-13983 ISBN 0-8414-8538-0 (lib. bdg.)
1. Eliot, George, pseud., i.e. Marian Evans, afterwards Cross, 1819-1880. I. Series: The Westminster biographies. BIP

Eliot, George, pseud., i.e. Marian Evans, afterwards Cross, 1819-1880—Biography.

BOURL'HONNE, P. 823'.8 B
George Eliot; essai de biographie intellectuelle et morale, 1819-1854, influences anglaises et etrangeres. Paris, H. Champion, 1933. [New York, AMS Press, 1973] 214 p. 23 cm. Original ed. issued as v. 88 of Bibliotheque de la Revue de litterature comparee. These—Lausanne. Bibliography: p. [213]-214. [PR4681.B6 1973] 76-148754 ISBN 0-404-08727-2
1. Eliot, George, pseud., i.e. Marian Evans, afterwards Cross, 1819-1880—Biography. I. Series: Bibliotheque de la Revue de litterature comparee, t. 88.

BROWNING, Oscar, 1837-1923. 823'.8 B
Life of George Eliot. Port Washington, N.Y., Kennikat Press [1972] 174, xiv p. 21 cm. Reprint of the 1890 ed. Bibliography: p. [i]-xiv. [PR4681.B7 1972] 75-160744 ISBN 0-8046-1557-8
1. Eliot, George, pseud., i.e. Marian Evans, afterwards Cross, 1819-1880—Biography. I. Title.

†DEAKIN, Mary Hannah. 823'.8 B
The early life of George Eliot / by Mary H. Deakin ; with an introductory note by C. H. Herford. Folcroft, Pa. : Folcroft Library Editions, 1976. xviii, 188 p. ; 23 cm. Reprint of the 1913 ed. published by the University Press, Manchester, which was issued as no. 4 of Publications of the University of Manchester, English series, and as no. 71 of Publications of the University of Manchester. Includes bibliographical references and index. [PR4682.D4 1976] 76-15232 ISBN 0-8414-3740-8 lib. bdg. : 25.00
1. Eliot, George, pseud., i.e. Marian Evans, afterwards Cross, 1819-1880—Biography. I. Title. II. Series: Victoria University of Manchester. Publications : English series ; no. 4. III. Series: Victoria University of Manchester. Publications ; no. 71. BIP

HAIGHT, Gordon Sherman. 823'.8 B
George Eliot; a biography [by] Gordon S. Haight. New York, Oxford University Press [1968] xvi, 616 p. ports. 22 cm. Bibliographical footnotes. [PR4681.H27] 68-9440 12.50
1. Eliot, George, pseud., i.e. Marian Evans, afterwards Cross, 1819-1880—Biography.

HALDANE, Elizabeth Sanderson, 1862-1937. 823'.8 B
George Eliot and her times; a Victorian study. New York, Haskell House Publishers, 1974. viii, 315 p. 22 cm. [PR4681.H3 1974] 74-11022 ISBN 0-8383-1848-7
1 Eliot, George, pseud., i.e. Marian Evans afterwards Cross, 1819-1880—Biography. I. Title.

HALDANE, Elizabeth Sanderson, 1862-1937. 823'.8 B
George Eliot and her times, a Victorian study. [Folcroft, Pa.] Folcroft Library Editions, 1974 [c1927] vii, 326 p. ports. 23 cm. Reprint of the ed. published by D. Appleton, New York. [PR4681.H3 1974b] 74-18416 ISBN 0-8414-4887-6 (lib. bdg.)
1. Eliot, George, pseud., i.e. Marian Evans afterwards Cross, 1819-1880—Biography. I. Title.

HANSON, Lawrence. 928.2
Marian Evans & George Eliot; a biography by Lawrence and Elisabeth Hanson. London, New York, Oxford University Press, 1952. xiv, 402 p. illus., ports. 22 cm Bibliography: p [319]-325. [PR4681.H37] 52-12318
1. Eliot, George, pseud., L. e. Marian Evans, afterwards Cross, 1819-1880. I. Hanson, Elisabeth M. joint author. II. Title.

LASKI, Marghanita, 1915- 823'.8 B
George Eliot and her world. London, Thames and Hudson, 1973. 128 p. illus., facsims., geneal. table, maps, ports. 24 cm. Bibliography: p. [124] [PR4681.L3] 73-169735 ISBN 0-500-13043-4
1. Eliot, George, pseud., Marian Evans, afterwards Cross, 1819-1880—Biography. I. Title.
Distributed by Transatlantic Arts; 8.25. BIP

LASKI, Marghanita, 1915- 823'.8 B
George Eliot and her world / Marghanita Laski. New York : Scribner, [1978] c1973. 119, [9] p. : ill. ; 24 cm. Includes index. Bibliography: p. [124] [PR4681.L3 1978] 77-83677 ISBN 0-684-15511-7 : 9.95
1. Eliot, George, pseud., i.e. Marion Evans afterwards Cross, 1819-1880—Biography. 2. Novelists, English—19th century—Biography. I. Title.

MOTTRAM, William. 823'.8
The true story of George Eliot in relation to "Adam Bede," giving the real life history of more prominent characters. With eighty-six illus., mainly from photos. by Allan P. Mottram and Vernon H. Mottram. [Folcroft, Pa.] Folcroft Library Editions, 1974. p. Reprint of the 1905 ed. published by F. Griffiths, London. [PR4656.M6 1974] 74-9899 ISBN 0-8414-6148-1 (lib. bdg.)
1. Eliot, George, pseud, i.e. Marion Evans, afterwards Cross, 1819-1880—Biography. 2. Eliot, George, pseud, i.e. Marion Evans, afterwards Cross, 1819-1880. Adam Bede. I. Title.

MURIEL, John St. Clair, 1909- 823'.8 B
Marian : the life of George Eliot / by Simon Dewes [i.e. J. St. Clair Muriel] New York : Haskell House, [1975] p. cm. Reprint of the 1939 ed. published by Rich & Cowan, London. [PR4681.M8 1975] 74-28384 ISBN 0-8383-1745-6 : 14.95
1. Eliot, George, pseud., i.e. Marian Evans, afterwards Cross, 1819-1880—Biography. I. Title. BIP

MURIEL, John St. Clair, 1910- 823'.8 B
Marian; the life of George Eliot, by Simon Dewes. [Folcroft, Pa.] Folcroft Library Editions, 1972. ix, 299 p. ports. 26 cm. 150 copies printed. Reprint of the 1939 ed. [PR4681.M8 1972] 72-187523
1. Eliot, George, pseud., i.e. Marian Evans, afterwards Cross, 1819-1880—Biography. I. Title.

ROMIEU, Emilie. 823'.8 B
The life of George Eliot, by Emilie and Georges Romieu. Translated from the French by Brian W. Downs. [1st ed.] [Folcroft, Pa.] Folcroft Library Editions, 1974 [c1932] p. Reprint of the ed. published by Dutton, New York. [PR4681.R62 1974] 74-11159 20.00
1. Eliot, George, pseud, i.e. Marian Evans, afterwards Cross, 1819-1880—Biography. I. Romieu, Georges, joint author. II. Title.

SPEAIGHT, Robert, 1904- 928.2
George Eliot. New York, Roy Publishers [1954] 128p. 19cm. (The English novelists) Bibliography: p126. [PR4688.S65] 53-13498
1. Eliot, George, pseud., ie. Morian Evans, a afterwards Cross, 1819-1880. I. Title. II. Series:The English novelists (London)

SPRAGUE, Rosemary, 1922- 823'.8 B
George Eliot; a biography. [1st ed.] Philadelphia, Chilton Book Co. [1968] xi, 337 p. 21 cm. Bibliography: p. [327]-328. [PR4681.S64 1968] 68-19179
1. Eliot, George, pseud., i.e. Marian Evans, afterwards Cross, 1819-1880—Biography.

Eliot, George, pseud., i.e. Marian Evans, afterwards Cross, 1819-1880—Biography—Juvenile literature.

FOULDS, Elfrida Vipont (Brown) 1902- 823'.8 B
Towards a high attic; the early life of George Eliot, 1819-1880 [by] Elfrida Vipont. [1st American ed.] New York, Holt, Rinehart and Winston [1971, c1970] 145 p. illus., ports. 24 cm. A biography of the Victorian author whose work and life defied many of the conventions of her time. [PR4682.F6 1971] 92 76-141012 ISBN 0-03-086238-8 (Holt library ed.) 4.59
1. Eliot, George, pseud., i.e. Marian Evans, afterwards Cross, 1819-1880—Biography—Juvenile literature. I. Title.

GAEDDERT, LouAnn Bigge. 823'.8 B
All-in-all : a biography of George Eliot / by LouAnn Gaeddert. 1st ed. New York : Dutton, c1976. 138 p. : port. ; 24 cm. Includes bibliographical references and index. A biography of Marian Evans, a victorian writer who adopted a male pen name to preserve her privacy. [PR4681.G3] 92 76-14791 ISBN 0-525-25440-4 : 7.95
1. Eliot, George, pseud., i.e. Marian Evans, afterwards Cross, 1819-1880—Biography—Juvenile literature. 2. Novelists, English—19th century—Biography—Juvenile literature. I. Title.

Eliot, John, 1604-1690.

BEALS, Carleton, 1893- 922.573
John Eliot, the man who loved the Indians (July 31, 1604-May 20, 1690) New York, Messner [1958, c1957] 192 p. 22 cm. Includes bibliography. [E78.M4E518] 58-6011
1. Eliot, John, 1604-1690.

FRANCIS, Convers, 1795-1863. 266'.022'0924 B
Life of John Eliot, the apostle to the Indians. New York, MSS Information Corp. [1972] vi, 184 p. 21 cm. Reprint of the 1854 ed. [E78.M4E523 1972] 72-8081 ISBN 0-13-676387-1 1.95
1. Eliot, John, 1604-1690. I. Title. BIP

WINSLOW, Ola Elizabeth. 285'.8'0924
John Eliot, apostle to the Indians. Boston, Houghton Mifflin, 1968. 225 p. illus., facsims. 22 cm. Bibliography: p. [213]-218. [E78.M4E595] 68-19633 5.95
1. Eliot, John, 1604-1690.

Eliot, Samuel Atkins, 1862-1950.

MCGIFFERT, Arthur Cushman, 1892- 288'.33'0924 B
Pilot of a liberal faith, Samuel Atkins Eliot, 1862-1950 / Arthur Cushman McGiffert, Jr. [Boston] : Beacon Press, 1976. 321 p. : ill. ; 23 cm. "A Skinner House book." Includes index. [BX9869.E37M28] 76-373984 12.95
1. Eliot, Samuel Atkins, 1862-1950. 2. Unitarian churches in the United States—Biography. I. Title.

Eliot, Sir John, 1592-1632.

HULME, Harold, 1898- 923.242
The life of Sir John Eliot, 1592 to 1632; struggle for parliamentary freedom. [1st U. S. ed.] New York, New York University Press [c1957] 423p. illus. 23cm. [DA396.E4H8 1957a] 57-5229
1. Eliot, Sir John, 1592-1632. I. Title.

THE life of Sir John Eliot, 1592 to 1632: struggle for parliamentary freedom. New York, New York University Press [1957] 423p. 4 ports. 23cm. Includes bibliography. v. 12
1. Eliot, Sir John, 1592-1632. I. Hulme, Harold, 1898-

Eliot, Thomas Stearns, 1888-1965.

BERGONZI, Bernard. 821'.9'12
T. S. Eliot. New York, Macmillan [1972] xiv, 207 p. 21 cm. (Masters of world literature series) Bibliography: p. [193]-195. [PS3509.L43Z643] 78-162337 6.95
1. Eliot, Thomas Stearns, 1888-1965.

FRYE, Northrop 821.912
T. S. Eliot. New York, Grove [c.1963] 106p. 18cm. (Evergreen pilot bks., EP26) Bibl. 63-9402 .95 pap.,
1. Eliot, Thomas Stearns, 1888- I. Title.

FRYE, Northrop 821.912
T. S. Eliot. [Gloucester, Mass., P. Smith, 1964, c.1963] 106p. 19cm. (Evergreen pilot bk, EP26 rebound) Bibl. 3.00
1. Eliot, Thomas Stearns, 1888- I. Title.

MARCH, Richard, ed. 928.2
T. S. Eliot; a symposium from Conrad Aiken [others] Comp. byRichard March and Tambimuttu. [New York, 10014] Tambimuttu & Mass, 86 Horatio St. [c.1965] 259p. ports., 23cm. [PS3509.L43Z73] 6.50
1. Eliot, Thomas Stearns, 1888-1964. I. Tambimuttu, M.J., joint ed. II. Title.

MARGOLIS, John D. 821'.9'12 B
T. S. Eliot's intellectual development, 1922-1939 [by] John D. Margolis. Chicago, University of Chicago Press [1972] xix, 226 p. 21 cm. Includes bibliographical references. [PS3509.L43Z734] 71-171071 ISBN 0-226-50518-9
1. Eliot, Thomas Stearns, 1888-1965. I. Title. BIP

READ, Herbert Edward, Sir, 1893-1968. 821.912
T. S. E., a memoir, by Herbert Read. [Middletown, Conn.] Center for Advanced Studies, Wesleyan University [1966] 31 p. 22 cm. (Monday evening papers, no. 5) Cover title. "Reprinted from T. S. Eliot

(1888-1965) edited by Alan Tate." [PS3509.L43Z823] 66-9541
1. Eliot, Thomas Stearns, 1888-1965. I. Title. II. Series: Wesleyan University, Middletown, Conn. Center for Advanced Studies in the Liberal Arts, Professions, and Sciences. Monday evening papers, no. 5.

ROBBINS, Rossell Hope, 1912- 810.81
The T. S. Eliot myth. New York, H. Schuman [1951] 226 p. 21 cm. [PS3509.L43Z825] 51-14190
1. Eliot, Thomas Stearns, 1888-1965. I. Title.

SENCOURT, Robert, 1890- 821'.9'12 [B]
T. S. Eliot, a memoir. Edited by Donald Adamson. [New York] [Dell] [1973, c.1971] xiv, 266 p. illus. 20 cm. (Delta Book) Bibliographical references. [PS3509.L43Z8638 1971] pap., 2.65
I. Eliot, Thomas Stearns, 1888-1965.

SENCOURT, Robert, 1890-1969. 821'.9'12 B
T. S. Eliot, a memoir. Edited by Donald Adamson. New York, Dodd, Mead [1971] xiv, 266 p. illus. 22 cm. Includes bibliographical references. [PS3509.L43Z8638 1971] 79-169732 ISBN 0-396-06347-0 8.95
1. Eliot, Thomas Stearns, 1888-1965. I. Title.

SIMPSON, Louis Aston Marantz, 1923- 811'.5'209
Three on the tower : the lives and works of Ezra Pound, T. S. Eliot, and William Carlos Williams / by Louis Simpson. New York : Morrow, 1975. ix, 373 p. ; 24 cm. Includes index. Bibliography: p. 356-362. [PS3531.O82Z836] 74-26952 ISBN 0-688-02899-3 : 12.50
1. Pound, Ezra Loomis, 1885-1972. 2. Eliot, Thomas Stearns, 1888-1965. 3. Williams, William Carlos, 1883-1963. I. Title. BIP

SPENDER, Stephen, 1909- 821'.9'12
T. S. Eliot / Stephen Spender. New York : Viking Press, 1976, c1975. xiii, 269 p. ; 22 cm. (Modern masters) Includes index. Bibliography: p. [255]-258. [PS3509.L43Z8694 1976] 72-78997 ISBN 0-670-29184-6 : 10.00 ISBN 0-670-01988-7 pbk. : 3.95
1. Eliot, Thomas Stearns, 1888-1965.

TATE, Allen, 1899- ed. 828.91209
T.S. Eliot: the man and his work. the man and his work; a critical evaluation by twenty-six distinguished writers. New York, Delacorte Press [1966] vi, 400 p. ports. 21 cm. "A Seymour Lawrence book." "The works of T. S. Eliot": p. [395]-397. [PS3509.L43Z874] 66-20994
1. Eliot, Thomas Stearns, 1888-1965.

THOMPSON, Eric, 1912- 821.912
T.S. Eliot: the metaphysical perspective With a pref. by Harry T. Moore. Carbondale, Southern Illinois University Press [1963] 186 p. 22 cm. (Crosscurrents: modern critiques) Includes bibliography. [PS3509.L43Z877] 62-16697
1. Eliot, Thomas Stearns, 1888-

UNGER, Leonard. 811.52
T. S. Eliot. Minneapolis, University of Minnesota Press [1961] 48 p. 21 cm. (University of Minnesota. Pamphlets on American writers, no. 8) Includes bibliography. [PS3509.L43Z882 1961] 61-62512
1. Eliot, Thomas Stearns, 1888-

UNGER, Leonard. 821.912
T.S. Eliot: moments and patterns. Minneapolis, University of Minnesota Press [1966] 196 p. 23 cm. Bibliography: p. 189-192. [PS3509.L43Z884] 66-27420
1. Eliot, Thomas Stearns, 1888-1965.

Eliot, Thomas Stearns, 1888-1965—Biography.

GORDON, Lyndall. 821'9'12 B
Eliot's early years / Lyndall Gordon. Oxford ; New York : Oxford University Press, 1977. xii, 174 p., [8] leaves of plates : ill. ; 22 cm. Includes index. Bibliography: p. [164]-167. [PS3509.L43Z679] 76-29809 ISBN 0-19-812078-8 : 10.00
1. Eliot, Thomas Stearns, 1888-1965—Biography. 2. Authors, American—20th century—Biography. I. Title. BIP

Eliot, Thomas Stearns, 1888-1965—Criticism and interpretation.

GEORGE, Arapara Ghevarghese, 1928- 828'.9'1209
T. S. Eliot: his mind and art [by] A. G. George. 2d rev. ed. Bombay, New York, Asia Pub. House [1969] xv, 310 p. 22 cm. Bibliography: p. 291-297. [PS3509.L43Z677 1969b] 74-906347 18.00
1. Eliot, Thomas Stearns, 1888-1965—Criticism and interpretation. I. Title.

WARD, David, 1932- 821'.9'12
T. S. Eliot between two worlds; a reading of T. S. Eliot's poetry and plays. London, Boston, Routledge & Kegan Paul, 1973. x, 304 p. 23 cm. Includes bibliographical references and index. [PS3509.L43Z892] 73-82371 ISBN 0-7100-7638-X 15.00
1. Eliot, Thomas Stearns, 1888-1965—Criticism and interpretation. I. Title.

Elisa, grand duchess of Tuscany, 1777-1820.

WEINER, Margery. 923.145
The parvenu princesses; the lives and loves of Napoleon's sisters. New York, Morrow [1964] xi, 274 p. illus., ports. 22 cm. Bibliography: p. 264-268. [DC216.W38] 64-22208
1. Elisa, grand duchess of Tuscany, 1777-1820. 2. Borghese, Maria Paolina (Bonaparte) principessa, 1780-1825. 3. Caroline Bonaparte, consort of Joachim Murat, King of Naples, 1782-1889. I. Title.

Elisabeth, consort of Francis Joseph I, Emperor of Austria, 1837-1898.

CARTLAND, Barbara, 1902- 923.1436
The private life of Elisabeth, empress of Austria. New York, Pyramid Books [1974, c1959] 285 p. illus. 18 cm. Bibliography: p. 279-280. [DB88.C3] ISBN 0-515-03373-1. 1.25 (pbk.)
1. Elisabeth, consort of Francis Joseph I, Emperor of Austria, 1837-1898. I. Title.
L.C. card number for original ed.: 59-3804.

HASLIP, Joan, 1911- 943.6040924
The lonely empress; a biography of Elizabeth of Austria. Cleveland, World Pub. Co. [1965] 462 p. illus., ports. 24 cm. Bibliography: p. 443-448. [DB88.H3] 65-17562
1. Elisabeth, consort of Francis Joseph I, Emperor of Austria, 1837-1898. 2. Habsburg, House of. I. Title.

LARISCH VON MOENNICH, Marie Luise Elisabeth (freiin von Wallersee) grafin, 1858-1940. 920.7
Her Majesty Elizabeth of Austria-Hungary, the beautiful, tragic empress of Europe's most brilliant court, by Marie Louise, countess Larisch von Wallersee-Wittelsbach, with Paul Maerker Branden and Elsa Branden. Garden City, N. Y., Doubleday, Doran & company, inc., 1934. x, 308p. incl. geneal. tab. front., ports. 24cm. 'This story appeared serially under the title of Aunt Sissy--and I.'--p. [iv] 'First edition.' [DB88.L3] 34-38322
1. Elisabeth, consort of Francis Joseph I, emperor of Austria, 1837-1898. 2. Austria—Court and courtiers. I. Branden, Albrecht Paul Maerker., 1888- joint author. II. Branden, Elsa (Weinberg) 1903- joint author. III. Title.

Elisabeth de la Trinite, Sister, 1880-1906.

BALTHASAR, Hans Urs von, 1905- 922.244
Elizabeth of Dijon; an interpretation of her spiritual mission. Translated and adapted by A. V. Littledale. [1st ed. New York] Pantheon [1956] 126p. 22cm. Translation of Elisabeth von Dijon und ihre geistliche Sendung. [BV5095.E5B313] 56-4229
1. Elisabeth de la Trinite, Sister, 1880-1906. I. Title.

Elisha, the prophet.

HARDINGE, Leslie. 221.92'4
Elisha, man of God. Washington, Review and Herald Pub. Association [1968] 128 p. 22 cm. [BS580.E5H3] 68-25113
1. Elisha, the prophet. I. Title.

Elisha, the prophet—Miracles.

PINK, Arthur Walkington, 1886-1952. 221.9'24 B
Gleanings from Elisha; his life and miracles. Chicago, Moody Press [1972] 254 p. 24 cm. Includes bibliographical references. [BS580.E5P55 1972] 79-181591 ISBN 0-8024-2962-9 5.95
1. Elisha, the prophet—Miracles. I. Title.

Elizabeth, consort of George VI, 1900-

DUFF, David, 1912- 942.0840924
Mother of the Queen; the life story of Her Majesty the Queen Mother Elizabeth. [1st Amer. ed.] New York, Hawthorn [1966, c.1965] 305p. ports. 24cm. [DA585.A2D8] 66-15242 5.95
1. Elizabeth, consort of George VI, 1900- I. Title.

ELLIS, Jennifer. 923.142
Royal mother; the story of Queen Mother Elizabeth and her family. New York, Prentice-Hall [1954] 219 p. illus. 21 cm. First published in 1958 under title: Elizabeth, the Queen Mother. [DA585.A2E4 1954] 54-10509
1. Elizabeth, consort of George VI, 1900- I. Title.

WAKEFORD, Geoffrey. 942.084'0924
Thirty years a queen; a study of H. M. Queen Elizabeth, the Queen Mother. [1st American ed.] South Brunswick [N.J.] A. S. Barnes [1968] 288 p. 22 cm. Bibliography: p. 281-282. [DA585.A2W3 1968] 68-31024 5.95
1. Elizabeth, consort of George VI, 1900- I. Title.

Elizabeth, Consort of Henry VII, King of England, 1465-1503.

HARVEY, Nancy Lenz. 942.05'1'0924 B
Elizabeth of York, the mother of Henry VIII. New York, Macmillan [1973] xiv, 241 p. illus. 22 cm. Bibliography: p. 227-233. [DA330.8.E44H37] 72-11952 6.95
1. Elizabeth, Consort of Henry VII, King of England, 1465-1503. I. Title.

Elizabeth, Empress of Russia, 1709-1762.

BAIN, Robert Nisbet, 1854-1909. 947'.06
The daughter of Peter the Great. New York, AMS Press [1970] xviii, 328 p. ports. 23 cm. Reprint of the 1899 ed. Bibliography: p. [xv]-xviii. [DK161.B18 1970] 72-136407 ISBN 0-404-00447-4
1. Elizabeth, Empress of Russia, 1709-1762. 2. Russia—History—Elizabeth, 1741-1762. I. Title. BIP

BAIN, Robert Nisbet, 1854-1909. 947'.06
The daughter of Peter the Great: a history of Russian diplomacy, and of the Russian court under the Empress Elizabeth Petrovna, 1741-1762. New York, Dutton, 1900. St. Clair Shores, Mich., Scholarly Press [1969?] xviii, 328 p. ports. 22 cm. Bibliography: p. [xv]-xviii. [DK161.B18 1969] 77-8456
1. Elizabeth, Empress of Russia, 1709-1762. 2. Russia—History—Elizabeth, 1741-1762. I. Title.

RICE, Tamara (Abelson) Talbot. 947'.06'0924 B
Elizabeth, Empress of Russia [by] Tamara Talbot Rice. New York, Praeger [1970] xvi, 231 p. illus., map, ports. 25 cm. Bibliography: p. 216-217. [DK161.R5 1970b] 73-100926 8.50
1. Elizabeth, Empress of Russia, 1709-1762.

Elizabeth, Empress, 1741-1762.

COUGHLAN, Robert, 1914- 947'.06'0922 B
Elizabeth and Catherine: empresses of all the Russias. Edited by Jay Gold. New York, Putnam [1974] 347 p. illus. 24 cm. Bibliography: p. 335-336. [DK161.C68] 73-87181 ISBN 0-399-11250-2 10.00
1. Elizabeth, Empress, 1741-1762. 2. Catharine II, Empress of Russia, 1729-1796. 3. Russia—History—1689-1800. I. Title.

Elizabeth, Grand Duchess of Russia, 1864-1918.

ALMEDINGEN, Martha Edith, 1898- 271.98
An unbroken unity; a memoir of Grand-Duchess Serge of Russia, 1864-1918. London, Bodley Head [Westminster, Md. 21157, Canterbury Pr., Court Place, 1965, c.1964] 144p. illus., ports. 23cm. [DK254.E6A7] 66-2779 3.95 bds.,
1. Elizabeth, Grand Duchess of Russia, 1864-1918. I. Title.

Elizabeth II, Queen of Great Britain, 1926-

BOCCA, Geoffrey. 923.142
Elizabeth and Philip; profusely illustrated with photos. [1st ed.] New York, Holt [1953] 248 p. illus. 22 cm. [DA590.B6] 53-5496
1. Elizabeth II, Queen of Great Britain, 1926- 2. Philip, Duke of Edinburgh, 1921- I. Title.

CAMPBELL, Judith. 942.085'092'2 B
Elizabeth & Philip; a royal love story. Chicago, H. Regnery Co. [1972] viii, 103 p. illus. 26 cm. [DA590.C247] 72-80920 5.95
1. Elizabeth II, Queen of Great Britain, 1926- 2. Philip, Duke of Edinburgh, 1921- I. Title.

CAMPBELL, Judith. 941.085'092'4 B
Queen Elizabeth II / Judith Campbell. New York : Crown Publishers, 1980, c1979. p. cm. [DA590.C249 1980] 79-16592 ISBN 0-517-53974-8 : 12.95
1. Elizabeth II, Queen of Great Britain, 1926- 2. Great Britain—History—George VI, 1936-1952. 3. Great Britain—History—Elizabeth II, 1952- 4. Monarchy, British. 5. Great Britain—Kings and rulers—Biography.

CAMPBELL, Judith 798.20922
The Queen rides. Photos. by Godfrey Argent. New York, Viking [c.1965] 95p. illus. (pt. col.) ports. (pt. col.) 29cm. [DA590.C25] 65-6876 7.50 bds.,
1. Elizabeth II, Queen of Great Britain, 1926- 2. Horses—Gt. Brit. I. Title.

CATHCART, Helen. 923.142
Her Majesty the Queen; the story of Elizabeth II. New York, Dodd, Mead, 1962. 207p. illus. 22cm. [DA590.C3] 62-146953
1. Elizabeth II, Queen of Great Britain, 1926- I. Queen of Great Britain, 1926- II. Title.

CATHCART, Helen. 942.085'0924
Her Majesty the Queen; the story of Elizabeth II. Illustrated with photos. Rev. ed. New York, Dodd, Mead, 1966. 215 p. plates, ports. 22 cm. [DA590.C3 1966] 66-24275
1. Elizabeth II, Queen of Great Britain, 1926- I. Title.

CATHCART, Helen. 942.085'0924 B
The married life of the Queen. London, New York, W. H. Allen, 1970. 198 p., 16 plates. ports. 23 cm. [DA590.C33 1970] 75-559401 ISBN 0-491-00465-6 42/-
1. Elizabeth II, Queen of Great Britain, 1926- I. Title.

CATHCART, Helen 798.40942
The Queen and the turf. London, S. Paul [stamped; distributed by Sportshelf, NewRochelle, N.Y., 1960 200p. illus. 22cm. 60-1235 5.75
1. Elizabeth II, Queen of Great Britain, 1926- 2. Horse-racing—Gt. Brit. I. Title.

CLARK, Stanley Frederick. 923.142
Palace diary; authorized account of the

crowded days of Queen Elizabeth's life from the time of her twenty-first birthday on April 21, 1947, compiled with full access to her engagement diaries. New York, Dutton [1958] 223p. illus. 2icm. [DA590.C545 1958a] 58-10820
1. Elizabeth II Queen of Great Britain, 1926- I. Title.

CLAY, Charles, 1906- 942.084
Long live the Queen, George VI to Elizabeth II. [1st ed.] Philadelphia, Winston [1953] 401p. illus. 22cm. [DA590.C55] 53-4418
1. Elizabeth II, Queen of Great Britain, 1926- I. Title.

CRAWFORD, Marion, 942.085'0924 B
1909-
Elizabeth the Queen; the story of Britain's new sovereign. Westport, Conn., Greenwood Press [1970, c1952] 236 p. illus., ports. 23 cm. [DA590.C7 1970] 74-97380
1. Elizabeth II, Queen of Great Britain, 1926-

CRAWFORD, Marion, 1909- 920.7
The little princesses. [1st ed.] New York, Harcourt, Brace [1950] 314 p. ports. 21 cm. [DA585.A4C7] 50-8077
1. Elizabeth II, Queen of Great Britain, 1926- 2. Margaret, Princess of Great Britain, 1930- I. Title.

DAVIS, Reginald. 941.085'092'4 B
Elizabeth, our Queen / Reginald Davis. London : Collins, 1976. 159 p. : col. ill., geneal. tables (on lining papers) ; 25 cm. [DA590.D38] 77-351693 ISBN 0-00-211233-7 : £3.95
1. Elizabeth II, Queen of Great Britain, 1926- 2. Great Britain—Kings and rulers—Biography. I. Title.

DIMBLEBY, 941.085'092'4 B
Richard.
Elizabeth, our Queen / Richard Dimbleby. Westport, Conn. : Greenwood Press, 1979. 187 p., [23] leaves of plates : ill. ; 22 cm. Reprint of the 1953 ed. published by Hodder and Stoughton, London. [DA590.D5 1979] 78-12304 ISBN 0-313-21096-9 lib. bdg. : 20.00
1. Elizabeth II, Queen of Great Britain, 1926- 2. Great Britain—Kings and rulers—Biography. I. Title. BIP

DUNCAN, Andrew, 942.085'0924
1940-
The Queen's year: the reality of monarchy. [1st ed.] Garden City, N.Y., Doubleday, 1970. viii, 345 p. geneal. tables, ports. 25 cm. London ed. (Heinemann) has title: The reality of monarchy. Includes bibliographical references. [DA590.D85 1970b] 79-113988 8.95
1. Elizabeth II, Queen of Great Britain, 1926- 2. Windsor, House of. I. Title.

FISHER, Graham. 923.142
Elizabeth, Queen & mother; the story of Queen Elizabeth II and the British royal family, by Graham and Heather Fisher. [1st ed.] New York, Hawthorn Books [1964] 212 p. ports. 24 cm. [DA590.F52 1964a] 64-20434
1. Elizabeth II, Queen of Great Britain, 1926- I. Fisher, Heather, joint author. II. Title.

JOHNSTON, Laurie. 923.142
Elizabeth enters, the story of a Queen. Photos. selected by Richard W. Johnston. New York, Scribner [1953] 185 p. illus. 21 cm. Includes bibliography. [DA590.J6] 53-9206
1. Elizabeth II, Queen of Great Britain, 1926- I. Title.

LACEY, Robert. 941.085'092'4
Majesty : Elizabeth II and the House of Windsor / Robert Lacey. New York : Avon, c1977. 416p. : ill. ; 18 cm. Bibliography:p.313-317. [DA590.L28] ISBN 0-380-01842-X pbk. : 1.75
1. Elizabeth II,Queen of Great Britain-1926- 2. Great britain-Kings and rulers-Bibliography. 3. Monarchy, british. I. Title. BIP

LACEY, Robert. 941.085'092'4 B
Majesty : Elizabeth II and the House of Windsor / Robert Lacey. New York : Harcourt Brace Jovanovich, c1977. xxxii, 349 p., [17] leaves of plates : ill. ; 24 cm. Includes index. Bibliography: p. 313-317. [DA590.L28] 76-27424 ISBN 0-15-155684-9 : 12.95
1. Elizabeth II, Queen of Great Britain, 1926- 2. Great Britain—Kings and rulers—Biography. 3. Monarchy, British. I. Title.

LAIRD, Dorothy. 923.142
How the Queen reigns; an authentic study of the Queen's personality and life work. [1st ed.] Cleveland, World Pub. Co. [1959] 367 p. illus. 25 cm. [DA590.L3] 59-7750
1. Elizabeth II, Queen of Great Britain, 1926- I. Title.

OUR royal family, 923.142
the record of a happy marriage. With a foreword by John Snagge London, Adhams Press [1960 label:Hollywood, Fla.,Transatlantic Arts, inc. 126p. illus. 26cm. 60-2317 4.50
1. Elizabeth II, Queen of Great Britain, 1926- I. Snagge, John. II. Odhams Press, ltd.

PARKER, Elinor Milnor, 923'.1'42
1906-
Most Gracious Majesty; the story of Queen Elizabeth II. New York, Crowell [1953?] 181 p. illus. 21 cm. [DA590.P3] 53-8422
1. Elizabeth II, Queen of Great Britain, 1926-

PARKER, Elinor Milnor, 923.142
1906-
Most Gracious Majesty; the story of Queen Elizabeth II. Rev. ed. New York, Crowell [1962] 197p. illus. 21cm. [DA590.P3 1962] 62-11005
1. Elizabeth II. Queen of Great Britain, 1926- I. Title.

SHERIDAN, Lisa. 923.142
The Queen and Princess Anne. Photos. by Studio Lisa. London, J.Murray [dist.Hollywood by-the-Sea,Florida, Transatlantic Arts 1959, i.e., 1960] 32p. (chiefly illus.) 25cm. 60-1545 1.50 bds.,
1. Elizabeth II, Queen of Great Britain, 1926- 2. Anne, Princess of Great Britain, 1950- I. Title.

WHITE, Ralphe M. 942.085'0924
The royal family; a personal portrait, by Ralphe M. White and Graham Fisher. New York, D. McKay Co. [1969] 275 p. illus. 22 cm. [DA590.W45] 78-79510 6.50
1. Elizabeth II, Queen of Great Britain, 1926- I. Fisher, Graham, joint author. II Title.

Elizabeth II, Queen of Great Britain, 1926- —Coronation.

BARKER, Brian, O. B. 394'.4'0941
E.
When the Queen was crowned / Brian Barker. 1st American ed. New York : D. McKay Co., 1976. xiii, 224 p., [4] leaves of plates : ill. ; 25 cm. Includes index. Bibliography: p. [217]-218. [DA590.B26 1976] 76-17491 ISBN 0-679-50693-4 : 10.95
1. Elizabeth II, Queen of Great Britain, 1926- —Coronation. 2. Great Britain—Kings and rulers—Biography. I. Title. BIP

Elizabeth II, Queen of Great Britain, 1926- —Juvenile literature.

LIVERSIDGE, 942.085'0924 B
Douglas, 1913-
The picture life of Elizabeth II. New York, F. Watts [1969] 39 p. illus., ports. 23 cm. Describes the private and public life of the woman whose official title is Her Majesty Queen Elizabeth II of the United Kingdom of Great Britain and Northern Ireland and her other realms and territories, Head of the Commonwealth, Defender of the Faith. [DA590.L5] 92 69-16982
1. Elizabeth II, Queen of Great Britain, 1926- —Juvenile literature. I. Title.

Elizabeth II, Queen of Great Britain, 1926—Portraits, caricatures, etc.

BROWN, Michele. 941.085'092'4
Queen Elizabeth II : the Silver Jubilee book 1952-1977 / Michele Brown. New York : St. Martin's Press, 1977, c1976. 104 p. : chiefly ill. ; 26 cm. [DA590.B76 1977] 76-29855 10.00
1. Elizabeth II, Queen of Great Britain, 1926—Portraits, caricatures, tc. 2. Great Britain—Kings and rulers—Portraits.

Elizabeth (Name)—Juvenile literature.

GLAZER, Tom. 929.4
All about your name, Elizabeth (Beth, Bette, Eliza, Betsy, Betty, Lizzie, Liz) / by Tom Glazer ; illustrated by Demi. 1st ed. Garden City, N.Y. : Doubleday, c1978. 43 p. : ill. ; 22 cm. Discusses the name Elizabeth and people of historical, literary, and theatrical significance who have held that name. [CS2391.E44G56] 77-82442 ISBN 0-385-06399-7 : 4.95. ISBN 0-385-06404-7 lib.bdg. : 5.90
1. Elizabeth (Name)—Juvenile literature. 2. Biography—Miscellanea—Juvenile literature. I. Hitz, Demi. II. Title.

Elizabeth of England, consort of Frederick I, King of Bohemia, 1596-1662.

ROSS, Josephine. 943.7'1'020924 B
The Winter Queen / by Josephine Ross. New York : St. Martin's Press, 1979. p. cm. Includes index. [D244.8.E4R67 1979] 79-7845 ISBN 0-312-88232-7 : 15.95
1. Elizabeth of England, consort of Frederick I, King of Bohemia, 1596-1662. 2. Bohemia—Queens—Biography. 3. Great Britain—Princes and princesses—Biography. I. Title.

Elizabeth, of Hungary, Saint, 1207-1231.

ANCELET-HUSTACHE, Jeanne
922.2439
Gold tried by fire; St. Elizabeth of Hungary. Tr. [from French] by Paul J. Oligny, Sister Venard O'Donnell. Chicago, Franciscan Herald Pr. [1963] xxx,313p. 21cm. Bibl. 63-21385 7.50 bds.
1. Elizabeth, of Hungary, Saint, 1207-1231. I. Title.

DE ROBECK, Nesta. 922.2439
Saint Elizabeth of Hungary; a story of twenty-four years. Milwaukee, Bruce Pub. Co. [1954] 211p. illus. 22cm. [BX4700.E4D4] 54-7549
1. Elizabeth, of Hungary, Saint, 1207-1231. I. Title.

Elizabeth, of Hungary, Saint, 1207-1231—Juvenile literature.

HARRIS, Mary Kathleen. 92
Elizabeth. Drawings by R. M Sak. New York, Sheed & Ward [1961] unpaged. illus. 21cm. (A Patron saint book) [BX4700.E4H3] 61-11801
1. Elizabeth, of Hungary, Saint, 1207-1231—Juvenile literature. I. Title.

Elizabeth, Queen consort of George VI, 1900-

CATHCART, Helen. 942.0840924 B
The Queen Mother; the story of Elizabeth, the commoner who became Queen. New York, Dodd, Mead [1966, c1965] 255 p. ports. 22 cm. Bibliography: p. [253]-255. [DA585.A2C3 1966] 66-2170
1. Elizabeth, Queen consort of George VI, 1900- I. Title.

Elizabeth, Queen of England, 1533-1603.

BECKINGSALE, B. W. 942.055
Elizabeth I. New York, Arco [1963] 159p. illus. 23cm. 63-17097 3.95
1. Elizabeth, Queen of England, 1533-1603. I. Title.

BEESLY, Edward 942.05'5'0924 B
Spencer, 1831-1915.
Queen Elizabeth. Freeport, N.Y., Books for Libraries Press [1972] vii, 243 p. 23 cm. Reprint of the 1892 ed. [DA355.B417 1972] 74-39408 ISBN 0-8369-9901-0
1. Elizabeth, Queen of England, 1533-1603.

BIGLAND, Eileen 923.142
Queen Elizabeth I. New York, Criterion [c.1965] 151p. 21cm. [DA357.B5] 65-15258 3.50
1. Elizabeth, Queen of England, 1533—1603—Juvenile literature. I. Title.

CAMDEN, William, 1551- 942.05'5
1623.
The history of the most renowned and victorious Princess Elizabeth, late Queen of England. Edited and with an introd. by Wallace T. MacCaffrey. Chicago, University of Chicago Press [1970] xxxix, 351 p. 23 cm. (Classics of British historical literature) Selected chapters from the 1688 ed. of the English translation of Annales rerum anglicarum et hibernicarum regnante Elizabetha. Bibliography: p. 334-336. [DA350.C22 1970] 74-115682 ISBN 0-226-09218-6
1. Elizabeth, Queen of England, 1533-1603. 2. Great Britain—History—Elizabeth, 1558-1603—Sources. I. Title. BIP

CAMMIADE, Audrey 942.055
Elizabeth the First. New York, Roy [1962] 79p. illus. map 22cm. 62-13283 3.25
1. Elizabeth, Queen of England, 1533-1603. I. Title.

CHIDSEY, Donald Barr, 942.055
1902-
Elizabeth I; a great life in brief. [1st ed.] New York, Knopf, 1955. 198 p. 19 cm. (Great lives in brief; a new series of biographies) Includes bibliography. [DA355.C45] 54-7216
1. Elizabeth, Queen of England, 1533-1603.

CRAWFORD, Marion, 1909- 923.142
Elizabeth the Queen, the story of Britain's new sovereign. [1st American ed.] New York, Prentice-Hall [1952] 236 p. illus. 21 cm. [DA590.C7] 52-8691
I. Elizabeth II. Queen of Great Britain, 1926- III. Title.

CREIGHTON, Mandel, 942.0550924
Bp. of London, 1843-1901
Queen Elizabeth. Introd. by G. R. Elton. New York, Apollo Eds. [1968,c.1966] xv, 200p. 20cm. (A-194) Reprinted from the ed. of 1899. [DA357.C9 1966] 1.95 pap.,
1. Elizabeth, Queen of England, 1533-1603. I. Title.

CREIGHTON, Mandell, 942.0550924
Bp. of London, 1843-1901
Queen Elizabeth. Introd. by G. R. Elton. New York, Crowell [c.1966] xv, 200p. 21cm. (Crowell hist. classical ser.) Reprinted from the ed. of 1899. Bibl. [DA357.C9 1966] 66-14619 2.75 pap.,
1. Elizabeth, Queen of England, 1533-1603. I. Title.

CREIGHTON, 942.0550924 (B)
Mandell, Bp. of London, 1843-1902.
Queen Elizabeth. With an introd. by G. R. Elton. New York, Crowell [1966] xv, 200 p. 21 cm. (The Crowell historical classical series) "Reprinted from the edition of 1899." Bibliographical footnotes. [DA357.C9 1966] 66-14619
1. Elizabeth, Queen of England, 1533-1608. I. Title.

ELIZABETH, Queen of 942.05'5'0924
England, 1533-1603.
Letters of Queen Elizabeth and King James VI. of Scotland; some of them printed from originals in the possession of the Rev. Edward Ryder, and others from a MS. which formerly belonged to Sir Peter Thompson, Kt. Edited by John Bruce. [1st AMS ed.] London, Printed for the Camden Society, 1849 New York, AMS Press [1968] xxii, 180, 6 p. 24 cm. Original ed. issued as no. 46 of the Camden Society's Publications. [DA355.E55 1968] 72-185534
I. James I, King of Great Britain, 1566-1625. II. Title. III. Series: Camden Society, London. Publications, no. 46.

ELIZABETH, Queen of 942.05'5'0924
England, 1533-1603.
The letters of Queen Elizabeth I. Edited by G. B. Harrison New York, Funk & Wagnalls [1968] xvi, 323 p. port. 22 cm. Reprint of the 1935 ed. Bibliography: p. [307]-313. [DA355.A18 1968b] 68-25020 6.95

I. Harrison, George Bagshawe, 1894- ed.

FFRENCH, Yvonne. 920.72'094
Six great Englishwomen : Queen Elizabeth I, Sarah Siddons, Charlotte Bronte, Florence Nightingale, Queen Victoria, Gertrude Bell / by Yvonne Ffrench. Folcroft, Pa. : Folcroft Library Editions, 1976. p. cm. Reprint of the 1953 ed. published by Hamilton, London. [DA28.7.F42 1976] 76-10646 ISBN 0-8414-4219-3 lib. bdg. : 17.50
1. Elizabeth, Queen of England, 1533-1603. 2. Siddons, Sarah Kemble, 1755-1831. 3. Bronte, Charlotte, 1816-1855. 4. Nightingale, Florence, 1820-1910. 5. Victoria, Queen of Great Britain, 1819-1901. 6. Bell, Gertrude Lowthian, 1868-1926. I. Title.

HANFF, Helene. 942.05'5'0924 B
Queen of England; the story of Elizabeth I. Illustrated by Ronald Dorfman. [1st ed.] Garden City, N.Y., Doubleday [1969] 144 p. illus. 22 cm. (Doubleday signal books) A biography of Queen Elizabeth I, who, without husband or sons, successfully ruled England for 45 years and made it the most powerful kingdom on the globe. [DA357.H3] 92 69-11004 3.50
1. Elizabeth, Queen of England, 1533-1603—Juvenile literature. I. Dorfman, Ronald, illus. II. Title.

JENKINS, Elizabeth 923.142
Elizabeth the Great. New York, Permabooks [dist. Pocket Bks.] [1960,c.1959] 388p. (Permabk. M5026) Bibl.: p.371-374 .50 pap.,
1. Elizabeth, Queen of England, 1533-1603. I. Title.

JENKINS, Elizabeth, 1907- v. 12
Elizabeth the Great. New York, Permabooks [1960] 388 p. 17 cm. 66-8317
1. Elizabeth, Queen of England, 1533-1603, I. Title. **BIP**

JENKINS, Elizabeth, 1907- 923.142
Elizabeth the Great. [1st American ed.] New York, Coward-McCann [1959, c1958] 336 p. illus. 22 cm. Includes bibliography. [DA355.J4] 59-5455
1. Elizabeth, Queen of England, 1533-1603. I. Title.

JOHNSON, Paul, 942.05'5'0924 B
1928-
Elizabeth I; a biography. New York, Holt, Rinehart and Winston [1974] 511 p. illus. 24 cm. Bibliography: p. 487-492. [DA355.J6] 74-55 ISBN 0-03-012936-2 12.95
1. Elizabeth, Queen of England, 1533-1603.

KENDALL, Alan. 942.05'5'0924 B
Elizabeth I / Alan Kendall. New York : St. Martin's Press, 1977. p. cm. (History makers series) Includes index. Bibliography: p. A biography of Elizabeth I, who secured her claim to the English throne by executing her cousin, Mary Stuart, Queen of the Scots. [DA355.K46 1977] 92 77-288 ISBN 0-312-24247-6 : 6.95
1. Elizabeth, Queen of England, 1533-1603—Juvenile literature. 2. Great Britain—Kings and rulers—Biography—Juvenile literature. 3. Great Britain—History—Elizabeth, 1558-1603—Juvenile literature. I. Title.

LEVINE, Joseph M., 942.05'5'0924
comp.
Elizabeth I, edited by Joseph M. Levine. Englewood Cliffs, N.J., Prentice-Hall [1969] viii, 177 p. 21 cm. (Great lives observed) (A Spectrum book.) "Bibliographical note": p. 170-173. [DA355.L46] 68-27490 4.95
1. Elizabeth, Queen of England, 1533-1603.

LININGTON, Elizabeth. 923.142
Forging an empire Queen Elizabeth I illustrated by Robert Boehmer Chicago, Kingston House [1961] 191 p. illus. 22 cm. (Bookshelf for young Americans) [DA355.L5] 61-9810
1. Elizabeth, Qeen of England, 1533-1603 — Juvenile literature. I. Title.

LININGTON, Elizabeth. 923.142
Forging an empire Queen Elizabeth I illustrated by Robert Boehmer Chicago, Encyclopaedia Britannica Press [1964? c 1961] 191 p. illus. (part col.) 22 cm. (Britannica bookshelf: Great lives series) [[DA355]] 64-57223
1. Elizabeth, Qeen of England, 1533-1603 — Juvenile literature. I. Title.

LUKE, Mary M. 942.05'2
A crown for Elizabeth [by] Mary M. Luke. New York, Coward-McCann [1970] 573 p. illus., ports. 24 cm. Sequel to Catherine, the queen. Sequel: Gloriana; the years of Elizabeth I. Bibliography: p. [541]-542. [DA317.1.L8] 70-113530 10.00
1. Mary I, Queen of England, 1516-1558. 2. Elizabeth, Queen of England, 1533-1603. 3. Edward VI, King of England, 1537-1553. I. Title.

MAYNARD, Theodore, 1890- 923.142
Queen Elizabeth. Milwaukee, Bruce Pub. Co. [1954] 306p. 21cm. Includes bibliography. [DA355.M35 1954] 54-10440
1. Elizabeth, Queen of England, 1533-1603. I. Title.

MORRISON, Nancy 942.05'092'2 B
Brysson.
King's quiver: the last three Tudors [by] N. Brysson Morrison. New York, St. Martin's Press [1973, c1972] vii, 212 p. illus. 23 cm. Bibliography: p. 203-204. [DA317.1.M67 1973] 73-80311 6.95
1. Mary I, Queen of England, 1516-1558. 2. Elizabeth, Queen of England, 1533-1603. 3. Edward VI, King of England, 1537-1553. I. Title.

NAUNTON, Robert, Sir, 820*.3*08
1563-1635.
Fragmenta regalia. Probably written about 1630. Reprinted from the 3d posthumous ed. of 1653. [Edited] by Edward Arber. London, 1870. [New York, AMS Press, 1966] 64 p. 22 cm. (English reprints, v. 5 [no. 20]) Bound with Visio monachi de Eynsham. The revelation to the monk of Evesham. [New York, 1966] Includes bibliographical references. [PR1121.V5 1966] 72-193036
1. Elizabeth, Queen of England, 1533-1603. 2. Great Britain—Court and courtiers. I. Title. II. Series.

NEALE, John Ernest, Sir 923.142
1890-
Queen Elizabeth I, a biography. New York, Doubleday, 1957. 424p. 18cm. (Doubleday anchor books, A105) [DA355] 57-4393
1. Elizabeth, Queen of England, 1533-1603. I. Title.

PLOWDEN, Alison. 942.05'5092'4 B
Marriage with my kingdom : the courtships of Elizabeth I / Alison Plowden. New York : Stein and Day, 1977. 216 p., [4] leaves of plates : ports. ; 24 cm. Includes index. Bibliography: p. [198]-200. [DA355.P568 1977] 77-8768 ISBN 0-8128-2338-9 : 10.00
1. Elizabeth, Queen of England, 1533-1603. 2. Great Britain—Kings and rulers—Biography. 3. Great Britain—History—Elizabeth, 1558-1603. I. Title.

ROSS, Josephine. 942.05'5'0924 B
Suitors to the Queen : the men in the life of Elizabeth I of England / Josephine Ross. 1st American ed. New York : Coward, McCann & Geohegan, 1975. [viii] , 198 p. [4] leaves of plates. : ports. ; 22 cm. Includes index. Bibliography: 7th-8th prelim. page. [DA356.R62 1975] 75-31864 ISBN 0-698-10698-9
1. Elizabeth, Queen of England, 1533-1603. I. Title. **BIP**

ROWSE, Alfred Leslie, 942.05'5
1903-
An Elizabethan garland, by A. L. Rowse. London, Macmillan, 1953. [New York, AMS Press, 1972] viii, 161 p. illus. 23 cm. [DA356.R65 1972] 76-161760 ISBN 0-404-07965-2
1. Elizabeth, Queen of England, 1533-1603. 2. Great Britain—History—Addresses, essays, lectures. I. Title. **BIP**

ROWSE, Alfred Leslie, 914.2'03'55
1903-
Queen Elizabeth and her subjects, by Alfred L. Rowse and George B. Harrison. Freeport, N.Y., Books for Libraries Press [1970] 139 p. ports. 23 cm. (Essay index reprint series) Reprint of the 1935 ed. [DA358.A1R6 1970] 79-76913
1. Elizabeth, Queen of England, 1533-1603. 2. Gt. Brit.—Court and courtiers. 3. Gt. Brit.—Biography. I. Harrison, George Bagshawe, 1894- joint author. II. Title. **BIP**

SITWELL, Edith, Dame 1887- v. 12
The queens and the hive. Boston, Little, Brown [c1962] 542 p. illus. 23 cm. 67-60580
1. Elizabeth, Queen of England, 1533-1603. 2. Gt. Brit. — Hist. — Elizabeth, 1558-1603. I. Title.

SMITH, Lacey 942.05'5'0924 B
Baldwin, 1922-
Elizabeth Tudor : portrait of a queen / Lacey Baldwin Smith. 1st ed. Boston : Little, Brown, [1975] xi, 234 p. : port. ; 21 cm. (The Library of world biography) Includes index. Bibliography: p. [223]-224. [DA355.S59] 75-19170 ISBN 0-316-80152-6 : 8.95
1. Elizabeth, Queen of England, 1533-1603. I. Title.

STEARNS, Monroe. 942.05'5'0924 B
Elizabeth I of England. New York, Franklin Watts [1970] xxvii, 227 p. illus., map, ports. 22 cm. (Immortals of history) Bibliography: p. 217-219. A biography of the Tudor Queen whose strong sense of responsibility to her subjects made her a much loved ruler during the forty-five years of her reign. [DA355.S75] 92 71-117181
1. Elizabeth, Queen of England, 1533-1603—Juvenile literature. I. Title.

STRONG, Roy C. 757'.0942
The cult of Elizabeth : Elizabethan portraiture and pageantry / Roy Strong. London : Thames and Hudson, 1977. 227 p. : ill. (some col.) ; 26 cm. Includes bibliographical references and index. [DA356.S83] 77-378494 ISBN 0-500-23263-6 : 24.95
1. Elizabeth, Queen of England, 1533-1603. 2. Great Britain—History—Elizabeth, 1558-1603. I. Title.
Distributed by W.W. Norton. **BIP**

STRONG, Roy C. 942.05'5'0924
Elizabeth R. Evocation [by] Roy Strong. Spectacle [by] Julia Trevelyan Oman. New York, Stein and Day [1971] 79 p. illus. 22 cm. [DA355.S85 1971b] 71-179699 ISBN 0-8128-1443-6 4.95
1. Elizabeth, Queen of England, 1533-1603. I. Oman, Julia Trevelyan. II. Title.

WALDMAN, Milton, 1895- 923.142
Queen Elizabeth. [New York, Collier bks., 1962] 127p. (AS135V: biography) .95 pap.,
1. Elizabeth, Queen of England, 1533-1603. I. Title.

WALDMAN, Milton, 942.0550924
1895-
Queen Elizabeth I. Hamden, Conn., Archon, 1966. 159p. ports. 21cm. (Markers of hist.) First pub. in 1952 under title: Queen Elizabeth. [DA355. W33 1966] 66-21095 4.00
1. Elizabeth, Queen ofEngland, 1533-1603. I. Title.

WALDMAN, Milton, 1895- 942.05
Some English dictators. Port Washington, N.Y., Kennikat Press [1970] vii, 253 p. illus., ports. 22 cm. Reprint of the 1940 ed. Includes bibliographical references. [DA315.W28 1970] 77-112820
1. Henry VIII, King of England, 1491-1547. 2. Elizabeth, Queen of England, 1533-1603. 3. Cromwell, Oliver, 1599-1658. 4. Gt. Brit.—History—Tudors, 1485-1603. 5. Gt. Brit.—History—Stuarts, 1603-1714. I. Title. **BIP**

WILLIAMS, 942.05'5'0922 B
Neville, 1924-
All the Queen's men; Elizabeth I and her courtiers. [1st American ed.] New York, Macmillan [1972] 272 p. illus. 26 cm. [DA355.W4816 1972] 72-84882 12.95
1. Elizabeth, Queen of England, 1533-1603. 2. Great Britain—Court and courtiers. I. Title.

WILLIAMS, 942.05'5'0924 B
Neville, 1924-
Elizabeth the First, Queen of England. New York, Dutton, 1968 [c1967] xii, 386 p. illus., geneal. table, ports. 25 cm. First published in 1967 under title: Elizabeth, Queen of England. Bibliography: p. [371]-374. [DA355.W482 1968.] 68-12449
1. Elizabeth, Queen of England, 1533-1603. I. Title.

WILLIAMS, 942.05'5'0924 B
Neville, 1924-
The life and times of Elizabeth I. Introd. by Antonia Fraser. Garden City, N.Y., Doubleday, 1972. 224 p. illus. 26 cm. Bibliography: p. 217-218. [DA355.W483 1972] 74-187567 10.00
1. Elizabeth, Queen of England, 1533-1603. I. Title.

Elizabeth, Queen of England, 1533-1603—Addresses, essays, lectures.

GREAVES, Richard 942.05'5'0924 B
L., comp.
Elizabeth I, Queen of England / edited and with an inrod. by Richard L. Greaves. Lexington, Mass. : Heath, [1974]. xvi, 197 p. : ill. ; 21 cm. (Problems in European civilization) Bibliography: p. 190-197. [DA355.G74] 73-19075 ISBN 0-669-86371-8 pbk. : 2.95
1. Elizabeth, Queen of England, 1533-1603—Addresses, essays, lectures. 2. Great Britain—Politics and government—1558-1603—Addresses, essays, lectures. I. Title. II. Series.

Elizabeth, Queen of England, 1533-1603—Juvenile literature.

HIBBERT, Eleanor, 1906- 92
The young Elizabeth [by] Jean Plaidy [pseud.] Illustrated by William Randell. New York, Roy Publishers [1961] 134p. illus. 21cm. [DA357.H5] 61-11043
1. Elizabeth, Queen of England, 1533-1603—Juvenile literature. I. Title.

LININGTON, Elizabeth. 923.142
Queen Elizabeth I; forging an empire. Illustrated by Robert Boehmer. Chicago, Kingston House [1961] 191p. illus. 22cm. (Bookshelf for young Americans) [DA357.A5] 61-9810
1. Elizabeth, Queen of England, 1533-1603—Juvenile literature. I. Title.

LININGTON, Elizabeth 923.142
Queen Elizabeth I; forging an empire. Illus. by Robert Boehmer. Chicago, Britannica Bks.,div. of Ency. Britannica [1963, c.1961] 191p. col. illus. 22cm. (Britannica bkshelf.: Great lives for young Amers.) 2.36 lib. ed.,
1. Elizabeth, Queen of England, 1533-1603—Juvenile literature. I. Title.

Elk Co, Pa. — Biog.

WHO'S who in Elk 920.0748
County, containing biographical sketches and photographic portraits. St. Marys, Pa., Lenze Commercial Studios, 1956. 133 p. illus. ports., maps. 28 cm. [F157.E4W5] 56-37626
1. Elk Co, Pa. — Biog.

Elkins, Opie Eldridge, 1894-1958.

ELKINS, Ada Mae 922.773
Thirty-eight years in the parsonage; the fruitful career of the Reverend Opie Eldridge Elkins in the Methodist ministry of rural and urban West Virginia--perceptively recounted by his wife and fellow worker. New York, William-Frederick Press [c.]1960. 101p. 60-11907 3.00
1. Elkins, Opie Eldridge, 1894-1958. I. Title.

Ellen.

LEVIT, Rose. 362.1'9'699400924 B
Ellen; a short life long remembered. San Francisco, Chronicle Books [1974] 156 p. 23 cm. [RC263.L4] 74-4398 ISBN 0-87701-051-X 6.95
1. Ellen. 2. Cancer—Personal narratives. I. Title.

Ellenborough, Jane Elizabeth Digby Law, Countess of, 1807-1881.

SCHMIDT, 301.41'76'330924 B
Margaret Fox.
Passion's child : the extraordinary life of Jane Digby / Margaret Fox Schmidt. 1st ed. New York : Harper & Row, c1976. p. cm. Includes index. Bibliography: p. [DA536.E45S35 1976] 74-15848 ISBN 0-06-013807-6 : 12.50
1. Ellenborough, Jane Elizabeth Digby Law, Countess of, 1807-1881. I. Title. BIP

Ellerman, John Reeves, Sir, bart., 1862-1933.

TAYLOR, James 387.5'06'541
Arnold.
Ellermans : a wealth of shipping / [by] James Taylor. London : Wilton House Gentry Ltd, 1976. 320 p., [8] p. of plates : ill. (some col.), maps, ports, ; 26 cm. Includes bibliographical references and index. [HE945.E54T39 1976] 77-359056 ISBN 0-905064-02-X : £6.95
1. Ellerman Lines Ltd.—History. 2. Ellerman, John Reeves, Sir, bart., 1862-1933. 3. Ellerman, John Reeves, Sir, bart., 1909- 4. Merchant marine—Great Britain—Biography. I. Title.

Ellerman Lines Ltd.—History.

TAYLOR, James 387.5'06'541
Arnold.
Ellermans : a wealth of shipping / [by] James Taylor. London : Wilton House Gentry Ltd, 1976. 320 p., [8] p. of plates : ill. (some col.), maps, ports, ; 26 cm. Includes bibliographical references and index. [HE945.E54T39 1976] 77-359056 ISBN 0-905064-02-X : £6.95
1. Ellerman Lines Ltd.—History. 2. Ellerman, John Reeves, Sir, bart., 1862-1933. 3. Ellerman, John Reeves, Sir, bart., 1909- 4. Merchant marine—Great Britain—Biography. I. Title.

Ellery, William, 1727-1820.

FOWLER, William M., 973.3'092'4 B
1944-
William Ellery: a Rhode Island politico and Lord of Admiralty, by William M. Fowler, Jr. Metuchen, N.J., Scarecrow Press, 1973. vi, 231 p. port. 22 cm. Bibliography: p. 197-214. [F83.E44F68] 72-12673 ISBN 0-8108-0576-6 6.50
1. Ellery, William, 1727-1820.

Ellet, Charles, 1810-1862.

LEWIS, Gene Dale, 620'.00924 B
1931-
Charles Ellet, Jr., the engineer as individualist, 1810-1862, by Gene D. Lewis. Urbana, University of Illinois Press, 1968. viii, 220 p. illus., maps, ports. 24 cm. Bibliographical footnotes. [TA140.E44L4] 68-18206 ISBN 0-252-72325-5 7.50
1. Ellet, Charles, 1810-1862. BIP

Elliff, Joseph Doliver.

TRACY, Lester L 1918- 353.008'5
Life and educational contributions of Joseph D. Elliff. [Columbia, Mo.] Published under the sponsorship of Gamma Chapter of Phi Delta Kappa [1953] 144p. ports. 27cm. 'Originally submitted ... in partial fulfillment of the requirement for the degree of doctor of education in the Graduate School [University of Missouri] may 1. 1951.' Bibliography: p.144. [LA2317.E46T7] 54-3608
1. Elliff, Joseph Doliver. I. Title.

Ellington, Duke, 1899-1974.

ELLINGTON, Duke, 785.4'2'0924 B
1899-
Music is my mistress, by Edward Kennedy Ellington. [1st ed.] Garden City, N.Y., Doubleday, 1973. xv, 522 p. illus. 27 cm. "Selected discography": p. 491-492; "compositions": p. 493-522. [ML410.E44A3] 73-83189 ISBN 0-385-02235-2 14.95
1. Ellington, Duke, 1899- 2. Musicians—Correspondence, reminiscences, etc. I. Title. BIP

ELLINGTON, Duke, 785.4'2'0924 B
1899-1974.
Music is my mistress / by Edward Kennedy Ellington ; with a rev. discography by Stanley Dance. New York : Da Capo Press, 1976. p. cm. (A Da Capo paperback) Reprint of the 1973 ed. published by Doubleday, Garden City, N.Y. Discography: p. [ML410.E44A3 1976] 75-31665 ISBN 0-306-80033-0 pbk. : 5.95
1. Ellington, Duke, 1899-1974. 2. Jazz musicians—Correspondence, reminiscences, etc. I. Title. BIP

ELLINGTON, Mercer. 785.4'2'0924 B
Duke Ellington in person : an intimate memoir / by Mercer Ellington with Stanley Dance. Boston : Houghton Mifflin Co., 1978. xii, 236 p., [12] leaves of plates : ill. ; 22 cm. Includes index. [ML410.E44E5] 77-18963 10.95
1. Ellington, Duke, 1899-1974. 2. Jazz musicians—United States—Biography. I. Dance, Stanley, joint author. II. Title. BIP

GAMMOND, Peter, ed. 927.8
Duke Ellington: his life and music. Contributions by Jeff Aldam [and others] Foreword by Hugues Panassie. New York, Roy Publishers [1958, i.e. 1960] 255p. illus., diagrs. 21cm. 59-12865 5.00
1. Ellington, Duke, 1899- I. Title.

GAMMOND, Peter, 785.4'2'0924 B
ed.
Duke Ellington : his life and music / edited by Peter Gammond ; contributions by Jeff Aldam ... [et al.] ; foreword by Hugues Panassie. New York : Da Capo Press, 1977. 255 p., [9] leaves of plates : ill. ; 21 cm. (The Roots of jazz) Reprint of the 1958 ed. published by Phoenix House, London. Discography: p. 217-255. [ML410.E44G3 1977] 77-1927 ISBN 0-306-70874-4 lib.bdg. : 17.50
1. Ellington, Duke, 1899-1974. 2. Jazz musicians—United States—Biography. BIP

JEWELL, Derek. 785.4'2'0924 B
Duke : a portrait of Duke Ellington / Derek Jewell. New York : Norton, c1977. 264 p. : ill. ; 24 cm. Includes index. Discography and bibliography: p. 251-253. [ML410.E44J5] 77-2271 ISBN 0-393-07512-5 : 8.95
1. Ellington, Duke, 1899-1974. 2. Jazz musicians—United States—Biography. BIP

ULANOV, Barry. 785.4'2'0924 B
Duke Ellington / by Barry Ulanov. New York : Da Capo Press, 1975, c1946. x, 322 p., [8] leaves of plates : ill. ; 22 cm. (The Roots of jazz) Reprint of the ed. published by Musicians Press Ltd., London. Includes index. Discography: p. [277]-311. [ML410.E44U4 1975] 74-31300 ISBN 0-306-70727-6 lib.bdg. : 15.95
1. Ellington, Duke, 1899-1974. BIP

Ellington, Duke, 1899-1974—Juvenile literature.

BARCLAY, Pamela. 785.4'2'0924 B
Duke Ellington; ambassador of music. Illustrated by Harold Henriksen. Mankato, Minn., Creative Education; [distributed by Childrens Press, Chicago, 1974] 29 p. col. illus. 25 cm. (Close-ups) A biography of the black musician who in fifty years has composed 2000 songs and performed them all over the world. [ML3930.E44B3] 92 74-8211 ISBN 0-87191-367-4
1. Ellington, Duke, 1899- —Juvenile literature. I. Henriksen, Harold, illus. II. Title.

GUTMAN, Bill. 785.4'2'0924 B
Duke : the musical life of Duke Ellington / by Bill Gutman. New York : Random House, c1977. 184, [1] p. : ill. ; 24 cm. Includes index. Discography: p. [185] A biography of the pianist, composer, and band leader who popularized jazz. [ML410.E44G9] 92 76-8136 ISBN 0-394-83097-0 : 6.95
1. Ellington, Duke, 1899-1974—Juvenile literature. 2. Composers—Biography—Juvenile literature. I. Title. BIP

MONTGOMERY, 785.4'2'0924 B
Elizabeth Rider.
Duke Ellington: king of jazz. Illustrated by Paul Frame. Champaign, Ill., Garrard Pub. Co. [1972] 96 p. illus. 24 cm. (Americans all) Biography of an internationally acclaimed jazz musician who as a young man was torn between a career in art and music. [ML3930.E44M6] 92 70-179401 ISBN 0-8116-4573-8
1. Ellington, Duke, 1899- —Juvenile literature. I. Frame, Paul, 1913- illus. II. Title.

Elliot, Elisabeth.

ELLIOT, Elisabeth. 248'.2 B
Love has a price tag / Elisabeth Elliot. Chappaqua, N.Y. : Christian Herald Books, [1979] p. cm. [BR1725.E46A34] 79-50944 ISBN 0-915684-50-0 : 7.95
1. Elliot, Elisabeth. 2. Christian biography—United States. I. Title. BIP

ELLIOT, Elisabeth. 980'.004'97
These strange ashes / Elisabeth Elliot. 1st ed. New York : Harper & Row, [1975] xi, 132 p. ; 21 cm. [F3722.1.C7E44 1975] 74-25684 ISBN 0-06-062233-4 : 6.95
1. Elliot, Elisabeth. 2. Colorado Indians (Ecuador) I. Title. BIP

Elliot, James, 1927-1956.

ELLIOT, Elisabeth. 922
Shadow of the Almighty; the life and testament of Jim Elliot. [1st ed.] New York, Harper [1958] 256 p. illus. 22 cm. [BV2853.E3E496] 58-10365
1. Elliot, James, 1927-1956. 2. Missions—Ecuador. I. Title. BIP

ELLIOT, James, 266'.023'0924 B
1927-1956.
The journals of Jim Elliot / edited by Elisabeth Elliot. Old Tappan, N.J. : F. H. Revell Co., c1978. 477 p. ; 24 cm. [BV2853.E3A34] 78-16298 ISBN 0-8007-0922-5 : 12.95
1. Elliot, James, 1927-1956. 2. Missionaries—Ecuador—Biography. 3. Missionaries—United States—Biography. I. Elliot, Elisabeth. II. Title. BIP

Elliot, Jared, 1685-1763.

THOMS, Herbert, 974.6'02'0924 (B)
1885-
Jared Eliot, minister, doctor, scientist, and his Connecticut. [Hamden, Conn.] Shoe String, 1967. xii, 156p. illus., ports. 21cm. Bibl. [F97.E4T47] 67-12392 6.00
1. Elliot, Jared, 1685-1763. I. Title. BIP

Elliott, Aaron Marshall, 1846-1910.

(ARMSTRONG, Edward Cooke, 920.1
1871-
A. Marshall Elliott, a retrospect. New York, Kraus Reprint, 1966. 16p. 23cm. (Elliott monographs in the Romance langs. & lit., no.15) Orig. pub. in 1923 by Princeton. 3.50 pap.,
1. Elliott, Aaron Marshall, 1846-1910. I. Title. II. Series.

Elliott, Bill, 1903-1965.

LEONARD, John W. 791.43'028'0924
Wild Bill Elliott / by John W. Leonard. [s.l. : s.n.], c1976. 95 p. : ill. ; 26 cm. [PN2287.E43L4] 76-151767
1. Elliott, Bill, 1903-1965.

Elliott, Edward Charles, 1874-1960.

BURRIN, Frank 378.1'12'0924 B
Kleiser, 1920-
Edward Charles Elliott, educator, by Frank K. Burrin. Lafayette, Ind., Purdue University Studies, 1970. xv, 187 p. illus., ports. 24 cm. Bibliography: p. 163-180. [LD4672.7 1922.B8] 69-11274 5.50
1. Elliott, Edward Charles, 1874-1960. BIP

Elliott, Errol T.

ELLIOTT, Errol T. 289.6'092'4 B
Life unfolding : the spiritual pilgrimage of a Quaker plainsman / by Errol T. Elliott. Richmond, Ind. : Friends United Press, [1975] xviii, 162 p. ; 21 cm. Autobiographical. [BX7795.E54A33] 75-9806 ISBN 0-913408-15-8 : 5.95 ISBN 0-913408-17-4 pbk. : 4.95
1. Elliott, Errol T. I. Title.

Elliott, John Lovejoy, 1868-1942.

HOHOFF, Tay. 923.673
A ministry to man; the life of John Lovejoy Elliott, a biography. [1st ed.] New York, Harper [c1959] 234p. 22cm. [BJ354.E43H6] 58-13240
1. Elliott, John Lovejoy, 1868-1942. 2. Ethical culture movement. I. Title.

Elliott, Maxine, 1868-1940.

FORBES-ROBERTSON, Diana. 927.92
My aunt Maxine; the story of Maxine Elliott. New York, Viking Press [1964] xii, 306 p. illus., ports. 22 cm. [PN2287.E45F6] 64-12228
1. Elliott, Maxine, 1868-1940. I. Title.

Ellis, Anne, 1875-1938.

ELLIS, Anne, 917.8'03'20924 B
1875-1938.
The life of an ordinary woman. New York, Arno Press, 1974 [c1929] xii, 300 p. illus. 21 cm. (Women in America: from colonial times to the 20th century) Reprint of the ed. published by Houghton Mifflin, Boston. [CT275.E38515A3 1974] 74-3946 ISBN 0-405-06092-0
1. Ellis, Anne, 1875-1938. I. Title. II. Series. BIP

Ellis, Arthur L.

ELLIS, Arthur L. 309.1'747'1
A mind on Harlem / Arthur L. Ellis. San Francisco : R & E Research Associates, 1978. vii, 104 p. : ill. ; 28 cm. Bibliography: p. 97-104. [HN80.N5E44] 78-62232 ISBN 0-88247-537-1 : 12.00
1. Ellis, Arthur L. 2. Harlem, New York (City) 3. New York (City)—Social conditions. 4. Social scientists—United States—Biography. I. Title. BIP

Ellis Co., Okla.—Biography.

OUR Ellis County 976.6'155
heritage, 1885-1974. [Gage, Okla.] : Ellis County Historical Society, c1974- v. : ill. ; 32 cm. Bibliography: v. 1, p. 9. [F693.O97] 75-317442
1. Ellis Co., Okla.—Biography. 2. Ellis Co., Okla.—History. I. Ellis County Historical Society.

Ellis, Dock.

HALL, Donald, 796.357'092'4 B
1928-
Dock Ellis in the country of baseball / by Donald Hall, with Dock Ellis. New York : Coward, McCann & Geoghegan, c1976. 254 p., [8] leaves of plates : ill. ; 22 cm. [GV865.E44H34 1976] 74-30602 ISBN 0-698-10658-X : 8.95
1. Ellis, Dock. 2. Baseball players—United States—Biography. I. Ellis, Dock, joint author. II. Title.

Ellis, Havelock, 1859-1939.

BROME, Vincent, 301.41'092'4 B
1910-
Havelock Ellis, philosopher of sex : a biography / Vincent Brome. London ; Boston : Routledge & K. Paul, 1979. xiv, 271 p., [3] leaves of plates : ports ; 24 cm. Includes index. Bibliography: p. 264-266. [HQ18.32.E44B76] 79-310649 ISBN 0-7100-0019-7 : 21.50
1. Ellis, Havelock, 1859-1939. 2. Sexologists—Great Britain—Biography. I. Title.

CALDER-MARSHALL, Arthur 928.2
The sage of sex; a life of Havelock Ellis. New York, Putnam [1960, c.1959] 292p. (3p. bibl.) illus. 23cm. 60-5269 5.00
1. Ellis, Havelock, 1859-1939. I. Title.

COLLIS, John Stewart, 1900- 928.2
Havelock Ellis: artist of life; a study of his life and work. New York, W. Sloane Associates, 1959. 223 p. 22 cm. "First

published in Great Britain under the title An artist of life." Includes bibliography. [PR6009.L8Z63 1959] 59-7409
1. Ellis, Havelock, 1859-1939.

ELLIS, Havelock, 1859-1939. 928.2
The unpublished letters of Havelock Ellis to Joseph Ishill. Introductory essay by Joseph Ishill. Berkeley Heights, N. J., Published and printed privately by the Oriole Press, 1954. xxviii, 232p. mounted illus., mounted ports. 22cm. 'Limited to 125 copies. Copy no. 10.' 'Bibliographical notes': p. [219)-226. [PR6009.L8Z54] 55-21719
I. Ishill, Joseph. II. Title.

ROBINSON, Paul A., 1940- 301.41'792'2
The modernization of sex : Havelock Ellis, Alfred Kinsey, William Masters, and Virginia Johnson / Paul Robinson. 1st ed. New York : Harper & Row, c1976. viii, 200 p. ; 22 cm. Includes bibliographical references and index. [HQ18.3.R6] 75-24500 ISBN 0-06-013583-2 : 8.95
1. Ellis, Havelock, 1859-1939. 2. Kinsey, Alfred Charles, 1894-1956. 3. Masters, William H. 4. Johnson, Virginia E. 5. Sexologists. I. Title.

Ellis, James Benton, 1870-1946.

ELLIS, James Benton, 1870-1946. 269'.2'0924 B
Blazing the Gospel trail / by James B. Ellis. Plainfield, N.J. : Logos International, c1976. 127 p. ; 21 cm. (A Logos classic) [BX7034.Z8E43] 76-2329 ISBN 0-88270-165-7 pbk. : 2.50
1. Ellis, James Benton, 1870-1946. I. Title. BIP

Ellis, James Tandy, 1868-1942.

JILLSON, Willard Rouse, 1890- 928.1
Rambo Flats; a sketch of the life, military service, and literary achievements of James Tandy Ellis (1869-1942) Frankfort, Ky., Perry Pub. Co., 1957. 95p. illus. 23cm. [PS3509.L598Z65] 57-2722
1. Ellis, James Tandy, 1868-1942. I. Title.

Ellis, Jim,

ELLIS, Jim, 1893- 659.1'0924 B
The jumping frog from Jasper County; Hoosier boy lands on Madison Avenue. London, New York, Abelard-Schuman [1970] 240 p. illus., facsims., group ports. 22 cm. First published in 1968 under title: Billboards to Buicks. [HF5810.E4A3 1970] 77-123211 6.95
I. Title.

Ellis, Marc H.

ELLIS, Marc H. 361.7'5
A year at the Catholic Worker / by Marc H. Ellis. New York : Paulist Press, c1978. 140 p. ; 18 cm. (A Deus book) [BX810.C393E44] 78-61722 ISBN 0-8091-2140-9 pbk. : 1.95
1. Ellis, Marc H. 2. The Catholic Worker Movement—Biography. 3. Catholic Worker Movement. I. Title. BIP

Ellis, Sydney Alberto, 1858-1915.

ELLIS, Lester N., 1891- 910.4'5'0924 B
True life story of a master mariner, by Lester N. Ellis. Philadelphia, Dorrance [1969] 161 p. illus., facsims., ports. 22 cm. [G540.E6] 68-57737 4.00
1. Ellis, Sydney Alberto, 1858-1915. 2. Seafaring life. I. Title.

Elliston, Robert William, 1774-1831.

RAYMOND, George. 792'.028'0924
Memoirs of Robert William Elliston. New York, B. Blom, 1969. 2 v. illus., facsims., port. 20 cm. Reprint of the 1846 ed. [PN2598.E5R3 1969] 77-81218
1. Elliston, Robert William, 1774-1831. BIP

Ellot, Jared, 1685-1763.

THOMAS, Herbert, 1885- 926.1
The Doctos Jared of Connecticut: Jared Eliot, Jared Potter, Jared Kirtland. Hamden, Conn., Shoe String Press, 1958. 76 p. illus. 22 cm. (Dept. of the History of Medicine, Yale University School of Medicine. Publication no. 35) [R153.T35] 58-59573
1. Ellot, Jared, 1685-1763. 2. Potter, Jared, 1742-1810. 3. Kirtland, Jared Potter, 1793-1877. I. Title.

Ellsworth, Ephraim Elmer, 1837-1861.

RANDALL, Ruth (Painter) 923.573
Colonel Elmer Ellsworth; a biography of Lincoln's friend and first hero of the Civil War. [1st ed.] Boston, Little, Brown [1960] 295p. illus. 22cm. Includes bibliography. [E467.1.E47R3] 60-6527
1. Ellsworth, Ephraim Elmer, 1837-1861. I. Title.

Ellsworth, Oliver, 1745-1807.

BROWN, William Garrott, 1868-1913. 347.99'24 B
The life of Oliver Ellsworth. New York, Da Capo Press, 1970. ix, 369 p. illus., ports. 24 cm. (Da Capo Press reprints in American constitutional and legal history) Reprint of the 1905 ed. [KF8745.E4B7 1970] 76-118028
1. Ellsworth, Oliver, 1745-1807. BIP

Ellwood, Craig.

MCCOY, Esther. 720'.924
Craig, Ellwood; architecture. Foreword by Peter Blake. New York, Walker [1968] 155 p. illus. (part col.), plans. 24 x 25 cm. [NA737.E36M3 1968b] 68-14007 15.00
1. Ellwood, Craig.

Ellyson, Theodore Gordon, 1885-1928.

VAN DEURS, George, 1901- 358.4'13'320924 B
Anchors in the sky : Spuds Ellyson, the first naval aviator / George van Deurs. San Rafael, Calif. : Presidio Press, [1978] p. cm. Includes index. Bibliography: p. [V63.E44V36] 78-74 ISBN 0-89141-034-1 : 8.95
1. Ellyson, Theodore Gordon, 1885-1928. 2. United States. Navy—Biography. 3. Air pilots, Military—United States—Biography. I. Title. BIP

Elmore, Bennie Carl, 1909-1973.

ELMORE, Inez K. 370'.92'4 B
The story of a great pioneer in Black education, Bennie Carl Elmore, 1909-1973 / Inez K. Elmore. 1st ed. Hicksville, N.Y. : Exposition Press, [1975] 79 p. : ports. ; 22 cm. Errata slip inserted. [LA2317.E47E46] 75-311783 ISBN 0-682-48194-7 : 4.00
1. Elmore, Bennie Carl, 1909-1973. I. Title: The story of a great pioneer in Black education, Bennie Carl Elmore ...

Elmslie, John, 1831-1907.

ELMSLIE, Jeannie Gibson, 1887- v. 12
John Elmslie, 1831-1907; he came from Bennachie. Christchurch, Printed at the Caxton press, 1963 [c1961] 97 p. illus., ports., map. 23 cm. 64-67920
1. Elmslie, John, 1831-1907. I. Title.

Elsasser, Walter M., 1904-

ELSASSER, Walter M., 1904- 530'.092'4 B
Memoirs of a physicist / Walter M. Elsasser. New York : Science History Publications, [1978] p. cm. Includes index. Bibliography: p. [QC16.E58A35] 77-16583 ISBN 0-88202-178-8 : 15.00
1. Elsasser, Walter M., 1904- 2. Physicists—United States—Biography. I. Title.

Elsenstein, Sergek Mikhallovich, 1896-1948.

SETON, Marie. 927.914
Sergie M. Eisenstein, a biography. New York, A.A. Wyn [1952] 533p. illus., ports. 22cm. [PN1998.A3E57] 52-11572
1. Elsenstein, Sergek Mikhallovich, 1896-1948. I. Title.

Elsheimer, Adam, 1578-1610.

ANDREWS, Keith. 760'.092'4
Adam Elsheimer : paintings, drawings, prints / Keith Andrews. New York : Rizzoli, 1977. 178 p. : ill. (some col.) ; 29 cm. Includes indexes. Bibliography: p. 171. [N6888.E63A5] 77-73365 ISBN 0-8478-0089-X : 60.00
1. Elsheimer, Adam, 1578-1610. 2. Artists—Italy—Rome (City)—Biography. 3. Artists—Germany—Biography. I. Elsheimer, Adam, 1578-1610.

Elssler, Fanny, 1810-1884.

†FANNY Elssler in America : comprising seven facsimilies of rare Americana—never before offered the public—depicting her astounding conquest of America in 1840-42, a memoir, a libretto, two verses, a penny-terrible blast, letters and journal, and an early comic strip—the sad tale of her impresario's courtship / [edited] with an introd. and notes by Allison Delarue. Brooklyn : Dance Horizons, 1976. 219 p. : ill. ; 26 cm. [GV1785.E4F36] 75-37381 ISBN 0-87127-084-6 : 17.50 792.8'092'4 B
1. Elssler, Fanny, 1810-1884. I. Delarue, Allison.

GUEST, Ivor Forbes. 792.8'0924 B
Fanny Elssler [by] Ivor Guest. [1st American ed.] Middletown, Conn., Wesleyan University Press [1970] 284 p. illus., ports. 24 cm. Bibliography: p. [265]-271. [GV1785.E4G8 1970] 74-105507 15.00
1. Elssler, Fanny, 1810-1884. I. Title. BIP

Elsynge, Henry, 1577 or 8-1636.

FOSTER, Elizabeth Read. 328.42'092'4 B
The painful labour of Mr. Elsyng. Philadelphia, American Philosophical Society, 1972. 69 p. 30 cm. (Transactions of the American Philosophical Society, new ser., v. 62, pt. 8) Bibliography: p. 3-4. [JN592.F67] 72-89400 ISBN 0-87169-628-2 3.00
1. Elsynge, Henry, 1577 or 8-1636. 2. Great Britain. Parliament—Rules and practice. 3. Great Britain. Parliament. House of Lords—History. I. Title. II. Series: American Philosophical Society, Philadelphia. Transactions, new ser. v. 62, pt. 8. BIP

Elwin, Verrier, 1902-1964.

MISRA, Bhabagrahi. 301.2'092'4
Verrier Elwin, a pioneer Indian anthropologist. With a foreword by Cora du Bois. New York, Asia Pub. House [1974, c1973] xii, 162 p. 23 cm. Bibliography: p. 149-159. [GN21.E48M57] 73-82274 ISBN 0-210-40556-2 7.95
1. Elwin, Verrier, 1902-1964. 2. Ethnology—India. BIP

Ely, Richard Theodore, 1854-1943.

ELY, Richard Theodore, 1854-1943. 330'.092'4 B
Ground under our feet : an autobiography / Richard T. Ely. New York : Arno Press, 1977. xi, 330 p., [8] leaves of plates : ill. ; 23 cm. (The Academic profession) Reprint of the 1938 ed. published by Macmillan, New York. Includes index. Bibliography: p. 309-323. [HB119.E5A3 1977] 76-55184 ISBN 0-405-10011-6 lib. bdg. : 20.00
1. Ely, Richard Theodore, 1854-1943. 2. Economists—United States—Biography. I. Title. II. Series. BIP

Elyot, Sir Thomas, 1490?-1546.

HOGREFE, Pearl. 942.05'2'0924 B
The life and times of Sir Thomas Elyot, Englishman. [1st ed.] Ames, Iowa State University Press [1967] xii, 410 p. 22 cm. Bibliography: p. 397-401. [DA334.E4H6] 67-10601
1. Elyot, Thomas, Sir, 1490?-1546. I. Title. BIP

LEHMBERG, Stanford E 923.242
Sir Thomas Elyot, Tudor humanist. Austin, University of Texas Press [1960] 218p. illus. 24cm. Includes bibliographies. [DA334.E4L4] 59-12858
1. Elyot, Sir Thomas, 1490?-1546. I. Title. BIP

LEHMBERG, Stanford E. 942.05'2'0924 B
Sir Thomas Elyot, Tudor humanist, by Stanford E. Lehmberg. New York, Greenwood Press [1969, c1960] xv, 218 p. illus. 23 cm. Bibliography: p. 201-207. [DA334.E4L4 1969] 73-90545
1. Elyot, Thomas, Sir, 1490?-1546. I. Title.

Elzear de Sabran, Saint, 1285-1328.

WRIGHT, Thomas, d.1624? 230'.2 S
Certaine articles or forcible reasons, 1600 / Thomas Wright ; [and] The lives and singular virtues of Saint Elzear ... and of his wife, 1638 / Etienne Binet. Ilkley, Eng. : Scolar Press, 1976. 461 p. ; 19 cm. (English recusant literature, 1558-1640 ; v. 301) (Series: Rogers, David Morrison, comp. English recusant literature, 1558-1640 ; v. 301.) "Reproduced with permission: 1. Thomas Wright, Certaine articles, 1600, from a copy in the library of St. Mary's Seminary, Oscott .... Reference: Allison and Rogers 920; not in STC. 2. Etienne Binet, The lives and singular virtues ..., 1638, from a copy in the Bodleian Library .... Reference: Allison and Rogers 111; not in STC." [BX1750.A1E5 vol. 301] [BX4700.E45] 282'.092'2 B 77-357172
1. Elzear de Sabran, Saint, 1285-1328. 2. Delphine, ca. 1284-ca. 1358. 3. Christian biography—France. 4. Protestantism—Controversial literature. I. Binet, Stephen, 1569-1639. The lives and singular virtues of Saint Elzear ... and of his wife. 1976. II. Title: Certaine articles or forcible reasons, 1600. III. Series.

Emerson, Peter Henry, 1856-1936.

NEWHALL, Nancy Wynne. 770'.92'4 B
P. H. Emerson : the fight for photography as a fine art / by Nancy Newhall. New York : Aperture, inc., c1975. 266 p. : ill. ; 24 x 27 cm. Also published as Aperture, v. 19, no. 3-4. Published to accompany an exhibition of British photographers prior to 1915 to be presented by the Alfred Stieglitz Center in 1978. Bibliography: p. 262-265. [TR140.E43N48] 74-76911 ISBN 0-912334-58-4 : 22.50. ISBN 0-912334-59-2 pbk. : 12.95
1. Emerson, Peter Henry, 1856-1936. 2. Photography, Artistic. BIP

TURNER, Peter. 770'.92'4 B
P. H. Emerson : photographer of Norfolk / Peter Turner and Richard Wood. Boston : D. R. Godine, [1975] c1974. 108 p. : ill. ; 30 cm. (Godine photographic monographs ; 2) Includes bibliographical references. [TR140.E43T87 1975] 74-81518 ISBN 0-87923-106-8 : 19.95
1. Emerson, Peter Henry, 1856-1936. 2. Photography, Artistic. 3. Norfolk, Eng. (County)—Description and travel—Views. I. Wood, Richard, joint author.

Emerson, Ralph Waldo, 1803-1882.

ALBEE, John, 1833-1915. 814'.3
Remembrances of Emerson. [Folcroft, Pa.] Folcroft Library Editions, 1974 [c1903]

202 p. port. 24 cm. Reprint of the ed. published by Gay & Bird, London. [PS1631.A59 1974] 73-11303 ISBN 0-8414-2877-8 (lib. bdg.)
1. Emerson, Ralph Waldo, 1803-1882. I. Title. **BIP**

BODE, Carl, 1911- comp. 818'.3'09
Ralph Waldo Emerson; a profile. [1st ed.] New York, Hill and Wang [1969, c1968] xvi, 201 p. 21 cm. (American profiles) "Selected bibliography": p. 201. Bibliographical footnotes. [PS1631.B57] 68-9298 5.95
1. Emerson, Ralph Waldo, 1803-1882.

BOLTON, Sarah Knowles, 814'.3 B
1841-1916.
Ralph Waldo Emerson. [Folcroft, Pa.] Folcroft Library Editions, 1973 [c1904] 27 p. illus. 23 cm. Reprint of the ed. published by Crowell, New York. [PS1631.B6 1973] 73-15752 10.00
1. Emerson, Ralph Waldo, 1803-1882.

BRUEL, Andree. 814'.3'09 B
Emerson et Thoreau. Folcroft, Pa., Folcroft Library Editions, 1974. p. cm. Reprint of the 1929 ed. published by Les Belles Lettres, Paris. Bibliography: p. [PS1631.B7 1974] 74-729 ISBN 0-8414-9899-7 (lib. bdg.)
1. Emerson, Ralph Waldo, 1803-1882. 2. Thoreau, Henry David, 1817-1862. I. Title.

BYRON, May Clarissa 814'.3 B
Gillington, d.1936.
A day with Ralph Waldo Emerson / By Maurice Clare [i.e. M. C. G. Byron]. Folcroft, Pa. : Folcroft Library Editions, 1979 p. cm. Reprint of the 1911 ed. published by Hodder & Stoughton, London. [PS163.B9 1978] 78-12781 ISBN 0-8414-9980-2 lib. bdg. : 8.50
1. Emerson, Ralph Waldo, 1803-1882. 2. Authors, American—19th century—Biography. I. Title.

CABOT, James Elliot, 1821- v. 12
1903.
A memoir of Ralph Waldo Emerson. New York, AMS Press, 1965. 2v. (vii, 809 p.) port. 20 cm. "Chronological list of lectures and addresses": p. 710-803. 68-46398
1. Emerson, Ralph Waldo, 1803-1882. I. Title. **BIP**

CABOT, James Elliot, 814'.3 B
1821-1903.
A memoir of Ralph Waldo Emerson. [Folcroft, Pa.] Folcroft Library Editions, 1973. p. Reprint of the 1887 ed. published by Macmillan, London, New York. [PS1631.C3 1973] 73-12366 24.50
1. Emerson, Ralph Waldo, 1803-1882. I. Title.

CARPENTER, Frederic 818'.3'09
Ives, 1903-
Emerson and Asia. New York, Haskell House, 1968 [c1930] xiii, 282 p. 22 cm. Bibliography: p. [265]-267. [PS1642.A7C3 1968] 67-30810
1. Emerson, Ralph Waldo, 1803-1882. 2. Literature, Comparative—Oriental and American. 3. Literature, Comparative—American and Oriental. I. Title. **BIP**

CARY, Elisabeth Luther, 814'.3 B
1867-1936.
Emerson, poet and thinker. [Folcroft, Pa.] Folcroft Library Editions, 1973 [c1904] p. Reprint of the ed. published by Putnam, New York. [PS1631.C35 1973] 73-12367 30.00
1. Emerson, Ralph Waldo, 1803-1882. I. Title.

COOKE, George Willis, 814'.3
1848-1923.
Ralph Waldo Emerson : his life, writings, and philosophy / by George Willis Cooke. Norwood, Pa. : Norwood Editions, 1975 [c1881] viii, 390 p. : port. ; 23 cm. Reprint of the 5th ed., 1882, published by J. R. Osgood, Boston. Includes bibliographical references and index. [PS1631.C65 1975] 75-35819 ISBN 0-88305-120-6 : 35.00
1. Emerson, Ralph Waldo, 1803-1882.

COOKE, George Willis, 814'.3 B
1848-1923.
Ralph Waldo Emerson: his life, writings, and philosophy. [Folcroft, Pa.] Folcroft Library Editions, 1974 [c1881] viii, 390 p. port. 23 cm. Reprint of the 1882 ed. published by J. R. Osgood, Boston. Includes bibliographical references. [PS1631.C65 1974] 74-8996 ISBN 0-8414-3367-4 (lib. bdg.)
1. Emerson, Ralph Waldo, 1803-1882.

DERLETH, August William, 814'.3 B
1909-
Emerson, our contemporary [by] August Derleth. [New York] Crowell-Collier Press [1970] viii, 168 p. 24 cm. "Bibliographical notes": p. 163-165. [PS1631.D4] 77-95175
1. Emerson, Ralph Waldo, 1803-1882. I. Title. **BIP**

DUGARD, Marie, 1862- 818'.3'09
Ralph Waldo Emerson, sa vie et son ouvre [par] M. Dugard. New York, AMS Press [1969] 418 p. illus., port. 23 cm. Reprint of the edition published in Paris, 1907. Includes bibliographical references. [PS1631.D7 1969] 76-100530
1. Emerson, Ralph Waldo, 1803-1882.

EMERSON, Ellen Louisa 920.7
(Tucker) 1809or10-1831
One first love; the letters of Ellen Louisa Tucker to Ralph Waldo Emerson. Ed. by Edith W. Gregg. Cambridge, Mass., Belknap Pr. of Harvard [c.]1962. xi, 208p. illus. 21cm. Bibl. 62-19215 4.00
1. Emerson, Ralph Waldo, 1803-1882. I. Title.

EMERSON, Ralph Waldo, 1803- 928.1
1882.
Journals. Abridged and edited, with an introd. by Robert N. Linscott. New York, Modern Library [1960] 463 p. 19 cm. (The Modern library of world's best books [192]) [PS1631.A3 1960a] 60-7685
I. Linscott, Robert Newton, 1886- ed. II. Title.

EMERSON, Ralph Waldo, 1803- 928.1
1882.
Journals and miscellaneous notebooks. Edited by William H. Gilman [and others] Cambridge, Belknap Press of Harvard University Press, 1960- v. illus., facsims. 25 cm. Bibliographical footnotes. [PS1631.A3 1960] 60-11554

FIRKINS, Oscar W. 1864- 818.3
1932.
Ralph Waldo Emerson. New York, Russell & Russell, 1965. 379p. front. 22cm. First pub. in 1915. Reissued, 1965. [PS1631.F5] 65-13958 7.50
1. Emerson, Ralph Waldo, 1803-1882. I. Title.

GARNETT, Richard, 1835- 814'.3 B
1906.
Life of Ralph Waldo Emerson. [Folcroft, Pa.] Folcroft Library Editions, 1973. p. Reprint of the 1888 ed. published by W. Scott, London and T. Whittaker, New York, in series: Great writers. [PS1631.G3 1973] 73-12352 12.50
1. Emerson, Ralph Waldo, 1803-1882. I. Title. **BIP**

GARNETT, Richard, 1835- 814'.3 B
1906.
Life of Ralph Waldo Emerson. New York, Haskell House Publishers, 1974. 207, xiv p. 23 cm. Reprint of the 1888 ed. published by W. Scott, London, in series: Great writers. "Bibliography, by John P. Anderson": p. [i]-xiv. [PS1631.G3 1974] 73-21630 ISBN 0-8383-1775-8 12.95
1. Emerson, Ralph Waldo, 1803-1882. I. Title.

HASKINS, David Greene, 929'.2
1818-1896.
Ralph Waldo Emerson; his maternal ancestors, with some reminiscences of him. Port Washington, N.Y., Kennikat Press [1971] xii, 151 p. illus., ports. 16 cm. (Kennikat Press scholarly reprints. Series on literary America in the nineteenth century) Reprint of the 1887 ed. [CS71.H351 1971] 929'.2'0973 76-122656
1. Emerson, Ralph Waldo, 1803-1882. 2. Haskins family.

HOLMES, Oliver Wendell, 818.4
1809-1894
Ralph Waldo Emerson. Detroit, Gale 1967. vii, 441p. port. 23cm. (Gale lib. of lives & letters. Amer. writers ser.) Title page includes orig. imprint: Boston, Houghton, Mifflin, 1885. [PS1631.H6 1967] 67-23884 7.80
1. Emerson, Ralph Waldo, 1803-1882. I. Title.

HOLMES, Oliver Wendell, 1809- 810
1894.
Ralph Waldo Emerson. Detroit, Gale Research Co., 1967. viii, 441 p. port. 23 cm. (The Gale library of lives and letters. American writers series) Title page includes original imprint: Boston, Houghton, Mifflin, 1885. [PS1631.H6 1967] 67-23884
1. Emerson, Ralph Waldo, 1803-1882.

HOLMES, Oliver Wendell, 814'.3 B
1809-1894.
Ralph Waldo Emerson. [Folcroft, Pa.] Folcroft Library Editions, 1973. p. Reprint of the 1885 ed. published by Houghton, Mifflin, Boston, which was issued as v. 7 of American men of letters. [PS1631.H6 1973] 73-12372 ISBN 0-8414-4732-2 (lib. bdg.)
1. Emerson, Ralph Waldo, 1803-1882. I. Series: American men of letters, v. 7.

IRELAND, Alexander, 814'.3 B
1810-1894.
Ralph Waldo Emerson: his life, genius, and writings; a biographical sketch to which are added personal recollections of his visits to England extracts from unpublished letters and miscellaneous characteristic records. 2d ed., largely augmented. Port Washington, N.Y., Kennikat Press [1972] xii, 338 p. 21 cm. First ed. published under title: In memoriam: Ralph Waldo Emerson. Reprint of the 1882 ed. Bibliography: p. 334-338. [PS1631.I6 1972] 72-160762 ISBN 0-8046-1581-0
1. Emerson, Ralph Waldo, 1803-1882.

PERRY, Bliss, 1860-1954. 814'.3
Emerson today / by Bliss Perry. Folcroft, Pa. : Folcroft Library Editions, 1977. 140 p. ; 24 cm. Reprint of the 1931 ed. published by Princeton University Press, Princeton, which was issued in seies: The Louis Clark Vanuxem Foundation lectures, Princeton University, 1931. Includes bibliographical references. [PS1638.P4 1977] 77-24261 ISBN 0-8414-6838-9 lib. bdg. : 25.00
1. Emerson, Ralph Waldo, 1803-1882. 2. Authors, American—19th century—Biography. I. Title. II. Series: Princeton University. Louis Clark Vanuxem Foundation. Lectures ; 1931. **BIP**

†PHILLIPS, George Searle, 814'.3
1815-1889.
Emerson, his life and writings / by January Searle [i.e. G. S. Phillips] Folcroft, Pa. : Folcroft Library Editions, 1976. 48 p. ; 23 cm. Reprint of the 1855 ed. published by Holyoake, London. [PS1631.P5 1976] 76-40142 ISBN 0-8414-7813-9 lib. bdg. : 8.50
1. Emerson, Ralph Waldo, 1803-1882. 2. Authors, American—19th century—Biography. I. Title.

PORTE, Joel. 818.309
Emerson and Thoreau; transcendentalists in conflict. [1st ed.] Middletown, Conn., Wesleyan University Press [1966] xi, 226 p. 22 cm. Bibliographical references included in "Notes" (p. [203]-218) [PS1631.P6] 66-14662
1. Emerson, Ralph Waldo, 1803-1882. 2. Thoreau, Henry David, 1817-1862. I. Title.

PORTE, Joel. 814'.3 B
Representative man : Ralph Waldo Emerson in his time / Joel Porte. New York : Oxford University Press, 1979 xxvi, 361 p. : port. ; 22 cm. Includes bibliographical references and index. [PS1631.P65] 78-5818 ISBN 0-19-502436-2 : 15.95
1. Emerson, Ralph Waldo, 1803-1882. 2. Authors, American—19th century—Biography. I. Title. **BIP**

RUSK, Ralph Leslie, 1888- 928.1
The life of Ralph Waldo Emerson. New York, Columbia University Press [1957, c1949] 592p. illus. 24cm. [PS1631.R78 1957] 57-14141
1. Emerson, Ralph Waldo, 1803-1882. I. Title.

SANBORN, Franklin 814'.3 B
Benjamin, 1831-1917.
The personality of Emerson. New York, Haskell House Publishers, 1971. 129 p. facsims., port. 23 cm. "First published in 1903." [PS1631.S35 1971] 72-156911 ISBN 0-8383-1290-X
1. Emerson, Ralph Waldo, 1803-1882. I. Title. **BIP**

SANBORN, Franklin 814'.3 B
Benjamin, 1831-1917.
Ralph Waldo Emerson. Boston, Small, Maynard, 1901. [Folcroft, Pa.] Folcroft Library Editions, 1972. p. Original ed. issued in series: The Beacon biographies of eminent Americans. Bibliography: p. [PS1631.S4 1972] 72-7220 ISBN 0-8414-0262-0 (lib. bdg.)
1. Emerson, Ralph Waldo, 1803-1882. I. Series: The Beacon biographies of eminent Americans.

SNIDER, Denton Jacques, 814'.3 B
1841-1925.
A biography of Ralph Waldo Emerson set forth as his life essay / by Denton J. Snider. Folcroft, Pa. : Folcroft Library Editions, 1977. p. cm. Reprint of the 1921 ed. published by W. H. Miner Co., St. Louis. [PS1631.S6 1977] 77-9617 ISBN 0-8414-7671-3 lib. bdg. : 40.00
1. Emerson, Ralph Waldo, 1803-1882. 2. Authors, American—19th century—Biography. I. Title.

STAEBLER, Warren. 814'.3
Ralph Waldo Emerson. New York, Twayne Publishers [1973] 268 p. 22 cm. (The Great American thinkers series) Bibliography: p. 245-254. [PS1631.S68] 79-161813 5.95
1. Emerson, Ralph Waldo, 1803-1882.

WAGENKNECHT, Edward 814'.3 B
Charles, 1900-
Ralph Waldo Emerson; portrait of a balanced soul [by] Edward Wagenknecht. New York, Oxford University Press, 1974. 307 p. port. 21 cm. Bibliography: p. [285]-295. [PS1631.W3] 73-87615 ISBN 0-19-501766-8 8.95
1 Emerson, Ralph Waldo, 1803-1882. **BIP**

WOOD, James Playsted, 814'.3 B
1905-
Trust thyself; a life of Ralph Waldo Emerson for the young reader. Illus. by Douglas Gorsline. [New York] Pantheon Books [1964] 182 p. illus. 22 cm. (A Pantheon portrait) A biography of the eighteenth century New England essayist, poet, and lecturer whose philosophy of self-reliance and individualism has continually influenced many people. [PS1631.W57] 92 AC 68
1. Emerson, Ralph Waldo, 1803-1882. I. Gorsline, Douglas W., 1913- illus. II. Title.

WOODBERRY, George 818'.03'09 B
Edward, 1855-1930.
Ralph Waldo Emerson. New York, Haskell House Publishers, 1968. 205 p. 23 cm. First published 1907. "Haskell House catalog item # 262." [PS1631.W6 1968] 68-24947
1. Emerson, Ralph Waldo, 1803-1882. **BIP**

Emerson, Ralph Waldo, 1803-1882—Addresses, essays, lectures.

HUSBAND, Thomas Fair. 814'.3 B
Emerson : a lecture given before the London Ethical Society / by T. F. Husband. Folcroft, Pa. : Folcroft Library Editions, 1977. 20 p. ; 23 cm. Reprint of the 1892 ed. published by Co-operative Print. Society, London. [PS1631.H8 1977] 77-23227 ISBN 0-8414-4947-3 lib. bdg. : 5.50
1. Emerson, Ralph Waldo, 1803-1882—Addresses, essays, lectures. 2. Authors, American—19th century—Biography—Addresses, essays, lectures.

Emerson, Ralph Waldo, 1803-1882—Biography.

BOLTON, Sarah Knowles, 814'.3 B
1841-1916.
Ralph Waldo Emerson / by Sarah K. Bolton. Norwood, Pa. : Norwood Editions, 1975 [c1904] 27 p., [8] leaves of plates : ill. ; 23 cm. Reprint of the ed. published by Crowell, New York. [PS1631.B6 1975] 75-40203 ISBN 0-88305-898-7 lib. bdg. : 12.00
1. Emerson, Ralph Waldo, 1803-1882—Biography.

Emerson, Ralph Waldo, 1803-1882—Criticism and interpretation.

RAMAKRISHNA Rao, V. 814'.3

Emerson, his muse and message / V. Ramakrishna Rao. Folcroft, Pa. : Folcroft Library Editions, 1979. p. cm. Originally presented as the author's thesis, University of Calcutta. Reprint of the 1938 1st ed. published by the University of Calcutta, Calcutta, India. Includes bibliographical references and index. [PS1638.R34 1979] 79-25801 ISBN 0-8414-7367-6 (lib. bdg.) : 12.50
1. Emerson, Ralph Waldo, 1803-1882—Criticism and interpretation. I. Title.

YODER, R. A. 814'.3
Emerson and the Orphic poet in America / R. A. Yoder. Berkeley : University of California Press, c1978. xvi, 240 p. ; 23 cm. Includes bibliographical references and index. [PS1638.Y6] 76-24599 ISBN 0-520-03317-5 : 13.50
1. Emerson, Ralph Waldo, 1803-1882—Criticism and interpretation. 2. Orphens in literature. 3. Romanticism—United States. I. Title. **BIP**

Emerson, Ralph Waldo, 1803-1882—Juvenile literature.

KEYES, Charlotte E. 920
The experimenter a biography of Ralph Waldo Emerson. College & Univ. Pr. [dist. New York, Twayne, c.1962] 156p. 21cm. Bibl. 62-13677 3.50
1. Emerson, Ralph Waldo, 1803-1882—Juvenile literature. I. Title.

KEYES, Charlotte E 92
The experimenter; a biography of Ralph Waldo Emerson. New Haven, College and University Press [1962] 156p. 21cm. Includes bibliography. [PS1631.K4] 62-13677
1. Emerson, Ralph Waldo, 1803-1882—Juvenile literature. I. Title.

WOOD, James Playsted, 1905- 920
Trust thyself; a life of Ralph Waldo Emerson for the young reader. Illus. by Douglas Gorsline [New York] Pantheon [c.1964] 182p. illus. 22cm. (Pantheon portrait) 64-18318 3.75; 3.29 lib. ed.,
1. Emerson, Ralph Waldo, 1803-1882—Juvenile literature. I. Title.

WOOD, James Playsted, 1905- j92
Trust thyself; a life of Ralph Waldo Emerson for the young reader. Illus. by Douglas Gorsline. [New York] Pantheon Books [1964] 182 p. illus. 22 cm. (A Pantheon portrait) [PS1631.W57] 64-18318
1. Emerson, Ralph Waldo, 1803-1882 — Juvenile literature. I. Title.

Emery, Sarah Smith, 1787-1879.

EMERY, Sarah Smith, 1787-1879. 974.4'5
Reminiscences of a Newburyport nonagenarian / [edited] by Sarah Anna Emery. Bowie, MD : Heritage Books, 1978. 344 p., [5] leaves of plates : ill. ; 23 cm. Reprint of the 1879 ed. printed by W. H. Huse, under title: Reminiscences of a nonagenarian. Includes index. [F74.N55E5 1978] 78-5010 ISBN 0-917890-09-4 : 20.50
1. Emery, Sarah Smith, 1787-1879. 2. Newburyport, Mass.—Biography. 3. Newbury, Mass.—Biography. I. Emery, Sarah Anna, 1821- II. Title. **BIP**

Emmerson, John K.

EMMERSON, John K. 327'.2'0924 B
The Japanese thread : a life in the U.S. Foreign Service / Joan K. Emmerson. 1st ed. New York : Holt, Rinehart and Winston, c1978. xii, 465 p., [4] leaves of plates : ill. ; 24 cm. Includes bibliographical references and index. [E748.E45A34] 77-26624 ISBN 0-03-041646-9 : 15.00
1. Emmerson, John K. 2. Diplomats—United States—Biography. 3. United States—Foreign relations—Japan. 4. Japan—Foreign relations—United States. I. Title. **BIP**

Emmet, Thomas Addis, 1828-1919.

MARR, James Pratt, 1898- 926.1
Pioneer surgeons of the Woman's Hospital; the lives of Sims, Emmet, Peaslee, and Thomas. Philadelphia, F. A. Davis Co., 1957. 148p. illus. 24cm. Includes bibliography. [RA982.N5W64] 57-8716
1. Sims, James Marlon, 1813-1883. 2. Emmet, Thomas Addis, 1828-1919. 3. Penslee, Edmund Randolph, 1814-1878. 4. Thomas, Theodore Gallard, 1832-1903. 5. New York. Woman's Hospital in the State of New York. I. Title.

Emmons, Chansonetta Stanley, 1858-1937.

PELADEAU, Marius B. 770'.92'4 B
Chansonetta : the life and photographs of Chansonetta Stanley Emmons, 1858-1937 / by Marius B. Peladeau ; introd. by Berenice Abbott. 1st ed. Waldoboro : Maine Antique Digest ; Dobbs Ferry, N.Y. : distributed by Morgan & Morgan, 1977. 96 p. : ill. ; 23 x 27 cm. Includes bibliographical references. [TR653.P44] 77-78057 ISBN 0-917312-01-5 pbk. : 8.95
1. Emmons, Chansonetta Stanley, 1858-1937. 2. Photography, Artistic. 3. Photographers—Maine—Biography. I. Emmons, Chansonetta Stanley, 1858-1937. II. Title. **BIP**

Empedocles.

BIDEZ, Joseph, 1867-1945. 182'.5 B
La biographie d'Empedocle. Hildesheim, New York, G. Olms, 1973. 176 p. 19 cm. (Recueil de travaux publies par la Faculte de philosophie et lettres de l'Universite de Gand, 12. fasc.) Reprint of the 1894 Ghent ed. Contents.Contents.—La vie d'Empedocle par Diogene Laerce (Hippobotos).—Histoire de la tradition.—Biographie d'Empedocle. Includes bibliographical references. [B218.Z7B5 1973] 73-166564 ISBN 3-487-04664-4
1. Empedocles. 2. Diogenes Laertius. I. Title. II. Series: Ghent. Rijksuniversiteit. Faculteit der Letteren en Wijsbegeerte. Werken, 12. fasc.

Empson, William, 1906-

WILLIAM Empson; 810'.95'0924 B
the man and his work; edited by Roma Gill. London, Boston, Routledge & K. Paul [1974] x, 244 p. 22 cm. Contents.Contents.—Auden, W. H. A toast.—Bradbrook, M. C. The ambiguity of William Empson.—Raine, K. Extracts from unpublished memoirs.—Fukuhara, R. Mr. William Empson in Japan.—Smith, J. A. A is B at 8,000 feet.—Miller, K. Empson Agonistes.—Bottrall, R. William Empson.—Fraser, G. The man within the name: William Empson as poet, critic, and friend.—Hough, G. An eighth type of ambiguity.—Richards, I. A. Semantic frontiersman.—Knights, L. C. All or nothing: a theme in John Donne.—Wain, J. Reflections on Johnson's life of Milton.—Stock, A. G. New signatures in retrospect.—Ricks, C. Empson's poetry.—Berry, F. William Empson.—Megaw, M. An Empson bibliography (p. [213]-244) Bibliography: p. [213]-244. [PR6009.M7Z9] 74-176927 ISBN 0-7100-7823-4 £4.95
1. Empson, William, 1906- I. Empson, William, 1906- II. Gill, Roma, ed.

WILLIS, John H., 1929- 801'.95'0924
William Empson, by J. H. Willis, Jr. New York, Columbia University Press, 1969. 48 p. 21 cm. (Columbia essays on modern writers, no. 39) Bibliography: p. 46-48. [PR6009.M7Z94] 74-76254 1.00
1. Empson, William, 1906- I. Title. II. Series. **BIP**

Encyclopedias and dictionaries.

NORTHROP, Henry Davenport, 1836-1909. 973'.09'7496
The college of life; or, Practical self-educator, a manual of self-improvement for the colored race, forming an educational emancipator and a guide to success, giving examples and achievements of successful men and women of the race as an incentive and inspiration to the rising generation, including Afro-American progress illustrated, the whole embracing, business, social, domestic, historical, and religious education. Miami, Fla., Mnemosyne Pub. Inc., 1969. iv, 17-160, [17]-656, [80] p. illus., ports. 27 cm. Reprint of the 1895 ed. [AG105.N848 1969] 71-79014
1. Encyclopedias and dictionaries. 2. Negroes—Education. 3. Negroes—Biography. I. Title.

Endecott, John, 1588?-1665.

MAYO, Lawrence Shaw, 1888-1947. 974.4'02'0924 B
John Endecott; a biography. Cambridge, Mass., Harvard University Press, 1936. St. Clair Shores, Mich., Scholarly Press, 1971 [c1936] 301 p. illus., facsims., map, port. 22 cm. Includes bibliographical references. [F67.E557 1971] 78-145171 ISBN 0-403-01099-3
1. Endecott, John, 1588?-1665. 2. Massachusetts—History—Colonial period, ca. 1600-1775. **BIP**

Engelbrecht, Jacob, 1797-1878.

ENGELBRECHT, Jacob, 1797-1878. 975.2'87'040924 B
The diary of Jacob Engelbrecht, 1818-1878 / edited by William R. Quynn. Frederick, Md. : Historical Society of Frederick County, 1976. 3 v. : port. ; 29 cm. Contents.Contents.—v. 1. 1818-1832, the railroad comes to Frederick.—v. 2. 1832-1858, the building of the clustered spires.—v. 3. 1858-1878, the Civil War. [F189.F8E53] 76-379531
1. Engelbrecht, Jacob, 1797-1878. 2. Frederick, Md.—Biography.

Engels, Friedrich, 1820-1895.

FREDERICK Engels; 335.4'092'4 B
a biography [by Heinrich Gemkow and others] Dresden, Verlag Zeit im Bild, 1972. 652 p. plates. 21 cm. Translation of Friedrich Engels; eine biographie. Includes bibliographical references. [HX273.E56F6913] 73-168066
1. Engels, Friedrich, 1820-1895. I. Gemkow, Heinrich.

MCLELLAN, David. 335.4'092'4 B
Friedrich Engels / David McLellan. New York : Penguin Books, [1978] p. cm. First published in 1977 under title: Engels. [HX273.E56M3 1978] 78-17161 ISBN 0-14-004935-5 pbk. : 1.95
1. Engels, Friedrich, 1820-1895. 2. Communists—Biography. I. Title. **BIP**

MCLELLAN, David. 335.4'092'4 B
Friedrich Engels / David McLellan ; edited by Frank Kermode. New York : Viking Press, 1978, c1977. 120 p. ; 19 cm. (Modern masters) First published in 1977 under title: Engels. Includes index. Bibliography: p. [111]-114. [HX273.E56M3 1978b] 78-64514 ISBN 0-670-32973-8 : 9.95
1. Engels, Friedrich, 1820-1895. 2. Communists—Biography. I. Kermode, John Frank.

NOVA, Fritz, 1915- 320.5'32'0924
Friedrich Engels; his contributions to political theory. New York, Philosophical Library [1967] xxi, 115 p. 23 cm. Bibliography: p. 113-115. [HX273.E56N6] 67-27268
1. Engels, Friedrich, 1820-1895. I. Title. **BIP**

Engelstad, Peder, 1857-1942.

ENGELSTAD, Melvin P., 1904- 977.6'04'0922 B
Peder and Mathilde : a biography / by Melvin P. Engelstad. Tucson : Alphagraphics, 1976. v, 328, 28 p., [5] leaves of plates : ill. ; 29 cm. [F614.R63E543] 76-151240
1. Engelstad, Peder, 1857-1942. 2. Engelstad, Mathilde, 1862-1944. 3. Rocksbury, Minn.—Biography. 4. Norwegian Americans—Minnesota—Rocksbury—Biography. 5. Pioneers—Minnesota—Rocksbury—Biography. I. Title.

Enger, Lenora Calsime, 1894-

GIMBEL, Ann Matterand. 286'.73 B
Lenora : story of a Norwegian girl whose guardian angle was on twenty-four-hour emergency alert / Ann Matterand Gimble [i.e. Gimbel]. Mountain View, Calif. : Pacific Press Pub. Association, c1977. 123 p. ; 22 cm. (A Destiny book ; D-162) [BX6193.E54G55] 77-71894 pbk. : 3.50
1. Enger, Lenora Calsime, 1894- 2. Seventy-Day Adventists—United States—Biography. I. Title.

Engineers.

HART, Ivor Blashka, 1889- 620'.00922
The great engineers, by Ivor B. Hart. Freeport, N.Y., Books for Libraries Press [1967] viii, 136 p. illus. 22 cm. (Essay index reprint series) First published in 1928. [TA139.H3 1967] 67-23226
1. Engineers. 2. Engineering—History. I. Title. **BIP**

MATSCHOSS, Conrad, 1871-1942. 620'.00924 B
Great engineers. Translated by H. Stafford Hatfield. Freeport, N.Y., Books for Libraries Press [1970] xi, 381 p. illus., ports. 23 cm. (Essay index reprint series) Translation of Grosse Ingenieure. Reprint of the 1939 ed. Bibliography: p. 369-374. [TA139.M3613 1970] 70-128278
1. Engineers. 2. Engineering—History. I. Title. **BIP**

SMILES, Samuel, 1812-1904. 620'.00922 B
Lives of the engineers: with an account of their principal works comprising, also, a history of inland communication in Britain. New York, A. M. Kelley, 1968. 3 v. illus., maps, plans, ports. 23 cm. Bibliographical footnotes. [TA139.S65 1968] 68-26161
1. Engineers. 2. Engineering—Great Britain. I. Title.

SMILES, Samuel, 1812-1904 624.0922
Selections from Lives of the engineers, with an account of their principal works. Ed. introd. by Thomas Parke Hughes. Cambridge, Mass., M.I.T. Pr. [c.1966] ix, 447p. illus., maps, ports. 21cm. Bibl. [TA139.S66] 66-19360 10.00
1. Engineers. 2. Roads—Gt. Brit. I. Hughes, Thomas Parke, ed. II. Smiles, Samuel, 1812-1904. Lives of the engineers. III. Title.

WATSON, Sara Ruth. 926.2
Famous engineers, by Sara Ruth and Emily Watson. New York, Dodd, Mead, 1950. viii, 152 p. ports. 23 cm. [Famous biographies for young people] [TA139.W3] 50-11963
1. Engineers. I. Watson, Emily Maria, joint author. II. Title.

ZINSSER, Hans, 1878-1940 926.1
As I remember him; the biography of R. S. Boston, Atlantic-Little [c.1939-1964] 443p., 20cm. (39) 2.45 pap.,
I. Title.

ZINSSER, Hans, 1878-1940 926.1
As I remember him; the biography of R. S. Introd. by Edward Weeks [Gloucester, Mass., P. Smith, 1965, c.1939-1964] ix, 443p. 21cm. (Atlantic-Little bk. rebound) [R154.S15Z5] 4.50
I. Title.

Engineers, American.

YOST, Edna, 1889- 926.2
Modern American engineers. [1st ed.] Philadelphia, Lippincott [1952] 182 p. 21 cm. [TA139.Y65] 52-5172
1. Engineers, American. I. Title.

YOST, Edna, 1889- 926.2
Modern American engineers. [Rev. Ed.] Philadelphia, Lippincott [1958] 182 p. 21 cm. [TA139.Y65 1958] 58-5979
1. Engineers, American. I. Title.

Engineers, British.

HALWARD, Leslie 926.2
Famous British engineers. [2d rev. ed.] [dist., label: Hollywood-by-the-Sea, Fla., Transatlantic Arts] 1959, c.1953] 206p. illus. 60-1480 4.00 bds.,
1. Engineers, British. 2. Engineering—Juvenile literature. I. Title.

Engineers—Great Britain—Biography.

BELL, S. Peter. 016.62'00092'2
A biographical index of British engineers in the 19th century / compiled by S. P. Bell. New York : Garland Pub., 1975. x, 246 p. , 22 cm. (Garland reference library of social science ; v. 5) [TA157.B44] 75-5114 ISBN 0-8240-1078-7 lib.bdg. : 22.00
1. Engineers—Great Britain—Biography. I. Title. BIP

KINGSFORD, Peter Wilfred 926
Engineers, inventors, and workers. New York, St. Martin's [c.]1964. 272p. illus., maps. 21cm. Bibl. 64-18790 4.95
1. Engineers—Gt. Brit. 2. Technology—Gt. Brit.—Hist. 3. Labor and laboring classes—Gt. Brit—Hist. I. Title.

Engineers—Juvenile literature.

EVANS, Idrisyn Oliver, 1894- 920
Engineers of the world. Illus. by Drake Brookshaw. New York, Warne [c.1963] 207p. illus. 22cm. 63-10572 2.95 bds.,
1. Engineers—Juvenile literature. I. Title.

EVANS, Idrisyn Oliver, 1894- 920
Engineers of the world. Illustrated by Drake Brookshaw. London, New York, Warne [1963] 207 p. illus. 22 cm. [[TA139]] 63-10572
1 Engineers — Juvenile literature. I. Title.

Engineers—United States—Biography.

NATIONAL Academy of 620'.0092'2 B Engineering.
Memorial tributes / National Academy of Engineering of the United States of America. Washington : National Academy of Engineering, 1979- v. : ports. ; 24 cm. [TA139.N34 1979] 79-21053 ISBN 0-309-02889-2 : 10.00
1. Engineers United States—Biography. I. Title.

Engineers—United States—Biography—Dictionaries.

ENGINEERS Joint 620'.00922 B Council.
Engineers of distinction, including scientists in related fields. 1st ed. New York [1970] xx, 457 p. ports. 29 cm. [TA139.E37] 75-21290
1. Engineers—United States Biography—Dictionaries. I. Title.

Engineers—United States—Biography—Juvenile literature.

LEIPOLD, L. Edmond, 620'.0092'2 B 1902-
Famous American engineers, by L. E. Leipold. Minneapolis, T. S. Denison [1972] 82 p. 25 cm. (His Famous American heroes and leaders series) Chronicles the achievements of ten engineers: Goethals, Turner, Davidson, Gilbreth, Roebling, Singstad, Bush, Suman, Mead, and Goddard. [TA139.L38] 920 78-174955 ISBN 0-513-01164-1
1. Engineers—United States—Biography—Juvenile literature. I. Title.

England—Biography.

KENIN, Richard. 920'.042
Return to Albion : Americans in England, 1760-1940 / Richard Kenin ; introd. by Alistair Cooke. 1st ed. New York : Holt, Rinehart and Winston, c1979. xv, 288 p. : ill. ; 26 cm. Bibliography: p. 279-282. Includes index. [CT775.K46] 78-1033 ISBN 0-03-042861-0. : 16.95
1. England—Biography. 2. Americans in England. I. Title. BIP

SUTHERLAND, James 942.1 Runcieman, 1900-
Background for Queen Anne / by James Sutherland. Folcroft, Pa. : Folcroft Library Editions, 1976. p. cm. Reprint of the 1939 ed. published by Methuen, London. Bibliography: p. [DA483.A1S87 1976] 76-29348 ISBN 0-8414-7600-4 lib. bdg. : 25.00
1. England—Biography. 2. London—Social life and customs. 3. England—Social life and customs—18th century. I. Title.
Contents omitted BIP

WEEKLEY, Montague. 927.6
Thomas Bewick. London, New York, Oxford University Press, 1953. x, 224p. illus. 23cm. 'Bewickiana: a supplementary note on manuscripts. personal relics. etc.':p. [218]-219. [NE1217.B4W4] 53-2758
I. Bewick, Thomas, 1753-1828. II. Title.

England—Biography—Bibliography.

PINTO, Vivian de 016.92'0042 Sola, 1895-
Seventeenth-century biographies / by V. de S. Pinto. Folcroft, Pa. : Folcroft Library Editions, 1977. 31 p. ; 26 cm. Reprint of the 1955 ed. published for the National Book League at the University Press, Cambridge, which was issued as Reader's guides, 2d ser., 5. Includes index. [Z2010.P56 1977] [CT781] 77-7564 ISBN 0-8414-6798-6 lib. bdg. : 5.50
1. England—Biography—Bibliography. I. Title. II. Series: National Book League, London. Reader's guides ; 2d ser., 5. BIP

England, John, Bp., 1786-1842.

GUILDAY, Peter 282'.0924 B Keenan, 1884-1947.
The life & times of John England. New York, Arno Press, 1969 [c1927] x, 596, 577 p. 24 cm. (Thought foundation: historical series, no. 1) Includes bibliographical references. [BX4705.E66G5 1969] 70-83422
1. England, John, Bp., 1786-1842. 2. Catholic Church in the United States. I. Title. II. Series. BIP

England—Nobility.

ASHDOWN, Dulcie M. 941'.00992 B
Ladies-in-waiting / Dulcie M. Ashdown. New York : St. Martin's Press, 1976. xii, 212 p., [4] leaves of plates : ill. ; 23 cm. Includes bibliographical references and index. [DA28.7.A83 1976b] 75-29609 7.95
1. England—Nobility. 2. Great Britain—Biography. I. Title.

ASHDOWN, Dulcie M. 941'.00922 B
Ladies-in-waiting / Dulcie M. Ashdown. London : Barker, c1976 xii, 212 p., [4] leaves of plates : ill. ; 23 cm. Includes bibliographical references and index. [DA28.7.A83] 76-362300 ISBN 0-213-16567-8 : £0.50
1. England—Nobility. 2. Great Britain—Biography. I. Title.

English diaries—Bibliography.

MATTHEWS, William, 1905- 016.92
British diaries; an annotated bibliography of British diaries written between 1442 and 1942. Berkeley, University of California Press, 1950. xxxiv, 339 p. 25 cm. [Z2014.D5M3] 50-5974
1. English diaries—Bibliography. I. Title. BIP

English diaries—History and criticism.

PONSONBY, Arthur 941'.00992 B Ponsonby, Baron, 1871-1946.
British diarists / by Arthur Ponsonby. Norwood, Pa. : Norwood Editions, 1975. 80 p. ; 23 cm. Reprint of the 1930 ed. published by E. Benn, London, in series: Benn's sixpenny library. Bibliography: p. 77-80. [PR908.P58 1975b] 75-44149 ISBN 0-88305-522-8 lib. bdg. : 12.50
1. English diaries—History and criticism. I. Title.

PONSONBY, Arthur 941'.00992 B Ponsonby, Baron, 1871-1946.
British diarists / by Arthur Ponsonby. Folcroft, Pa. : Folcroft Library Editions, 1975. p. cm. Reprint of the 1930 ed. published by E. Benn, London, in series: Benn's sixpenny library. Bibliography: [PR908.P58 1975] 75-1061 ISBN 0-8414-6703-X lib. bdg.
1. English diaries—History and criticism. I. Title. BIP

English drama—20th century—Bio-bibliography.

VINSON, James, 822'.9'1409 B 1921-
Contemporary dramatists / editor, James Vinson, associate editor, D. L. Kirkpatrick ; with a pref. by Ruby Cohn. 2d ed. London : St. James Press ; New York : St. Martin's Press, 1977. xiii, 1088 p. ; 25 cm. (Contemporary writers of the English language) Includes index. [PR106.V5 1977] 76-54628 ISBN 0-900997-86-9 : 35.00
1. English drama—20th century—Bio-bibliography. 2. American drama—20th century—Bio-bibliography. 3. English drama—20th century—History and criticism—Addresses, essays, lectures. 4. American drama 20th century—History and criticism—Addresses, essays, lectures. I. Kirkpatrick, D. L. II. Title. BIP

English fiction—20th century—Addresses, essays, lectures.

JOHNSON, Reginald 823'.9'1209 Brimley, 1867-1932.
Some contemporary novelists (women). Freeport, N.Y., Books for Libraries Press [1967] xxvii, 220 p. 22 cm. (Essay index reprint series) Reprint of the 1920 ed. Contents.Contents.—May Sinclair.—Eleanor Mordaunt.—Rose Macauley.—Sheila Kaye-Smith.—Ethel Sidgwick.—Amber Reeves.—Viola Meynell.—Dorothy Richardson.—Virginia Woolf.—Stella Benson.—E. M. Delafield.—Clemence Dane.—Mary Fulton.—Hope Mirrlees. [PR884.J6 1967] 67-26751
1. English fiction—20th century—Addresses, essays, lectures. 2. Women authors. I. Title.

English language—Eponyms—Dictionaries.

EPONYMS dictionaries index 423'.1 / edited by James A. Ruffner, associate editors, Jennifer Berger, Georgia Schoenung. Detroit : Gale Research Co., c1977. xxviii, 730 p. ; 29 cm. Bibliography: p. xiii-xxviii. [PE1596.E6] 76-20341 ISBN 0-8103-0688-3 : 45.00
1. English language—Eponyms—Dictionaries. 2. Biography. I. Ruffner, James A. II. Berger, Jennifer, III. Schoenung, Georgia.

EPONYMS dictionaries index 423'.1 / edited by James A. Ruffner, associate editors, Jennifer Berger, Georgia Schoenung. Detroit : Gale Research Co., c1977. xxviii, 730 p. ; 29 cm. Bibliography: p. xiii-xxviii. [PE1596.E6] 76-20341 ISBN 0-8103-0688-3 : 45.00
1. English language—Eponyms—Dictionaries. 2. Biography. I. Ruffner, James A. II. Berger, Jennifer. III. Schoenung, Georgia.

English language—Rhetoric.

MEASHAM, D. C., ed. 828.9140308
Fourteen: autobiography of an age-group [New York] Cambridge [c.]1965. viii, 94p. 23cm. [PE1413.M42] 65-19146 3.50
1. English language—Rhetoric. 2. Youth—Biog. 3. English language—Study and teaching. I. Title.

English letters.

FLOWER, Desmond, 1907- 821'.009 ed.
The pursuit of poetry; a book of letters about poetry written by English poets, 1550-1930. Collected and edited by Desmond Flower. [Folcroft, Pa.] Folcroft Press [1970] xv, 309 p. 24 cm. Reprint of the 1939 ed. Bibliography: p. 295-298. [PR1342.F6 1970] 72-194978
1. English letters. 2. Poetry. 3. Poets, English—Biography. I. Title.

English literature—Addresses, essays, lectures.

THOMSON, James, 1834-1882. 820.9
Biographical and critical studies, by James Thomson ("B. V.") Freeport, N.Y., Books for Libraries Press [1972] xi, 483 p. 23 cm. (Essay index reprint series) Reprint of the 1896 ed. Contents.Contents.—Rabelais.—Saint-Amant.—Ben Jonson.—The poems of William Blake.—Shelley.—Shelley's religious opinions.—Notice of "The life of Shelley."—A strange book.—John Wilson and the "Noctes ambrosianae."—James Hogg, the Ettrick shepherd.—Notes on the genius of Robert Browning.—"The ring and the book."—Browning's "Pacciarotto." [PR99.T48 1972] 77-37846 ISBN 0-8369-2630-7
1. English literature—Addresses, essays, lectures. I. B. V. II. V., B. III. Title. BIP

English literature—Bio-bibliography.

BIOGRAPHICAL dictionary of 013.82 *the living, authors of Great Britain and Ireland; (A)* comprising literary memoirs and anecdotes of their lives and a chronological register of their publications, with the number of editions printed; including notices of some foreign writers whose works have been occasionally published in England. Illus. by a variety of communications from persons of the first eminence in the world of letters. London. Printed for H. Colburn 1816. Detroit. Gate, 1966. vii, 449p. 24cm. Reprint of a work first pub. in 1816. Ascribed to John Watkins and Frederic Shoberl. of. Brit. Mus. cat. and Halkett & Laing. [Z2010.B61 1966] 66-16419 47.00
1. English literature—Bio-bibl. I. Watkins, John, fl, 1792-1831, supposed author. II. Shoberl, Frederic, 1775-1853, supposed author. III. Upcott, William, 1779-1845, supposed author. BIP

BROWNING, David Clayton, 928.2 1894- ed.
Everyman's dictionary of literary biography, English & American, compiled after John W. Cousin by D. C. Browning. New York, Dutton [1958] x, 752 p. 20 cm. (Everyman's reference library) "Superseding the Biographical dictionary of English literature compiled by John W. Cousin ... this ... is for all practical purposes a new work." [PR19.B7] A58
1. English literature—Bio-bibliography. 2. American literature—Bio-bibliography. I. Cousin, John William, 1849-1910. A short biographical dictionary of English literature. II. Title. III. Title: Dictionary of literary biography, English & American.

MYERS, Robin, fl.1967- 016.82
A dictionary of literature in the English language, from Chaucer to 1940, compiled and edited by Robin Myers, for the National Book League. [1st ed.] Oxford, New York, Pergamon Press [1970] 2 v. illus., facsim. 25 cm. [Z2010.M9] 68-18529 ISBN 0-08-012079-2
1. English literature—Bio-bibliography. 2. American literature—Bio-bibliography. I. National Book League, London. II. Title.

RIVERS, David. 016.8209'006
Literary memoirs of living authors of Great Britain. New York, Garland Pub., 1970. 2 v. 21 cm. "Facsimile ... made from a copy in the Yale University Library." Original t.p. reads: Literary memoirs of living authors of Great Britain, arranged according to an alphabetical catalogue of their names ... London, Printed for R. Faulder, New Bond Street. Sold also by T. Egerton, Whitehall, and W. Richardson, Royal Exchange, 1798. [Z2010.R62 1798a] 76-112225
1. English literature—Bio-bibliography. 2. Gt. Brit.—Bio-bibliography. I. Title.

SHARP, Robert Farquharson, 820'.9 1864-1945.
A dictionary of English authors / by R. Farquharson Sharp. Boston : Longwood

Press, 1977. p. cm. Reprint of the 1904 ed. published by Kegan Paul, Trench, Trubner, London, with title: A dictionary of English authors, biographical and bibliographical. [Z2010.S54 1977] [PR83] 77-20484 ISBN 0-89341-199-X lib.bdg. : 20.00
1. English literature—Bio-bibliography. 2. American literature—Bio-bibliography. I. Title. BIP

SHARP, Robert Farquharson, 1864-1945. 820'.9
A dictionary of English authors, biographical and bibliographical. Being a compendious account of the lives and writings of upwards of 800 British and American writers from the year 1400 to the present time. New ed., rev., with an appendix bringing the whole up to date and including a large amount of new matter. Boston, Milford House [1972] 363 p. 22 cm. Reprint of the new ed., rev., 1904. [Z2010.S54 1972] 74-186787 ISBN 0-87821-045-8
1. English literature—Bio-bibliography. 2. American literature—Bio-bibliography. I. Title.

SHARP, Robert Farquharson, 1864-1945. 016.82'08
A dictionary of English authors, biographical and bibliographical, being a compendious account of the lives and writings of upwards of 800 British and American writers from the year 1400 to the present time. New ed., rev., with an appendix bringing the whole up to date and including a large amount of new matter. Detroit : Gale Research, 1975. p. cm. Reprint of the 1904 ed. published by Kegan Paul, Trench, Trubner, London. [Z2010.S54 1975] [PR83] 75-35577 ISBN 0-8103-4281-2
1. English literature—Bio-bibliography. 2. American literature—Bio-bibliography. I. Title: A dictionary of English authors, biographical and bibliographical ...

SHARP, Robert Farquharson, 1864-1945. 820'.9
A dictionary of English authors, biographical and bibliographical, being a compendious account of the lives and writings of upwards of 800 British and American writers from the year 1400 to the present time / by R. Farquharson Sharp. New ed., rev., with an appendix bringing the whole up to date and including a large amount of new matter. Detroit : Gale Research, 1978. 363 p. ; 23 cm. Reprint of the 1904 ed. published by Kegan Paul, Trench, Trubner, London. [Z2010.S54 1975] [PR83] 75-35577 ISBN 0-8103-4281-2 : 15.00
1. English literature—Bio-bibliography. 2. American literature—Bio-bibliography. I. Title: A dictionary of English authors, biographical and bibliographical ...

English literature—History and criticism.

BRITISH writers / 820'.9
edited under the auspices of the British Council, Ian S. Scott-Kilvert, general editor. New York : Scribner, c1979- 1979. v. ; 29 cm. Includes bibliographies and index. [PR85.B688] 78-23483 ISBN 0-684-15798-5 : 50.00
1. English literature—History and criticism. 2. English literature—Bio-bibliography. 3. Authors, English—Biography. I. Scott-Kilvert, Ian. II. Great Britain. British Council.
Contents Deleted BIP

English literature—Irish authors—Dictionaries.

DICTIONARY of Irish literature / Robert Hogan, editor-in-chief ; Zack Bowen, William J. Feeney, James Kilroy, advisory editors ; Mary Rose Callaghan, Richard Burnham, associate editors. Westport, Conn. : Greenwood Press, 1979. p. cm. Includes index. Bibliography: p. [PR8706.D5] 78-20021 ISBN 0-313-20718-6 : 39.95 820'.9'9415 B
1. English literature—Irish authors—Dictionaries. 2. English literature—Irish authors—Bibliography. 3. Irish literature—Dictionaries. 4. Irish literature—Bibliography. 5. Authors, Irish—Biography. I. Hogan, Robert Goode, 1930- BIP

English literature—Outlines, syllabi, etc.

MANLY, John Matthews, 1865-1940. 820'.9
Contemporary British literature; bibliographies and study outlines, by John Matthews Manly and Edith Rickert. New York, Haskell House Publishers, 1974. xviii, 196 p. 20 cm. Reprint of the ed. published by Harrap, London. [PR87.M268 1974] 73-21795 ISBN 0-8383-1827-4 11.95
1. English literature—Outlines, syllabi, etc. 2. English literature—20th century—Bio-bibliography. I. Rickert, Edith, 1871-1938, joint author. II. Title.

English literature—20th century—History and criticism.

KIDD, Walter E. 820'.9'0091
British winners of the Nobel Literary Prize. [Edited] by Walter E. Kidd. [1st ed.] Norman, University of Oklahoma Press [1973] vii, 280 p. 22 cm. Bibliography: p. 266-274. [PR473.K5] 72-9270 ISBN 0-8061-1075-9 8.95
1. English literature—20th century—History and criticism. 2. Nobel prizes. 3. Authors, English—20th century—Biography. I. Title. BIP

English poetry — Bio-bibl.

NATIONAL Poetry Association. 016.821
Who's who in English speaking poets. Los Angeles, National Poetry Association [1958] 140 p. 23 cm. On spine: English speaking poets. [Z2014.P7W5] 58-38323
1. English poetry — Bio-bibl. I. Title. II. Title: English speaking poets.

English poetry—Early modern, 1500-1700—History and criticism.

CRUSE, Amy, 1870- 821'.04
The Elizabethan lyrists and their poetry. [Folcroft, Pa.] Folcroft Press [1969] 146, [1] p. 22 cm. Reprint of the 1919 ed., issued in series: Poetry and life series. Bibliography: p. [147] [PR531.C8 1969] 72-194435
1. English poetry—Early modern, 1500-1700—History and criticism. 2. Poets, English—Biography. I. Title. II. Series: Poetry and life series. BIP

TRICKETT, Rachel, 1923- 821.09
The honest muse: a study in Augustan verse. Oxford, Clarendon P., 1967. ix, 309 p. 22 1/2 cm. Bibliographical footnotes. [PR437.T7] 801'.95'0924 67-94468
1. English poetry—Early modern, 1500-1700—History and criticism. 2. English poetry—18th century—History and criticism. I. Title.

English poetry—History and criticism.

BLAKE, William 1757-1827. 821.09
William Blake; an introduction. Edited by Anne Malcolmson. With illus. from Blake's paintings and engravings. [1st American ed.] New York, Harcourt, Brace & World [1967] 127 p. illus. 21 cm. Bibliography: p. 123-124. An introduction and critical guide to William Blake's poetry, including a brief biography and fifteen reproductions of his paintings and engravings. [PR4142.M28 1967] AC 68
1. English poetry—History and criticism. I. Malcolmson, Anne (Burnett) 1910- ed. II. Title.

English poetry—20th century—Bio-bibliography.

CONTEMPORARY poets of the English language. With a pref. by C. Day Lewis. Editor: Rosalie Murphy. Deputy editor: James Vinson. Chicago, St. James Press [1970] xvii, 1243 p. 26 cm. Includes bibliographies. [Z2014.P7C63] 79-23734 25.00 821'.9'109
1. English poetry—20th century—Bio-bibliography. 2. American poetry—20th century—Bio-bibliography. I. Murphy, Rosalie, ed. BIP

CONTEMPORARY poets of the English language. With a pref. by C. Day Lewis. Editor: Rosalie Murphy. Deputy editor: James Vinson. New York, St. Martin's Press [1971, c1970] xvii, 1243 p. 26 cm. Includes bibliographies. [Z2014.P7C63 1971] 78-165556 25.00 821'.9'109
1. English poetry—20th century—Bio-bibliography. 2. American poetry—20th century—Bio-bibliography. I. Murphy, Rosalie, ed.

English poetry—20th century—History and criticism.

STURGEON, Mary C. 821'.9'1209
Studies of contemporary poets, by Mary C. Sturgeon. Rev. and enl. Port Washington, N.Y., Kennikat Press [1970] 439, [1] p. 21 cm. Reprint of the 1920 ed. Contents.Contents.—Lascelles Abercrombie.—Rupert Brooke.—William H. Davies.—Walter de la Mare.—Wilfrid Wilson Gibson.—Ralph Hodgson.—Ford Madox Hueffer.—An Irish group.—Rose Macaulay.—John Masefield.—Harold Monro.—Sarojini Naidu.—John Presland (Gladya Skelton).—James Stephens.—Margaret L. Woods.—John Drinkwater.—Michael Field (Katharine H. Bradley and Edith E. Cooper).—Thomas Hardy.—J. C. Squire.—Contemporary women poets.—W. B. Yeats.—Bibliography (p. 433-[440]) [PR610.S8 1970] 78-105839
1. English poetry—20th century—History and criticism. I. Title. BIP

English prose literature—19th century—History and criticism—Addresses, essays, lectures.

APPROACHES to Victorian autobiography / edited by George P. Landow. Athens, Ohio : Ohio University Press, c1978. p. cm. Includes bibliographical references. [PR788.A95A6] 77-91505 ISBN 0-8214-0400-8 : 16.00 820'.9'08
1. English prose literature—19th century—History and criticism—Addresses, essays, lectures. 2. Autobiography—Addresses, essays, lectures. 3. Authors, English—19th century—Biography—Addresses, essays, lectures. I. Landow, George P. BIP

Engstrom, John, 1869 or 70-1947.

ENGSTROM, Emil, 1879- 923.973
John Engstrom, the last frontiersman. [1st ed.] New York, Vantage Press [1957, c1956] 156 p. 21 cm. [F851.E5] 56-12311
1. Engstrom, John, 1869 or 70-1947. 2. Northwest, Pacific—Social life and customs. 3. Alaska—Social life and customs.

Enku, d. 1695.

GOTO, Hideo, 1910- 730.952
Enku, his life and work. Photos by Hideo Goto. Essay by Jun Ebara. [Dist. Los Angeles, Perkins, 1961] various p. illus., map. 27cm. J62 5.00
1. Enku, d. 1695. I. Ebara, Jun, pseud. II. Title.

Enos, Lizzie.

SIMPSON, Richard, 1931- 970'.004'97 B
Ooti / Richard Simpson. Millbrae, CA : Celestial Arts, 1977. p. cm. [E99.M18S55] 77-79888 ISBN 0-89087-213-9 : 4.95
1. Enos, Lizzie. 2. Maidu Indians. 3. Maidu Indians—Biography. I. Title. BIP

Enrique IV, King of Castile and Leon, 1425-1474.

MILLER, Townsend. 946.3'02'0924 B
Henry IV of Castile, 1425-1474. [1st ed.] Philadelphia, Lippincott, 1972 [c1971] viii, 306 p. illus., map. 23 cm. Bibliography: p. 292-295. [DP143.M5 1972] 70-163226 ISBN 0-397-00798-1
1. Enrique IV, King of Castile and Leon, 1425-1474. 2. Castile—History—Henry IV, 1454-1474. I. Title.

Ensor, James, baron, 1860-1949.

ENSOR, James, Baron, 1860-1949. 759.9493
Ensor / David Farmer. New York : G. Braziller, 1976. 48, p., [40] leaves of plates : ill. (some col.) ; 28 cm. [ND673.E6F37] 76-16639 ISBN 0-8076-0836-X : 9.95
1. Ensor, James, Baron, 1860-1949. 2. Painters—Belgium—Biography. I. Farmer, John David. II. Title.

GINDERTAEL, Roger van, 1899- 760'.092'4 B
Ensor / Roger Van Gindertael ; translated from French by Vivienne Menkes. Boston : New York Graphic Society, 1975. 157 p. : ill. (some col.) ; 30 cm. Includes index. Bibliography: p. 151. [ND673.E6G55 1975] 74-21493 ISBN 0-8212-0649-4 : 22.50
1. Ensor, James, Baron, 1860-1949. BIP

HAESAERTS, Paul, 1901- 759.9493
James Ensor. Pref. by Jean Cassou. [Translated from the French by Norbert Guterman] New York, Abrams [1959, c1957] 386p. illus. (part mounted col.) plates, ports. 30cm. Bibliography: p. 369-[374] [ND573.E6H313] 58-9032
1. Ensor, James, baron, 1860-1949. I. Title.

JANSSENS, Jacques. 759.9493 B
James Ensor / by Jacques Janssens. New York : Crown Publishers, c1978. 96 p. : ill. (some col.) ; 29 cm. Bibliography: p. 94-95. [ND673.E6J3613] 78-9884 ISBN 0-517-53284-0 pbk. : 5.95
1. Ensor, James, baron, 1860-1949. 2. Painters—Belgium—Biography.

Enters, Angna, 1907-

ENTERS, Angna, 1907- 927.933
Artist's life. New York, Coward-McCann [1958] 447 p. illus. 22 cm. Autobiographical. [GV1785.E5A34] 57-7059
I. Title.

ENTERS, Angna, 1907- 793.3'2'0924 B
First person plural / Angna Enters. New York : Da Capo Press, 1978. p. cm. (The Da Capo series in dance) Reprint of the 1937 ed. published by Stackpole, New York. [GV1785.E5A3 1978] 78-4687 ISBN 0-306-77594-8 pbk. : 22.50
1. Enters, Angna, 1907- 2. Dancers—Biography. I. Title. BIP

Entertainers—Biography.

FISHER, John, 1945- 791'.092'2 B
Call them irreplaceable / John Fisher. New York : Stein and Day, [1976] p. cm. [PN1583.A2F5] 75-37777 ISBN 0-8128-1927-6 : 14.95
1. Entertainers—Biography. I. Title. BIP

FISHER, John, 1945- 791'.092'2 B
Call them irreplaceable / by John Fisher ; drawings by Hirschfeld. London : Elm Tree Books, 1976. 224 p. : ports. ; 29 cm. Includes index. Bibliography: p. 219-220. [PN1583.F5 1976] 77-352901 ISBN 0-241-89201-5 : £6.95
1. Entertainers—Biography. I. Title.

HILGENSTUHLER, Ted. 927.8
Tennessee Ernie Ford. A heart warming book about America's favorite singing star of radio and TV; the long rocky road from Tennessee to Hollywood. [Los Angeles, Petersen Pub. Co., 1957] 96p. illus., ports. 28cm. Cover title.qaFord, Ernest Jennings, 1919- [ML420.F7H5] 57-3345
I. Title.

REED, Rex. 790.2'092'2 B
Valentines & vitriol / Rex Reed. New York : Delacorte Press, c1977. xvi, 280 p., [12] leaves of plates : ill. ; 24 cm. [PN1583.R4] 76-53002 ISBN 0-440-09336-8 : 8.95
1. Entertainers—Biography. I. Title.

REED, Rex. 790.2'092'2
Valentines & vitriol / Rex Reed. New York : Dell Pub. Co., 1978,c1977. 271 p. : ill. : 18 cm. Contents.Contents. [PN1583.R4] ISBN 0-440-19359-1 pbk. : 1.95
1. Entertainers—Biography. I. Title.

L.C. card no. for 1977 Delacorte Press ed.: 76-53002. BIP

Entertainers—Biography—Juvenile literature.

KLINGER, Gene. 791'.0922 B
The spectaculars. [Chicago] Reilly & Lee Books [1971] vi, 137 p. illus. 24 cm. Bibliography: p. 135-137. Brief biographies of the "Greatest Showmen on Earth"—Grock, Robert Houdin, Phineas T. Barnum, Dan Rice, Houdini, W. C. Fields, and the Ringling brothers. [GV1811.A1K56] 920 75-163273 5.95
1. Entertainers—Biography—Juvenile literature. I. Title.

Entertainers—Portraits.

ABBE, James 779'.9'791430280922
Edward, 1883-1973.
Stars of the twenties / observed by James Abbe ; text by Mary Dawn Earley ; introd. by Lillian Gish. New York : Viking Press, 1975. 32 p., [48] leaves of plates : ports. ; 29 cm. (A Studio book) [PN1583.A2A2 1975] 74-29487 ISBN 0-670-66836-2 : 10.00
1. Entertainers—Portraits. I. Earley, Mary Dawn. II. Title.

Entertainers—United States—Biography.

CARROLL, David, 1942- 791'.092'2
The matinee idols. New York, Arbor House [1972] 159 p. illus. 27 cm. [PN1583.A2C3] 72-184882 ISBN 0-87795-031-8 10.00
1. Entertainers—United States—Biography. I. Title. BIP

CARROLL, David, 1942- 791'.092'2
The matinee idols / David Carroll. New York : Galahad Books, [1974] c1972. 159 p. : ill. ; 26 cm. Includes index. [PN1583.A2C3 1974] 73-88099 ISBN 0-88365-101-7 : 10.00
1. Entertainers—United States—Biography. I. Title.

GEMME, Leila B. 791'.092'2
The new breed of performer / by Leila B. Gemme. New York : Washington Square Press : distributed by Simon & Schuster, 1976. 189 p. : ill. ; 18 cm. (Pocket books) [PN2285.G4] 76-353621 pbk. : 1.95
1. Entertainers—United States—Biography. I. Title. BIP

STELZER, Dick. 791.43'0922 B
The star treatment / by Dick Stelzer. Indianapolis : Bobbs-Merrill, [1977] p. cm. [PN2285.S719] 77-76868 ISBN 0-672-52290-X : 7.95
1. Entertainers—United States—Biography. 2. Authors, American—20th century—Biography. 3. Psychotherapy—Cases, clinical reports, statistics. I. Title. BIP

Entertainers—United States—Biography—Juvenile literature.

DAVIS, Sammy, 1925- 792.70924 B
Yes I can; [the story of Sammy Davis, Jr., by Sammy Davis, Jr., and Jane and Burt Boyar. New York, Farrar, Straus & Giroux, 1965] 612 p. ports. 22 cm. [PN2287.D322A3] 64-11456
I. Boyar, Jane, joint author. II. Boyar, Burt, joint author. III. Title. BIP

SIGNIFICANT American 791'.092'2 B
entertainers. Chicago : Childrens Press, [1976] p. cm. Includes index. Brief biographies of 187 entertainers arranged in chronological-alphabetical order. [PN1583.A2S5] 920 75-20677 ISBN 0-516-05302-7 lib.bdg. : 9.25
1. Entertainers—United States—Biography—Juvenile literature. I. Title: Entertainers.

Entomologists, American—Biography.

MALLIS, Arnold. 595.7'00922 B
American entomologists. New Brunswick, N.J., Rutgers University Press [1971] xvii, 549 p. illus. 25 cm. Bibliography: p. [519]-539. [QL26.M24 1971] 78-152316 ISBN 0-8135-0686-7 15.00
1. Entomologists, American—Biography. I. Title. BIP

Eon de Beaumont, Charles Genevieve Louis Auguste Andre Timothee d'. 1728-1810.

NIXON, Edna. 923.244
Royal spy, the strange case of the Chevalier d'Eon; dressed as a man he was none the less a woman; dressed as a woman she was none the less a man. New York, Reynal [1965] 260 p. illus., ports. 22 cm. Bibliography: p. [246]-248. [DC135.E6N5] 65-28909
1. Eon de Beaumont, Charles Genevieve Louis Auguste Andre Timothee d'. 1728-1810. I. Title.

Eotvos, Jozsef, baro, 1813-1871.

BODY, Paul. 320.9'439'04 B
Joseph Eotvos and the modernization of Hungary, 1840-1870; a study of ideas of individuality and social pluralism in modern politics. Philadelphia, American Philosophical Society, 1972. 134 p. illus. 30 cm. (Transactions of the American Philosophical Society, new ser., v. 62, pt. 2) Bibliography: p. 130-132. [DB933.3.E6B6] 71-184165 ISBN 0-87169-622-3 5.00
1. Eotvos, Jozsef, baro, 1813-1871. 2. Hungary—Politics and government—19th century. I. Title. II. Series: American Philosophical Society, Philadelphia. Transactions, new ser., v. 62, pt. 2.

Ephorus.

BARBER, Godfrey 938'.007'2024 B
Louis.
The historian Ephorus / by G. L. Barber. 1st AMS ed. New York : AMS Press, 1979. xii, 189, [1] p. ; 19 cm. Reprint of the 1935 ed. published by University Press, Cambridge, which was issued as the Prince Consort prize essay, 1934. Bibliography: p. 188-[190] [DF212.E7B3 1979] 76-29429 18.50
1. Ephorus. 2. Greece—History—To 146 B.C. I. Title. II. Series: Prince Consort prize essay ; 1934. BIP

Ephron, Phoebe Wolkind, 1914-1971—Biography.

EPHRON, Henry, 808.2'3'0924 B
1911-
We thought we could do anyting ; the life of screenwriters Phoebe and Henry Ephron / Henry Ephron. 1st ed. New York : Norton, c1977. 211 p. : ill. ; 22 cm. [PS3509.P46Z65] 76-54318 ISBN 0-393-07510-9 : 9.95
1. Ephron, Phoebe Wolkind, 1914-1971—Biography. 2. Ephron, Henry, 1911- —Biography. 3. Dramatists, American—20th century—Biography. 4. Screen writers—United States—Biography. I. Title.

Epicurus.

RIST, John M. 187
Epicurus; an introduction [by] J. M. Rist. Cambridge [Eng.] University Press, 1972 xiv, 185 p. 23 cm. Bibliography: p. 177-182. [B573.R57] 70-177939 ISBN 0-521-08426-1
1. Epicurus. BIP

Eppley, Eugene C., 1884-1958.

DALSTROM, 338.4'7'647940924 B
Harl Adams, 1936-
Eugene C. Eppley: his life and legacy, Lincoln, Neb., Johnsen Pub. Co. [1969] 177 p. illus., facsims., ports. 27 cm. (Nebraska heritage series) Bibliography: p. 133-164. [TX910.5.E65D3] 79-85815
1. Eppley, Eugene C., 1884-1958. I. Title.

Epstein, Jacob, Sir, 1880-1959.

BUCKLE, Richard 730.942
Jacob Epstein, sculptor. Cleveland, World [c.1963] 448p. illus., ports. 30cm. 63-11957 25.00
1. Epstein, Jacob, Sir 1880-1959. I. Title.

EPSTEIN, Jacob, 1880- 927.3
Epstein, an autobiography. [Rev. and extended ed.] New York, Dutton [1955] x, 294 p. plates, ports. 24 cm. First published in 1940 under title: Let there be sculpture. [NB497] 55-4439
1. Artists—Correspondence, reminiscences, etc. 2. Sculpture. I. Title.

EPSTEIN, Jacob, Sir, 730'.92'4 B
1880-1959.
Epstein, an autobiography / Jacob Epstein. [Rev. & extended ed.]. New York : Arno Press, 1975. x, 294 p., [47] leaves of plates : ill. ; 24 cm. (The Modern Jewish experience) Published in 1940 under title: Let there be sculpture. Reprint of the 1955 ed. published by Dutton, New York. Includes index. [NB497.E6A2 1975] 74-27978 ISBN 0-405-06707-0 : 26.00
1. Epstein, Jacob, Sir, 1880-1959. 2. Sculptors—Great Britain—Correspondence, reminiscences, etc. I. Title. II. Series.

EPSTEIN, Jacob, Sir, 709'.24
1880-1959.
The sculptor speaks, Jacob Epstein to Arnold L. Haskell; a series of conversations on art. New York, B. Blom, 1971. xiii, 200 p. illus. 24 cm. Reprint of the 1932 ed. [N7445.2.E6 1971] 73-172922
1. Art. I. Haskell, Arnold Lionel, 1903- II. Title.

Epstein, Kathie.

EPSTEIN, Kathie. 248'.2'0924 B
The quiet riot / Kathie Epstein. Old Tappan, N.J. : F. H. Revell Co., c1976. p. cm. [BR1725.E66A36] 76-2719 ISBN 0-8007-0789-3
1. Epstein, Kathie. I. Title. BIP

Epstein, Melech.

EPSTEIN, Melech. 914'.06'924 B
Pages from a colorful life; an autobiographical sketch. [Miami Beach, Fla., I. Block Pub. Co., 1971] 168 p. 22 cm. [E184.J5E615] 72-26623 5.95
I. Title.

Epstein, Perle S.

EPSTEIN, Perle S. 296.8'33 B
Pilgrimage : adventures of a wandering Jew / Perle Epstein. Boston : Houghton Mifflin, 1979. xi, 364 p. ; 22 cm. [BM755.E77A36] 79-15688 ISBN 0-395-27620-9 : 10.00
1. Epstein, Perle S. 2. Hasidim—New York (State)—Biography. 3. Mysticism—Judaism. 4. Mysticism—India. I. Title. BIP

Equiano, Olaudah,

EQUIANO, Olaudah, b.1745. 920
Equiano's travels; the interesting narrative of the life of Olaudah Equiano or Gustavus Vassa, the African. Abridged and edited by Paul Edwards. New York, Praeger [1967] xviii, 196 p. illus., port. 21 cm. First ed. published in 1789 under title: The interesting narrative of the life of Olaudah Equiano, or Gustavus Vassa, the African. Includes bibliographical references. [HT869.E6A3 1967] 66-15448
I. Title. II. Title: The interesting narrative of the life of Olaudah Equiano.

EQUIANO, Olaudah, 301.45'22 B
b.1745.
The life of Olaudah Equiano, or Gustavus Vassa, the African. Written by himself. New York, Negro Universities Press [1969] 294 p. illus., port. 23 cm. Reprint of the 1837 ed. [HT869.E6A3 1969] 76-88409 ISBN 0-8371-1839-5
I. Title. BIP

Equiano, Olaudah, b. 1745—Juvenile literature.

KENNERLY, Karen. 301.44'93'0924 B
The slave who bought his freedom; Equiano's story, adapted by Karen Kennerly. [1st ed.] New York, Dutton [1971] 121 p. 22 cm. (Black autobiographies) "A Richard W. Baron book." Adapted from O. Equiano's The interesting narrative of the life of Olaudah Equiano. The autobiography of a slave kidnapped from a West African tribe as a child who, during his voyages and trials in various parts of the world, educated himself and ultimately purchased his freedom. [HT869.E6K45 1971] 70-108969 ISBN 0-525-39455-9 4.50
1. Equiano, Olaudah, b. 1745—Juvenile literature. I. Equiano, Olaudah, b. 1745. The interesting narrative of the life of Olaudah Equiano. II. Title. III. Series. BIP

Erasmus, Desiderius, d. 1536.

BAINTON, Roland Herbert, 199'.492
1894-
Erasmus of Christendom [by] Roland H. Bainton. New York, Scribner [1969] xii, 308 p. illus., facsims., ports. 24 cm. Bibliography: p. 285-299. [B785.E64B3] 68-27788 6.95
1. Erasmus, Desiderius, d. 1536. I. Title. BIP

BROCKWELL, Maurice 759.9492
Walter, 1869-1958.
Erasmus, humanist and painter : a study of a triptych in a private collection / by Maurice W. Brockwell. Folcroft, Pa. : Folcroft Library Editions, 1979. 98 p., [6] leaves of plates : ill. ; 24 cm. Reprint of the 1918 ed. privately printed in New York. Includes bibliographical references and index. [ND653.E7A63 1979] 79-14635 ISBN 0-8414-9830-X lib. bdg. : 17.50
1. Erasmus, Desiderius, d. 1536. Christ on the Cross. I. Title.

ERASMUS and the age of 928.79
Reformation; [translated from the Dutch by F. Hopman] With a selection from the letters of Erasmus; [translated by Barbara Flower] New York, Harper [1957] 266p. illus. 21cm. (Harper torchbooks, TB19) [PA8518.H83 1957] 922.2492 57-10119
1. Erasmus, Desiderius, d. 1536. I. Huizinga, Johan, 1872- 1945.

FALUDY, Gyorgy. 199.492 B
Erasmus [by] George Faludy. New York, Stein and Day [1970] x, 298 p. illus., maps, ports. 25 cm. Bibliography: p. [274]-280. [B785.E64F3] 70-108315 10.00
1. Erasmus, Desiderius, d. 1536 BIP

FROUDE, James Anthony, 199'.492 B
1818-1894.
Life and letters of Erasmus. New York, AMS Press [1971] 433 p. 23 cm. Reprint of the 1895 ed. [PA8518.F7 1971] 70-155628 ISBN 0-404-02627-3
1. Erasmus, Desiderius, d. 1536. I. Title. BIP

HYMA, Albert, 1893- 199'.492 B
The life of Desiderius Erasmus. Assen, Van Gorcum, [1973 c1972] 140 p. 24 cm. Includes bibliographical references. [PA8518.H93] 73-153621 ISBN 9-02-320964-8
1. Erasmus, Desiderius, d. 1536. I. Title. Distributed by Humanities; pap. 7.75. BIP

HYMA, Albert, 1893- 199'.492 B
The youth of Erasmus. 2d ed., enl. New York, Russell & Russell [1968] xxii, 402 p. illus., facsims., port. 24 cm. "Appendix B, the Book against the barbarians" (p. 239-335), contains two Latin texts of the treatise. Bibliography: p. [387]-390. [PA8518.H95 1968] 68-10929
1. Erasmus, Desiderius, d 1536. 2. Brothers of the Common Life. I. Erasmus, Desiderius, d. 1536. Antibarbarorum liber. II. Title. BIP

JEBB, Richard 199'.492 B
Claverhouse, Sir, 1841-1905.
Erasmus; the Rede lecture delivered in the Senate House on June 11, 1890. Freeport, N.Y., Books for Libraries Press [1970] 55 p. 23 cm. Reprint of the 1890 ed. [PA8518.J4 1970] 70-114885
1. Erasmus, Desiderius, d. 1536. I. Title.

JONES, Rosemary 270.6'0922
Devonshire.
Erasmus and Luther, by R. Devonshire Jones. London, Oxford U.P., 1968. 96 p. 12 plates, illus., facsims., map (on lining paper), ports. 21 cm. (The Clarendon biographies, 13) Bibliography: p. 91-93. [BR350.E7J58] 74-355482 12/6
1. Erasmus, Desiderius, d. 1536. 2. Luther, Martin, 1483-1546.

MANGAN, John Joseph, 199'.492 B
1857-1935.
Life, character, & influence of Desiderius Erasmus of Rotterdam. New York, Macmillan, 1927. [New York, AMS Press, 1971] 2 v. ports. 23 cm. Bibliography: v. 2, p. 409-414. [PA8518.M35 1971] 73-147113 ISBN 0-404-04178-7
1. Erasmus, Desiderius, d. 1536. I. Title. BIP

MAY, Harry S. 199'.492 B
The tragedy of Erasmus : a psychohistoric

approach / Harry S. May. Saint Charles, Mo. : Piraeus Publishers, 1975. 180 p. : ill. ; 23 cm. Includes index. Bibliography: p. 167-171. [B785.E64M34] 75-11159 ISBN 0-913656-07-0 pbk. : 4.95
1. Erasmus, Desiderius, d. 1536. I. Title.

PHILLIPS, Margaret Mann. 922.2492
Erasmus and the northern Renaissance. New York, Macmillan, 1950. xxv, 236 p. map (on lining paper) 19 cm. (Teach yourself history) Bibliography: p. 228. [BR350.E7P5] 928.79 50-7057
1. Erasmus, Desiderius, d. 1536. 2. Reformation. I. Series: Teach yourself history library (New York)

SMITH, Preserved, 1880-1941. 922.2492
Erasmus: a study of his life, ideals, and place in history. New York, Ungar [1962] 477 p. 22 cm. [PA8518.S6 1962] 62-17092
1. Erasmus, Desiderius, d. 1536. I. Title. BIP

SMITH, Preserved, 1880-1941 922.2942
Erasmus; a study of his life, ideals and place in history [Gloucester, Mass., P. Smith, 1963] 479p. illus. 22cm. (Dover bk. rebound) Bibl. 4.00
1. Erasmus, Desiderius, d. 1536. I. Title.

SMITH, Preserved, 1880-1941 922.2942
Erasmus; a study of his life, ideals, and place in history. New York, Dover [1962] 479p. illus. 22cm. Unabridged and unaltered republication of the work first pub. by Harper in 1923. Bibl. 62-52883 2.00 pap.,
1. Erasmus, Desiderius, d. 1536. I. Title.

SMITH, Preserved, 1880-1941. 922.2492
Erasmus; a study of his life, ideals, and place in history. New York, Ungar [1962] 477 p. 22 cm. [PA8518.S6 1962] 62-17092
1. Erasmus, Desiderius, d. 1536.

SOWARDS, Jesse Kelley, 1924- 081 S
Erasmus and the "other" Pope Julius, by J. K. Sowards. Wichita, Kan., Wichita State University, 1972. 26 p. 23 cm. (Wichita State University. Bulletin, v. 48, no. 1. University studies, no. 90) Includes bibliographical references. [AS36.W62 no. 90] [BR350.E7] 262'.13'0924 72-610818
1. Erasmus, Desiderius, d. 1536. 2. Julius II, Pope, 1443-1513. I. Title. II. Series: Kansas. State University, Wichita. University studies, no. 90.

ZWEIG, Stefan, 1881-1942. v. 12
Erasmus of Rotterdam [by] Stefan Zweig; translated by Eden and Cedar Paul. New York, The Viking press, [1956] 247 p. 20 cm. (Compass books C13)
1. Erasmus, Desiderius, d. 1536. I. Title.

Erasmus, Desiderius, d. 1536—Correspondence.

ERASMUS, Desiderius, d.1536. 199'.492
The correspondence of Erasmus. Translated by R. A. B. Mynors and D. F. S. Thomson. Annotated by Wallace K. Ferguson. [Toronto, Buffalo] University of Toronto Press [1974- v. illus. 26 cm. (His Collected works of Erasmus v. 1) Translation of Opus epistolarum Des. Erasmi Roterdami. Contents.Contents.—[1] Letters 1 to 141, 1484-1500. Includes bibliographical references. [PA8511.A5E55 1974] 72-97422 ISBN 0-8020-1981-1 25.00
1. Erasmus, Desiderius, d. 1536—Correspondence. I. Title.

ERASMUS, Desiderius, d.1536. 199'.492
The correspondence of Erasmus. Translated by R. A. B. Mynors and D. F. S. Thomson. Annotated by Wallace K. Ferguson. [Toronto, Buffalo] University of Toronto Press [1974- v. illus. 26 cm. (His Collected works of Erasmus v. 1) Translation of Opus epistolarum Des. Erasmi Roterdami. Contents.Contents.—[1] Letters 1 to 141, 1484-1500.—[2] Letters 142 to 297, 1501-1514. Includes bibliographical references. [PA8511.A5E55 1974] 72-97422 ISBN 0-8020-1981-1 (v. 1) 25.00
1. Erasmus, Desiderius, d. 1536—Correspondence. I. Title.

ERASMUS, Desiderius, d.1536. 199'.492 B
Erasmus and his age; selected letters of Desiderius Erasmus. Edited by Hans J. Hillerbrand. Translated by Marcus A. Haworth. New York, Harper & Row [1970] xxvi, 305 p. 21 cm. (Harper torchbooks, TB 1461) Bibliography: p. [292]-294. [PA8511.A5E54] 71-119064 2.95
1. Erasmus, Desiderius, d. 1536—Correspondence. I. Hillerbrand, Hans Joachim, ed. II. Title.

Erasmus, Desiderius, d. 1536—Juvenile literature.

MEE, Charles L. 199'.492 B
Erasmus: the eye of the hurricane, by Charles L. Mee, Jr. New York, Coward, McCann & Geoghegan [1973, c1974] 128 p. illus. 22 cm. Bibliography: p. 124. A biography of the foremost Christian humanist of the Renaissance who devoted his life to uplifting man's condition through faith, reason, and education. [B785.E64M35 1974] 92 72-89768 ISBN 0-698-20251-1 5.95
1. Erasmus, Desiderius, d. 1536—Juvenile literature. I. Title.

Eratosthenes.

FRASER, Peter Marshall. 082 S
Eratosthenes of Cyrene, by P. M. Fraser. London, Oxford University Press, 1971. 35 p. 25 cm. (Lecture on a master mind, British Academy, 1970) (Proceedings of the British Academy, v. 56) Includes bibliographical references. [AS122.L5 vol. 56] [G87.E73] 520'.92'4 B 72-183166 ISBN 0-19-725661-9 £0.30
1. Eratosthenes. I. Title. II. Series: British Academy, London (Founded 1901) Annual lecture on a master-mind, Henriette Hertz Trust, 1970. III. Series: British Academy, London (Founded 1901) Proceedings, v. 56.

Erb, Paul, 1894-

GOOD, Phyllis Pellman, 1948- 289.7'092'2 B
Paul and Alta : living wisdom / Phyllis Pellman Good ; photography by Paul M. Schrock. Scottdale, Pa. : Herald Press, 1978. 114 p. : ill. ; 22 x 28 cm. [BX8143.E7G66] 78-2890 ISBN 0-8361-1853-7 pbk. : 7.95
1. Erb, Paul, 1894- 2. Erb, Alta Mae, 1891- 3. Mennonites—United States—Biography. I. Title.

Erdody, Anna Maria (Niczky) grof, 1780?-1837.

STEICHEN, Dana, 1894-1957. 927.8
Beethoven's beloved. [1st ed.] Garden City, N.Y., Doubleday, 1959. 526 p. illus. 24 cm. [ML410.B4S74] 59-13984
1. Erdody, Anna Maria (Niczky) grof, 1780?-1837. 2. Beethoven, Ludwig van, 1770-1827. I. Title.

Erdstein, Erich.

ERDSTEIN, Erich. 363.2'34'0924 B
Inside the Fourth Reich / by Erich Erdstein with Barbara Bean. New York : St. Martin's Press, c1977. 220 p. ; 22 cm. [D804.G4E75] 77-9153 ISBN 0-312-41885-X : 8.95
1. Erdstein, Erich. 2. Mengele, Josef, 1911- 3. War criminals—Germany. 4. Germans in South America. 5. Police—Brazil—Biography. I. Bean, Barbara, joint author. II. Title.

Erhard, Werner, 1936-

BARTLEY, William Warren, 1934- 158 B
Werner Erhard : the transformation of a man, the founding of est. / by William Warren Bartley, III. 1st ed. New York : C. N. Potter : distributed by Crown Publishers, c1978. xx, 279 p., [4] leaves of plates : ill. ; 24 cm. [RC339.52.E7B37 1978] 78-8990 ISBN 0-517-53502-5 : 10.00
1. Erhard, Werner, 1936- 2. Erhard seminars training. 3. Psychologists—United States—Biography.

Ericsson, Henry,

ERICSSON, Henry, 1861-1947. 690'.092'4 B
Sixty years a builder; the autobiography of Henry Ericsson. New York, Arno Press, 1972 [c1942] ix, 388 p. illus. 24 cm. (Technology and society) [TH140.E7A3 1972] 72-5046 ISBN 0-405-04698-7
I. Title. II. Series. BIP

Ericsson, John, 1803-1889.

LATHAM, Jean Lee. 623.80924 B
Man of the Monitor; the story of John Ericsson. Pictures by Leonard Everett Fisher. New York, Harper [1962] 231 p. illus. 22 cm. A biography of the Swedish-American engineer credited with over 2000 inventions as well as the design and construction of several types of boats. History remembers him for the construction of the Monitor, the little ironclad warship that held its own against the Merrimack. [PZ7.L348Mak] 92 AC 68
1. Ericsson, John, 1803-1889. I. Fisher, Leonard Everett, illus. II. Title. BIP

WHITE, Ruth (Morris) 926.2
Yankee from Sweden; the dream and the reality in the days of John Ericsson. [1st ed.] New York, Holt [1960] 290 p. 22 cm. Includes bibliography. [T40.E8W5] 60-5129
1. Ericsson, John, 1806-1889. I. Title.

Ericsson, John, 1803-1889—Juvenile fiction.

LATHAM, Jean Lee. 608.7'73
Man of the Monitor; the story of John Ericsson. Pictures by Leonard Everett Fisher. New York, Harper [1962] 231 p. illus. 22 cm. [PZ7.L348Mak] 62-8037
1. Ericsson, John, 1803-1889—Juvenile fiction. I. Title.

Ericsson, John, 1803-1889—Juvenile literature.

BURNETT, Constance (Buel) 926.2
Captain John Ericsson: father of the Monitor. New York, Vanguard Press [c1960] 255p. 21cm. [T40.E8B8] 60-15070
1. Ericsson, John, 1803-1889—Juvenile literature. I. Title. BIP

Erikson, Erik Homburger, 1902-

ROAZEN, Paul, 1936- 150'.19'50924 B
Erik H. Erikson : the power and limits of a vision / Paul Roazen. New York : Free Press, c1976. x, 246 p. ; 22 cm. Includes bibliographical references and index. [RC339.52.E74R6] 76-10497 ISBN 0-02-926450-2 : 8.95
1. Erikson, Erik Homburger, 1902- 2. Psychoanalysts—United States—Biography. BIP

Erikson, Erik Homburger, 1902- —Congresses.

ENCOUNTER with Erikson : historical interpretation and religious biography / edited by Donald Capps, Walter H. Capps, M. Gerald Bradford. Missoula, Mont. : Published by Scholars Press for the American Academy of Religion and the Institute of Religious Studies, University of California, Santa Barbara, c1977. xvi, 429 p. ; 24 cm. (Series on formative contemporary thinkers ; no. 2) Paper presented at a symposium to honor E. H. Erikson on the occasion of his seventieth birthday, held at La Casa de Maria Retreat Center near Santa Barbara, Calif., Feb. 17-19, 1972. "Erik Homburger Erikson: a bibliography of his books and articles": p. 421-429. [BL72.E5] 76-44434 200'.92'2 B
1. Erikson, Erik Homburger, 1902- —Congresses. 2. Religions—Biography—Congresses. 3. Psychohistory—Congresses. 4. Psychology, Religious—Congresses. I. Erikson, Erik Homburger, 1902- II. Capps, Donald. III. Capps, Walter H. IV. Bradford, Miles Gerald, 1938- V. American Academy of Religion. VI. California. University, Santa Barbara. Institute of Religious Studies. VII. Title. VIII. Series.

Erni, Hans, 1909-

ROY, Claude, 1915- v. 12
Hans Erni. Lausanne, Clairefontaine [1964] 168 p. illus. (part col.), plates. 65-86496
1. Erni, Hans, 1909- I. Erni, Hans, 1909- II. Title.

Ernst, Max, 1891-

DIEHL, Gaston. 759.4
Max Ernst. [Translated from the French by Eileen B. Hennessy] New York, Crown [1973] 95 p. illus. (part col.) 29 cm. Bibliography: p. 91-93. [ND588.E75D5313] 72-84222 ISBN 0-517-50004-3 3.95
1. Ernst, Max, 1891-

RUSSELL, John, 1919- 709'.44
Max Ernst: life and work. New York, H. N. Abrams [1967] 359 p. illus. (part col.) facsims., ports. 31 cm. Bibliography: p. 336-341. [N6888.E7R83] 67-22852
1. Ernst, Max, 1891- I. Title.

RUSSELL, John, 1919- 709'.44
Max Ernst: life and work. New York, H. N. Abrams [1967] 359 p. illus. (part col.), facsims., ports. 31 cm. Bibliography: p. 336-341. [N6888.E7R83 1967b] 67-22852
1. Ernst, Max, 1891-

SCHNEEDE, Uwe M. 759.4
Max Ernst [by] Uwe M. Schneede. Translated by R. W. Last. New York, Praeger [1973, c1972] 216 p. illus. (part col.) 22 cm. Bibliography: p. 204-205. [ND588.E75S3613 1973] 72-88535 10.00
1. Ernst, Max, 1891- BIP

Erskine, John, 1879-1951.

ERSKINE, John, 1879-1951. 780'.07 B
My life in music. Westport, Conn., Greenwood Press [1973, c1950] viii, 283 p. port. 22 cm. Reprint of the ed. published by Morrow, New York. [ML429.E7A3 1973] 73-8158 ISBN 0-8371-6950-X 12.50
1. Erskine, John, 1879-1951. 2. Musicians—Correspondence, reminiscences, etc. 3. Music—New York (City) I. Title. BIP

Erskine, Robert, 1735-1780.

HEUSSER, Albert Henry, 1886-1929. 973.3'0924 B
George Washington's map maker; a biography of Robert Erskine, by Albert H. Heusser. Edited with an introd. by Hubert G. Schmidt. New Brunswick, N.J., Rutgers University Press [1966] xix, 268 p. illus., facsims., maps (part fold.) 22 cm. First published in 1928 under title: The forgotten general. Bibliographical footnotes. [E207.E7H6 1966] 65-23231
1. Erskine, Robert, 1735-1780. I. Title.

HEUSSER, Albert Henry, 1886-1929. 92
George Washington's map maker; a biography of Robert Erskine, by Albert H. Heusser. Edited with an introd. by Hubert G. Schmidt. New Brunswick, N.J., Rutgers University Press [1966] xix, 268 p. illus., facsims., maps (part fold.) 22 cm. First published in 1928 under title: The forgotten general. Bibliographical footnotes. A biography of an engineer and inventor, born a Scotsman and died an American patriot, who served as geographer and surveyor-general for the American army in the Revolutionary War. [E207.E7H6 1966] AC 67
1. Erskine, Robert, 1735-1780. I. Title.

Erte.

ERTE. 745.4'49'24 B
Things I remember : an autobiography / Erte. New York : Quadrangle, [1975] p. cm. Includes index. [TT505.E78A34] 75-8286 ISBN 0-8129-0575-X : 12.50
1. Erte. I. Title.

Ervin, Samuel James, 1896-

CLANCY, Paul R., 1939- 328.73'092'4 B
Just a country lawyer; a biography of Senator Sam Ervin, by Paul R. Clancy. Bloomington, Indiana University Press [1974] 310 p. illus. 24 cm. Bibliography: p. [301]-304. [E840.8.E74C55] 73-16528 ISBN 0-253-14540-6 8.50
1. Ervin, Samuel James, 1896- I. Title. **BIP**

DABNEY, Dick. 973.924'092'4 B
A good man : the life of Sam J. Ervin / by Dick Dabney. Boston : Houghton Mifflin, 1976. x, 356 p., [6] leaves of plates : ill. ; 24 cm. Includes bibliographical references and index. [E748.E93D32] 75-42421 ISBN 0-395-20715-0 : 10.00
1. Ervin, Samuel James, 1896- I. Title.

Erving, Julius.

BELL, Marty. 796.32'3'0924 B
The legend of Dr. J. [New York] New American Library [1976 c1975] 180 p. 18 cm. (A Signet Book) Includes index. [GV884.E78B44] 1.25 (pbk.)
1. Erving, Julius. 2. Basketball. I. Title.
L.C. card no. of 1975 Coward, McCann & Geoghegan edition: 74-16636

BELL, Marty. 796.32'3'0924 B
The legend of Dr J / Marty Bell. New York : Coward, McCann & Geoghegan, [1975] 224 p. : ill. ; 22 cm. Includes index. A biography of the black basketball star who was voted the most valuable player by the ABA in 1974. [GV884.E78B44] 92 74-16636 ISBN 0-698-10639-3 : 7.95
1. Erving, Julius. 2. Basketball. I. Title.

Erving, Julius—Juvenile literature.

BRAUN, Thomas, 1944- 796.32'3'0924 B
Julius Erving / by Thomas Braun ; illustrated by John Keely. Mankato, Minn. : Creative Education, [1976] p. cm. A brief biography of the basketball star of the New York Nets. [GV884.E78B7] 92 75-37584 ISBN 0-87191-499-9
1. Erving, Julius—Juvenile literature. 2. Basketball—Juvenile literature. I. Keely, John. II. Title. **BIP**

BURCHARD, Marshall. 796.32'3'0924 B
Sports hero, Dr. J : the story of Julius Erving / by Marshall Burchard. New York : Putnam, c1976. p. cm. A biography of the basketball player whose agile movements on the court have made him famous. [GV884.E78B88 1976] 92 75-42914 ISBN 0-399-20495-4. ISBN 0-399-60985-7 lib. bdg.
1. Erving, Julius—Juvenile literature. 2. Basketball—Juvenile literature. I. Title.

HASKINS, James, 1941- 796.32'3'0924 B
Dr. J. : a biography of Julius Erving / James Haskins. 1st ed. Garden City, N.Y. : Doubleday, 1975. 88 p., [8] leaves of plates : ill. ; 22 cm. A biography of the black basketball star who was voted the most valuable player by the ABA in 1974. [GV884.E78H37] 92 74-33645 ISBN 0-385-09906-1 lib. bdg. : 4.95 ISBN 0-385-09905-3 : 4.95
1. Erving, Julius—Juvenile literature. 2. Basketball—Juvenile literature. I. Title.

JACOBS, Linda. 796.32'3'0924 B
Julius Erving : Doctor J and Julius W / by Linda Jacobs ; photos. by Jeffrey E. Blackman. St. Paul : EMC Corp., 1976. 38 p. : ill. ; 23 cm. (Black American athletes) A brief biography of the black basketball star who was voted the most valuable player by the ABA in 1974. [GV884.E78J32] 92 76-86 ISBN 0-88436-265-5 lib.bdg. : 4.95 ISBN 0-88436-266-3 pbk. :
1. Erving, Julius—Juvenile literature. 2. Basketball—Juvenile literature. I. Blackman, Jeffrey E. II. Title. III. Series. **BIP**

SABIN, Louis. 796.32'3'0924 B
The fabulous Dr. J. : all time all star / by Louis Sabin. New York : Putnam, c1976. p. cm. (Putnam sports shelf) Includes index. A biography of professional basketball player Julius Erving, known as Dr. J., who plays for the New York Nets. [GV884.E78S22 1976] 92 76-23124 ISBN 0-399-61042-1 lib. bdg. : 5.29
1. Erving, Julius—Juvenile literature. 2. Basketball—Juvenile literature. I. Title. **BIP**

Erwin, John Robert, 1930-

ERWIN, John Robert, 1930- 365'.66 B
The man who keeps going to jail / John R. Erwin [as told to Dell Coats Erwin]. Elgin, Ill. : D.C. Cook Pub. Co., c1978. 182 p., [4] leaves of plates : ill. ; 22 cm. [BV4340.E74] 77-88124 ISBN 0-89191-107-3 : 6.95
1. Erwin, John Robert, 1930- 2. Chicago. Cook County Jail. 3. Chaplains, Prison—Illinois—Chicago—Biography. 4. Church work with prisoners—Illinois—Chicago. I. Erwin, Dell Coats, joint author. II. Title. **BIP**

Erwitt, Elliott.

CALLAHAN, Sean. 770'.92'4
The private experience, Elliott Erwitt / text by Sean Callahan, with the editors of Alskog, inc. [New York] : T. Y. Crowell, [1974] 88 p. : ill. (some col.) ; 29 cm. (Masters of contemporary photography) [TR140.E78C34] 74-8232 ISBN 0-690-00623-3 : 7.95. ISBN 0-690-00624-1 pbk. : 3.95
1. Erwitt, Elliott. 2. Photography, Artistic. I. Alskog, inc. II. Erwitt, Elliott. III. Title.

Esberg, Milton Herman, 1875-1939.

[PERRY, Henry Lee] 1881- 923.373
A man and his friends; the life story of Milton H. Esberg, good citizen, successful business man, and warm hearted loyal friend: the tribute of a friend. [San Francisco, 1953] 163p. illus. 27cm. [CT275.E72P4] 53-36017
1. Esberg, Milton Herman, 1875-1939. I. Title.

Esbjorn, Lars Paul

RONNEGARD, Sam. 922.473
Prairie shepherd; Lars Paul Esbjorn and the beginnings of the Augustana Lutheran Church. A translation by G. Everett Arden. Rock Island, Ill., Augustana Book Concern [1952] 308 p. illus. 21 cm. [BX8080.E67R63] 52-2628
1. Esbjorn, Lars Paul 1808-1870. 2. Translation of Lars Paul Esbjorn och Augustana-aynödens uppkomst. 3. Augustana Evangelical Lutheran Church — Hist. I. Title.

Escalante-Dominguez Expedition, 1776—Personal narratives.

VELEZ de Escalante, Silvestre, fl.1768-1779. 917.8
The Dominguez-Escalante journal : their expedition through Colorado, Utah, Arizona, and New Mexico in 1776 / translated by Angelico Chavez ; edited by Ted J. Warner. Provo, Utah : Brigham Young University Press, c1976. xix, 203 p. : ill. ; 28 cm. English and Spanish. Bibliography: p. 201-203. [F799.V4413 1976] 76-44561 ISBN 0-8425-0037-5 : 12.95
1. Escalante-Dominguez Expedition, 1776—Personal narratives. 2. Velez de Escalante, Silvestre, fl. 1768-1779. 3. Dominguez, Francisco Atanasio, fl. 1776. 4. Explorers—Spain—Biography. I. Title.

Escher, Maurits Cornelis, 1898-

ESCHER, Maurits Cornelis, 1898- 769'.92'4
The world of M. C. Escher, with texts by M. C. Escher [and] J. L. Locher. [Edited by J. L. Locher] New concise NAL ed. New York, H. N. Abrams; distributed by New American Library [1974, c1971] 151 p. illus. (part col.) 31 cm. [NE670.E75L6 1974] 73-20290
1. Escher, Maurits Cornelis, 1898- I. Locher, J. L. II. Title. **BIP**

Escoffier, Auguste, 1846-1935—Juvenile literature.

SANGER, Majory Bartlett. 641.5'092'4 B
Escoffier, master chef / Marjory Bartlett Sanger. New York : Farrar Straus Giroux, c1976. 214 p. ; 21 cm. Includes index. Bibliography: p. 201-208. A biography of the world famous chef who changed the eating habits of nations. [TX649.E8S26 1976] 92 76-14810 ISBN 0-374-32227-9 : 6.95
1. Escoffier, Auguste, 1846-1935—Juvenile literature. I. Title. **BIP**

Esenin, Sergei Aleksandrovich, 1895-1925—Biography.

MCVAY, Gordon. 891.7'1'42 B
Esenin : a life / by Gordon McVay. Ann Arbor, Mich. : Ardis, c1976. 352 p., [31] leaves of plates : ill. ; 24 cm. Includes indexes. Bibliography: p. 312-332. [PG3476.E8Z774] 76-361860 ISBN 0-88233-182-5 : 10.00 ISBN 0-88233-183-3 pbk. : 3.95
1. Esenin, Sergei Aleksandrovich, 1895-1925—Biography.

MCVAY, Gordon. 891.7'1'42 B
Esenin : a life / by Gordon McVay. London : Hodder and Stoughton, 1976. 352 p., [2] leaves of plates, [60] p. of plates : ill., facsims., ports. ; 24 cm. Includes indexes. Bibliography: p. 312-332. [PG3476.E8Z774 1976b] 77-355924 ISBN 0-340-20461-3 : £8.95
1. Esenin, Sergei Aleksandrovich, 1895-1925—Biography. 2. Poets, Russian—20th century—Biography. **BIP**

Eshkol, Levi, 1895-1969.

PRITTIE, Terence Cornelius Farmer, Hon., 1913- 956.9405'0924 B
Eshkol; the man and the nation [by] Terence Prittie. New York, Pitman Pub. Corp. [1969] xiv, 368 p. illus., facsim., maps, ports. 25 cm. Bibliography: p. 351-354. [DS126.6.E8P7] 70-79051 7.95
1. Eshkol, Levi, 1895-1969.

Esparza, Carlos, 1828-1885.

LARRALDE, Carlos. 976.4'4 B
Carlos Esparza, a Chicano chronicle / by Carlos Larralde. San Francisco, Calif. : R & E Research Associates, 1977. viii, 123 p. ; 28 cm. Includes bibliographical references. [F392.R5E844] 76-26523 ISBN 0-88247-422-7 pbk. : 6.00
1. Esparza, Carlos, 1828-1885. 2. Mexican Americans—Rio Grande Valley—Biography. 3. Rio Grande Valley—History I. Title.

Espinel, Vincente, 1550?-1624.

HEATHCOTE, Antony A. 868'.3'09 B
Vincente Espinel / by Antony A. Heathcote. Boston : Twayne Publishers, c1977. p. cm. (Twayne's world authors series ; TWAS 440 : Spain) Includes index. Bibliography: p. [PQ6390.E56Z68] 76-53560 ISBN 0-8057-6169-1 lib.bdg. : 8.95
1. Espinel, Vincente, 1550?-1624. 2. Authors, Spanish—17th century—Biography.

Espionage, Russian.

[NEWMAN, Joseph] 327'.12'0922 B
Famous Soviet spies; the Kremlin's secret weapon. Washington, Books by U.S. News & World Report [1973] 223 p. illus. 23 cm. Bibliography: p. 212-213. [UB271.R9N46] 72-93237 2.95
1. Espionage, Russian. 2. Spies. I. Title.

Esposito, Phil, 1942- —Juvenile literature.

BURCHARD, Marshall. 796.9'62'0924 B
Sports hero, Phil Esposito / by Marshall and Sue Burchard. New York : Putnam, [1975] 95 p. : ill. ; 22 cm. A biography concentrating on the career of the star center of the Boston Bruins. [GV848.5.E68B87 1975] 74-21083 ISBN 0-399-60941-5 lib. bdg. : 4.69
1. Esposito, Phil, 1942- —Juvenile literature. 2. Hockey—Juvenile literature. I. Burchard, S. H., joint author. II. Title.

Esser, Grace Denton.

ESSER, Grace Denton. 790.2'092'4 B
Madame impresario; a personal chronicle of an epoch. Foreword by Merle Armitage. Yucca Valley, Calif., Manzanita Press [1974] 230 p. illus. 29 cm. [ML429.E8A3] 74-170907
1. Esser, Grace Denton. 2. Musicians—Correspondence, reminiscences, etc. I. Title.

Essex, Eng.—Biography.

BROWN, A. F. J., comp. 914.26'7'03
Essex people, 1750-1900 [compiled] from their diaries, memoirs and letters by A. F. J. Brown. Chelmsford [Eng.] Essex County Council [1972] viii, 215 p. illus. 26 cm. (Essex Record Office. Publications, no. 59) Includes bibliographical references. [DA670.E7A17 no. 59] 72-195059 ISBN 0-900360-14-3 £2.10
1. Essex, Eng.—Biography. I. Title. II. Series: Essex, Eng. Record Office. Publications, no. 59.

Essex, Robert Devereux, Earl of, 1566-1601.

BIRCH, Thomas, 1705-1766. 942.05'5
Memoirs of the reign of Queen Elizabeth, from the year 1581 till her death ... and the conduct of her favourite, Robert Earl of Essex, both at home and abroad ... London, Printed for A. Miller, 1754. [New York, Ams Press, 1970] 2 v. 24 cm. [DA355.B62 1970] 79-131513 ISBN 0-404-00909-3
1. Essex, Robert Devereux, Earl of, 1566-1601. 2. Gt. Brit.—History—Elizabeth, 1558-1603. I. Title.

HARRISON, George Bagshawe, 1894- 942.05'5'0924 B
The life and death of Robert Devereux, Earl of Essex, by G. B. Harrison. [Folcroft, Pa.] Folcroft Library Editions, 1973. xi, 359 p. illus. 26 cm. Reprint of the 1937 ed. published by Cassell, London. Bibliography: p. 326-327. [DA358.E8H3 1973] 73-14948 ISBN 0-8414-4774-8 (lib. bdg.)
1. Essex, Robert Devereux, Earl of, 1566-1601. I. Title. **BIP**

LACEY, Robert. 942.05'5'0924 B
Robert, Earl of Essex. [1st Amer. ed.] New York, Atheneum, 1971. xiii, 338 p. illus., maps, ports. 24 cm. Includes bibliographical references. [DA358.E8L3] 70-139313 8.95
1. Essex, Robert Devereux, Earl of, 1566-1601.

Essex, Robert Devereux, Earl of, 1591-1646.

SNOW, Vernon F., 1924- 943.06'1'0924 B
Essex the rebel; the life of Robert Devereux, the third Earl of Essex, 1591-1646, by Vernon F. Snow. Lincoln, University of Nebraska Press [1970] xv, 515 p. 23 illus., facsims., 7 maps, ports. 24 cm. Includes bibliographical references. [DA390.1.E8S6] 71-81542 15.00
1. Essex, Robert Devereux, Earl of, 1591-1646. 2. Gt. Brit.—History—Early Stuarts, 1603-1649. I. Title.

Essex (U.S. frigate)—Juvenile literature.

WERSTEIN, Irving. 973.5'0924 B
The cruise of the Essex; an incident from the War of 1812. Philadelphia, Macrae Smith [1969] 157 p. map. 22 cm. A biography of Captain David Porter and the U.S. frigate Essex which he commanded during its seventeen-month voyage so vital to the outcome of the War of 1812. [E360.W4] 69-18632 3.95
1. Essex (U.S. frigate)—Juvenile literature. 2. Porter, David, 1780-1843—Juvenile literature. 3. U.S.—History—War of 1812—Naval operations—Juvenile literature. I. Title. BIP

Estero.

DAMKOHLER, E. E., 1878- 975.9'48'06
Estero, Fla., 1882; memoirs of the first settler, by E. E. Damkohler. Fort Myers Beach, Fla., Island Press [1967] 32 p. port. 21 cm. [F319.E8D3] 67-19575
1. Estero.

Estevan, d. 1539.

TERRELL, John Upton, 1900- 979.1'01'0924 B
Estevanico the black. Los Angeles, Westernlore Press, 1968. 155 p. illus., map (on lining papers) 22 cm. (Westernlore Great West and Indian series, 36) Bibliography: p. 147-151. [E125.E8T4] 68-16505
1. Estevan, d. 1539. 2. Cibola. I. Title.

Estevan, d. 1539—Juvenile literature.

EDUCATIONAL Research Council of America. Social Science Staff. 973.1'6'0924 B
Explorers and discoverers, Estevan / prepared by the Social Science Staff of the Educational Research Council of America. Learner-verified ed. 2. Boston : Allyn and Bacon, [1974] 43 p. : ill. ; 21 cm. (Concepts and inquiry, the ERC social science program) An account of the travels of the sixteenth-century black man who explored for the Spanish in the New World and guided the search for the Seven Cities of Gold. [E125.E8E3 1974] 92 73-78341 pbk. : 1.76 pbk. : 1.76
1. Estevan, d. 1539—Juvenile literature. I. Title: Explorers and discoverers, Estevan. II. Series: Concepts and inquiry: the Educational Research Council social science program.

SHEPHERD, Elizabeth. 973.1'6'0924
The discoveries of Esteban the Black. With maps by William Steinel. New York, Dodd, Mead [1970] xi, 122 p. illus., maps. 24 cm. Bibliography: p. 117-118. Traces the adventures of the sixteenth-century black man who traveled with the conquistadors through the American southwest and guided the expedition in search of the Seven Cities of Gold. [E123.S5] 74-114240 3.95
1. Estevan, d. 1539—Juvenile literature. 2. America—Discovery and exploration—Spanish—Juvenile literature. I. Title. BIP

Esther, Queen of Persia.

KUMMEL, Sara B 221.92
Esther becomes a queen. Hal Just, illustrator. [New York] Union of American Hebrew Congregations, c1955. unpaged. illus. 16x24cm. [BS580.E8K8] 55-33687
1. Esther, Queen of Persia. I. Title.

MALVERN, Gladys. 221.92
Behold your queen! Decorations by Corinne Malvern. [1st ed.] New York, Longmans, Green, 1951. 218 p. 22 cm. [BS580.E8M3] 51-11613
1. Esther, Queen of Persia. I. Title.

Esther, Queen of Persia—Juvenile literature.

ARMSTRONG, William Howard, 1914- 221.9'24 B
Hadassah: Esther the orphan queen [by] William H. Armstrong. Illustrated by Barbara Ninde Byfield. [1st ed.] Garden City, N.Y., Doubleday [1972] 75 p. illus. 22 cm. Retells the Bible story of Esther who, as Queen of Persia and a Jew, was able to save her people from extermination. [BS580.E8A75] 72-76114 ISBN 0-385-08832-9 3.95
1. Esther, Queen of Persia—Juvenile literature. 2. Bible stories, English—O.T. Esther. I. Byfield, Barbara Ninde, illus. II. Title.

BRIN, Ruth Firestone. 222'.9'09505
The story of Esther / Ruth F. Brin ; illustrated by H. Hechtkopf. Minneapolis : Lerner Publications Co., 1976. [32] p. : col. ill. ; 31 cm. Retells the story of Esther, a young Jewish girl who became queen of Persia and used her influence to stop the murder of the Jews of her country. [BS580.E8B74 1976] 92 75-743 ISBN 0-8225-0364-6 lib.bdg. : 4.95
1. Esther, Queen of Persia—Juvenile literature. 2. Bible stories, English—O.T. Esther. I. Hechtkopf, H. II. Title. BIP

Estienne, Robert, 1503?-1559.

ARMSTRONG, Elizabeth (Tyler) 926.55
Robert Estienne, royal printer; an historical study of the elder Stephanus. Cambridge [Eng.] University Press, 1954. xx, 309p. illus., port., facsim. 27cm. Bibliography. p. 289-297. [Z232.E8A7] 55-1390
1. Estienne, Robert, 1503?-1559. I. Title.

Estrees, Gabrielle d', 1573?-1599.

GERSON, Noel Bertram, 1914- 920.7
Lady of France; a biography of Gabrielle d'Estrees, mistress of Henry the Great, by Paul Lewis [pseud.] New York, Funk & Wagnalls Co. [1963] x, 306 p. 22 cm. Bibliography: p. [293]-294. [DC122.9.E7G4] 63-16339
1. Estrees, Gabrielle d', 1573?-1599. I. Title.

Ethelred, Saint, 1109?-1166.

WALTER, Daniel, fl.1170. 922.242
The life of Ailred of Rievaulx, Translated from the Latin with introd. and notes by F. M. Powike. London, New York, Nelson [1950] cii, 81, 81. [82-]88 p. 23 cm. (Medieval classics) "Walter Daniel's apologia for his Life of Allred": p. 65-81. Latin and English on opposite pages. "Based upon...[the translator's] earlier work, 'Ailred of Rievauix and his biographer Walter Daniel.'" "Notes on Ailred's writings": p. xcv-cii. [BX4700.E7W3] 51-6360
1. Ethelred, Saint, 1109?-1166. I. Powicke, Sir Frederick Maurice, 1879- Ailred of Rievaulx and his biographer Walter Daniel. II. Title. III. Series.

Etherege, George, Sir, 1635?-1691.

DOBREE, Bonamy, 1891- 820.9'004
Essays in biography, 1680-1726 Freeport, N.Y., Books for Libraries Press [1967] x, 362 p. illus., ports. 21 cm. (Essay index reprint series) Reprint of the 1925 ed. Contents.Contents.—His Excellency, Sir George Etherege.—The architect of Blenheim, Sir John Vanbrugh.—The first Victorian, Joseph Addison.—Appendices: Godolphin's warrant to Vanbrugh. Mrs. Yarburgh. Secret. The Frenzy. Pope's letters.—Bibliography (p. [353]-357) [PR433.D6 1967] 67-23203
1. Etherege, George, Sir, 1635?-1691. 2. Vanbrugh, John, Sir, 1664-1726. 3. Addison, Joseph, 1672-1719. 4. Blenheim Palace. I. Title.

DOBREE, Bonamy, 1891- 821'.4 B
Rochester; a conversation between Sir George Etherege and Mr. Fitzjames. [Folcroft, Pa.] Folcroft Library Editions, 1973. p. Reprint of the 1926 ed. published by L. and V. Woolf, London, which was issued as no. 2 of The Hogarth essays. Second series. [DA447.R6D6 1973] 73-13531 6.50
1. Rochester, John Wilmot, 2d earl of, 1647-1680. 2. Etherege, George, Sir, 1635?-1691. 3. Berwick, James Fitz-James, 1st duke of, 1670-1734.

ETHEREGE, George, Sir, 1635?-1691. 822'.4 B
The letterbook of Sir George Etherege. Edited, with an introd. and notes, by Sybil Rosenfeld. New York, B. Blom, 1971. ix, 441 p. illus. 21 cm. Reprint of the 1928 ed. Includes bibliographical references. [PR3432.A83 1971] 79-173181
I. Title.

Etherege, George, Sir, 1635?-1691—Correspondence.

ETHEREGE, George, Sir, 1635?-1691. 822'.4 B
Letters of Sir George Etherege. Edited by Frederick Bracher. Berkeley, University of California Press [1973, c1974] xxv, 324 p. 24 cm. Includes bibliographical references. [PR3432.A83 1974] 70-187870 ISBN 0-520-02218-1 15.00
1. Etherege, George, Sir, 1635?-1691—Correspondence. I. Title. BIP

Ethiopia—Description and travel—To 1900.

WINSTANLEY, William. 916.3'04'4
A visit to Abyssinia; an account of travel in modern Ethiopia, by W. Winstanley. New York, Negro Universities Press [1969] 2 v. 23 cm. Reprint of the 1881 ed. [DT377.W78 1969] 75-82086
1. Ethiopia—Description and travel—To 1900. I. Title. BIP

Ethnology—India.

ELWIN, Verrier, 1902-1964. 923.654
The tribal world of Verrier Elwin, an autobiography. New York, Oxford University Press, 1964. ix, 356 p. illus., ports. 22 cm. [DS430.E52 1964] 64-4091
1. Ethnology—India. I. Title.

Ethnology—Papua New Guinea.

NIUGINI lives. 301.29'95
Milton, Q. : Jacaranda, 1974, c1973. vii, 109 p. ; 22 cm. (Pacific writers series) [GN671.N5N54 1974] 75-306327 ISBN 0-7016-8212-4 : 1.95
1. Ethnology—Papua New Guinea. 2. Acculturation. 3. Papua New Guinea—Biography.

Etienne, Charles Guillaume, 1777-1845.

WICKS, Charles Beaumont, 1907- 842'.7
Charles-Guillaume Etienne, dramatist and publicist (1777-1845) Baltimore, Johns Hopkins Press, 1940. [New York, Johnson Reprint Corp., 1973] 130 p. 22 cm. Original ed. issued as vol. 37 of the Johns Hopkins studies in Romance literatures and languages. Issued also as the author's thesis, Johns Hopkins University, 1935. Bibliography: p. 123-126. [PQ2240.E8W5 1973] 72-12579 ISBN 0-384-68273-1 7.50
1. Etienne, Charles Guillaume, 1777-1845. I. Series: The Johns Hopkins studies in Romance literatures and languages, v. 37. BIP

Etons, Ursula.

ETONS, Ursula. 362.2'93'0926 B
Angel dusted : A family's nightmare / Ursula Etons. New York : Macmillan, c1979. p. cm. [RC568.P45E76] 79-18915 ISBN 0-02-536600-9 : 8.95
1. Etons, Ursula. 2. Phencyclidine abuse—United States—Biography. 3. Psychoses—United States—Biography. I. Title. BIP

Etzel, Baptista.

ARENTH, Mary Aurelia, 1881- 922.273
As a living oak; biography of Mother Baptista Etzel, third Mother Superior of the Sisters of St. Francis, Pittsburgh, Pennsylvania. Milwaukee, Bruce Press [1956] 133p. illus. 23cm. (Catholic life publications) [BX4705.E74A7] 56-14691
1. Etzel, Baptista. I. Title.

Eudes, Jean, Saint, 1601-1680.

HERAMBOURG, Peter. 922.244
Saint John Eudes: a spiritual portrait. Translated by Ruth Hauser, edited and annotated by Wilfrid E. Myatt. Introd. by Edward A. Ryan. Westminster, Md., Newman Press, [c.]1960. xviii 318p. Bibl.: p.312 illus. 23cm. 60-14810 4.00
1. Eudes, Jean, Saint, 1601-1680. I. Title.

HERAMBOURG, Peter, 1661-1720. 922.244
Saint John Eudes: a spiritual portrait. Translated by Ruth Hauser, edited and annotated by Wilfrid E. Myatt., Introd. by Edward A. Ryan. Westminster, Md., Newman Press, 1960. 318p. illus. 23cm. Includes bibliography. [BX4700.E78H43] 60-14810
1. Eudes, Jean, Saint, 1601-1680. I. Title.

Eudocia, Aelia Augusta, consort of Theodorius II, Emperor of the East, d. 460.

†TSATSOU, Ioanna. 949.5'01'0924 B
Empress Athenais-Eudocia, a fifth century Byzantine humanist : women of Byzantium / by Jeanne Tsatsos ; translated by Jean Demos. Brookline, Mass. : Holy Cross Orthodox Press, c1977. 141 p. ; 22 cm. Translation of Athenais. Includes index. [DF562.6.T713] 77-77659 ISBN 0-916586-08-1 pbk. : 3.95
1. Eudocia, Aelia Augusta, consort of Theodorius II, Emperor of the East, d. 460. 2. Byzantine empresses—Biography. 3. Byzantine Empire—History—Theodorius II, 408-450. I. Title.
Publisher's address : 50 Goddard Ave., Brookline, MA 02146

Eugene, Prince of Savoie-Carignan, 1663-1736.

HENDERSON, Nicholas 923.5436
Prince Eugen of Savoy. New York, Praeger [1965, c.1964] xi, 324p. illus., facsims., geneal. table, maps, plans, ports. 22cm. Bibl. [D274.E8H4] 65-12157 6.95
1. Eugene, Prince of Savoie-Carrignan, 1663-1736. I. Title.

MCKAY, Derek. 943.6'03'0924 B
Prince Eugene of Savoy / Derek McKay. London : Thames and Hudson, c1977. 288 p., [8] leaves of plates : ill. ; 23 cm. (Men in office) Includes index. Bibliography: p. 263-269. [D274.E8M15] 78-306148 ISBN 0-500-87007-1 : 16.95
1. Eugene, Prince of Savoie-Carignan, 1663-1736. 2. Europe—History—1648-1789. 3. Marshals—Austria—Biography. 4. Statesmen—Austria—Biography. 5. Austria—History—Leopold I, 1657-1705. 6. Austria—History—Joseph I, 1705-1711. 7. Austria—History—Charles VI, 1711-1740. I. Title.
Distributed by W. W. Norton, New York BIP

Eugenie, consort of Napoleon III, 1826-1920.

KURTZ, Harold. 923.144
The Empress Eugenie, 1826-1920. Boston, Houghton Mifflin, 1964. xiii, 407 p. illus., ports. 23 cm. Bibliography: p. 387-392. [DC280.2.K85 1964a] 64-55895
1. Eugenie, consort of Napoleon III, 1826-1920. I. Title.

Eugenius IV, Pope, 1383-1447.

GILL, Joseph, 1901- 922.21
Eugenius iv, Pope of Christian union. Westminister, Md., Newman [c]1961. xi.

226p. front., maps. (Popes through hist., v.1) Bibl. 61-16572 3.75
1. Eugenius IV, Pope, 1383-1447. I. Title.

Eulenburg-Hertefeld, Philipp, Furst zu, 1847-1921.

HALLER, Johannes, 1865-1947. 943.08'4'0924 B
Philip Eulenburg; the Kaiser's friend. Translated from the German by Ethel Colburn Mayne. Freeport, N.Y., Books for Libraries Press [1971] 2 . illus., ports. 23 cm. Reprint of the 1930 ed. Translation of Aus dem Leben des Fursten Philipp zu Eulenburg-Hertefeld. Includes bibliographical references. [DD219.E8H32 1971] 72-148883 ISBN 0-8369-5651-6
1. Eulenburg-Hertefeld, Philipp, Furst zu, 1847-1921. 2. Germany—Politics and government—1871-1918. 3. Germany—Politics and government—1918-1933.

Euripides.

MELCHINGER, Siegfried. 882'.01
Euripides. Translated by Samuel R. Rosenbaum. New York, Ungar [1973] vi, 218 p. illus. 21 cm. (World dramatists) Bibliography: p. 209-210. [PA3978.M413] 72-79933 7.50
1. Euripides. BIP

MURRAY, Gilbert, 1866-1957. 882'.01 B
Euripides and his age / Gilbert Murray ; with a new introd. by H. D. F. Kitto. Westport, Conn. : Greenwood Press, 1979. p. cm. Reprint of the 1965 ed. published by Oxford University Press, London. Includes index. Bibliography: p. [PA3978.M8 1979] 79-4184 ISBN 0-313-20989-8 lib. bdg. : 15.50
1. Euripides. 2. Dramatists, Greek—Biography. I. Title. BIP

Europe—Biography.

BIRKHEAD, Alice. 920.04
Heroes of modern Europe. Freeport, N.Y., Books for Libraries Press [1966] 239 p. illus., ports. 21 cm. (Essay index reprint series) Reprint of the 1913 ed. Contents.Contents.—The two swords.—Dante, the divine poet.—Lorenzo the Magnificent.—The prior of San Marco.—Martin Luther, reformer of the church.—Charles V, holy Roman emperor.—The beggars of the sea.—William the Silent, father of his country.—Henry of Navarre.—Under the red robe.—The grand monarch.—Peter the Great.—The royal robber.—Spirits of the age.—The man from Corsica.—"God and the people."—"For Italy and Victor Emmanuel!"—The third Napoleon.—The reformer of the East.—The hero in history. [D106.B55 1966] 67-22073
1. Europe Biography. 2. Europe—History. I. Title. BIP

DARK, Sidney, 1874-1947. 920.04
Twelve bad men With ports. by Mabel Pugh. Freeport, N.Y., Books for Libraries Press [1968] 351 p. ports. 22 cm. (Essay index reprint series) Reprint of the 1929 ed. [D108.D3 1968] 68-54343
1. Europe—Biography. I. Title. BIP

HUDDLESTON, Sisley, 1883-1952. 920.02
Those Europeans; studies of foreign faces. Freeport, N.Y., Books for Libraries Press [1969] iv, 297 p. 23 cm. (Essay index reprint series) Reprint of the 1924 ed. [D412.6.H8 1969] 79-90647
1. Europe—Biography. 2. Statesmen. I. Title.

MACCALL, William, 1812-1888. 920'.04
Foreign biographies. Freeport, N.Y., Books for Libraries Press [1972] 2 v. 22 cm. (Essay index reprint series) Reprint of the 1873 ed. Contents.Contents.—v. 1. Joseph de Maistre. Samuel Vincent. Vincent de Paul. Paul Louis Courier. Vauvenargues. The Abbe de Saint-Pierre. St. Francis of Assisi. Ulrich von Hutten. Benedict Spinoza.—v. 2. Godfrey William Leibnitz. Louis Claude de Saint-Martin. Giordano Bruno. Vasco Nunez de Balboa. Alexander of Russia. Peter d'Aubusson. Martin Behaim. Cardinal Alberoni. President Boyer. Francis d'Almeida. George Cadoudal. Lazarus Carnot. [CT105.M17 1972] 72-5617 ISBN 0-8369-2999-3
1. Europe—Biography. I. Title. II. Series. BIP

MARCU, Valeriu, 1899-1943? 940.51'0922
Men and forces of our time. Translated by Eden and Cedar Paul. Freeport, N.Y., Books for Libraries Press [1968] 244 p. 22 cm. (Essay index reprint series) Reprint of the 1931 ed. Translation of Manner und Machte der Gegenwart. Contents.Contents.—Biography and biographers.—Georges Clemenceau between action and Nirvana.—Dogma and dialectic in Lenin.—Marshal Foch's ideas and the republic of civilians.—Kemal Pasha; or, From national farce to national revolution.—One head is more than three hundred vioces, or, Benedetto Croce in the Senate.—The "moderns" and their adversary, G. K. Chesterton.—Panait Istrati; or, Romance about Byzantium.—Hans Delbruck; or, The historian conquers the specialist.—Advertisement; or, Farewell to Europe.—Mythology of dictatorship (Georges Sorel) [D412.M313 1968] 68-29231
1. Europe—Biography. I. Title. BIP

TAYLOR, William Cooke, 1800-1849, ed. 940.2'3'0922 B
Romantic biography of the age of Elizabeth; or, Sketches of life from the bye-ways of history. By the Benedictine Brethren of Glendalough. Edited by William Cooke Taylor. Freeport, N.Y., Books for Libraries Press [1973] p. (Essay index reprint series) Reprint of the 1842 ed. Contents.Contents.—v. 1. Introduction. Margaret of Valois, Queen of Henry IV. Robert Dudley, Earl of Leicester. Castelnau, Ambassador from France. La Mothe Fenelon. La Mothe Fenelon and Castelnau. Thomas Howard, 4th duke of Norfolk. Hugh, Earl of Tyrone, and notices of Walter, 1st Earl of Essex. Dr. Dee.—v. 2. Calvin and the church of Geneva. William Whittingam and the Puritans. Archbishop Whitgift and Dr. Cartwright. John Darrel, the exorcist. Loyola and the order of the Jesuits. Robert Parsons, Edmund Campian, and the Jesuits in England. Pope Sixtus V. Charles de Valois, Duc d'Angouleme. Henry de la Tour d'Auvergne, Viscount Turenne and Duke de Bouillon. [D226.T3 1973] 72-14121 ISBN 0-518-10027-8 O
1. Europe—Biography. 2. Europe—History—1517-1648. I. Title. BIP

Europe—Biography—Dictionaries.

PEDLEY, Avril J. M., comp. 920.04
They looked like this (Europe); an assembly of authentic word-portraits of men and women in European history, art, and literature over 1900 years, compiled by Avril Pedley and Grant Uden. New York, Barnes & Noble [1967] xiii, 265 p. 23 cm. Includes bibliographical references. [D226.P4] 68-463
1. Europe—Biography—Dictionaries. I. Uden, Grant, joint comp. II. Title.

Europe—Description and travel—1800-1918.

BURR, Aaron, 1756-1836. 914.2'04'73
Private journal [of Aaron Burr, during his residence of four years in Europe; with selections from his correspondence. Edited by Matthew L. Davis.] Upper Saddle River, N.J., Literature House [1970, c1838] 2 v. 23 cm. Covers period 1808-1812. [E302.6.B9A25 1970] 72-104425 ISBN 0-8398-0182-3
1. Europe—Description and travel—1800-1918. I. Title.

CATHER, Willa Sibert, 1873-1947. 928.1
Willa Cather in Europe; her own story of the first journey. With an introd. and incidental notes by George N. Kates. [1st ed.] New York, Knopf, 1956. xii, 178p 22cm. [PS3505.A87Z53] 56-10906
1. Europe—Descr. & trav.—1800-1918. I. Title.

ELSON, Louis Charles, 1848-1920. 914'.03'287
European reminiscences, musical and otherwise. Being the recollections of the vacation tours of a musician in various countries. New York, Da Capo Press, 1972 [c1896] viii, 301 p. illus. 22 cm. (Da Capo Press music reprint series) [ML423.E492 1972] 72-125046 ISBN 0-306-70011-5 12.50
1. Europe—Description and travel—1800-1918. 2. Musicians—Correspondence, reminiscences, etc. I. Title.

IRVING, Washington, 1783-1859. 914
The journals of Washington Irving (hitherto unpublished) Edited by William P. Trent and George S. Hellman. New York, Haskell House, 1970. 3 v. illus., facsims., ports. 23 cm. Reprint of the 1919 ed. [PS2081.A2 1970] 71-92970
1. Europe—Description and travel—1800-1918. 2. U.S.—Description and travel—1783-1848. I. Trent, William Peterfield, 1862-1939, ed. II. Hellman, George Sydney, 1878- joint ed. III. Bibliophile society, Boston.

MENDELSSOHN-BARTHOLDY, Felix, 1809-1847 780'.924
Letters from Italy and Switzerland. Translated from the German by Lady Wallace. With a biographical notice by Julie de Marguerittes. 3d ed. Freeport, N.Y., Books for Libraries Press [1970] xv, 360 p. illus., music. 23 cm. Translation of Reisebriefe aus den Jahren 1830 bis 1832. Reprint of the 1865 ed. [ML410.M5A316 1970] 70-114866
1. Europe—Description and travel—1800-1918. BIP

TOPLIFF, Samuel, 1789-1864. 914'.04'282
Topliff's travels; letters from abroad in the years 1828 and 1829. Edited with a memoir and notes by Ethel Stanwood Bolton. New York, B. Blom, 1971. 245 p. illus. 21 cm. Fold. map inserted. Reprint of the 1906 ed. "From the original manuscript owned by the Boston Athenaeum." [D919.T67 1971] 78-173189
1. Europe—Description and travel—1800-1918. I. Title. BIP

Europe, Eastern—Biography.

PARTINGTON, Paul G. 920'.047
Who's who on the postage stamps of Eastern Europe / by Paul G. Partington. Metuchen, N. J. : Scarecrow Press, 1980 p. cm. Includes index. [CT759.P37] 79-22183 ISBN 0-8108-1257-6 : 29.50
1. Europe, Eastern—Biography. 2. Biography. 3. Postage-stamps—Europe, Eastern. I. Title. BIP

Europe—History.

HILT, Douglas. 940.2'7'0922
Ten against Napoleon / Douglas Hilt. Chicago : Nelson-Hall, [1975] xxix, 209 p. : ports. ; 23 cm. Includes index.

O'CONNOR, John T. 943'.044'0924 B
Negotiator out of season : the career of Wilhelm Egon von Furstenberg, 1629-1704 / by John T. O'Connor. Athens : University of Georgia Press, c1978. p. cm. Includes index. Bibliography: p. [DD177.F8O26] 77-23872 ISBN 0-8203-0436-0 : 20.00
1. Furstenberg, Wilhelm Egon, Graf von, Cardinal, 1629-1704. 2. Statesmen—Holy Roman Empire—Biography. 3. Holy Roman Empire—History—Leopold I, 1658-1705. I. Title. BIP

Europe—Kings and rulers—Biography.

CURLEY, Walter J. P. 929.7'094
Monarchs-in-waiting [by] Walter J. P. Curley, Jr. New York, Dodd, Mead [1973] xv, 238 p. illus. 24 cm. Bibliography: p. 229-230. [D412.7.C87] 73-11549 ISBN 0-396-06840-5 7.95
1. Europe—Kings and rulers. 2. Royal houses. I. Title.

FATTORUSSO, Joseph 923.14
Kings and queens of England and of France; a genealogical chronological history, with the names of contemporary popes and emperors from Charles the Great (Charlemagne) A.D. 800 to Napoleon the Great A.D. 1800. Notes by Rita Fattorusso [Rev. ed.] Florence, Medici Hist. Atlases [dist. New York, Heinman, 1963] 340p. illus. (pt. col.) ports. maps, geneal. tables. 23cm. (Medici hist. atlas, 1) 12.50
1. Europe—Kings and rulers. I. Title. II. Series.

MOHAMMED and Charlemagne. v. 12 [Translated by Bernard Miall] New York, Barnes & Noble [1958] 293p. 19cm. Bibliographical footnotes.
1. Europe—Hist.—476-1492. 2. Gaul—Hist. 3. Mohammedan countries—Hist. I. Pirenne, Henri, 1862-1935.

Europe—Politics—1918-1945.

FISCHER, Louis. 1896- 940.50924
Men and politics: Europe between the two World Wars. New York, Harper [1966, c.1941.1946] ix, 660p. 21cm. (Harper colophon bks., CN 96 Q) [D413.F5A3 1966] 66-21165 2.95 pap.,
1. Europe—Politics—1918-1945. 2. Journalists—Correspondence, reminiscences, etc. I. Title.

FENYVESI, Charles, 1937- 940'.0992 B
Splendor in exile : the ex-majesties of Europe / Charles Fenyvesi. Washington : New Republic Books, 1979. 281 p., [8] leaves of plates : ill. ; 24 cm. Bibliography: p. 281. [D107.F42] 79-20707 ISBN 0-915220-55-5 : 12.50
1. Europe—Kings and rulers—Biography. I. Title. BIP

Europe—Politics and government—1789-1815.

CZARTORYSKI, Adam Jerzy, ksiaze, 1770-1861. 947'.07'0924 B
Memoirs of Prince Adam Czartoryski. Edited by Adam Gielgud. New York, Arno Press, 1971. viii, 336, viii, 367 p. ports. 24 cm. (The Eastern Europe collection) Reprint of the 1888 ed. Translation of Memoires, first published in 1865 under title: Alexandre I et le prince Czartoryski. [DK435.5.C83A313 1971] 78-135808 ISBN 0-405-02750-8
1. Europe—Politics and government—1789-1815. 2. Russia—Foreign relations—1801-1825. 3. Polish question. I. Alexander I, Emperor of Russia, 1777-1825.

METTERNICH-WINNEBURG, Clemens Lothar Wenzel, Furst von, 1773-1859. 940.2'7'0924 B
Memoirs of Prince Metternich, 1773-1815. Edited by Prince Richard Metternich. The papers classified and arr. by M. A. de Klinkowstrom. Translated by Mrs. Alexander Napier. New York, H. Fertig, 1970. 5 v. facsims., port. 24 cm. Reprint of the 1880 ed. Translation of Aus Metternich's nach gelassenen papieren. Volume 5, 1830 1835 translated by Gerald W. Smith. [DB80.8.M52 1970] 68-9611
1. Europe—Politics and government—1789-1815. 2. Europe—Politics and government—1815-1848. 3. Austria—History—1789-1900. I. Metternich-Winneburg, Richard Clemens Lothar, Furst von, 1829-1895, ed. II. Klinkowstrom, Alfons, Freiherr von, 1818-1891, joint ed. III. Napier, Robina, trans. IV. Smith, Gerard W., trans. BIP

Europe—Politics and government—1918-1945.

FISCHER, Louis, 1896-1970. 940.5'0924
Men and politics: an autobiography. With an appendix of lectures from Eleanor Roosevelt added to the reprint ed. Westport, Conn., Greenwood Press [1970, c1946] ix, 672 p. 24 cm. [D413.F5A3 1970] 73-111498 ISBN 0-8371-4641-0
1. Europe—Politics and government—1918-1945. 2. Journalists—Correspondence, reminiscences, etc. I. Title. BIP

Europe—Politics—1789-1900.

BEUST, Friedrich 327'.2'0924 B
Ferdinand, Graf von, 1809-1886.
Memoirs of Friedrich Ferdinand, Count von Beust, written by himself. With an introd. containing personal reminiscences of Count Beust's career as prime minister of Austria and Austrian ambassador in London by Baron Henry de Worms. 2d ed. London, Remington, 1887. St. Clair Shores, Mich., Scholarly Press, 1972. p. Translation of Aus drei Viertel-Jahrhunderten. [D400.B5A32 1972] 70-144878 ISBN 0-403-00812-3
1. Europe—Politics—1789-1900. 2. Germany—Foreign relations—Austria. 3. Austria—Foreign relations—Germany. BIP

European federation.

COUDENHOVE-KALERGI, Richard 923.2
Nichlaus, Graf von, 1894-
An idea conquers the world, With a pref. by Sir Winston S. Churchill. New York, Roy Publishers [1954] 310p. illus. 22cm. Autobiographical. [D1060] 54-7134
1. European federation. 2. Europe—Politics. I. Title.

European literature—20th century—Bio-bibliography.

WHO was who among 809'.043 B
English and European authors, 1931-1949 : based on entries which frist appeared in The Author's and writer's who's who & reference guide originally compiled by Edward Martell and L. G. Pine and in Who's who among living authors of older nations, originally compiled by Alberta Lawrence. Detroit : Gale Research Co., c1978. 3 v. (1564 p.) ; 24 cm. (Gale composite biographical dictionary series ; no. 2) [PN451.W5] 77-280 96.00 per set
1. European literature—20th century—Bio-bibliography. I. The Author's & writer's who's who. II. Who's who among living authors of older nations. III. Title. IV. Series. V. An Omnigraphics book

European War, 1914-1918—Aerial operations.

JACKSON, Robert, 940.4'4'0922 B
1941-
Fighter pilots of World War I / Robert Jackson. New York : St. Martin's Press, [1977] p. cm. [D600.J33] 77-76641 ISBN 0-312-28874-3 : 8.95
1. European War, 1914-1918—Aerial operations. 2. Air pilots—Biography. I. Title. BIP

European War, 1914-1918—Biography.

DE WEERD, Harvey Arthur, 940.4 B
1902-
Great soldiers of the two World Wars. Freeport, N.Y., Books for Libraries Press [1969, c1941] 378 p. illus., maps, ports. 23 cm. (Essay index reprint series) Contents.Contents.—Schieffen.—Hindenburg.—Hoffmann.—Kitchener.—Lawrence.—Pershing.—Petain.—Gamelin.—Churchill.—Wavell.—Seeckt.—Hitler. [D507.D4 1969] 69-18926 ISBN 0-8369-1032-X
1. European War, 1914-1918—Biography. 2. World War, 1939-1945—Biography. 3. Military biography. 4. Generals. I. Title. BIP

JOHNSTON, Charles 940.4'1'0922
Haven Ladd, 1877-1943.
Famous generals of the Great War who led the United States and her Allies to a great victory. Freeport, N.Y., Books for Libraries Press [1970, c1919] xii, 310 p. ports. 23 cm. (Essay index reprint series) Contents.Contents.—The devil dogs.—"Papa" Joffre.—Sir John French.—King Albert of Belgium.—Ferdinand Foch.—Sir Douglas Haig.—John J. Pershing.—Henri P. Petain.—Armando Diaz.—Sir Edmund Allenby.—Sir Stanley Maude.—Franchet D'Esperey.—De Castelnau.—Jan Smuts.—Sir Julian H. Byng. [D507.J6 1970] 74-93349
1. European War, 1914-1918—Biography. 2. Generals. I. Title.

LIDDELL HART, Basil 940.4'1'0922
Henry 1895-
Reputations, ten years after, by B. H. Liddell Hart. Freeport, N.Y., Books for Libraries Press [1968] viii, 316 p. illus., maps, port. 23 cm. (Essay index reprint series) Reprint of the 1928 ed. Contents.Contents.—Marshal Joffre.—Erich von Falkenhayn.—Marshal Gallieni.—Haig of Bemersyde.—Ferdinand Foch.—Erich Ludendorff.—Petain.—Allenby of Megiddo.—Hunter Liggett.—"Black Jack" Pershing. [D507.L5 1968] 68-8478
1. European War, 1914-1918—Biography. 2. Generals. 3. Military biography. I. Title. BIP

MILITARY Order of the 940.4'6
World Wars. District of Columbia Chapter.
Historical record and fiftieth year who's who; golden anniversary commemoration, 1919-1969. [Washington? 1969] xxix, 186 p. illus., facsims., ports. 23 cm. [D570.A15M5427] 77-110345
1. European War, 1914-1918—Biography. 2. World War, 1914-1918—Biography. 3. Washington, D.C.,—Biography. I. Title.

SIMONDS, Frank 940.4'1'0922
Herbert, 1878-1936.
They won the war. Freeport, N.Y., Books for Libraries Press [1968, c1931] xi, 109 p. 23 cm. (Essay index reprint series) Contents.Contents.—Pershing; he made the A.E.F.—Foch, marshal of victory.—Petain, soldier of Verdum.—Haig, "the perfect ally."—Joffre, the miracle of the Marne.—Ludendorff; he almost won. [D507.S5 1968] 68-58813
1. European War, 1914-1918—Biography. 2. Generals. I. Title. BIP

European War, 1914-1918—Biography—Juvenile literature.

REEDER, Russell 940.3'092'2 B
Potter.
Bold leaders of World War I, by Red Reeder. [1st ed.] Boston, Little, Brown [1974] xiii, 252 p. illus. 21 cm. Contents.Contents.—The two world wars: the differences.—Erich Ludendorff, general at the gates.—Papa Joffre, and the German claw.—Edith Cavell, Red Cross nurse.—Fritz Kreisler, violinist at war.—Winston Churchill, the English bulldog.—Philippe Petain: "They shall not pass."—Bill Breckenridge, lady from hell.—Carl Mannerheim, the knight.—Manfred von Richthofen, the Red Baron.—Laurence Stallings, marine who never quit fighting.—George C. Marshall: the beginnings of a great American.—Ralph Eaton, American first-aid man.—Bibliography (p. 243-246) [D507.R37] 920. 74-13492 ISBN 0-316-73671-6 6.50
1. European War, 1914-1918—Biography—Juvenile literature. I. Title.
Contents omitted.

European War, 1914-1918—Campaigns—France.

SWINTON, Ernest Dunlop, 940.4'2
Sir, 1868-1951.
Eyewitness; being personal reminiscences of certain phases of the Great War, including the genesis of the tank. New York, Arno Press, 1972. xiii, 332 p. illus. 23 cm. (World affairs: national and international viewpoints) Reprint of the 1933 ed. [D544.S88 1972] 72-4304 ISBN 0-405-04594-8 17.00
1. European War, 1914-1918—Campaigns—France. 2. European War, 1914-1918—Personal narratives, English. 3. Tank warfare. I. Title. II. Series.

European War, 1914-1918—Conscientious objectors—U.S.

GRAY, Harold 355.2'24'0924 B
Studley, 1894-
Character "Bad"; the story of a conscientious objector, as told in the letters of Harold Studley Gray. Edited by Kenneth Irving Brown. With a new introd. for the Garland ed. by Charles Chatfield. New York, Garland Pub., 1971 [c1934] 11, ix, 258 p. illus. 22 cm. (The Garland library of war and peace) [UB342.U5G7 1971] 72-147634 ISBN 0-8240-0410-8
1. European War, 1914-1918—Conscientious objectors—U.S. 2. European War, 1914-1918—War work—Y.M.C.A. I. Brown, Kenneth Irving, 1896- ed. II. Title. III. Series.

European War, 1914-1918—Czechoslovak Republic.

BENES, Edvard, 943.7'03'0924
Pres. Czechoslovak Republic, 1884-1948.
My war memoirs, by Eduard Benes. Translated from the Czech by Paul Selver. Westport, Conn., Greenwood Press [1971] 512 p. port. 23 cm. Reprint of the 1928 ed. [DB217.B3A4 1971] 70-114467 ISBN 0-8371-4763-8
1. European War, 1914-1918—Czechoslovak Republic. BIP

European War, 1914-1918—Germany.

HANSSEN, Hans 940.3'43'0924 B
Peter, 1852-1936.
Diary of a dying empire. Translated by Oscar Osburn Winther. Edited by Ralph H. Lutz, Mary Schofield, and O. O. Winther. Introd. by Ralph H. Lutz. Port Washington, N.Y., Kennikat Press [1973, c1955] liii, 409 p. 22 cm. Translation of Fra krigstiden. Original ed. issued as no. 14 of Social science series (Bloomington, Ind.) [D531.H3213 1973] 72-85290 ISBN 0-8046-1726-0 17.50
1. European War, 1914-1918—Germany. I. Title. II. Series: Social science series (Bloomington, Ind.), no. 14. BIP

European War, 1914-1918—Greece.

NICHOLAS, Prince 949.5'06'0924 B
of Greece, 1872-1938.
Political memoirs, 1914-1917; pages from my diary. Freeport, N.Y., Books for Libraries Press [1972] 319 p. illus. 22 cm. Reprint of the 1927 ed. Bibliography: p. [DF832.A3A6 1972] 72-1274 ISBN 0-8369-6833-6 18.50
1. European War, 1914-1918—Greece. 2. Greece, Modern—History—Constantine I, 1913-1917. 3. Greece, Modern—Politics and government—1913-1917. 4. Greece, Modern—Foreign relations. I. Title.

European War, 1914-1918—Italy.

SPERANZA, Gino 940.4'81*73
Charles, 1872-1927.
The diary of Gino Speranza, Italy, 1915-1919. Edited by Florence Colgate Speranza Diary of Gino Speranza Italy nineteen fifteen-nineteen nineteen New York, AMS Press, 1966 [c1941] 2 v. illus. 23 cm. Contents.Contents.—v. 1. 1915-1916.—v. 2. 1917-1919. Bibliography: v. 1, p. xxv-xxvii. [D640.S72516 1966] 71-176000
1. European War, 1914-1918—Italy. 2. European War, 1914-1918—Personal narratives, American.

European War, 1914-1918—Negroes.

HUNTON, Addie D. 940.4'778'73
(Waite)
Two Colored women with the American Expeditionary Forces, by Addie W. Hunton and Kathryn M. Johnson. New York, AMS Press [1971] 256 p. illus. 19 cm. Cover title. Reprint of the 1920 ed. [D639.N4H8 1971] 75-155624 ISBN 0-404-00174-2
1. European War, 1914-1918—Negroes. 2. European War, 1914-1918—War work—Y.M.C.A. 3. European War, 1914-1918—Personal narratives, American. I. Johnson, Kathryn Magnolia, 1878- joint author. II. Title. BIP

European War, 1914-1918—Personal narratives, American.

GREENE, Warwick, 1879- 901.9 B
1929.
Letters of Warwick Greene, 1915-1928. Edited by Richard W. Hale. Freeport, N.Y., Books for Libraries Press [1971] xxiv, 309 p. illus. 23 cm. Reprint of the 1931 ed. [D570.9.G7 1971] 77-179522 ISBN 0-8369-6651-1
1. European War, 1914-1918—Personal narratives, American. 2. Baltic States—Description and travel. I. Title. BIP

LAHM, Frank Purdy, 940.4'4'0924 B
1877-1963.
The World War I diary of Col. Frank P. Lahm Air Service, A.E.F. Edited by Albert F. Simpson. Maxwell AFB, Ala., Historical Research Division, Aerospace Studies Institute, 1970. xvi, 271 p. illus. 27 cm. [D570.9.L25] 74-614829
1. European War, 1914-1918—Personal narratives, American. 2. European War, 1914-1918—Biography. I. Simpson, Albert Franklin, 1904- ed. II. Title.

European War, 1914-1918—Personal narratives, English.

A Place called 940.4'81'41 B
Armageddon : letters from the Great War / edited with an introduction by Michael Moynihan. Newton Abbot [Eng.] ; North Pomfret, Vt. : David & Charles, 1975. 191 p. : ill. ; 23 cm. [D640.A2P47] 75-318068 ISBN 0-7153-6959-8 : 9.95
1. European War, 1914-1918—Personal narratives, English. I. Moynihan, Michael.

European War, 1914-1918—Secret service.

COOK, Graeme. 940.4'86
Missions most secret / Graeme Cook. Blandford [Eng.] : Harwood-Smart, 1976. xi, 185, [1] p. ; 23 cm. Bibliography: p. [186] [D639.S7C58 1976] 77-356897 ISBN 0-904507-17-3 : £3.95
1. European War, 1914-1918—Secret service. 2. World War, 1939-1945—Secret service. 3. Spies—Biography. I. Title.

Eusebius Pamphili, Bp. of Caesarea.

WALLACE-HADRILL, David 922.133
Sutherland
Eusebius of Caesarea. Westminster, Md., Canterbury Pr., 1961 [c.1960] 224p. Bibl. 61-16285 7.50
1. Eusebius Pamphili, Bp. of Caesarea. I. Title.

Evangelical United Brethren Church—Clergy.

MILHOUSE, Paul William, 289.9 B
1910-
Nineteen bishops of the Evangelical United Brethren Church / by Paul W. Milhouse. [s.l.] : Milhouse, [1974] 118 p. : ports. ; 24 cm. Includes bibliographical references. [BX7556.Z8A28] 74-195206
1. Evangelical United Brethren Church—Clergy. 2. Evangelical United Brethren Church—Biography. I. Title.

Evangelistic work.

SMITH, Amanda 269'.2'0924 B
(Berry) 1837-1915.
An autobiography: the story of the Lord's dealings with Mrs. Amanda Smith, the colored evangelist; containing an account of her life work of faith, and her travels in America, England, Ireland, Scotland, India, and Africa, as an independent missionary. With an introd. by Bishop Thoburn, of India. Chicago, Afro-Am Press, 1969. 506 p. illus., ports. 22 cm. Reprint of the 1893 ed. Running title: Autobiography of Amanda Smith. [BV3785.S56A3 1969] 71-99407
1. Evangelistic work. I. Title: Autobiography of Amanda Smith.

Evangelists.

CLARKE, Charles. 269'.2'0922 B
Pioneers of revival. London and New Jersey (Central Hall, Durnsford Rd, SW19 8ED), Fountain Trust-Watchung Books, 1971. 71 p. 18 cm. [BV3780.C57] 72-190434 ISBN 0-901398-21-7 £0.35
1. Evangelists. 2. Revivals. I. Title.

Evangelists—Correspondence, reminiscences, etc.

GEESON, W G 1887- 922
Covenant by sacrifice; a story of true faith.

[1st ed.] NewYork, Exposition Press [c1955] 83p. 21cm. [BV3785.G42A3] 55-12464
1. Evangelists —Correspondence, reminiscences, etc. I. Title.

HARRINGTON, Bob, 1927- 269'.2
God's super salesman. Nashville, Broadman Press [1970] 176 p. illus., ports. 21 cm. [BV3785.H346A3] 73-117310 4.95
1. Evangelists—Correspondence, reminiscences, etc. 2. Evangelistic work. I. Title. BIP

HILL, Stanley. 922
A bullet stopped me, by Stanley Hill, as told to Dorothy C. Haskin. [Pasadena? 1954?] 96p. illus. 21cm. [BV3785.H5A3] 56-36208
1. Evangelists—Correspondence, reminiscences, etc. I. Haskin, Dorothy (Clark) 1905- II. Title.

HOUSMAN, Marzelius. 922
Under the Red star, by Marzelius Housman (Mark Houseman) [Reprinted, unabridged ed.] Williamsport, Pa. [1955] 144p. ills. 20cm. Autobiography. [BV3785.H59A3] 56-39332
1. Evangelists—Correspondence, reminiscences, etc. I. Title.

IRONSIDE, Henry Allan, 1876- 922
1951.
Random reminiscences from fifty years of ministry. Illustrated by Charles E. Pont. New York, Loizeaux Bros, 1939. 176p. illus. 20cm. [BV3785.I68A3] 56-55995
1. Evangelists—Correspondence, reminiscences, etc. I. Title.

KEYES, Charles A 1918- 922
The parson of the bills. [1st ed.] New York, Vantage Press [1956] 103p. illus. 21cm. An account of the author's missionary work in North Carolina, Kentucky, and Tennessee. [BV3785.K5A3] 56-8083
1 Evangelists—Correspondence, reminiscences, etc. 2. Missions—Southern States. I. Title.

KEYES, Charles A 1918- 922
The parson of the hills 1st ed. New York, Vantage Press [1956] 103p. illus. 21cm. An account of the author's missionary work in North Carolina, Kentucky, and Tennessee. [BV3785.K5A3] 56-8083
1. Evangelists—Correspondence, reminiscences, etc. 2. Missions—Southern States. I. Title.

ROBERTS, Oral. 922
My story. Tulsa, Okla., Summit Book Co., 1961. 213p. illus. 22cm. [BV3785.R58A28] 61-3683
1. Evangelists— Correspondence, reminiscences, etc. I. Title.

ROBERTS, Oral. 269'.2'0924
My twenty years of a miracle ministry. [Tulsa? Okla., 1967] 96 p. illus. (part col.), ports. (part col.) 28 cm. [BV3785.R58A29] 72-9283
1. Evangelists—Correspondence, reminiscences, etc. I. Title.

ROBERTS, Oral. 922
Oral Roberts' life story, as told by himself. Illus. by Eloise Gray. Tulsa, Okla, [1952] 160p. illus. 20cm. [BV3785.R58A3] 53-18797
1. Evangelists— Correspondence, reminiscences, etc. I. Title.

RUFF, Ethel, 1910- 922.673
When saints go marching; the memoirs of a Baptist evangelist. [1st ed.] New York, Exposition Press [1957] 260p. 21cm. [BV3785.R8A3] 58-74
1. Evangelists—Correspondence, reminiscences, etc. I. Title.

Evangelists—United States.

MORRIS, James, 269'.2'0922 B
1926-
The preachers. Illus. by Tom Huffman. New York, St. Martin's Press [1973] x, 418 p. illus. 25 cm. Includes bibliographical references. [BV3780.M67] 72-93927 8.95
1. Evangelists—United States. 2. Clergy—United States. I. Title.

WRIGHT, Melton. 922
Giant for God; a biography of the life of William Ashley ("Billy") Sunday. Boyce, Va., Distributed by Carr Pub. Co. [c1951] 168 p. illus. 24 cm. [BV3785.S8W7] 52-378
I. U. Sunday, William Ashley, 1862-1935. II. Title.

Evangelists—United States—Biography.

EVANS, William 269'.2'0922 B
Glyn.
Profiles of revival leaders / W. Glyn Evans. Nashville : Broadman Press, c1976. 128 p. ; 21 cm. Includes bibliographical references. [BV3780.E82] 76-4368 ISBN 0-8054-8604-6 : 2.50
1. Evangelists—United States—Biography. 2. Revivals—United States. I. Title.
Contents omitted BIP

Evans, Arthur John, Sir, 1851-1941.

EVANS, Joan, 913'.031'0924 B
1893-
Time and chance; the story of Arthur Evans and his forebears. Westport, Conn., Greenwood Press [1974] p. cm. Reprint of the 1943 ed. published by Longmans, Green, London, New York. [DF212.E82E8 1974] 70-114519 ISBN 0-8371-4737-9 19.75 (lib. bdg.)
1. Evans, Arthur John, Sir, 1851-1941. 2. Evans family. I. Title.

Evans, C. Burt.

EVANS, C. Burt. 917.86
Western pioneer, by C. B. Evans. [Berne? Ind.] [1965] 235 p. illus., facsims., ports. 21 cm. Autobiographical. [CT275.E82A3] 65-2216
I. Title.

Evans, Charles, 1850-1935.

HOLLEY, Edward G. 920.1
Charles Evans: American bibliographer. Urbana, Univ. of Ill. Pr. [c.]1963. xii, 343p. 24cm. (Ill. contributions to librarianship,no. 7) Bibl. 63-10315 7.50
1. Evans, Charles, 1850-1935. I. Title. II. Series.

Evans, Dick, 1905-

SKIDMORE, Ian. 363.1'23'81
Lifeboat VC : the story of coxswain Dick Evans and his many rescues / Ian Skidmore. Newton Abbot [Eng.] ; North Pomfret, Vt. : David & Charles, 1979. 140 p. : ill. ; 23 cm. [VK1430.E92S54] 79-322191 ISBN 0-7153-7691-8 : 14.50
1. Evans, Dick, 1905- 2. Lifeboat service—Wales—Moelfre—History. 3. Lifeboat crew members —Wales—Moelfre —Biography. 4. Moelfre, Wales—Biography.

Evans, Edith, Dame, 1888-1976.

FORBES, Bryan, 792'.028'0924 B
1926-
Dame Edith Evans, Ned's girl / Bryan Forbes. 1st American ed. Boston : Little, Brown, c1977. xvi, 297 p., [13] leaves of plates : ill. ; 24 cm. Includes index. [PN2598.E695F58 1977] 78-4419 ISBN 0-316-28875-6 : 10.95
1. Evans, Edith, Dame, 1888-1976. 2. Actors—Great Britain—Biography. I. Title. II. Title: Ned's girl.

Evans, Eli N.

EVANS, Eli N. 917.5'06'924
The provincials; a personal history of Jews in the South [by] Eli N. Evans. [1st ed.] New York, Atheneum, 1973. xiv, 369 p. 25 cm. Bibliography: p. 350-356. [F220.J5E82 1973] 73-80747 ISBN 0-689-10541-X 10.95
1. Evans, Eli N. 2. Jews in the Southern States. I. Title.

Evans, Frederick William, 1808-1893.

[EVANS, Frederick 289.8'092'4 B
William] 1808-1893.
Autobiography of a Shaker, and Revelation of the Apocalypse. With an appendix. New and enl. ed., with port. Glasgow, United Pub. Co.; New York, American News Co., 1888. [New York, AMS Press, 1973] xvi, 271 p. port. 19 cm. Appendix to new ed. (p. 120-271) includes essays on Shakers and Shakerism by the author and others. [BX9793.E8A3 1973] 72-2986 ISBN 0-404-10748-6 12.50
1. Evans, Frederick William, 1808-1893. 2. Shakers. 3. Bible. N.T. Revelation—Prophecies. I. Title. II. Title: Revelation of the Apocalypse.

[EVANS, Frederick 289.8'092'4 B
William] 1808-1893.
Autobiography of a Shaker, and Revelation of the Apocalypse. With an appendix. New and enl. ed., with port. Philadelphia, Porcupine Press, 1972. xvi, 271 p. port. 22 cm. (The American Utopian adventure) Reprint of the 1888 ed. [BX9793.E8A3 1972] 79-187481 ISBN 0-87991-002-X
1. Evans, Frederick William, 1808-1893. 2. Bible. N.T. Revelation—Prophecies. 3. Shakers. I. Title. II. Title: Revelation of the Apocalypse. BIP

Evans, Jerome, 1930-

JORDAN, Pat. 796.332'077'0924
Black coach. New York, Dodd, Mead [1971] 248 p. 22 cm. [GV939.E9J6] 79-173453 ISBN 0-396-06430-2 5.95
1. Evans, Jerome, 1930- I. Title.

JORDAN, Pat. 796.332'077'0924
Black coach. [New York] Warner Paperback Lib. [1973, c.1971] 190 p. 18 cm. [GV939.E9J6] 1.25 (pbk.)
1. Evans, Jerome, 1930- I. Title.
L.C. card no. for the hardbound edition: 79-173453. BIP

Evans, Jesse, 1853-

BARTHOLOMEW, Ed 923.4173
Ellsworth.
Jesse Evans, a Texas hide-burner. Houston, Frontier Press of Texas, 1955. 75 p. illus. 22 cm. [F391.E9B3] 56-17891
1. Evans, Jesse, 1853- 2. Crime and criminals—Texas.

Evans, Joan,

EVANS, Joan, 1893- 925.72
Prelude & fugue, an autobiography. London, Museum Pr. [New Rochelle, N. Y., SportShelf, 1965, c.]1964. 167p. illus., ports. 23cm. Bibl. [N8375.E9A2] 65-2191 5.75
I. Title.

Evans, Kay.

EVANS, Kay. 914.2'03'850924 B
This was yesterday. London, New York, Regency Press, 1972. 113 p. 23 cm. [CT788.E77A38] 73-150242 ISBN 0-7212-0142-3 £0.90
1. Evans, Kay. I. Title.

Evans, Norm, 1942-

EVANS, Norm, 796.332'.0924 B
1942-
On God's squad; the story of Norm Evans as told to Ray Didinger and Sonny Schwartz. [1st ed.] Carol Stream, Ill., Creation House [1971] 192 p. illus. 23 cm. [BR1725.E9A3] 73-182856 4.95
1. Evans, Norm, 1942- 2. Christian life—1960- 3. Football. I. Didinger, Ray. II. Schwartz, Sonny. III. Title.

EVANS, Norm, 796.33'2'0924 B
1942-
On God's squad; the story of Norm Evans as told to Ray Didinger and Sonny Schwartz. [2d ed.] Carol Stream, Ill., Creation House [1973] 241 p. 18 cm. (New leaf library) [BR1725.E9A3 1973] 74-152732 ISBN 0-88419-009-9 1.25 (pbk.).
1. Evans, Norm, 1942- 2. Christian life—1960- 3. Football. I. Didinger, Ray. II. Schwartz, Sonny. III. Title.

Evans, Oliver, 1755-1819.

BATHE, Greville, 620'.0092'4 B
1883-
Oliver Evans; a chronicle of early American engineering [by] Greville Bathe and Dorothy Bathe. New York, Arno Press, 1972 [c1935] xviii, 362 p. illus. 29 cm. (Technology and society) Bibliography: p. 344-345. [T40.E9B3 1972] 72-5031 ISBN 0-405-04684-7
1. Evans, Oliver, 1755-1819. I. Bathe, Dorothy, joint author. II. Title. III. Series. BIP

Evans, Robley Dunglison, 1846-1912.

FALK, Edwin 359.3'3'10924 B
Albert, 1894-
Fighting Bob Evans [by] Edwin A. Falk. Freeport, N.Y., Books for Libraries Press [1969] x, 495 p. illus., ports. 23 cm. (Select bibliographies reprint series) Reprint of the 1931 ed. [E182.E93F3 1969] 75-103651
1. Evans, Robley Dunglison, 1846-1912. I. Title. BIP

Evans, William, b. 1823.

LOWTHER, Winifred E 917.64
The sea was his mistress, by Winifred E. Lowther. San Antonio, Naylor Co. [1964] x, 170 p. illus., port. 22 cm. [F391.E915L6] 64-25416
1. Evans, William, b. 1823. I. Title.

Evans, William Gray, 1855 1924.

BRECK, Allen duPont. 923.873
William Gray Evans, 1855-1924; portrait of a Western executive. [1st ed. Denver] University of Denver, Dept. of History; [distributed to the trade by A. Swallow] 1964. 290 p. illus., geneal. table, map, ports. 23 cm. (The West in American history, no. 4) Bibliography: p. [277]-283. [CT275.E8526B7] 64-8678
1. Evans, William Gray, 1855-1924. I. Title. II. Series.

Evatt, Herbert Vere, 1894-1965.

DALZIEL, Allan J. 994'.05'0924
Evatt the enigma, by Allan Dalziel. [Melbourne] Lansdowne [1967] x, 186 p. illus., ports. 25 cm. Stamped on t.p.: Distributed by Sportshelf, New Rochelle, N.Y. Reference notes: p. [173]-181. [DU114.E88D3] 68-95254 5.50 Aust.
1. Evatt, Herbert Vere, 1894-1965. I. Title.

Everdingen, Allart van, 1621-1675.

DAVIES, Alice I., 760'.092'4
1943-
Allart van Everdingen / Alice I. Davies. New York : Garland Pub., 1979. p. cm. (Outstanding dissertations in the fine arts) Originally presented as the author's thesis, Harvard, 1973. Bibliography: p. [N6953.E93D38 1978] 77-94692 ISBN 0-8240-3223-3 lib bdg : 52.50
1. Everdingen, Allart van, 1621-1675. 2. Artists Netherlands—Biography. I. Everdingen, Allart van, 1621-1675. II. Title. III. Series.

Everest, Frank Kendall,

EVEREST, Frank Kendall, 926.2913
1920-
The fastest man alive, by Frank K. Everest, Jr., as told to John Guenther. Foreword by Albert Boyd. [1st ed.] New York, Dutton, 1958. 252 p. illus. 21 cm. [UG633.E85] 57-8998
I. Guenther, John, 1911- II. Title. BIP

Everest, Mount.

MCCALLUM, John 796.5220924
Dennis, 1924-
Everest diary; based on the personal diary of Lute Jerstad, one of the first five Americans to conquer Mount Everest. Chicago, Follett [c.1966] vi, 213p. illus., maps. 22cm. [DS486.E8M27] 66-16599 4.95
1. Everest, Mount. I. Jerstad, Lute. II. Title.

TENZING, Norkey, 1914- 915.42
Tiger of the snows; the autobiography of Tenzing of Everest, written collaboration with James Ramsey Ullman. New York, Putnam [1955] 294 p. illus. 22 cm. Published also under title: Tenzing: Tiger of Everest. [DS486.E8T45 1955a] 55-7740
1. Everest, Mount. I. Ullman, James Ramsey, 1907- II. Title.

Everett, Edward, 1794-1865.

FROTHINGHAM, Paul Revere, 1864-1926. 973.5'0924 B
Edward Everett, orator and statesman. Port Washington, N.Y., Kennikat Press [1971] x, 495 p. 22 cm. (Kennikat series on American history and culture in the nineteenth century) Reprint of the 1925 ed. Includes bibliographical references. [E340.E8F8 1971] 76-137910
1. Everett, Edward, 1794-1865.

Evers, Charles, 1922-

BERRY, Jason. 320.9'762'06 B
Amazing grace; with Charles Evers in Mississippi. New York, Saturday Review Press [1973] 370 p. 22 cm. Bibliography: p. [359]-362. [F345.B47 1973] 73-76488 ISBN 0-8415-0260-9 8.95
1. Evers, Charles, 1922- 2. Mississippi—Politics and government—1951- I. Title.

Evers, Medgar Wiley, 1925-1963.

SALTER, John R. 323.1'19'6073076251
Jackson, Mississippi : an American chronicle of struggle and schism / John R. Salter, Jr. ; with a foreword by R. Edwin King, Jr. 1st ed. Hicksville, N.Y. : Exposition Press, c1979. xxi, 248 p. ; 24 cm. (An Exposition-banner book) [F349.J13S25] 78-75356 ISBN 0-682-49353-8 : 10.00
1. Evers, Medgar Wiley, 1925-1963. 2. Salter, John R. 3. Afro-Americans—Civil rights—Mississippi—Jackson. 4. Jackson, Miss.—Race relations. 5. Civil rights workers—Mississippi—Jackson—Biography. BIP

Everson, William, 1912- —Addresses, essays, lectures.

BENCHMARK & blaze : 811'.5'2
the emergence of William Everson / edited by Lee Bartlett. Metuchen, N.J. : Scarecrow Press, 1979. xvii, 274 p. : port. ; 23 cm. Includes index. Bibliography: p. 263-265. [PS3509.V65Z57] 78-27137 ISBN 0-8108-1198-7 : 12.50
1. Everson, William, 1912- —Addresses, essays, lectures. 2. Poets, American—20th century—Biography—Addresses, essays, lectures. I. Bartlett, Lee, 1950- BIP

Evert, Chris—Juvenile literature.

BURCHARD, S. H. 796.34'2'0924 B
Chris Evert / S. H. Burchard. 1st ed. New York : Harcourt Brace Jovanovich, c1976. 64 p. : ill. ; 22 cm. (Sports hero) A biography of Chris Evert, a young American tennis player who won the Wimbledon championship in 1974. [GV994.E93B87] 92 76-18156 ISBN 0-15-278007-6 : 4.95 pbk. : 1.95
1. Evert, Chris—Juvenile literature. 2. Tennis—Juvenile literature. I. Title.

HANEY, Lynn. 796.34'2'0924 B
Chris Evert, the young champion / Lynn Haney. New York : Putnam, c1976. p. cm. Includes index. A biography of Chris Evert, a young American tennis player who has won numerous national and international titles. [GV994.E93H35 1976] 92 76-26716 ISBN 0-399-20548-9 : 7.95
1. Evert, Chris—Juvenile literature. 2. Tennis players—United States—Biography—Juvenile literature. I. Title.

JACOBS, Linda. 796.34'2'0924 B
Chris Evert, tennis pro. St. Paul, EMC Corp. [1974] 40 p. illus. 24 cm. (Her Women who win) A brief biography of the young, Florida tennis star noted for her coolness on the court. [GV994.E93J32 1974] 74-2300 ISBN 0-88436-128-4 3.95 (lib. bdg.)
1. Evert, Chris—Juvenile literature. I. Title.
Pbk. 1.75; ISBN 0-88436-129-2 BIP

O'SHEA, Mary Jo. 796.34'2'0924 B
Winning tennis star : Chris Evert / by Mary Jo O'Shea. [Mankato, Minn.] : Creative Education, c1977. 30 p. : ill. ; 19 cm. (The Allstars) Focuses on the life of the famous tennis player, who at twenty-one and as a mature player, faces new sets of problems. [GV994.E93O83] 92 76-44410 ISBN 0-87191-588-X lib.bdg. : 4.95
1. Evert, Chris—Juvenile literature. 2. Tennis players—United States—Biography—Juvenile literature. I. Title. BIP

PHILLIPS, Betty Lou. 796.34'2'0924 B
Chris Evert, first lady of tennis / Betty Lou Phillips. New York : J. Messner, c1977. p. cm. A biography of the star tennis player who has won every major tournament including Wimbledon and Forest Hills. [GV994.E93P48] 92 77-14398 ISBN 0-671-32890-5 lib.bdg. : 7.29
1. Evert, Chris—Juvenile literature. 2. Tennis players—United States—Biography—Juvenile literature. I. Title.

SABIN, Francene. 796.34'2'0924 B
Set point : the story of Chris Evert / by Francene Sabin. New York : Putnam, c1977. 127 p. ; 21 cm. (Putnam sports shelf) Includes index. A biography of Chris Evert, whose dedication to practice and hard work brought her to the top of the tennis world. [GV994.E93S2 1977] 92 76-41819 ISBN 0-399-61073-1 lib. bdg. : 5.29
1. Evert, Chris—Juvenile literature. 2. Tennis players—United States—Biography—Juvenile literature. I. Title. BIP

Evins, Joe Landon, 1910-

GRAVES, Susan B. 328.73'0924 B
Evins of Tennessee; twenty-five years in Congress, by Susan B. Graves. New York, Popular Library [1971] 128 p. ports. 18 cm. [E748.E9G7] 73-151662 0.75
1. Evins, Joe Landon, 1910-

Evolution.

DARWIN, Charles Robert, 1809-1882. 575.01'62
More letters of Charles Darwin; a record of his work in a series of hitherto unpublished letters. Edited by Francis Darwin and A. C. Seward. New York, Appleton, 1903. [New York, Johnson Reprint Corp., 1972] 2 v. illus. 22 cm. (The Sources of science, no. 137) [QH31.D2A4 1972] 72-2492
1. Evolution. I. Darwin, Francis, Sir, 1848-1925, ed. II. Seward, Albert Charles, Sir, 1863-1941, ed. III. Title.

SCOPES, John Thomas. 343'.3
Center of the storm; memoirs of John T. Scopes [by] John T. Scopes and James Presley. [1st ed.] New York, Holt, Rinehart and Winston [1967] vi, 277 p. 22 cm. [LAW] 66-22204
1. Evolution. I. Presley, James. II. Title.

Evtushenko, Evgenii Aleksandrovich

EVTUSHENKO, Evgenii Aleksandrovich 928.917
A precocious autobiography [by] Yevgeny Yevtushenko. Tr. from Russian by Andrew R. MacAndrew. New York, Dutton [1964, c.1963] 124p. illus. 18cm. (D150) 1.25 pap.,
I. Title.

EVTUSHENKO, Evgenil Aleksandrovich. 928.917
A precocious autobiography. Translated from the Russian by Andrew R. MacAndrew. [1st ed.] New York, Dutton [1963] 124 p. illus. 22 cm. [PG3476.E96Z52] 63-19740
I. Title.

Ewald, Johann von, 1744-1813.

EWALD, Johann von, 1744-1813. 973.3'42
Diary of the American War : a Hessian journal / Johann Ewald ; translated and edited by Joseph P. Tustin. New Haven : Yale University Press, 1979. p. cm. Includes index. Bibliography: p. [E268.E9213] 79-623 ISBN 0-300-02153-4 : 27.50
1. Ewald, Johann von, 1744-1813. 2. United States—History—Revolution, 1775-1783—German mercenaries—Biography. 3. United States—History—Revolution, 1775-1783—Personal narratives. I. Title.

Ewbank, Weeb.

ZIMMERMAN, Paul, 1903- 796.33'2'0924 B
The last season of Weeb Ewbank. New York, Farrar, Straus and Giroux [1974] viii, 326 p. illus. 22 cm. [GV939.E93Z55 1974] 74-11325 ISBN 0-374-18462-3 7.95
1. Ewbank, Weeb. 2. Football. 3. Football coaching. I. Title. BIP

Ex-nuns—Personal narratives.

HENDERSON, Nancy. 248.8'943'2
Out of the curtained world; the story of an American nun who left the convent. [1st ed.] Garden City, N.Y., Doubleday, 1972. 276 p. 22 cm. [BX4668.3.H45A35] 74-171297 6.95
1. Ex-nuns—Personal narratives. I. Title.

TURK, Midge. 271'.93
The buried life; a nun's journey. New York, World Pub. Co. [1971] 196 p. 22 cm. [BX4668.3.T87A3] 77-149415 6.95
1. Ex-nuns—Personal narratives. I. Title.

Ex-priests, Catholic.

MCLOUGHLIN, Emmett, 1907- 282'.0922
Famous ex-priests. New York, L. Stuart [1968] 224 p. 21 cm. Bibliography: p. 221-224. [BX4669.M3] 68-18759 4.95
1. Ex-priests, Catholic. I. Title. BIP

Executions and executioners—Personal narratives.

BERRY, James, 1852-1913. 364.6'6'0924 B
My experiences as an executioner; edited by H. Snowden Ward. [1st ed. reprinted]; with a new introduction and additional appendices by Jonathan Goodman. Newton Abbot, David and Charles, 1972. [12], 144 p. illus., form, plan., ports. 21 cm. Reprint of the 1st ed., London, Percy Lund, 1892. [HV8699.G8B47 1972] 72-187291
1. Executions and executioners—Personal narratives. I. Title.
Available from Gale, 6.50. BIP

Executives—Great Britain—Directories.

LEVIATHAN - the business who's who: 658.4'2'0922 B
a biographical dictionary of chairmen, chief executives and managing directors of British-registered companies, cross-referenced by an alphabetical index of the companies; edited by Ruth Dinning. London, New York, Leviathan House, 1972. [4], 501 p. 26 cm. [HF5500.3.G7L48] 73-165320 ISBN 0-900537-06-X 30.00
1. Executives—Great Britain—Directories.

Executives — U.S.

NEW York University. School of Commerce, Accounts and Finance. 926.5
Builders of enterprise; citations of candidates for the honorary degree of doctor of commercial science, conferred in conjunction with ceremonies marking the golden anniversary of the School of Commerce, Accounts, and Finance, New York University, 1900-1950. [New York, 1950?] 121 p. illus. 27 cm. [HC102.5.A2N4] 51-8069
1. Executives — U.S. 2. U.S. — Biog. I. Title.

Exeter, Eng.—Biog.

HELE'S School, Exeter, Eng. Historical Society. 920.042
Born in Exeter. Exeter, A. Wheaton [1950] 144 p. illus., ports. 22 cm. [DA690.E9H45] 50-37015
1. Exeter, Eng.—Biog. I. Title.

Exner, Judith, 1934-

EXNER, Judith, 1934- 973.922'092'4 B
My story / Judith Exner as told to Ovid Demaris. 1st ed. New York : Grove Press, 1977. 299 p. : ill. ; 22 cm. [CT275.E97A35] 76-49722 ISBN 0-8021-0139-9 : 8.95
1. Exner, Judith, 1934- 2. Kennedy, John Fitzgerald, Pres. U.S., 1917-1963—Relations with women. 3. United States—Biography. 4. Presidents—United States—Biography. I. Demaris, Ovid. II. Title.

EXNER, Judith, 1934- 973.922'092'4 B
My story / Judith Exner as told to Ovid Demaris. 1st ed. New York : Grove Press, 1977. 299 p. : ill. ; 22 cm. [CT275.E97A35] 76-49722 ISBN 0-8021-0139-9 : 8.95
1. Exner, Judith, 1934- 2. Kennedy, John Fitzgerald, Pres. U.S., 1917-1963—Relations with women. 3. United States—Biography. 4. Presidents—United States—Biography. I. Demaris, Ovid. II. Title.

Exon, John James, 1921-

HUTCHINSON, Duane. 978.2'03'0924 B
Exon: biography of a Governor. With drawings by the author. Lincoln, Neb., Foundation Books [1973] 243 p. illus. 23 cm. [F670.E93H87] 74-75044 5.95
1. Exon, John James, 1921- BIP

Expedition francaise a l'Himalaya, 1950.

TERRAY, Lionel, 1921- 927.9652
The borders of the impossible; from the Alps to Anna purna. Translated by Geoffrey Sutton [1st ed. in the U.S.A.] Garden City, N. Y., Doubleday, 1964. 350 p. illus., maps, ports. 22 cm. Autobiographical. Translation of Les conquerants de l'inutile. [G512.T45A313 1964] 64-19233
1. Expedition francaise a l'Himalaya, 1950. 2. Mountaineering. I. Title.

Explorers.

BAILEY, Bernardine (Freeman) 1901- 92
Famous modern explorers. New York, Dodd [1963] 156p. illus. 22cm. (Famous biogs. for young people) 63-10335 3.00
1. Explorers. I. Title.

BOLTON, Sarah Knowles, 1841-1916. 910.922 B
Famous voyagers and explorers. Freeport, N.Y., Books for Libraries Press [1972] vii, 509 p. map, ports. 23 cm. (Essay index reprint series) Reprint of the 1893 ed. Contents.Contents.—Christopher Columbus.—Marco Polo.—Ferdinand Magellan.—Sir Walter Raleigh.—Sir John Franklin, Dr. Kane, C. F. Hall, and others.—David Livingstone.—Matthew Calbraith Perry.—General A. W. Greely and other arctic explorers. Includes bibliographies. [G200.B57 1972] 70-39659 ISBN 0-8369-2751-6
1. Explorers. I. Title. BIP

HOFF, Rhoda. 923.9
They explored! Humboldt, Livingstone, Fremont, Hedin, Scott, Herzog. By Rhoda Hoff & Helmut de Terra. New York, H. Z. Walck, 1959. 120 p. illus. 25 cm. [G200.H6] 59-9629
1. Explorers. I. De Terra, Helmut, 1900- joint author. II. Title.

ROWLAND-ENTWISTLE, Theodore. 910'.92'2 B
Famous explorers [by] Theodore Rowland-Entwistle and Jean Cooke. Newton Abbot, David & Charles [1974, i.e.1975] 128 p. 22 cm. (Brief biographies) [G200.R67] 74-164702 ISBN 0-7153-6073-6 7.95
1. Explorers. I. Cooke, Jean, fl. 1974- joint author. II. Title.
Distributed by David and Charles, North Pomfret, Vermont.

WILCOX, Desmond. 910'.92'2
Ten who dared / by Desmond Wilcox ; pref. by Anthony Quinn. Boston : Little, Brown, c1977. 336 p. : ill. ; 26 cm. Original ed. published in 1975 under title: Explorers. "A Time-Life Television book." Includes index. Bibliography: p. 331. [G200.W54 1977] 76-46695 ISBN 0-316-94023-2 : 14.95
1. Explorers. 2. Discoveries (in geography) I. Title.

Explorers, American.

GREELY, Adolphus Washington, 1844-1935. 910'.92'2 B
Explorers and travellers. Freeport, N.Y., Books for Libraries Press [1973] p. (Essay index reprint series) Reprint of the 1893 ed., issued in series: Men of achievement. Contents.Contents.—Louis Joliet.—Peter Le Moyne, sieur d'Iberville.—Jonathan Carver.—Captain Robert Gray.—Captain Meriwether Lewis and Lieut. William Clark.—Zebulon Montgomery Pike.—Charles Wilkes.—John Charles Fremont.—Elisha Kent Kane.—Isaac Israel Hayes.—Charles Francis Hall.—George Washington De Long.—Paul Belloni Du Chaillu.—Stanley Africanus. [G222.G73 1973] 73-1167 ISBN 0-518-10042-1
1. Explorers, American. 2. Voyages and travels. I. Title.

WIBBERLEY, Leonard Patrick O'Connor, 1915- 920
Zebulon Pike, soldier and explorer. New York, Funk & Wagnalls [c.1961] 179p. 61-6817 2.95
I. Pike, Zebulon Montgomery, 1779-1813—Juvenile literature. II. Title.

Explorers—Biography.

FARWELL, Byron. 923.942
The man who presumed; a biography of Henry M. Stanley. [1st ed.] New York, Holt [1957] 334 p. illus. 22 cm. [DT351.S9F3] 57-6187
I. Stanley, Henry Morton, Sir 1841-1904. II. Title. BIP

PENNINGTON, Piers. 910'.92
The great explorers / Piers Pennington ; [editor, Mitzi Bales]. New York : Facts on File, c1979. 336 p. : ill. ; 30 cm. Includes index. [G200.P36 1979] 79-13413 ISBN 0-87196-411-2 lib. bdg. : 17.50
1. Explorers—Biography. I. Title. BIP

Explorers—Biography—Dictionaries.

THE Discoverers : 910'.92'2
an encyclopedia of explorers and exploration / edited by Helen Delpar. New York : McGraw-Hill, [1979] p. cm. Includes bibliographies and index. [G200.D53] 79-9259 ISBN 0-07-016264-6 : 29.95
1. Explorers—Biography—Dictionaries. I. Delpar, Helen. BIP

Explorers—Biography—Juvenile literature.

THE Discoverers. 910'.92'2 B
New York : Arco Pub., [1979] p. cm. (The Living past) Includes index. Discusses early explorers and the results of their exploration on the cultures and economies of both old and new worlds. [G200.D52] 920 79-11548 ISBN 0-668-04784-4 : 6.95
1. Explorers—Biography—Juvenile literature. BIP

Explorers—Juvenile literature.

DOLAN, Edward F., 1924- 910.09
Explorers; adventures in courage, by Edward F. Dolan, Jr. Chicago, Reilly & Lee Books [1970] 170 p. illus. 24 cm. Describes the conditions which challenged and beckoned eight explorers into unknown territory and how each dealt with the problems that confronted him. [G175.D64] 920 75-125375
1. Explorers—Juvenile literature. I. Title.

GILLESPIE, Moya. 910.09
How men discovered the world [by] Hans R. Hecke. With illus. by Nikolaus Plump. Freely translated by Moya Gillespie. Minneapolis, Lerner Publications Co. [1970] 43 p. col. illus., col. maps, ports. 27 cm. Brief accounts of the voyages and discoveries of various explorers from the Phoenicians of ancient times to Richard Byrd in the twentieth century. [G175.G5 1970] 75-113420 3.95
1. Explorers—Juvenile literature. 2. Discoveries (in geography)—Juvenile literature. I. Hecke, Hans R. Wie die Welt entdeckt wurde. II. Plump, Nikolaus, 1923- illus. III. Title.

KNIGHT, Frank, 1905- j 920
Stories of famous explorers by sea. Illustrated by Will Nickless. Philadelphia, Westminster Press [1966, c1964] 161 p. illus. (part col.) 21 cm. [G175.K6] 66-15521
1. Explorers—Juvenile literature. I. Title.

PRICE, Bruce D., 1941- 910.09'73
Into the unknown. Introd. by Maynard M. Miller. Illustrated by Mort Kunstler. New York, Platt & Munk [1968] xiii, 306 p. illus. 23 cm. Bibliography: p. [303]-306. [G175.P68] 68-19576 3.95
1. Explorers—Juvenile literature. I. Title.

Explorers, Women.

RITTENHOUSE, Mignon. 923.9
Seven women explorers. [1st ed.] Philadelphia, Lippincott [1964] 158 p. maps. 21 cm. Contents.Contents.—Alexine Tinne.—Florence von Sass Baker.—Delia J. Denning Akeley.—Fanny Bullock Workman.—Kathleen M. Kenyon.—Louise Arner Boyd.—Isabella Lucy Bird Bishop. [G200.R5] 64-19044
1. Explorers, Women. I. Title.

Eyck, Jan van, 1390-1440.

BOL, L. J. 739.9493
Jan van Eyck [by] L. J. Bol. [Translator: Albert J. Fransella] New York, Barnes & Noble [1965] 89 p. (p. 19-72, illus. (part col.)) 18 cm. (Barnes & Noble art series, 624) [ND673.E9B63] 66-141
1. Eyck, Jan van, 1390-1440. I. Title.

Eyck, Jan van, 1390-1440—Juvenile literature.

NUGENT, Frances Roberts 920
Jan van Eyck: master painter. Text, drawings by Frances Roberts Nugent. With reproductions from Van Eyck's paintings. Chicago, Rand McNally [c.1962] 64p. 24cm. 62-13168 2.95 bds.,
1. Eyck, Jan van, 1390-1440—Juvenile literature. I. Title.

Eyerly, Ray, 1894-

BLODGETT, Beverley. 760'.092'4
A picture or two : the story of Ray Eyerly / by Beverley Blodgett. ; with forward [sic] by Tom McCall. McMinnville, Or. : Oakwood Press, [1974] ix, 124, [3] p., [8] leaves of plates. : ill. (some col.) ; 23 cm. Bibliography: p. [125]-[127] [ND237.E84B55] 74-13705
1. Eyerly, Ray, 1894- I. Title.

Eyre, John, 1918-

EYRE, John, 1918- 133.8'092'4 B
The god trip : the story of a mid-century man / John Eyre. 1st British Commonwealth ed. London : P. Owen, 1976. 155 p. ; 22 cm. [BF1997.E95A33 1976] 76-372181 ISBN 0-7206-0294-7 : £4.50
1. Eyre, John, 1918- 2. Occult sciences—Biography. I. Title.

Eytinge, Bruce Swomley, 1893-

EYTINGE, Bruce Swomley, 1893- 629.13'092'4 B
Bruce Eytinge, actor, inventor, aviator : an autobiography. San Antonio : Naylor Co., [1975] ix, 191 p., [1] leaf of plates : ill. ; 22 cm. [TL540.E95A33] 74-34155 ISBN 0-8111-0555-5 : 7.95
1. Eytinge, Bruce Swomley, 1893-

Ezekiel, Moses, Sir, 1844-1917.

EZEKIEL, Moses, Sir, 1844-1917. 730'.92'4 B
Memoirs from the Baths of Diocletian / Moses Jacob Ezekiel ; edited by Joseph Gutmann and Stanley F. Chyet. Detroit : Wayne State University Press, 1975. 509 p. : ill. ; 26 cm. Includes index. Bibliography: p. 490-493. [NB237.E9A35] 74-28009 ISBN 0-8143-1525-9 : 25.00
1. Ezekiel, Moses, Sir, 1844-1917. 2. Sculptors—Virginia—Correspondence, reminiscences, etc. 3. Sculptors—Rome (City)—Correspondence, reminiscences, etc. I. Gutmann, Joseph, ed. II. Chyet, Stanley F., ed. III. Title.

Ezell, Uberto Desalx, 1867-1952.

MCDEARMON, Ray, 1894- 926.1
Without the shedding of blood; the story of Dr. U. D. Ezell and pioneer life at Old Kimball. San Antonio, Naylor [1953] 81p. 22cm. Includes bibliography. [R154.E9M2] 53-6796
1. Ezell, Uberto Desalx, 1867-1952. 2. Frontier and pioneer life—Texas—Kimball. I. Title.

Fenelon, Francois de Salignac de La Mothe-, Abp., 1651-1715.

JANET, Paul Alexandre Rene, 1823-1899. 282'.0924 B
Fenelon, his life and works. Translated and edited with introd., notes, and index by Victor Leuliette. Port Washington, N.Y., Kennikat Press [1970] xx, 307 p. port. 21 cm. Reprint of the 1914 ed. Bibliography: p. 294-301. [PQ1796.J313 1970] 78-113315
1. Fenelon, Francois de Salignac de La Mothe-, Abp., 1651-1715. I. Leuliette, Victor, ed.

ST. Cyres, Stafford Harry Northcote, Viscount, 1869- 282'.0924 B
Francois de Fenelon. Port Washington, N.Y., Kennikat Press [1970] viii, 311 p. illus., ports. 22 cm. Reprint of the 1901 ed. Includes bibliographical references. [PQ1796.S3 1970] 72-113319
1. Fenelon, Francois de Salignac de La Mothe-, Abp., 1651-1715. BIP

Faber, Petrus, 1506-1546.

BANGERT, William V 922.245
To the other towns; a life of Blessed Peter Favre, first companion of St. Ignatius. Westminster, Md., Newman Press, 1959. 331p. 23cm. Includes bibliography. [BX4705.F212B3] 58-11030
1. aFaber, Petrus, 1506-1546. I. Title.

Fabisch, Judith.

FABISCH, Judith. 248'.86 B
Not ready to walk alone / Judith Fabisch. Grand Rapids, Mich. : Zondervan Pub. House, c1978. 122 p. ; 22 cm. [BV4908.F32] 78-6724 ISBN 0-310-37070-1 : 5.95
1. Fabisch, Judith. 2. Widows—United States—Biography. 3. Christian biography—United States. 4. Consolation. I. Title. BIP

Fahrner, Mary, 1904-

FAHRNER, Mary, 1904- 271'.973'024 B
Way of the cross—where it led me : the story of a Franciscan nun / Mary Fahrner. Mountain View, Calif. : Pacific Press Pub. Association, c1977. 56 p., [2] leaves of plates : ports ; 18 cm. [BX6189.F33A38] 76-5072 pbk. : 0.75
1. Fahrner, Mary, 1904- 2. Converts, Seventh-Day Adventist—United States—Biography. 3. Ex-nuns—United States—Biography. I. Title.

Fahrni, Gordon S., 1887-

FAHRNI, Gordon S., 1887- 617'.0092'4 B
Prairie surgeon / by Gordon S. Fahrni. Winnipeg [Man.] : Queenston House Pub., c1976. vi, 138 p. : ill. ; 24 cm Bibliography: p. 136-138. [R464.F33A33] 76-375956 ISBN 0-919866-14-X
1. Fahrni, Gordon S., 1887- 2. Surgeons—Manitoba—Biography. I. Title.

Fahs, Sophia Blache (Lyon) 1876-

HUNTER, Edith Fisher, 1919- 288.320924
Sophia Lyon Fahs; a biography, by Edith F. Hunter. Boston, Beacon [1966] xi, 276p. 21cm. Bibl. [BX9869.F3H8] 66-23784 5.95 bds.,
1. Fahs, Sophia Blache (Lyon) 1876- I. Title.

Faiochild David, 1869-1954.

EPSTEIN, Beryl (Williams) 1910- 925.8
Plant explorer David Rairchild, by Beryl Williams, Samuel Epstein. New York, Messner [c.1961] 192p. 61-13824 2.95
1. Faiochild David, 1869-1954. 2. Plant introduction. I. Epsteim, Samuel, 1909- joint author. II. Title.

Fairbanks, Avard Tennyson, 1897-

FAIRBANKS, Eugene F. 730'.92'4
A sculptor's testimony in bronze and stone; the sacred sculpture of Avard T. Fairbanks, by Eugene F. Fairbanks. [Salt Lake City, Publishers Press, c1972] 101 p. illus. (part col.) 28 cm. [NB237.F3F34] 73-158695
1. Fairbanks, Avard Tennyson, 1897- I. Fairbanks, Avard Tennyson, 1897- II. Title.

Fairbanks, Douglas, 1883-1939.

CAREY, Gary. 791.43'028'0922 B
Doug & Mary : a biography of Douglas Fairbanks and Mary Pickford / by Gary Carey. 1st ed. New York : E. P. Dutton, c1977. vii, 248 p., [8] leaves of plates : ill. ; 22 cm. Includes index. Filmography: p. 229-241. [PN2287.F3C3] 77-8886 ISBN 0-525-09512-8 : 7.95
1. Fairbanks, Douglas, 1883-1939. 2. Pickford, Mary, 1893- 3. Moving-pictures actors and actresses—United States—Biography. I. Title. BIP

HANCOCK, Ralph, 1903- 927.92
Douglas Fairbanks, the fourth musketeer, by Ralph Hancock and Letitia Fairbanks. [1st ed.] New York, Holt [1953] 276 p. illus. 22 cm. [PN2287.F3H3] 53-5499
1. Fairbanks, Douglas, 1883-1939. I. Fairbanks, Letitia, joint author.

HERNDON, Booton. 791.43'028'0922
Mary Pickford and Douglas Fairbanks : the most popular couple the world has known / by Booton Herndon. 1st ed. New York : Norton, c1977. p. cm. Includes index. Bibliography: p. [PN2287.F3H4 1977] 77-12573 ISBN 0-393-07508-7 : 9.95
1. Fairbanks, Douglas, 1883-1939. 2. Pickford, Mary, 1893- 3. Moving-picture actors and actresses—United States—Biography. I. Title. BIP

SCHICKEL, Richard. 791.43'028'0924 B
Douglas Fairbanks : the first celebrity / by Richard Schickel. London : Elm Tree Books, 1976. 160 p. : ill., ports. ; 24 cm. American ed. published under title: His picture in the papers. Includes index. Filmography: p. 149-152. [PN2287.F3S3 1976] 77-364602 ISBN 0-241-89443-3 : £3.50
1. Fairbanks, Douglas, 1883-1939. 2. Moving-picture actors and actresses—United States—Biography.

Fairbanks, Douglas, 1909-

CONNELL, Brian. 927.92
Knight errant; a biography of Douglas Fairbanks, Jr. Garden City, N. Y., Doubleday, 1955. 255 p. illus. 22 cm. [PN2287.F32C6 1955a] 55-5497
1. Fairbanks, Douglas, 1909- I. Title.

Fairbrother, Lafayette I.

FAIRBROTHER, Lafayette I. 922.99
The hand of God in my life; my story and sermon of a crusade for souls. Dayton, Ohio, Fay-Ma-Sha-Press, P.O.Box 462, c.1962. 63p. illus. 23cm. 62-21920 1.50 pap.,
I. Title.

Fairbrother, Nan.

FAIRBROTHER, Nan. 920.7
The cheerful day. [1st ed.] New York, Knopf, 1960. 241 p. 25 cm. Autobiographical. [CT788.F2A28] 59-15949
I. Title.

FAIRBROTHER, Nan. 920.7
An English year. [1st American ed.] New York, Knopf [1954] 243 p. 25 cm. Autobiographical. [CT788.F2A3] 53-9462
I. Title.

Fairchild, David Grandison, 1869-1954.

DOUGLAS, Marjory Stoneman. 631.5'3 B
Adventures in a green world; the story of David Fairchild and Barbour Lathrop. Coconut Grove, Fla., Field Research Projects, 1973. 61 p. 26 cm. Title on spine: David Fairchild and Barbour Lathrop. [QK31.F2D68] 74-173654
1. Fairchild, David Grandison, 1869-1954. 2. Lathrop, Barbour, 1847-1927. 3. Plant introduction—United States. I. Title.

Fairchild, Lucius, 1831-1896.

ROSS, Sam, 1912- 923.273
The empty sleeve, a biography of Lucius Fairchild. Madison, State Hist. Soc. of Wisc. for the Wisc. Civil War Centennial Comm. [c.]1964. 291p. illus., facsim., map, ports. 24cm. Bibl. 64-63013 5.50
1. Fairchild, Lucius, 1831-1896. I. Title.

ROSS, Sam, 1912- 923.273
The empty sleeve, a biography of Lucius Fairchild. Madison, State Historical Society of Wisconsin for the Wisconsin Civil War Centennial Commission, 1964. 291 p. illus. ; facsim., map, ports. 24 cm. Includes bibliographical references. [F586.F3R6] 64-63013
1. Fairchild, Lucius, 1831-1896. I. Title.

Fairfax-Blakeborough, John, 1883-1976.

FAIRFAX-BLAKEBOROUGH, John, 1883-1976. 798.4'0092'4 B
"J. F-B" : the memoirs of Jack Fairfax-Blakeborough, O.B.E., M.C. / edited by Noel Fairfax-Blakeborough. London ; New York : J. A. Allen, 1978. 196 p., [4] leaves of plates : ill. ; 23 cm. Includes index. [SF336.F34A3] 78-320263 ISBN 0-85131-269-1 : 15.00
1. Fairfax-Blakeborough, John, 1883-1976. 2. Horse-racing—Great Britain—Biography. 3. Horsemen—Great Britain—Biography. I. Fairfax-Blakeborough, Noel. II. Title. III. Title: The memoirs of Jack Fairfax-Blakeborough.

Fairfax, Thomas Fairfax, 6th baron, 1692-1782.

BROWN, Stuart E 975.5020924
Virginia baron; the story of Thomas, 6th Lord Fairfax, by Stuart E. Brown, Jr. [Berryville, Va., Chesapeake Book Co., 1965] ix, 245 p. illus., fold. map, ports. 23 cm. Bibliography: p. 205-212. [F232.B86F33] 65-19262
1. Fairfax, Thomas Fairfax, 6th baron, 1692-1782. I. Title.

BROWN, Stuart E., Jr. 975.5020924
Virginia baron; the story of Thomas, 6th Lord Fairfax [Berryville, Va., Chesapeake Bk. c.1965] ix, 245p. illus., fold. map, ports. 23cm. Bibl. [F232.N86F33] 65-19262 7.50
1. Fairfax, Thomas Fairfax, 6th baron, 1692-1782. I. Title.

Faisal, King of Saudi Arabis, 1906-

DE GAURY, Gerald. 953'.8'050924
Faisal, King of Saudi Arabia. New York, Praeger [1967, 1966] xiv, 191 p. illus., map. ports. 25 cm. "A bibliography for Saudi Arabia in the twentieth century": p. 143-145. [DS244.6.D4 1967] 67-15606
1. Faisal, King of Saudi Arabis, 1906- I. Title.

Faith-cure.

KELSEY, Morton T. 248'.2
The age of miracles : seven journeys to faith / Morton Kelsey. Notre Dame, Ind. : Ave Maria Press, c1979. 77 p. ; 21 cm. [BT732.5.K38] 78-74095 ISBN 0-87793-169-0 pbk. : 2.45
1. Faith-cure. 2. Christian biography. I. Title.

Fakharzadeh, Mehdi.

ALEXANDER, Roy, 1925- 658.85
Mehdi : nothing is impossible / by Roy Alexander. Rockville Centre, N.Y. : Farnsworth Pub. Co., c1978. viii, 151 p. ; 24 cm. [HG8952.F3A43] 77-95190 ISBN 0-87863-157-7 : 8.95
1. Fakharzadeh, Mehdi. 2. Insurance, Life—Agents—United States—Biography. 3. Selling. BIP

Falco, Albert, 1927-

DIOLE, Philippe. 551.4'6'00924 B
The memoirs of Falco, chief diver of the Calypso / by Philippe Diole and Albert Falco ; translated from the French by Joseph Harriss. Woodbury, N.Y. : Barron's, c1977. p. cm. Translation of Les memoires de Falco, chef plongeur de la Calypso. [GV838.F28D5613] 77-376 ISBN 0-8120-5130-0 : 12.95
1. Falco, Albert, 1927- 2. Calypso (Ship) 3. Skin divers—Biography. 4. Marine biology. I. Falco, Albert, 1927- II. Title.

Falconer, Ruth Bishop, 1876-

NEWKIRK, Lyana June. 977.4'61
Back home with Ruth / by Lyana June Newkirk. 1st ed. New York : Vantage Press, c1976. 102 p. : ill. ; 22 cm. Bibliography: p. 101-102. [F574.S38F346] 76-375109 ISBN 0-533-01933-8 : 4.95
1. Falconer, Ruth Bishop, 1876- 2. Scottville, Mich.—Biography. I. Title.

Falk, Lisanne.

CAMERON, Betsy. 659.1'52 B
Lisanne, a young model / photos. by Betsy Cameron ; text by Diana Lewis Jewell ; foreword by Eileen Ford. 1st ed. New York : C. N. Potter : distributed by Crown, 1979. p. cm. Fourteen-year-old Lisanne Falk describes her career as a photographic model. [HD6073.M772U54 1979] 92 79-17322 ISBN 0-517-53866-0 : 10.95
1. Falk, Lisanne. 2. Models, Fashion—United States—Biography. 3. Youth—Employment—United States. I. Jewell, Diana Lewis. II. Title.

Falk, Louis Austin

FALK, Louis Austin 920
High windows, an autobiography. New York, Whittier Books [c.1959] x, 145p. illus. 24cm. 60-751 3.50
I. Title.

Falkenburg, Jinx,

FALKENBURG, Jinx, 1919- 927.92
Jinx. New York, Duell, Sloan and Pearce [1951] 273 p. illus. 22 cm. [CT275.F373A3] 51-10413
I. Title.

Falkenhausen, Alexander von.

LIANG, Hsi-huey, 1929- 301.29'51'043
The Sino-German connection : Alexander von Falkenhausen between China and Germany 1900-1941 / Hsi-Huey Liang. Assen : Van Gorcum, 1978. xv, 229 p., [2] leaves of plates : ill. ; 24 cm. (Van Gorcum's historical library ; no. 94) Includes index. Bibliography: p. 215-223. [DS740.5.G2L5] 78-364322 ISBN 9-02-321554-0 pbk. : 19.00
1. Falkenhausen, Alexander von. 2. China—Relations (general) with Germany. 3. Germany—Relations (general) with China. 4. Generals—Germany—Biography. 5. Generals—China—Biography. I. Title.
Distributed by Humanities Press, Atlantic Highlands, NJ

Falkland, Lucius Cary, 2d Viscount, 1610?-1643.

TEALE, William Henry, 1810-1878. 283'.092'2 B
Lives of English laymen, Lord Falkland, Izaak Walton, Robert Nelson. Freeport, N.Y., Books for Libraries Press [1972] p. (Essay index reprint series) Reprint of the 1842 ed. Includes bibliographical references. [CT781.T4 1972] 72-3363 ISBN 0-8369-2930-6
1. Falkland, Lucius Cary, 2d Viscount, 1610?-1643. 2. Walton, Izaak, 1593-1683. 3. Nelson, Robert, 1656-1715. I. Title.

Falkus, Hugh

FALKUS, Hugh 818.5403
The stolen vears. Illus by David Cobb. Cleveland, World [1966. c.1965] 130p. illus. 22cm. [CT788.F243A3 1966] 66-22868 3.95
I. Title.

FALKUS, Hugh. 818.5403
The stolen years. Illus. by David Cobb. Cleveland, World Pub. Co. [1966, c1965] 130 p. illus. 22 cm. Autobiographical. [CT788.F243A3 1966] 66-22868
I. Title.

Falla, Manuel de, 1876-1946.

DEMARQUEZ, Suzanne. 780'.924 B
Manuel de Falla. Translated from the French by Salvator Attanasio. [1st ed.] Philadelphia, Chilton Book Co. [1968] viii, 253 p. 21 cm. [ML410.F215D43] 68-25858
1. Falla, Manuel de, 1876-1946.

PAHISSA, Jaime, 1880- 780'.92'4 B
Manuel de Falla, his life and works / by Jaime Pahissa ; translated from the Spanish by Jean Wagstaff. Westport, Conn. : Hyperion Press, 1979. 190 p. : ill. ; 22 cm. (Encore music editions) Translation of Vida y obra de Manuel de Falla. Reprint of the 1954 ed. published by Museum Press, London. Includes index. Published works by Falla": p. 185-186. [ML410.F215P32 1979] 78-66917 ISBN 0-88355-756-8 : 17.50
1. Falla, Manuel de, 1876-1946. 2. Composers—Spain—Biography. BIP

Faludy, Gyorgy.

FALUDY, Gyorgy. 928.94511
My happpy days in hell. Translated by Kathleen Szasz. New York, Morrow [1963, c1962] 468 p. 22 cm. Autobiography. [PH3241.F2Z52 1963] 63-6039
I. Title.

Falwell, Jerry.

STROBER, Gerald S. 286'.1'0924 B
Aflame for God / Gerald Strober, Ruth Tomczak. Nashville, TN : T. Nelson Pub. Co., 1979. p. cm. Includes index. [BX6495.F3S8] 79-16248 ISBN 0-8407-5172-9 : 8.95
1. Falwell, Jerry. 2. Baptists—Clergy—Biography. 3. Thomas Road Baptist Church. 4. Clergy—United States—Biography. I. Tomczak, Ruth, joint author. II. Title.

Family—Mexico—Case studies.

LEWIS, Oscar, 1914- 309.172
The children of Sanchez, autobiography of a Mexican family. New York, Random House [1961] 499 p. 24 cm. [HQ562.L38] 61-6270
1. Family—Mexico—Case studies. 2. Mexico (City)—Poor. 3. Mexico—Social conditions. I. Title.

Fanning, David, 1756?-1825.

FANNING, David, 1756?-1825. 973.3'3'0924 B
The narrative of Colonel David Fanning. Spartanburg, S.C., Reprint Co. [1973] xxvi, 86 p. 22 cm. Reprint of the 1865 ed., which was issued as no. 1 of Historical documents relating to the Old North State, and as no. 1 of Sabin's reprints, 2d ser. Edited by T. H. Wynne. [E278.F2A25 1973] 73-2736 ISBN 0-87152-132-6
1. Fanning, David, 1756?-1825. 2. United States—History—Revolution, 1775-1783—Personal narratives—British. 3. North Carolina—History—Revolution, 1775-1783. I. Wynne, Thomas Hicks, d. 1875, ed. II. Title. III. Series: Historical documents relating to the Old North State, no. 1. IV. Series: Sabin's reprints, 2d ser., no. 1.

Fanon, Frantz, 1925-1961.

GEISMAR, Peter. 322'.42'0924 B
Fanon. New York, Dial Press, 1971. 214 p. illus., facsims., ports. 22 cm. Bibliography: p. [203]-206. [CT2750.F3G4] 70-144373 6.95
1. Fanon, Frantz, 1925-1961.

GENDZIER, Irene L. 322.4'2'0924 B
Frantz Fanon; a critical study [by] Irene L. Gendzier. New York, Vintage Books [1974, c1973] xvi, 300 p. 19 cm. Bibliography: p. [290]-292. [CT2628.F35G46 1974] 73-5699 ISBN 0-394-71969-7 1.95 (pbk.)

1. Fanon, Frantz, 1925-1961. **BIP**

GENDZIER, Irene L. 322.4'2'0924 B
Frantz Fanon: a critical study [by] Irene L. Gendzier. [1st ed.] New York, Pantheon Books [1973] xvi, 300 p. port. 25 cm. Bibliography: p. [290]-292. [CT2628.F35G46] 72-3414 ISBN 0-394-46205-X 10.00
1. Fanon, Frantz, 1925-1961. I. Title.

Fantin-Latour, Ignace Henri Jean Theodore, 1836-1904.

VERRIER, Michelle. 759.4
Fantin-Latour / Michelle Verrier. New York : Harmony Books, 1978. p. cm. Bibliography: p. [ND553.F3V47 1978] 78-1374 ISBN 0-517-53413-4 pbk. : 6.95
1. Fantin-Latour, Ignace Henri Jean Theodore, 1836-1904. 2. Painters—France—Biography. I. Fantin-Latour, Ignace Henri Jean Theodore, 1836-1904. II. Title. **BIP**

Faraday, Michael, 1791-1867.

AGASSI, Joseph. 530'.092'4 B
Faraday as a natural philosopher. Chicago, University of Chicago Press [1971] xiv, 359 p. illus. 23 cm. Bibliography: p. 333-350. [QC16.F2A64] 73-151130 ISBN 0-226-01046-5
1. Faraday, Michael, 1791-1867. I. Title. **BIP**

EPSTEIN, Samuel, 530'.0924 B
1909-
Michael Faraday, apprentice to science, by Sam and Beryl Epstein. Illustrated by Raymond Burns. Champaign, Ill., Garrard Pub. Co. [1971] 144 p. illus., ports. 22 cm. ([A People in the arts and sciences book]) The life of the British chemist who invented the electric generator and whose experiments in electricity opened a new scientific field. [QC16.F2E6] 92 76-141422 ISBN 0-8116-4511-8 2.59
1. Faraday, Michael, 1791-1867. I. Epstein, Beryl (Williams) 1910- joint author. II. Burns, Raymond, 1924- illus. III. Title.

KENDALL, James, 1889- 925.3
Michael Faraday, man of simplicity. New York, Roy Publishers [1955] 196p. illus. 21cm. [QC16] 55-9184
1. Faraday, Michael, 1791-1867. I. Title.

LUDWIG, Charles, 530'.092'4 B
1918
Michael Faraday, father of electronics / Charles Ludwig. Scottdale, Pa. : Herald Press, 1978. p. cm. Bibliography: p. [QC16.F2L82] 78-15028 ISBN 0-8361-1864-2 : 6.95
1. Faraday, Michael, 1791-1869. 2. Physicists—Great Britain—Biography. 3. Science—History. I. Title: Father of electronics **BIP**

MACDONALD, David Keith 925.3
Chalmers, 1920-
Faraday, Maxwell, and Kelvin. [1st ed.] Garden City, N.Y., Anchor Books, 1964. xvi, 143 p. illus., ports., facsims. 19 cm. (Science study series, S33) [QC15.M27] 64-11313
1. Faraday, Michael, 1791-1867. 2. Maxwell, James Clerk, 1831-1879. 3. Kelvin, William Thomson, baron, 1824-1907. I. Title. II. Series.

SOOTIN, Harry. 925.3
Michael Farraday: from errand boy to master physicist. New York, J. Messner [1954] 180 p. 22 cm. [QC16.F2S65] 54-6776
1. Faraday, Michael, 1791-1867.

TYNDALL, John, 2810-1893. 925.3
Faraday as a discover. Introd. and notes by Keith Gordon Irwin. New York, Crowell, [1961] 213 p. illus. 20 cm. [QC16.F1T9] 61-6143
1. Faraday, Michael, 1791-1867. I. Title.

WILLIAMS, Leslie Pearce, 925.3
1927-
Michael Faraday, a biography by L. Pearce Williams. New York, Basic Books [1965] xvi, 531 p. illus., facsims., ports. 25 cm. Includes bibliographical references. [QC16.F2W5] 65-19542
1. Faraday, Michael, 1791-1867. I. Title. **BIP**

Faraday, Michael, 1791-1867—Juvenile literature.

GUNSTON, David 925.3
Michael Faraday, father of electricity. London Wiendenfeld & Nicholson dist.NewRochelle,n.y., sportshelf, 1964. c.1962 Weidenfeld & Nicolson [dist. New Rochelle, N.Y., SportShelf, 1964, c.1962] 128p. illus., facsims., ports. 19cm. (Pathfinder biogs., 9) 64-3626 3.50 bds.,
1. Faraday, Michael, 1791-1867—Juveniline literature. I. Title.

HARVEY, Tad. 925.3
The quest of Michael Faraday. Illus. by Lee J. Ames. Garden City, N. Y., Garden City Books, [c.]1961. 56p. 32cm. 60-6176 2.50 bds.,
1. Faraday, Michael, 1791-1867—Juvenile literature. I. Title.

MAY, Charles Paul 925.3
Michae Faraday and the electric dynamo. Pictures by Geoffrey Biggs. New York, F. Watts [c.1961] 144p. illus. (First biography) 61-5279 1.95
1. Faraday, Michael, 1791-1867—Juvenile literature. I. Title.

MAY, Charles Paul. 925.3
Michael Faraday and the electric dynamo. Pictures by Geoffrey Biggs. New York, F. Watts [1961] 144p. illus. 22cm. (A First biography) [QC16.F2M35] 61-5279
1. Faraday, Michael, 1791-1867—Juvenile literature. I. Title.

PRINGLE, Patrick 92
The young Faraday. Illus. by Brian Liddle. New York, Roy [1965, c.1964] 122p. illus. 21cm. [QC16.F2P7] 64-23912 3.25 bds.,
1. Faraday, Michael, 1791-1867—Juvenile literature. I. Title.

VEGLAHN, Nancy. 530'.092'4 B
Coils, magnets, and rings : Michael Faraday's world / by Nancy Veglahn ; illustrated by Christopher Spollen. New York : Coward, McCann & Geoghegan, [1976] p. cm. A biography of the English scientist who believed that one should never stop asking questions. His questions led him to discoveries concerning electricity. [QC16.F2V43] 92 76-14385 ISBN 0-698-20384-4 : 5.95.
1. Faraday, Michael, 1791-1867—Juvenile literature. I. Spollen, Christopher J. II. Title. **BIP**

Farel, Guillaume, 1489-1565.

FLETCHER, Elaine J. 284'.2'0924 B
Farel the firebrand [by] Elaine Jessie Fletcher. Washington, Review and Herald Pub. Association [1972] 128 p. illus. 22 cm. [BR350.F3F43] 75-164936 2.95
1. Farel, Guillaume, 1489-1565. I. Title.

Farfan, Armando—Juvenile literature.

KREMENTZ, Jill. 791.3'4'0924 B
A very young circus flyer / written and photographed by Jill Krementz. 1st ed. New York : Knopf, 1979. ca. 100 p. : ill. (some col.) ; 32 cm. A nine-year-old trapeze artist tells about his life with a circus. [GV1811.F34K73 1979] 78-20546 ISBN 0-394-50574-3 : 9.95
1. Farfan, Armando—Juvenile literature. 2. Aerialist—Biography—Juvenile literature. I. Title. **BIP**

Fargo, William George, 1818-1880—Juvenile fiction.

WILKIE, Katharine Elliot, 920
1904-
William Fargo, young mail carrier. Illus. by James Ponter. Indianapolis, Bobbs [c.1962] 200p. col. illus. (Childhood of famous Amers.) 62-9257 2.25
1. Fargo, William George, 1818-1880—Juvenile fiction. I. Title.

Fargue, Leon Paul. 1878-1947.

BEUCLER, Andre, 1898- 928.4
The last of the Bohemians; twenty years with Leon-Paul Fargue. [Translated by Geoffrey Sainsbury] With an introd. by Archibald MacLeish. New York, W. Sloane Associates [1954] 237p. 22cm. Translation of Vingt and avec Leon-Paul Fargue. [PQ2611.A66Z613] 54-10608
1. Fargue, Leon Paul. 1878-1947. I. Title.

BEUCLER, Andre, 848'.9'1209 B
1898-
The last of the Bohemians; twenty years with Leon-Paul Fargue. With an introd. by Archibald MacLeish. Westport, Conn., Greenwood Press [1970, c1954] xii, 237 p 23 cm. Translation of Vingt ans avec Leon-Paul Fargue. [PQ2611.A66Z613 1970] 79-108841 ISBN 0-8371-3729-2
1. Fargue, Leon Paul, 1878-1947. I. Title. **BIP**

Farid-uddin, Shaikh, called Ganj-i Shakar, 1175?-1265.

NIZAMI, Khaliq 297'.64'0924
Ahmad.
The life and times of Shaikh Farid-ud-Din Gang-i-Shakar / by Khaliq Ahmad Nizami ; with a foreword by Sir Hamilton Gibb. 1st Pakistani ed. Lahore : Universal Books, 1976. x, 144 p. ; 24 cm. Reprint of the 1955 ed. published from Aligarh, India. Includes index. Running title: Life of Shaikh Farid-'ud-din Ganj-i Shakar. Bibliography: p. [125]-132. [BP80.F3N5 1976] 77-930059 Rs45.00
1. Farid-uddin, Shaikh, called Ganj-i Shakar, 1175?-1265. 2. Sufism—Biography. I. Title. II. Title: Life of Shaikh Farid-'ud-din Ganj-i Shakar.

Farieon, Eleanor, 1881-1965.

BOOK for Eleanor Farjeon juv
(A); a tribute to her life and work, 1881-1965. Introd. by Naomi Lewis. Illus. by Edward Ardizzone. [1st Amer. ed.] New York, Walck, [c]1966. 184p. illus. 23cm. [PZ5.B637] 66-14765 3.95
1. Farieon, Eleanor, 1881-1965. 1. Farjeon, Eleanor, 1881-1965. II. Ardizzone, Edward, 1900-illus.
Contentsomitted.

Farinacci, Roberto, 1893-1945.

FORNARI, Harry, 945.091'0924 B
1919
Mussolini's gadfly: Roberto Farinacci. Nashville, Vanderbilt University Press, 1971. xiv, 237 p. illus., ports. 23 cm. Bibliography: p. 217-220. [DG575.F37F67] 70-138986 ISBN 0-8265-1167-8 8.95
1. Farinacci, Roberto, 1893-1945. I. Title. **BIP**

Farington, Joseph, 1747-1821.

FARINGTON, Joseph, 1747 759.2 B
1821.
The diary of Joseph Farington / edited by Kenneth Garlick and Angus Macintyre. New Haven : Published for the Paul Mellon Centre for Studies in British Art by Yale University Press, 1978- v. ill. ; 23 cm. (Studies in British art) Contents.Contents.—v. 1. July 1793-December 1794.—v. 2. January 1795-August 1796. [N6797.F37A2 1978] 78-7056 ISBN 0-300-02294-8 : 60.00 set
1. Farington, Joseph, 1747-1821. 2. London. Royal Academy of Art. 3. Artists—England—Biography. 4. Arts, English. 5. England—Civilization—18th century. 6. England—Civilization—19th century. I. Garlick, Kenneth, 1916- II. Macintyre, Angus D. III. Paul Mellon Centre for Studies in British Art. IV. Title. V. Series.

Farjeon, Eleanor, 1881-1965.

BLAKELOCK, Denys, 1901- 828.91209
Eleanor; portrait of a Farjeon. London, Gollancz, 1966. 160p. front. (port.) 23cm. [PR6011.A67Z55] 66-73758 5.00 bds.,
1. Farjeon, Eleanor, 1881-1965. I. Title.
American distributor: Hillary House, New York.

COLWELL, Eileen H. 828.912
Eleanor Farjeon. New York, Walck [1962, c.1961] 94p. illus. 19cm. Bibl. 62-13176 2.50
1. Farjeon, Eleanor, 1881- I. Title.

Farm life.

CRAWFORD, Fred Erastus, 926.3
1857-1950.
The life and times of Oramel Crawford, a Vermont farmer, 1809-1888. [Cambridge? Mass.] Priv. Print., 1952 [i. e. 1953] 263p. illus. 27cm. Crawford, Oramel, 1809-1888 [S417.C64C7] 53-29379
I. Title.

PEDEN, Rachel. 630.1177
The land, the people. Drawings by Sidonie Coryn. [1st ed.] New York, Knopf, 1966. xv, 332 p. illus. 21 cm. Autobiographical. [S521.P357] 66-19395
1. Farm life. I. Title.

Farm life—Brazil—Sao Paulo.

GELD, Ellen Bromfield, 818.5
1932-
Strangers in the valley. Illustrated by Herbert Horn. New York, Dodd, Mead, 1957. 229 p. illus. 22 cm. Autobiographical. [PS3513.E43Z55] 57-10164
1. Farm life—Brazil—Sao Paulo. I. Title.

Farm life—U.S.

GUE, Benjamin F 1828- 630.173
1904.
Diary of Benjamin F. Gue in rural New York and pioneer Iowa, 1847-1856. Edited by Earle D. Ross. Ames, Iowa State University Press [c1962] 137p. 24cm. [CT234.G8] 62-15964
1. Farm life—U.S. I. Ross, Earle Dudley, 1885- ed. II. Title.

Farm life—Wales.

CRAGOE, Elizabeth. 942.9'65'085
Buttercups and daisy / Elizabeth Cragoe. New York : St. Martin's Press, 1977, c1976. 167 p. ; 23 cm. [S522.G7C7 1977] 76-62760 ISBN 0-312-11007-3 : 7.95
1. Farm life—Wales. 2. Cragoe, Elizabeth. 3. Penllwynplan Farm Nature Reserve, Wales. I. Title. **BIP**

Farmborough, Florence.

FARMBOROUGH, 940.4'81'42
Florence.
With the armies of the tsar : a nurse at the Russian front, 1914-18 / Florence Farmborough ; with 48 photos. by the author. New York : Stein and Day, [1975], c1974. p. cm. Originally published under title Nurse at the Russian front [D640 F287 1975] 74-26615 ISBN 0-8128-1793-1 : 10.00
1. Farmborough, Florence. 2. European War, 1914-1918—Personal narratives, English. 3. European War, 1914-1918—War work—Red Cross. 4. European War, 1914-1918—Russia. I. Title.

Farmer, Frances, 1914-1970.

ARNOLD, 791.43'028'0924 B
William, 1945-
Shadowland : William Arnold. New York : McGraw-Hill, c1978. 260 p. : ill. ; 22 cm. [PN2287.F34A7] 78-4593 ISBN 0-07-002311-5 : 9.95
1. Farmer, Frances, 1914-1970. 2. Moving-picture actors and actresses—United States—Biography. I. Title. **BIP**

FARMER, 791.43'028'0924 B
Frances, 1914-1970.
Will there really be a morning? An autobiography. New York, Putnam [1972] 318 p. illus. 22 cm [PN2287.F34A3 1972] 78-189885 ISBN 0-399-10913-7 7.95
I. Title.

FARMER, 791.43'028'0924 [B]
Frances, 1914-1970.
Will there really be a morning? An autobiography. [New York, Dell, 1973, c.1972] 379 p. 18 cm. [PN2287.F34A3] 1.50 (pbk.)
I. Title.

L.C. card no. for the hardbound edition: 78-189885.

Farmer's Brother, Seneca chief.

STONE, William Leete, 1792-1844. 970.3'0924
The life and times of Red-Jacket, or Sa-go-ye-wat-ha; being the sequel to the history of Six Nations. New York, Wiley and Putnam, 1841. St. Clair Shores, Mich., Scholarly Press, 1970. x, 484 p. illus., port. 24 cm. On spine: Life and letters of Red-Jacket. Includes bibliographical references. [E99.S3R4 1970] 71-108543
1. Red Jacket, Seneca chief, 1751?-1830. 2. Farmer's Brother, Seneca chief. 3. Cornplanter, Seneca chief, 1732?-1836. I. Title.

Farmington, Utah—History.

HESS, Margaret Steed, 1884- 979.2'27
My Farmington : a history of Farmington, Utah, 1847-1976 / by Margaret Steed Hess. [Farmington : Helen Mar Miller Camp, c1976] vii, 434 p., [1] leaf of plates : ill. ; 24 cm. Includes index. [F834.F2H47] 77-150337
1. Farmington, Utah—History. 2. Farmington, Utah—Genealogy. 3. Farmington, Utah—Biography. I. Title.

Farragut, David Glasgow, 1801-1870.

HOYT, Edwin Palmer. 973.75'0924 B
Damn the torpedos! the story of America's first admiral: David Glasgow Farragut, by Christopher Martin. London, New York, Abelard-Schuman [1970] 280 p. 22 cm. [E467.1.F23H6] 73-85799 6.95
1. Farragut, David Glasgow, 1801-1870. I. Title.

LATHAM, Jean Lee. JUV
Anchor's aweigh; the story of David Glasgow Farragut. Illus. by Eros Keith. New York, Harper & Row [1968] 273 p. illus., maps. 22 cm. A biography of David Farragut who received his commission in the United States Navy before he was ten and who in 1864 broke the back of the Confederate fleet in the Battle of Mobile Bay. [PZ7.L348An] 973.75'0924 B 92 AC 68
1. Farragut, David Glasgow, 1801-1870. I. Keith, Eros, illus. II. Title. **BIP**

MAHAN, Alfred Thayer, 1840-1914. 973.75'0924 B
Admiral Farragut. New York, Greenwood Press, 1968. 333 p. illus., port. 22 cm. "Originally published in 1895." [E467.1.F23M2 1968b] 69-10126
1. Farragut, David Glasgow, 1801-1870. I. Title. **BIP**

Farrell, Jeff.

HENNING, Jean M. 797.21'0924
Six days to swim; a biography of Jeff Farrell, by Jean M. Henning. North Hollywood, Calif., Swimming World [1970] xiii, 141 p. illus., ports. 22 cm. [GV838.F3H4] 71-103031 4.50
1. Farrell, Jeff. 2. Swimming—Biography. I. Title.

Farrer, Reginald John, 1880-1920.

COX, Euan Hillhouse Methven, 1893- 581.9'591
Farrer's last journey : Upper Burma, 1919-1920 / by E. H. M. Cox. Sakonnet, R.I. : Theophrastus, 1977. xix, 244 p., [25] leaves of plates, [1] fold. : ill. ; 24 cm. Reprint of the 1926 ed. published by Dulau, London. Includes index. [QK360.5.C69 1977] 76-48121 ISBN 0-913728-16-0 : 10.00
1. Farrer, Reginald John, 1880-1920. 2. Cox, Euan Hillhouse Methven, 1893- 3. Botany—Burma, Upper. 4. Burma, Upper—Description and travel. 5. Plant collectors—Great Britain—Biography. 6. Rhododendron. I. Title.

Farrier, Denis, 1921—

FARRIER, Denis, 1921- 636.089'092'4 B
Country vet. New York, Taplinger [1973, c1972] 196 p. 22 cm. Autobiographical. [SF613.F37A3 1973] 72-6615 ISBN 0-8008-1950-0 5.95
1. Farrier, Denis, 1921- 2. Veterinarians—Correspondence, reminiscences, etc. I. Title. **BIP**

Farson, Negley,

FARSON, Negley, 1890- 928.1
A mirror for Narcissus. [1st ed.] Garden City, N. Y., Doubleday, 1957. 330p. 22cm. A continuation of the author's autobiography, The way of a transgressor. [PS3511.A77Z514 1957] 57-5785
I. Title.

Faruk I, King of Egypt, 1920-1965.

MCBRIDE, Barrie St. Clair. 962'.05'0924 B
Farouk of Egypt; a biography. [1st American ed.] South Brunswick [N.J.] A. S. Barnes [1968, c1967] 238 p. 22 cm. Bibliography: p. 229-232. [DT107.82.M3 1968] 68-29863 5.95
1. Faruk I, King of Egypt, 1920-1965. I. Title.

MCLEAVE, Hugh. 962'.05'0924 B
The last Pharaoh: Farouk of Egypt. [1st American ed.] New York, McCall Pub. Co. [1970, c1969] 314 p. ports. 22 cm. Bibliography: p. [302]-304. [DT107.82.M33 1970] 79-104948 7.95
1. Faruk I, King of Egypt, 1920-1965. I. Title.

STERN, Michael 962.050924
Farouk. New York, Bantam [1965] 277p. 18cm. [DT107.82.S75] 65-23850 .75 pap.,
1. Faruk I, King of Egypt, I. Title.

Fashion—Biography.

KEENAN, Brigid, 1939- 391'.07'20922
The women we wanted to look like / by Brigid Keenan. New York : St. Martin's Press, [1978] p. cm. Includes index. Bibliography: p. [TT505.A1K43 1978] 78-4014 ISBN 0-312-88783-3 : 14.95
1. Fashion—Biography. 2. Fashion—History—20th century. I. Title. **BIP**

Fassbinder, Rainer Werner, 1946-

FASSBINDER / 791.43'0233'0924 B
edited by Tony Rayns. London : British Film Institute, 1976. vi, 62 p. ; 21 cm. Bibliography: p. 62. [PN1998.A3F274] 76-381160 ISBN 0-85170-052-7 : £0.55
1. Fassbinder, Rainer Werner, 1946- I. Rayns, Tony. **BIP**

Fathers of the church.

DEFERRARI, Roy Joseph, 1890- ed. 922.1
Early Christian biographies; lives of: St. Cyprian, by Pontius; St. Ambrose, by Paulinus; St. Augustine, by Possidius; St. Anthony, by St. Athanasius; St. Paul the first hermit, St. Hilarion, and Malchus, by St. Jerome; St. Epiphanius, by Ennodius; with a sermon on the life of St. Honoratus, by St. Hilary. Translated by Roy J. Deferrari [and others] [New York] Fathers of the Church [1952] xiv, 407 p. 22 cm. (The Fathers of the church, a new translation , v. 15) [BR60.F3D4] 52-12847
1. Fathers of the church. 2. Christian literature, Early (Selections: Extracts, etc.) I. Title. II. Series.

Fathers of the church—Biog.

HOARE, Frederick, russell, 1888-1951, ed. and tr. 922.1
The Western Fathers; being the lives of SS. Martin of Tours, Ambrose, Augustine of Hippo, Honoratus of Arles, and Germanus Auxerre. Translated and edited by F. R. Hoare. New York, Sheed and Ward, 1954. xxxii, 320p. 22cm. (The Makers of Christendom) Includes bibliographical references. [BR1705.A2H75] 54-11138
1. Fathers of the church— Biog. 2. Saints. I. Title. II. Series.

HOARE, Frederick Russell, 1888-1951, ed. and tr. 922.1
The Western Fathers; being the lives of Martin of Tours, Ambrose, Augustine of Hippo, Honoratus of Artes, and Germanus Auxerre by Sulpicius Severus [others] Harper [1965, c.1954] xxxii, 310p. 2ucm. (First pub. by Sheed under title Makers of Christendom. (Harper torch bk., Cathedral lib., TB309L) Bibl. [BR1705.A2H75] 1.95 pap.,
1. Fathers of the church—Biog. 2. Saints. I. Title. II. Series.

Fathers of the church, Greek.

CAMPBELL, James Marshall, 1895- 922.1
The Greek fathers. New York, Cooper Square Publishers, 1963. ix, 167 p. 19 cm. (Our debt to Greece and Rome) Bibliography: p. 163-167. [BR1705.C25 1963] 63-10279
1. Fathers of the church, Greek. I. Title. II. Series. **BIP**

CAMPENHAUSEN, Hans, Freiherr von, 1903- 922.1
The fathers of the Greek Church. Translated by Stanley Godman. [New York] Pantheon [1959] 170 p. 22 cm. Includes bibliography. [BR1705.C273] 59-8588
1. Fathers of the church, Greek.

Fathers of the Church, Latin.

CAMPENHAUSEN, Hans, Freiherr von, 1903- 281'.3'0922 B
The fathers of the Latin Church. Translated by Manfred Hoffman. Stanford, Calif., Stanford University Press [1969, c1964] vii, 328 p. 23 cm. Translation of Lateinische Kirchenvater. Contents.Contents.—Tertullian.—Cyprian.—Lactantius.—Ambrose.—Jerome.—Augustine.—Boethius.—Bibliography (p. 317-325) [BR1706.C313 1969] 76-75260 6.50
1. Fathers of the Church, Latin. I. Title.

Faulk, Laura E.

FAULK, Laura E. 919.4'04'6
The Australian alternative / Laura E. & Odie B. Faulk, with Nancy M. and Richard D. Faulk. New Rochelle, N.Y. : Arlington House, [1975] 183 p., [1] leaf of plates : ill. ; 24 cm. [DU105.F28] 75-6975 ISBN 0-87000-251-1 : 7.95
1. Faulk, Laura E. 2. Faulk, Odie B. 3. Australia—Description and travel—1951- I. Faulk, Odie B. II. Title. **BIP**

Faulkner, Barry, 1881-1966.

FAULKNER, Barry, 1881-1966. 759.13
Barry Faulkner; sketches from an artist's life. Dublin, N.H., W. L. Bauhan, 1973. xiv, 208 p. illus. 25 cm. Autobiography. [ND237.F267A22] 70-162875 ISBN 0-87233-023-0 10.00
1. Faulkner, Barry, 1881-1966. 2. Painters—United States—Correspondence, reminiscences, etc.

Faulkner, William, 1897-1962.

BEZZERIDES, Albert Isaac, 1908- 813'.5'2 B
William Faulkner, a life on paper / A. I. Bezzerides. Jackson : University Press of Mississippi, c1979. p. cm. [PS3511.A86Z6283] 79-15371 ISBN 0-87805-098-1 pbk. : 10.00
1. Faulkner, William, 1897-1962. 2. Authors, American—20th century—Biography. I. Title.

BLOTNER, Joseph Leo, 1923- 813'.5'2 B
Faulkner; a biography, by Joseph Blotner. [1st ed.] New York, Random House [1974] 2 v. illus. 24 cm. Includes bibliographical references. [PS3511.A86Z63] 72-11370 25.00
1. Faulkner, William, 1897-1962. **BIP**

BROOKS, Cleanth, 1906- 813.52
William Faulkner; the Yoknapatawpha country. New Haven, Yale University Press, 1963. xiv, 499 p. map, geneal. tables. 24 cm. Includes bibliographical references. [PS3511.A86Z64] 63-17023
1. Faulkner, William, 1897-1962. I. Title: The Yoknapatawpha country. **BIP**

COUGHLAN, Robert, 1914- 928.1
The private world of William Faulkner. [1st ed.] New York, Harper [1954] 151p. illus. 22cm. [PS3511.A86Z76] 54-8943
1. Faulkner, William, 1897- I. Title.

COUGHLAN, Robert, 1914- 813'.5'2 B
The private world of William Faulkner. New York, Cooper Square Publishers, 1972 [c1954] 151 p. illus. 23 cm. [PS3511.A86Z76 1972] 72-78474 ISBN 0-8154-0424-7
1. Faulkner, William, 1897-1962. I. Title.

COUGHLAN, Robert [John Robert Coughlan] 1914- 928.1
The private world of William Faulkner. New York, Avon [1962,c.1953,1954] 126p. illus. 17cm. (G-1144) .50 pap.,
1. Faulkner, William, 1897-1962. I. Title. **BIP**

COWLEY, Malcolm, 1898- 813'.5'2 B
The Faulkner-Cowley file : letters and memories, 1944-1962 / Malcolm Cowley. New York : Penguin Books, 1978, c1966. 184 p. ; 18 cm. Reprint of the ed. published by Viking Press, New York. [PS3511.A86Z77 1978] 77-23751 ISBN 0-14-004684-4 pbk. : 2.95
1. Faulkner, William, 1897-1962. 2. Faulkner, William, 1897-1962—Correspondence. 3. Cowley, Malcolm, 1898- —Correspondence. 4. Authors, American—20th century—Biography. I. Faulkner, William, 1897-1962. II. Title. **BIP**

FAULKNER, John, 1901-1963 928.1
My brother Bill; an affectionate reminiscence. New York, Pocket Bks. [1964, c.1963] 249p. 17cm. (50018) .50 pap.,
1. Faulkner, William, 1897-1962. I. Title.

FAULKNER, John, 1901-1963 928.1
My brother Bill: an affectionate reminiscence. New York, Trident [dist. S. & S., c.]1963. 277p. illus. 22cm. 63-13769 4.95
1. Faulkner, William, 1897-1962. I. Title.

FAULKNER, John, 1901-1963. 928.1
My brother Bill: an affectionate reminiscence. New York, Trident Press, 1963. 277 p. illus. 22 cm. [PS3511.A86Z783] 63-13769
1. Faulkner, William, 1897-1962. I. Title.

A Faulkner perspective 813'.5'2
: a companion-guide to the limited first edition of the Selected letters of William Faulkner. Franklin Center, Pa. : Franklin Library, 1976. 143 p. ; 24 cm. Contents.Contents.—Gardner, P. Faulkner remembered.—Reference materials for the Selected letters of William Faulkner.—Mottram, E. William Faulkner : an introduction to his writings. [PS3511.A86Z5462] 77-356487
1. Faulkner, William, 1897-1962. Selected letters of William Faulkner. 2. Faulkner, William, 1897-1962—Correspondence. 3. Novelists, American—20th century—Correspondence. I. Faulkner, William, 1897-1962. Selected letters of William Faulkner. II. Gardner, Paul, 1936- III. Mottram, Eric.

FAULKNER, William, 1897-1962. 813'.5'2 B
Faulkner at Nagano, edited by Robert A. Jelliffe. [Folcroft, Pa.] Folcroft Library Editions, 1973 [c1956] viii, 206 p. illus. 24 cm. Reprint of the ed. published by Kenkyusha, Tokyo. [PS3511.A86Z52 1973] 73-9952 ISBN 0-8414-2189-7 (lib. bdg.)
1. Faulkner, William, 1897-1962. I. Jelliffe, Robert Archibald, 1883- ed. II. Title.

HOFFMAN, Frederick John. v. 12
William Faulkner. New Haven, Conn., College and University Press, Paperback Division [c1961] 134 p. (Twayne's United States authors series, 1) NUC64

1. Faulkner, William, 1897-1962. I. Title. BIP

LEARY, Lewis Gaston, 1906- 813'.5'2 B
William Faulkner of Yoknapatawpha County, by Lewis Leary. New York, Crowell [1973] 214 p. 22 cm. (Twentieth-century American writers) Bibliography: p. 205-206. [PS3511.A86Z875] 72-7551 ISBN 0-690-89173-3 4.50
1. Faulkner, William, 1897-1962. I. Title. BIP

RICHARDSON, Harold Edward. 813'.5'2 B
William Faulkner; the journey to self-discovery, by H. Edward Richardson. Columbia, University of Missouri Press [1969] xii, 258 p. illus. 22 cm. Bibliography: p. 230-245. [PS3511.A86Z948] 76-80033 8.50
1. Faulkner, William, 1897-1962.

SATURDAY review. v. 12
William Faulkner: man and writer. [New York, 1962] 67 p. illus. 28 cm. Saturday review v. 45, no. 29, July 28, 1962. 63-57722
1. Faulkner, William, 1897-1962. I. Title.

WAGGONER, Hyatt Howe. 813.52
William Faulkner: from Jefferson to the world. [Lexington] University of Kentucky Press [1959] vi, 279 p. 24 cm. Bibliographical references included in "Notes" (p. [267]-274) [PS3511.A86Z985] 59-13268
1. Faulkner, William, 1897-1962.

WEBB, James W., ed. 813.52
William Faulkner of Oxford. Edited by James W. Webb and A. Wigfall Green. [Baton Rouge] Louisiana State University Press [1965] xi, 231 p. illus., facsims., ports. 24 cm. [PS3511.A86Z9854] 65-23763
1. Faulkner, William, 1897-1962. I. Green, Adwin Wigfall, 1900- joint ed. II. Title. BIP

Faulkner, William, 1897-1962—Correspondence.

COWLEY, Malcolm, 1898- 813'.5'2 B
The Faulkner-Cowley file : letters and memories, 1944-1962 / Malcolm Cowley. New York : Penguin Books, 1978, c1966. 184 p. ; 18 cm. Reprint of the ed. published by Viking Press, New York. [PS3511.A86Z77 1978] 77-23751 ISBN 0-14-004684-4 pbk. : 2.95
1. Faulkner, William, 1897-1962. 2. Faulkner, William, 1897-1962—Correspondence. 3. Cowley, Malcolm, 1898- —Correspondence. 4. Authors, American—20th century—Biography. I. Faulkner, William, 1897-1962. II. Title. BIP

FAULKNER, William, 1897-1962. 813'.5'2 B
Selected letters of William Faulkner / edited by Joseph Blotner. 1st trade ed. New York : Random House, c1977. xvii, 488 p. ; 24 cm. Includes bibliographical references and index. [PS3511.A86Z546 1976] 76-14163 ISBN 0-394-49485-7 : 15.00
1. Faulkner, William, 1897-1962—Correspondence. I. Blotner, Joseph Leo, 1923-

FAULKNER, William, 1897-1962. 813'.5'2 B
Selected letters of William Faulkner / edited by Joseph Blotner. Limited 1st ed. Franklin Center, Pa. : Franklin Library, 1976. xxiii, 594 p., [1] leaf of plates : geneal. table, port. ; 24 cm. At head of title: First Edition Society. "Privately printed." Includes index. [PS3511.A86Z546 1976b] 77-358923
1. Faulkner, William, 1897-1962—Correspondence. 2. Authors, American—20th century—Correspondence. I. First Edition Society.

Faulkner, William, 1897-1962—Criticism and interpretation.

WITTENBERG, Judith Bryant, 1938- 813'.5'2
Faulkner : the transfiguration of biography / Judith Bryant Wittenberg. Lincoln : University of Nebraska Press, c1979. p. cm. Includes bibliographical references and index. [PS3511.A86Z9858] 79-9230 ISBN 0-8032-4707-9 : 17.50
1. Faulkner, William, 1897-1962—Criticism and interpretation. 2. Psychology and literature. 3. Fiction, Autobiographic—History and criticism. BIP

Faulkner, William, 1897-1962—Relationship with women—Meta Carpenter Wilde.

WILDE, Meta Carpenter. 813'.5'2 B
A loving gentleman : the love story of William Faulkner and Meta Carpenter / by Meta Carpenter Wilde and Orin Borsten. New York : Simon and Schuster, c1976. 334 p., [12] leaves of plates : ill. ; 22 cm. [PS3511.A86Z98568] 76-21878 ISBN 0-671-22323-2 : 8.95
1. Faulkner, William, 1897-1962—Relationship with women—Meta Carpenter Wilde. 2. Wilde, Meta Carpenter. I. Borsten, Orin, joint author. II. Title.

Faure, Gabriel Urbain, 1845-1924.

KoCHLIN, Charles Louis Eugene, 1867-1950. 780'.92'4 B
Gabriel Faure, 1845-1924 / Charles Kocchlin. New York : AMS Press, 1976. viii, 98 p. : port. ; 23 cm. Reprint of the 1945 ed. published by D. Dobson, London. Includes index. Bibliography: p. 93. [ML410.F27K72 1976] 75-41167 ISBN 0-404-14679-1 : 8.50
1. Faure, Gabriel Urbain, 1845-1924. BIP

SUCKLING, Norman. 928.4
Faure. New York, Pellegrini & Cudahy, 1951. vii, 229p. illus., ports., facsim. 19cm. (The Master musicians) [ML410] 52-6483
1. Faure, Gabriel Urbain, 1845-1924. I. Title. II. Series. BIP

SUCKLING, Norman. 780'.92'4 B
Faure / by Norman Suckling. Westport, Conn. : Greenwood Press, 1979. vii, 229 p., [7] leaves of plates : ill. ; 23 cm. Reprint of the 1951 ed. published by Dent, London, in series: The Master musicians. Includes index. "Catalogue of works": p. 210-216. [ML410.F27S8 1979] 78-23842 ISBN 0-313-20667-8 lib. bdg. : 19.75
1. Faure, Gabriel Urbain, 1845-1924. 2. Composers—France—Biography. I. Series: Master musicians series.

SUCKLING, Norman. 780'.92'4 B
Faure / by Norman Suckling. Westport, Conn. : Hyperion Press, 1979. p. cm. (Encore music editions) Reprint of the 1946 ed. published by Dent, London; Dutton, New York, in series: The Master musicians. New series. "Catalogue of works": p. Includes index. Bibliography: p. [ML410.F27S8 1979b] 78-13797 ISBN 0-88355-745-2 : 21.00
1. Faure, Gabriel Urbain, 1845-1924. 2. Composers—France—Biography. I. Series: The Master musicians. New series.

Faust, Frederick, 1892-1944.

EASTON, Robert Olney. 813'.5'2 B
Max Brand, the big westerner, by Robert Easton. [1st ed.] Norman, University of Oklahoma Press [1970] xii, 330 p. illus., ports. (part col.) 24 cm. "A Faust filmography": p. 305-309. [PS3511.A87Z65] 69-16732 ISBN 8-06-108703- 7.95
1. Faust, Frederick, 1892-1944. 2. Faust, Frederick, 1892-1944—Bibliography.

Faust, Frederick, 1892-1944—Bibl.

RICHARDSON, Darrell Coleman, 1918 ed. 928.1
Max Brand, the man & his work; critical appreciations and bibliography. [1st ed.] Los Angeles, Fantasy Pub. Co. [1952] 198p. illus., ports. 20cm. Bibliography: p. [127]-198. [PS3511.A87Z85] 52-11930
1. Faust, Frederick, 1892-1944—Bibl. 2. Faust, Frederick, 1892-1944. I. Title.

Fawcett, Millicent Garrett, Dame, 1847-1929.

FAWCETT, Millicent Garrett, Dame, 1847-1929. 324'.3'0924 B
What I remember / by Millicent Garrett Fawcett. Westport, Conn. : Hyperion Press, 1975. p. cm. Reprint of the 1925 ed. published by T. F. Unwin, London. Includes index. [JN979.F26 1975] 75-33939 ISBN 0-88355-261-2
1. Fawcett, Millicent Garrett, Dame, 1847-1929. 2. Great Britain—Politics and government—20th century. 3. Women—Suffrage—Great Britain. I. Title.

FAWCETT, Millicent Garrett, Dame, 1847-1929. 324'.3'0924 B
What I remember / by Millicent Garrett Fawcett. Westport, Conn. : Hyperion Press, 1975. p. cm. Reprint of the 1925 ed. published by T. F. Unwin, London. Includes index. [JN979.F26 1975] 75-33939 ISBN 0-88355-261-2 : 18.50
1. Fawcett, Millicent Garrett, Dame, 1847-1929. 2. Great Britain—Politics and government—20th century. 3. Women—Suffrage—Great Britain. I. Title.

Fawick, Thomas L.

DEPKE, John E. 609'.2'4 B
The Tom Fawick story; a biography of Thomas L. Fawick [by] John E. Depke. Cleveland [Great Lakes Lithograph Co.] 1972. 71 p. illus. 29 cm. [T40.F35D46] 72-95743
1. Fawick, Thomas L.

Faye, Alice, 1915-

MOSHIER, W. Franklyn. 791 43'028'0924
The Alice Faye movie book [by] W. Franklyn Moshier. [Harrisburg, Pa.] Stackpole Books [1974] 192 p. illus. 29 cm. Published in 1971 and 1972 under title: The films of Alice Faye. Discography; p. 185. [PN2287.F36M6 1974] 74-4170 ISBN 0-8117-0086-0 9.95
1. Faye, Alice, 1915- I. Title.

Fayrfax, Robert, 1464-1521.

WARREN, Edwin Brady, 1910- 783'.0924 B
Life and works of Robert Fayrfax, 1464-1521, by Edwin B. Warren. [Dallas] American Institute of Musicology, 1969. 213 p. illus., music, 17 plates (facsims.) 26 cm. (Musicological studies and documents, 22) Bibliography: p. 195-208. [ML410.F28W3] 75-25963
1. Fayrfax, Robert, 1464-1521. I. Series: American Institute of Musicology. Studies and documents, 22

Fayssoux, Peter Dott, 1745-1795.

DAVIDSON, Chalmers Gaston, 1907- 926.1
Friend of the people; the life of Dr. Peter Fayssoux of Charleston, South Carolina. Columbia, Medical Association of South Carolina, 1950. vii, 151 p. 20 cm. Bibliography: p. 142-151. [R154 F42D3] 50-9230
1. Fayssoux, Peter Dott, 1745-1795. I. Title.

Feagin, Mabel Livingston (Lightner)

FEAGIN, Mabel Livingston (Lightner) 1875- 920.7
No rocking chair got me! I've been writing ... my book, by Mabel Lightner Feagin. [Nashville? 1964] 279 p. illus., geneal. tables, ports. 24 cm. Running title: My book. [CT275.F4277A3] 64-19128
I. Title. II. Title: My book.

Fechter, Charles Albert, 1824-1879.

FIELD, Kate, 1838-1896. 792'.028'0924 B
Charles Albert Fechter. New York, B. Blom [1969] 205 p. facsim., ports. 20 cm. Reprint of the 1882 ed. [PN2287.F4F5 1969] 70-82827
1. Fechter, Charles Albert, 1824-1879. I. Title. BIP

Federal Party.

FAY, Bernard, 1893- 070'.924 B
The two Franklins: fathers of American democracy. New York, AMS Press [1969] xvi, 397 p. illus., map. 23 cm. Reprint of the 1933 ed. Bibliography: p. 363-377. [E302.6.B14F3 1969] 70-93277
1. Bache, Benjamin Franklin, 1769-1798. 2. Franklin, Benjamin, 1706-1790. 3. Federal Party. 4. Democratic Party. 5. U.S.—Politics and government—Constitutional period, 1789-1809. I. Title.

FAY, Bernard, 1893- 070'.924 B
The two Franklins: fathers of American democracy. Boston, Little, Brown, 1933. St. Clair Shores, Mich., Scholarly Press [1971] xvi, 397 p. illus. 22 cm. Includes bibliographical references. [E302.6.B14F3 1971] 78-145009 ISBN 0-403-00961-8
1. Bache, Benjamin Franklin, 1769-1798. 2. Franklin, Benjamin, 1706-1790. 3. Federal Party. 4. Democratic Party. 5. U.S.—Politics and government—Constitutional period, 1789-1809. I. Title. BIP

Feelings, Tom.

FEELINGS, Tom. 741'.092'4 B
Black pilgrimage. New York, Lothrop, Lee & Shepard Co. [1972] 72 p. illus. 29 cm. A black artist describes his life, from his birthplace in Brooklyn to his adopted home, Ghana, and how various experiences helped him develop new aspects of his talent. [NC139.F36A2] 92 70-177328 5.95
I. Title. BIP

Feeney, Robert Earl, 1913-

FEENEY, Robert Earl, 1913- 598.2'1'920924 B
Professor on the ice / Robert E. Feeney. Davis, Calif. : Pacific Portals, c1974. 164 p. : ill. ; 22 cm. [QH84.2.F43] 75-307044
1. Feeney, Robert Earl, 1913- 2. Biology—Antarctic regions. 3. Antarctic regions. I. Title.

Fei, Hsiao-t'ung.

FEI Hsiao-t'ung : 301'.092'4
the dilemma of a Chinese intellectual / selected and translated by James P. McGough. White Plains, N.Y. : M. E. Sharpe, c1979. 159 p. ; 24 cm. Includes bibliographical references. [HM22.C62F442] 79-66094 ISBN 0-87332-141-3 : 17.50
1. Fei, Hsiao-t'ung. 2. Sociologists—China—Biography. 3. China—Intellectual life. I. Fei, Hsiao-t'ung. II. McGough, James P.

Feild, Reshad.

FEILD, Reshad. 297'.4'0924 B
The last barrier / Reshad Feild ; illustrated by Salik Chalom. 1st ed. New York : Harper & Row, c1976. 183 p. : ill. ; 21 cm. [BP189.6.F44 1976] 75-9345 ISBN 0-06-062585-6 : 8.95
1. Feild, Reshad. 2. Sufism. I. Title. BIP

FEILD, Reshad. 297'.4'0924 B
The last barrier / Reshad Feild ; illustrated by Salik Chalom. London : Turnstone Books, 1976. [7], 183 p. : ill. ; 20 cm. [BP189.6.F44 1976b] 77-362800 ISBN 0-85500-063-5 : £2.95
1. Feild, Reshad. 2. Sufism. 3. Sufism—Biography. I. Title.

Fejos, Pal.

DODDS, John Wendell, 1902- 301.2'092'4 B
The several lives of Paul Fejos; a Hungarian-American odyssey, by John W. Dodds. [New York] Wenner-Gren Foundation, 1973. ix, 113 p. illus. 25 cm. Includes bibliographical references. [GN21.F44D62] 73-89901
1. Fejos, Pal. 2. Wenner-Gren Foundation for Anthropological Research, New York. I. Title.

Felipe de Jesus, Saint, d. 1597.

MAGARET, Helene, 1906- 922.272
Felipe, being the little known history of the only canonized saint born in North America. Milwaukee, Bruce Pub. Co. [1962] 107p. illus. 22cm. [BX4700.F25M3] 62-19405
1. Felipe de Jesus, Saint, d. 1597. I. Title.

Felipe II, King of Spain, 1527-1598.

GRIERSON, Edward, 1914- 946'.04
The fatal inheritance; Philip II and the Spanish Netherlands. [1st ed.] Garden City, N.Y., Doubleday, 1969. xii, 390 p. maps. 25 cm. (The Crossroads of world history series) "Bibliographical note": p. [371]-373. [DP179.G7] 69-12199 6.95
1. Felipe II, King of Spain, 1527-1598. 2. Netherlands—History—Wars of Independence, 1556-1648. 3. Spain—History—Philip II, 1556-1598. I. Title.

GRIERSON, Edward, 946'.04'0924 B
1914-
King of two worlds : Philip II of Spain / Edward Grierson. New York : Putnam, [1974] 240 p. : ill. (some col.) ; 26 cm. Includes index. Bibliography: p. 233-234. [DP178.G74] 74-78401 ISBN 0-399-11384-3 : 12.95
1. Felipe II, King of Spain, 1527-1598. I. Title. **BIP**

HUME, Martin Andrew 946'.04'0924
Sharp, 1847-1910.
Philip II of Spain. Edited with notes by Henry Ketcham. New York, Haskell House, 1969. 325 p. illus., port. 23 cm. Reprint of the 1897 ed. Bibliography: p. 323-325. [DP178.H92 1969] 68-25245
1. Felipe II, King of Spain, 1527-1598. 2. Spain—History—Philip II, 1556-1598. I. Title.

HUME, Martin Andrew 946'.04'0924
Sharp, 1847-1910.
Philip II of Spain. Edited with notes by Henry Ketcham. Westport, Conn., Greenwood Press [1970] 325 p. illus., port. 23 cm. Reprint of the 1903 ed. Bibliography: p. 323-325. [DP178.H92 1970] 69-13940
1. Felipe II, King of Spain, 1527-1598. 2. Spain—History—Philip II, 1556-1598. I. Title.

MARIEJOL, Jean 946'.04'0924 B
Hippolyte, 1855-1934.
Philip II, the first modern king. Translated from the French by Warren B. Wells. Freeport, N.Y., Books for Libraries Press [1972] p. Reprint of the 1933 ed. (New York, Harper) Bibliography: p. [DP178.M3 1972] 72-7105 ISBN 0-8369-6948-0
1. Felipe II, King of Spain, 1527-1598. I. Title.

PARKER, Noel 946'.04'0924 B
Geoffrey.
Philip II / by Geoffrey Parker. 1st ed. Boston : Little, Brown, c1978. p. cm. (The Library of world biography) Includes bibliographical references and index. [DP178.P37] 78-17122 ISBN 0-316-69080-5 : 8.95
1. Felipe II, King of Spain, 1527-1598. 2. Spain—History—Philip II, 1556-1598. 3. Spain—Kings and rulers—Biography. I. Title.

PETRIE, Sir Charles 923.146
Alexander, bart., 1895-
Philip II of Spain. New York, Norton [1963] 318 p. illus., ports., maps, geneal table. 22 cm. Bibliographical footnotes. [DP178.P43] 62-12285
1. Felipe II, King of Spain, 1527-1598. I. Title.

PIERSON, Peter. 946'.04'0924 B
Philip II of Spain / Peter Pierson. London : Thames and Hudson, 1975. 240 p., [8] leaves of plates ; 23 cm. (Men in office) Includes index. Bibliography: p. [216]-223. [DP178.P64] 76-351952 ISBN 0-500-87003-9 : 15.00
1. Felipe II, King of Spain, 1527-1598. 2. Spain—History—Philip II, 1556-1598. I. Title.
Distributed by Transatlantic Arts

PRESCOTT, William 946'.04'0924 B
Hickling, 1796-1859.
History of the reign of Philip the Second, King of Spain. Edited by Wilfred Harold Munro and comprising the notes of the ed. by John Foster Kirk. Montezuma ed. New York, AMS Press [1968] 4 v. illus. 22 cm. (His The works of William H. Prescott, v. 16-19) Reprint of the 1904 ed. Includes bibliographies. [DP178.P8 1968] 72-186524
1. Felipe II, King of Spain, 1527-1598. 2. Spain—History—Philip II, 1556-1598. I. Title.

RULE, John C., ed. 923.146
The character of Philip II: the problem of moral judgements in history. Edited with an introd. by John C. Rule and John J. TePaske Boston, Heath [1963] 103 p. 24 cm. (Problems in European civilization) Includes bibliography. [DP179.R8] 63-12805
1. Felipe II, King of Spain, 1527-1598. I. TePaske, John J., joint ed. II. Title.

WALSH, William Thomas, 923.146
1891-1949.
Philip II New York, McMullen Books [1953, c1937] 770p. 24cm. Includes bibliography. [DP178] 53-11802
1. Felipe II King of Spain, 1527-1598. I. Title.

WILBUR, Marguerite 923.146
Knowlton Eyer, 1889-
The unquenchable flame; the life of Philip II. New York, Hastings House [1952] 342 p. 24 cm. [DP178.W5] 52-11806
1. Felipe II, King of Spain, 1527-1598. I. Title.

Felix, Elisa Rachel, 1821?-1858.

AGATE, James 792'.028'0924 B
Evershed, 1877-1947.
Rachel. New York, B. Blom [1969] 94 p. port. 23 cm. Reprint of the 1928 ed. Bibliography: p. 93-94. [PN2638.R3A5 1969] 72-84504
1. Felix, Elisa Rachel, 1821?-1858.

BEAUVALLET, Leon, 1829- 792'.0924
1885.
Rachel and the New World; translated and edited by Colin Clair. London, New York [etc.] Abelard-Schuman, 1967 224 p. cm. Translation of Rachel et le nouveau monde. [PN2638.R3B4 1967] 67-13457 unpriced
1. Felix, Elisa Rachel, 1821?-1858. 2. U.S.—Descr. & trav.—1848-1865. 3. Cuba—Descr. & trav. I. Title.

FALK, Bernard, 792'.028'0924 B
1882-1960.
Rachel the immortal: stage-queen, grande amoureuse, street urchin, fine lady; a frank biography. Twelve special plates by Frank C. Pape and numerous other illus. New York, B. Blom, 1972. 334 p. illus. 26 cm. Reprint of the 1935 ed. Bibliography: p. 317-322. [PN2638.R3F25 1972] 70-91900 12.50
1. Felix, Elisa Rachel, 1821-1858. I. Title.

GRIBBLE, Francis 792'.028'0924 B
Henry, 1862-1946.
Rachel, her stage life and her real life. New York, B. Blom, 1972. xii, 275 p. illus. 21 cm. Reprint of the 1911 ed. [PN2638.R3G8 1972] 70-93163
1. Felix, Elisa Rachel, 1821?-1858. I. Title.

RICHARDSON, Joanna. 927.92
Rachel. [1st U. S. A. ed.] New York, Putnam, 1957. 222p. illus. 23cm. Includes bibliographies. [PSn2638] 57-13758
1. Felix, Elisa Rachel, 1821?-1858. I. Title.

Fell, John, 1721-1798.

FELL, John, 1721- 973.3'12'0924
1798.
Delegate from New Jersey; the journal of John Fell. Edited with an introd. by Donald W. Whisenhunt. Port Washington, N.Y., Kennikat Press, 1973, [i.e. 1974] 212 p. 24 cm. (National University publications) Facsimile of t.p. of original ms.: Journal, kept by Judge John Fell—while member of Congress for the State of New Jersey, 1778. Bibliography: p. 204-205. [E302.6.F43A33] 73-83264 ISBN 0-8046-9041-3 9.50
1. Fell, John, 1721-1798. I. Title. **BIP**

Feller, Robert William Andrew, 1918-

SCHOOR, Gene 927.96357
Bob Feller, Hall of Fame strikeout star. Garden City, N.Y., Doubleday [c.1962] 191p. 22cm. 62-11452 2.95
1. Feller, Robert William Andrew, 1918- I. Title.

Fellig, Arthur, 1900-

[FELLIG, Arthur] 1900- 927.7
Weegee, by Weegee [pseud.] An autobiography. New York, Ziff-Davis [c.1961] 159p. illus. 61-14233 5.00
I. Title.

FELLIG, Arthur, 1900- 770'.92'4 B
1968.
Weegee : an autobiography / by Weegee [i.e. A. Fellig]. New York : Da Capo Press, 1975, c1961. 159 p., [28] leaves of plates : ill. ; 23 cm. Reprint of the ed. published by Ziff-Davis Pub. Co., New York. [TR140.F4A3 1975] 75-4885 ISBN 0-306-70737-3 lib.bdg. : 11.95
1. Fellig, Arthur, 1900-

Fellini, Federico.

FELLINI, 791.43'0233'0924 B
Federico.
Fellini on Fellini / edited by Anna Keel and Christian Strich ; translated by Isabel Quigly. London : Methuen, 1976. 180 p. ; 21 cm. Translation of Aufsatze und Notizen. Filmography: p. 167-175. [PN1998.A3F2913] 76-362770 ISBN 0-413-33640-9 : £4.50. ISBN 0-413-33650-6 pbk.
1. Fellini, Federico. I. Title. **BIP**

FELLINI, 791.43'0233'0924 B
Federico.
Fellini on Fellini / Federico Fellini ; translated from the Italian by Isabel Quigley. [New York] : Delacorte Press/S. Lawrence, c1976. 180 p. : ill. ; 21 cm. German translation has title: Aufsatze und Notizen. Includes index. Filmography: p. 167-175. [PN1998.A3F337] 76-363747 ISBN 0-440-02528-1 : 7.95
1. Fellini, Federico. I. Title.

KETCHAM, Charles 791.43'0233'0924
B.
Federico Fellini : the search for a new mythology / by Charles B. Ketcham. New York : Paulist Press, c1976. 94 p. ; 21 cm. (The Mythmakers) (An Exploration book) Includes bibliographical references. [PN1998.A3F339] 76-18045 ISBN 0-8091-1957-9 pbk. : 3.95
1. Fellini, Federico. **BIP**

SALACHAS, 791.43'0233'0924
Gilbert.
Federico Fellini. Translated by Rosalie Siegel. New York, Crown Publishers [1969] 224 p. illus., ports. 17 cm. (Editions Seghers' Cinema d'aujourd'hui) Contents.Contents.—Federico Fellini; an essay, by G. Salachas (p. [11]-89)—The cinema according to Federico Fellini.—The work of Federico Fellini; excerpts from screenplays and film treatments.—Critical spectrum [articles] by G. Agel and others.—Witnesses [articles] by D. Delouche and others. —Selected bibliography (p. 213-215)—Filmography (p. 215-221) [PN1998.A3F363] 68-9071 2.95
1. Fellini, Federico. 2. Moving-pictures—Italy.

SOLMI, Angelo. 704.092
Fellini; tr. [from Italian] by Elizabeth Greenwood. London, Merlin, 1967. 183p. front., 8 plates (incl. ports.) 26cm. Orig. pub. as "Storia di Federico Fellini. Milano, Rizzoli, 1962. Bibl. [PN1998.A3F3643] 67-89255 7.50
1. Fellini, Federico. I. Title.
Distributed by Humanities, New York.

WALL, James 796.43'092'2
McKendree, 1928-
Three European directors: Francois Truffaut [by] James M. Wall. Fellini's film journey [by] Roger Ortmayer. Luis Bunuel and the death of God [by] Peter P. Schillaci. Edited by James M. Wall. Grand Rapids, Eerdmans [1973] 224 p. 21 cm. Includes bibliographies. [PN1998.A2W33] 72-84010 ISBN 0-8028-1504-9 3.95
1. Truffaut, Francois. 2. Fellini, Federico. 3. Bunuel, Luis, 1900- I. Ortmayer, Roger. II. Schillaci, Peter P., 1927- III. Title.

Fels, Joseph, 1854-1914.

DUDDEN, Arthur Power, 330.15'5 B
1921-
Joseph Fels and the single-tax movement. Philadelphia, Temple University Press, 1971. xi, 308 p. ports. 22 cm. Includes bibliographical references. [HD1313.D8] 77-157738 ISBN 0-87722-010-7 10.00
1. Fels, Joseph, 1854-1914. 2. Single tax. I. Title. **BIP**

Felt, Jonathan, d. 1800.

FELT, E. J. 973.3'3'0924 B
The junior captain of the Massachusetts Line, 1775-1783 : a Bicentennial memorial / [by E. J. Felt]. [Uvalde, Tex.] : Felt, c1977. 26 p. ; 23 cm. [E263.M4F353] 77-371850
1. Felt, Jonathan, d. 1800. 2. Soldiers—United States—Biography. 3. United States—History—Revolution,1775-1783—Campaigns and battles. I. Title.

Female offenders—Biography.

MACCLURE, Victor, 364.3'74'0922 B
1887-
She stands accused : being a series of accounts of the lives and deeds of notorious women, murderesses, cheats, cozeners, on whom justice was executed, and of others, who, accused of crimes, were acquitted at least in law : drawn from authenticated sources / by Victor MacClure ; with ill. by the author. Westport, Conn. : Hyperion Press, 1975. 239 p., [6] leaves of plates : ill. ; 23 cm. Reprint of the 1935 ed. published by Lippincott, Philadelphia. Includes index. [HV6245.M23 1975] 74-10429 ISBN 0-88355-196-9 : 12.00
1. Female offenders—Biography. 2. Crime and criminals—Biography. I. Title. **BIP**

Female offenders—Great Britain.

JENKINS, Elizabeth, 364.1'0922 B
1907-
Six criminal women. Freeport, N.Y., Books for Libraries Press [1971, c1949] vii, 224 p. 23 cm. (Biography index reprint series) [HV6945.J4 1971] 76-142822 ISBN 0-8369-8069-7
1. Female offenders—Great Britain. I. Title. **BIP**

Female offenders—Great Britain—Case studies.

HARTMAN, Mary S. 364.1'523'0922
Victorian murderesses : a true history of thirteen respectable French and English women accused of unspeakable crimes / Mary S. Hartman. New York : Schocken Books, 1976. p. cm. Includes index. Bibliography: p. [HV6535.G4H29] 75-34877 ISBN 0-8052-3608-2 : 15.00
1. Female offenders—Great Britain—Case studies. 2. Female offenders—France—Case studies. 3. Murder—Great Britain—Case studies. 4. Murder—France—Case studies. I. Title. **BIP**

Feminists—United States—Biography.

LAGEMANN, Ellen 301.24'2'0922 B
Condliffe, 1945-
A generation of women : education in the lives of progressive reformers / Ellen Condliffe Lagemann. Cambridge, Mass. : Harvard University Press, 1979. p. cm. Includes bibliographical references and index. [HQ1412.L33] 79-13528 ISBN 0-674-34471-5 : 12.50
1. Feminists—United States—Biography. 2. Social reformers—United States—Biography. 3. Education of women—United States—Biography. I. Title. **BIP**

THESE modern women 301.41'2'0922 : autobiographies of women in the twenties / edited, with an introd. by Elaine Showalter. Old Westbury, N.Y. : Feminist Press, [1978] p. cm. Reprint of 17 essays and 3 responses by psychologists taken from The Nation, 1926-1927. Includes bibliographical references. [HQ1426.T5] 78-8750 ISBN 0-912670-46-0 pbk. : 4.95
1. Feminists—United States—Biography. 2. Women—Psychology—Addresses, essays, lectures. 3. United States—Social conditions—1918-1932. I. Showalter, Elaine. BIP

Feminists—United States—Biography—Juvenile literature.

DECLUE, Denise. 301.41'2'0922 B
Women shaping history / Denise DeClue; [ill. by Jackie Denison]. Milwaukee : Raintree Publishers, c1979. p. cm. Bibliography: p. Pesents brief biographies of women prominent in women's movements, including Lucretia Mott, Lucy Stone, Elizabeth Cady Stanton, and Gloria Steinam. [HQ1412.D4] 920 79-13734 ISBN 0-8172-1380-5 lib. bdg. : 7.49
1. Feminists—United States—Biography—Juvenile literature. 2. Women's rights—United States—Juvenile literature. I. Denison, Jackie. II. Title. BIP

Fenelon, Fania.

FENELON, Fania. 940.54'72'43
Playing for time / Fenia Fenelon with Marcelle Routier; translated from the French by Judith Landry. New York : Berkley Pub. Corp., 1979, c1976. 289p. ; 18 cm. (A Berkley Book) [M51429.F436A33] ISBN 0-425-04199-9 pbk. : 2.50
1. Fenelon, Fania. 2. Musicians — France — Biography 3. World War, 1939-1945 — Personal narratives, French. 4. World War 1939-1945 — Prisoners and prisons, German. I. Routier, Marcelle joint author. II. Title.
L.C. card no. for 1977 Atheneum Publishers ed.: 77-5502 BIP

Fenelon, Francois de Salignac de la Mothe-, Abp., 1651-1715.

LITTLE, Katharine Day. 928.4
Francois de Fenelon, study of a personality. [1st ed.] New York, Harper [1951] x, 273 p. port. 22 cm. Bibliography: p. 261-264. [PQ1796.L58] 51-2713
1. Fenelon, Francois de Salignac de la Mothe-, Abp., 1651-1715. I. Title.

Feng, Yu-hsiang, 1882-1948.

SHERIDAN, James E 951.040924
Chinese warlord; the career of Feng Yu-hsiang [by] James E. Sheridan. Stanford, Calif., Stanford University Press, 1966. x, 386 p. maps. 24 cm. Bibliography: p. [357]-372. [DS778.F45S45] 65-18978
1. Feng, Yu-hsiang, 1882-1948. I. Title. BIP

Fenians.

O'LEARY, John, 1830-1907. 941.5'8'0924
Recollections of Fenians and Fenianism. Introd. by Marcus Bourke. New York, Barnes & Noble [1969, c1968] 2 v. ports. 23 cm. On spine: Fenians and Fenianism. Reprint of the 1896 ed. [DA952.O5A2 1969] 78-4267
1. Fenians. 2. Ireland—History—1837-1901. I. Title. II. Title: Fenians and Fenianism. BIP

Fenlon, Thomas F.

ROARK, Garland. 910.45
Captain Thomas Fenlon, master mariner. New York, Messner [1958] 192 p. 22 cm. Includes bibliography. [G530.F38R6] 58-6022
1. Fenlon, Thomas F. 2. Seafaring life.

Fennell, James,

FENNELL, James, 1766-1816. 792'.028'0924 B
An apology for the life of James Fennell. New York, B. Blom [1969] 510 p. 21 cm. Reprint of the 1814 ed. [PN2598.F4A3 1969] 77-82826
I. Title.

Fenollosa, Ernest Francisco, 1853-1908.

CHISOLM, Lawrence W. 927
Fenollosa: the Far East and American culture. New Haven, Conn., Yale, 1963. xiii, 297p. illus., ports., facsims., plans. 25cm. (Yale pubns. in Amer. studies, 8) Bibl. 63-17024 7.50
1 Fenollosa, Ernest Francisco, 1853-1908. 2. U.S.—Relations (general) with the East (Far East) 3. East (Far East)—Relations (general) with the U.S. I. Title. II. Series.

Feodorov, Leonid Ivanovich, Exarch, 1879-1935.

MAILLEUX, Paul 922.247
Exarch Leonid Feodorov, bridgebuilder between Rome and Moscow. New York, Kenedy [c.1964] vi, 247p. illus., ports. 22cm. Bibl. 64-14560 4.95
1. Feodorov, Leonid Ivanovich, Exarch, 1879-1935. I. Title.

Ferber, Edna, 1887-1968—Biography.

FERBER, Edna, 1887-1968. 928.1
A peculiar treasure; [autobiography] Garden City, N. Y., Doubleday, 1960. 383 p. illus. 24 cm. [PS3511.E46Z5 1960] 60-8865
I. Title.

GILBERT, Julie Goldsmith. 813'.5'2 B
Ferber, a biography / Julie Goldsmith Gilbert. 1st ed. Garden City, N.Y. : Doubleday, 1978. 445 p. [16] leaves of plates : ill. ; 22 cm. Includes index. [PS3511.E46Z67] 76-57512 ISBN 0-385-03960-3 : 10.50
1. Ferber, Edna, 1887-1968—Biography. 2. Authors, American—20th century—Biography. I. Title.

Ferdinando II, King of the Two Sicilies, 1810-1859.

ACTON, Harold Mario Mitchell, 1904- 923.145
The last Bourbons of Naples (1825-1861) New York, St. Martin's Press [1962, c1961] 559 p. illus. 23 cm. Includes bibliography. [DG848.46.A25 1962] 62-7507
1. Ferdinando II, King of the Two Sicilies, 1810-1859. 2. Francesco II, King of the Two Sicilies, 1836-1894. I. Title.

Ferguson, George Howard, 1870-1946.

OLIVER, Peter N. 971.3'03'0924 B
G. Howard Ferguson : Ontario tory / Peter Oliver. Toronto ; Buffalo [N.Y.] : University of Toronto Press for the Ontario Historical Studies Series, c1977. xv, 501 p., [9] leaves of plates : ill. ; 24 cm. (Ontario historical studies series) ISSN 0380-9188) Includes index. Bibliography: p. [484]-486. [F1058.F466O43] 77-378936 ISBN 0-8020-3346-6 : 14.95
1. Ferguson, George Howard, 1870-1946. 2. Ontario—Politics and government. 3. Prime ministers—Ontario—Biography. I. Title. II. Series. BIP

Ferguson, Harry George, 1884-1960.

WYMER, Norman. v. 12
Harry Ferguson. London, Phoenix House; New York, Roy [1961] 103 p. front., 8 plates (incl. ports.) 19 cm. ("Living biographies" series)
1. Ferguson, Harry George, 1884- I. Title.

Ferguson, Harry, 1884-1960.

FRASER, Colin. 338.7'68'17631 B
Tractor pioneer; the life of Harry Ferguson. Athens, Ohio University Press [1973] vi, 294 p. illus. 23 cm. First published in 1972 under title: Harry Ferguson: inventor and pioneer. [TL140.F47F7 1973] 73-85451 ISBN 0-8214-0133-5 10.00
1. Ferguson, Harry, 1884-1960. I. Title. BIP

Ferguson, Hill.

HAMES, Carl Martin. 976.1'781'060924 B
Hill Ferguson, his life and works / by Carl Martin Hames. University : University of Alabama Press, c1977. p. cm. Includes index. Bibliography: p. [HV28.F4H35] 77-23109 ISBN 0-8173-5264-3 : 8.75
1. Ferguson, Hill. 2. Philanthropists—Alabama—Biography. I. Title.

Ferguson, Hugh, 1950-1974.

FERGUSON, Hugh, 1950-1974. 362.2'93'0924 B
Confessions of a long distance acid head / [by] Hugh Fergusson [i.e. Ferguson]. London : Mitre Press, 1976. 66 p. ; 23 cm. [HV5840.G7F47 1976] 76-676785 ISBN 0-7051-0232-7 : £2.00
1. Ferguson, Hugh, 1950-1974. 2. Narcotic addicts—Great Britain—Biography. 3. Lysergic acid diethylamide. I. Title.

Ferguson, Ira Lunan,

FERGUSON, Ira Lunan, 1904- 973.9'0924
I dug graves at night to attend college by day; the story of a West Indian Negro-American's first 30 years in the United States; an autobiography. Brooklyn, N.Y., Gaus [1967- c1968- v. facsims., ports. 24cm. [E185.97.F4] (B) 67-31239 6.95
I. Title.
Order from The Lunan-Ferguson Lib., 2219 Clement St., San Francisco, Calif. 94121.

Ferguson, John T.

DE KRUIF, Paul Henry, 1890- 926.1
A man against insanity. [1st ed.] New York, Harcourt, Brace [1957] 246 p. 21 cm. Includes bibliography. [R154.F47D4] 57-6218
1. Ferguson, John T. I. Title.

Ferguson, Max.

FERGUSON, Max. 791.44'0924
And now here's Max; [a funny kind of autobiography. With pictures by Doug Wright. Introd. by Allan McFee. New York, McGraw Hill Co. of Canada, c1967] 167 p. illus. 21 cm. [PN1991.4.F4A3] 67-26556
I. Title.

Ferguson, Samuel, 1874-1950.

KELLOGG, Charles Wetmore, 1880- 926.213
Samuel Ferguson, the man and his works; with appreciation by members of his family and some close associates. Hartford [Hartford Electric Light Co.] 1951. 95 p. illus. 25 cm. [HD9685.U7H35] 52-19935
1. Ferguson, Samuel, 1874-1950. 2. Hartford Electric Light Company. I. Title.

Ferguson, Sarah.

FERGUSON, Sarah. 942.084'092'4 B
To the place of shells / Sarah Ferguson. New York : St. Martin's Press, 1975. 171 p. ; 23 cm. [CT788.F35A33 1975] 75-7635 8.95
1. Ferguson, Sarah. I. Title.

Ferlinghetti, Lawrence—Biography.

CHERKOVSKI, Necli. 811'.5'4 B
Ferlinghetti, a biography / by Neeli Cherkovski. 1st ed. Garden City, N.Y. : Doubleday, 1979. 254 p., [12] leaves of plates : ill. ; 22 cm. Includes index. Bibliography: p. 243-244. [PS3511.E557Z6] 77-89876 ISBN 0-385-12312-4 : 10.95
1. Ferlinghetti, Lawrence—Biography. 2. Authors, American—20th century—Biography. I. Title.

Fermi, Enrico, 1901-1954.

EPSTEIN, Samuel, 1909- 539.7'0924 B
Enrico Fermi, father of atomic power, by Sam and Beryl Epstein. Illustrated by Raymond Burns. Champaign, Ill., Garrard Pub. Co. [1970] 95 p. illus. (part col.), ports. 24 cm. (Americans all) A biography of the Nobel prize-winning physicist who designed the first atomic piles, produced the first nuclear chain reaction, and aided in the development of the atomic bomb. [PZ10.E6En] 92 74-103955 ISBN 0-8116-4558-4 2.49
1. Fermi, Enrico, 1901-1954. I. Epstein, Beryl (William) 1910- joint author. II. Burns, Raymond, 1924- illus. III. Title.

FERMI, Laura 925.3
Atoms in the family my life with Enrico Fermi. [Chicago] Univ. of Chicago Pr. [1961, c.1954] 267p. illus. (Phoenix bk. P58) 1.65 pap.,
1. Fermi, Enrico, 1901- I. Title.

LATIL, Pierre de, 1905- 539.70924 B
Enrico Fermi; the man and his theories. Translated from the French by Len Ortzen. [1st American ed.] New York, P. S. Eriksson [1966, c1964] 178 p. illus., facsims., ports. 24 cm. (A Profile in science) Bibliography: p. [171]-173. [QC774.F4L313 1966] 66-17490
1. Fermi, Enrico, 1901-1954.

LICHELLO, Robert, 1926- 539.7'0924 B
Enrico Fermi, father of the atomic bomb. Charlotteville, N.Y., SamHar Press, 1971. 31 p. 22 cm. (Outstanding personalities, no 11) Bibliography: p. 30-31. [QC16.F46L52] 70-185667
1. Fermi, Enrico, 1901-1954. 2. Atomic bomb—History.

SEGRE, Emilio. 539.7'0924 B
Enrico Fermi: physicist. Chicago, University of Chicago Press [1970] x, 276 p. illus., ports. 23 cm. Bibliography: p. 251-268. [QC16.F46S4] 71-107424 ISBN 0-226-74472-8 6.95
1. Fermi, Enrico, 1901-1954. BIP

Fermi, Enrico, 1901-1954—Juvenile literature.

FABER, Doris, 1924- 92
Enrico Fermi, atomic pioneer. Illus. by David Hodges. Englewood Cliffs, N.J., Prentice [c.1966] 86p. illus. 21cm. [QC774.F4F3] 66-10563 3.50
1. Fermi, Enrico, 1901-1954—Juvenile literature. I. Title.

Fermor, Patrick Leigh.

FERMOR, Patrick Leigh. 914'.04'55
A time of gifts / Patrick Leigh Fermor. 1st U.S. ed. New York : Harper & Row, c1977. 291 p. ; 22 cm. "A Cass Canfield book." Includes index. [D923.F47 1977] 77-3747 ISBN 0-06-011224-7 : 10.95
1. Fermor, Patrick Leigh. 2 Europe—Description and travel—1971- 3. Central Europe—Description and travel. I. Title. BIP

Fernandez, Agustin, 1928-

FERNANDEZ, Agustin, 1928- 759.97291
Agustin Fernandez, by R. C. Kenedy. Joseph A. Novak, editor. [New York, Printed by Rapoport Print. Corp., 1973] 1 v. (unpaged) illus. 28 cm. Includes bibliography. [N6605.F47K46] 73-77897
1. Fernandez, Agustin, 1928- I. Kenedy, R. C.

Fernandez de Cordova y Aguilar, Gonzalvo, called El Gran Capitan, 1453-1515.

PURCELL, Mary. 923.546
The great captain: Gonzalo Fernandez de Cordoba. [1st ed.] Garden City, N.Y., Doubleday, 1962. 238 p. 22 cm. Includes bibliography. [DP166.F4P8] 62-15895
1. Fernandez de Cordova y Aguilar, Gonzalvo, called El Gran Capitan, 1453-1515. I. Title.

Fernow, Bernhard Eduard, 1851-1923.

RODGERS, Andrew Denny, 1900- 634.9'0924 B
Bernhard Eduard Fernow; a story of North American forestry, by Andrew Denny Rodgers, III. New York, Hafner Pub. Co., 1968 [c1951] 623 p. port. 24 cm. Bibliographical footnotes. [SD129.F4R6 1968] 68-58752 11.00
1. Fernow, Bernhard Eduard, 1851-1923. 2. Forests and forestry—North America. I. Title. BIP

Ferrari, Enzo, 1898-

TANNER, Hans, fl.1958- 629.22'8
Ferrari. New York, Drake Publishers [1974] p. cm. [TL236.T3 1974] 73-18458 ISBN 0-87749-618-8 14.95
1. Ferrari, Enzo, 1898- 2. Ferrari automobile.

Ferrari, Giuseppe, 1811-1876.

LOVETT, Clara Maria, 1939- 945'.08'0924
Giuseppe Ferrari and the Italian Revolution / by Clara M. Lovett. Chapel Hill : University of North Carolina Press, c1979. xiii, 278 p. : port. ; 22 cm. Includes index. Bibliography: p. 249-267. [DG552.8.F46L68] 78-24099 ISBN 0-8078-1354-0 : 15.00
1. Ferrari, Giuseppe, 1811-1876. 2. Italy—Politics and government—19th century. 3. France—Intellectual life. 4. Statesmen—Italy—Biography. 5. Intellectuals—Italy—Biography. I. Title. BIP

Ferraro, Norma Downey.

FERRARO, Norma Downey. 271.9
Few are chosen. [1st ed.] New York, Harper [1953] 307 p. 22 cm. Autobiographical. [BX4216.F4A3] 53-5367
I. Title.

Ferreira da Silva, Virgolino, known as Lampeao, 1900-1938.

CHANDLER, Billy Jaynes. 364.1'5'0924 B
The bandit king : Lampiao of Brazil / by Billy Jaynes Chandler. 1st ed. College Station : Texas A&M University Press, c1978. xii, 262 p., [6] leave of plates : ill. ; 24 cm. Includes index. Bibliography: p. [248]-254. [F2583.F472C48] 77-99275 ISBN 0-89096-050-X : 15.00
1. Ferreira da Silva, Virgolino, known as Lampeao, 1900-1938. 2. Brigands and robbers—Brazil, Northeast—Biography. 3. Brazil, Northeast—History. I. Title. BIP

Ferrier, Kathleen, 1912-1953.

CARDUS, Neville, 1889- ed. 927.8
Kathleen Ferner, a memoir. With contributions by Neville Cardus [and others] New York, Putnam [1955] 125 p. illus., ports. 23 cm. "Records made by Kathleen Ferrier": p. 120-125. [ML420.F35C3] 55-10098
1. Ferrier, Kathleen, 1912-1953. 2. Ferrier, Kathleen, 1912-1953—Discography.

Ferron, Marie Rose, 1902-1966.

BOYER, Onesimus Alfred, 1874- 922.273
She wears a crown of thorns Marie Rose Ferron (1902-1936) known as 'Little Rose,' the stigmatized ecstatic of Woonsocket, R. I. [4th ed.] New York, Benziger Bros., 1949. 364p. illus. 22cm. [BX4705.F445B6 1955] 55-36607
1. Ferron, Marie Rose, 1902-1966. 2. Stigmatization. I. Title.

BOYER, Onesimus Alfred, 1874- 922.273
She wears a crown of thorns; Marie Rose Ferron (1902-1936) known as 'Little Rose,' the stigmatized ecstatic of Woônsocket, R. I. By Rev. O. A. Boyer... 3d ed. Ellenburg, N. Y., The author, 1944. xv, 286p. front., plates(ports. 23cm. 'Some literature on mysticism' : p. 221-225. [BX4705.F445B6 1944] 44-31993
1. Ferron, Marie Rose, 1902-1936. 2. Stigmatixation. I. Title.

Ferry, Bryan.

BALFOUR, Rex. 784'.092'4 B
The Bryan Ferry story / as told by Rex Balfour. London : M. Dempsey, 1976. 128 p. : ill. ; 20 cm. [ML420.F36B3] 77-360344 ISBN 0-86044-015-X : £1.50
1. Ferry, Bryan. 2. Rock musicians—England—Biography. I. Title.

Ferry, Dexter Mason, 1833-1907.

FERRY, Marian Chapman. v. 12
Dexter Mason Ferry, a nineteenth century capitalist. [Detroit] 1957. vi, 158 p. illus., ports., maps. Bibliography: p. 155-158. 68-67453
1. Ferry, Dexter Mason, 1833-1907. 2. Michigan—Authors. I. Title.

Fersen, Hans Axel von, greve, 1755-1810.

BARTON, Hildor Arnold, 1929- 355'.0092'4 B
Count Hans Axel von Fersen : aristocrat in an age of revolution / H. Arnold Barton. Boston : Twayne Publishers, [1975] 530 p. : port. ; 24 cm. (The Library of Scandinavian studies ; v. 3) Includes index. Bibliography: p. 491-512. [DL750.F4B37] 74-22113 ISBN 0-8057-5363-X : 12.50
1. Fersen, Hans Axel von, greve, 1755-1810. I. Title. II. Series.

Fessenden, Reginald Aubrey, 1866-1932.

FESSENDEN, Helen May Trott. 621.3841'092'4 B
Fessenden, builder of tomorrows, by Helen M. Fessenden. Index by Ormond Raby. New York, Arno Press, 1974 [c1940] vi, 390 p. illus. 23 cm. (Telecommunications) Reprint of the ed. published by Coward-McCann, New York. Bibliography: p. 353-362. [TK6545.F4F4 1974] 74-4681 ISBN 0-405-06047-5
1. Fessenden, Reginald Aubrey, 1866-1932. I. Title. II. Series: Telecommunications (New York, 1974-

Fessenden, William Pitt, 1806-1869.

FESSENDEN, Francis, 1839-1906. 973.7'0924 B
LIfe and public services of William Pitt Fessenden. New York, Da Capo Press, 1970 [c1907] 2 v. ports. 24 cm. (A Da Capo Press reprint edition) [E415.9.F4F4 1970] 70-87532
1. Fessenden, William Pitt, 1806-1869. I. Fessenden, James D., ed. II. Title. BIP

JELLISON, Charles Albert. 923.273
Fessenden of Maine, Civil War Senator. Syracuse, N.Y., Syracuse University Press [1962] vi., 294 p. plates, ports. 24 cm. Bibliography: p. 274-284. [E415.9.F4J4] 62-10726
1. Fessenden, William Pitt, 1806-1869. BIP

Fetridge, William Harrison, 1906-

FETRIDGE, William Harrison, 1906- 973.91'092'4 B
With warm regards : a reminiscence / by William Harrison Fetridge. Chicago : Dartnell, c1976. 284 p., [10] leaves of plates : ill. ; 22 cm. [F546.2.F47A33] 75-35055 ISBN 0-85013-039-5 : 7.95
1. Fetridge, William Harrison, 1906- I. Title.

Feuchtwanger, Lion, 1884-1958.

KAHN, Lothar. 833'.9'12 B
Insight and action : the life and work of Lion Feuchtwanger / Lothar Kahn. Cranbury, N.J. : Associated University Presses, [1974] p. cm. Includes index. Bibliography: p. [PT2611.E85Z667] 73-2897 ISBN 0-8386-1314-4 : 15.00
1. Feuchtwanger, Lion, 1884-1958. I. Title. BIP

Few, William Preston,

FEW, William Preston, 1867-1940. 378'.00924
The papers and addresses. Edited, with a biographical appreciation, by Robert H. Woody. Freeport, N.Y., Books for Libraries Press [1968, c1951] xi, 369 p. ports. 22 cm. (Essay index reprint series) [LD1732.D817 1910b] 68-20299
I. Woody, Robert Hilliard, 1903- ed. BIP

Ffrench-Beytagh, Gonville Aubie.

FFRENCH-BEYTAGH, Gonville Aubie. 283'.092'4 B
Encountering darkness [by] Gonville Ffrench-Beytagh. New York, Seabury Press [1974, c1973] 283 p. 22 cm. "A Crossroad book." Autobiographical. [BX5700.6.Z8F473] 73-17895 ISBN 0-8164-1149-2 6.95
1. Ffrench-Beytagh, Gonville Aubie. 2. Church and race problems—Africa, South. I. Title.

Fiacre, Saint. d. ca. 670.

POND, Mariam Buckner, 1892- 922.244
Heaven in a wildflower. New York, Vantage Press [1954] 101p. illus. 22cm. [BX4700.F28P6] 54-7513
1. Fiacre, Saint. d. ca. 670. I. Title.

Fibonacci, Leonardo, fl. 1220.

GIES, Joseph. 510'.0924 B
Leonard of Pisa and the new mathematics of the Middle Ages, by Joseph and Frances Gies. Illustrated by Enrico Arno. New York, Crowell [1969] 127 p. illus. 21 cm. Bibliography: p. 115-121. [QA29.F5G5] 71-81952 3.95
1. Fibonacci, Leonardo, fl. 1220. 2. Mathematics—History. I. Gies, Frances, joint author. II. Arno, Enrico, illus. III. Title.

Fichte, Johann Gottlieb, 1762-1814.

ADAMSON, Robert, 1852-1902. 193 B
Fichte. Freeport, N.Y., Books for Libraries Press [1969] 222 p. 23 cm. (Select bibliographies reprint series.) (Philosophical classics for English readers) Reprint of the 1903 ed. [B2847.A3 1969] 76-94262 ISBN 8-369-50364-
1. Fichte, Johann Gottlieb, 1762-1814. I. Title. II. Series.

Fidrych, Mark.

FIDRYCH, Mark. 796.357'092'2 B
No big deal / Mark Fidrych and Tom Clark. 1st ed. Philadelphia : Lippincott, c1977. 251 p., leaves of plates : ill. ; 24 cm. An interview with Mark Fidrych in which he discusses his life and his baseball career. [GV865.F426A36] 92 77-8651 ISBN 0-397-01233-0 : 8.95
1. Fidrych, Mark. 2. Baseball players—United States—Biography. I. Clark, Tom, 1941- joint author. II. Title.

Fiedler, Arthur, 1894-

HOLLAND, James R. 785'.092'4 B
Mr. Pops, by James R. Holland. Barre, Mass., Barre Publishers, 1972. 96 p. illus. 26 cm. "Photographic essay." [ML422.F53H6] 72-186493 ISBN 0-8271-7232-X 4.95
1. Fiedler, Arthur, 1894- I. Title. BIP

MOORE, Robert Lowell. 785'.0924 B
Fiedler, the colorful Mr. Pops; the man and his music, by Robin Moore. [1st ed.] Boston, Little, Brown [1968] xv, 372 p. illus., facsim., ports. 22 cm. Discography: p. [293]-364. [ML422.F53M6] 68-17270 7.95
1. Fiedler, Arthur, 1894- 2. Music—Discography. I. Title.

MOORE, Robin. 785'.092'4 B
Fiedler, the colorful Mr. Pops : the man and his music / by Robin Moore. New York : Da Capo Press, 1980, c1968. p. cm. (Da Capo Press music reprint series) Reprint of the ed. published by Little, Brown, Boston. Includes index. Discography: p. [ML422.F53M6 1980] 79-24416 ISBN 0-306-76008-8 : 22.50
1. Fiedler, Arthur, 1894- 2. Conductors (Music)—United States—Biography. I. Title.

WILSON, Carol (Green) 1892- 785'.0924 B
Arthur Fiedler; music for the millions; the story of the conductor of the Boston Pops Orchestra. New York, Evans Pub. Co. [1968] 223 p. ports. 22 cm. [ML422.F53W5] 67-29134
1. Fiedler, Arthur, 1894-

Fiedler, Leslie A.

FIEDLER, Leslie A. 309.1'24 B
Being busted [by] Leslie A. Fiedler. New York, Stein and Day [1969] 255 p. 22 cm. [PS3556.I34B4 1969] 69-17946 5.95
I. Title. BIP

Field, Cyrus West, 1819-1892.

JUDSON, Isabella (Field) 1846- ed. 338.7'62'138280924 B
Cyrus W. Field, his life and work (1819-1892). New York, MSS Information Corp. [1972] p. "Reprint of the first edition published ... in 1896." [TK5611.F5J8 1972] 72-8168 ISBN 0-8422-8085-5
1. Field, Cyrus West, 1819-1892.

LATHAM, Jean Lee. 621.382'8'0924 B
Young man in a hurry; the story of Cyrus W. Field. Pictures by Victor Mays. New York, Harper [1958] 238 p. 21 cm. A biography of the man who rose from debt to amass a small fortune, and became the driving force behind the successful laying of the first transatlantic telegraph cable. [PZ7.L348Yo] 92 AC 68
1. Field, Cyrus West, 1819-1892. I. Mays, Victor, 1927- illus. II. Title. BIP

Field, Cyrus West, 1819-1892—Fiction.

LATHAM, jean Lee 926
Young man in a hurry; the story of Cyrus W. Field. Pictures by Victor Mays. New York, Harper [1963, c.1958] 238p. illus. 21cm. 3.27 lib. ed.,
1. Field, Cyrus West, 1819-1892—Fiction. I. Title.

Field, Eugene, 1850-1895.

DENNIS, Charles Henry, 1860-1943. 811'.4 B
Eugene Field's creative years. Garden City, N.Y., Doubleday, Page, 1924. St. Clair Shores, Mich., Scholarly Press, 1971 [c1924] iii [i.e viii] 339 p. port. 22 cm. [PS1668.D4 1971] 72-144971 ISBN 0-403-00939-1
1. Field, Eugene, 1850-1895. I. Title. BIP

Field, Eugene, 1850-1895—Biography.

CONROW, Robert. 811'.4 B
Field days; the life, times, & reputation of Eugene Field. New York, Scribner [1974] 244 p. illus. 24 cm. Bibliography: p. 231-239. [PS1668.C6] 73-19358 ISBN 0-684-13780-1 7.95
1. Field, Eugene, 1850-1895—Biography. I. Title. BIP

THOMPSON, Slason, 1849-1935. 811'.4 B
Eugene Field: a study in heredity and contradictions. New York, Beekman Publishers, 1974. 2 v. illus. 23 cm. (American newspapermen, 1790-1933) Reprint of the 1901 ed. published by Scribner, New York. [PS1668.T5 1974] 74-586 ISBN 0-8464-0005-7 37.50 (2 vol. set)
1. Field, Eugene, 1850-1895—Biography. BIP

Field, James Thomas, 1816-1881.

TRYON, Warren Stenson, 1901- 920.4
Parnassus Corner; a life of James T. Fields, publisher to the Victorians. Boston,

Houghton [c.]1963, xiv, 445p. illus., ports. 23cm. Bibl. 62-14207 7.00
1. Field, James Thomas, 1816-1881. 2. Boston—Intellectual life. 3. Authors and publishers—U.S. 4. Ticknor, firm, publishers, Boston. I. Title.

Field, John, 1782-1837.

NIKOLAEV, Aleksandr Aleksandrovich. 786.1'092'4 B
John Field, by Aleksandr Aleksandrovich Nikolayev. Translated from the Russian by Harold M. Cardello. 1st ed. in English. Foreword: David Doscher. New York, Musical Scope Publishers, 1973. 1 v. (various pagings) music. 29 cm. Includes bibliographies. [ML410.F445N53] 73-79275 ISBN 0-913000-99-X
1. Field, John, 1782-1837.
Publisher's Address: Box 125 Hudson Street N.Y. 10032.

PIGGOTT, Patrick, 1915- 786.1'092'4 B
The life and music of John Field, 1782-1837, creator of the nocturne. Berkeley, University of California Press, 1973. xvi, 287 p. illus. 26 cm. Bibliography: p. 271-275. [ML410.F445P5 1973b] 72-97741 ISBN 0-520-02412-5 22.00
1. Field, John, 1782-1837. I. Title.

Field, Maria Antonia.

FIELD, Maria Antonia. 920.7
Where Castilian roses bloom: memoirs. [San Francisco?] 1954. 142p. illus., ports., col. coats of arms, facsims. 30cm. 'Five hundred copies printed. [CT275.F374A3] 55-18412
I. Title.

Field, Marshall, 1893-1956.

BECKER, Stephen D., 1927- 923.373
Marshal Field III; a biography. New York, S. & S. [c.1964] 511p. ports. 23cm. Bibl. 63-19911 7.50
1. Field, Marshall, 1893-1956. I. Title.

BECKER, Stephen D 1927- 923.373
Marshall Field III; a biography, by Stephen Becker. New York, Simon and Schuster [1964] 511 p. ports. 23 cm. Bibliographical references included in "Notes" (p. 493-495) [CT275.F517B4] 63-19911
1. Field, Marshall, 1893-1956. I. Title.

Field, Michael, pseud.—Addresses, essays, lectures.

RICKETTS, Charles S., 1866-1931. 821'.9'12 B
Michael Field / by Charles Ricketts ; edited by Paul Delaney. Edinburgh : Tragara Press, 1976. vii, 12 p., [2] leaves of plates : ports ; 24 cm. Limited ed. of 125 numbered copies. No. 106. [PR4699.F5Z77 1976] 77-365380 ISBN 0-902616-32-3 : £6.00
1. Field, Michael, pseud.—Addresses, essays, lectures. 2. Bradley, Katherine Harris, 1846-1914—Biography—Addresses, essays, lectures. 3. Cooper, Edith Emma, 1862-1913—Biography—Addresses, essays, lectures. 4. Authors, English—19th century—Biography—Addresses, essays, lectures.

Field, Stephen Johnson, 1816-1899.

SWISHER, Carl Brent, 1897- 923.473
Stephen J. Field, craftsman of the law. Hamden, Conn., Archon [dist. Shoe String] 1963 [c.1930] 473p. illus. 22cm. 63-16037 12.00
1. Field, Stephen Johnson, 1816-1899. I. Title. BIP

SWISHER, Carl Brent, 1897-1968. 347.99'24 B
Stephen J. Field, craftsman of the law. With an introd. by Robert G. McCloskey. Chicago, University of Chicago Press [1969, c1930] xxii, 473 p. 21 cm. (The Court and the Constitution) Phoenix books. Bibliographical footnotes. [KF8745.F5S9 1969] 76-8437 2.95
1. Field, Stephen Johnson, 1816-1899.

Fielding, Henry, 1707-1754.

BANERJI, Hiran Kumar 828.5
Henry Fielding: playwright, journalist, and master of the art of fiction; his life and works. New York, Russell & Russell, 1962. 342p. 23cm. 62-13825 7.50
1. Fielding, Henry, 1707-1754. 2. Fielding, Henry, 1707-1754—Bibl. I. Title. BIP

BRISSENDEN, R F v. 12
Samuel Richardson, by R. F. Brissenden. Henry Fielding, by John Butt. Laurence Sterne, by D. W. Jefferson. Tobias Smollett, by Laurence Brander. Lincoln, University of Nebraska Press [c1965] 146 p. ports. 21 cm. (British writers and their work, no. 6) A Bison book, BB455. Includes bibliographies. 68-107263
1. Richardson, Samuel, 2. Fielding, Henry, 3. Sterne, Laurence, 4. Smollett, Tobias George, I. Butt, John Everett, 1906-1965. Henry Fielding. II. Jefferson, Douglas William, 1912- Laurence Sterne. III. Brander, Laurence, 1903- Tobias Smollett. IV. Title. V. Series.

CROSS, Wilbur Lucius, 1862-1948 928.2
The history of Henry Fielding. [3v.] New York, Russell & Russell, 1963[c.1918, 1945] 3v. (425; 437; 411p.) illus., ports., facsims. 23cm. Bibl. 64-10385 30.00 set,
1. Fielding, Henry, 1707-1754. I. Title.

DOBSON, Austin, 1840-1921. 823'.5 B
Fielding. New York, AMS Press [1968] ix, 205 p. 22 cm. (English men of letters) "Reprinted from the edition of 1889." [PR3456.D6 1968] 68-58376
1. Fielding, Henry, 1707-1754. BIP

GODDEN, Gertrude M. 823'.5 B
Henry Fielding: a memoir, including newly discovered letters and records with illustrations from contemporary prints, by G. M. Godden. [Folcroft, Pa.] Folcroft Library Editions, 1974. p. cm. Reprint of the 1909 ed. published by Barse & Hopkins, New York. [PR3456.G6 1974] 74-3417 ISBN 0-8414-4500-1 40.00 (lib. bdg.)
1. Fielding, Henry, 1707-1754. 2. Fielding, Henry, 1707-1754—Correspondence. I. Title.

LAWRENCE, Frederick, 1821-1867. 823'.5 B
The life of Henry Fielding : with notices of his writings, his times, and his contemporaries / by Frederick Lawrence. Folcroft, Pa. : Folcroft Library Editions, 1976. p. cm. Reprint of the 1855 ed. published by A. Hall, Virtue, London. [PR3456.L3 1976] 76-9795 ISBN 0-8414-5744-1 lib. bdg. : 40.00
1. Fielding, Henry, 1707-1754. I. Title.

Fielding, Henry, 1707-1754—Biography.

JENKINS, Elizabeth, 1907- 823'.5 B
Henry Fielding. [Folcroft, Pa.] Folcroft Library Editions, 1974. p. cm. Reprint of the 1948 ed. published by A. Swallow, Denver, in series: The English novelists. Bibliography: p. [PR3456.J3 1974] 74-8471 10.00 (lib. bdg.).
1. Fielding, Henry, 1707-1754—Biography. I. Title. II. Series: The English novelists (Denver) BIP

JONES, Benjamin Maelor. 823'.5 B
Henry Fielding, novelist and magistrate / by B. M. Jones ; with foreword by the Hon. Mr. Justice Du Parcq. Folcroft, Pa. : Folcroft Library Editions, 1978. 255 p. ; 23 cm. Reprint of th 1933 ed. published by G. Allen & Unwin, London. Includes index. Bibliography: p. 247-252. [PR3456.J6 1978] 78-8841 ISBN 0-8414-5294-6 lib. bdg. : 30.00
1. Fielding, Henry, 1707-1754—Biography. 2. Authors, English—18th century—Biography. 3. Justices of the peace—England—Biography. I. Title. BIP

ROGERS, Pat. 823'.5 B
Henry Fielding, a biography / Pat Rogers. New York : Scribner, c1979. 237 p. : ill. ; 25 cm. Includes index. Bibliography: p. [232]-233. [PR3456.R6] 79-84177 ISBN 0-684-16264-4 : 15.95
1. Fielding, Henry, 1707-1754—Biography. 2. Authors, English—18th century—Biography. I. Title.

WILLCOCKS, Mary Patricia, 1869- 823'.5 B
A true-born Englishman; being the life of Henry Fielding. [Folcroft, Pa.] Folcroft Library Editions, 1974. 288 p. illus. 26 cm. Reprint of the 1947 ed. published by Allen & Unwin, London. Bibliography: p. 280. [PR3456.W5 1974] 74-8472 20.00
1. Fielding, Henry, 1707-1754—Biography. I. Title. BIP

Fielding, William John,

FIELDING, William John, 1886- 301'.092'4 B
All the lives I have lived, by William J. Fielding. With an introd. by Jack Benjamin. Philadelphia, Dorrance [1972] x, 220 p. 22 cm. Bibliography: p. 209-212. [PS3511.I28Z5] 70-171932 ISBN 0-8059-1614-8 5.95
I. Title.

Fields, James Thomas, 1816-1881.

BONNER, Willard Hallam, 1899- ed. 828'.8'09 B
De Quincey at work. [Folcroft, Pa.] Folcroft Library Editions, 1973 [c1936] 111 p. illus. 26 cm. Reprint of the ed. published by Airport Publishers, Buffalo. Contents.Contents.—James T. Fields and the first American edition.—James Hogg and the first British edition. [PR4536.B6 1973] 73-9715 10.00
1. De Quincey, Thomas, 1785-1859. 2. Fields, James Thomas, 1816-1881. 3. Hogg, James, 1806-1888. 4. Hogg, James, 1830-1910, I. De Quincey, Thomas, 1785-1859. II. Title. BIP

Fields, W.C., 1880-1946.

FIELDS, W. C., 1879-1946. 818'.5'202
Fields' day; the best of W. C. Fields. [Kansas City, Mo., Hallmark Cards, 1972] [26] p. illus. 15 cm. [PN2287.F45A3 1972] 70-175035 ISBN 0-87529-266-6
I. Title.

FIELDS, W. C., 1879-1946. 791'.0924
Fields for President. Commentary and photo. selection by Michael M. Taylor. New York, Dodd, Mead [1971] xxiii, 163 p. illus. 24 cm. [PN2287.F45A3 1971] 70-173456 ISBN 0-396-06419-5 5.95
I. Taylor, Michael M. II. Title.

FIELDS, W. C., 1879-1946. 791'.092'4 B
W. C. Fields by himself; his intended autobiography. Commentary by Ronald J. Fields. Englewood Cliffs, N.J., Prentice-Hall [1973] xiv, 510 p. illus. 24 cm. [PN2287.F45A3 1973] 73-3086 ISBN 0-13-944462-9 10.00
I. Fields, W. C., 1879-1946. I. Fields, Ronald J., 1949- II. Title.

MONTI, Carlotta. 791.43'0924 [B]
W. C. Fields & me, by Carlotta Monti with Cy Rice. New York, Warner Paperback Lib. [1973, c.1971] 238 p. illus., ports. 18 cm. [PN2287.F45M6] pap., 1.25
1. Fields, W. C., 1879-1946. I. Rice, Cy.

MONTI, Carlotta. 791.43'0924 B
W. C. Fields & me, by Carlotta Monti with Cy Rice. Englewood Cliffs, N.J., Prentice-Hall [1971] 227 p. illus., ports. 24 cm. [PN2287.F45M6] 72-143032 ISBN 0-13-944454-8 6.95
1. Fields, W. C., 1879-1946. I. Rice, Cy.

TAYLOR, Robert Lewis 927.92
W. C. Fields, his follies and fortunes. Garden City. N.Y., Doubleday [1962, c.1949] viii, 340p. 22cm. 4.50
1. Fields, W. C., 1879-1946. I. Title.

TAYLOR, Robert Lewis. 791.43'0924 B
W. C. Fields, his follies and fortunes. [New York] New American Library [1967] 286 p. ports. 18 cm. (Signet books) "Q3064." [PN2287.F45T3 1967] 67-6917
1. Fields, W. C., 1879-1946. I. Title. II. Series.

Fields, W. C., 1880-1946—Juvenile literature.

FINKE, Blythe Foote. 791'.0924 B
W. C. Fields, renowned comedian of the early motion picture industry. Charlotteville, N.Y., SamHar Press, 1972. 30 p. 22 cm. (Outstanding personalities no. 48) Bibliography: p. 29-30. A biography of the actor whose life, through his stage and film performances, was "an attack against the phonies of the world." [PN2287.F45F5] 92 72-81898
1. Fields, W. C., 1880-1946—Juvenile literature. I. Title.

Fiesole, Giovanni da, called Fra Angelico, 1387-1455.

FIESOLE, Giovanni da, called Fra Angelico, 1387-1455. [759.5]
Fra Angelico, by John Pope-Hennessy. New York, Phaidon Publishers, distributed by Garden City Books, [1952.] 213p. illus., plates (part col.) 31 cm. Addendum slip inserted at p. 203. Catalogue: p. 165-207. Bibliography: p. 164. [ND623.F5P65] 927.5 55-7818
I. Pope-Hennessy, John, 1913- II. Title.

FIESOLE, Giovanni da, called Fra Angelico, 1387-1455. 759.5
Fra Angelico / Christopher Lloyd. Oxford : Phaidon ; New York : Dutton, 1979. 16 p., [24] leaves of plates : chiefly col. ill. ; 31 cm. Bibliography: p. 14. [ND623.F5A4 1979] 79-88174 ISBN 0-7148-1997-2 : 12.50
1. Fiesole, Giovanni da, called Fra Angelico, 1387-1455. I. Lloyd, Christopher Hamilton.

Figaro III (Yawl)

SNAITH, William, 1908- 910'.45 B
On the wind's way. New York, Putnam [1973] 256 p. illus. 22 cm. Taken, in part, from the log of the Figaro III. [G530.S92 1973] 73-82033 ISBN 0-399-11227-8 7.95
1. Figaro III (Yawl) 2. Atlantic Ocean. I. Figaro III (Yawl) II. Title.

Fighter pilots—United States—Biography.

TOLIVER, Raymond F. 358.4'3'0922 B
Fighter aces of the U.S.A. / by Raymond F. Toliver and Trevor J. Constable. Fallbrook, CA : Aero Publishers, c1979. p. cm. Includes index. [UG626.T64] 79-17845 ISBN 0-8168-5792-X : 24.95
1. Fighter pilots—United States—Biography. I. Constable, Trevor J., joint author. II. Title. BIP

Figl, Leopold, 1902-1965.

SELTENREICH, Susanne. 943.6050924(B)
Leopold Figl, Austrian patriot and statesman. [English language ed. prepared by Ritchie McEwen. Vienna, E. Metten, 1963?] 224, 159, 19 p. facsims., plates (part col.), ports. (part col.) 21 cm. Bibliography: p. 20 (1st group) [DB98.F5S413] 68-43575
1. Figl, Leopold, 1902-1965.

Filangieri, Gaetano, 1752-1788.

MAESTRO, Marcello T., 1907- 340'.092'4
Gaetano Filangieri and his Science of legislation / Marcello Maestro. Philadelphia : American Philosophical Society, 1976. 76 p. : ill. ; 30 cm. (Transactions of the American Philosophical Society ; new ser., v. 66, pt. 6 ISSN 0065-9746s) On spine: Filangieri and his Science of legislation. Includes index. Bibliography: p. 72-73. [K230.F52M3] 76-24256 ISBN 0-87169-666-5 pbk. : 6.00
1. Filangieri, Gaetano, 1752-1788. La scienza della legislazione. 2. Lawyers—Italy—Biography. I. Title. II. Title: Filangieri and his Science of legislation. III. Series: American Philosophical Society, Philadelphia. Transactions ; new ser., v. 66, pt. 6. BIP

Filipinos in the U.S.—Biog.

NICANOR, Precioso M. 920.0914
Profiles of notable Filipinos in the U.S.A. v.1. Introd. by Meliguiades Gamboa. Forward by Mauro Bavadi. New York 10, Pre-Mer Pub. Co., 175 Fifth Ave., [c.1963] ports., map. 24cm. 63-2269 10.00
1. Filipinos in the U.S.—Biog. I. Title.

NICANOR, Precioso M 920.0914
Profiles of notable Filipinos in the U.S.A. New York, Pre-Mer Pub. Co. [c1963- v. ports., map. 24 cm. [E184.F4N5] 63-22694
1. Filipinos in the U.S. — Biog. I. Title. II. Title: .... Introd. by Melquiades Gamboa. Foreward by Mauro Bavadi.

Filippo Neri, Saint, 1515-1595.

BOUYER, Louis, 1913- 922.245
The Roman Socrates; a portrait of St. Philip Neri. Translated from the French by Michael Day. Westminster, Md., Newman Press, 1958. 87p. 19cm. Translation of Saint Philippe Neri. [BX4700.F33B63] 58-4377
1. Filippo Neri, Saint, 1515-1595. I. Title.

JOUHANDEAU, Marcel 922.245
St. Philip Neri. Translated [from the French] by George Lamb. New York, Harper [1960] vi, 129p. 19cm. 60-16255 2.75
1. Filippo Neri, Saint, 1515-1595. I. Title.

NASH, Roy, 1929- 922.245
With flaming heart; a story of St. Philip Neri. Illus. by Brother Harold Ruplinger. Notre Dame, Ind., Dujarie Press [1956] 104p. illus. 24cm. [BX4700.F33N3] 57-16735
1. Filippo Neri, Saint, 1515-1595. I. Title.

Filley, William, 1832?-

FILLEY, William, 1832?- 973'.04'97 S
Life and adventures of William Filley. New York : Garland Pub., 1976 [c1867] p. cm. (The Garland library of narratives of North American Indian captivities ; v. 81) Issued with the 1837 ed. of Alden, T. An account of the captivity of Hugh Gibson. New York, 1976; with the reprint of the 1868 ed. of Ellet, E. F. L. Mary Nealy. New York, 1976; with the reprint of the 1869 ed. of General Sheridan's squaw spy and Clara Blynn's captivity. New York, 1976; and with the reprint of the 1869 ed. of Hood, J. E. Lost and found in the Rocky Mountains. New York, 1976. Reprint of the ed. published by Filley & Ballard, Chicago. [E85.G2 vol. 81] [E87.F48] 970'.004'97 B 75-40435 ISBN 0-8240-1705-6 lib.bdg. : 21.00
1. Filley, William, 1832?- 2. Indians of North America—Captivities. 3. Indians of North America—The West. I. Title. II. Series.

Fillmore, Charles, 1854-1948.

D'ANDRADE, Hugh. 289.9 B
Charles Fillmore: herald of the new age. [1st ed.] New York, Harper & Row [1974] xiv, 145 p. 21 cm. Bibliography: p. [144]-145. [BX9890.U5D36] 73-6337 ISBN 0-06-061682-2 5.95
1. Fillmore, Charles, 1854-1948. 2. Unity School of Christianity.

Fillmore, Millard, Pres. U.S., 1800-1874.

BARRE, W. L. 973.6'4'0924 B
The life and public services of Millard Fillmore, by W. L. Barre. New York, B. Franklin [1971] 408 p. port. 19 cm. (Burt Franklin research & source works series, 802. American classics in history and social science, 203) Reprint of the 1856 ed. [E427.B27 1971] 70-170962 ISBN 0-8337-4634-0
1. Fillmore, Millard, Pres. U.S., 1800-1874. I. Title. BIP

DIX, Dorothea Lynde, 1802-1887. 973.6'4'0924 B
The lady and the president : the letters of Dorothea Dix & Millard Fillmore / Charles M. Snyder. Lexington : University Press of Kentucky, c1975. 400 p., [4] leaves of plates : ill. ; 23 cm. Includes index. Bibliography: p. 387-392. [E427.D59 1975] 75-3551 ISBN 0-8131-1332-6 : 9.50
1. Fillmore, Millard, Pres. U.S., 1800-1874. 2. Dix, Dorothea Lynde, 1802-1887. I. Fillmore, Millard, Pres. U.S., 1800-1874. II. Snyder, Charles McCool. III. Title. BIP

RAYBACK, Robert J. 923.173
Millard Fillmore; biography of a President. [1st ed.] Buffalo, Published for the Buffalo Historical Society by H. Stewart, 1959. xiv, 470 p. plates, ports. 23 cm. (Publicatons of the Buffalo Historical Society, v. 40) Bibliography: p. [447]-457. [F129.B8B88 vol. 40] 58-14009
1. Fillmore, Millard, Pres. U.S., 1800-1874. I. Title. II. Series: Buffalo Historical Society. Publications, v. 40. BIP

SCARRY, Robert J. 973.6'4'0924 B
Millard Fillmore, 13th president, by Robert J. Scarry. [Moravia? N.Y., 1970] [58] p. (incl. cover) illus., ports. 24 cm. Cover title. 1965 ed. published under title: Millard Fillmore, the man and the cabin. Includes bibliographical references. [E427.S3 1970] 70-24063
1. Fillmore, Millard, Pres. U.S., 1800-1874.

Fillmore, Myrtle Page, d. 1931.

WITHERSPOON, Thomas E. 289.9 B
Myrtle Fillmore, mother of unity / by Thomas E. Witherspoon. 1st ed. Unity Village, Mo. : Unity Books, 1977. viii, 306 p. : ill. ; 24 cm. [BX9890.U58F548] 77-78221 5.95
1. Fillmore, Myrtle Page, d. 1931. 2. Unity School of Christianity—Biography.

Finch-Davies, Claude Gibney, 1875-1920.

KEMP, Alan C. 759.941
The biography of Claude Gibney Finch-Davies, 1875-1920 : observer, student and highly skilled illustrator of Southern African birds / text by A. C. Kemp. Pretoria : Transvaal Museum, c1976. 33 p., [30] leaves of plates : ill. (some col.), facsims. ; 36 cm. Includes bibliographical references. [QL31.F52K45] 77-368019 ISBN 0-620-02081-4
1. Finch-Davies, Claude Gibney, 1875-1920. 2. Ornithologists—South Africa—Biography. 3. Birds—Africa, Southern—Pictorial works. I. Title.

Finch family.

BROWN, Dorothy (Moulding) 1896- 917.75'8
The fighting Finches; tales of early pioneer freebooters in Rock and Jefferson Counties. [Madison? Wis., 1969?] 31 p. 20 cm. (Wisconsin folklore booklets publications) 1937 ed. issued by the Federal Writers' Project, Wisconsin. [F585.F5B7 1969] 79-4909
1. Finch family. 2. Frontier and pioneer life—Wisconsin. I. Federal Writers' Project, Wisconsin. II. Title. III. Series.

Finch Hatton, Denys George, 1887-1931.

TRZEBINSKI, Errol, 1936- 941.082'092'4 B
Silence will speak : a study of the life of Denys Finch Hatton and his relationship with Karen Blixen / by Errol Trzebinski. Chicago : University of Chicago Press, 1978. xix, 348 p., [8] leaves of plates : ill. ; 24 cm. Includes bibliographical references and index. [CT788.F47T79 1977b] 78-103580 ISBN 0-226-81286-3 : 15.00
1. Finch Hatton, Denys George, 1887-1931. 2. Blixen, Karen, 1885-1962—Friends and associates. 3. England—Biography. I. Title. BIP

Fink, Albert,

MILTON, Ellen (Fink) 1870- 923.873
A biography of Albert Fink. Rochester, N.Y., Printed [by] Commercial Controls Corp., 1951. 102 p. illus. 24 cm. [HE2754.F5M5] 52-25626
1. Fink, Albert, 1827-1897. I. Title.

Fink. Mike, 1770-1823?

BLAIR, Walter, 1900- ed. 923.973
Half horse, half alligator; the growth of the Mike Fink legend, edited with an introd. and notes by Walter Blair and Franklin J. Meine. [Chicago] University of Chicago Press [1956] 288p. illus. 23cm. Includes bibliography. [F353.F5B56] 56-10082
1. Fink. Mike, 1770-1823? I. Meine, Franklin Julius, 1896- joint ed. II. Title.

BLAIR, Walter, 1900- ed. 923.978
Half horse, half alligator; the growth of the Mike Fink legend, edited with an introd. and notes by Walter Blair and Franklin J. Meine. [Chicago] University of Chicago Press [1956] 288p. illus. 23cm. Includes bibliography. [F353.F5B56] 56-10082
1. Fink, Mike, 1770-1823? I. Meine, Franklin Julius, 1896- joint ed. II. Title.

BLAIR, Walter, 1900- 917.7'03'20924 B
Mike Fink, king of Mississippi keelboatmen, by Walter Blair and Franklin J. Meine. Westport, Conn., Greenwood Press [1971, c1933] xiv, 283 p. illus. 23 cm. Bibliography: p. 269-283. [F353.B62 1971] 74-138143 ISBN 0-8371-5600-9
1. Fink, Mike, 1770-1823? 2. Frontier and pioneer life—Mississippi Valley. 3. Frontier and pioneer life—Ohio Valley. 4. Frontier and pioneer life—Missouri Valley. 5. River life. I. Meine, Franklin Julius, 1896-1968, joint author. BIP

Fink, Mike, 1770-1823?—Juvenile literature.

FELTON, Harold W., 1902- 923.973
Mike Fink, best of the keelboatmen, being a revealing and trustworthy account of events in the life of the renowned riverman. Illustrated by Aldren A. Watson. New York, Dodd, Mead [1960] 159 p. illus. 23 cm. [F353.F5F4] 60-6178
1. Fink, Mike, 1770-1823?—Juvenile literature.

Finland—Hist.

TOKOI, Oskari. 923.2471
Sisu, 'even through a stone wall'; autobiography. Introd. by John I. Kolehmainen. [1st ed.] New York, R. Speller, 1957. 252p. illus. 22cm. (Makers of history series) [DK461.T63A34] 57-10593
1. Finland—Hist. 2. Finns in the U. S. I. Title.

Finley, Charles Oscar, 1918-

LIBBY, Bill. 796.357'092'4 B
Charlie O. and the angry A's / Bill Libby. 1st ed. Garden City, N.Y. : Doubleday, 1975. x, 324 p., [10] leaves of plates : ill. ; 22 cm. [GV865.F43L52] 74-12697 ISBN 0-385-09520-1 : 7.95
1. Finley, Charles Oscar, 1918- 2. Oakland Athletics (Baseball team) 3. Baseball—Biography. I. Title.

MICHELSON, Herb. 796.357'092'4 B
Charlie O / by Herb Michelson. Indianapolis : Bobbs-Merrill, [1975] xv, 331 p., [8] leaves of plates : ill. ; 24 cm. [GV865.F43M5] 74-17643 ISBN 0-672-52013-3 : 7.95
1. Finley, Charles Oscar, 1918- 2. Oakland Athletics (Baseball team) 3. Baseball. I. Title.

Finley, Robert, 1772-1817.

BROWN, Isaac Van Arsdale, 1784-1861. 973.5'0924 B
Biography of the Rev. Robert Finley. New York, Arno Press, 1969. 336 p. 23 cm. (The Anti-slavery crusade in America) Reprint of the 1857 ed. First published in 1819 under title: Memoirs of the Rev. Robert Finley. [E448.F5 1969] 73-82178
1. Finley, Robert, 1772-1817. 2. American Colonization Society. 3. Negroes—Colonization—Africa. 4. Slave-trade. I. Title. II. Series.

Finney, Ben, 1900-

FINNEY, Ben, 1900- 917.3'03'910924 B
Feet first. Foreword by John O'Hara. With five decades of personal photographs. New York, Crown [1971] 255 p. illus., ports. 22 cm. [CT275.F5544A3 1971] 78-151020 5.95
I. Title.

FINNEY, Ben, 1900- 359.9'6'0924 B
Once a marine-always a marine / Ben Finney ; foreword by Lem Shepard. New York : Crown Publishers, 1977. 128 p. : ill. ; 24 cm. [VE25.F56A34 1977] 77-15629 ISBN 0-517-53275-1 : 6.95
1. Finney, Ben, 1900- 2. United States. Marine Corps Reserve—Biography. 3. United States. Marine Corps—History. 4. Soldiers—United States—Biography. I. Title. BIP

Finney, Charles Grandison, 1792-1875.

FINNEY, Charles Grandison, 1792-1875. 285'.8'0924 B
The autobiography of Charles G. Finney / condensed & edited by Helen Wessel. Minneapolis : Bethany Fellowship, c1977. 230 p. ; 21 cm. Condensed version of Memoirs of Rev. Charles G. Finney, originally published in 1876. [BX7260.F47A352 1977] 77-2813 ISBN 0-87123-010-0 pbk. : 3.50
1. Finney, Charles Grandison, 1792-1875. 2. Congregational churches—Clergy—Biography. 3. Clergy—United States—Biography. 4. Evangelists—United States—Biography. I. Wessel, Helen Strain, 1924- II. Title. BIP

FINNEY, Charles Grandison, 1792-1875. 285'.8'0924 B
Memoirs of Rev. Charles G. Finney. New York, A. S. Barnes, 1876. [New York, AMS Press, 1973] p. [BX7260.F47A4 1973] 74-168025 ISBN 0-404-00047-9

Finney, Humphrey S., 1902-

FINNEY, Humphrey S., 1902- 798.4'092'4 B
Fair exchange; recollections of a life with horses, by Humphrey S. Finney, with Raleigh Burroughs. New York, Scribner [1974] x, 175 p. illus. 24 cm. Autobiography. [SF33.F56A33] 73-1339 ISBN 0-684-13707-0 10.00
1. Finney, Humphrey S., 1902- 2. Horsemen—Correspondence, reminiscences, etc. 3. Horse buying. I. Burroughs, Raleigh, joint author. II. Title.

Finnish Americans—Addresses, essays, lectures.

FINNISH American horizons / [compiled by the] Horizons Project of the Finnish-American Bi-Centennial Committee U.S.A. 1976 ; project chairman, John Ketonen. New York Mills, Minn. : R. Parta, [1976] vii, 503 p. : ill. ; 24 cm. English or Finnish. Includes index. [E184.F5F49] 76-670046 973'.04'94541
1. Finnish Americans—Addresses, essays, lectures. 2. Finnish Americans—Biography. 3. United States—Biography. I. Ketonen, John Emil, 1897- II. Finnish-American Bi-Centennial Committee U.S.A. 1976. Horizons Project.

Finta, Alexander, 1881-

LENGYEL, Alfonz. 730'.92'4
The life and art of Alexander Finta, Hungarian-American sculptor. Washington, Hungarian Reformed Federation of America, 1964. iii, 74 p. illus., port. 20 cm. (Hungarica Americans, 7) [NB237.F5L4] 66-50145
1. Finta, Alexander, 1881- I. Title. II. Series.

Firbank, Arthur Annesley Ronald, 1886-1926.

BENKOVITZ, Miriam J. 823'.9'12
Ronald Firbank; a biography [by] Miriam

J. Benkovitz. [1st ed.] New York, Knopf, 1969. xviii, 300, x p. illus., ports. 22 cm. Includes bibliographies. [PR6011.I7Z6] 69-10711 6.95
1. Firbank, Arthur Annesley Ronald, 1886-1926.

Firestone, Harvey Samuel, 1868-1938.

LIEF, Alfred, 1901- 926.78
Harvey Firestone, free man of enterprise; foreword by Allan Nevins. New York, McGraw-Hill [1951] xi, 324 p. illus., ports. 21 cm. [HD9161.U54F55] 51-11692
1. Firestone, Harvey Samuel, 1868-1938. 2. Firestone Tire and Rubber Company. I. Title.

PARADIS, Adrian A. 92 (J)
Harvey S. Firestone: young rubber pioneer, by Adrian Paradis. Illustrated by Fred M. Irvin. Indianapolis, Bobbs-Merrill [1968] 200 p. col. illus. 20 cm. (Childhood of famous Americans) [HD9161.U52P3] 68-17023 2.50
1. Firestone, Harvey Samuel, 1868-1938.

PARADIS, Adrian A. 338.7'6'6780924 B
Harvey S. Firestone: young rubber pioneer, by Adrian Paradis. Illustrated by Fred M. Irvin. Indianapolis, Bobbs-Merrill [1968] 200 p. col. illus. 20 cm. (Childhood of famous Americans) A biography concentrating on the childhood of Harvey Firestone, who was among the first to recognize the importance of rubber in making automobile tires and who founded the Firestone Tire and Rubber Company. [HD9161.U52P3] 92 AC 68
1. Firestone, Harvey Samuel, 1868-1938. I. Irvin, Fred M., illus. II. Title.

First Baptist Church, Hamlet, N.C.

NASII, Bessie Hursey, 286'.1756'34 1904-
From a mustard seed; a history of the First Baptist Church, Hamlet, North Carolina. [Raleigh, N.C., Printed by Sparks Press, 1973] xii, 153 p. illus. 24 cm. [BX6480.H315F576] 74-156960
1. First Baptist Church, Hamlet, N.C. 2. Hamlet, N.C.—Biography. I. Title.

First Christian Church, Greencastle, Ind.

OWENS, Harvey W., 286'.6'77249 1895-1968.
The history of First Christian Church, Greencastle, Indiana, 1830-1972, by Harvey W. Owens and associates. [Greencastle? Ind., 1973] 142 p. illus. 29 cm. [BX6781.G73F576] 73-174249
1. First Christian Church, Greencastle, Ind. 2. Greencastle, Ind.—Biography. I. Title.

First Congregational Society, Bedford, Mass.

MANSUR, Ina G. 285'.8744'4
A New England church, 1730-1834 / Ina Mansur. Freeport, Me. : Bond Wheelwright Co., 1974. xvii, 238 p. : ill. ; 23 cm. Includes indexes. Bibliography: p. 217-223. [BR560.B36M36] 74-76868 ISBN 0-87027-139-3. ISBN 0-87027-140-7 pbk. : 5.95
1. First Congregational Society, Bedford, Mass. 2. Bedford, Mass.—Church history. 3. Bedford, Mass.—Biography. I. Title.

MANSUR, Ina G. 285'.8744'4
A New England church, 1730-1834 / Ina Mansur. Freeport, Me. : Bond Wheelwright Co., 1974. xvii, 238 p. : ill. ; 23 cm. Includes indexes. Bibliography: p. 217-223. [BR560.B36M36] 74-76868 ISBN 0-87027-139-3 : 8.95 ISBN 0-87027-140-7 pbk. : 5.95
1. First Congregational Society, Bedford, Mass. 2. Bedford, Mass.—Church history. 3. Bedford, Mass.—Biography. I. Title.

First Presbyterian Church of Chester, New York.

PREDMORE, Helen R., 285'.1747'31 1893-
The Chester (N.Y.) Presbyterian Church : a history, 1799-1965 / Helen R. Predmore. Monroe, N.Y. : Library Research Associates, [1975] xii, 377 p. : ill. ; 24 cm. Includes index. Bibliography: p. 377. [BX9211.C36F576] 73-89297 ISBN 0-912526-11-4 : 9.45
1. First Presbyterian Church of Chester, New York. 2. Chester, N.Y.—Biography. I. Title. **BIP**

Firuz Shah

BANERJEE, Jamini 954'.56'0230924 Mohan.
History of Firuz Shah Tughluq Foreword by Banarsi Prasad Saksena. Delhi, Munshiram Manoharlal [1968, c.1967] x, 228p. 23 cm. Thesis approved for the degree of Doctor of Phil. of the Univ. of Allahabad. Bibl. [DS459.4.F5B3] (B) SA 68 6.00
1. Firuz Shah I. Taghlak, Sultan of Delhi, d. 1388. II. Title.
Distributed by Verry, Mystic Conn.

Fischer, Bobby, 1943-

BRADY, Frank Robert, 794.10924 1934-
Profile of a prodigy; the life and games of Bobby Fischer, by Frank Brady. New York, D. McKay Co. [1965] vi, 250 p. illus. 21 cm. [GV1439.F5B7] 65-18548
1. Fischer, Bobby, 1943- 2. Chess—Collections of games. I. Title.

BRADY, Frank Robert, 794.1'092'4 1934-
Profile of a prodigy; the life and games of Bobby Fischer, by Frank Brady. Rev. ed. New York, McKay [1973] ix, 435 p. illus. 21 cm. [GV1439.F5B7 1973] 72-96615 10.00
1. Fischer, Bobby, 1943- 2. Chess—Collections of games. I. Title.

DARRACH, Brad. 794.1'092'4 B
Bobby Fischer vs. the rest of the world / Brad Darrach. New York : Stein and Day, [1974] 240 p. ; 24 cm. [GV1439.F5D37 1974] 73-81322 ISBN 0-8128-1618-8 : 7.95
1. Fischer, Bobby, 1943- 2. Chess—Tournaments, 1972. I. Title. **BIP**

Fischer, Christian Wilhelm, 1789-1859.

WAGNER, Richard, 782.1'092'4 B 1813-1883.
Richard Wagner's letters to his Dresden friends, Tehodor Uhlig, Wilhelm Fischer, and Ferdinand Heine. Translated into English, with a pref. by J. S. Shedlock. And an etching of Wagner by C. W. Sherborn. New York, Vienna House [1972] xi, 512 p. port. 23 cm. "Originally published by Scribner and Welford, New York, 1890." [ML410.W1A38 1972] 72-163800 ISBN 0-8443-0006-3
1. Uhlig, Theodor, 1822-1853. 2. Fischer, Christian Wilhelm, 1789-1859. 3. Heine, Ferdinand. I. Shedlock, John South, 1843-1919, tr.

Fischer, Ernest G.

CROSTHWAIT, William 926.1 Lafayette, 1873-
The last stitch, by William L. Crosthwait and Ernest G. Fischer. [1st ed.] Philadelphia, Lippincott [1956] 250p. 21cm. [R154.C79A3] 56-8189
1. Fischer, Ernest G. I. Title.

Fischer, Joseph C

FISCHER, Joseph C 621.50924(B)
Engineering was my business, by Joseph C. Fischer. [1st ed.] New York, Exposition Press [1965] 84 p. illus. 21 cm. [TA140.F5A3] 65-9675
1. Title.

Fischer, Louis, 1896- ed.

FISCHER, Louis, 1896- 940.5'0924 1970.
Men and politics: an autobiography. With an appendix of lectures from Eleanor Roosevelt added to the reprint ed. Westport, Conn., Greenwood Press [1970, c1946] ix, 672 p. 24 cm. [D413.F5A3 1970] 73-111498 ISBN 0-8371-4641-0
1. Europe—Politics and government—1918-1945. 2. Journalists—Correspondence, reminiscences, etc. I. Title. **BIP**

GANDHI, Mohandas 923.254 Karamchand, 1869-1948
The essential Gandhi, his life, work, and ideas; an anthology. Ed. by Louis Fischer. New York, Random [1963, c.1962] 377p. 19cm. (Vintage Bk. V-225) Bibl. 1.95 pap.,
1. Fischer, Louis, 1896- ed. I. Title.

Fischer von Erlach, Johann Bernhard, 1656-1723.

AURENHAMMER, Hans. 720'.92'4
J. B. Fischer von Erlach. Cambridge, Mass., Harvard University Press, 1973. 193 p. illus. 26 cm. Includes bibliographical references. [NA1011.5.F57A94 1973b] 73-83421 ISBN 0-674-46988-7 15.95
1. Fischer von Erlach, Johann Bernhard, 1656-1723. I. Fischer von Erlach, Johann Bernhard, 1656-1723. **BIP**

Fish, Albert.

ANGELELLA, 364.1'523'0973 Michael.
Trail of blood / by Michael Angelella. Indianapolis : Bobbs-Merrill, [1979] p. cm. [HV6529.A54] 79-7461 ISBN 0-672-52380-9 : 10.00
1. Fish, Albert. 2. King, William Francis. 3. Murder—United States. 4. Crime and criminals—United States—Biography. 5. Detectives—United States—Biography. I. Title.

Fishbein, Morris,

FISHBEIN, Morris, 1889- 610'.924
Morris Fishbein, M.D.; an autobiography. [1st ed.] Garden City, N.Y., Doubleday, 1969. xii, 505 p. ports. 25 cm. [R154.F65A3] 69-15180 10.00
I. Title.

Fisher, Dorothea Frances (Canfield) 1879-1958.

YATES, Elizabeth, 813'.5'2 B 1905-
The lady from Vermont; Dorothy Canfield Fisher's life and world. Brattleboro, Vt., S. Greene Press [1971] 290 p. ports. 21 cm. 1958 ed published under title: Pebble in a pool. Bibliography: p. [285]-290. [PS3511.I7416Z9 1971] 74-148629 ISBN 0-8289-0127-9 3.95
1. Fisher, Dorothea Frances (Canfield) 1879-1958. I. Title. **BIP**

YATES, Elizabeth, 1905- 928.1
Pebble in a pool, the widening circles of Dorothy Canfield Fisher's life. Illustrated with photos. [1st ed.] New York, Dutton, 1958. 284 p. illus. 21 cm. Includes bibliography. [PS3511.I7416Z9] 58-9581
1. Fisher, Dorothea Frances (Canfield) 1879- I. Title.

Fisher, George, 1795-1873.

PARMENTER, Mary Fisher, 929.2 1895-
The life of George Fisher, 1795-1873, and the history of the Fisher family of Mississippi [by] Mary Fisher Parmenter Walter Russell Fisher [and] Lawrence Edward Mallette. Jacksonville, Fla., H. & W. B. Drew Co., 1959. 299p. illus. 23cm. Includes bibliography. [F390.F536] 59-4228
1. Fisher, George, 1795-1873. 2. Texas—Hist.—To 1846. 3. Fisher family. 4. Davis family. I. Title.

Fisher, Irving, 1867-1947.

FISHER, Irving Norton, 923.373 1900--
My father, Irving Fisher. New York, Comet Press Books [1956] 352p. illus. 21cm. (A Reflection book) [HB119.F5F5] 56-12157
1. Fisher, Irving, 1867-1947. I. Title.

Fisher, James Tucker,

FISHER, James Tucker, 1864- 926.1
A few buttons missing; the case book of a psychiatrist [by] James T. Fisher and Lowell S. Hawley. [1st ed.] Philadelphia, Lippincott [1951] 282 p. 22 cm. [R154.F66A3] 51-10666
I. Hawley, Lowell Stillwell, joint author. II. Title.

Fisher, John Arbuthnot Fisher, baron, 1841-1920.

BARKER, Dudley. 942.082'0922 B
Prominent Edwardians. [1st American ed.] New York, Atheneum, 1969. 254 p. ports. 22 cm. Contents.Contents.—Fisher of Kilverstone.—An episode in the life of William Butler Yeats.—The Marquess of Lansdowne.—Mrs. Emmeline Pankhurst. Bibliography: p. 247-248. [DA568.A1B34 1969] 68-27658 6.50
1. Fisher, John Arbuthnot Fisher, baron, 1841-1920. 2. Yeats, William Butler, 1865-1939. 3. Lansdowne, Henry Charles Keith Petty-Fitzmaurice, 5th marquis of, 1845-1927. 4. Pankhurst, Emmeline (Goulden) 1858-1928. I. Title.

HOUGH, Richard 359.3'3'10924 B Alexander, 1922-
Admiral of the fleet; the life of John Fisher [by] Richard Hough. [1st American ed. New York] Macmillan [1970, c1969] 392 p. illus., facsim., ports. 25 cm. "First published in Great Britain in 1969 by George Allen and Unwin Ltd. under the title: First sea lord." Includes bibliographical references. [DA89.1.F5H6 1970] 72-77970
1. Fisher, John Arbuthnot Fisher, Baron, 1841-1920. I. Title.

Fisher, John, Saint, Bp. of Rochester, 1469-1535.

REYNOLDS, Ernest Edwin, 922.242 1894-
Saint John Fisher. New York, Kenedy [1956?] 310p. illus. 23cm. [BX4700.F34R3] 56-5574
1. Fisher, John, Saint, Bp. of Rochester, 1469-1535. I. Title.

Fisher, Jonathan, 1768-1847.

FISHER, Jonathan, 1768- 759.13 1847.
Versatile Yankee; the art of Jonathan Fisher, 1768-1847 [by] Alice Winchester. [1st ed.] Princeton, Pyne Press [1973] 29, [15] p. illus., 40 col. plates. 32 cm. "List of works": p. [34]-[42] [ND237.F44W56] 73-79528 ISBN 0-87861-051-0 35.00
1. Fisher, Jonathan, 1768-1847. I. Winchester, Alice. II. Title.

Fisher, King. 1854-1884.

FISHER, Ovie 917.64030924 (B) Clark, 1903-
King Fisher; his life and times, by O. C. Fisher with J. C. Dykes. [1st ed.] Norman, Univ. of Okla. Pr. [1966] xvii, 157p. 20cm. (Western frontier lib., 32) [F392.D65F53] 66-22710 2.00 bds.,
1. Fisher, King. 1854-1884. I. Dykes, Jefferson Chenowth. 1900- II. Title. III. Series.

Fisher, Lois.

FISHER, Lois. 951'.156'05
A Peking diary : a westerner's life in China / by Lois Fisher. New York : St. Martin's Press, 1979. p. cm. [DS795.F57] 78-21424 ISBN 0-312-59997-8 : 10.95
1. Fisher, Lois. 2. Peking—Description. I. Title.

Fisher, Mary Frances (Kennedy)

FISHER, Mary Frances 917.94'93 B (Kennedy) 1908-
Among friends [by] M. F. K. Fisher. [1st ed.] New York, Knopf, 1971. 306 p. 22 cm. [TX649.F5A29 1971] 72-154925 ISBN 0-394-46899-6 6.95
I. Title.

Fisher, Ronald Aylmer, Sir, 1890-1962.

BOX, Joan Fisher, 1926- 519.5'092'4 B
R. A. Fisher, the life of a scientist / Joan Fisher Box. New York : Wiley, c1978. xii, 512 p., [13] leaves of plates : ill. ; 24 cm. (Wiley series in probability and mathematical statistics) "Bilbliography of R. A. Fisher": p. 486-503. [QA29.F57B68] 78-1668 ISBN 0-471-09300-9 : 20.00
1. Fisher, Ronald Aylmer, Sir, 1890-1962. 2. Statisticians—Great Britain—Biography. I. Title.

Fisher, Welthy (Honsinger)

FISHER, Welthy (Honsinger) 1880- 922.773
To light a candle. New York, McGraw [c.1962] 279p. illus. 62-11528 5.95
I. Title.

Fisheries—Massachusetts—Cape Cod.

SCHWIND, Phil. 639'.22'0924 B
Cape Cod fisherman / by Phil Schwind. Camden, Me. : International Marine Pub. Co., [1975] c1974. x, 224 p., [10] leaves of plates : ill. ; 24 cm. [SH20.S38A33 1975] 74-19999 ISBN 0-87742-045-9 : 8.95
1. Fisheries—Massachusetts—Cape Cod. 2. Fishing—Massachusetts—Cape Cod. 3. Fishermen—Massachusetts—Cape Cod—Correspondence, reminiscences, etc. 4. Schwind, Phil. I. Title. BIP

Fishermen—Correspondence, reminiscences, etc.

PIPER, Steven, d.1970. 639'.2'0924 B
The north ships; the life of a trawlerman. Newton Abbot, [Eng.] North Pomfret, Vt., David & Charles [1974] 161 p. illus. 23 cm. [SH344.6.T7P56 1974] 74-76187 ISBN 0-7153-6483-9 £3.95
1. Fishermen—Correspondence, reminiscences, etc. 2. Trawls and trawling—North Atlantic Ocean. I. Title. BIP

Fishermen—Massachusetts—Gloucester—Biography.

BARTLETT, Kim. 338.3'72'7097445
The finest kind : the fishermen of Gloucester / by Kim Bartlett ; ill. by Nubar. 1st ed. New York : Norton, c1977. p. cm. [SH20.A1B37 1977] 77-8800 ISBN 0-393-08797-2 : 8.95
1. Fishermen—Massachusetts—Gloucester—Biography. 2. Gloucester, Mass.—Biography. I. Title. BIP

Fishing—Anecdotes, facetiae, satire, etc.

HUGHES, Stephen Ormsby, 1924- 799.1'2
Tight lines and dragonflies. Drawings by Charles Saxon. [1st ed.] Philadelphia, Lippincott [1972] 155 p. illus. 22 cm. Autobiographical. [SH20.H8A3] 74-37612 ISBN 0-397-00865-1 5.95
1. Fishing—Anecdotes, facetiae, satire, etc. I. Title.

Fisk, Carlton, 1947- —Juvenile literature.

JACKSON, Robert B. 796.357'092'4 B
Fisk of Fenway Park : New England's favorite catcher / by Robert B. Jackson. New York : H. Z. Walck, c1976. 70 p. : ill. ; 21 cm. Focuses on the career of Carlton Fisk, catcher for the Boston Red Sox, who in 1972 was the first Rookie of the Year in the American League to be unanimously selected. [GV865.F44J32] 92 75-43039 ISBN 0-8098-5008-7 : 5.95
1. Fisk, Carlton, 1947- —Juvenile literature. 2. Baseball—Juvenile literature. I. Title.

Fisk, Clinton Bowen, 1828-1890.

HOPKINS, Alphonso Alva, 1843-1918. 973.8'0924 B
The life: Clinton Bowen Fisk, with a brief sketch of John A. Brooks. New York, Negro Universities Press [1969] x, 295 p. ports. 23 cm. On spine: Life of Clinton Bowen Fisk. Reprint of the 1888 ed. [E664.F53H7 1969] 75-78582
1. Fisk, Clinton Bowen, 1828-1890. 2. Brooks, John Anderson, 1836-

Fisk, James, 1835-1872.

SWANBERG, W A 1907- 923.373
Jim Fisk; the career of an improbable rascal. New York, Scribner [1959] 310 p. illus. 22 cm. [CT275.F565S8] 59-5787
1. Fisk, James, 1835-1872. I. Title.

Fisk, Pliny, 1792-1825.

BOND, Alvan, 1793-1882. 266'.009'24 B
Memoir of the Rev. Pliny Fisk, A.M. : late missionary to Palestine / Alvan Bond. New York : Arno Press, 1977 [c1827] 437 p. ; 21 cm. (America and the Holy Land) Reprint of the 1828 ed. published by Crocker and Brewster, Boston. [BV3202.F55B66 1977] 77-70683 ISBN 0-405-10230-5 : 25.00
1. Fisk, Pliny, 1792-1825. 2. Missionaries—Palestine—Biography. 3. Missionaries—United States—Biography. 4. Near East—Religion. 5. Near East—Description and travel. I. Fisk, Pliny, 1792-1825. II. Title. III. Series.

Fisk University, Nashville.

JONES, Thomas Elsa, 1888- 289.6'092'4 B
Light on the horizon; the Quaker pilgrimage of Tom Jones, by Thomas E. Jones. Richmond, Ind., Friends United Press [1973] vii, 225 p. illus. 22 cm. [BX7795.J58A34] 73-12707 ISBN 0-913408-08-5 4.95
1. Jones, Thomas Elsa, 1888- 2. Fisk University, Nashville. 3. Earlham College, Richmond, Ind. I. Title. BIP

Fiske, Bradley Allen, 1854-1942.

COLETTA, Paolo Enrico, 1916- 359.3'31'0924 B
Admiral Bradley A. Fiske and the American Navy / Paolo E. Coletta. Lawrence : Regents Press of Kansas, c1979. xiii, 306 p., [1] leaf of plates : port. ; 24 cm. Includes bibliographical references and index. [V63.F57C64] 78-16525 ISBN 0-7006-0181-3 : 20.00
1. Fiske, Bradley Allen, 1854-1942. 2. United States. Navy—History. 3. Admirals—United States—Biography. I. Title. BIP

Fiske, John, 1601-1677.

FISKE, John, 1601-1677. 917.44'03'208 S
The notebook of the Reverend John Fiske, 1644-1675 / edited and with an introd. by Robert G. Pope. Boston : Colonial Society of Massachusetts, 1974. xlii, 256 p. ; 25 cm. (Publications of the Colonial Society of Massachusetts ; v. 47 : Collections) Incudes index. [F61.C71 vol. 47] [BX7260.F535] 285'.8'0924 B 74-81447
1. Fiske, John, 1601-1677. 2. Wenham, Mass.—Church history—Sources. 3. Chelmsford, Mass.—Church history—Sources. I. Title. II. Series: Colonial Society of Massachusetts, Boston. Publications ; v. 47.

Fiske, Minnie Maddern (Davey)

FISKE, Minnie Maddern (Davey) 1865-1932. 792'.0924
Mrs. Fiske; her views on the stage. Recorded by Alexander Woollcott. New York, B. Blom [1968] 229 p. illus., facsims., ports. 20 cm. Reprint of the 1917 ed. [PN2287.F5A5 1968] 68-56482
I. Woollcott, Alexander, 1887-1943. II. Title.

Fitch, John, 1743-1798.

BOYD, Thomas Alexander, 1898-1935. 623.82'04'0924 B
Poor John Fitch, inventor of the steamboat. Freeport, N.Y., Books for Libraries Press [1971] 315 p. illus. 23 cm. Reprint of the 1935 ed. Bibliography: p. 303-307. [VM140.F5B6 1971] 75-150171 ISBN 0-8369-5684-2
1. Fitch, John, 1743-1798. 2. Steam-navigation. I. Title.

FITCH, John, 1743-1798. 081 S
The autobiography of John Fitch / edited with introd. and notes by Frank D. Prager. Philadelphia : American Philosophical, 1976. 215 p. : ill. ; 24 cm. (Memoirs of the American Philosophical Society ; v. 113 ISSN 0065-9738s) Includes bibliographical references and index. [Q11.P612 vol. 113] [VM140.F5] 623.82'04'0924 B 76-8596 ISBN 0-87169-113-2 pbk. : 7.00
1. Fitch, John, 1743-1798. 2. Inventors—United States—Biography. 3. Steam-navigation—United States—Biography. 4. Steam-navigation—United States—History—Sources. I. Title. II. Series: American Philosophical Society, Philadelphia. Memoirs ; v. 113. BIP

Fitch-Martin, Abby, 1850-1937.

LOUGHLIN, Kataryn [Gerin-La Joie] 1908- 920.7
Miss Abby Fitch-Martin. New York, Coward-McCann [1952] 179 p. 21 cm. [CT275.F57L6] 52-8028
1. Fitch-Martin, Abby, 1850-1937. I. Title.

Fitch, Ralph, fl. 1583-1606.

EDWARDES, Michael. 915.4'04'250924
Ralph Fitch, Elizabethan in the Indies. New York, Barnes & Noble Books [1973, c1972] 184 p. illus. 21 cm. (Great travellers) Bibliography: p. 173-174. [DS411.E38 1973] 73-168333 ISBN 0-06-491890-4 9.00
1. Fitch, Ralph, fl. 1583-1606. 2. East Indies—Description and travel. I. Title.

Fitch, Thomas, 1838-1923.

FITCH, Thomas, 1838-1923. 978'.02'0924
Western carpetbagger : the extraordinary memoirs of "Senator" Thomas Fitch / edited and with a foreword by Eric N. Moody. Reno : University of Nevada Press, 1978. x, 286 p. : ill. ; 21 cm. (A Bristlecone paperback) Includes index. [F594.F54A38 1978] 77-18257 ISBN 0-87417-050-8 pbk. : 5.25
1. Fitch, Thomas, 1838-1923. 2. Politicians—The West—Biography. 3. The West—History—1848-1950. 4. United States—Politics and government—1865-1900. I. Moody, Eric N. II. Title.

Fitz Gerald, Edward, 1809-1883—Biography.

FITZGERALD, Edward, 1809-1883. 928.2
Letters. Edited by J. M. Cohen. Carbondale, Southern Illinois University Press [1960] xxii, 275p. 19cm. (Centaur classics) 60-9249 4.75
1. Authors—Correspondence, reminiscences, etc. I. Title.

TERHUNE, Alfred McKinley, 1899- 821'.8 B
The life of Edward FitzGerald, translator of the Rubaiyat of Omar Khayyam / by Alfred McKinley Terhune. Westport, Conn. : Greenwood Press, 1980, c1947. p. cm. Reprint of the ed. published by G. Cumberlege, Oxford University Press, London. Includes index. Bibliography: p. [PR4703.T4 1980] 79-18964 ISBN 0-313-22108-1 : 31.00
1. Fitz Gerald, Edward, 1809-1883—Biography. 2. Authors, English—19th century—Biography. I. Title.

Fitz-Gibbon, Bernice.

FITZ-GIBBON, Bernice. 659.1'0924
Macy's, Gimbels, and me; how to earn $90,000 a year in retail advertising. New York, Simon and Schuster [1967] 880 p. illus. 22 cm. [HF5810.F5A3] 67-12922
I. Title.

Fitz Gibbon, Constantine.

FITZ GIBBON, Constantine. 828'.9'1403
Through the minefield; an autobiography. New York, W. W. Norton [1967] 266 p. ports. (on lining papers) 22 cm. [PR6011.I88Z5 1967b] 67-12435
I. Title.

FITZ Gibbon, Constantine. 828'.9'1403
Through the minefield; an autobiography. New York, W. W. Norton [1967] 266 p. ports. (on lining papers) 22 cm. [PR6011.I88Z5 1967b] 67-12435
I. Title.

Fitzgerald, Alice Louise Florence, 1874-1962.

NOBLE, Iris. 926.1
Nurse around the world: Alice Fitzgerald. New York, Messner [1964] 191 p. 22 cm. [RT37.F5N6] 64-11819
1. Fitzgerald, Alice Louise Florence, 1874-1962. I. Title.

Fitzgerald, Edward E., 1919- joint author.

UNITAS, John, 1933- 796.332'0924 B
Pro quarterback; my own story, by Johnny Unitas and Ed Fitzgerald. New York, Grosset & Dunlap [1968] 185 p. illus. 20 cm. (Grosset sports library) [GV939.U5A3 1968] 75-968 1.95
1. Fitzgerald, Edward E., 1919- joint author. I. Title. BIP

UNITAS, Johnny 796.332640924
Pro quarterback, my own story, by Johnny Unitas, Ed Fitzgerald. New York, S. & S. [c.1965] 188p. illus. 21cm. [GV939.U5A3] 65-22266 4.50
1. Fitzgerald, Edward E., I. Title.

Fitzgerald, Edward, Lord, 1763-1798.

MOLONY, John Chartres, 1877- 920.415
Ireland's tragic comedians. Freeport, N.Y., Books for Libraries Press [1970] ix, 313, [1] p. port. 23 cm. (Essay index reprint series) Reprint of the 1934 ed. "Bibliographical note": p. 313-[314] [DA948.6.A1M6 1970] 73-134117
1. Clare, John Fitzgibbon, 1st Earl of, 1749-1802. 2. Tone, Theobald Wolfe, 1763-1798. 3. Fitzgerald, Edward, Lord, 1763-1798. 4. Emmet, Robert, 1778-1803. I. Title. BIP

Fitzgerald, Edward, 1809-1883.

ADAMS, Morley. 821'.8 B
Omar's interpreter; a new life of Edward FitzGerald. With an essay on the letters by Canon Ainger. [Folcroft, Pa.] Folcroft Library Editions, 1973. 174 p. illus. 24 cm. Reprint of the 1911 ed. published by the Priory Press, London. [PR4703.A55 1973] 73-12993 ISBN 0-8414-2899-9 (lib. bdg.)
1. FitzGerald, Edward, 1809-1883. I. Ainger, Alfred, 1837-1904. II. Title. BIP

FITZGERALD, Edward, 1809-1883. 821'.8
A FitzGerald friendship, being hitherto unpublished letters from Edward FitzGerald to William Bodham Donne. Edited, with an introd. and notes, in collaboration with Catherine Bodham Johnson, by Neilson Campbell Hannay. [Folcroft, Pa.] Folcroft Library Editions, 1973 [c1932] p. Reprint of the ed. published by Faber and Faber, London. [PR4703.A4D6 1973] 73-12992 30.00
1. FitzGerald, Edward, 1809-1883. 2. Donne, William Bodham, 1807-1882. I. Donne, William Bodham, 1807-1882. II. Hannay, Neilson Campbell, 1880-1962, ed.

III. Johnson, Catharine Bodham (Donne) ed. IV. Title.

FITZGERALD, Edward, 1809-1883. 821'.8 B
Letters from Edward FitzGerald to Bernard Quaritch, 1853-1883. Edited by C. Quaritch Wrentmore. [Folcroft, Pa.] Folcroft Library Editions, 1973. p. Reprint of the 1926 ed. published by B. Quaritch, London. [PR4703.A4Q3 1973] 73-13547 40.00
1. FitzGerald, Edward, 1809-1883. 2. Quaritch, Bernard, 1819-1899. I. Quaritch, Bernard, 1819-1899. II. Title.

FITZGERALD, Edward, 1809-1883. 821'.8 B
Letters from Edward FitzGerald to Bernard Quaritch, 1853 to 1883. Edited by C. Quaritch Wrentmore. [Folcroft, Pa.] Folcroft Library Editions, 1973. viii, 135 p. illus. 24 cm. Reprint of the 1926 ed. published by B. Quaritch, London. [PR4703.A4Q3 1973] 73-13547 ISBN 0-8414-9428-2 (lib. bdg.)
1. FitzGerald, Edward, 1809-1883. 2. Quaritch, Bernard, 1819-1899. I. Quaritch, Bernard, 1819-1899. II. Title.

FITZGERALD, Edward, 1809-1883. 821'.8 B
Letters of Edward FitzGerald, edited by William A. Wright. Freeport, N.Y., Books for Libraries Press [1972] 2 v. illus. 22 cm. Consists of the letters first published in 1889 in Letters and literary remains of Edward FitzGerald, with some additional letters. Reprint of the 1894 ed., issued in series: Eversley series. Includes bibliographical references. [PR4703.A2 1972] 72-5597 ISBN 0-8369-6906-5
I. Wright, William Aldis, 1831-1914. II. FitzGerald, Edward, 1809-1883. Letters and literary remains of Edward FitzGerald. Letters. 1972. III. Series: Eversley series. BIP

FITZGERALD, Edward, 1809-1883. 821'.8 B
Letters of Edward Fitzgerald to Fanny Kemble, 1871-1883. Edited by William Aldis Wright. Freeport, N.Y., Books for Libraries Press [1972] 271 p. port. 22 cm. Reprint of the 1902 ed. Includes bibliographical references. [PR4703.A4K4 1972] 72-2502 ISBN 0-8369-6854-9 11.00
I. Kemble, Frances Anne, 1809-1893. II. Title.

FITZGERALD, Edward, 1809-1883. 821'.8 B
Letters of Edward FitzGerald to Fanny Kemble, 1871-1883. Edited by William Aldis Wright. [Folcroft, Pa.] Folcroft Library Editions, 1973. p. Reprint of the 1902 ed. published by Macmillan, London. Includes bibliographical references. [PR4703.A4K4 1973] 73-11420 10.50
1. FitzGerald, Edward, 1809-1883. I. Kemble, Frances Anne, 1809-1893. II. Title.

FITZGERALD, Edward, 1809-1883. 821'.8 B
Letters of Edward FitzGerald to Fanny Kemble, 1871-1883. Edited by William Aldis Wright. [Folcroft, Pa.] Folcroft Library Editions, 1973. p. Reprint of the 1902 ed. published by Macmillan, London. Includes bibliographical references. [PR4703.A4K4 1973] 73-11420 ISBN 0-8414-9372-3 (lib. bdg.)
1. FitzGerald, Edward, 1809-1883. I. Kemble, Frances Anne, 1809-1893. II. Title.

*HUSSEY, Frank. 623.88092
Old Fitz; Edward Fitzgerald and east coast sailing. Ipswich, Boydell Press, [1975 c1974] xii, 162 p. ill. maps on lining paper 23 cm. (Suffolk library) Includes index. Bibliography: p. [155]-156. [GV814] ISBN 0-85115-038-1
1. FitzGerald, Edward, 1809-1883. 2. Seafaring life. 3. Yachts and Yachting. 4. Sailing. I. Title.
Distributed by Rowman and Littlefield for 11.50.

WRIGHT, Thomas, 1859-1936. 821'.8 B
The life of Edward FitzGerald. London, Grant Richards, 1904. St. Clair Shores, Mich., Scholarly Press, 1971. 2 v. illus., facsims., geneal. tables, ports. 22 cm. Includes bibliographies. [PR4703.W8 1971] 70-108556 ISBN 0-403-00254-0
1. FitzGerald, Edward, 1809-1883. I. Title. BIP

Fitzgerald family.

MURRAY, Pauli, 1910- 301.45'19'6073
Proud shoes : the story of an American family / by Pauli Murray. New York : Harper & Row, c1978. xvii, 280 p., [10] leaves of plates : ill. ; 22 cm. [E185.97.F47M87] 77-11807 ISBN 0-06-013109-8 : 10.00. ISBN 0-06-090617-0 pbk. : 3.95
1. Fitzgerald family. 2. Murray, Pauli, 1910- 3. Afro-Americans—Biography. 4. Afro-Americans—Social life and customs. I. Title.

Fitzgerald, Francis Scott Key, 1896-1940.

ALLEN, Joan M., 1938- 813'.5'2 B
Candles and carnival lights : the Catholic sensibility of F. Scott Fitzgerald / Joan M. Allen. New York : New York University Press, 1978. xvi, 163 p. ; 24 cm. (The Gotham library of the New York University Press) Includes bibliographical references and index. [PS3511.I9Z5576] 77-82752 ISBN 0-8147-0563-4 : 15.00. ISBN 0-8147-0564-2 pbk. : 4.95
1. Fitzgerald, Francis Scott Key, 1896-1940. 2. Fitzgerald, Francis Scott Key, 1896-1940—Religion and ethics. 3. Novelists, American—20th century—Biography. I. Title. BIP

COWLEY, Malcolm, 1898- ed. 917.30391
Fitzgerald and the jazz age [by] Malcolm Cowley [and] Robert Cowley. New York, Scribner [1966] xvii, 192 p. 24 cm. (Scribner research anthologies) [E169.1.C795] 66-18182
1. Fitzgerald, Francis Scott Key, 1896-1940. 2. United States—Civilization—1918-1945. I. Cowley, Robert, joint ed. II. Title.

CROSS, K G W v. 12
Scott Fitzgerald. New York, Barnes & Noble [1966, c1964] 120 p. 19 cm. (Writers and critics) Bibliography: p. [116]-120. 68-91917
1. Fitzgerald, Francis Scott Key, 1896-1940. I. Title. II. Series.

CROSS, K. G. W. 813'.5'2 B
Scott Fitzgerald [by] K. G. W. Cross. New York, Capricorn Books [1971, c1964] 120 p. 19 cm. (A Capricorn book, CAP 168) (Writers and critics) Bibliography: p. [116]-120. [PS3511.I9Z58 1971] 72-172989 1.25
1. Fitzgerald, Francis Scott Key, 1896-1940. I. Title. II. Series.

EBLE, Kenneth Eugene. 813'.5'2 B
F. Scott Fitzgerald / by Kenneth Eble. Rev. ed. Boston : Twayne Publishers, c1977. 187 p. : port. ; 21 cm. (Twayne's United States authors series ; TUSAS 36) Includes index. Bibliography: p. 169-182. [PS3511.I9Z6 1977] 77-429 ISBN 0-8057-7183-2 lib.bdg. : 7.95
1. Fitzgerald, Francis Scott Key, 1896-1940. 2. Authors, American—20th century—Biography.

FAHEY, William A. 813'.5'2
F. Scott Fitzgerald and the American dream, by William A. Fahey. New York, Crowell [1973] 177 p. 21 cm. (Twentieth-century American writers) Bibliography: p. 165-167. [PS3511.I9Z616] 73-4523 ISBN 0-690-00078-2 4.50
1. Fitzgerald, Francis Scott Key, 1896-1940. I. Title. BIP

THE far side of paradise; v. 12
a biography of F. Scott Fitzgerald. New York, Vintage books, 1959. xxvi, 346p. 19cm. (Vintage book, K-77) 'First Vintage edition.' 'Fitzgerald's published work': p. [338]-346
1. Fitzgerald, Francis Scott Key, 1896-1940. I. Mizener, Arthur. II. Series. BIP

GRAHAM, Sheilah. v. 12
Beloved infidel; the education of a woman, by Sheilah Graham and Gerold Frank. New York, Bantam Books [1962, c1958] viii, 257 p. 19 cm. Autobiographical. This edition first published 1959. 67-49806
1. Fitzgerald, Francis Scott Key, 1896-1940. I. Frank, Gerold, 1907- II. Title.

GRAHAM, Sheilah. 928.1
Beloved infidel; the education of a woman, by Sheliah Graham and Gerold Frank. [1st ed.] New York, Holt [1958] 338 p. illus. 22 cm. Autobiography of Sheilah Graham. [PN4874.G67A3] 58-14130
1. Fitzgerald, Francis Scott Key, 1896-1940. I. Frank, Gerold, 1907- II. Title.

GRAHAM, Sheilah. 813'.5'2 B
College of one. New York, Viking Press [1967] viii, 245 p. facsims. 22 cm. "The story of a unique two-year liberal arts course—the student: Sheilah Graham; the teacher: F. Scott Fitzgerald."—Dust jacket. The appendices (p. [201]-245) contain facsims. of the corrected typescripts of "the curriculum," by F. Scott Fitzgerald, and the author's short story, Beloved infidel. [PS3511.I9Z64] 67-10218
1. Fitzgerald, Francis Scott Key, 1896-1940. I. Title.

GRAHAM, Sheilah. 920.5
The rest of the story. New York, Coward-McCann [1964] 317 p. ports., facsim. 22 cm. Autobiographical. [PN4874.G67A32] 64-13057
1. Fitzgerald, Francis Scott Key, 1896-1940. I. Title.

KAZIN, Alfred, 1915- ed. 928.1
F. Scott Fitzgerald: the man and his work. New York, Collier [1962, c.1961] 221p. 18cm. (AS 434X) Bibl. .95 pap.,
1. Fitzgerald, Francis Scott Key, 1896-1940. I. Title.

KAZIN, Alfred, 1915 ed. 928.1
F. Scott Fitzgerald: the man and his work. [1st ed.] Cleveland, World Pub. Co. [1951] 219 p. 22 cm. "The works of F. Scott Fitzgerald": p. [221] [PS3511.I9Z67] 51-10640
1. Fitzgerald, Francis Scott Key, 1896-1940.

KAZIN, Alfred, 1915- ed. v. 12
F. Scott Fitzgerald: the man and his work. [1st Collier Books ed.] New york. Collier Books [1962, c1951] 221, [2] p. 18 cm. "The works of F. Scott Fitzgerald": p. [223] 63-40941
1. Fitzgerald, Francis Scott Key, 1896-1840. I. Title.

LATHAM, Aaron. 813'.5'2 B
Crazy Sundays; F. Scott Fitzgerald in Hollywood. New York, Viking Press [1971] xi, 308 p. 23 cm. Includes bibliographical references. [PS3511.I9Z675] 70-132860 ISBN 0-670-24550-X 7.95
1. Fitzgerald, Francis Scott Key, 1896-1940. I. Title.

LEHAN, Richard Daniel, 1930- 813.52
F. Scott Fitzgerald and the craft of fiction [by] Richard D. Lehan. With a pref. by Harry T. Moore. Carbondale, Southern Illinois University Press [1966] xv, 206 p. 22 cm. (Crosscurrents: modern critiques) Bibliographical references included in "Notes" (p. [180]-195). Bibliography: p. [196]-198. [PS3511.I9Z68] 66-15059
1. Fitzgerald, Francis Scott Key, 1896-1940. BIP

MAYFIELD, Sara, 1905- 813'.5'2 B
Exiles from paradise: Zelda and Scott Fitzgerald. New York, Delacorte Press [1971] 309 p. 24 cm. Bibliography: p. 289-295. [PS3511.I9Z685] 76-137744 8.95
1. Fitzgerald, Francis Scott Key, 1896-1940. 2. Fitzgerald, Zelda (Sayre) I. Title.

MIZENER, Arthur. 928.1
The far side of paradise; a biography of F. Scott Fitzgerald. Boston, Houghton Mifflin, 1951. xx, 362 p. ports. 22 cm. "Notes and references": p. 315-349. "Fitzgerald's published work": p. 350-356. Full name: Arthur Moore Misener. [PS3511.I9Z7] 51-9185
1. Fitzgerald, Francis Scott Key, 1896-1940. I. Title.

MIZENER, Arthur. 928.1
The far side of paradise; a biography of F. Scott Fitzgerald. New York, Avon [1974, c1965] 408 p. illus. 18 cm. "Notes and references" p. 339-387. [PS3511.I9Z7] ISBN 0-380-00052-0. 1.50 (pbk.)
1. Fitzgerald, Francis Scott Key, 1896-1940. I. Title.
L.C. card number for hardbound ed.: 51-9185.

MIZENER, Arthur. 813'.5'2 B
Scott Fitzgerald and his world. [1st ed.] New York, Putnam [1972] 128 p. illus. 24 cm. Bibliography: p. 119. Presents the life of the flamboyant twentieth-century writer explaining the relationships between himself, his acquaintances, and the characters in his novels. [PS3511.I9Z72 1972b] 92 72-189992 6.95
1. Fitzgerald, Francis Scott Key, 1896-1940. I. Title.

SHAIN, Charles E. 813.52
F. Scott Fitzgerald. Minneapolis, University of Minnesota Press [1961] 48 p. 21 cm. (University of Minnesota pamphlets on American writers, no. 15) Includes bibliography. [PS3511.I9Z85 1961] 61-64010
1. Fitzgerald, Francis Scott Key, 1896-1940.

SKLAR, Robert. 813'.5'2
F. Scott Fitzgerald, the last Laocoon. New York, Oxford University Press, 1967. 376 p. 24 cm. Bibliographical references included in "Notes" (p. 347-369) [PS3511.I9Z86] 67-12387
1. Fitzgerald, Francis Scott Key, 1896-1940. I. Title.

TURNBULL, Andrew, 1921- 928.1
Scott Fitzgerald. New York, Scribner [1962] 364 p. illus. 24 cm. [PS3511.I9Z88] 62-9315
1. Fitzgerald, Francis Scott Key, 1896-1940. I. Title. BIP

Fitzgerald, Francis Scott Key, 1896-1940—Bibliography.

BRUCCOLI, Matthew Joseph, 1931- 016.813'52
F. Scott Fitzgerald; a descriptive bibliography [by] Matthew J. Bruccoli. [Pittsburgh] University of Pittsburgh Press, 1972. xxiii, 369 p. illus. 25 cm. (Pittsburgh series in bibliography) [Z8301.2.B69] 77-181395 ISBN 0-8229-3239-3 19.95
1. Fitzgerald, Francis Scott Key, 1896-1940—Bibliography. I. Title. II. Series. BIP

Fitzgerald, Francis Scott Key, 1896-1940—Biography.

BRUCCOLI, Matthew Joseph, 1931- comp. 813'.5'209 B
The romantic egoists : [Scott and Zelda Fitzgerald] / edited by Matthew J. Bruccoli, Scottie Fitzgerald Smith, and Joan P. Kerr ; art editor, Margareta F. Lyons. New York : Scribner, [1974] x, 246 p., [4] leaves of plates : ill. (some col.) ; 37 cm. Bibliography: p. 245-246. [PS3511.I9Z563] 74-14012 ISBN 0-684-13923-5 : 25.00.
1. Fitzgerald, Francis Scott Key, 1896-1940—Biography. 2. Fitzgerald, Zelda Sayre—Biography. 3. Fitzgerald, Francis Scott Key, 1896-1940—Miscellanea. 4. Fitzgerald, Zelda Sayre—Miscellanea. I. Smith, Scottie Fitzgerald, joint comp. II. Kerr, Joan Paterson, joint comp. III. Title.

BUTTITTA, Tony. 813.5'2
After the good gay times; Asheville, summer of '35, a season with F. Scott Fitzgerald. New York, Viking Press [1974] xii, 173 p. 22 cm. [PS3511.I9Z572] 73-16826 ISBN 0-670-10912-6 7.95
1. Fitzgerald, Francis Scott Key, 1896-1940—Biography. 2. Buttitta, Tony—Biography. 3. Authors—Correspondence, reminiscences, etc. I. Title.

Fitzgerald, Francis Scott Key, 1896-1940—Chronology.

FITZGERALD, Francis Scott Key, 1896-1940. 813'.5'2 B
F. Scott Fitzgerald's ledger : a facsimile / introd. by Matthew J. Bruccoli. Washington : NCR/Microcard Editions, 1972. 189 p. ; 39 cm. "A Bruccoli Clark book." Issued in case. Includes bibliograpiical references. [PS3511.I9Z52 1972] 72-87563 ISBN 0-910972-29-X

1. Fitzgerald, Francis Scott Key, 1896-1940—Chronology. 2. Fitzgerald, Francis Scott Key, 1896-1940—Bibliography. I. Title.

Fitzgerald, Francis Scott Key, 1896-1940—Correspondence.

BRUCCOLI, Matthew Joseph, 1931- 813'.5'209 B
Scott and Ernest : the authority of failure and the authority of success / Matthew J. Bruccoli. 1st ed. New York : Random House, c1978. xv 168 p. : ill. ; 25 cm. Bibliography: p. 167-168. [PS3511.I9Z565] 77-90250 ISBN 0-394-42889-7 : 8.95
1. Fitzgerald, Francis Scott Key, 1896-1940—Friends and associates. 2. Hemingway, Ernest, 1899-1961—Friends and associates. 3. Fitzgerald, Francis Scott Key, 1896-1940—Correspondence. 4. Hemingway, Ernest, 1899-1961—Correspondence. 5. Authors, American—20th century—Biography. I. Title. **BIP**

FITZGERALD, Francis Scott Key, 1896-1940. 813'.5'2 B
Dear Scott/Dear Max; the Fitzgerald-Perkins correspondence. Edited by John Kuehl and Jackson R. Bryer. New York, Scribner [1971] vi, 282 p. 25 cm. [PS3511.I9Z556] 76-143940 ISBN 0-684-12373-8 7.95
I. Perkins, Maxwell Evarts, 1884-1947. II. Title.

FITZGERALD, Francis Scott Key, 1896-1940 928.1
Letters. Ed. by Andrew Turnbull. New York. [Dell, 1966, c.1963] 638p. 18cm. (Laurel ed. 4745) [PS3511.I9Z54] 1.25 pap.,
I. Turnbull, Andrew, 1921- ed. II. Title.

Fitzgerald, Francis Scott Key, 1896-1940—Friends and associates.

BRUCCOLI, Matthew Joseph, 1931- 813'.5'209 B
Scott and Ernest : the authority of failure and the authority of success / Matthew J. Bruccoli. 1st ed. New York : Random House, c1978. xv 168 p. : ill. ; 25 cm. Bibliography: p. 167-168. [PS3511.I9Z565] 77-90250 ISBN 0-394-42889-7 : 8.95
1. Fitzgerald, Francis Scott Key, 1896-1940—Friends and associates. 2. Hemingway, Ernest, 1899-1961—Friends and associates. 3. Fitzgerald, Francis Scott Key, 1896-1940—Correspondence. 4. Hemingway, Ernest, 1899-1961—Correspondence. 5. Authors, American—20th century—Biography. I. Title. **BIP**

Fitzgerald, Francis Scott Key, 1896-1940—Homes and haunts—Minnesota.

KOBLAS, John J., 1942- 813'.5'2 B
F. Scott Fitzgerald in Minnesota : his homes and haunts / by John J. Koblas. St. Paul : Minnesota Historical Society Press, 1978. 41 p. : ill. ; 22 cm. (Minnesota historic sites pamphlet ; no. 18) (Publications of the Minnesota Historical Society) Includes bibliographical references. [PS3511.I9Z673] 78-21979 ISBN 0-87351-134-4 pbk. : 3.75
1. Fitzgerald, Francis Scott Key, 1896-1940—Homes and haunts—Minnesota. 2. Authors, American—20th century—Biography. 3. Minnesota—Biography. 4. Historical buildings—Minnesota. I. Title. II. Series: Minnesota Historical Society. Publications. III. Series: Minnesota historic sites pamphlet series ; no. 18. **BIP**

Fitzgerald, Francis Scott Key, 1896-1940—Juvenile literature.

GREENFELD, Howard. 813'.5'2 B
F. Scott Fitzgerald / by Howard Greenfeld. 1st ed. New York : Crown Publishers, [1974] 136 p., [1] leaf of plates : ill. ; 24 cm. Includes index. Bibliography: p. [127]-130. A biography of the author considered to be one of the most important American writers of the twentieth century. [PS3511.I9Z644] 92 73-91523 ISBN 0-517-51465-6 : 6.95
1. Fitzgerald, Francis Scott Key, 1896-1940—Juvenile literature.

Fitzgerald, Francis Scott Key, 1896-1940—Miscellanea.

BRUCCOLI, Matthew Joseph, 1931- comp. 813'.5'209 B
The romantic egoists : [Scott and Zelda Fitzgerald] / edited by Matthew J. Bruccoli, Scottie Fitzgerald Smith, and Joan P. Kerr ; art editor, Margareta F. Lyons. New York : Scribner, [1974] x, 246 p., [4] leaves of plates : ill. (some col.) ; 37 cm. Bibliography: p. 245-246. [PS3511.I9Z563] 74-14012 ISBN 0-684-13923-5 : 25.00.
1. Fitzgerald, Francis Scott Key, 1896-1940—Biography. 2. Fitzgerald, Zelda Sayre—Biography. 3. Fitzgerald, Francis Scott Key, 1896-1940—Miscellanea. 4. Fitzgerald, Zelda Sayre—Miscellanea. I. Smith, Scottie Fitzgerald, joint comp. II. Kerr, Joan Paterson, joint comp. III. Title.

Fitzgerald, John Francis, 1863-1950.

CUTLER, John Henry, 1910- 923.273
"Honey Fitz": three steps to the White House; the life and times of John F. (Honey Fitz) Fitzgerald. Indianapolis, Bobbs-Merrill [1962] 335 p. illus. 24 cm. [F73.5.F55C8] 62-10012
1. Fitzgerald, John Francis, 1863-1950.

Fitzgerald, Zelda Sayre—Biography.

BRUCCOLI, Matthew Joseph, 1931- comp. 813'.5'209 B
The romantic egoists : [Scott and Zelda Fitzgerald] / edited by Matthew J. Bruccoli, Scottie Fitzgerald Smith, and Joan P. Kerr ; art editor, Margareta F. Lyons. New York : Scribner, [1974] x, 246 p., [4] leaves of plates : ill. (some col.) ; 37 cm. Bibliography: p. 245-246. [PS3511.I9Z563] 74-14012 ISBN 0-684-13923-5 : 25.00.
1. Fitzgerald, Francis Scott Key, 1896-1940—Biography. 2. Fitzgerald, Zelda Sayre—Biography. 3. Fitzgerald, Francis Scott Key, 1896-1940—Miscellanea. 4. Fitzgerald, Zelda Sayre—Miscellanea. I. Smith, Scottie Fitzgerald, joint comp. II. Kerr, Joan Paterson, joint comp. III. Title.

MILFORD, Nancy. 813'.5'2 B
Zelda; a biography. New York, Harper & Row [1970] xiv, 424 p. illus., ports. 25 cm. Includes bibliographical references. [PS3511.I9234Z8 1970] 66-20742 10.00
1. Fitzgerald, Zelda Sayre—Biography. I. Title. **BIP**

Fitzherbert, Maria Anne (Smythe) 1756-1837.

LESLIE, Anita. 920.7
Mrs. Fitzherbert. New York, Scribner [1960] 239p. illus. 22cm. [DA538.F5L38 1960a] 60-12599
1. Fitzherbert, Maria Anne (Smythe) 1756-1837. I. Title.

LESLIE, Shane, Sir, bart., 1885- 920.042
Salutation to five. Freeport, N.Y., Books for Libraries Press [1970] v, 156 p. 23 cm. (Biography index reprint series) Reprint of the 1951 ed. Includes bibliographical references. [CT106.L4 1970] 75-126321 ISBN 8-369-80271-
1. Fitzherbert, Maria Anne (Smythe) 1756-1837. 2. Warre, Edmond, 1837-1920. 3. Butler, William Francis, Sir, 1838-1910. 4. Tolstoi, Lev Nikolaevich, graf, 1828-1910. 5. Sykes, Mark, Sir, bart., 1879-1919. I. Title.

Fitzherbert, William, Saint, d. 1154.

WHEELER, William Gordon. 282'.092'4 B
Saint William of York / by William G. Wheeler. London : Catholic Truth Society, 1976. [12] p. : ill. ; 19 cm. [BX4705.F567W47] 76-373767 ISBN 0-85183-168-0 : £0.12
1. Fitzherbert, William, Saint, d. 1154. 2. Christian saints—York, Eng.—Biography. 3. York, Eng.—Biography.

Fitzherbert, William Thomas.

FITZHERBERT, William Thomas. 920
The story of an American. Boston, Bruce Humphries [c1952] 252p. 21cm. Autobiographical. [CT275.F573A3] 52-14820
I. Title.

Fitzhugh, George, 1806-1881.

WISH, Harvey, 1909- 923.473
George Fitzhugh, propagandist of the old South. Gloucester, Mass., Peter Smith, 1962[c.1943] ix, 360p. illus. (Southern biog. ser; Louisiana State Univ. Pr. bk, rebound) 6.00
1. Fitzhugh, George, 1806-1881. 2. Slavery in the U. S. 3. Slavery—Justification. I. Title. **BIP**

Fitzpatrick, James Percy, Sir 1862-1931.

WALLIS, John Peter Richard. 1880- 923.2682
Fitz, the story of Sir Percy Fitzpatrick. London, Macmillan New York, St. Martin's Press, 1955. 278p. illus. 23cm. [DT776.F5W3] 55-3588
1. Fitzpatrick, James Percy, Sir 1862-1931. I. Title.

Fitzpatrick, John, ca. 1737-1791.

FITZPATRICK, John, ca.1737-1791. 976.3'03'0924
The merchant of Manchac : the letterbooks of John Fitzpatrick, 1768-1790 / edited with an introd. by Margaret Fisher Dalrymple. Baton Rouge : Published for the Baton Rouge Bicentennial Corp. by the Louisiana State University Press, c1978. p. cm. Includes index. Bibliography: p. [F373.F57 1978] 77-28801 ISBN 0-8071-0268-7 : 30.00
1. Fitzpatrick, John, ca. 1737-1791. 2. Louisiana—History—To 1803—Sources. 3. Pioneers—Louisiana—Biography. 4. Merchants—Louisiana—Biography. I. Dalrymple, Margaret Fisher. II. Title. **BIP**

Fitzpatrick, Thomas, 1799-1854.

GARST, Doris Shannon, 1899- 917.8'03'20924 B
Broken-Hand Fitzpatrick, greatest of mountain men. New York, J. Messner [1961] 190 p. 22 cm. Bibliography: p. 183-184. A biography of an Irish immigrant who left a clerking job in New York City to join a Missouri River expedition and, as a trapper and trailblazer discovered the South Pass through the Rockies, befriended the Arapahoes, and helped settle the West. [F593.F55G3] 92 AC 68
1. Fitzpatrick, Thomas, 1799-1854. I. Title.

HAFEN, Le Roy Reuben, 1893- 917.8'03'20924 B
Broken Hand; the life of Thomas Fitzpatrick: mountain man, guide, and Indian agent, by LeRoy R. Hafen. [1st rev. ed.] Denver, Colo., Old West Pub. Co. [1973] xiii, 359 p. illus. 25 cm. Includes bibliographical references. [F593.F55H33 1973] 73-81181 ISBN 0-912094-17-6 15.00
1. Fitzpatrick, Thomas, 1799-1854. 2. Frontier and pioneer life—The West. 3. The West—History—To 1848. I. Title. **BIP**

Fitzpatrick, Thomas, 1799-1854—Juvenile literature.

GARST, Doris Shannon, 1899- 923.573
Broken-Hand Fitzpatrick, greatest of mountain men. New York, Messner [c.1961] 190p. Bibl. 61-6369 2.95
1. Fitzpatrick, Thomas, 1799-1854—Juvenile literature. I. Title.

Fitzsimmons, James E., 1874-

BRESLIN, Jimmy. 927.98
Sunny Jim, the life of America's most beloved horseman, James Fitzsimmons. [1st ed.] Garden City, N. Y., Doubleday, 1962. 238p. illus. 22cm. [SF336.F5B7] 61-9484
1. Fitzsimmons, James E., 1874- I. Title.

Flack, Roberta—Juvenile literature.

JACOBS, Linda. 784'.092'4 B
Roberta Flack, sound of velvet melting / by Linda Jacobs. St. Paul : EMC Corp., 1975. p. cm. (Behind the bright lights) A biography of the versatile black singer whose voice has been described as the sound of velvet melting. [ML3930.F54J2] 75-15627 ISBN 0-88436-188-8 lib.bdg. : 4.95 ISBN 0-88436-189-6 pbk. : 2.95
1. Flack, Roberta—Juvenile literature. I. Title.

MORSE, Charles. 784'.092'4 B
Roberta Flack [by] Charles and Ann Morse. Illustrator: John Keely. Mankato, Minn., Creative Education [1974] p. cm. [ML3930.F54M7] 74-13938 ISBN 0-87191-396-8 4.95 (lib. bdg.)
1. Flack, Roberta—Juvenile literature. I. Morse, Ann, joint author. II. Keely, John, illus. III. Title. **BIP**

Flaget, Benedict Joseph, Bp., 1763-1850.

SPALDING, Martin John, Abp., 1810-1872. 282'.0924 B
Life, times, and character of the Right Reverend Benedict Joseph Flaget. New York, Arno Press, 1969. xvi, 406 p. 23 cm. (Religion in America) 1852 ed. published under title: Sketches of the life, times, and character of the Rt. Rev. Benedict Joseph Flaget, first Bishop of Louisville. Includes bibliographical references. [BX4705.F6S6 1969] 71-83441
1. Flaget, Benedict Joseph, Bp., 1763-1850. I. Title.

Flagler, Henry Morrison, 1830-1913.

REDDING, David A. 338.2'7'2820924 B
Flagler and his church, by David A. Redding. 1st ed. Jacksonville, Fla., Paramount Press [1970] 54 p. illus. (part col.), ports. 24 cm. [CT275.F582R4] 75-122479
1. Flagler, Henry Morrison, 1830-1913. 2. St. Augustine. Memorial Presbyterian Church. I. Title.

Flagstad, Kirsten, 1895-1962.

FLAGSTAD, Kirsten, 1895- 927.8
The Flagstad manuscript [by] Louis Biancolli. New York, Putnam [1952] 293 p. ports. 22 cm. An autobiography narrated to Louis Biancolli. [ML420.F55A3] 52-9828
1. Flagstad, Kirsten, 1895- I. Biancolli, Louis Leopold. II. Title.

FLAGSTAD, Kirsten, 1895-1962. 782.1'092'4 B
The Flagstad manuscript / Louis Biancolli. New York : Arno Press, 1977, c1952. xix, 293 p., [10] leaves of plates : ill. ; 23 cm. (Opera biographies) An autobiography narrated to Louis Biancolli. Reprint of the ed. published by Putnam, New York. Includes index. [ML420.F55A3 1977] 76-29935 ISBN 0-405-09677-1 : 20.00
1. Flagstad, Kirsten, 1895-1962. 2. Singers—Norway—Biography. I. Biancolli, Louis Leopold, joint author. II. Title.

Flaherty, Robert Joseph, 1884-1951.

CALDER-MARSHALL, Arthur, 1908- 791.430230924
The innocent eye; the life of Robert J. Flaherty, based on research material by Paul Rotha, Basil Wright. [1st Amer. ed.] New York, Harcourt [1966, c.1963] 303p. illus., ports. 22cm. Bibl. [PN1998.A3F47] 66-12357 6.95
1. Flaherty, Robert Joseph, 1884-1951. I. Rotha, Paul, 1907- II. Wright, Basil. III. Title.

FLAHERTY, Frances (Hubbard) 927.914
The odyssey of a film-maker; Robert Flaherty's story. Urbana, Ill., Beta Phi Mu, c/o Harold Lancour, Univ. of Ill. [c.]1960. 45p. 25cm. (Beta Phi Mu. Chapbook no. 4) 59-15964 3.00

1. Flaherty, Robert Joseph, 1884-1951. I. Title. BIP

FLAHERTY, Frances Hubbard. 791.43'023'0924 B
The odyssey of a film-maker : Robert Flaherty's story / by Frances Hubbard Flaherty. New York : Arno Press, 1972, c1960. 45 p., [8] leaves of plates : ill. ; 24 cm. (The Arno Press cinema program) Reprint of the ed. published by Beta Phi Mu, Urbana, Ill., as its Chapbook no. 4. Includes bibliographical references. [PN1998.A3F48 1972] 77-169343 ISBN 0-405-03918-2
1. Flaherty, Robert Joseph, 1884-1951. I. Title. II. Series. III. Series: Beta Phi Mu. Chapbook , no. 4. IV. The Literature of cinema.

GRIFFITH, Richard, 1912- 791.43'023'0924
The world of Robert Flaherty. Westport, Conn., Greenwood Press [1970, c1953] xxii, 165 p. illus. 23 cm. [PN1998.A3F5 1970] 78-98224
1. Flaherty, Robert Joseph, 1884-1951. I. Title.

GRIFFITH, Richard, 1912- 791.43'023'0924 B
The world of Robert Flaherty. New York, Da Capo Press, 1972 [c1953] xxii, 165 p. illus. 23 cm. [PN1998.A3F5 1972] 72-166104 ISBN 0-306-70296-7
1. Flaherty, Robert Joseph, 1884-1951. I. Title.

GRIFFITH, Richard, 1912- 927.914
The world of Robert Flaherty. With over 70 photos. [1st ed.] New York, Duell, Sloan and Pearce [1953] 165 p. illus. 25 cm. [PN1998.A3F5] 51-10886
1. Flaherty, Robert Joseph, 1884-1951. I. Title. BIP

Flanagan, Edward Joseph, 1886-1948.

OURSLER, Fulton, 1893- 922.273
Father Flanagan of Boys Town [by] Fulton Oursler, Will Oursler. Garden City, N.Y., Doubleday [1965, c.1949] 319p. 18cm. (Echo bk, E17) [HV876.F4O8] 49-10638 .95 pap.,
1. Flanagan, Edward Joseph, 1886-1948. 2. Father Flanagan's Boys' Home, Boys Town, Neb. I. Oursler, William Charles, 1913- joint author. II. Title.

Flanagan, Edward Joseph, 1886-1948—Juvenile literature.

GRAVES, Charles Parlin, 1911- 362.7'45'0924 B
Father Flanagan, founder of Boys Town, by Charles P. Graves. Illustrated by William Hutchinson. Champaign, Ill., Garrard Pub. Co. [1972] 95 p. illus. 24 cm. (Americans all) A biography of the priest who devoted his life to caring for homeless boys. [HV876.F4G73] 92 70-173448 ISBN 0-8116-4571-1
1. Flanagan, Edward Joseph, 1886-1948—Juvenile literature. 2. Father Flanagan's Boys' Home, Boys Town, Neb.—Juvenile literature. I. Hutchinson, William M., illus. II. Title.

ROBERTO, Brother, 1927- 922.273
There are no bad boys; a story of Father Edward Flanagan. Illus. by Carolyn Lee Jagodits. Notre Dame, Ind., Dujarie Press [1959] 94p. illus. 24cm. [HV876.F4R6] 60-352
1. Flanagan, Edward Joseph, 1886-1948—Juvenile literature. I. Title.

STEVENS, Clifford, 1926- 92
Father Flanagan; builder of boys. With drawings by Rus Anderson. New York, P. J. Kenedy [1967] 180, [2] p. illus. 22 cm. (American background books, 34) Bibliography: p. [182] [HV876.F4S73] 67-27370 2.50
1. Flanagan, Edward Joseph, 1886-1948—Juvenile literature. I. Title. II. Series.

STEVENS, Clifford, J. 92 (J)
Father Flanagan; builder of boys. With drawings by Rus Anderson. New York, P. J. Kenedy [1967] 180, [2] p. illus. 22 cm. (American background books, 34) Bibliography: p. [182] [HV876.F4S73] 67-27370 2.50
1. Flanagan, Edward Joseph, 1886-1948—Juvenile literature. I. Title. II. Series.

Flanders, Ralph Edward,

FLANDERS, Ralph Edward, 1880- 923.273
Senator from Vermont. [1st ed.] Boston, Little, Brown [1961] 312 p. 22 cm. Autobiography. [E748.F54A3] 60-5880
I. Title.

Flaubert, Gustave, 1821-1880.

BART, Benjamin F. 843'.8 B
Flaubert [by] Benjamin F. Bart. [1st ed.] Syracuse, N.Y.] Syracuse University Press [1967] xiii, 791 p. illus., ports. 24 cm. Bibliographical references included in "Notes" (p. 749-773) [PQ2247.B3] 67-27410
1. Flaubert, Gustave, 1821-1880. BIP

BUCK, Stratton, 1906- 843.8
Gustave Flaubert. [New York] Hippocrene Books [1973, c.1966] 153 p. 21 cm. (Hippocrene literary biographies) Bibliography: p. 149-150. [PQ2247.B8] 66-16120 ISBN 0-88254-039-4 2.95 (pbk.)
1. Flaubert, Gustave, 1821-1880. I. Title. L.C. card no. for the hardbound ed.: 66-16120. BIP

FLAUBERT, Gustave, 1821-1880. 928.4
Letters; selected, with an introd. by Richard Rumbold. Translated by J. M. Cohen. New York, Philosophical Library [1951] 248 p. 22 cm. "The French editions used in making this selection and translation are: Correspondance ... Paris, 1926-33 [and] Lettres inedites a Tourgeneff ... Monaco, 1946." [PQ2247.A23E53] 51-7113
I. Title.

FLAUBERT, Gustave, 1821-1880. 928.4
Selected letters, translated and edited with an introd. by Francis Steegmuller. New York, Farrar, Straus and Young, [1954, c1953] xxx, 281p. 22cm. (Great letters series) [PQ2247.A23E57] 53-7086
I. Title.

FLAUBERT, Gustave, 1821-1880. 843'.8 B
The selected letters of Gustave Flaubert. Translated and edited with an introd. by Francis Steegmuller. Freeport, N.Y., Books for Libraries Press [1971, c1953] xxx, 281 p. 23 cm. (Biography index reprint series) [PQ2247.A23E57 1971] 78-160919 ISBN 0-8369-8082-4
I. Steegmuller, Francis, ed. II. Title.

STARKIE, Enid. 843'.8
Flaubert: the making of the master. [1st American ed.] New York, Atheneum, 1967. xvii, 403 p. illus., facsim., ports. 25 cm. Sequel: Flaubert: the master. Bibliography: p. 365-358. [PQ2247.S77 1967b] 67-28968
1. Flaubert, Gustave, 1821-1880. I. Title.

STARKIE, Enid. 843'.8 B
Flaubert: the master; a critical and biographical study (1856-1880) [1st American ed.] New York, Atheneum, 1971. 390 p. illus. 25 cm. Sequel to Flaubert: the making of the master. Bibliography: p. 357-360. [PQ2247.S78 1971b] 75-139328 10.00
1. Flaubert, Gustave, 1821-1880. I. Title.

STEEGMULLER, Francis, 1906- 928.4
Flaubert and Madame Bovary; a double portrait. New York, Vintage Books, 1957 [1939] 365, viii p. 19 cm. (A Vintage book, K-16) Bibliography: p. 363-365. [[PQ2247]] 57-1095
1. Flaubert, Gustave, 1821-1880. 2. Flaubert, Gustave, 1821-1880. Madame Bovary. 3. Colet, Louise (Revoll) 1810-1876. I. Title.

STEEGMULLER, Francis, 1906 843'.8
Flaubert and Madame Bovary; a double portrait. Rev. ed. New York, Farrar, Straus and Giroux [1968, c1939] 365, viii p. 21 cm. Bibliography: p. [363]-365. [PQ2247.S8 1968] 68-1106
1. Flaubert, Gustave, 1821-1880—Relationship with women—Louise (Revoil) Colet. 2. Flaubert, Gustave, 1821-1880. Madame Bovary. 3. Colet, Louise (Revoil) 1810-1876. I. Title. BIP

TARVER, John Charles, 1854-1926. 843'.8
Gustave Flaubert as seen in his works and correspondence. Port Washington, N.Y., Kennikat Press [1970] xvi, 368 p. illus., port. 22 cm. Reprint of the 1895 ed. [PQ2247.T3 1970] 71-113324
1. Flaubert, Gustave, 1821-1880. I. Title. BIP

Flaubert, Gustave, 1821-1880—Relationship with women—Louise (Revoil) Colet.

STEEGMULLER, Francis, 1906- 843'.8
Flaubert and Madame Bovary; a double portrait. Rev. ed. New York, Farrar, Straus and Giroux [1968, c1939] 365, viii p. 21 cm. Bibliography: p. [363]-365. [PQ2247.S8 1968] 68-1106
1. Flaubert, Gustave, 1821-1880—Relationship with women—Louise (Revoil) Colet. 2. Flaubert, Gustave, 1821-1880. Madame Bovary. 3. Colet, Louise (Revoil) 1810-1876. I. Title. BIP

Flaxman, John, 1755-1826.

WHINNEY, Margaret Dickens 730'.924
The collection of models by John Flaxman, R.A. at University College London; a catalogue and introduction, by Margaret Whinney, Rupert Gunnis. London, Athlone Pr., 1967. viii, 72p. 24 plates. 26cm. [NB497.F5W5 1967] 67-101517 8.80
1. Flaxman, John, 1755-1826. I. Gunnis, Rupert, joint author. II. London, University, University College. III. Title.

Fleet, Maria Louisa Wacker.

FLEET, Maria Louisa Wacker. 975.5'04'0924 B
Green Mount after the war : the correspondence of Maria Louisa Wacker Fleet and her family, 1865-1900 / edited by Betsy Fleet. Charlottesville : University Press of Virginia, 1978. xi, 287 p. : ill. ; 24 cm. Includes index. [CT275.F5827A4 1978.] 77-24079 ISBN 0-8139-0730-6 : 12.50
1. Fleet, Maria Louisa Wacker. 2. Fleet family. 3. Virginia—Biography. I. Fleet, Betsy. II. Title. BIP

Fleg, Edmond, 1874-1963.

FLEG, Edmond, 1874-1963. 296.3
Why I am a Jew / by Emond Fleg. New York : Arno Press, 1975 [c1929] xvi, 84 p. ; 22 cm. (The Modern Jewish experience) Translation of Pourquoi je suis juif. Reprint of the 1945 ed. published by Bloch Pub. Co., New York. Includes bibliographical references. [BM560.F63 1975] 74-27984 ISBN 0-405-06711-9 : 9.00
1. Fleg, Edmond, 1874-1963. 2. Judaism. I. Title. II. Series.

Flegenheimer, Arthur, 1900 or 1-1935.

SANN, Paul. 364.1'0924 B
Kill the Dutchman! The story of Dutch Schultz. New Rochelle, N.Y., Arlington House [1971] 347 p. illus., ports. 22 cm. [HV6248.F55S3] 70-134849 ISBN 0-87000-109-4 8.95
1. Flegenheimer, Arthur, 1900 or 1-1935. I. Title.

Fleischer, Dave, 1894-

CABARGA, Leslie, 1954- 791.43'.092'2 B
The Fleischer story / by Leslie Cabarga. New York : Nostalgia Press, c1976. 183 p. : ill. ; 29 cm. [NC1766.U52F593] 73-94123 12.50
1. Fleischer, Max, 1888- 2. Fleischer, Dave, 1894- 3. Fleischer Studios, inc. 4. Animators—United States—Biography. I. Title. BIP

Fleischer, Max, 1888-

CABARGA, Leslie, 1954- 791.43'.092'2 B
The Fleischer story / by Leslie Cabarga. New York : Nostalgia Press, c1976. 183 p. : ill. ; 29 cm. [NC1766.U52F593] 73-94123 12.50
1. Fleischer, Max, 1888- 2. Fleischer, Dave, 1894- 3. Fleischer Studios, inc. 4. Animators—United States—Biography. I. Title. BIP

Fleischner, Louis—Juvenile literature.

APSLER, Alfred 923.973
Northwest pioneer; the story of Louis Fleschner. Illustrated by Morton Garchik. [New York] Farrar, Straus and Cudahy [c.1960] 180p. illus. 22cm. (Covenant books, 9) 60-9077 2.95
1. Fleischner, Louis—Juvenile literature. 2. Frontier and pioneer life—Northwest, Pacific—Juvenile literature. I. Title.

APSLER, Alfred. 923.973
Northwest pioneer; the story of Louis Fleischner. Illustrated by Morton Garehik. [New York] Farrar, Straus and Cudahy [1960] 180p. illus. 22cm. (Covenant books, 9) [F852.F55A75] 60-9077
1. Fleischner, Louis—Juvenile literature. 2. Frontier and pioneer life—Northwest, Pacific—Juvenile literature. I. Title.

Fleming, Alexander, Sir, 1881-1955.

LUDOVICI, Laurence James. 926.1
Fleming, discoverer of penicillin. Bloomington, Indiana University Press, 1955. 223p. illus. 22cm. [QR31] 55-533
1. Fleming, Alexander, Sir 1881- I. Title. BIP

MAUROIS, Andre, 1885- 926.1
The life of Sir Alexander Fleming, discoverer of penicillin. Translated from the French by Gerard Hopkins and with an introd. by Robert Cruickshank. [1st ed.] New York, Dutton [1959] 292p. illus. 22cm. Includes bibliography. [QR31.F5M353] 59-5817
1. Fleming, Aledander, Sir 1881-1955. I. Title.

ROWLAND, John, 1907- 926.1
The penicillin man; the story of Sir Alexander Fleming. New York, Roy Publishers [1957] 155 p. illus. 21 cm. Includes bibliography. [QR31.F5R7] 57-7195
1. Fleming, Alexander, Sir, 1881-1955. I. Title.

Fleming County, Ky.—Biography.

COOPER, Wade, 1908- 920'.0769'56
Early Fleming County Kentucky pioneers : historical facts / by Wade Cooper. [Flemingsburg, Ky.] : Cooper, [1974] 244 p. : ill. ; 23 cm. [F457.F4C66] 75-302425 6.95
1. Fleming County, Ky.—Biography. 2. Fleming County, Ky.—Genealogy. I. Title.

Fleming, Ian, 1908-1964.

GANT, Richard. v. 12
Ian Fleming: the fantastic 007 man. New York, Lancer Books, [1966] 174 p. 18 cm. (A Lancer book) 68-44709
1. Fleming, Ian, 1908-1964. I. Title.

Fleming, Peggy—Juvenile literature.

MORSE, Charles. 796.9'1'0924 B
Peggy Fleming, by Charles and Ann Morse. Illustrated by Harold Henriksen. Mankato, Minn., Creative Education; [distributed by Childrens Press, Chicago, 1974] 31 p. col. illus. 25 cm. (Superstars) A biography of the figure skater who went from winning two consecutive world championships in 1966 and 1967 to being the only Olympic gold medal winner for the United States in the 1968 winter games. [GV850.F55M67] 92 74-18429 ISBN 0-87191-380-1 4.95
1. Fleming, Peggy—Juvenile literature. 2. Skating—Juvenile literature. I. Morse, Ann, joint author. II. Henriksen, Harold, illus. III. Title. BIP

VAN STEENWYK, Elizabeth. 796.9'1'0924 B
Peggy Fleming : cameo of a champion / by Elizabeth Van Steenwyk. New York : McGraw-Hill, c1978. 132 p. : ill. ; 24 cm. Includes index. A biography of the figure skater who was the only American to win a gold medal at the 1968 winter Olympics and the youngest skater to be inducted into skating's Hall of Fame in 1975. [GV850.F55V36] 92 77-17060 ISBN 0-07-067167-2 : 7.95
1. Fleming, Peggy—Juvenile literature. 2. Skaters—United States—Biography—Juvenile literature. I. Title.

Fleming, Sandford, Sir, 1827-1915.

UNITT, Doris Joyce. 625.1'00924
Sir Sandford Fleming, compiled by Doris J. Unitt, Andrew Osler [and] Edward McCoy. Peterborough, Ont., Review Print Co., c1968. 159 p. map, facsims., ports. 23 cm. (A Clockhouse publication) Limited ed., 500 copies. Includes excerpts from the private diary of Sir Sandford Fleming. [TF140.F4U5] 78-358627 2.50
1. Fleming, Sandford, Sir, 1827-1915. I. Fleming, Sandford, Sir, 1827-1915. II. Osler, Andrew, joint author. III. McCoy, Edward, joint author. IV. Title.

Flesche, Mary Rose, 1824-1906.

BACKES, James Adam. 271.9730924(B)
If the grain does not die: a portrait of the life of the servant of God, Mother Mary Rose Flesch, foundress of the Franciscan Sisters of the Blessed Virgin Mary of the Angels. Translated by Isidore A. McCarthy. Chicago, Franciscan Herald Press [c1965] 61 p. illus. 18 cm. [BX4355.Z8B313] 65-16671
1. Flesche, Mary Rose, 1824-1906. 2. Franciscan Sisters of Our Lady of the Angels. I. Title.

Fletcher, Duncan Upshaw, 1859-1936.

FLYNT, Wayne, 1940- 328.73'0924 B
Duncan Upshaw Fletcher; Dixie's reluctant progressive. Tallahassee, Florida State University Press, 1971. ix, 213 p. 24 cm. Bibliography: p. 197-204. [E748.F55F55] 73-149954 10.00
1. Fletcher, Duncan Upshaw, 1859-1936. BIP

Fletcher, Grace (Nies)

FLETCHER, Grace (Nies) 915
Merry widow. New York, Morrow, 1970. viii, 255 p. 22 cm. [PS3556.L5Z5] 79-102190 5.95
I. Title.

Fletcher, Inglis Clark,

FLETCHER, Inglis Clark, 1888- 928.1
Pay, pack, and follow; the story of my life. [1st ed.] New York, Holt [1959] 308 p. illus. 22 cm. [PS3511.L449Z52] 59-8523
I. Title.

Fletcher, James Floyd, 1858-1946.

FLETCHER, Alfred Johnston, 1887- 266.6'1'0924 B
The story of a mountain missionary, Rev. James Floyd Fletcher, 1858-1946, by A. J. Fletcher. Raleigh, N.C., 1966. 39 l. 30 cm. [BX6379.F54F54] 78-17342
1. Fletcher, James Floyd, 1858-1946. I. Title.

Fletcher, John Gould, 1886-

SIMON, Charlie May (Hogue) 1897- 928.1
Johnswood. [1st ed] New York, Dutton, 1953. 249p. 22cm. Autobiographical. [PS3537.I64Z5] 53-6090
1. Fletcher, John Gould, 1886- I. Title.

Fleure, Herbert John, 1877-

PEATE, Iorwerth Cyfeiliog, 1901- ed. 910.03
Studies in regional consciousness and environment; essays presented to H. J. Fleure, edited by Iorwerth C. Peate. Freeport, N.Y., Books for Libraries Press [1968] xii, 220 p. illus., maps (part fold.) 24 cm. (Essay index reprint series) Reprint of the 1930 ed. Includes bibliographical references. [GF51.P4 1968] 68-26478
1. Fleure, Herbert John, 1877- 2. Anthropo-geography. 3. Man—Influence of environment. 4. Regionalism. 5. Moniezia. I. Title. BIP

Flick, Lawrence Francis, 1856-1968.

FLICK, Cecilia R 926.1
Dr. Lawrence F. Flick as I knew him. Philadelphia, Dorrance [1956] 177p. illus. 20cm. [R154.F678F46] 56-11550
1. Flick, Lawrence Francis, 1856-1968. I. Title.

Flinders, Matthew, 1774-1814.

DUDDING, John, Sir, 1915- 919.4'04'20924
Captain Matthew Flinders, RN : his life and place in the exploration of Australia / Sir John Dudding. [Lincoln : Lincolnshire and South Humberside Arts Association, 1973] [1], 16 p. : ill., maps, ports. ; 21 cm. Cover title. Bibliography: p. 16. [DU115.2.F57D82] 75-302196 £0.15
1. Flinders, Matthew, 1774-1814. 2. Australia—Discovery and exploration. I. Title.

MACK, James Decker, 1916- 994'.02'0924
Matthew Flinders, 1774-1814 [by] James D. Mack. [Melbourne, Nelson (Australia)] 1966. x, 270 p. illus., maps, ports. 22 cm. Bibliography: p. 254-262. [DU114.F6M3] 67-79832
1. Flinders, Matthew, 1774-1814.

Flint, Timothy, 1780-1840.

KIRKPATRICK, John Ervin, 1869-1931. 917.7'03'20924 B
Timothy Flint: pioneer, missionary, author, editor, 1780-1840; the story of his life among the pioneers and frontiersmen in the Ohio and Mississippi Valley and in New England and the South. New York, B. Franklin [1968] 331 p. illus. 23 cm. (Burt Franklin research and source works series, 267) (American classics in history & social science, 48.) Reprint of the 1911 ed. Bibliography: p. [305]-318. [F353.F64 1968] 68-56780
1. Flint, Timothy, 1780-1840. 2. Mississippi Valley.

Flood, Curt,

FLOOD, Curt, 1938- 796.357'0924 B
The way it is, by Curt Flood, with Richard Carter. New York, Trident Press [1971] 236 p. 21 cm. [GV865.F45A3] 70-143045 ISBN 0-671-27076-1 5.95
I. Carter, Richard, 1918- joint author. II. Title.

Flood, Henry, 1732-1791.

LECKY, William Edward Hartpole, 1838-1903. 941.57
Leaders of public opinion in Ireland. New York, Da Capo Press, 1973 [c1903] 2 v. 21 cm. (Europe 1815-1945) Reprint of the 1912 ed. Contents.—v. 1. Henry Flood. Henry Grattan.—v. 2. Daniel O'Connell. [DA948.A5L4 1973] 76-159800 ISBN 0-306-70556-7 29.50
1. Flood, Henry, 1732-1791. 2. Grattan, Henry, 1746-1820. 3. O'Connell, Daniel, 1775-1847. I. Title. II. Series. BIP

Florence — Hist.

WELLIVER, Warman, 1913- 923.1455
Lorenzo and Florence. Indianapolis, Clio Press [1961] 88 p. illus. 22 cm. [DG737.55.W4] 61-18214
1. Florence — Hist. 2. Medici, Lorence de', il Magnifico, 1449-1462. I. Title.

Florence—History.

MACHIAVELLI, Noccolo, 1469-1527. 914.5'03'60924 B
Machiavelli. With an introd. by Henry Cust. New York, AMS Press, 1967. 2 v. illus. 23 cm. Reprint of the 1905 ed., which was issued as no. 39-40 of the Tudor translations, 1st series. Contents.Contents.—v. 1. The art of war, translated by P. Whitehorne, 1560. The prince, translated by E. Dacres, 1640.—v. 2. The Florentine history, translated by T. Bedingfeld, 1595. [DG731.5.M325 1967] 73-153695
1. Florence—History. 2. Military art and science—Early works to 1800. 3. Political science—Early works to 1700. 4. Political ethics. I. Cust, Henry John Cockayne, 1861-1917. II. Series: The Tudor translations, no. 39-40.

Florence—History—Sources.

BRUCKER, Gene A., comp. 945.5'1'05
Two memoirs of Renaissance Florence; the diaries of Buonaccorso Pitti and Gregorio Dati. Translated by Julia Martines. Edited by Gene Brucker. New York, Harper & Row [1967] 141 p. map 21 cm. (Harper torchbooks, TB 1333) Both these memoirs have been abridged in this translation. Includes bibliographical references. [DG731.2.B7] 67-21565
1. Florence—History—Sources. I. Martines, Julia, tr. II. Pitti, Buonaccorso, 1354-ca. 1431. Cronica di Buonaccorso Pitti. English. 1967. III. Dati, Gregorio, 1362-1436. Il libro segreto di Gregorio Dati. English. 1967. IV. Title.

Florence—Intellectual life.

GARIN, Eugenio, 1909- 920'.45'51
Portraits from the Quattrocento. Translated by Victor A. and Elizabeth Velen. New York, Harper & Row [1972] xvii, 282 p. 21 cm. "HR 1568." Includes bibliographical references. [DG737.58.A1G3913] 73-159636 ISBN 0-06-138629-4
1. Florence—Intellectual life. 2. Florence—Biography. I. Title.

Florence, Lella Secor.

FLORENCE, Lella Secor. 301.41'2'0924
Lella Secor : a diary in letters, 1915-1922 / edited by Barbara Moench Florence ; foreword by Eleanor Flexner. New York : B. Franklin, c1978. xviii, 295 p. : ill. ; 24 cm. (American women's diary series ; 1) Includes index. Bibliography: p. 289-290. [HQ1413.F58A34] 78-8374 ISBN 0-89102-071-3 : 17.95
1. Florence, Lella Secor. 2. Feminists—United States—Biography. 3. Pacifists—United States—Biography. 4. Women journalists—United States—Biography. I. Florence, Barbara Moench. II. Title. III. Series. BIP

Florence, William Jermyn, 1831-1891.

UELAND, Alexander. 923.673
William Jermyn Florence, Shriner and humanitarian. Boston, Christopher Pub. House [1958] 89 p. illus. 23 cm. [HS835.6.U47] 58-8666
1. Florence, William Jermyn, 1831-1891. 2. Ancient Arabic Order of the Nobles of the Mystic Shrine for North America. I. Title.

Florey, Howard Walter, Sir, 1898-1968.

BICKEL, Lennard. 615'.329'230924 B
Rise up to life; a biography of Howard Walter Florey who gave penicillin to the world. With a foreword by R. G. MacFarlane. New York, Scribner [1973, c1972] xix, 314 p. illus. 23 cm. Includes bibliographical references. [R674.F54B5 1973] 73-1051 ISBN 0-684-13429-2 9.95
1. Florey, Howard Walter, Sir, 1898-1968. 2. Penicillin. I. Title.

Florida — Biog.

TRINKNER, Charles L ed. 920.0759
Florida lives; the Sunshine State who's who; a reference edition recording the biographies of contemporary leaders in Florida... written and prepared under the supervision of Charles L. Trinkner. Hopkinsville, Ky., Historical Record Association, 1966. 613 p. ports. 27 cm. [F310.T7] 66-27879
1. Florida — Biog. I. Title. II. Title: The Sunshine State who's who.

Florida—Biography.

COLLINS, LeRoy. 975.9'0922 B
Forerunners courageous; stories of frontier Florida. Drawings by Wallace Hughes. [Tallahassee] Colcade Publishers, 1971. xxi, 215 p. illus. 25 cm. Bibliography: p. 214-215. [F310.C57] 76-185182 8.50
1. Florida—Biography. 2. Florida—History. I. Title.

Florida—Biography—Dictionaries.

MARKS, Henry S. 920'.0759
Who was who in Florida. Written and compiled by Henry S. Marks. Huntsville, Ala., Strode Publishers [1973] 276 p. illus. 27 cm. Bibliography: p. [272]-276. [F310.M26] 73-83503 ISBN 0-87397-039-X 14.95
1. Florida—Biography—Dictionaries. I. Title. BIP

Florida—History—Juvenile literature.

SKINNER, Woodward B. 975.9
Adventurers in Florida history / written by W. B. (Woody) Skinner and W. George Gaines ; ill. by Jean Dahlstrom, maps by Guy Short, cover design by Jackie Taft, Robert Thornton, Robert Vandegrift. Pensacola, Fla. : Town and Country Books, [1974]. viii, 317 p. : ill. ; 24 cm. Includes index. Bibliography: p. 308-312. Traces the history of Florida through chronologically arranged biographies of the individuals instrumental in shaping it. [F311.3.S54] 74-196051
1. Florida—History—Juvenile literature. 2. Florida—Biography—Juvenile literature. I. Gaines, W. George, joint author. II. Dahlsrom, Jean, ill. III. Short, Guy, ill. IV. Title.

Florio, John, 1553?-1625.

ACHESON, Arthur, 1864-1930. 822.3'3 B
Shakespeare's lost years in London 1586-1592, giving new light on the pre-sonnet period; showing the inception of relations between Shakespeare and the Earl of Southampton and displaying John Florio as Sir John Falstaff. New York, Haskell House, 1971. vii, 261 p. 23 cm. Reprint of the 1920 ed. [PR2907.A4 1971] 79-152552 ISBN 0-8383-1235-7
1. Shakespeare, William, 1564-1616—Biography—London life. 2. Southampton, Henry Wriothesley, 3d Earl of, 1573-1624. 3. Florio, John, 1553?-1625. 4. Shakespeare, William, 1564-1616—Characters—Falstaff. I. Title.

Florsheim, Richard, 1924-

FREUNDLICH, August L. 759.13' B
Richard Florsheim / August L. Freundlich. South Brunswick [N.J.] : A. S. Barnes, c1976. p. cm. "This special edition is limited to 112 copies .... This is copy [ND237.F48F73] 74-30724 ISBN 0-498-01636-6 : 15.00. ISBN 0-498-01760-5 (lim. ed.) : 100.00
1. Florsheim, Richard, 1924- I. Florsheim, Richard, 1924- BIP

Flowers, Henry, 1904-

FLOWERS, Henry, 1904- 977.1'15'0924
Lantern on a windmill / by Henry Flowers. [Defiance, Ohio] : Flowers, c1976. 125 p. : ill. ; 22 cm. Includes index. [F497.H55F59] 76-23920
1. Flowers, Henry, 1904- 2. Henry Co.,

Ohio—Social life and customs. 3. Henry Co., Ohio—Biography. I. Title.

Flowers in art.

MITCHELL, Peter, 758'.42 B fl.1968-
Great flower painters; four centuries of floral art. Woodstock, N.Y., Overlook Press [1973] 272 p. illus. (part col.) 29 cm. Bibliography: p. 263-264. [ND2300.M57] 72-95231 ISBN 0-87951-008-0 27.95
1. Flowers in art. 2. Still-life painting. 3. Painters. I. Title. BIP

Floyd Co., Ind.—Biography.

†COTTOM, C. W. 977.2'19
1889 biographical and historical souvenir, Floyd County, Indiana / by C.W. Cotton i.e. Cottom Knightstown, Ind. : The Bookmark, 1977. 152 p. in various pagings : ports. ; 24 cm. Contains several parts of the work published in 1889 under title: Biographical and historical souvenir for the counties of Clark, Crawford, Harrison, Floyd, Jefferson, Jennings, Scott, and Washington, Indiana. Includes index. [F532.F6C67 1977] 78-103270 9.10
1. Floyd Co., Ind.—Biography. 2. Floyd Co., Ind.—History. I. Title. II. Title: Biographical and historical souvenir for the counties of Clark, Crawford, Harrison, Floyd, Jefferson, Jennings, Scott, and Washington, Indiana.

Floyd, William, 1734-1821.

MAXWELL, William 973.3'092'4 B Quentin.
A portrait of William Floyd, Long Islander, by William Q. Maxwell. [Setauket, N.Y., Privately printed by the] Society for the Preservation of Long Island Antiquities, 1956. 43 p. illus. 23 cm. Bibliography: p. 43. [F127.L8M29] 73-157713
1. Floyd, William, 1734-1821. I. Title.

Flury, Godfrey, 1864-1936.

FLURY, Dorothy 659.1'092'4 B Agnes, 1912-
Our father, Godfrey : a biography / by Dorothy Agnes Flury. [Austin, Tex.] : Flury, c1976. xi, 147 p., [5] leaves of plates (1 fold.) : ill. (some col.) ; 27 cm. [HF5810.F58F58] 75-40979
1. Flury, Godfrey, 1864-1936. 2. Advertising—Texas. I. Title.

Flying saucers—Biography.

WALTON, Travis. 001.9'42'0924 B
The Walton experience / by Travis Walton ; ill. by Michael Rogers. New York : Berkley Pub. Corp., 1978. ix, 181 p., [2] leaves of plates : ill. ; 18 cm. (A Berkley medallion book) [TL789.3.W34] 78-104973 ISBN 0-425-03675-8 pbk. : 1.95
1. Flying saucers—Biography. I. Title. BIP

Flynn, Edward Joseph,

FLYNN, Edward Joseph, 923.273 B 1891-1953.
You're the boss; the practice of American politics. With a new introd. by Eleanor Roosevelt. New York, Collier Books [1962] 255 p. 18 cm. (Collier books, AS233V) Autobiographical. [F128.5.F6 1962] 62-12296
I. Title.

Flynn, Elizabeth Gurley.

FLYNN, Elizabeth Gurley. 923.373
I speak my own piece; autobiography of 'The Rebel Girl.' New York, Massess& Mainstream [1955] 326p. illus. 21cm. [HX84.F5A3] 55-13980
I. Title.

FLYNN, Elizabeth 335'.0092'4 B Gurley.
The Rebel Girl; an autobiography, my first life (1906-1926). [New, rev. ed.] New York, International Publishers [1973] 351 p. illus. 21 cm. First ed. published in 1955 under title: I speak my own piece. [HX84.F5A3 1973] 72-94154 ISBN 0-7178-0367-8 8.50
1. Flynn, Elizabeth Gurley. I. Title.

Flynn, Errol Leslie, 1904-1959.

CONRAD, Earl. 791.43'028'0924 B
Errol Flynn : a memoir / by Earl Conrad. New York : Dodd, Mead, c1978. 222 p., [8] leaves of plates : ill. ; 22 cm. [PN2287.F55C6] 77-21870 ISBN 0-396-07502-9 : 8.95
1. Flynn, Errol Leslie, 1909-1959. 2. Moving-picture actors and actresses—United States—Biography. BIP

FLYNN, Errol Leslie, 1909- 927.92 1959.
My wicked, wicked ways. New York, Putnam [1960, c1959] 438 p. 23 cm. [PN2287.F55A3] 59-7849
1. Actors—Correspondence, reminiscences, etc. I. Title.

FLYNN, Errol 791.43'028'0924 B Leslie, 1909-1959.
My wicked, wicked ways. [New York] Berkley Pub Co. [1974, c1959] 383 p. 18 cm. (A Berkley medallion book) [PN2287.F55A3] ISBN 0-425-02512-8. 1.25 (pbk.)
1. Actors—Correspondence, reminiscences, etc. I. Title.
L.C. card number for original ed.: 59-7849.

FREEDLAND, 791.43'028'0924 B Michael, 1934-
The two lives of Errol Flynn / by Michael Freedland. 1st U.S. ed. New York : W. Morrow, 1979, c1978. x, 258 p., [10] leaves of plates : ill. ; 25 cm. [PN2287.F55F7 1979] 79-63012 ISBN 0-688-03465-9 : 9.95
1. Flynn, Errol Leslie, 1904-1959. 2. Moving-picture actors and actresses—United States—Biography. I. Title. BIP

GODFREY, 791.43'028'0924 B Lionel.
The life and crimes of Errol Flynn / Lionel Godfrey ; with ill. from the Rick Dodd Collection. New York : St. Martin's Press, [1977] p. cm. Includes index. Bibliography: p. [PN2287.F55G6 1977] 77-72302 ISBN 0-312-48385-6 : 7.95
1. Flynn, Errol Leslie, 1909-1959. 2. Moving-picture actors and actresses—United States—Biography. I. Title. BIP

HAYMES, Nora (Eddington) 927.92 Flynn, 1924-
Errol and me [by] Nora Eddington Flynn Haymes as told to Cy Rice. [New York] New American Library [c.1960] 176p. illus. (Signet books, D1875) 60-52186 .50 pap.,
1. Flynn, Errol Leslie, 1909-1959. I. Rice, Cy. II. Title.

THOMEY, Tedd. 927.92
The loves of Errol Flynn; the tempestuous life story of one of Hollywood's most flamboyant screen stars. Derby, Conn., Monarch Books [1962] 139 p. 19 cm. (Monarch books, K58) [PN2287.F55T4] 62-566
1. Flynn, Errol Leslie, 1909-1959. I. Title.

THOMEY, Tedd. 927.92
The loves of Errol Flynn; the tempestuous life story of one of Hollywood's most flamboyant screen stars. Derby, Conn., Monarch Books [1962] 139 p. 19 cm. (Monarch books, K58) [PN2287.F55T4] 62-566
1. Flynn, Errol Leslie, 1909-1959. I. Title.

Flynn, Wallace J.

FLYNN, Bethine. 636.089'092'4 B
The flying Flynns : the remarkable adventures of an animal doctor in the wilderness / Bethine Flynn. 1st ed. New York : Seaview Books, c1979. p. cm. [SF613.F58F59] 79-4877 ISBN 0-87223-538-6 : 9.95
1. Flynn, Wallace J. 2. Flynn, Behine. 3. Veternarians—Washington (State)—Biography. I. Title.

Flynt, Larry.

JONES, Larry. 248'.246
Hustler for the Lord / by Larry Jones, with C. A. Roberts. Plainfield, N.J. : Logos International, c1978. xii, 173 p. ; 18 cm. [BV4935.F59J66] 77-93653 ISBN 0-88270-309-9 : 1.95
1. Flynt, Larry. 2. Converts—United States—Biography. 3. Hustler. 4. Pornography—United States. I. Roberts, Cecil A., joint author. II. Title. BIP

Foch, Ferdinand, 1851-1929.

LIDDELL Hart, Basil 940.4 B Henry, Sir, 1895-1970.
Foch, the man of Orleans / by B. H. Liddell Hart. Westport, Conn. : Greenwood Press, [1980] c1932. p. cm. Reprint of the ed. published by Little, Brown, Boston. Includes index. Bibliography: p. [DC342.8.F6L5 1980] 79-22870 ISBN 0-313-22171-5 lib. bdg. : 35.00
1. Foch, Ferdinand, 1851-1929. 2. Marshals—France—Biography. I. Title. BIP

Foerster, Otfrid, 1873-1941.

ZULCH, Klaus Joachim, 610.924 (B) 1910-
Otfrid Foerster, Arzt und Naturforscher, 9. 11, 1873-15. 6. 1941. Berlin, New York, Springer-Verlag, 1966. viii, 103 p. illus., facsims., ports. 24 cm. "Auszuge aus Foersters wichtigsten Arbeiten": p. [27]-86. Bibliography of O. Foerster's works: p. 89-103. Includes bibliographical references. [R512.F6Z8] 66-19123
1. Foerster, Otfrid, 1873-1941. I. Title.

ZULCH, Klaus Joachim, 610.924 1910-
Otfrid Foerster, Arzt und Naturforscher. 9. 11. 1873-15. 6. 1941. New York, Springer-Verlag, [c.]1966. viii, 103p. illus., facsim., ports. 24cm. Bibl. [R512.F6Z8] 66-19123 4.00 pap.,
1. Foerster, Otfrid, 1873-1941. I. Title.

ZULCH, Klaus Joachim, 610'.924 B 1910-
Otfrid Foerster, physician and naturalist, November 9, 1873-June 15, 1941. Translated from the German by Adolf Rosenauer and Joseph P. Evans. Berlin, New York, Springer-Verlag, 1969. viii, 96 p. illus., ports. 24 cm. Translation of Otfrid Foerster, Arzt und Naturforscher. Bibliography: p. 83-96. [R512.F6Z83] 75-95563 unpriced
1. Foerster, Otfrid, 1873-1941. 2. Neurology. I. Title.

Fogarty family.

FOGARTY, Ollie Z., 917.59'62 1905-
They called it Fogartyville; a story of the Fogartys and Fogartyville, by Ollie Z. Fogarty. Brooklyn, N.Y., T. Gaus' Sons [1972] vi, 292 p. illus. 24 cm. Bibliography: p. 291-292. [CS71.F653 1972] 72-87088
1. Fogarty family. 2. Bradenton, Fla.—History. I. Title.

Fogazzaro, Antonio, 1842-1911.

GALLARATI-SCOTTI, 853'.8 B Tommaso, Conte, 1878-1966.
The life of Antonio Fogazzaro. Translated by Mary Prichard Agnetti. Port Washington, N.Y., Kennikat Press [1970] xii, 314 p. 22 cm. Reprint of the 1922 ed. Translation of La vita di Antonio Fogazzaro. [PQ4688.F6Z8513 1970] 73-113311
1. Fogazzaro, Antonio, 1842-1911. BIP

Fogerty, Elsie.

COLE, Marion. 792/.0924
Fogie: the life of Elsie Fogerty, C.B.E.; compiled and edited by one of her students, Marion Cole, from scraps of her memoirs and many other contributions from people who knew her. London, P. Davies, 1967 x, 229p. front., 4 plates (incl. port.). 23cm. [PN4059.F6C6] (B) 67-109098 8.50 bds.,
1. Fogerty, Elsie. I. Title.

American distributor: Hillary House, New York.

Fokker, Anthony Herman Gerard, 1890-1939.

FOKKER, Anthony 629.13'0092'4 B Herman Gerard, 1890-1939.
Flying Dutchman; the life of Anthony Fokker, by Anthony H. G. Fokker and Bruce Gould. [New York] Arno Press [1972, c1931] 282 p. illus. 23 cm. (Literature and history of aviation) [TL540.F6A3 1972] 70-169415 ISBN 0-405-03760-0
I. Gould, Bruce, joint author. II. Title. III. Series. BIP

WEYL, Alfred 629.13'00924 B Richard.
Fokker: the creative years [by] A. R. Weyl. Edited by J. M. Bruce. New York, Funk & Wagnalls [1968, c1965] 420 p. illus., ports. 23 cm. [TL540.F6W4 1968] 68-27366 17.50
1. Fokker, Anthony Herman Gerard, 1890-1939.

Foley, Ace.

FOLEY, Ace. 070.4'49'7960924 B
The first fifty years; the life and times of a sports writer. Windsor, N.S., Lancelot Press [1970] 101 p. ports. 21 cm. Autobiographical. [GV719.F6A3] 72-182643 2.50
I. Title.

Foley, Winifred, 1914-

FOLEY, Winifred, 942.083'092'4 B 1914-
As the twig is bent / Winifred Foley. New York : Taplinger Pub. Co., 1978, c1974. 254 p. ; 22 cm. Autobiographical. Originally published in 1974 under title: A child in the forest. [CT788.F64A33 1978] 77-92766 ISBN 0-8008-0421-X : 9.95
1. Foley, Winifred, 1914- 2. England—Biography. I. Title.

Folger, Walter, 1765-1849.

GARDNER, William Edward, 926.81 1872-
The clock that talks and what it tells; a portrait story of the maker: Hon. Walter Folger, Jr., astronomer, mathematician, navigator, lawyer, judge, legislator, congressman, philosopher; but he called himself: clock and watchmaker ... [Nantucket] Whaling Museum Publications; distributed by the Personal Book Shop, Boston [1954] viii, 143p. illus., ports, facsims. 21cm. [Nantucket, Mass. Whaling Museum. Publications] 'Books used by Walter Folger Jr.': p. 135-136. Bibliography: p. 119-120. [CT275.F652G3] 55-514
1. Folger, Walter, 1765-1849. I. Title. II. Series.

Folk art—United States—History—18th century.

BANK, Mirra. 745'.0973
Anonymous was a woman / Mirra Bank. New York : St. Martin's Press, [1979] p. cm. Bibliography: p. [NK806.B36] 79-16300 ISBN 0-312-04185-3 : 19.95 ISBN 0-312-04186-1 (pbk.) : 9.95
1. Folk art—United States—History—18th century. 2. Folk art—United States—History—19th century. 3. Women artists—United States—Biography. I. Title. BIP

Folk, Joseph Wingate, 1869-1923.

GEIGER, Louis George, 923.273 1913-
Joseph W. Folk of Missouri. Columbia, Curators of the University of Missouri, 1953. 206p. illus., port. 27cm. (The University of Missouri studies, v.25, no.2) Originally published as thesis, University of Missouri, 9n micorfil from, under title: The public career of Joseph W. Folk. Bibliography: p.[193]-199. [F466.F65] 53-7464
1. Folk, Joseph Wingate, 1869-1923. I.

Title. II. Series: Missouri. University. The University of Missouri studies, v.25, no.2

Folks, Homer, 1867-

TRATTNER, Walter I. 361'.9'73
Homer Folks, pioneer in social welfare [by] Walter I. Trattner. New York, Columbia University Press, 1968. xii, 355 p. 24 cm. Bibliographical references included in "Notes" (p. [265]-330) [HV28.F6T7] 67-29169
1. Folks, Homer, 1867- **BIP**

Follett, Barbara Newhall,

FOLLETT, Barbara Newhall, 1914- 818.5203
Barbara; the unconscious autobiography of a child genius. Edited by Harold Grier McCurdy in collaboration with Helen Follett. Chapel Hill, University of North Carolina Press [1966] xii, 146 p. illus., ports. 24 cm. [PS3511.O215Z5] 66-15507
I. McCurdy, Harold Grier, 1909- ed. II. Follett, Helen Thomas, ed. III. Title.

Folsom, James Elisha, 1908-

TWITTY, W. Bradley 923.273
Y'all come. Nashville, Hermitage Pr., P.O. Box 996 [c.1962] 169p. illus. 62-3014 5.00
1. Folsom, James Elisha, 1908- I. Title.

Fonda, Henry, 1905-

BROUGH, James, 1918- 791.43'028'0924 B
The fabulous Fondas. New York, McKay [1973] vii, 296 p. illus. 22 cm. [PN2285.B73] 73-84054 ISBN 0-679-50373-0 6.95
1. Fonda, Henry, 1905- 2. Fonda, Jane, 1937- 3. Fonda, Peter, 1940- I. Title.

*HANNA, David. 791.43'028'0924 B
Four giants of the West. New York, Belmont Tower [1976] 223 p. ill. 18 cm. [PN2287] 1.50 (pbk.)
1. Fonda, Henry, 1905- 2. Stewart, James, 1908- 3. Wayne, John, 1907- 4. Cooper, Gary, 1901-1961. I. Title.

Fonda, Jane, 1937-

BROUGH, James, 1918- 791.43'028'0924 B
The fabulous Fondas. New York, McKay [1973] vii, 296 p. illus. 22 cm. [PN2285.B73] 73-84054 ISBN 0-679-50373-0 6.95
1. Fonda, Henry, 1905- 2. Fonda, Jane, 1937- 3. Fonda, Peter, 1940- I. Title.

KIERNAN, Thomas. 791.43'028'0924 B
Jane: an intimate biography of Jane Fonda. New York, Putnam [1973] xvii, 358 p. 22 cm. [PN2287.F56K5] 73-78589 ISBN 0-399-11207-3 7.95
1. Fonda, Jane, 1937- I. Title.

Fonda, Jane, 1937- —Juvenile literature.

FOX, Mary Virginia. 791.43'028'0924 B
Jane Fonda : something to fight for / by Mary Virginia Fox ; illustrated by Mary Molina. Minneapolis : Dillon Press, 1980, c1979. p. cm. (Taking part) A biography of the award-winning actress who has been active in the antiwar movement and in recent protests against nuclear power. [PN2287.F56F6] 92 79-22102 ISBN 0-87518-189-9 lib. bdg. : 6.95 5.95
1. Fonda, Jane, 1937- —Juvenile literature. 2. Moving-picture actors and actresses—United States—Biography—Juvenile literature. I. Molina, Mary. II. Title.

Fontaine, Joan, 1917-

FONTAINE, Joan, 1917- 791.43'028'0924 B
No bed of roses / by Joan Fontaine. 1st ed. New York : Morrow, 1978. 319 p. : ill. ; 24 cm. Autobiographical. Includes index. [PN2287.F58A35] 78-7003 ISBN 0-688-03344-X : 9.95
1. Fontaine, Joan, 1917- 2. Moving-picture actors and actresses—United States—Biography. I. Title. **BIP**

Fontana, Lucio, 1899-1968.

BALLO, Guido, 1914- 709'.24
Lucio Fontana. New York, Praeger [1971] 268 p. illus. (part col.) 30 cm. Bibliography: p. 263-268. [NB623.F65B3 1971] 78-154353 30.00
1. Fontana, Lucio, 1899-1968.

Fontane, Theodor, 1819-1898.

ROBINSON, A. R. 838'.8'09
Theodor Fontane : an introduction to the man and his work / by A. R. Robinson. Cardiff : University of Wales Press, 1976. [7], 209 p., plate : port. ; 23 cm. Includes index. Bibliography: p. 206-208. [PT1863.Z7R6] 76-383573 ISBN 0-7083-0617-9 : £5.00
1. Fontane, Theodor, 1819-1898. 2. Authors, German—19th century—Biography. **BIP**

Fontbonne, Jeanne, 1759-1843.

MANNIX, Mary Dolorosa, Sister. 922.244
The living fountain; the story of Mother St. John Fontbonne. Illus. by Sister Francis Louise Russell. Los Angeles, Wetzel. Pub. Co. [1951] 150p. illus. 22cm. [BX4705.F62M3] 54-27097
1. Fontbonne, Jeanne, 1759-1843. I. Title.

Fonteyn, Margot, Dame, 1919-

BLAND, Alexander. 792.8'092'2 B
Fonteyn and Nureyev : the story of a partnership / Alexander Bland. New York : Times Books, [1979] p. cm. [GV1785.A1B57] 79-64452 ISBN 0-8129-0860-0 : 22.50
1. Fonteyn, Margot, Dame, 1919- 2. Nureyev, Rudolph Hametovitch, 1938- 3. Dancers—Biography. 4. Ballet. I. Title. **BIP**

FONTEYN, Margot, Dame, 1919- 792.8'028'0924 B
Margot Fonteyn : autobiography. 1st American ed. New York : Knopf : distributed by Random House, 1976. xii, 266, ix p., [40] leaves of plates : ill. ; 25 cm. Includes index. [GV1785.F63A35 1976] 75-36802 ISBN 0-394-48570-X : 12.50
1. Fonteyn, Margot, Dame, 1919- 2. Ballet. **BIP**

MONEY, Keith. 792.8'092'4 B
Fonteyn : the making of a legend / Keith Money. [New York] : Reynal, 1974, c1973. 318 p. : chiefly ill. ; 32 cm. Includes index. [GV1785.F63M65 1974] 74-3578 ISBN 0-688-61163-X : 25.00
1. Fonteyn, Margot, 1919- 2. Ballet. **BIP**

Fools Crow, Frank, 1890 or 91-

FOOLS Crow, Frank, 1890or91- 970'.004'97
Fools Crow / [recorded by] Thomas E. Mails, assisted by Dallas Chief Eagle ; with ill. by the author. 1st ed. Garden City, N.Y. : Doubleday, 1979. 278 p., [10] leaves of plates : ill. ; 24 cm. Includes index. Bibliography: p. [267] [E99.O3F664] 76-2803 ISBN 0-385-11332-3 : 12.95
1. Fools Crow, Frank, 1890 or 91- 2. Oglala Indians—Biography. 3. Oglala Indians. 4. Teton Indians. I. Mails, Thomas E. II. Chief Eagle, D., 1925-

Football.

PLIMPTON, George 796.332640924
Paper Lion. New York, Pocket Bks. [1967, c.1966] 303p. ports. 18cm. (95053) Autobiographical. [GV939.P6A3] .95 pap.,
1. Football. I. Title. **BIP**

PLIMPTON, George. 796.332640924
Paper Lion. [1st ed.] New York, Harper & Row [1966] 362 p. ports. 22 cm. Autobiographical. [GV939.P6A3] 64-20541
1. Football. I. Title.

PLIMPTON, George. 796.332'0924
Paper lion. Large type ed. New York, Harper & Row [1969, c1966] 362 p. 29 cm. [GV939] 72-4051 9.95
1. Football. 2. Sight-saving books. I. Title.

TITTLE, Yelberton Abraham, 1926- 796.3320924
Y. A. Tittle: I pass; my story as told to Don Smith. Rev. ed. New York, Watts [1966] ix, 300p. ports. 25cm. [GV939.T5A3 1966] 66-6245 5.95
1. Football. I. Smith, Don, 1926- II. Title. III. Title: I pass.

TITTLE, Yelberton Abraham, 1926- 927.96332
Y. A. Tittle: I pass! My story as told to Don Smith. New York, F. Watts [1964] x, 290 p. ports. 25 cm. [GV939.T5A3] 64-18950
1. Football. I. Smith, Don, 1926- II. Title. III. Title: I pass!

TITTLE, Yelberton Abraham, 1926- 927.96332
Y. A. Tittle: pass! My story as told to Don Smith. New York, F. W. Watts [1964] x. 290 p. ports. 25 cm. [GV939.T5A3] 64-18950
1. Football. I. Smith, Don, 1926- II. Title. III. Title: I pass!

Football—Biog.

DAVIS, Mac, 1905 796.33'64'0922
Pacemakers in football. Illus. by Sam Nisenson. Cleveland, World [1968] 126p. illus. 29cm. Holl bk. [GV939.A1D38] 68-13704 2.95 3.41 lib. ed.
1. Football—Biog.—Juvenile literature. I. Title.

HAND, Jack J 1912- 796.332'64'0922
Great running backs of the NFL, by Jack Hand. Illustrated with photos. New York, Random House [c1966] 184 p. illus., ports. 22 cm. (The Punt, pass, and kick library 5) [GV939.A1H29] 67-1944
1. Football—Biog.—Juvenile literature. I. Title. **BIP**

Football—Biography.

ANDERSON, Dave. 796.332'64'0922
Great defensive players of the NFL. New York, Random House [1967] x, 176 p. ports. 22 cm. (The Punt, pass, and kick library, 7) [GV939.A1A46] 67-20384
1. Football-Biog. I. Title.
Contents.--Sam Huff.--Willie Davis.--Larry Wilson.--Tommy Nobis.--Gino Marchetti.--Bob Lilly.--Joe Schmidt.--Dave "Deacon" Jones.--Chuck Bednarik.--Henry Jordan.--Dick "Night Train" Lane.--Dick Butkus.

ANDERSON, Dave. 796.332'64'0922
Great defensive players of the NFL. New York, Random House [1967] x, 176 p. ports. 22 cm. (The Punt, pass, and kick library, 7) Contents.Contents.—Sam Huff.—Willie Davis.—Larry Wilson.—Tommy Nobis.—Gino Marchetti.—Bob Lilly.—Joe Schmidt.—Dave "Deacon" Jones.—Chuck Bednarik.—Henry Jordan.—Dick "Night Train" Lane.—Dick Butkus. [GV939.A1A46] 67-20384
1. Football—Biography. I. Title.

ANDERSON, Dave. 796.332
Great defensive players of the NFL. New York, Random House [1967] x, 176 p. ports. 22 cm. (The Punt, pass, and kick library, 7) Brief sketches of the careers and great moments of ten defensive players of the National Football League: Sam Huff, Willie Davis, Larry Wilson, Tommy Nobis, Gino Marchetti, Bob Lilly, Joe Schmidt, Dave "Deacon" Jones, Chuck Bednarik, Henry Jordan, Dick "Night Train" Lane, and Dick Butkus. [GV939.A1A46] AC 68
1. Football—Biography. I. Title.

BERGER, Phil. 796.332'0922
Great running backs in pro football. New York, J. Messner [1970] 191 p. ports. 22 cm. Fifteen close-ups of pro football players including Hugh McElhenny, Paul Hornung, Don Perkins, Gale Sayers, Hoyle Granger, and Leroy Kelly. [GV939.A1B4] 70-100569 ISBN 0-671-32215-X 3.95
1. Football—Biography. I. Title.

CLARY, Jack T. 796.33'2'0922
Main men of the seventies : the quarterbacks / by Jack Clary. New York : National Football League Properties, 1975. 96 p. : ill. (some col.) ; 29 cm. [GV939.A1C52] 75-13796
1. Football—Biography. 2. Quarterback (Football) I. Title.

DALEY, Arthur. 796.33264092
Pro football's Hall of Fame; the official book. With a foreword by Dick McCann. Produced in co-operation with the Hall of Fame. Chicago, Quadrangle Books, 1963. 248 p. illus., ports. 22 cm. [GV939.A1D3] 63-18473
1. Football—Biography. I. Canton, Ohio. National Pro Football Hall of Fame. II. Title.

DALEY, Arthur. 796.332'64'0922
Pro football's Hall of Fame; the official book. With a foreword by Dick McCann. New York, Grosset & Dunlap [1968, c1963] 248 p. illus., ports. 22 cm. "Published in co-operation with the Hall of Fame." [GV939.A1D3 1968] 68-7622 3.95
1. Football—Biography. I. Canton, Ohio. National Pro Football Hall of Fame. II. Title.

DEVANEY, John 796.332640922
The pro quarterbacks. New York, Putman [1966] 222p. ports. 22cm. [GV939.A1D4] 66-7086 3.49 lib. ed.,
1. Football—Biog. I. Title.
Contents omitted.

KOWET, Don. 796.33'2'0922
Golden toes; football's greatest kickers. New York, St. Martin's Press [1972] 148 p. illus. 22 cm. [GV939.A1K68] 72-88046 5.95
1. Football—Biography. 2. Kicking (Football)—Biography. I. Title.

*LIBBY, Bill. 796.33263092
Champions of College football. New York, Hawthorn Books [1975] 205 p. ill. 21 cm. Includes index. [GV939] 74-31632 ISBN 0-8015-1196-8 7.95.
1. Football—Biography. I. Title.

LIBBY, Bill. 796.33'263'0922 B
Heroes of the Heisman trophy. New York, Hawthorn Books [1973] 211 p. illus. 22 cm. [GV939.A1L47 1973] 73-7180 5.95
1. Football—Biography. I. Title. II. Title: The Heisman trophy.

LISS, Howard. 796.332
The making of a rookie. Illustrated with photos. Glossary of pro football terms. New York, Random House [1968] xv, 172 p. illus., ports. 22 cm. (The Punt, pass, and kick library, 9) The rookie careers of four young major league football players—Gale Sayers, Jim Hart, Bubba Smith, and Paul Warfield—show how a rookie is chosen and what obstacles he must overcome to succeed in pro football. [GV959.L67] AC 68
1. Football—Biography. I. Title. **BIP**

LOWITT, Bruce. 796.33'2'0922 B
Profiles in football courage / Bruce Lowitt and Charles Morey. New York : Pyramid Books, 1975. 128 p. : ill. ; 18 cm. [GV939.A1L68] 75-4183 ISBN 0-515-03919-5 pbk. : 0.95
1. Football—Biography. I. Morey, Charles, 1916- joint author. II. Title.

PAUL, William Henry, 1948- 796.33'264'06273
The gray-flannel pigskin: movers and shakers of pro football. [1st ed.] Philadelphia, Lippincott [1974] 276 p. ports. 22 cm. [GV939.A1P37] 74-10669 ISBN 0-397-01025-7 7.95
1. Football—Biography. I. Title.

PRATT, John Lowell, comp. 927.9633
Pro, pro, pro; stories of pro football's greatest stars. New York, F. Watts [1963] vi, 181 p. 25 cm. [GV.939.A1P7] 63-16905
1. Football—Biog. I. Title.
Contents omitted

PRATT, John Lowell, comp. 927.9633
Pro, pro, pro; stories of pro football's greatest stars. New York, Author [dist. Kable News, 1964, c.1963] 181p. 18cm. (Amer. sports lib., F119) .50 pap.,
1. Football—Biog. I. Title.

*RUBIN, Bob. 796.33'2'0922 [B] *Football's toughest men.* New York, Lancer [1973] 159 p. 18 cm. [GV939] 0.95 (pbk)
1. Football—Biography. I. Title.

SCHAAP, Richard, 796.33'2'0922 B 1934- comp.
Quarterbacks have all the fun : the good life and hard times of Bart, Johnny, Joe, Francis, and other great quarterbacks / written and edited by Dick Schaap. Rev. ed. Chicago : Playboy Press, c1975. xx, 261 p. ; 18 cm. [GV939.A1S32 1975] 75-326050 pbk. : 1.75 1.75
1. Football—Biography. 2. Quarterback (Football) I. Title.

SIMPSON, O. J., 796.332'0924 B 1947-
O. J.: the education of a rich rookie, by O. J. Simpson, with Pete Axthelm. [New York] Macmillan [1970] 255 p. illus., ports. 21 cm. [GV939.S47A3] 70-126191
1. Football—Biography. I. Axthelm, Peter M. II. Title. BIP

STAINBACK, Berry. 796.332'64'0922 *Football stars.* New York, Pyramid Books [etc.] v. illus, ports. 18 cm. annual. Each vol. carries also in the title the year of issue, i.e., Football stars of 1967. [GV939.A1S72] 66-9834
I. Title.

STAINBACK, Berry 796.3320922 *Football stars of 1966.* New York [Pyramid 1966] 160p. illus., ports. 18cm. [GV939.A1S72] 66-9834 .50 pap.,
1. Football—Biog. I. Title.

SULLIVAN, George, 796.332'0922 B 1927-
The gamemakers; pro football's great quarterbacks—from Baugh to Namath. New York, Putnam [1971] 255 p. illus., ports. 24 cm. [GV939.A1S87 1971] 76-163418 7.95
1. Football—Biography. 2. Quarterback (Football) I. Title.

TARKENTON, Francis 796.332'0924 A.
Better scramble than lose, by Fran Tarkenton as told to Olsen. New York, Four Winds Press [1969] 126 p. illus., ports. 22 cm. Autobiographical. [GV939.T28A3] 73-81706 4.50
1. Football—Biography. I. Olsen, Jack. II. Title.

WEYAND, Alexander M., 927.96332 1892-
Football immortals. Foreword by Earl "Red" Blaik. New York, Macmillan [1962] 290 p. illus. 22 cm. [GV939.A1W4] 62-19433
1. Football-Biography. I. Title. BIP

Football—Biography—Dictionaries.

MENDELL, Ronald L., 796.33'2'0922 1943-
Who's who in football [by] Ronald L. Mendell [and] Timothy B. Phares. New Rochelle, N.Y., Arlington House [1974] 395 p. 24 cm. [GV939.A1M46] 74-17336 ISBN 0-87000-237-6
1. Football—Biography—Dictionaries. I. Phares, Timothy B., joint author. II. Title. BIP

Football—Biography—Juvenile literature.

ANDERSON, Dave. 796.332640922 *Great pass receivers of the NFL.* New York, Random House [1966] 180 p. illus., ports. 22 cm. (The Punt, pass, and kick library, 6) [GV939.A1A48] 66-31255
1. Football—Biography—Juvenile literature. I. Title. BIP

COAN, Howard, 796.332'09'22 B *Great pass catchers in pro football.* [Photos.] New York, J. Messner [1971] 192 p. illus., ports. 22 cm. Brief biographies of thirteen pass-catchers in pro football: Don Hutson, Elroy Hirsch, Raymond Berry, Tommy McDonald, Lance Alworth, Gary Collins, Bob Hayes, John Mackey, Don Maynard, George Sauer, Charley Taylor, Otis Taylor, and Paul Warfield. [GV939.A1C6] 920 78-160308 ISBN 0-671-32443-8 4.50
1. Football—Biography—Juvenile literature. I. Title.

DAVIS, Mac, 1905- 796.33'2'0922 B *100 greatest football heroes.* New York, Grosset & Dunlap [1973] 140 p. illus. 28 cm. (Illustrated true books) Brief biographies of coaches, players, trailblazers, innovators, record setters—all football immortals. [GV939.A1D37 1973] 920 73-822 4.95
1. Football—Biography—Juvenile literature. I. Title.
Library binding 5.49, ISBN 0-448-03932-X

DAVIS, Mac, 1905 796.33'64'0922 *Pacemakers in football.* Illus. by Sam Nisenson. Cleveland, World [1968] 126p. illus. 29cm. Holl bk. [GV939.A1D38] 68-13704 2.95 3.41 lib. ed.
1. Football—Biog.—Juvenile literature. I. Title.

DAVIS, Mac, 1905- 796.33'264'0922 *Pacemakers in football.* Illustrated by Sam Nisenson. Cleveland, World Pub. Co. [1968] 126 p. illus. 29 cm. "A Holly book." Brief biographies of thirty players and coaches who made and shaped football history. [GV939.A1D38] 920 68-13704
1. Football—Biography—Juvenile literature. I. Nisenson, Samuel, illus. II. Title.

GUTMAN, Bill. 796.33'2'0922 B *Football superstars of the '70s* / by Bill Gutman. New York : J. Messner, [1975] 191 p. : ports. ; 22 cm. Biographical sketches of twelve football stars: Archie Manning, Jack Tatum, Mike Reid, Franco Harris, Ted Kwalick, Bob Tucker, Bill Bradley, Chester Marcol, Greg Landry, Ron Johnson, O. J. Simpson, and Terry Bradshaw. [GV939.A1G86] 920 75-12751 ISBN 0-671-32750-X : 6.95 ISBN 0-671-32751-8 lib.bdg. : 6.29
1. Football—Biography—Juvenile literature. I. Title. BIP

GUTMAN, Bill. 796.33'2'0922 B *Modern football superstars* / Bill Gutman. New York : Dodd, Mead, [1974] 128 p. : ill. ; 22 cm. Includes index. Brief biographies emphasizing the careers of six professional football players: Fran Tarkenton, O. J. Simpson, Larry Brown, Gene Washington, Larry Csonka, and Joe Namath. [GV939.A1G877] 920 74-6799 4.50
1. Football—Biography—Juvenile literature. I. Title.

HAND, Jack J 796.332'64'0922 1912-
Great running backs of the NFL, by Jack Hand. Illustrated with photos. New York, Random House [c1966] 184 p. illus., ports. 22 cm. (The Punt, pass, and kick library 5) [GV939.A1H29] 67-1944
1. Football—Biog.—Juvenile literature. I. Title. BIP

HEUMAN, William. 796.332'64'0922 *Famous pro football stars.* New York, Dodd, Mead [1967] 153 p. ports. 22 cm. (Famous biographies for young people) [GV939.A1H4] 67-2408
1. Football—Biography—Juvenile literature. I. Title. BIP

LIBBY, Bill. 796.332'0922 B *Star running backs of the NFL.* New York, Random House [1971] viii, 144 p. illus., ports. 22 cm. (The Punt, pass, and kick library) Brief biographies of twenty-one running backs including O. J. Simpson, Larry Brown, Alvin Haymond, and Matt Snell. [GV939.A1L49] 920 77-158376 ISBN 0-394-92285-9 (library ed.)
1. Football—Biography—Juvenile literature. I. Title. BIP

LISS, Howard. 920 (J) *The making of a rookie.* Illustrated with photos. Glossary of pro football terms. New York, Random House [1968] xv, 172 p. illus., ports. 22 cm. (The Punt, pass, and kick library, 9) [GV959.L67] 68-26887
1. Football—Biography—Juvenile literature. I. Title.

RAINBOLT, 796.33'2'0922 B Richard.
Football's clever quarterbacks / Richard Rainbolt. Minneapolis : Lerner Publications Co., [1975] 72 p. : ill. ; 23 cm. (The Sports heroes library) Brief biographies emphasizing the careers of ten quarterbacks: Sammy Baugh, Sid Luckman, Bob Waterfield, Otto Graham, Norm Van Brocklin, Y. A. Tittle, Johnny Unitas, Bart Starr, Lenny Dawson, Joe Namath. [GV939.A1R34 1975] 920 74-27467 ISBN 0-8225-1051-0 lib.bdg. : 4.95
1. Football—Biography—Juvenile literature. 2. Quarterback (Football)—Juvenile literature. I. Title. BIP

RAINBOLT, 796.33'2'0922 B Richard.
Football's rugged running backs / Richard Rainbolt. Minneapolis : Lerner Publications Co., [1975] 71 p. : ill. ; 23 cm. (The Sports heroes library) Brief biographies emphasizing the careers of ten noted running backs: Jim Thorpe, Red Grange, Ernie Nevers, Steve Van Buren, Joe Perry, Ollie Matson, Hugh McElhenny, Lenny Moore, Jim Brown, and Gale Sayers. [GV939.A1R35 1975] 920 74-27469 ISBN 0-8225-1052-9
1. Football—Biography—Juvenile literature. 2. Backfield play (Football)—Juvenile literature. I. Title. BIP

STAINBACK, Berry. 796.33'2'0922 B *Pro football heroes of today.* New York, Random House [1973] 152 p. illus. 29 cm. (Landmark giant, 23) Profiles the lives of twenty-two champion football players including Joe Namath, Dick Butkus, Otis, Taylor, and Larry Brown. [GV939.A1S73 1973] 920 73-4434 ISBN 0-394-82629-9 5.49 (lib. bdg.)
1. Football—Biography—Juvenile literature. I. Title.

WAYNE, Bennett. 796.33'2'0922 B *Football replay; great games, coaches, players.* Edited with commentary by Bennett Wayne. Champaign, Ill., Garrard Pub. Co. [1973] 168 p. illus. 22 cm. (A Target book) (Target books) Anecdotes from football history and brief biographies of famous football players and coaches. [GV939.A1W35] 920 73-7871 ISBN 0-8116-4904-0 3.78
1. Football—Biography—Juvenile literature. I. Title.

ANDERSON, Dave. 796.332'64'0922 *Great defensive players of the NFL.* New York, Random House [1967] x, 176 p. ports. 22 cm. (The Punt, pass, and kick library, 7) [GV939.A1A46] 67-20384
1. Football-Biog. I. Title.
Contents.--Sam Huff.--Willie Davis.--Larry Wilson.--Tommy Nobis.--Gino Marchetti.--Bob Lilly.--Joe Schmidt.--Dave "Deacon" Jones.--Chuck Bednarik.--Henry Jordan.--Dick "Night Train" Lane.--Dick Butkus.

Football coaching—History.

COHANE, Tim. 796.33'2077 *Great college football coaches of the twenties and thirties.* New Rochelle, N.Y., Arlington House [1973] xv, 329 p. illus. 26 cm. [GV956.6.C63] 73-7543 ISBN 0-87000-152-3 11.95
1. Football coaching—History. 2. Football coaches. I. Title. II. Title: College football coaches.

Football—Defense.

OLDERMAN, Murray. 796.33'22 *The defenders.* Written and illustrated by Murray Olderman. Englewood Cliffs, N.J., Prentice-Hall [1973] 304 p. illus. (part col.) 29 cm. [GV951.1.O44] 73-7546 ISBN 0-13-197509-9 14.95
1. Football—Defense. 2. Football—Biography. I. Title.

Football—Dictionaries.

SULLIVAN, George, 796.33'2'0922 B 1927-
Pro football A to Z : a fully illustrated guide to America's favorite sport / George Sullivan. New York : Winchester Press, [1975] 341 p. : ill. ; 24 cm. [GV951.S898] 75-9259 ISBN 0-87691-202-1 : 10.00
1. Football—Dictionaries. 2. Football—Biography. I. Title.

SULLIVAN, George, 796.33'2'0922 B 1927-
Pro football A to Z : a fully illustrated guide to America's favorite sport / George Sullican. New York : Scribner, c1975. 341 p. : ill. ; 24 cm. [GV951.S898 1975] 75-43128 ISBN 0-684-14641-X pbk. : 3.95
1. Football—Dictionaries. 2. Football—Biography. I. Title. BIP

Football—History—Miscellanea.

NEFT, David S. 796.33'2'09 *The football scrapbook* / by David Neft. Indianapolis : Bobbs-Merrill, [1976] p. cm. [GV950.N43] 76-11613 ISBN 0-672-52029-X : 8.95
1. Football—History—Miscellanea. 2. Football—Biography—Miscellanea. I. Title.

Football—Juvenile literature.

HIRSHBERG, Albert, 796.332'0922 1909-
The glory runners, by Al Hirshberg. New York, Putnam [1968] 223 p. illus. 21 cm. [GV959.H57] 67-24155
1. Football—Juvenile literature. I. Title.

Football—Records—Juvenile literature.

PHILLIPS, Louis. 796.33'2'0922 B *Football, records, stars, feats, and facts* / by Louis Phillips and Arnie Markoe ; ill. by Paul Frame. 1st ed. New York : Harcourt, Brace, Jovanovich, c1979. p. cm. (A Handy book) Presents brief biographies of 35 outstanding football players, a compendium of notable football achievements, and an assortment of interesting facts. [GV955.P48] 920 79-87526 ISBN 0-15-228947-X pbk. : 2.95
1. Football—Records—Juvenile literature. 2. Football players—United States—Biography—Juvenile literature. I. Markoe, Arnie, joint author. II. Frame, Paul, 1913- III. Title.

Foote, Arthur William, 1853-1937.

FOOTE, Arthur 780'.92'4 B William, 1853-1937.
Arthur Foote, 1853-1937 : an autobiography ; with a new introd. and notes by Wilma Reid Cipolla. New York : Da Capo Press, 1978. xvii, 154 p. : port. ; 22 cm. (Da Capo Press music reprint series) Reprint of the 1946 ed. priv. print. at Plimpton Press, 1946. Includes bibliographical references and indexes. [ML410.F75A3 1978] 78-2021 ISBN 0-306-77531-X : 22.50
1. Foote, Arthur William, 1853-1937. 2. Composers—United States—Biography.

Foote, Mary (Hallock) 1847-1938.

FOOTE, Mary (Hallock) 813'.4 B 1847-1938.
A Victorian gentlewoman in the Far West; the reminiscences of Mary Hallock Foote. Edited, with an introd., by Rodman W. Paul. San Marino, Calif., Huntington Library, 1972. xiv, 416 p. illus. 25 cm. Includes bibliographical references. [PS1688.A4 1972] 72-86535
1. Foote, Mary (Hallock) 1847-1938. I. Paul, Rodman Wilson, 1912- ed. II. Title. BIP

Foote, Samuel, 1720-1777.

FITZGERALD, Percy 822'.6 B Hetherington, 1834-1925.
Samuel Foote; a biography. New York, B. Blom, 1972. vii, 382 p. port. 22 cm. Reprint of the 1910 ed. [PR3461.F6F5 1972] 72-84512 13.75
1. Foote, Samuel, 1720-1777. BIP

TREFMAN, Simon. 792'.028'0924 B *Sam. Foote, comedian, 1720-1777.* New York, New York University Press, 1971. xi, 302 p. illus. 24 cm. Bibliography: p. 283-291. [PR3461.F6T7] 70-171348 ISBN 0-8147-8153-5
1. Foote, Samuel, 1720-1777. I. Title. BIP

Forbes, Edward Waldo, 1873-1969.

EDWARD Waldo Forbes, 708'.00924 B *Yankee visionary*. [Cambridge, Mass.] Fogg Art Museum, Harvard University [1971] xi, 161 p. illus., maps, plans, ports. 22 cm. Includes the catalog of the exhibition held Jan. 16-Feb. 22, 1971, at the Fogg Art Museum. Contents.Contents.—Edward Waldo Forbes: art museum director, by J. Coolidge.—Edward Waldo Forbes: city planner, by B. A. Mandelbaum and M. K. Fitzsimons.—Edward Waldo Forbes: herald of conservation, by E. H. Jones.—Gifts and bequests of Edward Waldo Forbes. Includes bibliographical references. [N406.F6E3] 76-145673
1. Forbes, Edward Waldo, 1873-1969. I. Forbes, Edward Waldo, 1873-1969. II. Harvard University. William Hayes Fogg Art Museum.

Forbes, Malcolm S.

JONES, Arthur, 1936- 338.7'61'0705720924 B
Malcolm Forbes : peripatetic millionaire / Arthur Jones. 1st ed. New York : Harper & Row, c1977. x, 211 p., [8] leaves of plates : ill. ; 24 cm. Includes index. [HC102.5.F67J66 1977] 77-6885 ISBN 0-06-012204-8 : 10.00
1. Forbes, Malcolm S. 2. Forbes magazine. 3. Businessmen—United States—Biography. 4. Capitalists and financiers—United States—Biography. BIP

Ford, Arthur A.

FORD, Arthur A. 920.9133
Nothing so strange, autobiography. In collaboration with Margueritte Harmon Bro. [1st ed.] New York, Harper [1958] 250 p. 22 cm. [BF1027.F6A3] 57-9879
I. Bro, Margueritte (Harmon) 1894- II. Title.

SPRAGGETT, Allen. 133.9'1'0924 B
Arthur Ford, the man who talked with the dead, by Allen Spraggett, with William V. Rauscher. New York, New American Library; [distributed by W. W. Norton, 1973] xii, 301 p. illus. 22 cm. Bibliography: p. [288]-292. [BF1283.F63S66 1973] 72-9600 7.95
1. Ford, Arthur A. I. Title.

Ford, Barney L.—Juvenile literature.

TALMADGE, Marian. 978.8'83'030924 B
Barney Ford, Black baron [by] Marian Talmadge and Iris Gilmore. New York, Dodd, Mead [1973] xii, 237 p. illus. 22 cm. A biography of a former slave who overcame many misfortunes to become a leading citizen of Denver, a power in Republican politics, and one of Colorado's wealthiest men. Bibliography: p. 229-232. [E185.97.F69T34] 92 72-12020 ISBN 0-396-06751-4 4.50
1. Ford, Barney L.—Juvenile literature. I. Gilmore, Iris, joint author. II. Title. BIP

Ford, Betty, 1918-

CASSIDAY, Bruce. 973.925'092'4 B
Betty Ford : woman of courage / as written by Burce Cassiday. New York : Dale Books, c1978. 162 p. ; 18 cm. [E867.C37] 78-62319 ISBN 0-89559-116-2 pbk. : 1.95
1. Ford, Betty, 1918- 2. Presidents—United States—Wives—Biography. BIP

FEINMAN, Jeffrey. 973.925'092'4 B
Betty Ford / Jeffrey Feinman. New York : Award Books, 1976. 171 p. ; 18 cm. (An Award Bibliography ; AD1552) Includes bibliographical references. [E867.F67F44] 76-360648 1.50
1. Ford, Betty, 1918-

FORD, Betty, 1918- 973.925'092'4 B
The times of my life / Betty Ford, with Chris Chase. 1st ed. New York : Harper & Row, c1978. xi, 302 p., [12] leaves of plates : ill. ; 24 cm. Includes index. [E867.F66 1978] 78-2131 ISBN 0-06-011298-0 : 10.95
1. Ford, Betty, 1918- 2. Ford, Gerald R., 1913- 3. Presidents—United States—Wives—Biography. 4. Presidents—United States—Biography. I. Chase, Chris, joint author. II. Title. BIP

WEIDENFELD, Sheila Rabb. 973.925
First Lady's lady : with the Fords at the White House / by Sheila Rabb Weidenfeld. New York : Putnam, c1979. 419 p., [4] leaves of plates : ill. ; 24 cm. [E867.W43 1979] 78-10662 ISBN 0-399-12292-3 : 11.95
1. Ford family. 2. Ford, Betty, 1918- 3. Weidenfeld, Sheila Rabb. 4. Social secretaries—Washington, D.C.—Biography. I. Title. BIP

Ford, Charles Wilson, 1857-1884.

BREIHAN, Carl W., 1915- 364.1'55'0924 B
The man who shot Jesse James / Carl W. Breihan. South Brunswick [N.J.] : A. S. Barnes, c1978. p. cm. Includes index. [F594.B806] 77-84562 ISBN 0-498-02068-1 : 12.00
1. Ford, Robert Newton, 1862-1892. 2. Ford, Charles Wilson, 1857-1884. 3. James, Jesse Woodson, 1847-1882. 4. Outlaws—The West—Biography. 5. Frontier and pioneer life—The West. 6. The West—History—1848-1950. I. Title. BIP

Ford, Clara J. (Bryant)

CLANCY, Louise B 920.7
The believer; the life story of Mrs. Henry Ford, by Louise B. Clancy and Florence Davies. New York, Coward-McCann [1960] 215p. illus. 22cm. [CT275.F678C55] 60-11287
1. Ford, Clara J. (Bryant) I. Davies, Florence, joint author. II. Title.

Ford, Edward.

FORD, Edward. 796.357'092'2 B
Whitey and Mickey : a joint autobiography of the Yankee years / by Whitey [i.e. Edward] Ford, Mickey Mantle, and Joseph Durso. New York : Viking Press, 1977. 198 p., [12] leaves of plates : ill. ; 22 cm. [GV865.A1F6 1977] 75-46625 ISBN 0-670-76394-2 : 8.95
1. Ford, Edward. 2. Mantle, Mickey, 1931- I. Mantle, Mickey, 1931- joint author. II. Durso, Joseph, joint author. III. Title. BIP

SHAPIRO, Milton J. 927.96357
The Whitey Ford story. New York, Messner [c.1962] 190p. illus. 22cm. 62-16679 2.99
1. Ford, Edward. I. Title.

Ford family.

WEIDENFELD, Sheila Rabb. 973.925
First Lady's lady : with the Fords at the White House / by Sheila Rabb Weidenfeld. New York : Putnam, c1979. 419 p., [4] leaves of plates : ill. ; 24 cm. [E867.W43 1979] 78-10662 ISBN 0-399-12292-3 : 11.95
1. Ford family. 2. Ford, Betty, 1918- 3. Weidenfeld, Sheila Rabb. 4. Social secretaries—Washington, D.C.—Biography. I. Title. BIP

Ford, Ford Madox, 1873-1939.

FORD, Ford Madox, 1873-1939. 828'.9'1209 B
Your mirror to my times; the selected autobiographies and impressions of Ford Madox Ford. Edited, with an introd., by Michael Killigrew. [1st ed.] New York, Holt, Rinehart and Winston [1971] xxi, 392 p. illus. 24 cm. [PR6011.O53Z554] 74-138884 ISBN 0-03-085971-9 10.00
I. Title.

MACSHANE, Frank 828.91209
The life and work of Ford Madox Ford. New York, Horizon [c.1965] xx. 298p. illus., ports. 23cm. Bibl. [PR6011] 65-11858 6.50
1. Ford, Ford Madox, 1873-1939. I. Title.

Ford, Ford Madox, 1873-1939—Biography.

FORD, Ford Madox, 1873-1939. 828'.9'1209 B
It was the nightingale / Ford Madox Ford. New York : Octagon Books, 1975, c1933. 381 p. ; 24 cm. Autobiography. Reprint of the ed. published by Lippincott, Philadelphia. Includes index. [PR6011.O53Z55 1975] 75-5832 ISBN 0-374-92782-0 : 13.50
1. Ford, Ford Madox, 1873-1939—Biography. I. Title. BIP

Ford, Francis Xavier, Bp., 1892-1952.

DONOVAN, John F. 266'.023'0924
The pagoda and the cross; the life of Bishop Ford of Maryknoll [by] John F. Donovan. New York, Scribner [1967] xxvii, 223 p. illus., ports. 22 cm. [BX4705.F633D6] 67-17295
1. Ford, Francis Xavier, Bp., 1892-1952. 2. Missions—China. I. Title.

Ford, Francis Xavier, Bp., 1892-1952—Juvenile literature.

BETZ, Eva (Kelly) 1897- 92
To far places; the story of Francis X Ford. Illus. by Peter Landa. New York, Hawthorn [1962] 192p. illus. (pt. col.) 22cm. (Credo bks.) Bibl. 62-16229 2.95
1. Ford, Francis Xavier, Bp., 1892-1952—Juvenile literature. I. Title.

Ford, Gerald R., 1913-

AARON, Jan. 973.925'092'4 B
Gerald R. Ford, President of destiny / by Jan Aaron. New York : Fleet Press Corp., [1975] 103 p. : ill. ; 23 cm. Includes index. [E866.A27] 74-21356 ISBN 0-8303-0147-X : 5.95
1. Ford, Gerald R., 1913- I. Title.

FORD, Gerald R., 1913- 973.925'092'4 B
A time to heal : the autobiography of Gerald R. Ford. 1st ed. New York : Harper & Row, c1979. 454 p., [8] leaves of plates : ill. ; 24 cm. Includes index. [E866.F67 1979] 78-20162 ISBN 0-06-011297-2 : 12.95
1. Ford, Gerald R., 1913- 2. Presidents—United States—Biography. I. Title. BIP

HERSEY, John Richard, 1914- 973.925'092'4
The President / John Hersey. 1st ed. New York : Knopf, 1975. xi, 153 p. : ill. ; 21 cm. "This material first appeared in The New York Times Magazine April 20, 1975." [E866.H47 1975] 75-13675 ISBN 0-394-45986-5 6.95 6.95
1. Ford, Gerald R., 1913- I. Title.
Pbk. 2.95, ISBN 0-394-73148-4.

LEROY, Dave, 1920- 973.925'092'4 B
Gerald Ford—untold story. Arlington, Va., R. W. Beatty, 1974. viii, 120 p. illus. 22 cm. "A Scotty book." Bibliography: p. 120. [E866.L47] 74-81269 ISBN 0-87948-036-X 2.75
1. Ford, Gerald R., 1913-

NESSEN, Ron, 1934- 973.925
It sure looks different from the inside / Ron Nessen. 1st ed. Chicago : Playboy Press ; New York : trade distribution by Simon and Schuster, c1978. xv, 367 p., [4] leaves of plates : ill. ; 24 cm. Includes index. [E865.N47] 78-8185 ISBN 0-87223-500-9 : 12.95
1. Ford, Gerald R., 1913- 2. Nessen, Ron, 1934- 3. United States—Politics and government—1974-1977. 4. Journalists—Washington, D.C.—Biography. I. Title. BIP

REEVES, Richard. 973.925'092'4 B
A Ford, not a Lincoln / Richard Reeves. 1st ed. New York : Harcourt Brace Jovanovich, [1975] xi, 212 p. ; 25 cm. Includes index. [E866.R46] 75-22195 ISBN 0-15-132302-X : 8.95
1. Ford, Gerald R., 1913- I. Title. BIP

SIDEY, Hugh. 973.925'092'4 B
Portrait of a President / text Hugh Sidey ; photos. Fred Ward. 1st ed. New York : Harper & Row, [1975] 189 p. : ill. ; 27 cm. [E866.S56 1975] 74-28795 ISBN 0-06-013869-6 : 12.95
1. Ford, Gerald R., 1913- I. Ward, Fred, 1935- II. Title.

VESTAL, Bud. 973.925'092'4 B
Jerry Ford, up close : an investigative biography / by Bud Vestal. New York : Coward, McCann & Geoghegan, [1974] ix, 214 p., [8] leaves of plates : ports. ; 22 cm. Includes index. [E866.V47] 74-78008 ISBN 0-698-10606-7 : 7.95
1. Ford, Gerald R., 1913- I. Title.

Ford, Gerald R., 1913——Juvenile literature.

MERCER, Charles E. 973.925'092'4
Gerald Ford / by Charles Mercer ; illustrated by George Loh. New York : Putnam, [1975] 63 p. : ill. ; 23 cm. (A See and read biography) A simple biography of the thirty-eighth President, who was first to be sworn into office as a result of a Presidential resignation. [E866.M47] 74-24332 ISBN 0-399-60944-X lib.bdg. : 3.96
1. Ford, Gerald R., 1913-—Juvenile literature. I. Loh, George. BIP

Ford, Henry Lewis,

ROGERS, Fred Blackburn, 1889- 923.573
Bear Flag lieutenant; the life story of Henry L. Ford, 1822-1860. Together with some reproductions of related and contemporary paintings by Alexander Edouart. San Francisco, California Historical Society, 1951. 87 p. illus., port. 27 cm. "Two hundred and fifty numbered copies printed ... No. 78." "Reprinted with some changes and additions from California Historical Society quarterly, volume xxix, numbers 2, 3, and 4; volume xxx, numbers 1 and 2." Bibliographical references included in "Notes" (p. 69-79) [F864.F64R6] 52-529
1. Ford, Henry Lewis, 2. Bear Flag Revolt, 1846. I. Title.

Ford, Henry, 1863-1947.

AIRD, Hazel Blair. 923.373
Henry Ford, boy with ideas, by Hazel B. Aird and Catherine Ruddiman. Illustratedby Wallace Wood. Indianapolis, Bobbs-Merrill [1960] 192p. illus. 20cm. (Childhood of famous Americans) [CT275.F68A6] 59-14006
1. Ford, Henry, 1863-1947. I. Ruddiman, Catherine, joint author. II. Title.

BENNETT, Harry Herbert, 1892- 923.373
We never called him Henry, by Harry Bennett, as told to Paul Marcus. New York, Fawcett Publications [1951] 180 p. 18 cm. (Gold medal books. 185) [CT275.F68B37] 51-36122
1. Ford. Henry. 1863-1947. I. Marcus. Paul. II. Title.

BRADFORD, Gamaliel, 1863-1932. 920.02
The quick and the dead. Port Washington, N.Y., Kennikat Press [1969, c1931] x, 282 p. ports. 22 cm. (Essay and general literature index reprint series) Contents.Contents.—Theodore Roosevelt.—Woodrow Wilson.—Thomas Alva Edison.—Henry Ford.—Nikolai Lenin.—Benito Mussolini.—Calvin Coolidge. Bibliographical references included in "Notes" (p. [259]-[274]) [CT120.B65 1969] 70-85991
1. Roosevelt, Theodore, Pres. U.S., 1858-1919. 2. Wilson, Woodrow, Pres. U.S., 1856-1924. 3. Edison, Thomas Alva, 1847-1931. 4. Ford, Henry, 1863-1947. 5. Lenin, Vladimir Il'ich, 1870-1924. 6. Mussolini, Benito, 1883-1945. 7. Coolidge, Calvin, Pres. U.S., 1872-1933. I. Title.

BURLINGAME, Roger, 1889- v. 12
Henry Ford, a great life in brief. New York, Knopf, 1964 [c1954] 194, vii p. 19 cm. (Great lives in brief) 68-85057
1. Ford, Henry, 1863-1947. I. Title.

BURLINGAME, Roger, 1889-1967. 923.373
Henry Ford, a great life in brief. [1st ed.] New York, Knopf, 1955 [i.e. 1954] 194, vii

p. 19 cm. (Great lives in brief) "Advance copy." [CT275.F68B78] 54-5268
1. Ford, Henry, 1863-1947.

BUTTERFIELD, Roger Place, 1907- v. 12
Henry Ford, the Wayside Inn, and the problem of "history is bunk". [Boston, 1965]C53-66 p. 25 cm. "Separate from the Proceedings of the Massachusetts Historical Society, v, 77, 1965." Bibliographical footnotes. 68-104774
1. Ford, Henry, 1863-1947. I. Title. II. Title: Wayside Inn.

DAHLINGER, John Cote. 629.2'092'4 B
The secret life of Henry Ford / by John Cote Dahlinger as told to Frances Spatz Leighton. Indianapolis : Bobbs-Merrill, c1978. 243 p., [12] leaves of plates : ill. ; 24 cm. Includes index. [HD9710.U52F663] 77-15422 ISBN 0-672-52377-9 : 10.95
1. Ford, Henry, 1863-1947. 2. Businessmen—United States—Biography. I. Leighton, Frances Spatz, joint author. II. Title. **BIP**

EDISON Institute (Henry Ford Museum and Greenfield Village) Dearborn, Mich. v. 12
Henry Ford; a personal history, 1863-1947. a guide to an exhibition. 2d ed. [Dearborn] 1960. vi, 64 p. illus. 23 cm. 64-35577
1. Ford, Henry, 1863-1947. I. Title.

EDISON Institute (Henry Ford Museum and Greenfield Village) Dearborn, Mich. 629.2'092'4 B
Henry Ford, a personal history, 1863-1947 : a guide to an exhibition. 2nd ed. Dearborn, Mich. : Henry Ford Museum, 1960. vi, 64 p. : ill. ; 23 cm. [TL140.F6E34 1953] 74-196972
1. Ford, Henry, 1863-1947.

EDISON Institute (Henry Ford Museum and Greenfield Village) Dearborn, Mich. 629.2'092'4 B
Henry Ford, a personal history, 1863-1947 : a catalogue of a permanent exhibition. 3d rev. ed. / by Henry E. Edmunds. Dearborn, Mich. : Edison Institute, 1973 55 p. : ill. ; 26 cm. Page 55 is p. [3] of cover. Bibliography: p. 54-55. [TL140.F6E34 1973] 74-196973
1. Ford, Henry, 1863-1947. I. Edmunds, Henry Everett, 1912-

FORD, Henry, 1863-1947. 629.2'092'4 B
My life and work, by Henry Ford [in collaboration with Samuel Crowther] New York, Arno Press, 1973 [c1922] 289 p. 23 cm. (Big business: economic power in a free society) Reprint of the ed. published by Doubleday, Page, Garden City, N.Y. [HD9710.U54F58] 73-2507 ISBN 0-405-05088-7 15.00
1. Ford, Henry, 1863-1947. I. Crowther, Samuel, 1880-1947. II. Title. III. Series. **BIP**

GARRETT, Garet, 1878- 923.373
The wild wheel. New York, Pantheon Books [1952] 220 p. illus. 21 cm. [CT275.F68G3] 52-7392
1. Ford, Henry, 1863-1947. I. Title.

HENRY Ford. v. 12
[New York] New American Library [1956] 143p. 19cm. (A Signet key book) Bibliographical references included in 'Notes;'p. [132]-138
1. Ford, Henry, 1863-1947. I. Burlingame, Roger, 1889-

HERNDON, Booton. 338.7'62'0922
Ford; an unconventional biography of the men and their times. New York, Weybright and Talley [1969] 408 p. illus., ports. 24 cm. Bibliography: p. 397. [HD9710.U52F664] 72-87068 8.95
1. Ford, Henry, 1863-1947. 2. Ford, Henry, 1917- 3. Ford Motor Company. I. Title.

JARDIM, Anne. 629.2'0924
The first Henry Ford: a study in personality and business leadership. Cambridge, MIT Press [1970] ix, 278 p. 21 cm. Includes bibliographical references. [CT275.F68J3] 74-122259 6.95
1. Ford, Henry, 1863-1947. I. Title. **BIP**

KIMES, Beverly Rae. 629.22'22
The cars that Henry Ford built : a 75th anniversary tribute to America's most remembered automobiles / by Beverly Rae Kimes. Princeton, N.J. : Princeton Pub. ; [New York : distribution by E. P. Dutton], c1978. 136 p. : ill. ; 22 x 28 cm. (An Automobile quarterly library series book) Includes indexes. [TL140.F6K55 1978] 78-51029 ISBN 0-915038-08-0 : 19.95
1. Ford, Henry, 1863-1947. 2. Ford automobile. 3. Automobile industry and trade—United States—Biography. I. Title.

THE last billionaire v. 12
Henry Ford. New abridged ed. New York, Bantom Books, 1956. 300p. 18cm. (A Bantam biography)
1. Ford, Henry, 1863-1947. I. Richards, William C journalist.

THE last billionaire: Henry Ford. New abridged ed. New York, Bantom Books, 1956. 300p. 18cm. (A Bantam biography) v. 12
1. Ford, Henry, 1863-1947. I. Richards, William C 1886 or 7-1956.

NEVINS, Allan, 1890- 923.373
Ford. By Allan Nevins with the collaboration of Frank Ernest Hill. New York, Scribner, 1954- v. illus., ports., maps, facsims., geneal. table. 24cm. Contents.1. The times, the man, the company.--2. Expansion and challenge, 1915-1933, by A. Nevins and F. E. Hill. Bibliographical footnotes. Bibliography: v.1, p.653-664. [CT275.F68N37] 54-6305
1. Ford. Henry, 1863-1947. 2. Ford Motor Company. I. Hill, Frank Ernest, 1888- II. Title.

NEVINS, Allan, 1890- 923.973
Ford. By Allan Nevins with the collaboration of Frank Ernest Hill. New York, Scribner, 1954-[63] 3 v. illus., ports., maps, facsims., geneal. table. 24 cm. Full name: Joseph Allan Nevins. Contents. -- 1. The times, the man, the company. -- 2. Expansion and challenge, 1915-1933, by A. Nevins and F. E. Hill. -- [3] Decline and rebirth, 1933-1962. by A. Nevins and F. E. Hill. Bibliographical footnotes. Bibliography: v. 1. p. 653-664. [CT275.F68N37] 54-6305
1. Ford, Henry, 1863-1947. 2. Ford Motor Company. I. Hill, Frank Ernest, 1888- II. Title. **BIP**

NEVINS, Allan, 1890-1971. 629.2'092'4 B
Ford / Allan Nevins, with the collaboration of Frank Ernest Hill. New York : Arno Press, 1976, c1954-c1963. p. cm. (companies and men, business enterprise in America) Contents—v. 1. The times, the man, the company.—v. 2. Expansion and challenge, 1915-1933.—v. 3. Decline and rebirth, 1933-1962. Bibliography: v. 1, p. [HD9710.U54F654 1976] 75-41775 ISBN 0-405-08062-X (set)
1. Ford, Henry, 1863-1947. 2. Ford Motor Company. I. Hill, Frank Ernest, 1888-1969, joint author. II. Title. III. Series.

NYE, David E., 1946- 629.2'092'4 B
Henry Ford, ignorant idealist / David E. Nye. Port Washington, N.Y. : Kennikat Press, 1979. ix, 147 p. ; 23 cm. (Series in American studies.) (National university publications) Includes index. Bibliography: p. 139-143. [TL140.F6N93] 79-464 ISBN 0-8046-9242-4 : 12.50
1. Ford, Henry, 1863-1947. I. Title.

OLSON, Sidney. 923.373
Young Henry Ford: a picture history of the first forty years. Detroit, Wayne State University Press, 1963. 188 p. illus., ports., facsims. 29 cm. Errata slip inserted. [CT275.F68O4] 63-20162
1. Ford, Henry, 1863-1947. I. Title.

PARADIS, Adrian A. 629.2'0924 B
Henry Ford, by Adrian Paradis. Illustrated by Paul Frame. New York, Putnam [1968] 64 p. col. illus. 23 cm. (A See and read beginning to read biography) An easy-to-read biography of the man whose natural mechanical ability enabled him to realize his childhood dream and make a fortune by building an engine that would replace the horse. [CT275.F68P3] 92 AC 68
1. Ford, Henry, 1863-1947. I. Frame, Paul, illus. II. Title.

RAE, John Bell, 1911- comp. 629.2'0924 B
Henry Ford, edited by John B. Rae. Englewood Cliffs, N.J., Prentice-Hall [1969] ix, 180 p. 21 cm. (Great lives observed) (A Spectrum book.) Includes bibliographical references. [CT275.F68R28 1969] 69-15348 4.95
1. Ford, Henry, 1863-1947. I. Title. **BIP**

SIMONHOFF, Harry. v. 12
The first Henry Ford and his Dearborn Independent. New York, Bloch [1964] 20 p. 21 cm. Cover title. 67-12801
1. Ford, Henry. 2. Dearborn independent. I. Title.

SWARD, Keith, 1904- 629.2'0924
The legend of Henry Ford. With a new pref. by William Greenleaf. New York, Russell & Russell [1968, c1948] xviii, 550 p. 22 cm. Bibliography: p. [513]-534. [CT275.F68S9 1968] 68-10947
1. Ford, Henry, 1863-1947. I. Title. **BIP**

SWARD, Keith, 1904- 629.2'0924 B
The legend of Henry Ford. With a new pref. by William Greenleaf. New York, Atheneum, 1968 [c1948] xviii, 550 p. 21 cm. (Atheneum paperbacks, 129) Bibliography: p. 515-534. [CT275.F68S9 1968b] 68-16412 3.95
1. Ford, Henry, 1863-1947. I. Title.

WIK, Reynold M. 629.2'092'4 B
Henry Ford and grass-roots America [by] Reynold M. Wik. Ann Arbor, University of Michigan Press [1972] viii, 266 p. illus. 24 cm. Includes bibliographical references. [HD9710.U52F669] 76-163627 ISBN 0472-06193-3 3.95 (pbk.)
1. Ford, Henry, 1863-1947. 2. United States—Rural conditions. I. Title. **BIP**

Ford, Henry, 1863-1947—Juvenile literature.

BARRY, James P. 629.2'092'4 B
Henry Ford and mass production; an inventor builds a car that millions can afford, by James P. Barry. New York, F. Watts, 1973. 89 p. illus. 22 cm. (A Focus book) Bibliography: p. 84-85. The life of Henry Ford emphasizing the creation and growth of the Ford Motor Company and its impact on the American economy. [TL140.F6B37] 92 73-5760 ISBN 0-531-01045-7 3.95
1. Ford, Henry, 1863-1947—Juvenile literature. 2. Ford Motor Company—Juvenile literature. I. Title.

KELLY, Regina (Zimmerman) 1898- 629.2'0924 B
Henry Ford, by Regina Z. Kelly. Chicago, Follett Pub. Co. [1970] 191 p. illus., facsim., ports. 23 cm. Bibliography: p. 188. A biography of the man remembered as "father of assembly-line production" and as an innovator in labor practices. [CT275.F68K4] 92 68-14583 3.50
1. Ford, Henry, 1863-1947—Juvenile literature. I. Title.

KURLAND, Gerald, 1942- 629.2'092'4 B
Henry Ford, a pioneer in the automobile industry. Charlotteville, N.Y., SamHar Press, 1972. 32 p. 22 cm. (Outstanding personalities, no. 42) Includes bibliographical references. A biography of the engineering genius whose pioneering efforts in industrial mass production made it possible for Americans to enjoy consumer items once regarded as luxuries. [HD9710.U54F64] 92 72-81900
1. Ford, Henry, 1863-1947—Juvenile literature. 2. Ford Motor Company—Juvenile literature. I. Title.

MONTGOMERY, Elizabeth Rider. 629.2'0924 B
Henry Ford: automotive pioneer. Illustrated by Russell Hoover. Champaign, Ill., Garrard Pub. Co. [1969] 96 p. illus. (part col.), ports. 24 cm. (Americans all) A biography of the farm boy whose desire to tinker rather than do chores led to the design of the horseless carriage that eventually made him a billionaire. [CT275.F68M65] 92 72-83487 ISBN 8-11-645568- 2.49
1. Ford, Henry, 1863-1947—Juvenile literature. I. Hoover, Russell, illus. II. Title.

PARADIS, Adrian A. 92
Henry Ford, by Adrian Paradis. Illus. by Paul Frame. New York, Putnam [1968] 64p. col. illus. 23cm. (See & read beginning to readbiog.) [CT275.F68P3] 67-14809 2.52 lib. ed.,
1. Ford, Henry, 1863-1947—Juvenile literature. I. Title.

QUACKENBUSH, Robert M. 629.2'092'4 B
Along came the Model T! : How Henry Ford put the world on wheels / Robert Quackenbush. New York : Parents' Magazine Press, c1978. [38] p. : ill. (some col.) ; 27 cm. A biography of the developer of the first lightweight, inexpensive automobile. [HD9710.U52F666] 92 77-10057 ISBN 0-8193-0952-4 : 5.95. ISBN 0-8193-0953-2 lib. bdg. : 5.41
1. Ford, Henry, 1863-1947—Juvenile literature. 2. Automobile industry and trade—United States—Biography—Juvenile literature. I. Title. **BIP**

RICHARDS, Kenneth G 1926- 629.2'0924 (B)
Henry Ford, by Kenneth Richards. Chicago, Childrens Press [1967] 93 p. illus., ports. 29 cm. (People of destiny: a humanities series) Bibliography: p. 90-91. [TL140.F6R5] 67-20104
1. Ford, Henry, 1863-1947—Juvenile literature. I. Title.

Ford, Henry, 1917-

HERNDON, Booton. 338.7'62'0922
Ford; an unconventional biography of the men and their times. New York, Weybright and Talley [1969] 408 p. illus., ports. 24 cm. Bibliography: p. 397. [HD9710.U52F664] 72-87068 8.95
1. Ford, Henry, 1863-1947. 2. Ford, Henry, 1917- 3. Ford Motor Company. I. Title.

Ford, John Charles, 1929-

SCHWABACHER, Ethel K. 709'.2'4
John Ford, conquistador / Ethel K. Schwabacher ; with an introd. by Naomi Bliven. New York : Published for the Country Art Gallery Locust Valley, L.I., N.Y., by Nadelstein Press, 1974. 39 p. : ill. ; 28 cm. Includes bibliographical references. [N6537.F67S38] 74-84492 5.50
1. Ford, John Charles, 1929-

Ford, John, 1895-1973.

BOGDANOVICH, Peter, 1939- 791.43'0233'0924 B
John Ford / Peter Bogdanovich. New rev. and enl. ed. Berkeley : University of California, [1978] c1967. 149 p. : ill. ; 18 cm. (Movie paperbacks) Ford's career filmography: p. 113-149. [PN1998.A3F568 1978] 77-77522 ISBN 0-520-03498-8 pbk. : 4.95
1. Ford, John, 1895-1973. 2. Moving-picture producers and directors—United States—Biography. **BIP**

FORD, Dan, 1945- 791.43'0233'0924 B
Pappy : the life of John Ford / Dan Ford. Englewood Cliffs, N.J. : Prentice Hall, c1979. ix, 324, [16] leaves of plates : ill. ; 24 cm. Includes index. [PN1998.A3F566] 79 14988 ISBN 0-13-648493-X : 12.95
1. Ford, John, 1895-1973. 2. Moving-picture producers and directors—United States—Biography. I. Title. **BIP**

SINCLAIR, Andrew. 791.43'0233'0924 B
John Ford / Andrew Sinclair. New York : Dial Press/J. Wade, c1979. viii, 305 p., [16] leaves of plates : ill. ; 24 cm. "Filmography": p. 229-291. [PN1998.A3F6255] 78-10427 ISBN 0-8037-4826-4 : 11.95
1. Ford, John, 1895-1973. 2. Moving-picture producers and directors—United States—Biography. **BIP**

Ford, Marolyn.

FORD, Marolyn. 286'.1'0924 B
These blind eyes now see / Marolyn Ford with Phyllis Boykin. Wheaton, Ill. : Victor Books, c1977. 126 p. ; 18 cm. [BX6495.F665A37] 76-62742 ISBN 0-88207-657-4 pbk. : 1.75
1. Ford, Marolyn. 2. Baptists—United States—Biography. 3. Blind—United

States—Biography. I. Boykin, Phyllis, joint author. II. Title.

Ford, Patrick, 1835-1913.

RODECHKO, James Paul. 070.4'092'4 B
Patrick Ford and his search for America : a case study of Irish-American journalism, 1870-1913 / James Paul Rodechko. New York : Arno Press, 1976, c1968. viii, 294 p. ; 23 cm. (The Irish-Americans) Reprint of the author's thesis, University of Connecticut, 1967. Bibliography: p. 274-294. [PN4874.F52R6 1976] 76-6362 ISBN 0-405-09354-3 : 20.00
1. Ford, Patrick, 1835-1913. 2. Irish question. I. Title. II. Series. BIP

Ford, Phoeba Louvicy Swink, 1859-1945.

FORD, Zerno Matthew. 286'.0924 (B)
Phoeba Granny Ford [by Z. M. Ford] Owensboro, Ky., Messenger Job Print. Co. [1967] 105 p. illus., ports. 23 cm. [CT275.F6815F6] 67-9511
1. Ford, Phoeba Louvicy Swink, 1859-1945. I. Title.

Ford, Robert Newton, 1862-1892.

BREIHAN, Carl W., 1915- 364.1'55'0924 B
The man who shot Jesse James / Carl W. Breihan. South Brunswick [N.J.] : A. S. Barnes, c1978. p. cm. Includes index. [F594.B806] 77-84562 ISBN 0-498-02068-1 : 12.00
1. Ford, Robert Newton, 1862-1892. 2. Ford, Charles Wilson, 1857-1884. 3. James, Jesse Woodson, 1847-1882. 4. Outlaws—The West—Biography. 5. Frontier and pioneer life—The West. 6. The West—History—1848-1950. I. Title. BIP

Foreign correspondents—Correspondence, reminiscences, etc.

MARCOSSON, Isaac Frederick, 1876- 920.5
Before I forget; a pilgrimage to the past. New York, Dodd, Mead, 1959. 587p. illus. 22cm. Autobiographical. [PN4874.M4835A3] 59-7978
1. Foreign correspondents—Correspondence, reminiscences, etc. I. Title.

PARTON, Margaret. 920.5
The leaf and the flame. [1st ed.] New York, Knopf, 1959. 277p. 22cm. The author's five years experience in India as a staff correspondent of the New York herald tribune and as the wife of a British correspondent. [PN4874.P352A3] 59-6227
1. Foreign correspondents—Correspondence, reminiscences, etc. 2. India—Descr. & trav.—1947- 3. India—Soc. life & cust. I. Title.

SHEPARD, Elaine. 920.5
Forgive us our press passes. Englewood Cliffs, N. J., Prentice-Hall [1962] 301 p. illus. 22 cm. [PN4874.S47A3] 62-16320
1. Foreign correspondents—Correspondence, reminiscences, etc. I. Title.

Foreman, Chuck, 1950- —Juvenile literature.

DEROSIER, John. 796.33'2'0924 B
Chuck Foreman / by John deRosier ; photographs by Carl Skalak, Jr. Mankato, Minn. : Creative Education, c1977. 31 p. : col. ill. ; 25 cm. (Creative education sports superstars) A brief biography of the star running back of the Minnesota Vikings football team. [GV939.F67D47] 92 76-49561 ISBN 0-87191-543-X : 4.95
1. Foreman, Chuck, 1950- —Juvenile literature. 2. Football players—United States—Biography—Juvenile literature. I. Shalak, Carl. II. Title.

DEROSIER, John. 796.33'2'0924 B
Chuck Foreman / by John deRosier ; photographs by Carl Skalak, Jr. Mankato, Minn. : Creative Education, c1977. 31 p. : col. ill. ; 25 cm. (Creative education sports superstars) A brief biography of the star running back of the Minnesota Vikings football team. [GV939.F67D47] 92 76-49561 ISBN 0-87191-543-X : 4.95
1. Foreman, Chuck, 1950- —Juvenile literature. 2. Football players—United States—Biography—Juvenile literature. I. Shalak, Carl. II. Title. BIP

Foreman, Percy, 1902-

DORMAN, Michael. 343'.0924 B
King of the courtroom; Percy Foreman for the defense. New York, Delacorte Press [1969] xiii, 327 p. 22 cm. [KF373.F6D6] 68-19468 5.95
1. Foreman, Percy, 1902- I. Title.

Forestdale Evangelical United Brethren Church, Knoxville, Tenn.

MCDANIEL, Harold W., 1920- 289.9
History of Forestdale Evangelical United Brethren Church, by Harold W. McDaniel. Foreword by Fred L. Dennis. Knoxville, Tenn., Forestdale E.U.B. Church, 1956. 138 p. illus. 21 cm. [BX7556.Z7K55] 75-303350
1. Forestdale Evangelical United Brethren Church, Knoxville, Tenn. 2. Knoxville, Tenn.—Biography. I. Title.

Foresters—Correspondence, reminiscences, etc.

MOOMAW, Jack Clifford, 1892- 926.3
Recollections of a Rocky Mountain ranger. [Longmont, Colo., Times-Call Pub. Co., 1963] 216p. illus. 23cm. 63-5479 apply.
1. Foresters—Correspondence, reminiscences, etc. I. Title.

Forgan, James Berwick, 1852-1924.

FORGAN, James Berwick, 1852-1924. 332.1'092'4 B
Recollections of a busy life / James B. Forgan. New York : Arno Press, 1975 [c1924] 335 p., [13] leaves of plates : ill. ; 23 cm. (Wall Street and the security markets) Reprint of the ed. published by Bankers Pub. Co., New York. [HG2463.F6A3 1975] 75-2632 ISBN 0-405-06957-X : 21.00
1. Forgan, James Berwick, 1852-1924. 2. Bankers—United States—Correspondence, reminiscenes, etc. I. Title. II. Series.

Forgery—United States—Biography.

BOYER, Brian D. 364.1'63 B
Prince of thieves : the memoirs of the world's greatest forger / by Brian David Boyer. New York : Dial Press, 1975. ix, 239 p. ; 24 cm. [HV6679.B68] 75-15569 ISBN 0-8037-5387-X 8.95
1. Forgery—United States—Biography. 2. Crime and criminals—United States—Biography. I. Title. BIP

Forman, Simon, 1552-1616.

ROWSE, Alfred Leslie, 1903- 309.1'42'055
The case books of Simon Forman : sex and society in Shakespeare's age / [by] A. L. Rowse. London : Pan Books, 1976. 320 p. ; 20 cm. (Picador) Originally published under title: Simon Forman. Includes bibliographical references and index. [PR2910.R76 1976] 77-370736 ISBN 0-330-24784-0 : £1.25
1. Shakespeare, William, 1564-1616—Contemporary England. 2. Forman, Simon, 1552-1616. 3. Shakespeare, William, 1564-1616—Contemporaries. 4. England—Social life and customs—16th century. 5. Physicians—England—Biography. I. Title.

Fornander, Abraham, 1812-1887.

DAVIS, Eleanor H. 996.9'02'0924 B
Abraham Fornander : a biography / Eleanor Harmon Davis. Honolulu : University Press of Hawaii, c1979. xiv, 322 p. : ill. ; 22 cm. Includes index. Bibliography: p. [299]-314. [DU627.17.F67D38] 78-31368 ISBN 0-8248-0459-7 : 12.95
1. Fornander, Abraham, 1812-1887. 2. Hawaii—Politics and government—To 1893. 3. Statemen—Hawaii—Biography. 4. Historians—Hawaii—Biography. 5. Sweden—Biography. BIP

Forrest, Edwin, 1806-1872.

ALGER, William Rounseville, 1822-1905. 792'.028'0924 B
Life of Edwin Forrest, the American tragedian. New York, B. Blom, 1972. 2 v. ports. 22 cm. Reprint of the 1877 ed. [PN2287.F6A5 1972] 76-84505
1. Forrest, Edwin, 1806-1872.

BARRETT, Lawrence, 1838-1891. 792'.028'0924 B
Edwin Forrest. New York, B. Blom [1969] 171 p. illus., ports. 21 cm. (American actor series) Reprint of the 1887 ed. [PN2287.F6B3 1969b] 71-91894
1. Forrest, Edwin, 1806-1872. I. Title. II. Series.

BARRETT, Lawrence, 1838-1891. 792'.028'0924 B
Edwin Forrest. Boston, J. R. Osgood, 1881. St. Clair Shores, Mich., Scholarly Press [1969?] 171 p. illus., facsims., ports. 22 cm. (American actor series) [PN2287.F6B3 1969] 74-8817
1. Forrest, Edwin, 1806-1872. I. Title. II. Series. BIP

MOODY, Richard, 1911- 927.92
Edwin Forrest, first star of the American stage. [1st ed.] New York, Knopf, 1960. 415p. illus. 25cm. [PN2287.F6M57] 60-6648
1. Forrest, Edwin, 1806-1872. I. Title.

MOODY, Richard [Anselm] 927.92
Edwin Forrest, first star of the American stage. New York, Knopf, [c.]1960. 415p. illus. 25cm. 60-6648 6.95
1. Forrest, Edwin, 1806-1872. I. Title.

REES, James, 1802-1885. 792'.028'0924 B
The life of Edwin Forrest / by James Rees. Boston : Longwood Press, 1978. p. cm. Reprint of the 1874 ed. published by T. B. Peterson, Philadelphia. [PN2287.F6R4 1978] 77-92447 ISBN 0-89341-376-3 lib.bdg. : 40.00
1. Forrest, Edwin, 1806-1872. 2. Actors—United States—Biography. BIP

Forrest, Nathan Bedford, 1821-1877.

HENRY, Robert Selph, 1889- ed. 923.573
As they saw forest some recollections and comments of contemporaries. Jackson, Tenn., McCowat-Mercer Press, 1956. xvi, 306p. illus., ports., 2 maps (on fold. leaf) facsims. 24cm. (Monographs, sources, and reprints in Southern history, no. 3) [E467.1.F72H39] 55-9808
1. Forrest, Nathan Bedford, 1821-1877. I. Title. II. Series.

HENRY, Robert Selph, 1889- ed. 923.573
As they saw Forest; some recollections and comments of contemporaries. Jackson, Tenn., McCowat-Mercer Press, 1956. xvi, 306p. illus., ports., 2 maps (on fold. leaf) facsims. 24cm. (Monographs, sources, and reprints in Southern history, no. 3) [E467.1.F72H39] 55-9808
1. Forrest, Nathan Bedford, 1821-1877. I. Title. II. Series.

WILLIAMS, Edward F. 973.73'0924 B
Fustest with the mostest; the military career of Tennessee's greatest Confederate, Lt. Gen. Nathan Bedford Forrest [by Edward F. Williams III. Memphis sesquicentennial ed. Memphis? Distributed by Southern Books, 1969] 32 p. illus., maps, ports. 28 cm. [E467.1.F72W5] 73-21252 1.50
1. Forrest, Nathan Bedford, 1821-1877. I. Title.

LYTLE, Andrew Nelson, 1902- 923.573
Bedford Forrest and his critter company. Rev. ed. with an introd. by the author. New York, McDowell, Obolensky [1960] 402 p. illus. 24 cm. Includes bibliography. [E467.1.F72L9 1960] 60-9040
1. Forrest, Nathan Bedford, 1821-1877. 2. U.S.—History—Civil War—Campaigns and battles. 3. Forrest's Cavalry Corps (C. S. A.)

WYETH, John Allan, 1845-1922. 923.573
That devil Forrest; life of General Nathan Bedford Forrest. Foreward by Henry Steele Commager. Maps by Jean Treniblay. Original illus. by T. de Thulstrup [and others] New York, Harper [1959] xxvi, 614 p. illus., ports., maps (1 fold. col.) 22 cm. First published in 1899 under title: Life of General Nathan Bedford Forrest. [E467.1.F72W92] 58-12458
1. Forrest, Nathan Bedford, 1821-1877. I. Title.

Forrestal, James, 1892-1949.

ROGOW, Arnold A. 923.273
James Forrestal, a study of personality, politics, and policy. New York, Macmillan [1964, c.1963] xv, 397p. ports. 21cm. Bibl. 63-16126 6.95
1. Forrestal, James, 1892-1949. I. Title.

ROGOW, Arnold A 973.9170924
Victim of duty: a study of James Forrestal, by Arnold A. Rogow. London, Hart-Davis, 1966. [21], 324 p. 4 plates (ports) 22 1/2 cm. 45/- Originally published as James Forrestal: a study of personality, politics, and policy. New York, Macmillan, 1964. Bibliographical footnotes. [E748.F68R6] 67-72955
1. Forrestal, James, 1892-1949. I. Title.

Forsberg, Vivian.

FELL, Doris Elaine. 266'.009599'7
Lady of the Tboli / Doris Fell. Chappaqua, N.Y. : Christian Herald Books, c1979. 201 p. ; 21 cm. [BV3382.A1F44] 79-50950 ISBN 0-915684-28-4 : 7.95
1. Forsberg, Vivian. 2. Lindquist, Alice. 3. Missionaries—United States—Biography. 4. Missionaries—Philippine Islands—Biography. 5. Missions to Tboli (Philippine people) I. Title. BIP

Forster, Edward Morgan, 1879-1970—Biography.

FURBANK, Philip Nicholas. 823'.9'12
E. M. Forster : a life / by P. N. Furbank. New York : Harcourt Brace Jovanovich, [1978] p. cm. Includes index. Bibliography: p. [PR6011.O58Z655 1978] 78-54671 ISBN 0-15-128759-7 : 19.95
1. Forster, Edward Morgan, 1879-1970—Biography. 2. Authors, English—20th century—Biography. BIP

GODFREY, Denis, 1912- 823'.9'12
E. M. Forster's other kingdom. New York, Barnes & Noble [1968] vii, 228 p. 23 cm. (Biography and criticism) Bibliography: p. [224]-225. [PR6011.O58Z67 1968] 74-90 7.50
1. Forster, Edward Morgan, 1879- I. Title.

KELVIN, Norman. 823'.9'12
E. M. Forster. With a pref. by Harry T. Moore. Carbondale, Southern Illinois University Press [1967] ix, 196 p. 22 cm. (Crosscurrents: modern critiques) Bibliographical references included in "Notes" (p. [175]-183) Bibliography: p. [184]-190. [PR6011.O58Z69] 67-10282
1. Forster, Edward Morgan, 1879- BIP

KING, Francis Henry. 823'.9'12 B
E. M. Forster and his world : with 122 illustrations / Francis King. New York : Scribner, c1978. 128 p. : ill. ; 24 cm. Includes index. Bibliography: p. 120-121. [PR6011.O58Z7] 78-53935 ISBN 0-684-15868-X : 10.95
1. Forster, Edward Morgan, 1879-1970—Biography. 2. Authors, English—20th century—Biography. I. Title.

TRILLING, Lionel, 1905- 823.912
E. M. Forster. [2d rev. ed. New Directions, dist. Philadelphia, Lippincott, 1965, c.1943, 1964] 194p. 18cm.

(NDP189) Bibl. [PR6011.O58Z85] 64-23845 1.50 pap.,
1. Forster, Edward Morgan, 1879- I. Title.

Forster, Minnie Jane (Wyatt)

FORSTER, Minnie Jane (Wyatt) 920
1875-
Was the hill barren? The story of an American family. [1st ed.] New York, Exposition Press [1953] 173p. 21cm. [CT275.F6824A35] 53-11261
I. Title.

Forster-Nietzsche, Elisabeth, 1846-1935.

MY sister and I; v. 12
translated and introduced by Oscar Levy. New York, Bridgehead Books [1957] 254p. illus., port. 21cm. The authorship of this work and responsibility for the translation and editorship by Levy are under dispute. Cf. Saturday review of literature, Apr. 5 and May 24, 1952; Aufbau, May 30, 1952, etc.
1. Forster-Nietzsche, Elisabeth, 1846-1935. I. Nietzsche, Friedrich Wilhelm, 1844-1900, supposed author.

NIETZSCHE, Friedrich 921.3
Wilhelm, 1844-1900.
My sister and I; translated and introduced by Oscar Levy. New York, Boar's Head Books, 1951. [B3316.A224] 52-6752
1. Forster-Nietzsche, Elisabeth, 1846-1935. 2. 254 p. illus., port. 21 cm. I. Title.

Forster, William Edward, 1818-1886.

REID, Wemyss, 914.2'03'810924 B
Sir, 1842-1905.
Life of the Rt. Hon. W. E. Forster [by] T. Wemyss Reid. With an introd. by Valerie E. Chancellor. New York, A. M. Kelley, 1970. 2 v. in 1. illus., ports. 23 cm. (Documents of social history) Reprint of the 1888 ed. [DA565.F7R3 1970b] 73-108853 ISBN 6-7807-7630-
1. Forster, William Edward, 1818-1886. I. Title.

Forsyth-Grant, Osbert Clare, 1880-1911.

FRASER, Robert J. 910'.09'1632 B
Arctic adventurer; Grant and the Seduisante, by Robert J. Fraser and William F. Rannie. Lincoln, Ont., W. F. Rannie, 1972. 175 p. ill., fold. maps. 21 cm. [G530.F572F72] 73-179425 6.00
1. Forsyth-Grant, Osbert Clare, 1880-1911. 2. Seduisante (Schooner) I. Rannie, William F., joint author. II. Title.

Forsyth, John, 1780-1841.

DUCKETT, Alvin Laroy 923.273
John Forsyth, political tactician. Athens, Univ. of Ga. Pr. [c.1962] 263 front. port. 25cm. Bibl. 62-12497 5.00
1. Forsyth, John, 1780-1841. I. Title.

Forsyth. Peter Taylor, 1848-1921.

BROWN, Robert McAfee, 922.542
1920-
P. T. Forsyth: prophet for today. Philadelphia, Westminster Press [1952] 191 p. 21 cm. [BX7260.F583B7] 52-8862
1. Forsyth. Peter Taylor, 1848-1921. I. Title.

Forsythe, Hilda Josephine (Nelson)

FORSYTHE, Hilda 818.5403
Josephine (Nelson)
The fragments, by Hilda J. Forsythe. With. Illus. by the author. [Washington? 1965] 90 p. illus. 24 cm. Autobiographical. "Fragments, of the [author's] book, Grandeur in simplicity." [CT275.F6828A32] 65-27042
I. Title.

FORSYTHE, Hilda Josephine 920.7
(Nelson)
Grandeur in simplicity, by Hilda J. Forsythe. [1st ed.] New York, Vantage Press [1963] 108 p. 21 cm. Autobiographical. [CT275.F6828A3] 64-7286
I. Title.

Fort, Charles, 1874-1932.

KNIGHT, Damon 001'.9'0924 B
Francis, 1922-
Charles Fort; prophet of the unexplained, by Damon Knight. [1st ed.] Garden City, N.Y., Doubleday, 1970. xvi, 224 p. ports. 22 cm. Includes bibliographical references. [Q143.F67K57] 70-111340 6.95
1. Fort, Charles, 1874-1932.

Fort Henry, 1863-1947.

NEYHART, Louise 923.373
(Albright)
Henry Ford, engineer. Boston, Houghton Mifflin, 1950. x. 210 p. illus. 24 cm. [CT275.F68N4] 50-8859
1. Fort Henry, 1863-1947. I. Title.

Forten, Charlotte L.

DOUTY, Esther 371.1'00924 B
(Morris)
Charlotte Forten, free Black teacher, by Esther M. Douty. Champaign, Ill., Garrard Pub. Co. [1971] 144 p. illus. 22 cm. A biography of the nineteenth-century black woman who taught newly-freed slaves. [LA2317.F67D67] 92 73-151993 ISBN 0-8116-4512-6 2.79
1. Forten, Charlotte L. I. Title.

FORTEN, Charlotte L. 325.26
Journal; with an introd. and notes by Ray Allen Billington. New York, Dryden Press [1953] 248 p. maps. 25 cm. Bibliographical references included in "Notes" (p. [205]-244) [LA2317.F67A3] 53-6301

LONGSWORTH, Polly. 371.1'00924 B
I, Charlotte Forten, Black and free. New York, Crowell [1970] 248 p. 21 cm. Based on the Journal of Charlotte L. Forten, with introd. and notes by R. A. Billington, published 1953. Bibliography: p. 234-237. A biography of the black woman from a prosperous Philadelphia family who devoted herself to educating newly freed slaves after the Civil War. [LA2317.F67L6 1970] 92 79-109901 4.50
1. Forten, Charlotte L. I. Title. BIP

Forten, James—Juvenile literature.

DOUTY, Esther 326'.0924 B
(Morris)
Forten, the sailmaker; pioneer champion of Negro rights, by Esther M. Douty. Chicago, Rand McNally [1968] 208 p illus., ports. 22 cm. Bibliography: p. 200-201. [E185.97.F717D6] 68-23534 4.95
1. Forten, James—Juvenile literature. I. Title.

JOHNSTON, Brenda 322.4'4'0924 B
A.
Between the devil and the sea; the life of James Forten, by Brenda A. Johnston. Illus. by Don Miller. [1st ed.] New York, Harcourt Brace Jovanovich [1974] 125 p. illus. 24 cm. Bibliography: p. 125. A biography of the free black man who became a wealthy Philadelphia sailmaker and active abolitionist. [E185.97.F717J64] 92 74-5603 ISBN 0-15-206965-8 6.75
1. Forten, James—Juvenile literature. I. Miller, Don, 1923- illus. II. Title. BIP

Forth, Elizabeth (Denison) d. 1866.

SWAN, Isabella 920.7
Lisette, [1st ed.] Grosse Ile, Mich., 1965. 83 p. illus., ports. 23 cm. Bibliography: p. [79]-83. [E185.97.F72S9] 65-19209
1. Forth, Elizabeth (Denison) d I. Title.

SWAN, Isabella E. 920.7
Lisette. Grosse Ile, Mich., Author, 27740 Southpointe [c.]1965. 83p. illus., ports. 23cm. Bibl. [E185.97.F7259] 65-19209 3.00 pap.,
1. Forth, Elizabeth (Denison) d. 1866. I. Title.

Fortune, Amos, 1709 or 10-1801.

MAGOUN, F. Alexander, 326.92
1896-
Amos Fortune's choice; the story of a Negro slave's struggle for self-fulfillment. Photos. by the author. Freeport, Me., Bond Wheelwright Co. [1964] xi, 237 p. illus., maps, facsims. 25 cm. Bibliographical footnotes. [E185.97.F73M3] 64-12190
1. Fortune, Amos, 1709 or 10-1801. I. Title.

Fortune, Amos, 1709 or 10-1801—Juvenile literature.

YATES, Elizabeth, 1905- 326.92
Amos Fortune, free man. Illustrated by Nora S. Unwin. [1st ed.] New York, Aladdin Books, 1950. 181 p. illus. 21 cm. [E185.97.F73Y3] 50-7154
1. Fortune, Amos, 1709 or 10-1801—Juvenile literature. I. Title. BIP

Fortune hunters—Biography.

MOATS, Alice Leone. 301.41'1
The million dollar studs / Alice-Leone Moats. New York : Delacorte Press, c1977. 282 p. : photos. ; 22 cm. [HQ756.M63] 76-47346 ISBN 0-440-05683-7 : 8.95
1. Fortune hunters—Biography. 2. Marriages, International—Case studies. I. Title. BIP

Fortune, Timothy Thomas, 1856-1928.

THORNBROUGH, Emma 070.4'092'4 B
Lou.
T. Thomas Fortune; militant journalist. Chicago, University of Chicago Press [1972] xi, 388 p. 23 cm. (Negro American biographies and autobiographies) Bibliography: p. 371-374. [PN4874.F574T5] 73-175305 ISBN 0-226-79832-1
1. Fortune, Timothy Thomas, 1856-1928. I. Title. II. Series. BIP

Forwards (Basketball)—United States—Biography—Juvenile literature.

O'REILLY, Sean, 796.32'3'0922 B
1922-
Meet the forwards / by Sean O'Reilly. Mankato, Minn. : Creative Education, [c1977] 30 p. : ill. ; 20 cm. (Creative Education early sports books) Biographical sketches of basketball forwards Rick Barry, Julius Erving, George McGinnis, and John Havlicek. [GV884.A1O745] 920 76-52952 ISBN 0-87191-603-7 lib.bdg. : 4.95
1. Forwards (Basketball)—United States—Biography—Juvenile literature. I. Title. BIP

Foscolo, Ugo, 1778-1827—Homes and haunts—England.

VINCENT, Eric 858'.6'09 B
Reginald Pearce, 1894-
Ugo Foscolo, an Italian in Regency England, by E. R. Vincent. [Folcroft, Pa.] Folcroft Library Editions, 1973. p. Reprint of the 1953 ed. published by the University Press, Cambridge, Eng. Includes bibliographical references. [PQ4691.V55 1973] 73-13602 7.50
1. Foscolo, Ugo, 1778-1827—Homes and haunts—England.

Fosdick, Harry Emerson,

FOSDICK, Harry Emerson, 922.673
1878-1969.
The living of these days, an autobiography. [1st ed.] New York, Harper [1956] 324 p. 22 cm. [BX6495.F68A3] 56-10207
I. Title.

Fosdick, Raymond Blaine,

FOSDICK, Raymond Blaine, 923.273
1883-
Chronicle of a generation; an autobiography. [1st ed.] New York, Harper [1958] 306 p. 22 cm. [E748.F69A3] 58-11047
I. Title.

Foss, Joseph Jacob, 1915-

FOSS, Joseph Jacob, 940.54'49'73
1915-
Joe Foss, flying marine : the story of his flying circus in World War II / as told to Walter Simmons. Washington : Zenger Pub., [1979] c1943. p. cm. Reprint of the 1st ed. published by Dutton, New York. [D790.F6 1979] 79-19902 ISBN 0-89201-080-0 : 8.95
1. Foss, Joseph Jacob, 1915- 2. World War, 1939 1945—Aerial operations, American. 3. World War, 1939-1945—Personal narratives, American. 4. World War, 1939-1945—Campaigns—Solomon Islands. 5. Fighter pilots—United States—Biography. I. Simmons, Walter. II. Title.

Foster, Abigail Kelley, 1810-1887—Juvenile literature.

BACON, Margaret 322.4'4'0924 B
Hope.
I speak for my slave sister: the life of Abby Kelley Foster. New York, Crowell [1974] viii, 235 p. illus. 21 cm. (Women of America) Bibliography: p. [222]-226. A biography of Abby Kelley Foster, pacifist, abolitionist, and campaigner for women's rights in the 1840s. [E449.F742B32 1974] 92 74-4042 ISBN 0-690-00515-6 5.50
1. Foster, Abigail Kelley, 1810-1887—Juvenile literature. 2. Slavery in the United States—Anti-slavery movements—Juvenile literature. 3. Abolitionists—Juvenile literature. I. Title.

Foster, Dora.

FOSTER, Dora. 917.88'03'3
My childhood days in Colorado sunshine. Colorado Springs, Printed by Dentan-Berkeland Print. Co., 1967] 84 p. illus., group ports. 23 cm. [CT275.F6835A3] 67-9672
I. Title.

FOSTER, Dora. 917.88'03'3
My childhood days in Colorado sunshine. [Colorado Springs, Printed by Dentan-Berkeland Print. Co., 1967] 84 p. illus., group ports. 23 cm. [CT275.F6835A3] 67-9672
I. Title.

Foster, Dorothy F.

FOSTER, 917.47'1'0340924 B
Dorothy F.
The noisesome day, the stilly night; an autobiography: fact and fancy [by] Dorothy F. Foster. [1st ed.] New York, Exposition Press [1973] 93 p. 22 cm. [CT275.F6837A33] 73-165447 ISBN 0-682-47660-9 4.00
1. Foster, Dorothy F. I. Title.

Foster, George, 1948 (Dec. 1)- —Juvenile literature.

DRUCKER, Malka.
The George Foster story / by Malka Drucker, with George Foster ; introd. by George Foster. New York : Holiday House, c1979. 111 p. : ill. ; 22 cm. Includes index. A biography of one of the few National League baseball players to hit over 50 home runs in a single season. [GV865.F62D78] 78-20616 ISBN 0-8234-0351-3 : 7.95
1. Foster, George, 1948 (Dec. 1)- —Juvenile literature. 2. Baseball players—United States—Biography—Juvenile literature. I. Foster, George, 1948 (Dec. 1)- joint author. II. Title. BIP

Foster, Gregory, 1949-1972.

SILVERMAN, Al. 363.2'092'2 B
Foster and Laurie. [1st ed.] Boston, Little, Brown [1974] 303 p. 22 cm. [HV7911.F68S55] 73-16232 ISBN 0-316-79116-4 7.95
1. Foster, Gregory, 1949-1972. 2. Laurie, Rocco, 1948-1972. I. Title. BIP

Foster, Jack, 1932-

FOSTER, Jack, 1932- 796.4'2 B
Tale of the ancient marathoner : Jack

Foster's own story / cover photo by Stan Pantovic. Mountain View, Calif. : World Publications, 1974. 48 p. : ill. ; 22 cm. (Runner's monthly booklet ; no. 41) [GV697.F67A37] 74-83661 ISBN 0-89037-049-4 : 1.50
1. Foster, Jack, 1932- 2. Marathon running. I. Title.

Foster, Malcolm Cecil.

FOSTER, Malcolm Cecil. 971.6'33'030924 B
Annapolis Valley saga / by Malcolm Cecil Foster ; as edited and with foreword by Howard L. Trueman. Windsor, N.S. : Lancelot Press, 1976. 224 p. : ill. ; 22 cm. [F1039.A2F673] 76-382382
1. Foster, Malcolm Cecil. 2. Annapolis Valley—Biography. I. Title.

Foster, Michael, Sir, 1836-1907.

GEISON, Gerald L., 1943- 591.1'092'4
Michael Foster and the Cambridge School of Physiology : the scientific enterprise in late Victorian society / Gerald L. Geison. Princeton, N.J. : Princeton University Press, c1978. xix, 401 p. : ill. ; 24 cm. Based on the author's thesis, Yale, 1970. Includes bibliographical references and indexes. [QP26.F66G44] 77-85539 ISBN 0-691-08197-2 : 27.50
1. Foster, Michael, Sir, 1836-1907. 2. Physiologists—England—Biography. 3. Physiology—England—History. 4. Heart beat—History. I. Title. BIP

Foster, Nathaniel, 1767?-1840.

CURTISS, Arthur Lester Byron- 1871- 974.7'03 B
The life and adventures of Nat Foster, trapper and hunter of the Adirondacks / by A. L. Byron-Curtiss. Harrison, N.Y. : Harbor Hill Books, 1976. p. cm. Reprint of the 1897 ed. published by Press of T. J. Griffiths, Utica, N.Y. [F127.A2F572 1976] 75-45337 ISBN 0-916346-19-6 : 13.95
1. Foster, Nathaniel, 1767?-1840. 2. Frontier and pioneer life—New York (State)—Adirondack Mountains. 3. Adirondack Mountains—History. I. Title.

Foster parents—United States—Biography.

DICKERSON, Martha Ufford. 301.42'7
Our four boys : foster parenting retarded teenagers / Martha Ufford Dickerson. 1st ed. Syracuse, N.Y. : Syracuse University Press, 1978. xix, 222 p. ; 24 cm. [HQ759.7.D5] 78-5642 ISBN 0-8156-0146-8 : 11.95
1. Foster parents—United States—Biography. 2. Mentally handicapped children—United States—Biography. I. Title. BIP

Foster, Stephen Collins, 1826-1864.

GAUL, Harvey Bartlett, 1881-1945. 928.1
The minstrel of the Alleghenies. [Pittsburgh, Issued by Friends of Harvey Gaul, 195-] 86 p. illus. 24 cm. [ML410.F78G4] [ML410.F78G4] 927.8 53-25056 53-25056
1. Foster, Stephen Collins, 1826-1864. I. Title.

HODGES, Fletcher, 1906- 927.8
Swanee Ribber and a biographical sketch of Stephen Collins Foster. White Springs, Fla., Stephen Foster Memorial Association, c1958. [56]p. illus., ports. 21cm. [ML410.F78H548] 58-3903
1. Foster, Stephen Collins, 1826-1864. I. Title.

HOWARD, John Tasker, 1890- 927.8
Stephen Foster, America's troubadour. [Gloucester, Mass., Peter Smith, 1962, c.1934, 1953] 433p. 21cm. (Crowell bk. rebound.) Bibl. 4.00
1. Foster, Stephen Collins, 1826-1864. I. Title. BIP

HOWARD, John Tasker, 1890- 927.8
Stephen Foster America's troubadour. New York [Apollo Eds., 1962, c.1934, 1953] xv, 433p. (A-32) Bibl. 1.95 pap.,
1. Foster, Stephen Collins, 1826-1864. I. Title.

HOWARD, John Tasker, 1890- 928'.1
Stephen Foster, America's troubadour. [Rev. ed.] New York, Crowell [1953] xv, 433 p. illus., ports. 23 cm. "The published works of Stephen Foster": p. 403-412. [ML410.F78H6 1954] 927'.8 53-11133
1. Foster, Stephen Collins, 1826-1864.

HOWARD, John Trasker, 1890- v. 12
Stephen Foster, America's troubadour. New York, T.Y. Crowell [1962, c1953] 433 p. (Apollo editions, A32) "The published works of Stephen Foster": p. 403-412. 64-19891
1. Foster, Stephen Collins, 1826-1864. I. Title.

MILLIGAN, Harold Vincent, 1888-1951. 784'.092'4 B
Stephen Collins Foster : a biography of America's folk-song composer / by Harold Vincent Milligan. New York : Gordon Press, 1977, c1920. p. cm. Reprint of the ed. published by G. Schirmer, New York. [ML410.F78M4 1977] 77-7593 ISBN 0-87968-313-9 lib.bdg. : 39.95
1. Foster, Stephen Collins, 1826-1864. 2. Composers—United States—Biography.

PEARE, Catherine Owens. [928.1] 927.8
Stephen Foster, his life; illustrated by Margaret Ayer. [1st ed.] New York, Holt [1952] 87 p. illus. 21 cm. [ML3930.F6P4] 52-9037
1. Foster, Stephen Collins, 1826-1864. 2. Music — Juvenile literature. I. Title.

Foster, Stephen Collins, 1826-1884—Fiction.

DOUTY, Esther (Morris) 927.8
The story of Stephen Foster; illustrated by Jo Polseno. New York, Grosset & Dunlap [1954] 180p. illus. 22cm. (Signature books, 81) [ML3925.F57D7] 54-5863
1. Foster, Stephen Collins, 1826-1884—Fiction. 2. Music—Juvenile literature. 3. Musical I. Title.

Foster, Tom, 1902-

FOSTER, Tom, 1902- 385'.09'24 B
Forty-five years on the Rock Island line : being a true story of my life as I lived and remembered it, beginning at the age of three, and including forty-five years working on the railroad as an engine watchman, and ending with my retirement at age sixty-five / by Tom Foster. [Malvern? Ark.] : Foster, [1974] 188 p. : ill. ; 22 cm. [HD8039.R12U63] 74-81923 2.95
1. Foster, Tom, 1902- 2. Railroads—United States—Employees—Personal narratives. I. Title.

Foster, Wilbur Fisk, 1834-1922.

CREIGHTON, Wilbur Foster. v. 12
The life of Major Wilbur Fisk Foster, a civil engineer, Confederate soldier, builder, churchman and Free Mason; with personal recollections. [Nashville, Ambrose Printing Co., 1961] 58 p. ports., maps. 19 cm. 63-10833
1. Foster, Wilbur Fisk, 1834-1922. 2. Tennessee—Biography. I. Title.

Fotedar, S. N.

KATJU, Shiva Nath. 294.5'6'10924 B
Review on the biography of Bhagawan Gopinath Ji of Kashmir : and ... letters expounding Shiva-Sakhti [sic] philosophy / by S. N. Katju. Srinagar : Bhagawan Gopinath Ji Trust, 1976. 39 p., [2] leaves of plates : ports. ; 23 cm. Cover title. [BL1175.G625F6734] 77-901796 Re1.00
1. Fotedar, S. N. Bhagawan Gopinath Ji of Kashmir. 2. Gopinath, 1898-1968. I. Title.

Foucauld, Charles Eugene, vicomte de, 1858-1916.

BODLEY, Ronald Victor Courtenay, 1892- 922.261
The warrior saint. [1st ed.] Boston, Little, Brown [1953] 302 p. illus. 21 cm. [BX4705.F65B6] 53-5261
1. Foucauld, Charles Eugene, vicomte de, 1858-1916. I. Title.

CARROUGES, Michel, 1910- 922.261
Soldier of the spirit; the life of Charles de Foucauld. Translated from the French by Marie-Christine Hellin; with an introd. by Anne Fremantle. New York, Putnam [1956] 300 p. 21 cm. Translation of Charles de Foucauld, explorateur mystique. [BX4705.F65C32] 56-6615
1. Foucauld, Charles Eugene, vicomte de, 1858-1916. I. Title.

CARROUGES, Michel, 1910- 922.261
Solider of the spirit; the life of Charles de Foucauld. Translated from the French by Marie-Christine Hellin; with an introd. by Anne Fremantle. New York, Putnam [1956] 300p. 21cm. Translation of Charles de Foucauld, explorateur mystique. [BX4705.F65C32] 56-6615
1. Foucauld, Charles Eugene, vicomte de, 1858-1916. I. Title.

PREMINGER, Marion Mill 922.261
The sands of Tamanrasset; the story of Charles de Foucauld. True hero of God. Garden City, N.Y., Doubleday [1963, c.1961] 264p. 18cm. (Image bk., D160) Bibl. .85 pap.,
1. Foucauld, Charles Eugene, vicomte de, 1858-1916. I. Title.

PREMINGER, Marion Mill. 922.261
The sands of Tamanrasset; the story of Charles de Foucauld. [1st ed.] New York, Hawthorn Books [1961] 279 p. illus. 24 cm. Includes bibliography. [BX4705.F65P7] 61-12656
1. Foucauld, Charles Eugene, vicomte de, 1858-1916. I. Title.

ROBERTO, Brother, 1927- 922.261
The heart in the desert; a story of Father Charles deFoucauld, Illus. by Anthony Joyce. Notre Dame, Ind., Dujarie Press [1956] 94p. illus. 24cm. [BX4705.F65R64] 56-42845
1. Foucauld, Charles Eugene, vicomte de, 1858-1916. I. Title.

SIX, Jean Francois 922.244
Witness in the desert; the life of Charles de Foucauld. Tr. [from French] by Lucie Noel. New York, Macmillan [c.1965] vii, 276p. map. 22cm. [BX4705.F65S53] 65-15571 5.00
1. Foucauld, Charles Eugene, vicomte de, 1858-1916. I. Title. II. Title: The life of Charles de Foucauld.

Foucauld, Charles Eugene, vicomte de, 1858-1916—Juvenile literature.

GARNETT, Emmeline, 1924- 920
Charles de Foucauld; adventurer of the desert. Illus. by Leo Summers. New York, Farrar [c.1962] 192p. illus. 22cm. (Vision bks., 56) 62-15298 2.25
1. Foucauld, Charles Eugene, vicomte de, 1858-1916—Juvenile literature. I. Title.

Fouche, Joseph, Duc d'Otrante, 1759-1820.

COLE, Hubert. 944.05'0924 B
Fouche: the unprincipled patriot. [1st American ed.] New York, McCall Pub. Co. [1971] 347 p. illus., maps, ports. 22 cm. Bibliography: p. [317]-328. [DC198.F7C63 1971] 74-144812 ISBN 0-8415-0106-8 8.95
1. Fouche, Joseph, Duc d'Otrante, 1759-1820. I. Title.

FORSSELL, Nils, 1889-1969. 944.05'0924 B
Fouche, the man Napoleon feared. Translated from the Swedish by Anna Barwell. New York, AMS Press [1970] 255 p. illus., ports. 23 cm. Reprint of the 1928 ed. Translation of Fouche, revolutionsmannen og polisministern. Bibliography: p. 248-253. [DC198.F7F613 1970] 71-112299
I. Fouche, Joseph, duc d'Otrante, 1759-1820. II. Title. BIP

Fountain, Albert Jennings, 1838-1896.

GIBSON, Arrel Morgan 923.273
The life and death of Colonel Albert Jennings Fountain Norman, Univ. of Okla. Pr. [c.1965] xi, 301p. illus., map, ports. 23cm. Bibl. [F801.F6G5] 65-11229 5.95
1. Fountain, Albert Jennings, 1838-1896. I. Title. BIP

GIBSON, Arrell Morgan. 923.273
The life and death of Colonel Albert Jennings Fountain, by A. M. Gibson. Norman, University of Oklahoma Press [1965] xi, 301 p. illus., map, ports. 23 cm. Bibliography: p. 289-293. [F801.F6G5] 65-11229
1. Fountain, Albert Jennings, 1838-1896. I. Title.

Four Winds (Schooner)

LIPSCOMB, James. 910'.45
Cutting loose. Photos. by Chuck Bangert [and others] Illus. by Dennis Lasker. [1st ed.] Boston, Little, Brown [1974] 304 p. illus. 22 cm. [G530.F65L56] 74-5146 ISBN 0-316-52733-5 8.95
1. Four Winds (Schooner) 2. Pacific Ocean. I. Title. BIP

Fourier, Francois Marie Charles, 1772-1837.

RIASANOVSKY, Nicholas Valentine, 1923- 335.2'0924 B
The teaching of Charles Fourier [by] Nicholas V. Riasanovsky. Berkeley, University of California Press, 1969. xii, 256 p. port. 23 cm. Bibliography: p. 244-251. [HX704.F9R5] 77-84043 6.50
1. Fourier, Francois Marie Charles, 1772-1837. I. Title. BIP

Fourier, Jean Baptiste Joseph, baron, 1768-1830.

GRATTAN-GUINNESS, I. 510'.924 B
Joseph Fourier, 1768-1830; a survey of his life and work, based on a critical edition of his monograph on the propagation of heat, presented to the Institut de France in 1807 [by] I. Grattan-Guinness, in collaboration with J. R. Ravetz. Cambridge, MIT Press [1972] x, 516 p. illus. 27 cm. Includes Fourier's original unpublished text of 1807 with title: Theorie de la propagation de la chaleur dans les solides. The first separately published version appeared in 1822 under title: Theorie analytique de la chaleur. Bibliography: p. [491]-502. [QA29.F68G7] 76-128538 ISBN 0-262-07041-3 20.00
1. Fourier, Jean Baptiste Joseph, baron, 1768-1830. 2. Heat. I. Fourier, Jean Baptiste Joseph, baron, 1768-1830. Theorie analytique de la chaleur. 1972.

HERIVEL, John. 510'.92'4 B
Joseph Fourier : the man and the physicist / by John Herivel. Oxford : Clarendon Press, 1975. xi, 350 p. : ill. ; 24 cm. Includes index. Bibliography: p. [334]-342. [QA29.F68H47] 75-318175 ISBN 0-19-858149-1 : 31.75
1. Fourier, Jean Baptiste Joseph, baron, 1768-1830.
Distributed by Oxford University Press, N.Y. BIP

Fournier-Aubry, Fernand.

FOURNIER-AUBRY, Fernand. 910'.41'0924 B
Don Fernando; the story of Fernand Fournier-Aubry. Recorded by Andre Voisin and translated from the French by Xan Fielding. [1st American ed.] New York, Putnam [1974] vii, 246 p. illus. 24 cm. Autobiographical. [CT9971.F68A3313 1974] 73-78590 ISBN 0-399-11206-5 7.95
1. Fournier-Aubry, Fernand. I. Voisin, Andre, 1923-

Fowell, Edith Anne.

FOWELL, Edith Anne. 920.7
Mama was a drummer. [1st ed.] New

York, Vantage Press [1956] 66p. 21cm. Autobiographical. [CT275.F687A3] 56-11213
I. Title.

Fowler, Gene, 1890-1960.

FOWLER, Will, 1922- 928.1
The young man from Denver. [1st ed.] Garden City, N.Y., Doubleday, 1962. 310 p. illus. 22 cm. [PS3511.O93Z54] 62-11320
1. Fowler, Gene, 1890-1960. I. Title.

Fowler, Gene, 1890-1960—Biography.

SMITH, Harry Allen, 1907- 818'.5'209 B
The illegitimate son of Buffalo Bill / by H. Allen Smith. Indianapolis : Bobbs-Merrill, [1976] p. cm. [PS3511.O93Z88] 75-6391 ISBN 0-672-52053-2
1. Fowler, Gene, 1890-1960—Biography. I. Title.

SMITH, Harry Allen, 1907- 818'.5'209 B
The life and legend of Gene Fowler / H. Allen Smith. New York : Morrow, 1977. 319 p. : ill. ; 24 cm. Includes index. [PS3511.O93Z884] 76-30544 ISBN 0-688-03188-9 : 10.00
1. Fowler, Gene, 1890-1960—Biography. 2. Authors, American—20th century—Biography. I. Title. **BIP**

Fowler, James Lowry.

ROBB, R. H. v. 12
A biographical sketch of Rev. James Lowry Fowler, the hero of the reorganization in Georgia. Cincinnati, Press of the Western Methodist Book Concern [n.d.] 106 p. 18 cm. 67-1481
1. Fowler, James Lowry. 2. Methodist Church in Georgia. I. Title.

Fowles, Edward.

FOWLES, Edward. 706'.5 B
Memories of Duveen Brothers / [by] Edward Fowles ; introduction by Sir Ellis Waterhouse. London : Times Books, 1976 [7], 215 p., [16] p. of plates : ill., facsim., ports. ; 24 cm. "Abridged by Michael Glover." Includes index. [N8660.F67A25 1976] 77-359790 ISBN 0-7230-0155-3 : £7.95
1. Fowles, Edward. 2. Duveen Brothers. 3. Duveen, Joseph Duveen, Baron, 1869-1939. 4. Art dealers—Great Britain—Biography. I. Title.

Fowlie, Wallace, 1908-

FOWLIE, Wallace, 1908- 840'.9 B
Journal of rehearsals : a memoir / by Wallace Fowlie. Durham, N.C. : Duke University Press, 1977. xi, 219 p. ; 25 cm. Includes index. [PQ67.F65A34] 77-79809 ISBN 0-8223-0401-5 : 12.75
1. Fowlie, Wallace, 1908- 2. French philology—Study and teaching (Higher)—United States. 3. Philologists—United States—Biography. I. Title. **BIP**

FOWLIE, Wallace, 1908 927.92
Pantomine, a journal of rehearsals. Chicago, H. Regnery Co., 1951. 246 p. 22 cm. Autobiography. [PS3511.O94Z5 1951] 51-2808
I. Title.

Fowlie, Wallace, 1908- —Biography.

FOWLIE, Wallace, 1908- 818'.5'209 B
Pantomime : a journal of rehearsals / by Wallace Fowlie. Westport, Conn. : Greenwood Press, 1975, c1951. 246 p. ; 22 cm. Autobiography. Reprint of the ed. published by H. Regnery Co., Chicago. Includes index. [PS3511.O94Z5 1975] 74-29632 ISBN 0-8371-7981-5 lib.bdg. : 13.25
1. Fowlie, Wallace, 1908- —Biography. I. Title.

Fowling—Great Britain.

HAWKER, Peter, 1786-1853. 799.2'4
The diary of Colonel Peter Hawker. [1st ed.] republished; with a new introduction. Richmond, Publishing Company Ltd., 1971. [7], xi, 366, [5], 393 p., 10 plates. illus., map, ports. 22 cm. Reprint of the London, Longmans, 1893 ed., published in 2 v. [SK17.H3A3 1971] 72-192283 ISBN 0-85546-010-5 £5.50
1. Fowling—Great Britain. I. Title.

Fox, Barclay, 1817-1855.

FOX, Barclay, 1817-1855. 942.3'78'0750924 B
Barclay Fox's Journal / edited by R. L. Brett. Totowa, N.J. : Rowman and Littlefield, 1979. 426 p., [2] leaves of plates : ill. ; 25 cm. Includes bibliographical references and index. [DA690.F19F69 1979] 79-120186 ISBN 0-8476-6187-3 : 23.50
1. Fox, Barclay, 1817-1855. 2. Friends, Society of—England—Falmouth—Biography. 3. Falmouth, Eng.—Biography. 4. England—Social life and customs—19th century. I. Brett, R. L. II. Title. **BIP**

Fox, Charles James, 1749-1806.

DERRY, John Wesley. 942.07'3'0924 B
Charles James Fox [by] John W. Derry. New York, St. Martin's Press [1972] 454 p. illus. 23 cm. Bibliography: p. [445]-446. [DA506.F7D47 1972b] 73-176065 12.50
1. Fox, Charles James, 1749-1806.

MITCHELL, Leslie George. 942.07'3'0924
Charles James Fox and the disintegration of the Whig Party, 1782-1794, by L. G. Mitchell. London, Oxford University Press, 1971. x, 318 p. 23 cm. (Oxford historical monographs) Bibliography: p. [303]-313. [DA506.F7M55] 70-560328 ISBN 0-19-821838-9 £3.75
1. Fox, Charles James, 1749-1806. 2. Whig Party (Gt. Brit.) 3. Great Britain—Politics and government—1760-1820. I. Title. **BIP**

OLIVER, Robert Tarbell, 1909- 942.07'3'0922
Four who spoke out: Burke, Fox, Sheridan, Pitt, by Robert T. Oliver. Freeport, N.Y., Books for Libraries Press [1969, c1946] x, 196 p. 23 cm. (Biography index reprint series) Bibliography: p. 184-196. [DA522.A1O55 1969] 75-101831
1. Burke, Edmund, 1729?-1797. 2. Fox, Charles James, 1749-1806. 3. Sheridan, Richard Brinsley Butler, 1751-1816. 4. Pitt, William, 1759-1806. 5. Orators, English. I. Title.

REID, Loren Dudley, 1905- 942.07'3'0924 B
Charles James Fox: a man for the people [by] Loren Reid. [Columbia] University of Missouri Press [1969] xiv, 475 p. illus. 23 cm. Bibliography: p. 447-457. [DA506.F7R38 1969] 69-19319 7.50
1. Fox, Charles James, 1749-1806. 2. Gt. Brit.—Politics and government—1760-1820.

TREVELYAN, George Otto, Sir, bart., 1838-1928. 942.07'3'0924 B
The early history of Charles James Fox. New York, AMS Press [1971] viii, 470 p. port. 23 cm. Reprint of the 1880 ed. [DA506.F7T7 1971] 79-158852 ISBN 0-404-06524-4
1. Fox, Charles James, 1749-1806. I. Title. **BIP**

Fox, Charles James, 1749-1806—Juvenile literature.

NOBLE, Iris. 942.07'0922
Rivals in Parliament; William Pitt and Charles Fox. New York, J. Messner [1970] 191 p. 22 cm. Bibliography: p. 185-186. Brief biographies emphasizing the parliamentary careers of two rival and influential English statesmen of the late eighteenth-century. [DA506.F7N62] 920 76-123180 3.50
1. Fox, Charles James, 1749-1806—Juvenile literature. 2. Pitt, William, 1759-1806—Juvenile literature. I. Title.

Fox, Debbie Diane, 1955-

FOX, Debbie Diane, 1955- 362.7'8'19752 B
A face for me / Debbie Diane Fox, with Jean Libman Block. 1st ed. New York : Wyden Books : trade distribution by Simon and Schuster, c1978. vi, 197 p. ; 22 cm. [QM695.F32F69] 78-10266 ISBN 0-88326-156-1 : 7.95
1. Fox, Debbie Diane, 1955- 2. Face—Abnormalities—Biography. I. Block, Jean Libman, joint author. II. Title. **BIP**

Fox, Emmet.

GAZE, Harry. 920.91313
Emmet Fox, the man and his work. [1st ed.] New York, Harper [1952] 150 p. illus. 20 cm. [BF648.F6G3] 52-5437
1. Fox, Emmet.

WOLHORN, Herman. 248'.4'0924
Emmet Fox's golden keys to successful living & reminiscences / Herman Wolhorn. 1st ed. New York : Harper & Row, c1977. viii, 229 p. ; 21 cm. [BF648.F6W64 1977] 76-62930 ISBN 0-06-069670-2 : 6.95
1. Fox, Emmet. 2. New Thought. 3. Clergy—United States—Biography. I. Title.

Fox, George Lansing, 1900-1943.

FOX, Isadore (Hurlbut) 287.60924
The immortal chaplain; the story of Rev. George L. Fox, 1900-1943, by Isadore H. Fox. Introd. by Arthur Wentworth Hewitt. New York, Exposition [c.1965] 84p. port. 21cm. [UH23.F68] 65-4883 4.00
1. Fox, George Lansing, 1900-1943. I. Title.

Fox, George, 1624-1691.

BRINTON, Howard Haines, 1884- 289.6'0924
The religion of George Fox, 1624-1691, as revealed by his epistles [by] Howard H. Brinton [Wallingford, Pa., Pendle Hill Publications, 1968] 32 p. 20 cm. (Pendle Hill pamphlet 161) Bibliographical footnotes. [BX7795.F7B75] 68-57978 0.55
1. Fox, George, 1624-1691. I. Title. **BIP**

FOGELKLOU, Emilia, 1878- 289.6'0922
The atonement of George Fox [by] Emilia Fogelklou Norlind. Edited by Eleanore Price Mather. [Wallingford, Pa., Pendle Hill Publications, 1969] 31 p. 20 cm. (Pendle Hill pamphlet 166) Bibliography: p. 30-31. [BX7676.2.F6] 75-84675 0.55
1. Friends, Society of—History 2. Fox, George, 1624-1691. 3. Nayler, James, 1617?-1660. I. Title. **BIP**

FOX, George, 1624-1691. 922.86
Journal. Edited with an introd. and notes by Rufus M. Jones. With an essay on the influence of the Journal by Henry J. Cadbury. New York, Capricorn Books [1963] 578 p. port. (on cover) 19 cm. (A Capricorn book, Cap81) [BX7795.F7A23 1963] 63-4585

FOX, George, 1624-1691. 289.6'092'4 B
The journal of George Fox. Edited from the mss. by Norman Penney. With an introd. by T. Edmund Harvey. New York, Octagon Books, 1973. 2 v. ports. 24 cm. Reprint of the 1911 ed. published by the University Press, Cambridge. [BX7795.F7A2 1973] 73-8978 ISBN 0-374-92826-6 40.00 (2 vol. set)
1. Fox, George, 1624-1691. I. Penney, Norman, 1858-1933, ed. II. Title. **BIP**

FOX, George, 1624-1691. 289.6'092'4
A journal or historical account of the life, travels, sufferings, Christian experiences, and labour of love in the work of the ministry, of that ancient, eminent, and faithful servant of Jesus Christ, George Fox. New York : AMS Press, 1975. 2 v. ; 22 cm. (The works of George Fox ; v. 1-2) Reprint of the 1831 ed. published by M. T. C. Gould, Philadelphia. Includes index. [BX7617.F54 1975 vol. 1-2] [BX7795.F7] 289.6'092'4 B 75-16194 ISBN 0-404-09351-5 : 30.00
1. Fox, George, 1624-1691. I. Title: A journal or historical account of the life, travels, sufferings, Christian experiences ...

NOBLE, Wilfred Vernon, 1908- 922.86
The man in leather breeches; the life & times of George Fox. New York, Philosophical Library [1953] 298p. illus. 23cm. [BX7795] 53-11997
1. Fox, George, 1624-1691. I. Title.

ROBERTS, Arthur O 922.86
Through flaming sword; a spiritual biography of George Fox. Illus. by Stanley Putman. Portland, Or., Barclay Press [1959] 113p. illus. 22cm. Includes bibliography. [BX7795.F7R6] 59-14084
1. Fox, George, 1624-1691. I. Title.

WILDES, Harry Emerson, 1890- 922.8642
Voice of the Lord; a biography of George Fox. Philadelphia, University of Pennsylvania Press [1965] 473 p. 22 cm. Bibliography: p. 437-449. [BX7795.F7W5 1965] 64-10896
1. Fox, George, 1624-1691. I. Title. **BIP**

Fox, George, 1624-1691—Juvenile literature.

YOLEN, Jane H. 289.6'092'4 B
Friend: the story of George Fox and the Quakers, by Jane Yolen. New York, Seabury Press [1972] x, 179 p. map. 24 cm. Bibliography: p. [173]-175. A biography of the English pacifist who founded the Quaker movement in the seventeenth century. [BX7795.F7Y65] 92 74-171865 5.95
1. Fox, George, 1624-1691—Juvenile literature. 2. Friends, Society of—Juvenile literature. I. Title. **BIP**

Fox, John, 1862-1919.

MOORE, Elizabeth (Fox) 928.1
John Fox, Jr.: personal and family letters and papers. [Lexington, Ky., 1955] ii, 92p. port. 28cm. On cover: University of Kentucky Library Associates. [PS1703.M6] 55-13720
1. Fox, John, 1862-1919. I. University of Kentucky Library Associates. II. Title.

Fox, Josephine Clardy, 1881-1970.

BURNS, Ruby. 917.64'96 B
Josephine Clardy Fox: traveler, opera-goer, collector of art, benefactor. El Paso, Texas Western Press, 1973. xvi, 143 p. illus. 27 cm. [CT275.F6893B87] 73-83925 ISBN 0-87404-042-6 10.00
1. Fox, Josephine Clardy, 1881-1970.

Fox, Lawrence Webster, 1853-1931.

GRIFFITH, Beatrice Fox, 1890- 926.1
Pennsylvania doctor. [1st ed.] Harrisburg, Stackpole. [1957] 239p. illus. 23cm. Includes bibliography. [R154.F74G7] 57-6994
1. Fox, Lawrence Webster, 1853-1931. I. Title.

Fox, Lydia Mantle,

FOX, Lydia Mantle, 1861- 920.7
Eighty plus; 1861 to 1945. Boston, Christopher Pub. House [1950] 330 p. port. 21 cm. [CT275.F6895A3] 50-11643
I. Title.

Fox, Margaret Askew Fell, 1614-1702.

BARBOUR, Hugh. 289.6'092'4 B
Margaret Fell speaking / Hugh Barbour. [Wallingford, Pa. : Pendle Hill Publications], 1976. 32 p. ; 20 cm. (Pendle Hill pamphlet ; 206 ISSN 0031-4250s) Includes bibliographical references. [BX7795.F75B37] 76-4224 ISBN 0-87574-206-8 : 0.95
1. Fox, Margaret Askew Fell, 1614-1702. I. Fox, Margaret Askew Fell, 1614-1702. Margaret Fell speaking. 1976. II. Title. **BIP**

Fox, Margaret, 1833-1893.

JACKSON, Herbert G. 133.9'2'0922 B
The spirit rappers [by] Herbert G. Jackson, Jr. [1st ed.] Garden City, N.Y., Doubleday, 1972. 226 p. 22 cm. Bibliography: p. [221]-226. [BF1283.F7J33] 71-171300 6.95
1. Jencken, Catherine Fox, 1836-1892. 2. Fox, Margaret, 1833-1893. 3. Underhill, Ann Leah, 1814-1890. 4. Spiritualism—History. I. Title.

Fox, Maude A (Thiesen)

FOX, Maude A (Thiesen) 917.9495
Both sides of the mountain. Palm Desert, Calif., Printed by Desert Magazine Press [1954] 132p. illus. 24cm. Autobiographical. [CT275.F6897A3] 54-1782
I. Title.

Fox (Steam yacht)

M'CLINTOCK, Francis Leopold, Sir, 1819-1907. 919.8
The voyage of the "Fox" in the Arctic seas; a narrative of the discovery of the fate of Sir John Franklin and his companions, by Captain M'Clintock. Rutland, Vt., C. E. Tuttle Co. [1972] xl, 375 p. illus. 20 cm. [G665 1857.M255] 79-170104 ISBN 0-8048-1010-9 8.25
1. Fox (Steam yacht) 2. Franklin, John, Sir, 1786-1847. 3. Arctic regions. I. Title. II. Title: A narrative of the discovery of the fate of Sir John Franklin and his companions.

Fox, Stephen, Sir, 1627-1716.

CLAY, Christopher. 332'.092'4 B
Public finance and private wealth : the career of Sir Stephen Fox, 1627-1716 / Christopher Clay. Oxford : Clarendon Press ; New York : Oxford University Press, 1978. xvi, 362 p. : port. ; 23 cm. Includes index. Bibliography: p. 336-343. [HG172.F69C56] 78-40071 ISBN 0-19-822467-2 : 32.50
1. Fox, Stephen, Sir, 1627-1716. 2. Capitalists and financiers—England—Biography. I. Title. BIP

Foxworth, Jo.

FOXWORTH, Jo. 658.4'0092'4 B
Boss lady : an executive woman talks about making it / Jo Foxworth. 1st ed. New York : Crowell, c1978. x, 224 p. ; 24 cm. Includes index. [HF5500.3.U54F68 1978] 78-2514 ISBN 0-690-01398-1 : 9.95
1. Foxworth, Jo. 2. Women executives—Biography. 3. Women executives—United States. I. Title. BIP

Foyt, A. J., 1935-

ENGEL, Lyle Kenyon. 796.7'2'0924 B
The incredible A. J. Foyt / produced by Lyle Kenyon Engel. Rev. ed. New York : Arco Pub. Co., 1977. 187 p. : ill. ; 24 cm. [GV1032.F66E5 1977] 76-47614 ISBN 0-668-02195-0 lib. bdg. : 6.95. ISBN 0-668-04097-1 pbk. : 4.95.
1. Foyt, A. J., 1935- 2. Automobile racing drivers—United States—Biography. I. Title. BIP

LIBBY, Bill. 796.7'2'0924 B
Foyt / Bill Libby. New York : Hawthorn Books, 1974. 218 p. : ill. ; 24 cm. Includes index. [GV1032.F66L52 1974] 73-21314 7.95
1. Foyt, A. J., 1935- 2. Automobile racing.

Foyt, A. J., 1935- —Juvenile literature.

BRAUN, Thomas, 1944- 796.7'2'0924
Racing's Indy winner, A. J. Foyt / by Thomas Braun. [Mankato, Minn.] : Creative Education/Childrens Press, c1976. 30 p. : ill. (some col.) ; 19 cm. Briefly describes the dramatic auto race, the Indianapolis 500, focusing on A. J. Foyt, the driver who hopes to be the first person in history to win that race four times. [GB1032.F66B73] 92 76-45632 ISBN 0-87191-582-0 lib.bdg. : 4.95
1. Foyt, A. J., 1935- —Juvenile literature. 2. Indianapolis Speedway Race—Juvenile literature. 3. Automobile racing drivers—United States—Biography—Juvenile literature. I. Title.

LIBBY, Bill. 796.7'2'0924 B
A. J. Foyt : racing champion / by Bill Libby. New York : Putnam, c1978. 189 p. : ill. ; 21 cm. (Putnam sport shelf) Includes index. A biography of the race driver who "has won more kinds of races in more kinds of cars on more kinds of tracks than any other other driver ever." [GV1032.F66L519 1978] 92 78-767 ISBN 0-399-61123-1 lib. bdg. : 5.69
1. Foyt, A. J., 1935- —Juvenile literature. 2. Automobile racing drivers—United States—Biography—Juvenile literature. I. Title. BIP

OLNEY, Ross Robert, 1929-
A. J. Foyt, the only four time winner / by Ross R. Olney. New York : Harvey House, c1978. 54 p. : ill. ; 23 cm. A biography of the four time winner of the annual 500-mile Indianapolis Speedway race. [GV1032.F66O46 1978] 78-105549 ISBN 0-8178-5792-3 lib bdg : 4.99
1. Foyt, A. J., 1935-—Juvenile literature. 2. Indianapolis Speedway Race—Juvenile literature. 3. Automobile racing drivers—United States—Biography—Juvenile literature. I. Title.

OLSEN, James T. 796.7'2'0924 B
A. J. Foyt; "fancypants" at the wheel, by James T. Olsen. Illustrated by John Keely. [Mankato, Minn., Creative Education; distributed by Childrens Press, Chicago, 1973, c1974] 29 p. illus. (part col.) 25 cm. (Creative's superstars) "Prepared for the publisher by Educreative Systems, inc." A brief biography of the American race car driver who has won the United States Auto Club Championship five times and the Indy 500 three times. [GV1032.F66O47] 92 73-13938 ISBN 0-87191-282-1 4.95
1. Foyt, A. J., 1935- —Juvenile literature. I. Keely, John, illus. II. Educreative Systems, inc. III. Title. IV. Title: Fancypants at the wheel.

Fraenkel, Michael, 1896-1957.

LOWENFELS, Walter, 1897- 818'.5'209
The life of Fraenkel's death; a biographical inquest, by Walter Lowenfels and Howard McCord. Assisted by Lillian Lowenfels and Will Slotnikoff. [Pullman, Wash.] Washington State University Press [1970] 92 p. illus. 23 cm. [PS3511.R13Z7] 71-11331 3.00
1. Fraenkel, Michael, 1896-1957. I. McCord, Howard, 1932- joint author. II. Title.

Fragonard, Jean Honore, 1732-1806.

THUILLIER, Jacques. 759.4
Fragonard; biographical and critical study. Translated from the French by Robert Allen. [Geneva] Skira [distributed in the U.S. by the World Pub. Co., Cleveland, 1967] 156 p. col. plates. 19 cm. (The Taste of our time [v. 46]) Bibliography: p. 143-[146] [ND553.F7T413 1967] 66-30307
1. Fragonard, Jean Honore, 1732-1806.

Frakes, Hiram, 1888-

FISHER, Lee. 287'.6'0924 B
Fire in the hills; the story of Parson Frakes and the Henderson Settlement. Introd. by Billy Graham. Nashville, Abingdon Press [1971] 158 p. illus., ports. 21 cm. [BX8495.F75F54] 73-134247 ISBN 0-687-13080-8 4.95
1. Frakes, Hiram, 1888- 2. Henderson Settlement. I. Title.

Frampton, Peter.

ADLER, Irene. 784'.092'4 B
Peter Frampton / by Irene Adler. New York : Quick Fox, c1979. 96 p. : ill. ; 26 cm. [ML420.F76A65] 79-63526 ISBN 0-8256-3933-6 pbk. : 4.95
1. Frampton, Peter. 2. Rock musicians—England—Biography. BIP

DALY, Marsha. 784'.092'4 B
Peter Frampton / by Marsha Daly ; edited by Barbara Williams Prabhu. New York : Grosset & Dunlap, c1979. 92 p. : ill. ; 21 cm. "Tempo books." Abridgement of the 1978 ed. [ML410.F816D3 1978] 78-64951 ISBN 0-448-17026-4 : 1.95 lib. bdg. : 8.45
1. Frampton, Peter. 2. Rock musicians—England—Biography. I. Prabhu, Barbara Williams. BIP

KATZ, Susan. 784'.092'4 B
Frampton! : an unauthorized biography / by Susan Katz ; designed by Paul Gamarello. 1st ed. New York : Jove Publications, 1978. 190 p. : ports. ; 18 cm. "A Jove/HBJ book." Discography: p. 188-190. [ML410.F816K4] 77-91246 ISBN 0-515-04603-5 : 1.75
1. Frampton, Peter. 2. Rock musicians—Biography.

Francois I, King of France, 1494-1547.

HACKETT, Francis, 1883-1962. 944'.028'0924 B
Francis the First. New York, Greenwood Press, 1968 [c1935] 448 p. 22 cm. [DC113.H3 1968] 68-8334
1. Francois I, King of France, 1494-1547. BIP

SEWARD, Desmond, 1935- 944.028'092'4 B
Prince of the Renaissance; the golden life of Francois I. [1st American ed.] New York, Macmillan [1973] 264 p. illus. (part col.) 26 cm. Bibliography: p. [254]-255. [DC113.S48 1973b] 73-2331 14.95
1. Francois I, King of France, 1494-1547. I. Title.

WILKINSON, Burke, 1913- 944'.028'0924 B
Francis in all his glory. [1st ed.] New York, Farrar, Straus & Giroux [1972] xii, 234 p. illus. 22 cm. Bibliography: p. [225]-227. [DC113.W54 1972] 70-182106 ISBN 0-374-32457-3 5.95
1. Francois I, King of France, 1494-1547. I. Title. BIP

France—Biog.

DES Reaux, Tallemant gedeon 1619-1692 920.044
Portraits and anecdotes (historiettes) Tr. [from French] by Hamish Miles, Revs, introd. by F. J. Barnett. New York, Oxford [c.]1965. xiv, 191p. 19cm. (Oxford lib. of French classics) Tr. of 25 selections from Historiettes. First pub. in 1925 under title: Miniature portraits. [DC130.T2A433] 65-8635 3.40
1. France—Biog. 2. France—Hist.—Louis XI II, 1610-1643. 3. France—Hist.—Louis XIV, 1643-1715. I. Miles, Hamish, 1894-1937, tr. II. Title. III. Title: Historiettes.

DICTIONNAIRE biographique francais contemporain. [2. ed.] Paris, Pharos; agent pour les Etats-Unis: Stechert-Hafner, New York [1954] 708p. ports. 27cm. [DC406.D5 1954] 54-4253 v. 12
1. France—Biog.

GOOCH, George Peabody, 1873- 920.0944
French profiles; prophets and pioneers [London] Longmans [dist. Mystic, Conn., Verry, 1965, c.1961] viii, 291p. 23cm. [DC36.1.G6] 65-7084 6.50 bds.,
1. France—Biog. I. Title.

SAINT-BEUVE, Charles Augustin, 1804-1869 920.044
Portraits of the seventeenth century, historic and literary. v.1& 2 [Tr. by Katharine P. Wormeley] Introd. by Ruth Mulhauser. New York, Ungar [c.1964] 2v. (461; 446p.) ports. 22cm. Contents.v.1. Cardinal de Richelieu. Henri, Duc de Rohan, Cardinal Mazarin, Francois, Duc de la Rochefoucauld. Anne-Genevieve de Bourbon (1619-1679) Cardinal de Retz. Mademoiselle de l'Enclos. Tallemant des Reaux and Bussy-Rabutin. The Abbe de Rance. Anne-Genevieve de Bourbon (1627-1963) Marie-Madeleine de la Vergne, Henrietta Ann of England., Louis XIVa Louise de la Beaume Le Blanc.--v.2. History of the French Academy. Corneille, Mademoiselle de Scudery.. Moliere. La Fontaine. Pascal. Madame of Sevigne. Bossuet, Boileau. Racine. Madame de Caylus. Fenelon. Comte Antoine Hamilton. The Princess des Ursins. 15.00 set,
1. France—Biog. 2. Biography—17th cent. I. Title.

SAINTE-BEUVE, Charles Augustin, 1804-1869 920.044
Portraits of the eighteenth century, historic and literary. v.1& 2 [Tr. from French by Katharine P. Wormeley] Introd. by Ruth Mulhauser. New York, Ungar [c.1964] 2v. (474; 478p.) illus. 22cm. Contents.v.1. Introduction: Saint-beuve, by E. Scherer. Duchesse du Maine. Madame de Staal-Delumay. Le Sage, Montesquieu. Adrienne Le Couvreur. Voltaire. Marquise du Deffand. Earl of Chesterfield. Benjamin Franklin. Madame Geoffrin. The Abbe Barthelemy. Louis VX.--v.2. Abbe Prevost. Madame de Lambert and Madame Necker. Denis Diderot. Jean-Jacques Rousseau. Friedrich Melchior Grimm. Madame d'Epinay. Buffon. Bernardin de Saint-Pierre. Frederick the Great. Wilhelmina, Margravine of Baireuth. Beaumarchais. Jacques Necker. Marie-Antoinette. 64-15699 15.00 set,
1. France—Biog. 2. Biography—18th cent. I. Title.

WEDGWOOD, Cicely Veronica, 1910- 923.244
Richelieu and the French monarchy New, rev. ed. New York, Collier Books [1962] 155 p. 18 cm. (Men and history, BS130V) Includes bibliography. [DC123.9.R5W4 1962] 62-19197
1. Richelieu, Armand Jean du Plessis, Cardinal, duc de, 1585-1642 II. Title. BIP

France, Anatole, 1844-1924.

MAY, James Lewis, 1873- 843'.8 B
Anatole France: the man and his work; an essay in critical biography. Port Washington, N.Y., Kennikat Press [1970] xi, 262 p. illus., ports. 22 cm. Reprint of the 1924 ed. [PQ2254.Z5M3 1970] 70-103205
1. France, Anatole, 1844-1924. I. Title.

STEWART, Herbert Leslie, 1882-1953. 848'.8'09
Anatole France, the Parisian. Freeport, N.Y., Books for Libraries Press [1972] xiv, 394 p. 22 cm. Reprint of the 1927 ed. "Bibliography: of Anatole France's chief works": p. 385-386. [PQ2254.Z5S7 1972] 72-1324 ISBN 0-8369-6837-9 14.50
1. France, Anatole, 1844-1924.

France. Armee. Legion etrangere.

REEVES, Peter. 355.3'52'0944
Legion of outcasts; the autobiography of Peter Reeves as told to Hurk Davis. Los Angeles, Holloway House Pub. Co. [1968] 313 p. 18 cm. [U55.R38A3] 68-58867 ISBN 0-87067-161-8
1. France. Armee. Legion etrangere. I. Davis, Hurk. II. Title.

France—Biography.

COCTEAU, Jean, 1889-1963. 920.044
My contemporaries. [Translated from the French]; edited and introduced by Margaret Crosland. [1st ed.] Philadelphia, Chilton Book Co. [1968] xii, 146 p. illus., ports. 21 cm. [PQ2605.O15M89 1968] 68-31695
1. France—Biography. 2. France—Civilization—1901- I. Crosland, Margaret, 1920- ed. II. Title.

OLIVER, Alfred Richard. 1912- 928.4
Charles Nodier, pilot of romanticism. [Syracuse, N.Y.] Syracuse Univ. Pr. [c.] 1964. xi, 276 p. illus., ports. 22cm. Bibl. [PQ2376.N6Z66] 64-8670 5.95
1. Nodier, Charles, 1780-1844. II. Title.

SAROLEA, Charles, 1870-1953. 920.044
The French renascence. Port Washington, N.Y., Kennikat Press [1970] 302 p. ports. 24 cm. Reprint of the 1916 ed. Contents.Contents.—Montaigne.—Montaigne and Nietzsche.—Pascal's

Thoughts.—Pascal and Newman.—Madame de Maintenon.—Liselotte: A German princess at the Court of Louis XIV.—Sir Arthur Conan Doyle on the French Huguenots.—Rousseau's Emile.—Marie Antoinette before the Revolution.—Mirabeau.—Robespierre.—The real Napoleon.—Napoleon as a socialist.—Balzac.—Gustave Flaubert.—Maurice Maeterlinck.—The condemnation of Maeterlinck.—Professor Bergson.—Mons. Poincare.—The new France. [CT1005.S3 1970] 73-110920
1. France—Biography. 2. French literature—History and criticism. I. Title. BIP

SICHEL, Edith Helen, 1862-1914. 920.044
Women and men of the French Renaissance. Port Washington, N.Y., Kennikat Press [1970] xx, 395 p. illus., ports. 23 cm. Reprint of the 1901 ed. Includes bibliographical references. [DC33.3.S57 1970] 74-110923
1. France—Biography. 2. Renaissance—France. I. Title. BIP

France—Civilization—1789-1830.

MORGAN, Sydney (Owenson) Lady, 1783?-1859. 914.4'03'60924
Lady Morgan in France; edited by Elizabeth Suddaby and P. J. Yarrow. Newcastle upon Tyne, Oriel Press, 1971. [9], 339 p., plate. port. 23 cm. "The three books in which Lady Morgan records her impressions of France, and which are the source of the present volume are: France, 2 vols., London, Colburn, 1817. France in 1829-30, 2 vols., London, Saunders & Othey, 1830. Passages from my autobiography, London, Bentley, 1859." [DC33.5.M89] 74-133983 ISBN 0-85362-103-9 £3.00
1. France—Civilization—1789-1830. I. Suddaby, Elizabeth, ed. II. Yarrow, Philip John, ed. III. Title. BIP

France combattante.

THOMPSON, Robert Smith. 940.53'44'0924 B
Pledge to destiny: Charles de Gaulle and the rise of the free French. New York, McGraw-Hill [1974] 282 p. illus. 24 cm. Bibliography: p. [263]-274. [D761.9.F7T4] 73-19695 ISBN 0-07-064390-3 9.95
1. France combattante. 2. Gaulle, Charles de, Pres. France, 1890-1970. I. Title.

France. Convention nationale, 1792-1795.

PATRICK, Alison. 944.04'2
The men of the First French Republic; political alignments in the National Convention of 1792. Baltimore, Johns Hopkins University Press [1972] xviii, 407 p. 23 cm. Bibliography: p. 379-393. [DC176.P37] 72-4018 ISBN 0-8018-1305 0 16.50 16.50
1. France. Convention nationale, 1792-1795. 2. France—History—Revolution—Biography. I. Title. BIP

France—Description and travel.

PIOZZI, Hester Lynch (Salusbury) Thrale, 1741-1821. 914.4
The French journals of Mrs. Thrale and Doctor Johnson. Edited from the original manuscripts in the John Rylands library and in the British Museum, with introd. and notes, by Moses Tyson and Henry Guppy. New York, Haskell House, 1973. vii, 274 p. ports. 23 cm. Reprint of the 1932 ed. published by Manchester University Press, Manchester, Eng. Includes bibliographical reference. [DC25.P5 1973] 72-1263 ISBN 0-8383-1430-9 11.95
1. France—Description and travel. I. Johnson, Samuel, 1709-1784. II. Title.

France—History—House of Valois, 1328-1589.

COMINES, Philippe de, Sieur d'Argenton, 1445?-1511. 944'.027'0924 B
The memoirs of Philippe de Commynes. Edited by Samuel Kinser. Translated by Isabelle Cazeaux. [1st ed.] Columbia, University of South Carolina Press [1969-1973] 2 v. (xv, 665 p.) illus., map, ports. 27 cm. Translation of Memoires. Bibliography: v. 1, p. 81-85. [DC106.9.C7323 1969] 68-9363 ISBN 0-87249-130-7 (v. 1) 10.00 (v. 1)
1. France—History—House of Valois, 1328-1589. I. Kinser, Samuel, ed. II. Title. BIP

France—History—Louis XIV, 1643-1715.

JUDGE, Harry George, ed. 944.0330924
Louis XIV. [London] Longmans [New York, Barnes & Noble, 1966, c1965] x, 150p. port. 22cm. [Problems and perspectives in hist.) Bibl. [DC124.5.J8] 66-4880 2.00 pap.,
1. France—Hist.—Louis XIV. 1643-1715—Sources. I. Title.

ORLEANS, Elisabeth Charlotte, duchesse d', 1652-1722. 914.4'03'330924 B
Letters from Liselotte. Translated and edited by Maria Kroll. [1st American ed.] New York, McCall Pub. Co. [1971, c1970] 269 p. illus., facsim., geneal. table, ports. 25 cm. Bibliography: p. [249] [DC130.O7A253 1971] 76-141213 ISBN 0-8415-0090-8 8.95
1. France—History—Louis XIV, 1643-1715. 2. France—Court and courtiers. I. Kroll, Maria, ed. II. Title.

France—History—Louis XVI, 1774-1793.

SEGUR, Louis Philippe, comte de, 1753-1830. 944.04'0924
Memoirs and recollections of Count Louis Philippe de Segur. New York, Arno Press, 1970. 1 v. (various pagings) facsim., fold map, port. 23 cm. (Russia observed) Reprint of the 1825-27 ed. published under title: Memoirs and recollections of Count Segur. Translation of Memoires. [DC146.S37A423 1970] 73-115584 ISBN 0-405-03061-4
1. France—History—Louis XVI, 1774-1793. 2. United States—History—Revolution, 1775-1783—French participation. I. Title. BIP

France—History—Revolution—Biography.

THOMPSON, James Matthew, 1878-1956. 923.244
Leaders of the French Revolution. New York, Barnes & Noble, 1962. 272 p. illus. 22 cm. [DC145.T5 1962] 62-4275
1. France—History—Revolution—Biography. I. Title.

France—History—Revolution, 1789-1799.

MORRIS, Gouverneur, 1752-1816. 973.4'0924
The diary and letters of Gouverneur Morris. Edited by Anne Cary Morris. New York, Da Capo Press, 1970. 2 v. ports. 24 cm. Reprint of the 1888 ed. [E302.6.M7M8 1970] 70-98691 ISBN 0-306-71835-9 47.50
1. France—History—Revolution, 1789-1799. 2. France—Foreign relations—United States. 3. United States—Foreign relations—France. I. Morris, Anne Cary, ed. BIP

WHITHAM, John Mills, 1883- 944.04'0922
Men and women of the French Revolution, by J. Mills Whitham. Freeport, N.Y., Books for Libraries Press [1968] x, 419 p. illus., ports. 22 cm. (Essay index reprint series) Reprint of the 1933 ed. Bibliography: p. 401-403. [DC145.W53 1968] 68-20346
1. France—History—Revolution, 1789-1799. 2. France—History—Revolution, 1789-1799—Biography. I. Title. BIP

France—History—Revolution, 1789-1799—Biography.

BERAUD, Henri, 1885-1958. 944.04'0922
Twelve portraits of the French Revolution. Translated by Madeleine Boyd. Wood engravings by Bertrand Zadig. Freeport, N.Y., Books for Libraries Press [1968] 331 p. ports. 22 cm. (Essay index reprint series) Reprint of the 1928 ed. Contents.Contents.—Mirabeau.—Danton.—Robespierre.—Saint-Just.—Marat.—Camille Desmoulins.—Vergniaud.—The King.—The women.—Soldiers and generals.—Leaders of the mob.—Secondary figures. [DC145.B54 1968] 68-16909
1. France—History—Revolution, 1789-1799—Biography. I. Title. BIP

MADELIN, Louis, 1871-1956. 944.04'0922
Figures of the Revolution. Translated from the French by Richard Curtis. Illustrated from linoleum blocks by Karl S. Woerner. Port Washington, N.Y., Kennikat Press [1968, c1929] vii, 342 p. ports. 22 cm. (Essay and general literature index reprint series) Translation of Les hommes de la Revolution. Contents.Contents.—La Fayette and his delusions.—Mirabeau, or the revolutionary despite himself.—Talleyrand, revolutionary.—The Constituent Assembly.—The Girondins and Madame Roland.—Danton.—Robespierre and his friends.—Soldiers of the Revolution.—The Thermidorians.—Sieyes. [DC145.M32 1968] 68-16297
1. France—History—Revolution, 1789-1799—Biography. I. Title.

†MANCERON, Claude. 944.04'092'2
The French revolution Claude Manceron ; translated from the French by Patricia Wolf. 1st American ed. New York : Knopf, 1977, c1976- v. : ill. ; 25 cm. Translation of Les hommes de la liberte. Contents.Contents.—v. 1. Twilight of the old older 1774-1778. Includes bibliographical references and index. [DC145.M3513 1977] 76-46398 15.95
1. France—History—Revolution, 1789-1799—Biography. 2. Revolutionists—France—Biography. I. Title.

†MANCERON, Claude. 944.04'092'2 S
Twilight of the old order 1774-1778 / Claude Manceron ; translated from the French by Patricia Wolf. 1st American ed. New York : Knopf, 1977. xvii, 650 p. : ill. ; 25 cm. (The French revolutions ; 1) Translation of Les vingt ans du roi. Includes bibliographical references and index. [DC145.M3513 1977 vol. 1] 944'.035'0922 76-46399 ISBN 0-394-48902-0 : 15.95
1. France—History—Revolution, 1789-1799—Biography. 2. France History—Louis XVI, 1774-1793. 3. France—History—Revolution, 1789-1799—Causes and character. 4. Revolutionists—France—Biography. I. Title. BIP

THOMPSON, James Matthew, 1878-1956. 944.04'0922
Leaders of the French Revolution. New York, Harper & Row [1967] xii, 272 p. ports. 21 cm. (Harper colophon books) Contents.Contents.—Sieyes.—Mirabeau.—Lafayette.—Brissot.—Louvet.—Danton.—Fabre d'Eglantine.—Marat.—Saint Just.—Robespierre.—Dumouriez. Includes bibliographies. [DC145.T5 1967] 67-21590
1. France—History—Revolution, 1789-1799—Biography. I. Title.

France—History—1789-1815.

LAVALETTE, Antoine Marie Chamant, comte de, 1769-1830. 944.04'092'4 B
Memoirs of Count Lavallette, written by himself. Freeport, N.Y., Books for Libraries Press [1973] p. Translation of Memoires et souvenirs. Reprints of the 1831 ed. [DC198.L4A23 1973] 72-12770 ISBN 0-8369-7145-0
1. France—History—1789-1815. I. Title.

PASQUIER, Etienne Denis, duc, 1767-1862. 944.05'0924 B
The memoirs of Chancellor Pasquier, 1767-1815. Translated by Douglas Garman. Introd. and notes by Robert Lacour-Gayet. [1st American ed.] Rutherford [N.J.] Fairleigh Dickinson University Press [1968, c1967] xv, 292 p. illus., ports. 23 cm. Translation of Souvenirs du Chancelier Pasquier. Bibliographical footnotes. [DC255.P3A353 1968] 68-9353 10.00
1. France—History—1789-1815. I. Lacour-Gayet, Robert, ed. II. Title. BIP

France—History—1789-1900.

TALLEYRAND-PERIGORD, Charles Maurice de, prince de Benevent, 1754-1838. 944.04'092'4 B
Memoirs of the Prince de Talleyrand. Edited, with a pref. and notes, by the duc de Broglie. Translated by Raphael Ledos de Beaufort. With an introd. by Whitelaw Reid. New York, Putnam, 1891. [New York, AMS Press, 1973] 5 v. illus. 22 cm. Vol. 3-5 translated by Mrs. Angus Hall. Includes bibliographical references. [DC255.T3A222] 78-176452 ISBN 0-404-07510-X 75.00
1. France—History—1789-1900. BIP

France—History—1848-1870—Sources.

NAPOLEON III, Emperor of the French, 1808-1873. 944.07'092'4
Oeuvres de Napol III. New York : AMS Press, [1976] p. cm. Reprint of the 1869 ed. published by Plon, Paris. [DC275.2.N3 1976] 74-173015 ISBN 0-404-07380-8
1. France—History—1848-1870—Sources. 2. France—Politics and government—1848-1870—Sources. 3. Military history.

France—Kings and rulers.

FLEUR de lys : 944'.00992
the kings and queens of France [compiled] by Joy Law. New York : McGraw-Hill, c1976. [DC36.6.F58 1976] 75-28501 ISBN 0-07-036695-0 : 19.95
1. France—Kings and rulers. 2. France—Queens. I. Law, Joy.

France—Kings and rulers—Biography.

CASTRIES, Rene de La Croix, duc de, 1908- 944'.00992 B
The lives of the kings and queens of France / Duc de Castries ; translated by Anne Dobell. 1st American ed. New York : Knopf : distributed by Random House, 1979. p. cm. Translation of Les vies des rois et des reines de la France. [DC36.6.C38513 1979] 79-2205 ISBN 0-394-50734-7 : 20.00
1. France—Kings and rulers—Biography. 2. France—Queens—Biography. I. Title. BIP

DENIEUL-CORMIER, Anne. 944'.025
Wise and foolish kings : the first house of Valois, 1328-1498 / Anne Denieul-Cormier. 1st ed. Garden City, N.Y. : Doubleday, 1979. p. cm. Translation of Rois fous et sages de la premiere maison de Valois. Includes index. Bibliography: p. [DC36.6.D4613] 77-175365 ISBN 0-385-04903-X : 11.95
1. France—Kings and rulers—Biography. 2. France—History—House of Valois, 1328-1589. I. Title.

FLEUR de lys : 944'.00992
the kings and queens of France / [compiled by] Joy Law. London : Hamilton, 1976. 256 p., [8] p. of plates : ill., facsims., geneal. tables, ports. (some col.) ; 28 cm. Bibliography: p. [252]-255. [DC36.6.F58 1976b] 76-380877 ISBN 0-241-89297-X : £6.95
1. France—Kings and rulers—Biography. 2. France—Queens—Biography. I. Law, Joy.

FLEUR de lys : 944'.00992
the kings and queens of France / [compiled by] Joy Law. London : Hamilton, 1976. 256 p., [8] p. of plates : ill., facsims., geneal. tables, ports. (some col.) ; 28 cm. Bibliography: p. [252]-255. [DC36.6.F58 1976b] 76-380877 ISBN 0-241-89297-X : £6.95
1. France—Kings and rulers—Biography. 2. France—Queens—Biography. I. Law, Joy.

France—Politics and government—20th century.

BIDAULT, Georges. 944.082'0924
Resistance; the political autobiography of Georges Bidault. Translated from the French by Marianne Sinclair. New York, F.A. Praeger [1967] xx, 348 p. illus., ports. 25 cm. Translation of D'une resistance a l'autre. [DC373.B395A33 1967b] 67-20471
1. France—Politics and government—20th century. I. Title.

GAULLE, Charles de, Pres. v. 12
France, 1890-
De Gaulle: implacable ally [edited by] Roy C. Macridis. With a special introd. by Maurice Duverger. New York, Harper & Row [1966] xxxv. 248 p. 21 cm.
1. France — Pol. & govt. — 20th cent. 2. France — For. rel. — 1945- I. Macridis, Roy C., ed. II. Title.

France—Queens.

CHALLICE, Annie Emma 920.72'0944
(Armstrong) 1821-1875.
Illustrious women of France, 1790-1873. Freeport, N.Y., Books for Libraries Press [1973] p. (Essay index reprint series) Reprint of the 1873 ed. Contents.—Madame Tallien.—Empress Josephine, Queen Hortense, and Caroline Bonaparte.—Duchesse d'Angouleme and Duchesse de Berri.—Queen Marie Amelie and Duchesse d'Orleans.—Empress Eugenie and Princess Mathilde. [DC36.7.C47 1973] 72-10852 ISBN 0-8369-7212-0
1. France—Queens. 2. France—Princes and princesses. I. Title.

MORRIS, David D 923.144
The greatest queen of France, her life and times, written and illustrated by David D. Morris. Albion, Mich. c1956. 103 l. illus. 30cm. [DC91.6.B5M6] 56-9535
1. Blanche de Castille, consort of Louis VIII, King of France, 1188-1252. II. Title.

France—Social life and customs.

LA Tour du Pin 914.4'03'40924 B
Gouvernet, Henriette Lucie (Dillon) marquise de, 1770-1853.
Memoirs of Madame de La Tour du Pin. Edited and translated by Felice Harcourt. With an introd. by Peter Gay. [1st American ed.] New York, McCall Pub. Co. [1971, c1969] 468 p. illus., coat of arms, geneal. tables, ports. 22 cm. "Mrs. Harcourt has based her translation of the 1913 edition which she has abridged." Full version originally published as Journal d'une femme de cinquante ans, 1778-1815. Paris, 1970. [DC146.L3A2213 1971] 70-122144 ISBN 0-8415-0050-9 8.95
1. France—Social life and customs. 2. U.S.—Social life and customs—1783-1865. I. Title.

Frances Mary, Sister.

WAYLEN, Barbara, 133.9'092'4 B
1906-
The story of Frances Banks; the great seeker. London, New York, Regency Press, 1972. [2], 121, [8] p. illus., facsim., plan, ports. 23 cm. [BX5199.F64W38] 74-159385 ISBN 0-7212-0268-3 £1.20
1. Frances Mary, Sister. I. Title.

Francesca, Saint, 1384-1440.

KAUMANS, Gregory, Sister. 922.245
Golden tapestries; the story of the life and times of St. Frances of Rome. New York, St. Paul Publications [1960] 247p. illus. 21cm. [BX4700.F43K3] 60-8947
1. Francesca, Saint, 1384-1440. I. Title.

KEYES, Frances Parkinson 922.22
(Wheeler) 1885-
Three ways of love. New York, Hawthorn, [c1933] 299p. illus. 24cm. Bibl. 63-16770 5.00
1. Agnes, Saint, 3d cent. 2. Francesca, Saint, 1384-1440. 3. Caterina da siena, Saint, 1347-1380. 4. Saints, Italian. I. Title.
BIP

KEYES, Frances Parkinson 922.22
(Wheeler) 1885-1970.
Three ways of love. [1st ed.] New York, Hawthorn Books [1963] 299 p. illus. 24 cm. Errata slip inserted. Bibliography: p. 286-290. [BX4659.I8K46] 63-16770
1. Agnes, Saint, 3d century. 2. Francesca, Saint, 1384-1440. 3. Caterina da Siena, Saint, 1347-1380. 4. Christian saints—Italy. I. Title.

ROBERTO, Brother, 1927- 922.245
I saw an angel; a story of St. Frances of Rome. Illus. by William Pero. Notre Dame, Ind., Dujarie Press [1955] 93p. illus. 24cm. [BX4700.F43R6] 55-12872
1. Francesca, Saint, 1384-1440. I. Title.

Francesco d'Assisi, Saint, 1182-1226.

ALMEDINGEN, Martha 271'.3'0924 B
Edith, 1898-
St. Francis of Assisi; a great life in brief, by E. M. Almedingen. New York, A. A. Knopf, 1967. ix, 229, ix p. 19 cm. (Great lives in brief) First published in London in 1967 under title: Francis of Assisi; a portrait. Bibliography: p. 227-229. [BX4700.F6A725 1967b] 67-11143
1. Francesco d'Assisi, Saint, 1182-1226.

ARMSTRONG, April 271.30924 B
(Oursler)
St. Francis of Assisi; a concise biography. New York, American R.D.M. Corp. [1966] 70 p. port. 21 cm. (A Study master publication, 960) Bibliography: p. 70. [BX4700.F6A77] 66-28702
1. Francesco d'Assisi, Saint, 1182-1226.

ARMSTRONG, Edward 271'.3'024 B
Allworthy.
Saint Francis: nature mystic; the derivation and significance of the nature stories in the Franciscan Legend [by] Edward A. Armstrong. Berkeley, University of California Press, 1973. 270 p. illus. 24 cm. (Hermeneutics studies in the history of religions, v. 2) Bibliography: p. 253-254. [BX4700.F6A78] 74-149949 ISBN 0-520-01966-0 12.00
1. Francesco d'Assisi, Saint, 1182-1226. Legend. 2. Francesco d'Assisi, Saint, 1182-1226—Legends—History and criticism. 3. Animals, Legends and stories of. I. Title. II. Series.

BACH, Lester. 248'.48'2
Take time for sunsets / Lester Bach. Chicago : Franciscan Herald Press, [1975] 233 p. ; 21 cm. [BX2350.2.B27] 75-1496 ISBN 0-8199-0565-8
1. Francesco d'Assisi, Saint, 1182-1226. 2. Christian life—Catholic authors. I. Title.
BIP

BEATTY, Hetty Burlingame. 922.245
Saint Francis and the wolf. Boston, Houghton Mifflin, 1953. 29 p. illus. 26 cm. [BX4700.F6B38] 52-5912
1. Francesco d'Assisi, Saint, 1182-1226. I. Title.

BERNHART, Joseph, 271'.3'024
1881-1969.
A short life of Saint Francis / by Joseph Bernhart ; translated by Matthew J. O'Connell. Chicago : Franciscan Herald Press, 1977. vi, 96 p. : ill. ; 21 cm. Translation of Franz von Assisi, Leben und Wort. [BX4700.F6B4813] 77-6702 ISBN 0-8199-0675-1 pbk. : 4.95
1. Francesco d'Assisi, Saint, 1182-1226. 2. Christian saints—Italy—Assisi—Biography. 3. Assisi—Biography. I. Title.

BISHOP, Morris, 282'.092'4 B
1893-1973.
Saint Francis of Assisi. [1st ed.] Boston, Little, Brown [1974] xii, 227 p. port. 21 cm. (The Library of world biography) Bibliography: p. [215]-217. [BX4700.F6B52 1974] 74-10757 ISBN 0-316-09665-2 6.95
1. Francesco d'Assisi, Saint, 1182-1226.

BOASE, Thomas 271'.3'0924 B
Sherrer Ross, 1898-
St. Francis of Assisi [by] T. S. R. Boase. With 16 lithographs by Arthur Boyd. Bloomington, Indiana University Press [1968] 120 p. illus. 25 cm. Bibliography: p. [117] [BX4700.F6B55 1968b] 68-15550
1. Francesco d'Assisi, Saint, 1182-1226. I. Boyd, Arthur, 1920- illus. II. Title.

BULLA, Clyde Robert. 271'.3'024 B
Song of St. Francis; illustrated by Valenti Angelo. New York, Crowell [1952] 71 p. illus. 21 cm. A short biography of St. Francis telling how his father wanted him to become a rich prince but how Francis became a princely person who cared for the sick and needy and loved all animals. [PZ7.B912So] 92 AC 68
1. Francesco d'Assisi, Saint, 1182-1226. I. Angelo, Valenti, 1897- illus. II. Title.

CAPOZZI, Francis Clement, 922.245
1885-
God's fool, a new portrait of St. Francis of Assisi. New York, Morehouse-Gorham Co. [1956] 222p. 21cm. [BX4700.F6C326] 56-9170
1. Francesco d'Assisi, Saint, 1182-1226. I. Title.

CAPOZZI, Francis 271'.3'0924(B)
Clement, 1885-
A new portrait of Francis of Assisi, by Francis C. Capozzi. Northridge, Calif., Voice Christian Publications [1967] 222 p. 22 cm. First published in 1956 under title: God's fool. [BX4700.F6C326] 67-8551
1. Francesco d'Assisi, Saint, 1182-1226. I. Title.

CHESTERTON, Gilbert Keith, 270
1874-1936.
St. Francis of Assisi. Garden City, N.Y., Image Books [1957, c1924] 158 p. 19 cm. (A Doubleday image book, D50) [BX4700] 57-1230
1. Francesco d'Assisi, Saint, 1182-1226. I. Title.

CHESTERTON, Gilbert 922.245
Keith, 1874-1936.
St. Francis of Assisi. Garden City, N. Y., Image Books [1957, c1924] 158p. 19cm. (A Doubleday image book, D50) [BX4700] 57-1230
1. Franceso d'Assisi, Saint, 1182-1226. I. Title.
BIP

CORSTANJE, Auspicius 271'3'024 B
van.
Francis, Bible of the poor / by Auspicius van Corstanje ; translated by David Smith ; introd. by L. A. M. Goossens. Chicago : Franciscan Herald Press, [1977] p. cm. Translation of Franciscus, Bijbel der armen. Includes bibliographical references. [BX4700.F6C77313] 77-24188 ISBN 0-8199-0661-1 : 5.95
1. Francesco d'Assisi, Saint, 1182-1226. 2. Christian saints—Italy—Assisi—Biography. 3. Assisi—Biography. I. Title.

CRISTIANI, Leon, 271'.3'024 B
1879-
Saint Francis of Assisi, 1182-1226 / by Leon Cristiani; translated from the French by M. Angeline Bouchard. Boston : St. Paul Editions, c1975. 164 p., [12] leaves of plates : ill. ; 22 cm. Translation of Saint Francois d'Assise, 1182-1226. [BX4700.F6C77913] 74-79802 4.95
1. Francesco d'Assisi, Saint, 1182-1226. 2. Franciscans.

CUNNINGHAM, 271'.3'024 B
Lawrence, comp.
Brother Francis; an anthology of writings by and about St. Francis of Assisi. [1st ed.] New York, Harper & Row [1972] xxii, 201 p. illus. 22 cm. [BX4700.F6C784 1972] 72-78080 ISBN 0-06-061647-4 5.95
1. Francesco d'Assisi, Saint, 1182-1226. I. Title.

CUNNINGHAM, 271'.3'024 B
Lawrence.
Saint Francis of Assisi / by Lawrence S. Cunningham. Boston : Twayne Publishers, c1976. p. cm. (Twayne's world authors series ; TWAS 409) Includes index. Bibliography: p. [BX4700.F6C785] 76-14219 ISBN 0-8057-6249-3 lib. bdg. : 7.95
1. Francesco d'Assisi, Saint, 1182-1226.
BIP

CUTHBERT, Father, 1866- 922.22
1939(Secularname:LawrenceAnthonyHess]
Life of St. Francis of Assisi [London] Longmans [Mystic, Conn., Verry, 1965] xiv, 464p. front. port. 20cm. [BX4700.F6C8] 3.25 bds.,
1. Francesco d'Assisi, Saint, 1182-1226. I. Title.

DE LA BEDOYERE, Michael, 922.245
1900-
Francis, a biography of the Saint of Assisi. Garden City, N. Y., Doubleday [1964,c.1962] 280p. 18cm. (Image bk. D175) .85 pap.,
1. Francesco d'Assisi, Saint, 1182-1226. I. Title.

DE LA BEDOYERE, Michael, 922.245
1900-
Francis, a biography of the Saint of Assisi. [1st ed.] New York, Harper & Row [1962] 288 p. illus. 22 cm. [BX4700.F69D45] 62-11124
1. Francesco d'Assisi, Saint, 1182-1226. I. Title.

DE LA BEDOYERE, Michael, v. 12
1900-
Francis, a biography of the Saint of Assisi. Garden City, New York, Doubleday [1964, c1962] 280 p. 19 cm. "Image Books Edition, 1964." 66-14112
1. Francesco d'Assisi, Saint, 1182-1226. I. Title.

DOORNIK, Nicolaas 271'.302'4 B
Gerardus Maria van.
Francis of Assisi : a prophet for our time / by N. C. van Doornik ; translated by Barbara Potter Fasting. Chicago : Franciscan Herald Press, [1978] p. cm. Translation of Franciscus van Assisi. Bibliography: p. [BX4700.F6D6413] 78-671 ISBN 0-8199-0695-6 : 7.95
1. Francesco d'Assisi, Saint, 1182-1226. 2. Christian saints—Italy—Assisi—Biography. 3. Assisi—Biography.
BIP

ENGLEBERT, Omer, 1893- 922.245
Saint Francis of Assisi; a biography. Translated and edited by Edward Hutton. New York, Longmans, Green, 1950. 352 p. illus., ports. 23 cm. Translation of Vie de saint Francois d'Assise. Includes bibliographies. [BX4700.F6E613 1950a] 50-14456
1. Francesco d'Assisi, Saint, 1182-1226. I. Hutton, Edward, 1875- tr. & ed. II. Title.

ENGLEBERT, Omer, 1893- 271.30924
Saint Francis of Assisi; a biography New tr. [from French] by Eve Marie Cooper. 2d English ed., rev., augm. by Ignatius Brady, Raphael Brown. Chicago, Franciscan Herald [1966, c.1965] xii, 616p. 21cm. Bibl. [BX4700.F6E612] 64-14252 8.50
1. Francesco d'Assisi, Saint, 1182-1226. 2. Francesco d'Assisi, Saint, 1182-1226—Bibl. I. Brown, Beverly Holladay, 1912- II. Title.

ERIKSON, Joan Mowat. 271'.3'0924
Saint Francis et his four ladies. [1st ed.] New York, Norton [1970] 140 p. illus. 25 cm. Includes bibliographical references. [BX4700.F6E74 1970] 71-127178 5.00
1. Francesco d'Assisi, Saint, 1182-1226. I. Title.
BIP

ERNEST, Brother, 1897- 922.245
A story of Saint Francis of Assisi. Pictures by Carolyn Lee Jagodits. Notre Dame, Ind., Dujarie Press [1957] unpaged. illus. 21cm. [BX4700.F6E73] 57-4982
1. Francesco d'Assisi, Saint, 1182-1226. I. Title.

FRANCESCO d'Assisi, 922.245
Saint. Legend. Fioretti.
The little flowers of St. Francis. 1st complete ed. An entirely new version with twenty additional chapters. Also The considerations on the holy stigmata, The life and sayings of Brother Giles [and] The life of Brother Juniper. A modern English translation from the Latin and the Italian, with introd., notes and biographical sketches, by Raphael Brown [pseud.] Garden City, N.Y., Hanover House [1958] 357 p. map, diagr. 22 cm. Bibliography: p. [351]-357. [BX4700.F63E43] 58-11308
I. Brown, Beverly Holladay, 1912- ed. and tr. II. Title.
BIP

FRANCESCO D'ASSISI, 271.30924
Saint. Legend Fioretti
The little flowers of Saint Francis of Assisi. in the 1st Eng. tr., rev., emended by Roger Hudleston; Introd. by Arthur Livingston. New York, Heritage [Dist. Dial, c.1965] xviii, 261p. illus. 29cm. [BX4700.F63E5] 66-829 6.50
I. Hudleston, Gilbert Roger, 1874- ed. II. Title.

FRANCESCO D'ASSISI, 922.22
Saint. Legend. Fioretti.
The little flowers of St. Francis, and other Franciscan writings. Newly translated and with an introd. by Serge Hughes. [New York] New American Library [1964] 222 p. 18 cm. (A Mentor-Omega book, MT593) "Bibliographical note:" p. 221-222. [BX4700.F63E52] 64-25657
I. Hughes, Serge, tr. II. Title.

FRANCESCO D'ASSISI, 922.245
Saint. Legend. Fioretti.
The little flowers of St. Francis. The mirror of perfection. St. Bonaventure's Life of St. Francis. Introd. by Hugh McKay. London, Dent; New York, Dutton [1963] xi, 397 p. 19 cm. (Everyman's library, no. 485) [BX4700.F63E474] 63-5437
I. Francesco d'Assisi, Saint. Legend. Speculum perfectionis. II. Francesco d'Assisi, Saint. Legend. Legenda Bonaventurae. III. Title. IV. Title: The mirror of perfection.

FRANCESCO D'ASSISI, 922.22
Saint. Legend. Fioretti.
The little flowers of Saint Francis of Assisi. Translated by Abby Langdon Alger. Edited by Louise Bachelder. Illustrated by Valenti Angelo. Mount Vernon, N.Y., Peter Pauper Press [c1964] [BX4700.F63E32] 67-6651
I. Alger, Abby Langdon, b. 1850, tr. II. Bachelder, Louise, ed. III. Title.

FRANCESCO D ASSISI, 922.245
Saint. Legend. Fioretti.
The little flowers of St. Francis of Assisi, in the first English translation, rev. and emended by Dom Roger Hudleston. With an introd. by Paulinus Lavery. Westminster, Md., Newman Press [1953] xxii, 245p. 20cm. Based on the English version edited by Cardinal Manning (London, 1864) [BX4700.F63E5 1953] 53-11048
I. Hudleston, Gilbert Roger, 1874- ed. II. Title.

FRANCESCO D'ASSISI, 922.245
Saint. Legend. Fioretti.
The mirror of perfection. London, Dent; New York, Dutton [1963] xi, 397 p. 19 cm. (Everyman's library, no. 485) [BX4700.F63E474] 63-5437
I. Francesco d'Assisi, Saint. Legend. Speculum perfectionis. II. Francesco d'Assisi, Saint. Legend. Legenda Bonaventurae. III. Title.

FRANCESCO D'ASSISI, 922.245
saint legend vita Thomae celanensis
St. Francis of Assisi: frist and second life of St. Francis, with selections from Treatise on the miracles of Blessed Francis. Tr. from Latin, introd., footnotes by Placid Hermann. Chicago, Franciscan Herald [c.1963] xxx, 245p. illus., ports., map, facsims. 29cm. Bibl. 62-22288 11.95
I. Hermann, Placid, ed. and tr. II. Title.

FRANCESCO D'ASSISI, 922.245
Saint. Legend. Vita Thomae Celanensis.
St. Francis of Assisi: first and second life of St. Francis, with selections from Treatise on the miracles of Blessed Francis. Translated from the Latin with introd. and footnotes by Placid Hermann. Chicago, Franciscan Herald Press [1963] xxx, 245 p. illus., ports., map, facsims. 29 cm. Bibliography: p. 237. [BX4700.F68E49] 62-22288
I. Hermann, Placid, ed. and tr. II. Title.

FRANCIS of Assisi 271'.3'024 B
: an essay / by Walter Nigg, with extracts from the lives of Bonaventure, Thomas of Celano, and the Three Companions ; and 71 color photos. by Toni Schneiders ; translated by William Neil. Chicago : Franciscan Herald Press, 1975. 132 p. : ill. ; 25 cm. Translation of Der Mann von Assisi. The extracts constitute captions for tho photos. [BX4700.F6N5413] 75-25662 ISBN 0-8199-0586-0 : 12.95
1. Francesco d'Assisi, Saint, 1182-1226. I. Schneiders, Toni.

FULOP-MILLER, Rene, 1891- 922
The saints that moved the world; Anthony, Augustine, Francis, Ignatius, Theresa. Tr(by Alexander Gode, Erika Fulop-Miller. New York, Collier [1962, c.1945] 511p. 18cm. (AS268 9) Bibl. .95 pap.,
1. Augustinus, Aurelius, Saint, bp. of Hippo. 2. Francesco d'Assisi, Saint, 1182-1226. 3. Loyola, Ignacio de, saint, 1491-1556. 4. Teresa, Saint, 1515-1582 5. Antonius, Saint, 'the Great.' I. Gode, Alexander, tr. II. Eulop-Miller, Erika, joint tr. III. Title. BIP

GALLI, Mario von. 271'.3'024 B
Living our future: Francis of Assisi and the Church tomorrow. With color photos by Dennis Stock. Translated by Maureen Sullivan and John Drury. Chicago, Franciscan Herald Press [1972] 234 p. illus. (part col.) 21 cm. Translation of Gelebte Zukunft: Franz von Assisi. Bibliography: p. 236-239. [BX4700.F6G2513] 72-77444 ISBN 0-8199-0439-2 6.95
1. Francesco d'Assisi, Saint, 1182-1226. I. Stock, Dennis, illus. II. Title.

GHILARDI, Agostino. 271'.3'0924 B
The life and times of St Francis; text by Agostino Ghilardi; translator [from the Italian] Salvator Attanasio. Revised ed. London, New York, Hamlyn, 1969. 2-75 p. illus. (some col.), facsims. (some col.), ports. 30 cm. (Portraits of greatness) Col. illus. on lining papers. [BX4700.F69G49 1969] 79-541923 ISBN 0-600-03140-3 17/6
1. Francesco d'Assisi, Saint, 1182-1226. 2. Francesco d'Assisi, Saint, 1182-1226 Art. I. Title.

HABIG, Marion 271'.3'024 B
Alphonse, 1901- comp.
St. Francis of Assisi : writings and early biographies : English omnibus of the sources for the life of St. Francis / edited by Marion A. Habig ; translations by Raphael Brown ... [et al.]. 3d rev. ed., including A new Fioretti / by John R. H. Moorman. Chicago : Franciscan Herald Press, [1977] p. cm. Bibliography: p. [BX4700.F6H27 1977] 76-58903 ISBN 0-8199-0658-1 : 18.95
1. Francesco d'Assisi, Saint, 1182-1226. 2. Christian saints—Italy-Assisi—Biography. 3. Assisi—Biography. I. Moorman, John Richard Humpidge, Bp. of Ripon. A new Fioretti. 1977. II. Title.

HABIG, Marion Alphonse, 271'.3
1901- comp.
St. Francis of Assisi: writings and early biographies; English omnibus of the sources for the life of St. Francis, edited by Marion A. Habig. Chicago, Franciscan Herald Press [1973] xx, 1808 p. maps (on lining papers) 22 cm. "Translations by Raphael Brown, Benen Fahy, Placid Hermann, Paul Oligny, Nesta de Robeck, Leo Sherley-Price, with a research bibliography by R. Brown." Bibliography: p. 1667-1760. [BX4700.F6H27] 72-11257 ISBN 0-8199-0440-6 18.95
1. Francesco d'Assisi, Saint, 1182-1226.

HERMANN, Placid, ed. 922.22
Via seraphica; selected readings from the early documents and writings pertaining to Saint Francis and the Franciscan Order. Chicago, Franciscan Herald Press [1959] 221p. 22cm. In Latin. Includes bibliography. [BX4700.F6H44] 59-4913
1. Francesco d'Assisi, Saint, 1182-1226. 2. Franciscans. I. Title.

HERMANN, Placid. 922.245
The way of St. Francis. Chicago, Franciscan Herald Press [1964] 172 p. 21 cm. Bibliography: p. 169-172. [BX4700.F6H443] 64-17584
1. Francesco d'Assisi, Saint, 1182-1226. I. Title.

HOMAN, Helen Mary 922.245
(Walker) 1893-
Francis and Clare, Saints of Assisi. Illus. by Hamilton Greene. New York, Guild [dist. Golden c.1956,1962] 76p. illus. (pt. col.) 24cm. (Jr. vision bk., 30800) 2.50 bds.,
1. Francesco d'Assisi, Saint, 1182-1226. 2. Clara, of Assisi, Saint, d. 1253. I. Title.

HOMAN, Helen (Walker) 922.245
1893-
Francis and Clare, Saints of Assisi. Illus. by John Lawn. New York, Farrar, Straus & Cudahy [1956] 190p. illus. 22cm. (Vision books, 15) [BX4700.F6H54] 56-9812
1. Francesco d'Assisi, Saint, 1182-1226. 2. Clars, of Assisi, Saint, d. 1253. I. Title.

JAEGER, Muriel. 920.02
Adventures in living, from Cato to George Sand. Freeport, N.Y., Books for Libraries Press [1970] viii, 216 p. 23 cm. (Essay index reprint series) Reprint of the 1932 American ed. Published in London in 1932 under title: Experimental lives. Includes bibliographical references. [CT105.J3 1970] 79-121480 ISBN 8-369-17588-
1. Cato, Marcus Porcius, Uticensis. 2. Francesco d'Assisi, Saint, 1182-1226. 3. Chesterfield, Philip Dormer Stanhope, 4th Earl of, 1694-1773. 4. Day, Thomas, 1748-1789. 5. Sand, George, pseud. of Mme. Dudevant, 1804-1876. I. Title. BIP

JEWETT, Sophie, 1861- 922.245
1909.
God's trobadour; the story of Saint Francis of Assisi. With paintings by Giotto. [3d ed.] New York, Crowell [1957] 115p. illus. 22cm. [BX4700.F6J4 1957] 57-5087
1. Francesco d'Assisi, Saint, 1182-1226. I. Title.

JEWETT, Sophie, 1861- 922.245
1909.
God's troubadour; the story of Saint Francis of Assisi. With paintings by Giotto, [3d ed.] New York, Crowell [1957] 115p. illus. 22cm. [BX4700.F6J4 1957] 57-5087
1. Francesco d Assisi, Saint, 1182-1226. I. Title.

JORGENSEN, Johannes, 922.245
1866-1956.
Saint Francis of Assisi; a biography. Translated from the Danish with the author's sanction by T. O'Conor Sloane. Garden City, N. Y., Image Books [1955, c1939] 354p. 18cm. (A doubleday Image book, D22) Translation of Den heliige Frans af Assisi. [BX4700] 55-14905
1. Francesco d'Assisi, Saint, 1182-1226 I. Title.

KANN, Jean Marie 922.245
I found Francis in Assisi. With a foreword by Richard Cardinal Cushing. Chicago, Franciscan Herald Press [c.1960] xv, 80p. illus. 21cm. 60-11994 1.95 bds.,
1. Francesco d'Assisi, Saint, 1182-1226. I. Title.

KYBAL, Vlastimil, 1880- 922.245
Francis of Assisi. Notre Dame, Ind., Ave Maria Press [1954] xiv, 217p. 24cm. 'Prepared on the basis of a literal translation from the Czech original ,,, [which] has been thoroughly revised, corrected, and partly abridged.' [BX4700.F6K912] 53-12278
1. Francesco d'Assisi, Saint, 1182-1226. I. Title.

LECLERC, Eloi 922.22
Exile and tenderness. Tr. by Germain Marc'hadour. Chicago, Franciscan Herald Pr. [c.1965] xiii, 174p. 22cm. [BX4700.F6L363] 65-16676 3.95
1. Francesco d'Assisi, Saint, 1182-1226. I. Title.

LINE, Francis R. 271'.3'024 B
Man with a song : some major & minor notes in the life of Francis of Assisi / by Francis Raymond Line and Helen E. Line. Chicago : Franciscan Herald Press, [1978] p. cm. [BX4700.F6L548] 78-15316 ISBN 0-8199-0756-1 : 7.95
1. Francesco d'Assisi, Saint, 1182-1226. 2. Christian saints—Italy—Assisi—Biography. 3. Assisi—Biography. I. Line, Helen E., joint author. II. Title.

LIVERSIDGE, 271'.3'0924 B
Douglas, 1913-
Saint Francis of Assisi. New York, F. Watts [1968] v, 164 p. map. 22 cm. (Immortals of philosophy and religion) A biography of the man whose life and deeds were a quiet protest against man's inhumanity to man and to animals. [BX4700.F6L62] 92 AC 68
1. Francesco d'Assisi, Saint, 1182-1226. I. Title. BIP

MATT, Leonard von 922.245
St. Francis of Assisi [by] Leonard von Matt, Walter Hauser [Tr. from German] New York, Universe [c.1963] 48p. 72 illus. (incl. ports., facsims.) 18cm. (Orbis bks., 3) Summary of St. Francis of Assisi, a pictorial biography, orig. pub. in German under title: Franz von Assisi. 63-18344 1.75 pap.,
1. Francesco d'Assisi, Saint, 1182-1226. I. Hauser, Walter, 1902- II. Title.

MATT, Leonard von. 922.245
St. Francis of Assisi, a pictorial biography. [Photos.] by Leonard von Matt and [text by] Walter Hauser. Translated from the German by Sebastian Bullough. Chicago. H. Regnery Co. [1956] vi, 106p., 200p. of illus, maps. 25cm. Bibliography: p. 105. [BX4700.F6M3535] 56-58128
1. Francesco d'Assisi, Saint, 1182-1226. I. Hauser, Walter, 1902- II. Title.

MAYNARD, Theodore, 1890- 922.245
Richest of the poor; the life of Saint Francis of Assisi. Garden City, N. Y., Doubleday [1967, c.1948] 280p. 18cm. (Echo bks., E43) [BX4700.F6M364] 48-6640 .95 pap.,
1. Francesco d'Assisi, Saint, 1182-1226. I. Title.

MOCKLER, Anthony. 271'.3'024 B
Francis of Assisi : the wandering years / Anthony Mockler. Oxford : Phaidon, 1976. 256 p. : ill. ; 24 cm. Includes bibliographical references and index. [BX4700.F6M56] 76-15923 ISBN 0-7148-1715-5 : 8.95
1. Francesco d'Assisi, Saint, 1182-1226. 2. Christian saints—Italy—Assisi—Biography. 3. Assisi—Biography. I. Title.
Distributed by E.P. Dutton, N.Y.

MOORMAN, John 271'.3'024 B
Richard Humpidge, Bp. of Ripon.
Saint Francis of Assisi / [by] John R. H. Moorman. New ed. London : S.P.C.K., 1976. x, 118 p. ; 19 cm. Bibliography: p. 117-118. [BX4700.F6M648 1976] 76-384065 ISBN 0-281-02946-6 : £0.95
1. Francesco d'Assisi, Saint, 1182-1226. 2. Christian saints—Italy—Assisi—Biography. 3. Assisi—Biography.

O'BRIEN, Isidore, 271'.3'024 B
1895-1953.
Francis of Assisi : mirror of Christ / by Isidore O'Brien. Chicago : Franciscan Herald Press, c1978. vii, 205 p. : port. ; 23 cm. Published in 1944 under title: Mirror of Christ: Francis of Assisi. [BX4700.F6O25 1978] 77-26212 ISBN 0-8199-0691-3 : 6.95
1. Francesco d'Assisi, Saint, 1182-1226. 2. Christian saints—Italy—Assisi—Biography. 3. Assisi—Biography. I. Title: Mirror of Christ. BIP

POLITI, Leo, 1908- 271'.3'0924 B
Saint Francis and the animals. New York, Scribner, c1959. [32] p. illus. 26 cm. Tells of St. Francis' friendship with various animals—birds, a little hare, doves, a pheasant, a fish, a lamb, and the wolf of Gubbio. [BX4700.F69P6] 92 AC 68
1. Francesco d'Assisi, Saint, 1182-1226. I. Title.

RAYMOND, Ernest, 271'.3'024 B
1888-
In the steps of St. Francis. Illustrated with photos. by the author. Chicago, Franciscan Herald Press [1975] p. cm. Reprint of the 1939 ed. published by H. C. Kinsey, New York. [BX4700.F6R3 1975] 74-17076 ISBN 0-8199-0551-8
1. Francesco d'Assisi, Saint, 1182-1226. 2. Franciscans. 3. Italy—Description and travel—1901-1944. 4. Levant—Description and travel. I. Title. BIP

SABATINI, Rafael, 1875- 920.02
1950.
Heroic lives; Richard I: Saint Francis of Assisi: Joan of Arc: Sir Walter Ralegh: Lord Nelson: Florence Nightingale. Freeport, N.Y., Books for Libraries Press [1971, c1934] 416 p. 23 cm. (Essay index reprint series) [D106.S28 1971] 70-99648 ISBN 0-8369-2071-6
1. Richard I, King of England, 1157-1199. 2. Francesco d'Assisi, Saint, 1182-1226. 3. Jeanne d'Arc, Saint, 1412-1431. 4. Raleigh,

Walter Sir, 1552?-1618. 5. Nelson, Horatio Nelson, Viscount, 1758-1805. 6. Nightingale, Florence, 1820-1910. I. Title.

ST. Francis of Assisi, 922.245
his holy life and love of poverty: The legend of the three companions, translated by Nesta de Robeck, and the Sacrum commercium; or, Francis and his Lady Poverty, translated by Placid Hermann. Chicago, Franciscan Herald Press [1964] ix, 204 p. 21 cm. Bibliographical footnotes. [BX4700.F6S257] 64-4324
1. Francesco d'Assisi, Saint, 1182-1226. I. De Robeck, Nesta, tr. II. Hermann, Placid, tr. III. Francesco d'Assisi, Saint. Legend. Legenda trium sociorum. IV. Sacrum commercium beati Francisci cum Domina Paupertate.

SCHMITT, Myles. 922.245
Francis of the Crucified. Milwaukee, Bruce Pub. Co. [1956] 152p. 22cm. [BX4700.F6S279] 56-13235
1. Francesco dAssisi, Saint, 1182-1226. I. Title.

SCHNEIDER, Reinhold, 1903- 922.245
The hour of St. Francis of Assisi; translated from the 2d ed., and supplied with an introd., by James Meyer. Prefatory note by Richard J. Cushing, Archbishop of Boston. Chicago, Franciscan Herald Press [1953] 113p. 20cm. [BX4700.F6S2933] 53-9208
1. Francesco d'Assisi, Saint, 1182-1226. I. Title.

SMITH, John Holland. 271'.3'024 [B]
Francis of Assisi. New York, Scribner [1974 c1972] 210 p. illus. 21 cm. Bibliography: [p. 204]-206. [BX4700.F6S56] 72-1439 ISBN 0-684-13697-X. 2.95 (pbk.)
1. Francesco d'Assisi, Saint, 1182-1226. I. Title.

STICCO, Maria, 1891- 922.245
The peace of St. Francis. Translated from the Italian by Salvator Attanasio. With an introd. by Agostino Gemelli. [1st ed.] New York, Hawthorn Books [1962] 283 p. illus. 24 cm. Translation of San Francesco d'Assissi. [BX4700.F6S683] 62-9034
1. Francesco d'Assisi, Saint, 1182-1226. I. Title.

TIMMERMANS, Felix, 1886-1947. 922.245
The perfect joy of St. Francis; translated from the Flemish by Raphael Brown. Garden City, N. Y., Image Books [1955, c1952] 277p. 18cm. (A Doubleday image book, D11) Translation of De harp van Saint Franciscus. [BX4700] 55-822
1. Francesco d'Assisi, Saint, 1182-1226. I. Title.

TIMMERMANS, Felix, 1886-1947. 922.245
The perfect joy of St. Francis; translated from the Flemish. New York, Farrar, Straus and Young [1952] 344 p. 22 cm. Translation of De harp van Sint Franciscus. Full name: Felix Leopoldus Maximillianus Maria Timmermans. [BX4700.F6T513] 52-10903
1. Francesco d'Assisi, Saint, 1182-1226. I. Title. BIP

TIMMERMANS, Felix, 1886-1947. 922.22
The perfect joy of St. Francis. Translated from the Flemish by Raphael Brown. Garden City, N.Y., Doubleday [1974? c.1952] 276 p. 18 cm. (Image Book, D11) Translation of De harp van Sint Franciscus. [BX4700] ISBN 0-385-02378-2 1.95 (pbk.)
1. Francesco d'Assisi, Saint, 1182-1226 I. Title.

TRETTEL, Efrem. 271'.3'024 B
Francis, Saint of Assisi and of the world / by Efrem Trettel. Chicago : Franciscan Herald Press, c1975. xxii, 224 p., [19] leaves of plates : ill. ; 21 cm. Translation of Francesco d'Assisi. [BX4700.F6T6513] 75-23336 ISBN 0-8199-0587-9 pbk. : 4.95
1. Francesco d'Assisi, Saint, 1182-1226. I. Title.

VORREUX, Damien. 271'.3'024 B
First encounter with Francis of Assisi / by Damien Vorreux ; translated by Paul Schwartz and Paul Lachance. Chicago : Franciscan Herald Press, [1978] p. cm. (Tau series) Translation of Premiere rencontre avec Francois d'Assise. Bibliography: p. [BX4700.F6V6413] 78-16300 ISBN 0-8199-0698-0 pbk. : 3.95
1. Francesco d'Assisi, Saint, 1182-1226. 2. Christian saints—Italy—Assisi—Biography. 3. Assisi—Biography. I. Title. BIP

WROBLEWSKI, Sergius. 271'.3'0924 (B)
The real Francis, Poetry by M. Angela Sassak. Pulaski, Wis., Franciscan Publishers [1967] 128 p. 19 cm. Bibliographical references included in "Notes" (p. 125-128) [BX4700.F6W7] 67-7411
1. Francesco of Assisi, Saint, 1182-1226. 2. Franciscans — Spiritual life. I. Title.

Francesco d'Assisi, Saint, 1182-1226—Juvenile literature.

BRUCE, Janet 92
The life of Saint Francis of Assisi. Pictures by Emile Probst. New York, Herder & Herder [1965] c.1964. 1v. (unpaged) col. illus. 19cm. (Men of God, 1) [BX4700.F69B7] 65-13484 1.50 bds.,
1. Francesco d'Assisi, Saint, 1182-1226—Juvenile literature. I. Probst, Emile, illus. II. Title. III. Series.

CHAVEZ, Angelico, 1910- 271'.3'024 B
The song of Francis. Illus. by Judy Graese. [1st ed.] Flagstaff, Ariz., Northland Press [1973] 59 p. illus. (part col.) 21 cm. Recounts the life of St. Francis of Assisi, who gave all his riches to the poor and devoted the rest of his life to the service of Lady Poverty. [BX4700.F69C47] 92 73-75205 ISBN 0-87358-105-9 6.50
1. Franceso d'Assisi, Saint, 1182-1226—Juvenile literature. I. Graese, Judy, illus. II. Title.

DAUGHTERS of St. Paul. 271'.3'024 B
Gentle revolutionary : the life of St. Francis of Assisi / written and illustrated by the Daughters of St. Paul. Boston : St. Paul Editions, c1978. 115 p. : ill. ; 22 cm. (Encounter books) Recounts the life of St. Francis of Assisi who gave up his wealth in order to devote his life to serving and teaching the poor. [BX4700.F69D37 1978] 92 77-17206 1.95
1. Francesco d'Assisi, Saint, 1182-1226—Juvenile literature. 2. Christian saints—Italy—Assisi—Biography—Juvenile literature. 3. Assisi—Biography—Juvenile literature. I. Title.
Publisher's address : St. Paul's Catholic Book and Film Center, 172 Tremont St., Boston, MA

DOANE, Pelagie 922.245
St. Francis. New York, H. Z. Walck [c.] 1960. 62p. illus. (col.) 27cm. 60-6421 3.75
1. Francesco d'Assisi, Saint, 1182-1226—Juvenile literature. I. Title.

HEGENER, Mark. 922.245
St. Francis of Assisi, the poverello. [Chicago, Franciscan Herald Press, 1956] 92p. illus. 18cm. (Herald books) [BX4700.F6H37] 56-4537
I. Francesco d'Assisi, Saint, 1182-1226. II. Title.

JOHNSON, Jan. 271'.3'024 B
Brother Francis : a story about Saint Francis of Assisi / written by Jan Johnson ; illustrated by Kathryn E. Shoemaker. Minneapolis, MN : Winston Press, c1977. [32] p. : ill. (some col.) ; 21 cm. (Stories about Christian heroes) A simple retelling of the life and deeds of the young Italian who gave up his comfortable, carefree life to devote himself to preaching God's word and caring for the poor. [BX4700.F69J64] 92 77-77684 ISBN 0-03-022131-5 pbk. : 1.50
1. Francesco d'Assisi, Saint, 1182-1226—Juvenile literature. 2. Christian saints—Italy—Assisi—Biography—Juvenile literature. 3. Assisi—Biography—Juvenile literature. I. Shoemaker, Kathryn E. II. Title. III. Series. BIP

MOORSELAAR, Corinne van. 271'.3'024 B
Francis and the animals / by Corinne van Moorselaar. Chicago : Franciscan Herald Press, [1977] p. cm. Translation of Franciscus en de dieren. Recounts the life of St. Francis of Assisi and his special relationship with animals. [BX4700.F69M6613] 92 77-7391 ISBN 0-8199-0677-8 : 2.95
1. Francesco d'Assisi, Saint—Juvenile literature. 2. Christian saints—Italy—Assisi—Biography. 3. Assisi—Biography—Juvenile literature. I. Title. BIP

POLITI, Leo, 1908- 922.245
Saint Francis and the animals. New York, Scribner, c1959. unpaged. illus. 26 cm. [BX4700.F68P6] 59-6620
1. Francesco d'Assisi, Saint, 1182-1226—Juvenile literature.

SCHMITT, Myles. 922.245
Francis of the Crucified. Milwaukee, Bruce Pub. Co. [1956] 152p. 22cm. [BX4700.F6S279] 56-13235
1. Francesco dAssisi, Saint, 1182-1226. I. Title.

TIFFANY, Kathleen S. 920
The story of St. Francis. Pictures by Johannes Troyer. New York, Golden Pr. [dist. Affiliated Pubs.] c.1961 unpaged. col. illus. (Guild Pr.; Catechetical guild bk., First bk. for little Catholics) .25 bds.,
I. Title.

Franciabigio, 1484-1525.

MCKILLOP, Susan Regan. 708.5'5
Franciabigio / Susan Regan McKillop. Berkeley : University of California Press, c1974. xvii, 322 p., [38] leaves of plates : ill. ; 32 cm. (California studies in the history of art ; 16) Includes indexes. Bibliography: p. 275-290. [ND623.F783M32] 76-107661 ISBN 0-520-01688-2 : 40.00
1. Franciabigio, 1484-1525. I. Title. II. Series. BIP

Francis, Arlene.

FRANCIS, Arlene. 791'.092'4 B
Arlene Francis : a memoir / by Arlene Francis, with Florence Rome. New York : Simon & Schuster, c1978. 204 p., [3] leaves of plates : ill. ; 25 cm. Includes index. [PN2287.F67A32] 77-13701 ISBN 0-671-22808-0 : 9.95
1. Francis, Arlene. 2. Actors—United States—Biography. I. Rome, Florence, joint author. BIP

Francis, Dick.

FRANCIS, Dick. 798'.4'00924 B
The sport of queens; the autobiography of Dick Francis. [1st U.S. ed.] New York, Harper & Row [1969] 247 p. illus., ports. 22 cm. [SF359.F7 1969] 69-14574 5.95
1. Francis, Dick. 2. Steeplechasing. 3. Jockeys—Correspondence, reminiscences, etc. I. Title.

Francis family.

UPSHAW, Sophie W., 1904- 929'.2'0973
Captain William Upshaw, gent., planter of Virginia : some of his Georgia descendants and allied families, Francis, Wright, MacAllen, Bardwell, Daves, Chalmers / compiled by Sophie W. Upshaw. Baltimore : Gateway Press, 1975. xii, 500 p., [14] leaves of plates (1 fold.) : ill. ; 24 cm. Includes index. [CS71.U68 1975] 75-27313
1. Upshur family. 2. Francis family. 3. Wright family. 4. Virginia—Genealogy. I. Title.

Francis, Joseph, 1801-1893.

EHRHARDT, John Bohne. 926.238
Joseph Francis, 1801-1893: shipbuilder, father of the U. S. Life-Saving Service. New York, Newcomen Society in North America, 1950. 36 p. illus., mounted port. 23 cm. "Address, memorializing the centenary of Ocean County, New Jersey ... delivered during the '1950 New Jersey luncheon' of the Newcomen Society of England, held ... near Toms River, New Jersey .... July 27, 1950." Bibliography: p. 31. [VM140.F7E4] 50-13980
1. Francis, Joseph, 1801-1893. 2. U. S. Life-Saving Service. I. Title.

Francis, Robert,

FRANCIS, Robert, 1901- 811'.5'2 B
The trouble with Francis; an autobiography. [Amherst] University of Massachusetts Press, 1971. 246 p. illus., maps, ports. 24 cm. [PS3511.R237Z5] 75-150313 7.50
I. Title.

Francis, Sam, 1923-

SELZ, Peter Howard, 1919- 759.13
Sam Francis, by Peter Selz. New York, H. N. Abrams [1976 i.e.,1975] p. cm. [ND237.F67S44] 74-16096 ISBN 0-8109-0265-6 37.50
1. Francis, Sam, 1923- BIP

Francis-Williams, Edward Francis Williams,

FRANCIS-WILLIAMS, Edward Francis Williams, Baron, 1903-1970. 070.4'0924
Nothing so strange. New York, American Heritage Press [1970] ix, 354 p. 22 cm. Autobiography. [PN5123.F63A3 1970b] 77-95727 ISBN 0-8281-0044-6 8.95
I. Title.

Franciscan Sisters of Christian Charity, Manitowoc, Wis.—History.

NUGENT, Rosamond. 271'.973'0924 B
Buried wheat. Milwaukee, Bruce Publishing Co. [1967] vii, 165 p. 22 cm. Bibliography: p. 161-162. [BX4354.N8] 70-4822
1. Franciscan Sisters of Christian Charity, Manitowoc, Wis.—History. 2. Gabriel, Mother, 1842-1914. I. Title.

Franciscans—Biog.

HABIG, Marion Alphonse, 1901- 922.22
The Franciscan book of saints. First published as The Poverello's round table, by Sister M. Aquina Barth. Now completely rev. and greatly augm. Chicago, Franciscan Herald Press [1959] 1006p. illus. 24cm. Includes bibliography. [BX3655.H3] 59-9333
1. Franciscans—Biog. 2. Meditations. 3. Devotional calendars—Catholic Church. I. Title.

Franciscans in Central America—Bio-bibl.

ADAMS, Eleanor Burnham. 013.2713
A bio-bibliography of Franciscan authors in colonial Central America. Washington, Academy of American Franciscan History, 1953. xxi, 97p. 26cm. (Publications of the Academy of American Franciscan History. Bibliographical series, v.2) Bibliography: p. xix-xxi. [Z1437.A65] 53-3645
1. Franciscans in Central America—Bio-bibl. 2. Central America—Bio-bibl. I. Title. II. Series: Academy of American Franciscan History. Bibliographical series, v. 2 BIP

Franciscans. Third Order—Biog.

HALLACK, Cecily Rosemary, 1898-1938. 922.2
These made peace; studies in the lives of the beatified and canonized members of the Third Order of St. Francis of Assisi, by Cecily Hallack and Peter F. Anson. Rev. and edited by Marion A. Habig. Paterson, N. J., St. Anthony Guild Press [c1957] 268p. illus. 24cm. Includes bibliography. [BX3651.H2 1957] 58-2198
1. Franciscans. Third Order—Biog. I. Anson, Peter Frederick, 1889- joint author. II. Title.

Francisco de Borja, Saint, 1510-1572.

ROBERTO, Brother, 1927- 922.246
I serve the King, a story of Saint Francis

Borgia. Illus. by Anthony Joyce. Notre Dame, Ind., Dujarie Press [1954] 95p. illus. 24cm. [BX4700.F75R6] 54-2594
1. Francisco de Borja, Saint, 1510-1572. I. Title.

Francisco, Peter, d. 1831.

HAMILTON, Charles Henry. 973.3'3'0924 B
Peter Francisco, soldier extraordinary : most famous private soldier of the Revolutionary War / by Charles Henry Hamilton. [s.l. : s.n.], c1976 (Richmond : Whittet & Shepperson) 142 p. : ill. ; 24 cm. Includes bibliographical references and index. [F230.F79H35] 77-360580 14.25
1. Francisco, Peter, d. 1831. 2. United States. Army. Continental Army—Biography. 3. Soldiers—United States—Biography. 4. Virginia—Biography. I. Title.

Francisco Xavier, Saint, 1506-1552.

BRODRICK, James, 1891- 922.246
Saint Francis Xavier, 1506-1552. New York, Wicklow Press [1952] 548 p. 22 cm. [BX4700.F8B74] 52-9459
1. Francisco Xavier, Saint, 1506-1552. I. Title.

BRODRICK, James, 1891- 922.246
Saint Francis Xavier, 1506-1552. [Condensed version] Garden City, N. Y., Image Books [1957] 359p. 18cm. (A Doubleday image book, D49) [BX4700.F8B74 1957] 57-5782
1. Francisco Xavier, 1506-1552. I. Title.

BRODRICK, James, 1891- 922.246
Saint Francis Xavier, 1506-1552. [Condensed version] Garden City, N. Y., Image Books [1957] 359p. 18cm. (A Doubleday image book, D49) [BX4700.F8B74 1957] 57 5782
1. Francisco Xavier, 1506-1552. I. Title.

LANGIOIS-BERTHELOT, Jean Marc. 922.246
St. Francis Xavier [by] Jean-Marc Montguerre [pseud.] Translated by Ruth Murdoch. [1st American ed.] Garden City, N.Y., Doubleday, 1963. 165 p. 22 cm. Translation of Francois Xavier au Quartier latin and Francois Xavier dans les chemins d'Orient. Includes bibliography. [BX4700.F8L27 1963] 63-18222
1. Francisco Xavier, Saint, 1506-1552. I. Title.

LANGLOIS-BERTHELOT, Jean Marc. 922.246
St. Francis Xavier [by] Jean-Marc Montguerre [pseud.] Translated by Ruth Murdoch. [1st American ed.] Garden City, N.Y., Doubleday, 1963. 165 p. 22 cm. Translation of Francois Xavier au Quartier latin and Francois Xavier dans les chemins d'Orient. Includes bibliography. [BX4700.F8L27 1963] 63-18222
1. Francisco Xavier, Saint, 1506-1552.

MCGRATTY, Arthur R., 1909- 922.246
The fire of Francis Xavier; the story of an apostle. Milwaukee, Bruce Pub. Co. [1952] 295 p. 23 cm. [BX4700.F8M32] 52-4717
1. Francisco Xavier, Saint, 1506-1552. I. Title.

MAYNARD, Theodore, 1890- 922.246
The Odyssey of Francis Xavier. [1st ed.] Westminster, Md., Newman Press, [1950]. vii, 364 p. map (on lining paper) 21 cm. Bibliography: p. 349-355. [BX4700.F8M35 1950] 51-1230
1. Francisco Xavier, Saint, I. Title.

PURCELL, Mary. 922.246
Don Francisco; the story of St. Francis Xavier. Westminster, Md., Newman Press, 1954. 319p. illus. 22cm. [BX4700.F8P8] 53-5591
1. Francisco Xavier, Saint, I. Title.

SCHURHAMMER, Georg, 1882-1971. 282'.092'4 B
Francis Xavier; his life, his times. Translated by M. Joseph Costelloe. Rome, Jesuit Historical Institute, 1973- v. illus. 25 cm. Translation of Franz Xaver, sein Leben und seine Zeit. Contents.Contents.—v. 1. Europe, 1506-1541. Bibliography: v. 1, p. [744]-758. [BX4700.F8S2313] 72-88247 20.00 (U.S.) (v. 1)
1. Francisco Xavier, Saint, 1506-1552. Publisher's address: Creighton University, Omaha, Neb. 60131. BIP

TORSELLINO, Orazio, 1545-1599. 230'.2 S
The admirable life of S. Francis Xavier, 1632 / Orazio Torsellino Ilkley [Eng.] : Scolar Press, 1976. 616 p. : ill. ; 21 cm. (English recusant literature, 1558-1640 ; v. 299) (Series: Rogers, David Morrison, comp. English recusant literature, 1558-1640 ; v. 299.) "Reproduced (original size) from a copy in Cambridge University Library ... References: Allison and Rogers 824; STC 24140" Reprint of the 1632 ed. [BX1750.A1E5 vol. 299] [BX4700.F8] 282'.092'4 B 76-377650
1. Francisco Xavier, Saint, 1506-1552. 2. Christian saints—Biography. I. Title. II. Series.

Franck, Cesar Auguste, 1822-1890.

DAVIES, Laurence. 780'.0924 B
Cesar Franck and his circle. [1st American ed.] Boston, Houghton Mifflin Co., 1970. 380 p. illus., facsims., music, ports. 23 cm. Bibliography: p. [369]-374. [ML410.F82D29] 73-108305 10.00
1. Franck, Cesar Auguste, 1822-1890. I. Title. BIP

DAVIES, Laurence. 780'.092'4 [B]
Cesar Franck and his circle / Laurence Davies. New York : Da Capo Press, 1977, c1970. 380 p., [5] leaves of plates : ill. ; 24 cm. (Da Capo Press music reprint series) Reprint of the 1st American ed. published by Houghton Mifflin, Boston. Includes index. Bibliography: p. [369]-374. [ML410.F82D29 1977] 77-4231 ISBN 0-306-77410-0 19.50
1. Franck, Cesar Auguste, 1822 1890. 2. Composers—France—Biography. I. Title.

INDY, Vincent d', 1851-1931. 780.92
Cesar Franck; a translation from the French. With an introd. by Rosa Newmarch New York, Dover Publications [1965] 286 p. illus., music, ports. 21 cm. (Dover books on music) "An unabridged and unaltered republication of the work first published by John Lane, The Bodley Head, London, in 1910." Bibliography: p. 271-273. [ML410.F82I63 1965] 65-14031
1. Franck, Cesar Auguste, 1822-1890.

VALLAS, Leon, 1879-1956. 780'.92'4 B
Cesar Franck. Translated by Hubert Foss. Westport, Conn., Greenwood Press [1973] 283 p. illus. 22 cm. Translation of La veritable histoire de Cesar Franck. Reprint of the 1951 ed. published by Harrap, London. Includes bibliographical references. [ML410.F82V33 1973] 73-5210 ISBN 0-8371-6873-2 12.25
1. Franck, Cesar Auguste, 1822-1890. BIP

Franck, Ira Stoner,

FRANCK, Ira Stoner, 1896- 248.50924
My search for an anchor. Philadelphia, Dorrance [c.1966] 129p. illus., ports. 21cm Autobiographical. [BX5995.F67A3] 66-18610 3.00
I. Title.

FRANCK, Ira Stoner, 1896- 248.50924
My search for an anchor, by Ira S. Franck. Philadelphia, Dorrance [1966] 129 p. illus., ports. 21 cm. Autobiographical. [BX5995.F67A3] 66-18610
I. Title.

Franco Bahamonde, Francisco, 1892-

COLES, Sydney Frederick Arthur, 1896- 923.546
Franco of Spain; a full-length biography. [Westminster, Md.] Newman Press [1956] 264p. illus. 23cm. Includes bibliography. [DP264.F7C6 1956] 56-4151
1. Franco Bahamonde, Francisco, 1892- I. Title.

CROZIER, Brian. 946.082'0924 (B)
Franco. [1st American ed.] Boston, Little, Brown [c1967] xx, 589 p. illus., maps, ports. 25 cm. Bibliography: p. [526]-558. [DP264.F7C75 1967] 68-13880
1. Franco Bahamonde, Francisco, 1892- I. Title.

HILLS, George. 946.082'0924 (B)
Franco; the man and his nation. [1st American ed.] New York, Macmillan [1967] 464 p. illus., maps, ports. 21 cm. Bibliography: p. [449]-456. [DP264.F7H54 1967b] 68-11428
1. Franco Bahamonde, Francisco, 1892- I. Title.

HILLS, George. 946.082'0924 B
Franco; the man and his nation. [1st American ed.] New York, Macmillan [1967] 464 p. illus., maps, ports. 21 cm. Bibliography: p. [449]-456. [DP264.F7H54 1967b] 68-11428
1. Franco Bahamonde, Francisco, 1892- I. Title.

LLOYD, Alan, 1927- 946.082'0924 B
Franco. [1st ed.] Garden City, N.Y., Doubleday, 1969. 256 p. 22 cm. Bibliography: p. [243]-247. [DP264.F7L55] 69-20066 5.95
1. Franco Bahamonde, Francisco, 1892-

TRYTHALL, John William Donald, 1944- 946.082'0924 B
El Caudillo; a political biography of Franco, by J. W. D. Trythall. New York, McGraw-Hill [1970] 304 p. illus., maps. 23 cm. London ed. (Hart-Davis) has title: Franco: a biography. Includes bibliographical references. [DP264.F7T78 1970] 70-107298 7.95
1. Franco Bahamonde, Francisco, 1892- I. Title.

Franco-German War, 1870-1871.

FRIEDRICH III, German Emperor, 1831-1888. 943.08'2
The war diary of the Emperor Frederick III, 1870-1871. Translated and edited by A. R. Allinson. Westport, Conn., Greenwood Press [1971] xi, 355 p. illus., map, ports. 23 cm. Translation of Das Kriegstagebuch von 1870/71. Reprint of the 1926 ed. [DC285.F7513 1971] 77-114529 ISBN 0-8371-4824-3
1. Franco-German War, 1870-1871.

Francois de Sales, Saint, Bp. of Geneva, 1567-1622.

BEAHN, John Edward, 1910- 922.244
A man of good zeal; a biographical novel based on the life of St. Francis de Sales. Westminster, Md., Newman Press, 1958. 236p. 23cm. [BX4700.F85B4] 58-11029
1. Francois de Sales, Saint, Bp of Geneva, 1567-1622. I. Title.

CHANTAL, Jeanne Francoise (Fremiot) de Rabutin, Baronne de, Saint, 1572-1641. 282'.0924
St. Francis de Sales; a testimony, by St. Chantal. Newly edited in translation with an introd. by Elisabeth Stopp. Hyattsville, Md. Institute of Salesian Studies [1967] 181 p. illus., port. 23 cm. Bibliography: p 175-176. [BX4700.F85C53 1967a] 67 6454
1. Francois de Sales, Saint, Bp. of Geneva, 1567-1622. I. Stoop, Elisabeth, ed. II. Title.

CHANTAL, Jeanne Francoise (Fremiot) de Rabutin, Baronne de, 1572-1641 282'.0924
St. Francis de Sales; a testimony, by St. Chantal. Newly ed. in tr. with an introd. by Elisabeth Stopp. Hyattsville, Md. Inst. of Salesian Studies [1967] 181p. illus., port. 23cm. Bibl. [BX4700.F85C53 1967a] 67-6454 3.75
1. Francois de Sales, Saint, Bp. of Geneva, 1567-1622. I. Stopp, Elizabeth, ed. II. Title.

DE LA BEDOYERE, Michael [Anthony Maurice] 1900- 922.244
Francois de Sales. New York, Harper [c.1960] 254p. illus. endpaper map 22cm. 60-15268 4.00
1. Francois de Sales, Saint, Bp. of Geneva, 1567-1622. I. Title.

FLAVIUS, brother 1927- 922.244
Proudly we hail; a story of St. Francis de Sales. Illus. by Aloysius Tiedt. Notre Dame, Ind., Dujarie Press [1956] 88p. illus. 24cm. [BX4700.F85F5] 56-59254
1. Francois de Sales, Saint, Bp. of Geneva, 1567-1622. I. Title.

HENRY, Couannier, Maurice. 1887-1921 922.224
Saint Francis de Sales and his friends. Tr. [from French] by Veronica Morrow. Staten Island, N.Y., Alba House [1964] 413p. illus., facsim., ports. 23cm. Bibl. 64-62101 7.95
1. Francois de Sales, Bp. of Geneva, 1567-1622. I. Title.

PALMER, Christopher Harold. 282'.092'4 B
The prince bishop; a life of St. Francis de Sales [by] C. H. Palmer. IlFracombe; Stockwell, [1975 c1974] 204 p. port. 22 cm. [BX4700.F85Q3] 75-321845 ISBN 0-7223-0409-9
1. Francoes de Sales, Saint, 8p. of Geneva, 1567-1622. I. Title.
Distributed by Christian Classics for 7.95. BIP

WOODGATE, Mildred Violet, 1904- 922.244
Saint Francis de Sales. Westminster, Md., Newman Press [1961] 138 p. 19 cm. Includes bibliography. [BX4700.F85W6] 61-8977
1. Francois de Sales, Saint, Bp. of Geneva, 1567-1622. I. Title.

Francois de Sales, Saint, Bp. of Geneva, 1567-1622 — Juvenile literature.

THOMPSON, Blanche Jennings, 1887-. 92
St. Francis de Sales. Illustrated by Charles Walker. New York, Vision Books [1965] x, 182 p. (p. [180]-182 advertising matter) illus. 22 cm. [BX4700.F85T45] 65-20918
1. Francois de Sales, Saint, Bp. of Geneva, 1567-1622 — Juvenile literature. I. Title.

Franesco d'Assisi, Saint, 1182-1226— Juvenile literature.

LLOYD, Teresa 92
The poor man of Assisi: Saint Francis. Illus. in colour by T. J. Bond. Chicago, Franciscan Herald [1963] 116p. illus. 23cm. 62-2230 2.95 bds.,
1. Franesco d'Assisi, Saint, 1182-1226—Juvenile literature. I. Title.

Frank. Anne, 1929-1945.

ANNE Frank: 949.2
a portrait in courage. Translated from the German by Richard and Clara Winston. [1st American ed.] New York, Harcourt, Brace [1958] 192p. illus. 22cm. Translation of Anne Frank: Spur eines Kindes. [D810.J4S32] 940.53492 58-12702
1. Frank. Anne, 1929-1945. 2. World War, 1939-1945—Jews. 3. Netherlands—Hist.—German. I. Schnabel, Ernst, 1913-

FRANK, Anne, 1929-1945. 940.53492
The diary of a young girl; translated from the Dutch by B. M. Mooyaart-Doubleday, with an introd. by Eleanor Roosevelt. [1st ed.] Garden City, N.Y., Doubleday, 1952. 285 p. illus. 20 cm. Translation of Het achterhuis. [D810.J4F715] 949.2 52-6355
1. World War, 1939-1945—Jews. 2. Netherlands—History—German occupations, 1940-1945. I. Title.

FRANK, Anne, 1929-1945. 940.531'5
The diary of a young girl. Translated from the Dutch by B. M. Mooyaart-Doubleday. With an introd. by Eleanor Roosevelt. Garden City, N.Y., Doubleday [1967] 308 p. illus., port. (on lining papers) 22 cm. Translation of Het achterhuis. [D810.J4F715 1967] 67-66285
1. World War, 1939-1945—Jews. 2. Netherlands—History—German occupation, 1940-1945. I. Title.

FRANK, Anne, 1929-1945. 940.53'1503'924 B
The works of Anne Frank. Introd. by Ann Birstein and Alfred Kazin. Westport, Conn., Greenwood Press [1973, c1959] 332 p. illus. 22 cm. Reprint of the ed. published by Doubleday, Garden City, N.Y. [PT5834.F78A25 1973] 73-16643

ISBN 0-8371-7206-3 13.50

Frank, Glenn, 1887-1940.

LARSEN, Lawrence H 378.110924
The president wore spats; a biography of Glenn Frank [by] Lawrence H. Larsen. Madison, State Historical Society of Wisconsin, 1965. ix, 198 p. illus., Ports. 23 cm. Bibliographical references included in "Notes to the test" (p. 171-187) "Sources": p. 188-190. [LD6125 1925.L3] 65-63009
1. Frank, Glenn, 1887-1940. I. Title. BIP

Frank, Jerome, 1889-1957.

ROSENBERG, Jehiol 340.1'0924
Mitchell.
Jerome Frank: jurist and philosopher, by J. Mitchell Rosenberg. New York, Philosophical Library [1970] xviii, 274 p. 22 cm. A revision of the author's thesis, New School for Social Research. Bibliography: p. 163-179. [KF373.F7R6] 76-100581 8.75
1. Frank, Jerome, 1889-1957. I. Title.

Frank, Waldo David, 1889-1967.

FRANK, Waldo David, 813'.5 B
1889-1967.
Memoirs of Waldo Frank. Edited by Alan Trachtenberg. Introd. by Lewis Mumford. [Amherst] University of Massachusetts Press, 1973. xxxv, 268 p. ports. 25 cm. Bibliography: p. 255-256. [PS3511.R258Z52] 73-123541 15.00
1. Frank, Waldo David, 1889-1967. I. Title. BIP

Frankel, Emily.

JACKSON, Teague. 792.8'2'0924 B
Encore : the private and professional triumph of Emily Frankel / by Teague Jackson. Englewood Cliffs, N.J. : Prentice-Hall, c1978. p. cm. [GV1785.F74J3] 78-17259 ISBN 0-13-275032-5 : 8.95
1. Frankel, Emily. 2. Dancers—Biography. I. Title. BIP

Frankel, Haskel.

BERLE, Milton. 791.0924
Milton Berle, with Haskel Frankel. New York, Dell [1975 c1974] 366 p., illus. 18 cm. [PN2287.B436A52] 1.95 (pbk.)
1. Frankel, Haskel. I. Title.

Franken, Rose,

FRANKEN, Rose, 1895- 818.52
When all is said and done, an autobiography. [1st ed. in the U.S.A.] Garden City, N. Y., Doubleday, 1963. 397 p. illus. 22 cm. [PS3511.R264Z5 1963] 62-11372
I. Title.

Frankfurter, Felix, 1882-1965.

BAKER, Liva. 347.99'24 B
Felix Frankfurter. New York, Coward-McCann [1969] 376 p. illus., ports. 24 cm. Bibliography: p. [335]-339. [KF8745.F7B2] 69-11057 8.95
1. Frankfurter, Felix, 1882-1965.

FRANKFURTER, 347'.73'2634 B
Felix, 1882-1965.
Felix Frankfurter reminisces / recorded in talks with Harlan B. Phillips. Westport, Conn. : Greenwood Press, 1978, c1960. ix, 310 p. ; 23 cm. Reprint of the ed. published by Reynal, New York. Includes index. [KF8745.F7P45 1978] 78-5896 ISBN 0-313-20466-7 lib. bdg. : 22.00
1. Frankfurter, Felix, 1882-1965. 2. Judges—United States—Biography. I. Phillips, Harlan Buddington, 1920- II. Title. BIP

FRANKFURTER, 347'.73'2634 B
Felix, 1882-1965.
From the diaries of Felix Frankfurter : with a biographical essay and notes / by Joseph P. Lash ; assisted by Jonathan Lash. 1st ed. New York : Norton, [1975] xiii, 366 p. ; 24 cm. Includes bibliographical references and index. [KF8745.F7A33] 75-8675 ISBN 0-393-07488-9 : 12.50
1. Frankfurter, Felix, 1882-1965. 2. Judges—United States—Correspondence, reminiscences, etc. I. Lash, Joseph P., 1909- II. Title.

KURLAND, Philip B. 347'.7326'34 B
Mr. Justice Frankfurter and the Constitution [by] Philip B. Kurland. Chicago, University of Chicago Press [1971] xiv, 235 p. 23 cm. [KF8745.F7K85] 77-133259 ISBN 0-226-46405-9
1. Frankfurter, Felix, 1882-1965. I. Title. BIP

MENDELSON, Wallace, ed. 923.473
Felix Frankfurter. New York, Reynal, 1964. 2 v. 22 cm. Contents.CONTENTS. -- [1] A tribute. --[2] The judge. Bibliographical references included in "Notes" (v. 1, p. 229-242; v. 2, p. 229-285) 64-20512
1. Frankfurter, Felix, 1882- 2. Law — U.S. — Addresses, essays, lectures. I. Frankfurter, Felix, 1882- II. Title.

THOMAS, Helen Shirley. 923.473
Felix Frankfurter, scholar on the bench. Baltimore, Johns Hopkins Press [c.1960] xiv, 381p. (Bibl. footnotes) 24cm. 60-11571 6.50
1. Frankfurther, Felix, 1882- I. Title.

Franklin, Aretha—Juvenile literature.

OLSEN, James T. 784'.092'4 B
Aretha Franklin [by] James T. Olsen. Illustrator: John Keely. Mankato, Minn., Creative Education [1974] p. cm. A brief biography emphasizing the career of Aretha Franklin. [ML3930.F68O5] 92 74-14672 ISBN 0-87191-390-9 4.95 (lib. bdg.)
1. Franklin, Aretha—Juvenile literature. I. Keely, John, illus. II. Title. BIP

Franklin, Benjamin, 1706-1790.

ALDRIDGE, Alfred Owen, 973.30924
1915-
Benjamin Franklin, philosopher & man. Philadelphia, Lippincott [c.1965] xii, 438p. port. 25cm. Bibl. [E302.6.F8A46] 65-20586 7.95
1. Franklin, Benjamin, 1706-1790. I. Title.

ALDRIDGE, Alfred 973.30924(B)
Owen, 1915-
Benjamin Franklin, philosopher & man. [1st ed.] Philadelphia. Lippincott [1965] xii. 438 p. port. 25 cm Bibliographical references included in "Notes" (p. 418-427) [E302.6.F8A46] 65-20586
1. Franklin, Benjamin, 1706-1790. I. Title.

ALDRIDGE, Alfred Owen, 923.273
1915-
Franklin and his French contemporaries. [New York] New York University Press, 1957. 260p. 25cm. Includes bibliography. [E302.6.F8A47] 56-10778
1. Franklin, Benjamin, 1706-1790. I. Title. BIP

ALDRIDGE, Alfred 973.3'092'4 B
Owen, 1915-
Franklin and his French contemporaries / Alfred Owen Aldridge. Westport, Conn. : Greenwood Press, 1976. p. cm. Reprint of the 1957 ed. published by New York University Press, New York. Includes index. Bibliography: p. [E302.6.F8A47 1976] 76-21244 ISBN 0-8371-9007-X lib.bdg. : 17.00
1. Franklin, Benjamin, 1706-1790. 2. Franklin, Benjamin, 1706-1790, in literature. I. Title.

BENJAMIN Franklin. v. 12
[250th anniversary ed.] New York, Viking Press, 1956. xvii, 845p. illus. 22cm.
1. Franklin, Benjamin, 1706-1790. I. Van Doren, Carl Clinton, 1885-1950.

BLINDERMAN, Abraham, 370'.92'2
1916-
Three early champions of education : Benjamin Franklin, Benjamin Rush, and Noah Webster / by Abraham Blinderman. Bloomington, Ind. : Phi Delta Kappa Educational Foundation, c1976. 34 p. ; 18 cm. (Fastback - Phi Delta Kappa Educational Foundation ; 74) (Bicentennial series) [LA2311.B57] 76-362357 ISBN 0-87367-074-4 : 0.50
1. Franklin, Benjamin, 1706-1790. 2. Rush, Benjamin, 1745-1813. 3. Webster, Noah, 1758-1843. 4. Education—United States—History. I. Title. II. Series: Phi Delta Kappa. Educational Foundation. Fastback ; 74. BIP

BOWEN, Catherine 973.3'2'0924 B
Drinker, 1897-
The most dangerous man in America: scenes from the life of Benjamin Franklin. [1st ed.] Boston, Little, Brown [1974] xiv, 274 p. port. 24 cm. "An Atlantic Monthly Press book." Bibliography: p. 252-261. [E302.6.F8B79] 74-10658 ISBN 0-316-10396-9 8.95
1. Franklin, Benjamin, 1706-1790. I. Title.

BURLINGAME, Roger, 1889- 923.273
Benjamin Franklin, the first Mr. American. New York, New American Library [1955] 127p. 19cm. (A Signet key book, K 321) [E302.6.F8B894] 55-6661
1. Franklin, Benjamin, 1706-1790. I. Title.

BURLINGAME, Roger, 973.3'0924 B
1889-1967.
Benjamin Franklin, envoy extraordinary. New York, Coward-McCann [1967] 255 p. illus., map, ports. 22 cm. Includes bibliographical references. [E302.6.F8B8938] 67-10561
1. Franklin, Benjamin, 1706-1790.

BUXBAUM, Melvin H. 277.3
Benjamin Franklin and the zealous Presbyterians [by] Melvin H. Buxbaum. University Park, Pennsylvania State University Press [1975] 265 p. ports. 24 cm. Includes bibliographical references. [E302.6.F8B94] 74-14932 ISBN 0-271-01176-9
1. Franklin, Benjamin, 1706-1790. 2. Presbyterians in the United States. I. Title.

BUXBAUM, Melvin H. 973.3'2'0924 B
Benjamin Franklin and the zealous Presbyterians [by] Melvin H. Buxbaum. University Park, Pennsylvania State University Press [1975, i.e.1974] p. cm. Includes bibliographical references. [E302.6.F8B94] 74-14932 ISBN 0-271-01176-9 11.50.
1. Franklin, Benjamin, 1706-1790. 2. Presbyterians in the United States. I. Title. BIP

COHEN, I. Bernard, 1914- 923.273
Benjamin Franklin: his contribution to the American tradition. [1st ed.] Indianapolis, Bobbs-Merrill [1953] 320 p. illus. 23 cm. (Makers of the American tradition series) Includes bibliography. [E302.6.F8C67] 53-9874
I. Franklin, Benjamin, 1706-1790.

COHEN, I. Bernard, 530'.092'4 B
1914-
Benjamin Franklin, scientist and statesman / I. Bernard Cohen. New York : Scribner, c1975. 95 p. : ill. ; 21 cm. (DSB editions) Includes index. Bibliography: p. 85-89. [QC16.F68C63] 75-7595 ISBN 0-684-14251-1 : 6.95. ISBN 0-684-14252-X pbk. : 2.65
1. Franklin, Benjamin, 1706-1790. I. Title.

CONNER, Paul W. 320.50924
Poor Richard's politicks; Benjamin Franklin and his new American order [by] Paul W. Conner. New York, Oxford University Press, 1965. xiv, 285 p. 22 cm. Bibliography: p. 263-277. [E302.6.F8C72] 65-25056
1. Franklin, Benjamin, 1706-1790. I. Title.

COUSINS, Margaret, 1905- 923.273
Ben Franklin of old Philadelphia; illustrated by Fritz Eichenberg. New York, Random House [1952] 184 p. illus. 22 cm. (Landmark books, 28) [E302.6.F8C74] 52-72318
1. Franklin, Benjamin, 1706-1790. I. Title.

CRANE, Verner Winslow, 923.273
1889-
Benjamin Franklin and a rising people. Ed. by Oscar Handlin, Boston, Little [1962, c.1954] 219p. 20cm. (Lib. of Amer. biog.) Bibl. 1.65 pap.,
1. Franklin, Benjamin, 1706-1790. I. Title.

CRANE, Verner Winslow, 923.273
1889-
Benjamin Franklin and a rising people. [1st ed.] Boston, Little, Brown [1954] 219 p. 21 cm. (The Library of American biography) Includes bibliography. [E302.6.F8C77 1954] 54-5136

ELIOT, Charles 973'.0992 B
William, 1834-1926.
Four American leaders. [Folcroft, Pa.] Folcroft Library Editions, 1973. p. Reprint of the 1907 ed. published by P. Green, London. Contents.Contents.—Franklin.—Washington.—Channing.—Emerson. [E176.E42 1973] 73-14550 ISBN 0-8414-3916-8 (lib. bdg.)
1. Franklin, Benjamin, 1706-1790. 2. Washington, George, Pres. U.S., 1732-1799. 3. Channing, William Ellery, 1780-1842. 4. Emerson, Ralph Waldo, 1803-1882. I. Title. BIP

EPSTEIN, Samuel, 1909- 923.273
The real book about Benjamin Franklin [by] Samuel Epstein and Beryl Williams; illustrated by Herbert Danska. [1st ed.] Garden City, N. Y., Garden City Books, by arrangement with F. Watts [New York, 1952] 192 p. illus. 21 cm. (Real books) [E302.6.F8E6] 52-8114
1. Franklin. Benjamin, 1706-1790. I. Title.

EPSTEIN, Samuel, 1909- 923.273
The real book about Benjamin Franklin [by] Samuel Epstein and Beryl Williams; illustrated by Herbert Danska. [1st ed.] Garden City, N. Y., Garden City Books, by arrangement with F. Watts [New York, 1952] 192 p. illus. 21 cm. (Real books) [E302.6.F8E6] 52-8114
1. Franklin. Benjamin, 1706-1790. I. Title.

FAY, Bernard, 1893- 070'.924 B
The two Franklins: fathers of American democracy. New York, AMS Press [1969] xvi, 397 p. illus., map. 23 cm. Reprint of the 1933 ed. Bibliography: p. 363-377. [E302.6.B14F3 1969] 70-93277
1. Bache, Benjamin Franklin, 1769-1798. 2. Franklin, Benjamin, 1706-1790. 3. Federal Party. 4. Democratic Party. 5. U.S.—Politics and government—Constitutional period, 1789-1809. I. Title.

FAY, Bernard, 1893- 070'.924 B
The two Franklins: fathers of American democracy. Boston, Little, Brown, 1933. St. Clair Shores, Mich., Scholarly Press [1971] xvi, 397 p. illus. 22 cm. Includes bibliographical references. [E302.6.B14F3 1971] 78-145009 ISBN 0-403-00961-8
1. Bache, Benjamin Franklin, 1769-1798. 2. Franklin, Benjamin, 1706-1790. 3. Federal Party. 4. Democratic Party. 5. U.S.—Politics and government—Constitutional period, 1789-1809. I. Title. BIP

FLEMING, Thomas J. 973.32'0924 B
The man who dared the lightning; a new look at Benjamin Franklin, by Thomas Fleming. New York, Morrow, 1971. x, 532 p. illus., ports. 25 cm. Bibliography: p. 515-520. [E302.6.F8F57] 79-133289 12.50
1. Franklin, Benjamin, 1706-1790. I. Title.

FORD, Paul 973.3'2'0924 B
Leicester, 1865-1902.
The many-sided Franklin. Freeport, N.Y., Books for Libraries Press [1972] xx, 516 p. illus. 23 cm. "First published 1898." [E302.6.F8F7 1972] 73-38353 ISBN 0-8369-6770-4
1. Franklin, Benjamin, 1706-1790. I. Title. BIP

*FRANKLIN, Benjamin. 973.38.
1706-1790.
Benjamin Franklin; A biography in his own words, edited by Thomas Fleming;with an introduction by Whitfield J. Bell, Jr. New York, Newsweek [1975c1972] 416p. col. ill., col. por., 26 cm. Includes index. Bibliography: p.408. [E275] [B] 72-75999 ISBN 006-011286-7. 15.00.
1. Franklin, Benjamin, 1706-1790. I. Fleming, Thomas, comp. II. Title. BIP

FRANKLIN, 973.3'2'0924 B
Benjamin, 1706-1790.
Benjamin Franklin; a biography in his own words. Edited by Thomas Fleming. With an introd. by Whitfield J. Bell, Jr. Joan Paterson Kerr, picture editor. New York, Newsweek [1972] 2 v. (416 p.) illus. 27 cm. (The Founding fathers) Bibliography:

p. 408. [E302.6.F7A23 1972b] 72-171612 6.95
1. Franklin, Benjamin, 1706-1790. I. Fleming, Thomas J., ed. II. Title.
Deluxe ed. 8.95.

FRANKLIN, Benjamin, 1706- 923.273 1790.
The Benjamin Franklin papers, by Frank Donovan. New York, Dodd, Mead [1962] ix, 306 p. ports., facsims. 22 cm. (The Papers of the Founding Fathers) [E302.F83 1962] 62-17351
I. Donovan, Frank Robert, 1906-

FRANKLIN, Benjamin, 1706- v. 12 1790.
Benjamin Franklin's autobiography. Edited with an introduction and supplementary account of Franklin's later life by W. Macdonald. Dent, London; New York, Dutton [1964] xvi, 240 p. (Everyman's library. 316) 67-17961
1. Franklin, Benjamin, 1706-1790. I. Macdonald, W., ed. II. Title.

FRANKLIN, Benjamin, 1706- 923.273 1790.
The letters of Benjamin Franklin & Jane Mecom, edited with an introd., by Carl Van Doren. [Princeton] Published for the American Philosophical Society by Princeton University Press, 1950. xx, 380 p. illus., port., facsims. 25 cm. (Memoirs of the AmericanPhilosophical Society, v. 27) [E302.6.F75A185] 50-10857
I. Mecom. Jane (Franklin), 1712-1794. II. Van Doren, Carl Clinton, 1885-1950. ed. III. Title. IV. Series: American Philosophical Society, Philadelphia. Memoirs. v. 27

FRANKLIN, Benjamin, 973.3'092'4 B 1706-1790.
The spirit of early America : the life and words of Benjamin Franklin. Fort Atkinson, Wis. : Home Library Pub. Co., c1976. 96 p. : ill. (some col.) ; 32 cm. "The Franklin text for this book has been excerpted from The life and writings of Benjamin Franklin, edited by Albert Henry Smyth." [E302.6.F7A23 1976] 76-371321 ISBN 0-87294-093-4 : 4.98
1. Franklin, Benjamin, 1706-1790. 2. Statesmen—United States—Biography. I. Home Library Publishing Company. II. Title.

GREENE, Jay Elihu, 1914- 920.02 ed.
Four biographies. [School ed.] New York, Globe Book Co. [1956] 499p. illus. 21cm. [CT106.G65] 56-2582
1. Franklin, Benjamin, 1706-1790. 2. Blackwell, Elizabeth, 1821-1910. 3. Pupin, Michael Idvorsky, 1858-1965. 4. Rogers, Will, 1879-1935. I. Title.
Contents omitted.

GRIGGS, Edward Howard, 1868- 973 1951.
American statesmen; an interpretation of our history and heritage. Freeport, N.Y., Books for Libraries Press [1970] 364 p. 24 cm. (Essay index reprint series) Reprint of the 1927 ed. Contents.Contents.—Washington: the first American.—Franklin: the practical American.—Jefferson: the democratic American.—Hamilton and the making of our government.—Lee: the American warrior.—Lincoln: the prophetic American.—Bibliography: p. 348-355. [E176.G852 1970] 76-121474
1. Washington, George, Pres. U.S., 1732-1799. 2. Franklin, Benjamin, 1706-1790. 3. Jefferson, Thomas, Pres. U.S., 1743-1826. 4. Hamilton, Alexander, 1757-1804. 5. Lee, Robert Edward, 1807-1870. 6. Lincoln, Abraham, Pres. U.S., 1809-1865. 7. Statesmen, American. I. Title. **BIP**

GROVER, Eulalie Osgood, 923.273 1873-
Benjamin Franklin, the story of Poor Richard; illustrated by Edwin L. Schmidt. New York, Dodd, Mead, 1953. 267p. illus. 21cm. [E302.6.F8G83] 52-14117
1. Franklin, Benjamin, 1706-1790. I. Title.

HAWKE, David 973.3'092'4 B Freeman.
Franklin / by David Freeman Hawke. 1st ed. New York : Harper & Row, c1976. ix, 436 p. ; 24 cm. Includes index. Bibliography: p. 407-416. [E302.6.F8H38 1976] 75-23886 ISBN 0-06-011779-6 : 17.50

1. Franklin, Benjamin, 1706-1790. I. Title. **BIP**

JUDSON, Clara (Ingram) 923.273 1879-
Benjamin Franklin. Illustrated by Robert Frankenberg. Chicago, Follett Pub. Co. [1957] 204p. illus. 25cm. [E302.6.F8J8] 57-11030
1. Franklin, Benjamin, 1706-1790. I. Title.

JUDSON, Clara Ingram, 923.273 1879-1960.
Benjamin Franklin. Illustrated by Robert Frankenberg. Chicago, Follett Pub. Co. [1957] 204 p. illus. 25 cm. [E302.6.F8J8] 57-11030
1. Franklin, Benjamin, 1706-1790.

JUDSON, Clara 973.32'0924 B (Ingram) 1879-1960.
Benjamin Franklin. Illustrated by Robert Frankenberg. Chicago, Follett Pub. Co. [1957] 204 p. illus. 25 cm. A biography of the American printer, inventor, scientist, and statesman, which concentrates upon his service to his new nation. [E302.6.F8J8] 92 AC 68
1. Franklin, Benjamin, 1706-1790. I. Frankenberg, Robert C., illus. II. Title.

KETCHAM, Ralph Louis, 973.30924 B 1927-
Benjamin Franklin [by] Ralph L. Ketcham. New York, Washington Square Press [1965] xiv, 226 p. 18 cm. (The Great American thinkers) Bibliography: p. 213-220. [E302.6.F8K43] 65-5126
1. Franklin, Benjamin, 1706-1790.

KEYES, Nelson Beecher, 923.273 1894-
Ben Franklin, an affectionate portrait. Kingswood, Surrey. World's Work [1956] 318p. 23cm. Includes bibliography. [E302.6.F8K45 1956a] 57-20301
1. Franklin Benjamin, 1706-1790. I. Title.

KEYES, Nelson, Beecher, 923.273 1894-
Ben Franklin, an affectionate portrait. [1st ed.] Garden City, N. Y., Hanover House [c1956] 318p. 22cm. Includes bibliography. [E302.6.F8K45] 56-5408
1. Franklin, Benjamin, 1706-1790. I. Title.

KEYES, Nelson Beecher, 923.273 1894-
Ben Franklin, an affectionate portrait. 1st ed. Garden City, N.Y., Hanover House [c1956] 318p. 22cm. Includes bibliography. [E302.6.F8K45] 56-5408
1. Franklin, Benjamin, 1706-1790. I. Title.

LOPEZ, Claude Anne. 973.3'092'4 B
The private Franklin : the man and his family / by Claude-Anne Lopez and Eugenia W. Herbert. 1st ed. New York : Norton, [1975] xv, 361 p., [8] leaves of plates : ill. ; 24 cm. Includes index. Bibliography: p. 338-344. [E302.6.F8L82 1975] 75-17530 ISBN 0-393-07496-X : 11.95
1. Franklin, Benjamin, 1706-1790. I. Herbert, Eugenia W., joint author. II. Title. **BIP**

MCMASTER, John 973.32'0924 B Bach, 1852-1932.
Benjamin Franklin as a man of letters. [New York] Arno [1970, c1887] ix, 293 p. port. 23 cm. (The American journalists) (American men of letters) Includes bibliographical references. [PS751.M3 1970] 70-125706 ISBN 0-405-01687-5
1. Franklin, Benjamin, 1706-1790. I. Title. II. Series. **BIP**

MEADOR, Roy. 530'.092'4 B
Franklin, revolutionary scientist / Roy Meador. Ann Arbor, Mich. : Ann Arbor Science Publishers, c1975. xii, 436 p. : ill. ; 24 cm. Includes index. Bibliography: p. 411-415. [QC16.F68M4] 75-34501 ISBN 0-250-40121-5 : 15.00
1. Franklin, Benjamin, 1706-1790. I. Title.

MEADOWCROFT, Enid (La 923.273 Monte) 1898-
Benjamin Franklin. Illus. by Donald McKay. New York, Scholastic Bk. Servs. [1962, c.1941] 186p. 20cm. (TX 328) .50 pap.,
1. Franklin, Benjamin, 1706-1790. I. Title.

MEADOWCROFT, Enid 973.32'0924 B (La Monte) 1898-
The story of Benjamin Franklin; illustrated by Edward A. Wilson. New York, Grosset & Dunlap [1952] 182 p. illus. 22 cm. (Signature books) A biography of Benjamin Franklin: printer, journalist, and statesman, as well as inventor who, by flying a kite, discovered that lightning is electricity. [PZ7.M506St] 92 AC 68
1. Franklin, Benjamin, 1706-1790. I. Wilson, Edward Arthur, 1886- illus. II. Title.

*MEADOWCROFT, Enid LaMonte 92
Benjamin Franklin. Illus. by Donald McKay. New York, Scholastic [1965, c.1941] 186p. illus. 21cm. (TX328) .50 pap.,
1. Franklin, Benjamin, 1706-1790. I. Title.

MORSE, John Torrey, 973.32'0924 B 1840-1937.
Benjamin Franklin. Boston, Houghton, Mifflin. [New York, AMS Press, 1972] xx, 444 p. illus. 18 cm. (American statesmen, v. 1) Reprint of the 1898 ed. [E302.6.F8M87 1972] 74-128926 ISBN 0-404-50851-0
1. Franklin, Benjamin, 1706-1790. I. Title. II. Series.

MORSE, John Torrey, 973.32'0924 B 1840-1937.
Benjamin Franklin [by] John T. Morse, Jr. New Rochelle, N.Y., Arlington House [1970] 444 p. illus., ports. 21 cm. (Giants of America. The Founding Fathers) Originally published in 1889. Includes bibliographical references. [E302.6.F8M87 1970] 74-111222 ISBN 0-87000-086-1
1. Franklin, Benjamin, 1706-1790.

NEWCOMB, Benjamin 973.3'2'0924 B H.
Franklin and Galloway: a political partnership, by Benjamin H. Newcomb. New Haven, Yale University Press, 1972. 332 p. 23 cm. Bibliography: p. 299-308. [F152.N43] 72-75205 ISBN 0-300-01506-2 12.50
1. Franklin, Benjamin, 1706-1790. 2. Galloway, Joseph, 1731-1803. 3. Pennsylvania—Politics and government—Colonial period. 4. United States—History—Revolution—Causes. I. Title.

OSWALD, John Clyde, 973.32'0924 B 1872-1938.
Benjamin Franklin, printer. Ann Arbor, Mich., Gryphon Books, 1971. xv, 244 p. facsims., port. 22 cm. "Facsimile reprint of the 1917 edition." [Z232.F8O8 1917a] 71-143632
1. Franklin, Benjamin, 1706-1790. **BIP**

OSWALD, John Clyde, 070.5'092'4 B 1872-1938.
Benjamin Franklin, printer. Published by Doubleday, Page for the Associated Advertising Clubs of the World, 1917. Detroit, Gale Research Co., 1974. xv, 244 p. illus. 22 cm. [Z232.F8O8 1974] 74-3020 ISBN 0-8103-3642-1 12.50
1. Franklin, Benjamin, 1706-1790.

PARTON, James, 973.32'0924 B 1822-1891.
Life and times of Benjamin Franklin. New York, Da Capo Press, 1971. 2 v. ports. 23 cm. (The American scene: comments and commentators) "Dissertation on liberty and necessity, pleasure and pain," by B. Franklin: v. 1, p. [605]-617. Reprint of the 1864 ed. Includes bibliographical references. [E302.6.F8P27 1971] 72-126603 ISBN 0-306-70048-4
1. Franklin, Benjamin, 1706-1790. I. Franklin, Benjamin, 1706-1790. Dissertation on liberty and necessity, pleasure and pain. 1970. II. Title. **BIP**

ROSS, Frank Xavier, 1914- 923.273
Ben Franklin, scientist; illustrated with line drawings by Ava Morgan. New York, Lothrop, Lee & Shepard [1952] 128 p. illus. 21 cm. [Q143.F8R6] 52-14139
1. Franklin, Benjamin, 1706-1790.

SCARF, Maggi. 973.32'0924 B
Meet Benjamin Franklin. Illustrated by Harry Beckhoff. New York, Random House [1968] 60 p. col. illus., map (on lining papers) 22 cm. (Step-up books) An easy-to-read biography of the Boston printer who became a scientist, inventor, writer, and leader of the American Revolution. [E302.6.F8S35 1968] 92 AC 68
1. Franklin, Benjamin, 1706-1790. I. Beckhoff, Harry, illus. II. Title. **BIP**

SCHOENBRUN, David. 973.3'2'0924 B
Triumph in Paris : the exploits of Benjamin Franklin / David Schoenbrun. 1st ed. New York : Harper & Row, c1976. x, 420 p. ; 24 cm. Includes index. Bibliography: p. 397-405. [E302.6.F8S38 1976] 76-9199 ISBN 0-06-013854-8 : 15.00
1. Franklin, Benjamin, 1706-1790. 2. Paris, Treaty of, 1783. 3. United States—Foreign relations—Revolution, 1775-1783. 4. United States—Foreign relations—France. 5. France—Foreign relations—United States. I. Title. **BIP**

SCUDDER, Evarts 973.32'0924 B Seelye, 1896-
Benjamin Franklin; a biography, by Evarts S. Scudder. Freeport, N.Y., Books for Libraries Press [1971] 328 p. illus., ports. 23 cm. Reprint of the 1939 ed. Bibliography: p. 318-320. [E302.6.F8S4 1971] 79-150199 ISBN 0-8369-5712-1
1. Franklin, Benjamin, 1706-1790.

SKAGGS, Merrill 973.3'0924 B Maguire.
Benjamin Franklin: The autobiography of Benjamin Franklin. Prepared for Barnes & Noble. New York, Barnes & Noble [1969] 80 p. 21 cm. (Barnes & Noble book notes, 870) Bibliography: p. 80. [E302.6.F7L86] 73-84026 1.00 (1.10 Can.)
1. Franklin, Benjamin, 1706-1790. The autobiography. I. Barnes & Noble, inc., New York.

STEVENSON, Augusta. 973.32'0924 B
Ben Franklin, boy printer. Illustrated by Ray Quigley. Indianapolis, Bobbs-Merrill [1962] 200 p. illus. 20 cm. (Childhood of famous Americans) The boyhood of the printer, inventor, author, and statesman whose patriotism helped the thirteen colonies to attain independence. [PZ7.S8467Be6] 92 AC 68
1. Franklin, Benjamin, 1706-1790. I. Quigley, Ray, illus. II. Title.

STOURZH, Gerald. 327.73
Benjamin Franklin and American foreign policy. 2d ed. Chicago, University of Chicago Press [1969] xvi, 335 p. 23 cm. Bibliographical references included in "Notes" (p. 261-318) [E249.S88 1969] 71-10594
1. Franklin, Benjamin, 1706-1790. 2. United States—Foreign relations. 3. United States—Foreign relations—Revolution, 1775-1783. I. Title. **BIP**

TOURTELLOT, Arthur 973.3'092'4 B Bernon.
Benjamin Franklin : the shaping of genius, 1706-1723 / Arthur Bernon Tourtellot. 1st ed. Garden City, N.Y. : Doubleday, 1977. p. cm. Includes index. Bibliography: p. [E302.6.F8T7] 76-12054 ISBN 0-385-03230-7 : 8.95
1. Franklin, Benjamin, 1706-1790. 2. Statesmen—United States—Biography.

VAN DOREN, Carl Clinton, v. 12 1885-1950.
Benjamin Franklin. [250th anniversary ed.] New York, Viking Press, 1956. xvii, 845 p. illus. 22 cm.
1. Franklin, Benjamin, 1706-1790. I. Title.

VAN DOREN, Carl Clinton, 923.273 1885-1950
Benjamin Franklin. New York, Viking [1964, c.1938] xvii, 845p. 20cm. (Compass bks.; C163) Bibl. 64-6593 2.95 pap.,
1. Franklin, Benjamin, 1706-1790. I. Title.

VAN DOREN, Carl 973.3'2'0924 B Clinton, 1885-1950.
Benjamin Franklin. Westport, Conn., Greenwood Press [1973, c1938] xix, 845 p. ports. 22 cm. Reprint of the ed. published by Viking Press, New York. Bibliography: p. [785]-788. [E302.6.F8V36 1973] 73-8566 ISBN 0-8371-6964-X 27.50
1. Franklin, Benjamin, 1706-1790. I. Title.

VAN DOREN, Carl Clinton, 920.7 1885-1950.
Jane Mecom, the favorite sister of Benjamin Franklin: her life here first fully narrated from their entire surviving correspondence. New York, Viking Press, 1950. vii, 255 p. illus., ports., maps. 22 cm.

Mecom, Jane (Franklin) 1712-1794. [CT275.M46553V3] 50-14626
1. Franklin, Benjamin, 1706-1790. I. Title.

WECHSLER, Louis K. 973.3'092'4 B
Benjamin Franklin : American and world educator / by Louis K. Wechsler. Boston : Twayne Publishers, c1976. p. cm. (Twayne's world leaders series ; TWLS 56) Includes index. Bibliography: p. [E302.6.F8W3] 76-2679 ISBN 0-8057-7667-2 lib. bdg. : 8.50
1. Franklin, Benjamin, 1706-1790.

WEIR, Ruth Cromer, 1912- 923.273
Benjamin Franklin, printer and patriot. Illustrated by Rus Anderson. Nashville, Abingdon Press [1955] 127 p. illus. 21 cm. (Makers of America) [E302.6.F8W55] 55-14994
1. Franklin, Benjamin, 1706-1790.

WENDEL, Thomas. 917.3'03'30924 B
Benjamin Franklin & the politics of liberty; a biography with readings. Woodbury, N.Y., Barron's Educational Series, inc. [1974] xiv, 454 p. illus. 19 cm. (Shapers of history series) Bibliography: p. [435]-442. [E302.6.F8W56] 73-7133 ISBN 0-8120-0459-0 2.95 (pbk.)
1. Franklin, Benjamin, 1706-1790. I. Title.

Franklin, Benjamin, 1706-1790—Juvenile literature.

FRIEDMAN, Estelle 92
Ben Franklin. Illus. by James Caraway. New York, Putnam [c.1961] 45p. col. illus. (See and read biography) 61-8241 2.00; 2.19 lib. ed.,
1. Franklin, Benjamin, 1706-1790—Juvenile literature. I. Title.

GRAVES, Charles Parlin, 1911- 92
Benjamin Franklin, man of ideas Illus. by Gerald McCann. New York, Grosset [1962, c.]1960. 79p. illus. 23cm. (Garrard; Discovery bk.) A62 1.00 lib. ed.,
1. Benjamin Franklin, 1706-1790—Juvenile literature. I. Title.

MCKOWN, Robin 920
Benjamin Franklin. New York, Putnam [c.1963] 192p. 21cm. (Lives to remember ser.) Bibl. 63-9688 3.25
1. Franklin, Benjamin, 1706-1790—Juvenile literature. I. Title.

Franklin, Benjamin, 1706-1790—Women.

LOPEZ, Claude Anne 973.30924
Mon cher Papa, Franklin and the ladies of Paris. New Haven, Yale, 1966. xv, 404p. illus., facsims., ports. 23cm. Bibl. [E302.6.F8L8] 66-12507 7.50
1. Franklin, Benjamin, 1706-1790—Women. 2. Paris—Soc. life & cust. I. Title.
BIP

Franklin, Benjamin, 1706-1790—Addresses, essays, lectures.

JACOBS, Wilbur R., comp. 973.32'0924 B
Benjamin Franklin: statesman-philosopher or materialist? Edited by Wilbur R. Jacobs. New York, Holt, Rinehart and Winston [1971, c1972] 114 p. illus. 24 cm. (American problem studies) Bibliography: p. 112-114. [E302.6.F8J33] 72-162862 ISBN 0-03-078045-4
1. Franklin, Benjamin, 1706-1790—Addresses, essays, lectures. I. Title.

WRIGHT, Esmond, comp. 973.32'0924 B
Benjamin Franklin; a profile. [1st ed.] New York, Hill and Wang [1970] xxvii, 227 p. 21 cm. (American profiles) [E302.6.F8W87] 75-106968 6.50
1. Franklin, Benjamin, 1706-1790—Addresses, essays, lectures.

Franklin, Benjamin 1706-1790. Autobiography.

FOWLER, Austin 973.30924
benjamin Franklin's Autobiography. New York, Monarch Pr [c]1966 71p. 22cm. (Monarch notes & study gds., 832-6) Bibl [E302.6] 66-27281 pap, 1.00
1. Franklin, Benjamin 1706-1790. Autobiography. I. Title.

*FRANKLIN, Benjamin 923.273
The autobiography of Benjamin Franklin. [Introd. by J. William Bigoness.] New York, Airmont [c.1965] 159p. illus. 19cm. (Classics ser., CL71) .50 pap.,
I. Title.

FRANKLIN, Benjamin, 1706-1790 923.273
Autobiography. New introd. by Lewis Leary. New York, Collier Bks. [c.1962] 160p. (Classic Collier bks., HS5) Bibl. 62-10135 .65 pap.,
I. Title.

FRANKLIN, Benjamin, 1706-1790. 973.2'0924 (B)
Autobiography. Edited by C. Merton Babcock and illustrated by Erwin Schachner. Mount Vernon, N. Y., Peter Pauper Press [1967] 62 p. col. illus. 19 cm. [E302.6.F7A2 1967] 67-66299
I. Title.

FRANKLIN, Benjamin, 1706-1790. 923.273
Autobiography. With an introd. by Verner W. Crane. New York, Harper [1956] xvii, 231p. 21cm. (Harper's modern classics) 'Bibliographical note': p. xvii. [E302.6.F7A2 1956] 56-6982
I. Title.

FRANKLIN, Benjamin, 1706-1790. 973.2'0924 B
Autobiography. Edited by C. Merton Babcock and illustrated by Erwin Schachner. Mount Vernon, N.Y., Peter Pauper Press [1967] 62 p. col. illus. 19 cm. [E302.6.F7A2 1967] 67-66299

FRANKLIN, Benjamin, 1706-1790. 923.273
Autobiography. Introd. by Thomas Yoseloff. New York, Fine Editions Press [1957] viii, 240p. 22cm. 'Historical sketch of the fortunes and misfortunes of the autograph manuscript of Franklin's memoirs of his own life [by J. Bigelow]': p. 1-48. [E302.6.F7A2 1957] 57-59154
I. Title.

FRANKLIN, Benjamin, 1706-1790. 818.1
The autobiography, and other writings. With selections from Poor Richard's almanac and papers relating to the Junto, together with sixteen pages of illus. and commentary by Frank Donovan. New York, Dodd, Mead [1963] xvi, 312 p. illus., ports. 22 cm. (Great illustrated classics) [PS745.A2 1963] 63-20471
I. Donovan, Frank Robert, 1906- ed.

FRANKLIN, Benjamin, 1706-1790. 973.32'0924 B
Autobiography and other pieces; edited with an introd. by Dennis Welland. [London] Oxford University Press, 1970. xxx, 183 p. 20 cm. (Classic American texts) Bibliography: p. xxx. [E302.6.F7A2 1970] 70-499083
I. Welland, Dennis Sydney Reginald, ed.

FRANKLIN, Benjamin, 1706-1790 923.273
The autobiography and other writings. Selected ed., introd. by L. Jesse Lemisch. [New York] New Amer. Lib. [c.1961] 350p. (Signet classic CC74) Bibl. .50 pap.,
I. Title.

FRANKLIN, Benjamin, 1706-1790. 923.273
Autobiography, now printed for the first time from the manuscript as Franklin wrote it, and including his preliminary outline; with an introd. by Carl Van Doren and drawings by William Sharp. New York, Heritage Press [1951] xix, 233 p. illus., ports. 26 cm. [E302.6.F7A2 1951] 51-4833
I. Title.

*FRANKLIN, Benjamin, 1706-1790 923.273
Autobiography of Benjamin Franklin. Large type ed. New York, Watts [1966] 300p. port. 29cm. (Keith Jennison bk.) 6.95
I. Title.

*FRANKLIN, Benjamin. 1706-1790 923.273
The autobiography of Benjamin Franklin. Post-script by Richard B. Morris [New York] Washington Sq. [1966. c.1955] 215p. illus. 17cm. (Collateral classic, CC501) With 48-page Reader's supplement. .50 pap.,
I. Title.

FRANKLIN, Benjamin, 1706-1790. 973.2'0924
The autobiography of Benjamin Franklin. Edited by Margaret K. Soifer. [Unabridged school ed.] New York, Macmillan [1967] ix, 217 p. 21 cm. (Literary heritage series) [E302.6.F7A2 1967] 67-5155
I. Soifer, Margaret K., ed. II. Title. **BIP**

FRANKLIN, Benjamin, 1706-1790. 923.273
The autobiography of Benjamin Franklin, edited by Leonard W. Labaree [and others] New Haven, Yale University Press, 1964. 351 p. col. illus., facsim., col. port. 27 cm. Bibliography: p. 323-325. [E302.6.F7A2 1964] 64-12653
I. Labaree, Leonard Woods, 1897- ed. **BIP**

FRANKLIN, Benjamin, 1706-1790. 923.273
The autobiography of Benjamin Franklin & selections from his other writings. With an introd. by Henry Steele Commager. New York, Modern Library [1950] xxi, 264 p. 19 cm. (Modern Library college editions, T18) Contents.Contents.—Chief events in Franklin's life.—Franklin's draft scheme.—The autobiography.—The Dogood papers.—Poor Richard's almanack, 1749.—From Poor Richard's almanack, 1756.—From Poor Richard's almanack, 1757.—The way to wealth.—On the price of corn & management of the poor.—Advice to a young tradesman, 1748.—Journal of a voyage. Bibliography: p. xiv-xvi. [E302.6.F7A2 1950] 51-106

FRANKLIN, Benjamin, 1706-1790. 923.273
Benjamin Franklin: the Autobiography and selections from his other writings; edited with an introd. by Herbert W. Schneider. New York, Liberal Arts Press [1952] xx, 218 p. 21 cm. (The American heritage series, no. 2) Bibliography: p. xv-xvii. [E302.6.F7A2 1952] 52-14644

FRANKLIN, Benjamin, 1706-1790. 973.2'0924 B
Benjamin Franklin; an autobiographical portrait. Edited by Alfred Tamarin. [New York] Macmillan [1969] xi, 276 p. illus., maps, ports. 24 cm. Includes excerpts from Franklin's Autobiography (p. [1]-128), letters, and others writings. Bibliography: p. [272]-273. [E302.6.F7A23 1969] 78-78091
I. Tamarin, Alfred H., ed. II. Franklin, Benjamin, 1706-1790. Autobiography. III. Title.

Franklin, Benjamin, 1706-1790—Humor, satire, etc.

BLOCK, Seymour Stanton, 1918- 973.3'2'0924 B
Benjamin Franklin : his wit, wisdom, and women / by Seymour Stanton Block. New York : Hastings House, [1975] ix, 406 p. : ill. ; 22 cm. Includes index. Bibliography: p. [392]-394. [PS751.B56] 75-6561 ISBN 0-8038-0767-8 : 12.95
1. Franklin, Benjamin, 1706-1790—Humor, satire, etc. **BIP**

FRANKLIN, Benjamin, 1706-1790. 973.3'2'0924
On the choice of a mistress & other satires & hoaxes of Dr. Benjamin Franklin. New York, Gordon Press, 1974. 93 p. illus. 22 cm. Cover title: Advice to a young man on the choice of a mistress. [PS746.G6] 73-16625 ISBN 0-87968-097-0
I. Title. II. Title: Advice to a young man on the choice of a mistress.
Contents omitted.

Franklin, Benjamin, 1706-1790—Juvenile literature.

ALIKI. 973.3'092'4 B
The many lives of Benjamin Franklin / by Aliki. Englewood Cliffs, N.J. : Prentice-Hall, c1977. p. cm. A simple biography of Benjamin Franklin emphasizing his contributions to American literature, politics, and science. [E302.6.F8A48] 92 77-5508 ISBN 0-13-556019-5 lib.bdg. : 6.95
1. Franklin, Benjamin, 1706-1790—Juvenile literature. 2. Statesmen—United States—Biography—Juvenile literature. I. Title. **BIP**

AULAIRE, Ingri (Mortenson) d', 1904- 923.273
Benjamin Franklin [by] Ingri & Edgar Parin d'Aulaire. Garden City, N.Y., Doubleday, c1950. [48] p. illus. (part col.) 29 cm. [E302.6.F8A9] 50-10503
1. Franklin, Benjamin, 1706-1790—Juvenile literature. I. Aulaire, Edgar Parin d', 1898- joint author.

AULAIRE, Ingri (Mortenson) d', 1904- 92
Benjamin Franklin [by] Ingri & Edgar Parin d'Aulaire. Garden City, N.Y., Doubleday [1966]c. 1950. 48p. illus. (pt. col.) 29cm. [E302.6.F8A9 1966] 66-4602 3.50
1. Franklin, Benjamin, 1706-1790—Juvenile literature. I. Aulaire, Edgar Parin d', 1898- joint author. II. Title.

CUNEO, John R. 973.30924 B
Benjamin Franklin, ingenious diplomat, by John Cuneo. New York, McGraw-Hill [1969] 159 p. illus., ports. 24 cm. (Saratoga cluster) Bibliography: p. 155-157. A biography of the diplomat whose skillful negotiations brought France to the aid of the colonies in the Revolutionary War. [E302.6.F8C79] 92 74-88324
1. Franklin, Benjamin, 1706-1790—Juvenile literature. I. Title.

EBERLE, Irmengarde, 1898- 923.273
Benjamin Franklin, man of science. Pictures by Henry S. Gillette. New York, F. Watts [c.1961] 145p. illus. 61-5179 1.95
1. Franklin, Benjamin, 1706-1790—Juvenile literature. I. Title.

FLEMING, Thomas J. 973.3'2'0924 B
Benjamin Franklin, by Thomas Fleming. New York, Four Winds Press [1972, c1973] 166 p. illus. 24 cm. The life of the printer, inventor, and statesman who played an influential role in the early history of the United States. [E302.6.F8F56] 92 72-77809 5.62 (lib. bdg.)
1. Franklin, Benjamin, 1706-1790—Juvenile literature. I. Title.

FRITZ, Jean. 973.3'092'4 B
What's the big idea, Ben Franklin? / By Jean Fritz ; illustrated by Margot Tomes. New York : Coward, McCann & Geoghegan, c1976. 46 p. : ill. (some col.) ; 24 cm. A brief biography of the eighteenth-century printer, inventor, and statesman who played an influential role in the early history of the United States. [E302.6.F8F88 1976] 92 75-25902 ISBN 0-698-20365-8 : 6.95.
1. Franklin, Benjamin, 1706-1790—Juvenile literature. I. Tomes, Margot. II. Title. **BIP**

*GRAVES, Charles Parlin, 1911- 92
Benjamin Franklin, man of ideas. Illus. by Gerald McCann. New York, Dell [1968,c. 1960] 79p. illus. 19cm. (Yearling, Discovery bk. 0499) .50 pap.,
1. Benjamin Franklin, 1706-1790—Juvenile literature. I. Title.

JOHNSON, Spencer. 973.3'092'4 B
The value of saving : the story of Benjamin Franklin / by Spencer Johnson. La Jolla, Calif. : Value Communications, c1978. p. cm. (ValueTales series) A brief biography of the outstanding eighteenth-century printer, inventor, and statesman, emphasizing the value of saving in his life. [E302.6.F8J56] 78-8652 ISBN 0-916392-17-1 : 5.95
1. Franklin, Benjamin, 1706-1790—Juvenile literature. 2. Statesmen—United States—Biography—Juvenile literature. 3. Saving and thrift—Juvenile literature. I. Title. **BIP**

KURLAND, Gerald, 1942- 973.3'2'0924 B
Benjamin Franklin, America's universal man. Charlotteville, N.Y., SamHar Press, 1972. 32 p. 22 cm. (Outstanding personalities, no. 33) Bibliography: p. 32. A biography of the eighteenth-century American printer, inventor, scientist, statesman, and diplomat. [E302.6.F8K94] 92 72-190250
1. Franklin, Benjamin, 1706-1790—Juvenile literature. I. Title.

LEE, Susan. 973.3'2'0924 B
Benjamin Franklin, by Susan & John Lee. Illustrated by Richard Wahl. Chicago, Childrens Press [1974] 47 p. col. illus. 24 cm. (Heroes of the Revolution) A simple biography of a man whose many accomplishments in science, writing, social reform, and politics still influence America today. [E302.6.F8L42] 92 73-17358 ISBN 0-516-04651-9 5.25 (lib. bdg.)
1. Franklin, Benjamin, 1706-1790—Juvenile literature. I. Lee, John, joint author. II. Wahl, Richard, 1939- illus. III. Title.

MERRIAM, Eve, 1916- 92
The story of Ben Franklin. Pictures by Brinton Turkle. New York, Four Winds Pr. [dist. Scholastic, 1965] 78p. col. illus. 22cm. [E302.6.F8M52] 65-9483 2.95
1. Franklin, Benjamin, 1706-1790—Juvenile literature. I. Turkle, Brinton, illus. II. Title.

SANDERLIN, George William, 1915- 973.32'0924 B
Benjamin Franklin as others saw him, by George Sanderlin. New York, Coward, McCann & Geoghegan [1972, c1971] 95 p. illus. 21 cm. Bibliography: p. 94. A brief biography of Franklin accompanies excerpts from his own writings and from works about him by prominent men of the eighteenth, nineteenth, and twentieth centuries. [E302.6.F8S317 1972] 92 72-157060 4.95
1. Franklin, Benjamin, 1706-1790—Juvenile literature. I. Title.

SCARF, Maggi. 92 (J)
Meet Benjamin Franklin. Illustrated by Harry Beckhoff. New York, Random House [1968] 60 p. col. illus., map (on lining papers) 22 cm. (Step-up books) [E302.6.F8S35 1968] 68-10747
1. Franklin, Benjamin, 1706-1790—Juvenile literature. I. Title.

STEIN, R. Conrad. 973.3'2'0924 B
Benjamin Franklin: inventor, statesman, and patriot, by R. Conrad Stein. Chicago, Rand McNally [1972] 69 p. illus. (part. col.) 29 cm. A biography of the printer, inventor, and statesman who played an influential role in the early history of the United States. [E302.6.F8S875] 92 72-3884 ISBN 0-528-82478-3
1. Franklin, Benjamin, 1706-1790—Juvenile literature. I. Jacobson, William, illus. II. Title.

WAYNE, Bennett. 973.3'092'2 B
The Founding Fathers. Edited, with commentary, by Bennett Wayne. Champaign, Ill., Garrard Pub. Co. [1975] 166 p. illus. 22 cm. (A Target book) Biographies of three contemporaries who helped establish the United States as an independent nation: Benjamin Franklin, George Washington, and Thomas Jefferson. [E302.5.W39] 920 74-19112 ISBN 0-8116-4912-1 3.98 (lib. bdg.).
1. Franklin, Benjamin, 1706-1790—Juvenile literature. 2. Washington, George, Pres. U.S., 1732-1799—Juvenile literature. 3. Jefferson, Thomas, Pres. U.S., 1743-1826—Juvenile literature. I. Title. **BIP**

WISE, Winifred Esther, 1906- 973.32'0924 B
Benjamin Franklin, by Winifred E. Wise. Illustrated by Ronald Dorfman. New York, Putnam [1970] 95 p. illus. 24 cm. (A World pioneer biography) Bibliography: p. 94. A biography of the statesman, scientist, inventor, and writer well-known in America and Europe during his lifetime. [E302.6.F8W83] 92 77-92820 3.29
1. Franklin, Benjamin, 1706-1790—Juvenile literature. I. Dorfman, Ronald, illus. II. Title. **BIP**

Franklin, Benjamin, 1706-1790—Liberary art—Addresses, essays, lectures.

BENJAMIN Franklin : 973.3'092'4
a collection of critical essays / edited by Brian M. Barbour. Englewood Cliffs, N.J. : Prentice-Hall, c1979. viii, 179 p. ; 21 cm. (Twentieth century views) (A Spectrum book) Bibliography: p. 176-179. [E302.6.F8B46] 79-12443 ISBN 0-13-074856-0 : 9.95 ISBN 0-13-074849-8 pbk. : 3.95
1. Franklin, Benjamin, 1706-1790—Liberary art—Addresses, essays, lectures. 2. Franklin, Benjamin, 1706-1790. The Autobiography—Addresses, essays, lectures. 3. American literature—Colonial period, ca. 1600-1775—History and criticism—Addresses, essays, lectures. 4. American literature—1783-1850—History and criticism—Addresses, essays, lectures. I. Barbour, Brian M., 1943- **BIP**

Franklin, George E.

FRANKLIN, George E. 189- 818.5403
i
From Cotswolds to high Sierras. Caldwell. Idaho, Caxton [c.] 1966 167p. illus., map, ports. 22cm. Autobiographical. [CT275.F6944A3] 66-20373 4.00
I. Title.

FRANKLIN, George E 1890- 818.5403
From Cotswolds to high Sierras, by George E. Franklin. Caldwell, Idaho, Caxton Printers, 1966. 167 p. illus., map, ports. 22 cm. Autobiographical. [CT275.F6944A3] 66-20373
I. Title.

Franklin, Isaac, 1789-1846.

STEPHENSON, Wendell Holmes, 1899- 917.63'03'50924
Isaac Franklin, slave trader and planter of the Old South, with plantation records. Gloucester, Mass., P. Smith, 1968 [c1938] xi, 368 p. illus., facsim., map (on lining papers) 21 cm. Bibliography: p. 340-348. [F213.F73 1968] 73-2581
1. Franklin, Isaac, 1789-1846. 2. Slave-trade—U.S. 3. Plantation life.—Southern States. I. Title.

Franklin, Joe.

FRANKLIN, Joe. 791.45'092'4 B
A gift for people / Joe Franklin. New York : M. Evans ; Philadelphia : distributed in the U.S. by Lippincott, c1978. 246 p., [4] leaves of plates ; ill. ; 22 cm. [PN1990.72.F7A33] 77-26258 ISBN 0-87131-244-1 ; 7.95
1. Franklin, Joe. 2. Broadcasters—United States—Biography. I. Title. **BIP**

Franklin, John, Sir, 1786-1847.

NEATBY, Leslie H. 971.2'9'010924
The search for Franklin [by] Leslie H. Neatby. New York, Walker [1970] 280 p. illus., maps, ports. 23 cm. Bibliography: p. 271-272. [G660 N4 1970f] 73-99977 7.50
1. Franklin, John, Sir, 1786-1847. 2. Northwest Passage. I. Title.

Franklin, Lyn.

FRANKLIN, Lyn. 363.2'092'4 B
Sawed off justice / by Lyn Franklin, with Maury Green. New York : Putnam, c1976. 254 p. ; 22 cm. [HV7911.F73A37 1976] 76-20562 7.95
1. Franklin, Lyn. 2. Detectives—California—Beverly Hills—Biography. I. Green, Maury, joint author. II. Title.

Franklin, Rosalind, 1920-1958.

SAYRE, Anne. 574.8'732'0924 B
Rosalind Franklin and DNA / Anne Sayre. 1st ed. New York : Norton, [1975] 221 p. ; 21 cm. Includes bibliographical references. [QP26.F68S29 1975] 75-11737 ISBN 0-393-07493-5 : 8.95
1. Franklin, Rosalind, 1920-1958. 2. Deoxyribonucleic acid. I. Title. **BIP**

Franklin, Sidney,

FRANKLIN, Sidney, 1903- 927.918
Bullfighter from Brooklyn, an autobiography; with an evaluation of Sidney Franklin from Death in the afternoon, by Ernest Hemingway. [New York] Prentice-Hall [1952] 245 p. illus. 24 cm. [GV1108.F7A3] 52-10661
I. Title.

Franklin, Sir John, 1786-1847.

SUTTON, Ann 923.998
Journey into ice; John Franklin and the Northwest Passage, by Ann and Myron Sutton. Chicago, Rand McNally [c.1965] 268p. illus., maps, ports. 22cm. Bibl. [G660.S9] 65-10761 4.50
1. Franklin, Sir John, 1786-1847. 2. Northwest Passage. I. Sutton, Myron, joint author. II. Title.

Franson, Fredrik, 1852- 1908.

WOODWARD, David B. 269'.2'0924(B)
Aflame for God: biography of Fredrik Franson, founder of The Evengelical ,alliance Mission, by David B. Woodward. Chicago. Moody [1966] 190p. 22cm. [BV3705.F7W6] 66-16225 3.50
1. Franson, Fredrik, 1852- 1908. 2. The Evangelical Alliance Mission. I. Title.

Frantz, Adolf Ingram.

FRANTZ, Adolf Ingram. 830'.92'4 B
Water from the well : the recollections of a former plowboy / by Adolf Ingram Frantz. Philadelphia : Dorrance, c1978. xv, 411 p. : ill. ; 24 cm. Includes bibliographical references. [PT67.F7A38] 78-104568 ISBN 0-8059-2469-8 : 10.00
1. Frantz, Adolf Ingram. 2. Teachers—United States—Biography. I. Title.

Franz Ferdinand, Archduke of Austria, 1863-1914.

PAULI, Hertha Ernestine, 1909- 943.6040924
The secret of Sarajevo; the story of Franz Ferdinand and Sophie, by Hertha Pauli. [1st ed.] New York, Appleton-Century [1965] ix, 309 p. illus., ports. 21 cm. Bibliography: p. 300-304. [DB89.F7P3] 65-21675
1. Franz Ferdinand, Archduke of Austria, 1863-1914. 2. Hohenberg, Sophie, Herzogin von, 1868-1914. I. Title.

Franz Ferdinand, Archduke of Austria 1863-1914—Assassination.

GILFOND, Henry. 940.3'112
The Black Hand at Sarajevo / by Henry Gilfond. Indianapolis : Bobbs-Merrill, c1975. xi, 176 p. ; 22 cm. [DB89.F7G54] 74-17690 ISBN 0-672-52070-2 : 6.95
1. Franz Ferdinand, Archduke of Austria 1863-1914—Assassination. 2. Ujedinjenje ili smrt. 3. European War, 1914-1918—Causes. I. Title.

Franz Joseph I, Emperor of Austria, 1830-1916.

FRANZ JOSEPH, I, 943.6040924
Emperor of Austria, 1830-1916
The incredible friendship; the letters of Emperor Franz Joseph to Frau Katharina Schratt. Orig. ed. by Jean de Bourgoing. Tr. from German. ed. by Evabeth Miller Kienast, Robert Rie. [Albany] State Univ. of N.Y. [1966] x, 399p. illus., map (on lining papers) ports. 24cm. Tr. of Briefe Kaiser Franz Josephs an Frau Katharina Schratt. [DB87.A2613] 66-63789 10.00
I. Bourgoing, Jean Baron de, 1877- II. Schratt, Katharina, 1855-1940. III. Title. Distributed by Antioch.

MURAD, Anatol, 1904- 943'.604'0924 B
Franz Joseph i of Austria and his Empire New York, Twayne Publishers [1968] x, 259 p. geneal. table. 21 cm. Includes bibliographical references. [DB85.M83] 68-17233
1. Franz Joseph I, Emperor of Austria, 1830-1916. 2. Austria—History—Francis Joseph, 1848-1916. I. Title. **BIP**

REDLICH, Josef, 1869-1936 943.6040924
Emperor Francis Joseph of Austria; a biography. Hamden, Conn., Archon [dist. Shoe String] 1965 [c.1929] xvi, 547p. illus., ports. 22cm. [DB87.R45] 65-25394 11.00
1. Franz Joseph I, Emperor of Austria, 1830-1916. 2. Austria—Hist.—Francis Joseph, 1848-1916. I. Title.

Fraser, Alexander Garden, 1873-1962.

WARD, William Ernest Frank, 1900- 266'.023'
Fraser of Trinity and Achimota [by] W. E. F. Ward. [Accra?] Ghana Universities Press; [sole distributors outside Ghana, Oxford University Press, London] 1965. vii, 328 p. ports. 23 cm. [BV3625.G62F79] 65-2962
1. Fraser, Alexander Garden, 1873-1962. I. Title.

Fraser, Amy Stewart.

FRASER, Amy Stewart. 941.1082'092'4 B
In memory long / Amy Stewart Fraser. London ; Boston : Routledge and Kegan Paul, 1977. xi, 305 p. : ill. ; 23 cm. [CT828.F65A34 1977] 77-369622 ISBN 0-7100-8586-9 : 12.25
1. Fraser, Amy Stewart. 2. Scotland—Biography. I. Title. **BIP**

Fraser, Andrew Henderson Leith, Sir, 1848-1919.

FRASER, Andrew Henderson Leith, Sir, 1848-1919. 954'.3
Among Indian rajahs and ryots : a civil servant's recollections & impressions of thirty-seven years of work & sport in the Central Provinces & Bengal / by Sir Andrew H. L. Fraser. 3d & rev. ed. Allahabad : Chugh Publications, 1975. 375 p., [24] leaves of plates : ill., map. ; 22 cm. "Indian edition." Reprint of the 1912 ed. Includes index. [DS485.C3F7 1975] 75-901839 15.50
1. Fraser, Andrew Henderson Leith, Sir, 1848-1919. 2. Madhya Pradesh, India—Description and travel. 3. Madhya Pradesh, India—Politics and government. 4. Bengal—Description and travel. 5. Bengal—Politics and government. I. Title. Distributed by South Asia Books, Columbia, Mo.

Fraser, Charles, 1782-1860.

SMITH, Alice Ravenel Huger, 1876- 759.157
Charles Fraser, by Alice R. Huger Smith and D. E. Huger Smith. Charleston, S.C., Garnier [1967] ix, 58 p. ports. 25 cm. "Unabridged and unaltered republication of the limited edition (325) originally published ... in 1924." [ND1337.U6F71967] 68-23427
1. Fraser, Charles, 1782-1860. I. Smith, Daniel Elliott Huger, joint author.

Fraser, Dawn,

FRASER, Dawn, 1937- 927.972
Below the surface; confessions of an Olympic champion, by Dawn Fraser with Harry Gordon. New York, Morrow, 1965. 250 p. ports. 24 cm. "Published in Australia under title, Gold medal girl." [GV838.F7A3 1965a] 65-18518
I. Gordon, Harry, 1926- II. Title.

Fraser family.

FRASER, Thomas Layton, 1899- 929'.2'0973
Back when : a biography of Joseph Bacon Fraser and Maria Boulineau Fraser of Hinesville, Georgia, and their children / by Layton Fraser. Clinton, S.C. : Fraser, c1976. v, 179 p., [1] leaf of plates : ill. ; 24 cm. [CS71.F848 1976] 76-151518
1. Fraser family. 2. United States—Genealogy. 3. Georgia—Genealogy. I. Title.

Fraser, Malcolm.

KELLY, Paul. 320.9'94'06
The unmaking of Gough / [by] Paul Kelly. [Sydney] : Angus & Robertson, 1976. 361 p. ; 23 cm. [DU117.2.F72K44] 77-365901 ISBN 0-207-13400-6
1. Fraser, Malcolm. 2. Whitlam, Edward Gough, 1916- 3. Prime ministers—Australia—Biography. I. Title.

Frassinetti, Paola Angela Maria, 1809-1882.

CASHIN, Helen, Sister, 1918- 922.245
A great servant of God, Mother Paola Frassinetti, foundress of the Sisters of St. Dorothy, 1803 [i. e. 1809]-1882; compiled by a Sister of St. Dorothy. S[taten] I[sland] N. Y., '1951. 62 p. illus. 22 cm. [BX4705.F736C3] 52-18340
1. Frassinetti, Paola Angela Maria, 1809-1882. I. Title.

Frazier, Jane, b. 1735.

FRAZIER, Jane, b.1735. 973'.04'97 S
Narrative of the captivity of Jane Frazier / Jane Frazier. New York : Garland Pub., 1977. 13 leaves, [2] leaves of plates : ill. ; 23 cm. (The Garland library of narratives of North American Indian captivities ; v. 109) Issued with the reprint of the 1927 ed. of Meredith, G. E. Girl captives of the Cheyennes. New York, 1977. Reprint of the 1930 ed. published under title: Narrative of the captivity of Mrs. Jane Frazier. "Taken from Thomas' History of Allegheny County, Pennsylvania." [E85.G2 vol. 109] [E99.M48] 970'.004'97 76-51255 ISBN 0-8240-1733-1 lib.bdg. : 25.00 (set)
1. Frazier, Jane, b. 1735. 2. Miami Indians—Captivities. 3. Indians of North America—Captivities. 4. United States—Biography. I. Title. II. Series.

FRAZIER, Jane, b.1735. 973'.04'97 S
Narrative of the captivity of Jane Frazier / Jane Frazier. New York : Garland Pub., 1977. 13 leaves, [2] leaves of plates : ill. ; 23 cm. (The Garland library of narratives of North American Indian captivities ; v. 109) Issued with the reprint of the 1927 ed. of Meredith, G. E. Girl captives of the Cheyennes. New York, 1977. Reprint of the 1930 ed. published under title: Narrative of the captivity of Mrs. Jane Frazier. "Taken from Thomas' History of Allegheny County, Pennsylvania." [E85.G2 vol. 109] [E99.M48] 970'.004'97 76-51255 ISBN 0-8240-1733-1 lib.bdg. : 25.00 (set)
1. Frazier, Jane, b. 1735. 2. Miami Indians—Captivities. 3. Indians of North America—Captivities. 4. United States—Biography. I. Title. II. Series.

Frazier, Joe, 1944-

PEPE, Phil. 796.8'3'0924
Come out smokin'. Joe Frazier - the champ nobody knew. New York, Coward, McCann & Geoghegan [1972] 224 p. illus. 23 cm. "An Associated Features book." [GV1132.F7P4] 70-172628 6.95
1. Frazier, Joe, 1944- I. Title.

Frazier, Walt,

FRAZIER, Walt, 1945- 796.32'3'0924
Clyde, by Walt Frazier and Joe Jares. [1st ed.] New York, Rutledge Book [1970] 286 p. illus., ports. 22 cm. Autobiographical. [GV884.F7A3 1970] 77-98177 6.95
I. Jares, Joseph Frank, 1937- joint author. II. Title.

Frazier, Walt, 1945-—Juvenile literature.

BATSON, Larry, 1930- 796.32'3'0924 B
Walt Frazier. Illustrated by Harold Henriksen. Mankato, Minn., Amecus Street; [distributed by Childrens Press, Chicago, 1974] 31 p. col. illus. 25 cm. (Superstars) Follows the basketball career of "Clyde" Walt Frazier, star of the New York "Knicks" whose skill in the sport has made him a millionaire. [GV884.F7B37] 92 74-2013 ISBN 0-87191-348-8 4.95
1. Frazier, Walt, 1945-—Juvenile literature. I. Henriksen, Harold, illus. BIP

BURCHARD, S. H. 796.32'3'0924 B
Sports star, Walt Frazier / S. H. Burchard ; illustrated with photos. 1st ed. New York : Harcourt Brace Jovanovich, [1975] p. cm. A simple biography of Walt Frazier, guard for the New York Knickerbockers basketball team. [GV884.F7B87] 92 75-11781 ISBN 0-15-277999-X : 4.95
1. Frazier, Walt, 1945- —Juvenile literature. 2. Basketball—Juvenile literature. I. Title.

SABIN, Louis 796.3230924
Walt Frazier, no. 1 guard of the NBA / Louis Sabin New York : Putnam, 1976 124 p. ; 21 cm. (Putnam sports shelf) Includes index [GV884.F7S23] 75-23458 ISBN 0-399-60975-X lib.bdg. : 5.29
1. Frazier, Walt, 1945-—Juvenile literature 2. Basketball—Biography. I. Title.

Frear, Edwin D.

HAWKINS, Cora Frear, 1887- 610'.924 B
Buggies, blizzards, and babies. [1st ed.] Ames, Iowa State University Press [1971] x, 191 p. illus., ports. 24 cm. [R154.F824H3] 74-137091 ISBN 0-8138-0395-0 5.95
1. Frear, Edwin D. I. Title. BIP

Freas, Frank Kelly, 1922-

FREAS, Frank Kelly, 1922- 741.9'73
Frank Kelly Freas : the art of science fiction / by Frank Kelly Freas ; introd. by Isaac Asimov. Norfolk, Va. : Donning Co., c1977. p. cm. [NC975.5.F74A45] 77-8644 ISBN 0-915442-30-2 collector's ed. : 29.95. ISBN 0-915442-37-X pbk. : 7.95. ISBN 0-915442-38-8 lib. ed. : 12.95
1. Freas, Frank Kelly, 1922- 2. Illustrators—United States—Biography. 3. Science fiction—Illustrations. I. Title. BIP

Fred, Edwin Broun, 1887-

JOHNSON, Diane, 1929- 589.9'0092'4 B
Edwin Broun Fred: scientist, administrator, gentleman. [Madison] Published for the Trustees of the Wisconsin Alumni Research Foundation by University of Wisconsin Press [1974] x, 179 p. illus. 22 cm. "Chronological listing of Edwin B. Fred's scientific publications": p. 129-144. [QR31.F68J63] 74-5904 ISBN 0-299-06580-4 10.00
1. Fred, Edwin Broun, 1887- I. Wisconsin Alumni Research Foundation.

Frederic, Harold, 1856-1898—Correspondence.

FREDERIC, Harold, 1856-1898. 813'.4 S
The correspondence of Harold Frederic / edited by George E. Fortenberry, Stanton Garner, Robert H. Woodward ; text established by Charlyne Dodge. Fort Worth : Texas Christian University Press, 1977. xxv, 615 p. : ill. ; 24 cm. (The Harold Frederic edition ; v. 1) Includes bibliographical references and index. [PS1705.A2 1977 vol. 1] [PS1708.A44] 813'.4 76-8562
1. Frederic, Harold, 1856-1898—Correspondence. 2. Authors, American—19th century—Correspondence. I. Fortenberry, George E., 1920- II. Garner, Stanton. III. Woodward, Robert Hanson, 1925- IV. Dodge, Charlyne.

Frederic, M. Catherine,

FREDERIC, M. Catherine, sister 922.273
Beneath the lamp's rays, memoirs. New York, Pageant [c.1961] 158p. 2.75
I. Title.

Frederics, Diana, pseud.

FREDERICS, Diana, pseud. 301.41'57'0924 B
Diana : a strange autobiography / by Diana Fredericks. New York : Arno Press, 1975, c1939. x, 284 p. ; 22 cm. (Homosexuality) Reprint of the ed. published by Dial Press, New York. [HQ76.F7 1975] 75-12315 ISBN 0-405-07359-3 : 15.00
1. Frederics, Diana, pseud. 2. Lesbianism—Personal narratives. I. Title. II. Series. BIP

Free Methodist Church—Biog.

BLEWS, Richard R 922.773
Master workmen; biographies of the late bishops of the Free Methodist Church during her first century, 1860-1960. Centennial ed. Winona Lake, Ind., Light and Life Press [1960] 303p. ports. 23cm. [BX8412.B55] 60-11570
1. Free Methodist Church—Biog. I. Title.

Free, Mickey, 1851-1913.

GRIFFITH, A. Kinney. 979.1'03'0924
Mickey Free, manhunter, by A. Kinney Griffith. Caldwell, Idaho, Caxton Printers, 1969. 239 p. illus., ports. 24 cm. Includes bibliographical references. [E90.F7G7] 79-76337 6.50
1. Free, Mickey, 1851-1913. I. Title.

Free Will Baptists (Founded in N.C.)—Clergy—Biography.

HARRISON, Harrold D. 285'.2'0922
Who's who among Free Will Baptists, and encyclopedia of denominational information / edited by Harrold D. Harrison. Nashville : Randall House Publications, 1978. 493 p. : ill. ; 27 cm. [BX6493.H34] 78-107973 ISBN 0-89265-052-4 : write for information
1. Free Will Baptists (Founded in N.C.)—Clergy—Biography. 2. Free Will Baptists (Founded in N.C.)—History. 3. Free Will Baptists (Founded in N.C.)—Societies, etc. 4. Clergy—United States—Biography. I. Title.

Free Will Baptists (Founded in N.C.)—History.

HARRISON, Harrold D. 285'.2'0922
Who's who among Free Will Baptists, and encyclopedia of denominational information / edited by Harrold D. Harrison. Nashville : Randall House Publications, 1978. 493 p. : ill. ; 27 cm. [BX6493.H34] 78-107973 ISBN 0-89265-052-4 : write for information
1. Free Will Baptists (Founded in N.C.)—Clergy—Biography. 2. Free Will Baptists (Founded in N.C.)—History. 3. Free Will Baptists (Founded in N.C.)—Societies, etc. 4. Clergy—United States—Biography. I. Title.

Freeling, Nicolas.

FREELING, Nicolas. 642'.56'0924 B
The kitchen; a delicious account of the author's years as a grand hotel cook. Woodcuts by Gail Garraty. [1st U.S. ed.] New York, Harper & Row [1970] xviii, 152 p. illus. 22 cm. [TX649.F7A3 1970] 78-122887 6.00
I. Title.

Freeman, Daniel, 1826-1908.

KAPLAN, Beverly S. 917.82'03'3 B
Daniel and Agnes Freeman, homesteaders, by Beverly S. Kaplan. Lincoln, Neb., Johnsen Pub. Co. [1971] xvi, 179, [8] p. 22 cm. Bibliography: p. [181]-[187] [F666.F7K3] 73-180504 ISBN 0-910814-37-6
1. Freeman, Daniel, 1826-1908. 2. Freeman, Agnes S., 1843-1931. 3. Frontier and pioneer life—Nebraska. I. Title.

Freeman, Elizabeth, 1744-1829—Juvenile literature.

FELTON, Harold W., 1902- 917.44'1'0330924 B
Mumbet; the story of Elizabeth Freeman [by] Harold W. Felton. Illustrated by Donn Albright. New York, Dodd, Mead [1970] 63 p. illus. 24 cm. A biography of the first Negro slave to win her freedom in the courts of Massachusetts. [E444.F87F4] 92 74-108785 3.75
1. Freeman, Elizabeth, 1744-1829—Juvenile literature. I. Albright, Donn, illus. II. Title. BIP

Freeman, Lawrence, 1906-

FREEMAN, Lawrence, 1906- 785.4'2
If you know of a better life please tell me / Bud Freeman. Dublin : B. Eaves, [1976] 61 p. ; 18 cm. [ML419.F74A28] 77-351045 ISBN 0-902638-02-5 : £0.80
1. Freeman, Lawrence, 1906- 2. Jazz musicians—United States—Biography. I. Title.

Freeman, Legh Richmond.

HEUTERMAN, Thomas H., 1934- 070.5'092'4 B
Movable type : biography of Legh R. Freeman / Thomas H. Heuterman. 1st ed. Ames : Iowa State University Press, 1979. viii, 172 p. : ill. ; 24 cm. Includes index. Bibliography: p. 159-165. [PN4874.F64H4] 79-15511 ISBN 0-8138-0890-1 : 9.95
1. Freeman, Legh Richmond. 2. Journalists—United States—Biography. I. Title. BIP

WRIGHT, Elizabeth, 1909- 070.5'092'4 B
Independence in all things, neutrality in nothing; the story of a pioneer journalist of the American West. [San Francisco, Miller Freeman Publications, 1973] 255 p. illus. 24 cm. Bibliography: p. [254]-255. [PN4874.F64W7] 73-88669 ISBN 0-87930-023-X 10.00
1. Freeman, Legh Richmond. I. Title.

Freeman, Lucy—Biography.

FREEMAN, Lucy, ed. 616.89092
Troubled women, ed., introd., notes by Lucy Freeman. [New York] New American Lib. [1961, c.1959, 1961] 254p. (Signet bk. D1925) Bibl. .50pap.,
I. Title.

FREEMAN, Lucy. 813'.5'4 B
Who is Sylvia? / By Lucy Freeman. New York : Arbor House, c1979. x, 307 p. : ill. ; 22 cm. [PS3556.R392Z477] 78-57327 ISBN 0-87795-197-7 : 9.95
1. Freeman, Lucy—Biography. 2. Greenbaum, Sylvia Sobel. 3. Mothers and daughters. 4. Authors, American—20th century—Biography. I. Title. BIP

Freeman, Mary Eleanor (Wilkins) 1852-1930.

FOSTER, Edward. 928.1
Mary E. Wilkins Freeman. New York, Hendricks House, 1956. 229p. 22cm. [PS1713.F6] 56-4024
1. Freeman, Mary Eleanor (Wilkins) 1852-1930. I. Title. BIP

Freeman, Miller, 1875-1955.

WRIGHT, Elizabeth, 1909- 070.5'092'4 B
Miller Freeman : man of action / Elizabeth Wright. San Francisco : M. Freeman Publications, c1977. 253 p. : ill. ; 23 cm. [Z473.F75W75] 76-29566 ISBN 0-87930-060-4 pbk. : 10.00
1. Freeman, Miller, 1875-1955. 2. Publishers and publishing—Washington (State)—Biography. 3. Journalists—Washington (State)—Biography.

Freeman, Richard Austin, 1862-1943.

DONALDSON, Norman. 823'.9'12
In search of Dr. Thorndyke; the story of R. Austin Freeman's great scientific investigator and his creator. Bowling

Green, Ohio, Bowling Green University Popular Press [1971] xii, 288 p. illus. 24 cm. Bibliography: p. 242-274. [PR6011.R43Z6] 72-147819
1. Freeman, Richard Austin, 1862-1943. I. Title.

Freemasons, Hannibal, N.Y. Hannibal Lodge, no. 550.

STURGE, Gordon W comp. v. 12
Biographical sketches of the past masters of Hannibal Lodge no. 550, F. & A. M. from 1824-1960. [Red Creek, N.Y., Press of the Community Newspapers, 1960] 87 p. illus., ports. 22 cm. 63-76161
1. Freemasons, Hannibal, N.Y. Hannibal Lodge, no. 550. 2. Freemasons — Biog. I. Title.

Freemasons. U. S.—Biog.

HEATON, Ronald E 1898- 923.173
Masonic membership of the general officers of the Continental Army. Washington, Masonic Service Association [1960] viii, 56p. ports., facsims. 28cm. Includes bibliography. [HS509.H5] 60-06420
1. Freemasons. U. S.—Biog. 2. Generals—U. S. 3. U. S. Army— Biog. 4. U. S.—Hist.—Revolution—Biog. I. Title.

Freemasons. United States—History.

POLLARD, Ralph J. 366'.1'0922 B
Famous American Freemasons, by Ralph J. Pollard. Silver Spring, Md., Masonic Service Association [1971] 22 p. 28 cm. [HS517.P64] 73-170592
1. Freemasons. United States—History. I. Title.

Freer, Charles Lang, 1856-1919.

MEYER, Agnes Elizabeth (Ernst) 1887- 709'.24
Charles Lang Freer and his gallery, by Agnes E. Meyer. Washington, Freer Gallery of Art, 1970. 23 p. col. illus., port. 23 cm. [N857.5.M48] 70-124106
1. Freer, Charles Lang, 1856-1919. 2. Freer Gallery of Art, Washington, D.C.

Freestone family.

FREESTONE, John Wilford. v. 12
I remember. Glendale, Calif., A. H. Clark Co., 1963. 85 p. illus. 22 cm. Autobiographical [CT276.F6954A3] 63-18083
1. Freestone family. 2. Mormons and Mormonism in Arizona. I. Title.

Frei Montalva, Eduardo, Pres. Chile, 1911-

GROSS, Leonard. 983'.064'0924
The last, best hope: Eduardo Frei & Chilean democracy. New York, Random House [1967] xiii, 240 p. 22 cm. [F3099.F72G7] 66-23500
1. Frei Montalva, Eduardo, Pres. Chile, 1911- 2. Chile—Politics and government 1920- I. Title.

Freidberg, Carl, 1872-1955.

SMITH, Julia Frances, 1911- 927.8
Master pianist; the career and teaching of Carl Friedberg. New York, Philosophical Library [1963] 183 p. illus. 21 cm. Includes bibliographical notes. [ML417.F74S6] 62-18548
1. Freidberg, Carl, 1872-1955. I. Title.

Freiligrath, Ferdinand, 1810-1876.

FERDINAND Freiligrath v. 12
1876/1976 / edited by Josef Ruland ; translation, Patricia Crampton. Bonn Bad Godesberg : Inter Nationes, 1976. 86 p. : ill. ; 21 cm. Translation of Ferdinand Freiligrath. Includes bibliographical references. [PT1867.Z5F4713] 77-459596
1. Freiligrath, Ferdinand, 1810-1876. 2. Authors, German—19th century—Biography. I. Ruland, Josef.

Freire, Paulo, 1921-

COLLINS, Denis E. 370.1'092'4
Paulo Freire, his life, works, and thought / by Denis E. Collins. New York : Paulist Press, c1977. 94 p. ; 19 cm. (A Deus book) Includes bibliographical references. [LB775.F7632C64] 77-83567 pbk. : 2.45
1. Freire, Paulo, 1921- 2. Education—Philosophy. I. Title.

Fremont. Jessie (Benton) 1824-1902—Juvenile literature.

RANDALL, Ruth (Painter) 920
I, Jessie; a biography of the girl who married John Charles Fremont, famous explorer of the West. Boston, Little [c.1963] 223p. illus. 21cm. 63-13463 3.95
1. Fremont. Jessie (Benton) 1824-1902—Juvenile literature. I. Title.

RANDALL, Ruth (Painter) 92
I, Jessie: a biography of the girl who married John Charles Fremont, famous explorer of the West. [1st ed.] Boston, Little, Brown [1963] 223 p. illus. 21 cm. [E415.9.F79R3] 63-13463
1. Fremont, Jessie (Benton) 1824-1902 — Juvenile literature. I. Title.

Fremont, John Charles, 1813-1890.

BURT, Olive (Woolley) 1894- 973.6'6'0924 B
John Charles Fremont, trial marker of the Old West (January 21, 1813-July 13, 1890) Illustrated by Albert Orbaan. New York, J. Messner [1955] 192 p illus. 22 cm. A biography of John Charles Fremont whose many careers included those of explorer, soldier, Senator, Governor of the territory of Arizona, and the first Republican candidate for President. [PZ7.B9456Jo] 92 AC 68
1. Fremont, John Charles, 1813-1890. I. Orbaan, Albert, illus. II. Title.

EGAN, Ferol. 979'.02'0924 B
Fremont, explorer for a restless nation / Ferol Egan. 1st ed. Garden City, N.Y. : Doubleday, 1977. xv, 582 p., [16] leaves of plates : ill. ; 24 cm. Includes index. Bibliography: p. [559]-561. [E415.9 F8E33] 76-2770 ISBN 0-385-01775-8 : 14.95
1. Fremont, John Charles, 1813-1890. I. Title.

NEVINS, Allan, 1890- 923.973
Fremont, Pathmarker of the West. New York, Ungar [1962, c1955] 2 v. illus. 24 cm. (American classics) Full name: Joseph Allan Nevins. [E415.9] 61-7088
1. Fremont, John Charles, 1813-1890. I Title BIP

NEVINS, Allan, 1890- 923.973
Fremont, pathmarker of the West. [New ed.] New York, Longmans, Green, 1955. xiv, 689p. illus., ports., maps. 22cm. 'Bibliographical note': p. 671-673. [E415.9.F8N46 1955] 55-1552
1. Fremont, John Charles, 1813-1890. I. Title.

PHILLIPS, Fred M. 979'.02
Desert people and mountain men : exploration of the Great Basin, 1824-1865 / Fred M. Phillips. Bishop, Calif. : Chalfant Press, c1977. 62 p. : ill. ; 23 cm. Bibliography: p. 62. [F592.P47] 77-2335 ISBN 0-912494-25-5 pbk. : 3.95
1. Fremont, John Charles, 1813-1890. 2. Ogden, Peter Skene, 1790-1854. 3. Smith, Jedediah Strong, 1799-1831. 4. Walker, Joseph Reddeford, 1798-1876. 5. Great Basin—Discovery and exploration. 6. Explorers—Great Basin—Biography. 7. Indians of North America—Great Basin. I. Title. BIP

Fremont, John Charles, 1813-1890—Juvenile literature.

SMITH, Fredrika Shumway. 917.300924 (B)
Fremont; soldier, explorer, statesman. Chicago, Rand McNally [1966] 256 p. illus., maps, ports. 22 cm. [E415.9.F8S58] 66-10944
1. Fremont, John Charles, 1813-1890 — Juvenile literature. I. Title.

SMITH, Fredrika Shumway 917.300924
Fremont-soldier, explorer, statesman. Chicago, Rand McNally [c.1966] 256p. illus., maps, ports. 22cm. [E415.9.F8S58] 66-10944 4.50
1. Fremont, John Charles, 1813-1890—Juvenile literature. I. Title.

SYME, Ronald, 1910- 979'.02'0924 B
John Charles Fremont: the last American explorer. Illustrated by Richard Cuffari. New York, Morrow, 1974. 190 p. illus. 21 cm. Bibliography: p. 189-190. A biography of the nineteenth-century soldier, politician, and explorer whose many expeditions helped open up the western territories to settlers. [E415.9.F8S95 1974] 92 74-4198 ISBN 0-688-20120-2 4.95
1. Fremont, John Charles, 1813-1890—Juvenile literature. I. Cuffari, Richard, 1925- illus. II. Title.
Library Binding 4.59

Fremstad, Anna Olivia, 1870-1951.

CUSHING, Mary Fitch Watkins. 927.8
The Rainbow Bridge. New York, Putnam [1954] 318 p. illus. 22 cm. Account of the author's life as a companion to primadonna Olive Fremstad. [ML420.F84C8] 54-10494
1. Fremstad, Anna Olivia, 1870-1951. I. Title.

CUSHING, Mary Fitch Watkins. 782.1'092'4 B
The rainbow bridge / Mary Watkins Cushing ; with a discography by W. R. Moran. New York : Arno Press, 1977. 318, vi p., [4] leaves of plates : ill. ; 23 cm. (Opera biographies) Account of the author's life as a companion to prima donna Olive Fremstad. Reprint of the 1954 ed. published by Putnam, New York. Discography: p. i-iv. [ML420.F84C8 1977] 76-29932 ISBN 0-405-09674-7 : 20.00
1. Fremstad, Anna Olivia, 1870-1951. 2. Singers—Biography. I. Title.

French, Alice, 1850-1934.

MCMICHAEL, George L., 1927- 813.4
Journey to obscurity; the life of Octave Thanet. Lincoln, Univ. of Neb. Pr. [c.1965] v, 259p. illus., ports. 24cm. [PS1718.M3] 64-19852 5.00
1. French, Alice, 1850-1934. I. Title.

French Americans—Texas.

INSTITUTE of Texan Cultures. 976.4'004'41
The French Texans / [prepared by the staff of the University of Texas, Institute of Texan Cultures]. [San Antonio] : The Institute, [1973] 32 p. : ill. ; 22 x 28 cm. (The Texians and the Texans) Cover title. [F395.F8157 1973] 74-622566
1. French Americans—Texas. 2. Texas—Biography. I. Title. II. Series.

French-Canadians.

VALLIERES, Pierre. 322'.42'0924 B
White niggers of America; the precocious autobiography of a Quebec "terrorist". Translated by Joan Pinkham. New York, [Monthly Review Press, 1971] 288 p. 21 cm. Translation of Negres blancs d'Amerique. Includes bibliographical references. [F1027.V313] 76-142986 7.50
1. French-Canadians. 2. Quebec (Province)—History—Autonomy and independence movements. 3. Quebec (Province)—Social conditions. I. Title. BIP

French, Daniel Chester, 1850-1931.

RICHMAN, Michael Tingley. 730'.92'4
The early career of Daniel Chester French, 1869-1891. [Newark? Del.] 1974. vii, 353 l. 30 cm. Thesis—University of Delaware. Bibliography: leaves 303-315. [NB237.F7R52] 74-174387
1. French, Daniel Chester, 1850-1931. I. Title.

French literature—History and criticism.

SAINTSBURY, George Edward Bateman, 1845-1933. 840'.9
French literature and its masters. Edited by Huntington Cairns. Westport, Conn., Greenwood Press [1972, c1946] ix, 326, xxx p. port. 22 cm. Bibliography: p. 318-326. [PQ119.S18 1972] 77-163540 ISBN 0-8371-6202-5
1. French literature—History and criticism. I. Title. BIP

French literature—19th century—Collected works.

†JAMES, Henry, 1843-1916. 840'.9
French poets and novelists / by Henry James. Folcroft, Pa. : Folcroft Library Editions, 1977. 344 p. ; 24 cm. Reprint of the 1893 ed. published by Macmillan, London and New York. [PQ286.J3 1977] 77-13419 ISBN 0-8414-5284-9 lib. bdg. : 30.00
1. French literature—19th century—Collected works. 2. Authors, French—Biography. I. Title.
contents omitted BIP

French literature—19th century—History and criticism.

JAMES, Henry, 1843-1916. 840.9
French poets and novelists. Freeport, N.Y., Books for Libraries Press [1972] 439 p. 23 cm. (Essay index reprint series) Reprint of the 1878 ed. Contents.Contents.—Alfred de Musset.—Theophile Gautier.—Charles Baudelaire.—Honore de Balzac.—Balzac's letters.—George Sand.—Charles de Bernard and Gustave Flaubert.—Ivan Turgenieff.—The two Amperes.—Madame de Sabran. Merimee's letters.—The theatre francais. [PQ286.J3 1972] 70-38773 ISBN 0-8369-2660-9
1. French literature—19th century—History and criticism. 2. Authors, French—Biography. I. Title.

French, Parker H.

MCGOWAN, Edward, 1813-1893. 923.973
The strange eventful history of Parker H. French. With introd., notes, and comments by Kenneth M. Johnson. Los Angeles, G. Dawson, 1958. v, 63p. illus., facsim. 19cm. (Early California travel series, 43) Bibliography: p.61-63. [F856.E174 vol. 43] 58-3575
1. French, Parker H. I. Title. II. Series.

French, Stanley.

FRENCH, Stanley. 345'.421'01 B
Crime every day / by Stanley French. Chichester : Rose, 1976. 156 p. ; 23 cm. [KD632.F7A3] 77-371132 ISBN 0-85992-029-1 : £4.50
1. French, Stanley. 2. Clerks of court—Great Britain—Biography. I. Title.

Freneau, Philip Morin, 1752-1832.

BOWDEN, Mary Weatherspoon. 811'.2 B
Philip Freneau / by Mary Weatherspoon Bowden. Boston : Twayne Publishers, c1976. 194 p. ; 21 cm. (Twayne's United States authors series ; TUSAS 260) Includes index. Bibliography: p. 181-185. [PS758.B6] 75-30651 ISBN 0-8057-7161-1 lib.bdg. : 7.95
1. Freneau, Philip Morin, 1752-1832. BIP

FORMAN, Samuel Eagle, 1858-1941. 811'.2 B
The political activities of Philip Freneau. [New York] Arno [1970, c1902] 105 p. 23 cm. (The American journalists) (Johns Hopkins University. Studies in historical and political science, ser. 20, no. 9-10) "The publications of Philip Freneau": p. [103]-105. [PS758.F6 1970] 77-125693 ISBN 0-405-01670-0
1. Freneau, Philip Morin, 1752-1832. I. Title. II. Series. BIP

LEARY, Lewis Gaston, 1906- 928.1
That rascal Freneau; a study in literary failure. New York, Octagon, 1964[c.1941] x, 501p. 24cm. Bibl. 64-16380 10.00
1. Freneau, Philip Morin, 1752-1832. I. Title.

MARSH, Philip Merrill, 1893- 818'.2'09
Philip Freneau, poet and journalist, by Philip M. Marsh. Minneapolis, Dillon Press [1968, c1967] v, 444 p. illus., facsims., ports. 23 cm. Bibliography: p. [369]-394. [PS758.M3] 67-28331
1. Freneau, Philip Morin, 1752-1832.

Freneau, Philip Morin, 1752-1832—Political and social views.

AXELRAD, Jacob. 811'.2 B
Philip Freneau, champion of democracy. Austin, University of Texas Press [1967] xii, 480 p. 24 cm. Bibliography: p. [437]-459. [PS758.A9] 66-15699
1. Freneau, Philip Morin, 1752-1832—Political and social views.

FORMAN, Samuel Eagle, 1858-1941. 330.9'73 S
The political activities of Philip Freneau. Baltimore, Johns Hopkins Press, 1902. [New York, Johnson Reprint Corp., 1973] p. Original ed. issued as no. 9-10 of Colonial and economic history, which forms the 20th series of Johns Hopkins University studies in historical and political science. "The publications of Philip Freneau": p. Bibliography: p. [HC101.C58 no. 9-10] [PS758] 973.3'11'0924 B 73-3254 ISBN 0-384-16430-7 pap. 5.50
1. Freneau, Philip Morin, 1752-1832—Political and social views. I. Title. II. Series: Johns Hopkins University. Studies in historical and political science, 20th ser., 9-10. III. Series: Colonial and economic history, no. 9-10.

Freud, Sigmund, 1856-1939.

ALDINGTON, Hilda (Doolittle) 1886- 928.1
Tribute to Freud, by H. D. With unpublished letters by Freud to the author. [New York] Pantheon [1956] 180p. 21cm. [PS3501.L373T68] 56-10063
1. Freud, Sigmund, 1856-1969. 2. Psychoanaysis—Cases. clinical reports, statistics. I. Title.

AN autobiographical study; authorized translation by James Strachey. New York, Norton [1952] 141 p. 20 cm. "Appeared originally in 1925 in volume IV of Die Medizin der Gegenwart in Selbstdarstellungen (Leipzig: Felix Melner)" [BF173.F85A3 1952] 926.1 52-12426 [921.36]
1. Psychoanalysis. I. Freud, Sigmund, 1856-1939.

BAKER, Rachel (Mininberg), 1903- 921.36
Sigmund Freud. New York, J. Messner [1952] 201 p. 22 cm. [BF173.F85B25] 926.1 52-13547
1. Freud, Sigmund, 1856-1939. 2. Psychoanalysis—Dictionaries. I. Title.

BLANTON, Smiley, 1882-1966. 150.19'52'0924 B
Diary of my analysis with Sigmund Freud. With biographical notes and comments by Margaret Gray Blanton. Introd. by Iago Galdston. New York, Hawthorn Books [1971] 141 p. 22 cm. [BF173.F85B57 1971] 75-158015 7.95
1. Freud, Sigmund, 1856-1939. 2. Psychoanalysis. I. Title.

CLOUZET, Maryse (Choisy) 1903- 926.1
Sigmund Freud: a new appraisal. New York, Citadel [c.1963] 141p. 22cm. (C122) Bibl. 63-2294 1.75 pap.,
1. Freud, Sigmund, 1856-1939. I. Title. BIP

CLOUZET, Maryse Choisy, 1903- 150'.19'52 B
Sigmund Freud: a new appraisal, by Maryse Choisy. Westport, Conn., Greenwood Press [1974, c1963] 141 p. 22 cm. Reprint of the ed. published by Philosophical Library, New York. Includes bibliographical references. [BF173.F85C6 1974] 72-9606 ISBN 0-8371-6593-8
1. Freud, Sigmund, 1856-1939.

COSTIGAN, Giovanni. 926.1
Sigmund Freud, a short biography. New York, Macmillan [1965] xiv, 306 p. 21 cm. [BF173.F85C68 1965] 65-14957
1. Freud, Sigmund, 1856-1939.

DOOLITTLE, Hilda, 1886-1961. 616.8'917
Tribute to Freud / HD ; foreword by Norman Holmes Pearson ; introd. by Kenneth Fields. Boston : D. R. Godine, c1974. xlv, 194 p. : port. ; 23 cm. Originally published in 1956 in a shorter version that contained only "Writing on the wall." This updated version also includes its sequel, "Advent," published here for the first time. "Freud's letters to H. D.": p. 189-194. Includes bibliographical references. [RC504.D66 1974] 73-81064 ISBN 0-87923-074-6 : 10.00
1. Freud, Sigmund, 1856-1939. 2. Psychoanalysis—Cases, clinical reports, statistics. I. H. D. II. D., H. III. Title. BIP

DUKE, Michael Hare. 150'.19'52 B
Sigmund Freud. Valley Forge, Pa., Judson Press [1972] 56 p. 19 cm. (Makers of modern thought) Bibliography: p. 56. [BF173.F85D8 1972] 76-182460 ISBN 0-8170-0558-7 1.50
1. Freud, Sigmund, 1856-1939. 2. Psychoanalysis.

FINE, Reuben, 1914- 131.3462
Freud: a critical re-evaluation of his theories. New York, D. McKay Co. [1962] 307 p. 22 cm. Includes bibliography. [BF173.F85F5] 62-18462
1. Freud, Sigmund, 1856-1939.

FREEMAN, Lucy. 150.19'52'0924
Exploring the mind of man; Sigmund Freud and the age of psychology. New York, Grosset & Dunlap [1969] 150 p. illus. 24 cm. (Crosscurrents of the twentieth century) Bibliography: p. 146. [BF173.F85F67] 68-29976 4.50
1. Freud, Sigmund, 1856-1939. 2. Psychoanalysis—History. I. Title.

FREUD: v. 12
the mind of the moralist. Garden City, Doubleday, 1961. xxvi, 441p. 18cm. (Anchor book A278) Includes bibliography.
1. Freud, Sigmund, 1856-1939. I. Rieff, Philip, 1922- II. Title: The mind of the moralist. BIP

FREUD, Sigmund, 1856-1939 926.1
An autobiographical study; authorized tr. by James Strachev. New York, Norton [c.1952, 1963] 141p. 20cm. (N146) 1.25 pap.,
1. Psychoanalysis. I. Title.

FREUD, Sigmund, 1856-1939. v. 12
An autobiographical study. Authorized translation by James Strachey. New York, Norton [1963] 141 p. 20 cm. (The Norton Library, N146) "Appeared originally in 1925 in volume IV of Die Medizin der Gegenwart in Selbstdarstellungen (Leipzig: Felix Meiner)" 64-28772
1. Freud, Sigmund, 1856-1939. 2. Psychoanalysis. I. Title. BIP

FREUD, Sigmund, 1856-1939 926.1
Letters. Selected, ed. by Ernst L. Freud. Tr. by Tania & James Stern. New York, McGraw [1964, c.1960] viii, 470p. illus., ports., facsims. 21cm. Bibl. 2.95 pap.,
I. Title.

FREUD, Sigmund, 1856-1939. 926.1
Letters. Selected and edited by Ernst L. Freud. Translated by Tania & James Stern. [1st ed.] New York, Basic Books [1960] viii, 470 p. illus., ports, facsims. 25 cm. "Bibliography and acknowledgments": p. 461-462. [BF173.F85A43] 60-13282
I. Title.

FREUD, Sigmund, 1856-1939. 150'.19'52 B
Letters of Sigmund Freud / selected and edited by Ernst L. Freud ; translated by Tania & James Stern ; introd. by Steven Marcus. New York : Basic Books, 1975, c1960. p. cm. Translation of Briefe 1873-1939. Includes bibliographical references. [BF173.F85A43 1975] 74-28069 ISBN 0-465-09704-9 pbk. : 5.95
1. Freud, Sigmund, 1856-1939. 2. Psychoanalysts—Correspondence, reminiscences, etc. I. Freud, Ernst L., 1892-1970, ed. II. Title. BIP

FREUD, the fusion of science and humanism : the intellectual history of psychoanalysis / edited by John E. Gedo and George H. Pollock. New York : International Universities Press, c1976. 447 p. ; 23 cm. (Psychological issues ; v. 9, no. 2/3 : Monograph ; 34-35) Includes index. Bibliography: p. 426-438. [BF173.F85F742] 75-792 ISBN 0-8236-2030-1 : 12.50 150'.19'52
1. Freud, Sigmund, 1856-1939. 2. Psychoanalysis—History—Addresses, essays, lectures. I. Gedo, John E. II. Pollock, George H. III. Series.
Contents omitted BIP

GRINSTEIN, Alexander. 154.6'3'0924
On Sigmund Freud's dreams. Detroit, Wayne State University Press, 1968. 475 p. illus., ports. 24 cm. [BF1078.F762G7] 68-10321 17.50
1. Freud, Sigmund, 1856-1939. Die Traumdeutung. 2. Freud, Sigmund, 1856-1939. Uberden Traum. 3. Dreams—Case studies. I. Title. BIP

JONES, Ernest, 1879- 921.36
The life and work of Sigmund Freud. [1st ed.] New York, Basic Books [1953-57] 3v. illus., ports. 24cm. Contents.v. 1. The formative years and the great discoveries, 1856-1900.-- v. 2. Years of maturity, 1901-1919.--v. 3. The last phase, 1919-1939. Includes bibliographical references. [BF173.F85J6] 926.1 53-8700
1. Freud, Sigmund, 1856-1939. I. Title.

JONES, Ernest, 1879-1958. 926.1
The life and work of Sigmund Freud. Edited and abridged by Lionel Trilling & Steven Marcus. With an introd. by Lionel Trilling. New York, Basic Books [1961] 541 p. illus. 25 cm. [BF173.F85J612] 61-15950
1. Freud, Sigmund, 1856-1939.

JONES, Ernest, 1879-1958. v. 12
The life and work of Sigmund Freud. Edited and abridged by Lionel Trilling & Steven Marcus. With an introd. by Lionel Trilling. Garden City, New York, Doubleday [1963] 532 p. illus. 25 cm. (Anchor books) 64-13232
1. Freud, Sigmund, 1856-1939. I. Title. BIP

JONES, Ernest, 1879-1958. 926.1
The life and work of Sigmund Freud. [1st ed.] New York, Basic Books [1953-57] 3 v. illus., ports. 24 cm. Contents.Contents.—v. 1. The formative years and the great discoveries, 1856-1900.—v. 2. Years of maturity, 1901-1919.—v. 3. The last phase, 1919-1939. Includes bibliographical references. [BF173.F85J6] 921.36 53-8700
1. Freud, Sigmund, 1856-1939.

JONES, Ernest [Alfred Ernest Jones] 1879-1958 926.1
The life and work of Sigmund Freud. Ed., abridged by Lionel Trilling, Stevens Marcus. Introd. by Lionel Trilling. Garden City, N. Y., Doubleday [1963, c.1953-1961] 532p. illus. 18cm. (Anchor bk., A340) 1.95 pap.,
1. Freud, Sigmund, 1856-1939. I. Title.

KLAGSBRUN, Francine. 92
Sigmund Freud. New York, F. Watts [1967] ix, 150 p. 22 cm. (Immortals of science) Bibliography: p. vii-ix. Biography of the Viennese doctor, who through exploration of the mind, found a new method for treating emotional and mental disturbances. [BF173.F85K55] AC 67
1. Freud, Sigmund, 1856-1939.

KUSHNER, Martin D. 150.19'52
Freud, a man obsessed, by Martin D. Kushner. Philadelphia, Dorrance [1967] 151 p. 21 cm. [BF173.F85K8] 67-12228
1. Freud, Sigmund, 1856-1939. I. Title.

LAUZON, Gerard 926.1
Sigmund Freud, the man and his theories. Tr. [from French] by Patrick Evans [1st Amer. ed.] New York, Eriksson [dist. Taplinger, 1965, c.1962] 224p. illus., facsims., ports. 24cm. (Profile in sci.) Bibl. [BF173.F85L313] 64-22733 5.00
1. Freud, Sigmund, 1856-1939. I. Title.

*LUDWIG, Emil, 1881-1948. 150.195'2
Doctor Freud [by] Emil Ludwig. [New York] Manor Books [1973] 317 p. 18 cm. [BF173] 1.25 (pbk)
1. Freud, Sigmund, 1856-1939. I. Title. BIP

MANNONI, O. 150'.19'52
Freud [by] O. Mannoni. Translated from the French by Renaud Bruce. New York, Vintage Books [1974, c1971] 215 p. 19 cm. Includes bibliographical references. [BF173.F85M2813 1974] 73-14946 ISBN 0-394-71006-1 1.95 (pbk.)
1. Freud, Sigmund, 1856-1939. 2. Psychoanalysis.

MILLER, Jonathan, 1934- 150'.19'52 B
Freud: the man, his world, his influence, edited by Jonathan Miller. [1st American ed.] Boston, Little, Brown [1972] xi, 180 p. illus. 26 cm. Includes bibliographical references. [BF173.F85M47 1972] 72-3607 14.95
1. Freud, Sigmund, 1856-1939. I. Title.

MORRIS, Nat. 150'.19'52 B
A man possessed; the case history of Sigmund Freud. Los Angeles, Regent House [1974] viii, 160 p. 23 cm. Includes bibliographical references. [BF173.F85M63] 73-92383 ISBN 0-911238-53-0 7.95
1. Freud, Sigmund, 1856-1939. I. Title. II. Title: The case history of Sigmund Freud. BIP

NELSON, Benjamin N., 1911- ed. 131.3462
Freud and the 20th century. New York, Meridian Books, 1957. 314 p. illus. 19 cm. (Meridian books, M45) Includes bibliography. [BF173.F85N37] 57-6682
1. Freud, Sigmund, 1856-1939. I. Title.

THE psychoanalytic revolution; Sigmund Freud's life and achievement. Tr. by Kenneth Morgan. New York, Avon [1968, c.1966] 384p. 18cm. (Discus Bks. W127) Orig. pub. by Payot, Paris, 1964 under the title La revolution psychanalytique. [BF173.F85R633 1966] (B) 1.25 pap., 616.89170924
1. Freud, Sigmund, 1856-1939. I. Robert, Marthe.

PUNER, Helen Walker. v. 12
Freud, his life and his mind; a biography. Laurel ed. New York, Dell, [1947:1961] 288 p. 16 cm. (Dell LC137) Includes bibliography. 65-81084
1. Freud, Sigmund, 1856-1939 I. Title.

ROAZEN, Paul, 1936- 150.19'52'0922
Brother animal: the story of Freud and Tausk. [1st ed.] New York, Knopf; [distributed by Random House] 1969. xx, 221, v p. facsim., ports. 22 cm. Bibliographical references included in "Notes" (p. 207-221) [BF173.F85R56 1969] 77-79333 5.95
1. Freud, Sigmund, 1856-1939. 2. Tausk, Victor, 1879-1919. I. Title.

ROAZEN, Paul, 1936- 150'.19'52
Freud and his followers. [1st ed.] New York, Knopf, 1975 [c1974] xxxiv, 602, xiii p. illus. 24 cm. Includes bibliographical references. [BF173.R55 1975] 73-20782 ISBN 0-394-48896-2
1. Freud, Sigmund, 1856-1939. 2. Psychoanalysis. I. Title. BIP

ROAZEN, Paul, 1936- comp. 300'.92'4
Sigmund Freud. Englewood Cliffs, N.J., Prentice-Hall [1973] vi, 186 p. 21 cm. (A Spectrum book) (Makers of modern social science) Bibliography: p. 182-184. [BF173.F85R585] 73-14880 ISBN 0-13-332361-7 6.95
1. Freud, Sigmund, 1856-1939. 2. Social sciences—Addresses, essays, lectures. I. Title. II. Series.
Pbk. 2.95, ISBN 0-13-332353-6.

ROBERT, Marthe. 150'.19'52
From Oedipus to Moses : Freud's Jewish identity / by Marthe Robert ; translated by Ralph Manheim. 1st ed. Garden City, N.Y. : Anchor Books, 1976. 229 p. ; 18 cm. Translation od D'Odipe a Moise. Includes bibliographical references and index. [BF173.F85R6213] 76-3125 ISBN 0-385-00064-2 pbk. : 2.95

1. Freud, Sigmund, 1856-1939. 2. Jews—Psychology. 3. Psychoanalysis. I. Title.

ROBERT, Marthe. 616.89170924
The psychoanalytic revolution; Sigmund Freud's life and achievement. Translated by Kenneth Morgan. [1st American ed.] New York, Harcourt, Brace & World [1966] 396 p. 22 cm. Bibliographical footnotes. [BF173.F85R633] 66-15017
1. Freud, Sigmund, 1856-1939. I. Title.

ROBERT, Marthe. 616.89170924 B
The psychoanalytic revolution; Sigmund Freud's life and achievement. Translated by Kenneth Morgan. [1st American ed.] New York, Harcourt, Brace & World [1966] 396 p. 22 cm. Bibliographical footnotes. [BF173.F85R633 1966] 88-15017
1. Freud, Sigmund, 1856-1939. I. Title.

ROBERT, Marthe. 131.3463
The psychoanalytic revolution: Sigmund Freud's life and achievement; translated [from the French] by Kenneth Morgan. London, Allen & Unwin [1966] 3-396 p. 22 1/2 cm. 50/ -- Bibliographical footnotes. [BF173.F85R633] [616.89170924 (B)] 66-67719
1. Freud, Sigmund, 1856-1939. I. Title.

SACHS, Hanns, 1881-1947. 150.19'52'0924 B
Freud, master and friend. Freeport, N.Y., Books for Libraries Press [1970, c1944] 192 p. illus., ports. 23 cm. [BF173.F85S2 1970] 78-133531
1. Freud, Sigmund, 1856-1939. I. Title. BIP

SCHOENWALD, Richard L 1927- 131.3462
Freud, the man and his mind, 1856-1956. [1st ed.] New York, Knopf, 1956. 250p. illus. 22cm. [BF173.F89S35] 56-5798
1. Freud, Sigmund. 1856-1939. I. Title.

SCHUR, Max. 150'.19'52 B
Freud: living and dying. New York, International Universities Press [1972] xiii, 587 p. 24 cm. Bibliography: p. 568-573. [BF109.F74S38] 71-143379 ISBN 0-8236-2025-5 20.00
1. Freud, Sigmund, 1856-1939. I. Title.

SIGMUND Freud: 921.36
reminiscences of a friendship. Translated by Norbert Guterman. New York, Grune & Stratton, 1957. 106p. illus. 23cm. Translation of Erinnerungen an Sigmund Freud. [BF173.F85B52] [BF173.F85B52] 926.1 57-8360 57-8360
1. Freud, Sigmund, 1856-1939. I. Binswanger, Ludwig, 1881-

SIGMUND Freud : 150'.19'52 B
his life in pictures and words / edited by Ernst Freud, Lucie Freud, and Ilse Grubrich-Simitis ; with a biographical sketch by K. R. Eissler ; translation by Christine Trollope ; design by Willy Fleckhaus. New York : Harcourt Brace Jovanovich, c1978. 350 p. : ill. ; 30 cm. "A Helen and Kurt Wolff book." Includes bibliographical references and index. [BF173.F85S537] 78-110889 ISBN 0-15-182546-7 : 39.95
1. Freud, Sigmund, 1856-1939. 2. Psychoanalysts—Austria—Biography. I. Freud, Ernst L., 1892-1970. II. Freud, Lucie, 1896- III. Grubrich-Simitis, Ilse. BIP

SPECTOR, Jack J. 150'.19'52
The aesthetics of Freud; a study in psychoanalysis and art [by] Jack J. Spector. New York, Praeger [1973, c1972] xiv, 242 p. illus. 24 cm. Bibliography: p. [226]-237. [BF173.F85S62] 70-168347 8.95
1. Freud, Sigmund, 1856-1939. 2. Psychoanalysis and art. I. Title. BIP

STOUTENBURG, Adrien. 926.1
Explorer of the unconscious: Sigmund Freud, by Adrien Stoutenburg and Laura Nelson Baker. New York, Scribner [1965] 202 p. port. 21 cm. Bibliography: p. 191-192. [BF173.F85S76] 65-14772
1. Freud, Sigmund, 1856-1939. I. Baker, Laura Nelson, 1911- joint author. II. Title.

Freud, Sigmund, 1856-1939—Comic books, strips, etc.

APPIGNANESI, Richard. 150'.19'52
Freud for beginners / text by Richard Appignanesi, ill. by Oscar Zarate. 1st American ed. New York : Pantheon Books, c1979. 174 p. : ill. ; 21 cm. Bibliography: p. 174. [BF173.F85A63 1979] 79-1891 ISBN 0-394-50590-5 : 8.95. ISBN 0-394-73800-4 pbk. : 2.95
1. Freud, Sigmund, 1856-1939—Comic books, strips, etc. 2. Psychoanalysts—Austria—Biography—Comic books, strips, etc. 3. Psychoanalysis—Comic books, strips, etc. I. Zarate, Oscar, 1942- joint author. II. Title. BIP

Freud, Sigmund, 1856-1939—Juvenile literature.

KLAGSBRUN, Francine. 616.891700924 B
Sigmund Freud. New York, F. Watts [1967] ix, 150 p. 22 cm. (Immortals of science) Bibliography: p. vii-ix. [BF173.F85K55] 67-10229
1. Freud, Sigmund, 1856-1939—Juvenile literature.

MANN, John Harvey 920
Sigmund Freud. doctor of secrets and dreams, by John H. Mann. Illus. by Clare Romano Ross, John Ross. New York, Macmillan [c.1964. 48]p. col. illus. 24cm. (Sci. story lib.) 63-16368 2.95
1. Freud, Sigmund, 1856-1939—Juvenile literature. I. Title.

MCGLASHAN, Agnes M. 150'.19'52
Sigmund Freud; founder of psychoanalysis [by] Agnes M. McGlashan and Christopher J. Reeve. New York, Praeger Publishers [1970] ix, 148 p. illus., ports. 23 cm. (Praeger pathfinder biographies) Bibliography: p. 143-144. [BF173.F85M225 1970] 69-12716 4.95
1. Freud, Sigmund, 1856-1939—Juvenile literature. I. Reeve, Christopher J., joint author.

NEIMARK, Anne E. 150'.19'52
Sigmund Freud : the world within / Anne E. Neimark. 1st ed. New York : Harcourt Brace Jovanovich, c1976. 120 p. : port. ; 22 cm. Includes index. Bibliography: p. [115]-116. A biography of the world-famous Austrian doctor who spent his life analyzing the mind and its illnesses. [BF173.F85N35] 92 76-18713 ISBN 0-15-274164-X : 6.95
1. Freud, Sigmund, 1856-1939—Juvenile literature. I. Title. BIP

Freund, Ernst, 1864-1932.

KRAINES, Oscar, 1916- 340'.0973
The world and ideas of Ernst Freund: the search for general principles of legislation and administrative law. University, University of Alabama Press [1974] ix, 221 p. port. 22 cm. "Bibliography; the published writings of Ernst Freund": p. 168-173. [KF373.F75K7] 73-22719 ISBN 0-8173-4819-0 8.00
1. Freund, Ernst, 1864-1932. 2. Legislation—United States. 3. Administrative law—United States. I. Title. Pbk. 3.50, ISBN 0-8173-4822-0 BIP

Frewen, Moreton, 1853-1924.

ANDREWS, Allen. 942.081'0924 B
The splendid pauper. Philadelphia, Lippincott [1968] 255 p. illus., facisms., ports. 21 cm. [DA565.F85A6 1968b] 68-13320
1. Frewen, Moreton, 1853-1924. I. Title.

Freyberg, Bernard Cyril, baron, 1889-

STEVENS, William George 1893- 923.5931
Freyberg, V. C.; the man, 1939-1945. Wellington, A. H. & A. W. Reed [dist. San Francisco, Tri-Ocean, c.1965] 130p. ports. 23cma. Bibl. [DA69.3.F7S58] 65-8637 3.35 bds.,
1. Freyberg, Bernard Cyril, baron, 1889- I. Title.

Friars

SMALLEY, Beryl. 922.42
English friars and antiquity in the early fourteenth century. New York, Barnes & Noble [1961,c.1960] xvi, 398p. facsim. Bibl. 61-3057 9.00
1. Friars 2. Latin literature—hist. & crit. I. Title.

Fricker, E. G., 1910-

FRICKER, E. G., 1910- 615'.852'0924 B
God is my witness : the story of the World-fanous healer / E. G. Fricker. New York : Stein and Day, 1977. 190 p. ; 22 cm. Autobiography. [RZ408.F74A33] 76-50557 8.95
1. Fricker, E. G., 1910- 2. Healers—England—Biography. 3. Mental healing. I. Title.

Friedberg, Carl, 1872-1955.

SMITH, Julia Frances, 1911- 927.8
Master pianist; the career and teaching of Carl Friedberg. New York, Philosophical [c.1963] 183p. illus. 21cm. Bibl. 62-18548 4.50
1. Friedberg, Carl, 1872-1955. I. Title.

Friedenwald, Hary, 1864-1950.

LEVIN, Alexandra Lee 926.1
Vision; a biography of Hary Friedenwald. Philadelphia, Jewish Pubn. Soc. [c.]1964. xviii, 469p. illus., geneal. table, ports. 22cm. (Jacob R. Schiff lib. of Jewish contributions to Amer. democracy, no. 21) Bibl. 64-16758 5.00
1. Friedenwald, Hary, 1864-1950. I. Title. II. Series.

Friedlander, Saul, 1932—

FRIEDLANDER, Saul, 1932- 944'.004'924 B
When memory comes / Saul Friedlander ; translated from the French by Helen R. Lane. New York : Farrar, Straus, Giroux, [1979] p. cm. Translation of Quand vient le souvenir ... [DS135.F9F74513] 79-12005 ISBN 0 374-28898-4 : 8.95
1. Friedlander, Saul, 1932- 2. Jews in France—Biography. 3. Holocaust, Jewish (1939-1945)—France—Personal narratives. 4. France—Biography. I. Title. BIP

Friedman, Samuel, 1874 or 5-1947.

FRIEDMAN, Leonard Seymour 610.924
The angel cometh; a biography of Samuel Friedman, M. D. New York, Living Bks. [c.1966] 157p. facsims., ports. 23cm. [R154.F855F7] 65-28416 4.95
1. Friedman, Samuel, 1874 or 5-1947. I. Title.

Friedman, William Frederick, 1891-1969.

CLARK, Ronald William. 358'.24 B
The man who broke Purple : a life of the world's greatest cryptographer, Colonel William F. Friedman / by Ronald Clark. 1st American ed. Boston : Little, Brown, c1977. p. cm. Includes index. [UB290.C58 1977] 77-10004 ISBN 0-316-14595-5 : 8.95
1. Friedman, William Frederick, 1891-1969. 2. Cryptographers—United States—Biography. I. Title.

Friedreich's ataxia—Biography.

SCHUT, Henry J. 616.8'3 B
Ten years to live / Henry J. Schut. Grand Rapids : Baker Book House, c1978. 162 p., [4] leaves of plates : ill. ; 22 cm. [RC406.F7S38] 78-103036 ISBN 0-8010-8127-0 : 7.95
1. Friedreich's ataxia—Biography. I. Title. BIP

Friedrich August I, der Starke, Elector of Saxony and King of Poland, 1670-1733.

POLLNITZ, Karl Ludwig, Freiherr von, 1692-1775. 943.8'02 B
La Saxe galante; or, The amorous adventures and intrigues of Frederick-Augustus II. With a new introd. for the Garland ed. by Josephine Grieder. [Translated from the French, by a gentleman of Oxford]. New York, Garland Pub., 1972. 12, 307 p. 22 cm. (Foundations of the novel) Reprint of the 1734 ed. [DD801.S396P72 1972] 78-170589 ISBN 0-8240-0571-6 22.00 ea.
1. Friedrich August I, der Starke, Elector of Saxony and King of Poland, 1670-1733. I. Title. II. Series.
Part of 71 vol. series 1400.00 set.

Friedrich, Caspar David, 1774-1840.

FRIEDRICH, Caspar David, 1774-1840. 759.3
Caspar David Friedrich / edited by Jorg Traeger. New York : Rizzoli, c1976. 97 p. : ill. (some col.) ; 25 cm. English, German and French. [ND588.F75T7] 76-151002 ISBN 0-8478-0033-4 : 16.50
1. Friedrich, Caspar David, 1774-1840. 2. Painters—Germany—Biography. I. Traeger, Jorg, 1942- BIP

FRIEDRICH, Caspar David, 1774-1840. 759.3
Caspar David Friedrich / hrsg. von Jorg Traeger ; [transl. into Engl. by Gillian Turner ; trad. francaise par Denise Baumann]. Munchen : Bruckmann, 1976. 97 p. : chiefly ill. (some col.) ; 25 cm. English, French, and German. [ND588.F75T7 1976b] 77-484085 ISBN 3-7654-1649-5 : DM35.00
1. Friedrich, Caspar David, 1774-1840. 2. Painters—Germany—Biography. I. Traeger, Jorg, 1942-

JENSEN, Jens Christian. 759.3 B
Caspar David Friedrich : life and work / Jens Christian Jensen ; translated from the German by Joachim Neugroschel. 1st English-language ed. Woodbury, N.Y. : Barron's Educational Series, 1979. p. cm. Includes index. Bibliography: p. [ND588.F75J4613 1980] 80-10830 ISBN 0-8120-2102-9 pbk : 2.95
1. Friedrich, Caspar David, 1774-1840. 2. Painters—Germany—Biography.

Friedrich I, Barbarossa, Emperor of Germany, 1121-1190.

PACAUT, Marcel. 943'.024'0924
Frederick Barbarossa. Translated by A. J. Pomerans. New York, Scribner [1970] 223 p. 2 geneal. tables, 4 maps. 23 cm. Translation of Frederic Barberousse "The first three chapters ... have been abridged from the original French edition." Bibliography: p. 213-215. [DD149.P314 1970b] 78-114083 6.95
1. Friedrich I, Barbarossa, Emperor of Germany, 1121-1190.

Friedrich II, der Grosse, King of Prussia, 1712-1786.

CARLYLE, Thomas, 1795-1881. 943'.053'0924 B
History of Friedrich II. of Prussia, called Frederick the Great. New York, Scribner. St. Clair Shores, Mich., Scholarly Press, 1972. p. (The works of Thomas Carlyle, v. 12-19) Reprint of the 1900 ed. [PR4420.F72 vol. 12-19] [DD404] 72-10645
1. Friedrich II der Grosse, King of Prussia, 1712-1786. 2. Prussia—History—Frederick II, the Great, 1740-1786. I. Title.

CARLYLE, Thomas, 1795-1881. 943'.053'0924
History of Friedrich II of Prussia, called Frederick the Great. Edited, and with an introd., by John Clive. Chicago, University of Chicago Press [1969] xl, 479 p. 21 cm. (Classic European historians) Selections from the original work. Includes bibliographical references. [DD404.C3423] 79-82375 ISBN 2-260-92968-
1. Friedrich II, der Grosse, King of Prussia, 1712-1786. 2. Prussia—History—Frederick II, the Great, 1740-1786. I.

Clive, John Leonard, 1924- ed. II. Title. III. Series.

CARLYLE, Thomas, 1795- 824'.8 S 1881.
History of Friedrich II. of Prussia, called Frederick the Great. New York, AMS Press [1974] 8 v. illus. 23 cm. (The works of Thomas Carlyle, v. 12-19) (Series: Carlyle, Thomas, 1795-1881. Works. 1974. vols. 12-19.) Reprint of the 1897-98 ed. published by Chapman and Hall, London. Includes bibliographical references. [PR4420.F74 vols. 12-19] [DD404] 943'.053'0924 B 74-3165 17.50 per vol.
1. Friedrich II, der Grosse, King of Prussia, 1712-1786. 2. Prussia—History—Frederick II, the Great, 1740-1786. I. Title. II. Series.

DODGE, Theodore 355.3'32'0922 Ayrault, 1842-1909.
Great captains; showing the influence on the art of war of the campaigns of Alexander, Hannibal, Caesar, Gustavus Adolphus, Frederick, and Napoleon. Port Washington, N.Y., Kennikat Press [1968, c1889] xiii, 219 p. illus., maps. 21 cm. [U51.D6 1968] 67-27591
1. Alexander the Great—Campaigns. 2. Hannibal. 3. Caesar, C. Julius. 4. Gustaf II Adolf, King of Sweden, 1594-1632. 5. Friedrich II, der Grosse, King of Prussia, 1712-1821. 6. Napoleon I, Emperor of the French, 1769-1821. 7. Military biography. I. Title.

GAXOTTE, Pierre. 943'.053'0924 B
Frederic the Great / by Pierre Gaxotte ; translated by R. A. Bell. Westport, Conn. : Greenwood Press, 1975, c1942. p. cm. Translation of Frederic II. Reprint of the ed. published by Yale University Press, New Haven. Bibliography: p. [DD404.G32 1975] 75-16845 ISBN 0-8371-8269-7 lib.bdg. : 21.00
1. Friedrich II, der Grosse, King or Prussia, 1712-1786. 2. Friedrich Wilhelm I, King of Prussia, 1688-1740. 3. Prussia—History—Frederick II, the Great, 1740-1786.

GAXOTTE, Pierre. 943'.053'0924 B
Frederic the Great / by Pierre Gaxotte ; translated by R. A. Bell. Westport, Conn. : Greenwood Press, 1975, c1942. 420 p., [8] leaves of plates : ill. ; 22 cm. Translation of Frederic II. Reprint of the ed. published by Yale University Press, New Haven. Includes index. Bibliography: p. [397]-410. [DD404.G32 1975] 75-16845 ISBN 0-8371-8269-7
1. Friedrich II, der Grosse, King or Prussia, 1712-1786. 2. Friedrich Wilhelm I, King of Prussia, 1688-1740. 3. Prussia—History—Frederick II, the Great, 1740-1786.

GOOCH, George Peabody, 923.143 1873-1968.
Frederick the Great; the ruler, the writer, the man. Hamden, Conn., Archon Books [1962] 363 p. illus. 22 cm. [DD403.G6 1962] 62-16045
1. Friedrich II, der Grosse, King of Prussia, 1712-1786.

HORN, David Bayne, 943'.053 B 1901-
Frederick the Great and the rise of Prussia, by D. B. Horn. New York, Harper & Row [1969, c1964] 180 p. 19 cm. (Perennial library, P143) [DD403] 77-7554 1.25
1. Friedrich II, der Grosse, King of Prussia, 1712-1786. 2. Prussia—History—Frederick II, the Great, 1740-1786. I. Title.

HUBATSCH, Walther. 320.9'43'053 1915-
Frederick the Great of Prussia : absolutism and administration / Walther Hubatsch. London : Thames and Hudson, c1975. 303 p., [8] leaves of plates : ill. ; 23 cm. (Men in office) Translation of Friedrich der Grosse und die preussische Verwaltung. Includes index. Bibliography: p. [256]-257. [DD403.H813] 76-352146 15.00
1. Friedrich II, der Grosse, King of Prussia, 1712-1786. 2. Prussia—Politics and government—1740-1786.
Distributed by Transatlantic Arts

LAVISSE, Ernest, 943'.053'0924 B 1842-1922.
The youth of Frederick the Great. Translated from the French by Mary Bushnell Coleman. Chicago, S. C. Griggs, 1892. [New York, AMS Press, 1972] xv, 445 p. front. 19 cm. Translation of La jeunesse du Grand Frederic. [DD404.L413 1972] 71-172308 ISBN 0-404-03891-3 12.50
1. Friedrich II, der Grosse, King of Prussia, 1712-1786. I. Title. BIP

MACAULAY, Thomas 943'.053'0924 B Babington Macaulay, Baron, 1800-1859.
An essay on Frederic the Great / by Thomas Babington Macaulay ; with biographical sketch of Macaulay and with explanatory and biographical notes. New York : AMS Press, 1975. 103 p. ; 19 cm. Originally published in 1878 under title: Frederic the Great. Reprint of the 1893 ed. published by Maynard, Merrill, New York, which was issued as no. 108-109 of English classic series. [DD404.M2 1975] 73-137257 ISBN 0-404-04100-0 : 6.00
1. Friedrich II, der Grosse, King of Prussia, 1712-1786. I. Title. BIP

PARET, Peter, comp. 943'.05300994
Frederick the Great; a profile. [1st ed.] New York, Hill and Wang [1972] xxi, 249 p. 22 cm. (World profiles) Bibliography: p. 241-244. [DD404.P18 1972] 72-184945 ISBN 0-8090-4678-4 7.95
1. Friedrich II, der Grosse, King of Prussia, 1712-1786.
Pap. $2.95, ISBN0-8090-1402-5 BIP

REDDAWAY, William 943'.053'0924 B Fiddian, 1872-1949.
Frederick the Great and the rise of Prussia. New York, Haskell House, 1969. xi, 368 p. illus., maps, ports. 23 cm. Reprint of the 1904 ed. [DD404.R3 1969] 68-25262
1. Friedrich II, der Grosse, King of Prussia, 1712-1786. 2. Prussia—History—Frederick II, the Great, 1740-1786. I. Title.

REDDAWAY, William 943'.053'0924 B Fiddian, 1872-1949.
Frederick the Great and the rise of Prussia. London, Putnam [1904] St. Clair Shores, Mich., Scholarly Press [1969?] xi, 368 p. illus., maps (part col.), ports. 22 cm. [DD404.R3 1969c] 70-8340
1. Friedrich II, der Grosse, King of Prussia, 1712-1786. 2. Prussia—History—Frederick II, the Great, 1740-1786. I. Title. BIP

REINERS, Ludwig, 1896- 923.143 1957.
Frederick the Great, a biography. Translated and adapted from the German by Lawrence P. R. Wilson. New York, Putnam [1960] 304 p. illus. 22 cm. Translation of Friedrich. [DD404.R373 1960a] 60-13438
1. Friedrich II, der Grosse, King of Prussia, 1712-1786.

RITTER, Gerhard 943.0530924
Frederick the Great; a historical profile. Translated with an introduction, by Peter Paret. Berkeley, University of California Press [1974, c1968] xiv, 207 p. 22 cm. [DD404.R513] 68-15815 ISBN 0-520-02775-2 2.85 (pbk.)
1. Friedrich II, der Grosse, King of Prussia, 1712-1786 I. Title. BIP

SIMON, Edith 923.143
The making of Frederick the Great. Boston, Little, [c.1963] 296p. illus., maps. 22cm. Bibl. 63-8963 6.50
1. Friedrich II, der Grosse, King of Prussia, 1772-1786. I. Title. BIP

SIMON, Edith, 943'.053'0924 B 1917-
The making of Frederick the Great / by Edith Simon. Westport, Conn. : Greenwood Press, [1977, c1963] p. cm. Reprint of the ed. published by Little, Brown, Boston. Includes index. Bibliography: p. [DD404.S57 1977] 76-51768 ISBN 0-8371-9440-7 lib.bdg. : 19.00
1. Friedrich II, der Grosse, King of Prussia, 1712-1786. 2. Prussia—Kings and rulers—Biography. 3. Prussia—History—Frederick II, the Great, 1740-1786. I. Title.

SNYDER, Louis 943'.053'0924 B Leo, 1907- comp.
Frederick the Great. Edited by Louis L. Snyder. Englewood Cliffs, N.J., Prentice-Hall [1971] viii, 182 p. 21 cm. (Great lives observed) (A Spectrum book.) Includes bibliographical references. [DD404.S59] 79-133053
1. Friedrich II, der Grosse, King of Prussia, 1712-1786. I. Title. BIP

SNYDER, Louis 943'.053'0924 B Leo, 1907-
Frederick the Great; Prussian warrior and statesman, by Louis L. Snyder and Ida Mae Brown. New York, F. Watts [1968] 177 p. illus., facsim., map, ports. 22 cm. (Immortals of history) [DD404.S6] 68-24122
1. Friedrich II, der Grosse, King of Prussia, 1712-1786. I. Brown, Ida Mae, joint author.

WRIGHT, Constance. 923.143
A royal affinity; the story of Frederick the Great and his sister, Wilhelmina of Bayreuth. New York, Scribner [1965] viii, 309 p. illus., geneal. table, ports. 24 cm. Bibliography: p. 295-299. [DD404.W86] 65-13663
1. Friedrich II, der Grosse, King of Prussia, 1712-1786. 2. Wilhelmine, consort of Frederick William, margrave of Bayreuth, 1709-1758. I. Title.

Friedrich II, Emperor of Germany, 1194-1250.

KANTOROWICZ, Ernst, 1895- 923.143
Frederick the Second, 1194-1250. Authorized English version by E. O. Lorimer. New York, F. Ungar Pub. Co. [1957] xxvii, 724p. maps (part fold.) 22cm. Bibliography: p.xxv-xxvii. [DD151.K33 1957] 57-9408
1. Friedrich II, Emperor of Germany, 1194-1250. 2. Germany—Hist.— Frederick II, 1215-1250. 3. Holy Roman Empire—Hist.—Frederick II, 1215-1250. I. Title.

KANTOROWICZ, Ernst 923.143 Hartwig, 1895-
Frederick the Second, 1194-1250. Authorized English version by E. O. Lorimer. New York, Ungar [1957] xxvii, 724p. maps (part fold.) 22cm. Bibliography: p. xxv-xxvii. [DD151.K33 1957] 57-9408
1. Friedrich II, Emperor of Germany, 1194-1250. 2. Germany—Hist.—Frederick II, 1215- 1250. 3. Holy Roman Empire—Hist.—Frederick II, 1215-1250. I. Title.

MASSON, Georgina. 943'.025'0924 B
Frederick II of Hohenstaufen, a life New York, Octagon Books, 1973 [c1957] 376 p. illus. 23 cm. Reprint of the ed. published by Secker & Warburg, London. Bibliography: p. 368-370. [DD151.M3 1973] 73-5939 ISBN 0-374-95297-3 15.00
1. Friedrich II, Emperor of Germany, 1194-1250.

VAN CLEVE, Thomas 943'.025'0924 B Curtis, 1888
The Emperor Frederick II of Hohenstaufen, immutator mundi. Oxford, Clarendon Press, 1972. xx, 607 p. illus. 24 cm. Bibliography: p. [556]-598. [DD151.V34] 73-150754 ISBN 0-19-822513-X 19.95
1. Friedrich II, Emperor of Germany, 1194-1250. I. Title.
Distributed by Oxford University Press N.Y.

Friedrich III, German Emperor, 1831-1888.

ARONSON, Theo. 943.08'3'0922
The kaisers. Indianapolis, Bobbs-Merrill [1971] xii, 276 p. illus., ports. 22 cm. Bibliography: p. [261]-269. [DD370.A7 1971b] 74-142483 8.95
1. Wilhelm I, German Emperor, 1797-1888. 2. Friedrich III, German Emperor, 1831-1888. 3. Wilhelm II, German Emperor, 1859-1941. I. Title.

FRIEDRICH III, German 943.08'2 Emperor, 1831-1888.
The war diary of the Emperor Frederick III, 1870-1871. Translated and edited by A. R. Allinson. Westport, Conn., Greenwood Press [1971] xi, 355 p. illus., map, ports. 23 cm. Translation of Das Kriegstagebuch von 1870/71. Reprint of the 1926 ed. [DC285.F7513 1971] 77-114529 ISBN 0-8371-4824-3
1. Franco-German War, 1870-1871.

POSCHINGER, 943.08'4'0924 B Margarete (Landau) Edle von, 1862-
Life of the Emperor Frederick. Edited from the German of Margaretha von Poschinger. With an introd. by Sidney Whitman. New York, AMS Press [1971] xiv, 459 p. port. 23 cm. Translation of Kaiser Friedrich. Reprint of the 1901 ed. Includes bibliographical references. [DD224.P85 1971] 72-151599 ISBN 0-404-05089-1
1. Friedrich III, German Emperor, 1831-1888. 2. Germany—History—1789-1900. BIP

Friedrich Wilhelm, Elector of Brandenburg, called the Great Elector, 1620-1688.

SCHEVILL, Ferdinand, 923.143 1868-1954
The Great Elector. [Reprinted in an unaltered, unabridged ed.] Hamden. Conn., Archon [dist. Shoe String, 1965, c.1947] ix, 442p. illus., maps, ports. 23cm. Bibl. [DD394.S4] 65-16972 12.00
1. Friedrich Wilhelm, Elector of Brandenburg, called the Great Elector, 1620-1688. I. Title.

Friedrich Wilhelm I, King of Prussia, 1688-1740.

ERGANG, Robert 943'.052'0924 B Reinhold, 1898-
The Potsdam fuhrer: Frederick William I, father of Prussian militarism, by Robert Ergang. New York, Octagon Books, 1973 [c1941] 290 p. 23 cm. Bibliography: p. [257]-270. [DD399.E7 1972] 72-8922 ISBN 0-374-92623-9 10.25
1. Friedrich Wilhelm I, King of Prussia, 1688-1740. 2. Militarism—Prussia. I. Title.

Friend, J. B. B.

FRIEND, J. B. B. 269'.2'0924 B
Gipsy for Jesus / [by] J. B. B. Friend. Stoke-on-Trent : M.O.V.E. Press, 1976. 67 p. ; 19 cm. [BR1725.F63A33] 76-380849 ISBN 0-9504136-3-1 : £0.50
1. Friend, J. B. B. 2. Christian biography—South Africa. I. Title.

Friends, Society of.

WATKINS, Owen C. 285'.9
The Puritan experience; studies in spiritual autobiography [by] Owen C. Watkins. New York, Schocken Books [1972, c1971] x, 270 p. 23 cm. Bibliography: p. 241-260. [BX9322.W36 1972b] 70-150987 ISBN 0-8052-3425-X
1. Friends, Society of. 2. Puritans. 3. Witness bearing (Christianity) I. Title. BIP

Friends, Society of — Biog.

BRINTON, Anna (Cox) 922.86
Quaker profiles, pictorial and biographical, 7850-1850 [Wallingford, Pa.] Pendle Hill Pubns. [c.1964] viii, 55p. illus., ports. 13x19cm. (Pendle Hill pubns.: art hist., PH. P2) [BX7791.B7] 64-8697 1.50 pap.,
1. Friends, Society of—Biog. 2. Silhouettes. I. Title.

BRINTON, Anna (Cox) 922.86
Quaker profiles, pictorial and biographical, 1750-1850. [Wallingford, Pa.] Pendle Hill Publications [1964] viii, 55 p. illus., ports. 13 x 10 cm. (Pendle Hill publications: art history, PH. P2) [BX7791.B7] 64-8697
1. Friends, Society of — Biog. 2. Silhouettes. I. Title.

FOULDS, Elfrida Vipont 922.86 (Brown) 1902-
A faith to live by [by] Elfrida Vipont [pseud.] Philadelphia, Religious Education Committee, Friends General Conference, [c1962] 199 p. 21 cm. [BX7791.F6] 63-626
1. Friends, Society of — Biog. I. Title.

Friends, Society of—Biography.

BEST, Mary Agnes, 289.6'0922 d.1942.
Rebel saints. Freeport, N.Y., Books for Libraries Press [1968] 333 p. illus. ports. 23 cm. (Essay index reprint series) Reprint

of the 1925 ed. Bibliography: p. 333. [BX7791.B4 1968] 68-55839
1. Friends, Society of—Biography. 2. Friends, Society of—History. I. Title. BIP

ELLIOTT, Errol T. 289.6'092'4 B
Quaker profiles from the American West, by Errol T. Elliott. Richmond, Ind., Friends United Press [1972] xxii, 172 p. illus. 22 cm. [BX7791.E47] 72-5126
1. Friends, Society of—Biography. I. Title.

HAINES, Marie. 289.6'092'2 B
Brave rebels. Newberg, Or., Barclay Press [1972] xiii, 160 p. illus. 21 cm. Bibliography: p. 159-160. [BX7791.H25] 72-88677 ISBN 0-913342-02-5 4.50
1. Friends, Society of—Biography. I. Title.

JACOB, Caroline Nicholson. 922.86
Builders of the Quaker road 1652-1952 Chicago, H. Regnery Co., 1953. 233 p. 22 cm. [BX7791.J2] 53-6892
1. Friends, society of—Biography. 2. Friends, society of—History. I. Title.

Friends, Society of—Collected works.

FOX, George, 1624-1691. 289.6'092'4 S
A collection of many select and Christian epistles, letters and testimonies / written on sundry occasions by that ancient, eminent, faithful Friend, and minister of Christ Jesus, George Fox. New York : AMS Press, 1975. 2 v. ; 23 cm. (The works of George Fox ; v. 7-8) On spine: Epistles. Reprint of the 1831 ed. published by M. T. C. Gould, Philadelphia. [BX7617.F54 1975 vol. 7-8] 230'.9'6 75-16207 ISBN 0-404-09357-4 : 30.00
1. Friends, Society of—Collected works. 2. Fox, George, 1624-1691. I. Title.

WOOLMAN, John, 1720-1772. 289.6'0924 B
The works of John Woolman. 2d ed. Philadelphia, Printed by J. Crukshank, 1775. Miami, Fla., Mnemosyne Pub. Co. [1969] 2 v. in 1 (xiv, 432 p.) 23 cm. [BX7617.W6 1969] 78-83893
1. Friends, Society of—Collected works. BIP

Friends, Society of—History.

FOGELKLOU, Emilia, 1878- 289.6'0922
The atonement of George Fox [by] Emilia Fogelklou Norlind. Edited by Eleanore Price Mather. [Wallingford, Pa., Pendle Hill Publications, 1969] 31 p. 20 cm. (Pendle Hill pamphlet 166) Bibliography: p. 30-31. [BX7676.2.F6] 75-84675 0.55
1. Friends, Society of—History. 2. Fox, George, 1624-1691. 3. Nayler, James, 1617?-1660. I. Title. BIP

Friends, Society of—Missions.

HADLEY, Martha E., 1852-1915. 266.9'6'0924 B
The Alaskan diary of a pioneer Quaker missionary. [Mt. Dora, Fla., Loren S. Hadley, 1969] 210 p. illus., facsims., fold. map, ports. 28 cm. Cover title. [BV2803.A4H26 1969] 73-12622 3.75
1. Friends, Society of—Missions. 2. Missions—Alaska. I. Title.

Friends, Society of. Pennsylvania.

MYERS, Albert Cook, 1874-1960. 929.3
Quaker arrivals at Philadelphia, 1682-1750; being a list of certificates of removal received at Philadelphia Monthly Meeting of Friends. Baltimore, Genealogical Pub. Co., 1969. vi, 131 p. 23 cm. Reprint of the 1902 ed. [F152.M985 1969] 70-77321
1. Friends, Society of. Pennsylvania. 2. Pennsylvania—Biography. 3. Philadelphia—Biography. I. Friends, Society of. Philadelphia Monthly Meeting. II. Title.

Friends, Society of—United States—Biography.

ELLIOTT, Errol T. 289.6'092'4 B
R. Ernest Lamb, Irish-American Quaker : the life, work, and wit of a world Friend / by Errol T. Elliott. Richmond, IN : Friends United Press, c1977. xiv, 140 p. : ill. ; 22 cm. [BX7795.L28E44] 77-70184 ISBN 0-913408-29-8 : 4.95
1. Lamb, Richard Ernest, 1887-1973. 2. Friends, Society of—United States—Biography. 3. Friends, Society of—Clergy—Biography. I. Title.

Friermood, Elisabeth Hamilton—Biography.

FRIERMOOD, Elisabeth Hamilton. 813'.5'4 B
Frier and Elisabeth, sportsman and storyteller / by Elisabeth Hamilton Friermood ; consultant, Harold Thomas Friermood. 1st ed. New York : Vantage Press, c1979. 386 p. : ill. ; 22 cm. Includes index. [PS3556.R567Z405] 79-104543 ISBN 0-533-03711-5 : 10.00
1. Friermood, Elisabeth Hamilton—Biography. 2. Friermood, Harold T. 3. Authors, American—20th century—Biography. 4. Librarians—United States—Biography. 5. Physical education teachers—United States—Biography. I. Title.

Friese-Greene, William, 1855-1921.

FORTH, Muriel, 1907- 608'.7'24 B
Friese-Greene; close-up of an inventor [by] Ray Allister. New York, Arno Press, 1972. 192 p. illus. 23 cm. (The Arno Press cinema program. The literature of cinema) Reprint of the 1948 ed. published by Marsland Publications, London. [TR140.F7F6 1972] 71-169339 ISBN 0-405-03908-5
1. Friese-Greene, William, 1855-1921. I. Series: The Arno Press cinema program. II. Series: The Literature of cinema.

Friesen, Heinrich B., 1837-1926.

FRIESEN, Heinrich B., 1837-1926. 973'.04'9171 B
The autobiography of H. B. Friesen, 1837-1926 / translated from the German by August Schmidt. Newton, Kan. : [A. Schmidt], 1974. 121 p. : group port. ; 30 cm. Label mounted on cover: H. B. Friesen diary, 1837-1926. [CT275.F718A313] 75-329065
1. Friesen, Heinrich B., 1837-1926.

Frisch, Max, 1911 —Biography.

FRISCH, Max, 1911- 838'.9'1209 B
Montauk / Max Frisch ; translated by Geoffrey Skelton. 1st ed. New York : Harcourt Brace Jovanovich, c1976. 143 p. ; 22 cm. "A Helen and Kurt Wolff book." [PT2611.R814Z513 1976] 76-70 ISBN 0-15-162100-4 : 7.95
1. Frisch, Max, 1911- —Biography. I. Title. BIP

FRISCH, Max, 1911- 838'.9'1209 B
Montauk / Max Frisch ; translated by Geoffrey Skelton. New York : Harcourt Brace Jovanovich, [1978] c1976. p. cm. (A Harvest/HBJ book) "A Helen and Kurt Wolff book." [PT2611.R814Z513 1978] 77-16016 ISBN 0-15-661990-3 : 7.95
1. Frisch, Max, 1911- —Biography. 2. Authors, Swiss—Biography. I. Title.

Frisch, Otto Robert, 1904-

FRISCH, Otto Robert, 1904- 530'.092'4 B
What little I remember / Otto R. Frisch. Cambridge, [Eng.] ; New York : Cambridge University Press, 1979. xi, 227 p. : ill. ; 22 cm. Includes index. Bibliography: p. 220. [QC16.F75A38] 78-18096 ISBN 0-521-22297-4 : 14.95
1. Frisch, Otto Robert, 1904- 2. Physicists—Great Britain—Biography. I. Title. BIP

Fritchman, Stephen Hole, 1902-

FRITCHMAN, Stephen Hole, 1902- 288'.33'0924 B
Heretic : a partisan autobiography / by Stephen H. Fritchman. [Boston] : Beacon Press, c1977. 362 p., [4] leaves of plates : ports. ; 22 cm. "A Skinner House book." Includes bibliographical references. [BX9869.F815A34] 77-70244 pbk. : 3.95
1. Fritchman, Stephen Hole, 1902- 2. Unitarian churches—Clergy—Biography. 3. Clergy—United States—Biography. I. Title.

Frodsham, Stanley Howard, 1882-1969.

CAMPBELL, Faith, 1913- 289.9 B
Stanley Frodsham, prophet with a pen. Springfield, Mo., Gospel Pub. House [1974] 146, [1] p. 18 cm. (Radiant books) "Books by Stanley H. Frodsham": p. [147] [BX6198.A7F763] 74-77406 1.25
1. Frodsham, Stanley Howard, 1882-1969. I. Title.

Froebel, Friedrich Wilhelm August, 1782-1852.

DOWNS, Robert Bingham, 1903- 370'.92'4 B
Friedrich Froebel / by Robert B. Downs. Boston : Twayne Publishers, c1978. 126 p. : port. ; 21 cm. (Twayne's world leaders series : TWLS 74) Includes index. Bibliography: p. 119-124. [LB638.D68] 77-13512 ISBN 0-8057-7668-0 : 8.50
1. Froebel, Friedrich Wilhelm August, 1782-1852. 2. Teachers—Germany—Biography. 3. Education—Philosophy. I. Title. BIP

LAWRENCE, Evelyn Mary, 1892- ed. 372.2
Friedrich Froebel and English education [by] P. Woodham-Smith [and others]. New York, Philosophical Library [1953] 248 p. illus., ports. 23 cm. Bibliography: p. 234-237. [LB639.L38 1953] 53-7911
1. Froebel, Friedrich Wilhelm August, 1782-1852. 2. Education—Great Britain—History. I. Title.

Froissart, Jean, 1338?-1410?

COULTON, George Gordon, 1858-1947. 940.1'7'072024 B
The chronicler of European chivalry / by G. G. Coulton. Folcroft, Pa. : Folcroft Library Editions, 1976. x, 133 p. : ill. ; 34 cm. The illustrations are reproduced from manuscripts Harley 4379 and 4380 in the British Museum Reprint of the 1930 ed. published by The Studio, ltd., London, which was originally issued as a special winter no. of Studio. Includes bibliographical references. [DC36.98.F7C68 1976] 76-58028 ISBN 0-8414-3444-1 lib. bdg. : 30.00
1. Froissart, Jean, 1338?-1410? 2. Illumination of books and manuscripts - Specimens, reproductions, etc. 3. Historians—France—Biography. I. British Museum. MSS. (Harleian 4379-4380) II. Title. BIP

SHEARS, Frederick Sidney. 940.1'7072024 B
Froissart, chronicler and poet, by F. S. Shears. [Folcroft, Pa.] Folcroft Library Editions, 1972. xiii, 244 p. illus. 24 cm. "Limited to 150 copies." Reprint of the 1930 ed. Includes bibliographical references. [DC36.98.F7S5 1972] 72-187238
1. Froissart, Jean, 1338?-1410? BIP

Fromm, Erich, 1900-

EVANS, Richard Isadore, 1922- 150.1957
Dialogue with Erich Fromm, by Richard I. Evans. [1st ed.] New York, Harper & Row [1966] xix, 136 p. 22 cm. (His Dialogues with notable contributors to personality theory, v. 2) Bibliography: p. 123-126. "Bibliography: selected works of Erich Fromm": p. 127-128. [BF173.F89E9] 66-13939
1. Fromm, Erich, 1900- 2. Psychoanalysis. I. Title.

GLEN, John Stanley, 1907- 208
Erich Fromm; a Protestant critique, by J. Stanley Glen. Philadelphia, Westminster Press [1966] 224 p. 21 cm. Bibliography: p. [213]-224. [BX4817.G5] 66-21807
1. Fromm, Erich, 1900- 2. Protestantism.

Frontenac, Louis de Buade, comte de, 1620-1698 — Juvenile literature.

SWAYZE, Fred. 923.271
Frontenac and the Iroquois; the fighting Governor of New France. Illustrated by Huntley Brown. New York, St Martin's Press, 1950. 158 p. illus. 22 cm. (Great stories of Canada [19]) [F1030.F935] 59-4747
1. Frontenac, Louis de Buade, comte de, 1620-1698 — Juvenile literature. I. Title.

Frontenac, Louis de Buade, comte de, 1620-1698—Juvenile literature.

SYME, Ronald, 1910- 971.01'6'0924 B
Frontenac of New France. Illustrated by William Stobbs. New York, Morrow [1969] 190 p. illus. 21 cm. A biography of the governor of seventeenth-century New France and a history of the territory he governed relating how he welded an isolated people into a united colony capable of self-defense. [F1030.F936] 92 76-78341 3.95
1. Frontenac, Louis de Buade, comte de, 1620-1698—Juvenile literature. I. Stobbs, William, illus. II. Title. BIP

Frontier and pioneer life—Arizona.

BANTA, Albert Franklin, 1843-1924. 923.973
Albert Franklin Banta: Arizona pioneer; [memoirs] Edited by Frank D. Reeve. Albuquerque [1953] 143p. port. 23cm. (Historical Society of New Mexico. Publications in history, v.14) [F791.N45 vol.14] 56-62983
1. Frontier and pioneer life—Arizona. I. Title. II. Series: New Mexico. Historical Society. Publications in history, v.14

Frontier and pioneer life — Kansas.

WELLS, William Morris, 1857- 923.973
A story of the magic West; the life-story of a man of the American people. [Los Angeles, 1934] 234 p. plates, ports., map. 21 cm. First published in 1934 under title: The desert's hidden wealth. [F686.W47 1934a] 34-25355
1. Frontier and pioneer life — Kansas. 2. Frontier and pioneer life — The West. I. Title.

Frontier and pioneer life — Oklahoma.

FRONTIER adventurers 976.6'03 B : American exploration in Oklahoma / edited by Joseph A. Stout, Jr. 1st ed. Oklahoma City : Oklahoma Historical Society, 1976. vii, 158 p. : ill. ; 24 cm. (The Oklahoma series ; v. 4) Includes bibliographical references and index. [F697.F76] 76-23590
1. Frontier and pioneer life—Oklahoma. 2. Oklahoma—History. 3. Pioneers—Oklahoma—Biography. 4. Oklahoma—Biography. I. Stout, Joseph Allen. II. Title. III. Series.

WALLACE, Allie B 917.66
Frontier life in Oklahoma [by] Allie B. Wallace. With an introd. by A. S. Mike Monroney. Washington, Public Affairs Press [1964] vi, 136 p. 24 cm. Autobiographical. [CT275.W2523A3] 64-23869
1. Frontier and pioneer life — Oklahoma. I. Title.

Frontier and pioneer life—Southwest, New.

FLIPPER, Henry Ossian, 1856-1940. 923.5
Negro frontiersman: the Western memoirs of Henry O. Flipper, first Negro graduate of West Point. Ed., introd. by Theodore D. Harris. El Paso, Texas Western College Pr. [c.]1960. x, 54p. ports. 24cm. 63-2609 6.00; 3.00 pap.,
1. Frontier and pioneer life—Southwest, New. 2. Frontier and pioneer life—Mexico. I. Title.

RYNNING, Thomas Harbo, 1866- 978'.02'0924 B
Gun notches; a saga of frontier lawman Captain Thomas H. Rynning, as told to Al Cohn and Joe Chisholm. Foreword by Rupert Hughes. San Diego, Calif., Frontier Heritage Press, 1971. xiii, 332 p. illus., ports. 23 cm. Reprint of the 1931 ed. [F786.R98 1971] 75-157992 ISBN 0-87896-002-3 9.50
1. Frontier and pioneer life—Southwest, New. I. Cohn, Alfred Abraham, 1880- II. Chisholm, Joseph Francis, 1875-1937. III. Title.

Frontier and pioneer life—The West.

BECKWOURTH, James Pierson, 1798-1866. 917.8'04'20924 B
The life and adventures of James P. Beckwourth [edited by] T. D. Bonner. New York, Arno Press, 1969. viii, 537 p. illus., ports. 20 cm. (The American Negro, his history and literature) Reprint of the 1856 ed. [F592.B388 1969] 69-18563
1. Frontier and pioneer life—The West. 2. Crow Indians. I. Bonner, T. D., ed. II. Title. III. Series. **BIP**

BECKWOURTH, James Pierson, 1798-1866 917.80320924
The life and adventures of James P. Beckwourth, mountaineer, scout, and pioneer, and chief of the Crow Nation of Indians. Written from his own dictation, by T. D. Bonner [New introd. by Stan Nelson] Minneapolis, Ross & Haines [1965] xii, 547p. illus., ports. 23cm. Orig. pub. in 1856. [F592.B394] 65-9475 8.75
1. Frontier and pioneer life—The West. 2. Crow Indians. I. Bonner, T. D., ed. II. Title.

BECKWOURTH, James Pierson, 1798-1866. 917.8'03'20924 B
The life and adventures of James P. Beckwourth as told to Thomas D. Bonner. Introduced and with notes and an epilogue by Delmont R. Oswald. Lincoln, University of Nebraska Press [1972] xiii, 649 p. 24 cm. Reprint of the 1856 ed. Includes bibliographical references. [F592.B39 1972] 73-88092 ISBN 0-8032-0724-7 9.75
1. Frontier and pioneer life—The West. 2. Crow Indians. I. Bonner, T. D.

BECKWOURTH, James Pierson, 1798-1866. 917.8'03'20924 B
Mountain man, Indian chief; the life and adventures of Jim Beckwourth. Written from his own dictation by T. D. Bonner, edited with an introd. and epilogue by Betty Shepard. New York, Harcourt, Brace & World [1968] viii, 184 p. illus., maps. 21 cm. Abridged edition of The life and adventures of James P. Beckwourth. [F592.B3943] 68-25196 3.95
1. Frontier and pioneer life—The West. 2. Crow Indians. I. Bonner, T. D. II. Shepard, Betty, ed. III. Title.

CANTON, Frank M. 1849-1927 363.30924
Frontier trails; the autobiography of Frank M. Canton. Ed. by Edward Exerett Dale. [New ed.] Norman. Univ. of Okla. Pr. [c.1966] xix, 236p. 20cm. (Western frontier lib., V.30) [F595.C23] 66-13415 2.00 bds.,
1. Frontier and pioneer life—The West. I. Dale. Edward Exerett. 1879- ed. II. Title.

CARSON, Christopher, 1809-1868 923.973
Kit Carson's autobiography, ed. by Milo Milton Quaife. Lincoln. Univ. of Neb. Pr. [1966] xxxii, 192p. port. 21cm. (Bison bk., BB325) Orig. pub. by R. R. Donelley in 1935. [F592.C31] 1.50 pap.,
1. Frontier and pioneer life—The West. I. Quaife, Milo Milton, 1880- ed. II. Title.

CARSON, Christopher, 1809-1868. 978.020924 (B)
Kit Carson's autobiography, edited by Milo Milton Quaife. Lincoln, University of Nebraska Press [1966] xxxii, 192 p. facsim., port. 21 cm. (A Bison book BB325) Includes bibliographical references. [F592.C314] 66-4130
1. Frontier and pioneer life — The West. I. Quaife, Milo Milton, 1880-1959, ed. II. Title. **BIP**

CARSON, Christopher, 1809-1868 923.973
Kit Carson's autobiography, ed. by Milo Milton Quaife [Gloucester, Mass., P. Smith, 1966] xxxii, 192p. port. 21cm. (Bison bk., BB325 rebound.) First pub. in 1935 by R. R. Donnelley by arrangement with Lakeside Pr. First pub. in 1935 by R. R. Donnelley by arrangement with Lakeside Pr. [F592.C31] 3.50
1. Frontier and pioneer life—The West. I. Quaife, Milo Milton, 1880- ed. II. Title.

CLYMAN, James, 1792-1881. 923.973
James Clyman, frontiersman; the adventures of a trapper and covered-wagon emigrant as told in his own reminiscences and diaries. Edited by Charles L. Camp. Definitive ed. Portland, Or., Champoeg Press [1960] 352 p. illus., ports., maps (part fold.) 27 cm. At head of title: 1792-1881. Bibliographical references included in "Notes" (p. 306-342) [F592.C65 1960] 61-1845
1. Frontier and pioneer life—The West. I. Camp, Charles Lewis, 1893- ed.

EATON, Frank, 1860- 917.66
Pistol Pete, veteran of the Old West. [1st ed.] Boston, Little, Brown, 1952. 278 p. illus. 21 cm. Autobiography. "Eva Gillhouse wrote this book ... just the way I told it to her." [F594.E17] 52-5509
1. Frontier and pioneer life—The West. I. Gillhouse, Eva Olenna. II. Title.

GUERIN, Elsa Jane. 917.8
Mountain Charley; or, The adventures of Mrs. E. J. Guerin, who was thirteen years in male attire; an autobiography comprising a period of thirteen years life in the States, California, and Pike's Peak. With an introd. by Fred W. Mazzulla and William Kostka. [New ed.] Norman, University of Oklahoma Press [1968] xv, 112 p. 19 cm. (The Western frontier library) First published in Dubuque, Iowa, in 1861. [F593.G9 1968] 68-15671
1. Frontier and pioneer life—The West. I. Title. II. Title: The adventures of Mrs. E. J. Guerin. **BIP**

HERRON, Jim, 1866-1949. 917.8'03'20924 B
Fifty years on the Owl Hoot Trail; Jim Herron, the first sheriff of No Man's Land, Oklahoma Territory [edited] by Harry E. Chrisman from an original manuscript by Jim Herron. Introd. by Edward Everett Dale. [1st ed.] Chicago, Sage Books [1969] xxii, 355 p. illus., maps (on lining papers), ports. 24 cm. Bibliography: p. 335-341. [F596.H4 1969] 73-75735 8.50
1. Frontier and pioneer life—The West. I. Chrisman, Harry E., ed. II. Title.

MAJORS, Alexander, 1814-1900. 978.0924
Seventy years on the frontier; Alexander Majors' memoirs of a lifetime on the border. Pref. by 'Buffalo Bill' (General W. F. Cody) Ed. by Prentiss Ingraham. Minneapolis, Ross & Haines [c.]1965. 325p. illus., ports. 23cm. [F591.M23] 65-6282 7.50
1. Frontier and pioneer life—The West. I. Title.

MERRIAM, Harold Guy, 1883- comp. 917.8'03'2
Way out West; recollections and tales, collected and edited by H. G. Merriam. [1st ed.] Norman, University of Oklahoma Press [1969] xi, 296 p. 23 cm. Bibliographical footnotes. [F591.M43] 68-31372
1. Frontier and pioneer life—The West. I. Title. **BIP**

METCALF, P. Richard, comp. 917.8'03'2
The American people on the Western Frontier. Edited by P. Richard Metcalf. West Haven, Conn., Pendulum Press [1973] 175 p. 20 cm. (The American people) Excerpts from personal accounts reveal the social life, customs, attitudes, and goals of the people who settled the western frontier. [F591.M434 1973] 72-95871 ISBN 0-88301-089-5 5.95
1. Frontier and pioneer life—The West. 2. The West—Social life and customs. I. Title. II. Series.
Pbk. 1.95; ISBN 0-88301-073-9 **BIP**

MYERS, John Myers, 1906- 978.02'0922
The Westerners; a roundup of pioneer reminiscences. Compiled and annotated [by] John Myers Myers. Englewood Cliffs, N.J., Prentice-Hall [1969] xiv, 258 p. map (on lining papers) 24 cm. Consists of interviews with 24 persons. [F596.M9] 69-14552 7.95
1. Frontier and pioneer life—The West. 2. The West—Biography. I. Title.

WAREHAM, John, 1844- 917.8'03
1870 diary of John Wareham [edited] by jean Wareham Owens. [Fort Worth? Tex., c1968] 38 l. maps. 28 cm. [F594.W27] 71-3358
1. Frontier and pioneer life—The West. I. Owens, Jean Wareham, 1925- ed. II. Title.

WOOTTON, Richens Lacy, 1816-1893. 923.973
Uncle Dick Wootton, the pioneer frontiersman of the Rocky Mountain region, by Howard Louis Conard. Edited by Milo Milton Quaife. Chicago, R. R. Donnelly, 1957. xxvii, 465 p. illus., ports., map. 18 cm. (The Lakeside classics. 55) "Instead of writing his narrative ... [Wootton] related it in a series of interviews, which Conard, his interviewer, noted down ... and subsequently recast." [F593.W92 1957] 58-1715
1. Frontier and pioneer life — The West. I. Conrad, Howard Louis. II. Title.

WOOTTON, Richens Lacy, 1816-1893. 923.973
"Uncle Dick" Wootton, the pioneer frontiersman of the Rocky Mountain region; an account of the adventures and thrilling experiences of the most noted American hunter, trapper, guide, scout, and Indian fighter now living, by Howard Louis Conard. With an introd. by Joseph Kirkland. Chicago, W. E. Dibble, 1890. Columbus, Reprinted by Long's College Book Co., 1950. 472 p. illus., ports. 24 cm. "Limited to 500 copies." "Instead of writing his narrative ... [Wootton] related it in a series of interviews, which Conard, his interviewer, noted down ... and subsequently recast." -- Historical introd. to 1957 ed. [F593.W92 1950] 52-66007
1. Frontier and pioneer life — The West. I. Conard, Howard Louis. II. Title.

Frontier and pioneer life— Wyoming.

HUNTON, John, 1839-1928. 923.973
Diary. [Lingle?Wyo., 1956- v. illus. 16cm. [F761.H85] 59-33178
1. Frontier and pioneer life— Wyoming. 2. Ranch life. I. Title.

LEONARD, Peg Layton, 1931- 978.7
West of yesteryear : profiles of early Wyoming people and places / by Peg Layton Leonard. Limited ed. [Douglas? Wyo. : s.n.], c1976 (Boulder, Colo. : Johnson Pub. Co.) xviii, 222 p. : ill. ; 24 cm. Includes index. Bibliography: p. 209. [F761.L54] 76-374898 17.95
1. Frontier and pioneer life—Wyoming. 2. Wyoming—Biography. 3. Wyoming—History. I. Title.

Frontier and pioneer life—Africa, South.

BUTLER, Guy, 1918- comp. 916.8'09'742
When boys were men. Cape Town, New York, Oxford University Press, 1969. xi, 275 p. illus., maps, ports. 22 cm. Includes bibliographical references. [DT767.B83] 72-464184 4.50
1. Frontier and pioneer life—Africa, South. 2. British in South Africa. I. Title. **BIP**

Frontier and pioneer life—Alaska.

BERTO, Hazel Dunaway. 923.973
North to Alaska's shining river. [1st ed.] Indianapolis, Bobbs-Merrill [1959] 224 p. 22 cm. Autobiographical. [F909.B495] 59-14296
1. Frontier and pioneer life—Alaska. 2. Eskimos—Alaska. 3. Eskimos—Education. I. Title.

HADMAN, Ballard. 917.98
As the sailor loves the sea. Illus. by the author. [1st ed.] New York, Harper [1951] 232 p. illus. 21 cm. Autobiographical. [F909.H2] 51-12679
1. Frontier and pioneer life—Alaska. I. Title.

MCGARVEY, Lois, 1885-1959. 917.98
Along Alaska trails. [1st ed.] New York, Vantage Press [1960] 200 p. illus. 21 cm. Autobiography. [F909.M155] 60-3760
1. Frontier and pioneer life—Alaska. I. Title.

MARTIN, Martha, of Alaska. 917.98
O rugged land of gold. New York, Macmillan, 1953. 223 p. 22 cm. Autobiographical. [F909.M378] 53-7034
1. Frontier and pioneer life—Alaska. I. Title. **BIP**

SHORT, Wayne. 917.98
The cheechakoes. Drawings by Peter Parnall. New York, Random House [1964] 244 p. illus., map. 22 cm. Autobiographical. [F909.S498] 63-16853
1. Frontier and pioneer life—Alaska. I. Title. **BIP**

Frontier and pioneer life—Alberta.

FREDRICKSON, Olive A. 917.11'03'30924 B
The silence of the North, by Olive A. Fredrickson with Ben East. New York, Crown Publishers [1972] xii, 209 p. illus. 22 cm. [F1078.F717 1972] 73-185089 5.95
1. Frontier and pioneer life—Alberta. 2. Frontier and pioneer life—British Columbia. 3. Alberta—Biography. 4. British Columbia—Biography. I. East, Ben. II. Title.

FREDRICKSON, Olive A. 917.11'03'60924 [B]
The silence of the North, by Olive A. Fredrickson with Ben East. [New York] Warner Paperback Lib. [1973, c.1972] 222 p. illus. 18 cm. [F1078.F717] 1.50 (pbk.)
1. Frontier and pioneer life—Alberta. 2. Frontier and pioneer life—British Columbia. 3. Alberta—Biography. 4. British Columbia—Biography. I. East, Ben. II. Title.
L.C. card no. for the hardbound edition: 73-185089.

ROBERTS, Sarah Ellen. 917.123'03'20922 B
Alberta homestead; chronicle of a pioneer family. Edited by Lathrop E. Roberts. Austin, University of Texas Press [1971] x, 272 p. map. 24 cm. (The M. K. Brown range life series, no. 10) 1968 ed. published under title: Of us and the oxen. [F1078.R6 1971] 75-165909 ISBN 0-292-70143-8 7.50
1. Frontier and pioneer life—Alberta. I. Title. **BIP**

Frontier and pioneer life—Colorado.

HALL, Mabel (Wilson) 1893- 917.88'58
Upper Beaver Creek; pioneer life in Colorado [by] Mabel Hall. [1st ed.] New York, Exposition Press [1972] 159 p. illus. 21 cm. (An Exposition-Lochinvar book) [F776.H2] 72-188398 ISBN 0-682-47502-5 6.00
1. Frontier and pioneer life—Colorado. 2. Colorado—History. I. Title.

Frontier and pioneer life—Colorado—Moffat Co.

FITZPATRICK, V. S., 1886- 978.8'12
The last frontier / by V. S. FitzPatrick. Steamboat Springs, Colo. : Steamboat Pilot, c1976- v. : ill. ; 23 cm. Includes indexes. [F782.M65F57] 76-374232
1. Frontier and pioneer life—Colorado—Moffat Co. 2. Moffat Co., Colo.—History. 3. Moffat Co., Colo.—Biography. I. Title.

FITZPATRICK, V. S., 1886- 978.8'12
The last frontier / by V. S. FitzPatrick. Steamboat Springs, Colo. : Steamboat Pilot, c1976- v. : ill. ; 23 cm. Includes indexes. [F782.M65F57] 76-374232
1. Frontier and pioneer life—Colorado—Moffat Co. 2. Moffat Co., Colo.—History. 3. Moffat Co., Colo.—Biography. I. Title.

Frontier and pioneer life—Iowa.

OLNEY, Warren, 1841-1921. 923.473
Warren Olney, 1841-1921. [Santa Barbara? Calif., 1961] 103p. illus. 24cm. 'Papers of Warren Olney . . . reprinted primarily for . . . his descendants.' [CT275.O515A3] 61-28319
1. Frontier and pioneer life—Iowa. 2. Shiloh, Battle of, 1862. I. Title.

ORR, Ellison. 917.77'33'0320924
Reminiscences of a pioneer boy. Edited with an introd. by Marshall McKusick. [Iowa City? Iowa, 1971] 68 p. illus. 24 cm. Reprinted from the Annals of Iowa, issue no. 7, winter, 1971, p. 530-560; and issue no. 8, spring, 1971, p. 593-630. [F621.5.O7] 72-191341
1. Frontier and pioneer life—Iowa. I. McKusick, Marshall Bassford, 1930- ed. II. Title.

THE way it was : 977.7'03
as told by Iowans / researched & compiled by Betty Putnam & Kathryn Love. [Des Moines?] : s.n., c1976. 166 p. : ill. ; 23 cm. Includes index. [F621.T47] 76-372258
1. Frontier and pioneer life—Iowa. 2. Iowa—Biography. 3. Iowa—History, Local. I. Putnam, Betty. II. Love, Kathryn.

Frontier and pioneer life—Minnesota.

DAUGHTERS of the 977.6'04
American Revolution. Minnesota. Old Trails and Historic Spots Committee.
Old rail fence corners : frontier tales told by Minnesota pioneers / edited by Lucy Leavenworth Wilder Morris. Reprint ed. / with an introd. by Marjorie Kreidberg. St. Paul : Minnesota Historical Society Press, 1976. p. cm. (Publications of the Minnesota Historical Society) Reprint of the 2d ed., 1915, printed by F. H. McCulloch Print. Co., Austin, Minn., under title: Old rail fence corners : the A.B.C.'s of Minnesota history. Includes bibliographical references and index. [F606.D34 1976] 76-30262 ISBN 0-87351-108-5 : 8.50 ISBN 0-87351-109-3 pbk. : 4.50
1. Frontier and pioneer life—Minnesota. 2. Minnesota—History, Local. 3. Pioneers—Minnesota—Biography. 4. Minnesota—Biography. I. Morris, Lucy Leavenworth Wilder, 1865-1935. II. Title. III. Series: Minnesota Historical Society. Publications.

Frontier and pioneer life-Montana.

MY unseen world; v. 12
the personal chronicle of a westerner's pioneer hardships, on the road to spiritual understanding. [1st ed.] New York, Exposition Press [c1958] 108p. 21cm.
1. Frontier and pioneer life-Montana. 2. Spiritualism. I. Jones, Arthur L 1887-

Frontier and pioneer life—Nebraska.

JACKSON, Charles Tenney, 917.82
1874-
The buffalo wallow, a prairie boyhood, by Charles Tenney Jackson, "Jack Tennison." [1st ed.] Indianapolis, Bobbs-Merrill [1953] 253 p. 22 cm. Autobiographical. [F666.J2] 52-14022
1. Frontier and pioneer life—Nebraska. I. Title. BIP

Frontier and pioneer life—North America.

SPECK, Gordon. 970.1
Breeds and half-breeds. [1st ed.] New York, C. N. Potter; distributed by Crown Publishers [1969] xvi, 361 p. illus., maps, plans, ports. 24 cm. Bibliography: p. 350-356. [E71.S67 1969] 69-11686 7.50
1. Frontier and pioneer life—North America. 2. Indians of North America. I. Title.

Frontier and pioneer life—Oklahoma—Wichita Mountains region.

HOWENSTINE, Papa Jack. 976.6'48
Papa Jack, cowman from the Wichitas / [edited] by Paul McClung ; illustrated by Robert A. Gartland. Norman : University of Oklahoma Press, 1976. p. cm. "First appeared as a three-part series in the Great Plains journal (spring, 1973, fall, 1973, and spring, 1974)." Includes index. [F702.W55H67 1976] 76-19071 ISBN 0-8061-1321-9 : 9.95 pbk. : 3.95
1. Frontier and pioneer life—Oklahoma—Wichita Mountains region. 2. Howenstine, Papa Jack. 3. Wichita Mountians region, Okla.—Biography. I. McClung, Paul. II. Title.

Frontier and pioneer life—South Dakota.

WYMAN, Walker 917.83'03'30924 B
Demarquis, 1907-
Frontier woman; the life of a woman homesteader on the Dakota frontier. Retold from the original notes and letters of Grace Fairchild, a Wisconsin teacher, who went to South Dakota in 1898, by Walker D. Wyman. Illustrated by Helen B. Wyman. [River Falls] University of Wisconsin-River Falls Press [1972] ix, 115 p. illus. 23 cm. [F656.W9] 72-185705
1. Frontier and pioneer life—South Dakota. 2. South Dakota—History. I. Fairchild, Grace, 1881- II. Title.

Frontier and pioneer life—Southwest, New—Juvenile literature.

FARNSWORTH, Harriett. 917.91
Pioneers of the Western frontier. San Antonio, Tex., Naylor Co. [1968] xvi, 127 p. illus., facsims., ports. 22 cm. [F786.F28] 68-20145
1. Frontier and pioneer life—Southwest, New—Juvenile literature. 2. Southwest, New—Biography—Juvenile literature. I. Title.

Frontier and pioneer life—Texas.

HARDIN, John Wesley, 923.4173
1853-1895.
The life of John Wesley Hardin, as written by himself. With an introd. by Robert G. McCubbin. Norman, University of Oklahoma Press [c.1961] 152p. illus. (Western frontier library, 16) 61-6493 2.00 bds.,
1. Frontier and pioneer life—Texas. 2. Crime and criminals—Texas. I. Title.

JENKINS, John Holland, 976.4 [B]
1822-1890.
Recollections of early Texas; the memoirs of John Holland Jenkins, edited by John Holmes Jenkins, III. Foreword by J. Frank Dobie. Austin, University of Texas Press [1974, c.1958] xxvi, 307 p. illus. 22 cm. Includes bibliography [F390.J4] 58-7234 ISBN 0-292-73347-X 8.50
1. Frontier and pioneer life—Texas. 2. Texas—History—Republic, 1836-1846. I. Title. BIP

MAUDSLAY, Robert, 917.64'03'6
1855-1939.
Texas sheepman; the reminiscences of Robert Maudslay. Edited by Winifred Kupper. Illus. by Hilda Wilcox Phelps. Freeport, N.Y., Books for Libraries Press [1971, c1951] xi, 138 p. illus., facsim., ports. 23 cm. Includes bibliographical references. [F391.M46 1971] 78-157347 ISBN 0-8369-5808-X
1. Frontier and pioneer life—Texas. 2. Shepherds—Texas. I. Title.

RHAT, Carlysle 917.64'03'60924
Graham.
Old Buck and I, our golden years, 1886-1898; a cow country idyl. Ed. deluxe. Drawings by Loys Raymer. Odessa, Tex., Rahtbooks Co. [1964] xv, 208 p. illus., port. 20 cm. [F391.R15] 68-2544
1. Frontier and pioneer life—Texas. I. Title.

SIMS, Orland L. 917.64'7'036
Cowpokes, nesters, & so forth, by Orland L. Sims. [1st ed.] Austin, [Tex.] Encino Press, 1970. xii, 297 p. illus., ports. 24 cm. [F391.S6] 76-24839 8.50
1. Frontier and pioneer life—Texas. 2. Cowboys—Texas. 3. Ranch life—Texas. I. Title.

Frontier and pioneer life—United States.

JOHNSTON, Charles 917.3'04'0922
Haven Ladd, 1877-1943.
Famous scouts, including trappers, pioneers, and soldiers of the frontier; their hazardous and exciting adventures in the mighty drama of the white conquest of the American continent. Freeport, N.Y., Books for Libraries Press [1972, c1910] ix, 340 p. illus. 23 cm. (Essay index reprint series) [E176.J65 1972] 79-38743 ISBN 0-8369-2661-7
1. Frontier and pioneer life—United States. 2. Pioneers—United States. 3. Scouts and scouting. I. Title.

Frontier and pioneer life—Utah.

HAMBLIN, Jacob, 266.93'792 B
1819-1886.
Jacob Hamblin, a narrative of his personal experience, as a frontiersman, missionary to the Indians and explorer, disclosing interpositions of Providence, severe privations, perilous situations and remarkable escapes, by James A. Little. Freeport, N.Y., Books for Libraries Press [1971] 140 p. 23 cm. Reprint of the 1881 ed. [F826.H19 1971] 72-164615 ISBN 0-8369-5899-3
1. Frontier and pioneer life—Utah. 2. Mormons and Mormonism. 3. Indians of North America—Utah. I. Little, James A.

Frontier and pioneer life—Victoria, Australia.

MIDGLEY, Sarah, 1831- 919.4'5'033
1893.
The diaries of Sarah Midgley and Richard Skilbeck; a story of Australian settlers, 1851-1864. Edited by H. A. McCorkell. [Melbourne] Cassell, Australia [1967] viii, 208 p. illus., maps (lining-papers), ports. 25 cm. [DU222.M5A3] 68-96037 6.25 Aust.
1. Frontier and pioneer life—Victoria, Australia. I. Skilbeck, Richard, 1838-1924. II. Title.

Frontier and pioneer life—Wisconsin.

STEPHENSON, 977.5'03'0924 B
Isaac, 1829-1918.
Recollections of long life, 1829-1915. Freeport, N.Y., Books for Libraries Press [1972] p. Reprint of the 1915 ed. [E664.S83A3 1972] 72-8416 ISBN 0-8369-6991-X
1. Frontier and pioneer life—Wisconsin. 2. Wisconsin—Politics and government—1848-1950. 3. Lumbering—Wisconsin. I. Title.

Frontier and pionneer life—The West.

OAKS, George Washington, 923.973
1840-1917.
Man of the West; reminiscences of George Washington Oaks. 1840-1917. Recorded by Ben Jaastad; edited and annotated by Arthur Woodward. 3Tucson, Arizona Pioneers Historical Society, c1956]c67p. plate. port. 22cm. (Arizona Pioneers' Historical Society. Pamphlet series, no. 1) '400 copies' Bibliographical references included in 'Notes' (p. 49-65) [F591.O22] 59-30577
1. Frontier and pionneer life—The West. I. Jaastad, Ben. II. Title. III. Series.

Frontier Nursing Service, Inc.

BRECKINRIDGE, Mary, 1881- 926.1
Wide neighborhoods; a story of the Frontier Nursing Service. [1st ed.] New York, Harper [1952] 366 p. 22 cm. Autobiography. [RT37.B72A3] 52-5423
1. Frontier Nursing Service, Inc. I. Title.

Frontinus, Sextus Julius.

FRONTINUS, Sextus 628.1'0937'6
Julius.
The two books on the water supply of the city of Rome of Sextus Julius Frontinus, water commissioner of the city of Rome, A.D. 97. A translation into English, and explanatory chapters by Clemens Herschel. Introd. by Russell H. Babock and James J. Matera. [Boston] New England Water Works Association, 1973. v, 252 p. illus. 24 cm. Translation of De aquae ductibus urbis Romae. Includes bibliographical references. [TD216.F72 1973] 73-91138
1. Frontinus, Sextus Julius. 2. Herschel, Clemens, 1842-1930. 3. Rome (City)—Water-supply. I. Herschel, Clemens, 1842-1930, ed. II. Title.

Fronto, Marcus Cornelius.

FRONTO, Marcus 875'.01 B
Cornelius.
M. Cornelii Frontonis Epistulae adnotatione critica instructae / edited by Michael Petrus Iosephus van den Hout. New York : Arno Press, 1975. xciii, 262 p., [2] leaves of plates : ill. ; 24 cm. (Roman history) Reprint of the 1954 ed. published by E. J. Brill, Leiden. Originally published as the editor's thesis, Nijmegen. Includes index. Bibliography: p. [lxiii]-xciii. [PA6389.F7A4 1975] 75-7349 ISBN 0-405-07070-5
1. Fronto, Marcus Cornelius. I. Hout, M. P. J. van den. II. Title. III. Series. BIP

Frooks, Dorothy, 1899-

FROOKS, Dorothy, 340'.092'4 B
1899-
Lady lawyer. [1st ed.] New York, R. Speller [1975] 201 p. illus. 24 cm. Autobiographical. [KF373.F76A33] 74-8881 ISBN 0-8315-0141-3
1. Frooks, Dorothy, 1899- I. Title. BIP

Frost, David.

FRISCHAUER, Willi, 791.45'0924 B
1906-
Will you welcome now ... David Frost. New York, Hawthorn Books [1971] vii, 248 p. illus. 24 cm. "A Martin Dale book." Bibliography: p. 239. [PN1992.4.F7F7] 79-158032 6.93
1. Frost, David. I. Title.

Frost, Robert. 1874

MUNSON, Gorham Bert, 1896- 920
Robert Frost; making poems for America. Illus. by by Dan Siculan. Chicago, Ency. Britannica [1963,c.1962] 190p. col. illus. 22cm. (Britannica bkshelf: Great lives for young Amers.) 62-10427 2.36 lib. ed.,
1. Frost, Robert, 1874 —Juvenile literature. I. Title.

Frost, Robert, 1874-1963.

CLEMENS, Cyril, 1902- 811'.5'2
A chat with Robert Frost / Cyril Clemens ; with a foreword by Hamlin Garland. Folcroft, Pa. : Folcroft Library Editions, 1977. 14 p., [1] leaf of plates : ports. ; 23 cm. Reprint of the 1940 ed. published by the International Mark Twain Society, Webster Groves, Mo., which was issued as no. 9 of its Biographical series. [PS3511.R94Z56 1977] 77-860 ISBN 0-8414-3567-7 lib. bdg. : 6.50
1. Frost, Robert, 1874-1963. I. Frost, Robert, 1874-1963. II. Title. III. Series: International Mark Twain Society. Biographical series ; no. 9.

COX, Sidney, 1889-1952 928.1
A swinger of birches; a portrait of Robert Frost. Introd. by Robert Frost. New York, Collier Bks. [1962,c.1957] 123p. (AS124) .95 pap.,
1. Frost, Robert, 1875- I. Title.

COX, Sidney, 1889-1952. 928.1
A swinger of birches; a portrait of Robert Frost. With an introd. by Robert Frost. New York, New York University Press, 1957. 177p. 21cm. [PS3511.R94Z59] 57-6372
1. Frost, Robert, 1873- I. Title.

FRANCIS, Robert, 1901- 811'.5'2 B
Frost: a time to talk; conversations & indiscretions recorded by Robert Francis. [Amherst] University of Massachusetts Press [1972] 100 p. 24 cm. Includes bibliographical references. [PS3511.R94Z653] 72-77570 7.50
1. Frost, Robert, 1874-1963. I. Title.

FROST, Robert, 1874-1963. 928.1
The letters of Robert Frost to Louis Untermeyer. [1st ed.] New York, Holt, Rinehart and Winston [1963] ix, 388 p. 25 cm. [PS3511.R94Z53] 63-15383
I. Untermeyer, Louis, 1885- II. Title.

FROST, Robert, 1874-1963. 811'.9'12 B
Robert Frost, a tribute to the source / poems by Robert Frost ;photos. by Dewitt Jones ; text by David Bradley. 1st ed. New York : Holt, Rinehart and Winston, c1979. 165 p. : ill. ; 29 cm. [PS3511.R94Z518 1979] 78-10444 ISBN 0-03-046326-2. : 20.00
1. Frost, Robert, 1874-1963. 2. Poets, American—20th century—Biography. I. Bradley, David, 1915- II. Jones, Dewitt. III. Title. **BIP**

FROST, Robert, 1874-1963. 928.1
Selected letters. Edited by Lawrance Thompson. [1st ed.] New York, Holt, Rinehart and Winston [1964] lxiv, 645 p. facsims. 25 cm. [PS3511.R94Z52 1964] 64-10767
I. Thompson, Lawrance Roger, 1906- ed.

GOULD, Jean, 1909- 928.1
Robert Frost; the aim was song. New York, Dodd, Mead [1964] xi, 302 p. 24 cm. [PS3511.R94Z68] 64-16193
1. Frost, Robert, 1874-1963.

LATHEM, Edward Connery. 818'.5'209
Robert Frost and the Lawrence, Massachusetts, High School Bulletin; the beginning of a literary career, by Edward Connery Lathem and Lawrance Thompson. New York, Grolier Club, 1966. 94 p. facsims., port. 31 cm. "The facsimile section ... reproduces in full each of the four issues of the Lawrence High School bulletin for the period of Robert Frost's editorship." Bibliographical references included in "Notes" (p. 81-94) [PS3511.R94Z7642] 66-29452
1. Frost, Robert, 1874-1963. I. Thompson, Lawrance Roger, 1906- joint author. II. Lawrence, Mass High School. High School bulletin. III. Title. **BIP**

MERTINS, Marshall Louis, 1885- 811.52 B
Robert Frost; life and talks-walking, by Louis Mertins. [1st ed.] Norman, University of Oklahoma Press [1965] xiii, 450 p. illus., ports. 23 cm. [PS3511.R94Z786] 65-11238
1. Frost, Robert, 1874-1963.

ORTON, Vrest, 1897- 811'.5'2
Vermont afternoons with Robert Frost. Rutland, Vt., Tuttle [1971] 63 p. illus., ports. 20 cm. [PS3565.R8V4] 70-134029 4.00
1. Frost, Robert, 1874-1963. I. Title. **BIP**

SIMPSON, Lewis P., comp. 811'.5'2
Profile of Robert Frost. Compiled by Lewis P. Simpson. Columbus, Ohio, Merrill [1971] x, 118 p. 23 cm. (Charles E. Merrill profiles) Contents.Contents.—Robert Frost: the popular and the central poetic images, by L. N. Dendinger.—Robert Frost and the edge of the clearing, by J. M. Cox.—Robert Frost: some divisions in a whole man, by I. Traschen.—Frost and Emerson: voice and vision, by A. S. Ryan.—The themes of Robert Frost, by R. P. Warren.—An approach to Robert Frost's nature poetry, by N. Baym.—Diminished nature, by W. H. Pritchard.—The strength of Robert Frost, by A. Kazin. Includes bibliographical references. [PS3511.R94Z923] 78-143449 ISBN 0-675-09234-5
1. Frost, Robert, 1874-1963. I. Title.

THOMPSON, Lawrance Roger, 1906- 811.52
Fire and ice; the art and thought of Robert Frost. New York, Russell & Russell, 1961 [c1942] 241 p. 22 cm. [PS3511.R94Z93 1961] 61-15326
1. Frost, Robert, 1874-1963. I. Title. **BIP**

THOMPSON, Lawrance Roger, 1906- 811.52 B
Robert Frost, by Lawrance Thompson. [1st ed.] New York, Holt, Rinehart and Winston [1966- v. illus., ports. 24 cm. Contents.Contents.—[1] The early years, 1874-1915.—[2] The years of triumph, 1915-1938. Includes bibliographical references. [PS3511.R94Z953] 66-20523
1. Frost, Robert, 1874-1963. **BIP**

WILSON, Ellen Janet (Cameron) j92
Robert Frost, boy with promises to keep, by Ellen Wilson. Illustrated by Al Fiorentino. Indianapolis, Bobbe-Merrill [1967] 200 p. col. illus. 20 cm. (Childhood of famous Americans) [PS3511.R94Z99] 67-17740
1. Frost, Robert, 1874-1963 — Juvenile literature. I. Title.

Frost, Robert, 1874-1963—Addresses, essays, lectures.

FROST, centennial essays 811'.5'2
III / edited by Jac Tharpe. Jackson : University Press of Mississippi, 1978. p. cm. Includes index. Bibliography: p. [PS3511.R94Z6545] 78-3548 ISBN 0-87805-047-7 : 15.00
1. Frost, Robert, 1874-1963—Addresses, essays, lectures. 2. Poets, American—20th century—Biography—Addresses, essays, lectures. I. Tharpe, Jac.

ROBERT Frost : 811'.5'2
read and remembered : his centennial celebration at Agnes Scott College / edited by Margret G. Trotter. Decatur, Ga. : The College, 1976. 82 p. ; 23 cm. Includes bibliographical references. [PS3511.R94Z918] 76-369793
1. Frost, Robert, 1874-1963—Addresses, essays, lectures. I. Trotter, Margret G. II. Agnes Scott College, Decatur, Ga.

Frost, Robert, 1874-1963—Biography.

MORRISON, Kathleen, 1898- 811'.5'2 B
Robert Frost; a pictorial chronicle. New York, Holt, Rinehart and Winston [1974] viii, 133 p. illus., facsim. 26 cm. [PS3511.R94Z795] 74-3383 ISBN 0-03-012601-0 10.95
1. Frost, Robert, 1874-1963—Biography. 2. Frost, Robert, 1874-1963—Portraits, etc.

Frost, Robert, 1874-1963—Biography—Teaching career.

VOGEL, Nancy. 807'.11'73 B
Robert Frost, teacher. [Bloomington, Ind.] Phi Delta Kappa [1974] vii, 99 p. 23 cm. Bibliography: p. 93-94. [PS3511.R94Z98] 73-89797 3.95 (pbk.)
1. Frost, Robert, 1874-1963—Biography—Teaching career. **BIP**

Frost, Robert, 1874-1963—Juvenile literature.

FABER, Doris, 1924- j92
Robert Frost, America's poet. Illustrated by Paul Frame. Englewood Cliffs, N.J., Prentice-Hall [1964] 79 p. illus., ports. 22 cm. (P-H junior research books) [PS3511.R94Z64] 64-16441
1. Frost, Robert, 1874-1963 — Juvenile literature. I. Title.

LONGO, Lucas. 811'.5'2 B
Robert Frost, twentieth century American poet laureate. Charlotteville, N.Y., SamHar Press, 1972. 32 p. 22 cm. (Outstanding personalities, no. 21) Bibliography: p. 31-32. A brief biography of the first American poet to recite at a presidential inauguration. [PS3511.R94Z7646] 92 70-190239 pap. .98
1. Frost, Robert, 1874-1963—Juvenile literature. I. Title.
Library Edition 1.98.

Frost, Robert, 1874-1963—Manuscripts—Facsimiles.

FROST, Robert, 1874-1963. 811'.5'2
Robert Frost, a remembrance. [Amherst? Mass.] : Friends of the Amherst College Library, 1974. [6] p. : facsim. ; 23 cm. "An edition of five hundred copies." [PS3511.R94Z516 1974] 74-188848
1. Frost, Robert, 1874-1963—Manuscripts—Facsimiles. I. Amherst College. Library. Friends. II. Title. III. Title: A remembrance.

Frothingham, Octavius Brooks, 1822-1895.

CARUTHERS, J. Wade. 288'.092'4 B
Octavius Brooks Frothingham, gentle radical / J. Wade Caruthers. University : University of Alabama Press, c1977. ix, 279 p., [3] leaves of plates : ill. ; 25 cm. Includes index. Bibliography: p. [262]-268. [BX9869.F83C37] 76-18079 ISBN 0-8173-5166-3 12.50
1. Frothingham, Octavius Brooks, 1822-1895. I. Title.

Froude, James Anthony, 1818-1894.

DUNN, Waldo Hilary, 1882- 928.2
James Anthony Froude, a biography. [New York] Oxford [c.]1961[ ] 261p. illus. Contents.[1] 1818-1856. Bibl. 61-65218 5.60
1. Froude, James Anthony, 1818-1894. I. Title.

DUNN, Waldo Hilary, 1882- 928.2
James Anthony Froude, a biography [v.2. New York] Oxford [1964, c.1963] v illus., ports. 23cm. Contents.--v.2. 1857-1894. Bibl. 61-65218 8.80
1. Froude, James Anthony, 1818-1894. I. Title.

WILSON, David Alec, 1864-1933. 824'.8 B
Mr. Froude and Carlyle. New York, Haskell House Publishers, 1970. viii, 360 p. 23 cm. Reprint of the 1898 ed. [PR4433.W45 1970] 75-122460
1. Froude, James Anthony, 1818-1894. 2. Carlyle, Thomas, 1795-1881. I. Title.

Fry, Christopher—Biography—Ancestry.

FRY, Christopher. 822'.9'14 B
Can you find me : a family history / Christopher Fry. London ; New York : Oxford University Press, 1978. p. cm. [PR6011.R9Z465] 77-30728 ISBN 0-19-211751-3 : 13.95
1. Fry, Christopher—Biography—Ancestry. 2. Fry family. 3. Hammond family. 4. Dramatists, English—20th century—Biography. 5. England—Biography. I. Title.

Fry, Edwin Maxwell, 1899-

FRY, Edwin Maxwell, 1899- 720'.92'4
Autobiographical sketches / [by] Maxwell Fry ; with twenty-six illustrations by the author. London : Elek, 1975. 167 p. : ill. ; 23 cm. [NA997.F78A22] 76-361717 ISBN 0-236-40010-X : 14.95
1. Fry, Edwin Maxwell, 1899- 2. Architects—Great Britain—Correspondence, reminiscences, etc. I. Title.
Distributed by Technical Impex **BIP**

Fry, Elizabeth Gurney, 1780-1845.

FRY, Elizabeth Gurney, 1780-1845. 365'.92'4 B
Memoir of the life of Elizabeth Fry, with extracts from her journal and letters. Edited by her daughters, Katharine Fry and Rachel Elizabeth Cresswell. 2d ed., rev. & enl. Montclair, N.J., Patterson Smith, 1974. xxviii, 521, viii, 561 p. illus. 23 cm. (Patterson Smith series in criminology, law enforcement, and social problems, publication no. 187) Reprint of the 1848 ed. published by J. Hatchard, London; with the addition of genealogical tables and an index. [HV8978.F7A3 1974] 70-172597 ISBN 0-87585-187-8
1. Fry, Elizabeth Gurney, 1780-1845. I. Fry, Katharine, 1801-1886, ed. II. Cresswell, Rachel Elizabeth Fry, ed.

KENT, John, 1923- 923.642
Elizabeth Fry. New York, ARCO Pub. Co. [1963] 144 p. illus. 23 cm. (Makers of world history) Includes bibliography. [HV8978.F7K4 1963] 63-17094
1. Fry, Elizabeth (Gurney) 1780-1845.

PITMAN, Emma Raymond. 635'.924 B
Elizabeth Fry. New York, Greenwood Press [1969] vi, 269 p. 18 cm. Reprint of the 1884 ed. [HV8978.F7P6 1969] 69-14036
1. Fry, Elizabeth (Gurney) 1780-1845. I. Title. **BIP**

PRINGLE, Patrick. 923.642
The prisoners' friend; the story of Elizabeth Fry. New York, Roy Publishers [1954] 143p. illus., ports. 19cm. [HV8978.F7P75] 54-5223
1. Fry, Elizabeth (Gurney) 1780-1845. I. Title.

PRINGLE, Patrick 92
The young Elizabeth Fry. Illus. by Denise Brown. New York, Roy [1965, c.1963] 126p. illus. 21cm. [HV8978.F7P76] 64-23911 3.25 bds.,
1. Fry, Elizabeth (Gurney) 1780-1845. I. Title.

WHITNEY, Janet (Payne) 1894- 365'.924 B
Elizabeth Fry, Quaker heroine, by Janet Whitney. New York, B. Blom, 1972. 327 p. illus. 21 cm. Reprint of the 1937 ed. Bibliography: p. 313-315. [HV8978.F7W5 1972] 72-83752
1. Fry, Elizabeth (Gurney) 1780-1845.

Fry, Elizabeth Gurney, 1780-1845—Juvenile literature.

JOHNSON, Jan. 365'.92'4 B
Angel of the prison : a story about Elizabeth Fry / written by Jan Johnson ; illustrated by Vera Rosenberry. Minneapolis : Winston Press, c1977. [32] p. : ill. (some col.) ; 21 cm. (Stories about Christian heroes) A brief biography of the woman who was responsible for prison reform throughout England during the nineteenth century. [HV8978.F7J62] 77-77673 ISBN 0-03-022121-8 pbk. : 1.50
1. Fry, Elizabeth Gurney, 1780-1845—Juvenile literature. 2. Prison reformers—Biography—Juvenile literature. I. Rosenberry, Vera. II. Title. III. Series. **BIP**

JOHNSON, Spencer. 365'.92'4 B
The value of kindness : the story of Elizabeth Fry / by Spencer Johnson ; illustrated by Pileggi. 2d ed. La Jolla, Calif. : Value Communications, c1976. 62 p. : col. ill. ; 29 cm. (ValueTales) First ed. published in 1975 under title: The ValueTale of Elizabeth Fry. Discusses the work of the English woman whose pioneering efforts in improving the lot of prisoners were based on the premise that prisoners' behaviour would improve if they were treated more kindly. [HV8978.F7J63 1976] 92 76-55339 ISBN 0-916392-09-0 : 4.95
1. Fry, Elizabeth Gurney, 1780-1845—Juvenile literature. 2. Prisoners and prisons—Great Britain—Juvenile literature. I. Pileggi, Steve. II. Title. **BIP**

Fry family.

FRY, Christopher. 822'.9'14 B
Can you find me : a family history / Christopher Fry. London ; New York : Oxford University Press, 1978. p. cm. [PR6011.R9Z465] 77-30728 ISBN 0-19-211751-3 : 13.95
1. Fry, Christopher—Biography—Ancestry. 2. Fry family. 3. Hammond family. 4. Dramatists, English—20th century—Biography. 5. England—Biography. I. Title.

FRYE, George Walter, 1909- 929'.2'0973
Colonel Joshua Fry of Virginia and some of his descendants and allied families, by George W. Frye. Cincinnati, 1966. 59, 531, 54, 91 p. illus., ports. 22 cm. Bibliographical footnotes. [CS71.F947 1966] 66-31313

1. Fry family. I. Title.

Fry, Jane.

FRY, Jane, 1945- 362.2'092'4 B
Being different: the autobiography of Jane Fry. Collected, compiled, and edited, with an introd. and conclusion by Robert Bogdan. New York, Wiley [1974] xii, 235 p. 23 cm. "A Wiley-Interscience publication." Includes bibliographical references. [RC557.F78] 73-20155 ISBN 0-471-08570-7 9.95
1. Fry, Jane. 2. Sexual deviation—Personal narratives. 3. Psychiatric hospitals. 4. United States—Social conditions. I. Bogdan, Robert, ed. II. Title.

Fry, Margery, 1874-1958.

JONES, Enid Huws. 365.924
Margery Fry; the essential amateur. London, New York [etc.] Oxford U.P., 1966. [10] 256 p. front., plates (ports.) 22 1/2 c.m. 42/ Bibliography: p. [246]-247. [HV8978.F73J6] 66-76635
1. Fry, Margery, 1874-1958. I. Title.

Fry, Roger Eliot, 1866-1934.

WOOLF, Virginia 709'.2'4 B
Stephen, 1882-1941.
Roger Fry : a biography / Virginia Woolf. New York : Harcourt Brace Jovanovich, 1976, c1940. 303 p., [8] leaves of plates : ill. ; 21 cm. (A Harvest book ; HB338) Includes index. [N7483.F79W66 1976] 75-34023 ISBN 0-15-678520-X pbk. : 4.50
1. Fry, Roger Eliot, 1866-1934. **BIP**

Fry, William Henry, 1813-1864.

UPTON, William Treat, 1870- 927.8
William Henry Fry, American journalist and composer-critic. New York, Crowell [1954] xv, 346p. port., music. 22cm. 'Musical works of William Henry Fry in the collections of the Library Company of Philadelphia': p. [308]-328. [ML410.F965U62] 54-5533
1. Fry, William Henry, 1813-1864. I. Title.

UPTON, William Treat, 780'.92'4 B
1870-1961.
William Henry Fry, American journalist and composer-critic. New York, Da Capo Press, 1974 [c1954] xv, 346 p. illus. 22 cm. (Da Capo Press music reprint series) Reprint of the ed. published by T. Y. Crowell Co., New York. "Musical works of William Henry Fry in the collections of the Library Company of Philadelphia": p. [303]-323. [ML410.F965U62 1974] 73-20224 ISBN 0-306-70625-3 15.00
1. Fry, William Henry, 1813-1864.

Frydland, Rachmiel.

FRYDLAND, 940.53'1503'924
Rachmiel.
When being Jewish was a crime / by Rachmiel Frydland. Nashville : T. Nelson, c1978. p. cm. Includes index. [DS135.P63F783] 78-16689 ISBN 0-8407-5659-3 pbk. : 3.95
1. Frydland, Rachmiel. 2. Jews Poland—Biography. 3. Holocaust, Jewish (1939-1945)—Personal narratives. 4. Converts from Judaism—Biography. 5. Poland—Biography. I. Title. **BIP**

Frye, Walter, 15th century.

KENNEY, Sylvia W. 784.0942
Walter Frye and the contenance angloise [by] Sylvia W. Kenney. New Haven, Yale University Press, 1964 [c1965] xxv, 227 p. illus., music. 24 cm. (Yale studies in the history of music, v. 3) Bibliography: p. [201]-218. [ML410.F9654K5] 65-11183
1. Frye, Walter, 15th century. 2. Music—History and criticism—Medieval, 400-1500. 3. Music, English—History and criticism. I. Title. II. Series. **BIP**

Fuchs, Klaus Emil Julius, 1911-

MOOREHEAD, Alan, 1910- 364.13
The traitors. With a new pref. [Rev. ed.] New York, Harper & Row [1963] 236 p. illus. 22 cm. Includes bibliography. [HD9698.A28M6 1963] 63-10606
1. Fuchs, Klaus Emil Julius, 1911- 2. Pontecorvo, Bruno, 1913- 3. May, Allan Nunn, 1911- 4. Atomic energy. I. Title.

Fuchs, Sir Vivian.

LEHRBURGER, Egon, 1904- 923.942
Sir Vivian Fuchs, by Egon Larsen [pseud.] New York, Roy Publishers [1960, c1959] 110p. illus. 19cm. (The Living biographies series) [G246.F8L4 1960] 60 7679
1. Fuchs, Sir Vivian. I. Title.

Fudge, Bob, 1862-1933.

RUSSELL, Jim. 917.8
Bob Fudge, Texas trail driver, Montana-Wyoming cowboy, 1862-1933. Denver, Big Mountain Press [1962] 135 p. illus. 23 cm. [CT275.F728R8] 63-130
1. Fudge, Bob, 1862-1933. 2. Frontier and pioneer life—The West. I. Title.

Fuentes, Rafael L. (Tony Fuentes)

FUENTES, Rafael L. (Tony 920
Fuentes)
My diary. New York, Comet Press [c.] 1960. 89p. 21cm. 2.75
I. Title.

Fuertes, Louis Agassiz,

FUERTES, Louis Agassiz, 759.13
1874-1927.
Louis Agassiz Fuertes: his life briefly told and his correspondence edited by Mary Fuerles Boynton. New York, Oxford University Press, 1956. 317p. illus. 24cm. [ND237.F78A3] [ND237.F78A3] 927.5 56-5705 56-5705
I. Boynton, Mary (Fuertes) 1906- ed. II. Title.

Fugate, Caril Ann.

BEAVER, Ninette. 364.1'523'0924 B
Caril, by Ninette Beaver, B. K. Ripley, and Patrick Trese. [1st ed.] Philadelphia, Lippincott [1974] 320 p. illus. 25 cm. [HV6248.F83B43] 74-9843 ISBN 0-397-00997-6 8.95
1. Fugate, Caril Ann. 2. Starkweather, Charles. 3. Crime and criminals—Biography. I. Ripley, B. K., joint author. II. Trese, Patrick, joint author. **BIP**

Fugger, Jakob, 1459-1525.

STRIEDER, Jacob, 1877- 332.0924
1936
Jacob Fugger the Rich, Merchant and banker of Augsburg, 1459-1525. Tr. by Mildred L. Hartsough. Ed. by N. S. B. Gras. [Hamden, Conn.] Archon 1966 [c.1931] xxiv, 227p. illus., geneal. table, port. 22cm. Bibl. [HF442.F7S745 1966] 66-23448 6.00
1. Fugger, Jakob, 1459-1525. I. Title.

Fukuzawa, Yukichi,

FUKUZAWA, Yukichi, 378.520924
1835-1901
Autobiography, Rev. tr. by Eiichi Kiyooka. Foreword by Carmen Blacker [1st Amer. ed.] New York, Columbia [c.1960,1966] xv,407p. illus., ports. 21cm. [LG271.K44F83] 66-15468 7.50
I. Kiyooka, Eiichi, 1902- ed. and tr. II. Title.

Fulbert, Bp. of Chartres, 960 (ca.)-1028.

FULBERT, Bp. of 282'.092'4 B
Chartres, 960(ca.)-1028.
The letters and poems of Fulbert of Chartres / edited and translated by Frederick Behrends. Oxford : Clarendon Press, 1976. xciii, 297 p. ; 22 cm. (Oxford medieval texts) Introd. and notes in English, parallel text in English and Latin. Includes indexes. Bibliography: p. [x]-xii. [BX4705.F88A4 1976] 76-379876 ISBN 0-19-822233-5 : 27.50
1. Fulbert, Bp. of Chartres, 960 (ca.)-1028. 2. Bishops—France—Chartres—Correspondence. 3. Chartres, France—Biography. I. Behrends, Frederick. II. Title. III. Series.
Dist. by Oxford University Press NY NY **BIP**

Fulbright, James William, 1905-

COFFIN, Tristram, 973.90924 B
1912-
Senator Fulbright, portrait of a public philosopher. [1st ed.] New York, Dutton, 1966. 378 p. illus., ports. 22 cm. Bibliography: p. [371]-372. [E748.F88C6] 67-11358
1. Fulbright, James William, 1905- I. Title.

JOHNSON, Haynes 973.9'0924 B
Bonner, 1931-
Fulbright; the dissenter [by] Haynes Johnson and Bernard M. Gwertzman. [1st ed.] Garden City, N.Y., Doubleday, 1968. x, 321 p. illus., ports. 25 cm. [E748.F88J6] 68-17789
1. Fulbright, James William, 1905- I. Gwertzman, Bernard M., joint author.

Fulco.

FULCO. 945.8'23
The happy summer days : a Sicilian childhood / by Fulco. London : Weidenfeld and Nicolson, c1976. 160 p., [4] leaves of plates : ill. ; 23 cm. [DG865.6.F84] 77-360702 ISBN 0-297-77200-7 : £4.95
1. Fulco. 2. Sicily—Social life and customs. 3. Sicily—Nobility—Biography. 4. Children in Sicily—Biography. I. Title.

Fuldheim, Dorothy.

FULDHEIM, Dorothy. 070.1'9'0924
A thousand friends. [1st ed.] Garden City, N.Y., Doubleday, 1974. 183 p. 22 cm. Contents.Contents.—What is TV really like?—Aunt Molly.—Talk shows and hosts.—A tragic story.—In a German garden.—I threw Jerry Rubin off my show.—Kent.—Man's destiny.—Mrs. O'Grady.—Lilacs.—Jane Fonda and the Duke of Windsor.—Six days.—I hate eggs.—A Roman fountain. A wonderful engine.—Americans are different.—Paris.—A September afternoon.—Television sucks a performer dry.—$3,400. [PN4874.F77A38] 73-10805 ISBN 0-385-01701-4 5.95
1. Fuldheim, Dorothy. 2. Journalists—Correspondence, reminiscences, etc. I. Title.
Contents omitted.

Fulkerson, Jasbo, 1904-1949.

INGRAM, Wayne 927.913
Jasbo, by Wagne Ingram and Jane Pattie. San Antonio, Naylor Co. [1960, c.1959] vii, 89p. plates, ports. 22cm. 59-14816 3.50
1. Fulkerson, Jasbo, 1904-1949. I. Pattie, Jane, joint author. II. Title.

Fuller, Alfred Carl, 1885

ALLEN, Edward, 1929- 926.58
Alfred C. Fuller; selling door to door. Chicago, Encyclopaedia Britannica Press [1964] 174 p. illus., ports. 22 cm. (Britannica bookshelf: Great lives) [HD9999.B865F83] 63-22506
1. Fuller, Alfred Carl, 1885-

Fuller, Charles Edward, 1887-1968.

FULLER, Daniel P. 269'.2'0924 B
Give the winds a mighty voice; the story of Charles E. Fuller, by Daniel P. Fuller. Waco, Tex., Word Books [1972] 247 p. illus. 23 cm. [BV3785.F8F84] 72-83342 5.95
1. Fuller, Charles Edward, 1887-1968. I. Title.

FULLER, Grace (Payton) comp. 922
Heavenly sunshine; letters to the 'Old fashioned revival hour,'complied by Mrs. Charles E. Fuller. [Westwood, N. J.] Revell [1956] 156p. 20cm. [BV3785.F8A4] 56-13217
1. Fuller, Charles Edward, 1887- 2. Old fashioned revival hour (Radio program) I. Title.

Fuller, Claude Albert, 1876-

BEALS, Frank Lee, 1881- 923.473
Backwoods baron; the life story of Claude Albert Fuller. Wheaton. Ill., Morton Pub. Co. [1951] 146 p. illus. 20 cm. 51-8745
1. Fuller, Claude Albert, 1876- I. Title.

Fuller, George Warren, 1868-1934.

WOLMAN, Abel, 1892- 628'.092'4 B
George Warren Fuller, a reminiscence / Abel Wolman. Washington : Public Works Historical Society, 1976. 30 p. : port. ; 22 cm. (Essays in public works history ; essay no. 2) Includes a paper, Recent developments in sewage treatment, presented by Fuller at the 1922 meeting of the American Society of Municipal Improvements, and a partial list of his publications and clients. [TD140.F84W64] 77-150482 1.00
1. Fuller, George Warren, 1868-1934. 2. Sanitary engineers United States—Biography. I. Fuller, George Warren, 1868-1934. Recent developments in sewage treatment. 1976. II. Title. III. Series.

Fuller, John Frederick Charles, 1878-1966.

TRYTHALL, Anthony 355'.0092'4 B
John, 1927-
"Boney" Fuller : soldier, strategist, and writer, 1878-1966 / Anthony John Trythall. New Brunswick, N.J. : Rutgers University Press, 1977. xiii, 314 p., [6] leaves of plates : ill. ; 23 cm. "Books published by Major-General Fuller": p. [301]-303. [U55.F86T78 1977] 77-76775 ISBN 0-8135-0844-4 : 13.95
1. Fuller, John Frederick Charles, 1878-1966. 2. Generals—Great Britain—Biography.

Fuller, Melville Weston, 1833-1910.

KING, Willard Leroy, 347'.73'2634
1893-
Melville Weston Fuller, Chief Justice of the United States, 1888-1910. New York, Macmillan, 1950. x, 394 p. ports. 22 cm. Bibliography: p. 343-347. [KF8745.F8K5 1950] 50-8032
1. Fuller, Melville Weston, 1833-1910. I. Title.

KING, Willard Leroy, 347.99'24
1893-
Melville Weston Fuller, Chief Justice of the United States, 1888-1910 [by] Willard L. King. With an introd. by Phil C. Neal. Chicago, University of Chicago Press [1967] xvi, 394 p. ports. 21 cm. (The Court and the Constitution) (Phoenix books.) Includes bibliographical references. [KF8745.F8K5 1967] 67-12152
1. Fuller, Melville Weston, 1833-1910. I. Title

Fuller, Millard, 1935-

FULLER, Millard, 266'.0096751
1935-
Bokotola / Millard Fuller. New York : Association Press, c1977. v, 174 p. ; 22 cm. [BV3625.C6F8] 77-1277 ISBN 0-8096-1924-5 pbk. : 4.25
1. Fuller, Millard, 1935- 2. Missions—Zaire. 3. Labor and laboring classes—Dwellings—Zaire. 4. Missionaries—Zaire—Biography. I. Title. **BIP**

Fuller, Richard Buckminster, 1895-

FULLER, Richard Buckminster, 926
1895-
Ideas and integrities, a spontaneous autobiographical disclosure. Edited by Robert W. Marks. Englewood Cliffs, N.J., Prentice-Hall [1963] 318 p. illus. 24 cm. [T40.F86A3] 63-11571
I. Title.

HATCH, Alden, 1898- 620'.0092'4 B
Buckminster Fuller; at home in the universe. New York, Crown Publishers

[1974] vii, 279 p. illus. 24 cm. [TA140.F9H37 1974] 73-91509 7.95
1. Fuller, Richard Buckminster, 1895-

KENNER, Hugh. 620 B
Bucky; a guided tour of Buckminster Fuller. New York, Morrow, 1973. 338 p. illus. 21 cm. Bibliography: p. 327-331. [TA140.F9K46] 79-182966 ISBN 0-688-00141-6 7.95
1. Fuller, Richard Buckminster, 1895- I. Title. BIP

MARKS, Robert W. 624.17
The Dymaxion world of Buckminster Fuller. New York, Reinhold Pub. Corp. [1960] 232 p. illus., ports., maps, diagrs. 27 cm. [TA140.F9M3] 60-5487
1. Fuller, Richard Buckminster, 1895- I. Title.

SNYDER, Robert. 620'.0092'4 B
Buckminster Fuller : an auto-biographical monologue/scenario / Robert Synder. New York : St. Martin's Press, 1979. p. cm. [TA140.F9S64] 79-16323 ISBN 0-312-24547-5 : 15.95
1. Fuller, Richard Buckminster, 1895- 2. Engineers—United States—Biography. 3. Architects—United States—Biography. I. Title. BIP

Fuller, Richard Buckminster, 1895- — Juvenile literature..

LORD, Athena V. 620'.0092'4 B
Pilot for Spaceship Earth : R. Buckminster Fuller, architect, inventor, and poet / Athena V. Lord. New York : Macmillan, c1978. 168 p. : ill. ; 24 cm. Includes index. Bibliography: p. [161]-163. A biography of R. Buckminster Fuller, the architect and inventor whose investigations into the principles of nature influenced his designs and helped revolutionize our world. [T40.F86L67] 92 77-12629 ISBN 0-02-417670-2 : 7.95
1. Fuller, Richard Buckminster, 1895- — Juvenile literature.. 2. Inventors—United States—Biography—Juvenile literature. 3. Architects—United States—Biography—Juvenile literature. I. Title. BIP

Fuller, Samuel Michael, 1911-

GARNHAM, Nicholas. 791.43'0232'0924
Samuel Fuller. New York, Viking Press [1972, c1971] 176 p. illus. 20 cm. (Cinema one,15) [PN1998.A3F843 1972] 75-173870 ISBN 0-670-61663-X 6.95
1. Fuller, Samuel Michael, 1911-

Fuller, Thomas, 1608-1661.

ADDISON, William. 283'.0924 B
Worthy Dr. Fuller. Westport, Conn., Greenwood Press [1971] xxi, 298 p. illus. 23 cm. Reprint of the 1951 ed. Bibliography: p. 290-294. [BX5199.F8A6 1971] 71-106707 ISBN 0-8371-3437-4
1. Fuller, Thomas, 1608-1661. I. Title. BIP

Fuller, William, 1670-1733.

CAMPBELL, George Archibald, 1900- 923.4142
Impostor at the bar: William Fuller, 1670-1733. London, Hodder & Stoughton [dist. Mystic, Conn., Verry, 1964, c.1961] New york Collier Books 1958 [c.1933] 250p. illus. 23cm. 18 cm 183 p. 63-5512 5.00
1. Fuller, William, 1670-1733. I. Title.

Fullingim, Archer.

FULLINGIM, Archer. 320.9'764'06
Archer Fullingim : a country editor's view of life / edited, with an introd., by Roy Hamric. 1st ed. Austin, Tex. : Heidelberg Publishers, 1975. p. cm. [F386.F84] 75-29497 ISBN 0-913206-07-5 : 8.95
1. Fullingim, Archer. 2. Texas—Politics and government—Collected works. 3. United States—Politics and government—1945- —Collected works. 4. Big Thicker National Park, Tex.—Collected works. BIP

Fullman, Terry.

SLOSSER, Bob. 283'.092'4 B
Miracle in Darien / Bob Slosser. Plainfield, N.J. : Logos International, c1979. 268 p. ; 22 cm. [BX5995.F78S58] 79-83791 ISBN 0-88270-355-2 : 6.95
1. Fullman, Terry. 2. St. Paul's Episcopal Church, Darien, Conn. 3. Protestant Episcopal Church in the U.S.A.—Clergy—Biography. 4. Clergy—United States—Biography. I. Title. BIP

Fulton Co., Ind.—Biography.

FULTON County folks / 917.72'87
edited by Shirley Willard. [Rochester, Ind.] : Fulton County Historical Society, [1974- v. : ill. ; 29 cm. Cover title. [F532.F9F84] 73-94273 7.50 (v. 1)
1. Fulton Co., Ind.—Biography. I. Willard, Shirley, ed. II. Fulton County Historical Society (Ind.)

Fulton County, Ill.—Biography.

RAMBLIN' thru 917.73'48'03'30922
Spoon River country via the rambler's notes. Produced by the Publication Committee of the Spoon River Scenic Drive Associates. Canton, Ill., Canton daily ledger, 1970 [c1969] 107 p. illus., map, ports. 23 cm. Based on interviews recorded by James K. P. White and published in the Canton weekly register during the years 1904-1910. [F547.F8R3] 71-19888
1. Fulton County, Ill.—Biography. I. White, James P. K. II. Spoon River Scenic Drive Associates. Publication Committee.

Fulton, Eileen.

FULTON, Eileen. 791.45'028'0924 B
How my world turns [by] Eileen Fulton as told to Brett Bolton. New York, Taplinger Pub. Co. [1970] 208 p. illus., ports. 22 cm. [PN2287.F8A3 1970] 73-125302 5.95
I. Bolton, Brett. II. Title. BIP

FULTON, Eileen. 791.45'028'0924 [B]
How my world turns [by] Eileen Fulton as told to Brett Bolton. [New York] Warner Paperback Lib. [1973 c.1970] 285 p. illus., ports. 18 cm. [PN2287.F8A3 1973] 73-125302 1.25 (pbk)
I. Bolton, Brett. II. Title.

Fulton, John Edwin, 1869-1945.

HARE, Eric B. 266.6'7'0924 B
Fulton's footprints in Fiji [by] Eric B. Hare. Washington, Review and Herald Pub. Association [1969] 252 p. illus., map (on lining papers), ports. 22 cm. [BV3680.F6F8] 77-84993
1. Fulton, John Edwin, 1869-1945. 2. Seventh-Day Adventists—Missions. 3. Seventh-Day Adventists—Missions. 4. Missions—Fiji Islands. I. Title.

Fulton, Len.

FULTON, Len. 658.8'09'0705730924 B
American odyssey, a bookselling travelogue / by Len Fulton, with Ellen Ferber. Paradise, CA. : Dustbooks, 1975. p. cm. [HF5456.B8F844] 75-25600 ISBN 0-913218-47-2 pbk. : 4.50. ISBN 0-913218-46-4 : 7.95.
1. Fulton, Len. The grassman. 2. Booksellers and bookselling—United States—Colportage, subscription trade, etc. 3. United States—Description and travel—1960- I. Ferber, Ellen, 1939- joint author. II. Title.

Fulton, Robert, 1765-1815.

DICKINSON, Henry Winram, 1870-1952. 623.8'0924 B
Robert Fulton, engineer and artist; his life and works. Freeport, N.Y., Books for Libraries Press [1971] xiv, 333 p. illus., facsims., ports. 23 cm. Reprint of the 1913 ed. "Appendix C: List of writings by Robert Fulton," p. 282-283. [VM140.F9D5 1971] 73-148878 ISBN 0-8369-5649-4
1. Fulton, Robert, 1765-1815.

HILL, Ralph Nading, 1917- 926.238
Robert Fulton and the steamboat; illustrated by Lee J. Ames. New York, Random House [1954] 181 p. illus. 22 cm. (Landmark books, 45) [VM140.F9H5 1954] 54-7020
1. Fulton, Robert, 1765-1815.

MORGAN, John Smith, 1921- 623.82'4'0924 B
Robert Fulton / by John S. Morgan. New York : Mason/Charter, 1977. xi, 235 p., [4] leaves of plates : ill. ; 24 cm. Includes index. Bibliography: p. 224-227. [VM140.F9M67] 77-633 ISBN 0-88405-438-1 : 8.95
1. Fulton, Robert, 1765-1815. 2. Marine engineers—United States—Biography. 3. Inventors—United States—Biography. I. Title.

PARSONS, William Barclay, 1859- v. 12
Robert Fulton and the submarine. New York, AMS Press, 1967. 154 p. illus. Reprint of 1922 ed., Columbia University Press, New York. 68-67745
1. Fulton, Robert, 1765-1815. 2. Submarine boats. I. Title. BIP

Fulton, Robert, 1765-1815—Juvenile literature.

HENRY, Joanne Landers. 623.82'4'0924 B
Robert Fulton, steamboat builder. Illustrated by Tran Mawicke. Champaign, Ill., Garrard Pub. Co. [1975] 80 p. col. illus. 23 cm. (A Discovery book) A brief biography of the portrait painter and inventor of the submarine and steamboat. [VM140.F9H4] 92 74-18326 ISBN 0-8116-6317-5 3.12 (lib. bdg.)
1. Fulton, Robert, 1765-1815—Juvenile literature. 2. Steamboats—History—Juvenile literature. I. Mawicke, Tran, illus. II. Title.

RADFORD, Ruby Lorraine, 1891- 623.8'0924 B
Robert Fulton, by Ruby L. Radford. Illustrated by Salem Tamer. New York, Putnam [1970] 64 p. illus. (part col.) 23 cm. (A See and read beginning to read biography) An easy-to-read biography of the portrait painter and inventor of the submarine and steamboat. [PZ10.R15Ro] 92 74-90860 2.68
1. Fulton, Robert, 1765-1815—Juvenile literature. I. Tamer, Salem, illus. II. Title. BIP

Fundamentalism.

RUSSELL, Charles Allyn. 230'.092'2 B
Voices of American fundamentalism : seven biographical studies / by C. Allyn Russell. Philadelphia : Westminster Press, c1976. p. cm. Includes index. Bibliography: p. [BT82.2.R87] 76-5886 ISBN 0-664-20814-2 : 12.50
1. Fundamentalism. 2. Christian biography. I. Title. BIP

Funk, Casimir, 1884-

HARROW, Benjamin, 1888- 926.1
Casimir Funk, pioneer in vitamins and hormones. New York, Dodd, Mead, 1955. 209 p. illus. 21 cm. [QP26.F8H3] 55-6935
1. Funk, Casimir, 1884-

Funk, Isaac, 1797-1865.

CAVANAGH, Helen Marie, 1904- 328.7730924 B
Funk of Funk's Grove, by Helen M. Cavanagh. Springfield, Illinois State Historical Society, 1968 [c1952] v, 208 p. illus., ports. 20 cm. Bibliography: p. 195-203. [F545.F95 1968] 78-634853
1. Funk, Isaac, 1797-1865. 2. Illinois—History—1778-1865. I. Title. BIP

CAVANAGH, Helen Marie, 1904- 923.273
Funk of Funk's Grove: farmer, legislator, and cattle king of the Old Northwest, 1797-1865. Bloomington, Ill., Pantagraph Print. Co., 1952. v. 208 p. illus., ports., fold. map. 20 cm. Bibliography: p. 195-206. [F545.F95] 52-29660
1. Funk, Isaac, 1797-1865. 2. Illinois—Hist.—1778-1865. I. Title.

Funk, John Fretz, Bp., 1835-1930.

GATES, Helen Litchfield (Kolb) 1895-1961. 922.8773
Bless the Lord, O my soul; a biography of Bishop John Fretz Funk, 1835-1930, creative pioneer for Christ and Mennonite leader, by Helen Kolb Gates [others] Ed. by J. C. Wenger. Scottdale, Pa., Herald Pr. [c.1964] 261p. illus., ports. 23cm Bibl. [BX8143.F8G3] 64-23375 4.75
1. Funk, John Fretz, Bp., 1835-1930. I. Title.

Funkhouser, Lloyd.

HERRERA, Barbara Hand. 248'.2'0924 B
Funky / Barbara Hand Herrera. Mountain View, Calif. : Pacific Press Pub. Association, c1978. 128 p. ; 22 cm. (A Destiny book ; D-167) [BX6193.F86H47] 77-80685 pbk. : 3.50
1. Funkhouser, Lloyd. 2. Seventh-Day Adventists—Biography. I. Title. BIP

Furman, James Clement.

FURMAN, James Clement. 286'.1'0924 B
From movies to ministry (and victory over alcohol) / by James Clement Furman. Raleigh : Christian Action League of N.C., c1977. 121 p., [8] leaves of plates : ill. ; 22 cm. Autobiographical. [BX6495.F84A34] 77-70572 ISBN 0-918648-01-7 pbk. : 2.95
1. Furman, James Clement. 2. Baptists—Clergy—Biography. 3. Clergy—South Carolina—Biography. I. Title.

Furnas. William Carlyle, 1886-1962.

LORZ, Robert Michael, 1922- 338.7'62'130420976178
Shadow of a man, by Robert Lorz. [Batavia? Ill., 1964] 70 p. illus., ports. 24 cm. [HD9695.U54F8] 65-44644
1. Furnas. William Carlyle, 1886-1962. I. Title.

Furniture—U. S.—Hist.

ORMSBEE, Thomas Hamilton, 1890- 749.211
Early American furniture makers; a social and biographical study. With 122 illus. New York, Archer House [1957] 185p. illus. 22cm. [NK2405.O7 1957] 57-13366
1. Furniture—U. S.—Hist. 2. Cabinet-workers. I. Title.

ORMSBEE, Thomas Hamilton, 1890- 749.2'13
Early American furniture makers, a social and biographical study. New York, Crowell. Detroit, Gale Research Co., 1974. p. cm. Reprint of the 1930 ed. Bibliography: p. [NK2405.O7 1974] 70-174089 ISBN 0-8103-4086-0
1. Furniture—United States—History. 2. Furniture workers—United States. I. Title.

Furuseth, Andrew, 1854-1938.

WEINTRAUB, Hyman. 923.373
Andrew Furuseth, emancipator of the seamen. Berkeley, University of California Press, 1959. 267 p. illus. 25 cm. At head of title: Publications of the Institute of Industrial Relations, University of California. Includes bibliography. [HD8073.F8W4] 59-3747
1. Furuseth, Andrew, 1854-1938. 2. Merchant seamen — U.S. I. Title. BIP

WEINTRAUB, Hyman. 331.88'11'38750924 B
Andrew Furuseth, emancipator of the seamen / Hyman Weintraub. New York : Arno Press, 1979, c1959. p. cm. (Scandinavians in America) Includes index. Reprint of the ed. published by University of California Press, Berkeley. Bibliography: p. [HD8073.F8W4 1979] 78-15860 ISBN 0-405-11664-0 : 20.00

1. Furuseth, Andrew, 1854-1938. 2. Merchant seamen—United States—Biography. 3. Trade-unions—Merchant seamen—United States—Officials and employees—Biography. I. Title. II. Series.

Fuseli, Henry, 1741-1825.

TOMORY, P. A., 1922- 759.2
The life and art of Henry Fuseli [by] Peter Tomory. New York, Praeger [1972] 255 p. illus. (part col.) 30 cm. Bibliography: p. 238-239. [ND853.F87T65] 72-77546 25.00
1. Fuseli, Henry, 1741-1825. I. Title. BIP

Fussing, Ellen Munroe,

FUSSING, Ellen Munroe, 1913- 920.7
... and the streets are covered with gold. New York, Willard Pub. Co. [1950] 194 p. 22 cm. Autobiographical. [CT275.F88A3] 50-989
I. Title.

Fyodorova, Victoria, 1946-

FYODOROVA, Victoria, 1946- 947.084'092'2 B
The admiral's daughter / Victoria Fyodorova and Haskel Frankel. New York : Delacorte Press, c1979. 372 p., [8] leaves of plates : ill. ; 24 cm. Includes index. [CT1218.F88A33] 78-26664 ISBN 0-440-00366-0 : 10.95
1. Fyodorova, Victoria, 1946- 2. Russia—Biography. 3. United States—Biography. I. Frankel, Haskel, joint author. II. Title. BIP

Gag, Wanda, 1893-1946—Juvenile literature.

DUIN, Nancy E. 741'.092'4 B
Wanda Gag, author and illustrator of children's books, by Nancy E. Duin. Charlotteville, N.Y., SamHar Press, 1973. 32 p. 22 cm. (Outstanding personalities, no 57) Bibliography: p. 31-32. A biography of the painter, author, and illustrator, famous for such children's books as Millions of Cats. [NC975.5.G34D84] 92 73-77601 1.98 (lib. bdg.)
1. Gag, Wanda, 1893-1946—Juvenile literature. I. Title. BIP

Galvez, Bernardo de Galvez, conde de, 1746-1786.

CAUGHEY, John Walton, 1902- 976.3'02'0924
Bernardo de Galvez in Louisiana, 1776-1783. Foreword by Jack D. L. Holmes. Gretna [La.] Pelican Pub. Co., 1972. xiii, 290 p. port. 24 cm. Reprint of the 1934 ed., which was issued as v. 4 of Publications of the University of California at Los Angeles in social sciences. Bibliography: p. 259-272. [F373.G252C38 1972] 72-86562 ISBN 0-911116-78-8 15.00
1. Galvez, Bernardo de Galvez, conde de, 1746-1786. 2. Louisiana—History—Colonial period. 3. United States—History—Revolution—Spanish participation. I. Title. II. Series: California. University. University at Los Angeles. Publications ... in social sciences, v. 4. BIP

Gericault, Jean Louis Andre Theodore, 1791-1824.

CLEMENT, Charles, 1821-1887. 760'.092'4 B
Gericault : a biographical and critical study with a catalogue raisonne of the master's works / Charles Clement ; introd. by Lorenz Eitner ; the catalogue of Gericault's work brought up to date by Lorenz Eitner in a new suppl. ; [suppl. translated by Regis Annequin]. New York : Da Capo, 1974. xv, iii, 472 p., [29] leaves of plates : ill. ; 24 cm. Text in French; introd. in English. Reprint of the 1879 ed. published by Didier, Paris. Includes bibliographical references. [ND553.G45C6 1974] 73-83834 ISBN 0-306-70643-1
1. Gericault, Jean Louis Andre Theodore, 1791-1824.

Gokalp, Ziya, 1876-1924.

HEYD, Uriel. 949.6'1'02072024
Foundations of Turkish nationalism : the life and teachings of Ziya Gokalp / by Uriel Heyd. Westport, Conn. : Hyperion Press, 1979. 174 p. ; 22 cm. Reprint of the 1950 ed. published by Luzac, London. "Based on a study, originally written in Hebrew, which was accepted by the Hebrew University in Jerusalem as a PH.D. thesis." Bibliography: p. 171-174. [DR438.9.G63H49 1979] 78-59025 ISBN 0-88355-698-7 : lib.bdg. : 14.50
1. Gokalp, Ziya, 1876-1924. 2. Historians—Turkey—Biography. 3. Nationalism—Turkey. I. Title. BIP

Gomez Morel, Alfredo.

GOMEZ Morel, Alfredo. 364.1'092'4 B
The river / by Alfredo Gomez Morel. Milbrae, Calif. : Celestial Arts, 1976. p. cm. Translation of El rio. [HV6248.G46A3713] 76-11356 ISBN 0-89087-166-3 pbk. : 4.95
1. Gomez Morel, Alfredo. 2. Crime and criminals—Biography. I. Title.

Goring, Hermann, 1893-1946.

GRITZBACH, Erich, 1896- 943.086'092'4 B
Hermann Goering: the man and his work; the only authorised biography. Translated from the German by Gerald Griffin. With a pref. by R. H. Bruce Lockhart. London, Hurst & Blackett, 1939. [New York, AMS Press, 1973] 256 p. illus. 23 cm. [DD247.G67G73 1973] 75-180404 ISBN 0-404-56128-4 12.50
1. Goring, Hermann, 1893-1946. I. Title.

LEE, Asher. 943.086'092'4 B
Goering: air leader. New York, Hippocrene Books [1972] 256 p. illus. 23 cm. Bibliography: p. [251]-252. [DD247.G67L37 1972] 72-81241 ISBN 0-88254-015-7 8.95
1. Goring, Hermann, 1893-1946.

MANVELL, Roger, 1909- 943.086'092'4 B
Goring [by] Roger Manvell. Advised by Heinrich Franenkel [i.e. Fraenkel. New York, Ballantine Books, 1972] 160 p. illus. 21 cm. (Ballantine's illustrated history of the violent century. War leader book no. 8) [DD247.G67M3 1972] 72-181439 ISBN 0-345-02460-5 1.00
1. Goring, Hermann, 1893-1946.

MOSLEY, Leonard, 1913- 943.086'092'4 B
The Reich Marshal; a biography of Hermann Goering. [1st ed.] Garden City, N.Y., Doubleday, 1974. xi, 394 p. illus. 25 cm. Includes bibliographical references [DD247.G67M67] 73-20825 ISBN 0-385-04961-7 12.50
1. Goring, Hermann, 1893-1946. I. Title.

Guemes, Martin Miguel, 1785-1821.

HAIGH, Roger M. 982'.4 B
Martin Guemes: tyrant or tool? A study of the sources of power of an Argentine caudillo, by Roger M. Haigh. Fort Worth, Texas Christian University Press, 1968. ix, 77 p. illus. 23 cm. (Texas Christian University monographs in history and culture, no. 3) Bibliography: p. 72-73. [F2845.G93H3] 68-8359
1. Guemes, Martin Miguel, 1785-1821. I. Title. II. Series.

Gable, Clark, 1901-1960.

CARPOZI, George, Jr. 927.92
Clark Gable. New York, Pyramid Books [c.1961] 160p. illus. (Pyramid books, R620) 61-3400 .50 pap.,
1. Gable, Clark, 1901-1960. I. Title.

GABLE, Kathleen (Williams) 927.92
Clark Gable; a personal portrait. Englewood Cliffs, N. J., Prentice-Hall [c.1961] 151p. illus. 26cm. 61-14694 3.95 bds.,
1. Gable, Clark, 1901-1960. I. Title.

GARCEAU, Jean. 927.92
"Dear Mr. G—"; the biography of Clark Gable, by Jean Garceau with Inez Cocke. [1st ed.] Boston, Little, Brown [1961] 297 p. illus. 22 cm. [PN2287.G3G35] 61-13898
1. Gable, Clark, 1901-1960. I. Cocke, Inez, joint author. II. Title.

GARCEAU, Jean. 791'.092'4 B
Gable : a pictorial biography / Jean Garceau with Inez Cocke. New York : Grosset & Dunlap, [1977] c1961. 202 p. : ill. ; 28 cm. "Adapted from Dear Mr. G—." Includes index. [PN2287.G3G35 1977] 77-378455 ISBN 0-448-14359-3 pbk : 6.95
1. Gable, Clark, 1901-1960. 2. Moving-picture actors and actresses—United States—Biography. I. Cocke, Inez, joint author. II. Title.

JORDAN, Rene. 791.43'028'0924 B
Clark Gable. New York, Pyramid Publications [1973] 159 p. illus. 20 cm. (A Pyramid illustrated history of the movies) Bibliography: p. 143-144. [PN2287.G3J6] 72-93669 ISBN 0-515-02929-7 1.45 (pbk.)
1. Gable, Clark, 1901-1960.

JORDAN, Rene. 791.43'028'0924 B
Clark Gable / by Rene Jordan ; general editor, Ted Sennett. New York : Galahad Books, c1973. 158 p. : ill. ; 22 cm. (The Pictorial treasury of film stars) Includes index. Bibliography: p. 143-144. [PN2287.G3J6 1973b] 73-90212 ISBN 0-88365-160-2 : 4.95
1. Gable, Clark, 1901-1960.

MORELLA, Joe. 791.43'028'0922 B
Cable & Lombard & Powell & Harlow / [by] Joe Morella & Edward Z. Epstein. 1st British ed. London : W. H. Allen, 1976. 204 p., [8] p. of plates : ill., ports. ; 23 cm. [PN1998.A2M56 1976] 76-383446 ISBN 0-491-01975-0 : £3.50
1. Gable, Clark, 1901-1960. 2. Lombard, Carole, 1908-1942. 3. Powell, William, 1892- 4. Harlow, Jean, 1911-1937. 5. Moving-picture actors and actresses—United States—Biography. I. Epstein, Edward Z., joint author. II. Title.

SAMUELS, Charles. 927.92
The king, a biography of Clark Gable. New York, Coward-McCann [1962] c315p. 22cm. [PN2287.G3S3 1962] 62-8861
1. Gable, Calrk, 1901-1960. I. Title.

SAMUELS, Charles 927.92
The king, a biography of Clark Gable. New York, Popular Lib. [1963, c.1961, 1962] 262p. 18cm. (M2019) .60 pap.,
1. Gable, Clark, 1901-1960. I. Title.

SCAGNETTI, Jack. 791.43'028'0924 B
The life and loves of Gable / by Jack Scagnetti. Middle Village, N.Y. : J. David Publishers, c1976. 160 p. : ill. ; 29 cm [PN2287.G3S35] 75-43842 ISBN 0-8246-0205-6 : 12.95
1. Gable, Clark, 1901-1960. I. Title. BIP

TORNABENE, Lyn. 791.43'028'0924 B
Long live The King : a biography of Clark Gable / by Lyn Tornabene. New York : Putnam, c1976. 396 p., [16] leaves of plates : ill. ; 24 cm. Includes index. [PN2287.G3T6] 76-43227 ISBN 0-399-11863-2 : 10.95
1. Gable, Clark, 1901-1960. 2. Moving-picture actors and actresses—United States—Biography. I. Title. BIP

Gabor, Jolie.

GABOR, Jolie. 791.43'028'0924 B
Jolie Gabor / as told to Cindy Adams. New York : Mason/Charter, 1975. xvii, 315 p., [22] leaves of plates : ill. ; 25 cm. [PN2287.G323A34] 75-19176 ISBN 0-88405-125-0 : 9.95
1. Gabor, Jolie. I. Adams, Cindy (Heller)

Gabor, Zsa Za

GABOR, Zsa Za 927.92
Zsa Zsa Gabor, my story, written for me by Gerold Frank. Greenwich, Conn., Fawcett [1961, c.1960] 286p. illus. (Crest giant d455) .50 pap.,
I. Frank, Gerold. II. Title.

GABOR, Zsa Zsa 927.92
Zsa Zsa Gabor, my story, written for me by Gerold Frank. Cleveland, World Pub. Co. [c.1960] 308p. illus. 22cm. 60-11458 3.95
I. Frank, Gerold. II. Title.

Gabriel, Philip Louis,

GABRIEL, Philip Louis, 1908- 923.873
I found America. New York, Vantage Press [1952] 141 p. 22 cm. [CT275.G22A3] 52-6955
I. Title.

Gabriel, Roman.

GABRIEL, Roman. 796.332'0924
Player of the year: Roman Gabriel's football journal, by Roman Gabriel, with Bob Oates. New York, World Pub. Co. [1970] xiv, 225 p. illus., ports. 22 cm. [GV939.G27A3 1970] 77-128494 6.95
I. Title.

Gabriel, Roman—Juvenile literature.

GUSTKEY, Earl. 796.33'2'0924 B
Roman Gabriel, outstanding pro / by Earl Gustkey. New York : Putnam, [1974] 159 p. ; 21 cm. (Putnam sports shelf) Includes index. A biography of the North Carolina State football sensation who became star quarterback of the Los Angeles Rams and later of the Philadelphia Eagles. [GV939.G27G87 1974] 92 73-88523 ISBN 0-399-20388-5. ISBN 0-399-60878-8 lib. bdg. : 4.97
1. Gabriel, Roman—Juvenile literature. 2. Football—Juvenile literature. I. Title.

Gabriele, Saint, 1838-1892.

BURKE, Edmund, 1904- 922.245
Happy was my youth; a study of Saint Gabriel of Our Lady of Sorrows, Passionist student. Westminster, Md., Newman, 1962[c.1961] 267p. illus. Bibl. 62-16056 4.95
1. Gabriele, Saint, 1838-1862. I. Title.

ERNEST, Brother, 1897- 922.245
Just one of us, a story of Saint Gabriel, C. P. Notre Dame, Ind., Dujarie Press [1956] 143p. illus. 22cm. Published in 1940 under title: That boy: [BX4700.G2E7 1956] 56-34613
1. Gabriele. Saint, 1838-1892. I. Title.

HOLLOBOUGH, Camillus J 1879-1935. 922.245
Saint Gabriel, Passionist, by Father Camillus New ed. Union City, N. J., Passionist Fathers, 1953. 278p. 19cm. [BX4700.G2H6 1953] 53-26461
1. Gabriele, Saint, 1838-1862. I. Title.

POAGE, Godfrey Robert, 1920- 922.245
Son of the Passion; the story of Gabriel Francis Possenti, the new patron of Catholic youth for the universal church. Milwaukee, Bruce Pub. Co. [1962] 120p. illus. 22cm. [BX4700.G2P6] 62-16840
1. Gabriele, Saint, 1838-1862. I. Title.

Gabrielson, Gabrielle.

GABRIELSON, Catherine. 920
The story of Gabrielle. [1st ed.] Cleveland, World Pub. Co. [c1956] 113p. 22cm. [CT275.G223G3] 56-12384
1. Gabrielson, Gabrielle. I. Title.

Gabrilowitsch, Ossip, 1878-1936.

CLEMENS, Clara. 786.1'092'4 B
My husband, Gabrilowitsch / by Clara Clemens. New York : Da Capo Press, 1979, c1938. 351 p., [8] leaves of plates : ill. ; 23 cm. (Da Capo Press music reprint series) Reprint of the ed. published by Harper, New York. Includes index. [ML417.G11C4 1979] 79-11316 ISBN 0-306-79563-9 : 22.95
1. Gabrilowitsch, Ossip, 1878-1936. 2. Pianists—Biography. I. Title.

Gacy, John Wayne.

LINEDECKER, Clifford L. 364.1'523'0924 B
The man who killed boys / by Clifford Linedecker. New York : St. Martin's Press, [1980] p. cm. [HV6248.G24L56] 79-23030 ISBN 0-312-51157-4 : 8.95
1. Gacy, John Wayne. 2. Crime and criminals—Illinois—Biography. 3. Murder—Illinois—Chicago—Case studies. I. Title. BIP

Gadgil, Dhananjaya Ramchandra.

GOKHALE Institute of Politics and Economics, Poona, India. 330'.0924
Dhananjaya Ramchandra Gadgil: making of the man. Poona, Gokhale Institute of Politics and Economics; 57 p. port. 24 cm. Rs 2.50 Bombay, New York, ISSN [1967]) Bibliography of Gadgil's works: p. [25]-52. [HB126.I43G3] S A
1. Gadgil, Dhananjaya Ramchandra. I. Title. II. Series.

Gaffney, Evangelista, Mother.

BATES, Rita, Sister. 922.242
Living His theme song; virtues of Mother M. Evangelista Gaffney, first superior general of the Congregation of the Sisters of St. Joseph of Newark. [Spring Lake, N. J.] Congregation of the Sisters of St. Joseph of Newark [1953] 88p. illus. 20cm. [BX4705.G1115B3] 53-35197
1. Gaffney, Evangelista, Mother. 2. Sisters of St. Joseph of Newark. I. Title.

MCDERMOTT, Rosarii. 922.242
The undivided heart; the life of Mother Evangelista, first Mother General of the Sisters of St. Joseph of Newark. With a foreword by Thomas A. Boland. [Newark, N. J., Sisters of St. Joseph of Newark [1961] 236p. illus. 21cm. Includes bibliography. [BX4705.G1115M3] 61-41336
1. Gaffney, Evangelista, 1855-1920. 2. Sisters of St. Joseph of Newark. I. Title.

Gagarin, IUrii Alekseevich, 1934-1968—Juvenile literature.

SHARPE, Mitchell R. 629.4'0924 B
Yuri Gagarin; first man in space, by Mitchell R. Sharpe. [Huntsville, Ala.] Strode Publishers [1969] 119 p. illus., ports. 22 cm. (Heroes of space series) Bibliography: p. [115] A biography of the Russian cosmonaut who was the first man to leave earth and to orbit the planet in a spacecraft on April 12, 1961. [TL789.85.G3S5] 92 74-75841
1. Gagarin, IUrii Alekseevich, 1934-1968—Juvenile literature. I. Title. BIP

Gagarine, Marie.

GAGARINE, Marie. 914.7'03'80924 B
From Stolnoy to Spartanburg; the two worlds of a former Russian princess. [1st ed.] Columbia, S.C., Sandlapper Press [1971] 138 p. illus., ports. 22 cm. [CT1218.G17A3] 76-143041 ISBN 0-87844-001-1
I. Title. BIP

Gage family.

GAGE, Clyde Van Tassel, 1887- 929'.2'0973
John Gage of Ipswich, Mass., and his descendants; an historical, genealogical and biographical record, as developed from sources explained herein; compiled, documented and edited by Clyde V. Gage. Worcester, N.Y. [1964] 125 l. 29 cm. [CS71.G133 1964a] 65-51586
1. Gage family. I. Title.

Gage, Thomas, 1721-1787.

ALDEN, John Richard, 1908- 973.33'0924 B
General Gage in America; being principally a history of his role in the American Revolution. New York, Greenwood Press [1969, c1948] xi, 313 p. map., ports. 23 cm. "Bibliographical note": p. 299-303. [E207.G23A6 1969] 77-90459 ISBN 0-8371-2264-3
1. Gage, Thomas, 1721-1787. 2. United States—History—Revolution, 1775-1783—British forces. I. Title.

Gaine, Hugh, 1726 or 7-1807.

LORENZ, Alfred Lawrence, 1937- 070.5'092'4
Hugh Gaine: a Colonial printer-editor's odyssey to loyalism. Foreword by Howard Rusk Long. Carbondale, Southern Illinois University Press [1972] xii, 192 p. 23 cm. (New horizons in journalism) Bibliography: p. 163-176. [Z232.G2L6] 72-75335 ISBN 0-8093-0588-7 6.95
1. Gaine, Hugh, 1726 or 7-1807. I. Title.

Gains, Larry, 1900-

GAINS, Larry, 1900- 796.8'3'0924 B
The impossible dream / [by] Larry Gains. London : Leisure Publications, [1976] 141 p., [16] p. of plates : ports. ; 22 cm. Includes index. [GV1132.G28A35 1976] 77-354243 ISBN 0-900518-00-6 : £3.50
1. Gains, Larry, 1900- 2. Boxers (Sports)—Biography. I. Title.

Gainsborough, Thomas, 1727-1788.

GAINSBOROUGH, Thomas, 1727-1788 927.5
Letters. Ed. by Mary Woodall [Rev. ed.] Greenwich, Conn., N.Y. Graphic [c.1963] 184p. illus., ports., facsims. 29cm. Bibl. 63-25404 15.00, lim. ed.
I. Woodall, Mary, ed. II. Title.

WORMAN, Isabelle. 759.2 B
Thomas Gainsborough : a biography 1727-1788 / by Isabelle Worman. Lavenham [Eng.] : T. Dalton, 1976. 148 p. : ill. (some col.) ; 24 cm. Includes index. Bibliography: p. 145. [ND497.G2W65] 77-355134 ISBN 0-900963-69-7 : £4.80
1. Gainsborough, Thomas, 1727-188. 2. Painters—Great Britain—Biography. I. Gainsborough, Thomas, 1727-1788.

Gainsborough, Thomas, 1727-1788—Juvenile literature.

RIPLEY, Elizabeth 927.5
Gainsborough, a biography. Philadelphia, Lippincott [c.1964] 72p. illus.,ports. 27cm. Bibl. 64-15236 3.50
1. Gainsborough, Thomas, 1727-1788—Juvenile literature. I. Title.

Gaitan, Jorge Eliecer, 1902-1948.

SHARPLESS, Richard. 986.1'062'0924 B
Gaitan of Colombia : a political biography / Richard Sharpless. Pittsburgh : University of Pittsburgh Press, 1977c1978. p. cm. (Pitt Latin American series) Includes index. Bibliography: p. [F2277.G24S48] 77-74552 ISBN 0-8229-3354-3 : 13.95
1. Gaitan, Jorge Eliecer, 1902-1948. 2. Politicians—Colombia—Biography. 3. Populism—Colombia. I. Title. BIP

Gaither, Alonzo S.

CURRY, George E. 796.33'2'0924 B
Jake Gaither, America's most famous Black coach / by George E. Curry ; illustrated with photographs and diagrams. New York : Dodd, Mead, c1977. ix, 209 p., [4] leaves of plates : ill. ; 22 cm. [GV939.G3C87] 76-50580 ISBN 0-396-07381-6 : 7.95
1. Gaither, Alonzo S. 2. Football coaches—United States—Biography. I. Title.

Gaither, Alonzo S.—Juvenile literature.

BLASSINGAME, Wyatt. 796.332'0924 B
Jake Gaither: winning coach. Illustrated by Raymond Burns. Champaign, Ill., Garrard Pub. Co. [1969] 95 p. illus. (part col.), ports. 24 cm. (Americans all) A biography of the head football coach at Florida A & M College whose teams' successes have made him the "winningest" coach in football. [GV939.G3B55] 92 69-12140 ISBN 0-8116-4552-5 2.49
1. Gaither, Alonzo S.—Juvenile literature. I. Burns, Raymond, 1924- illus. II. Title.

Gaither, Gloria.

GAITHER, Gloria. 248
Because He lives / Gloria Gaither. Old Tappan, N.J. : F. H. Revell Co., 1977. 202 p. ; 22 cm. [ML420.G13A3] 77-10336 ISBN 0-8007-0881-4 : 5.95
1. Gaither, Gloria. 2. Gospel musicians—United States—Biography. 3. Christian biography—United States. I. Title.

GAITHER, Gloria. 248
Because He lives / Gloria Gaither. Old Tappan, N.J. : F. H. Revell Co., 1977. 202 p. ; 22 cm. [ML420.G13A3] 77-10336 ISBN 0-8007-0881-4 : 5.95
1. Gaither, Gloria. 2. Gospel musicians—United States—Biography. 3. Christian biography—United States. I. Title. BIP

Gaitskell, Hugh Todd Naylor, 1906-1963.

MCDERMOTT, Geoffrey, 1912- 942.085'0924 B
Leader lost; a biography of Hugh Gaitskell. Princeton, Vertex Book [1971] vii, 218 p. 22 cm. Bibliography: p. 217-218. [DA566.9.G3M3] 73-124628 ISBN 0-87769-037-5 6.95
1. Gaitskell, Hugh Todd Naylor, 1906-1963. I. Title.

Gaius.

HONORE, Antony Maurice, 1921- 923.437
Gaius. Oxford, Clarendon [dist. New York, Oxford, 1963, c.1962] xviii, 183p. Tables. 23cm. Bibl. 63-1413 6.75
1. Gaius. I. Title.

Galbraith, John Kenneth, 1908-

GAMBS, John Sake, 1899- 330'.092'4 B
John Kenneth Galbraith [by] Johns S. Gambs. Boston, Twayne Publishers [1975] 131 p. port. 22 cm. (Twayne's world leaders series) Bibliography: p. 121-123. [HB119.G33G35] 74-14590 ISBN 0-8057-3681-6 6.95 (lib. bdg.)
1. Galbraith, John Kenneth, 1908- I. Title. BIP

MUNRO, C. Lynn. 330'.092'4
The Galbraithian vision : the cultural criticism of John Kenneth Galbraith / C. Lynn Munro. Washington : University Press of America, c1977. v, 236 p. ; 22 cm. Includes index. Bibliography: p. 217-231. [HB119.G33M85] 78-100360 ISBN 0-8191-0255-5 pbk. : 9.00
1. Galbraith, John Kenneth, 1908- 2. Economists—United States—Biography. I. Title.

Galbraith, John Kenneth, 1908- — Addresses, essays, lectures.

GALBRAITH, John Kenneth, 1908- 330'.092'4 B
Annals of an abiding liberal / John Kenneth Galbraith ; edited by Andrea D. Williams. Boston : Houghton Mifflin, 1979. xiv, 384 p. ; 22 cm. Includes bibliographical references and index. [HB119.G33A32] 79-15782 ISBN 0-395-27617-9 : 12.95
1. Galbraith, John Kenneth, 1908- — Addresses, essays, lectures. 2. Economists—United States—Biography—Addresses, essays, lectures. 3. Economics—Addresses, essays, lectures. I. Williams, Andrea D. II. Title. BIP

Gale, John M.,

GALE, John M., 1925- 070.924
Clean young Englishman [by] John Gate. [1st American ed.] New York, Coward-McCann [1966, c1965] 192 p. 23 cm. Autobiographical. [CT788.G225A3 1966] 66-13119
I. Title.

Galgani, Gemma, Saint, 1878-1903.

ERNEST, Brother, 1897- 922.245
A story of Saint Gemma. Pictures by Carolyn Lee Jagodits. Notre Dame, Ind., Dujarie Press [1957] unpaged. illus. 21cm. [BX4700.G22E7] 57-4990
1. Galgani, Gemma, Saint, 1878-1906. I. Title.

GALGANI, Gemma, Saint, 1878-1903. 922.245
Portrait of Saint Gemma, a stigmatic, by Sister Saint Michael. Foreword by J. F. Minihan. New York, Kenedy [1950] xviii, 248 p. ports., facsim. 21 cm. Bibliography: p. 247-248. [BX4700.G22A44] 51-45
I. Saint Michael, Sister. II. Title.

GREENE, Genard, 1921- 922.245
All on fire; a story of St. Gemma Galgani. Illus. by Brother Bernard Howard. Notre Dame, Ind., Dujarie Press [1953] 96p. illus. 24cm. [BX4700.G22G7] 53-2904
1. Galgani, Gemma, Saint, 1878-1903. I. Title.

Galiani, Ferdinando, 1728-1787.

GAUDEMET, Eugene, 1872-1933. 330'.92'4 B
L'abbe Galiani et la question du commerce des bles a la fin du regne de Louis XV. New York, B. Franklin [1972] 233 p. 22 cm. (Burt Franklin research & source works series. Selected studies in history, economics & social science, n.s. 13. (c) Modern European studies) Reprint of the 1899 ed. These—Dijon. Includes bibliographical references. [HD9042.5.G2 1972] 72-87294 ISBN 0-8337-1294-2 15.00
1. Galiani, Ferdinando, 1728-1787. 2. Grain trade—France. I. Title.

Galilei, Galileo, 1564-1642.

ACKER, Helen. 920.045
Five sons of Italy. New York, Nelson [1950] 191 p. 21 cm. Bibliography: p. 190-191. [DG463.A28] 50-8995
1. Leonardo da Vinci, 1452-1519. 2. Buonarroti, Michel Angelo, 1475-1564. 3. Galilei, Galileo, 1564-1642. 4. Paganini, Nicolo, 1782-1840. 5. Verdi, Giuseppe, 1813-1901. I. Title.

BRODERICK, James, 1891- v. 12
Galileo; the man, his work, his misfortunes. New York, Harper & Row [1964] 152 p. illus., ports. 21 cm. 66-79148
1. Galilei, Galileo, 1564-1642. I. Title.

BRODRICK, James, 1891- 925.2
Galileo; the man, his work, his misfortunes. New York, Harper [1965, c.1964] 152p. illus., ports. 21cm. [QB36.G2B65] 65-3622 3.50
1. Galilei, Galileo, 1564-1642. I. Title.

DE SANTILLANA, Giorgio, 1902- 925.2
The crime of Galileo. [Chicago] University of Chicago Press [1955] xx, 338 p. ports., diagrs. 24 cm. Bibliographical footnotes. [QB36.G2D4 1955] 55-7400
1. Galilei, Galileo, 1564-1642. I. Title.

DIBNER, Bern. 520'.924 B
A letter from Galileo: Galileo, the innovator [by] Bern Dibner. A long-lost letter from Galileo to Peiresc on a magnetic clock [by] Stillman Drake. Norwalk, Conn., Burndy Library, 1967. 56 p. illus., facsims., ports. 28 cm. (Burndy Library. Publication no. 24) Bibliographical footnotes. [QB36.G2D5] 68-6534
1. Galilei, Galileo, 1564-1642. I. Burndy Library, Norwalk, Conn. II. Drake, Stillman. A long-lost letter from Galileo to Peiresc on a magnetic clock. 1967. III. Title. IV. Title: Galileo, the innovator. V. Title: A long-lost letter from Galileo to Peiresc on a magnetic clock.

DRAKE, Stillman. 520'.92'4 B
Galileo at work : his scientific biography / Stillman Drake. Chicago : University of Chicago Press, 1978. p. cm. Includes bibliographical references and index.

[QB36.G2D69] 78-5239 ISBN 0-226-16226-5 : 25.00
1. Galilei, Galileo, 1564-1642. 2. Astronomers—Italy—Biography. I. Title. BIP

GALILEI, Galileo, 1564-1642. 520.924
Men of physics: Galileo Galilei, his life and his works, by Raymond J. Seeger, [1st ed.] Oxford. New York, Pergamon Press [1966] xi, 286 p. illus., port. 20 cm. (The Commonwealth and international library. Selected reading in physics) 66-23858
I. Seeger, Raymond John, 1906- II. Title.

GALILEI, Galileo, 1564-1642 520.924
Men of physics: Galielo Galilei, his life and his works. [1sted.] Oxford, New York, pergamon [1966] xi. 286 p. illus., port. 20 cm. [Commonwealth & intl. lib. Selected readings in physics] [QB36.62A233 1966] 66-23858 price unreported.
I. Seeger,Raymond John, 1906- II. Title.

GALILEO, man of science. 520'.924 B Edited by Ernan McMullin. New York, Basic Books [1968, c1967] xiv, 455, cii p. illus. 24 cm. Consists chiefly of papers delivered at the Galileo Quatercentenary Congress held at the University of Notre Dame in 1964. "Bibliografia Galileiana, 1940-1964; being the second supplement to the original Carli-Favaro Bibliografia Galileiana": p. [i]-lxxxii (3d group) [QB36.G2G62] 68-11203
1. Galilei, Galileo, 1564-1642. I. McMullin, Ernan, 1924- ed. II. McMullin, Ernan, 1924- Bibliografia Galileiana, 1940-1964. III. Carli, Alarico. Bibliografia Galileiana (1568-1895) IV. Galileo Quatercentenary Congress, University of Notre Dame, 1964.

GEBLER, Karl von, 1850-1878. 520'.92'4 B
Galileo Galilei and the Roman Curia : from authentic sourves / by Karl von Gebler ; translated with the sanction of the author by Mrs. George Sturge. Merrick, N.Y. : Richwood Pub. Co., [1977] p. cm. Reprint of the 1879 ed., published by C. K. Paul, London. Translation of Galileo Galilei und die Romische Curie. Includes index. Bibliography: p. [QB36.G2G653 1977] 76-1124 ISBN 0-915172-11-9 lib.bdg. : 25.00
1. Galilei, Galileo, 1564-1642. 2. Catholic Church. Curia romana. 3. Religion and science—History of controversy. 4. Astronomers—Italy—Biography. I. Title.

GEYMONAT, Ludovico. 925.2
Galileo Galilei; a biography and inquiry into his philosophy of science. Foreword by Giorgio de Santillana. Text translated from the Italian with additional notes and appendix by Stillman Drake. New York, McGraw-Hill [1965] xii, 260 p. 22 cm. Bibliographical references included in "Notes" (p. 227-251) [QB36.G2G655] 64-8549
1. Galliei, Galileo, 1564-1642. I Title.

LAUBER, Patricia. 925.2
The quest of Galileo. Illustrated by Lee J. Ames. [1st ed.] Garden City, N. Y., Garden City Books [1959] 56 p. illus. 32 cm. [QB36.G2L33] 58-7792
1. Galilei, Galileo, 1564-1642. I. Title.

LEVINGER, Elma (Ehrlich), 1887- 925.2
Galileo first observer of marvelous things. New York, Messner [1952] 180 p. illus. 22 cm. [QB36.G2L65] 52-13550
1. Galilei, Galileo, 1564-1642. I. Title.

LEVINGER, Elma (Ehrlich) 1887-1958. v. 12
Galileo, first observer of marvelous things. New York, J. Messner [1963, c1952] 180 p. Bibliography: p. 171-173. 66-70820
1. Galilei, Galileo, 1564-1642. I. Title.

RONAN, Colin A. 520'.92'4 B
Galileo / Colin A. Ronan. New York : Putnam, [1974] 264 p. : ill. (some col.) ; 26 cm. Includes index. Bibliography: p. 258-259. [QB36.G2R58] 74-76233 ISBN 0-399-11364-9 : 14.95
1. Galilei, Galileo, 1564-1642. BIP

SANTILLANA, George de. 925.2
The crime of Galileo. [Chicago] University of Chicago Press [1955] xv, 338p. ports., diagrs. 24cm. Bibliographical footnotes. [QB36.G2S3] 55-7400
1. Galliel, Galileo, 1564-1642. I. Title. BIP

SHEA, William R. 520'.92'4 B
Galileo's intellectual revolution; middle period, 1610-1632 [by] William R. Shea. New York, Science History Publications [1972] xii, 204 p. illus. 25 cm. Bibliography: p. [190]-197. [QB36.G2S46] 72-89852 ISBN 0-88202-006-4 15.95
1. Galilei, Galileo, 1564-1642. I. Title. BIP

†SHEA, William R. 520'.92'4 B
Galileo's intellectual revolution : middle period, 1610-1632 / William R. Shea. 2d ed. New York : Science History Publications, 1977. xi, 204 p. : ill. ; 23 cm. Includes index. Bibliography: p. [190]-197. [QB36.G2S46 1977] 77-155980 pbk. : 6.95
1. Galilei, Galileo, 1564-1642. 2. Astronomers—Italy—Biography. I. Title.

Galilei, Galileo, 1564-1642—Juvenile literature.

COBB, Vicki. 520'.92'4 B
Truth on trial : the story of Galileo Galilei / by Vicki Cobb ; illustrated by George Ulrich. New York : Coward, McCann & Geoghegan, c1979. 63 p. : ill. ; 21 cm. Bibliography: p. 63. A biography of the 16th-century Italian mathematician, physicist, and astronomer who questioned the accepted scientific theories of his time and was tried by the Inquisition for his ideas. [QB36.G2C65 1979] 92 79-237 ISBN 0-698-30709-7 lib.bdg. : 5.49
1. Galilei, Galileo, 1564-1642—Juvenile literature. 2. Astronomers—Italy—Biography—Juvenile literature. I. Ulrich, George. II. Title. BIP

GREGOR, Arthur S. 92
Galileo. Illus. by George Giusti. New York, Scribners [c.1965] 191p. illus. 21cm. Bibl. [QB36.G2G75] 65-14768 3.50; 3.31 lib. ed.,
1. Galilei, Galileo, 1564-1642—Juvenile literature. I. Title.

GREGOR, Arthur S j92
Galileo, by Arthur S. Gregor. Illustrated by George Giusti. New York, Scribner [1965] 191 p. illus. 21 cm. Bibliography: p. 183. [QB36.G2G75] 65-14768
1. Galilei, Galileo, 1564-1642 — Juvenile literature. I. Title.

MARCUS, Rebecca B 925.2
Galileo and experimental science. Pictures by Richard Mayhew. New York, F. Watts [1961] 134p. illus. 22cm (A First biography) [QB36.G2M29] 61-5277
1. Galilei, Galileo, 1564-1642—Juvenile literature I. Title.

SHIRLEY, Jean. 92 (J)
Galileo. Pictures by Raymond Renard. Adapted by Jean Shirley from the original text. St. Louis, Webster Division, McGraw-Hill [1967] 1 v. (unpaged) col. illus., port. 19 x 21 cm. (Men of genius books) Around the world library. [QB36.G2S47] 67-4552
1. Galilei, Galileo, 1564-1642—Juvenile literature. I. Renard, Raymond, fl. 1967- illus.

Galinsky, Ellen.

GALINSKY, Ellen. 649'.15
Beginnings : a young mother's personal account of two premature births / Ellen Galinsky. Boston : Houghton Mifflin, 1976. 147 p. ; 22 cm. [RG525.G28] 75-32510 ISBN 0-395-24079-4
1. Galinsky, Ellen. 2. Pregnancy—Personal narratives. 3. Infants (Premature) I. Title.

Galitzine, Irina, Princess, 1900-

GALITZINE, Irina, Princess, 1900- 947.084'092'4 B
Spirit to survive : the memoirs of Princess Nicholas Galitzine. London : Kimber, 1976. 199 p., [16] p. of plates : ill., geneal. table, ports. ; 25 cm. [CT1218.G19A35] 77-359448 ISBN 0-7183-0394-6 : £4.95
1. Galitzine, Irina, Princess, 1900- 2. Golitsyn family. 3. Russia—Nobility—Biography. 4. Russia—History—Revolution, 1917-1921—Personal narratives. 5. Russia—Genealogy. I. Title.

Gall, Franz Josef. 1758-1828.

ACKERKNECHT, Erwin Heinz, 1906- 920.9139
Franz Joseph Gall, inventor of phrenology, and his collection, by Erwin H. Ackerknecht and Henri V. Vallois. Translated from the French by Claire St. Leon. Pref. by John Z. Bowers. Madison, Dept. of History of Medicine, University of Wisconsin Medical School, 1956. 86p. illus. 23cm. (Wisconsin studies in medical history, no. 1) Translation of François Joseph Gall et sa collection. Bibliographical footnotes. [BF869.G3A613] 56-63425
1. Gall, Franz Joseph, 1758-1828. I. Vallois, Henri Victor, 1889- II. Title. III. Series.

ACKERKNECHT, Erwin Heinz, 1906- 920.9139
Franz Joseph Gall, inventor of phrenology, and his collection, by Erwin H, Ackerkneecht and Henri V. Vallois. Translated from the French by Claire St. Leon. Pref. by John Z. Bowers. Madison. Dept. of History of Medicine. University of Wisconsin Medical School, 1956. 86p. illus. 23cm. (Wisconsin studies in medical history, no. 1) Translation of Francois Joseph Gall et sa collection. Bibliographical footnotes. [BFS69.G3A613] 56-63425
1. Gall, Franz Josef. 1758-1828. I. Vallois, Henri Victor, 1889- II. Title. III. Series.

Galla Placidia, 389 (ca.)-450.

OOST, Stewart Irvin, 1922- 937'.09'0924 B
Galla Placidia Augusta; a biographical essay. Chicago, University of Chicago Press [1968] xi, 346 p. illus., map, ports. 24 cm. Includes bibliographical references. [DG312.5.G3O5] 68-25090
*1. Galla Placidia, 389 (ca.)-450. I. Title.*BIP

Gallahue, Edward,

GALLAHUE, Edward, 1902- 368'.00924 B
Edward's odyssey; an autobiography of Edward Gallahue. [1st ed.] Garden City, N.Y., Doubleday, 1970. 216 p. 22 cm. Bibliography: p. [215]-216. [HG9970.A5G33] 75-116205 5.95
I. Title.

Gallatin, Albert, 1761-1849.

STEVENS, John Austin, 1827-1910. 973.4'0924 B
Albert Gallatin. Boston, Houghton, Mifflin. [New York, AMS Press, 1972] x, 423 p. illus. 19 cm. (American statesmen, v. 13) Reprint of the 1898 ed. [E302.6.G16S8 1972] 74-128977 ISBN 0-404-50863-4 15.00
1. Gallatin, Albert, 1761-1849. I. Title. II. Series. BIP

WALTERS, Raymond, 1912- 923.273
Albert Gallatin: Jeffersonian financier and diplomat. New York, Macmillan, 1957. 461 p. 22 cm. Includes bibliography. [E302.6.G16W3] 57-8267
1. Gallatin, Albert, 1761-1849. I. Title.

WALTERS, Raymond, 1912- 923.273
Albert Gallatin: Jeffersonian financier and diplomat. New York, Macmillan, 1957. 461p. 22cm. Includes bibliography. [E302.6.G16W3] 57-8267
1. Gallatin, Albert, 1761-1849. I. Title. BIP

Gallatin, James, 1796-1876.

GALLATIN, James, 1796-1876. 973.5'092'4
The diary of James Gallatin, secretary to Albert Gallatin, a great peace maker, 1813-1827 / edited by Count Gallatin ; with an introd. by Viscount Bryce. New ed. West Port, Conn. : Greenwood Press, 1979, c1916. xiii, 314 p., [10] leaves of plates : ill. ; 23 cm. Reprint of the ed. published by Scribner, New York, which was originally published under title: A great peace maker. Includes index. [E302.6.G17A33 1979] 78-12126 ISBN 0-313-21098-5 : 20.00
1. Gallatin, James, 1796-1876. 2. Gallatin, Albert, 1761-1849. 3. Ghent, Treaty of, 1814. 4. France—Social life and customs—19th century. 5. Great Britain—Social life and customs—19th century. 6. Diplomats—United States—Biography. I. Gallatin, James Francis, 1853-1915. II. Title.

Gallaudet, Edward Miner, 1837-1917.

BOATNER, Maxine Tull. 923.773
Voice of the deaf; a biography of Edward Miner Gallaudet. Introd. by John S. Brubacher. Washington, Public Affairs Press [1959] 190p. illus. 24cm. [HV2561.D858B6] 59-6972
1. Gallaudet, Edward Miner, 1837-1917. 2. Gallaudet College, Washington, D. C. I. Title.

Gallaudet. Thomas Hopkins, 1787-1851.

DEGERING, Etta. 92
Gallaudet, frined of the deaf. Illustrated by Emil Weiss. New York, D. McKay Co. [1964] xi, 177 p. illus. 21 cm. Bibliography: p. 173-177. [HV2534.G3D4] 64-22095
1. Gallaudet. Thomas Hopkins, 1787-1851. I. Title.

DEGERING, Etta. 92
Gallaudet, friend of the deaf. Illustrated by Emil Weiss. New York, D. McKay Co. [1964] xi, 177 p. illus. 21 cm. Bibliography: p. 173-177. [HV2534.G3D4] 64-22095
1. Gallaudet, Thomas Hopkins, 1787 1851. I. Title.

Gallenga, Antonio Carlo Napoleone, 1810 1895.

CERUTTI, Toni. 945'.08'0924 B
Antonio Gallenga : an Italian writer in Victorian England / Toni Cerutti. London ; New York : published for the University of Hull by Oxford University Press, 1974. viii, 204 p., [5] leaves of plates : 9 ill. ; 23 cm. (University of Hull Publications) Includes index. "Bibliography of Antonio Gallenga's writings": p. [185]-189. [CT1138.G3C47] 74-189213 ISBN 0-19-713419-X : 13.00
1. Gallenga, Antonio Carlo Napoleone, 1810-1895.

Galli-Curci, Amelita, 1889-1963.

*LE Massena, C.E. 782.1'09'24 [B]
Galli-Curci's life of song / C.E. Le Massena. Beverly Hills, CA : Monitor Book Co., c1978. 280p. : ill., photos ; 24 cm. (An Opera Classics Book) Includes index. Discography: p. 267-272. [ML420] 76-46603 ISBN 0-917734-00-9 : 14.95
*1. Galli-Curci, Amelita, 1882-1963. 2 Singers — Italian — Biography. I. Title.*BIP

LE MASSENA, Clarence, Edward, 1868- 782.1'092'4 B
Galli-Curci's life of song / C. E. Le Massena. Beverly Hills, Calif. : Monitor Book Co., c1978. 280 p., [8] leaves of plates : ill. ; 24 cm. (An Opera classics book) Originally published by The Paebar Co., New York, 1945. Includes index. Discography: p. 267-273. [ML420.G17L4 1978] 76-46603 ISBN 0-917734-00-9 : 15.95
1. Galli-Curci, Amelita, 1889-1963. 2. Singers—Biography. I. Title.

Gallier, James.

GALLIER, James. 720'.92'4 B
Autobiography of James Gallier, architect. With a new introd. by Samuel Wilson, Jr., and a supplement of illus. New York, Da Capo Press, 1973. xi, 150, [42] p. illus. 23 cm. (Da Capo Press series in architecture and decorative art, v. 25) Reprint of the 1864 ed. [NA737.G34A2 1973] 69-13715 ISBN 0-306-71247-4 15.00
1. Gallier, James. BIP

Gallo, Joey, 1929-1972.

GODDARD, Donald. 364.1'092'4 B
Joey. [New York, Dell, 1975, c1974] 442 p. 18 cm. [HV6248.G28G6 1975] 1.75 (pbk.)
1. Gallo, Joey, 1929-1972. I. Title.
L.C. card number for original ed.: 73-14262

GODDARD, Donald. 364.1'092'4 B
Joey. [1st ed.] New York, Harper & Row [1974] viii, 450 p. 24 cm. [HV6248.G28G6 1974] 73-14262 ISBN 0-06-011570-X 10.00
1. Gallo, Joey, 1929-1972. I. Title.

Galloway, Joseph, 1731-1803.

FERLING, John E. 973.3'2'0924
The Loyalist mind : Joseph Galloway and the American Revolution / John E. Ferling. University Park : Pennsylvania State University Press, c1977. 157 p. ; 24 cm. Includes bibliographical references and index. [E278.G14F47] 77-22369 ISBN 0-271-00514-9 : 10.00
1. Galloway, Joseph, 1731-1803. 2. American loyalists—Biography. I. Title. BIP

Gallup family.

WALKER, Louise G. 929.2'0973
Back to William Gallop, revolutionary soldier, by Louise E. Gallup. [Chicago, c1954] [30] l. 29 cm. Caption title. Cover title: William Gallop, revolutionary soldier. Includes bibliographical references. [CS71.G175 1954] 75-269135
1. Gallup family. 2. Gallop, William, b. ca. 1738. I. Title.

WALKER, Louise G. 929'.2'0973
William Gallop, revolutionary soldier, by Louise G. Walker. [Chicago, 1973] iv, 279 p. 29 cm. [CS71.G175 1973] 73-166347
1. Gallup family. I. Title.

Gally, Martha.

LEWIS, Marvin, 1923-1971. 979.3'02'0924 B
Martha and the Doctor : a frontier family in central Nevada / by Marvin Lewis ; edited by B. Betty Lewis. Reno : University of Nevada Press, 1977. p. cm. (A Bristlecone paperback) [F841.L47] 77-24964 ISBN 0-87417-049-4 pbk. : 5.00
1. Gally, Martha. 2. Gally, James W. 3. Pioneers—Nevada—Biography. 4. Nevada—Frontier and pioneer life. I. Title. BIP

Galois, Evariste, 1811-1832.

INFELD, Leopold, 1898-1968. 510'.92'4 B
Whom the gods love : the story of Evariste Galois / Leopold Infeld. Reston, Va. : National Council of Teachers of Mathematics, 1978, c1948. xv, 323 p., [1] leaf of plates : ill. ; 24 cm. (Classics in mathematics education ; v. 7) Reprint, with new introductory material, of the ed. published by Whittlesey House, New York. Bibliography: p. [318]-323. [QA29.G25I5 1978] 78-3709 ISBN 0-87353-125-6 : 11.00
1. Galois, Evariste, 1811-1832. 2. Mathematicians—France—Biography. I. Title. BIP

Galsworthy, John, 1867-1933.

BARKER, Dudley. 928.2
The man of principle: a view of John Galsworthy. New York, London House & Maxwell [1963] 240 p. illus. 23 cm Full name: Dudley Raymond Barker. Includes bibliography. [PR6013.A5Z54] 63-14352
1. Galsworthy, John, 1867-1933. I. Title.

BARKER, Dudley. 823'.9'12 B
The man of principle; a biography of John Galsworthy. New York, Stein and Day [1969, c1963] 240 p. group port. 22 cm. Bibliography: p. [7] [PR6013.A5Z54 1969] 69-17943 6.95
1. Galsworthy, John, 1867-1933. I. Title. BIP

BARKER, Dudley Ramymond 928.2
The man of principle: a view of John Galsworthy. New York, London House [c.1963,54 240p. illus. 23cm. Bibl. 63-14352 6.25
1. Galsworthy, John, 1867-1933. I. Title.

GINDIN, James Jack, 1926- 823'.9'12 B
The English climate : an excursion into a biography of John Galsworthy / by James Gindin. Ann Arbor : University of Michigan Press, c1979. viii, 230 p., [1] leaf of plates : port. ; 24 cm. Includes index. [PR6013.A5Z5673] 79-9860 ISBN 0-472-08349-X lib. bdg. : 12.00 12.00
1. Galsworthy, John, 1867-1933. 2. Authors, English—20th century—Biography. 3. England—Description and travel—1971- I. Title. BIP

Galsworthy, John, 1867-1933—Biography.

DUPRE, Catherine. 823'.9'12 B
John Galsworthy : a biography / Catherine Dupre. 1st American ed. New York : Coward, McCann & Geoghegan, 1976. 315 p., [4] leaves of plates : ill. ; 24 cm. Includes index. Bibliography: p. 291-292. [PR6013.A5Z5655 1976] 76-13473 ISBN 0-698-10715-2 : 9.95
1. Galsworthy, John, 1867-1933—Biography. 2. Authors, English—20th century—Biography. BIP

MARROT, Harold Vincent. 823'.9'12 B
The life and letters of John Galsworthy, by H. V. Marrot. Clifton [N.J.] A. M. Kelley, 1973 [c1936] xv, 819 p. illus. 22 cm. (Scribner reprint editions) Reprint of the ed. published by Scribner, New York. [PR6013.A5Z63 1973] 78-128060 ISBN 0-678-02759-5
1. Galsworthy, John, 1867-1933—Biography. BIP

Galt, John, 1779-1839—Biography.

GORDON, Ian Alistair, 1908- 823'.9'12 B
John Galt: the life of a writer [by] Ian A. Gordon. Toronto, University of Toronto Press, 1972. ix, 170 p., [3] l. of plates. ill. 23 cm. Includes index. Bibliography: p. 157-163. [PR4708.G2Z69 1972b] 74-180821 ISBN 0-8020-1941-2 9.00
1. Galt, John, 1779-1839—Biography. BIP

Galton, Francis, Sir, 1822-1911.

FORREST, Derek William. 509'.2'4 B
Francis Galton : the life and work of a Victorian genius / D. W. Forrest. New York : Taplinger Pub. Co., 1974. x, 340 p., [8] leaves of plates : ill. ; 24 cm. "Bibliography of Galton's published work": p. [303]-317. [Q143.G3F67 1974] 74-5819 ISBN 0-8008-2682-5 : 14.95
1. Galton, Francis, Sir, 1822-1911. BIP

GALTON, Francis, Sir, 1822-1911. 509'.2'4 B
Memories of my life. London, Methuen, 1908. [New York, AMS Press, 1974] viii, 339 p. illus. 23 cm. "Books and memoirs by the author": p. 325-331. [Q143.G3A3 1974] 72-1639 ISBN 0-404-08128-2
1. Galton, Francis, Sir, 1822-1911. BIP

Galvin, Paul, 1885-1959.

PETRAKIS, Harry Mark 338.47621384
The founder's touch: the life of Paul Galvin of Motorola. New York, McGraw [c.1965] ix, 240p. illus. (pt. col.) 22cm. [HD9696.U54M6] 65-17495 4.95
1. Galvin, Paul, 1885-1959. 2. Motorola, inc. I. Title.

Galway Blazer II (Boat)

KING, William Donald Aelian, 1910- 910'.41'0924 B
Adventure in depth / William King. New York : Putnam, [1975] 250 p., [4] leaves of plates : ill. ; 22 cm. [GV822.G36K49 1975] 74-30558 ISBN 0-399-11493-9 : 7.95
1. Galway Blazer II (Boat) 2. King, William Donald Aelian, 1910- 3. Voyages around the world—1951- I. Title.

Galway, James.

GALWAY, James. 788'.51'0924 B
An autobiography / James Galway. New York : St. Martin's Press, c1979. 181 p., [4] leaves of plates : ill. ; 22 cm. [ML419.G28A3 1979] 78-21403 ISBN 0-312-43965-2 : 8.95
1. Galway, James. 2. Flute-players—Biography.

Gama, Vasco da, 1469-1524.

HART, Henry Hersch, 1886- 910.9'469
Sea road to the Indies; an account of the voyages and exploits of the Portuguese navigators, together with the life and times of Dom Vasco da Gama, Capitao-Mor, Viceroy of India and Count of Vidigueira, by Henry H. Hart. Westport, Conn., Greenwood Press [1971, c1950] xii, 296 p. map. 23 cm. Bibliography: p. 275-291. [G286.G2H3 1971] 70-135246 ISBN 0-8371-5165-1
1. Gama, Vasco da, 1469-1524. 2. Explorers—Portugal. I. Title. BIP

SYME, Ronald, 1910- 923.9469
Vasco da Gama, sailor toward the sunrise. Illustrated by William Stobbs. New York, Morrow, 1959. 95 p. illus. 22 cm. [G286.G2S9] 59-5018
I. Gama, Vasco da, 1469-1524. II. Title.

SYME, Ronald, 1910- 923.9469
Vasco da Gama, sailor toward the sunrise. Illustrated by William Stobbs. New York, Morrow, 1959. 95 p. illus. 22 cm. [G286.G2S9] 59-5018
1. Gama, Vasco da, 1469-1524.

Gambino, Richard.

GAMBINO, Richard. 973'.04'51
Blood of my blood : the dilemma of the Italian-Americans / Richard Gambino. Garden City, N.Y. : Anchor Press, 1975, c1974. viii, 388 p. ; 18 cm. Includes index. [E184.I8G35 1975] 75-307228 ISBN 0-385-07564-2 pbk. : 3.50
1. Gambino, Richard. 2. Italian Americans. I. Title. BIP

Gambling, John A.,

GAMBLING, John A., 1930- 791.44'7 B
Rambling with Gambling [by] John Gambling. Edited by Robert Saffron. Englewood Cliffs, N.J., Prentice-Hall [1972] 191 p. illus. 23 cm. Autobiography. [PN1991.4.G28A3] 72-3732 ISBN 0-13-752899-X
I. Title.

Gambling—United States—Biography.

BRADSHAW, Jon. 301.5'7
Fast company / Jon Bradshaw. 1st ed. New York : Harper's Magazine Press, 1975. 239 p. ; 22 cm. [HV6715.B65 1975] 74-3892 ISBN 0-06-120455-2 : 7.95
1. Gambling—United States—Biography. I. Title. BIP

Game protection—Kenya—Personal narratives.

ADAMSON, George, 1906- 639'.9'0924 B
A lifetime with lions. [1st ed. in the U.S.A.] Garden City, N.Y., Doubleday, 1968. 286 p. illus., col. map (on lining papers) 24 cm. Autobiography. London ed. (Collins & Harvill Press) has title: Bwana game. [SK575.K4A65 1968b] 67-11733
1. Game protection—Kenya—Personal narratives. 2. Lions—Behavior. I. Title.

Gamekeepers—Correspondence, reminiscences, etc.

TUFTS, Robie W. 639'.97'829715
Looking back : recollections of a migratory bird officer / by Robie W. Tufts. Windsor, N.S. : Lancelot Press, 1975. 72 p. ; 20 cm. [SK354.T83A34] 75-329915
1. Gamekeepers—Correspondence, reminiscences, etc. 2. Game and game-birds—Maritime Provinces. I. Title.

Gamow, George,

GAMOW, George, 1904-1968. 539.7'0924 B
My world line; an informal autobiography. Foreword by Stanislaw M. Ulam. New York, Viking Press [1970] xii, 178 p. illus., ports. 22 cm. "Publications by George Gamow": p. 165-172. Includes bibliographical references. [QC16.G37A3 1970] 79-94855 5.95
I. Title.

Gandhi, Indira Nehru, 1917-

ALEXANDER, Mithrapuram K. 954'.04'0924 B
Madame Gandhi; a political biography, by Mithrapuram K. Alexander. North Quincy, Mass., Christopher Pub. House [1969] 226 p. 21 cm. Bibliography: p. 217-220. [DS481.G23A83] 71-78033 5.00
1. Gandhi, Indira (Nehru) 1917- I. Title.

ARORA, Jagdish. 954.04'092'4 B
Indira Gandhi, harbinger of peace / Jagdish Arora. 1st ed. Lucknow : Puri Publishers, 1976. 174, [9] p., [9] leaves of plates : ill. ; 23 cm. [DS481.G23A86] 76-903069 Rs20.00
1. Gandhi, Indira Nehru, 1917- 2. Prime Ministers—India—Biography. 3. India—Politics and government—1947-

BHATIA, Krishan, 1925- 954.04'092'4 B
Indira: a biography of Prime Minister Gandhi. New York, Praeger [1974] x, 290 p. illus. 24 cm. Bibliography: p. 283-284. [DS481.G23B48] 72-92880 ISBN 0-275-19900-2 10.00
1. Gandhi, Indira Nehru, 1917- 2. India—Politics and government—1947- I. Title.

HARRIETT. 954.04'0924 B
First Lady of India; the story of Indira Gandhi [by] Harriett Willcoxen. [1st ed.] Garden City, N.Y., Doubleday [1969] 143 p. illus., map, ports. 22 cm. (A Doubleday signal book) A biography of Indira Gandhi, India's Prime Minister, which emphasizes her part in India's long non-violent struggle for independence from England. [DS481.G23H3] 92 69-10999 3.50
1. Gandhi, Indira (Nehru) 1917- I. Title.

HEREDIA, Susana. 954.04'092'4 B
No kin to the Mahatma : a study of Indira Gandhi / Susana Heredia. 1st ed. New York : Vantage Press, c1976. 127 p. ; 21 cm. Bibliography: p. 127. [DS481.G23H47] 76-150453 ISBN 0-533-02092-1 : 6.50
1. Gandhi, Indira Nehru, 1917- 2. Prime Ministers—India—Biography. I. Title.

INDIRA a study. 954.04'0924
[1st ed.] Delhi, Sterling Pubs. [1967] vi, 112p. port. 23cm. Bibl. [DS481.G23S2] [PL480.I-E-7862] 67-2732 4.50
1. Gandhi, Indira (Nehru) 1917- I. Sahni, Naresh Chander
American distributor: Verry, Mystic, Conn.

KHOSLA, Gopal Das, 1901- 954.04'092'4 B
Indira Gandhi. Text: G. D. Khosla; picture editors: T. S. Nagarajan [and] P. D. Chandwadkar. [Delhi] Thomson Press (India), Publication Division, 1974. 152 p. (chiefly illus.) 25 cm. [DS481.G23K53] 74-900843 ISBN 0-8002-0037-3 15.00
1. Gandhi, Indira Nehru, 1917- I. Nagarajan, T. S., ed. II. Chandwadkar, P. D., ed. III. Title.
Distributed by International Publications Service. BIP

MASANI, Zareer. 954.04'092'4 B
Indira Gandhi : a biography / Zareer Masani. New York : T. Y. Crowell, [1976] 341 p., [4] leaves of plates : ill. ; 24 cm. Includes index. Bibliography: p. [334]-335. [DS481.G23M37] 75-20149 ISBN 0-690-00169-X : 10.95
1. Gandhi, Indira Nehru, 1917- BIP

MOHAN, Anand, fl.1967- 954.04'0924
Indira Gandhi, a personal and political

York, Philosophical Library [1955] 350p. 23cm. [DS481] 56-13588
1. Gandhi, Mohandras Karamchand, 1869-1948. I. Title.

REYNOLDS, Reginald, 1905- 923.254
A quest for Gandhi. Garden City, N.Y., Doubleday, 1952. 215 p. 23 cm. "Published in England under the title To live in mankind: a quest for Gandhi." -- Dust jacket. Full name: Reginald Arthur Reynolds. [DS481.G3R4] 52-8047
1. Gandhi, Mohandas Karamchand, 1869-1948. I. Title.

REYNOLDS, Reginald, 1905- 954.03'5'0924 B
The true story of Gandhi, man of peace. [American ed.] Chicago, Childrens Press [1964] 141 p. col. illus. 23 cm. First published in London in 1960 under title: The true book about Mahatma Gandhi. A biography of the father of India, who used nonviolent civil disobedience to win his country's independence and social and economic reforms. [DS481.G3R42 1964] 92 AC 68
1. Gandhi, Mohandas Karamchand, 1869-1948. I. Title.

REYNOLDS, Reginald [Arthur] 923.254
The true book about Mahatma Gandhi, Illustrated by N. G. Wilson. London, F. Muller [1960, c.1959; stamped: distributed by Sportshelf, New Rochelle, N.Y. 144p. illus. 20cm. 60-888 2.75 bds.,
1. Gandhi, Mohandas Karamchand, 1869-1948. I. Title.

ROLLAND, Romain, 1866-1944. 954.03'5'0924 B
Mahatma Gandhi: the man who became one with the Universal Being. Translated by Catherine D. Groth. With a new introd. for the Garland ed. by Margaret W. Fisher. New York, Garland Pub., 1973 [c1924] 36, 250 p. port. 22 cm. (The Garland library of war and peace) Reprint of the ed. published by the Century Co., New York. Bibliography: p. 249-250. [DS481.G3R613 1973] 73-15941 ISBN 0-8240-0498-1 11.00
1. Gandhi, Mohandas Karamchand, 1869-1948. 2. India—Politics and government—1919-1947. I. Title. II. Series. BIP

ROSENTHAL, Newman Hirsch. 954.03'5'0924 B
The uncompromising truth; Mahatma Gandhi 1869-1948 [by] Newman Rosenthal. [Melbourne] Nelson [1969] xv, 151 p. illus., ports. 18 cm. (Nelson's Australian paperbacks) [DS481.G3R66] 75-487830 1.00
1. Gandhi, Mohandas Karamchand, 1869-1948. I. Title.

SHAHANI, Ranjee Gurdarsing, 1904- 923.254
Mr. Gandhi. New York, Macmillan, 1961. 211 p. 22 cm. [DS481.G3S475] 61-8110
1. Gandi, Mohandas Karamchand, 1869-1948.

SHEEAN, Vincent, 1899- 923.254
Lead, kindly light. New York, Random House [1949] viii, 374 p. 24 cm. "That life work of Gandhi." Full name: James Vincent Sheean. Bibliography: p. 365-369. [DS481.G3S48 1949] 49-9824
1. Gandhi, Mohandas Karamchand, 1869-1948. 2. Evil, Non-resistance to. I. Title. BIP

SHEEAN, Vincent, 1899- v. 12
Mahatma Gandhi, a great life in brief. New York, Knopf, 1965 [c1954] 204 p. 19 cm. (Great lives in brief, a new series of biographies) 68-67607
1. Gandhi, Mohandas Karamchand, 1869-1948. I. Title.

SHEEAN, Vincent, 1899- 923.254
Mahatma Gandhi, a great life in brief. [1st ed.] New York, Knopf, 1955 [c1954] 204 p. 19 cm. (Great lives in brief, a new series of biographies) [DS481.G3S483] 54-7222
1. Gandhi, Mohandas Karamchand, 1869-1948. I. Title.

SHIRER, William Lawrence, 1904- 954.03'5'0924 B
Gandhi, a memoir / William L. Shirer. New York : Simon and Schuster, c1979. p. cm. Includes index. [DS481.G3S487] 79-17359 ISBN 0-671-25079-5 : 9.95
1. Gandi, Mohandas Karamchand, 1869-1948. 2. Shirer, William Lawrence, 1904- 3. Statesmen—India—Biography. 4. Journalists—United States—Biography. I. Title.

SLADE, Madeleine. 923.254
The spirit's pilgrimage. New York, Coward-McCann [1960] 318 p. illus. 22 cm. Autobiographical. [DS481.G3S55] 59-11030
1. Gandhi, Mohandas Karamchand, 1869-1948. I. Title.

WATSON, Francis, 1907- 954.03'5'0924
Gandhi. London, Oxford Univ. Pr., 1967. 64p. 8 plates (incl. ports.) 21cm. (Clarendon biogs., 18) Bibl. [DS481.G3W29 1967] (B) 68-91660 1.55 bds.,
1. Gandhi, Mohandas Karamchand, 1869-1948. I. Title.
Available from the publisher's New York office.

WOODCOCK, George, 1912- 954.03'5'0924
Mohandas Gandhi. New York, Viking Press [1971] 133 p. 19 cm. (Modern masters, M15) Bibliography: p. [119]-123. [DS481.G3W65] 79-161060 ISBN 0-670-48429-6 1.95
1. Gandhi, Mohandas Karamchand, 1869-1948.

ZINKIN, Taya. 92
The story of Gandhi. Illustrated by Robert Hales. [1st American ed.] New York, Criterion Books [1966, c1965] 190 p. illus., ports. 21 cm. Includes bibliographical references. A biography of the great economic and social reformer whose leadership in passive resistance brought independence to India. [DS481.G3Z58 1966] AC 67
1. Gandhi, Mohandas Karamchand, 1869-1948. I. Title.

Gandhi, Mohandas Karamchand, 1869-1948

LENGYEL, Emil, 1895- 92 (J)
Mahatma Gandhi; the great soul. New York, F. Watts [1966] 216 p. ports. 22 cm. (Immortals of history) Bibliography: p. 211-213. [DS481.G3L34] 67-10167
1. Gandhi, Mohandas Karamchand, 1869-1948—Juvenile literature. I. Title.

MONTGOMERY, Elizabeth Rider. 954.03'5'0924 B
Gandhi; peaceful fighter. Champaign, Ill., Garrard Pub. Co. [1970] 174 p. illus., ports. 24 cm. (A Century book) The life of the twentieth-century Indian leader who helped gain independence for his country through passive resistance and non-violence. [DS481.G3M62] 92 75-116039 2.98
1. Gandhi, Mohandas Karamchand, 1869-1948—Juvenile literature. I. Title.

PEARE, Catherine Owens. 954.03'5'0924
Mahatma Gandhi, father of nonviolence. [1st ed.] New York, Hawthorn Books [1969] 301 p. illus. 22 cm. Bibliography: p. 285-288. A biography of Gandhi, whose philosophy of nonviolence helped India gain independence from British rule. [DS481.G3P42 1969] 92 72-80111 5.95
1. Gandhi, Mohandas Karamchand, 1869-1948—Juvenile literature. I. Title.

ZINKIN, Taya. 954.0350924 (B)
The story of Gandhi. Illustrated by Robert Hales. [1st American ed.] New York, Criterion Books [1966, c1965] 190 p. illus., ports. 21 cm. Includes bibliographical references. [DS481.G3Z58] 66-22774
1. Gandhi, Mohandas Karamchand, 1869-1948 — Juvenile literature. I. Title.

ZINKIN TOYA 954.0350924 (B)
The story of gandhi Illus. by Robert Hales. [1st Amer. ed.] New York, Criteron Bks [1966.c.1965] 190p. illus. ports. 21 cm. Bibl. [DS481.G3Z58] 66-22774 3.50
1. Gandhi Mohandas Karemchand, 1869-1948—Juvenile literature. I. Title.

Gandhi, Mohandas Karamchand, 1869-1948—Addresses, essays, lectures.

THE Americanization of Gandhi : images of the Mahatma / edited, with an introductory essay, by Charles Chatfield. New York : Garland Pub. Co., 1976. p. cm. (The Garland Library of war and peace) Includes bibliographical references. [DS481.G3A574] 79-147747 ISBN 0-8240-0446-9 lib.bdg.: 25.00 954.03'5'0924
1. Gandhi, Mohandas Karamchand, 1869-1948—Addresses, essays, lectures. 2. India—Politics and government—1919-1947—Addresses, essays, lectures. 3. Passive resistance. 4. India—Foreign opinion, American—Addresses, essays, lectures. 5. Public opinion—United States—Addresses, essays, lectures. 6. Afro-Americans—Civil rights—Addresses, essays, lectures. I. Chatfield, Charles, 1934- II. Series.

MAHADEVAN, Thopil Krishnan. 320.9'54'04
Gandhi, my refrain; controversial essays, 1950-1972 [by] T. K. Mahadevan. [1st ed.] Bombay, Popular Prakashan [1973, i.e. 1974] 223 p. 22 cm. [DS481.G3M234] 73-905552
1. Gandhi, Mohandas Karamchand, 1869-1948—Addresses, essays, lectures. 2. India—Politics and government—1947- —Addresses, essays, lectures. I. Title.
Distributed by International Publications Service, 11.25 BIP

Gandhi, Mohandas Karamchand, 1869-1948—Juvenile literature.

REYNOLDS, Reginald, 1905- 92
The true story of Gandhi, man of peace. [American ed.] Chicago, Childrens Press [1964] 141 p. col. illus. 23 cm. First published in London in 1960 under title: The true book about Mahatma Gandhi. [DS481.G3R42 1964] 64-12907
1. Gandhi, Mohandas Karamchand, 1869-1948—Juvenile literature. I. Title.

Gandler, Alfred, 1861-1932.

DOW, John, 1885- 922.573
Alfred Gandier, man of vision and achievement. Toronto, United Church Pub. House [1951] 138 p. illus. 21 cm. [BX9883,G3D6] 52-27464
1. Gandler, Alfred, 1861-1932. I. Title.

Gann, Ernest Kellogg, 1910- —Biography.

GANN, Ernest Kellogg, 1910- 813'.5'4
A hostage to fortune / Ernest K. Gann. 1st ed. New York : Knopf, 1978. 504 p. ; 25 cm. [PS3513.A56Z466 1978] 78-54908 ISBN 0-394-49984-0 : 12.95
1. Gann, Ernest Kellogg, 1910- —Biography. 2. Novelists, American—20th century—Biography. 3. Air pilots—United States—Biography. I. Title.

Gannett, Deborah (Sampson) 1760-1827.

MANN, Herman, 1772-1833. 973.3'3'0924 B
The female review: Life of Deborah Sampson; the female soldier in the Revolution. With an introd. and notes by John Adams Vinton. Boston, J. K. Wiggin.& W. Parsons Lunt, 1866. New York, Arno Press, 1972. 267 p. front. (port.) 23 cm. (American women: images and realities) [E275.G22 1972] 72-2603 ISBN 0-405-04476-3 12.00
1. Gannett, Deborah (Sampson) 1760-1827. 2. United States—History—Revolution—Personal narratives. I. Title. II. Series.

Gannett, Deborah Sampson, 1760-1827—Juvenile fiction.

CLAPP, Patricia. JUV
I'm Deborah Sampson : a soldier in the War of the Revolution / Patricia Clapp. New York : Lothrop, Lee & Shepard, c1977. 176 p. ; 22 cm. Relates the experiences of the woman who disguised herself as a man in order to enlist and fight in the American Revolution. [PZ7.C5294Ian] [FIC] 76-51770 ISBN 0-688-41799-X : 5.95 ISBN 0-688-51799-4 lib.bdg. : 5.21
1. Gannett, Deborah Sampson, 1760-1827—Juvenile fiction. I. Title. BIP

Gannett, Deborah Sampson, 1760-1827—Juvenile literature.

FELTON, Harold W. 973.3'3'0924 B
Deborah Sampson, soldier of the Revolution / Harold W. Felton ; illustrated by John Martinez. New York : Dodd, Mead, c1976. 111 p. : ill. ; 24 cm. Includes index. Biography of Deborah Sampson Gannett, a young woman who, disguised as a man, served in the army during the American Revolution. [E275.G193] 76-13438 ISBN 0-396-07343-3 : 4.95
1. Gannett, Deborah Sampson, 1760-1827—Juvenile literature. I. Martinez, John. II. Title. BIP

MCGOVERN, Ann. 973.3'3'0924 B
The secret soldier : the story of Deborah Sampson / by Ann McGovern ; illustrated by Ann Grifalconi. New York : Four Winds Press, [1975] 62 p. : ill. ; 23 cm. A brief biography of the woman who disguised herself as a man and joined the Continental Army during the Revolutionary War. [E275.G2] 92 75-15819 ISBN 0-590-07432-6 : 5.95
1. Gannett, Deborah Sampson, 1760-1827—Juvenile literature. I. Grifalconi, Ann. II. Title. BIP

Gannett, Ezra Stiles, 1801-1871.

GANNETT, William Channing, 1840-1923. 288'.0924 B
Ezra Stiles Gannett, Unitarian minister in Boston, 1824-1871; a memoir, by his son William C. Gannett. Port Washington, N.Y., Kennikat Press [1971] xv, 572 p. illus., ports. 22 cm. (Kennikat Press scholarly reprints. Series on literary America in the nineteenth century) Reprint of the 1875 ed. Bibliography: p. [565]-572. [BX9869.G3G3 1971] 79-122654
1. Gannett, Ezra Stiles, 1801-1871.

Gannett, Guy Patterson, 1881-1954.

ZUVER, Dudley. 920.5
The lengthened shadow of a Maine man, a biography of Guy P. Gannett. [Freeport, Me.] Bond Wheelwright Co. [c1956] 128 p. 24 cm. (American saga series) [PN4874.G313Z8] 56-13471
1. Gannett, Guy Patterson, 1881-1954. I. Title.

Gantt family.

TERRY, Jessie B. Gantt, 1899- 978'.03'0924 B
Bud and Sis at the turn of the century / Jessie B. Gantt Terry. San Antonio, Tex. : Naylor Co., c1976. p. cm. [CS71.G195 1976] 76-28789 ISBN 0-8111-0636-5 : 5.95
1. Gantt family. 2. Terry, Jessie B. Gantt, 1899- 3. Great Plains—Genealogy. I. Title.

Garbo, Greta, 1905-

AFFRON, Charles. 791.43'028'0922
Star acting : Gish, Garbo, Davis / Charles Affron. New York : Dutton, c1977. x, 354 p. : ill. ; 23 cm. Includes index. Bibliography: p. [345]-347. [PN1995.A27] 76-8039 ISBN 0-525-20968-9 : 16.95
1. Gish, Lillian, 1896- 2. Garbo, Greta, 1905- 3. Davis, Bette, 1908- 4. Moving-picture acting. I. Title. BIP

BAINBRIDGE, John. 927.92
Garbo. [1st ed.] Garden City, N. Y., Doubleday, 1955. 256 p. illus. 22 cm. Biography. [PN2778.G3B3] 55-5589
1. Garbo, Greta, 1905-

BAINBRIDGE, John. 791.43'028'0924 B
Garbo. [1st ed.] New York, Holt, Rinehart and Winston [1971] 320 p. illus. 27 cm.

[PN2778.G3B3 1971] 73-117282 ISBN 0-03-085045-2 10.95
1. Garbo, Greta, 1905-

BAINBRIDGE, John. 791.43'028'0924 B
Garbo : the famous biography, lavishly illustrated / by John Bainbridge. New York : Galahad Books, [1975] c1971. 320 p. : ill. ; 26 cm. Includes index. [PN2778.G3B3 1975] 74-29492 ISBN 0-88365-286-2 : 14.95
1. Garbo, Greta, 1905-

BILLQUIST, Fritiof 927.92
Garbo, a biography. Translated by Maurice Michael. New York, Putnam [c.1960] 255p. illus. 60-16682 4.50 half cloth,
1. Garbo, Greta, 1905- I. Title.

CARR, Larry. 791.43'028'0922
Four fabulous faces : Swanson, Garbo, Crawford, Dietrich / Larry Carr. New York : Penguin Books, 1978. 492 p. : ill. ; 28 cm. Reprint of the 1970 ed. published by Arlington House, New Rochelle, N.Y. [PN1998.A2C34 1978] 78-18862 ISBN 0-14-004988-6 : 12.95
1. Garbo, Greta, 1905- 2. Swanson, Gloria. 3. Crawford, Joan, 1908-1977. 4. Dietrich, Marlene, 1905- 5. Moving-picture actors and actresses—United States—Biography. I. Title. BIP

PAYNE, Pierre Stephen Robert, 1911- 791.43'028'0924 B
The great Garbo / Robert Payne. New York : Praeger, 1976. 297 p. : ill. ; 26 cm. Includes index. Filmography: p. 289-290. [PN2778.G3P37] 73-11784 ISBN 0-275-34000-7 : 12.95
1. Garbo, Greta, 1905- I. Title.

SANDS, Frederick. 791.43'028'0924 B
The divine Garbo / Frederick Sands and Sven Broman. New York : Grosset & Dunlap, c1979. 243 p. : ill. ; 28 cm. Includes index. [PN2778.G3S2] 78-58096 ISBN 0-448-16245-8 : 17.95
1. Garbo, Greta, 1905- 2. Moving-picture actors and actresses—Sweden—Biography. I. Broman, Sven, joint author. II. Title. BIP

SJOLANDER, Ture, 1937- 791.43'028'0924 B
Garbo. [1st ed.] New York, Harper & Row [1971] 135 p. (chiefly illus.) 31 cm. [PN2778.G3S5] 73-160651 ISBN 0-06-013926-9 12.00
1. Garbo, Greta, 1905- I. Title.

ZIEROLD, Norman J. 791.43'028'0924 B
Garbo [by] Norman Zierold. New York, Stein and Day [1969] 196 p. illus., ports. 23 cm. Bibliography: p. 188-190. [PN2778.G3Z5 1969] 69-17936 5.95
1. Garbo, Greta, 1905-

Garcia Diego y Moreno, Francisco, Bp., 1785-1946.

GARCIA Diego y Moreno, Francisco, Bp., 1785-1846. 282'.092'4 B
The writings of Francisco Garcia Diego y Moreno, Obispo de Ambas Californias / translated and edited by Francis J. Weber. Los Angeles : Weber, 1976. xiii, 192 p. : group port. ; 27 cm. Includes bibliographical references. [BX4705.G244.G37] 76-21434
1. Garcia Diego y Moreno, Francisco, Bp., 1785-1846. 2. Catholic Church—Bishops—Biography. 3. Catholic Church in California—History—Sources. 4. Bishops—California—Biography.

WEBER, Francis J. 922.2794
A biographical sketch of Right Reverend Francisco Garcia Diego y Moreno, first bishop of the California, 1785-1846. Los Angeles, Borromeo Guild [1961] 50 p. illus. 22 cm. Includes bibliography. [BX4705.G244W4] 61-10808
1. Garcia Diego y Moreno, Francisco, Bp., 1785-1946. I. Title.

WEBER, Francis J. 282'.092'4 B
Francisco Garcia Diego, California's transition bishop, by Francis J. Weber. Los Angeles, Dawson's Book Shop, 1972 [c1971] x, 63 p. illus. 22 cm. "Limited to a press run of 250 copies." Includes bibliographical references. [BX4705.G244W42] 78-167849
1. Garcia Diego y Moreno, Francisco, Bp., 1785-1846.

Garcia, Ector.

GARCIA, Ector. 363.2 B
Portraits of crime / Ector Garcia and Charles E. Pike. New York : Condor, 1977. xiii, 271 p. : ill. ; 18 cm. [HV8073.4.G37] 77-83872 ISBN 0-89516-010-2 pbk. : 2.25
1. Garcia, Ector. 2. Police artists—Biography. 3. Crime and criminals—California—Los Angeles—Case studies. I. Pike, Charles E., joint author. II. Title. BIP

Garcia Lorca, Federico, 1899-1936.

ADAMS, Mildred, 1894- 868'.6'209 B
Garcia Lorca : playwright, poet, and traveller / Mildred Adams. New York : G. Braziller, 1977. p. cm. Bibliography: p. [PQ6613.A763Z528] 77-77561 ISBN 0-8076-0873-4 : 8.95
1. Garcia Lorca, Federico, 1898-1936. 2. Authors, Spanish—20th century—Biography.

HONIG, Edwin 861.62
Garcia Lorca. [Rev. ed. New Directions, dist. Philadelphia, Lippincott, c.1944, 1963] 239p. 19cm. (102) 62-12396 1.65 pap.,
1. Garcia Lorca, Federico, 1899-1936. I. Title.

TEXTOS y documentos lorquianos / Daniel Eisenberg. Tallahassee, Fla. : Eisenberg, [1975] 52 p. ; 22 cm. Chiefly Spanish; some French or English. The texts attributed to Garcia Lorca were previously published in the periodical Gallo. Contents.Contents.—Textos en prosa atribuidos a Lorca: Los pintores de Granada. La construccion urbana. Resena. Falla en Paris. Recepcion de Gallo. Advertencias sin importancia.—Lorca en Nueva York: La matricula de Columbia University. Documentos de los dormitorios de Columbia University. La conferencia de Vassar College. La conferencia de Columbia University.—Una visita con Jean-Louis Schonberg. Includes bibliographical references. [PQ6613.A763Z886] 75-12438 ISBN 0-9600866-1-7 : 2.50 861'.6'2
1. Garcia Lorca, Federico, 1898-1936—Biography. I. Garcia Lorca, Federico, 1898-1936. II. Eisenberg, Daniel. III. Schonberg, Jean Louis.

Garcia, Manuel, 1805-1906.

MACKINLAY, Malcolm Sterling, 1876- 782.1'092'4 B
Garcia the centenarian and his times / by M. Sterling Mackinlay. New York : Da Capo Press, 1976. xii, [3], 335 p., [17] leaves of plates : ill. ; 23 cm. (Da Capo Press music reprint series) Reprint of the 1908 ed. published by D. Appleton, New York. Includes index. Bibliography: 15th prelim. page. [ML420.G24M2 1976] 75-40206 ISBN 0-306-70671-7 : 19.50
1. Garcia, Manuel, 1805-1906. I. Title. BIP

Garcilaso de la Vega, el Inca, 1539-1616.

VARNER, John Grier. 985'.03'0924 B
El Inca; the life and times of Garcilaso de la Vega. Austin, University of Texas Press [1968] xiv, 413 p. illus., facsims. 24 cm. (Texas pan-American series) Bibliography: p. [391]-400. [F3444.G4] 68-55059 ISBN 0-292-78375-2 10.00
1. Garcilaso de la Vega, el Inca, 1539-1616. I. Title.

Gard, Wayne, 1899-

ADAMS, Ramon Frederick, 1889- 978'.0072'024
Wayne Gard, historian of the West, by Ramon F. Adams. Austin, Tex., Steck-Vaughn Co. [1970] ii, 44 p. 21 cm. (Southwest writers series, no. 31) Bibliography: p. 40-44. [E175.5.G3A62] 73-123044 ISBN 0-8114-3894-5
1. Gard, Wayne, 1899- I. Title. II. Series.

GARD, Wayne, 1899- 636.2'01'0922
Reminiscences of range life. Austin, Tex., Steck-Vaughn Co. [1970] ii, 52 p. 21 cm. (Southwest writers series, no. 30) Biographies. Bibliography: p. 49-52. [PS277.G26] 71-120004 ISBN 8-11-438937-
1. Authors, American—Southwest, New. I. Title. II. Series.

Garden, Alexander, 1730-1791.

BERKELEY, Edmund. 574'.0924 B
Dr. Alexander Garden of Charles Town, by Edmund Berkeley and Dorothy Smith Berkeley. Chapel Hill, University of North Carolina Press [1969] xiv, 379 p. illus. 24 cm. Bibliography: p. 359-370. [QH31.G32B47] 70-80925 10.00
1. Garden, Alexander, 1730-1791. I. Berkeley, Dorothy Smith, joint author. II. Title.

Gardens.

LEES, Carlton B. 635.9
Gardens, plants, and man, by Carlton B. Lees. Englewood Cliffs, N.J., Prentice-Hall [1970] 251 p. illus. (part col.), ports. 29 cm. "A Rutledge book." [SB453.L43] 67-10531 19.95
1. Gardens. 2. Botanists. I. Title.

Gardiner, Glenn Lion,

GARDINER, Glenn Lion, 1896- 920
Sin, fiddles, and buggy wheels. Ridgewood, N.J., Knollwood House [1955] 129p. 21cm. Autobiographical. [CT275.G268A3] 55-34493
I. Title.

Gardiner, Leslie, 1921-

GARDINER, Leslie, 1921- 914.96'04
Curtain calls : travels in Albania, Romania and Bulgaria / Leslie Gardiner. London : Duckworth, 1976. 206 p. ; 23 cm. Includes index. [DR16.G37] 77-351201 ISBN 0-7156-1026-0 : £6.95
1. Gardiner, Leslie, 1921- 2. Balkan Peninsula—Description and travel. 3. Balkan Peninsula—Social life and customs. I. Title. BIP

Gardner, Ava, 1922-

HANNA, David. 927.92
Ava, a portrait of a star. New York, Putnam [1960] 256p. illus. 22cm. [PN2287.G37H3] 60-13669
1. Gardner, Ava, 1922- I. Title.

HANNA, David 927.92
Ava, a portrait of a star. New York, Putnam [c.1960] 256p. illus. 3.95 half cloth,
1. Gardner, Ava, 1922- I. Title.

HIGHAM, Charles, 1931- 791.430280
Ava: a life story [New York] Dell [1975 c1974] 208 p. 18 cm [PN2287.G37H5] 1.50 (pbk.)
1. Gardner, Ava, 1922- I. Title.
L.C. card no. for original edition: 74-8106

HIGHAM, Charles, 1931- 791.43'028'0924 B
Ava: a life story. New York, Delacorte Press [1974] xii, 267 p. illus. 22 cm. "Ava Gardner films": p. [251]-255. [PN2287.G37H5] 74-8106 ISBN 0-440-01394-1 7.95
1. Gardner, Ava, 1922- I. Title.

Gardner, Erle Stanley, 1889-1970—Biography.

HUGHES, Dorothy Belle Flanagan, 1904- 813'.5'2 B
Erle Stanley Gardner : the case of the real Perry Mason / by Dorothy B. Hughes. 1st ed. New York : Morrow, 1978. 350 p. : ill. ; 25 cm. Includes index. "Bibliography of Erle Stanley Gardner, compiled by Ruth Moore": p. [311]-341. [PS3513.A6322Z68] 77-16845 ISBN 0-688-03282-6 : 15.00
1. Gardner, Erle Stanley, 1889-1970—Biography. 2. Authors, American—20th century—Biography. I. Title. BIP

Gardner, Isabella (Stewart) 1840-1924.

PALFFY, Eleanor. 920.7
The lady and the painter; an extravaganza, based on incidents in the lives of the two principal characters: Mrs. John Lowell Gardner of the Isabella Stewart Gardner Museum, and the artist, John Singer Sargent. Decorations by Alanson Hewes. New York, Coward-McCann [1951] 263 p. illus. 21 cm. [N8384.G3P3] 51-13732
1. Gardner, Isabella (Stewart) 1840-1924. 2. Sargent, John Singer, 1856-1924. I. Title.

THARP, Louise (Hall) 1898- 708.144610924
Mrs. Jack; a biography of Isabella Stewart Gardner. Boston, Little [c.1965] xii, 365p. illus., ports. 23cm. Bibl. [N8384.G3T5] 65-18129 6.95
1. Gardner. Isabella (Stewart) 1840-1924. I. Title.

THARP, Louise (Hall) 1898- 706'.5
Mrs. Jack; a biography of Isabella Stewart Gardner. [1st ed.] Boston, Little, Brown [1965] xii, 365 p. illus., ports. 22 cm. Bibliographical references included in "Chapter notes" (p. [329]-345) [N8384.G3T5] 65-18129
1. Gardner, Isabella (Stewart) 1840-1924. I. Title.

Gardner, Oliver Max, 1882-1947.

MORRISON, Joseph L. 973.917'0924 B
Governor O. Max Gardner; a power in North Carolina and New Deal Washington, by Joseph L. Morrison. Chapel Hill, University of North Carolina Press [1971] xii, 323 p. illus., group ports. 24 cm. Includes bibliographical references. [F259.G23M6 1971] 74-132253 ISBN 0-8078 1153-X 10.00
1. Gardner, Oliver Max, 1882-1947. BIP

Gardner, William Alexander, 1859-1916.

COOK, Willamine A (Gardner) 1897- 923.873
The W. A. Gardner story; his life, his family, the times and the town they lived in. [Evanston, Ill., c1956] 199p. illus. 24cm. [HE2754.G3C6] 57-21789
1. Gardner, William Alexander, 1859-1916. I. Title.

Garfield, Harry Augustus, 1863-1942.

COMER, Lucretia (Garfield) 350.000924 (B)
Harry Garfield's first forty years; man of action in a troubled world, [1st ed,] New York, Vantage Press [1965] 270 p. illus., ports. 21 cm. Bibliographical references included in "Notes" (p. 264-265) [LD6072.7 1908.C58] 65-5563
1. Garfield, Harry Augustus, 1863-1942. I. Title.

Garfield, James Abram, Pres. U.S., 1831-1881.

CALDWELL, Robert Granville 923.173
James A. Garfield, party chieftain [Unaltered, unabridged ed.] Hamden, Conn., Archon [dist. Shoe String, 1965, c.1931] xi, 383p. illus., ports. 23cm. Bibl. [E687.C25] 65-15014 10.00
1. Garfield, James Abram, Pres. U.S., 1831-1881. I. Title.

FEIS, Ruth Stanley-Brown. 92
Mollie Garfield in the White House. Chicago, Rand McNally [1963] 128 p. illus., ports. 22 cm. [E687.F4] 63-12329
1. Stanley-Brown, Mary Garfield, b. 1867. 2. Garfield, James Abram, Pres. U.S., 1831-1881. 3. Garfield family.

GARFIELD, James Abram, Pres. U.S., 1831-1881. 973.8'4'0924 B
The diary of James A. Garfield. Edited with an introd. by Harry James Brown [and] Frederick D. Williams. [East Lansing] Michigan State University, 1967- v. illus., facsim., port. 25 cm.

Contents.Contents.——v. 1. 1848-1871.— Bibliographical footnotes. [E660.G223] 67-12577 ISBN 0-87013-169-9 (v. 3) 22.50 (v. 3)
I. Brown, Harry James, ed. II. Williams, Frederick D., ed. III. Title.

LEECH, Margaret, 973.8'4'0924 B 1893-1974.
The Garfield orbit / Margaret Leech and Harry J. Brown. 1st ed. New York : Harper & Row, c1978. xi, 369 p., [16] leaves of plates : ill. ; 24 cm. Includes bibliographical references and index. [E687.L43 1978] 76-5140 ISBN 0-06-012551-9 : 15.00
1. Garfield, James Abram, Pres. U.S., 1831-1881. 2. United States—Politics and government—Civil War, 1861-1865. 3. United States—Politics and government—1865-1883. 4. Presidents—United States—Biography. I. Brown, Harry James, joint author. II. Title.

PESKIN, Allan. 973.8'4'0924 B
Garfield : a biography / by Allan Peskin. Kent, Ohio : Kent State University Press, c1978. x, 716 p. : port. ; 25 cm. Includes index. Bibliography: p. [691]-704. [E687.P47] 77-15630 ISBN 0-87338-210-2 : 20.00
1. Garfield, James Abram, Pres. U.S., 1831-1881. 2. Presidents—United States—Biography. 3. United States—Politics and government—1849-1877. 4. United States—Politics and government—1877-1881.

SMITH, Theodore 973.8'4'0924 Clarke, 1870-1960
The life and letters of James Abram Garfield. [Hamden, Conn.] Archon, 1968. 2v. (ix, 1283p.) ports. 24cm. Reprint of 1925 ed. Contents.v. 1. 1831-1877.--v.2. 1877-1882. Bibl. footnotes. [E687S66 1968] (B) 68-26935 25.00 set,
1. Garfield, James Abram, Pres. U.S., 1831-1881. I. Title. BIP

TAYLOR, John M., 973.8'4'0924 1930-
Garfield of Ohio, the available man [by] John M. Taylor. New York, Norton [1970] 336 p. illus., ports. 25 cm. Bibliography: p. 309-312. [E687.T22 1970] 75-111974 8.50
1. Garfield, James Abram, Pres. U.S., 1831-1881. I. Title.

WASSON, Woodrow W 1919- 923.173
James A. Garfield; his religion and education; a study in the religious and educational thought and activity of an American statesman. Nashville, Tennessee Book Co., 1952. xi, 155 p. 22 cm. Bibliography: p. 142-150. [E687.W3] 52-3628
1. Garfield, James Abram, Pres. U.S., 1831-1881. 2. Disciples of Christ. I. Title.

Garfield, James Abram, Pres. U.S.,1831-1881—Juvenile literature

HOYT, Edwin Palmer 923.173
James A. Garfield. Chicago, Reilly & Lee [c.1964] 165p. 21cm. Bibl. 64-22918 3.95
1. Garfield, James Abram, Pres. U.S., 1831-1881—Juvenile literature. I. Title.

SEVERN, William 923.173
Teacher, soldier, President: the life of James A. Garfield, by Bill Severn. New York, Washburn [dist. McKay, c.1964] 176p. port. 21cm. 64-21634 3.50
1. Garfield, James Abram, Pres. U.S.,1831-1881—Juvenile literature I. Title.

SEVERN, William. 923.173
Teacher, soldier, President: the life of James A. Garfield, by Bill Severn. New York, I. Washburn [1964] 176 p. port. 21 cm. [E687.S4] 64-21634
1. Garfield, James Abram, Pres. U. S., 1831-1881—Juvenile literature. I. Title.

FARLEY, Karin 973.8'4'0924 B Clifford.
Canal boy / Karin Clifford Farley ; illustrated by Dennis Bellile. Elgin, Ill. : D. C. Cook Pub. Co., c1978. 158 p. : ill. ; 18 cm. Relates the experiences of the 20th President of the United States during the two teenage years he spent as a canal boy guiding barges from New York to Illinois. [E687.F34] 77-94010 ISBN 0-89191-106-5 pbk. : 1.95
1. Garfield, James Abram, Pres. U.S., 1831-1881—Childhood and youth—Juvenile literature. 2. Presidents—United States—Biography—Juvenile literature. I. Title. BIP

BEAVER, James N., 791.43'028'0924 1950-
John Garfield / James N. Beaver, Jr. South Brunswick, N.J. : A. S. Barnes, c1977. p. cm. Includes index. [PN2287.G377B4 1977] 75-38450 ISBN 0-498-01890-3 : 17.50
1. Garfield, John.

MORRIS, George, 791.43'028'0924 B 1943-
John Garfield / by George Morris. New York : Jove Publications, [1977] p. cm. (An illustrated history of the movies) (A Harvest/HBJ book) Includes index. Filmography: p. [PN2287.G377M6] 77-76444 ISBN 0-15-646250-8 : 2.50
1. Garfield, John. 2. Moving-picture actors and actresses—United States—Biography. BIP

SWINDELL, Larry. 791'.092'4 B
Body and soul, the story of John Garfield / by Larry Swindell. New York : Morrow, 1975. 288 p., [12] leaves of plates : ill. ; 21 cm. Includes index. Filmography: p. 275-279. [PN2287.G377S9] 74-31470 ISBN 0-688-02907-8
1. Garfield, John. I. Title.

Gargan, William,

GARGAN, William, 1905- 791'.0924
Why me?; an autobiography. [1st ed.] Garden City, N.Y., Doubleday, 1969. 311 p. illus. 22 cm. [PN2287.G38A3] 68-10310 5.95
I. Title.

Garibaldi, Annita, ca. 1821-1849.

SERGIO, Lisa, 945'.08'0924 B 1905-
I am my beloved; the life of Anita Garibaldi. New York, Weybright and Talley [1969] x, 273 p. ports. 24 cm. Bibliography: p. 265-268. [DG552.8.G18S45] 73-82746 6.95
1. Garibaldi, Annita, ca. 1821-1849. I. Title.

Garibaldi, Giuseppe, 1807-1882.

DE POLNAY, Peter, 1906- 923.245
Garibaldi; the man and the legend. New York, T. Nelson [1961] 255 p. 22 cm. Includes bibliography. [DG552.8.G2D4] 61-15050
1. Garibaldi, Giuseppe, 1807-1882.

DE POLNAY, Peter, 945'.08'0924 B 1906-
Garibaldi : the legend and the man / by Peter de Polnay. Westport, Conn. : Greenwood Press, 1976, c1960. 234 p., [5] leaves of plates : ill. ; 22 cm. Reprint of the ed. published by Hollis & Carter, London. Includes index. Bibliography: p. [227]-229. [DG552.8.G2D4 1976] 75-22641 ISBN 0-8371-8361-8 lib.bdg. : 14.50
1. Garibaldi, Giuseppe, 1807-1882. BIP

GARIBALDI, 945'.08'0924 B Giuseppe, 1807-1882.
Autobiography of Giuseppe Garibaldi. Translated by A. Werner. With an introd. by A. William Salomone. Supplement by Jessie White Mario. New York, H. Fertig, 1971. 3 v. facsims., port. 21 cm. Reprint, with new introd., of the 1889 translation of Memorie autobiografiche. Contents.—v. 1. 1807-1849.—v. 2. 1849-1872.—v. 3. Supplement. Includes bibliographical references. [DG552.8.G2A2 1971] 68-9597
I. Werner, Alica, 1859-1935, tr. II. Mario, Jessie (White) 1832-1906. III. Title. BIP

HIBBERT, Christopher, 945.080924 1924-
Garibaldi and his enemies; the clash of arms and personalities in the making of Italy [1st Amer. ed.] Boston, Little [c.1965, 1966] xiv, 423p. illus., maps, ports. 25cm. Bibl. [DG552.G2H5] 66-10974 7.50
1. Garibaldi, Giuseppe, 1807-1882. 2. Italy—Hist.—19th cent. I. Title.

HIBBERT, Christopher, 945.080924 1924-
Garibaldi and his enemies: The clash of arms and personalities in the making of Italy. [1st American ed.] Boston, Little, Brown [1966] xvi, 423 p. illus., maps, ports. 25 cm. Bibliography: p. [394]-407. [DG552.8.G2H5] (B) 66-10974
1. 1. Garibaldi, Giuseppi, 1807-1882. 2. Italy — Hist. — 19th Cent. I. Title.

LARG, David Glass. 945'.08'0924 B
Giuseppe Garibaldi; a biography, by David Larg. Port Washington, N.Y., Kennikat Press [1970] xiii, 352 p. maps, ports. 22 cm. Reprint of the 1934 ed. Includes bibliographies. "Garibaldi's memoirs and other writings": p. 322-324. [DG552.8.G2L3 1970] 73-112811
1. Garibaldi, Giuseppe, 1807-1882. BIP

MACK Smith, Denis, 1920- 923.245
Garibaldi, a great life in brief. [1st ed.] New York, Knopf, 1956. 207 p. illus. 19 cm. (Great lives in brief; a new series of biographies) [DG552.8.G2M24] 56-5804
1. Garibaldi, Giuseppe, 1807-1882.

MACK Smith, Denis, 945'.08'0924 1920- comp.
Garibaldi. Englewood Cliffs, N.J., Prentice-Hall [1969] x, 182 p. map. 21 cm. (Great lives observed) (A Spectrum book.) "Bibliographical note": p. 176-178. [DG552.8.G2M24 1969] 69-15335 4.95
1. Garibaldi, Giuseppe, 1807-1882.

MACK SMITH, Denis, 1920- 923.245
Garibaldi, a great life in brief. [1st ed.] New York, Knopf, 1956. 207p. illus: 19cm. (Great lives in brief: a new series of biographies) [DG552.8.G2M24] 56-5804
1. Garibaldi, Giuseppe, 1807-1882. I. Title.

PARRIS, John 923.245
The Lion of Caprera; a biography of Giuseppe Garibaldi. New York, McKay [c.1962] 352p. front. port. 23cm. Bibl. 61-17451 5.00
1. Garibaldi, Giuseppe, 1807-1882. I. Title.

PARRIS, John. 923.245
The Lion of Caprera: a biography of Giuseppe Garibaldi. New York, D. McKay Co. [1962] 352p. illus. 23cm. Includes bibliography. [DG552.8.G2P3] 61-17451
1. Garibaldi, Gluseppe, 1807-1882. I. Title.

RIDLEY, Jasper 945'.08'0924 B Godwin.
Garibaldi / Jasper Ridley. New York : Viking Press, 1976, c1974. xvii, 718 p., [6] leaves of plates : ill. ; 25 cm. Includes index. Bibliography: p. 639-652. [DG552.8.G2R52 1976] 75-41366 ISBN 0-670-33548-7 : 15.00
1. Garibaldi, Giuseppe, 1807-1882.

Garibaldi, Giuseppe, 1807-1882—Juvenile literature.

SYME, Ronald, 1910- juv
Garibaldi, the man who made a nation. Illustrated by William Stobbs. New York, Morrow, 1967. 190, [1] p. illus., maps. 21 cm. Bibliography: p. [191] [DG552.8.G2S9] 67-15148
1. Garibaldi, Giuseppe, 1807-1882—Juvenile literature. I. Title.

Garland, Hamlin, 1860-1940.

GARLAND, Hamlin 928.1
A daughter of the middle border. [Gloucester, Mass. Peter Smith(1960, c.1951] xii, 337p 21cm. (Sagamore Press paperback rebound in cloth. American century series, S-11) A continuation of the author's autobiography, A son of the middle border. 3.50
I. Title. BIP

GARLAND, Hamlin, 1860- 813'.5'2 B 1940.
Back-trailers from the middle border. Illus. by Constance Garland. New York, Macmillan, 1928. St. Clair Shores, Mich., Scholarly Press, 1974. x, 379 p. illus. 22 cm. Autobiographical. [PS1733.A38 1974] 72-84727 ISBN 0-403-02986-4 15.50 (lib. ed.)
1. Garland, Hamlin, 1860-1940. I. Title.

GARLAND, Hamlin, 1860- 813'.5'2 B 1940.
Companions on the trail; a literary chronicle. Decorations by Constance Garland. St. Clair Shores, Mich., Scholarly Press [1974, c1931] p. Reprint of the ed. published by Macmillan, New York. Sequel to the author's Roadside meetings. [PS1733.A39 1974] 72-84728 ISBN 0-403-02978-3
1. Garland, Hamlin, 1860-1940. 2. Authors, English—Correspondence, reminiscences, etc. I. Title.

GARLAND, Hamlin, 1860- 813'.5'2 B 1940.
A daughter of the middle border. New York, Macmillan, 1922. St. Clair Shores, Mich., Scholarly Press [1974, c1921] xv, 405 p. ports. 22 cm. A continuation of the author's autobiography, A son of the middle border. [PS1733.A42 1974] 72-84723 ISBN 0-403-02968-6
1. Garland, Hamlin, 1860-1940. I. Title.

GARLAND, Hamlin, 1860- 818'.5'203 1940.
My friendly contemporaries; a literary log. Decorations by Constance Garland. New York, Macmillan, 1932. St. Clair Shores, Mich., Scholarly Press, 1971. xvi, 544 p. 22 cm. [PS1733.A4255 1971] 79-145036 ISBN 0-403-00982-0
1. Garland, Hamlin, 1860-1940. 2. Authors, English—Correspondence, reminiscences, etc. I. Title.

GARLAND, Hamlin, 1860- 813'.5'2 1940.
Roadside meetings. Decorations by Constance Garland. St. Clair Shores, Mich., Scholarly Press [1974, c1930] p. Autobiographical. Reprint of the ed. published by Macmillan, New York. [PS1733.A45 1974] 72-145037 ISBN 0-403-02982-1 19.50 (lib. ed.)
1. Garland, Hamlin, 1860-1940. 2. Authors—Correspondence, reminiscences, etc. I. Title.

GARLAND, Hamlin, 1860-1940. 082
A son of the middle border. Edited and with an introd. by Henry M. Christman. New York, Macmillan, 1962. 401 p. 22 cm. [PS1733.A47 1962] 62-11916
1. Garland, Hamlin, 1860-1940. 2. Frontier and pioneer life—Northwestern States. I. Title. BIP

GARLAND, Hamlin, 1860- 813'.5'2 B 1940.
A son of the middle border. With illus. by Alice Barber Stephens. St. Clair Shores, Mich., Scholarly Press [1974, c1917] p. cm. Reprint of the 1920 ed. published by Macmillan, New York. [PS1733.A47 1974] 72-84722 ISBN 0-403-02998-8
1. Garland, Hamlin, 1860-1940. 2. Frontier and pioneer life—Northwestern States. I. Title.

GARLAND, Hamlin, 1860- 818'.5'208 1940.
Trail-makers of the middle border. With Illus. by Constance Garland. Grosset & Dunlap. St. Clair Shores, Mich., Scholarly Press, 1971 [c1926] 426 p. illus. 22 cm. [PS1733.A49 1971] 76-145038 ISBN 0-403-00984-7
I. Title.

HOLLOWAY, Jean. 813'.5'2 B
Hamlin Garland, a biography. Freeport, N.Y., Books for Libraries Press [1971, c1960] xii, 346 p. illus., ports. 22 cm. Bibliography: p. [314]-334. [PS1733.H6 1971] 70-157342 ISBN 0-8369-5802-0
1. Garland, Hamlin, 1860-1940.

his French friends, by Frank A. Hedgcock. New York, B. Blom [1969] 442 p. illus., ports. 24 cm. Reprint of the 1912 ed. An adaptation of the author's thesis, University of Paris. Includes bibliographical references. [PN2598.G3H4 1969] 70-81976
1. Garrick, David, 1717-1779. I. Title.

KNIGHT, Joseph, 1829-1907. 792'.028'0924 B
David Garrick. With etched port. by W. Boucher. New York, B. Blom [1969] vi, 346 p. port. 21 cm. Reprint of the 1894 ed. [PN2598.G3K5 1969] 74-91904
1. Garrick, David, 1717-1779. BIP

MURPHY, Arthur, 1727-1805. 792'.028'0924 B
The life of David Garrick. New York, B. Blom, 1969. 2 v. front. 21 cm. Reprint of the 1801 ed. [PN2598.G3M8 1969] 76-84521
1. Garrick, David, 1717-1779. I. Title.

PARSONS, Florence Mary (Wilson) 1864-1934. 792'.028'0924 B
Garrick and his circle, by Mrs. Clement Parsons. 2d ed. New York, B. Blom [1969] xxiii, 417 p. illus., ports. 23 cm. Reprint of the 1906 ed. Includes bibliographical references. [PN2598.G3P3 1969] 78-82837
1. Garrick, David, 1717-1779. 2. London—Intellectual life. I. Title. BIP

STEIN, Elizabeth P. 822'.6
David Garrick, dramatist, by Elizabeth P. Stein. New York, B. Blom [1967] xx, 315 p. illus., facsim., ports. 20 cm. (Revolving Fund series, 7) Reprint of 1938 ed. "Bibliography of various editions of Garrick's plays": p. 289-300. [PR3469.S8 1967] 67-23859
1. Garrick, David, 1717-1779. I. Title. II. Series: Modern Language Association of America. Revolving Fund series, 7. BIP

Garrison, William Lloyd, 1805-1879.

CHAPMAN, John Jay, 1862-1933. 322.4'4'0924 B
William Lloyd Garrison. New York, Beekman Publishers, 1974. xii, 289 p. port. 23 cm. (American newspapermen, 1790-1933) Reprint of the 1921 ed. published by Atlantic Monthly Press, Boston. [E449.G25 1974] 74-589 ISBN 0-8464-0027-8 16.00
1. Garrison, William Lloyd, 1805-1879. 2. Abolitionists. 3. Slavery in the United States—Anti-slavery movements.

CHERTKOV, Vladimir Grigor'evich, 1854-1936. 326'.092'4 B
A short biography of William Lloyd Garrison, by V. Tchertkoff and F. Holah. With an introductory appreciation of his life and work by Leo Tolstoy. Westport, Conn., Negro Universities Press [1970] xiv, 176 p. port. 23 cm. [E449.G253 1970] 73-111569 ISBN 0-8371-4590-2
1. Garrison, William Lloyd, 1805-1879. I. Holah, Florence, joint author. BIP

CROSBY, Ernest Howard, 1856-1907. 322.4'4'0924
Garrison, the non-resistant. Chicago, Public Pub. Co. [New York, J. S. Ozer, 1972, c1905] 141 p. port. 22 cm. (The Peace movement in America) Facsim. reprint. [E449.G2535 1972] 72-137534 7.50
1. Garrison, William Lloyd, 1805-1879. I. Title. II. Series. BIP

FREDRICKSON, George M., 1934- comp. 973.71'14'0924 B
William Lloyd Garrison, edited by George M. Fredrickson. Englewood Cliffs, N.J., Prentice-Hall [1968] vii, 182 p. 21 cm. (Great lives observed) (A Spectrum book.) "Bibliographical note": p. 180. [E449.F78] 68-27491 4.95
1. Garrison, William Lloyd, 1805-1879.

GARRISON, Wendell Phillips, 1840-1907. 973.71'14'0924 B
William Lloyd Garrison, 1805-1879: the story of his life, told by his children Wendell Phillips Garrison and Francis Jackson Garrison New York, Negro Universities Press [1969] 4 v. facsims., ports. 23 cm. Reprint of the 1885 ed. [E449.G2548 1969] 79-88431
1. Garrison, William Lloyd, 1805-1879. I. Garrison, Francis Jackson, 1848-1916, joint author.

GRIMKE, Archibald Henry, 1849-1930. 322.4'0924 B
William Lloyd Garrison; the abolitionist. New York, Negro Universities Press [1969] 405 p. port. 23 cm. Reprint of the 1891 ed. [E449.G255 1969] 75-92746
1. Garrison, William Lloyd, 1805-1879.

GRIMKE, Archibald Henry, 1849-1930. 322.44'092'4 B
William Lloyd Garrison, the abolitionist. New York, Funk & Wagnalls, 1891. [New York, AMS Press, 1974] 405 p. port. 19 cm. [E449.G255 1974] 73-168207 ISBN 0-404-00057-6
1. Garrison, William Lloyd, 1805-1879. BIP

JOHNSON, Oliver, 1809-1889. 973.71'14'0924 B
W. L. Garrison and his times. Miami, Fla., Mnemosyne Pub. Co. [1969] xxvi, 490 p. illus., facsim., port. 23 cm. Reprint of the 1881 ed. [E449.G2555 1969] 74-89400
1. Garrison, William Lloyd, 1805-1879. BIP

KORNGOLD, Ralph, 1886- 923.673
Two friends of man; the story of William Lloyd Garrison and Wendell Phillips, and their relationship with Abraham Lincoln. [1st ed.] Boston, Little, Brown, 1950. xii, 425 p. ports. 23 cm. Selected bibliography": p. [401]-410. [E449.G2556] 49-49461
1. Garrison, William Lloyd, 1805-1879. 2. Phillips, Wendell, 1811-1884. 3. Lincoln, Abraham, Pres. U.S., 1809-1865. 4. Slavery in the U.S.—Anti-slavery movements. I. Title.

MERRILL, Walter McIntosh 923.673
Against wind and tide, a biography of Wm. Lloyd Garrison. Cambridge, Mass., Harvard [c.]1963. xvi, 391p. illus., ports. 24cm. Bibl. 63-10871 8.75
1. Garrison, William Lloyd, 1805-1879. I. Title.

NYE, Russel Blaine, 1913- 923.673
William Lloyd Garrison and the humanitarian reformers. [1st ed.] Boston, Little, Brown [1955] 215 p. 21 cm. (The Library of American biography) Includes bibliography. [E449.G2558] 55-7470
1. Garrison, William Lloyd, 1805-1879. BIP

THOMAS, John L. 923.673
The liberator, William Lloyd Garrison, a biography. [1st ed.] Boston, Little Brown [1963] 502 p. illus. 22 cm. Includes bibliography. [E449.G26] 63-8310
1. Garrison, William Lloyd, 1805-1879. I. Title.

Garrison, William Lloyd, 1805-1879—Juvenile literature.

ARCHER, Jules. 973.71'14'0924 B
Angry abolitionist: William Lloyd Garrison. New York, J. Messner [1969] 191 p. 22 cm. Bibliography: p. 185-186. A biography of the journalist who became famous in the 1830's for his denunciations of slavery and whose printed attacks on slave dealers caused his arrest. [E449.G248] 92 72-83148 3.50
1. Garrison, William Lloyd, 1805-1879—Juvenile literature. I. Title.

FABER, Doris, 1924- 973.71'14'0924
I will be heard; the life of William Lloyd Garrison. New York, Lothrop, Lee and Shepard [1970] 127 p. illus., ports. 22 cm. Bibliography: p. [122]-123. A biography of the controversial abolitionist who founded the antislavery newspaper, The Liberator, thirty years before the Civil War. [E449.G2483] 92 B 75-101472 3.75
1. Garrison, William Lloyd, 1805-1879—Juvenile literature. I. Title. BIP

SPENCER, Philip, 1925- 326'.092'2 B
3 against slavery: Denmark Vesey, William Lloyd Garrison, Frederick Douglass. [New York] Scholastic Book Services [1972] 128 p. illus. 21 cm. (Firebird biographies) (Firebird books) Brief biographies of three nineteenth-century men—two black, one white—who led the struggle for the abolition of slavery. [E449.S75617] 920 76-187885
1. Vesey, Denmark, 1769 (ca.)-1822—Juvenile literature. 2. Garrison, William Lloyd, 1805-1879—Juvenile literature. 3. Douglass, Frederick, 1817?-1895—Juvenile literature. I. Title.

Garrity, Richard G.

GARRITY, Richard G. 386'.4042'40924 B
Canal boatman : my life on upstate waterways / Richard Garrity. 1st ed. Syracuse, N.Y. : Syracuse University Press, 1977. p. cm. (A York State book) [HE569.G37A32] 77-21909 ISBN 0-8156-0139-5 : 14.00
1. Garrity, Richard G. 2. Boatmen—New York (State)—Biography. 3. Canals—New York (State)—History. I. Title.

GARRITY, Richard G. 386'.4042'40924 B
Canal boatman : my life on upstate waterways / Richard Garrity. 1st ed. Syracuse, N.Y. : Syracuse University Press, 1977. p. cm. (A York State book) [HE569.G37A32] 77-21909 ISBN 0-8156-0139-5 : 14.00
1. Garrity, Richard G. 2. Boatmen—New York (State)—Biography. 3. Canals—New York (State)—History. I. Title. BIP

Garry, Charles R., 1909-

GARRY, Charles R., 1909- 345'.73'00924 B
Streetfighter in the courtroom : the people's advocate / Charles Garry and Art Goldberg ; foreword by Jessica Mitford. 1st ed. New York : Dutton, c1977. xi, 268 p. ; 25 cm. [KF373.G33A35] 77-2319 ISBN 0-525-21110-1 : 10.95
1. Garry, Charles R., 1909- 2. Lawyers—United States—Biography. I. Goldberg, Art, joint author. II. Title.

GARRY, Charles R., 1909- 345'.73'00924 B
Streetfighter in the courtroom : the people's advocate / Charles Garry and Art Goldberg ; foreword by Jessica Mitford. 1st ed. New York : Dutton, c1977. xi, 68 p. ; 25 cm. [KF373.G33A35] 77-2319 ISBN 0-525-21110-1 : 10.95
1. Garry, Charles R., 1909- 2. Lawyers—United States—Biography. I. Goldberg, Art, joint author. II. Title.

Garry, Spokane, 1811?-1892.

JESSETT, Thomas Edwin, 1902- 970.2
Chief Spokan Garry, 1811-1892, Christian, statesman, and friend of the white man. Minneapolis, T. S. Denison [1960] 232 p. illus. 22 cm. Includes bibliography. [E99.S68G3] 60-12059
1. Garry, Spokane, 1811?-1892. 2. Spokan Indians. I. Title.

*Garst, Shannon

*GARST, Shannon 92
The picture story and biography of Daniel Boone. Illus. Bill Barss. Chicago, Follett [c.1965] 140p. illus. col. illus. 22cm. (Lib, of Amer. heroes) 65-14467 1.95 bds.,
I. Title.

*GARST, Shannon 92
The picture story and biography of Red Cloud. Illus. by Art Seiden. Chicago, Follet [c.1965] 141p. col. illus. 22cm. Lib. of Amer. heroes) 65-14467 1.95 bds.,
I. Title.

Garvey, Marcus, 1887-1940.

CRONON, Edmund David. 920.932526
Black Moses; the story of Marcus Garvey and the Universal Negro Improvement Association. Madison, University of Wisconsin Press, 1955. 278 p. illus. 23 cm. [E185.97.G3C7] 54-6931
1. Garvey, Marcus, 1887-1940. 2. Universal Negro Improvement Association. I. Title. BIP

CRONON, Edmund David, comp. 320.5'4'0924 B
Marcus Garvey, edited by E. David Cronon. Englewood Cliffs, N.J., Prentice-Hall [1973] x, 176 p. 21 cm. (Great lives observed) (A Spectrum book) Bibliography: p. 170-172. [E185.97.G3C72 1973] 73-9796 ISBN 0-13-556068-3 6.95
1. Garvey, Marcus, 1887-1940.
Pbk. 2.45; ISBN 0-13-556050-0. BIP

FAX, Elton C. 301.45'19'6024 B
Garvey: the story of a pioneer Black nationalist [by] Elton C. Fax. Foreword by John Henrik Clarke. New York, Dodd, Mead [1972] xxii, 305 p. illus. 22 cm. Bibliography: p. 291-296. [E185.97.G3F3] 77-38520 ISBN 0-396-06521-X 7.95
1. Garvey, Marcus, 1887-1940.

GARVEY, Amy Jacques. 301.45'19'60924 B
Garvey and Garveyism / Amy Jacques Garvey ; introd. by John Henrik Clarke. New York : Octagon Books, 1978, c1968. xv, 336 p. ; 22 cm. Reprint of the 1970 ed. published by Collier Books, New York. Includes index. [E185.97.G3G3 1978] 77-26846 ISBN 0-374-93015-5 lib.bdg. : 14.50
1. Garvey, Marcus, 1887-1940. 2. Afro-Americans—Biography. 3. Black nationalism—United States—History. 4. Intellectuals—United States—Biography. I. Title. BIP

VINCENT, Theodore G. 322'.43
Black power and the Garvey movement, by Theodore G. Vincent. [Berkeley, Calif.] Ramparts Press [1971] 299 p. illus., ports. 22 cm. Includes bibliographical references. [E185.97.G3V5] 75-158626 ISBN 0-87867-007-6 5.95
1. Garvey, Marcus, 1887-1940. 2. Universal Negro Improvement Association. I. Title. BIP

Garvey, Marcus, 1887-1940—Juvenile literature.

DAVIS, Daniel S. 320.5'4 B
Marcus Garvey, by Daniel S. Davis. Illustrated with photos. New York, F. Watts, 1972. 179 p. illus. 23 cm. Bibliography: p. 169-170. A biography of the controversial Negro leader who advocated black nationalism in the early twentieth century. [E185.97.G3D3] 92 72-3992 ISBN 0-531-02577-2
1. Garvey, Marcus, 1887-1940—Juvenile literature. BIP

STERLING, Philip. 301.45'19'6070922 B
The question of color; Marcus Garvey, Malcolm X. New York, Scholastic Book Services [1973] 128 p. illus. 21 cm. (Firebird books) [E185.97.G3S83] 73-76239 3.95
1. Garvey, Marcus, 1887-1940—Juvenile literature. 2. Little, Malcolm, 1925-1965—Juvenile literature. I. Title.
Pbk. 1.65.

Garvey, Steve, 1948- —Juvenile literature.

COHEN, Joel H. 796.357'092'4 B
Steve Garvey : storybook star / by Joel H. Cohen. New York : Putnam, c1977. 158 p. : ill. ; 21 cm. (Putnam sports shelf) Includes index. A biography of the popular first baseman for the Los Angeles Dodgers. [GV865.G34C64 1977] 92 77-2648 ISBN 0-399-61099-5 lib. bdg. : 5.29
1. Garvey, Steve, 1948- —Juvenile literature. 2. Baseball players—United States—Biography—Juvenile literature. I. Title. BIP

VASS, George. 796.357'092'4 B
Steve Garvey, the bat boy who became a star / by George Vass. Chicago : Childrens Press, 1979. p. cm. (Sportstars) A brief biography of the star batter for the Los Angeles Dodgers. [GV865.G34V37] 92 78-11041 ISBN 0-516-04304-8 lib.bdg. : 6.00
1. Garvey, Steve, 1948- —Juvenile literature. 2. Los Angeles. Baseball club (National League)—Juvenile literature. 3. Baseball players—United States—Biography—Juvenile literature. I. Title. II. Series.

Gary, Elbert Henry, 1846-1927.

TARBELL, Ida Minerva, 1857-1944. 338.7'67'20924
The life of Elbert H. Gary; a story of steel. New York, Greenwood Press [1969,

c1925] xii, 361 p. illus., facsims., ports 23 cm. [HD9520.G3T3 1969] 69-14106
1. Gary, Elbert Henry, 1846-1927. 2. United States Steel Corporation. I. Title. BIP

Gascoigne, George, 1542?-1577.

PROUTY, Charles Tyler. 828.309
George Gascoigne, Elizabethan courtier, soldier, and poet, by C. T. Prouty. New York, B. Blom [1966, c1942] xii, 351 p. facsim., geneal. tables. 23 cm. Bibliography: p. [329]-333. [PR2278.P7 1966] 65-19620
1. Gascoigne, George, 1542?-1577.

SCHELLING, Felix 828'.3'09
Emmanuel, 1858-1945.
The life and writings of George Gascoigne; with three poems heretofore not reprinted. New York, Russell & Russell [1967] 131 p. 23 cm. Reprint of the 1893 ed. Bibliography: p. 117-123. [PR2278.S4 1967] 67-27852
1. Gascoigne, George, 1542?-1577.

Gaskell, Elizabeth Cleghorn Stevenson, 1810-1865—Biography.

GASKELL, Elizabeth 828'.8'08
Cleghorn (Stevenson) 1810-1865.
The letters of Mrs. Gaskell, edited by J. A. V. Chapple and Arthur Pollard. Cambridge, Harvard University Press, 1967 [c1966] xxix, 1010 p. 23 cm. [PR4711.A4 1967] 67-3154
I. Chapple, J. A. V., ed. II. Pollard, Arthur, ed. III. Title. BIP

GASKELL, Elizabeth 823'.8 B
Cleghorn (Stevenson) 1810-1865.
Letters of Mrs Gaskell and Charles Eliot Norton, 1855-1965. Edited with an introd. by Jane Whitehill. [Folcroft, Pa.] Folcroft Library Editions, 1973. xxxi, 131 p. facsims. 24 cm. Reprint of the 1932 ed. published by Oxford University Press, London. [PR4711.A5 1973] 73 14667 ISBN 0-8414-9450-9 (lib. bdg.)
1. Gaskell, Elizabeth Cleghorn (Stevenson) 1810-1865. 2. Norton, Charles Eliot, 1827-1908. I. Norton, Charles Eliot, 1827-1908.

GASKELL, Elizabeth 823'.8 B
Cleghorn (Stevenson) 1810-1865.
Letters to Mrs. Gaskell and Charles Eliot Norton, 1855-1965. Edited with an introd. by Jane Whitehill. [Folcroft, Pa.] Folcroft Library Editions, 1973. p. Reprint of the 1932 ed. published by Oxford University Press, London. [PR4711.A5 1973] 73-14667 20.00
1. Gaskell, Elizabeth Cleghorn (Stevenson) 1810-1865. 2. Norton, Charles Eliot, 1827-1908. I. Norton, Charles Eliot, 1827-1908. BIP

GERIN, Winifred. 823'.8 B
Elizabeth Gaskell : a biography / Winifred Gerin. Oxford : Clarendon Press, 1976. xiv, 318 p., [9] leaves of plates : ill. ; 22 cm. Includes index. Bibliography: p. [309]-311. [PR4711.G4] 76-375703 ISBN 0-19-812070-2 : 12.50
1. Gaskell, Elizabeth Cleghorn Stevenson, 1810-1865—Biography. 2. Novelists, English—19th century—Biography. Distributed by Oxford University Press N.Y. N.Y. BIP

HALDANE, Elizabeth 823'.8 B
Sanderson, 1862-1937.
Mrs. Gaskell and her friends. Freeport, N.Y., Books for Libraries Press [1970] vii, 318 p. ports. 23 cm. Reprint of the 1931 ed. [PR4711.H3 1970] 73-140356 ISBN 0-8369-5599-4
1. Gaskell, Elizabeth Cleghorn (Stevenson) 1810-1865. I. Title. BIP

HOPKINS, Annette Brown, 823'.8 B
1879-
Elizabeth Gaskell, her life and work [by] A. B. Hopkins. New York, Octagon Books, 1971. 383 p. illus., ports. 24 cm. Reprint of the 1952 ed., with an added leaf, 340A: "Bibliographical items of significance that have appeared since 1952." Bibliography: p. 333-340A. [PR4711.H6 1971] 71-120631
1. Gaskell, Elizabeth Cleghorn (Stevenson) 1810-1865. I. Title.

PAYNE, George Andrew. 823'.8 B
Mrs. Gaskell : a brief biography / by George A. Payne. Folcroft, Pa. : Folcroft Library Editions, 1976. 94 p. [4] leaves of plates : ports. ; 23 cm. Reprint of the 1929 ed. published by Sherratt & Hughes, Manchester, Eng. Includes bibliographical references and index. [PR4711.P3 1976] 76-9117 ISBN 0-8414-6749-8 lib. bdg. : 12.50
1. Gaskell, Elizabeth Cleghorn Stevenson, 1810-1865—Biography. I. Title. BIP

POLLARD, Arthur 823.8
Mrs. Gaskell: novelist and biographer. Cambridge, Mass., Harvard, 1966 [c.1965] xii, 268p. front., 3 plates (ports.) 21cm. [PR4711.P6] 66-2594 5.50
1. Gaskell, Elizabeth Cleghorn (Stevenson) 1810-1865. I. Title. BIP

POLLARD, Arthur. 823.8
Mrs. Gaskell, novelist and biographer. Cambridge, Mass., Harvard University Press, 1966[c1965] xii, 268 p. ports. 21 cm. Bibliographical footnotes. [PR4711] 66-6073
1. Gaskell, Elizabeth Cleghorn (Stevenson) 1810-1865. I. Title.

RUBENIUS, Aina. 823'.8
The woman question in Mrs. Gaskell's life and works. New York, Russell & Russell [1973] viii, 396 p. 23 cm. (Essays and studies on English language and literature, no. 5) Reprint of the 1950 ed. published by Harvard University Press, Cambridge. Bibliography: p. [373]-386. [PR4711.R8 1973] 72-90568 ISBN 0-8462-1717-1 20.00
1. Gaskell, Elizabeth Cleghorn (Stevenson) 1810-1865. 2. Women in literature. 3. Women in England. 4. Woman—Rights of women. I. Title. II. Series: Uppsala. Universitet. Engelska seminariet. Essays and studies on English language and literature, no. 5. BIP

SANDERS, Gerald DeWitt. 823'.8 B
Elizabeth Gaskell. With a bibliography by Clark S. Northup. New York, Russell & Russell [1971] xvii, 267 p. 22 cm. (Cornell studies in English, no. 14) Reprint of the 1929 ed. Bibliography: p. [163]-262. [PR4711.S3 1971] 71-139938
1. Gaskell, Elizabeth Cleghorn (Stevenson) 1810-1865. 2. Gaskell, Elizabeth Cleghorn (Stevenson) 1810-1865—Bibliography. I. Series: Cornell University. Cornell studies in English, no. 14

SANDERS, Gerald DeWitt. 823'.8 B
Elizabeth Gaskell. With a bibliography by Clark S. Northup. New Haven, Published for Cornell University [by] Yale University Press, 1929. St. Clair Shores, Mich., Scholarly Press, 1971. xvii, 267 p. 22 cm. Bibliography: p. 167-262. [PR4711.S3 1971b] 74-131824 ISBN 0-403-00711-9
1. Gaskell, Elizabeth Cleghorn (Stevenson) 1810-1865. 2. Gaskell, Elizabeth Cleghorn (Stevenson) 1810-1865—Bibliography. I. Northup, Clark Sutherland, 1872-1952. BIP

WHITFIELD, Archie Stanton, 823'.8
1899-
Mrs. Gaskell, her life and work, by A. Stanton Whitfield [Folcroft, Pa.] Folcroft Library Editions, 1973. p. Reprint of the 1929 ed. published by G. Routledge, London. Bibliography: p. [PR4711.W5 1973] 73-14820 27.50
1. Gaskell, Elizabeth Cleghorn (Stevenson) 1810-1865. I. Title.

WHITFIELD, Archie Stanton, 823'.8
1899-
Mrs. Gaskell, her life and work, by A. Stanton Whitfield. [Folcroft, Pa.] Folcroft Library Editions, 1973. vii, 258 p. port. 23 cm. Reprint of the 1929 ed. published by G. Routledge, London. Bibliography: p. 221-253. [PR4711.W5 1973] 73-14820 ISBN 0-8414-9462-2 (lib. bdg.)
1. Gaskell, Elizabeth Cleghorn (Stevenson) 1810-1865. I. Title.

Gaspard, Leon, 1882-1964.

WATERS, Frank, 1902- 927.5
Leon Gaspard. Flagstaff, Ariz., Northland Press, 1964. 114 p. illus. (part col.) port. 32 cm. [ND237.G285W3] 64-20419
1. Gaspard, Leon, 1882-1964. I. Title.

WATERS, Frank, 1902- 927.5
Leon Gaspard. Flagstaff, Ariz., Northland Pr. [c.] 1964. 114p. illus. (pt. col.) port. 32cm. [ND237.G285W3] 64-20419 14.50
1. Gaspard, Leon, 1882-1964. I. Title.

Gasquet, Francis Aldan, Cardinal, 1846-1929.

LESLIE, Shane, Sir 1885- 922.242
Cardinal Gasquet, a memoir. New York, P. J. Kenedy [1953] 273p. illus. 22cm. [BX4705.G258L4] 53-11512
1. Gasquet, Francis Aldan, Cardinal, 1846-1929. I. Title.

Gastiglione, Baldassare, conte, 1478-1529.

ROEDER, Ralph, 1890- 945'.05'0922
1970.
The man of the Renaissance : four lawgivers, Savonarola, Machiavelli, Castiglione, Aretino / by Ralph Roeder. Clifton, N.J. : A. M. Kelley, 1975, c1933. p. cm. (Viking reprint editions) Reprint of the ed. published by Viking Press, New York. Bibliography: p. [DG533.R6 1975] 78-122059 ISBN 0-678-03171-1
1. Savonarolda, Girolamo Maria Francesco Matteo, 1452-1498. 2. Machiavelli, Niccolo, 1469-1527. 3. Gastiglione, Baldassare, conte, 1478-1529. 4. Aretino, Pietro, 1492-1556. 5. Renaissance—Italy. I. Title. BIP

Gaston, Arthur George,

GASTON, Arthur 338'.04'0924 B
George, 1892-
Green power, the successful way of A. G. Gaston. [Birmingham, Ala., Southern University Press, c1968] 175 p. illus. 23 cm. [F334.B6G37] 68-54896
I. Title.

Gaston, William, 1778-1844 — Juvenile literature

BETZ, Eva (Kelly) 1897- 92
William Gaston, fighter for justice, by Eva K. Betz. Illustrated by Salem Tamer. New York, P. J. Kenedy [1964] 190 p. illus. 22 cm. (American background books, 27) [F340.G2B4] 64-21180
1. Gaston, William, 1778-1844 — Juvenile literature I. Title. II. Series.

Gates, Adelia.

ORPEN, Adela 910'.92'4 B
Elizabeth Richards.
The chronicles of the Sid; or, The life and travels of Adelia Gates, by Adela E. Orpen. Freeport, N.Y., Books for Libraries Press, 1972. 413 p. illus. 22 cm. (The Black heritage library collection) Reprint of the 1897 ed. [G463.O74 1972] 72-5585 ISBN 0-8369-9145-1
1. Gates, Adelia. 2. Voyages and travels. I. Title. II. Series.

Gates, Arthur Irving, 1890-1972.

THORNDIKE, Robert 378.1'2'0924 B
Ladd, 1910-
Arthur I. Gates (1890-1972) : a biographical memoir / by Robert L. Thorndike. [Washington] : National Academy of Education, c1973. 10 p. : port. ; 22 cm. Bibliography: p. 8-10. [LA2317.G28T46] 75-325493
1. Gates, Arthur Irving, 1890-1972.

Gates, Frederick Taylor, 1853-1929.

GATES, Frederick 361.7'6'0924 B
Taylor, 1853-1929.
Chapters in my life / Frederick Taylor Gates ; with the Frederick Taylor Gates lectures by Robert Swain Morison. New York : Free Press, c1977. xi, 305 p., [4] leaves of plates : ill. ; 24 cm. Includes index. [HV28.G3A33 1977] 76-47956 ISBN 0-02-911350-4 : 10.95
1. Gates, Frederick Taylor, 1853-1929. 2. Rockefeller Foundation. 3. Philanthropists—United States—Biography. I. Morison, Robert S., 1906- Frederick Taylor Gates lectures. 1977. II. Title.

GATES, Frederick 361.7'6'0924 B
Taylor, 1853-1929.
Chapters in my life / Frederick Taylor Gates ; with the Frederick Taylor Gates lectures by Robert Swain Morison. New York : Free Press, c1977. xi, 305 p., [4] leaves of plates : ill. ; 24 cm. Includes index. [HV28.G3A33 1977] 76-47956 ISBN 0-02-911350-4 : 10.95
1. Gates, Frederick Taylor, 1853-1929. 2. Rockefeller Foundation. 3. Philanthropists—United States Biography. I. Morison, Robert S., 1906- Frederick Taylor Gates lectures. 1977. II. Title. BIP

Gates, Horatio, 1728-1806.

NELSON, Paul 973.3'3'0924 B
David, 1941-
General Horatio Gates : a biography / Paul David Nelson. Baton Rouge : Louisiana State University Press, c1976. xiii, 319 p. : ill. ; 24 cm. Includes index. Bibliography: p. 299-312. [E207.G3N44] 74-27191 ISBN 0-8071-0159-1 : 17.50
1. Gates, Horatio, 1728-1806. I. Title.

Gates, Horatio, 1728-1806—Juvenile literature.

MCKOWN, Robin. 973.33'0922 B
Horatio Gates & Benedict Arnold, American military commanders. Illustrated with old prints. New York, McGraw-Hill [1969] 160 p. illus., plans, ports. 24 cm. (Saratoga cluster) Bibliography: p. 157. Biographies of two American military commanders of the Revolutionary War. [E207.G3M3] 920 79-88328
1. Gates, Horatio, 1728-1806 —Juvenile literature. 2. Arnold, Benedict, 1741-1801—Juvenile literature. 3. Saratoga Campaign, 1777—Juvenile literature. I. Title.

Gatti-Casazza, Giulio, 1869-1940.

GATTI-CASAZZA, 782.1'092'4 B
Giulio, 1869-1940.
Memories of the opera. New York, Vienna House, 1973. xxvi, 326 p. illus. 22 cm. Reprint of the 1941 ed. published by Scribner, New York; with new introd. [ML429.G17A3 1973] 71-183334 ISBN 0-8443-0022-5 12.50
1. Gatti-Casazza, Giulio, 1869-1940. 2. Musicians—Correspondence, reminiscences, etc. 3. Opera—New York (City) I. Title. BIP

Gaudi y Cornet, Antonio, 1852-1926.

DESCHARNES, Robert. 720'.924 B
Gaudi; the visionary [by] Robert Descharnes. [Photos. by] Clovis Prevost. Pref. by Salvador Dali. Translation from the French by Frederick Hill. Followed by "Gaudi's artistic and religious vision" by Francesc Pujols. Introd. by Joan Alavedra. Translation from the Catalan by Judith C. Rohrer. Editor: George R. Collins. New York, Viking Press [1971] 247 p. illus. (part col.), ports. 31 cm. (A Studio book) Translation of La vision artistique et religieuse de Gaudi and La visio artistica i religiosa d'en Gaudi. "Selected bibliography, by George R. Collins": p. 246-247. [NA1313.G3D413] 71-101778 ISBN 0-670-33586-X
1. Gaudi y Cornet, Antonio, 1852-1926. I. Prevost, Clovis, illus. II. Pujols, Francisco, 1882-1962. La visio artistica i religiosa d'en Gaudi. English. 1971.

MARTINELL y Brunet, 720'.92'4
Cesar, 1888-1973.
Gaudi : his life, his theories, his work / Cesar Martinell ; translated from the Spanish by Judith Rohrer ; edited by George R. Collins. Cambridge, Mass. : MIT Press, [1975] p. cm. Translation of Gaudi: su vida, su teoria, su obra. Includes indexes. Bibliography: p. [NA1313.G3M2813 1975] 74-109 ISBN 0-262-13087-4 : 45.00
1. Gaudi y Cornet, Antonio, 1852-1926. I. Title.

SWEENEY, James Johnson, 720'.924
1900-
Antoni Gaudi [by] James Johnson Sweeney and Josep Lluis Sert. Rev. ed. New York, Praeger [1970, c1960] 191 p.

illus. (part col.), facsims., plans, ports. 29 cm. Bibliography: p. 187-191. [NA1313.G3S9 1970] 70-125363 18.50
1. Gaudi y Cornet, Antonio, 1852-1926. I. Sert, Jose Luis, 1902- joint author.

Gaudier-Brzeska, Henri, 1891-1915.

EDE, Harold Stanley, 1895- 730'.92'4
Savage messiah, by H. S. Ede. New York, Outerbridge & Lazard; distributed by Dutton [1972, c1971] 160 p. illus. 22 cm. [NB553.G35E4 1972] 72-84263 ISBN 0-87690-081-3 6.95
1. Gaudier-Brzeska, Henri, 1891-1915. 2. Brzeska, Sophie Suzanne. I. Title. **BIP**

GAUDIER-BRZESKA, Henri, 1891-1915. 730'.92'4 B
Burning to speak : the life and art of Henri Gaudier Brzeska / [text by] Roger Cole. Oxford : Phaidon ; New York : E. P. Dutton, 1978. 141 p. : chiefly ill., facsims., ports. ; 29 cm. Includes index. Bibliography: p. 137. [NB553.G35A4 1978] 78-55006 ISBN 0-7148-1805-4 : 30.00
1. Gaudier-Brzeska, Henri, 1891-1915. 2. Sculptors—France—Biography. I. Cole, Roger. II. Title. **BIP**

HARRIS, Frank, 1855-1931. 920.042
Contemporary portraits (third series). New York, Greenwood Press [1969] viii, 233 p. illus., ports. 23 cm. Reprint of the 1920 ed. Contents.Contents.—H. G. Wells.—Upton Sinclair.—John Galsworthy.—Cunninghame Graham.—Gilbert K. Chesterton.—Arthur Symons.—Winston Churchill.—Russel Wallace.—Thomas Huxley.—Louis Wilkinson.—W. L. George.—Gaudier-Brzeska.—Earl St. Aldwyn.—Augustus John.—Coventry Patmore.—Walt Whitman. [PN761.H23 1969] 79-95103 ISBN 8-371-25774-
1. Gaudier-Brzeska, Henri, 1891-1915. 2. St. Aldwyn, Michael Edwayd Hicks-Beach, 1st earl, 1837-1916. 3. John, Augustus Edwin, 1878- 4. Authors, English. 5. Authors, American. I. Title.

POUND, Ezra Loomis, 1885- 730'.924
Gaudier-Brzeska, a memoir [by] Ezra Pound. [New York, New Directions Pub. Corp., 1970] 147 p. illus., ports. 21 cm. (A New Directions book) Includes bibliographical references. [NB553.G35P6 1970] 78-107490 7.50
1. Gaudier-Brzeska, Henri, 1891-1915. **BIP**

POUND, Ezra Loomis, 1885- 730.944
Gaudier-Brzeska, a memoir. [New York] New Directions [1961] 147p. illus. 60-9893 8.25
1. Gaudier-Brzeska, Henri, 1891-1915. I. Title.

Gauguin, Paul, 1848-1903.

ANDERSEN, Wayne V. 759.4 B
Gauguin's paradise lost [by] Wayne Andersen. With the assistance of Barbara Klein. New York, Viking Press [1971] xii, 371 p. illus. 25 cm. Bibliography: p. 355-362. [ND553.G27A74 1971] 72-135347 ISBN 0-670-33593-2 12.50
1. Gauguin, Paul, 1848-1903. I. Klein, Barbara. II. Title.

GAUGUIN, Paul, 1848-1903. v. 12
Gauguin, [by] Ronald Alley. New York, Marboro Books [c1961] 95 p. (p. [45]-[92] col. plates) illus. 28 cm. 63-70445
1. Gauguin, Paul, 1848-1903. I. Allen, Ronald. II. Title. **BIP**

GAUGUIN, Paul, 1848-1903. 759.4 B
Noa Noa / by Paul Gauguin ; translated from the French by O. F. Theis. Danbury, CT : Archer Editions Press, 1976, c1919. p. cm. Reprint of the ed. published by N. L. Brown, New York. [ND553.G27A25 1976] 76-16128 ISBN 0-89097-006-8 : 15.00
1. Gauguin, Paul, 1848-1903. 2. Tahiti. 3. Painters—France—Correspondence, reminiscences, etc. I. Title. **BIP**

GAUGUIN, Paul, 1848-1903. 759.4 B
The writings of a savage / Paul Gauguin ; edited by Daniel Guerin ; with an introduction by Wayne Andersen ; translated by Eleanor Levieux. New York : Viking Press, [1977] p. cm. Includes index. [ND553.G27A4813] 76-53574 ISBN 0-670-53309-2 : 15.00
1. Gauguin, Paul, 1848-1906. 2. Painters—France—Biography. I. Title. **BIP**

HANSON, Lawrence. 759.4
Noble savage; the life of Paul Gauguin, by Lawrence and Elisabeth Hanson. New York, Random House [1955, c1954] 299p. illus. 24cm. [ND553.G27H33 1955] 927.5 55-5792
1. Gauguin, Paul, 1848-1903. I. Hanson, Elisabeth M., joint author. II. Title.

HANSON, Lawrence 927.5
The seekers: Gauguin, Van Gogh, Cezanne [by] Lawrence, Elisabeth Hanson. New York, Random [c.1963] xv, 334p. illus., ports. 25cm. Bibl. 63-11619 6.95
1. Gauguin, Paul, 1848-1903. 2. Gogh, Vincent van, 1853-1890. 3. Cezanne, Paul, 1839-1906. 4. Post-impressionism (Art) I. Hanson, Elizabeth M., joint author. II. Title.

MARCHIORI, Giuseppe. 759.4
Gauguin. [1st American ed. Translated from the Italian by Caroline Beamish] New York, Grosset & Dunlap [1967] 39, [80] p. col. illus. 18 cm. (The New Grosset art library, 11) On cover: Gauguin; the life and work of the artist. [ND553.G27M323 1967] 68-12745
1. Gauguin, Paul, 1848-1903.

PERRUCHOT, Henri, 1917- 927.5
Gauguin. Translated by Humphrey Hare. Edited by Jean Ellsmoor. [1st ed.] Cleveland, World Pub. Co. [1964, c1963] 398 p. illus., ports., facsim. 23 cm. (His Art and destiny, v. 4) Translation of La vie de Gaugin. Bibliography: p. 371-389. [ND553.G27P433] 64-12463
1. Gauguin, Paul, 1848-1903.

Gauguin, Paul, 1848-1903—Juvenile literature.

PETER, Adeline. 759.4 B
Paul Gauguin, by Adeline Peter and Ernest Raboff. Edited by Bradley Smith. Garden City, N.Y., Doubleday [1974] [31] p. illus. (part col.) 29 cm. (Art for children) (A Gemini-Smith book) A brief biography of this nineteenth-century French artist accompanies reproductions and analyses of several of his works. [ND553.G27P45] 73-75360 ISBN 0-385-05012-7 4.95
1. Gauguin, Paul, 1848-1903—Juvenile literature. I. Raboff, Ernest Lloyd, joint author. II. Title.
Library binding; 5.70, ISBN 0-385-06994-4

Gaulle, Charles de, Pres. France, 1890-

CLARK, Stanley Frederick. 923.144
The man who is France; the story of General Charles de Gaulle. Rev. ed. New York, Dodd, Mead, 1963. 262 p. 21 cm. [DC373.G3C55] 63-1061
1. Gaulle, Charles de, Pres. France, 1890- I. Title.

HARRITY, Richard 923.144
Man of destiny: De Gaulle of France [by] Richard Harrity, Ralph G. Martin. New York, Duell [c.1961] unpaged. illus. 26cm. 61-16833 6.95
1. Gaulle, Charles de, Pres. France, 1890—-Portraits, caricatures, etc. I. Martin, Ralph G. 1920- joint author. II. Title.

MAN of destiny: 944.083'092'4
De Gaulle of France [by] Richard Harrity and Ralph G. Martin. [1st ed.] New York, Duell, Sloan and Pearce [1961] unpaged. illus. 26cm. 3G315 [DC373.]
1. Gaulle, Charles de, Pres France, 1890-—Portraits, caricatures, etc. I. Harrity, Richard. II. Martin, Ralph G., 1920- joint author.

Gaulle, Charles de, Pres. France, 1890-1970.

ARON, Robert, 1898- 944.080924
An explanation of De Gaulle. Translated from the French by Marianne Sinclair. [1st ed.] New York, Harper & Row [1966] xiv, 210 p. 22 cm. [DC373.G3A713] 65-14647
1. Gaulle, Charles de, Pres. France, 1890-1970. I. Title.

BRICHANT, Colette Dubois, 1926- 944.08'0924 B
Charles de Gaulle artiste de l'action. New York, McGraw-Hill [1969] 284 p. illus., maps, ports. 23 cm. Bibliography: p. 271-275. [DC373.G3B67] 68-25647
1. Gaulle, Charles de, Pres. France, 1890-

CLARK, Stanley Frederick 923.144
The man who is France; the story of General Charles de Gaulle. Rev. ed. New York [Apollo, 1964, c.1960] 1963. 262p. 20cm. (A-83) 1.95 pap.,
1. Gaulle, Charles de, 1890- I. Title.

CLARK, Stanley Frederick. 923.144
The man who is France; the story of General Charles de Gaulle. New York, Dodd, Mead, 1960. 240 p. 21 cm. [DC373.G3C55] 60-9656
1. Gaulle, Charles de, Pres. France, 1890-1970. I. Title.

CRAWLEY, Aidan. 944.08'0924 B
De Gaulle; a biography. Indianapolis, Bobbs-Merrill Co. [1969] 510 p. illus., ports. 24 cm. Bibliography: p. 487-493. "Works of General de Gaulle": p. 495-496. [DC373.G3C7 1969b] 75-81996 10.00
1. Gaulle, Charles de, Pres. France, 1890-1970.

CROZIER, Brian. 944.083'092'4 B
De Gaulle. New York, Scribner [1973] ix, 726 p. 25 cm. Includes bibliographical references. [DC373.G3C762] 72-1190 ISBN 0-684-12996-5 12.50
1. Gaulle, Charles de, Pres. France, 1890-1970.

EUNSON, Roby. 944.083'092'4 B
When France was de Gaulle. New York, Watts [1971] 184 p. illus. 25 cm. Bibliography: p. 175. A biography of the controversial Frenchman who was a prominent figure in the history and government of his country for thirty years. [DC373.G3E85] 71-161838 ISBN 0-531-02005-3 5.95
1. Gaulle, Charles de, Pres. France, 1890-1970. 2. France—Politics and government—1945- I. Title. **BIP**

GAULLE, Charles de, Pres. France, 1890- v. 12
De Gaulle: implacable ally [edited by] Roy C. Macridis. With a special introd. by Maurice Duverger. New York, Harper & Row [1966] xxxv. 248 p. 21 cm.
1. France — Pol. & govt. — 20th cent. 2. France — For. rel. — 1945- I. Macridis, Roy C., ed. II. Title.

GRINNELL-MILNE, Duncan William. 923.144
The triumph of integrity; a portrait of Charles de Gaulle. New York, Macmillan, 1962. 334 p. illus. 22 cm. Includes bibliography. [DC373.G3G67 1962] 62-9294
1. Gaulle, Charles de, Pres. France, 1890-1970. 2. France—Politics and government—1940-1945. I. Title.

HATCH, Alden, 1898- 923.144
The De Gaulle nobody knows; an intimate biography of Charles de Gaulle. [1st ed.] New York, Hawthorn Books [1960] 277p. illus. 24cm. [DC373.G3H32] 60-10342
1. Gaulle, Charles de, Pres. France, 1890- I. Title.

HILTERMANN, G. B J 944.083'092'4
Charles de Gaulle en de Fransen. [Door] G.B.J. Hiltermann. Baarn [In den Toren, 1968] 168 p. 20 1/2 cm. (Torenboeken) fl 8.90 Bibliography: p. 165-166. [DC373.G3H5] 68-77886
1. Gaulle, Charles de, Pres. France, 1890- I. Title.

LACOUTURE, Jean. 944.080924 B
De Gaulle. Translated by Francis K. Price. [New York] New American Library [1966] 215 p. 22 cm. [DC373.G3L2513] 66-24425
1. Gaulle, Charles de, Pres. France, 1890-

LAUNAY, Jacques de. 944.08'0924
De Gaulle and his France; a psychopolitical and historical portrait. Translated by Dorothy Albertyn. New York, Julian Press [1968] x, 316 p. ports. 24 cm. Bibliography: p. [293]-296. [DC373.G3L353] 68-19017 7.50
1. Gaulle, Charles de, Pres. France, 1890- I. Title.

MAURIAC, Claude, 1910- 944.082'092'4 B
The other de Gaulle; diaries 1944-1954. Translated by Moura Budberg and Gordon Latta. New York, John Day Co. [1973] 378 p. illus. 23 cm. Translation of Un autre de Gaulle. [DC373.G3M36713] 73-7413 ISBN 0-381-98253-X 12.95
1. Gaulle, Charles de, Pres. France, 1890-1970. 2. Mauriac, Claude, 1910- 3. France—Politics and government—1945- I. Title.

MAURIAC, Francois, 1885 944.080924
De Gaulle. Tr. from French by Richard Howard. [1st ed. in the U.S.A.] Garden City, N.Y., Doubleday, 1966 [c.1955-1960] 229p. 22cm. [DC373.G3M373] 65-13978 4.50
1. Gaulle, Charles de, Pres. France, 1890- I. Title.

MONTICONE, Ronald C. 944.083'092'4 B
Charles de Gaulle, Ronald C. Monticone Boston, Twayne Publishers [1975] 176 p. port. 22 cm. (Twayne's world leaders series) Includes bibliographical references. [DC373.G3M63] 74-16412 ISBN 0-8057-3663-8 7.50
1. Gaulle, Charles de, Pres. France, 1890-1970. 2. France—Foreign relations—1945- **BIP**

SCHOENBRUN, David. 944.080924 B
The three lives of Charles de Gaulle. [1st ed.] New York, Atheneum, 1966. 373 p. 25 cm. Bibliographical footnotes. [DC373.G3S36] 65-15921
1. Gaulle, Charles de, Pres. France, 1890- I. Title.

WERTH, Alexander, 1901- 944.080924
De Gaulle; a political biography. New York, Simon and Schuster [1966] 416 p. 23 cm. "Bibliographical note": p; 408-411. [DC373.G3W4] 66-21828
1. Gaulle, Charles de, Pres. France, 1890- 2. France—Politics and government—20th century.

WERTH, Alexander, 1901- 944.08'0924
De Gaulle; a political biography. [New ed.] Baltimore, Penguin Books [1967] 437 p. port. 18 cm. (Political leaders of the twentieth century) (Pelican book, A793.) Bibliography: p. [425]-428. [DC373.G3W4 1967] 68-337
1. Gaulle, Charles de, Pres. France, 1890- 2. France—Politics and government—20th century. I. Title.

Gaulle, Charles de, Pres. France, 1890-1970—Assassination attempts.

DEMARET, Pierre, fl.1972- 944.083'092'4 B
Target de Gaulle : the true story of the 31 attempts on the life of the French president / Pierre Demaret and Christian Plume ; translated from the French by Richard Barry. New York : Dial Press, 1975, c1974. 293 p. ; 24 cm. Translation of Objectif de Gaulle. [DC373.G3D4513 1975] 74-20658 ISBN 0-8037-8514-3 : 10.00
1. Gaulle, Charles de, Pres. France, 1890-1970—Assassination attempts. I. Plume, Christian, fl. 1973- joint author. II. Title.

DEMARET, Pierre, fl.1972- 944.083'092'4 B
Target de Gaulle : the thirty-one attempts to assassinate the General / [by] Christian Plume and Pierre Demaret ; translated from the French by Richard Barry. London : Corgi, 1976. 410 p., [8] p. of plates : ill., ports ; 18 cm. Translation of Objectif de Gaulle. [DC373.G3D4513 1976] 77-367410 ISBN 0-552-10143-5 : £0.95
1. Gaulle, Charles de, Pres. France, 1890-1970—Assassination attempts. 2. Assassins—France—Biography. I. Plume, Christian, fl. 1973- joint author. II. Title.

Gaulle, Charles de, Pres. France, 1890-1970—Juvenile literature.

APSLER, Alfred. 944.083'092'4 B
"Vive de Gaulle," the story of Charles de Gaulle. New York, J. Messner [1973] 191 p. 21 cm. Bibliography: p. 184-185. A biography of the Frenchman who served his country in the military during World Wars I and II and later as President for ten years. [DC373.G3A65] 92 72-11818 ISBN 0-671-32583-3 4.95
1. Gaulle, Charles de, Pres. France, 1890-1970—Juvenile literature. I. Title.
Library Edition 4.79

EPSTEIN, Samuel, 944.083'092'4 B
1909-
Charles de Gaulle, defender of France, by Sam and Beryl Epstein. Champaign, Ill., Garrard Pub. Co. [1973] 175 p. illus. 22 cm. (A Century book) The life of the French soldier, liberator, and statesman, stressing the events and political maneuverings during his career as President of the Republic. [DC373.G3E67] 92 72-6254 ISBN 0-8116-4756-0 3.68
1. Gaulle, Charles de, Pres. France, 1890-1970—Juvenile literature. I. Epstein, Beryl (Williams) 1910- joint author. II. Title.

LESTER, John. 944.08'0924 B
De Gaulle; king without a crown. [1st ed.] New York, Hawthorn Books [1968] 192 p. ports. 22 cm. A biography of the French leader whose name literally means Charles of France, who led the resistance movement of his country during World War II, and who restored order to France when the war ended. [DC373.G3L44] 92 68-27645 4.95
1. Gaulle, Charles de, Pres. France, 1890-—Juvenile literature. I. Title: King without a crown.

Gauss, Karl Friedrich, 1777-1855.

DUNNINGTON, Guy Waldo, 925.1
1906-
Carl Friedrich Gauss, Titan of science; a study of his life and work. [1st ed.] New York, Exposition Press, 1955. xi, 479p. illus., ports. 21cm. (Exposition--University book) Bibliography: p. [420]-447. Bibliographical footnotes. [QA29.G3D8] 55-10291
1. Gauss, Karl Friedrich, 1777-1855. I. Title.

DUNNINGTON, Guy Waldo, 925.1
1906-
Carl Friedrich Gauss, Titan of science a study of his life and work. New York, Hafner Pub. Co. [1960, c.1955] 479p. illus. 479p. illus. Bibl. 5.00
1. Gauss, Karl Friedrich, 1777-1855. I. Title.

HALL, Tord. 510'.924 B
Carl Friedrich Gauss, a biography. Translated by Albert Froderberg. Cambridge, M.I.T. Press [1970] 175 p. 22 cm. Translation of Gauss, matematikernas konung. Bibliography: p. [171]-[172] [QA29.G3H353] 71-110227 ISBN 2-620-80400-
1. Gauss, Karl Friedrich, 1777-1855.

Gauss, Karl Friedrich, 1777-1855—Juvenile literature.

SCHAAF, William Leonard, 925.1
1897-
Carl Freidrich Gauss, prince of mathematicians. New York, Watts [c.1964] vii, 168p. illus., ports., maps, facsims. 22cm. (Immortals of sci.) Bibl. 64-11913 2.95
1. Gauss, Karl Friedrich, 1777-1855—Juvenile literature. I. Title.

Gautama Buddha.

FOUCHER, Alfred Charles 294.3
Auguste, 1865-1952.
The life of the Buddha, according to the ancient texts and monuments of India. Abridged translation by Simone Brangier Boas. [1st ed.] Middletown, Conn., Wesleyan University Press [1963] xiv, 272 p. illus. 25 cm. Bibliography: p. [269]-272. [BL1470.F623] 63-17795
1. Gautama Buddha. I. Title.

FOUCHER, Alfred 294.3'63 B
Charles Auguste, 1865-1952.
The life of the Buddha, according to the ancient texts and monuments of India. Abridged translation by Simone Brangier Boas. Westport, Conn., Greenwood Press [1972, c1963] xiv, 272 p. 24 cm. Bibliography: p. [269]-272. [BQ884.F6813 1972] 72-6195 ISBN 0-8371-6476-1
1. Gautama Buddha. I. Title.

GAUTAMA; the story of Lord v. 12
Buddha. Illustrated by Nena von Leyden. New York, Macmillan [1956] 118p. illus. 19cm.
1. Buddha and Buddhism. I. Masani, Shakuntala.

†IKEDA, Daisaku. 294.3'63 B
The living Buddha : an interpretive biography / by Daisaku Ikeda ; translated by Burton Watson. 1st English ed. New York : Weatherhill, 1976. x, 148 p., [4] leaves of plates : ill. ; 24 cm. Translation of Watakushi no Shakuson kan. [BQ886.I3813] 75-40446 ISBN 0-8348-0117-5 : 7.95
1. Gautama Buddha. I. Title. **BIP**

KELEN, Betty. 294.3'63 B
Gautama Buddha in life and legend. New York, Lothrop, Lee & Shepard Co. [1967] xiv, 192 p. ports. 22 cm. Bibliography: p. [187]-188. [BL1470.K4] 67-22598
1. Gautama Buddha. I. Title.

KELEN, Betty. 294.3'63'0924 B
Gautama Buddha in life and legend. New York, Lothrop, Lee & Shepard Co. [1967] xiv, 192 p. ports. 22 cm. Bibliography: p. [187]-188. Combines archeological fact and Buddhist theological legend to recount the life of Gautama Buddha, from the traditional story of his birth, through his quest for wisdom, the years as a sage and teacher, and his death. [BL1470.K4] 92 AC 68
1. Gautama Buddha. 2. Buddha and Buddhism. I. Title.

MASANI, Shakuntala. v. 12
Gautama; the story of Lord Buddha. Illustrated by Nena von Leyden. New York, Macmillan [1956] 118p. illus. 19cm.
1. Buddha and Buddhism. I. Title.

†NAKAMURA, Hajime, 294.3'63 B
1912-
Gotama Buddha / by Hajime Nakamura. Los Angeles : Buddhist Books International, c1977. p. cm. Translation of Gotama Budda no shogai, pt. 1 of the author's Gotama Budda. Includes bibliographical references and index. [BQ886.N34213] 77-8589 ISBN 0-914910-05-1 : 8.95
1. Gautama Buddha. 2. Buddhists—India—Biography. **BIP**

PERCHERON, Maurice, 1891- 922.94
The marvelous life of the Buddha. Translated by Adrienne Foulke. New York, St. Martin's Press [1960] 250 p. illus. 24 cm. [BL1470.P413] 60-13878
1. Gautama Buddha. I. Title.

Gautama Buddha—Biography.

MARSHALL, George N. 294.3'6'3
Buddha, the quest for serenity : a biography / George N. Marsahll ; introd. by Houston Smith. Boston : Beacon Press, c1978. xx, 239 p. ; 21 cm. Bibliography: p. 237-239. [BQ882.M37 1978] 78-53787 ISBN 0-8070-1346-3 : 10.95
1. Gautama Buddha—Biography. 2. Buddhists—India—Biography. I. Title.

Gautama Buddha—Biography—Juvenile literature.

RAWDING, F. W. 294.3'63 B
The Buddha / F. W. Rawding. Minneapolis : Lerner Publications Co., 1979, c1975. 51 p. : ill. ; 21 x 23 cm. (A Cambridge topic book) Includes index. Examines the life, teachings, and followers of Gautama Buddha. [BQ892.R38 1979] 92 78-56789 ISBN 0-8225-1212-2 : 4.95
1. Gautama Buddha—Biography—Juvenile literature. 2. Buddhists—India—Biography—Juvenile literature. 3. Buddhism—Juvenile literature. I. Title. **BIP**

Gautama Buddha—Footprints.

BYLES, Marie 294.3'6'3
Beuzeville.
Footprints of Gautama the Buddha; being the story of the Buddha his disciples knew, describing portions of his ministerial life. Wheaton, Ill., Theosophical Pub. House [1967, c1957] 227 p. illus., map. 20 cm. (A Quest book) Includes bibliographical references. [BL1470.B9 1967] 68-5855 1.50
1. Gautama Buddha—Footprints. I. Title.

Gautier, Theophile, 1811-1872.

DU CAMP, Maxime, 848'.7'09 B
1822-1894.
Theophile Gautier. Translated by J. E. Gordon. Pref. by Andrew Lang. Freeport, N.Y., Books for Libraries Press [1971] xviii, 231 p. port. 23 cm. [PQ2258.Z5D83 1971] 76-152980 ISBN 0-8369-5732-6
1. Gautier, Theophile, 1811-1872. **BIP**

DU CAMP, Maxime, 1822- 848'.7'09
1894.
Theophile Gautier. Translated by J. E. Gordon. Pref. by Andrew Lang. Port Washington, N.Y., Kennikat Press [1972] xviii, 231 p. illus. 20 cm. Reprint of the 1893 ed. Includes bibliographical references. [PQ2258.Z5D83 1972] 74-153268 ISBN 0-8046-1564-0
1. Gautier, Theophile, 1811-1872. I. Gordon, J. E., tr.

GRANT, Richard B. 848'.7'09 B
Theophile Gautier / by Richard B. Grant. New York : Twayne Publishers, [1975] 179 p. : port. ; 21 cm. (Twayne's world authors series ; TWAS 362 : France) Includes index. Bibliography: 169-1973. [PQ2258.Z5G7] 75-4819 ISBN 0-8057-6213-2 lib.bdg. : 7.50
1. Gautier, Theophile, 1811-1872.

RICHARDSON, Joanna. 928.4
Theophile Gautier, his life & times. [1st American ed.] New York, Coward-McCann [1959, c1958] 335 p. illus. 22 cm. Includes bibliography. [PQ2258.Z5R49 1959] 59-8739
1. Gautier, Theophile, 1811-1872.

TENNANT, Philip 848'.7'09 B
Ernest.
Theophile Gautier / by P. E. Tennant. London : Athlone Press, 1975. x, 150 p. ; 21 cm. (Athlone French poets) Distributed in the U.S.A. by Humanities Press, Atlantic Highlands, New Jersey. Includes index. Bibliography: p. 143-146. [PQ2258.Z5T4] 75-317249 ISBN 0-485-14604-5 : 13.50 ISBN 0-485-12204-9 pbk. : 5.25
1. Gautier, Theophile, 1811-1872. **BIP**

Gauvreau, Emile Henry, 1891-1956.

GAUVREAU, Emile 070'.92'4 B
Henry, 1891-1956.
My last million readers. New York, Arno Press, 1974 [c1941] 488 p. 23 cm. (Popular culture in America) Reprint of the ed. published by E. P. Dutton, New York. Autobiographical. [PN4874.G33A3 1974] 74-15741 ISBN 0-405-06376-8 27.00
1. Gauvreau, Emile Henry, 1891-1956. 2. Journalists—Correspondence, reminiscences, etc. I. Title. II. Series. **BIP**

Gay, Edward, 1837-1928.

COKER, Richard G. 759.13 B
Portrait of an American painter: Edward Gay, 1837-1928, by Richard G. Coker. [1st ed.] New York, Vantage Press [1973] 115 p. illus. 21 cm. Includes bibliographical references. [ND237.G318C64] 74-157761 ISBN 0-533-00777-1 3.95
1. Gay, Edward, 1837-1928. I. Title.

Gay, Edwin Francis, 1867-1946.

HEATON, Herbert, 330'.072'024 B
1890-
A scholar in action, Edwin F. Gay. New York, Greenwood Press, 1968 [c1952] vi, 260 p. port. 23 cm. [HB119.G38H4 1968] 68-9543
1. Gay, Edwin Francis, 1867-1946. I. Title. **BIP**

Gay, George H., 1917-

GAY, George H., 1917- 940.54'26
Sole survivor : the Battle of Midway and its effect on his life / George Gay. Naples, Fla. : Naples Ad/Graphics Services, c1979. 320 p. : ill. ; 23 cm. [D774.M5G39] 79-121637 14.00
1. Gay, George H., 1917- 2. United States. Navy. Torpedo Squadron 8—Biography. 3. Midway, Battle of, 1942—Personal narratives, American. 4. Seamen—United States—Biography. I. Title.
Publisher's address: 1015 5th Ave. North, Naples, FL.

Gay, John, 1685-1732.

BENJAMIN, Lewis Saul, 821'.5 B
1874-1932.
Life and letters of John Gay (1685-1732), author of "The beggar's opera," by Lewis Melville. Folcroft, Pa., Folcroft Press [1969] xii, 167 p. port. 23 cm. Reprint of the 1921 ed. [PR3474.B4 1969] 72-194432
1. Gay, John, 1685-1732.

Gay-Lussac, Joseph Louis, 1778-1850.

CROSLAND, Maurice P. 540'.92'4 B
Gay-Lussac, scientist and bourgeois / Maurice Crosland. Cambridge ; New York : Cambridge University Press, 1978. p. cm. Includes index. Bibliography: p. [QD22.G35C76] 77-91084 ISBN 0-521-21979-5 : 36.00
1. Gay-Lussac, Joseph Louis, 1778-1850. 2. Chemists—France—Biography. I. Title.

Gayatri Devi, Maharani of Jaipur, 1919-

GAYATRI Devi, 954.03'5'0924
Maharani of Jaipur, 1919-
A princess remembers : the memoirs of the Maharani of Jaipur / by Gayatri Devi of Jaipur and Santha Rama Rau. 1st ed. Philadelphia : Lippincott, c1976. 335 p. : ill. ; 24 cm. Includes index. [DS481.G36A33] 75-33293 ISBN 0-397-01103-2 : 12.50
1. Gayatri Devi, Maharani of Jaipur, 1919- 2. India—Princes and princesses. I. Rama Rau, Santha, 1923- joint author. II. Title.

Gaye, Laura B.

GAYE, Laura B. 917.3
Laugh on Friday, weep on Sunday; one woman's reminiscence [by] Laura B. Gaye. Illustrated by Laine Liska. [Calabasas, Calif., Loma Palaga Press, 1968] 172 p. illus., ports. 22 cm. [CT275.G2995A3] 68-16781
I. Title.

Gayle, Addison, 1932-

GAYLE, Addison, 1932- 813'.5'4 B
Wayward child : a personal odyssey / Addison Gayle, Jr. 1st ed. Garden City, N.Y. : Anchor Press, 1977. 182 p. ; 22 cm. [PS29.G3] 76-42329 ISBN 0-385-08873-6 : 7.95
1. Gayle, Addison, 1932- 2. Critics—United States—Biography. I. Title. **BIP**

Gaylord, Katherine Cole, 1745-1840.

MUZZY, Florence 978.7'01'0924 B
Emlyn (Downs) 1851-1939.
Katherine Gaylord, heroine; first prize biographical sketch, National Society Daughters of the American Revolution. Written and illustrated by Florence E. D. Muzzy (as copied from the hand-written notes of Marjorie Gaylord) Bristol, Conn., Bristol Press Pub. Co., 1898. [Coldwater? Kan., 1971?] 16 p. ports. 29 cm. [E241.W9M9 1971] 72-176713
1. Gaylord, Katherine Cole, 1745-1840. 2. Wyoming Massacre, 1778. I. Title.

Gaynor, William Jay, 1851-1913.

PINK, Louis 974.71'04'0924 B
Heaton, 1882-1955.
Gaynor, the Tammany mayor who swallowed the tiger; lawyer, judge, philosopher. Freeport, N.Y., Books for Libraries Press [1970] 256 p. illus., ports. 23 cm. Reprint of the 1931 ed. [F128.5.G293 1970] 77-124251
1. Gaynor, William Jay, 1851-1913. 2. New York (City)—Politics and government—1898-1951. I. Title.

SMITH, Mortimer Brewster, 923.273
1906-
William Jay Gaynor, mayor of New York. Chicago, H. Regnery Co., 1951. 192 p. illus. 22 cm [F128.5.G294] 51-12724
1. Gaynor, William Jay, 1851-1913. 2. New York (City)—Pol. & govt. I. Title.

STEELE, Robert 974.7'1'040924 B
V. P.
The mayor who mastered New York; the life & opinions of William J. Gaynor, by Lately Thomas. New York, Morrow, 1969. 516 p. illus., facsims., ports. 25 cm. Bibliography: p. 499-505. [F128.5.G295] 70-83690 12.50
1. Gaynor, William Jay, 1851-1913. I. Title.

Gayoso de Lemos, Manuel, 1747-1799.

HOLMES, Jack David 976.3030924
Lazarus, 1930-
Gayoso; the life of a Spanish governor in the Mississippi Valley, 1789-1799 [Baton Rouge] Pub. by La. State Univ. Pr. for the La. Hist. Assn. [1966, c.1965] x, 305p. map, port. 23cm. Bibl. [F373.G3H6] 65-24680 7.50
1. Gayoso de Lemos, Manuel, 1747-1799. 2. Louisiana—Hist.—Colonial period. I. Louisiana Historical Association. II. Title.

HOLMES, Jack David 976.3'03'0924
Lazarus, 1930-
Gayoso; the life of a Spanish Governor in the Mississippi Valley 1789-1799 [by] Jack D. L. Holmes. Gloucester, Mass., Peter Smith, 1968 [c1965] x, 305 p. geneal. table, map, port. 21 cm. Bibliography: p. 285-291. [F373.G3H6 1968] 74-2785
1. Gayoso de Lemos, Manuel, 1747-1799. 2. Louisiana—History—Colonial period. BIP

Gebelein, George Christian, 1878-1945.

LEIGHTON, 739.2'3'724 B
Margaretha Gebelein.
George Christian Gebelein, Boston silversmith, 1878-1945 : a biographical sketch / by Margaretha Gebelein Leighton, in collaboration with Esther Gebelein Swain and J. Herbert Gebelein. Boston : [Gebelein], 1976. xix, 118 p., [4] leaves of plates : ill. ; 25 cm. Includes bibliographical references. [NK7198.G35L44] 76-52871
1. Gebelein, George Christian, 1878-1945. 2. Silversmiths—Massachusetts—Boston—Biography. 3. Silverwork—Massachusetts—Boston. I. Swain, Esther Gebelein, joint author. II. Gebelein, J. Herbert, joint author. III. Title.

Geddes, Norman Bel [Norman Melancton Geddes]

GEDDES, Norman Bel [Norman 927.4
Melancton Geddes]
Miracle in the evening, an autobiography. Edited by William Kelley. Garden City, N. Y., Doubleday [c.]1960. 352p. 25cm. 60-11371 4.95 half cloth,
I. Title.

Geddes, Patrick, Sir, 1854-1932.

BOARDMAN, Philip. 711'.092'4 B
The worlds of Patrick Geddes : biologist, town planner, re-educator, peace-warrior / Philip Boardman. London ; Boston : Routledge and K. Paul, 1978. x, 528 p. : ill. ; 24 cm. Includes index. Bibliography: p. 500-508. [CT828.G42B62] 78-313806 ISBN 0-7100-8548-6 : 31.50
1. Geddes, Patrick, Sir, 1854-1932. 2. Scotland—Biography. I. Title. BIP

KITCHEN, Paddy. 309.2'62'0924 B
A most unsettling person : the life and ideas of Patrick Geddes, founding father of city planning and environmentalism / by Paddy Kitchen. 1st American ed. [New York] : Saturday Review Press, c1975. 351 p., [4] leaves of plates : ill. ; 22 cm. Includes bibliographical references and index. [HT166.K57 1975] 75-33591 ISBN 0-8415-0409-1 : 10.95
1. Geddes, Patrick, Sir, 1854-1932. I. Title.

MAIRET, Philippe, 301'.092'4 B
1886-
Pioneer of sociology : the life and letters of Patrick Geddes / by Philip Mairet. Westport, Ct. : Hyperion Press, [1979] p. cm. Reprint of the 1957 ed. published by L. Humphries, London. Includes index. [HM22.G8G4 1979] 78-20482 ISBN 0-88355-859-9 : 21.00
1. Geddes, Patrick, Sir, 1854-1932. 2. Sociologists—Great Britain—Biography. 3. City planners—Great Britain—Biography. I. Title. BIP

Geelong Grammar School.

JUDD, Tom. 377'.8'30924 B
Fifty years will be long enough!: a school porter's story. Melbourne, National Press, 1971. 208 p. front. 23 cm. [LG720.M44J82] 73-153488 ISBN 0-909470-05-7 4.00
1. Geelong Grammar School. I. Title.

Gehlen, Reinhard, 1902-

GEHLEN, 327'.12'0924 [B]
Reinhard.
The Service; the memoirs of General Reinhard Gehlen. Translated by David Irving. Introd. by George Bailey. New York, Popular Lib. [1972] xxvii, 386 p. illus. 18 cm. Translation of Der Dienst. [DD247.G37A313 1972] pap., 1.50
1. World War, 1939-1945—Secret Service. 2. Organisation Gehlen. I. Title.

SPIRO, Edward. 327'.12'0924 B
Gehlen; spy of the century, by E. H. Cookridge. [1st American ed.] New York, Random House [1972, c1971] xxii, 402 p. illus. 25 cm. Bibliography: p. 384-393. [DD247.G37S65 1972] 72-177225 ISBN 0-394-47313-2 10.00
1. Gehlen, Reinhard, 1902- I. Title.

Gehman, Clayton H., 1909-

GEHMAN, Clayton H., 286'.5 B
1909-
Children of the Conestoga / by Clayton H. Gehman. Elgin, Ill. : Brethren Press ; New York : distributed by Two Continents Publishing Group, c1978. 116 p. ; 21 cm. [BX7843.G43A33] 78-7255 ISBN 0-87178-133-6 pbk. : 3.95
1. Gehman, Clayton H., 1909- 2. Church of the Brethren—Clergy—Biography. 3. Clergy—Pennsylvania—Conestoga Valley—Biography. 4. Pennsylvania Germans—Biography. 5. Conestoga Valley, Pa.—Biography. I. Title. BIP

Gehrig, Lou, 1903-1941.

GEHRIG, Eleanor. 796.357'092'4
My Luke and I / Eleanor Gehrig and Joseph Durso. New York : Crowell, c1976. 229 p. : ports. ; 21 cm. [GV865.G4G44 1976] 75-44457 ISBN 0-690-01109-1 : 7.95
1. Gehrig, Lou, 1903-1941. 2. Gehrig, Eleanor. 3. Baseball. I. Durso, Joseph, joint author. II. Title. BIP

Gehrig, Lou, 1903-1941—Juvenile literature.

GRAHAM, Frank, 796.357'092'4 B
1893-
Lou Gehrig: a quiet hero. New York, Putnam [1969? c1942] 186 p. illus. 22 cm. (Putnam sports shelf) A biography of the Yankee player voted "the greatest first baseman of all time" by the Baseball Writer's Association. [GV865.G4G7 1969] 92 69-15080 ISBN 0-399-60431-6
1. Gehrig, Lou 1903-1941—Juvenile literature. I. Title.

LUCE, Willard. 796.357'0924 B
Lou Gehrig: iron man of baseball, by Willard and Celia Luce. Illustrated by Dom Lupo. Champaign, Ill., Garrard Pub. Co. [1970] 95 p. col. illus., ports. 24 cm. (Americans all) The life of the Yankee player voted "the greatest first baseman of all time" by the Baseball Writers' Association. [GV865.G4L8] 92 78-103956 2.49
1. Gehrig, Lou, 1903-1941—Juvenile literature. I. Luce, Celia, joint author. II. Lupo, Dom, illus. III. Title.

RUBIN, Robert, 796.357'092'4 B
1941-
Lou Gehrig, courageous star / by Robert Rubin. New York : Putnam, c1979. 160 p. : ill. ; 21 cm. (Putnam sport shelf.) Includes index. A biography of the "Iron Horse", remembered for playing 2,130 consecutive games for the New York Yankees. [GV865.G4R82 1979] 92 78-31604 ISBN 0-399-61135-5 lib.bdg. : 5.96
1. Gehrig, Lou, 1903-1941—Juvenile literature. 2. New York (City). Baseball Club (American League) 3. Baseball players—United States—Biography—Juvenile literature. I. Title.

Geiger, Jacob Casson, 1885-

MARSHALL, Max Skidmore, 926.1
1897-
Crusader undaunted: Dr. J. C. Geiger, private physician to the public. New York, Macmillan, 1958. 246p. illus. 22cm. [RA424.5.G4M3] 58-14055
1. Geiger, Jacob Casson, 1885- I. Title.

Geiger, Maynard J., 1901-

WEBER, Francis J. 282'.07'2024 B
Maynard J. Geiger, O.F.M., Franciscan & historian: a 70th birthday tribute, by Francis J. Weber and Doyce B. Nunis, Jr. Foreword by W. W. Robinson. Santa Barbara, Friends of the Santa Barbara Mission Archive-Library, 1971. viii, 53 p. ports. 23 cm. 300 copies printed. "A Geiger bibliography": p. 19-52. [E175.5.G4W4] 71-173908
1. Geiger, Maynard J., 1901- I. Nunis, Doyce Blackman.

Geiger, Oscar Harold, 1873-1934.

CLANCY, Robert, 1904- 923.373
A seed was sown; the life, philosophy, and writings of Oscar H. Geiger, founder of the Henry George School of Social Science. 2d ed. New York, Henry George School of Social Science, 1954, c1952] 124p. illus. 28cm. [HD1313] 54-1081
1. Geiger, Oscar Harold, 1873-1934. 2. Henry George School of Social Science, New York. 3. George, Henry, 1839-1897. I. Title.

Geiger, Roy Stanley, 1885-1947.

WILLOCK, Roger. 359.9'6'0924 B
Unaccustomed to fear; a biography of the late General Roy S. Geiger, U.S.M.C. Princeton, N.J., [1968] xiii, 321 p. illus., ports. 23 cm. Bibliography: p. 318-321. [U53.G4W5] 68-22840
1. Geiger, Roy Stanley, 1885-1947. I. Title.

Geiser, Peter, 1826-1901.

GEISER, Peter, 1826- 631.3'6 B
1901.
Autobiography of Peter Geiser, inventor; the Geiser Separator, patented 1852-1855. [Waynesboro, Pa., Printed by Caslon Press, 1968] 45 p. illus. 24 cm. Cover title. [TJ140.G44A33] 73-155901
1. Geiser, Peter, 1826-1901. 2. Threshing machines. I. Title.

Geist, Otto William.

KEIM, Charles J. 970.4'98 B
Aghvook, white Eskimo; Otto Geist and Alaskan archaeology, by Charles J. Keim. Foreword by Olaus J. Murie. [1st ed.] College, University of Alaska Press; distributed by University of Washington Press, Seattle [1969] xix, 313 p. illus., ports. 23 cm. [QH31.G36K4] 68-28823 7.95
1. Geist, Otto William. 2. Natural history—Alaska. I. Title.

Gelee, Claude, called Claude Lorrain, 1600-1682.

COTTE, Sabine. 741.9'44
Claude Lorrain. [Translated by Helen Sebba] New York, G. Braziller [1971, c1970] 96 p. illus. 25 cm. (The Great draughtsmen) Translation of L'univers de Claude Lorrain. [NC248.G3C613 1971] 76-137220 ISBN 0-8076-0594-8 7.95
1. Gelee, Claude, called Claude Lorrain, 1600-1682. BIP

Gelb, Donald M.

GELB, Donald M. 362.1'9'6123
Heart attack—you can survive! / By Donald M. Gelb. Los Alamitos, CA. : Hwong Pub. Co., c1979. vii, 107 p. ; 21 cm. [RC685.I6G35] 79-63532 ISBN 0-89260-128-0 : 2.95
1. Gelb, Donald M. 2. Heart—Infarction—Biography. 3. Surgeons—California—Biography. I. Title.

Geller, Uri, 1946-

THE *Amazing Uri* 133.8'092'4 B
Geller / edited by Martin Ebon. New York : New American Library, 1975. xxi, 168 p., [4] leaves of plates : ill. ; 18 cm. (A Signet Book) [BF1283.G4A65] 75-31387 pbk. : 1.50
1. Geller, Uri, 1946- I. Ebon, Martin
Contents omitted BIP

GELLER, Uri, 1946- 133.9
Uri Geller, my story. New York : Praeger, 1975. 282 p., [8] leaves of plates : ill. ; 22 cm. [BF1283.G4A36] 74-25462 ISBN 0-275-33170-9 : 8.95
1. Geller, Uri, 1946- I. Title.

GELLER, Uri, 1946- 133.9
Uri Geller, my story. New York : Praeger, 1975. 282 p., [8] leaves of plates : ill. ; 22 cm. [BF1283.G4A36] 74-25462 ISBN 0-275-33170-9 : 8.95
1. Geller, Uri, 1946- I. Title.

GELLER, Uri 1946- 133.9
Uri Geller, my story. [New York] Warner Books [1976 c1975] 287 p., 8 leaves of plates illus. 18 cm. [BF1283.G4A36] ISBN 0-446-89025-1 1.95 (pbk.)
1. Geller, Uri, 1946- I. Title.
L.C. card no. of 1975 Praeger edition: 74-25462.

PUHARICH, Andrija. 133.8'092'4
Uri; a journal of the mystery of Uri Geller. [1st ed.] Garden City, N.Y., Anchor Press, 1974. 285 p. 22 cm. [BF1283.G4P83] 73-17770 ISBN 0-385-00992-5 7.95
1. Geller, Uri, 1946- I. Title.

Geller, Uri, 1946- —Juvenile literature.

COLLINS, Jim. 133.8'092'4
The strange story of Uri Geller / by Jim Collins. New York : Contemporary Perspectives ; Milwaukee, Wis. : distributor, Raintree Publishers, c1977. 48 p. : ill. (some col.) ; 24 cm. Describes the psychic powers and abilities of Israeli-born Uri Geller and presents the doubts of

people who insist he is only a magician. [BF1283.G4C64] 92 B 77-24501 ISBN 0-8172-1037-7 lib. bdg. : 4.95
1. Geller, Uri, 1946- —Juvenile literature. 2. Psychical research—Biography—Juvenile literature. 3. Magicians—Biography—Juvenile literature. I. Title. **BIP**

Genealogy.

JONASSON, Eric. 929'.1'0971
The Canadian genealogical handbook / by Eric Jonasson. 1st ed. Winnipeg : Wheatfield Press, 1976. 110 p. : ill. ; 28 cm. Includes bibliographies. [CS16.J66] 77-372669 12.50
1. Genealogy. 2. Canada—Genealogy—Handbooks, manuals, etc. I. Title.

General Motors Corporation.

SLOAN, Alfred Pritchard, 1875- v. 12
My years with General motors. Edited by John McDonald with Catharine Stevens. [N.Y., Macfadden-Bartell Corp., 1965, c1963] 467 p. illus. 19 cm. (A Macfadden-Bartell Book, 135-100) 66-7208
1. General Motors Corporation. 2. Corporations — Hist. — General Motors Corporation. I. Title.

SLOAN, Alfred Pritchard, 1875-1966. 338.7'62'920924 B
Adventures of a white-collar man [by] Alfred P. Sloan, Jr., in collaboration with Boyden Sparkes. Freeport, N.Y., Books for Libraries Press [1970, c1941] xv, 208 p. illus., ports. 23 cm. [CT275.S5233A3 1970] 74-126258
1. General Motors Corporation. I. Sparkes, Boyden, 1890-1954. II. Title. **BIP**

SLOAN, Alfred Pritchard, 1875-1966. 658.96292
My years with General Motors. Edited by John McDonald, with Catharine Stevens. [1st ed.] Garden City, N.Y., Doubleday, 1964 [c1963] xxv, 472 p. illus., ports. 24 cm. [CT275.S5233A35] 64-11306
1. General Motors Corporation. I. Title. **BIP**

Generalic, Ivan.

GENERALIC, Ivan. 759.9497 B
The magic world of Ivan Generalic / [edited] by Nebojsa Tomasevic ; translated from the Italian by John Shepley. New York : Rizzoli, 1976, c1975. 223 p. : ill. (some col.) ; 31 cm. Translation of Il mondo magico di Ivan Generalic. [ND953.G4T6513 1976] 76-11251 ISBN 0-8478-0044-X : 27.50
1. Generalic, Ivan. 2. Painters—Yugoslavia—Biography. 3. Primitivism in art—Yugoslavia. I. Tomasevic, Nebojsa. II. Title.

Generals.

GELLERMANN, Josef Egmond, 1909- 923.5
Generals as statesmen. [1st ed.] New York, Vantage Press [1959] 150 p. 23 cm. [D412.6.G39] 58-14022
1. Generals. 2. Statesmen.

MCSPADDEN, Joseph Walker, 1874- 923.5
Boys' book of famous soldiers. Edited by Jockey Kaplan. Cleveland, World Pub. Co. [1951] 220 p. illus. 19 cm. (Falcon books, A-53) [CT107.M4 1951] 51-8382
1. Generals. I. Title.

YOUNG, Desmond 923.543
Rommel, the desert fox. New ed. [New York] Berkley [1961, c.1950] 250p. maps (Berkley Medallion BG522) .50 pap.,
I. Title.

Generals—Confederate States of America—Juvenile literature.

REEDER, Russell Potter 973.742
The Southern generals, by Red Reeder. Maps by Ned Glattauer. New York, Duell, [dist. Meredith, c.1965] xiii, 237p. maps, plans. ports. 22cm. Bibl. [E467.R44] 65-14408 4.50 bds.,
1. Generals—Confederate States of America—Juvenile literature. 2. U.S.—Hist.—Civil War—Biog.—Juvenile literature. 3. U.S.—Hist.—Civil War—Campaigns and battles—Juvenile literature. I. Title.

Generals — U.S.

ANDERS, Curtis, 1927- 355.3320922
Fighting generals, by Curt Anders. New York, Putnam [1965] 320 p. 22 cm. Bibliography: p. 300-310. [E181.A52] (B)
1. Generals — U.S. 2. U.S. Army — Biog. I. Title.

WARNER, Ezra J. 973.741
Generals in blue; lives of the Union commanders, by Ezra J. Warner. [Baton Rouge] Louisiana State University Press [1964] xxiv, 679, [1] p. ports. 24 cm. Bibliography: p. 673-[680] [E467.W29] 64-21593
1. Generals — U.S. 2. U.S. — Hist. — Civil War — Biog. I. Title. **BIP**

WARNER, Ezra J. 973.741
Generals in blue lives of the Union commanders [Baton Rouge] La State Univ. Pr. [c.1964] xxiv, 679, [1] p. ports. 24cm. Bibl. 64-21593 15.00; 12.50 before Dec. 31,
1. Generals—U. S. 2. U. S.—Hist.—Civil War—Biog. I. Title.

WARNER, Ezra J. 973.742
Generals in gray; lives of the Confederate commanders. [1st ed.] [Baton Rouge] Louisiana State University Press [1959] xxvii, 420 p. ports. 25 cm. Bibliography: p. 401-420. [E467.W3] 58-7551
1. Generals—Confederate States of America. 2. U.S.—History—Civil War, 1861-1865—Biography. I. Title. II. Title: Confederate commanders. **BIP**

Genet, Jean, 1910-

SARTRE, Jean Paul, 1905- 928.4
Saint Genet, actor and martyr. Tr. from French by Bernard Frechtman [New York] New Amer. Lib. [1964, c.1963] 669p. 18cm. (Mentor bk. MY595) 1.25 pap.,
1. Genet, Jean, 1910- I. Title.

SARTRE, Jean Paul, 1905- 928.4
Saint Genet, actor and martyr. Translated from the French by Bernard Frechtman. New York, G. Braziller, 1965. 625 p. 25 cm. [PQ2613.E53Z883] 63-15828
1. Genet, Jean, 1910- I. Title.

Genghis Khan, 1162-1227.

MACKENZIE, Franklin, 1910- 950.2
The ocean and the steppe; the life and times of the Mongol conqueror Genghis Khan, 1155-1227. New York, Vantage [c.1963] ix, 357p. 22cm. Bibl. 63-23755 6.00
1. Genghis Khan, 1162-1227. I. Title.

Genlis, Stephanie Felicite Ducrest de Saint-Aubin, comtesse de, afterwards marquise de Sillery, 1746-1830.

WYNDHAM, Violet 928.4
Madame de Genlis a biography. New York, Roy Publishers [1960] 304p. Bibl.: p.287-290 illus. 22cm. 60-10796 4.00
1. Genlis, Stephanie Felicite Ducrest de Saint-Aubin, comtesse de, afterwards marquise de Sillery, 1746-1830. I. Title.

Genovese, Vito, 1897-

FRANCA, Dom. 364.15
Vito Genovese: king of crime. Rev. ed. New York, Avon Books, 1963] 159 p. ports. 18 cm. "G1196." Published in 1959 under title: King of crime. [HV6248.G34F7 1963] 64-196
1. Genovese, Vito, 1897- 2. Mafia. I. Title.

FRASCA, Dom. 364.15
Vito Genovese: king of crime. [Rev. ed. New York, Avon Books, 1963] 159 p. ports. 18 cm. [HV6248.G34F7 1963] 64-196
1. Genovese, Vito, 1897- 2. Mafia. I. Title.

Gent, Thomas, 1693-1778.

GENT, Thomas, 1693-1778. 686.2'092'4 B
The life of Mr. Thomas Gent, printer, of York, written by himself. New York, Garland Pub., 1974. iv, 208 p. 22 cm. (The English book trade, 1660-1853) Reprint of the 1832 ed. printed for T. Thorpe, London. [Z232.G33G46 1974] 74-7445 ISBN 0-8240-0984-3
1. Gent, Thomas, 1693-1778. I. Title. II. Series.

Genthe, Arnold, 1869-1942.

GENTHE, Arnold, 1869-1942. 770'.92'4 B
As I remember / Arnold Genthe. New York : Arno Press, 1979, c1936. p. cm. (The Sources of modern photography) Reprint of the ed. published by Reynal & Hitchcock, New York. Includes index. [TR140.G4A3 1979] 76-24684 ISBN 0-405-09660-7 : 28.00
1. Genthe, Arnold, 1869-1942. 2. Photographers—United States—Biography. I. Title. II. Series.

Gentry, Byron

GENTRY, Byron 927.9633
The way the ball bounces. San Antonio, Naylor [c.1962] 191p. 22cm. 62-20523 4.95
I. Title.

Gentz, Friedrich von, 1764-1832.

MANN, Golo, 1909- 940.2'7'0924 B
Secretary of Europe; the life of Friedrich Gentz, enemy of Napoleon. Translated by William H. Woglom. [Hamden, Conn.] Archon Books, 1970 [c1946] xvi, 323 p. illus., ports. 23 cm. Translation of Friedrich von Gentz; Geschichte eines europaischen Staatsmannes. [DB80.8.G4M3 1970] 77-122395 ISBN 0-208-00957-4
1. Gentz, Friedrich von, 1764-1832. 2. Europe—Politics and government—1789-1900. I. Title. **BIP**

SWEET, Paul Robinson, 1907- 940.2'7'0924 B
Friedrich von Gentz, defender of the old order, by Paul R. Sweet. Westport, Conn., Greenwood Press [1970, c1941] viii, 326 p. port. 23 cm. Includes bibliographical references. [DB80.8.G4S9 1970] 74-97321
1. Gentz, Friedrich von, 1764-1832. 2. Europe—Politics and government—1789-1900. **BIP**

Geography—Dictionaries.

THE New Century cyclopedia of names, edited by Clarence L. Barnhart with the assistance of William D. Halsey and a staff of more than 350 consulting scholars, special editors, and other contributors. New York, Appleton-Century-Crofts [1954] 3v. (xxviii, 4342 p.) 28cm. [PE1625.C43 1954] 52-13879 929.4
1. Geography—Dictionaries. 2. Biography—Dictionaries. 3. Names—Dictionaries. I. Barnhart, Clarence Lewis, 1900- ed.

Geologists.

FENTON, Carroll Lane, 1900- 925.5
Giants of geology, by Carroll Lane Fenton and Mildred Adams Fenton. Garden City, N.Y., Doubleday, 1952. 333 p. illus. 22 cm. "A revised and enlarged edition of ... [the authors'] The story of the great geologists." [QE21.F4 1952] 52-5125
1. Geologists. 2. Geology—History. I. Title.

FENTON, Carroll Lane, 1900- 550'.0922
The story of the great geologists [by] Carroll Lane Fenton and Mildred Adams Fenton. Freeport, N.Y., Books for Libraries Press [1969, c1945] xvi, 301 p. illus., ports. 23 cm. (Essay index reprint series) Bibliography: p. 287-294. [QE21.F4 1969] 73-84306
1. Geologists. 2. Geology—History. I. Fenton, Mildred (Adams) 1899- joint author. II. Title. **BIP**

George, Henry, 1839-1897.

BARKER, Charles Albro, 1904- 330'.092'4 B
Henry George. Westport, Conn., Greenwood Press [1974, c1955] xvii, 696 p. 22 cm. Reprint of the ed. published by Oxford University Press, New York. Includes bibliographical references. [HB119.G4B3 1974] 74-12949 ISBN 0-8371-7775-8
1. George, Henry, 1839-1897. **BIP**

CORD, Steven B., 1928- 330.1530924
Henry George: dreamer or realist? Philadelphia, Univ. of Pa. Pr. [1965] 272p. 22cm. Bibl. [HB119.G4C65] 65-21733 6.00
1. George, Henry, 1839-1897. I. Title. **BIP**

DE MILLE, Anna Angela George, 1877- 923.373
Henry George, citizen of the world; edited by Don C. Shoemaker, with an introd. by Agnes de Mille. Chapel Hill, University of North Carolina Press [1950] xv, 276 p. illus., ports. 25 cm. Bibliographical references included in "Notes" (p. 243-267) [HB119.G4D4] 50-6148
1. George, Henry, 1839-1897.

DE MILLE, Anna Angela (George) 1877-1947. 330.15'3'0924 B
Henry George, citizen of the world, by Anna George de Mille. Edited by Don C. Shoemaker. With an introd. by Agnes de Mille. Westport, Conn., Greenwood Press, [1972, c1950] xv, 276 p. illus. 22 cm. [HB119.G4D4 1972] 79-138218 ISBN 0-8371-5575-4
1. George, Henry, 1839-1897. **BIP**

GEORGE, Henry, 1862-1916. v. 12
The life of Henry George. New York, Robert Schalkenbach Foundation, 1960. 634 p. 64-27274
1. George, Henry, 1839-1897. I. Title. **BIP**

GEORGE, Henry, 1862-1916. 330'.092'4 B
The life of Henry George. Garden City, N.Y., Doubleday, Page, 1911. [New York, AMS Press, 1973] 2 v. (634 p.) illus. 23 cm. (The complete works of Henry George, v. 9-10) Contents.Contents.—[1] Formation of the character. Formulation of the philosophy.—[2] Propagation of the philosophy. Includes bibliographical references. [HB119.G4G4 1973] 73-12762 ISBN 0-404-02809-8 (v. 9)
1. George, Henry, 1839-1897.

LAWRENCE, Elwood Parsons. 923.373
Henry George in the British Isles. East Lansing, Michigan State University Press [1957] 203p. 22cm. Includes bibliographical references. [HB171.G4L3] 57-9034
1. George, Henry, 1839-1897. I. Title. **BIP**

ROSE, Edward J. 330.15'3'0924
Henry George, by Edward J. Rose. New York, Twayne Publishers [1968] 176 p. 21 cm. (Twayne's United States authors series, 128) Bibliography: p. 170-172. [HB119.G4R6] 67-28858
1. George, Henry, 1839-1897.

George I, King of Great Britain, 1660-1727.

HATTON, Ragnhild Marie. 941.07'1'0924 B
George I, elector and king / by Ragnhild M. Hatton. Cambridge, MA : Harvard University Press, [1978] p. cm. Includes index. [DA501.A2H4] 77-15058 ISBN 0-674-34935-0 : 15.00
1. George I, King of Great Britain, 1660-1727. 2. Great Britain—Kings and rulers—Biography. 3. Great Britain—History—George I, 1714-1727.

IMBERT-TERRY, Henry Machu, Sir, bart., 1854-1938. 942.07'1'0924 B
A constitutional king: George the First. Port Washington, N.Y., Kennikat Press

[1972] x, 397 p. illus. 23 cm. Reprint of the 1927 ed. Bibliography: p. 387-390. [DA501.A2I6 1972] 77-153223 ISBN 0-8046-1533-0
1. George I, King of Great Britain, 1660-1727. 2. Gt. Brit.—History—George I, 1714-1727. I. Title.

George II, King of Great Britain, 1683-1760.

HERVEY, John Hervey, baron, 1696-1743. 942.072
Memoirs. Edited by Romney Sedgwick. [Rev. ed.] New York, Macmillan [1963] 278 p. illus. 21 cm. [DA501.A3H46] 63-15935
1. George II, King of Great Britain, 1683-1760. I. Title.

HERVEY, John Hervey, Baron, 1696-1743. 942.07'2
Some materials towards memoirs of the reign of King George II. Edited by Romney Sedgwick. New York, AMS Press [1970] 3 v. (lx, 1003 p.) ports. 23 cm. Title on spine: Memoirs. Originally published in 1848 under title: Memoirs of the reign of George the Second. Reprint of the 1931 ed. Includes bibliographical references. [DA501.A3H47 1970] 79-119102 ISBN 4-04-033008-
1. George II, King of Great Britain, 1683-1760. 2. Gt. Brit.—History—George II, 1727-1760. I. Sedgwick, Romney, 1894- ed. II. Title.

HERVEY, John Hervey, baron, 1696-1743 942.072
Memoirs. Ed. by Romney Sedgwick. [Rev. ed.] New York, Macmillan [c.1963] 278p. illus. 21cm. 63-15935 4.00: 1.95 pap.,
1. George II, King of Great Britain, 1683-1760. I. Title.

George III, King of Great Britain, 1738-1820.

ANDREWS, Allen. 941.07'3'0924 B
The King who lost America : George III and independence / by Allen Andrews. London : Jupiter Books, 1976. 182 p. : ill. ; 26 cm. Bibliography: p. 179-182. [DA506.A2A83] 76-380926 ISBN 0-904041-54-9 : £5.50
1. George III, King of Great Britain, 1738-1820. 2. Great Britain—Kings and rulers—Biography. 3. United States—History—Revolution, 1775-1783—Causes. I. Title.

AYLING, Stanley Edward. 942.07'3'0924 B
George the Third, by Stanley Ayling. [1st American ed.] New York, Knopf, 1972. 510 p. illus. 25 cm. Bibliography: p. [487]-493. [DA506.A2A9 1972] 72-2325 ISBN 0-394-48169-0 12.50
1. George III, King of Great Britain, 1738-1820.

BROOKE, John. 942.07'3'0924 B
King George III. With a foreword by H. R. H. the Prince of Wales. New York, McGraw-Hill [1972] xix, 411 p. col. front., illus. 26 cm. (American Revolution bicentennial program) Includes bibliographical references. [DA506.A2B75] 72-2011 ISBN 0-07-008059-3
1. George III, King of Great Britain, 1738-1820. I. Title. II. Series. **BIP**

DELANY, Mary Granville Pendarves, 1700-1788. 942.07'3'0924 B
The autobiography and correspondence of Mary Granville, Mrs. Delany: with interesting reminiscences of King George the Third and Queen Charlotte. Edited by Lady Llanover. [1st-2d series] London, R. Bentley, 1861-62. [New York, AMS Press, 1974] 6 v. illus. 23 cm. [DA483.D3A2 1974] 75-163683 ISBN 0-404-02080-1 180.00 (6 vols.)
1. Delany, Mary Granville Pendarves, 1700-1788. 2. George III, King of Great Britain, 1738-1820. 3. Charlotte, Queen consort of George III, 1744-1818. I. Llanover, Augusta Waddington Hall, Lady, d. 1896, ed. II. Title. **BIP**

GEORGE III, King of Great Britain, 1738-1820 942.07'3'0924
The letters. Edited by Bonamy Dobree. New York, Funk & Wagnalls [1968] xvi, 293 p. geneal. table, port. 22 cm. Bibliography: p. 275-283. [DA506.A2A25 1968b] 68-25024 6.95
I. Dorbee, Bonamy, 1891- ed.

LLOYD, Alan, 1927- 942.07'3'0924 B
The King who lost America; a portrait of the life and times of George III. [1st ed.] Garden City, N.Y., Doubleday, 1971. x, 369 p. 22 cm. Bibliography: p. 354-357. [DA506.A2L58] 73-139042 7.95
1. George III, King of Great Britain, 1738-1820. I. Title.

LONG, John Cuthbert, 1892- 923.142
George III; the story of a complex man. [1st ed.] Boston, Little, Brown [1961, c1960] 372 p. illus. 22 cm. [DA505.L6] 60-5878
1. George III, King of Great Britain, 1738-1820.

George III, King of Great Britain, 1738-1820—Juvenile literature.

FRITZ, Jean. 941.07'3'0924 B
Can't you make them behave, King George? / By Jean Fritz ; pictures by Tomie de Paola. New York : Coward, McCann & Geoghegan, c1977. 45 p. : ill. ; 24 cm. A biography of George the Third, King of Great Britain at the time of the American Revolution. [DA506.A2F74 1977] 92 75-33722 ISBN 0-698-20315-1 ISBN 0-698-20315-1 : 6.95
1. George III, King of Great Britain, 1738-1820—Juvenile literature. 2. Great Britain—History—George III, 1760-1820—Juvenile literature. 3. Great Britain—Kings and rulers—Biography—Juvenile literature. I. De Paola, Thomas Anthony. II. Title.

FRITZ, Jean. 941.07'3'0924 B
Can't you make them behave, King George? / By Jean Fritz ; pictures by Tomie de Paola. New York : Coward, McCann & Geoghegan, c1977. 45 p. : ill. ; 24 cm. A biography of George the Third, King of Great Britain at the time of the American Revolution. [DA506.A2F74 1977] 92 75-33722 ISBN 0-698-20315-1 ISBN 0-698-20315-1 : 6.95
1. George III, King of Great Britain, 1738-1820—Juvenile literature. 2. Great Britain—History—George III, 1760-1820—Juvenile literature. 3. Great Britain—Kings and rulers—Biography—Juvenile literature. I. De Paola, Thomas Anthony. II. Title. **BIP**

George IV, King of Great Britain, 1762-1830.

FULFORD, Roger, 1902- v. 12
George the fourth. [Rev. and enig. ed.] New York, Capricorn Books [1963] 240 p. (Capricorn Books, 78) 64-27585
1. George IV, King of Great Britain, 1762-1830. I. Title.

GEORGE IV King of Great Britain. 923.142
The correspondence of George, Prince of Wales, 1770-1812.
I. Title.
Volume 5 for the years 1804-1806 is now available from Oxford Univ. Pr., New York, for $23.50. L.C. card order no.: 64-237.

HIBBERT, Christopher, 1924- 942.07'4'0924 B
George IV: Prince of Wales, 1762-1811. [1st U. S. ed.] New York, Harper & Row [1974, c1972] xiii, 338 p. illus. 25 cm. (A Cass Canfield book) Bibliography: p. 311-319. [DA538.A1H5 1974] 72-9122 ISBN 0-06-011884-9 10.00
1. George IV, King of Great Britain, 1762-1830.

HIBBERT, Christopher, 1924- 941.07'4'0924 B
George IV, regent and king, 1811-1830 / Christopher Hibbert. 1st U. S. ed. New York : Harper & Row, [1975] c1973. xiv, 430 p., [8] leaves of plates : ill. ; 25 cm. Includes index. Bibliography: p. 389-403. [DA538.A1H53 1975] 75-313668 ISBN 0-06-011886-5 : 15.00
1. George IV, King of Great Britain, 1762-1830.

RICHARDSON, Joanna 942.074
The disastrous marriage; a study of George IV and Caroline of Brunswick. London, Cape [dist. Mystic, Conn., Verry, 1964, c.1960] 255p. illus. 23cm. Bibl. 61-982 5.00
1. George IV, King of Great Britain, 1762-1830. 2. Caroline Amelia Elizabeth, consort of George IV, 1768-1821. I. Title. **BIP**

RICHARDSON, Joanna. 941.07'4'0924 B
The disastrous marriage : a study of George IV and Caroline of Brunswick / by Joanna Richardson. Westport, Conn. : Greenwood Press, 1975, c1960. 255 p., [7] leaves of plates : ill. ; 23 cm. Reprint of the ed. published by J. Cape, London. Includes index. Bibliography: p. 246-252. [DA538.A1R5 1975] 75-31823 ISBN 0-8371-8439-8
1. George IV, King of Great Britain, 1762-1830. 2. Caroline Amelia Elizabeth, consort of George IV, 1768-1821. I. Title.

RICHARDSON, Joanna. 942.0740924
George the Magnificent; a portrait of King George IV. [1st American ed.] New York, Harcourt, Brace & World [1966] xvii, 410 p. illus., ports. 22 cm. London ed. has title: George IV, a portrait. Bibliography: p. 394-404. [DA538.A1R53 1966a] 66-22284
1. George IV, King of Great Britain, 1762-1830. I. Title.

George, marguerite Josephine Weitner. called Mlle, 1787-1867.

SAUNDERS, Edith. 927.92
Napoleon and Madmoiselle George [1st ed.] London, New York, Longmans. Green [1958] 248p. illus. 23cm. Includes bibliographies. [PN2638.G37S3 1958] 59-1325
1. George, marguerite Josephine Weitner. called Mlle, 1787-1867. 2. Napoeon I. Emperor of the French, 1769-1821. I. Title.

George Peabody College for Teachers, Nashville—History.

†CRABB, Alfred Leland, 1884- 378.768'55
Peabody and Alfred Leland Crabb : the story of Peabody as reflected in selected writings of Alfred Leland Crabb / edited by John E. Windrow. Nashville : Williams Press, c1977. x, 382 p., [4] leaves of plates : ill. ; 24 cm. [LB1960.N42C72] 77-85734 8.95
1. George Peabody College for Teachers, Nashville—History. 2. Crabb, Alfred Leland, 1884- 3. Educators—United States—Biography. I. Windrow, John Edwin, 1899- II. Title.
Publishers's address : 417 Commerce St., Nashville, TN, 37219

George, Saint, d. 303.

BARCLAY, Alexander, 1475?-1552. 398.22
The life of St. George. Edited by William Nelson. London, Published for the Early English Text Society by Oxford University Press, 1955. xxvi, 120 p. front. 23cm. (Early English Text Society. [Publications] Original series, no. 230. 1955 (for 1948)) Erratum slip mounted on front. [PR1119.A2 no.230] 55-13523
1. George, Saint, d. 303. I. Title. II. Series.

ERNEST, Brother, 1897- 922.1
The story of Saint George. Pictures by Brother Hilarion. Notre Dame, Ind., Dujarie Press [1956] unpaged. illus. 22cm. Abridgment of the author's The dragon killer. [BR1720.G4E73] 56-34889
1. George, Saint, d. 303. I. Title.

George, Stefan Anton, 1868-1933.

METZGER, Michael M. 831'.8
Stefan George, by Michael M. Metzger and Erika A. Metzger. New York, Twayne Publishers [1972] 208 p. 21 cm. (Twayne's world authors series, TWAS 182. Germany) Bibliography: p. 199-205. [PT2613.E47Z747] 75-153453
1. George, Stefan Anton, 1868-1933. I. Metzger, Erika Alma, joint author.

George V, King of Great Britain, 1865-1936.

GORE, John, 1885- 942.083'092'4 B
King George V: a personal memoir. Freeport, N.Y., Books for Libraries Press [1972] p. Reprint of the 1941 ed. Bibliography: p. [DA573.G55 1972] 72-7077 ISBN 0-8369-6938-3
1. George V, King of Great Britain, 1865-1936.

*JUDD, Denis 941.082
The House of Windsor New York, St. Martins, [1974 c1973] [223 p.] illus. 25 cm. [DA566] 73-91378 10.95
1. Edward VII, King of Great Britain, 1841-1910 2. George V, King of Great Britain, 1865-1936 3. George VI, King of Great Britain, 1895-1952 4. Elizabeth II, Queen of Great Britain, 1926- I. Title.

NICOLSON, Harold George, Sir, 1886-1968. 923.142
King George the Fifth; his life and reign. Garden City, N. Y., Doubleday, 1953. xxiii, 570 p. plates, ports., geneal. tables. 25 cm. Erratum slip inserted. Bibliography: p. 535-539. [DA573.N5 1953] 53-9100
1. George V, King of Great Britain, 1865-1936.

George VI, King of Great Britain, 1895-1952.

BUXTON, Aubrey. 923.142
The King in his country. Woodstock, Vt., Countryman Press [1956] 139p. illus. 22cm. [DA584.B8] 56-13814
1. George VI, King of Great Britain, 1895-1952. 2. Hunting—Gt. Brit. I. Title.

BUXTON, Aubrey. 923.142
The King in his country. London, New York, Longmans, Green [1955] 139p. illus. 23cm. [DA584.B8 1955] 56-3362
1. George VI, King of Great Britain, 1895-1952. 2. Hunting—Gt. Brit. I. Title.

DONALDSON, Frances Lonsdale, Lady. 941.084'092'2 B
King George VI and Queen Elizabeth / Philadelphia : Lippincott, c1977. 127 p., [4] leaves of plates : ill. ; 28 cm. Includes index. [DA584.D6 1977] 77-5122 ISBN 0-397-01229-2 : 12.95
1. George VI, King of Great Britain, 1895-1952. 2. Elizabeth, consort of George VI, 1900- 3. Great Britain—Kings and rulers—Biography. 4. Great Britain—Queens—Biography. I. Title. II. Title: ..Frances Donaldson. **BIP**

*JUDD, Denis 941.082
The House of Windsor New York, St. Martins, [1974 c1973] [223 p.] illus. 25 cm. [DA566] 73-91378 10.95
1. Edward VII, King of Great Britain, 1841-1910 2. George V, King of Great Britain, 1865-1936 3. George VI, King of Great Britain, 1895-1952 4. Elizabeth II, Queen of Great Britain, 1926- I. Title.

TOWNSEND, Peter, 1914- 909'.09'71241082
The last emperor : an intimate account of George VI and the fall of his empire / Peter Townsend. New York : Simon and Schuster, c1976. p. cm. Includes index. Bibliography: p. [DA16.T68 1976] 76-18059 ISBN 0-671-22328-3 : 9.95
1. George VI, King of Great Britain, 1895-1952. 2. Great Britain—Colonies—History. 3. Commonwealth of Nations—History. I. Title.

WHEELER-BENNETT, John Wheeler 1902- 923.142
King George VI, his life and reign. New York, St. Martin's Press [1958] xii, 891 p. illus., ports. (part col.) geneal. table. 24 cm. Bibliography: p. 830-834. [DA584.W45] 58-13050
1. George VI, King of Great Britain, 1895-1952.

George, 2d duke of Cambridge, 1819-1904.

ST. Aubyn, Giles. 923.542
The Royal George, 1819-1904; the life of H. R. H. Prince George, duke of Cambridge. [1st American ed. New York, Knopf, 1964. xi, 393, xv p. illus., geneal. table, ports. 23 cm. Bibliographical

references included in "Notes for chapters" (p. 372-391) Bibliography: p. 392-393. [DA559.G4S3 1964] 64-12317
1. George, 2d duke of Cambridge, 1819-1904. 2. Gt. Brit.—History, Military—19th century. I. Title.

Georges-Picot, Jacques.

GEORGES-PICOT, Jacques. 962'.15'05
The real Suez crisis : the end of a great nineteenth century work / Jacques Georges-Picot ; translated from the French by W. G. Rogers. 1st ed. New York : Harcourt Brace Jovanovich, c1978. xii, 200 p. ; 22 cm. Translation of La veritable crise de Suez. [DT107.83.G3913] 77-84388 ISBN 0-15-175963-4 : 10.95
1. Georges-Picot, Jacques. 2. Egypt—History—Intervention, 1956. 3. Suez Canal—History. 4. Suez Canal—Biography. I. Title.

Georgia—Biography.

HISTORIC Georgia mothers, 1776-1976. 920.72 1st ed. [Atlanta? : Georgia Mothers Association], 1976. 157 p. : ports. : 24 cm. Includes index. Bibliography: p. 134-137. [CT230.H57] 76-2335
1. Georgia—Biography 2. Mothers—Georgia—Biography. I. Georgia Mothers Association.

NORTHEN, William J., 1835-1913, ed. 920'.0758
Men of mark in Georgia; a complete and elaborate history of the State from its settlement to the present time, chiefly told in biographies and autobiographies of the most eminent men of each period of Georgia's progress and development. Spartanburg, S.C., Reprint Co., 1974 [c1906-12] 7 v. ports. 22 cm. Reprint of the ed. published by A. B. Caldwell, Atlanta, with a new index. [F285.N872] 74-2193 150.00 (7 vols.)
1. Georgia—Biography. 2. Georgia—History. I. Title. BIP

Georgia—Biography—Portraits.

BUNNEN, Lucinda. 920'.0758
Movers and shakers in Georgia / Lucinda Bunnen and Frankie Coxe. New York : Simon and Schuster, [1978] p. cm. [CT230.B86] 78-16229 ISBN 0-671-24043-9 : 12.95
1. Georgia—Biography—Portraits. I. Coxe, Frankie, joint author. II. Title. BIP

Georgia. Institute of Technology, Atlanta.

WALLACE, Robert B. 620'.0071'1758231
Dress her in white and gold; a biography of Georgia Tech and of the men who led her, by Robert B. Wallace, Jr. Rev. ed. Atlanta, Georgia Tech Foundation, 1969. x, 484 p. illus., ports. 23 cm. Bibliography: p. 461-462. [T171.G595W3 1969] 73-15119
1. Georgia. Institute of Technology, Atlanta. I. Title.

Georgius Trapezuntius, d. 1484.

MONFASANI, John. 185
George of Trebizond : a biography and a study of his rhetoric and logic / by John Monfasani. Leiden : Brill, 1976. 414 p. ; 25 cm. (Columbia studies in the classical tradition ; v. 1) Includes indexes. Bibliography: p. [381]-391. [PA5317.G43Z8] 76-372617 ISBN 9-00-404370-5 : fl 96.00
1. Georgius Trapezuntius, d. 1484. 2. Humanists—Italy—Biography. I. Title. II. Series.

Gerard de Nerval, Gerard Labrunie, known as, 1808-1855.

RHODES, Solomon Alhadef, 1895- 928.4
Gerard de Nerval, 1808-1855, poet, traveler, dreamer New York, Philosophical Library [1951] ix, 416 p. port. 23 cm. Bibliography: p. 401-408. [PQ2260.G36Z74] 50-11176
1. Gerard de Nerval, Gerard Labrunie, known as, 1808-1855. I. Title.

Gerard, James Watson,

GERARD, James Watson, 1867- 923.273
My first eighty-three years in America; the memoirs of James W. Gerard. [1st ed.] Garden City, N. Y., Doubleday, 1951. xi, 372 p. port. 22 cm. [E748.G3A3] 51-1103
I. Title.

Gerard, John,

GERARD, John, 1564-1637. 922.242
The autobiography of a hunted priest; translated from the Latin by Philip Caraman, with an introd. by Graham Greene. New York, Pellegrini & Cudahy [1952] 287 p. illus. 22 cm. [BX4705.G418A33] 51-12758
I. Title.

Gerardo Majella, Saint, 1726-1755.

CARR, John 922.245
Saint Gerard Majella. Westminster, Md., Newman Press [1959] 238p. 19cm. 60-48 2.75
1. Gerardo Majella, Saint, 1726-1755. I. Title.

ERNEST, Brother, 1897- 922.245
He's man; a story of Saint Gerard Majella. Notre Dame, Ind., Dujarie Press [1956] 141p. illus. 22cm. High school ed. of the author's The miracle man of Muro. [BX4700.G47E7 1956] 57-15548
1. Gerardo Majella, Saint, 1726-1755. I. Title.

ERNEST, Brother, 1897- 922.245
The miracle man of Muro, a story of St. Gerard Mejella. Illus. by Mary Barnet. Notre Dame, Dujarie Press [1950] 103 p. illus. 24 cm. [BX4700.G47E7] 50-2412
1. Gerardo Majella, Saint, 1726-1755. I. Title.

Geraway, William R.

GERAWAY, William R. 364.1'092'4 B
There's $50,000 on my head / 1st ed. Theres fifty thousand dollars on my head Hicksville, N.Y. : Exposition Press, c1976. 280 p. ; 22 cm. [HV6248.G355A35] 77-354971 ISBN 0-682-48465-2 . 7.50
1. Geraway, William R. 2. Crime and criminals—United States—Biography. 3. Mafia. I. Title.

Gerhardinger, Theresia von Jesus, 1797-1879.

MAST, Dolorita. 922.243
Through Caroline's consent; life of Mother Teresa of Jesus Gerhardinger, foundress of the School Sisters of Notre Dame, 1797-1879. Baltimore, School Sisters of Notre Dame, [c1958] 276p. illus. 24cm. [BX4705.G425M3] 59-31014
1. Gerhardinger, Theresia von Jesus, 1797-1879. I. Title.

Germaine Cousin, Saint, 1579-1601.

CANTONI, Louise Bellucci. 282'.0924 B
The girl in the stable; the life of St. Germaine. Illustrated by the Daughters of St. Paul under the direction of Guy R. Pennisi. [Boston] St. Paul Editions [1967] 55 p. illus. 22 cm. A brief biography of the young shepherd girl who, in spite of poor health and a cruel stepmother, showed great love and charity to all she met and is remembered for these qualities more than for the miracles attributed to her. [BX4700.G5C3] 92 AC 68
1. Germaine Cousin, Saint, 1579-1601. I. Title.

STAIRWAY to the stars; a story of St. Germaine Cousin. v. 12 Illustrations by Carolyn Lee Jagodits. Notre Dame, Ind., Dujarie Press [c1958] 95p. illus. 22cm.
1. Germain Counsin, Couisn, Saint, 1579-1601. I. Roberto, Brother, 1927-

Germaine Cousin, Saint, 1579-1601—Juvenile literature.

BETZ, Eva K. 920
Saint Germaine and the sheep. Illus. by Charles B. Vukovich. Paterson, N.J., St. Anthony Guild Press [c.1961] 48p. (Easy reading books of saints and friendly beasts) 61-10679 1.75 bds.,
1. Germaine Cousin, Saint, 1579-1601—Juvenile literature. I. Title.

CANTONI, Louise Bellucci. 92 (J)
The girl in the stable; the life of St. Germaine. Illustrated by the Daughters of St. Paul under the direction of Guy R. Pennisi. [Boston] St. Paul Editions [1967] 55 p. illus. 22 cm. [BX4700.G5C3] 68-20525
1. Germaine Cousin, Saint, 1579-1601—Juvenile literature. I. Title.

German Americans—Biography.

WILK, Gerard. 973'.004'31
Americans from Germany / by Gerard Wilk. New York : German Information Center, c1976. xii, 81 p. : ports. ; 22 cm. [E184.G3W46] 77-151401
1. German Americans—Biography. I. German Information Center. II. Title.

German Americans—History.

TOLZMANN, Don Heinrich, 1945- 973'.04'31
America's German heritage : Bicentennial minutes / by Don Heinrich Tolzmann. Cleveland : German-American National Congress, Chapter of Greater Cleveland, c1976. 124 p. : ill. ; 22 cm. On spine: Bicentennial minutes. Based on the radio program German-American Bicentennial minutes. Bibliography: p. 9. [E184.G3T64] 76-374910
1. German Americans—History. 2. German Americans—Biography. I. Title. II. Title: Bicentennial minutes.

German literature—20th century—Bio-bibliography.

UNGAR, Frederick, comp. 830'.9'9436
Handbook of Austrian literature. Introduced and edited by Frederick Ungar. New York, F. Ungar Pub. Co. [1973] xvi, 296 p. 24 cm. Most of the articles were originally published in Handbuch der deutschen Gegenwartsliteratur, by H. Kunisch. Includes bibliographies. [PT155.U5] 71-125969 ISBN 0-8044-2929-4 12.50
1. German literature—20th century—Bio-bibliography. 2. German literature—Austrian authors—Bio-bibliography. I. Title. BIP

Germans in Michigan.

SCHMID, Friedrich, 1807-1883. 922.473
The Schmid letters; a translation of letters written between the years 1833 and 1879 by Pastor Friedrich Schmid, pioneer German missionary, from Ann Arbor, Michigan, to his seminary in Basel, Switzerland, by Emerson E. Hutzel. [St. Louis. 1953] 87p. 5 1. illus. 28cm. [BX8080.S27A4] 53-26245
1. Germans in Michigan. 2. Lutherans in Michigan. I. Title.

Germans in the U.S.—Juvenile literature.

CUNZ, Dieter, 1910-1969. 301.45130730922
They came from Germany; the stories of famous German-Americans. New York, Dodd, Mead [1966] 178 p. illus., facsim., ports. 22 cm. Bibliography: p. 167-170. [E184.G3C85] 66-11458
1. Germans in the U.S.—Juvenile literature. I. Title.

Germany

RAEDER, Erich, 1876- 923.543
My life; translated from the German by Henry W. Drexel. Annapolis, United States Naval Institute, 1960. 430p. illus. 24cm. [DD231.R17A313] 60 9236
1. Germany—History, Naval— 20th cent. I. Title.

Germany—Court and courtiers.

WILHELM II, German Emperor, 1859-1941. 943'.08'4'0924 B
My early life. Translated from the German. New York, G. H. Doran Co. [1971] xii, 353 p. illus., facsim., ports. 23 cm. Reprint of the 1926 ed. Translation of Aus meinem Leben. [DD229.A5 1971] 71-137306 ISBN 0-404-06947-9
1. Germany—Court and courtiers. I. Title. BIP

Germany (Federal Republic, 1949-)—Biog.

HENKELS, Walter. 923.243
Zeitgenossen: funfziig Bonner Kopfe. Portratskizzen von Mirko Szewczuk. Hamburg, Rowohlt [1953] 238p. illus. 20cm. [DD259.63.H4] 56-44451
1. Germany (Federal Republic, 1949-)—Biog. I. Title.

Germany. Heer—Biography.

BRETT-SMITH, Richard, 1923- 355.3'31'0922 B
Hitler's generals / Richard Brett-Smith. San Rafael, Calif. : Presidio Press, 1978,c1976 viii, 306 p., [8] leaves of plates : ill. ; 24 cm. Includes index. Bibliography: p. 297-299. [D757.B73 1977] 77-85481 ISBN 0-89141-044-9 : 12.95
1. Germany. Heer—Biography. 2. Germany. Luftwaffe—Biography. 3. World War, 1939-1945—Germany. I. Title. BIP

BRETT-SMITH, Richard, 1923 355.3'31'0922 B
Hitler's generals / [by] Richard Brett-Smith. London : Osprey Publishing, 1976. viii, 306 p., [16] p. of plates : maps, ports. ; 24 cm. Includes index. Bibliography: p. 297-299. [D757.B73] 77-363801 ISBN 0-85045-073-X : £5.95
1. Germany. Heer—Biography. 2. Germany. Luftwaffe Biography. 3. World War, 1939-1945—Germany. 4. Generals—Germany—Biography. I. Title.

HART, W. E., pseud. 940.54'13'43 B
Hitler's generals. Plainview, N.Y., Books for Libraries Press [1974] p. cm. (Essay index reprint series) Reprint of the 1944 ed. published by Doubleday, Doran, Garden City, N.Y. [D736.H37 1974] 74-2414 ISBN 0-518-10165-7 15.00
1. Germany. Heer—Biography. 2. World War, 1939-1945—Biography. 3. Generals—Germany. I. Title.
Contents omitted. BIP

Germany—History—1789-1900.

BISMARCK, Otto, Furst von, 1815-1898. 943'.08'0924 B
Reflections and reminiscences. Edited with an introd. by Theodore S. Hamerow. New York, Harper & Row [1968] 274 p. 21 cm. (Harper torchbooks, TB 1357) (European perspectives.) Compiled from translations of the author's Gedanken und Erinnerungen. [DD218.A2 1968] 68-25436
1. Germany—History—1789-1900. 2. Germany—Politics and government—1789-1900. 3. Prussia—Politics and government—1815-1870. 4. Europe—Politics and government—1789-1900. I. Title.

Germany—History—1848-1870.

HOHENLOHE-SCHILLINGSFURST, Chlodwig Karl Viktor, Furst zu, 1819-1901. 943'.07'0924
Memoirs of Prince Chlodwig of Hohenlohe-Schillingsfuerst, authorised by Prince Alexander of Hohenlohe-Schillingsfuerst and edited by Friedrich Curtius. English ed. supervised by George W. Chrystal. New York, AMS Press [1970] 2 v. facsim., ports. 23 cm. Reprint of the 1906 ed. Translation of the author's Denkwurdigkeiten. [DD205.H7A213 1970] 75-111765 ISBN 0-404-03306-7 (v. 1)
1. Germany—History—1848-1870. 2. Germany—History—1871-1918. I. Curtius, Friedrich, 1851-1933, ed. II. Chrystal, George William, Sir, 1880-1944. III. Title. BIP

Germany. Kriegsmarine.

TIRPITZ, Alfred Peter Friedrich von, 1849-1930. 940.4'512'0924
My memoirs. New York, AMS Press [1970] 2 v. 23 cm. Reprint of the 1919 ed. [DD231.T5A5 1970] 77-111779 ISBN 0-404-06464-7
1. Germany. Kriegsmarine. 2. European War, 1914-1918—Germany. 3. European War, 1914-1918—Naval operations, German. I. Title.

Germany. Luftwaffe—Biography.

CONSTABLE, Trevor J. 940.544'9'430922
Horrido! Fighter aces of the Luftwaffe [by] Trevor J. Constable and Raymond F. Toliver. Introd. by Adolph Galland. New York, Macmillan [1968] xv, 348 p. illus., ports. 24 cm. [D787.C63] 69-10046
1. Germany. Luftwaffe—Biography. 2. World War, 1939-1945—Aerial operations, German. I. Toliver, Raymond F., joint author. II. Title. III. Title: Fighter aces of the Luftwaffe.

TOLIVER, Raymond F. 940.54'49'430922
Fighter aces of the Luftwaffe / Raymond F. Toliver and Trevor J. Constable ; introd. by Adolph Galland. Fallbrook, Calif. : Aero Publishers, c1977. 432 p. : ill. ; 29 cm. First ed. published in 1968 under title: Horrido! Fighter aces of the Luftwaffe. Includes index. [D787.C63 1977] 77-79516 ISBN 0-8168-5790-3 : 17.95
1. Germany. Luftwaffe—Biography. 2. World War, 1939-1945—Aerial operations, German. 3. World War, 1939-1945—Biography. I. Constable, Trevor J., joint author. II. Title.

Germany. Luftwaffe—History.

SUCHENWIRTH, Richard, 1896- 358.4'00943
Command and leadership in the German Air Force. Edited by Harry R. Fletcher, with an introd. by Telford Taylor. [Maxwell Air Force Base, Ala.] USAF Historical Division, Aerospace Studies Institute, Air University, 1969. New York, Arno Press [1970] xix, 351 p. illus., ports. 29 cm. (USAF historical studies, no. 174) Includes bibliographical references. [UG633.A37784 no. 174 1970] 71-111598
1. Germany. Luftwaffe—History. 2. Germany. Luftwaffe—Biography. I. Title. II. Series. BIP

Germany—Politics and government—1871-1918.

BULOW, Bernhard Heinrich Martin Karl, Furst von, 1849-1929. 943.08'4'0924 B
Memoirs of Prince von Bulow. [Translated from the German by F. A. Voigt] New York, AMS Press [1972] 4 v. illus. 24 cm. Translation of Denkwurdigkeiten. Reprint of the 1931-32 ed. Contents.Contents.—v. 1. From Secretary of State to Imperial Chancellor, 1897-1903.—v. 2. From the Morocco crisis to resignation, 1903-1909.—v. 3. The World War and Germany's collapse, 1909-1919.—v. 4. Early years and diplomatic service, 1849-1897. [DD231.B8A17 1972] 77-127900 ISBN 0-404-01230-2 80.00
1. Germany—Politics and government—1871-1918. 2. Germany—Foreign relations—1871-1918.

Germany—Politics and government—1918-1933.

KLOTZ, Helmut, ed. 943.085
The Berlin diaries, May 30, 1932-January 30, 1933. Edited by Helmut Klotz. With a foreword by Edgar Ansel Mowrer. New York, Morrow, 1934. [New York, AMS Press, 1972] 303 p. 23 cm. "This volume purports to be the true story of the betrayal of the German Republic by its chosen leaders. In the form of a personal diary that conceals a compilation, the supposed author reveals how the German democracy was done to death by a group of 'gentlemen' ... The writers ... are clearly insiders." Translation of Von Weimer, uber Potsdam, nach ... [DD251.K45 1972] 70-180408 ISBN 0-404-56132-2 16.00
1. Germany—Politics and government—1918-1933. I. Title.

Germany—Politics and government—1933-1945.

HITLER, Adolf, 1889-1945. 943.086'092'4 B
Secret conversations, 1941-1944. [Translated by Norman Cameron and R. H. Stevens] With an introductory essay on The mind of Adolf Hitler, by H. R. Trevor-Roper. New York, Octagon Books, 1972 [c1953] xxx, 597 p. 23 cm. "The original Bormann-Vermerke ... translated in full." [DD247.H5A685 1972] 72-9820 ISBN 0-374-93919-5 19.00
1. Germany—Politics and government—1933-1945. 2. National socialism. 3. World War, 1939-1945—Germany. I. Trevor-Roper, Hugh Redwald. II. Title.

RECK-MALLECZEWEN, Fritz Percy, 1884-1945. 943.086'0924
Diary of a man in despair [by] Friedrich Percyval Reck-Malleczewen. Translated by Paul Rubens. [1st American ed. New York] Macmillan [1970] 219 p. 21 cm. Translation of Tagebuch eines Verzweifelten. Includes bibliographical references. [DD256.5.R3813 1970] 74-85783
1. Germany—Politics and government—1933-1945. 2. World War, 1939-1945—Germany. I. Title. BIP

Germany—Politics and government—20th century.

BRECHT, Arnold, 1884- 320.9'43 B
The political education of Arnold Brecht; an autobiography, 1884-1970. Princeton, N.J., Princeton University Press, 1970. xvii, 544 p. 24 cm. Abridged version of the author's autobiography originally issued in German in 1966-67 in two volumes: Aus nachster Nahe and Mit der Kraft des Geistes. Includes bibliographical references. [DD247.B67A33] 77-100994 15.00
1. Germany—Politics and government—20th century. I. Brecht, Arnold, 1884- Aus nachster Nahe. English. 1970. II. Brecht, Arnold, 1884- Mit der Kraft des Geistes. English. 1970. III. Title.

Geronimo, Apache chief, 1829-1909.

ADAMS, Alexander B. 970.3 B
Geronimo; a biography [by] Alexander B. Adams. New York, Putnam [1971] 381 p. illus. 22 cm. Bibliography: p. 367-372. [E99.A6G14 1971] 77-163402 8.95
1. Geronimo, Apache chief, 1829-1909. 2. Apache Indians—History.

CLUM, Woodworth. 970'.004'97
Apache agent : the story of John P. Clum / by Woodworth Clum. Lincoln : University of Nebraska Press, 1978, c1936. xiv, 296 p., [8] leaves o fplates : ports. ; 21 cm. "A Bison book." Reprint of the ed. published by Houghton Mifflin, New York. Includes index. [E99.A6C52 1978] 77-14135 ISBN 0-8032-0967-3 : 13.95 ISBN 0-8032-5886-0 pbk. : 4.95
1. Clum, John Philip, 1851-1932. 2. Geronimo, Apache chief, 1829-1909. 3. United States. Bureau of Indian Affairs—Officials and employees—Biography. 4. Apache Indians. 5. Apache Indians—Government relations. 6. San Carlos Indian Reservation, Arizona. I. Title. BIP

DAVIS, Britton, 1860- v. 12
The truth about Geronimo. Edited by M. M. Quaife, with a foreword by Robert M. Utley. New Haven, Yale University Press [1963, c1929] xxix, 253 p. illus., ports., maps. 20 cm. (Yale Western Americana paperbound, YW-7) 64-37845
1. Geronimo, Apache chief, 1829-1909. 2. Indians — North America — Wars — 1883-1886. I. Quaife, Milo Milton, 1880- ed. II. Title.

DAVIS, Britton, 1860- 970'.004'97 B
The truth about Geronimo / by Britton Davis ; edited by M. M. Quaife ; with a foreword by Robert M. Utley. Lincoln : University of Nebraska Press, [1976] c1929. xxix, 253 p., [6] leaves of plates : ill. ; 21 cm. "A Bison book." Reprint of the ed. published by Yale University Press, New Haven. Includes bibliographical references and index. [E99.A6G323 1976] 75-37958 ISBN 0-8032-0877-4. pbk. : 3.75
1. Geronimo, Apache chief, 1829-1909. 2. Apache Indians—Wars, 1883-1886. I. Title. BIP

DEBO, Angie, 1890- 970'.004'97 B
Geronimo : the man, his time, his place / by Angie Debo. 1st ed. Norman : University of Oklahoma Press, [1976], c1975. p. cm. (Civilization of the American Indian series) Bibliography: [E99.A6G324 1976] 76-13858 ISBN 0-8061-1333-2 : 14.95
1. Geronimo, Apache chief, 1829-1909. I. Title. II. Series. BIP

GERONIMO, Apache Chief, 1829-1909. 973.8'0924 B
Geronimo: his own story. Edited by S. M. Barrett. Newly edited with an introd. and notes by Frederick W. Turner, III. New York, Dutton, 1970. 190, [1] p. illus., map, ports. 25 cm. First published in 1906 under title: Geronimo's story of his life. Bibliography: p. [191] [E99.A6G3 1970] 72-113457 ISBN 5-251-13088- 6.95
1. Apache Indians. I. Barrett, Stephen Melvil, 1865- ed. II. Turner, Frederick W., 1937- ed. III. Title.

KJELGAARD, James Arthur, 1910-1959. 970.3 B
The story of Geronimo. Illustrated by Charles Banks Wilson. New York, Grosset & Dunlap [1958] 179 p. illus. 22 cm. (Signature books, 44) A biography of Geronimo, chief of the southern Chiricahua band of Apache Indians, who rose to leadership through the ranks and [who] plundered the Arizona countryside for many years before accepting the white man's treaty. [PZ7.K675St] 92 AC 68
1. Geronimo, Apache chief, 1829-1909. I. Wilson, Charles Banks, illus. II. Title.

MOODY, Ralph, 1898- 970.2
Geronimo, wolf of the warpath. Illustrated by Nicholas Eggenhofer. New York, Random House [1958] 186 p. illus. 22 cm. (Landmark books [81]) [E99.A6M6] 58-6180
1. Geronimo, Apache Chief, 1829-1909.

WYATT, Edgar. *970.1
Geronimo, the last Apache war chief; illustrated by Allan Houser, direct descendant of Geronimo. New York, Whittlesey House [1952] 188 p. illus. 21 cm. [E99.A6W9] W 970.2 51-13610
1. Geronimo, Apache chief, 1829-1909. 2. Apache Indians — Wars, 1883-1886. I. Title.

Geronimo, Apache chief, 1829-1909.—Juvenile literature.

GRANT, Matthew G. 970.3 B
Geronimo, Apache warrior [by] Matthew G. Grant. Illustrated by John Keely and Dick Brude. [Mankato, Minn., Creative Education; distributed by Childrens Press, Chicago, 1973, c1974] 28 p. illus. (part col.) 25 cm. (His Gallery of great Americans series. Indians of America) A brief biography of the last of the Apache war chiefs to be subdued by the United States Army. [E99.A6G72] 92 73-12203 ISBN 0-87191-267-8 3.95
1. Geronimo, Apache chief, 1829-1909—Juvenile literature. I. Keely, John, illus. II. Brude, Dick, illus. III. Title.

SYME, Ronald, 1910- 970.3 B
Geronimo, the fighting Apache. Illustrated by Ben F. Stahl. New York, Morrow, 1975. 95 p. illus. 22 cm. Bibliography: p. 95. A biography of the Apache chief who rose to leadership through the ranks and led one of the last great Indian uprisings in the nineteenth century. [E99.A6S95] 92 74-16337 ISBN 0-688-22013-4 4.50
1. Geronimo, Apache chief, 1829-1909—Juvenile literature. I. Stahl, Ben F., illus. II. Title.
Lib. bdg. 4.14, ISBN 0-688-32013-9.

WILSON, Charles Morrow, 1905- 970.3 B
Geronimo. Minneapolis, Dillon Press [1973] 74 p. illus. 23 cm. (The Story of an American Indian) A biography of Apache Indian chief Geronimo, who rose to leadership through the ranks and led one of the last great Indian uprisings. [E99.A6G328] 92 73-9513 ISBN 0-87518-059-0 4.95
1. Geronimo, Apache chief, 1829-1909.—Juvenile literature. BIP

Gerry, Elbridge, 1744-1814.

AUSTIN, James Trecothick, 1784-1870. 973.3'0924
The life of Elbridge Gerry, with contemporary letters to the close of the American Revolution. New York, Da Capo Press, 1970. 2 v. facsim., port. 24 cm. Reprint of the 1828-29 ed. Includes bibliographical references. [E302.6.G37A92] 77-99470 ISBN 3-06-718413-
1. Gerry, Elbridge, 1744-1814. I. Title.

BILLIAS, George Athan, 1919- 973.3'092'4 B
Elbridge Gerry, founding father and republican statesman / by George Athan Billias. New York : McGraw-Hill, c1976. xviii, 442 p., [3] leaves of plates : ill. ; 24 cm. Includes index. Bibliography: p. 431-433. [E302.6.G37B54] 76-13481 ISBN 0-07-005269-7 : 20.00
1. Gerry, Elbridge, 1744-1814. I. Title.

Gershwin, George, 1898-1937.

ALTMAN, Frances. 780'.924 B
George Gershwin, master composer. Minneapolis, T. S. Denison [1968] 235 p. 22 cm. (Men of Achievement series) Bibliography: p. 233-235. A biography of the son of New York ghetto immigrants, who blended the sounds and moods of America into popular songs, musical comedies, folk opera, and serious compositions. [ML410.G288A4] 92 AC 68
1. Gershwin, George, 1898-1937. I. Title.

ARMITAGE, Merle, 1893- 927.8
George Gershwin, man and legend. With a note on the author by John Charles Thomas. [1st ed.] New York, Duell, Sloan and Pearce [1958] 188p. illus., facsims., music. 21cm. Bibliography: p. 179. George Gerahwin's works: p. 181-185. 'A Gershwin discography': p. 186-188. [ML410.G288A76] 58-12265
1. Gershwin, George, 1898-1937. I. Title.

EWEN, David, 1907- 780'.92'4 B
George Gershwin : his journey to greatness / by David Ewen. Westport, Conn. : Greenwood Press, 1977. p. cm. "Completely rewritten edition" of the author's A journey to greatness, 1956. Reprint of the 1970 ed. published by Prentice-Hall, Englewood Cliffs, N.J. Includes index. [ML410.G288E87 1977] 77-6821 ISBN 0-8371-9663-9 lib.bdg. : 19.75
1. Gershwin, George, 1898-1937. 2. Composers—United States—Biography. BIP

EWEN, David, 1907- 780'.92'4 B
George Gershwin, his journey to greatness. Englewood Cliffs, N.J., Prentice-Hall [1970] xxx, 354 p. illus., facsims., ports. 24 cm. "Completely rewritten edition" of the author's A journey to greatness, 1956. [ML410.G288E87 1970] 77-107605 7.95
1. Gershwin, George, 1898-1937.

EWEN, David, 1907- 927.8
A journey to greatness; the life and music

of George Gershwin.Illustrated with photos. [1st ed.] New York, Holt [c1956] 384p. illus., ports., facsims. (music) 22cm. Lists of the composer's works: p.330-355. Discography: p.356-362. Bibliography: p. 363-368. [ML410.G288E9] 56-6192
1. Gershwin, George, 1898-1937. 2. Gershwin, George, 1898-1937—Discography. I. Title.

JABLONSKI, Edward. 927.8
George Gershwin. With an introd. by Harold Arlen. New York, Putnam [1962] 190 p. 21 cm. (Lives to remember) Bibliography: p. 179-180. [ML410.G288J28] 62-10973
1. Gershwin, George, 1898-1937.

JABLONSKI, Edward. 780'.924 B
George Gershwin. With an introd. by Harold Arlen. New York, Putnam [1962] 190 p. 21 cm. (Lives to remember) Discography: p. 161-177. A biography of a successful song writer, from the early influence of his boyhood friend, a violin prodigy, to his untimely death at age thirty-nine. [ML410.G288J28] 92 AC 68
1. Gershwin, George, 1898-1937. I. Title.

JABLONSKI, Edward. 927.8
The Gershwin years, by Edward Jablonski and Lawrence D. Stewart. With an introd. by Carl Van Vechten. [1st ed.] Garden City, N. Y., Doubleday, 1958. 313 p. illus., ports., facsims., music. 27 cm. "The works of George and Ira Gershwin": p. 285-302. [ML410.G288J3] 58-11317
1. Gershwin, George, 1898-1937. 2. Gershwin, Ira, 1896- I. Stewart, Lawrence Delbert, 1926- joint author. II. Title. **BIP**

JABLONSKI, Edward. 782.8'1'0922 B
The Gershwin years, by Edward Jablonski and Lawrence D. Stewart. With an introd. by Carl Van Vechten. [2d ed.] Garden City, N.Y., Doubleday, 1973. 416 p. illus. 27 cm. Discography: p. 359-387. [ML410.G288J3 1973] 73-78334 ISBN 0-385-02847-4 12.95
1. Gershwin, George, 1898-1937. 2. Gershwin, Ira, 1896- I. Stewart, Lawrence Delbert, 1926- joint author. II. Title.

PAYNE, Pierre Stephen Robert, 927.8
Gershwin. New York, Pyramid Books [c.1960] 157p. illus. 18cm. (Pyramid books, R500) 60-2588 .50 pap.,
1. Gershwin, George, 1898-1937. I. Title.

PAYNE, Pierre Stephen Robert, 1911- 927.8
Gershwin. New York, Pyramid Books [1960] 157p. illus. 18cm. (Pyramid books, R500) [ML410.G288P4] 60-2588
1. Gershwin, George, 1898-1937. I. Title.

RUSHMORE, Robert. 780.924
The life of George Gershwin. New York, Crowell-Collier Press [1966] 177 p. illus., facsims., ports 22 cm. (America in the making) [ML410.G288R9] 66-7516
1. Gershwin, George, 1898-1937. **BIP**

SCHWARTZ, Charles. 780'.92'4 B
Gershwin, his life and music / by Charles Schwartz. New York : Da Capo Press, 1979, c1973. p. cm. (A Da Capo paperback) Reprint of the ed. published by Bobbs-Merrill, Indianapolis. "Compositions by George Gershwin": p. [ML410.G288S33 1979] 78-20838 ISBN 0-306-80096-9 pbk. : 7.95
1. Gershwin, George, 1898-1937. 2. Composers—United States—Biography. **BIP**

Gershwin, George, 1898-1937—Juvenile fiction.

BRYANT, Bernice Morgan, 1908- JUV
George Gershwin, young composer, by Bernice Bryant. Illus. by Nathan Goldstein. Indianapolis, Bobbs [c.1965] 200p. col. illus. 20cm. (Childhood of famous Amers.) Bibl. [PZ7.B834Ge] 780.92 65-23666 2.25
1. Gershwin, George, 1898-1937—Juvenile fiction. I. Title.

Gerstein, Kurt, 1905-1945.

JOFFROY, Pierre. 940.548'2'43
A spy for God; the ordeal of Kurt Gerstein. Translated by Norman Denny. [1st American ed.] New York, Harcourt Brace Jovanovich [1971, c1970] 319 p. 22 cm. "A Helen and Kurt Wolff book." Translation of L'espion de Dieu. Bibliography: p. 309-312. [DD247.G39J613 1971] 73-142089 ISBN 0-15-184800-9
1. Gerstein, Kurt, 1905-1945. I. Title.

Gertler, Mark, 1891-1939.

WOODESON, John. 759.2
Mark Gertler; biography of a painter, 1891-1939. [Toronto, Buffalo] University of Toronto Press [1973] xii, 413 p. illus. (part col.) 24 cm. Includes bibliographical references. [ND497.G47W66 1973] 73-79294 ISBN 0-8020-2060-7 15.00
1. Gertler, Mark, 1891-1939.

Gertrude, Saint, surnamed the Great, 1256-1302.

MARY, Jeremy, Sister, 1907 922.143
Scholars and mystics. Chicago, Regnery [c.]1962 213p. 22 cm. 62-15229 4.50
1. Gertrude, Saint, surnamed the Great, 1256-1302? I. Title.

MARY Jeremy, Sister, 1907- 922.143
Scholars and mystics. Chicago, H. Regnery Co., 1962. 213p. 22cm. [BX4700.G6M3] 62-15229
1. Gertrude, Saint, surnamed the Great, 1256-1302. I. Title.

Gertz, Elmer, 1906-

MILLER, Henry, 1891- 818'.5'209 B
Henry Miller : years of trail & triumph, 1962-1964 : the correspondence of Henry Miller and Elmer Gertz / edited by Elmer Gertz and Felice Flanery Lewis. Carbondale : Southern Illinois University Press, c1978. xxiii, 345 p., [8] leavesof plate : ill ; 25 cm. Includes bibliographical references and index. [PS3525.I5454Z552] 78-3547 ISBN 0-8093-0860-6 : 17.50
1. Miller, Henry, 1891- —Correspondence. 2. Gertz, Elmer, 1906- 3. Miller, Henry, 1891- Tropic of Cancer. 4. Authors, American—20th century—Correspondence. 5. Lawyers—United States—Correspondence. 6. Censorship—United States. I. Gertz, Elmer, 1906- joint author. II. Lewis, Felice Flanery.

Gervasutti, Giusto, 1909-1946.

GERVASUTTI, Giusto, 1909-1946. 796.5'22'0924 B
Gervasutti's climbs / Giusto Gervasutti ; translated by Nea Morin and Janet Adam Smith. Seattle : The Mountaineers, c1979. 201 p., [9] leaves of plates : ill. ; 22 cm. Translation of Scalate nelle Alpi. Reprint of the 1957 ed. published by Hart-Davis, London. [GV199.92.G47A3313 1979] 78-70839 ISBN 0-916890-67-8 pbk. : 6.95
1. Gervasutti, Giusto, 1909-1946. 2. Mountaineers—Italy—Biography. 3. Mountaineering—Alps. 4. Alps—Description and travel. I. Title. **BIP**

Gessner, Salomon, 1730-1788—Criticism and interpretation.

HIBBERD, John. 831'.6 B
Salomon Gessner : his creative achievement and influence / John Hibberd. Cambridge [Eng.] ; New York : Cambridge University Press, 1976. vii, 183 p., [4] leaves of plates : ill. ; 23 cm. (Anglica Germanica : Series 2) Includes index. Bibliography: p. 171-180. [PT1886.Z84] 76-7139 ISBN 0-521-21234-0 : 14.95
1. Gessner, Salomon, 1730-1788—Criticism and interpretation. I. Title. II. Series.

Gesualdo, Carlo, principe di Venosa, 1560 (ca.)-1613.

GRAY, Cecil, 1895-1951. 784'.0924 B
Carlo Gesualdo, Prince of Venosa, musician and murderer, by Cecil Gray and Philip Heseltine. Westport, Conn., Greenwood Press [1971] xiv, 145 p. music, 8 plates. 23 cm. Reprint of the 1926 ed. Contents.Contents.—The life of Carlo Gesualdo, by C. Gray.—Carlo Gesualdo considered as a murderer, by C. Gray.—Gesualdo the musician, by P. Heseltine. Includes bibliographies. [ML410.G29G71 1971] 76-104268 ISBN 0-8371-3934-1
1. Gesualdo, Carlo, principe di Venosa, 1560 (ca.)-1613. I. Heseltine, Philip, 1894-1930. **BIP**

WATKINS, Glenn Elson, 1927- 784'.092'4 B
Gesualdo, the man and his music [by] Glenn Watkins. Pref. by Igor Stravinsky. Chapel Hill, University of North Carolina Press [1974, c1973] xxiv, 334 p. illus. 25 cm. Bibliography: p. [311]-321. [ML410.G29W4] 72-78154 ISBN 0-8078-1201-3 17.50
1. Gesualdo, Carlo, principe di Venosa, 1560 (ca.)-1613. **BIP**

Getty, Jean Paul, 1892-1976.

GETTY, Jean Paul, 1892-1976. 332'.092'4 B
As I see it : the autobiography of J. Paul Getty. Englewood Cliffs, N.J. : Prentice-Hall, c1976. 360 p., [16] leaves of plates : ill. ; 24 cm. [HD9570.G4A26 1976] 76-22639 ISBN 0-13-049593-X : 10.95
1. Getty, Jean Paul, 1892-1976. I. Title.

GETTY, Jean Paul, 1892-1976. 332'.092'4 B
As I see it : the autobiography of J. Paul Getty. London : W. H. Allen, 1976. 361 p., [16] leaves of plates : ill. ; 24 cm. Includes index. [HD9570.G4A26 1976b] 76-376029 ISBN 0-491-01756-1 : £6.00
1. Getty, Jean Paul, 1892-1976. 2. Businessmen—Biography. I. Title.

HEWINS, Ralph. 923.373
The richest American: J. Paul Getty. [1st ed.] New York, Dutton, 1960. 404 p. illus. 22 cm. [HD9569.T55H4] 60-5064
1. Getty, Jean Paul, 1892- I. Title.

Geyer, M. E. (Buchholtz)

GEYER, M. E. (Buchholtz) 914.38'03'40924
The way it was over there, by M. E. Geyer. Philadelphia, Dorrance [1969] 86 p. 22 cm. Autobiographical. [CT1232.G44A3] 69-19898 3.95
I. Title.

Ghana—Hist.

THE autobiography of Kwame Nkrumah. Edinburgh, T. Nelson, 1957 310p. illus. v. 12
1. Ghana—Hist. I. Nkrumah, Kwame, 1909-

Ghana—Politics and government—To 1957.

NKRUMAH, Kwame, Pres. Ghana, 1909- 966.7'05'0924 B
Ghana; the autobiography of Kwame Nkrumah. New York, International Publishers [1971, c1957] xiii, 310 p. maps, port. 21 cm. [DT510.6.N5A33 1971] 70-148514 ISBN 0-7178-0293-0 7.50
1. Ghana—Politics and government—To 1957. **BIP**

Gharibadasa, 1717-1782?

GUPTA, K. C., 1924- 891'.43'13
Sri Garib Das, Haryana's saint of humanity / K. C. Gupta. New Delhi : Impex India, c1976. xx, 216 p. ; 22 cm. Includes index. Bibliography: p. [210]-213. [PK2096.G5Z68] 76-905419 Rs40.00 ($8.00 U.S.)
1. Gharibadasa, 1717-1782? 2. Poets, Hindi—18th century—Biography. 3. Mystics—India—Biography. I. Title.

Ghika, Marie Chassaigne, princesse, 1869-1950.

GHIKA, Marie Chassaigne, princesse, 1869-1950. 944.08'092'4 B
My blue notebooks / Liane de Pougy [i.e. M. C. Ghika] ; pref. by R. P. Rzewuski ; translated by Diana Athill. New York : Harper & Row, c1979. p. cm. Translation of Mes cahiers bleus. Includes index. [CT1018.G48A3513 1979] 79-1659 ISBN 0-06-011083-X : 15.00
1. Ghika, Marie Chassaigne, princesse, 1869-1950. 2. France—Prices and princesses—Biography. I. Title.

Ghilberti, Lorenzo, 1378-1455.

LORENZO Ghiberti, 734.45
by Richard Krautheimer in collaboration with Trude Krautheimer-Hess. Princeton, Princeton University Press, 1956. viii, 457p. illus., plates. 31cm. (Princeton monographs in art and archaeology, 31) 'Sources [documents]': p. 359-421. Bibliography: p. 425-438. [NB623.G45K7] 927.3 56-8383
1. Ghilberti, Lorenzo, 1378-1455. I. Krautheimer, Richard, 1897- II. Series.

Ghormley, James Grant, 1925-1967.

GHORMLEY, Ruby Pearl (Foreman) 1901- 686.2'092'4 B
Ghormley and offset; a biography, by Pearl Ghormley. [Austin, Tex., Rupegy Pub. Co., 1972] xvi, 222 p. illus. 24 cm. [Z249.G47] 73-178281 6.95
1. Ghormley, James Grant, 1925-1967. I. Title.

Ghose, Aurobindo, 1872-1950.

FEYS, Jan, 1933- 181'.45 B
The life of a yogi / J. Feys. Calcutta : Firma KLM, 1976. 54 p., [1] leaf of plates : ill. ; 22 cm. Includes bibliographical references. [B5134.G42F47] 76-903907 ISBN 0-88386-863-6 : 5.50
1. Ghose, Aurobindo, 1872-1950. 2. Philosophers—India—Biography. I. Title. Distributed by South Asia Books **BIP**

GOKAK, Vinayak Krishna. 181'.45
Sri Aurobindo, seer and poet. New Delhi, Abhinav Publications, 1973. 183 p. 22 cm. [PR9480.9.G4Z67] 73-900907
1. Ghose, Aurobindo, 1872-1950. I. Title. Available from International Publications Service, New York, for 9.50. **BIP**

SATPREM, 1923- 181'.45 B
Sri Aurobindo : or, The adventure of consciousness / Satprem ; translated from the French by Tehmi. 1st U.S. ed. New York : Harper & Row, [1974], c1968 381 p. : ill., ports. ; 21 cm. "A Lindisfarne book." Bibliography: p. 377-381. [BL1270.G4S248 1968] 74-6770 ISBN 0-06-013772-X : 7.95 ISBN 0-06-013773-8 pbk : 3.95
1. Ghose, Aurobindo, 1872-1950. I. Title: The adventure of consciousness.

Ghose, Aurobindo, 1872-1950—Addresses, essays, lectures.

GANDHI, Kishor, comp. 181'.45 B
Contemporary relevance of Sri Aurobindo. Edited by Kishore Gandhi. Delhi, Vivek Pub. House [1973] xx, 343 p. 22 cm. Bibliography: p. [328]-336. [B5134.G42G36] 73-900086
1. Ghose, Aurobindo, 1872-1950—Addresses, essays, lectures. I. Title. Distributed by Humanities Press, New York, 10.00.

Ghose, Surendra Mohan, 1893-

BHATTACHARJEE, Adhir. 954.03'5'0924 B
Great revolutionary leader Surendra Mohan Ghose / by Adhir Bhattacharjee. Calcutta : Surendra Mohan Ghose Birthday Celebrations Committee, 1976. iii, 64 p., [2] leaves of plates : ports. ; 23 cm. [DS481.G413B45] 76-902975 Rs5.00
1. Ghose, Surendra Mohan, 1893- 2. Statesmen—India—Biography. 3. India—Politics and government—1919-1947. I. Title.

Giacometti, Alberto, 1901-1966.

GIACOMETTI, Alberto, 1901-1966. 730'.92'4
Alberto Giacometti. [New York] Praeger in association with the Solomon R. Guggenheim Museum [1974] p. cm.

Catalog of a retrospective exhibition held at the Solomon R. Guggenheim Museum. Includes bibliographical references. [NB553.G4S64] 74-77334 25.00
1. Giacometti, Alberto, 1901-1966. I. Solomon R. Guggenheim Museum, New York.

HOHL, Reinhold. 730'.92'4 B
Alberto Giacometti. New York, H. N. Abrams [1972, c1971] 328 p. illus. (part col.) 31 cm. Translated from German. Bibliography: p. 311-324. [NB553.G4H613] 70-160216 ISBN 0-8109-0139-0 30.00
1. Giacometti, Alberto, 1901-1966.

NEW YORK. MUSEUM OF MODERN ART. 927
Alberto Giacometti. Introd. by Peter Selz and an autobiographical statement by the artist [Catalog] Mus. of Mod. Art, New York in collaboration with the Art Inst. of Chicago [others] Dist. Garden City, N.Y., Doubleday [c.1965] 119p. illus. (pt. col.) facsims., port. 27cm. Catalog of a comprehensive exhibition of Giacometti's work org. by the Mus. of Mod. Art, N.Y. in 1965. Bibl. [N7153.G47N4] 65-23847 7.95; 3.75 pap.,
1. Giacometti, Alberto, 1901- I. Selz, Peter. II. Title.

Giacomin, Eddie.

DELANO, Hugh. 796.9'62'0924 B
Eddie / Hugh Delano. 1st ed. New York : Atheneum, 1976. xviii, 320 p. : ill. ; 22 cm. A biography of hockey player Eddie Giacomin, all-star goalie of the New York Rangers. [GV848.5.G52D44] 92 75-38345 ISBN 0-689-10715-3 : 8.95
1. Giacomin, Eddie. 2. Hockey. I. Title.

DELANO, Hugh. 796.9'62'0924 B
Eddie / Hugh Delano. 1st ed. New York : Atheneum, 1976. p. cm. A biography of hockey player Eddie Giacomin, all-star goalie of the New York Rangers. [GV848.5.G52D44] 92 75-43599 ISBN 0-689-10715-3 : 7.95
1. Giacomin, Eddie. 2. Hockey. I. Title. BIP

Gian Galeazzo Visconti, duke of Milan, 1351-1402.

CHAMBERLIN, Eric Russell. 945.050924 B
The count of virtue; Giangaleazzo Visconti, duke of Milan, by E. R. Chamberlin. New York, Scribner [1966, c1965] 244 p. illus., map (on lining papers) ports. 22 cm. Bibliography: p. 233-236. [DG657.7.C45 1966] 66-15977
1. Gian Galeazzo Visconti, duke of Milan, 1351-1402. I. Title.

Giancana, Sam, 1908-1975.

BRASHLER, William. 364.1'092'4 B
The don : the life and death of Sam Giancana / William Brashler. 1st ed. New York : Harper & Row, c1977. ix, 341 p., [3] leaves of plates : ill. ; 22 cm. [HV6248.G38B72 1977] 76-5113 ISBN 0-06-010447-3 : 10.95
1. Giancana, Sam, 1908-1975. 2. Crime and criminals—United States—Biography. 3. Mafia. I. Title.

BRASHLER, William. 364.1'092'4
The don : the life and death of Sam Giancana / William Brashler. 1st ed. New York : Ballantine Books, 1978,c1977. 371p. : ill. ; 18 cm. [HV6248.G38B72 1977] ISBN 0-345-27326-5 pbk. : 1.95
1. Giancana, Sam, 1908-1975. 2. Crime and criminals — United States — Biography. 3. Mafia. I. Title.
L.C. card no. for 1977 Harper & Row ed.: 76-5113. BIP

Gianci, Carlo, 1881-1968.

LO Gatto-Perry, Joseph J. T. 282'.0924 B
An Italian pioneer in America [by Joseph J. T. Lo Gatto-Perry. Netcong, N.J., 1969] 110 p. illus. 23 cm. [BX4705.G484L6] 75-81350
1. Gianci, Carlo, 1881-1968. I. Title.

Giannini, Amadeo Peter, 1870-1949.

RINK, Paul, 1912- 923.373
Building the Bank of America: A. P. Giannini. Illus. by Robert Boehmer. Chicago, Encyclopaedia Britannica [c.1963] 192p. illus. 22cm. (Britannica bkshelf.: Great lives) 63-13514 2.95; 2.36 lib. ed.,
1. Giannini, Amadeo Peter, 1870-1949. 2. Bank of America National Trust and Savings Association. I. Title.

RINK, Paul, 1912- 923.373
Building the Bank of America: A. P. Giannini. Illustrated by Robert Boehmer. Chicago, Encyclopedia Britannica Press [1963] 192 p. illus. 22 cm. (Britannica bookshelf: Great lives) [HG2613.S54B277] 63-13514
1. Giannini, Amadeo Peter, 1870-1949. 2. Bank of America National Trust and Savings Association. I. Title.

Gibault, Pierre, 1737-1804.

DISPENZA, Joseph 253.0924
Forgotten patriot; a story of Father Pierre Gibault, by Brother Joseph Dispenza. Decorations by Carolyn Lee Jagodits. Notre Dame, Ind., Dujarie [1966] 95p. illus. 24cm. [BX4705.G49D5] 66-22270 2.25
1. Gibault, Pierre. 1737-1804. I. Title.

DONNELLY, Joseph P. 973.33'4'0924 B
Pierre Gibault, missionary, 1737-1802 [by] Joseph P. Donnelly. Chicago, Loyola University Press [1971] viii, 199 p. 24 cm. Bibliography: p. 181-193. [F597.G42D6] 77-156371 ISBN 0-8294-0203-9 8.00
1. Gibault, Pierre, 1737-1804. 2. Northwest, Old—History. I. Title. BIP

Gibbon, Edward, 1737-1794.

BLUNDEN, Edmund Charles, 1896- 937'.06'072024 B
Edward Gibbon and his age [by] Edmund Blunden. [Folcroft, Pa.] Folcroft Library Editions, 1974. p. cm. Reprint of the 1935 ed. printed for the University of Bristol by J. W. Arrowsmith, Bristol, which was issued as the 1935 Arthur Skemp memorial lecture. [DG206.G574b] 74-14702 ISBN 0-8414-3287-2 (lib. bdg.)
1. Gibbon, Edward, 1737-1794. I. Title. II. Series: Arthur Skemp memorial lecture, 1935.

BLUNDEN, Edmund Charles, 1896-1974. 937'.06'0924
Edward Gibbon and his age / Edmund Blunden. Norwood, Pa. : Norwood Editions, 1976. p. cm. Reprint of the 1935 ed. printed for the University of Bristol by J. W. Arrowsmith, Bristol, which was issued as the 1935 Arthur Skemp memorial lecture. [DG206.G5B6 1976] 76-15391 ISBN 0-8482-0161-2 lib. bdg. : 6.50
1. Gibbon, Edward, 1737-1794. I. Title. II. Series: Arthur Skemp memorial lecture ; 1935. BIP

DEBEER, Gavin Rylands, Sir 1899- 828.6
Gibbon and his world, by Sir Gavin DeBeer. New York, Viking [1968] 144p. illus., map, ports. 24cm. (Studio bk.) Bibl. [PR3476.D4 1968] 68-31922 6.95
1. Gibbon, Edward, 1737-1794. I. Title.
Published in Britain by Thames & Hudson.

DEBEER, Gavin Rylands, Sir, 1899- 907'.2'022
Gibbon and his world, by Sir Gavin DeBeer. New York, Viking Press [1968] 144 p. illus., map, ports. 24 cm. (A Studio book) Includes bibliographical references. [PR3476.D4 1968] 68-31922
1. Gibbon, Edward, 1737-1794. I. Title.

GAY, Peter, 1923- 907'.2'022
Style in history. New York, Basic Books [1974] xiii, 242 p. illus. 22 cm. Bibliography: p. 219-238. [D14.G39] 73-91076 ISBN 0-465-08304-8 8.95
1. Gibbon, Edward, 1737-1794. 2. Ranke, Leopold von, 1795-1886. 3. Macaulay, Thomas Babington Macaulay, Baron, 1800-1859. 4. Burckhardt, Jakob Christoph, 1818-1897. 5. Historiography. I. Title. BIP

GIBBON, Edward, 1737-1794. 928.2
Autobiography. Ed., introduced by Dero A. Saunders. [New, rev. ed.] New York, Meridian Books [c.1961] 224p. illus. (M111) 59-12140 1.35 pap.,
I. Title.

GIBBON, Edward, 1737-1794. 928.2
Autobiography, as originally edited by Lord Sheffield. With an introd. by J. B. Bury. London, Oxford University Press [1959] 339 p. 16 cm. (The World's classics, 139) [[PR3476]] A 63
I. Title.

GIBBON, Edward, 1737-1794. 928.2
Autobiography, as originally edited by Lord Sheffield. With an introd. by J. B. Bury. London, Oxford University Press [1959] 339 p. 16 cm. (The World's classics, 139) [[PR3476]] A 63
I. Title.

GIBBON, Edward, 1737-1794. v. 12
The autobiography of Edward Gibbon. Edited by Bernard Groom. London, Macmillan; New York, St. Martin's press, 1956. xii, 198 p. (English literature series) 65-107768
1. Gibbon, Edward, 1737-1794. I. I. Groom, Bernard, 1892- ed. II. Title. BIP

GIBBON, Edward, 1737-1794. 828.603
Memoirs of my life; edited from the manuscripts by Georges A. Bonnard. Funk & Wagnalls, 1969. xxxvi, 346 p. front. (port.) 7 plates (incl. facsims.) 24 cm. Bibliography: p. 229. [PR3476.A82 1966]
I. Bonnard, Georges Alfred, 1886- ed. II. Title.

GIBBON, Edward, 1737-1794. 937'.0072'024 B
Memoirs of my life, edited from the manuscripts by Georges A. Bonnard. [1st American ed.] New York, Funk & Wagnalls [1969, c1966] xxxv, 346 p. illus., facsims, port. 24 cm. Bibliography: p. 229. Bibliographical references included in "Editor's notes" (p. 231-340) [PR3476.A82 1969] 72-90029 10.00
I. Bonnard, Georges Alfred, 1886- ed. II. Title.

GIBBON, Edward, 1737-1794. 937'.06'072024 B
Private letters of Edward Gibbon (1753-1794). With an introd. by the Earl of Shellfield. Edith by Rowland E. Prothero. [New York, AMS Press, 1971] 2 v. illus. 24 cm. Includes bibliographical references. [PR3476.A83 1971] 71-151596 ISBN 0-404-02751-2
I. Title.

GIBBONIANA. 907'.2'024
New York, Garland Pub., 1974- p. cm. (The Life & times of seven major British writers) [DG206.G5G52] 74-14849 22.00
1. Gibbon, Edward, 1737-1794. BIP

JOYCE, Michael. v. 12
Edward Gibbon. London, New York, Longmans, Green [1953] ix, 176p. plate, ports., facsim. 19cm. (Men and books) Bibliography: p. 172-173. A 53
1. Gibbon, Edward, 1737-1794. I. Title. II. Series. BIP

MORISON, James Augustus Cotter, 1832-1888. 937'.0072'024 B
Gibbon. New York, AMS Press [1968] vi, 184 p. 22 cm. (English men of letters) Reprint of the 1887 ed. [PR3476.M7 1968] 68-58387
1. Gibbon, Edward, 1737-1794. BIP

QUENNELL, Peter, 1905- 920.042
Four portraits; studies of the eighteenth century. [Rev.ed.] Hamden, Conn., Archon [dist. Shoe String c.1965] 256p. illus., ports. 22cm. First ed. pub. in 1945 under title: The profane virtues. [DA506.A1Q4] 65-21845 6.00
1. Boswell, James 1740-1795. 2. Gibbon, Edward, 1737-1794. 3. Sterne, Laurence, 1713-1768. 4. Wilkes, John, 1727-1797. I. Title.
Contents omitted.

QUENNELL, Peter, 1905- 920.042
Four portraits; studies of the eighteenth century, [Rev. ed.] Hamden, Conn., Archon Books, 1965. 256 p. illus., ports. 22 cm. First ed. published in 1945 under title: The profane virtues. Contents.James Boswell,--Edward Gibbon.--Laurence Sterne.--John Wilkes. [DA506.A1Q4] 65-21845
1. Boswell, James, 1740-1795. 2. Gibbon, Edward, 1737-1794 3. Sterne, Laurence, 1713-1768. 4. Wilkes, John, 1727-1797. I. Title. BIP

QUENNELL, Peter, 1905- 920'.041
The profane virtues : for studies of the eighteenth century / Peter Quennell. Westport, Conn. : Greenwood Press, 1979, c1945. 220 p., [8] leaves of plates : ill. ; 23 cm. Reprint of the ed. published by Viking, New York. Contents.Contents.—James Boswell.—Edward Gibbon.—Laurence Sterne.—John Wilkes. [DA506.A1Q4 1979] 78-11551 ISBN 0-313-21039-X lib. bdg. : 18.75
1. Boswell, James, 1740-1795. 2. Gibbon, Edward, 1737-1794. 3. Sterne, Laurence, 1713-1768. 4. Wilkes, John, 1727-1797. 5. Great Britain—Biography. I. Title.

TRAVIS, George, 1741-1797. 907'.2'024 S
Letters to Edward Gibson, esq., 1785. New York, Garland Pub., 1974. p. cm. (The Life & times of seven major British writers. Gibboniana 13) Reprint of the 1785 ed. printed by C. F. and J. Rivington, London. [DG206.G5G52 vol. 13] [BT112] 231 74-14851 ISBN 0-8240-1349-2 22.00
1. Gibbon, Edward, 1737-1794. History of the decline and fall of the Roman empire. 2. Benson, George, 1699-1762. 3. Newton, Isaac, Sir, 1642-1727. 4. Bible. N.T. 1 John V, 7—Criticism, Textual. 5. Trinity—Biblical teaching. I. Gibbon, Edward, 1737-1794. II. Title. III. Series: Gibboniana 13.

YOUNG, George Malcolm, 1882-1959. 937'.06'072024 B
Gibbon. New York, D. Appleton, 1933. St. Clair Shores, Mich., Scholarly Press, 1974. p. cm. Original ed. issued in series: Appleton biographies. Bibliography: p. [PR3476.Y6 1974] 74-4068 ISBN 0-403-03085-4
1. Gibbon, Edward, 1737-1794. I. Series: Appleton biographies. BIP

Gibbons, Floyd Phillips, 1887-1939.

GIBBONS, Edward. 920.5
Floyd Gibbons, your headline hunter; a biography. [1st ed.] New York, Exposition Press [1953] 350 p. illus. 21 cm. "A Banner book." [PN4874.G36G5] 53-6714
1. Gibbons, Floyd Phillips, 1887-1939.

Gibbons, James, Cardinal, 1834-1921.

ELLIS, John Tracy, 1905- 922.273
The life of James Cardinal Gibbons. Popular ed., ed. by Francis L. Broderick. Milwaukee, Bruce [c.1963] v, 223p. 22cm. 63-21344 4.50
1. Gibbons, James, Cardinal, 1834-1921. I. Title.

ELLIS, John Tracy, 1905- 922.273
The life of James Cardinal Gibbons, Archbishop of Baltimore, 1834-1921. Milwaukee, Bruce Pub. Co. [1952] 2v. plates. ports. 23cm. 'An essay on the sources': v. 2, p. 651-669. Bibliographical footnotes. [BX4705.G5E4] 52-14973
1. Gibbons, James, Cardinal, 1834-1921. I. Title.

TEHAN, Arline (Boucher) 922.273
Prince of democracy, James Cardinal Gibbons [by] Arline Boucher, John Tehan. Garden City, N.Y., Hanover [c.1962] 308p. 22cm. Bibl. 62-7605 4.95
1. Gibbons, James, Cardinal, 1834-1921. I. Tehan, John, joint author. II. Title.

TEHAN, Arline (Boucher) 922.273
Prince of democracy, James Cardinal Gibbons [by] Arline Boucher & John Tehan. [1st ed.] Garden City, Hanover House [1962] 308 p. 22 cm. [BX4705.G5T4] 62-7605
1. Gibbons, James, Cardinal, 1834-1921. I. Tehan, John, joint author. II. Title.

TEHAN, Arline (Boucher) 922.273
Prince of democracy: James Cardinal Gibbons, by Arline Boucher. John Tehan. Garden City, N.Y., Doubleday [1966, c.1962] x, 307p. 18cm. (Image bk., D214) Bibl. .95 pap.,

1. Gibbons, James, Cardinal, 1834-1921. I. Tehan, John, joint author. II. Title.

Gibbons, Orlando, 1583-1625.

FELLOWES, Edmund Horace, 1870- 927.8
Orlando Gibbons and his family; the last of the Tudor School of musicians. 2d ed. London, New York, Oxford University Press, 1951. 109 p. illus., port., geneal. table. 23 cm. First published in 1925 under title: Orlando Gibbons; a short account of his life and work. [ML410.G295F4 1951] 52-209
1. Gibbons, Orlando, 1583-1625. 2. Gibbon family. I. Title.

Gibbs, Anthony, 1902-

GIBBS, Anthony, 1902- 823'.9'14 B
In my own good time. Boston, Gambit, 1970. 321 p. 22 cm. Autobiography. 1969 ed. has title: In my time. [PR6013.I245Z5 1970] 77-107404 6.95
I. Title.

GIBBS, Anthony, 1902- 796.7'7'0924 B
A passion for cars / Anthony Gibbs. New York : Scribner, [1974] 202 p., [12] leaves of plates : ill. ; 23 cm. Includes index. [TL140.G52A33 1974b] 73-11587 ISBN 0-684-13636-8 : 10.00
1. Gibbs, Anthony, 1902- I. Title. BIP

Gibbs, Jane DeBow.

LEVESCONTE, Lillie Gibbs. 917.47'92
Little bird that was caught; the story of the early years of Jane DeBow Gibbs. [St. Paul? Ramsey County Historical Society, 1968] 54 p. illus. 23 cm. [CT275.G378L4] 68-3839
1. Gibbs, Jane DeBow. I. Title.

Gibbs, Josiah Willard, 1839-1903.

LEERBURGER, Benedict A. 925
Josiah W. Gibbs, American theoretical physist. New York, Watts [c.1963] 118p. illus., port. 22cm. (Immortals of sci.) 63-16917 2.95
1. Gibbs, Josiah Willard, 1839-1903. I. Title.

LEERBURGER, Benedict A 925
Josiah W. Gibbs American theoretical physicist. New York, F. Watts [1963] 118 p. illus., port. 22 cm. (Immortals of science) [QC16.G5L4] 63-16917
1. Gibbs, Josiah Willard, 1839-1903. I. Title.

RUKEYSER, Muriel, 1913- 925
Willard Gibbs. New York, Dutton, 1964 [c.1942] 465p. illus. 19cm. (D156) Bibl. 1.95 pap.,
1. Gibbs, Josiah Willard, 1839-1903. I. Title.

WHEELER, Lynde Phelps. 925
Josiah Willard Gibbs, the history of a great mind. New Haven, Yale University Press, 1951. viii, 264 p. illus., ports., geneal. table. 25 cm. Bibliography: p. [251]-256. [QA29.G5W5] 51-1738
1. Gibbs, Josiah Willard, 1839-1903.

WHEELER, Lynde Phelps. 925
Josiah Willard Gibbs; the history of a great mind. Rev. ed. New Haven, Yale University Press, 1952. viii, 270p. illus., ports., geneal. table. 25cm. Bibliography: p. [251]-256. [QA29.G5W5 1952] 52-14822
1. Gibbs, Josiah Willard, 1839-1908. I. Title.

WHEELER, Lynde Phelps. 925
Josiah Willard Gibbs, the history of a great mind. With a foreword by A. Whitney Griswold. New Haven, Yale University Press [1962] 270 p. illus. 21 cm. (A Yale paperbound, Y-70) [QC16.G5W45 1962] 62-6570
1. Gibbs, Josiah Willard, 1839-1903. I. Title.

WHEELER, Lynde Phelps. 530'.0924 B
Josiah Willard Gibbs: the history of a great mind. With a foreword by A. Whitney Griswold. [Hamden, Conn.] Archon Books, 1970 [c1962] xiii, 270 p. illus., geneal. table, ports. 22 cm. Bibliography: p. [251]-256. [QC16.G5W45 1970] 76-113021
1. Gibbs, Josiah Willard, 1839-1903. I. Title. BIP

Gibbs, Mifflin Wistar.

GIBBS, Mifflin Wistar. 973.8'0924 B
Shadow and light; an autobiography. New York, Arno Press, 1968 [c1902] xv, 372 p. ports. 22 cm. (The American Negro: his history and literature) [E185.97.G44 1968] 68-28998
I. Title. II. Series. BIP

Gibert, Pierre, ca. 1755-1815.

GIBERT, Anne C., 1930- 975.7'35
Pierre Gibert, Esq., the devoted Huguenot : a history of the French settlement of New Bordeaux, South Carolina / by Anne C. Gibert. [s.l.] : Gibert, c1976. iv, 131 p., [3] leaves of plates : ill. ; 23 cm. Includes index. Bibliography: p. 124-126. [F279.B7G5] 77-150141
1. Gibert, Pierre, ca. 1755-1815. 2. Gibert family. 3. Huguenots—South Carolina—Bordeaux—History. 4. Huguenots—South Carolina—Bordcaux—Genealogy. 5. Huguenots—South Carolina—Bordeaux—Biography. 6. Bordeaux, S.C.—History. 7. Bordeaux, S.C.—Genealogy. I. Title.

Gibney, Virgil Pendleton, 1847-1927.

GIBNEY, Robert A., 1889-1957. 617'.0924 B
Gibney of the Ruptured & Crippled. Edited by Alfred R. Shands, Jr. New York, Appleton-Century-Crofts [1969] xiv, 152 p. illus., ports. 25 cm. "Bibliography of Virgil Pendleton Gibney, 1876 to 1920": p. 145-152. [R154.G45G5] 69-19447
1. Gibney, Virgil Pendleton, 1847-1927. I. Shands, Alfred Rives, 1899- ed. II. Title.

Gibran, Kahlil, 1883-1931.

GIBRAN, Kahlil, 1883-1931. 892.76
Kahlil Gibran, a self-portrait. Translated from the Arabic & edited by Anthony R. Ferris. New York, Citadel Press [1959] 94 p. illus. 21 cm. Letters. [PJ826.I2Z54] 59-14062
I. Title. BIP

GIBRAN, Kahlil, 1883-1931. 811'.5'2 B
The letters of Kahlil Gibran and Mary Haskell; visions of life as expressed by the author of The prophet". [Arr. and edited by Annie Salem Otto. Houston? Tex., A. S. Otto? 1970] 677 p. illus., facsims. 23 cm. Added t.p. has title: The love letters of Kahlil Gibran and Mary Haskell. Bibliography: p. 677. [PS3513.I25Z54 1970] 71-119616
I. Haskell, Mary, 1873-1964. II. Otto, Annie Salem, ed. III. Title.

NAIMY, Mikhail, 1889- 928.1
Kahlil Gibran: his life and his work. Beirut, Khayats [dist. Mystic. Conn., Verry 1965, c.1964] xii, 267p. illus., ports. 22cm. [PJ7741] 65-7762 6.50
1. Gibran, Kahlil, 1883-1931. I. Title.

NAIMY, Mikhail, 1889- 928.1
Kahlil Gibran: a biography. With a pref. by Martin L. Wolf. New York, Philosophical Library [1950] xviii, 267 p. illus., ports. 23 cm. [PJ7741.G54Z8] 50-12146
1. Gibran, Kahlil, 1883-1931.

Gibran, Kahlil, 1883-1931—Biography.

GIBRAN, Jean. 811'.5'2 B
Kahlil Gibran, his life and world / Jean Gibran and Kahlil Gibran. Boston : New York Graphic Society, 1974. 442 p. : ill. ; 26 cm. Includes index. Bibliography: p. 432-437. [PJ7826.I2Z615] 73-80368 ISBN 0-8212-0510-2 : 12.50
1. Gibran, Kahlil, 1883-1931—Biography. I. Gibran, Kahlil, 1922- joint author. II. Title.

Gibson, Althea

GIBSON, Althea 927.9634
I always wanted to be somebody. Edited by Ed Fitzgerald. New York, Pyramid Bks. [1960, c.1958] 160p. 18cm. (G478) .35 pap.,
I. Title.

GIBSON, Althea, 1927- 927.9634
I always wanted to be somebody. Edited by Ed Fitzgerald. [1st ed.] New York, Harper [1958] 176 p. illus. 23 cm. Autobiography. "A condensed version ... was published in the Saturday evening post, under the title of I wanted to be somebody." [GV994.G5A3] 58-12447
I. Title. BIP

GIBSON, Althea, 1927- 796'.0924 B
So much to live for, by Althea Gibson with Richard Curtis. New York, Putnam [1968] 160 p. 21 cm. (Putnam sports shelf) A biography of the Negro athlete who made a name for herself by winning the major women's amateur tennis championships and who then retired from tennis to turn to professional golf. [GV697.G5A3] 92 68-24514 3.49
I. Curtis, Richard. II. Title.

Gibson, Bob, 1935 —Juvenile literature.

GIBSON, Bob, 1935- 796.357'0924 B
From ghetto to glory; the story of Bob Gibson [by] Bob Gibson with Phil Pepe. Englewood Cliffs, N.J., Prentice-Hall [1968] 200 p. ports. 22 cm. [GV865.G5A3] 68-30699 5.95
I. Pepe, Phil. II. Title.

LIPMAN, David. 796.357'092'4 B
Bob Gibson, pitching ace / by David Lipman and Ed Wilks. New York : Putnam, [1975] 191 p. ; 21 cm. Includes index. A biography emphasizing the career of the star pitcher of the St. Louis Cardinals who won seven consecutive World Series games. [GV865.G5L56] 92 73-93755 ISBN 0-399-60896-6 lib. bdg. : 5.29
1. Gibson, Bob, 1935- —Juvenile literature. 2. Baseball—Juvenile literature. 3. Pitching (Baseball)—Juvenile literature. I. Wilks, Ed, joint author. II. Title.

Gibson, Francis E.

GIBSON, Francis E. 798.2'092'4 B
Gibby : the recollections of a horsey man / Francis Gibson. London ; New York : J. A. Allen, 1978. 126 p. ; 21 cm. Includes index. Bibliography: p. 122. [SF284.52.G53A34] 78-317479 ISBN 0-85131-277-2 : 7.50
1. Gibson, Francis E. 2. Horsemen—Great Britain—Biography. I. Title.
Distributed by Sporting Book Center, Inc., Canaan, N.Y.

Gibson, John Frederic.

GIBSON, John Frederic. 928.2
Memory bay. [1st ed.] New York, Longmans, Green [1950] v, 172 p. 21 cm. [PR6013.I 2847S2] 50-9414
I. Title.

GIBSON, John Frederic. 301.45'19'70711
A small and charming world / John Frederic Gibson. Don Mills, Ont. : Totem Books, 1976, c1972. 220 p. ; 18 cm. "A Totem book." [E78.B9G52 1976] 77-370801 ISBN 0-00-211596-4 : 1.95
1. Gibson, John Frederic. 2. Indians of North America—British Columbia—Social life and customs. 3. Indians of North America—British Columbia—Social conditions. 4. Social workers—British Columbia—Biography. I. Title.

Gibson, John, 1740-1822.

HANKO, Charles William, 1920- 923.273
The life of John Gibson, soldier, patriot, statesman. Daytona Beach, Fla., College Pub. Co [c1955] 89p. 24cm. [Americans of distinction series] Includes bibliography. [E302.6.G4H3] 57-3090
1. Gibson, John, 1740-1822. I. Title.

Gibson, John, 1911-1947.

BRASHLER, William. 796.357'092'4 B
Josh Gibson : a life in the Negro Leagues / William Brashler. 1st ed. New York : Harper & Row, c1978. xviii, 201 p., [4] leaves of plates : ill. ; 22 cm. Includes index. [GV865.G53B7 1978] 77-83861 ISBN 0-06-010446-5 : 10.00
1. Gibson, John, 1911-1947. 2. Baseball players—United States—Biography. I. Title: Negro Leagues. BIP

Gibson, Maud, 1885-1970.

RICHARDSON, Michael. 361.7'4'0924 B
Maud Gibson: a quiet philanthropist. With a foreword by her nephew, Peter Howson. [Clayton, Australia, Printed by Wilke and Co., 1970?] [14] p. 20 cm. [HV28.G44R5] 73-180731
1. Gibson, Maud, 1885-1970.

Gibson, Walter Murray.

GIBSON, Walter Murray. 996.9'02'0924 B
The diaries of Walter Murray Gibson: 1886, 1887. Edited with introd. and notes by Jacob Adler and Gwynn Barrett. [Honolulu] University Press of Hawaii, 1973. xvii, 199 p. illus. 27 cm. Includes bibliographical references. [DU627.17.G5A3] 75-188977 ISBN 0-8248-0211-X 10.00
1. Gibson, Walter Murray. I. Adler, Jacob, 1913- ed. II. Barrett, Gwynn, ed. III. Title.

Gide, Andre Paul Guillaume. 1869-1951

GIDE, Andre Paul Guillaume, 1869-1951. 848'.9'1209
The correspondence of Andre Gide and Edmund Gosse, 1904-1928 / edited with translations introd., and notes by Linette F. Brugmans. Westport, Conn. : Greenwood Press, 1977, [c1959] p. cm. Reprint of the ed. published by New York University Press, New York, which was issued as no. 2 of New York University studies in Romance languages and literatures. Includes index. Bibliography: p. [PQ2613.I2Z564 1977] 77-22618 ISBN 0-8371-9736-8 lib.bdg. : 16.50
1. Gide, Andre Paul Guillaume, 1869-1951—Correspondence. 2. Gosse, Edmund William, Sir, 1849-1928—Correspondence. 3. Authors, French—20th century—Correspondence. 4. Authors, English—20th century—Correspondence. I. Gosse, Edmund William, Sir, 1849-1928. II. Title. III. Series: New York University. Studies in Romance languages and literatures ; 2.

GIDE, Andre Paul Guillaume, 1869-1951. 848'.9'1209
The correspondence of Andre Gide and Edmund Gosse, 1904-1928 / edited, with translations, introd., and notes by Linette F. Brugmans Westport, Conn. : Greenwood Press, 1977, [c1959] p. cm. Reprint of the ed. published by New York University Press, New York, which was issued as no. 2 of New York University studies in Romance languages and literatures. Includes index. Bibliography: p. [PQ2613.I2Z564 1977] 77-22618 ISBN 0-8371-9736-8 lib.bdg. : 16.50
1. Gide, Andre Paul Guillaume, 1869-1951—Correspondence. 2. Gosse, Edmund William, Sir, 1849-1928—Correspondence. 3. Authors, French—20th century—Correspondence. 4. Authors, English—20th century—Correspondence. I. Gosse, Edmund William, Sir, 1849-1928. II. Title. III. Series: New York University. Studies in Romance languages and literatures ; 2. BIP

Gide, Andre Paul Guillaume, 1869-1951.

DELAY, Jean Paul Louis, 1907- 928.4
The youth of Andre Gide. Abridged, tr. [from French] June Guicharnaud. Chicago, Univ. of Chic. Pr. [c.1963] 498p. illus. 24cm. 63-13063 7.95
1. Gide, Andre Paul Guillaume, 1869-1951. I. Title.

FOWLIE, Wallace, 1908- 848.912
Andre Gide: his life and art. New York, Macmillan [c.1965] 217p. 21cm. Bibl. [PQ2613.I2Z6275] 64-20739 4.95
1. Gide, Andre Paul Guillaume, 1869-1951. I. Title.

FOWLIE, Wallace, 1908- v. 12
Andre Gide; his life and art. New York, Collier Books [1966] 217 p. 21 cm. (Collier books, 00287) Bibliography: p. 209-212. 67-92904
1. Gide, Andre Paul Guillaume, 1869-1951. I. Title.

GIDE, Andre Paul Guillaume, 928.4
The correspondence of Andre Gide and Edmund Gosse, 1904-1928. Edited, with translations, introd., and notes, by Linette F. Brugmans. [New York] New York University Press, [c.] 1959. ix, 220p. Bibliography: p. port., facsims. 22cm. (New York University. Studies in Romance languages and literature, 2) 59-11772 4.50
I. Gosse, Edmund William, Sir II. Brugmans, Linette Fisher, ed. III. Title. IV. Series.

GIDE, Andre Paul 848'.9'1203 B
Guillaume, 1869-1951.
The journals of Andre Gide / translated from the French, with an introd. and notes, by Justin O'Brien. New York : H. Fertig, 1975, c1947-[1951] p. cm. Reprint of the ed. published by Knopf, New York. Includes index. Contents.Contents.—v. 1. 1889-1913.—v. 2. 1914-1927.—v. 3. 1928-1939.—v. 4. 1939-1949. [PQ2613.I2Z526 1975] 74-22297 16.00(v.1)
1. Gide, Andre Paul Guillaume, 1869-1951—Biography.
17.00 (v. 2); 17.00 (v.3); 15.00 (v. 4)

GIDE, Andre Paul Guillaume, 928.4
1869-1951.
The journals of Andre Gide, 1889-1949. Edited, translated, abridged, and with an introd. by Justin O'Brien. [1st Vintage ed.] New York, Vintage Books, 1956. 2v. 19cm. (A Vintage book, K33A-B) [PQ2613.I2Z527] 56-58321
1. Authors—Correspondence, reminiscences, etc. I. Title.

GUERARD, Albert Joseph, 843.91
1914-
Andre Gide. Cambridge, Harvard University Press, 1951. xvii, 263 p. 22 cm. Bibliographical references included in "Notes" (p. [243]-254) [PQ2613.I 2Z634] 51-11673
1. Gide, Andre Paul Guillaume, 1869-1951. I. Title.

GUERARD, Albert Joseph, v. 12
1914-
Andre Gide. Intro. by Thomas Mann. New York, Dutton, 1963. 263 p. (Dutton paperback, D131) 64-22217
1. Gide, Andre Paul Guillaume, 1869-1951. I. Title.

GUERARD, Labert Joseph, 843.912
1914-
Andre Gide. New York, Dutton, 1963 [c.1951] 254p. 18cm. (D131) Bibl. 1.35 pap.,
1. Gide, Andre Paul Guillaume, 1869-1951. I. Title.

HARRIS, Frederick 848'.9'1209
John, 1943-
Andre Gide and Romain Rolland: two men divided. New Brunswick, N.J., Rutgers University Press [1973] ix, 282 p. 21 cm. Bibliography: p. 259-272. [PQ2613.I2Z635] 73-5991 ISBN 0-8135-0716-2 10.00
1. Gide, Andre Paul Guillaume, 1869-1951. 2. Rolland, Romain, 1866-1944. I. Title.

HYTIER, Jean. v. 12
Andre Gide. Translated by Richard Howard. New York, F. Ungar Pub. Co. [1967] 239 p. 21 cm. 68-41202
1. Gide, Andre Paul Gulliaume, 1869-1951. I. Title. BIP

HYTIER, Jean 848.912
Andre Gide. Tr. by Richard Howard. New York, Ungar [1967, c.1962] 239p. 21cm. (Lit. in tr.) Bibl. [PQ2613.I2Z6433] 5.00; 1.95 pap.,
1. Gide, Andre Paul Guillaume, 1886-1961. I. Title.

HYTIER, Jean. 848.912
Andre Gide. Translated by Richard Howard. [1st ed.] Garden City, N. Y., Doubleday, 1962. 239p. 19cm. (Anchor books, A307) [PQ2613.I2Z6433] 62-10462
1. Gide, Andre Paul Guillaume, 1869-1951. I. Title.

IRELAND, George William 843.912
Andre Gide. New York, Grove [c.1963] 120p. 18cm. (Evergreen pilot bks., EP21) Bibl. 62-10149 .95 pap.,
1. Gide, Andre Paul Guillaume, 1869-1951. I. Title.

IRELAND, George William. 843.912
Andre Gide. [1st ed.] New York, Grove Press [1963] 120 p. 18 cm. (Evergreen pilot books,EP21) Includes bibliography. [PQ2613.I2Z644] 62-10149
1. 1. Gide, Andre Paul Guillaume, 1869-1951. I. Title.

MANN, Klaus, 1906- 848.91209 B
1949.
Andre Gide and the crisis of modern thought / by Klaus Mann. New York : Octagon Books, 1978, c1943. viii, 331 p. ; 23 cm. Reprint of the ed. published by Creative Age Press, New York. Bibliography: p. 327-331 [PQ2613.I2Z654 1978] 77-26702 ISBN 0-374-95266-3 lib.bdg. : 15.00
1. Gide, Andre Paul Guillaume, 1869-1951. 2. Authors, French—20th century—Biography. I. Title. BIP

MARTIN DU GARD, Roger, 928.4
1881-
Recollections of Andre Gide. [Translated by John Russell] New York, Viking Press, 1953. 134p. 20cm. Translation of Notes sur Andre Gide. [PQ2613.I 2Z654623] 53-5724
1. Gide, Andre Paul Guillaume, 1869-1951. I. Title.

O'BRIEN, Justin, 1906- v. 12
Portrait of Andre Gide; a critical biography. New York, McGraw-Hill [1964] 390, xiv p. port. (McGraw-Hill paperbacks) Includes bibliographies. 65-44982
1. Gide, Andre, 1869-1951. I. Title.

O'BRIEN, Justin, 1906- 928.4
Portrait of Andre Gide, a critical biography. [1st ed.] New York, Knopf, 1953. 390p. illus., ports. 25cm. 'The works of Andre Gide': p. [388]-390. [PQ2613.I2Z6568] 52-12192
1. Gide, Andre Paul Guillaume, 1869-1951. I. Title.

O'BRIEN, Justin, 848'.9'1209
1906-1968.
Portrait of Andre Gide : a critical biography / by Justin O'Brien. New York : Octagon Books, 1977, c1953. xii, 390, xiv p., [5] leaves of plates : ill. ; 24 cm. Reprint of the ed. published by Knopf, New York. Includes bibliographical references and index. [PQ2613.I2Z6568 1977] 76-56751 lib.bdg. : 18.00
1. Gide, Andre Paul Guillaume, 1869-1951—Biography. 2. Authors, French—20th century—Biography. I. Title.

O'BRIEN, Justin McCortney, 928.4
1906-
Portrait of Andre Gide, a critical biography. New York, McGraw [1964, c.1953] 390p. port. 21cm. (47604) Bibl. 2.95 pap.,
1. Gide, Andre Paul Guillaume, 1869-1951. I. Title.

PAINTER, George Duncan, 843'.9'12
1914-
Andre Gide; a critical biography [by] George D. Painter. [1st American ed.] New York, Atheneum [1968] viii, 147 p. ports. 23 cm. Bibliography: p. [135]-142. [PQ2613.I2Z657 1968b] 67-16541
1. Gide, Andre Paul Guillaume, 1869-1951.

Gide, Madeleine Louise Mathilde (Rondeaux) 1867 (ca.)-1938.

GIDE, Andre Paul Guillame, 928.4
1869-1951
Madeleine (Et nunc manet in te) Tr. from French, introd., notes, by Justin O'Brien. New York, Bantam [1968,c.1952] xxii, 87p. 18cm. (SX4014) .75 pap.,
1. Gide, Madeleine Louise Mathilde (Rondeaux) 1867 (ca.)-1938. I. Title.

GIDE, Andre Paul Guillaume, 928.4
1869-1951.
Madeleine (Et nunc manet in te) Translated from the French, with an introd. and notes, by Justin O'Brien. [1st American ed.] New York, Knopf, 1952. 98p. illus. 20cm. [PQ2613.I2Z523] 52-6417
1. Gide, Madeleine Louise Mathilde (Rondeaux) 1867 (ca.)-1933. I. Title.

Gielgud, John, Sir, 1904-

GIELGUD, John, 792'.028'0922
Sir, 1904-
Distinguished company. [1st ed. in the U.S.A.] Garden City, N.Y., Doubleday, 1973. xii, 179 p. illus. 22 cm. [PN2597.G5 1973] 72-96237 ISBN 0-385-04563-8 5.95
1. Actors—Great Britain—Correspondence, reminiscences, etc. I. Title.

GIELGUD, John, 792'.028'0924 B
Sir, 1904-
Early stages / John Gielgud. Rev. ed. New York : Taplinger Pub. Co., 1976, c1974. xiv, 210 p., [8] leaves of plates : ill. ; 23 cm. Includes index. [PN2598.G45A3 1976] 75-24663 ISBN 0-8008-2351-6 : 9.50
1. Gielgud, John, Sir, 1904- 2. Actors—England—Correspondence, reminiscences, etc. I. Title.

GIELGUD, John, Sir, 1904- 792
Stage directions / John Gielgud. Westport, Conn. : Greenwood Press, 1979, c1963. xiv, 146 p., [5] leaves of plates : ill. ; 23 cm. Reprint of the ed. published by Random House, New York. [PN2598.G45A33 1979] 78-23580 ISBN 0-313-21035-7 lib. bdg. : 16.50
1. Gielgud, John, Sir, 1904- 2. Actors—Great Britain—Biography. I. Title. BIP

Gifford, Frank, 1930-

SMITH, Don, 1926- 927.96332
The Frank Gifford story. New York, Putnam, c1960. 192 p. illus. 21 cm. Full name: Donald Gregory Smith. [GV939.G5S6] 61-5823
1. Gifford, Frank, 1930- I. Title.

SMITH, Don [Donald 927.96332
Gregory Smith]
The Frank Gifford story. New York, Putnam, c.1960. 192p. illus. 61-5823 2.95
1. Gifford, Frank, 1930- I. Title.

WALLACE, William 796.332'0924 B
N.
Frank Gifford, by William N. Wallace. Englewood Cliffs, N.J., Prentice-Hall [1969] viii, 130 p. illus., ports. 22 cm. (The Golden year, 1956) [GV939.G5W3] 73-80768 4.95
1. Gifford, Frank, 1930-

Gifford, Sanford Robinson, 1823-1880.

WEISS, Ila, 1939- 759.13 B
Sanford Robinson Gifford (1823-1880) / Ila Weiss New York : Garland Pub., 1977. ca. 600 p. : ill. ; 21 cm. (Outstanding dissertations in the fine arts) Reprint of the author's thesis, Columbia, 1968; with a new pref. Includes bibliographical references. [ND237.G4W44 1977] 76-23655 lib.bdg. : 57.50
1. Gifford, Sanford Robinson, 1823-1880. 2. Landscape painters—United States—Biography. I. Title. II. Series. BIP

Gigli, Beniamino, 1890-1957.

GIGLI, Beniamino, 782.1'092'4 B
1890-1957.
The memoirs of Beniamino Gigli / translated by Darina Silone. New York : Arno Press, 1977, c1957. x, 277 p., [12] leaves of plates : ill. ; 24 cm. (Opera biographies) Translation of Memorie. Reprint of the 1957 ed. published by Cassell, London. Includes index. Discography: p. 236-270. [ML420.G43A313 1977] 76-29937 ISBN 0-405-09679-8 : 20.00
1. Gigli, Beniamino, 1890-1957. 2. Singers—Biography. I. Title. BIP

Giglio, Giovanni.

GIGLIO, Giovanni. 320.9'45'091
The triumph of Barabbas. Translated from the Italian by Eric Mosbacher. London, V. Gollancz, 1937. [New York, AMS Press, 1973] 317 p. 23 cm. [DG575.G48A33 1973] 74-180401 ISBN 0-404-56125-X 16.00
1. Giglio, Giovanni. 2. Italy—Politics and government—1914-1945. I. Title. BIP

Gikow, Ruth,

GIKOW, Ruth, 1915- 759.13
Ruth Gikow. Introd. by Matthew Josephson. New York, Maecenas Press [1970] [30] p., 131 plates (part col.) illus. 29 cm. [ND237.G44A57 1970] 71-127537 14.95

Gilbert, Alfred Carlton,

GILBERT, Alfred Carlton, 920
1884-
The man who lives in paradise; the autobiography of A. C. Gilbert, with Marshall McClintock. New York, Rinehart [1954] 374 p. illus. 22 cm. [CT275.G3917A3 1954] 54-9126
I. Title.

Gilbert-Carter, Humphrey, 1884-1969.

HUMPHREY Gilbert- 581'.092'4
Carter : a memorial volume / edited by J. S. L. Gilmour and S. M. Walters, assisted by C. J. King. Cambridge : University Botanic Garden, 1975. xv, 132 p., leaf of plate, [8] p. of plates : facsims., ports. ; 20 cm. Includes index. Bibliography: p. 123. [QK31.G54H85] 76-357302
1. Gilbert-Carter, Humphrey, 1884-1969. 2. Botany—Addresses, essays, lectures. I. Gilbert-Carter, Humphrey, 1884-1969. II. Gilmour, John Scott Lennox, 1906- III. Walters, Stuart Max. IV. King, Clive John.

Gilbert, Humphrey, Sir, 1539?-1583.

GOSLING, William 973.1'7'0924 B
Gilbert, 1863-
The life of Sir Humphrey Gilbert, England's first empire builder. Westport, Conn., Greenwood Press [1970] x, 304 p. illus. 23 cm. Reprint of the 1911 ed. [DA358.G5G7 1970] 76-109737
1. Gilbert, Humphrey, Sir, 1539?-1583. I. Title. BIP

Gilbert, John Gibbs, 1810-1889.

WINTER, William, 792'.028'0924 B
1836-1917.
A sketch of the life of John Gilbert, together with extracts from his letters and souvenirs of his career. New York, B. Franklin [1970] 55 p. illus., facsims. (1 fold.) 19 cm. (Burt Franklin research & source works series, 573. Theatre and drama series, 12) Reprint of the 1890 ed. [PN2287.G52W5 1970] 72-130087 ISBN 0-8337-3827-5
1. Gilbert, John Gibbs, 1810-1889. I. Gilbert, John Gibbs, 1810-1889. II. Title.

Gilbert, Sir William Schwenck, 1836-1911.

PEARSON, Hesketh, 1887- 927.8
Gilbert, his life and strife. New York, Harper [1957] 276p. illus. 22cm. [PR4714.P4 1957a] 57-8176
1. Gilbert, Sir William Schwenck, 1836-1911. I. Title. BIP

PEARSON, Hesketh, 1887- 927.8
1964.
Gilbert, his life and strife. New York, Harper [1957] 276 p. illus. 22 cm. [PR4714.P4 1957a] 57-8176
1. Gilbert, Sir William Schwenck, 1836-1911.

Gilbert, Virginia (Johnson).

GILBERT, Virginia 927.92
(Johnson).
Virginia reel. [1st ed.] Philadelphia, Lippincott [1950] 254 p. 21 cm.

Autobiographical. [PN2287.G53A3] 50-8017
I. Title.

Gilbert, William Schwenck, Sir, 1836-1911.

ABRAHAMS, Doris Caroline, 1901- 782.8'1'0924
Gilbert and Sullivan : lost chords and discords / Caryl Brahms [i.e. D. C. Abrahams]. 1st American ed. Boston : Little, Brown, c1975. 264 p. : ill. (some col.) ; 26 cm. Includes index. [ML410.S95A65 1975b] 75-4233 15.00
1. Gilbert, William Schwenk, Sir, 1836-1911. 2. Sullivan, Arthur Seymour, Sir, 1842-1900. I. Title.

BAILY, Leslie. 782.8'1'0924 B
Gilbert and Sullivan; their lives and times. New York, Viking Press [1974, c1973] 119, [1] p. illus. 24 cm. (A studio book) London edition (Thames and Hudson) has title: Gilbert and Sullivan and their world. Bibliography: p. [120] [ML410.S95B28 1974] 73-20669 ISBN 0-670-33990-3 7.95
1. Gilbert, William Schwenck, Sir, 1836-1911. 2. Sullivan, Arthur Seymour, Sir, 1842-1900. I. Title.

BAILY, Leslie. 782.8'1'0924 B
Gilbert and Sullivan, their lives and times / Leslie Baily. Harmondsworth, Eng. ; New York : Penguin Books, 1979, c1973. 119 [1] p. : ill. ; 24 cm. Reprint of the 1974 ed. published by Viking Press, New York, in series: A Studio book; London ed. published under title: Gilbert and Sullivan and their world. Bibliography: p. [120] [ML410.S95B28 1979] 78-16312 ISBN 0-14-005106-6 pbk. : 5.95
1. Gilbert, William Schwenck, Sir, 1836-1911. 2. Sullivan, Arthur Seymour, Sir, 1842-1900. 3. Dramatists, English—19th century—Biography. 4. Composers—England—Biography.

DARK, Sidney, 1874-1947. 782.8'1'0924 B
W. S. Gilbert; his life and letters, by Sidney Dark and Rowland Grey. New York, B. Blom, 1972. ix, 269 p. illus. 21 cm. Reprint of the 1923 ed. "The Gilbert and Sullivan operas": p. 265-266. Bibliography: p. 261-264. [PR4714.D3 1972] 76-177509
1. Gilbert, William Schwenck, Sir, 1836-1911. I. Rowland-Brown, Lilian Kate, joint author. BIP

DARK, Sidney, 1874-1947. 782.8'1'0924 B
W. S. Gilbert; his life and letters, by Sidney Dark and Rowland Grey. London, Methuen. Ann Arbor, Mich., Gryphon Books, 1971. ix, 269 p. illus. 22 cm. Reprint of the 1923 ed. "The Gilbert and Sullivan operas": p. 265-266. Bibliography: p. 261-264. [PR4714.D3 1971] 71-164210
1. Gilbert, William Schwenck, Sir, 1838-1911. I. Rowland-Brown, Lilian Kate, joint author.

DARLINGTON, William Aubrey, 1890- 782.6
The world of Gilbert and Sullivan. New York, Crowell [1950] xiii, 209 p. illus. 21 cm. "Dictionary-index of opera characters": p. 197-204. [ML410.S95D3] 50-7010
1. Gilbert, William Schwenck, Sir, 1836-1911. 2. Sullivan, Arthur Seymour, Sir, 1842-1900. I. Title.

DARLINGTON, William Aubrey, 1890- 782.1
The world of Gilbert and Sullivan, by W. A. Darlington. Freeport, N.Y., Books for Libraries Press [1970] 167 p. illus., ports. 23 cm. Reprint of the 1951 ed. [ML410.S95D3 1970] 78-137372
1. Gilbert, William Schwenck, Sir, 1836-1911. 2. Sullivan, Arthur Seymour, Sir, 1842-1900. I. Title.

GOLDBERG, Isaac, 1887-1938. 782.8'1'0922 B
The story of Gilbert and Sullivan; or, The compleat Savoyard. New York, AMS Press [1970, c1928] xviii, 588 p. illus., facsims., music, ports. 23 cm. Bibliography: p. 569-573. [ML410.S95G7 1970] 76-113194 ISBN 0-404-02858-6
1. Gilbert, William Schwenck, Sir, 1836-1911. 2. Sullivan, Arthur Seymour, Sir, 1842-1900. I. Title.

LAVINE, Sigmund A. 927.8
Wandering minstrels we; the story of Gilbert and Sullivan. New York, Dodd, Mead, 1954. 303 p. illus. 21 cm. [ML410.S95L27] 54-12090
1. Gilbert, William Schwenck, Sir, 1836-1911. 2. Sullivan, Arthur Seymour, Sir, 1842-1900. I. Title.

PEARSON, Hesketh, 1887-1964. 782.8'1'0924 B
Gilbert and Sullivan; a biography. Freeport, N.Y., Books for Libraries Press [1971, c1962] 317 p. ports. 23 cm. Bibliography: p. 309-312. [ML410.S95P4 1971] 70-175706 ISBN 0-8369-6621-X
1. Gilbert, William Schwenck, Sir, 1836-1911. 2. Sullivan, Arthur Seymour, Sir, 1842-1900. I. Title.

WYMER, Noramn 927.8
Gilbert and Sullivan. Portraits by John Pimlott. New York, Dutton [1963, c.1962] 157p. illus. 21cm. Bibl. 63-8597 3.00
1. Gilbert, William Schewenck, Sir 1836-1911. 2. Sullivan, Arthur Seymour, Sr. 1842-1900. I. Title.

Gilbert, William Schwenck, Sir 1836-1911—Juvenile literature.

HARRIS, Paula 782.810922
The young Gilbert and Sullivan. Illus. by Gloria Timbs. New York, Roy [1966. c. 1965] 128p. illus. 21cm. [ML3930.S95H4] 65-22984 3.25 bds.,
1. Gilbert. William Schwenck, Sir 1836-1911—Juvenile literature. 2. Sullivan, Arthur Seymour, Sir 1842-1900—Juvenile literature. I. Title.

PEARSON, Hesketh, 1887-1964. 782.8'1'0924 B
Gilbert, his life and strife / Hesketh Pearson. Westport, Conn. : Greenwood Press, 1978. 276 p., [8] leaves of plates : ill. ; 23 cm. Reprint of the 1957 ed. published by Methuen, London. Includes index. [PR4714.P4 1978] 78-3698 ISBN 0-313-20364-4 lib. bdg. : 20.25
1. Gilbert, William Schwenck, Sir, 1836-1911—Biography. 2. Dramatists, English—19th century—Biography. 3. Librettists—England—Biography. I. Title.

Gilbreth, Frank Bunker, 1868-1924.

GILBRETH, Frank B., Jr. 920.9
Cheaper by the dozen, by Frank B. Gilbreth, Jr., Ernestine Gilbreth Carey. Illus. by Donald McKay. New York, Bantam [1963, c.1948] 179p. 18cm. (Pathfinder ed., JP35) .40 pap.,
I. Carey, Ernestine Gilbreth, joint author. II. Title.

GILBRETH, Frank Bunker. 926.58
Cheaper by the dozen [by] Frank B. Gilbreth, Jr., Ernestine Gilbreth Carey; illus. by Donald McKay. Large type ed. New York, Watts [1968,c.1948] x, 237p. 28cm. (Keith Jennison bk.) Reminiscences of the Gilbreth family. [T40.G5G5] 6.95
1. Gilbreth, Frank Bunker, 1868-1924 2. Gilbreth, Lillian Evelyn (Moller) 1878- I. Carey, Ernestine Moller (Gilbreth). joint author. II. Title.

GILBRETH, Frank Bunker, Jr., 1911- 926.58
Cheaper by the dozen [by] Frank B. Gilbreth, Jr., Ernestine Gilbreth Carey. Drawings by Vasiliu. New York, Corwell [c.1948, 1963] ix, 245p. illus. 21cm. 63-20411 4.50
1. Gilbreth, Frank Bunker, 1868-1924. 2. Gilbreth, Lillian Evelyn (Moller) 1878- I. Carey, Ernestine Moller (Gilbreth) 1908- joint author. II. Title.

GILBRETH, Frank Bunker, 1911- 926.58
Cheaper by the dozen [by] Frank B. Gilbreth and Ernestine Gilbreth Carey. A school ed., by Frederick Houk Law. New York, Globe Book Co. [1953] 264p. illus. 21cm. [T40.G5G5 1953] 53-20866
1. Gilbreth, Frank Bunker, 1868-1924. 2. Gilbreth, Lillian Evelyn (Moller) 1878- I. Carey, Ernestine Moller (Gilbreth) 1908- joint author. II. Title.

GILBRETH, Frank Bunker, 1911-. 621.3819'5'0924
Cheaper by the dozen [by] Frank B. Gilbreth, Jr., and Ernestine Gilbreth Carey. Drawings by Vasiliu. New York, Crowell [1963] ix, 245 p. illus. 21 cm. [T40.G5G5] 63-20411
1. Gilbreth, Frank Bunker, 1868-1924. 2. Gilbreth, Lillian Evelyn (Moller) 1878- I. Carey, Ernestine Moller (Gilbreth) 1908- joint author. II. Title. BIP

GILBRETH, Lilliam Evelyn Moller 1878-1972. 658.5'4'0924 B
The quest of the one best way; a sketch of the life of Frank Bunker Gilbreth. Easton [Pa.] Hive Pub. Co., 1973. 64 p. illus. 23 cm. (Hive management history series, no. 21) Reprint of the 1954? ed. [T55.85.G64G64 1973] 73-1170 ISBN 0-87960-032-2 10.00 (lib. bdg.)
1. Gilbreth, Frank Bunker, 1868-1924. I. Title.

Gilbreth, Lillian Evelyn Moller, 1878-1972.

GILBRETH, Frank Bunker, 1911- 926.58
Belles on their toes [by] Frank B. Gilbreth, Jr. and Ernestine Gilbreth Carey; illustrated by Donald McKay. New York, Crowell [1950] 237 p. illus. 21 cm. [T40.G53G5] 50-13907
1. Gilbreth, Lillian Evelyn Moller, 1878-1972. I. Carey, Ernestine Moller Gilbreth, 1908- joint author. II. Title. BIP

Gilchrist, Anne (Burrows) 1828-1885.

GILCHRIST, Anne (Burrows) 1828-1885 820'.9'008 B
Anne Gilchrist, her life and writings. Edited by Herbert Harlakenden Gilchrist, with a prefatory notice by William Michael Rossetti. 2d ed. London, T. F. Unwin, 1887. [New York, AMS Press, 1973] xxi, 368 p. illus. 19 cm. [PR4715.G5Z6 1973] 74-148783 ISBN 0-404-02767-9 15.50
1. Gilchrist, Anne (Burrows) 1828-1885. I. Gilchrist, Herbert Harlakenden, 1857- ed.

GILCHRIST, Anne (Burrows) 1828-1885. 811'.3 B
The letters of Anne Gilchrist and Walt Whitman, edited, with an introd. by Thomas B. Harned. New York, Haskell House Publishers, 1973. xxxviii, 241 p. illus. 23 cm. [PR4715.G5Z55 1973] 72-6286 ISBN 0-8383-1630-1 10.95 (Lib. ed.)
I. Whitman, Walt, 1819-1892. BIP

Gilchrist, Sidney.

ARCHIBALD, Frank E. 266'.7'92 B
Salute to Sid; the story of Dr. Sidney Gilchrist, by Frank E. Archibald. Windsor, N.S., Lancelot Press [1970] 127 p. illus., ports. 21 cm. [R464.G54A72] 73-177690 2.50
1. Gilchrist, Sidney. 2. Missions, Medical—Angola. I. Title.

Gilcrease, Thomas, 1890-1962.

MILSTEN, David Randolph. 704'.36 B
Thomas Gilcrease. San Antonio, Tex., Naylor Co. [1969] xxii, 468 p. illus., ports. 23 cm. Bibliography: p. 451-458. [CT275.G399M5] 74-84447 12.95
1. Gilcrease, Thomas, 1890-1962.

Gilder, Richard Watson,

GILDER, Richard Watson, 1844-1909. 811'.4 B
Letters of Richard Watson Gilder. Edited by his daughter Rosamond Gilder. Freeport, N.Y., Books for Libraries Press, 1973. p. Reprint of the 1916 ed. [PS1743.A4 1973] 72-12814 ISBN 0-8369-7137-X

Gildersleeve, Virginia Crocheron,

GILDERSLEEVE, Virginia Crocheron, 1877- 923.773
Many a good crusade; memoirs. New York, Macmillan, 1954. 434 p. illus. 22 cm. [LB875.G54A3] 54-12954
I. Title.

Giles, Alfred, 1853-1920.

JUTSON, Mary Carolyn Hollers. 720'.92'4
Alfred Giles: an English architect in Texas and Mexico. Photography by Joe S. Lawrie. San Antonio, Trinity University Press [1972] xviii, 178 p. illus. 29 cm. (San Antonio Conservation Society series, no. 1) Bibliography: p. 167-172. [NA997.G54J87] 72-75338 ISBN 0-911536-42-6
1. Giles, Alfred, 1853-1920. 2. Architecture—Texas. 3. Architecture—Mexico. I. Title. II. Series: San Antonio Conservation Society. San Antonio Conservation Society series, no. 1.

Giles, Ernest, d. 1897.

DUTTON, Geoffrey. 919.4
Australia's last explorer: Ernest Giles. New York, Barnes & Noble [1970] 175 p. illus., maps (2 fold.), ports. 21 cm. (Great travellers) Bibliography: p. 170. [DU114.G5D88 1970] 70-16394 5.50
1. Giles, Ernest, d. 1897. 2. Australia—Discovery and exploration. I. Title.

Giles, Janice (Holt)

GILES, Janice (Holt) 813'.5'4 B
The Kinta years. Boston, Houghton Mifflin, 1973. xii, 337 p. illus. 22 cm. Autobiographical. [PS3513.I4628Z52] 72-9016 ISBN 0-395-14011-0 7.95
1. Giles, Janice (Holt) I. Title. BIP

Gilford, Jack.

MOSTEL, Kate. 792'.028'0922 B
170 years of show business / Kate Mostel and Madeline Gilford, with Jack Gilford and Zero Mostel. 1st ed. New York : Random House, c1978. xi, 175 p., [16] leaves of plates : ill. ; 24 cm. [PN2285.M63] 77-90300 ISBN 0-394-41181-1 : 8.95
1. Mostel, Kate. 2. Gilford, Madeline. 3. Gilford, Jack. 4. Mostel, Zero, 1915-1977. 5. Actors—United States—Biography. I. Gilford, Madeline, joint author. II. Title.

Gilford, Madeline.

MOSTEL, Kate. 792'.028'0922 B
170 years of show business / Kate Mostel and Madeline Gilford, with Jack Gilford and Zero Mostel. 1st ed. New York : Random House, c1978. xi, 175 p., [16] leaves of plates : ill. ; 24 cm. [PN2285.M63] 77-90300 ISBN 0-394-41181-1 : 8.95
1. Mostel, Kate. 2. Gilford, Madeline. 3. Gilford, Jack. 4. Mostel, Zero, 1915-1977. 5. Actors—United States—Biography. I. Gilford, Madeline, joint author. II. Title.

Gill, Brendan, 1914- —Biography.

GILL, Brendan, 1914- 818'.5'209 B
Here at the New Yorker / Brendan Gill. 1st ed. New York : Random House, [1975] 406 p. : ill. ; 25 cm. Autobiographical. Includes index. [PS3513.I468Z52] 74-23927 ISBN 0-394-48989-6 : 12.95
1. Gill, Brendan, 1914- —Biography. 2. The New Yorker. I. Title. BIP

Gill, Eric [Arthur Eric Rowton Peter Joseph Gill]

GILL, Eric [Arthur Eric Rowton Peter Joseph Gill] 927.3
Autobiography. London, J. Cape [dist. Chester Springs, Pa., Dufour, 1964] 283p. front., plates, ports., facsim. 21cm. 41-51646 3.50
I. Title.

Gill, Eric, 1882-1940.

ATTWATER, Donald, 1892- ed. 270.8'1'0922
Modern Christian revolutionaries; an

introduction to the lives and thought of: Kierkegaard, Eric Gill, G. K. Chesterton, C. F. Andrews [and] Berdyaev. Edited by Donald Attwater. Freeport, N.Y., Books for Libraries Press [1971, c1947] xiii, 390 p. illus., ports. 23 cm. (Essay index reprint series) Contents.Contents.—Soren Kierkegaard, by M. Chaning-Pearce.—G. K. Chesterton, by F. A. Lea.—Eric Gill, by D. Attwater.—C. F. Andrews, by N. MacNichol.—Nicolas Berdyaev, by E. Lampert.—Bibliography (p. [383]-390) [BR1700.A8 1971] 76-156608 ISBN 0-8369-2304-9
1. Kierkegaard, Soren Aabye, 1813-1855. 2. Chesterton, Gilbert Keith, 1874-1936. 3. Gill, Eric, 1882-1940. 4. Andrews, Charles Freer, 1871-1940. 5. Berdiaev, Nikolai Aleksandrovich, 1874-1948. I. Title.

BRADY, Elizabeth A., 1914- 686.2'24 B
Eric Gill: twentieth century book designer, by Elizabeth A. Brady. Rev. ed. Metuchen, N.J., Scarecrow Press, 1974. vii, 142 p. illus. 22 cm. Bibliography: p. 127-135. [Z232.G47B7 1974] 73-18453 ISBN 0-8108-0640-1 5.00
1. Gill, Eric, 1882-1940.

GILL, Eric, 1882-1940. 709'.24 B
Autobiography. New York, Biblo and Tannen, 1968 [c1941] xv, 300, [33] p. illus., ports. 22 cm. "Illustrations": p. [301]-[333] [NB497.G55A3 1968] 68-54231

KINDERSLEY, David. 730'.924 B
Mr. Eric Gill; recollections of David Kindersley. [San Francisco] Book Club of California, 1967. 24 p. illus., port. 19 cm. [NB497.G55K5] 67-66314
1. Gill, Eric, 1882-1940. I. Book Club of California, San Francisco.

THE Life and works of 741'.0924
Eric Gill; papers read at a Clark Library symposium, 22 April 1967, by Cecil Gill, Beatrice Warde & David Kindersley. Introd. by Albert Sperisen. Los Angeles, William Andrews Clark Memorial Library, University of California, 1968. ix, 67 p. illus., facsims., port. 26 cm. (William Andrews Clark Memorial Library seminar papers) [NB497.G55L5] 77-630232
1. Gill, Eric, 1882-1940. I. Gill, Cecil. II. Warde, Beatrice Lamberton (Becker) 1900- III. Kindersley, David. IV. California. University. University at Los Angeles. William Andrews Clark Memorial Library. V. Title. VI. Series.

SPEAIGHT, Robert, 1904- 730.924
The life of Eric Gill. New York, Kenedy [1966] xvii, 323p. illus., ports. 24cm. Bibl. [NB497.G55S6 1966a] 66-25003 6.95
1. Gill, Eric, 1882-1940. I. Title.

Gill, William H., 1886-

GILL, William H., 1886- 355.3'32'0924 B
Always a commander; the reminiscences of Major General William H. Gill, as told to Edward Jaquelin Smith. Colorado Springs, Colorado College, 1974. 124 p. illus. 22 cm. [E745.G54A32] 74-176063
1. Gill, William H., 1886- I. Smith, Edward Jaquelin. II. Title.

Giller, Norman M.

GILLER, Norman M. 720'.92'4 B
An adventure in architecture / Norman M. Giller. Miami Beach, Fla. : Virgo Press, c1976. 248 p. : ill. ; 26 cm. Includes index. [NA737.G534A43] 76-28287 12.50
1. Giller, Norman M. 2. Architects—United States—Biography. I. Title. BIP

Gillespie, Angela, 1824-1887.

BETZ, Eva (Kelly) 1897- 922.273
Stout hearts and gentle hands; the life of Mother Angela, of the Sisters of the Holy Cross [by] Eva K. Betz. Valatie, N.Y., Holy Cross Press, 1964. 106 p. 23 cm. [BX4496.Z8B4] 64-8534
1. Gillespie, Angela, 1824-1887. 2. Sisters of the Holy Cross. I. Title.

Gillespie, Janet.

GILLESPIE, Janet. 974'.04'0924 B
With a merry heart / Janet Gillespie. 1st ed. New York : Harper & Row, c1976. 231 p. ; 22 cm. [BX9225.G49A34 1976] 76-5125 ISBN 0-06-011537-8 : 8.95
1. Gillespie, Janet. 2. Wicks, Robert Russell, 1882- 3. Wickes family. 4. Presbyterians—United States—Biography. I. Title. BIP

GILLESPIE, Janet. 974'.04'0924 B
With a merry heart / Janet Gillespie. Boston : G. K. Hall, 1977, c1976. 467 p. ; 24 cm. Large print ed. [BX9225.G49A34 1977] 77-5585 lib.bdg. : 12.95
1. Gillespie, Janet. 2. Wicks, Robert Russell, 1882- 3. Wickes family. 4. Presbyterians—United States—Biography. 5. Large type books. I. Title.

Gillies, Robert Pearse, 1788-1858.

GILLIES, Robert Pearse, 1788-1858. 828'.8'03 B
Memoirs of a literary veteran; including sketches and anecdotes of the most distinguished literary characters from 1794 to 1849. London, R. Bentley, 1851. [New York, AMS Press, 1973] 3 v. 19 cm. [PR4715.G7Z5 1973] 71-148785 ISBN 0-404-07650-5 40.00
1. Gillies, Robert Pearse, 1788-1858. I. Title. BIP

Gillingham family.

GILLINGHAM, George Oliver, 1895- 929.2
The story of Gillingham. Washington, 1967. 32 p. 28 cm. Cover title. Bibliography: p. 52. [CS71.G481 1967] 79-5677
1. Gillingham family. I. Title.

Gilman, Charlotte Perkins Stetson, 1860-1935.

GILMAN, Charlotte (Perkins) Stetson, 1860-1935. 309.1'2'4 B
The living of Charlotte Perkins Gilman; an autobiography. New York, Arno Press, 1972 [c1935] xxxviii, 341 p. ports. 23 cm. (American women: images and realities) [PS1744.G57Z5 1972] 72-2604 ISBN 0-405-04459-3 17.00
I. Title. II. Series. BIP

HILL-PETERS, Mary. 301.41'2'0924 B
Charlotte Perkins Gilman : the making of a radical feminist, 1860-1896 / Mary Hill-Peters. Philadelphia : Temple University Press, [1979] p. cm. Includes index. Bibliography: p. [HQ1413.G54H54] 79-22395 ISBN 0-87722-160-X : 14.95
1. Gilman, Charlotte Perkins Stetson, 1860-1935. 2. Feminists—United States—Biography. BIP

Gilman, Charlotte Perkins Stetson, 1860-1935—Biography.

GILMAN, Charlotte Perkins Stetson, 1860-1935. 309.1'2'4 B
The living of Charlotte Perkins Gilman : an autobiography / by Charlotte Perkins Gilman ; foreword by Zona Gale. New York : Harper & Row, 1975, c1935. xxxviii, 341 p. : port. ; 21 cm. (Harper colophon books ; CN 422) (Women's studies) Includes index. [PS1744.G57Z5 1975] 75-324195 ISBN 0-06-090422-4 pbk. : 3.95
1. Gilman, Charlotte Perkins Stetson, 1860-1935—Biography. I. Gale, Zona, 1874-1938. II. Title.

Gilman, Dorothy—Homes and haunts—Nova Scotia.

GILMAN, Dorothy, 1923- 813'.5'4 B
A new kind of country / by Dorothy Gilman. 1st ed. Garden City, N.Y. : Doubleday, 1978. 125 p. ; 22 cm. [PS3557.I433Z47] 77-12852 ISBN 0-385-13628-5 : 6.95
1. Gilman, Dorothy—Homes and haunts—Nova Scotia. 2. Novelists, American—20th century—Biography. 3. Nova Scotia—Social life and customs. I. Title. BIP

Gilman, James Franklin, 1850-1929.

DAWSON, Adele Godchaux, 1905- 759.13
James Franklin Gilman, nineteenth century painter / by Adele Godchaux Dawson. Canaan, N.H. : Phoenix Pub., c1975. vii, 159 p. : ill. (some col.) ; 32 cm. Includes index. Bibliography: p. 146-147. [ND237.G46D38] 75-20929 ISBN 0-914016-20-2 : 15.00
1. Gilman, James Franklin, 1850-1929. I. Title.

Gilmer Co., W. Va.—Biography.

BICENTENNIAL 920'.0754'27
biographies, Gilmer County, West Virginia / edited by the Gilmer County Historical Society ; cover design by Deborah Ann Erwin. Glenville, W. Va. : The Society, 1976. ix, 142 p. ; 21 cm. Errata slip inserted. Includes index. [F247.G5B5] 76-53133
1. Gilmer Co., W. Va.—Biography. 2. Pioneers—West Virginia—Gilmer Co.—Biography. 3. Gilmer Co., W. Va.—Genealogy. I. Gilmer County Historical Society.

Gilmore, Mary (Cameron) Dame, 1865-1962.

LAWSON, Sylvia Thomas. 821
Mary Gilmore [by] Sylvia Lawson. Melbourne, New York [etc.] Oxford University Press [1966, i.e. 1967] 30 p. illus., ports. 19 cm. (Great Australians) [PR6013.I4Z8] 75-407282 0.55
1. Gilmore, Mary (Cameron) Dame, 1865-1962.

Gilmore, Patrick Sarsfield, 1829-1892.

DARLINGTON, Marwood, 1912- 927.8
Irish Orpheus, the life of Patrick S. Gilmore, bandmaster extraordinary. Philadelphia, Olivier-Maney-Klein [1950] 130 p. illus., ports. 21 cm. [ML422.G48D3] 50-2756
1. Gilmore, Patrick Sarsfield, 1829-1892. I. Title.

Gilpin, William, 1724-1804.

TEMPLEMAN, William Darby, 1903-. 928.2
The life and work of William Gilpin (1724-1804) master of the picturesque and vicar of Boldre, by William D. Templeman. Urbana, The University of Illinois press, 1939. 336 p. front. (port.) plates. 26 cm. (Added t.-p.: [Illinois, University] Illinois studies in language and literature. vol. xxiv, no. 3-4) Bibliography: p. 307-325. [PR3478.G47Z8] 39-28551
1. Gilpin, William, 1724-1804. I. Title.

Gilpin, William, 1822-1894.

KARNES, Thomas L. 978.8'02'0924 B
William Gilpin, western nationalist, by Thomas L. Karnes. Austin, University of Texas Press [1970] 383 p. illus., facsims., ports. 24 cm. Bibliography: p. [351]-370. [F593.G48K3] 77-105398 7.50
1. Gilpin, William, 1822-1894.

Gilroy, Beryl.

GILROY, Beryl. 372.1'1'00924 B
Black teacher / [by] Beryl Gilroy. London : Cassell, 1976. ix, 196 p. ; 23 cm. [LA2375.G72G534] 77-356286 ISBN 0-304-29733-X : £4.50
1. Gilroy, Beryl. 2. Black teachers—Great Britain. 3. Teachers—Great Britain—Biography. I. Title.

Gimson, Ernest, 1864-1919.

ERNEST Gimson, his life 749.2'2 B
& work. New York : Garland Pub., 1978. vii, 47 v p., [60] leaves of plates : ill. ; 29 cm. (The Aesthetic movement & the arts and crafts movement) Three articles on Gimson, with notes on the 60 plates. Reprint of the 1924 ed. published by the Shakespeare Head Press, Stratford-upon Avon. [NK942.G5E7 1978] 76-17779 ISBN 0-8240-2485-0 : lib.bdg. : 35.00
1. Gimson, Ernest, 1864-1919. 2. Art industries ad trade—England—Biography. I. Title. II. Series.

Ginastera, Alberto Evaristo, 1916-

LOWENS, Irving, 1916- 781.7'7 S
Beatrix Cenci. Washington, Organization of American States [1972] 11 p. illus. 28 cm. (Inter-American Music bulletin, no. 82) [ML1.I717 no. 82] 782.1'073 73-170826
1. Ginastera, Alberto Evaristo, 1916- Beatrix Cenci. I. Title. II. Series.

Gingras, Gustave, 1918-

GINGRAS, Gustave, 1918- 617'.3'00924 B
Feet was I to the lame / by Gustave Gingras ; translated by Joan Chapman. London : Souvenir Press, 1977. 262 p., [4] leaves of plates : ill. ; 23 cm. (Human horizons series) (A Condor book) Translation of Combats pour la survie. [R464.G56A3413] 78-318484 ISBN 0-285-64836-5 : 14.95
1. Gingras, Gustave, 1918- 2. Physicians—Quebec (Province)—Biography. 3. Physically handicapped—Rehabilitation. I. Title. BIP

Ginsberg, Allen, 1926-

MOTTRAM, Eric. 811'.5'4 B
Allen Ginsberg in the sixties. Brighton, Seattle, Unicorn Bookshop, 1972. [1], 26 p. 21 cm. Includes bibliographical references. [PS3513.I74Z75] 72-197858 ISBN 0-85659-003-7 1.25
1. Ginsberg, Allen, 1926- I. Title.

Ginsberg, Allen, 1926- —Aesthetics.

PORTUGES, Paul, 1945- 811'.5'4
The visionary poetics of Allen Ginsberg / by Paul Cornel Portuges. Santa Barbara, CA : Ross-Erikson, 1978. xiv, 181 p. ; 23 cm. Includes index. Bibliography: p. 175-177. [PS3513.I74Z84] 78-6094 ISBN 0-915520-17-6 lib. bdg. : 11.95
1. Ginsberg, Allen, 1926- —Aesthetics. 2. Ginsberg, Allen, 1926- —Interviews. 3. Blake, William, 1757-1827—Influence—Ginsberg. 4. Poets, American—20th century—Biography. I. Title. BIP

Ginsberg, Allen, 1926- —Diaries.

GINSBERG, Allen, 1926- 818'.5'403
Journals : early fifties, early sixties / Allen Ginsberg ; edited by Gordon Ball. 1st ed. New York : Grove Press : distributed by Random House, 1977. xxx, 302 p. : ill. ; 25 cm. Includes bibliographical references. [PS3513.I74Z516] 76-54581 ISBN 0-8021-0134-8 : 10.00
1. Ginsberg, Allen, 1926- —Diaries. 2. Poets, American—20th century—Biogrpahy. I. Ball, Gordon.

GINSBERG, Allen, 1926- 818'.5'403
Journals : early fifties, early sixties / Allen Ginsberg ; edited by Gordon Ball. 1st ed. New York : Grove Press : distributed by Random House, 1977. xxx, 302 p. : ill. ; 25 cm. Includes bibliographical references. [PS3513.I74Z516] 76-54581 ISBN 0-8021-0134-8 : 10.00
1. Ginsberg, Allen, 1926- —Diaries. 2. Poets, American—20th century—Biogrpahy. I. Ball, Gordon. BIP

GINSBERG, Allen, 1926- 818'.5'403
Journals : early fifties, early sixties / Allen Ginsberg ; edited by Gordon Ball. 1st Evergreen ed. New York : Grove Press : distributed by Random House, 1978, c1977. xxx, 313 p. : ill. ; 24 cm. (An Evergreen book) Includes bibliographical references and index. [PS3513.I74Z516 1978] 78-50785 ISBN 0-394-17034-2 pbk. : 6.95
1. Ginsberg, Allen, 1926- —Diaries. 2. Poets, American—20th century—Biography. I. Ball, Gordon.

Ginsberg, Allen, 1926- —Interviews.

PORTUGES, Paul, 1945- 811'.5'4
The visionary poetics of Allen Ginsberg / by Paul Cornel Portuges. Santa Barbara, CA : Ross-Erikson, 1978. xiv, 181 p. ; 23 cm. Includes index. Bibliography: p. 175-177. [PS3513.I74Z84] 78-6094 ISBN 0-915520-17-6 lib. bdg. : 11.95
1. Ginsberg, Allen, 1926- —Aesthetics. 2. Ginsberg, Allen, 1926- —Interviews. 3. Blake, William, 1757-1827—Influence—Ginsberg. 4. Poets, American—20th century—Biography. I. Title. BIP

Ginther, John Robert, 1922-

GINTHER, John Robert, 1922- 616.8'34'00926
But you look so well / John R. Ginther. Chicago : Nelson Hall, c1978. ix, 153 p. ; 23 cm. Includes index. [RC377.G56] 77-26009 10.95
1. Ginther, John Robert, 1922- 2. Multiple sclerosis—Biography. I. Title. BIP

Ginzberg, Asher, 1856-1927.

SIMON, Leon, Sir 1881- 923.25693
Ahad ha-am, Asher Ginzberg; a biography. Philadelphia, Jewish Publication Society of America [c.1960] 348p. illus. Bibl.: p.331-332. 60-9794 4.50
1. Ginzberg, Asher, 1856-1927. I. Title.

SIMON, Leon Sir, 1881- 923.25693
Ahad ha-am, Asher Ginzberg; a biography. [1st ed.] Philadelphia, Jewish Publication Society of America [1960] 348 p. illus. 22 cm. Includes bibliography. [DS151.G5S54] 60-9794
1. Ginzberg, Asher, 1856-1927. I. Title.

Ginzberg, Louis, 1873-1953.

GINZBERG, Eli, 1911- 296.610924
Keeper of the law: Louis Ginzberg. Philadelphia, Jewish Pubn. Soc. [c.]1966. x, 348p. illus., ports. 22cm. Bibl. [BM755.G5G5] 66-11720 6.00
1. Ginzberg, Louis, 1873-1953. I. Title.

Ginzberg, Louis, 1877-1965

GINZBERG, Eli, 1911- 296.610924
Keeper of the law: Louis Ginzberg. [1st ed.] Philadelphia, Jewish Publication Society of America, 1966. x. 348 p. illus., ports. 22 cm. Bibliography: p. 335-336. [BM755.G5G5] 66-11720
1. Ginzberg, Louis, 1877-1965 I. Title.

Giolitti, Giovanni, 1842-1928.

GIOLITTI, Giovanni, 1842-1928. 945.09'092'4 B
Memoirs of my life. Translated from the Italian by Edward Storer. With an introd. by O. Malagodi. New York, H. Fertig, 1973. ix, 472 p. port. 22 cm. Translation of Memorie della mia vita. Reprint of the 1923 ed. [DG575.G5A4 1973] 72-80619 14.50
1. Giolitti, Giovanni, 1842-1928. 2. Italy—Politics and government—1870-1915—Sources. I. Title. BIP

Giono, Jean, 1895-

REDFERN, W. D. 843'.9'12
The private world of Jean Giono [by] W. D. Redfern. Durham, N.C., Duke University Press, 1967. xiv, 203 p. 23 cm. Bibliography: p. 197-203. [PQ2613.I57Z79] 67-20396
1. Giono, Jean, 1895- I. Title. BIP

Giorgione, Giorgio Barbarelli, known as, 1477-1511.

BALDASS, Ludwig von, 1887-1963 759.5
Giorgione. Notes on the plates by Gunther Heinz. [Tr. from from German by J. Maxwell Brownjohn] New York, Abrams [1965] 188p. illus., plates (26 mounted col.) 34cm. Bibl. [ND623.G5B33] 65-23171 25.00
1. Giorgione, Giorgio Barbarelli, known as, 1477-1511. I. Heinz, Gunther. II. Title.

Giotto di Bondone, 1266?-1337.

BATTISTI, Eugenio 759.5
Giotto. biographical and critical study. Translated from the Italian by James Emmons. [Lausanne] Skira; [distributed in the U. S. by World Pub. Co., Cleveland, 1960] 146p. (Bibl: p. 133-[138]) (The Taste of our time, v. 32) 60-8730 5.75
1. Giotto di Bondone, 1266?-1337. 2. ounted col. illus. 19cm. I. Title.

Giotto di Bondone, 1266?-1337—Juvenile literature.

ROCKWELL, Anne F. 759.5 B
The boy who drew sheep [by] Anne Rockwell. [1st ed.] New York, Atheneum, 1973. 37 p. illus. 25 cm. Based on the biography of Giotto di Bondone as written down by G. Vasari in the sixteenth century. A brief biography of the early Renaissance artist who was the most famous of his time and introduced a new way of painting. [ND623.G6R62 1973] 92 72-86948 4.50
1. Giotto di Bondone, 1266?-1337—Juvenile literature. I. Title. BIP

Giovanni, Nikki.

GIOVANNI, Nikki. 811'.5'4 B
Gemini: an extended autobiographical statement on my first twenty-five years of being a Black poet. Indianapolis, Bobbs-Merrill [1972, c1971] xii, 149 p. group port. 22 cm. [PS3557.I55Z5 1972] 75-161244 5.95
I. Title.

GIOVANNI, Nikki 811'.5'4[B]
Gemini: an extended autobiographical statement on my first twenty-five years of being a black poet. [New York,] [Viking Press] [1973, c1971] 149 p. 20 cm. [PS3557.155Z5 1973] 72-11674 ISBN 0-670-00325-5 1.95 (pbk)

*GIOVANNI, Nikki 811.'5'4
Gemini : an extended autobiographical statement on my first twenty-five years of being a black poet / Nikki Giovanni. New York : Penguin, 1976 c1971. x, 149 p. ; 19 cm. [PS3557.I55Z5] ISBN 0-14-004264-4 pbk. : 1.95
I. Title.
L.C. card no. for 1971 Bobbs Merrill edition: 72-11674. BIP

Gipp, George, 1895-

CHELLAND, Patrick, 1928- 796.33'2'0924 B
One for the Gipper George Gipp, Knute Rockne, and Notre Dame. Chicago, H. Regnery Co. [1973] xi, 212 p. illus. 22 cm. [GV939.G53C47] 73-6453 7.95
1. Gipp, George, 1895- I. Title.

Gippius, Zinaida Nikolaevna, 1869-1945—Diaries.

GIPPIUS, Zinaida Nikolaevna, 1869-1945. 891.7'1'3 B
Between Paris and St. Petersburg : selected diaries of Zinaida Hippius / translated and edited by Temira Pachmuss. Urbana : University of Illinois Press, [1975] xiii, 329 p. : port. ; 24 cm. Includes bibliographical references and index. [PG3460.G5Z514 1975] 75-4857 ISBN 0-252-00307-1 : 12.50
1. Gippius, Zinaida Nikolaevna, 1869-1945—Diaries. I. Pachmuss, Temira, 1927- ed. II. Title. BIP

Girard, Fred.

GIRARD, Fred. 978.8'29 B
Durango : the end of the trail / by Fred Girard. Santa Fe, N.M. : Sleeping Fox Enterprises, c1975. 101 p., [12] leaves of plates : ill. ; 23 cm. [F784.D9G57] 76-357957 pbk. : 4.95
1. Girard, Fred. 2. Durango, Colo.—Biography. I. Title.

Girard, Joe.

GIRARD, Joe. 658.85
How to sell anything to anybody / Joe Girard with Stanley Hi Brown. New York : Warner Books, 1979,c1977. 238p. ; 18 cm. [HI5439.5.G57A33] ISBN 0-446-82957-9 pbk. : 2.25
1. Girard, Joe. 2. Sales personnel — Biography. 3. Selling. I. Title.
L.C. card no. for 1977 Simon and Schuster ed.:77-21683.

GIRARD, Joe. 658.85
How to sell anything to anybody / Joe Girard with Stanley H. Brown. New York : Simon and Schuster, c1977. p. cm. Includes index. [HF5439.5.G57A33] 77-21683 7.95
1. Girard, Joe. 2. Sales personnel—Biography. 3. Selling. I. Brown, Stanley H., joint author. II. Title.

GIRARD, Joe. 658.85
How to sell anything to anybody / Joe Girard with Stanley H. Brown. New York : Simon and Schuster, c1977. p. cm. Includes index. [HF5439.5.G57A33] 77-21683 7.95
1. Girard, Joe. 2. Sales personnel—Biography. 3. Selling. I. Brown, Stanley H., joint author. II. Title. BIP

Girard, Stephen, 1750-1831.

MINNIGERODE, Meade, 1887-1967. 650'.0922 B
Certain rich men; Stephen Girard, John Jacob Astor, Jay Cooke, Daniel Drew, Cornelius Vanderbilt, Jay Gould, Jim Fisk. Freeport, N.Y., Books for Libraries Press [1970] xi, 210 p. illus., facsim., ports. 23 cm. (Essay index reprint series) Reprint of the 1927 ed. Bibliography: p. ix-xi. [CT219.M55 1970] 71-121489
1. Girard, Stephen, 1750-1831. 2. Astor, John Jacob, 1763-1848. 3. Cooke, Jay, 1821-1905. 4. Drew, Daniel, 1797-1879. 5. Vanderbilt, Cornelius, 1794-1877. 6. Gould, Jay, 1836-1892. 7. Fisk, James, 1835-1872. I. Title.

Giraudoux, Jean, 1882-1944.

LE SAGE, Laurent, 1913- 840.81
Jean Giraudoux; his life and works. [University Park] Pennsylvania State University, 1959. 238p. 24cm. Bibliographical references included in 'Notes' (p. 211-234) [PQ2613.I74Z68] 59-12342
1. Giraudoux, Jean, 1882-1944. I. Title.

REILLY, John H. 848'.9'1209
Jean Giraudoux / by John H. Reilly. Boston : Twayne Publishers, 1978. p. cm. (Twayne's world authors series ; TWAS 513 : France) Includes index. Bibliography: p. [PQ2613.I74Z784] 78-19156 ISBN 0-8057-6354-6 lib. bdg. : 9.95
1. Giraudoux, Jean, 1882-1944. 2. Authors, French—20th century—Biography. BIP

Giri Varahagiri Venkata, 1894-

GIRI, Varahagiri Venkata, 1894- 954.04'092'4 B
My life and times / V. V. Giri. Delhi ; Macmillan Co. of India, 1976- v. : ill. ; 25 cm. Includes index. "Appendix: A comparison between the Irish and Indian independence movements and its leaders": v. 1, p. [207]-212. [DS481.G5A35] 76-904258 Rs70.00 (v. 1)
1. Giri Varahagiri Venkata, 1894- 2. Presidents—India—Biography. 3. India—History—20th century. I. Title.

Girls.

A Young girl's diary. 301.43'15
Prefaced with a letter by Sigmund Freud. Translated by Eden and Cedar Paul. Boston, Milford House [1971] 284 p. 22 cm. Reprint of the 1921 ed. [HQ798.Y57 1971] 73-165118 ISBN 0-87821-043-1
1. Girls. 2. Adolescence.

Girls—Biography—Juvenile literature.

KIRKLAND, Winifred Margaretta, 1872-1943. 920.072
Girls who made good, by Winifred and Frances Kirkland. Freeport, N.Y., Books for Libraries Press [1971, c1930] 120 p. 23 cm. (Essay index reprint series) Contents.Contents.—Rosa Bonheur, painter and tomboy.—Anna Howard Shaw, pioneer.—Gertrude Bell, the girl who had "been there."—Sarojini Naidu, poet and patriot.—Alice Freeman Palmer, the country girl who became a college president.—Marie Curie, the light-bringer.—Florence Nightingale, the wish that waited.—Jane Adams, the girl who wanted to live in a big house.—Nance Astor, the girl who had two countries.—Lucy Larcom, a poet of the mills.—Maude Royden, woman and preacher.—Mary Slessor, only one missionary.—Florence Allen, woman and citizen.—Alice Foote McDougall, doing the next thing next.—Mary Martin Sloop, what she built out of old clothes. [CT3205.K5 1971] 71-152183 ISBN 0-8369-2235-2
1. Girls—Biography—Juvenile literature. I. Kirkland, Frances, joint author. II. Title. BIP

Gish, Lillian, 1896-

AFFRON, Charles. 791.43'028'0922
Star acting : Gish, Garbo, Davis / Charles Affron. New York : Dutton, c1977. x, 354 p. : ill. ; 27 cm. Includes index. Bibliography: p. [345]-347. [PN1995.A27] 76-8039 ISBN 0-525-20968-9 : 16.95
1. Gish, Lillian, 1896- 2. Garbo, Greta, 1905- 3. Davis, Bette, 1908- 4. Moving-picture acting. I. Title. BIP

GISH, Lillian, 1896- 791.43'028'0922
Dorothy and Lillian Gish. Edited by James E. Frasher. New York, Scribner [1973] 311 p. illus. 32 cm. [PN2287.G55A3 1973] 73-1111 ISBN 0-684-13571-X 19.95
1. Gish, Lillian, 1896- 2. Gish, Dorothy.

GISH, Lillian, 1896- 791.43'028'0924 B
Lillian Gish; the movies, Mr. Griffith, and me, by Lillian Gish with Ann Pinchot. Englewood Cliffs, N.J., Prentice-Hall [1969] xii, 388 p. illus. 24 cm. [PN2287.G55A3] 69-16169 7.95
I. Pinchot, Ann. II. Title. III. Title: The movies, Mr. Griffith, and me.

GISH, Lillian, 1896- 791.43'028'0924 B
Lillian Gish; the movies, Mr. Griffith & me [by] Lillian Gish with Ann Pinchot. [New York] Avon [1970, c1969] xii, 388 p. illus., ports. 18 cm (Avon/W190) [PN2287.G55A3 1970] 70-14685 1.25
I. Pinchot, Ann. II. Title. III. Title: The movies, Mr. Griffith & me.

Gissing, George Robert, 1857-1903.

†COLLIE, Michael. 823'.8 B
George Gissing : a biography / Michael Collie. Folkestone, Eng. : Dawson ; Hamden, Conn. : Archon Books, 1977. 189 p. ; 23 cm. Includes index. Bibliography: p. [182]-186. [PR4717.C58] 78-309185 ISBN 0-7129-0770-X : 13.50
1. Gissing, George Robert, 1857-1903. 2. Novelists, English—19th century—Biography. BIP

DONNELLY, Mabel Collins. 928.2
George Gissing, grave comedian. Cambridge, Harvard University Press, 1954. 245p. 22cm. Bibliography: p. [225]-229. [PR4717.D6] 53-10869
1. Gissing, George Robert, 1857-1906. I. Title.

GISSING, George Robert, 1857-1903 928.2
George Gissing and H. G. Wells, their friendship and correspondence. Ed. by Royal A. Gettmann. Urbana, Univ. of Ill. Pr. [c.]1961 285p. illus., (H. G. Wells papers at the Univ. Ill.) Bibl. 61-17275 3.50
I. Wells, Herbert George, 1866-1946. II. Title. III. Series.

GISSING, George Robert, 1857-1903. 928.2
The letters of George Gissing to Eduard Bertz, 1887-1903. Ed. by Arthur C. Young. New Brunswick, N.J., Rutgers, 1961. 337p. 60-14209 6.00
I. Bertz, Eduard, 1853-1931. II. Title.

GISSING, George Robert, 1857-1903. 823'.8 B
Letters of George Gissing to members of his family. Collected and arr. by Algernon and Ellen Gissing. With a pref. by his son. New York, Haskell House, 1970. vii, 414 p. facsim., port. 23 cm. "Chronological list of works": p. [407] [PR4717.A3 1970] 77-130257 ISBN 0-8383-1158-X
1. Gissing, Algernon, 1860-1937, ed. II. Gissing, Ellen, 1867- ed. BIP

KORG, Jacob. 828.8
George Gissing: a critical biography. Seattle, University of Washington Press, 1963. 311 p. illus. 24 cm. Includes bibliography. [PR4717.K6] 63-9938
1. Gissing, George Robert, 1857-1903. I. Title. BIP

ROBERTS, Morley, 1857-1942 928.2
The private life of Henry Mitland; a portrait of George Gissing. Ed. introd. by Morchard Bishop. London, Richards pr. [dist. Chester Springs, Pa., Dufour, 1964] 253p. port. 23cm. 58-4682 4.50
1. Gissing, George Robert, 1857-1903. I. Title.

TINDALL, Gillian. 823'.8 B
The born exile; George Gissing. [1st American ed.] New York, Harcourt Brace Jovanovich [1974] 295 p. illus. 21 cm. Includes bibliographical references. [PR4717.T5 1974] 74-6387 ISBN 0-15-113594-0 10.00
1. Gissing, George Robert, 1857-1903. I. Title. BIP

Gissing, George Robert, 1857-1903—Diaries.

GISSING, George Robert, 1857-1903. 828'.8'03 B
London and the life of literature in late Victorian England : the diary of George Gissing, novelist / edited by Pierre Coustillas. 1st American ed. Lewisburg [Pa.] : Bucknell University Press, 1978. vii, 617 p., [1] leaf of plates : port. ; 25 cm. Includes bibliographical references and index. [PR4717.A24 1978b] 77-72970 ISBN 0-8387-2145-1 : 30.00
1. Gissing, George Robert, 1857-1903—Diaries. 2. Novelists, English—19th century—Biography. I. Coustillas, Pierre. II. Title. BIP

Gissing, George Robert, 1857-1903—Knowledge and learning.

GAPP, Samuel Vogt, 1902- 823'.8
George Gissing, classicist / by Samuel Vogt Gapp. Philadelphia : R. West, 1978. 210 p. ; 25 cm. Reprint of the 1936 ed. published by the University of Pennsylvania Press, Philadelphia. Originally presented as the author's thesis, University of Pennsylvania, 1934. Includes index. Bibliography: p. 199-205. [PR4717.G3 1978] 78-57535 ISBN 0-8492-0918-8 : 25.00
1. Gissing, George Robert, 1857-1903—Knowledge and learning. 2. Novelists, English—19th century—Biography. 3. Classicists—England—Biography. I. Title. BIP

Gist, Christopher, d. 1759.

BAILEY, Kenneth P., 1912- 973.2'6'0924 B
Christopher Gist : colonial frontiersman, explorer, and Indian agent / by Kenneth P. Bailey. Hamden, Conn. : Archon Books, 1976. 264 p. : ill. ; 24 cm. Includes index. Bibliography: p. 219-239. [F229.G532B34] 75-30810 ISBN 0-208-01564-7 : 15.00
1. Gist, Christopher, d. 1759.

Giuliano, Salvatore, 1922-1950.

MAXWELL, Gavin. 923.4145
Bandit. [1st ed.] New York, Harper [c1956] 274p. illus. 22cm. 'Published in England under the title of God protect me from my friends.' [HV6453.I82S627 1956] 55-8027
1. Giuliano, Salvatore, 1922-1950. 2. Mafia. I. Title.

Glackens, William J, 1870-1938.

GLACKENS, Ira, 1907 v. 12
William Glackens and the Ashcan group. New York, Grosset & Dunlap [1957] 260 p. illus. 24 cm. (The Universal Library) 67-100209
1. Glackens, William J, 1870-1938. 2. Painters, American. 3. Realism in art. I. Title. II. Series.

Gladilin, Anatolii Tikhonovich—Biography.

GLADILIN, Anatolii Tikhonovich. 891.7'3'44 B
The making and unmaking of a Soviet writer : my story of the "Young prose" of the sixties and after / Anatoly Gladilin ; translated by David Lapeza. Ann Arbor : Ardis, c1979. 166 p. ; 21 cm. [PG3481.L24Z4713] 78-74199 ISBN 0-88233-354-2 : 10.00 ISBN 0-8352-0001-9 pbk. : 3.50
1. Gladilin, Anatolii Tikhonovich—Biography. 2. Gladilin, Anatolii Tikhonovich—Friends and associates. 3. Authors, Russian—20th century—Biography. 4. Literature and state—Russia. I. Title.

Gladstone family.

CHECKLAND, S. G. 929.2'0942
The Gladstones: a family biography, 1764-1851 [by] S. G. Checkland. Cambridge [Eng.] University Press, 1971. xvi, 448 p. illus., ports. 24 cm. Bibliography: p. 418-425. [CS439.G547 1971] 72-134611 ISBN 0-521-07966-7
1. Gladstone family. I. Title.

Gladstone, William Ewart, 1809-1898.

DREW, Mary (Gladstone) 1847-1927. 914.2'081'0922
Acton, Gladstone, and others. Port Washington, N. Y., Kennikat Press [1968] 147 p. 19 cm. (Essay and general literature index reprint series) Reprint of the 1924 ed. Contents.--Acton and Gladstone.--Mr. Gladstone's books.--Henry Scott Holland.--Mr. Ruskin and Rose.--Tennyson and Laura Tennant.--"Here's me." Bibliographical footnotes. [DA531.1.D7] 68-16292
1. Acton, John Emerich Edward Dalberg Acton, Baron, 1834-1902. 2. Gladstone, William Ewart, 1809-1898. 3. Holland, Henry Scott, 1874-1918 I. Title.

DREW, Mary (Gladstone) 1847-1927. 920.042
Acton, Gladstone, and others. Freeport, N.Y., Books for Libraries Press [1968] 147 p. 22 cm. (Essay index reprint series) Reprint of the 1924 ed. Contents.—Acton and Gladstone.—Mr. Gladstone's books.—Henry Scott Holland.—Mr. Ruskin and Rose.—Tennyson and Laura Tennant.—Here's me. Bibliographical footnotes. [DA531.1.D7 1968b] 68-20294
1. Acton, John Emerich Edward Dalberg Acton, Baron, 1834-1902. 2. Gladstone, William Ewart, 1809-1898. 3. Holland, Henry Scott, 1847-1918. I. Title. BIP

EYCK, Erich, 1878-1964. 942.081'0924 B
Gladstone, Translated by Bernard Miall. New York, A. M. Kelley, 1968. 505 p. port. 23 cm. (Reprints of economic classics) Reprint of the 1938 ed. Bibliography: p. 465-487. [DA563.4.E82 1968] 68-56055
1. Gladstone, William Ewart, 1809-1898. 2. Gt. Brit.—Politics and government—1837-1901.

FEUCHTWANGER, E. J. 941.081'092'4 B
Gladstone / E. J. Feuchtwanger. New York : St. Martin's Press, 1975. x, 315 p. ; 23 cm. (British political biography) Includes index. Bibliography: p. [291]-298. [DA563.4.F48 1975b] 75-7712 13.95
1. Gladstone, William Ewert, 1809-1898. 2. Great Britain—Politics and government—1837-1901. BIP

GLADSTONE, a biography. v. 12
New York, E. Dutton [1960] 482p. illus. 23cm. Bibliography: p. 449-451.
1. Gladstone, William Ewart, 1809-1898. I. Magnus, Philip Montefiore, Sir bart., 1906-

GLADSTONE, William Ewart. 941.081'092'4
The Gladstone diaries : Vol. 5 1855-1860; [and] Vol. 6, 1861-1868 / William Ewart Gladstone. Oxford : Clarendon Press, 1978. 1251 p. ; 24 cm. [DA563.4] ISBN 0-19-822445-1 : 92.00
1. Gladstone, William Ewert. I. Matthew, Henry Colin Grlay ed. II. Title.
Distributed by Oxford University Press, New York.

MAGNUS, Philip Montefiare, Sir, bart., 923.242
Gladstone, a biography. New York, Dutton, 1964. 482p. illus. 19cm. (D155) Bibl. 2.25 pap.,
1. Gladstone, William Ewart, 1809-1898. I. Title.

MAGNUS, Philip Montefiore, Sir, bart., 1906- 923.242
Gladstone, a biography. New York, Dutton [1954] 482 p. illus. 22 cm. Includes bibliography. [DA563.4.M3 1954a] 54-11697
1. Gladstone, William Ewart, 1809-1898.

MARLOW, Joyce. 941.081'092'2 B
The oak and the ivy : an intimate biography of William and Catherine Gladstone / Joyce Marlow. 1st ed. Garden City, N.Y. : Doubleday, 1977. 324 p., [8] leaves of plates : ill. ; 24 cm. Includes index. Bibliography: p. [302]-310 [DA563.4.M37] 76-18362 ISBN 0-385-11290-4 : 8.95
1. Gladstone, William Ewart, 1809-1898. 2. Gladstone, Catherine Glynne, 1812-1900. 3. Great Britain—Politics and government—1837-1901. 4. Prime ministers—Great Britain—Biography. 5. Prime ministers' wives—Great Britain—Biography. I. Title.

MORLEY, John Morley, Viscount, 1838-1923. 942.081'092'4 B
The life of William Ewart Gladstone. New York, Greenwood Press [1968, c1903] 3 v. illus. 24 cm. Contents.Contents.—v. 1. 1809-1859.—v. 2. 1859-1880.—v. 3. 1880-1898. Includes bibliographical references. [DA563.4.M8 1968] 68-57630
1. Gladstone, William Ewart, 1809-1898. 2. Great Britain—Politics and government—1837-1901. I. Title.

MORLEY, John Morley, Viscount, 1838-1923. 942.081'092'4 B
The life of William Ewart Gladstone. New York, Macmillan, 1903. St. Clair Shores, Mich., Scholarly Press, 1972. 3 v. illus. 22 cm. Contents.Contents.—v. 1. 1809-1859.—v. 2. 1859-1880.—v. 3. 1880-1898. [DA563.4.M8 1972] 70-145193 59.50
1. Gladstone, William Ewart, 1809-1898. 2. Great Britain—Politics and government—1837-1901. BIP

STANSKY, Peter. 941.081'092'4 B
Gladstone, a progress in politics / by Peter Stansky. 1st ed. Boston : Little, Brown, c1979. xxiv, 201 p. ; 21 cm. (The Library of world biography) Includes index. Bibliography: p. [191]-194. [DA563.4.S73] 79-586 ISBN 0-316-81058-4 : 9.95
1. Gladstone, William Ewart, 1809-1898. 2. Great Britain—Politics and government—1837-1901. 3. Prime ministers—Great Britain—Biography. I. Title.

WILLIAMS, William Evan. 320.9'42'081 B
The rise of Gladstone to the leadership of the Liberal Party, 1859 to 1868, by W. E. Williams. With a new pref. by the authors. New York, Octagon Books, 1973. xxi, 188 p. 21 cm. Reprint of the 1934 ed. published by the University Press, Cambridge, Eng. Includes bibliographical references. [DA563.5.W5 1973] 73-17482 ISBN 0-374-98614-2 9.00
1. Gladstone, William Ewart, 1809-1898. 2. Liberal Party (Gt. Brit.) 3. Great Britain—Politics and government—1837-1901. I. Title. BIP

Gladwyn, Hubert Myles Gladwyn Jebb,

GLADWYN, Hubert Myles Gladwyn Jebb, Baron, 1900- 327'.2'0924 B
The memoirs of Lord Gladwyn. [1st American ed.] New York, Weybright and Talley [1972] x, 422 p. 24 cm. [D413.G57A3 1972b] 72-87144 9.95

Glanvill, Joseph, 1636-1680.

COPE, Jackson I 922.342
Joseph Glanvill, Anglican apologist. St. Louis [Committee on Publications, Washington University] 1956. 179p. 25cm. (Washington University studies) Bibliographical footnotes. [B1201.G54C6] 56-14710
1. Glanvill, Joseph, 1636-1680. 2. Apologetics—17th cent. I. Title. II. Series: Washington University, St. Louis. Washington University studies

Glasgow, Ellen Anderson Gholson, 1873-1945.

FIELD, Louise Maunsell. 813'.5'2
Ellen Glasgow, novelist of the Old and the new South; an appreciation. Together with a critical essay and an index to her works. [Folcroft, Pa.] Folcroft Library Editions, 1974 [c1923] 20 p. 23 cm. Reprint of the ed. published by Doubleday, Page, Garden City, N.Y., in series: Little biographies of great writers series. [PS3513.L34Z655 1974] 74-11118 ISBN 0-8414-4214-2 (lib. bdg.)
1. Glasgow, Ellen Anderson Gholson, 1873-1945.

GLASGOW, Ellen Anderson Gholson, 1873-1945. 928.1
The woman within. [1st ed.] New York, Harcourt, Brace [1954] xii, 397 p. illus., ports., facsim. 22 cm. Autobiography. "The works of Ellen Glasgow": p. 302. [PS3513.L34Z5] 54-11329
I. Title. BIP

GLASGOW, Ellen Anderson Gholson, 1874-1945. 928.1
Letters. Compiled and edited with an introd. and commentary by Blair Rouse. [1st ed.] New York, Harcourt, Brace [1958] 384 p. 25 cm. [PS3513.L34Z53] 58-5473
1. Authors—Correspondence, reminiscences, etc.

GLASGOW, Ellen Anderson Gholson, 1874-1945. 928.1
The woman within. [1st ed.] New York, Harcourt, Brace [1954] xii, 307p. illus., ports., facsim, 22cm. Autobiography. 'The works of Ellen Glasgow: p. 308. [PS3513.L34Z5] 54-11329
I. Title.

GODBOLD, E. Stanly. 813'.5'2 B
Ellen Glasgow and The woman within [by] E. Stanly Godbold, Jr. Baton Rouge, Louisiana State University Press [1972] xiii, 322 p. illus. 23 cm. Bibliography: p. 303-313. [PS3513.L34Z665] 71-165068 ISBN 0-8071-0040-4 10.95
1. Glasgow, Ellen Anderson Gholson, 1873-1945. I. Title. BIP

Glasgow school of painting.

MARTIN, David, artist. 759.9414'43 B
The Glasgow School of painting / David Martin. Edinburgh : P. Harris, 1976. [7], 72 p., [12] p. of plates : ill., ports. ; 16 cm. Reprint of the 1897 ed. published by G. Bell & Sons, London. [ND481.G5M4 1976] 77-375308 ISBN 0-904505-15-4 : £2.00
1. Glasgow school of painting. 2. Painting, Modern—19th century—Scotland—Glasgow. 3. Painters—Scotland—Biography. I. Title.

Glass, Carter, 1858-1946.

SMITH, Rixey, 1892- 973.9'0924 B
Carter Glass; a biography, by Rixey Smith and Norman Beasley. Introd. by Harry Flood Byrd. Pref. by Douglas Southall Freeman. New York, Da Capo Press, 1972 [c1939] xv, 519 p. illus. 22 cm. (Franklin

D. Roosevelt and the era of the New Deal) [E748.G53S6 1972] 72-172012 ISBN 0-306-70392-0
1. Glass, Carter, 1858-1946. 2. United States—Politics and government—1901-1953. I. Beasley, Norman, joint author. II. Title. III. Series. BIP

Glass, Charlie, d. 1937.

WYMAN, Walker Demarquis, 1907- 978.8'03'0924 B
The legend of Charlie Glass, Negro cowboy on the Colorado-Utah Range, by Walker D. Wyman and John D. Hart. Including "The ballad of Charlie Glass," words and music by William L. Clark. Illus. by Helen B. Wyman. River Falls, Wis., River Falls State University Press [1970] [20] p. illus. 23 cm. "The legend of Charlie Glass' originally appeared in the Colorado magazine of history, winter 1969." [E185.97.G55W95] 73-172048
1. Glass, Charlie, d. 1937. I. Hart, John D., joint author. II. Title.

Glass, Hugh, ca. 1780-ca. 1833.

MYERS, John Myers, 1906- 978'.02'0924 B
The saga of Hugh Glass : pirate, pawnee, and mountain man / by John Myers Myers. Lincoln : University of Nebraska Press, [1976] c1963. 237 p. ; 21 cm. Reprint of the ed. published by Little, Brown, Boston under title: Pirate, pawnee, and mountain man. Bibliography: p. 233-237. [F592.G55M9 1976] 75-38613 ISBN 0-8032-0867-7. ISBN 0-8032-5834-8 pbk. 3.25
1. Glass, Hugh, ca. 1780-ca. 1833. I. Title. BIP

Glass, Hugh, ca. 1780-ca. 1833—Juvenile literature.

TRIPP, Jenny. 613.6'9
The man who was left for dead / Jenny Tripp ; ill., Charles Shaw. Milwaukee : Raintree Publishers, c1980. p. cm. The true story of a man's survival after being attacked by a grizzly bear and left to die by his companions. [GV200.5.T74] 79-21519 ISBN 0-8172-1556-5 (lib. bdg.) : 7.99
1. Glass, Hugh, ca. 1780-ca. 1833—Juvenile literature. 2. Wilderness survival—Juvenile literature. 3. Grizzly bear—Legends and stories—Juvenile literature. 4. Pioneers The West—Biography—Juvenile literature. I. Shaw, Charles, 1941- II. Title. BIP

Glass painting and staining—New York (State)

SORACI, Carmelo. 748.59747
The convict and the stained glass windows. New York, John Day Co. [1961] 253 p. illus. 21 cm. Autobiography. [NK5398.S6A2] 61-8285
1. Glass painting and staining—New York (State) 2. Prisons—New York (State) I. Title.

Glass, Wiley B.

CAUTHEN, Eloise Glass. 266'.023'0924 B
Higher ground : biography of Wiley B. Glass, missionary to China / Eloise Glass Cauthen. Nashville, Tenn. : Broadman Press, c1978. 224 p. : ill. ; 21 cm. [GV3427.G56C38] 77-82402 ISBN 0-8054-7221-5 pbk. : 3.95
1. Glass, Wiley B. 2. Missionaries—China—Biography. 3. Missionaries—United States—Biography. 4. Baptists—Biography—United States. I. Title.

Glass, William.

GLASS, William. 796.3320924 B
Get in the game, by Bill Glass. [Waco, Tex.] Word Books [1965] xi, 150 p. illus., ports. 21 cm. [GV939.G55A3] 65-9767
I. Title.

Glatzer, Norbert, 1903-ed.

ROSENZWEIG, Franz, 1886-1929. 922.96
Franz Rosenzweig: his life and thought, presented by Nahum N. Glatzer. [2d rev. ed.] New York, Schocken Books [c1961] 404p. 21cm. (Schocken paperbacks, SB21) Includes bibliography. [BM755.R6A5 1961] 62-4143
1. Glatzer, Norbert, 1903-ed. I. Title.

Gleason. Jackie. 1916-

BISHOP, James Alonzo, 1907- 927.92
The golden ham; a candid biography of Jackie Gleason. New York, Simon and Schuster, 1956. 208p. 22cm. [PN1992.4.G6B5] 56-6680
1. Gleason. Jackie. 1916- I. Title.

Glegg, Lindsay, 1882-1975.

DOUGLAS, James Dixon. 269'.2'0924 B
Completing the course : the story of Lindsay Glegg / by J. D. Douglas. London : Pickering and Inglis, 1976. 128 p., [8] p. of plates : ill., ports. ; 19 cm. [BV3785.G54D68] 77-350974 ISBN 0-7208-0386-1 : £1.00
1. Glegg, Lindsay, 1882-1975. 2. Evangelists—England—Biography. I. Title.

Gleig, George Robert, 1796-1888.

GLEIG, George Robert, 1796-1888. 973.5'23
The campaigns of the British army at Washington and New Orleans. With a new foreword by Robin Reilly. Totowa, N.J., Rowman and Littlefield [1972] x, 208 p. 24 cm. Reprint of the 1847 ed. published by J. Murray, London. First published, London, 1821, with title: A narrative of the campaigns of the British army at Washington and New Orleans [E355.6.G567] 73-155140 ISBN 0-87471-023-5 10.00
1. Gleig, George Robert, 1796-1888. 2. United States—History—War of 1812—Campaigns and battles. 3. United States—History—War of 1812—Personal narratives. 4. Washington, D.C.—History—Capture by the British, 1814. 5. New Orleans, Battle of, 1815. I. Title. BIP

Glen Flora, Wis.—History.

GUSTAFSON, Walter. 917.75'19
Glen Flora pioneers. Chicago, Adams Press [1971] xviii, 292 p. maps, ports. 22 cm. [F589.G55G8] 68-9198
1. Glen Flora, Wis.—History. 2. Glen Flora, Wis.—Biography. I. Title.

Glendenning, Maurice Lerrie, Bp.

BEESTON, Blanche W 922.8373
Now my servant; a brief biography of a firstborn son of Aaron. [Caldwell Idaho, 1957. 216p. illus. 22cm. [BX8695.G57B4] 58-44407
1. Glendenning, Maurice Lerrie, Bp. I. Title.

Glendower, Owen, 1359?-1416?

BRADLEY, Arthur Granville, 1850-1943. 942.9'041'0924 B
Owen Glyndwr and the last struggle for Welsh independence : with a brief sketch of Welsh history / by Arthur Granville Bradley. New York : AMS Press, 1978. xvii, 357 p., [32] leaves of plates : ill. ; 18 cm. Reprint of the 1901 ed. published by Putnam, New York, which was issued in series: Heroes of the nations. Includes index. [DA716.G5B8 1978] 73-14435 ISBN 0-404-58253-2 : 30.00
1. Glendower, Owen, 1359?-1416? 2. Wales—History—To 1536. 3. Wales—Kings and rulers—Biography. I. Title. II. Series: Heroes of the nations.

WILLIAMS, Glanmor 942.90410924
Owen Glendower [New York] Oxford [c.] 1966. 64p. 8 plates (incl. ports., map) 21cm. (Clarendon biogs.) [DA716.G5W5] 66-70035 1.55 bds.,
1. Glendower, Owen, 1359?-1416? I. Title.

Glenn, John Herschel, 1921-

EDUCATIONAL Research Council of America. Social Science Staff. 629.4'0924
Explorers and discoverers: John Glenn. Boston, Allyn and Bacon [1970] 44 p. illus. (part col.), ports. (part col.) 21 cm. (Concepts and inquiry: the ERC social science program) Describes in simple terms the flight of John Glenn—the first American to orbit Earth. [PZ10.E25Exd] 92 73-97101
1. Glenn, John Herschel, 1921- 2. Astronautics—Juvenile literature. I. Title. II. Series: Concepts and inquiry: the Educational Research Council social science program

Glenn, John Herschel, 1921- —Juvenile literature.

AKENS, David S. 629.4'0924 B
John Glenn, first American in orbit, by David S. Akens. [Huntsville, Ala.] Strode Publishers [1969] 128 p. illus., ports. 22 cm. (Heroes of space series) A biography of the first American astronaut to orbit the earth on February 20, 1962. [TL789.85.G6A64] 92 78-75842
1. Glenn, John Herschel, 1921- —Juvenile literature. 2. Project Mercury—Juvenile literature.

PIERCE, Philip N., 1917- 920
John H. Glenn, astronaut, by Philip N. Pierce, Karl Schuon. New York, Watts [c.1962] 208p illus. 22cm. 62-16284 3.95
1. Glenn, John Herschel, 1921- —Juvenile literature. 2. Project Mercury—Juvenile literature. I. Schuon, Karl, joint author. II. Title.

WESTMAN, Paul. 629.45'092'4 B
John Glenn : around the world in 90 minutes / by Paul Westman. Minneapolis : Dillon Press, c1979. p. cm. (Taking part ; 4) A biography of the first American to orbit the earth who is now a United States Senator from his native Ohio. [TL789.85.G6W47] 79-19515 ISBN 0-87518-186-4 lib. bdg. : 6.95 6.95
1. Glenn, John Herschel, 1921- —Juvenile literature. 2. Astronauts—United States—Biography—Juvenile literature.

Glenn, Mabelle, 1881-

HOLGATE, George Jackson. v. 12
The life of Mabelle Glenn, music educator. West Yarmouth Mass., Rainbow Press [1965] 150 p. 65-101601
1. Glenn, Mabelle, 1881- I. Title.

Glennon, John Joseph, 1862-1946.

SCHNEIDER, Nicholas A. 262'.135'0924 B
The life of John Cardinal Glennon, Archbishop of St. Louis [by] Nicholas Schneider. Liguori, Mo., Liguori Publications [1971] 224 p. illus. 18 cm. Bibliography: p. 223-224. [BX4705.G557S35] 78-165974 1.75
1. Glennon, John Joseph, 1862-1946. I. Title.

Glesler, Jerry, 1886-1962.

ROEBURT, John. 923.473
Get me Giesler. New York, Belmont Books [1962] 191p. 18cm. 62-5530
1. Glesler, Jerry, 1886-1962. I. Title.

Glessner, Chloe (Holt)

GLESSNER, Chloe (Holt) 917.66'03'50924 B
I'm a Sooner born. San Antonio, Naylor Co. [1969] ix, 211 p. 22 cm. Autobiographical. [CT275.G52A33] 69-12500 4.95
I. Title.

Glickman, Harry.

GLICKMAN, Harry. 796'.092'4 B
Promoter ain't a dirty word / Harry Glickman. Forest Grove, Or. : Timber Press, c1978. xiv, 186 p. : ill. ; 22 cm. Label mounted on t.p.: Exclusive distributor: ISBS, Forest Grove, OR. [GV719.G56A36] 78-5604 ISBN 0-917304-35-7 : 9.95 pbk : 6.95 pbk : 6.95
1. Glickman, Harry. 2. Promoters—United States—Biography. 3. Sports—Organization and administration—United States. 4. Public relations—Sports. I. Title. BIP

Glieberman, Herbert A.

GLIEBERMAN, Herbert A. 346'.773'01660924 B
Confessions of a divorce lawyer / Herbert A. Glieberman, with Paul Neimark. Chicago : H. Regnery Co., [1975] 182 p. ; 24 cm. Autobiographical. [KF373.G58A33] 74-32210 ISBN 0-8092-9020-0 : 7.95
1. Glieberman, Herbert A. 2. Lawyers—Illinois—Correspondence, reminiscences, etc. I. Neimark, Paul G., joint author. II. Title. BIP

Glinka, Mikhail Ivanovich, 1804-1857.

BROWN, David, 1929- 780'.92'4 B
Mikhail Glinka; a biographical and critical study. London, New York, Oxford University Press, 1974 [i.e. 1973] 340 p. illus., music. 23 cm. Bibliography of works by and about M. Glinka: p. [316]-332. [ML410.G46B76] 74-153057 ISBN 0-19-315311-4 22.50
1. Glinka, Mikhail Ivanovich, 1804-1857. I. Title.

GLINKA, Mikhail Ivandvich, 1804-1857. 927.8
Memoirs. Tr. from Russian by Richard B. Mudge. Norman, Univ. of Okla. Pr. [c.1963] xi, 264p. illus., ports, music, 24cm. 63 8993 5.95
1. Musicians—Correspondence, reminiscences,etc. I. Title.

GLINKA, Mikhail Ivanovich, 1804-1857. 927.8
Memoirs, Translated from the Russian by Richard B. Mudge. [1st ed.] Norman, University of Oklahoma Press [1963] xi, 264 p. illus., ports., music. 24 cm. [ML410.G46A25] 63-8993 MN
1. Musicians — Correspondence, reminiscences, etc. I. Title.

MONTAGU-NATHAN, Montagu. 780'.92'4 B
Glinka / by M. Montagu-Nathan. New York : AMS Press, 1976. 85 p. ; 19 cm. Reprint of the 1917 ed. published by Duffield, New York, in series: Masters of Russian music. Includes index. "List of principal works": p. 81-82. [ML410.G46M7] 74-24156 ISBN 0-404-13049-6 : 10.00
1. Glinka, Mikhail Ivanovich, 1804-1857. 2. Composers—Russia—Biography. BIP

Gloethe, Johann Wolfgang von—Contemporaries.

ODYNIEC, Antoni Edward, 1804-1885. 928.3
Besuch in Weimar, Goethes achtzigster Geburtstag; Brief-berichte enines jungen polnischen Dichters, ubertragen von F. Th. Bratranck. Neu hrsg. von Max Mell. Wien, Pilgram Verlag [c1949] 189 p. 20 cm. Letters from Odyniec to Juljan Koraak. [PT2101.045] 50-24821
1. Gloethe, Johann Wolfgang von—Contemporaries. I. Korsak, Juljan 1807-1855. II. Mell, Max, 1882- ed. III. Title.

Gloucester, Mass.—History—Sources.

PARSONS, Peter. 917.44'5
When Gloucester was Gloucester; toward an oral history of the city [by] Peter Parsons and Peter Anastas. Photos. by Mark Power. Gloucester, Mass., Gloucester 350th Anniversary Celebration, inc., 1973. x, 82 p. illus. 23 cm. [F74.G5P37] 73-76939 2.95
1. Gloucester, Mass.—History—Sources. 2. Gloucester, Mass.—Biography. I. Anastas, Peter, joint author. II. Title.

Glovanni da Capistrano, Saint, 1385 or 6-1456.

ROBERTO, Brother, 1927- 922.245
A torch in the darkness; a story of St. John Capistran.Illus. by Brother Eagan. Notre Dame, Ind., Dujarie Press [1956] 92p. illus. 24cm. [BX4700.G72R6] 56-1599
1. Glovanni da Capistrano, Saint, 1385 or 6-1456. I. Title.

ROBERTO, Brother, 1927- 922.245
A torch in the darkness; a story of St. John Capistran, Illus. by Brother Eagan. Notre Dame, Ind., Dujarie Press [1956] 92p. illus. 24cm. [BX4700.G72R6] 56-1599
1. Glovanni da Capistrano, Saint, 1385 or 6-1456. I. Title.

Glover, Cato D.,

GLOVER, Cato D., 359.3'3'20924
1897-
Command performance, with guts, by Cato D. Glover. [1st ed. New York, Greenwich Book Publishers, 1969] 215 p. illus., maps, ports. 22 cm. Autobiographical. [V63.G55A3] 69-18089 7.50
I. Title.

Glover, Terrot Reaveley, 1869-1943.

WOOD, Herbert George, 922.642
1879-
Terrot Reaveley Glover; a biography. Cambridge [Eng.] University Press, 1953. 233p. illus. 22cm. [BX6495.G58W6] 53-9512
1. Glover, Terrot Reaveley, 1869-1943. I. Title.

Gluck, Christoph Willibald, Ritter von, 1714-1787.

EINSTEIN, Alfred, 1880- v. 12
1952.
Gluck; translated by Eric Blom. New York, Collier Books [1962] 254 p. music. 18 cm. (Great composers series) Collier book AS 377X.
1. Gluck, Christoph Willibald, Ritter von, 1714-1787. I. Title.

EINSTEIN, Alfred, 782.1'092'4 B
1880-1952.
Gluck. Translated by Eric Blom. New York, McGraw-Hill Book Co. [1972, c1964] ix, 238 p. music, port. 21 cm. (McGraw-Hill paperbacks) Translation of Gluck, sein Leben, seine Werke. Bibliography: p. 225-226. [ML410.G5E5 1972] 72-189735 ISBN 0-07-019530-7 2.95
1. Gluck, Christoph Willibald, Ritter von, 1714-1787.

EINSTEIN, Alfred, 1880- v. 12
1952.
Gluck. Translated by Eric Blom. With eight pages of plates and music examples in the text. London, J. M. Dent; New York, Farrar, Straus and Cudahy [1964] 238 p. illus. 20 cm. (The Master Musicians Series) "Catalogue of works": p. 216-218. "First published 1936; reprinted (with revisions) 1964." Bibliography: p. 225-226. 64-32584
1. Gluck, Christoph Willibald, Ritter von, 1714-1787. I. Title.

NEWMAN, Ernest, 782.1'092'4 B
1868-1959.
Gluck and the opera : a study in musical history / by Ernest Newman. 1st AMS ed. New York : AMS Press, 1978. xxiv, 300 p. ; 19 cm. (Music and theater in France in the 17th and 18th centuries) Reprint of the 1895 ed. published by B. Dobell, London. Includes bibliographical references and index. [ML410.G5N3 1978] 76-43929 18.00
1. Gluck, Christoph Willibald, Ritter von, 1714-1787. 2. Composers—Biography. 3. Opera—History and criticism. I. Title. II. Series. **BIP**

Glueck, Eleanor Touroff, 1898-1972.

GLUECK, Sheldon, 364'.092'2 B
1896-
Lives of labor, lives of love : fragments of friendly autobiographies / Sheldon Glueck. 1st ed. Hicksville, N.Y. : Exposition Press, c1977. 222 p., [4] leaves of plates : ill. ; 22 cm. (An Exposition-Banner book) "Chronological bibliography of Glueck writings": p. 169-210. [HV6023.G55A34] 76-24259 ISBN 0-682-48632-9 : 8.50
1. Glueck, Eleanor Touroff, 1898-1972. 2. Glueck, Sheldon, 1896- 3. Criminologists—United States—Biography. I. Title. **BIP**

Glyn, Elinor (Sutherland) 1864-1948.

DAVSON, Geoffrey Leo Simon, 928.2
bart., Sir 1922-
Elinor Glyn: a biography, by Anthony Glyn [pseud. 1st ed.] Garden City, N. Y., Doubleday 1955. 348p. illus. 22cm. [PS3513.L69Z65] 55-5507
1. Glyn, Elinor (Sutherland) 1864-1948. I. Title.

Glynn, Patrick McMahon, 1855-1931.

O'COLLINS, Gerald 994.0924
Patrick McMahon Glynn, a founder of Australin Federation. [Carlton, Australia] Melbourne Univ. Pr.; New York, Cambridge [1966] xv, 281p. ports. 23cm. [DU114.G55O25] 65-25719 12.00
1. Glynn, Patrick McMahon, 1855-1931. I. Title.

Gnanananda Sarasvathi, Swami, 1929-

THE Divine descent 294.5'6'1 B
: the life and mission of Her Holiness Sadguru Swami Sri Gnanananda Sarasvathi. Madras : Sri Gnana Advaitha Peetam, 1976. 73 p., [13] leaves of plates : ill. ; 24 cm. [BL1175.G587D58] 76-904735 Rs7.00
1. Gnanananda Sarasvathi, Swami, 1929- 2. Hindus—Biography.

God—Will.

GRACE, John Patrick, 1942- 269 B
Hearing His voice / John Patrick Grace. Notre Dame, Ind. : Ave Maria Press, c1979. 157 p. : ill. ; 21 cm. [BV4501.2.G69] 79-54696 ISBN 0-87793-187-9 pbk. : 3.50
1. God—Will. 2. Pentecostalism—United States. 3. Christian biography—United States. I. Title. **BIP**

Goddard, George Henry, 1817-1906.

SHUMATE, Albert. 709'.24
The life of George Henry Goddard, artist, architect, surveyor, and map maker, written by Albert Shumate. With a pref. by Francis P. Farquhar. [Berkeley] Friends of the Bancroft Library, University of California, 1969. 13 p. fold. map (in pocket) 36 cm. (The Series of keepsakes issued by the Friends of the Bancroft Library, no. 17) Bibliography: p. 11-13. [N6537.G6S5] 79-631610
1. Goddard, George Henry, 1817-1906. I. Title. II. Series: Friends of the Bancroft Library. Keepsakes, no. 17

Goddard, Robert Hutchings. 1882-1945.

GODDARD, Robert 629.134'354'0924
Hutchings, 1882-1945.
The autobiography of Robert Hutchings Goddard, father of the space age; early years to 1927. Worcester, Mass., A. J. St. Onge, 1966. 85 p. illus., ports. 74 mm. [TL781.85.G6A3] 67-4344

LEHMAN, Milton. 926.294
This high man; the life of Robert H. Goddard. With a pref. by Charles A. Lindbergh. New York, Farrar, Straus [1963] xv, 430 p. illus., ports. 22 cm. Includes bibliographical references. [TL781.85.G6L4] 63-15815
1. Goddard, Robert Hutchings. 1882-1945. I. Title.

Goddard, Robert Hutchings, 1882-1945—Juvenile literature.

DAUGHERTY, Charles Michael 92
Robert Goddard, trail blazer to the stars. Illus. by James Daugherty. New York, Macmillan [c.1964. 48]p. col. illus. 24cm. (Sci. story lib.) 63-15667 2.95
1. Goddard, Robert Hutchings, 1882-1945—Juvenile literature. I. Title.

DEWEY, Anne Perkins 92
Robert Goddard, space pioneer. Boston, Little, [c.1962] 154p. illus. Bibl. 62-8309 3.50
1. Goddard, Robert Hutchings, 1882-1945—Juvenile literature. I. Title.

LOMASK, Milton. 629.4'092'4 B
Robert H. Goddard; space pioneer. Illustrated by Al Fiorentino. Champaign, Ill., Garrard Pub. Co. [1972] 80 p. col. illus. 23 cm. (A Discovery book) A brief biography of the scientist whose inventions led to the bazooka, the jet engine, and the space rocket. [TL781.85.G6L65] 92 70-182847 ISBN 0-8116-6308-6 2.59
1. Goddard, Robert Hutchings, 1882-1945—Juvenile literature. I. Fiorentino, Al, illus. II. Title. **BIP**

QUACKENBUSH, Robert 629.4'092'4 B
M.
The boy who dreamed of rockets : how Robert Goddard became the father of the space age / Robert Quackenbush. New York : Parents' Magazine Press, c1978. [36] p. : col. ill. ; 27 cm. A biography of the American physicist responsible for many of the underlying principles of modern rocketry. Includes instructions for a model multistage rocket and an explanation of rocket flight. [TL781.85.G6Q32] 92 78-21882 ISBN 0-8193-0995-8 : 6.50 ISBN 0-8193-0996-6 lib. bdg.: 5.99
1. Goddard, Robert Hutchings, 1882-1945—Juvenile literature. 2. Rocketry—United States—Biography—Juvenile literature. I. Title.

VERRAL, Charles Spain 920
Robert Goddard: father of the space age. Illus. by Paul Frame. Englewood Cliffs, N.J., Prentice [1963] 80p. illus. 22cm. (P-H jr. res. bks.) 63-101444 2.95
1. Goddard, Robert Hutchings, 1882-1945—Juvenile literature. I. Title.

WINDERS. GERTRUDE (HECKER) 920
Robert Goddard: father of rocketry. New York, John Day [c.1963] 189p. illus. 21cm. Bibl. 63-10235 3.50
1. Goddard, Robert Hutchings, 1882-1945—Juvenile literature. I. Title.

WINDERS, Gertrude (Hecker) 92
Robert Goddard, father of rocketry. New York, John Day Co. [1963] 180 p. illus. 21 cm. Includes bibliography. [TL781.85.G6W5] 63-10235
1. Goddard, Robert Hutchings, 1882-1945 — Juvenile literature. I. Title.

Goddard, Will, b. 1819.

MCVEY, Frances 976.9'485'030924
Jewell.
Uncle Will of Wildwood : nineteenth century life in the Bluegrass / Frances Jewell McVey & Robert Berry Jewell ; with an introd. by Thomas D. Clark ; ill. by Robert James Foose. Lexington : University Press of Kentucky, [1974] xxi, 99 p. : ill. ; 21 cm. (The Kentucky bicentennial bookshelf) [CT275.G5517M32] 74-7877 ISBN 0-8131-0206-5 pbk. : 3.95
1. Goddard, Will, b. 1819. I. Jewell, Robert Berry, 1896- joint author. II. Title. III. Series. **BIP**

Goddard, William, 1740-1817.

MINER, Ward L 920.5
William goddard, newspaperman. Durham, N. C., Duke University Press, 1962. 223p. 24cm. [PN4874.G49M5] 62-14873
1. Goddard, William, 1740-1817. 2. Journalism—U. S. 3. Postal service— U. S.—Hist. I. Title. **BIP**

Godfrey, Arthur, 1903-

O'BRIAN, Jack. 927.914
Godfrey the great. New York, Cross Publications, 1951. 66 p. illus., ports. 28 cm. [PN1991.4.G6O2] 51-3300
1. Godfrey, Arthur, 1903- I. Title.

Godfrey, Mary.

NARRATIVE of the 973'.04'97 S
Seminole War and the miraculous escape of Mary Godfrey. New York : Garland Pub., 1977. 24 p. ; 23 cm. (The Garland library of narratives of North American Indian captivities ; v. 52) Issued with the reprint of the 1833 ed. of Priest, J. The captivity and sufferings of Gen. Freegift Patchin. New York, 1977. Reprint of the 1836 ed. published by D. F. Blanchard, Providence, under title: An authentic narrative of the Seminole War, and of the miraculous escape of Mrs. Mary Godfrey, and her four female children. [E85.G2 vol. 52] [E83.835] 973.5'7 76-51449 ISBN 0-8240-1676-9(set) lib.bdg. : 25.00
1. Godfrey, Mary. 2. Seminole War, 2d, 1835-1842. 3. Seminole Indians—Captivities. 4. Indians of North America—Captivities. 5. Florida—Biography. I. Series.

Godkin, Edwin Lawrence, 1831-1902.

ARMSTRONG, William 070.4'092'4 B
M.
E. L. Godkin : a biography / William M. Armstrong. Albany : State University of New York Press, 1978. xix, 287 p., [4] leaves of plates : ill. ; 24 cm. Includes index. Bibliography: p. 249-263. [PN4874.G5A87] 77-12918 ISBN 0-87395-371-1 : 30.00
1. Godkin, Edwin Lawrence, 1831-1902. 2. Journalists—United States—Biography. I. Title. **BIP**

GODKIN, Edwin 070.4'12'0924 B
Lawrence, 1831-1902.
Life and letters of Edwin Lawrence Godkin. Edited by Rollo Ogden. Westport, Conn., Greenwood Press [1972, c1907] 2 v. ports. 22 cm. [PN4874.G5O3 1972] 70-137055 ISBN 0-8371-5516-9 (set)
1. Godkin, Edwin Lawrence, 1831-1902. **BIP**

Godolphin, Margaret (Blagge) 1652-1678.

EVELYN, John, 942.06'6'0924 B
1620-1706.
The life of Mrs. Godolphin. Now first published and edited by Samuel Lord Bishop of Oxford. Freeport, N.Y., Books for Libraries Press [1972] xvii, 265 p. port. 22 cm. Reprint of the 1847 ed. [DA447.G6E9 1972] 72-5552 ISBN 0-8369-6905-7
1. Godolphin, Margaret (Blagge) 1652-1678. I. Title. **BIP**

Godoy Alcayaga, Lucila, 1889-1957.

ARCE de Vazquez, Margot. 861.62
Gabriela Mistral, the poet and her work. Translated by Helene Masslo Anderson. [New York] New York University Press, 1964. 158 p. 22 cm. Bibliography: p. [149] -152. [PQ8097.G6Z5253] 64-16899
1. Godoy Alcayaga, Lucila, 1889-1957. **BIP**

Godoy Alcayaga, Lucila, 1889-1957—Biography.

GAZARIAN-GAUTIER, Marie- 861 B
Lise.
Gabriela Mistral, the teacher from the Valley of Elqui / by Marie-Lise Gazarian-Gautier. Chicago : Franciscan Herald Press, [1975] xxiii, 168 p., [8] leaves of plates : ill. ; 22 cm. Translation of Gabriela Mistral, la maestra de Elqui. Includes bibliographical references. [PQ8097.G6Z56413] 75-4764 ISBN 0-8199-0544-5 : 7.50
1. Godoy Alcayaga, Lucila, 1889-1957—Biography. I. Title.

Godoy Alvarez de Faria Rios Sanchez y Zarzosa, Manuel de, principe de la Paz, 1767-1851.

CHASTENET, 946.058'0924 B Jacques, 1893-
Godoy: master of Spain, 1792-1808. Translated by J. F. Huntington. Port Washington, N.Y., Kennikat Press [1972] 249 p. ports. 22 cm. Reprint of the 1953 ed. [DP200.8.G7C513 1972] 70-153205 ISBN 0-8046-1515-2
1. Godoy Alvarez de Faria Rios Sanchez y Zarzosa, Manuel de, principe de la Paz, 1767-1851. I. Title.

Godwin, Edward William, 1833-1886.

HARBRON, Dudley, 1880- 720'.924 B
The conscious stone; the life of Edward William Godwin. New York, B. Blom, 1971. xviii, 190 p. illus., ports. 22 cm. Reprint of the 1949 ed. [NA997.G6H3 1971] 79-172551
1. Godwin, Edward William, 1833-1886. I. Title.

Godwin, Mary Wollstonecraft, 1759-1797.

WARDLE, Ralph Martin, 1909- 928.2
Mary Wollstonecraft, a critical biography. Lawrence, University of Kansas Press, 1951. 366 p. 24 cm. Bibliographical references included in "Notes" (p. [342]-359) [PR4719.G5Z9] 51-12250
1. Godwin, Mary Wollstonecraft, 1759-1797. BIP

WARDLE, Ralph Martin, 1909- 928.2
Mary Wollstonecraft, a critical biography. London, Richards Press: Lawrence, University of Kansas Press, 1951 [i. e. 1952] 366p. 25cm. Bibliographical references included in 'Notes' p. [342]-350) [PR4719.G5Z9 1952] 53-19723
1. Godwin, Mary (Wollstonecraft) 1739-1797. I. Title.

Godwin, Mills Edwin, 1914-

ANDREWS, Miner 975.5'04'0924 B Carl.
No higher honor; the story of Mills E. Godwin, Jr., by M. Carl Andrews. Richmond, Dietz Press [1970] xix, 207 p. illus., ports. 24 cm. [F231.3.G6A7] 73-20070
1. Godwin, Mills Edwin, 1914- I. Title.

Godwin, William, 1756-1836.

BROWN, Ford Keeler. 828'.6'09 B
The life of William Godwin, by Ford K. Brown. [Folcroft, Pa.] Folcroft Library Editions, 1972. xv, 387 p. ports. 26 cm. Reprint of the 1926 ed. published by Dent, London, and Dutton, New York. Includes bibliographical references. [PR4723.B7 1972] 72-10170 ISBN 0-8414-0641-3 (lib. bdg.)
1. Godwin, William, 1756-1836. BIP

FLEISHER, David. 320.5'1'0924
William Godwin; a study in liberalism [Folcroft, Pa.] Folcroft Library Editions, 1974. p. cm. Reprint of the 1951 ed. published by Allen & Unwin, London. Bibliography: p. [HN388.G7F55 1974] 74-11152 17.50
1. Godwin, William, 1756-1836. BIP

GODWIN, William, 1756- 826'.6 1836.
Godwin & Mary; letters of William Godwin and Mary Wollstonecraft. Edited by Ralph M. Wardle. Lawrence, University of Kansas Press, 1966. viii, 125 p. illus., ports. 22 cm. Bibliographical footnotes. [PR4720.A5W3 1966] 66-27700
I. Wollstonecraft, Mary, 1759-1797. II. Wardle, Ralph Martin, 1909- ed. III. Title.

GRYLLS, Rosalie 828'.6'09 B Glynn, 1905-
William Godwin & his world. [Folcroft, Pa.] Folcroft Library Editions, 1974. 256 p. ports. 24 cm. Reprint of the 1953 ed. published by Odhams Press, London. Bibliography: p. 250-252. [PR4723.G7 1974] 74-13753 ISBN 0-8414-4525-7 (lib. bdg.)
1. Godwin, William, 1756-1836. I. Title. BIP

RODWAY, Allan Edwin, 320.5'092'4 ed.
Godwin and the age of transition / edited by A. E. Rodway. Brooklyn, N.Y. : Haskell House, 1977. 231 p. ; 21 cm. Reprint of the 1952 ed. published by G. C. Harrap, London, in series: Life, literature, and thought library. Bibliography: p. [229]-231. [JC176.G85R6 1977] 76-52953 ISBN 0-8383-2146-1 : 11.95
1. Godwin, William, 1756-1836. I. Title. II. Series. Life, literature, and thought library. BIP

Godwin, William, 1756-1836—Addresses, essays, lectures.

ROBINSON, Victor, 328'.6'09 B 1886-1947.
William Godwin and Mary Wollstonecraft / by Victor Robinson. Folcroft, Pa. : Folcroft Library Editions, 1978. p. cm. Reprint of the 1907 ed. which was published by The Altrurians, New York, in the series: Lives of great altrurians. [PR4723.R57 1978] 78-31579 ISBN 0-8414-7361-7 : 10.00
1. Godwin, William, 1756-1836—Addresses, essays, lectures. 2. Wollstonecraft, Mary, 1759-1979—Addresses, essays, lectures. 3. Authors, English—Biography—Addresses, essays, lectures. I. Title. II. Series: Lives of grat altrurians. BIP

Godwin, William, 1756-1836—Biography.

WOODCOCK, George, 828' 6'09 B 1912-
William Godwin : a biographical study / by George Woodcock ; with a foreword by Herbert Read. Folcroft, Pa. : Folcroft Library Editions, 1975. x, 265 p., [3] leaves of plates : ill. ; 26 cm. Reprint of the 1946 ed. published by Porcupine Press, London. Includes index. Bibliography: p. 259-260. [PR4723.W6 1975] 75-14023 ISBN 0-8414-9433-9 lib. bdg. : 20.00
1. Godwin, William, 1756-1836—Biography. BIP

Goebbels, Joseph, 1897-1945.

GOEBBELS, Joseph 1897- 923.243 1945
The early Goebbels diaries, 1925-1926. Pref. by Alan Bullock. Ed. by Helmut Heiber. Tr. from German by Oliver Watson. New York, Praeger [1963, c.1962] 156p. 23cm. Bibl. 63-750 5.50
I. Heiber, Helmut, 1924- ed. II. Title.

GOEBBELS, Joseph 1897- 923.243 1945
The Goebbels diaries, tr., ed. by Louis P. Lochner. New York, Popular Lib. [1965, c.1948] 638p. 18cm. (Eagle bks., Z24) [DD247.G6A25] 1.25 pap.,
I. Lochner, Louis Paul, 1887- ed. and tr. II. Title.

GOEBBELS, Joseph, 1897- 923.243 1945
The Goebbels diaries [1942-1943] Ed., tr. & introd. by Louis P. Lochner. New York, Popular Lib. [1968,c.1948] 638p. 18cm. (Eagle bks., 125-59) [DD247.G6A25] 1.25 pap.,
I. Lochner, Louis Paul, 1887- ed. and tr. II. Title.

GOEBBELS, Joseph, 943.086'0924 1897-1945.
The Goebbels diaries, 1942-1943. Edited, translated, and with an introd. by Louis P. Lochner. Westport, Conn., Greenwood Press [1970, c1948] ix, 566 p. group port. 23 cm. Translation of Goebbels Tagebucher. [DD247.G6A25 1970] 74-108391
I. Lochner, Louis Paul, 1887- ed. and tr. II. Title.

GOEBBELS, Joseph, 943.085'092'4 B 1897-1945.
My part in Germany's fight / by Joseph Goebbels ; translated by Kurt Fiedler. New York : H. Fertig, 1978 p. cm. Reprint of the 1935 ed. published by Hurst & Blackett, London. Translation of Vom Kaiserhof zur Reichskanzlei. [DD247.G6A32 1976] 76-27871 13.50
1. Goebbels, Joseph, 1897-1945. 2. Nationalsozialistische Deutsche Arbeiter-Partei. 3. Statesmen—Germany—Biography. 4. Germany—History—1918-1933. I. Title. BIP

HEIBER, Helmut, 943.086'092'4 B 1924-
Goebbels. Translated by John K. Dickinson. New York, Hawthorn Books [1972] v, 387 p. illus. 24 cm. Translation of Joseph Goebbels. Bibliography: p. 367-372. [DD247.G6H413 1972] 70-130728 9.95
1. Goebbels, Joseph, 1897-1945.

MANVELL, Roger 923.243
Dr. Goebbels, his life and death, by Roger Manvell and Heinrich Fraenkel. New York, Simon. and Schuster, [c.]1960. xi, 306p. Includes bibliographies. illus. 23cm. 59-13878 4.50
1. Goebbels, Joseph, 1897-1945. I. Fraenkel, Heinrich, 1897- joint author. II. Title.

MANVELL, Roger 1909- 923.243
Dr. Goebbels, his life and death, by Roger Manvell, Heinrich Fraenkel. New York, Pyramid Books [1961, c.1960] 287p. (R587) Bibl. .50 pap.,
1. Goebbels, Joseph, 1897-1945. I. Fraenkel, Heinrich, 1897- joint author. II. Title.

MANVELL, Roger, 1909- 923.243
Dr. Goebbels, his life and death, by Roger Manvell and Heinrich Fraenkel. New York, Simon and Schuster, 1960. 306p. illus. 23cm. Includes bibliographies. [DD247.G6M33] 59-13878
1. Goebbels, Joseph, 1897-1945. I. Fraenkel, Heinrich, 1897- joint author. II. Title.

REIMANN, Viktor. 943.086'092'4 B
Goebbels / by Viktor Reimann ; translated from the German by Stephen Wendt. 1st ed. Garden City, N.Y. : Doubleday, 1976. 352 p., [4] leaves of plates : ill. ; 24 cm. Translation of Dr. Joseph Goebbels. Includes index. Bibliography: p. [338]-340. [DD247.G6R4813] 74-2723 ISBN 0-385-01713-8 : 12.50
1. Goebbels, Joseph, 1897-1945. I. Title.

Goebel, William, 1856-1900.

KLOTTER, James C. 976.9'04'0924 B
William Goebel : the politics of wrath / James C. Klotter. [Lexington] : University Press of Kentucky, c1977. ix, 137 p. : ill. ; 21 cm. (The Kentucky Bicentennial bookshelf) Bibliography: p. 133-137. [F456.G64K57] 77-76335 ISBN 0-8131-0240-5 : 4.95
1. Goebel, William, 1856-1900. 2. Kentucky—Governors—Biography. 3. Kentucky—Politics and government—1865-1950. I. Title. II. Series. BIP

Goering, Hermann, 1893-1946

MOSLEY, Leonard 943.086092 B
The Reich Marshal, a biography of Hermann Goering [New York] Dell [1975 c1974] 476 p. illus. 18 cm. Includes bibliographical references [DD247G67M67] 1.75 (pbk.)
1. Goering, Hermann, 1893-1946 I. Title. L.C. card no. for original edition: 73-20825 BIP

Goeritz, Mathias, 1915-

ZUNIGA, Olivia 709.43
Mathias Goeritz. [Tr. from Spanish by Sonia Levy-Spira] Mexico, Editorial Intercontinental [dist. New York, Wittenborn, 1964] 211p. illus., plates (pt. mounted col.) port. 23cm. Bibl. [N6888.G6Z83] 65-17 7.00
1. Goeritz, Mathias, 1915- I. Title.

Goeth, Ottilie,

GOETH, Ottilie, 929.2'0973 b.1836.
Memoirs of a Texas pioneer grandmother (Was Grossmutter erzaehlt), 1805-1915, by Ottilie Goeth, nee Fuchs. Translated from the German by Irma Goeth Guenther. Austin, Tex., 1969. 183 p. illus., ports. 28 cm. Includes various poems in German. Bibliography: p. 167-169. [CT275.G5524A3] 70-17639
I. Title. II. Title: Was grossmutter erzaehlt.

Goethals, George Washington, 1858-1928—Juvenile literature.

LATHAM, Jean Lee 92
George W. Goethals, Panama Canal engineer. Panama Canal engineer. Illus. by Hamilton Greene. Champaign, Ill., Garrard [c.1965] 80p. col. illus. 23cm. (Discovery bk.) [TA140.G58L3] 65-14547 1.98
1. Goethals, George Washington, 1858-1928—Juvenile literature. I. Title.

Goethe, Johann Wolfgang von, 1749-1832.

ANCELET-HUSTACHE, Jeanne. 830.81
Goethe. Translated [from the French] by Cecily Hastings. New York, Grove Press [1960] 191p. illus., ports., facsims. 18cm. (Evergreen profile book 5) 59-7437 1.35 pap.,
1. Goethe, Johann Wolfgang von, 1749-1832. I. Title. II. Series.

BROWN, Peter Hume, 1849- 831'.6 B 1918.
Life of Goethe. With a prefatory note by Viscount Haldane. New York, Haskell House, 1971. 2 v. (xi, 817 p.) illus. 23 cm. Chapter 23 is by Viscount Haldane, who, with his sister's aid, revised v. 2. Reprint of the 1920 ed. [PT2049.B57 1971] 77-163114 ISBN 0-8383-1307-8 29.95
1. Goethe, Johann Wolfgang von, 1749-1832. I. Haldane, Richard Burdon Haldane, 1st Viscount, 1856-1928. II. Title. BIP

CITATI, Pietro 831'.6 B
Goethe. Translated by Raymond Rosenthal. New York, Dial Press, 1974. xviii, 469 p. 24 cm. Includes bibliographical references. [PT1982.C5 1974] 74-11839 ISBN 0-8037-3006-3
1. Goethe, Johann Wolfgang von, 1749-1832. Wilhelm Meisters Lehrjahre. 2. Goethe, Johann Wolfgang von, 1749-1832. Faust II.

CROCE, Benedetto, 1866- 831'.6 1952.
Goethe. With an introd. by Douglas Ainslie and a portrait. Port Washington, N.Y., Kennikat Press [1970] xxi, 208 p. port. 20 cm. "First published in 1923." Translated by Emily Anderson. [PT2177.C6 1970] 78-103179
1. Goethe, Johann Wolfgang von, 1749-1832.

CROCE, Benedetto, 1866- 831'.6 1952.
Goethe. With an introd. by Douglas Ainslie. [Folcroft, Pa.] Folcroft Library Editions, 1973. xxi, 208 p. port. 20 cm. Reprint of the 1923 ed. published by Methuen, London. [PT2177.C6 1973] 73-12548 ISBN 0-8414-3441-7 (lib. bdg.)
1. Goethe, Johann Wolfgang von, 1749-1832.

FAIRLEY, Barker, 1887- 831'.6 B
A study of Goethe / by Barker Fairley. Westport, Conn. : Greenwood Press, 1977. vii, 280 p. ; 23 cm. Reprint of the 1947 ed. published by Clarendon Press, Oxford. Includes index. [PT2049.F33 1977] 76-56253 ISBN 0-8371-9330-3 lib.bdg. : 17.00
1. Goethe, Johann Wolfgang von, 1749-1832. 2. Authors, German—18th century—Biography. I. Title.

FAIRLEY, Barker, 1887- 831'.6 B
A study of Goethe / by Barker Fairley. Westport, Conn. : Greenwood Press, 1977. vii, 280 p. ; 23 cm. Reprint of the 1947 ed. published by Clarendon Press, Oxford. Includes index. [PT2049.F33 1977] 76-56253 ISBN 0-8371-9330-3 lib.bdg. : 17.00
1. Goethe, Johann Wolfgang von, 1749-1832. 2. Authors, German—18th century—Biography. I. Title. BIP

FRIEDENTHAL, Richard, 1896- 838.6
Goethe, his life and times. Cleveland, World [1965, c.1963] 561p. illus., ports.

24cm. Bibl. [PT2051.F713] 65-18292 8.50
1. Goethe, Johann Wolfgang von, 1749-1832. I. Title.

GOETHE, Johann Wolfgang von, 1749-1832. 831'.6 B
The autobiography of Johann Wolfgang von Goethe. Translated by John Oxenford. Introd. by Gregor Sebba. New York, Horizon Press [1969] 2 v. in 1. illus., ports. 25 cm. Translation of Aus meinem Leben: Dichtung und Wahrheit. Includes bibliographical references. [PT2027.A8O8 1969] 77-78789 15.00
I. Oxenford, John, 1812-1877, tr. II. Title. **BIP**

GOETHE, Johann Wolfgang von, 1749-1832 928.3
Conversation with Goethe [by] J. P. Eckermann. Selected, introd. annotated index, by Hans Kohn. Tr. [from German] by Gisela C. O'Brien [abridged] New York, Ungar [c.1964] xvi, 271p. 21cm. (Milestones of thought) (Series, Milestones of thought in the history of ideas) 64-15294 5.00; 1.45 pap.,
I. Eckermann, Johann Peter, 1792-1854. Gesprache mit Goethe. II. Kohn, Hans, 1891- ed. III. Title. IV. Series.

GOETHE, Johann Wolfgang von, 1749-1832. 928.3
Conversations with Goethe [by] J. P. Eckermann. Selected, with an introd. and annotated index, by Hans Kohn. Translated by Gisela C. O'Brien. New York, Ungar [1964] xvi, 271 p. 21 cm. (Milestones of thought) [PT2027.C5O2 1964] 64-15294
I. Eckermann, Johann Peter, 1792-1854. Gesprache mit Goethe. II. Kohn, Hans, 1891- ed. III. Title. IV. Series: Milestones of thought in the history of ideas

GRIMM, Herman Friedrich, 1828-1901. 831'.6
The life and times of Goethe. Translated by Sarah Holland Adams. Freeport, N.Y., Books for Libraries Press [1971] viii, 559 p. port. 23 cm. Translation of Goethe. Reprint of the 1880 ed. [PT2051.G73 1971] 78-152986 ISBN 0-8369-5738-5
1. Goethe, Johann Wolfgang von, 1749-1832. I. Title. **BIP**

HOYER, Walter 928.326
Goethe's life in pictures [Tr. from German of the biographical texts: Edith Anderson. [dist. New York, Heinman, 1965, c.1963] dist. New York, Heinman, 1965, c.1963 1v. (unpaged) illus., facsims., maps (1 fold.) ports. 20cm. [PT2143.A2H6] 64-5235 4.50 bds.
1. Goethe, Johann Wolfgang von—Portraits, etc. 2. Goethe, Johann Wolfgang von—Biog. I. Title.

KLENZE, Camillo von, 1865- 830.9
From Goethe to Hauptmann; studies in a changing culture. New York, Biblo and Tannen, 1966. 321 p. 21 cm. "Originally published 1926." Contents.Contents.—A Renaissance vision: Goethe's Italy.—A romantic view of art: German predecessors of Ruskin.—Realism and romanticism in two great narrators: Keller and Meyer.—Naturalism in German drama from Schiller to Hauptmann.—Hauptmann's treatment of the lower classes: a twentieth century vision.—Bibliography (p. 279-314) [PT343.K5 1966] 66-23519
1. Goethe, Johann Wolfgang von, 1749-1832. Italienische Reise. 2. Hauptmann, Gerhart Johann Robert, 1862-1946. 3. German literature—19th century—History and criticism. 4. German drama—19th century—History and criticism. I. Title. **BIP**

NEVINSON, Henry Woodd, 1856-1941. 831'.6 B
Goethe: man and poet. Written for the centenary of Goethe's death on March 22nd, 1832. Freeport, N.Y., Books for Libraries Press [1971] 264 p. illus., ports. 23 cm. Reprint of the 1931 ed. Bibliography: p. 259-260. [PT2049.N4 1971] 77-164619 ISBN 0-8369-5902-7
1. Goethe, Johann Wolfgang von, 1749-1832. I. Title.

ROBERTSON, John George, 1867-1933. 831'.6 B
The life and work of Goethe, 1749-1832. New York, Haskell House Publishers, 1973. xii, 350 p. illus. 23 cm. Reprint of the 1932 ed. Bibliography: p. 327-339. [PT2049.R6 1973] 72-8646 ISBN 0-8383-1671-9 11.95
1. Goethe, Johann Wolfgang von, 1749-1832.

ROBERTSON, John George, 1867-1933. 831'.6 B
The life and work of Goethe, 1749-1832. Freeport, N.Y., Books for Libraries Press [1971] xii, 350 p. illus. 23 cm. Reprint of the 1932 ed. Bibliography: p. 327-339. [PT2049.R6 1971] 79-179536 ISBN 0-8369-6665-1
1. Goethe, Johann Wolfgang von, 1749-1832. **BIP**

SIME, James, 1843-1895. 831'.6 B
Life of Johann Wolfgang Goethe. Port Washington, N.Y., Kennikat Press [1972] 194, xliv p. 21 cm. Reprint of the 1888 ed. "Bibliography, by John P. Anderson": p. [i]-xliv. [PT2049.S5 1972] 77-160782 ISBN 0-8046-1614-0
1. Goethe, Johann Wolfgang von, 1749-1832. I. Title. **BIP**

STEARNS, Monroe 831'.6(B)
Goethe, pattern of genius. New York, Watts [1967] 310p. 22cm. (Immortals of lit.) Bibl. [PT2049.S84] 67-16871 2.95
1. Goethe, Johann Wolfgang von. 1749-1832. I. Title.

Goethe, Johann Wolfgang von, 1749-1832—Biography.

ANGELLOZ, Joseph Francois. 928.3
Goethe. Translated from the French by R. H. Blackley. New York, Orion Press; distributed by Crown Publishers [1958] 317p. illus. 22cm. [PT2050.A713] 58-7922
1. Goethe, Johann Wolfgang von—Biog. I. Title.

BIELSCHOWSKY, Albert, 1847-1902. 831'.6
The life of Goethe. Authorised translation from the German by William A. Cooper. New York, Haskell House Publishers, 1969. 3 v. illus., ports. 23 cm. Reprint of the 1905-08 ed. The author's work, left unfinished by his death, was completed by T. Ziegler. Chapter 3 entitled The naturalist, was written by S. Kalischer; Goethe's poems set to music (v. 3, p. 374-376) by M. Friedlaender. Contents.—v. 1. 1749-1788: from birth to the return from Italy.—v. 2. 1788-1815: from the Italian journey to the wars of liberation.—v. 3. 1815-1832: from the Congress of Vienna to the poet's death. Includes bibliographical references. [PT2051.B55 1969] 70-92935
1. Goethe, Johann Wolfgang von, 1749-1832—Biography. I. Ziegler, Theobald, 1846-1918. II. Kalischer, Salomon, 1845-1924. III. Friedlaender, Max, 1852-1934. IV. Title.

BIELSCHOWSKY, Albert, 1847-1902. 831'.6
The life of Goethe. Authorised translation from the German by William A. Cooper. New York, Haskell House Publishers, 1969. 3 v. illus., ports. 23 cm. Reprint of the 1905-08 ed. The author's work, left unfinished by his death, was completed by T. Ziegler. Chapter 3 entitled The naturalist, was written by S. Kalischer; Goethe's poems set to music (v. 3, p. 374-376) by M. Friedlaender. Contents.Contents.—v. 1. 1749-1788: from birth to the return from Italy.—v. 2. 1788-1815: from the Italian journey to the wars of liberation. -v. 3. 1815-1832: from the Congress of Vienna to the poet's death. Includes bibliographical references. [PT2051.B55 1969] 70-92935
1. Goethe, Johann Wolfgang von, 1749-1832—Biography. I. Ziegler, Theobald, 1846-1918. II. Kalischer, Salomon, 1845-1924. III. Friedlaender, Max, 1852-1934. IV. Title.

DEQUINCEY, Thomas, 1785-1859. 809 B
Biographies of Shakspeare, Pope, Goethe, and Schiller, and on the policial parties of modern England. New York, AMS Press [1972] vii, 376 p. port. 19 cm. Reprint of the ed. issued in 1862 by A. and C. Black, Edinburgh, as: De Quincey's works, v. 15. [PN452.D4 1972] 75-164822 ISBN 0-404-02079-8 17.50
1. Shakespeare, William, 1564-1616—Biography. 2. Pope, Alexander, 1688-1744. 3. Goethe, Johann Wolfgang von, 1749-1832—Biography. 4. Schiller, Johann Christoph Friedrich von, 1759-1805—Biography. 5. Political parties—Great Britain.

HAILE, Harry Gerald, 1931- 831'.6 B
Artist in chrysalis; a biographical study of Goethe in Italy [by] H. G. Haile. Urbana, University of Illinois Press [1973] viii, 201 p. 21 cm. Includes bibliographical references. [PT2066.H3] 72-92632 ISBN 0-252-00326-8 7.95
1. Goethe, Johann Wolfgang von, 1749-1832—Biography. I. Title. **BIP**

Goethe, Johann Wolfgang von, 1749-1832—Biography—Theatrical career.

CARLSON, Marvin A., 1935- 832'.6 B
Goethe and the Weimar theatre / Marvin Carlson. Ithaca, N.Y. : Cornell University Press, 1978. 328 p. : ill. ; 23 cm. Includes index. Bibliography: p. [319]-321. [PT2116.C3] 78-6866 ISBN 0-8014-1118-1 : 5.50
1. Goethe, Johann Wolfgang von, 1749-1832—Biography—Theatrical career. 2. Authors, German—18th century—Biography. 3. Authors, German—19th century—Biography. 4. Theater—Germany—Weimar—History. I. Title. **BIP**

Goethe, Johann Wolfgang von, 1749-1832—Biography—Youth.

BROWN, Peter Hume, 1849-1918. 831'.6 B
The youth of Goethe. New York, Haskell House Publishers, 1970. xvi, 304 p. 23 cm. Reprint of the 1913 ed. [PT2060.B7 1970] 77-133283
1. Goethe, Johann Wolfgang von, 1749-1832—Biography—Youth. I. Title. **BIP**

Goethe, Katharina Elisabeth Textor, 1731-1808.

GOETHE, Katharina Elisabeth Textor, 1731-1808. 831'.6 B
Goethe's mother : correspondence of Catharine Elizabeth Goethe with Goethe, Lavater, Wieland, Duchess Anna Amalia of Saxe-Weimar, Friedrich von Stein, and others / translated from the German, with the addition of biographical sketches and notes, by Alfred S. Gibbs ; with an introductory note by Clarence Cook. New York : AMS Press, 1975. xxxiv, 265 p. : ill. ; 19 cm. (Women of letters) Reprint of the 1880 ed. published by Dodd, Mead, New York. Includes bibliographical references. [PT2077.B66 1975] 73-37695 ISBN 0-404-56752-5 : 16.00
1. Goethe, Katharina Elisabeth Textor, 1731-1808. I. Goethe, Johann Wolfgang von, 1749-1832. II. Title.

Goff, Nathan,

SMITH, Gerald Wayne. 923.273
Nathan Goff, Jr., a biography; with some account of Guy Despard Goff and Brazilla Carroll Reece. Charleston, W. Va., Education Foundation, 1959. 375 p. illus. 24 cm. [E664.G62S55] 60-41553
1. Goff, Nathan, I. Title.

Gogarty, Oliver St. John, 1878-1957.

GOGARTY, Oliver St. John, 1878-1957. 928.2
It isn't this time of year at all! An unpremeditated autobiography. [1st ed.] Garden City, Doubleday, 1954. 256 p. 22 cm. [PR6013.O28Z5] 54-5360
I. Title.

GOGARTY, Oliver St. John, 1878-1957. 821'.9'12 B
It isn't this time of year at all! An unpremeditated autobiography. Westport, Conn., Greenwood Press [1970, c1954] 256 p. 23 cm. [PR6013.O28Z5 1970] 78-108392 ISBN 0-8371-3814-0
I. Title.

O'CONNOR, Ulick 928.2
The times I've seen; Oliver St. John Gogarty, a biography. New York, Obolensky [1964] 365p. ports. 24cm. Bibl. 63-12375 1.95
1. Gogarty, Oliver St. John, 1878-1957. I. Title.

Gogh, Vincent van, 1853-1890.

ABELES, Ehvn, 1909- 927.5
The man who painted the sun; the story of Vincent Van Gogh, by Kerwin Bowles [pseud.] Illustrated by Henry Kallem. New York, Stravon Publishers [1951] 31 p. illus. 22 x 28 cm. (A Child's book of great artists) [ND653.G7A6] 51-14728
1. Gogh, Vincent van, 1853-1890. 2. Art—Juvenile literature. I. Title.

BURRA, Peter, 1909- v. 12
Van Gogh, by Peter Burra. New York, Collier Books [1962] 127 p. (Collier Books AS65Y) 67-23933
1. Gogh, Vincent van, 1853-1890. I. Title.

CABANNE, Pierre. 927.5
Van Gogh. [Translated from the French by Mary I. Martin. 1st American ed.] Englewood Cliffs, N.J., Prentice-Hall [1963] 288 p. illus. (part col.) 22 cm. Bibliography: p. 280. [ND653.G7C33 1963] 63-4334
1. Gogh, Vincent van, 1853-1890. I. Title.

CABANNE, Pierre. 759.9492 B
Van Gogh. [Translated from the French by Daphne Woodward] New York, H. N. Abrams [1971?] 288 p. illus. (part col.) 22 cm. Bibliography: p. 286. [ND653.G7C33 1971] 71-143482 ISBN 0-8109-0523-X
1. Gogh, Vincent van, 1853-1890.

CABANNE, Pierre. 759.9492 B
Van Gogh / Pierre Cabanne; translated from the French by Daphne Woodward New York : Praeger Publishers, 1975, c1963. 288 p. : ill. (some col.) ; 21 cm. (Praeger world of art paperbacks) (A Praeger world of art profile) Includes bibliographical references and index. [ND653.G7C33 1975] 74-8443 ISBN 0-275-71680-5 pbk. : 5.95
1. Gogh, Vincent van, 1853-1890.

ELGAR, Frank. 927.5
Van Gogh, a study of his life and work. [Translated from the French by James Cleugh] New York, Praeger [1958] 256, [60] p. illus. (part col.) 21 cm. Bibliography: p. [35]-[38] (2d group) [ND653.G7E523] 759.9492 58-12092
1. Gogh, Vincent van, 1853-1890.

ELGAR, Frank. 759.9492 B
Van Gogh; a study of his life and work. [Translated from the French by James Cleugh] New York, Praeger [1966, c1958] 239 [55] p. illus. (part col.) 22 cm. (A Praeger world of art profile) Bibliography: p. [33]-[36] (2d group) [ND653.G7E533 1966] 66-9326
1. Gogh, Vincent van, 1853-1890.

GOGH, Vincent van, 1835-1890. 759.9492
Van Gogh: a self-portrait; letters revealing his life as a painter(selected by W. H. Auden. New York, Dutton, 1963. 398p. illus. 21cm. (Dutton paperback D116) 2.75 pap.,
1. Artist—Correspondence, reminiscences, etc. I. Auden, Wystan Hugh, 1907- II. Title.

GOGH, Vincent van, 1853-1890 927.5
Letters. Selected, ed., introd. by Mark Roskill. New York, Atheneum, 1963[c.1927-1963] 351p. plates. 18cm. (39) 63-13689 1.95 pap.,
I. Title.

GOGH, Vincent van, 1853-1890. 759.9492
Van Gogh. [New York] St. Martin's Press [1972] [4] p., 13 col. plates. 34 cm. [ND653.G7A4878] 72-76959 4.95 (pbk.)

GOGH, Vincent van, 1853-1890. 759.9492
Van Gogh. Text and notes by Gerald E.

Finley. New York, Tudor Pub. Co. [1966] 36 p. 91 col. plates. 18 cm. Bibliography: p. 15. [ND653.G7F53] 66-10490
I. Finley, Gerald E.

GOGH, Vincent van, 1853-1890. v. 12
Van Gogh: a self-portrait; letters revealing his life as a painter, selected by W. H. Auden. New York, E. P. Dutton, 1963. 652 p. illus. (A Dutton paperback D-116) "Newly translated...by Cornelius de Dood and Mrs. J. van Gogh-Bonger." 64-23987
1. Artist — Correspondence, reminiscences, etc. I. Auden, Wystan Hugh, 1907- II. Title.

GOGH, Vincent van, 1853-1890. 759.9492
Van Gogh's "diary"; the artist's life in his own words and art. Edited by Jan Hulsker. New York, Morrow, 1971 [c1970] 168 p. illus. (part col.) 27 cm. Translation of "Dagboek" van Van Gogh. [ND653.G7A2813] 70-158078 12.50
1. Painters—Netherlands—Correspondence, reminiscences, etc. I. Hulsker, Jan, ed. II. Title.

HAMMACHER, Abraham Marie, 1897- 759.9492
Genius and disaster; the ten creative years of Vincent van Gogh [by] A. M. Hammacher. New York, H. N. Abrams [1968] 188 p. illus. (part col.) 28 x 30 cm. [ND653.G7H24] 68-11540
1. Gogh, Vincent van, 1853-1890. I. Title.

HANSON, Lawrence. 927.5
Passionate pilgrim; the life of Vincent van Gogh, by Lawrence and Elisabeth Hanson. New York, Random House [1955] 300p. illus. 24cm. [ND653.G7H275] 55-8162
1. Gogh, Vincent van, 1853-1890. I. Hanson, Elisabeth M., joint author. II. Title.

HANSON, Lawrence 927.5
The seekers: Gauguin, Van Gogh, Cezanne [by] Lawrence, Elisabeth Hanson. New York, Random [c.1963] xv, 334p. illus., ports. 25cm. Bibl. 63-11619 6.95
1. Gauguin, Paul, 1848-1903. 2. Gogh, Vincent van, 1853-1890. 3. Cezanne, Paul, 1839-1906. 4. Post-impressionism (Art) I. Hanson, Elizabeth M., joint author. II. Title.

HUYGHE, Rene. 759.9492
Van Gogh. [Translated by Helen C. Slonim] New York, Crown Publishers, 1958. 95 p. illus. (part mounted col.) plates (part col.) 29 cm. Bibliography: p. 92-94. [ND653.G7H93] 58-12881
1. Gogh, Vincent van, 1853-1890. **BIP**

JASPERS, Karl, 1883-1969. 616.8'982'09 B
Strindberg and Van Gogh : an attempt of a pathographic analysis with reference to parallel cases of Swedenborg and Holderlin / Karl Jaspers ; translated by Oskar Grunow and David Woloshin. Tucson, Ariz. : University of Arizona Press, [1977] p. cm. Translation of Strindberg und Van Gogh. Includes index. Bibliography: p. [PT9815.J313 1977] 77-9394 ISBN 0-8165-0608-6 : 12.50. ISBN 0-8165-0434-2 pbk. : 4.95
1. Strindberg, August, 1849-1912. 2. Gogh, Vincent van, 1853-1890. 3. Swedenborg, Emanuel, 1688-1772. 4. Holderlin, Friedrich, 1770-1843. 5. Psychology, Pathological—Cases, clinical reports, statistics. I. Title.

JONES, Jack Raymond. 759.9492 (B)
The man who loved the sun: the life of Vincent Van Gogh. London, Evans Bros., 1966. 176 p. 16 plates. 22 1/3 cm. 21/- Bibliography: p. 172-173. [ND653.G7J6] 66-78334
1. Gogh, Vincent van, 1853-1890. I. Title.

KELLER, Horst. 759.9492
Vincent van Gogh; the final years. [New York, H. N. Abrams, 1970] 81 p. illus. (part col.) 30 cm. Translation of Die Jahre der Vollendung. [ND653.G7K413] 78-125783 ISBN 0-8109-0526-4
1. Gogh, Vincent van, 1853-1890.

KNUTTEL, Gerhardus, 1889- 759.9492
Vincent van Gogh. [Translation: Corry van Alphen] New York, Barnes & Noble [1962, c1961] 89 p. illus. (part col.) 18 cm. (Barnes & Noble art series) [ND653.G7K573] 62-52811
1. Gogh, Vincent van, 1853-1890.

LASSAIGNE, Jacques, 1910- 759.9492
Van Gogh. [1st U.S. ed.] Garden City, N.Y., Doubleday [1973] 95 p. illus. (part col.) 34 cm. (The Great impressionists) Bibliography: p. 94. [ND653.G7L36 1973] 73-82258 ISBN 0-385-08365-3 9.95
1. Gogh, Vincent van, 1853-1890. I. Title.

LEYMARIE, Jean. 759.9492 B
Van Gogh / [text by Jean Leymarie ; translated from the French by James Emmons]. New ed. New York : Rizzoli International Publications, 1977. 210 p. : ill. (some col.) ; 35 cm. (Discovering the nineteenth century) Translation of Qui etait van Gogh? Includes index. Bibliography: p. 199-[200] [ND653.G7L463 1977] 78-100029 ISBN 0-8478-0119-5 : 45.00
1. Gogh, Vincent van, 1853-1890. 2. Painters—Netherlands—Biography. I. Title. II. Series.

LUBIN, Albert J. 759.9492 B
Stranger on the earth; a psychological biography of Vincent van Gogh [by] Albert J. Lubin. [1st ed.] New York, Holt, Rinehart Winston [1972] xxii, 265 p. illus. 24 cm. Bibliography: p. 255-256. [ND653.G7L75 1972] 75-182772 ISBN 0-03-091352-7 8.95
1. Gogh, Vincent van, 1853-1890. I. Title.

MASINI, Lara Vinca. 759.9'492
Van Gogh. [Translated from the Italian by Caroline Moorehead. 1st American ed.] New York, Grosset & Dunlap [1967] 39 [80] p. illus. (part col.) 18 cm. (The New Grosset art library, 2) On cover: Van Gogh; the life and work of the artist. [ND653.G7M333 1967] 67-24229
1. Gogh, Vincent van, 1853-1890.

MEIER-GRAEFE, Julius, 1867-1935. 759.9492
Vincent van Gogh; a biographical study. Translated by John Holroyd-Reece. Westport, Conn., Greenwood Press [1970] xvi, 239 p. 61 plates. 23 cm. Reprint of the 1933 ed. [ND653.G7M5 1970] 76-109788 ISBN 8-371-42784-
1. Gogh, Vincent van, 1853-1890. **BIP**

NAGERA, Humberto. 759.9492
Vincent Van Gogh; a psychological study. Foreword by Anna Freud. New York, International Universities Press [1967] 182 p. illus. (part col.) 23 cm. [ND653.G7N3 1967b] 67-31967
1. Gogh, Vincent van, 1853-1890. **BIP**

NEW York (City) Museum of Modern Art. 760'.0924
Vincent van Gogh: with an introd. and notes selected from the letters of the artist, edited by Alfred H. Barr, Jr. And A bibliography comprising a catalogue of the literature published from 1890 through 1940; with an introductory essay and notes, by Charles Mattoon Brooks, Jr. New York, Published for the Museum of Modern Art by Arno Press, 1966. 193, xviii, 58 p. illus. 27 cm. Reprint of 2 works previously published separately. Includes bibliographies. [ND653.G7N4 1966] 66-261217
1. Gogh, Vincent van, 1853-1890. I. Barr, Alfred Hamilton, 1902- ed. II. Brooks, Charles Mattoon, 1908- Vincent van Gogh, a bibliography. III. Title.

NORDENFALK, Carl Adam Johan, 1907- 927.5
The life and work of van Gogh. New York, Philosophical Library [1953] 206 p. plates (incl. ports.; part col.) 26 cm. Translated by Lawrence Wolfe. Bibliography: p. 198-204. [ND653.G7N614] 53-7906
1. Gogh, Vincent van, 1853-1890.

PACH, Walter, 1883-1958. 759.9492
Vincent van Gogh, 1853-1890; a study of the artist and his work in relation to his times. Freeport, N.Y., Books for Libraries Press [1969] 55 p. 30 plates (incl. ports.) 24 cm. (Select bibliographies reprint series) Reprint of the 1936 ed. [ND653.G7P3 1969] 78-99666
1. Gogh, Vincent van, 1853-1890.

POLLOCK, Griselda. 759.9492 B
Vincent van Gogh : artist of his time / [by] Griselda Pollack and Fred Orton. Oxford : Phaidon, 1978. 80 p. : ill. (some col.), facsim., ports. (some col.) ; 29 cm. Bibliography: p. 6. [ND653.G7P64 1978b] 79-303710 ISBN 0-7148-1883-6 : 12.95 ISBN 0-7148-1906-9 pbk. : 6.95
1. Gogh, Vincent van, 1853-1890. 2. Painters—Netherlands—Biography. I. Orton, Fred, joint author. II. Gogh, Vincent van, 1853-1890.
Available from Dutton, N.Y., N.Y. **BIP**

POLLOCK, Griselda. 759.9492 B
Vincent van Gogh, artist of his time / Griselda Pollock and Fred Orton. New York : Dutton, 1978. 80 p. : ill. (some col.) ; 29 cm. Bibliography: p. 6 [ND653.G7P64] 78-56652 ISBN 0-7148-1883-6 : 12.95. ISBN 0-7148-1906-9 pbk : 6.95
1. Gogh, Vincent van, 1853-1890. 2. Painters—Netherlands—Biography. I. Orton, Fred, joint author. II. Gogh, Vincent van, 1853-1890. III. Title.

RIPLEY, Elizabeth, 1906- 927.5
Vincent van Gogh, a biography. With drawings and paintings by Vincent van Gogh. New York, Oxford University Press, 1954. 68 p. illus. 26 cm. [ND653.G7R5] 54-10010
1. Gogh, Vincent van, 1853-1890.

TRALBAUT, Mark Edo. 759.9492
Van Gogh; a pictorial biography. [Translated by Margaret Shenfield] New York, Viking Press [1959] 143 p. illus. (part col.) ports., maps, facsims. 24 cm. (A Studio book) [ND653.G7T673] 60-10086
1. Gogh, Vincent van, 1853-1890.

TRALBAUT, Mark Edo. 759.9492 B
Vincent van Gogh [by] Marc Edo Tralbaut. New York, Viking Press [1969] 350 p. illus. (part col.), facsims., ports. (part col.) 31 cm. (A Studio book) Translation of Van Gogh, le mal aime. Bibliography: p. 350. [ND653.G7T67453 1969] 76-87251 ISBN 6-7074-2783- 40.00
1. Gogh, Vincent van, 1853-1890. I. Title.

VAN Gogh. v. 12
New York, Macmillan [1957] 142p. port. 19cm. (Great lives) 'First published in 1934. ... First published in the United States in 1957.'
1. Gogh, Vincent van, 1853-1890. I. Burra, Peter, 1909-

VINCENT van Gogh in full colour. [927.5] 50 plates. [London] Phaidon Publishers; distributed by Oxford University Press, New York [195] unpaged, illus. 31 cm [ND653.G7A53] 759.9422 51-14044
1. Gogh, Vincent van, 1853-1890.

WALLACE, Robert, 1919- 759.9492 B
The world of Van Gogh, 1853-1890, by Robert Wallace and the editors of Time-Life Books New York, Time-Life Books [1969] 192 p. illus. (part col.), ports. 32 cm. (Time-Life library of art) Bibliography: p. 184. [ND653.G7W34] 70-78988
1. Gogh, Vincent van, 1853-1890. 2. Time-Life Books. I. Title. **BIP**

WELSH-OVCHAROV, Bogomila. 759.9492 B
Vincent van Gogh : his Paris period 1886-1888 / Bogomila Welsh-Ovcharov. Utrecht : Editions Victorine, 1976. xi, 302 p. : ill. ; 28 cm. Thesis—Toronto. Includes index. Bibliography: p. 255-261. [ND653.G7W43] 77-465148
1. Gogh, Vincent van, 1853-1890. 2. Painters—Netherlands—Biography. 3. Painters—France—Paris—Biography.

WILKIE, Kenneth, 1942- 759.9492 B
The van Gogh assignment / Kenneth Wilkie. New York : Paddington Press : distributed by Grosset & Dunlap, c1978. 207 p. : ill. ; 22 cm. [ND653.G7W54] 77-20966 ISBN 0-448-23167-0 : 7.95
1. Gogh, Vincent van, 1853-1890. 2. Painters—Netherlands—Biography. I. Title. **BIP**

Gogh, Vincent van, 1853-1890—Juvenile literature.

ABELES, Elvin, 1909- 927.5
The man who painted the sun; the story of Vincent Van Gogh, by Kerwin Bowles. Illustrated by Henry Kallem. New York, Stravon Publishers [1951] 31 p. illus. 22 x 28 cm. (A Child's book of great artists) [ND653.G7A6] 51-14728
1. Gogn, Vincent van, 1853-1890 — Juvenile literature. I. Title.

DOBRIN, Arnold. 759.9492 B
I am a stranger on the earth : the story of Vincent Van Gogh / by Arnold Dobrin. New York : F. Warne, c1975. 95 p. : ill. (some col.) ; 22 x 23 cm. Includes index. Bibliography: p. 90. A biography of the nineteenth-century Dutch artist emphasizing the interrelationship of his life and his art. [ND653.G7D56] 92 75-8105 ISBN 0-7232-6121-0 lib.bdg. : 7.95
1. Gogh, Vincent van, 1853-1890—Juvenile literature. I. Gogh, Vincent van, 1853-1890. II. Title. **BIP**

LUCHNER, Laurin. 759.9492
A child's story of Vincent van Gogh [by] Laurin Luchner and George Kaye. Pictures by Vincent van Gogh. [New York] Scroll Press [1971, c1965] [32] p. illus. (part. col.) 26 cm. Translation of Der Maler Vincent. Describes a day in the life of the artist van Gogh illustrated with many of his paintings. [ND653.G7L7613 1971] 92 71-140318 4.95
1. Gogh, Vincent van, 1853-1890—Juvenile literature. I. Kaye, George, joint author. II. Gogh, Vincent van, 1853-1890. III. Title.

PETER, Adeline. 759.9492 B
Vincent Van Gogh, by Adeline Peter and Ernest Raboff. Garden City, N.Y., Doubleday [1974] [31] p. illus. (part col.) 29 cm. (Art for children) (A Gemini-Smith book) A brief biography of this nineteenth-century Dutch painter accompanies reproductions and analyses of several of his works. [ND653.G7P43] 73-75362 ISBN 0-385-05009-7 4.95
1. Gogh, Vincent van, 1853-1890—Juvenile literature. I. Raboff, Ernest Lloyd, joint author. II. Title.
Library binding, 5.70, ISBN 0-385-06695-5

Gogol', Nikolai Vasil evich, 1809-1852.

GIPPIUS, Vasilii Vasil'evich, 1890- 891.783
Gogol'. [in Russian, dist.] Providence, R. I., Brown Univ. Pr., 1963. 237p. 21cm. (Brown Univ. Slavic reprint ser., no. 1) Bibl. 63-7522 3.50 pap.,
1. Gogol', Nikolai Vasil'evich, 1809-1852. I. Title. II. Series.

LAVRIN, Janko, 1887- 891.7081
Nikolai Gogol, 1809-1852. New York, Collier [1962] 160p. 18cm. (AS241Y) .95 pap.,
1. Gogol', Nikolai Vasil'evich, 1809-1852. I. Title.

NIKOLAI Gogol. v. 12
[New York New Directions 1961] 172p. 19cm. (A New Directions paper-book 78) 'First published in 1959 as New Directions corrected edition, 1961.'
1. Gogol', Nikolai Vasil evich, 1809-1852. I. Nabokov, Vladimir Vladimirovich, 1899- **BIP**

SETSCHKAREFF, Vsevolod 891.733
Gogol: his life and works. Tr. by Robert Kramer [NewYork] N.Y.U. [c.]1965. vii. 264p. 22cm. Bibl. [PG3335.S4213] 65-19518 6.00; 2.25 pap.,
1. Gogol', Nikolai Vasil'evich, 1809-1852. I. Title.

Gogol, Nikolai Vasil'evich, 1809-1852.

LAVRIN, Janko, 1887- v. 12
Nikolai Gogol, 1809-1852. [1st Collier Books ed.] New York, Collier Books [1962] 160 p. (Collier books, no. AS241Y) 63-50029
1. Gogol, Nikolai Vasil'evich, 1809-1852. I. Title.

MAGARSHACK, David. 928.917
Gogol, a life. New York, Grove Press [1957] 329 p. illus. 23 cm. [PG3335.M25 1957a] 57-5155
1. Gogol', Nikolavi Vasil'evich, 1809-1852.

MAGARSHACK, David. 928.917
Gogol, a life. New York, Grove Press [1957] 329p. illus. 23cm. [PG3335.M25 1957a] 57-5155
1. Gogol', Nikolai Vasil'evich, 1809-1852. I. Title.

TROYAT, Henri, 1911- 891.7'8'309 B
Divided soul; the life of Gogol. Translated from the French by Nancy Amphoux. [1st ed.] Garden City, N.Y., Doubleday, 1973. vi, 489 p. illus. 24 cm. Translation of Gogol. Bibliography: p. [439]-441. [PG3335.T713] 73-79722 ISBN 0-385-05190-5 12.95
1. Gogol', Nikolai Vasil'evich, 1809-1852. I. Title.

Gogolak, Pete.

GOGOLAK, Pete. 796.33'2'0924 B
Nothing to kick about; the autobiography of a modern immigrant, by Peter Gogolak with Joseph Carter. New York, Dodd, Mead [1973] 274 p. illus. 22 cm. [GV939.G63A36] 73-3904 ISBN 0-396-06820-0 6.95
1. Gogolak, Pete. 2. Football. I. Carter, Joseph. II. Title. **BIP**

Gokhale, Gopal Krishna, 1866-1915.

NANDA, Bal Ram. 954.03'5'0924 B
Gokhale : the Indian moderates and the British raj / B. R. Nanda. Princeton, N.J. : Princeton University Press, c1977. x, 520 p., [4] leaves of plates : ill. ; 25 cm. Includes index. Bibliography: p. [495]-505. [DS479.1.G6N36 1977b] 77-72129 ISBN 0-691-03115-0 : 25.00
1. Gokhale, Gopal Krishna, 1866-1915. 2. India—Politics and government—1765-1947. 3. Statesmen—India—Biography. **BIP**

Golbeck, Kay.

GOLBECK, Kay. 248'.2'0924 B
"Lord, how will you get me out of this mess?" / Kay Golbeck, with Irene Burk Harrell. Lincoln, Va. : Chosen Books ; Waco, Tex. : distributed by Word Books, c1978. 156 p. ; 23 cm. [BX6495.G59A33] 78-17395 ISBN 0-912376-34-1 (vol. 1) : 6.95
1. Golbeck, Kay. 2. Baptists—Canada—Biography. 3. Arthritis—Biography. 4. Death, Apparent. 5. Faith-cure. 6. Missionaries—Canada—Biography. 7. City missions—Ontario—Hamilton—Biography. 8. Hamilton, Ont.—Biography. I. Harrell, Irene Burk, joint author. II. Title.

Gold, Herbert,

GOLD, Herbert, 1924- 813'.5'4
My last two thousand years. [1st ed.] New York, Random House [1972] 246 p. 22 cm. Autobiographical. [PS3557.O34Z5] 72-4087 ISBN 0-394-47098-2 6.95
I. Title. **BIP**

Gold mines and mining—California—Mariposa Co.

COFFEY, Jesse L. 917.94'46
Bacon and beans from a gold pan [by] Jesse L. Coffey and George Hoeper. [1st ed.] Garden City, N.Y., Doubleday, 1972. x, 177 p. 22 cm. [F868.M4C6] 76-171284 5.95
1. Gold mines and mining—California—Mariposa Co. 2. Gold mines and mining—California—Sierra Co. I. Hoeper, George, joint author. II. Title.

Goldberg, Dorothy Kurgans.

GOLDBERG, Dorothy Kurgans. 973.92'092'4 B
A private view of a public life / Dorothy Goldberg. New York : Charterhouse, [1975] vi, 274 p. ; 22 cm. Includes index. [E840.8.G58A34] 75-22221 ISBN 0-88327-047-1 : 9.95
1. Goldberg, Dorothy Kurgans. 2. Goldberg, Arthur J. I. Title. **BIP**

Goldberg, Howard Ellner.

GOLDBERG, Howard Ellner. 741.9'73
Howard Ellner Goldberg. [Hastings-on-Hudson, N.Y., Printed by the Morgan Press, 1973] [22] l. illus. (part col.) 35 cm. [NC139.G58A47] 73-75290
1. Goldberg, Howard Ellner.

Goldberg, Reuben Lucius, 1883-1970.

DO it the hard way; 741.5973
Rube Goldberg and modern times. [Washington] National Museum of History and Technology, [1970] [32] p. illus., port. 21 cm. Cover title. Articles written by D. J. Boorstin, A. C. Golovin, and R. Goldberg for an exhibition at the National Museum of History and Technology. [NC1429.G46D6] 79-144126
1. Goldberg, Reuben Lucius, 1883-1970. I. Boorstin, Daniel Joseph, 1914- II. Golovin, Anne Castrodale. III. Goldberg, Reuben Lucius, 1883-1970. IV. National Museum of History and Technology.

MARZIO, Peter C. 741'.092'4 B
Rube Goldberg; his life and work [by] Peter C. Marzio. [1st ed.] New York, Harper & Row [1973] xiii, 322 p. illus. 22 x 26 cm. Bibliography: p. 307-315. [NC1429.G46M3 1973] 73-4108 ISBN 0-06-012830-5 12.50
1. Goldberg, Reuben Lucius, 1883-1970.

Golden, Clinton Strong, 1888-1961.

BROOKS, Thomas R. 331.88'16'900924 B
Clint : a biography of a labor intellectual, Clinton S. Golden / by Thomas R. Brooks. 1st ed. New York : Atheneum, 1978. p. cm. Includes index. Bibliography: p. [HD8073.G58B76 1978] 78-3152 ISBN 0-689-10923-7 : 13.95
1. Golden, Clinton Strong, 1888-1961. 2. Labor and laboring classes—United States—Biography. 3. Trade-unions—United States—Officials and employees—Biography. 4. Industrial relations—United States—History. I. Title. **BIP**

Golden, Harry Lewis, 1902-

GOLDEN, Harry Lewis, 1902- 070.924 B
The right time; an autobiography, by Harry Golden. New York, Putnam [1969] 450 p. illus., ports. 23 cm. [PN4874.G535A32] 69-18176 6.95
I. Title.

LEVIN, Martin, ed. 818.082
Five boyhoods: Howard Lindsay, Harry Golden, Walt Kelly, William K. Zinsser and John Updike. [1st ed.] New York, Doubleday, 1962. 198 p. illus. 22 cm. [PS221.L4] 61-9527
1. Lindsay, Howard, 1889- 2. Golden, Harry Lewis, 1902- 3. Kelly, Walt. 4. Zinsser, William Knowlton. 5. Updike, John. I. Title.

Golden, Jerry.

GOLDEN, Jerry. 248'.246'0924 B
Too tough for God / by Jerry Golden. Waco, Tex. : Word Books, c1977. 128 p. : ill. ; 21 cm. [BV4935.G6A37] 77-75460 ISBN 0-8499-0007-7 : 5.95
1. Golden, Jerry. 2. Converts—Louisiana—Biography. 3. Prisoners—Louisiana—Biography. 4. Clergy—Louisiana—Biography. I. Title.

Goldie, George Dashwood Taubman, Sir, 1846-1925.

WELLINGTON, Dorothy Violet Ashton Wellesley, Duchess of. 966.9'03'0924 B
Sir George Goldie, founder of Nigeria / Dorothy Wellesley Wellington. New York : Arno Press, 1977, c1934. p. cm. (European business) Reprint of the ed. published by Macmillan, London. Bibliography: p. [DT515.72.G6W44 1977] 76-29765 ISBN 0-405-09779-4 : 13.00
1. Goldie, George Dashwood Taubman, Sir, 1846-1925. 2. Royal Niger Company. 3. Nigeria—History. 4. Colonial administrators—Nigeria—Biography. 5. Capitalists and financiers—Great Britain—Colonies—Biography. I. Title. II. Series.

Goldman, Emma, 1869-1940.

DRINNON, Richard 923.347
Rebel in paradise; a biography of Emma Goldman. [Chicago] Univ. of Chic. Pr. [c.1961] 349p. Bibl. 61-17074 5.95
1. Goldman, Emma, 1869-1940. I. Title.

DRINNON, Richard. 335.4'092'4 [B]
Rebel in paradise; a biography of Emma Goldman. New York, Bantam [1973, c.1961] [xv] 431 p. 18 cm. (Bantam Book, Y7655) "Bibliographical essay": p. [392]-412. [HX843.D7] pap., 1.95
1. Goldman, Emma, 1869-1940 I. Title.
L.C. card no. for original ed.: 61-17074.

DRINNON, Richard 3359830924
Rebel in paradise a biography of Emma Goldman. New York Harper and Row [1976 c1961] xv, 349 p. ill.; 20 cm. (Harper colophon books) Includes index. Bibliography: p. 315-333. [HX843.D7] ISBN 0-06-090469-0 pbk.: 4.95
1. Goldman, Emma, 1869-1940. I. Title.
L.C. card no. for original edition: 61-17074.

SHULMAN, Alix Kates. 335'.83'0924 B
To the barricades; the anarchist life of Emma Goldman. New York, Crowell [1971] vii, 255 p. illus., ports. 21 cm. (Women of America) Bibliography: p. [236]-239. [HX843.S5] 72-132302 ISBN 0-690-83280-X 4.50
1. Goldman, Emma, 1869-1940. I. Title. **BIP**

Goldman, Pierre, 1944-

GOLDMAN, Pierre, 1944- 364.1'523'0924 B
Dim memories of a Polish Jew born in France / Pierre Goldman ; translated by Joan Pinkham. New York : Viking Press, [1977] p. cm. Translation of Souvenirs obscurs d'un juif polonais ne en France. "A Richard Seaver book." [HV6248.G45A3313] 76-55345 ISBN 0-670-27273-6 : 10.00
1. Goldman, Pierre, 1944- 2. Crime and criminals—France—Biography. I. Title. **BIP**

Goldman, Sylvan Nathan, 1898-

WILSON, Terry P., 1941- 381 B
The cart that changed the world : the career of Sylvan Nathan Goldman. 1st ed. Norman : Published for the Oklahoma Heritage Association by the University of Oklahoma Press, c1978. p. cm. (Oklahoma trackmaker series) "Outgrowth of a dissertation written at Oklahoma State University." Includes index. Bibliography: p. [HF5469.W55] 78-58074 ISBN 0-8061-1496-7 : 9.75
1. Goldman, Sylvan Nathan, 1898- 2. Supermarkets—United States. 3. Businessmen—United States—Biography. 4. Inventors—United States—Biography. I. Title. II. Series.

Goldmann, Nachum, 1894-

GOLDMANN, Nachum, 1894- 956.94'001'0924 B
The Jewish paradox / Nahum Goldmann ; translated by Steve Cox. New York : Grosset & Dunlap, c1978. 218 p. ; 22 cm. Translation of Le paradoxe juif. "Fred Jordan books." [DS151.G585A2913 1978] 78-58073 ISBN 0-448-15166-9 : 12.95
1. Goldmann, Nachum, 1894- 2. Zionists—Biography. I. Title. **BIP**

Goldmark, Peter C., 1906-

GOLDMARK, Peter C., 1906- 621.38'092'4 B
Maverick inventor; my turbulent years at CBS [by] Peter C. Goldmark with Lee Edson. New York, Saturday Review Press [1973] 278 p. 22 cm. [TK7807.G64A33 1973] 73-122126 ISBN 0-8415-0046-0 7.95
1. Goldmark, Peter C., 1906- I. Edson, Lee. II. Title.

Goldoni, Carlo, 1707-1793.

GOLDONI, Carlo, 1707-1793. 852'.6
Memoirs of Carlo Goldoni / written by himself ; translated from the original French by John Black ; edited, with an introd. by William A. Drake. Westport, Conn. : Greenwood Press, 1976, c1926. xxxii, 484 p. ; 23 cm. Translation of Memoires de M. Goldoni. Reprint of the ed. published by Knopf, New York, in series: Blue jade library. [PQ4698.A6E5 1976] 76-8013 ISBN 0-8371-8871-7 lib.bdg. : 25.00
1. Goldoni, Carlo, 1707-1793. I. Series: Blue jade library. **BIP**

Goldoni, Carlo, 1707-1793—Biography.

HOLME, Timothy. 852'.6 B
A servant of many masters : the life and times of Carlo Goldoni / Timothy Holme. London : Jupiter, 1976. 200 p., [8] leaves of plates : ill. ; 25 cm. Includes index. Bibliography: p. [195]-196. [PQ4699.H6] 76-377401 ISBN 0-904041-61-1 : £5.50
1. Goldoni, Carlo, 1707-1793—Biography. 2. Dramatists, Italian—18th century—Biography. I. Title.

Goldovsky, Boris.

GOLDOVSKY, Boris. 782.1'092'4 B
My road to opera : the recollections of Boris Goldovsky / as told to Curtis Cate. Boston : Houghton Mifflin, 1979. x, 401 p., [8] leaves of plates : ill. ; 24 cm. Includes index. [ML422.G613A3] 78-20846 ISBN 0-395-27760-4 : 12.50
1. Goldovsky, Boris. 2. Opera—Biography. I. Cate, Curtis, 1924- II. Title.

Goldschmidt, Meir, 1819-1887.

OBER, Kenneth H. 839.8'1'36 B
Meir Goldschmidt / by Kenneth H. Ober. Boston : Twayne Publishers, c1976. 146 p. : port. ; 21 cm. (Twayne's world authors series ; TWAS 414 : Denmark) Includes index. Bibliography: p. 135-141. [PT8129.G5Z79] 76-16525 ISBN 0-8057-6253-1 lib.bdg. 7.95
1. Goldschmidt, Meir, 1819-1887. **BIP**

Goldschmidt, Richard Benedict

GOLDSCHMIDT, Richard Benedict 925.9
In and out of the ivory tower; the autobiography of Richard B. Goldschmidt. Seattle, University of Washington Press [c.] 1960. xiii, 352p. (bibl.: p.327-342) illus. 25cm. 60-5653 5.75 bds.,
I. Title.

Goldsmith, John,

GOLDSMITH, John, 1909- 940.548'6'42'0924
Accidental agent. New York, Scribner [1971] 192 p. ports. 22 cm. [UB271.G72G6] 78-158884 ISBN 0-684-12449-1
I. Title.

Goldsmith, Oliver, 1728-1774.

DOBSON, Austin, 1840-1921. 828'.6'09 B
Life of Oliver Goldsmith. Port Washington, N.Y., Kennikat Press [1972] 214, xxiii, [1] p. 20 cm. Reprint of the 1888 ed. Bibliography, by J. P. Anderson: p. [i]-[xxiv] [PR3493.D6 1972] 79-160753 ISBN 0-8046-1570-5
1. Goldsmith, Oliver, 1728-1774. I. Title. **BIP**

FREEMAN, William, 1880- 928.2
Oliver Goldsmith. New York, Philosophical Library [c1952] 286p. illus. 23cm. [PR3493] 52-13334
1. Goldsmith, Oliver, 1728-1774. I. Title.

GWYNN, Stephen Lucius, 1864-1950. 828'.6'09 B
Oliver Goldsmith. [Folcroft, Pa.] Folcroft Library Editions, 1974. p. cm. Reprint of the 1935 ed. published by T. Butterworth,

ltd., London. [PR3493.G8 1974] 74-9728 ISBN 0-8414-4511-7 (lib. bdg.)
1. Goldsmith, Oliver, 1728-1774.

GWYNN, Stephen 828'.6'09 B
Lucius, 1864-1950.
Oliver Goldsmith. [Folcroft, Pa.] Folcroft Library Editions, 1974. p. cm. Reprint of the 1935 ed. published by T. Butterworth, ltd., London. [PR3493.G8 1974] 74-9728 25.00 (lib. bdg.)
1. Goldsmith, Oliver, 1728-1774.

GWYNN, Stephen 828'.6'09 B
Lucius, 1864-1950.
Oliver Goldsmith / by Stephen Gwynn. New York : Haskell House Publishers, [1975] p. cm. Reprint of the 1935 ed. published by T. Butterworth, London. [PR3493.G8 1975] 74-30338 ISBN 0-8383-1843-6 : 15.95
1. Goldsmith, Oliver, 1728-1774.

HILLEGASS, Clifton K v. 12
The vicar of Wakefield; notes. [Rev.] Lincoln, Neb., Cliff's Notes [1959] 95 p. 21 cm. 67-102925
1. Goldsmith, Oliver, 1728-1774. The vicar of Wakefield. I. Title.

IRVING, Washington, 828'.6'09 B
1783-1859.
Oliver Goldsmith; a biography. New York, Putnam. [New York, AMS Press, 1973] 448 p. illus. 18 cm. (The works of Washington Irving, v. 9) At head of title: Hudson edition. "The author's revised edition." Reprint of the 1889 ed. [PR3493.I7 1973b] 73-8736 ISBN 0-404-03519-1 20.00
1. Goldsmith, Oliver, 1728-1774.

IRVING, Washington, 828'.6'09 B
1783-1859.
Oliver Goldsmith, a biography. New York, Haskell House Publishers, 1973. 427 p. front. 23 cm. Reprint of the 1882 ed. [PR3493.I7 1973] 72-1507 ISBN 0-8383-1446-5 14.95
1. Goldsmith, Oliver, 1728-1774. I. Title.

JACKSON, Robert Wyse. 828'.6'09 B
Oliver Goldsmith; essays towards an interpretation, by R. Wyse Jackson. Plainview, N.Y., Books for Libraries Press [1974] 47 p. 22 cm. (Biography index reprint series) Reprint of the 1951 ed. distributed by A.P.C.K., Dublin. [PR3493.J3 1974] 74-680 ISBN 0-8369-8199-5 8.00
1. Goldsmith, Oliver, 1728-1774. **BIP**

KENT, Elizabeth 658.8'090705'73
Eaton.
Goldsmith and his booksellers, by Elizabeth E. Kent. Clifton, A. M. Kelley, 1973. vii, 119 p. illus. 22 cm. (The English book trade) Reprint of the 1933 ed., which was issued as v. 20 of Cornell studies in English. Bibliography: p. 113-116. [Z325.K37 1973] 76-107925 ISBN 0-678-00725-X 8.50
1. Goldsmith, Oliver, 1728-1774. 2. Booksellers and bookselling—London—Biography. 3. London—Biography. I. Title. II. Series: Cornell University. Cornell studies in English, 20.

KENT, 658.8'09'0705730942
Elizabeth Eaton.
Goldsmith and his booksellers / by Elizabeth Eaton Kent. Folcroft, Pa. : Folcroft Library Editions, 1977 [c1933] vii, 119 p. ; 26 cm. Reprint of the ed. published by Cornell University Press, Ithaca, N.Y., which was issued as v. 20 of Cornell studies in English. Includes index. Bibliography: p. 113-116. [Z325.K37 1977] 77-3411 ISBN 0-8414-5545-7 lib. bdg. : 17.50
1. Goldsmith, Oliver, 1728-1774. 2. Booksellers and bookselling—England—London—Biography. 3. London—Biography. I. Title. II. Series: Cornell University. Cornell studies in English ; v. 20. **BIP**

NEAL, Minnie Mills. 928.2
Oliver Goldsmith. [1st ed.] New York, Pageant Press [1955] 86p. 21cm. [PR3493.N4] 55-11414
1. Goldsmith, Oliver, 1728-1774. I. Title.

SELLS, Arthur Lytton, 828'.6'09 B
1895-
Oliver Goldsmith : his life and works / A. Lytton Sells. New York : Barnes & Noble Books, 1974. 423 p., [4] leaves of plates : 11 ill. ; 23 cm. Includes index. Bibliography: p. [411]-412. [PR3493.S4] 74-15174 ISBN 0-06-496168-0 : 23.50
1. Goldsmith, Oliver, 1728-1774.

SHERWIN, Oscar 928.2
The life and times of Oliver Goldsmith. New York, Collier [1962, c.1961] 351p. (AS228) 'Originally pub. under title: Goldy: the life and times of Oliver Goldsmith.' Bibl. .95 pap.,
1. Goldsmith, Oliver, 1728-1774. I. Title.

SHERWIN, Oscar, 1902- 928.2
Goldy; the life and times of Oliver Goldsmith. New York, Twayne [c.1961] 367p. illus. Bibl. 61-15093 6.00
1. Goldsmith, Oliver, 1728-1774. I. Title.

SHERWIN, Oscar, 1902- v. 12
The life and times of Oliver Goldsmith. New York, Collier Books [1962, c1961] 351 p. 18 cm. "AS 228". "First Collier Books edition, 1962." "Orginally appeared under the title: Goldy: The life and times of Oliver Goldsmith." Bibliography: p. 337-343. 68-104753
1. Goldsmith, Oliver, 1728-1774. I. Title. II. Title: Goldy: The life and times of Oliver Goldsmith.

WARDLE, Ralph Martin, 1909- 928.2
Oliver Goldsmith. Lawrence, University of Kansas Press, 1957. 330 p. 24 cm. Includes bibliography. [PR3493.W3] 57-8924
1. Goldsmith, Oliver, 1728-1774. I. Title.

WARDLE, Ralph Martin, 828'.6'09 B
1909-
Oliver Goldsmith, by Ralph M. Wardle. [Unaltered and unabridged ed. Hamden, Conn.] Archon Books, 1969 [c1957] 330 p. illus., ports. 23 cm. [PR3493.W3 1969] 69-13631
1. Goldsmith, Oliver, 1728-1774.

Goldsmith, Oliver, 1728-1774—Bibliography.

SCOTT, Temple, 1864- 016.828'6'09
1939.
Oliver Goldsmith bibliographically and biographically considered; based on the collection of material in the library of W. M. Elkins, Esq. With an introd. by A. Edward Newton. [Folcroft, Pa.] Folcroft Library Editions, 1974 [c1928] xix, 368 p. illus. 26 cm. Reprint of the ed. published by Bowling Green Press, New York. [Z8353.S43 1974] 74-2487 50.00
1. Goldsmith, Oliver, 1728-1774—Bibliography. 2. Goldsmith, Oliver, 1728-1774—Biography. I. Elkins, William McIntire, 1882-1947. II. Title.

Goldsmith, Oliver, 1728-1774—Biography.

DOBSON, Austin, 1840- 828'.6'09 B
1921.
Life of Oliver Goldsmith. New York, Lemma Pub. Corp., 1972. 214, xxiii p. 23 cm. Reprint of the 1888 ed., issued in series: Great writers. "Bibliography, by John P. Anderson": p. [i]-xxiii. [PR3493.D6 1972b] 73-180764 ISBN 0-87696-025-5
1. Goldsmith, Oliver, 1728-1774—Biography. **BIP**

DOBSON, Austin, 1840- 828'.6'09 B
1921.
Life of Oliver Goldsmith. Freeport, N.Y., Books for Libraries Press [1972] 214, xxiii p. 23 cm. Reprint of the 1888 ed., issued in series: Great writers. Bibliography, by John P. Anderson: p. [i]-[xxiv] [PR3493.D6 1972c] 72-38350 ISBN 0-8369-6767-4
1. Goldsmith, Oliver, 1728-1774—Biography. I. Title.

FORSTER, John, 1812- 828'.6'09 B
1876.
The life and times of Oliver Goldsmith. London, Ward, Lock, 1890. St. Clair Shores, Mich., Scholarly Press, 1971 [i.e. 1972] xxxii, 472 p. illus. 22 cm. Original ed. issued in series: The Minerva library of famous books. [PR3493.F6 1972] 70-145020 ISBN 0-403-00967-7 19.50
1. Goldsmith, Oliver, 1728-1774—Biography. I. Title. II. Series: The Minerva library of famous books.

FORSTER, John, 1812- 828'.6'09 B
1876.
The life of Oliver Goldsmith. Abridged and newly edited with notes, etc. Westport, Conn., Greenwood Press [1971] 460 p. illus. 16 cm. Reprint of the 1903 ed. [PR3493.F6 1971] 78-98835 ISBN 0-8371-3100-6
1. Goldsmith, Oliver, 1728-1774—Biography. I. Title.

FREEMAN, William, 828'.6'09 B
1880-
Oliver Goldsmith. [Folcroft, Pa.] Folcroft Library Editions, 1974 [c1952] p. cm. Reprint of the ed. published by the Philosophical Library, New York. Bibliography: p. [PR3493.F7 1974] 74-5386 20.00
1. Goldsmith, Oliver, 1728-1774—Biography.

FREEMAN, William, 828'.6'09 B
1880-
Oliver Goldsmith. [Folcroft, Pa.] Folcroft Library Editions, 1974 [c1952] p. cm. Reprint of the ed. published by the Philosophical Library, New York. Bibliography: p. [PR3493.F7 1974] 74-5386 ISBN 0-8414-4185-5 (lib. bdg.)
1. Goldsmith, Oliver, 1728-1774—Biography.

FREEMAN, William, 828'.6'09 B
1880-
Oliver Goldsmith / by William Freeman. Norwood, Pa. : Norwood Editions, 1976 [c1952] p. cm. Reprint of the ed. published by Philosophical Library, New York. Includes bibliographical references and index. [PR3493.F7 1976] 76-13622 ISBN 0-8482-0756-4 lib. bdg. : 25.00
1. Goldsmith, Oliver, 1728-1774—Biography.

IRVING, Washington, 828'.6'09 B
1783-1859.
Oliver Goldsmith : a biography ; Biography of the late Margaret Miller Davidson / Washington Irving ; edited by Elsie Lee West. Boston : Twayne Publishers, 1978. xlviii, 654 p. : ports. ; 25 cm. (The complete works of Washington Irving ; v. 17) Includes bibliographical references and indexes. [PR3493.I7 1978] 78-2957 ISBN 0-8057-8521-3 lib. bdg. : 25.00
1. Goldsmith, Oliver, 1728-1774—Biography. 2. Davidson, Margaret Miller, 1823-1838—Biography. 3. Authors, English—18th century—Biography. 4. Poets, American—19th century—Biography. I. West, Elsie Lee. II. Irving, Washington, 1783-1859. Biography of the late Margaret Miller Davidson. 1978. III. Title.

KING, Richard Ashe, 828'.6'09 B
1839-1932.
Oliver Goldsmith / by Richard Ashe King. Folcroft, Pa. : Folcroft Library Editions, 1976. xxix, 295 p., [1] leaf of plates : ports. ; 23 cm. Reprint of the 1910 ed. published by Methuen, London. Includes index. [PR3493.K5 1976] 76-53568 ISBN 0-8414-5534-1 lib. bdg. : 30.00
1. Goldsmith, Oliver, 1728-1774—Biography. 2. Authors, Irish—18th century—Biography.

PERCY, Thomas, Bp. 828'.6'09 B
of Dromore, 1729-1811.
Thomas Percy's Life of Dr. Oliver Goldsmith / edited with an introd. and notes by Richard L. Harp. Salzburg, Austria, : Institut fur Englische Sprache und Literatur, Universitat Salzburg, 1976. xxviii, 205 p. ; 21 cm. (Romantic reassessment ; 52) Reprinted from v. 1 of The miscellaneous works of Oliver Goldsmith, London, 1801. Bibliography: p. 202-205. [PR3493.P4 1976] 77-354163 pbk. : 17.50
1. Goldsmith, Oliver, 1728-1774—Biography. 2. Authors, Irish—18th century—Biography. I. Harp, Richard L. II. Goldsmith, Oliver, 1728-1774. Selected works. 1801. III. Title. IV. Title: Life of Dr. Oliver Goldsmith. V. Series. VI. Salzburg studies in English literature
Distributed by Humanities Press

Goldsmith, Oliver, 1728-1774—Correspondence.

GOLDSMITH, Oliver, 828'.6'09 B
1728-1774.
The collected letters of Oliver Goldsmith / edited by Katharine C. Balderston. Folcroft, Pa. : Folcroft Library Editions, 1975. li, 189 p. ; 23 cm. Reprint of the 1928 ed. published at the University Press, Cambridge, Eng. Includes index. Contents.Contents.—Introduction — Letters.—Appendices (p. 141-178);—1. Doubtful letters.—2. Forged letters.—3. The text of Mrs. Hodson's narrative of Goldsmith's early life.—List of correspondents. [PR3493.A3 1975b] 75-42214 ISBN 0-8414-3334-8 lib. bdg. : 17.50
1. Goldsmith, Oliver, 1728-1774—Correspondence. I. Balderston, Katharine Canby, 1895- II. Title.
Contents omitted **BIP**

Goldsmiths—England.

LEVER, Christopher, 739.2'092'2 B
1932-
Goldsmiths and silversmiths of England / Christopher Lever. London : Hutchinson, 1975. 256 p., leaf of plate, [32] p. of plates : ill., facsim., geneal. tables, ports. ; 25 cm. Includes index. Bibliography: p. [243]-248. [NK7143.L48] 75-314072 ISBN 0-09-121220-0 : 12.00
1. Goldsmiths—England. 2. Silversmiths—England. I. Title.
Distributed by Humanities Press **BIP**

Goldsmiths—England—London—Registers.

GRIMWADE, Arthur. 739.2'09421
London goldsmiths, 1697-1837 : their marks and lives from the original registers at Goldsmiths' Hall and other sources / by Arthur G. Grimwade. London : Faber, 1975 ix, 728 p. : ill. ; 26 cm. [NK7144.L66G74] 76-358285 ISBN 0-571-10550-5 : 79.95
1. Goldsmiths—England—London—Registers. 2. Hall-marks. I. Title.
Distributed by Rowman & Littlefield

Goldstein, Andrew.

GOLDSTEIN, 917.3'03'920924 B
Andrew.
Becoming; an American odyssey. New York, Saturday Review Press [1973] 118 p. 22 cm. [CT275.G5576A3 1973] 72-88650 ISBN 0-8415-0219-6 4.95
1. Goldstein, Andrew. I. Title.

Goldstone, Lafayette Anthony, 1876-1958

GOLDSTONE, Aline May 720'.924
(Lewis) 1878- comp.
Lafayette A. Goldstone; a career in architecture, a record compiled by Aline Lewis Goldstone and Harmon H. Goldstone. New York, 1964. 148 p. illus., port. 22 cm. "Limited to 200 copies .. Number 175." [Na737.G58G6] 64-3364
1. Goldstone, Lafayette Anthony, 1876-1958. I. Goldstone, Harmon Hendricks, 1911- joint comp. II. Title.

Goldsworthy, Bill, 1944-

RAINBOLT, 796.9'62'0924 B
Richard.
The Goldy shuffle; the Bill Goldsworthy story, by Richard Rainbolt and Ralph Turtinen. Minneapolis, T. S. Denison [1971] 236 p. illus. 22 cm. [GV848.5.G6R3] 70-180924 ISBN 0-513-01227-3 6.95
1. Goldsworthy, Bill, 1944- I. Turtinen, Ralph, joint author. II. Title.

Goldszmit, Henryk, 1878-1942.

GOLDSZMIT, 940.53'1503'924
Henryk, 1878-1942.
Ghetto diary / Janusz Korczak [i.e. H. Goldszmit]. New York : Holocaust Library, c1978. 191 p. : ill. ; 23 cm. On dust jacket : Distributed by Schocken

Books, New York. [DS135.P62W272 1978] 77-91911 ISBN 0-89604-004-6 : 8.95
1. Goldszmit, Henryk, 1878-1942. 2. Jews in Warsaw—Persecutions. 3. Holocaust, Jewish (1939-1945)—Poland—Warsaw. 4. Educators—Poland—Warsaw—Biography. 5. Warsaw—Politics and government. I. Title.

HYAMS, Joseph. 362.7'32'0924
A field of buttercups. Englewood Cliffs, N.J., Prentice-Hall [1968] 273 p. map (on lining papers) 22 cm. [DS135.P62W275] 68-27840 6.95
1. Goldszmit, Henryk, 1878-1942. 2. Jews in Warsaw. 3. Holocaust, Jewish (1939-1945) I. Title.

Goldwater, Barry Morris, 1909-

BELL, Jack, 1904- 923.273
Mr. Conservative: Barry Goldwater. [New York] Macfadden [1964, c.1962, 1963] 239p. 18cm. (60-149) .60 pap.,
1. Goldwater, Barry Morris, 1909- I. Title.

BELL, Jack, 1904- 923.273
Mr. Conservative: Barry Goldwater. [1st ed.] Garden City, N.Y., Doubleday, 1962. 312p. 22cm. [E748.G64B4] 62-11443
1. Goldwater, Barry Morris, 1909- I. Title.

DONOVAN, Frank Robert, 1906- 923.273
The Americanism of Barry Goldwater. [New York, Macfadden, 1964] 176p. 18cm. (MB60-163) 64-3506 .60 pap.,
1. Goldwater, Barry Morris, 1909- 2. U. S.—Social policy. 3. U. S.—Hist.—Philosophy. I. Title.

GOLDWATER, Barry Morris, 1909- 328.73'092'4 B
With no apologies : the personal and political memoirs of United States Senator Barry M. Goldwater. 1st ed. New York : Morrow, 1979. 320 p., [8] leaves of plates : ill. ; 25 cm. Includes index. [E748.G64A37] 79-16823 ISBN 0-688-03547-7 : 12.95
1. Goldwater, Barry Morris, 1909- 2. United States. Congress. Senate—Biography. 3. Conservatism—United States. 4. United States—Politics and government—1945- 5. Legislators—United States—Biography. I. Title. BIP

MCDOWELL, Edwin 923.273
Barry Goldwater; portrait of an Arizonan. Chicago, Regnery, 1964. 269p. illus., ports. 21cm. 64-14594 4.95
1. Goldwater, Barry Morris, 1909- I. Title.

PERRY, James Moorhead. 923.273
Barry Goldwater; a new look at a presidential candidate, by James M. Perry. Silver Spring, Md., The National Observer [1964] 159 p. illus., ports. 28 cm. (The National observer [Silver Spring, Md.] Newsbook) [E748.G64P4] 64-25216
1. Goldwater, Barry Morris, 1909- I. Series.

SHADEGG, Stephen C. 923.273
Barry Goldwater: freedom is his flight plan. Foreword by Clarence Budington Kelland. New York, Fleet Pub. Corp. [1962] 304 p. illus. 21 cm. [E748.G64S5] 61-14556
1. Goldwater, Barry Morris, 1909-

WOOD, Rob, 1927- 923.273
Barry Goldwater; [the biography of a conservative by] Rob Wood and Dean Smith. New York, Avon Book Division, Hearst Corp. [1961] 175 p. illus. 19 cm. [E748.G64W6] 61-66488
1. Goldwater, Barry Morris, 1900- I. Smith, Dean, 1923- joint author. II. Title.

Goldwyn, Samuel, 1882-1974.

EASTON, Carol. 791.43'0232'0924 B
The search for Sam Goldwyn ; a biography / by Carol Easton. New York : Morrow, 1976, c1975. 304 p., [8] leaves of plates : ill. ; 24 cm. Includes index. Bibliography: p. 292-296. [PN1998.A3G64 1976] 75-28167 ISBN 0-688-03007-6 : 8.95
1. Goldwyn, Samuel, 1882-1974. I. Title.

JOHNSTON, Alva. 791.43'0232'0924 B
The great Goldwyn / Alva Johnston. New York : Arno Press, 1978 [c1937] p. cm. (Aspects of film) Reprint of the ed. published by Random House, New York. [PN1998.A3G66 1978] 77-11377 ISBN 0-405-11133-9 : 15.00
1. Goldwyn, Samuel, 1882-1974. 2. Moving-picture producers and directors—United States—Biography. I. Title. II. Series. BIP

MARILL, Alvin H. 791.43'0232'0924 B
Samuel Goldwyn presents / Alvin H. Marill. South Brunswick : A. S. Barnes, c1976. p. cm. [PN1998.A3G667] 75-20598 ISBN 0-498-01658-7 : 19.95
1. Goldwyn, Samuel, 1882-1974. I. Title. BIP

MARX, Arthur, 1921- 791.43'0232'0924 B
Goldwyn : a biography of the man behind the myth / by Arthur Marx. 1st ed. New York : Norton, c1976. viii, 376 p., [4] leaves of plates : ill. ; 24 cm. Includes index. Bibliography: p. 360. [PN1998.A3G67 1976] 75-37906 ISBN 0-393-07497-8 : 9.95
1. Goldwyn, Samuel, 1882-1974. I. Title. BIP

Golf—Biography.

ALFANO, Pete. 796.352'092'2 B
Grand slam! [New York] Stadia Sports Pub. [1973] 160 p. illus. 20 cm. (Sport-spectrum classic) [GV964.A1A43] 73-75001 1.50
1. Golf—Biography. I. Title.

AULTMAN, Richard. 796.352'092'2
The methods of golf's masters : how they played, and what you can learn from them / Dick Aultman & Ken Bowden ; illustrated by Anthony Ravielli ; introd. by Herbert Warren Wind ; research associate, Barbara Kelly. New York : Coward, McCann & Geoghegan, c1975. 191 p. : ill. ; 29 cm. Bibliography: p. 189-191. [GV964.A1A84 1975] 74-30605 ISBN 0-698-10651-2 : 12.95
1. Golf—Biography. 2. Swing (Golf) I. Bowden, Ken, joint author. II. Title.

BEARD, Frank, 1939- 796.352'0924 B
Pro; Frank Beard on the golf tour. Edited by Dick Schaap. New York [Maddick Manuscripts, inc.; distributed by] World Pub. Co. [1970] xv, 323 p. illus., ports. 22 cm. [GV964.B4A35] 77-115806 6.95
1. Golf—Biography. I. Title.

ELLIOTT, Len, 1902- 796.352'092'2 B
Who' who in golf / Len Elliott, Barbara Kelly. New Rochelle, N.Y. : Arlington House, c1976. 208 p. ; 24 cm. Includes index. [GV964.A1E44] 76-21059 ISBN 0-87000-225-2 : 8.95
1. Golf—Biography. I. Kelly, Barbara, 1945- joint author. II. Title.

HEAGER, Ronald. 796.352'0922
Kings of clubs. London, S. Paul, 1968. 159p. 12 plates, illus., ports 22cm. [GV964.A1H4] 68-74793 6.75 bds.,
1. Golf—Biog. I. Title.
Distributed by SportShelf, New Rochelle, N.Y.

JONES, Robert Tyre, 1902- 927.96352
Golf is my game. [1st ed.] Garden City, N.Y., Doubleday, 1960. 255 p. illus. 25 cm. Autobiographical. [GV965.J63] 60-13386
1. Golf. I. Title.

MCDONNELL, Michael 796.352'0922 B
Golf: the great ones. New York, Drake Publishers [1973, c1971] 147 p. illus. 23 cm. [GV964.A1M3 1973] 72-3805 ISBN 0-87749-318-9 5.95
1. Golf—Biography. I. Title.

PROFESSIONAL Golfers' Association of America. Tournament Players Division. 796.352'092'2
The tour book: 1973 tournament schedule, current player biographies, 1972 tournament results. New York [1973] 1 v. (unpaged) illus. 23 cm. [GV964.A1P72 1973] 73-163832
1. Golf—Biography. 2. Golf—Tournaments. I. Title.

SCOTT, Tom, 1906- 796.352'0922
The gold immortals [by] Tom Scott & Geoffrey Cousins. New York, Hart Pub. Co. [1969] 272 p. illus., ports. 24 cm. [GV964.A1S35 1969] 68-29530 6.95
1. Golf—Biography. I. Cousins, Geoffrey, 1900- joint author. II. Title.

Golf—Biography—Juvenile literature.

LARDNER, Rex. 796.352'0922
The great golfers. New York, Putnam [1970] 160 p. 21 cm. Profiles of ten great golfers of the past sixty years. [GV964.A1L3 1970] 920 76-113510 3.64
1. Golf—Biography—Juvenile literature. I. Title. BIP

Golf players—Biography.

GOODNER, Ross. 796.352'092'2 B
Golf's greatest : the legendary world golf hall of famers / by Ross Goodner ; foreword by Don Collett. Norwalk, Conn. : Golf Digest ; New York : distribution by Simon and Schuster, c1978. xv, 240 p. : ill. ; 26 cm. Bibliography: p. 238-239. [GV964.A1G66] 78-62344 ISBN 0-914178-17-2 : 11.95
1. Golf players—Biography. I. Title.

Golf players—United States—Biography.

SEITZ, Nick, 1939- 796.352'092'2 B
Superstars of golf / by Nick Seitz ; swing studies / by Bob Toski. Norwalk, Conn. : Golf Digest, c1978. 192 p. : ill. ; 26 cm. [GV964.A1S43] 77-92910 ISBN 0-914178-13-X : 10.95
1. Golf players—United States—Biography. I. Toski, Bob. II. Title. BIP

Golinick, Albert F

GOLINICK, Albert F 928.1
Autobiography. [1st ed.] New York, Exposition Press [1954] 171p. 21cm. [PS3513.O36Z5] 54-9993
I. Title.

Golitsyn, Dmitril Dmitrievich, kniaz', 1770-1840.

GLASS, Fides, Sister, 1889- 922.273
Prince Dimitri's mountaineers, by Sister Mary Fides Glass and Cecilia Glass Bard; illus. by Stephen Grout. St. Meinrad, Ind. [1951] 199 p. illus. 22 cm. "Grall Publication." [BX4705.G57G68] 51-13715
1. Golitsyn, Dmitril Dmitrievich, kniaz', 1770-1840. I. Title.

Gollancz, Victor,

GOLLANCZ, Victor, 1893- 920.4
My dear Timothy, an autobiographical letter to his grandson, by Victor Gollancz. New York, Simon and Schuster, 1953 [c1952] 438p. illus. 23cm. [DS135.E6G63] 53-5818
I. Title.

GOLLANCZ, Victor, 1893-1967. 828'.9'1203
Reminiscences of affection. With a foreword by Livia Gollancz. [1st American ed.] New York, Atheneum, 1968. 287 p. illus. (part col.), facsims., ports. 22 cm. [CT788.G595A3 1968b] 68-31638
I. Title.

Gomez, Juan Vicente, Pres. Venezuela, 1859-1935.

CLINTON, Daniel Joseph, 1900- 987'.063'0924 B
Gomez, tyrant of the Andes, by Thomas Rourke. New York, Greenwood Press [1969, c1936] xvi, 320 p. illus., map, ports. 23 cm. Bibliography: p. 314-315. [F2325.G6323 1969] 70-97833
1. Gomez, Juan Vicente, Pres. Venezuela, 1859-1935. 2. Venezuela—Politics and government—1830- I. Title. BIP

LAVIN, John. 923.187
A halo for Gomez. [1st ed.] New York, Pageant Press [1954] 471p. illus. 24cm. Includes bibliography. [F2325.G63523] 54-12341
1. Gomes, Juan Viconte, Pres. Venesuela, 1859-1935 I. Title.

Gompers, Samuel, 1850-1924.

CHASAN, Will. 331.88'0924 B
Samuel Gompers: leader of American labor. New York, Praeger Publishers [1971] 159 p. illus., ports. 22 cm. (Praeger pathfinder biographies) Includes bibliographical references. [HD8073.G6C46] 70-86511 5.50
1. Gompers, Samuel, 1850-1924. I. Title.

HARVEY, Rowland Hill. 331.88'32'0924 B
Samuel Gompers, champion of the toiling masses / by Rowland Hill Harvey. New York : Octagon Books, 1975, c1935. vii, 376 p. : port. ; 24 cm. Reprint of the ed. published by Stanford University Press, Stanford University, Calif. Includes index. Bibliography: p. 360-364. [HD8073.G6H3 1975] 75-1386 ISBN 0-374-93730-3 : 14.50
1. Gompers, Samuel, 1850-1924. 2. American Federation of Labor.

KAUFMAN, Stuart Bruce. 331.88'32'0924 B
Samuel Gompers and the origins of the American Federation of Labor, 1848-1896. Westport, Conn., Greenwood Press [1973] xiv, 274 p. port. 21 cm. (Contributions in economics and economic history, no. 8) Bibliography: p. 253-265. [HD8073.G6K38 1973] 76-176430 ISBN 0-8371-6277-7 11.50
1. Gompers, Samuel, 1850-1924. 2. American Federation of Labor. I. Title. BIP

MANDEL, Bernard, 1920- 923.273
Samuel Gompers, a biography. Introd.: Samuel Gompers. labor statesman or labor faker? by Louis Filler [Yellow Springs, Ohio] Antioch [c.]1963. xxii, 566p. illus., ports. 24cm. Bibl. 63-14380 8.00
1. Gompers, Samuel, 1850-1924 I. Title.

REED, John, 1887-1920. 331.88'32'0924 B
Labor's grand old man / John Reed. London : Slienger, 1976. 44 p. ; 20 cm. Limited ed. of 250 copies. No. 17. Written 1917; first published 1976. [HD6509.G57R43 1976] 77-363575 ISBN 0-904758-07-9 : £2.10
1. Gompers, Samuel, 1850-1924. 2. Trade-unions—United States—Officials and employees—Biography. I. Title.

SELVIN, David F 923.273
Sam Gompers: labor's pioneer. London, New York, Abelard-Schuman [1964] 159 p. illus., ports. 21 cm. [HD8073.G6S4 1964] 64-13161
1. Gompers, Samuel, 1850-1924. I. Title.

SELVIN, David F. 923.273
Sam Gompers: labor's pioneer. London, New York, Abelard-Schuman [1964] 159 p. illus., ports. 21 cm. [HD8073.G6S4 1964] 64-13161
1. Gompers, Samuel, 1850-1924. I. Title: Labor's pioneer.

STEARN, Gerald Emanuel, comp. 331.88'0924 B
Gompers. Englewood Cliffs, N.J., Prentice-Hall [1971] x, 178 p. 22 cm. (Great lives observed) (A Spectrum book) Includes bibliographical references. [HD8073.G6S74] 79-140273 ISBN 0-13-360206-0 5.95
1. Gompers, Samuel, 1850-1924. 2. Trade-unions—U.S.—History. 3. Labor and laboring classes—U.S.—History.

THORNE, Florence Calvert. 923.273
Samuel Gompers, American statesman. New York, Philosophical Library [1957] 175p. illus. 22cm. [HD8073.G6T5] 57-2741
1. Gompers, Samuel, 1850-1924. I. Title. BIP

THORNE, Florence 331.88'0924 Calvert.
Samuel Gompers, American statesman. New York, Greenwood Press [1969, c1957] xi, 175 p. port. 23 cm. Bibliography: p. 175. [HD8073.G6T5 1969] 70-90710
1. Gompers, Samuel, 1850-1924.

WEISBERGER, Bernard A 331.88'0924 1922-
Samuel Gompers, by Bernard A. Weisberger and the editors of Silver Burdett. Editor in charge: Sam Welles. Morristown, N.J., Silver Burdett Co. [1967] 240 p. illus. (part col.) facsims., ports. (part col.) 27 cm. (Illustrious Americans) Bibliography: p. 232-234. [HD8073.G6W4] 67-15872
1. Gompers, Samuel. 1850-1924. I. Title.

Gompers, Samuel, 1850-1924—Juvenile literature.

KURLAND, Gerald, 331.88'32'0924 B 1942-
Samuel Gompers, founder of the modern American labor movement. Charlotteville, N.Y., SamHar Press, 1972. 32 p. 22 cm. (Outstanding personalities, no. 24) Bibliography: p. 32. Biography of an American labor leader instrumental in union organization and labor legislation from 1880 to 1920. [HD8073.G6K87] 92 72-190242
1. Gompers, Samuel, 1850-1924—Juvenile literature. I. Title.

Gomulka, Wladyslaw, 1906-

BETHELL, Nicholas 943.8'05'0924 B William, Baron Bethell, 1938-
Gomulka: his Poland and his Communism [by] Nicholas Bethell. Revised ed. Harmondsworth, Penguin, 1972. [10], 307, [8] p. illus., facsims., maps, ports. 18 cm. (Pelican books) (Political leaders of the twentieth century) Bibliography: p. 296-299. [DK443.5.G6B47 1972] 73-155261 ISBN 0-14-021470-4
1. Gomulka, Wladyslaw, 1906- 2. Poland—Politics and government—1945- I. Title. Distributed by Penguin, Baltimore, 2.65 (pbk).

BETHELL, Nicholas 943.8'05'0924 B William, Baron Bethell, 1938-
Gomulka: his Poland, his communism, by Nicholas Bethell. [1st ed.] New York, Holt, Rinehart and Winston [1969] 296 p. illus., facsims., maps, ports. 22 cm. Includes bibliographical references. [DK443.B4 1969b] 70-84679 ISBN 0-03-082873-2 5.95
1. Gomulka, Wladyslaw, 1906- 2. Poland—Politics and government—1945-

Goncharov, Ivan Aleksandrovich, 1812-1891.

EHRE, Milton, 1933- 891.7'3'3
Oblomov and his creator; the life and art of Ivan Goncharov. Princeton, N.J., Princeton University Press [1974, c1973] ix, 295 p. 23 cm. (Studies of the Russian Institute, Columbia University) Bibliography: p. 280-287. [PG3337.G6Z633] 72-5378 ISBN 0-691-06245-5 14.50
1. Goncharov, Ivan Aleksandrovich, 1812-1891. I. Title. II. Series: Columbia University. Russian Institute. Studies. **BIP**

Goncourt, Edmond Louis Antoine Huot de, 1822-1896.

BILLY, Andre 928.4
The Goncourt brothers. Translated [from the French] by Margaret Shaw. New York, Horizon Press [c.1960] 352p. illus. 23cm. 60-12855 6.50
1. Goncourt, Edmond Louis Antoine Huot de, 1822-1896. 2. Goncourt, Jules Alfred Huot de, 1830-1870. I. Title.

BILLY, Andre, 1882- 928.4
The Goncourt brothers. Translated by Margaret Shaw. [1st American ed.] New York, Horizon Press [1960] 352p. illus. 23cm. [PQ2261.Z5B53] 60-12855
1. Goncourt, Edmond Louis Antonie Huot de, 1822-1896. 2. Goncourt, Jules Alfred Huct de, 1830—1870. I. Title.

GONCOURT, Edmond Louis 848'.8'03 Antoine Huot de, 1822-1896.
The Goncourt journals, 1851-1870. Edited and translated from the Journal of Edmund and Jules de Goncourt. With an introd., notes and a biographical repertory by Lewis Galantiere, New York, Greenwood Press, 1968 [c1937] xv, 377 p. 21 cm. [PQ2261.Z5A225 1968] 69-10099
I. Goncourt, Jules Alfred Huot de, 1830-1870, joint author. II. Title. **BIP**

GONCOURT, Edmond Louis 928.4 Antoine Huot de, 1822-1896.
Pages from the Goncourt journal. Ed., tr., introd. by Robert Baldick. New York, Oxford [c.]1962. xxii, 434p. illus. 22cm. Bibl. 62-6393 8.75
I. Goncourt, Jules Alfred Huot de, 1830-1870, joint author. II. Baldick, Robert, ed. and tr. III. Title.

Gonzales, Henry Barbosa, 1916- —Juvenile literature.

WHEELOCK, Warren. 973'.04'68 S
Henry B. Gonzales, greater justice for all ; Trini Lopez, the Latin sound ; Edward Roybal, awaken the sleeping giant / written by Warren H. Wheelock and J. O. "Rocky" Maynes, Jr. ; consultants, Jorge Valdivieso, Amalia Perez, Fabiola Franco. St. Paul : EMC Corp., 1976. 48 p. : ill. ; 23 cm. (Their Hispanic heroes of U.S.A. ; 2) Brief biographies of three Spanish Americans: two United States Congressmen and a popular singer. [E184.S75W5 vol. 2] 920'.0092'68 920 75-40232 ISBN 0-88436-242-6. pbk. : 2.95 lib.bdg. : 4.95
1. Gonzales, Henry Barbosa, 1916- —Juvenile literature. 2. Lopez, Trini—Juvenile literature. 3. Roybal, Edward Ross, 1916- —Juvenile literature. I. Maynes, J. O., joint author. II. Title. III. Title: Trini Lopez, the latin sound. IV. Title: Edward Roybal, awaken the sleeping giant.

WHEELOCK, Warren H. 973'.04'68 S
Henry B. Gonzalez, mas justicia para todos. Trini Lopez, et ritmo latino. Edward Roybal, despierten al gigante dormido / Warren H. Wheelock ; adaptacion, J. O. "Rocky" Maynes ; consultantes, Jorge Valdivieso, Amalia Perez, Ruben A. Soruco B. St. Paul, Minn. : EMC, 1976. p. cm. (His Ilustres hispanos de los EE. UU. ; 2) Translation of Henry B. Gonzalez, greater justice for all. Brief biographies of three Spanish Americans: two United States Congressmen and a popular singer. [E184.S75W517 vol. 2] 920'.0092'6873 920 76-2418 ISBN 0-88436-250-7. ISBN 0-88436-251-5 pbk.
1. Gonzalez, Henry Barbosa, 1916- —Juvenile literature. 2. Lopez, Trini—Juvenile literature. 3. Roybal, Edward Ross, 1916- —Juvenile literature. I. Maynes, J. O. II. Title. III. Title: Trini Lopez, el ritmo latino. IV. Title: Edward Roybal, despierten al gigante dormido.

Gonzalez, Justo.

SHACKLOCK, 972.91'06'0924 B Floyd.
Man of two revolutions; the story of Justo Gonzalez. New York, Friendship Press [1969] 63 p. group port. 19 cm. (Bold believers series) [BR1725.G57S5] 72-4812 ISBN 3-7784-1617- 1.50
1. Gonzalez, Justo. I. Title.

Gonzaga, Brother, 1912?-1952.

LYONS, Francis X. 922.284
Something for God: the life of Maryknoll's Brother Gonzaga. New York, Kenedy [c.1960] xiii, 206p. 21cm. 60-12057 3.50
1. Gonzaga, Brother, 1912?-1952. I. Title.

Gonzales, Pancho, 1928- —Juvenile literature.

GONZALES, Pancho, 1928- 927.96342
Man with a racket; the autobiography of Pancho Gonzales as told to Cy Rice. New York, Barnes [1959] 254 p. illus. 22 cm. [GV994.G65A3] 59-7068
I. Rice, Cy. II. Title.

MORSE, Charles. 796.34'2'0924 B
Pancho Gonzales, by Charles and Ann Morse. Illustrated by Harold Henriksen. Mankato, Minn., Amecus Street; [distributed by Childrens Press, 1974] 31 p. col. illus. 25 cm. (Superstars) A biography of Pancho Gonzales, tennis champion, whose serve was once clocked in excess of one hundred miles per hour. [GV994.G65M67] 92 74-1359 ISBN 0-87191-341-0
1. Gonzales, Pancho, 1928- —Juvenile literature. I. Morse, Ann, joint author. II. Henriksen, Harold, illus. III. Title. **BIP**

Gonzales, Ramon, 1922—

GONZALES, 301.45'19'68720794 B Ramon, 1922-
Between two cultures; the life of an American-Mexican, as told to John J. Poggie, Jr. Tucson, University of Arizona Press [1973] xiv, 94 p. map. 23 cm. [E184.M5G64] 72-84765 ISBN 0-8165-0334-6 2.50 (pbk.)
1. Gonzales, Ramon, 1922- 2. Mexicans in the United States. 3. United States—Emigration and immigration. 4. Mexico—Emigration and immigration. I. Poggie, John J. II. Title.

Gonzalez, Julio, 1876-1942.

WITHERS, Josephine. 730'.92'4 B
Julio Gonzalez : sculpture in iron / by Josephine Withers. New York : New York University Press, 1977. p. cm. Includes index. Bibliography: p. [NB813.G6W57] 76-26798 ISBN 0-8147-9171-9 : 40.00
1. Gonzalez, Julio, 1876-1942. 2. Sculptors—Spain—Biography. **BIP**

Gonzaullas, Manuel Trazazas, 1891-1977.

MALSCH, Brownson, 363.2'092'4 B 1910-
Captain M. T. Lone Wolf Gonzaullas, the only Texas Ranger captain of Spanish descent / by Brownson Malsch. 1st ed. Austin, Tex. : Shoal Creeek Publishers, c1979. p. cm. Includes index. Bibliography: p. [F391.G65M34] 79-23228 ISBN 0-88319-047-8 : 12.50
1. Gonzaullas, Manuel Trazazas, 1891-1977. 2. Texas Rangers—Biography. I. Title.

Good, Paul.

GOOD, Paul. 322.4'4'0973
The trouble I've seen; white journalist/Black movement. Washington, Howard University Press, 1975 [c1974] 272 p., 24 cm. [E185.615.G66 1975] 74-10923 ISBN 0-88258-020-5 8.95
1. Good, Paul. 2. Negroes—Civil rights. 3. United States—Race question. I. Title. **BIP**

Goode, Tom.

LEVITT, Zola. 796.33'2'0924 B
Guts, god, and the Superbowl : the exciting sports biography of Tom Goode, offensive lineman, Miami Dolphins / by Zola Levitt. Grand Rapids, Mich. : Zondervan Pub. House, [1974] 119 p. : ill. ; 18 cm. [GV939.G66L49] 74-4961 pbk. : 1.25
1. Goode, Tom. 2. Football. 3. Christian life—1960- I. Title.

Goodenough, Luman Webster,

GOODENOUGH, Luman 923.473 Webster, 1873-1947.
Lumber, lath, and shingles; an autobiographical sketch written for his children during his retirement years, 1939-1946, by Luman W. Goodenough. [Detroit?] c1954. 252p. illus. 26cm. [CT275.G558A3] 54-41894
I. Title.

Goodgame, Louis R., 1927-

GOODGAME, Louis R., 1927- 649'.1
Delightful discipline : humorous stories of woodshed wisdom and Biblical principles / Louis R. Goodgame. Milford, MI : Mott Media, c1977. 184 ; 19 cm. [BJ1581.2.G58] 77-22560 ISBN 0-915134-43-8 : 2.50
1. Goodgame, Louis R., 1927- 2. Conduct of life. 3. Self-control. 4. Christian biography—United States. I. Title. **BIP**

Goodman, Benny, 1909-

CAEN, Herbert 788'.62'0924 B Eugene, 1916-
Benny Goodman : an album / text by Herb Caen. New York : G. P. Putnam's Sons, 1976. p. cm. [ML422.G65C3] 76-8286
1. Goodman, Benny, 1909- I. Title.

GOODMAN, Benny [Benjamin 927.8 David Goodman] 1909-
The kingdom of swing [by] Benny Goodman, Irving Kolodin. New York, Ungar [1961, c.1939]; 263p. illus. 61-17562 4.75
1. Jazz music. I. Kolodin, Irving, 1908- II. Title.

Goodman, Cardell, 1653-ca. 1713.

WILSON, John Harold, 1900- 927.92
Mr. Goodman, the player. [Pittsburgh] University of Pittsburgh Press [1964] viii, 153 p. ports. 23 cm. Bibliography: p. [136]-137. [PN2598.G57W5] 64-16153
1. Goodman, Cardell, 1653-ca. 1713. 2. Theater — London — Hist. I. Title.

WILSON, John Harold, 1900- 927.92
Mr. Goodman, the player [Pittsburgh] Univ. of Pittsburgh Pr. [c.1964] viii, 153p, ports. 23cm. Bibl. 64-16153 4.00
1. Goodman, Cardell, 1653-ca. 1713. 2. Theater— London—Hist. I. Title.

Goodman, Happy.

BUCKINGHAM, Jamie. 783.7 B
O happy day; the Happy Goodman story. Waco, Tex., Word Books [1973] 224 p. illus. 23 cm. [ML420.G73B8] 76-144361 5.95
1. Goodman, Happy. I. Title.

Goodnough, Robert, 1917-

BUSH, Martin H. 759.13
Goodnough, by Martin H. Bush and Kenworth Moffett. Wichita, University Art Museum, Wichita State University; [distributed by McCormick-Armstrong Co., 1973] 112 p. illus. (part col.) 24 cm. "A McKnight Fine Arts Center book." Pages [108]-112 blank. Bibliography: p. 102-104. [ND237.G612B87] 73-620039 7.50
1. Goodnough, Robert, 1917- I. Moffett, Kenworth joint author.

GUEST, Barbara 759.13
Goodnough [by] Barbara Guest, B. H. Friedman. Paris, G. Fall [dist. New York, Efron, 1963, c.1962] 63p. illus. (pt. ol.) 19cm. (Pocket museum) 63-5300 1.95 pap.,
1. Goodnough, Robert, 1917- I. Friedman, Bernard Harper, 1926- joint author. II. Title.

Goodpasture family.

GOODPASTURE, Robert 929'.2'0973 Abraham, 1909-
Captain James Goodpasture, Tennessee pioneer, son of Abraham and Martha (Hamilton) Goodpasture, with some descendants [by] Robert A. Goodpasture. [Sunnyvale, Calif., 1972?] 9 l. 29 cm. Includes bibliographical references. [CS71.G6548 1972] 73-170661
1. Goodpasture family. I. Title.

Goodrich, Annie Warburton, 1866-

KOCH, Harriett Rose 926.1 (Berger).
Militant angel. New York, Macmillan, 1951. xviii, 167 p. illus., ports. 21 cm. Bibliography: p. 158-163. [RT37.G6K6] 51-9863
1. Goodrich, Annie Warburton, 1866- I. Title.

Goodspeed, Charles Eliot, 1867-

GOODSPEED, Charles Eliot, 1867- 658.8'09'0705730924 B
Yankee bookseller; being the reminiscences of Charles E. Goodspeed. Westport, Conn., Greenwood Press [1974, c1937] xiii, 325 p. illus. 22 cm. Reprint of the ed. published by Houghton Mifflin, Boston. Includes bibliographical references. [Z473.G57 1974] 73-15401 ISBN 0-8371-7173-3 17.50
1. Goodspeed, Charles Eliot, 1867- 2. Booksellers and bookselling—United States—Correspondence, reminiscences, etc. I. Title.

Goodwin, Ruby Berkley.

GOODWIN, Ruby Berkley. 301.45'19'6073024 B
It's good to be black / Ruby Berkley Goodwin. Carbondale : Southern Illinois University Press, 1976, c1953. 256 p. ; 20 cm. (Arcturus paperbacks ; AB133) Reprint of the 1954 ed. published by Doubleday, Garden City, N.Y. Autobiographical. [E185.97.G64A3 1976] 75-44673 ISBN 0-8093-0757-X pbk. : 2.95
1. Goodwin, Ruby Berkley. I. Title. BIP

Goodwin, William, 1756-1836.

FLEISHER, David. 320.5'1'0924 B
William Goodwin: a study in liberalism. Westport, Conn., Greenwood Press [1973] p. Reprint of the 1951 ed. Bibliography: p. [HN388.G7F55 1973] 73-1838 ISBN 0-8371-6807-4
1. Goodwin, William, 1756-1836. I. Title.

FLEISHER, David. 320.5'1'0924 B
William Goodwin: a study in liberalism. Westport, Conn., Greenwood Press [1973] 154 p. port. 22 cm. Reprint of the 1951 ed. Bibliography: p. 152. [HN388.G7F55 1973] 73-1838 ISBN 0-8371-6807-4 8.50
1. Goodwin, William, 1756-1836. I. Title.

Goodyear Tire and Rubber Company, Akron, Ohio.

LITCHFIELD, Paul Weeks, 1875- 926.78
Industrial voyage; my life as an industrial lieutenant. Illus. by Richard Bartlett. [1st ed.] Garden City, N. Y., Doubleday, 1954. 347p. illus. 22cm. [HD9161.U54G65] 54-10455
1. Goodyear Tire and Rubber Company, Akron, Ohio. I. Title.

Goolagong, Evonne, 1951-

GOOLAGONG, Evonne, 1951- 796.34'2'0924
Evonne! On the move. By Evonne Goolagong with Bud Collins. [1st ed.] New York, Dutton, 1975. 190 p. illus. 22 cm. [GV994.G67A34 1975] 74-3245 ISBN 0-525-10115-2
1. Goolagong, Evonne, 1951- 2. Tennis. I. Collins, Bud, joint author. II. Title.

Goolagong, Evonne, 1951- —Juvenile literature.

†HERDA, D. J., 1948- 796.34'2'0924 B
Free spirit, Evonne Goolagong / author, D. H. Herda ; photography, Bruce Curtis, Melchior DiGiacomo, Jo Anne Kalish. Milwaukee : Raintree Editions ; Chicago : distributed by Childrens Press, c1976. 47 p. : ill. (some col.) ; 23 cm. A biography of Evonne Goolagong, an Australian who has become an international tennis champion. [GV994.G67H47] 92 76-16197 ISBN 0-8172-0146-7 : 4.95.
1. Goolagong, Evonne, 1951- —Juvenile literature. 2. Tennis—Juvenile literature. I. Curtis, Bruce. II. Di Giacomo, Melchior. III. Kalish, Jo Anne. IV. Title.

JACOBS, Linda. 796.34'2'0924 B
Evonne Goolagong : smiles and smashes / by Linda Jacobs. St. Paul : EMC Corp., [1975] p. cm. (Her Women who win 2) A biography of the Australian woman who won Wimbledon in 1971, becoming one of the youngest players ever to become world champion. [GV994.G67J32] 74-31267 ISBN 0-88436-158-6 lib.bdg. : 4.95 ISBN 0-88436-159-4 pbk. : 2.95
1. Goolagong, Evonne, 1951- —Juvenile literature. 2. Tennis—Juvenile literature. I. Title. BIP

MORSE, Charles. 796.34'2'0924 B
Evonne Goolagong, by Charles and Ann Morse. Illustrated by Harold Henriksen. Mankato, Minn., Amecus Street; distributed by Childrens Press, Chicago [1974] 31 p. illus. (part col.) 25 cm. (Superstars) Biography of the champion Australian tennis player of part Aboriginal heritage. [GV994.G67M67] 92 74-796 ISBN 0-87191-339-9 4.95
1. Goolagong, Evonne, 1951- —Juvenile literature. I. Morse, Ann, joint author. II. Henriksen, Harold, illus. III. Title. BIP

Goose, Roscoe.

RUBY, Earl. 798'.4'00924 B
The golden Goose; story of the jockey who won the most stunning Kentucky Derby and then became a millionaire. With foreword by Eddie Arcaro. Verona, Wis., Edco-Vis Associates [1974] ix, 174 p. illus. 23 cm. [SF336.G64R8] 74-177242 7.95
1. Goose, Roscoe. 2. Kentucky Derby. I. Title.

Gor'kii, Maksim,

GOR'KII, Maksim, 1868-1936. 928.917
Autobiography. With a new introd. by Avraham Yarmolinsky. New York, Collier Books [1962] 630 p. 18 cm. (Collier books. Russian classics. BS68V) Real name: Aleksel Maksimovich Peshkov. Contents.Contents. -- Childhood. -- My apprenticeship. -- My universities. -- [PG3465] 62-13161
I. Title.

GOR'KII, Maksim, 1868-1936. 928.917
Childhood. [Translated from the Russian by Margaret Wettlin] Moscow, Foreign Languages Pub. House, 1950. 442 p. port. 17 cm. (Library of selected Soviet literature) [PG3465.A32W4] 52-40588
I. Title.

GORKII, Maksim, 1868-1936 928.917
Childhood [by] Maxim Gorki. Tr by Gertrude M. Foakes. Abridged, ed for use in schs. by David Holbrook. [New York] Cambridge [c.]1965. 154p. geneal. tables. 23cm. (The Broadstream books, 4) [PG3465] 65-10498 1.95 bds.,
I. Holbrook, David, ed. II. Title.

GORKII, Maksim, 1868-1936.[Realname:alekseiMaksimovichPeshkov.] 928.917
My childhood [by] Maxim Gorky; translated [from the Russian] by Isidor Schneider. New York, Grove Press [c.1960] 171p. 21cm. (An Evergreen book, E-246) 60-11105 1.75 pap.,
I. Title.

GOR KII, Maksim [Aleksei Maksimovich Peshkov] 928.917
The autobiography of Maxim Gorky. New intrd. by Avrahm Yarmolinsky. New York, Collier [c.1962] 639p. 18cm. (Collier bks. Russian classics, BS68V) 62-13161 1.50 pap.,
I. Title.

GOR'KII, Maksim [Aleksei Maksimovich Peshkov] 928.917
The autobiography of Maxim Gorky. New Introd. by Avrahm Yarmolinski [Gloucester, Mass., P. Smith, 1963, c.1962] 639p. 19cm. (Collier Russian classics, BS68V rebound) Bibl. 3.50
I. Title.

GOR'KII, Maksim, [Real name: Aleksei Maksimovich Peshkov] 928.917
Gorky [by] Nina Gourfinkel. Translated [from the Russian] by Ann Feshbach. New York, Grove Press [1960] 192p. illus. ports. (Evergreen profile book, 17) Bibl.: p.190-191. 60-7387 1.35 pap.,
I. Gourfinkel. Nina, 1898- ed. II. Title.

GOR'KII, Maksim [Real name: Aleksei Maksimovich Peshkov] 1868-1936 928.917
Childhood. Tr. [from Russian] by Margaret Wettlin. Tr. rev. by Jessie Coulson. Introd. by C. P. Snow. [New York] Oxford [c.] 1961[ ] 330p. 16cm. (World's classics, 581) 61-65560 1.85bds.,
I. Title.

GOR'KII, Maksim [Real name: Aleksei Maksimovich Peshkov] 1868-1936. 928.917
My childhood. Tr. [from Russian] by Isidor Schneider. [Gloucester, Mass., Peter Smith, 1960] 171p. (Evergreen ed. rebound in cloth) 3.75
I. Title.

LEVIN, Dan 928.917
Stormy Petrel; the life and work of Maxim Gorky. New York, Appleton-Century [dist. New York, Meredith, c.1965] 332p. 25cm. [PG3465.L38] 65-14403 7.95 bds.,
1. Gor'kii, Maksim, 1868-1936. I. Title.

Gorse, France.

GORSE, France. 730'.92'4
Sculptor France Gorse [by] John A. Arnez [and] Rudy Vecerin. New York, Studia Slovenica, 1971. xvi, 72 p. illus. 24 cm. (Studia Slovenica 8) [NB953.G6A89] 73-156911 10.00
1. Gorse, France. I. Arnez, John A. II. Vecerin, Rudy. III. Title. IV. Series. BIP

Gorbatov, Aleksandr Vasil'evich.

GORBATOV, Aleksandr Vasil'evich. 923.547
Years off my life; The memoirs of General of the Soviet Army, A. V. Gorbatov. Translated by Gordon Clough and Anthony Cash. [1st American Ed.] New York, W. W. Norton [1965, c1965] 222 p. port. 22 cm. "An abridged edition of the excerpts from Gorbatov's autobiography published in Novy mir. March-May 1964." [U55.G64A3] 65-11621
I. Title.

GORBATOV, Aleksandr Vassil'evich 923.547
Years off my life; the memoirs of General of the Soviet Army. Tr. [from Russian] by Gordon Clough, Anthony Cash [1st Amer. ed.] New York, Norton [1965, c.1964] 222p. port. 22cm. Abridged ed. of the excerpts from Gorbatov's autobiography pub. in Novy mir, March-May 1964. [U55.G64A3] 65-11621 3.95
I. Title.

Gordon, Aaron David, 1856-1922.

ROSE, Herbert H., 1929- 956.94
The life and thought of A. D. Gordon: pioneer, philosopher, and prophet of modern Israel. New York, Bloch [c.1964] 2x, 151p. 21cm. Bibl. 64-19142 3.50
1. Gordon, Aaron David, 1856-1922. I. Title.

Gordon, Adam Lindsay, 1833-1870.

GORDON, Adam Lindsay, 1833-1870. 821 B
The last letters 1868-1870, Adam Lindsay Gordon to John Riddoch. Edited, with an introduction by Hugh Anderson. Melbourne, Hawthorn Press [1970] 75 p. illus., facsims., port. 23 cm. [PR4725.G3Z546 1970] 74-552424 ISBN 0-7256-0010-1 3.95
I. Riddoch, John. II. Anderson, Hugh, ed. III. Title.

HUTTON, Geoffrey William, 1909- 821 B
Adam Lindsay Gordon : the man and the myth / by Geoffrey Hutton. London ; Boston : Faber and Faber, 1978. 217 p. ; 23 cm. Includes index. Bibliography: p. 209-212. [PR9619.2.G68Z7] 78-318751 ISBN 0-571-10921-7 : 12.95
1. Gordon, Adam Lindsay, 1833-1870. 2. Poets, Australian—19th century—Biography. BIP

Gordon, Anna Adams, 1853-1931.

DEANE, Julia Freeman. v. 12
Anna Adams Gordon; a story of her life. Evanston, Ill., National Woman's Christian Temperance Union [n.d.] 67 p. illus., ports. 23 cm. 65-38542
1. Gordon, Anna Adams, 1853-1931. I. Title.

Gordon, Barbara, 1935-

GORDON, Barbara, 1935- 362.2'9
I'm dancing as fast as I can / Barbara Gordon. 1st ed. New York : Harper & Row, c1979. 313 p. ; 22 cm. [RM146.5.G67 1979] 78-20165 ISBN 0-06-011499-1 : 10.95
1. Gordon, Barbara, 1935- 2. Medication abuse—Biography. 3. Drug withdrawal symptoms. 4. Diazepam. I. Title. BIP

Gordon, Benjamin Lee,

GORDON, Benjamin Lee, 1875- 926.1
Between two worlds; the memoirs of a physician. New York, Bookman Associates [1952] 354 p. illus. 24 cm. [R154.G67A3] 52-9400
I. Title.

Gordon, Charles George, 1833-1885.

*CHARRIER, Paul 923.542
Gordon of Khartoum [1st Amer. ed.] New York, Lancer [1966, c.1965] 223p. 18cm. (73-486) .60 pap.,
1. Gordon, Charles George, 1833-1885. I. Title.

CHENEVIX Trench, Charles Pocklington, 1914- 962.4'03'0924 B
The road to Khartoum : a life of General Charles Gordon / Charles Chenevix Trench. 1st American ed. New York : Norton, 1979, c1978. p. cm. Includes index. Bibliography: p. [DA68.32.G6C46 1979] 78-21043 ISBN 0-393-01237-9 : 13.95
1. Gordon, Charles George, 1833-1885. 2. Great Britain. Army—Biography. 3. Generals—Great Britain—Biography. 4. Colonial administrators—Africa—Biography. 5. Egypt—History—British occupation, 1882-1936. 6. Sudan—History—1862-1899. I. Title.

CRABITES, Pierre, 1877-1943. 962.4'03'0924 B
Gordon, the Sudan, and slavery. New York, Negro Universities Press [1969] x, 334 p. port. 23 cm. Reprint of the 1933 ed. Includes bibliographical references. [DT108.3.C75 1969] 72-88999
1. Gordon, Charles George, 1833-1885. 2. Sudan—History—1862-1899. 3. Egypt—History—British occupation, 1862-1936. 4. Slave-trade—Africa. I. Title. BIP

ELTON, Godfrey Elton, baron, 1892- 923.542
Gordon of Khartoum; the life of General Charles George Gordon. [1st American ed.] New York, Knopf, 1955 [c1954] 376 p. illus. 25 cm. First published in London in 1954 under title: General Gordon. [DA68.32.G6E48 1955] 54-8761
1. Gordon, Charles George, 1833-1885. I. Title.

HANSON, Lawrence. 923.542
Chinese Gordon: the story of a hero [by] Lawrence and Elisabeth Hanson. New York, Funk & Wagnalls Co., 1954. 256 p. illus. 22 cm. [DA68.32.G6H35 1954] 54-6420
1. Gordon, Charles George, 1833-1885. I. Hanson, Elisabeth M., joint author. II. Title.

NUTTING, Anthony 335.3320924
Gordon of Khartoum, martyr and misfit. New York, Potter [1966] 338p. illus., facsims., maps, ports. 23cm. [DA68.32.G6N8 1966a] 66-17887 6.00 bds.,

1. Gordon, Charles George, 1833-1885 I. Title.*

SPARROW, Gerald, 1903- 923.242
Gordon: mandarin and pasha. [London] Jarrolds [1962] 192 p. illus. 22 cm. Full name: John Walter Gerald Sparrow. Includes bibliography. [DA68.32.G6S6] 63-1979
1. Gordon, Charles George, 1833-1885. I. Title.

Gordon, Charles George, 1833-1885—Juvenile literature.

ORRMONT, Arthur 355.3320924
Chinese Gordon, hero of Khartoum. New York, Putnam [1966] 187p. illus. 21cm. (Lives to remember ser.) Bibl. [DA68.32.G6O7] 66-7215 3.29 lib. ed.,
1. Gordon, Charles George, 1833-1885—Juvenile literature. I. Title.

Gordon, Emilie Olga Mary Anne, 1871-1963.

GORDON, Huntly. 941.1'081'0924 B
The minister's wife / by Huntly Gordon. London ; Boston : Routledge & K. Paul, 1978. x, 216 p. : ill. ; 23 cm. [CT828.G59A35] 77-30624 ISBN 0-7100-8846-9 : 11.50
1. Gordon, Huntly. 2. Gordon, Emilie Olga Mary Anne, 1871-1963. 3. Gordon family. 4. Scotland—Biography. I. Title. **BIP**

Gordon, George, Lord, 1751-1793.

COLSON, Percy, 1873-1952. 920.71
Their ruling passions. Foreword by James Laver. Freeport, N.Y., Books for Libraries Press [1970] 221 p. illus., ports. 24 cm. (Biography index reprint series) Reprint of the 1949 ed. Contents.Contents.—Baron Stockmar, a study in wire-pulling.—Lord George Gordon, a study in fanaticism.—Dr. Samuel Parr, a study in egoism.—Joseph Nollekens, a study in avarice.—The young Disraeli, a study in ambition. Includes bibliographies. [DA531.2.C78 1970] 70-136645
1. Stockmar, Christian Friedrich, Freiherr von, 1787-1863. 2. Gordon, George, Lord, 1751-1793. 3. Parr, Samuel, 1747-1825. 4. Nollekens, Joseph, 1737-1823. 5. Beaconsfield, Benjamin Disraeli, 1st Earl of, 1804-1881. I. Title. **BIP**

Gordon, George, 1818-1869.

SHUMATE, Albert. 338'.092'4 B
The California of George Gordon, and the 1849 sea voyages of his California association : a San Francisco pioneer rescued from the legend of Gertrude Atherton's first novel / by Albert Shumate ; with foreword by Richard H. Dillon. Glendale, Calif. : A. H. Clark Co., 1976. 271 p. : ill. ; 25 cm. Includes index. [HC102.5.G67S48] 76-17948 ISBN 0-87062-118-1 : 9.50
1. Gordon, George, 1818-1869. 2. Atherton, Gertrude Franklin Horn, 1857-1948. 3. Businessmen—California—Biography. 4. San Francisco—History. I Title.

Gordon, Huntly.

GORDON, Huntly. 941.1'081'0924 B
The minister's wife / by Huntly Gordon. London ; Boston : Routledge & K. Paul, 1978. x, 216 p. : ill. ; 23 cm. [CT828.G59A35] 77-30624 ISBN 0-7100-8846-9 : 11.50
1. Gordon, Huntly. 2. Gordon, Emilie Olga Mary Anne, 1871-1963. 3. Gordon family. 4. Scotland—Biography. I. Title. **BIP**

Gordon, John Brown, 1882-1904.

TANKERSLEY, Allen P 1908- 923.573
John B. Gordon: a study in gallantry. Atlanta, Whitehall Press, 1955. xii, 400p. illus., ports. 24cm. Bibliography: p. 377-390. [E467.1.G66T3] 55-12593
1. Gordon, John Brown, 1882-1904. I. Title.

Gordon, Kermit, 1916-1976—Addresses, essays, lectures.

IN memoriam, Kermit 330'.092'4
Gordon, July 3, 1916-June 21, 1976 / tributes by John Chandler ... [et al.] ; together with a memorial resolution of the Board of Trustees of the Brookings Institution. Washington : The Institution, 1977. 37 p. ; 23 cm. Cover title: Kermit Gordon. "Tributes ... delivered at memorial services at Williams College in Williamstown, Massachusetts, on June 27 and at the Brookings Institution in Washington, D.C., on June 30, 1976." [HB119.G6415] 77-150194
1. Gordon, Kermit, 1916-1976—Addresses, essays, lectures. 2. Economists—United States—Biography—Addresses, essays, lectures. I. Gordon, Kermit, 1916-1976. II. Chandler, John H. III. Brookings Institution, Washington, D.C.

Gordon, Philip B., 1885-1948.

DELFELD, Paula. 282'.092'4 B
The Indian priest, Father Philip B. Gordon, 1885-1948 / by Paula Delfeld. Chicago : Franciscan Herald Press, [1977] p. cm. [E99.C6G643] 76-44869 ISBN 0-8199-0650-6 : 5.95
1. Gordon, Philip B., 1885-1948. 2. Catholic Church—Clergy—Biography. 3. Chippewa Indians—Biography. 4. Clergy—United States—Biography. I. Title.

Gordon, Ruth, 1896-

GORDON, Ruth, 792'.028'0924 B 1896-
My side : the autobiography of Ruth Gordon. 1st ed. New York : Harper & Row, 1977,c1976. 502 p., [12] leaves of plates : ill. ; 25 cm. Errata slip inserted. [PN2287.G64A295 1976] 76-5124 ISBN 0-06-011618-8 : 12.95
1. Gordon, Ruth, 1896- I. Title.

GORDON, Ruth, 792'.028'0924 B 1896-
My side : the autobiography of Ruth Gordon. 1st ed. New York : Harper & Row, 1977,c1976. 502 p., [12] leaves of plates : ill. ; 25 cm. Errata slip inserted. [PN2287.G64A295 1976] 76-5124 ISBN 0-06-011618-8 : 12.95
1. Gordon, Ruth, 1896- I. Title. **BIP**

GORDON, Ruth, 792'.028'0924 B 1896-
Myself among others. [1st ed.] New York, Atheneum, 1971. 389 p. 25 cm. [PN2287.G64A3] 74-139309 10.00
1. Actors—Correspondence, reminiscences, etc. I. Title.

Gordon, Taylor, 1893-

GORDON, Taylor, 1893- 783.6'7 B
Born to be / by Taylor Gordon ; with an introd. by Muriel Draper ; a foreword by Carl Van Vechten ; and illustrated by Covarrubias ; new introd. by Robert Hemenway. Seattle : University of Washington Press, [1975] c1929. p. cm. Reprint of the ed. published by Covici-Friede, New York. [E185.97.G66A33 1975] 75-26561 ISBN 0-295-95352-7 : 10.00 ISBN 0-295-95428-0 pbk. : 3.95
1. Gordon, Taylor, 1893- I. Title. **BIP**

Gordon, Walter Lockhart, 1906-

GORDON, Walter 971.06'43'0924 B Lockhart, 1906-
A political memoir / Walter L. Gordon. Toronto : McClelland and Stewart, c1977. 395 p. : ill. ; 25 cm. Includes index. [F1034.3.G67A35] 78-303536 ISBN 0-7710-3440-7 : 15.95
1. Gordon, Walter Lockhart, 1906- 2. Statesmen—Canada—Biography. 3. Canada—Politics and government—1945- 4. Canada—Economic policy. I. Title. Distributed by J. B. Lippincott Philadelphia, PA 19105

Gordy, Berry, 1888-1978—Juvenile literature.

GORDY, Berry, 301.45'19'6073024 B 1888-1978.
Movin' up, Pop Gordy tells his story / by Berry Gordy, Sr. ; introd. by Alex Haley. 1st ed. New York : Harper & Row, c1979. p. cm. The autobiography of Berry Gordy, Sr., son of a slave and father of the founder of Motown Records. [F574.D49N4433 1979] 92 78-22493 ISBN 0-06-022053-8 : 7.95 ISBN 0-06-022054-6 (lib. bdg.) : 7.89
1. Gordy, Berry, 1888-1978—Juvenile literature. 2. Afro-Americans—Michigan—Detroit—Biography—Juvenile literature. 3. Afro-Americans—Georgia—Biography—Juvenile literature. 4. Detroit—Biography—Juvenile literature. 5. Georgia—Biography—Juvenile literature. 6. Country life—Georgia—Juvenile literature. I. Title.

Gordy, John.

PLIMPTON, George. 796.33'2'0922
Mad ducks and bears. [1st ed.] New York, Random House [1973] vii, 421 p. 22 cm. Based on the contributions of the author, J. Gordy, and A. Karras. [GV939.A1P55] 73-85563 ISBN 0-394-48847-4 6.95
1. Plimpton, George. 2. Gordy, John. 3. Karras, Alex. 4. Football—Biography. I. Gordy, John. II. Karras, Alex. III. Title.

Gore, Art, 1926-

GORE, Art, 1926- 779'.92'4
Images of yesterday / by Art Gore. Palo Alto, Calif. : American West Pub. Co., [1975] [103] p. : chiefly ill. ; 24 x 32 cm. [TR140.G65A32] 75-6322 ISBN 0-910118-67-1 : 12.95
1. Gore, Art, 1926- 2. Photographers—Correspondence, reminiscences, etc. 3. Country life—United States. I. Title. **BIP**

Gore-Browne, Stewart, Sir, 1883-1967.

ROTBERG, Robert 968.9'4'040924 B I.
Black heart : Gore-Browne and the politics of multiracial Zambia / Robert I. Rotberg. Berkeley : University of California Press, c1977. xviii, 359 p. : ill. ; 25 cm. (Perspectives on southern Africa ; 20) Includes index. Bibliography: p. 337-340. [DT963.76.G67R67] 75-40666 ISBN 0-520-03164-4 : 15.00
1. Gore Browne, Stewart, Sir, 1883-1967. 2. Zambia—History. 3. Zambia—Race relations. 4. Statesmen—Zambia—Biography. I. Title. II. Series. **BIP**

Gore, Christopher, 1758-1827.

PINKNEY, Helen 328.73'092'4 B (Reisinger) 1912-
Christopher Gore, Federalist of Massachusetts, 1758-1827 [by] Helen R. Pinkney. Waltham, Mass., Gore Place Society, 1969. 180 p. illus. 23 cm. Bibliography: p. 147-148. [F69.G652P56] 71-154539
1. Gore, Christopher, 1758-1827. I. Title.

Gore, Thomas Pryor, 1870-1949.

BILLINGTON, Monroe 973.91'0924 Lee.
Thomas P. Gore; the blind Senator from Oklahoma. Lawrence, University of Kansas Press, 1967. 229 p. illus., port. 25 cm. Bibliographical references included in "Notes" (p. 191-214) [E748.G69B5] 67-14432
1. Gore, Thomas Pryor, 1870-1949. I. Title.

Gorgas, Amelia Gayle.

JOHNSTON, Mary 027.7'092'4 B Tabb.
Amelia Gayle Gorgas : a biography / Mary Tabb Johnston, with Elizabeth Johnston Lipscomb. University : University of Alabama Press, c1978. p. cm. [Z720.G67J64] 77-18889 ISBN 0-8173-5235-X : 11.50
1. Gorgas, Amelia Gayle. 2. Alabama. University. Library—Biography. 3. College librarians—Alabama—Biography. I. Lipscomb, Elizabeth Johnston. **BIP**

Gorgas, William Crawford, 1854-1920.

DOLAN, Edward F., 617'.0924 B 1924-
William Crawford Gorgas, warrior in white, by Edward F. Dolan, Jr., and H. T. Silver. New York, Dodd, Mead [1968] x, 269 p. illus., ports. 21 cm. [R154.G674D6] 68-14243
1. Gorgas, William Crawford, 1854-1920. I. Silver, H. T., 1924- joint author.

EPSTEIN, Beryl (Williams) 926.1 1910-
William Crawford Gorgas:tropic fever fighter, by Beryl Williams and Samuel Epstein; illustrated by Robert Burns. New York, J. Messner [1953] 184 p. illus. 23 cm. [RA424.5.G6E6] 53-8196
1. Gorgas, William Crawford, 1854-1920. I. Epstein, Samuel, 1909- joint author. II. Title.

GIBSON, John Mendinghall. 926.1
Physician to the world; the life of General William C. Gorgas. Durham, N.C., Duke University Press, 1950. ix, 315 p. ports. 24 cm. (Duke University publications) Bibliography: p. [295]-307. [RA424.5.G6G5] 50-10881
1. Gorgas, William Crawford, 1854-1920. I. Title.

Gorges, Thomas, 1618-1670.

GORGES, Thomas, 974.1'02'0924 1618-1670.
The letters of Thomas Gorges, Deputy Governor of the Province of Maine, 1640-1643 / edited by Robert E. Moody. Portland : Maine Historical Society, 1978. xxii, 148 p. : ill. ; 26 cm. Bibliography: p. xv-xx. [F23.G69A4 1978] 78-52565 ISBN 0-915592-30-4 : 20.00
1. Gorges, Thomas, 1618-1670. 2. Maine—History—Colonial period, ca. 1600-1775—Sources. 3. Colonial administrators—Maine—Biography. 4. Maine—Governors. I. Moody, Robert Earle, 1901- II. Title. **BIP**

Gorham, Abigail Wakeman, 1735-1810 or 11.

HALSTEAD, Vera 917.46'9'0320924 B Colton.
New Fairfield (Sherman) Conn. early days and the life of a pioneer woman, Abigail Wakeman Gorham. [New Fairfield, Conn., 1971] 18, [2] l. 29 cm. Bibliography: leaves [19]-[20] [F104.N54H3] 73 170691
1. Gorham, Abigail Wakeman, 1735-1810 or 11. 2. New Fairfield, Conn.—History 3. New Fairfield, Conn.—Genealogy. I. Title.

Gorham, Ethel Bloehm, 1912-

GORHAM, Ethel 248'.092'4 B Bloehm, 1912-
Love you Abigali ... always did / Ethel Gorham. 1st ed. Garden City, N.Y. : Doubleday, 1978. 206 p. ; 22 cm. [CT275.G594A34] 77-11778 ISBN 0-385-13643-9 : 7.95
1. Gorham, Ethel Bloehm, 1912- 2. Gorham, Abigail, 1943-1976. 3. United States—Biography. I. Title.

Goring, Hermann, 1893- 1946.

MANVELL, Roger, 1909- 923.243
Goering, by Roger Manvell and Heinrich Fraenkel. New York, Simon and Schuster, 1962. 442p. illus. 22cm. Includes bibliography. [DD247.G67M3] 62-16707
1. Goring, Hermann, 1893- 1946. I. Fraenkel, Heinrich, 1897- joint author. II. Title.

Gorky, Arshile, 1904-1946.

ROSENBERG, Harold. 759.13
Arshile Gorky: the man, the time, the idea. New York, Horizon Press [1962] 144 p. illus. 22 cm. [ND237.G613R6] 62-11237
1. Gorky, Arshile, 1904-1946.

ROSENBERG, Harold 759.13
Arshile Gorky: the man, the time, the idea. New York, Grove [1963, c.1962] 144p. illus. 21cm. (E-365) 2.95 pap.,
1. Gorky, Arshile, 1904-1948. I. Title.

Gorman, Arthur Pue, 1839-1906.

LAMBERT, John R. 923.273
Arthur Pue Gorman. Baton Rouge, Louisiana State University Press [1953] ix, 397 p. illus., ports. 22 cm. (Southern biography series) "Begun in 1939 as a doctoral dissertation [Princeton University] " Bibliography: p. [378]-388. [E664.G67L3] 53-13452
1. Gorman, Arthur Pue, 1839-1906. I. Series.

Gorman, Lawrence, 1846-1917.

IVES, Edward D. 784.4973
Larry Gorman: the man who made the songs. Bloomington, Ind. Univ. Pr. [c.] 1964. xv, 225p. 24cm. Bibl. 64-63000 5.00
1. Gorman, Lawrence, 1846-1917. I. Title.
BIP

IVES, Edward D. 78'.092'4 B
Larry Gorman : the man who made the songs / Edward Dawson Ives. New York : Arno Press, 1977. p. cm. Reprint of the 1964 ed. published by Indiana University Press, Bloomington. Includes index. [ML410.G64519 1977] 77-70601 ISBN 0-405-10100-7 : 14.00
1. Gorman, Lawrence, 1846-1917. 2. Composers—United States—Biography. I. Title.

Gorman, Patrick Emmet, 1892-

HANNA, Hilton E. 923.3173
Picket and the pen; the Pat Gorman story, by Hilton E. Hanna and Joseph Belsky. Yonkers, N. Y., American Institute of Social Science [1960] 416 p. illus. 24 cm. Inlcudes bibliography. [HD6509.G6H3] 60-3982
1. Gorman, Patrick Emmet, 1892- 2. Amalgamated Meat Cutters and Butcher Workmen of North America. I. Belsky, Joseph, 1902- joint author. II. Title.

Gorman, Rudolph Carl, 1932-

MONTHAN, Doris Born, 769'.92'4 B
1924-
R. C. Gorman : the lithographs / by Doris Monthan ; with a foreword by Jules Heller. 1st ed. Flagstaff [Ariz.] : Northland Press, c1978. xix, 170 p., [1] leaf of plates : ill. (some col.) ; 32 cm. Includes bibliographies and index. [NE2312.G67M67] 78-58469 ISBN 0-87358-179-2 : 35.00
1. Gorman, Rudolph Carl, 1932- 2. Lithographers—United States—Biography. 3. Navaho Indians—Biography. I. Gorman, Rudolph Carl, 1932-
BIP

Gorman, Tom, 1919-

GORMAN, Tom, 796.357'092'4 B
1919-
Three and two! / by Tom Gorman, as told to Jerome Holtzman. New York : Scribner, c1979. 216 p. : ill. ; 22 cm. Includes index. [GV865.G63A36] 79-84382 ISBN 0-684-16169-9 : 8.95
1. Gorman, Tom, 1919- 2. National League of Professional Baseball Clubs. 3. Baseball—Umpires—Biography. I. Holtzman, Jerome. II. Title.
BIP

Gortner, Marjoe.

GAINES, Stephen S. 269'.2'0924
Marjoe [by] Stephen S. Gaines. [New York, Dell, 1974 c.1973] 236 p. 18 cm. [BV3785.G64G34] [[B]] 1.50 (pbk.)
1. Gortner, Marjoe. I. Title.
L.C. number for hardbound ed.: 72-9118.
BIP

GAINES, Steven S. 269'.2'0924 B
Marjoe: the life of Marjoe Gortner [by] Steven S. Gaines. [1st ed.] New York, Harper & Row [1973] 238 p. illus. 22 cm. [BV3785.G64G34] 72-9118 ISBN 0-06-011401-0 6.95
1. Gortner, Marjoe. I. Title.

Gorton, John Grey, 1911-

TRENGOVE, Alan. 329.9'94'0924 B
John Grey Gorton; an informal biography. [Melbourne] Cassell Australia [1969] 251 p. illus., ports. 22 cm. [DU114.G66T7] 77-462700 4.95
1. Gorton, John Grey, 1911-

Gor'kii, Maksim, 1868-1936.

GOR'KII, Maksim, 891.7'8'309 B
1868-1936.
Gorky / Nina Gourfinkel ; translated by Ann Feshbach. Westport, Conn. : Greenwood Press, 1975. p. cm. Reprint of the 1960 ed. published by Grove Press, New York, which was issued as no. 17 in the series: Evergreen profile book. Bibliography: p. [PG3465.A3F4 1975] 75-11423 ISBN 0-8371-8190-9 lib.bdg. : 16.00
1. Gor'kii, Maksim, 1868-1936—Biography. I. Gourfinkel, Nina, 1898-

GOR'KII, Maksim, 891.7'8'309 B
1868-1936.
My apprenticeship / Maxim Gorky ; translated with an introd. by Ronald Wilks. Harmondsworth, Eng. ; Baltimore : Penguin Books, 1974. 362 p. ; 18 cm. (Penguin classics ; L291) Translation of V liudiakh. [PG3465.A33W4 1974] 74-186322 ISBN 0-14-044291-X pbk. : 2.25.
1. Gor'kii, Maksim, 1868-1936—Biography. I. Title.
BIP

GOR'KII, Maksim, 1868-1936.
My universities / Maxim Gorky ; translated with an introd. by Ronald Wilks. Harmondsworth, Eng. ; New York : Penguin Books, 1979. 156 p. ; 18 cm. (Penguin classics) Translation of Moi universitety. [PG3465.A34W54] 79-320468 ISBN 0-14-044302-9 pbk. : 2.95
1. Gor'kii, Maksim, 1868-1936—Biography. 2. Authors, Russian—20th century—Biography. I. Title.
BIP

HABERMANN, Gerhard 891.7'8'309 B
E.
Maksim Gorki [by] Gerhard Habermann. Translated by Ernestine Schlant. New York, F. Ungar Pub. Co. [1971] 105 p. 20 cm. (Modern literature monographs) Bibliography: p. 97-98. [PG3465.H2813] 75-129114 ISBN 0-8044-2326-1
1. Gor'kii, Maksim, 1868-1936.
BIP

HARE, Richard. 891.7'8'09 B
Maxim Gorky, romantic realist and conservative revolutionary / Richard Hare. Westport, Conn. : Greenwood Press, 1978, c1962. 156 p., [3] leaves of plates : ill. ; 23 cm. Reprint of the ed. published by Oxford University Press, London, New York. Includes bibliographical references and index. [PG3465.H3 1978] 78-3868 ISBN 0-313-20365-2 lib.bdg. : 14.75
1. Gor'kii, Maksim, 1868-1936. 2. Authors, Russian—20th century—Biography. I. Title.

WOLFE, Bertram David, 891.7'8'309
1896-
The bridge and the abyss; the troubled friendship of Maxim Gorky and V. I. Lenin, by Bertram D. Wolfe. New York, Published for the Hoover Institution on War, Revolution and Peace, Stanford University, Stanford, Calif. [by] F. A. Praeger [1967] x, 180 p. illus., facsims., ports. 21 cm. Bibliography: p. 166-174. [PG3465.Z9L48] 67-27953
1. Gor'kii, Maksim, 1868-1936—Friends and associates. 2. Lenin, Vladimir Il'ich, 1870-1924—Friends and associates. I. Stanford University. Hoover Institution on War, Revolution, and Peace. II. Title.

Goschen, George Joachim Goschen, Viscount, 1831-1907.

SPINNER, Thomas J. 942.081'092 B
George Joachim Goschen; the transformation of a Victorian liberal [by] Thomas J. Spinner, Jr. Cambridge [Eng.] University Press, 1973. xii, 263 p. 23 cm. (Conference on British studies biographical series) Bibliography: p. 246-250. [DA565.G5S67] 73-77263 ISBN 0-521-20210-8
1. Goschen, George Joachim Goschen, Viscount, 1831-1907. I. Title. II. Series.
Distributed by Cambridge University Press, New York, 14.50
BIP

Gospel musicans—United States—Biography.

BAXTER, Clarice 783.7'0922 B
(Howard) comp.
Gospel song writers biography. Compiled by J. R. (Ma) Baxter and Videt Polk. Dallas, Stamps-Baxter Music & Print. Co. [1971] 306 p. ports. 21 cm. [ML390.B37] 73-28237 5.00
1. Gospel musicians—United States—Biography. 2. Gospel music—United States. I. Polk, Videt, joint comp. II. Title.

HALL, Jacob Henry, 783.9'0922 B
b.1855.
Biography of Gospel song and hymn writers. New York, AMS Press [1971] 419 p. ports. 19 cm. Reprint of the 1914 ed. [ML390.H25 1971] 70-144626 ISBN 0-404-07226-7
1. Gospel musicans—United States—Biography. 2. Gospel music—United States. I. Title.
BIP

Gosse, Edmund William, Sir, 1849-1928.

CHARTERIS, Evan 828'.8'09 B
Edward, Hon. Sir, 1864-1940.
The life and letters of Sir Edmund Gosse. New York, Haskell House Publishers, 1973. 524 p. illus. 23 cm. Bibliography of Gosse's more important writings, by Norman Gullick: p. 507-515. [PR4725.G7Z64 1973] 72-2097 ISBN 0-8383-1456-2 21.95
1. Gosse, Edmund William, Sir, 1849-1928. I. Gullick, Norman. II. Title.
BIP

Gosse, Edmund William, Sir, 1849-1928—Biography—Youth.

GOSSE, Edmund 828'.8'09 B
William, Sir, 1849-1928.
Father and son / a study of two temperaments / Sir Edmund Gosse ; edited with an introduction by James Hepburn. London ; New York : Oxford University Press, 1974. xxviii, 192 p., [12] p. of plates : ill., ports. ; 25 cm. (Oxford English memoirs and travels) Originally published in 1907 by Heinemann, London. Bibliography: p. xxi-xxiii. [PR4725.G7Z52 1974] 75-323249 ISBN 0-19-255401-8 : £4.95
1. Gosse, Edmund William, Sir, 1849-1928—Biography—Youth. 2. Gosse, Philip Henry, 1810-1888. I. Title. II. Series.

Gosse, Philip Henry, 1810-1888.

GOSSE, Edmund William, 928.2
Sir, 1849-1928
Father and son; a study of two temperaments. New York, Norton [1963] 249p. 20cm. (Norton lib. N195) 1.25 pap.,
1. Gosse, Philip Henry, 1810-1888. I. Title.

GOSSE, Edmund William, Sir 928.2
1849-1928.
Father and son; a study of two temperaments. With an introd. and notes by William Irvine. Boston, Houghton Mifflin [1965, c1907] xiii, 227 p. 21 cm. (Riverside editions, B88) Bibliographical footnotes. [PR4715.G6Z52] 65-4606
1. Gosse, Philip Henry, 1810-1888. I. Irvine, William, 1906- ed. II. Title.

Gosselin, Joshua, 1739-1813.

MCCLINTOCK, 942.3'42'0720924 B
David.
The life of Joshua Gosselin of Guernsey, 1739-1813 : greffier and soldier, antiquary and artist, plantsman and natural historian / by David McClintock. [St Peter Port] : Toucan Press, 1976. [1], 2-32 p. : ill., facsim., geneal. tables, plans, port. ; 23 cm. Cover title: Joshua Gosselin of Guernsey, botanist and antiquary. [CT788.G675M3] 77-362631 ISBN 0-85694-086-0 : £0.75
1. Gosselin, Joshua, 1739-1813. 2. Guernsey—Biography. I. Title. II. Title: Joshua Gosselin of Guernsey, botanist and antiquary.

Gosselink, Marion Gerard.

GOSSELINK, Marion 917.77'5'030924
Gerard.
Corn town kid: a horse and buggy boyhood. Brooklyn, N.Y., T. Gaus' Sons [1972] 159 p. 23 cm. [CT275.G597A3] 72-78465 4.95
I. Title.

Gosson, Stephen, 1554-1624.

RINGLER, William A., 828'.3'09 B
1912-
Stephen Gosson; a biographical and critical study, by William Ringler. New York, Octagon Books, 1972 [c1942] 151 p. 24 cm. Original ed. issued as vol. 25 of Princeton studies in English series. A revision of the author's thesis, Princeton University, 1937. Bibliography: p. [139]-151. [PR2279.G6Z7 1972] 79-159222 ISBN 0-374-96814-4
1. Gosson, Stephen, 1554-1624. I. Series: Princeton University. Princeton studies in English, v. 25.

Gothard, Bill.

BOCKELMAN, 267'.61'0924 B
Wilfred.
Gothard : the man and his ministry : an evaluation / by Wilfred Bockelman. Santa Barbara, CA : Quill Publications ; Milford, Mich. : distributed by Mott Media, c1976. 150 p., [4] leaves of plates : ill. ; 21 cm. [BR1725.G7B6] 76-43001 ISBN 0-916608-07-7 pbk. : 3.50
1. Gothard, Bill. 2. Clergy—United States—Biography. 3. Church work with youth. 4. Youth—Religious life.

Gotsch, Friedrich Karl, 1900-

FLEMING, Hanns Theodor. 741.973
F. K. Gotsch, eine Monographie. Geleitwort von Alfred Hentzen. Hamburg, H. Christian, 1963. 135 p. illus., plates (part col.) port 25 cm. Bibliography: p. 128-133. [ND588.G635F5] 66-48336
1. Gotsch, Friedrich Karl, 1900- I. Title.

Gottehrer, Barry.

GOTTEHRER, 352'.0083'097471 B
Barry.
The mayor's man / Barry Gottehrer. 1st ed. Garden City, N.Y. : Doubleday, 1975. x, 326 p. ; 22 cm. Includes index. [F128.52.G67] 73-10538 ISBN 0-385-08468-4 : 8.95
1. Gottehrer, Barry. 2. Lindsay, John Vliet. 3. New York (City)—Politics and government—1951- I. Title.

Gottschalk, Louis Moreau, 1829-1869.

GOTTSCHALK, Louis 786.1'092'4 B
Moreau, 1829-1869.
Notes of a pianist / Louis Moreau Gottschalk ; edited, with a prelude, a postlude, and explanatory notes, by Jeanne Behrend. New York : Da Capo Press, 1979, c1964. xxxviii, 420, xiii p., [4] leaves of plates : ill. ; 23 cm. (Da Capo Press music reprint series) Reprint of the ed. published by Knopf, New York. Includes index. Bibliography: p. [415]-420. [ML410.G68A3 1979] 79-1260 ISBN 0-306-79508-6 : 27.50
1. Gottschalk, Louis Moreau, 1829-1869. 2. Pianists—United States—Biography. I. Behrend, Jeanne, 1911- II. Title.

LOGGINS, Vernon, 1893- 927.8
Where the word ends; the life of Louis Moreau Gottschalk. Baton Rouge, Louisiana State University Press [1958] 273p. illus. 23cm. [ML410.G68L6] 58-7553
1. Gottschalk, Louis Moreau, 1829-1869. I. Title.
BIP

Goudge, Elizabeth, 1900- — Biography.

GOUDGE, Elizabeth, 1900- 823'.9'12 B
The joy of the snow / Elizabeth Goudge. New York : Coward, McCann & Geoghegan, c1974. 319 p., [8] leaves of plates : ill. ; 22 cm. Includes index. [PR6013.O74Z52 1974] 73-93757 ISBN 0-698-10605-9 : 8.95
1. Goudge, Elizabeth, 1900- —Biography. I. Title. BIP

Gough, Hubert,

GOUGH, Hubert, Sir 1870- 923.542
Soldiering on; being the memoirs of General Sir Hubert Gough ... With an introd. by Sir Arthur Bryant. New York, R. Speller [1957] 260p. illus. 22cm. [DA69.3] 57-2982
I. Title.

Gould, Franklin Farrar.

GOULD, Franklin Farrar. 917.41
A Maine man in the making. [1st ed.] New York, Harper [1950] viii, 212 p. 21 cm. [CT275.G598A3] 50-6639
I. Title.

Gould, Jay, 1836-1892.

MINNIGERODE, Meade, 1887-1967. 650'.0922 B
Certain rich men; Stephen Girard, John Jacob Astor, Jay Cooke, Daniel Drew, Cornelius Vanderbilt, Jay Gould, Jim Fisk. Freeport, N.Y., Books for Libraries Press [1970] xi, 210 p. illus., facsim., ports. 23 cm. (Essay index reprint series) Reprint of the 1927 ed. Bibliography: p. ix-xi. [CT219.M55 1970] 71-121489
1. Girard, Stephen, 1750-1831. 2. Astor, John Jacob, 1763-1848. 3. Cooke, Jay, 1821-1905. 4. Drew, Daniel, 1797-1879. 5. Vanderbilt, Cornelius, 1794-1877. 6. Gould, Jay, 1836-1892. 7. Fisk, James, 1835-1872. I. Title.

O'CONNOR, Richard, 1915- 332'.092'4 B
Gould's millions. Westport, Conn., Greenwood Press [1973, c1962] 335 p. illus. 22 cm. Reprint of the ed. published by Doubleday, Garden City, N.Y. Bibliography: p. [321]-323. [HE2754.G6O27 1973] 73-5271 ISBN 0-8371-6875-9 14.25
1. Gould, Jay, 1836-1892. I. Title. BIP

Gould, Joseph, 1808-1886.

HIGGINS, W. H. 917.3'55'020924 B
The life and times of Joseph Gould, by W. H. Higgins, with a new introd. by William F. E. Morley. Belleville, Ont., Mika Silk Screening, 1972. xvi, 304 p. port. 24 cm. (Canadiana reprint series, no. 25) [F1059.O5G6 1972] 74-159405 ISBN 0-919302-34-3 10.00
1. Gould, Joseph, 1808-1886. 2. Ontario Co., Ont.—History. 3. Uxbridge, Ont. 4. Ontario—Politics and government. I. Title. II. Series

Gould, Milton S.

GOULD, Milton S. 340'.092'4 B
The witness who spoke with God and other tales from the courthouse / Milton S. Gould. New York : Viking Press, 1979. xxvi, 309 p. ; 22 cm. Includes index. [KF373.G64A35] 79-10038 ISBN 0-670-69158-5 : 10.00
1. Gould, Milton S. 2. Lawyers—United States—Biography. 3. Law—United States—Anecdotes, facetiae, satire, etc. I. Title.

Gould, Ronald, Sir, 1904-

GOULD, Ronald, Sir, 1904- 331.88'11'371100924 B
Chalk up the memory : an autobiography of Sir Ronald Gould. Birmingham : George Philip Alexander, 1976. x, 176 p., [8] p. of plates : ill., ports. ; 23 cm. [LA2375.G72G664] 77-354433 ISBN 0-540-09836-1 : £3.50. ISBN 0-540-09714-4 pbk.
1. Gould, Ronald, Sir, 1904- 2. National Union of Teachers. 3. Teachers—Great Britain—Biography. 4. Education—Great Britain. I. Title.

Gould, Shane—Juvenile literature.

JACOBS, Linda. 797.2'1'0924 B
Shane Gould, Olympic swimmer. St. Paul, EMC Corp. [1974] 38 p. illus. 24 cm. (Her Women who win) A biography of the fifteen-year-old Australian swimmer who won five medals—three gold, one silver, and one bronze—at the 1972 Olympics. [GV838.G68J32 1974] 92 74-2228 ISBN 0-88436-126-8 3.95 (lib. bdg.)
1. Gould, Shane—Juvenile literature. I. Title.
Pbk. 1.75; ISBN 0-88436-129-2 BIP

Gournay, Marie le Jars de,

ILSLEY, Marjorie Henry. 842'.4
A daughter of the Renaissance, Marie le Jars de Gournay, her life and works. The Hague, Mouton, 1963. 317 p. illus. 25 cm. Includes bibliography. [PQ1799.G65Z7] 63-24008
1. Gournay, Marie le Jars de, 2. France — Intellectual life. I. Title.

Government attorneys—U. S.—Correspondence, reminiscences.

HOFFMANN, Malcolm A 923.473
Government lawyer. New York City, Federal Legal Publications, 1956. 242p. 24cm. 57-13869
1. Government attorneys—U. S.—Correspondence, reminiscences.

HOFFMANN, Malcolm A 923.473
Government lawyer. New York, Bookman Associates, 1956. 242p. 24cm. 56-58700
1. Government Attorneys— U. S.—Correspondence, reminiscences, etc. I. Title.

Government executives—United States.

STANLEY, David T. 353
Men who govern; a biographical profile of Federal political executives [by] David T. Stanley, Dean E. Mann [and] Jameson W. Doig. Washington, Brookings Institution [1967] xiv, 169 p. illus., map. 24 cm. Bibliographical footnotes. [JK723.E9S82] 67-25422
1. Government executives—United States. I. Mann, Dean E., joint author. II. Doig, Jameson W., joint author. III. Brookings Institution, Washington, D.C. IV. Title. BIP

Governors—United States—Biography.

BIOGRAPHICAL 973'.0992 B
directory of the governors of the United States, 1789-1978 / edited by Robert Sobel and John Raimo. Westport, Conn. : Meckler Books, 1978. 4 v. (xviii, 1785 p.) ; 24 cm. Includes bibliographical references and indexes. [E176.B573] 77-10435 ISBN 0-913672-17-3 : 195.00
1. Governors—United States—Biography. I. Sobel, Robert, 1931 (Feb. 19)- II. Raimo, John, 1946- BIP

Govinda Simha, 10th guru of the Sikhs, 1666-1708.

GURU Gobind 294.5'53'0924(B)
Singh, a biography [by] Srinder Singh Johar. [1st ed.] Delhi, Sterling [1967] 266p. 23cm. Bibl. [BL2017.9.G6J6] [PL480: I-E- 7867] SA 67 7.50
1. Govinda Simha, 10th guru of the Sikhs, 1666-1708. I. Johar, Surinder Sigh
American distributor: Verry, Mystic, Conn.

Gowan, Stella B.

GOWAN, Stella B. 920.7
Wildwood: a story of pioneer life. New York, Vantage Press [c.1959] 155p. 22cm. 3.50 bds.,
I. Title.

Gowanlock, Theresa.

GOWANLOCK, Theresa. 973'.04'97 S
Two months in the camp of Big Bear : the life and adventures of Theresa Gowanlock and Theresa Delaney. New York : Garland Pub., 1976. p. cm. (The Garland library of narratives of North American Indian captivities ; v. 95) Pt. 2 by T. Delaney. Reprint of the 1885 ed. published by the Times Office, Parkdale. Issued with the reprint of the 1886 ed. of De Shields, James T. Cynthia Ann Parker. New York, 1976. [E85.G2 vol. 95] [E99.C88] 970'.004'97 B 75-40244 ISBN 0-8240-1719-6 lib.bdg. : 21.00
1. Gowanlock, Theresa. 2. Delaney, Theresa Fulford. 3. Cree Indians—Captivities. 4. Indians of North America—Captivities. I. Delaney, Theresa Fulford. II. Title. BIP

Gowdy, Curtis.

GOWDY, Curtis. 791.440924
Cowboy at the mike [by] Gowdy with Al Hirshberg. [1st ed.] Garden City, N.Y., Doubleday, 1966. 213 p. 22 cm. [PN4874.G56A3] 64-13818
I. Hirshberg, Albert, 1900- II. Title.

Gower, Herschel.

MCGAVOCK, Randal William, 1826-1863. 920
Pen and sword; the life and journals of Randal W. McGavock. The biography [by] Herschel Gower. The early journals. 1848-1851; Herschel Gower, editor. The political and Civil War journals, 1853-1862; Jack Allen, editor. Nashville, Tennessee Historical Commission, 1959. 695p. illus., ports., map. 25cm. Bibliographical footnotes. [F436.M135] 60-9243
1. Gower, Herschel. I. Title.

Goya y Lucientes, Francisco Jose de, 1746-1828.

ABBRUZZESE, Margherita. 759.6
Goya. [Translated from the Italian by Caroline Beamish]. [1st American ed.] New York, Grosset & Dunlap [1967] 39, [80] p. illus. (part col.) 18 cm. (The New Grosset art library, 6) On cover: Goya; the life and work of the artist. Bibliography: p. 31. [ND813.G7A62 1967] 67-25790
1. Goya y Lucientes, Francisco Jose de, 1746-1828.

CHABRUN, Jean Francois, 1920- 759.6 (B)
Goya. [Translated from the French by J. Maxwell Brownjohn] New York, Tudor Pub. Co. [c1965] 278 p. illus. (part col.) ports. (part col) 22 cm. Bibliography: p. 273. [[ND813]] 66-8622
1. Goya y Lucientes, Francisco Jose de, 1746-1828. I. Title.

DESPARMET FITZ-GERALD, Xaviere. 759.6
goya. New York, Scribner, 1956. 44[1] p. 36col. plates. 38cm. (The Gallery of masterpieces) Bibliography: p. 0--[45] [ND813.G7D43] 57-539
1. Goya y Luctentes, FranciscO Jose de. 1746-1828. I. Title.

DIEHL, Gaston. 759.6
Goya. [Translated from the French by Anne Ross] New York, Crown Publishers [1966] 45 p. illus. (part col.) 19 cm. (Basic art library) [ND813.G7D513] 66-26179
1. Goya y Lucientes, Francisco Jose de, 1746-1828.

GASSIER, Pierre. 927.5
Goya; [biographical and critical study. Translated by James Emmons. New York] Skira [1955?] 139 p. 57 mounted col. illus. 19 cm. (The Taste of our time, v. 13) Bibliography: p. 127-129. [ND813.G7G324] 759.6 55-10594
1. Goya y Lucientes, Francisco Jose de, 1746-1828.

GERSON, Noel Bertram, 1914- 759.6
The double lives of Francisco de Goya, by Samuel Edwards. New York, Grosset & Dunlap [1973] 248 p. illus. 22 cm. Bibliography: p. 243. [ND813.G7G47] 73-6901 ISBN 0-448-01377-0 7.95
1. Goya y Lucientes, Francisco Jose de, 1746-1828. I. Title.

HARRIS, Enriqueta. 759.6
Goya. [New York] Phaidon; [distributed in the U.S. by F. A. Praeger, 1969] 92 p. illus., 50 col. plates. 31 cm. Bibliography: p. 91. [ND813.G7H3] 69-12788 5.95
1. Goya y Lucientes, Francisco Jose de, 1746-1828. BIP

HOLLAND, Vyvyan Beresford, 1886- 927.5
Goya, a pictorial biography. New York, Viking Press [1962, c1961] 144 p. illus., 3 col. plates, facsim. 22 cm. (A Studio book) [ND813.G7H6] 61-15436
1. Goya y Lucientes, Francisco Jose de, 1746-1828.

HORWITZ, Sylvia L. 759.6 B
Francisco Goya, painter of kings and demons / by Sylvia L. Horwitz ; pref. by Elizabeth Borton de Trevino. 1st ed. New York : Harper & Row, [1974] xii, 194 p. : ill. ; 22 cm. Includes index. Bibliography: p. 189-191. [ND813.G7H64 1974] 74-2613 ISBN 0-06-022594-7 : 5.95. ISBN 0-06-022595-5 lib.bdg. : 5.79
1. Goya y Lucientes, Francisco Jose de, 1746-1828. I. Title.

LEWIS, Dominic Bevan Wyndham, 1894-1969. 759.6 B
The world of Goya. [1st American ed.] New York, C. N. Potter [1968] 256 p. illus. (part col.), col. plates, ports. (part col.) 26 cm. Bibliography: p. 249. [ND813.G7L55 1968b] 67-20542 10.00
1. Goya y Lucientes, Francisco Jose de, 1746 1828. I. Title.

SCHICKEL, Richard. 760'.0924
The world of Goya, 1746-1828, New York, Time-Life Books [1968] 192 p. illus. (part fold., part col.), map, ports. (part col.) 32 cm. (Time-Life library of art) Bibliography: p. 187. [ND813.G7S35] 68-56432
1. Goya y Lucientes, Francisco Jose de, 1746-1828. I. Time-Life Books. II. Title. III. Title: ..by Richard Schickel and the editors of Time-Life Books BIP

VALLENTIN, Antonina, 1893-1957. 759.6 B
This I saw; the life and times of Goya. Translated from the French by Katherine Woods. Westport, Conn., Greenwood Press [1971, c1949] 371 p. illus. 23 cm. Translation of Goya. Bibliography: p. 361-363. [ND813.G7V2913 1971] 78-152612 ISBN 0-8371-6047-2
1. Goya y Lucientes, Francisco Jose de, 1746-1828. I. Title. BIP

Goyens, William, 1794-1856.

PRINCE, Diane Elizabeth, 1943- 976.4'18'0924 B
William Goyens, free Negro on the Texas frontier. [Nacogdoches, Tex.] Stephen F. Austin State College, 1967. vi, 98 l. illus., maps. 29 cm. Thesis (M.A.)—Stephen F. Austin State College. Bibliography: leaves 92-98. [E185.97.G68P7] 70-2646
1. Goyens, William, 1794-1856.

Gozzi, Carlo, conte,

GOZZI, Carlo, conte, 1722-1806 928.5
Useless memoirs of Carlo Gozzi. The tr. of John Addington Symonds, ed., rev., abridged by Philip Horne. Introd. by Harold Acton. New York, Oxford, 1962. 285p. 19cm. 62-51297 4.75
I. Title.

Gregoire, Henri, Constitutional Bp. of Blois, 1750-1831.

NECHELES, Ruth F., 1936- 282.0924 B
The Abbe Gregoire, 1787-1831; the odyssey of an egalitarian [by Ruth F.

Necheles Westport, Conn., Greenwood Pub. Corp. [1971] xviii, 333 p. port. 22 cm. (Contributions in Afro-American and African studies, no. 9) "A Negro Universities Press publication." Bibliography: p. [291]-317. [DC146.G84N4] 75-105987 ISBN 0-8371-3312-2
1. Gregoire, Henri, Constitutional Bp. of Blois, 1750-1831. I. Title. II. Series. **BIP**

Grunewald, Mathias, 16th cent.

BURKHARD, Arthur. 759.3
Matthias Grunewald : personality and accomplishment / by Arthur Burkhard. New York : Hacker Art Books, 1976. x, 123 p., [90] leaves of plates : ill. ; 28 cm. Reprint of the 1936 ed. published by Harvard University Press, Cambridge, Mass. Bibliography: p. [95]-111. [ND588.G7B9 1976] 75-10712 ISBN 0-87817-186-X : 35.00
1. Grunewald, Mathias, 16th cent. **BIP**

Grabbe, Paul, 1902-

GRABBE, Paul, 1902- 947.08 B
Windows on the River Neva : a memoir / by Paul Grabbe. New York : Pomerica Press, c1977. 187 p., [8] leaves of plates : ill. ; 24 cm. [CT1218.G67A38] 77-84876 ISBN 0-918732-03-4 : 8.95
1. Grabbe, Paul, 1902- 2. Russia—Nobility—Biography. I. Title.

Gracchus, G. Sempronius.

RICHARDSON, Keith, 1936- 937'.05'0922 B
Daggers in the Forum : the revolutionary lives and violent deaths of the Gracchus brothers / [by] Keith Richardson. London : Cassell, 1976. xii, 244 p. : geneal. tables, 3 maps ; 23 cm. Includes index. Bibliography: p. [236]-239. [DG254.5.R48] 77-357065 ISBN 0-304-29540-X : £4.95
1. Gracchus, G. Sempronius. 2. Gracchus, Tiberius Sempronius. 3. Rome—History—Servile Wars, 135-71 B.C. 4. Reformers—Rome—Biography. I. Title.

Gracchus, Tiberius Sempronius.

RIDDLE, John M., comp. 937'.05'0924
Tiberius Gracchus: destroyer or reformer of the Republic? Edited with an introd. by John M. Riddle. Lexington, Mass., Heath [1970] xvii, 94 p. 24 cm. (Problems in European civilization) Contents.Contents.—The life of Tiberius, by Plutarch.—The events of 133 B.C., by Appian.—A well-meaning conservative who leads a revolution, by T. Mommsen.—Poor sources for Tiberius, by E. Meyer.—The first sign of a great awakening, by A. H. J. Greenidge.—The difficulty of interpreting the sources on Tiberius, by M. Gelzer.—Plutarch's and Appian's sources, by P. Fraccaro.—An uncompromising reformer who may have acted legally, by F. B. Marsh.—The need for agricultural reform and the illegality of Octavius' removal, by H. M. Last.—The political origins of the agrarian program, by J. Carcopino.—Tiberius' purpose: include all Italians in the land bill, by J. Gohler.—Purely a social reformer for the Romans, by D. Kontchalovsky.—The urban side of the Gracchan economic crisis, by H. C. Boren.—A pOTiberius Gracchus: destroyer or reformer of the Republic? Edited with an introd. by John M. Riddle. Lexington, Mass., Heath [1970] xvii, 94 p. 24 cm. (Problems in European civilization) Contents.Contents.—The life of Tiberius, by Plutarch.—The events of 133 B.C., by Appian.—A well-meaning conservative who leads a revolution, by T. Mommsen.—Poor sources for Tiberius, by E. Meyer.—The first sign of a great awakening, by A. H. J. Greenidge.—The difficulty of i
1. Gracchus, Tiberius Sempronius. I. Title. II. Series.

Grace, Dick,

GRACE, Dick, 1898- 926.2913
Visibility unlimited. Decorations by Avery F. Johnson. [1st ed.] New York, Longmans, Green, 1950. 276 p. illus., port. 22 cm. Autobiographical. [TL540.G67A32] 50-5826
I. Title.

Grace, Henry, b. 1730?

GRACE, Henry, b.1730? 973'.04'97 S
History of the life and sufferings of Henry Grace / Henry Grace. New York : Garland Pub. Co., 1977. 56 p. : 23 cm. (The Garland Library of narratives of North American Indian captivities ; v. 10) Reprint of the 1764 ed. printed for the author in Reading, Eng. [E85.G2 vol. 10] [E87.G7] 973.2'6 77-402 ISBN 0-8240-1634-3 : 25.00
1. Grace, Henry, b. 1730? 2. Indians of North America—Captivities. 3. England—Biography. 4. Indians of North America—Social life and customs. 5. United States—History—French and Indian War, 1755-1763—Personal narratives. I. Title. II. Series.

GRACE, Henry, b.1730? 973'.04'97 S
History of the life and sufferings of Henry Grace / Henry Grace. New York : Garland Pub. Co., 1977. 56 p. : 23 cm. (The Garland Library of narratives of North American Indian captivities ; v. 10) Reprint of the 1764 ed. printed for the author in Reading, Eng. [E85.G2 vol. 10] [E87.G7] 973.2'6 77-402 ISBN 0-8240-1634-3 : 25.00
1. Grace, Henry, b. 1730? 2. Indians of North America—Captivities. 3. England—Biography. 4. Indians of North America—Social life and customs. 5. United States—History—French and Indian War, 1755-1763—Personal narratives. I. Title. II. Series.

Grace, Princess of Monaco, 1929-

GAITHER, Gant, 1917- 923.144949
Princess of Monaco; the story of Grace Kelly. [1st ed.] New York, Holt [1957] 176p. illus. 22cm. [DC943.G7G3] 56-10509
1. Grace, Princess of Monaco, 1929- I. Title.

KATZ, Marjorie P. 944.9'49'0924 B
Grace Kelly, by Marjorie P. Katz. New York, Coward-McCann [1970] 96 p. 22 cm. A biography of the Philadelphia girl who became an actress, won an Academy Award, and married Prince Rainier of Monaco. [DC943.G7K37] 92 72-97606 3.95
1. Grace, Princess of Monaco, 1929- I. Title.

NEWMAN, Robert 923.144949
Princess Grace Kelly; the fascinating life story of a girl who made the leap from the Philadelphia suburb to a royal palace. Derby, Conn., Monarch [c.1962] 138p. (K60) 62-1414 .35 pap.,
1. Grace, Princess of Monaco, 1929- I. Title.

ROBYNS, Gwen. 944'.949'080924 B
Princess Grace / by Gwen Robyns. New York : McKay, c1976. ix, 276 p., [20] leaves of plates : ill. ; 24 cm. Includes index. [DC943.G7R6] 76-17294 ISBN 0-679-50612-8 : 8.95
1. Grace, Princess of Monaco, 1929- I. Title. **BIP**

Grace, Richard Virgil,

GRACE, Richard Virgil, 1898- 926.2913
Visibility unlimited. Decorations by Avery F. Johnson. [1st ed.] New York, Longmans, Green, 1950. 276 p. illus., port. 22 cm. Autobiographical. [TL540.G67A32] 50-5826
I. Title.

Grady, Henry Woodfin, 1850-1889.

HARRIS, Joel Chandler, 1848-1908. 070'.924 B
Life of Henry W. Grady, including his writings and speeches. A memorial volume compiled by Henry W. Grady's co-workers on "The Constitution," and edited by Joel Chandler Harris. New York, Haskell House Publishers, 1972. xiii, 628 p. illus. 23 cm. Reprint of the 1890 ed. [E664.G73H3 1972] 70-39490 ISBN 0-8383-1402-3
1. Grady, Henry Woodfin, 1850-1889.

NIXON, Raymond Blalock, 1903- 070.9'24 B
Henry W. Grady, spokesman of the New South, by Raymond B. Nixon. New York, Russell & Russell [1969, c1943] x, 360, xiv p. illus., ports. 23 cm. Bibliography: p. [351]-360. [E664.G73N5 1969] 68-27076
1. Grady, Henry Woodfin, 1850-1889. **BIP**

Grafton, Augustus Henry FitzRoy, 3d Duke of, 1735-1811.

GRAFTON, Augustus Henry FitzRoy, 3d Duke of, 1735-1811. 942.07'3'0924 B
Autobiography and political correspondence of Augustus Henry, Third Duke of Grafton, K. G., from hitherto unpublished documents in the possession of his family. Edited by Sir William R. Anson, bart. London, J. Murray, 1898. Millwood, N.Y., Kraus Reprint Co., 1973. xii, 417 p. ports. 24 cm. [DA512.G7A2 1973] 72-13791
1. Grafton, Augustus Henry FitzRoy, 3d Duke of, 1735-1811.

GRAFTON, Augustus Henry FitzRoy, 3d Duke of, 1735-1811. 942.07'3'0924 B
Autobiography and political correspondence of Augustus Henry, Third Duke of Grafton, K. G., from hitherto unpublished documents in the possession of his family. Edited by Sir William R. Anson, bart. London, J. Murray, 1898. Millwood, N.Y., Kraus Reprint Co., 1973. xii, 417 p. ports. 24 cm. [DA512.G7A2 1973] 72-13791 16.00
1. Grafton, Augustus Henry FitzRoy, 3d Duke of, 1735-1811.

Graham, Brenda Knight.

GRAHAM, Brenda Knight. 975.8 B
Stone Gables / Brenda Knight Graham. Nashville : Broadman Press, c1978. 167 p. ; 21 cm. Relates the life of the Graham family, parents and 10 children, at their home in a 150-acre pine forest in north Georgia during the 1940's and 50's. [F294.P48G72] 920 78-52615 ISBN 0-8054-7222-3 : 5.95
1. Graham, Brenda Knight. 2. Graham family. 3. Pinedale, Ga.—Biography. I. Title. **BIP**

Graham, Eric, Bp. of Brechin, 1888-1964.

ERIC Graham. 1888-1964: 283/.09214 Dean of Oriel, Principal of Cuddeson, Bishop of Brechin [by] Robert T. Holtby London, New York Oxford Univ. Pr., 1967. xi, 160p. 4 plates (ports.) 22cm. Bibl. [BX5199.G69H6] (B) 67-114881 2.90 pap.,
1. Graham, Eric, Bp. of Brechin, 1888-1964. I. Holtby, Robert Tinsley.

HOLTBY, Robert Tinsley. 283'.09214(B)
Eric Graham, 1888-1964: Dean of Oriel, Principal of Cuddesdon, Bishop of Brechin [by] Robert T. Holtby. London, New York [etc.] Oxford U. P., 1967. xii, 160 p. 4 plates (ports.) 22 cm. Bibliographical footnotes. [BX5199.G69H6] 67-114881
1. Graham, Eric, Bp. of Brechin, 1888-1964. I. Title.

Graham, James Robert George, Sir, bart., 1792-1861.

ERICKSON, Arvel B. 942.081'092'4 B
The public career of Sir James Graham, by Arvel B. Erickson. Westport, Conn., Greenwood Press [1974] vii, 433 p. 22 cm. Reprint of the 1952 ed. published by Blackwell, Oxford, and Press of Western Reserve University, Cleveland. Bibliography: p. 407-422. [DA536.G65E7 1974] 74-382 ISBN 0-8371-7383-3 17.50
1. Graham, James Robert George, Sir, bart., 1792-1861. 2. Great Britain—History—Victoria, 1837-1901. I. Title. **BIP**

Graham, Jerry.

GRAHAM, Jerry. 248'.246'0924 B
Where flies don't land : the story of a junkie, jailhouses, and Jesus / by Jerry Graham & M. L. Johnson. Plainfield, N.J. : Logos International, c1977. 141 p. ; 21 cm. [BV4935.G68A38] 76-57902 ISBN 0-88270-222-X : 2.95
1. Graham, Jerry. 2. Converts—California—Sacramento—Biography. 3. Sacramento, Calif.—Biography. 4. Church work with prisoners—California. I. Johnson, Mary L., joint author. II. Title.

Graham, Kerri.

DOWN, Goldie M. 610.73'07'11 B
Kerri and company : nurses in training on hospital duty / Goldie Down. [Washington] : Review and Herald Pub. Association, c1978. 125 p. ; 21 cm. A biography of a student nurse whose Christian faith and desire to serve help her through many rough moments during her training. [RT37.G7D68] 92 77-83626 pbk. : 3.95
1. Graham, Kerri. 2. Nursing students—Biography. 3. Christian biography. I. Title.

Graham, Martha.

ARMITAGE, Merle, 1893- ed. 793.30924
Martha Graham, edited and with a foreword by Merle Armitage. Articles by John Martin [and others. New York, Dance Horizons, 1966] 132 p. illus., music, ports. 21 cm. [GV1785.G7A7 1966] 66-26859
1. Graham, Martha. I. Martin, John Joseph, 1893-

LEATHERMAN, Le Roy. 793.30924
Martha Graham; portrait of the lady as an artist. Photos. by Martha Swope. [1st ed.] New York, Knopf, 1966. 178 p. illus., ports. 29 cm. [GV1785.G7L43] 66-19377
1. Graham, Martha.

MCDONAGH, Don. 793.3'092'4 B
Martha Graham: a biography. New York, Praeger [1973] x, 341 p. illus. 24 cm. Bibliography: p. 333-334. [GV1785.G7M32] 72-87297 10.95
1. Graham, Martha.

Graham, Martha—Juvenile literature.

TERRY, Walter. 793.3'092'4 B
Frontiers of dance ; the life of Martha Graham / by Walter Terry. New York : Crowell, [1975] p. cm. (Women of America series) Includes index. Bibliography: p. A biography of the dancer, choreographer, and teacher who is generally considered to be one of America's greatest pioneers of modern dance. [GV1785.G7T47] 92 75-9871 ISBN 0-690-00920-8 : 5.95
1. Graham, Martha—Juvenile literature. 2. Modern dance—Juvenile literature. I. Title. **BIP**

Graham, Morrow C., 1892-

GRAHAM, Morrow C., 1892- 269'.2'0924 B
They call me Mother Graham / Morrow C. Graham. Old Tappan, N.J. : F. H. Revell Co., c1977. 64 p. : ports. ; 18 cm. (New life ventures) Autobiographical. [BX6495.G663A35] 77-5617 ISBN 0-8007-9000-6 pbk. : 0.95
1. Graham, Morrow C., 1892- 2. Graham, William Franklin, 1918- 3. Baptists—North Carolina—Charlotte—Biography. 4. Charlotte, N.C.—Biography. I. Title.

GRAHAM, Morrow C., 1892- 269'.2'0924 B
They call me Mother Graham / Morrow C. Graham. Old Tappan, N.J. : F. H. Revell Co., c1977. 64 p. : ports. ; 18 cm. (New life ventures) Autobiographical. [BX6495.G663A35] 77-5617 ISBN 0-8007-9000-6 pbk. : 0.95
1. Graham, Morrow C., 1892- 2. Graham, William Franklin, 1918- 3. Baptists—North Carolina—Charlotte—Biography. 4. Charlotte, N.C.—Biography. I. Title. **BIP**

Graham, Sheilah

GRAHAM, Sheilah 920.5
The rest of the story. New York, Bantam [1965, c.1964] 215p. 18cm. (H2951) .60 pap.,
I. Title.

Graham, Virginia,

GRAHAM, Virginia, 1912- 791.45 B
There goes what's her name; the continuing saga of Virginia Graham, by Virginia Graham and Jean Libman Block. Englewood Cliffs, N. J., Prentice-Hall [1965] viii, 246 p. ports. 22 cm. [PN1992.4.G7A3] 65-25237
I. Block, Jean Libman, joint author. II. Title.

Graham, William Franklin, 1918-

AMERICA'S hour of decision; 922
featuring a life story of Billy Graham, and stories of his evangelistic campaigns in Portland, Ore., Minneapolis, Atlanta, Fort Worth, Shreveport, La., Memphis, and the Rose Bowl, Pasadena, California. Includes four of the evangelist's sermons. Wheaton, Ill., Van Kampen Press [1951] 158 p. illus. 20 cm. [BV3785.G69A5] 51-6987
1. Graham, William Franklin, 1918- 2. Revivals—U. S. 3. Evangelistic sermons. I. Graham, William Franklin, 1918-

ASHMAN, Chuck. 269'.2092'4 B
The gospel according to Billy / by Chuck Ashman ; with an introd. by Rod McKuen. 1st ed. Secaucus, N.J. : Lyle Stuart, c1977. 240 p. ; 24 cm. [BV3785.G69A8 1977] 77-23027 ISBN 0-8184-0251-2 : 8.95
1. Graham, William Franklin, 1918- I. Title. BIP

BARNHART, Joe E., 1931- 269'.2
The Billy Graham religion, by Joe E. Barnhart. Philadelphia, United Church Press [1972] 255 p. 22 cm. "A Pilgrim Press book." Includes bibliographical references. [BV3785.G69B28] 72-8447 ISBN 0-8298-0242-8 6.95
1. Graham, William Franklin, 1918- 2. Evangelicalism—United States. 3. United States—Religion. I. Title.

BILLY Graham, 269'.2'0924 B
performer?, Politician?, Preacher?, Prophet? : A chronological record compiled from public sources by the Church League of America, 1951 through 1978. Wheaton, Ill. : The League, [1979] 152 p. ; 18 cm. [BV3785.G69B52] 79-53090 ISBN 0-89601-024-4 pbk. : 3.00
1. Graham, William Franklin, 1918- 2. Evangelists—United States—Biography. I. Church League of America.

BURNHAM, George. 922
Billy Graham: a mission accomplished. [Westwood, N. J.] Revell [1955] 158p. 22cm. [BV3785.G69B8] 55-12219
1. Graham, William Franklin, 1918- I. Title.

BURNHAM, George. 922
To the far corners, with Billy Graham in Asia, including excerpts from Billy Graham's diary. [Westwood, N. J.] Revell [1956] 160p. 22cm. [BV3785.G69B82] 56-10891
1. Graham, William Franklin, 1918- 2. Revivals-Asia. I. Title.

COOK, Charles Thomas, 1886- 922
The Billy Graham story, 'One thing I do.' Wheaton, Ill., Van Kampen Press [1954] 128p. illus. 19cm. [BV3785] 54-10720
1. Graham, William Franklin, 1918- I. Title.

DANIELS, Glenn 922.673
The man who walks with God [Orig. title: The inspiring life and thoughts of Billy Graham] New York, Paperback Lib. [1964, c.1961] 152p. 18cm. (52-330) .50 pap.,
1. Graham, William Franklin, 1918- I. Title.

FRADY, Marshall. 269'.2'0924 B
Billy Graham, a parable of American righteousness / Marshall Frady. 1st ed. Boston : Little, Brown, c1979. xi, 546 p. ; 24 cm. Includes bibliographical references and index. [BV3785.G69F7] 79-9947 ISBN 0-316-29130-7 : 12.95
1. Graham, William Franklin, 1918- 2. Evangelists—United States—Biography. I. Title.

GRAHAM, William Franklin, 208
1918-
The faith of Billy Graham. Compiled and edited by T. S. Settel. Introd. by Cort R. Flint. [1st ed.] Anderson, S.C., Droke House [1968] 127 p. 24 cm. [BV3785.G69A25 1968] 68-28781 3.95
1. Graham, William Franklin, 1918- 2. Bible—Homiletical use. I. Settel, Trudy S., ed. II. Title.

GRAHAM, William Franklin, 243
1918-
The wit and wisdom of Billy Graham. Edited and compiled by Bill Adler. New York, Random House [1967] 165 p. 22 cm. [BV3797.G675] 66-21481
I. Adler, Bill, ed. II. Title.

HIGH, Stanley, 1895- 922
Billy Graham: the personal story of the man, his message, and his mission. New York, McGraw-Hill [1956] 274 p. illus. 22 cm. [BV3785.G69H5] 56-11952
1. Graham, William Franklin, 1918-

HIGH, Stanley, 1895- 922
Billy Graham: the personal story of the man, his message, and his mission. New York, McGraw-Hill [1956] 274p. illus. 22cm. [BV3785.G69H5] 56-11952
1. Graham, William Franklin. 1918- I. Title.

MCLOUGHLIN, William Gerald. 922
Billy Graham, revivalist in a secular age. New York, Ronald Press Co. [1960] 269p. 21cm. Includes bibliography. [BV3785.G69M3] 59-12122
1. Graham, William Franklin, 1918- I. Title.

MCLOUGHLIN, William Gerald 922
Billy Graham, revivalist in a secular age. New York, Ronald Press Co. [c.1960] xi, 269p. Bibl. notes p.232-259. 21cm. 59-12122 4.50
1. Graham, William Franklin I. Title.

MITCHELL, Curtis. 269.20924
Billy Graham; the making of a crusader. Foreword by George M. Wilson. [1st ed.] Philadelphia, Chilton Books [1966] x, 288 p. 21 cm. [BV3785.G69M47] 65-25659
1. Graham, William Franklin, 1918-

PAUL, Ronald C. 269'.2'0924 B
Billy Graham, prophet of hope / Ronald C. Paul. 1st ed. New York : Ballantine Books, 1978. 218 p. ; 18 cm. Bibliography: p. 215-218. [BV3785.G69P38] 78-67474 ISBN 0-345-27818-6 pbk. : 1.95
1. Graham, William Franklin, 1918- 2. Evangelists—United States—Biography. I. Title.

POLING, David, 269'.2'0924 B
1928-
Why Billy Graham? / By David Poling. Grand Rapids, Mich. : Zondervan Pub. House, c1977. p. cm. [BV3785.G69P59] 77-13195 ISBN 0-310-36350-0 : 6.95
1. Graham, William Franklin, 1918- 2. Evangelists—United States—Biography. I. Title. BIP

POLLOCK, John 269'.2'0924
Charles.
Billy Graham; the authorized biography, by John Pollock. Grand Rapids, Zondervan [1967, c.1966] ix, 277p. illus., ports. 18cm. Bibl. [BV3785.G69P6 1967] 67-17236 .95 pap.,
1. Graham, William Franklin, 1918- I. Title.

POLLOCK, John 296'.2'0924 B
Charles.
Billy Graham, evangelist to the world : an authorized biography of the decisive years / John Pollock. 1st ed. San Francisco : Harper & Row, c1979. x, 324 p., [8] leaves of plates : ill. ; 24 cm. Includes index. [BV3785.G69P597 1979] 76-62949 ISBN 0-06-066691-9. : 10.00
1. Graham, William Franklin, 1918- 2. Evangelists—United States—Biography.

POLLOCK, John 269.20924 B
Charles.
Billy Graham; the authorized biography, by John Pollock. New York, McGraw-Hill [1966] ix, 277 p. 21 cm. "Notes on sources": p. 270. [BV3785.G69P6 1966a] 66-19465
1. Graham, William Franklin, 1918-

STREIKER, Lowell D. 269'.2'0924 B
Religion and the new majority: Billy Graham, Middle America, and the politics of the 70s [by] Lowell D. Streiker and Gerald S. Strober. New York, Association Press [1972] 202 p. 22 cm. Includes bibliographical references. [BR515.S76] 79-189009 ISBN 0-8096-1844-3 5.95
1. Graham, William Franklin, 1918- 2. United States—Religion—1945- 3. Fundamentalism. 4. United States—Politics and government—1969-1974. I. Strober, Gerald S., joint author. II. Title.

Graham, William Franklin, 1918- — Juvenile literature.

STROBER, Gerald S. 269'.2'0924 B
Billy Graham, his life and faith / Gerald S. Strober. Waco, Tex. : Word Books, c1977. 144 p. ; 23 cm. A biography of the world-famous evangelist who has advised presidents and kings. [BV3785.G69S86] 92 76-56484 ISBN 0-87680-445-8 : 4.95
1. Graham, William Franklin, 1918- — Juvenile literature. 2. Evangelists—United States—Biography Juvenile literature. I. Title.

Graham, William Franklin, 1918- — Portraits, etc.

SPILLMAN, Sandy. 269'.2'0924 B
Billy Graham : a photobiography / written by Sandy Spillman. Houston : Epps-Praxis Publishers, c1976. [80] p. : chiefly ill. ; 28 cm. [BV3785.G69S68] 76-151099 2.95
1. Graham, William Franklin, 1918- — Portraits, etc. 2. Evangelists—United States—Portraits, etc.

Grahame, Iain.

GRAHAME, Iain. 636.5'9
Flying feathers / Iain Grahame ; foreword by Gerald Durrell ; ill. by Timothy Greenwood. New York : St. Martin's Press, c1977. 148 p. : ill., map (on lining paper) ; 23 cm. Continued by: Ruffled feathers. [SF510.W3G7] 77-71324 ISBN 0-312-29690-8 : 7.95
1. Grahame, Iain. 2. Daw's Hall Wildfowl Farm, Eng. 3. Bird breeders—England—Biography. I. Greenwood, Timothy. II. Title.

GRAHAME, Iain. 636.5'9
Ruffled feathers / Iain Grahame ; foreword by Gerald Durrell ; ill. by Timothy Greenwood. New York : St. Martin's Press, 1978. vi, 170 p. : ill. ; 23 cm. Continues the author's Flying feathers. [SF510.W3G72 1978] 78-52207 ISBN 0-312-69561-6 : 8.95
1. Grahame, Iain. 2. Daw's Hall Wildfowl Farm, Eng. 3. Bird breeders—England—Biography. I. Title. BIP

Grahame, Kenneth, 1859-1932.

CHALMERS, Patrick 828'.8'09 B
Reginald, 1872-1942.
Kenneth Grahame; life, letters and unpublished work. Port Washington, N.Y., Kennikat Press [1972] xvii, 321 p. illus. 23 cm. Reprint of the 1933 ed. [PR4727.C5 1972] 76-160747 ISBN 0-8046-1560-8
1. Grahame, Kenneth, 1859-1932.

GRAHAM, Eleanor, 1896- 823.912
Kenneth Grahame. New York, Walck [1963] 72p. port. 19cm. Bibl. 63-14497 2.50
1. Grahame, Kenneth, 1859-1932. I. Title.

GREEN, Peter, 1924- 928.2
Kenneth Grahame, a biography. [1st ed.] Cleveland, World Pub. Co. [1959] 400p. illus. 23cm. Includes bibliography. [PR4727.G7] 59-7751
1. Grahame, Kenneth, 1859-1932. I. Title.

Grainger, Percy Aldridge, 1882-1961.

BIRD, John. 786.1'092'4 B
Percy Grainger / John Bird. London : P. Elek, 1976. xv, 317 p., [8] leaves of plates : ill. ; 24 cm. Includes index. Bibliography: p. [258]-260. [ML410.G75B6] 77-355788 ISBN 0-236-40004-5 : 19.95
1. Grainger, Percy Aldridge, 1882-1961. 2. Composers—Biography.
Distributed by Paul Elek, Salem, New Hampshire BIP

SLATTERY, Thomas C. 786.1'092'4 B
Percy Grainger : the inveterate innovator / by Thomas C. Slattery. Evanston, Ill. : Instrumentalist Co., [1974] xi, 308 p., [8] leaves of plates : ill. ; 22 cm. Bibliography: p. 299-308. [ML410.G75S55] 73-87230 8.95
1. Grainger, Percy Aldridge, 1882-1961. BIP

Grammar, Comparative and general— Phonology—Biobibliography.

A Biographical 414'.092'2 B
dictionary of the phonetic sciences / edited by Arthur J. Bronstein, Lawrence J. Raphael, Cj Stevens. New York : Press of Lehman College, c1977. xxv, 255 p. ; 26 cm. Includes index. Bibliography: p. 239-241. [P83.B5] 77-87592 14.95
1. Grammar, Comparative and general—Phonology—Biobibliography. 2. Phonetics—Biobibliography. 3. Dialectology—Biobibliography. I. Bronstein, Arthur J. II. Raphael, Lawrence J. III. Stevens, Cj.

Gramont, Antoine, duc de, 1604-1678.

LEWIS, Warren Hamilton. 923.244
Assault on Olympus; the rise of the house of Gramont between 1604 and 1678. [1st American ed.] New York, Harcourt, Brace [1958] 240p. 23cm. Includes bibliography. [DC123.9.G74L4] 57-6212
1. Gramont, Antoine, duc de, 1604-1678. 2. Gramont family. I. Title.

Gramsci, Antonio, 1891-1937.

CAMMETT, John McKay, 335.40945
1927-
Antonio Gramsci and the origins of Italian Communism [by] John M. Cammett. Stanford, Calif., Stanford University Press, 1967. xiv, 306 p. 24 cm. Bibliography: p. [274]-297. [HX288.G7C27] 66-22983
1. Gramsci, Antonio, 1891-1937. BIP

DAVIDSON, Alastair, 335.4'092'4 B
1939-
Antonio Gramsci : towards an intellectual biography / by Alastair Davidson. Atlantic Highlands, N.J. : Humanities Press, 1977. xvi, 337 p. ; 23 cm. Includes index. Bibliography: p. 310-319. [HX288.G7D32 1977] 76-42190 ISBN 0-391-00671-1 : 14.50
1. Gramsci, Antonio, 1891-1937. 2. Communists—Italy—Biography. I. Title. BIP

FIORI, Giuseppe, 335.43'0924 B
1923-
Antonio Gramsci: life of a revolutionary. [Translated by Tom Nairn. 1st ed.] New York, Dutton, 1971 [c1970] 304 p. 24 cm. Translation of Vita di Antonio Gramsci. Bibliography: p. [293]-297. [DG575.G69F513 1971] 70-148475 ISBN 0-525-05625-4 8.95
1. Gramsci, Antonio, 1891-1937. I. Title.

FIORI, Giuseppe, 335.43'0924 [B]
1923-
Antonio Gramsci: life of a revolutionary. Translated by Tom Nairn New York, Schocken Books [1973, c.1970] 304 p. 20 cm. (Schocken paperback, SB388) Translation of Vita di Antonio Gramsci. Bibliography: p. [293]-297. [DG575.G69F513 1971] ISBN 0-8052-0388-5 pap., 3.45
1. Gramsci, Antonio, 1891-1937. I. Title.

GRAMSCI, Antonio, 335.43'092'4 B
1891-1937.
Letters from prison. Selected, translated from the Italian, and introduced by Lynne Lawner. [1st ed.] New York, Harper & Row [1973] 292 p. illus. 22 cm. Translated from Lettere dal carcere. Bibliography: p. 283-284. [HX288.G7A4213] 74-156531 ISBN 0-06-012539-X 10.00
1. Gramsci, Antonio, 1891-1937. 2. Communists—Correspondence, reminiscences, etc. I. Title.

GRAMSCI, Antonio, 1891- v. 12 B 1937
Letters from prison. Selected, translated from the Italian, and introduced by Lynne Lowner. New York, Harper and Row [1975 c1973] 292 p. illus. 21 cm. (A Harper Colophon Book) Translated from lettere dal carcere. Bibliography: p. 283-284 [HX288.G7A4213] 335.43'092'4 B ISBN 0-06-090452-6 3.95 (pbk.)
1. Communists—Correspondence, reminiscences, etc. I. Title.
L.C. card no. for original edition: 74-156531 **BIP**

JOLL, James. 335.43'092'4 B
Antonio Gramsci / James Joll. New York : Penguin Books, [1978] p. cm. (Penguin modern masters) Includes index. Bibliography: p. [HX288.G7J65] 78-7417 ISBN 0-14-004934-7 pbk. : 2.95
1. Gramsci, Antonio, 1891-1937. 2. Communists—Italy—Biography. **BIP**

JOLL, James. 335.43'092'4 B
Antonio Gramsci / James Joll ; edited by Frank Kermode. New York : Viking Press, 1979,c1977. 160 p. ; 19 cm. (Modern masters) Includes index. Bibliography: p. [151]-153. [HX288.G7J65 1977] 78-64513 ISBN 0-670-12942-9 : 9.95
1. Gramsci, Antonio, 1891-1937. 2. Communists—Italy—Biography. I. Kermode, John Frank.

Granatelli, Anthony,

GRANATELLI, Anthony, 1923- 796.7'2'0924 B
They call me Mister 500, by Anthony (Andy) Granatelli Chicago, H. Regnery Co. [1969] ix, 341 p. illus., ports. 24 cm. Autobiographical. [GV1032.G7A3] 72-76023 6.95
I. Title. **BIP**

Grand prix racing—Biography.

HEGLAR, Mary Schnall. 796.7'2'0922 B
The grand prix champions. [Newport Beach, Calif., Bond/Parkhurst Publications, 1973] 234 p. illus. 24 cm. [GV1032.A1H43] 72-96300 ISBN 0-87880-014-X 7.95
1. Grand prix racing—Biography. I. Title. **BIP**

Grandison, Otho de, d. Sir 1328.

CLIFFORD, Esther Rowland. 923.542
A knight of great renown; the life and times of Othon de Grandson. [Chicago] University of Chicago Press [1961] 312p. illus. 23cm. Includes bibliographies. [DA229.C5] 60-14361
1. Grandison, Otho de, d. Sir 1328. 2. Thirteenth century. I. Title.

Grandjany, Marcel, 1891-1975.

INGLEFIELD, Ruth K. 787'.5'0924 B
Marcel Grandjany : concert harpist, composer, and teacher / Ruth K. Inglefield. Washington : University Press of America, c1977. vi, 119 p. : ill. ; 22 cm. [ML419.G7I6] 78-301889 ISBN 0-8191-0348-9 pbk. : 7.40
1. Grandjany, Marcel, 1891-1975. 2. Musicians—Biography.

Grange, Harold Edward, 1904-

COLLINS, David R. 796.33'2'0922 B
Football running backs : three ground gainers / by David R. Collins. Champaign, Ill. : Garrard Pub. Co., c1976. 96 p. : ill. (some col.) ; 24 cm. Biographies of three running backs who helped popularize football: Red Orange, Bronko Nagurski, and Gale Sayers. [GV939.A1C64] 75-23346 ISBN 0-8116-6677-8 : 3.58
1. Grange, Harold Edward, 1903- —Juvenile literature. 2. Nagurski, Bronko, 1908- —Juvenile literature. 3. Sayers, Gale, 1943- —Juvenile literature. 4. Football—Biography—Juvenile literature. I. Title. **BIP**

GRANGE, Harold Edward 1904- 927.9633
The Red Grange story, the autobiography of Red Grange, as told to Ira Morton. New York, Putnam [1953] 180 p. illus. 22 cm. [Putnams sports series] [GV939.G7A3] 53-8161
I. Morton, Ira. II. Title.

PETERSON, James Andrew, 1897- 927.9633
Grange of Illinois. [Chicago, Hinckley & Schmitt, 1956 unpaged. illus. 24cm. On cover: 77: Grange of Illinois. [GV939.G7P4] 56-58181
1. Grange, Harold Edward, 1904- I. Title. II. Title: 77: Grange of Illiniois.

PETERSON, James Andrew, 1897- 927.9633
Grange of Illinois. [Chicago, Hinckley & Schmitt, 1956] unpaged. illus. 24cm. On cover: 77: Grange of Illinois. [GV939.G7P4] 56-58181
1. Grange, Harold Edward, 1904- I. Title. II. Title: 77; Grange of Illinois.

Graniteville Company

MITCHELL, Broadus, 1892- 338.40924
William Gregg, factory master of the Old South. New York, Octagon. 1966 [c.1928] xi, 331p. port. 21cm. Bibl. [CT275.G774M5 1966] 66-18028 8.00
1. Graniteville Company 2. Gregg, William, 1800-1867. 3. Gregg, William, 1800-1867. 4. Graniteville Company. I. Title.

Grant, Anne (MacVicar) 1755-1838—Juvenile literature.

BOBBE, Dorothie (De Bear) 828'.7'09 B
The New World journey of Anne MacVicar, by Dorothie Bobbe. New York, Putnam [1971] 127 p. front. 21 cm. Bibliography: p. [126] A girl from Scotland learns much about colonial and Indian ways of life when she and her mother spend eleven years following her father, a British officer, around the American Frontier. [PR4728.G113Z6] 92 70-150585 3.86
1. Grant, Anne (MacVicar) 1755-1838—Juvenile literature. I. Title.

Grant, Bernice Echols, 1898-

ECHOLS, Katie Sue. 630'.924 B
Bernice Echols Grant—4-H pioneer. [Harrisonburg, Va.] 1971. viii, 53 p. illus., ports. 22 cm. [S533.F66E25] 74-635474
1. Grant, Bernice Echols, 1898- 2. 4-H clubs—Georgia. I. Title.

Grant, Cary, 1904-

GOVONI, Albert. 791.43'028'0924 B
Cary Grant; an unauthorized biography. Chicago, H. Regnery Co. [1972, c1971] 233 p. illus. 22 cm. [PN2287.G675G6 1972] 73-163251 5.95
1. Grant, Cary, 1904-

GUTHRIE, Lee. 791.43'028'0924 B
The life and loves of Cary Grant / a biography by Lee Guthrie. New York : Drake Publishers, 1977. 239 p., [8] leaves of plates : ill. ; 24 cm. Includes index. Filmography: p. 227-234. [PN2287.G675G8] 77-6201 ISBN 0-8473-1613-0 : 9.95
1. Grant, Cary, 1904- 2. Moving-picture actors and actresses—United States—Biography. I. Title. **BIP**

VERMILYE, Jerry. 791.43'028'0924
Cary Grant / by Jerry Vermilye ; general editor Ted Sennett. New York : Galahad Books, c1973. 160 p. : ill. ; 22 cm. (The Pictorial treasury of film stars) Includes index. Bibliography: p. 152-153. [PN2287.G675V4 1973b] 74-33232 ISBN 0-88365-291-9 : 5.95
1. Grant, Cary, 1904- **BIP**

Grant, Heber Jeddy, 1856-1945.

HINCKLEY, Bryant S, 1867- 922.8373
Heber J. Grant; highlights in the life of a great leader. [Salt Lake City, Deseret Book Co., '1951] 264 p. illus. 23 cm. [BX8695.G7H5] 52-25579
1. Grant, Heber Jeddy, 1856-1945. I. Title.

Grant, James Richard, 1880-1951.

HALL, Harriet (Grant) 1922- 923.773
Green shoot from Gum Log; a biography of James Richard Grant, college president and American humorist. New York, William-Frederick Press, 1953. 126p. 22cm. [LD4431.O717 1934.H3] 53-5033
1. Grant, James Richard, 1880-1951. I. Title.

Grant, Joan (Marshall)

GRANT, Joan (Marshall) 1907- 928.2
Far memory, autobiography. [1st ed.] New York, Harper [c1956] 272p. 22cm. London ed. (Barker) has title: Time out of mind. [PR6013.R2737Z52 1956a] 56-12226
I. Title.

Grant, Julia Dent, 1826-1902.

FLEMING, Alice (Mulcahey) 1928- 973.8'2'0924 B
General's lady; the life of Julia Grant, by Alice Fleming. Illustrated by Richard Lebenson. [1st ed.] Philadelphia, Lippincott [1971] 155 p. illus. 21 cm. The life of the wife of the Commander of the Union Forces during the Civil War and First Lady during her husband's eight years as President of the United States. [E672.F55] 92 76-141457 4.75
1. Grant, Julia (Dent) 1826-1902—Juvenile literature. I. Lebenson, Richard, illus. II. Title.

GRANT, Julia Dent, 1826-1902. 973.8'2'0924 B
The personal memoirs of Julia Dent Grant (Mrs. Ulysses S. Grant) / edited, with notes and foreword by John Y. Simon ; with introd. by Bruce Catton ; and The First Lady as an author, by Ralph G. Newman. 1st ed. New York : Putnam, [1975] 346 p., [9] leaves of plates : ill. ; 24 cm. Includes bibliographical references and index. [E672.G758 1975] 74-79648 ISBN 0-399-11386-X : 12.50
1. Grant, Julia Dent, 1826-1902. I. Title.

ROSS, Ishbel, 1897- 920.7
The general's wife; the life of Mrs. Ulysses S. Grant. New York, Dodd, Mead, 1959. 372p. illus. 22cm. Includes bibliography. [E672.R77] 59-12212
1. Grant, Julia (Dent) 1826-1902. I. Title.

Grant, Robert Lee,

GRANT, Robert Lee, 1938- 301.45'19'6073024 B
The star spangled hustle [by] Robert Lee Grant, with Carl Gardner. [1st ed.] Philadelphia, Lippincott [1972] 240 p. 22 cm. Autobiography. [E185.97.G73A3] 72-6325 ISBN 0-397-00944-5
I. Gardner, Carl, 1931- II. Title.

Grant, Ulysses Simpson, Pres. U.S., 1822-1885.

ARNOLD, Matthew, 1822- 1888 973.730924
General Grant. With a rejoinder by Mark Twain. Ed. with an introd. by John Y. Simon. Carbondale, Ill., Southern Ill. Univ. Pr. [c.1966] 58p. 21cm. Bibl. [E672.A75] 65-19775 4.25
1. Grant, Ulysses Simpson, Pres. U.S., 1822-1885. I. Clemens, Samuel Langhorne, 1835-1910. II. Simon, John Y., ed. III. Title.

ARNOLD, Matthew, 1822- 1888. 973.730924
General Grant. With a rejoinder by Mark Twain. Edited with an introd. by John Y. Simon. Carbondale, Southern Illinois University Press [1966] 58 p. 21 cm. Bibliographical footnotes. [E672.A75] 65-19775
1. Grant, Ulysses Simpson, Pres. U.S., 1822-1885. I. Clemens, Samuel Langhorne, 1835-1910. II. Simon, John Y., ed. III. Title.

BROOKS, William Elizabeth, 1875- 973.73'0924
Grant of Appomattox; a study of the man, by William E. Brooks. Westport, Conn., Greenwood Press [1971, c1942] 347 p. 23 cm. Bibliography: p. 315-320. [E672.B872 1971] 73-138577 ISBN 0-8371-5776-5
1. Grant, Ulysses Simpson, Pres. U.S., 1822-1885. I. Title.

CATTON, Bruce, 1899- 923.173
U.S. Grant and the American military tradition. [1st ed.] Boston, Little, Brown [1954] x, 201 p. 22 cm. (The Library of American biography) "A note on the sources": p. [191]-193. [E672.C3 1954] 54-6860
1. Grant, Ulysses Simpson, Pres. U.S., 1822-1885. I. Title. II. Series.

CONGER, Arthur Latham, 1872-1951. 973.73'0924
The rise of U. S. Grant. Freeport, N.Y., Books for Libraries Press [1970] xi, 390 p. illus., maps, ports. 23 cm. Reprint of the 1931 ed. Bibliography: p. 379-382. [E672.C734 1970] 74-137371
1. Grant, Ulysses Simpson, Pres. U.S., 1822-1885. I. Title. **BIP**

COOLIDGE, Louis Arthur, 1861-1925. 973.8'2'0924 B
Ulysses S. Grant. Boston, Houghton Mifflin. [New York, AMS Press, 1972] xix, 596 p. illus. 19 cm. (American statesmen, v. 32) Reprint of the 1917 ed. [E672.C74 1972] 75-128953 ISBN 0-404-50894-4
1. Grant, Ulysses Simpson, Pres. U.S., 1822-1885. I. Title. II. Series.

DODGE, Grenville Mellen, Maj.-Gen. 1831-1916 923.73
Personal recollections of President Abraham Lincoln, General Ulysses S. Grant, and General William T. Sherman. Denver. Sage [dist. Swallow, 1966] 237p. illus., ports. 23cm. Reprinted from a private ed. (Western Sage paperbk.) [E467.D64] 65-14621 1.85 pap.,
1. Lincoln. Abraham. Pres. U.S., 1809-1865. 2. Grant, Ulysses Simpson, Pres. U.S., 1822-1885. 3. Sherman, William Tecumseh, 1820-1891. I. Title.

DODGE, Grenville Mellen, 1931-1916 923.173
Personal recollections of President Abrahm Lincoln, General Ulysses S. Grant, and General William T. Sherman. Denver, Sage [dist. Swallow, 1965] 237p. illus., ports. 23cm. Reprinted from a private ed. with the imprint: Council Bluffs, Iowa, The Monarch Printing Company, 1914. [E467.D64] 65-14621 6.00
1. Lincoln, Abraham, Pres. U.S., 1809-1865. 2. Grant, Ulysses Simpson, Pres. U.S., 1822-1885. 3. Sherman, William Tecumseh, 1820-1891. I. Title.

FROST, Lawrence A. 973.8'2'0924 B
U.S. Grant Album; a pictorial biography of Ulysses S. Grant from leather clerk to the White House, by Lawrence A. Frost. [1st ed.] Seattle, Superior Pub. Co. [1966] 192 p. illus., facsims., ports. 28 cm. Bibliography: p. 188-189. [E672.F76] 66-25419
1. Grant, Ulysses Simpson, Pres. U.S., 1822-1885. I. Title.

GOLDHURST, Richard. 973.8'2'0924 B
Many are the hearts : the agony and the triumph of Ulysses S. Grant / Richard Goldhurst. New York : Reader's Digest Press : distributed by Crowell, 1975. xxii, 297 p., [16] leaves of plates : ill. ; 24 cm. Includes index. Bibliography: p. 279-282. [E672.G64] 75-8698 ISBN 0-88349-050-1 : 10.00
1. Grant, Ulysses Simpson, Pres. U.S., 1822-1885. I. Title.

GRANT, Ulysses S., 1881-1968. 973.8'2'0924
Ulysses S. Grant; warrior and statesman. New York, Morrow, 1969. 480 p. illus., maps, ports. 25 cm. Bibliography: p. [459]-466. [E672.G7654 1969] 68-57446 12.50
1. Grant, Ulysses Simpson, Pres. U.S., 1822-1885. I. Title.

GRANT, Ulysses Simpson, Pres. U.S., 1822-1885. 973.8'2'0924 B
General Grant's letters to a friend, 1861-1880. With introd. and notes by James Grant Wilson. New York, Crowell, 1897.

[New York, AMS Press, 1973] x, 132 p. ports. 19 cm. Letters addressed to Hon. E. B. Washburne. [E672.G757 1973] 73-168179 ISBN 0-404-04598-7 6.00
1. Grant, Ulysses Simpson, Pres. U.S., 1822-1885. 2. Washburne, Elihu Benjamin, 1816-1887. I. Washburne, Elihu Benjamin, 1816-1887. II. Title. **BIP**

HESSELTINE, William Best, 1902- 923.173
Ulysses S. Grant, politician. New York, F. Ungar Pub. Co. [1957, c1935] xiii, 480p. plates, ports., facsim. 35cm. (American classics) Bibliography: p. 453-460. [E672.H46 1957] 57-12323
1. Grant, Ulysses Simpson, Pres. U. S., 1822-1885. 2. U. S.—Pol. & govt.—1869-1877. I. Title. **BIP**

HESSELTINE, William Best, 1902-1963. 923.173
Ulysses S. Grant, politician. New York, F. Ungar Pub. Co. [1957, c1935] xiii, 480 p. plates, ports., facsim. 25 cm. (American classics) Bibliography: p. 453-460. [E672.H46 1957] 57-12323
1. Grant, Ulysses Simpson, Pres. U.S., 1822-1885. 2. United States—Politics and government—1869-1877.

LEWIS, Lloyd, 1891-1949. 923.173
Captain Sam Grant. [1st ed.] Boston, Little, Brown, 1950. viii, 512 p. port. 23 cm. Bibliography: p. [473]-484. [E672.L48 1950] 50-7939
1. Grant, Ulysses Simpson, Pres. U.S., 1822-1885. I. Title. **BIP**

MACARTNEY, Clarence Edward Noble, 1879- 973.741
Grant and his generals. [1st ed.] New York, McBride Co. 1953] 352p. illus. 22cm. Includes bibliography. [E467.M114] 53-9749
1. Grant, Ulysses Simpson, Pres. U. S., 1822-1885. 2. Generals—U. S. 3. U.S.—Hist.—Civil War—Biog. I. Title.

MACARTNEY, Clarence Edward Noble, 1879-1957. 973.7'41
Grant and his generals. Freeport, N.Y., Books for Libraries Press [1971, c1953] xiv, 352 p. illus., ports. 23 cm. (Essay index reprint series) Includes bibliographical references. [E467.M114 1971] 75-142660 ISBN 0-8369-2171-2
1. Grant, Ulysses Simpson, Pres. U.S., 1822-1885. 2. Generals—United States. 3. United States—History—Civil War, 1861-1865—Biography. I. Title. **BIP**

MEYER, Howard N. 973.820924
Let us have peace; the story of Ulysses S. Grant [by] Howard N. Meyer. New York, Collier Books [1966] xi, 244 p. illus., map, ports. 21 cm. (America in the making) [E672.M613] 64-24353
1. Grant, Ulysses Simpson, Pres. U.S., 1822-1885. I. Title.

OKIE, Howard S. 973.8'2'0924
General U. S. Grant: a defense [by] Howard S. Okie. [1st ed.] New York, Vantage Press [1970] 72 p. maps. 21 cm. [E672.O35] 79-15951 2.95
1. Grant, Ulysses Simpson, Pres. U.S., 1822-1885. I. Title.

PARK, Clyde William, 1880- v. 12
That Grant boy. [Cincinnati, C.J. Krehbiel co., 1957] 4 p. l., 52 p. illus., ports. 16 cm. Presentation copy of the C.J. Krehbiel company, Christmas, 1957. 63-60721
1. Grant, Ulysses Simpson, Pres. U.S., 1822-1885. I. Krehbiel (C.J.) Company, Cincinnati. II. Title.

PITKIN, Thomas M., ed. 973.730924
Grant, the soldier. [Washington. D.C. Acropolis Bks.] [dist Colortone Pr., 1966, c.1965] ix, 88p. illus., facsims., maps, ports. 23cm. Bibl. [E672.P6] 65-28302 4.50
1. Grant, Ulysses Simpson, Pres. U. S., 1822-1885. I. Title. **BIP**

STEVENSON, Augusta. 973.8'2'0924 B
U. S. Grant, young horseman. Illustrated by James Ponter. Indianapolis, Bobbs-Merrill [1962] 200 p. illus. 20 cm. (Childhood of famous Americans) The boyhood of the leader of the Union forces during the Civil War and eighteenth President of the United States. [PZ7.S8467U2] 92 AC 68
1. Grant, Ulysses Simpson, Pres. U.S., 1822-1885. I. Ponter, James, illus. II. Title.

WOODWARD, William E 1874-1950. 973.8'2'0924 (B)
Meet General Grant. [Black & gold ed.] New York, Liveright [c1925] 524 p. port. 22 cm. A reissue with the exception of some illus. of the 1946 ed., with a new foreword by James A. Rawley. Bibliography:p. 305-506. [E672.W873 1965] 65-21894
1. Grant, Ulysses Simpson, Pres. U.S., 1822-1885. I. Title.

Grant, Ulysses Simpson, Pres. U.S., 1822-1885 — Juvenile literature.

GRANT, Matthew G. 973.8'2'0924 B
Ulysses S. Grant; general and President [by] Matthew G. Grant. Illustrated by John Nelson. [Mankato, Minn., Creative Education; distributed by Childrens Press, Chicago, 1974] 30 p. illus. (part col.) 25 cm. (His Gallery of great Americans series. War heroes of America) A brief biography stressing the personal and political turmoil in the career of the Civil War leader who became the eighteenth President. [E672.G7653] 92 73-18213 ISBN 0-87191-298-8 3.95 (lib. bdg.)
1. Grant, Ulysses Simpson, Pres. U.S., 1822-1885—Juvenile literature. I. Nelson, John, illus. II. Title.

GRANT, Ulysses Simpson, Pres. U.S., 1822-1885. 923.173
Mr. Lincoln's general; U. S. Grant, an illustrated autobiography. Edited and arr. by Roy Meredith. [1st ed.] New York, Dutton, 1959. 252 p illus., ports., maps. 29 cm. "Consists largely of literary material drawn from General Grant's [Personal memoirs]" [E672.G7618] 59-9795
I. Meredith, Roy, 1908- ed. II. Title.

OLGIN, Joseph. 92 (J)
Ulysses S. Grant: general and President. Illustrated by William Moyers. Boston, Houghton Mifflin [1967] 191 p. col. illus. 23 cm. (Piper books) [E672.O4] 67-10460
1. Grant, Ulysses Simpson, Pres. U.S., 1822-1885—Juvenile literature. I. Moyers, William, illus. II. Title.

REEDER, Russell Potter. 92
U.S. Grant, horseman and fighter. Illustrated by Ken Wagner Champaign, Ill., Garrard Pub. Co. [c1964] 80 p. col. illus. 23 cm. (A Discovery book) [E672.R4] 64-10069
1. Grant, Ulysses Simpson, Pres. U.S., 1822-1885 — Juvenile literature. I. Title.

REEDER, Russell Potter 920
U. S. Grant, horseman and fighter. Illus. by Ken Wagner. Champaign, Ill., Garrard [c.1964] 80p. col. illus. 23cm. (Discovery bk.) 64-10069 2.50
1. Grant, Ulysses Simpson, Pres. U. S., 1822-1885 Juvenile literature. I. Title.

THOMAS, Henry, 1886- j92
Ulysses S. Grant. New York, Putnam [1961] 192 p. 21 cm. (Lives to remember) Includes bibliography. [E672.T45] 61-8246
1. Grant, Ulysses Simpson, Pres. U.S., 1822-1885 — Juvenile literature. I. Title.

YOUNG, Bob, 1916-1969. 973.8'2'0924 B
Reluctant warrior: Ulysses S. Grant, by Bob & Jan Young. New York, J. Messner [1971] 191 p. 22 cm. Bibliography: p. 185. A biography of the Union general who served two terms as the eighteenth President of the United States. [E672.Y68] 92 77-160305 ISBN 0-671-32439-X 3.95
1. Grant, Ulysses Simpson, Pres. U.S., 1822-1885—Juvenile literature. I. Young, Jan, 1919- joint author. II. Title.

Grant-Whyte, Harry.

GRANT-WHYTE, Harry. 617'.96'0924 B
Between life and death / Harry Grant-Whyte. Pietermaritzburg : Shuter and Shooter, 1976. 135 p., [1] col. plate : ill. ; 22 cm. [RD80.62.G7A32] 77-372095 ISBN 0-86985-331-7 : R6.45
1. Grant-Whyte, Harry. 2. Anesthetists—South Africa—Biography. I. Title.

Grant, Wilson W., 1941-

GRANT, Wilson W., 1941- 248'.48'6
The search for me / Wilson Wayne Grant. Nashville : Broadman Press, c1977. 152 p. ; 20 cm. Includes bibliographical references. [BX6495.G672A37] 77-73453 ISBN 0-8054-5252-4 pbk. : 3.25
1. Grant, Wilson W., 1941- 2. Baptists—United States—Biography. 3. Identification (Religion) I. Title. **BIP**

Granville-Barker, Harley Granville, 1877-1946.

PURDOM, Charles Benjamin, 1883- 790.2'0924
Harley Granville Barker, man of the theatre, dramatist, and scholar. Cambridge, Harvard University Press, 1956. xiv, 822p. illus., ports. 22cm. 'List of writings, compiled by Frederick May and Margery M. Morgan : p. 293-309. [PN2598.G655P] A56
1. Granville-Barker, Harley Granville, 1877-1946. 2. Theater—England—Hist. I. Title. **BIP**

PURDOM, Charles Benjamin, 1883- 792'.0924 B
Harley Granville Barker, man of the theatre, dramatist, and scholar, by C. B. Purdom. Westport, Conn., Greenwood Press [1971] xiv, 322 p. illus. 23 cm. Reprint of the 1956 ed. "List of writings, compiled by Frederick May and Margery M. Morgan": p. 293-309. [PN2598.G655P8 1971] 72-156205 ISBN 0-8371-6155-X
1. Granville-Barker, Harley Granville, 1877-1946. 2. Theater—England—History. I. Title. **BIP**

Graphology—Biography.

LANDRUM, Paul W. 137'.7'025
Who's who in graphology worldwide / by Paul W. Landrum and Betty Tucker. [1st ed.]. Hixson, Tenn. : Unique Books, 1975. 1 v. : forms ; 23 cm. Loose-leaf for updating. Includes index. [BF891.L32] 74-24600 ISBN 0-915286-01-7 : 12.95
1. Graphology—Biography. I. Tucker, Betty, joint author. II. Title.

Grattan, Henry, 1746-1820.

GWYNN, Stephen Lucius, 1864-1950. 941.5'7'0924 B
Henry Grattan and his times. Westport, Conn., Greenwood Press [1971] viii, 402 p. illus., facsims., ports. 23 cm. Reprint of the 1939 ed. [DA948.3.G7G87 1971] 76-114534 ISBN 0-8371-4828-6
1. Grattan, Henry, 1746-1820. 2. Ireland—Politics and government—1760-1820. 3. Irish question. 4. Catholic emancipation. I. Title.

GWYNN, Stephen Lucius, 1864-1950. 941.5'7'0924 B
Henry Grattan and his times. Freeport, N.Y., Books for Libraries Press [1971] viii, 402 p. illus. 23 cm. Reprint of the 1939 ed. [DA948.3.G7G87 1971b] 78-175699 ISBN 0-8369-6614-7
1. Grattan, Henry, 1746-1820. 2. Ireland—Politics and government—1760-1820. 3. Irish question. 4. Catholic emancipation. I. Title. **BIP**

LECKY, William Edward Hartpole, 1838-1903. 941.57
Leaders of public opinion in Ireland. New York, Da Capo Press, 1973 [c1903] 2 v. 21 cm. (Europe 1815-1945) Reprint of the 1912 ed. Contents.Contents.—v. 1. Henry Flood. Henry Grattan.—v. 2. Daniel O'Connell. [DA948.A5L4 1973] 76-159800 ISBN 0-306-70556-7 29.50
1. Flood, Henry, 1732-1791. 2. Grattan, Henry, 1746-1820. 3. O'Connell, Daniel, 1775-1847. I. Title. II. Series. **BIP**

Grattidge, Harry,

GRATTIDGE, Harry, 1890- 923.842
Captain of the Queens; the autobiography of Captain Harry Grattidge, former Commodore of the Cunard Line, as told to Richard Collier. [1st ed.] New York, Dutton, 1956. 313 p. illus. 22 cm. [VK140.G7A3] 56-6309
I. Collier, Richard, 1924- II. Title.

Gratz, Rebecca, 1781-1869.

GRATZ, Rebecca, 1781-1869. 296'.092'4 B
Letters of Rebecca Gratz / David Philipson, editor. New York : Arno Press, 1975, c1929. xxiv, 454 p. : port. ; 23 cm. (The Modern Jewish experience) Reprint of the ed. published by the Jewish Publication Society of America, Philadelphia. Includes index. [F158.9.J5G7 1975] 74-27987 ISBN 0-405-06714-3 : 29.00
1. Gratz, Rebecca, 1781-1869. I. Title. II. Series. **BIP**

Graves, Robert, 1895-

KIRKHAM, Michael. 821'.9'12
The poetry of Robert Graves. New York, Oxford University Press, 1969. viii, 284 p. 23 cm. Bibliography: p. 275-278. [PR6013.R35Z73] 70-3328 6.75
1. Graves, Robert, 1895- **BIP**

Gray, Asa, 1810-1888.

GRAY, Asa, 1810-1888. 581'.092'4 B
Letters of Asa Gray. Edited by Jane Loring Gray. New York, B. Franklin [1973] 2 v. (838 p.) illus. 22 cm. (Burt Franklin research and source works series. Science classics series 13) Reprint of the 1893 ed. published by Houghton Mifflin, Boston. [QK31.G8A4 1973] 73-170952 ISBN 0-8337-1430-9 25.00 (2 vols.)
1. Gray, Asa, 1810-1888. **BIP**

Gray, Barry, 1916-

GRAY, Barry, 1916- 070.4'3'0924 B
My night people / Barry Gray. New York : Simon and Schuster, [1975] 191 p. ; 22 cm. Autobiographical. [PN1991.4.G69A35] 75-14039 ISBN 0-671-22090-X : 7.95
1. Gray, Barry, 1916- I. Title.

Gray, Blanche,

GRAY, Blanche, 1872- 920.7
Ruffled petticoat days. [1st ed.] Culver City, Calif., Murray & Gee [1953] 147p. illus. 20cm. Autobiographical. [CT275.G688A3] 54-305
I. Title.

Gray, Charles Glass, b. 1820.

GRAY, Charles Glass, b.1820. 978'.02
Off at sunrise : the overland journal of Charles Glass Gray / edited with an introduction by Thomas D. Clark. San Marino, Calif. : Huntington Library, c1976. xxx, 182 p. : ill. ; 24 cm. Original ms. has title: Journal of an overland passage, from Independence Mo to San Francisco, Cala in 1849. Includes index. Bibliography: p. 171-182. [F593.G73 1976] 76-9350 ISBN 0-87328-069-5 : 12.00
1. Gray, Charles Glass, b. 1820. 2. Overland journeys to the Pacific. 3. Pioneers—The West—Biography. 4. The West—Biography. I. Title. **BIP**

Gray, David Benjamin.

WINCHESTER, Barry. 940.4'72'43
Beyond the tumult. With a foreword by Douglas Bader and an introd. by L. G. Nixon. New York, Scribner [1972, c1971] xv, 207 p. illus. 23 cm. [D627.G3W53 1972] 76-38528 ISBN 0-684-12848-9 6.95
1. Blain, Cecil. 2. Gray, David Benjamin. 3. Kennard, Casper. 4. European War, 1914-1918—Prisoners and prisons, German. 5. Escapes. I. Title.

Gray, Edward Whitaker, 1748-1806.

GUNTHER, Albert Edward. 574'.08 S
Edward Whitaker Gray (1748-1806), Keeper of Natural Curiosities at the British Museum / by Albert E. Gunther. London : British Museum (Natural History), 1976. p. 191-210, [5] leaves of plates : ill. ; 25 cm. (Bulletin of the British Museum (Natural History) : Historical series ; v. 5, no. 2. ISSN 0068-2306s) Bibliography: p. 208-210..[QH15.B73 vol. 5, no. 2] X[QH31.G72]I069'.5'0924 B 77-363894 £3.00
1. Gray, Edward Whitaker, 1748-1806. 2. Naturalists—Great Britain—Biography. I. Series: British Museum (Natural History). Bulletin : Historical series ; v. 5, no. 2.

Gray, George Morris, 1856-1958.

SPEER, Robert Leland. v. 12
The incredible Dr. George Morris Gray. [n.p.] 1964. 13 [i.e., 17] l. 29 cm. "History of Kansas, Dr. George L. Anderson." Xeroxed copy of typescript. Bibliography: 3 l. at end. 66-58331
1. Gray, George Morris, 1856-1958. 2. Kansas. University. School of Medicine — Hist. I. Title.

Gray, Hector.

GRAY, Hector. 791'.092'4 B
Memories of a variety artist / [by] Hector Gray. Melbourne : Hawthorn Press, 1975. 106 p. : ill. ; 22 cm. [PN2598.G663A36] 75-324497 ISBN 0-7256-0133-7
1. Gray, Hector. 2. Actors—Correspondence, reminiscences, etc. 3. Music-halls (Variety-theaters, cabarets, etc.) I. Title.

Gray, Martin.

DUNCAN, David Douglas. 944'.004'924 B
The fragile miracle of Martin Gray : photographs and text / by David Douglas Duncan. New York : Abbeville Press, c1979. p. cm. [DS135.F9D86] 79-88970 ISBN 0-89659-073-9 : 6.95
1. Gray, Martin. 2. Jews in France—Biography. 3. Holocaust, Jewish (1939-1945)—Poland—Personal narratives. 4. France—Biography. I. Title.

Gray, Mary Montgomery (Dunklin) 1873-

BLACKWELL, Harriet (Gray) 920.7
A candle for all time. Richmond, Dietz Press, 1959. 339p. 24cm. [CT275.G69B55] 60-975
1. Gray, Mary Montgomery (Dunklin) 1873- I. Title.

Gray, Pete—Juvenile literature.

NICHOLSON, William G. 796.357'092'4 B
Pete Gray : one-armed major leaguer / by William G. Nicholson ; illustrated by Ray Abel. Englewood Cliffs, N.J. : Prentice-Hall, c1976. [32] p. : col. ill. ; 24 cm. A biography of the baseball player who played for several years in the minor leagues and one year in the majors in spite of the fact that he had only one arm. [GV865.G66N5] 92 75-42034 ISBN 0-13-363481-7 : lib. bdg. : 5.95
1. Gray, Pete—Juvenile literature. 2. Baseball—Juvenile literature. I. Abel, Raymond. II. Title.

Gray, Thomas, 1716-1771.

GRAY, Thomas, 1716-1771. 821'.6
Correspondence of Thomas Gray, edited by Paget Toynbee and Leonard Whibley. With corrections and additions by H. W. Starr. Oxford, Clarendon Press [1971] 3 v. illus., fold. maps. 23 cm. Reprint of 1935 ed. Contents.—v. 1. 1734-1755.—v. 2. 1756-1765.—v. 3. 1766-1771. [PR3503.A3 1971] 78-24999
I. Toynbee, Paget Jackson, 1855-1932, ed. II. Whibley, Leonard, 1862 or 3-1941, ed. III. Starr, Herbert Willmarth, 1916- ed. IV. Title. BIP

GRAY, Thomas, 1716-1771. 928.2
Selected letters; edited with an introd, by Joseph Wood Krutch. New York, Farrar, Straus and Young [1952] xxxiv, 170 p. 22 cm. (Great letters series) [PR3503.A3 1952] 52-6980
I. Title.

KETTON-CREMER, Robert Wyndham, 1906- 928.2
Thomas Gray; a biography. Cambridge [Eng.] University Press, 1955. 309 p. illus. 23 cm. Includes bibliography. [PR3503.K4 1955] 55-14583
1. Gray, Thomas, 1716-1771.

ROBERTS, Sydney Castle, Sir, 1887-1966. 821'.6 B
Thomas Gray of Pembroke. [Folcroft, Pa.] Folcroft Library Editions, 1973. 31 p. 24 cm. Reprint of the 1952 ed. published by Jackson, Son, Glasgow, which was issued as the 13th W. P. Ker memorial lecture, and as no. 93 of the Glasgow University publications. [PR3503.R6 1973] 73-11384 4.50
1. Gray, Thomas, 1716-1771. I. Series: Glasgow. University. W. P. Ker memorial lecture, 13. II. Series: Glasgow. University. Glasgow University publications, 93. BIP

Gray, Thomas, 1716-1771—Correspondence.

GRAY, Thomas, 1716-1771. 821'.6
Gray, poetry & prose / with essays by Johnson, Goldsmith, and others ; with an introd. and notes by J. Crofts. New York : AMS Press, [1980] i.e. 1979. p. cm. Reprint of the 1926 ed. published by the Clarendon Press, Oxford. [PR3501.C7 1980] 76-29472 ISBN 0-404-15304-6 : 18.50
1. Gray, Thomas, 1716-1771—Correspondence. 2. Poets, English—18th century—Correspondence. I. Crofts, John Ernest Victor, 1887- II. Title.

Gray, Wil Lou, 1883-

MONTGOMERY, Mabel 923.773
South Carolina's Wil Lou Gray: pioneer in adult education, a crusader, modern model [Columbia, S.C., Vogue Pr., 1223 Franklin St. [c.]1963. xvi, 103p. illus., ports. 24cm. 63-23433 3.00 bds.,
1. Gray, Wil Lou, 1883- 2. Illiteracy—South Carolina. I. Title.

Grayson, John.

GRAYSON, John. 910'.45 B
Life at sea : a nineteenth century voyage to New Zealand : the diary of John Grayson / edited with an introduction by John Fines. Old Woking : Unwin Brothers Ltd, 1976. xviii, 50 p. : ill., port. ; 21 cm. (Looking back series ; v. 3) [G540.G72] 77-367397 ISBN 0-9502121-9-9 : £1.55
1. Grayson, John. 2. Seafaring life. I. Title. II. Series.

Graziano, Rocky,

GRAZIANO, Rocky, 1921- 927.9681
Somebody up there likes me; the story of my life until today. Written with Rowland Barber. New York, Simon and Schuster, 1955. 375p. illus. 22cm. [GV1132.G62A3] 54-12365
I. Barber, Rowland. II. Title.

Greacen, Robert.

GREACEN, Robert. 821 B
Even without Irene; an autobiography. With an introd. by Clifford Dyment. [Dublin] Dolmen Press; [distributed in the U.S.A. by Dufour Editions, Chester Springs, Pa., 1969] 116 p. 23 cm. [PR6013.R4Z5] 72-5852 6.00
I. Title.

Great Awakening.

WHITEFIELD, George 922.542
Journals. [London] Banner of Truth Trust, 1960[ ] Stamped on t. p.: Distributed by Bible Truth Depot, Swengel, Pa. 594p. illus., maps (1 fold.) facsims. 23cm. 'A new edition containing fuller material than any hitherto published.' Stamped on t.p.: Distributed by Bible Truth Depot, Swengel, Pa. 60-2891 5.00
1. Great Awakening. I. Title.

Great Britain. Army—Biography.

FITCHELL, William Henry, 1845-1928. 940.2'7'0922 B
Wellington's men : some soldier autobiographies : Kincaid's Adventures in the Rifle Brigade; Rifleman Harris; Anton's Military life; Mercer's Waterloo / edited by W. H. Fitchett. Wakefield : EP Publishing, 1976. vi, 419 p. ; 20 cm. Photoreprint of the 1900 ed. published by Smith, Elder, London. Includes index. Contents.—The soldier in literature.—From Torres Vedras to Waterloo.—One of Cranfield's veterans.—A Royal Highlander.—With the guns at Waterloo. [DC232.F54 1976] 77-366810 ISBN 0-7158-1151-7 : £5.50
1. Great Britain. Army—Biography. 2. Peninsular War, 1807-1814—Personal narratives, English. 3. Waterloo, Battle of, 1815—Personal narratives, English. 4. Soldiers—Great Britain—Biography. I. Title.

Great Britain—Bio-bibliography.

WRIGHT, Thomas, 1810-1877. 829
Biographia Britannica literaria; or, Biography of literary characters of Great Britain and Ireland, arranged in chronological order. London, J. W. Parker, 1842-46. Detroit, Gale Research Co., 1968. 2 v. 22 cm. "Published under the superintendence of the Council of the Royal Society of Literature." Contents.Contents.—v. 1. Anglo-Saxon period.—v. 2. Anglo-Norman period. Includes bibliographies. [Z2012.W952] 68-22061
1. Great Britain—Bio-bibliography. 2. Anglo-Saxon literature—Bio-bibliography. 3. Anglo-Norman literature—Bio-bibliography. I. Royal Society of Literature of the United Kingdom, London. II. Title. III. Title: Biography of literary characters of Great Britain and Ireland.

Great Britain—Biography.

ABBOTT, Wilbur Cortez, 1869-1947. 920.042
Adventures in reputation; with an essay on some new history and historians. Port Washington, N.Y., Kennikat Press [1969, c1935] 264 p. illus., ports. 22 cm. (Essay and general literature index reprint series) [DA28.4.A28 1969] 69-16486
1. Gt. Brit.—Biography. 2. Historiography. I. Title.

ANTIQUITIES 914.2'03 S
biographical and miscellaneous. London, Printed by and for J. Nichols, 1790. New York, Kraus Reprint Co., 1968. 1 v. (various pagings) illus. 27 cm. (Bibliotheca topographica Britannica v. 6) [DA620.B543 vol. 6] [DA28] 914.2'03 73-157003
1. Great Britain—Biography. 2. Great Britain—History—Addresses, essays, lectures. I. Nichols, John, 1745-1826, ed. II. Title. III. Series.

BAYNE, Peter, 1830-1896. 942.06'092'2 B
The chief actors in the Puritan revolution. 2d ed. Freeport, N.Y., Books for Libraries Press [1973] p. (Essay index reprint series) Reprint of the 1879 ed. published by J. Clarke, London. Contents.Contents.—Three centuries ago.—The transition period: James the First.—The Anglo-Catholic reaction: Archbishop Laud.—Henrietta Maria.—Charles the First.—The covenanters, Charles II., and Argyle.—Montrose.—Milton.—Sir Henry Vane.—Oliver Cromwell.—Clarendon. [DA407.A1B3 1973] 73-4573 ISBN 0-518-10073-1
1. Great Britain—Biography. 2. Great Britain—History—Stuarts, 1603-1714. I. Title.

BIRKENHEAD, Frederick Edwin Smith, 1st earl of, 1872-1930. 942.083'0922
Contemporary personalities. With frontispiece and photos. and 30 half-tone plates from cartoons by Matt. Freeport, N.Y., Books for Libraries Press [1969] x, 325 p. illus., ports. 22 cm. (Essay index reprint series) Reprint of the 1924 ed. [DA566.9.A1B5 1969] 69-17562
1. Gt. Brit.—Biography. I. Title. BIP

BLYTH, Henry. 914.2'03 B
The rakes. New York, Dial Press, 1971 [c1970] 257 p. ports. 24 cm. First published in 1970 under title: The high tide of pleasure. Contents.Contents.—The restoration rake: John Wilmot, 2d Earl of Rochester.—The elegant rake: Beau Nash of Bath.—The political rake: John Montague, 4th Earl of Sandwich.—The upstart rake: Colonel Dennis O'Kelly.—The eccentric rake: Richard Barry, 7th Earl of Barrymore.—The millionaire rake: Francis Charles Seymour-Conway, 3d Marquess of Hertford.—The potential rake: Albert Edward, Prince of Wales.—Bibliography (p. 245-248) [DA28.9.B58 1971] 74-103431 7.95
1. Gt. Brit.—Biography. I. Title.

BUCHAN, John, 1875-1940. 920'.042
Some eighteenth century byways, and other essays. [Folcroft, Pa.] Folcroft Library Editions, 1972. 345 p. 23 cm. Reprint of the 1908 ed. [DA483.A1B8 1972] 72-13299 20.00
1. Great Britain—Biography. 2. Great Britain—History—18th century—Addresses, essays, lectures. I. Title.

BUCHAN, John, 1875-1940. 920'.041
Some eighteenth century byways, and other essays. [Folcroft, Pa.] Folcroft Library Editions, 1972. 345 p. 23 cm. Reprint of the 1908 ed. [DA483.A1B8 1972] 72-13299 ISBN 0-8414-1178-6 (lib. bdg.)
1. Great Britain—Biography. 2. Great Britain—History—18th century—Addresses, essays, lectures. I. Title.

THE Compact edition of the Dictionary of national biography : 920'.041 complete text reproduced micrographically. London : Oxford University Press, 1975. 2 v. (3149 p.) ; 31 cm. "Includes the complete and unaltered text of the 22 volumes of the main D.N.B. and of the six volumes which make up the twentieth-century D.N.B." In slip case. [DA28.C64] 76-351877 ISBN 0-19-865102-3
1. Great Britain—Biography. I. Title: Dictionary of national biography.

COSTIGAN, Giovanni. 942.0922
Makers of modern England; the force of individual genius in history. New York, Macmillan [1966, c1967] xii, 334 p. ports. 21 cm. Contents.Contents.—Jeremy Bentham (1748-1832).—John Stuart Mill (1806-73).—John Henry Newman (1801-90).—Benjamin Disraeli (1804-81).—William Ewart Gladstone (1801-98).—Beatrice & Sidney Webb (1858-1943 and 1859-1947).—David Lloyd George (1863-1945).—Sir Winston Churchill (1874-1965) Bibliography: p. 315-319. [DA531.1.C6] 66-26144
1. Great Britain—Biography. I. Title.

COURTNEY, William Prideaux, 1845-1913. 920'.042
Eight friends of the great. [Folcroft, Pa.] Folcroft Library Editions, 1974. xiv, 192 p. 23 cm. Reprint of the 1910 ed. published by Constable, London. Contents.Contents.—Dr. Thomas Rundle, friend of Pope and Swift.—Philip Metcalfe, M.P., friend of Johnson and Reynolds.—The Rev. John Warner, D.D., friend of George Selwyn.—"Jack" Taylor of the "Sun," friend of Sheridan.—Scrope Davies, friend of Lord Byron.—Lord Webb Seymour, friend of Sydney Smith and John Playfair.—Lydia White, friend of Tom Moore and Sir Walter Scott.—Lord John Townshend, M.P., friend of Charles Fox. [CT775.C68 1974] 74-1376 25.00
1. Great Britain—Biography. I. Title.
Contents omitted. BIP

CUST, Edward, Sir, bart., 1794-1878. 942.06'0922 B
Lives of the warriors of the civil wars of France and England. Warriors of the seventeenth century. Freeport, N.Y., Books for Libraries Press [1972] 2 v. (xiv, 650 p.) map. 23 cm. (Essay index reprint series) Reprint of the 1867 ed. [D244.6.C94 1972] 76-38737 ISBN 0-8369-2642-0
1. Great Britain—Biography. 2. France—

Biography. 3. Great Britain—History, Military—Stuarts, 1603-1714. 4. France—History, Military—1610-1643. 5. France—History, Military—1643-1715. I. Title. **BIP**

DE SELINCOURT, Aubrey, 1894-1962. 920'.042
Six great Englishmen: Drake, Dr. Johnson, Nelson, Marlborough, Keats, Churchill. [Folcroft, Pa.] Folcroft Library Editions, 1973. p. Reprint of the 1953 ed. published by H. Hamilton, London. [DA28.D35 1973] 73-12820 ISBN 0-8414-3658-4 (lib. bdg.)
1. Great Britain—Biography I. Title.

DOBREE, Bonamy, 1891- ed. 920.042
From Anne to Victoria; essays by various hands. Freeport, N.Y., Books for Libraries Press [1967] x, 630 p. 22 cm. (Essay index reprint series) [CT781.D6 1967] 67-30184
1. Great Britain—Biography. I. Title.

DOBREE, Bonamy, 1891- ed. 920'.042
From Anne to Victoria; essays by various hands. [Folcroft, Pa.] Folcroft Library Editions, 1973. x, 630 p. 22 cm. Reprint of the 1971 ed. published by Folcroft Library Editions, Folcroft, Pa. [CT781.D6 1973] 73-12828 15.00
1. Great Britain Biography. I. Title. **BIP**

ERSKINE, Stuart Ruaraidh Joseph, Hon., 1869- 920.042
King Edward VII, & some other figures [by] Ruavaidh Erskine of Marr. Freeport, N.Y., Books for Libraries Press [1966] xv, 194 p. 22 cm. (Essay index reprint series) Reprint of the 1936 ed. Contents.Contents.—King Edward VII.—Gladstone.—John Redmond.—Henry Asquith.—Charles Stewart Parnell.—Lord Granville.—Arthur James Balfour.—Lord Rosebery.—History and personality. [DA562.E67 1966] 67-22092
1. Great Britain—Biography.

FEILING, Keith Grahame, Sir, 1884- 920.042
Sketches in nineteenth century biography. Freeport, N.Y., Books for Libraries Press [1970] vii, 181 p. 23 cm. (Essay index reprint series) Reprint of the 1930 ed. Contents.Contents.—Pitt.—Lord Liverpool.—Canning.—Croker.—Southey and Wordsworth.—Coleridge.—Newman.—Bulwer Lytton. Walter Bagehot.—Curzon.—Monypenny and Buckle's Disraeli. [CT782.F4 1970] 73-107698
1. Gt. Brit.—Biography. I. Title. II. Title: Nineteenth century biography.

FEILING, Keith Grahame, Sir, 1884- 920'.042
Sketches in nineteenth century biography, by Keith Feiling. London, New York, Longmans, Green, 1930. [Folcroft, Pa.] Folcroft Library Editions, 1972. p. Contents.Contents.—Pitt.—Lord Liverpool. Canning.—Croker.—Southey and Wordsworth.—Coleridge.—Newman.—Bulwer Lytton.—Walter Bagehot.—Curzon.—Monypenny and Buckle's "Disraeli." [CT782.F4 1972] 72-10137 ISBN 0-8414-0654-5
1. Great Britain—Biography. I. Title II. Title. Nineteenth century biography. **BIP**

FOSS, Michael. 920'.042
Tudor portraits: success and failure of an age. New York, Barnes & Noble [1974, c1973] 239 p. illus. 23 cm. Bibliography: p. 229-232. [DA317.F67 1974] 74-10393 ISBN 0-06-492175-1 8.50
1. Great Britain—Biography. 2. Great Britain—History—Tudors, 1485-1603. I. Title.

FREEMAN, Arthur, 1938- 920'.042
Unworthies of England: ten brief lives. New York, Garland Pub., 1974. p. cm. Includes bibliographical references. [CT775.F74] 74-2067 ISBN 0-8240-1051-5 12.00
1. Great Britain—Biography. I. Title.

GARDINER, Alfred George, 1865-1946. 920.042
Portraits and portents. Freeport, N.Y., Books for Libraries Press [1971, c1926] vi, 306 p. ports. 23 cm. (Essay index reprint series) [DA566.9.A1G26 1971] 79-167344 ISBN 0-8369-2499-1
1. Great Britain—Biography. 2. Biography—20th century. I. Title. **BIP**

GARVIN, Katherine, 1904- ed. 920'.042
The great Tudors. [Folcroft, Pa.] Folcroft Library Editions, 1974. p. cm. Reprint of the 1935 ed. published by I. Nicholson & Watson, London. [DA317.G3 1974] 74-8259 40.00
1. Great Britain—Biography. 2. Great Britain—History—Tudors, 1485-1603. I. Title.

*GLENTON, William 923.1
Tony's room: the secret love story of Princess Margaret [New York] Geis [dist.] Pocket Bks. [c.1965] 183p. illus. 18cm. (75134) .75 pap.,
I. Title.

HARMSWORTH, Cecil Bisshopp Harmsworth, Baron, 1869-1948. 920'.042
Immortals at first hand; famous people as seen by their contemporaries. [Folcroft, Pa.] Folcroft Library Editions, 1974. p. Reprint of the 1933 ed. published by D. Harmsworth, London. Quotations from contemporaries about a number of famous figures in English literature and history. [CT774.H3 1974] 920 74-9764 ISBN 0-8414-4802-7 (lib. bdg.)
1. Great Britain—Biography. 2. Authors, English—Biography. I. Title. **BIP**

HUTCHINSON, Horace Gordon, 1859-1932. 914.2'03'810922 B
Portraits of the eighties. [Folcroft, Pa.] Folcroft Library Editions, 1974. p. cm. Reprint of the 1920 ed. published by T. F. Unwin, London. Contents.Contents.—G. W. E. Russell.—W. E. Gladstone.—Lord Hartington (later Duke of Devonshire)—Charles Stewart Parnell.—John Bright.—Joseph Chamberlain.—Sir William Vernon Harcourt.—The members for Northampton.—General Gordon.—Lord Wolseley and Lord Roberts.—Archbishop Temple, Archdeacon Farrar, and some other churchmen.—Professor Huxley and the evolutionists.—Sir John Lubbock (later Lord Avebury)—Sir Thomas Brassey (later Earl Brassey)—Lord Elcho and Lord Wemyss.—William Morris.—Swinburne and George Meredith.—Spencer Walpole and Andrew Lang.—G. F. Watts, J. E. Millais, and E. Burne Jones.—Nellie Farren and some other players.—W. S. Gilbert and the Savoyards.—The "Aesthetes" and Oscar Wilde.—W. C. Grace.—The "Souls". [DA562.H8 1974] 74-13913 ISBN 0-8414-4854-X (lib. bdg.)
1 Great Britain—Biography. 2. Great Britain—Intellectual life—19th century. I. Title. **BIP**

HUTCHINSON, Horatio Gordon, 1859-1932. 920'.042
Portraits of the eighties. Freeport, N.Y., Books for Libraries Press [1970] xv, 301 p. ports. 23 cm. (Essay index reprint series) Reprint of the 1920 ed. Contents.Contents.—G. W. E. Russell.—W. E. Gladstone.—Lord Hartington (later Duke of Devonshire).—Charles Stewart Parnell.—John Bright.—Joseph Chamberlain.—Sir William Vernon Harcourt.—The members for Northampton.—General Gordon.—Lord Wolseley and Lord Roberts.—Archbishop Temple, Archdeacon Farrar, and some other churchmen.—Professor Huxley and the evolutionists.—Sir John Lubbock (later Lord Avebury).—Sir Thomas Brassey (later Earl Brassey).—Lord Elcho and Lord Wemyss.—William Morris.—Swinburne and George Meredith.—Spencer Walpole and Andrew Lang.—G. F. Watts, J. E. Millais, and E. Burne-Jones.—Nellie Farren and some other players.—W. S. Gilbert and the savoyards.—The Aesthetes and Oscar Wilde.—W. G. Grace.—The Souls.—Index. [DA562.H8 1970] 72-105020
1. Gt. Brit.—Biography. 2. Gt. Brit.—Intellectual life—19th century. I. Title.

INNES, Arthur Donald, 1863-1938. 942.05'0922
Leading figures in English history, Tudor and Stewart period. Freeport, N.Y., Books for Libraries Press [1967] viii, 361 p. 22 cm. (Essay index reprint series) Reprint of the 1931 ed. Contents.Contents.—Henry VII.—Cardinal Wolsey.—Sir Thomas More.—Thomas Cromwell.—Protector Somerset.—Queen Elizabeth.—Francis Drake.—Sir Walter Ralegh.—William Shakespeare.—James I.—Captain John Smith.—Strafford.—Oliver Cromwell.—Robert Blake.—John Milton.—Charles II.—James II.—John and Sarah Churchill.—Daniel Defoe.—Chronology. [DA304.I6 1967] 67-23233
1. Great Britain—Biography. 2. Great Britain—History—Tudors, 1485-1603. 3. Great Britain—History—Stuarts, 1603-1714. I. Title.

KIRCHER, Rudolf. 942
Englander; the public men of England through a German's eyes. Translated from the German by Constance Vesey, with revisions and additions. Freeport, N.Y., Books for Libraries Press [1968] x, 310 p. illus., ports. 22 cm. (Essay index reprint series) Reprint of the 1928 ed. [DA566.9.A1K5 1968] 68-8476
1. Great Britain—Biography. 2. Statesmen—Great Britain. I. Vesey, Constance, tr. II. Title.

KRAUS, Rene, 1902- 942.084'0922
The men around Churchill. Freeport, N.Y., Books for Libraries Press [1971] 339 p. ports. 23 cm. (Essay index reprint series) Reprint of the 1941 ed. Contents.Contents.—Enigma: Lord Halifax.—Prince charming: Anthony Eden.—Churchill's man Friday: Sir Archibald Sinclair.—Miraculous metamorphosis: Sir Kingsley Wood.—Boss: Ernest Bevin.—Lord of London: Herbert Morrison.—The gentleman vanishes: Clement Attlee.—A lord who rules the water: Albert Victor Alexander.—Empire builder, new style: Arthur Greenwood.—The King's first soldier: Sir John Greer Dill.—The general and the desert: General Sir Archibald Wavell.—A Canadian yankee at King George's court: Lord Beaverbrook.—Ambassador most extraordinary: Sir Stafford Cripps.—The life of King Geroge VI. [DA585.A1K7 1971] 79-142653 ISBN 0-8369-2056-2
1. Gt. Brit—Biography. 2. Statesmen, British. I. Title. **BIP**

LAURENCE Urdang Associates. 920'.041
Lives of the Georgian age, 1714-1837 / compiled by Laurence Urdang Associates ; editor, William Gould, managing editor, Patrick Hanks. New York : Barnes & Noble Books, 1978. xi, 516 p. : ports. ; 24 cm. Includes bibliographies and indexes. [CT781.L35 1978] 77-2684 25.00
1. Great Britain—Biography. 2. Great Britain—History—1714-1837—Biography. I. Gould, William. II. Title. **BIP**

LAURENCE Urdang Associates. 920'.041
Lives of the Stuart age, 1603-1714 / compiled by Laurence Urdang Associates ; editor, Edwin Riddell, managing editor, Patrick Hanks. London ; Osprey Publishing, 1976. xi, 500 p. : ports. ; 24 cm. Includes bibliographies and indexes. [CT781.L35 1976a] 77-353392 ISBN 0-85045-087-X : £12.50
1. Great Britain—Biography. I. Riddell, Edwin. II. Title.

LEE, Sidney, Sir, 1859-1926. 914.2'03'5
Great Englishmen of the sixteenth century. Freeport, N.Y., Books for Libraries Press [1970] xxiii, 337 p. ports. 23 cm. (Essay index reprint series) Based on eight lectures delivered at the Lowell Institute, Boston, 1903. Includes bibliographical references. [DA317.L5 1970] 77-128269
1. Gt. Brit.—Biography. 2. Renaissance—England. I. Title. **BIP**

LEE, Sidney, Sir, 1859-1926. 914.2'03'5
Great Englishmen of the sixteenth century. Port Washington, N.Y., Kennikat Press [1972] xxiii, 333 p. ports. 22 cm. (Essay and general literature index reprint series) Reprint of the 1904 ed. Based on eight lectures delivered at the Lowell Institute, Boston, 1903. Includes bibliographical references. [DA317.L5 1972] 77-159708 ISBN 0-8046-1655-8
1. Gt. Brit.—Biography. 2. Renaissance—England. I. Title.

LUDWIG, Charles, 1918- 267'.15'0924
The lady general. Grand Rapids, Baker Book House, 1962. 93p. illus. 20cm. (Valor series, sBooth, Evangeline Cory, 1865-1950--Juvenile literature:. [BX9743.B63L8] 62-18416
I. Title.

MCCARTHY, Justin, 1830-1912. 920.042
Portraits of the sixties. Freeport, N.Y., Books for Libraries Press [1971] v, 339 p. illus., facsims., ports. 23 cm. (Essay index reprint series) Reprint of the 1903 ed. [DA562.M15 1971] 79-142661 ISBN 0-8369-2061-9
1. Gt. Brit.—Biography. 2. Gt. Brit.—Civilization—19th century. I. Title. **BIP**

MACDONALD, Hugh, 1885- ed. 920.042
Portraits in prose; a collection of characters, chosen by Hugh Macdonald. Freeport, N.Y., Books for Libraries Press [1969] xxiii, 350 p. 23 cm. (Biography index reprint series) Reprint of the 1946 ed. [DA28.M25 1969] 71-101830
1. Gt. Brit.—Biography. I. Title. **BIP**

MANSBRIDGE, Albert, 1876-1952. 920.042
Fellow men; a gallery of England, 1876-1946. Freeport, N.Y., Books for Libraries Press [1970] xi, 116 p. ports. 23 cm. (Biography index reprint series) Reprint of the 1948 ed. [CT782.M35 1970] 73-117329
1. Gt. Brit.—Biography. I. Title.

MARTINDALE, Hilda, 1875-1952. 920.042
Some Victorian portraits and others. Freeport, N.Y., Books for Libraries Press [1970] 106 p. ports. 23 cm. (Biography index reprint series) Reprint of the 1948 ed. [CT782.M37 1970] 76-126324
1. Gt. Brit.—Biography. I. Title. **BIP**

MASSINGHAM, Harold John, 1888- ed. 942.081'0922
The great Victorians. Edited by Harold John Massingham and Hugh Massingham. Freeport, N.Y., Books for Libraries Press [1971] xxi, 507 p. 23 cm. (Essay index reprint series) Reprint of the 1932 ed. Includes bibliographical references. [DA562.M3 1971] 70-156692 ISBN 0-8369-2284-0
1. Gt. Brit.—Biography. 2. Gt. Brit.—Intellectual life 19th century. 3. English literature—19th century—History and criticism. I. Massingham, Hugh, joint ed. II. Title. **BIP**

MURRAY, Grace A. 920'.042
Personalities of the eighteenth century, by Grace A. Murray; with a foreword by Nigel Playfair. [Folcroft, Pa.] Folcroft Library Editions, 1972. 230 p. illus. 24 cm. Reprint of the 1927 ed. [CT781.M87 1972] 72-7299 17.50
1. Great Britain—Biography. 2. Great Britain—Social life and customs—18th century. I. Title. **BIP**

NICHOLS, John, 1745-1826. 920.042
Minor lives; a collection of biographies. Annotated and with an introd. on John Nichols and the antiquarian and anecdotal movements of the late eighteenth century, Edward L. Hart, editor. Cambridge, Mass., Harvard University Press, 1971. xxxii, 367 p. ports. 25 cm. [CT781.N5 1971] 73-131470 ISBN 0-674-57630-6 12.50
1. Gt. Brit.—Biography. I. Hart, Edward LeRoy, 1916- ed. II. Title.

NOTESTEIN, Wallace, 1878-1969. 920.042
English folk; a book of characters. Freeport, N.Y., Books for Libraries Press [1970, c1938] xxvii, 328 p. ports. 23 cm. (Essay index reprint series) Contents.Contents.—Frederick Bettesworth, 1837 (circa)-1905.—Lucy Lyttelton (Lady Frederick Cavendish), 1841-1925.—Thomas Coke of Holkham (finally Earl of Leicester), 1754-1842.—Thomas Bewick, 1753-1828.—Parson Woodforde and Nancy, 1740-1803.—Thomas Tyldesley, 1657-1715.—Alice Thornton, 1626-1707.—Leonard Wheatcroft, 1627-1706.—Roger Lowe, 1643 (probably)-1679.—Adam Eyre, 1614-1661.—Brilliana, Lady Harley, 1598-1643.—Nicholas Assheton, 1590-1625.—Henry, Lord Berkeley, Elizabethan period. [CT774.N6 1970] 72-99643
1. Gt. Brit.—Biography. 2. England—

Social life and customs. 3. National characteristics, English. I. Title.

POLLITT, Ronald. 920'.041
Portraits in British history / Ronald Pollitt, Herbert F. Curry. Homewood, Ill. : Dorsey Press, 1975. xi, 328 p. : ports. ; 23 cm. (The Dorsey series in history) Includes bibliographies. [DA28.P64] 74-24454 ISBN 0-256-01679-8 : 5.95
1. Great Britain—Biography. I. Curry, Herbert Franklin, 1928- joint author. II. Title. BIP

THE Post 942.08'0922
Victorians. With an introd. by W. R. Inge. Freeport, N.Y., Books for Libraries Press [1972] xi, 648 p. 23 cm. (Essay index reprint series) Reprint of the 1933 ed. [CT783.P6 1972] 77-37791 ISBN 0-8369-2618-8
1. Great Britain—Biography.

THE Post Victorians. 920'.042
With an introd. by W. R. Inge. [Folcroft, Pa.] Folcroft Library Editions, 1973, [i.e.1974] p. Reprint of the 1933 ed. published by I. Nicholson & Watson, London. [CT783.P6 1973] 73-13736 21.45 (lib. bdg.).
1. Great Britain—Biography. I. Inge, William Ralph, 1860-1954. BIP

REVALUATIONS : 920'.041
studies in biography / by Lascelles Abercrombie ... [et al.]. New York : Haskell House, [1976] p. cm. Reprint of the 1931 ed. published by Oxford University Press, London. [CT774.R4 1976] 75-30773 ISBN 0-8383-2106-2 lib.bdg. : 12.95
1. Great Britain—Biography. I. Abercrombie, Lascelles, 1881-1938.
Contents omitted BIP

REVALUATIONS; studies in 920.042
biography, by Lascelles Abercrombie [and others] Freeport, N.Y., Books for Libraries Press [1967] xi, 245 p. 22 cm. (Essay index reprint series) "First published 1911." Contents.Contents.—Introduction, by A. C. Ward.—Mary, Queen of Scots, by G. K. Chesterton.—Oliver Goldsmith, by S. Gwynn.—Charles James Fox, by Lord David Cecil.—Tennyson, by L. Abercrombie.—W. E. Gladstone, by E. Marjoribanks.—George Frederick Watts, by J. Laver.—William Morris, by G. D. H. Cole.—Elizabeth Garrett Anderson, by N. Mitchison.—Walter Pater, by T. E. Welby.—Ferdinand Foch, by Capt. L. Hart. [CT774.R4 1967] 67-23264
1. Great Britain—Biography. I. Abercrombie, Lascelles, 1881-1938.

ROSENBAUM, Robert A., 920'.042
1926-
Earnest Victorians; six great Victorians as portrayed in their own words and those of their contemporaries, by Robert A. Rosenbaum. Westport, Conn., Greenwood Press [1974, c1961] 383 p. illus. 23 cm. Reprint of the ed. published by Hawthorn Books, New York. Contents.Contents.—Lord Ashley, 1801-1885.—John Henry Newman, 1801-1890.—Elizabeth Barrett Browning, 1806-1861.—Dante Gabriel Rossetti, 1828-1882.—Charles Darwin, 1809-1882. Includes bibliographical references. [CT782.R6 1974] 74-9043 ISBN 0-8371-7607-7 17.00
1. Great Britain—Biography. I. Title.
Contents omitted.

RUPP, Ernest Gordon. 274.2 B
Six makers of English religion, 1500-1700, by Gordon Rupp. Plainview, N.Y., Books for Libraries Press [1974, c1957] p. cm. (Essay index reprint series) Reprint of the ed. published by Harper, New York. [BR767.R8 1974] 74-849 ISBN 0-518-10159-2 9.75
1. Great Britain—Biography. 2. Christian biography. I. Title.
Contents omitted.

RUSSELL, George 942.081'0922
William Erskine, 1853-1919.
Portraits of the seventies. Freeport, N.Y., Books for Libraries Press [1970] 485 p. ports. 23 cm. (Essay index reprint series) "First published 1916." [DA562.R9 1970] 73-117834
1. Gt. Brit.—Biography. 2. Gt. Brit.—History—Victoria, 1837-1901. I. Title. BIP

TAYLOR, William Cooke, 920'.042
1800-1849.
The modern British Plutarch; or, Lives of men distinguished in the recent history of England for their talents, virtues, or achievements. Freeport, N.Y., Books for Libraries Press [1972] iv, 365 p. 22 cm. (Essay index reprint series) Reprint of the 1846 ed. [DA506.A1T3 1972] 72-1264 ISBN 0-8369-2866-0
1. Great Britain—Biography. I. Title. II. Title: Lives of men distinguished in the recent history of England. BIP

THOMPSON, Edward Raymond, 920.042
1872-
Portraits of the new century (the first ten years) by Edward Raymond Thompson (E. T. Raymond). Freeport, N.Y., Books for Libraries Press [1970] 336 p. 23 cm. (Essay index reprint series) Reprint of the 1928 ed. Contents.Contents.—King Edward VII.—Sir Henry Campbell-Bannerman.—Literary swashbucklers and sentimentalists.—George Wyndham.—The "Prancing pro-consuls."—Some divines.—Press magnates.—Tree and Alexander.—Alfred Lyttelton.—Roberts and Kitchener.—William Hesketh Lever.—Tariff reformers and free traders.—Lord Strathcona.—Five editors.—Two admirals.—Henry James and Max Beerbohm.—Certain Irishmen.—Ministers for war.—Men of the law.—Labour leaders. [DA568.A1T5 1970] 74-117853 ISBN 8-369-16859-
1. Gt. Brit.—Biography. 2. Gt. Brit.—History—20th century. 3. Gt. Brit.—Intellectual life—20th century. I. Title.

THOMPSON, Edward Raymond, 920.042
1872-
Portraits of the nineties. Freeport, N.Y., Books for Libraries Press [1970] 319 p. 20 ports. 23 cm. (Essay index reprint series) Reprint of the 1921 ed. Includes bibliographical references. [CT782.T5 1970] 78-117854
1. Gt. Brit.—Biography. 2. Gt. Brit.—Intellectual life—19th century. I. Title.

THOMPSON, Edward Raymond, 920.042
1872-
Uncensored celebrities. Freeport, N.Y., Books for Libraries Press [1970] 220 p. 23 cm. (Essay index reprint series) Reprint of the 1919 ed. [DA566.9.A1T6 1970] 71-117855
1. Gt. Brit.—Biography. I. Title. BIP

TIMPSON, George Frederick. 920.71
Kings and commoners; studies in British idealism, by George F. Timpson. Freeport, N.Y., Books for Libraries Press [1969] xvi, 190 p. illus., ports. 23 cm. (Essay index reprint series) Reprint of the 1936 ed. [CT774.T5 1969] 70-80401 ISBN 0-8369-1051-6
1. Gt. Brit.—Biography. I. Title.

TOYNBEE, Arnold Joseph, 920.02
1889-
Acquaintances [by] Arnold J. Toynbee. London, Oxford U.P., 1967. viii, 312 p. 12 plates (ports.) facsim. 23 cm. [CB19.T575] 67-83072 35/-
1. Great Britain—Biography. 2. Statesmen. I. Title. BIP

VALENTINE, Alan Chester, 920.042
1901-
The British establishment, 1760-1784; an eighteenth-century biographical dictionary, by Alan Valentine. [1st ed.] Norman, University of Oklahoma Press [1970] 2 v. (xii, 960 p.) 24 cm. [CT781.V3] 69-16734
1. Gt. Brit.—Biography. I. Title.

VAUGHAN, Herbert 920.042
Millingchamp, 1870-1948.
From Anne to Victoria; fourteen biographical studies between 1702 and 1901. Port Washington, N.Y., Kennikat Press [1967] ix, 260 p. ports. 22 cm. First published in 1931. Contents.Contents.—James Edward Francis Stuart.—Charles Edward Stuart.—William Hogarth.—Benjamin Hoadly.—John Gambold.—Horace Walpole.—Captain James Cook.—Admiral Arthur Phillip.—Sir Robert, Jane, and Maria Porter.—Sir J. E. Millais and W. H. Hunt.—Richard Jefferies.—Samuel Butler.—John Percival.—Marianne North.—Francis Thompson. [CT774.V3 1967] 66-25950
1. Great Britain—Biography. I. Title. BIP

WARD, Wilfrid Philip, 920.042
1856-1916.
Ten personal studies. Freeport, N.Y., Books for Libraries Press [1970] xvii, 300 p. ports. 23 cm. (Essay index reprint series) Reprint of the 1908 ed. Contents.Contents.—Arthur James Balfour: a political Fabius Maximus.—Three notable editors: Delane, Hutton, Knowles.—Some characteristics of Henry Sidgwick.—Robert, Earl of Lytton, statesman and poet.—Father Ignatius Ryder: a reminiscence.—Sir M. E. Grant Duff's diaries.—Leo XIII.—The genius of Cardinal Wiseman.—John Henry Newman: an address.—Newman and Manning. Includes bibliographical references. [DA562.W3 1970] 73-107742
1. Gt. Brit.—Biography. 2. Catholics in Great Britain. I. Title. BIP

WHIBLEY, Charles, 1859- 920.042
1930.
Essays in biography. Freeport, N.Y., Books for Libraries Press [1968] 311 p. 22 cm. (Essay index reprint series) Reprint of the 1913 ed. Contents.Contents.—Sir Thomas Overbury.—George Buchanan.—Edward Hall.—John Tiptoft.—John Stow.—The admirable Crichton.—A princely woman.—Sir Thomas Browne. [CT774.W3 1968] 68-57343
1. Great Britain—Biography. I. Title. BIP

WRIGHT, Ronald Selby, 920.042
1908-
Great men; being short impressions of "X," H. H. Almond, W. A. Smith, A. H. Stanton, Kingsley Fairbridge [and] Alexander Paterson. Freeport, N.Y., Books for Libraries Press [1970] 32 p. 23 cm. (Biography index reprint series) Reprint of the 1951 ed. Includes bibliographical references. [CT782.W74 1970] 74-126329 ISBN 8-369-80352-
1. Gt. Brit.—Biography. I. Title. BIP

Great Britain—Biography—Bibliography.

MATTHEWS, William, 016.920042
1905-
British autobiographies; an annotated bibliography of British autobiographies published or written before 1951. [Hamden, Conn.] Archon Books, 1968 [c1955] xiv, 376 p. 23 cm. [Z2027.A9M3 1968] 68-21691
1. Great Britain—Biography—Bibliography. I. Title. BIP

REEL, Jerome V. 016.92'0042
Index to biographies of Englishmen, 1000-1485, found in dissertations and theses / Jerome V. Reel, Jr. Westport, Conn. : Greenwood Press, 1975. xiii, 689 p. ; 25 cm. Bibliography: p. 679-688. [Z5305.G7R43] [CT774] 74-19807 ISBN 0-8371-7846-0 lib.bdg. : 30.00
1. Great Britain—Biography—Bibliography. 2. Great Britain—Biography—Indexes. 3. Dissertations, Academic—Bibliography. 4. Dissertations, Academic—Indexes. I. Title.

Great Britain-Biography-Dictionaries.

BOASE, Frederic, 1843- 920.042
1916
Modern English biography: containing many thousand concisememoirs of persons who have died between the years 1851-1900, with an index of the most interesting matter [6v.] New York, Barnes & Noble [1965] 6v. (various p.) 26cm. [CT773.B6] 65-8551 135.00 set,
1. Gt. Brit.—Biog.—Dictionaries. I. Title.

*LAURENCE Urdang 920.'042
Associates comp.
Lives of the Stuart age, 1603-1714 / compiled by Laurence Urdang Associates. New York : Barnes & Noble Books, 1976. v : ports ; 24 cm. (Lives before the Tudors) Includes index. [CT773] 75-39126 ISBN 0-06-494330-5 : 27.50
1. Great Britain-Biography-Dictionaries. I. Title. BIP

Great Britain—Biography—Quotations, maxims, etc.

THE Dictionary of 920'.041
biographical quotation of British and American subjects / edited by Richard Kenin and Justin Wintle. 1st American ed. New York : Knopf : distributed by Random House, 1978. xviii, 860 p. ; 26 cm. Includes index. [CT773.D38 1978] 78-452 ISBN 0-394-50027-X : 25.00
1. Great Britain—Biography—Quotations, maxims, etc. 2. United States—Biography—Quotations, maxims, etc. I. Kenin, Richard. II. Wintle, Justin.

Great Britain—Civilization—Addresses, essays, lectures.

LUNN, Hugh Kingsmill, 914.2'03
1889-1949, comp.
What they said at the time, an anthology [by] Hugh Kingsmill. London, Wisnart Books, 1935. [Folcroft, Pa.] Folcroft Library Editions, 1973. [DA110.L76 1973] 73-93 ISBN 0-8414-1392-4 (lib. bdg.)
1. Great Britain—Civilization—Addresses, essays, lectures. 2. Authors, English—Biography. I. Title.

Great Britain—Description and travel—1701-1800.

DAVIES, Samuel, 1723- 253'.0924
1761.
The Reverend Samuel Davies abroad; the diary of a journey to England and Scotland, 1753-55. Edited, with an introd., by George William Pilcher. Urbana, University of Illinois Press, 1967. xv, 176 p. 24 cm. Bibliographical footnotes. [BX9225.D33A3] 67-12991
1. Great Britain—Description and travel—1701-1800. I. Pilcher, George William, ed. II. Title.

Great Britain—Economic conditions—19th century.

BAMFORD, Samuel, 331'.0924 B
1788-1872.
The autobiography of Samuel Bamford. Edited and with an introd. by W. H. Chaloner. New ed. New York, A. M. Kelly, 1967. 2 v. port. 23 cm. (Reprints of economic classics) Previously published separately. Contents.Contents.—v. 1. Early days. 3d ed. An account of the arrest and imprisonment of Samuel Bamford ... on suspicion of high treason. 2d ed.—v. 2. Passages in the life of a radical. 6th ed. [DA536.B2A3 1967] 67-23461
1. Great Britain—Economic conditions—19th century. I. Title: Early days. II. Title: An account of the arrest and imprisonment of Samuel Bamford ... on suspicion of high treason. III. Title: Passages in the life of a radical. BIP

Great Britain—Foreign relations—1603-1625.

DORCHESTER, Dudley 320.9'42'061
Carleton, 1st Viscount, 1573-1632.
Dudley Carleton to John Chamberlain, 1603-1624; Jacobean letters. Edited with an introd. by Maurice Lee, Jr. New Brunswick, N.J., Rutgers University Press [1972] x, 335 p. port. 24 cm. [DA46.D65A43] 76-185391 ISBN 0-8135-0723-5 12.50
1. Great Britain—Foreign relations—1603-1625. I. Chamberlain, John, 1554?-1628. II. Title.

Great Britain—Foreign relations—1936-1945.

CADOGAN, 940.53'12'0924 B
Alexander, Sir, 1884-1968.
The diaries of Sir Alexander Cadogan, O.M., 1938-1945. Edited by David Dilks. [1st American ed.] New York, Putnam [1972, c1971] 881 p. illus. 24 cm. Bibliography: p. 817-823. [DA566.9.C2A3 1972] 70-183915 15.00
1. Great Britain—Foreign relations—1936-1945. I. Dilks, David, 1938- ed.

Great Britain—History—Charles I, 1625-1649—Biography.

BENCE-JONES, 942.06'2'0922 B
Mark.
The Cavaliers / [by] Mark Bence-Jones. London : Constable, 1976. xi, 206 p., leaf of plate, [16] p. of plates : ill., map (on

lining papers) ports. (1 col.) ; 23 cm. Includes index. Bibliography: p. 196-200. [DA396.A1B46 1976] 77-367367 ISBN 0-09-461260-9 : £5.25
1. Great Britain—History—Charles I, 1625-1649—Biography. 2. Great Britain—Biography. I. Title.

Great Britain—History—Elizabeth, 1558-1603—Sources.

MONMOUTH, 914.2'03'550924 B
Robert Carey, 1st Earl of, 1560?-1639.
The memoirs of Robert Carey; edited by F. H. Mares. Oxford, Clarendon Press, 1972. xxxvi, 99 p. 23 cm. (Series of studies in Tudor and Stuart literature) Includes bibliographical references. [DA358.M7A33] 72-172651 ISBN 0-19-812440-6 £1.75
1. Great Britain—History—Elizabeth, 1558-1603—Sources. I. Mares, Francis Hugh, ed. II. Title. III. Series.

MONMOUTH, 914.2'03'550924 B
Robert Carey, 1st Earl of, 1560?-1639.
The memoirs of Robert Carey; edited by F. H. Mares. Oxford, Clarendon Press, 1972. xxxvi, 99 p. 23 cm. (Series of studies in Tudor and Stuart literature) Includes bibliographical references. [DA358.M7A33] 72-172651 ISBN 0-19-812440-6 5.75
1. Great Britain—History—Elizabeth, 1558-1603—Sources. I. Mares, Francis Hugh, ed. II. Title. III. Series.
Distributed by Oxford University Press N.Y.

Great Britain—History—Puritan Revolution, 1642-1660—Biography.

RIDLEY, Jasper 942.06'2'0922 B
Godwin.
The Roundheads / [by] Jasper Ridley. London : Constable, 1976. xi, 276 p., leaf of plate, [16] p. of plates : ill., map (on lining papers), ports. (1 col.) ; 23 cm. Includes index. Bibliography: p. 261-269. [DA407.A1R53 1976] 77-363465 ISBN 0-09-461230-7 : £5.50
1. Great Britain—History—Puritan Revolution, 1642-1660—Biography. 2. Great Britain—Biography. 3. Roundheads—Biography. I. Title.

Great Britain—History—To 1485.

HARDYNG, John, 1378-1465? 942
The chronicle of Iohn Hardyng. Containing an account of public transactions from the earliest period of English history to the beginning of the reign of King Edward the Fourth. Together with the continuation by Richard Grafton, to the thirty fourth year of King Henry the Eighth. The former part collated with two manuscripts of the author's own time; the last, with Grafton's duplicate edition. To which are added a biographical and literary preface, and an index, by Henry Ellis. London, Printed for F. C. and J. Rivington [etc.] 1812. [New York, AMS Press, 1974] xxi, 607 p. 26 cm. Includes bibliographical references. [DA130.H35 1974] 75-178538 ISBN 0-404-56621-9 75.00
1. Great Britain—History—To 1485. 2. Great Britain—History—Tudors, 1485-1603. I. Grafton, Richard, d. 1572?

Great Britain—History—Tudors, 1485-1603—Biography.

HOFFMANN, Ann. 942.05'092'2 B
Lives of the Tudor age, 1485-1603 / by Ann Hoffmann. New York : Barnes & Noble Books, 1977. xi, 500 p. : ports. ; 24 cm. Includes bibliographical references and indexes. [DA317.H65] 76-15685 ISBN 0-06-494331-3 : 25.00
1. Great Britain—History—Tudors, 1485-1603—Biography. 2. Great Britain—Biography. I. Title. BIP

Great Britain—History—Victoria, 1837-1901—Biography.

†ESCOTT, Thomas Hay 920.041 B
Sweet, 1844-1924.
Great Victorians : memories and personalities / by T. H. S. Escott. Folcroft, Pa. : Folcroft Library Editions, 1976. 383 p. : port. ; 26 cm. Reprint of the 1916 ed. published by Scribner, New York. Includes index. [DA562.E69 1976] 76-45373 ISBN 0-8414-3943-5 lib. bdg. : 35.00
1. Great Britain—History—Victoria, 1837-1901—Biography. 2. Great Britain—Biography. I. Title. BIP

Great Britain—History—William I, 1066-1087.

WACE, fl.1170. 942.02'1'0924
Master Wace, his chronicle of the Norman conquest from the Roman de Rou / translated with notes and ill. by Edgar Taylor. New York : AMS Press, 1975. xxix, 314 p., [1] leaf of plates : ill. ; 19 cm. Reprint of the 1837 ed. published by W. Pickering, London. Includes index. [DA190.W3213 1975] 78-178501 ISBN 0-404-56682-0 : 25.00
1. Great Britain—History—William I, 1066-1087. I. Title.

Great Britain—History—1714-1837.

PLUMB, John 942.07'092'2 B
Harold, 1911-
The first four Georges / J. H. Plumb. Boston : Little, Brown, 1975, c1956. 208 p. : ill. (some col.) ; 31 cm. Includes index. Bibliography: p. 205. [DA480.P55 1975] 74-12150 17.50
1. Great Britain—History—1714-1837. 2. Great Britain—Kings and rulers—Biography. I. Title. BIP

PLUMB, John Harold, 941.07'092'2
1911-
The first four Georges / J. H. Plumb. Revised ed. London ; New York : Hamlyn, 1974. 208 p. : ill (some col.), ports. (some col.) ; 31 cm. Includes index. Bibliography: p. 205. [DA480.P55 1974] 75-308654 ISBN 0-600-38702-X : £3.95
1. Great Britain—History—1714-1837. 2. Great Britain—Kings and rulers—Biography. I. Title.

Great Britain—History—1760-1789.

WALPOLE, Horace, 4th 942.07'3
Earl of Orford, 1717-1797.
The last journals of Horace Walpole during the reign of George III from 1771-1783. With notes by Dr. Doran. Edited with an introd. by A. Francis Steuart. London, New York, J. Lane, 1910. London, New York, J. Lane, 1910. [New York, AMS Press, 1973] 2 v. illus. 23 cm. [DA506.W2A154 1973] 71-177879 ISBN 0-404-06815-4 32.50 (set)
1. Great Britain—History—1760-1789. I. Title.

Great Britain—History—19th century.

LEAN, Edward Tangye. 914.2'03
The Napoleonists: a study in political disaffection, 1760-1960, by E. Tangye Lean. London, New York, Oxford U.P., 1970. xiv, 402 p., 28 plates. illus., facsims., maps, ports. (some col.) 25 cm. Bibliography: p. 371-378. [DA530.L4 1970] 79-537520 ISBN 0-19-215184-3 70/-
1. Great Britain—History—19th century. 2. Great Britain—History—20th century. 3. Great Britain—Biography. 4. Authoritarianism. I. Title. BIP

Great Britain—History—19th century—Sources.

CROKER, John 942.07'3'0924 B
Wilson, 1780-1857.
The Croker papers; the correspondence and diaries of ... John Wilson Croker, Secretary to the Admiralty from 1809 to 1830. Edited by Louis J. Jennings. London, J. Murray, 1885. 2d ed., rev. [New York, AMS Press, 1972] 3 v. port. 23 cm. [DA536.C94A4 1972] 77-154125 ISBN 0-404-01880-7 52.00
1. Great Britain—History—19th century—Sources. I. Jennings, Louis John, 1836-1893, ed. II. Title.

CROKER, John Wilson, 1780- 942.07
1857.
The Croker papers, 1808-1857. Edited by Bernard Pool. [New and abridged ed.] New York, Barnes & Noble [1967] vii, 277 p. illus., ports. 25 cm. First published in 1884. [DA536.C94A4 1967] 67-1244
1. Great Britain—History—19th century—Sources. I. Poole, Bernard, ed. II. Title. BIP

Great Britain—Kings and rulers—Biography.

ANDREWS, Allen. 941'.00992 B
Kings & queens of England & Scotland / Allen Andrews ; with an introduction by Dulcie M. Ashdown. London ; New York : Marshall Cavendish, 1976. 184 p. : chiefly ill. (some col.), coats of arms (1 col.), facsims., geneal. table, map, ports. (some col.) ; 29 cm. Includes index. [DA28.1.A63] 77-371685 ISBN 0-85685-136-1 : £3.95
1. Great Britain—Kings and rulers—Biography. I. Title. BIP

BROOKS, Janice Young. 942'.00992
Kings and queens : the Plantagenets of England / by Janice Young Brooks. 1st ed. Nashville : T. Nelson, [1975] p. cm. Includes index. [DA177.B76] 75-17843 ISBN 0-8407-6438-3 : 6.50
1. Great Britain—Kings and rulers—Biography. 2. Great Britain—History—Medieval period, 1066-1485. I. Title. BIP

CAMPBELL, Judith. 929.7'2
Royalty on horseback / Judith Campbell. Garden City, N.Y. : Doubleday, [1975] c1974. 141 p. : ill. (some col.) ; 25 cm. [DA28.1.C35 1975] 74-17703 ISBN 0-385-08851-5 : 12.95
1. Great Britain—Kings and rulers—Biography. 2. Horsemanship—Great Britain. I. Title.

HUDSON, Mildred, 1902- 941'.00992
1961.
Crown of a thousand years : a millenium of British history presented as a pageant of kings and queens / by M. E. Hudson and Mary Clarke. New York ; Crown Publishers, 1978. 152 p. : ill. ; 25 cm. Includes index. [DA28.1.H83 1978] 78-4466 ISBN 0-517-53452-5 : 10.00
1. Great Britain—Kings and rulers—Biography. 2. Great Britain—Kings and rulers—Portraits. I. Clarke, Mary, 1944- joint author. II. Title.

JENNER, Heather. 942'.099
Royal wives. New York, St. Martin's Press [1971, c1967] 247, [1] p. illus., map, ports. 23 cm. Bibliography: p. 245-[248] [DA28.1.J4 1971] 79-142428
1. Great Britain Kings and rulers—Biography. 2. Great Britain—Queens—Biography. I. Title.

THE Lives of the kings & 929.7'2
queens of England / edited by Antonia Fraser ; heraldic consultant, J. P. Brooke-Little. 1st American ed. New York : Knopf, 1975. 360 p. : ill. ; 26 cm. Includes index. [DA28.1.L58 1975b] 74-29035 17.50
1. Great Britain—Kings and rulers—Biography. I. Fraser, Antonia Pakenham, Lady, 1932-

LONDON. National 941'.00992 B
Portrait Gallery.
Royal faces : 900 years of British monarchy / [text by Hugh Clayton ; picture selection and captions by Mary Pettman and Richard Ormond]. London : H.M.S.O., 1977. [1], 56 p. : col. geneal. table, ports. (some col.) ; 28 cm. Obtainable in U.S.A. from Pendragon House, Palo Alto, Calif. [DA28.1.L63 1977] 77-374773 ISBN 0-11-290209-X : £1.95
1. Great Britain—Kings and rulers—Biography. 2. Great Britain—History. I. Clayton, Hugh. II. Title.

MARLOW, Joyce. 941'.00992 B
Kings & queens of Britain / Joyce Marlow. New York : Arco Pub. Co., [1978] p. cm. Includes index. [DA28.1.M327] 77-7067 ISBN 0-668-04357-1 : 15.00
1. Great Britain—Kings and rulers—Biography. I. Title. II. Title: Kings & queens of England & Scotland.

MORRIS, Jean, 1924- 941'.00992 B
The monarchs of England / by Jean Morris. New York : Charterhouse, c1975. xii, 457 p. : ill., maps (on lining papers) ; 24 cm. Includes index. Bibliography: p. 434-439. [DA28.1.M56] 74-82977 ISBN 0-88327-043-9 : 17.50
1. Great Britain—Kings and rulers—Biography. I. Title.

MURRAY, Jane. 942'.00992 B
The kings and queens of England; a tourist guide. New York, Scribner [1974] xi, 337 p. 22 cm. Bibliography: p. [243]-252. [DA28.1.M8] 74-8019 ISBN 0-684-13889-1 7.95
1. Great Britain—Kings and rulers—Biography. I. Title.

PALMER, Alan 941'.00992 B
Warwick.
Kings and queens of England / [by] Alan Palmer. London : Octopus Books, 1976. 5-157 p. : chiefly ill. (some col.), facsims., ports. (some col.) ; 31 cm. Ill. on lining papers. Includes index. [DA28.1.P26 1976] 77-362010 ISBN 0-7064-0542-0 : 2.95
1. Great Britain—Kings and rulers—Biography. 2. Great Britain—History. I. Title.

ROSS, Josephine. 942.04'092'2 B
The Tudors : Englands golden age / Josephine Ross. 1st American ed. New York : Putnam, 1979. 184 p. : ill. ; 31 cm. Includes index. Bibliography: p. 179. [DA317.1.R67 1979] 79-84036 ISBN 0-399-12417-9 : 15.95
1. Great Britain—Kings and rulers—Biography. 2. Great Britain—History—Tudors, 1485-1603. I. Title. BIP

Great Britain—Kings and rulers—Biography—Juvenile literature.

DELDERFIELD, Eric R. 942'.00992 B
Kings and queens of England. Devised and edited by Eric R. Delderfield. Parts one and three written by D. V. Cook. [Rev. ed.] New York, Stein and Day [1972, c1971] 160 p. illus. 19 cm. First published in 3 v. (later combined into one vol.) under title: A brief guide to Kings & Queens of England and Great Britain. Discusses the characters, careers, and influence on history of each English king and queen from the early Saxons to Elizabeth II. [DA28.1.D42 1972] 920 72-79138 ISBN 0-8128-1493-2 5.95
1. Great Britain—Kings and rulers—Biography—Juvenile literature. 2. Great Britain—History—Juvenile literature. I. Cook, D. V. II. Title.

SCOTT Moncrieff, Martha 929.72
Christian.
Kings and queens of England [by] M. C. Scott Moncrieff. Including an essay on royal portraiture by Richard Ormond. New York, Macmillan [1966] 159 p. illus., geneal. tables, map., ports. (part col.) 23 cm. Bibliography: p. 155. [DA28.1.S3 1966a] 66-29032
1. Great Britain—Kings and rulers—Biography—Juvenile literature. I. Title.

SCOTT Moncrieff, 941'.00992 B
Martha Christian.
Kings and queens of England / M. C. Scott Moncrieff ; including an essay on royal protraiture by Richard Ormond. New York : Hippocrene Books, 1975. 159 p. : ill. (some col.) ; 23 cm. Includes index. Bibliography: p. 155. The historical tradition of the British Monarchy is outlined through the lives of her kings and queens, as well as through the depiction of surrounding rituals and historical events. [DA28.1.S3 1975] 74-18969 ISBN 0-88254-313-X 5.95
1. Great Britain—Kings and rulers—Biography—Juvenile literature. I. Title.

Great Britain. Lord Chancellor's Departments.

CAMPBELL, John 347'.42'04 B
Campbell, Baron, 1779-1861.
Lives of the Lord Chancellors and Keepers of the Great Seal of England, from the earliest times till the reign of King George IV. 4th ed. London, J. Murray, 1856-57. [New York, AMS Press, 1973] p. [KD620.C34 1973] 74-39877 ISBN 0-404-01380-5 25.00 each
1. Great Britain. Lord Chancellor's Departments. 2. Judges—Great Britain—Biography. I. Title.
10 volumes set 250.00.

Great Britain. Navy—Biography.

HUMBLE, Richard. 359.1'334'0924 B
Captain Bligh / Richard Humble. London : A. Barker, c1976. xii, 212 p., [4] leaves of plates : ill. ; 23 cm. Includes index. [DA87.1.B6H85] 76-383726 ISBN 0-213-16584-8 : £4.95
1. Bligh, William, 1754-1817. 2. Great Britain. Navy—Biography. 3. Bounty (Ship) 4. Admirals—Great Britain—Biography. I. Title.

RALFE, James, 359'.0092'2 B
fl.1820-1829.
The naval biography of Great Britain: consisting of historical memoirs of those officers of the British Navy who distinguished themselves during the reign of His Majesty George III. With a new introd. and pref. by George Athan Billias. Boston, Gregg Press, 1972. 4 v. illus. 27 cm. (The American Revolutionary series. British accounts of the American Revolution) Reprint of the 1828 ed. published by Whitmore & Fenn, London. [DA87.1.A1R35 1972] 72-10833 ISBN 0-8398-1773-8
1. Great Britain. Navy—Biography. 2. Great Britain—History, Naval—18th century. 3. United States—History—Revolution, 1775-1783—Naval operations. I. Title. II. Series: British accounts of the American Revolution. BIP

Great Britain Navy-History

TANNER, Joseph Robson, 359.3'0924
1860-1931.
Samuel Pepys and the Royal Navy. New York, Haskell House, 1971. 83 p. 23 cm. (Lees Knowles lectures, 1919) Reprint of the 1920 ed. Includes bibliographical references. [VA454.T33 1971] 79-163207 ISBN 0-8383-1314-0
1. Gt. Brit. Navy—History. 2. Pepys, Samuel, 1633-1703. I. Title. II. Series. BIP

Great Britain. Navy—History.

TANNER, Joseph Robson, 359.3'0924
1860-1931.
Samuel Pepys and the Royal Navy. [Folcroft, Pa.] Folcroft Library Editions, 1974. 83 p. 24 cm. "Delivered at Trinity College in Cambridge, 6, 13, 20, and 27 November." Reprint of the 1920 ed. published by the University Press, Cambridge, Eng., which was issued as the 1919 Lees Knowles lectures. Includes bibliographical references. [VA454.T33 1973] 73-13909 ISBN 0-8414-8532-1 (lib. bdg.)
1. Great Britain. Navy—History. 2. Pepys, Samuel, 1633-1703. I. Title. II. Series: The Lees Knowles lectures, 1919.

Great Britain—Nobility.

KINNEY, Arthur F., 1933- 929.7'2
Titled Elizabethans; a directory of Elizabethan state and church officers and knights, with peers of England, Scotland, and Ireland, 1558-1603 [by] Arthur F. Kinney. [Hamden, Conn.] Archon Books, 1973. ix, 89 p. port. 23 cm. [CS420.K56] 73-5700 ISBN 0-208-01334-2 5.00
1. Great Britain—Nobility. 2. Statesmen, British. 3. Great Britain—Peerage. 4. Orders of knighthood and chivalry—Great Britain. I. Title. BIP

SANFORD, John Langton, 929.72
1824-1877.
The great governing families of England, by John Langton Sanford and Meredith Townsend. Freeport, N.Y., Books for Libraries Press [1972] 2 v. fold. map. 23 cm. (Essay index reprint series) Reprint of the 1865 ed. [DA305.S2 1972] 77-37862 ISBN 0-8369-2623-4
1. Great Britain—Nobility. I. Townsend, Meredith White, 1831-1911, joint author. II. Title. BIP

Great Britain. Parliament—Biography.

DAVIDSON, John 328.42'0922 B
Morrison.
Eminent English liberals in and out of Parliament. Freeport, N.Y., Books for Libraries Press [1972] vii, 300 p. 23 cm. (Essay index reprint series) Reprint of the 1880 ed. [DA562.D27 1972] 70-37521 ISBN 0-8369-2542-4
1. Great Britain. Parliament—Biography. 2. Great Britain—Biography. I. Title. BIP

Great Britain. Parliament. House of Commons—Registers.

JUDD, Gerrit 328.42'0922 B
Parmele, 1915-
Members of Parliament, 1734-1832, by Gerrit P. Judd, IV. [Hamden, Conn.] Archon Books, 1972 [c1955] vii, 389 p. 23 cm. Originally issued as no. 61 of the Yale historical publications, Miscellany series. Includes bibliographical references. [JN672.J8 1972] 73-179572 ISBN 0-208-01230-3 12.00
1. Great Britain. Parliament. House of Commons—Registers. 2. Great Britain—Biography. I. Title. II. Series: Yale historical publications. Miscellany 61. BIP

Great Britain Parliament House Of Commons Speaker.

DASENT, Arthur Irwin, 328.42'07'2
1859-1939.
The speakers of the House of Commons, from the earliest times to the present day, with a topographical description of Westminster at various epochs & a brief record of the principal constitutional changes during seven centuries. With notes on the illus. by John Lane & a portrait of every speaker where one is known to exist. New York, B. Franklin [1966] xl, 455 p. illus., ports. 24 cm. (Burt Franklin research and source work series, 104) Reprint of the 1911 ed. On spine: Speakers of the House of Commons to 1850. Bibliographical footnotes. [JN678.D3 1966] 71-6297
1. Gt. Brit. Parliament. House of Commons—Speaker. 2. Gt. Brit. Parliament. House of Commons—History. 3. Gt. Brit.—Politics and government. 4. Westminster, Eng. I. Title.

Great Britain. Parliament—Rules and practice.

FOSTER, Elizabeth 328.42'092'4 B
Read.
The painful labour of Mr. Elsyng. Philadelphia, American Philosophical Society, 1972. 69 p. 30 cm. (Transactions of the American Philosophical Society, new ser., v. 62, pt. 8) Bibliography: p. 3-4. [JN592.F67] 72-89400 ISBN 0-87169-628-2 3.00
1. Elsynge, Henry, 1577 or 8-1636. 2. Great Britain. Parliament—Rules and practice. 3. Great Britain. Parliament. House of Lords—History. I. Title. II. Series: American Philosophical Society, Philadelphia. Transactions, new ser. v. 62, pt. 8. BIP

Great Britain—Politics and government—1461-1483.

ROSS, Charles 942.04'4'0924 B
Derek.
Edward IV / Charles Ross. Berkeley : University of California Press, 1974. xvi, 479 p., [12] leaves of plates : ill. (1 col.) ; 25 cm. Includes index. Bibliography: p. [443]-456. [DA258.R67] 74-79771 ISBN 0-520-02781-7 : 25.00
1. Great Britain—Politics and government—1461-1483.

Great Britain—Politics and government—1485-

GRAINGER, J. H. 329'.00922
Character and style in English politics, by J. H. Grainger. London, Cambridge U.P., 1969. viii, 291 p. 23 cm. Bibliographical footnotes. [DA42.G7] 69-10428 ISBN 0-521-07350-2 50/-
1. Great Britain—Politics and government—1485- 2. Statesmen—Great Britain. I. Title.

Great Britain—Politics and government—1760-1820.

STANTON, Henry Brewster, 309.1'42
1805-1887.
Sketches of reforms and reformers of Great Britain and Ireland. New York, Wiley, 1849. Miami, Fla., Mnemosyne Pub. Co. [1969] 393 p. 23 cm. [DA535.S75 1969] 75-89446
1. Great Britain—Politics and government—1760-1820. 2. Great Britain—Politics and government—19th century. 3. Great Britain—Social conditions—19th century. 4. Social reformers—Great Britain. I. Title. BIP

Great Britain—Politics and government—1936-

GEORGE-BROWN, 942.085'092'4 B
George Alfred Brown, Baron, 1914-
In my way, by George Brown. New York, St Martin's Press [1971] 299 p. 24 cm. "The political memoirs of Lord George-Brown." [DA591.G45A3 1971b] 75-165558 8.95
1. Great Britain—Politics and government—1936- I. Title.

Great Britain—Politics and government—20th century.

CAMPBELL-JOHNSON, Alan, 923.242
1913-
Eden; the making of a statesman. New York, Washburn [1955] 306p. illus. 22cm. First published in 1938 under title: Anthony Eden. [DA566.9.E28C3 1955] 55-2908
1. Gt. Brit.—Pol. & govt.—20th cent. I. Title. BIP

CHURCHILL, Winston 942.080924
Leonard Spencer, Sir 1874-1965
Churchill. Ed. by Martin Gilbert. Englewood Cliffs, N. J., Prentice [1967] ix, 180p. 21cm. (Great lives observed) Bibl. [DA566.9.C5A3593] 67-28397 4.95; 1.95 pap.,
1. Gt. Brit.—Pol. & govt.—20th cent. I. Gilbert, Martin, 1936- ed. II. Title.

CHURCHILL, Winston 942.08'0924
Leonard Spencer, Sir 1874-1965.
Churchill. Edited by Martin Gilbert. Englewood Cliffs, N.J., Prentice-Hall [1967] ix, 180 p. 21 cm. (Great lives observed) "Bibliographical note": p. 173-175. [DA566.9.C5A3593] 67-28397
1. Gt. Brit.—Pol. & govt.—20th cent. I. Gilbert, Martin, 1936- ed. II. Title.

COOPER, Duff, 1st 923.242
viscount Norwich, 1890-1954.
Old men forget; the autobiography of Duff Cooper (Viscount Norwich) [1st American ed.] New York, Dutton, 1954. 399p. illus. 22cm. [DA566.9.C64A3 1954] 54-11701
1. Gt. Brit.—Pol. & govt.—20th cent. I. Title.

MACMILLAN, Harold, 942.0820924 B
1894-
Winds of change, 1914-1939. [1st U.S. ed. New York, Harper & Row [1966] vi, 584 p. illus., ports. 24 cm. First vol. of the author's memoirs. Bibliographical footnotes. [DA566.9.M33A3 1966a] 66-21710
1. Great Britain—Politics and government—20th century. 2. Great Britain—Foreign relations—20th century. I. Title.

Great Britain—Princes and princesses—Biography.

ASHDOWN, Dulcie M. 942.9'00992
Princess of Wales / Dulcie M. Ashdown. New York : Scribner, c1979. 240 p. : ill. ; 25 cm. Includes index. Bibliography: p. 230-234. [DA28.3.A84] 78-24618 ISBN 0-684-16153-2 : 15.95
1. Great Britain—Princes and princesses—Biography. 2. Great Britain—History—Medieval period, 1066-1485. 3. Great Britain—History—Modern period, 1485- I. Title. BIP

PINE, Leslie Gilbert. 942
Princes of Wales, by L. G. Pine. [1st ed.] Rutland, Vt., C. E. Tuttle Co. [1970] 208 p. illus., geneal. table, ports. 22 cm. Reprint of the 1959 ed. with an additional chapter on the present Prince of Wales. Bibliography: p. 201-202. [DA28.3.P5 1970] 72-104216 ISBN 0-8048-0896-1 5.00
1. Great Britain—Princes and princesses—Biography. I. Title. BIP

Great Britain—Queens—Biography.

ARGY, Josy, 1927- 941'.00992
Britain's royal brides / Josy Argy and Wendy Riches. New York : St. Martin's Press, 1975. p. cm. Bibliography: p. [DA28.2.A73 1975] 74-33900 10.00
1. Great Britain—Queens—Biography. 2. Great Britain—Princes and princesses—Biography. 3. Weddings—Great Britain. I. Riches, Wendy, 1944- joint author. II. Title.

LOFTS, Norah 941'.00992 B
Robinson, 1904-
Queens of England / North Lofts. 1st ed. in the United States of America. Garden City, N.Y. : Doubleday, 1977. 192 p., [4] leaves of plates : ill. ; 25 cm. [DA28.2.L6 1977] 76-40576 ISBN 0-385-12780-4 : 12.50
1. Great Britain—Queens—Biography. 2. Great Britain—Princes and princesses—Biography. I. Title.

SOFTLY, Barbara. 941'.00992 B
Queens of England / Barbara Softly. New York : Stein and Day, [1976] p. cm. Bibliography: p. [DA28.2.S63 1976] 76-14851 ISBN 0-8128-2096-7
1. Great Britain—Queens—Biography. I. Title. BIP

Great Britain Royal Air Force—Biography.

VOSS, Vivian. 940.4'4'0924 B
Flying minnows : memoirs of a World War One fighter pilot, from training in Canada to the front line, 1917-1918 / Roger Vee (Vivian Voss). [2d ed.]. London : Arms and Armour Press ; New York : Hippocrene Books, 1977. 306 p., [6] leaves of plates : ill. ; 23 cm. Reprint of the 1935 ed. published by J. Hamilton, London. [D602.V67 1977] 76-13831 ISBN 0-88254-410-1 (Hippocrene) : 12.50 (U.S.)
1. Great Britain Royal Air Force—Biography. 2. Voss, Vivian. 3. European War, 1914-1918—Aerial operations, British. 4. European War, 1914-1918—Personal narratives, English. I. Title.

Great Britain. Royal Air Force. 19 Squadron.

MONTGOMERY-MOORE, 940.54'49'41
Cecil
"That's my bloody plane" : the World War I experiences of Major Cecil Montgomery-Moore, as told to Peter Kilduff / foreword by Sir John W. Baker. Chester, Conn. : Pequot Press, c1975. ix, 157 p. : ill., map (on lining papers) ; 23 cm. Includes index. [D602.M674] 75-18036 ISBN 0-87106-057-4 : 9.95
1. Great Britain. Royal Air Force. 19 Squadron. 2. Montgomery-Moore, Cecil. 3. European War, 1914-1918—Aerial operations, British. 4. European War, 1914-1918—Personal narratives, American. I. Kilduff, Peter. II. Title.

Great Britain—Social life and customs—17th century.

PEPYS, Samuel, 1633- 914.2'03'6
1703.
The diary of Samuel Pepys. A new and complete transcription edited by Robert Latham and William Matthews. Contributing editors: William A. Armstrong [and others] Berkeley, University of California Press [1970]- v. illus., facsims., maps, ports. 23 cm. Contents.Contents.—v. 1. 1660.—v. 2. 1661.—v. 3. 1662.—v. 4. 1663.—v. 5. 1664. [DA447.P4A4 1970] 70-96950 ISBN 0-520-01575-4 (v. 1) varies 27.00 (v. 1-3)
1. Great Britain—Social life and customs—17th century. I. Latham, Robert, 1912- ed. II. Matthews, William, 1905- ed. III. Title. BIP

Great Western Railway (Gt. Brit.)—History.

GASSON, Harold. 385'.092'4 B
Footplate days : more reminiscences of a Great Western fireman / by Harold

Gasson. Oxford : Oxford Publishing, 1976. vi, 112 p., [32] p. of plates : ill., port. ; 22 cm. [TJ603.4.G72G73165] 77-361914 ISBN 0-902888-51-X : £1.80
1. Great Western Railway (Gt. Brit.)—History. 2. Gasson, Harold. 3. Locomotives—Great Britain—History. 4. Locomotive firemen—Great Britain—Biography. I. Title.

Greathouse, Charles H.,

GREATHOUSE, Charles H., 1883- 917.8'03'0924 B
Ranch life in the Old West, by Charles H. Greathouse. Hollywood, Calif., Asgard House [1971] 286 p. illus. 23 cm. Autobiography. [CT275.G74A3] 70-171726 10.00
I. Title.

Greave, Peter.

GREAVE, Peter. 954.03'5'0924 B
The seventh gate / [by] Peter Greave. London : Temple Smith, 1976. 217 p. ; 23 cm. [RC154.G73 1976] 76-375955 ISBN 0-85117-078-1 : £3.75
1. Greave, Peter. 2. Leprosy—Biography. I. Title.

Grebel, Konrad, 1498-1526.

RUTH, John L. 284'.3 B
Conrad Grebel, son of Zurich : commissioned by Conrad Grebel College, Waterloo, Ontario, in observance of the 450th anniversary of the Mennonites / John L. Ruth. Scottdale, Pa. : Herald Press, 1975. 160 p. : ill. ; 26 cm. [BX4946.G7R87] 75-8829 ISBN 0-8361-1767-0 : 6.95
1. Grebel, Konrad, 1498-1526. I. Title.

Greco, Jose.

GRECO, Jose. 793.3'2'0924 B
The gypsy in my soul : the autobiography of Jose Greco / by Jose Greco, with Harvey Ardman. 1st ed. Garden City, N.Y. : Doubleday, 1977. 279 p., [16] leaves of plates : ill. ; 22 cm. Includes index. [GV1785.G712A34] 76-23765 ISBN 0-385-11504-0 : 10.00
1. Greco, Jose. 2. Dancers—Biography. I. Ardman, Harvey, joint author. II. Title. BIP

Greece—Biography.

HOPKINSON, Leslie White. 938
Greek leaders. Under the editorship of William Scott Ferguson. Freeport, N.Y., Books for Libraries Press [1969, c1918] vii, 259 p. 23 cm. (Essay index reprint series) Contents.Contents.—Solon.—Themistocles.—Pericles.—Alcibiades.—Socrates.—Agesilaus.—Dionysius the Elder.—Epaminondas.—Demosthenes.—Alexander the Great.—Aratus.—Summary of Greek history. [DF208.H6 1969] 75-76904
1. Greece—Biography. I. Title. BIP

PLUTARCHUS. 920'.038
The age of Alexander: nine Greek lives. Translated [from the Latin] and annotated by Ian Scott-Kilvert; introduction by G. T. Griffith. Harmondsworth, Penguin, 1973. 443 p. maps. 18 cm. (Penguin classics, L286) Contents.Contents.—Agesilaus.—Pelopidas.—Dion.—Timoleon.—Demosthenes.—Phocion.—Alexander.—Demetrius.—Pyrrhus. Includes bibliographical references. [DF208.P5513 1973] 73-175995 ISBN 0-14-044286-3 £0.60
1. Greece—Biography. I. Scott-Kilvert, Ian, ed. II. Title.

PLUTARCHUS 920.03
Eight great lives. The Dryden translation, rev. by Arthur Hugh Clough. Edited with an introd. by Charles Alexander Robinson, Jr. New York, [Holt] Rinehart [& Winston, c.1960] xv, [3], 364p. map. (Rinehart editions, 105) 'Bibliographical note': p.[xvi] Partial contents. -- Pericles. -- Alcibiades. -- Gaius Marcius Coriolanus. -- Demosthenes. -- Cicero. -- Alexander. Caesar. -- Antony. 60-6497 1.25 pap.,
1. Greece—Biog. 2. Rome—Biog. I. Roinson, Charles Alexander, 1900- ed. II. Title.

PLUTARCHUS 920.03
Eight great lives. The Dryden translation, rev. by Arthur Hugh Clough. Edited with an introd. by Charles Alexander Robinson, Jr. New York, [Holt] Rinehart [& Winston, c.1960] xv, [3], 364p. map. (Rinehart editions, 105) 'Bibliographical note': p.[xvi] Partial contents. -- Pericles. -- Alcibiades. -- Gaius Marcius Coriolanus. -- Demosthenes. -- Cicero. -- Alexander. Caesar. -- Antony. 60-6497 1.25 pap.,
1. Greece—Biog. 2. Rome—Biog. I. Roinson, Charles Alexander, 1900- ed. II. Title.

PLUTARCHUS. 920.03
Everybody's Plutarch. Arr. and edited for the modern reader from the "Parallel lives" and with an introd. by Raymond T. Bond. New York, Dodd, Mead [1962, c1931] ix, 780 p. illus., ports. 22 cm. (Great illustrated classics: Titan editions) "The translation used is that called Dryden's, corrected from the Greek and revised by Arthur Hugh Clough." [DE7.P5 1962] 62-9722
1. Greece—Biography. 2. Rome—Biography. I. Dryden, John, 1631-1700, tr. II. Clough, Arthur Hugh, 1819-1861, ed. III. Bond, Raymond Tostevin, 1893- ed. IV. Title.

PLUTARCHUS 920.9'38
Lives from Plutarch. The modern Amer. ed. of Twelve lives ed. abridged, introd., by John W. McFarland, Pleasant & Audrey Graves. New York, Random [1967, c.1966] xx, 284p. 22cm. [DE7.P7M3] 66-12018 5.95
1. Greece—Biog. I. McFarland, John W., ed. II. Title.
Contents omitted.

PLUTARCHUS 920.03
The lives of the noble Grecians and Romans. Translated by John Dryden. Rev. by Arthur Hugh Clough. Chicago, Encyclopædia Britannica [1955, c1952] vii, 897 p. 25 cm. (Great books of the Western World, v. 14) [AC1.G72 vol. 14] 888.8 55-10323
1. Greece—Biography. 2. Rome—Biography. I. Dryden, John, 1631-1700, tr. II. Clough, Arthur Hugh, 1819-1861, ed.

PLUTARCHUS. 920.038
Lives of the noble Greeks; a selection edited by Edmund Fuller. [New York] [Dell Pub. Co.] [1959] 383 p. 17 cm. (A Laurel classic, LC138) [DE7.P7F8] 60-22730
1. Greece Biography. I. Fuller, Edmund, 1914- ed. II. Title.

PLUTARCHUS 920
Plutarch's "Lives." Selected and edited [by] John S. White. New York, Biblo and Tannen, 1966. xv, 468 p. illus. 24 cm. Reprint of the 1883 ed. published under title: The boys' and girls' Plutarch. Running title: Plutarch's Lives. "Selections from the ... translation called 'Dryden's,' made by many different scholars, corrected and revised ... by Professor Clough." Character studies comparing statesmen and generals of pre-Christian Greece and Rome. [PZ8.1.P746LWh3] AC 67
1. Greece—Biography. 2. Rome—Biography. I. White, John Stuart, 1847-1922, comp. II. Title.

PLUTARCHUS. 920'.038
Plutarch's Lives of the noble Grecians and Romans. Englished by Sir Thomas North, anno 1579. With an introd. by George Wyndham. New York, AMS Press, 1967. 6 v. 23 cm. On spine: North's Plutarch. Includes the lives of Annabal and Scipio African, attributed to Donoto Acciaiolus; translated into French by Charles de La Sluce and into English by Thomas North. Reprint of the 1895-96 translation, which was originally issued as v. 7-12 of the 1st ser. of the Tudor translations. [DE7.P55 1967] 73-154517
1. Greece—Biography. 2. Rome—Biography. I. North, Thomas, Sir, 1535?-1602? tr. II. Acciaiolus, Donatus, 1429-1478. III. Title. IV. Title: North's Plutarch. V. Series: The Tudor translations, 1st ser., v. 7-12.

PLUTARCHUS. 938.00992 B
The rise and fall of Athens : nine Greek lives / by Plutarch ; translated with an introd. by Ian Scott-Kilvert. Harmondsworth, Eng. ; Baltimore : Penguin Books, c1960, 1975 printing. 318 p., [1] leaf of plates : maps ; 18 cm. (Penguin classics) "L102." [DE7.P7S3 1975] 75-332292
1. Greece—Biography. I. Scott-Kilvert, Ian. II. Title.

PLUTARCHUS. 920.03
Ten famous lives. The Dryden translation rev. by Arthur Hugh Clough; further rev. and edited for young readers and with an introd. by Charles Alexander Robinson, Jr. [1st ed.] New York, Dutton [1962] 170 p. illus. 22 cm. [DE7.P7R62] 62-14703
1. Greece—Biography. 2. Rome—Biography. I. Robinson, Charles Alexander, 1900- ed. II. Title.

TOYNBEE, Arnold Joseph, 1889- ed. and tr. 920.038
Twelve men of action in Graeco-Roman history. Boston, Beacon Press [1952] 108 p. 20 cm. [DE7.T6] 52-11114
1. Greece—Biography. 2. Rome—Biography. I. Title. BIP

TOYNBEE, Arnold Joseph, 1889- ed. and tr. 938 B
Twelve men of action in Graeco-Roman history. Translated with an introd. by Arnold J. Toynbee. Freeport, N.Y., Books for Libraries Press [1969, c1952] 108 p. 23 cm. (Essay index reprint series) Contents.Contents.—Themistocles, from Thucydides.—Pericles, from Thucydides.—Cyrus the Younger, from Xenophon.—Five condottieri, from Xenophon.—Cleomenes the last of Sparta, from Plutarch and Polybius.—Cato the Elder, from Plutarch.—Scipio the Younger, from Polybius.—Cato the Younger, from Plutarch. [DE7.T6 1969] 69-17592
1. Greece—Biography. 2. Rome—Biography. I. Title.

Greece, Modern—History—War of Independence, 1821-1829.

HOWE, Samuel Gridley, 1801-1876. 371.9'11'0924 B
Letters and journals of Samuel Gridley Howe. Edited by his daughter, Laura E. Richards. With notes by F. B. Sanborn. Boston, D. Estes, 1909. [New York, AMS Press, 1973] 2 v. illus. 23 cm. Contents.Contents.—[1] The Greek revolution.—[2] The servant of humanity. [HV1624.H7A3 1973] 75-169451 ISBN 0-404-03357-1
1. Greece, Modern—History—War of Independence, 1821-1829. 2. Charities—United States. BIP

MAKRYGIANNES, Ioannes, 1797-1864 355.3320924
The memoirs of General Makriyannis. 1797-1864; ed., tr. [from the Greek] by H. A. Lidderdale; foreword by C. M. Woodhouse. London, Oxford 1966. xxi, 234p. front., 17 plates (incl. ports. maps) 23cm. [DF803.9.M3A313] 66-74119 7.20
1. Greece, Modern—Hist.—War of Independence, 1821-1829. 2. Greece, Modern Hist.—Otho I, 1832-1862. I. Title.
Available from the publisher's New York office.

Greek Indians—History.

TODD, Helen, 1908- 970'.004'97 B
Tomochichi Indian friend of the Georgia Colony / by Helen Todd. Atlanta : Cherokee Pub. Co., 1977. xiii, 182 p. : ill. ; 19 cm. Includes index. Bibliography: p. 167-176. [E99.Y22T657] 77-75268 ISBN 0-87797-040-8 : 7.95
1. Tomo-chi-chi, d. 1739. 2. Yamassee Indians—Biography. 3. Greek Indians—History. 4. Oglethorpe, James Edward, 1696-1785. 5. Georgia—History—Colonial period, ca. 1600-1775. I. Title.

Greeks in Turkey.

THEODORE, Demetrios E. 949.5'06
The sacrificials; part of an autobiography depicting the life of minorities in a war torn country, by D. E. Theodore. Boston, Branden Press [1970] 127 p. illus. 23 cm. Autobiographical. [DR589.T46] 79-93046 ISBN 0-8283-1267-2 5.00
1. Greeks in Turkey. 2. Turkey—History—Revolution, 1918-1923. I. Title.

Greeley, Andrew M., 1928-

KOTRE, John N. 282'.092'4 B
The best of times, the worst of times : Andrew Greeley and America Catholicism, 1950-1975 / John N. Kotre. Chicago : Nelson-Hall Co., [1978] p. cm. "Books by Andrew M. Greeley": p. Includes index. Bibliography: p. [BX4705.G6185K67] 78-14224 ISBN 0-88229-380-X. ISBN 0-88229-597-7 pbk. : 11.95
1. Greeley, Andrew M., 1928- 2. Catholic Church—Clergy—Biography. 3. Catholic Church in the United States—History. 4. Clergy—United States—Biography. I. Title.

Greeley, Horace, 1811-1872.

ARCHER, Jules. 071.4710924 B
Fighting journalist: Horace Greeley. New York, J. Messner [1966] 192 p. 22 cm. Bibliography: p. 185-186. [PN4874.G677A88] 66-7394
1. Greeley, Horace, 1811-1872. I. Title.

GREELEY, Horace, 1811-1872. 070.924 B
Recollections of a busy life. Miami, Fla., Mnemosyne Pub. Co. [1969] 624 p. illus., ports. 23 cm. Reprint of the 1868 ed. [E415.9.G8G83 1969] 74-83912
I. Title. BIP

GREELEY, Horace, 1811-1872. 070'.924 B
Recollections of a busy life. [New York] Arno [1970, c1868] xv, 624 p. illus., facsims., port. 23 cm. (The American journalists) [E415.9.G8G83 1970] 74-125695 ISBN 0-405-01674-3
I. Title.

GREELEY, Horace, 1811-1872. 070'.924 B
Recollections of a busy life. A new ed., with a memoir of Mr. Greeley's later years and death. Port Washington, N.Y., Kennikat Press [1971] 2 v. illus., ports. 22 cm. (Kennikat Press scholarly reprints. Series in American history and culture in the nineteenth century) Reprint of the 1873 ed. [E415.9.G8G83 1971] 77-137913 ISBN 0-8046-1481-4
I. Title.

HALE, William Harlan, 1910- 920.5
Horace Greeley, voice of the people. [1st ed.] New York, Harper [1950] xiii, 377 p. port. 22 cm. Bibliography: p. 355-367. [E415.9.G8H17] 50-9784
1. Greeley, Horace, 1811-1872. I. Title.

INGERSOLL, Lurton Dunham. 071'.47'1 B
The life of Horace Greeley. New York, Beekman Publishers, 1974. 688 p. illus. 23 cm. (American newspapermen, 1790-1933) Reprint of the 1873 ed. published by Union Pub. Co., Chicago. [E415.9.G814 1974] 74-587 ISBN 0-8464-0018-9 25.00
1. Greeley, Horace, 1811-1872.

PARTON, James, 1822-1891. 070'.924 B
The life of Horace Greeley. [New York] Arno [1970] xviii, 442 p. illus., facsim., port. 23 cm. (The American journalists) Reprint of the 1855 ed. [E415.9.G8P233] 70-125711 ISBN 0-405-01692-1
1. Greeley, Horace, 1811-1872. BIP

SEITZ, Don Carlos, 1862-1935. 070.4'0924 B
Horace Greeley; founder of the New York tribune. New York, AMS Press [1970] 433 p. illus., facsims., port. 23 cm. Reprint of the 1926 ed. [E415.9.G8S4 1970] 74-112297
1. Greeley, Horace, 1811-1872.

TRIETSCH, James H 920.5
The printer and the prince; a study of the influence of Horace Greeley upon Abraham Lincoln as candidate and President. [1st ed.] New York, Exposition Press [1955] 332p. 21cm. (Exposition-university book) Includes bibliography. [E415.9.G8T7 1955] 54-13410
1. Greeley, Horace, 1811-1872. 2. Lincoln, Abraham, Pres. U. S. 1809-1865. I. Title.

VAN DEUSEN, Glyndon Garlock 920.5
1897-
Horace Greeley, nineteenth-century crusader. New York, Hill & Wang [1964, c.1953] 444p. illus., ports. 21cm. (Amer. cent. ser., AC72) Bibl. 64-55560 2.45 pap.,
1. Greeley, Horace, 1811-1872. I. Title.

VAN DEUSEN, Glyndon 920.5
Garlock, 1897-
Horace Greeley, nineteenth-century crusader. Philadelphia, University of Pennsylvania Press, 1953. 445p. illus., ports. 23cm. Bibliography: p. [431]--437. [E415.9.G8V3] 53-9554
1. Greeley, Horace, 1811-1872. I. Title.

VAN DEUSEN, Glyndon 920.5
Garlock, 1897-
Horace Greeley, nineteenth-century crusader, by Glyndon G. Van Deusen. New York, Hill and Wang [1964, c1953] 444 p. illus., ports. 21 cm. (American century series, AC72) Bibliography: p. [431]-437. [E415.9.G8V3] 64-55560
1. Greeley, Horace, 1811-1872. I. Title.

ZABRISKIE, Francis 071'.47'1
Nicoll, 1832-1891.
Horace Greeley, the editor. New York, Beekman Publishers, 1974. 398 p. port. 23 cm. (American newspapermen, 1790-1933) Reprint of the 1890 ed. published by Funk & Wagnalls, New York, in series: American reformers. [E415.9.G8Z32 1974] 74-923 ISBN 0-8464-0000-6 18.00
1. Greeley, Horace, 1811-1872. I. Series: American reformers. BIP

Greeley, Horace, 1811-1872—Juvenile literature.

FABER, Doris, 1924- 92
Horace Greeley: the people's editor. Illus. by Paul Frame. Englewood Cliffs, N.J., Prentice [1964] 78p. illus. 22cm. (Jr. res. bk.) 64-10846 2.95; 2.84 bds., lib. ed.,
1. Greeley, Horace, 1811-1872—Juvenile literature. I. Title.

WINDERS, Gertrude (Hecker) 920
Horace Greeley; newspaperman. New York, John Day [c.1962] 153p. illus. 21cm. Bibl. 62-10959 3.25
1. Greeley, Horace, 1811-1872—Juvenile literature. I. Title.

WINDERS, Gertrude (Hecker) j92
Horace Greeley: newspapermen. New York, John Day Co. [1962] 153 p. illus. 21 cm. Includes bibliography. [PN4874.G677W5] 62-10059
1. Greeley, Horace, 1811-1872 — Juvenile literature. I. Title.

WINDERS, Gertrude (Hecker) 92
Horace Greeley: newspaperman. New York, John Day Co. [1962] 153 p. port. 21 cm. Bibliography: p. 149-150. [PN4874.G677W5] 62-10959
1. Greeley, Horace, 1811-1872—Juvenile literature. I. Title.

Greeley, Horace, 1811-1872—Homes—New York (State)—Chappaqua.

GRUBER, Dorothy 070.9'2'4
Whitney.
The Chappaqua life of Horace Greeley : an illustrated history of his farm, his family, and his houses / [prepared for the Chappaqua Historical Society by Dorothy Whitney Gruber]. New Castle, N.Y. : Chappaqua Historical Society, [1974] [27] p. : ill. : 22 cm. Cover title. Bibliography: p. [26] [E415.9.G8G92] 74-191725
1. Greeley, Horace, 1811-1872—Homes—New York (State)—Chappaqua. 2. Chappaqua, N.Y.—Buildings. I. Chappaqua Historical Society, Chappaqua, N.Y. II. Title.

Greeley, William Buckhout, 1879-1955.

MORGAN, George Thomas, 926.3
1931-
William B. Greeley, a practical forester, 1879-1955. St. Paul, Forest History Society, c1961. 82 p. illus. 24 cm. Includes bibliography. [SD129.G7M6] 61-15568
1. Greeley, William Buckhout, 1879-1955.

Greely, Adolphys Washington, 1844-1935—Juvenile literature.

WERSTEIN, Irving 923.973
Man against the elements: Adolphus W. Greely. New York, J. Messner [c.1960] 191p. Bibl.: p.181 22cm. (Julian Messner shelf of Biogrpahies) 60-13264 2.95
1. Greely, Adolphys Washington, 1844-1935—Juvenile literature. I. Title. BIP

Green Bay, Wis. Football Club (National League)

KRAMER, Jerry, 1936- 796.332'0924
Instant replay; the Green Bay diary of Jerry Kramer. Edited by Dick Schaap. Photos. by John and Vernon J. Biever. New York, World Pub. Co. [1968] xvi, 286 p. illus. 22 cm. Cover title: The Green Bay diary of Jerry Kramer. [GV956.G7K7] 68-31469 5.95
1. Green Bay, Wis. Football Club (National League) I. Title. II. Title: The Green Bay diary of Jerry Kramer. BIP

Green, Ben K.

WILSON, Robert A., 636.1'0092'4 B
1912-
Ben K. Green : a descriptive bibliography of writings by and about him / compiled by Robert A. Wilson ; with a foreword by Jenkins Garrett. 1st ed. Flagstaff : Northland Press, c1977. xix, 158 p. : ill. ; 25 cm. Includes index. [SF613.G74W54] 76-52541 ISBN 0-87358-160-1 : 10.50
1. Green, Ben K. 2. Veterinarians—Texas—Biography. 3. Horsemen—Texas—Biography. BIP

Green, David, 1956-

GREEN, Gerald. 813'.5'4 B
My son the jock / Gerald Green. New York : Praeger, 1975. 192 p. ; 22 cm. [PS3513.R4493M9] 74-15677 ISBN 0-275-19820-0 : 6.95
1. Green, David, 1956- 2. Football. I. Title.

Green, George, 1743(ca.)-1808.

WORDSWORTH, Dorothy, 828'.7'07
1771-1855.
George & Sarah Green; a narrative. Edited from the original ms. with a pref. by E. de Selincourt. [Folcroft, Pa.] Folcroft Press [1969] 91 p. 23 cm. Reprint of the 1936 ed. [PR5849.A7 1969] 72-196429
1. Green, George, 1743(ca.)-1808. 2. Green, Sarah, 1763(ca.)-1808. I. Title.

Green, Hetty Howland (Robinson) 1834-1916.

LEWIS, Arthur H. 923.373
The day they shook the plum tree: New York, Bentam [1964, c.1963] 247p. 18cm. (S2761) .75 pap.,
1. Green, Hetty Howland (Robinson) 1834-1916. I. Title. BIP

LEWIS, Arthur H., 1906- 923.373
The day they shook the plum tree [by] Arthur H. Lewis. New York, Pocket Books [1975, c1963] 247 p. 18 cm. [CT275.G755L4] 63-8101 ISBN 0-671-78492-7 1.50 (pbk.)
1. Green, Hetty Howland (Robinson) 1834-1916. I. Title.

Green, Julien, 1900- —Biography.

GREEN, Julien, 1900- 843'.9'12 B
Memories of evil days / Julien Green ; edited, with an introd., by Jean-Pierre J. Piriou. Charlottesville : University Press of Virginia, 1976. xxi, 140 p., [5] leaves of plates : ill. ; 24 cm. Includes index. Bibliography: p. [135]-136. [PQ2613.R3Z498] 75-44037 ISBN 0-8139-0553-2 : 12.50
1. Green, Julien, 1900- —Biography. I. Title. BIP

Green, Paul, 1894-

ADAMS, Agatha Boyd. 928.1
Paul Green of Chapel Hill; edited by Richard Walser. Chapel Hill, University of North Carolina Library, 1951. vil, 116 p. port. 23 cm. (The University of North Carolina. Library extension publication, v. 16, no. 2) [PS3513.R452Z58] 51-62187
1. Green, Paul, 1894- I. Title. II. Series: North Carolina. University. Library. Extension Dept. Library extension publication, v. 16, no. 2

CLARK, Barrett Harper, 812'.5'2
1890-1953.
Paul Green. New York, R. M. McBride, 1928. New York, Haskell House Publishers [1974] p. cm. [PS3513.R452Z6 1974] 74-1164 ISBN 0-8383-2016-3 14.95
1. Green, Paul, 1894- BIP

Green, Robert B., 1865-1907.

GREEN, Mary Rowena 920*.0764*3
(Maverick) 1874-
Robert B. Green: a personal reminiscence [by] Rena Maverick Green. San Antonio, 1962. 1 v. (unpaged) illus., port. 21 cm. Cover title. [C] [CT275.G7613G7] 70-8698
1. Green, Robert B., 1865-1907.

Green, Samuel Swett, 1837-1918.

SHAW, Robert Kendall, 020'.92'4
1871-1956.
Samuel Swett Green. Boston, Gregg Press, 1972 [c1926] 92 p. illus. 23 cm. (The Library reference series. Library history and biography.) Reprint of the ed. published by American Library Association, Chicago, which was issued as no. 2 of American Library pioneers. Bibliography: p. 83-86. [Z720.G8S5 1972] 72-8743 ISBN 0-8398-1885-8 6.25
1. Green, Samuel Swett, 1837-1918. 2. Worcester, Mass. Free Public Library. I. Title. II. Series: Library history and biography. III. Series: American Library pioneers, no. 2.

Green, Ted.

GREEN, Ted. 796.9'62
High stick, by Ted Green, with Al Hirshberg. New York, Dodd, Mead [1971] viii, 211 p. illus. 22 cm. [GV848.5.G7A3] 77-179695 ISBN 0-396-06427-2 5.95
I. Hirshberg, Albert, 1909- II. Title. BIP

Green, Theodore Francis, 1867-1966.

LEVINE, Erwin L. 328.73'0924 B
Theodore Francis Green. Providence, Brown University Press [1963] ix, 222 p. port. 24 cm. (Brown University bicentennial publications: studies in the fields of general scholarship) Bibliography: p. 216-217. [E748.G8L4] 63-18096
1. Green, Theodore Francis, 1867-1966. I. Title.

Green, Thomas Hill, 1836-1882.

CACOULLOS, Ann R. 192 B
Thomas Hill Green: philosopher of rights [by] Ann R. Cacoullos. New York, Twayne Publishers [1974] 189 p. port. 21 cm. (Twayne's world leaders series) Bibliography: p. 184-186. [B1636.C3] 73-21997 ISBN 0-8057-3683-2 8.50 (lib. bdg.)
1. Green, Thomas Hill, 1836-1882.

Green, Thomas, 1814-1864.

FAULK, Odie B 923.973
General Tom Green, fightin' Texan, by Odie Faulk. Introd. by Rupert N. Richardson. Waco, Tex., Texian Press, 1963. ix, 77 p. illus., ports. 23 cm. Bibliography: p. [74]-75. [F390.G788] 67-181
1. Green, Thomas, 1814-1864. 2. Texas — History, Military. I. Title.

Green, William, 1872-

DANISH, Max D., 1895- 923.373
William Green, a pictorial biography. New York, Inter-Allied Publications [1952] 190 p. illus. 26 cm. [HD8073.G7D3] 52-13271
1. Green, William, 1872- I. Title.

Greenaway, Kate, 1846-1901.

HOLME, Bryan, 1913- 741'.092'4 B
The Kate Greenaway book / Bryan Holme. New York : Penguin Books, [1977] p. cm. Includes index. Bibliography: p. [NC978.5.G7H64 1977] 77-6330 ISBN 0-14-004519-8 pbk. : 4.95
1. Greenaway, Kate, 1846-1901. I. Greenaway, Kate, 1846-1901. II. Title.

HOLME, Bryan, 1913- 741.9'42 B
The Kate Greenaway book / Bryan Holme. New York : Viking Press, [1976] p. cm. (A Studio book) Includes index. Bibliography: p. [NC978.5.G7H64] 76-7904 ISBN 0-670-41183-3 : 8.95
1. Greenaway, Kate, 1846-1901. I. Greenaway, Kate, 1846-1901. II. Title.

SPIELMANN, Marion 709'.24 B
Harry, 1858-1948.
Kate Greenaway, by M. H. Spielmann and G. S. Layard. New York, B. Blom [1969] xix, 299 p. illus., facsims., ports. 25 cm. Reprint of the 1905 ed. "List of books, etc., illustrated ... by Kate Greenaway": p. 285-289. [ND1942.G8S7 1969] 68-58917
1. Greenaway, Kate, 1846-1901. I. Layard, George Somes, 1857-1925, joint author. II. Title. BIP

Greenberg, Clement, 1909-

KUSPIT, Donald Burton. 709'.2'4
Clement Greenberg, art critic / Donald B. Kuspit. Madison : University of Wisconsin Press, 1979. p. cm. Bibliography: p. [N7483.G73K87] 79-3967 ISBN 0-299-07900-7 : 15.00
1. Greenberg, Clement, 1909- I. Title. BIP

Greenberg, David, 1943-

GREENBERG, David, 363.2'092'2 B
1943-
Play it to a bust : the super cops / Dave Greenberg. New York : Hawthorn Books, [1975] viii, 247 p. ; 22 cm. [HV7911.A1G7] 74-18685 ISBN 0-8015-5890-5 : 7.95
1. Greenberg, David, 1943- 2. Hantz, Robert. I. Title.

WHITTEMORE, L. H. 363.2'092'2[B]
The super cops; the true story of the cops called Batman and Robin. New York, Bantam Books [1973] 394 p. 18 cm. [HV7911.A1W5 1973] 1.50 (pbk.)
1. Greenberg, David, 2. Hantz, Robert. I. Title.
L.C. card no. for the hardbound edition: 72-96377.

Greenberg, Samuel Bernard, 1893-1917.

SIMON, Marc, 1938- 811'.5'2
Samuel Greenberg, Hart Crane, and the lost manuscripts / by Marc Simon. Atlantic Highlands, N.J. : Humanities Press, 1978. viii, 149 p. ; 22 cm. Includes index. Bibliography: p. 135-143. [PS3513.R4582Z88] 78-6248 ISBN 0-391-00558-8 : 7.50
1. Greenberg, Samuel Bernard, 1893-1917. 2. Crane, Hart, 1899-1932—Criticism and interpretation. 3. Poets, American—20th century—Biography. I. Title. BIP

Greenburg, Dan.

GREENBURG, Dan. 818'.5'409 B
Scoring; a sexual memoir. [1st ed.] Garden City, N.Y., Doubleday, 1972. 223 p. 22 cm. [PS3557.R379Z5] 78-173268 6.95
I. Title.

Greenburger, Ingrid, 1913-

GREENBURGER, 838'.9'1209 B
Ingrid, 1913-
A private treason: a German memoir. [1st ed.] Boston, Little, Brown [1973] 308 p. 21 cm. [PT3919.G7Z52] 73-10046 ISBN 0-316-32666-6 7.95
1. Greenburger, Ingrid, 1913- I. Title.

Greene, A. C., 1923-

GREENE, A. C., 1923- 917.64'8'0360924
A personal country [by] A. C. Greene. Illustrated by Ancel Nunn. [1st ed.] New York, A. Knopf, 1969. 328 p. illus. 22 cm. Autobiographical. [PN4874.G679A3] 69-10674 6.95
I. Title. BIP

GREENE, A. C., 1923- 976.4'06
A personal country / A. C. Greene ; foreword by Larry L. King ; illustrated by Ancel Nunn. [Rev. and updated]. College Station : Texas A&M University Press, 1979. p. cm. [F391.2.G66 1979] 79-7410 ISBN 0-89096-077-1 : 12.95
1. Greene, A. C., 1923- 2. Texas—Description and travel—1951- 3. Texas—Social life and customs. 4. Texas—Biography. I. Title.

Greene, Clarence Wilson,

GREENE, Clarence Wilson, 1873- 923.773
Life at Greene's Corners. Boston, Meador Pub. Co. [1956] 148p. 21cm. [CT275.G768A3] 56-14247
I. Title.

Greene Co., Pa.—Biography.

BATES, Samuel Penniman, 1827-1902. 920'.0748'83
A biographical history of Greene County, Pennsylvania / by Samuel P. Bates. Baltimore : Genealogical Pub. Co., 1975. vii, p. [561]-898 ; 22 cm. Reprint of Biographical sketches, excerpted from the 1888 ed. of the author's History of Greene County, Pennsylvania, published by Nelson, Rishforth & Co., Chicago. [F157.G8B3 1975] 75-7875 ISBN 0-8063-0676-9 : 15.00
1. Greene Co., Pa.—Biography. I. Title. BIP

Greene, Graham, 1904-

DE VITIS, A. A. 828.912
Graham Greene, by A. A. De Vitis. New York, Twayne Publishers [1964] 175 p. 21 cm. (Twayne's English authors series, 3) Bibliography: p. 161-171. [PR6013.R44Z632] 64-19028
1. Greene, Graham, 1904- BIP

GREENE, Graham, 1904- 828'.9'1209 B
A sort of life. New York, Simon and Schuster [1971] 220 p. 22 cm. [PR6013.R44Z52] 77-156146 ISBN 0-671-21010-6 6.95
I. Title. BIP

GREENE, Graham, 1904- 828'.9'1209 B
A sort of life. New York, Simon and Schuster [1971] 220 p. 22 cm. [PR6013.R44Z52] 77-156146 ISBN 0-671-21010-6 6.95
I. Title. BIP

Greene, Joe—Juvenile literature.

BURCHARD, S. H. 796.33'2'0924 B
"Mean" Joe Greene / S. H. Burchard. 1st ed. New York : Harcourt Brace Jovanovich, c1976. 64 p. : ill. ; 22 cm. (Sports star) A biography of "Mean" Joe Greene, a defensive tackle for the Pittsburgh Steelers who is part of their powerful "front four" defense. [GV939.G74B87] 92 76-18130 ISBN 0-15-278009-2 : 4.95 ISBN 0-15-278010-6 pbk. : 1.95
1. Greene, Joe—Juvenile literature. 2. Football—Juvenile literature. I. Title.

Greene, Nathanael, 1742-1786.

ABBAZIA, Patrick. 973.3'3'0924 B
Nathanael Greene, Commander of the American Continental Army in the South / by Patrick Abbazia. Charlotteville, N.Y. : SamHar Press, 1976. p. cm. (Outstanding personalities ; no. 87) Bibliography: p. [E207.G9A57] 76-40920 lib.bdg. : 2.45 pbk. : 1.25
1. Greene, Nathanael, 1742-1786. 2. United States. Army. Continental Army—Biography. 3. Generals—United States—Biography. 4. United States—History—Revolution, 1775-1783. I. Title. BIP

GREENE, Francis Vinton, 1850-1921. 973.33'0924 B
General Greene. New York, D. Appleton, 1893. New York, Research Reprints [1970] 332 p. illus., maps, port. 20 cm. (Great commanders) [E207.G9G7 1970] 70-124801
1. Greene, Nathanael, 1742-1786. I. General Greene.

GREENE, Francis Vinton, 1850-1921. 973.33'0924 B
General Greene. Port Washington, N.Y., Kennikat Press [1970] 332 p. illus., maps, port. 21 cm. (Kennikat American bicentennial series) Reprint of the 1893 ed. [E207.G9G7 1970b] 72-120878 ISBN 8-04-612714-
1. Greene, Nathanael, 1742-1786. I. Title. BIP

GREENE, George Washington, 1811-1883. 973.3'3'0924 B
The life of Nathanael Greene, major-general in the Army of the Revolution. Freeport, N.Y., Books for Libraries Press [1972] 3 v. illus. 22 cm. Reprint of the 1867-71 ed. [E207.G9G74 1972] 72-5507 ISBN 0-8369-6910-3
1. Greene, Nathanael, 1742-1786. I. Title.

JOHNSON, William, 1771-1834. 973.3'3'0924 B
Sketches of the life and correspondence of Nathanael Greene. New York, Da Capo Press, 1973. 2 v. illus. 26 cm. (The Era of the American Revolution) Reprint of the 1st ed., published in 1822. Includes bibliographical references. [E207.G9J5 1973] 78-119063 ISBN 0-306-71953-3 39.50
1. Greene, Nathanael, 1742-1786.

THANE, Elswyth, 1900- 973.3'3'0924 B
The fighting Quaker: Nathanael Greene. New York, Hawthorn Books [1972] xvi, 304 p. illus. 24 cm. Bibliography: p. 289-291. [E207.G9T46 1972] 79-39278 8.95
1. Greene, Nathanael, 1742-1786. I. Title.

THAYER, Theodore George, 1904- 923.573
Nathanael Greene; strategist of the American Revolution. New York, Twayne Publishers, 1960. 500 p. illus. 24 cm. Includes bibliography. [E207.G9T48] 60-8546
1. Greene, Nathanael, 1742-1786. I. Title.

Greene, Nathanael, 1742-1786—Juvenile literature.

BAILEY, Ralph Edgar, 1893- 973.33'0924(B)
Guns over the Carolinas; the story of Nathanael Greene. Maps by James MacDonald. Front by Franz Altschuler. New York, Morrow, 1967. 224p. illus., maps 22cm. Bibl. [E207.G9B3] 67-15147 3.75
1. Greene, Nathanael, 1742-1786—Juvenile literature. I. Title.

Greene, Ruth Altman, 1896

GREENE, Ruth Altman, 1896- 266'.7'60924 B
Hsiang-Ya journal / by Ruth Altman Greene. Hamden, Conn. : Archon Books, 1977. xvi, 171 p. : map (on lining papers) ; 22 cm. Includes index. [R722.32.G73A34] 76-28526 ISBN 0-208-01614-7 : 10.00
1. Greene, Ruth Altman, 1896- 2. Hsiang Ya i hsueh yuan, Ch'ang-sha, China. 3. Missionaries' wives—China—Biography. 4. Missions, Medical—China. I. Title.
Distributed by Shoe String Press BIP

Greene, William Cornell, 1853-1911.

SONNICHSEN, Charles Leland, 1901- 338.7'62'23430924 B
Colonel Greene and the copper skyrocket; the spectacular rise and fall of William Cornell Greene: copper king, cattle baron, and promoter extra-ordinary in Mexico, the American Southwest, and the New York financial district [by] C. L. Sonnichsen. Tucson, University of Arizona Press [1974] x, 325 p. illus. 23 cm. Bibliography: p. 307-315. [HD9539.C7U573] 74-77205 ISBN 0-8165-0429-6 9.50
1. Greene, William Cornell, 1853-1911. 2. Copper industry and trade—United States. I. Title.
Pbk. 4.95, ISBN 0-8165-0465-2.

Greenfeld, Noah Jiro, 1966-

GREENFELD, Josh. 362.7'8'2 B
A place for Noah / Josh Greenfeld. New York : Holt, Rinehart and Winston, c1978. 310 p. ; 24 cm. Continues the author's A child called Noah. [RJ496.B7G73] 77-13354 ISBN 0-03-089896-X : 10.00
1. Greenfeld, Noah Jiro, 1966- 2. Brain-damaged children—Biography. I. Title. BIP

GREENFELD, Josh. 362.7'8'2 [B]
A place for Noah / Josh Greenfeld. New York : Pocket books, 1979,c1978. 295p. ; 18 cm. Continues the author's A child called Noah. [RJ496B7G73] ISBN 0-671-82650-6 pbk. : 2.25
1. Greenfeld Noah Jiro, 1966- 2. Brain damaged children — Biography. I. Title.
L.C. card no. for 1978 Holt,Rinehart and Winston ed.:77-13354.

Greenhill. David, 1876-1947.

LEECH, Miriam (Greenhill) 1908- 926.55
David Greehill, master printer by his daughter Miriam Leech, in collaboration with Charles F. Cook [Watford? Herts.] Published privately [1951] xiv, 137p. illus., ports. (part col.) 25cm. [Z232.G825L4] 53-16428
1. Greenhill. David, 1876 1947. I. Title.

Greenhow, Rose (O'Neal) 1814-1864

FABER, Doris, 1924- 92 (J)
Rose Greenhow, spy for the Confederacy. New York, Putnam [1968, c1967] 128 p. illus. 21 cm. (Spies of the world) Bibliography: p. 124-125. [E608.G83F3] 68-11362
1. Greenhow, Rose (O'Neal) 1814-1864—Juvenile literature.

FABER, Doris, 1924- 973.78'6'0924 B
Rose Greenhow, spy for the Confederacy. New York, Putnam [1968, c1967] 128 p. illus. 21 cm. (Spies of the world) Bibliography: p. 124-125. A biography of the southern woman who, as a leading figure in Washington society during the Civil War, was able to conduct a valuable spy ring for the Confederates and to harass Union leaders even after her arrest. [E608.G83F3] 92 AC 68
1. Greenhow, Rose (O'Neal) 1814-1864. I. Title.

GRANT, Dorothy (Fremont) 1900- 920
Rose Greenhow, Confederate secret agent. Illus. by Douglas Grant. New York, Kenedy [c.19614 188p. (Amer. background bks.) 61-15565 2.50
1. Greenhow, Rose (O'Neal) 1814-1861—Juvenile literature. I. Title.

ROSS, Ishbel, 1897- 920.7
Rebel Rose; life of Rose O'Neal Greenhow, Confederate spy. [1st ed.] New York, Harper [1954] 294p. illus. 22cm. Includes bibliography. [E608.G83R6] 54-8986
1. Greenhow, Rose (O'Neal) d. 1864. I. Title.

Greenland—Description and travel.

FREUCHEN, Peter, 1886-1957. 998'.2 B
Arctic adventure : my life in the frozen North / by Peter Freuchen. New York : AMS Press, 1976. xi, 467 p. : ill. ; 23 cm. Reprint of the 1935 ed. published by Farrar & Rinehart, New York. [G743.F7 1976] 74-5833 ISBN 0-404-11638-8 : 32.50
1. Greenland—Description and travel. 2. Arctic regions. 3. Eskimos. I. Title.

Greenlaw, Georgia (Faye) 1883-1949.

GREENLAW, Lowell Mason. 920.7
Georgia Eaye; story of an American family. [1st ed.] New York, Exposition Press [1954] 614p. illus. 21cm. [CT275.G7733G7] 54-8266
1. Greenlaw, Georgia (Faye) 1883-1949. I. Title.

Greenman, Frances Cranmer.

GREENMAN, Frances Cranmer. 927.5
Higher than the sky. Illustrated by the author. [1st ed.] New York, Harper [1954] 305 p. illus. 22 cm. Autobiography. [ND237.G62A2] 54-8953
I. Title.

Greenman, Jeremiah, 1758-1828.

GREENMAN, Jeremiah, 1758-1828. 973.3'3'0924 B
Diary of a common soldier in the American Revolution, 1775-1783 : an annotated edition of the military journal of Jeremiah Greenman / edited by Robert C. Bray & Paul E. Bushnell. DeKalb : Northern Illinois University Press, 1978. xliv, 333 p., [2] leaves of plates : ill. ; 24 cm. Includes index. Bibliography: p. 309-320. [E275.G78 1977] [.G78 19789] 77-18528 17.50
1. Greenman, Jeremiah, 1758-1828. 2. United States. Army. Continental Army—Biography. 3. United States—History—Revolution, 1775-1783—Personal narratives. 4. Soldiers—United States—Biography. 5. United States—History—Revolution, 1775-1783—Campaigns and battles. I. Bray, Robert C. II. Bushnell, Paul E. III. Title.

Greenough, Henry, 1807-1883.

GREENOUGH, Horatio, 1805-1852. 730'.924 B
Letters of Horatio Greenough. Edited by Frances B. Greenough. New York, Kennedy Graphics, 1970. 250 p. facsim., port. 22 cm. (Library of American art) Reprint of the 1887 ed. Includes letters to Henry Greenough. [NB237.G8G8 1970] 70-96437
1. Greenough, Henry, 1807-1883. I. Greenough, Frances Boott, ed. BIP

GREENOUGH, Horatio, 1805-1852. 730'.92'4 B
Letters of Horatio Greenough to his brother, Henry Greenough. With biographical sketches and some contemporary correspondence. Edited by Frances Boott Greenough. Boston, Ticknor, 1887. [New York, AMS Press, 1973] 250 p. port. 19 cm. [NB237.G8A35 1973] 78-168199 ISBN 0-404-02897-7 8.00
1. Greenough, Henry, 1807-1883. I. Title.

Greenough, Horatio, 1805-1852.

CRANE, Sylvia E. 730'.973
White silence; Greenough, Powers, and Crawford, American sculptors in nineteenth-century Italy [by] Sylvia E. Crane. Coral Gables [Fla.] University of Miami Press [1972] xviii, 499 p. illus. 27 cm. Bibliography: p. [459]-489. [NB236.C72] 79-156141 ISBN 0-87024-199-0 9.95
1. Greenough, Horatio, 1805-1852. 2. Powers, Hiram, 1805-1873. 3. Crawford, Thomas, 1813-1857. I. Title.

GREENOUGH, Horatio, 1805-1852. 730'.92'4
Letters of Horatio Greenough, American sculptor. Edited by Nathalia Wright. [Madison] University of Wisconsin Press [1972] xxix, 456 p. 24 cm. Includes bibliographical references. [NB237.G8W72] 77-176417 ISBN 0-299-06070-5 22.50
I. Title. BIP

WRIGHT, Nathalia. 927.3
Horatio Greenough, the first American

sculptor. Philadelphia, University of Pennsylvania Press [1963] 382 p. illus., ports. 22 cm. Bibliographical references included in "Notes" (p. 307-358) [NB237.G8W7] 62-11261
1. Greenough, Horatio, 1805-1852. I. Title. BIP

WRIGHT, Nathalia 927.3
Horation Greenough, the first American sculptor. Philadelphia, Univ. of Pa. Pr. [c.1963] 382p. illus., ports. 22cm. Bibl. 62-11261 8.50
1. Greenough, Horatio, 1805-1852. I. Title.

Greenspun Herman Milton.

GREENSPUN, Herman Milton. 070.924 1909-
Where I stand; the record of a reckless man. by Hank Greenspun with Alex Pelle. New York, McKay [1966] xv. 304p. 21cm. Autobiographical. [PN4874.G69A3] 66-24423 5.50
I. Pelle, Alex, joint author. II. Title.

Greenstein, Harry.

KAPLAN, Louis L. 360'.924 B
Justice, not charity; a biography of Harry Greenstein, by Louis L. Kaplan and Theodor Schuchat, with a foreword by Herbert H. Lehman. New York, Crown [1967] xiii, 176 p. illus., ports. 22 cm. Bibliographical references included in "Notes on sources" (p. 153-155) [HV28.G75K3] 66-26200
1. Greenstein, Harry. I. Schuchat, Theodor, joint author. II. Title.

Greenstein, Joseph L.

SPIELMAN, Ed. 791.3'5'0924 B
The Mighty Atom : the life and times of Joseph L. Greenstein / Ed Spielman. New York : Viking Press, 1979. xv, 236 p., [1] leaf of plates : ill. ; 25 cm. [CT9997.G73S65] 79-12911 ISBN 0-670-47564-5 : 10.95
1. Greenstein, Joseph L. 2. Strong men—United States—Biography. I. Title. BIP

Greenway, Francis Howard, 1777-1837.

ELLIS, Malcolm Henry 720'.924
Francis Greenway, his life and times, by M. H. Ellis. [2nd ed. Sydney] Angus & Robertson; San Francisco, Tri-Ocean [1966] xxv, 231p. illus., diagrs., port. 23cm. Bibl. [NB1105.G7E55 1966] 67-77527 6.95
1. Greenway, Francis Howard, 1777-1837. I. Title.

Greenwich Village, New York (City)

HUMPHREY, Robert E. 974.7'1
Children of fantasy : the first rebels of Greenwich Village / Robert E. Humphrey. New York : Wiley, c1978. ix, 267 p. : ill. ; 24 cm. "A Ronald Press publication." Includes index. Bibliography: p. 256-263. [HN80.N5H85] 77-28242 ISBN 0-471-42100-6 : 15.00
1. Greenwich Village, New York (City) 2. Bohemianism—New York (City)—Greenwich Village. 3. Intellectuals—New York (City)—Greenwich Village—Biography. I. Title. BIP

Greenwich Village, New York (City)—Social life and customs.

MANLEY, Seon. 917.471
My heart's in Greenwich Village. New York, Funk & Wagnalls [1969] 221 p. 22 cm. Reminiscenes of life in Greenwich Village in the early forties when the author and her sister shared an apartment and many experiences. [F128.68.G8M25] 75-80704 4.95
1. Greenwich Village, New York (City)—Social life and customs. I. Title.

Greenwood, Harold W.

LEIPOLD, L. Edmond, 332'.0924 B 1902-
Harold W. Greenwood, Jr., financier, by L. E. Leipold. Minneapolis, T. S. Denison [1970] 205 p. illus., ports. 23 cm. (Men of achievement series) A biography of the Minneapolis financier and businessman. [HG172.G7L43] 92 71-114810
1. Greenwood, Harold W.

Greenwood, Marianne.

GREENWOOD, Marianne. 839.7874
The tattoed heart of Livingston. New York, Stein and Day [1965] 187 p. illus., ports. 25 cm. Autobiographical. Translation of Det tatuerade hjartat. [CT1328.G7A33] 65-14400
I. Title.

Greer, Howard.

GREER, Howard. 926.46
Designing male. New York, Putnam [1951] 310 p. illus. 22 cm. Autobiographical. [TT505.G7A3] 51-66411
I. Title.

Gregg, John Robert, 1867-1948.

SYMONDS, Francis Addington, 926.5 1893-
John Robert Gregg, the man and his work. Foreword by Paul S. Lomax. New York, Gregg-McGraw [c.1963] 72p. illus. 22cm. 63-9826 3.00
1. Gregg, John Robert, 1867-1948. I. Title.

SYMONDS, Francis Addington, 926.5 1893-
John Robert Gregg, the man and his work. With a foreword by Paul S. Lomax. New York, Gregg Pub. Division [1963] 72 p. illus. 22 cm. 63-9826
1. Gregg, John Robert, 1867-1948. I. Title.

Gregg, Troy.

DAVIS, 364.1'523'0924 B Christopher, 1928-
Waiting for it / by Christopher Davis. 1st ed. New York : Harper & Row, c1980. p. cm. [HV6248.G725D38 1980] 79-2617 ISBN 0-06-010973-4 : 9.95
1. Gregg, Troy. 2. Crime and criminals—United States—Biography. 3. Capital punishment—United States. I. Title.

Gregorie, Anne King.

SURLES, Flora 975.7'0072'024 B Belle, 1887-
Anne King Gregorie. Columbia, S. C., Printed for the author by R. L. Bryan Co., 1968. xii, 218 p. illus., ports. 24 cm. "An edition of 500 copies." Bibliographical footnotes. [CT275.G7744S8] 68-59318
1. Gregorie, Anne King.

Gregorius I, the Great, Saint, Pope, 540 (ca.)-604.

DUDDEN, Frederick 262'.13'0924 Homes, 1874-1955.
Gregory the Great, his place in history and thought, by F. Homes Dudden. New York, Russell & Russell [1967] 2 v. port. 22 cm. Reprint of the 1905 ed. Authorities cited in "Preface" (v. 1, p. viii-xv) [BX1076.D8 1967] 66-24687
1. Gregorius I, the Great, Saint, Pope, 540 (ca)-604. I. Title.

THE Earliest life 262'.13'0924 B *of Gregory the Great,* by an anonymous monk of Whitby. Text, translation & notes by Bertram Colgrave. Lawrence, University of Kansas Press, 1968. ix, 180 p. 22 cm. Cover title: Gregory the Great. Latin text and English translation on opposite pages. The text is based on the only surviving copy of the original MS. which is part of Codex 567 of the Stiftsbibliothek of St. Gall, Switzerland. Bibliography: p. [166]-167. [BX1076.E2] 67-24360
1. Gregorius I, the Great, Saint, Pope, 540 (ca.)-604. I. An anonymous monk of Whitby. II. Colgrave, Bertram. III. St. Gall, Switzerland. Stiftsbibliothek. MSS. (567)

JONES, Charles 270.2'0922 Williams, 1905-
Saints' lives and chronicles in early England. Together with first English translations of The oldest life of Pope St. Gregory the Great by a monk of Whitby and The life of St. Guthlac of Crowland by Felix. By Charles W. Jones. [Hamden, Conn.] Archon Books, 1968 [c1947] xiii, 232 p. facsims. 23 cm. The translation of the life of Gregory the Great is from Cardinal Gasquet's transcription of the original MS. which is part of Codex 567 of the Stiftsbibliothek of St. Gall, Switzerland. Bibliographical references included in "Notes" (p. [200]-220) [BX4662.J6 1968] 68-26934
1. Gregorius I, the Great, Saint, Pope, 540 (ca.)-604. 2. Guthlac, Saint, 673?-714. 3. Hagiography. I. Felix, 8th cent. Vita Sancti Guthlaci. English. 1968. II. The Oldest life of Pope St. Gregory the Great. Vita Sancti Gregorii I Popae. English. 1968. III. Title.

Gregorius I, the Great Saint, Pope, 540 (ca.)-604—Juvenile literature.

SANDERLIN, George William, 922.21 1915-
St. Gregory the Great, consul of God. Illus. by Christopher Curtis. New York, Farrar [c.1964] xii, 180p. illus. 22cm. (Vision bk., 61) 64-11633 2.25
1. Gregorius I, the Great Saint, Pope, 540 (ca.)-604—Juvenile literature. I. Title.

Gregorius Nazianzenus, Saint, Patriarch of Constantinople.

BENOIT, Alphonse. 281'.4'0924 B
Saint Gregoire de Nazianze; sa vie, ses ouvres et son epoque. Hildesheim, New York, G. Olms, 1973. vi, 788 p. port. 20 cm. "Nachdruck der Ausgabe Marseille und Paris 1876." Includes bibliographical references. [BR1720.G7B46 1973] 73-168647 ISBN 3-487-04695-4
1. Gregorius Nazianzenus, Saint, Patriarch of Constaninople. I. Title.

RUETHER, Rosemary Radford. 189'.2
Gregory of Nazianzus, rhetor and philosopher. Oxford, Clarendon P., 1969. viii, 184 p. 23 cm. Bibliography: p. 181-182. [BR1720.G7R8] 70-399576 40/-
1. Gregorius Nazianzenus, Saint, Patriarch of Constantinople. I. Title.

Gregorius VII, Saint, Pope, 1015 (ca.)-1085.

MACDONALD, Allan 262'.13'0924 B John Macdonald, 1887-
Hildebrand : a life of Gregory VII / by A. J. Macdonald. Merrick, N.Y. : Richwood Pub. Co., 1976. ix, 254 p. ; 23 cm. Reprint of the 1932 ed. published by Methuen, London, in series: Great medieval churchmen. Includes bibliographical references and index. [BX1187.M25 1976] 76-30354 ISBN 0-915172-26-7 : 15.00
1. Gregorius VII, Saint, Pope, 1015 (ca.)-1085. 2. Popes—Biography. I. Title. II. Series: Great medieval churchmen.

Gregory Co., S.D.—History.

GNIRK, Adeline S., 978.3'59 B 1914-
The saga of the Sully Flats : comprising Lucas, Scissons, Turney, Turgeon and parts of Burke, Rhoades, Huston, and Landing Creek Townships in Gregory County, South Dakota / compiled and written by Adeline S. Gnirk. Gregory, S.D. : Gregory times-advocate, 1976. 356 p. : ill. ; 28 cm. Includes index. [F657.G8G59] 77-151396
1. Gregory Co., S.D.—History. 2. Gregory Co., S.D.—Biography. I. Title.

Gregory, Cynthia.

PERES, Louis. 792.8'092'4
Cynthia Gregory / [photos. and text by Louis Peres]. [Brooklyn, N.Y. : Dance Horizons, 1975] 23 p. : ill. ; 23 cm. (Dance Horizons spotlight series) [GV1785.G713P47] 75-321038
1. Gregory, Cynthia. 2. Ballet.

Gregory, Dick.

GREGORY, Dick 927.92
Nigger, an autobiography, by Dick Gregory with Robert Lipsyte. New York, Pocket Bks. [1965, c.1964] 209p. illus. 18cm. (75091) .75 pap.,
1. Negroes—Civil rights. I. Title.

GREGORY, Dick. 818'.5'409 B
Up from Nigger / by Dick Gregory. New York : Stein and Day, [1975] p. cm. [PN2287.G68A37] 75-12817 ISBN 0-8128-1832-6 : 8.95
1. Gregory, Dick. 2. Negroes—Civil rights. I. Title. BIP

Gregory, Horace,

GREGORY, Horace, 1898- 811'.5'2
The house on Jefferson Street; a cycle of memories. [1st ed.] New York, Holt, Rinehart and Winston [1971] 276 p. port. 22 cm. [PS3513.R558Z5] 68-12208 ISBN 0-03-068485-4 6.95
I. Title.

Gregory, Isabella Augusta Persse, Lady, 1852-1932.

COXHEAD, Elizabeth [Eileen 928.2 Elizabeth Coxhead] 1909-
Lady Gregory, a literary portrait. New York, Harcourt [c.1961] 241p. illus. 61-13965 5.95
1. Gregory, Isabella Augusta (Persse) Lady, 1852-1932. I. Title. BIP

GREGORY, Isabella 822'.9'12 B Augusta (Persse), Lady, 1852-1932.
Coole. Completed from the manuscript and edited by Colin Smythe, with a foreword by Edward Malins. [Dublin, Dolmen Press, 1972] 105 p. plan (on lining papers) 29 cm. (Dolmen editions, 10) Label on t.p.: Distributed in the U.S.A. by Humanities Press, New York. Original ed. published in 1931 contained chapters 3, 4, and 5 of this text. Includes bibliographical references. [PR4728.G5C65 1971b] 72-189307 ISBN 0-85105-189-8 13.50
I. Title. BIP

KOPPER, Edward A. 822'.9'12 B
Lady Isabella Persse Gregory / by Edward A. Kopper, Jr. Boston : Twayne Publishers, c1976. p. cm. (Twayne's English authors series ; TEAS 194) Includes index. Bibliography: p. [PR4728.G5Z63] 76-24845 ISBN 0-8057-6658-8 lib.bdg. : 8.95
1. Gregory, Isabella Augusta Persse, Lady, 1852-1932. BIP

Gregory, Isabella Augusta Persse, Lady, 1852-1932—Biography.

GREGORY, Isabella 822'.9'12 B Augusta Persse, Lady, 1852-1932.
Seventy years : being the autobiography of Lady Gregory / edited and with a foreword by Colin Smythe. 1st American ed. New York : Macmillan, 1976 [i.e., 1975], c1974 p. cm. Includes index. [PR4728.G5Z534 1976] 75-23329 ISBN 0-02-545550-8 : 10.00
1. Gregory, Isabella Augusta Persse, Lady, 1852-1932—Biography. I. Title.

LADY Gregory : 822'.9'12 B interviews and recollections / [edited by] E. H. Mikhail. Totowa, N.J. : Rowman and Littlefield, 1977. p. cm. Includes index. [PR4728.G5Z64] 77-1322 ISBN 0-87471-961-5 : 12.50
1. Gregory, Isabella Augusta Persse, Lady, 1852-1932—Biography. 2. Authors, Irish—19th century—Biography. I. Mikhail, E. H. BIP

Gregory, Isabella Augusta Persse, Lady, 1852-1932—Diaries.

GREGORY, Isabella 822'.9'12 B Augusta Persse, Lady, 1852-1932.
Lady Gregory's journals / edited by Daniel J. Murphy. New York : Oxford University Press, 1978- v. : ill. ; 23 cm. Contents.Contents.—v. 1. Book one to twenty-nine, 10 October 1916-24 February 1925. Includes bibliographical references and index. [PR4728.G5Z53 1978] 78-3869 ISBN 0-19-519886-7 (v. 1) : 40.00
1. Gregory, Isabella Augusta Persse, Lady, 1852-1932—Diaries. 2. Authors, Irish—20th century—Biography. I. Murphy, Daniel Joseph, 1921- II. Title.

Gregory, John Milton, 1822-1898.

KERSEY, Harry A., 378.773'66 B
1935-
John Milton Gregory and the University of Illinois, by Harry A. Kersey, Jr. Urbana, University of Illinois Press, 1968. ix, 252 p. port. 23 cm. Bibliography: p. 230-238. [LD2369.K4] 67-21854
1. Gregory, John Milton, 1822-1898. 2. Illinois. University—History. I. Title. **BIP**

Gregory, Maundy, 1877-1941.

CULLEN, Tom A. 364.1'32 B
A playful panther : the story of J. Maundy Gregory, con-man / Tom Cullen ; illustrated with photos. 1st American ed. Boston : Houghton Mifflin, 1975, c1974. 255 p., [4] leaves of plates : ill. ; 22 cm. First published in 1974 under title: Maundy Gregory, purveyor of honours. Includes index. Bibliography: p. 249-250. [HV6248.G73C85 1975] 75-302492 ISBN 0-395-19410-5 : 6.95
1. Gregory, Maundy, 1877-1941. I. Title.

Gregory, Sir Richard Arman, bart., 1864-1952.

ARMYTAGE W. H. G. 925
Sir Richard Gregory, his life and work. London, Macmillan; New York, St. Martin's Press, 1957. 240p. illus. 23cm. [Q143.G84A7] 57-4009
1. Gregory, Sir Richard Arman, bart., 1864-1952. I. Title.

Grellet, Stephen, 1773-1855.

DALGLISH, Doris N. 289.6'0922
People called Quakers, by Doris N. Dalglish. Freeport, N.Y., Books for Libraries Press [1969] 169 p. 23 cm. (Essay index reprint series) Reprint of the 1938 ed. Contents.Contents.—The first Quaker poet.—An American saint.—A digression on women and the eighteenth century.—A neighbour of Wordsworth.—A friend from France.—Convert and critic. [BX7791.D3 1969] 78-90628
1. Story, Thomas, 1662-1742. 2. Woolman, John, 1720-1772. 3. Wilkinson, Thomas, 1751-1836. 4. Grellet, Stephen, 1773-1855. 5. Stephen, Caroline Emelia, 1834-1909. 6. Friends, Society of—Biography. I. Title.

GARRETT, Alfred Cope, 289.6'0924
1867-1946.
A short life of Stephen Grellet (1773-1855) [Pocket ed.] Philadelphia, Friends' Book Store [19--] 128 p. port. 17 cm. "Reprinted from vol. iv of Quaker biographies." [BX7795.G7G3] 51-31299
1. Grellet, Stephen, 1773-1855. I. Title.

Grenfell, George St. Leger, 1808-1868.

STARR, Stephen Z. 973.7'0924
Colonel Grenfell's wars; the life of a soldier of fortune [by] Stephen Z. Starr. Baton Rouge, Louisiana State University Press [1971] vii, 352 p. front. 24cm. Bibliography: p. 333-340. [E458.8.S8] 71-142339 ISBN 0-8071-0921-5 10.95
1. Grenfell, George St. Leger, 1808-1868. 2. Northwestern Conspiracy, 1864. I. Title. **BIP**

Grenfell, Joyce, 1910-

GRENFELL, Joyce, 791'.092'4 B
1910-
Joyce Grenfell requests the pleasure. London : Macmillan, 1976. 295 p. : ill., ports. ; 25 cm. Facsims. on lining papers. Includes index. [PN2598.G674A34] 77-351310 ISBN 0-333-19428-4 : £4.95
1. Grenfell, Joyce, 1910- 2. Entertainers—Great Britain—Biography. I. Title.

GRENFELL, Joyce, 791'.092'4 B
1910-
Joyce Grenfell requests the pleasure / by Joyce Grenfell. New York : St. Martin's Press, [1977] p. cm. Includes index. [PN2598.G674A34 1977] 77-76636 ISBN 0-312-44528-8 : 10.95
1. Grenfell, Joyce, 1910- 2. Entertainers—Great Britain—Biography. I. Title.

Grenfell, Julian Henry Francis, 1888-1915.

MOSLEY, Nicholas, 941.082'092'4 B
1923-
Julian Grenfell, his life and the times of his death, 1888-1915 / by Nicholas Mosley. New York : Holt, Rinehart and Winston, c1976. p. cm. [DA574.G8M6 1976] 76-4720 ISBN 0-03-017596-8 : 12.95
1. Grenfell, Julian Henry Francis, 1888-1915.

MOSLEY, Nicholas, 941.082'092'4 B
1923-
Julian Grenfell, his life and the times of his death 1888-1915 / Nicholas Mosley. London : Weidenfeld and Nicolson, c1976. x, 275 p., [9] leaves of plates : ill. ; 24 cm. Includes index. [DA574.G8M6 1976b] 76-366587 ISBN 0-297-77093-4 : £6.50
1. Grenfell, Julian Henry Francis, 1888-1915.

Grenfell, Wilfred Thomason, Sir, 1865-1940.

KERR, James Lennox, 1899- 926.1
Wilfred Grenfell, his life and work. With sketches reproduced from letters of Dr. Grenfell. New York, Dodd, Mead, 1959. 270 p. illus. 22 cm. Includes bibliography. [F1137.G7K4] 59-13340
1. Grenfell, Wilfred Thomason, Sir, 1865-1940. **BIP**

KERR, James Lennox, 266'.025'0924
1899-
Wilfred Grenfell, his life and work / by J. Lennox Kerr ; with a foreword by Lord Grenfell of Kilvey. Westport, Conn. : Greenwood Press, 1977, c1959. 272 p. : ill. ; 23 cm. Reprint of the ed. published by Harrap, London. Includes index. Bibliography: p. [261]-262. [R722.32.G75K47 1977] 73-21177 ISBN 0-8371-6068-5 lib.bdg. : 18.75
1. Grenfell, Wilfred Thomason, Sir, 1865-1940. 2. Missionaries, Medical—Newfoundland—Biography. 3. Newfoundland—Description and travel. 4. Labrador—Description and travel. I. Title.

MILLER, Basil William, 926.1
1897-
Wilfred Grenfell, Labrador's dogsled doctor. Grand Rapids, Mich., Zondervan [1965, c.1948] 120p. i0cm. [F1136.G88] 48-8078 1.00 pap.,
1. Grenfell, Sir Wilfred Thomason, 1865-1940. I. Title.

Grenfell, Wilfred Thomason, Sir 1865-1940—Juvenile literature.

BLACKBURN, Joyce 92
Wilfred Grenfell: doctor, explorer. Illus. by David Cunningham. Grand Rapids, Mich., Zondervan [c.1966] 152p. illus., port. 23cm. (People you should know) [F1137.G7B5] 65-25956 2.95 bds.,
1. Grenfell, Wilfred Thomason, Sir 1865-1940—Juvenile literature. I. Title.

PUMPHREY, George H. 926.1
Grenfell of Labrador. New York, Dodd, Mead.1959 [c.1958] 171 p. illus. 21 cm. [F1137.G7P8] 60-12047
1. Grenfell, Wilfred Thomason, sir, 1865-1940—Juvenile literature. Grenfell Wilfred Thomason 1865 1940 Juvenile literature

Gresham, Thomas, Sir, 1519?-1579.

BURGON, John William, 1813- v. 12
1888.
The life and times of Sir Thomas Gresham, Knt., founder of the Royal Exchange; including notices of many of his contemporaries. With illus. [2d. ed.] New York, B. Franklin [1964] 2 v. illus. 23 cm. (Research and source work series no. 123) Originally published in 1839. 68-74422
1. Gresham, Sir Thomas, 1519?-1579 2. Finance, Public—Gt. Brit.—Hist. 3. London. Royal Exchange. I. Title.

BURGON, John 336.41*092*4
William, 1813-1888.
The life and times of Sir Thomas Gresham, knt., founder of the Royal Exchange; including notices of many of his contemporaries. New York, B. Franklin [1965] 2 v. illus. 24 cm. (Burt Franklin research and source work series #123) First published 1839. Includes bibliographical references. [HJ1003.G7B8 1965] 72-184036
1. Gresham, Thomas, Sir, 1519?-1579. 2. London. Royal Exchange. 3. Finance, Public—Great Britain—To 1688.

THE lives of the 378.101'1
professors of Gresham college: to which is prefixed the life of the founder, Sir Thomas Gresham by John Ward. London, Printed by J. Moore for the author, 1740; New York, Johnson Reprint, 1967. 2p. 1., xxiv, 338, [2], 156p. 4p1., port. 29cm (Sources of sci., no. 71) Facsimile: reprint of the London ed. of 1740, with orig. t.p. [LF795.G84A2] (B) 20.00
1. Gresham, Sir Thomas, 1519?-1579. 2. Gresham college. London. I. Ward, John, 1679?-1758

Gresham, Walter Quintin, 1832-1895.

GRESHAM, Matilda 973.8'0924 B
(McGrain) b.1839.
Life of Walter Quintin Gresham, 1832-1895. Freeport, N.Y., Books for Libraries Press [1970] 2 v. (xxxiii, 875 p.) ports. 23 cm. Reprint of the 1919 ed. [E664.G82G8 1970] 70-137378
1. Gresham, Walter Quintin, 1832-1895. **BIP**

Gresley, Herbert Nigel, Sir, 1876-1941.

BELLWOOD, John. 625.2'61'0922
Gresley and Stanier : a centenary tribute / [by] John Bellwood and David Jenkinson. London : H.M.S.O. [for the] National Railway Museum, York, 1976. ii-vii, 100 p. : ill., ports. ; 28 cm. Bibliography: p. 99. [TJ603.49.B44] 77-356305 ISBN 0-11-290253-7 : £3.00
1. Gresley, Herbert Nigel, Sir, 1876-1941. 2. Stanier, William Arthur, Sir, 1876- 3. Locomotive engineers—Great Britain—Biography. I. Jenkinson, D., joint author. II. Title.

Grew, Joseph Clark, 1880-1965.

HEINRICHS, Waldo H. 327.20924 B
American ambassador; Joseph C. Grew and the development of the United States diplomatic tradition, by Waldo H. Heinrichs, Jr. [1st ed.] Boston, Little, Brown [1966] xii, 460 p. ports. 24 cm. Bibliography: p. 441-446. [E748.G835H4] 66-21993
1. Grew, Joseph Clark, 1880-1965. 2. United States—Foreign relations—20th century. 3. United States—Foreign relations—Japan. 4. Japan—Foreign relations—United States. 5. United States—Diplomatic and consular service. I. Title.

Grey, Beryl, 1927-

ANTHONY, Gordon. 927.933
Beryl Grey. with an introd. by Arnold L. Haskell. London, Phoenix House [1952] 95p. illus. 25cm. [GV1785.G72A55] 53-18576
1. Grey, Beryl, 1927- I. Title.

Grey Owl, 1888-1938.

DICKSON, Lovat, 1902- 970.3 B
Wilderness man; the strange story of Grey Owl. [1st American ed.] New York, Atheneum, 1973. 283 p. illus. 24 cm. Bibliography: p. 273-274. [E90.G75D52 1973] 73-81707 ISBN 0-689-10580-0 10.00
1. Grey Owl, 1888-1938. I. Title.

Grey, Zane, 1872-1939.

GRUBER, Frank. 813'.5'2 B3
Zane Grey : a biography / by Frank Gruber. New York : Belmont Tower Books, 1978. 286p. 18 cm. Includes index. [PS3513.R6545Z65] pbk
1. Grey, Zane, 1872-1939 I. Title.
L.C. card no. for 1970 World Pub. Co ed.: 75-75879

GRUBER, Frank, 1904- 813'.5'2 B
1969.
Zane Grey; a biography. New York, World Pub. Co. [1970] xi, 284 p. illus., ports. 22 cm. Bibliography: p. [255]-273. [PS3513.R6545Z65 1970] 75-75879 6.95
1. Grey, Zane, 1872-1939.

RONALD, Ann, 1939- 813'.5'2 B
Zane Grey / by Ann Ronald. Boise, Idaho : Boise State University, 1976c1975 46 p. ; 21 cm. (Boise State University Western writers series ; no 17) Bibliography. p. 43-46. [PS3513.R6545Z85] 75-7010 ISBN 0-88430-016-1 pbk. : 1.50
1. Grey, Zane, 1872-1939. 2. Novelists, American—20th century—Biography. I. Series: Boise State University. Boise State University Western writers series ; no. 17. **BIP**

Grieg, Edvard Hagerup, 1843-1907.

ACKER, Helen. 920.0481
Four sons of Norway. Illustrated by Nils Hogner. Freeport, N.Y., Books for Libraries Press [1970, c1948] 255 p. illus., ports. 23 cm. (Biography index reprint series) Contents.Contents.—The story of Ole Bull (1810-1880)—The story of Henrik Ibsen (1828-1906)—The story of Edvard Grieg (1843-1907)—The story of Fridtjof Nansen (1861-1930)—Bibliography (p. [256]) [DL504.A2A2] 72-117318
1. Bull, Ole Bornemann, 1810-1880. 2. Grieg, Edvard Hagerup, 1843-1907. 3. Ibsen, Henrik, 1828-1906. 4. Nansen, Fridtjof, 1861-1930. I. Title. **BIP**

FINCK, Henry 780'.924 B
Theophilus, 1854-1926.
Grieg and his music New York, D. Blom, 1971. xxxv, 317 p. illus. 22 cm. Reprint of the 1910 ed. (London) Bibliography: p. 304-307. [ML410.G9F44 1971] 79-173165
1. Grieg, Edvard Hagerup, 1843-1907. I. Title.

Grieg, Edvard Hagerup, 1843-1907—Juvenile literature.

DUNLOP, Agnes Mary 780'.924 B
Robertson.
Song of the waterfall; the story of Edward and Nina Grieg, by Elisabeth Kyle. [1st ed.] New York, Holt, Rinehart and Winston [1970] 233 p. 22 cm. A biography of the Norwegian composer, Edvard Grieg, concentrating on his relationship with his wife and their efforts to establish a place for Norwegian music. [ML3930.G8D85] 92 71-80328 ISBN 0-03-081608-4 4.50
1. Grieg, Edvard Hagerup, 1843-1907—Juvenile literature. 2. Grieg, Nina (Hagerup) 1845-1935—Juvenile literature. I. Title.

Grierson, John, 1898-1972.

JOHN Grierson, 791.43'023'0924 B
film master / [compiled] by James Beveridge. New York : Macmillan, c1978. xix, 361 p. : ill. ; 24 cm. Interviews and essays, most of which were done for the film, Grierson. [PN1998.A3G7135] 77-17799 ISBN 0-02-510530-2 : 17.95
1. Grierson, John, 1898-1972. 2. Grierson. [Motion picture] 3. Moving-picture producers and directors—Great Britain—Biography. I. Beveridge, James A.

Griese, Bob—Juvenile literature.

BURCHARD, S. H. 796.33'2'0924 B
Sports star, Bob Griese / S. H. Barchard ; illustrated with photos. and with drawings by Paul Frame. 1st ed. New York : Harcourt Brace Jovanovich, [1975] 63 p. : ill. ; 21 cm. An easy-to-read biography of the quarterback who led the Miami Dolphins from being a last place team to one of the strongest teams in pro football. [GV939.G76B87] 92 75-11779 ISBN 0-15-277997-3 : 4.95
1. Griese, Bob—Juvenile literature. 2. Football—Juvenile literature. I. Title.

MORSE, Charles. 796.33'2'0924 B
Bob Griese, by Charles and Ann Morse. Illustrated by Harold Henriksen. Mankato, Minn., Amecus Street; [distributed by Childrens Press, Chicago, 1974] 31 p. col. illus. 25 cm. (Superstars) A brief biography

of the Miami Dolphin quarterback emphasizing his plays in various football games. [GV939.G76M67] 92 74-4426 ISBN 0-87191-345-3 4.95 (lib. bdg.)
1. Griese, Bob—Juvenile literature. 2. Football—Juvenile literature. I. Morse, Ann, joint author. II. Henriksen, Harold, illus. III. Title. BIP

Griesse, Rosalie.

GRIESSE, Rosalie. 362.4'3'0926 B
The crooked shall be made straight / by Rosalie Griesse. Atlanta : John Knox Press, c1979. 240 p. ; 21 cm. [RD771.S3G74] 78-10408 ISBN 0-8042-1101-9 : 10.00
1. Griesse, Rosalie. 2. Scoliosis—Biography. I. Title. BIP

Grieve, Alexander James, 1874-1952.

SURMAN, Charles E 922.542
Alexander James Grieve, M. A., D. D., 1874-1952; a biographical sketch. Manchester, Lancashire Independent College [1953] 100p. illus. 20cm. [BX7260.G768S8] 54-25712
1. Grieve, Alexander James, 1874-1952. I. Title.

Griffin, Archie, 1954-

GRIFFIN, Archie, 796.33'2'0924 B 1954-
Archie : the Archie Griffin story / Archie Griffin with Dave Diles. 1st ed. Garden City, N.Y. : Doubleday, 1977. 192 p., [6] leaves of plates : ill. ; 22 cm. [GV939.G77A33] 76-51691 ISBN 0-385-12442-2 : 7.95
1. Griffin, Archie, 1954- 2. Football players—United States—Biography. I. Diles, David L., joint author. II. Title.

Griffin, Archie, 1954- —Juvenile literature.

DOLAN, Edward F., 796.33'2'0924 B 1924-
Archie Griffin / Edward F. Dolan, Jr., and Richard B. Lyttle. 1st ed. Garden City, N.Y. : Doubleday, c1977. 95 p., [12] leaves of plates : ill. ; 22 cm. (A Doubleday Signal book) A biography of Archie Griffin, star player for Ohio State University's football team and two-time winner of the Heisman Trophy. [GV939.G77D64] 92 76-56279 ISBN 0-385-12524-0 5.95
1. Griffin, Archie, 1954- —Juvenile literature. 2. Football players—United States—Biography—Juvenile literature. I. Lyttle, Richard B., joint author.

DOLAN, Edward F., 1924- 796.33'2'924 [B]
Archie Griffin / Edward F. Doland Jr. and Richard B. Lyttle. New York : Pocket Books, 1978, c1977. 113p., [12] leaves of plates : ill. ; 18 cm. (Archway paperbacks) A biography of Archie Griffin, star for Ohio State University's football team and two-time winner of the Heisman Trophy. [GV939.G77D64] ISBN 0-671-29904-2 pbk.: 1.25
1. Griffin Archie,1954 — Juvenile literature. 2. Football players — United States — Biography—Juvenile literature. I. Lyttle, Richard B., joint author. II. Title. L.C. card no. for 1977 Doubleday ed.:76-56279. BIP

Griffin, Gerald, 1803-1840.

CRONIN, John, 1928- 823'.7 B
Gerald Griffin, 1803-1840 : a critical biography / John Cronin. Cambridge ; New York : Cambridge University Press, 1978. xx, 163 p., [2] leaves of plates : ill. ; 23 cm. Includes index. Bibliography: p. 152-160. [PR4728.G8Z58] 77-80831 ISBN 0-521-21800-4 : 16.95
1. Griffin, Gerald, 1803-1840. 2. Authors, Irish—19th century—Biography. BIP

MANNIN, Ethel Edith, 1900- 928.2
Two studies in integrity: Gerald Griffin and the Rev. Francis Mahony ('Father Prout') New York, Putnam [1954] 271p. illus. 22cm. [PR4728] 54-11801
1. Griffin, Gerald, 1808-1840. 2. Mahony, Francis Sylvester, 1804-1866. I. Title.

Griffin, John Howard, 1920-

GRIFFIN, John Howard, 1920- 301.45'19'6073076 B
Black like me / by John Howard Griffin. 2d ed. / with a new epilogue by the author. Boston : Houghton Mifflin, 1977. 208 p. ; 22 cm. [E185.61.G8 1977] 76-47690 ISBN 0-395-25102-8 : 8.95
1. Griffin, John Howard, 1920- 2. Afro-Americans—Southern States. 3. Southern States—Race question. 4. Texas—Biography. I. Title. BIP

Griffin, John Howard, 1920- —Juvenile literature.

GRIFFIN, John Howard, 1920- 301.45'1
A time to be human / by John Howard Griffin. New York : Macmillan, c1977. 102 p. : ill. ; 22 cm. One man's account of the prejudice and racism in the United States. [R185.98.G74A33] 76-47468 6.95
1. Griffin, John Howard, 1920- —Juvenile literature. 2. Texas—Biography—Juvenile literature. 3. United States—Race relations—Juvenile literature. 4. Afro-Americans—Civil rights—Juvenile literature. I. Title. BIP

Griffin, Mary Annarose, Sister.

GRIFFIN, Mary Annarose, Sister. 271'.91 B
The courage to choose : an American nun's story / by Mary Griffin. 1st ed. Boston : Little, Brown, [1975] ix, 214 p. ; 22 cm. Autobiographical. Includes bibliographical references. [BX4705.G62245A33] 75-9636 ISBN 0-316-32864-2 : 7.95
1. Griffin, Mary Annarose, Sister. 2. Monastic and religious life of women. 3. Ex-nuns—Personal narratives. I. Title. BIP

Griffin, Robert.

GRIFFIN, Robert, 1925- 282'.092'4 B
In the kingdom of the lonely God. New York, Paulist Press [1973] 128 p. illus. 18 cm. Autobiographical. [BX4705.G6225A33] 72-94181 ISBN 0-8091-1747-9 2.95
1. Griffin, Robert. I. Title. BIP

Griffis, Stanton.

GRIFFIS, Stanton. 923.273
Lying in state. [1st ed.] New York, Doubleday, 1952. 315 p. illus. 22 cm. Autobiographical. [E748.G875A3] 52-11622
I. Title.

Griffis, William Elliot, 1843-1928.

BEAUCHAMP, Edward R., 1933- 915'.03 S
An American teacher in early Meiji Japan / Edward R. Beauchamp. [Honolulu] : University Press of Hawaii, c1976. xiii, 154 p. : ill. ; 23 cm. (Asian studies at Hawaii ; no. 17) Originally presented as the author's thesis, University of Washington, 1973, under title: William Elliot Griffis: an American yatoi in Meiji Japan. Bibliography: p. [149]-154. [DS3.A2A82 no. 17] [LA2317.G66] 370'.952 75-45222 ISBN 0-8248-0404-X pbk. : 4.75
1. Griffis, William Elliot, 1843-1928. 2. Education—Japan—History. 3. Japan—History—Meiji period, 1868-1912. I. Title. II. Series. BIP

Griffith, David Wark, 1875-1948.

BARRY, Iris, 1895- 791.430973
D. W. Griffith, American film master. With an annotated list of films by Eileen Bowser. New York, Museum of Modern Art; distributed by Doubleday, Garden City, N.Y. [1965] 88 p. illus., facsim., ports. 24 cm. [PN1998.A3G72 1965] 65-21928
1. Griffith, David Wark, 1875-1948. 2. Moving-pictures—United States.

BROWN, Karl. 791.43'0233'0924 B
Adventures with D. W. Griffith. New York, Farrar, Straus and Giroux [1973] xi, 251 p. illus. 24 cm. [PN1998.A3G7216] 72-97001 ISBN 0-374-10093-4 10.00
1. Griffith, David Wark, 1875-1948. 2. Brown, Karl. 3. Cinematographers—Correspondence, reminiscences, etc. I. Title. BIP

BROWN, Karl. 791.43'0233'0924 B
Adventures with D. W. Griffith / Karl Brown. New York : Da Capo Press, 1976, c1973. xi, 251 p., [18] leaves of plates : ill. ; 23 cm. (A Da Capo paperback) Reprint of the ed. published by Farrar, Straus and Giroux, New York. Includes index. [PN1998.A3G7216 1976] 75-31755 ISBN 0-306-80032-2 pbk. : 4.95
1. Griffith, David Wark, 1875-1948. 2. Brown, Karl. 3. Cinematographers—Correspondence, reminiscences, etc. I. Title.

CROY, Homer, 1883- 927.92
Star maker; the story of D. W. Griffith. Introd. by Mary Pickford. [1st ed.] New York, Duell, Sloan and Pearce [1959] 210 p. illus. 21 cm. [PN1998.A3G73] 59-6691
1. Griffith, David Wark, 1875-1948. I. Title.

GRIFFITH, David Wark, 1875-1948. 791.43'0233'0924 B
The man who invented Hollywood; the autobiography of D. W. Griffith. Edited and annotated by James Hart. Louisville, Ky., Touchstone Pub. Co. [1972] xiv, 170 p. illus. 29 cm. [PN1998.A3A715 1972] 75-178948 ISBN 0-87963-001-9 9.95
I. Hart, James, 1908- ed. II. Title.

HENDERSON, Robert M. 791.43'0233'0924 B
D. W. Griffith: his life and work [by] Robert M. Henderson. New York, Oxford University Press, 1972. ix, 326 p. illus. 24 cm. Includes bibliographical references. [PN1998.A3G748] 75-182425 10.95
1. Griffith, David Wark, 1875-1948. I. Title.

O'DELL, Paul. 791.43'0233'0924
Griffith and the rise of Hollywood, by Paul O'Dell, with the assistance of Anthony Slide. New York, A. S. Barnes [1971] 163 p. illus., ports. 16 cm. (The International film guide series) Includes bibliographical references. [PN1998.A3G77] 71-119640 ISBN 0-498-07718-7 2.95
1. Griffith, David Wark, 1875-1948. I. Slide, Anthony. II. Title. BIP

SLIDE, Anthony. 791.43'0233'0924
The Griffith actresses. South Brunswick, A. S. Barnes [1973] 181 p. illus. 27 cm. Bibliography: p. 179-181. [PN1998.A3G78] 72-6373 ISBN 0-498-01018-X 8.95
1. Griffith, David Wark, 1875-1948. 2. Moving-picture actors and actresses—United States—Biography. I. Title.

Griffith, George P.

GRIFFITH, George P. 336'.02'73 B
Life and adventures of revenooer number one / by George P. Griffith. Birmingham, Ala. : Gander Publishers, [1975] p. cm. Autobiographical. [HJ4652.G77] 74-31105 8.95
1. Griffith, George P. 2. United States. Internal Revenue Service—Officials and employees—Correspondence, reminiscences, etc. I. Title.

Griffith, Samuel Walker, Sir, 1845-1920.

FORWARD, Roy. 347'.94'03534 B
Samuel Griffith [by] R. K. Forward. Melbourne, New York, Oxford University Press [1964] 30 p. illus. 19 cm. (Great Australians) Bibliography: p. 30. [LAW] 74-164283
1. Griffith, Samuel Walker, Sir, 1845-1920.

Griffith, William Brandford,

GRIFFITH, William Brandford, Sir 1858-1939. 923.4667
The far horizon; portrait of a colonial judge. Ilfracombe, Devon., A. H. Stockwell, 1951. 317 p. illus. 19 cm. 52-19537
I. Title.

Griffiths, Ann Thomas, 1776-1805.

ALLCHIN, A. M. 891.6'6'12 B
Ann Griffiths / [by] A. M. Allchin. [Cardiff] : University of Wales Press [for] the Welsh Arts Council, 1976. [3], 72 p., plate : port. ; 25 cm. (Writers of Wales) Bibliography: p. 67-68. [PB2297.G7Z57] 77-350048 ISBN 0-7083-0628-4 : £1.00
1. Griffiths, Ann Thomas, 1776-1805. 2. Authors, Welsh—Biography. BIP

Griffiths, Harry, 1895-

GRIFFITHS, Harry, 1895- 266'.7'0924 B
An Australian adventure / [by] Harry Griffiths. Adelaide : Rigby, 1978, c1975. 198 p., [6] leaves of plates : ill. ; 18 cm. [BV3667.G74A32 1978] 79-316790 ISBN 0-7270-0568-5 pbk. : 3.95
1. Griffiths, Harry, 1895- 2. Missionaries—Australia—Biography. 3. Missionaries—England—Biography. I. Title.

Griffiths, John, 1826-1891.

GRIFFITHS, Iris. 289.3'3 B
The vindicator / Iris Griffiths. Independence, Mo. : Herald Pub. House, c1977. 214 p. : port. ; 20 cm. A biography of the Welsh immigrant to Utah whose disillusionment leads him to California where he finds the Reorganized Church and serves as its missionary to Wales. [BX8678.G74G74] 92 77-1808 ISBN 0-8309-0172-8 : 6.50
1. Griffiths, John, 1826-1891. 2. Mormons and Mormonism in the United States—Biography. 3. Missionaries—Wales—Biography. 4. Missionaries—United States—Biography. I. Title.

Griffon (Ship)

MACLEAN, Harrison John. 917.7'04'10924
The fate of the Griffon / by Harrison John MacLean. Chicago : Sage Books, [1975] c1974. [10], 118 p. : ill. ; 23 cm. Bibliography: 8th prelim. page. [F1030.5.M32 1975] 74-14399 ISBN 0-8040-0674-1 : 8.95
1. La Salle, Robert Cavelier, sieur de, 1643-1687. 2. Griffon (Ship) 3. MacLean, Harrison John. 4. Great Lakes—Discovery and exploration. I. Title. BIP

Griffs, Stanton.

GRIFFS, Stanton. 923.273
Lying in state. [1st ed.] Garden City, N. Y., Doubleday, 1952. 315p. illus. 22cm. Autobiographical. [E748.G875A3] 52-11622
I. Title.

Grigg, David Henry,

GRIGG, David Henry, 1883- 920
From one to seventy. [1st American ed.] New York, Vantage Press [1957, c1956] 262p. 21cm. Autobiography. [CT310.G74A3 1957] 56-12199
I. Title.

Griggs, Laura A. (Tressel) 1884-1956.

GRIGGS, Robert F v. 12
We two together; an autobiography and biography. Pittsburgh, Boxwood Press, c1961. 320 p. front. plates (part col.) 22 cm. 64-22142
1. Griggs, Laura A. (Tressel) 1884-1956. I. Title.

Grignon de Montfort, Louis Marie, Saint, 1673-1716.

WINDEATT, Mary Fabyan, 1910- 922.244
Our Lady's slave; the story of Saint Louis Mary Grignion de Montfort. Illustrated by Paul A. Grout. St. Meinrad, Ind. [1950]

201 p. illus. 22 cm. "A Grail publication." [BX4700.G83W5] 50-58045
1. Grignon de Montfort, Louis Marie, Saint, 1673-1716. I. Title.

Grigorenko, Petr Grigor'evich, 1907-

GRIGORENKO, Petr Grigor'evich, 1907- 320.9'47'084
The Grigorenko papers / by Peter Grigorenko ; introd. by Edward Crankshaw. Boulder, Colo. : Westview Press, 1976. vi, 187 p. : ill. ; 23 cm. Translation of Mysli sumasshedshego. Includes index. [DK274.G7313 1976] 76-5912 ISBN 0-89158-603-2 : 14.75
1. Grigorenko, Petr Grigor'evich, 1907- 2. Russia (1923- U.S.S.R.). Armiia—Biography. 3. Russia—Politics and government—1917- —Addresses, essays, lectures. 4. Generals—Russia—Biography. 5. Political prisoners—Russia—Personal narratives. I. Title.

Grillparzer, Franz, 1791-1872—Biography.

YATES, Douglas. 832'.6 B
Franz Grillparzer; a critical biography. [Folcroft, Pa.] Folcroft Library Editions, 1974. viii, 188 p. ports. 24 cm. Reprint of the 1946 ed. published by Blackwell, Oxford, in series: Modern language studies. No more published. Includes bibliographical references. [PT2265.Y3 1974] 74-9599 ISBN 0-8414-9764-8 (lib. bdg.)
1. Grillparzer, Franz, 1791-1872—Biography. BIP

Grimaldi, Joseph, 1779-1837.

FINDLATER, Richard, 1921- 791.3'3'0924 B
Joe Grimaldi, his life and theatre / Richard Findlater. 2d ed. Cambridge, [Eng.] ; New York : Cambridge University Press, 1978. 260 p., [6] leaves of plates : ill. ; 22 cm. First published in 1955 under title: Grimaldi, king of clowns. Includes bibliographical references and index. [GV1811.G7F56 1978] 78-7465 ISBN 0-521-22221-4 : 34.50 ISBN 0-521-29407-X pbk. : 9.95
1. Grimaldi, Joseph, 1779-1837. 2. Clowns—Great Britain—Biography. I. Title.

GRIMALDI, Joseph, 1779-1837. 792'.0924
Memoirs of Joseph Grimaldi, by Charles Dickens. Edited by Richard Findlater, with new notes and introd. With illus. by George Cruikshank. NewYork, Stein and Day [1968] 311 p. illus. (part col.), ports. 22 cm. The original manuscript was rewritten in the third person by Charles Dickens. [PN2598.G68A3 1968] 68-13245
I. Dickens, Charles, 1812-1870, ed. II. Bain, Kenneth Bruce Findlater, 1921- ed.

Grimke, Angelina Emily, 1805-1879.

LERNER, Gerda, 1920- 973.71'14'0922
The Grimke sisters from South Carolina; rebels against slavery. Illustrated with photos. Boston, Houghton Mifflin, 1967. xiv, 479 p. illus., facsim., ports. 22 cm. Bibliography: p. [437]-457. [E449.G89] 67-25218
1. Grimke, Angelina Emily, 1805-1879. 2. Grimke, Sarah Moore, 1792-1873. I. Title.

LUMPKIN, Katharine Du Pre, 1897- 322.4'4'0924 B
The emancipation of Angelina Grimke. Chapel Hill, University of North Carolina Press [1974] xv, 265 p. ports. 24 cm. Bibliography: p. 247-255. [E449.G865L85] 74-8914 ISBN 0-8078-1232-3
1. Grimke, Angelina Emily, 1805-1879. I. Title. BIP

Grimke, Archibald Henry, 1849-1930—Juvenile literature.

STEVENSON, Janet. 340'.0924 B
Spokesman for freedom; the life of Archibald Grimke. Illus. by John Wagner. [New York] Crowell-Collier Press [1969] 100 p. illus. 21 cm. A biography of a spokesman for the Negro people in the late eighteen hundreds, founder of a newspaper, and lawyer who defended many black brothers. [E185.97.G8S7] 92 73-82561
1. Grimke, Archibald Henry, 1849-1930—Juvenile literature. I. Wagner, John, illus. II. Title. BIP

Grimke, Sarah Moore, 1792-1873.

BIRNEY, Catherine H. 322'.4
The Grimke sisters: Sarah and Angelina Grimk[e], the first American women advocates of abolition and woman's rights. New York, Haskell House, 1970. 319 p. 23 cm. Reprint of the 1885 ed. [E449.G88 1970b] 68-24971
1. Grimke, Sarah Moore, 1792-1873. 2. Grimke, Angelina Emily, 1805-1879. I. Title.

BIRNEY, Catherine H. 326'.0922
The Grimke sisters; Sarah and Angelina Grimke, the first American women advocates of abolition and woman's rights, by Catherine H. Birney. Westport, Conn., Greenwood Press [1969] 319 p. 23 cm. Reprint of the 1885 ed. [E449.G88 1969] 69-13828
1. Grimke, Sarah Moore, 1792-1873. 2. Grimke, Angelina Emily, 1805-1879.

BIRNEY, Catherine H. 322'.4
The Grimke sisters: Sarah and Angelina Grimke, the first American women advocates of abolition and woman's rights, by Catherine H. Birney. Boston, Lee and Shepard, 1885. St. Clair Shores, Mich., Scholarly Press, 1970. 319 p. 22 cm. [E449.G88 1970] 70-108461
1. Grimke, Sarah Moore, 1792-1873. 2. Grimke, Angelina Emily, 1805-1879. I. Title.

Grimke, Sarah Moore, 1792-1873—Juvenile literature.

WILLIMON, William H. 326'.092'2 B
Turning the world upside down; the story of Sarah and Angelina Grimke [by] William and Patricia Willimon. With drawings by G. Hoyt Simmons. [1st ed.] Columbia [S.C.] Sandlapper Press, 1972. 128 p. illus. 23 cm. A biography of two sisters from a wealthy southern family who devoted their lives to the causes of abolition and women's rights. [E449.G895] 920 72-86901 ISBN 0-87844-011-9 4.95
1. Grimke, Sarah Moore, 1792-1873—Juvenile literature. 2. Grimke, Angelina Emily, 1805-1879—Juvenile literature. I. Willimon, Patricia, joint author. II. Simmons, Hoyt, illus. III. Title.

Grimm, Charlie.

GRIMM, Charlie. 796.357'0924 B
Jolly Cholly's story: Baseball, I love you! [by] Charlie Grimm with Ed Prell. Introd. by Bill Veeck. Chicago, Regnery [1968] xiv, 242 p. illus., ports. 22 cm. [GV865.G7A3] 68-18274
I. Prell, Ed. II. Title. III. Title: Baseball, I love you!

Grimm, Jakob Ludwig Karl, 1785-1863.

MICHAELIS-JENA, Ruth. 398.21'0922 B
The brothers Grimm. New York, Praeger [1970] xvi, 212 p. illus., geneal. table, ports. 26 cm. Bibliography: p. 198-204. [PD64.G7M5 1970b] 72-109480 8.95
1. Grimm, Jakob Ludwig Karl, 1785-1863. 2. Grimm, Wilhelm Karl, 1786-1859. I. Title.

PEPPARD, Murray B., 1917- 398.21'0922 B
Paths through the forest; a biography of the brothers Grimm [by] Murray B. Peppard. [1st ed.] New York, Holt, Rinehart and Winston [1971] xvi, 266 p. group port. 22 cm. Bibliography: p. [252]-255. [PD64.G7P4] 72-117271 ISBN 0-03-085076-2 7.95
1. Grimm, Jakob Ludwig Karl, 1785-1863. 2. Grimm, Wilhelm Karl, 1786-1859. I. Title.

Grimwade, Russell, Sir, 1879-1955.

POYNTER, John Riddoch. 919.4'03'40924 B
Russell Grimwade [by] J. R. Poynter. [Melbourne] Melbourne University Press at the Miegunyah Press [1967] xiv, 321 p. illus., geneal. table, ports. (part col.) 25 cm. Bibliographical references included in "Notes" (p. 313-315) [CT2808.G73P68] 67-30709 8.35 Aust.
1. Grimwade, Russell, Sir, 1879-1955. BIP

Grindal, Edmund, Abp. of Canterbury, 1519?-1583.

COLLINSON, Patrick. 283'.092'4
Archbishop Grindal, 1519-1583 : the struggle for a reformed Church / Patrick Collinson. Berkeley : University of California Press, 1979. 368 p., [4] leaves of plates : ill. ; 24 cm. Includes bibliographical references and index. [BX5199.G74C64] 78-65474 ISBN 0-520-03831-2 : 27.50
1. Grindal, Edmund, Abp. of Canterbury, 1519?-1583. 2. Church of England—Bishops—Biography. 3. Bishops—England—Biography.

STRYPE, John, 1643-1737. 283'.092'4
The history of the life and acts of the Most Reverend Father in God, Edmund Grindal ... To which is added an appendix of original mss. ... New York, B. Franklin [1974] xxi, 607 p. port. 23 cm. (Burt Franklin research and source work series. Philosophy and religious history monographs, 145) Reprint of the ed. published in 1821 by Clarendon Press, Oxford, Eng. [BX5199.G74S8 1974] 78-183700 ISBN 0-8337-3445-8 50.00 (2 volumes)
1. Grindal, Edmund, Abp. of Canterbury, 1519?-1583. I. Title. II. Series.

Grinnan, Randolph Bryan, 1860-1942.

HILLDRUP, Robert Leroy. 266.5'1'0924 B
An American missionary to Meiji Japan. [Norfolk, Va.] 1970. 138 p. illus., port. 24 cm. Includes bibliographical references. [BV3457.G7H5] 72-17090
1. Grinnan, Randolph Bryan, 1860-1942. 2. Missions—Japan. I. Title.

Grinnell Expedition, 2d, 1853-1855.

KANE, Elisha Kent, 1820-1857. 910.09'1632
Arctic explorations in 1853, 1854, 1855. New York, Arno Press, 1971. 2 v. illus., maps, ports. 23 cm. (Physician travelers) Reprint of the 1856 ed., originally published under title: Arctic explorations: the second Grinnell Expedition in search of Sir John Franklin, 1853, '54, '55. [G665 1853.K33] 74-115615 ISBN 0-405-01735-9
1. Grinnell Expedition, 2d, 1853-1855. 2. Northwest Passage. I. Title.

Grisham, Noel.

GRISHAM, Noel. 370.11'092'4
Beyond the schoolhouse / by Noel Grisham. San Antonio, Tex. : Naylor Co., [1974] xi, 118 p. ; 22 cm. Autobiographical. [LA2317.G73A32] 74-23712 ISBN 0-8111-0543-1 : 6.95
1. Grisham, Noel. I. Title.

Grissom, Virgil I.

CHAPPELL, Carl L. 629.4'0924 B
Seven minus one; the story of the Gus Grissom, by Carl L. Chappell. Mitchell, Ind. [1968] xii, 284 p. illus., facsim., ports. 23 cm. (His A New frontier publication) Bibliography: p. 275-276. [TL789.85.G7C45] 68-6185
1. Grissom, Virgil I. I. Title.

GRISSOM, Betty. 629.4'092'4 B
Starfall [by] Betty Grissom and Henry Still. Developed by Whitehall, Hadlyme & Smith, Inc. New York, Crowell [1974] 276 p. illus. 24 cm. Bibliography: p. 261. [TL789.85.G7G74 1974] 74-7285 ISBN 0-690-00473-7 7.95
1. Grissom, Virgil I. I. Still, Henry, joint author. II. Title.

Griswold, Thomas.

GRISWOLD, Thomas. 338.7'66'00924 B
The time of my life. [Midland, Mich., Northwood Institute, 1973] xii, 201 p. 24 cm. [HD9651.95.G74A33] 73-76876 ISBN 0-87359-001-5 5.00
1. Griswold, Thomas. 2. Dow Chemical Company. I. Title.

Grivas, George, 1898-

BARKER, Dudley [Raymond] 923.5495
Grivas: portrait of a terrorist. New York. Harcourt, Brace [1960, c.1959] 202p. illus. 21cm. 60-7424 3.95
1. Grivas, George, 1898- I. Title.

Groat, Dick.

GROAT, Dick. 796.357'092'4 B
Groat : I hit and ran / by Dick Groat, with Frank Dascenzo. Durham : Moore Pub. Co., c1978. 110 p., [14] leaves of plates : ill. ; 24 cm. [GV865.G73A33] 78-65167 ISBN 0-87716-094-5 : 7.95
1. Groat, Dick. 2. Baseball players—United States—Biography. I. Dascenzo, Frank, joint author. II. Title. BIP

Grobart, Fabio.

KOZOLCHYK, Boris. 920.07291
The political biographies of three Castro officials. Santa Monica, Calif., Rand Corp., 1966. x, 95 p. 28 cm. ([Rand Corporation. Research] memorandum, RM-4994-RC) Bibliographical footnotes. [Q180.A1R36 no. 4994] 67-2990
1. Grobart, Fabio. 2. Anillo, Rene. 3. Roa, Raul. I. Title. II. Series.

Groddeck, Georg Walther, 1866-1934.

GROSSMAN, Carl M 926.1
The wild analyst; the life and work of Georg Groddeck, by Carl M. Grossman and Sylva Grossman. New York, G. Braziller [1965] 222 p. 22 cm. Bibliography: p. 207-210. [R512.G7G7] 65-12573
1. Groddeck, Georg Walther, 1866-1934. I. Grossman, Sylva, joint author. II. Title.

Groell, Clara, 1882-

GROELL, Clara, 1882- 266'.2'0924 B
White wings in bamboo land. [Emmitsburg, Md., Saint Joseph's Provincial House Press, 1973] 207 p. illus. 22 cm. Autobiographical. [BV3427.G74A3] 73-83504
1. Groell, Clara, 1882- 2. Daughters of Charity of St. Vincent de Paul, Emmitsburg, Md.—Missions. 3. Missions—China. I. Title.

Groesbeck, Alexander Joseph, 1873-1953.

WOODFORD, Frank Bury, 1903- 923.273
Alex J. Groesbeck; portrait of a public man. With a foreword by Murray D. Van Wagoner and an introd. by Roscoe O. Bonisteel. Detroit, Wayne State University Press, 1962. 366 p. illus. 24 cm. Includes bibliography. [F566.G8W6] 62-7209
1. Groesbeck, Alexander Joseph, 1873-1953. I. Title. BIP

Grogan, Emmett.

GROGAN, Emmett. 301.2'2'0924 B
Ringolevio; a life played for keeps. [1st ed.] Boston, Little, Brown [1972] 498 p. illus. 24 cm. [CT275.G7784A3] 78-186970 7.95
I. Title.

Groom, W. H. A.

GROOM, W. H. A. 940.4'81'4 B
Poor bloody infantry : a memoir of the First World War / [by] W. H. A. Groom. London : Kimber, 1976. 185 p., [8] p. of plates : ill., maps ; 24 cm. [D640.G7773] 77-355598 ISBN 0-7183-0384-9 : £3.95
1. Groom, W. H. A. 2. Great Britain. Army. Infantry—Biography. 3. European War, 1914-1918—Personal narratives, English. 4. Soldiers—Great Britain—Biography. I. Title.

Gropius, Walter, 1883-1969.

GIEDION, Sigfried, 1888- 927.2
Walter Gropius, work and teamwork. New York, Reinhold Pub. Corp. [1954] 249 p. illus., ports., plans. 26 cm. Bibliography: p. 237-243. [NA1088.G85G52] 54-14245
1. Gropius, Walter, 1883-1969.

Gropius, Walter, 1883-1969—Bibliography.

GROPIUS, Wren, Latrobe, Wright. 016.72 S
Charlottesville, Published for the American Association of Architectural Bibliographers [by the] University Press of Virginia [1972] 132 p. 24 cm. (American Association of Architectural Bibliographers. Papers, v. 9) [Z5941.A5 vol. 9] [Z8369.43] 016.72'092'2 72-195645 ISBN 0-8139-0391-2 7.50
1. Gropius, Walter, 1883-1969—Bibliography. 2. Wren, Christopher, Sir, 1632-1723—Bibliography. 3. Latrobe, Benjamin Henry, 1764-1820—Bibliography. 4. Wright, Frank Lloyd, 1867-1959—Bibliography. I. American Association of Architectural Bibliographers. II. Title. III. Series.

Gross, Chaim, 1904-

GROSS, Chaim, 1904- 730'.92'4
Chaim Gross, by Frank Getlein. New York, H. N. Abrams [1974] 235 p. illus. (part col.) 28 x 30 cm. Bibliography: p. 233-235. [NB237.G85G47] 73-13807 ISBN 0-8109-0160-9
1. Gross, Chaim, 1904- I. Getlein, Frank.

Gross, Fred W., 1895-

GROSS, Fred W., 1895- 285'.8'0924 B
The pastor; the life of an immigrant [by] Fred W. Gross. Philadelphia, Dorrance [1973] 182 p. illus. 21 cm. Bibliography: p. 181-182. [BX7260.G785A3] 73-76214 ISBN 0-8059-1843-4 4.95
1. Gross, Fred W., 1895- I. Title.

Gross, Mary.

GROSS, Mary. 920
Mariska in forgive and forget. Boston, Bruce Humphries [1961] 160p. 21cm. Autobiographical. [CT275.G779A3] 61-2013
I. Title.

Gross, Samuel David,

GROSS, Samuel David, 1805-1884. 610'.92'4 B
Autobiography of Samuel D. Gross, with sketches of his contemporaries. Edited by his sons. New York, Arno Press, 1972 [c1887] 2 v. ports. 23 cm. (Medicine & society in America) [R154.G77A3 1972] 71-180576 ISBN 0-405-03953-0
I. Title. II. Series.

Grosseteste, Robert, bp. of Lincoln, 1175?-1253.

CROMBIE, Alistair Cameron, 1915- v. 12
Robert Grosseteste and the origins of experimental science, 1100-1700. Oxford, Clarendon Press [1962] xi, 371 p. illus., port. 23 cm. First published 1953; reprinted with corrections ... 1962. Bibliography: p. [320-352] 64-38825
1. Grosseteste, Robert, Bp. of Lincoln, 1175?-1253. 2. Science—Hist. I. Title. **BIP**

STEVENSON, Francis Seymour, 1862- v. 12
Robert Grosseteste, Bishop of Lincoln; a contribution to the religious, political and intellectual history of the thirteenth century. Dubuque, Iowa, W. C. Brown Reprint Library [1962] xvi, 348 p. 24 cm. 64-45654
1. Grosseteste, Robert, bp. of Lincoln, 1175?-1253. 2. Gt. Brit. — Hist. — 13th cent. — Sources. I. Title. **BIP**

Grossinger, Jennie (Grossinger) 1892-

POMERANTZ, Joel. 647'.94'0924 B
Jennie and the story of Grossinger's. New York, Grosset & Dunlap [1970] 325 p. illus. 22 cm. [TX910.5.G75P6] 71-106313 6.95
1. Grossinger, Jennie (Grossinger) 1892- 2. The Grossinger, Ferndale, N.Y. I. Title.

Grotius, Hugo, 1583-1645.

DUMBAULD, Edward, 1905- 340'.0924
The life and legal writings of Hugo Grotius. [1st ed.] Norman, University of Oklahoma Press [1969] xiii, 206 p. illus., ports. 19 cm. Bibliography: p. 181-199. [LAW] 68-31373 4.95
1. Grotius, Hugo, 1583-1645. I. Title. **BIP**

Grouard, Frank, 1850-

DE BARTHE, Joseph. 923.973
Life and adventures of Frank Grouard. Edited and with an introd. by Edgar I. Stewart. [New ed.] Norman, University of Oklahoma Press [1958] 268 p. illus. 24 cm. [E83.866.G88 1958] 58-11651
1. Grouard, Frank, 1850- 2. Indians of North America—Wars—1866-1895. **BIP**

Grove, Frederick Philip, 1879-1948—Correspondence.

GROVE, Frederick Philip, 1879-1948. 813'.5'2 B
The letters of Frederick Philip Grove / edited with an introd. and notes by Desmond Pacey. Toronto ; Buffalo : University of Toronto Press, [1975] p. cm. Includes index. [PR9199.3.G77Z53 1975] 74-75828 ISBN 0-8020-5311-4 : 25.00
1. Grove, Frederick Philip, 1879-1948—Correspondence. **BIP**

Grove, George, Sir, 1820-1900.

GRAVES, Charles Larcom, 1856-1944. 780'.92'4 B
The life & letters of Sir George Grove / by Charles L. Graves. Boston : Longwood Press, 1977. xi, 484 p. ; 22 cm. Reprint of the 1903 ed. published by Macmillan, London. Includes index. [ML423.G8G7 1977] 77-75177 ISBN 0-89341-059-4 lib.bdg. : 50.00
1. Grove, George, Sir, 1820-1900. 2. Musicians—England—Biography. I. Title.

GRAVES, Charles Larcom, 1856-1944. 780'.92'4 B
The life & letters of Sir George Grove / by Charles L. Graves. Boston : Longwood Press, 1977. xi, 484 p. ; 22 cm. Reprint of the 1903 ed. published by Macmillan, London. Includes index. [ML423.G8G7 1977] 77-75177 ISBN 0-89341-059-4 lib.bdg. : 50.00
1. Grove, George, Sir, 1820-1900. 2. Musicians—England—Biography. I. Title. **BIP**

Grove, Merlin, 1929-1962.

EBY, Omar, 1935- 266.97'0924 B
A whisper in a dry land; a biography of Merlin Grove, martyr for Muslims in Somalia. Scottdale, Pa., Herald Press [1968] 174 p. illus. 21 cm. [BV3625.S62G7] 68-12027
1. Grove, Merlin, 1929-1962. 2. Missions—Somalia. I. Title.

Grubbe, Emil Herman, 1875-1960.

HODGES, Paul Chesley, 1893- 926.1
M.D., *The life and times of Emil H. Grubbe.* Chicago, Univ. of Chic. Pr. [c.1964] xi, 135p. illus., facsims., ports. 23cm. Bibl. 64-24977 3.95
1. Grubbe, Emil Herman, 1875-1960. I. Title.

Gruber, Frank,

GRUBER, Frank, 1904- 818'.9'1203
The pulp jungle. Los Angeles, Sherbourne Press [1967] 189 p. 22 cm. Autobiographical. [PS3513.R866Z5] 67-21873
I. Title.

GRUBER, Frank, 1904-1969. 818'.5'203
The pulp jungle. Los Angeles, Sherbourne Press [1967] 189 p. 22 cm. Autobiographical. [PS3513.R866Z5] 67-21873
I. Title.

Gruening, Ernest Henry, 1887-

GRUENING, Ernest Henry, 1887- 329'.0092'4
Many battles; the autobiography of Ernest Gruening. New York, Liveright [1973] x, 564 p. illus. 24 cm. [E748.G898A35] 72-97492 ISBN 0-87140-565-2 12.95
1. Gruening, Ernest Henry, 1887- I. Title.

ROSS, Sherwood. 979.8'04'0924 B
Gruening of Alaska. New York, Best Books [1968] 224 p. illus., ports. 18 cm. [E748.G898R6] 68-5235
1. Gruening, Ernest Henry, 1887- I. Title.

Gruffydd, William John, 1881-1954—Biography.

GRUFFYDD, William John, 1881-1954. 891.6'6'12 B
The years of the locust / by W. J. Gruffydd ; a translation from the Welsh by D. Myrddin Lloyd. Llandysul : Gomer Press, 1976, i.e.1978 [1], 207 p. ; 23 cm. Translation of Hen atgofion. Includes index. [PB2298.G78Z5213 1976] 77-550390 ISBN 0-85088-342-3 : pbk. : 11.00
1. Gruffydd, William John, 1881-1954—Biography. 2. Authors, Welsh—20th century—Biography. I. Title.
Distributed by British Book Ctr. **BIP**

Grum, Zeljko.

MESTROVIC, Ivan, 1883-1962 730.9497
Ivan Mestrovic [by] Zeljko Grum. Photos. by Toso Dabac. Zagreb, Matica Hrvatska [dist. New York, Vanous, 1963] xxxvi, 189p. chiefly illus. 29cm. 63-3936 14.90
1. Grum, Zeljko. I. Title.

Grundling, Beulah.

GUNDLING, Beulah. 797.2'03
Dancing in the water / by Beulah Gundling. Cedar Rapids, Iowa : Gundling, c1976. viii, 253 p. : ill. ; 23 cm. Includes index. Bibliography: p. 236. [GV838.G86A32] 76-357950
1. Grundling, Beulah. 2. Synchronized swimming. I. Title.

Grundtvig, Nikolai Frederik Severin, 1783-1872.

ARDEN, Gothard Everett, 1905- 922.448
Four northern lights; men who shaped Scandinavian churches, by G. Everett Arden. Illus. by Hordan Lang. Minneapolis, Augsburg Pub. House [1964] 165 p. ports. 21 cm. "Originally presented as a series of lectures in connection with the twenty-fourth Luther Academy, held at Wartburg Theological Seminary, Dubuque, Iowa, during the summer of 1963." Includes bibliographies. [BX8079.A7] 64-21502
1. Ruotsalainen, Paavo, 1777-1852. 2. Hauge, Hans Nielsen, 1771-1824. 3. Grundtvig, Nikolai Frederik Severin, 1783-1872. 4. Rosenius, Carl Olof, 1916-1868. I. Title.

KNUDSEN, Johannes, 1902- 922.4489
Danish rebel: a study of N. F. S. Grundtvig. Philadelphia, Muhlenberg Press [1955] 242p. 20cm. [BX8080.G76K55] 55-7763
1. Grundtvig, Nicolai Frederik Severin, 1783-1872. I. Title.

Grundy, Joseph Ridgway, 1863-1961.

HUTTON, Ann (Hawkes) 923.273
The Pennsylvanian: Joseph R. Grundy. Philadelphia, Dorrance [1962] 241p. illus. 21cm. Includes bibliography. [F154.G83] 62-21713
1. Grundy, Joseph Ridgway, 1863-1961. I. Title.

Grunebaum, Ernest,

GRUNEBAUM, Ernest, 1861-1944. 920.043
Memoirs. Translated by Edith A. Simons and Norbert Guterman. Scarsdale, N. Y. [L. H. Grunebaum] 1960. 182p. illus. 29cm. [CT1098.G76A33] 61-34402
I. Title.

Grunewald, Mathias, 16th cent.

SCHMITT, Pierre 759.3
Mathias Grunewald and other old masters in Colmar. Introd. by Pierre Schmitt. [Tr. from German by Gladys Wheelhouse] With 28 color plates by E. Ohresser. New York, A. S. Barnes [1963, c.1961] 67p. mounted col. illus. 22cm. [Metropolis bks.] 63-6133 4.95
1. Grunewald, Mathias, 16th cent. 2. Painters, German—Colmar. I. Title.

Grunwell, Charles Vanderwerken,

GRUNWELL, Charles Vanderwerken, 1880- 923.473
All in a lifetime. Philadelphia, Dorrance [1961] 301p. 21cm. Autobiography. [CT275.G8A3] 61-11804
I. Title.

Grzegorczyk, Ignacy, 1888-1959—Biography.

GRZEGORCZYK, Ignacy, 1888-1959. 891.8'5'17 B
Poems and autobiography of Ignacy Grzegorczyk = Poezje i zyciorys Ignacego Grzegorczyka / translation into English poetry by Adele Cisniewicz and Daniel E. Grzegorczyk. Clearwater, Fla. : D. Grzegorczyk, c1977. 108 p. : port. ; 23 cm. [PG7399.G74A23 1977] 77-554382
1. Grzegorczyk, Ignacy, 1888-1959—Biography. 2. Poets, Polish—United States—Biography. I. Cisniewicz, Adele M. II. Grzegorczyk, Dan, 1929- III. Title. IV. Title: Poezje i zyciorys Ignacego Grzegorczyka.

Gt. Brit.

WHO'S who, 1963, 920.01
an annual biographical dictionary, with which is incorporated 'Men and women of the time.' 115th ed. London, A. and C. Black Dist. New York, St. Martin's [c.1963] 3390p. 23cm. annual. Absorbed Men and women of the time with v. 53, 1901. Subtitle varies. Imprint varies. 4-16933 23.00; 30, 25.00 after Mar. 30,
1. Gt. Brit.—Bidg. 2. Biography—Dictionaries.

Gt. Brit.—Biog.

AUBREY, John, 1626-1697. 920.042
Brief lives. Edited from the original manuscripts and with a life of John Aubrey by Oliver Lawson Dick. Foreword by Edmund Wilson. Ann Arbor, University of Michigan Press [1957] cvi, 341p. 24cm. [DA447.A3A8 1957] 57-13981
1. Gt. Brit.—Biog. I. Dick, Oliver Lawson, 1920-ed II. Title.

EDGAR, F. T. R. 942.06'2'0924
Sir Ralph Hopton: the King's man in the

West [1642-1652): a study in character and command, by F. T. R. Edgar. Oxford, Clarendon Pr., 1968. xx, 248p. plate, table, map, 4 plans, port. 23cm. Bibl: p. [213]-236. [DA802.H6E3] 68-107889 8.80; 7.48 text,
1. Hopton, Ralph Hopton, Baron, 1598-1652. II. Title.
Available from Orford Univ., Pr., New York.

FULLER, Thomas, 1608-1661 920.042
The worthies of England. Ed. with introd. and notes by John Freeman. [abridged ed., dist. New York, Barnes & Noble, 1962, c.1952] xvii, 716p. front. port. Bibl. 10.00
1. Gt. Brit.—Biog. 2. England—Descr. & trav. 3. Gt. Brit. —History, Local. I. Title.

GARVIN, Katharine Garvin, ed. 920.042
The great Tudors. Chester Springs, Pa., Dufour [1962, c.1961] 296p. 22cm. 61-14086 500; 1.95 pap.,
1. Gt. Brit.—Biog. 2. Gt. Brit.—Hist. — Tudors, 1485-1603. I. Title. **BIP**

JONES, Howard, 1906- 920.042
Men of courage: Bunyan, Wilson, Penn, Lister, Shaftesbury, Grenfell. London, G. Bell, 1957. 179p. illus. 20cm. [DA307.J6 1957] 57-2579
1. Gt. Brit.—Biog. I. Title.

JONES, Howard, 1906- 920.042
Men of courage: Bunyan, Wilson, Penn, Lister, Shaftesbury, Grenfell. New York, St. Martin's Press [1957] 179p. illus. 20cm. [DA307.J6 1957a] 57-10599
1. Gt. Brit.— Biog. I. Title.

MEADOWS, Denis. 920.042
Elizabethan quintet. London, New York, Longmans, Green [1956] xv, 304p. 19cm. [DA358.A1M4 1956] 57-703
1. Gt. Brit.—Biog. I. Title.
Contents omitted.

PEARSON, Hesketh, 1887-1964 920.042
Extraordinary people. New York, Harper [c.1965] 267p. illus., ports. 22cm. [DA28.P4] 65-14656 5.95
1. Gt. Brit.—Biog. I. Title.

ROSENBAUM, Robert A., 1926- 920.042
Earnest Victorians; six great Victorians as portrayed in their own words and those of their contemporaries New York, Hawthorn [1965, c.1961] 383p. illus. 21cm. [CT782.R6] 61-5955 2.45 pap.,
1. Gt. Brit.—Biog. I. Title.
Contents omitted.,

ROUTH, Charles Richard Nairne, ed. 920.042
Who's who in history. General editor: C. R. N. Routh. New York, Barnes & Noble [196] v. illus., geneal. table, ports. 22 cm. Contents.v. 3. England, 1603-1714, by C. P. Hill. [DA28.W619] 68-2859
1. Gt. Brit.—Biog. 2. Gt Brit. Hist.— Chronology. I. Title.

ROUTH, Charles Richard Nairne, ed. 920.042
Who's who in history. General editor: C. R. N. Routh. Oxford, Blackwell, 1960- v. illus., ports., maps (on lining papers) geneal. tables. 23 cm. Contents.v. 1. British Isles, 55 B.C. to 1485, by W. O. Hassall. [DA28.W618] 61-66758
1. Gt. Brit. — Biog. 2. Gt. Brit. — Hist. — Chronology. I. Title.

STERN, Gladys Bronwyn, 1890- 928.2
And did he stop and speak to you? Chicago, II. Regnery Co., 1958. 202 p. 21 cm. [PR6037.T453A77] 58-11699
1. Gt. Brit. — Biog. I. Title.

WHO was who, 920.042
v.5, 1951-1960; a companion volume to Who's who, containing the biographies of those who died during the decade 1951-1960. New York, Macmillan [1962, c.1961] 1206p. 20-14622 17.50
1. Gt. Brit.—Biog. 2. Biography—Dictionaries.

WHO'S who ... 920'.01
an annual biographical dictionary, with which is incorporated Men and women of our time. 120th issue. 1968-1969 [London. A. & C. Black] New York, St. Martin's v. 13-22cm. Subtitle varies: [DA28.W6] 4-16933 30.00
1. Gt. Brit.—Biog. 2. Biography—Dictionaries. I. Addison, Henry Robert, 1805?-1876. ed. II. Oakes, Charles Henry, 1810-1864, ed. III. Lawson, William John. ed. IV. Sladen, Douglas Brooke Wheelton, 1856-1947, ed.

WHO'S who 1960, 920.042
an annual biographical dictionary, to which is incorporated 'Men and women of the time'; one hundred and twelfth year of issue New York, Macmillan [1960] 351p. 22cm. 4-16933 20.00
1. Gt. Brit.—Biog. 2. Biography—Dictionaries. I. Addison, Henry Robert, 1805?-1876. ed. II. Oakes,Charles Henry, 1810-1864, ed. III. Lawson, William John, ed. IV. Sladen, Douglas Brooke Wheelton, 1856-1947, ed.

WHO'S who, 1964, 920.01
an annual biographical dictionary with which is incorporated 'Men and women of the time.' 116th ed. London, A. & C. Black; dist. New York, St. Martin's [c.1964] 3390p. 23cm. annual. Absorbed Men and women of the time with v.53, 1901. Subtitle varies. Imprint varies. 4-16933 25.00
1. Gt. Brit.—Biog. 2. Biography—Dictionaries.

WHO'S who, 1965; 920.01
an annual biographical dictionary with which is incorporated Men and women of our time.' 117th year of issue London, A. & C. Black, New York, St Martin's [c.1965] 3407p. 23cm. annual. 4-16933 25.00
1. Gt. Brit.—Biog. 2. Biography—Dictionaries.

WHO'S who, 1967-1968; 920.01
an annual biographical dictionary, 119th year of issue NewOrk. St. Martin's [1967] v. 23cm. Incorporates Men & Women of our time. 4-16933 3o.00
1. Gt. Brit.—Biog. 2. Biography—Dictionaries.

WHO'S who in history. 920.042
General ed.: C. R. N Routh. New York, Barnes & Noble [196 v. illus., geneal. table, ports. 22cm. Contents.V. 3. England, 1603-1714, by C. P. Hill. [DA28.W619] 68-2859 7.50
1. Gt. Brit.—Biog. 2. Gt. Brit.—Hist.—Chronology. I. Routh, Charles Richard Nairne. ed.

WHO'S who in history, 920.042
v.3. Gen. ed.: C. R. N. Routh. New York, Barnes & Noble [1966, c.1965] xvi, 443p. illus., ports., geneal. tables. 23cm. Contents.v.3. England, 1603 to 1714, by C. P, Hill [DA28.W618] 7.50 bds.,
1. Gt. Brit.—Biog. 2. Gt. Brit.—Hist — Chronology. I. Routh, Charles Richard Nairne, ed.

WHO'S who in history. 920.042
General ed.: C.R.N. Routh. Oxford, Blackwell [dist. New York, Barnes & Noble, 1964,c.] 1960. v. illus., ports., maps (on lining papers) geneal. tables. Contents.v.1 British Isles, 55 B.C. to 1485, by W.O, Hassall 61 66758
1. Gt. Brit.-Biog. 2. Gt Brit. Hist.—Chronology. I. Routh, Charles Richard Nairne, ed.

WHO'S who in history; 920.042
v.2. Gen. ed.: [Oxford, Blackwell] New York, Barnes & Noble [c. 1964] . R. N. Routh 476p. illus., ports., maps (onlining papers) general. tables. 23cm. Contents.v.2.England, 1485-1603, by C. R. N. Routh. 61-66758 7.50 bds.,
1. Gt. Brit.—Biog. 2. Gt. Brit.—Hist.—Chronology. I. Routh, Charles Richard Nairne, ed.

Gt. Brit.—Hist.—George III, 1760-1820

GEORGE III, King of Great Britain, 1738-1820 George the third 942.07/3/0924
The correspondence of King George the Third from 1760 to December 1783, printed from the original papers in the Royal Archives at Windsor Castle: arranged, ed. by Sir John Fortescue. 1st ed., new impression. London, Cass. 1967. dist. in the U.S.A. by Barnes & Noble 6v. tables. 23cm Contents.v. 1. 1760-1767. v. 2. 1768-June 1773.--v. 3. July 1773-December 1777.--v. 4. 1778-1779.--v. 5.1780.April 1782.--v. 6. May 1782-December 1783. [DA506.A2A2 1967] 68-72568 135.00 set,
1. Gt. Brit.—Hist.—George III, 1760-1820 I. Fortescue, John William, Sir 1859-1933. ed. II. Title.

Gt. Brit.—Hist.—George III, 1760-1820—Sources.

GEORGE, IV, King of Great Britain 1762-1830 George the fourth 923.142
The correspondence of George, Prnce of Wales, 1770-1812. Ed. by A. Aspinall. New York, Oxford Univ. Pr. [1967] v. illus., ports., facsims., geneal. tables. 26cm. Contents.v. 4. 1799-1804 [DA538.A1A3] 64-237 26.90
1. Gt. Brit. — Hist. — George III, 1760-1820 — Sources. 2. Gt. Brit. — Court and courtiers. I. Aspinall, Arthur, 1901- ed. II. Title.

GEORGE I V, King of Great Britain 1762-1930. 923.142
The correspondence of George, Prince of Wales, 1770-1812. Edited by A. Aspinall. New York, Oxford University Press [c1963- v. illus., ports., facsims, geneal. tables. 26 cm. 64-237
1. Gt. Brit.—Hist.—George III, 1760-1820—Sources. 2. Gt. brit.—Court and courtiers. I. Aspinall, Arthur, 1901- ed. II. Title.

GEORGE IV, King of Great Britain, 1762-1830 923.142
The correspondence of George, Prince of Wales, 1770-1812; v.3. Ed. by A. Aspinall. New York, Oxford [c.1965] x, 519p. illus., ports., facsims., fold. geneal. tables. 26cm. Contents.v.3. 1795-1798. 64-237 19.20
1. Gt. Brit.—Hist.—George III, 1760-1820—Sources. 2. Gt. Brit. Court and courtiers. I. Aspinall, Arthur, 1901- ed. II. Title.

GEORGE III, King of Great Britain, 1738-1820. 942.07'3'0924
The correspondence of King George the Third with Lord North 1768 to 1783. Edited with an introd. and notes by W. Bodham Donne New York, Da Capo Press, 1971. 2 v. 24 cm. (The Era of the American Revolution) Running title: Letters to Lord North. Reprint of the 1867 ed. Includes bibliographical references. [DA506.A2A45 1971] 76-154697 ISBN 0-306-70155-3
1. Gt. Brit.—History—George III, 1760-1820—Sources. I. North, Frederick North, Baron, 1732-1792.

GEORGE IV, King of Great Britain, 1762-1830 923.142
The correspondence of George, Prince of Wales, 1770-1812; v.2. Ed. by A. Aspinall. New York, Oxford [c.1964] 559p. illus., ports., facsims., geneal. tables. 26cm. Contents.v.2. 1789-1794. 64-237 19.20
1. Gt. Brit.—Hist.— George III, 1760-1820—Sources. 2. Gt. Brit. Court and courtiers. I. Aspinall, Arthur, 1901- ed. II. Title.

GEORGE IV, King of Great Britain 1762-1830 George the fourth 1762-1830 923.142
The correspondence of George, Prince of Wales, 1770-1812; v.1. Ed. by A. Aspinall. New York, Oxford [c.1963] 528p. illus., ports., facsims., geneal. tables. 26cm. Contents.v.1. 1770-1789. 64-237 16.80
1. Gt. Brit.—Hist.—George III, 1760-1820—Sources. 2. Gt. Brit. — Court and courtiers. I. Aspinal, Arthur, 1901- ed. II. Title.

Gt. Brit.—Hist.—Stuarts, 1603-1714.

EVELYN, John 928.2
Diary. Edited by E. S. de Beer. London, New York Oxford University Press, 1959[i.e. 1960] xii, 1307p. (bibl. footnotes) 19cm. (Oxford standard authors) 60-79 7.00
1. Gt. Brit.—Hist.—Stuarts, 1603-1714. 2. Gt. Brit.—Court and couriers. I. Title.

EVELYN, John, 1620-1706 942.060924
The diary of John Evelyn; ed. by William Bray, preface by Valerie Cromwell. Rev. ed. reprinted. London, Dent; New York, Dutton, 1966. 2 v. 19cm. (Everyman's lib., 220-221) Bibl. [DA447.E9A42 1966] 66-78089 2.25 ea.,
1. Gt. Brit.—Hist.—Stuarts, 1603-1714. 2. Gt. Brit.—Court and courtiers. I. Bray, William, 1736-1832, ed. II. Title.

PEPYS, Samuel 928.2
The diary of Samuel Pepys. Selections edited by O. F. Morshead. Illus. by Ernest H. Shepard. New York, Harper [1960, c.1926] xxi, 548p. illus., maps 21 cm. (Harper Torchbooks; Academy lib. TB1007) 2.45 pap.,
1. Gt. Brit.—Hist.—Stuarts, 1603-1714—Sources. 2. Gt. Brit.—Soc. life & cust. I. Morshead, O.F., ed. II. Title.

PEPYS, Samuel, 1633-1703 928.2
Diary. Based on the Mynors Bright ed. of 1875. Ed., abridged, introd. by John D. Jump. New York, Washington Sq. [c.1964] 336p. 18cm. (W504) .60 pap.,
1. Gt. Brit.—Hist.—Stuarts, 1603-1714—Sources. 2. Gt. Brit.—Sec. life & cust. I. Jump, John D., ed. II. Title.

PEPYS, Samuel, 1633-1793 928.2
Diary. Ed. by J. P. Kenyon. [Rev. ed.] New York, Macmillan [c.1963] x, 246p. illus., ports. 21cm. 63-17296 4.00; 1.95 pap.,
1. Gt. Brit.—Hist.—Stuarts, 1603-1714—Sources. 2. Gt. Brith.—Soc. life & cust. I. Kenyon, John Philipps, 1927- ed. II. Title.

SELECTIONS from the diary of Samuel Pepys 1660-1669 923.242
Introd. by Thomas Yoseloff. New York, Fine Editions Press [1957] ix, 306p. 22cm. [DA447.P4A5 1957] 928.2 57-59365
1. Gt. Brit.—Hist.—Stuarts, 1603-1714—Sources. 2. Gt. Brit.—Soc. —life & cust. I. Pepys, Samuel, 1633-1703.

Gt. Brit.—Hist.—20th cent.

CHURCHILL, Winston Leonard Spencer Sir 1874-1965 942.0820924
A man of destiny: Winston S. Churchill, by the eds. of Country beautiful. Waukesha, Wis. 53186, 24198 W. Bluemound Rd. Country Beautiful Found., [1966] 96p. illus. (pt. col.) facsim., ports. 32cm. [DA566.9.C5A373] 65-21475 5.95
1. Gt. Brit.—Hist.—20th cent. 2. Painting. I. Country beautiful. II. Title.
Content omitted

Gt. Brit.—Hist. 1714-1837.

PLUMB, John Harold, 1911- 942.07'0922
The first four Georges, [by] J. H. Plumb. New York, Wiley [1967, c.1956] 188p. illus., ports. 21cm. (Sci. eds.) Bibl [DA480.P55 1966] 1.95 pap.,
1. Gt. Brit.—Hist. 1714-1837. I. Title.

Gt. Brit.—History, Military—1789-1820.

WHEELER, William, b.1784or5. 923.542
The letters of Private Wheeler, edited and with a foreword by B.H. Liddell Hart. Boston, Houghton Mifflin, 1952 [c1951] viii, 342 p. map (on lining paper) 22 cm. [DA68.12.W5A4] 52-6921
1. Gt. Brit.—History, Military—1789-1820. 2. Gt. Brit. Army. King's Own Yorkshire Light Infantry. I. Title.

Gt. Brit.—Intellectual life.

JEBB, Caroline Lane (Reynolds) Slemmer, Lady. 920.7
With dearest love to all, the life and letters of Lady Jebb, by Mary Reed Bobbitt. Chicago, H. Regnery Co. [1960] 277p. illus. 22cm. [CT788.J32A3] 60-7919
1. Gt. Brit.—Intellectual life. I. Bobbitt, Mary Reed, ed. II. Title.

JEBB, Caroline Lane (Reynolds) Slemmer, Lady. 920.7
With dearest love to all, the life and letters of Lady Jebb, by Mary Reed Bobbitt.

Chicago, H. Regnery Co. [c.1960] 277p. illus. 22cm. 60-7919 5.00
1. Gt. Brit.—Intellectual life. I. Bobbitt, Mary Reed, ed. II. Title.

Gt. Brit.—Kings and rulers—Juvenile literature.

DELDERFIELD, Eric R. 929.7'2
Kings and Queens of England and Great Britain, devised and edited by Eric R. Delderfield. [New ed.] New York, Taplinger Pub. Co. [1967, 1966] 160 p. illus., coats of arms, geneal. tables, ports. 21 cm. First published in 1962-63 under title: A brief guide to Kings & Queens of England and Great Britain. [DA28.1.D42 1967] 67-14050
1. Gt. Brit. — Kings and rulers — Juvenile literature. 2. Gt. Brit. — Hist. — Juvenile literature. I. Title.

SCOTT, Moncrieff, martha Christian 929.72
Kings and queens of England [by] M.C. Scott Moncrieff. Including an essay on royal portraiture by Richard Ormond. New York, Macmillan [1966] 159 p. illus., geneal. tables, map., ports. (part col.) 23 cm. Bibliography: p. 155. [DA28.1.S3 1966a] 66-29032
1. Gt. Brit.—Kings and rulers—Juvenile literature. I. Title.

Gt. brit.—Pol. & Govt.—1800-1837.

CREEVEY, Thomas, 1768-1838 923.242
The Creevey papers. Ed. by John Gore. [Rev. ed.] New York, Macmillan [c.1963] 280p. illus. 21cm. 63-15932 1.95 pap.,
1. Gt. brit.—Pol. & Govt.—1800-1837. I. Title.

Gt. Brit.—Pol. & govt.—1906-1945.

HERBERT, Alan Patrick, 1890- 923.242
Independent Member. [1st American ed.] Garden City, N. Y., Doubleday, 1951. x, 363 p. 22 cm. Autobiographical. [DA585.H4A3 1951] 51-11287
1. Gt. Brit.—Pol. & govt.—1906-1945. 2. Gt. Brit.—Pol. & govt.—1945- I. Title.

Gt. Brit.— Pol. & govt.—1910-1936.

WEBB, Beatrice (Potter) 1858-1943. 923.342
Diaries, edited by Margaret I. Cole, with an introd. by Lord Beveridge. London, New York, Longmans, Green [1952- v. ports. 23cm. Contents.[1] 1912-1924.--[2] 1924-1932. [HX246.W33] 50-11654
1. Gt. Brit.— Pol. & govt.—1910-1936. I. Title.

WEBB, Beatrice (Potter) 1858-1943. 923.342
Diaries, 1912-1924, edited by Margaret I. Cole with an introd. by Lord Beveridge. London, New York, Longmans, Green [1952] xxvi, 272 p. ports. 22 cm. [HX246.W33] 52-11654
1. Gt. Brit. — Pol. & govt. — 1910-1936. I. Title.

Gt. Brit.—Pol. & govt.—1945—

EDEN, Anthony Sir 923.242
Full circle; the memoirs of Anthony Eden. Boston, Houghton Mifflin, [c.]1960. 676p. illus. 22cm. 59-8856 6.75
1. Gt. Brit.—Pol. & govt.—1945- I. Title.

Gt. Brit.—Addresses, essays, lectures.

ROSEBERY, Archibald Philip Primrose, 5th Earl of, 1847-1929. 920.042
Miscellanies: literary & historical. Freeport, N.Y., Books for Libraries Press [1971] 2 v. port. 23 cm. (Essay index reprint series) "First published in 1921." [DA27.R75 1971] 71-152211 ISBN 0-8369-2253-0
1. Gt. Brit.—Addresses, essays, lectures. 2. Gt. Brit.—Biography. I. Title.

Gt. Brit.—Biography—Juvenile literature.

GRICE, Frederick. 920.042
Rebels & fugitives. Drawings by William Stobbs. [1st American ed.] New York, Norton [1964] 160 p. illus. 22 cm. [DA28.G85 1964] 64-9835
1. Gt. Brit.—Biography—Juvenile literature. I. Title.

Gt. Brit.—Colonies.

MACGREGOR, Lewis R., 1886- 327'.2'0924 B
British imperialism; memories and reflections, the autobiography of Lewis R. McGregor. 1st ed. Millbrook, N.Y., Dymer Communications, 1968. 968 p. illus., ports. 24 cm. [D413.M23A3] 68-58517
1. Gt. Brit.—Colonies. 2. Diplomats—Correspondence, reminiscences, etc. I. Title.

Gt. Brit.—Defenses.

HORE-BELISHA, Leslie Hore-Belisha, baron, 1893-1957. 923.242
The private papers of Hore-Belisha [edited by] R. J. Minney. [1st American ed.] Garden City, N. Y., Doubleday, 1961 [c1960] 320 p. illus. 22 cm. [DA585.H6A3 1961] 61-5472
1. Gt. Brit.—Defenses.

Gt. Brit.—Description and travel—1801-1900.

BROWN, William Wells, 1815-1884. 914.2'04'81
The American fugitive in Europe; sketches of places and people abroad. With a memoir of the author. New York, Negro Universities Press [1969] 320 p. port. 23 cm. "Originally published in 1855." An enlarged edition of the author's Three years in Europe, published in London, 1852. [DA625.B881 1969] 72-88424
1. Gt. Brit.—Description and travel—1801-1900. I. Title.

Gt. Brit.—Foreign relations.

SPRING Rice, Cecil Arthur, Sir, 1859-1918. 327'.2'0924 B
The letters and friendships of Sir Cecil Spring Rice; a record. Edited by Stephen Gwynn. Freeport, N.Y., Books for Libraries Press [1972] 2 v. illus. 22 cm. Reprint of the 1929 ed. [DA566.9.S65A3 1972] 79-37912 ISBN 0-8369-6750-X
1. Great Britain—Foreign relations. 2. European War, 1914-1918. I. Gwynn, Stephen Lucius, 1864-1950, ed. II. Title. BIP

SPRING Rice, Cecil Arthur, Sir, 1859-1918. 327'.2'0924 B
The letters and friendships of Sir Cecil Spring Rice; a record. Edited by Stephen Gwynn. Westport, Conn., Greenwood Press [1971] 2 v. illus. 23 cm. Reprint of the 1929 ed. [DA566.9.S65A3 1971] 73-110868 ISBN 0-8371-4545-7
1. Gt. Brit.—Foreign relations. 2. European War, 1914-1918.

Gt. Brit. — Hist. — Henry VIII, 1509-1547.

SITWELL, Edith, Dame, 1887- v. 12
Fanfare for Elizabeth. New York, The Macmillan company, 1962. 6 p. l., 227 p. illus. 21 cm. (Macmillan paperbacks, 90) "First printing." 63-74229
1. Gt. Brit. — Hist. — Henry VIII, 1509-1547. 2. Elizabeth, queen of England, 1533-1603. 3. Gt. Brit. — Court and courtiers. I. Title.

Gt. Brit.—History—Anglo-Saxon period, 449-1066.

GILES, John Allen, 1808-1884, comp. 942.01
Vita quorundum Anglo-Saxonum. Original lives of Anglo-Saxons and others who lived before the conquest. New York, Franklin [1967] iv, 396 p. 23 cm. (Burt Franklin research & source works series, no. 154) Reprint of the 1854 ed. Originally issued as a Publication of the Caxton Society, v. 16. Contents.Contents.—Vita et passio Waldevi Comitis.—Excerptum de familia Herwardi.—Story found in the Isle of Ely.—Vita Haroldi Regis.—Vita Beda Venerabilis, auctore anonymo pervetusto.—Vita alia Venerabilis Beda.—Vita Aldhelmi, Faricio auctore.—De vita vel passione beati martyris Bonifacii, auctore Willibaldo.—Vita Sancti Wilfridi Episcopi Eboracensis, auctore Eddio.—De inventione Sancta Crucis Walthamensis.—Vita Sancti Gilda, auctore, ut fertur, Caradoco Lancarvanensi.—Alia vita Gidla, auctore incerto.—Vita Sancti Egwini Wigorniensis Episcopi per Brithwaldum Glastoniensem Monachum anno 731; incipit epilogus episcopi et confessoris. [DA150.G53 1967] 73-6276
1. Gt. Brit.—History—Anglo-Saxon period, 449-1066. 2. Anglo-Saxons. I. Title. II. Title: Original lives of Anglo-Saxons and others who lived before the conquest. BIP

Gt. Brit. — History, Naval.

RICHMOND, Sir Herbert William, 1871-1946. 923.542
Portrait of an admiral; the life and papers of Sir Herbert Richmond, by Arthur J. Marder. Cambridge, Harvard University Press [1952] 407 p. port. 22 cm. [DA89.1.R] A52
1. Gt. Brit. — History, Naval. I. Marder, Arthur Jacob. II. Title.

Gt. Brit.—History—Stuarts, 1603-1714.

EVELYN, John, 1620-1706. 928.2
Diary. Now first printed in full from the mss. belonging to John Evelyn, and edited by E. S. de Beer. Oxford, Clarendon Press, 1955. 6v. illus., ports., fold. map, facsims., geneal. tables. 23 cm. Contents.Contents.—v. 1. Introduction and De vita propria.—v. 2 Kalendarium, 1620-1649.—v. 3. Kalendarium, 1650-1672.—v. 4. Kalendarium, 1673-1689.—v. 5. Kalendarium, 1690-1706.—v. 6. Additions & corrections. Index. Includes bibliographies. [DA447.E9A44] 56-13545
1. Gt. Brit.—History—Stuarts, 1603-1714. 2. Gt. Brit.—Court and courtiers.

Gt. Brit.—History—Victoria, 1837-1901.

BRIGGS, Asa, 1921- 914.2'03'810922 B
Victorian people; a reassessment of persons and themes, 1851-67. Rev. ed. [Chicago] University of Chicago Press [1970] ix, 312 p. illus. 21 cm. [DA560.B84 1970] 71-16973
1. Gt. Brit.—History—Victoria, 1837-1901. 2. Gt. Brit.—Biography. I. Title. BIP

BRIGGS, Asa, 1921- 914.2'03'810922 B
Victorian people; a reassessment of persons and themes, 1851-67. Rev. and illustrated ed. [Chicago] University of Chicago Press [1973] x, 312 p. illus. 23 cm. Bibliography: p. 300-306. [DA560.B84 1973] 74-176141 ISBN 0-226-07487-0 9.75
1. Great Britain—History—Victoria, 1837-1901. 2. Great Britain—Biography. I. Title.

Gt. Brit.—Kings and rulers.

BARTON, John, 1928- comp. 914.2'03'0922 B
The hollow crown; the follies, foibles and faces of the kings and queens of England. Devised by John Barton. Picture research by Joy Law. [1st American ed.] New York, Dial Press [1971] 272 p. illus. 27 cm. "Originated as ... a stage anthology composed of prose, verse and music by and about the kings and queens of England." [DA28.1.B362 1971] 72-167704 12.50
1. Gt. Brit.—Kings and rulers. I. Title.

DELDERFIELD, Eric R. 929.7
Kings and queens of England and Great Britain, revised and edited by Eric R. Delderfield. [New ed.] New York, Taplinger Pub. Co. [1967, c1966] 160 p. illus., coats of arms, geneal. tables, ports. 21 cm. First published in 1962-63 under title: A brief guide to Kings & Queens of England and Great Britain. A brief history of England presented in a summary of the ruling personality of each English monarch and the main events of their reign. Includes coats of arms and geneological trees of the royal families. [DA28.1.D42 1967] AC 67
1. Great Britain—Kings and rulers. 2. Great Britain—History. 3. Heraldry—Great Britain. I. Title.

MACDONAGH, Michael, 1862-1946. 301.44'2
The English king; a study of the monarchy and the royal family, historical, constitutional, and social. Port Washington, N.Y., Kennikat Press [1971] 318 p. 22 cm. Reprint of the 1929 ed. [DA28.1.M3 1971] 78-118484 ISBN 0-8046-1233-1
1. Gt. Brit.—Kings and rulers. 2. Gt. Brit.—Politics and government. 3. Monarchy, British. I. Title.

MILLES, Thomas, 1550?-1627? 929.7'2
A catalogue of the kings of England; a genealogical history of the monarchs of Great Britain from Egbert in the year 800 A.D. to James I in 1603, originally published in the The catalogue of honour in 1610. Cottonport, Polyanthos, 1972. 241 p. illus. 32 cm. The work was begun by R. Glover and left with Milles, who translated the Latin manuscripts and reduced them to a printable form. [DA28.1.M45 1972] 70-168572 15.00
1. Great Britain—Kings and rulers. 2. Heraldry—Great Britain. I. Glover, Robert, 1544-1588. II. Title.

SCOTT Moncrieff, Martha Christian. 920
Kings and queens of England [by] M. C. Scott Moncrieff. Including an essay on royal portraiture by Richard Ormond. New York, Macmillan [1966] 159 p. illus., geneal. tables, map, ports. (part col.) 23 cm. Bibliography: p. 155. A panorama of the rulers of Great Britain giving basic details of the lives and personalities of the kings and queens set against a background of history and civilization. [DA28.1.S3 1966a] AC 67
1. Great Britain—Kings and rulers. I. Title. BIP

SMITH, Varrel. 942'.00922
Their majesties and other folk. South Brunswick [N.J.] A. S. Barnes [1970, c1969] 343 p. illus. 24 cm. [DA28.1.S57] 68-27215 7.50
1. Gt. Brit.—Kings and rulers. 2. Gt. Brit.—History, Comic, satirical, etc. I. Title.

Gt. Brit.—Politics and government—1837-1901.

BAUMANN, Arthur Anthony, 1856-1936. 942.08'0922
The last Victorians. Freeport, N.Y., Books for Libraries Press [1970] 315 p. facsim., ports. 23 cm. (Essay index reprint series) Reprint of the 1927 ed. Contents.Contents.—Queen Victoria's middle years.—Disraeli's meridian.—The Marquis of Salisbury.—Sir William Harcourt.—Viscount Goschen.—The Balfour-Chamberlain partnership.—Lord Randolph Churchill.—Walter Bagehot.—Anthony Trollope.—Benjamin Jowett.—Mr. Jim Lowther.—George Wyndham.—Lord Chief Justice Coleridge.—Sir Henry Fowler.—Sir John Gorst.—Sir Michael Hick-Beach.—Henry Labouchere.—Charles Stewart Parnell.—Viscount Grey.—The Earl of Oxford.—The statesman's end. [DA550.B3 1970] 70-104991
1. Gt. Brit.—Politics and government—1837-1901. 2. Gt. Brit.—Politics and government—20th century. 3. Statesmen, British. I. Title. BIP

Gt. Brit.—Politics and government—1910-1936.

DAVIDSON, John Colin Campbell Davidson, 1st Viscount, 1889- 942.083
Memoirs of a Conservative; J. C. C. Davidson's memoirs and papers, 1910-37 [edited by] Robert Rhodes James. [1st American ed. New York] Macmillan [1970, c1969] xiii, 446 p. illus., facsim., ports. 25 cm. Bibliography: p. 431. [DA574.D35A3 1970] 76-88835 9.95

1. Gt. Brit.—Politics and government—1910-1936. I. James, Robert Rhodes, 1933- ed. II. Title.

Gt. Brit.—Politics and government—1964-

WILSON, Harold, 942.085'0924 B
1916-
A personal record: the Labour Government, 1964-1970. [1st American ed.] Boston, Little, Brown [1971] 836 p. illus. 25 cm. "An Atlantic Monthly Press book." First published under title: The Labour Government, 1964-1970; a personal record. [DA592.W49 1971b] 70-170166 15.00
1. Gt. Brit.—Politics and government—1964- I. Title. II. Title: The Labour Government, 1964-1970.

Gt. Brit.—Princes and princesses.

JOELSON, Annette, 1903- 929.72
England's Princes of Wales. [1st ed.] Philadelphia, Chilton Books [1966] 254 p. ports. 21 cm. Bibliography: p. 235-242. [DA28.3.J6] 66-15054
1. Gt. Brit.—Princes and princesses. I. Title.

THORNTON-COOK, Elsie 929.7'2
(Prentys) 1889-
Kings in the making; the princes of Wales, by E. Thornton Cook. Freeport, N.Y., Books for Libraries Press [1968] xvi, 345 p. illus., ports. 22 cm. (Essay index reprint series) Reprint of the 1931 ed. Bibliography: p. [329]-338. [DA28.3.T45 1968] 68-22951
1. Great Britain—Princes and princesses. 2. Great Britain—History. I. Title. II. Title: The princes of Wales. **BIP**

Gt. Brit.—Queens.

THORNTON-COOK, Elsie 942
(Prentys) 1889-
Her Majesty; the romance of the queens of England, 1066-1910, by Elsie Thornton Cook. Freeport, N.Y., Books for Libraries Press [1970] xiv, 404 p. illus., ports. 23 cm. (Essay index reprint series) Reprint of the 1926 ed. Bibliography: p. 390-394. [DA28.2.T5 1970] 78-105043
1. Gt. Brit.—Queens. I. Title.

TREASE, Geoffrey, 1909- 923.142
The seven queens of England. New York, Vanguard Press [1953] 254 p. 22 cm. [DA28.2.T7] 53-6900
1. Gt. Brit.—Queens. I. Title. **BIP**

Gt. Brit.—Social life and customs.

FIELDING, Daphne Vivian, 920.7
1904-
Mercury presides. [1st American ed.] New York, Harcourt, Brace [1955] 256 p. illus. 23 cm. Autobiographical. [C1788.F434A3 1955] 55-5318
1. Gt. Brit.—Social life and customs. I. Title.

WILSON, Harriette, 1786- 920.7
1846.
The game of hearts; Harriette Wilson's memoirs, interspersed with excerpts from the Confessions of Julia Johnstone, her rival. Edited and with an introd. by Lesley Blanch. New York, Simon and Schuster, 1955. 532 p. illus. 24 cm. [DA536.W7A32] 55-7134
1. Gt. Brit.—Social life and customs. 2. Gt. Brit.—Court and courtiers. 3. Gt. Brit.—Moral conditions. I. Title.

Gt. Brit. Army—Military life.

CHURCHILL, Winston 923.242
Leonard Spencer, 1874-
A roving commission; the story of my early life. New York, Scribner, 1951 1939] 370 p. illus. 22 cm. First published in 1930 under title: My early life; a roving commission. [DA566.9.C5A3 1951] 52-1113
1. Gt. Brit. Army—Military life. I. Title.

Gt. Brit. Navy— Biog.

JAMESON, William, Sir 923.542
1899-
The fleet that Jack built: nine men who made a modern navy. [1st American ed.] New York, Harcourt, Brace & World [1962] 344p. illus. 23cm. [DA88.1.A1J3 1962a] 62-15423
1. Gt. Brit. Navy—Biog. 2. Gt. Brit.—History, Naval. I. Title.

JAMESON, William 923.542
Scarlett, Sir 1899-
The fleet that Jack built: nine men who made a modern navy. New York, Harcourt [c.1962] 344p. illus. 23cm. 62-15423 5.95
1. Gt. Brit. Navy— Biog. 2. Gt. Brit.—History, Naval. I. Title.

Gt. Britain—History—Victoria, 1837-1901—Sources.

VICTORIA, Queen of Great 923.142
Britain, 1819-1901.
Early letters. Edited by John Raymond. [Rev. ed.] New York, Macmillan [1963] 310 p. illus. 21 cm. [DA552.E3 1963] 63-15934
1. Gt. Britain—History—Victoria, 1837-1901—Sources. I. Title.

Gt. Brit. Royal Air Force—History.

SLESSOR, John Cotesworth, 358
Sir 1897-
The central blue; autobiography. New York, Praeger [1957] 709 p. illus. 22 cm. [DA585.S58A3] 358.4 57-5288
1. Gt. Brit. Royal Air Force—History. I. Title.

Gt. Brit. Royal Marine Forces.

BASSETT, Samuel John 923.542
Woodruff.
Royal Marine; the autobiography of Colonel Sam Bassett. With a foreword by His Royal Highness Prince Philip, and an introd. by General Lemuel C. Shepard, Jr. New York, Stein and Day [1965, c1962] 224 p. 22 cm. [DA88.1.B29A3 1965] 65-13604
1. Gt. Brit. Royal Marine Forces. 2. Gt. Brit.—History, Naval—20th century. I. Title.

Guerin, Theodore, Mother, 1798-1856.

JOSEPH, Eleanor, 271'.979 B
Sister, S.P.
Call to courage; a story of Mother Theodore Guerin. Illustrated by Carolyn Lee Jagodits. Notre Dame, Dujarie Press [1968] 94 p. port. 22 cm. [BX4705.G65J6] 68-23381
1. Guerin, Theodore, Mother, 1798-1856. I. Title.

Guadalupe, Nuestra Senora de.

LEIES, Herbert F. 232.9317
Mother for a new world: Our Lady of Guadalupe. Westminster, Md., Newman, [c.]1964 xi, 125p. col. front. 22cm. Bibl. [BT660.G8L44] 64-66034 5.95
1. Guadalupe, Nuestra Senora de. I. Title.

Guanella, Luigi, 1842-1915.

DAUGHTERS of Saint Mary 922.245
of Providence.
The pilgrim of love; a short popular sketch of the life of the servant of God, Father Aloysius Guanella, founder of the Servants of Charity and of the Daughters of Saint Mary of Divine Providence. [Chicago, 1952] 117p. illus. 22cm. [BX4705.G626D3] 53-181990
1. Guanella, Luigi, 1842-1915. 2. Servants of Charity. I. Title.

Guardi, Francesco, 1712-1793.

BINION, Alice. 741'.092'2
Antonio and Francesco Guardi, their life and milieu : with a catalogue of their figure drawings / Alice Binion. New York : Garland Pub., 1976. 466 p. : ill. ; 21 cm. (Outstanding dissertations in the fine arts) Originally presented as the author's thesis, Columbia University, 1971. Bibliography: p. [333]-348. [NC257.G8B56 1976] 75-23782 ISBN 0-8240-1979-2 lib.bdg. : 32.50
1. Guardi, Francesco, 1712-1793. 2. Guardi, Giovanni Antonio, 1698-1760. 3. Figure drawing—Catalogs. I. Title. II. Series. **BIP**

Guards (Basketball)—United States—Biography—Juvenile literature.

ARMSTRONG, 796.32'3'0922 B
Robert, 1938-
The guards / by Robert Armstrong. Mankato, Minn. : Creative Education, c1977. 47 p. : col. ill. ; 28 cm. (Stars of the NBA) Biographical sketches of five professional basketball guards: Walt Frazier, Nate Archibald, Doug Collins, Pete Maravich, and Dave Bing. [GV884.A1A75] 920 76-45861 ISBN 0-87191-564-2 lib.bdg. : 5.95
1. Guards (Basketball)—United States—Biography—Juvenile literature. I. Title. **BIP**

O'REILLY, Sean, 796.32'3'0922 B
1922-
Meet the guards / by Sean O'Reilly. Mankato, Minn. : Creative Education, [c1977] 30 p. : col. ill. ; 19 cm. Short career biographies of basketball guards Walt Frazier, Nate Archibald, Pete Maravich, and Dave Bing. [GV884.A1O75] 920 76-51833 ISBN 0-87191-602-9 lib.bdg. : 4.95
1. Guards (Basketball)—United States—Biography—Juvenile literature. I. Title. **BIP**

Guareschi, Giovanni,

GUARESCHI, Giovanni, 1908- 858.34
1968.
My home, sweet home. [Translated from the Italian by Joseph Green] New York, Farrar, Straus and Giroux [1966] 214 p. 21 cm. Autobiographical. Translation of Corrierino delle famiglie. [PQ4817.U193Z53] 66-25133
I. Title. **BIP**

Guarneri, Giuseppe, b. 1686?

PETHERICK, Horace. 787'.12'0924 B
Joseph Guarnerius : his work and his master / by Horace Petherick. Boston : Longwood Press, 1977. p. cm. Reprint of the 1906 ed. published by The Strad, London; Scribner, New York, which was issued as no. 16 of The Strad library. [ML424.G8P3 1977] 77-75187 ISBN 0-89341-092-6 : 30.00
1. Guarneri, Giuseppe, b. 1686? 2. Gisalberti, Andreas. 3. Violin makers—Italy—Biography.

Guarneri, Giuseppe, b. 1686?—Juvenile literature.

WIBBERLEY, Leonard Patrick JUV
O'Connor, 1915-
Guarneri: story of a genius [by] Leonard Wibberley. New York, Farrar, Straus, Giroux [1974] viii, 151 p. 22 cm. A fictionalized biography of the Italian violin maker whose instruments, unappreciated in his lifetime, were deemed among the greatest many years after his death. [PZ7.W625Gr] 813'.5'4 FIC 74-8142 ISBN 0-374-32822-6
1. Guarneri, Giuseppe, b. 1686?—Juvenile literature. I. Title.

Guderian, Heinz, 1888-1954.

MACKSEY, Kenneth 358'.18'0924 B
John.
Guderian, creator of the blitzkrieg / by Kenneth Macksey. New York : Stein and Day, [1976] p. cm. [U55.G8M3] 75-37758 ISBN 0-8128-1844-X : 9.95
1. Guderian, Heinz, 1888-1954. I. Title.

Gudmundson, Moses S.

CULMSEE, Carlton 289.3'0924 B
Fordis, 1904-
A modern Moses at West Tintic; essay, by Carlton Culmsee. Logan, Utah State University Press, 1967. 40 p. 24 cm. (Utah State University. Monograph series, v. 14, no. 1) [BX8680.S88G8] 67-65621
1. Gudmundson, Moses S. 2. Church of Jesus Christ of Latter-Day Saints. I. Title. II. Series: Utah. State University of Agriculture and Applied Science, Logan. Monograph series, v. 14, no. 1

Guenther, Carl Hilmar.

GUENTHER, Carl Hilmar. 926.79131
Literal translation of diary and letters of Carl Hilmar Guenther, by Regina Beckmann Hurst. San Antonio, Lithographed [by] the Clegg Co., '1952. 1 v. illus. 23 cm. [CT275.G817A4] 52-25960
I. Title.

Guernsey Co., Ohio—Biography.

PORTRAIT and 977.1'92'00992
biographical record of Guernsey County, Ohio : containing biographical sketches of prominent and representative citizens of the county, together with biographies and portraits of all the Presidents of the United States. Evansville, Ind. : Unigraphic, 1974. 545, 61 p. : ports. ; 29 cm. Reprint of the 1895 ed. published by C. O. Owen, Chicago. Includes indexes. [F497.G93P67 1974] 75-309968
1. Guernsey Co., Ohio—Biography. 2. Presidents—United States—Biography. 3. United States—Biography.

Guerrant, Edward Owings, 1838-1916.

MCALLISTER, James Gray, 922.573
1872-
Edward O. Guerrant: apostle to the southern highlanders, by J. Gray McAllister and Grace Owings Guerrant. Richmond, Richmond Press, 1950. viii, 238 p. illus., ports. 24 cm. [BX9225.G829M2] 50-12449
1. Guerrant, Edward Owings, 1838-1916. I. Guerrant, Grace Owings (Guerrant) 1875- joint author. II. Title.

Guerrillas.

BEALS, Carleton, 909.82'0922
1893-
Great guerrilla warriors. Englewood Cliffs, N.J., Prentice-Hall [1970] 246 p. 24 cm. [D25.5.B33] 71-84997 7.95
1. Guerrillas. 2. Guerrilla warfare. I. Title.

Guess, George, or Sequoyah, Cherokee Indian, 1770?-1843.

COBLENTZ, Catherine (Cate) v. 12
1897-
Sequoya; decorations by Ralph Ray, Jr. New York, David McKay [1962, c1946] viii, 199 p. illus. 21 cm. 66-32761
1. Guess, George, or Sequoyah, Cherokee Indian, 1770?-1843. I. Title.

Guest, Edgar Albert, 1881-

HOWES, Royce. 928.1
Edgar A. Guest, a biography. [Chicago] Reilley & Lee, 1953. 248p. illus. 22cm. [PS3513.U45Z65] 53-13255
1. Guest, Edgar Albert, 1881- I. Title.

Guevara, Ernesto, 1928-1967.

DEBRAY, Regis. 322.4'2'0984
Che's guerrilla war / [by] Regis Debray ; translated [from the French] by Rosemary Sheed. Harmondsworth ; Baltimore [etc.] : Penguin, 1975(i.e.1976) 157 p. : maps ; 18 cm. Translation of La guerilla du Che. Includes bibliographical references. [F3326.D39213 1975b] 76-356594 ISBN 0-14-021884-X pbk. : 2.50
1. Guevara, Ernesto, 1928-1967. 2. Guerrillas—Bolivia. 3. Bolivia—History—1938- I. Title. **BIP**

EBON, Martin. 323.2'0924
Che: the making of a legend. [New York] Universe books [1969] 216 p. illus., ports. 22 cm. Bibliography: p. [209]-211. [F2849.22.G85E2] 70-90938 5.95
1. Guevara, Ernesto, 1928-1967. I. Title.

EBON, Martin. 323.2'0924
Che: the making of a legend. [New York] New American Library [1969] 176 p. illus., facsims., map, ports. 18 cm. (A Signet book) Bibliography: p. [174]-176. [F2849.22.G85E2 1969b] 74-7678 0.75
1. Guevara, Ernesto, 1928-1967. I. Title.

GADEA, Hilda. 980'.03'0924 B
Ernesto: a memoir of Che Guevara. Translated from the Spanish by Carmen Molina and Walter I. Bradbury. [1st ed.] Garden City, N.Y., Doubleday, 1972. xiii, 222 p. illus. 22 cm. [F2849.22.G85G27] 76-160869 6.95
1. Guevara, Ernesto, 1928-1967. I. Title.

GRIGULEVICH, Iosif Romual'dovich, 1913- 980'.03'0924 B
Ernesto Che Guevara / I. Lavretsky [i.e. I. R. Grigulevich] ; [translated from the Russian by A. B. Eklof]. Moscow : Progress Publishers, 1976. 310 p., [24] leaves of plates : ill. ; 21 cm. Translation of Ernesto Che Gevara. Errata slip inserted. Includes bibliographical references. [F2849.22.G85G713] 77-480353
1. Guevara, Ernesto, 1928-1967. 2. Guerrillas—Latin America—Biography.

JAMES, Daniel. 980'.03'0924 B
Che Guevara; a biography. New York, Stein and Day [1969] 380 p. illus., ports. 25 cm. Bibliographical footnotes. [F2849.22.G85J3] 68-19566 7.95
1. Guevara, Ernesto, 1928-1967.

JAMES, Daniel, comp. 984'.05'0922
The complete Bolivian diaries of Che Guervara, and other captured documents. Edited and with an introd. by Daniel James. New York, Stein and Day [1968] 330 p. illus., facsims., maps, ports. 21 cm. Contents.Contents.—Chronology of the Bolivian campaign.—Che Guevara's diary.—Rolando's diary.—Pombo's diary.—Braulio's diary.—Appendices (p. 323-330) :1. A list of the querrilla forces.—2. Others mentioned in the diaries. Bibliographical footnotes. [F3326.J3] 68-55642 6.95
1. Bolivia—History—1938- 2. Guerrillas—Bolivia. 3. Subversive activities—Bolivia. I. Guevara, Ernesto, 1928-1967. II. Title.

RESNICK, Marvin D. 980'.03'0924 B
The black beret: the life and meaning of Che Guevara [by] Marvin D. Resnick. New York, Ballantine Books [1970, c1969] 306 p. 18 cm. Includes bibliographical references. [F1788.22.G8R4] 79-18673 1.25
1. Guevara, Ernesto, 1928-1967. I. Title.

ROJO, Ricardo, 1923- 972.91'064'0924 B
My friend Che. Translated from the Spanish by Julian Casart. New York, Dial Press, 1968. 220 p. illus., facsims., ports. 22 cm. Translation of mi amigo el Che. [F2849.22.G85R613] 68-9461 4.95
1. Guevara, Ernesto, 1928-1967. I. Title.

SAUVAGE, Leo. 980'.03'0924 B
Che Guevara; the failure of a revolutionary. Translated from the French by Raoul Fremont. Englewood Cliffs, N.J., Prentice-Hall [1973] 282 p. 22 cm. Translation of Le cas Guevara. Includes bibliographical references. [F2849.22.G85S2813] 73-9516 ISBN 0-13-128330-8 6.95
1. Guevara, Ernesto, 1928-1967.

SINCLAIR, Andrew. 980'.03'0924 B
Che Guevara. New York, Viking Press [1970] 115 p. 20 cm. (Modern masters) Bibliography: p. 109. [F1788.22.G8S5 1970] 79-104144 4.95
1. Guevara, Ernesto, 1928-1967. 2. Cuba—History—1959-

Guevara, Ernesto, 1928-1967—Juvenile literature.

MALLIN, Jay. 980'.03'0924 B
Ernesto "Che" Guevara, modern revolutionary, guerilla theorist. Charlotteville, N.Y., SamHar Press, 1973. 31 p. 22 cm. (Outstanding personalities, no. 53) Bibliography: p. 31. A biography of the Latin American revolutionary and guerrilla warrior who led guerrilla movements in Africa, Latin America, and Cuba. [F2849.22.G85M34] 92 73-77604 ISBN 0-87157-556-6 1.98 (lib. bdg.)
1. Guevara, Ernesto, 1928-1967—Juvenile literature. I. Title.
Pbk. 0.98; ISBN 0-87157-056-4

Guggenheim family.

DAVIS, John Hagy, 1929- 338'.092'2 B
The Guggenheims : an American epic / by John H. Davis. 1st ed. New York : Morrow, 1978. 608 p., [16] leaves of plates : ill. ; 25 cm. Includes index. Bibliography: p. [577]-588. [HC102.5.G8D38] 77-20069 ISBN 0-688-03273-7 : 14.95
1. Guggenheim family. 2. Businessmen—United States—Biography. 3. Art patrons—United States—Biography. 4. Jews in the United States—Biography. I. Title. **BIP**

HOYT, Edwin Palmer. 332'.0922
The Guggenheims and the American dream [by] Edwin P. Hoyt, Jr. [New York] Funk & Wagnalls [1967] 382 p. 22 cm. Bibliographical references included in "Notes" (p. 355-364) [HC102.5.G8H6] 67-25415
1. Guggenheim family. I. Title.

LOMASK, Milton. 923.673
Seed money: the Guggenheim story. New York, Farrar, Straus [1964] viii, 307 p. illus., ports. 22 cm. Bibliographical references included in "Notes" (p. 279-289) [HV28.G78L6] 63-22088
1. Guggenheim family. I. Title.

O'CONNOR, Harvey, 1897- 338.7'62'20922 B
The Guggenheims : the making of an American dynasty / Harvey O'Connor. New York : Arno Press, 1976, c1937. p. cm. (American business abroad) Reprint of the ed. published by Covici, Friede, New York. Includes index. [TN139.O22 1976] 76-5026 ISBN 0-405-09292-X : 30.00
1. Guggenheim family. 2. Mining industry and finance—United States. I. Title. II. Series. **BIP**

Guggenheim, Marguerite, 1898-

GUGGENHEIM, Marguerite, 1898- 704'.7 B
Out of this century : confessions of an art addict / Peggy Guggenheim ; foreword by Gore Vidal ; introd. by Alfred H. Barr. New York : Universe Books, c1979. p. cm. Autobiographical. Updated and combined ed. of the author's Out of this century and Confessions of an art addict, with new material added. Includes index. [N5220.G886A36 1979] 78-68475 ISBN 0-87663-337-8 : 17.50
1. Guggenheim, Marguerite, 1898- 2. Art patrons—United States—Biography. I. Guggenheim, Marguerite, 1898- Confessions of an art addict. II. Title. **BIP**

Guggenheimer, Minnie (Schaefer).

UNTERMEYER, Sophie (Guggenheimer) 927.8
Mother is Minnie, by Sophie Guggenheimer Untermeyer and Alix Williamson. Garden City, N. Y., Doubleday. [c.]1960. 213p. 22cm. 60-10672 3.95
1. Guggenheimer, Minnie (Schaefer). 2. Concerts—New York (City) I. Williamson, Alix, joint author. II. Title.

Guicciardini, Francesco, 1483-1540.

BONDANELLA, Peter E., 1943- 945'.06'0924 B
Francesco Guicciardini / by Peter E. Bondanella. Boston : Twayne Publishers, c1976. 160 p. : port. ; 21 cm. (Twayne's world authors series) Includes index. Bibliography: p. 153-157. [DG738.14.G9B66] 75-41388 ISBN 0-8057-6231-0 lib.bdg. : 7.50
1. Guicciardini, Francesco, 1483-1540. 2. Italy—Historiography. **BIP**

RIDOLFI, Roberto, 1895- 945'.06'0924 B
The life of Francesco Guicciardini. Translated from the Italian by Cecil Grayson. [1st American ed.] New York, Knopf, 1968. ix, 336 p. port. 25 cm. Translation of Vita di Francesco Guicciardini. Includes bibliographies. [DG738.14.G9R513 1968] 68-13645
1. Guicciardini, Francesco, 1483-1540.

Guidry, Mary Babriella, Sr., 1914-

*GUIDRY, Mary Gabriella, Sister. 922.2763 B
The southern negro nun; an autobiography 1st. ed. [Jericho] N.Y. Exposition Press [1974] 156 p. illus. 22 cm. [BX2511] ISBN 0-682-47888-1 6.50
1. Guidry, Mary Gabriella, Sr. I. Title.

GUIDRY, Mary Gabriella, 1914- 271'.97 B
The Southern Negro nun : an autobiography / by Mary Gabriella Guidry. 1st ed. New York : Exposition Press, c1974. 156 p., [4] leaves of plates : ill. ; 22 cm. [BX4705.G717A35] 75-321162 ISBN 0-682-47888-1 : 6.50
1. Guidry, Mary Gabriella, 1914- I. Title.

Guilbert, Yvette, 1865-1944.

KNAPP, Bettina (Liebowitz) 1926- 927.8
That was Yvette; the biography of Yvette Guilbert, the great diseuse, by Bettina Knapp, Myra Chipman. New York, Holt [c.1964] 380p. illus., facsims., ports. 22cm. Bibl. 64-14788 5.95
1. Guilbert, Yvette, 1865-1944. I. Chapman, Myra joint author. II. Title.

Guilford Greene Gallery, Guilford, Conn.

WASHBURN, Robert Collyer. 658.87
Gallery on the green. New York, Washburn [1957] 152 p. illus. 21 cm. Autobiographical. [HF5483.W3] 57-6609
1. Guilford Greene Gallery, Guilford, Conn. 2. Gift shops. I. Title.

Guilfoyle, William Robert, 1840-1912.

PESCOTT, Richard Thomas Martin, 1905- 712'.5 B
W. R. Guilfoyle, 1840-1912 : the master of landscaping / [by] R. T. M. Pescott. Melbourne ; New York : Oxford University Press, 1974. xvii, 153 p., 13 p. of plates : ill., facsims., front., map on lining papers ; 25 cm. Includes index. Bibliography: p. 143-145. [SB470.G84P47] 75-320160 ISBN 0-19-550454-2 : 9.75
1. Guilfoyle, William Robert, 1840-1912. 2. Melbourne. Botanic Garden. 3. Landscape gardening—Australia—Melbourne.

Guillaume de Machaut, d. 1377.

LEAVARIE, Siegmund, 1914- 927.8
Guillaume de Machaut. New York, Sheed and Ward, 1954. 114p. illus. 22cm. (Great religious composers) [ML410.G966L4] 54-11137
1. Guillaume de Machaut, d. 1377. I. Title.

LEVARIE, Siegmund, 1914- 783'.0924 B
Guillaume de Machaut. Edited by John J. Becker. New York, Da Capo Press, 1969 [c1954] 114 p. illus. 24 cm. (Da Capo Press music reprint series) "This Da Capo Press edition is an unabridged republication of the first edition published in 1954." Bibliography: p. [111]-114. Discography: p. 114. [ML410.G966 1969] 70-98309
1. Guillaume de Machaut, d. 1377. **BIP**

REANEY, Gilbert. 784'.0924
Guillaume de Machaut. London, New York, Oxford University Press, 1971. 76 p. music. 22 cm. (Oxford studies of composers, 9) Bibliography: p. 75-76. [ML410.G966R4] 79-32092 ISBN 0-19-315218-5 £0.90
1. Guillaume de Machaut, d. 1377. Works. I. Title. II. Series. **BIP**

Guillaume de Saint-Thierry, 1085 (ca)-1148?

DECHANET, Jean Marie. 230'.2'0924 B
William of St. Thierry the man and his work. Translated by Richard Strachan. Spencer, Mass., Cistercian Publications, 1972. x, 172 p. 23 cm. (Cistercian studies series, no. 10) Translation of Guillaume de Saint-Thierry: l'homme et son oeuvre. Bibliography: p. 165-166. [BX4705.G7464D413 1972] 73-152485 ISBN 0-87907-810-3 10.95
1. Guillaume de Saint-Thierry, 1085 (ca)-1148? I. Title. II. Series. **BIP**

Guillot, Luis.

BUCKLEY, Peter. 914.6
Luis of Spain, written and photographed by Peter Buckley. New York, F. Watts [c1955] 87p. illus. 27cm. (His The around the world today books) [DP48.B8] 54-10913
1. Guillot, Luis. 2. Spain—Soc. life & cust. I. Title.

Guinea—Politics and government.

MORROW, John H. 327.66'52'073
First American ambassador to Guinea [by] John H. Morrow. New Brunswick, N.J., Rutgers University Press [1967, c1968] xiv, 291 p. illus., group ports. 25 cm. Autobiographical. [DT543.8.M67] 67-31172
1. Guinea—Politics and government.

Guinea—Social life and customs.

LAYE, Camara, 1928- 916.652
The dark child. With an introd. by Philippe Thoby-Marcellin. Translated by James Kirkup, Ernest Jones [and] Elaine Gottlieb. New York, Noonday Press, 1954. 188 p. 21 cm. Autobiographical story. [DT543.L313] 54-11726
1. Guinea—Social life and customs. I. Title.

Guiney, Louise Imogen, 1861-1920.

FAIRBANKS, Henry George, 1914- 811'.4 B
Louise Imogen Guiney; laureate of the lost, by Henry G. Fairbanks. Albany, N.Y., Magi Books [1973, c1972] xiv, 315 p. port. 24 cm. Bibliography: p. 293-302. [PS1768.F3 1973] 73-176128 ISBN 0-87343-039-5
1. Guiney, Louise Imogen, 1861-1920. **BIP**

GUINEY, Louise Imogen, 1861-1920. 811'.4 B
Letters of Louise Imogen Guiney. Edited by Grace Guiney, with a pref. by Agnes Repplier. Freeport, N.Y., Books for Libraries Press [1972] p. Reprint of the 1926 ed. [PS1768.A45 1972] 72-8455 ISBN 0-8369-6975-8
I. Guiney, Grace Cecily, ed.

Guion, Connie M., 1882-

CAMPION, Nardi (Reeder) 926.1
Look to this day. The lively education of a great woman doctor: Connie Guion, M.D., by Nardi Reeder Campion, with Rosamond Wilfley Stanton. [1st ed.] Boston, Little, Brown [1965] xii, 308 p. ports. 22 cm. [R154.G82C3] 65-10582
1. Guion, Connie M., 1882- I. Stanton, Rosamond Wilfley. II. Title.

Guiseppe, Francesco, 1887-

*GIGLIOZZI, Giovanni 271.36
Padre Pio, a pictorial biography. Tr. [from Italian] by Oscar DeLiso. New York, Pocket Bks. [1966, c.1965] 128p. illus., ports. 18cm. (75177) First pub. in 1965 by Phaedra under the title: I monili dello sposo (Cardinal ed., 75177) .75 pap.,
1. Guiseppe, Francesco, 1887- 2. Stigmata. I. Title.

Guitarists.

BONE, Philip James. 927.8
The guitar and mandolin; biographies of celebrated players andcomposers. [2d ed., enl.] London, New York, Schott, 1954. 388p. ports., facsims., music. 22cm. [ML399.B6 1954] 55-20252
1. Guitarists. 2. Mandolinists. 3. Composers. 4. Music—Bio-bibl. I. Title.

Guitarists—Biography.

BONE, Philip James. 787'.61'0922 B
The guitar and mandolin; biographies of celebrated players and composers, by Philip J. Bone. London, Schott. St. Clair Shores, Mich., Scholarly Press, 1973. p. Reprint of the 1954 ed. [ML399.B6 1973] 73-4829 ISBN 0-403-01910-9
1. Guitarists—Biography. 2. Mandolinists. 3. Composers—Biography. 4. Music—Bio-bibliography. I. Title. BIP

TOBLER, John. 787'.61'0922 B
Guitar heroes / John Tobler. New York : St. Martin's Press, 1978. 88 p. : ports. (some col.) ; 30 cm. [ML399.T65] 78-439 ISBN 0-312-35320-0 : 8.95
1. Guitarist—Biography. 2. Rock musicians—Biography. BIP

Guitry, Sacha, 1885-1957.

HARDING, James. 842'.9'12 B
Sacha Guitry: the last boulevardier. New York, Scribner [1968] ix, 277 p. illus., facsim., ports. 25 cm. Bibliography: p. 266-268. [PN2638.G8H3 1968b] 68-27786 6.95
1. Guitry, Sacha, 1885-1957.

Gulab Singh, Maharajah of Kashmir, 1792-1857.

BAWA Satinder Singh, 1932- 954'.6'0310924 B
The Jammu Fox; a biography of Maharaja Gulab Singh of Kashmir, 1792-1857, by Dawa Satinder Singh. Carbondale, Southern Illinois University Press [1974] xiv, 263 p. illus. 24 cm. Bibliography: p. 239-252. [DS475.2.G8S56] 73-23023 ISBN 0-8093-0652-2 15.00
1. Gulab Singh, Maharajah of Kashmir, 1792-1857. I. Title. BIP

PANIKKAR, Kavalam Madhava, 1896- 923.1564
The founding of the Kashmir State; a biography of Maharajah Gulab Singh, 1782-1858. London, Allen & Unwin [Mystic, Conn., Verry, 1964] 172p. port. fold. map. First ed. pub. in 1960 under title: Gulab singh, 1792-1858, founder of Kashmir. 61-48873 3.25 bds.,
1. Gulab Singh, Maharajah of Kashmir, 1792-1858. 2. India—Hist 3. Kashmir—Hist. I. Title.

Gulbenkian, Calouste Sarkis.

LODWICK, John, 1916- 923.3496
Gulbenkian; an interpretation of the richest man in the world, by John Lodwick in collaboration with D. H. Young, [1st American ed.] Garden City, N. Y., Doubleday, 1958. 289p. 22cm. [CT3150.G8L6 1958a] 58-8101
1. Gulbenkian, Calouste Sarkis. I. Title.

Gulbenkian, Nubar S.

GULBENKIAN, Nubar S. 338.272820924
Portrait in oil; the autobiography of Nubar Gulbenkian. New York, S. & S. [c.1965] 383p. illus., ports. 24cm. First pub. under title: Pantaraxia: the autobiography of Nubar Gulbenkian [CT3150.G85A3] 65-24833 6.50
I. Title.

Gulick, Luther Halsey, 1865-1918.

DORGAN, Ethel Josephine, 1894- 613.7'092'4 B
Luther Halsey Gulick, 1865-1918. New York, Bureau of Publications, Teachers College, Columbia University, 1934. [New York, AMS Press, 1973, c1972] vii, 180 p. 22 cm. Reprint of the 1934 ed., issued in series: Teachers College, Columbia University. Contributions to education, no. 635. Originally presented as the author's thesis, Columbia. Bibliography: p. 155-171. [GV333.G8D6 1972] 75-176726 ISBN 0-404-55635-3 10.00
1. Gulick, Luther Halsey, 1865-1918. 2. Physical education and training—United States. I. Series: Columbia University. Teachers College. Contributions to education, no. 635. BIP

Gumberg, Alexander, 1887-1939.

LIBBEY, James K. 327'.73'047 B
Alexander Gumberg & Soviet-American relations, 1917-1933 / James K. Libbey. Lexington : University Press of Kentucky, c1977. xiv, 229 p. ; 24 cm. Includes bibliographical references and index. [E183.8.R9L5] 77-73704 ISBN 0-8131-1361-X : 13.50
1. Gumberg, Alexander, 1887-1939. 2. United States—Foreign relations—Russia. 3. Russia—Foreign relations—United States. 4. United States—Foreign economic relations—Russia. 5. Russia—Foreign economic relations—United States. 6. Businessmen—United States—Biography. I. Title. BIP

Gumilev, Nikolai Stepanovich, 1886-1921.

SAMPSON, Earl D. 891.7'1'42 B
Nikolay Gumilev / by Earl D. Sampson. Boston : Twayne Publishers, 1979. 192 p. : port. ; 21 cm. (Twayne's world authors series ; TWAS 500 : Russia) Includes index. Bibliography: p. 185-188. [PG3476.G85Z88] 78-18006 ISBN 0-8057-6341-4 : 12.95
1. Gumilev, Nikolai Stepanovich, 1886-1921. 2. Poets, Russian—20th century—Biography.

Gunn, John Angus Lancaster, 1892-1962.

GUNN, Dorothy Ruth (Bodell) 910'.4
A light that shone; a portrait of J. A. L. Gunn, by Dorothy Ruth Gunn. [Brisbane] Jacaranda Press [1964] 116 p. ports. 22 cm. [CT2808.G8G8] 65-66223
1. Gunn, John Angus Lancaster, 1892-1962. I. Title.

Gunn, Neil Miller, 1891-1973.

NEIL M. Gunn; 823'.9'12
the man and the writer. Edited by Alexander Scott & Douglas Gifford. New York, Barnes & Noble, 1973. vii, 397 p. illus. 23 cm. Erratum slip inserted. [PR6013.U64Z8 1973b] 73-161519 13.50
1. Gunn, Neil Miller, 1891-1973. I. Gunn, Neil Miller, 1891-1973. II. Scott, Alexander, ed. III. Gifford, Douglas, 1920- ed.
Contents Omitted.

Gunn, Paul Irvin, 1900-1957.

KENNEY, George Churchill, 1889- 923.573
The saga of Pappy Gunn. [1st ed.] New York, Duell, Sloan and Pearce [1959] 133p. 21cm. [UG633.K45] 59-6694
1. Gunn, Paul Irvin, 1900-1957. 2. World War, 1939-1945—Aerial operations, American. I. Title.

Gunn, Thomas Franklin.

GUNN, Thomas Franklin. 923.373
Good folks, by Thomas F. Gunn. Denver, Big Mountain Press [1964] 327 p. illus., coat of arms, ports. 23 cm. Autobiographical. [CT275.G853A3] 65-1237
I. Title.

Gunsmiths—Ohio.

HUTSLAR, Donald A. 338.7'68'140025771
Gunsmiths of Ohio, 18th & 19th centuries, by Donald A. Hutslar. Edited by Nancy Bagby. York, Pa., G. Shumway [1973- v. illus. 32 cm. (Longrifle series) Contents.Contents.—v. 1. Biographical data. Bibliography: v. 1, p. 417-426. [TS533.3.O3H87] 72-87114 29.50 (v. 1)
1. Gunsmiths—Ohio. I. Title.

HUTSLAR, Donald A. 338.7'68'340025771
Gunsmiths of Ohio, 18th & 19th centuries, by Donald A. Hutslar. Edited by Nancy Bagby. York, Pa., G. Shumway [1973- v. illus. 32 cm. (Longrifle series) Contents.Contents.—v. 1. Biographical data. Bibliography: v. 1, p. 417-426. [TS533.3.O3H87] 72-87114 ISBN 0-87387-026-3 (v. 1) 29.50 (v. 1)
1. Gunsmiths—Ohio. I. Title.

Gunsmiths—Vermont.

HORN, Warren R. 683.4'009743
Gunsmiths and gunmakers of Vermont : a partial checklist from the early years through 1900 / by Warren R. Horn. Burlington, Vt. : Horn Co., c1975. iii, 75 p. : ill. ; 23 cm. Bibliography: p. 73-75. [TS533.3.V5H67] 75-21180
1. Gunsmiths—Vermont. 2. Vermont—Biography. I. Title.

Gunstone, John Thomas Arthur.

†GUNSTONE, John Thomas Arthur. 283'.092'4 B
Living together : the warm and candid story of one man's experience in a Christian community / John Gunstone ; drawings by Sylvia Lawton. 1st American ed. Minneapolis : Bethany Fellowship, 1976. 125 p. : ill. ; 18 cm. (Dimension books) [BX5186.B37G86 1976] 76-57794 ISBN 0-87123-325-8 pbk. : 1.95
1. Barnabas Fellowship. 2. Gunstone, John Thomas Arthur. 3. Church of England—Clergy—Biography. 4. Pentecostalism—Church of England. 5. Clergy—England—Biography. I. Title.

Gunther, John, 1929-1947.

GUNTHER, John, 1901- 616.9'94'810924
Death be not proud; a memoir. Large type ed. New York, Harper & Row [1966, c1949] 261 p. 29 cm. [[CT275.G]] 68-1552
1. Gunther, John, 1929-1947. I. Title.

GUNTHER, John, 1901- 920
Death be not proud, a memoir. New York, Harper [1965, c.1949] 161p. 18cm. (Perennial classic, P 3049 A) [CT275.G855] .50 pap.,
1. Gunther, John, 1929-1947 I Title. BIP

GUNTHER, John, 1901- 920
Death be not proud, a memoir. Large Type ed. New York, Harper [1966, c.1949] 261p. 29cm. [CT275.G855G8] 5.79 lib. ed.,
1. Gunther, John, 1929-1947 2. Gunther, John, 1929-1947 I. Title.

GUNTHER, John, 1901- 920.02
Procession. New York, Harper [c.1933-1965] xiv, 514p. 25cm. [CT120.G8] 65-16257 6.95
1. Biography—20th cent. I. Title.

GUNTHER, John, 1901-1970. 920
Death be not proud, a memoir; with an introd. by the author. New York, Modern Library [1953] 261 p. 19 cm. (The Modern library of the world's best books [286]) [CT275.G855G8 1953] 53-5344
1. Gunther, John, 1929-1947. I. Title.

GUNTHER, John, 1901-1970. 616.9'94'810924 B
Death be not proud. Pref. by Cass Canfield. Memorial ed. New York, Harper & Row [1971] 264 p. port. 21 cm. Memoir. [CT275.G855G8 1971] 75-138730 ISBN 0-06-011634-X 6.95
1. Gunther, John, 1929-1947. I. Title. BIP

GUNTHER, John, 1901-1970. 920.02
Procession. [1st ed.] New York, Harper & Row [1965] xiv, 514 p. 25 cm. [CT120.G8] 65-16257
1. Biography—20th century. I. Title.

Gunther, Robert William Theodore, 1869-1940.

GUNTHER, Albert Everard, 1903- v. 12
Robert T. Gunther; a pioneer in the history of science, 1869-1940. Oxford [University Press] for the subscribers, 1967. xiii, 520 p. 22 cm. (Early science in Oxford, v. 15) 68-44119
1. Gunther, Robert William Theodore, 1869-1940. I. Title. II. Series.

Gupta, Chandra Bhanu, 1902-

SARIN, L. N. 954.03'5'0924
Chandra Bhanu Gupta; a profile in courage, by L. N. Sarin. Delhi, S. Chand, 1967. 80p. port. 22cm. [DS481.G79S2] [PL 480: I-E-9252] SA 68 4.00
1. Gupta, Chandra Bhanu, 1902- I. Title.
American distributor: Verry, Mystic, Conn.

Gurdjieff, Georges Ivanovitch, 1872-1949.

BENNETT, John Godolphin, 1897- 197.20924
Gurdjieff making a new world /J. G. Bennett New York Harper and Row [1976 c1973] 320 p. ill.; 20 cm. (Harper colophon books) Includes index. [B4249.G84B463] ISBN 0-06-090474-7 pbk.: 3.95
1. Gurdjieff, Georges Ivanovitch, 1872-1949. I. Title.
L.C. card no. for original edition: 73-18675. BIP

BENNETT, John Godolphin, 1897- 133'.092'4 B
Gurdjieff, a very great enigma; three lectures, by J. G. Bennett. New York, S. Weiser, 1973 [c1969] 100 p. 21 cm. "Given at Denison House, summer 1963." [B4249.G84B46 1973] 72-91951 ISBN 0-87728-216-1 2.50
1. Gurdjieff, Georges Ivanovitch, 1872-1949.

BENNETT, John Godolphin, 1897- 133'.092'4 B
Gurdjieff: making a new world [by] J. G. Bennett. [1st U.S. ed.] New York, Harper & Row [1974, c1973] 320 p. illus., maps (on lining papers) 22 cm. Includes bibliographical references. [B4249.G84B463 1973b] 73-18675 ISBN 0-06-060778-5 8.95
1. Gurdjieff, Georges Ivanovitch, 1872-1949. I. Title.

HARTMANN, Thomas Aleksandrovich, 1883- 133'.092'4
Our life with Mr. Gurdjieff [by] Thomas de Hartmann. New York, Cooper Square Publishers, 1964. xiii, 130 p. map, ports. 24 cm. [B4249.G84H3] 64-22661
1 Gurdjieff, Georges Ivanovitch, 1872-1949. I. Title.

LEFORT, Rafael. 133'.092'4
The teachers of Gurdjieff. New York, S. Weiser, 1973 [c1966] 157 p. 23 cm. [B4249.G84L4 1973] 72-91193 ISBN 0-87728-213-7 5.00
1. Gurdjieff, Georges Ivanovich, 1872-1949. 2. Sufism. I. Title. BIP

PAUWELS, Louis, Aug.2,1920- 133'.092'4
Gurdjieff. With paintings by Felix Labisse, Georges Rohner [and] Ferro. [1st American ed.] New York, S. Weiser, 1972 [c1964] xxi, 456 p. illus. 21 cm. Translation of Monsieur Gurdjieff. [B4249.G84P33 1972] 71-188373 ISBN 0-87728-178-5 5.00
1. Gurdjieff, Georges Ivanovitch, 1872-1949. BIP

PETERS, Arthur Anderson, 1913- 197'.2
Gurdjieff remembered, by Fritz Peters. [1st American ed.] New York, S. Weiser, 1971 [c1965] 159 p. 21 cm. [B4249.G84P42 1971] 70-152854 ISBN 0-87728-142-4 2.50
1. Gurdjieff, Georges Ivanovitch, 1872-1949. I. Title.

POPOFF, Irmis B. 133'.092'4 B
Gurdjieff : his work on myself, with others, for the work / Irmis B. Popoff. Rev. ed. New York : S. Weiser, 1973. 198 p. ; 24 cm. Includes index. Bibliography: p. 195.

[B4249.G84P66 1973] 73-79122 ISBN 0-87728-224-2 : 5.95
1. Gurdjieff, Georges Ivanovitch, 1872-1949. 2. Uspenskii, Petr Dem'ianovich, 1878-1947. I. Title. **BIP**

WEBB, James, 1946- 133'.092'4 B
The harmonious circle : an exploration of the lives and work of G. I. Gurdjieff, P. D. Ouspensky, A. R. Orage, Maurice Nicoll, Jean Toomer, Rodney Collin-Smith, J. G. Bennett and others / by James Webb. New York : Putnam, c1978. p. cm. [B4249.G84W4 1978] 77-16261 ISBN 0-399-11465-3 : 19.95
1. Gurdjieff, Georges Ivanovitch, 1872-1949. 2. Philosophers—Russia—Biography. 3. Mystics—Russia—Biography. I. Title.

WOLFE, Edwin. 133'.092'4 B
Episodes with Gurdjieff / Edwin Wolfe. [Millerton, N.Y.] : Far West Press, 1974, c1973. 38 p. ; 22 cm. [B4249.G84W64 1974] 75-313599
1. Gurdjieff, Georges Ivanovitch, 1872-1949. I. Title.

Gurney, Ivor, 1890-1937—Biography.

MOORE, Charles Willard, 1925- 821'.9'12 B
Maker and lover of beauty : Ivor Gurney, poet and songwriter / [by] Charles W. Moore ; with decorations by Richard Walker ; and an introduction by Herbert Howells. Rickmansworth : Triad Press, 1976. 28 p. : ill., music, port. ; 28 cm. Cover title: Ivor Guerney, poet and songwriter. Limited ed. of 200 numbered copies. No. 182. Includes bibliographical references. [PR6013.U693Z8] 76-365730 ISBN 0-902070-16-9 : £2.65
1. Gurney, Ivor, 1890-1937—Biography. I. Title.

Gurney, Joseph John, 1788-1847.

SWIFT, David E. 922.8642
Joseph John Gurney: banker, reformer, and Quaker. Middletown, Conn., Wesleyan Univ. Pr. [c.1962] xvii, 304p. illus. 24cm. Bibl. 62-18346 6.50
1. Gurney, Joseph John, 1788-1847. I. Title.

SWIFT, David E 922.8642
Joseph John Gurney: banker, reformer, and Quaker. [1st ed.] Middletown, Conn., Wesleyan University Press [1962] xvii, 304 p. illus., ports. 24 cm. Bibliographical references included in "Notes" (p. [259]-275) Bibliography: p. [279]-294. [BX7795.G85S9 1962] 62-18346
1. Gurney, Joseph John, 1788-1847. I. Title.

Gurvitch, Georges, 1894-1965.

BALANDIER, Georges. 301'.092'4 B
Gurvitch, translated from the French by Margaret A. Thompson; with the assistance of Kenneth A. Thompson. New York, Harper & Row, [1975 c1974] vi, 110, [1] p. 23 cm. (Explorations in interpretative sociology) Translation of Gurvitch. Includes extracts from Gurvitch's works. "The works of Gurvitch" p. [40]-42. Bibliography: p. [111] [HM22.F8G8313] 75-329852 ISBN 0-06-136171-2 12.50.
1. Gurvitch, Georges, 1894-1965. 2. Sociology. I. Title.

Gusman, Maurice, 1888-

ERLICH, Lillian. 338'.092'4 B
Money isn't important : the life of Maurice Gusman / with a foreword by Efrem Zimbalist, Jr. Miami : E. A. Seemann Pub., c1976. 186 p. : ill. ; 24 cm. [HC102.5.G87E74] 76-14508 ISBN 0-912458-76-3 : 9.95
1. Gusman, Maurice, 1888- 2. Businessmen—United States—Biography. I. Title. **BIP**

Gusstaf Adolf, King of Sweden, 1594-1632.

LIDDELL HART, Basil Henry, 1895- 909'.00922
Great captains unvelied. by B. H. Liddell Hart. Freeport, N.Y., Bks. for Libs. Pr. [1967] 274p. maps. 22cm. (Essay index reprint ser.) Reprint of the 1928 ed. [D106.L5 1967] 67-23240 8.50
1. Jenghis Khan, 1162-1227. 2. Saxe, Maurice, comte de, 1696-1750. 3. Gusstaf Adolf, King of Sweden, 1594-1632. 4. Wallenstein, Alberecht Wenzel Eusebius von. Herzog zu Friendland. 1583-1634. 5. Wolfe, James, 1727-1759. I. Title.
Contents omitted.

Gust, Peter.

TAUSSIG, Ellen M., 1906- 338.7'61'6479574797
Your host, Peter Gust of the Park Lane Restaurant, his story / by Ellen M. Taussig. Boston : Herman Pub., c1979. p. cm. Includes index. [TX910.5.G86T38] 79-17799 ISBN 0-89047-033-2 : 12.95
1. Gust, Peter. 2. Park Lane Restaurant, Buffalo. 3. Restaurateurs—New York (State)—Buffalo—Biography. I. Title.

Gustaf II, Adolf, King of Sweden, 1594-1632.

DODGE, Theodore Ayrault, 1842-1909. 355.3'32'0922
Great captains; showing the influence on the art of war of the campaigns of Alexander, Hannibal, Caesar, Gustavus Adolphus, Frederick, and Napoleon. Port Washington, N.Y., Kennikat Press [1968, c1889] xiii, 219 p. illus., maps. 21 cm. [U51.D6 1968] 67-27591
1. Alexander the Great—Campaigns. 2. Hannibal. 3. Caesar, C. Julius. 4. Gustaf II Adolf, King of Sweden, 1594-1632. 5. Friedrich II, der Grosse, King of Prussia, 1712-1821. 6. Napoleon I, Emperor of the French, 1769-1821. 7. Military biography. I. Title.

FLETCHER, Chalres Robert Leslie, 1857-1934. 923.1485
Gustavus Adolphus and the Thirty Years War, by C.R.L. Fletcher. New York, Capricorn Books [1963] xiii, 316 p. port. 18 cm. Publisher on spine: Peter Smith. [DL706.F62 1963] 64-4278
1. Gustaf II, Adolf, King of Sweden, 1594-1632. 2. Thirty Years' War, 1618-1648. I. Title.

FLETCHER, Charles Robert Leslie, 1857-1934 923.1485
Gustavus Adolphus and the Thirty Years War [Gloucester, Mass., P. Smith, 1964] xii, 316p. front port. 19cm. (Capricorn bk. rebound) 3.65
1. Gustaf, II, Adolf, King of Sweden, 1594-1632. 2. Thirty Years War, 1618-1648. I. Title.

Gustaf v. King of Sweden, 1858-1950.

AMERICAN-SWEDISH News Exchange, inc., New York. 923.1485
Gustaf v, in memoriam; hail, Gustaf VI Adolf! Clippings from American newspapers. New York [1950?] [64] p. illus., ports. 28 cm. Cover title. [DL867.A5] 51-30363
1. Gustaf v. King of Sweden, 1858-1950. 2. Gustaf VI Adolf, King of Sweden, 1882- I. Title.

Gutenberg, Johann, 1397?-1468.

MCMURTRIE, Douglas Crawford, 1888-1944. 686'.1'0924 B
Wings for words; the story of Johann Gutenberg and his invention of printing. With the collaboration of Don Farran. Illustrated by Edward A. Wilson. New York, Rand McNally, 1940. Detroit, Tower Books, 1971. 175 p. illus. 24 cm. A biography of the man who developed the process of printing from moveable type in the fifteenth century. [Z126.Z7M32 1971] 92 78-167061
1. Gutenberg, Johann, 1397?-1468. 2. Printing—History—Origin and antecedents. I. Wilson, Edward Arthur, 1886- illus. II. Title. **BIP**

Gutenberg, Johann, 1397?-1468—Juvenile literature.

HARRIS, Brayton. 686.1'092'4 B
Johann Gutenberg and the invention of printing. New York, Watts, 1972. xv, 144 p. illus. 22 cm. (A Franklin Watts biography) Bibliography: p. 141-142. A biography of the man who developed printing from moveable type in the fifteenth century. [Z126.Z7H37] 92 73-150377 ISBN 0-531-00967-X
1. Gutenberg, Johann, 1397?-1468—Juvenile literature. 2. Printing—Invention—Juvenile literature. I. Title.

Guthlad, Legend. Vita Felicis. Latin.

GUTHLAD, Legend. Vita Felicis. Latin. Saint. 922.22
Felix's Life of Saint Guthlac; introd., text, translation, and notes, by Bertram Colgrave. Cambridge [Eng.] University Press, 1956. xv. 205p. 23cm. Bibliography: p. [xiii]-xv. [PR1722.A2C6] A57
I. Colgrave. Bertram, ed. and tr. II. Guthlad, Saint. Legend. Vita Felicis. English. III. Title.

Guthrie, Janet, 1938- —Juvenile literature.

DOLAN, Edward F., 1924- 796.7'2'0924 B
Janet Guthrie, first woman driver at Indianapolis / Edward F. Dolan, Jr., and Richard B. Lyttle. 1st ed. Garden City, N.Y. : Doubleday, c1978. 80 p., [12] leaves of plates : ill. ; 22 cm. (A Doubleday signal book) Includes index. A biography of the physicist who broke into the all-male world of the Indianapolis 500. [GV1032.G87D64] 92 77-12848 ISBN 0-385-12526-7 : 5.95
1. Guthrie, Janet, 1938- —Juvenile literature. 2. Indianapolis Speedway Race—Juvenile literature. 3. Automobile racing drivers—United States—Biography—Juvenile literature. I. Lyttle, Richard B., joint author. II. Title.

HAHN, James. 796.7'2'0924 B
Janet Guthrie : champion racer / by James and Lynn Hahn. St. Paul : EMC Corp., 1978. p. cm. (Their Champions and challengers 2) A biography of the first woman driver to qualify for the annual Indianapolis 500-mile auto race. [GV1032.G87H33] 78-12670 ISBN 0-88436-476-3 : 5.95
1. Guthrie, Janet, 1938- —Juvenile literature. 2. Automobile racing drivers—United States—Biography—Juvenile literature. I. Hahn, Lynn, joint author. II. Title. III. Series. **BIP**

OLNEY, Ross Robert, 1929- 796.7'2'0924 B
Janet Guthrie, first woman at Indy / by Ross R. Olney. New York : Harvey House, c1978. 54 p. : ill. ; 23 cm. A biography of the first woman ever to attempt to race at the Indianapolis Motor Speedway. [GV1032.G87O46 1978] 92 78-111983 ISBN 0-8178-5882-2 : 4.99
1. Guthrie, Janet, 1938- —Juvenile literature. 2. Indianapolis Speedway Race—Juvenile literature. 3. Automobile racing drivers—United States—Biography—Juvenile literature. I. Title.

ROBISON, Nancy. 796.7'2'0924 B
Janet Guthrie, race car driver / by Nancy Robison. Chicago : Children's Press, c1979. 43 p. : ill. ; 21 cm. (Sports stars) Traces the racing career of the first woman to complete the Indianapolis 500. [GV1032.G87R62] 92 78-23648 ISBN 0-516-04301-3 : 6.00
1. Guthrie, Janet, 1938- —Juvenile literature. 2. Automobile racing drivers—United States—Biography—Juvenile literature. I. Title. II. Series.

Guthrie, Jimmy.

GUTHRIE, Jimmy. 796.334'092'4 B
Soccer rebel : the evolution of the professional footballer / [by] Jimmy Guthrie ; with Dave Caldwell. Pinner : Pentagon, 1976. 5-180 p. : ill., facsim., ports. ; 23 cm. [GV942.7.G87A37] 76-383044 ISBN 0-904288-08-0 : £3.50
1. Guthrie, Jimmy. 2. Soccer players—England—Biography. 3. Soccer—England—History. I. Caldwell, Dave. II. Title.

Guthrie, Tyrone, Sir, 1900-1971.

FORSYTH, James, 1913- 792'.023'0924 B
Tyrone Guthrie : a biography / [by] James Forsyth. London : Hamilton, 1976. xi, 372 p., [12] p. of plates : ill., ports. ; 23 cm. Includes index. Bibliography: p. [355] [PN2598.G85F6] 77-373471 ISBN 0-241-89471-9 : £7.95
1. Guthrie, Tyrone, Sir, 1900-1971. 2. Theatrical producers and directors—Great Britain—Biography.

GUTHRIE, Tyrone, Sir, 1900-1971. 927.92
A life in the theatre. [1st ed.] New York, McGraw-Hill [1959] 357 p. 22 cm. Autobiography. [PN2598.G85A3] 59-14450
1. Actors—Correspondence, reminiscences, etc. I. Title.

ROSSI, Alfred. 792'.023'0924 B
Astonish us in the morning : Tyrone Guthrie remembered / Alfred Rossi. London : Hutchinson, 1977, i.e.1978 309 p., [4] leaves of plates : ports. ; 23 cm. Includes index. "A representative listing of stage productions directed by Tyrone Guthrie": p. 297-[302] [PN2598.G85R67] 77-376106 ISBN 0-09-128860-6 : 16.95
1. Guthrie, Tyrone, Sir, 1900-1971. 2. Theatrical producers and directors—Great Britain—Biography. I. Title.
Distributed by Hutchinson, Salem, N.H **BIP**

Guthrie, Woody, 1912-1967.

GUTHRIE, Woody, 1912- 927.8
Bound for glory; Illus. with sketches by the author. Garden City, N.Y., Doubleday [1961, c.1943] 353p. illus. (Dolphin bk., C248) .95 pap.,
I. Title.

GUTHRIE, Woody, 1912-1967. 784.4'92'4 B
Seeds of man : an experience lived and dreamed Woody Guthrie. by Woody Guthrie. 1st ed. New York : Dutton, c1976. 401 p. ; 24 cm. [ML429.G95A37] 76-6556 11.95
1. Guthrie, Woody, 1912-1967. 2. Musicians—United States—Biography. I. Title.

YURCHENCO, Henrietta. 784.4'9'24
A mighty hard road; the Woody Guthrie story, by Henrietta Yurchenco, assisted by Marjorie Guthrie. Introd. by Arlo Guthrie. New York, McGraw-Hill [1970] 159 p. illus., ports. 24 cm. "Discography": p. 155-156. [ML410.G978Y9] 73-110963
1. Guthrie, Woody, 1912-1967. I. Guthrie, Marjorie. II. Title.

Guyer family.

THOMPSON, Goldianne. 929.2'0973
Biography of the Guyers. [1st ed.] Denver, Monitor Publications [1968] 147 p. port. 25 cm. [CS71.G987 1968] 68-20553 10.00
1. Guyer family. I. Title.

Guynemer, Georges Marie Ludovic, 1894-1917.

BORDEAUX, Henry, 1870-1963. 940.4'49'440924 B
Georges Guynemer, knight of the air. [Translated from the French by Louise Morgan Sill. New York] Arno Press [1972, c1918] 256 p. illus. 22 cm. (Literature and history of aviation) Translation of Le chevalier de l'air; vie heroique de Guynemer. Includes bibliographical references. [D603.B66 1972] 73-169405 ISBN 0-405-03751-1
1. Guynemer, Georges Marie Ludovic, 1894-1917. I. Title. II. Series. **BIP**

Guyon, Jeanne Marie (Bouvier de La Motte) 1648-1717.

DE LA BEDOYERE, Michael, 1900- 928.4
The archbishop and the lady; the story of Fenelon and Madame Guyon. [New York] Pantheon [1956] 256p. illus. 22cm. [BX4705.F3D4 1956a] 56-7910
1. Guyon, Jeanne Marie (Bouvier de La Motte) 1648-1717. 2. Fenelon, Francois de

Salignac de La Mothe, Abp., 1651-1715. I. Title.

Guzman Blanco, Antonio, Pres. Venezuela, 1828-1899.

WISE, George 987'.061'0924 Schneiweis, 1906-
Caudillo, a portrait of Antonio Guzman Blanco, by George S. Wise. Westport, Conn., Greenwood Press [1970, c1951] xii, 190 p. map, ports. 23 cm. Revision of the author's thesis, Columbia, published in microfilm form in 1950 under the title: Antonio Guzman Blanco; a study of caudillismo. Bibliography: p. [179]-184. [F2325.W76 1970] 72-104232 ISBN 0-8371-3349-1
1. Guzman Blanco, Antonio, Pres. Venezuela, 1828-1899. 2. Venezuela—Politics and government—1830- I. Title.

Guzman, Nicomedes, 1914—

PEARSON, Lon, 1939- 863 B
Nicomedes Guzman, proletarian author in Chile's literary generation of 1938 / by Lon Pearson. Columbia : University of Missouri Press, [1976] p. cm. Includes index. Bibliography: p. [PQ8097.G85Z8] 75-19334 ISBN 0-8262-0178-4 : 13.00
1. Guzman, Nicomedes, 1914- I. Title.

Guzman Bianco, Antonio, Pres. Venezuela, 1828-1899.

WISE, George Schneiweis, 923.187 1906-
Caudillo, a portrait of Antonio Guzman Blanco. New York, Columbia University Press, 1951. xii, 190 p. ports., map. 23 cm. Revision of thesis, Columbia University, published in microfilm form in 1950 under title: Antonio Guzman Bianco; a study of caudillismo. Bibliography: p. [179]-184. [F2325.G994] 51-14336
1. Guzman Bianco, Antonio, Pres. Venezuela, 1828-1899. 2. Venezuela — Pol. & govt. — 1830- I. Title.

Gwinnett, Button, 1735-1777.

JENKINS, Charles 973.3'13'0924 B Francis, 1865-1951.
Button Gwinnett, signer of the Declaration of Independence. Spartanburg, S.C., Reprint Co., 1974 [c1926] xvi, 291 p. illus. 22 cm. Reprint of the ed. published by Doubleday, Page, Garden City, N.Y. Includes bibliographical references. [E302.6.G95J38 1974] 74-2194 ISBN 0-87152-171-7 15.00
1. Gwinnett, Button, 1735-1777. I. Title.

Gwyn, Nell, 1650-1687.

BAX, Clifford, 792'.028'0924 B 1886-
Pretty witty Nell; an account of Nell Gwyn and her environment. New York, B. Blom [1969] xii, 261 p. illus. 22 cm. Reprint of the 1932 ed. Bibliography: p. 256-257. [DA447.G9B3 1969] 76-83871
1. Gwyn, Nell, 1650-1687. I. Title. BIP

BEVAN, Bryan. 942.06'6'0924 B
Nell Gwynn, vivacious mistress of Charles II. New York, Roy Publishers [1970, c1969] 190 p. illus., facsim., ports. 23 cm. Bibliography: p. 181-184. [DA447.G9B44 1970] 75-96221 5.95
1. Gwyn, Nell, 1650-1687.

CUNNINGHAM, 942.06'6'0924 B Peter, 1816-1869.
The story of Nell Gwyn, and the sayings of Charles the Second, related and collected by Peter Cunningham. New ed., with an introd. by John Drinkwater. New York, B. Blom [1969] 194 p. illus., ports. 22 cm. Reprint of the 1927 ed., originally published in the Gentleman's magazine for 1851. Includes bibliographical references. [DA447.G9C9 1969] 77-82554
1. Gwyn, Nell, 1650-1687. 2. Charles II, King of Great Britain, 1630-1685. I. Title.

DASENT, Arthur 792'.028'0924 B Irwin, 1859-1939.
Nell Gwynne, 1650-1687; her life story from St. Giles's to St. James's with some account of Whitehall and Windsor in the reign of Charles the Second. New York, B. Blom [1969] xi, 322 p. illus., plan, ports. 22 cm. Reprint of the 1924 ed. [DA447.G9D3 1969] 70-82824
1. Gwyn, Nell, 1650-1687. 2. Theater—England. 3. Gt. Brit.—Court and courtiers.

WILSON, John Harold, 1900- 920.7
Nell Gwyn, Royal mistress. New York, Pellegrini & Cudahy [1952] 309 p. illus. 22 cm. Includes bibliography. [DA447.G9W5] 51-12757
1. Gwyn, Nell, 1650-1687. 2. Charles II, King of Great Britain, 1680-1686. 3. Theater—England—History.

Gyllensten, Lars Johan Wictor, 1921-

ISAKSSON, Hans, 1942- 839.7'3'74
Lars Gyllensten / by Hans Isaksson ; translated from the Swedish by Katy Lissbrant. Boston : Twayne Publishers, c1978. 194 p. : port. ; 21 cm. (Twayne's world authors series ; TWAS 473 : Sweden) Includes index. Bibliography: p. 189-192. [PT9875.G95Z74 1978] 77-15551 ISBN 0-8057-6314-7 : 9.50
1. Gyllensten, Lars Johan Wictor, 1921- 2. Authors, Swedish—20th century—Biography. BIP

Gymnastics—Addresses, essays, lectures.

THE Gymnastics 796.4'1'0922 B *guide /* edited by Hal Straus. Mountain View, Calif. : World Publications, [1978] p. cm. Includes index. [GV461.G9] 78-55790 ISBN 0-89037-139-3 : pbk. : 4.95
1. Gymnastics—Addresses, essays, lectures. 2. Gymnastics—Biography—Addresses, essays, lectures. I. Straus, Hal. BIP

Gymnasts—Biography—Juvenile literature.

LITSKY, Frank 796.4'1'0922 B
Winners in Gymnastics / by Frank Litsky. New York : F. Watts, 1978. 48 p. : ill. ; 22 cm. (A Picture life book) Biographical sketches of gymnasts Nadia Comaneci, Olga Korbut, Nelli Kim, Cathy Rigby Mason, Nikolai Andrianov, Mitsuo Tsukahara, and Bart Conner. [GV460.L57] 920 77-17535 ISBN 0-531-01460-6 lib.bdg. : 4.90
1. Gymnasts—Biography—Juvenile literature. I. Title. BIP

Gysi, Lydia.

GYSI, Lydia. 271'.98 B
Mother Maria, her life in letters / selected, edited, and introduced with a brief biography by Sister Thekla. New York : Paulist Press, c1979. xlviii, 144 p. : port. ; 23 cm. [BX395.G94A35 1979] 79-63455 ISBN 0-8091-0286-2 : 12.95
1. Gysi, Lydia. 2. Nuns—England—Correspondence. I. Thekla, Sister. II. Title.

H

SIEVERS, Harry Joseph, 923.173 1920-
Benjamin Harrison. Introd. by Hilton U. Brown. Chicago, H. Regnery Co., 1952- v. illus., ports., maps. 24 cm. Contents.Contents.—1. Hoosier warrior, 1833-1865. Bibliography: v. 1, p. [321]-331. [E702.S54] 52-12674
1. H 2. Harrison, Benjamin, Pres. U.S., 1833-1901.

Handel, Georg Friedrich, 1685-1759.

BARNE, Kitty, 1883- 927.8
Introducing Handel. With drawings by J. J. Crockford. New York, Roy Publishers [1957] 90p. illus. 19cm. [ML3930] 57-10085
1. Handel, Georg Friedrich. 1685-1759. 2. Music—Juvenile literature. I. Title.

CLARKE, Eliza. 780'.924 B
Handel. [New York, Haskell House Publishers, 1972] 128 p. port. 23 cm. Reprint of the 1885 ed. Originally issued in series: The World's workers. [ML410.H13C38 1972] 70-158201 ISBN 0-8383-1250-0
1. Handel, Georg Friedrich, 1685-1759. BIP

CUDWORTH, Charles. 780'.92'4 B
Handel; a biography, with a survey of books, editions, and recordings. [Hamden, Conn.] Linnet Books [1972] 112 p. 23 cm. (The Concertgoer's companions) [ML410.H13C88] 72-176705 ISBN 0-208-01068-8 4.00
1. Handel, Georg Friedrich, 1685-1759. BIP

DEAN, Winton. 782.1'0924
Handel and the opera seria. London, Oxford U.P., 1970. xiii, 220 p. music, plan. 27 cm. (The Ernest Bloch lectures, 1) [MT100.H3D4 1970] 72-527318 £5/-/-
1. Handel, Georg Friedrich, 1685-1759. Operas. 2. Opera. I. Title. II. Series. BIP

DEAN, Winton. 782.1'0924
Handel and the opera seria. Berkeley, University of California Press, 1969. xi, 220 p. music, plan. 26 cm. (The Ernest Bloch lectures, 1) [MT100.H3D4] 79-78567 8.50
1. Handel, Georg Friedrich, 1685-1759. Operas. 2. Opera. I. Title. II. Series.

DENT, Edward Joseph, 780'.924 B 1876-1957.
Handel. Port Washington, N.Y., Kennikat Press [1972] 140 p. port. 21 cm. Reprint of the 1948 ed. Bibliography: p. 135-136. [ML410.H13D4 1972] 76-154709 ISBN 0-8046-1603-5
1. Handel, Georg Friedrich, 1685-1759.

DEUTSCH, Otto Erich, 1883- 927.8
Handel, a documentary biography. New York, W. W. Norton [1955] xiv, 942p. illus., ports., facsims. 24cm. Bibliography: p.863-886. [ML410.H13D47 1955a] A55
1. Handel, George Friedrich, 1685-1759. I. Title. BIP

DEUTSCH, Otto Erich, 780'.92'4 B 1883-1967.
Handel, a documentary biography. New York, Da Capo Press, 1974. xiv, 942 p. illus. 23 cm. (Da Capo Press music reprint series) Reprint of the 1955 ed. published by W. W. Norton, New York. Bibliography: p. 863-886. [ML410.H13D47 1974] 74-3118 ISBN 0-306-70624-5 37.50
1. Handel, Georg Friedrich, 1685-1759.

FLOWER, Newman [Walter 927.8 Newman Flower Sir 1879-
Geoge Frederic Handel, his personality and his times. New and rev. ed. London, Cassell [dist. Chester Springs, Pa., Dufour , 1964] 399p. illus. 26cm. 59 2628 6.50
1. Handel, Georg Friedrich, 1685-1759. I. Title.

†HADDEN, James 780'.92'4 B Cuthbert, 1861-1914.
Life of Handel / J. C. Hadden. New York : AMS Press, 1976. 157 p. ; 19 cm. Reprint of the 1904 ed. published by J. J. Keliher, London, in series: The Kelkel series of volumes relative to song, music, and biology. Includes index. [ML410.H13H2 1976] 74-24096 ISBN 0-404-12941-2 : 10.00
1. Handel, Georg Friedrich, 1685-1759. 2. Composers England—Biography.

HANDEL, Georg 780'.924 Friedrich, 1685-1759.
The letters and writing of George Frideric Handel. Edited by Erich H. Muller. Freeport, N.Y., Books for Libraries Press [1970] viii,98 p. 23 cm. In English, French or German; "translations of those letters appearing in the text in French and German": p. 78-92. Reprint of the 1935 ed. [ML410.H13A3 1970] 70-114882

LANG, Paul Henry, 780'.92'4 B 1900-
George Frideric Handel / by Paul Henry Lang. New York : Norton, 1977, c1966. p. cm. (The Norton library) Includes index. Bibliography: p. [ML410.H13L16 1977] 77-3977 ISBN 0-393-00815-0 pbk. : 7.95
1. Handel, Georg Friedrich, 1685-1759. 2. Composers—Biography.

LANG, Paul Henry, 780.924 B 1901-
George Frideric Handel. [1st ed.] New York, W. W. Norton [1966] xviii, 731 p. music, 16 plates (incl. facsims., ports.) 24 cm. "Bibliographical note": p. [711]-714. [ML410.H13L16] 66-11793
1. Handel, Georg Friedrich, 1685-1759.

PAULI, Hertha 780'.924 B Ernestine, 1909-
Handel and the Messiah story, by Hertha Pauli. [1st ed.] New York, Meredith Press [1968] ix, 112 p. illus., ports. 21 cm. Handel's work at London's Foundling Hospital and the first and famous performance there of his Messiah are the focal points of this biography of the well-known German born musician. [ML3930.H25P4] 92 AC 68
1. Handel, Georg Friedrich, 1685-1759. Messiah. I. Title.

ROLLAND, Romain, 1866- 780'.924 B 1944.
Handel. [Translated by A. Eaglefield Hull] New York, AMS Press [1971] xi, 210 p. illus., port., music. 19 cm. "Reprinted from the edition of 1916, London." "List of Handel's works": p. 193-200. [ML410.H13R673 1971] 75-151597 ISBN 0-404-05388-2
1. Handel, Georg Friedrich, 1685-1759. I. Hull, Arthur Eaglefield, 1876-1928, tr.

SADIE, Stanley 780.924
Handel. London, J. Calder [New York, Hillary House, 1966, c.1962] 192p. illus., facsims., music, ports. 21cm. (Illus. Calderbk., CB. 60) Bibl. [ML410.H13S13] 66-4818 4.00
1. Handel, George Friedrich, 1685-1759. I. Title.

SADIE, Stanley. 780'.924 B
Handel. New York, T. Y. Crowell Co. [1969, c1968] 95 p. illus. 26 cm. (The great composers) Bibliography: p. 90. A biography of the composer of more than forty operas, nineteen oratorios, and hundreds of other vocal and instrumental works. [ML410.H13S13 1969] 92 68-29474 4.50
1. Handel, Georg Friedrich, 1685-1759.

SCHoLCHER, Victor, 780'.92'4 B 1804-1893.
The life of Handel / by Victor Scholcher. New York : Da Capo Press, 1979. xxxii, 443 p. ; 23 cm. (Da Capo Press music reprint series) Reprint of the 1857 ed. published by R. Cocks, London. Includes index. Bibliography: p. [ix]-xv. [ML410.H13S3 1979] 79-12290 ISBN 0-306-79572-8 : 29.50
1. Handel, Georg Friedrich, 1685-1759. 2. Composers—Biography. I. Title.

STREATFEILD, Richard 927.8 Alexander, 1866-1919
Handel. Introd. to the Da Capo ed. by J. Merrill Knapp. [Rev. 2d ed.] New York, Da Capo Pr. [dist. Plenum] 1964. xvii, 366p. illus., facsim. (music) 23cm. (Da Capo reprint ed.) Bibl. 64-18991 6.95 bds.,
1. Handel, Georg Friedlich, 1685-1759. I. Title

STREATFEILD, Richard 780'.92'4 B Alexander, 1866-1919.
Handel / by R. A. Streatfeild. Westport, Conn. : Greenwood Press, 1978. xvii, 366 p., [12] leaves of plates : ill. ; 23 cm. (The New library of music) Reprint of the 1909 ed. published by Methuen, London. Includes index. [ML410.H13S7 1978] 77-28261 ISBN 0-313-20248-6 lib. bdg. : 24.00
1. Handel, Georg Friedrich, 1685-1759. 2. Composers—Biography. I. Title. II. Series.

WEINSTOCK, Herbert, 784'.092'4 1903-
Handel. 2d ed., rev. New York, Knopf, 1959. xv, 328, xxxiii p. plates, ports., facsims, music 25 cm. "Letters of Handel": p. 308-317. Bibliography :p. 325-328. [ML410.H13W27 1957] 59-7221
1. Handel, Georg Friedrich, 1685-1759. I. Title.

WEINSTOCK, Herbert, 780'.92'4 B 1905-
Handel / by Herbert Weinstock. Westport, Conn. : Greenwood Press, 1979, c1959. xv, 328, xxxiii p., [11] leaves of plates : ill. ; 24 cm. Reprint of the 2d ed. publisshed by Knopf, New York. Includes indexes. Bibliography: p. 325-328. [ML410.H13W27 1979] 78-11991 ISBN 0-313-21109-4 lib. bdg. : 25.50
1. Handel, Georg Friedrich, 1685-1759. 2. Composers—Biography.

YOUNG, Percy, Marshall, 1912- 927.8
Handel. New, rev. ed. New York, Collier [1963, c.1962] 288p. facsims., music. 18cm. (Great composers ser.; BS164V) Catalogue of works. Bibl. 62-21615 1.50 pap.,
1. Handel, Georg Friedrich, 1685-1759. I. Title.

Hebert, Felix Edward, 1901—

CONRAD, Glenn R. 973.917'0924
Creed of a congressman: F. Edward Hebert of Louisiana. Edited and evaluated by Glenn R. Conrad, with a biographical sketch by Virginea R. Burguieres. [1st ed.] Lafayette, La., The USL History Series, University of Southwestern Louisiana, 1970 [c1971] xvi, 216 p. ports. (1 col.) 24 cm. Includes excerpts from Hebert's speeches and addresses, and Hebert's correspondence. Includes bibliographical references. [E748.H3895C6] 70-633180 5.95
1. Hebert, Felix Edward, 1901- I. Hebert, Felix Edward, 1901- II. Burguieres, Virginea R. III. Title.

HEBERT, Felix Edward, 1901- 328.73'092'4 B
"Last of the titans" : the life and times of Congressman F. Edward Hebert of Louisiana / by F. Edward Hebert, with John McMillan ; pref. by Bascom N. Timmons ; edited by Glenn R. Conrad. 1st ed. Lafayette : Center for Louisiana Studies, University of Southwestern Louisiana, 1976. xviii, 478 p., [33] leaves of plates : ill. ; 24 cm. Includes index. [E748.H3895A35] 76-15774 10.00
1. Hebert, Felix Edward, 1901- 2. Legislators—United States—Biography. 3. United States—Politics and government—1945- 4. Louisiana—Politics and government. I. McMillan, John, 1937- joint author. II. Title.

Helias, Pierre Jakez.

HELIAS, Pierre Jakez. 944'.11
The horse of pride : life in rural Brittany / Pierre-Jakez Helias ; translated and abridged by June Guicharnaud. New Haven : Yale University Press, 1978. p. cm. Translation of Le cheval d'orgueil. [DC611.B9173H4413] 78-6929 ISBN 0-300-02036-8 : 15.00
1. Helias, Pierre Jakez. 2. Brittany—Social life and customs. 3. Brittany—Biography. I. Guicharnaud, June. II. Title.

Helion, Jean, 1904—

MICHA, Rene. 759.4
Jean Helion / by Rene Micha ; [translated from the French by Alice Sachs]. New York : Crown Publishers, [1979] p. cm. [ND553.H34M5213] 79-14537 ISBN 0-517-53791-5 pbk. : 6.95
1. Helion, Jean, 1904- BIP

Heloise, 1101-1164.

PERNOUD, Regine, 1909- 282'.092'2 B
Heloise and Abelard. Translated by Peter Wiles. New York, Stein and Day [1973] 256 p. illus. 24 cm. Bibliography: p. 246-247. [BX4705.H463P4613 1973] 72-95915 ISBN 0-8128-1558-0 8.95
1. Heloise, 1101-1164. 2. Abailard, Pierre, 1079-1142. I. Title.

Heritte-Viardot, Louise Pauline Marie, 1841-1918.

HERITTE-VIARDOT, Louise Pauline Marie, 1841-1918. 784'.092'4 B
Memories and adventures / by Louise Heritte-Viardot ; translated from the German ms. and arranged by E. S. Buchheim. New York : Da Capo Press, 1977. p. cm. (Da Capo Press music reprint series) Reprint of the 1913 ed. published by Mills & Boon, London. [ML423.H57A3 1977] 77-22220 ISBN 0-306-77515-8 lib.bdg. : 22.50
1. Heritte-Viardot, Louise Pauline Marie, 1841-1918. 2. Musicians—Biography. BIP

Ho Chi Minh, 1890-1969—Juvenile literature.

ARCHER, Jules. 959.7'04'0924
Ho chi Minh: legend of Hanoi. New York, Crowell-Collier Press [1971] 199 p. port. 21 cm. Bibliography: p. [191]-193. A biography of the Vietnamese peasant who led his people in a successful revolution for independence from France and in the war with South Vietnam. [DS557.A76H6716] 92 B 79-151161
1. Ho Chi Minh, 1890-1969—Juvenile literature. I. Title.

Hurlimann, Bettina, 1909—

HURLIMANN, Bettina, 1909- 070.5'092'4 B
Seven houses : my life with books / Bettina Hurlimann ; translated from the German by Anthea Bell. New York : Crowell, 1977, c1976. 262 p. : ill. ; 21 cm. Translation of Sieben Hauser. [Z430.H85A3413] 76-48889 ISBN 0-690-01353-1 : 7.95
1. Hurlimann, Bettina, 1909- 2. Publishers and publishing—Switzerland—Biography. I. Title. BIP

Haakon VII, king of Norway.

HAAKON, v. 12
king of Norway. New York, Macmillan [1958] 207p. illus.
1. Haakon VII, king of Norway. 2. Norway- Biography. I. Michael, Maurice.

Haase, Hugo, 1863-1919.

CALKINS, Kenneth R. 943.08'4'0924 B
Hugo Haase, democrat and revolutionary / Kenneth R. Calkins. Durham, N.C. : Carolina Academic Press, 1979. x, 254 p. ; 24 cm. Bibliography: p. 247-254. [DD231.H18C34] 77-88657 ISBN 0-89089-075-7 : 14.95 ISBN 0-89089-073-0 (pbk.) : 7.50
1. Haase, Hugo, 1863-1919. 2. Politicians—Germany—Biography. 3. Germany—Politics and government—1888-1918. I. Title.

Habeler, Peter.

HABELER, Peter. 796.5'22'0924 B
The lonely victory : Mt. Everest '78 / Peter Habeler ; translated from the German by David Heald. New York : Simon and Schuster, c1979. 224 p., [8] leaves of plates : ill. ; 25 cm. Translation of Der einsame Sieg. [GV199.92.H32A3413] 79-13741 ISBN 0-671-24842-1 : 9.95
1. Habeler, Peter. 2. Messner, Reinhold. 3. Mountaineer—Austria—Biography. 4. Everest, Mount—Description. I. Title.

Haber, Fritz, 1868-1934.

GORAN, Morris Herbert, 1916- 540'.924 B
The story of Fritz Haber [by] Morris Goran. [1st ed.] Norman, University of Oklahoma Press [1967] xi, 212 p. 22 cm. Bibliography: p. 191-206. [QD22.H15G6] 67-24615
1. Haber, Fritz, 1868-1934. I. Title. BIP

Habsburg, House of—History.

CRANKSHAW, Edward. 943.6
The Habsburgs: portrait of a dynasty. New York, Viking Press [1971] 272 p. illus. 27 cm. (A Studio book) [DB36.1.C7] 72-156753 ISBN 0-670-36134-8 16.95
1. Habsburg, House of—History. 2. Austria—Politics and government. I. Title.

Hachard, Marie Madeleine.

HACHARD, Marie Madeleine. 271'.974'024 B
The letters of Marie Madeleine Hachard, 1727-28 / translated by Myldred Masson Costa. 1st ed. New Orleans : [s.n.], 1974. 66 p. ; 19 cm. Translation of Relation du voyage des dames religieuses Ursulines de Rouen a la Nouvelle Orleans. On spine: Letters of an Ursuline, 1727-1728. [BX4705.H13A413 1974] 74-193362
1. Hachard, Marie Madeleine. 2. New Orleans—History. I. Title: Letters of an Ursuline, 1727-1728.

Hackett, Frank Sutliff, 1877-1952.

HACKETT, Allen, 1905- 923.773
Quickened spirit; a biography of Frank Sutliff Hackett, by his son. [New York] Riverdale Country School, 1957. 212p. illus. 24cm. [LD7501.R58H3] 57-36834
1. Hackett, Frank Sutliff, 1877-1952. 2. Riverdale Country School, Riverdale, N. Y. I. Title.

Hackett, John Winthrop, Sir, 1910-

HACKETT, John Winthrop, Sir, 1910- 940.54'12'41 B
I was a stranger / John Winthrop Hackett. 1st American ed. Boston : Houghton Mifflin Co., 1978. 219 p. : map ; 22 cm. [D811.H22 1978] 78-108003 ISBN 0-395-27087-1 : 8.95
1. Hackett, John Winthrop, Sir, 1910- 2. Great Britain. Army. 1st Airborne Division—Biography. 3. World War, 1939-1945—Personal narratives, English. 4. Generals—Great Britain—Biography. 5. World War, 1939-1945—Netherlands—Ede. 6. World War, 1939-1945—Underground movements—Netherlands. 7. Ede, Netherlands—History. I. Title.

Hackett, Marie.

HACKETT, Marie. 616.8982
The cliff's edge. New York, McGraw-Hill [1954] 245 p. 21 cm. Autobiographical. [RC464.H29A3] 54-6733
I. Title.

Haden, Pat.

HADEN, Pat. 796.33'2'0924 B
Pat Haden : my rookie season with the Los Angeles Rams / by Pat Haden, with Robert Blair Kaiser. New York : Morrow, 1977. 223 p. : ill. ; 22 cm. Includes index. [GV939.H24A36] 77-9441 ISBN 0-688-03224-9 : 8.95
1. Haden, Pat. 2. Los Angeles. Football club (National League) 3. Football players—United States—Biography. I. Kaiser, Robert Blair, joint author. BIP

Hadley, James,

HADLEY, James, 1821-1872. 924.8
Diary (1843-1852) of James Hadley, tutor and professor of Greek in Yale College, 1845-1872; edited with a foreword by Laura Hadley Moseley New Haven, Yale University Press [1951] xii, 334 p. illus., ports., facsim. 25 cm. [LD6331.H3A3] 51-9832
I. Title.

Hadley, Paul, 1880-1971.

HARDIN, Becky. 759.13 B
The Indiana State flag, its designer : biography of Paul Hadley with anthology of his paintings / [by Becky Hardin]. [Mooresville, IN : Hardin, c1976] 40 p. : ill. (some col.) ; 28 cm. Cover title. Includes bibliographical references and index. [ND1839.H3H37] 76-12963 4.00
1. Hadley, Paul, 1880-1971. 2. Painters—United States—Biography. I. Title.

Hadlock, Adah,

HADLOCK, Adah, 1883- 917.6496
My life in the Southwest; the memoir of Adah Hadlock, early day El Pasoan, amateur artist, champion golfer, avid wildcatter and gold seeker. Introduced and annotated by Kenneth A. Goldblatt. [El Paso] Texas Western Press, 1969. xviii, 113 p. illus., ports. 25 cm. [CT275.H237A3] 75-97793 5.00
I. Goldblatt, Kenneth A., ed. II. Title.

Hadrianus, Emperor of Rome, 76-138.

PEROWNE, Stewart, 1901- 937.07
Hadrian. New York, Norton [1962, c.1960] 192p. illus. map. Bibl. 61-17683 5.00
1. Hadrianus, Emperor of Rome, 76-138. I. Title. BIP

PEROWNE, Stewart, 1901- 937'.07'0924 B
Hadrian / by Stewart Perowne. Westport, Conn. : Greenwood Press, 1976, c1960. 192 p., [15] leaves of plates : ill. ; 22 cm. Reprint of the ed. published by Hodder and Stoughton, London. Includes bibliographical references and index. [DG295.P38 1976] 75-43946 ISBN 0-8371-8723-0 lib.bdg. : 14.50
1. Hadrianus, Emperor of Rome, 76-138.

Hafen, Le Roy Reuben, 1893-

HAFEN, Le Roy Reuben, 1893- 917.8'03'0924 B
The joyous journey of LeRoy R. and Ann W. Hafen; an autobiography. Glendale, Calif., A. H. Clark Co., 1973. 334 p. illus. 25 cm. [E175.5.H26A34] 72-90517 11.50
1. Hafen, Le Roy Reuben, 1893- 2. Hafen, Ann (Woodbury) 1893-1970. I. Hafen, Ann (Woodbury) 1893-1970, joint author. II. Title.

Haffkine, Waldemar Mordecai Wolff, 1860-1930.

WAKSMAN, Selman Abraham, 1888- 925.8
The brilliant and tragic life of W. M. W. Haffkine, bacteriologist. New Brunswick, N.J., Rutgers, 1964. 86p. illus., port. 22cm. Bibl. 64-17676 price unreported
1. Haffkine, Waldemar Mordecai Wolff, 1860-1930. I. Title.

Hagen, Walter,

HAGEN, Walter, 1892- 927.96352
The Walter Hagen story, by The Haig, himself, as told to Margaret Seaton Heck. New York, Simon and Schuster, 1956. 342 p. illus. 24 cm. [GV964.H3A3] 56-7487
I. Heck, Margaret Seaton.

Hagey family.

HAGEY, Henry D., 1868-1935. 974.8'12
Some local history of Franconia Township : including six hundred acres in Franconia Township, daily happenings, historical datas, life in Elroy, 1918-1935, history and historical facts of Elroy, a genealogical record of the descendents of Daniel Hagey / by Henry D. Hagey ; edited by Joyce Clemmer Munro. [Telford, Pa.] : Munro, c1979. xiv, 385 p. [1] fold. leaf of plates : ill. ; 23 cm. Errata slip inserted. Includes bibliographical references and index. [F159.F8H33 1979] 79-114363 8.95
1. Hagey family. 2. Hagey, Henry D., 1868-1935. 3. Franconia Township, Pa.—Biography. 4. Elroy, Pa.—Biography. 5. Franconia Township, Pa.—History. 6. Elroy, Pa.—History. I. Munro, Joyce Clemmer, 1947- II. Title.

Haggai, John Edmund, 1950-1975.

HAGGAI, John Edmund. 362.7'8'1968588
My son Johnny / John Edmund Haggai. Wheaton, Ill. : Tyndale House, c1978. 238 p., [4] leaves of plates : ill. ; 21 cm. [RJ496.B7H33] 75-7229 ISBN 0-8423-4647-3 pbk. : 4.95
1. Haggai, John Edmund, 1950-1975. 2. Brain-damaged children—Georgia—Atlanta—Biography. 3. Christian biography—Georgia—Atlanta. I. Title. BIP

Haggard, Henry Rider, Sir 1856-1925.

COHEN, Morton Norton, 1921- 928.2
Rider Haggard, his life and works. New York, Walker, [1961, c.1960] 327p. illus. Bibl. 61-8136 6.00
1. Haggard, Henry Rider, Sir 1856-1925. I. Title.

Haggard, Henry Rider, Sir, 1856-1925.

ELLIS, Peter Berresford. 823'.8 B
H. Rider Haggard : a voice from the infinite / Peter Berresford Ellis. London : Routledge & K. Paul, 1978. xiv, 291 p., [8] leaves of plates : ill. ; 22 cm. Bibliography: p. 268-291. [PR4732.E4] 78-325562 ISBN 0-7100-0026-X : 19.50
1. Haggard, Henry Rider, Sir, 1856-1925. 2. Novelists, English—19th century—Biography. 3. Agriculturists—England—Biography. BIP

Haggard, Rice, 1776-1819.

HALL, Colby Dixon, 1875- 922.673
Rice Haggard, the American frontier evangelist who revived the name Christian. [Fort Worth, Tex., University Christian Church] 1957. 75p. illus. 23cm. [BX7343.H3H34] 57-20947
1. Haggard, Rice, 1776-1819. 2. Christian (The word) 3. Haggard family. I. Title.

Hagstotz, Hannah Yanke, 1908-

OSMUNSON, Robert Lee. 286'.73 B
Hannah : true story of a spirited Oklahoma girl's struggle for life, love, and peace with God / by Robert L. Osmunson. Mountain View, Calif. : Pacific Press Pub. Association, c1976. 112 p. ; 22 cm. (A Destiny book) [BX6193.H26O8] 76-22295 pbk. : 3.50
1. Hagstotz, Hannah Yanke, 1908- 2. Seventh-Day Adventists—Oklahoma—Biography.

Hagstrom, Gustave Arvid, 1867-1953.

ERIKSON, Martin, 1901- 922.673
A chosen vessel; the life story of G. Arvid Hagstrom, by Martin Erikson and K. William Hagstrom. Chicago, Baptist Conference Press [1954] 136p. illus. 20cm. [BX6495.H23E7] 54-31231
1. Hagstrom, Gustave Arvid, 1867-1953. I. Hagstrom, Kenneth William, 1919- joint author. II. Title.

Hague, Frank, 1876-1956.

CONNORS, Richard J., 1927- 974.9'27'040924 B
A cycle of power; the career of Jersey City Mayor Frank Hague, by Richard J. Connors. Metuchen, N.J., Scarecrow Press, 1971. 226 p. 22 cm. Bibliography: p. 212-222. [F144.J5C6] 71-168603 ISBN 0-8108-0435-2
1. Hague, Frank, 1876-1956. 2. Jersey City—Politics and government. 3. Politics, Practical. I. Title. BIP

MCKEAN, Dayton David, 1904- 974.9'27'040924 B
The boss; the Hague machine in action. New York, Russell & Russell [1967, c1940] xvii, 284 p. port. 23 cm. Bibliographical footnotes. [F144.J5H3 1967] 66-24726
1. Hague, Frank, 1876- 2. Jersey City—Politics and government. 3. Politics, Practical. I. Title.

Hague. Gemeentemuseum.

CAVALIERE, Alik, 1926- 730'.924
Alik Cavaliere. [Tentoonstelling] Haags Gemeentemuseum 17 juni t. m. 30 juli, 1967. 's-Gravenhage, 1967. 1 v. (unpaged) 23cm. Bibl. [NB623.C245A42] 67-68416 15.00
1. Hague. Gemeentemuseum. I. Title.

Hahn, Emily, 1905- —Biography.

HAHN, Emily, 1905- 813'.5'2 B
China to me : a partial autobiography / by Emily Hahn. New York : Da Capo Press, 1975, c1944. 429 p. ; 22 cm. (China in the 20th century) Reprint of the ed. published by Doubleday, Doran, Garden City, New York. Includes index. [PS3515.A2422C5 1975] 74-23432 ISBN 0-306-70695-4 : 25.00.
1. Hahn, Emily, 1905- —Biography. 2. China—Description and travel—1901-1948. I. Title. BIP

HAHN, Emily, 1905- 813'.5'2
Times and places. New York, Crowell [1970] 304 p. 22 cm. "The material in this book appeared originally in The New Yorker." [PS3515.A2422Z525] 70-132312 ISBN 6-908249-98- 6.95
I. Title.

Hahn, Otto,

HAHN, Otto, 1879- 541.380924
Otto Hahn: a scientific autobiography. Translated and edited by Willy Ley. Introd. by Glenn T. Seaborg. New York, C. Scribner's Sons [1966] xxiv, 296 p. illus., ports. 24 cm. Translation of Vom Radiothor zur Uranspaltung. "Publications by Otto Hahn": p. [286-292. Bibliographical footnotes. [QD22.H2A313] 66-25149
I. Ley, Willy, 1906-1969. ed. and tr.

HAHN. OTTO, 1879- 541.380924
Otto Hahn: a scientific autobiography. Tr., ed. by Willy Ley. Introd. by Glenn T. Seaborg. New York, Scribners [1966] xxiv. 296p. illus., ports. 24cm. Tr. of Vom Radiothor zur Uranspaltung. Bibl. [QD22.H2A313] 66-25149 7.95
I. Ley. Willy, 1906- ed. and tr. II. Title.

HAHN, Otto, 1879-1968. 541'.38'0924 B
My life; the autobiography of a scientist. Translated by Ernst Kaiser and Eithne Wilkins. [New York] Herder and Herder [1970] 240 p. 22 cm. Translation of Mein Leben. [QD22.H2A2813] 71-110791 6.50
I. Title.

Haig, Douglas Haig, 1st earl, 1861-1928.

DUNCAN, George Simpson, 1884-1965. 940.41440924
Douglas Haig as I knew him, by G. S. Duncan; foreword by Sir Arthur Bryant. London, Allen & Unwin, 1966. 141p. front. (port.) 21cm. [DA69.3.H3D8] 66-78032 5.00 bds.,
1. Haig, Douglas Haig, 1st earl, 1861-1928. I. Title.
Distributed by Hillary House, New York.

SIXSMITH, Eric Keir Gilborne. 355.3'31'0924 B
Douglas Haig / [by] E. K. G. Sixsmith. London : Weidenfeld and Nicolson, 1976. xi, 212 p., [8] p. of plates : ill., maps, plans, ports. ; 23 cm. Includes index. Bibliography: p. 203-206. [DA69.3.H3S59] 76-381448 ISBN 0-297-77149-3 : £5.95
1. Haig, Douglas Haig, 1st Earl, 1861-1928. 2. Great Britain. Army—Biography. 3. Generals—Great Britain—Biography.

***Haigh, Gilbert W., M.D.**

*HAIGH, Gilbert W., M.D. 926.1
Ye olde G.P.; fifty years of general practice. New York, Vantage [c.1965] 88p. 21cm. 2.50 bds.,
I. Title.

Haile Selassie I, Emperor of Ethiopia, 1891-1975.

GORHAM, Charles Orson, 1911- 963.050924
The Lion of Judah: a life of Haile Selassie I, Emperor of Ethiopia. [New York, Farrar, c.1966] 152p. map. 22cm. (Ariel bks.) Bibl. [DT387.7.G6] 6671170 3.25
1. Haile Selassi I, Emperor of Ethiopia, 1891- I. Title.

GORHAM, Charles Orson, 1911- 963.050924 B
The Lion of Judah; a life of Haile Selassie I, Emperor of Ethiopia [by] Charles Gorham. [New York] Ariel Books [1966] 152 p. map. 22 cm. Bibliography: p. [151]-152. [DT387.7.G6] B 66-11707
1. Haile Selassie I, Emperor of Ethiopia, 1891- I. Title.

HAILE Selassie I, Emperor of Ethiopia, 1891-1975. 963'.05'0924 B
My life and Ethiopia's progress, 1892-1937 : the autobiography of Emperor Haile Sellassie I / translated and annotated by Edward Ullendorf Oxford [Eng.] : Oxford University Press, 1976. xxxii, 335 p., [5] leaves of plates : ill. ; 23 cm. Spine title: The autobiography of Emperor Haile Sellassie I. Translation of Heyewatena Ya'Ityopya 'ermeja. Includes index. Bibliography: p. [314]-315. [DT387.7.H2513 1976] 76-366562 ISBN 0-19-713589-7 : 15.50
1. Haile Selassie I, Emperor of Ethiopia, 1891-1975. 2. Ethiopia—History—1889-1974. I. Ullendorff, Edward. II. Title. III. Title: The autobiography of Emperor Haile Sellassie I.
Distributed by Oxford University Press N.Y. N.Y.

MOSLEY, Leonard Oswald, 1911- 923.163
Haile Selassie: the Conquering Lion [by] Leonard Mosley. [1st American ed.] Englewood Cliffs, N. J., Prentice-Hall [1965, c1964] 288 p. illus., ports. 24 cm. Bibliography: p. 281-282. [DT387.7.M64 1965] 65-11882
1. Haile Selassie I, Emperor of Ethiopia, 1891- I. Title.

SANDFORD, Christine (Lush) 963'.056
The Lion of Judah hath prevailed, being the biography of HisImperial Majesty Haile Selassie I. Illustrated with 16 pages of photos. New York, MacMillan [1955] 192p. illus. 22cm. [DT387.7.S] A56
1. Haile Selassie I, Emperor of Ethiopia, 1891- I. Title. BIP

SCHWAB, Peter, 1940- 963'.05'0924 B
Haile Selassie I : Ethiopia's Lion of Judah / Peter Schwab. Chicago : Nelson-Hall, c1979. viii, 192 p., [6] leaves of plates : ill. ; 23 cm. Includes index. Bibliography: p. 181-185. [DT387.7.S372] 79-9897 ISBN 0-88229-342-7 : 13.95
1. Haile Selassie I, Emperor of Ethiopia, 1891-1975. 2. Ethiopia—History—1899-1974. 3. Ethiopia—History—Revolution, 1974. 4. Ethiopia—Kings and rulers—Biography. BIP

Hailey, Arthur—Biography—Marriage.

HAILEY, Sheila, 1927- 813'.5'4 B
I married a best seller / Sheila Hailey. 1st ed. Garden City, N.Y. : Doubleday, 1978. 287 p. ; 22 cm. [PR9199.3.H3Z7] 77-76235 ISBN 0-385-12337-X : 8.95
1. Hailey, Arthur—Biography—Marriage. 2. Hailey, Sheila, 1927- 3. Authors, Canadian—20th century—Biography. 4. Wives Biography. I. Title. BIP

Hailton, William, 1704-1754

BUSHNELL, Nelson Sherwin. v. 12
William Hamilton of Bangour, poet and Jacobite. Aberdeen, University Press, 1957. xi, 164p. ports., facsims. 22cm. 'Bibliography of the published writings of William Hamilton': p. 150- 153. Includes bibliographical references. A58
1. Hailton, William, 1704-1754. I. Title.

Haimo, Oscar.

HAIMO, Oscar. 926.4795
Nothing lasts forever, an autobiography; illustrated by The author. [New York? 1953] 282p. illus. 21cm. [TX950.5.H3A3] 53-39105
I. Title.

Haines, Connie, 1921-

*HAINES, Connie. 784.0924 B
For once in my life by Connie Haines, as told to Robert B. Stone. [New York] Warner Books [1976] 223 p. illus. 18 cm. [ML420] 1.50 (pbk.)
1. Haines, Connie 2. Singers—Correspondence, reminiscences, etc. I. Title. BIP

HAINES, Connie, 1921- 784'.092'4 B
For once in my life / by Connie Haines, as told to Robert B. Stone. New York : Warner Books, 1976. 223 p., [8] leaves of plates : ill. ; 18 cm. [ML420.H116A3] 76-361077 ISBN 0-446-78799-X : 1.50
1. Haines, Connie, 1921- 2. Musicians—Correspondence, reminiscences, etc. I. Stone, Robert B., joint author. II. Title.

Haiti—Hist.

CHRISTOPHE, Henri, King of Haiti, 1767-1820. 923.17294
Henry Christophe & Thomas Clarkson, a correspondence edited by Earl Leslie Griggs and Clifford H. Prator. Berkeley, University of California Press, 1952. 287 p. illus., ports., maps, facsim. 24 cm. Bibliography: p. 281-282. [F1924.C46] 52-901
1. Haiti—Hist. I. Clarkson, Thomas, 1760-1846. II. Griggs, Earl Leslie, 1899- ed. III. Title.

CHRISTOPHE, Henri, King of Haiti, 1767-1820. 972'.94'040924
Henry Christophe & Thomas Clarkson; a correspondence, edited by Earl Leslie Griggs and Clifford H. Prator. New York, Greenwood Press, 1968 [c1952] 287 p. illus., facsim., maps, ports. 24 cm. Bibliography: p. 281-282. [F1924.C46 1968] 68-23281
1. Haiti—History. I. Clarkson, Thomas, 1760-1846. II. Griggs, Earl Leslie, 1899- ed. III. Prator, Clifford Holmes, ed. IV. Title.

Hake, Gordon,

HAKE, Gordon, 1809-1895. 821'.8 B
Memoirs of eighty years. New York, AMS Press [1970] xx, 304 p. 23 cm. Reprint of the 1892 ed. [PR4735.H2Z5 1970] 73-131509 ISBN 0-404-03025-4
I. Title. BIP

Halas, George Stanley, 1895-

HALAS, George Stanley, 1895- 796.33'2'0924 B
Halas / by Halas, with Gwen Morgan and Arthur Veysey. New York : McGraw-Hill, c1979. p. cm. [GV939.H26A33] 79-13554 ISBN 0-07-025549-0 : 12.95
1. Halas, George Stanley, 1895- 2. Chicago. Foot-ball club (National League) 3. Sports team owners United States—Biography. I. Morgan, Gwen, joint author. II. Veysey, Arthur, joint author. III. Title.

Halberstam, Michael.

HALBERSTAM, Michael. 616.1'23'09
A coronary event / by Michael Halberstam and Stephan Lesher. 1st ed. Philadelphia : Lippincott, c1976. 208 p. ; 24 cm. [RC685.C6H28] 76-914 ISBN 0-397-01119-9 : 8.95
1. Halberstam, Michael. 2. Lesher, Stephen. 3. Coronary heart disease—Personal narratives. I. Lesher, Stephan, joint author. II. Title. BIP

Halbert, Frederic, 1945-

HALBERT, Frederic, 1945- 636.2'08'9431
Bitter harvest / Frederic and Sandra Halbert. Grand Rapids : W. B. Eerdmans Pub. Co., c1978. p. cm. [SF203.H25] 78-23531 ISBN 0-8028-7039-2 : 8.95
1. Halbert, Frederic, 1945- 2. Halbert, Sandra, 1943- 3. Cattle—Feeding and feeds. 4. Feed contamination—Michigan. 5. Polybrominated biphenyls—Toxicology—Michigan. 6. Farmers—Michigan—Battle Creek region—Biography. I. Halbert, Sandra, 1943- joint author. II. Title.

Halbert, Sara.

HALBERT, Sara. 340'.092'4
Call me counselor / by Sara Halbert, with Florence Stevenson. 1st ed. Philadelphia : Lippincott, c1977. 251 p. ; 24 cm. [KF373.H23A3] 77-21054 ISBN 0-397-01239-X : 8.95
1. Halbert, Sara. 2. Lawyers—United

States—Biography. I. Stevenson, Florence, joint author. II. Title. BIP

Halbouty, Michel Thomas, 1909-

DONAHUE, Jackson. 622'.33'80924 B
Wildcatter : the story of Michel T. Halbouty and the search for oil / Jack Donahue. New York : McGraw-Hill, c1979. 268 p. ; 22 cm. Includes index. [TN140.H24D66] 79-561 ISBN 0-07-017542-X : 10.95
1. Halbouty, Michel Thomas, 1909- 2. Petroleum engineers—United States—Biography. I. Title.

Haldane, John Burdon Sanderson, 1892-1964.

CLARK, Ronald William. 575.00924 B
JBS: the life and work of J. B. S. Haldane [by] Ronald W. Clark. [1st American ed.] New York, Coward-McCann [1969, c1968] 326 p. ports. 23 cm. Bibliography: p. [305]-318. [QH31.H27C55 1969] 68-11875 6.95
1. Haldane, John Burdon Sanderson, 1892-1964. I. Title.

Haldane, Richard Burdon Haldane, 1st viscount, 1856-1928.

SOMMER, Dudley 923.242
Haldane of Cloan: his life and times, 1856-1928. [dist. Hollywood-by-the-Sea, Fla., Transatlantic Arts, c.1960] 448p. illus. 60-4669 10.50
1. Haldane, Richard Burdon Haldane, 1st viscount, 1856-1928. I. Title.

Haldeman-Julius, Emanuel

HALDEMAN-JULIUS, Emanuel. 926.55
The world of Haldeman-Julius. With foreword of Harry Golden; compiled by Albert Mordell. New York, Twayne Publishers [c.1960] 288p. 23cm. 60-8550 4.00 bds.,
I. Title.

Hale, Edward Everett, 1822-1909.

HOLLOWAY, Jean. 922.8173
Edward Everett Hale, a biography. Austin, University of Texas Press, 1956. xi, 275p. ports., facsim. 24cm. Bibliographical footnotes. [PS1773.H6] 55-8474
1. Hale, Edward Everett, 1822-1909. I. Title.

Hale, George Ellery, 1868-1938.

WRIGHT, Helen, 1914- 520.924
Explorer of the universe; a biography of George Ellery Hale. Introd. by Ira S. Bowen. New York, Dutton [c.]1966. 480p. illus., ports. 22cm. Bibl. [QB36.H14W7] 66-11542 10.00
1. Hale, George Ellery, 1868-1938. I. Title.

WRIGHT, Helen, 1914- 520.924 (B)
Explorer of the universe; a biography of George Ellery Hale. With an introd. by Ira S. Bowen. [1st ed.] New York, Dutton, 1966. 480 p. illus., ports. 22 cm. "Biographical articles on George Ellery Hale": p. [465] [QB36.H14W7] 66-11542
1. Hale, George Ellery, 1868-1938. I. Title.

Hale, John Parker, 1806-1873.

SEWELL, Richard H. 923.273
John P. Hale and the politics of abolition. Cambridge, Mass., Harvard [c.]1965. viii, 290p. port. 22cm. Bibl. [E415.9.H15S4] 65-13849 6.50
1. Hale, John Parker, 1806-1873. 2. Slavery in the U. S.—Anti-slavery movements. I. Title.

Hale, Matthew Blagdon.

ROBIN, Arthur de Quetteville. 283'.092'4 B
Mathew Blagden Hale : the life of an Australian pioneer bishop / [by] A. de Q. Robin. Melbourne : Hawthorn Press, 1976. iv, 227 p., 2 leaves of plates, (ports.) ; 22 cm. Includes index. Bibliography: p. 216-221. [BX5199.H215R6] 77-362808 ISBN 0-7256-0167-1 : 14.95
1. Hale, Matthew Blagdon. 2. Church of England—Bishops—Biography. 3. Bishops—Australia—Biography.

Hale, Matthew, Sir, 1609-1676.

BURNET, Gilbert, Bp. of Salisbury, 1643-1715. 347'.42'0234 B
The life and death of Sir Matthew Hale, Kt., sometime Lord Chief Justice of His Majesties Court of Kings Bench, written by Gilbert Burnett. South Hackensack, N.J., Rothman Reprints, 1972. 128 p. port. 20 cm. Reprint of the 1682 ed. "A catalogue of all his [Hale's] books": p. 112-123. [LAW] 70-181890
1. Hale, Matthew, Sir, 1609-1676. I. Title.

Hale, Nathan, 1755-1776.

STEVENSON, Augusta. 973.3850924 B
Nathan Hale, Puritan boy. Illustrated by Leslie Goldstein. Indianapolis, Bobbs-Merrill [1959] 192 p. illus. 20 cm. (Childhood of famous Americans) Describes the strict Puritan upbringing that made Nathan Hale a brave and honest boy and a loyal patriot who gave his life for his country. [PZ7.S8467Nat] 92 AC 68
1. Hale, Nathan, 1755-1776. I. Goldstein, Leslie, illus. II. Title.

Hale, Nathan, 1755-1776 — Fiction.

STEVENSON, Augusta. JUV
Nathan Hale, Puritan oby. Illustrated by Leslie Goldstein. Indianapolis, Bobbs-Merrill [1959] 192 p. illus. 20 cm. (Childhood of famous Americans) [PZ7.S8467Nat] fic 59-14007
1. Hale, Nathan, 1755-1776 — Fiction. I. Title.

Hale, Nathan, 1755-1776 — Juvenile literature.

GERSON, Noel Bertram, 1914-. 923.573
Nathan Hale, espionage agent. Garden City, N. Y., Doubleday [1960] 55 p. illus. 21 cm. (The Living history program) [E280.H2G4] 60-51890
1. Hale, Nathan, 1755-1776 — Juvenile literature. I. Title.

POOLE, Susan D. 973.3'85'0924 B
Nathan Hale / by Susan Poole ; illustrated by Drina Karp. New York : Dandelion Press, 1979. [29] p. : col. ill. ; 23 cm. A brief biography of the young schoolteacher who was arrested by the British and hanged for spying during the American revolution. [E280.H2P66] 92 78-64421 ISBN 0-89799-128-1 : 3.50 ISBN 0-89799-035-8 (pbk.) : 1.50
1. Hale, Nathan, 1755-1776—Juvenile literature. 2. United States—History—Revolution, 1775-1783—Secret service—Juvenile literature. 3. Spies—United States—Biography—Juvenile literature. 4. Soldiers—United States—Biography—Juvenile literature. I. Karp, Drina. II. Title. BIP

VOIGHT, Virginia Frances. 973.3
Nathan Hale. Illustrated by Frank Aloise. New York, Putnam [1965] 63 p. illus. 23 cm. (A See and read beginning to read biography) [E280.H2V6] 65-10872
1. Hale, Nathan, 1755-1776—Juvenile literature. BIP

Hale, Philip Leslie, 1865-1931.

HALE, Nancy, 1908- 759.13
The life in the studio. [1st ed.] Boston, Little, Brown [1969] xiv, 209 p. 21 cm. Autobiographical. [ND236.H3] 69-16965 5.95
1. Hale, Philip Leslie, 1865-1931. 2. Hale, Lillian Westcott, 1881-1963. I. Title. BIP

Hale, Sarah Josepha (Buell) 1788-1879.

BURT, Olive [Frank] (Woolley) 920.5
First woman editor, Sara J. Hale. New York, Messner [c.1960] 191p. (bibl.: p. 185-186) 22cm. (Julian Messner shelf of biographies) 60-7818 2.95
1. Hale, Sarah Josepha (Buell) 1788-1879. I. Title.

BURT, Olive (Woolley) 1894- 920.5
First woman editor, Sarah J. Hale. New York, Messner [1960] 191p. 22cm. Includes bibliographies. [PN4874.H22B8] 60-7818
1. Hale, Sarah Josepha (Buell) 1788-1879. I. Title.

BURT, Olive (Woolley) 1894- 070.4'8347'0924 B
First woman editor, Sarah J. Hale. New York, Messner [1960] 191 p. 22 cm. Includes bibliographies. A biography of the New Hampshire woman who wrote "Mary Had a Little Lamb," persuaded Lincoln to make Thanksgiving a national holiday, and edited nineteenth-century women's magazines, including Godey's Lady's Book. [PN4874.H22B8] 92 AC 68
1. Hale, Sarah Josepha (Buell) 1788-1879. I. Title.

HALE, Nancy, 1908- 759.13
The life in the studio. [1st ed.] Boston, Little, Brown [1969] xiv, 209 p. 21 cm. Autobiographical. [ND236.H3] 69-16965 5.95
1. Hale, Philip Leslie, 1865-1931. 2. Hale, Lillian Westcott, 1881-1963. I. Title. BIP

*Hale, Yvonne Tilly

*HALE, Yvonne Tilly 920.7
Laugh and cry. New York, Exposition [c.1965] 64p. 21cm. (EP43023) 3.00
I. Title.

Hales, Stephen, 1677-1761.

CLARK-KENNEDY, Archibald Edmund, 1893- 509'.2'2
Stephen Hales, D.D., F. R. S.; an eighteenth century biography, by A. E. Clark-Kennedy. Ridgewood, N.Y., Gregg Press, 1965. xii, 256 p. illus., map. port. 20 cm. Reprint of the 1929 ed. Bibliographical footnotes. [Q143.H3C5 1965] 67-3093
1. Hales, Stephen, 1677-1761. I. Title.

Halevy, Daniel, 1872-1962.

SILVERA, Alain 944.0810924[B]
Daniel Halevy and his times; a genteleman-commoner in the Third Republic. Ithaca, N.Y., Cornell Univ. Pr. [1966] xi, 251p. port. 23cm. Bibl. [DC36.98.H28S5] 66-20130 6.50
1. Halevy, Daniel, 1872-1962. I. Title.

Halevy, Isaak, 1847-1914.

REICHEL, O. Asher, 1921- 296'.072'024 B
Isaac Halevy, 1847-1914: spokesman and historian of Jewish tradition, by O. Asher Reichel. New York, Yeshiva University Press. 1969. 176 p. facsims., port. 24 cm. Includes, in Hebrew, "Facsimiles of Halevy's letters" (p. 129-158) Bibliography: p. 160-170. Bibliographical footnotes. [BM755.H225R4] 70-85704
1. Halevy, Isaak, 1847-1914. 2. Orthodox Judaism—Germany.

Haley, Alex.

HALEY, Alex. 929'.2'0973
Roots / Alex Haley. 1st ed. Garden City, N.Y. : Doubleday, 1976. viii, 587 p. ; 24 cm. "A condensed version of a portion of this work first appeared in Reader's digest." [E185.97.H24A33] 72-76164 ISBN 0-385-03787-2 : 12.50
1. Haley, Alex. 2. Haley family. 3. Kinte family. I. Title. BIP

Haley family.

HALEY, Alex. 929'.2'0973
Roots / Alex Haley. 1st ed. Garden City, N.Y. : Doubleday, 1976. viii, 587 p. ; 24 cm. "A condensed version of a portion of this work first appeared in Reader's digest." [E185.97.H24A33] 72-76164 ISBN 0-385-03787-2 : 12.50
1. Haley, Alex. 2. Haley family. 3. Kinte family. I. Title. BIP

HALEY, James Evetts, 1901- 976.4'00992 B
Rough times, tough fiber : a fragmentary family chronicle / by J. Evetts Haley. Canyon, Tex. : Palo Duro Press, 1976. ix, 196 p., [15] leaves of plates : ill. ; 25 cm. Includes index. [F385.H325] 77-152563
1. Haley family. 2. Evetts family. 3. Pioneers—Texas—Biography. 4. Frontier and pioneer life—Texas. 5. Texas—Biography. I. Title.

Haliburton, Thomas Chandler, 1796-1865.

CHITTICK, Victor Lovitt Oakes, 1882- v. 12
Thomas Chandler Haliburton ("Sam Slick"): a study in provincial Toryism, by V.L.O. Chittick. New York, AMS Press, 1966. xi, 695 p. front. (port.) Bibliography: p. 655-686. 68-29071
1. Haliburton, Thomas Chandler, 1796-1865. I. Title.

Hall, Abraham Oakey, 1826-1898.

BOWEN, Croswell. 923.273
The elegant Oakey. New York, Oxford University Press, 1956. 292p. illus. 22cm. Includes bibliography. [F128.47.H19B6] 56-10456
1. Hall, Abraham Oakey, 1826-1898. I. Title.

Hall, Carl Mitchel, 1899-

HALL, Carl Mitchel, 1899- 620'.0092'4 B
A personal memoir : an unforgettable autobiography / by C. Mitchel Hall. Baltimore : Gateway Press, 1976. xxvii, 639 p. : ill. ; 24 cm. [TA140.H29A35] 76-25362
1. Hall, Carl Mitchel, 1899- 2. Engineers—United States—Biography. I. Title.

Hall, Charles Francis, 1821-1871.

LOOMIS, Chauncey C., 1930- 919.8'03 B
Weird and tragic shores; the story of Charles Francis Hall, explorer [by] Chauncey C. Loomis. [1st ed.] New York, Knopf, 1971. xiv, 367, xii p. illus., maps, ports. 22 cm. Bibliography: p. [363]-367. [G635.H2L6 1971] 70-111253 ISBN 0-394-45131-7 8.95
1. Hall, Charles Francis, 1821-1871. 2. Arctic regions—History. I. Title.

Hall, Charles Martin, 1863-1914.

YOUNG, Rosamond McPherson. 669.7220924 (B)
Made of aluminum; a life of Charles Martin Hall. New York, D. McKay Co., 1965. 213 p. 21 cm. Bibliography: p. 207-210. [TN140.H25Y6] 65-22567
1. Hall, Charles Martin, 1863-1914. I. Title.

Hall, Donald, 1928- —Friends and associates.

HALL, Donald, 1928- 818'.03
Remembering poets : reminiscences and opinions : Dylan Thomas, Robert Frost, T. S. Eliot, Ezra Pound / by Donald Hall. 1st ed. New York : Harper & Row, c1978. xv, 253 p. : ports. ; 24 cm. Includes index. [PS3515.A3152Z526 1978] 76-47266 ISBN 0-06-011723-0 : 10.00
1. Hall, Donald, 1928- —Friends and associates. 2. Poets, American—20th century—Biography. I. Title.

Halle, Charles, Sir, 1819-1895.

HALLE, Charles, Sir, 1819-1895. 785'.092'4 B
The autobiography of Charles Halle, with correspondence and diaries. Edited with an introd. by Michael Kennedy. New York, Barnes & Noble [1973] 215 p. illus. 23 cm. Selected from The life and letters of Sir Charles Halle; edited by C. E. Halle and Marie Halle. London, Smith, Elder, 1896. [ML422.H18A3 1973] 73-161153 ISBN 0-06-493634-1 10.75
1. Halle, Charles, Sir, 1819-1895. 2. Musicians—Correspondence, reminiscences, etc.

Hall, Edwin Presley.

HALL, Edwin Presley. 617'.092'4 B
A doctor reminisces / Edwin Presley Hall. Huntsville, Ala. : Strode Publishers, c1978. 332 p. ; 24 cm. [RD27.35.H34A33] 77-94279 ISBN 0-87397-133-7 : 9.95
1. Hall, Edwin Presley. 2. Surgeons—United States—Biography. I. Title. BIP

Hall, Ennen Reaves.

HALL, Ennen Reaves. 248.2'0924 B
Break the glass wall. Waco, Tex., Word Books [1971] 129 p. 23 cm. [BR1725.H19A3] 75-144369 3.95
I. Title.

Hall, Glenn, 1931- —Juvenile literature.

ETTER, Les. 796.9'62'0922
Hockey's masked men : three great goalies / by Les Etter ; illustrated by Larry Noble. Champaign, Ill. : Garrard Pub. Co., c1976. 96 p. : ill. ; 24 cm. Biographies of three men who brought a new style of goaltending to hockey: Terry Sawchuk, Glenn Hall, and Jacques Plante. [GV848.5.A1E87] 920 75-28413 ISBN 0-8116-6676-X : 3.58
1. Hall, Glenn, 1931- —Juvenile literature. 2. Plante, Jacques, 1929- —Juvenile literature. 3. Sawchuk, Terry, 1929- —Juvenile literature. 4. Hockey—Biography—Juvenile literature. I. Noble, Larry. II. Title. BIP

Hall, Granville Stanley, 1844-1924.

†HALL, Granville Stanley, 1844-1924. 150'.92'4 B
Life and confessions of a psychologist / by G. Stanley Hall. New York : Arno Press, 1977, c1923. ix, 622 p., [8] leaves of plates : ill. ; 24 cm. (The Academic profession) Reprint of the 1924 issue of the ed. first published in 1923 by D. Appleton, New York, London. Includes index. Bibliography: p. 597-[616]. [BF109.H3A35 1977] 76-55180 ISBN 0-405-10008-6 : 36.00
1. Hall, Granville Stanley, 1844-1924. 2. Psychologists—United States—Biography. I. Title. II. Series. BIP

ROSS, Dorothy, 1936- 150'.92'4 B
G. Stanley Hall: the psychologist as prophet. Chicago, University of Chicago Press [1972] xix, 482 p. illus. 23 cm. Based on the author's thesis, Columbia. Bibliography: p. [439]-468. [BF109.H3R67] 75-165180 ISBN 0-226-72821-8
1. Hall, Granville Stanley, 1844-1924. BIP

Hall, James Norman,

HALL, James Norman, 1887-1951. 813'.5'2 B
My island home; an autobiography. Westport, Conn., Greenwood Press [1970, c1952] x, 374 p. illus., ports. 23 cm. [PS3515.A363Z5 1970] 78-109306 ISBN 8-371-35818-
I. Title.

HALL, James Norman, 1887-1951. 928.1
My island home, an autobiography. [1st ed.] Boston, Little, Brown [1952] 374 p. illus. 22 cm. "An Atlantic Monthly Press book." [PS3515.A363Z5] 52-9089
I. Title.

Hall, James, 1793-1868.

BURTSCHI, Mary. 818'.2'09 B
James Hall of Lincoln's frontier world / by Mary Burtschi ; with ill. by Josephine Burtschi. Vandalia, Ill. : Little Brick House, c1977. 202 p. : ill. ; 23 cm. Includes index. Bibliography: p. 190-194. [PS1779.H16Z58] 77-87957 8.95
1. Hall, James, 1793-1868. 2. Authors, American—19th century—Biography. 3. Frontier and pioneer life in literature. I. Title.
Publishers address 621 Saint Clair St., Vandalia, Ill.,62471 BIP

Hall, James, 1811-1898.

CLARKE, John Mason, 1857-1925. 551.7'0092'4 B
James Hall of Albany, geologist and palaeontologist, 1811-1898 / John Mason Clarke. New York : Arno Press, 1978. 565 p., [13] leaves of plates : ill. : 21 cm. (History of geology) Reprint of the 1923 ed. priv. print. in Albany. Includes bibliographical references and index. [QE22.H25C5 1978] 77-6512 ISBN 0-405-10435-9 : 35.00
1. Hall, James, 1811-1898. 2. Geologists—United States—Biography. I. Title. II. Series.

Hall, John, 1575-1635.

JOSEPH, Harriet. 926.1
Shakespeare's son-in-law: John Hall, man and physician. With a facsimile of the 2d ed. of Hall's Select observations on English bodies. Hamden, Conn., Archon Books, 1964. xv, 328 p. illus., facsims. 21 cm. The facsimile ends with p. 179 of the original 2d ed. Bibliography: p. [101]-102. [R489.H21J6] 64-9810
1. Hall, John, 1575-1635. I. Hall, John, 1575-1635. Select observations on English bodies. II. Title.

MITCHELL, C Martin. 610'.92'4 B
The Shakespeare circle : a life of Dr. John Hall, Shakespeare's son-in-law, with glimpses of their intimate friends and relations / by C. Martin Mitchell. Brooklyn, N.Y. : Haskell House, 1977. 116 p. ; 21 cm. Reprint of the 1947 ed. published by Cornish Bros., Birmingham. [PR2912.H3M5 1977] 76-30693 lib. bdg. : 9.95
1. Hall, John, 1575-1635. 2. Shakespeare, William, 1564-1616—Friends and associates. 3. Physicians—England—Biography. I. Title.

Hall, Joseph, Bp. of Norwich, 1574-1656.

HUNTLEY, Frank Livingstone, 1902- 283'.092'4
Bishop Joseph Hall, 1574-1656 : a biographical and critical study / Frank Livingstone Huntley. Cambridge [Eng.] : D. S. Brewer, 1979. viii, 180 p. ; 22 cm. Includes bibliographical references and index. [BX5199.H25H86] 79-309300 ISBN 0-85991-035-0 : 21.50
1. Hall, Joseph, Bp. of Norwich, 1574-1656. 2. Church of England—Bishops—Biography. 3. Bishops—England—Biography. I. Title.
Available from Rowman & Littlefield, Totowa, NJ 07511 BIP

Hall, Kenneth George, 1901-

HALL, Kenneth George, 1901- 791.43'023'0924 B
Directed by Ken G. Hall : autobiography of an Australian film maker. Melbourne : Lansdowne Press, 1977. 216 p. : ill. ; 27 cm. [PN1998.A3H29] 77-375571 ISBN 0-7018-0670-2
1. Hall, Kenneth George, 1901- 2. Moving-picture producers and directors—Australia—Biography.

Hall, Loran.

HALL, Loran. 364.1'524'0924 B
Jackal for the CIA / by Loran Hall. New York : Drake Pub., [1976] p. cm. Includes index. Bibliography: p. [HV6278.H27] 76-16383 ISBN 0-8473-1263-1 : 8.95
1. Hall, Loran. 2. Assassins—Biography. I. Title.

Hall, Lyman, 1724-1790.

HALL, James William. 923.273
Lyman Hall, Georgia patriot. Savannah, Pigeonhole Press [1959] 113p. illus. 24cm. Includes bibliography. [E263.G3H23] 59-4971
1. Hall, Lyman, 1724-1790. I. Title.

Hall, Prince, 1748-1807.

WESLEY, Charles Harris, 1891- 366'.1'0924 B
Prince Hall : life and legacy / by Charles H. Wesley. 1st ed. Washington : United Supreme Council, Southern Jurisdiction, Prince Hall Affiliation, 1977. xvii, 237 p. : ill. ; 23 cm. Includes index. Bibliography: p. 221-228. [HS883.W47] 76-53127
1. Hall, Prince, 1748-1807. 2. Freemasons, Afro-American.

Hall, Radclyffe.

DICKSON, Lovat, 1902- 821'.9'12 B
Radclyffe Hall at The well of loneliness : a sapphic chronicle / Lovat Dickson. New York : Scribner, c1975. 236 p., [4] leaves of plates : ill. ; 22 cm. Includes bibliographical references and index. [PR6015.A33Z64 1975b] 76-358643 ISBN 0-684-14530-8 : 7.95
1. Hall, Radclyffe—Relationship with women—Una Troubridge. 2. Troubridge, Una Elena Taylor, Lady. I. Title.

TROUBRIDGE, Una Elena (Taylor) Lady 928.2
The life of Radclyffe Hall. New York, Citadel [1963, c.1961] 189p. illus. 21cm. First pub. in England in 1961 under title: The life and death of Radcyffe Hall. 63-11768 4.00 bds.,
1. Hall, Radolyffe. I. Title.

Hall, Radclyffe—Biography.

TROUBRIDGE, Una Elena Taylor, Lady. 821'.9'12 B
The life of Radclyffe Hall / by Una, Lady Troubridge [Vincenzo]. New York : Arno Press, 1975, c1961. p. cm. (Homosexuality) First published under title: The life and death of Radclyffe Hall. Reprint of the ed. published by Citadel Press, New York. [PR6015.A33Z87 1975] 75-12350 ISBN 0-405-07355-0 : 10.00
1. Hall, Radclyffe—Biography. I. Title. II. Series.

Hall, Ralph J.,

HALL, Ralph J., 1891- 266.5'0924 B
The main trail, by Ralph J. Hall. Edited by Vic Jameson. San Antonio, Tex., Naylor [1971] xiii, 193 p. illus. 22 cm. Autobiographical. [BX9225.H312A3] 76-185994 ISBN 0-8111-0448-6 7.95
I. Title.

Hall, Raymond C

HALL, Raymond C 1897- 920
A Vermonter's way. [1st ed.] New York, Pageant Press [1954] 181p. 21cm. Autobiography. [CT275.H2855A3] 54-12947
I. Title.

Hall, Richard Smith, 1855-1910.

HALL, Dorothy, ed. 340.0924
Life and letters of Richard Smith Hall, selected and compiled by Dorothy Hall. [1st ed.] New York, Printed by the Comet Press [1965] 216 p. facsims., ports. 24cm. Errata slip included. [KF373.H25H3] 65-29053
1. Hall, Richard Smith, 1855-1910.

Hall, Sarah C., 1832-1926.

MALIN, James Claude, 1893- 978.1'97
Doctors, devils, and the woman : Fort Scott, Kansas, 1870-1890 / by James C. Malin. Lawrence, Kan. : Coronado Press, 1975. 122 p. ; 22 cm. Includes bibliographical references. [F689.F7M34] 75-328474 ISBN 0-87291-074-1 : 8.50
1. Hall, Sarah C., 1832-1926. 2. Fort Scott, Kan.—History. I. Title. BIP

Hall, William Henry Harrison, 1823-1907.

HALL, William Henry Harrison, 1823-1907. 917.8'04'20924
The private letters and diaries of Captain Hall; an epic of an argonaut in the California gold rush, Oregon Territories, Civil War, and Oil City. Edited by Eric Schneirsohn. Glendale, Calif., London Book Co. [1974] xi, 270 p. illus. 29 cm. Errata sheet inserted. [F865.H172 1974] 74-182284
1. Hall, William Henry Harrison, 1823-1907. 2. California—Gold discoveries. 3. Voyages to the Pacific Coast. 4. United States—Description and travel—1848-1865. 5. United States—Description and travel—1865-1900. I. Schneirsohn, Eric, ed.

Hall, William Preston, 1918-

HALL, William Preston, 1918- 286'.1'0924 B
Admired and condemned / by William Preston Hall, Jr. 1st ed. Honea Path, S.C. : Hall, 1974. 300 p. : ill. ; 21 cm. [BX6495.H263A32] 74-75519
1. Hall, William Preston, 1918- I. Title.

Hallahan, Margaret Mary, 1806-1868.

MARY Catherine, Sister, of the English Dominioan Congregation of Saint Catherins of Siena. 922.242
Steward of souls; a portrait of Mother Margaret Hallahan, by S. M. C. London, New York, Longmans, Green [1952] 181p. illus. 19cm. [BX4705.H23M3] 52-13871
1. Hallahan, Margaret Mary, 1806-1868. I. Title.

Hallam, Arthur Henry, 1811-1833—Correspondence.

HALLAM, Arthur Henry, 1811-1833. 824'.7 B
The letters of Arthur Henry Hallam / edited by Jack Kolb. Columbus : Ohio State University Press, [1979] p. cm. Includes index. [PR4735.H4Z53 1979] 79-13490 ISBN 0-8142-0300-0 : 30.00
1 Hallam, Arthur Henry, 1811-1833—Correspondence. 2. Poets, English—19th century—Correspondence. I. Kolb, Jack, 1946- BIP

HALLAM, Arthur Henry, 1811-1833. 824'.7 B
The love story of In memoriam : letters from Arthur Hallam to Emily Tennyson / [with a foreword by] Clement Shorter. Folcroft, Pa. : Folcroft Library Editions, 1977. p. cm. Reprint of the 1916 ed. printed by C. Shorter, London. [PR4735.H4Z544 1977] 77-8199 ISBN 0-8414-7688-8 lib. bdg. : 10.00
1. Hallam, Arthur Henry, 1811-1833—Correspondence. 2. Jesse, Emily Tennyson, 1811-1887. 3. Tennyson, Alfred Tennyson, Baron, 1809-1892. In memoriam. 4. Poets, English—19th century—Correspondence. I. Jesse, Emily Tennyson, 1811-1887. II. Title.

Halleck, Charles A., 1900-

SCHEELE, Henry Z., 1933- 973.90924
Charlie Halleck; a political biography, by Henry Z. Scheele. With a foreword by Dwight D. Eisenhower and an introd. by Everett McKinley Dirksen. [1st ed.] New York, Exposition Press [1966] 287 p. 21 cm. (An Exposition-Banner book) Bibliographical footnotes. [E748.H29S3] 66-28844
1. Halleck, Charles A., 1900-

Haller, Lelia.

SCOTT, Harold George. 792.8'092'4 B
Lelia : the compleat ballerina / Harold George Scott. Gretna, La. : Pelican Pub. Co., 1975. 230 p. : ill. ; 30 cm. Includes index. [GV1785.H26S36] 75-8768 ISBN 0-88289-075-1 : 19.95
1. Haller, Lelia. 2. Ballet. I. Title.

Halley, Edmond, 1656-1742.

HALLEY, Edmond, 1656-1742. 520'.92'4 B
Correspondence and papers of Edmond Halley / arranged and edited by Eugene Fairfield MacPike. New York : Arno Press, 1975. xiv, 300 p., [5] leaves of plates : ill. ; 24 cm. (History, philosophy, and sociology of science) Reprint of the 1932 ed. published by the Clarendon Press, Oxford, which was issued as no. 2 of History of Science Society publications, new series. English, French, or Latin. Includes index. "Halleiana: I-XXI": p. [171]-289. [QB36.H25A25 1975] 74-26268 ISBN 0-405-06596-5 : 18.00
1. Halley, Edmond, 1656-1742. I. Title. II. Series. III. Series: History of Science Society. Publications. New series ; New series ; BIP

Halliburton, Richard, 1900-1939.

ROOT, Jonathan 910.40924
Halliburton, the magnificent myth; a biography. New York, Coward [c.1965] 288p. illus., ports. 22cm. [CT275.H28555R6] 65-20408 5.50
1. Halliburton, Richard, 1900-1939. I. Title.

Halliday, Jerry.

HALLIDAY, Jerry. 248'.83
Spaced out and gathered in; a sort of an autobiography of a Jesus freak. Old Tappan, N.J., F. H. Revell Co. [1972] 126 p. 18 cm. [BV4935.H26A3] 78-186536 ISBN 0-8007-0511-4 0.95 (pbk)
I. Title. BIP

Hallock, Gerard, 1800-1866.

HALLOCK, William H. 070.4'0924 B
Life of Gerard Hallock, editor of the New York Journal of commerce [by] William H. Hallock. [New York] Arno [1970] vi, 287 p. port. 23 cm. (The American journalists) Reprint of the 1869 ed. [E340.H17H3 1970] 78-125696 ISBN 0-405-01675-1
1. Hallock, Gerard, 1800-1866. 2. Journal of commerce and commercial (New York) 3. United States—Politics and government—1815-1861.

Hallwas family.

HALLWAS, Rudolph, 1912- 929'.2'0971
Canadian branch of the Hal(l) was family : record book / by Rudolph Hallwas. Vernon, B.C. : R. Hallwas, 1974. 30 p. : map ; 22 cm. "With brief historical events, origin of family name, and genealogical record from the early 1800's to the 1970's." Limited ed. of 200 copies. Bibliography: p. 29. [CS90.H24 1974] 75-325905
1. Hallwas family. I. Title.

Halperin, Samuel William.

HISTORIANS of modern 940'.072'022
Europe. Edited by Hans A. Schmitt. Baton Rouge, Louisiana State University Press [1971] xviii, 338 p. 25 cm. Papers written in honor of S. William Halperin. Contents.Contents.—Introduction, by H. A. Schmitt.—Arnold J. Toynbee: the paradox of prophecy, by E. W. Fox.—Carlton J. H. Hayes, by C. Jefferson.—Oscar Halecki, by K. L. Lewalski.—Hans Kohn: historian of nationalism, by L. L. Snyder.—A. J. P. Taylor, by H. R. Williams.—J. L. Hammond, by H. R. Winkler.—Adolfo Omodeo: historian of the "religion of freedom," by C. F. Delzell.—Gerhard Ritter, by W. H. Maehl.—Gaetano Salvemini: Meridionalista, by G. T. Peck.—Ernest Labrousse, by P. Renouvin.—Frederico Chabod: portrait of a master historian, by A. W. Salomone.—The France of M. Chastenet, by W. Savage.—Gioacchino Volpe, by E. R. Tannenbaum. Includes bibliographical references. [D14.H52] 71-140961 ISBN 0-8071-0836-7 11.00
1. Halperin, Samuel William. 2. Historians. I. Halperin, Samuel William. II. Schmitt, Hans A., ed.

Hals, Frans, 1584-1666.

BEEREN, Willem A. L. 759.9492
Frans Hals. [Tr.: Albert J. Fransella] New York, Barnes &Noble [1963, c.1962] 90p. illus. (pt. col.) 18cm. (Barnes & Noble art ser., 609) 63-5387 .75 pap.,
1. Hals, Frans, 1584-1666. I. Title.

DESCARGUES, Pierre. 759.9492
Hals. Biographical and critical study. Translated from the French by James Emmons. [Geneva] Skira [1968] 145 p. col. plates. 19 cm. (The Taste of our time) "Distributed in the United States by the World Publishing Company ... Cleveland." Bibliography: p. 134-[136] [ND653.H2D393] 68-20497
1. Hals, Frans, 1584-1666.

Hals, Frans, 1584-1666—Addresses, essays, lectures.

FRANS Hals, his life, 759.9492
his paintings, a critique of his art / [edited by] Georg van der Groot. Albuquerque, N.M. : Gloucester Art Press, [1978] leaves [21]-33, [7] leaves of plates : ill. ; 28 cm. (A GRreat masters art book) Cover title. [ND653.H2F73] 78-27332 ISBN 0-930582-27-6 : 14.50
1. Hals, Frans, 1584-1666—Addresses, essays, lectures. 2. Painters—Netherlands—Addresses, essays, lectures. I. Van der Groot, Georg. II. Series.

Halsell, William Electious, 1850-1934-

HOLDEN, William Curry, 1896- 976.4'06'0922 B
A ranching saga : the lives of William Electious Halsell and Ewing Halsell / by William Curry Holden ; drawings by Jose Cisneros. San Antonio : Trinity University Press, c1976. 2 v. (568 p.) : ill. ; 27 cm. Includes bibliographical references and index. [F391.H185H64] 75-9300 ISBN 0-911536-59-0 : 25.00
1. Halsell, William Electious, 1850-1934- 2. Halsell, Ewing, 1877-1965. 3. Ranchers—Texas—Biography. 4. Ranchers—Oklahoma—Biography. 5. Texas—Biography. 6. Oklahoma—Biography. I. Title.

Halsey, Margaret, 1910-

HALSEY, Margaret, 1910- 974.7'04'0924 B
No laughing matter : the autobiography of a WASP / Margaret Halsey. 1st ed. Philadelphia : Lippincott, c1977. 250 p. ; 22 cm. An autobiographical account of what it meant to be a WASP in America during four decades encompassing the Depression, World War II, McCarthyism, and Watergate. [CT275.H28743A36] 92 77-22949 ISBN 0-397-01240-3 : 8.95
1. Halsey, Margaret, 1910- 2. United States—Biography. I. Title. BIP

Halsey, William Frederick, 1882-1859.

HALSEY, William Frederick, 1882-1959. 940.54'26'0924 B
Admiral Halsey's story / William F. Halsey and J. Bryan III. New York : Da Capo Press, 1976, c1947. p. cm. (The Politics and strategy of World War II) Reprint of the ed. published by Whittlesey House, New York. [E746.H3A3 1976] 76-13462 ISBN 0-306-70770-5 ; 22.50
1. Halsey, William Frederick, 1882-1959. 2. World War, 1939-1945—Personal narratives, American. 3. World War, 1939-1945—Naval operations, American. 4. World War, 1939-1945—Pacific Ocean. I. Bryan, Joseph, 1904- joint author. BIP

KEATING, Lawrence A. 1903- 940.545
Fleet Admiral; the story of William F. Halsey, by Lawrence A. Keating. Philadelphia, Westminster Press [1965] 191 p. illus., maps, ports. 23 cm. Bibliography: p. [190]-191. [E746.H3K4] 65-10580
1. Halsey, William Frederick, 1882-1959. I. Title. II. Title: The story of William F. Halsey. BIP

MERRILL, James M. 940.54'26'0924 B
A Sailor's admiral : a biography of William F. Halsey / by James M. Merrill. New York : Crowell, c1976. ix, 271 p. : ill. ; 24 cm. Includes index. Bibliography: p. 259-261. [V63.H34M47 1976] 76-8880 ISBN 0-690-01163-6 : 9.95
1. Halsey, William Frederick, 1882-1959. I. Title. BIP

PEARL, Jack 923.573
Admiral 'Bull' Halsey. Derby, Conn., Monarch [c.1962] 139p. 18cm. (MA328) Bibl. 63-395 .35 pap.,
1. Halsey, William Frederick, 1882-1859. I. Title.

Halsey, William Frederick, 1882-1959—Juvenile literature.

BLASSINGAME, Wyatt. 940.542'6'0924 B
William F. Halsey, five star admiral. Illustrated by Pers Crowell. Champaign, Ill., Garrard Pub. Co. [1970] 112 p. illus. (part col.), col. map, ports. 24 cm. (A Defenders of freedom book) The biography of a leading naval commander of World War II, whose maneuvers in the South Pacific helped secure victory for the United States. [E746.H3B55] 92 73-101304 2.69
1. Halsey, William Frederick, 1882-1959—Juvenile literature. I. Crowell, Pers, illus. II. Title.

WHIPPLE, Chandler. 940.542'6'0924 B
William F. Halsey: fighting admiral. New York, Putnam [1968] 222 p. 22 cm. (Lives to remember) Bibliography: p. 8-9. [E746.H3W5] 67-24180 3.49
1. Halsey, William Frederick, 1882-1959—Juvenile literature.

Halsted, William Stewart, 1832-1922.

BECKHARD, Arthur J. 926.1
Cancer, cocaine and courage; the story of Dr. William Halsted, by Arthur J. Beckhard and William D. Crane. New York, Messner [1960] 191 p. 22 cm. Includes bibliography. [R154.H235B4] 60-13268
1. Halsted, William Stewart, 1852-1922. I. Crane, William Dwight, joint author. II. Title.

CROWE, Samuel James, 1883-1955. 926.1
Halsted of Johns Hopkins: the man and his men. Springfield, Ill., Thomas [1957] ix, 247p. illus., ports. 24cm. [R154.H235C7] 56-11481
1. Halsted, William Stewart, 1832-1922. I. Title.

Ham, Mordecal Fowler, 1877-

HAM, Edward Everett, 1916- 922.673
50 years on the battle front with Christ; a biography of Mordecai F. Ham. [Louisville?] Old Kentucky Home Revivalist [1950] xiv, 312 p. illus., ports. 21 cm. [BX6495.H264H3] 50-35185
1. Ham, Mordecal Fowler, 1877- I. Title.

Hamada, Shoji, 1894—

LEACH, Bernard Howell, 1887- 738.3'092'4 B
Hamada, potter / Bernard Leach. London : Thames and Hudson, 1976. 306 p. : ill. (some col.), ports. ; 31 cm. Text in form of dialogue between the author and Hamada. Includes index. [NK4210.H32L4 1976] 76-377126 ISBN 0-500-23222-9 : £20.00
1. Hamada, Shoji, 1894- 2. Potters—Japan—Biography. I. Hamada, Shoji, 1894- II. Title. BIP

Hambledon, Eng. (Hampshire)—History.

GOLDSMITH, John, 1924- 914.22'7
Hambledon: the biography of a Hampshire village. Winchester (32 High St., Winchester, Hants.), Winton Publications Ltd, 1971. 119 p., 8 plates (1 fold.). illus., map. 24 cm. Bibliography: p. 117. [DA690.H196G63] 72-183401 ISBN 0-901565-03-2 £2.40
1. Hambledon, Eng. (Hampshire)—History. I. Title.

Hamblen, Stuart, 1908-

HAMBLEN, Oberis, 1905- 927.8
My brother Stuart Hamblen. Los Angeles, Cowman Publications [1950] vi, 130 p. illus., ports. 20 cm. [ML420.H117H3] 50-10980
1. Hamblen, Stuart, 1908- I. Title.

Hamblin, Jacob, 1819-1886.

BAILEY, Paul Dayton, 1906- v. 12
Jacob Hamblin, buckskin apostle. Los Angeles, Westernlore Press, 1961 [c1948] 408 p. illus., port., map (on lining-papers) 23 cm. Bibliography: p. 401-402. NUC64
1. Hamblin, Jacob, 1819-1886. 2. Mormons and Mormonism. I. Title.

CORBETT, Pearson Harris, 1900- 922.8373
Jacob Hamblin, the peacemaker. Salt Lake City, Deseret Book Co. [1952] 538p. illus. 24cm. Includes bibliography. [F826.H2C6] 53-26139
1. Hamblin, Jacob, 1819-1886. 2. Mormons and Mormonism. 3. Indians of North America—Missions. I. Title.

HAMBLIN, Jacob 922.8373
Jacob Hamblin, buckskin apostle. Los Angeles, Westernlore Pr. [1961, c.1948] 408p. illus. Bibl. 7.50
1. Hamblin, Jacob, 1819-1886. 2. Mormons and Mormonism. I. Title.

Hamburg—Biography.

HAMBURGER, wie sie keiner 943.423
kennt : Portrats aus e. Weltstadt. Hamburg : Gloss, 1975. 159 p. : ill. ; 25 cm. Originally published as a series in the Hamburger Abendblatt. [DD901.H235H25] 75-517493 ISBN 3-87261-007-4 : DM24.80
1. Hamburg—Biography. I. Hamburger Abendblatt.

Hameln, Gluckel of, 1646-1724.

HAMELN, Gluckel of, 1646-1724. 943'.044'0924 B
The memoirs of Gluckel of Hameln / translated by Marvin Lowenthal ; introd. by Norma and Robert Rosen. New York : Schocken Books, 1977. p. cm. Translation of Zikhroynes. Reprint of the 1932 ed. published by Harper, New York. [DS135.G5H33813 1977] 77-75290 ISBN 0-8052-0572-1 pbk. : 6.95
1. Hameln, Gluckel of, 1646-1724. 2. Jews in Germany—Biography. 3. Germany—Biography. I. Title. BIP

HAMELN, Gluckel of, 1646-1724 922.96
The life of Gluckel of Hamelin, 1646-1724, written by herself. Tr. from theorig. Yiddish, ed. by Beth-Zion Abrahams. New York, Yoseloff [1963, c.1962] 190p. illus. 23cm. 63-1721 5.95
1. Jews in Germany—Hist.—1096-1800. I. Abrahams, Beth-Zion, ed. and tr. II. Title.

Hamer, Fannie Lou—Juvenile literature.

JORDAN, June, 1936- 324'.241'0924 B
Fannie Lou Hamer. Illustrated by Albert Williams. New York, Crowell [1972] 39 p. illus. 24 cm. (A Crowell biography) A brief

biography of one of the first black organizers of voter registration in Mississippi. [E185.97.H35J67] 92 70-184982 ISBN 0-690-28893-X 3.75
1. Hamer, Fannie Lou—Juvenile literature. I. Williams, Albert, 1947- illus. II. Title. BIP

Hamer, Frank, 1884-1955.

FROST, H. Gordon. 363.2'32'0924 B
I'm Frank Hamer; the life of a Texas peace officer, by H. Gordon Frost and John H. Jenkins. Austin, Pemberton Press, 1968. 305 p. illus., ports. 26 cm. Bibliography: p. 295-297. [HV7911.H35F7] 68-31953
1. Hamer, Frank, 1884-1955. 2. Barrow, Clyde, 1909-1934. 3. Parker, Bonnie, 1909-1934. I. Jenkins, John Holmes, joint author. II. Title. BIP

Hamil, Harold.

HAMIL, Harold. 978.8'75'03
Colorado without mountains : a high plains memoir / by Harold Hamil ; illustrated by James R. Hamil. 1st ed. Kansas City, Mo. : Lowell Press, c1976. p. cm. [F782.L8H35] 76-21134 ISBN 0-913504-33-5 : 10.95
1. Hamil, Harold. 2. Logan Co., Col.—History. 3. Ranch life—Logan Co., Col. 4. Logan Co., Col.—Biography. I. Title.

Hamill, Dorothy—Juvenile literature.

BURCHARD, S. H. 796.9'1'0924 B
Dorothy Hamill / S. H. Burchard. 1st ed. New York : Harcourt Brace Jovanovich, c1978. 62 p. : ill. ; 22 cm. (Sports star) A brief biography of the American figure skater who won a gold medal at the 1976 Winter Olympics. [GV850.H3B87] 92 77-88960 ISBN 0-15-278014-9 : 4.95 pbk. : 1.95
1. Hamill, Dorothy—Juvenile literature. 2. Skaters—United States—Biography—Juvenile literature. I. Title.

DOLAN, Edward F., 796.9'1'0924 B
1924-
Dorothy Hamill, Olympic skating champion / Edward F. Dolan, Jr. and Richard B. Lyttle. 1st ed. Garden City, N.Y. : Doubleday, c1979. 95 p., [12] leaves of plates : ill. ; 22 cm. (A Doubleday signal book) Includes index. A biography of the 1976 Olympic Gold Medalist in figure skating who originated a manuever known as the "Hamill Camel." [GV850.H3D64] 92 78-18558 ISBN 0-385-14096-7 : 5.95
1. Hamill, Dorothy—Juvenile literature. 2. Skaters—United States—Biography—Juvenile literature. I. Lyttle, Richard B., joint author. II. Title.

PHILLIPS, Betty 796.9'1'0924 B
Lou.
The picture story of Dorothy Hamill / Betty Lou Phillips. New York : J. Messner, c1978. 63 p. : ill. ; 22 cm. A biography of a champion ice skater and star of the Ice Capades. [GV850.H3P47] 92 78-18543 ISBN 0-671-32936-7 : 6.95
1. Hamill, Dorothy—Juvenile literature. 2. Skaters—United States—Biography—Juvenile literature. I. Title.

SMITH, Miranda. 796.9'1'0924 B
Dorothy Hamill / by Miranda G. Smith ; photos. by UPI. Mankato, Minn. : Creative Education, c1977. 31 p. : ill. (some col.) ; 25 cm. (Creative education sports superstars) A biography of the nineteen-year-old American who overcame her stage fright to win the world championship in figure skating in the 1976 Olympics. [GV850.H3S55] 92 76-48057 ISBN 0-87191-546-4 lib.bdg. : 4.95
1. Hamill, Dorothy—Juvenile literature. 2. Skaters—Biography—Juvenile literature. I. United Press International. II. Title. BIP

†VAN STEENWYK, 796.9'1'0924 B
Elizabeth.
Dorothy Hamill : Olympic champion / by Elizabeth Van Steenwyk ; photos. (except where noted) by David Leonardi. New York : Harvey House, c1976. 55 p. : ill. ; 23 cm. Traces the ice skating career of Dorothy Hamill who won a gold medal at the 12th Winter Olympic Games. [GV850.H3V36 1976] 92 76-10046 ISBN 0-8178-5522-X lib.bdg. : 4.99
1. Hamill, Dorothy—Juvenile literature. 2. Skaters—United States—Biography—Juvenile literature. I. Title. BIP

Hamilton, Alexander, 1757-1804.

ALEXANDER Hamilton. v. 12 New York, Barnes & Co. [1961] vi, 488p. (Perpetua book. P4027)
1. Hamilton, Alexander, 1757-1804. I. Schachner, Nathan, 1895-1955. BIP

ALEXANDER, Holmes 973.4'092'4 B
Moss, 1906-
To covet honor : a biography of Alexander Hamilton / by Holmes Alexander. Belmont, Mass. : Western Islands, c1977. xxvii, 473 p. ; 21 cm. Includes index. Bibliography: p. [447]-455. [E302.6.H2A39] 77-75276 ISBN 0-88279-232-6 : 12.00
1. Hamilton, Alexander, 1757-1804. 2. United States—Politics and government—1783-1809. 3. Statesmen—United States—Biography. I. Title.

BROWN, Stuart Gerry, 973.4'0924 B
1911-
Alexander Hamilton. New York, Washington Square Press [1967] 183 p. 18 cm. (The Great American thinkers series) "Bibliographical note": p. 176-178. [E302.6.H2B84] 68-1987
1. Hamilton, Alexander, 1757-1804.

CANTOR, Milton, comp. 973.4'0924
Hamilton. Englewood Cliffs, N.J., Prentice-Hall [1971] vii, 184 p. 21 cm. (Great lives observed) (A Spectrum book) Bibliography: p. 180-182. [E302.6.H2C3] 72-133054 ISBN 0-13-372292-9 5.95
1. Hamilton, Alexander, 1757-1804. I. Hamilton, Alexander, 1757-1804.

COLEMAN, William, 973.4'6'0924 B
1766-1829.
A collection of facts and documents, relative to the death of Major-General Alexander Hamilton; with comments: together with the various orations, sermons, and eulogies, that have been published or written on his life and character ... By the editor of the Evening post. A Shoal Creek facsim. reproduction of the 1804 ed., with an introd. by Dorman H. Winfrey. [Austin, Tex., Shoal Creek Publishers, 1972 or 3] 238 p. 22 cm. On spine: Alexander Hamilton: a collection of facts and documents. Reprint of the ed. printed by Hopkins and Seymour for I. Riley, New York. [E302.6.H2C6 1972] 72-95422
1. Hamilton, Alexander, 1757-1804. I. Title. II. Title: Alexander Hamilton: a collection of facts and documents. BIP

COLEMAN, William, 973.4'6'0924
1766-1829.
A collection of the facts and documents, relative to the death of Major-General Alexander Hamilton, with comments; together with the various orations, sermons, and eulogies, that have been published or written on his life and character ... By the editor of the Evening post. Freeport, N.Y., Books for Libraries Press [1969] vi, 276 p. 23 cm. (Select bibliographies reprint series) Reprint of the 1904 ed. [E302.6.H2C6 1969] 72-95068
1. Hamilton, Alexander, 1757-1804. I. Title.

FLEXNER, James 973.4'092'4 B
Thomas, 1908-
The young Hamilton : a biography / James Thomas Flexner. 1st ed. Boston : Little, Brown, c1978. xiv, 497 p. : ill. ; 24 cm. Includes index. Bibliography: p. 458-466. [E302.6.H2F58] 77-13877 ISBN 0-316-28594-3 : 15.00
1. Hamilton, Alexander, 1757-1804. 2. Soldiers—United States—Biography. 3. United States—History—Revolution, 1775-1783. 4. Legislators—United States—Biography. I. Title. BIP

GRIGGS, Edward Howard, 1868- 973
1951.
American statesmen; an interpretation of our history and heritage. Freeport, N.Y., Books for Libraries Press [1970] 364 p. 24 cm. (Essay index reprint series) Reprint of the 1927 ed. Contents.Contents.—Washington: the first American.—Franklin: the practical American.—Jefferson: the democratic American.—Hamilton and the making of our government.—Lee: the American warrior.—Lincoln: the prophetic American.—Bibliography: p. 348-355. [E176.G852 1970] 76-121474
1. Washington, George, Pres. U.S., 1732-1799. 2. Franklin, Benjamin, 1706-1790. 3. Jefferson, Thomas, Pres. U.S., 1743-1826. 4. Hamilton, Alexander, 1757-1804. 5. Lee, Robert Edward, 1807-1870. 6. Lincoln, Abraham, Pres. U.S., 1809-1865. 7. Statesmen, American. I. Title. BIP

HACKER, Louis Morton, 923.273
1899-
Alexander Hamilton in the American tradition. New York, McGraw-Hill [1957] 273 p. 21 cm. Includes bibliography. [E302.6.H2H15] 57-6393
1. Hamilton, Alexander, 1757-1804. BIP

HAMILTON, Alexander, 923.273
1757-1804.
Alexander Hamilton: selections representing his life, his thought, and his style. Edited with an introd. by Bower Aly. New York, Liberal Arts Press [1957] xxvi, 261p. 21cm. (The American heritage series, no. 20) Bibliography: p. xxiii-xxvi. [E302.H25734] 57-2414
I. Title. BIP

HAMILTON, 973.4'092'4 B
Alexander, 1757-1804.
Alexander Hamilton; a biography in his own words. Edited by Mary-Jo Kline. With an introd. by Harold C. Syrett. Picture editor: Joan Paterson Kerr. New York, Newsweek [1973] 2 v. (416 p.) illus. 27 cm. (The Founding fathers) Based on the Columbia University Press ed. of The Papers of Alexander Hamilton, v. 1-19. Bibliography: v. 2, p. 408. [E302.6.H2A125] 72-92140 ISBN 0-88225-043-4
1. Hamilton, Alexander, 1757-1804. 2. United States—History—Revolution—Sources. 3. United States—History—Confederation, 1783-1789—Sources. 4. United States—History—Constitutional period, 1789-1809—Sources. I. Kline, Mary-Jo, ed.
Available from Harper & Row, 15.00. BIP

HAMILTON, Alexander, 973.4'0924 B
1757-1804.
Alexander Hamilton and the founding of the Nation. Edited by Richard B. Morris. New York, Harper & Row [1969] xxii, 617 p. 21 cm. (Harper torchbooks, 1448) Reprint of the 1957 ed. Bibliographical footnotes. [E302.H2573 1969] 72-5371 3.95
I. Morris, Richard Brandon, 1904- ed. II. Title.

HAMILTON, Alexander, 923.273
1757-1804.
The mind of Alexander Hamilton. Arr. and with an introd. by Saul K. Padover. [1st ed.] New York, Harper [1958] 461 p. 22 cm. [E302.H28] 58-54328
I. Padover, Saul Kussiel, 1905- II. Title.

HENDRICKSON, Robert 973.4'092'4 B
A., 1923-
Hamilton / Robert Hendrickson. New York : Mason/Charter, 1976- v. : ill. ; 26 cm. Includes index. Contents.Contents. 1. 1757-1789. Bibliography: v. 1, p. [593]-616. [E302.6.H2H44] 75-45436 ISBN 0-88405-139-0 : 19.95
1. Hamilton, Alexander, 1757-1804.

LODGE, Henry Cabot, 973.3'0924 B
1850-1924.
Alexander Hamilton. New York, Greenwood Press [1969] viii, 317 p. 23 cm. (American statesmen [v. 7]) Reprint of the 1917 ed. [E302.6.H2L8 1969] 69-13974
1. Hamilton, Alexander, 1757-1804. I. Title. II. Series.

LODGE, Henry Cabot, 973.4'0924 B
1850-1924.
Alexander Hamilton. Boston, Houghton, Mifflin. [New York, AMS Press, 1972] viii, 317 p. illus. 19 cm. (American statesmen, v. 7) Reprint of the 1898 ed. [E302.6.H2L8 1972] 72-128971 ISBN 0-404-50857-X
1. Hamilton, Alexander, 1757-1804. I. Title. II. Series.

LODGE, Henry Cabot, 973.4'0924 B
1850-1924.
Alexander Hamilton. New Rochelle, N.Y., Arlington House [1970] 317 p. illus., ports. 21 cm. (Giants of America. The Founding Fathers) Originally published in 1882. [E302.6.H2L8 1970] 71-111224 ISBN 0-87000-088-8
1. Hamilton, Alexander, 1757-1804.

MCDONALD, Forrest. 973.4'092'4 B
Alexander Hamilton : a biography / Forrest McDonald. 1st ed. New York : Norton, c1979. p. cm. Includes bibliographical references and index. [E302.6.H2M32 1979] 78-26554 ISBN 0-393-01218-2 : 15.00
1. Hamilton, Alexander, 1757-1804. 2. United States—Politics and government—1783-1809. 3. United States—Economic conditions—To 1865. 4. Statesmen—United States—Biography. BIP

MILLER, John Chester, 923.273
1907-
Alexander Hamilton: portrait in paradox. [1st ed.] New York, Harper [1959] 659 p. illus. 25 cm. Includes bibliography. [E302.6.H2M58] 59-10587
1. Hamilton, Alexander, 1757-1804.

MILLER, John 973.4'092'4 B
Chester, 1907-
Alexander Hamilton, portrait in paradox / by John C. Miller. Westport, Conn. : Greenwood Press, [1979] c1959. p. cm. Reprint of the ed. published by Harper & Row, New York. Includes index. Bibliography: p. [E302.6.H2M58 1979] 78-27607 ISBN 0-313-20908-1 lib. bdg. : 38.75
1. Hamilton, Alexander, 1757-1804. 2. Statesmen—United States—Biography. 3. United States—Politics and government—1789-1797. I. Title.

MITCHELL, Broadus, 1892- 923.273
Alexander Hamilton. New York, Macmillan, 1957-62. 2 v. illus. 22 cm. Contents.Contents.—[1] Youth to maturity, 1755-1788.—[2] The national adventure, 1788-1804. Includes bibliography. [E302.6.H2M6] 57-5506
1. Hamilton, Alexander, 1757-1804.

MITCHELL, Broadus, 973.4'092'4 B
1892-
Alexander Hamilton : a concise biography / Broadus Mitchell. New York : Oxford University Press, 1976. viii, 395 p. : ill. ; 22 cm. Includes index. Bibliography: p. 377-382. [E302.6.H2M6 1976] 75-16899 ISBN 0-19-501735-8 : 12.95
1. Hamilton, Alexander, 1757-1805. BIP

SCHACHNER, Nathan, 1895- 923.273
Alexander Hamilton, nation builder. Drawings by Gillett Griffin. New York, McGraw-Hill [1952] vii, 229 p. illus., maps (on lining papers) 21 cm. (They. made America) Bibliography: p. 223-224. [E302.6H2S26] 52-9765
1. Hamilton, Alexander, 1757-1804.

SCHACHNER, Nathan, 1895- 923.273
1955.
Alexander Hamilton. New York, T. Yoseloff [1957] 488 p. 24 cm. Includes bibliography. [E302.6.H2S25 1957] 57-7645
1. Hamilton, Alexander, 1757-1804.

STOURZH, Gerald. 321.8'0924
Alexander Hamilton and the idea of republican government. Stanford, Stanford University Press, 1970. viii, 278 p. 23 cm. Bibliography: p. [207]-268. [E302.6.H2S8] 69-18496 8.50
1. Hamilton, Alexander, 1757-1804. I. Title. BIP

WISE, William. j92
Alexander Hamilton. New York, Putnam [1963] 191 p. 21 cm. (Lives to remember) Includes bibliography. [E302.6.H2W76] 63-7761
1. Hamilton, Alexander, 1757-1804 —Juvenile literature. I. Title.

Hamilton, Alexander, 1757-1804—Juvenile literature.

ORRMONT, Arthur 920
The amazing Alexander Hamilton. New York, Messner [c.1964] 191p. 22cm. 64-11816 3.25;3.19 lib. ed.,
1. Hamilton, Alexander, 1757-1804—Juvenile literature. I. Title.

WISE, William 920
Alexander Hamilton. New York, Putnam [c.1963] 191p. 21cm. (Lives to remember) Bibl. 63-7761 2.95
1. Hamilton, Alexander, 1757-1804—Juvenile literature. I. Title.

Hamilton, Alexander, 1757-1804—Juvenile literature.

KURLAND, Gerald, 1942- 973.4'092'4 B
Alexander Hamilton, architect of American nationalism. Charlotteville, N.Y., SamHar Press, 1972. 32 p. 22 cm. (Outstanding personalities, no. 27) Bibliography: p. 32. A biography of the first Secretary of the Treasury of the United States who was killed in a duel with Aaron Burr. [E302.6.H2K87] 92 73-190245 ISBN 0-87157-527-2
1. Hamilton, Alexander, 1757-1804—Juvenile literature. I. Title.
PLB 1.98, pap. .98.

LOMASK, Milton. 973.4'0924 B
Odd destiny; a life of Alexander Hamilton. New York, Farrar, Straus & Giroux [1969] 180 p. 21 cm. Bibliography: p. [173]-176. The controversial life of the man who was the first Secretary of the Treasury of the newly formed United States and who was killed in a duel with Aaron Burr. [E302.6.H2L86] 92 69-14974 3.75
1. Hamilton, Alexander, 1757-1804—Juvenile literature. I. Title.

Hamilton, Alice, 1869-

GRANT, Madeleine Parker, 1895- 610'.924
Alice Hamilton; pioneer doctor in industrial medicine by Madeleine P. Grant. London, New York [etc.] Abelard-Schuman [1967] 223 p. illus., facsims., ports. 22 cm. Bibliography: p. 218. [R154.H238G7] 67-13612 unpriced
1. Hamilton, Alice, 1869- I. Title.

GRANT, Madeleine Parker, 1895- 616.9'8030924 B
Alice Hamilton; pioneer doctor in industrial medicine, by Madeleine P. Grant. London, New York [etc.] Abelard-Schuman [1967] 223 p. illus., facsims., ports. 22 cm. Bibliography: p. 218. A biography of the woman doctor whose foresight of and crusade against "industrial diseases" revolutionized factory conditions and saved thousands of workingmen from paralysis and painful death. [R154.H238G7] 92 AC 68
1. Hamilton, Alice, 1869- I. Title.

Hamilton, Andrew Jackson, 1815-1875.

WALLER, John Leroy, 1889- 976.4'05'0924 B
Colossal Hamilton of Texas; a biography of Andrew Jackson Hamilton, militant Unionist and Reconstruction governor, by John L. Waller. [El Paso] Texas Western Press, 1968. xii, 152 p. illus., ports. 24 cm. Bibliographical footnotes. [F391.H19W3] 68-30890 5.00
1. Hamilton, Andrew Jackson, 1815-1875. I. Title.

Hamilton, Andrew, 1676 (ca.)-1741.

KONKLE, Burton Alva, 1861-1944. 973.3'0924 B
The life of Andrew Hamilton, 1676-1741, "the Day-star of the American Revolution." Freeport, N.Y., Books for Libraries Press [1972] 168 p. illus. 23 cm. Reprint of the 1941 ed. Includes bibliographical references. [F152.H2K6 1972] 72-27 ISBN 0-8369-9962-2
1. Hamilton, Andrew, 1676 (ca.)-1741. 2. Pennsylvania—History—Colonial period, ca. 1600-1775. 3. Liberty of the press—New York (State) I. Title.

Hamilton, Anne, Duchess of, 1632-1716.

MARSHALL, Rosalind Kay. 914.1'03'6
The days of Duchess Anne; life in the household of the Duchess of Hamilton, 1656-1716 [by] Rosalind K. Marshall. New York, St. Martin's Press [1974, c1973] 256 p. illus. 24 cm. Bibliography: p. 233-235. [DA802.H35M37 1974] 73-86558 12.50
1. Hamilton, Anne, Duchess of, 1632-1716. 2. Hamilton family. 3. Scotland—Social life and customs—17th century. I. Title.

Hamilton, Edith, 1867-1963.

REID, Doris Fielding. 818'.5'208
Edith Hamilton; an intimate portrait. [1st ed.] New York, W. W. Norton [1967] 174 p. illus., ports. 22 cm. [CT275.H2893R4] 67-12449
1. Hamilton, Edith, 1867-1963.

Hamilton, Elizabeth,

HAMILTON, Elizabeth, 1906- 928.2
A river full of stars. New York, Norton [1955, c1954] 223p. illus. 22cm. Autobiographical. [CT788.H263A3 1955] 54-13517
I. Title.

Hamilton, Emma, Lady, 1761-1815.

HAMILTON, Gerald, 1890- 920.7
Emma in blue; a romance of friendship, by Gerald Hamilton and Desmond Stewart. New York,Roy Publishers [1958] 157p. illus. 23cm. [DA483.H3H3 1958] 58-7717
1. Hamilton, Emm, Lady, 1761-1815. I. Stewart, Desmond Stirling, joint author. II. Title.

HARDWICK, Mollie. 942.07'3'0924 B
Emma, Lady Hamilton. [1st ed.] New York, Holt, Rinehart and Winston [1970, c1969] viii, 312 p. illus., coat of arms, ports. 22 cm. Bibliography: p. 297-299. [DA483.H3H34 1970] 72-80363 7.95
1. Hamilton, Emma, Lady, 1761?-1815. I. Title.

LOFTS, Norah Robinson, 1904- 941.07'3'0924 B
Emma Hamilton / Norah Lofts. 1st American ed. New York : Coward, McCann & Geoghegan, c1978. 192 p., [8] leaves of plates : ill. ; 26 cm. [DA483.H3L63 1978] 77-26868 ISBN 0-698-10912-0 : 15.00
1. Hamilton, Emma, Lady, 1761?-1815. 2. Nelson, Horatio Nelson, Viscount, 1758-1805. 3. Mistresses—England—Biography. BIP

RUSSELL, Jack, 1928- 942.07'3'0922
Nelson and the Hamiltons. New York, Simon and Schuster [1969] 448 p. illus., ports. 25 cm. Bibliography: p. 427-435. [DA87.1.N4R77 1969b] 70-79638 10.00
1. Nelson, Horatio Nelson, Viscount, 1758-1805. 2. Hamilton, Emma, Lady, 1761?-1815. 3. Hamilton, William, Sir, 1730-1803. I. Title. BIP

TOURS, Hugh 920.72
The life and letters of Emma Hamilton. London. V. Gollanez [New York, Hillary. House. 1965, c.1963] 288p. port. 23cm. Bibl. [DA483.H3T67] 65-69513 6.00
1. Hamilton, Emma, Lady, 1761?-1815. I. Hamilton, Emma, Lady, 1761?-1815. II. Title.

Hamilton, James, 1st Duke of, 1606-1649.

RUBINSTEIN, Hilary L. 941.106'2'0924 B
Captain Luckless : James, first Duke of Hamilton, 1606-1649 / Hilary L. Rubinstein. Totowa, N.J. : Rowman and Littlefield, 1976. viii, 307 p., [6] leaves of plates : ill. ; 23 cm. Includes index. Bibliography: p. [282]-290. [DA803.7.H2R8 1976] 76-378865 ISBN 0-87471-806-6 : 15.00
1. Hamilton, James, 1st Duke of, 1606-1649. 2. Scotland—History—Charles I, 1625-1649. 3. Scotland—Court and courtiers—Biography. I. Title. BIP

Hamilton, Max.

HAMILTON, Max. 659.2'0207
Throw away the key. Indianapolis, Bobbs-Merrill [1967, c1966] 256 p. 22 cm. Autobiographical. [TX910.5.H3A3] 66-29905
I. Title.

Hamilton, Ont.—Biography.

BAILEY, Thomas Melville, 1912- 971.3'52
Hamilton famous and fascinating : two centuries of a colourful city / by Thomas Melville Bailey and Charles Ambrose Carter. Hamilton, Ont. : W. L. Griffin, 1972. 72 p. : ill., ports. ; 28 cm. Includes index. [F1059.5.H2B26] 75-321201
1. Hamilton, Ont.—Biography. I. Carter, Charles Ambrose, joint author. II. Title.

BAILEY, Thomas Melville, 1912- 920'.0713'52
Hamilton firsts / by Thomas Melville Bailey and Charles Ambrose Carter. Hamilton, Ont. : T. M. Bailey and C. A. Carter, 1973. 72 p. : ill., facsims., ports. ; 28 cm. Includes index. [F1059.5.H2B27] 75-302668
1. Hamilton, Ont.—Biography. 2. Hamilton, Ont.—History—Miscellanea. I. Carter, Charles Ambrose, joint author. II. Title.

Hamilton, Richard R., 1924-

HAMILTON, Richard R., 1924- 628.9'2'0924 B
20,000 alarms : the memoirs of New York's most decorated fireman / Richard R. Hamilton, with Charles N. Barnard. 1st ed. Chicago : Playboy Press, c1975. 249 p. ; 22 cm. [TH9118.H35A33] 74-33553 ISBN 0-87223-427-4 : 9.50 ISBN 0-87223-427-4 pbk. : 0.95
1. Hamilton, Richard R., 1924- I. Barnard, Charles N., joint author. II. Title.

Hamilton, William Rowan, Sir, 1805-1865.

GRAVES, Robert Perceval. 510'.92'4 B
Life of Sir William Rowan Hamilton / by Robert Perceval Graves. New York : Arno Press, 1975. p. cm. (History, philosophy, and sociology of science) Reprint of the ed. published in 1882-1889 by Hodges, Figgis, Dublin, in series: Dublin University Press series. [QA29.H2G8 1975] 74-26266 ISBN 0-405-06594-9 : 120.00
*1. Hamilton, William Rowan, Sir, 1805-1865. 2. Quaternions. I. Title. II. Series.*BIP

Hamilton, William, Sir, 1730-1803.

FOTHERGILL, Brian. 327.2'0924 B
Sir William Hamilton, envoy extraordinary. [1st American ed.] New York, Harcourt, Brace & World [1969] 459 p. illus., ports. 23 cm. "A Helen and Kurt Wolff book." Bibliography: p. 445-449. [DA483.H32F6 1969b] 76-76765 10.00
1. Hamilton, William, Sir, 1730-1803.

Hamlin, George John, 1868-1923.

HAMLIN, Anna M. 784'.092'4 B
Father was a tenor / Anna M. Hamlin. 1st ed. Hicksville, N.Y. : Exposition Press, c1978. 96 p., [2] leaves of plates : ill. ; 21 cm. [ML420.H12H3] 78-302891 ISBN 0-682-48956-5 : 5.00
1. Hamlin, George John, 1868-1923. 2. Singers—United States—Biography. I. Title. BIP

Hamlin, Hannibal, 1809-1891.

HAMLIN, Charles Eugene. 973.7'0924 B
The life and times of Hannibal Hamlin. Port Washington, N.Y., Kennikat Press [1971] 2 v. (xi, 627 p.) illus., ports. 23 cm. (Kennikat Press scholarly reprints. Series in American history and culture in the nineteenth century) Reprint of the 1899 ed. [E415.9.H2H2 1971] 70-137914 ISBN 0-8046-1482-2
1. Hamlin, Hannibal, 1809-1891. I. Title. BIP

HUNT, Harry Draper. 973.7'0924 B
Hannibal Hamlin of Maine, Lincoln's first Vice-President [by] H. Draper Hunt. [1st ed. Syracuse, N.Y.] Syracuse University Press [1969] ix, 292 p. port. 24 cm. Bibliography: p. 277-284. [E415.9.H2H8] 70-88709 9.00
1. Hamlin, Hannibal, 1809-1891. I. Title.

Hamlin, James D., 1871-1950.

HAMLIN, James D., 1871-1950. 976.4'825 B
The flamboyant judge: James D. Hamlin. A biography as told to J. Evetts Haley and Wm. Curry Holden. Canyon, Tex., Palo Duro Press, 1972. xxiii, 312 p. illus. 24 cm. Includes bibliographical references. [KF373.H28A34] 73-157074 10.00
1. Hamlin, James D., 1871-1950. 2. Amarillo, Tex.—History. I. Haley, James Evetts, 1901- II. Holden, William Curry, 1896- III. Title.
Publisher's Address: Box 390, Canyon Texas 79015.

Hammarskjold, Dag, 1905-1961.

BESKOW, Bo, 1906- 341.13'7'0924
Dag Hammarskjold: strictly personal; a portrait. [1st ed.] Garden City, N.Y., Doubleday, 1969. 191 p. illus., ports. 25 cm. [D839.7.H3B4513 1969] 69-10804 5.95
1. Hammarskjold, Dag, 1905-1961. I. Title.

GAVSHON, Arthur L. 967.5
The mysterious death of Dag Hammarskjold. New York, Walker [c.1962] 243p. map. 22cm. 62-12739 4.50
1. Hammarskjold, Dag, 1905-1961. I. Title.

HAMMARSKJOLD, Dag, 1905-1961. 341.13'7'0924
Hammarskjold: the political man. Ed. by Emery Kelen. New York, Funk & Wagnalls [1968] xii, 236p. 22cm. Bibl. [D413.H3A25 1968] 67-31254 5.95
1. Kelen, Emery, 1896- ed. II. Title.

HERSHEY, Burnet, 1898- 923.2485
Dag Hammarskjold, soldier of peace. Chicago, Encyclopaedia Britannica Press [1961] 191p. illus. 22cm. (Britannica bookshelf: Great lives for young Americans) [D839.7.H3H4] 61-13231
1. Hammarskjold, Dag, 1905-1961. I. Title.

HERSHEY, Burnet, 1898- 923.2485
Dag Hammarskjold, soldier of peace. Chicago, Britannica Bks., div. of Ency. Britannica [1963, c.1961] 191p. col. illus. 22cm. (Britannica bkshelf: Great lives for young Amers.) 2.36 lib. ed.,
1. Hammarskjold, Dag, 1905-1961. I. Title.

KELEN, Emery, 1896- 341.23'2 B
Dag Hammarskjold: a biography. [1st ed.] New York, Meredith Press [1969] 117 p. 21 cm. Bibliography: p. 108. A biography of the Swedish economist who, as Secretary General of the United Nations, held one of the most important diplomatic posts in the world. [D839.7.H3K4 1969] 92 69-16296 3.95
1. Hammarskjold, Dag, 1905-1961. I. Title.

LASH, Joseph P., 1909- 923.2485
Dag Hammarskjold, custodian of the brushfire peace. [1st ed.] Garden City, N.Y., Doubleday, 1961. 304 p. 22 cm. [D839.7.H3L3] 61-12546
1. Hammarskjold, Dag, 1905-1961.

LASH, Joseph P., 1909- 341.23'2 B
Dag Hammarskjold: custodian of the brushfire peace [by] Joseph P. Lash. Westport, Conn., Greenwood Press [1974, c1961] 304 p. 22 cm. Reprint of the ed. published by Doubleday, Garden City, N.Y. [D839.7.H3L3 1974] 73-22637 ISBN 0-8371-6995-X 13.25
1. Hammarskjold, Dag, 1905-1961.

LEVINE, Israel E. 923.2485
Champion of world peace: Dag Hammarskjold. New York, Messner [c.1962] 190p. 22cm. Bibl. 62-15418 2.99
1. Hammarskjold, Dag, 1905—Juvenile literture. I. Title.

MAYER, Ann Margaret. 341.23'2 B
Dag Hammarskjold, the peacemaker.

Illustrated by Harold Henriksen. Mankato, Minn., Creative Education [inc.; distributed by Childrens Press, Chicago, 1974] 36 p. illus. (part col.) 25 cm. (Creative Education close-ups) A brief biography of the Swedish diplomat who became Secretary-General of the United Nations in 1953 and held that post until his death in 1961. [D839.7.H3M38] 92 74-1498 ISBN 0-87191-322-4 4.95 (lib. bdg.).
1. Hammarskjold, Dag, 1905-1961—Juvenile literature. I. Henriksen, Harold, illus. II. Title.

MONTGOMERY, Elizabeth Rider. 341.23'2 B
Dag Hammarskjold: peacemaker for the U.N. Champaign, Ill., Garrard Pub. Co. [1973] 176 p. illus. 22 cm. (A Century book) A biography of the second Secretary-General of the United Nations who died in a plane crash on a peace mission to the Congo in 1961. [D839.7.H3M65] 92 73-570 ISBN 0-8116-4757-9 3.68
1. Hammarskjold, Dag, 1905-1961—Juvenile literature. I. Title.

RICHARDS, Norman. 341.13'7'0924 B
Dag Hammarskjold. Chicago, Childrens Press [1969, c1968] 95 p. illus., ports. 29 cm. (People of destiny; a humanities series) Bibliography: p. 92. A biography of the man whose tact and leadership made the United Nations, for the first time, an effective force for peace in the world. [D839.7.H3R5] 92 68-31303
1. Hammarskjold, Dag, 1905-1961—Juvenile literature. I. Title.

SIMON, Charlie May (Hogue) 1897- 341.13'7'0924 B
Dag Hammarskjold, by Charlie May Simon. [1st ed.] New York, Dutton [1967] 192 p. illus., ports. 21 cm. Bibliography: p. 186. [D839.7.H3S5] 67-2111
1. Hammarskjold, Dag, 1905-1961.

SODERBERG, Sten Valdemar, 1908- 923.2485
Hammarskjold, a pictorial biography. New York, Viking Press [1962] 144 p. illus. 24 cm. (A Studio book) [D839.7.H3S6] 62-15846
1. Hammarskjold, Dag, 1905-1961. I. Title.

STOLPE, Sven, 1905- 248.2
Dag Hammarskiold, a spiritual portrait. English tr. by Naomi Walford. New York, Scribners [1967, c.1966] 127p. 21cm. (Scribner lib., SL138) Tr. of Dag Hammarskjold's andliga vag. [D839.7.H3S753] 67-12027 1.25 pap.,
1. Hammarskjold, Dag, 1905-1961. I. Title.

STOLPE, Sven, 1905- 248.2
Dag Hammarskjold, a spiritual portrait. English tr. by Naomi Walford. New York, Scribners [c.1966] 127p. port. 22cm. [D839.7.H3S753] 66-12027 3.95
1. Hammarskjold, Dag, 1905-1961. I. Title.

URQUHART, Brian. 341.23'2 B
Hammarskjold. [1st ed.] New York, Knopf, 1972. xv, 630, xxv p. illus. 25 cm. Includes bibliographical references. [D839.7.H3U7] 72-2255 ISBN 0-394-47960-2 12.50
1. Hammarskjold, Dag, 1905-1961. **BIP**

VAN DUSEN, Henry Pitney, 1897- 341.1370924 B
Dag Hammarskjold; the statesman and his faith, by Henry P. Van Dusen. [1st ed.] New York, Harper & Row [1967] xv, 240 p. illus., ports. 22 cm. [D839.7.H3V3] 67-11503
1. Hammarskjold, Dag, 1905-1961.

VAN DUSEN, Henry Pitney, 1897- 341.13'7'0924 B
Dag Hammarskjold, the man and his faith, by Henry P. Van Dusen. Rev. ed. New York, Harper & Row [1969] xv, 244 p. illus., ports. 21 cm. (Harper colophon books, CN 160) Originally published as Dag Hammarskjold: the statesman and his faith, New York, Harper, 1967. Bibliographical footnotes. [D839.7.H3V3 1969] 72-7191 1.75
1. Hammarskjold, Dag, 1905-1961.

Hammarskjold, Dag, 1905-1961—Juvenile literature.

LEVINE, Israel E 923.2485
Champion of world peace: Dag Hammarskjold. New York, J. Messner [1962] 190p. 22cm. Includes bibliography. [D839.7.H3L4] 62-15418
1. Hammarskjold, Dag, 1905-1961—Juvenile literature. I. Title.

Hammer, Armand, 1897-

CONSIDINE, Robert Bernard, 1906- 338'.092'4 B
The remarkable life of Dr. Armand Hammer / Bob Considine. 1st ed. New York : Harper & Row, [1975] xii, 287 p., [8] leaves of plates : ill. ; 25 cm. (A Cass Canfield book) Errata slip inserted. Includes index. [HC102.5.H35C65] 74-20400 ISBN 0-06-010836-3 : 12.50
1. Hammer, Armand, 1897- I. Title. **BIP**

CONSIDINE, Robert Bernard, 1906- 338'.092'4 B
The remarkable life of Dr. Armand Hammer / Bob Considine. 1st ed. New York : Harper & Row, [1975] xii, 287 p., [8] leaves of plates : ill. ; 25 cm. (A Cass Canfield book) Errata slip inserted. Includes index. [HC102.5.H35C65] 74-20400 ISBN 0-06-010836-3 : 12.50
1. Hammer, Armand, 1897- I. Title. **BIP**

Hammer family—Pictorial works.

LIEBERMAN, Archie. 917.73'03'4
Farm boy. New York, H. N. Abrams [1974] 360 p. illus. 29 cm. [S521.L467] 73-12231 ISBN 0-8109-0148-X 18.50
1. Hammer family—Pictorial works. 2. Farm life—Pictorial works. 3. Jo Davies Co., Ill.—Pictorial works. I. Title.

Hammerstein, Oscar, 1847-1910.

SHEEAN, Vincent, 1899- 927.8
Oscar Hammerstein I the life and exploits of an impresario. With a pref. by Oscar Hammerstein II. New York, Simon and Schuster, 1956. 363 p. illus. 23 cm. [ML429.H25S5] 56-7495
1. Hammerstein, Oscar, 1847-1910. I. Title.

Hammerstein, Oscar, 1895-1960.

FORDIN, Hugh, 1935- 782.8'1'0924 B
Getting to know him : a biography of Oscar Hammerstein II / by Hugh Fordin. 1st ed. New York : Random House, c1977. p. cm. Includes index. Bibliography: p. [ML423.H24F7] 77-6021 ISBN 0-394-49441-5 : 5.00
1. Hammerstein, Oscar, 1895-1960. 2. Librettists—United States—Biography. I. Title. **BIP**

Hammes, Romy.

HOFFMAN, Bernard. 338'.0092'4 B
The man from Kankakee : the story of Romy Hammes, twentieth-century pioneer / by Bernard Hoffman. 1st ed. Hicksville, N.Y. : Exposition Press, [1974] 224 p. : ill. ; 24 cm. Includes index. [HV28.H28H64] 74-80679 ISBN 0-682 47909-8 . 10.00
1. Hammes, Romy. I. Title.

Hammett, Dashiell, 1894-1961.

NOLAN, William F., 1928- 813'.5'2
Dashiell Hammett; a casebook [by] William F. Nolan. With an introd. by Philip Durham. Santa Barbara [Calif.] McNally & Loftin [1969] xvi, 189 p. 23 cm. "A Lionshead book." "A Dashiell Hammett check-list": p. [129]-165. Bibliography: p. [167]-180. [PS3515.A4347Z79] 68-8393 6.95
1. Hammett, Dashiell, 1894-1961. **BIP**

Hammett, Minnie Lee, 1915-

HAMMETT, Minnie Lee, 1915- 362.4'1'0924 B
Angel with a broken wing / by Minnie Lee Hammett. Austin, Tex. : Hammett : distribution, Ginny's Copying Service, 1976. 81 p., [1] leaf of plates : ports. ; 21 cm. [CT9983.H35A33] 76-46141
1. Hammett, Minnie Lee, 1915- 2. Delafield, Marjorie Anne, 1922-1974. 3. Physically handicapped—United States—Biography. I. Title.

Hammon, Jupiter, 1711-ca. 1800—Juvenile literature.

CLARK, Margaret Goff. 810'.9'896073 B
Their eyes on the stars: four Black writers. Champaign, Ill., Garrard Pub. Co. [1973] 174 p. illus. 22 cm. (Toward freedom series) Traces the lives of four black writers who wrote of the Negro experience in eighteenth-and nineteenth-century America. [PS153.N5C5] 920 73-3499 ISBN 0-8116-4804-4 3.78
1. Hammon, Jupiter, 1711-ca. 1800—Juvenile literature. 2. Horton, George Moses, 1798?-ca. 1880—Juvenile literature. 3. Brown, William Wells, 1815-1884—Juvenile literature. 4. Chesnutt, Charles Waddell, 1858-1932—Juvenile literature. I. Cary, Louis F., 1915- illus. II. Title. III. Series.

Hammond, John Hays, 1855-1936.

HAMMOND, John Hays, 1855-1936. 622'.092'4 B
The autobiography of John Hays Hammond. New York, Arno Press, 1974 [c1935] xiii, 813 p. illus. 24 cm. (Gold: historical and economic aspects) Reprint of the ed. published by Farrar & Rinehart, New York. Bibliography: p. 779-782. [CT275.H3585A3 1974] 74-351 ISBN 0-405-05913-2 44.00
1. Hammond, John Hays, 1855-1936. I. Title. II. Series. **BIP**

Hammond, John, 1910-

HAMMOND, John, 1910- 780'.9'2
John Hammond on record : an autobiography with Irving Townsend. New York : Summit Books, c1977. p. cm. Includes index Discography: p. [ML429.H26A] 77-8789 ISBN 0-671-40003-7 : 12.50
1. Hammond, John, 1910- 2. Impresarios—United States—Biography. 3. Jazz music. I. Townsend, Irving. II. Title.

Hammond, Laurence.

HAMMOND, Laurence. 209'.2'2 B
Beyond love / Laurence Hammond. Carol Stream, Ill. : Creation House, c1976. 287 p. ; 21 cm. Autobiographical. [BX5995.H285A32] 76-14542 ISBN 0-88419-000-5 : 6.95
1. Hammond, Laurence. 2. Hammond, Merikay. 3. Christian biography. 4. Conversion. I. Title.

Hampden, John, 1594-1643.

ADAIR, John Eric, 1934- 941.06'2'0924 B
A life of John Hampden, the patriot (1594-1643) / [by] John Adair. London : Macdonald and Jane's, 1976. [viii], 261 p., [16] p. of plates : ill., maps, plan, ports. ; 23 cm. Spine title: John Hampden, the patriot. Includes index. Bibliography: p. [253]-254. [DA396.H18A7] 77-364076 ISBN 0-354-04014-6 : £5.95
1. Hampden, John, 1594-1643. 2. Statesmen—Great Britain—Biography. 3. Great Britain—History—Charles I, 1625-1649. I. Title. II. Title: John Hampden, the patriot.

PHILLIPS, Cecil Ernest Lucas, 1898- 942.06'3'0922 B
Cromwell's captains, by Cecil E. Lucas Phillips. Freeport, N.Y., Books for Libraries Press [1972] ix, 426 p. illus. 23 cm. Reprint of the 1938 ed. Bibliography: p. 399. [DA419.A1P45 1972] 73-37908 ISBN 0-8369-6746-1
1. Hampden, John, 1594-1643. 2. Skippon, Philip, d. 1660. 3. Blake, Robert, 1598-1657. 4. Lambert, John, 1619-1684. 5. Great Britain—History—Puritan Revolution, 1642-1660. I. Title. **BIP**

Hampton, Joseph Wade, 1813-1855.

TYLER, Ronnie C. 070.4'1'0924 B
Joseph Wade Hampton, editor and individualist, by Ronnie C. Tyler. [El Paso, Texas Western Press, 1969] 39 p. illus., ports. 23 cm. (Southwestern studies, v. 6, no. 3) Cover title. Bibliographical references included in "References" (p. 35-39) [PN4874.H224T9] 74-6725 2.00
1. Hampton, Joseph Wade, 1813-1855. I. Title. II. Series.

Hampton, Wade, 1818-1902—Juvenile literature.

WILLIMON, William H. 975.7'03'0924 B
Lord of the Congaree, by William H. Willimon. Illustrated by Hoyt Simmons. [1st ed. Columbia, S.C.] Sandlapper Press [1972] 106 p. illus. 23 cm. A biography of the Confederate general from South Carolina who devoted himself to rebuilding the South after the Civil War. [E467.1.H19W5] 92 72-76382 ISBN 0-87844-010-0 4.50
1. Hampton, Wade, 1818-1902—Juvenile literature. I. Simmons, Hoyt, illus. II. Title.

Hamsun, Knut, 1859-1952.

HAMSUN, Marie (Andersen) 1881- v. 12
Varaviksne; Knuta Hamsuna vetraina dzive. Tulkojusi Lizete Skalbe. Dzejojus atdzejojusi Veronika Strelerte. [Brooklyn, N.Y.] Gramatu draugs, 1962. 319 p.port. Translation of Regnbuen. 65-1466
1. Hamsun, Knut, 1859-1952. I. Title.

Han-shan, 1546-1623.

HSU, Sung-peng. 294.3'6'10924
A Buddhist leader in Ming China : the life and thought of Han-shan Te-ch'ing / Sung-peng Hsu. University Park : Pennsylvania State University Press, 1978. p. cm. A revision of the author's thesis, University of Pennsylvania, 1970. Includes index Bibliography: p. [BQ962.A557H78 1978] 78-50068 ISBN 0-271-00542-4: 16.95
1. Han-shan, 1546-1623. 2. Priests, Buddhist—China—Biography. I. Title. **BIP**

Han, Suyin,

HAN, Suyin, pseud. 920.7
A many-splendored thing. [1st American ed.] Boston, Little, Brown [1952] 366 p. 22 cm. [CT1828.H3A33 1952a] 52-10950
I. Title.

Hancock, Cornelia, 1840-1926—Juvenile literature.

MCCONNELL, Jane Tompkins, 1898- 926.1
Cornelia; the story of a Civil War nurse. Illustrated by Dorothy Bayley Morse. New York, Crowell [1959] 184 p. illus. 21 cm. [E621.H295] 58-14266
1. Hancock, Cornelia, 1840-1926—Juvenile literature. I. Title.

Hancock, Gordon Blaine, 1884-1970.

GAVINS, Raymond. 301.45'19'6073075 B
The perils and prospects of Southern Black leadership : Gordon Blaine Hancock, 1884-1970 / by Raymond Gavins. Durham, N.C. : Duke University Press, 1977. x, 221 p. ; 23 cm. Includes index. Bibliography: p. 191-209. [F234.R53H363] 76-44090 ISBN 0-8223-0381-7 : 11.75
1. Hancock, Gordon Blaine, 1884-1970. 2. College Teachers—Virginia—Richmond—Biography. 3. Baptists—Clergy—Biography. 4. Clergy—Virginia—Richmond—Biography. 5. Afro-Americans—Virginia—Richmond—Biography. 6. Richmond—Biography. 7. Afro-Americans—Civil Rights—Southern States. 8. Afro-American leadership—Virginia—Richmond. I. Title. **BIP**

Hancock, John, 1737-1793.

FOWLER, William M. 973.3'092'4 B
The Baron of Beacon Hill : a biography of John Hancock / William M. Fowler, Jr. Boston : Houghton Mifflin, 1980, c1979. p. cm. Includes index. Bibliography: p.

[E302.6.H23F65 1980] 79-22268 ISBN 0-395-27619-5 : 15.00
1. Hancock, John, 1737-1793. 2. United States. Declaration of independence—Signers—Biography. 3. Statesmen—United States—Biography. I. Title. **BIP**

LEE, Susan. 973.3'092'4 B
John Hancock, by Susan & John Lee. Illustrated by Chuck Mitchell. Chicago, Childrens Press [1974] 47 p. col. illus. 24 cm. (Heroes of the Revolution) An easy-to-read biography of the man whose prominent signature on the Declaration of Independence was indicative of his dedication to the revolutionary cause. [E302.6.H23L43] 92 73-19971 ISBN 0-516-04653-5
1. Hancock, John, 1737-1793. I. Lee, John, joint author. II. Mitchell, Chuck, illus. III. Title.

SEARS, Lorenzo, 1838-1916. 973.3'092'4 B
John Hancock, the picturesque patriot. With a new introd. and pref. by George Athan Billias. Boston, Gregg Press, 1972. x, x, 351 p. port. 23 cm. (The American Revolutionary series. American and French accounts of the American Revolution) Reprint of the 1912 ed. published by Little, Brown, Boston. [E302.6.H23S4 1972] 72-8733 ISBN 0-8398-1880-7 15.00 (Lib. ed.)
1. Hancock, John, 1737-1793. I. Series: American and French accounts of the American Revolution. **BIP**

UMBREIT, Kenneth Bernard. 973.3'0922
Founding fathers; man who shaped our tradition, by Kenneth Umbreit. Port Washington, N.Y., Kennikat Press [1969, c1941] viii, 344 p. ports. 22 cm. (Essay and general literature index reprint series) Contents.Contents.—Thomas Jefferson.—John Adams.—John Hancock.—Samuel Adams.—Patrick Henry.—George Washington. [E302.5.U55 1969] 68-26228
1. Jefferson, Thomas, Pres. U.S., 1743-1826. 2. Adams, John, Pres. U.S., 1735-1826. 3. Hancock, John, 1737-1793. 4. Adams, Samuel, 1722-1803. 5. Henry, Patrick, 1736-1799. 6. Washington, George, Pres. U.S., 1732-1799. I. Title.

WAGNER, Frederick, 1928- 923.273
Patriot's choice; the story of John Hancock. New York, Dodd, Mead [1964] xi, 179 p. illus., map, ports. 24 cm. Bibliography: p. 165-173. [E302.6.H23W3] 64-18658
1. Hancock, John, 1737-1793. I. Title.

Hancock, John, 1737-1793 — Juvenile literature.

NOLAN, Jeannette (Covert) 1896- j92
John Hancock, friend of freedom [by] Jeannette C. Nolan. Illustrated by Louis F. Cary. Boston, Houghton Mifflin [1966] 191 p. col. illus. 22 cm. (Piper books) [E302.6.H23N6] 66-10881
1. Hancock, John, 1737-1793 — Juvenile literature. I. Title.

NOLAN, Jeannette (Covert) 1896- j92
John Hancock, friend of freedom [by] Jeannette C. Nolan. Illustrated by Louis F. Cary. Boston, Houghton Mifflin [1966] 191 p. col. illus. 22 cm. (Piper books) [E302.6.H23N6] 66-10881
1. Hancock, John, 1737-1793 — Juvenile literature. I. Title.

Hancock, Langley George, 1909-

PHILLIPSON, Neill. 338.2'092'4 B
Man of iron / [by] Neill Phillipson. Melbourne : Wren, 1974. x, 206 p., [8] leaves of plates : ill. ; 22 cm. On spine: Hancock, man of iron. Includes index. Bibliography: p. [199]-200. [HD9528.A8H36] 75-313815 ISBN 0-85885-079-6 : 6.75
1. Hancock, Langley George, 1909- 2. Iron industry and trade—Australia. I. Title. II. Title: Hancock, man of iron.

Hancock, Lyn.

HANCOCK, Lyn. 500.9'795
There's a raccoon in my parka / Lyn Hancock. Toronto : Doubleday Canada ; Garden City, N.Y. : Doubleday, 1977. viii, 231 p., [8] leaves of plates : ill. ; 22 cm. [QL31.H28A33] 76-42333 ISBN 0-385-12755-3 : 8.95
1. Hancock, Lyn. 2. Animals, Legends and stories of. 3. Northwest, Pacific—Description and travel. 4. Zoologists—Canada—Biography. I. Title. **BIP**

Hancock, Ralph, 1903—

BROWN, Joe Evan, 1892- 927.92
Laughter is a wonderful thing, by Joe E. Brown, as told to Ralph Hancock. New York, Barnes [1956] 312 p. illus. 22 cm. Autobiographical. [PN2287.B72A3] 56-5554
1. Hancock, Ralph, 1903- I. Title.

Hancock, William Keith, Sir, 1898-

HANCOCK, William Keith, Sir, 1898- 907'.2
Professing history / W. K. Hancock. Sydney : Sydney University Press, 1977. vi, 173 p. ; 22 cm. Continues Country and calling. Distributed in North America by International Scholarly Book Services, Forest Grove, Or. Includes bibliographical references and index. [DA3.H3A35] 77-365527 ISBN 0-424-00024-5 : 10.50
1. Hancock, William Keith, Sir, 1898- 2. Historians—Great Britain—Biography. 3. Historians—Australia—Biography. I. Title. **BIP**

HANCOCK, William Keith, 1898- 923.568
Smuts. Cambridge [Eng.] Univ. Pr., 1962- v. ports. fold. maps (pt. col.) facsim. 24cm. Contents.2. The fields of force. 1919-1950 Bibl. [DT779.8.S6H28] 62-52102 12.50
I. Smuts, Jan Christiaan, 1870-1950. II. Title.
Available from Cambridge Univ. Pr., New York. **BIP**

Hancock, Winfield Scott, 1824-1886.

TUCKER, Glenn. 923.573
Hancock the Superb. Maps by Dorothy Thomas Tucker, [1st ed.] Indianapolis, Bobbs-Merrill [1960] 368 p. illus 22 cm. [E467.1.H2T8] 60-7154
1. Hancock, Winfield Scott, 1824-1886. I. Title. **BIP**

TUCKER, Glenn. 973.573
Hancock the Superb. Maps on Dorothy Thomas Tucker. [1st ed.] Indianapolis, Bobbs-Merrill [1960] 368 p. illus., maps, ports. 22 cm. Bibliography: p. 343-350. [E467.1.H2T8] 60-7154
1. Hancock, Winfield Scott, 1824-1886.

Hand, Daniel, 1801-1891.

DANIEL Hand of 361.7'4'0924 B
Madison, Connecticut, 1801-1891. Edited by Howard T. Oedel. Researched by Florence B. Holbrook [and others] Madison, Conn., Madison Historical Society, 1973. 58 p. illus. 23 cm. Includes bibliographical references. [HV28.H3D35] 73-15862
1. Hand, Daniel, 1801-1891. I. Oedel, Howard T., ed. II. Holbrook, Florence B.

Hand, Edward, 1744-1802—Juvenile literature.

SHELLEY, Mary Virginia. 973.3'092'4 B
Dr. Ed. : the story of General Edward Hand / by Mary Virginia Shelley ; with ill. by Regina Weatherlow. Lititz, Pa. : Sutter House, c1978. 36 p. : ill. ; 21 cm. [E207.H32S53] 78-10331 ISBN 0-915010-24-0 : 5.75
1. Hand, Edward, 1744-1802—Juvenile literature. 2. Generals—United States—Biography—Juvenile literature. 3. Lancaster Co., Pa.—History—Revolution, 1775-1783—Juvenile literature. I. Weatherlow, Regina. II. Title. **BIP**

Hand—Surgery—History.

BOYES, Joseph H. 617'.575'0922
On the shoulders of giants : notable names in hand surgery / by Joseph H. Boyes. Philadelphia : Lippincott, 1976. p. cm. Includes index. [RD559.B69] 76-25807 ISBN 0-397-50357-1 : 15.00
1. Hand—Surgery—History. 2. Surgeons—Biography. I. Title. **BIP**

Hand, William Flowers, 1873-1948.

HILBUN, Ben, 1890- 925.4
William Flowers Hand; the life and philosophy of a Mississippi scientist and educator, 1873-1948. State College, Miss., 1952. 200p. illus. 22cm. [QD22.H25H5] 53-62189
1. Hand, William Flowers, 1873-1948. I. Title.

Handcock, William Keith, Sir, 1898-

HANCOCK, William Keith, Sir, 1898- 907'.2'024
Country and calling / by W. K. Hancock. Westport, Conn. : Greenwood Press, 1978. 246 p. ; 23 cm. Autobiographical. Continued by Professing history. Reprint of the 1954 ed. published by Faber and Faber, London. [DA3.H3A3 1978] 78-6026 ISBN 0-313-20447-0 lib.bdg. : 18.00
1. Handcock, William Keith, Sir, 1898- 2. Historians—Great Britain—Biography. 3. Historians—Australia—Biography. I. Title. **BIP**

Handel, Georg Friedrich, 1685-1759.

STREATFEILD, Richard Alexander, 1866-1919. 784'.092'4
Handel, by R. A. Streatfeild. With an introd. to the Da Capo ed. by J. Merrill Knapp. [Rev. 2d ed.] New York, Da Capo Press, 1964. xvii, 366 p. illus., ports., facsim. (music) 28 cm. (A Da Capo reprint edition) Bibliographical footnotes. [ML410.H13S7] 64-18991
1. Handel, Georg Friedrich, 1685-1759. I. Title.

Handel, Georg Friedrich, 1685-1759—Iconography.

RACKWITZ, Werner 927.8
George Frideric Handel: a biography in pictures [by] Werner Rackwitz, Helmut Steffens [Leipzig] Edition Leipzio i[New York, Heinman, 1964, c.1962] 191p. illus., facsims., music, 179 plates, ports. 29cm. Bibl. 64-55004 10.00
1. Handel, Georg Friedrich, 1685-1759—Iconography. I. Steffens, Helmut, joint author. II. Title.

Handel, Georg Friedrich, 1685-1759 — Juvenile literature.

YOUNG, Percy Marshall, 1912- j 92
Handel [by] Percy M. Young. New York, D. White [c1966] viii, 70 p. illus., music. 23 cm. (Masters of music) [ML3930.H25Y7] 67-16967
1. Handel, Georg Friedrich, 1685-1759 — Juvenile literature. I. Title. **BIP**

Handicapped—Biography.

EBY, Lois Christine. 920.02
Marked for adventure. Philadelphia, Chilton Co., Book Division [c.1960]*v, 122p. 21cm. 60-6223 3.50
1. Handicapped-Biog. I. Title.

LOTZ, Philip Henry, 1889- ed. 920.073
Unused alibis. Freeport, N.Y., Books for Libraries Press [1970, c1951] vi, 120 p. 23 cm. (Biography index reprint series) "Originally published as volume VII of [his] Creative personalities series." Contents.Contents.—Louise Baker, an athletic uniped, by M. E. Moxcey.—Betsey Barton, a girl who learned to live again, by M. E. Moxcey.—Charles Guy Bolte, something new in veterans, by C. Bowman.—"Elizabeth Bowers", polio victim, yet always rejoicing, by G. C. Auten.—"Ida Brown," through unmarried motherhood to social service, by G. H. Groves.—"John Carlton," a man who stopped drinking, by G. C. Auten.—Emma Clement, America's mother of 1946, by F. G. Lankard.—Paul Davis, explorer of the air, by D. B. Hamill.—Bayard Dodge, builder of human bridges, by H. B. Hunting.—Clarence Hawkes, taller than the night, by H. Faust.—Robert W. Irwin, bringer of light into darkened lives, by H. Faust.—Edward J. Kuncel, one who seeks no special favors, by F. G. Lankard.—Charles Fletcher Lummis, OUnused alibis. Freeport, N.Y., Books for Libraries Press [1970, c1951] vi, 120 p. 23 cm. (Biography index reprint series) "Originally published as volume VII of [his] Creative personalities series." Contents.Contents.—Louise Baker, an athletic uniped, by M. E. Moxcey.—Betsey Barton, a girl who learned to live again, by M. E. Moxcey.—Charles Guy Bolte, something new in vetera
1. Handicapped—Biography. I. Title.

Handicapped—Biography—Juvenile literature.

GELFAND, Ravina. 920 (j)
They wouldn't quit; stories of handicapped people, by Ravina Gelfand and Letha Patterson. Illustrated by Chet Sullivan. Minneapolis, Lerner Publications Co. [1962] 56 p. illus. 24 cm. (Medical books for young people) [CT9983.A1G4] 62-16852
1. Handicapped—Biography—Juvenile literature. I. Patterson, Letha, joint author. II. Title.

LYTTLE, Richard B. 362.4'0922 B
Challenged by handicap; adventures in courage, by Richard B. Lyttle. Chicago, Reilly & Lee Books [1971] 160 p. ports. 24 cm. Profiles of eleven Americans who attained success despite physical limitations. Includes John Wesley Powell, Roy Campanella, Joseph Pulitzer, Washington A. Roebling, and Laura Bridgman. [CT9983.A1L9] 920 73-143871
1. Handicapped—Biography—Juvenile literature. I. Title.

Handicraft—Kentucky.

ROYCE, Craig Evan. 745'.092'2 B
Country miles are longer than city miles / by Craig Evan Royce ; photographs by Jeffrey Gitlin. Pasadena, Calif. : W. Ritchie Press, c1976. 125 p. : ill. ; 26 cm. [TT24.K4R68] 75-18098 ISBN 0-378-07897-6 ISBN 0-378-07892-5 pbk. : 6.95
1. Handicraft—Kentucky. 2. Artisans—Kentucky—Biography. I. Gitlin, Jeffrey. II. Title.

Handke, Peter.

HANDKE, Peter. 838'.9'1409 B
A sorrow beyond dreams : a life story / Peter Handke ; translated by Ralph Manheim. New York : Farrar, Straus and Giroux, 1975, c1974. 69 p. ; 21 cm. Translation of Wunschloses Ungluck. [PT2668.A5W813 1975] 75-1183 ISBN 0-374-26680-8 : 5.95
I. Title.

Handley, Thomas, 1894-1949.

GRUNDY, Bill. 791.44'028'0924 B
That man : a memory of Tommy Handley / by Bill Grundy. London : Elm Tree Books, 1976. 95 p. : ill., facsims., ports. ; 21 cm. Includes index. [PN1991.4.H3G7] 77-352244 ISBN 0-241-89344-5 : £3.50
1. Handley, Thomas, 1894-1949. 2. Radio broadcasters—Great Britain—Biography. 3. Comedians—Great Britain—Biography. I. Title.

Handy, William Christopher, 1873-1958.

HANDY, William Christopher, 1873-1958. 784'.092'4 B
Father of the blues, an autobiography. Edited by Arna Bontemps, with a foreword by Abbe Niles. [New York] Collier Books [1970, c1941] xvi, 333 p. illus. 18 cm. "Compositions, arrangements and books by W. C. Handy": p. 317-321. [ML410.H18B6 1970] 73-172170 1.95

1. Handy, William Christopher, 1873-1958. 2. Jazz music. I. Bontemps, Arna Wendell, 1902- ed. II. Title.

MONTGOMERY, Elizabeth Rider. 780'.924 B
William C. Handy; father of the blues. Illustrated by David Hodges. Champaign, Ill., Garrard Pub. Co. [1968] 95 p. col. illus., ports. 24 cm. (Americans all series) A biography of musician W. C. Handy who first wrote and introduced the blues and whose famous contributions included "Saint Louis Blues" and "Memphis Blues." [ML3930.H27M7] 92 AC 68
1. Handy, William Christopher, 1873-1958. I. Hodges, David, illus. II. Title. BIP

Handy, William Christopher, 1873-1958—Juvenile literature.

MONTGOMERY, Elizabeth Rider. 92 (J)
William C. Handy; father of the blues. Illustrated by David Hodges. Champaign, Ill., Garrard Pub. Co. [1968] 95 p. col. illus., ports. 24 cm. (American all series) [ML3930.H27M7] 68-22639
1. Handy, William Christopher, 1873-1958—Juvenile literature.

Hanff, Helene.

HANFF, Helene. 914.21'03'85
The Duchess of Bloomsbury Street. [1st ed.] Philadelphia, Lippincott [1973] 137 p. 21 cm. [PS3515.A4853Z5] 73-1801 ISBN 0-397-00976-3 5.95
1. Hanff, Helene. 2. London—Description—1951- I. Title. BIP

Hangen, Welles, 1930-

HANGEN, Patricia. 070'.92'4 B
Tell him that I heard / Patricia Hangen. 1st ed. New York : Harper & Row, c1977. 217 p. ; 22 cm [PN4874.H224H3] 76-40581 ISBN 0-06-011788-5 : 8.95
1. Hangen, Welles, 1930- 2. Hangen, Patricia. 3. Journalists—United States—Biography. 4. Wives—United States—Biography. I. Title. BIP

Hankey, Maurice Pascal Alers Hankey, Baron, 1877-1963.

ROSKILL, Stephen Wentworth. 941.082'092'4 B
Hankey, man of secrets / Stephen Roskill. Annapolis, Md. : Naval Institute Press, [1979- c1970- v. : ill. ; 24 cm. Contents.Contents.—v. 1. 1877-1918.—v. 2. 1919-1931. Includes bibliographical references. [DA566.9.H286R6 1970b] 78-56140 ISBN 0-87021-934-0 (v. 1) ISBN 0-87021-935-9 (v. 2) 38.95 (set)
1. Hankey, Maurice Pascal Alers Hankey, Baron, 1877-1963. 2. Great Britain—Political and government—20th century. 3. Great Britain—Foreign relations—20th century. 4. Statesmen—Great Britain—Biography. I. Title.

Hanks, Lucey, d. 1825.

PETERSON, James Andrew, 1897- 929.2'0973
In re Lucey Hanks / compiled and written by James A. Peterson. 1st ed. Yorkville, Ill. : Peterson, 1973. 42 [i.e. 71] leaves : ill. ; 24 cm. No. 91 of 150 copies printed. Includes bibliographical references. [E457.32.P44] 75-324177
1. Hanks, Lucey, d. 1825. 2. Lincoln, Nancy Hanks, 1784-1818. 3. Lincoln, Abraham, Pres. U.S., 1809-1865—Family. I. Title.

Hanks, Stedman Shumway, 1889-

CORRIE, Ivan. 973.9'092'4 B
Making an American / Ivan Corrie. 1st ed. New York : Vantage Press, c1976. x, 181 p. : ill. ; 21 cm. Includes bibliographical references and index. [CT275.H3612C67] 76-382998 ISBN 0-533-02095-6 : 9.95
1. Hanks, Stedman Shumway, 1889- 2. United States—Biography. I. Title.

Hanlan, Archie J.

HANLAN, Archie J. 362.1'9'83
Autobiography of dying / Archie J. Hanlan ; postscript by Mary S. Hanlan ; edited by Muriel E. Nelson. 1st ed. Garden City, N.Y. : Doubleday, 1979. 193 p. ; 22 cm. [RC406.A24H36] 78-7755 ISBN 0-385-14481-4 : 8.95
1. Hanlan, Archie J. 2. Amyotrophic lateral sclerosis—Biography. 3. Death—Psychological aspects. I. Title. BIP

Hanley, Tullah Innes.

HANLEY, Tullah Innes. 301.41'76'330924 B
Love of art & art of love : Tullah Hanley's autobiography : an educational book, according to the gospel of Tullah. 1st ed. Blue Earth, Minn. : Piper, c1975. 455 p., [24] leaves of plates : ill. ; 24 cm. [CT275.H3613A33] 75-24839 ISBN 0-87832-017-2 : 10.95
1. Hanley, Tullah Innes. I. Title.

Hanna, Marcus Alonzo, 1837-1904.

BEER, Thomas, 1889-1940. 328.73'092'4 B
Hanna. New York, Octagon Books, 1973 [c1929] xi, 325, xii p. 23 cm. [E664.H24B4 1973] 73-3036 ISBN 0-374-90518-5 12.25 (lib. bdg.)
1. Hanna, Marcus Alonzo, 1837-1904. 2. United States—Politics and government—1865-1900. BIP

CROLY, Herbert David, 1869-1930. 923.273
Marcus Alonzo Hanna, his life and work, by Herbert Croly. Hamden, Conn., Archon Books, 1965 [c1912] xiii, 495 p. facsims., plates, ports. 22 cm. [E664.H24C9 1965] 65-15015
1. Hanna, Marcus Alonzo, 1837-1904. I. Title.

THOMPSON, Charles Willis, 1871-1946. 973.9'0922
Presidents I've known and two near Presidents. Freeport, N.Y., Books for Libraries Press [1970, c1956] 386 p. 23 cm. (Essay index reprint series) Contents.Contents.—Hanna-McKinley.—Bryan.—Roosevelt.—Taft.—Wilson.—Harding.—Coolidge. [E176.1.T45 1970] 71-93383
1. Hanna, Marcus Alonzo, 1837-1904. 2. McKinley, William, Pres. U.S., 1843-1901. 3. Bryan, William Jennings, 1860-1925. 4. Roosevelt, Theodore, Pres. U.S., 1858-1919. 5. Taft, William Howard, Pres. U.S., 1857-1930. 6. Wilson, Woodrow, Pres. U.S., 1856-1924. 7. Harding, Warren Gamaliel, Pres. U.S., 1865-1923. 8. Coolidge, Calvin, Pres. U.S., 1872-1933. I. Title. BIP

Hannah (Biblical character)—Juvenile literature.

NEFF, LaVonne. 222'.43'0905
God's gift baby : 1 Samuel 1-2 for children / written by LaVonne Neff ; illustrated by Don Kueker. St. Louis : Concordia Pub. House, 1977c1976 p. cm. (Arch books ; ser. 14) Retells the story of Hannah's years-long desire for a child and how after she finally gave birth to a son, Samuel, she returned him to God. [BS580.H3N44] 76-27752 ISBN 0-570-06113-X pbk. : 0.59
1. Hannah (Biblical character)—Juvenile literature. 2. Samuel, judge of Israel—Juvenile literature. 3. Bible. O.T.—Biography—Juvenile literature. I. Kueker, Don. II. Title.

Hannam, Charles.

HANNAM, Charles. 943'.004'924 B
A boy in that situation : an autobiography / by Charles Hannam. 1st American ed. New York : Harper & Row, [1978] 215 p. ; 21 cm. First published in 1977 under title: A boy in your situation. The author describes his growing-up years in Nazi Germany and his subsequent life at school in England. [DS135.G5H34 1977b] 92 77-11857 ISBN 0-06-022218-2 : 6.95. ISBN 0-06-022219-0 lib. bdg. : 6.79
1. Hannam, Charles. 2. Jews in Germany—Biography. 3. Jews in Germany—History—1933-1945. 4. High school students—Great Britain—Biography. 5. Germany—Biography. I. Title. BIP

Hannay, James, 1827-1873.

WORTH, George John, 1929- 928.2
James Hannay: his life and works, Lawrence, Univ. of Kan. Pr. [c.]1964. 191p. port. 24cm. Also issued in the Univ. of Kan. humanistic studies, no. 37. Bibl. 64-18493 4.00
1. Hannay, James, 1827-1873. I. Title.

WORTH, George John, 1929- 928.2
James Hannay: his life and works, by George J. Worth. Lawrence, University of Kansas Press, 1964. 191 p. port. 24 cm. "Also issued in the University of Kansas humanistic studies, no. 37." Bibliography: p. 177-186. [PR4739.H49Z94] 64-18493
1. Hannay, James, 1827-1873. I. Title.

Hannibal.

BAKER, George Philip, 1879-1951. 937'.04'0924
Hannibal. New York, Barnes & Noble [1967] xv, 332 p. illus., maps. 23 cm. First published 1930. Bibliographical footnotes. [DG249.B3 1967] 67-9118
1. Hannibal.

DODGE, Theodore Ayrault, 1842-1909. 355.3'32'0922
Great captains; showing the influence on the art of war of the campaigns of Alexander, Hannibal, Caesar, Gustavus Adolphus, Frederick, and Napoleon. Port Washington, N.Y., Kennikat Press [1968, c1889] xiii, 219 p. illus., maps. 21 cm. [U51.D6 1968] 67-27591
1. Alexander the Great—Campaigns. 2. Hannibal. 3. Caesar, C. Julius. 4. Gustaf II Adolf, King of Sweden, 1594-1632. 5. Friedrich II, der Grosse, King of Prussia, 1712-1821. 6. Napoleon I, Emperor of the French, 1769-1821. 7. Military biography. I. Title.

LAMB, Harold. 923.53973
5 hannibal New York : Pinnacle Books, 1976c1958. 294p. ; 18 cm. Includes index. [DG249.L33] ISBN 0-523-00901-1 pbk. : 1.50
1. Hannibal. 2. Punic War, 2nd, 218-201 B.C.
L.C. card no. of 1958 Doubleday edition: 58-13282.

LAMB, Harold, 1892-1962. 923.53973
Hannibal: one man against Rome. [1st ed.] Garden City, N.Y., Doubleday, 1958. 310 p. illus. 22 cm. [DG249.L33] 58-13282
1. Hannibal. 2. Punic War, 2d, 218-201 B.C.

LAMB, Harold Albert, 1892- 923.53973
Hannibal: one man against Rome. New York, Bantam [1963, c.1958] 276p. 18cm. (Bantam pathfinder ed. FP18) Bibl. .50 pap.,
1. Hannibal. 2. Punic War, 2d, 218-201 B.C. I. Title.

MORRIS, William O'Connor, 1824-1904. 937'.04'0924 B
Hannibal, soldier, statesman, patriot, and the crisis of the struggle between Carthage and Rome / by William O'Connor Morris. New York : AMS Press, [1978] p. cm. Reprint of the 1897 ed. published by Putnam, New York, which was issued in series: Heroes of the nations. Includes index. [DG249.M87 1978] 73-14457 ISBN 0-404-58275-3 : 30.00
1. Hannibal. 2. Generals—Carthage—Biography. 3. Punic wars. I. Title. II. Series: Heroes of the nations.

Hannibal— Juvenile literature.

JACOBS, William Jay. 937'.04'0924 B
Hannibal, an African hero [by] William J. Jacobs. Content consultant: Richard F. W. Whittemore. New York, McGraw-Hill [1973] 96 p. illus. 24 cm. A biography of Hannibal whose military tactics baffled the Roman Empire's finest generals and whose campaigns are still studied with interest by military strategists. [DG249.3.J3] 92 72-13165 ISBN 0-07-032157-4 4.72
1. Hannibal—Juvenile literature. I. Title.

JOHNSTON, Johanna. 923.53973
The story of Hannibal. Illustrated by W. T. Mars. [1st ed.] Garden City, N. Y., Garden City Books [1960] 87p. illus. 32cm. [DG249.J6] 59-11600
1. Hannibal— Juvenile literature. I. Title.

WEBB, Robert N. 939/.73/0924
Hannibal, invader from Carthage, by Robert N. Webb. New York, Watts [c.1968] vi, 134p. map. 22cm. (Immortals of hist.) Bibl. [DG249.W4] (B) 68-10512 2.95 lib. ed.,
1. Hannibal—Juvenile literature. I. Title.

WEBB, Robert N 939'.73'0924 (B)
Hannibal, invader from Carthage, by Robert N. Webb. New York, F. Watts [c1968] vi, 134 p. map. 22 cm. (Immortals of history) Bibliography: p. 133. [DG249.W4] 68-10512
1. Hannibal—Juvenile literature. I. Title.

Hannington, James, Bp., 1847-1885.

DAWSON, Edwin Collas, 1849-1925. 283'.0924 B
James Hannington, D.D., F.L.S., E.R.G.S., first bishop of eastern equatorial Africa; a history of his life and work, 1847-1885. New York, Negro Universities Press [1969] x, 451 p. illus., map, port. 23 cm. Reprint of the 1887 ed. [BV3522.H3D3 1969] 69-19355
1. Hannington, James, Bp., 1847-1885.

Hanover, House of.

FULFORD, Roger, 1902- 942.07'0922
The wicked uncles; the father of Queen Victoria and his brothers. Freeport, N.Y., Books for Libraries Press [1968] 320 p. ports. 23 cm. (Essay index reprint series) Reprint of the 1933 ed. Bibliography: p. 312-317. [DA480.F8 1968] 68-8461
1. Hanover, House of. 2. Great Britain—Princes and princesses—Biography. 3. Great Britain—Court and courtiers. I. Title. BIP

REDMAN, Alvin. 942.07
The House of Hanover. [1st American ed.] New York, Coward-McCann [1961, c1960] 471 p. illus. 23 cm. [DA480.R35 1961] 61-5429
1. Hanover, House of.

REDMAN, Alvin. 942.07
The House of Hanover. New York, Funk & Wagnalls [1969, c1968] 471 p. geneal. table, ports. 23 cm. Bibliography: p. 443-449. [DA480.R35 1969] 68-31550 6.95
1. Hanover, House of.

Hansberry, Lorraine, 1930-1965—Biography—Juvenile literature.

SCHEADER, Catherine. 812'.5'4 B
Lorraine Hansberry / by Catherine Scheader. Chicago : Childrens Press, [1977] p. cm. (The found a way) A biography of the playwright who was the first black person and the youngest American to receive the best play of the year award. [PS3515.A515Z87] 92 77-7279 ISBN 0-516-01851-5 lib.bdg. : 6.60
1. Hansberry, Lorraine, 1930-1965—Biography—Juvenile literature. 2. Dramatists, American—20th century—Biography—Juvenile literature. I. Title. II. Series.

Hansen, Martin Alfred, 1909-1955—Criticism and interpretation.

INGWERSEN, Faith. 839.8'1'372 B
Martin A. Hansen / by Faith and Niels Ingwersen. Boston : Twayne Publishers, c1976. p. cm. (Twayne's world authors series ; TWAS 419 : Denmark) Includes index. Bibliography: p. [PT8175.H33Z7] 76-21278 ISBN 0-8057-6259-0 lib.bdg. : 9.50
1. Hansen, Martin Alfred, 1909-1955—Criticism and interpretation. I. Ingwersen, Niels, joint author. BIP

Hanskamp, Minka, 1922-1974.

THOMPSON, Phyllis. 266'.023'0922 B
Minka and Margaret : the heroic story of two women missionaries martyred by bandits / by Phyllis Thompson. London : Hodder and Stoughton : Overseas Missionary Fellowship, 1976. 188 p. ; 18 cm. (Hodder Christian paperbacks) [R722.3.T49] 77-371656 ISBN 0-340-20741-8 : £0.80
1. Hanskamp, Minka, 1922-1974. 2. Morgan, Margaret, 1934-1974. 3. Missionaries, Medical—Thailand—Biography. 4. Kidnapping—Thailand. I. Title.

Hanson, Elizabeth, 1684-1737.

HANSON, Elizabeth, 1684-1737. 973'.04'97 S
God's mercy surmounting man's cruelty / Elizabeth Hanson. New York : Garland Pub., 1977. 40 p. ; 23 cm. (The Garland library of narratives of North American Indian captivities ; v. 6) The account recorded by Samuel Bownas. Reprint of the 1728 ed. printed and sold by S. Keimer, Philadelphia. Issued with the reprint of the 1760 ed. of Hanson, E. An account of the captivity of Elizabeth Hanson, taken by S. Bownas. New York, 1977. The reprint of the 1736 ed. of Gyles, J. Memoirs of odd adventures, strange deliverances, etc. New York, 1977. The reprint of the 1748 ed. of How, N. A narrative of the captivity of Nehemiah How. New York, 1977. The reprint of the 1748 ed. of Norton, J. The redeemed captive. New York, 1977. [E85.G2 vol. 6] [E87] 970'.004'97 77-4696 ISBN 0-8240-1630-0 : 29.50
1. Hanson, Elizabeth, 1684-1737. 2. Indians of North America—Captivities. 3. United States—Biography. I. Bownas, Samuel, 1676-1753. II. Title. III. Series.

Hanson, Ola, 1864-1929.

SWORD, Gustaf A 922.6592
Light in the jungle; life story of Dr. Ola Hanson of Burma. Chicago, Baptist Conference Press [1954] 189p. illus. 20cm. [BV3271.H3S8] 54-13154
1. Hanson, Ola, 1864-1929. I. Title.

Hapgood, Hutchins,

HAPGOOD, Hutchins, 1869-1944. 070'.924 B
A Victorian in the modern world. Introd. by Robert Allen Skotheim. Seattle, University of Washington Press [1972, c1967] xxiii, 604 p. 23 cm. (Americana library, AL-24) [PS3515.A538Z5 1972] 72-172903 ISBN 0-295-95183-4 12.50
I. Title. **BIP**

Hapgood, Norman, 1868-1937.

MARCACCIO, Michael D., 1946- 301.24'2'0922 B
The Hapgoods, Michael D. Marcaccio. Charlottesville : University Press of Virginia, [1977] p. cm. A revision of the author's thesis, University of Virginia. Includes index. Bibliography: p. [HN64.M32 1977] 77-5102 ISBN 0-8139-0693-8 : 15.00
1. Hapgood, Norman, 1868-1937. 2. Hapgood, Hutchins, 1869-1944. 3. Hapgood, William Powers. 4. Social reformers—United States—Biography. 5. Intellectuals—United States—Biography. I. Title.

Harald, Crown Prince of Norway, 1937-

LANGE-NIELSEN, Sissel. v. 12
Kronprins Harald av Norge / [tekstforfatter, Sissel Lange-Nielsen ; billedredaktor, Eeva-Liisa Jor]. [Oslo : Norsk kunstforlag, 1976] 380, [2] p. : ill. ; 27 cm. Captions and summary in English. Bibliography: p. [382] [DL535.A3L36] 77-476105 ISBN 8-290-06973-1 : kr148.00
1. Harald, Crown Prince of Norway, 1937- 2. Norway—Princes and princesses—Biography. I. Title.

Harald III Haroraoi, King of Norway, 1015-1066.

SNORRI, Sturluson 1178-1241 839.8209001
King Harald's saga; Harald Hardradi of Norway. From Snorri Sturluson's Heimskringla. Tr., introd. by Magnus Magnusson, Hermann Palsson. Baltimore, Penguin [1966] 180p. general. table, maps. 18cm. (Penguin classics, L183) [PT7278.5.H32 E55 1966a] 67-2064 1.25 pap.,
1. Harald III Haroraoi, King of Norway, 1015-1066. I. Magnusson, Magnus, tr. II. Palsson, Hermann, tr. III. Title.

SNORRI, Sturluson 1178-1241. 839.61
King Harald's Sage: Harald Hardradi of Norway, from Snorri Sturuluson's 'Heimskringla'; transalted with an introduction by Magnus Magnusson and Hermann Palsson. Harmondsworth, Penguin, 1966. 187 o. maps, diagrs. 18 cm. (Penguin classics) (B66-19063) [PT278.5.H32E55] 67-72570
1. Harald III Haroraol, King of Norway, 1015-1066. I. Magnusson, Magnus, ed. and trans. II. Palsson, Hermann, ed. and trans. III. Title.

STURLUSON, Smorri, 1178-1241. 839.8209001
King Harald's saga; Harald Hardradi of Norway. from Snorri Sturuson's Heimskringla. Translated with an introd. by Magnus Magnusson and Hermann Palsson. Baltimore, Penguin Books [1966] 180 p. geneal. table, maps. 18 cm. (Penguin classics, L183) [PT7278.5.H32E55 1966a] 67-2064
1. Harald III Haroraol, King of Norway, 1015-1066. I. Magnusson, Magnus, tr. II. Palsson, Hermann tr. III. Title.

Haraszthy, Agostin, 1812-1869.

HARASZTHY, Agostin, 1812-1869. 641.2'2'094
Father of California wine, Agoston Haraszthy : including Grape culture, wines & wine-making / edited by Theodore Schoenman ; foreword by Robert L. Balzer. Santa Barbara, Calif. : Capra Press, 1979. 45, xxv, 126 p., [3] leaves of plates : ill. ; 24 cm. Includes reprint of the 1862 ed. author's Grape culture, wines, and wine making published by Harper, New York. Bibliography: p. 41-45 (1st group) [TP547.H37A33 1979] 79-200 ISBN 0-88496-092-7 : 10.00
1. Haraszthy, Agostin, 1812-1869. 2. Vintners—California—Biography. 3. Viticulturists—California—Biography. 4. Viticulture—Europe. 5. Wine and wine making—Europe. 6. Viticulture—California. 7. Wine and wine making—California. I. Schoenman, Theodore. II. Haraszthy, Agostin, 1812-1869. Grape culture, wines, and wine-making. 1979. III. Title.

Harbin family.

GILBERT, Mary Harbin, 1911- 929'.2'0973
Music, medicine, and memories : a family history of Edith Lester Harbin and William Pickens Harbin, M.D. / compiled by Mary Harbin Gilbert ; edited by Mary E. Lane. [Rome? Ga.] : Gilbert, 1976. viii, 127 p. : ill. ; 27 cm. Cover title: A family history. Bibliography: p. 125-127. [CS71.H2564 1976] 77-356608
1. Harbin family. 2. Georgia—Genealogy. 3. United States—Genealogy. I. Title. II. Title: A family history.

Harbison, Massy White, b. 1770.

HARBISON, Massy White, b.1770. 973'.04'97 S
A narrative of the sufferings of Massy Harbison / Massy Harbison. New York : Garland Pub., c1977. vi, 66 p. ; 19 cm. (The Garland library of narratives of North America Indian captivities ; v. 42) Reprint of the 1st ed. printed in 1825 by S. Engles, Pittsburgh. Issued with the reprint of the 1836 ed. of this work, New York, 1977. [E85.G2 vol. 42] [E83.79] 973.4'2 B 76-30391 ISBN 0-8240-1666-1 lib.bdg. : 25.00
1. Harbison, Massy White, b. 1770. 2. Indians of North America—Wars—1790-1794. 3. Indians of North America—Captivities. 4. St. Clair's Campaign, 1791. 5. United States—Biography. I. Title. II. Series.

Harcourt, Brace and Company.

LEWIS, Sinclair, 1885-1951. 928.1
From Main Street to Stockholm; letters of Sinclair Lewis, 1919-1930. Edited and with an introd. by Harrison Smith. [1st ed.] New York, Harcourt, Brace [1952] xii, 307 p. port. 24 cm. [PS3523.E94Z53] 52-6449
1. Harcourt, Brace and Company. I. Harcourt, Alfred, 1881- II. Smith, Harrison, 1888- ed. III. Title.

Hardee, William Joseph, 1815-1873.

HUGHES, Nathaniel Cheairs. 973.730924 (B)
General William J. Hardee; Old Reliable. Baton Rouge, Louisiana State University Press [1965] ix. 329 p. port. 24 cm. (Southern biography series) "Critical essay on authorities": p. 317-321. Bibliographical footnotes. [E467.1.H23H8] 65-12841
1. Hardee, William Joseph, 1815-1873. I. Title. II. Series.

Hardeman, Nicholas Brodie, 1874-

POWELL, James Marvin, 1907- v. 12
N.B.H.; a biography of Nicholas Brodie Hardeman, by James Marvin Powell and Mary Nelle Hardeman Powers. Introd. by B.C. Goodpasture. Nashville, Gospel Advocate Co., c1964] [ix], 387 p., 1 l., [24] p. of illus., facsims., ports. 65-91172
1. Hardeman, Nicholas Brodie, 1874- I. Powers, Mary Nelle (Hardeman) joint author. II. Title.

Hardie, James Keir, 1856-1915.

MORGAN, Kenneth O. 329.9/42
Keir Hardie, by Kenneth O. Morgan. London, Oxford Univ. Pr., 1967. 64p. 8 plates (incl. ports., facsims.), table. 21cm. (Clarendon biographies) Bibl. [HD8393.H3M6] (B) 67-108727 1.55 bds.,
1. Hardie, James Keir, 1856-1915. I. Title. Available from publisher's New York office.

STEWART, William, 1856-1947. 329.9'42 B
J. Keir Hardie, a biography. With an introd. by J. Ramsay Macdonald. Westport, Conn., Greenwood Press [1970] xxv, 387 p. ports. 23 cm. Reprint of the 1921 ed. [HD8393.H3S7 1970] 79-100208
1. Hardie, James Keir, 1856-1915. **BIP**

Hardin, John Wesley, 1853-1895.

NORDYKE, Lewis. 923.4173
John Wesley Hardin, Texas gunman. New York, Morrow, 1957. 278 p. illus. 22 cm. [F391.H27N6] 57-6085
1. Hardin, John Wesley, 1853-1895.

PLENN, Jaime Harrysson, 1905- 923.4173
The fastest gun in Texas, by J. H. Plenn and C. J. LaRoche. [New York] New American Library [1956] 128p. 19cm. (A Signet book, 1312) [F391.P68] 56-9785
1. Hardin, John Wesley, 1853-1895. I. La Roche, Clarence J., joint author. II. Title.

Harding, Warren Gamaliel, Pres. U.S., 1865-1923.

ADAMS, Samuel Hopkins, 1871- v. 12
Incredible era; the life and times of Warren Gamaliel Harding. New York, Capricorn Books [1964] 441 p. "CAP 103." NUC66
1. Harding, Warren Gamaliel, Pres. U.S., 1865-1923. 2. U.S. — Pol. & govt. — 1921-1923. I. Title.

ADAMS, Samuel Hopkins, 1871-1958. 973.91'4'0924 B
Incredible era : the life and times of Warren Gamaliel Harding / by Samuel Hopkins Adams. New York : Octagon Books, 1979, c1939. vii, 456 p., [13] leaves of plates : ill. ; 21 cm. Reprint of the ed. published by Houghton Mifflin, Boston. Includes index. Bibliography: p. 443-[445] [E786.A34 1979] 78-27383 ISBN 0-374-90051-5 lib.bdg. : 22.50
1. Harding, Warren Gamaliel, Pres. U.S., 1865-1923. 2. United States—Politics and government—1921-1923. 3. Presidents—United States—Biography. I. Title.

BRITTON, Nan, 1896- 973.91'4'0924 B
The President's daughter. Freeport, N.Y., Books for Libraries Press [1973] p. Reprint of the 1927 ed. [E786.B86 1973] 72-12799 ISBN 0-8369-7132-9
1. Harding, Warren Gamaliel, Pres. U.S., 1865-1923. I. Title.

COTTRILL, Dale E., 1930- 973.91'4'0924 B
The conciliator, by Dale E. Cottrill. Philadelphia, Dorrance [1969] xix, 343 p. illus., facsims., maps, ports. 22 cm. "Chronological list of Harding's speeches": p. 259-301. Bibliography: p. 339-343. [E786.C7] 68-29903 6.95
1. Harding, Warren Gamaliel, Pres. U.S., 1865-1923. I. Title.

DAUGHERTY, Harry Micajah, 1860-1941. 973.91'4'0924 B
The inside story of the Harding tragedy. In collaboration with Thomas Dixon. Freeport, N.Y., Books for Libraries Press [1971] viii, 323 p. illus., ports. 23 cm. Reprint of the 1932 ed. [E786.D28 1971] 70-160965 ISBN 0-8369-5833-0
1. Harding, Warren Gamaliel, Pres. U.S., 1865-1923. I. Dixon, Thomas, 1864-1946, joint author. II. Title. **BIP**

DAUGHERTY, Harry Micajah, 1860-1941. 973.91'4'0924 B
The inside story of the Harding tragedy / by Harry M. Daugherty, in collaboration with Thomas Dixon ; with an introd. by William P. Fall. Boston : Western Islands, [1975] xl, 312 p., [7] leaves of plates : ill. ; 21 cm. Reprint of the 1932 ed. published by Churchill Co., New York. [E786.D28 1975] 75-27054 ISBN 0-88279-118-4 pbk. : 2.00
1. Harding, Warren Gamaliel, Pres. U.S., 1865-1923. 2. Daugherty, Harry Micajah, 1860-1941. I. Dixon, Thomas, 1864-1946, joint author. II. Title.

GROSS, Edwin K. 973.9140924
Vindication for Mr. Normalcy; a 100th-birthday memorial Buffalo,N.Y. 14225 Amer. Soc. for the Faithful Recording of Hist. 56 Hillsboro Rd., c.1965. 98p. illus., facsims., ports. 28cm. Cover title. [E786.G7] 65-9317 2.95 pap.,
1. Harding, Warren Gamaliel, Pres. U. S., 1865-1923. I. Title.

KURLAND, Gerald, 1942- 973.91'4'0924 B
Warren Harding, a president betrayed by friends. Charlotteville, N.Y., SamHar Press, 1971. 32 p. 22 cm. (Outstanding personalities, no. 6) Bibliography: p. 32. A biography of the twenty-ninth President whom historians rate as one of the least successful to hold that office. [E786.K8] 92 72-185662
1. Harding, Warren Gamaliel, Pres. U.S., 1865-1923. **BIP**

MORAN, Philip R., comp. 973.91'4'0924
Warren G. Harding, 1865-1923: chronology, documents, bibliographical aids. Edited by Philip R. Moran. Dobbs Ferry, N.Y., Oceana Publications, 1970. 120 p. 24 cm. (Oceana presidential chronology series [14]) Bibliography: p. 115-119. [E785.M73] 78-95013 ISBN 0-379-12064-X 3.00
1. United States—History—1919-1933—Sources. I. Harding, Warren Gamaliel, Pres. U.S., 1865-1923. II. United States. President, 1921-1923 (Harding) III. Title. **BIP**

RUSSELL, Francis, 1910- 973.91'4'0924 B
The shadow of Blooming Grove; Warren G. Harding in his times. [1st ed.] New York, McGraw-Hill [1968] xvi, 691 p. 23 cm. Bibliographical references included in "Notes" (p. 667-672) [E786.R95] 68-29916
1. Harding, Warren Gamaliel, Pres. U.S., 1865-1923. I. Title.

SINCLAIR, Andrew 923.173
The available man; the life behind the masks of Warren Gamaliel Harding. New York, Macmillan [c.1965] viii, 344p. illus., ports. 22cm. Bibl. [E786.S5] 65-14332 6.95
1. Harding, Warren Gamaliel, Pres. U.S., 1865-1923. I. Title.

THOMPSON, Charles Willis, 1871-1946. 973.9'0922
Presidents I've known and two near Presidents. Freeport, N.Y., Books for Libraries Press [1970, c1956] 386 p. 23 cm. (Essay index reprint series) Contents.Contents.—Hanna-McKinley.—Bryan.—Roosevelt.—Taft.—Wilson.—Harding.—Coolidge. [E176.1.T45 1970] 71-93383
1. Hanna, Marcus Alonzo, 1837-1904. 2. McKinley, William, Pres. U.S., 1843-1901. 3. Bryan, William Jennings, 1860-1925. 4. Roosevelt, Theodore, Pres. U.S., 1858-1919. 5. Taft, William Howard, Pres. U.S., 1857-1930. 6. Wilson, Woodrow, Pres. U.S., 1856-1924. 7. Harding, Warren Gamaliel, Pres. U.S., 1865-1923. 8. Coolidge, Calvin, Pres. U.S., 1872-1933. I. Title. BIP

TRANI, Eugene P. 973.91'4'0924 B
The Presidency of Warren G. Harding / by Eugene P. Trani and David L. Wilson. Lawrence : Regents Press of Kansas, c1977. ix, 232 p., [1] leaf of plates : port. ; 24 cm. (American Presidency series) Includes index. Bibliography: p. 205-221. [E785.T7] 76-26110 ISBN 0-7006-0152-X : 12.00
1. Harding, Warren Gamaliel, Pres. U.S., 1865-1923. 2. United States—Politics and government—1921-1923. I. Wilson, David L., 1943- joint author. II. Title. III. Series. BIP

Hardinge of Penshurst, George Edward Charles Hardinge, Baron, 1921-

HARDINGE of Penshurst, George Edward Charles Hardinge, Baron, 1921- 799.1'7'55
An incompleat angler : a fishing autobiography / Lord Hardinge of Penshurst ; ill. by Garth Tapper. London : M. Joseph, 1976. 160 p. : ill. , 23 cm. [SH685.H23] 76-381284 ISBN 0-7181-1481-7 : £4.25
1. Hardinge of Penshurst, George Edward Charles Hardinge, Baron, 1921- 2. Salmon fishing—Great Britain. 3. Trout fishing—Great Britain. 4. Fishermen—Great Britain—Biography. I. Title.

Hardwicke, Philip Yorke, 1st Earl of, 1690-1764.

YORKE, Philip Chesney, 1865- 347'.42'03334 B
The life and correspondence of Philip Yorke, Earl of Hardwicke, Lord High Chancellor of Great Britain / by Philip C. Yorke. New York : Octagon Books, 1977. 3 v. : ill. ; 24 cm. Reprint of the 1913 ed. published by Cambridge University Press, Cambridge, Eng. Includes bibliographical references and index. [KD621.H37Y67 1977] 77-1381 ISBN 0-374-98837-4 : 100.00
1. Hardwicke, Philip Yorke, 1st Earl of, 1690-1764. 2. Judges—Great Britain—Biography. 3. Judges—Great Britain—Correspondence. 4. Great Britain—Politics and government—1727-1760. I. Title: The life and correspondence of Philip Yorke ...

Hardy, Emma Lavinia Gifford, 1840-1912.

KAY-ROBINSON, Denys. 823'.8 B
The first Mrs. Thomas Hardy / Denys Kay-Robinson. New York : St. Martin's Press, 1979. x, 278 p., [4] leaves of plates : ill. ; 23 cm. Includes bibliographical references and index. [PR4753.K3] 79-14065 ISBN 0-312-29246-5 : 18.50
1. Hardy, Emma Lavinia Gifford, 1840-1912. 2. Hardy, Thomas, 1840-1928—Biography—Marriage. 3. Authors, English—19th century—Biography. 4. Wives—England—Biography. I. Title. BIP

Hardy, Thomas, 1840-1928.

BRENNECKE, Ernest, 1896-1969. 823'.8 B
The life of Thomas Hardy. [New York, Haskell House Publishers, 1973] viii, 259 p. illus. 23 cm. [PR4753.B7 1973] 72-8648 ISBN 0-8383-1672-7 12.95
1. Hardy, Thomas, 1840-1928. BIP

BROWN, Douglas, 1921- 928.2
Thomas Hardy. London, New York, Longmans, Green [1954] 196p. illus. 20cm. (Men and books) Includes bibliography. [PR4754.B75] 55-479
1. Hardy, Thomas, 1840-1928. I. Title.

GUERARD, Albert Joseph, 1914- 823.8
Thomas Hardy [New Directions, dist. Philadelphia, Lippincott, 1964] xi, 207p. 21cm. (NDP185) Bibl. [PR4754.G8 1964] 64-23651 1.95 pap.,
1. Hardy, Thomas, 1840-1928. I. Title.

HARDY, Evelyn, 1902- 928.2
Thomas Hardy, a critical biography. New York, St. Martin's Press, 1954. x, 342p. illus., port., facsim., geneal. table. 23cm. Bibliographical footnotes. [PR4753] 54-12021
1. Hardy, Thomas, 1840-1928. I. Title.

HARDY, Evelyn, 1902- 823'.8 B
Thomas Hardy; a critical biography. [Folcroft, Pa.] Folcroft Library Editions, 1973. p. Reprint of the 1953 ed. published by Hogarth Press, London. Includes bibliographical references. [PR4753.H28 1973] 73-12879 14.50
1. Hardy, Thomas, 1840-1928.

HARDY, Florence Emily, 1881-1937. 823'.8 B
The life of Thomas Hardy, 1840-1928; compiled largely from contemporary notes, letters, diaries, and biographical memoranda, as well as from oral information in conversations extending over many years. Hamden, Conn., Archon Books, 1970 [c1962] xiii, 470 p. illus., facsim., plan, ports. 23 cm. "Brings together ... The early life of Thomas Hardy, 1840-1891, and The later years of Thomas Hardy, 1892-1928 ... originally published in 1928 and 1930 respectively." [PR4753.H35 1970] 72-12496 12.00
1. Hardy, Thomas, 1840-1928.

HARDY, Florence Emily (Dugdale) d.1937. 928.2
The life of Thomas Hardy, 1840-1928. Comp. largely from contemporary notes, letters, diaries, and biographical memoranda, as well as from oral information in conversations extending over many years. New York, St. Martin's [c.]1962. 470p. illus. 23cm. 62-4705 7.00
1. Hardy, Thomas, 1840-1928. I. Title.

HARDY, Florence Emily (Dugdale) d.1937. v. 12
The life of Thomas Hardy, 1840-1928. Compiled largely from contemporary notes, letters, diaries, and biographical memoranda, as well as from oral information in conversations extending over many years. London, Macmillan; New York, St. Martin's Press [c1962] 470 p. illus. 23 cm. "Brings together ... The early life of Thomas Hardy, 1840-1891, and The later years of Thomas Hardy, 1892-1928." 63-18336
1. Hardy, Thomas, 1840-1928. I. Title.

HARDY, Florence Emily (Dugdale) d. 1937. 928.2
The life of Thomas Hardy, 1840-1928. Compiled largely frfrom contemporary notes, letters, diaries, and biographical memoranda, as well as from oral information in conversations extending over many years. New York, St. Martin's Press, 1962. 470p. illus. 23cm. 'Brings together ... The early life of Thomas Hardy, 1840-1891, and The later years of Thomas Hardy, 1892-1928.' [PR4753.H35 1962] 62-4705
1. Hardy, Thomas, 1840-1928. I. Title.

HARDY, Thomas, 1840-1928. 928.2
Letters; transcribed from the original autographs now in the Colby College Library, and edited with an introd. and notes by Carl J. Weber. Waterville, Me., Colby College Press, 1954. 126p. illus., ports. 26cm. Bibliographical footnotes. [PR4753.A42] 53-7346
I. Weber, Carl Jefferson, 1894- ed. II. Colby College, Waterville, Me. Library. III. Title.

HARDY, Thomas, 1840-1928. 823'.8 B
One rare fair woman; Thomas Hardy's letters to Florence Henniker, 1893-1922. Edited by Evelyn Hardy and F. B. Pinion. [London] Macmillan [1972] xl, 221 p. illus. 22 cm. Bibliography: p. [213] [PR4753.A43 1972b] 72-193887 ISBN 0-333-13182-7
I. Henniker, Florence Ellen Hungerford. II. Hardy, Evelyn, 1902- ed. III. Pinion, F. B., ed. IV. Title.
Available from Univ. of Miami Pr., 12.50, 0-87024-236-9. BIP

HOLLAND, Clive, 1866-1959. 730'.92'4
Thomas Hardy, O. M.; the man, his works, and the land of Wessex. Illustrated by Douglas Snowden. New York, Haskell House, 1966. 320 p. illus., port. 23 cm. Reprint of the 1933 ed. [PR4753.H55 1966] 68-952
1. Hardy, Thomas, 1840-1928. I. Title.

HOLLAND, Clive, 1866-1959. 822.8
Thomas Hardy, O.M.; the man, his works, and the land of Wessex. Illustrated by Douglas Snowden. New York, Haskell House, 1966. 320 p. illus., port. 23 cm. Reprint of the 1933 ed. [PR4753.H55 1966] 730'.92'4 68-952
1. Hardy, Thomas, 1840-1928.

HOLLAND, Clive, 1866-1959. 823'.8
Thomas Hardy's Wessex scene. New York, Haskell House Publishers, 1971. 230 p. illus., port. 23 cm. [PR4757.L3H6 1971] 79-119090 ISBN 0-8383-1086-9
1. Hardy, Thomas, 1840-1928. 2. Dorset, Eng. 3. Literary landmarks—Gt. Brit. I. Title. BIP

HOWE, Irving. 823'.8
Thomas Hardy. New York, Macmillan [1967] xii, 206 p. 21 cm. (Masters of world literature series) Bibliography: p. [195]-196. [PR4753.H65] 67-16710
1. Hardy, Thomas, 1840-1928.

MACDONELL, Annie. 823'.8 B
Thomas Hardy / by Annie Macdonell. New York : AMS Press, [1975] p. cm. Reprint of the 1895 ed. published by Dodd, Mead, New York. [PR4753.M3 1975] 77-148276 ISBN 0-404-08885-6 : 15.00
1. Hardy, Thomas, 1840-1928.

NEVINSON, Henry Woodd, 1856-1941. 823'.8 B
Thomas Hardy / by Henry W. Nevinson. Folcroft, Pa. : Folcroft Library Editions, 1974. p. cm. Reprint of the 1941 ed. published by G. Allen & Unwin, London, which was issued in series: P.E.N. books. [PR4753.N37 1974] 74-23622 ISBN 0-8414-6283-6 lib. bdg. : 8.75
1. Hardy, Thomas, 1840-1928. I. Series: P.E.N. books.

OREL, Harold, 1926- 823'.8 B
The final years of Thomas Hardy, 1912-1928 / Harold Orel Lawrence : University Press of Kansas, c1976. 151 p.,[4] leaves of plates : ill. ; 22 cm. Includes bibliographical references and index. [PR4753.O7] 76-381217 14.00
1. Hardy, Thomas, 1840-1928. 2. Authors, English—20th century—Biography. I. Title.

OREL, Harold, 1926- 823'.8 B
The final years of Thomas Hardy, 1912-1928 / Harold Orel London : Macmillan, 1976. vii, 151 p., [4] leaves of plates : ports. ; 23 cm. Includes bibliographical references and index. [PR4754.O7] 76-376725 ISBN 0-333-19454-3 : £7.95
1. Hardy, Thomas, 1840-1928. 2. Authors, English—19th century—Biography. I. Title.

O'SULLIVAN, Timothy, 1945- 823'.8 B
Thomas Hardy : an illustrated biography / Timothy O'Sullivan. New York : St. Martin's Press, 1976, c1975. 192 p. : ill. (some col.) ; 29 cm. Includes index. Bibliography: p. [187]-188. [PR4753.O8 1976] 75-27159 12.50
1. Hardy, Thomas, 1840-1928.

SIME, Jessie Georgina, 1880- 823'.8 B
Thomas Hardy of the Wessex novels; an essay & bibliographical note, by J. G. Sime. [Folcroft, Pa.] Folcroft Library Editions, 1974. p. cm. Reprint of the 1928 ed. published by L. Carrier, Montreal, New York. [PR4753.S5 1974] 74-10581 6.50
1. Hardy, Thomas, 1840-1928. I. Title.

STEWART, John Innes Mackintosh, 1906- 823'.8
Thomas Hardy; a critical biography [by] J. I. M. Stewart. New York, Dodd, Mead [1971] 249 p. 23 cm. Bibliography: p. [237]-239. [PR4754.S7 1971b] 78-159830 ISBN 0-396-06338-1 5.95
1. Hardy, Thomas, 1840-1928. BIP

THOMAS Hardy. v. 12
London, New York, Macmillan, 1958. ix, 286p. 18cm.
1. Hardy, Thomas, 1840-1928. I. Blunden, Edmund Charles, 1896-

THOMAS Hardy; notes on his life and work. 823'.8 B
[Folcroft, Pa.] Folcroft Library Editions, 1974. 32 p. 24 cm. Reprint of the 1925 ed. published by Harper, New York. Contents.Contents.—Canby, H. S. The novelist of pity.—Tributes from American and English writers.—Biographical.—Courtney, W. L. "The most modern of the moderns".—Bibliography (p. 27-32) [PR4753.T53 1974] 74-11144 5.50
1. Hardy, Thomas, 1840-1928.
Contents omitted.

TOMLINSON, Henry Major, 1873-1958. 823'.8
Thomas Hardy. New York, Haskell House, 1971. xxx p. port. 23 cm. Reprint of the 1929 ed. [PR4753.T6 1971] 70-160129 ISBN 0-8383-1283-7
1. Hardy, Thomas, 1840-1928.

TOMLINSON, Henry Major, 1873-1958. 823'.8
Thomas Hardy. [Folcroft, Pa.] Folcroft Library Editions, 1973. p. Reprint of the 1929 ed. published by C. Gaige, New York. [PR4753.T6 1973] 73-11383 5.75
1. Hardy, Thomas, 1840-1928.

WEBER, Carl Jefferson, 1894- 730'.92'4
Hardy of Wessex, his life and literary career. Hamden, Conn., Archon Books [1962, c1940] 302 p. illus. 23 cm. [PR4753] A62
1. Hardy, Thomas, 1840-1928. I. Title.

WEBER, Carl Jefferson, 1894-1966. 823.8 B
Hardy of Wessex, his life and literary career, by Carl J. Weber. [Rev. ed.] New York, Columbia University Press [1965] x, 324 p. port. 23 cm. "Notes and references": p. 296-311. [PR4753.W27 1965] 65-20474
1. Hardy, Thomas, 1840-1928. I. Title.

WING, George Douglas. 823.8
Thomas Hardy. New York, Grove Press [1963] 119 p. 18 cm. (Evergreen pilot books, EP22) Includes bibliography. [PR4753.W55 1963] 62-18144
1. Hardy, Thomas, 1840-1928. I. Title.

Hardy, Thomas, 1840-1928—Biography.

GITTINGS, Robert. 823'.8 B
Thomas Hardy's later years / by Robert Gittings. 1st American ed. Boston : Little, Brown, c1978. xv, 244 p., [8] leaves of plates : ill. ; 24 cm. "An Atlantic Monthly Press book." Includes index. Bibliography: p. 231-233. [PR4753.G49 1978] 77-19236 ISBN 0-316-31454-4 : 12.50
1. Hardy, Thomas, 1840-1928—Biography. 2. Authors, English—20th century—Biography. I. Title. BIP

HARDY, Florence Emily, 1881-1937. 823'.8 B
The early life of Thomas Hardy, 1840-1891. Compiled largely from contemporary notes, letters, diaries, and biographical memoranda, as well as from oral information in conversations extending over many years. New York, MacMillan, 1928. St. Clair Shores, Mich., Scholarly Press, 1971. xii, 327 p. illus., facsims., ports. 22 cm. [PR4753.H3 1971] 78-145068
1. Hardy, Thomas, 1840-1928—Biography. I. Title. BIP

Hardy, Thomas, 1840-1928—Biography—Youth.

GITTINGS, Robert. 823'.8 B
Young Thomas Hardy / by Robert Gittings. 1st American ed. Boston : Little, Brown, [1975] p. cm. "An Atlantic Monthly Press book." [PR4753.G5 1975] 75-5555 ISBN 0-316-31453-6 : 10.95
1. Hardy, Thomas, 1840-1928—Biography—Youth. I. Title. BIP

Hardy, Thomas, 1840-1928—Correspondence.

HARDY, Thomas, 1840-1928. 823'.8 B
The collected letters of Thomas Hardy / edited by Richard Little Purdy and Michael Millgate. Oxford [Eng.] ; New York : Clarendon Press, 1978- xxi, 293 p., [1] leaf of plates : 1 ill. ; 24 cm. Includes index. Contents.Contents.—v. 1. 1840-1892. [PR4753.A42 1978] 77-30355 ISBN 0-19-812470-8 (v. 1) : 28.75
1. Hardy, Thomas, 1840-1928—Correspondence. 2. Novelists, English—19th century—Correspondence. I. Purdy, Richard Little, 1904- II. Millgate, Michael. III. Title.
Distributed by Oxford University Press, New York, NY BIP

Hardy, Thomas, 1840-1928—Interviews.

HARDY, Thomas, 1840-1928. 823'.8
Talks with Thomas Hardy at Max Gate, 1920-1922 / by Vere H. Collins. Folcroft, Pa. : Folcroft Library Editions, 1974. p. cm. Reprint of the 1928 ed. published by Doubleday, Doran, Garden City, N.Y. [PR4753.A4 1974] 74-28383 ISBN 0-8414-3615-0 lib. bdg. : 15.00
1. Hardy, Thomas, 1840-1928—Interviews. I. Collins, Vere Henry. II. Title.

Hare, Augustus John Cuthbert, 1834-1903.

LESLIE, Shane, Sir bart., 1885- 920.042
Men were different; five studies in late Victorian biography. Freeport, N. Y., Books for Libraries Press [1967] 288 p. 22 cm. (Essay index reprint series) Reprint of the 1937 ed. Contents.CONTENTS.--Randolph Churchill, 1849-1895.--Augustus Hare, 1834-1903.--Arthur Dunn, 1860-1902.--George Wyndham, 1863-1913.--Wilfrid Blunt, 1840-1922. Includes bibliographies. [DA562.L46] 67-26754
1. Churchill, Lord Randolph Henry Spencer, 1849-1895. 2. Hare, Augustus John Cuthbert, 1834-1903. 3. Dunn, Arthur Tempest Blakiston, 1860-1902. 4. Wyndham, George, 1863-1913. 5. Blunt, Wilfrid Scawen, 1840-1922. I. Title. BIP

LESLIE, Shane, Sir, bart., 1885-1971. 920.042
Men were different; five studies in late Victorian biography. Freeport, N.Y., Books for Libraries Press [1967] 288 p. 22 cm. (Essay index reprint series) Reprint of the 1937 ed. Contents.Contents.—Randolph Churchill, 1849-1895.—Augustus Hare, 1834-1903.—Arthur Dunn, 1860-1902.—George Wyndham, 1863-1913.—Wilfrid Blunt, 1840-1922. Includes bibliographies. [DA562.L46 1967] 67-26754
1. Churchill, Randolph Henry Spencer, Lord, 1849-1895. 2. Hare, Augustus John Cuthbert, 1834-1903. 3. Dunn, Arthur Tempest Blakiston, 1860-1902. 4. Wyndham, George, 1863-1913. 5. Blunt, Wilfrid Scawen, 1840-1922. I. Title.

Hare, Francis Hutcheson, 1904-

HARE, Francis Hutcheson, 1904- 345'.761'00924 B
My learned friends : memories of a trial lawyer / by Francis Hutcheson Hare. Cincinnati : Anderson Pub. Co., c1976. 121 p. ; 24 cm. [KF373.H355A3] 76-21592 ISBN 0-87084-346-X
1. Hare, Francis Hutcheson, 1904- 2. Lawyers—Alabama—Biography. I. Title.

Hare, James H., 1856-1946.

GOULD, Lewis L. 770'.92'4 B
Photojournalist : the career of Jimmy Hare / by Lewis L. Gould & Richard Greffe. Austin : University of Texas Press, c1977. 157 p. : ill. ; 26 cm. Includes bibliographical references and index. [TR140.H37G68] 76-52920 ISBN 0-292-74004-2 : 12.95
1. Hare, James H., 1856-1946. 2. Photography, Journalistic. 3. Photographers—United States—Biography. I. Greffe, Richard, 1947- joint author. II. Title.

GOULD, Lewis L. 770'.92'4 B
Photojournalist : the career of Jimmy Hare / by Lewis L. Gould & Richard Greffe. Austin : University of Texas Press, c1977. 157 p. : ill. ; 26 cm. Includes bibliographical references and index. [TR140.H37G68] 76-52920 ISBN 0-292-74004-2 : 12.95
1. Hare, James H., 1856-1946. 2. Photography, Journalistic. 3. Photographers—United States—Biography. I. Greffe, Richard, 1947- joint author. II. Title. BIP

Hare, Julius Charles, 1795-1855.

DISTAD, N. Merrill. 283'.092'4 B
Guessing at truth : the life of Julius Charles Hare (1795-1855) / by N. Merrill Distad. Shepherdstown, W. Va. : Patmos Press, 1979. xii, 258 p. ; 22 cm. Bibliography: p. 239-247. [BX5199.H35D57] 78-11625 17.50
1. Hare, Julius Charles, 1795-1855. 2. Church of England—Clergy—Biography. 3. Clergy—England—Biography. I. Title. BIP

Hare, Robert, 1850-1953.

HARE, Eric B 286.73 (B)
An Irish boy and God; The biography of Robert Hare [by] Eric B. Hare. Washington, Review and Herald Pub. Association [1965] 192 p. illus., ports. 22 cm. [BX6193.H3H3] 65-18677
1. Hare, Robert, 1850-1953. I. Title.

Hargis, Billy James, 1925-

REDEKOP, John Harold. 323.2'0973
The American far right; a case study of Billy James Hargis and Christian Crusade. Grand Rapids, W. B. Eerdmans Pub. Co. [1968] 232 p. 23 cm. Bibliography: p. 209-226. [E743.R38] 67-28375
1. Hargis, Billy James, 1925- 2. Christian Crusade. 3. United States—Politics and government—1945- 4. Right and left (Political science) I. Title.

Hargrave, Lawrence, 1850-1916.

GRAINGER, Elena. 629.13'0092'4 B
Hargrave and son : a biography of John Fletcher Hargrave and his son Lawrence Hargrave / [by] Elena Grainger. St. Lucia, Q. : University of Queensland Press ; Hemel Hempstead, Eng. : distributed by Prentice-Hall International, 1978. 202 p. : ill. ; 22 cm. Includes index. Bibliography: p. [193]-196. [TL540.H254G73] 79-310059 ISBN 0-7022-1077-3 : 18.75
1. Hargrave, Lawrence, 1850-1916. 2. Hargrave, John Fletcher, 1815-1885. 3. Aeronautics—Australia—Biography. 4. Judges—Australia—Biography. I. Title.

Harington, John, d. 1582.

HUGHEY, Ruth Willard, 1899- 821'.3 B
John Harington of Stepney: Tudor gentleman; his life and works, by Ruth Hughey. Columbus, Ohio State University Press [1971] xi, 343 p. facsim., ports. 25 cm. Includes Harington's translation, The booke of freendeship of Marcus Tullie Cicero. Includes bibliographical references. [PR2283.H9 1971] 71-125863 ISBN 0-8142-0150-4 15.00
1. Harington, John, d. 1582. I. Harington, John, d. 1582. John Harington of Stepney: Tudor gentleman; his life and works. 1971. II. Cicero, Marcus Tullius. Laelius de amicitia. English. 1971.

Hariot, Thomas, 1560-1621.

STEVENS, Henry, 1819-1886. 510'.92'4 B
Thomas Hariot, the mathematician, the philosopher, and the scholar; developed chiefly from dormant materials, with notices of his associates, including biographical and bibliographical disquisitions upon the materials of the history of 'Ould Virginia.' New York, B. Franklin [1973, c1972] 213 p. 18 cm. (Burt Franklin research works series. Science classics series, 10) Reprint of the 1900 ed. [F229.H297 1972] 72-82483 ISBN 0-8337-3399-0 19.50
1. Hariot, Thomas, 1560-1621. I. Title.

THOMAS Harriot Symposium, University of Delaware, 1971. 510'.92'4 B
Thomas Harriot; Renaissance scientist, edited by John W. Shirley. Oxford [Eng.] Clarendon Press, 1974. viii, 181 p. illus. 25 cm. Held 5th-7th April 1971. Bibliography: p. [166]-174. [Q143.H36T47 1971] 74-176704 ISBN 0-19-858140-8
1. Hariot, Thomas, 1560-1621. I. Shirley, John William, 1908- ed.
Distributed by Oxford University Press, New York; 21.00.

Harker, Ronald W.

HARKER, Ronald W. 338.7'62'37460924 B
Rolls-Royce from the wings : military aviation, 1925-71 / Ronald W. Harker. Oxford [Eng.] : Oxford Illustrated Press, c1976. vii, 165 p. : ill. ; 26 cm. [TL540.H2548A34] 76-382949 ISBN 0-902280-38-4 : £4.95
1. Harker, Ronald W. 2. Rolls-Royce, Ltd. 3. Aeronautics—Great Britain—Biography. I. Title. II. Title: From the wings.

Harkreader, Sidney J.

HARKREADER, Sidney J. 784'.092'4 B
Fiddlin' Sid's memoirs : the autobiography of Sidney J. Harkreader / edited by Walter D. Haden. Los Angeles : John Edwards Memorial Foundation, 1976. vii, 37 p., [6] leaves of plates : ill. ; 25 cm. (JEMF special series ; no. 9) Discography: p. 35-37. [ML418.H3A3] 76-151217
1. Harkreader, Sidney J. 2. Country musicians—United States—Biography. I. Haden, Walter Darrell. II. Series: John Edwards Memorial Foundation. JEMF special series ; no. 9.

Harlan, John Marshall, 1833-1911.

LATHAM, Frank Brown, 1910- 347.99'24 B
The great dissenter, John Marshall Harlan, 1833-1911 [by] Frank B. Latham. [1st ed.] New York, Cowles Book Co. [1970] xvi, 175 p. illus., ports. 22 cm. Bibliography: p. 167-168. [KF8745.H3L3] 79-104353 ISBN 4-02-141415- 4.95
1. Harlan, John Marshall, 1833-1911. I. Title.

Harlan, John Marshall, 1833-1911—Juvenile literature.

STILLER, Richard. 323.42'3'0922
The white minority : pioneers for racial equality / Richard Stiller. 1st ed. New York : Harcourt Brace Jovanovich, c1977. 120 p. : ill. ; 22 cm. Includes index. Bibliography: p. [114]. Biographical sketches of three early fighters for racial equality. [E185.98.A1S73] 77-76442 ISBN 0-15-295877-0 : 6.95
1. Cable, George Washington, 1844-1925—Juvenile literature. 2. Harlan, John Marshall, 1833-1911—Juvenile literature. 3. Tourgee, Albion Winegar, 1838-1905—Juvenile literature. 4. Social reformers—United States—Biography—Juvenile literature. 5. Reconstruction—Juvenile literature. 6. Afro-Americans—Civil rights—History—Juvenile literature. BIP

Harlan, Silas, 1753-1782.

GREENE, James S 917.69'53'03
Major Silas Harlan; his life and times. [Cleveland? 1964] 83 p. 24 cm. Bibliography: p. [81]-83. [F454.H28G7] 65-79843
1. Harlan, Silas, 1753-1782. I. Title.

Harland, John.

HARLAND, John. 973.92'092'4 B
Brave new world : a different projection / by John Harland. Rochester, WA : Sovereign Press, c1978. 151 p. ; 18 cm. Bibliography: p. 150-151. [CT275.H3838A33] 77-83061 ISBN 0-914752-08-1 pbk. : 2.00
1. Harland, John. 2. United States—Biography. 3. United States—Civilization—1945- I. Title. BIP

Harlem. New York (City)—Biog.

TROTTMAN, Beresford Sylvester Briggs, comp. 920.0747
Who's who in Harlem. 1st- ed.; New York, Magazine & Periodical Print, & Pub. Co. 1949/50. v. illus., ports. 24 cm. Compiler: 1949/50- B.S.B. Trottman. [F128.68.H3W5] 51-30549
1. Harlem. New York (City)—Biog. I. Title.

Harlem, New York (City)—Social conditions.

BROWN, Claude, 1937- 309.17471
Manchild in the promised land. New York, Macmillan [1965] 415 p. 22 cm. Autobiographical. [E185.97.B86A3] 65-16938
1. Harlem, New York (City)—Social conditions. I. Title. BIP

Harlin, John, 1935-1966.

ULLMAN, James Ramsey, 1907- 796.5'22'0924 B
Straight up; the life and death of John Harlin. Garden City, N.Y., Doubleday, 1968. 288 p. illus., ports. 24 cm. [G512.H3U4] 68-12193
1. Harlin, John, 1935-1966. I. Title.

Harlow, Jean, 1911-1937.

BROWN, Curtis F. 791.43'028'0924 B
Jean Harlow / by Curtis F. Brown ; general editor, Ted Sennett. New York : Pyramid Publications, 1977. 160 p. : ill. ; 20 cm. (A Pyramid illustrated history of the movies) Includes index. Bibliography: p. 149-150. [PN2287.H24B7] 76-57806 ISBN 0-515-04247-1 pbk. : 1.75
1. Harlow, Jean, 1911-1937. 2. Moving-picture actors and actresses—United States—Biography. BIP

PASCAL, John. 792.0924 (B)
The Jean Harlow story. New York, Popular Library [1964] 158 p. ports. 18 cm. [PN2287.H24P37] 65-3578
1. Harlow, Jean, 1911-1937. I. Title.

*SHULMAN, Irving 927.92
Harlow, an intimate biography [New York] Dell [c.1964] 352p. illus., ports. 18cm. (3443) .95 pap.,
1. Harlow, Jean, 1911-1937. I. Title.

SHULMAN, Irving. 927.92
Harlow, an intimate biography. [New York] Bernard Geis Associates; distributed by Random House [1964] 408 p. illus., ports. 22 cm. [PN2287.H24S48] 64-16544
1. Harlow, Jean, 1911-1937. I. Title.

TRUE story of Jean Harlow, 927.92
(The) Hollywood's all-time sex goddess. Bob Nystedt, senior ed. Skokie, Ill., Publishers' Development Corp. [dist. Transamerican & Export News, 8150 N. Central Ave., 1965, c.1964] 66p. illus., ports. 28cm. Deluxe collector's ed. [PN2287.H24T7] 65-1106 1.00 pap.,
1. Harlow, Jean, 1911-1937. I. Nystedt, Bob.

Harlow, Le Roy F.

HARLOW, Le Roy F. 352'.0084'0924 B
Without fear or favor : odyssey of a city manager / Le Roy F. Harlow. Provo, Utah : Brigham Young University Press, c1977. x, 350 p. : ill. ; 24 cm. Includes index. [JS344.C5H28] 76-40172 ISBN 0-8425-1461-9 : 11.95. ISBN 0-8425-1458-9 pbk. : 7.95
1. Harlow, Le Roy F. 2. City managers—United States—Biography. I. Title.

Harmon, Byron, 1876-1934.

HARMON, Byron, 1876-1934. 779'.9'97110924
Great days in the rockies : the photographs of Byron Harmon, 1906-1934 / edited by Carole Harmon and the Peter Whyte Foundation ; with a biography by Bart Robinson ; and an appreciation by Jon Whyte. Toronto ; New York : Oxford University Press, 1978. 86p. : ill. ; 23 x 28 cm. [TR787.H37 1978] 78-325354 ISBN 0-19-540288-X : 15.95
1. Harmon, Byron, 1876-1934. 2. Photography of mountains. 3. Photographers — Northwest Territories, Can. — Biography. 4. Rocky Mountains, Can. — Description and travel — Views. I. Harmon, Carole, 1947- II. Peter Whyte Foundation. III. Title. BIP

Harmon, Ernest N.

HARMON, Ernest N. 940.548'1'73 B
Combat commander; autobiography of a soldier [by] E. N. Harmon, with Milton MacKaye and William Ross Mackaye. Englewood Cliffs, N.J., Prentice-Hall [1970] 352 p. illus., maps, ports. 24 cm. [U53.H3A3] 74-100630 8.95
I. MacKaye, Milton, 1901- II. MacKaye, William Ross. III. Title.

Harnack, Adolf von, 1851-1930.

PAUCK, Wilhelm, 1901- 230'.0924
Harnack and Troeltsch; two historical theologians. New York, Oxford University Press, 1968. x, 131 p. 21 cm. (Drew University, Madison, N.J. Drew lectureship in biography, 1967) Contents.Contents.—Adolf von Harnack.—Ernst Troeltsch.—Appendix. Adolf von Harnack and Ferdinand Christian von Baur; Troeltsch's contribution to a Festschrift dedicated to Harnack.—Ernst Troeltsch; a funeral address delivered by A. von Harnack. Bibliographical footnotes. [BX4827.H3P3] 68-17617
1. Harnack, Adolf von, 1851-1930. 2. Troeltsch, Ernst, 1865-1923. I. Title. II. Series.

Harner, Marietta Fisher

HARNER, Marietta Fisher 920
Perseverance wins victory, my life story. New York, Carlton [c.]1962. 65p. 21cm. (Reflection Bk.) 2.00
I. Title.

Harnett, William Michael, 1848-1892.

FRANKENSTEIN, Alfred Victor, 1906- 927.5
After the hunt; William Harnett and other American still life painters, 1870-1900. Berkeley, University of California Press, 1953. xiii, 189 p. plates (1 col.) 29 cm. Bibliographical footnotes. [ND237.H315F7] 759.13 53-11237
1. Harnett, William Michael, 1848-1892. 2. Painters, American. 3. Still-life painting. 4. Painting, American. I. Title.

Harney, William Selby, 1800-1889—Juvenile literature.

ARCHER, Jules. 970.5 B
Indian foe, Indian friend; the story of William S. Harney. [New York] Crowell-Collier Press [1970] 185 p. illus., facsim., ports. 22 cm. Bibliography: p. [184]-185. A biography of the nineteenth-century military officer who devoted his life to gain just treatment and adequate compensation for the Indians from the United States Government. [E181.H28A76] 92 72-93280
1. Harney, William Selby, 1800-1889—Juvenile literature. 2. Indians of North America—Wars—Juvenile literature. I. Title.

Harper, John C.

HARPER, John C. 283'.092'4 B
Sunday: a minister's story [by] John C. Harper. [1st ed.] Boston, Little, Brown [1974] xi, 238 p. 21 cm. Autobiographical. [BX5995.H33A35] 74-4401 ISBN 0-316-34709-4 6.95
1. Harper, John C. I. Title.

Harper, Robert Goodloe, 1765-1825.

COX, Joseph W. 328.757'092'4 B
Champion of Southern federalism; Robert Goodloe Harper of South Carolina [by] Joseph W. Cox. Port Washington, N.Y., Kennikat Press, 1972. x, 230 p. port. 24 cm. (Kennikat Press national university publications. Series in American studies) Includes bibliographical references. [E302.6.H29C69] 78-189554 ISBN 0-8046-9025-1 12.50
1. Harper, Robert Goodloe, 1765-1825. 2. Federal Party. South Carolina. I. Title. BIP

Harper's bazaar.

SNOW, Carmel (White) 1887?-1961 926.59
The world of Carmel Snow, by Carmel Snow, Mary Louise Aswell. Design by Alexey Brodovitch. New York, McGraw [c.1962] 212p. illus. 26cm. 62-12095 6.95
1. Harper's bazaar. I. Aswell, Mary Louise (White) 1902- II. Title.

SNOW, Carmel (White) 1887?-1961. 926.59
The world of Carmel Snow by Carmel Snow,with Mary Louise As well;design by Alexey Brodo vitch New York, McGraw-Hill [1962] 212 p. illus 26 cm. [PN4874.S57A3] 62-12095
1. Harper's bazaar. I. Aswell, Mary Louise (White) 1902- II. Title.

Harper, Valerie—Juvenile literature.

JACOBS, Linda. 791'.092'4 B
Valerie Harper, the unforgettable snowflake / by Linda Jacobs. St. Paul : EMC Corp., [1975] p. cm. (Behind the bright lights) A biography of a once-aspiring dancer who instead gained fame as a comedienne in the television series Rhoda. [PN2287.H244J3] 92 75-15661 ISBN 0-88436-190-X lib.bdg. : 4.95 ISBN 0-88436-191-8 pbk. : 2.95
1. Harper, Valerie—Juvenile literature. I. Title.

Harper, William Rainey, 1856-1906.

YOUNG man in a hurry; v. 12
the story of William Rainey Harper, first president of the University of Chicago. Chicago, University of Chicago Alumni Association [foreword 1957] 81p. illus., port. 21cm. 'Published originally as a supplement to the University of Chicago magazine, June, 1941.'
1. Harper, William Rainey, 1856-1906. I. Mayer, Milton Sanford, 1908-

Harper, Winfred Ozell.

FLETCHER, Jesse C. 266'.023'0924
Wimpy Harper of Africa [by] Jesse C. Fletcher. Nashville, Broadman Press [1967] 142 p. 22 cm. [BV3625.T32H338] 67-18170
1. Harper, Winfred Ozell. 2. Missions—Tanganyika. I. Title.

Harrelson, Bud, 1944- —Juvenile literature.

LIBBY, Bill. 796.357'092'4 B
Bud Harrelson : super shortstop / by Bill Libby. New York : Putnam, [1975] 159 p. ; 21 cm. (Putnam sports shelf) Includes index. A biography of the baseball player who gained renown as a shortstop for the New York Mets. [GV865.H27L52] 74-78899 ISBN 0-399-60901-6 lib. bdg. : 4.97
1. Harrelson, Bud, 1944- —Juvenile literature. 2. Baseball—Juvenile literature. I. Title. BIP

Harriman, Edward Henry, 1848-1909.

KENNAN, George, 1845-1924. 385'.0924 B
E. H. Harriman; a biography. Freeport, N.Y., Books for Libraries Press [1969] 2 v. illus., fold. col. map, ports. 23 cm. (Select bibliographies reprint series) Reprint of the 1922 ed. [HE2754.H2K36 1969] 77-99663
1. Harriman, Edward Henry, 1848-1909.

Harriman, Mary Williamson Averell.

CAMPBELL, Persia Crawford, 1898- v 12 [B]
Mary Williamson Harriman. With a foreword by Grayson Kirk. New York [Columbia University Press] 1960. 84 p. illus. 21 cm. [CT275.H38567C3] 60-4635
1. Harriman, Mary Williamson Averell.

CAMPBELL, Persia Crawford, 1898- v. 12 [B]
Mary Williamson Harriman. With a foreword by Grayson Kirk. New York [Columbia University Press] 1960. 84 p. illus. 21 cm. [CT275.H38567C3] 60-4635
1. Harriman, Mary Williamson Averell.

Harrington, Bob,

HARRINGTON, Bob, 1927- 286'.1'0924 B
The chaplain of Bourbon Street. With Walter Wagner. [1st ed.] Garden City, N.Y., Doubleday, 1969. 214 p. 22 cm. Autobiography. [BX6495.H267A3] 69-10969 4.95
I. Wagner, Walter, 1927- II. Title.

HARRINGTON, Bob, 1927- 286'.1'0924 B
The chaplain of Bourbon Street. With Walter Wagner. [1st ed.] Garden City, N.Y., Doubleday, 1969. 214 p. 22 cm. Autobiography. [BX6495.H267A3] 69-10969 4.95
I. Wagner, Walter, 1927- II. Title.

ROBERTS, Cecil A. 286'.1'0924 B
Bob Harrington: God's happy hero, by C. A. Roberts. Nashville, T. Nelson [1974] 188 p. illus. 22 cm. [BX6495.H267R6] 74-4354 ISBN 0-8407-5078-1
1. Harrington, Bob, 1927-

Harrington, John Peabody.

LAIRD, Carobeth, 1895- 301.2'092'4
Encounter with an angry God : recollections of my life with John Peabody Harrington / by Carobeth Laird ; foreword by Harry Lawton ; decorations by Don Perceval. Banning, Calif. : Malki Museum Press, 1975. xxii, 190 p. ; 24 cm. [GN21.H27L35] 73-88700
1. Harrington, John Peabody. 2. Laird, Carobeth, 1895- 3. Anthropologists—United States. I. Title. BIP

LAIRD, Carobeth, 1895- 301.2'092'4
Encounter with an angry God : recollections of my life with John Peabody Harrington / Carobeth Laird ; foreword by Harry Lawton ; decorations by Don Perceval. New York : Ballantine Books, 1977c1975. xviii, 220p. ; 18 cm. [GN21.H27L35] ISBN 0-345-26075-9 pbk. : 1.95
1. Harrington, John Peabody. 2. Laird, Carobeth, 1895- 3. Anthropologists-United States. I. Title.
L.C. card no. for c1975 Malki Museum ed.:73-88700.

Harrington, Michael.

HARRINGTON, Michael. 309.1'73'092
Fragments of the century. [1st ed.] New York, Saturday Review Press, 1973. 246 p. 22 cm. Autobiographical. [HN58.H24 1973] 73-76509 ISBN 0-8415-0283-8 7.95
1. Harrington, Michael. 2. United States—Social conditions—1945- 3. United States—Politics and government—1945- I. Title. BIP

Harris, Caroline.

BARKER, Joseph, 1747?-1824? 973'.04'97 S
Interesting narrative of the sufferings of Joseph Barker and his wife. New York : Garland Pub., 1977. p. cm. (The Garland library of narratives of North American Indian captivities ; v. 63) "The history of the captivity and providential release of Mrs. Caroline Harris": p. Reprint of the 1848 ed. published by Cunningham & Brooks, Rochester, N.Y. Issued with the reprint of the 1848 ed. of An Indian tradition, no fiction. New York, 1977. The reprint of the 1850 ed. of Adam, G. The dreadful sufferings and thrilling adventures of an overland party of emigrants to California. New York, 1977. The reprint of the 1851 ed. of Brice, J. R. History of the Revolutionary War. New York, 1977. The reprint of the 1851 ed. of Butterfield, D.C. Life and adventures of David C. Butterfield. New York, 1977. [E85.G2 vol. 63] 973.3'8 B 75-7087 ISBN 0-8240-1687-4(set) lib. bdg. : 25.00
1. Barker, Joseph, 1747?-1824? 2. Harris, Caroline. 3. Plummer, Clarissa. 4. Indians of North America—Captivities. 5. United States—History—Revolution, 1775-1783—Personal narratives. 6. Comanche Indians—Captivities. 7. United States—Biography. I. Harris, Caroline. History of the captivity and providential release therefrom of Mrs. Caroline Harris. 1977 II. Title. III. Series.

HARRIS, Caroline. 973'.04'97 S
History of the captivity of Caroline Harris, 1838. New York : Garland Pub., 1977 [c1838] 23 p. : ill. ; 23 cm. (The Garland library of narratives of North American Indian captivities ; 54) Reprint of the ed. published by Perry and Cooke, New York, under title: History of the captivity and providential release therefrom of Mrs. Caroline Harris. Issued with the reprint of the 1838 ed. of Plummer, C. Narrative of the captivity of Clarissa Plummer. New York, 1977. [E85.G2 vol. 54] [E99.C85] 970'.004'97 76-51848 lib.bdg. : 25.00
1. Harris, Caroline. 2. Plummer, Charissa. 3. Comanche Indians—Captivities. 4. Indians of North America—Captivities. 5. United States—Biography. I. Title. II. Series.

Harris, Clifton.

[HARRIS, Clifton] 615'.852'0924 B
From medicine to miracles / Kathryn Kuhlman. Minneapolis, Minn. : Bethany Fellowship, c1978. 96 p. : ill. ; 18 cm. (Dimension books) "The story of Clifton Harris, M.D., as told to a reporter of the Kathryn Kuhlman Foundation." [RC931.O67H37] 78-67100 ISBN 0-87123-383-5 : 1.50
1. Harris, Clifton. 2. Osteoarthritis—Biography. 3. Faith-cure. 4. Christian life—1960- 5. Physicians (General practice)—

Louisiana—Pineville—Biography. I. Kuhlman, Kathryn. II. Title. BIP

Harris, Corra May (White), 1869-1935.

TALMADGE, John Erwin, 1899- 813'.5'2
Corra Harris, lady of purpose, by John E. Talmadge. Athens, University of Georgia Press [1968] xi, 179 p. ports. 25 cm. Bibliographical references included in "Notes" (p. 151-166) Bibliography: p. 167-176. [PS3515.A725Z9] 68-28362 6.00
1. Harris, Corra May (White), 1869-1935. I. Title.

Harris, Franco, 1950-

KOWET, Don. 796.33'2'0924 B
Franco Harris. New York : Coward, McCann & Geoghegan, c1977. p. cm. [GV939.H33K68 1977] 77-7508 ISBN 0-698-10778-0 : 8.95
1. Harris, Franco, 1950- 2. Pittsburgh Steelers (Football club) 3. Football players—United States—Biography. BIP

Harris, Franco, 1950-—Juvenile literature.

BRAUN, Thomas, 1944- 796.33'2'0924 B
Football's powerful runner, Franco Harris / by Thomas Braun. [Mankato, Minn.] : Creative Education, [c1977] 30 p. : ill. ; 19 cm. (The All-stars) A portrait of an outstanding running back who holds the record for yardage gained during a rookie season. [GV939.H33B7] 92 76-44440 ISBN 0-87191-585-5 lib.bdg. 4.95
1. Harris, Franco, 1950- —Juvenile literature. 2. Football players—United States—Biography—Juvenile literature.

BRAUN, Thomas, 1944- 796.33'2'0924 B
Franco Harris / by Thomas Braun ; illustrated by Harold Henriksen. Mankato, Minn. : Creative Education, inc., [1975] p. cm. A brief biography of a running back of the Pittsburgh Steelers who was Super Bowl IX's Most Valuable Player in 1974. [GV939.H33B72] 75-23174 ISBN 0-87191-473-5 lib.bdg. : 4.95
1. Harris, Franco, 1950- —Juvenile literature. 2. Pittsburgh Steelers (Football club) 3. Football—Juvenile literature. I. Henriksen, Harold. II. Title.

BURCHARD, S. H. 796.33'2'0924 B
Franco Harris / S. H. Burchard ; illustrated with photos. 1st ed. New York : Harcourt Brace Jovanovich, c1976. 64 p. : ill. ; 22 cm. (Sports star) An easy-to-read biography of the big, speedy fullback who helped turn the Pittsburgh Steelers into Super Bowl champions. [GV939.H33B87] 92 75-35527 ISBN 0-15-278000-9 : 4.95 pbk. : 1.95
1. Harris, Franco, 1950- —Juvenile literature. 2. Football—Juvenile literature. I. Title.

HAHN, James. 796.33'2'0924 B
Franco Harris : the quiet ironman / by James and Lynn Hahn. St. Paul : EMC Corp., 1978. p. cm. (Their Champions and challengers 2) A biography emphasizing the career of the star running back for the Pittsburgh Steelers. [GV939.H33H33] 92 78-12841 ISBN 0-88436-447-X : 5.95
1. Harris, Franco, 1950-—Juvenile literature. 2. Football players—United States—Biography—Juvenile literature. I. Hahn, Lynn, joint author. II. Title. III. Series. BIP

Harris, Frank,

HARRIS, Frank, 1855-1931. 928.2
My life and loves. Edited, and with an introd. by John F. Gallagher. New York, Grove Press [1963] 5 v. in 1 (xviii, 983 p.) port. 24 cm. Bibliographical references included in footnotes. [PR4759.H37Z5] 63-16996
I. Title. BIP

Harris. Frank, 1855-1931.

BROME, Vincent [Herbert Vincent Brome] 928.2
Frank Harris; the life and loves of a scoundrel. New York, T. Yoseloff [1960, c.1959] 246p. (7p. bibl.) illus. 22cm. 60-6829 5.00
1. Harris. Frank, 1855-1931. I. Title.

HARRIS, Frank, 1855-1931. 928.2
My life and loves. Edited, and with an introd. by John F. Gallagher. New York, Grove Press [1963] 5 v. in 1 (xviii, 983 p.) port. 24 cm. Bibliographical references included in footnotes. [PR4759.H37Z5] 63-16996
I. Title. BIP

TOBIN, A. I. 828'.9'1209 B
Frank Harris: a study in black and white, by A. I. Tobin and Elmer Gertz. New York, Haskell House Publishers, 1970. xii, 393 p. illus., ports. 23 cm. "An 'authorized' biography." Reprint of the 1931 ed. Bibliography: p. 357-379. [PR4759.H37Z85 1970] 71-133279 ISBN 0-8383-1178-4
1. Harris, Frank, 1855-1931. I. Gertz, Elmer, 1906- joint author. II. Title.

Harris, Frank, 1855-1931—Biography.

PULLAR, Philippa, 1935- 828'.9'1209 B
Frank Harris : a biography / by Philippa Pullar. New York : Simon and Schuster, [1975] p. cm. Includes index. Bibliography: p. [PR4759.H37Z735] 75-23352 ISBN 0-671-22091-8 : 9.95
1. Harris, Frank, 1855-1931—Biography.

Harris, Franklin Stewart, 1884-1960.

FRANKLIN Stewart Harris: educator, administrator, father, friend; 378.1'12'0924 B vignettes of his life. Provo, Utah, Brigham Young University [1965] vi, 95 p. illus. 23 cm. "Published to coincide with the dedication of the Franklin S. Harris Fine Arts Center, April 3, 1965." [LD571.B6717 1921.F72] 73-153318
1. Harris, Franklin Stewart, 1884-1960. I. Harris, Franklin Stewart, 1884-1960. II. Brigham Young University, Provo, Utah.

Harris, Fred R., 1930-

HARRIS, Fred R., 1930- 328.73'092'4 B
Potomac fever / Fred R. Harris. 1st ed. New York : Norton, c1977. x, 214 p. ; 22 cm. Includes index. [E840.8.H28A37 1977] 76-30675 ISBN 0-393-05610-4 : 8.95
1. Harris, Fred R., 1930- 2. Legislators—United States—Biography. 3. United States—Politics and government—1945- I. Title. BIP

Harris, Grace McAdams.

HARRIS, Grace McAdams. 629.13'092'4 B
West to the sunrise / Grace McAdams Harris. 1st ed. Ames : Iowa State University Press, 1979. p. cm. [TL540.H2555A38] 79-16183 9.95
1. Harris, Grace McAdams. 2. Women air pilots—United States—Biography. 3. Aeronautics—United States—History. I. Title. BIP

Harris, Howel, 1714-1773.

NUTTALL, Geoffrey Fillingham, 1911- 283.420924
Howel Harris, 1714-1773; the last enthusiast. Cardiff, Univ. of Wales Pr. [Mystic, Conn., Verry, 1965] x, 87p. 22cm. Bibl. [BX5207.H3N8] 65-29739 3.00
1. Harris, Howel, 1714-1773. I. Title.

Harris, Jeremiah C., 1790-1876.

HARRIS, Jeremiah C., 1790-1876. 371.1'0092'4
An old field school teacher's diary : life and times of Jeremiah C. Harris / edited by Charles W. Turner. Verona, Va. : McClure Press, [1975] 87 p., [4] leaves of plates : ill. ; 24 cm. Includes index. [LA2317.H424A33] 75-322326
1. Harris, Jeremiah C., 1790-1876. 2. Teachers—Virginia—Correspondence, reminiscences, etc. I. Title.

Harris, Joel Chandler, 1848-1908.

COUSINS, Paul M. 817'.4 B
Joel Chandler Harris; a biography, by Paul M. Cousins. Baton Rouge, Louisiana State University Press [1968] xiv, 237 p. illus., ports. 24 cm. (Southern literary studies) Bibliography: p. 225-234. [PS1813.C6] 68-13452
1. Harris, Joel Chandler, 1848-1908. I. Title. II. Series. BIP

HARRIS, Julia Florida (Collier) 1875- 818'.4'09 B
The life and letters of Joel Chandler Harris, by Julia Collier Harris. Boston, Houghton Mifflin, 1918. [New York, AMS Press, 1973] ix, 620 p. illus. 23 cm. Bibliography: p. 603-[610] [PS1813.H3 1973] 72-168247 ISBN 0-404-00059-2 21.00
1. Harris, Joel Chandler, 1848-1908. I. Title. BIP

Harris, John Will, 1876-1956.

HARRIS, John Will, 1876-1956. 370'.92'4 B
Riding & roping : the memoirs of J. Will Harris / edited by C. Virginia Matters. San Juan : Inter-American University of Puerto Rico, [1977] xix, 211 p., [22] leaves of plates : ill. ; 26 cm. Includes bibliographical references and indexes. [LA2317.H425A37] 74-78373 ISBN 0-913480-23-1 : 20.00. ISBN 0-913480-34-7 pbk. : 6.00
1. Harris, John Will, 1876-1956. 2. San German, Puerto Rico. Inter American University of Puerto Rico—History. 3. Educators—Puerto Rico—Biography. 4. Puerto Rico—Biography. I. Title. BIP

Harris, Lawren Stewart, 1885-1970.

HARRIS, Lawren Stewart, 1885-1970. 759.11
Lawren Harris / edited by Bess Harris and R. G. P. Colgrove ; and with an introd. by Northrop Frye. Toronto : Macmillan of Canada, 1976, c1969. xii, 146 p. : ill. (some col.) ; 22 x 28 cm. [ND249.H28H3 1976] 77-368957 ISBN 0-7705-1453-7 : 14.95
1. Harris, Lawren Stewart, 1885-1970. 2. Painters—Canada—Biography. I. Harris, Bess, ed. II. Colgrove, R. G. P., ed.

Harris, Mark, 1922- —Biography.

HARRIS, Mark, 1922- 818'.5'409 B
Best father ever invented : the autobiography of Mark Harris. New York : Dial Press, 1976. x, 276 p. ; 24 cm. [PS3515.A757Z52] 75-33854 9.95
1. Harris, Mark, 1922- —Biography. I. Title.

Harris, Patricia Roberts, 1924-

BLACK Americans in government. 973.92'0922 [Text and exercises by Sheila Hobson and Harvey D. Goldenberg. General editor: Saunders Redding]. Produced by Buckingham Learning Corporation. [Jamaica, N.Y., Buckingham Learning Corp., 1969] 5 v. illus., ports. 28 cm. Cover title. Contents.Contents.—[1] The three wars of Edward Brooke; the story of the first black U.S. Senator since Reconstruction.—[2] Fighting Shirley Chisholm; the story of the first black U.S. Congresswoman.—[3] Ambassador for progress; the story of Patricia Harris, former U.S. Ambassador to Luxembourg.—[4] Equal under the law; the story of Supreme Court Justice Thurgood Marshall.—[5] Robert Weaver sees a new city; the story of the first Secretary of Housing and Urban Development. [E185.96.B53] 79-20085
1. Brooke, Edward William, 1919- 2. Chisholm, Shirley, 1924- 3. Harris, Patricia Roberts, 1924- 4. Marshall, Thurgood, 1908- 5. Weaver, Robert Clifton, 1907- I. Hobson, Sheila. II. Goldenberg, Harvey D.

Harris, Radie.

HARRIS, Radie. 070.4'3'0924 B
Radie's world / by Radie Harris. 1st American ed. New York : Putnam, 1975. 288 p., [16] leaves of plates : ill. ; 22 cm. Includes index. [PN4874.H24A35 1975b] 75-29667 ISBN 0-399-11667-2 : 8.95
1. Harris, Radie. 2. Journalists—United States—Correspondence, reminiscences, etc. 3. Moving-pictures—Biography. I. Title. BIP

Harris, Reginald Hargreaves.

HARRIS, Reginald Hargreaves. 796.6 B
Two wheels to the top : an autobiography / by Reg Harris, with Gregory Houston Bowden. London : Allen, 1976. 218 p., [8] leaves of plates : ill. ; 23 cm. Includes index. [GV1051.H3A35] 77-354442 ISBN 0-491-01957-2 : £4.50
1. Harris, Reginald Hargreaves. 2. Cyclists—England—Biography. I. Bowden, Gregory Houston, joint author. II. Title.

Harris, Roy, 1898-

*STRASSBURG, Robert, comp. 780.92
Roy Harris; a catalog of his works, published by California State University, Los Angeles, as a tribute to the outstanding American composer. [Los Angeles, California State Univ., Los Angeles Foundation, 1974] 46 p. illus. 27 cm. [ML134] 74-77114 3.95 (pbk.)
1. Harris, Roy, 1898- 2. Musicians—Biography & works. I. Title.

Harris, Seymour Edwin,

HARRIS, Seymour Edwin, 1897- 330'.0924
Schumpeter, social scientist. Freeport, N.Y., Books for Libraries Press [1969, c1951] x, 142 p. ports. 29 cm. (Essay index reprint series) Contents.Contents.—Introductory remarks, by S. E. Harris.—Some personal reminiscences on a great man, by R. Frisch.—Memorial: Joseph Alois Schumpeter, 1883-1950, by A. Smithies.—Joseph Alois Schumpeter, 1883-1950, by G. Haberler.—Schumpeter as a teacher and economic theorist, by P. A. Samuelson.—Schumpeter's early German work, 1906-1917, by E. Schneider.—Schumpeter and quantitative research in economics, by J. Tinbergen.—The monetary aspects of the Schumpeterian system, by A. W. Marget.—Schumpeter's theory of interest, by G. Haberler.—Schumpeter's contribution to business cycle theory, by A. H. Hansen.—The impact of recent monopoly theory on the Schumpeterian system, by E. H. Chamberlin.—Schumpeter on monopoly and the large firm, by E. S. Mason.—Schumpeter's economic methodology, by F. Machlup.—Reflections on Schumpeter's writings, by WOSchumpeter, social scientist. Freeport, N.Y., Books for Libraries Press [1969, c1951] x, 142 p. ports. 29 cm. (Essay index reprint series) Contents.Contents.—Introductory remarks, by S. E. Harris.—Some personal reminiscences on a great man, by R. Frisch.—Memorial: Joseph Alois Schumpeter, 1883-1950, by A. Smithies.—Joseph Alois Schumpeter, 1883-1950, by G. Haberler.—Schumpeter
I. Schumpeter, Joseph Alois, 1883-1950. II. Title.

Harris, Steve

HARRIS, Steve 926.4
Don't let it happen to you; memoirs of a Greek-American. New York, Exposition [c.1961] 118p. 3.00
I. Title.

Harris, Thomas Lake, 1823-1906.

CUTHBERT, Arthur A. 289.9 B
The Life and world-work of Thomas Lake Harris, written from direct personal knowledge / by Arthur A. Cuthbert. New York : AMS Press, 1975. 413, xix p. ; 18 cm. (Communal societies in America) Reprint of the 1909 ed. published by C. W. Pearce, Glasgow, Scot. Includes index.

[PS1819.H6Z6 1975] 72-2954 ISBN 0-404-10719-2 : 27.50
1. Harris, Thomas Lake, 1823-1906. I. Title. BIP

Harris, Thomas Mealey, 1817-1906.

MATHENY, H. E. 923.573
Major General Thomas Maley Harris, a member of the military commission that tried the President Abraham Lincoln assassination conspirators, and Roster of the 10th West Virginia Volunteer Infantry Regiment, 1861-1865. Parsons, W. Va., McClain Print. Co., [c.]1963. 296p. illus. (pt. col.) ports. 23cm. Bibl. 63-13186 9.00
1. Harris, Thomas Mealey, 1817-1906. 2. U. S.—Hist. —Civil War—Regimental histories—West Virginia Infantry—10th. 3. West Viriginia Infantry. 10th Regt., 1861-1865. 4. Lincoln, President U. S.—Assassination. I. Title. II. Title: Roster of the 10th West Viriginia Volunteer Infantry Regiment, 1861-1865.

Harris, Thomas Spencer, 1836-1893.

LINGENFELTER, Richard E 920.5
The 'Nonpareil' press of T. S. Harris, by Richard E. Lingenfelter and Richard A. Dwyer. Los Angeles, G. Dawson, 1957. xii, 59p. illus., facsims. 19cm. (Early California travels series, 39) '250 copies.' 'Papers known to have been published by T. S. Harris and some locations of extart copies;: p. 56-59. [F856.E174 vol.39] 58-661
1. Harris, Thomas Spencer, 1836-1893. I. Dwyer, Richard A., joint author. II. Title. III. Series.

Harris, Townsend, 1804-1878.

CROW, Carl, 1883-1945. 327'.2'0924 B
He opened the door of Japan; Townsend Harris and the story of his amazing adventures in establishing American relations with the Far East. Westport, Conn., Greenwood Press [1974, c1939] p. cm. Reprint of the 1st ed. published by Harper, New York. Bibliography: p. [E183.8.J3C76 1974] 74-5552 ISBN 0-8371-7512-7 14.00
1. Harris, Townsend, 1804-1878. 2. United States—Foreign relations—Japan. 3. Japan—Foreign relations—United States. I. Title.

GRIFFIS, William Elliot, 1843-1928. 327'.2'0924 B
Townsend Harris: first American envoy in Japan. Freeport, N.Y., Books for Libraries Press [1971] xii, 351 p. port. 23 cm. Reprint of the 1895 ed. Includes bibliographical references. [DS881.3.G8 1971] 74-175698 ISBN 0-8369-6613-9
1. Harris, Townsend, 1804-1878. 2. Japan—History—Restoration, 1853-1870. 3. U.S.—Foreign relations—Japan. 4. Japan—Foreign relations—U.S.

LEVINE, Israel E. 923.273
Behind the silken curtain; the story of Townsend Harris. New York, Messner [c.1961] 192p. Bibl. 61-7993 2.95
1. Harris, Townsend, 1804-1878. I. Title.

LEVINE, Israel E 923.273
Behind the silken curtain; the story of Townsend Harris. New York, Messner [1961] 192p. 22cm. Includes bibliography. [DS8813.L4] 61-7993
1. Harris, Townsend, 1804-1878. I. Title.

Harrison, Barbara Grizzuti.

HARRISON, Barbara Grizzuti. 289.9
Visions of glory : a history and a memory of Jehovah's Witnesses / Barbara Grizzuti Harrison. New York : Simon and Schuster, c1978. 413 p. ; 24 cm. Includes index. Bibliography: p. [395]-[397] [BX8525.7.H37] 77-29024 ISBN 0-671-22530-8 : 12.95
1. Jehovah's Witnesses—History. 2. Harrison, Barbara Grizzuti. 3. Jehovah's Witnesses—United States—Biography. 4. Converts, Catholic—Biography. I. Title.

Harrison, Benjamin, Pres. U.S., 1833-1901.

SIEVERS, Harry Joseph, 1920-. 923.173
Benjamin Harrison. Introd. by Hilton U. Brown. [2d ed., rev] New York, University Publishers [c1960-] v. illus. 24 cm. Includes bibliography. [E702.S55] 60-12711
1. Harrison, Benjamin, Res. U.S. 1833-1901. 2. Hoosier warrior: through the Civil War years, 1833-1865. I. Title.

SIEVERS, Harry Joseph, 1920- 973.8'6'0924 B
Benjamin Harrison. Introd. by Hilton U. Brown. Chicago, H. Regnery Co., 1952-[68] 3 v. illus., ports., maps. 24 cm. Vol. 2 has imprint: New York, University Publishers; vol. 3 has imprint, Indianapolis, Bobbs-Merrill. Contents.Contents.—1. Hoosier warrior, 1833-1865.—2. Hoosier statesman; from the Civil War to the White House, 1865-1888.—3. Hoosier President; the White House and after. Includes bibliographies. [E702.S54] 67-27226
1. Harrison, Benjamin, Pres. U.S., 1833-1901.

SIEVERS, Harry Joseph, 1920- 973.8'6'0924 B
Benjamin Harrison. Introd. by Hilton U. Brown. Chicago, H. Regnery Co., 1952-[68] 3 v. illus., ports., maps. 24 cm. Vol. 2 has imprint: New York, University Publishers; vol. 3 has imprint, Indianapolis, Bobbs-Merrill. Contents.Contents.—1. Hoosier warrior, 1833-1865.—2. Hoosier statesman; from the Civil War to the White House, 1865-1888.—3. Hoosier President; the White House and after. Includes bibliographies. [E702.S54] 67-27226
1. Harrison, Benjamin, Pres. U.S., 1833-1901.

Harrison, Benjamin, Pres. U.S., 1833-1901—Juvenile literature.

MYERS, Elisabeth P. 973.8'6'0924 B
Benjamin Harrison, by Elisabeth P. Myers. Chicago, Reilly & Lee Books [1969] 165 p. illus., ports. 22 cm. (Reilly & Lee President series) Bibliography: p. 158-159. A biography of the Republican elected President in 1888, the first man in that office to enact an anti-trust bill, the Sherman Anti-Trust Law. [E702.M9] 92 72-88720 4.95
1. Harrison, Benjamin, Pres. U.S., 1833-1901—Juvenile literature. I. Title.

Harrison Co., Ind.—Biography.

†PERRIN, William Henry, d.1892? 920'.0772'21
1889 biographical and historical souvenir, Harrison County, Indiana / by W.B. Perrin. Knightstown, Ind. : The Bookmark, 1977. 190 p. in various pagings : ill. ; 24 cm. Contains several parts of the work published in 1889 under title: Biographical and historical souvenir for the counties of Clark, Crawford, Harrison, Floyd, Jefferson, Jennings, Scott, and Washington, Indiana. Includes index. [F532.H4P47 1977] 78-103272 12.85
1. Harrison Co., Ind.—Biography. 2. Harrison Co., Ind.—History. I. Title. II. Title: Biographical and historical souvenir for the counties of Clark, Crawford, Harrison, Floyd, Jefferson, Jennings, Scott, and Washington, Indiana.

Harrison, Frederick, 1831-1923.

HARRISON, Austin, 1873-1928. 192 B
Frederic Harrison : thoughts and memories / by Austin Harrison. New York : AMS Press, 1977. v, 220 p. : port. ; 19 cm. Reprint of the 1927 ed. published by Putnam, New York. [B1646.H24H3 1977] 75-30024 ISBN 0-404-14029-7 : 14.50
1. Harrison, Frederic, 1831-1923. 2. Philosophers—England—Biography. BIP

HARRISON, Frederic, 1831-1923. 192 B
Autobiographic memoirs / by Frederic Harrison. New York : AMS Press, 1977. 2 v. ; 23 cm. Reprint of the 1911 ed. published by Macmillan, London. Includes indexes. Contents.Contents.—v. 1. 1831-1870.—v. 2. 1870-1910. Bibliography: v. 2, p. 335-345. [B1646.H24A33 1977] 75-30025 ISBN 0-404-13990-6 : 42.50
1. Harrison, Frederic, 1831-1923. 2. Philosophers—England—Biography. 3. Lawyers—England—Biography. I. Title. BIP

Harrison, George, 1943-

MICHAELS, Ross. 784'.092'4 B
George Harrison : yesterday and today / by Ross Michaels. New York : Flash Books, c1977. 96 p. : ill. ; 26 cm. Discography: p. [90]-96. [ML410.H206M5] 77-78536 ISBN 0-8256-3913-1 pbk. : 3.95
1. Harrison, George, 1943- 2. Rock musicians—England—Biography.
Publisher's address : 33 W. 60 St., NY 10023

Harrison, Jane Irwin.

*BOWERS, Dorothy W. 920.72 B
The Irwins and the Harrisons, by Dorothy W. Bowers. Mercersburg, Pa., Irwinton Publishers [1974, c1973] 156 p. illus. (part. col.) 24 cm. Bibliography: p. 153-156. [E176.2] 73-88914 10.00
1. Harrison, Jane Irwin. 2. Harrison, Elizabeth Irwin. 3. Presidents—U.S.—Wives. I. Title.
Publisher's address: Route 2 Mercersburg, Pa. 17236 BIP

Harrison, John, 1693-1776.

LAYCOCK, William S. 681'.11'0924 B
The lost science of John "Longitude" Harrison / by W. S. Laycock. Ashford, Kent. : Brant Wright Associates Ltd, 1976. 159 p. : ill., facsim., port. ; 26 cm. Includes index. Bibliography: p. 153. [TS544.8.H37L39] 77-365991 ISBN 0-903512-07-6 : £18.75
1. Harrison, John, 1693-1776. 2. Clock and watchmakers—England—Biography. I. Title.

QUILL, Humphrey. 681'.118
John Harrison: the man who found longitude. With a foreword by Sir Richard Wooley. New York, Humanities Press [1966] xiv, 255 p. illus., geneal. table, port. 23 cm. Bibliography: p. [240]-247. [QB107.Q5 1966a] 67-12246
1. Harrison, John, 1693-1776.

Harrison, Marvin Bradley, 1847-1933.

SWIFT, Grace (Harrison) 922.573
M. B. Harrison, Nebraska Puritan. Lincoln, University of Nebraska Press [1954] 174p. illus. 23cm. [BX7260.H23S9] 54-12559
1. Harrison, Marvin Bradley, 1847-1933. I. Title.

Harrison, Pat, 1881-1941.

SWAIN, Martha. 328.73'092'4 B
Pat Harrison : the New Deal years / Martha Swain. Jackson : University Press of Mississippi, c1978. p. cm. Based on the author's thesis. Includes index. Bibliography: p. [E748.H385S9] 78-7919 ISBN 0-87805-076-0 : 15.00
1. Harrison, Pat, 1881-1941. 2. United States. Congress. Senate—Biography. 3. Legislators—United States—Biography. 4. Mississippi—Politics and government—1865-1950. 5. United States—Politics and government—1933-1945. BIP

Harrison, Paul Wilberforce, 1883-

HARRISON, Ann M 922
A tool in his hand. New York, Friendship Press [1958] 170p. 21cm. Experiences of the author and her husband, a medical missionary, in Arabia. [BV3182.H3H3] 58-7033
1. Harrison, Paul Wilberforce, 1883- 2. Missions—Arabia. I. Title.

Harrison, Rex.

HARRISON, Rex. 791.0924
Rex / Rex Harrison. New York : Dell, 1976c1974. 224p. : ?ill. ; 18 cm. Includes list of plays and films. Includes index. [PN2598.H336A37] pbk. : 1.75
1. Harrison, Rex. I. Title.
L.C. card no. for 1975 Morrow edition: 74-16451

Harrison, William Henry, Pres. U.S., 1773-1841.

CLEAVES, Freeman, 1904- 973.5'8'0924 B
Old Tippecanoe; William Henry Harrison and his time. Port Washington, N.Y., Kennikat Press [1969, c1939] xiv, 422 p. illus., maps, ports. 23 cm. Bibliographical references included in "Notes" (p. 345-391) Bibliography: p. 392-401. [E392.C64 1969] 68-26263
1. Harrison, William Henry, Pres. U.S., 1773-1841. 2. United States—History—1783-1865. I. Title.

GOEBEL, Dorothy Burne, 1898- 973.5'8'0924 B
William Henry Harrison: a political biography. Philadelphia, Porcupine Press, 1974. xi, 456 p. illus. 22 cm. (Perspectives in American history, no. 11) Originally presented as the author's thesis, Columbia University, 1926. Reprint of the 1926 ed. published by Historical Bureau of the Indiana Library and Historical Dept., Indianapolis, in series: Indiana historical collection, v. 14. Biographical series, v. 2. Bibliography: p. [381]-422. [E392.G59 1974] 73-20129 17.50 (lib. bdg.)
1. Harrison, William Henry, Pres. U.S., 1773-1841. I. Title. II. Series. III. Series: Indiana historical collections, v. 14. BIP

HALL, James, 1793-1868. 973.5'0924 B
A memoir of the public services of William Henry Harrison of Ohio. Freeport, N.Y., Books for Libraries Press [1970] 323 p. port. 23 cm. Reprint of the 1836 ed. [E392.H17 1970] 70-117879
1. Harrison, William Henry, Pres. U.S., 1773-1841. BIP

PECKHAM, Howard Henry, 1910- 923.173
William Henry Harrison, young Tippecanoe: illustrated by Paul Laune. [1st ed.] Indianapolis, Bobbs-Merrill [1951] 190 p. illus. 20 cm. (The Childhood of famous Americans series) [E392.P33] 51-10356
1. Harrison, William Henry, Pres. U.S., 1773-1841. I. Title. BIP

YOUNG, Stanley, 1906- 923.173
Tippecanoe and Tyler, too- Illustrated by Warren Chappell. New York, Random House [1957] 177p. illus. 22cm. (Landmark books, 76) [E702.Y6] 56-5456
1. Harrison, William Henry, Pres. U. S., 1773-1841. I. Title.

Harrison, William K.

LOCKERBIE, D. Bruce. 355.3'31'0924 B
A man under orders : Lieutenant General William K. Harrison, Jr. / D. Bruce Lockerbie. 1st ed. San Francisco : Harper & Row, c1979. xii, 194 p., [4] leaves of plates : ill. ; 22 cm. Includes index. [U53.H34L6 1979] 78-15838 ISBN 0-06-065257-8. : 8.95
1. Harrison, William K. 2. United States. Army—Biography. 3. Generals—United States—Biography. I. Title.

Harrod, James,

MASON, Kathryn Harrod. 976.9
James Harrod of Kentucky. Baton Rouge, Louisiana State University Press [1951] xxii, 266 p. illus., port., 3 fold. maps, facsims. 23 cm. Southern biography series) Bibliography: p. [245]-254. [F454.H3M3] 51-10080
1. Harrod, James, I. Title. II. Series.

Harsono, Ganis.

HARSONO, Ganis. 327'.2'0924 B
Recollections of an Indonesian diplomat in

the Sukarno era / Ganis Harsono ; edited by C. L. M. Penders and B. B. Hering. St. Lucia [Australia] : University of Queensland Press ; Hemel Hempstead, Eng. : distributed by Prentice-Hall International, 1977. xiv, 324 p. : ill. ; 23 cm. (Sources of modern Indonesian history and politics) Includes index. [DS644.1.H36A35] 78-306003 ISBN 0-7022-1440-X : 23.75
1. Harsono, Ganis. 2. Sukarno, Pres. Indonesia, 1901-1970. 3. Indonesia—Politics and government—20th century. 4. Diplomats—Indonesia—Biography. I. Penders, Christian Lambert Maria. II. Hering, B. B. III. Title. IV. Series.
Distributed by Technical Impex, 5 South Union St., Lawrence, MA 01843 **BIP**

Hart, Abraham, 1810-1885.

GINSBERG, Louis, 1920- 070.5'092'4
A. Hart, Philadelphia publisher (1829-1854) Petersburg, Va., 1972. ii, 53 p. illus. 22 cm. Includes bibliographical references. [Z473.H33G55] 72-81128
1. Hart, Abraham, 1810-1885. 2. Philadelphia—Industries.

Hart, James H., 1825-1906.

HART, Edward LeRoy, 1916- 289.3'092'4 B
Mormon in motion : the life and journals of James H. Hart, 1825-1906, in England, France, and America / by Edward L. Hart. [s.l.] : Windsor Books, 1978. xix, 313 p. : ill. ; 24 cm. Includes bibliographical references and index. [BX8695.H34H34] 78-60386 ISBN 0-932100-00-7 : 15.00
1. Hart, James H., 1825-1906. 2. Mormons and Mormonism—Biography. I. Hart, James H., 1825-1906. II. Title.
Publisher's address: PO Box 280, Brightwaters, NY 11718

Hart, Jim, 1944-

BARNIDGE, Tom. 796.33'2'0924 B
The Jim Hart story / by Tom Barnidge and Douglas Grow. St. Louis : Bethany Press, c1977. 176 p. : ill. ; 24 cm. Includes index. [GV939.H334B37] 77-12538 ISBN 0-8272-1705-6 : 9.95. ISBN 0-8272-1704-8 pbk. : 6.95
1. Hart, Jim, 1944- 2. Football players—United States—Biography. I. Grow, Douglas, joint author. II. Title. **BIP**

Hart, Jim, 1944- —Juvenile literature.

LIPMAN, David. 796.33'2'0924 B
Jim Hart, underrated quarterback / by David and Marilyn Lipman. New York : Putnam, c1977. p. cm. (Putnam sports shelf) Includes index. Discusses the life and career of quarterback Jim Hart of the St. Louis Cardinals. [GV939.H334L56 1977] 92 76-42275 ISBN 0-399-61057-X lib.bdg. : 5.29
1. Hart, Jim, 1944- —Juvenile literature. 2. Football players—Biography—Juvenile literature. I. Lipman, Marilyn, joint author. II. Title.

Hart, Joel Tanner, 1810-1877.

COLEMAN, John Winston, 1898- 709'.2'2
Three Kentucky artists—Hart, Price, Troye / J. Winston Coleman, Jr. Lexington : University Press of Kentucky, [1974] 76 p., [4] leaves of plates : ill. ; 21 cm. (The Kentucky bicentennial bookshelf) "Partial list of portraits by Samuel Price": p. 44-[48] [N6530.K4C64] 74-7873 ISBN 0-8131-0202-2 pbk. : 3.95
1. Hart, Joel Tanner, 1810-1877. 2. Price, Samuel Woodson, 1828-1918. 3. Troye, Edward, 1808-1874. 4. Art—Kentucky. I. Title. II. Series.

Hart, John, 1708-1780.

HAMMOND, Cleon E. 973.3'092'4 B
John Hart : the biography of a signer of the Declaration of Independence / by Cleon E. Hammond. Bicentennial ed. Newfane, Vt. : Pioneer Press, 1977. xv, 357 p. : ill. ; 24 cm. Includes index. Bibliography: p. 334-340. [E302.6.H33H35] 77-70992 15.45
1. Hart, John, 1708-1780. 2. Declaration of Independence—Signers—Biography. 3. Legislators—New Jersey—Biography. 4. New Jersey—History—Revolution, 1775-1783.

Hart, Lorenz Milton, 1895-1943.

HART, Dorothy. 784'.092'4 B
Thou swell, thou witty : the life and lyrics of Lorenz Hart / edited and with a memoir by Dorothy Hart. 1st ed. New York : Harper & Row, 1976. 191 p. : ill. ; 31 cm. Erratum slip inserted. [ML423.H32H4] 75-23885 ISBN 0-06-011776-1 : 25.00
1. Hart, Lorenz Milton, 1895-1943. 2. Songs—Texts. I. Title. **BIP**

Hart, Moss, 1904-1961.

HART, Moss, 1904-1961. 818.52
Act one, an autobiography. New York, Random House [1959] 444 p. 24 cm. [PN2287.H27A3] 59-10813
1. Hart, Moss, 1904-1961. Once in a lifetime. I. Title.

HART, Moss, 1904-1961. 812'.5'2 B
Act one : an autobiography / Moss Hart. New York : Vintage Books, 1976, c1959. p. cm. [PS3515.A7943Z52 1976] 75-28169 ISBN 0-394-72044-X pbk. : 2.95
1. Hart, Moss, 1904- —Biography. I. Title.

Hart, Moss, 1904-1961. Once in a lifetime.

HART, Moss 818.52
Act one, an autobiography. [New York] New American Library, [1960, c.1959] 383p. 18cm. (Signet Book, T1849) .75 pap.,
1. Hart, Moss. Once in a lifetime. I. Title.

HART, Moss, 1904-1961. v. 12
Act one, an autobiography. New York, Modern Library [1959] 444 p. 19 cm. 68-91937
1. Hart, Moss, 1904-1961. Once in a lifetime. I. Title.

Hart, Oliver, 1723-1795.

OWENS, Loulie (Latimer) 286'.1'0924 B
Oliver Hart, 1723-1795; a biography. Art work by Leonard Cave. Greenville, S.C., Printed and distributed by the South Carolina Baptist Historical Society, 1966. 41 p. illus. 23 cm. Bibliography: p. 36-41. [BX6495.H275O9] 73-172381
1. Hart, Oliver, 1723-1795.

Hart, Sylvan.

PETERSON, Harold, 1939- 917.96'82 B
The last of the mountain men. New York, Scribner [1969] 160 p. illus., maps (on lining papers), ports. 25 cm. [F752.S35H35] 68-57081 5.95
1. Hart, Sylvan. 2. Salmon Valley, Idaho. I. Title.

Harte, Bret, 1836-1902.

BOYNTON, Henry Walcott, 1869-1947. 813'.4 B
Bret Harte. Freeport, N.Y., Books for Libraries Press [1970] 117 p. port. 23 cm. Reprint of the 1903 ed. [PS1833.B6 1970] 70-133513
1. Harte, Bret, 1836-1902. **BIP**

HARTE, Bret, 1836-1902. 813'.4 B
The letters of Bret Harte, assembled and edited by Geoffrey Bret Harte. Boston, Houghton Mifflin, 1926. [New York, AMS Press, 1973] xviii, 515 p. illus. 23 cm. [PS1833.A5 1973] 70-161761 ISBN 0-404-09024-9 25.00
1. Harte, Bret, 1836-1902. **BIP**

MERWIN, Henry Childs, 1853-1929. 813'.4 B
The life of Bret Harte, with some account of the California pioneers. Detroit, Gale Research Co., 1967 [c1911] xii, 362 p. illus., ports. 22 cm. (The Gale library of lives and letters. American writers series) Title page includes original imprint: Boston, Houghton Mifflin, 1911. [PS1833.M4 1967] 67-23887
1. Harte, Bret, 1836-1902. I. Title.

O'CONNOR, Richard, 1915- 813.4
Bret Harte; a biography. Boston, Little [c.1966] 331p. illus., ports. 22cm. Bibl. [PS1833.O3] 66-10981 6.95 bds.,
1. Harte, Bret, 1836-1902. I. Title.

PEMBERTON, Thomas Edgar, 1849-1905. 813'.4 B
The life of Bret Harte. Freeport, N.Y., Books for Libraries Press [1970] vii, 357 p. illus., map, ports. 23 cm. Reprint of the 1903 ed. Bibliography: p. 346-354. [PS1833.P5 1970] 74-133530
1. Harte, Bret, 1836-1902. I. Title.

PEMBERTON, Thomas Edgar, 1849-1905. 813'.4 B
The life of Bret Harte. [Folcroft, Pa.] Folcroft Library Editions, 1973. p. Reprint of the 1903 ed. published by C. A. Pearson, London. Bibliography: p. [PS1833.P5 1973] 73-13955 12.00
1. Harte, Bret, 1836-1902. I. Title. **BIP**

STEWART, George Rippey, Jr., 1895- 928.1
Bret Harte, argonaut and exile, being an account of the life of the celebrated American humorist . . . comp. from New and original sources. Port Washington, N.Y., Kennikat [1964, c.1935] xi, 384p. illus., facsims., ports. 23cm. Bibl. 64-24470 10.00
1. Harte, Br)0et, 1836-1902. I. Title.

Harte, Bret, 1836-1902—Bibliography.

GAER, Joseph, 1897- ed. 016.813'4
Bret Harte; bibliography and biographical data. New York, B. Franklin [1968] 189 p. 24 cm. (Burt Franklin bibliography and reference series, #162) Reprint of the 1935 ed. [Z8388.65.G13 1968] 79-6465
1. Harte, Bret, 1836-1902—Bibliography. 2. Harte, Bret, 1836-1902. **BIP**

Harte, Bret, 1836-1902—Biography.

STEWART, George Rippey, 1895- 813'.4 B
Bret Harte, Argonaut and exile : being an account of the life of the celebrated American humorist ... / by George R. Stewart, Jr. 1st AMS ed. New York : AMS Press, 1979, c1931. xi, 384 p., [7] leaves of plates : ill. ; 23 cm. Reprint of the ed. published by Houghton Mifflin, Boston. Includes index. Bibliography: p. 337-[340] [PS1833.S7 1979] 76-6593 ISBN 0-404-15298-8 : 30.00
1. Harte, Bret, 1836-1902—Biography. 2. Authors, American—19th century—Biography. I. Title.

Harte, Bret, 1836-1902—Juvenile literature.

BRANHAM, Janet. 813'.4 B
Bret Harte; young storyteller. Illustrated by Robert Doremus. Indianapolis, Bobbs-Merrill [1969] 200 p. col. illus. 20 cm. (Childhood of famous Americans) Bibliography: p. 198. A biography stressing the childhood of the nineteenth-century American author who became internationally famous for his stories about California gold mining days. [PS1833.B75] 92 77-89981
1. Harte, Bret, 1836-1902—Juvenile literature. I. Doremus, Robert, illus. II. Title.

Harthoorn, Antonie Marinus.

HARTHOORN, Susanne. 639'.96'0924 B
Life with Daktari: two vets in East Africa, by Susanne Hart. [1st American ed.] New York, Atheneum, 1969. 224 p. illus. (part col.), map, ports. (part col.) 23 cm. Autobiographical. [SF613.H33A28 1969] 74-75746 7.95
1. Harthoorn, Antonie Marinus. 2. Zoology—Africa, East. 3. Veterinarians—Correspondence, reminiscences, etc. I. Title.

Hartley, Al.

HARTLEY, Al. 248'.2'0924 B
Come meet my friend / Al Hartley. Old Tappan, N.J. : F. H. Revell, c1977. 61 p. ; 18 cm. (New life ventures) [BV4935.H355A33] 77-5921 ISBN 0-8007-9001-4 pbk : 0.95
1. Hartley, Al. 2. Converts—United States—Biography. 3. Cartoonists—United States—Biography. I. Title. **BIP**

Hartley, Leslie Poles.

BIEN, Peter 813.52
L. P. Hartley. University Park, Penn. State [c.] 1963. 288p. 23cm. Bibl. 63-16500 6.00
1. Hartley, Leslie Poles. I. Title.

Hartley, Marsden, 1877-1943.

MCCAUSLAND, Elizabeth, 1899- 759.13
Marsden Hartley. Minneapolis, University of Minnesota Press [1952] xi, 80 p. illus. 26 cm. Bibliography: p. 76-80. [ND237.H3435M3] 52-7483
1. Hartley, Marsden, 1877-1943. I. Title.

Hartman—Homecrest, New York.

HARTMAN, May (Weisser) 923.673
I gave my heart. [by] Mrs. Gustave Hartman, New York, Citadel Press [c.1960] 350p. illus. 22cm. 60-12348 5.00 half cloth,
1. Hartman—Homecrest, New York. I. Title.

Hartman, David, 1949-

HARTMAN, David, 1949- 616.8'9'00924 B
White Coat, white cane / David Hartman and Bernard Asbell. 1st ed. Chicago : Playboy Press ; New York : trade distribution by Simon and Schuster, c1979. p. cm. [RC339.52.H37A33] 78-26127 ISBN 0-87223-516-5 : 8.95
1. Hartman, David, 1949- 2. Psychiatrists—Pennyslvania—Biography. 3. Blind—Pennsylvania—Biography. I. Asbell, Bernard, joint author. II. Title.

Hartmann, Erich, 1922-

TOLIVER, Raymond F. 940.544'943'0924 B
The blond knight of Germany [by] Raymond F. Toliver and Trevor J. Constable. Introd. by Adolf Galland. [1st ed.] Garden City, N.Y., Doubleday, 1970. xv, 318 p. illus., ports. 25 cm. Title on spine: The blonde knight of Germany. [TL540.H257T6] 74-89076
1. Hartmann, Erich, 1922- I. Constable, Trevor J., joint author. II. Title. III. Title: The blonde knight of Germany.

Hartsfield, William Berry.

MARTIN, Harold H. 975.8'231'040924 B
William Berry Hartsfield, Mayor of Atlanta / Harold H. Martin. Athens : University of Georgia Press, c1978. xv, 230 p., [8] leaves of plates : ill. ; 24 cm. Includes bibliographical references and index. [F294.A853H375] 78-1550 ISBN 0-8203-0445-X : 7.50
1. Hartsfield, William Berry. 2. Atlanta—Mayors—Biography. 3. Atlanta—Politics and government. I. Title. **BIP**

Hartshorne, Charles, 1897-

GRAGG, Alan. 230'.092'4 B
Charles Hartshorne. Waco, Tex., Word Books [1973] 127 p. 23 cm. (Makers of the modern theological mind) Bibliography: p. 124-127. [B945.H354G72] 70-188063 3.95
1. Hartshorne, Charles, 1897-

Harvard University—Biog.

SIBLEY'S Harvard graduates; biographical sketches of those who attended Harvard College . . . with bibliographical and other notes, v.12, 1746- 378.7444

1750. Boston, Mass. Historical Soc. [c.] 1962. illus. 26cm. Title varies. 7-1440 7.50
1. Harvard University—Biog. I. Sibley, John Langdon, 1804-1885. II. Massachusetts Historical Society, Boston.

SIBLEY'S Harvard 378.744
graduates; bibliographical sketches of those who attended Harvard College in the classes 1756-1760 with bibliographical and other notes by Clifford K. Shipton. Boston, Mass. Hist. Soc., 1968 v. ports. 25cm. [LD2139.S5] 7-1440 17.50
1. Harvard University—Biog. I. Sibley, John Longdon, 1804-1885. II. Shipton, Clifford Kenyon, 1902- III. Massachusetts Historical Society, Boston.

SIBLEY'S Harvard 378.7444
graduates; bibliographical sketches of those who attended Harvard College; v.13. Bibliograpical and other notes by Clifford K. Shipton. Boston, Mass., Mass. Hist. Soc. [c.]1965. 725p. illus., ports. 26cm. Title varies. Contents.v.13. Classes [of] 1751-1755. [LD2139.S5] 7-1440 10.00
1. Harvard University—Biog. I. Sibley, John Langdon, 1804-1885. II. Shipton, Clifford Kenyon, 1902- III. Massachusetts Historical Society, Boston.

SIBLEY'S Harvard 378.744
graduates; biographical sketches of those who attended Harvard College . . . with bibliographical and other notes. v. 1-3 1642-58-- Boston, Massachusetts Hist. Soc., 1873-19; New York,, Johnson Reprint, 1967. v illus. ports. 26cm. Title. varies: v. 1-3, 1642-58--1678-89, Biographical sketches of graduates of Harvard University; in Cambridge, Massachusetts. Vols. 1-3 by J. L. Sibley; v. 4- by C. K. Shipton. Imprint varies. v. 1-3, Cambridge, C. W. Sever, 1873-85.--v. 4, Cambridge, Harvard Univ. Pr. 1933 Vol. 1 includes an appendix, containing an abstract of the steward's accounts, and notices of non-graduates, from 1649-50 to 1659. [LD2139.S5] 7-1440 82.00, 27.50 set., ea.,
1. Harvard University—Biog. I. Sibley, John Longdon, 1804-1885. II. Shipton, Clifford Kenyon, 1902- III. Massachusetts Historical Society, Boston.

Harvey, Charles Thompson, 1829-

RATIGAN, William. 926.2
Young Mister Big; the story of Charles Thompson Harvey, the young traveling salesman who built the world's mightiest canal. Grand Rapids, Eerdmans, 1955. 152p. 23cm. [TC140.H3R3] 55-14765
1. Harvey, Charles Thompson, 1829- I. Title.

Harvey, William, 1578-1657.

CHAUVOIS, Louis, 1881- 926.1
William Harvey: his discoveries, his methods. Foreword by Zachary Cope. New York, Philosophical Library [1957] 271p. illus. 24cm. Translated from the French. Includes bibliography. [QP26.H3C52] 57-2717
1. Harvey, William, 1578-1657. I. Title.

CHAUVOIS, Louis, 1881- 926.1
William Harvey: his life and times, his discoveries, his methods. Foreword by Zachary Cope. New York, Philosophical Library [1957] 271 p. illus. 24 cm. Translated from the French. Includes bibliography. [QP26.H3C52] 57-2717
1. Harvey, William, 1578-1657.

FRANKLIN, Kenneth James, 926.1
1897-
William Harvey, Englishman, 1578-1657. [Dist. Chester Springs, Pa., Dufour, 1962, c.]1961. 151p. illus. 23cm. Bibl. 62-6373 3.95
1. Harvey, William, 1578-1657. I. Title.

KEYNES, Geoffrey 610.924 (B)
Langdon, Sir 1887-
The life of William Harvey by Geoffrey Keynes. Oxford, Clarendon Pr., 1966. xviii, 484p. col. front., 32 plates (incl. ports., facsims.) plan, maps. 26cm. Bibl. [QP26.H3K4] 66-73575 14.40
1. Harvey, William, 1578-1657. I. Title.
Available from Oxford in New York.

MARCUS, Rebecca B. 926.1
William Harvey, trailblazer of scientific medicine. Picutes by Richard Mayhew. New York, F. Watts [1962] 127 p. illus. 22 cm. (Immortals of science) [QP26.H3M34] 62-7423
1. Harvey, William, 1578-1657.

PAGEL, Walter, 1898- 591.1'0924
William Harvey's biological ideas; selected aspects and historical background. New York, Hafner Pub. Co., 1967. 394 p. illus. 25 cm. Bibliographical footnotes. [QP26.H3P3 1967a] 67-2133
1. Harvey, William, 1578-1657. I. Title.

WILLIAM Harvey and 612'.1'0924 B
his age : the professional and social context of the discovery of the circulation / edited by Jerome J. Bylebyl. Baltimore : Johns Hopkins University Press, c1979. xii, 154 p. : ill. ; 24 cm. (The Henry E. Sigerist supplements to the Bulletin of the history of medicine ; new ser., no. 2) Papers from a conference held in Kansas City, May 13, 1978, at the annual meeting of the American Association for the History of Medicine. Includes bibliographical references and index. [QP26.H3W544] 78-20526 ISBN 0-8018-2213-0. : 12.50
1. Harvey, William, 1578-1657. 2. Blood—Circulation—History—Congresses. 3. Physiologists—England—Biography. 4. Physicians—England—Biography. I. Bylebyl, Jerome J. II. American Association for the History of Medicine. III. Title. IV. Series.

Harzfeld, Abraham, 1888-

KUSHNIR, Simon, 1896- 338.095694
The village builder, a biography of Abraham Harzfeld, by Shimon Kushnir. Translated from the Hebrew by Abraham Regelson and Gertrude Hirschler. New York, Herzl Press [c1967] 346 p. ports. 22 cm. Translation of Sadot va-lev [DS126.6.H36K863] 67-19869
1. Harzfeld, Abraham, 1888- I. Title.

KUSHNIR, Simon, 956.94'04'0924
1896-
The village builder; a biography of Abraham Harzfeld, by Shimon Kushnir. Tr. from Hebrew by Abraham Regelson, Gertrude Hirschler. New York, Herzl Pr. [c.1967] 346p. ports. 22cm. (romanized: Sadot va-lev) Tr. of [DS126.6.H36K863] (B) 67-19869 5.95
1. Harzfeld, Abraham, 1888- I. Title.
Distributed by Yoseloff.

Hasek, Jaroslay, 1883-1923.

FRYNTA, Emanuel 891.868509
Hasek, the creator of Schweik, [Tr. by Jean Layton, George Theiner. Prague] Artia [c1965] 145p. illus., ports. 28cm. [PG5038.H28Z72] 66-8392 6.00
1. Hasek, Jaroslay, 1883-1923. I. Title.
Available from Vanous in New York.

Haskell, Stephen Nelson.

ROBINSON, Ella May 286'.7'0924
(White) 1882-
S. N. Haskell, man of action. Washington, Review and Herald Pub. Association [1967] 256 p. illus., ports. 22 cm. Bibliographical footnotes. [BX6193.H32R6] 67-21869
1. Haskell, Stephen Nelson. I. Title.

Hassam, Childe, 1859-1935.

HOOPES, Donelson F. 759.13
Childe Hassam / Donelson Hoopes. New York : Watson-Guptill, 1979. p. cm. [ND237.H345H66] 79-15232 ISBN 0-8230-0622-0 : 20.00
1. Hassam, Childe, 1859-1935. 2. Painters—United States—Biography. I. Title. BIP

Hassan II, King of Morocco, 1929-

LANDAU, Rom, 1899- 923.164
Hassan II, King of Morocco. London, Allen & Unwin [dist. Mystic, Conn., Verry, 1965, c.1962] 95p. illus. 23cm. [DT324.3.H3L3] 63-1007 3.00 bds.,
1. Hassan II, King of Morocco, 1929- I. Title.

Hastings, Beatrice.

CARSWELL, John. 820'.9'00912
Lives and letters : A. R. Orage, Beatrice Hastings, Katherine Mansfield, John Middleton Murry, S. S. Koteliansky : 1906-1957 / by John Carswell. New York : New Directions Pub. Corp., 1978. p. cm. Includes index. Bibliography: p. [PR106.C37] 77-15986 ISBN 0-8112-0681-5 : 15.00
1. Orage, Alfred Richard, 1873-1934. 2. Hastings, Beatrice. 3. Mansfield, Katherine, 1888-1923. 4. Murry, John Middleton, 1889-1957. 5. Koteliansky, Samuel Solomonovitch, 1880-1955. 6. Authors, English—20th century—Biography. I. Title. BIP

CARSWELL, John. 820'.9'00912
Lives and letters : A. R. Orage, Beatrice Hastings, Katherine Mansfield, John Middleton Murry, S. S. Koteliansky, 1906-1957 / by John Carswell. London ; Boston : Faber and Faber, 1978. 306 p., [4] leaves of plates : ill. ; 23 cm. Includes index. Bibliography: p. 294-297. [PR106.C37 1978] 78-313376 ISBN 0-571-10596-3 : 15.00
1. Orage, Alfred Richard, 1873-1934. 2. Hastings, Beatrice. 3. Mansfield, Katherine, 1888-1923. 4. Murry, John Middleton, 1889-1957. 5. Koteliansky, Samuel Solomonovitch, 1880-1955. 6. Authors, English—20th century—Biography. I. Title.
Distributed by New Directions Publishing Corp., 333 Ave of the Americas, New York, NY 10014

Hastings, Henry Weysford Charles Plantagenet, 4th marquis of, 1842-1868.

BLYTH, Henry. 942.081'0922
The Pocket Venus, a Victorian scandal. New York, Walker [1967, c1966] xv, 301 p. illus., ports. 22 cm. Bibliography: p. 285-289. [DA565.H33B5 1967] 67-14564
1. Hastings, Henry Weysford Charles Plantagenet, 4th marquis of, 1842-1868. 2. Paget, Florence Cecilia, Lady, 1842-1907. 3. Chaplin, Henry Chaplin, 1st viscount, 1841-1923. 4. Horse-racing—Great Britain. I. Title.

Hastings, Warren, 1732-1818.

EDWARDES, 954.03'1'0924 B
Michael.
Warren Hastings : king of the Nabobs / Michael Edwardes. London : Hart-Davis, MacGibbon, 1976. 208 p., [1] leaf of plates : ill. ; 24 cm. Includes index. Bibliography: p. 200-201. [DS473.E38 1976] 77-351202 ISBN 0-246-10622-0 : £5.95
1. Hastings, Warren, 1732-1818. 2. Statesmen—India—Biography.

FEILING, Keith Grahame, 923.254
1884-
Warren Hastings. London, Macmillan; New York, St. Martin's Press, 1954. xi, 419p. illus., ports. 23cm. Bibliography: p.400-404. [DS473.F4] 54-3898
1. Hastings, Warren, 1732-1818. I. Title.

FEILING, Keith 954.03'1'0924 B
Grahame, Sir, 1884-
Warren Hastings, by Keith Feiling. Hamden, Conn., Archon Books, 1967. ix, 419 p. illus., map, ports. 23 cm. Bibliography: p. 400-404. [DS473.F4 1967] 67-1677
1. Hastings, Warren, 1732-1818.

LYALL, Alfred 954.03'1'0924
Comyn, Sir, 1835-1911.
Warren Hastings. Freeport, N.Y., Books for Libraries Press [1970] vi, 235 p. port. 23 cm. First published 1889. [DS473.L96 1970] 73-140364 ISBN 0-8369-5607-9
1. Hastings, Warren, 1732-1818.

MOON, Penderel [Full 923.254
name: Edward Penderel Moon] 1905-
Warren Hastings and British India. New York, Collier [1962] 224p. 18cm. (AS451V) Bibl. .95 pap.,
1. Hastings, Warren, 1732-1818. I. Title.

TROTTER, Lionel 954.03'1'0924 B
James, 1827-1912.
Warren Hastings. Freeport, N.Y., Books for Libraries Press [1972] 219 p. front. (fold. map) 23 cm. Reprint of the 1890 ed., issued in the series: Rulers of India. [DS473.T8 1972] 70-39407 ISBN 0-8369-9922-3
1. Hastings, Warren, 1732-1818. 2. India—History—British occupation, 1765-1947. I. Series: Rulers of India. BIP

Hatano, Satomi, 1931-

HATANO, Isoko (Hatakeyama) 920
1905-
Mother and son; the wartime correspondence of Isoko and Ichiro Hatano. [Tr. from the French ed. by Margaret Shenfield] Boston, Houghton [c.] 1962. 195p. illus. 22cm. 62-8141 3.75
1. Hatano, Satomi, 1931- I. Title.

Hatcher, Doris,

HATCHER, Doris, 917.4'03'40924
1904-
The education of Victoria Speyer. [1st ed.] Upper Black Eddy, Pa., Tinicum Press, 1969. 246 p. illus. 22 cm. Autobiography. [CT275.H443A3] 71-91468 5.00
I. Title.

Hatfield, Emmanuel, b. 1805.

HATFIELD, Emmanuel, 976 B
b.1805.
Stories of Hatfield, the pioneer, embracing a detailed account of his experience in the wilderness of east Tennessee, Kentucky, and southern Indiana / by Emmanuel Hatfield as told to E. Inman ; with a foreword by Fontella Hatfield Singley. Philadelphia : Dorrance, c1978. 130 p. : ill. ; 22 cm. Origianally published in 1889 by G. Fishback, New Albany, Ind. [F534.O97H3 1978] 78-105817 ISBN 0-8059-2524-4 : 6.95
1. Hatfield, Emmanuel, b. 1805. 2. Owensburg, Ind.—Biography. 3. Pioneers—Indiana—Owensburg—Biography. 4. Frontier and pioneer life—Ohio Valley. I. Inman, E. II. Title.

Hatfield, Mark O., 1922-

EELLS, Robert. 973.92'092'4 B
Lonely walk : the life of Senator Mark Hatfield / Robert Eells & Bartell Nyberg. Chappaqua, N.Y. : Christian Herald Books, c1979. 201 p. ; 24 cm. Includes index. Bibliography: p. 195-197. [E840.8.H3E34] 79-50942 ISBN 0-915684-49-7 : 8.95
1. Hatfield, Mark O., 1922- 2. United States. Congress. Senate—Biography. 3. Christianity and politics. 4. United States—Politics and government—1945- 5. Legislators—United States—Biography. 6. Baptists—United States—Biography. I. Nyberg, Bartell, joint author. II. Title. BIP

HATFIELD, Mark O., 973.92'092'4 B
1922-
Between a rock and a hard place / Mark Hatfield. Waco, Tex. : Word Books, c1976. 224 p. ; 23 cm. Includes bibliographical references. [E840.8.H3A27] 75-42906 ISBN 0-87680-427-X : 7.95
1. Hatfield, Mark O., 1922- 2. Christianity and politics. I. Title. BIP

Hathaway, David.

HATHAWAY, David. 266'.3'0924 B
Czech mate / David Hathaway. Old Tappan, N.J. : F. H. Revell Co., c1974. 187 p. ; 18 cm. Autobiographical. [BR1725.H245A33 1974] 75-6552 ISBN 0-8007-0742-7 pbk. : 1.95
1. Hathaway, David. 2. Bible—Publication and distribution—Europe, Eastern. 3. Prisoners—Czechoslovak Republic. I. Title.

Hathaway, Maggie (Smith) 1867-

TASCHER, Harold, 1900- 923.273
Maggie and Montana; the story of Maggie Smith Hathaway. [1st ed.] New York, Exposition Press [1954] 134p. illus. 21cm. [F731.H3T3] 54-5559

1. Hathaway, Maggie (Smith) 1867- I. Title.

Hatshepsut, Queen of Egypt.

WELLS, Evelyn. 932'.01'0924 B
Hatshepsut. [1st ed.] Garden City, N.Y., Doubleday [1969] 287 p. illus. 24 cm. Bibliography: p. 269-272. [DT87.2.W4] 69-10980 6.95
1. Hatshepsut, Queen of Egypt.

Hattersley, Roy.

HATTERSLEY, Roy. 942.8'1 B
Goodbye to Yorkshire / by Roy Hattersley. London : Gollancz, 1976. 163 p., [16] p. of plates : ill., map (on lining papers) ; 24 cm. Includes index. [DA670.Y6H37] 77-356811 ISBN 0-575-02201-9 : £4.75
1. Hattersley, Roy. 2. Yorkshire, Eng.—Description and travel. 3. Yorkshire, Eng.—Biography. I. Title.

Hatton, Christopher, Sir, 1540-1591.

VINES, Alice Gilmore. 942.05'5'0924 B
Neither fire nor steel : Sir Christopher Hatton / by Alice Gilmore Vines. Chicago : Nelson-Hall, [1977] p. cm. Includes index. Bibliography: p. [DA358.H3V56] 77-21424 ISBN 0-88229-372-9 : 13.95
1. Hatton, Christopher, Sir, 1540-1591. 2. Statesmen—Great Britain—Biography. 3. Great Britain—History—Elizabeth, 1558-1603. I. Title. **BIP**

Hauge, Hans Nielsen, 1771-1824.

ARDEN, Gothard Everett, 1905- 922.448
Four northern lights; men who shaped Scandinavian churches, by G. Everett Arden. Illus. by Hordan Lang. Minneapolis, Augsburg Pub. House [1964] 165 p. ports. 21 cm. "Originally presented as a series of lectures in connection with the twenty-fourth Luther Academy, held at Wartburg Theological Seminary, Dubuque, Iowa, during the summer of 1963." Includes bibliographies. [BX8079.A7] 64-21502
1. Ruotsalainen, Paavo, 1777-1852. 2. Hauge, Hans Nielsen, 1771-1824. 3. Grundtvig, Nikolal Frederik Severin, 1783-1872. 4. Rosenius, Carl Olof, 1916-1868. I. Title.

SHAW, Joseph M 922.4481
Pulpit under the sky; a life of Hans Nielsen Hauge. Minneapolis, Augsburg Pub. House [1955] 250p. 22cm. [BX8080.H3S44] 55-9787
1. Hauge, Hans Nielsen, 1771-1824. I. Title.

SHAW, Joseph M. 284'.1'0924 B
Pulpit under the sky : a life of Hans Nielsen Hauge / by Joseph M. Shaw. Westport, Conn. : Greenwood Press, 1979, c1955. xii, 250 p. ; 23 cm. Reprint of the ed. published by Augsburg Pub. House, Minneapolis. Includes index. Bibliography: p. 245-246. [BX8080.H3S44 1979] 78-12391 ISBN 0-313-21123-X lib. bdg. : 18.50
1. Hauge, Hans Nielsen, 1771-1824. 2. Lutherans—Norway—Biography. 3. Evangelists—Norway—Biography. I. Title.

Haughery, Margaret (Gaffney) 1813-1882—Juvenile literature.

STROUSSE, Flora, 1897- 923.673
Margaret Haughery; bread woman of New Orleans. Illus. by Lili Rethi. New York, P. J. Kenedy [c.1961] 190p. (American background books [17]) Bibl. 61-7971 2.50
1. Haughery, Margaret (Gaffney) 1813-1882—Juvenile literature. I. Title.

Hauk, Minnie, 1852-1929.

HAUK, Minnie, 1852-1929. 782.1'092'4 B
Memories of a singer / Minnie Hauk. New York : Arno Press, 1977. 295, [15] leaves of plates : ill. ; 23 cm. (Opera biographies) Reprint of the 1925 ed. published by A. M. Philpot, London. [ML420.H23A3 1977] 76-29938 ISBN 0-405-09680-1 : 20.00
1. Hauk, Minnie, 1852-1929. 2. Singers—Biography. I. Title. **BIP**

Haupt, Herman, 1817-1905.

WARD, James Arthur, 1941- 625.1'0092'4 B
That man Haupt; a biography of Herman Haupt [by] James A. Ward. Baton Rouge, Louisiana State University Press [1973] xvi, 278 p. 24 cm. Bibliography: p. [251]-272. [TA140.H38W37] 73-82420 ISBN 0-8071-0225-3 11.95
1. Haupt, Herman, 1817-1905. I. Title. **BIP**

Hauptmann, Bruno Richard, 1899-1936.

SCADUTO, Anthony. 364.1'54'0924 B
Scapegoat : the lonesome death of Bruno Richard Hauptmann / by Anthony Scaduto. New York : Putnam, c1976. 512 p., [8] leaves of plates : ill. ; 24 cm. Includes index. [HV6603.L5S3] 76-15205 ISBN 0-399-11660-5 12.50
1. Hauptmann, Bruno Richard, 1899-1936. 2. Lindbergh, Charles Augustus, 1930-1932. 3. Kidnapping—New Jersey. I. Title. **BIP**

Hauptmann, Gerhart Johann Robert, 1862-1946.

GERHART Hauptmann, v. 12
his life and work. Translated by Helen Taubert. Wurzburg, Holzner [1956] 60p. 19cm. (Goettingen Research Committee. Publication no. 153)
1. Hauptmann, Gerhart Johann Robert, 1862-1946. I. Behl, Carl Friedrich Wilhelm, 1889- II. Series: Gottinger Arbeiterkreis. Publications, no. 153

HOLL, Karl, 1886- 832'.8
Gerhart Hauptmann; his life and his work, 1862-1912. Freeport, N.Y., Books for Libraries Press [1972] x, 112 p. port. 22 cm. Reprint of the 1913 ed. Bibliography: p. 105-108. [PT2616.Z9H6 1972] 72-7083 ISBN 0-8369-6941-3
1. Hauptmann, Gerhart Johann Robert, 1862-1946. I. Title.

HOLL, Karl, 1886- 832'.8
Gerhart Hauptmann; his life and his work, 1862-1912. [Folcroft, Pa.] Folcroft Library Editions, 1973. x, 112 p. ports. 24 cm. Reprint of the 1913 ed. published by A. C. McClurg, Chicago. Bibliography: p. 105-108. [PT2616.Z9H6 1973] 73-4013 ISBN 0-8414-2078-5
1. Hauptmann, Gerhart Johann Robert, 1862-1946.

POHL, Gerhart, 1902- 928.3
Gerhart Hauptmann and Silesia; a report on the German dramatist's last days in his occupied homeland. Tr. from German by William I. Morgan. Introd. by Erich Funke. Grand Forks, Univ. of N. Dak. Pr., [c.]1962. xii, 82p. illus., map 24cm. 62-3926 1.50
1. Hauptmann, Gerhart Johann Robert, 1862-1946. I. Title.

Hauptmann, Moritz, 1792-1868.

HAUPTMANN, Moritz, 1792-1868. 780'.92'4 B
The letters of a Leipzig cantor; being the letters of Moritz Hauptmann to Franz Hauser, Ludwig Spohr, and other musicians. Edited by Alfred Schone and Ferdinand Hiller. Translated and arranged by A. D. Coleridge. New York, Vienna House, 1972. 2 v. 23 cm. Reprint of the 1892 ed. "A catalogue of the published compositions of Moritz Hauptmann": v. 2, p. [288]-296. [ML410.H37H6 1972] 75-163789 ISBN 0-8443-0008-X (v. 2)
1. Hauptmann, Moritz, 1792-1868. 2. Composers—Correspondence, reminiscences, etc. I. Title.

Hausman, Jim.

HAUSMAN, Jim. 977.1'78'040924 B
When I was a boy / by Jim Hausman. Lincoln, Neb. : Centennial Press, c1976. 48 p. : ill. ; 23 cm. Portions originally appeared in the Cincinnati enquirer in 1973. [F499.C5H37] 76-375578 ISBN 0-8220-1624-9 pbk. : 1.95
1. Hausman, Jim. 2. Cincinnati—Biography. I. Title. **BIP**

Havemann, Robert.

HAVEMANN, Robert. 322.4'4'0924 B
Questions, answers, questions; from the biography of a German Marxist. Translated from the German by Salvator Attanasio. [1st ed.] Garden City, N.Y., Doubleday, 1972. 255 p. 22 cm. Translation of Fragen, Antworten, Fragen. [HX273.H3713] 70-182839 7.95
I. Title.

Haven, Gilbert, Bp., 1821-1880.

GRAVELY, William, 1939- 287'.632'0924 B
Gilbert Haven, Methodist abolitionist; a study in race, religion, and reform, 1850-1880. Edited by the Commission on Archives and History of the United Methodist Church. Nashville, Abingdon Press [1973] 272 p. illus. 24 cm. Bibliography: p. 258-263. [BX8495.H28G7] 72-14179 ISBN 0-687-14702-6 8.95
1. Haven, Gilbert, Bp., 1821-1880. 2. Slavery in the United States. 3. Church and race problems—United States. I. United Methodist Church (United States). Commission on Archives and History.

Havlicek, John, 1940-

HAVLICEK, John, 1940- 796.32'3'0924 B
Hondo : Celtic man in motion / by John Havlicek and Bob Ryan. Englewood Cliffs, N.J. : Prentice-Hall, c1977. 192 p., [16] leaves of plates : ill. ; 22 cm. [GV884.H27A34] 76-53719 ISBN 0-13-394601-0 : 8.95
1. Havlicek, John, 1940- 2. Basketball players—United States—Biography. 3. Basketball. I. Ryan, Bob. II. Title.

Havlicek, John, 1940- —Juvenile literature.

BRAUN, Thomas, 1944- 796.32'3'0924 B
John Havlicek / by Thomas Braun ; illustrated by John Keely. Mankato, Minn. : Creative Education, [1976] p. cm. A brief biography of the Boston Celtic whose sports versatility almost led him into a football career. [GV884.H27B72] 92 75-34489 ISBN 0-87191-498-0
1. Havlicek, John, 1940- —Juvenile literature. 2. Boston Celtics (Basketball team)—Juvenile literature. 3. Basketball—Juvenile literature. I. Keely, John. II. Title. **BIP**

Havner, Vance,

HAVNER, Vance, 1901- 286'.1'0924 B
Three-score & ten. Old Tappan, N.J., F. H. Revell Co. [1973] 127 p. front. 21 cm. Autobiographical. [BX6495.H288A33] 72-10390 ISBN 0-8007-0578-5 4.95
I. Title. **BIP**

Havner, Vance, 1901-

WHITE, Douglas Malcolm, 1909- 286'.1'0924 B
Vance Havner, journey from Jugtown : a biography / by Douglas M. White. Old Tappan, N.J. : F. H. Revell Co., c1977. 192 p. ; ill. ; 21 cm. [BV3785.H392W48] 77-9458 ISBN 0-8007-0893-8 : 6.95
1. Havner, Vance, 1901- 2. Evangelists—United States—Biography. I. Title.

Havoc, June

HAVOC, June 927.92
Early Havoc. [New York] Dell [1960, c.1959] 319p. (F110) .50 pap.,
I. Title.

HAVOC, June. 927.92
Early Havoc. New York, Simon and Schuster, 1959. 313 p. illus. 21 cm. [PN2287.H33A3] 59-6012
I. Title.

Hawaii—Biog.—Juvenile literature.

CURTIS, Caroline 996.9020922
Builders of Hawaii. Honolulu, Kamehameha Schools Pr., 1966. x, 266p. illus., ports. 23cm. [DU624.9.C8] 66-6314 4.25
1. Hawaii—Biog.—Juvenile literature. 2. Missions—Hawaii—Juvenile literature. I. Title.

Hawaii—Kings and rulers.

BAILEY, Paul Dayton, 1906- 996.9'00992 B
Those kings and queens of old Hawaii : a mele to their memory / by Paul Bailey. Los Angeles : Westernlore Books, 1975. 381 p. : ill., ports. ; 24 cm. Includes index. Bibliography: p. 373-374. [DU624.9.B34] 75-259 ISBN 0-87026-035-9 : 11.95
1. Hawaii—Kings and rulers. 2. Hawaii—History. I. Title.

Hawes, Hampton, 1928-

HAWES, Hampton, 1928- 786.1'092'4 B
Raise up off me / by Hampton Hawes and Don Asher. New York : Coward, McCann & Geoghegan, [1974] 179 p. ; 22 cm. [ML417.H27A3] 73-93765 ISBN 0-698-10590-7 : 7.95
1. Hawes, Hampton, 1928- 2. Musicians—Correspondence, reminiscences, etc. I. Asher, Don, joint author. II. Title.

Hawes, Jerome. 1876-1956.

ANSON, Peter Frederick, 1880- 922.242
The hermit of Cat Island; the life of Fra Jerome Hawes. New York, P. J. Kenedy [1957] 286p. illus. 21cm. [BX4705.H336A6] 57-10096
1. Hawes, Jerome. 1876-1956. I. Title.

ANSON, Peter Frederick, 1889- 922.242
The hermit of Cat Island; the life of Fra Jerome Hawes. New York, P.J.Kenedy [1957] 286p. illus. 21cm. [BX4705.H336A6] 57-10096
1. Hawes, Jerome, 1876-1956. I. Title.

Hawk, John Chrisman.

SAUNDERS, Mary Ellen Hawk. 266'.87'1
Unfinished business in China. Pacific Palisades, Calif., Pan Pacific Centers 1972, [i.e. 1973] xii, 238 p. illus. 20 cm. Bibliography: p. 234-238. [BV3427.H27S28] 73-163413 3.25
1. Hawk, John Chrisman. 2. Hawk, Jean Buchanan. I. Title.

Hawker, Beatrice,

HAWKER, Beatrice, 1910- 922
Look back in love. Illustrated by Rosemary Haughton. London, New York, Longmans, Green [1958] 149p. illus. 21cm. Autobiographical. [BR1725.H25A3] 59-2029
I. Title.

Hawker, Charles Allan Seymour—Juvenile literature.

PIKE, Douglas Henry, 1908- 994'.2'040924 B
Charles Hawker. Melbourne, New York [etc.] Oxford University Press [1968] 30 p. illus. 19 cm. (Great Australians) A profile of Australian statesman, Charles Hawker, who despite a severe physical handicap lived a productive life as a public and private citizen. [DU322.H3P5] 92 74-409418 unpriced
1. Hawker, Charles Allan Seymour—Juvenile literature. I. Title.

Hawker, Lanoe George, 1890-1916.

HAWKER, Tyrrel Mann 940.449420924
Hawker, V. C.; the biography of the late Major Lanoe George Hawker, V. C., D. S. O., Royal Engineers and Royal Flying Corps. London, Mitre Pr. [New York, Heinman, 1965] xiv,253p. illus., ports. 23cm. [TL540.H32H3] 65-82746 8.50
1. Hawker, Lanoe George, 1890-1916. I. Title.

Hawkes, Herbert Edwin, 1872-1943.

WELD, William Ernest, 923.773
1881-
Herbert E. Hawkes, dean of Columbia College, 1918-1943, by William Ernest Weld and Kathryn W. Sewny. New York, Columbia University Press, 1958. 171 p. illus. 21 cm. [LD1246.H3W4] 58-13991
1. Hawkes, Herbert Edwin, 1872-1943. I. Sewny, Kathryn W., joint author. II. Title.

Hawkins, Anthony Hope, Sir, 1863-1933.

MALLET, Charles Edward, v. 12
Sir, 1862-1947.
Anthony Hope and his books; being the authorized life of Sir Anthony Hope Hawkins. Port Washington, N.Y., Kennikat Press [1968] 290 p. illus., ports. 22 cm. Reprint of the 1935 ed. [PR4763.M3 1968] 68-16280
1. Hawkins, Anthony Hope, Sir, 1863-1933.

Hawkins, Connie, 1942-

WOLF, Dave. 796.32'3'0924 B
Foul! The Connie Hawkins story, by David Wolf. [1st ed.] New York, Holt, Rinehart and Winston [1972] xi, 400 p. 24 cm. [GV884.H3W6] 71-117279 7.95
1. Hawkins, Connie, 1942- I. Title. BIP

Hawkins, Jack, 1910-1973.

HAWKINS, Jack, 791.43'028'0924
1910-1973.
Anything for a quiet life; the autobiography of Jack Hawkins. With a postscript by Doreen Hawkins. New York, Stein and Day [1974, c1973] 180 p. illus. 24 cm. [PN2598.H346A3 1974] 74-78527 ISBN 0-8128-1708-7 7.95
1. Hawkins, Jack, 1910-1973. I. Title.

Hawkins, John, Sir, 1532-1595.

WILLIAMSON, James 942.05'5'0924 B
Alexander, 1886-
Hawkins of Plymouth; a new history of Sir John Hawkins and of the other members of his family prominent in Tudor England, by James A. Williamson. 2d ed. New York, Barnes & Noble [1969] xi, 348 p. illus., facsims., maps, ports. 23 cm. Bibliographical footnotes. [DA86.22.H3W49 1969b] 72-7944
1. Hawkins, John, Sir, 1532-1595. I. Title.

WILLIAMSON, James 359.3'3'10924
Alexander, 1886-
Sir John Hawkins; the time and the man, by James A. Williamson. Westport, Conn., Greenwood Press [1970] xii, 542 p. illus., facsims., maps, ports. 23 cm. Reprint of the 1927 ed. Includes bibliographical references. [DA86.22.H3W5 1970] 77-110885 ISBN 0-8371-4569-4
1. Hawkins, John, Sir, 1532-1595. 2. Gt. Brit.—History, Naval—Tudors, 1485-1603.

Hawkins, John, Sir, 1719-1789.

DAVIS, Bertram 828'.6'09 B
Hylton.
Johnson before Boswell; a study of Sir John Hawkin's Life of Samuel Johnson, by Bertram H. Davis. Westport, Conn., Greenwood Press [1973, c1957] xi, 222 p. 22 cm. Reprint of the ed. published by Yale University Press, New Haven. Bibliography: p. 198-206. [PR3533.H32D3 1973] 72-12309 ISBN 0-8371-6691-8 10.25
1. Hawkins, John, Sir, 1719-1789. The life of Samuel Johnson, LL.D. 2. Johnson, Samuel, 1709-1784. I. Hawkins, John, Sir, 1719-1789. The life of Samuel Johnson, LL.D. II. Title.

DAVIS, Bertram 347'.42'0234 B
Hylton.
A proof of eminence; the life of Sir John Hawkins [by] Bertram H. Davis. Bloomington, Indiana University Press [1972, c1973] xii, 436 p. illus. 25 cm. Includes bibliographical references. [CT788.H378D38 1973] 72-75389 ISBN 0-253-34617-7 10.00
1. Hawkins, John, Sir, 1719-1789. I. Title. BIP

SCHOLES, Percy 780'.92'4 B
Alfred, 1877-1958.
The life and activities of Sir John Hawkins, musician, magistrate, and friend of Johnson / Percy A. Scholes. New York : Da Capo Press, 1978, c1953. xiii, 287 p., [8] leaves of plates : ill. ; 23 cm. (Da Capo Press music reprint series) Reprint of the ed. published by Oxford University Press, London, New York. "Books and articles by Hawkins and his family": p. [231]-237. [ML423.H3964S3 1978] 77-26652 ISBN 0-306-77571-9 : 22.50
1. Hawkins, John, Sir, 1719-1789. 2. Musician—England—Biography.

Hawkins, Latitia Matilda, 1760-1835.

HAWKINS, Latitia 941.07'3'0924 B
Matilda, 1760-1835.
Gossip about Dr. Johnson and others : being chapters from the memoirs of Miss Latitia Matilda Hawkins / edited by Francis Henry Skrine. Folcroft, Pa. : Folcroft Library Editions, 1977. p. cm Reprint of the 1926 ed. published by E. Nash and Grayson, London. [CT788.H38A25 1977] 77-10159 ISBN 0-8414-7876-7 lib. bdg. : 25.00
1. Hawkins, Latitia Matilda, 1760-1835. 2. Johnson, Samuel, 1709-1784—Biography. 3. England—Biography. 4. Authors, English—18th century—Biography. I. Title.

Hawkins, Sir John, 1719-1789.

SCHOLES, Percy Alfred, 927.8
1877-
The life and activities of Sir John Hawkins, musician, magistrate, and friend of Johnson. London, New York, Oxford University Press, 1953. xiii, 287p. illus., ports., facsims. 23cm. 'Books and articles by Hawkins and his family': p.[231]-237. [ML423.H3964S3] 53-7827
1. Hawkins, Sir John, 1719-1789. I. Title. BIP

Hawks, Howard, 1896-

WOOD, Robin. 791.43'0233'0924
Howard Hawks. Garden City, N.Y., Doubleday, 1968. 200 p. illus., port. 20 cm. (Cinema world, 7) [PN1998.A3H355 1968b] 68-23754 4.95
1. Hawks, Howard, 1896-

Hawksworth, Henry.

HAWKSWORTH, Henry. 616.8'523 B
The five of me : the autobiography of a multiple personality / Henry Hawksworth, with Ted Schwarz ; introduction by Ralph Allison. Chicago : Regnery, c1977. viii, 289 p. ; 24 cm. [RC569.5.M8H38 1977] 76-55662 ISBN 0-8092-7869-3 : 9.95
1. Hawksworth, Henry. 2. Multiple personality—Biography. I. Schwarz, Theodore, joint author. II. Title.

HAWKSWORTH, Henry. 616.8'523 B
The five of me : the autobiography of a multiple personality / Henry Hawksworth, With Ted schwarz ; introduction by Ralph Allison. New York : Pocket Books, 1978,c1977. 238 p. ; 18 cm. [RC569.5M8H38] ISBN 0-671-81880-5 pbk. : 1.95
1. Hawksworth, Henry. 2. Multiple personality- -Biography. I. Schwarz, Ted, joint author. II. Title.
L.C. card no. for 1977 Regnery ed. [i.e.] Contemporary Books ed 76-55662 BIP

Hawley, James Henry, 1847-1929.

MACLANE, John Fisher, 923.473
1878-
A sagebrush lawyer. [New York] Priv. print. [1953] 177p. illus. 24cm. 53-24150
1. Hawley, James Henry, 1847-1929. 2. Lawyers—Idaho—Correspondence, reminiscences, etc. 3. Idaho—Pol. & govt. I. Title.

Hawley, Joseph,

BROWN, Ernest Francis, v. 12
1903-
Joseph Hawley, colonial radical. New York, AMS Press, 1966 [1931] 213 p. Bibliography: p. [193]-207. 68-85753
1. Hawley, Joseph, 2. Massachusetts—Hist.—Colonial period. I. Title. BIP

Hawley, Nero, d. 1817.

BEACH, E. Merrill. 973.3'092'4 B
From Valley Forge to freedom : a story of a Black patriot / by E. Merrill Beach. 1st ed. Chester, Conn. : Pequot Press, [1975] 69 p. : ill. ; 24 cm. Bibliography: p. 67-69. [E444.H38B42] 75-5028 ISBN 0-87106-056-6 : 6.00
1. Hawley, Nero, d. 1817. 2. Valley Forge, Pa. 3. United States—History—Revolution, 1775-1783—Afro-American soldiers. I. Title.

Hawthorne, Charles Webster, 1872-1930.

HAWTHORNE retrospective. v. 12
[Exhibition] June 16 through September 17, 1961. Provincetown, 1961. 72p. illus. Introduction by E. P. Richardson.
1. Hawthorne, Charles Webster, 1872-1930. I. Chrysler Art Museum, Provincetown, Mass. II. Richardson, Edgar Preston, 1902-

Hawthorne, Julian, 1846-1934.

BASSAN, Maurice. 813'.4 B
Hawthorne's son: the life and literary career of Julian Hawthorne. Columbus, Ohio State University Press [1970] xix, 284 p. geneal. table, port. 24 cm. Bibliography: p. 259-274. [PS1848.B3] 70-83142 10.00
1. Hawthorne, Julian, 1846-1934. I. Title. BIP

Hawthorne, Nathaniel, 1804-1864.

ARVIN, Newton [Frederic 928.1
Newton Arvin] 1900-
Hawthorne. New York, Russell & Russell, 1961 [c.1929, 1956] 303p. illus. 61-12123 7.50
1. Hawthorne, Nathaniel, 1804-1864. I. Title. BIP

BRIDGE, Horatio, 1806- 818'.3'09
1893.
Personal recollections of Nathaniel Hawthorne. New York, Haskell House, 1968. ix, 200 p. illus., ports. 23 cm. Reprint of the 1893 ed. Based on three papers first published in Harper's magazine. [PS1881.B7 1968] 68-24931
1. Hawthorne, Nathaniel, 1804-1864. I. Title. BIP

CONWAY, Moncure Daniel, 813'.3 B
1832-1907.
Life of Nathaniel Hawthorne. New York, Haskell House, 1968. 224, xiii p. port. 23 cm. Reprint of the 1890 ed. "Bibliography by John P. Anderson": p. [i]-xiii. [PS1881.C6 1968] 68-24935
1. Hawthorne, Nathaniel, 1804-1864. I. Title. BIP

CROWLEY, Joseph Donald. 813'.3
Nathaniel Hawthorne, by J. Donald Crowley. New York, Humanities Press [1971] x, 101 p. 19 cm. (The Profiles in literature series) Bibliography: p. 96-101. [PS1881.C74] 70-24190 ISBN 0-391-00164-7 3.75
1. Hawthorne, Nathaniel, 1804-1864.

DHALEINE, L., 1870- 813'.3
N. Hawthorne, sa vie et son ouvre, par L. Dhaleine. Paris, Hachette, 1905. [New York, AMS Press, 1972] 510 p. 23 cm. These—Paris. [PS1881.D5 1972] 77-164828 ISBN 0-404-02122-0 18.50
1. Hawthorne, Nathaniel, 1804-1864.

HAWTHORNE, Nathaniel, 813'.3 S
1804-1864.
The American notebooks / Nathaniel Hawthorne ; edited by Claude M. Simpson. [Columbus] : Ohio State University Press, c1972. xiii, 835 p., [2] leaves of plates : ill. ; 25 cm. (The Centenary edition of the works of Nathaniel Hawthorne ; v. 8) Includes bibliographical references and index. [PS1850.F63 vol. 8] [PS1865] 818'.3'03 70-150222 ISBN 0-8142-0159-8
1. Hawthorne, Nathaniel, 1804-1864. 2. New England—Description and travel—1775-1865. I. Simpson, Claude Mitchell, 1910- II. Title. BIP

HAWTHORNE, Nathaniel, 813'.3
1804-1864.
Letters of Hawthorne to William D. Ticknor, 1851-1864. Foreword by C. E. Frazer Clark, Jr. Newark, N.J., Carteret Book Club, 1910. [Washington] NCR Microcard Editions, 1972. x, 123, 130 p. facsims. 24 cm. "A Bruccoli-Clark book." [PS1881.A4 1972] 72-76250 ISBN 0-910972-19-2 10.00
1. Hawthorne, Nathaniel, 1804-1864. 2. Ticknor, William Davis, 1810-1864. I. Ticknor, William Davis, 1810-1864. BIP

HAWTHORNE, Nathaniel, 813'.3 B
1804-1864.
Love letters of Nathaniel Hawthorne, 1839-1863. Foreword by C. E. Frazer Clark, Jr. Chicago, Priv. print., Society of the Dofobs, 1907 [Washington] NCR Microcard Editions, 1972. 2 v. in 1. port. 24 cm. "A Bruccoli-Clark book." [PS1881.A3 1972] 72-76251 ISBN 0-910972-18-4
1. Hawthorne, Nathaniel, 1804-1864. 2. Hawthorne, Sophia Amelia (Peabody) 1811-1871. BIP

HOELTJE, Hubert H., 1898- 928.1
Inward sky; the mind and heart of Nathaniel Hawthorne. Durham, N.C., Duke University Press, 1962. 579 p. illus. 24 cm. Includes bibliography. [PS1881.H6 1962] 62-10052
1. Hawthorne, Nathaniel, 1804-1864. I. Title.

JAMES, Henry, 1843-1916. 813'.3 B
Hawthorne. New York, AMS Press [1968] vi, 183 p. 22 cm. (English men of letters) [PS1881.J3 1968b] 68-58383
1. Hawthorn, Nathaniel, 1804-1864.

JAMES, Henry, 1843-1916. v. 12
Hawthorne. With an introd. by Quentin Anderson. New York, Collier Books [1966] 155 p. 67-104677
1. Hawthorne, Nathaniel, 1804-1864. I. Title. BIP

LATHROP, George Parsons, 813'.3
1851-1898.
A study of Hawthorne. New York, AMS Press [1969] 350 p. 23 cm. Reprint of the 1876 ed. [PS1881.L35 1969] 70-86168
1. Hawthorne, Nathaniel, 1804-1864. I. Title. BIP

MANLEY, Seon. 813'.3 B
Nathaniel Hawthorne; captain of the imagination. New York, Vanguard Press [1968] 257 p. illus., ports. 24 cm. Bibliography: p. [245]-253. [PS1881.M27] 69-10907 4.95
1. Hawthorne, Nathaniel, 1804-1864.

MATHER Jackson, Edward 813'.3 B
Arthur, 1899-
Nathaniel Hawthorne, a modest man [by] Edward Mather. Westport, Conn., Greenwood Press [1970, c1940] viii, 356 p. illus., ports. 23 cm. Bibliography: p. [341]-345. [PS1881.M3 1970] 77-110834 ISBN 0-8371-2594-4
1. Hawthorne, Nathaniel, 1804-1864. BIP

MORRIS, Lloyd R., 1893- 813'.3
1954.
The rebellious Puritan; portrait of Mr. Hawthorne. Port Washington, N.Y., Kennikat Press [1969, c1955] viii, 369 p. illus., ports. 22 cm. Bibliography: p. vii-viii. [PS1881.M6 1969] 77-86048 ISBN 8-04-606315-

1. Hawthorne, Nathaniel, 1804-1864. I. Title.

PICKARD, Samuel Thomas, 1828-1915. 818'.3'03 B
Hawthorne's first diary, with an account of its discovery and loss. Boston, Houghton, Mifflin, 1897. New York, Haskell House Publishers, 1972. vi, 115 p. illus. 23 cm. [PS1882.A3 1972] 72-285 ISBN 0-8383-1408-2 6.95
1. Hawthorne, Nathaniel, 1804-1864. I. Title.

†STEARNS, Frank Preston, 1846-1917. 813'.3 B
The life and genius of Nathaniel Hawthorne / by Frank Preston Stearns. Folcroft, Pa. : Folcroft Library Editions, 1976. 463 p., [9] leaves of plates : ill. ; 23 cm. Reprint of the 1906 ed. published by Lippincott, Philadelphia. Includes bibliographical references and index. [PS1881.S65 1976] 76-40459 ISBN 0-8414-7710-8 lib. bdg. : 35.00
1. Hawthorne, Nathaniel, 1804-1864. 2. Novelists, American—19th century—Biography. I. Title. **BIP**

STEWART, Randall, 1896- v. 12
Nathaniel Hawthorne, a biography. New Haven, Yale University Press [1961] 279 p. 20 cm. (A Yale paperbound) Bibliography: p. [266]-268.
1. Hawthorne, Nathaniel, 1804-1864. I. Title.

STEWART, Randall, 1896-1964. 813'.3 B
Nathaniel Hawthorne, a biography. [Hamden, Conn.] Archon Books, 1970, [c1948] 279 p. 22 cm. Bibliography: p. [266]-268. [PS1881.S67 1970] 74-114425
1. Hawthorne, Nathaniel, 1804-1864. **BIP**

VAN DOREN, Mark, 1894- v. 12
Nathaniel Hawthorne. New York, Viking Press [1957] 279 p. port. 22 cm. (Compass Books edition) "Bibliographical note": p. 268-272.
1. Hawthorne, Nathaniel, 1804-1864. I. Title. II. Series. **BIP**

WAGENKENCHT, Edward [Charles] 1900- 928.1
Nathaniel Hawthorne: man and writer. New York, Oxford University Press [c.] 1961. 233p. Front. Bibl. 61-6301 5.50
1. Hawthrone, Nathaniel, 1804-1864. I. Title.

WOODBERRY, George Edward, 1855-1930. 813'.3 B
Nathaniel Hawthorne. Detroit, Gale Research Co., 1967 [c1902] 302 p. port. 23 cm. (The Gale library of lives and letters. American writers series) Title page includes original imprint: Boston, Houghton. Mifflin [1902] [PS1881.W6 1967] 67-23888
1. Hawthorne, Nathaniel, 1804-1864. **BIP**

Hawthorne, Nathaniel, 1804-1864—Biography.

FIELDS, Annie Adams, 1834-1915. 813'.3 B
Nathaniel Hawthorne. [Folcroft, Pa.] Folcroft Library Editions, 1974 [c1899] xv, 136 p. illus. 21 cm. Reprint of the ed. published by Small, Maynard, Boston, in series: The Beacon biographies of eminent Americans. Bibliography: p. [133]-136. [PS1881.F5 1974b] 74-11032 ISBN 0-8414-4224-X (lib. bdg.)
1. Hawthorne, Nathaniel, 1804-1864—Biography. I. Series: The Beacon biographies of eminent Amerians. (Boston)

HAWTHORNE, Julian, 1846-1934. 813'.3 B
Nathaniel Hawthorne and his wife; a biography. [Hamden, Conn.] Archon Books, 1968. 2 v. illus., ports. 21 cm. Reprint of the 1884 ed. [PS1881.H35 1968] 68-20383
1. Hawthorne, Nathaniel, 1804-1864—Biography. 2. Hawthorne, Sophia Amelia (Peabody) 1811-1871. I. Title. **BIP**

HAWTHORNE, Julian, 1846-1934. 813'.3
Nathaniel Hawthorne and his wife; a biography. 2d ed. Boston, J. R. Osgood, 1885 [c1884]; Grosse Pointe, Mich., Scholarly Press, 1968. 2 v. illus., ports. 20 cm. [PS1881.H35 1968] 72-3665
1. Hawthorne, Nathaniel, 1804-1864—Biography. 2. Hawthorne, Sophia Amelia (Peabody) 1811-1871. I. Title.

LEWIN, Walter. 813'.3 B
Nathaniel Hawthorne / by Walter Lewin. Folcroft, Pa. : Folcroft Library Editions, 1977. 44 p. : port. ; 18 cm. Reprint of the 1906 ed. published by Hodder and Stoughton, London. [PS1881.L46 1977] 77-9015 ISBN 0-8414-5822-7 lib. bdg. : 10.00
1. Hawthorne, Nathaniel, 1804-1864—Biography. 2. Novelists, American—19th century—Biography. I. Title.

Hawthorne, Nathaniel, 1804-1864—Juvenile literature.

WOOD, James Playsted, 1905- 813'.3 B
The unpardonable sin; a life of Nathaniel Hawthorne. [New York] Pantheon Books [1970] 180 p. illus., ports. 22 cm. (A Pantheon portrait) Bibliography: p. 179-180. The life of the early nineteenth-century author whose New England heritage served as a theme for his works. [PS1881.W57] 92 71-117461
1. Hawthorne, Nathaniel, 1804-1864—Juvenile literature. I. Title. **BIP**

Hay, David, 1909-

HAY, David, 1909- 942.7'86
Mardale, the drowned village : being a Lakeland journey into yesterday / by David and Joan Hay. [Kendal] : Friends of the Lake District, 1976. 80, [1] p., [12] p. of plates : ill., maps, ports. ; 22 cm. Bibliography: p. 76-77. [DA690.M418H38] 77-370255 ISBN 0-9504629-0-X : £1.50
1. Hay, David, 1909- 2. Hay, Joan Frances Doulton. 3. Mardale, Eng.—History. 4. Mardale, Eng.—Biography. I. Hay, Joan Frances Doulton, joint author. II. Title.

Hay, John,

HAY, John, 1838-1905. 973.8'0924
Letters of John Hay and extracts from diary. New York, Gordian Press, 1969. 3 v. 24 cm. "Printed but not published, 1908." [E664.H41A4 1969] 71-93245

Hay, John, 1838-1905.

BROWN University. Library. 923.273
The life and works of John Hay, 1838-1905; a commemorative catalogue of the exhibition shown at the John hay Library of Brown University in honor of the centennial of his graduation at the commencement of 1858. Providence, R. I. [Brown Univ. Press, c.1961] xii, 51p. illus. 61-3289 2.00 bds.,
1. Hay, John, 1838-1905. I. Title.

CLYMER, Kenton J. 327'.2'0924 B
John Hay : the gentleman as diplomat / Kenton J. Clymer. Ann Arbor : University of Michigan Press, c1975. ix, 314 p. : ill. ; 24 cm. Includes index. Bibliography: p. 287-302. [E664.H41C55 1975] 74-78986 ISBN 0-472-23400-5 : 15.00
1. Hay, John, 1838-1905. **BIP**

GALE, Robert L. 818'.4'09
John Hay / by Robert L. Gale. Boston : Twayne Publishers, c1978. 164 p. : port. ; 22 cm. (Twayne's United States authors series ; TUSAS 296) Includes index. Bibliography: p. 147-155. [PS1903.G3] 77-27650 ISBN 0-8057-7199-9 : 9.50
1. Hay, John, 1838-1905. 2. Authors, American—19th century—Biography. 3. Statesmen—United States—Biography. **BIP**

HAY, John, 1838-1905. 973.8'0924
Letters of John Hay and extracts from diary. New York, Gordian Press, 1969. 3 v. 24 cm. "Printed but not published, 1908." [E664.H41A4 1969] 71-93245

KUSHNER, Howard I. 327'.2'0924 B
John Milton Hay / Howard I. Kushner and Anne Hummel Sherrill. Boston : Twayne Publishers, c1977. p. cm. (Twayne's world leaders series ; TWLS 69) Includes bibliographical references and index. [E664.H41K87] 77-7955 ISBN 0-8057-7186-7 lib.bdg. : 9.95
1. Hay, John, 1838-1905. 2. Statesmen—United States—Biography. 3. United States—Foreign relations—1865-1921. 4. United States—Politics and government—1865-1900. I. Sherrill, Anne Hummel, joint author. II. Title. III. Series. **BIP**

Hayden, Melissa.

GUSTAITIS, Rasa. 792.82'0924 B
Melissa Hayden, ballerina. London, New York, Nelson [1967] 127 p. illus., ports. 22 cm. "A Rutledge book." [GV1785.H35G8] 67-3192
1. Hayden, Melissa. I. Title.

Hayden, Sterling.

HAYDEN, Sterling 927.92
Wanderer. New York, Bantam [1964, c.1963] 407p. 18cm. (W2864) .85 pap.,
1. Actors—Correspondence, reminiscences, etc. I. Title. **BIP**

HAYDEN, Sterling. 791.43'028'0924 B
Wanderer / Sterling Hayden. New York : Norton, [1977] c1963. p. cm. [PN2287.H34A3 1977] 77-14097 10.95
1. Hayden, Sterling. 2. Actors—United States—Biography. I. Title.

HAYDEN, Sterling. 791.43'028'0924
Wanderer / Sterling Hayden. New York : Avon Books, 1978,c1977. 407p. ; 18 cm. [PN2287.H34A3] [[B]] ISBN 0-380-39834-6 pbk. : 2.50
1. Hayden, Sterling. 2. Actors — United States — Biography. I. Title.
L.C. card no. for 1977 W.W. Norton ed.: 77-14097.

Hayden, William,

HAYDEN, William, b.1785. 301.45'22'0924 B
Narrative of William Hayden, containing a faithful account of his travels for a number of years, whilst a slave, in the South. Written by himself. [Philadelphia, Rhistoric Publications, 1969] 156 p. illus., port. 22 cm. (Rhistoric publication no. 220.) (Afro-American history series) Cover title. Reprint of the 1846 ed. with "William Hayden, untypical slave; a bibliographical note, by Maxwell Whiteman" added. [E444.H4 1969] 70-77057
I. Title. II. Series.

Haydn, Hiram Collins, 1907-1973.

HAYDN, Hiram Collins, 1907-1973. 070.4'092'4 B
Words & faces. [1st ed.] New York, Harcourt Brace Jovanovich [1974] 346 p. 22 cm. Autobiographical. [PS3515.A934Z52 1974] 74-7184 ISBN 0-15-198460-3 8.95
1. Haydn, Hiram Collins, 1907-1973. I. Title. **BIP**

Haydn, Joseph, 1732-1809.

BEYLE, Marie Henri, 1783-1842. 780'.92'2 B
Haydn, Mozart and Metastasio, by Stendhal. Translated, introduced & edited by Richard N. Coe. New York, Grossman Publishers, 1972. xxxii, 370 p. illus. 23 cm. London ed. (Calder & Boyars) has title: Lives of Haydn, Mozart and Metastasio. Translation of Vies de Haydn, de Mozart et de Metastase. Bibliography: p. 283-291. [ML390.B555V53 1972b] 77-188310 ISBN 0-670-36417-7 15.00
1. Haydn, Joseph, 1732-1809. 2. Mozart, Johann Chrysostom Wolfgang Amadeus, 1756-1791. 3. Metastasio, Pietro Antonio Domenico Buonaventura, 1698-1782. I. Coe, Richard N., ed. II. Title.

BOBILLIER, Marie, 1858-1918. 780'.924 B
Haydn, by Michel Brenet. Translated by C. Leonard Leese, with a commentary by Sir W. H. Hadow. Freeport, N.Y., Books for Libraries Press [1972] xii, 143 p. music. 23 cm. Reprint of the 1919 ed. Bibliography: p. 127-135. [ML410.H4B83 1972] 79-39688 ISBN 0-8369-9930-4
1. Haydn, Joseph, 1732-1809.

BOBILLIER, Marie, 1858-1918. 780'.92'4 B
Haydn, by Michel Brenet. Translated by C. Leonard Leese. With a commentary by W. H. Hadow. New York, B. Blom, 1972. xii, 143 p. illus. 21 cm. Translated from the 2d ed., 1919. Bibliography: p. 127-135. [ML410.H4B83 1972b] 72-80497
1. Haydn, Joseph, 1732-1809. I. Leese, Charles Leonard, 1895- tr.

FRANCISCUS, Brother, 1922- 927.8
The merry music maker, a story of Joseph Haydn. Illus. by Brother Bernard Howard. Notre Dame, Ind., Dujarie Press [1952] 93 p. illus. 24 cm. [ML3930.H3F7] 52-3977
1. Haydn, Joseph, 1732-1809. 2. Music—Juvenile literature. I. Title.

GEIRINGER, Karl, 1899- 927.8
Haydn; a creative life in music, by Karl Geiringer in collaboration with Irene Geiringer. 2d ed. rev. and enl. Garden City, N.Y., Doubleday, 1963. vii, 430 p. music. 18 cm. (Anchor books, A361) Bibliography: p. [405]-417. [ML410.H4G4 1963] 63-18035
1. Haydn, Joseph, 1732-1809. I. Geiringer, Irene. **BIP**

GEIRINGER, Karl, 1899- 780'.924 B
Haydn; a creative life in music, by Karl Geiringer in collaboration with Irene Geiringer. Berkeley, University of California Press, 1968 [c1963] vii, 434 p. illus., facsims., music, ports. 21 cm. "Reprinted with revisions 1968." Bibliography: p. [407]-417. [ML410.H4G4 1968] 68-2371
1. Haydn, Joseph, 1732-1809. I. Geiringer, Irene.

GRIESINGER, Georg August, d.1828. 927'.8
Joseph Haydn: eighteenth-century gentleman and genius. A translation with introd. and notes by Vernon Gotwals of the Biographische Notizen uber Joseph Haydn, by G. A. Griesinger, and the Biographische Nachrichten von Joseph Haydn, by A. C. Dies. Madison, University of Wisconsin Press, 1963. xviii, 275 p. illus., ports., music. 23 cm. "Catalogue of those works of J. Haydn from the ages of eighteen to seventy-three that he recalled" (compiled by A. D. Dies): p. 206-209. Bibliography: p. 267-268. [ML410.H4G713] 62-17399
1. Haydn, Joseph, 1732-1809. I. Dies, Albert Christoph, 1755-1822. Biographische Nachrichten. II. Gotwals, Vernon, tr.

HADDEN, James Cuthbert, 1861-1914. 780'.92'4 B
Haydn / by J. Cuthbert Hadden. New York : AMS Press, 1977. xv, 237 p., [8] leaves of plates : ill. ; 19 cm. Reprint of the 1934 ed. published by Dent, London, in series: The Master musicians. Includes index. Bibliography: p. 193-194. [ML410.H4H27 1977] 74-24267 ISBN 0-404-12940-4 : 18.00
1. Haydn, Joseph, 1732-1809. 2. Composers—Austria—Biography. I. Series: The Master musicians.

HAYDN, Joseph, 1732-1809. 927.8
Collected correspondence, and London notebooks. [By] H. C. Robbins Landon. Fair Lawn, N. J., Essential Books, 1959. xxix, 367p. illus., ports., facsims, music. 23cm. Bibliography: p. xxix, 317. [ML410.H4A4] 59-3697
I. London, Howard Chandler Robbins, 1926- ed. II. Title. III. Title: London notebooks.

HUGHES, Rosemary. v. 12
Haydn. New York, Collier [1950, 1963] 254 p. music. (The great composers series) 64-20909
1. Haydn, Joseph, 1732-1809. I. Title. **BIP**

HUGHES, Rosemary. 927.8
Haydn. London, Dent; New York, Pellegrini and Cudahy [1950] xi, 244 p. illus., ports., music. 19 cm. (The Master musicians. New series) Bibliography: p. 231-234. [ML410.H4H8] 50-13620
1. Haydn, Joseph, 1732-1809. I. Title. II. Series.

JACOB, Heinrich Eduard, 1889- 927.8
Joseph Haydn; his art, times, and glory [translated by Richard and Clara Winston] New York, Rinehart [1950] xv, 368 p. illus., ports., music. 24 cm. Bibliography: p. 354-359. [ML410.H4J32] 49-49600
1. Haydn, Joseph, 1732-1809. I. Title.

JACOB, Heinrich Eduard, 1889-1967. 780'.924 B
Joseph Haydn; his art, times, and glory. Westport, Conn., Greenwood Press [1971, c1950] xv, 368 p. illus. 23 cm. Bibliography: p. 354-359. [ML410.H4J32 1971] 76-138591 ISBN 0-8371-5792-7
1. Haydn, Joseph, 1732-1809. BIP

LANDON, Howard Chandler Robbins, 1926- 780'.92'4 B
Haydn : chronicle and works / H. C. Robbins Landon. Bloomington : Indiana University Press, 1976- p. cm. Contents.Contents.— —v. 3. Haydn in England, 1791-1795. Includes bibliographies and indexes. [ML410.H4L26] 76-14630 ISBN 0-253-37003-5 : 37.50
1. Haydn, Joseph, 1732-1809. BIP

LANDON, Howard Chandler Robbins, 1926- 780'.92'4 B
Haydn, by H. C. Robbins Landon, in association with Henry Raynor. New York, Praeger [1972] 107 p. illus. 26 cm. (The Great composers) Bibliography: p. 101. A biography of the eighteenth-century Austrian composer responsible for the creation of the modern orchestra and numerous advances in musical techniques. [ML410.H4L27 1972b] 92 70-185336 6.95
1. Haydn, Joseph, 1732-1809. I. Raynor, Henry, joint author. II. Title.

NOHL, Ludwig, 1831-1885. 780'.924 B
Life of Haydn, by Louis Nohl. Translated from the German by George P. Upton. New York, AMS Press [1971] 195 p. port. 19 cm. Reprint of the 1902 ed. [ML410.H4N8 1971] 73-173796 ISBN 0-404-04786-6
1. Haydn, Joseph, 1732-1809.

NOHL, Ludwig, 1831-1885. 780'.924 B
Life of Haydn, by Louis Nohl. Translated from the German by George P. Upton. St. Clair Shores, Mich., Scholarly Press, 1970. 195 p. port. 21 cm. Reprint of the 1902 ed. [ML410.H4N8 1970] 75-115259
1. Haydn, Joseph, 1732-1809. BIP

PEYSER, Herbert Francis, 1886- 927.8
Joseph Haydn, servant and master. [New York, Philharmonic-Symphony Society of New York, c1950] 64 p. illus. 16 cm. [ML410.H4P4] 51-7954
1. Haydn. Joseph, 1732-1890. I. Title.

REDFERN, Brian L. 780'.924 B
Haydn; a biography, with a survey of books, editions & recordings, by Brian Redfern. [Hamden, Conn.] Archon Books [1970] 111 p. 23 cm. (The Concertgoer's companions) [ML410.H4R26] 70-132000 ISBN 2-08-008861-
1. Haydn, Joseph, 1732-1809. BIP

Haydn, Joseph, 1732-1809—Juvenile literature.

HAYDN, Joseph, 1732-1809. 927.8
Collected correspondence, and London notebooks. [By] H. C. Robbins Landon. Fair Lawn, N. J., Essential Books, 1959. xxix, 367p. illus., ports., facsims, music. 23cm. Bibliography: p. xxix, 317. [ML410.H4A4] 59-3697
I. London, Howard Chandler Robbins, 1926- ed. II. Title. III. Title: London notebooks.

KAUFMANN, Helen (Loeb) 92
The story of Haydn. Illustrated by John Leone. Supervising editor: Enid Lamonte Meadowcroft. New York, Grosset & Dunlap [1962] 179p. illus. 22cm. (Signature books [49]) [ML3930.H3K4] 62-52033
1. Haydn, Joseph, 1732-1809—Juvenile literature. I. Title.

Haydn, Joseph, 1732-1809 — Juvenile literature.

KAUFMANN, Helen Babette (Loeb) 920
The story of Hayden Illus. by John Leone. Supervising ed.: Enid Lamonte Meadowcroft. New York, Grosset [c.1962] 179p. illus. 22 cm. (Signature bks. [49]) 62-52033 1.95
1. Haydn, Joseph, 1732-1809—Juvenile literature. I. Title.

MIRSKY, Reba Paeff. 927.436
Haydn. Illustrated by W. T. Mars. Chicago, Follett Pub. Co. [1963] 160 p. illus. 25 cm. [ML3930.H3M6] 63-9612
1. Haydn, Joseph, 1732-1809—Juvenile literature.

WILLETT, Franciscus. j92
The merry music maker, a story of Joseph Haydn. Illus. by Brother Bernard Howard. Notre Dame, Ind., Dujarie Press [1952] 98 p. illus. 24 cm. [ML3930.H3W55] 52-3977
1. Haydn, Joseph, 1732-1809 — Juvenile literature. I. Title.

Haydn, Joseph, 1732-1809—Iconography.

SOMFAI, Laszlo, comp. 780'.924
Joseph Haydn; his life in contemporary pictures. Collected and supplied with a commentary and an iconography of authentic Haydn pictures. [Translated by Mari Kuttna and Karoly Ravasz] New York, Taplinger Pub. Co. [1969] xxii, 244 p. illus., facsims., music, ports. 30 cm. "List of sources and annotations": p. 227-235. [ML88.H37S63 1969] 68-10725 12.95
1. Haydn, Joseph, 1732-1809—Iconography. BIP

Haydon, Benjamin Robert, 1786-1846.

GEORGE, Eric. 759.2
The life and death of Benjamin Robert Haydon, historical painter, 1786-1846. 2nd ed. with additions by Dorothy George. Oxford, Clarendon Pr., 1967. xiii, 400p. front., 20 plates (incl. ports.). 23cm. Bibl. [ND497.H4G4 1967] 67-113552 7.20
1. Haydon. Benjamin Robert. 1786-1846. I. George, Mary Dorothy (Gordon) II. Title. Available from Oxford Univ. Pr., New York.

HAYDON, Benjamin Robert 927.5
Diary. Edited by Willard Bissell Pope. Cambridge, Mass., Harvard University Press [c.]1960 xxvi, 495: 553p. (Bibl. footnotes.) illus., ports., facsims. 25cm. Contents.v.1.1808-1815.--v.2.1816-1824. 60-5394 20.00 set,
I. Title.

HAYDON, Benjamin Robert, 1786-1846. 927.5
Diary [v.3,4,5] Ed. by Willard Bissell Pope. Cambridge, Mass., Harvard [c.]1963. 3v. (660;664;688p.) illus., ports. 25cm. Bibl. 60-5394 35.00 set,
I. Title.

HAYDON, Benjamin Robert, 1786-1846. 927.5
Diary. Edited by Willard Bissell Pope. Cambridge, Harvard University Press, 1960-63. 5 v. illus., ports., facsims. 25 cm. Contents.CONTENTS. -- v. 1. 1808-1815. -- v. 2. 1816-1824. -- v. 3. 1825-1832. -- v. 4. 1832-1840. -- v. 5. 1840-1846. Bibliographical footnotes. [ND497.H4A37] 60-5394
I. Title.

OLNEY, Clarke, 1901- 927.5
Benjamin Robert Haydon, historical painter. Athens, University of Georgia Press [1952] xiv, 309 p. illus., ports. 24 cm. Bibliography: p. 272-280. [ND497.H4O43] 52-14773
1. Haydon, Benjamin Robert, 1786-1846. I. Title.

SYMONDS, Emily Morse, d.1936. 920.042
Little memoirs of the nineteenth century. Freeport, N.Y., Books for Libraries Press [1969] ix, 375 p. ports. 23 cm. (Essay index reprint series) Reprint of the 1902 ed. Contents.Contents.—Benjamin Robert Haydon.—Lady Morgan (Sydney Owenson)—Nathaniel Parker Willis.—Lady Hester Stanhope.—Prince Puckler-Muskau in England.—William and Mary Howitt. [DA531.1.S9 1969] 70-86787 ISBN 8-369-11970-
1. Puckler-Muskau, Hermann Ludwig Heinrich, furst von, 1785-1871. 2. Morgan, Sydney (Owenson) lady, 1783?-1859. 3. Haydon, Benjamin Robert, 1786-1846. 4. Willis, Nathaniel Parker, 1806-1867. 5. Stanhope, Hester Lucy, Lady, 1776-1839. 6. Howitt, William, 1792-1879. 7. Howitt, Mary (Botham) 1799-1888. I. Title. BIP

Hayek, Friedrich August von, 1899-

ESSAYS on Hayek / 330'.092'4
William F. Buckley, Jr. ... [et al.] ; edited by Fritz Machlup ; foreword by Milton Fiedman. New York : New York University Press, 1976. xxiv, 182 p. : port. ; 24 cm. Delivered at a special regional meeting of the Mont Pelerin Society, held from August 24 to 28, 1975, at Hillsdale College in Hillsdale, Michigan. Includes bibliographical references and index. [HB103.H3E77] 76-8360 ISBN 0-8147-5409-0 : 10.00
1. Hayek, Friedrich August von, 1899- 2. Ecnomists Biography—Addresses, essays, lectures. I. Buckley, William Frank, 1925- II. Machlup, Fritz, 1902- III. Mont Pelerin Society.

Hayes, Bob, 1942- —Juvenile literature.

LIPMAN, David. 796.332'0924 B
The speed king: Bob Hayes of the Dallas Cowboys. By David Lipman and Ed Wilks. New York, Putnam [1971] 188 p. 22 cm. (Putnam sports shelf) A biography of the track athlete and football star who was the first man to run 100 yards in 9.1 seconds. [GV939.H34L5 1971] 92 73-146108 3.96
1. Hayes, Bob, 1942- —Juvenile literature. I. Wilks, Ed, joint author. II. Title. BIP

Hayes, Carlton Joseph Huntley, 1882-1964.

HAYES, Carlton Joseph Huntley, 1882-1964. 940.53'22'73
Wartime mission in Spain, 1942-1945 / by Carlton J. H. Hayes. New York : Da Capo Press, 1976, c1945. viii, 313 p. ; 23 cm. (The Politics & strategy of World War II) Reprint of the 1st 1946 ed. published by Macmillan, New York. [D754.S7H3 1976] 76-18191 22.50
1. Hayes, Carlton Joseph Huntley, 1882-1964. 2. World War, 1939-1945—Diplomatic history. 3. World War, 1939-1945—Spain. 4. United States—Foreign relations—Spain. 5. Spain—Foreign relations—United States. I. Title. BIP

Hayes, Elvin, 1945-

HAYES, Elvin, 1945- 796.32'3'0924 B
They call me "The Big E" / Elvin Hayes and Bill Gilbert. Englewood Cliffs, N.J. : Prentice-Hall, c1978. x, 169 p., [8] leaves of plates : ill. ; 22 cm. [GV884.H32A34] 77-26321 ISBN 0-13-917054-5 : 8.95
1. Hayes, Elvin, 1945- 2. Basketball players—United States—Biography. 3. Religion and sports. I. Gilbert, Bill, 1931- joint author. II. Title. BIP

Hayes, Helen,

HAYES, Helen, 1900- 792'.028'0924 B
On reflection; an autobiography [by] Helen Hayes with Sandford Dody. [1st ed.] New York, M. Evans; distributed by Lippincott, Philadelphia [1968] 253 p. ports. 22 cm. [PN2287.H35A32] 68-54122 5.95
I. Dody, Sandford. II. Title.

Hayes, Raymond Lee.

THOMAS, Cal. 248'.246 B
A freedom dream / Cal Thomas. Waco, Tex. : Word Books, c1977. 144 p. : ill. ; 23 cm. [BX6495.H34T48] 76-48492 ISBN 0-87680-506-3 : 5.95
1. Hayes, Raymond Lee. 2. Thomas, Cal. 3. Converts—Texas—Biography. 4. Prisoners—Texas—Biography. 5. Baptists—Texas—Biography. 6. Texas—Biography. I. Title. BIP

Hayes, Roland, 1887-

HELM, MacKinley, 1896- 784'.0924 B
Angel Mo' and her son, Roland Hayes. New York, Greenwood Press [1969, c1942] viii, 289 p. port. 23 cm. [ML420.H25H3 1969] 73 95123
1. Hayes, Roland, 1887- I. Title. BIP

Hayes, Rutherford Birchard, Pres. U.S., 1822-1893.

BARNARD, Harry, 1906- 923.173
Rutherford B. Hayes, and his America. [1st ed.] Indianapolis, Bobbs-Merrill [1954] 606 p. illus., ports., facsim. 25 cm. Bibliographical references included in "Notes" (p. 525-570) "Selected bibliography": p. 571-588. [E682.B3] 54-11942
1. Hayes, Rutherford Birchard, Pres. U.S., 1822-1893.

DAVISON, Kenneth E. 973.8'3'0924 B
The Presidency of Rutherford B. Hayes [by] Kenneth E. Davison. Westport, Conn., Greenwood Press, [1972] xvii, 266 p. illus. 25 cm. (Contributions in American studies, no. 3) Bibliography: p. 239-251. [E682.D38] 79-176289 ISBN 0-8371-6275-0 $12.00
1. Hayes, Rutherford Birchard, Pres. U.S., 1822-1893. I. Title. BIP

ECKENRODE, Hamilton James, 1881- 923.173
Rutherford B. Hayes; statesman of reunion, assisted by Pocahontas Wilson Wight. Port Washington, N.Y., Kennikat Press [1963, c1957] 363 p. illus., ports., facsim. 22 cm. Bibliography: p. 345-349. [E682.E19 1963] 63-20590
1. Hayes, Rutherford Birchard, Pres. U.S., 1822-1893.

HAYES, Rutherford Birchard, Pres. U.S., 1822-1893. 973.83
Hayes: the diary of a president 1875-1881, covering the disputed election, the end of reconstruction, and the beginning of civil service. Edited by T. Harry Williams. New York, D. McKay Co. [1964] xliv, 329 p. 21 cm. [E682.H48] 64-10784
1. United States—Politics and government—1877-1881. I. Williams, Thomas Harry, 1909- ed. II. Title: The diary of a president, 1875-1881.

HAYES, Rutherford Birchard, Pres. U.S., 1822-1893. 973.8'3'0924
Rutherford B. Hayes, 1822-1893; chronology, documents, bibliographical aids. Edited by Arthur Bishop Dobbs

Ferry, N.Y., Oceana Publications, 1969. 90 p. 24 cm. (Oceana presidential chronology series, 12) Bibliography: p. 83-87. [E681.B59] 69-15394 3.00
1. United States—History—1865-1898—Sources. I. Bishop, Arthur, ed. II. United States. President, 1877-1881 (Hayes) BIP

†HOWELLS, William Dean, 1837-1920. 973.8'3'0924 B
Sketch of the life and character of Rutherford B. Hayes : also a biographical sketch of William A. Wheeler / by Wm. D. Howells. Folcroft, Pa. : Folcroft Library Editions, 1977 [c1876] p. cm. Reprint of the ed. published by Hurd and Houghton, New York. [E682.H85 1977] 77-19043 ISBN 0-8414-4786-1 lib. bdg. : 25.00
1. Hayes, Rutherford Birchard, Pres. U.S., 1822-1893. 2. Wheeler, William Almon, 1819-1887. 3. United States. Congress. House—Biography. 4. Presidents—United States—Biography. 5. Legislators—United States—Biography. 6. United States—Politics and government—1865-1883. I. Title.

WILLIAMS, Charles Richard, 1853-1927. 973.8'3'0924 B
The life of Rutherford Birchard Hayes, nineteenth president of the United States. New York, Da Capo Press, 1971 [c1914] 2 v. illus., ports. 23 cm. (The American scene) [E682.W7 1971] 79-87678 ISBN 0-306-71714-X
1. Hayes, Rutherford Birchard, Pres. U.S., 1822-1893.

Hayes, Rutherford Birchard, Pres. U.S., 1822-1893—Juvenile literature.

MYERS, Elisabeth P. 973.8'3'0924
Rutherford B. Hayes, by Elisabeth P. Myers. Chicago, Reilly & Lee [1969] 121 p. illus. 22 cm. Bibliography: p. 115-116. A biography of the man declared the nineteenth President of the United States by the electoral college in the disputed election of 1876. [E682.M9] 92 B 69-17432 4.50
1. Hayes, Rutherford Birchard, Pres. U.S., 1822-1893—Juvenile literature. I. Title.

Hayes, Rutherford Birchard, Press. U.S., 1822-1893.

BARNARD, Harry, 1906- 973.8'3'0924
Rutherford B. Hayes and his America. New York, Russell & Russell [1967, c1954] 606 p. illus., facsim., ports. 22 cm. Bibliographical references included in "Notes" (p. 525-570) Bibliography: p. 571-588. [E682.B3] 66-24667
1. Hayes, Rutherford Birchard, Press. U.S., 1822-1893. I. Title. BIP

Haygood, Atticus Greene, Bp., 1839-1896.

MANN, Harold W. 922.773
Atticus Greene Haygood, Methodist bishop, editor, and educator. Athens, Univ. of Ga. Pr. [c.1965] viii, 254p. port. 25cm. Bibl. [BX8495.H269M3] 65-19380 6.00
1. Haygood, Atticus Greene, Bp., 1839-1896. I. Title.

Haykal, Muhammad Hasanayn.

NASSER, Munir K., 1936- 070.4'092'4 B
Press, politics, and power : Egypt's Heikal and Al-Ahram / Munir K. Nasser. 1st ed. Ames : Iowa State University Press, 1979. viii, 175 p. ; 22 cm. Includes index. Bibliography: p. 169-172. [PN5465.H3N3] 79-11924 15.50 pbk. : 9.50
1. Haykal, Muhammad Hasanayn. 2. al-Ahram, Cairo. 3. Egypt—Politics and government—1952- 4. Journalists—Egypt—Biography. 5. Statesmen—Egypt—Biography. I. Title.

Haylett, William, 1778-1830—Biography.

†STODDARD, Richard Henry, 1825-1903, ed. 828'.7'09 B
Personal recollections of Lamb, Hazlitt, and others / edited by Richard Henry Stoddard. Folcroft, Pa. : Folcroft Library Editions, 1976 [c1875] xxii, 322 p. [4] leaves of plates : ill. ; 24 cm. Selections from My friends and acquaintance, by P. G. Patmore. Reprint of the ed. published by Scribner, Armstrong, New York, which was issued as no. 9 of the Bric-a-brac series. Includes index. [PR105.S74 1976] 76-17557 ISBN 0-8414-7623-3 lib. bdg. : 27.50
1. Lamb, Charles, 1775-1834—Biography. 2. Haylett, William, 1778-1830—Biography. 3. Campbell, Thomas, 1777-1844—Biography. 4. Blessington, Marguerite Power Farmer Gardiner, Countess of, 1789-1849—Biography. 5. Authors, English—19th century—Correspondence, reminiscences, etc. I. Patmore, Peter George, 1786-1855. My friends and acquaintance. Selections. 1976. II. Title. III. Series: Bric-a-brac series ; no. 9. BIP

Hayley, William, 1745-1820.

STONOR, Oliver, 1903- 821'.6
Blake's Hayley; the life, works, and friendships of William Hayley, by Morchard Bishop. Freeport, N.Y., Books for Libraries Press [1972, c1951] 372 p. illus. 22 cm. (Biography index reprint series) Bibliography: p. 357-360. [PR3506.H9S8 1972] 72-5490 ISBN 0-8369-8133-2
1. Hayley, William, 1745-1820. 2. Blake, William, 1757-1827. I. Title. BIP

STONOR, Oliver, 1903- 928.2
Blake's Hayley; the life, works, and friendships of William Hayley, by Morchard Bishop [pseud.] London, V. Gollancz, 1951. 372 p. illus., ports. 23 cm. Bibliography: p. 357-360. [PR3506.H9S8] 51-6798
1. Hayley, William, 1745-1820. 2. Blake, William, 1757-1827. I. Title.

Haymerle, Heinrich, Freiherr von, 1828-1881.

BROWN, Marvin Luther. 327'.2'0924 B
Heinrich von Haymerle; Austro-Hungarian career diplomat, 1828-81, by Marvin L. Brown, Jr. [1st ed.] Columbia, University of South Carolina Press [1973] xii, 238 p. illus. 23 cm. Bibliography: p. 221-228. [D352.8.H38B76] 73-2586 ISBN 0-87249-243-5 12.95 (lib. bdg.)
1. Haymerle, Heinrich, Freiherr von, 1828-1881. I. Title.

Hayne, Donald,

HAYNE, Donald, 1908- 922.273 B
Batter my heart. [1st ed.] New York, Knopf, 1963. 303 p. 22 cm. Autobiographical. [BX4705.H36A3] 62-15563
I. Title.

Hayne, Isaac, 1745-1781.

BOWDEN, David K. 973.3'81 B
The execution of Isaac Hayne / by David K. Bowden. 1st ed. Lexington, S.C. : Sandlapper Store, c1977. 102 p. : ill. ; 24 cm. Includes index. Bibliography: p. 87-97. [E263.S7H392] 76-20850 ISBN 0-87844-037-2 : 9.95
1. Hayne, Isaac, 1745-1781. 2. United States—History—Revolution, 1775-1783—Prisoners and prisons. 3. United States—History—Revolution, 1775-1783—Biography. 4. South Carolina—History—Revolution, 1775-1783. I. Title. BIP

Hayne, Paul Hamilton, 1830-1886.

MOORE, Rayburn S., 1920- 811'.3
Paul Hamilton Hayne, by Rayburn S. Moore. New York, Twayne Publishers [1972] 193 p. 21 cm. (Twayne's United States authors series, TUSAS 202) Bibliography: p. 181-183. [PS1908.M6] 73-125818
1. Hayne, Paul Hamilton, 1830-1886. BIP

Hayne, Robert Young, 1791-1839.

JERVEY, Theodore Dehon, 1859- 328.73'0924
Robert Y. Hayne and his times, by Theodore D. Jervey. New York, Da Capo Press, 1970 [c1909] xix, 555 p. 24 cm. (The American scene) (A Da Capo Press reprint series.) Includes bibliographical references. [E340.H4J5 1970] 73-104330
1. Hayne, Robert Young, 1791-1839. 2. U.S.—Politics and government—1815-1861. 3. South Carolina—Politics and government—1775-1865. BIP

Haynes, Eliza, 1850-1930.

SURMAN, Phyl. 942.5'73
Eliza of Otmoor / [by] Phyl Surman. Oxford : Oxprint, 1976. [9], 49 p. : ill., geneal. table, map, ports. ; 21 cm. Bibliography: p. 49. [CT788.H383S97] 77-362180
1. Haynes, Eliza, 1850-1930. 2. Oxfordshire, Eng.—Biography. I. Title.

Haynes, Lemuel, 1753-1833.

COOLEY, Timothy Mather, 1772-1859. 285'.8'0924 B
Sketches of the life and character of the Rev. Lemuel Haynes, A.M., for many years pastor of a church in Rutland, Vt., and late in Granville, New York. With some introductory remarks by William B. Sprague. New York, Negro Universities Press [1969] 345 p. port. 23 cm. "Originally published in 1837." [BX7260.H315C6 1969] 70-88426
1. Haynes, Lemuel, 1753-1833. I. Title.

Haynes, Raleigh Rutherford, 1851-1917.

HAYNES, Ina (Fortune) 923.373
Raleigh Rutherford Haynes: a history of his life and achievements, by Mrs. Grover C. Haynes, Sr. [Cliffside? N. C., 1954] 99p. illus. 24cm. [HC107.N8H39] 54-36710
1. Haynes, Raleigh Rutherford, 1851-1917. I. Title.

Hays, John Coffee, 1817-1883.

GREER, James Kimmins, 1896- 923.573
Colonel Jack Hays, Texas frontier leader and California builder. [1st ed.] New York, Dutton, 1952. 428 p. ports., maps. 22 cm. Bibliography: p. 405-410. [F391.H44G7] 52-5314
1. Hays, John Coffee, 1817-1883. 2. Texas Rangers. 3. Frontier and pioneer life—Texas. 4. Frontier and pioneer life—California. I. Title.

HENDERSON, Harry McCorry. 923.573
Colonel Jack Hays, Texas ranger. San Antonio, Naylor Co. [1954] 115p. illus. 22cm. Includes bibliography. [F391.H44H4] 54-3079
1. Hays, John Coffee, 1817-1883. I. Title.

Hays, John Coffee, 1817-1883—Juvenile literature.

BISHOP, Curtis Kent, 1912- 923.573
The first Texas ranger, Jack Hays. New York, J. Messner [1959] 192p. 22cm. Includes bibliography. [F391.H44B5] 59-12755
1. Hays, John Coffee, 1817-1883—Juvenile literature. I. Title.

Hays, John Jacob, 1770?-1836.

LEVINE, Joseph, 1907- 917.72'74'06924 B
John Jacob Hays: the first known Jewish resident of Fort Wayne. Fort Wayne, Indiana Jewish Historical Society, 1973. 13 p. port. 22 cm. Bibliography: p. 13. [F534.F7L48] 74-172940
1. Hays, John Jacob, 1770?-1836. 2. Jews in Fort Wayne.

Hays, Will H.,

HAYS, Will H., 1879-1954. 923.273
Memoirs. [1st ed.] Garden City, N. Y., Doubleday, 1955. 600 p. illus. 22 cm. [E748.H388A3] 55-8402

Hayter, Stanley William, 1901-

LIMBOUR, Georges, 1902- 759.2
Hayter. [Paris, G. Fall, dist. New York, Efron] c.1962. 77p. col. illus. 19cm. (Le Musee de poche) 62-52313 1.50 pap.,
1. Hayter, Stanley William, 1901- I. Title.

Hayward family.

HAYWARD, Brooke, 1937- 792'.092'2 B
Haywire / by Brooke Hayward. 1st ed. New York : Knopf, 1977. 325 p. : ill. ; 24 cm. [PN2287.H377H3] 76-40989 ISBN 0-394-49325-7 : 10.00
1. Hayward family. I. Title. BIP

Hayward, Susan

*MCCLELLAND, Doug. 791.43'028'0924 B
The complete life story of Susan Hayward ... immortal screen star. New York, Pinnacle Books 1975 c1973 ix, 213 p. illus. 18 cm. [PN2287] ISBN 0-523-00706-X 1.50 (pbk.)
1. Hayward, Susan I. Title.

MORENO, Eduardo, 791.43'028'0924 B
The films of Susan Hayward / by Eduardo Moreno. Secaucus, N.J. : Citadel Press, [1979] p. cm. [PN2287.H378M67] 79-17937 ISBN 0-8065-0682-2 : 14.95
1. Hayward, Susan. 2. Moving-picture actors and actresses—United States—Biography. I. Title. BIP

Haywood, Harry, 1898-

HAYWOOD, Harry, 1898- 335.43'092'4 B
Black Bolshevik : autobiography of an Afro-American Communist / Harry Haywood. Chicago : Liberator Press, c1978. x, 700 p., [7] leaves of plates : ill. ; 23 cm. Includes bibliographical references and index. [HX84.H38A32] 77-77464 ISBN 0-930720-52-0 : 15.00.
1. Haywood, Harry, 1898- 2. Communists—United States—Biography. 3. Afro-Americans—Biography. 4. Communism—United States—History. I. Title.

Haywood, Spencer, 1949-

LIBBY, Bill. 796.32'3'0924
Stand up for something; the Spencer Haywood story, by Bill Libby and Spencer Haywood. New York, Grosset & Dunlap [1972] 248 p. illus. 22 cm. [GV884.H33L42] 75-183012 ISBN 0-448-01143-3 6.95
1. Haywood, Spencer, 1949- I. Haywood, Spencer, 1949- joint author. II. Title.

Haywood, William Dudley, 1869-1928.

CONLIN, Joseph Robert. 331.88'6 B
Big Bill Haywood and the radical union movement [by] Joseph R. Conlin. [1st ed. Syracuse, N.Y.] Syracuse University Press [1969] xii, 244 p. ports. 21 cm. (Men and movements) Includes bibliographical references. [HD6509.H3C65] 79-80015 6.95
1. Haywood, William Dudley, 1869-1928. I. Title. II. Series: Men and movements (Syracuse) BIP

Hayworth, Rita, 1919-

KOBAL, John. 791.43'028'0924 B
Rita Hayworth : the time, the place, and the woman / by John Kobal. 1st American ed. New York : Norton, 1978, c1977. p. cm. Includes index. [PN2287.H38K6 1978] 77-18124 ISBN 0-393-07526-5 : 12.95

1. Hayworth, Rita, 1919- 2. Moving picture actors and actresses—United States—Biography. **BIP**

Hazen, William Babcock, 1830-1887.

KROEKER, Marvin 355.3'31'0924 B E., 1928-
Great Plains command : William B. Hazen in the frontier West / by Marvin E. Kroeker. 1st ed. Norman : University of Oklahoma Press, c1976. xv, 216 p., [4] leaves of plates : ill. ; 22 cm. Includes index. Bibliography: p. 199-207. [F594.H422K76] 75-17709 ISBN 0-8061-1318-9 : 9.95
1. Hazen, William Babcock, 1830-1887. 2. The West—History—1848-1950. 3. Indians of North America—The West. I. Title. **BIP**

Hazlitt, Sarah (Stoddart)

HAZLITT, Sarah (Stoddart) 928.2
The journals of Sarah and William Hazlitt, 1822-1831. Edited by Willard Hallam Bonner. [Buffalo] University of Buffalo, 1959. 172-281p. 23cm. (The University of Buffalo studies. v. 24, no. 3) [AS36.B95 vol. 24, no.3] 59-16173
I. Hazlitt, William, 1778-1830. II. Bonner, Willard Hallam, 1899- ed. III. Title. IV. Series: Buffalo. University. Th

Hazlitt, William, 1778-1830.

HAZLITT, William 824'.7'09 B Carew, 1834-1913.
Lamb and Hazlitt; further letters and records hitherto unpublished, edited by William Carew Hazlitt. [Folcroft, Pa.] Folcroft Library Editions, 1973. liv, 161 p. 19 cm. Reprint of the 1900 ed. published by E. Mathews, London. [PR4773.A46L3 1973] 73-17226 ISBN 0-8414-4785-3 (lib. bdg.)
1. Hazlitt, William, 1778-1830. 2. Lamb, Charles, 1775-1834. I. Title.

HOWE, Percival Presland, 824'.7 B 1886-1944.
The life of William Hazlitt. With an introd. by Frank Swinnerton. Westport, Conn., Greenwood Press [1972] xxvi, 433 p. illus. 22 cm. Reprint of the 1947 ed. Includes bibliographical references. [PR4773.H6 1972] 72-7505 ISBN 0-8371-6512-1 17.25
1. Hazlitt, William, 1778-1830. I. Title. **BIP**

KINNAIRD, John William, 824'.7 1924-
William Hazlitt, critic of power / John Kinnaird. New York : Columbia University Press, 1978. xv, 429 p. : ill. ; 24 cm. Includes bibliographical references and index. [PR4773.K5] 78-14523 ISBN 0-231-04600-6 . 22.50
1. Hazlitt, William, 1778-1830. 2. Hazlitt, William, 1778-1830—Knowledge—Literature. 3. Criticism—England—History. 4. Authors, English—19th century—Biography. I. Title. **BIP**

ROBINSON, Robert 944.05'092'4 B E.
William Hazlitt's Life of Napoleon Buonaparte; its sources and characteristics [by] Robert E. Robinson. [Folcroft, Pa.] Folcroft Library Editions, 1973. p. Reprint of the 1959 ed. published by E. Droz, Geneve. Bibliography: p. [DC203.H433R6 1973] 73-14519 25.00
1. Hazlitt, William, 1778-1830. The life of Napoleon Buonaparte.

Hazlitt, William, 1778-1830—Correspondence.

HAZLITT, William, 1778- 824'.7 1830.
The letters of William Hazlitt / edited by Herschel Moreland Sikes, assisted by Willard Hallam Bonner and Gerald Lahey. New York : New York University Press, 1978. p. cm. (The Gotham library of the New York University Press) Includes bibliograpical references. [PR4773.A44 1978] 78-54079 ISBN 0-8147-4986-0 : 20.00. ISBN 0-8147-4987-9 pbk. : 6.95
1. Hazlitt, William, 1778-1830—Correspondence. 2. Author, English—19th century—Correspondence. I. Sikes, Herschel Moreland. II. Bonner, Willard Hallam, 1899- III. Lahey, Gerald B. **BIP**

Hazlitt, William, 1778-1830. Life of Napoleon Buonaparte.

ROBINSON, Robert E. 923.144
William Hazlitt's Life of Napoleon Buonaparte, its sources and characteristics. Geneve, E. Droz [dist. New York, Gregory Lounz, 1959, i.e., 1960] 108p. Bibliography: p. [107]-108. 25 cm. A60 3.25 pap.,
1. Hazlitt, William, 1778-1830. Life of Napoleon Buonaparte. I. Title.

Head, Edmund Walker, Sir, bart., 1805-1868.

KERR, Donald Gordon 922.271 Grady, 1913-
Sir Edmund Head, a scholorly governor, by D. G. G. Kerr, with the assistance of J. A. Gibson. [Toronto] University of Toronto Press, 1954. xi, 259 p. port. 24 cm. Bibliography: p. 243-247. [F1032.H4K4] 55-4927
1. Head, Edmund Walker, Sir, bart., 1805-1868.

Heade, Martin Johnson, 1819-1904.

STEBBINS, Theodore E. 759.13
The life and works of Martin Johnson Heade / Theodore E. Stebbins, Jr. New Haven : Yale University Press, 1975. xix, 303 p., [4] leaves of plates : ill. (some col.) ; 29 cm. (Yale publications in the history of art ; 26) Includes index. Bibliography: p. 198-201. [ND237.H39S68] 74-83794 ISBN 0-300-01808-8 : 30.00
1. Heade, Martin Johnson, 1819-1904. I. Title. II. Series. **BIP**

Heads of state—Biography.

LONGFORD, Frank Pakenham, 920'.02 7th Earl of, 1905-
The history makers; leaders and statesmen of the 20th century. Edited by Lord Longford & Sir John Wheeler-Bennet. Chronologies and editorial assistance by Christine Nicholls. New York, St. Martin's Press [1973] 448 p. illus. 24 cm. Includes bibliographical references. [D412.7.L66 1973b] 73-79066 10.95
1. Heads of state—Biography. 2. Statesmen—Biography. I. Wheeler-Bennett, John Wheeler, Sir, 1902- joint author. II. Title.

Healy, Fleming.

HEALY, Fleming. 818.54
With sunshiny faces. [1st ed.] Philadelphia, Lippincott [1963] 220 p. 21 cm. Story of the author's childhood. [CT275.H4859A3] 63-8890
I. Title.

Healy, George W.

HEALY, George W. 070.4'092'4 B
A lifetime on deadline / George W. Healy, Jr. ; foreword by Turner Catledge. Gretna, La. : Pelican Pub. Co., 1975. p. cm. [PN4874.H36A33] 75-22404 ISBN 0-88289-076-X : 12.50
1. Healy, George W. I. Title. **BIP**

Healy, James Augustine, Bp., 1830-1900.

BISHOP Healy, beloved v. 12 *outcast;* the story of a great priest whose life has become a legend. Dublin, Clonmore and Reynolds [1956] 199p.
1. Healy, James Augustine, Bp., 1830-1900. I. Foley, Albert Sidney, 1912-

ERNEST, Brother, 1897- v. 12
The children's bishop; a story of Bishop James A. Healy. Illus. by Carolyn Lee Jagodits. Notre Dame, Ind., Dujarie Press [1962] 95 p. illus. 22 cm. 64-31738
1. Healy, James Augustine, Bp., 1830-1930 — Juv. lit. I. Title.

FOLEY, Albert Sidney, 282'.0924 B 1912-
Bishop Healy: beloved outcaste [by] Albert S. Foley. New York, Arno Press, 1969 [c1954] viii, 248 p. port. 21 cm. (The American Negro, his history and literature) [BX4705.H37F6 1969] 79-94130
1. Healy, James Augustine, Bp., 1830-1900. I. Title. II. Series.

KELLY, Josephine. 282'.0924 B
Dark shepherd Paterson, N.J., St. Anthony Guild Press [1967] v, 169 p. illus. 20 cm. Biography of the first Negro bishop in the United States. [BX4705.H37K4] 92 67-19690
1. Healy, James Augustine, Bp., 1830-1900. I. Title.

Healy, Katherine—Juvenile literature.

KREMENTZ, Jill. 796.9'1
A very young skater / written and photographed by Jill Krementz. 1st ed. New York : Knopf : distributed by Random House, 1979. p. cm. A 10-year-old relates her experiences as a skater. [GV849.K73] 79-2209 ISBN 0-394-50833-5 : 9.95
1. Healy, Katherine—Juvenile literature. 2. Skating—Juvenile literature. 3. Skaters—Biography—Juvenile literature. I. Title. **BIP**

Healy-Murphy, Margaret Mary, 1833-1907.

TURLEY, Mary 271'.979 B Immaculata.
Mother Margaret Mary Healy-Murphy; a biography. San Antonio, Tex., Naylor Co. [1969] xviii, 228 p. illus., maps (on lining paper), ports. 22 cm. Bibliography: p. 219-223. [BX4705.H383T87] 74-92518 7.95
1. Healy-Murphy, Margaret Mary, 1833-1907. I. Title.

Heard, George W

HEARD, George W 1867- 926.1
Man versus toothache. [Milwaukee, Lee Foundation for Nutritional Research, c1952] 183p. illus. 24cm. Autobiographical. [RK43.H4A3] 54-29505
I. Title.

Hearn, Lafcadio,

HEARN, Lafcadio, 1850- 816'.4 1904.
Letters from the Raven, being the correspondence of Lafcadio Hearn with Henry Watkin. With introd. and critical comment by the editor, Milton Bronner. Freeport, N.Y., Books for Libraries Press [1972] p. Contents.Contents.—Letters from the Raven.—Letters to a lady.—Letters of Ozias Midwinter. [PS1918.A46W3 1972] 72 8454 ISBN 0-8369-6977-4

HEARN, Lafcadio, 1850- 816'.4 1904.
Letters from the Raven, being the correspondence of Lafcadio Hearn with Henry Watkin. With introd. and critical comment by the editor, Milton Bronner. Freeport, N.Y., Books for Libraries Press [1972] p. Contents.Contents.—Letters from the Raven.—Letters to a lady.—Letters of Ozias Midwinter. [PS1918.A46W3 1972] 72-8454 ISBN 0-8369-6977-4

KOIZUMI, Kazuo, 1893- 928.1
Re-echo. Edited by Nancy Jane Fellers. Illustrated with photos and with original, hitherto unpublished pen and watercolor sketches by Lafcadio Hearn. Caldwell, Idaho, Caxton Printers, 1957. 161p. illus. 25cm. Memories of the author's early years with his father, Lafcadio Hearn. [PS1918.K62] 56-7263
1. Hearn, Lafcadio, 1850-1904. I. Title.

MCWILLIAMS, Vera Seeley. 813'.4 B
Lafcadio Hearn [by] Vera McWilliams. New York, Cooper Square Publishers, 1970 [i.e. 1971, c1946] ix, 464 p. 22 cm. Bibliography: p. [447]-[453] [PS1918.M3 1971] 79-129462 ISBN 0-8154-0350-X 12.50
1. Hearn, Lafcadio, 1850-1904.

STEVENSON, Elizabeth, 1918- 928.1
Lafacdio Hearn. New York, Macmillan [c.] 1961. 362p. front. 61-10337 6.95
1. Hearn, Lafacadio, 1850-1904- I. Title.

STEVENSON, Elizabeth, 1919- 928.1
Lafcadio Hearn. New York, Macmillan, 1961. 302 p. illus. 24 cm. [PS1918.S75] 61-10337
1. Hearn, Lafcadio, 1850-1904. I. Title.

Hearn, Lafcadio, 1850-1904—Biography.

HEARN, Setsu Koizumi. 813'.4 B
Reminiscences of Lafcadio Hearn / by Setsuko Koizumi (Mrs. Hearn) ; translated from the Japanese by Paul Kiyoshi Hisada and Frederick Johnson. Folcroft, Pa. : Folcroft Library Editions, 1978 [c1978] viii, 87 p. ; 23 cm. Reprint of the ed. published by Houghton Mifflin, Boston. [PS1918.H4 1978] 78-16202 ISBN 0-8414-2226-5 : 17.50
1. Hearn, Lafcadio, 1850-1904—Biography. 2. Authors, American—19th century—Biography. 3. Hearn, Setsu Koizumi. 4. Wives—Japan—Biography. I. Title. **BIP**

STEVENSON, Elizabeth, 813'.4 B 1919-
Lafcadio Hearn / by Elizabeth Stevenson. New York : Octagon Books, 1979, c1961. p. cm. Reprint of the ed. published by Macmillan Co., New York. Includes index. Bibliography: p. [PS1918.S75 1979] 79-17313 ISBN 0-374-97625-2 lib. bdg. : 17.50
1. Hearn, Lafcadio, 1850-1904—Biography. 2. Authors, American—19th century—Biography.

TEMPLE, Jean. 813'.4 B
Blue ghost; a study of Lafcadio Hearn. New York, Haskell House, 1974. 228 p. 21 cm. [PS1918.T4 1974b] 74-16485 ISBN 0-8383-2027-9
1. Hearn, Lafcadio, 1850-1904—Biography. I. Title.

TEMPLE, Jean. 813'.4 B
Blue ghost; a study of Lafcadio Hearn. [Folcroft, Pa.] Folcroft Library Editions, 1974. p. Reprint of the 1931 ed. published by J. Cape, London; J. Cape & H. Smith, New York. [PS1918.T4 1974] 74-11119 12.75
1. Hearn, Lafcadio, 1850-1904 Biography. I. Title.

THOMAS, Edward, 1878- 813'.4 B 1917.
Lafcadio Hearn / by Edward Thomas. Folcroft, Pa. : Folcroft Library Editions, 1977. p. cm. Reprint of the 1912 ed. published by Constable, London, and Houghton Mifflin, Boston, in series: Modern biographies. [PS1918.T5 1977] 77-7488 ISBN 0-8414-8630-1 lib.bdg. : 10.00
1. Hearn, Lafcadio, 1850-1904—Biography. 2. Authors, American—19th century—Biography. I. Series: Modern biographies. **BIP**

Hearn, Lafcadio, 1850-1904—Correspondence.

HEARN, Lafcadio, 1850- 813'.4 B 1904.
Letters / Lafcadio Hearn ; [editors, Hojin Yano, Tadanobu Kawai, Hiroyishi Kishimoto]. New York : AMS Press, 1975. p. cm. Reprints of letters in the Tenri University Library, Tenri, Japan. Contents.Contents.—v. 1. To and from various persons.—v. 2. To and from B. H. Chamberlain. [PS1918.A45 1975] 75-25954 ISBN 0-404-13210-3 (v. 1)
1. Hearn, Lafcadio, 1850-1904—Correspondence. 2. Hearn, Lafcadio, 1850-1904—Manuscripts—Facsimiles. 3. Toyama, Masakazu, 1848-1900. 4. Chamberlain, Basil Hall, 1850-1935. I. Chamberlain, Basil Hall, 1850-1935.

Hearn, Lafcadio, 1850-1904—Homes and haunts—Japan.

NOGUCHI, Yone, 1875- 813'.4 B 1947.
Lafcadio Hearn in Japan / by Yone Noguchi ; with Mrs. Lafcadio Hearn's reminiscences ; frontispiece by Shoshu Saito, with sketches by Genjiro Kataoka and Mr. Hearn himself. Folcroft, Pa., : Folcroft Library Editions, 1978. vii, 117 p., [4] leaves of plates : ill. ; 23 cm. Reprint of the 1910 ed. published by E. Mathews, London. [PS1918.N6 1978] 78-2870 ISBN 0-8414-0284-1 lib. bdg. : 25.00
1. Hearn, Lafcadio, 1850-1904—Homes and haunts—Japan. 2. Hearn, Lafcadio, 1850-1904—Appreciation—Japan. 3. Authors, American—19th century—Biography. 4. Japan—Description and travel—1801-1900. I. Title. **BIP**

Hearn, Lafcadio, 1850-1904—Manuscripts—Facsimiles.

HEARN, Lafcadio, 1850- 813'.4 B 1904.
Letters / Lafcadio Hearn ; [editors, Hojin Yano, Tadanobu Kawai, Hiroyishi Kishimoto]. New York : AMS Press, 1975. p. cm. Reprints of letters in the Tenri University Library, Tenri, Japan. Contents.Contents.—v. 1. To and from various persons.—v. 2. To and from B. H. Chamberlain. [PS1918.A45 1975] 75-25954 ISBN 0-404-13210-3 (v. 1)
1. Hearn, Lafcadio, 1850-1904—Correspondence. 2. Hearn, Lafcadio, 1850-1904—Manuscripts—Facsimiles. 3. Toyama, Masakazu, 1848-1900. 4. Chamberlain, Basil Hall, 1850-1935. I. Chamberlain, Basil Hall, 1850-1935.

Hearne, Samuel, 1745-1792.

LAUT, Agnes Christina, 971.2'01 1871-1936.
Pathfinders of the West; being the thrilling story of the adventures of the men who discovered the great Northwest, Radisson, La Verendrye, Lewis, and Clark. Illus. by Remington, Goodwin, Marchand and others. Freeport, N.Y., Books for Libraries Press [1969] xxv, 380 p. illus., maps, ports. 23 cm. (Essay index reprint series) "First published 1904." [F1060.7.L38 1969] 74-90651
1. Radisson, Pierre Esprit, 1620?-1710. 2. La Verendrye, Pierre Gaultier de Varennes, sieur de, 1685-1749. 3. Hearne, Samuel, 1745-1792. 4. Mackenzie, Alexander, Sir, 1763-1820. 5. Lewis and Clark Expedition. 6. Northwest, Canadian—Discovery and exploration. I. Title.

Hearne, Samuel, 1745-1792 — Juvenile literature.

SYME, Ronald, 1910- 923.942
On foot to the Arctic; the story of Samuel Hearne. Illustrated by William Stobbs. New York, W. Morrow, 1959. 187 p. illus. 21 cm. [F1060.7.H497] 59-5530
1. Hearne, Samuel, 1745-1792 — Juvenile literature. I. Title.

SYME, Ronald, 1910- 923.942
On foot to the Arctic; the story of Samuel Hearne. Illustrated by William Stobbs. New York, W. Morrow, 1959. 187 p. illus. 21 cm. [F1060.7.H497] 59-5530
1. Hearne, Samuel, 1745-1792—Juvenile literature. I. Title.

Hearne, Samuel, 1745-1792 — Juvenile literature. Full name: Neville Ronald Syme.

SYME, Ronald, 1910- 923.942
On foot to the Arctic; the story of Samuel Hearne. Illustrated by William Stobbs. New York, W. Morrow, 1959. 187 p. illus. 21 cm. [F1060.7.H497] 59-5530
1. Hearne, Samuel, 1745-1792 — Juvenile literature. Full name: Neville Ronald Syme. I. Title.

Hearst. George, 1820-1891.

OLDER, Fremont, 1856- 622.0924 1935
George Hearst, California pioneer. by Mr. and Mrs. Fremont Older. Front. and headbands from the orig. ed. by William Wilke. Los Angeles, Westernlore Pr. [c.] 1966 240p. illus. ports. 21cm. (Westernlore great West and Indian series. 31) Pub. orig. in 1933, for private dist. only. [E664.H43O4] 66-16725 7.50
1. Hearst. George, 1820-1891. I. Older, Cora Miranda (Baggerly) joint author. II. Title.

Hearst, Patricia, 1954-

BAKER, Marilyn. 322.4'2'0924 B
Exclusive! The inside story of Patricia Hearst and the SLA [by] Marilyn Baker with Sally Brompton. New York, Macmillan [1974] ix, 246 p. illus. 24 cm. [F866.2.H42B34] 74-16300 ISBN 0-02-506400-2 8.95
1. Hearst, Patricia, 1954- 2. Symbionese Liberation Army. I. Brompton, Sally, joint author. II. Title. **BIP**

WEST, Don, 1928- 322.4'2'0924 B
Patty/Tania/ Don West and Jerry Belcher. New York : Pyramid Books, 1975. 347 p. ; 18 cm. [F866.2.H42W47] 74-25050 ISBN 0-515-03727-3 : 1.25
1. Hearst, Patricia, 1954- 2. Symbionese Liberation Army. I. Belcher, Jerry, joint author. II. Title.

Hearst, William Randolph,

HEARST, William Randolph, 923.247 Jr.
Khrushchev and the Russian challenge. Original title: Ask me anything--our adventures with Khrushchev. [By] William Randolph Hearst, Jr., Frank Conniff, Bob Considine. With new chapters added. New York, Avon [c.1960, 1961] 255p. (G1060) .50 pap.,
I. Title.

HEARST, William Randolph, 920.5 1863-1951.
William Randolph Hearst, a portrait in his own words; edited by Edmond D. Coblentz. New York, Simon and Schuster, 1952. 309 p. illus. 22 cm. [PN4874.H4A3] 52-10863
I. Coblentz, Edmond D. ed. II. Title.

Hearst, William Randolph, 1863-1951.

HEARST, William Randolph, 923.247 Jr.
Khrushchev and the Russian challenge. Original title: Ask me anything--our adventures with Khrushchev. [By] William Randolph Hearst, Jr., Frank Conniff, Bob Considine. With new chapters added. New York, Avon [c.1960, 1961] 255p. (G1060) .50 pap.,
I. Title.

HEARST, William Randolph, 920.5 1863-1951.
William Randolph Hearst, a portrait in his own words; edited by Edmond D. Coblentz. New York, Simon and Schuster, 1952. 309 p. illus. 22 cm. [PN4874.H4A3] 52-10863
I. Coblentz, Edmond D. ed. II. Title.

LUNDBERG, Ferdinand, 070.4'0924 B 1902-
Imperial Hearst; a social biography. With a pref. by Charles A. Beard. Westport, Conn., Greenwood Press [1970] 406 p. 23 cm. Reprint of the 1936 ed. Bibliography: p. 382-390. [PN4874.H4L8 1970] 74-98850
1. Hearst, William Randolph, 1863-1951. I. Title.

MURRAY, Ken, 1903- 917.94'78
The golden days of San Simeon. Foreword by Ronald Reagan. [1st ed.] Garden City, N.Y., Doubleday, 1971. xi, 163 p. illus., ports. 27 cm. [F868.S18M8] 73-130962 10.00
1. Hearst, William Randolph, 1863-1951. 2. Hearst-San Simeon State Historical Monument. I. Title. **BIP**

OLDER, Cora Miranda 070.5'092'4 B (Baggerly)
William Randolph Hearst, American. With a foreword by Fremont Older. Freeport, N.Y., Books for Libraries Press [1972] p. Reprint of the 1936 ed. [PN4874.H4O5 1972] 72-7195 ISBN 0-8369-6951-0
1. Hearst, William Randolph, 1863-1951.

SWANBERG, W. A., 1907- 920.5
Citizen Hearst, a biography of William Randolph Hearst. New York, Bantam [1963, c.1961] 653p. 18cm. (N2507) Bibl. .95 pap.,
1. Hearst, William Randolph, 1863-1951. I. Title.

SWANBERG, W A 1907- 920.5
Citizen Hearst, a biography of William Randolph Hearst. New York, Scribner [1961] 555 p. illus. 24 cm. Includes bibliography. [PN4874.H4S83] 61-7220
1. Hearst, William Randolph, 1863-1951. I. Title.

SWANBERG, W. A 1907- 920.5
Citizen Hearst, a biography of William Randolph Hearst. New York, Bantam [1967.c.1961] xv, 653 p. 18cm (Matrix ed, QM 1048) Bibl. [PN4874.H4S83] pap. 1.25
1. Hearst, William Randolph, 1863-1951. I. Title.

SWANBERG, W. A., 1907- 920.5
Citizen Hearst, a biography of William Randolph Hearst. New York, Scribner [1961] 555 p. illus. 24 cm. Includes bibliography. [PN4874.H4S83] 61-7220
1. Hearst, William Randolph, 1863-1951. I. Title.

TEBBEL, John 920.5
The life and good times of William Randolph Hearst. New York, Paperback Lib. [1962, c.1952] 346p. (Gold ed. 54-132) .75 pap.,
1. Hearst, William Randolph, 1863-1961. I. Title.

TEBBEL, John William, 1912- 920.5
The life and good times of William Randolph Hearst. [1st ed.] New York, Dutton, 1952. 386 p. 22 cm. [PN4874.H4T4] 52-8258
1. Hearst, William Randolph, 1863-1951.

TEBBEL, John William, 1912- v. 12
The life and good times of William Randolph Hearst. New York, Paperback Library [1962] 349 p. (Paperback library. 54-132) 65-21829
1. Hearst, William Randolph, 1863-1951. I. Title.

WINKLER, John K. 920.5
William Randolph Hearst, a new appraisal. New York, Avon [1962, c.1955] 384p. illus. (V-2045) .75 pap.,
1. Hearst, William Randolph, 1863-1961. I. Title.

WINKLER, John Kennedy, 920.5 1891-
William Randolph Hearst, a new appraisal. New York, Hastings House [1955] 325p. illus. 24cm. [PN4874.H4W52] 55-11639
1. Hearst, William Randolph, 1863-1951. I. Title.

Heart—Diseases.

STUART, Jesse, 1907- 616.12
The year of my rebirth. Illus. by Barry Martin. New York, McGraw-Hill [1956] 342 p. illus. 22 cm. [RC682.S8] 56-12275
1. Heart—Diseases. I. Title.

Heart—Diseases—Personal narratives.

GRAHAM, Marion 616.1'2'06520924 B Francis, 1919-
The conquest of fear [by] M. F. Graham. Nashville, Broadman Press [1973] 124 p. illus. 21 cm. Bibliography: p. 122-124. [RC682.G68] 72-97600 ISBN 0-8054-8228-8 1.50 (pbk.)
1. Heart—Diseases—Personal narratives. 2. Faith-cure. I. Title. **BIP**

Heart—Transplantation.

BARNARD, Christiaan 617'.0924 B Neethling.
Christiaan Barnard: one life [by] Christiaan Barnard and Curtis Bill Pepper. [1st American ed. New York] Macmillan [1970, c1969] 402 p. 24 cm. [RD598.B37 1970] 78-99020
1. Heart—Transplantation. I. Pepper, Curtis Bill, joint author. II. Title.

Heath, Edward.

HEATH, Edward. 780'.92'4 B
Music : a joy for life / Edward Heath. London : Sidgwick & Jackson, 1976. 208 p. : ill. (some col.), ; 26 cm. Includes index. [ML429.H35A3] 77-351585 ISBN 0-283-98349-3 : £5.95
1. Heath, Edward. 2. Musicians—England—Biography. I. Title. **BIP**

HEATH, Edward. 797.1'4'0924 B
Sailing : a course of my life / Edward Heath. New York : Stein and Day, [1976] p. cm. [DA591.H4A36] 75-29912 ISBN 0-8128-1886-5 : 14.95
1. Heath, Edward. 2. Sailing. I. Title.

LAING, Margaret 942.085'092'4 B Irene.
Edward Heath, Prime Minister [by] Margaret Laing. New York, Third Press [1973, c1972] x, 258 p. illus. 24 cm. "A Joseph Okpaku book." Includes bibliographical references. [DA591.H4L34 1973] 72-95089 ISBN 0-89388-086-8 10.00
I. Heath, Edward. I. Title.

Heath, Lawrence Seymour,

HEATH, Lawrence Seymour, 920 1869-
My footsteps on the sands of time, an autobiography. [Robinson? Ill.] c1955. 71p. illus. 28cm. [CT275.H4867A3] 56-15250
I. Title.

Hebbel, Friedrich, 1813-1863.

KUH, Emil, 1828-1876. 838'.7'09 B
Biographie Friedrich Hebbel's. Wien, W. Braumuller, 1877. [New York, AMS Press, 1972] 2 v. port. 19 cm. Reprint of the 1877 ed. Includes bibliographical references. [PT2296.K8 1972] 75-171632 ISBN 0-404-03784-4
1. Hebbel, Friedrich, 1813-1863. I. Title. **BIP**

PURDIE, Edna, 1894- 832'.7
Friedrich Hebbel: a study of his life and work. [London] Oxford University Press [1969] 276 p. 23 cm. First published in 1932. Bibliography: p. [272]-273. [PT2296.P8 1969] 74-428330 unpriced
1. Hebbel, Friedrich, 1813-1863.

Hebblethwaite, Roger.

HEBBLETHWAITE, 338.4'7'910924 Roger.
Just the ticket; the travel industry, with a foreword by Eric A. L. Sutherland. Reading, Educational Explorers, 1973. 136 p. illus. 22 cm. (My life and my work series) [G154.5.H42A34] 74-163196 ISBN 0-85225-751-1 £1.50
1. Hebblethwaite, Roger. 2. Travel agents. I. Title.

Hebrew literature—Italy.

MORAIS, Sabato, 892.4'09'945 1823-1897.
Italian Hebrew literature. Edited by Julius H. Greenstone. With a foreword by Henry S. Morais. New York, Hermon Press [1970] vi, 244 p. port. 24 cm. Reprint of the 1926 ed. "A critical and hermeneutical introduction to the Pentateuch," by S. D. Luzzatto: p. [93]-152. Includes bibliographical references. [PJ5049.I8M6 1970] 70-76171 9.75
1. Bible. O.T. Pentateuch—Criticism, interpretation, etc. 2. Hebrew literature—Italy. 3. Jews in Italy—Biography. I. Luzzatto, Samuele Davide, 1800-1865. II. Title. **BIP**

Hecht, Ben,

HECHT, Ben, 1893- 928.1
A child of the century. [New York] Simon and Schuster, 1954. 654p. illus. 22cm. Autobiography. [PS3515.E18Z5] 53-9699
I. Title.

Hecht, Darwin,

HECHT, Darwin, M.D., 1889- 926.1
This is my life; a vivid true story of seventy years experience. Brooklyn, N.Y., Darem Pub., 1368 President St. 1963[c.] 1961. 63-23105 3.75
I. Title.

Hecker, Isaac Thomas, 1819-1888.

ELLIOTT, Walter, 1842-1928. 271'.64'024 B
The life of Father Hecker. New York, Arno Press, 1972. xvii, 428 p. port. 24 cm. (Religion in America, series II) Reprint of the 1891 ed. [BX4705.H4E6 1972] 75-38446 ISBN 0-405-04065-2
1. Hecker, Isaac Thomas, 1819-1888. I. Title. BIP

HOLDEN, Vincent F. 271'.64'024
The early years of Isaac Thomas Hecker (1819-1844), by Vincent F. Holden. Washington, Catholic University of America Press, 1939. [New York, AMS Press, 1974] ix, 257 p. 23 cm. Reprint of the author's thesis, Catholic University of America, 1939, which was issued as v. 29 of the Catholic University of America. Studies in American church history. Bibliography: p. 247-252. [BX4705.H4H6 1974] 73-3583 ISBN 0-404-57779-2 11.00
1. Hecker, Isaac Thomas, 1819-1888. I. Title. II. Series: Catholic University of America. Studies in American church history, v. 29. BIP

HOLDEN, Vincent F 922.273
The Yankee Paul: Isaac Thomas Hecker. Milwaukee, Bruce Pub. Co. [1958] 508p. illus. 23cm. Includes bibliography. [BX4705.H4H63] 58-12230
1. Hecker, Isaac Thomas, 1819-1888. I. Title.

MCSORLEY, Joseph, 1874- 922.273
Father Hecker and his friends; studies and reminiscences. Introd. by John F. O'Hara. St. Louis, B. Herder Book Co., 1952. 304p. illus. 21cm. [BX4705.H4M25] 52-12994
1. Hecker, Issac Thomas, 1819-1888. I. Title.

Hecker, Isaac Thomas, 1819-1888—Drama.

AMERICAN portrait; v. 12
the story of Father Hecker. A new kind of 'reading' play-for a stage without scenery, by Emmet Lavery, with music by Robert E. Moonan. New York, French [1959] 70p. Without music.
1. Hecker, Isaac Thomas, 1819-1888-Drama. I. Moonan, Robert E II. Lavery, Emmet, 1902

Heckscher, August, 1913-

HECKSCHER, August, 1913- 352'.73'092
Alive in the city: memoir of an ex-commissioner. New York, Scribner [1974] viii, 294 p. illus. 24 cm. [SB470.H4H43] 73-11588 8.95
1. Heckscher, August, 1913- 2. New York (City)—Parks. 3. New York (City)—Politics and government—1951- I. Title.

Hedderich family.

HETRICK, Martha Louise, 1907- 929'.2'0973
The Hetrick family, 1651-1955; historical and biographical sketch of the Hedderich, Heddrich, Hedrick, Heidenrich, Heidrich, Hetrich, Hetrick family [Harrisburg? Pa., 1955] xvi, 165p. illus., ports., map, coat of arms. 25cm. Bibliography: p. 161. [CS71.H59 1955] 55-36305
1. Hedderich family. I. Title.

Hefner, Hugh Marston, 1926-

BRADY, Frank. 070.5'092'4 B
Hefner. New York, Macmillan [1974] 231 p. illus. 21 cm. [Z473.H44B7] 74-13739 ISBN 0-02-514600-9 7.95
1. Hefner, Hugh Marston, 1926-

BRADY, Frank. v. 12 B
Hefner. New York, Ballantine Books [1975 c1974] 272 p., 18 cm. [Z473.H44B7] 070.50924 1.75 (pbk.)
1. Hefner, Hugh Marston, 1926. I. Title.
L.C. card no. for original edition: 74-13739. BIP

Hefner, Robert Alexander, 1874-1971.

TRAFZER, Clifford E. 347'.766'03534 B
The judge : the life of Robert A. Hefner / by Clifford Earl Trafzer. 1st ed. Norman : Published for the Oklahoma Heritage Association by the University of Oklahoma Press, [1975] xviii, 298 p. : ill. ; 22 cm. (Oklahoma trackmaker series ; no. 1) Includes index. Bibliography: p. 287-291. [KF373.H43T73] 75-16741 ISBN 0-8061-1307-3 : 9.95
1. Hefner, Robert Alexander, 1874-1971. I. Title. II. Series. BIP

Hegel, Georg Wilhelm Friedrich, 1770-1831.

CAIRD, Edward, 1835-1908. 193 B
Hegel. [Hamden, Conn.] Archon Books, 1968. viii, 224 p. port. 19 cm. Reprint of the 1883 ed. [B2947.C3 1968] 68-8015 ISBN 0-208-00720-2
1. Hegel, Georg Wilhelm Friedrich, 1770-1831. BIP

FINDLAY, John Niemayer. v. 12
Hegel; a re-examination. New York, Collier Books [1962] 382 p. (BS110V) Bibliographical footnotes. 63-15924
1. Hegel, Georg Wilhelm Friedrich, 1770-1831. I. Title. BIP

LUQUEER, Frederic Ludlow, 1870- v. 12
Hegel as educator. New York, AMS Press, 1967. 185 p. 24 cm. Reprint of the 1896 ed. 68-51496
1. Hegel, Georg Wilhelm Friedrich, 1770-1831. I. Title. BIP

TAYLOR, Charles, 1931- 193
Hegel / Charles Taylor. Cambridge [Eng.] ; New York : Cambridge University Press, 1975. xii, 580 p. ; 24 cm. Includes index. Bibliography: p. 574-577. [B2948.T39] 74-25642 ISBN 0-521-20679-0 : 36.00
1. Hegel, Georg Wilhelm Friedrich, 1770-1831. I. Title. BIP

WIEDMANN, Franz, 1927- 193 B
Hegel; an illustrated biography. Translated from the German by Joachim Neugroschel. New York, Pegasus [1968] 140 p. illus., ports. 21 cm. Translation of Georg Wilhelm Friedrich Hegel in Selbstzeugnissen und Bilddokumenten. Bibliography: p. 135. [B2947.W513] 68-21037 5.00
1. Hegel, Georg Wilhelm Friedrich, 1770-1831.

Hegener, Mark.

HEGENER, Mark. 922.245
St. Francis of Assisi, the poverello. [Chicago, Franciscan Herald Press, 1956] 92p. illus. 18cm. (Herald books) [BX4700.F6H37] 56-4537
I. Francesco d'Assisi, Saint, 1182-1226. II. Title.

Heidenreich, Steve.

HEIDENREICH, Steve. 796.4'26 B
Running back / Steve Heidenreich and Dave Dorr. New York : Hawthorn Books, c1979. 219 p. ; 24 cm. [GV697.H39A37 1979] 78-71020 ISBN 0-8015-6494-8 : 11.95
1. Heidenreich, Steve. 2. Runners (Sports)—United States—Biography. I. Dorr, Dave, joint author. II. Title. BIP

Heimler, Eugene.

HEIMLER, Eugene. 940.54'72'43
Night of the mist / Eugene Heimler. Westport, Conn. : Greenwood Press, 1978, c1959. 191 p. ; 23 cm. Autobiographical. Reprint of the ed. published by Vanguard Press, New York. [D805.G3H37 1978] 77-28508 ISBN 0-313-20229-X lib.bdg. : 15.25
1. Heimler, Eugene. 2. World War, 1939-1945—Prisoners and prisons, German. 3. World War, 1939-1945—Personal narratives, English. 4. Prisoners of war—Germany—Biography. I. Title. BIP

Heine, Heinrich, 1797-1856.

BROD, Max, 1884- 928.3
Heinrich Heine; the artist in revolt. Tr. from German by Joseph Witriol. New York, Collier [1962, c.1957] 381p. (BS53) 1.50 pap.,
1. Heine, Heinrich, 1797-1856 I. Title.

BROD, Max, 1884- 928.3
Heinrich Heine; the artist in revolt. Translated from the German by Joseph Witriol. [1st U. S. ed.] New York, New York University Press, 1957. 355p. illus. 22cm. [PT2328.B652] 57-10138
1. Heine, Heinrich; 179-1856. I. Title.

BROD, Max, 1884- v. 12
Heinrich Heine: [the artist in revolt] Translated from the German by Joseph Witriol. New York, Collier Books [1962, c1957] 381 p. 18 cm. (Collier books, BS53) 63-7052
1. Heine, Heinrich, 1797-1856. I. Title.

BUTLER, Eliza Marian, 1885- 928.3
Heinrich, Heine; a biography. New York, Philosophical Library [1957] 291 p. illus. 23 cm. [PT2328.B8 1957] 57-14229
1. Heine, Heinrich, 1797-1856.

BUTLER, Eliza Marian, 1885-1959. 831'.6 B
Heinrich Heine, a biography. Westport, Conn., Greenwood Press [1970, c1956] xii, 291 p. illus., ports. 23 cm. Bibliography: p. 277-280. [PT2328.B8 1970] 70-106684
1. Heine, Heinrich, 1797-1856. I. Title.

FEJTO, Francois, 1909- 831'.7 B
Heine; a biography. Translated by Mervyn Savill. Port Washington, N.Y., Kennikat Press [1970] 300 p. illus., ports. 23 cm. Reprint of the 1946 ed. Bibliography: p. 291-294. [PT2328.F42 1970] 78-103187
1. Heine, Heinrich, 1797-1856.

HEINE, Heinrich, 1797-1856. 928.3
Heinrich Heine; a biographical anthology, edited by Hugo Bieber. English translations made or selected by Moses Hadas. [1st ed.] Philadelphia, Jewish Publication Society of America, 1956. viii, 452p. 24cm. (The Gitelson library) [PT2316.A3B5] 56-7782
I. Bieber, Hugo, 1883-1950, ed. II. Title.

HEINE, Heinrich, 1797-1856. 831'.7 B
Memoirs, from his works, letters, and conversations. Edited by Gustav Karpeles. [English translation by] Gilbert Cannan. New York, Arno Press, 1973. viii, 299, vi, 303 p. ports. 23 cm. (The Jewish people: history, religion, literature) Reprint of the 1910 ed. published by J. Lane Co., New York. [PT2329.A1K32 1973] 73-2204 ISBN 0-405-05269-3 30.00
1. Heine, Heinrich, 1797-1856. I. Karpeles, Gustav, 1848-1909, ed. II. Title. III. Series.

VALLENTIN, Antonina, 1893- 928.3
Heine; poet in exile. Translated by Harrison Brown. Garden City, n.y., Doubleday, 1956. 320 p. 22 cm. [PT2328.V32] 56-5490
1. Heine, Heinrich, 1797-1856. I. Title.

VALLENTIN, Antonina, 1893-1957. 928.3
Heine: poet in exile. Translated by Harrison Brown. Garden City, N. Y., Doubleday, 1956. 320 p. 22 cm. [PT2328.V32 1956] 56-5490
1. Heine, Heinrich, 1797-1856.

VALLENTIN, Antonina, 1893-1957. 831'.7 B
Poet in exile; the life of Heinrich Heine. Translated by Harrison Brown. Port Washington, N.Y., Kennikat Press [1970] 320 p. 22 cm. Reprint of the 1934 ed. Translation of Henri Heine. [PT2328.V32 1970] 72-113327
1. Heine, Heinrich, 1797-1856. I. Title.

Heine, Heinrich, 1797-1856—Biography.

BROD, Max, 1884-1968. 831'.7 B
Heinrich Heine : the artist in revolt / by Max Brod ; translated from the German by Joseph Witriol. Westport, Conn. : Greenwood Press, 1976. p. cm. Reprint of the 1957 ed. published by New York University Press, New York. [PT2328.B652 1976] 76-21292 ISBN 0-8371-8992-6 lib.bdg. : 19.75
1. Heine, Heinrich, 1797-1856—Biography. BIP

HEINE, Heinrich, 1797-1856. 928.3
Heinrich Heine; a biographical anthology, edited by Hugo Bieber. English translations made or selected by Moses Hadas. [1st ed.] Philadelphia, Jewish Publication Society of America, 1956. viii, 452p. 24cm. (The Gitelson library) [PT2316.A3B5] 56-7782
I. Bieber, Hugo, 1883-1950, ed. II. Title.

SAMMONS, Jeffrey L. 831'.7 B
Heinrich Heine / by Jeffrey L. Sammons. Princeton, N.J. : Princeton University Press, c1980. p. cm. Includes index. Bibliography: p. [PT2328.S2] 79-84015 ISBN 0-691-06321-4 : 27.50 ISBN 0-06-910081-0 (pbk.) : 9.75
1. Heine, Heinrich, 1797-1856—Biography. 2. Authors, German—19th century—Biography.

Heinich, Edward Oscar.

BLOCK, Eugene B. 923.673
The wizard of Berkeley. New York, Coward-McCann [1958] 254 p. 21 cm. [HV6023.H4B6] 58-5691
1. Heinich, Edward Oscar. I. Title.

Heinkel, Ernst,

HEINKEL, Ernst, 1888- 926.2913
Stormy life; memoirs of a pioneer of the air age. Edited by Jurgen Thorwald. Translated from the German. [1st American ed.] New York, Dutton, 1956. 256 p. illus. 22 cm. [TL540.H4A33 1956a] 56-8300
I. Title.

Heinrich, Prince of Prussia, 1726-1802.

EASUM, Chester Verne. 943'.053'0924
Prince Henry of Prussia, brother of Frederick the Great, by Chester V. Easum. Westport, Conn., Greenwood Press [1971, c1942] 403 p. illus., facsims., geneal. table, fold. map, ports. 23 cm. Bibliography: p. 381-385. [DD402.H4E2 1971] 75-113061 ISBN 0-8371-4697-6
1. Heinrich, Prince of Prussia, 1726-1802. BIP

Heinsheimer, Hans, W.

HEINSHEIMER, Hans W. 780'.92'4 B
Menagerie in F sharp / H. W. Heinsheimer. Westport, Conn. : Greenwood Press, 1979, c1947. 275 p. ; 23 cm. Reprint of the ed. published by Doubleday, Garden City, N.Y. [ML427.H4A3 1979] 78-12062 ISBN 0-313-21004-7 lib. bdg. 19.75
1. Heinsheimer, Hans, W. 2. Musicians—Biography. I. Title. BIP

Heinsohn, A. G., 1896-

HEINSOHN, A. G., 1896- 338.7'67'700924 B
Cousin Mercedes and the White Russian / by A. G. Heinsohn, Jr. Boston : Western Islands, [1974] 262 p. : ill. ; 21 cm. [HD3616.U47H43] 74-18736 ISBN 0-88279-231-8 : 7.00
1. Heinsohn, A. G., 1896- 2. Industry and state—United States. 3. Bureaucracy. I. Title. BIP

Heinsohn, Tommy.

HEINSOHN, Tommy. 796.32'3'0924 B
Heinsohn, don't you ever smile? : The life & times of Tommy Heinsohn & the Boston Celtics / by Tommy Heinsohn, with Leonard Lewin. 1st ed. Garden City, N.Y. : Doubleday, 1976. 213 p., [12] leaves of plates : ill. ; 22 cm. [GV884.H44A33] 75-29885 ISBN 0-385-11336-6 : 7.95
1. Heinsohn, Tommy. 2. Boston Celtics (Basketball team) 3. Basketball. I. Lewin, Leonard, joint author. II. Title.

Heintzelman, Samuel Peter, 1805-1880.

NORTH, Diane M. T. 338.7'62'20924 B
Samuel Peter Heintzelman and the Sonora Exploring and Mining Company / Diane M. T. North. Tucson : University of Arizona Press, 1980, c1979 p. cm. Includes index. Bibliography: p. [HD9506.U62N67] 79-15307 ISBN 0-8165-0679-5 : 12.50 pbk. : 7.95 pbk.
1. Heintzelman, Samuel Peter, 1805-1880. 2. Sonora Exploring and Mining Company—History. 3. Businessmen—United States—Biography. 4. Arizona—Industries—History. I. Title. BIP

Heinz, Hans Joachim.

HEINZ, Hans Joachim. 301.29'68'1 B
Namkwa : life among the Bushmen / Hans-Joachim Heinz and Marshall Lee ; with a foreword by Margaret Mead. 1st American ed. Boston : Houghton Mifflin, 1979, c1978. xiii, 272 p., [6] leaves of plates : ill. ; 22 cm. Includes index. [DT797.H44 1979] 79-346 ISBN 0-395-27611-X : 10.95
1. Heinz, Hans Joachim. 2. San (African people) 3. Anthropologists—Biography. 4. Namkwa. 5. San (African people)—Biography. I. Lee, Marshall, joint author. II. Title. BIP

Heinz, Henry John, 1844-1919.

ALBERTS, Robert C. 338.7'66'40280924 B
The good provider: H. J. Heinz and his 57 varieties [by] Robert C. Alberts. Boston, Houghton Mifflin, 1973. xvi, 297 p. illus. 24 cm. Bibliography: p. [279]-283. [HD9321.9.H4A65] 73-9625 ISBN 0-395-17126-1 10.00
1. Heinz, Henry John, 1844-1919. 2. Heinz (H. J.) Company. I. Title.

Heinze, Frederick Augustus, 1869-1914.

NCNELIS, Sarah. 338.7'62'23430924 B
Copper king at war; the biography of F. Augustus Heinze. [Missoula] University of Montana Press, 1968. xi, 230 p. illus., ports. 24 cm. Bibliography: p. [217]-219. [HD9539.C6H364] 73-1462
1. Heinze, Frederick Augustus, 1869-1914. 2. Copper industry and trade—Montana. I. Title.

Heinzl, Brigitte Franziska,

HEINZL, Brigitte Franziska, 1937- 769'.92'4
Durer; [the life and work of the artist, illustrated with 80 full-color plates, by] Brigitte Heinzl. [Translated from Italian by Diane Goldrei. 1st American ed.] New York, Grosset & Dunlap [1969, c1968] 39 p. illus., col. plates. 18 cm. (The New Grosset art library, 19) Bibliography: p. 26-28. [ND588.D9H463 1969] 69-13391
1. Durer, Albrecht, 1471-1528. II. Title.

Heisman, John William, 1869-1936—Juvenile literature.

VAN RIPER, Guernsey, Jr. 1909- 920
Yea, coach! Three great football coaches. Illus. by Robert Doremus. Champaign, Ill., Garrard [c.1966] 94p. illus. (pt. col.) ports. 24cm. (Sports lib. bks.) [GV939.A1V3] 66-12389 2.19 bds.,
1. Warner, Glenn Scobey, 1871-1954—Juvenile literature. 2. Heisman, John William, 1869-1936—Juvenile literature. 3. Rockne, Knute Kenneth, 1888-1931—Juvenile literature. I. Title.

Heiss, Carol, 1940-

BOLSTAD, Helen Cambria 927.9691
Golden skates; the story of Carol Heiss, teen-age champion. New York, Published for Scholastic Book Service by Ridge Press [dist. Rutledge Bks.] [1960] 64p. ports. 20cm. (A Rutledge book, RP9) 60-1129 .25 pap.,
1. Heiss, Carol, 1940- I. Title.

Heiss, Carol, 1940- —Juvenile literature.

PARKER, Robert 927.9691
Carol Heiss, Olympic queen. Garden City, N. Y., Doubleday [c.1961] 128p. illus. "Text based on Golden skates, by Helen Bolstad." (Signal book) 61-8289 2.50 bds.,
1. Heiss, Carol, 1940- —Juvenile literature. I. Title.

PARKER, Robert. 927.9691
Carol Heiss: Olympic queen. [1st ed.] Garden City, N. Y., Doubleday [1961] 128p. illus. 22cm. (A Signal book) 'Text based on Golden skates, by Helen Bolstad. [GV850.H38P3] 61-8289
1. Heiss, Carol, 1940—Juvenile literature. I. Title.

Heiss, Michael, Abp., 1818-1890.

BLIED, Benjamin Joseph, 1908- 922.273
Three archbishops of Milwaukee: Michael Heiss (1818-1890) Frederick Katzer (1844-1903) Sebastian Messmer (1847-1930) Milwaukee, 1955. 160p. 23cm. [BX1417.M5B5] 55-30113
1. Heiss, Michael, Abp., 1818-1890. 2. Katzer, Friedrich Xaver, Abp., 1844-1903. 3. Messmer, Sebastian Gebhard, Abp., 1847-1930. 4. Bishops—U. S.—Milwaukee. I. Title.

LUDWIG, Mileta, Sister. 271'.3'0924 (B)
Right-hand glove uplifted; a biography of Archbishop Michael Heiss, by Sister M. Mileta Ludwig. [1st ed.] New York, Pageant Press [1968] 567 p. illus., ports. 24 cm. $7.50 Includes bibliographical references. [BX4705.H4527L8] 67-30506
1. Heiss, Michael, Abp., 1818-1890. I. Title.

Heizer, Dorothy Wendell, 1881-

KRECHNIAK, Helen Bullard, 1902- 745.59'22
Dorothy Heizer, the artist and her dolls [by] Helen Bullard. New York, National Institute of American Doll Artists, 1972. v, 78 p. illus. 23 cm. Bibliography: p. 76. [NK4894.2.H34K73] 71-190747
1. Heizer, Dorothy Wendell, 1881- I. Title.

Held, Anna, 1877?-1918.

HELD, Anna, 1877?-1918. 791'.092'4 B
Anna Held and Flo Ziegfeld / Liane Carrera ; translated from the French by Guy Daniels. 1st American ed. Hicksville, N.Y. : Exposition Press, c1979. 175 p., [16] leaves of plates : ill. ; 22 cm. Translation of Memoires, une etoile francaise au ciel de l'Amerique. [PN2287.H42A313 1979] 79-50382 ISBN 0-682-49309-0 : 10.00
1. Held, Anna, 1877?-1918. 2. Entertainers—United States—Biography. 3. Entertainers—France—Biography. I. Carrera, Liane. II. Title.

Helen of Troy.

POLLARD, John 808.8027
Helen of Troy. New York, Roy [1966, c.1965] 192p. illus. 23cm. [PN57.H4P6] 66-18819 5.25 bds.,
1. Helen of Troy. I. Title.

POLLARD, John Richard Thornhill, 1914- 808.8027
Helen of Troy. New York, Roy Publishers [1965] 192 p. illus. 23 cm. [PN57.H4P6] 66-18819
1. Helen of Troy. I. Title.

Helena, Saint, 246 (ca.)-326?.

DAUGHTERS of St. Paul. JUV
Noble lady; the life of St. Helen, written and illustrated by the Daughters of St. Paul. [Boston] St. Paul Editions [1966] 73 p. illus. 22 cm. (Their Encounter books) The life story of Helena, mother of the Emperor Constantine, who persuaded him to lift the ban on Christianity in the Roman Empire. [PZ7.D264No] 92 AC 67
1. Helena, Saint, 246 (ca.)-326?. I. Title.

Helena, Saint, 246 (ca.)-326?—Juvenile literature.

HARRIS, Mary Kathleen 92
Helena. Drawings by Michael A. Hampshire. New York, Sheed [1964] 1v. (unpaged) illus. (pt. col.) 21cm. (Patron saint bks.) [BX4700.H45H3] 64-18774 2.50
1. Helena, Saint, 246 (ca.)-326?—Juvenile literature. I. Title.

SMARIDGE, Norah Antoinette 920
Saint Helena. Drawings by James T. Andrews. Paterson, N. J., St. Anthony Guild [1962] 28p. col. illus. 23cm. 62-15583 1.39 bds.,
1. Helena, Saint, 246 (ca.)-326? —Juvenile literature. I. Title.

Helfferich, Karl Theodor, 1872-1924.

WILLIAMSON, John G., 1933- 330'.0924 B
Karl Helfferich, 1872-1924: economist, financier, politician [by] John G. Williamson. Princeton, N.J., Princeton University Press, 1971. xviii, 439 p. illus. 25 cm. Bibliography: p. 415-424. [DD231.H35W5] 74-132245 ISBN 0-691-05145-3 13.50
1. Helfferich, Karl Theodor, 1872-1924. 2. Germany—Economic policy.

Hell's Angels.

HENDERSON, Wild Bill. 364.14'3'0924 B
A place in hell; the autobiography of Wild Bill Henderson as told to H. R. Kaye. Los Angeles, Holloway House Pub. Co. [1968] 312 p. 18 cm. [HV6489.C2H4] 68-23186
1. Hell's Angels. I. Kaye, H. R. II. Title.

Heller, Stephen, 1813-1888.

BARBEDETTE, Hippolyte, 1827-1901. 786.1'092'4 B
Stephen Heller : his life and works / by Hippolyte Barbedette ; translated by Robert Brown-Borthwick ; with new introd. by Ronald E. Booth. Detroit : Detroit Reprints in Music, 1974. xvi, 89, xii p. : ill. ; 19 cm. Reprint of the 1877 ed. published by Ashdown & Parry, London. "Catalogue of pianoforte works by Stephen Heller": xii p. at end. Includes bibliographical references. [ML410.H47B3 1974] 74-75886 ISBN 0-911772-69-3 : 6.50
1. Heller, Stephen, 1813-1888.
A Division of Information Coordinators BIP

Hellerman, Michael.

HELLERMAN, Michael. 364.1'63'0924 B
Wall Street swindler / by Michael Hellerman, with Thomas C. Renner. 1st ed. Garden City, N.Y. : Doubleday, 1977. xi, 367 p. ; 22 cm. [HV6248.H398A38] 76-42335 ISBN 0-385-11284-X : 10.00
1. Hellerman, Michael. 2. Swindlers and swindling—United States—Biography. 3. Securities theft—United States. 4. White collar crimes—United States. I. Renner, Thomas C., joint author. II. Title.

Hellestad, Oscar.

JURGENSEN, Barbara 266.410924
All the bandits of China; adventures of a missionary in a land ravaged by bandits and war lords. Illus. by Robert Friedericksen. Minneapolis, Augsburg [c.1965] 184p. illus. 22cm. [BV3427.H35J8] 65-22839 3.95
1. Hellestad, Oscar. 2. Missions—China. I. Title.

Hellman, Lillian,

HELLMAN, Lillian, 1905- 812'.5'2 B
An unfinished woman; a memoir. [1st ed.] Boston, Little, Brown [1969] 280 p. ports. 25 cm. Autobiographical. [PS3515.E343Z5] 76-75019 7.50
I. Title.

HELLMAN, Lillian, 1905- 812'.5'2 B
Pentimento. [1st ed.] Boston, Little, Brown [1973] 297 p. 25 cm. [PS3515.E343Z498] 73-7747 ISBN 0-316-35520-8 7.95
1. Hellman, Lillian, 1905- I. Title.

HELLMAN, Lillian, 1905- 812'.5'2 B
Pentimento. [New York] New American Library [1974, c1973] 245 p. 18 cm. (A Signet book) [PS3515.E343Z498] 1.95 (pbk.)
1. Hellman, Lillian, 1905- I. Title.
L.C. card number for original ed.: 73-7747.

HELLMAN, Lillian, 1905- 812'.5'2 B
An unfinished woman; a memoir. [1st ed.] Boston, Little, Brown [1969] 280 p. ports. 25 cm. Autobiographical. [PS3515.E343Z5] 76-75019 7.50
I. Title.

MOODY, Richard, 1911- 812'.5'2
Lillian Hellman, playwright. New York, Pegasus [1972] xv, 372 p. illus. 21 cm. (Pegasus American authors) Bibliography: p. 357-361. [PS3515.E343Z78] 76-175224 6.95
1. Hellman, Lillian, 1905-

Hellman, Lillian, 1905- —Biography.

HELLMAN, Lillian, 1905- 812'.5'2 B
Scoundrel time / by Lillian Hellman ; introd. by Gary Wills. Boston : G. K. Hall, 1977, c1976. 211 p. ; 24 cm. "Published in large print." [PS3515.E343Z499 1977] 76-51378 ISBN 0-8161-6446-0 lib.bdg. : 8.95
1. Hellman, Lillian, 1905- —Biography. 2. Dramatists, American—20th century—Biography. 3. Sight-saving books. I. Title. BIP

HELLMAN, Lillian, 1905- 812'.5'2 B
Three / by Lillian Hellman, with new commentaries by the author ; introd. by Richard Poirier. 1st ed. Boston : Little, Brown, c1979. xxv, 726 p., [12] leaves of plates : ill. ; 25 cm. Contents.Contents.—An unfinished woman.—Pentimento.—Scoundrel time. [PS3515.E343Z4994] 79-108376 ISBN 0-316-35514-3 : 16.95
1. Hellman, Lillian, 1905- —Biography. 2. Dramatists, American—20th century—Biography. I. Title.

Helmholtz, Hermann Ludwig Ferdinand von, 1821-1894.

KOENIGSBERGER, Leo, 1837-1921 509.24
Hermann von Helmholtz. Tr. [from German] by Frances A. Welby. Pref. by Lord Kelvin. New York, Dover [1965] xvii, 400p. ports. 22cm. Unabridged, unaltered repubn. of the work orig. pub. in 1906 [Q143.H5K813] 65-27993 2.25 pap.,
1. Helmholtz, Hermann Ludwig Ferdinand von, 1821-1894. I. Title.

KOENIGSBERGER, Leo, 1837- 1921 509.24
Hermann von Helmholtz. Tr. [from German] by Frances A. Welby. Preface by Lord Kelvin [Gloucester, Mass., P. Smith, 1966] xvii, 440p. ports. 22cm. (Dover bk. rebound) The Eng. ed. is a slightly abridged version of the orig. German work. [Q143.H5K813] 4.25
1. Helmholtz, Hermann Ludwig Ferdinand von, 1821-1894. I. Title.

KOENIGSBERGER, Leo, 1837- 1921. 509.24
Hermann von Helmholtz. Translated by Frances A. Welby. With a pref. by Lord Kelvin. New York, Dover Pulbications [1965] xvii, 440 p. ports. 22 cm. "Unabridged and unaltered republication of the work originally published ... in 1906." [Q143.H5K813] 65-27993
1. Helmholtz, Hermann Ludwig Ferdinand von, 1821-1894. I. Title. BIP

Helmreich, William B.

HELMREICH, William B. 974.7'1'04924024 B
Wake up, wake up, to do the work of the creator / William B. Helmreich. 1st ed. New York : Harper & Row, c1976. 210 p. ; 22 cm. [BM755.H33A33 1976] 76-5129 ISBN 0-06-011823-7 : 8.95
1. Helmreich, William B. 2. Orthodox Judaism—United States—Biography. 3. Jewish way of life. 4. New York (City)—Biography. I. Title. BIP

Helms, Edgar James, 1863-

PLUMB, Beatrice, 1886- 923.673
Edgar James Helms, the Goodwill man. Minneapolis, T. S. Denison [1965] 231 p. 22 cm. (Men of achievement series) Bibliography: p. 230-231. [HD7256.U5P58] 64-22880
1. Helms, Edgar James, 1863- 2. Goodwill Industries of America.

PLUMB, Beatrice, 1886- 923.673
Edgar James Helms, the Goodwill man. Minneapolis, Denison [1965] 231p. 22cm. (Men of achievement ser.) Bibl. [HD7256.U5P58] 64-22880 price unreported
1. Helms, Edgar James, 1863- 2. Goodwill Industries of America. I. Title.

Helms, Tom.

HELMS, Tom. 362.4'3'0926 B
Against all odds / Tom Helms. 1st ed. New York : Crowell, c1978. p. cm. [RC406.T4H44 1978] 78-3302 ISBN 0-690-01763-4 : 9.95
1. Helms, Tom. 2. Tetraplegia—Biography. I. Title. BIP

Helper, Hinton Rowan, 1829-1909.

BAILEY, Hugh C 973.71140924 (B)
Hinton Rowan Helper, abolitionist-racist [by] Hugh C. Bailey. University, University of Alabama Press [1965] xi. 256 p. port. 22 cm. (Southern historical publications, no. 7) Bibliography: p. 221-229. [E449.H485] 65-16384
1. Helper, Hinton Rowan, 1829-1909. I. Title. II. Series.

Helpern, Milton, 1902-1977.

HELPERN, Milton, 1902-1977. 614'.19'0924 B
Autopsy : the memoirs of a medical detective / Milton Helpern, with Bernard Knight. New York : St. Martin's Press, [1977] p. cm. Includes index. [RA1025.H4A3] 77-76639 ISBN 0-312-06211-7 : 10.00
1. Helpern, Milton, 1902-1977. 2. Medical examiners (Law)—New York (City)—Biography. I. Knight, Bernard, joint author. II. Title. BIP

HELPERN, Milton, 1902-1977. 614'.19'0924
Autopsy : the memoirs of a medical detective / Milton Helpern, with Bernard Knight. New York : New American Library, 1979, c1977. 272p. ; 18 cm. (A Signet book) [RA1025.H4A3] ISBN 0-451-08607-4 pbk. : 2.50
1. Helpern, Milton, 1902-1977 2. Medical examiners (Law) — New York City — Biography. I. Knight, Bernard, joint author. II. Title.
L.C. card no. for 1977 St. Martin's Press ed.: 77-76639.

Helphand, Alexander, 1867-1924.

ZEMAN, Z. A. B. 335.430924
The merchant of revolution; the life of Alexander Israel Helphand (Parvus) 1867-1924 [by] Z. A. B. Zeman, W. B. Scharlau [Tr. from German] New York, Oxford [c.] 1965. 306p. ports. 23cm. Bibl. [HX312.H44Z43] 65-6995 7.20
1. Helphand, Alexander, 1867-1924. I. Scharlau, Winfried B., 1934- II. Title.

ZEMAN, Z A B 335.430924
The merchant of revolution; the life of Alexander Israel Helphand (Parvus) 1867-1924 [by] Z. A. B. Zeman and W. B. Scharlau. London, New York, Oxford University Press, 1965. 306 p. ports. 23 cm. Translation of Freibeuter der Revolution, Parvus-Helphand. Bibliography: p. [282]-290. [HX312.H44Z43] 65-6995
1. Helphand, Alexander, 1867-1924. I. Scharlau, Winfried B., 1934- II. Title.

ZEMAN, Zbynek A B 335.430924
The merchant of revolution; the life of Alexander Israel Helphand (Parvus) 1867-1924 [by] Z. A. B. Zeman and W, B. Scharlau. London, New York, Oxford University Press, 1965. 306 p. ports. 23 cm. Also written in German and published under title: Freibeuter der Revolution...[von] Winfried B. Scharlau, [und] Zbynek A. Zeman. Bibliography: p. [282]-290. [HX312.H44Z43] 65-6995
1. Helphand, Alexander, 1867-1924. I. Scharlau, Winfried B., 1934- joint author. II. Title.

Hemenway, Ruth V., 1894-1974.

HEMENWAY, Ruth V., 1894-1974. 951.04'2'0924 B
Ruth V. Hemenway, M.D. : a memoir of Revolutionary China, 1924-1941 / edited with an introd. by Fred W. Drake. Amherst : University of Massachusetts Press, 1977. viii, 220 p. : ill. ; 21 cm. [R722.32.H45A37 1977] 76-45245 ISBN 0-87023-230-4 : 12.50
1. Hemenway, Ruth V, 1894-1974. 2. Missionaries, Medical—China—Biography. 3. China—Description and travel—1901-1948. BIP

Hemery, David.

HEMERY, David. 796.4'2'0924 B
Another hurdle / David Hemery. London : Heinemann, 1976. viii, 216 p., [13] leaves of plates : ports. ; 23 cm. Includes index. [GV697.H44A33] 76-373779 ISBN 0-434-32630-5 : £4.50
1. Hemery, David. 2. Athletes—Great Britain—Biography. I. Title.

Hemingway, Ernest, 1899-1961.

ARNOLD, Lloyd R. 813'.5'2
High on the wild with Hemingway, by Lloyd R. Arnold. Illustrated with photos. Caldwell, Idaho, Caxton Printers, 1968. xiv, 343 p. illus., facsims., ports. 29 cm. [PS3515.E37Z557] 68-15029 9.95
1. Hemingway, Ernest, 1899-1961. I. Title.

ARONOWITZ, Alfred G. 928.1
Ernest Hemingway; the life and death of a man, by Alfred G. Aronowitz and Peter Hamill. New York, Lancer Books [c1961] 222 p. 10 cm. (A Lancer original) "72-611." [PS3515.E37Z56] 61-18105
1. Hemingway, Ernest, 1899-1961. I. Hamill, Peter, joint author. II. Title.

BURGESS, Anthony, 1917- 813'.5'2
Ernest Hemingway and his world / Anthony Burgess. New York : Scribner, c1978. 128 p. : ill. ; 24 cm. Includes index. Bibliography: p. 117-118. [PS3515.E37Z58416] 77-93899 ISBN 0-684-15661-X : 10.95
1. Hemingway, Ernest, 1899-1961. 2. Novelists, American—20th century—Biography. I. Title. BIP

DONALDSON, Scott. 813'.5'2 B
By force of will : the life and art of Ernest Hemingway / Scott Donaldson. New York : Viking Press, c1977. xiv, 367 p. ; 24 cm. Includes bibliographical references and index. [PS3515.E37Z5857] 76-18306 ISBN 0-670-19824-2 : 12.50
1. Hemingway, Ernest, 1899-1961. I. Title. BIP

DONALDSON, Scott. 813'.5'2 B
By force of will : the life and art of Ernest Hemingway / Scott Donaldson. New York : Penguin Books, 1978, c1977. xiv, 367 p. ; 20 cm. Includes bibliographical references and index. [PS3515.E37Z5857 1978] 77-17210 ISBN 0-14-004689-5 pbk. : 3.95
1. Hemingway, Ernest, 1899-1961. 2. Novelists, American—20th century—Biography. I. Title.

FENTON, Charles A. 928.1
The apprenticeship of Ernest Hemingway: the early years. [New York] New Amer. Lib. [1961, c.1954] 240p. (Mentor bk. MP385) Bibl. .60 pap.,
1. Hemingway, Ernest, 1898-1961. I. Title.

FENTON, Charles A. 928.1
The apprenticeship of Ernest Hemingway: the early years. New York, Farrar, Straus & Young [1954] xi, 302 p. 22 cm. Bibliographical references included in "Notes" (p. [265]-290) [PS3515.E37Z59] 54-7968
1. Hemingway, Ernest, 1899-1961. I. Title.

HEMINGWAY, Leicester, 1915- 928.1
My brother, Ernest Hemingway. [1st ed.] Cleveland, World Pub. Co. [1962] 283p. illus. 22cm. [PS3515.E37Z62] 62-9043
1. Hemingway, Ernest, 1898-1961. I. Title.

HEMINGWAY, Leicester, 1915- 928.1
My brother, Ernest Hemingway. Cleveland, World Pub. Co. [c.1961, 1962] 283p. illus. 62-9043 4.95
1. Hemingway, Ernest, 1898-1961. I. Title.

HEMINGWAY, Leicester, 1915- v. 12
My brother, Ernest Hemingway. Greenwich, Conn., Fawcett Publications [1963] 256 p. illus. 18 cm. (Crest book, T593) 67-34468
1. Hemingway, Ernest, 1899-1961. I. Title.

HERRMANN, Lazar, 1896- 928.1
Hemingway; a pictorial biography, by Leo Lania [pseud.] New York, Viking Press [1961] 141 p. illus., ports. 24 cm. (A Studio book) [PS3515.E37Z63] 61-8826
1. Hemingway, Ernest, 1899-1961.

KILEY, John Gerald, 1889- 1962. 928.1
Hemingway: an old friend remembers [by] Jed Kiley. [1st ed.] New York, Hawthorn Books [1965] 198 p. illus., ports. 21 cm. [PS3515.E37Z666 1965] 65-12039
1. Hemingway, Ernest, 1899-1961. I. Title.

MCCAFFERY, John K. M., ed. 813.5
Ernest Hemingway, the man and his work. Cleveland, World Pub. Co. [1950] 351 p. 22 cm. [PS3515.E37Z7] 50-10036
1. Hemingway, Ernest, 1899-1961.

MCCAFFERY, John K. M., ed. 813'.5'2
Ernest Hemingway: the man and his work. Edited by John K. M. McCaffery. New York, Cooper Square Publishers, 1969 [c1950] 351, [1] p. 23 cm. "The works of Ernest Hemingway": p. [352] [PS3515.E37Z7 1969] 69-17516 7.50
1. Hemingway, Ernest, 1899-1961.

MACHLIN, Milt 928.1
The private hell of hemigway. New York, Paperback Lib. [c.1962] 222p. (Silver ed. 52-128) .50 pap.,
1. Hemingway, Ernest, 1898-1961. I. Title.

MACHLIN, Milton. 812.5
The private hell of Hemingway. New York, Paperback Library [1962] 222p. 18cm. (Paperback Library original) [PS3515.E37Z74] 62-38898
1. Hemingway, Ernest, 1898-1961. I. Title.

MCLENDON, James. 813'.5'2 B
Papa; Hemingway in Key West. Miami, Fla., E. A. Seemann Pub. [1972] 222 p. illus. 23 cm. Bibliography: p. [213]-215. [PS3515.E37Z7413] 72-82925 ISBN 0-912458-16-X 7.95
1. Hemingway, Ernest, 1899-1961. I. Title.

MCLENDON, James. 813'.5'2 B
Papa; Hemingway in Key West. Miami, Fla., E. A. Seemann Pub. [1972] 222 p. illus. 23 cm. Bibliography: p. [213]-215. [PS3515.E37Z7413] 72-82925 ISBN 0-912458-16-X 7.95
1. Hemingway, Ernest, 1899-1961. I. Title. BIP

RICHARDS, Norman. 813'.5'2 B
Ernest Hemingway. Chicago, Children's Press [1968] 94 p. illus., ports. 29 cm. (People of destiny: a humanities series) Bibliography: p. 90-91. The life of the twentieth-century American writer, whose accounts of his adventures and new style of writing brought him worldwide recognition. [PS3515.E37Z755] 92 AC 68
1. Hemingway, Ernest, 1899-1961. I. Title.

ROSS, Lillian 928.1
Portrait of Hemingway [New York, Avon, 1964, c.1950, 1961] 94p. illus. 18cm. (Originated as a Profile in the New Yorker, pub. May 13, 1950) [PS3515.E37Z77] .60 pap.,
1. Hemingway, Ernest, 1899-1961. I. Title.

ROSS, Lillian. 928.1
Portrait of Hemingway. New York, Simon and Schuster, 1961. 65 p. illus. 22 cm. "Originated as a Profile in the New Yorker, published May 13, 1950." [PS3515.E37Z77] 61-17707
1. Hemingway, Ernest, 1899-1961. I. Title.

SANFORD, Marcelline (Hemingway) 1898- 928.1
At the Hemingways, a family portrait. Boston, Atlantic-Little [c.1961, 1962] 244p. illus. 21cm. 62-10529 4.95 bds.,
1. Hemingway, Ernest, 1898-1961. 2. Hemingway family. I. Title.

SATURDAY review, v. 12
Hemingway, a world view. [New York, 1961] 58 p. illus. 28 cm. Issued as v. 44, no. 30, July 29, 1961. 63-57721
1. Hemingway, Ernest, 1898-1961. I. Title.

SEWARD, William Ward, 1913- 813'.5'2
My friend, Ernest Hemingway; an affectionate reminiscence, by William Seward. South Brunswick, A. S. Barnes [1969] 69 p. illus., ports. 22 cm. [PS3515.E37Z826] 69-14869 4.50
1. Hemingway, Ernest, 1899-1961. I. Title.

SINGER, Kurt D 1911- 928.1
Ernest Hemingway, man of courage; a biographical sketch of a Nobel prize winner in literature, by Kurt Singer and Jane Sherrod. Minneapolis, T. S. Denison [1963] 200 p. 22 cm. (Men of achievement series) [PS3515.E37Z83] 62-22239
1. Hemingway, Ernest, 1899-1961. I. Sherrod, Jane, joint author. II. Title.

SINGER, Kurt D., 1911- 928.1
Ernest Hemingway, man of courage; a biographical sketch of a Nobel prize winner in literature, by Kurt Singer(Jane Sherrod. Minneapolis Denison ,53c.1963] 200p. 22cm. (Men of achievement ser.) 62-22239 3.00
1. Hemingway(Ernest, 1899-1961. I. Sherrod, Jane, joint author. II. Title.

SINGER, Kurt D 1911- 928.1
Hemingway: life and death of a giant. Cover by Chet Collom; illus. by Ben Kudo. Los Angeles, Holloway House Pub. Co. [1961] 223 p. illus. 19 cm. [PS3515.E37Z84] 61-18898
1. Hemingway, Ernest, 1898-1961. I. Title.

Hemingway, Ernest, 1899-1961-Biography.

BAKER, Carlos Heard, 1909- 813'.5'2 B
Ernest Hemingway; a life story, by Carlos Baker. New York, Scribner [1969] xvi, 697 p. illus., ports. 23 cm. Bibliographical references included in "Notes" (p. 567-668) [PS3515.E37Z575 1969] 68-57079 10.00
1. Hemingway, Ernest, 1899-1961—Biography.

BARGER, James. 813'.5'2 B
Ernest Hemingway : American literary

giant / James Barger. Charlotteville, N.Y. : SamHar Press, 1975. p. cm. (Outstanding personalities ; 80) Bibliography: p. [PS3515.E37Z5823] 75-33830 lib.bdg. : 2.29 pbk. : 0.98
1. Hemingway, Ernest, 1899-1961—Biography. BIP

BUCKLEY, Peter. 813'.5'2
Ernest / by Peter Buckley. New York : Dial Press, [1978] p. cm. [PS3515.E37Z58414] 78-17729 ISBN 0-8037-2392-X : 9.95
1. Hemingway, Ernest, 1899-1961—Biography. 2. Novelists, American—20th century—Biography. I. Title. BIP

FENTON, Charles A. 813'.5'2 B
The apprenticeship of Ernest Hemingway : the early years / by Charles A. Fenton. New York : Octagon Books, 1975, c1954. xi, 302 p. ; 23 cm. Includes bibliographical references and index. [PS3515.E37Z59 1975] 75-11784 ISBN 0-374-92737-5 : 13.00
1. Hemingway, Ernest, 1898-1961—Biography—Journalistic career. 2. Hemingway, Ernest, 1898-1961—Biography—Youth. I. Title.

HEMINGWAY, Gregory, 813'.5'2 B 1931-
Papa : a personal memoir / Gregory Hemingway ; with a foreword by Norman Mailer. Boston : Houghton Mifflin, 1976. p. cm. [PS3515.E37Z617] 76-6933 ISBN 0-395-24348-3
1. Hemingway, Ernest, 1899-1961—Biography. I. Title. BIP

HEMINGWAY, Gregory H. 813'.5'2 B
Papa : a personal memoir / [by]Gregory H. Hemingway ; with a preface byNorman Mailer. New York : Pocket Books, 1977,c1976. 157, [7]p. : photos. ; 18 cm. (A Kangaroo Book) [PS3515.E37Z617] ISBN 0-671-80936-9 pbk. : 1.75
1. Hemingway, Ernest, 1899-1961-Biography. I. Title.
L.C. card no. for Houghton Mifflin ed.:76-8186

HEMINGWAY, Gregory H., 813'.5'2 B 1931-
Papa : a personal memoir / Gregory H. Hemingway ; with a pref. by Norman Mailer. Boston : Houghton Mifflin, 1976. p. cm. [PS3515.E37Z617] 76-8186 ISBN 0-395-24348-3 : 7.95
1. Hemingway, Ernest, 1899-1961—Biography. I. Title.

HOTCHNER, A. E. 813.52
Papa Hemingway; a personal memoir, by A. E. Hotchner. New York, Random House [1966] x, 304 p. ports. 22 cm. [PS3515.E37Z635] 66-12017
1. Hemingway, Ernest, 1899-1961—Biography. I. Title.

MILLER, Madelaine 813'.5'2 B Hemingway.
Ernie : Hemingway's sister "Sunny" remembers / by Madelaine Hemingway Miller ; pref. by Robert Traver. More than 100 personal photos. New York : Crown Publishers, [1975] ix, 146 p. : ill. ; 27 cm. [PS3515.E37Z742 1975] 74-28109 ISBN 0-517-51894-5 : 7.95
1. Hemingway, Ernest, 1899-1961—Biography. I. Title.

Hemingway, Ernest, 1899-1961—Biography—Last years and death.

NOLAN, William F., 813'.5'2 B 1928-
Hemingway, last days of the lion : including Now never there (a poem) and Hemingway, a biographical checklist / by William F. Nolan. Santa Barbara, Calif. : Capra Press, 1974. 38 p. ; 18 cm. (Yes! Capra chapbook series ; no. 24) Caption title: Last days of the lion. [PS3515.E37Z747] 75-318149 ISBN 0-88496-012-9. ISBN 0-88496-011-0 pbk. : 2.50
1. Hemingway, Ernest, 1899-1961—Biography—Last years and death. 2. Hemingway, Ernest, 1899-1961, in fiction, drama, poetry, etc. 3. Hemingway, Ernest, 1899-1961—Bibliography. I. Title. II. Title: Last days of the lion.

Hemingway, Ernest, 1899-1961—Biography—Marriage.

HEMINGWAY, Mary Welsh, 813'.5'2 1908-
How it was / Mary Welsh Hemingway. 1st ed. New York : Knopf : distributed by Random House, 1976. vi, 537, xi p., [12] leaves of plates : ill. ; 25 cm. Autobiographical. Includes index. [PS3515.E37Z6175] 76-13672 ISBN 0-394-40109-3 : 12.95
1. Hemingway, Ernest, 1899-1961—Biography—Marriage. 2. Hemingway, Mary Welsh, 1908- I. Title. BIP

Hemingway, Ernest, 1899-1961—Biography—Youth.

ERNEST Hemingway, 813'.5'2 B
as recalled by his high school contemporaries. Edited by Ina Mae Schleden and Marion Rawls Herzog. Design and production by Harry Knaphurst. [1st ed. Oak Park, Ill.] Historical Society of Oak Park and River Forest [1973] 47 p. illus. 23 cm. (Historical Society of Oak Park and River Forest. Monograph no. 1) Based on a panel discussion presented by the Historical Society of Oak Park and River Forest, Oct. 29, 1971. [PS3515.E37Z5867] 74-155371 1.70
1. Hemingway, Ernest, 1899-1961—Biography—Youth. I. Schleden, Ina Mae, ed. II. Herzog, Marion Rawls, ed.

Hemingway, Ernest, 1899-1961—Friends and associates.

BRUCCOLI, Matthew 813'.5'209 B Joseph, 1931-
Scott and Ernest : the authority of failure and the authority of success / Matthew J. Bruccoli. 1st ed. New York : Random House, c1978. xv 168 p. : ill. ; 25 cm. Bibliography: p. 167-168. [PS3511.I9Z565] 77-90250 ISBN 0-394-42889-7 : 8.95
1. Fitzgerald, Francis Scott Key, 1896-1940—Friends and associates. 2. Hemingway, Ernest, 1899-1961—Friends and associates. 3. Fitzgerald, Francis Scott Key, 1896-1940—Correspondence. 4. Hemingway, Ernest, 1899-1961—Correspondence. 5. Authors, American—20th century—Biography. I. Title. BIP

CALLAGHAN, Morley, 818'.5'203 B 1903-
That summer in Paris : memories of tangled friendships with Hemingway, Fitzgerald, and some others / Morley Callaghan. Harmondsworth ; New York : Penguin Books, 1979. 255 p. ; 18 cm. Reprint of the 1963 ed. published by By Coward-McCann, New York. [PR9199.3.C27Z52 1978] 79-193 ISBN 0-14-005074-4 pbk. : 3.95
1. Callaghan, Morley, 1903- —Friends and associates. 2. Hemingway, Ernest, 1899-1961—Friends and associates. 3. Fitzgerald, Francis Scott Key, 1896-1940—Friends and associates. 4. Novelists Canadian—20th century—Biography. 5. Novelists American—20th century—Biography. I. Title. BIP

Hemingway, Ernest, 1899-1961—Homes and haunts—France—Paris.

HEMINGWAY'S Paris / 813'.5'2
[compiled] by Robert E. Gajdusek. New York : Scribner, c1978. 182 p. : ill. ; 28 cm. Includes index. Bibliography: p. 177-178. [PS3515.E37Z626] 78-17214 ISBN 0-684-15799-3 : 15.00
1. Hemingway, Ernest, 1899-1961—Homes and haunts—France—Paris. 2. Hemingway, Ernest, 1899-1961—Quotations. 3. Authors, American—20th century—Biography. 4. Paris—Description—Views. I. Hemingway, Ernest, 1899-1961. II. Gajdusek, Robert E.

Hemingway, Ernest, 1899-1961—Homes and haunts—Idaho—Sun Valley.

ARNOLD, Lloyd R. 813'.5'2 B
Hemingway : high on the wild / Lloyd R. Arnold. New York : Grosset & Dunlap, 1977. 163 p. : ill. ; 29 cm. Published in 1968 under title: High on the wild Hemingway. Includes index. [PS3515.E37Z557 1977] 77-71746 ISBN 0-448-14290-2 : 17.95
1. Hemingway, Ernest, 1899-1961—Homes and haunts—Idaho—Sun Valley. 2. Novelists, American—20th century—Biography. 3. Sun Valley, Idaho—Biography. BIP

Hemingway, Ernest, 1899-1961—Homes and haunts—Spain.

CASTILLO Puche, Jose 813'.5'2 Luis.
Hemingway in Spain; a personal reminiscence of Hemingway's years in Spain by his friend. Translated from the Spanish by Helen R. Lane. [1st ed.] Garden City, N.Y., Doubleday, 1974. xv, 388 p. illus. 25 cm. Translation of Hemingway, entre la vida y la muerte. [PS3515.E37Z584413] 73-22150 ISBN 0-385-08337-8 10.95
1. Hemingway, Ernest, 1899-1961—Homes and haunts—Spain. 2. Hemingway, Ernest, 1899-1961—Biography. I. Title.

Hemingway, Ernest, 1899-1961, in fiction, drama, poetry, etc.

NOLAN, William F., 813'.5'2 B 1928-
Hemingway, last days of the lion : including Now never there (a poem) and Hemingway, a biographical checklist / by William F. Nolan. Santa Barbara, Calif. : Capra Press, 1974. 38 p. ; 18 cm. (Yes! Capra chapbook series ; no. 24) Caption title: Last days of the lion. [PS3515.E37Z747] 75-318149 ISBN 0-88496-012-9. ISBN 0-88496-011-0 pbk. : 2.50
1. Hemingway, Ernest, 1899-1961—Biography—Last years and death. 2. Hemingway, Ernest, 1899-1961, in fiction, drama, poetry, etc. 3. Hemingway, Ernest, 1899-1961—Bibliography. I. Title. II. Title: Last days of the lion.

Hemingway, Ernest, 1899-1961—Juvenile literature.

RICHARDS, Norman. 92 (J)
Ernest Hemingway. Chicago, Childrens Press [1968] 94 p. illus., ports. 29 cm. (People of destiny: a humanities series) Bibliography: p. 90-91. [PS3515.E37Z755] 68-15564
1. Hemingway, Ernest, 1899-1961—Juvenile literature.

RINK, Paul, 1912- 928.1
Ernest Hemingway; remaking modern fiction. Illus. by Robert Boehmer. Chicago, Ncy. Britannica [c.1962] 191p. col. illus. 22cm. (Britannica bkshelf: Great lives for young Amers.) 62-19373 2.36 lib. ed.,
1. Hemingway, Ernest, 1899-1961—Juvenile literature. I. Title. II. Title: Remaking modern fiction.

Hemingway, Ernest, 1899-1961—Relationship with women.

SOKOLOFF, Alice Hunt. 813'.5'2 B
Hadley, the first Mrs. Hemingway. Illustrated with photos. New York, Dodd, Mead [1973] 111 p. illus. 24 cm. Includes bibliographical references. [PS3515.E37Z867] 72-11253 ISBN 0-396-06768-9 6.95
1. Hemingway, Ernest, 1899-1961—Relationship with women. 2. Mowrer, Hadley Richardson Hemingway, 1891- I. Title.

Hemphill, John, 1803-1862.

CURTIS, Rosalee 347'.73'2634 B Morris.
John Hemphill, first chief justice of the State of Texas. Austin, Tex., Jenkins Pub. Co., 1971. xv, 122 p. illus. 23 cm. Includes bibliographical references. [KF368.H4C8] 72-184821
1. Hemphill, John, 1803-1862. I. Title.

Hemphill, La Breeska Rogers, 1940-

HEMPHILL, La Breeska 783.7 B Rogers, 1940- Hemphill LaBreeska Rogers
La Breeska : an autobiography / by La Breeska Rogers Hemphill. Nashville : Hemphill Music Co., c1976. xii, 220 p. : ill. ; 21 cm. [ML420.H37A3] 75-42869 4.95
1. Hemphill, La Breeska Rogers, 1940- 2. Gospel musicians—Correspondence, reminiscences, etc. I. Title.

Hemphill, Paul, 1936-

HEMPHILL, Paul, 917.5'03'40924 1936-
The good old boys. New York, Simon and Schuster [1974] 255 p. 22 cm. [F209.H44] 74-373 ISBN 0-671-21771-2 7.95
1. Hemphill, Paul, 1936- 2. Southern States—Addresses, essays, lectures. 3. Country music—Southern States—Addresses, essays, lectures. I. Title. BIP

Henderson, Ernest

HENDERSON, Ernest 926.4
The world of 'Mr. Sheraton.' New York, Popular Lib. [1962, c.1960] 237p. (PC1013) .50 pap.,
I. Title.

Henderson, James Pinckney, 1808-1858.

WINCHESTER, 976.4'04'0924 B Robert Glenn.
James Pinckney Henderson, Texas' first governor. San Antonio, Naylor Co. [1971] xiii, 116 p. coat of arms, plates, ports. 22 cm. Bibliography: p. 106-109. [F391.W7] 70-143463 ISBN 0-8111-0396-X 4.95
1. Henderson, James Pinckney, 1808-1858.

Henderson, Randall.

MCKENNEY, J. Wilson. 070.4'0924 B
Desert editor; the story of Randall Henderson and Palm Desert, by J. Wilson McKenney. Georgetown [Calif.] Wilmac Press, 1972. 188 p. illus. 24 cm. Bibliography: p. 188. [PN4874.H457M3] 79-190619 7.95
1. Henderson, Randall. 2. Deserts—Southwest, New. I. Title.

Hendrickson, John Jefferson.

HENDRICKSON, John 923.773 Jefferson.
Through the years in photos with John J. Hendrickson. New York, New Voices Pub. Co. [1955] 64p. illus. 23cm. [LA2317.H52A3] 55-4071
I. Title.

Hendrix, Eugene Russell, Bp., 1847-1927.

HOLT, Ivan Lee, Bp., 922.773 1886-
Eugene Russell Hendrix, servant of the kingdom. Nashville, Parthenon Press [1950] 221 p. illus., ports. 22 cm. [BX8495.H39H6] 50-14977
1. Hendrix, Eugene Russell, Bp., 1847-1927. I. Title.

Hendrix, Jimi.

HENDERSON, David, 784'.092'4 B 1942-
Jimi Hendrix : voodoo child of the Aquarian age / David Henderson. 1st ed. Garden City, N.Y. : Doubleday, 1978. 514 p., [11] leaves of plates : ill. ; 22 cm. [ML410.H476H46] 76-56299 ISBN 0-385-07357-7 : 12.50
1. Hendrix, Jimi. 2. Rock musicians—United States—Biography. BIP

KNIGHT, Curtis. 784'.092'4 B
Jimi; an intimate biography of Jimi Hendrix. New York, Praeger [1974] 223 p. illus. 22 cm. "A Jimi Hendrix discography, compiled by John McKellar"; p. [209] [ML410.H476K6] 73-9394 7.95
1. Hendrix, Jimi. I. Title.

KNIGHT, Curtis. 784'.092'4 B
Jimi; an intimate biography of Jimi Hendrix. London, New York, W. H. Allen, 1974. 223 p., [32] p. of plates. ports. 23 cm. Includes index. Discography: p. [209]-218. [ML410.H476K6 1974b] 74-180135 ISBN 0-491-01132-6 £2.50
1. Hendrix, Jimi.

WELCH, Chris, 1941- 784'.092'4 B
Hendrix; biography. New York, Flash Books [1973] 104 p. illus. 27 cm. Discography: p. 102-103. [ML410.H476W5 1973] 73-83767 ISBN 0-8256-3901-8 2.95
1. Hendrix, Jimi. 2. Hendrix, Jimi—Discography.

Heney, Michael John, 1864-1910.

HERRON, Edward Albert, 1912- 926.25
Alaska's railroad builder, Mike Heney. New York, Messner [1960] 192 p. 22 cm. Includes bibliography. [TF140.H36H4] 60-7816
1. Heney, Michael John, 1864-1910. I. Title.

Henle, Gunter,

HENLE, Gunter, 1899- 914.3'087'0924 B
Three spheres: a life in politics, business and music; the autobiography of Guenter Henle. [Translated from the German by Annette Jacobsohn] Chicago, H. Regnery, 1971 [c1970] 277 p. illus., facsims., maps, music, ports. 24 cm. Translation of Weggenosse des Jahrhunderts. [DD259.7.H35A313] 77-126150 10.00
I. Title.

Henley, John, 1692-1756.

MIDGLEY, Graham. 283'.092'4 B
The life of Orator Henley. Oxford, Clarendon Press, 1973. ix, 297 p. illus. 22 cm. "A list of Henley's writings" (p. [288]-291) [BX5199.H444M53 1973] 73-162280 ISBN 0-19-812032-X
1. Henley, John, 1692-1756. I. Title.
Distributed by Oxford University Press N.Y. 19.25. BIP

Henley, William Ernest, 1849-1903.

BUCKLEY, Jerome Hamilton. 828'.8'09 B
William Ernest Henley; a study in the "counter-decadence" of the 'nineties. New York, Octagon Books, 1971 [c1945] xi, 234 p. illus., ports. 23 cm. Bibliography: p. 214-224. [PR4784.B8 1971] 74-120238
1. Henley, William Ernest, 1849-1903.

ROBERTSON, John Henry, 1909-1965 828'.8'09 B
W. E. Henley [by] John Connell. Port Washington, N.Y., Kennikat Press [1972] xix, 385 p. illus. 23 cm. Reprint of the 1949 ed. Includes bibliographical references. [PR4784.R6 1972] 78-160750 ISBN 0-8046-1566-7
1. Henley, William Ernest, 1849-1903.

WILLIAMSON, Kennedy, 1892- 828'.8'09 B
W. E. Henley : a memoir / by Kennedy Williamson. New York : Haskell House Publishers, 1974. 296 p. : port. ; 21 cm. Reprint of the 1930 ed. published by H. Shaylor, London. Includes index. Bibliography: p. 287-290. [PR4784.W5 1974] 74-30419 ISBN 0-8383-1751-0
1. Henley, William Ernest, 1849-1903.

Henn, Desmond, 1929-1964.

HENN, Enid. 364.15220924 B
Desmond: December 28th, 1929-December 29th, 1964; a memoir. Cambridge, Golden Head P., 1967. 152 p. 6 plates, illus., ports. 23 cm. [CT788.H435H4] 68-75874 15/-
1. Henn, Desmond, 1929-1964. I. Title.

Hennacy, Ammon,

HENNACY, Ammon, 1893- 920
The book of Ammon. [Salt Lake City, 1964?] 473 p. illus., ports. 24 cm. Revision and expansion of his Autobiography of a Catholic anarchist. Includes bibliographies. [CT275.H564A3 1964] 65-8979
I. Title.

Hennacy, Ammon, 1893-1970.

HENNACY, Ammon, 1893- 920
The book of Ammon. [Salt Lake City, 1964?] 473 p. illus., ports. 24 cm. Revision and expansion of his Autobiography of a Catholic anarchist. Includes bibliographies. [CT275.H564A3 1964] 65-8979
I. Title.

THOMAS, Joan, 1934- 322.4'4 B
The years of grief and laughter : a "biography" of Ammon Hennacy / by Joan Thomas. Phoenix, Ariz. : Hennacy Press, 1974. ix, 342 p. : ill. ; 22 cm. [CT275.H564T48] 75-332747 ISBN 0-89019-002-X : 5.95
1. Hennacy, Ammon, 1893-1970. I. Title.

Henni, Johann Martin, Abp., 1805-1881.

JOHNSON, Peter Leo. 922.273
Crosier on the frontier; a life of John Martin Henni, Archbishop of Milwaukee. Madison, State Historical Society of Wisconsin, 1959. xiii, 240p. illus., ports. 20cm. (State Street books, 1) Bibliography: p. 225-231. [BX4705.H47J6] 59-62972
1. Henni, Johann Martin, Abp., 1805-1881. I. Title.

Henrey, Robert, Mrs., 1906- Biography.

HENREY, Robert, Mrs., 1906- 944'.22083'0924 B
The golden visit / by Mrs. Robert Henrey. London : J. M. Dent, 1979. 232 p. ; 23 cm. Continues She who pays. [PR6015.E46Z517] 79-323077 ISBN 0-460-04433-8 : 10.00
1. Henrey, Robert, Mrs., 1906- Biography. 2. Authors, English—20th century—Biography. I. Title.
Distributed by Biblio Distribution Centre, Totowa, NJ BIP

Henri IV, King of France, 1553-1610.

MAHONEY, Irene. 944'.031'0924 B
Royal cousin; the life of Henri IV of France. [1st ed.] Garden City, N.Y., Doubleday, 1970. xiv, 451 p. map (on lining paper), ports. 24 cm. Includes bibliographical references. [DC122.8.M3] 77-123700 10.00
1. Henri IV, King of France, 1553-1610. I. Title.

PEARSON, Hesketh, 1887- 923.144
Henry of Navarre, the King who dared. New York, Harper [1964, c.1963] xiv, 249p. ports., map, geneal. table. 22cm. London ed.(Heinmann) has title:Henry of Navarre, his life. Bibl. 63-20296 5.00
1. Henri IV, King of France, 1553-1610. I. Title. BIP

PEARSON, Hesketh, 1887-1964. 944'.031'0924 B
Henry of Navarre, the King who dared / by Hesketh Pearson. Westport, Conn. : Greenwood Press, 1976. p. cm. Reprint of the 1963 ed. published by Harper & Row, New York. Includes index. Bibliography: p. [DC122.8.P37 1976] 76-23244 ISBN 0-8371-9015-0 lib.bdg. : 17.25
1. Henri IV, King of France, 1553-1610. I. Title.

RUSSELL, Edward Frederick Langley Russell, Baron, 1895- 944'.031'0924 B
Henry of Navarre; Henry IV of France [by] Lord Russell of Liverpool. New York, Praeger Publishers [1970, c1969] 206 p. illus., geneal. table, maps, ports. 23 cm. Bibliography: p. 200. [DC122.8.R88 1970] 77-112027 6.95
1. Henri IV, King of France, 1553-1610. I. Title.

SEWARD, Desmond, 1935- 944'.031'0924 B
The first Bourbon: Henri iv, King of France and Navarre. Boston, Gambit, 1971. 235 p. illus. 22 cm. Bibliography: p. [203]-211. [DC122.8.S45 1971b] 73-167959 ISBN 0-87645-051-6 7.95
1. Henri IV, King of France, 1553-1610. I. Title.

Henri IV, King of France, 1553-1610 — Juvenile literature.

WILKINSON, Burke, 1913- j92
The helmet of Navarre. Illustrated by James W. Williamson. New York, Macmillan [1965] 162 p. illus. 21 cm. Bibliography: p. 155-156. [DC122.8.W48] 65-15167
1. Henri IV, King of France, 1553-1610 — Juvenile literature. I. Title. BIP

Henrichsen, Margaret

HENRICHSEN, Margaret 922.773
Seven steeples; illus. by William Barss. New York, Harper [1967, c.1953] 238p. illus. 21cm. (Chapel Bk., CB36) Autobiographical. [BX8495.A3] 1.50
I. Title.

HENRICHSEN, Margaret. 922.773
Seven steeples; illustrated by William Barss. Boston, Houghton Mifflin, 1953. 238 p. illus. 22 cm. Autobiographical. [BX8495.H397A3] 53-9251
I. Title. BIP

HENRICHSEN, Margaret 922.773
Seven steeples; illus. by William Barss. New York, Harper [1967, c.1953] 238p. illus. 21cm. (Chapel Bk., CB36) Autobiographical. [BX8495.A3] 1.50
I. Title.

HENRICHSEN, Margaret. 922.773
Seven steeples; illustrated by William Barss. Boston, Houghton Mifflin, 1953. 238 p. illus. 22 cm. Autobiographical. [BX8495.H397A3] 53-9251
I. Title. BIP

HENRICHSEN, Margaret. 287'.6'0924 B
Seven steeples / Margaret Henrichsen ; illustrated by William Barss. Thorndike, Me. : Thorndike Press, [1978] c1953. 238 p. : ill. ; 20 cm. Reprint of the ed. published by Houghton Mifflin, Boston. [BX8495.H397A3 1978] 78-26203 ISBN 0-89621-023-5 lib. bdg.: 11.50 ISBN 0-89621-022-7 pbk. : 4.95
1. Henrichsen, Margaret. 2. Methodist Church—Clergy—Biography. 3. Clergy—United States—Biography. I. Title.

Henrici, Arthur Trautwein, 1889-1943.

HENRICI Society for Microbiologists 925.7
Henrici: recollections by some close friends and associates. Minneapolis, Burgess Pub. Co. [c.1960] 32p. illus. 23cm. 60-12525 1 00 bds.,
1. Henrici, Arthur Trautwein, 1889-1943. I. Title.

Henrietta Maria, Consort of Charles I, King of Great Britain, 1609-1669.

BONE, Quentin Blane, 1918- 942.06'2'0924 B
Henrietta Maria: Queen of the Cavaliers, by Quentin Bone. Urbana, University of Illinois Press [1972] x, 287 p. port. 24 cm. Based on the author's thesis, University of Illinois. Bibliography: p. 253-271. [DA396.A5B65] 70-172250 ISBN 0-252-00198-2 10.00
1. Henrietta Maria, Consort of Charles I, King of Great Britain, 1609-1669. I. Title. BIP

HAMILTON, Elizabeth, Lady, 1928- 941.06'2'0924 B
Henrietta Maria / Elizabeth Hamilton. London : H. Hamilton, 1976. xiv, 290 p., [8] leaves of plates : ill. ; 24 cm. Includes index. Bibliography: p. 261-264. [DA396.A5H35 1976b] 76-367116 ISBN 0-241-89336-4 : £6.95
1. Henrietta Maria, consort of Charles I, King of Great Britain, 1609-1669.

HAMILTON, Elizabeth, Lady, 1928- 941.06'2'0924 B
Henrietta Maria / by Elizabeth Hamilton. 1st American ed. New York : Coward, McCann & Geoghegan, 1976. xii, 290 p., [8] leaves of plates : ill. ; 24 cm. Includes index. Bibliography: p. 261-264. [DA396.A5H35 1976] 76-206 ISBN 0-698-10713-6 : 8.95
1. Henrietta Maria, consort of Charles I, King of Great Britain, 1609-1669.

Henrique, O Navegador, Infante of Portugal, 1394-1460.

BEAZLEY, Charles Raymond, Sir, 1868-1955. 910.09'469'0924
Prince Henry the Navigator, the hero of Portugal and of modern discovery, 1394-1460 A.D.; with an account of geographical progress throughout the Middle Ages as the preparation for his work. New York, B. Franklin [1968] xxvii, 336 p. illus., maps, ports. 23 cm. (Burt Franklin research & source works series, 316) (The Literature of discovery, exploration & geography, 1.) Reprint of the 1895 ed. Bibliography: p. xix-xxi. [G286.H5] 68-57121
1. Henrique, o Navegador, Infante of Portugal, 1394-1460. 2. Discoveries (in geography) I. Title.

BRADFORD, Ernle Dusgate Selby. 923.9469
A wind from the north; the life of Henry the Navigator. New York, Harcourt, Brace [1960] 277 p. illus. 22 cm. [G286.H5B66] 60-12730
1. Henrique, O Navegador, Infante of Portugal, 1394-1460. I. Title.

SANCEAU, Elaine. 946.9'02'0924 B
Henry the Navigator; the story of a great prince and his times. [Hamden, Conn.] Archon Books, 1969 [c1947] 318 p. illus., port., map. 22 cm. Bibliography: p. 309-312. [G286.H5S32 1969] 69-11549 ISBN 2-08-006818-
1. Henrique, o Navegador, Infante of Portugal, 1394-1460. I. Title. BIP

Henrique, o Navegador, Infante of Portugal, 1394-1460—Juvenile literature.

ANDERSON, Helen Jean, 1929- 910.09'4690924 B
Henry the Navigator, Prince of Portugal, by Jean Anderson. Philadelphia, Westminster Press [1969] 124 p. 24 cm. Bibliography: p. [117]-118. A biography of Portugal's national hero whose advanced ideas on geography and navigation opened the way for Columbus and other explorers. [G286.H5A6] 92 69-20339 4.50
1. Henrique, o Navegador, Infante of Portugal, 1394-1460—Juvenile literature I Title.

BUEHR, Walter 910.09
The Portuguese explorers. New York, Putnam [c.1966] 95p. col. illus. 23cm. [DP583.B85] 66-10452 2.86 lib. ed.,
1. Henrique, o Navegador, Infante of Portugal, 1394-1460—Juvenile literature. 2. Portugal—Hist.—Period of discoveries, 1385-1580—Juvenile literature. 3. Explorers, Portuguese—Juvenile literature. I. Title. BIP

CHUBB, Thomas Caldecot, 1899- 910.09'469'0924 B
Prince Henry the Navigator and the highways of the sea. [1st ed.] New York, Viking Press [1970] 160 p. illus., map. 25 cm. "Chapter head drawings and map ... by Laurel Brown." Bibliography: p. [155]-156. Describes the age of Prince Henry and the explorations and methods he pioneered and financed which changed the course of navigation history. [G286.H5C46 1970] 78-106923 ISBN 6-7057-6247- 4.95
1. Henrique, o Navegador, infante of Portugal, 1394-1460—Juvenile literature. I. Brown, Laurel, illus. II. Title.

JACOBS, William Jay. 910'.92'4 B
Prince Henry, the Navigator, by W. J. Jacobs. With authentic prints, documents, and maps. New York, F. Watts, 1973. 53 p. illus. 26 cm. (A Visual biography) Bibliography: p. 53. A biography of the Portuguese prince who made sailing safer by his navigational maps and who designed

the caravel—a type of sailing ship. [G286.H5J32] 92 72-11511 ISBN 0-531-00972-6 4.50 (Lib. ed.)
1. Henrique, o Navegador, Infante of Portugal, 1394-1460—Juvenile literature. I. Title. BIP

Henriques, Basil Lucas Quixano, 1890-1961.

LOEWE, Lionel Louis. 369.4'092'4 B
Basil Henriques : a portrait / L. L. Loewe ; foreword by Viscount Amory. London ; Boston : Routledge & K. Paul, 1976. x, 181 p., [5] leaves of plates : ill. ; 23 cm. "Based on his diaries, letters, and speeches as collated by his widow, Rose Henriques." Includes bibliographical references. [HV28.H435L63] 76-382679 ISBN 0-7100-8439-0 : 12.50
1. Henriques, Basil Lucas Quixano, 1890-1961. 2. Social workers—Great Britain—Biography. I. Henriques, Rose Louise Loewe. BIP

Henry, Alexander, 1739-1824.

HENRY, Alexander, 1739-1824. 973'.04'97 S
Travels and adventures in Canada and the Indian territories / Alexander Henry. New York : Garland Pub., 1976. vi, 330 p. ; 23 cm. (The Garland library of narratives of North American Indian captivities ; v. 31) Reprint of the 1809 ed. published by I. Riley, New York. [E85.G2 vol. 31] [F1013] 917.1'04'2 75-7053 ISBN 0-8240-1655-6 lib.bdg. : 21.00
1. Henry, Alexander, 1739-1824. 2. Canada—Description and travel—1763-1867. 3. Mackinac region—Description and travel. 4. Indians of North America—Canada. 5. Indians of North America—Michigan. I. Title. II. Series.

Henry, Duke of Lancaster, 1299?-1361.

FOWLER, Kenneth Alan. 942.03'7'0924 B
The King's lieutenant: Henry of Grosmont, First Duke of Lancaster, 1310-1361 [by] Kenneth Fowler. New York, Barnes & Noble [1969] 312 p. illus., maps, ports. 23 cm. Bibliography: p. 241-254. [DA237.H4F6 1969] 70-7473
1. Henry, Duke of Lancaster, 1299?-1361. I. Title.

Henry, Edward Lamson, 1841-1919.

MCCAUSLAND, Elizabeth, 1899-1966. 759.13
The life and work of Edward Lamson Henry, N. A., 1841-1919. New York, Kennedy Graphics, 1970. 381 p. illus., ports. 24 cm. (Library of American art) Reprint of the 1945 ed. "A catalog of the work of E. L. Henry, 1858-1919": p. 147-254. "A memorial sketch: E. L. Henry, N.A.; his life and his life work, by Frances L. Henry": p. 311-346. Bibliography: p. 363-367. [ND237.H52M3 1970] 74-100614
1. Henry, Edward Lamson, 1841-1919. I. Henry, Frances Livingston (Wells) 1845-1928. II. Title. BIP

Henry Frederick, Prince of Wales, 1594-1612.

WILLIAMSON, Jerry Wayne, 1944- 941.06'1'0924 B
The myth of the conqueror : Prince Henry Stuart, a study of 17th century personation / by J. W. Williamson. 1st ed. New York : AMS Press, 1978. x, 219 p., [9] leaves of plates : ill. ; 23 cm. Includes index. Bibliography: p. 197-211. [DA391.1.H5W47] 77-78318 ISBN 0-404-16004-2 : 21.00
1. Henry Frederick, Prince of Wales, 1594-1612. 2. Great Britain—Princes and princesses—Biography. 3. Great Britain—History—James I, 1603-1625. I. Title. BIP

Henry George School of Social Science, New York.

CLANCY, Robert, 1904- 923.373
A seed was sown; the life, philosophy, and writings of Oscar H. Geiger, founder of the Henry George School of Social Science. 2d ed. New York, Henry George School of Social Science, 1954, c1952] 124p. illus. 28cm. [HD1313] 54-1081
1. Geiger, Oscar Harold, 1873-1934. 2. Henry George School of Social Science, New York. 3. George, Henry, 1839-1897. I. Title.

Henry, Harold, 1909—

FISCHER, Edward. 266'.2'0924 B
Light in the Far East : Archbishop Harold Henry's forty-two years in Korea / Edward Fischer. New York : Seabury Press, c1976. p. cm. "A Crossroad book." [BV3462.H38F57] 76-22466 ISBN 0-8164-0307-4 : 8.95
1. Henry, Harold, 1909- 2. Missions—Korea. I. Title. BIP

Henry, Horace Chapin, 1844-1928.

HOGGSON, Noble, 1899- 926.9
A biography of Horace Chapin Henry, 1844-1928. Seattle, 1960. 185 p. illus. 23 cm. [HD9715.U52H5] 60-31559
1. Henry, Horace Chapin, 1844-1928.

Henry II, King of England, 1133-1189.

BARBER, Richard W. 942.0310924 B
Henry Plantagenet; a biography [by] Richard Barber. New York, Roy Publishers [1967, c1964] 278 p. illus. 23 cm. Bibliography: p. [250]-260. [DA206.B35 1967] 67-10509
1. Henry II, King of England, 1133-1189. 2. Gt. Brit.—History—Henry II, 1154-1189. I. Title. BIP

BARBER, Richard W. 942.03'1'0924 B
Henry Plantagenet [by] Richard Barber. [Totowa, N.J.] Rowman & Littlefield [1972, c1964] 278 p. illus. 23 cm. Bibliography: p. [250]-260. [DA206.B35 1972] 72-180451 8.50
1. Henry II, King of England, 1133-1189. 2. Great Britain—History—Henry II, 1154-1189. I. Title.

SALZMAN, Louis Francis, 1878- 942'.03'1'0924 B
Henry II, by L. F. Salzman. New York, Russell & Russell [1967] viii, 267 p. illus., map. 22 cm. Reprint of the 1914 ed. Bibliography: p. 236-240. [DA206.S3 1967] 66-27144
1. Henry II, King of England, 1133-1189. 2. Great Britain—History—Henry II, 1154-1189.

SCHLIGHT, John. 942.03'1'0924 B
Henry II Plantagenet. New York, Twayne Publishers [1973] 219 p. maps. 22 cm. (Twayne's rulers and statesmen of the world series, TROW 19) Bibliography: p. 195-209. [DA206.S36] 74-187638 4.95
1. Henry II, King of England, 1133-1189.

WARREN, Wilfred Lewis. 942.03'1'0924 B
Henry II [by] W. L. Warren. Berkeley, University of California Press, 1973. 693 p. illus. 25 cm. Bibliography: p. [637]-668. [DA206.W37 1973] 72-82220 ISBN 0-520-02282-3 20.00
1. Henry II, King of England, 1133-1189. 2. Great Britain—Politics and government—1154-1189.

WARREN, Wilfred Lewis. 942.03'1'0924
Henry II / [by] W.L. Warren. Berkely : University of California Press, 1977,c1973. 693p. : ill. ; 23 cm. Bibliography: p. [637]-668. [DA206.W37] ISBN 0-520-03494-5 pbk. : 8.95
1. Henry II, King of England, 1133-1189. 2. Great Britain — Politics and government — 1154-1189. I. Title.
L.C. card no. for 1973 University of California Press ed.: 72-82220.

Henry IV, King of England, 1367-1413.

MCFARLANE, Kenneth Bruce. 942.04'1'08
Lancastrian kings and Lollard knights [by] K. B. McFarlane. Oxford, Clarendon P., 1972. [5], 261 p. 23 cm. Bibliography: p. [239]-247. [DA255.M3] 72-186052 ISBN 0-19-822344-7 £2.75
1. Henry IV, King of England, 1367-1413. 2. Henry V, King of England, 1387-1422. 3. Great Britain—Politics and government—1399-1485. 4. Lollards. I. Title. BIP

Henry, Joseph, 1797-1878.

COULSON, Thomas, 1886- 925.3
Joseph Henry, his life and work. Princeton, Princeton University Press, 1950. 352 p. illus., ports. 24 cm. Bibliography: p. 344-346. [QC16.H37C6] 50-7249
1. Henry, Joseph, 1797-1878. I. Title.

RIEDMAN, Sarah Regal, 1902- 925.3
Trailblazer of American science; the life of Joseph Henry. Chicago, Rand McNally [1961] 224 p. illus. 22 cm. [QC16.H37R5] 61-6844
1. Henry, Joseph, 1797-1878. I. Title.

Henry, Joseph, 1797-1878—Juvenile literature.

JAHNS, Patricia. 537'.0924 B
Joseph Henry, father of American electronics. Illustrated by Dave Hodges. Englewood Cliffs, N.J., Prentice-Hall [1970] 143 p. illus. 22 cm. (Hall of Fame books) "A Rutledge book." Bibliography: p. 143. A biography of the first secretary of the Smithsonian Institution whose experiments laid the basis for modern electronics. [Q143.H6J3] 92 69-10333 4.50
1. Henry, Joseph, 1797-1878—Juvenile literature. I. Hodges, David, illus. II. Title. III. Series.

Henry, King of England, 1491-1547—Juvenile literature.

FLETCHER, David. 942.05'2'0924 B
Henry VIII / [by] David Fletcher. Hove : Wayland, [1976] 96 p. : ill., facsim., ports. ; 22 cm. (Wayland kings and queens) Includes index. Bibliography: p. 96. [DA332.F56] 76-383296 ISBN 0-85340-430-5 : £2.95
1. Henry, King of England, 1491-1547—Juvenile literature. 2. Great Britain—Kings and rulers—Biography—Juvenile literature.

Henry, Matthew, 1662-1714.

THE lives of Philip and Matthew Henry / J. B. Williams. 283'.092'2 B
Edinburgh ; Carlisle, Pa. : Banner of Truth Trust, 1974. 2 v. in 1 : ports. ; 23 cm. Includes The life of the Rev. Philip Henry, A.M. with funeral sermons for Mr. and Mrs. Henry, by Matthew Henry, corrected and enlarged by J. B. Williams, 1825, and Memoirs of the life, character and writings of the Rev. Matthew Henry, by J. B. Williams, 1828. Includes indexes. [BX5207.H38L58] 75-327558 ISBN 0-85151-178-3 : £2.95
1. Henry, Philip, 1631-1696. 2. Henry, Matthew, 1662-1714. 3. Henry, Katharine, 1629-1707. I. Williams, John Bickerton, Sir, 1792-1855. II. Henry, Matthew, 1662-1714. The life of the Rev. Philip Henry. 1974. III. Williams, John Bickerton, Sir, 1792-1855. Memoirs of the life, character and writings of the Rev. Matthew Henry. 1974.

Henry, Patrick, 1736-1799.

AXELRAD, Jacob. 973.3'092'4 B
Patrick Henry, the voice of freedom / by Jacob Axelrad. Westport, Conn. : Greenwood Press, 1975, c1947. p. cm. Reprint of the ed. published by Random House, New York. Bibliography: p. [E302.6.H5A9 1975] 75-22310 ISBN 0-8371-8331-6 lib.bdg. : 16.50
1. Henry, Patrick, 1736-1799.

BARTON, Thomas Frank, 1905- 973.3'0924 B
Patrick Henry, boy spokesman. Illustrated by Mel Bolden. Indianapolis, Bobbs-Merrill [1960] 192 p. illus. 20 cm. (Childhood of famous Americans) A biography which stresses the boyhood of Patrick Henry who grew up to be known as the "Father of Virginia," as well as a great orator for the cause of freedom. [PZ7.B2856Pat] 92 AC 68
1. Henry, Patrick, 1735-1799. I. Bolden, Mel, illus. II. Title.

BEEMAN, Richard R. 973.3'092'4 B
Patrick Henry; a biography [by] Richard R. Beeman. New York, McGraw-Hill [1974] xvi, 229 p. illus. 24 cm. Bibliography: p. 215-218. [E302.6.H5B44] 74-11445 ISBN 0-07-004280-2 8.95
1. Henry, Patrick, 1736-1799. 2. Virginia—History—Revolution, 1775-1783. BIP

FRANTZ, Mabel (Goode) 923.273
The voice: Patrick Henry of Virginia. Philadelphia, Dorrance [1954] 251p. 20cm. [E302.6.H5F7] 53-10194
1. Henry, Patrick, 1736-1799. I. Title.

MEADE, Robert Douthat, 1903- 923.273
Patrick Henry: patriot in the making. [1st ed.] Philadelphia, Lippincott [1957- v. illus. 24cm. Includes bibliography. [E302.6.H5M4] 57-9501
1. Henry, Patrick. 1736-1799. I. Title.

MEADE, Robert Douthat, 1903- 973.3'0924 B
Patrick Henry. [1st ed.] Philadelphia, Lippincott [1957-69] 2 v. illus., facsims., ports. 24 cm. Contents.Contents.—[1] Patriot in the making.—[2] Practical revolutionary. Includes bibliographies. [E302.6.H5M4] 57-9501
1. Henry, Patrick, 1736-1799.

TYLER, Moses Coit, 1835-1900. 923.273
Patrick Henry, Ithaca, N.Y., Great Seal Books [1962] 454 p. 19 cm. Includes bibliography. [E302.6.H5T94] 62-17475
1. Henry, Patrick, 1736-1799. I. Title. BIP

TYLER, Moses Coit, 1835-1900 973.30924
Patrick Henry. New York, Ungar [1966] x. 454p. illus., ports. 21cm. (Amer. classics) Reprinted from the ed. of 1898. Bibl. [E302.6.H5T92 1966] 66-22989 6.50
1. Henry, Patrick, 1736-1799. I. Title.

TYLER, Moses Coit, 1835-1900. 973.3'0924 B
Patrick Henry. [Rev. ed.] New Rochelle, N.Y., Arlington House [1970?] 454 p. ports. 21 cm. (Giants of America. The Founding Fathers) Originally published in 1887. [E302.6.H5T92 1970b] 75-111225 ISBN 0-87000-091-8
1. Henry, Patrick, 1736-1799.

TYLER, Moses Coit, 1835-1900. 973.3'0924 B
Patrick Henry. Boston, Houghton, Mifflin. [New York, AMS Press, 1972] x, 454 p. illus. 19 cm. (American statesmen, v. 3) Reprint of the 1898 ed. Bibliography: p. [424]-429. [E302.6.H5T92 1972] 71-128936 ISBN 0-404-50853-7
1. Henry, Patrick, 1736-1799. I. Title. II. Series.

UMBREIT, Kenneth Bernard. 973.3'0922
Founding fathers; man who shaped our tradition, by Kenneth Umbreit. Port Washington, N.Y., Kennikat Press [1969, c1941] viii, 344 p. ports. 22 cm. (Essay and general literature index reprint series) Contents.Contents.—Thomas Jefferson.—John Adams.—John Hancock.—Samuel Adams.—Patrick Henry.—George Washington. [E302.5.U55 1969] 68-26228
1. Jefferson, Thomas, Pres. U.S., 1743-1826. 2. Adams, John, Pres. U.S., 1735-1826. 3. Hancock, John, 1737-1793. 4. Adams, Samuel, 1722-1803. 5. Henry, Patrick, 1736-1799. 6. Washington, George, Pres. U.S., 1732-1799. I. Title.

WILLISON, George Findlay, 1897- 973.3'0924 B
Patrick Henry and his world, by George F. Willison. [1st ed.] Garden City, N.Y., Doubleday, 1969. xii, 498 p. port. 25 cm.

Bibliographical footnotes. [E302.6.H5W67] 67-27847 7.95
1. Henry, Patrick, 1736-1799. I. Title.

WIRT, William, 1772- 1834. 973.3'0924 B
Sketches of the life and character of Patrick Henry. 9th ed., corr. by the author. Freeport, N.Y., Books for Libraries Press [1970] 468 p. 2 ports. 23 cm. Reprint of the 1836 ed. Includes bibliographical references. [E302.6.H5W7893 1970] 72-130568
1. Henry, Patrick, 1736-1799. I. Title. **BIP**

Henry, Patrick, 1736-1799—Juvenile literature.

HENRY, William Wirt, 1831-1900. 973.3'0924 B
Patrick Henry; life, correspondence and speeches. New York, B. Franklin [1969] 3 v. 24 cm. (Burt Franklin research and source works series, 407) (American classics in history and social science, 92.) Reprint of the 1891 ed. [E302.6.H5H5 1969] 71-108350
1. Henry, Patrick, 1736-1799. **BIP**

JONES, William Percival. 923.273
Patrick Henry: voice of liberty. Illustrated by Louis F. Cary. Boston, Houghton Mifflin [1960] 191p. illus. 22cm. (Piper books) [E302.6.H5J6] 60-13066
1. Henry, Patrick, 1736-1799—Juvenile literature. I. Title.

Henry, Patrick, 1736-1799—Juvenile literature.

CAMPION, Nardi Reeder. 923.273
Patrick Henry, firebrand of the Revolution. Illustrated by Victor Mays. [1st ed.] Boston, Little, Brown [1961] 261 p. illus. 21 cm. Includes bibliography. [F302.6.H5C27] 61-5329
1. Henry, Patrick, 1736-1799—Juvenile literature.

DAVIS, Burke. 973.3'092'2 B
Three for revolution / Burke Davis ; with prints and portraits of the period. 1st ed. New York : Harcourt Brace Jovanovich, [1975] 160 p. : ill. ; 21 cm. Includes index. Bibliography: p. [154]-155. Brief biographies of the three Virginians who became "the trumpet, the pen, and the sword of the Revolution." [E302.5.D35] 920 74-24320 ISBN 0-15-286653-1 : 6.25
1. Henry, Patrick, 1736-1799—Juvenile literature. 2. Jefferson, Thomas, Pres. U.S., 1743-1826—Juvenile literature. 3. Washington, George, Pres. U.S., 1732-1799—Juvenile literature. I. Title. **BIP**

FRITZ, Jean. 973.3'092'4 B
Where was Patrick Henry on the 29th of May? / By Jean Fritz ; illustrated by Margot Tomes. New York : Coward, McCann & Geoghegan, [1975] 47 p. : ill. (some col.) ; 24 cm. A brief biography of Patrick Henry tracing his progress from planter to statesman. [E302.6.H5F74 1975] 92 74-83014 ISBN 0-698-20307-0 : 5.95. ISBN 0-698-30339-0 lib. bdg.
1. Henry, Patrick, 1736-1799—Juvenile literature. I. Tomes, Margot. II. Title. **BIP**

Henry, Philip, 1631-1696.

THE lives of Philip and Matthew Henry / J. B. Williams. 283'.092'2 B Edinburgh ; Carlisle, Pa. : Banner of Truth Trust, 1974. 2 v. in 1 : ports. ; 23 cm. Includes The life of the Rev. Philip Henry, A.M. with funeral sermons for Mr. and Mrs. Henry, by Matthew Henry, corrected and enlarged by J. B. Williams, 1825, and Memoirs of the life, character and writings of the Rev. Matthew Henry, by J. B. Williams, 1828. Includes indexes. [BX5207.H38L58] 75-327558 ISBN 0-85151-178-3 : £2.95
1. Henry, Philip, 1631-1696. 2. Henry, Matthew, 1662-1714. 3. Henry, Katharine, 1629-1707. I. Williams, John Bickerton, Sir, 1792-1855. II. Henry, Matthew, 1662-1714. The life of the Rev. Philip Henry. 1974. III. Williams, John Bickerton, Sir, 1792-1855. Memoirs of the life, character and writings of the Rev. Matthew Henry. 1974.

Henry, Ralph L

HENRY, Ralph L 1902- 920
My life and death story; from life to death and back again. Los Angeles, Wetzel [1953] 59p. illus. 21cm. [CT275.H568A3] 54-7773
I. Title.

Henry, Sarah Winston Syme, 1710-1784.

HARTLESS, Eva C. 973.3'092'2 B
Sarah Winston Syme Henry, mother of Patrick Henry / by Eva C. Hartless. Boston : Branden Press, c1977. 138 p., [4] leaves of plates : ill. ; 23 cm. [F229.H5H37] 76-47414 ISBN 0-8283-1688-0 : 10.00
1. Henry, Sarah Winston Syme, 1710-1784. 2. Henry, Patrick, 1736-1799. 3. Virginia—Biography. 4. Legislators—Virginia—Biography. I. Title.

Henry, Sarepta Myrenda (Irish) 1839-1900.

WHITE, Margaret Rossiter, 1901- 922
The whirlwind of the Lord; story of Mrs. S. M. I. Henry. Washington, Review and Herald Pub. Association [1953] 320p. illus. 21cm. [BR1725.H45W5] 53-33642
1. Henry, Sarepta Myrenda (Irish) 1839-1900. I. Title.

Henry V, King of England, 1387-1422.

HUTCHISON, Harold Frederick. 942.04'2'0924 B
King Henry V; a biography [by] Harold F. Hutchison. [1st American King Henry the fifth]. New York, John Day Co. [1967] 287 p. illus., maps, ports. 24 cm. "Appendix: The siege of Rouen, by John Page": p. [227]-250. Bibliographical references included in "Notes" (p. 251-279) [DA256.H8 1967b] 67-29803
1. Henry V, King of England, 1387-1422. I. Page, John, fl. 1419. The siege of Rouen. 1967.

†LABARGE, Margaret Wade. 942.04'2'0924 B
Henry V : the cautious conqueror / Margaret Wade Labarge. New York : Stein and Day, 1976, c1975. xii, 219 p., [4] leaves of plates : ill. ; 24 cm. Includes index. Bibliography: p. [207] [DA256.L3] 75-15238 ISBN 0-8128-1869-5 : 10.00
1. Henry V, King of England, 1387-1422. 2. Great Britain—History—Henry V, 1413-1422. I. Title.

LABARGE, Margaret Wade. 942.04'2'0924 B
King Henry V : the cautious conqueror / Margaret wade Larbarge. New York : Stein and Day, [1976] p. cm. [DA256.L3] 75-16408 ISBN 0-8128-1869-5 : 10.00
1. Henry V, King of England, 1387-1422. 2. Great Britain—History—Henry V, 1413-1422. I. Title.

Henry V, King of England, 1387-1422—Drama.

SHAKESPEARE, William, 1564-1616. 822.33
The life of Henry the Fifth. Edited by R. J. Dorius. [Rev. ed.] New Haven, Yale University Press [1955] x, 166 p. 18 cm. (The Yale Shakespeare) Bibliography: p. 166. [PR2812.A2D6 1955] 55-11035
1. Henry V, King of England, 1387-1422—Drama. I. Darius, Raymond Joel, 1919- ed.

SHAKESPEARE, William, 1564-1616. 822.3'3
The life of King Henry the Fifth. Edited by Alfred Harbage. [Rev. ed.] Baltimore, Penguin Books [1971, c1972] 144 p. 18 cm. (The Pelican Shakespeare) [PR2812.A2H3 1972] 79-98365 ISBN 0-14-071409-X 1.65
1. Henry V, King of England, 1387-1422—Drama. I. Harbage, Alfred, 1901- ed. II. Title.

SHAKESPEARE, William, 1564-1616. 822.3'3
The life of King Henry the Fifth. Edited by George Lyman Kittredge. Rev. by Irving Ribner. Waltham, Mass., Blaisdell Pub. Co. [1967] xiv, 128 p. 21 cm. (A Blaisdell book in the humanities) "The Kittredge Shakespeares." [PR2812.A2K5 1967] 67-18320
1. Henry V, King of England, 1387-1422—Drama. I. Kittredge, George Lyman, 1860-1941, ed. II. Ribner, Irving, ed.

Henry VII, King of England, 1457-1509.

CHRIMES, Stanley Bertram, 1907- 942.05'1'0924 B
Henry VII [by] S. B. Chrimes. Berkeley, University of California Press, 1972. xv, 373 p. illus. 24 cm. Bibliography: p. [345]-354. [DA330.C48 1972b] 72-78947 ISBN 0-520-02266-1 16.00
1. Henry VII, King of England, 1457-1509. 2. Great Britain—Politics and government—1485-1509.

GAIRDNER, James, 1828-1912. 942.05'1'0924 B
Henry the Seventh. New York, AMS Press [1970] vi, 219 p. 23 cm. Reprint of the 1889 ed. [DA330.G14 1970] 70-112639
1. Henry VII, King of England, 1457-1509. 2. Gt. Brit.—History—Henry VII, 1485-1509. **BIP**

SIMONS, Eric N. 942.05'1'0924 B
Henry VII, the first Tudor king [by] Eric N. Simons. New York, Barnes & Noble [1968] xiii, 322 p. facsim., geneal. table, ports. 23 cm. Bibliography: p. [308]-311. [DA330.S5 1968] 68-1171
1. Henry VII, King of England, 1457-1509. I. Title.

TEMPERLEY, Gladys. 942.05'1'0924
Henry VII. With an introd. by James T. Showell. Westport, Conn., Greenwood Press [1971] xiv, 453 p. illus., plan, ports. 23 cm. Reprint of the 1914 ed. Bibliography: p. 431-435. [DA330.T4 1971] 75-110871 ISBN 0-8371-4550-3
1. Henry VII, King of England, 1457-1509. 2. Gt. Brit.—History—Henry VII, 1485-1509.

Henry VIII, King of England, 1491-1547.

BAGLEY, John J., 1908- 942.052
Henry VII and his times. New York, Arco [1963, c.1962] 154p. illus. 23cm. 63-17098 3.95
1. Henry VIII, King of England, 1491-1547. I. Title.

BOWLE, John. 923.142
Henry VIII, a biography. [1st American ed. Boston, Little, Brown [1965, c1964] 316 p. illus., geneal. tables, ports. 22 cm. "Note on sources": p. [301]-303. [DA332.B6 1965] 65-15237
1. Henry VIII, King of England, 1491-1547.

HACKETT, Francis, 1883-1962. 942.05'2'0924 B
Henry the Eighth. New York, Liveright [1970, c1957] x, 452 p. 21 cm. [DA332.H15 1970] 77-114379 2.95
1. Henry VIII, King of England, 1491-1547.

LACEY, Robert. 942.05'2'0924 B
The life and times of Henry VIII. Introd. by Antonia Fraser. New York, Praeger [1974, c1972] 224 p. illus. 26 cm. Bibliography: p. 220-221. [DA332.L3 1974] 73-12896 10.95
1. Henry VIII, King of England, 1491-1547. I. Title.

MORRISON, Nancy Brysson. 923.142
The private life of Henry VIII, by N. Brysson Morrison. New York, Vanguard Press [1964] 205 p. illus., ports. 23 cm. [DA332.M6 1964a] 63-13796
1. Henry VIII, King of England, 1491-1547. I. Title.

THE personal history of Henry the Eighth. v. 12 New York, Bantam Books [1956] 303p. 18cm. (A Bantam biography B401)
1. Henry VIII, King of England, 1491-1547. I. Hackett, Francis, 1883-

POLLARD, Albert Frederick, 1869- 923.142
Henry VIII. a[Illustrated ed.] London, New York, Longmans, Green [1951] xv. 385 p. ports. 22 cm. Bibliographical footnotes. [DA332.P78 1951] 52-6999
1. Henry viii, King of England, 1491-1547. I. Title.

POLLARD, Albert Frederick, 1869-1948 923.142
Henry VIII. Introd. to Torchbk. d.: A. G. Dickens. Henry the eighth New York, Harper [c.1966] xxx, 385p. front. port. 21cm. First pub. in 1902 (Torchbk. Acad. Lib., TB1249Q) Bibl. [DA332.P78] 2.95 pap.,
1. Henry VIII, King of England, 1491-1547. I. Title.

SCARISBRICK, J. J. 942.05'2'0924 B
Henry VIII, by J. Scarisbrick. Berkeley, University of California Press, 1968. xiv, 561 p. illus., ports. (1 col.) 24 cm. [DA332.S25 1968b] 68-10995
1. Henry VIII, King of England, 1491-1547.

SMITH, Lacey Baldwin, 1922- 942.05'2'0924 B
Henry VIII; the mask of royalty Boston, Houghton, 1973 [c.1971] xii, 335 p. illus. 21 cm. (Sentry edition, 74) Bibl.: p. [313]-323. [DA332.S63 1971b] 70-162004 ISBN 0-395-13694-6 3.20 (pbk.)
1. Henry VIII, King of England, 1491-1547. I. Title.

TREE, Herbert Beerbohm, Sir, 1853-1917. 942.05'2'0924 B
Henry VIII and his court / by Herbert Beerbohm Tree. 6th ed. Folcroft, Pa. : Folcroft Library Editions, 1977. p. cm. "Chronology of public events during the lifetime of King Henry VIII" : p. [DA332.T8 1977] 77-4446 ISBN 0-8414-8545-3 lib. bdg. : 17.50
1. Henry VIII, King of England, 1491-1547. 2. Henry VIII, King of England, 1491-1547—Wives—Biography. 3. Shakespeare, William, 1564-1616. King Henry VIII. 4. Great Britain—Kings and rulers—Biography. I. Title. **BIP**

VANCE, Marguerite. 923.142
Six queens; the wives of Henry VIII. Illustrated by J. Luis Pellicer. [1st ed.] New York, Dutton [1965] 190 p. illus. 21 cm. Bibliographical references included in "Acknowledgment" (p. [11]) [DA333.A2V3] 65-12186
1. Henry VIII, King of England, 1491-1547 — Wives — Juvenile literature. I. Title.

WALDMAN, Milton, 1895- 942.05
Some English dictators. Port Washington, N.Y., Kennikat Press [1970] vii, 253 p. illus., ports. 22 cm. Reprint of the 1940 ed. Includes bibliographical references. [DA315.W28 1970] 77-112820
1. Henry VIII, King of England, 1491-1547. 2. Elizabeth, Queen of England, 1533-1603. 3. Cromwell, Oliver, 1599-1658. 4. Gt. Brit.—History—Tudors, 1485-1603. 5. Gt. Brit.—History—Stuarts, 1603-1714. I. Title. **BIP**

Henry VIII, King of England, 1491-1547—Drama.

SHAKESPEARE, William, 1564-1616. 822'.3'3
The life of King Henry the Eighth. Edited by F. David Hoeniger. Baltimore, Penguin Books [1966] 153 p. 18 cm. (The Pelican Shakespeare, AB36) [PR2817.A2H6] 66-13631
1. Henry VIII, King of England, 1491-1547—Drama. I. Hoeniger, F. David, ed.

Henry VIII, King of England, 1491-1547—Juvenile literature.

FEUERLICHT, Roberta Strauss. 942.05'2'0924 B
The life and world of Henry VIII. [New York] Crowell-Collier Press [1970] 161 p. illus., map, ports. 24 cm. Bibliography: p. 153-155. The life and reign of the

sixteenth-century English monarch who effected the separation of the English Church from Rome. [DA332.F47 1970] 92 72-114324
1. Henry VIII, King of England, 1491-1547—Juvenile literature. I. Title.

FLETCHER, David, 942.05'2'0924 B
1940-
Henry VIII / David Fletcher. New York : St. Martin's Press, [1977] p. cm. (History makers series) Includes index. Bibliography: p. The life and reign of the sixteenth-century English monarch who effected the separation of England from the Church of Rome. [DA332.F56 1977] 92 77-283 ISBN 0-312-36802-X : 6.95
1. Henry VIII, King of England, 1491-1547—Juvenile literature. 2. Great Britains—Kings and rulers—Biography—Juvenile literature. 3. Great Britain—History—Henry VIII, 1509-1547—Juvenile literature. I. Title.

PITTENGER, 942.05'2'0924 B
William Norman, 1905-
Henry VIII, by W. Norman Pittenger. London, New York, Franklin Watts Ltd., 1970. viii, 3-184 p. illus., maps, port. 23 cm. Bibliography: p. 179-180. [DA332.P53 1970b] 73-876516 ISBN 0-85166-311-7 £1.25
1. Henry VIII, King of England, 1491-1547—Juvenile literature. I. Title.

PITTENGER, 942.05'2'0924 B
William Norman, 1905-
Henry VIII of England, by W. Norman Pittenger. New York, Watts [1970] viii, 184 p. illus., map, ports. 22 cm. (Immortals of history) Bibliography: p. 179-180. A biography of the sixteenth-century English monarch who effected the separation of England from the Church of Rome. [DA332.P53] 92 76-110472
1. Henry VIII, King of England, 1491-1547—Juvenile literature. I. Title.

SOUTHWORTH, John 942.05'2'0924 B
Van Duyn, 1904-
Monarch and conspirators; the wives and woes of Henry VIII. New York, Crown Publishers [1973] 234 p. illus. 24 cm. Bibliography: p. 227-228. Details the historical events of the reign of Henry VIII of England with emphasis on his six marriages. [DA332.S68 1973] 92 72-92387 ISBN 0-517-50261-5 5.95
1. Henry VIII, King of England, 1491-1547—Juvenile literature. 2. Great Britain—History—Henry VIII, 1509-1547—Juvenile literature.

Henry VIII, King of England, 1491-1547—Wives—Biography.

TREE, Herbert 942.05'2'0924 B
Beerbohm, Sir, 1853-1917.
Henry VIII and his court / by Herbert Beerbohm Tree. 6th ed. Folcroft, Pa. : Folcroft Library Editions, 1977. p. cm. "Chronology of public events during the lifetime of King Henry VIII" : p. [DA332.T8 1977] 77-4446 ISBN 0-8414-8545-3 lib. bdg. : 17.50
1. Henry VIII, King of England, 1491-1547. 2. Henry VIII, King of England, 1491-1547—Wives—Biography. 3. Shakespeare, William, 1564-1616. King Henry VIII. 4. Great Britain—Kings and rulers—Biography. I. Title. BIP

Henry, Waights Gibbs.

HENRY, Mary (Davis) 1878- 922.773
One mile from Trinity. [Nashville? 1955] 249p. 24cm. [BX8495.H42H4] 55-37449
1. Henry, Waights Gibbs. I. Title.

Henry, William Wirt,

HENRY, William Wirt, 973.3'0924 B
1831-1900.
Patrick Henry; life, correspondence and speeches. New York, B. Franklin [1969] 3 v. 24 cm. (Burt Franklin research and source works series, 407) (American classics in history and social science, 92.) Reprint of the 1891 ed. [E302.6.H5H5 1969] 71-108350
I. Henry, Patrick, 1736-1799. BIP

Henryson, Robert, 1430?-1506?

STEARNS, Marshall Winslow. 820'.2
Robert Henryson, by Marshall W. Stearns. New York, AMS Press, 1966 [c1949] viii, 155 p. 23 cm. Bibliography: p. [137]-148. [PR1990.A4Z8 1966] 73-182718
1. Henryson, Robert, 1430?-1506? BIP

Henschel, George, Sir, 1850-1934.

HENSCHEL, George, 780'.92'4 B
Sir, 1850-1934.
Musings and memories of a musician / by Sir George Henschel ; with a new table of contents prepared by Roy Chernus. New York : Da Capo Press, 1979. 400 p. ; 24 cm. (Da Capo Press music reprint series) Reprint of the 1919 ed. published by Macmillan, New York. Includes index. [ML410.H48A3 1979] 78-27074 ISBN 0-306-79540-X : 29.50
1. Henschel, George, Sir, 1850-1934. 2. Musicians—Biography. I. Title. BIP

Hensel, William Uhler, 1851-1915.

GIRVIN, J Barry. 974.8'15'040924
The life of William Uhler Hensel, by J. Barry Girvin. Lancaster, Pa., Lancaster County Historical Society, 1966. viii, 138-248 p. illus. 23 cm. (Journal of the Lancaster County Historical Society, v. 70, no. 4) Cover title. Includes bibliographical references. [F157.L2L5 vol.70,no.4] 68-4129
1. Hensel, William Uhler, 1851-1915. I. Title. II. Series: Lancaster County (Pa.) Historical Society. Journal, v. 70, no. 4

Henson, Josiah,

HENSON, Josiah, 301.44'93'0924 B
1789-1883.
An autobiography of the Reverend Josiah Henson. With an introd. by Robin W. Winks. Reading, Mass., Addison-Wesley Pub. Co. [1969] xxxiv, 190 p. 21 cm. (Addison-Wesley's fugitive slave narratives, 1) First published in 1849 under title: The life of Josiah Henson. Reprint of the 1881 ed. Includes bibliographical references. [E444.H52 1969] 69-10343
I. Title. II. Series. BIP

HENSON, Josiah, 301.44'93'0924 B
1789-1883.
Father Henson's story. Upper Saddle River, N.J., Literature House [1970] xii, 212 p. port. 23 cm. "First published as The life of Josiah Henson" in 1849. Reprint of the 1858 ed. [E444.H52 1970] 78-104480 ISBN 0-8398-0776-7
I. Title. BIP

HENSON, Josiah, 301.44'93'0924 B
1789-1883.
Father Henson's story of his own life. With an introd. by H. B. Stowe. Northbrook, Ill., Metro Books, 1972. xii, 212 p. port. 23 cm. At head of title: Truth stranger than fiction. First published in 1849 under title: The life of Josiah Henson. Reprint of the 1858 ed. [E444.H52 1972] 70-99381 ISBN 0-8411-0052-7
I. Title. BIP

HENSON, Josiah, 301.44'93'0924 B
1789-1883.
Father Henson's story of his own life. Introd. by Walter Fisher. New York, Corinth Books [1962] 212 p. illus. 19 cm. (The American experience series, AE18) At head of title: Truth stranger than fiction. First published in 1849 under title: The life of Josiah Henson. [E444.H523 1962] 62-10048
I. Title. II. Title: Truth is stranger than fiction.

Henson, Josiah, 1789-1883.

BLEBY, Henry, 301.45'22'0924 B
1809-1882.
Josiah, the maimed fugitive; a true tale. London, Sold at the Wesleyan Conference Office, 1873. Miami, Fla., Mnemosyne Pub. Co. [1969] 187 p. illus., port. 23 cm. [E444.H526B56 1969] 76-89422
1. Henson, Josiah, 1789-1883. I. Title.

HENSON, Josiah, 301.44'93'0924 B
1789-1883.
An autobiography of the Reverend Josiah Henson. With an introd. by Robin W. Winks. Reading, Mass., Addison-Wesley Pub. Co. [1969] xxxiv, 190 p. 21 cm. (Addison-Wesley's fugitive slave narratives, 1) First published in 1849 under title: The life of Josiah Henson. Reprint of the 1881 ed. Includes bibliographical references. [E444.H52 1969] 69-10343
I. Title. II. Series. BIP

HENSON, Josiah, 301.44'93'0924 B
1789-1883.
Father Henson's story. Upper Saddle River, N.J., Literature House [1970] xii, 212 p. port. 23 cm. "First published as The life of Josiah Henson" in 1849. Reprint of the 1858 ed. [E444.H52 1970] 78-104480 ISBN 0-8398-0776-7
I. Title. BIP

HENSON, Josiah, 301.44'93'0924 B
1789-1883.
Father Henson's story of his own life. With an introd. by H. B. Stowe. Northbrook, Ill., Metro Books, 1972. xii, 212 p. port. 23 cm. At head of title: Truth stranger than fiction. First published in 1849 under title: The life of Josiah Henson. Reprint of the 1858 ed. [E444.H52 1972] 70-99381 ISBN 0-8411-0052-7
I. Title. BIP

HENSON, Josiah, 301.44'93'0924 B
1789-1883.
Father Henson's story of his own life. Introd. by Walter Fisher. New York, Corinth Books [1962] 212 p. illus. 19 cm. (The American experience series, AE18) At head of title: Truth stranger than fiction. First published in 1849 under title: The life of Josiah Henson. [E444.H523 1962] 62-10048
I. Title. II. Title: Truth is stranger than fiction.

Henson, Josiah, 1789-1883—Juvenile literature.

CAVANAH, 301.44'93'0924 B
Frances.
The truth about the man behind the book that sparked the War Between the States / Frances Cavanah. Philadelphia : Westminster Press, [1975] 187 p. ; 21 cm. A biography of the former slave who after escaping to Canada with his family became a well-known minister and active power in the Underground Railroad and served as model for Harriet Beecher Stowe's famous book. [E444.H526C38] 92 75-11566 ISBN 0-664-32572-6 : 6.95
1. Henson, Josiah, 1789-1883—Juvenile literature. I. Title. BIP

Henson, Matthew Alexander, 1866-1955.

MILLER, Floyd. 923.973
Ahdoolo: The biography of Matthew A. Henson. [1st ed.] New York, Dutton, 1963. 221 p. illus. 21 cm. [G635.H4M5 1963] 63-15771
1. Henson, Matthew Alexander, 1866-1955. I. Title.

ROBINSON, Bradley. v. 12
Dark companion; the story of Matthew Henson, by Bradley Robinson with Matthew Henson. Rev. ed. Greenwich, Conn., Fawcett Publications, Inc. [1967] 238 p. 18 cm. (A Fawcett Premier Book) Map and illustration on lining-papers. 68-15113
1. Henson, Matthew Alexander, 1866- I. Title.

ROBINSON, Bradley. 998 B
Dark companion; the story of Matthew Henson, by Bradley Robinson with Matthew Henson. Rev. ed. Greenwich, Conn., Fawcett Publications [1969, c1967] 238 p. map. 18 cm. (A Fawcett premier book) [G635.H4R6 1969] 67-20947 0.75
1. Henson, Matthew Alexander, 1866-1955. I. Title.

*ROBINSON, Bradley 998
Dark companion: the story of Matthew Henson by Bradley Robinson, with Matthew Henson. Rev. ed. Greenwich, Conn., Fawcett [1967,c.1947] 238p. 18cm. (Premier bk., t341) .75 pap.,
1. Henson. Matthew, 1867-1955. I. rctic exploration—U.S. II. Title.

Henson, Matthew Alexander, 1866-1955—Juvenile literature.

DOLAN, Edward F., 1924- 919.8 B
Matthew Henson, Black explorer / Edward F. Dolan, Jr. New York : Dodd, Mead, [1979] p. cm. Includes index. Bibliography: p. A biography of the black explorer who accompanied Robert E. Peary to the North Pole in 1909. [G635.H4D64] 79-52053 ISBN 0-396-07728-5 : 7.95
1. Henson, Matthew Alexander, 1866-1955—Juvenile literature. 2. North Pole—Juvenile literature. 3. Explorers—United States—Biography—Juvenile literature. I. Title.

GRAVES, Charles Parlin, 919.8 B
1911-
Matthew A. Henson, by Charles P. Graves. Illustrated by Ronald Dorfman. New York, Putnam [1971] 62 p. illus. (part col.) 23 cm. (A See and read beginning to read biography) An easy-to-read biography of the black explorer who accompanied Robert Peary to the North Pole. [G635.H4G7 1971] 92 77-133922 2.97
1. Henson, Matthew Alexander, 1866-1955—Juvenile literature. I. Dorfman, Ronald, illus. II. Title. BIP

RIPLEY, Sheldon N. 92 (J)
Matthew Henson, arctic hero [by] Sheldon N. Ripley. Illustrated by E. Harper Johnson. Boston, Houghton Mifflin [1966] 191 p. col. illus. 23 cm. (Piper books) [G635.H4R5] 66-10883
1. Henson, Matthew Alexander, 1866-1955—Juvenile literature. I. Johnson, E. Harper, illus.

Hepburn, John Stuart, 1803-1860.

QUINLAN, Lucille M. 994'.5 B
Here my home; the life and times of Captain John Stuart Hepburn, 1803-1860, master mariner, overlander and founder of Smeaton Hill, Victoria [by] Lucille M. Quinlan. Melbourne, New York [etc.] Oxford University Press, 1967. xii, 212 p. illus., maps, ports. 22 cm. Bibliography: p. 203-205. [DU222.H4Q5 1967] 68-104483 7.75 Aust.
1. Hepburn, John Stuart, 1803-1860. I. Title.

Hepburn, Katharine, 1909-

CAREY, Gary. 791.43'028'0924 B
Katherine Hepburn : a biography / by Gary Carey. New York : Pocket Books, 1975. 238 p., [8] leaves of plates : ill. ; 18 cm. [PN2287.H45C3 1975] 75-328521 ISBN 0-671-80209-7 pbk. : 1.95
1. Hepburn, Katherine, 1909- I. Title.

HIGHAM, 791.43'028'0924 B
Charles, 1931-
Kate : the life of Katharine Hepburn / by Charles Higham. 1st ed. New York : Norton, [1975] xix, 244 p., [6] leaves of plates : ill. ; 22 cm. Includes index. [PN2287.H45H54] 74-32145 ISBN 0-393-07486-2 : 7.95
1. Hepburn, Katharine, 1909- I. Title. BIP

HIGHAM, Charles, 791.43'028'0924
1931-
Kate the life of Katherine Hepburn [New York] New American Library [1976 c1975] xvi, 237 p., 4 leaves of plates illus. 18 cm. (A Signet Book) Includes index. [PN2287.H45H54] 1.95 (pbk.)
1. Hepburn, Katharine, 1909- I. Title.
L.C. card no. of 1975 Norton edition: 74-32145. BIP

MARILL, Alvin H. 791.43'028'0924
Katharine Hepburn, by Alvin H. Marill. General editor: Ted Sennett. New York, Pyramid Publications [1973] 160 p. illus. 20 cm. (Pyramid illustrated history of the movies) Bibliography: p. 140-141. [PN2287.H45M3] 72-93665 ISBN 0-515-02931-9 1.45 (pbk.)
1. Hepburn, Katharine, 1907-

MARILL, Alvin H. 791.43'028'0924
Katharine Hepburn / by Alvin H. Marill ;

general editor, Ted Sennett. New York : Galahad Books, [1974] c1973. 160 p. : ill. ; 22 cm. (The Pictorial treasury of film stars) Includes index. Bibliography: p. 140-141. [PN2287.H45M3 1973] 73-90219 ISBN 0-88365-166-1 : 4.95
1. Hepburn, Katharine, 1907- BIP

Hephurn, Emily (Eaton)

SAVELL, Isabelle Keating, 1905- 920.7
Daughter of Vermont: a biography of Emily Eaton Hepburn. New York, North River Press, 1952. 184p. illus. 24cm. [CT275.H5862S3] 53-5741
1. Hephurn, Emily (Eaton) I. Title.

Hepworth, Barbara,

HEPWORTH, Barbara, Dame, 1903- 730'.924 B
A pictorial autobiography [by] Barbara Hepworth. New York, Praeger [1970] 127 p. illus., facsims., ports. 28 cm. [NB497.H4A2 1970] 73-99496 12.50
I. Title. BIP

Heraldry.

PINE, Leslie Gilbert 929.6
The story of heraldry. Wood engravings by K. F. Rowland. [2d rev. ed] London, Country Life, Ltd. [dist. Hollywood-by-the-Sea, Transatlantic, c.1963] 164p. illus. 23cm. 63-40449 7.50
1. Heraldry. I. Title.

PINE, Leslie Gilbert. 929.6
The story of heraldry, by L. G. Pine. With wood engravings by K. F. Rowland. Rutland, Vt., C. E. Tuttle Co. [1967, c1963] 164 p. coats of arms. 23 cm. "What to read": p. 149-153. [CR27.P48 1967] 66-26840
1. Heraldry. I. Title.

SCOTT-GILES, Charles Wilfrid, 1893- 929.6
Looking at heraldry. New York, Roy [c.1962] 166p. illus. (pt. col.) 19cm. 62-16753 3.00 bds.,
1. Heraldry. I. Title.

Herbert, Alan Patrick, Sir, 1890-1971—Biography.

HERBERT, Alan Patrick, 1890- 923.242
Independent Member. [1st American ed.] Garden City, N. Y., Doubleday, 1951. x, 363 p. 22 cm. Autobiographical. [DA585.H4A3 1951] 51-11287
1. Gt. Brit.—Pol. & govt.—1906-1945. 2. Gt. Brit.—Pol. & govt.—1945- I. Title.

POUND, Reginald. 828'.9'1209 B
A. P. Herbert : a biography / Reginald Pound. London : Joseph, 1976. 312 p., [4] leaves of plates : ill. ; 23 cm. Includes index. [PR6015.E58Z8] 76-380185 ISBN 0-7181-1390-X : £7.25
1. Herbert, Alan Patrick, Sir, 1890-1971—Biography. 2. Authors, English—20th century—Biography.

Herbert, Edward Herbert,

HERBERT, Edward Herbert, Baron, 1583-1648. 942.05'5'0924 B
The autobiography of Edward, Lord Herbert of Cherbury. With introd., notes, appendices, and a continuation of the life, by Sidney Lee. 2d ed., rev. Westport, Conn., Greenwood Press [1970] xli, 214 p. geneal. table, port. 23 cm. Reprint of the 1906 ed. Includes bibliographical references. [DA391.1.H6A2 1970] 76-109745 ISBN 0-8371-4235-0
I. Lee, Sidney, Sir, 1859-1926, ed. II. Title. BIP

Herbert, George, 1593-1633—Biography.

CHARLES, Amy Marie. 821'.3 B
A life of George Herbert / Amy M. Charles. Ithaca, N.Y. : Cornell University Press, 1977. 242 p. : ill. ; 23 cm. Includes bibliographical references and index. [PR3508.C48] 77-3116 ISBN 0-8014-1014-2 : 15.00
1. Herbert, George, 1593-1633—Biography. 2. Poets, English—Early modern, 1500-1700—Biography. I. Title. BIP

Herbert, Victor, 1859-1924.

KAYE, Joseph. 780'.924 B
Victor Herbert: the biography of America's greatest composer of romantic music. Freeport, N.Y., Books for Libraries Press [1970] 271 p. illus., facsims., music, ports. 23 cm. Reprint of the 1931 ed. "Published compositions of Victor Herbert": p. 259-266. [ML410.H52K2 1970] 74-109628
1. Herbert, Victor, 1859-1924. I. Title.

WATERS, Edward Neighbor, 1906- 927.8
Victor Herbert; a life in music. New York, Macmillan, 1955. xvi, 653p. port. 21cm. Foreword by Ella Herbert Bartlett. 'Compositions by Victor Herbert': p. 577-592. 'Phonograph recordings made by Victor Herbert': p. 596-595. Bibliographical annotations included in 'Notes' (p. 597-612) [ML410.H52W3] 55-1675
1. Herbert, Victor, 1859-1924. 2. Herbert, Victor, 1859-1924—Discorgraphy. I. Title. BIP

WATERS, Edward Neighbor, 1906- 782.8'1'0924 B
Victor Herbert : a life in music / by Edward N. Waters. New York : Da Capo Press, 1978, c1955. xvi, 653 p. ; 23 cm. (Da Capo Press music reprint series) Reprint of the ed. published by Macmillan, New York. "Compositions by Victor Herbert": p. 577-592. "Phonograph recordings made by Victor Herbert": p. 593-595. Includes bibliographical references and index. [ML410.H52W3 1978] 78-9597 ISBN 0-306-79502-7 lib.bdg. : 35.00
1. Herbert, Victor, 1859-1924. 2. Composers—United States—Biography.

Herbert, Victor, 1859-1924—Discography.

WATERS, Edward Neighbor, 1906- 927.8
Victor Herbert; a life in music. New York, Macmillan, 1955. xvi,653 p. port. 21cm. Foreword by Ella Herbert Bartlett.'Compositions by 'Victor Herbert': p. 577-592. 'Phonograph recordings made by Victor Herbert': p. 596-595 Bibliographical annotations included in 'Notes' (p. 597-612,)sHerbert, Victor, 1859-1924. [ML410.H32W3] 55-1675
1. Herbert, Victor, 1859-1924—Discography. I. Title.

Herder, Johann Gottfried von, 1744-1803.

CLARK, Robert Thomas, 1906- 830.81
Herder: his life and thought. Berkeley, University of California Press, 1955. vi, 501 p. ports. 25 cm. Bibliography: p. 455-478. [PT2353.C6] 55-6267
1. Herder, Johann Gottfried von, 1744-1803. BIP

Hereford Cathedral—Organs.

SHAW, Harold Watkins, 1911- 786.6'22'2 B
The organists and organs of Hereford Cathedral / by Watkins Shaw ; with a note by Roy Massey. Hereford : Friends of Hereford Cathedral Publications Committee, 1976. 47 p., leaf of plate, iv p. of plates : ill., facsim., ports. ; 22 cm. Bibliography: p. 46-47. [ML594.H45H47] 77-368384 ISBN 0-904642-01-1 : £0.50
1. Hereford Cathedral—Organs. 2. Organists, English. I. Title.

Heresies and heretics.

BAINTON, Roland Herbert 922.8146
Hunted heretic; the life and death of Michael Servetus, 1511-1553. With a new foreword by the author. [Gloucester, Mass., Peter Smith, c.1953, 1960] xiv, 270p. (Bibl. p. 230-241; bibl. notes p. 242-264) 21cm. (Beacon paperback LR2 rebound in cloth) illus. 3.75
I. Title.

SHRIVER, George H., ed. 273.0922
American religious heretics; formal and informal trials, edited by George H. Shriver. Nashville, Abingdon Press [1966] 240 p. 23 cm. Includes bibliographical references. [BR517.S44] 66-21972
1. Heresies and heretics. 2. Trials (Heresy)—United States. 3. United States—Church history. I. Title.

Herff, Adolph, 1858-1952.

HERFF, Ferdinand Peter, 1883-1965. 610'.92'22 B
The doctors Herff: a three-generation memoir. Edited by Laura L. Barber. San Antonio, Trinity University Press, 1973. 2 v. (xiii, 519 p.) illus. 25 cm. Issued in a case. [R154.H377A35 1973] 78-128375 ISBN 0-911536-40-X 18.00
1. Von Herff, Ferdinand Ludwig, 1820-1912. 2. Herff, Adolph, 1858-1952. 3. Herff, Ferdinand Peter, 1883-1965. I. Title. BIP

Herget, Charles A.

HERGET, Charles A. 359.3'38'0924 B
Dear shipmates / by Charles A. Herget. San Diego, Calif. : Grossmont Press, c1977. xv, 156 p. : ill. ; 18 cm. [V63.H47A33] 77-78386 ISBN 0-913182-94-X pbk. : 3.95
1. Herget, Charles A. 2. United States. Navy—Biography. 3. Seamen—Unites States—Biography. I. Title. BIP

Hermann, Nina,1943-

HERRMANN, Nina, 1943- 248'.5'0924
Go out in joy! / Nina Herrmann. New York : Pocket Books, 1978,c1977. viii, 257p. ; 18 cm. (A Kangaroo Book) [BV4335.H38] ISBN 0-671-81424-9 pbk. : 1.95
1. Hermann, Nina,1943- 2. Chicago — Biography. 3. Sick children. 4. Chaplains Hospital — Illinois — Chicago — Biography. I. Title.
L.C. card no. for 1977 John Knox Press ed.: 76-44972. BIP

Hermannsson, Halldor, 1878-1958.

MITCHELL, Phillip Marshall, 1916- 839'.67'072024 B
Halldor Hermannsson / by P. M. Mitchell. Ithaca, N.Y. : Cornell University Press, 1978. 167 p. : ill. ; 22 cm. (Islandica ; 41) Includes index. "A bibliography of the writings of Halldor Hermannsson" p. 123-163. [PT7127.H4M5] 77-14665 ISBN 0-8014-1085-1 : 20.00
1. Hermannsson, Halldor, 1878-1958. 2. Cornell University. Libraries. 3. Literary historians—Biography. 4. Librarians—Biography. 5. Icelandic and Old Norse literature—History and criticism. I. Title. II. Series. BIP

Hermetic Order of the Golden Dawn.

COLQUHOUN, Ithell, 1906- 135.4'3'0924
Sword of wisdom : MacGregor Mathers and the Golden Dawn / Ithell Colquhoun. 1st. American ed. New York : Putnam, 1975. 307 p., [6] leaves of plates : ill. ; 23 cm. Includes index. [BF1623.R7C784 1975] 76-351557 8.95
1. Hermetic Order of the Golden Dawn. 2. Mathers, S. Liddell MacGregor. 3. Mathers, Moina MacGregor, 1865-1928. 4. Colquhoun, Ithell, 1906- I. Title.

Herndon, Angelo,

HERNDON, Angelo, 1913- 364.13'1 B
Let me live. New York, Arno Press, 1969. x, 409 p. ports. 23 cm. (The American Negro, his history and literature) Reprint of the 1937 ed., with new introd. by H. N. Meyer. [E185.97.H47 1969] 69-18566
I. Title. II. Series. BIP

Herne, James A., 1839-1901—Biography.

PERRY, John, 1937- 812'.4
James A. Herne : The American Ibsen / John Perry. Chicago : Nelson-Hall, c1978. x, 343 p., [12] leaves of plates : ill.; 24 cm. A revision of the author's thesis, Southern Illinois University. Includes bibliographical references and index. [PS1919.H75Z8] 77-17931 ISBN 0-88229-265-X : 15.95 ISBN 0-88229-561-6 pbk. : 7.95
1. Herne, James A., 1839-1901—Biography. 2. Dramatists, American—19th century—Biography. 3. Actors—United States—Biography. 4. Theater—United States—History—19th century. BIP

Herod Antipas, tetrarch of Galilee.

HARLOW, Victor Emmanuel, 1876- 923.233
The destroyer of Jesus; the story of Herod Antipas, tetrarch of Galilee. Oklahoma City, Modern Publishers, 1954. 256p. illus. 24cm. [DS122.5.H37 1954] 54-29040
1. Herod Antipas, tetrarch of Galilee. I. Title.

HOEHNER, Harold W. 933'.0099'4 B
Herod Antipas, by Harold W. Hoehner. Cambridge [Eng.] University Press, 1972. xvi, 436 p. map. 23 cm. (Society for New Testament Studies. Monograph series, 17) Bibliography: p. 353-398. [DS122.5.H64 1972] 79-158548 ISBN 0-521-08132-7
1. Herod Antipas, Tetrarch of Galilee. I. Series: Studiorum Novi Testamenti Societas. Monograph series, 17.

Herod I, the Great, King of Judea, d. 4 B.C.

GRANT, Michael, 1914- 933 B
Herod the Great. New York, American Heritage Press [1971] 272 p. illus. 25 cm. Bibliography: p. 265-[266] [DS122.3.G66 1971b] 78-130781 ISBN 0-07-024073-6 12.95
1. Herod I, the Great, King of Judea, d. 4 B.C.

GROSS, William Joseph, 1894- 923.133
Herod the Great. Baltimore, Helicon Press [1962] 370 p. 23 cm. [DS122.3.G7] 62-18775
1. Herod I, the Great, King of Judea, d. 4 B.C.

MINKIN, Jacob Samuel, 1885- 923.133
Herod, King of the Jews. [New ed.] New York, T. Yoseloff [1956, c1936] 277 p. 22 cm. First published in 1936 under title: Herod, a biography. [DS122.3.M5 1956] 56-58674
1. Herod I, the Great, King of Judea, d. 4 B. C.

SANDMEL, Samuel. 933
Herod; profile of a tyrant. [1st ed.] Philadelphia, Lippincott [1967] 282 p. geneal, table, map. 22 cm. Bibliographical references included in "To the scholar" (p. 269-271) [DS122.3.S27] 67-16920
1. Herod I, the Great King of Judea, d. 4 B. C. I. Title.

Heroes.

CHURCHILL, Winston Leonard Spencer, Sir, 1874-1965. 920
Heroes of history. Pictures by Robert MacLean. New York, Dodd, Mead [1968] 192 p. col. illus., maps, ports. 26 cm. Sketches of sixteen of Churchill's favorite historical characters selected from his four-volume A History of the English-speaking Peoples, followed by a profile of Sir Winston drawn from autobiographical writings and speeches. [D107.C63 1968] AC 68
1. Heroes. I. MacLean, Robert, illus. II. Title.

HADAS, Moses, 1900-1966. 291.2'13
Heroes and gods; spiritual biographies in antiquity, by Moses Hadas and Morton Smith. Freeport, N.Y., Books for Libraries Press [1970, c1965] xiv, 266 p. 23 cm.

(Essay index reprint series) [BL325.H46H3 1970] 77-117800
1. Heroes. 2. Biography (as a literary form) I. Smith, Morton, 1915- II. Title. BIP

HEIDERSTADT, Dorothy. 920.02
A book of heroes; great Europeans who live in the hearts of their people. Drawings by Harry Lees. [1st ed.] Indianapolis, Bobbs-Merrill [1954] 192 p. illus. 21 cm. [CT107.H4] 54-6061
1. Heroes.

HEROES of our time. 920
By Lord Shackleton [others] New York, Dutton [1962, c.1961] 181p. 21cm. 62-14708 3.50
1. Heroes. 2. Biography—20th cent. I. Shackelton, Edward, baron

*KELLY, Regina (Zimmerman) 920 1898-
The picture story and biography of Marquette and Joliet, Illus. by W. T. Mars. Chicago, Follett [c.1965] 144p. illus. (pt. col.) 22cm. (Lib. of Amer heroes) 65-14479 1.95 bds.,
I. Title.

Heroes—Juvenile literature.

EDMONDS, I. G. 920
Our heroes' heroes. New York, Criterion [c.1966] 159p. ports. 22cm. [CT107.E4] 66-15171 3.95
1. Heroes—Juvenile literature. I. Title.

EDMONDS, I G j 920
Our heroes' heroes, by I. G. Edmonds. New York, Criterion Books [1966] 159 p. ports. 22 cm. [CT107.E4] 66-15171
1. Heroes — Juvenile literature. I. Title.

Herold, Amos Lee,

HEROLD, Amos Lee, 1885- 923.773
I chose teaching; a life record of self-reliance and devotion to scholarship and democracy. [1st ed.] San Antonio, Tex., Printed by Naylor Co., 1958. 255p. illus. 23cm. [LA2317.H53A3] 58-7540
I. Title.

Herold, David E., 1844-1865.

HEROLD, David E., 345'.73'02524 1844-1865, defendant.
The assassination of President Lincoln and the trial of the conspirators; the courtroom testimony as originally compiled by Benn Pitman. With an introd. by Philip Van Doren Stern. Westport, Conn., Greenwood Press [1974, c1954] xxiv, 421 p. illus. 26 cm. Trial of David E. Herold, Mary E. Surratt, Samuel A. Mudd, and others, before a Military Commission at Washington, D.C. Reprint of the 1954 facsim. ed., published by Funk & Wagnalls, New York, of the 1865 ed. published by Moore, Wilstach & Baldwin, New York. [KF223.H4P5 1974] 73-8568 ISBN 0-8371-6963-1 22.00
1. Herold, David E., 1844-1865. 2. Lincoln, Abraham, Pres. U.S., 1809-1865—Assassination. 3. Booth, John Wilkes, 1838-1865. I. Surratt, Mary Eugenia (Jenkins) 1826-1865, defendant. II. Mudd, Samuel Alexander, 1833-1883, defendant. III. Pitman, Benn, 1822-1910, reporter. IV. United States. Army. Military Commission. Lincoln's assassins. 1865. V. Title.

Herr, Ethel L.

HERR, Ethel L. 301.42'7
Growing up is a family affair / by Ethel L. Herr. Chicago : Moody Press, c1978. 160 p. ; 22 cm. Includes bibliographical references. [HQ535.H46] 78-17581 ISBN 0-8024-3357-X pbk. : 3.95
1. Herr, Ethel L. 2. Parent and child—Biography. 3. Family—United States. I. Title. BIP

Herr, Michael.

HERR, Michael. 959.704'33
Dispatches / Michael Herr. 1st ed. New York : Knopf, 1977. p. cm. Contents.Contents.—Breathing in.—Hell sucks.—Khe Sanh.—Illumination rounds.—Colleagues.—Breathing out. [DS559.5.H47] 77-74994 ISBN 0-394-41788-7 8.95
1. Herr, Michael. 2. Vietnamese Conflict, 1961-1975—Personal narratives, American. I. Title.
Contents omitted BIP

Herreshoff family.

CARTER, Samuel, 338.4'7'623823 B 1904-
The boatbuilders of Bristol; the story of the amazing Herreshoff family of Rhode Island/inventors, individualists, yacht designers, and America's Cup defenders, by Samuel Carter, III. [1st ed.] Garden City, N.Y., Doubleday, 1970. xvii, 215 p. illus., facsim., geneal. table, map, fold. plan, ports. 22 cm. [VM139.C36] 73-121949 7.95
1. Herreshoff family. I. Title.

Herreshoff, Nathanael Greene, 1848-1938.

BURNETT, Constance (Buel) 926.238
Let the best boat win; the story of America's greatest yacht designer. Illustrated by John O'Hara Cosgrave, II. Boston, Houghton Mifflin, 1957. 266p. illus. 22cm. [VM140.H4B8] 57-7204
1. Herreshoff, Nathanael Greene, 1848-1968. I. Title.

HERRESHOFF, Lewis 926.238 Francis, 1890-
Capt. Nat Herreshoff, the wizard of Bristol; the life and achivements of Nathanael Greene Herreshoff, together with an account of some of the yachts he designed. New York, Sheridan House [1953] 349p. illus. 24cm. [VM140.H4H4] 53-12493
1. Herreshoff, Nathanael Greene, 1848-1938. I. Title.

Herrgesell, Oscar, 1926-1972.

HERRGESELL, Oscar, 959.704'38 1926-1972.
Dear Margaret, today I died ... letters from Vietnam. Compiled by Margaret Rowton Herrgesell. San Antonio, Naylor Co. [1974] vii, 93 p. illus. 22 cm. [DS557.A69H37] 73-23044 ISBN 0-8111-0526-1 6.95
1. Herrgesell, Oscar, 1926-1972. 2. Herrgesell, Margaret Rowton. 3. Vietnamese Conflict, 1961-1975—Personal narratives, American. I. Herrgesell, Margaret Rowton. II. Title.

Herrick, Clara Belle (James) 1871-1966.

HERRICK, Cheesman Abiah, 923.773 1866-
Clara James Herrick; a memoir. Philadelphia, Priv. print. 1939. viii, 192p. plate, ports. 22cm. [LD7501.P5G5832] 52-57708
1. Herrick, Clara Belle (James) 1871-1966. I. Title.

Herrick, Clarence Luther, 1858-1904.

HERRICK, Charles Judson, 595.78 1868-
Clarence Luther Herrick, pioneer naturalist, teacher, and psychobiologist. Philadelphia, American Philosophical Society, 1955. 85p. illus., port. 30cm. (Transactions of the American Philosophical Society, new ser., v. 45, pt. 1) Bibliographical footnotes. Bibliography: p. 80-83. [Q11.P6 n. s., vol. 45, pt.1] 55-5431
1. Herrick, Clarence Luther, 1858-1904. I. Title. II. Series: American Philosophical Society, Philadelphia. Transactions, new ser., v. 45, pt. 2 BIP

WINDLE, William 591.1'88'0924 B Frederick, 1898-
The pioneering role of Clarence Luther Herrick in American neuroscience / William Frederick Windle. 1st ed. Hicksville, N.Y. : Exposition Press, c1979. 140 p., [2] leaves of plates : ill. ; 22 cm. (An Exposition-university book) Includes index. Bibliography: p. 135. [QP26.H48W56] 78-75284 ISBN 0-682-49340-6 : 7.50
1. Herrick, Clarence Luther, 1858-1904. 2. Physiologists—United States—Biography. 3. Neurologists—United States—Biography. I. Title. BIP

Herrick, Manuel, 1876-1952.

ALDRICH, Gene. 328.73'092'4 B
The Okie Jesus Congressman (the life of Manuel Herrick). Oklahoma City, Times-Journal Pub. Co. [1974] 290 p. illus. 23 cm. Bibliography: p. 271-278. [F700.H47A42] 74-159851
1. Herrick, Manuel, 1876-1952. 2. Oklahoma—Politics and government—1907- I. Title.

Herrick, Robert, 1591-1674.

MOORMAN, Frederic William, 821.4 1872-1919.
Robert Herrick, a biographical & critical study. New York, Russell & Russell, 1962. 343p. illus. 23cm. [PR3513.M6 1962] 62-13843
1. Herrick, Robert, 1591-1674. I. Title.

SCOTT, George Walton. 821'.4 B
Robert Herrick, 1591-1674. New York, St. Martin's Press [1974] 200 p. illus. 23 cm. Bibliography: p. 189-193. [PR3513.S3 1974] 73-94380 10.00
1. Herrick, Robert, 1591-1674. BIP

Herrick, Smith, Donald, Farley & Ketchum.

CONNOLLY, Eugene 340'.065'74461 T., 1891-
History of the Boston law firm of Herrick, Smith, Donald, Farley & Ketchum, 1890-1970. Compiled and edited by Eugene T. Connolly. [Boston, Mass., Printed by George H. Dean Co., 1971] ix, 164 p. port. 24 cm. [KF355.B6C65] 71-30719
1. Herrick, Smith, Donald, Farley & Ketchum. 2. Lawyers—Boston. I. Title.

Herridge, Herbert Wilfred, 1895-1972.

HODGSON, Maurice, 328.71'092'4 B 1934-
The Squire of Kootenay West : a biography of Bert Herridge / by Maurice Hodgson. Saanichton, B.C. : Hancock House, c1976. 232 p., [8] leaves of plates : ill. ; 23 cm. Includes index. [F1034.H48H6] 77-353347 ISBN 0-919654-45-2
1. Herridge, Herbert Wilfred, 1895-1972. 2. Legislators—Canada—Biography. 3. West Kootenay, B.C.—History. I. Title.

Herring, Ethel.

HERRING, Ethel. 975.6'8
Echoes of a log cabin / by Ethel Herring. Winston-Salem, N.C. : Herring, c1976. 94 p. : ill. ; 22 cm. [S521.5.N8H47] 76-374533
1. Herring, Ethel. 2. Country life—North Carolina. 3. Country life—Blue Ridge Mountains. 4. Log cabins. 5. North Carolina—Biography. I. Title.

Herriot, Edouard, 1872-1957.

JESSNER, Sabine. 944.081'092'4 B
Edouard Herriot, patriarch of the Republic. New York, Haskell House Publishers, 1974. 165 p. 23 cm. Bibliography: p. 155-165. [DC373.H4J47] 73-20352 ISBN 0-8383-1808-8 11.95 (lib. bdg.)
1. Herriot, Edouard, 1872-1957. I. Title.

Herriot, James.

HERRIOT, James. 636.089'092'4 [B]
All creatures great and small. New York, Bantam Books [1973, c.1972] 499 p. 18 cm. [SF613.H44A28] 1.75 (pbk.)
1. Vetenarians—Correspondence, reminiscences, etc. I. Title.
L.C. card no. for the hardbound edition: 72-79632. BIP

HERRIOT, James. 636.089'092'4 B
All things bright and beautiful / James Herriot. Boston : G. K. Hall, 1975, c1974. 2 v. (798 p.) ; 24 cm. "Published in large print." [SF613.H44A283 1975] 74-32391 ISBN 0-8161-6269-7
1. Herriot, James. 2. Veterinarians—Correspondence, reminiscences, etc. 3. Sight-saving books. I. Title. BIP

HERRIOT, James. 636.089'092'4 B
All things wise and wonderful / James Herriot. New York : St. Martin's Press, c1977. 432 p. ; 22 cm. [SF613.H44A285] 77-76640 ISBN 0-312-02031-7 : 10.00
1. Herriot, James. 2. Veterinarians—Biography. I. Title. BIP

HERRIOT, James. 636.089'.092'4
All things wise and wonderful / James Herriot. New York : Bantam Books, 1978,c1977. 440p. ; 18 cm. [SF613.H44.A285] [[B]] ISBN 0-553-11746-7 pbk. : 2.75
1. Herriot, James. 2. Veterinarians-Biography. I. Title.
L.C. card no. for 1977 St. Martin's Press ed.: 77-76640. BIP

HERRIOT, James. 636.089'392'4 B
All things wise and wonderful / James Herriot. New York : St. Martin's Press, 1977. 2 v. (900 p.) ; 24 cm. "Published in large print." [SF613.H44A285 1977] 77-15495 ISBN 0-312-02031-7 : 10.00
1. Herriot, James. 2. Veterinarians—England—Biography. 3. Large type books. I. Title.

HERRIOT, James. 636.089'092'4 B
If only they could talk / James Herriot. Boston : G. K. Hall, 1977, c1970. 398 p. ; 25 cm. "Published in large print." [SF613.H44A29 1977] 76-47508 ISBN 0-8161-6415-0 lib. bdg. : 10.95
1. Herriot, James. 2. Veterinarians—Great Britain—Biography. 3. Sight-saving books. I. Title.

HERRIOT, James. 636.089'092'4 B
Vets might fly / [by] James Herriot ; drawings by Larry. London : Joseph, 1976. 255 p. : ill. ; 22 cm. [SF658.H47 1976] 77-354805 ISBN 0-7181-1512-0 : £3.50
1. Herriot, James. 2. Veterinary medicine—Great Britain—Yorkshire, Eng. 3. Veterinarians—Great Britain—Biography. I. Title.

Herschel, Caroline Lucretia, 1750-1848—Juvenile literature.

HIGGINS, Frances 520'.924 B Lowry.
Sweeper of the skies; a story of the life of Caroline Herschel, astronomer. Chicago, Follett Pub. Co. [1967] 127 p. 23 cm. [QB36.H58H65] 67-21170
1. Herschel, Caroline Lucretia, 1750-1848—Juvenile literature. I. Title.

Herschel, John Frederick William, Sir, bart., 1792-1871.

BUTTMANN, Gunther. 520'.924 B
The shadow of the telescope; a biography of John Herschel. Translated by B. E. J. Pagel. Edited and with an introd. by David S. Evans. New York, Scribner [1970] xiv, 219 p. illus., facsim., ports. 24 cm. Translation of John Herschel; Lebensbild eines Naturforschers. Bibliography: p. 207-211. [QB36.H59B813] 72-85256 7.95
1. Herschel, John Frederick William, Sir, bart., 1792-1871. I. Evans, David Stanley, ed. II. Title.

Herschel, William, Sir 1738-1822.

ARMITAGE, Angus, 1902- 925.2
William Herschel. Garden City, N.Y., Doubleday 1963[c.1962] 158p. illus. 21cm. (British men of sci.) 63-7962 3.95
1. Herschel, William, Sir 1738-1822. I. Title.

CRAWFORD, Deborah. 520'.924 B
The king's astronomer, William Herschel. With a foreword by Willy Ley. New York, J. Messner [1968] 191 p. 22 cm. Bibliography: p. 187. A life of the musician and astronomer who discovered the planet Uranus and infrared radiation, and through his development of and work with the high

powered telescope, proved that a star's brightness is not necessarily proof of its nearness. [QB36.H6C7] 92 AC 68
1. Herschel, William, Sir, 1738-1822. I. Title.

HOSKIN, Michael A. 925.2
William Herschel, pioneer of sidereal astronomy. New York, Sheed and Ward [1960, c.1959] 79p. Includes bibliography. 19cm. (The Philosophy of science series) 60-12882 .95 pap.,
1. Herschel, William, Sir 1738-1832. I. Title.

Herschensohn, Wes, 1928-

HERSCHENSOHN, Wes, 1928- 791.43'7
Resurrection in Cannes : the making of the Picasso summer / Wes Herschensohn. South Brunswick, [N.J.] : A. S. Barnes, 1979. p. cm. Includes index. [PN1997.P4783H47 1979] 76-24621 ISBN 0-498-01942-X : 14.50
1. Herschensohn, Wes, 1928- 2. Picasso summer (Motion picture) 3. Moving-picture producers and directors—United States—Biography. I. Title. BIP

Hersey, Harold Brainerd, 1893-

HERSEY, Harold Brainerd, 051 1893-
Pulpwood editor; the fabulous world of the thriller magazines revealed by a veteran editor and publisher. Westport, Conn., Greenwood Press [1974, c1937] viii, 301 p. 22 cm. Reprint of the ed. published by F. A. Stokes Co., New York. [PN4877.H4 1974] 74-4841 ISBN 0-8371-7490-2 14.75
1. Hersey, Harold Brainerd, 1893- 2. American periodicals. 3. Journalists—Correspondence, reminiscences, etc. I. Title.

Hershey, Jean, 1902-

HERSHEY, Jean, 301.42'86'0924 1902-
A widow's pilgrimage / by Jean Hershey. New York : Seabury Press, 1979. 114 p. ; 22 cm. (A Continuum book) [HQ1058.5.U5H47] 79-16776 ISBN 0-8164-9118-6 : 12.95
1. Hershey, Jean, 1902- 2. Widows—United States—Biography. I. Title.

Hershey, Lewis Blaine, 1893-

SEIVERLING, 355.2'25'0924 B Richard E., 1920-
Lewis B. Hershey, a pictorial and documentary biography, written, designed, and produced, by Richard F. Seiverling. Drawings by Walter F. Halleck. Photos. by Bartlett J. Hawkins. Hershey, Pa., Keystone Enterprises [1969] 64 p. illus., ports. 28 cm. [E745.H4S4] 78-14296 1.50
1. Hershey, Lewis Blaine, 1893-

Hershey, Milton Snavely, 1857-1945.

HERSHEY Chocolate 926.6 Corporation, Hershey, Pa.
The story of Hershey, the chocolate town. Hershey, Pa., Hershey Dept. Store, 1963. 59p. illus., ports. 28cm. 63-24875 .50 pap.,
1. Hershey, Milton Snevely, 1857-1945. 2. Hershey, Pa. I. Title.

MALONE, Mary. 338.7'66'41530924 B
Milton Hershey, chocolate king. Illustrated by William Hutchinson. Champaign, Ill., Garrard Pub. Co. [1971] 95 p. illus. (part col.), ports. 24 cm. (Americans all) A biography of the man whose faltering beginnings in candy making eventually resulted in a chocolate business known throughout the world. [CT275.H5863M33] 92 74-131020 ISBN 0-8116-4565-7 2.49
1. Hershey, Milton Snavely, 1857-1945. I. Hutchinson, William M., illus. II. Title.

SNAVELY, Joseph Richard. 926.4185
The Hershey story. Hershey, Pa., 1950. xv, 384 p. illus., ports. 26 cm. First ed. published in 1935 under title: Milton S. Hershey, builder. [CT275.H5863S5 1950] 50-13942
1. Hershey, Milton Snavely, 1857-1945. 2. Hershey, Pa. — Hist. I. Title.

SNAVELY, Joseph Richard. 926.4185
An intimate story of Milton S. Hershey. Hershey, Pa., 1957. 549 p. illus. 26 cm. [CT275.H5863S45] 57-4679
1. Hershey, Milton Snavely, 1857-1945. 2. Hershey, Pa. — Hist. I. Title.

SNAVELY, Joseph Richard. 926.4185
The story of Hershey, the chocolate town; commemorating the 50th anniversary of Hershey. Hershey, Pa., 1953. 63p. illus. 28cm. [CT275.H5863S52] 53-1596
1. Hershey, Milton Snavely, 1837-1945. 2. Herahey, Pa.—Hist. I. Title.

Herskovits, Melville Jean, 1895-1963.

SIMPSON, George 301.2'092'4 B Eaton, 1904-
Melville J. Herskovits. New York, Columbia University Press, 1973. viii, 200 p. illus. 23 cm. (Leaders of modern anthropology series) "Selections from the writings of Melville J. Herskovits": p. 105-188. Bibliography: p. 189-200. [GN21.H47S55] 73-5966 ISBN 0-231-03385-0 10.00
1. Herskovits, Melville Jean, 1895-1963. 2. Ethnology—Africa, West—Addresses, essays, lectures. I. Herskovits, Melville Jean, 1895-1963. II. Title. III. Series.

Herter, Christian Archibald, 1895-1966.

NOBLE, George 973.92'0924 Bernard, 1892-
Christian A. Herter, by G. Bernard Noble. New York, Cooper Square Publishers, 1970. xii, 333 p. port. 22 cm. (The American Secretaries of State and their diplomacy, v. 18) (Series: Bemis, Samuel Flagg, 1891- ed. The American Secretaries of State and their diplomacy, v. 18) Includes bibliographical references. [E183.7.B462 vol. 18] 73-122753 7.95
1. Herter, Christian Archibald, 1895-1966. 2. United States—Foreign relations—1953-1961. I. Title. II. Series. BIP

Hertzen, Aleksandr Ivanovich, 1812-1870.

ACTON, Edward. 947'.07'0924 B
Alexander Herzen and the role of the intellectual revolutionary / Edward Acton. Cambridge [Eng.] ; New York : Cambridge University Press, 1979. x, 194 p. : port. ; 24 cm. Includes index. Bibliography: p. [179]-188. [DK209.6.H4A64] 78-56747 ISBN 0-521-22166-8 : 18.95
1. Hertzen, Aleksandr Ivanovich, 1812-1870. 2. Intellectual—Russia—Biography. I. Title. BIP

CARR, Edward 335'.83'0922 Hallett, 1892-
The romantic exiles : a nineteenth-century portrait gallery / by Edward Hallett Carr. New York : Octagon Books, 1975. 391 p. : port. ; 21 cm. Reprint of the 1933 ed. published by V. Gollancz, London. Bibliography: p. [389]-391. [HX914.C3 1975] 75-15595 ISBN 0-374-91297-1 lib.bdg. : 15.50
1. Hertzen, Aleksandr Ivanovich, 1812-1870. 2. Herwegh, Georg, 1817-1875. 3. Ogarev, Nikolai Platonovich, 1813-1877. 4. Anarchism and anarchists—Russia. I. Title.

HERTZEN, Aleksandr 947'.07'0924 B Ivanovich, 1812-1870.
The memoirs of Alexander Herzen, parts I and II. Translated from the Russian by J. D. Duff. New York, Russell & Russell [1967] xvi, 384 p. 22 cm. "First published in 1923." [DK209.6.H4A325] 66-27098

HERTZEN, Aleksandr 947'.07'0924 B Ivanovich, 1812-1870.
My past and thoughts; the memoirs of Alexander Herzen. Translated by Constance Garnett. Rev. by Humphrey Higgens. With an introd. by Isaiah Berlin. New York, Knopf, 1968. 4 v. (xlvi, 1908 p.) 23 cm. Translation of Byloe i dumy (romanized form) A revision of the translation first published 1924-27. Bibliographical footnotes. [DK209.6.H4A33 1968] 68-12684
I. Garnett, Constance (Black) 1862-1946, tr. II. Higgens, Humphrey. III. Title.

Hertzen, Aleksandr Ivanovich, 1812-1870—Biography.

HERTZEN, Aleksandr 947'.07'0924 B Ivanovich, 1812-1870.
The memoirs of Alexander Herzen, parts I and II translated from the Russian by J. D. Duff. Westport, Conn. : Greenwood Press, 1976. xvi, 384 p. ; 23 cm. Translation of Byloe i dumy. Reprint of the 1923 ed. published by Yale University Press, New Haven. [DK209.6.H4A325 1976] 76-48971 ISBN 0-8371-9319-2 lib. bdg. : 20.00
1. Hertzen, Aleksandr Ivanovich, 1812-1870—Biography. 2. Revolutionists—Russia—Biography. 3. Socialists—Russia—Biography. 4. Authors, Russian—Biography. I. Title.

HERTZEN, Aleksandr 947'.07'0924 B Ivanovich, 1812-1870.
My past and thoughts: the memoirs of Alexander Herzen. Translated by Constance Garnett; rev. by Humphrey Higgens. Introd. by Isaiah Berlin. Abridged, with a pref. and notes by Dwight Macdonald. [1st ed.] New York, Knopf; [distributed by Random House] 1973. xlix, 684, xi p. 22 cm. Translation of Byloe i dumy. Includes bibliographical references. [DK209.6.H4A353] 72-11034 ISBN 0-394-48308-1 12.50
1. Hertzen, Aleksandr Ivanovich, 1812-1870—Biography. I. Macdonald, Dwight. II. Title.

Hertzler, Arthur Emanuel, 1870-1946.

HASHINGER, Edward Hagerman, 926.1 1892-
Arthur E. Hertzler, the Kansas horse-and-buggy doctor. Lawrence, Univ. of Kansas Press [c.]1961. 37p. illus. (Logan Clendening lectures on the history and philosophy of medicine, ser. 9) Bibl. 61-9329 2.00
1. Hertzler, Arthur Emanuel, 1870-1946. I. Title.

Hervey, John Hervey, Baron, 1696-1743.

HALSBAND, Robert, 942.07'2'0924 B 1914-
Lord Hervey; eighteenth-century courtier. New York, Oxford University Press, 1974 [c1973] xiv, 380 p. illus. 22 cm. Includes bibliographical references. [DA501.H47H34 1974] 73-87774 ISBN 0-19-501731-5 12.50
1. Hervey, John Hervey, Baron, 1696-1743. I. Title. BIP

HALSBAND, Robert, 942.07'2'0924 B 1914-
Lord Hervey; eighteenth century courtier. Oxford, Clarendon P., 1973. xiv, 380 p., 16 leaves. illus., facsims., ports. 22 cm. Includes bibliographical references and index. [DA501.H47H34] 73-180803 ISBN 0-19-812045-1
1. Hervey, John Hervey, Baron, 1696-1743. I. Title.
Distributed by Oxford University Press, New York, 12.50.

Herwegh, Georg, 1817-1875.

CARR, Edward 335'.83'0922 Hallett, 1892-
The romantic exiles : a nineteenth-century portrait gallery / by Edward Hallett Carr. New York : Octagon Books, 1975. 391 p. : port. ; 21 cm. Reprint of the 1933 ed. published by V. Gollancz, London. Bibliography: p. [389]-391. [HX914.C3 1975] 75-15595 ISBN 0-374-91297-1 lib.bdg. : 15.50
1. Hertzen, Aleksandr Ivanovich, 1812-1870. 2. Herwegh, Georg, 1817-1875. 3. Ogarev, Nikolai Platonovich, 1813-1877. 4. Anarchism and anarchists—Russia. I. Title.

Herz, Alice.

HERZ, Alice. 327'.172'0924
Phoenix: letters and documents of Alice Herz : the thought and practice of a modern-day martyr / edited by Shingo Shibata. Amsterdam : Gruner, 1977,c1976. xiii, 216p., : ill.,[23] leaves of plates ; 24 cm. (Philosophical currents ; v.11) Includes bibliographical references. [JX1962.H46A34] 74-84133 ISBN 90-6032-027-1 pbk. : 17.00
1. Herz, Alice. 2. Pacifists-United States-Correspondence. I. Shibata, Shingo, 1930- II. Title. III. Series.
Distributed by Humanities Press.

Herz, Max.

CLARKE, Joan. 617'.3'00924 B
Dr. Max Herz, surgeon extraordinary : the human price of civil and medical bigotry in Australia / by Joan Clarke. Sydney : Alternative Pub. Co-operative, 1976. xv, 188 p., [4] leaves of plates : ill., ports. ; 22 cm. Includes bibliographical references and index. [RD728.H47C57] 77-372406 ISBN 0-909188-00-9
1. Herz, Max. 2. Orthopedists—Australia—Biography. 3. Political prisoners—Australia—Biography. 4. European War, 1914-1918—Australia.

Herzel, Catherine

HERZEL, Catherine 920
Great Christians, their response and witness. Illus. by Harold Minton. Gustav K. Wiencke, ed. Philadelphia, Lutheran Church Pr. [c.1964] 127p. col. illus. 22cm. 1.25
I. Title.

Herzen, Natalie, 1844-1936.

CONFINO, Michael, 335'.83'0924 B 1926- comp.
Daughter of a revolutionary; Natalie Herzen and the Bakunin-Nechayev circle. Edited with an introd. by Michael Confino. Translated by Hilary Sternberg and Lydia Bott. LaSalle, Ill., Library Press, 1973. 416 p. illus., ports. 23 cm. [DK209.6.H43C66 1973] 73-86555 ISBN 0-912050-15-2 10.95
1. Herzen, Natalie, 1844-1936. 2. Anarchism and anarchists—Russia. I. Herzen, Natalie, 1844-1936. II. Hertzen, Aleksandr Ivanovich, 1812-1870. III. Bakunin, Mikhail Aleksandrovich, 1814-1876. IV. Nechaev, Sergei Gennadievich, 1847-1882. V. Title.

Herzl, Theodor,

HERZL, Theodor, 1860- 923.25693 1904.
Herzl speaks his mind on issues, events, and men. Edited by Herbert Parzen. New York, Herzl Press, 1960. 104p. 17cm. (Herzl Institute pamphlet no. 16) [DS151.H4A252] 60-50587
I. Title.

Herzl, Theodor Benjamin,

HERZL, Theodor 923.25693 [Benjamin]
Herzl speaks his mind on issues. events, and men. Edited by Herbert Parzen. New York, Herzl Press [c.]1960. 104p. 17cm. (Herzl Institute pamphlet no. 16) 60-50587 .75 pap.,
I. Title.

HERZL, Theodor Benjamin, 1860-1904. 923.25693
Complete diaries. Ed. by Raphael Patai. Tr. by Harry Zohn. New York, Herzl Press [dist.] Yoseloff [1961, c.1960] 5 v. (vi, 1961p.) ports. 60-8594 25.00 bxd.
I. Title.

Herzl, Theodor, 1860-1904.

BAKER, Nina (Brown), 1888- 922.96
Next year in Jerusalem; the story of Theodor Herzl. [1st ed.] New York, Harcourt, Brace [1950] 186 p. port. 21 cm. Bibliography: p. 183. [DS151.H4B3] 50-5812
1. Herzl. Theodor. 1860-1904. I. Title.

COHEN, Israel, 1879- 922.96
Theodor Herzl, founder of political Zionism. New York, T. Yoseloff [1959] 399 p. illus. 22 cm. Includes bibliography. [DS151.H4C6] 58-9743
1. Herzl, Theodor, 1860-1904.

ELON, Amos. 956.94'001'0924 B
Herzl. [1st ed.] New York, Holt, Rinehart and Winston [1975] viii, 448 p. illus. 24 cm. Bibliography: p. 413-417. [DS151.H4E57] 74-5128 ISBN 0-03-013126-X 12.95
1. Herzl, Theodor, 1860-1904.

HERZL, Theodor, 1860-1904. 923.25693
Herzl speaks his mind on issues, events, and men. Edited by Herbert Parzen. New York, Herzl Press, 1960. 104p. 17cm. (Herzl Institute pamphlet no. 16) [DS151.H4A252] 60-50587
I. Title.

HERZL, Theodor, 1860-1904. 922.96
Theodor Herzl: a portrait for this age, edited and with an introd. by Ludwig Lewisohn. Pref. by David Ber. Gurion. [1st ed.] Cleveland, World Pub. Co. [1955] 345p. illus. 22cm. [DS149.H523] 55-6226
1. Zionism— Addresses, essays, lectures. I. Lewisohn, Ludwig, 1882- A portrait for this age. II. Title.
Contents omitted.

HERZL, Theodor [Benjamin] 923.25693
Herzl speaks his mind on issues. events, and men. Edited by Herbert Parzen. New York, Herzl Press [c.]1960. 104p. 17cm. (Herzl Institute pamphlet no. 16) 60-50587 .75 pap.,
I. Title.

HERZL, Theodor Benjamin, 1860-1904. 923.25693
Complete diaries. Ed. by Raphael Patai. Tr. by Harry Zohn. New York, Herzl Press [dist.] Yoseloff [1961, c.1960] 5 v. (vi, 1961p.) ports. 60-8594 25.00 bxd.
I. Title.

JOINT Committee of the Government of Israel and the World Zionist Organisation for the Observance of the Herzl Centennial. 923.25693
Herzl's life in pictures. New York, Herzl Press 1960. [2]p., 40 plates (in portfolio) 29cm. Cover title. Legends in Hebrew and English. Title transliterated: Yalkut temunot. 60-50622 6.00, pap., bxd.
1. Herzl, Theodor, 1860-1904 I. Title.

NEUMANN, Emanuel 923.25693
Theodor Herzl; the birth of Jewish statesmanship. New York, Herzl Press [c.] 1960. 62p. 17cm. (Herzl Institute pamphlet no. 17) First published in 1940 under title: The birth of Jewish statesmanship. 60-50584 .50 pap.,
1. Herzl, Theodor, 1860-1904. I. Title.

NEUMANN, Emanuel, 1893- 923.25693
Theodor Herzl; the birth of Jewish statesmanship. New York, Herzl Press, 1960. 62p. 17cm. (Herzl Institute pamphlet no. 17) First published in 1940 under title: The birth of Jewish statesmanship. [DS151.H4N37 1960] 60-50584
1. Herzl, Theodor, 1860-1904. I. Title.

ROSENBERGER, Erwin, 1875- 922.96
Herzl as I remember him. Translated from the German and abridged by Louis Jay Herman. New York, Herzl Press, 1959. 251p. illus. 22cm. [DS151.H4R613] 59-9713
1. Herzl. Theodor, 1860-1904. I. Title.

STEWART, Desmond Stirling. 956.94'001'0924 B
Theodor Herzl [by] Desmond Stewart. [1st ed.] Garden City, N.Y., Doubleday, 1974. xi, 395 p. illus. 24 cm. Bibliography: p. [379]-385. [DS151.H4S74] 73-83676 ISBN 0-385-08896-5 12.50
1. Herzl, Theodor, 1860-1904.

Heschel, Abraham Joshua, 1907-

SHERMAN, Franklin. 296.3'0924
The promise of Heschel. [1st ed.] Philadelphia, Lippincott [1970] 103 p. 22 cm. (The Promise of theology) Bibliography: p. 101-103. [BM755.H37S47] 70-105549 3.95
1. Heschel, Abraham Joshua, 1907- I. Title.

Heseltine, Philip, 1894-1930.

TOMLINSON, Fred. 780'.92'4 B
Warlock and Delius / [by] Fred Tomlinson. London : Thames Publishing [for the Peter Warlock Society], 1976. 31 p. : facsims., music, ports. ; 24 cm. "Basically the script of a talk given to the Delius Society in London on 29th January 1976." [ML410.H585T7] 76-383440 ISBN 0-905210-05-0 : £1.50
1. Heseltine, Philip, 1894-1930. 2. Delius, Frederich, 1862-1934. 3. Composers—England—Biography. I. Title.

Hess, Moses, 1812—1875.

BERLIN, Isaiah. Sir 923.343
The and opinions of Moses Hess. Cambridge, Published for the Jewish Historical Society of England [by] W. Heffer [1959] 49p. illus. 26cm. (The Lucien Wolf memorial lecture, Dec. 1957) [DS151.H43B4] 60-4833
1. Hess, Moses, 1812—1875. I. Title.

Hess, Moses, 1812-1875.

BERLIN, Isaiah. Sir 923.343
The and opinions of Moses Hess. Cambridge, Published for the Jewish Historical Society of England [by] W. Heffer [1959] 49p. illus. 26cm. (The Lucien Wolf memorial lecture, Dec. 1957) [DS151.H43B4] 60-4833
1. Hess, Moses, 1812—1875. I. Title.

WEISS, Horace John, 1927- 923.343
Moses Hess, utopian socialist. Detroit, Wayne State University Press, 1960. 77 p. 21 cm. (Wayne State University studies, no. 8) Includes bibliography. [HX273.H47W4] 60-16551
1. Hess, Moses, 1812-1875. I. Title.

WEISS, John 923.343
Moses Hess, utopian socialist. Detroit, Wayne State University Press [c.]1960. 77p. (Bibl. and bibl. notes: p.68-77) 21cm. (Wayne State University studies, no. 8) 60-16551 1.95 pap.,
1. Hess, Moses, 1812-1875. I. Title.

Hess, Myra, 1890- 1965.

LASSIMONNE, Denise. comp. 786.1/0924
Myra Hess, by her friends. Ed., an introd. by Howard Ferguson. New York, Vanguard [1967,c.1966] 121p. plates (ports.) 24cm. [ML417.H4L4 1966b] 67-29444 5.95
1. Hess, Myra, 1890- 1965. I. Ferguson Howard, 1908- ed. II. Title.
Contents Omitted.

Hess, Rudolf, 1894-

BIRD, Eugene K., 1926- 943.086'092'4 B
Prisoner 7, Rudolf Hess : the thirty years in jail of Hitler's deputy Fuhrer / by Eugene K. Bird. New York : Viking Press, 1974. viii, 270 p. : ill. ; 24 cm. [DD247.H37B57 1974] 73-19479 ISBN 0-670-57831-2 : 10.00
1. Hess, Rudolf, 1894- I. Title.

HUTTON, Joseph Bernard. 940.548'2'43
Hess: the man and his mission [by] J. Bernard Hutton. Introd. by Airey Neave. [1st American ed.] New York, Macmillan [1971, c1970] xv, 262 p. illus., facsim., ports. 21 cm. [DD247.H37H88 1971] 78-138030 6.95
1. Hess, Rudolf, 1894- I. Title.

Hess, Rudolph, 1894-

LEASER, James 923.243
The uninvited envoy. New York, McGraw [c.1962] 249p. illus. 22cm. Bibl. 62-17643 5.95
1. Hess, Rudolph, 1894- I. Title.

MANVELL, Roger, 1909- 943.086'092'4 B
Hess: a biography [by] Roger Manvell and Heinrich Fraenkel. New York, Drake Publishers [1973] 256 p. illus. 23 cm. Bibliography: p. 219-220. [DD247.H37M3 1973] 72-10526 ISBN 0-87749-428-2 7.95
1. Hess, Rudolf, 1894- I. Fraenkel, Heinrich, 1897- joint author. II. Title.

THOMAS, Walter Hugh. 943.086'092'4 B
The murder of Rudolf Hess / by W. Hugh Thomas. New York : Harper & Row, [1979] p. cm. Includes index. Bibliography: p. [DD247.H37T48 1979] 79-2237 ISBN 0-06-014251-0 : 9.95
1. Hess, Rudolf, 1894- 2. National socialism—Biography. I. Title. **BIP**

Hesse, Eva, 1936-1970.

HESSE, Eva, 1936-1970. 709'.2'4
Eva Hesse: a memorial exhibition. New York, Solomon R. Guggenheim Foundation [1972] 1 v. (unpaged) illus. (part col.) 22 cm. Catalog of an exhibition held at Solomon R. Guggenheim Museum, New York. Includes bibliographical references. [N6537.H4S64] 72-95105
1. Hesse, Eva, 1936-1970. I. Solomon R. Guggenheim Museum, New York.

Hesse, Hermann, 1877-1962.

HESSE, Hermann, 1877-1962. 838'.9'1209 B
Autobiographical writings. Edited, and with an introd. by Theodore Ziolkowski. Translated by Denver Lindley. New York, Farrar, Straus and Giroux [1972] xxvii, 291 p. 22 cm. Contents.—Childhood of the magician.—from my schooldays.—About my grandfather.—Life story briefly told.—Remembrance of India.—Pidurutalagala.—A guest at the spa.—Journey to Nuremberg.—On moving to a new house.—Notes on a cure in Baden.—For Marulla.—Events in the Engadin. [PT2617.E85Z5213] 75-165401 ISBN 0-374-10733-5 8.95

HESSE, Hermann, 1877-1962. 838'.9'1209
The Hesse-Mann letters : the correspondence of Hermann Hesse and Thomas Mann, 1910-1955 / edited by Anni Carlsson and Volker Michels ; translated from the German by Ralph Manheim ; annotations by Wolfgang Sauerlander ; foreword by Theodore Ziolkowski. London : P. Owen, 1976, c1975. xxii, 196 p. : ill. ; 23 cm. Translation of Der Briefwechsel Hermann Hesse-Thomas Mann. Includes index. Bibliography: p. 181-182. [PT2617.E85Z54513 1976] 77-368005 ISBN 0-7206-0284-X : £5.75
1. Hesse, Hermann—Correspondence. 2. Mann, Thomas, 1875-1955—Correspondence. 3. Authors, German—20th century—Correspondence. I. Mann, Thomas, 1875-1955. II. Carlsson, Anni. III. Michels, Volker. IV. Title.

MILECK, Joseph, 1922- 838'.9'1209 B
Hermann Hesse : life and art / Joseph Mileck. Berkeley : University of California Press, c1978. xiii, 397 p. : ill. ; 25 cm. Includes indexes. Bibliography: p. [307]-371. [PT2617.E85Z833] 76-48020 ISBN 0-520-03351-5 : 14.95
1. Hesse, Hermann, 1877-1962. 2. Authors, German—20th century—Biography. **BIP**

SORELL, Walter, 1905- 838.9
Hermann Hesse: the man who sought and found himself. London: Wolff, [1975 c1974] 143 p., plate: port; 20 cm. (Modern German authors; new series, v.2) Bibliography: p. 140-143. [PT2617.E85Z93] 74-192897 ISBN 0-85496-049-X
1. Hesse, Hermann, 1877-1962. I. Title. II. Series.
Distributed by Humanities Press for 6.75. **BIP**

ZELLER, Bernhard. 838'.9'1209 B
Portrait of Hesse; an illustrated biography. Translated by Mark Hollebone. [New York] Herder and Herder [1971] 176 p. illus., facsims., ports. 21 cm. Translation of Hermann Hesse in Selbstzeugnissen und Bilddokumenten. Bibliography: p. 176. [PT2617.E85Z98613] 77-150142 6.95
1. Hesse, Hermann, 1877-1962. I. Title.

Hesse, Hermann, 1877-1962—Bibliography.

MILECK, Joseph, 1922- 016.838'9'1209
Hermann Hesse : biography bibliography / by Joseph Mileck. Berkeley : University of California Press, c1977. 2 v. (xxiv, 1402 p.) : ill. ; 27 cm. Includes indexes. [Z8401.3.M48] [PT2617.E85] 74-77727 ISBN 0-520-02756-6 : 50.00
1. Hesse, Hermann, 1877-1962—Bibliography. 2. Hesse, Hermann, 1877-1962—Biography. 3. Authors, German—20th century—Biography.

Hesse, Hermann, 1877-1962—Biography.

FREEDMAN, Ralph, 1920- 838'.9'1209 B
Hermann Hesse : pilgrim of crisis a biography / by Ralph Freedman. 1st ed. New York : Pantheon Books, c1978. xii, 432 p., [12] leaves of plates : ill. ; 25 cm. Includes bibliographical references and index. [PT2617.E85Z6955] 78-51795 ISBN 0-394-41981-2 : 15.00
1. Hesse, Hermann, 1877-1962—Biography. 2. Authors, German—20th century—Biography.

Hesse, Hermann, 1877-1962—Iconography.

MICHELS, Volker. 838'.9'1209
Hermann Hesse, a pictorial biography / edited by Volker Michels ; translated by Theodore and Yetta Ziolkowski. Including Hermann Hesse's "Life story briefly told" / translated by Denver Lindley. 1st ed. New York : Farrar, Straus and Giroux, 1975. 238 p. : ill. ; 22 cm. Translation of Hermann Hesse, Leben und Werk im Bild. Includes index. [PT2617.E85Z82513 1975] 75-9625 ISBN 0-374-16988-8 : 10.00 ISBN 0-374-51228-0 pbk. : 2.95
1. Hesse, Hermann, 1877-1962—Iconography. I. Title.

Hesse, Hermann, 1877-1962—Juvenile literature.

FLEISSNER, Else (Mentz) 1900- 838'.9'1209 B
Hermann Hesse, modern German poet and writer, by Else M. Fleissner. Charlotteville, N.Y., SamHar Press, 1972. 31 p. 22 cm. (Outstanding personalities, no. 26) Bibliography: p. 31. Biography of a Nobel

prize winner whose works portray man's inner struggles and search for peace. [PT2617.E85Z695] 92 70-190244 ISBN 0-87157-526-4 1.98
1. Hesse, Hermann, 1877-1962—Juvenile literature. I. Title.
Pap. 0.98, ISBN 0-87159-026-2

Hession, Roy.

HESSION, Roy. 269'.2'0924 B
My Calvary road / Roy Hession. Grand Rapids : Zondervan Pub. House, c1978. 192 p. ; 21 cm. [BV3785.H44A35] 78-1284 ISBN 0-310-26031-0 pbk. : 3.95
1. Hession, Roy. 2. Evangelists—England—Biography. I. Title. BIP

Heston, Charlton.

DRUXMAN, Michael B., 1941- 791.43'028'0924 B
Charlton Heston / by Michael B. Druxman. New York : Pyramid Publications, 1976. 159 p. : ill. ; 20 cm. (A Pyramid illustrated history of the movies) Includes index. Bibliography: p. 143. [PN2287.H47D7] 76-41108 ISBN 0-515-04189-0 : 1.75
1. Heston, Charlton. 2. Actors—United States—Biography. I. Title. BIP

HESTON, Charlton. 791.43'028'0924 B
The actor's life : journals, 1956-1976 / Charlton Heston ; edited by Hollis Alpert. 1st ed. New York : E. P. Dutton, c1978. xvi, 482 p., [6] leaves of plates : ill. ; 24 cm. "A Henry Robbins book". [PN2287.H47A32 1978] 78-14910 ISBN 0-525-05030-2 : 12.50
1. Heston, Charlton. 2. Moving-picture actors and actresses—United States—Biography. I. Alpert, Hollis, 1916- II. Title. BIP

Heth, Henry, 1825-1899.

HETH, Henry, 1825-1899. 973.7'42'0924 B
The memoirs of Henry Heth. Edited by James L. Morrison, Jr. Westport, Conn., Greenwood Press [1974] lxxvi, 303 p. illus. 21 cm. (Contributions in military history, no. 6) Bibliography: p. 281-291. [E181.H47A35] 72-820 ISBN 0-8371-6389-7
1. Heth, Henry, 1825-1899. 2. United States—History—Civil War, 1861-1865—Personal narratives—Confederate side. I. Morrison, James L., 1923- ed. II. Title. III. Series. BIP

Hewes, David, 1822-1915.

FRIIS, Leo J. 979.4'04'0924 B
David Hewes : more than the golden spike / by Leo J. Friis. 1st ed. Santa Ana, Calif. : Friis-Pioneer Press, 1974. 92 p., [12] leaves of plates : ill. ; 23 cm. (Orange County pioneer series ; no. 3) Includes bibliographical references and index. [CT275.H5885F7] 73-82832 12.50
1. Hewes, David, 1822-1915. I. Title. II. Series.

LAMPSON, Robin, 1900- 979.4'61'040924 B
The man who gave the golden spike. [1st ed.] Richmond, Calif., Chimes Press, 1969. 17 p. illus., ports. 23 cm. [CT275.H5885L3] 73-6521
1. Hewes, David, 1822-1915. I. Title.

Hewitt, Abram Stevens, 1822-1903.

NEVINS, Allan, 1890- 920.073
Abram S. Hewitt, with some account of Peter Cooper. New York, Octagon Books, 1967 [1935] xiii, 623 p. illus., facsims., map, ports. 24 cm. "A note upon sources": p. 603. [E664.H523N4] 67-18777
1. Hewitt, Abram Stevens, 1822-1903. 2. Cooper, Peter, 1791-1883. 3. New York (City)—Pol. & govt.—To 1898. I. Title.

Hewitt, Arthur Wentworth,

HEWITT, Arthur Wentworth, 1883- 253.0924
The old brick manse. New York, Harper [c.1966] vi, 246p. 22cm. Autobiography. [BX8495.H52A3] 66-10674 4.95
I. Title.

Hewitt, Joe.

HEWITT, Joe. 289.9 B
I was raised a Jehovah's Witness / Joe Hewitt. Denver : Accent Books, c1979. 191 p. ; 21 cm. [BX8526.H396] 78-73255 ISBN 0-89636-018-0 pbk. : 3.95
1. Hewitt, Joe. 2. Jehovah's Witnesses—Doctrinal and controversial works. 3. Baptists—Clergy—Biography. 4. Clergy—United States—Biography. I. Title. BIP

Heydrich, Reinhard, 1904-1942.

WIGHTON, Charles. 923.543
Heydrich, Hitler's most evil henchman. [1st American ed.] Philadelphia, Chilton Co., Book Division [1962] 288 p. illus. 23 cm. [DD247.H42W5 1962] 62-5538
1. Heydrich, Reinhard, 1904-1942. I. Title.

WYKES, Alan. 940.54'05'0924 B
Heydrich. [New York, Ballantine Books, 1973] 158, [2] p. illus. 21 cm. (Ballantine's illustrated history of the violent century. War leader book no. 22) Bibliography: p. [160] [DD247.H42W9] 74-158436 ISBN 0-345-23573-8 1.50 (pbk.)
1. Heydrich, Reinhard, 1904-1942. 2. Germany—Politics and government—1933-1945.

Heydrich, Reinhard, 1904-1942—Assassination.

IVANOV, Miroslav. 940.54'05'0924 B
Target: Heydrich. Translated from French by Patrick O'Brian. New York, Macmillan [1974, c1973] 292 p. illus. 22 cm. Translation of L'attentat contre Heydrich. [DD247.H42I8813 1974] 72-11277 7.95
1. Heydrich, Reinhard, 1904-1942—Assassination. I. Title.

Heyerdahl, Thor.

HEYERDAHL, Thor. 919.6'31 B
Fatu-Hiva : back to nature / Thor Heyerdahl. 1st American ed. Garden City, N.Y. : Doubleday, 1975, c1974. viii, 276 p., [32] leaves of plates : ill. ; 25 cm. Includes bibliographical references and index. [DU701.F3H47 1975] 74-33646 ISBN 0-385-08921-X : 10.00
1. Heyerdahl, Thor. 2. Fatuhiva Island—Description and travel. I. Title.

JACOBY, Arnold, 1913- 910.09'18'230924 B
Senor Kon-Tiki; the biography of Thor Heyerdahl. [Chicago] Rand McNally [1967] 424 p. illus., ports. 22 cm. [G306.H47J3] 67-24915
1. Heyerdahl, Thor. I. Title.

Heymanns, Betty, 1932-

HEYMANNS, Betty, 1932- 362.4'3'0926 B
Bittersweet triumph / Betty Heymanns. 1st ed. Garden City, N.Y. : Doubleday, 1977. 191 p. ; 22 cm. [RC388.H49] 76-22997 ISBN 0-385-12456-2 : 6.95
1. Heymanns, Betty, 1932- 2. Cerebral palsy—Biography. I. Title. BIP

Heysen, Hans, Sir, 1877-1968.

THIELE, Colin. 760'.092'4
Heysen's early Hahndorf / [Text by] Colin Thiele ; illustrated with early works by Sir Hans Heysen, including drawings from his sketchbooks selected by David Heysen. Adelaide : Rigby, 1976. 63 p. : ill. (some col.) ; 24 cm. [N7405.H4T45] 76-379632 ISBN 0-7270-0066-7
1. Heysen, Hans, Sir, 1877-1968. 2. Artists—Australia—Biography. 3. Hahndorf, Australia, in art. I. Title.

Heyward, Carter.

HEYWARD, Carter. 283'.092'4 B
A priest forever / Carter Heyward. 1st ed. New York : Harper & Row, c1976. 146 p. : ill. ; 21 cm. Includes bibliographical references. [BX5995.H46A34 1976] 75-36736 ISBN 0-06-063893-1 : 6.95
1. Heyward, Carter. 2. Ordination of women—Protestant Episcopal Church in the U.S.A. I. Title. BIP

Heyward, Du Bose, 1885-1940.

DURHAM, Frank 813.52
Du Bose Heyward, the man who wrote Porgy. Port Washington, N.Y., Kennikat [1965, c.1954] 152p. illus., ports. 22cm. [PS3515.E98Z6] 65-27111 6.00
1. Heyward, Du Bose, 1885-1940. I. Title.

DURHAM, Frank. 813.52
DuBose Heyward, the man who wrote Porgy. Port Washington, N. Y., Kennikat Press [1965, c1954] 152 p. illus., ports. 22 cm. [PS3515.E98Z6 1965] 65-27111
1. Heyward, Du Bose, 1885-1940. I. Title.

Heyward, Du Bose, 1885-1940—Addresses, essays, lectures.

ALLEN, Hervey, 1889-1949. 818'.5'209
Du Bose Heyward; a critical and biographical sketch. [Folcroft, Pa.] Folcroft Library Editions, 1973. 19 p. 24 cm. Reprint of the ed. published by G. H. Doran Co., New York. Bibliography: p. [2] [PS3515.E98Z57 1973] 73-5974 ISBN 0-8414-1731-8 (lib. bdg.)
1. Heyward, Du Bose, 1885-1940—Addresses, essays, lectures. BIP

Heywood, John 1497?-1580?

BOLWELL, Robert George Whitney, 1891- v. 12
The life and works of John Heywood. New York, AMS Press, 1966. xiii, 188 p. geneal. table. 23 cm. Reprint of edition published by Columbia University Press, New York, in 1921. Bibliography: p. [175]-182. 66-79460
1. Heywood, John 1497?-1580? I. Title. BIP

Heywood, Thomas, d. 1641.

BOAS, Frederick Samuel, 1862-1957. 822'.3
Thomas Heywood. [Folcroft, Pa.] Folcroft Library Editions, 1974. 159 p. illus. 23 cm. Reprint of the 1950 ed. published by Williams & Norgate, London. [PR2576.B6 1974b] 74-5032 ISBN 0-8414-9938-1 (lib. bdg.)
1. Heywood, Thomas, d. 1641.

BOAS, Frederick Samuel, 1862-1957. 822'.3 B
Thomas Heywood. St. Clair Shores, Mich., Scholarly Press [1974] p. cm. Reprint of the 1950 ed. published by Williams & Norgate, London. [PR2576.B6 1974] 74-3153 ISBN 0-403-02292-4
1. Heywood, Thomas, d. 1641. BIP

Hiawatha, Iroquois Indian.

HENRY, Thomas Robert, 1893- 970.3
Wilderness messiah; the story of Hiawatha and the Iroquois. New York, W. Sloane Associates, 1955. 285 p. 22 cm. Includes bibliography. [E99.I7H4] 55-5312
1. Hiawatha, Iroquois Indian. 2. Iroquois Indians. I. Title.

Hiawatha, Iroquois Indian—Juvenile literature.

MALKUS, Alida Sims, 1895- 970.2
There really was a Hiawatha. Illus. by Jon Neilson. New York, Grosset [c.1963] ix, 180p. illus. map (on lining pap.) 22cm. (4931) 63-18976 2.95 bds.,
1. Hiawatha, Iroquois Indian—Juvenile literature. 2. Iroquois Indians—Juvenile literature. I. Title.

Hibbard, Aldro Thompson, 1886-

COOLEY, John L. 760'.0924
A. T. Hibbard, N.A.; artist in two worlds [by] John L. Cooley. With a commentary by Aldren A. Watson. [1st ed.] Concord, N.H., Rumford Press [1968] 174 p. illus. 27 cm. [ND237.H57C6] 68-7465
1. Hibbard, Aldro Thompson, 1886- I. Title: Artist in two worlds.

*Hickerson, Vivian

*HICKERSON, Vivian 922.673
Thy kingdom come. New York, Vantage [c.1964] 102p. 21cm. 2.5 bds.,
I. Title.

Hickes, Michael, Sir, 1543-1612.

SMITH, Alan Gordon Rae. 942.05'5'0924 B
Servant of the Cecils : the life of Sir Michael Hickes, 1543-1612 / Alan G. R. Smith. Totowa, N.J. : Rowman and Littlefield, 1977. 220 p., [4] leaves of plates : ports. ; 23 cm. Includes bibliographical references and index. [DA358.H5S63 1977] 77-150677 ISBN 0-87471-933-X : 15.00
1. Hickes, Michael, Sir, 1543-1612. 2. Cecil family. 3. Great Britain—Court and courtiers—Biography. I. Title. BIP

Hickey, William, b.

HICKEY, William, b. 1749 920
The prodigal rake; memoirs of William Hickey. Ed. by Peter Quennell. New York, Dutton, 1962 [c.1960] 452p. illus. Previous ed. pub. under title: Memoirs. 62-8217 6.50
I. Title.

Hickey, William, b. 1749.

HICKEY, William, b.1749. 941'.073'0924 B
Memoirs of William Hickey / edited by Peter Quennell. London ; Boston : Routledge & K. Paul, 1975. xvii, 447 p., [8] leaves of plates : ill. ; 24 cm. Includes index. [CT788.H5A35 1975] 76-352318 ISBN 0-7100-8129-4
1. Hickey, William, b. 1749. I. Title. BIP

HICKEY, William, b. 1749 920
The prodigal rake; memoirs of William Hickey. Ed. by Peter Quennell. New York, Dutton, 1962 [c.1960] 452p. illus. Previous ed. pub. under title: Memoirs. 62-8217 6.50
I. Title.

Hickford, Jessie.

HICKFORD, Jessie. 362.4'1'0924 B
I never walked alone / Jessie Hickford. New York : St. Martin's Press, 1977. 125 p. ; 23 cm. [HV1946.H5A34 1977] 76-10556 6.95
1. Hickford, Jessie. 2. Blind—Biography. 3. Guide dogs. I. Title. BIP

Hickin, Norman Ernest

HICKIN, Norman Ernest 595.700924
Forest refreshed; the autobiographical notes of a biologist. London, Hutchinson [New York, Intl. Pubns. Serv., c.1965] 184p. illus. 24cm. Bibl. [QL31.H6A3] 65-5613 6.25 bds.,
I. Title.

Hickok, James Butler, 1837-1876.

*BUEL, J. W. 978.020924
The life of Wild Bill Hickok / J. W. Buel New York : Leisure Books ,1976 176 p. ; 18 cm. (Golden west series) [F594.H622] pbk. : 1.25
1. Hickok, James Butler, 1837-1876 I. Title.

CONNELLEY, William Elsey, 1855-1930. 917.8'03'20924 B
Wild Bill and his era; the life & adventures of James Butler Hickok. With introd. by Charles Moreau Harger. New York, Cooper Square Publishers, 1972. xii, 229 p. illus. 24 cm. Reprint of the 1933 ed. Includes bibliographical references. [F594.H622 1972] 76-187842 ISBN 0-8154-0413-1

1. Hickok, James Butler, 1837-1876. 2. Frontier and pioneer life—The West. I. Title. BIP

FIELDER, Mildred 917.80320924
Wild Bill and Deadwood. Seattle, Superior Pub. [c.1965] 160p. illus. 28cm. Bibl. [F594.F47] 65-23449 12.95
1. Hickok, James Butler, 1837-1876. 2. Frontier and pioneer life—South Dakota—Deadwood. I. Title.

FIELDER, Mildred. 917.80320924 (B)
Wild Bill and Deadwood. [1st ed.] Seattle, Superior Pub. Co. [1965] 160 p. illus. 28 cm. Bibliography: p. 148-[150] [F594.F47] 65-23449
1. Hickock, James Butler, 1837-1876. 2. Frontier and pioneer life — South Dakota — Deadwood. I. Title.

GARST, Doris Shannon, 1899- 923.973
Wild Bill Hickok [by] Shannon Garst with Warren Garst. New York, J. Messner [1952] 183 p. illus. 22 cm. [F594.H626] 52-8210
1. Hickok. James Butler, 1837-1876. I. Title.

GARST, Doris Shannon, 1899- 917.8'03'20924 B
Wild Bill Hickok [by] Shannon Garst with Warren Garst. New York, J. Messner [1952] 183 p. illus. 22 cm. Bibliography: p. 179-180. A biography of the frontiersman who was a teamster, Civil War soldier, Indian fighter, Scout, and Marshall of several rough frontier towns. [F594.H626] 92 AC 68
1. Hickok, James Butler, 1837-1876. I. Garst, Warren Edward, 1922- joint author. II. Title.

KNIGHT, Edward. 923.973
Wild Bill Hickok; the contemporary portrait of a Civil War hero. Franklin, N. H., Hillside Press, 1959. 61p. 23cm. Includes bibliography. [F594.H6265] 59-39672
1. Hickok, James Butler, 1837-1876. I. Title.

O'CONNOR, Richard, 1915- 923.973
Wild Bill Hickok. [1st ed.] Garden City, N.Y., Doubleday, 1959. 282 p. 22 cm. Includes bibliography. [F594.H6267] 59-10683
1. Hickok, James Butler, 1837-1876.

ROSA, Joseph G. 923.973
They called him Wild Bill; the life and adventures of James Butler Hickok. [1st ed.] Norman, University of Oklahoma Press [1964] xvii, 278 p. illus., ports. 24 cm. Bibliography: p. 261-267. [F594.H627] 64-11319
1. Hickok, James Butler, 1837-1876. I. Title.

ROSA, Joseph G. 917.8'03'20924 B
They called him Wild Bill: the life and adventures of James Butler Hickok, by Joseph G. Rosa. 2d ed., rev. and enl. Norman, University of Oklahoma Press [1974] xxi, 377 p. illus. 24 cm. Bibliography: p. 354-363. [F594.H627 1974] 74-5958 ISBN 0-8061-1217-4 12.50
1. Hickok, James Butler, 1837-1876. I. Title.

Hickok, Lorena A.

HICKOK, Lorena A. 920
The road to the White House; F.D.R.: the pre-presidential years. New York, Scholastic [1963, c.1962] 212p. 17cm. (T479) .45 pap.,
I. Roosevelt, Franklin Delano, Pres. U.S.—Juvenile literature. II. Title.

Hicks, Edward, 1780-1849.

FORD, Alice Elizabeth, 1906- [759.13]
Edward Hicks, painter of the Peaceable Kingdom. Philadelphia, University of Pennsylvania Press, 1952. xvi, 161 p. plates (part col.) porta, geneal. table. 29 cm. Bibliography: p. 123-126. [ND237.H58F6] 927.5 52-13392
1. Hicks, Edward, 1780-1849. I. Title.

HAYNES, George Emerson. 289.6'092'4 B
Edward Hicks, Friends' minister / by George Emerson Haynes. Doylestown, Pa. : C. Ingerman at the Quixott Press, 1974. xi, 60 p. : ill. ; 23 cm. [BX7795.H48H38] 74-189464
1. Hicks, Edward, 1780-1849.

PULLINGER, Edna S. 759.13
A dream of peace; Edward Hicks of Newtown, by Edna S. Pullinger. Philadelphia, Dorrance [1973] 93 p. illus. 22 cm. Bibliography: p. 91-93. [ND237.H58P84] 73-76215 ISBN 0-8059-1848-5 3.95
1. Hicks, Edward, 1780-1849. I. Title.

Hicks, Elias,

HICKS, Elias, 1748-1830. 289.6'0924 B
Journal of the life and religious labours of Elias Hicks. New York, Arno Press, 1969. 451 p. 23 cm. (Religion in America) Reprint of the 1832 ed. [BX7795.H5A3 1969] 78-83424
I. Title.

Hicks, Elias, 1748-1830.

FORBUSH, Bliss, 1896- 922.8673
Elias Hicks, Quaker liberal. With a foreword by Frederick B. Tolles. New York, Columbia University Press, 1956. xxii, 355p. illus., ports., maps, fascism., geneal. table. 24cm. Bibliographical references included in 'Notes' (p. [297]-337) [BX7795.H5F6] 56-6250
1. Hicks, Elias, 1748-1830. I. Title.

Hicks, Granville,

HICKS, Granville, 1901- 928.1
Part of the truth. [1st ed.] New York, Harcourt, Brace & World [1965] 314 p. 21 cm. [PS3515.I253P3] 65-19058
I. Title.

Hicks, Isaac, 1767-1820.

DAVISON, Robert A. 923.873
Isaac Hicks; New York merchant and Quaker, 1767-1820. Cambridge, Mass., Harvard [c.]1964. 217p. illus. 22cm. (Harvard studies in bus. hist., 22) Bibl. 64-11128 4.75
1. Hicks, Isaac, 1767-1820. I. Title. II. Series.

DAVISON, Robert A 338.7'67'700924
Isaac Hicks; New York merchant and Quaker, 1767-1820. Cambridge, Harvard University Press, 1964. 217 p. illus. 22 cm. (Harvard studies in business history, 22) Bibliography: p. [171]-180. [HF3023.H5D3] 64-11128
1. Hicks, Isaac, 1767-1820. I. Title.

Hicks, Jean Johnson.

HICKS, Jean Johnson. 917'.04'530924 B
Where next, Lady Thuppence? Philadelphia, Dorrance [1973] 251 p. illus. 22 cm. Autobiographical. [CT275.H5957A33] 72-96802 ISBN 0-8059-1824-8 5.95
1. Hicks, Jean Johnson. I. Title.

Hicks, John Donald,

HICKS, John Donald, 1890- 973'.071'124 B
My life with history; an autobiography, by John D. Hicks. Lincoln, University of Nebraska Press [1968] ix, 366 p. illus., ports. 24 cm. [E175.5.H48A3] 68-25154 5.95
I. Title.

Hicks, Ruby Sheppeard.

HICKS, Ruby Sheppeard. 976.2'47'060924 B
The song of the Delta / by Ruby Sheppeard Hicks. 1st ed. Jackson, Miss. : Howick House, 1976. 127 p. : ill. ; 24 cm. [F347.S9H524] 76-150063
1. Hicks, Ruby Sheppeard. 2. Sunflower Co., Miss.—Biography. I. Title.

Hidalgo, Francisco, 1659?-1726.

CARTER, Robert F. 266'.2'0924 B
The tarnished halo; story of Fray Francisco Hidalgo, by Robert F. Carter. Chicago, Franciscan Herald Press [1973] p. Bibliography: p. [E78.T4C37] 73-8669 ISBN 0-8199-0457-0
1. Hidalgo, Francisco, 1659?-1726. 2. Indians of North America—Texas—Missions. 3. Indians of Mexico—Missions. I. Title.

Hidalgo y Costilla, Miguel, 1753-1811.

NOLL, Arthur Howard, 1855-1930. 972'.03'0924 B
The life and times of Miguel Hidalgo y Costilla, by Arthur Howard Noll and A. Philip McMahon. New York, Russell & Russell [1973] vii, 200 p. 20 cm. "First published in 1910." [F1232.H63 1973] 72-85003 ISBN 0-8462-1687-6 12.00
1. Hidalgo y Costilla, Miguel, 1753-1811. 2. Mexico—History—War of Independence, 1810-1821. I. McMahon, Amos Philip, 1890-1947, joint author. II. Title. BIP

Hidalgo y Costilla, Miguel, 1753-1811—Juvenile literature.

LIEBERMAN, Mark, 1942- 972'.03'0924 B
Hidalgo; Mexican revolutionary. New York, Praeger Publishers [1970] vi, 161 p. map. 22 cm. (Praeger pathfinder biographies) Bibliography: p. 157. A biography of the Mexican priest who helped organize the revolution that won Mexico's independence from Spain. [F1232.H627 1970] 92 78-124857 5.50
1. Hidalgo y Costilla, Miguel, 1753-1811—Juvenile literature. I. Title.

Hides, Jack Gordon, 1906-1938.

SINCLAIR, James Patrick, 1928- 919.5 B
The outside man, Jack Hides of Papua [by] James Sinclair. [Melbourne] Lansdowne [1969] xiii, 266 p. illus., map (fold. in pocket) 25 cm. Bibliography: p. 262-266. [DU746.H5S5] 70-492721 5.95
1. Hides, Jack Gordon, 1906-1938. I. Title.

Hiebert, Paul Gerhardt, 1892-

HIEBERT, Paul Gerhardt, 1892- 209'.2'4 B
Doubting castle / Paul Hiebert. Winnipeg : Queenston House, c1976. 120 p. ; 24 cm. [BR1725.H456A33] 77-366899 ISBN 0-919866-15-8
1. Hiebert, Paul Gerhardt, 1892- 2. Christian biography—Manitoba. I. Title.

Hiero II, King of Syracuse, d. 215? B.C.

KINCAID, Charles Augustus, 1870-1954. 930'.4
Successors of Alexander the Great. Chicago, Argonaut, 1969. 182 p. maps. 24 cm. (The Argonaut library of antiquities) Reprint of the 1930 ed. Bibliographical footnotes. [DF235.K5 1969] 73-7841
1. Ptolemaeus I Soter, King of Egypt, d. 283 B.C. 2. Pyrrhus, King of Epirus, 318-272 B.C. 3. Hiero II, King of Syracuse, d. 215? B.C. 4. Antiochus III, the Great, King of Syria, 238 (ca)-187 B.C. I. Title.

Hieronymus, Saint.

KELLY, John Norman Davidson. 270.2'092'4 B
Jerome : his life, writings, and controversies / J. N. D. Kelly. 1st U.S. ed. New York : Harper & Row, c1975. xi, 353 p. : map (on lining papers) ; 24 cm. Includes bibliographical references and index. [BR1720.J5K44 1975b] 75-36732 ISBN 0-06-064333-1 : 15.00
1. Hieronymus, Saint. I. Title. BIP

MIEROW, Charles Christopher, 1883- 922.1
Saint Jerome, the sage of Bethlehem. Milwaukee, Bruce Pub. Co. [1959] 142p. illus. 22cm. [BR1720.J5M5] 59-13488
1. Hieronymus, Saint. I. Title.

PERNOUD, Regine, 1909- 922.137
Saint Jerome, by Regine and Madeleine Pernoud. Tr. by Rosemary Sheed. New York, Macmillan, 1962 [c.1960, 1962] 98p. 18cm. (Your name-- Your saint ser.) Bibl. 62-13438 2.50
1. Hieronymus, Saint. I. Pernoud, Madeleine, joint author. II. Title.

STEINMANN, Jean. 922.1
Saint Jerome and his times. Translated by Ronald Matthews. Notre Dame, Ind., Fides Publishers [1959?] 358 p. 23 cm. [BR1720.J5S753] 60-1807
1. Hieronymus, Saint. I. Title.

Hieronymus, Saint—Juvenile literature.

SANDERLIN, George William. 1915- 922.1
St. Jerome and the Bible. Illus. by Harry Barton. New York, Vision Bks [dist. Farrar, c.1961] 192p. (Vision bks 51) 61-11324 1.95
1. Hieronvmus. Saint—Juvenile literature. I. Title.

Higginbottom, Sam, 1874-1958.

HESS, Gary R. 630'.924 B
Sam Higginbottom of Allahabad, pioneer of point four to India [by] Gary R. Hess. Charlottesville, University Press of Virginia [1967] 177 p. illus., maps, ports. 25 cm. Bibliography: p. [165]-173. [S532.H5H4] 67-17631
1. Higginbottom, Sam, 1874-1958. 2. Allahabad. University. Agricultural Institute.

Higgins, Thomas Gilbert McQuiston,

HIGGINS, Thomas Gilbert McQuiston, 1900- 657.0924
Thomas G. Higgins, CPA; an autobiography. New York, 1965. xvi, 347 p. ports. 24 cm. [HF5604.H5A3] [(B)] 65-25763
I. Title.

Higginson, Henry Lee,

HIGGINSON, Henry Lee, 1834-1919. 332.1'0924 B
Life and letters of Henry Lee Higginson, by Bliss Perry. Freeport, N.Y., Books for Libraries Press [1972] viii, 557 p. illus. 23 cm. Reprint of the 1921 ed. Includes bibliographical references. [CT275.H5965A3 1972] 72-37905 ISBN 0-8369-6743-7
I. Perry, Bliss, 1860-1954. BIP

Higginson, Thomas Wentworth,

HIGGINSON, Thomas Wentworth, 1823-1911. 301.153'0924
Letters and journals of Thomas Wentworth Higginson, 1846-1906. Edited by Mary Thacher Higginson. New York, Da Capo Press, 1969 [c1921] 358 p. 24 cm. (A Da Capo Press reprint edition) [PS1928.A4 1969] 73-87489
I. Higginson, Mary Potter (Thacher) 1844-1941, ed.

HIGGINSON, Thomas Wentworth, 1823-1911. 301.153'0924 B
Letters and journals of Thomas Wentworth Higginson, 1846-1906. Edited by Mary Thacher Higginson. New York, Negro Universities Press [1969] 358 p. 23 Reprint of the 1921 ed. [PS1928.A4 1969b] 73-88435
I. Higginson, Mary Potter (Thacher) 1844-1941, ed. II. Title. BIP

Higginson, Thomas Wentworth, 1823-1911.

EDELSTEIN, Tilden G., 1931- 301'.15'30924 B
Strange enthusiasm; a life of Thomas Wentworth Higginson, by Tilden G.

Edelstein. New Haven, Yale University, 1968. ix, 425 p. port. 25 cm. "Books published by Higginson": p. [403-404] [PS1928.E2] 68-27752 11.00
1. Higginson, Thomas Wentworth, 1823-1911. I. Title. BIP

HIGGINSON, Mary 818'.4'09 B
Potter (Thacher) 1844-1941.
Thomas Wentworth Higgins; the story of his life. Freeport, N.Y., Books for Libraries Press [1972] x, 435 p. illus. 23 cm. Reprint of the 1914 ed. Bibliography: p. [403]-428. [PS1928.H5 1972] 76-37886 ISBN 0-8369-6723-2
1. Higginson, Thomas Wentworth, 1823-1911.

HIGGINSON, Mary 818'.4'09 B
Potter (Thacher) 1844-1941.
Thomas Wentworth Higginson; the story of his life. Port Washington, N.Y., Kennikat Press [1971] x, 435 p. illus., ports. 22 cm. (Kennikat Press scholarly reprints. Series on literary America in the nineteenth century) Reprint of the 1914 ed. Bibliography: p. [403]-428. [PS1928.H5 1971] 70-122657
1. Higginson, Thomas Wentworth, 1823-1911.

HIGGINSON, Thomas 301.153'0924
Wentworth, 1823-1911.
Letters and journals of Thomas Wentworth Higginson, 1846-1906. Edited by Mary Thacher Higginson. New York, Da Capo Press, 1969 [c1921] 358 p. 24 cm. (A Da Capo Press reprint edition) [PS1928.A4 1969] 73-87489
I. Higginson, Mary Potter (Thacher) 1844-1941, ed.

HIGGINSON, Thomas 301.153'0924 B
Wentworth, 1823-1911.
Letters and journals of Thomas Wentworth Higginson, 1846-1906. Edited by Mary Thacher Higginson. New York, Negro Universities Press [1969] 358 p. 23 Reprint of the 1921 ed. [PS1928.A4 1969b] 73-88435
I. Higginson, Mary Potter (Thacher) 1844-1941, ed. II. Title. BIP

WELLS, Anna Mary 928.1
Dear preceptor; the life and times of Thomas Wentworth Higginson. Boston, Houghton [c.]1963. 363p. illus. 22cm. Bibl. 63-7197 6.00
1. Higginson, Thomas Wentworth, 1823-1911. I. Title.

WELLS, Anna Mary. 928.1
Dear preceptor; the life and times of Thomas Wentworth Higginson. Boston, Houghton Mifflin, 1963. 363 p. illus. 22 cm. Includes bibliography. [PS1928.W4] 63-7197
1. Higginson, Thomas Wentworth, 1823-1911. I. Title.

High school students—New York (City)—Political activity.

REEVES, Donald, 373.1'8'1097471
1952-
Notes of a processed brother. [1st ed.] New York, Pantheon Books [1972, c1971] xiii, 480 p. 22 cm. Autobiographical. [LA229.R4 1972] 75-162564 ISBN 0-394-47101-6 8.95
1. High school students—New York (City)—Political activity. 2. Negroes—Education. I. Title. BIP

Higham, David—Biography.

HIGHAM, David. 070.5'2'0924 B
Literart gebt / David Higham. New York : Coward, McCann & Geoghegan, 1978. 334 p. ; 23 cm. Includes index. [PR6058.I35Z47 1978] 78-648 ISBN 0-698-10852-3 : 12.50
1. Higham, David—Biography. 2. Authors, English—20th century—Biography. 3. Literary agents—Great Britain—Biography. I. Title.

Highlands of Scotland—Description and travel.

VICTORIA, Queen of 942.081'0924
Great Britain, 1819-1901.
Victoria in the Highlands; the personal journal of Her Majesty Queen Victoria, with notes and introductions, and a description of the acquisition and rebuilding of Balmoral Castle, by David Duff. New York, Taplinger Pub. Co. [1969, c1968] 397 p. illus., fold. geneal. table, maps, ports. 23 cm. Selections from Leaves from the journal of our life in the Highlands, and More leaves. Bibliography: p. 381-383. [DA552.V5 1969] 76-79854 12.50
1. Highlands of Scotland—Description and travel. I. Duff, David, 1912- II. Title.

Hiigel, Friedrich, Freiherr von, 1852-1925.

DE LA BEDOYERE, Michael, 922.242
1900-
The life of Baron von Hiigel. London, Dent [dist. Mystic, Conn., Verry, 1965] xviii, 366p. ports. facsims. 22cm. [BX4705.H77D4] 51-8513 5.00
1. Hiigel, Friedrich, Freiherr von, 1852-1925. I. Title.

Hijab, Sayyid.

HIJAB, Sayyid. 892.7'1'6 B
A new Egyptian; the autobiography of a young Arab [by] Sayed Hegab. New York, Praeger Publishers [1971] 160 p. map. 22 cm. [PJ7832.I384Z5] 70-159410 5.95
I. Title.

Hilgenstuhler, Ted.

HILGENSTUHLER, Ted. 927.8
Tennessee Ernie Ford. A heart warming book about America's favorite singing star of radio and TV; the long rocky road from Tennessee to Hollywood. [Los Angeles, Petersen Pub. Co., 1957] 96p. illus., ports. 28cm. Cover title.qaFord, Ernest Jennings, 1919- [ML420.F7H5] 57-3345
I. Title.

Hill, Ambrose Powell, 1823-1865.

HASSLER, William Woods. 923.573
A. P. Hill; Lee's forgotten general. Richmond, Garrett Massie [1957] 249p. illus. 24cm. [E467.1.H56H3] 57-13027
1. Hill, Ambrose Powell, 1823-1865. I. Title. BIP

Hill, Barry.

HILL, Archie. 301.42'7 B
Closed world of love / Archie Hill. New York : Simon and Schuster, c1976. 136 p. ; 25 cm. [RJ496.S6H54] 77-3048 ISBN 0-671-22845-5 : 6.95
1. Hill, Barry. 2. Hill, Archie. 3. Paralysis, Spastic—Biography. 4. Children, Adopted—Biography. 5. Love, Paternal. 6. Stepfathers—Biography. I. Title.

HILL, Archie. 301.42'7
Closed world of love / Archie Hill. New York : Avon Books, 1978,c1976. 125p. ; 18 cm. [RJ496.S6H54] [[B]] ISBN 0-380-39917-2 pbk. : 1.75
1. Hill, Barry. 2. Hill, Archie. 3. Paralysis, Spastic — Biography. 4. Children, Adopted — Biography. 5. Love, Paternal. 6. Stepfathers — Biography. I. Title.
L.C. card no. for 1976 Simon and Schuster ed.: 77-3048 BIP

Hill, Benjamin Harvey, 1823-1882.

PEARCE, Haywood 328.73'0924
Jefferson, 1893-
Benjamin H. Hill, secession and reconstruction [by] Haywood J. Pearce, Jr. New York, Negro Universities Press [1969] ix, 330 p. illus., ports. 23 cm. Reprint of the 1928 ed. Bibliography: p. 310-318. [E664.H53P3 1969] 70-97434
1. Hill, Benjamin Harvey, 1823-1882. 2. Georgia—Politics and government. 3. Reconstruction—Georgia. I. Title.

Hill, Clifton D.

HILL, Clifton 917.74'81'0340924
D.
Father was first, by Clifton D. Hill. Philadelphia, Dorrance [1973] 60 p. 22 cm. Autobiographical. [CT275.H5977A3] 73-82563 ISBN 0-8059-1887-6 4.95
1. Hill, Clifton D. I. Title.

Hill, Daniel Harvey, 1821-1889.

BRIDGES, Leonard Hal, 923.573
1918-
Lee's maverick general. Daniel Harvey Hill. New York, McGraw [c.1961] 323p. illus. Bibl. 61-13163 7.50 bds.,
1. Hill, Daniel Harvey, 1821-1889. I. Title.

Hill, Dave, 1937-

HILL, Dave, 1937- 796.352'092'4 B
Teed off / by Dave Hill and Nick Seitz. Englewood Cliffs, N.J. : Prentice-Hall, c1977. ix, 217 p., [8] leaves of plates : ill. ; 22 cm. [GV964.H46A37] 76-30769 ISBN 0-13-902247-3 : 8.95
1. Hill, Dave, 1937- 2. Golf—United States. 3. Golfers—United States—Biography. I. Seitz, Nick, 1939- joint author. II. Title.

Hill, David Octavius, 1802-1870.

BRUCE, David, 1939- 779'.2'0922
comp.
Sun pictures; the Hill-Adamson calotypes. Greenwich, Conn., New York Graphic Society [1974, c1973] 247 p. illus. 30 cm. Bibliography: p. 243. [TR651.B78 1974] 73-87361 ISBN 0-8212-0588-9 17.50
1. Hill, David Octavius, 1802-1870. 2. Adamson, Robert, 1821-1848. 3. Photography, Artistic. 4. Calotype. I. Hill, David Octavius, 1802-1870. II. Adamson, Robert, 1821-1848. III. Title.

Hill, Eva Esther, 1898-

BARRETT, John, 1914- 610'.92'4 B
Cancer and cure : a doctor's story / John Barrett. London : Bachman & Turner, 1976. 135 p. : port. ; 23 cm. (Debate) [RC271.H47B37] 76-676714 ISBN 0-85974-040-4 : £3.50
1. Hill, Eva Esther, 1898- 2. Herbs—Therapeutic use. 3. Cancer—Chemotherapy. 4. Physicians—New Zealand—Biography. I. Title.

Hill, Graham, 1929-1975.

HILL, Graham, 1929- 796.7'2'0924
Life at the limit. [1st American ed.] New York, Coward-McCann [1970, c1969] 255 p. illus., ports. 22 cm. [GV1032.H48A3 1970] 73-117921 5.95
1. Automobile racing—Biography. I. Title.

HILL, Graham, 796.7'2'0924 B
1929-1975.
Graham Hill / by Graham Hill, with Neil Ewart ; afterword by Bette Hill ; with a foreword by H. R. H. the Prince of Wales. New York : St. Martin's Press, [1977] p. cm. [GV1032.H48A34] 77-72299 ISBN 0-312-34212-8 : 8.95
1. Hill, Graham, 1929-1975. 2. Automobile racing drivers—Great Britain—Biography. I. Ewart, Neil. II. Title.

Hill, Harold, 1905-

HILL, Harold, 1905- 248'.4
How to be a winner / Harold Hill, with Irene Burk Harrell. Plainfield, N.J. : Logos International, c1976. xix, 196 p. ; 22 cm. [BR1725.H47A32] 76-31676 ISBN 0-88270-178-9 : 5.95. ISBN 0-88270-179-7 pbk. :
1. Hill, Harold, 1905- 2. Christian life—1960- 3. Christian biography—United States. I. Harrell, Irene Burk, joint author. II. Title. BIP

Hill, Hubert M.,

HILL, Hubert M., 1918- 818.5
The golden trek. [1st ed.] New York, Pageant Press [1955] 68 p. 21 cm. Autobiographical. [CT275.H5984A3] 55-12149
I. Title.

Hill, James Jerome, 1838-1916.

HOLBROOK, Stewart Hall, 923.873
1893-1964.
James J. Hill, a great life in brief. [1st ed.] New York, Knopf, 1955. 205 p. 20 cm. (Great lives in brief; a new series of biographies) [HE2754.H5H6] 54-7220
1. Hill, James Jerome, 1838-1916.

MARTIN, Albro. 385'.092'4 B
James J. Hill and the opening of the Northwest / Albro Martin. New York : Oxford University Press, 1976. xii, 676 p. : ill. ; 24 cm. Includes bibliographical references and index. [HE2754.H5M37] 75-46362 ISBN 0-19-502070-7 : 19.50
1. Hill, James Jerome, 1838-1916. 2. Great Northern Railway. 3. Businessmen—United States—Biography. I. Title. BIP

Hill, James Jerome, 1838-1916—Juvenile literature.

COMFORT, Mildred 385'.0924 B
Houghton, 1886-
James J. Hill: young empire builder, by Mildred Comfort. Illustrated by William K. Plummer. Indianapolis, Bobbs-Merrill, [1968] 200 p. col. illus. 20 cm. (Childhood of famous Americans) A biography of James J. Hill concentrating on his boyhood years when thrift and hard work laid the foundations for his future reputation as empire builder and wealthy railroad tycoon. [HE2754.H5C65] 92 68-55147
1. Hill, James Jerome, 1838-1916—Juvenile literature. I. Plummer, William K., illus. II. Title.

COMFORT, Mildred 385'.092'4 B
Houghton, 1886-
James Jerome Hill, railroad pioneer. Minneapolis, Denison [1973] 124 p. 23 cm. (Men of achievement series) A biography of the man who built his fortune as he built the Great Northern Railroad and used it to help settle the West. [TF140.H54C65] 92 72-92119 ISBN 0-513-01305-9 4.98 (lib. bdg.)
1. Hill, James Jerome, 1838-1916—Juvenile literature. I. Title.

Hill, Jim Dan,

HILL, Jim Dan, 1897- 923.573
Sea dogs of the sixties. Farragut and seven contemporaries [Gloucester, Mass., P. Smith, 1963,c.1935] 265p. illus., map. 21cm. (Perpetua bk. rebound) Bibl. 4.00
I. Title.

Hill, Joan Olive Robinson, 1931-1969.

THOMPSON, 364.1'523'0922 B
Thomas.
Blood and money / Thomas Thompson. 1st ed. Garden City, N.Y. : Doubleday, 1976. 450 p. ; 24 cm. [HV6534.H8T48] 75-36632 ISBN 0-385-09685-2 : 10.00
1. Hill, Joan Olive Robinson, 1931-1969. 2. Hill, John Robert, 1931-1972. 3. Murder—Texas—Houston. I. Title. BIP

Hill, John.

HILL, John Ensign, 1887-1950. 920
Diaries and biographical material. Compiled and edited by Ivy Hooper Blood Hill. Logan, Utah, J. P. Smith, 1962. 213 p. illus. 24 cm. [CT275.H59864A3] 63-673
I. Hill, Ivy Hooper (Blood) 1888- II. Title.

KURTH, Ann. 364.15230924
Prescription: murder : a true story Ann Kurth. New York : New American Library ,1976. 184 p. : ill. ; 18 cm. (Signet Book) [HV6248] pbk. : 1.50
1. Hill, John. 2. Kurth, Ann. 3. Murder. I. Title.

Hill, John Ensign,

HILL, John Ensign, 1887-1950. 920
Diaries and biographical material. Compiled and edited by Ivy Hooper Blood Hill. Logan, Utah, J. P. Smith, 1962. 213 p. illus. 24 cm. [CT275.H59864A3] 63-673
I. Hill, Ivy Hooper (Blood) 1888- II. Title.

Hill, Philip Toll, 1927-

NOLAN, William F. 1928- 927.9672
Phil Hill: Yankee champion; first American to win the driving championship of the world. New York, Putnam [1963, c1962] 256 p. illus. 22 cm. [GV1032.H5N6] 62-20492
1. Hill, Philip Toll, 1927-

Hill, Rick.

HILL, Rick. 362.1'9'6994630924
Too young to die / by Rick Hill ; [editor, Ray Bartholomew]. 1st ed. Grand Rapids : Hill Publications, 1979. vii, 96 p. : ill. ; 21 cm. Bibliography: p. 95. [RC280.T4H54] 79-87783 ISBN 0-9602704-0-X : 3.00
1. Hill, Rick. 2. Testicle—Cancer—Biography. 3. Cancer—Diet therapy. 4. Laetrile. I. Bartholomew, Ray. II. Title.

Hill, Robert Thomas, 1858-1941.

ALEXANDER, Nancy, 1933- 551'.092'4 B
Father of Texas geology, Robert T. Hill / Nancy Alexander. Dallas : SMU Press, c1976. xii, 317 p., [8] leaves of plates : ill. ; 24 cm. (Bicentennial series in American studies ; 4) Includes bibliographical references and index. [QE22.H47A75] 76-2621 ISBN 0-87074-152-7 : 12.50
1. Hill, Robert Thomas, 1858-1941. 2. Geology—Texas—History. I. Title.

Hill, Stephen Spencer.

JOLLY, John, 1823-1899. 917.94'45'0330924
Gold Spring diary; the journal of John Jolly. Edited and annotated by Carlo M. De Ferrari, and including a brief history of Stephen Spencer Hill. 1st ed. Sonora, Calif., Tuolumne County Historical Society, c1966. 160 p. illus., port. 16 cm. 500 copies. Includes bibliographical references. [F868.T9J6] 66-30618
1. Hill, Stephen Spencer. 2. Frontier and pioneer life—California—Tuolumne Co. 3. Gold mines and mining—California—Tuolumne Co. I. De Ferrari, Carlo M., ed. II. Title.

Hill, Virginia

*HANNA, David. 364'.092'2B
Virginia Hill; queen of the underworld. New York, Belmont Tower Books [1975] 201 p. illus. 18 cm. [HV6785] 1.25 (pbk.)
1. Hill, Virginia 2. Crime and criminals—United States—Biography. I. Title.

Hillary, Edmund, Sir.

HILLARY, Edmund, Sir. 796.5'22'0924 B
Nothing venture, nothing win / by Sir Edmund Hillary. 1st American ed. New York : Coward, McCann & Geoghegan, 1975. 319 p., [16] leaves of plates : ill. ; 24 cm. Autobiographical. Includes index. [GV199.92.H54A36 1975] 74-24330 ISBN 0-698-10649-0 : 12.95
1. Hillary, Edmund, Sir. 2. Mountaineering. I. Title. BIP

Hillary, Edmund, Sir—Juvenile literature.

KNOOP, Faith Yingling. 796.5'22'0924 B
A world explorer: Sir Edmund Hillary. Illustrated by William Hutchinson. Champaign, Ill., Garrard Pub. Co. [1970] 96 p. illus. (part col.), col. maps (on lining papers) 24 cm. (World explorer books) A biography of the New Zealand explorer emphasizing his conquest of Mt. Everest, his exploration of Antarctica, and his search for the Abominable Snowman. [DS486.E8K56] 92 71-111906
1. Hillary, Edmund, Sir—Juvenile literature. I. Hutchinson, William M., illus. II. Title.

Hilleary, William M

HILLEARY, William M 1840-(ca.)1917. 355.3510924
A webfoot volunteer; the diary of William M. Hilleary, 1884-1866. Edited by Herbert B. Nelson and Preston E. Onstad, in cooperation with the Oregon Historical Society. Corvallis, Oregon State University Press [c1965] viii, 240 p. illus., facsim., maps, ports. 24 cm. (Oregon State monographs. Studies in history, no. 5) Bibliography: p. 229-234. [U53.H5A3] 65-65228
I. Nelson, Herbert B., ed. II. Onstad, Preston E., ed. III. Title. IV. Series. BIP

Hillel, the elder,

GLATZER, Nahum Norbert, 1903- 296.60924
Hillel, the elder; the emergence of classical Judaism. Rev. ed. New York, Schocken [1966, c.1956] 100p. 21cm. (Hillel bk.; SB123) [BM755.H45G54] 66-14870 1.25 pap.,
1. Hillel, the elder, d. ca. 10. I. Title.

GLATZER, Nahum Norbert, 1903- 922.96
Hillel the elder; the emergence of classical Judaism. New York, B'nai B'rith Hillel Foundations, 1956. 100p. 19cm. (Hillel little books, v. 3) [BM755.H45G54] 56-13000
1. Hillel, the elder, d. ca. 10. I. Title.

PILCHIK, Ely Emanuel. 922.96
Hillel, the book against the sword. Wood engravings by Ilya Schor. New York, Schuman [1951] 127 p. illus. 21 cm. [BM755.H45P5] 51-6986
1. Hillel, the elder, d. ca. 10. I. Title.

Hillenbrand, John A.

DALGLISH, Garvan. 923.873
Of this heritage; the biography of John A. Hillenbrand. [Crawfordsville ? Ind.] 1954. 205 p. illus. 24 cm. [CT275.H5987D3] 55-16404
1. Hillenbrand, John A. I. Title.

Hillhouse, James Abraham, 1789-1841.

HAZELRIGG, Charles Tabb. 928.1
American literary pioneer: a biographical study of James A. Hillhouse. New York, Bookman Associates, 1953. 226p. illus., port. 25cm. 'In its original form, written ... for the PH. D. degree ... Yale University.' Bibliography: p. 185-191. [PS1929.H68Z65] 53-1841
1. Hillhouse, James Abraham, 1789-1841. I. Title. BIP

Hilliard, Marion.

ROBINSON, Marion O. 926.1
Give my heart: the Dr. Marion Hilliard story [by] Marion O. Robinson. [1st ed.] Garden City, N.Y., Doubleday, 1964. x, 348 p. illus., ports. 22 cm. [R464.H5R6] 64-19257
1. Hilliard, Marion. I. Title.

Hillinger, Brad.

HILLINGER, Brad. 973.92'092'4 B
The wings are gone / by Brad Hillinger with Henry S. Bloomgarden. New York : W. Morrow, 1976. 156 p. ; 22 cm. [HD6073.A43H54] 75-45050 ISBN 0-688-03037-8 : 6.95
1. Hillinger, Brad. 2. Air lines—Flight attendants—Biography. I. Bloomgarden, Henry S. II. Title. BIP

Hillman, Sidney, 1887-1946.

GOULD, Jean, 1909- 923.373
Sidney Hillman, great American. Boston, Houghton Mifflin, 1952. 342 p. illus. 22 cm. Includes bibliography. [HD6509.H5G6] 52-5904
1. Hillman, Sidney, 1887-1946. 2. Amalgamated Clothing Workers of America.

JOSEPHSON, Matthew, 1899- 923.373
Sidney Hillman, statesman of American labor. [1st ed.] Garden City, N. Y., Doubleday, 1952. 701 p. 22 cm. [HD6509.H5J6] 52-11080
1. Hillman, Sidney, 1887-1946.

Hillquit, Morris, 1869-1933.

PRATT, Norma Fain. 335'.0092'4 B
Morris Hillquit : a political history of an American Jewish socialist / Norma Fain Pratt. Westport, Conn. : Greenwood Press, 1979. xi, 272 p. : ports. ; 22 cm. (Contributions in political science ; no. 20) ISSN 0147-1066) Includes index. Bibliography: p. [251]-258. [HX84.H5P7] 78-55349 ISBN 0-313-20526-4 lib.bdg. : 18.50
1. Hillquit, Morris, 1869-1933. 2. Socialists—United States—Biography. 3. Socialists, Jewish—United States—Biography. 4. Jews in the United States—Biography. I. Title. II. Series. BIP

Hillstrom, Joseph, 1879-1915.

FONER, Philip Sheldon, 1910- 343.523
The case of Joe Hill. New York, Intl. Pubs. [1966, c.1965] 127p. illus., port. 21cm. Bibl. 65-26742 3.50; 1.45 pap.,
1. Hillstrom, Joseph, 1879-1915. I. Title. BIP

Hilo Hattie.

SINGLETARY, Milly, 1918- 784'.092'4
Hilo Hattie, a legend in our time : a biography / by Milly Singletary. Honolulu : Singletary, c1979. p. cm. [ML420.H43S5] 79-16172 ISBN 0-9601256-5-5 : 10.00 ISBN 0-9601256-6-3 pbk. : 6.95
1. Hilo Hattie. 2. Singers—Hawaii—Biography. I. Title.

Hilsenrad, Helen,

HILSENRAD, Helen, 1895- 818.5408
Brown was the Danube. With an introd. by Harry Golden. New York, T. Yoseloff [1966] 492 p. illus., ports. 22 cm. Autobiography. [CT275.H59925A3] 65-17828
I. Title.

HILSENRAD, Helen, 1895- 818.5408
Brown was the Danube. With an introd. by Harry Golden. New York, T. Yoseloff [1966] 492 p. illus., ports. 22 cm. Autobiography. [CT275.H59925A3] 65-17828
I. Title.

Hilton, Conrad Nicholson,

HILTON, Conrad Nicholson, 1887- 926.4794
Be my guest. Englewood Cliffs, N.J., Prentice-Hall, [1957] 372 p. illus. 22 cm. Autobiography. [TX910.5.H5A3] 57-12418
I. Title.

Hilton, Conrad Nicholson, 1887-

BOLTON, Whitney. 926.4794
The silver spade; the Conrad Hilton story. With a foreword by Conrad Hilton. New York, Farrar, Straus and Young [1954] 230 p. illus. 22 cm. [TX910.5.H5B6] 54-9988
1. Hilton, Conrad Nicholson, 1887- I. Title. BIP

BOLTON, Whitney. 338.7'61'647940924 B
The silver spade; the Conrad Hilton story. With a foreword by Conrad Hilton. Freeport, N.Y., Books for Libraries Press [1973] p. (Biography index reprint series) Reprint of the 1954 ed. [TX910.5.H5B6 1973] 72-13265 ISBN 0-8369-8142-1
1. Hilton, Conrad Nicholson, 1887- I. Title.

COMFORT, Mildred Houghton 1886- 926.4794
Conrad N. Hilton, hotelier: a biography. Minneapolis, T. S. Denison [1946] 240 p. 23 cm. (Men of achievement series) [TX910.5H5C6] 64-14544
1. Hilton, Conrad Nicholson, I. Title.

DABNEY, Thomas Ewing. 926.4794
The man who bought the Waldorf; the life of Conrad N. Hilton. New York, Duell, Sloan and Pearce [1950] 272 p. 21 cm. [TX910.5.H5D3] 50-5058
1. Hilton, Conrad Nicholson, 1887- I. Title.

HILTON, Conrad Nicholson, 1887- 926.4794
Be my guest. Englewood Cliffs, N.J., Prentice-Hall, [1957] 372 p. illus. 22 cm. Autobiography. [TX910.5.H5A3] 57-12418
I. Title.

Hilton, Eugene,

HILTON, Eugene, 1889- 289.3'0924 B
My second estate; the life of a Mormon. [Oakland, Calif., Hilton Family, 1968] 245 p. illus., facsims., ports. 28 cm. Cover title. "Volume of family lore and pictures ... prepared especially for the families descended from Eugene Hilton and Ruth Naomi Savage." Bibliographical footnotes. [BX8695.H5A3] 70-11040
I. Title.

Hilton, John W.

AINSWORTH, Katherine, 1908- 759.13 B
The man who captured sunshine : episodes in the life of John W. Hilton, botanist, gemologist, zoologist, and gifted painter of the desert scene / as garnered during long years of friendship by Katherine Ainsworth. Palm Springs, Calif. : ETC Publications, c1978. xiv, 274 p., [8] leaves of plates : ill. (some col.) ; 24 cm. Includes index. [CT275.H59914A46] 77-21823 ISBN 0-88280-054-X : 15.00
1. Hilton, John W. 2. United States—Biography. I. Title.

Himes, Chester B.,

HIMES, Chester B., 1909- 813'.5'4 B
The quality of hurt; the autobiography of Chester Himes. [1st ed.] Garden City, N.Y., Doubleday, 1972- v. 22 cm. [PS3515.I713Z5] 71-157601 7.95
I. Title. BIP

Himmler, Heinrich, 1900-1945.

FRISCHAUER, Willi, 1906- 923.243
Himmler; the evil genius of the Third Reich. Boston, Beacon Press, 1953. 269p. illus. 22cm. [DD247] 53-12575
1. Himmler, Heinrich, 1900-1945. I. Title.

FRISCHAUER, Willi, 1906- 923.243
Himmler; the evil genius of the Third Reich. New York, Belmont [1962, c.1953] 221p. (Belmont documentary, L92-526) Bibl. .50 pap.,
1. Himmler, Heinrich, 1900-1945. I. Title.

KERSTEN, Felix, 1898-1960. 320.9'43
Samtal med Himmler; minnen fran Tredje riket, 1839-1945. Stockholm, New York, Ljus [1947] 320 p. illus. 20 cm. [DD247.H46K4] 63-37823
1. Himmler, Heinrich, 1900-1945. I. Title.

MANVELL, Roger, 1909- 923.243
Himmler [by] Roger Manvell and Heinrich Fraenkel. [1st American ed.] New York, Putnam [1965] xvii, 285 p. illus., ports. 23 cm. First published in London under title: Heinrich Himmler. Bibliography: p. [275]-278. [DD247.H46M3 1965a] 64-18020
1. Himmler, Heinrich, 1900-1945. I. Fraenkel, Heinrich, 1897- joint author.

WYKES, Alan. 943.086'092'4 B
Himmler. [New York, Ballantine Books, 1972] 158 p. illus. 21 cm. (Ballantine's illustrated history of the violent century. War leader book no. 14) [DD247.H46W9] 72-188993 1.00

1. Himmler, Heinrich, 1900-1945.

Hinchman, Walter Swain,

HINCHMAN, Walter Swain, 1879- 923.773
The only paradise. Wakefield, Mass., Murray Print. Co. [1952] 192 p. illus. 23 cm. Autobiography. [CT275.H5994A3] 52-32355
I. Title.

Hinckley, Anita W., 1884-

HINCKLEY, Anita W., 1884- 917.45'9
Wickford memories, by Anita W. Hinckley. Boston, Branden Press [1972] 118 p. illus. 23 cm. Autobiographical. [CT275.H59944A3] 72-83723 ISBN 0-8283-1360-1 6.95
1. Hinckley, Anita W., 1884- 2. Wickford, R.I.—History. I. Title. BIP

Hinckley, Robert H., 1891-

HINCKLEY, Robert H., 1891- 979.2'03'0924 B
"I'd rather be born lucky than rich" : the autobiography of Robert H. Hinckley / Robert H. Hinckley and JoAnn Jacobsen Wells. Provo, Utah : Brigham Young University Press, c1977. xii, 160 p. : ill. ; 23 cm. (Charles Redd monographs in western history ; no. 7) Includes index. Bibliography: p. 153. [F826.H66A34] 77-153897 ISBN 0-8425-0859-7 : 4.95
1. Hinckley, Robert H., 1891- 2. Politicians—Utah—Biography. 3. Businessmen—United States—Biography. 4. Utah—Biography. 5. United States—Politics and government—1933-1945. 6. Utah—History. I. Wells, JoAnn Jacobsen, joint author. II. Title. III. Series.

Hindemith, Paul, 1895-1963.

KEMP, Ian. 780'.92'4
Hindemith. London, New York, Oxford University Press, 1970. 59 p. music. 22 cm. (Oxford studies of composers, 6) Bibliography: p. 59. [ML410.H685K4] 784'.092'4 75-18053 15/- ($2.50 U.S.)
1. Hindemith, Paul, 1895-1963. Works. I. Title. II. Series. BIP

Hindenburg, Paul von, Pres. germany, 1847-1934.

DUPUY, Trevor Nevitt, 1916- 940.4'143'0922
The military lives of Hindenburg and Ludendorff of Imperial Germany. New York, Watts [1970] xv, 200 p. illus., maps, ports. 23 cm. Interwoven biographies of the two German soldiers whose collaboration during World War I nearly enabled Germany to win the war against great odds. [DD231.H5D8] 920 72-80895 3.95
1. Hindenburg, Paul von, Pres. Germany, 1847-1934. 2. Ludendorff, Erich, 1865-1937. I. Title. BIP

GOLDSMITH, Margaret Leland, 1894- 943.085'092'4 B
Hindenburg: the man and the legend, by Margaret Goldsmith and Frederick Voigt. Freeport, N.Y., Books for Libraries Press [1972] 304 p. illus. 22 cm. Reprint of the 1930 ed. [DD231.H5G6 1972] 72-1289 ISBN 0-8369-6826-3 12.50
1. Hindenburg, Paul von, Pres. Germany, 1847-1934. I. Voigt, Fritz August, 1892- joint author. II. Title.

HINDENBURG, Paul von, Pres. Germany, 1847-1934. 943.085'092'4 B
Out of my life / by Marshal von Hindenburg ; translated by F. A. Holt. New York : H. Fertig, 1975, c1921. p. cm. Translation of Aus meinem Leben. Reprint of the ed. published by Harper, New York. Includes index. [D531.H4813 1975] 74-22303 19.50
1. Hindenburg, Paul von, Pres. Germany, 1847-1934. 2. European War, 1914-1918—Germany. 3. European War, 1914-1918—Campaigns. 4. European War, 1914-1918—Personal narratives, German. I. Title.

WHEELER-BENNETT, John Wheeler, Sir 1902- 943.085'0924
Hindenburg: the wooden Titan [by] John W. Wheeler-Bennett. London, Melbourne, Macmillan; New York, St. Martin's 1967. xviii, 507p. front., 8 plates (incl. ports.) 23cm. Orig. Amer. ed. (New York, Morrow 1936) has title: Wooden titan, Hindenburg in twenty years of German history, 1914-1934. Bibl. [DD231.H5W5 1967] 67-15778 11.50
1. Hindenburg, Paul von, Pres. germany, 1847-1934. 2. Germany—Hist.—20th cent. I. Title.

Hindman, Thomas Carmichael, 1818-1868.

NASH, Charles Edward. 973.7'42'0924 B
Biographical sketches of Gen. Pat Cleburne and Gen. T. C. Hindman, together with humorous anecdotes and reminiscences of the late Civil War / by Charles Edward Nash. Dayton, Ohio : Press of Morningside Bookshop, 1977. 300 p., [4] leaves of plates : ill., ports. ; 21 cm. "Facsimile 39." "Malthus theory": p. [289]-300. Reprint of the 1898 ed. printed by Tunnah & Pittard, Little Rock, Ark.; with new introd. [E496.4.C55N37 1977] 77-153871 15.00
1. Cleburne, Patrick Ronayne, 1828-1864. 2. Hindman, Thomas Carmichael, 1818-1868. 3. Confederate States of America. Army—Biography. 4. Arkansas—History—Civil War, 1861-1865. 5. Generals—Confederate States of America—Biography. I. Title: Biographical sketches of Gen. Pat Cleburne and Gen. T. C. Hindman ...

Hinduism—Biography.

CHINMOY. 294.5'6'4
Mother India's lighthouse: India's spiritual leaders; flame-heights of the West, by Sri Chinmoy. Blauvelt, N.Y., R. Steiner Publications [1973] vii, 277 p. 18 cm. (Steinerbooks, 1732) [BL1170.C46] 74-189998 1.95 (pbk.)
1. Hinduism—Biography. 2. India—Biography. I. Title.

Hiner, John, 1742-1814.

FORBES, Amanda Arbogast. 929.2'09755
A man of the bullpasture; John Hiner, 1742-1814. 2d ed. Monterey, Va., Printed by Highland Recorder [1966] 9 l. 28 cm. Cover title. Bibliography: leaves 8-9. [CT275.H5997F6 1966] 68-5099
1. Hiner, John, 1742-1814. I. Title.

Hines, Earl, 1905-

DANCE, Stanley. 786.2'1'0924 B
The world of Earl Hines / Stanley Dance. New York : Scribner, c1977. ix, 324 p. : ill. ; 28 cm. (The world of swing ; v. 2) Includes index. Bibliography: p. 312. [ML417.H5D4] 77-2269 ISBN 0-684-14935-4 . 14.95. ISBN 0-684-15030-1 pbk. : 7.95
1. Hines, Earl, 1905- 2. Jazz musicians—United States—Biography. I. Title. BIP

Hinsdale, Burke Aaron, 1837-1900.

DAVIS, Harold Eugene, 1902- 370'.924 B
Hinsdale of Hiram: the life of Burke Aaron Hinsdale, pioneer educator, 1837-1900. [Washington] University Press of Washington, D.C., 1971. ix, 238 p. 24 cm. Includes bibliographical references. [LD2241.H617D38 1869] 73-139846 ISBN 0-87419-028-2 7.00
1. Hinsdale, Burke Aaron, 1837-1900. I. Title. BIP

Hippocrates—Juvenile literature.

GOLDBERG, Herbert S. 92
Hippocrates, father of medicine. New York, F. Watts [1963] 107 p. 22 cm. (Immortals of science) [R126.H8G55] 62-10378
1. Hippocrates—Juvenile literature.

Hiquily, Philippe, 1925-

JOUFFROY, Alain 730.944
Hiquily. [Paris] G. Fall [dist. New York, Efron. c.1962] 89p. illus. (pt. col.) 23cm. French and English. 62-52235 4.50
1. Hiquily, Philippe, 1925- I. Title.

Hirohito, Emperor of Japan, 1901-

MOSLEY, Leonard, 1913- 952.0330924 B
Hirohito, Emperor of Japan. Englewood Cliffs, N.J., Prentice-Hall [1966] ix, 371 p. illus., ports. 24 cm. Bibliography: p. 357-361. [DS889.8.M6 1966] 66-15138
1. Hirohito, Emperor of Japan, 1901-

MOSLEY, Leonord Oswald, 1911- 952.033'0924 (B)
Hirohito, Emperor of Japan. [New York] Avon [1967, c.1966] vii, 381p. illus., ports. 18cm. (N163) Bibl. [DS889.8.M6 1966] .95 pap.,
1. Hirohito, Emperor of Japan, 1901- I. Title.

Hirota, Koki, 1878-1948.

†SHIROYAMA, Saburo. 952.03'092'4 B
War criminal : the life and death of Hirota Koki / Saburo Shiroyama ; translated by John Bester. 1st ed. Tokyo ; New York : Kodansha International ; New York : distributed through Harper & Row, 1977. 301 p., [5] leaves of plates : ill. ; 22 cm. Translation of Rakujitsu moyu. Bibliography: p. 300-301. [DS885.5.H58S5313] 76-9361 ISBN 0-87011-275-9 : 10.00
1. Hirota, Koki, 1878-1948. 2. Statesmen—Japan—Biography. 3. Japan—Politics and government—1912-1945. I. Title. BIP

Hirsch, Emil Gustav, 1851-1923.

HIRSCH, David Einhorn. 296.8'346'0924 B
Rabbi Emil G. Hirsch, the reform advocate. Chicago, Whitehall Co. [1968] ii, 191 p. 24 cm. [BM755.H47H5] 68-24717
1. Hirsch, Emil Gustav, 1851-1923. 2. Jesus Christ—Crucifixion. 3. Sermons, American—Jewish authors. 4. Sermons, Jewish—U.S.

Hirsch, Ernest A., 1924-

HIRSCH, Ernest A., 1924- 362.1'9'683400924 B
Starting over : the autobiographical account of a psychologist's experience with multiple sclerosis / by Ernest A. Hirsch ; with a foreword by Karl A. Menninger. North Quincy, Mass. : Christopher Pub. House, c1977. 169 p. ; 22 cm. [RC377.H57] 77-78030 ISBN 0-8158-0348-6 : 6.95
1. Hirsch, Ernest A., 1924- 2. Multiple sclerosis—Biography. I. Title.

Hirsch, Moritz, Freiherr auf Gereuth, 1831-1896.

GRUNWALD, Kurt, 1901- 956.940010924(B)
Turkenhirsch; a study of Baron Maurice de Hirsch, entrepreneur and philanthropist. [Jerusalem] Israel Program for Scientific Translations, Imprint on mounted label. New York, D. Davey. 1966. New York, Imprint on mounted label: D. Davey. 1966. xviii, 139p. illus., coat of arms, map (on lining pap.) ports. 25cm. Bibl. [DS135.G5H49] 66-8842 5.50 bds.,
1. Hirsch, Moritz, Freiherr auf Gereuth, 1831-1896. I. Title.

LEE, Samuel James. 956.94'001'0924 B
Moses of the new world; the work of Baron de Hirsch [by] Samuel J. Lee. New York, T. Yoseloff [1970] 313 p. port. 22 cm. [DS135.G5H52] 79-88281 ISBN 0-498-07378-5 8.50
1. Hirsch, Moritz, Freiherr auf Gereuth, 1831-1896. 2. Jews—History—1789-1945. I. Title.

*Hirsch, Phil,

*HIRSCH, Phil, ed. 920.073
The Kennedy courage, ed. by Phil Hirsch, Edward Hymoff. New York, Pyramid [c.1965] 128p. 18cm. (X-1238) .60 pap.,
I. Title.

Hirschmann, Ira Arthur,

HIRSCHMANN, Ira Arthur, 1902- 923.873 B
Caution to the winds. New York, D. McKay Co. [1962] 312 p. 21 cm. Autobiographical. [CT275.H6248A3] 62-20006
I. Title.

Hirschmann, Maria Anne.

HIRSCHMANN, Maria Anne. 248'.2'0924 B
Please don't shoot! : I'm already wounded : the story of a heartbreak and a ministry / Maria Anne Hirschmann. Wheaton, Ill. : Tyndal House Publishers, 1979. 149 p. ; 21 cm. [BX6193.H54A35] 78-58744 ISBN 0-8423-4837-9 : 3.95
1. Hirschmann, Maria Anne. 2. Seventh-Day Adventists—United States—Biography. I. Title.

Hirschvogel, Augustin, 1503-1553.

SCHWARZ, Karl, 1885- 741'.092'4
Augustin Hirschvogel. New York, Collectors Edition [1971] 2 v. illus. 26 cm. "The text volume [(in German)] is a reprint of the 1917 Berlin edition, pp. i-xi and 1-215. All the works illustrated in the Berlin edition are to be found in the plate volume accompanying this new edition." Plate volume contains new English text by B. A. Rifkin. Vol. 2 has title: Plates accompanying Augustin Hirschvogel. Bibliography: v. 1, p. [209]-215. [NC251.H5S3 1971] 741.9'43 78-130958 ISBN 0-87681-052-0
1. Hirschvogel, Augustin, 1503-1553.

Hirshberg, Albert, 1909-

GOWDY, Curtis 791.440924
Cowboy at the mike [by] Curt Gowdy with Al Hirshberg. Garden City, N.Y., Doubleday [c.]1966. 213p. 22cm. [PN4874.G56A3] 64-13818 4.50
1. Hirshberg, Albert, 1909- I. Title.

Hisle, Larry.

*GUTMAN, Bill. 796.357'092'2 [B]
Grand slammers : Rice, Luzinski, Foster, Hisle / by Bill Gutman. New York : Tempo Books, 1979. 182p. ; 18 cm. [GV865] ISBN 0-448-17344-1 pbk. : 1.50
1. Rice, Jim. 2. Luzinski, Greg. 3. Hisle, Larry. 4. Foster, George. 5. Baseball players — United States — Biography. I. Title.

Hiss, Alger.

CHAMBERS, Whittaker. 351.74
Witness. New York, Random House [1952] 808 p. 22 cm. Autobiographical. [E743.5.C47] 364.13* 52-5149
1. Hiss, Alger. 2. Communism—United States—1917- I. Title.

HISS, Anthony. 364.1'31'0924 B
Laughing last : Alger Hiss / by Tony Hiss. Boston : Houghton Mifflin, 1977. 194 p. ; 22 cm. [E748.H59H57] 76-49940 ISBN 0-395-24899-X : 8.95
1. Hiss, Alger. 2. United States. Department of State—Officials and employees—Biography. 3. Communism—United States—1917- I. Title. BIP

SMITH, John Chabot. 364.1'31'0924
Alger Hiss : the true story / John Chabot Smith. New York : Penguin Books, 1977. xii, 495 p., [11] leaves of plates : ill. ; 20 cm. Includes index. Bibliography: p. 453-458. [E748.H59S6 1977] 76-49973 ISBN 0-14-004427-2 pbk. : 2.95
1. Hiss, Alger. 2. United States. Department of State—Officials and employees—Biography. 3. Communism—United States—1917- BIP

ZELIGS, Meyer A. 973.918
Friendship and fratricide; an analysis of Whittaker Chambers and Alger Hiss, by Meyer A. Zeligs. New York, Viking Press [1967] xiv, 476 p. illus., facsims., ports. 25 cm. Bibliography: p. 451-464. [E743.5.H55Z4] 66-23822
1. Hiss, Alger. 2. Chambers, Whittaker. I. Title.

Historians.

HALPERIN, Samuel William, ed. 928
Some 20th-century historians; essays on eminent Europeans. Contributors James L. Cate, others. [Chicago] University of Chicago Press [c.1961] xxiv, 298p. Bibl. 61-5608 5.95
1. Historians. 2. Schmitt, Bernadotte Everly, 1886- I. Title.

Historians, American.

CUNLIFFE, Marcus. 973'.072'073
Pastmasters; some essays on American historians. Edited by Marcus Cunliffe and Robin W. Winks. [1st ed.] New York, Harper & Row [1969] xv, 492 p. 22 cm. Bibliographical references included in "Appendix" (p. 409-477) [E175.45.C8] 77-81380 10.00
1. Historians, American. I. Winks, Robin W., joint author. II. Title. **BIP**

Historians, British.

LAWRENCE, Eugene, 1823-1894. 942'.007'2024
The lives of the British historians. Freeport, N.Y., Books for Libraries Press [1973] p. (Essay index reprint series) Reprint of the 1855 ed. [DA3.A1L4 1973] 72-14122 ISBN 0-518-10016-2
1. Historians, British. I. Title.

Historians—Czechoslovak Republic.

LUTZOW, Franz Heinrich Hieronymus Valentin, Graf von, 1849-1916. 914.37'1'03072022
Lectures on the historians of Bohemia, by the Count Lutzow. New York, B. Blom, 1971. vii, 120 p. 22 cm. (Ilchester lectures, 1904) [DB203.A4L83 1971] 72-173174
1. Historians—Czechoslovak Republic. I. Title. II. Series. **BIP**

Historians. English.

ANGUS-BUTTERWORTH LIONEL MILNER 928.2
Ten master historians. [dist. Chester Springs, Pa., Dufour, c.1961] 182p. illus. 61-65398 5.95
1. Historians. English. I. Title.

BOUCHER, Sharon. 922.673
Luther Warren, man of prayer and power. Illustrated by Stanley Dunlap, Jr. Washington, Review and Herald Pub. Association [1959] 191p. illus. 22cm. [BX6193.W3B6] 59-3746
I. Warren, Luther Willis 1864- II. Title.

CLARKE, Martin Lowther 928.2
George Grote, a biography. [Dist. New York, Oxford, c.]1962. 196p. illus. 23cm. Bibl. 62-6655 5.60
I. Grote, George, 1794-1871. II. Title.

Historians—Great Britain.

BELL, Henry Esmond 342.420924
Maitland; a critical examination and assessment. Cambridge, Mass., Harvard [c.] 1965. 150p. 23cm. Bibl. 65-25077 4.00
I. Maitland, Frederick William, 1850-1906. II. Title. **BIP**

SAKLATVALA, Beram. 941.01'07'2022
Dark Age Britain; some sources of history [by] Henry Marsh. [Hamden, Conn.] Archon Books, 1970. 221 p. facsims., maps. 23 cm. Includes bibliographical references. [DA3.A1S24 1970b] 76-20245 ISBN 0-208-01153-6
1. Historians—Great Britain. 2. Great Britain—History—To 1066. I. Title.

Historians—United States—Biography.

CUNLIFFE, Marcus. 973'.07'2022 B
Pastmasters : some essays on American historians / edited by Marcus Cunliffe and Robin W. Winks. Westport, Conn. : Greenwood Press, 1979, c1969. xv, 492 p. ; 22 cm. Reprint of the ed. published by Harper & Row, New York. Includes bibliographies and index. [E175.45.C8 1979] 78-27918 ISBN 0-313-20938-3 lib. bdg. : 29.75
1. Historians—United States—Biography. I. Winks, Robin W., joint author. II. Title.

Historians—United States—Biography—Juvenile literature.

SIGNIFICANT 973'.07'2022 B
American historians and educators. Chicago : Childrens Press, [1976] p. cm. Includes index. Brief biographies of 163 prominent American historians and educators arranged in chronological and alphabetical order. [E175.45.S47] 920 75-20690 ISBN 0-516-05301-9 : 6.95
1. Historians—United States—Biography—Juvenile literature. 2. Educators—United States—Biography—Juvenile literature. I. Title: Historians and educators.

Historic buildings—England—London.

HALL, Martin. 942.1'00992 B
The blue plaque guide to London homes / [by] Martin Hall. London : Queen Anne Press, 1976. 159 p. : ill., facsims., ports. ; 25 cm. Includes index. Bibliography: p. 153. [DA689.H48H34 1976] 76-372190 ISBN 0-362-00287-8 : £5.95
1. Historic buildings—England—London. 2. London—Dwellings. 3. England—Biography. I. Title.

Historiography.

SCHOULER, James, 1839-1920. 907'.2'024 B
Historical briefs. With a biography. Freeport, N.Y., Books for Libraries Press [1972] 310 p. port. 22 cm. (Essay index reprint series) Reprint of the 1896 ed. [E175.S4 1972] 72-4586 ISBN 0-8369-2974-8 11.75
1. Historiography. 2. United States—Historiography. I. Title. **BIP**

History—Biog.

SCHU, Pierre 909.00922
The world of great men; history told through the lives of the men who made it. / Illus. by Dorothy Koch. North Easton, Mass., Holy Cross Pr. [1967] 134p. ports. 24cm. [D33.S3] 67-25217 3.50
1. History—Biog. I. Title.

History, Modern—19th century—Biography.

CONN, Nathan A. 920.02
Modern prophets, true and false, by Nathan A. Conn. [1st ed.] New York, Exposition Press [1967] 113 p. 21 cm. Bibliography: p. [111]-113. [D352.5.C6] 67-3276
1. History, Modern—19th century—Biography. 2. History, Modern—20th century—Biography. I. Title.

Hitch, Henry Charles, 1884-1921.

GREEN, Donald Edward, 1936- 976.6'135'050924 B
Panhandle pioneer : Henry C. Hitch, his ranch, and his family / by Donald E. Green. 1st ed. Norman : Published for the Oklahoma Heritage Association by the University of Oklahoma Press, c1979. xvii, 294 p. : ill. ; 22 cm. (Oklahoma trackmaker series ; [v. 7]) Includes index. Bibliography: p. 269-277. [F702.T4H574] 78-21390 ISBN 0-8061-1529-7 : 9.75
1. Hitch, Henry Charles, 1884-1921. 2. Ranch life—Oklahoma—Texas Co. 3. Texas Co., Okla.—Biography. 4. Pioneers—Oklahoma—Texas Co.—Biography. I. Title. II. Series. **BIP**

Hitchcock, Alfred Joseph, 1899-

TAYLOR, John Russell. 791.43'0233'0924 B
Hitch : the life and times of Alred Hitchcock. / John Russell Taylor. 1st American ed. New York : Berkley Publishing Corp., 1979, c1978. 322 p. : ill. ; 18 cm. [PN1998.A3H567] ISBN 0-425-04436-X pbk. : 2.75
1. Hitchcock, Alfred Joseph, 1899- 2. Moving-picture producers and directors — Great Britain — Biography. I. Title.
L.C. card no. for 1978 Pantheon ed.: 78-53501

TAYLOR, John Russell. 791.43'0233'0924 B
Hitch : the life and times of Alfred Hitchcock / by John Russell Taylor. 1st American ed. New York : Pantheon Books, c1978. 320 p., [8] leaves of plates : ill. ; 22 cm. Includes index. [PN1998.A3H567 1978] 78-53501 ISBN 0-394-49996-4 : 10.00
1. Hitchcock, Alfred Joseph, 1899- 2. Moving-picture producers and directors—Great Britain—Biography. I. Title. **BIP**

Hitchcock, Ethan Allen, 1798-1870.

COHEN, I. Bernard, 1914- 540.1
Ethan Allen Hitchcock, soldier, humanitarian, scholar, discoverer of the "true subject" of the hermetic art. Worcester, Mass., The Society, 1952. 30-136 p. 25 cm. At head of title: American Antiquarian Society. Includes a "facsimile reprint of the sale catalogue of Hitchcock's library" (p. 93-116) "Hitchcock's major publications": p. 117-122. "Bibliography and guide to further reading": p. 123-129. "Reprinted from the Proceedings of the American Antiquarian Society for April 1951." [QD24.H5C6 1952] 52-36583
1. Hitchcock, Ethan Allen, 1798-1870. 2. Alchemy—Bibl.—Catalogs. I. Title.

Hitchcock, Lambert, 1795-1852.

KENNEY, John Tarrant. 338.7'68'41
The Hitchcock chair; the story of a Connecticut Yankee—L. Hitchcock of Hitchcocks-ville—and an account of the restoration of his 19th-century manufactory. [1st ed.] New York, C. N. Potter; distributed by Crown Publishers [1971] x, 339 p. illus. 29 cm. Bibliography: p. 333-334. [NK2439.H5K4 1971] 79-150696 12.50
1. Hitchcock, Lambert, 1795-1852. I. Title.

Hitler, Adolf, 1889-1945.

BULLOCK, Alan Louis Charles. 923.143
Hitler; a study in tyranny. New York, Harper [1952] 776p. illus. 23cm. Includes bibliography. [DD247.H5B85 1952a] 52-12040
1. Hitler, Adolf, 1889- I. Title.

BULLOCK, Alan Louis Charles 923.143
Hitler, a study of tyranny. Completely rev. ed. [Harmondsworth, Eng.] Penguin Books [1962] 848 . illus. 18 cm. (Pelican books, A564) Includes bibliography. [DD247.H5B85] 63-5065
1. Hitler, Adolf, 1880-1945. I. Title.

FEST, Joachim C., 1926- 943.086'092'4 B
Hitler [by] Joachim C. Fest. Translated from the German by Richard and Clara Winston. [1st ed.] New York, Harcourt Brace Jovanovich [1974] xiii, 844 p. illus. 24 cm. "A Helen and Kurt Wolff book." Bibliography: p. 817-829. [DD247.H5F4713] 73-18154 ISBN 0-15-141650-8 15.00
1. Hitler, Adolf, 1889-1945.

HITLER, Adolf, 1889- 923.143
Secret conversations, 1941-1944 [translated by Norman Cameron and R. H. Stevens] With an introductory essay on The mind of Adolf Hitler, by H. R. Trevor-Roper. New York, Farrar, Straus and Young [1953] 597p. 22cm. London ed. (Weidenfeld and Nicolson) has title: Table talk, 1941-1944. 'The original Bormann-Vermerke ... translated in full.' [DD247.H5A685 1953a] 53-9116
I. Title.

HITLER, Adolf, 1889- 923.143
Secret conversations, 1941-1944 [tr. from German by Norman Cameron, R.H.Stevens]Introductory essay on The mind of Adolph Hitler, by R.Trevor-Roper. [New York.] New American Lib. [1961, c. 1953] 672p. (Signet T20151) .75 pap.,
I. Title.

JENKS, William Alexander 923.143
Vienna and the young Hitler. New York, Columbia University Press, [c.] 1960. 252p. (4p. bibl.) 24cm. 60-5285 5.00
1. Hitler, Adolf—1889-1945. 2. Vienna—Soc. condit. 3. Vienna—Intellectual life. I. Title. **BIP**

KUBIZEK, August. 923.143
The young Hitler I knew. Translated from the German by E. V. Anderson; with an introd. by H. R. Trevor-Roper. Boston, Houghton Mifflin, 1955 [c1954] 296p. illus. 22cm. Translation of Adolf Hitler, mein Jugendfreund. [DD247.H5K813 1955] 55-5301
1. Hitler, Adolf, I. Title.

KUBIZEK, August. 943.086'092'4 B
The young Hitler I knew / by August Kubizek ; translated from the German by E. V. Anderson ; with an introd. by H. R. Trevor-Roper. Westport, Conn. : Greenwood Press, 1976, c1954. xv, 298 p., [11] leaves of plates : ill. ; 23 cm. Translation of Adolf Hitler, mein Jugendfreund. Reprint of the ed. published by Houghton Mifflin, Boston. [DD247.H5K813 1976] 75-38385 ISBN 0-8371-8664-1 lib. bdg. : 21.00
1. Hitler, Adolf, 1889-1945. I. Title. **BIP**

LANGER, William Charles, 1899- 943.086'092'4 [B]
The mind of Adolf Hitler; the secret wartime report [by] Walter C. Langer. Foreword by William L. Langer. Afterword by Robert G. L. Waite. [New York] New American Lib. [1973, c.1972] 286 p. illus. 18 cm. (Signet, W5523) Originally prepared in 1943 for the U.S. office of Strategic Services; know in that office as The Hitler source-book. Bibliography: p. 257-279. [DD247.H5L29] 1.50 (pbk.)
1. Hitler, Adolf, 1889-1945. I. United States. Office of Strategic Services. II. Title. III. Title: The Hitler source-book.
L.C. card no. for the hardbound edition: 72-86336.

MASER, Werner, 1922- 943.086'092'4 B
Hitler: legend, myth & reality. Translated from the German by Peter and Betty Ross. [1st U.S. ed.] New York, Harper & Row [1973] viii, 433 p. illus. 25 cm. Translation of Adolf Hitler. Bibliography: p. [400]-422. [DD247.H5M28413 1973] 72-9136 ISBN 0-06-012831-3 12.50
1. Hitler, Adolf, 1889-1945.

Hitler, Adolf, 1889-1945.

BULLOCK, Alan Louis Charles. 923.143
Hitler; a study in tyranny. New York,

Harper [1952] 776 p. illus. 23 cm. Includes bibliography. [DD247.H5B85 1952] 52-12040
1. Hitler, Adolf, 1889-1945. BIP

TREVOR-ROPER, Hugh Redwald 923.143
The last days of Hitler. 3d ed., with a new pref. by the author. New York, Berkley [1960] 318 p. illus. 18 cm. [DD247.H5T7 1962] 62-17496
1. Hitler, Adolf, 1889-1945. I. Title.

WALDMAN, Morris David, 1879- 923.143
Sieg heil! the story of Adolf Hitler. Introd. by George N. Shuster. Dobbs Ferry, N.Y., Oceans. Publications, 1962. 318 p. 22 cm. [DD247.H5W28] 62-11854
I. Title.

Hitler, Adolf, 1889-1945.

APPEL, Benjamin, 1907- 943.086
Hitler, from power to ruin. New York, Grosset & Dunlap [1964] 91 p. illus., ports. 27 cm. [DD247.H5A84] 64-24442
1. Hitler, Adolf, 1889-1945. 2. National socialism. I. Title.

APPEL, Benjamin, 1907- 943.086
Hitler, from power to ruin. New York, Grosset & Dunlap [1964] 91 p. illus., ports. 27 cm. Records the background and twelve-year history of the Third Reich, from Hitler's legal ascendency to power in 1933 to the defeat of the Axis powers in 1945. [DD247.H5A84] AC 68
1. Hitler, Adolf, 1889-1945. 2. National socialism. I. Title.

BREITING, Richard, 1882-1937. 943.086'0924 B
Secret conversations with Hitler; the two newly-discovered 1931 interviews. Edited by Edouard Calic. With a foreword by Golo Mann. Translated from the German by Richard Barry. [1st American ed.] New York, John Day Co. [1971] 191 p. 21 cm. "Transcript of Richard Breiting's shorthand notes": p. 17-93. Translation of Ohne Maske. Bibliography: p. 180-186. [DD247.H5B723 1971] 79-155022 6.95
1. Hitler, Adolf, 1889-1945. I. Hitler, Adolf, 1889-1945. II. Calic, Edouard, ed. III. Title.

BULLOCK, Alan Louis Charles. 923.143
Hitler, a study in tyranny. Authorized abridgment. New York, Bantam Books [1958] 415p. 18cm. (Bantam books, F1896/6) [DD247.H5B86] 58-11780
1. Hitler, Adolf, 1889-1945. I. Title.

BULLOCK, Alan Louis Charles. 923.143
Hitler, a study in tyranny. Rev. ed. New York, Harper [1960] 776 p. illus. 22 cm. Includes bibliography. [DD247.H5B85 1960] 60-13434
1. Hitler, Adolf, 1889-1945.

BULLOCK, Alan Louis Charles 923.143
Hitler, a study in tyranny. Completed rev. ed. New York, Harper [1964, c.1962] 848p. illus., ports., maps, geneal. table. 22cm. Bibl. 63-21045 8.95
1. Hitler, Adolf, 1889-1945. I. Title. II. Title: A study in tyranny.

BULLOCK, Alan Louis Charles, Sir. 923.143
Hitler, a study in tyranny. Completely rev. ed. [Harmondsworth, Eng.] Penguin Books [1962] 848 p. illus. 18 cm. (Pelican books, A564) Includes bibliography. [DD247.H5B85 1962] 63-5065
1. Hitler, Adolf, 1889-1945.

BULLOCK, Alan Louis Charles, Sir. 943.086'0924 B
Hitler, a study in tyranny, by Alan Bullock. Abridged ed. New York, Harper & Row [1971] ix, 489 p. 19 cm. (Perennial library, P216) [DD247.H5B86 1971] 79-159640 ISBN 0-06-080216-2 (pbk) 1.50 (pbk)
1. Hitler, Adolf, 1889-1945. I. Title.

CARR, William, 1921- 943.086'092'4 B
Hitler : a study in personality and politics / William Carr. New York : St. Martin's Press, 1979. x, 200 p. ; 24 cm. Includes index. Bibliography: p. 182-189. [DD247.H5C32155 1979] 78-10354 ISBN 0-312-38818-7 : 18.50
1. Hitler, Adolf, 1889-1945. 2. Heads of state—Germany—Biography. 3. Germany—History—1933-1945. BIP

DAVIDSON, Eugene, 1902- 943.086'092'4 B
The making of Adolf Hitler / by Eugene Davidson. New York : Macmillan, c1977. xi, 408 p., [16] leaves of plates : ill. ; 25 cm. Includes index. Bibliography: p. 389-396. [DD247.H5D38] 77-6761 ISBN 0-02-529700-7 : 15.95
1. Hitler, Adolf, 1889-1945. 2. Statesmen—Germany—Biography. I. Title.

DIETRICH, Otto, 1897-1952. 923.143
Hitler. Translated by Richard and Clara Winston. Chicago, H. Regnery Co., 1955. 277 p. 22 cm. Translation of 12 Jahre mit Hitler. [DD247.H5D565] 55-10826
1. Hitler, Adolf, 1889-1945.

ELLIOTT, Brendan John. 943.086
Hitler and Germany. Foreword by William J. Jacobs. New York, McGraw-Hill [1968] viii, 134 p. illus., maps, ports. 24 cm. Bibliography: p. [128]-129. Chronicles the rise of Hitler from a poor worker in Vienna to the powerful dictator of Germany who influenced the course of world history. [DD256.5.E43 1968] AC 68
1. Hitler, Adolf, 1889-1945. 2. World War, 1939-1945—Germany. I. Title.

FEST, Joachim C., 1926- 943.086'092'4 B
Hitler / Joachim C. Fest ; translated from the German by Richard and Clara Winston. New York : Vintage Books, 1975, c1974. vii, 844 p. ; 21 cm. Reprint of the ed. published by Harcourt Brace Jovanovich, New York. Includes index. Bibliography: p. 817-829. [DD247.H5F4713 1975] 75-8975 ISBN 0-394-71530-6 pbk. : 5.95
1. Hitler, Adolf, 1889-1945.

HEIDEN, Konrad, 1901-1966. 943.086'092'4 B
Hitler : a biography / by Konrad Heiden. New York : AMS Press, [1975] viii, 416 p. ; 18 cm. Reprint of the 1936 ed. published by Constable, London. [DD247.H5H34 1975] 79-180665 ISBN 0-404-56401-1 : 20.00
1. Hitler, Adolf, 1889-1945. 2. Nationalsozialistische Deutsche Arbeiter-Partei. 3. Germany—Politics and government—1918-1933. 4. Germany—Politics and government—1933-1945. I. Title. BIP

HERZSTEIN, Robert Edwin. 943.086'092'4 B
Adolf Hitler and the German trauma, 1913-1945; an interpretation of the Nazi phenomenon New York, Putnam [1974] xiv, 294 p. illus. 22 cm. Bibliography: p. 271-283. [DD247.H5H3685] 73-87193 ISBN 0-399-11286-3 7.95
1. Hitler, Adolf, 1889-1945. 2. National socialism—History. 3. Germany—Politics and government—1933-1945. I. Title.

HITLER'S war machine 940.54'43 / [editor Simon Goodenough ; maps Richard Natkiel ; drawings John W. Wood]. London : Manlyn, 1976. 248 p. : ill. (some col.), map, col. plans, ports. (some col.) ; 31 cm. (A Salamander book) Includes bibliographies and index. [D757.1.H58] 76-376159 ISBN 0-600-34500-9 : £4.95
1. Hitler, Adolf, 1889-1945. 2. Germany—Armed Forces. 3. World War, 1939-1945—Germany. 4. Germany—History—1933-1945. 5. Heads of State—Germany—Biography. I. Goodenough, Simon.

INFIELD, Glenn B. 943.086'092'4 B
Eva and Adolf / Glenn B. Infield. New York : Grosset & Dunlap, [1974] x, 330 p., [12] leaves of plates : ill. ; 24 cm. Errata slip inserted. Includes index. Bibliography: p. [323]-324. [DD247.H5I54] 73-22735 10.00
1. Hitler, Adolf, 1889-1945. 2. Braun, Eva. I. Title.

INFIELD, Glenn B. 943.086'092'4 B
Hitler's secret life : the mysteries of the Eagle's Nest / by Glenn B. Infield. Briarcliff Manor, N.Y. : Stein & Day, c1979. p. cm. Includes index. Bibliography: p. [DD247.H5I543] 79-65109 ISBN 0-8128-2674-4 : 12.95
1. Hitler, Adolf, 1889-1945. 2. Heads of state—Germany—Biography. I. Title.

INFIELD, Glenn B. 943.086'092'2 B
The private lives of Eva & Adolf : adapted from Eva and Adolf / by Glenn B. Infield. New York : Grosset & Dunlap, c1978. 137 p. : ill. ; 28 cm. Includes index. [DD247.H5I55] 77-95180 ISBN 0-448-14716-5 : 15.95 ISBN 0-448-14730-0 pbk. : 6.95
1. Hitler, Adolf, 1889-1945. 2. Braun, Eva. 3. Heads of state—Germany—Biography. I. Title.

IRVING, David John Cawdell, 1938- 940.54'0943
Hitler's war / David Irving. New York : Viking Press, 1977. xxxiii, 926 p. : maps (on lining papers) ; 25 cm. Includes index. Bibliography: p. 824-828. [D757.I69 1977] 76-18195 ISBN 0-670-37412-1 : 17.50
1. Hitler, Adolf, 1889-1945. 2. World War, 1939-1945—Germany. 3. Heads of state—Germany—Biography. I. Title.

IRVING, David John Cawdell, 1938- 940.54'0943
Hitler's war / David Irving. New York : Viking Press, 1977. xxxiii, 926 p. : maps (on lining papers) ; 25 cm. Includes index. Bibliography: p. 824-828. [D757.I69 1977] 76-18195 ISBN 0-670-37412-1 : 17.50
1. Hitler, Adolf, 1889-1945. 2. World War, 1939-1945—Germany. 3. Heads of state—Germany—Biography. I. Title. BIP

JENKS, William Alexander, 1918- 943.086'092'4 B
Vienna and the young Hitler / by William A. Jenks. New York : Octagon Books, 1976, c1960. viii, 252 p. ; 24 cm. Reprint of the ed. published by Columbia University Press, New York. Includes index. Bibliography: p. [237]-241. [DD247.H5J38 1976] 75-42454 ISBN 0-374-94206-4 lib.bdg. : 12.50
1. Hitler, Adolf, 1889-1945. 2. Vienna—Social conditions. 3. Vienna—Intellectual life. I. Title.

JETZINGER, Franz. 943.08'4'0924 B
Hitler's youth / Franz Jetzinger ; translated from the German by Lawrence Wilson ; foreword by Alan Bullock. Westport, Conn. : Greenwood Press, 1976. 200 p., [1] leaf of plates : port. ; 23 cm. Translation of Hitlers Jugend. Reprint of the 1958 ed. published by Hutchinson, London. Includes index. Bibliography: p. 192-193. [DD247.H5J453 1976] 75-36096 ISBN 0-8371-8617-X : 14.25
1. Hitler, Adolf, 1889-1945. 2. Heads of state—Germany—Biography. I. Title. BIP

KATZ, Robert, 1933- 943.0860924 (B)
Adolf Hitler; a biography, by Robert Holland. Edited by Edna Goldwater. New York, Distributed by Monarch Press [c1966] 116 p. 22 cm. (Monarch notes and study guides, 896-1) Bibliography: p. 111-112. [[DD247.H5]] 66-27294 CD
1. Hitler, Adolf, 1889-1945. I. Title.

LANGER, Walter Charles, 1899- 943.086'092'4 B
The mind of Adolf Hitler; the secret wartime report [by] Walter C. Langer. Foreword by William L. Langer. Afterword by Robert G. L. Waite. New York, Basic Books [1972] ix, 269 p. illus. 24 cm. Originally prepared in 1943 for the U.S. Office of Strategic Services; known in that office as The Hitler source-book. Bibliography: p. 250-263. [DD247.H5L29] 72-86336 ISBN 0-465-04620-7 10.00
1. Hitler, Adolf, 1889-1945. I. United States. Office of Strategic Services. II. Title. III. Title: The Hitler source-book.

LEWIS, Wyndham, 1882-1957. 320.5'33
Hitler. New York, Gordon Press, 1972. ix, 202 p. illus. 20 cm. Reprint of the 1931 ed. published by Chatto & Windus, London. [DD253.L43 1972] 72-82189 ISBN 0-87968-005-9 15.00
1. Hitler, Adolf, 1889-1945. 2. National socialism.

PAYNE, Pierre Stephen Robert, 1911- 943.086'092'4 B
The life and death of Adolf Hitler [by] Robert Payne. New York, Praeger [1973] xiii, 623 p. 25 cm. Bibliography: p. 607-612. [DD247.H5P29] 72-92891 12.95
1. Hitler, Adolf, 1889-1945. I. Title. BIP

SCHRAMM, Percy Ernst, 1894-1970. 943.086'0924 B
Hitler: the man and the military leader. Translated, edited, and with an introd. by Donald S. Detwiler. Chicago, Quadrangle Books, 1971. viii, 214 p. 22 cm. (A Quadrangle paperback original, QP 310) Portions of this book were first published in 1963 and 1965 in Hitlers Tischgesprache im Fuhrerhauptquartier 1941-1942 by H. Picker, edited by P. E. Schramm, et al.; and in 1961 in Kriegstagebuch des Oberkommandos der Wehrmacht (Wehrmachtfuhrungsstab) 1940-1945, introduced and edited by P. E. Schramm. Includes bibliographical references. [DD247.H5S34 1971] 72-78316 ISBN 0-8129-0166-5
1. Hitler, Adolf, 1889-1945. 2. Germany—Politics and government—1933-1945.

SMITH, Bradley F 943.08'4'0924
Adolf Hitler; his family, childhood, and youth, by Bradley F. Smith. Stanford, Calif., Hoover Institution on War, Revolution, and Peace [1967] 180 p. ports., geneal. table. 24 cm. (Hoover Institution publications) Bibliography: p. [168]-176. [DD247.H5S55] 66-25727
1. Hitler, Adolf, 1889-1945. I. Title. BIP

SMITH, Bradley F. 943.08'4'0924
Adolf Hitler; his family, childhood, and youth, by Bradley F. Smith. Stanford, Calif., Hoover Institution on War, Revolution, and Peace [1967] 180 p. ports., geneal. table. 24 cm. (Hoover Institution publications) Bibliography: p. [168]-176. [DD247.H5S55] 66-25727
1. Hitler, Adolf, 1889-1945. I. Series: Stanford University. Hoover Institution on War, Revolution, and Peace. Publications

SMITH, Gene. 943.086'092'4 B
The horns of the moon; a short biography of Adolf Hitler. New York, Charterhouse [1974, c1973] xi, 209 p. illus. 21 cm. Includes bibliographical references. [DD247.H5S56 1974] 73-84081 5.95
1. Hitler, Adolf, 1889-1945. I. Title. BIP

SNYDER, Louis Leo, 1907- 923.143
Hitler and Nazism. New York, F. Watts [1961] 182 p. illus. 22 cm. [DD247.H5S59] 61-9593
1. Hitler, Adolf, 1889-1945. 2. Germany—History—1933-1945.

SPEER, Albert, 1905- 943.086'0924 B
Inside the Third Reich: memoirs, Translated from the German by Richard and Clara Winston. Introd. by Eugene Davidson. [New York] Macmillan [1970] xviii, 596 p. illus., facsims., plans, ports. 24 cm. Translation of Erinnerungen. Includes bibliographical references. [DD247.S63A313 1970] 70-119132
1. Hitler, Adolf, 1889-1945. 2. Germany—Politics and government—1933-1945. I. Title.

TOLAND, John. 943.086'092'4 B
Adolf Hitler / by John Toland. 1st ed. Garden City, N.Y. : Doubleday, 1976. xx, 1035 p., [32] leaves of plates : ill. ; 25 cm. Includes index. Bibliography: p. [906]-923. [DD247.H5T56] 74-25126 ISBN 0-385-03724-4 : 17.50
1. Hitler, Adolf, 1889-1945. BIP

TREVOR-ROPER, Hugh Redwald 923.143
The last days of Hitler [New ed. New York] Berkeley Publishing Co. [1960, c.1947] 249p. (Berkely Medallion S485) .75 pap.,
1. Hitler, Adolf, 1889-1945. I. Title.

TREVOR-ROPER, Hugh Redwald. 923.143
The last days of Hitler. 3d ed. London, Macmillan; New York, St. Martin's Press, 1956. 283p. illus. 20cm. [DD247.H5T7 1956] 57-3490
1. Hitler, Adolf, 1889-1945. I. Title.

TREVOR-ROPER, Hugh Redwald. 923.143
The last days of Hitler. 3d ed., with a new pref. by the author. New York, Collier

Books [1962] 318 p. illus. 18 cm. (Collier books, AS369V) [DD247.H5T7] 62-17496
1. Hitler, Adolf, 1889-1945. I. Title. BIP

WAITE, Robert George Leeson, 1919- 443.086'092'4 B
The psychopathic god : Adolf Hitler / Robert G. L. Waite. New York : Basic Books, c1977. xx, 482 p., [4] leaves of plates : ill. ; 24 cm. Includes bibliographical references and index. [DD247.H5W23] 76-43484 ISBN 0-465-06743-3 : 15.95
1. Hitler, Adolf, 1889-1945. 2. Heads of state—Germany—Biography. I. Title. BIP

WALDMAN, Morris David, 1879- 923.143
Sieg heil!the story of Adolph Hitler. Introd. by George N. Shuster. Dobbs Ferry, N.Y., Oceana [c.] 1962. 318p. 22cm. Bibl. 62-11854 6.00
1. Hitler, Adolf, 1889-1945. I. Title.

WOLFE, Burton H. 943.086'0924 B
Hitler and the Nazis [by] Burton H. Wolfe. New York, Putnam [1970] 253 p. 23 cm. Bibliography: p. 245-246. Recounts Hitler's rise from obscurity to power as head of the Nazi Party and the German nation. [DD247.H5W58 1970] 70-102394 3.96
1. Hitler, Adolf, 1889-1945. 2. Nationalsozialistische Deutsche Arbeiter-Partei—History. 3. Germany—Politics and government—1933-1945. I. Title. BIP

Hitler, Adolf, 1889-1945—Addresses, essays, lectures.

CIGARETTEN-BILDERDIENST, G.m.b.H. 943.086'092'4 B
Adolf Hitler, pictures from the life of the Fuhrer, 1931-1935 / encomium, Hermann Goring ; foreword, Joseph Goebbels ; text, Joseph Goebbels ... [et al.] ; translated from the 1936 edition, Carl Underhill Quinn ; introd. and commentary, Julius Rosenthal. New York : Peebles Press ; Indianapolis : distributed by Bobbs Merrill, 1978. xiv, 145 p. : ill. ; 29 cm. Translation of Adolf Hitler, Bilder aus dem Leben des Fuhrers. [DD247.H5C5 1978] 77-20715 ISBN 0-85690-065-6 : 14.95
1. Hitler, Adolf, 1889-1945—Addresses, essays, lectures. 2. Heads of state—Germany—Biography—Addresses, essays, lectures. I. Goebbels, Joseph, 1897-1945. II. Quinn, Carl Underhill. III. Title.

Hitler, Adolf, 1889-1945—Bibliography.

PHILLIPS, Leona. 016.943086'092'4
Adolf Hitler and the Third Reich : an annotated bibliography / by Leona R. Phillips. New York : Gordon Press, 1977 p. cm. (Gordon Press bibliographies for librarians series) [Z8409.6.P47] [DD247.H5] 76-46939 ISBN 0-8490-1355-0 lib.bdg. 39.95
1. Hitler, Adolf, 1889-1945—Bibliography. 2. Germany—History—1933-1945—Bibliography. I. Title.

Hitler, Adolf, 1889-1945—Juvenile literature.

DEVANEY, John. 943.086'092'4 B
Hitler, mad dictator of World War II / by John Devaney. New York : Putnam, c1978. 222 p. : ill. ; 23 cm. Includes index. Traces the life of Adolf Hitler from his youth to his self-destruction in a Berlin bunker. [DD247.H5D4775 1978] 92 77-21057 ISBN 0-399-20627-2 : 7.95
1. Hitler, Adolf, 1889-1945—Juvenile literature. 2. Heads of state—Germany—Biography—Juvenile literature. 3. Germany—Politics and government—1933-1945—Juvenile literature. I. Title.

SHIRER, William Lawrence, 1904- 943.086 J
The rise and fall of Adolf Hitler. New York, Random House [1961] 185 p. illus. 22 cm. (World landmark books [W-47]) [DD247.H5S5] 61-7317
1. Hitler, Adolf, 1889-1945—Juvenile literature. I. Title. BIP

Hitler, Adolf, 1889-1945—Portraits, caricatures, etc.

DAYTON, Eldorous L. 923.143
The secret life of Adolf Hitler. Based on the television documentary film produced for WPIX, inc., by William L. Cooper, Jr. and Walter D. Engels. With text adapted from Eldorous L. Dayton's television script. New York, Citadel Press [c.]1960. unpaged. illus. 26cm. 60-13933 3.95; 1.95 pap.,
1. Hitler, Adolf, 1889-1945—Portraits, caricatures, etc. I. Title.

ADOLF Hitler: faces 943.086'0924
of a dictator. Text and captions by Jochen von Lang. With an introd. by Constantine FitzGibbon. [1st ed.] New York, Harcourt, Brace & World [1969] xiii, [172] p. (chiefly illus., ports.) 30 cm. Translation of Adolf Hitler: Gesichter eines Diktators. [DD247.H5A75853] 68-24392
1. Hitler, Adolf, 1889-1945—Portraits, caricatures, etc. I. Lang, Jochen von.

Ho-chi-Minh, Pres. Democratic Republic of Vietnam, 1894?-1969.

FENN, Charles, Captain. 959.704'092'4 B
Ho Chi Minh; a biographical introduction. New York, Scribner [1973] 144 p. maps. 22 cm. (Leaders of modern thought) Bibliography: p. [139]-140. [DS557.A76H6774 1973b] 72-12153 ISBN 0-684-13348-2 5.95
1. Ho Chi Minh, 1890-1969.

HALBERSTAM, David. 959.7'04'0924 B
Ho. New York, Random House [1971] 118, [1] p. 22 cm. Bibliography: p. [119] [DS557.A782H65 1971b] 77-140708 ISBN 0-394-46275-0 4.95
1. Ho Chi Minh, 1890-1969. BIP

HUYEN, N. Khac. 959.7'04'0924
Vision accomplished? The enigma of Ho Chi Minh [by] N. Khac Huyen. New York, Collier Books [1971] xviii, 377 p. maps. 22 cm. Bibliography: p. [365]-372. [DS557.A76H679 1971] 78-147929 7.95
1. Ho Chi Minh, 1890-1969. I. Title. BIP

LACOUTURE, Jean. 959.7'04'0924 B
Ho Chi Minh; a political biography. Translated from the French by Peter Wiles. Translation edited by Jane Clark Seitz. New York, Vintage Books [1968] 313 p. 19 cm. Bibliographical footnotes. [DS557.A76H68 1968c] 74-2308 1.95
1. Ho Chi Minh, 1890-1969. I. Title.

LACOUTURE, Jean. 959.7'04'0924 B
Ho Chi Minh; a political biography. Translated from the French by Peter Wiles. Translation edited by Jane Clark Seitz. [1st American ed.] New York, Random House [1968] 313 p. 22 cm. Bibliographical footnotes. [DS557.A76H643] 68-14527
1. Ho-chi-Minh, Pres. Democratic Republic of Vietnam, 1894?-1969.

NEUMANN-HODITZ, Reinhold, 1926- 959.704'092'4 B
Portrait of Ho Chi Minh, an illustrated biography. Translated by John Hargreaves. [1st ed. New York] Herder and Herder [1972] 187 p. illus. 21 cm. Translation of Ho Chi Minh in Selbstzeugnissen und Bildokumenten. Bibliography: p. 185. [DS557.A76H68613] 72-2904 ISBN 0-07-073788-6 6.95
1. Ho Chi Minh, 1890-1969. I. Title.

Ho, Hsin-yin, 1517-1579.

DIMBERG, Ronald. 181'.11 B
The sage and society : the life and thought of Ho Hsin-yin / Ronald G. Dimberg. [Honolulu] : University Press of Hawaii, 1974. 175 p. ; 23 cm. (Monograph of the Society for Asian and Comparative Philosophy ; no. 1) Bibliography: p. [157]-171. [PL2698.H56Z63] 74-11085 ISBN 0-8248-0347-7 pbk. : 4.75
1. Ho, Hsin-yin, 1517-1579. 2. Philosophy, Chinese. I. Title. II. Series: Society for Asian and Comparative Philosophy. Monograph of the Society for Asian and Comparative Philosophy ; no. 1. BIP

Hoan, Daniel Webster, 1881-1961.

KERSTEIN, Edward S 1911- 352.077595 (B)
Milwaukee's all-American mayor; portrait of Daniel Webster Hoan [by] Edward S. Kerstein. Englewood Cliffs, N. J., Prentice-Hall [1966] xviii, 237 p. ports. 24 cm. Bibliography: p. 219-220. [F589.M6H65] 66-13187
1. Hoan, Daniel Webster, 1881-1961. I. Title.

Hoard, Edison, 1933- —Juvenile literature.

HOARD, Edison, 1933- 340'.092'4 B
Curse not the darkness, by Edison Hoard, with Michael Reuben. [Chicago, Childrens Press, 1970] 64 p. illus., ports. 19 cm. (Open door books) A black lawyer relates the events in his life that inspired him to become a lawyer and help his people. [KF373.H53A32] 92 73-107497
1. Hoard, Edison, 1933- —Juvenile literature. I. Reuben, Michael. II. Title.

Hobart, Alice Tisdale Nourse,

HOBART, Alice Tisdale Nourse, 1882- 928.1
Gusty's child. [1st ed.] New York, Longmans, Green, 1959. 343 p. 22 cm. [PS3515.O134Z52] 59-12750
I. Title.

Hobbes, Thomas, 1588-1679.

JAMES, David Gwilym, 1905-1968. 192
The life of reason; Hobbes, Locke, Bolingbroke. Freeport, N.Y., Books for Libraries Press [1972] xiii, 272 p. 24 cm. (Biography index reprint series) Reprint of the 1949 ed., which was issued as v. 1 of the author's The English Augustans. [B1131.J3 1972] 76-38378 ISBN 0-8369-8122-7
1. Hobbes, Thomas, 1588-1679. 2. Locke, John, 1632-1704. 3. Bolingbroke, Henry Saint-John, 1st viscount, 1678-1751. I. Title. BIP

REIK, Miriam M., 1938- 192 B
The golden lands of Thomas Hobbes / Miriam M. Reik. Detroit : Wayne State University Press, 1977. 239 p. : ports. ; 24 cm. Includes index. Bibliography: p. 226-234. [B1246.R44] 77-3594 ISBN 0-8143-1574-7 : 15.95
1. Hobbes, Thomas, 1588-1679. 2. Philosophers—England—Biography. I. Title. BIP

ROBERTSON, George Croom, 1842-1892. 192
Hobbes. Cheap ed. Edinburgh, W. Blackwood, 1910. St. Clair Shores, Mich., Scholarly Press, 1970. vii, 240 p. 22 cm. Includes bibliographical references. [B1246.R65 1970] 75-107188
1. Hobbes, Thomas, 1588-1679.

ROBERTSON, George Croom, 1842-1892. 192 B
Hobbes. New York, AMS Press [1971] vii, 240 p. port. 19 cm. Reprint of the 1886 ed., which was issued as v. 10 in the Philosophical classics for English readers series. Includes bibliograpical references. [B1246.R65 1971] 70-137283 ISBN 0-404-05359-9 7.50
1. Hobbes, Thomas, 1588-1679. BIP

STEPHEN, Leslie, Sir 1832-1904. 921.2
Hobbes. [Ann Arbor] Univ. of Michigan Press [1961] 243p. (Ann Arbor paperbacks, AA54) 61-16055 4.40 lib. ed.,
1. Hobbes, Thomas, 1588-1679. I. Title.

TAYLOR, Alfred Edward, 1869-1945. 192 B
Thomas Hobbes. Port Washington, N.Y., Kennikat Press [1970] vii, 127, [1] p. 18 cm. "First published in 1908." "Books useful to the student of Hobbes": p. 127-[128] [B1247.T3 1970] 76-102586
1. Hobbes, Thomas, 1588-1679. BIP

THOMAS Hobbes in his time / 192
edited by Ralph Ross, Herbert W. Schneider, Theodore Waldman. Minneapolis : University of Minnesota Press, [1974, i.e.1975] x, 150 p. ; 23 cm. Includes index. Bibliography: p. 136-139. [B1247.T45 1974] 74-83134 ISBN 0-8166-0727-3 : 7.50
1. Hobbes, Thomas, 1588-1679. I. Ross, Ralph Gilbert, 1911- II. Schneider, Herbert Wallace, 1892- III. Waldman, Theodore. BIP

Hobbs, Anne.

HOBBS, Anne. 371.1'0092'4
Tisha : the story of a young teacher in the Alaska wilderness / as told to Robert Specht. New York : St. Martin's Press, c1976. 358 p. ; 24 cm. [LA2317.H59A37] 75-40789 8.95
1. Hobbs, Anne. 2. Education—Alaska. I. Specht, Robert, 1928- joint author. II. Title.

Hobbs, May, 1938-

HOBBS, May, 1938- 331.4'81'64850924 B
Born to struggle / May Hobbs. 1st American ed. Plainfield, Vt. : Daughters, 1975, c1973. 164 p. ; 22 cm. [HD8393.H55A3 1975] 75-16511 ISBN 0-913780-10-3 pbk. : 3.50
1. Hobbs, May, 1938- 2. London—Social conditions. I. Title. BIP

Hobby, William Pettus, 1878-

CLARK, James Anthony, 1907- 928.273
The tactful Texan: a biography of Governor Will Hobby, by James A. Clark with Weldon Hart. New York, Random House [1958] 211p. illus. 22cm. [F391.H75C5] 58-8764
1. Hobby, William Pettus, 1878- I. Title.

Hobhouse, Charles Edward Henry, Sir, bart., 1862-1941.

HOBHOUSE, Charles Edward Henry, Sir, bart., 1862-1941. 941.083'092'4
Inside Asquith's cabinet : from the diaries of Charles Hobhouse / edited by Edward David. New York : St. Martin's Press, 1978, c1977. x, 295 p., [6] leaves of plates : ill. ; 23 cm. Includes index. [DA566.9.H59A34 1977b] 77-84941 ISBN 0-312-41868-X : 16.95
1. Hobhouse, Charles Edward Henry, Sir, bart., 1862-1941. 2. Oxford and Asquith, Herbert Henry Asquith, 1st Earl of, 1852-1928. 3. Great Britain—Politics and government—1837-1901. 4. Great Britain—Politics and government—1901-1936. 5. Statesmen—Great Britain—Biography. I. David, Edward. II. Title.

Hobhouse, Leonard Trelawney, 1864-1929.

OWEN, John E. 301'.092'4
L. T. Hobhouse, sociologist [by] John E. Owen. Columbus, Ohio State University Press [1975, c1974] xiii, 225 p. 23 cm. (The making of sociology series) Bibliography: p. 215-222. [HM22.G8H68 1975] 74-18457 ISBN 0-8142-0235-7 11.00
1. Hobhouse, Leonard Trelawney, 1864-1929. 2. Sociology—History. I. Title. BIP

Hobhouse, Stephen Henry,

HOBHOUSE, Stephen Henry, 1881- 923.642
The autobiography of Stephen Hobhouse, reformer, pacifist, Christian. Boston, Beacon Press [1952] 216 p. 23 cm. London ed. (J. Clarke) has title: Forty years and an epilogue. [HV28.H614A3] 52-8381
I. Title.

Hobson, Elizabeth Christophers (Kimball)

HOBSON, Elizabeth Christophers (Kimball) 1831-1912. 901.93'4 B
Recollections of a happy life. Freeport,

N.Y., Books for Libraries Press [1972] p. Reprint of the 1914 ed. [CT275.H628A3 1972] 72-8463 ISBN 0-8369-6978-2
I. Title.

Hobson, Joshua, 1810-1876.

CHADWICK, Stanley. 070.4'092'4 B
A bold and faithful journalist : Joshua Hobson, 1810-1876 / [by] Stanley Chadwick. Huddersfield : Kirklees Libraries and Museums Service, 1976. 82 p. : ill., facsims., map, ports. ; 24 cm. At head of title: Centenary memorial. Includes index. Bibliography: p. 79. [PN5123.H54C5] 77-363591 ISBN 0-9502568-3-8 : £1.00
1. Hobson, Joshua, 1810-1876. 2. Journalists—Great Britain—Biography. I. Title.

Hockey.

GILBERT, Rod. 796.9'62'0924
Goal! My life on ice, by Rod Gilbert with Stan Fischler and Hal Bock. [1st ed.] New York, Hawthorn Books [1968] 181 p. plan, ports. 24 cm. A Stuart L. Daniels book. [GV847.G5] 68-30719 4.95
1. Hockey. I. Fischler, Stan, joint author. II. Bock, Hal, joint author. III. Title.

Hockey—Biography.

*BOCK, Hal. 796.9'62'0922 B
Save! Hockey's brave goalies. New York, Avon [1974] 256 p. illus. 18 cm. [GV848.5] ISBN 0-380-00135-7. 1.25 (pbk.)
1. Hockey—Biography. I. Title.

FISCHLER, Stan. 796.9'62'0922 B
Fire on ice; hockey's superstars. Photography [by] Melchior Di Giacomo. Englewood Cliffs, N.J., Prentice-Hall [1974] 143 p. illus. 28 cm. (Reward books) "A Stuart L. Daniels book." [GV848.5.A1F47] 73-7236 ISBN 0-13-317552-9 3.95 (pbk.).
1. Hockey—Biography. I. Di Giacomo, Melchior, illus. II. Title.

FISCHLER, Stan. 796.9'62'0922 B
Heroes of pro hockey. New York, Random House [1971] ix, 141 p. illus., ports. 22 cm. (Pro hockey library, 2) [GV848.5.A1F48] 70-158374 ISBN 0-394-92146-1 (library ed.)
1. Hockey—Biography. I. Title. BIP

FISCHLER, Stan. 796.9'62'0922
Up from the minor leagues of hockey [by] Stan & Shirley Fischler. [Chicago] Cowles Book Co. [1971] xvi, 174 p. illus. 22 cm. [GV848.5.A1F53] 71-163280 5.95
1. Hockey—Biography. I. Fischler, Shirley, joint author. II. Title.

FRAYNE, Trent. 796.9'62'0922 B
Famous hockey players. New York, Dodd, Mead [1973] 160 p. illus. 22 cm. [GV848.5.A1F68] 73-7095 ISBN 0-396-06848-0 4.95
1. Hockey—Biography. I. Title. BIP

FRAYNE, Trent. 796.9'62'0922 B
The mad men of hockey / by Trent Frayne. New York : Dodd, Mead, c1974. 191 p., [8] leaves of plates : ill. ; 24 cm. [GV848.5.A1F72] 75-304579 ISBN 0-396-07060-4 : 8.95
1. Hockey—Biography. I. Title. BIP

HUNT, James R. 796.9'62'0922
The men in the nets [by] Jim Hunt. Chicago, Follett Pub. Co. [1967] 133 p. ports. 21 cm. Contents.Contents.—None but the brave.—Glenn Hall.—Jacques Plante.—Durnan and the Turk.—The Stanley cup.—Johnny Bower.—Terry Sawchuk.—Gump Worsley.—Roger Crozier.—Ed Giacomin.—Charlie Hodge.—The new wave.—Vezina trophy winners. [GV847.H83] 67-30086
1. Hockey—Biography. I. Title.

KARIHER, Harry C., 1932- 796.9'62'0922 B
Who's who in hockey [by] Harry C. Kariher. New Rochelle, N.Y., Arlington House [1973] 189 p. 24 cm. [GV848.5.A1K37] 73-11868 ISBN 0-87000-221-X 7.95
1. Hockey—Biography. I. Title. BIP

LISS, Howard. 796.9'62'0922
Hockey's greatest all-stars. New York, Hawthorn Books [1972] xi, 144 p. illus. 22 cm. [GV848.5.A1L57 1972] 79-179126 5.95
1. Hockey—Biography. I. Title.

O'BRIEN, Andy, 1910- 796.9'62'0922 B
Superstars; hockey's greatest players. Toronto, New York, McGraw-Hill Ryerson [1973] 187 p. illus. 24 cm. Accounts of the life and career of each of nineteen of hockey's greatest stars. [GV848.5.A1O18] 920 73-10910 ISBN 0-07-077620-2 6.95 (U.S.)
1. Hockey—Biography. I. Title.

O'BRIEN, Andy, 1910- 796.9'62'0922
Young hockey champions. [1st ed.] New York, Norton [1969] xii, 105 p. ports. 21 cm. Interviews with and observations on thirteen of hockey's superstars, all of whom competed in National League hockey before the age of twenty. [GV848.5.A1O2] 920 69-12621 3.95
1. Hockey—Biography. 2. Hockey—Juvenile literature. I. Title.

ORR, Frank. 796.9'62'0922
Hockey's greatest stars. New York, Putnam [1970] 224 p. ports. 21 cm. (Sports shelf books) Brief biographies stressing the hockey careers of twenty-two players from the early days of the National Hockey League to the present. [GV848.5.A1O7 1970] 920 73-113512 3.86
1. Hockey—Biography. 2. Hockey—Juvenile literature. I. Title. BIP

Hockey—Biography—Juvenile literature.

GUTMAN, Bill. 796.9'62'0922 B
Modern hockey superstars / Bill Gutman. New York : Dodd, Mead, [1976] p. cm. Includes index. [GV848.5.A1G87] 76-13420 ISBN 0-396-07368-9 : 4.95
1. Hockey—Biography—Juvenile literature. I. Title. BIP

LIBBY, Bill. 796.9'62'0922 B
Pro hockey heroes of today. New York, Random House [1974] 150 p. illus. 29 cm. (Landmark giant 25) Profiles of twenty-four hockey stars including goalies, scoring leaders, and defensemen. [GV848.5.A1L52 1974] 920 74-4929 ISBN 0-394-82761-9 3.95
1. Hockey—Biography—Juvenile literature. I. Title.

MACPEEK, Walt, 1942- 796.9'62'0922 B
Hot shots of pro hockey / by Walt MacPeek. New York : Random House, [1975] 151 p. : ill. ; 22 cm. (Pro hockey library ; 9) Includes index. Profiles of eight professional hockey stars include Bobby Clarke, Denis Potvin, Marcel Dionne, Mark Howe, Gil Perreault, Syl Apps, Rick Martin, and Guy Lafleur. [GV848.5.A1M32] 920 75-8079 ISBN 0-394-83104-7 : 2.50. ISBN 0-394-93104-1 lib. bdg. : 3.69
1. Hockey—Biography—Juvenile literature. I. Title. BIP

MOHN, Peter B. 796.9'62'0922 B
Meet the defensemen / written by Pete Mohn ; photos. from the National Hockey League. Mankato, Minn. : Creative Education, [1976] p. cm. Biographical sketches of four hockey defensemen: Brad Parks, Ed Van Impe, Bobby Orr, and Denis Potvin. [GV848.5.A1M635] 920 76-24912 ISBN 0-87191-535-9 lib.bdg. : 4.95
1. Hockey—Biography—Juvenile literature. I. Title.

MOHN, Peter B. 796.9'62'0922 B
Meet the wingmen / written by Pete Mohn ; photos. from the National Hockey League. Mankato, Minn. : Creative Education, [1976] p. cm. Biographical sketches of four hockey wingmen: Wayne Cashman, Yvan Cournoyer, Dave Schultz, and Rick Martin. [GV848.5.A1M64] 920 76-20745 ISBN 0-87191-536-7 : 4.95
1. Hockey—Biography—Juvenile literature. I. Title.

ORR, Frank. 796.9'62'0922 B
Great goalies of pro hockey. Illustrated with photos. New York, Random House [1973] 153 p. illus. 22 cm. (Pro hockey library, 5) [GV848.5.A1O67 1973] 920 73-5896 ISBN 0-394-82539-X 1.95
1. Hockey—Biography—Juvenile literature. I. Title.
Library binding 3.37, ISBN 0-394-92539-1. Contents omitted. BIP

ORR, Frank. 796.9'62'0922
Hockey stars of the 70s. New York, Putnam [1973] 192 p. 22 cm. (Putnam sports shelf) Brief biographies emphasize the careers of seventeen hockey stars, including Ken Dryden, Bobby Orr, Tony Esposito, and Marcel Dionne. [GV848.5.A1O69 1973] 920 72-94262 ISBN 0-399-60831-1 4.89
1. Hockey—Biography—Juvenile literature. I. Title. BIP

ORR, Frank. 796.9'62'0922 B
Tough guys of pro hockey. New York, Random House [1974] 152 p. illus. 22 cm. (Pro hockey library) Brief biographies concentrating on the careers of such hockey stars as Gordie Howe, the Plager brothers, John Ferguson, and others. [GV848.5.A1Q72 1974] 920 74-4931 ISBN 0-394-82821-6 1.95
1. Hockey—Biography—Juvenile literature. I. Title.
Library binding 3.77, ISBN 0-394-92821-0.

RAINBOLT, Richard. 796.9'62'0922 B
Hockey's top scorers / Richard Rainbolt. Minneapolis : Lerner Publications Co., [1975] 67 p. : ill. ; 23 cm. (The Sports heroes library) Brief biographies focusing on the careers of ten hockey stars : Maurice Richard, Ted Lindsay, Bernie Geoffrion, Jean Beliveau, Bobby Orr, Bobby Hull, Gordie Howe, Stan Mikita, Frank Mahovlich, and Phil Esposito. [GV848.5.A1R34 1975] 920 74-27471 ISBN 0-8225-1056-1 lib.bdg. : 4.95
1. Hockey—Biography—Juvenile literature. I. Title. BIP

THOMAS, Linda, 1947- 796.9'62'0922 B
Meet the centers / written by Linda Thomas ; photos. from the National Hockey League. Mankato, MN : Creative Education, 1976. p. cm. (Meet the players) Biographical sketches of four hockey centers: Phil Esposito, Stan Gvath, Bobby Clarke, and Gil Perrault. [GV848.5.A1T42] 920 76-20743 ISBN 0-87191-534-0 : 4.95
1. Hockey—Biography—Juvenile literature. I. National Hockey League. II. Title. BIP

THORNE, Ian. 796.9'62'0922 B
The great goalies / by Ian Thorne ; photos. from the National Hockey League. Mankato, Minn. : Creative Education, c1976. 47 p. : col. ill. ; 28 cm. (Stars of the National Hockey League) Brief biographies of outstanding goalies of the National Hockey League: Ken Dryden, Tony Esposito, Bernie Parent, and Gilles Gilbert. [GV848.5.A1T46] 920 75-34479 ISBN 0-87191-491-3 : 5.95
1. Hockey—Biography—Juvenile literature. I. National Hockey League. II. Title. BIP

Hockey—Dictionaries.

BVB: Research (Organization) 796.9'62'03
The pocket hockey encyclopedia; a complete and illustrated handbook on hockey. Records, rules, statistics, and results. [Compiled by B. V. Brown, David Spencer, and Barbara Spencer] New York, Scribner [1972] 254 p. illus. 19 cm. (The Scribner library. Emblem editions) "A Pagurian Press book." [GV847.B22 1972] 72-2775 3.50
1. Hockey—Dictionaries. 2. Hockey—Biography—Dictionaries. I. Brown, B. V. II. Spencer, David. III. Spencer, Barbara. IV. Title.

SPENCER, David, fl.1972- 796.9'62'03
The pocket hockey encyclopedia / by David and Barbara Spencer. Rev. and updated. New York : Scribner, c1976. 210 p. ; 23 cm. (The Scribner library : Sports) (Emblem editions) Ed. for 1972 entered under BVB: Research. [GV847.B22 1976] 77-352786 ISBN 0-684-14783-1 : 4.95
1. Hockey—Dictionaries. 2. Hockey players—Biography. I. Spencer, Barbara, fl. 1972- joint author. II. BVB: Research (Organization) The pocket hockey encyclopedia. III. Title. IV. Title: Hockey encyclopedia.

Hockey—Juvenile literature.

MIKITA, Stan. 796.9'62'0924 B
I play to win. New York, Morrow, 1969. 223 p. ports. 22 cm. Biography of a professional hockey player for the Chicago Black Hawks who has won many awards for scoring and sportsmanship. [GV848.5.M5A3] 92 73-95308 5.95
1. Hockey—Juvenile literature. I. Title.

Hockey players—Biography—Juvenile literature.

HOCKEY hotshots 796.9'62'0922 B
/ edited, with commentary, by Bennett Wayne. Champaign, Ill. : Garrard Pub. Co., c1977. 167 p. : ill. ; 22 cm. (Target) Includes index. Brief biographies of great offensive and defensive hockey players and goalies include Howie Morenz, Maurice Richard, Bobby Hull, Bobby Orr, Terry Sawchuk, Glenn Hall, and Jacques Plante. [GV848.5.A1H6] 920 76-47478 ISBN 0-8116-4917-2 lib. bdg. : 4.84
1. Hockey players—Biography—Juvenile literature. I. Wayne, Bennett. BIP

Hocknell, John, 1723?-1799.

EVANS, Frederick William, 1808-1893. 289.8
Shakers : compendium of the origin, history, principles, rules and regulations, government, and doctrines of the United Society of Believers in Christ's Second Appearing ... / by F. W. Evans. 4th ed. New York : AMS Press, 1975. 190 p. ; 19 cm. (Communal societies in America) Reprint of the 1867 ed. published in New Lebanon, N.Y. Bibliography: p. [188]-190. [BX9771.E85 1975] 72-2985 ISBN 0-404-10747-8
1. Shakers. 2. Shakers—Biography. 3. Lee, Ann, 1736-1784. 4. Lee, William, 1740-1784. 5. Whittaker, James, 1751-1787. 6. Hocknell, John, 1723?-1799. 7. Meacham, Joseph, 1742-1796. 8. Wright, Lucy, 1760-1821. I. Title: Compendium of the origin, history, principles, rules and regulations, government, and doctrines of the United Society of Believers in Christ's Second Appearing. BIP

Hockney, David.

HOCKNEY, David. 759.2 B
David Hockney / by David Hockney ; edited by Nikos Stangos ; introductory essay by Henry Geldzahler. New York : H. N. Abrams, 1977, c1976. 312 p. : ill. (some col.) ; 28 cm. Includes index. [N6797.H57A42 1977] 76-11721 ISBN 0-8109-1058-6 : 35.00
1. Hockney, David. 2. Artists—Great Britain—Biography. BIP

HOCKNEY, David. 759.2 B
David Hockney / by David Hockney ; edited by Nikos Stangos ; introductory essay by Henry Geldzahler. London : Thames & Hudson, c1976. 312 p. : with 414 ill. ; 27 cm. Includes index. [N6797.H57S7 1976] 77-354409 ISBN 0-500-09108-0 : £10.00
1. Hockney, David. 2. Artists—Great Britain—Biography. I. Stangos, Nikos.

Hodge, Charles, 1797-1878.

HODGE, Archibald Alexander, 1823-1886. 285'.1'0924 B
The life of Charles Hodge [by] Alexander A. Hodge. New York, Arno Press, 1969. viii, 620 p. port. 23 cm. (Religion in America) Reprint of the 1881 ed. With selections from the reminiscences, letters, and writings of Charles Hodge. [BX9225.H6H6 1969] 71-83425
1. Hodge, Charles, 1797-1878. I. Hodge, Charles, 1797-1878.

Hodges, Edward, 1796-1867.

HODGES, Faustina Hasse, d.1895. 786.6'2'24 B
Edward Hodges, Doctor in Music of Sydney Sussex College, Cambridge; organist of the Churches of St. James and St. Nicholas, Bristol, England, 1819-1838; organist and director in Trinity Parish, New York, 1839-1859. New York, AMS Press [1970] xviii, 302 p. illus., ports. 23 cm. Reprint of the 1896 ed. [ML416.H68 1970] 73-135733 ISBN 0-404-03289-3
1. Hodges, Edward, 1796-1867.

Hodges, Gil, 1924-

SHAPIRO, Milton J. 927.96357
The Gil Hodges story. New York, J. Messner [1960] 192 p. illus. 22 cm. [GV865.H5S5] 60-12453
1. Hodges, Gil, 1924- I. Title.

Hodges, Gil, 1924-1972—Juvenile literature.

DEVANEY, John. 796.357'092'4 B
Gil Hodges: baseball miracle man. New York, Putnam [1973] 191 p. port. 22 cm. (Putnam sports shelf) A biography of the star of two championship Dodger teams and the manager of the championship New York Mets. [GV865.H57D4 1973] 92 72-95560 ISBN 0-399-20351-6 4.89 (guaranteed bdg.)
1. Hodges, Gil, 1924-1972—Juvenile literature. I. Title.

Hodges, William, 1744-1797.

STUEBE, Isabel Combs, 1943- 759.2
The life and works of William Hodges / Isabel Combs Stuebe. New York : Garland Pub., 1979. xxiv, 388 p., [75] leaves of plates : ill. ; 21 cm. (Oustanding dissertations in the fine arts) Originally presented as the author's thesis, New York University, 1978. Bibliography: p. 375-388. [ND497.H65S75 1979] 78-74383 ISBN 0-8240-3969-6 : 45.00
1. Hodges, William, 1744-1797. 2. Painters—England—Biography. I. Title. II. Series. **BIP**

Hodgins, Eric, 1899-

HODGINS, Eric, 1899- 813'.5'4 B
Trolley to the moon; an autobiography. New York, Simon and Schuster [1973] ix, 467 p. 25 cm. [PS3515.O1714Z524] 72-90396 ISBN 0-671-21440-3 10.00
1. Hodgins, Eric, 1899- I. Title.

Hodgson, Francis, 1781-1852.

HODGSON, James Thomas, 1845-1880. 821'.6 B
Memoir of the Rev. Francis Hodgson, B.D., scholar, poet, and divine : with numerous letters from Lord Byron and others / by his son, James T. Hodgson. Folcroft, Pa. : Folcroft Library Editions, 1975- v. : port. ; 24 cm. Reprint of the 1878 ed. published by Macmillan, London. [PR4790.H65Z7 1975] 75-26864 ISBN 0-8414-4804-3 : 75.00
1. Hodgson, Francis, 1781-1852. 2. Byron, George Gordon Noel Byron, Baron, 1788-1824—Correspondence. 3. Authors, English—Correspondence, reminiscences, etc. I. Byron, George Gordon Noel Byron, Baron, 1788-1824. II. Title.

HODGSON, James Thomas, 1845-1880. 821'.6 B
Memoir of the Rev. Francis Hodgson, B. D., scholar, poet, and divine : with numerous letters from Lord Byron and others / by James T. Hodgson. New York : AMS Press, 1977. 2 v. ; 19 cm. Reprint of the 1878 ed. published by Macmillan, London. Includes bibliographical references and index. [PR4790.H65Z7 1977] 76-169470 ISBN 0-404-07374-3 : 57.50
1. Hodgson, Francis, 1781-1852. 2. Byron, George Gordon Noel Byron, Baron, 1788-1824—Correspondence. 3. Poets, English—19th century—Biography. 4. Authors, English—19th century—Correspondence. I. Byron, George Gordon Noel Byron, Baron, 1788-1824. II. Title.

Hodgson, Vere.

HODGSON, Vere. 942.1'084'0924
Few eggs and no oranges : a diary showing how unimportant people in London and Birmingham lived through the war years 1940-1945 / written in the Notting Hill area of London by Vere Hodgson. London : D. Dobson, 1976. 480 p., [4] leaves of plates : ill. ; 22 cm. Includes index. [D811.5.H615 1976] 77-351559 ISBN 0-234-77202-6 : £6.25
1. Hodgson, Vere. 2. World War, 1939-1945—Personal narratives, English. 3. London—Biography. I. Title.

Hodson family.

SNYDER-HODSON, Katie, 1863-1958. 929.2'0973
Snyder-Hodson family; a story of Katie's pioneer days in northeast Kansas. Edited by Lena Hodson-Brown. [Atchison? Kan., 1969] 26 p. ports. 23 cm. Cover title: Snyder-Hodson family, pioneers to Kansas. Autobiographical. [CS71.H6962 1969] 70-8071
1. Hodson family. I. Hodson-Brown, Lena, ed. II. Title.

Hofer, Jesse W., 1910-

HOFER, Jesse W., 1910- 289.7'3'0924 B
An Amish boy remembers: from behind those fences, by Jesse W. Hofer. San Antonio, Naylor Co. [1973] xiii, 225 p. illus. 22 cm. [CT275.H6285A33] 73-10014 ISBN 0-8111-0500-8
1. Hofer, Jesse W., 1910- I. Title.

Hoff, Charles W., 1863-1956.

THE farther sky; v. 12
the life of Charles W. Hoff, by Hazel MacClintock and Doris Flynn Taylor. [1. ed.] New York, Vantage press [1960] 98p. illus., ports. 22cm. One of 300 copies printed.
1. Hoff, Charles W., 1863-1956. I. MacClintock, Hazel (Hoff) II. Taylor, Doris Flynn, joint author.

Hoffa, James Riddle, 1913-

CLAY, James. 923.3173
Hoffa! Ten angels swearing; an authorized biography by Jim Clay. Beaverdam, Va., Beaverdam Books [1965] vii, 182 p. 28 cm. [HD6515.T3C55] 65-23945
1. Hoffa, James Riddle, 1913- I. Title.

CLAY, James 923.3173
Hoffa! Ten angels swearing; an authorized biography. Beaverdam, Va. 23015. Beaverdam Bks. [c.1965] vii, 182p. 28cm. [HD6515.T3C55] 65-23945 4.95
1. Hoffa, James Riddle, 1913- I. Title.

HOFFA, James Riddle, 1913- 331.88'11'3883240924 B
Hoffa / by James R. Hoffa ; edited by Oscar Fraley. New York : Stein and Day, 1975. p. cm. [HD6509.H6A3] 75-28207 ISBN 0-8128-1885-7 : 8.95
1. Hoffa, James Riddle, 1913-

Hoffa, James Riddle, 1913——Juvenile literature.

KURLAND, Gerald, 1942- 331.88'11'388240924 B
James Hoffa; convicted leader of the Teamsters Union. Charlotteville, N.Y., SamHar Press, 1972. 32 p. 23 cm. (Outstanding personalities, no. 44) Bibliography: p. 32. A biography of the teamsters president who is considered by many to be "the most controversial American labor leader of recent years." [HD6509.H6K87] 92 72-89208
1. Hoffa, James Riddle, 1913-—Juvenile literature. I. Title.

Hoffman, Charles Fenno, 1806-1884.

BARNES, Homer Francis, 1895- v. 12
Charles Fenno Hoffman. New York, AMS Press, 1966. 361 p. Reprint of the original edition published in 1930. Includes bibliography. 68-51653
1. Hoffman, Charles Fenno, 1806-1884. I. Title. **BIP**

Hoffman, Elizabeth, 1921- —Juvenile literature.

HOFFMAN, Elizabeth, 1921- 133.1'29'74814
This house is haunted! / By Elizabeth P. Hoffman. New York : Contemporary Perspectives ; Milwaukee, Wis. : distributor, Raintree Publishers, c1977. 48 p. : ill. (some col.) ; 24 cm. The author describes the house she and her family moved into, only to discover it was haunted. [BF1472.U6H635] 77-10981 ISBN 0-8172-1033-4 lib. bdg. : 4.95
1. Hoffman, Elizabeth, 1921- —Juvenile literature. 2. Ghosts—Pennsylvania—Beechwood—Juvenile literature. 3. Beechwood, Pa.—Biography—Juvenile literature. I. Title. **BIP**

Hoffman, Malvina,

HOFFMAN, Malvina, 1887- 730.924
Yesterday is tomorrow, a personal history. New York, Crown [c.1965] 378p. illus., facsims., ports. 27cm. [NB237.H55A32] 65-15847 7.50
I. Title.

HOFFMAN, Malvina, 1887-1966. 730.924
Yesterday is tomorrow, a personal history. New York, Crown Publishers [1965] 378 p. illus., facsims., ports. 27 cm. [NB237.H55A32] 65-15847
I. Title.

Hoffman, Paul Gray, 1891-

HAUSSAMEN, Crane. 973.9'0924
The story of Paul G. Hoffman. [Santa Barbara, Calif., Center for the Study of Democratic Institutions, 1966] 63 p. ports. 23 cm. Cover title: A man who shaped his age. "A tribute by the Center for the Study of Democratic Institutions to its honorary chairman." [E748.H63H3] 67-3008
1. Hoffman, Paul Gray, 1891- I. Center for the Study of Democratic Institutions. II. Title. III. Title: A man who shaped his age.

Hoffman, Richard, 1831-1909.

HOFFMAN, Richard, 1831-1909. 786.1'092'4 B
Some musical recollections of fifty years / by Richard Hoffman ; with biographical sketch by his wife ; and introductions by Frank E. Kirby and John G. Doyle. Detroit : Information Co-ordinators, 1976. xvi, viii, 168 p., [25] leaves of plates : ill. ; 22 cm. (Music for the Bicentennial) (Detroit reprints in music) [ML417.H74A3 1976] 74-75890 ISBN 0-911772-79-0 : 9.50
1. Hoffman, Richard, 1831-1909. 2. Pianists—England—Biography. 3. Pianists—United States—Biography. **BIP**

Hoffmann, Charles, 1891-1971.

STARR, Harvey E. 355.3'32'0924 B
Colonel Charles Hoffmann, 1891-1971, by Harvey E. Starr. [Los Angeles, Calif.] Los Angeles Corral of the Westerners [1972] 16 p. illus. 21 cm. ([The Westerners. Los Angeles Corral] Publication 104) "Special keepsake for 1972." [CT275.H6289S7] 72-195925
1. Hoffmann, Charles, 1891-1971. I. Title. II. Series.

Hoffmann, Ernst Theodor Amadeus, 1776-1822.

HEWETT-THAYER, Harvey Waterman, 1873- 833'.6 B
Hoffmann: author of the tales, by Harvey W. Hewett-Thayer. New York, Octagon Books, 1971 [c1948] viii, 416 p. illus., ports. 24 cm. "List of Hoffmann's literary works": p. [399]-401. [PT2361.Z5H44 1971] 73-120629
1. Hoffmann, Ernst Theodor Amadeus, 1776-1822. I. Title.

Hofmann, Hans, 1880-1966.

WIGHT, Frederick Stallknecht, 1902- 927.5
Hans Hofmann. Berkeley, University of California Press, 1957. 66 p. illus. (part col.), port. 28 cm. Bibliography: p. 64-65. [ND237.H667W5] 57-7593
1. Hofmann, Hans, 1880-1966.

Hofmann, Josef, 1876-1957.

BARINOVA, Mariia Nikolaevna, 1878- v. 12
Vospominaniia o I. Gofmane i F. Buzoni. Moskva, Muzyka, 1964. 159 p. illus. 17 cm. In Cyrillic characters. NUC68
1. Hofmann, Josef, 1876-1957. 2. Busoni, Ferruccio Benvenuto, 1866-1924. I. Title.

Hofmeyr, Jan Hendrik, 1804-1948

PATON, Alan. 968.050924 (B,
South African tragedy; the life and times of Jan Hofmeyr. Abridgement by Dudley C. Lunt. New York, Scribner [1965] xxii. 424 p. col. maps (on lining papers) ports. 24 cm. First published in 1964 under title: Hofmeyr. [DT779.8.H6P35] 65-25406
1. Hofmeyr, Jan Hendrik, 1804-1948 2. Africa, South—Pol. & govt. 1909- I. Title.

Hofstadter, Richard, 1916-1970.

CREMIN, Lawrence Arthur, 1925- 973'.07'2024 B
Richard Hofstadter (1916-1970); a biographical memoir, by Lawrence A. Cremin. [Syracuse, N.Y.] National Academy of Education [1972] 12 p. front. 22 cm. Bibliography: p. 11-12. [E175.5.H55C73] 73-172431
1. Hofstadter, Richard, 1916-1970.

Hogan, Ben, 1912-

DEMARET, Jimmy. 927.96352
My partner, Ben Hogan. Drawings by Murray Olderman. New York, McGraw-Hill [1954] 214 p. illus. 21 cm. [GV964.H6D4] 54-7467
1. Hogan, Ben, 1912- I. Title.

GREGSTON, Gene, 1925- 796.352'092'4 B
Hogan : the man who played for glory / by Gene Gregston. Englewood Cliffs, N.J. : Prentice-Hall, c1978. 192 p., [4] leaves of plates : ill. ; 24 cm. Includes index. Bibliography: p. 185-186. [GV964.H6G73] 77-27421 ISBN 0-13-392464-5 : 8.95
1. Hogan, Ben, 1912- 2. Golfers—United States—Biography. **BIP**

Hogan, Frank S.

CUNNINGHAM, Barry. 345'.7471'01 B
Mr. District Attorney / by Barry Cunningham, with Mike Pearl. New York : Mason/Charter, 1977. 290 p., [8] leaves of plates : ill. ; 25 cm. Includes index. [KF373.H56C8] 77-879 ISBN 0-88405-465-9 : 10.95
1. Hogan, Frank S. 2. Public prosecutors—New York (City)—Biography. 3. New York (City)—History—1951- I. Pearl, Mike, joint author. II. Title.

CUNNINGHAM, Barry. 345'.7471'01 B
Mr. District Attorney / by Barry Cunningham, with Mike Pearl. New York : Mason/Charter, 1977. 290 p., [8] leaves of plates : ill. ; 25 cm. Includes index. [KF373.H56C8] 77-879 ISBN 0-88405-465-9 : 10.95
1. Hogan, Frank S. 2. Public prosecutors—New York (City)—Biography. 3. New York (City)—History—1951- I. Pearl, Mike, joint author. II. Title.

Hogarth. Georgina, 1827-1917.

ADRIAN, Arthur A 928.2
Georgina Hogarth and the Dickens circle. London, New York, Oxford University Press, 1957. 320p. illus. 22cm. [PR4586.A2] 57-14175
1. Hogarth. Georgina, 1827-1917. 2. Dickens. Charles, 1812-1870. I. Title. **BIP**

Hogarth Press.

KENNEDY, Richard, 1910- 338.7'61'0705092 B
A boy at the Hogarth Press / [by] Richard Kennedy ; illustrated by the author ; with an introduction by Bevis Hillier. Harmondsworth ; New York [etc.] : Penguin, 1978. 104 p. : ill. ; 20 cm. [PR6021.E712Z463 1978] 79-306749 ISBN 0-14-004862-6 pbk. : 1.95
1. Kennedy, Richard, 1910- 2. Hogarth Press. 3. Woolf, Virginia Stephen, 1882-1941—Biography. 4. Woolf, Leonard Sidney, 1880-1969—Biography. 5. Authors, English—20th century—Biography. I. Title. BIP

Hogarth, William,

HOGARTH, William, 1697-1764. 759.2
Hogarth [by] R. B. Beckett. Boston, Boston Book & Art Shop [1955] vii, 80p. 142plates. 26cm. (English master painters) 'Catalogue of Hogarth's paintings': p. [35]-75. [ND497] 927.5 55-9578
I. Beckett, Ronald Brymer. II. Title. III. Series.

Hogarth, William, 1697-1764.

JARRETT, Derek. 942.07
England in the age of Hogarth / Derek Jarrett. New York : Viking Press, 1974. 256 p. : ill. ; 26 cm. Includes index. Bibliography: p. 248-250. [DA485.J37] 74-5538 ISBN 0-670-29624-4 : 15.00
1. Hogarth, William, 1697-1764. 2. England—Civilization—18th century. I. Title. BIP

JARRETT, Derek. 760'.092'4 B
The ingenious Mr Hogarth / Derek Jarrett. London : M. Joseph, 1976. 223 p., [12] leaves of plates : ill. ; 24 cm. Includes index. Bibliography: p. [214]-217. [ND497.H7J37] 76-380637 ISBN 0-7181-1489-2 : £7.00
1. Hogarth, William, 1697-1764. 2. Painters—Great Britain—Biography. I. Title.

LICHTENBERG, Georg Christoph, 1742-1799. 769.924
The world of Hogarth; Lichtenberg's commentaries on Hogarth's engravings. Translated from the German and with an introd. by Innes and Gustav Herdan. Boston, Houghton Mifflin, 1966. xxiii, 297 p. illus. 26 cm. Translation of Lfg. 1-4 of Ausfuhrliche Erklarung der Hogarthischen Kupferstiche, an enl., rev. version of a series of commentaries which appeared originally in the Gottinger Taschenkalender, 1784-96. [NE642.H6L53 1966a] 66-27492
1. Hogarth, William, 1697-1764. I. Title.

LINDSAY, Jack, 1900- 760'.092'4 B
Hogarth : his art and his world / Jack Lindsay. New York : Taplinger Pub. Co., 1979, c1977. x, 277 p., [16] leaves of plates : ill. ; 24 cm. Includes index. Bibliography p. 260-268. [ND497.H7L77 1979] 78-21289 ISBN 0-8008-3916-1 : 14.95
1. Hogarth, William, 1697-1764. 2. Painters—England—Biography. BIP

PAULSON, Ronald. 759.2 B
Hogarth: his life, art, and times [by] Ronald Paulson. Abridged by Anne Wilde. [Abridged ed.] New Haven, Yale University Press, 1974. xiii, 461 p. illus. 24 cm. Bibliography: p. 443-444. [ND497.H7P39] 73-91338 ISBN 0-300-01766-9 20.00
1. Hogarth, William, 1697-1764. I. Wilde, Anne.
Pbk. 8.95, ISBN 0-300-01763-4. BIP

QUENNELL, Peter, 1905- 927.5
Hogarth's progress. New York, Viking Press, 1955. 318p. 25cm. [ND497.H7Q4 1955a] 55-7378
1. Hogarth, William, 1696-1764. I. Title.

Hogg, Ima.

ISCOE, Louise Kosches. 976.4'06'0924 B
Ima Hogg, first lady of Texas : reminiscences and recollections of family and friends / by Louise Kosches Iscoe. [Austin] : Hogg Foundation for Mental Health, c1976. 47 p. : ill. ; 22 x 25 cm. [F394.H8I82] 76-363299
1. Hogg, Ima. 2. Houston, Tex.—Biography. I. Title.

Hogg, James, 1770-1835.

BATHO, Edith Clara, 1895- 821'.7 B
The Ettrick Shepherd, by Edith C. Batho. New York, Greenwood Press [1969] xi, 233 p. 18 cm. Reprint of the 1927 ed. Revised and expanded edition of the author's master's thesis, University of London. Includes bibliographies. [PR4792.B3 1969] 69-13809
1. Hogg, James, 1770-1835. 2. Hogg, James, 1770-1835—Bibliography. I. Title. BIP

CARSWELL, Donald, 1882-1940. 828'.7'09 B
Sir Walter: a four-part study in biography (Scott, Hogg, Lockhart, Joanna Baillie) [Folcroft, Pa.] Folcroft Library Editions, 1973. p. cm. Reprint of the 1930 ed. published by J. Murray, London, American ed. originally published in 1930 under: Scott and his circle. Bibliography: p. [PR5332.C3 1973] 73-20091 ISBN 0-8414-3532-4 (lib. bdg.)
1. Scott, Walter, Sir, Bart., 1771-1832—Biography. 2. Hogg, James, 1770-1835—Biography. 3. Lockhart, John Gibson, 1794-1854—Biography. 4. Baillie, Joanna, 1762-1851—Biography. I. Title.

DOUGLAS, George Brisbane, Sir, bart., 1856-1935. 821'.7 B
James Hogg. [Folcroft, Pa.] Folcroft Library Editions, 1974. 154 p. 23 cm. Contains also brief essays on Robert Tannahill, William Motherwell, and William Thom. Reprint of the 1899 ed. published by O. Anderson & Ferrier, Edinburgh, issued in series: Famous Scots series. Includes bibliographical references. [PR4792.D6 1974] 74-10889 ISBN 0-8414-3762-9 (lib. bdg.)
1. Hogg, James, 1770-1835—Biography. 2. Tannahill, Robert, 1774-1810—Addresses, essays, lectures. 3. Motherwell, William, 1797-1835—Addresses, essays, lectures. 4. Thom, William, 1798?-1848—Addresses, essays, lectures.

HOGG, James, 1770-1835. 821'.7 B
Memoir of the author's life, and Familiar anecdotes of Sir Walter Scott. Edited by Douglas S. Mack. New York, Barnes & Noble [1972] xviii, 145 p. 23 cm. [PR4792.A3 1972] 73-151174 ISBN 0-389-04606-X 8.50
1. Hogg, James, 1770-1835—Biography. 2. Scott, Walter, Sir, 1771-1832—Biography. I. Mack, Douglas S., ed. II. Hogg, James, 1770-1835. Familiar anecdotes of Sir Walter Scott. 1972. III. Title. IV. Title: Familiar anecdotes of Sir Walter Scott.

Hogg, James, 1806-1888.

BONNER, Willard Hallam, 1899- ed. 828'.8'09 B
De Quincey at work. [Folcroft, Pa.] Folcroft Library Editions, 1973 [c1936] 111 p. illus. 26 cm. Reprint of the ed. published by Airport Publishers, Buffalo. Contents.Contents.—James T. Fields and the first American edition.—James Hogg and the first British edition. [PR4536.B6 1973] 73-9715 10.00
1. De Quincey, Thomas, 1785-1859. 2. Fields, James Thomas, 1816-1881. 3. Hogg, James, 1806-1888. 4. Hogg, James, 1830-1910. I. De Quincey, Thomas, 1785-1859. II. Title. BIP

Hogg, Thomas Jefferson, 1792-1862.

HOGG, Thomas Jefferson, 1792-1862. 821'.7 B
After Shelley; the letters of Thomas Jefferson Hogg to Jane Williams. Edited with a biographical introduction by Sylva Norman. [Folcroft, Pa.] Folcroft Library Editions [1973] p. Reprint of the 1934 ed. published by Oxford University Press, London, New York. [PR4793.H4A8 1973] 72-14369 ISBN 0-8414-1359-2 (lib. bdg.)
1. Hogg, Thomas Jefferson, 1792-1862. 2. Williams, Jane, 1798-1884. 3. Shelley, Percy Bysshe, 1792-1822. I. Williams, Jane, 1798-1884. II. Title.

HOGG, Thomas Jefferson, 1792-1862. 821'.7 B
After Shelley : the letters of Thomas Jefferson Hogg to Jane Williams / edited, with a biographical introd., by Sylva Norman. Folcroft, Pa. : Folcroft Library Editions, 1975. xlvi, 94 p. : port. ; 26 cm. Reprint of the 1934 ed. published by Oxford University Press, London. [PR4793.H4A8 1975] 75-11764 ISBN 0-8414-6286-0 lib. bdg. : 17.50
1. Hogg, Thomas Jefferson, 1792-1862. 2. Williams, Jane, 1798-1884. 3. Shelley, Percy Bysshe, 1792-1822. I. Norman, Sylva, 1901- II. Title.

HOGG, Thomas Jefferson, 1792-1862. 821'.7 B
The Athenians, being correspondence between Thomas Jefferson Hogg and his friends, Thomas Love Peacock, Leigh Hunt, Percy Bysshe Shelley, and others. Edited by Walter Sidney Scott. [Folcroft, Pa.] Folcroft Library Editions, 1973. p. Reprint of the 1943 ed. published by the Golden Cockerel Press, London. [PR4793.H4A75 1973] 73-14724 25.00
1. Hogg, Thomas Jefferson, 1792-1862. I. Peacock, Thomas Love, 1785-1866. II. Hunt, Leigh, 1784-1859. III. Shelley, Percy Bysshe, 1792-1822. IV. Scott, Walter Sidney, 1900- ed. V. Title.

Hogg, Will Clifford, 1875-1930.

LOMAX, John Avery, 1872-1948. 923.373
Will Hogg, Texan. Austin, Published for the Hogg Foundation [by] University of Texas Press, 1956 [c1940] 51p. illus. 24cm. [CT275.H638L6] 57-13519
1. Hogg, Will Clifford, 1875-1930. I. Title.

Hogren, Charles V., 1936-

CLAERBAUT, David. 345'.77311'01
The reluctant defender : a big-city attorney defends desperate people / by David Claerbaut ; [foreword by Chuck Colson]. Wheaton, Ill. : Tyndale House Publishers, 1978. 263 p., [4] leaves of plates : ill. ; 21 cm. [KF373.H57C58] 78-55983 ISBN 0-8423-5425-5 : 4.95
1. Hogren, Charles V., 1936- 2. Cabrini-Green Legal Aid Clinic. 3. Lawyers—Illinois—Biography. 4. Criminal justice, Administration of—Illinois—Chicago. I. Title.

Hohenlohe-Waldenburg-Schillingsfurst, Stephanie Juliana, Prinzessin zu, 1896-1972.

HOHENLOHE, Franz, Prinz zu, 1914- 943.6'05'0924 B
Steph, the fabulous princess / [by] Prince Franz Hohenlohe. London : New English Library, 1976. 205 p., [16] p. of plates : facsims., ports. ; 22 cm. [CT3150.H56H63 1976] 77-371538 ISBN 0-450-02594-2 : £4.95
1. Hohenlohe-Waldenburg-Schillingsfurst, Stephanie Juliana, Prinzessin zu, 1896-1972. 2. Princesses—Biography. I. Title.

Hohn, Caesar

HOHN, Caesar 926.3
Dutchman on the Brazos; reminiscences. Foreword by Agnes Meyer. Drawings by E. M. Schiwetz. Austin, Univ. of Tex. Pr. [c.1963] xii, 194p. illus., ports. 23cm. 63-16064 4.50 bds.,
I. Title.

Holand, Hjalmar Rued,

HOLAND, Hjalmar Rued, 1872- 928.1
My first eighty years. New York, Twayne Publishers [1957] 256p. illus. 23cm. [E175.5.H6A3] 57-3665
I. Title.

Holbein, Hans, the Younger, 1497-1543.

HOLBEIN, Hans, the Younger, 1497-1543. 759.3
Holbein / [by] Helen Langdon. Oxford : Phaidon, 1976. 16 p., [48] p. of plates : col. ill., col. ports. ; 31 cm. [ND588.H7L28] 77-352859 ISBN 0-7148-1748-1 : 6.95
1. Holbein, Hans, the Younger, 1497-1543. I. Langdon, Helen.
Distributed by E.P. Dutton, New York

Holbrook, Donald,

HOLBROOK, Donald, 1897- 614.84'3'0924
An unlikely firemaster; the dual life of a financier and fire chief. Fitzwilliam, N.H., Fire Protection Research International, 1968. xvii, 170 p. illus., port. 24 cm. [TH140.H64A3] 68-58955
I. Fire Protection Research International. II. Title.

Holden, Edith.

HOLDEN, Edith, 1871-1920. 500.9'424'8
The country diary of an Edwardian lady, 1906 : a facsimile reproduction of a naturalist's diary / Edith Holden New York : Holt, Rinehart and Winston, c1977. 176 p. : col. ill. ; 24 cm. "A Webb & Bower book." [QH138.W37H64 1977] 77-71198 ISBN 0-03-021026-7 : 14.95
1. Holden, Edith. 2. Natural history—England—Warwickshire. 3. Country life—England—Warwickshire. 4. Illustrators—England—Biography. I. Title.

Holden, Horace, b. 1810.

HOLDEN, Horace, b.1810. 919.6
A narrative of the shipwreck, captivity & sufferings of Horace Holden & Benj. H. Nute / Horace Holden. Fairfield, Wash. : Ye Galleon Press, 1975. p. cm. Reprint of the 1836 ed. published by Russell, Shattuck, Boston. [G530.H6 1975] 75-25567 ISBN 0-87770-147-4 : 6.00
1. Holden, Horace, b. 1810. 2. Nute, Benjamin H. 3. Pelew Islands. 4. Lord North (Island) I. Title. BIP

Holder, Maryse.

HOLDER, Maryse. 301.41'2'0924
Give sorrow words : Maryse Holder's letters from Mexico ; introd. by Kate Millet. 1st ed. New York : Grove Press : distributed by Random House, 1979. p. cm. [HV6250.4.W65H643] 78-74551 ISBN 0-8021-0185-2 : 10.00
1. Holder, Maryse. 2. Victims of crimes—Biography. I. Title.

Holgate, Edwin H.

REID, Dennis R. 759.11
Edwin Holgate / Dennis Reid. Ottawa : National Gallery of Canada, 1976. 87 p. : chiefly ill. (some col.) ; 24 cm. (Canadian artists series ; no 4) Bibliography: p. 85 [ND249.H7R44] 77-358365 ISBN 0-88884-314-3
1. Holgate, Edwin H. 2. Painters—Canada—Biography. I. Holgate, Edwin H. II. Title. III. Series.

Holiday, Billie, 1915-1959.

CHILTON, John, 1931or2- 784'.092'4 B
Billie's blues : a survey of Billie Holiday's career, 1933-1959 / John Chilton ; foreword by Buck Clayton. New York : Stein and Day, 1975. p. cm. Includes bibliographies, discographies, and index. [ML420.H58C5] 75-8837 ISBN 0-8128-1821-0 : 8.95
1. Holiday, Billie, 1915-1959. I. Title.

HOLIDAY, Billie, 1915- 927.8
Lady sings the blues [by] Billie Holiday with William Dufty. [1st ed.] Garden City, N. Y., Doubleday, 1956. 250p. illus. (on linning papers) 22cm. Autobiography. [ML420.H58A3] 56-5962

1. Musicians—Correspondence, reminiscences, etc. I. Title.

HOLIDAY, Billie, 1915- v. 12
Lady sings the blues by Billie holiday with William Dufty. New York, Lancer Books [1965] 191 p. 18 cm. (A Lancer book, 74-839) Autobiography. "Complete and unabridged." 67-18956
1. Musicians — Correspondence, reminiscences, etc. I. Title. **BIP**

HOLIDAY, Billie, 1915- 927.8
Lady sings the blues [by] Billie Holiday with William Dufty. [New lYork] Avon [1976 c1956] 192 p. 18 cm. [ML420.H58A3] ISBN 0-380-00491-7 1.50 (pbk.)
1. Musicians—Correspondence, reminiscences, etc. I. Title.
L.C. card no. of 1956 Doubleday edition: 56-5962.

Holiday, Chico.

HOLIDAY, Chico. 784'.092'4 B
Holiday in hell / Chico Holiday & Bob Owen. Springdale, Pa. : Whitaker House, c1976. 179 p. : ill. ; 18 cm. [ML420.H583A3] 73-92387 ISBN 0-88368-067-X pbk. : 1.75
1. Holiday, Chico. 2. Singers—United States—Biography. 3. Witness bearing (Christianity) I. Title.

Holiday, John Henry, 1852?-1887.

MYERS, John Myers, 1906- 923.4173
Doc Holliday. [1st ed.] Boston, Little, Brown [c1955] 287p. illus. 21cm. [F594.h74M9] 55-5528
1. Holiday, John Henry, 1852?-1887. 2. Crime and criminals—The West. 3. Outlaws. I. Title.

Holladay, Ben, 1819-1887.

LUCIA, Ellis. 923.873
The saga of Ben Holladay, giant of the Old West. New York, Hastings House [1959] 374 p. illus. 21 cm. Includes bibliography. [F594.H73L8] 59-13551
1. Holladay, Ben, 1819-1887. 2. Transportation—The West.

Holland, Alice Moseman (Peck)

HOLLAND, Alice Moseman (Peck) 621.3000924
Reflections; a duobiography by Alice & Walter Holland. Tucson, Ariz., [Palo Verde Press] 1965. 80 p. facsim., ports. 20 cm. [CT275.H642A3] 66-910
I. Holland, Walter Elam, 1884- joint author. II. Title.

Holland, Henry Richard Vassall Fox, Baron, 1773-1840.

HOLLAND, Henry Richard Vassall Fox, Baron, 1773-1840. 941.07'5'0924 B
The Holland House diaries 1831-1840 : the diary of Henry Richard Vassall Fox, third Lord Holland, with extracts from the diary of Dr. John Allen / edited with introductory essay and notes by Abraham D. Kriegel London ; Boston : Routledge & Kegan Paul, 1977. lxiv, 513. ; 24 cm. Includes bibliographical references index. [DA541.H64A34 1977] 77-365888 ISBN 0-7100-8406-4 : 31.25
1. Holland, Henry Richard Vassall Fox, Baron, 1773-1840. 2. Statesmen—Great Britain—Biography. 3. Great Britain—Politics and government—1830-1837—Sources. I. Allen, John, 1771-1843. II. Kriegel, Abraham D. III. Title.

Holland, Henry, 1745-1806.

STROUD, Dorothy. 720'.924
Henry Holland; his life and architecture. South Brunswick [N.J.] A. S. Barnes [1967, c1966] 159 p. illus., plans, ports. 26 cm. Bibliographical footnotes. [NA997.H6S79] 67-13085
1. Holland, Henry, 1745-1806. I. Title.

STROUD, Dorothy. 720'.924
Henry Holland; his life and architecture. South Brunswick [N.J.] A. S. Barnes [1967, c1966] 159 p. illus., plans, ports. 26 cm. Bibliographical footnotes. [NA997.H6S79 1966a] 67-13085
1. Holland, Henry, 1745-1806.

Holland, John Philip, 1842-1914.

MORRIS, Richard Knowles. 623.82570924 B
John P. Holland, 1841-1914, inventor of the modern submarine Annapolis, Md., United States Naval Institute [1966] xviii, 211 p. illus., maps, fold. plans, ports. 24 cm. Bibliography: p. 197-202. [VM140.H6M57] 66-20239
1. Holland, John Philip, 1842-1914. I. Title.

Holland, Vyvyan Beresford, 1886-1967.

HOLLAND, Vyvyan Beresford, 1886-1967. 828'.9'1209 B
Son of Oscar Wilde. Westport, Conn., Greenwood Press [1973, c1954] xv, 237 p. illus. 22 cm. Reprint of the ed. published by Dutton, New York. [PR6015.O4115S6 1973] 73-5267 ISBN 0-8371-6884-8
1. Holland, Vyvyan Beresford, 1886-1967. 2. Wilde, Oscar, 1854-1900. 3. Wild family. I. Title.

Hollander, Else von, 1885-1932.

ARNOLD, Eberhard, 1883-1935. 289.7'3'0924 B
Else von Hollander, January 1932, by Eberhard Arnold, and others. [Translated from the German and edited by the Society of Brothers]. Rifton, N.Y., Plough Pub. House [1972, c1973] xii, 111 p. illus. 20 cm. [BX8143.H64A83] 72-96191 ISBN 0-87486-111-X 3.00
1. Hollander, Else von, 1885-1932. I. Title.

Hollar, Wenceslaus, 1607-1677.

VAN EERDE, Katherine S., 1920- 769'.924
Wenceslaus Hollar: delineator of his time [by] Katherine S. Van Eerde. Charlottesville, Published for Folger Shakespeare Library [by] University Press of Virginia [1970] ix, 122 p. illus. (2 fold.), facsims., maps, plans, ports. 28 cm. "Bibliographical essay": p. [111]-115. [NE642.H7V3] 70-110753 ISBN 8-13-902975- 15.00
1. Hollar, Wenceslaus, 1607-1677. I. Folger Shakespeare Library, Washington, D.C.

Hollaway, Ida Nelle.

HOLLAWAY, Ida Nelle. 362.2'092'4 B
When all the bridges are down / Ida Nelle Hollaway. Nashville : Broadman Press, c1975. 128 p. ; 18 cm. Autobiographical. [RC464.H58A33] 76-351354 ISBN 0-8054-5416-0 pbk. : 1.95 pbk. : 1.95 1.95
1. Hollaway, Ida Nelle. 2. Psychotherapy patients—Biography. I. Title. **BIP**

Holley, Mary (Austin) 1784-1846.

LEE, Rebecca (Smith) 920.7
Mary Austin Holley, a biography. Austin, Univ. of Tex. Pr. [c.1962] xii, 447p. illus. 24cm. (Elma Dill Russell Spencer Found. ser., no. 2) Bibl. 62-9787 7.50
1. Holley, Mary (Austin) 1784-1846. I. Title. II. Series.

LEE, Rebecca Washington (Smith) 1894- 920.7
Mary Austin Holley, a biography. Austin, University of Texas Press [1962] xii, 447 p. illus., ports., maps, facsims., geneal, tables. 24 cm. (The Elma Dill Russell Spencer Foundation series, no. 2) Bibliography: p. [410]-424. [F389.H78L4] 62-9787
1. Holley, Mary (Austin) 1784-1846. I. Title. II. Series.

Holliday, John Henry, 1852?-1887.

JAHNS, Patricia. 923.4173
The frontier world of Doc Holliday, faro dealer from Dallas to Deadwood. New York, Hastings House [1957] 305 p. 22 cm. Includes bibliography. [F594.H74J3] 57-12798
1. Holliday, John Henry, 1852?-1887. 2. Crime and criminals—The West. **BIP**

JAHNS, Patricia. 923.4173
The frontier world of Doc Holliday, faro dealer from Dallas to Deadwood. New York, Hastings House [1957] 305p. 22cm. Includes bibliography. [F594.H74J3] 57-12798
1. Holliday, John Henry, 1852?-1887. 2. Crime and criminals—The West. I. Title.

JAHNS, Patricia. 364.11'523'0924 B
The frontier world of Doc Holliday, faro dealer from Dallas to Deadwood / by Pat Jahns. Lincoln : University of Nebraska Press, [1979] c1957. xiii, 305 p. ; 21 cm. "A Bison book." Reprint of the ed. published by Hastings House, New York. Includes index. Bibliography: p. 287-293. [F594.H74J3 1979] 78-26811 ISBN 0-8032-7550-1 pbk. : 4.50
1. Holliday, John Henry, 1852?-1887. 2. Crime and criminals—The West—Biography. I. Title.

MYERS, John Myers, 1906- 923.4173
Doc Holliday. New York, Bantam [c.1963, c.1955] 184p. 18cm. (J2586) .40 pap.,
1. Holliday, John Henry, 1825?-1887. 2. Crime and criminals—The West. 3. Outlaws. I. Title. **BIP**

MYERS, John Myers, 1906- 923.41'78
Doc Holliday. Lincoln, Univ. of Nebraska Pr. [1973, c.1955] 224 p. port. 21 cm. (Bison Book) [F594.H74M9] 55-5528 ISBN 0-8032-5781-3 1.95 (pbk.)
1. Holliday, John Henry, 1852?-1887. 2. Crime and criminals—The West. 3. Outlaws. I. Title.

Hollings, Michael.

HOLLINGS, Michael. 253'.2
Living priesthood / Michael Hollings. Huntington, Ind. : Our Sunday Visitor, 1978 262 p. ; 21 cm. [BX4705.H727A34 1977] 78-58590 ISBN 0-87973-708-5 pbk. : 3.95
1. Hollings, Michael. 2. Catholic Church—Clergy—Biography. 3. Clergy—England—Biography. I. Title. **BIP**

*Hollis, Verdon La Mont

*HOLLIS, Verdon La Mont 364.1620924
My chains fell off. New York, Carlton [c.1966] 155p. 21cm. (Reflection bk.) 3.50
I. Title.

Holloway, Gilbert N.

HOLLOWAY, Gilbert N. 133
This way up : a psychic autobiography and guide to spiritual development / Gilbert N. Holloway. Chicago : H. Regnery, [1975] x, 278 p. ; 22 cm. [BF1027.H64A34 1975] 74-26978 ISBN 0-8092-8290-9 : 9.95
1. Holloway, Gilbert N. 2. Psychical research. I. Title.

Holm, Hanya, 1893-

SORELL, Walter, 1905- 793.3'2'0924 B
Hanya Holm : the biography of an artist / by Walter Sorell. Middletown, Conn. : Wesleyan University Press, [1979] p. cm. Includes bibliographies and index. [GV1785.H6S6 1979] 79-3110 ISBN 0-8195-6060-X : 7.50
1. Holm, Hanya, 1893- 2. Choreographers—United States—Biography. 3. Modern dance. **BIP**

SORELL, Walter, 1905- 793.3'2'0924 B
Hanya Holm; the biography of an artist. [1st ed.] Middletown, Conn., Wesleyan University Press [1969] x, 226 p. illus., ports. 22 cm. Includes bibliographies. [GV1785.H6S6] 69-17796 7.95
1. Holm, Hanya, 1893-

Holman-Hunt, Diana.

HOLMAN-HUNT, Diana. 828.914
My grandmother and I. [dist American bd.] New York, W. W. Norton [1960] 208p. illus. 22cm. [CT788.H745A3 1960] 61-5620
I. Title.

Holmes, Burton.

HOLMES, Burton, 1870- 923.973
The world is mine. [An autobiography] [1st ed.] Culver City, Calif., Murray & Gee [1953] 267 p. illus. 24 cm. [G226.H6A35] 53-3181
I. Title.

HOLMES, Burton, 1870- 779'.9'910924
Burton Holmes : the man who photographed the world : travelogues, 1892-1938 / photos. and text by Burton Holmes ; selected and edited by Genoa Caldwell ; introd. by Irving Wallace. New York : Abrams, [1977] p. cm. Includes index. [G226.H6A32] 77-8075 ISBN 0-8109-1059-4 : 25.00
1. Holmes, Burton, 1870- 2. Travelers—United States—Biography. I. Caldwell, Genoa. II. Title.

HOLMES, Burton, 1870- 923.973
The world is mine. [An autobiography] [1st ed.] Culver City, Calif., Murray & Gee [1953] 267 p. illus. 24 cm. [G226.H6A35] 53-3181
I. Title.

Holmes, Emma, 1838-1910.

HOLMES, Emma, 1838-1910. 975.7'91 B
The diary of Miss Emma Holmes, 1861-1866 / edited, with an introd. and notes by John F. Marszalek. Baton Rouge : Louisiana State University Press, c1979. p. cm. (Library of Southern civilization) Includes index. [F279.C453H643] 78-25924 ISBN 0-8071-0386-1 : 35.00
1. Holmes, Emma, 1838-1910. 2. Charleston, S.C.—History—Civil War, 1861-1865—Sources. 3. Charleston, S.C.—Biography. 4. United States—History—Civil War, 1861-1865—Personal narratives—Confederate side- I. Marszalek, John F. II. Title. **BIP**

Holmes, Ernest Shurtleff.

HOLMES, Fenwicke Lindsay, 1883- 289.9 B
Ernest Holmes: his life and times [by] Fenwicke L. Holmes. New York, Dodd, Mead [1970] x, 308 p. illus., ports. 22 cm. [BF648.H6H58] 70-96765 6.95
1. Holmes, Ernest Shurtleff. I. Title.

Holmes, Ezekiel, 1801-1865.

DAY, Clarence Albert. 630'.924 B
Ezekiel Holmes, father of Maine agriculture [by] Clarence A. Day. Orono, University of Maine Press, 1968. vii, 185 p. illus., facsim., ports. 23 cm. (University of Maine studies, 2d ser. no. 86) (University of Maine bulletin.) Bibliography: p. [177]-180. [S417.H68D3] 68-66729 2.50
1. Holmes, Ezekiel, 1801-1865. 2. Agriculture—Maine—History. I. Series: Maine. University. University of Maine studies, 2d ser., no. 86 **BIP**

Holmes, George Frederick, 1820-1897.

GILLESPIE, Neal C., 1933- 917.5'03'30924 B
The collapse of orthodoxy; the intellectual ordeal of George Frederick Holmes [by] Neal C. Gillespie. Charlottesville, University Press of Virginia [1972] x, 273 p. port. 25 cm. Bibliography: p. [249]-267. [CT275.H6447G55] 70-163978 ISBN 0-8139-0345-9
1. Holmes, George Frederick, 1820-1897. I. Title. **BIP**

Holmes, James, 1804-1883.

HOLMES, James, 975.8'03'0924 B
1804-1883.
"Dr. Bullie's" notes : reminiscences of early Georgia and of Philadelphia and New Haven in the 1800s / by James Holmes ; compiled, edited, and with an introduction by Delma Eugene Presley. Atlanta : Cherokee Pub. Co., 1976. xxxvii, 247 p. : ill. ; 24 cm. Includes index. Bibliography: p. 229-234. [F291.H774] 76-14370 ISBN 0-87797-038-6 : 10.00
1. Holmes, James, 1804-1883. 2. Legislators—Georgia—Biography. 3. Physicians—Georgia—Biography. I. Presley, Delma Eugene. II. Title.

Holmes, Jesse Herman, 1864-

WAHL, Albert J. 289.6'092'4 B
Jesse Herman Holmes, 1864-1942 : a Quaker's affirmation for man / by Albert J. Wahl. Richmond, Ind. : Friends United Press, c1979. xvii, 447 p. : ill. ; 23 cm. An outgrowth of the author's thesis, Temple University, 1951. [BX7795.H74W33] 79-63127 ISBN 0-913408-50-6 : 10.95.
1. Holmes, Jesse Herman, 1864- 2. Friends, Society of—United States—Biography.

Holmes, John,

HOLMES, John, 1812-1899. 816'.4 B
Letters of John Holmes to James Russell Lowell and others. Edited by William Roscoe Thayer. With an introd. by Alice M. Longfellow. Freeport, N.Y., Books for Libraries Press [1972] xlvii, 290 p. illus. 23 cm. Reprint of the 1917 ed. [CT275.H6455A4 1972] 72-21 ISBN 0-8369-9973-8
I. Title.

Holmes, John Haynes,

HOLMES, John Haynes, 922.8173
1879-1964.
I speak for myself; the autobiography of John Haynes Holmes. [1st ed.] New York, Harper [1959] 308 p. illus. 22 cm. [BX9869.H535A33] 59-5220
I. Title.

HOLMES, John Haynes, 1879- 208
1964.
A summons unto men; an anthology of the writings of John Haynes Holmes. Edited, with foreword by Carl Hermann Voss. Pref. by James Luther Adams, Dana MacLean Greeley [and] Donald Szantho Harrington. New York, Simon and Schuster [1971] 255 p. 21 cm. Bibliography: p. 241-243. [BX9869.H535A2 1971] 74-139664 ISBN 0-671-20995-7 7.95
I. Title.

Holmes, Oliver Wendell, 1809-1894.

KENNEDY, William 818'.3'09 B
Sloane, 1850-1929.
Oliver Wendell Holmes; poet, litterateur, scientist. [Folcroft, Pa.] Folcroft Library Editions, 1974 [c1883] p. cm. Reprint of the ed. published by S. E. Cassino, Boston. Bibliography: p. [PS1981.K4 1974] 74-13969 ISBN 0-8414-5514-7 (lib. bdg.)
1. Holmes, Oliver Wendell, 1809-1894.

KENNEDY, William 818'.3'09 B
Sloane, 1850-1929.
Oliver Wendell Holmes; poet, litterateur, scientist. [Folcroft, Pa.] Folcroft Library Editions, 1974 [c1883] p. cm. Reprint of the ed. published by S. E. Cassino, Boston. Bibliography: p. [PS1981.K4 1974] 74-13969 35.00 (lib. bdg.).
1. Holmes, Oliver Wendell, 1809-1894. **BIP**

SCHROEDER, William 818'.3'09 B
Lawrence.
Oliver Wendell Holmes : an appreciation / by William Lawrence Schroeder. Folcroft, Pa. : Folcroft Library Editions, 1976. 120 p. ; 23 cm. Reprint of the 1909 ed. published by P. Green, London. [PS1981.S3 1976] 76-5423 ISBN 0-8414-7640-3 lib. bdg.
1. Holmes, Oliver Wendell, 1809-1894. **BIP**

TOWNSEND, Lewis W. 818'.3'09 B
Oliver Wendell Holmes / by Lewis W. Townsend. Folcroft, Pa. : Folcroft Library Editions, 1974. p. cm. At head of title: Centenary biography. Reprint of the 1895 ed. published by Headley Bros., London. [PS1981.T6 1974] 74-31155 ISBN 0-8414-8612-3 lib. bdg. : 15.00
1. Holmes, Oliver Wendell, 1809-1894. **BIP**

Holmes, Oliver Wendell, 1809-1894—Biography.

HOYT, Edwin Palmer. 818'.3'09 B
The improper Bostonian : Dr. Oliver Wendell Holmes / by Edwin P. Hoyt. 1st ed. New York : Morrow, 1979. 319 p. : ill. ; 24 cm. Includes bibliographical references and index. [PS1981.H64] 78-21275 ISBN 0-688-03429-2 : 10.95
1. Holmes, Oliver Wendell, 1809-1894—Biography. 2. Authors, American—19th century—Biography. 3. Physicians—Massachusetts—Biography. I. Title. **BIP**

TILTON, Eleanor 818'.3'09 B
Marguerite, 1913-
Amiable autocrat : a biography of Dr. Oliver Wendell Holmes / by Eleanor M. Tilton. New York : Octagon Books, 1978, c1947. xi, 470 p., [5] leaves of plates : ill. ; 23 cm. Reprint of the ed. published by H. Schuman, New York. Originally presented as the author's thesis, Columbia University, 1947. Includes bibliographical references and index. [PS1981.T5 1978] 78-924 ISBN 0-374-97945-6 lib.bdg. : 18.50
1. Holmes, Oliver Wendell, 1809-1894—Biography. 2. Authors, American—19th century—Biography. 3. Physicians—Massachusetts—Biography. I. Title.

Holmes, Oliver Wendell, 1841-1935.

BOWEN, Catherine 923.473
(Drinker) 1897-
Yankee from Olympus; Justice Holmes and his family New York, Bantam Books [1960, c.1943, 1944] 432p. (Bantam classic, SC95) Bibl. .75 pap.,
1. Holmes, Oliver Wendell, 1841-1935. I. Title.

BOWEN, Catherine 923.473
(Drinker) 1897-
Yankee from Olympus. Edited and abridged by Bessie Charlotte Stenhouse. [Educational ed.] New York, Globe Book Co. [1956] 491p. illus. 21cm. 57-16778
1. Holmes, Oliver Wendell, 1841-1935. I. Title.

BOWEN, Catherine 923.473
(Drinker) 1897-
Yankee from Olympus; Justice Holmes and his family. Introd. written for this ed. by Catherine Drinker Bowen. Suggestions for reading and discussion by Helen Tangeman. School ed. Boston, Pub. for Little by Houghton [c.1943-1962] 473p. illus. 22cm. (Riverside literature ser., R-20) 62-51682 1.64 pap.,
1. Holmes, Oliver Wendell, 1841-1935. I. Title.

BURTON, David 347'.73'2634 B
Henry, 1925-
Oliver Wendell Holmes, what manner of liberal? / David H. Burton. Huntington, N.Y. : R. E. Krieger Pub. Co., 1979. p. cm. Bibliography: p. [KF8745.H6B8] 78-23645 ISBN 0-88275-793-8 pbk. : 4.95
1. Holmes, Oliver Wendell, 1841-1935. 2. Judges—United States—Biography. I. Title.

*FEUERLICHT, Roberta 923.473
Strauss
Oliver Wendell Holmes; a concise biography. New York, Amer. R.D.M. [c.1965] 71p. illus. 21cm. (Study master pubn., 900) Bibl. 1.00 pap.,
1. Holmes, Oliver Wendell, 1841-1935. I. Title.

FRANKFURTER, Felix, 1882- 923.473
1965
Mr. Justice Holmes and the Supreme Court. 2d ed. New York, Antheneum, 1965[c.1938, 1961] 111p. front port. 18cm. (Atheneum 72) 1.25 pap.,
1. Holmes, Oliver Wendell, 1841-1935. 2. U.S.—Constitutional law. 3. U.S.—Supreme Court. 4. Law—Addresses, essays, lectures. I. Title.

FRANKFURTER, Felix, 1882- 923.473
1965.
Mr. Justice Holmes and the Supreme Court. 2d ed. Cambridge, Mass., Belknap Press of Harvard University Press, 1961. 112 p. port. 22 cm. [KF8745.H6F73 1961] 61-16693
1. Holmes, Oliver Wendell, 1841-1935. 2. United States. Supreme Court. 3. United States—Constitutional law. 4. Law—Addresses, essays, lectures. I. Title.

FULLER, Edmund Maybank, 920.073
1914- ed.
4 American biographies [by] Edmund Fuller, O. B. Davis. New York, Harcourt, [c.1961] 779p. illus. (Adventures in good bks.) 61-19640 3.75
1. Lincoln, Abraham, Pres. U. S., 1809-1865. 2. Holmes, Oliver Wendell, 1841-1935. 3. Clemens, Samuel Langhorne, 1835-1910. 4. Keller, Helen Adams, 1880- I. Davis, O. B., joint ed. II. Title.
Content omitted.

HOWE, Mark De Wolfe, 923.473
1906-
Justice Oliver Wendell Holmes; v. 2. Cambridge, Mass., Belknap Pr. of Harvard [c.]1963. 295p. illus., ports. 24cm. Contents.2. The proving years 1870-1882. Bibl. 57 5.00
1. Holmes, Oliver Wendell, 1841-1935. I. Title.

HOWE, Mark DeWolfe, 1906- v. 12
Justice Oliver Wendell Holmes: the proving years, 1870-1882. Cambridge, Mass., Belknap Press [1963] 295 p. 65-43101
1. Holmes, Oliver Wendell, 1841-1935. I. Title.

JUDSON, Clara (Ingram) 923.473
1879-
Mr. Justice Holmes; illustrated by Robert Todd. Chicago, Follett Pub. Co. [1956] 192p. illus. 25cm. 56-11218
1. Holmes, Oliver Wendell, 1841-1935. I. Title.

JUDSON, Clara 347'.7326'0924 B
(Ingram) 1879-1960.
Mr. Justice Holmes; illustrated by Robert Todd. Chicago, Follett Pub. Co. [1956] 192 p. illus. 25 cm. A biography of Oliver Wendell Holmes, Jr., describing his early education at dame and latin schools and Harvard College, his years of military service during the Civil War, his study of law, his work on The Common Law and his years as lawyer and judge in Massachusetts and as justice of the Supreme Court. 92 AC 68
1. Holmes, Oliver Wendell, 1841-1935. I. Todd, Robert, illus. II. Title.

MEYER, Edith 347.99'73 B
Patterson.
That remarkable man: Justice Oliver Wendell Holmes. [1st ed.] Boston, Little, Brown [1967] 189 p. illus., ports. 21 cm. Bibliography: p. [181]-182. [KF8745.H6M4] 67-19797
1. Holmes, Oliver Wendell, 1841-1935. I. Title.

MR. Justice Holmes and the v. 12
Supreme Court. 2d ed. New York, Atheneum, 1965 [c1961] 111 p. port. 19 cm. (Atheneum paperbacks) 67-5700
1. Holmes, Oliver Wendell, 1841-1935. 2. U.S. — Constitutional law. 3. U.S. Supreme Court. 4. Law — Addresses, essays, lectures.

Holmes, Wilfred Jay, 1900-

HOLMES, Wilfred 940.54'886'73
Jay, 1900-
Double-edged secrets : U.S. naval intelligence operations in the Pacific during World War II / W. J. Holmes. Annapolis : Naval Institute Press, c1979. x, 231 p., [4] leaves of plates : ill. ; 24 cm. Includes index. [D810.S7H637] 78-70779 ISBN 0-87021-162-5 : 11.95
1. Holmes, Wilfred Jay, 1900- 2. United States. Navy—Biography. 3. World War, 1939-1945—Secret service—United States. 4. World War, 1939-1945—Personal narratives, American. 5. World War, 1939-1945—Pacific area. 6. Seamen—United States—Biography. I. Title.

Holocaust, Jewish (1939-1945)—Juvenile literature.

NOBLE, Iris. 364.12'092'4 B
Nazi hunter, Simon Wiesenthal / by Iris Noble. New York : J. Messner, c1979. p. cm. Includes index. Presents an account of the activities of Simon Wiesenthal who has been instrumental in locating and prosecuting members of the Nazi SS, many of whom disappeared at the end of World War II. [D810.J4W55] 92 79-15783 ISBN 0-671-32964-2 : 7.29
1. Holocaust, Jewish (1939-1945)—Juvenile literature. 2. Wiwsenthal, Simon—Juvenile literature. 3. War criminals—Juvenile literature. I. Title. **BIP**

Holocaust, Jewish (1939-1945)—Personal narratives.

EARTH be not 940.53'1503'924
silent : personal and eyewitness accounts of the holocaust, resistance, and rebirth / [edited by] Azriel Eisenberg. New York : Sanhedrin Press, c1979. p. cm. Includes bibliographical references. [D810.J4E17] 79-25880 ISBN 0-88482-911-1 : 12.50 pbk. : 6.95
1. Holocaust, Jewish (1939-1945)—Personal narratives. 2. Refugees, Jewish—Biography. I. Eisenberg, Azriel Louis, 1903-

Holovak, Mike.

HOLOVAK, Mike. 796.332'077'0924
Violence every Sunday; the story of a professional football coach, by Mike Holovak and Bill McSweeny. New York, Coward-McCann [1967] 220 p. illus. 22 cm. [GV939.H58A3] 67-21508
I. Mc Sweeny, Bill, joint author. II. Title.

Holsey, Lucius Henry, Bp., 1842-1920.

CADE, John Brother 922.773
Holsey, the incomparable. New York, Pageant [c.1964] 221p. 21cm. Bibl. 63-21706 4.00
1. Holsey, Lucius Henry; Bp., 1842-1920. I. Title.

CADE, John Brother. 922.773
Holsey, the incomparable. [1st ed.] New York, Pageant Press [1964] 221 p. 21 cm. Bibliography: p. 208-211. [BX8473.H58C3] 63-21706
1. Holsey, Lucius Henry, Bp., 1842-1920. I. Title.

Holst, Gustav, 1874-1934.

HOLST, Imogen, 1907- 780'.924 B
Gustav Holst; a biography, with a note by R. Vaughan Williams. 2nd ed. London, New York, Oxford University Press, 1969. xvi, 209 p. illus., facsims., plates, ports. 23 cm. "List of compositions": p. [170]-177. [ML410.H748H6 1969] 71-432960 unpriced
1. Holst, Gustav, 1874-1934. **BIP**

Holst, Gustav, 1874-1934—Bibliography.

SHORT, Michael. 016.78'092'4
Gustav Holst, 1874-1934 : a centenary documentation / Michael Short. London ; New York : White Lion Publishers, 1974. [3], iv, 285 p. ; 26 cm. Includes index. Bibliography: p. 206-233. [ML134.H75S5] 75-317503 ISBN 0-7285-0000-0 : £15.00
1. Holst, Gustav, 1874-1934—Bibliography. 2. Holst, Gustav, 1874-1934—Discography. I. Title. **BIP**

Holt family.

JONES, Viva Mary 929'.2'0973
(Peterson) 1919-
The wheel of time; the story of Mary Holt and her husbands, with historical, genealogical and biographical data on thier ancestry and descendants, compiled by Viva M. P. Jones. [Salt Lake City?] 1964 [c1965] 388 p. illus., maps, ports. 24 cm. [CS71.H7578 1965] 66-477
1. Holt family. 2. Hulett, Mary Matilda (Holt) 1829-1920. I. Title.

MARSHALL, Maudie 929.2'09764
Marie Holt, 1908-
My father and the bride he took, compiled by Mrs. Arch Bruce Marshall (Maudie Marie Holt) [Houston, Tex., c1967] 106 p. illus., map (on lining papers), ports. 26 cm. Bibliography: p. 100-101. [CS71.H7575] 68-20082
1. Holt family. I. Title.

RAINEY, Buck. 791.43'028'0922 B
The fabulous Holts : a tribute to a favorite movie family / by Buck Rainey. Nashville : Western Film Collector Press, c1976. 215 p. : ill. ; 22 cm. "Filmographies": p. 177-210. [PN1998.A2R33] 77-150222
1. Holt family. 2. Moving-picture actors and actresses—United States—Biography. 3. Western films—History and criticism. I. Title.

Holt, Hamilton, 1872-1951.

KUEHL, Warren F. 923.773
Hamilton Holt: journalist, internationalist, educator. Gainesville, University of Florida Press, [c.]1960. 303p. illus., ports. Bibl. 60-15787 7.50
1. Holt, Hamilton, 1872-1951. I. Title. BIP

KUEHL, Warren F 1924- 923.773
Hamilton Holt: journalist, internationalist, educator. Gainesville, University of Florida Press, 1960. 303p. illus. 24cm. [LD4721.R717 1925] 60-15787
1. Holt, Hamilton, 1872-1951. I. Title.

Holt, Harold Edward, 1908-1967.

HOLT, Zara, Dame. 994'.05'0924 B
My life and Harry; an autobiography. Melbourne, The Herald [1968] 256 p. illus., ports. 25 cm. [DU114.H63H6] 75-374941 5.50
1. Holt, Harold Edward, 1908-1967. I. Title.

Holt, Harry Quentin,

HOLT, Harry Quentin, 370'.924 (B)
1806-
Historical autobiography of a Hoosier hillbilly, by Harry Q. Holt. With special section on Klondike, Medaryville, Otterbein [and] Remington. [Oxford? Ind., 1967] ix, 288 p. illus., ports. 24 cm. Bibliographical footnotes. [LA2317.H64A3] 68-1059
I. Title.

HOLT, Harry Quentin, 370'.924 B
1896-
Historical autobiography of a Hoosier hillbilly, by Harry Q. Holt. With special section on Klondike, Medaryville, Otterbein [and] Remington. [Oxford? Ind., 1967] ix, 288 p. illus., ports. 24 cm. Bibliographical footnotes. [LA2317.H64A3] 68-1059
I. Title.

Holt, Henry, 1840-1926.

MADISON, Charles 655.5920924
Allan
The owl among colophons: Henry Holt as publisher and editor. New York. Holt [c.1966] x, 197p. facsim. 22cm. [Z473.H75M3] 66-17596 7.50
1. Holt, Henry, 1840-1926. I. Title.

Holt, John Caldwell, 1923-

HOLT, John Caldwell, 780'.92'4 B
1923-
Never too late : my musical life story / John Holt. New York : Delacorte Press, c1978. x, 245 p. ; 22 cm. "A Merloyd Lawrence book." [ML419.H64A3] 78-18380 ISBN 0-440-06641-7 : 10.00
1. Holt, John Caldwell, 1923- 2. Musicians—United States— Biography. I. Title.

Holt, Luther Emmett, 1855-1924.

DUFFUS, Robert 618.9'2'000924 B
Luther, 1888-
L. Emmett Holt; pioneer of a children's century [by] R. L. Duffus and L. Emmett Holt, Jr. New York, Arno Press, 1974 [c1940] xiv, 295 p. illus. 23 cm. (Children and youth: social problems and social policy) Reprint of the ed. published by Appleton-Century, New York. [RJ43.H6D8 1974] 74-1683 ISBN 0-405-05960-4 18.00
1. Holt, Luther Emmett, 1855-1924. I. Holt, Luther Emmett, 1895- joint author. II. Title. III. Series. BIP

Holt, Thomas, 1811-1888.

HOLT, Henry 994.403'092'4 B
Thomas Eulert.
An energetic colonist; a biographical account of the activities of the late Hon. Thomas Holt, by Henry E. Holt. Melbourne, Hawthorn Press, 1972. 202 p. illus., maps, ports. 25 cm. Includes bibliographical references. [CT2808.H65H64] 73-169932 ISBN 0-7256-0068-3 6.95
1. Holt, Thomas, 1811-1888. I. Title.

Holtkamp, Walter, 1874-1962.

FERGUSON, John 786.6'22'4 B
Allen, 1941-
Walter Holtkamp, American organ builder / John Allen Ferguson. Kent, Ohio : Kent State University Press, c1978. p. cm. Bibliography: p. [ML424.H77F5] 78-26500 9.50
1. Holtkamp, Walter, 1874-1962. 2. Organ-builders—United States—Biography. 3. Organs—United States.

Holtzclaw, William Henry, 1870?-1943.

HOLTZCLAW, R. Fulton, 370'.92'4 B
1903-
William Henry Holtzclaw, scholar in ebony, founder of Utica Junior College / by R. Fulton Holtzclaw ; introd., Richard D. Morrison. Cleveland : Dillon/Liederbach, c1977. xii, 251 p. : ill. ; 23 cm. [LA2317.H66H64] 76-29278 ISBN 0-913228-19-2 : 10.00
1. Holtzclaw, William Henry, 1870?-1943. 2. Teachers—United States—Biography.

Holtzmann, Fanny E., 1903-

BERKMAN, Ted. 340'.092'4 B
The lady and the law : the remarkable life of Fanny Holtzmann / by Ted Berkman. 1st ed. Boston : Little, Brown, c1976. xi, 403 p. : ill. ; 24 cm. Includes index. [KF373.H616B4] 75-33891 ISBN 0-316-09175-8 : 10.95
1. Holtzmann, Fanny E., 1903- I. Title.

Holy Roman Empire—Kings and rulers—Biography.

INGRAO, Charles 943'.044'0924 B
W.
In quest and crisis : Emperor Joseph I and the Habsburg monarchy / by Charles W. Ingrao. West Lafayette, Ind. : Purdue University Press, 1979. xi, 278 p. : maps ; 24 cm. Includes bibliographical references and index. [DB68.I53] 77-88358 ISBN 0-911198-53-9 : 12.95
1. Joseph I, Emperor of Germany, 1678-1711. 2. Holy Roman Empire—Kings and rulers—Biography. 3. Rakozi, Ferenc II, Prince of Transylvania, 1676-1735. 4. Austria—History—Joseph I, 1705-1711. 5. Hungary—History—1683-1848. I. Title. BIP

Holyoake, George Jacob, 1817-1906.

GRUGEL, Lee 309.1'41'0810924 B
E., 1940-
George Jacob Holyoake : a study in the evolution of a Victorian radical / Lee E. Grugel. Philadelphia : Porcupine Press, 1976. x, 189 p. : ill. ; 22 cm. Includes index. Bibliography: p. 177-182. [HD8393.H57G78] 76-8241 ISBN 0-87991-619-2 lib.bdg. : 12.50
1. Holyoake, George Jacob, 1817-1906. 2. Labor and laboring classes—Great Britain—Biography. 3. Labor and laboring classes—Great Britain—Political activity—History. 4. Great Britain—Social conditions—19th century. BIP

Holzer, Adela.

HOLZER, Adela. 792'.0232'0924 B
If at first ... / Adela Holzer. New York : Stein and Day, 1977. 214 p. ; 22 cm. [PN2287.H62A34] 77-9610 ISBN 0-8128-2145-9 : 8.95
1. Holzer, Adela. 2. Theatrical producers and directors—United States—Biography. I. Title. BIP

Home, Alexander Frederick Douglas-Home, 14th earl of, 1903-

DICKIE, John, 1923- 923.242
The uncommon commoner; a study of Sir Alec Douglas-Home. London, New York, F. A. Praeger [1964] xv, 224 p. illus., ports. 22 cm. Bibliography: p. [216] [DA591.H6D5] 64-20446
1. Home, Alexander Frederick Douglas-Home, 14th earl of, 1903- I. Title.

Home, Daniel Dunglas, 1833-1886.

EDMONDS, I. G. 133.9'1'0924 B
D. D. Home, the man who talked with ghosts / I. G. Edmonds. 1st ed. Nashville : T. Nelson, c1978. 192 p. : ill. ; 21 cm. Includes index. Bibliography: p. 181-182. [BF1283.H7E35] 78-7579 ISBN 0-8407-6584-3 : 6.95
1. Home, Daniel Dunglas, 1833-1886. 2. Mediums—Great Britain—Biography. I. Title.

HOME, Daniel Dunglas, Mrs. 133.9
D. D. Home, his life and mission / Mme. Dunglas Home. New York : Arno Press, 1976. p. cm. (The Occult) Reprint of the 1888 ed. published by Trubner & Co., London. [BF1027.H65H6 1976] 75-36844 ISBN 0-405-07956-7 : 24.00
1. Home, Daniel Dunglas, 1833-1886. 2. Spiritualism—Controversial literature. I. Title. II. Series: The Occult (New York, 1976-)

Home of the Hirsel, Alexander Frederick Douglas Home, Baron, 1903-

HOME of the 941.085'6'0924 B
Hirsel, Alexander Frederick Douglas Home, Baron, 1903-
The way the wind blows : an autobiography / by Alec Douglas-Home. New York : Quadrangle/New York Times Book Co., 1976. 320 p., [8] leaves of plates : ill. ; 24 cm. Includes index. [DA566.9.H65A38] 76-47153 ISBN 0-8129-0665-9 : 10.95
1. Home of the Hirsel, Alexander Frederick Douglas Home, Baron, 1903- 2. Prime ministers—Great Britain—Biography. 3. Great Britain—Politics and government—20th century. I. Title.

Home, William Douglas.

HOME, William Douglas. 928.2
Half-term report; an autobiography. London, New York, Longmans, Green [1954] 209p. illus. 23cm. [PR6015.O524Z5] 55-480
I. Title.

Homer, Louise Dilworth Beatty, 1871-1947.

HOMER, Anne. 782.1'092'4 B
Louise Homer and the golden age of opera. New York, W. Morrow, 1974 [c1973] 439 p. illus. 25 cm. Bibliography: p. 432-434. [ML420.H6H6] 73-11250 10.00
1. Homer, Louise Dilworth (Beatty) 1871-1947. I. Title.

VERMORCKEN, 782.1'092'4 B
Elizabeth Moorhead.
These too were here : Louise Homer and Willa Cather / by Elizabeth Moorhead. Folcroft, Pa. : Folcroft Library Editions, 1976. 62 p. ; 21 cm. Reprint of the 1950 ed. published by University of Pittsburgh, Press, Pittsburgh. [ML420.H6V4 1976] 76-30901 ISBN 0-8414-6061-2 lib. bdg. : 15.00
1. Homer, Louise Dilworth Beatty, 1871-1947. 2. Cather, Willa Sibert, 1873-1947. I. Title.

Homer, Sidney, 1864-1953.

HOMER, Sidney, 1864- 784'.092'2 B
1953.
My wife and I : the story of Louise and Sidney Homer / by Sidney Homer. New York : Da Capo Press, 1977, [c1939] xii, 269 p. [18] leaves of plates : ill. ; 24 cm. (Da Capo Press music reprint series) Reprint of the ed. published by Macmillan, New York. [ML410.H77A2 1977] 77-10561 ISBN 0-306-77526-3 : 22.50
1. Homer, Sidney, 1864-1953. 2. Homer, Louise Dilworth Beatty, 1875-1947. 3. Composers—United States—Biography. 4. Singers—United States—Biography. I. Title. BIP

Homer, Winslow, 1836-1910.

DOWNES, William Howe, 759.13 B
1854-1941.
The life and works of Winslow Homer. New York, B. Franklin [1974] xxviii, 306 p. illus. 23 cm. (Burt Franklin research & source works series. Art history & reference series, 49) Reprint of the 1911 ed. published by Houghton Mifflin, Boston. Bibliography: p. [293]-295. [ND237.H7D6 1974] 72-81983 ISBN 0-8337-5127-1 19.50 (lib. bdg.)
1. Homer, Winslow, 1836-1910. I. Title. BIP

GOULD, Jean 927.5
Winslow Homer, a portrait. New York, Apollo [1963, c.1962] 305p. 20cm. (A-72) 1.95 pap.,
1. Homer, Winslow, 1836-1910. I. Title.

GOULD, Jean, 1909- 927.5
Winslow Homer, a portrait. New York, Dodd, Mead [1962] 305 p. illus. 24 cm. [ND237.H7G65] 62-10146
1. Homer, Winslow, 1836-1910.

HENDRICKS, Gordon. 759.13 B
The life and work of Winslow Homer / Gordon Hendricks. New York : H. N. Abrams, 1979. 345 p. : ill. (some col.) ; 31 x 35 cm. Includes index. Bibliography: p. 330-333. [ND237.H7H46] 79-210 ISBN 0-8109-1063-2 : 45.00
1. Homer, Winslow, 1836-1910. 2. Painters—United States—Biography. I. Title. BIP

Homer, Winslow, 1836-1910—Juvenile literature.

HYMAN, Linda. 759.13
Winslow Homer: America's old master. [1st ed.] Garden City, N.Y., Doubleday [1973] 95 p. illus. (part col.) 25 cm. A biography and analysis of the major works of the nineteenth-century American painter often called America's "Old Master." [ND237.H7H95 1973] 92 72-92225 ISBN 0-385-03488-1 4.95
1. Homer, Winslow, 1836-1910—Juvenile literature. I. Title.

Homerus.

BLACKWELL, Thomas, 1701- 883'.01
1757.
An enquiry into the life and writings of Homer. New York, Garland Pub., 1970. 335 p. illus., fold. map. 21 cm. "Facsimile ... made from a copy in the Harvard University Library [originally published in 1735]" Includes bibliographical references. [PA4037.A2B5 1735a] 77-112078
1. Homerus. I. Title.

BOWRA, Cecil Maurice, 883'.01
Sir, 1898-1971.
Homer. New York, Scribner [1972] viii, 191 p. illus. 23 cm. (Classical life and letters) Bibliography: p. [183]-184. [PA4037.B618 1972b] 72-890 ISBN 0-684-12986-8 8.95
1. Homerus.

MICHALOPOULOS, Andre, 883'.01
1897-
Homer / by Andre Michalopoulos. New York : St. Martin's Press, [1975] c1966. 217 p. ; 21 cm. (The Griffin author series) Includes index. Bibliography: p. 211-214. [PN4037.M46 1975] 74-80026 pbk. : 14.95 3.95
1. Homerus. BIP

Homosexuality.

GERBER, Israel Joshua 301.41'57'0922
Man on a pendulum; a case history of an invert. [1st ed.] New York, American Press [c1955] 320p. 22cm. [HQ76.G4] 55-12201
1. Homosexuality. I. Title.

MILLER, Merle, 1919- 301.41'57'0924
On being different what it means to be a homosexual. New York Popular Library [1972] 126 p. 18 cm. [HQ76.M55] 70-162391 Pap. .95 (445-00377-095)
1. Homosexuality. I. Title.

Homosexuality and Christianity.

PHILPOTT, Kent. 261.8'34'157
The gay theology / by Kent Philpott. Plainfield, N.J. : Logos International, c1977. x, 194 p. ; 18 cm. [BR115.H6P48] 77-10171 ISBN 0-88270-241-6 pbk. : 1.95
1. Homosexuality and Christianity. 2. Converts—United States—Biography. 3. Homosexuals—United States—Biography. I. Title. BIP

Homosexuality—Personal narratives.

PERRY, Troy D. 301.41'57'0924 B
The Lord is my shepherd and he knows I'm gay; the autobiography of the Rev. Troy D. Perry, as told to Charles L. Lucas. With a foreword by Edith Perry. Los Angeles, Nash Pub. [1972] ix, 232 p. 23 cm. [BR1725.P45A3] 72-186895 ISBN 0-8402-1249-6 7.95
1. Homosexuality—Personal narratives. I. Lucas, Charles L. II. Title.

Homosexuality—United States—Personal narratives.

AARON, William. 301.41'57
Straight; a heterosexual talks about his homosexual past. [1st ed.] Garden City, N.Y., Doubleday, 1972. 216 p. 22 cm. [HQ76.A23] 71-163938 6.95
1. Homosexuality—United States—Personal narratives. I. Title.

LIND, Earl, pseud. 301.41'57'0924 B
Autobiography of an androgyne / by Earl Lind ("Ralph Werther"—"Jennie June"). New York : Arno Press, 1975 [c1919] p. cm. (Homosexuality) Continued by The female-impersonators, by R. Werther. Reprint of the ed. published by the Medico-legal journal, New York. [HQ76.3.U5L56 1975] 75-12333 ISBN 0-405-07400-X : 15.00
1. Homosexuality—United States—Personal narratives. 2. Homosexuality—New York (City) I. Werther, Ralph, pseud. The female-impersonators. II. Title. III. Series. BIP

WERTHER, Ralph, pseud. 301.41
The female-impersonators / by Ralph Werther—Jennie June ("Earl Lind"). New York : Arno Press, 1975 [c1922] p. cm. (Homosexuality) Continues Autobiography of an androgyne, by E. Lind. Reprint of the ed. published by Medico-legal journal, New York. [HQ76.3.U5W47 1975] 75-12334 ISBN 0-405-07358-5 : 18.00
1. Homosexuality—United States—Personal narratives. 2. Impersonators, Female. 3. Homosexuality—New York (City) I. Lind, Earl, pseud. Autobiography of an androgyne. II. Title. III. Series.

Homosexuals, Male—Biography.

ROWSE, Alfred Leslie, 1903- 301.41'57'09
Homosexuals in history : a study of ambivalence in society, literature, and the arts / by A. L. Rowse. 1st American ed. New York : Macmillan, 1977. xiii, 346 p., [8] leaves of plates : ports. ; 25 cm. Includes index. [HQ75.7.R68 1977] 77-1682 ISBN 0-02-605620-8 12.95
1. Homosexuals, Male—Biography. 2. Homosexuality, Male—History. I. Title.

Honami, Koetsu, 1558-1637.

LEACH, Bernard Howell, 1887- 709.52
Kenzan and his tradition: the lives and times of Koetsu, Sotatsu, Korin and Kenzan. New York, Transatlantic Arts [1967] 3-173p. col. front., illus., 108 plates (incl. ports., facsims.) table, diagr. 26cm. [corrected entry] [ND1059.035 L4] 27.50
1. Honami, Koetsu, 1558-1637. 2. Ogata, Korin, 1658-1716. 3. Ogata, Kenzam, 1663-1743. 4. Tawaraya, Sotatsu, d. 1643. I. Title.

Honcharenko, Ahapius, 1832-1916.

LUCIW, Theodore. 281.9'0924 B
Father Agapius Honcharenko; first Ukrainian priest in America. Introd. by Walter Dushnyck. New York, Ukrainian Congress Committee of America, 1970. xx, 223 p. illus., facsims., ports. 24 cm. Bibliography: p. 209-216. [E184.U5L77] 78-115892 7.50
1. Honcharenko, Ahapius, 1832-1916. 2. Ukrainians in the United States. I. Title.

Honda, Soichiro, 1906—

SANDERS, Sol W. 338.7'62'922750924 B
Honda : the man and his machines / Sol Sanders. 1st ed. Boston : Little, Brown, [1975] xvi, 208 p. : ill. ; 22 cm. [TL140.H56S247] 75-16235 ISBN 0-316-77007-8 : 7.95
1. Honda, Soichiro, 1906- 2. Honda motorcycle. BIP

Hone, William, 1780-1842.

HACKWOOD, Frederick William, 1851- 827'.7 B
William Hone: his life and times. New York, A M. Kelley, 1970. 373 p. illus., facsims., ports. 22 cm. Reprint of the 1912 ed. Bibliography: p. 357-368. [PR4794.H5Z7 1970] 71-114025
1. Hone, William, 1780-1842.

Hong Kong—Biog.

ENDACOTT, G. B. 920.05
A biographical sketch-book of early Hong Kong. Singapore, Pub. by D. Moore for Eastern Universities Pr. [dist. Detroit. Cellar Bk. Shop, 1963, c.1962] xii, 171p. ports. 22cm. Bibl. 3.75
1. Hong Kong—Biog. I. Title.

Honie, John, 1901-

CARLSON, Vada F. 970.3 B
Black Mountain boy; a story of the boyhood of John Honie, written by Vada Carlson and Gary Witherspoon. Illustrated by Andy Tsinajinnie. [Rough Rock, Ariz., Navaho Curriculum Center] 1968. 80 p. illus. 23 cm. "Prepared by the Navaho Curriculum Center, Rough Rock Demonstration School, Rough Rock, Arizona." Recounts the life of a Navajo boy in Arizona at the beginning of the century as he grew to manhood as the adopted son of a childless couple. [PZ7.C2168Bl] 92 AC 68
1. Honie, John, 1901- 2. Navaho Indians. I. Witherspoon, Gary, joint author. II. Navaho Curriculum Center. III. Tsinajinnie, Andy, illus. IV. Title.

Honigsheim, Paul,

HONIGSHEIM, Paul, 1885-1963 320'.0924
On Max Weber. Tr. by Joan Rytina. New York, Free Pr. [1968] ix, 155p. 23cm. Bibl. ref. [HM22.G3W444] 67-63230 4.95
1. Weber, Max, 1864-1920. II. Title.

Honiss, William Henry, 1858-1940.

HONISS, William Tibbits, 1897- 621.0924 (B)
Patents unlimited a biography of William Henry Honiss, 1858-1940. [Hartford, Conn.] Bond Press, 1965. xiii, 158 p. illus., facsims., geneal, tables, ports. 23 cm. 66-1135
1. Honiss, William Henry, 1858-1940. I. Title.

Honolulu Marathon.

OSMUN, Mark, 1952- 796.4'26
The Honolulu Marathon / by Mark Osmun. 1st ed. New York : Lippincott, c1979. 255 p. ; 22 cm. [GV1065.22.H66O83] 79-9726 ISBN 0-397-01322-1 : 12.95
1. Honolulu Marathon. 2. Runners (Sports)—Biography. I. Title.

Honorat, Sister, 1898-1961.

ECCLESINE, Margaret Wyvill. 271.07'0924
A touch of radiance; Sister Honorat of the Bon Secours Sisters. Milwaukee, Bruce Pub. Co. [1966] xiv, 226 p. illus., ports. 22 cm. [BX4705.H742E25] 67-1650
1. Honorat, Sister, 1898-1961. I. Title.

Hood, John Bell, 1831-1879.

HOOD, Cavalier general v. 12
1st ed. New York, Prentice-Hall [1959] x, 316p. port., plans. 24cm. 'Bibliographical note: p. 305-309.
1. Hood, John Bell, 1831-1879. 2. U. S.-Hist.-Civil War-Campaigns and battles. I. O'Connor, Richard, 1915-

Hood, Raymond Mathewson, 1881-1934.

KILHAM, Walter Harrington, 1904- 720'.92'4
Raymond Hood, architect; form through function in the American skyscraper, by Walter H. Kilham, Jr. New York, Architectural Book Pub. Co. [1974, c1973] 200 p. illus. 26 cm. Bibliography: p. 193-195. [NA737.H57K54] 73-12395 ISBN 0-8038-0218-8
1. Hood, Raymond Mathewson, 1881-1934.

Hood, Thomas,

HOOD, Thomas, 1799-1845. 821'.7 B
Letters of Thomas Hood, from the Dilke papers in the British Museum. Edited with an introd. and notes by Leslie A. Marchand. New York, Octagon Books, 1972 [c1945] viii, 104 p. 23 cm. Letters written to Mr. and Mrs. Dilke. Original ed. issued as v. 4 of Rutgers University studies in English. [PR4798.A44 1972] 75-159193 ISBN 0-374-93936-5
1. Dilke, Charles Wentworth, 1789-1864. II. Dilke, Maria Dover (Walker) d. 1850. III. Series: Rutgers University, New Brunswick, N.J. Rutgers studies in English, no. 4.

Hood, Thomas, 1799-1845.

CLUBBE, John. 821'.7
Victorian forerunner, the later career of Thomas Hood. Durham, N.C., Duke University Press, 1968. x, 255 p. illus. 23 cm. Includes bibliographical references. [PR4798.C5] 68-28520 7.50
1. Hood, Thomas, 1799-1845. I. Title. BIP

HOOD, Thomas, 1799-1845. 821'.7 B
The letters of Thomas Hood. Edited by Peter F. Morgan. [Toronto, Buffalo] University of Toronto Press [1973] xxviii, 703 p. 24 cm. (University of Toronto Dept. of English. Studies and Texts, 18) [PR4798.A44 1973] 76-185726 ISBN 0-8020-5222-3 15.00
1. Hood, Thomas, 1799-1845. I. Morgan, Peter F., ed. II. Title. III. Series: Toronto. University. Dept. of English. Studies and texts, 18. BIP

JEFFREY, Lloyd N. 821'.7
Thomas Hood, by Lloyd N. Jeffrey. New York, Twayne Publishers [1972] 176 p. 21 cm. (Twayne's English authors series, TEAS 137) Bibliography: p. 167-170. [PR4799.J4] 72-185453 5.50
1. Hood, Thomas, 1799-1845.

JERROLD, Walter Copeland, 1865-1929. 821'.7
Thomas Hood: his life and times. New York, Greenwood Press [1969] ix, 420 p. illus., ports. 23 cm. Reprint of the 1907 ed. [PR4798.J5 1969] 69-13953
1. Hood, Thomas, 1799-1845.

JERROLD, Walter Copeland, 1865-1929. 821'.7 B
Thomas Hood, his life and times. New York, Haskell House Publishers, 1968. ix, 420 p. illus., ports. 24 cm. Reprint of the 1907 ed. [PR4798.J5 1968] 68-24911
1. Hood, Thomas, 1799-1845. I. Title.

REID, John Cowie 821.7
Thomas Hood. London, Routledge & K. Paul [dist. New York, Hillary, 1964, c.1963] vii, 286p ports. 23cm. Bibl. 63-25790 6.50
1. Hood, Thomas, 1799-1845. I. Title.

Hooe family.

FADNER, Lawrence Trever. 929'.2'0973
Who was Fannie Hooe? / By Lawrence Trever Fadner. [s.l.] : Fadner, c1976. 77 leaves ; 30 cm. [CS71.H778 1976] 76-373457
1. Hooe family. 2. White, Fannie Seymour Hooe, ca. 1827-1882. 3. Virginia—Genealogy. I. Title.

Hook, Charles Ruffin, 1880-

TEBBEL, John William, 1912- 926.5
The human touch in business; the story of Charles R. Hook, who rose from office boy to internationally-known business leader. Dayton, Ohio, Otterbein Press [1963] 196 p. illus. 22 cm. [HD9520.H6T4] 63-1582
1. Hook, Charles Ruffin, 1880- . I. Title.

Hook, Theodore Edward, 1788-1841.

BRIGHTFIELD, Myron Franklin, 1897-1964. 823'.7
Theodore Hook and his novels. Cambridge, Harvard University Press, 1928. St. Clair Shores, Mich., Scholarly Press, 1971. 381 p. port. 22 cm. A revision of the author's thesis, Harvard. Bibliography: p. [365]-372. [PR4803.H2Z7 1971] 78-144900 ISBN 0-403-00814-X
1. Hook, Theodore Edward, 1788-1841. I. Title. BIP

HOOK, Theodore Edward, 1788-1841. 823'.7 B
The life and remains of Theodore Edward Hook / by R. H. Dalton Barham. New York : AMS Press, 1975. 2 v. : ports. ; 19 cm. Reprint of the 1849 ed. published by R Bentley, London. [PR4803.H2A6 1975] 73-170045 ISBN 0-404-07907-5 : 52.50
1. Barham, Richard Harris Dalton, 1815-1886. II. Title. BIP

Hooke, Robert, 1635-1703.

'ESPINASSE, Margaret 925
Robert Hooke. Berkeley, Calif., Univ. of Calif. Pr [1962] 192p. illus. 21cm. (Cal 65) Bibl. 1.95 pap.,
1. Hooke, Robert, 1635-1703. I. Title.

ESPINASSE, Margaret. v. 12
Robert Hooke, [1st paper-bound ed.] vii, 192 p. illus. 21 cm. Berkeley University of California Press, 1962) 63-21482
1. Hooke, Robert, 1635-1703. I. Title. II. Series.

ESPINASSE, Margaret 925
Robert Hooke [Gloucester, Mass., P. Smith, 1964] 192p. illus. 21cm. (Univ. of Calif. paperback 65 rebound) Bibl. 4.00
1. Hooke, Robert, I. Title. BIP

ESPINASSE, Margaret. 925
Robert Hooke. Berkeley, Calif., University of California Press, 1956. 192p. illus. 23cm. Includes bibliography. [Q143.H7E8] 56-58211
1. Hooke, Robert, 1635-1703. I. Title.

HOOKE, Robert, 1635-1703. 551.2'1
Lectures and discourses of earthquakes and subterraneous eruptions / Robert Hooke. New York : Arno Press, 1978. p. 172-181, xxviii, p. 279-450 : ill. ; 26 cm. (History of geology) Reprint of a chapter originally presented in the 1705 ed. of the author's The posthumous works of Robert Hooke, published by R. Waller, London. Also includes The first English geologist by A. P. Rossiter, reprinted from the Durham University journal, v. 29, 1935 (p. 172-181) and The life of Robert Hooke by R. Waller, reprinted from The post humous works of Robert Hooke, London, 1705 (p. i-xxviii) [QE521.H66 1978] 77-6521 ISBN 0-405-10443-X : 15.00
1. Hooke, Robert, 1635-1703. 2. Earthquakes. 3. Volcanism. 4. Geology—England—History. 5. Geologists—England—Biography. I. Waller, Richard. The life of Robert Hooke. 1978. II. Rossiter, Arthur Percival. The first English geologist. 1977. III. Title. **BIP**

Hooker, Joseph Dalton, Sir, 1817-1911.

HOOKER, Joseph Dalton, Sir, 1817-1911. 581'.092'4 B
Life and letters of Sir Joseph Dalton Hooker / Leonard Huxley. New York : Arno Press, 1978. p. cm. (Biologists and their world) Based on materials collected and arranged by Lady Hooker. Reprint of the 1918 ed. published by J. Murray, London. Appendices (v. 2, p.): A. Jorgen Jorgensen.—B. List of works by the late Sir Joseph Hooker.—C. List of degress, appointments, societies, and honours. Includes index. [QK31.H66A4 1978] 77-81130 ISBN 0-405-10726-9 : 70.00
1. Hooker, Joseph Dalton, Sir, 1817-1911. 2. Botanists—Great Britain—Biography. I. Huxley, Leonard, 1860-1933. II. Hooker, Hyacinth Symonds, Lady. III. Title. IV. Series.

Hooker, Richard, 1553 or 4-1600.

DAVIES, Ebenezer Thomas. 230'.5'20924 B
The political ideas of Richard Hooker [by] E. T. Davies. With a pref. by R. H. Malden. New York, Octagon Books, 1972. xii, 98 p. 21 cm. Reprint of the 1946 ed. Includes bibliographical references. [JC137.H7D3 1972] 75-159177 ISBN 0-374-92073-7
1. Hooker, Richard, 1553 or 4-1600. I. Title. **BIP**

Hooker, Thomas, 1586-1647.

HOOKER, Thomas, 1586-1647. 230'.5'8
Thomas Hooker : writings in England and Holland, 1626-1633 / edited, with introductory essays, by George H. Williams ... [et al.]. Cambridge : Harvard University Press, 1975. viii, 435 p., [1] leaf of plates : ill. ; 24 cm. (Harvard theological studies ; 28) Includes indexes. "A bibliography of the published writings of Thomas Hooker": p. 390-425. [BX7117.H58 1975] 75-30570 ISBN 0-674-88520-1 : 10.00
1. Hooker, Thomas, 1586-1647. 2. Hooker, Thomas, 1586-1647—Bibliography. 3. Theology—Collected works—17th century. 4. Congregational churches—Collected works. I. Williams, George Huntston, 1914- II. Title. III. Series.
Contents omitted **BIP**

SHUFFELTON, Frank, 1940- 285'.8'0924 B
Thomas Hooker, 1586-1647 / Frank Shuffelton. Princeton, N.J. : Princeton University Press, c1977. xii, 324 p. ; 23 cm. Includes index. Bibliography: p. 309-317. [BX7260.H596S55] 76-45912 ISBN 0-691-05249-2 : 17.50
1. Hooker, Thomas, 1586-1647. 2. Congregationalists—Connecticut—Hartford—Biography. 3. Clergy—Connecticut—Hartford—Biography. 4. Hartford—Biography. **BIP**

Hookworm infection—Hist.

ROUNTREE, Moses. v. 12
Hookworm doctor; the life story of Dr. C.F. Strosnider, a practicing physician for over a half a century. Goldsboro, N.C., Nash [1967?] ii, 111 p. port. 68-61901
1. Hookworm infection—Hist. 2. Strosnider, Charles Franklin, 1881- I. Title.

Hooper, Claude Ernest, 1898-1956.

'HOOP' of Hooperatings; v. 12
the man and his work. Norwalk, Conn., 1957. 132p. illus., ports.
1. Hooper, Claude Ernest, 1898-1956. I. Nye, Frank Wilson, 1887-

Hooper, George, Bp. of Bath and Wells, 1640-1727.

MARSHALL, William M. 283'.092'4 B
George Hooper, 1640-1727, Bishop of Bath and Wells / [by] William M. Marshall. Sherborne : Dorset Publishing Co., 1976. [8], 221 p. : ill., facsims., ports. ; 22 cm. Includes index. Bibliography: p. 204-212. [BX5199.H814M37 1976] 76-377651 ISBN 0-902129-27-9 : £4.50
1. Hooper, George, Bp. of Bath and Wells, 1640-1727. 2. Church of England—Bishops—Biography. 3. Bishops—England—Biography. I. Title.

Hooper, Johnson Jones, 1815?-1863.

HOOLE, William Stanley, 1903- 928.1
Alias Simon Suggs; the life and times of Johnson Jones Hooper. University, Ala., University of Alabama Press, 1952. xxiii, 283 p. port. 23 cm. Bibliography: p. [252]-271. [PS1999.H25Z6] 52-8066
1. Hooper, Johnson Jones, 1815?-1863. I. Title. **BIP**

HOOLE, William Stanley, 1903- 813'.3 B
Alias Simon Suggs; the life and times of Johnson Jones Hooper, by W. Stanley Hoole. Westport, Conn., Greenwood Press [1970, c1952] xxiii, 283 p. port. 23 cm. Bibliography: p. [252]-271. [PS1999.H25Z6 1970] 78-106694 ISBN 0-8371-3367-X
1. Hooper, Johnson Jones, 1815?-1863. I. Title.

Hooten, William J.

HOOTEN, William J. 070.4'092'4 B
Fifty-two years a newsman / by William J. Hooten; edited by Joseph M. Ray. [El Paso] : Texas Western Press, 1974. 193 p. : ill. ; 24 cm. Includes index. [PN4874.H63A34] 73-91959 ISBN 0-87404-047-7 : 10.00
1. Hooten, William J. 2. El Paso, Tex.—History. I. Title. **BIP**

Hoover, Herbert Clark,

HOOVER, Herbert Clark, Pres. U.S., 1874-1964. 923.173
Memoirs. New York, Macmillan, 1951- v. illus. ports. 25 cm. Contents.Contents.—v. 1. Years of adventure, 1874-1920.—[v. 2] The Cabinet and the Presidency, 1920-1933.—[v. 3] The great depression, 1929-1941. [E802.H7] 51-13301

Hoover, Herbert Clark, Pres. U.S., 1874-1964.

BURNER, David, 1937- 973.91'6'0924 B
Herbert Hoover, the public life / David Burner. 1st ed. New York : Knopf, 1978. p. cm. Includes bibliographical references and index. [E802.B87 1978] 78-54912 ISBN 0-394-46134-7 : 15.95
1. Hoover, Herbert Clark, Pres. U.S., 1874-1964. 2. Presidents—United States—Biography. I. Title.

COMFORT, Mildred Houghton, 1886- 923.173
Herbert Hoover, humanitarian; a biographical sketch of the former President of the United States. Minneapolis, T.S.Denison [c.1960] 186p. 60-53022 3.00
1. Hoover, Herbert Clark, Pres. U. S., 1874- I. Title.

HINSHAW, David, 1882- 923.173
Herbert Hoover, American Quaker. New York, Farrar, Straus [1950] xx, 469 p. illus., ports. 22 cm. Bibliography: p. 461-462. [E802.H65] 50-7271
1. Hoover, Herbert Clark, Pres. U. S., 1874- I. Title.

HOOVER, Herbert Clark, Pres. U.S., 1874-1964. 923.173
Memoirs. New York, Macmillan, 1951- v. illus. ports. 25 cm. Contents.Contents.—v. 1. Years of adventure, 1874-1920.—[v. 2] The Cabinet and the Presidency, 1920-1933.—[v. 3] The great depression, 1929-1941. [E802.H7] 51-13301

HOOVER Presidential Library Association. 973.91'6'0924 B
Herbert Hoover, the uncommon man. [West Branch, Iowa] : Hoover Presidential Library Association, 1974. 59 p. : ill. (some col.) ; 29 cm. [E802.H784 1974] 76-351205
1. Hoover, Herbert Clark, Pres. U.S., 1874-1964. I. Title.

JOHNSON, Lyndon Baines, Pres. U.S., 1908-1973. 973.91'6'0924
Oral history interview with Lyndon B. Johnson by Raymond Henle, director, January 8, 1971 at LBJ Ranch, Johnson City, Texas. For the Herbert Hoover Presidential Library, West Branch, Iowa, and the Hoover Institution on War, Revolution and Peace, Stanford, California. [n.p.] c1972. 22, [4] l. 28 cm. "Appendix": leaves [23]-[26] [E802.J65] 73-160702
1. Hoover, Herbert Clark, Pres. U.S., 1874-1964. 2. Johnson, Lyndon Baines, Pres. U.S., 1908-1973. 3. United States—Politics and government—20th century. I. Henle, Raymond, 1899- II. Title.

JOSLIN, Theodore Goldsmith, 1890-1944. 973.91'6'0924 B
Hoover off the record. Freeport, N.Y., Books for Libraries Press [1971] vi, 367 p. 23 cm. Reprint of the 1934 ed. [E801.J65 1971] 71-165644 ISBN 0-8369-5953-1
1. Hoover, Herbert Clark, Pres. U.S., 1874-1964. 2. U.S.—Politics and government—1929-1933. I. Title. **BIP**

KILLION, George L. 973.91'6'0924
Oral history interview with George L. Killion by Raymond Henle, director, January 25, 1970 at San Francisco, California. For the Herbert Hoover Presidential Library, West Branch, Iowa, and the Hoover Institution on War, Revolution and Peace, Stanford, California. [Rockford? Ill.] c1972. 17 l. 28 cm. [E802.K54] 73-160703
1. Hoover, Herbert Clark, Pres. U.S., 1874-1964. I. Henle, Raymond, 1899- II. Title.

LYONS, Eugene, 1898- 923.173
Herbert Hoover, a biography. [1st ed.] Garden City, N. Y., Doubleday, 1964. xii, 444 p. ports. (on lining papers) 24 cm. Bibliography: p. 443-444. [E802.L82] 64-15934
1. Hoover, Herbert Clark, Pres. U.S., 1874-1964.

LYONS, Eugene, 1898- v. 12
Herbert Hoover, a biography. Garden City, N.Y., Doubleday, 1964. xii, 468 p. ports. (on lining papers) 24 cm. Bibliography: p. 443-444. 65-90756
1. Hoover Herbert Clark, Pres. U.S., 1874- I. Title.

LYONS, Eugene, 1898- 923.173
The Herbert Hoover story. Washington, Human Events, 1959. 358p. 21cm. First published in 1948 under title: Our unknown ex-President, a portrait of Herbert Hoover. Includes bibliography. [E802.L85 1959] 59-4494
1. Hoover, Herbert Clark, Pres. U. S., 1874- I. Title.

MCGEE, Dorothy Horton 973.9160924
Herbert Hoover: engineer, humanitarian, statesman. New York, Dodd, 1965. x, 325p. illus., ports. 21cm. [E802.M2] 65-26316 3.75
1. Hoover, Herbert Clark, Pres., U.S., 1874-1964. I. Title.

MCGEE, Dorothy Horton. 923.173
Herbert Hoover: engineer, humanitarian, statesman. New York, Dodd, Mead, 1959. 307p. illus. 21cm. Includes bibliography. [E802.M2] 59-9621
1. Hoover, Herbert Clark, Pres. U. S., 1874- I. Title.

MILLER, Walter L. 973.91'6'0924 B
The life and accomplishments of Herbert Hoover [by] Walter L. Miller. Durham, N.C., Moore Pub. Co. [1970] 141 p. illus. 23 cm. Bibliography: p. 140-141. [E802.M54] 78-99300 ISBN 0-87716-024-4 6.95
1. Hoover, Herbert Clark, Pres. U.S., 1874-1964. I. Title. **BIP**

ROBINSON, Edgar Eugene, 1887- 973.9'16'0924 B
Herbert Hoover, President of the United States / Edgar Eugene Robinson and Vaughn Davis Bornet. Stanford, Calif. : Hoover Institution Press, Stanford University, 1975. xii, 398 p., [10] leaves of plates : ill. ; 24 cm. (Hoover Institution publications ; 149) Includes index. Bibliography: p. 307-331. [E801.R57] 75-18666 ISBN 0-8179-1491-9
1. Hoover, Herbert Clark, Pres. U.S., 1874-1964. 2. United States—Politics and government—1929-1933. I. Bornet, Vaughn Davis, 1917- joint author. II. Series: Stanford University. Hoover Institution on War, Revolution, and Peace. Publications ; 149.

STEINBERG, Alfred, 1917- 92
Herbert Hoover. New York, Putnam [1967] 255 p. 21 cm. (The Lives to remember series) Bibliography: p. 247-249. Biography of Herbert Hoover who spent forty-three years as a civil servant and whose career covered from the organization of relief programs during the first world war to his tour of duty as our thirty-first president. [E802.S84] AC 67
1. Hoover, Herbert Clark, Pres. U.S., 1874-1964. I. Title.

WEYANDT, Dorothy E. 799.1'2
I was a guide for three U.S. Presidents : as taken from the log of a famous Brule guide, Steve Weyandt I / by Dorothy E. Weyandt. [Brule, Wis.] : Weyandt, c1976. 298 p., [4] leaves of plates : ill. ; 24 cm. [SH415.W47] 75-25219
1. Weyandt, Steve, 1905- 2. Coolidge, Calvin, Pres. U.S., 1872-1933. 3. Hoover, Herbert Clark, Pres. U.S., 1874-1964. 4. Eisenhower, Dwight David, Pres. U.S., 1890-1969. 5. Trout fishing—Wisconsin—Brule River. 6. Guides for hunters, fishermen, etc.—Biography. I. Weyandt, Steve, 1905- II. Title.

WILSON, Joan Hoff, 1937- 973.91'6'0924 B
Herbert Hoover, forgotten progressive / Joan Hoff Wilson. Boston : Little, Brown, [1975] viii, 307 p. ; 20 cm. (Library of American biography) Includes bibliographical references and index. [E802.W53] 74-25676 pbk. : 3.95
1. Hoover, Herbert Clark, Pres. U.S., 1874-1964. I. Title. II. Series.

Hoover, Herbert Clark, Pres. U.S., 1874-1964—Juvenile literature.

EMERY, Anne, 1907- 973.91'6'0924 (B)
American Friend; Herbert Hoover. [New York] Rand McNally [1967] 232 p. illus., ports. 22 cm. Bibliography: p. 221-222 [E802.E4] 67-11955
1. Hoover, Herbert Clark, Pres. U.S., 1874-1964 — Juvenile literature. I. Title.

EMERY, Anne, 1907- 973.91'6'0924
America's Friend; Herbert Hoover. [New York] Rand McNally [1967] 232 p. illus., ports. 22 cm. Bibliography: p. 221-222. [E802.E4] 67-11955
1. Hoover, Herbert Clark, Pres. U.S., 1874-1964—Juvenile literature. I. Title.

PEARE, Catherine Owens 92
The Herbert Hoover story. New York, Crowell [c.1965] 247p. 21cm. Bibl. [E802.P4] 65-21418 3.75
1. Hoover, Herbert Clark, Pres. U.S., 1874-1964—Juvenile literature. I. Title. **BIP**

TERZIAN, James P. 92
The many worlds of Herbert Hoover, by

James P. Terzian. New York, Messner [1966] 191p. 22cm. [E802.T4] 66-8600 3.25; 3.19 lib. ed.,
1. Hoover, Herbert Clark, Pres. U.S., 1874-1964—Juvenile literature. I. Title.

Hoover, Irwin Hood, 1871-1933.

HOOVER, Irwin Hood, 1871-1933. 973'.0992 B
Forty-two years in the White House. Westport, Conn., Greenwood Press [1974, c1934] p. cm. Reprint of the ed. published by Houghton Mifflin, New York. [E176.1.H78 1974] 74-7938 ISBN 0-8371-7602-6
1. Hoover, Irwin Hood, 1871-1933. 2. Presidents—United States—Biography. 3. Washington, D.C. White House. I. Title. **BIP**

Hoover, John Edgar, 1895-1972.

DEMARIS, Ovid. 353.007'4'0924 B
The Director : an oral biography of J. Edgar Hoover / by Ovid Demaris. New York : Harper's Magazine Press, [1975] p. cm. Includes index. [HV7911.H6D45] 75-9361 ISBN 0-06-121951-7 : 12.95
1. Hoover, John Edgar, 1895-1972. 2. United States. Federal Bureau of Investigation. I. Title.

DE TOLEDANO, Ralph, 1916- 364.12'092'4 B
J. Edgar Hoover; the man in his time. New Rochelle, N.Y., Arlington House [1973] 384 p. port. 24 cm. [HV7911.H6D48] 72-91217 ISBN 0-87000-188-4 8.95
1. Hoover, John Edgar, 1895-1972. **BIP**

MESSICK, Hank. 364'.092'4 B
John Edgar Hoover; an inquiry into the life and times of John Edgar Hoover, and his relationship to the continuing partnership of crime, business, and politics. New York, McKay [1972] 276 p. 22 cm. Includes bibliographical references. [HV7911.H6M46] 70-188259 6.95
1. Hoover, John Edgar, 1895-

NASH, Jay Robert. 364.12'092'4 B
Citizen Hoover; a critical study of the life and times of J. Edgar Hoover and his FBI. Chicago, Nelson-Hall [1972] 298 p. illus. 23 cm. Includes bibliographical references. [HV7911.H6N36] 72-76266 ISBN 0-911012-60-5 7.95
1. Hoover, John Edgar, 1895-1972. I. Title. **BIP**

Hoover, Lou (Henry)

PRYOR, Helen (Brenton) 1897- 973.91'6'0924 B
Lou Henry Hoover: gallant First Lady, by Helen B. Pryor. Illustrated with photos. and a map. New York, Dodd, Mead [1969] xiii, 271 p. illus. 21 cm. Bibliography: p. 257-261. A biography of the woman who, in addition to serving for four years as First Lady in the White House, accompanied her husband all over the world, nursed the wounded on the battlefront of China's Boxer Rebellion, participated in many World War I relief movements, and served as President of the Girl Scouts of America. [E802.1.P7] 92 69-16201 4.50
1. Hoover, Lou (Henry) I. Title. **BIP**

Hope.

THE Guideposts treasury of hope. 248'.2 B Garden City, N.Y. : Doubleday, 1979, c1976. 305 p. ; 22 cm. [BV4638.G83] 79-114012 ISBN 0-385-14975-1 : 8.95
1. Hope. 2. Christian biography. **BIP**

Hope, Ashley Guy, 1914-

HOPE, Ashley Guy, 1914- 327'.2'0924 B
Journal of a journey : adventures in life, 1914-1974 / by Ashley Guy Hope. [Richmond] : Hope, c1976. 451 p. ; 24 cm. [E748.H666A34] 76-18330
1. Hope, Ashley Guy, 1914- 2. Diplomats—United States—Biography. I. Title.

Hope—Biblical teaching.

DEEN, Edith. 220.9'2 B
All the Bible's men of hope. [1st ed.] Garden City, N.Y., Doubleday, 1974. xxiv, 310 p. 22 cm. Bibliography: p. [297]-299. [BS571.D4] 73-22786 ISBN 0-385-05100-X 7.95
1. Bible—Biography. 2. Hope—Biblical teaching. I. Title.

Hope, Bob, 1903-

HOPE, Bob, 1903- 791'.092'4 B
The road to Hollywood : my 40-year love affair with the movies / by Bob Hope and Bob Thomas. 1st ed. Garden City, N.Y. : Doubleday, 1977. 271 p. : ill. ; 29 cm. [PN2287.H63A325] 73-81988 ISBN 0-385-02292-1 : 12.50
1. Hope, Bob, 1903- 2. Comedians—United States—Biography. I. Thomas, Bob, 1922- joint author. II. Title. **BIP**

MORELLA, Joe. 790.2'092'4 B
The amazing careers of Bob Hope; from gags to riches, by Joe Morella, Edward Z. Epstein, and Eleanor Clark. New Rochelle, N.Y., Arlington House [1973] 256 p. illus. 25 cm. [PN2287.H63M6] 73-10745 ISBN 0-87000-191-4 8.95
1. Hope, Bob, 1903- I. Epstein, Edward Z., joint author. II. Clark, Eleanor, joint author. III. Title.

MORELLA, Joe. 791'.092'4 B
The amazing careers of Bob Hope : from gags to riches / by Joe Morella, Edward Z. Epstein and Eleanor Clark. London ; New York : W. H. Allen, 1974. 256 p. : ill., ports. ; 24 cm. Includes index. Bibliography: p. 249. [PN2287.H63M6 1974] 75-317498 ISBN 0-491-01242-X : £3.00
1. Hope, Bob, 1903- I. Epstein, Edward Z., joint author. II. Clark, Eleanor, joint author. III. Title.

Hope, Bob, 1903- —Juvenile literature.

TAYLOR, Paula. 790.2'092'4 B
Bob Hope, master of entertainment. Illustrated by Harold Henriksen. Mankato, Minn., Creative Education; [distributed by Childrens Press, Chicago, 1974] 29 p. col. illus. 25 cm. (Creative Education close-ups) A brief biography of the entertainer and comedian emphasizing the events of his more than forty-year career in show business. [PN2287.H63T3] 92 74-19116 ISBN 0-87191-408-5 4 (lib. bdg.)
1. Hope, Bob, 1903- —Juvenile literature. I. Henriksen, Harold, illus. II. Title.

Hope, John, 1868-1936.

TORRENCE, Frederic Ridgely, 1875-1950. 378.1'1'0924
The story of John Hope. New York, Arno Press, 1969. 398 p. port. 23 cm. (The American Negro, his history and literature) Reprint of the 1948 ed. Bibliography: p. 379-380. [E185.97.H8T6 1969] 69-18568
1. Hope, John, 1868-1936. I. Title. II. Series. **BIP**

Hopekirk, Helen, 1856-1945.

HALL, Constance Huntington, 1886- comp. 927.8
Helen Hopekirk, 1856-1945. Cambridge, Mass., , 1954. 41p. illus. 24cm. Foreword signed: Constance Huntington Hall [and] Helen Ingersoll Tetlow. [ML417.H78H3] 54-25161
1. Hopekirk, Helen, 1856-1945. I. Tetlow, Helen Ingersoll, 1877- joint comp. II. Title.

Hopkins, Esek, 1718-1802.

MILLER, Charles Hazelius, 1887- 923.573
Admiral number one, some incidents in the life of Esek Hopkins, 1718-1802, first admiral of the Continental Navy. New York, William-Frederick Press, 1962. 74p. illus. 23cm. [E207.H7M5] 62-9234
1. Hopkins, Esek, 1718-1802. I. Title.

Hopkins, Gerard Manley, 1844-1889.

BERGONZI, Bernard. 821'.8 B
Gerard Manley Hopkins / Bernard Bergonzi. New York : Collier Books, 1977. p. cm. (Masters of world literature series) Includes index. Bibliography: p. [PR4803.H44Z584 1977b] 76-46330 ISBN 0-02-509950-7 : 8.95 ISBN 0-02-048590-5 pbk. 4.95
1. Hopkins, Gerard Manley, 1844-1889. 2. Poets, English—19th century—Biography.

DOWNES, David Anthony, 1927- 928.2
Victorian portraits; Hopkins and Pater. New York, Bkman [c.1965] 176p. 22cm. Bibl. [PR4803.H44Z624] 65-14412 4.50
1. Hopkins, Gerard Manley, 1844-1889. 2. Pater, Walter Horatio, 1839-1894. I. Title.

DOWNES, David Anthony, 1927- 928.2
Victorian portraits; Hopkins and Pater. New York, Bookman Associates [1965] 176 p. 22 cm. Bibliographical references included in "Notes" (p. 161-171) [PR4803.H44Z624] 65-14412
1. Hopkins, Gerard Manley, 1844-1889. 2. Pater, Walter Horatio, 1839-1894. I. Title.

HEUSER, Alan. 821.89
The shaping vision of Gerard Manley Hopkins. London, New York, Oxford University Press, 1958. 128p. 23cm. Includes bibliography. [PR4803.H44Z648] 58-14998
1. Hopkins, Gerard Manley, 1844-1889. I. Title. **BIP**

HEUSER, Alan. 821'.8
The shaping vision of Gerard Manley Hopkins. [Hamden, Conn.] Archon Books, 1968. viii, 128 p. 22 cm. Reprint of the 1958 ed. Bibliography: p. 119-122. [PR4803.H44Z648 1968] 68-15346
1. Hopkins, Gerard Manley, 1844-1889. I. Title.

HOPKINS, Gerard Manley, 1844-1889. 928.2
The correspondence of Gerard Manley Hopkins and Richard Watson Dixon. Edited with notes & an introd. by Claude Colleer Abbott. London, New York, Oxford University Press [1955] xxxi, 194p. ports., facsims. 23cm. This work is referred to as v. 2 in 'The letters of Gerard Manley Hopkins to Robert Bridges,' and contains the appendixes and index to both volumes. Includes bibliographical references. [PR4803.H44Z57 1955] 55-14511
I. Dixon, Richard Watson, 1833-1900. II. Title.

HOPKINS, Gerard Manley, 1844-1889. 928.2
The letters of Gerard Manley Hopkins to Robert Bridges. Edited with notes & an introd. by Claude Colleer Abbott. London, New York, Oxford University Press [1955] xivii, 324p. illus., ports., facsims, 23cm. 'The correspondence of Gerard Manley Hopkins and Richard Watson Dixon is referred to throughout as volume II. The appendixes, and also the index to both volumes ... will be found there.' Includes bibliographical references. [PR4803.H44Z55 1955] 55-14502
I. Bridges, Robert Seymour, 1844-1980. II. Title.

PICK, John, 1911- v. 12
Gerard Manley Hopkins; priest and poet. 2d ed. New York, Oxford University Press, 1966. xii, 169 p. front., plate (port.) 20 cm. (Galaxy book, GB171) 68-6180
1. Hopkins, Gerard Manley, 1844-1889. I. Title. **BIP**

PICK, John, 1911- 821.8
Gerard Manley Hopkins; priest and poet. 2nd ed. London, Oxford, 1966. xii, 169p. front., plate (port.) 20cm. (Oxford paperbacks) [PR4803.H44Z77 1966] 66-736501 1.25 pap.,
1. Hopkins, Gerard Manley, 1844-1889 I. Title.
Available from the pub's New York office, Galaxy bk., GB171.

PICK, John, 1911- 821'.8
Gerard Manley Hopkins, priest and poet / John Pick. 2d ed. Westport, Conn. : Greenwood Press, 1978, c1966. xii, 169 p. : port. ; 23 cm. Reprint of the ed. published by Oxford University Press, New York, which was issued as GB171 in series: A Galaxy book. Includes bibliographical references and index. [PR4803.H44Z77 1978] 78-14838 ISBN 0-313-20589-2
1. Hopkins, Gerard Manley, 1844-1889. 2. Jesuits—Great Britain—Biography. 3. Poets, England—19th century—Biography. I. Title.

SRINIVASA Iyengar, K. R. 821'.8 B
Gerard Manley Hopkins : the man and the poet / by K. R. Srinivasa Iyengar ; with a foreword by Jerome D'Souza. [Folcroft, Pa.] : Folcroft Library Editions, 1976. p. cm. Reprint of the 1948 ed. published by Indian Branch, Oxford University Press, Calcutta, New York. Bibliography: p. [PR4803.H44Z85 1976] 76-29030 ISBN 0-8414-5061-7 lib. bdg. : 20.00
1. Hopkins, Gerard Manley, 1844-1889. 2. Poets, English—19th century—Biography. **BIP**

SRINIVASA Iyengar, K. R. 821'.8
Gerard Manley Hopkins, the man and the poet, by K. R. Srinivasa Iyengar. With a foreword by Jerome D'Souza. New York, Haskell House Publishers, 1971. xv, 191 p. 23 cm. First published in 1948. Includes bibliographical references. [PR4803.H44Z85 1971] 71-117591 ISBN 0-8383-1024-9
1. Hopkins, Gerard Manley, 1844-1889

Hopkins, Gerard Manley, 1844-1889—Biography.

KITCHEN, Paddy. 821'.8 B
Gerard Manley Hopkins / Paddy Kitchen. 1st American ed. New York : Atheneum, 1979, c1978. 243 p., [4] leaves of plates : ill. ; 22 cm. Includes index. Bibliography: p. [233]-234. [PR4803.H44Z692 1979] 78-56337 ISBN 0-689-10930-X : 10.95
1. Hopkins, Gerard Manley, 1844-1889—Biography. 2. Jesuits—England—Biography. 3. Poets, English—19th century—Biography. I. Title.

LAHEY, Gerald F. 821'.8 B
Gerard Manley Hopkins, by G. F. Lahey. New York, Octagon Books, 1970. viii, 172 p. 23 cm. Reprint of the 1930 ed. [PR4802.H44Z7 1970] 77-120638
1. Hopkins, Gerard Manley, 1844-1889—Biography. **BIP**

LAHEY, Gerald F. 821'.8 B
Gerard Manley Hopkins, by G. F. Lahey. New York, Gordon Press, 1972. 172 p. illus. 23 cm. Reprint of the 1930 ed. published by H. Milford, Oxford University Press, London. [PR4803.H44Z7 1972] 72-88304 ISBN 0-87968-030-X 14.95
1. Hopkins, Gerard Manley, 1844-1889—Biography.

LAHEY, Gerald F. 821'.9'12 B
Gerard Manley Hopkins, by G. F. Lahey. New York, Haskell House Publishers, 1969. viii, 172 p. port. 23 cm. "First published 1930." "Juvenile prose extracts [by G. M. Hopkins]": p. [149]-158. "Prose extracts on clouds [by G. M. Hopkins]": p. [159]-169. Bibliographical footnotes. [PR4803.H44Z7 1969] 72-95435 ISBN 0-8383-0986-0
1. Hopkins, Gerard Manley, 1844-1889—Biography.

RUGGLES, Eleanor, 1916- 821'.8
Gerard Manley Hopkins; a life. Port Washington, N.Y., Kennikat Press [1969, c1944] 305 p. port. 22 cm. Bibliography: p. [293]-300. [PR4803.H44Z8 1969] 68-8213
1. Hopkins, Gerard Manley, 1844-1889—Biography.

Hopkins, Hampton Colvard, 1903-1956.

HOPKINS, Eva(Elliot) 922.673
He had to preach; an informal biography of Hampton C. Hopkins. With a foreword by Leon Macon. New York, Greenwich [c.1959] 127p. 21cm. 59-14759 2.75
1. Hopkins, Hampton Colvard, 1903-1956. I. Title.

HOPKINS, Eva (Elliott) 922.673
1913-
He had to preach;an informal biography of Hampton C. Hopkins. With a foreword by Leon Macon. [1st ed.] New York, Greenwich [1959] 127p. 21cm. [BX6495.H58H6] 59-14759
1. Hopkins, Hampton Colvard, 1903-1956. I. Title.

Hopkins, Harry Lloyd, 1890-1946.

ADAMS, Henry H. 973.917'092'4 B
Harry Hopkins : a biography / by Henry H. Adams ; foreword by W. Averell Harriman. New York : Putnam, c1977. 448 p., [8] leaves of plates : ill. ; 24 cm. Includes index. Bibliography: p. 427-433. [E748.H67A63 1977] 76-48985 ISBN 0-399-11833-0 : 15.00
1. Hopkins, Harry Lloyd, 1890-1946. 2. Statesmen—United States—Biography. **BIP**

Hopkins, John Henry, 1820-1891.

SWEET, Charles 283'.0924 B
Filkins, 1854or5-1927.
A champion of the cross. New York, AMS Press [1971] ix, 374 p. illus., port. 23 cm. Reprint of the 1894 ed. [BX5995.H67S8 1971] 76-144692 ISBN 0-404-07202-X
1. Hopkins, John Henry, 1820-1891. I. Title. **BIP**

Hopkins, Mark, 1813-1878.

LATTA, Estelle Cothran. 923.373
Controversial Mark Hopkins, by Estelle Latta, in collaboration with Mary L. Allison. New York, Greenberg [1953] 195 p. illus. 21 cm. [CT275.H64562L3] 52-10872
1. Hopkins, Mark, 1813-1878. I. Title. **BIP**

LATTA, Estelle (Cothran) 923.373
Controversial Mark Hopkins, by Estelle Latta, with Mary L Allison. 2d rev. ed. Sacramento, Calif., Cothran Historical and Research Found. [1963] 257p. illus. 21cm. 63-2043 Apply
1. Hopkins, Mark, 1813-1878. I. Title.

Hopkins, Pryns,

HOPKINS, Pryns, 1885- 920
Both hands before the fire, by Prynce Hopkins. Penobscot, Me., Traversity [c.1962] 205p. illus. 23cm. 62-18886 4.95
I. Title.

HOPKINS, Pryns, 1885- 920
Both hands before the fire, by Prynce Hopkins. Penobscot, Me., Traversity Press [1962] 205p. illus. 23cm. [CT275.H645624A3] 62-18886
I. Title.

Hopkins, Sarah Winnemucca, 1844?-1891.

GEHM, Katherine. 973'.04'97 B
Sarah Winnemucca : most extraordinary woman of the Paiute nation / by Katherine Gehm. Phoenix : O'Sullivan Woodside, [1975] 196 p. : ill. ; 25 cm. Bibliography: p. 195-196. A biography of an Indian princess who spent her life working for better treatment for her people by the United States government. [E99.P2H698] 92 75-12600 ISBN 0-89019-030-5
1. Hopkins, Sarah Winnemucca, 1844?-1891. 2. Paiute Indians. I. Title.

Hopkins, Stephen, 1581-1644.

HODGES, Margaret. 910'.453
Hopkins of the Mayflower; portrait of a dissenter. [1st ed.] New York, Farrar, Straus and Giroux [1972] 274 p. illus. 22 cm. Bibliography: p. 259-264. [F68.H8H62 1972] 72-81485 ISBN 0-374-33324-6 5.95
1. Hopkins, Stephen, 1581-1644. I. Title. **BIP**

Hopkinson, James,

HOPKINSON, James, 684.1'00924 B
1819-1894.
Victorian cabinet maker; the memoirs of James Hopkinson, 1819-1894. Edited by Jocelyne Baty Goodman. [New York] A. M. Kelley [1969] xiii, 138 p. illus., map, ports. 23 cm. Bibliographical references included in "Notes on the text": (p. 120-138) [TT140.H6A3 1969] 69-17113
I. Goodman, Jocelyne Baty, ed. II. Title. **BIP**

Hoppe, Willie, 1887-1959.

HOPPE, Willie, 794.7'2'0924 B
1887-1959.
Thirty years of billiards / by Willie Hoppe ; edited by Thomas Emmett Crozier. New York : Dover Publications, 1975. xiv, 254 p., [10] leaves of plates : ill. ; 21 cm. Reprint of the 1925 ed. published by Putnam, New York. Includes index. [GV891.H6 1975] 74-15003 ISBN 0-486-23126-7 pbk. : 3.00
1. Hoppe, Willie, 1887-1959. 2. Billiards. I. Title. **BIP**

Hopper, Hedda, 1890-1966.

EELLS, George. 070.4'49'791430922
Hedda and Louella. New York, Putnam [1972] 360 p. ports. 22 cm. [PN4874.H64E3] 70-174638 7.95
1. Hopper, Hedda, 1890-1966. 2. Parsons, Louella (Oettinger) 1885- I. Title.

EELLS, George. 070.4'49'791430922
Hedda and Louella. [New York] Warner Paperback Lib. [1973, c.1972] 382 p. ports. 18 cm. [PN4874.H64E3] 1.75 (pbk)
1. Hopper, Hedda, 1890-1966. 2. Parsons, Louella (Oettinger) 1885-1972 I. Title.
L.C. card no. for the hardbound edition: 70-174638.

ROSENSTEIN, Jaik, 1910- 791.4
Hollywood leg man. Los Angeles, Madison Press [1950] 212 p. 22 cm. [PN1993.5.U65R58] 50-14234
1. Hopper, Hedda, 2. Moving-pictures. 3. Hollywood, Calif. I. Title.

Hopper, Isaac Tatem, 1771-1852—Juvenile literature.

BACON, Margaret Hope. 326'.0924 B
Lamb's warrior; the life of Isaac T. Hopper. New York, Crowell [1970] xiii, 207 p. 21 cm. Bibliography: p. 193-197. A biography of the Quaker abolitionist who devoted his life to the defense of freedmen and escaping slaves. [E449.H7978] 92 72-101920 4.50
1. Hopper, Isaac Tatem, 1771-1852—Juvenile literature. I. Title.

Horatius Flaccus, Quintus.

CONWAY, Robert 913.3'7'0350922
Seymour, 1864-1933.
Makers of Europe. Freeport, N.Y., Books for Libraries Press [1967] 89 p. 24 cm. (The James Henry Morgan lectures in Dickinson College, 1930) Essay index reprint series. Reprint of the 1931 ed. Bibliographical footnotes. [DB203.C6] 67-28748
1. Caesar, C Julius. 2. Cicero, Marcus Tullius. 3. Horatius Fiaccus, Quintus. 4. Vergilius Maro. Publius. I. Title. II. Series.

CONWAY, Robert 913.3'7'0350922
Seymour, 1864-1933.
Makers of Europe. Freeport, N.Y., Books for Libraries Press [1967] 89 p. 24 cm. (Essay index reprint series.) (The James Henry Morgan lectures in Dickinson College 1930) Reprint of the 1931 ed. Bibliographical footnotes. [DG203.C6 1967] 67-28748
1. Caesar, C. Julius. 2. Cicero, Marcus Tullius. 3. Horatius Flaccus, Quintus. 4. Vergilius Maro, Publius. I. Title. II. Series.

FRAENKEL, Eduard, 1888- 874.5
Horace. Oxford, Clarendon Pr., 1957. xiv, 463p. 20cm. Bibl. [PA6411.F67] 58-37 3.50 pap.,
1. Horatius Flaccus Quintus. I. Title.
Available from Oxford in New York. **BIP**

FRAENKEL, Eduard, 1888- 874.01
Horace. Oxford, Clarendon P., 1966. xiv, 464 p. 20 cm. (Oxford paperback no. 105) Bibliographical footnotes. [PA6411.F67 1966] 68-94576 13/6
1. Horatius Flaccus, Quintus.

PERRET, Jacques, 1901- 878
Horace. Translated by Bertha Humez. [New York] New York University Press, 1964. vii, 212 p. 22 cm. Bibliography: p. 190-206. [PA6411.P4413] 64-21812
1. Horatius Flaccus, Quintus.

SEDGWICK, Henry Dwight, 874'.01
1861-1957.
Horace; a biography. New York, Russell & Russell [1967, c1947] ix, 182 p. 23 cm. Bibliography: p. [178]-179. [PA6411.S5 1967] 66-27146
1. Horatius Flaccus, Quintus. **BIP**

WILLIAMS, Gordon Willis. 874'.01
Horace. Oxford, Clarendon Press, 1972. 49 p. 24 cm. (Greece & Rome. New surveys in the classics, no. 6) Includes bibliographical references. [PA6411.W55] 73-163573
1. Horatius Flaccus, Quintus. I. Title. II. Series.

Horden, John, Bp. of Moosonee, 1828-1893.

BATTY, Beatrice 266'.3'0924 B
(Stebbing)
Forty-two years amongst the Indians and Eskimo; pictures from the life of the Right Reverend John Horden, first bishop of Moosonee, by Beatrice Batty. With a new series introd. by Sidney Forman. Boston, Gregg Press, 1973. p. (History of minority education) Reprint of the 1893 ed. [E78.C2B38 1973] 73-1811 ISBN 0-8398-0196-3
1. Horden, John, Bp. of Moosonee, 1828-1893. 2. Indians of North America—Canada—Missions. 3. Northwest Territories, Can. I. Title. II. Series.

LETTERS from James 266'.3'0924 B
Bay / commentary by James Scanlon ; drawings by Cecil Dunn ; foreword by J. A. Watton. Colbalt, Ont. : Highway Book Shop, 1976. 56 p., [3] p. : ill. ; 22 cm. Bibliography: p. [59] [E99.C88H674] 77-369946 ISBN 0-88954-094-2
1. Horden, John, Bp. of Moosonee, 1828-1893. 2. Missionaries—Canada—Biography. 3. Missionaries—England—Biography. 4. Cree Indians—Missions. 5. Indians of North America—Canada—Missions. I. Scanlon, James.

Horgan, Paul, 1903-

DAY, James M 818'.5'209
Paul Horgan, by James M. Day. Austin, Tex., Steck-Vaughn Co [1967] ii, 44 p. 21 cm. (Southwest writers series, no. 8) Bibliography: p. 39-44. [PS3515.O6583Z6] 67-24561
1. Horgan, Paul, 1903- I. Title. II. Series.

Hormizd, Rabban, 7th cent.

BUDGE, Ernest 281'.4'0924 B
Alfred Thompson Wallis, 1857-1834, ed.
The histories of Rabban Hormizd the Persian and Rabban Bar-'Idta : the Syriac texts edited with English translations / by E. A. Wallis Budge. New York : AMS Press, 1976. 2 v. ; 23 cm. Reprint of the 1902 ed. published by Luzac, London. The life of Hormizd was written by Rabban Mar Simon, the disciple of Mar Yozadhak. The life of Bar-'Idta was written by Abraham, a priest, at the command of 'Abhd-Isho, metropolitan of Adiabene, and is based upon that which was written by Mar John, a disciple of Bar-'Idta, who flourished about A.D. 660. Contents.Contents.—[v. 1] The Syriac texts.—v. 2, pt. 1. English translations. pt. 2. The metrical life of Rabban Hormizd by Mar Sergius of Adhorbjaijan. [BR1720.H82B8 1976] 73-18847 ISBN 0-404-11336-2 : 46.00 (2 vol set)
1. Hormizd, Rabban, 7th cent. 2. Bar-'Idta, ca. 509-612. I. Shem'on, Rabban Mar, 7th cent. Tash'ita de-'amlauhi alahaye ve-dubbarauhi temihe de-Rabban Hormizd. English & Syriac. 1976. II. Abraham, a priest. Tash'ita mekallasta de-abun zahya ve-kaddisha Rabban Bar 'Idta. English & Syriac. 1976. III. Sargis bar Wahle. Memerona. English. 1976. IV. Title.

Horn, Joshua S.

HORN, Joshua S. 362.1'0951
Away with all pests ... ; an English surgeon in People's China, by Joshua S. Horn. With an introduction by Edgar Snow. London, New York, Hamlyn [1969] 192 p., 32 plates. illus., ports. 23 cm. Includes bibliographical references and index. [R601.H56 1969] 74-182740 ISBN 0-600-10019-7 35/-
1. Horn, Joshua S. 2. Medicine—China. 3. Physicians—Correspondence, reminiscences, etc. I. Title. **BIP**

Horn, Sylvia Hall, 1813-1899.

SCANLAN, Charles 973'.04'97 S
Martin, 1854-1940.
Indian Creek massacre and captivity of Hall girls / Charles Martin Scanlan. New York : Garland Pub., 1975. 119 p. : ill. ; 23 cm. (The Garland library of narratives of North American Indian captivities ; v. 49) Reprint of the 2d ed., 1915, published by the Reic Pub. Co., Milwaukee. Bound with the reprint of the 1832 ed. of Narrative of the capture and providential escape of Misses Frances and Almira Hall. Includes bibliographical references and index. [E85.G2 vol. 49] [E83.83] 973.5'6 75-7071 ISBN 0-8240-1673-4 lib.bdg. : 21.00
1. Horn, Sylvia Hall, 1813-1899. 2. Munson, Rachel Hall, d. 1870. 3. Black Hawk War, 1832. 4. Indians of North America—Captivities. I. Title. II. Series.

Horn, Tom, 1860-1903.

CAESAR, Gene, 1927- 923.4173
Rifle for rent, a dramatic true story of one of the most colorful figures of the untamed Southwest. Derby, Conn., Monarch [c.1963] 141p. 19cm. (Monarch Americana bk., MA338) 63-2628 .35 pap.,
1. Horn, Tom, 1860-1903. I. Title.

HORN, Tom, 1860- 979'.03'0924 B
1903.
Life of Tom Horn : government scout and interpreter : a vindication / written by himself, together with his letters and statements by his friends. Glorieta, N.M. : Rio Grande Press, [1976], c1904. p. cm. (A Rio Grande classic) Reprint of the ed. published for J. C. Cole by the Louthan Book Co., Denver. [E83.88.H67 1976] 76-49944 ISBN 0-87380-119-9 lib.bdg. : 12.00
1. Horn, Tom, 1860-1903. 2. Apache Indians—Wars, 1883-1886. 3. Frontier and pioneer life—Southwest, New. 4. Scouts and scouting—Southwest, New—Biography. I. Title.

HORN, Tom, 1860-1903. 923.4173
Life of Tom Horn, Government Scout and interpreter written by himself, together with his letters and statements by his friends; a vindication. With an introd. by Dean Krakel. [New ed.] Norman, University of Oklahoma Press [1964] xviii, 277 p. 20 cm. (The Western frontier library, 26) [F595.H797 1964] 64-20758
1. Apache Indians. 2. Apache Indians—Wars, 1883-1886. 3. Frontier and pioneer life—Arizona. I. Title. **BIP**

HORN, Tom, 1860-1903. 979'.03'0924 B
Life of Tom Horn, Government scout and interpreter : a vindication / written by himself, together with his letters and statements by his friends ; with an introd. by James D. Horan. New York : Jingle Bob/Crown Publishers, [1977] p. cm. (Jingle Bob series) Reprint of the 1904 ed. published for J. C. Cole by the Louthan Book Co., Denver, with a new introd. [E83.88.H67 1977] 77-3998 ISBN 0-517-53114-3 : 6.95 ISBN 0-517-53115-1 pbk. : 3.95
1. Horn, Tom, 1860-1903. 2. Apache Indians—Wars, 1883-1886. 3. Frontier and pioneer life—Southwest, New. 4. Scouts and scouting—Southwest, New—Biography. I. Title.

KRAKEL, Dean Fenton, 1923- 923.4173
The saga of Tom Horn; the story of a cattlemen's war with personal narratives, newspaper accounts, and official documents and testimonies. Illustrated with The pageant of personalities. [Laramie, Wyo., Powder River Publishers 1954] ix, 277p. illus., ports. 24cm. Bibliography: p. [267]-269. [F595.H8K7] 54-31950
1. Horn, Tom, I. Title.

PAINE, Lauran. 923.4173
Tom Horn; man of the West. [1st American ed.] Barre, Mass., Barre Pub. Co., 1963. vi, 186 p. 22 cm. [F595.H8P3 1963] 63-18870
1. Horn, Tom, 1860-1903.

PAINE, Lauran 923.4173
Tom Horn: man of the West. Barre, Mass., Barre Pub. [dist. Barre Gazette, c.]1963. vi, 186p. 22cm. 3.95
1. Horn, Tom, 1860-1903. I. Title.

Hornaday, William Temple, 1854-1937.

FORBES, John Ripley. 92
In the steps of the great American zoologist: William Temple Hornaday. Illus. by Kathleen Elgin. New York, Published by M. Evans and distributed in association with Lippincott, Philadelphia [1966] 128 p. illus. 21 cm. ([In the steps of the great American naturalists]) Bibliography: p. 128. A biography of a zoologist and taxidermist who found a better way to stuff and preserve animals and subsequently aided in the development of natural history museums. [PZ10.F565In] AC 67
1. Hornaday, William Temple, 1854-1937. 2. Taxidermy. 3. Zoology. I. Elgin, Kathleen, 1923- illus. II. Title. **BIP**

Hornburg family.

ELKINS, Edna Hornburg, 1912- 929'.2'0973
The Hornburg story / by Edna Hornburg Elkins, Annie Mae Turner Hornburg, Ruth Smith Brady. Austin, Tex. : J. G. Garcia, [1974] ix, 468 p., [19] leaves of plates : ill. ; 29 cm. Includes index. Bibliography: p. 446-447. [CS71.H8155 1974] 75-305240
1. Hornburg family. I. Hornburg, Annie Mae Turner, 1909- joint author. II. Brady, Ruth Smith, 1910- joint author. III. Title.

Hornby, John, 1880-1927.

WHALLEY, George, 1915- 923.971
The legend of John Hornby. London, Murray [dist. Leavittown, L. I., N. Y., Transatlantic, c.1965] 367p. illus. 23cm. [F1096.H6W5] 63-4838 9.50
1. Hornby, John, 1880-1927. 2. Mackenzie District—Descr. & trav. I. Title.

Horne, Donald.

HORNE, Donald. 994'.04'0924
The education of young Donald. [Sydney] Angus & Robertson [1967] 331p. 21cm. [DU114.H64A3] 68-80459 6.95
I. Title.
Distributed by Tri-Ocean, San Francisco.

Horne, Joseph, 1812-1897.

PARK, Clara (Horne) v. 12
Joseph Horne, pioneer of 1847. [Salt Lake City, 1961] 68 p. illus. 23 cm. Cover title. 65-48159
1. Horne, Joseph, 1812-1897. I. Title.

Horner, Henry, 1878-1940.

LITTLEWOOD, Thomas B. 977.3'04'0924 B
Horner of Illinois [by] Thomas B. Littlewood. Evanston, Northwestern University Press, 1969. xi, 273 p. illus., ports. 24 cm. Bibliography: p. 256-259. [F546.H67L5] 70-78329
1. Horner, Henry, 1878-1940. I. Title. **BIP**

Horney, Karen, 1885-1952.

RUBINS, Jack L. 616.8'917'0924
Karen Horney : gentle rebel of psychoanalysis / Jack L. Rubins. New York : Dial Press, c1978. xviii, 362 p., [8] leaves of plates : ill. ; 24 cm. Includes index. Bibliography: p. 349-350. [RC339.52.H67R8] 78-9339 ISBN 0-8037-4425-0 : 9.95
1. Horney, Karen, 1885-1952. 2. Psychoanalysts—Biography. I. Title. **BIP**

Hornibrook, Manuel Richard, Sir, 1893-1970.

BROWNE, Waveney. 338.7'62'40924 B
A man of achievement : Sir Manuel Hornibrook, Kt, Q.B.E., Hon. F.L.O.B., F.I.A.B., F.R. Hist. S.Q. / by Waveney Browne. Brisbane : P.E.P. Enterprises, 1974. xiv, 154 p. : ill., front. ; 26 cm. Includes index. [TA140.H65B76 1974] 75-327804 ISBN 0-9598168-0-1 : 7.50
1. Hornibrook, Manuel Richard, Sir, 1893-1970. I. Title.

Hornsby, Rogers, 1896- —Juvenile literature.

FINLAYSON, Ann. 796.357'092'2
Champions at bat; three power hitters. Illustrated by Paul Frame. Champaign, Ill., Garrard Pub. Co. [1970] 96 p. illus., ports. 24 cm. (Garrard sports library) Biographical sketches of three baseball players renowned for their batting skill: Rogers Hornsby, Joe DiMaggio, Ted Williams. [GV865.A1F5] 74-113838 ISBN 0-8116-6661-1 2.59
1. Hornsby, Rogers, 1896- —Juvenile literature. 2. Di Maggio, Joseph Paul, 1914- —Juvenile literature. 3. Williams, Theodore Samuel, 1918- —Juvenile literature. I. Frame, Paul, 1913- illus. II. Title. **BIP**

Hornung, Paul,

HORNUNG, Paul, 1935- 796.3320924
Football and the single man, by Paul Hornung as told to Al Silverman. Garden City, N.Y., Doubleday [c.]1965. 252p. ports. 22cm. Autobiographical. [GV939.H6A3] 65-23789 4.95
I. Silverman, Al. II. Title.

Horoscopes.

COOPER, Michael, 1943- 133.5'48
An astrological index to the world's famous people / by Michael Cooper and Andrew Weaver. 1st ed. Garden City, N.Y. : Doubleday, 1975. 290 p. ; 22 cm. [BF1728.A2C66] 74-3545 ISBN 0-385-00507-5
1. Horoscopes. 2. Biography—Miscellanea. I. Weaver, Andrew, 1946- joint author. II. Title.

PENFIELD, Marc. 133.5'48
An astrological who's who. [1st ed.] York Harbor, Me., Arcane Publications [1972] xxv, 543 p. illus. 24 cm. Bibliography: p. 543. [BF1728.A2P45] 74-188580 ISBN 0-912240-08-3 10.00
1. Horoscopes. I. Title. **BIP**

Horowitz, Jacob Isaac, d. 1815.

WIESEL, Elie, 1928- 296.8'33
Four Hasidic masters and their struggle against melancholy / by Elie Wiesel ; foreword, Theodore M. Hesburgh. Notre Dame [Ind.] : University of Notre Dame Press, c1978. xix, 131 p., [1] leaf of plates : ill. ; 21 cm. (Ward-Phillips lectures in English language and literature ; v. 9) [BM198.W5125] 78-1419 ISBN 0-268-00944-9 : 7.95
1. Phinehas ben Abraham, of Korets, 1726 or 8-1791. 2. Baruch, of Tul'chin, 1757 (ca.)-1811. 3. Horowitz, Jacob Isaac, d. 1815. 4. Horowitz, Naphtali Zebi, 1760-1827. 5. Hasidim—Biography. I. Title. II. Series. **BIP**

Horowitz, Steve.

HOROWITZ, Steve. 610'.92'4 B
Calling Dr. Horowitz / Steve Horowitz and Neil Offen. New York : Morrow, 1977. 251 p. ; 22 cm. [R154.H662A33] 76-40225 ISBN 0-688-03140-4 : 8.95
1. Horowitz, Steve. 2. Residents (Medicine)—New York (City)—Biography. 3. Hospital care. I. Offen, Neil, joint author. II. Title. **BIP**

Horrocks, Brian, Sir, 1895-

HORROCKS, Brian, Sir, 1895- 940.54'21
Corps commander / Sir Brian Horrocks, with Eversley Belfield and H. Essame. New York : Scribner, c1977. xvi, 256 p. : ill. ; 25 cm. Includes index. [D756.H66 1977b] 77-79221 ISBN 0-684-15324-6 : 14.95
1. Horrocks, Brian, Sir, 1895- 2. World War, 1939-1945—Campaigns—Western. 3. World War, 1939-1945—Personal narratives, English. 4. Generals—Great Britain—Biography. I. Belfield, Eversley Michael Gallimore, joint author. II. Essame, Hubert, 1896-1976, joint author. III. Title. **BIP**

Horror films—Biography.

BROSNAN, John. 791.43'0909'16
The horror people / John Brosnan. New York : St. Martin's Press, c1976. 304 p. : ill. ; 25 cm. Includes bibliographical references and indexes. [PN1998.A2B6866] 75-26173 11.95
1. Horror films—Biography. I. Title. **BIP**

BROSNAN, John. 791.43'0909'16
The horror people / [by] John Brosnan. London : Macdonald and Jane's, 1976. vi, 304 p. : ill., ports. ; 25 cm. Includes bibliographical references and indexes. [PN1998.A2B6866 1976b] 76-383391 ISBN 0-356-08394-2 : £6.50
1. Horror films—Biography. I. Title.

Horse racing.

MONOLULU, Ras. 927.984
I gotta horse, the autobiography of Ras prince Monolulu, as told to Sidney H. White. London, New York, Hurst & Blackett [1950] 184 p. ports. 22 cm. [SF336.M6A3] 52-64463
1. Horse racing. I. White, Sidney H. II. Title.

Horse-shows.

HANSON, Christilot 1947- 798'.2'0924
Canadian entry. Pref. by Waldemar Seunig. Chicago, Follett Pub. Co. [c1966] 140 p. illus., ports. 23 cm. Autobiographical. [SF295.H28] 66-30000
1. Horse-shows. I. Title.

Horsemen.

BOWMAR, Dan M 927.98
Giants of the turf: the Alexanders, the Belmonts, James R. Keene, the Whitneys. Lexington, Ky., The Blood-horse, 1960. 224p. illus. 24cm. [SF31.B6] 61-1836
1. Horsemen. 2. U. S.—Biog. 3. Race horses. I. Title.

Horsemen—Correspondence, reminiscences, etc.

BLOODGOOD, Lida (Fleitmann) 1894- 927.98
Hoofs in the distance. Foreword by A. Henry Higginson. Decorations by Lida Lacey Bloodgood. New York, Van Nostrand [1953] 131p. illus. 27cm. [SF309.B617] 53-10092
1. Horsemen—Correspondence, reminiscences, etc. I. Title.

SMYTHE, Pat, 1928- 927.98
Jump for joy. [1st American ed.] New York, Dutton, 1955. 253 p. illus. 21 cm. [SF301.S58 1955] 55-9655
1. Horsemen—Correspondence, reminiscences, etc. I. Title.

Horsemen—United States—Biography.

PHILLIPS, Lance. 798'.23
Folks I knowed and horses they rode / by Lance Phillips. Ashland, Va. : Plantation Press, 1975. 223 p. : ill. ; 26 cm. Includes indexes. [SF336.A2P47] 74-33878 12.95
1. Horsemen—United States—Biography. 2. American saddle horse. 3. Horse-shows. I. Title.

Horses.

EVANS, Edna Hoffman, 1913- 636.1
Famous horses and their people / Edna H. Evans. Brattleboro, Vt. : S. Greene Press, [1975] viii, 168 p. : ill. ; 22 cm. Bibliography: p. 165-168. [SF285.E93] 74-31238 ISBN 0-8289-0231-3 : 7.95
1. Horses. 2. Statesmen—Biography. 3. Horsemen—Biography. I. Title. **BIP**

Horses—Legends and stories.

GREEN, Ben K. 636.1'00924
Horse tradin', by Ben K. Green. Illus. by Lorence Bjorklund. [1st ed.] New York, Knopf, 1967. xiv, 304 p. illus. 22 cm. Autobiographical. [SF301.G73] 66-19378
1. Horses—Legends and stories. I. Title. **BIP**

Horsley, Albert E.,

HORSLEY, Albert E., 1866-1954. 922
Harry Orchard, the man God made again, by Harry Orchard [pseud.] in collaboration with Le Roy Edwin Froom. Nashville, Southern Pub. Association [1952] 200 p. illus. 21 cm. [BV4935.H65A3] 52-25949
I. Title.

Horsley, Albert E., 1866-1954.

†GRIMMETT, Robert G., 1931- 364.1'523'0924 B
Cabal of death : Harry Orchard and his associates in murder in the western mining wars / by Robert G. Grimmett. Moscow : University Press of Idaho, c1977. 292 p., 12 leaves of plates : ill. ; 22 cm. (A GEM book) Bibliography: p. 285-291. [F595.H815G74] 77-15675 ISBN 0-89301-047-2 pbk. : 7.50
1. Horsley, Albert E., 1866-1954. 2. Outlaws—The West—Biography. 3. Mines and mining—The West—History. 4. Frontier and pioneer life—The West. I. Title.

HORSLEY, Albert E., 1866-1954. 922
Harry Orchard, the man God made again, by Harry Orchard [pseud.] in collaboration with Le Roy Edwin Froom. Nashville, Southern Pub. Association [1952] 200 p. illus. 21 cm. [BV4935.H65A3] 52-25949
I. Title.

Hortense, consort of Louis, King of Holland, 1783-1837.

HORTENSE, consort 949.2'05'0924 B of Louis, King of Holland, 1783-1837. *The memoirs of Queen Hortense.* Published by arrangement with Prince Napoleon. Edited by Jean Hanoteau. Translated by Arthur K. Griggs. Freeport, N.Y., Books for Libraries Press [1973] p. Translation of Memoires de la reine Hortense. Reprint of the 1927 ed. published by Cosmopolitan Book Corp., New York. [DC216.4.A35 1973] 73-5999 ISBN 0-518-19050-1
1. Hortense, consort of Louis, King of Holland, 1783-1837. 2. Napoleon I, Emperor of the French, 1769-1821. 3. Bonaparte family. 4. France—History—1789-1815.

WRIGHT, Constance. 923.1492 *Daughter to Napoleon;* a biography of Hortense, Queen of Holland. [1st ed.] New York, Holt, Rinehart and Winston [1961] 436 p. illus. 22 cm. Includes bibliography. [DC216.4.W95] 61-14680
1. Hortense, consort of Louis, King of Holland, 1783-1837. I. Title.

Horticulture—Biography.

WEBBER, Ronald. 635'.0922 *The early horticulturists.* New York, A. M. Kelley [1968] 224 p. illus., ports. 23 cm. Contents.Contents.—Commercial horticulture until 1900.—Richard Harris of Teynham.—Gardener Cawsway of Houndsditch.—Seedsman Child of Pudding Lane.—John Tradescant of Lambeth.—Sarah Sewell of Convent Garden.—James Lee of Hammersmith.—William Forsyth of St. James's.—Andrew Knight of Ludlow.—The Rochfords of Tottenham.—The Pouparts of Twickenham.—John Wills of Kensington.—Thomas Smith of Mayland.—Alfred Smith of Feltham.—Appendix: Where the plants came from.—Bibliography: (p. 210-215) [SB61.W4] 68-23823
1. Horticulture—Biography. 2. Horticulture—England—History. I. Title.

Horton, George Moses, 1798?-ca. 1880.

WALSER, Richard Gaither, 811.3(B) 1908- *The black poet;* being the remarkable story (partly told my [sic] himself) of George Moses Horton, a North Carolina slave, by Richard Walser. Drawings by Claude Howell. New York, Philosophical Lib. [1966] vii, 120p. illus. 22cm. [PS1999.H473Z9] 66-18817 3.50
1. Horton, George Moses, 1798?-ca. 1880. I. Title.

Horton, George Moses, 1798?-ca. 1880—Juvenile literature.

CLARK, Margaret 810'.9'896073 B Goff. *Their eyes on the stars: four Black writers.* Champaign, Ill., Garrard Pub. Co. [1973] 174 p. illus. 22 cm. (Toward freedom series) Traces the lives of four black writers who wrote of the Negro experience in eighteenth-and nineteenth-century America. [PS153.N5C5] 920 73-3499 ISBN 0-8116-4804-4 3.78
1. Hammon, Jupiter, 1711-ca. 1800—Juvenile literature. 2. Horton, George Moses, 1798?-ca. 1880—Juvenile literature. 3. Brown, William Wells, 1815-1884—Juvenile literature. 4. Chesnutt, Charles Waddell, 1858-1932—Juvenile literature. I. Cary, Louis F., 1915- illus. II. Title. III. Series.

Horton, James Africanus Beale.

FYFE, 916.6'03'0924 B Christopher. *Africanus Horton, 1835-1883, West African scientist and patriot* New York, Oxford University Press, 1972. xi, 169 p. illus. 21 cm. Bibliography: p. 160-163. [DT504.H67F9] 71-170259 ISBN 0-19-501501-0 6.75
1. Horton, James Africanus Beale.

Horton, Lester, 1906-1953.

WARREN, Larry. 793.3'2'0924 B *Lester Horton, modern dance pioneer /* Larry Warren. New York : M. Dekker, c1977. xvi, 265 p. : ill. ; 24 cm. ([The Dance program ; v. 3]) Includes bibliographical references and index. [GV1785.H64W37] 76-23364 ISBN 0-8247-6503-6 : 12.75
1. Horton, Lester, 1906-1953. 2. Choreographers—United States—Biography. 3. Modern dance. I. Title. II. Series.

Horton, Marilee.

HORTON, Marilee. 248'.2 B *Dear mamma please don't die /* Marilee Horton. Nashville : Thomas Nelson, c1979. 160 p. ; 21 cm. [BR1725.H664A33] 79-13455 ISBN 0-8407-5689-5 pbk. : 3.50
1. Horton, Marilee. 2. Chritian biography—United States. 3. Multiple sclerosis—Biography. 4. Depression, Mental—Biography. I. Title. **BIP**

Horton, Willie, 1942-

BUTLER, Hal. 796.357'0924 B *The Willie Horton story.* New York, J. Messner [1970] 187 p. illus., ports. 22 cm. A biography of the star Detroit Tiger outfielder who spends his off-field time helping young people in the slums. [GV865.H63B8 1970] 92 72-123171 3.95
1. Horton, Willie, 1942- I. Title.

Horwitz, Simi.

HORWITZ, Simi. 792'.092'4 B *South of the navel.* New York, Crowell [1973] ix, 194 p. 21 cm. [CT275.H64585A3] 73-10056 ISBN 0-690-00082-0 5.95
1. Horwitz, Simi. I. Title.

Hosack, David, 1769-1835.

ROBBINS, Christine Chapman 926.1 *David Hosack, citizen of New York.* Philadelphia, Amer. Phil. Soc. [c.]1964. vii, 246p. illus., geneal. table, map, ports. 25cm. (Mems. of the Amer. Phil. Soc., v.62) Bibl. [R154.H667R6] 64-8747 3.50
1. Hosack, David, 1769-1835. I. Title. II. Series: American Philosophical Society, Philadelphia. Memoirs, v.62

Hosey, William J., 1854-1937.

FORT Wayne. Public v. 12 Library. *William J. Hosey;* Fort Wayne's dedicated mayor. [Fort Wayne] Public Library of Fort Wayne and Allen County, 1957. 60 p. illus., port. 23 cm. 68-69083
1. Hosey, William J., 1854-1937. I. Title.

FORT Wayne. Public 977.2'74 Library. *William J. Hosey; Fort Wayne's dedicated mayor.* Prepared by the staff of the Public Library of Fort Wayne and Allen County. [Fort Wayne] 1957. 60 p. illus., ports. 21 cm. [F534.F7F63] 977.2'65 75-270528
1. Hosey, William J., 1854-1937. 2. Fort Wayne—History. I. Title.

Hosford, Henry Hallock, 1859-1965.

HOSFORD, 917.7'03'0924 (B) Herbert Chamberlain, 1894- *This good life;* a biography of Henry Hallock Hosford, and A boyhood in old Hudson, by Henry Hallock Hosford. Erie, Pa. [1966] 99 p. illus., ports. 23 cm. [CT275.H6459H6] 67-3423
1. Hosford, Henry Hallock, 1859-1965. I. Hosford, Henry Hallock, 1859-1965. A boyhood in old Hudson. II. Title.

Hosking, Eric John.

HOSKING, Eric John. 770'.92'4 B *An eye for a bird; the autobiography of a bird photographer* [by] Eric Hosking, with Frank W. Lane. Foreword by Prince Philip, Duke of Edinburgh. [1st American ed.] New York, P. S. Eriksson [1973, c1970] xviii, 302 p. illus. 24 cm. [TR140.H67A3 1973] 72-93312 ISBN 0-8397-0290-6 10.00
1. Hosking, Eric John. 2. Photography of birds. I. Lane, Frank Walter. II. Title.

Hoskins, John, 1566-1638.

OSBORN, Louise Brown. 828'.3'07 *The life, letters, and writings of John Hoskyns, 1566-1638.* [Hamden, Conn.] Archon Books, 1973 [c1937] viii, 321 p. illus. 22 cm. Original ed. issued as v. 87 of Yale studies in English. A revision of the author's thesis, Yale, 1930. Includes bibliographical references. [PR2294.H58O8 1973] 72-8893 ISBN 0-208-01132-3
1. Hoskins, John, 1566-1638. I. Series: Yale studies in English, v. 87. **BIP**

Hosmer, Horace, 1830-1894.

HOSMER, Horace, 1830- 818'.3'09 B 1894. *Remembrances of Concord and the Thoreaus :* letters of Horace Hosmer to Dr. S. A. Jones / edited by George Hendrick. Urbana : University of Illinois Press, 1977. p. cm. Includes bibliographical references and index. [PS3053.H58 1977] 77-24232 ISBN 0-252-00660-7 : 10.00
1. Thoreau, Henry David, 1817-1862—Biography—Sources. 2. Thoreau family. 3. Hosmer, Horace, 1830-1894. 4. Jones, Samuel Arthur, 1834-1912—Correspondence. 5. Concord, Mass.—Social life and customs. 6. Authors, American—19th century—Correspondence. I. Jones, Samuel Arthur, 1834-1912. II. Hendrick, George. III. Title.

Hostetler, David, 1926-

ADAMS, Phillip D 730'.924 *David Hostetler,* the carver from Coolville Ridge, by Phillip D. Adams. Kalamazoo, School of Graduate Studies, Western Michigan University, 1967. 52 p. 36 illus. 23 cm. (Western Michigan University, Kalamazoo. School of Graduate Studies. Faculty contributions, ser. 10, no. 1) Bibliographical footnotes. [LB5.M56 ser. 10, no. 1] 68-2654
1. Hostetler, David, 1926- I. Title. II. Series: Michigan. Western Michigan University, Kalamazoo. School of Graduate Studies. Faculty contributions, ser. 10, no. 1

ADAMS, Phillip D. 730'.924 *David Hostetler, the carver from Coolville Ridge,* by Phillip D. Adams. Kalamazoo, School of Graduate Studies, Western Michigan University, 1967. 52 p. 36 illus. 23 cm. (Western Michigan University, Kalamazoo. School of Graduate Studies. Faculty contributions, ser. 10, no. 1) Bibliographical footnotes. [LB5.M56 ser. 10, no. 1] 68-2654
1. Hostetler, David, 1926- I. Title. II. Series: Michigan. Western Michigan University, Kalamazoo. School of Graduate Studies. Faculty contributions, ser. 10, no. 1

Hotel management—United States—Biography.

WHO'S who among 647'.94'0922 *inkeepers* a biographical reference work about hotel, motel, and resort managers and owners in America. 1st ed., 1974-1975. [New York, Rating Publications, 1974] 210 p. 23 cm. [TX910.3.W48] 73-89548 ISBN 0-914472-01-1 30.00 (lib. bdg.).
1. Hotel management—United States—Biography. 2. Motel management—United States—Biography.

Hotman, Francois, sieur de Villiers Saint Paul, 1524-1590.

KELLEY, Donald R. 284'.5'0924 B *Francois Hotman;* a revolutionary's ordeal, by Donald R. Kelley. [Princeton, N.J.] Princeton University Press [1973] xvi, 370 p. illus. 23 cm. Bibliography: p. 347-359. [DC112.H67K44] 72-735 13.50
1. Hotman, Francois, sieur de Villiers Saint Paul, 1524-1590. 2. France—Politics and government—16th century. **BIP**

Houck, Louis 1840-1925.

DOHERTY, William T 923.873 *Louis Houck,* Missouri historian and entrepreneur. Columbia, Univ. of Missouri Press. [1961 c1960] 153 p. map. (Univ. of Missouri studies) Bibli. 60-15511 5.50
1. Houck, Louis 1840-1925. I. Title. **BIP**

Houdini, Harry, 1874-1926.

THE Amazing Randi. 793.8'092'4 B *Houdini, his life and art /* by The Amazing Randi and Bert Randolph Sugar. New York : Grosset & Dunlap, c1976. 191 p. : ill. ; 28 cm. Cover title: Presenting Houdini, his life and art. Includes index. [GV1545.H8A46] 76-15709 ISBN 0-448-12546-3 lib.bdg. : 12.95 ISBN 0-448-12552-8 pbk. : 6.95
1. Houdini, Harry, 1874-1926. 2. Conjuring. 3. Magicians—United States—Biography. I. Sugar, Bert Randolph, joint author. II. Title. III. Title: Presenting Houdini, his life and art.

CANNELL, John 793.8'092'4 B Clucas. *The secrets of Houdini,* by J. C. Cannell. London, Hutchinson. Detroit, Gale Research Co., 1974. 279 p. illus. 22 cm. Facsim. reprint of the 1931 ed. [GV1545.H8C3 1931a] 74-10523 ISBN 0-8103-3725-8 14.00
1. Houdini, Harry, 1874-1926. 2. Conjuring. I. Title. **BIP**

CHRISTOPHER, 793.8'092'4 B Milbourne. *Houdini :* a pictorial life / Milbourne Christopher. New York : Crowell, 1977, c1976 218 p. : ill. ; 29 cm. Includes index. Bibliography: p. 212-215. [GV1545.H8C49 1976] 76-18234 ISBN 0-690-01152-0 : 14.95
1. Houdini, Harry, 1874-1926. 2. Conjuring. **BIP**

CHRISTOPHER, 793.8'0924 B Milbourne. *Houdini; the untold story.* New York, Crowell [1969] 281 p. illus., facsims., ports. 22 cm. "Bibliography of works by Houdini": p. 266-267. Bibliography: p. 268-272. [GV1545.H8C5] 69-11829 6.95
1. Houdini, Harry, 1874-1926. **BIP**

EPSTEIN, Beryl (Williams) 920.9 1910- *The great Houdini,* magician extraordinary, by Beryl Williams and Samuel Epstein. New York, Messner [1950] viii, 182 p. port. 22 cm. Bibliography: p. 177-178. [GV1545.H8E6] 50-7035
1. Houdini, Harry, 1874-1926. I. Epstein, Samuel, 1909- joint author.

ERNST, Bernard Morris 793.8'092'4 Lee, 1879-1938. *Houdini and Conan Doyle;* the story of a strange friendship, by Bernard M. L. Ernst and Hereward Carrington. Foreword by J. C. Cannell. New York, B. Blom, 1972. 255 p. illus. 21 cm. Reprint of the 1933 ed. [GV1545.H8E7 1972] 72-174861 12.75
1. Houdini, Harry, 1874-1926. 2. Doyle, Arthur Conan, Sir, 1859-1930. 3. Spiritualism. I. Carrington, Hereward, 1880- joint author. II. Title. **BIP**

GRESHAM, William Lindsay, 927.91 1909- *Houdini, the man who walked through walls.* [1st ed.] New York, Holt [1959] 306 p. illus. 22 cm. [GV1545.H8G7] 59-10470
1. Houdini, Harry, 1874-1926.

†HENNING, Doug. 793.8'092'4 B *Houdini :* his legend and his magic / by Doug Henning, with Charles Reynolds. New York : Times Books, c1977. 190 p. : ill. (some col.) ; 29 cm. [GV1545.H8H4 1977] 76-52817 ISBN 0-8129-0686-1 : 14.95
1. Houdini, Harry, 1874-1926. 2. Magicians—United States—Biography. I. Reynolds, Charles R., joint author. **BIP**

MEYER, Bernard C. 793.8'092'4 B *Houdini :* a mind in chains : a psychoanalytic portrait / Bernard C. Meyer. 1st ed. New York : Dutton, c1976.

xix, 197 p., [4] leaves of plates : ill. ; 25 cm. Includes index. Bibliography: p. 191-192. [GV1545.H8M48 1976] 76-12631 ISBN 0-8415-0448-2 : 10.00
1. Houdini, Harry, 1874-1926. 2. Conjuring.

THE original Houdini scrapbook / [compiled] by Walter B. Gibson. New York : Corwin Sterling Pub. Co., c1976. 224 p. : ill. ; 29 cm. Includes index. [GV1545.H8O74] ISBN 0-8069-8049-4 lib.bdg. : ISBN 0-8069-8050-8 pbk. : 12.95 796.8'092'4
1. Houdini, Harry, 1874-1926. 2. Magicians—Biography. 3. Conjuring. I. Gibson, Walter Brown, 1897-

STOUTENBURG, Adrien. 927.91
Houdini, master of escape [by] Lace Kendall [pseud.] Philadelphia, Macrae Smith [1960] 187 p. illus. 22 cm. [GV1545.H8S8] 60-14035
1. Houdini, Harry, 1874-1926.

Houdini, Harry, 1874-1926—Juvenile literature.

BORLAND, Kathryn Kilby. 793.8'0924 B
Harry Houdini, young magician, by Kathryn Kilby Borland and Helen Ross Speicher. Illustrated by Fred Irvin. Indianapolis, Bobbs-Merrill [1969] 200 p. col. illus. 20 cm. (Childhood of famous Americans) On spine: Harry Houdini, boy magician. Bibliography: p. 198. A biography of Harry Houdini concentrating on his earlier years and the training that made him a master magician and escape artist. [GV1545.H8B6] 92 70-89982
1. Houdini, Harry, 1874-1926—Juvenile literature. I. Speicher, Helen Ross, joint author. II. Irvin, Fred M., illus. III. Title.

EDWARDS, Anne, 1927- 793.8'092'4 B
The great Houdini / written by Anne Edwards ; illustrated by Joseph Ciardiello. New York : Putnam, c1977. 62 p. : ill. ; 23 cm. (A See and read book) A biography of the man reputed to be the greatest magician and escape artist of all time. [GV1545.H8E38 1977] lib.bdg. : 4.29
1. Houdini, Harry, 1874-1926—Juvenile literature. 2. Conjuring—Juvenile literature. I. Ciardiello, Joseph. II. Title. **BIP**

EDWARDS, Anne, 1927- 793.8'092'4 B
Houdini / by Anne Edwards ; ill. by Joseph Ciardiello. New York : Putnam, c1976. p. cm. (A See and read biography) A biography of the man reputed to be the greatest magician and escape artist of all time. [GV1545.H8E38 1976] 92 76-8472 ISBN 0-399-20530-6. ISBN 0-399-61020-0 lib. bdg.
1. Houdini, Harry, 1874-1926—Juvenile literature. 2. Conjuring—Juvenile literature. I. Ciardiello, Joseph. II. Title.

ERNST, John, 1940- 793.8'092'4 B
Escape king: the story of Harry Houdini. Illustrated by Stefan Martin. Englewood Cliffs, N.J., Prentice-Hall [1974, c1973] p. A simple biography of the famous magician describing his major tricks. [GV1545.H8E73] 92 73-15696 ISBN 0-13-283416-2 4.95
1. Houdini, Harry, 1874-1926—Juvenile literature. I. Martin, Stefan, illus. II. Title. **BIP**

HENNING, Doug. 793.8'092'4 B
Houdini, his legend and his magic / by Doug Henning, with Charles Reynolds. New York : Warner Books, 1978,c1977. 190 p. : ill. ; 28 cm. A biography of the magician who became famous for his ability to escape almost any form of restraint. Describes his 10 greatest illusions as they appeared to audiences in the early 1900's. [GV1545.H8H4 1977b] 92 79-109627 ISBN 0-446-87328-4 : 8.95
1. Houdini, Harry, 1874-1926—Juvenile literature. 2. Magicians—United States—Biography—Juvenile literature. I. Reynolds, Charles R., joint author. II. Title.

KRASKE, Robert. 791'.092'2 B
Daredevils do amazing things / by Robert Kraske ; illustrated by Ivan Powell. New York : Random House, c9178. 69 p. : ill. ; 22 cm. (Step-up books ; 26) Describes the daring feats of adventures Blondin, Harry Houdini, Annie Oakley, Harry Rieseberg, and Evel Knievel. [GV1811.A1K7] 920 77-90194 ISBN 0-394-83623-5 : 2.95. ISBN 0-394-93623-X lib. bdg. : 3.99
1. Houdini, Harry, 1874-1926—Juvenile literature. 2. Oakley, Annie, 1860-1926—Juvenile literature. 3. Rieseberg, Harry Earl—Juvenile literature. 4. Knievel, Evel, 1938- —Juvenile literature. 5. Blondin, Jean Francois Gravelet, known as, 1824-1897—Juvenile literature. 6. Entertainers—United States—Biography—Juvenile literature. I. Powell, Ivan. II. Title. **BIP**

KRASKE, Robert. 793.8'092'4 B
Harry Houdini, master of magic. Illustrated by Victor Mays. Champaign, Ill., Garrard Pub. Co. [1973] 96 p. illus. (part col.) 24 cm. (Americans all) A brief biography of Ehrich Weiss, who gained renown as Harry Houdini, master magician and escape artist. [GV1545.H8K72] 92 72-3446 ISBN 0-8116-4578-9 2.79
1. Houdini, Harry, 1874-1926—Juvenile literature. I. Mays, Victor, 1927- illus. II. Title. **BIP**

WARREN, David. 793.8'092'4 B
The great escaper / by David Warren ; ill. by Annabel Large. Milwaukee : Raintree Publishers, c1979. p. cm. Relates the dramatic stage life of magician and escape artist Harry Houdini. [GV1545.H8W37] 92 78-26629 ISBN 0-8393-0152-9 lib. bdg. : 6.95
1. Houdini, Harry, 1874-1926—Juvenile literature. 2. Magicians—United States—Biography—Juvenile literature. I. Large, Annabel. II. Title. **BIP**

WAYNE, Bennett. 793.8'092'4
The super showmen, edited with commentary by Bennett Wayne. Champaign, Ill., Garrard Pub. Co. [1974] 167 p. illus. 22 cm. (A Target book) Biographies of three men who achieved fame for their ability to entertain one as a magician, one as a cowboy comedian and philosopher, and one as a producer of motion pictures and animated cartoons. [PN1583.A2W35] 920 74-2282 ISBN 0-8116-4909-1 4.75
1. Houdini, Harry, 1874-1926—Juvenile literature. 2. Rogers, Will, 1879-1935—Juvenile literature. 3. Disney, Walt, 1901-1966—Juvenile literature. I. Title. **BIP**

WHITE, Florence Meiman, 1910- 793.8'092'4 B
Escape! : The life of Harry Houdini / by Florence Meiman White ; illustrated with photos. New York : J. Messner, c1979. 112 p. : ill. ; 22 cm. Includes index. Highlights the life and career of one of the world's greatest escape artists and magicians. [GV1545.H8W47] 92 78-26248 ISBN 0-671-32937-5 : 7.79
1. Houdini, Harry, 1874-1926—Juvenile literature. 2. Magicians—United States—Biography—Juvenile literature. **BIP**

Hough, Donald,

HOUGH, Donald, 1895- 818.52
The streetcar house. [1st ed.] New York, Duell, Sloan and Pearce [1960] 180 p. 21 cm. Autobiographical. [CT275.H6469A3] 60-5445
I. Title.

Hough, Emerson, 1857-1923.

WYLDER, Delbert E. 813'.5'2
Emerson Hough, by Delbert E. Wylder. Austin, Tex., Steck-Vaughn [1969] ii, 43 p. 21 cm. (Southwest writers series, no. 19) Bibliography: p. 39-43. [PS3515.O7593Z9] 69-18409 1.00
1. Hough, Emerson, 1857-1923. I. Title. II. Series.

Hough, Henry Beetle

HOUGH, Henry Beetle 928.1
Melville in the South Pacific. Illustrated by Frank Nicholas. Boston, Houghton Mifflin [c.]1960. 179p. Includes bibliography. illus. (part col.) 22cm. (North Star books [22]) 60-6386 1.95
I. Melville, Herman, 1819-1891—Juvenile literature. II. Title.

Hough, Henry Beetle, 1896- —Biography.

HOUGH, Henry Beetle 928.1
Melville in the South Pacific. Illustrated by Frank Nicholas. Boston, Houghton Mifflin [c.]1960. 179p. Includes bibliography. illus. (part col.) 22cm. (North Star books [22]) 60-6386 1.95
I. Melville, Herman, 1819-1891—Juvenile literature. II. Title.

HOUGH, Henry Beetle, 1896- 070.4'092'4 B
To the Harbor Light / Henry Beetle Hough ; drawings by Donald Carrick. Boston : Houghton Mifflin, 1976. 210 p. : ill. ; 22 cm. [PS3515.O75933Z52] 76-20534 ISBN 0-395-24774-8 : 7.95
1. Hough, Henry Beetle, 1896- —Biography. I. Title. **BIP**

HOUGH, Henry Beetle, 1896- 070.40924 B
To the harbor light / Henry Beetle Hough. Boston : G. K. Hall, 1976. 347 p. ; 24 cm. "Published in large print." [PS3515.O75933Z52 1976b] 76-47608 ISBN 0-8161-6435-5 lib. bdg. : 9.95
1. Hough, Henry Beetle, 1896- —Biography. 2. Authors, American—20th century—Biography. 3. Journalists—United States—Biography. 4. Sight-saving books. I. Title.

Houghton, Aianson Bigelow, 1863-1941.

HOUGHTON, Adelaide Louise (Wellington) 1867- 914.21
The London years; the diary of Adelaide Wellington Houghton, 1925-1929. [New York?] 1963. 274 p. plates, ports. 25 cm. "Fifty copies ... were printed." [DA578.H65A3] 63-22574
1. Houghton, Aianson Bigelow, 1863-1941. 2. Gt. Brit. — Soc. life & cust. 3. Diplomats — Correspondence, reminiscences, etc. I. Title.

Houghton, Douglass, 1809-1845.

RINTALA, Edsel Kenneth, 1924- 925.5
Douglass Houghton, Michigan's pioneer geologist. Detroit, Wayne University Press, 1954. vi, 119p. port. 23cm. Bibliography: p. [113]-115. [QE22.H83R5] 54-6983
1. Houghton, Douglass, 1809-1845. I. Title.

Houghton, Richard Monckton Milnes, Baron, 1809-1885.

REID, Wemyss, Sir, 1842-1905. 821'.8 B
The life, letters, and friendships of Richard Monckton Milnes, first Lord Houghton. 3d ed. Boston, Milford House [1973] p. Reprint of the 1891 ed. published by Cassell, London. [PR4808.R4 1973] 76-165124 ISBN 0-87821-090-3 55.00
1. Houghton, Richard Monckton Milnes, baron, 1809-1885. I. Title.

REID, Wemyss, Sir, 1842-1905. 821'.8 B
The life, letters, and friendships of Richard Monckton Milnes, first Lord Houghton / by T. Wemyss Reid. Boston : Longwood Press, 1977. p. cm. Reprint of the 3d ed. published in 1891 by Cassell, London. [PR4808.R4 1977] 77-88581 ISBN 0-89341-463-8 lib.bdg. : 55.00
1. Houghton, Richard Monckton Milnes, Baron, 1809-1885. 2. Poets, English—19th century—Biography. I. Title. **BIP**

Houghton, Will Henry, 1886 or 7-1947.

SMITH, Wilbur Moorehead, 1894- 922.673
A watchman on the wall; the life story of Will H. Houghton. Grand Rapids, Eerdmans, 1951. 191 p. ports. 21 cm. Bibliography: p. [175]-191. [BX6495.H64S5] 51-11419
1. Houghton, Will Henry, 1886 or 7-1947. I. Title.

House, Edward Mandell, 1858-1938.

RICHARDSON, Rupert Norval, 1891- 923.273
Colonel Edward M. House. [Abilene? Tex., 1964- v. illus., ports. 24 cm. (Hardin-Simmons University. Publications in history, v. 1. Contents.1. The Texas years, 1858-1912. Bibliography: v. 1, p. 318-332. [E748.H77R5] 64-56263
1. House, Edward Mandell, 1858-1938. I. Title. II. Series. III. Series: Hardin-Simmons University, Abilene, Tex. Publications in history, v. 1

Household, Geoffrey,

HOUSEHOLD, Geoffrey, 1900- 928.2
Against the wind. [1st American ed.] Boston, Little, Brown [1959, c1958] 238p. 21cm. Autobiographical. [PR6015.O7885Z54 1959] 59-5158
I. Title.

Houselander, Frances Caryll.

HOUSELANDER, Frances Caryll. 928.2
A rocking-horse Catholic. New York, Sheed & Ward [1955] 148p. illus. 20cm. Autobiography. [PR6015.O79Z5] 55-9445
I. Title.

WARD, Maisie, 1889- 928.2
Caryll Houselander, that divine eccentric. New York, Sheed and Ward [1962] 329 p. 22 cm. [PR6015.O79Z9] 62-9100
1. Houselander, Frances Caryll. I. Title.

WARD, Maisie [Mary Josephine (Ward) Sheed] 1889- 928.2
Caryll Houselander, that divine eccentric. New York, Sheed & Ward [c.1962] 329p. 62-9100 4.95
1. Houselander, Frances Caryll. I. Title.

Houseman, John.

HOUSEMAN, John. 792'.023'0924 B
Front and center / John Houseman. New York : Simon and Schuster, c1979. p. cm. [PN2287.H7A295] 79-17482 ISBN 0-671-24328-4 : 11.95
1. Houseman, John. 2. Theatrical producers and directors—United States—Biography. I. Title. **BIP**

HOUSEMAN, John. 792'.0232'0924 B
Run-through; a memoir. New York, Simon and Schuster [1972] 507 p. illus. 23 cm. "Portions of this work have appeared in Audience." [PN2287.H7A3] 70-179582 ISBN 0-671-21034-3 9.95
I. Title.

Houser, Hentz, 1933-1955.

HOUSER, Harriet Hentz. 920
Hentz, of things not seen. New York, Macmillan, 1955. 235 p. 22 cm. [CT275.H64717H6] 55-13566
1. Houser, Hentz, 1933-1955. I. Title.

Housman, Alfred Edward,

HOUSMAN, Alfred Edward, 1859-1936. 821'.9'12 B
The letters of A. E. Housman, edited by Henry Maas. Cambridge, Harvard University Press, 1971. xxi, 458 p. facsims., ports. 24 cm. Bibliography: p. 439-441. [PR4809.H15A8 1971] 70-142222 ISBN 0-674-52581-7 11.50
I. Maas, Henry, ed. II. Title. **BIP**

Housman, Alfred Edward, 1859-1936.

GOW, Andrew Sydenham 821'.9'12
Farrar, 1886-
A. E. Housman; a sketch together with a list of his writings and indexes to his classical papers, by A. S. F. Gow. New York, Haskell House, 1972. xiii, 136 p. illus. 23 cm. Reprint of the 1936 ed. [PR4809.H15G6 1972] 72-699 ISBN 0-8383-1423-6
1. Housman, Alfred Edward, 1859-1936. 2. Housman, Alfred Edward, 1859-1936—Bibliography. 3. Housman, Alfred Edward, 1859-1936—Concordances.

GOW, Andrew Sydenham 821'.9'12
Farrar, 1886-
A. E. Housman; a sketch together with a list of his writings and indexes to his classical papers, by A. S. F. Gow. [Folcroft, Pa.] Folcroft Library Editions, 1973. p. Reprint of the 1936 ed. published by the University Press, Cambridge, Eng. [PR4809.H15G6 1973] 73-12520 8.75
1. Housman, Alfred Edward, 1859-1936. 2. Housman, Alfred Edward, 1859-1936—Bibliography. 3. Housman, Alfred Edward, 1859-1936—Concordances.

GOW, Andrew Sydenham 821'.9'12
Farrar, 1886-
A. E. Housman; a sketch together with a list of his writings and indexes to his classical papers, by A. S. F. Gow. [Folcroft, Pa.] Folcroft Library Editions, 1973. p. Reprint of the 1936 ed. published by the University Press, Cambridge, Eng. [PR4809.H15G6 1973] 73-12520 ISBN 0-8414-4416-1 (lib. bdg.)
1. Housman, Alfred Edward, 1859-1936. 2. Housman, Alfred Edward, 1859-1936—Bibliography. 3. Housman, Alfred Edward, 1859-1936—Concordances.

GOW, Andrew Sydenham 821'.9'12
Farrar, 1886-
A. E. Housman; a sketch together with a list of his writings and indexes to his classical papers, by A. S. F. Gow. [Folcroft, Pa.] Folcroft Library Editions, 1973. p. Reprint of the 1936 ed. published by the University Press, Cambridge, Eng. [PR4809.H15G6 1973] 73-12520 ISBN 0-8414-4416-1 (lib. bdg.)
1. Housman, Alfred Edward, 1859-1936. 2. Housman, Alfred Edward, 1859-1936—Bibliography. 3. Housman, Alfred Edward, 1859-1936—Concordances.

HAMILTON, John Robert, 821'.9'12
1908-
Housman the poet, by Robert Hamilton. [Folcroft, Pa.] Folcroft Library Editions, 1971. 74 p. 24 cm. Reprint of the 1953 ed. [PR4809.H15H3 1971] 72-187522
1. Housman, Alfred Edward, 1859-1936. I. Title. BIP

HAWKINS, Maude M 928.2
A. E. Housman: man behind a mask. Chicago, H. Regenery Co., 1958. 202p. illus. 22cm. Includes bibliography. [PR4809.H15H33] 58-6752
1. Housman, Alfred Edward, 1859-1936. I. Title.

HOUSMAN, Alfred 821'.9'12 B
Edward, 1859-1936.
The letters of A. E. Housman, edited by Henry Maas. Cambridge, Harvard University Press, 1971. xxi, 458 p. facsims., ports. 24 cm. Bibliography: p. 439-441. [PR4809.H15A8 1971] 70-142222 ISBN 0-674-52581-7 11.50
I. Maas, Henry, ed. II. Title. BIP

MARLOW, Norman. 821.91
A. E. Housman; scholar and poet. Minneapolis, University of Minnesota Press [1958] 192p. 22cm. [PR4809.H15M3] 58-14825
1. Housman, Alfred Edward, 1859-1936. I. Title.

RICHARDS, Grant, 821'.9'12 B
1872-1948.
Housman, 1897-1936. With an introd. by Mrs. E. W. Symons and appendices by G. B. A. Fletcher and others. New York, Octagon Books, 1973 [c1942] xxii, 493 p. illus. 23 cm. Reprint of the ed. published by Oxford University Press, New York. Includes bibliographical references. [PR4809.H15R5 1973] 73-17090 ISBN 0-374-96799-7 16.00
1. Housman, Alfred Edward, 1859-1936.

WATSON, George L. 928.2
A. E. Housman; a divided life. Boston, Beacon Press [1958] 235 p. illus. 23 cm. Includes bibliography. [PR4809.H15W3 1958] 58-14988
1. Housman, Alfred Edward, 1859-1936.

WITHERS, Percy, 1867- 821'.9'12 B
1945.
A buried life; personal recollections of A. E. Housman. [Folcroft, Pa.] Folcroft Library Editions, 1971. 133 p. port. 24 cm. "Limited to 150 copies." Reprint of the 1940 ed. [PR4809.H15W5 1971] 72-193678 10.00
1. Housman, Alfred Edward, 1859-1936. I. Title. BIP

Housman, Alfred Edward, 1859-1936—Bibliography.

GOW, Andrew Sydenham 821'.9'12
Farrar, 1886-
A. E. Housman; a sketch together with a list of his writings and indexes to his classical papers, by A. S. F. Gow. New York, Haskell House, 1972. xiii, 136 p. illus. 23 cm. Reprint of the 1936 ed. [PR4809.H15G6 1972] 72-699 ISBN 0-8383-1423-6
1. Housman, Alfred Edward, 1859-1936. 2. Housman, Alfred Edward, 1859-1936—Bibliography. 3. Housman, Alfred Edward, 1859-1936—Concordances.

GOW, Andrew Sydenham 821'.9'12
Farrar, 1886-
A. E. Housman; a sketch together with a list of his writings and indexes to his classical papers, by A. S. F. Gow. [Folcroft, Pa.] Folcroft Library Editions, 1973. p. Reprint of the 1936 ed. published by the University Press, Cambridge, Eng. [PR4809.H15G6 1973] 73-12520 8.75
1. Housman, Alfred Edward, 1859-1936. 2. Housman, Alfred Edward, 1859-1936—Bibliography. 3. Housman, Alfred Edward, 1859-1936—Concordances.

GOW, Andrew Sydenham 821'.9'12
Farrar, 1886-
A. E. Housman; a sketch together with a list of his writings and indexes to his classical papers, by A. S. F. Gow. [Folcroft, Pa.] Folcroft Library Editions, 1973. p. Reprint of the 1936 ed. published by the University Press, Cambridge, Eng. [PR4809.H15G6 1973] 73-12520 ISBN 0-8414-4416-1 (lib. bdg.)
1. Housman, Alfred Edward, 1859-1936. 2. Housman, Alfred Edward, 1859-1936—Bibliography. 3. Housman, Alfred Edward, 1859-1936—Concordances.

GOW, Andrew Sydenham 821'.9'12
Farrar, 1886-
A. E. Housman; a sketch together with a list of his writings and indexes to his classical papers, by A. S. F. Gow. [Folcroft, Pa.] Folcroft Library Editions, 1973. p. Reprint of the 1936 ed. published by the University Press, Cambridge, Eng. [PR4809.H15G6 1973] 73-12520 ISBN 0-8414-4416-1 (lib. bdg.)
1. Housman, Alfred Edward, 1859-1936. 2. Housman, Alfred Edward, 1859-1936—Bibliography. 3. Housman, Alfred Edward, 1859-1936—Concordances.

Houssaye, Arsene,

HOUSSAYE, Arsene, 848'.8'09
1815-1896.
Man about Paris; the confessions of Arsene Houssaye. Translated and edited by Henry Knepler. New York, Morrow, 1970. xiii, 350 p. port. 25 cm. Translation of selections from Les confessions. Bibliography: p. 339-341. [PQ2276.H7Z5213] 78-107971 15.00
I. Knepler, Henry W., ed. II. Title. BIP

Houston, Fred F., 1912-

HOUSTON, Fred F., 359.3'38'0924 B
1912-
Sam Houston's Navy / Fred F. "Sam" Houston. 1st ed. New York : Grossmont Press, c1976. 135 p. : ill. ; 22 cm. [V63.H68A34] 76-5597 ISBN 0-913182-59-1 lib.bdg. : 5.95 p pbk. : 2.25
1. Houston, Fred F., 1912- 2. United States. Navy—Biography. 3. Seamen—United States—Biography. I. Title. BIP

Houston, John, 1906-

NOLAN, William F., 791.4302330924
1928-
John Huston, king rebel. Los Angeles, Sherbourne [c.1965]c247p. illus., ports. 22cm. Bibl. [PN1998.A3H8] 65-15790 5.95
1. Houston, John, 1906- I. Title.

Houston, Margaret Lea, 1819-1867.

SEALE, William. 976'.03'0924 B
Sam Houston's wife: a biography of Margaret Lea Houston. Norman, University of Oklahoma Press [1970] xv, 287 p. illus., ports. 22 cm. A revision of the author's thesis, Duke University. Bibliography: p. 264-273. [F390.H824S4] 77-123341
1. Houston, Margaret Lea, 1819-1867. I. Title. BIP

Houston, Samuel, 1758-1839.

DIEHL, George West. 285'.1'0924 B
The Rev. Samuel Houston, V.D.M. [Verona, Va., McClure Press, 1970.] 123 p. illus., map, port. 24 cm. Includes bibliographical references. [BX9225.H75D5] 70-133502 5.95
1. Houston, Samuel, 1758-1839.

Houston, Samuel, 1793-1863.

BRAIDER, Donald, 976'.03'0924 B
1923-
Solitary star; a biography of Sam Houston. New York, Putnam [1974] 344 p. maps. 24 cm. Bibliography: p. 327-332. [F390.H8378 1974] 73-78619 ISBN 0-399-11160-3 10.00
1. Houston, Samuel, 1793-1863. I. Title.

CRANE, William 976'.03'0924 B
Carey, 1816-1885.
Life and select literary remains of Sam Houston, of Texas. Freeport, N.Y., Books For Libraries Press [1972] 672 p. illus. 24 cm. Reprint of the 1884 ed. [F390.H844 1972] 74-38348 ISBN 0-8369-6765-8
1. Houston, Samuel, 1793-1863. I. Houston, Samuel, 1793-1863. Life and select literary remains of Sam Houston, of Texas. 1972. II. Title. BIP

FRIEND, Llerena, 1903- 923.273
Sam Houston, the great designer. Austin, University of Texas Press, 1954. xiv, 394 p. illus., ports. 24 cm. "Under a similar title and in only a slightly different form, this biography ... was prepared as a doctoral dissertation in history at the University of Texas." Bibliography: p. 357-368. [F390.H8472] 54-13252
1. Houston, Samuel, 1793-1863. BIP

GREGORY, Jack. 976'.03'0924
Sam Houston with the Cherokees, 1829-1833, by Jack Gregory and Rennard Strickland. Austin, University of Texas Press [1967] xx, 206 p. illus., map, ports. 24 cm. Bibliography: p. [165]-182. [F390.H84725] 67-25326
1. Houston, Samuel, 1793-1863. I. Strickland, Rennard, joint author. BIP

HOLLANDER, Paul. 976'.03'0924 B
Sam Houston. Illustrated by Salem Tamer. New York, Putnam [1968] 61 p. col. illus., col. maps, col. ports. 23 cm. (A See and read beginning to read biography) A simple biography of the soldier and politician responsible for the statehood of Texas. [F390.H84736] 92 AC 68
1. Houston, Samuel, 1793-1863. I. Tamer, Salem, illus. II. Title.

HOUSTON, Samuel, 1793- 923.273
1863.
The autobiography of Sam Houston, edited by Donald Day & Harry Herbert Ullom. [1st ed.] Norman, University of Oklahoma Press [1954] xviii, 298p. illus., ports., maps. 25cm. Bibliography: p. 283-289. [F390.H8474] 54-10051
1. Texas—Hist.—Sources. I. Day, Donald, 1899- ed. II. Ullom, Harry Herbert, ed. III. Title.

HOUSTON, Samuel, 976'.03'0924 B
1793-1863.
Ever thine truly : love letters from Sam Houston to Anna Raguet. Austin, Tex. : Jenkins Garrett Press, c1975. 157 p. : facsims. ; 32 cm. "A portion of an extensive collection of the papers of Dr. Robert Anderson Irion, now in the Jenkins Garrett Library at the University of Texas at Arlington." Includes index. Bibliography: p. [143]-153. [F390.H83] 75-7013
1. Houston, Samuel, 1793-1863. 2. Raguet, Anna. I. Raguet, Anna. II. Title. BIP

*JAMES, Marquis 976.4'04'0924
The raven : the story of Sam Houston by Marquis James, ; introduction by Henry Steele Commager. New York : Bobbs-Merrill, 1976 c1929. 489 p. : ill. ; 24 cm. Includes bibliographical references & index. [F390] 75-33436 ISBN 0-672-52215-2 : 10.00
1. Houston, Samuel, 1793-1863. I. Title.

JAMES, Marquis, 1891- 923.273
The Raven, a biography of Sam Houston. New York, Paperback Lib. [1962, c.1929, 1956] 384p. 18cm. (Gold ed., 54-144) Bibl. .75 pap.,
1. Houston, Samuel, 1793-1863. I. Title. BIP

JAMES, Marquis, 1891-1955. v. 12
The Raven, a biography of Sam Houston. New York, Paperback Library [1962] 384 p. (Paperback library gold ed., 54-144) 67-76687
1. Houston, Samuel, 1793-1863. I. Title.

JAMES, Marquis, 976'.03'0924 B
1891-1955.
The raven; a biography of Sam Houston. Dunwoody, Ga., N. S. Berg [1968, c1929] 489 p. illus., maps, ports. 23 cm. Includes bibliographical references. [F390.H8494] 68-2545
1. Houston, Samuel, 1793-1863. I. Title.

JOHNSON, William, 1909- 923.273
Sam Houston, the tallest Texan; illustrated by William Reusswig. New York, Random House [1953] 185 p. illus. 22 cm. (Landmark books, 32) [F390.H8495] 53-6256
1. Houston, Samuel, 1793-1863.

JOHNSON, William 976.03'0924 B
Weber, 1909-
Sam Houston, the tallest Texan; illustrated by William Reusswig. New York, Random House [1953] 185 p. illus. 22 cm. (Landmark books, 32) A biography of a leader in Texas' fight for independence who became a governor of the new state and a United States Senator. [F390.H8495] 92 AC 68
1. Houston, Samuel, 1793-1863. I. Reusswig, William, illus. II. Title.

KENNEDY, John 328.73'0924 B
Fitzgerald, Pres. U.S., 1917-1963.
Sam Houston & the Senate. Illus. by Tom Lea. Austin, Pemberton Press [1970] 33 l. ports. 29 cm. First published as chapter 5 of the author's Profiles in courage. [F390.H8496 1970] 79-14422 9.50
1. Houston, Samuel, 1793-1863. I. Title. BIP

LATHAM, Jean Lee. 976'.03'0924 B
Retreat to glory; the story of Sam Houston. [1st ed.] New York, Harper & Row [1965] viii, 274 p. map. 21 cm. The childhood, military career, and political life of the man who fought for the statehood of Texas. [PZ7.L348Re] 92 AC 68
1. Houston, Samuel, 1793-1863. I. Title. BIP

LATHAM, Jean Lee. 976'.03'0924 B
Sam Houston, hero of Texas Champaign, Ill., Garrard Pub. Co. [1965] 80 p. col. illus. 23 cm. (A Discovery book) A brief account of Sam Houston who served as a Congressman and Governor of Tennessee before his association with Texas began. [F390.H8498] 92 AC 68
1. Houston, Samuel, 1793-1863. I. Title. BIP

LESTER, Charles 976'.03'0924 B
Edwards, 1815-1890.
The life of Sam Houston. (The only authentic memoir of him ever published) Freeport, N.Y., Books for Libraries Press [1972] xi, 402 p. illus. 23 cm. First ed., 1846, published under title: Sam Houston

and his republic. Reprint of the 1855 ed. [F390.H85 1972] 70-38360 ISBN 0-8369-6777-1
1. Houston, Samuel, 1793-1863. 2. Texas—History—Republic, 1836-1846. I. Title.

LOCKHART, John Washington, v. 12
1824-1900.
Sixty years on the Brazos, the life and letters of Dr. John Washington Lockhart, 1824-1900, by Mrs. Jonnie Lockhart Wallis in association with Laurance L. Hill. New York, Published for University Microfilms, Ann Arbor, by Argonaut Press, 1966 [c1930] 336 p. plates, ports. 25 cm. 67-104598
1. Houston, Samuel, 1793-1863. 2. Pioneer life — U.S. — Texas. 3. Texas — Hist. — To 1846. I. Wallis, Mrs. Jonnie (Lockhart) comp. II. Hill, Laurance Landreth, comp. III. Title.

MCCALEB, Walter Flavius, 923.273
1873-
Sam Houston. [San Antonio] Naylor Co. [1958] 128p. illus. 20cm. [F390.H8582] 58-2829
1. Houston, Samuel, 1793-1863. I. Title.

MCNUTT, Walter Scott. 923.273
Sam Houston, the empire builder; his love affairs and political entanglements. [Rev.] Jefferson, Tex., Four States Pub. House [1956] 69p. illus. 16cm. [F390.H8586 1956] 56-38454
1. Houston, Samuel, 1796-1863. I. Title.

MCNUTT, Walter Scott. 923.273
Sam Houston, the empire builder; his love affairs and political entanglements. [Rev.] Jefferson, Tex., Four States Pub. House [1956] 69p. illus. 16cm. [F390.H8586 1956] 56-38454
1. Houston, Samuel, 1793-1863. I. Title.

THE Raven; v. 12
a biography of Sam Houston. New York, Grosset & Dunlap [1956, c1929] 489p. illus. 22cm. (Biographies of distinction) [AJames, Marquis,] 1891
1. Houston, Samuel, 1793-1863.

STEVENSON, 976'.03'0924 B
Augusta.
Sam Houston, boy chieftain Illustrated by Katharine Sampson. Indianapolis, Bobbs-Merrill [1962] 200 p. illus. 20 cm. (Childhood of famous Americans) A biography of the man who helped make Texas a part of the United States, emphasizing his boyhood in Virginia and his friendship with the Cherokee Indians. [PZ7.S8467Sam6] 92 AC 68
1. Houston, Samuel, 1793-1863. I. Sampson, Katharine, illus. II. Title. **BIP**

TURNER, Martha Anne 976.40924
Sam Houston and his twelve women; the ladies who influenced the life of Texas' greatest statesman. Austin [Tex.] Pemberton Pr., 1966. 96p. illus., port. 24cm. Bibl. [F390.H8595] 66-6999 6.95
1. Houston, Samuel, 1793-1863. I. Title.

WISEHART, Marion Karl, 923.273
1889-
Sam Houston, American giant. Washington, R. B. Luce [1962] 712 p. illus. 22 cm. Includes bibliography. [F390.H868] 62-20000
1. Houston, Samuel, 1793-1863.

WRIGHT, Frances 923.273
(Fitzpatrick) 1897-
Sam Houston, fighter and leader; illustrated by Robert Burns. Nashville, Abingdon-Cokesbury Press [1953] 128p. illus. 22cm. [Makers of America] [F390.H869] 53-11616
1. Houston, Samuel, 1793-1863. I. Title.

Houston, Samuel, 1793-1863—Juvenile literature.

BISHOP, Curtis Kent, 923.273
1912-
Lone Star leader; Sam Houston. New York, J. Messner [c.1961] 192p. Bibl. 61-7994 2.95
1. Houston, Samuel, 1793-1863—Juvenile literature. I. Title.

GRANT, Matthew G. 976.4'04'0924 B
Sam Houston of Texas [by] Matthew G. Grant. Illustrated by Harold Henriksen. [Mankato, Minn., Creative Education; distributed by Childrens Press, Chicago, 1974] 29 p. illus. (part col.) 25 cm. (His Gallery of great Americans series. War heroes of America) An easy-to-read-biography of the soldier and politician who helped gain Texas independence from Mexico and became first president of the new Republic of Texas in 1836. [F390.H84723] 92 73-18080 ISBN 0-87191-299-6 3.95
1. Houston, Samuel, 1793-1863—Juvenile literature. I. Henricksen, Harold, illus. II. Title.

HOLLANDER, Paul. 92 (J)
Sam Houston. Illustrated by Salem Tamer. New York, Putnam [1968] 61 p. col. illus., col. maps, col. ports. 23 cm. (A See and read beginning to read biography) [F390.H84736] 68-15055
1. Houston, Samuel, 1793-1863—Juvenile literature.

JOHNSON, William Weber, 923.273
1909-
Sam Houston, the tallest Texan; illustrated by William Reusswig. New York, Random House [1953] 185p. illus. 22cm. (Landmark books, 32) [F390.H8495] 53-6256
1. Houston, Samuel, 1793-1863—Juvenile literature. I. Title.

LATHAM, Jean Lee. j92
Sam Houston, hero of Texas. Champaign, Ill., Garrard Pub. Co. [1965] 80 p. col. illus. 23 cm. (A Discovery book) [F390.H8498] 65-10101
1. Houston, Samuel, 1793-1803 — Juvenile literature. I. Title.

LATHAM, Jean Lee 92
Sam Houston. Illus. by Ernest Kurt Barth, Hobe Hays [New York, Dell, 1966, c.1965] 80p. illus. 20cm. (Discovery bk., Dell yearling bk., 7597) 50 pap.,
1. Houston, Samuel 1793-1863—Juvenile literature. I. Title.

MCCALEB, Walter Flavius 1873- 920
1967
Sam Houston [Rev., enl. ed.] San Antonio, Naylor [1967] xiii, 129 p. col. illus., col. map. 20 cm. [F390.H8582 1967] 67-26251 2.95
1. Houston, Samuel, 1793-1863—Juvenile litterture. I. Title.

MCCALEB, Walter Flavius, 92 (J)
1873-1967.
Sam Houston. [Rev. and enl. ed.] San Antonio, Naylor Co. [1967] xiii, 129 p. col. illus., col. map. 20 cm. [F390.H8582 1967] 67-26251
1. Houston, Samuel, 1793-1863—Juvenile literature.

MOONEY, Booth, 1912- j92
Sam Houston. Illustrated by George Roth. Chicago, Follett Pub. Co. [c1966] 144 p. col. illus. 22 cm. (Library of American heroes) [F390.H8588] 67-1748
1. Houston, Samuel, 1798-1863 — Juvenile literature. I. Title.

Hovaness, Alan Scott, 1911- —Bibl.

PETERS (C.F.) Corporation. v. 12
Hovhaness. New York [1965?] 66 p. ports. 23 cm. (Peters Edition) 68-88092
1. Hovaness, Alan Scott, 1911- —Bibl. I. Title.

Hovey, Byron P.

HOVEY, Byron P. 922.7
One jump ahead; memories of a yankee. New York, Exposition [c.1962] 45p. 2.50
I. Title.

HOVEY, Byron P. 922.7
A Yankee out West; a minister's reminiscences. New York, Exposition Press [c.1961] 113p. 3.00
I. Title.

Hovey, Richard, 1864-1900.

MACDONALD, Allan Houston, 928.1
1901-1951.
Richard Hovey, man & craftsman. [Durham, N. C.] Duke University Press, 1957. xiii, 265p. port. 24cm. 'A bibliography of the first editions of books by Richard Hovey . . . compiled by Edward Connery Lathem': p.[229]-250. 'Works consulted': p.[251]-254. [PS2008.M3] 57-7647
1. Hovey, Richard, 1864-1900. I. Title.

MACDONALD, Allan Houston, 928.1
1901-1951.
Richard Hovey, man & craftsman. [Durham, N. C.] Duke University Press, 1957. xiii, 265p. port. 24cm. A bibliography of the first editions of books by Richard Hovey ... coiplled by Edward Connery Lathem': p. [229]-250. 'Works consulted': p. [251]-254. [PS2008.M3] 57-7647
1. Hovey, Richard, 1864-1900. I. Title. **BIP**

MACDONALD, Allan 811'.4 B
Houston, 1901-1951.
Richard Hovey, man & craftsman. New York, Greenwood Press, 1968 [c1957] xiii, 265 p. port. 24 cm. "A bibliography of the first editions of books by Richard Hovey ... compiled by Edward Connery Lathem": p. [229]-250. Bibliography: p. [251]-254. [PS2008.M3 1968] 68-29745
1. Hovey, Richard, 1864-1900.

Howard, Dorothy, 1902-

HOWARD, 976.4'275'060924 B
Dorothy, 1902-
Dorothy's world : childhood in Sabine Bottom, 1902-1910 / Dorothy Howard. Englewood Cliffs, N.J. : Prentice-Hall, c1977. xi, 298 p. : ill. ; 24 cm. [GR55.H69A33] 76-48735 ISBN 0-13-218602-0 : 10.00
1. Howard, Dorothy, 1902- 2. Rains Co., Tex.—Social life and customs. 3. Children in Texas. 4. Folklorists—Biography. I. Title.

HOWARD, Dorothy, 248'.246'0924 B
1912-
No longer alone / Dorothy Howard. Elgin, Ill. : D. C. Cook Pub. Co., c1976. 170 p. ; 18 cm. [BR1725.H687A34] 74-32603 ISBN 0-912692-60-X pbk. : 1.50
1. Howard, Dorothy, 1912- 2. Christian life—1960- I. Title. **BIP**

Howard, Ebenezer, Sir, 1850-1928.

MOSS-ECCARDT, John, 711'.4'0924 B
1930-
Ebenezer Howard, an illustrated life of Sir Ebenezer Howard, 1850-1928. Aylesbury, Shire Publications, 1973. 48 p. illus., facsims., maps, ports. 21 cm. (Lifelines, 18) Includes bibliographical references and index. [HT161.H7M67] 74-155513 ISBN 0-85263-205-3
1. Howard, Ebenezer, Sir, 1850-1928. 2. Garden cities.
Distributed by International Publication Service, 3.00 pbk.

Howard, Frank, 1936- —Juvenile literature.

HIRSHBERG, 796.357'092'4 B
Albert, 1909-1973.
Frank Howard, the gentle giant, by Al Hirshberg. New York, Putnam [1973] 190 p. 21 cm. (Putnam sports shelf) A biography of the baseball player who began to set batting records after a long period of unspectacular play. [GV865.H66H57] 92 72-88401 ISBN 0-399-20314-1 4.69 (lib. bdg.)
1. Howard, Frank, 1936- —Juvenile literature. I. Title. **BIP**

Howard, Harriet, 1823-1865.

MAUROIS, Simone Arman de 920.7
Caillavet.
Miss Howard and the emperor; translated from the French by Humphrey Hare. [1st American ed.] New York, Knopf [1957] 224 p. illus. 22 cm. Translation of Miss Howard, la femme qui fit un empereur. [DC280.5.H6M32 1957a] 57-59392
1. Howard, Harriet, 1823-1865.

Howard, John, 1726?-1790.

GODBER, Joyce. 365'.92'4 B
John Howard, the philanthropist / by Joyce Godber. [Bedford, Eng.] : Arts and Recreation Dept., Bedfordshire County Council, 1977. 17 p., [2] leaves of plates : ill. ; 22 cm. [HV8978.H8G62] 77-373993 £0.30
1. Howard, John, 1726?-1790. 2 Philanthropists—England—Biography. I. Title.

HOWARD, Derek Lionel. 923.642
John Howard: prison reformer. With a foreword by Hugh J. Klare. New York City, Archer House [1963, c.1958] 186 p. illus., port. 23 cm. [HV8978.H8H6] 63-14441
1. Howard, John, 1726?-1790. I. Title.

HOWARD, Drrek Lionel 923.642
John Howard: prison reformer. Foreword by Hugh J. Klare. New York, Archer House [1963, c.1958] 186p. illus., port. 23cm. 63-14441 4.50 bds.,
1. Howard, John, 1726?-1790. I. Title.

THE story of John Howard, v. 12
the eighteenth century humanitarian, in whose honor the Howard Savings Institution was named. [Newark, author, 1957] 1v. (unpaged) illus. 'Published on the occasion of the one hundredth anniversary of the Howard Savings Institution ... 1857-1957.'
1. Howard, John 1726-1790. I. Howard Savings Institution, Newark, N. J.

Howard, Katherine Graham, 1898-

HOWARD, Katherine 329'.0092'4 B
Graham, 1898-
With my shoes off / Katherine G. Howard. 1st ed. New York : Vantage Press, c1977. 347 p. : ill. ; 21 cm. [E748.H785A38] 77-74556 ISBN 0-533-02950-3 : 10.00
1. Howard, Katherine Graham, 1898- 2. United States. Federal Civil Defense Administration—Officials and employees—Biography. 3. Republican Party. National Convention. 25th, Chicago, 1952. 4. Eisenhower, Dwight David, Pres. U.S., 1890-1969. 5. Presidents—United States—Election—1952. 6. United States—Civil defense. I. Title. **BIP**

Howard, Leslie, 1893-1943.

HOWARD, Leslie Ruth, 1924- 927.92
A quite remarkable father. [1st ed.] New York, Harcourt, Brace [1959] 307 p. illus. 21 cm. [PN2598.H73H6] 59-7538
1. Howard, Leslie, 1893-1943. I. Title.

Howard, Linda.

HOWARD, Linda. 248'.2 B
The secret life of a housewife / by Linda Howard. Plainfield, N.J. : Logos International, c1978. v, 149 p. ; 21 cm. [BR1725.H688A37] 78-60946 ISBN 0-88270-296-3 pbk. : 2.95
1. Howard, Linda. 2. Christian biography—United States. 3. Wives—Religious life. I. Title.

Howard, Luke, 1772-1864.

HOWARD, Luke, 1772- 551.5'092'4
1864.
Luke Howard (1772-1864) : his correspondence with Goethe and his continental journey of 1816 / edited with a commentary by D. F. S. Scott. York : William Sessions Limited, 1976. viii, 99 p., [2] p. of plates : ill., facsims. ; 21 cm. Bibliography: p. 99. [QC858.H68A34] 76-372721 ISBN 0-900657-36-7 : £2.25
1. Howard, Luke, 1772-1864. 2. Goethe, Johann Wolfgang von, 1749-1832. 3. Meteorologists—England—Biography. I. Goethe, Johann Wolfgang von, 1749-1832. II. Scott, Douglas Frederick Schumacher.

Howard, Mary,

HOWARD, Mary, 1907- FIC
Duchess / Josephine Edgar [i.e. M.

Howard]. New York : St. Martin's Press, 1976. p. cm. [PZ3.H8344Du3] [PR6015.O857] 823'.9'12 B 76-10551 7.95
I. Title.

Howard, Maureen, 1930- — Biography.

HOWARD, Maureen, 1930- 813'.5'4 B
Facts of life / by Maureen Howard. 1st ed. Boston : Little, Brown, c1978. 182 p. ; 24 cm. Autobiographical. [PS3558.O8823Z465] 78-17656 ISBN 0-316-37469-5 : 8.95
1. Howard, Maureen, 1930- —Biography. 2. Novelists, American—20th century—Biography. I. Title. BIP

Howard, Moe.

HOWARD, Moe. 791.43'028'0924 B
Moe Howard & the 3 Stooges : the Pictorial biography of the wildest trio in the history of American entertainment / by Moe Howard. 1st ed. Secaucus, N.J. : Citadel Press, c1977. 208 p. : ill. ; 29 cm. Includes index. Filmography: p. 196-205. [PN2287.H73A35 1977] 76-58430 ISBN 0-8065-0554-0 : 14.00
1. Howard, Moe. 2. The Three Stooges. 3. Comedians—United States—Biography. I. Title.

Howard, Oliver Otis, 1830-1909.

MCFEELY, William S. 973.71'4'0924
Yankee stepfather: General O. O. Howard and the freedmen, by William S. McFeely. New Haven, Yale University Press, 1968. 351 p. port. 22 cm. (Yale publications in American studies, 15) Bibliography: p. [329]-346. [E467.1.H8M3] 68-27761 10.00
1. Howard, Oliver Otis, 1830-1909. 2. United States. Bureau of Refugees, Freedmen and Abandoned Lands. 3. Freedmen. I. Title. II. Series.

Howard, Oscar C.

HOWARD, Oscar C. 338.7'61'642470924 B
Oscar C. Howard, master of challenges; an autobiography. With an introd. by Frederick D. Patterson. Minneapolis, T. S. Denison [1974] 211 p. 23 cm. (Men of achievement series) The author, a black man from the South, relates his determined efforts to get an education and establish a successful food catering business. [TX910.5.H58A33] 92 73-87049 ISBN 0-513-01348-2 6.95
1. Howard, Oscar C. I. Title.

Howard, Peter James,

HOWARD, Peter James, 1891- 920
Life of an orphan boy. [1st ed.] New York, Pageant Press [1952] 194 p. 21 cm. [CT275.H6483A3] 52-14923
I. Title.

Howard, Robert Ervin, 1906-1936—Bibliography.

THE Last Celt : 016.813'52
a bio-bibliography of Robert Ervin Howard / edited and compiled by Glenn Lord. New York : Berkley Pub. Corp., 1977, c1976. 415 p. : ill. ; 20 cm. (A Berkley windhover book) Bibliography: p. 105-352. [Z8419.5.L37 1977] [PS3515.O842] 77-154974 ISBN 0-425-03630-8 pbk. : 5.95
1. Howard, Robert Ervin, 1906-1936—Bibliography. 2. Howard, Robert Ervin, 1906-1936—Addresses, essays, lectures. 3. Authors, American—20th century—Biography—Addresses, essays, lectures. I. Lord, Glenn.

Howard, Robert West,

HOWARD, Robert West, 1908- 92
Eli Whitney. Illustrated by David Cunningham. Chicago, Follett Pub. Co. [c1966] 144 p. col. illus. 22 cm. (Library of American heroes) [Whitney, Eli, 1765-1825--Juvenile literature.] [TS1570.W4H6] 67-1526
I. Title.

Howard, Sir Robert, 1626-1698.

OLIVER, Harold James 928.2
Sir Robert Howard, 1626-1698; a critical biography. Durham, N.C., Duke [c.]1963. xii, 346p. 24cm. Bibl. 63-17327 9.25
1. Howard, Robert, Sir 1626-1698. I. Title. BIP

OLIVER, Harold James. 928.2
Sire Robert Howard, 1626-1698; a critical biography. Durham, N.C., Duke University Press, 1963. xii, 346 p. 24 cm. Bibliography: p. [318]-327. [PR3517.H3Z75] 63-17327
1. Howard, Sir Robert, 1626-1698. I. Title.

Howard, Thomas.

HOWARD, Thomas. 248.2
Christ the tiger; a postscript to dogma. [1st ed.] Philadelphia, Lippincott [1967] 160 p. 21 cm. Autobiographical. [BR1725.H69A3] 67-24008
I. Title.

Howe, Edgar Watson, 1853-1937.

PICKETT, Calder M. 070'.924 B
Ed Howe, country town philosopher, by Calder M. Pickett. Lawrence, University Press of Kansas [1969, c1968] ix, 401 p. illus., facsims., ports. 23 cm. Bibliography: p. [385]-392. [PS2014.H5Z8] 68-25821 10.00
1. Howe, Edgar Watson, 1853-1937.

SACKETT, Samuel John, 1928- 813'.4
E. W. Howe [by] S. J. Sackett. New York, Twayne Publishers [1972] 189 p. 21 cm. (Twayne's United States authors series, TUSAS 195) Bibliography: p. 177-182. [PS2014.H5Z85] 79-153454
1. Howe, Edgar Watson, 1853-1937.

Howe, Edgar Watson, 1853-1937—Biography.

HOWE, Edgar Watson, 1853-1937. 070.4'092'4 B
Plain people. New York, Dodd, Mead, 1929. St. Clair Shores, Mich., Scholarly Press, 1974. 317 p. port. 22 cm. Autobiography. [PS2014.H5Z5 1974] 72-84686 ISBN 0-403-02963-5 12.95 (lib. ed.)
1. Howe, Edgar Watson, 1853-1937—Biography. I. Title.

Howe family.

HOWE, Daniel Dunbar. 929'.2'0973
Listen to the mockingbird; the life and times of a pioneer Virginia family. [Boyce, Va., Carr Pub. Co., 1961] 373p. illus. 24cm. [CS71.H855 1961] 62-25095
1. Howe family. I. Title.

Howe, Frederic Clemson,

HOWE, Frederic Clemson, 1867-1940 923.6
The confessions of a reformer, by Frederic C. Howe. Introd. by John Braeman. [Magnolia, Mass., P. Smith, 1967] xxx, 352p. 21cm. (Quadrangle bk. rebound). [H59.H6A3] 4.75
I. Title.

Howe, George, 1886-1955.

WEST, Helen Howe. 720'.92'4 B
George Howe, architect, 1886-1955; recollections of my beloved father. [Philadelphia, Produced by W. Nunn Co., 1973] 114 p. illus. 27 cm. Includes bibliographical references. [NA737.H65W47] 73-88249
1. Howe, George, 1886-1955.

Howe, Gordie, 1928-

FISCHLER, Stan. 796.9'62'0924
Gordie Howe. New York, Grosset & Dunlap [1969, c1967] 160 p. illus. 18 cm. (Tempo books, 5317) [GV847] 76-88894 0.75
1. Howe, Gordie, 1928-

FISCHLER, Stan. 796.9'62'0924
Gordie Howe. New York, Grosset & Dunlap [1967] 152 p. illus., group port. 20 cm. (Grosset sports library) [GV847.F46] 67-23790
1. Howe, Gordie, 1928-

FISCHLER, Stan. 92
Gordie Howe. New York, Grosset & Dunlap [1967] 152 p. illus., group port. 20 cm. (Grosset sports library) Portrait of the hockey player who has won more honors than any other player in the game—Gordie Howe of the Detroit Red Wings. [GV847.F46] AC 67
1. Howe, Gordie, 1928- I. Title.

HOWE, Colleen. 796.9'62'0922 B
My three hockey players / Colleen Howe. New York : Hawthorn Books, c1975. xi, 192 p., [9] leaves of plates : ill. ; 22 cm. [GV848.5.H58A35 1975] 74-33591 ISBN 0-8015-5294-X : 8.95
1. Howe, Gordie, 1928- 2. Howe, Marty, 1954- 3. Howe, Mark. 4. Hockey. I. Title.

O'REILLY, Don. 796.9'62'0924 B
Mr. Hockey : the world of Gordie Howe / Don O'Reilly. Chicago : Regnery, c1975. 197 p., [8] leaves of plates : ill. ; 22 cm. [GV848.5.H6O73 1975] 75-13237 ISBN 0-8092-8273-9
1. Howe, Gordie, 1928- 2. Hockey. I. Title.

Howe, Gordie, 1928—Juvenile literature.

BATSON, Larry, 1930- 796.9'62'0924 B
Gordie Howe. Illustrated by Harold Henriksen. Mankato, Minn., Amecus Street; [distributed by Children's Press, Chicago, 1974] 31 p. col. illus. 25 cm. (Superstars) A biography of the hockey star considered by some "the finest all-around hockey player the game has ever seen." [GV848.5.H6B37] 74-895 ISBN 0-87191-347-X 4.95
1. Howe, Gordie, 1928—Juvenile literature. I. Henricksen, Harold, illus. II. Title.

Howe, Jemimah Sartwell, 1713?-1805.

THE Affecting history of Mrs. Howe. 973'.04'97 S
New York : Garland Pub., 1977. p. cm. (The Garland library of narratives of North American Indian captivities ; v. 19) Reprint of the 1815 ed. published by J. Bailey, London. Issued with the reprint of the 1788 ed. of Humphryes, D. An essay on the life of the Honorable Major-General Israel Putnam. New York, 1977. [E85.G2 vol. 19] [E199] 973.2'6 B 75-7040 ISBN 0-8240-1643-2 lib.bdg. : 25.00
1. Howe, Jemimah Sartwell, 1713?-1805. 2. United States—History—French and Indian War, 1755-1763. 3. Indians of North America—Captivities. I. Series.

Howe, Joseph, 1804-1873.

FERGUSSON, Charles Bruce, 1911- 971.6'03'0924 B
Joseph Howe of Nova Scotia / by Bruce Fergusson. Windsor, N.S. : Lancelot Press, 1973. 132 p. ; 21 cm. [F1038.H83] 75-305141 2.95
1. Howe, Joseph, 1804-1873.

Howe, Julia (Ward) 1819-1910.

THARP, Louise (Hall) 1898- 929'.2'0973
Three saints and a sinner; Julia Ward Howe, Louisa, Annie, and Sam Ward. [1st ed.] Boston, Little, Brown [1956] 406 p. illus. 23 cm. Includes bibliography. [CS71.W26 1956] 56-10638
1. Howe, Julia (Ward) 1849-1910. 2. Terry, Louisa (Ward), 1823-1897. 3. Mailliard, Anne Eliza (Ward) 1824-1895. 4. Ward, Samuel, 1814-1884. I. Title.

THARP, Louise (Hall) 1898- 929'.2'0973
Three saints and a sinner: Julia Ward Howe, Louisa, Annie, Sam Ward. [1st ed.] Boston, Little, Brown [1956] 406 p. illus. 23 cm. Includes bibliography. [CS71.W26 1956] 56-10638
1. Howe, Julia (Ward) 1819-1910. 2. Terry, Louisa (Ward) 1823-1897. 3. Mailliard, Anne Eliza (Ward) 1824-1895. 4. Ward, Samuel, 1814-1884. I. Title.

Howe, Julia Ward, 1819-1910—Biography.

CLIFFORD, Deborah Pickman. 818'.4'09 B
Mine eyes have seen the glory : a biography of Julia Ward Howe / by Deborah Pickman Clifford. 1st ed. Boston : Little, Brown, c1979. 313 p., [4] leaves of plates : ill. ; 24 cm. "An Atlantic Monthly Press book." Includes index. Bibliography: p. 298-303. [PS2018.C55] 78-10379 ISBN 0-316-14747-8 : 15.00
1. Howe, Julia Ward, 1819-1910—Biography. 2. Authors, American—19th century—Biography. I. Title. BIP

Howe, Louis McHenry, 1871-1936.

STILES, Lela. 923.273
The man behind Roosevelt; the story of Louis McHenry Howe. [1st ed.] Cleveland, World Pub. Co. [1954] 311 p. 22 cm. [E748.H787S8] 54-5340
1. Howe, Louis McHenry, 1871-1936. 2. Roosevelt, Franklin Delano, Pres. U.S., 1882-1945. I. Title.

Howe. Mark Antony De Wolfe, 1864-1960.

HOWE, Helen Huntington, 1905- 818.520924
The gentle Americans, 1864-1960; biography of a breed. New York, Harper [c.1965] xix, 458p. illus., ports. 22cm. Bibl. [F73.5.H84] 65-20431 6.95
1. Howe. Mark Antony De Wolfe, 1864-1960. 2. Boston—Intellectual life. 3. Authors—Correspondence, reminiscences, etc. I. Title.

HOWE, Helen Huntington, 1905- 818.520924 B
The gentle Americans, 1864-1960; biography of a breed [by] Helen Howe. [1st ed.] New York, Harper & Row [1965] xix, 458 p. illus., ports. 22 cm. Bibliography: p. 445-446. [F73.5.H84] 65-20431
1. Howe, Mark Antony De Wolfe, 1864-1960. 2. Boston—Intellectual life. 3. Authors—Correspondence, reminiscences, etc. I. Title.

HOWE, Mark Antony De Wolfe, 1864-1960. 070.4'0924 B
A venture in remembrance. Westport, Conn., Greenwood Press [1970, c1941] viii, 319 p. 23 cm. [PS3515.O858Z5 1970] 71-109307 ISBN 0-8371-3582-6
I. Title. BIP

Howe, Mark Antony De Wolfe, 1864-1960.— Biography.

HOWE, Helen Huntington, 1905- 811'.5'2 B
The gentle Americans, 1864-1960 : biography of a breed / Helen Howe. Westport, Conn. : Greenwood Press, 1979, c1965. xix, 458 p., [8] leaves of plates : ill. ; 23 cm. Reprint of the 1st ed. published by Harper & Row, New York. Includes index. Bibliography: p. 447-449. [PS3515.O858Z68 1979] 78-24027 ISBN 0-313-20826-3 lib. bdg. : 29.75
1. Howe, Mark Antony De Wolfe, 1864-1960.— Biography. 2. Authors, America—20th century—Biography. 3. Boston—Intellectual life. I. Title.

Howe, Marty, 1954-

HOWE, Colleen. 796.9'62'0922 B
My three hockey players / Colleen Howe.

New York : Hawthorn Books, c1975. xi, 192 p., [9] leaves of plates : ill. ; 22 cm. [GV848.5.H58A35 1975] 74-33591 ISBN 0-8015-5294-X : 8.95
1. Howe, Gordie, 1928- 2. Howe, Marty, 1954- 3. Howe, Mark. 4. Hockey. I. Title.

Howe, Oscar, 1915-

PENNINGTON, Robert. 759.13
Oscar Howe. artist of the Sioux. [Sioux Falls, S. D.] Dakota Territory Centennial Commission, 1961. 61p. illus. 21cm. [ND237.H79P4] 62-4299
1. Howe, Oscar, 1915- I. Title.

Howe, Oscar, 1915-—Juvenile literature.

MILTON, John R. 759.13 B
Oscar Howe, by John R. Milton. Minneapolis, Dillon Press [1972] 56 p. illus. 24 cm. A biography of the Yanktonai Sioux who despite many obstacles became a prominent artist and teacher. [E99.Y26H65] 92 74-172870 ISBN 0-87518-043-4
1. Howe, Oscar, 1915-—Juvenile literature. I. Title. BIP

Howe, Samuel Gridley, 1801-1876.

MELTZER, Milton, 1915- 923.673
A light in the dark; the life of Samuel Gridley Howe. New York, Crowell [1964] 239 p. 21 cm. Bibliography: p. 228-231. [HV1624.H7M4] 64-16533
1. Howe, Samuel Gridley, 1801-1876. I. Title.

SCHWARTZ, Harold. 923.673
Samuel Gridley Howe, social reformer, 1801-1876. Cambridge, Harvard University Press, 1956. viii, 348p. 22cm. (Harvard historical studies, v. 67) Bibliographical footnotes. [HV1624.H7S35] 56-11286
1. Howe, Samuel Gridley, 1801-1876. II. Title. III. Series.

WILKIE, Katharine Elliott, 1904- 371.9110924
Teacher of the blind: Samuel Gridley Howe, by Katharine E. Wilkie, Elizabeth R. Moseley. New York, Messner [c.1965] 191p. 22cm. Bibl. [HV1624.H7W5] 65-21607 3.25; 3.19 lib. ed.,
1. Howe, Samuel Gridley, 1801-1876. I. Moseley, Elizabeth Robards, joint author. II. Title.

WILKIE, Katharine Elliott, 1904- 371.9110924 (B)
Teacher of the blind: Samuel Gridley Howe, by Katharine E. Wilkie and Elizabeth R. Moseley. New York, J. Messner [1965] 191 p. 22 cm. Bibliography: p. [183] [HV1624.H7W5] 65-21607
1. Howe, Samuel Gridley, 1801-1876. I. Moseley, Elizabeth Robards, joint author. II. Title.

Howe, William F.

ROVERE, Richard H. 343.23
Howe and Hummel. Introd. by the author. Illus. by Reginald Marsh. New York, Paperback Lib. [1963, c.1947] 157p. illus. 18cm. (Silver ed., 52-202) .50 pap.,
1. Howe, William F. 2. Hummel, Abraham H. 3. Crime and criminals. I. Title.

Howe, William H., d. 1864.

ALOTTA, Robert I. 973.7'4
Stop the evil : a Civil War history of desertion and murder / Robert I. Alotta. San Rafael, Calif. : Presidio Press, c1978. p. cm. Includes index. Bibliography: p. [E527.5 116th.H68A44] 78-10425 ISBN 0-89141-018-X : 14.95
1. Howe, William H., d. 1864. 2. United States—History—Civil War, 1861-1865—Desertions. 3. Desertion, Military—United States. 4. Trials (Military offenses)—United States. 5. Soldiers—United States—Biography. I. Title.

Howell, Elizabeth (Lloyd) b. 1811.

WHITTIER, John Greenleaf, 1809-1892. 811'.3 B
Whittier's unknown romance; letters to Elizabeth Lloyd. With an introd. by Marie V. Denervaud. Boston, Houghton Mifflin, 1922. New York, Haskell House, 1973. x, 72 p. illus. 23 cm. [PS3281.A35 1973] 73-8938 ISBN 0-8383-1707-3 9.95
1. Howell, Elizabeth (Lloyd) b. 1811. I. Title. BIP

Howell family.

LANPHIER, Beatrice Howell. 929'.2'0973
The Alexander and Howell families. Dixon, Ill., 1964. 237 p. illus., facsims., ports. 24 cm. [CS71.H858 1964] 65-4571
1. Howell family. 2. Alexander family. I. Title.

Howell, George, 1833-1910.

LEVENTHAL, F. M., 1938- 323.3 B
Respectable radical: George Howell and Victorian working class politics [by] F. M. Leventhal. Cambridge, Mass., Harvard University Press, 1971. xv, 276 p. 23 cm. A rewritten and shortened version of the author's dissertation submitted to Harvard, 1967, with title: George Howell, 1833-1910: a career in radical politics. Bibliography: p. [255]-267. [HD8393.H6L45 1971] 77-135190 ISBN 0-674-76540-0 7.75
1. Howell, George, 1833-1910. 2. Labor and laboring classes—Gt. Brit.—History. I. Title. BIP

Howell, Robert Beecher, 1864-1933.

O'BRIEN, Patrick G. 328.73'0924 B
Senator Robert B. Howell: a Midwestern progressive and insurgent during "normalcy", by Patrick G. O'Brien. Emporia, Kansas State Teachers College, 1970. 28 p. port. 23 cm. (The Emporia State research studies v. 19, no. 2) Includes bibliographical references. [E748.H79O2] 75-634524
1. Howell, Robert Beecher, 1864-1933. I. Title. II. Series.

Howell, Robert Boyte Crawford, 1801-1868.

BURTON, Joe Wright, 1907- 286'.132'0924 B
Road to Augusta : R. B. C. Howell and the formation of the Southern Baptist Convention / Joe W. Burton. Nashville : Broadman Press, c1976. 186 p. : ill. ; 20 cm. Bibliography: p. 184-186. [BX6495.H68B87] 75-16581 ISBN 0-8054-6520-0 . 6.95
1. Howell, Robert Boyte Crawford, 1801-1868. 2. Southern Baptist Convention—History. 3. Baptists—Southern States—Biography. 4. Southern States—Biography. I. Title.

Howells, William Dean,

HOWELLS, William Dean, 1837-1920. 818'.4'09 B
My literary passions. New York, Greenwood Press [1969] 261 p. 18 cm. Reprint of the 1895 ed. [PS2033.A63 1969] 68-57612
I. Title. BIP

HOWELLS, William Dean, 1837-1920. 818'.4'09 B
Years of my youth. Freeport, N.Y., Books for Libraries Press [1971, c1916] 238 p. 23 cm. [PS2033.A65 1971] 70-146859 ISBN 0-8369-5626-5
I. Title. BIP

Howells, William Dean, 1837-1920.

BENNETT, George N. 813.4
William Dean Howells; the development of a novelist. Norman, University of Oklahoma Press [1959] 220 p. illus. 24 cm. [PS2033.B4] 59-7487
1. Howells, William Dean, 1837-1920.

BROOKS, Van Wyck, 1886- 928.1
Howells, his life and world. [1st ed.] New York, Dutton, 1959. 296p. illus. 22cm. [PS2033.B7] 59-10782
1. Howells, William Dean, 1837-1920. I. Title.

CADY, Edwin Harrison. 928.1
The realist at war; the mature years, 1885-1920, of William Dean Howells. [Syracuse] Syracuse University Press [1958] 299 p. 24 cm. Includes bibliography. [PS2033.C23] 58-13106
1. Howells, William Dean, 1837-1920. I. Title.

CADY, Edwin Harrison. 928.1
The road to realism; the early years, 1837-1885, of William Dean Howells. [Syracuse] Syracuse University Press [1956] x, 283p. 24cm. 'Bibliographical notes': p. 247-276. [PS2033.C25] 56-11892
1. Howells, William Dean, 1837-1920. I. Title.

GIBSON, William Merriam, 1912- 818'.4'09
William D. Howells, by William M. Gibson. Minneapolis, University of Minnesota Press [1967] 48 p. 20 cm. (University of Minnesota pamphlets on American writers, no. 63) Bibliography: p. 45-48. [PS2033.G5] 67-26663
1. Howells, William Dean, 1837-1920. I. Series: Minnesota. University. Pamphlets on American writers, no. 63 BIP

HOWELLS, William Dean, 1837-1920. 818'.4'09 B
My literary passions. New York, Greenwood Press [1969] 261 p. 18 cm. Reprint of the 1895 ed. [PS2033.A63 1969] 68-57612
I. Title. BIP

HOWELLS, William Dean, 1837-1920. 818'.4'09 B
Years of my youth. Freeport, N.Y., Books for Libraries Press [1971, c1916] 238 p. 23 cm. [PS2033.A65 1971] 70-146859 ISBN 0-8369-5626-5
I. Title. BIP

KIRK, Clara (Marburg) 1898- 818.4
William Dean Howells, by Clara M. Kirk and Rudolf Kirk. New York, Twayne Publishers [1962] 223 p. 21 cm. (Twayne's United States authors series, 16) Includes bibliography. [PS2033.K5] 61-18070
1. Howells, William Dean, 1837-1920. I. Kirk, Rudolf, 1898- joint author.

LYNN, Kenneth Schuyler. 818'.4'09 B
William Dean Howells; an American life [by] Kenneth S. Lynn. [1st ed.] New York, Harcourt Brace Jovanovich [1971] 372 p. illus., ports. 26 cm. Includes bibliographical references. [PS2033.L9] 71-142091 ISBN 0-15-142177-3
1. Howells, William Dean, 1837-1920

WAGENKNECHT, Edward Charles, 1900- 818'.4'09
William Dean Howells; the friendly eye [by] Edward Wagenknecht. New York, Oxford University Press, 1969. x, 340 p. port. 21 cm. Bibliography: p. 317-324. [PS2033.W3] 70-83055 7.50
1. Howells, William Dean, 1837-1920.

Howells, William Dean, 1837-1920. A traveler from Altruria.

KIRK, Clara (Marburg) 1898- 814.4
W. D. Howells, Traveler from Altruria, 1889-1894. New Brunswick, N.J., Rutgers [c.1962] 148p. illus. 22cm. 62-13762 5.00
1. Howells, William Dean, 1837-1920. A traveler from Altruria. I. Title.

Howells, William Dean, 1837-1920—Biography—Youth.

HOWELLS, William Dean, 1837-1920. 818'.4'09 B
Years of my youth, and three essays. Introd. and notes to the text by David J. Nordloh. Text established by David J. Nordloh. Bloomington, Indiana University Press, 1975. xxvii, 420 p. port. 24 cm. (His A selected edition of W. D. Howells, v. 29) Includes bibliographical references. [PS2020.F68 vol. 29] [PS2033] 78-166119 ISBN 0-253-36850-2 20.00
1. Howells, William Dean, 1837-1920—Biography—Youth. I. Title. BIP

Howerd, Frankie.

HOWERD, Frankie. 791'.092'4 B
On the way I lost it : an autobiography / Frankie Howerd. London : Allen, 1976. 288 p., [16] leaves of plates : ports. ; 23 cm. [PN2598.H75A35] 77-350065 ISBN 0-491-01807-X : £4.50
1. Howerd, Frankie. 2. Comedians—Great Britain—Biography. I. Title.

Howes, John.

HOWES, John. 910'.4 B
Second time lucky / John Howes. Ilfracombe : Stockwell, 1976. 220 p., [16] p. of plates : ill., 2 maps, music, ports. ; 23 cm. [CT2808.H69A37] 77-361937 ISBN 0-7223-0814-0 : £3.00
1. Howes, John. 2. Australia—Biography. I. Title.

Howitt, Mary (Botham) 1799-1888.

HOWITT, Mary (Botham) 1799-1888. 828'.8'09 B
Mary Howitt; an autobiography. Edited by her daughter, Margaret Howitt. Boston, Houghton Mifflin, 1889. [New York, AMS Press, 1973] p. (Women of letters) [PR4809.H2A8 1973] 70-37697 ISBN 0-404-56754-1 37.00 (2 vols.)
1. Howitt, Mary (Botham) 1799-1888. I. Howitt, Margaret, 1839- ed. II. Title. III. Series. BIP

Howitt, William, 1792-1879.

LEE, Amice (Macdonell) 928.2
Laurels & rosemary; the life of William and Mary Howitt. London. New York, Oxford University Press, 1955. 330p. illus. 23cm. [PR4809.H3Z7] 55-14707
1. Howitt. William. 1792-1879. 2. Howitt, Mary (Botham) 1799-1888. I. Title.

SYMONDS, Emily Morse, d.1936. 920.042
Little memoirs of the nineteenth century. Freeport, N.Y., Books for Libraries Press [1969] ix, 375 p. ports. 23 cm. (Essay index reprint series) Reprint of the 1902 ed. Contents.Contents.—Benjamin Robert Haydon.—Lady Morgan (Sydney Owenson)—Nathaniel Parker Willis.—Lady Hester Stanhope.—Prince Puckler-Muskau in England.—William and Mary Howitt. [DA531.1.S9 1969] 70-86787 ISBN 8-369-11970-
1. Puckler-Muskau, Hermann Ludwig Heinrich, furst von, 1785-1871. 2. Morgan, Sydney (Owenson) lady, 1783?-1859. 3. Haydon, Benjamin Robert, 1786-1846. 4. Willis, Nathaniel Parker, 1806-1867. 5. Stanhope, Hester Lucy, Lady, 1776-1839. 6. Howitt, William, 1792-1879. 7. Howitt, Mary (Botham) 1799-1888. I. Title. BIP

Howland, Bette.

HOWLAND, Bette. 362.2'1'0924 B
W-3. New York, Viking Press [1974] 206 p. 22 cm. Autobiographical. [RC463.H68 1974] 73-15475 ISBN 0-670-74863-3 7.95
1. Howland, Bette. 2. Mental illness—Personal narratives. I. Title.

Howland, Emily, 1827-1929.

BREAULT, Judith Colucci, 1946- 301.24'2'0924 B
The world of Emily Howland : odyssey of a humanitarian / by Judith Colucci Breault. Millbrae, Calif. : Les Femmes Pub., 1976. xiii, 173 p. : ill. ; 22 cm. Includes index. Bibliography: p. 165-168. [HQ1413.H68B73] 75-10580 ISBN 0-89087-987-7 : 9.95. ISBN 0-89087-904-4 pbk. : 5.95
1. Howland, Emily, 1827-1929. 2. United States—Social conditions—To 1865. 3. United States—Social conditions—1865-1918. I. Title.

Howland, Larry O.

HOWLAND, Larry O. 269'.2'0924 B
Going straight / [Larry O. Howland]. Irvine, Calif. : Harvest House Publishers, c1979. 142 p. ; 18 cm. [BV3785.H64A34] 79-84766 ISBN 0-89081-198-9 : 2.25
1. Howland, Larry O. 2. Evangelists—United States—Biography. I. Title.

Howser, James Wilson, 1840-1926.

[HOUSER, Martin Luther] 1871- 920 comp.
Grandfather and Grandmother Howser and some friends;their lives and times. Compiled by M. L. H. Peoria, Ill., 1926. 64p. illus., ports. 24cm. [CT275.H659H6] 53-51935
1. Howser, James Wilson, 1840-1926. I. Howser, Frances Amanda (Summers) 1840-1922. II. Title.

Howson, John, 1865-1956.

GWILLIAM, Elizabeth 623.820924 B Caroline.
Sunset and evening star. [1st ed.] New York, Vantage Press [1967, c1966] 68 p. illus., ports. 21 cm. [VM140.H68G9] 67-179
1. Howson, John, 1865-1956. I. Title.

Hoxie, Vinnie (Ream) 1847-1914.

HALL, Gordon Langley 920
Vinnie Ream; the story of the girl who sculptured Lincoln. New York, Holt [c.1963] 149p. 22cm. Bibl. 63-12746 3.50; 3.27 bds., lib. ed.,
1. Hoxie, Vinnie (Ream) 1847-1914. I. Title.

HALL, Gordon Langley. j92
Vinnie Ream; the story of the girl who sculptured Lincoln. [1st ed.] New York, Holt, Rinehart and Winston [1963] 149 p. 22 cm. Includes bibliography. [NB237.H7H3] 63-12746
1. Hoxie, Vinnie (Ream) 1847-1914. I. Title.

Hoy, David.

•GODWIN, John. 133.8
Super-psychic; the incredible Dr. Hoy. New York, Pocket Books, [1974] 239 p. illus. 18 cm. [BF1127] ISBN 0-671-78463-3 1.25 (pbk.)
1. Hoy, David. 2. Extrascensory perception. I. Title.

GODWIN, John, 1928- 133.8'092'4 B
Super-psychic : the incredible Dr. Hoy / by John Godwin. New York : Pocket Books, 1974. 239 p., [8] leaves of plates : ill. ; 18 cm. Includes index. [BF1027.H69G6] 74-192049 ISBN 0-671-78463-3 pbk. 1.25
1. Hoy, David. I. Title.

Hoyland, Eric.

HOYLAND, Eric. 791.3'3'0924 B
Tickey : the story of Eric Hoyland / as told by him to T. V. Bulpin ; illustrated by Penny Miller. Cape Town : Bulpin, c1976. 241 p. : ill. (some col.) ; 29 cm. [GV1811.H69A36] 77-356978
1. Hoyland, Eric. 2. Clowns—Biography. I. Bulpin, Thomas Victor. II. Title.

Hoyos, Bernardo Francisco de, 1711-1735.

BECHARD, Henri. 922.246
The visions of Bernard Francis de Hoyos, S. J., apostle of the Sacred Heart in Spain a biography. [1st ed.] New York, Vantage Press[1959] 178p. illus. 21cm. Includes bibliography. [BV5095.H6B4] 59-8423
1. Hoyos, Bernardo Francisco de, 1711-1735. 2. Sacred Heart, Devotion to. 3. Visions. I. Title.

Hoyt, Adelia M.

HOYT, Adelia M. 920.96177
Unfolding years; the events of a lifetime. [Washington, W. Conway, 1950] 125 p. 24 cm. [HV1624.H75A3] 51-24213
I. Title.

Hoyt, Sally Foresman.

HOYT, Sally Foresman. 925.982
In memoriam: J. Southgate Y. Hoyt; the life of an ornithologist, with excerpts from his journals, collected and edited by his wife. [n.p., 1958] 163p. illus. 23cm. [QL31.H845H6] 59-17141
I. Hoyt, John Southgate Yeaton, 1913-1951. II. Title.

Hoyt, Samuel Leslie, 1888-

HOYT, Samuel 669'.0092'4 B Leslie, 1888-
Men of metals : an exciting career among the pathfinders of modern metallurgy / Samuel L. Hoyt. Metals Park, Ohio : American Society for Metals, c1979. iv, 315 p. ; 24 cm. [TN140.H754A34] 78-31521 ISBN 0-87170-059-X : 12.50
1. Hoyt, Samuel Leslie, 1888- 2. Metallurgists—United States—Biography. 3. Metallurgy—History—20th century. I. Title.

Hsu-yun, 1839-1959.

HSU-YUN, 1839-1959. 294.3'6'1 B
Empty Cloud : the autobiography of the Chinese Zen Master, Hsu Yun / translated by Upasaka Lu K'uan Yu (Charles Luk). Rochester, N.Y. : Empty Cloud Press, c1974. 120 p. ; 21 cm. Abridged translation of Hsu-yun ho shang nien p'u. [BQ962.S87A33213] 75-313534
1. Hsu-yun, 1839-1959. I. Title.

Hsuan-tsang, 596 (ca.)-664.

HUI-LI. 294.3'61 B
The life of Hiuen-Tsiang, by the shaman Hwui Li. With an introd. containing an account of the works of I-tsing, by Samuel Beal. With a pref. by L. Cranmer-Byng. New ed. Westport, Conn., Hyperion Press [1973] xlvii, 218 p. 23 cm. Reprint of the 1911 translation of Ta T'ang ta tz'u en ssu San Tsang fa shih chuan published by K. Paul, Trench, Trubner, London in series: Trubner's oriental series. Includes bibliographical references. [BQ8149.H787H813 1973] 73-880 ISBN 0-88355-074-1
1. Hsuan-tsang, 596 (ca.)-664. 2. I-ching, 635-713. I. Beal, Samuel, 1825-1889, tr. II. Title. BIP

HUI-LI. 294.3'61'0924 B
The life of Hiuen-Tsiang, by the shaman Hwui Li. With an introd. containing an account of the works of I-tsing, by Samuel Beal. With a pref. by L. Cranmer-Byng. New ed. Westport, Conn., Hyperion Press [1973] xlvii, 218 p. 23 cm. Reprint of the 1911 translation of Ta T'ang ta tz'u en ssu San Tsang fa shih chuan published by K. Paul, Trench, Trubner, London in series: Trubner's oriental series. Includes bibliographical references. [BQ8149.H787H813 1973] 73-880 ISBN 0-88355-074-1 12.75
1. Hsuan-tsang, 596 (ca.)-664. 2. I-ching, 635-713. I. Beal, Samuel, 1825-1889, tr. II. Title.

Hsun, Yueh, 148-209.

CHEN, Chi-yun, 181'.09'512 B 1933-
Hsun Yueh (A.D. 148-209) : the life and reflections of an early medieval Confucian / by Chi-yun Chen. Cambridge [Eng.] ; New York : Cambridge University Press, 1975. x, 242 p. ; 24 cm. (Cambridge studies in Chinese history : Literature and institutions) Originally presented as the author's thesis, Harvard. Includes index. Bibliography: p. 214-229. [B128.H54C47 1975] 74-79135 ISBN 0-521-20394-5 : 22.50
1. Hsun, Yueh, 148-209. I. Title.

Hsieh, Ping-ying, 1906- —Biography.

HSIEH, Ping-ying, 1906- 322.4'2 B
Girl rebel : the autobiography of Hsieh Pingying, with extracts from her New war diaries / translated by Adet and Anor Lin ; with an introd. by Lin Yutang. New York : Da Capo Press, 1975, c1940. xviii, 270 p., [1] leaf of plates ; 22 cm. (China in the 20th century) Translation of I ko nu ping ti tzu chuan. Reprint of the ed. published by John Day Co., New York. [PL2765.I45Z5213 1975] 74-34583 ISBN 0-306-70691-1 : 18.00
1. Hsieh, Ping-ying, 1906- —Biography. I. Title. BIP

Hsin, Ch'i-chi, 1140-1207.

LO, Irving Yucheng, 895.1'1'4 B 1922-
Hsin Ch'i-chi. New York, Twayne Publishers [1971] 194 p. 22 cm. (Twayne's world authors series, TWAS 169: China) Bibliography: p. 173-178. [PL2680.Z5L6] 70-120509
1. Hsin, Ch'i-chi, 1140-1207.

Huang, Ch'ao, d. 884.

OU-YANG, Hsiu, 1007-1072. 923.551
Biography of Huang Ch'ao [Hsin Tang-shu 225C.la-9a] Translated and annotated by Howard S. Levy. Berkeley, University of California Press, 1955. 144p. 3 fold. maps (in pocket) 24cm. (Institute of East Asiatic Studies, University of California. Chinese Dynastic histories translations, no. 5) Part of the editor's thesis--University of California. The Hsin Tang shu is by Ou-yang Hslu, Sung Ch'l, and others. Cf. Wylle. Notes on Chinese literature. Bibliography: p. 130-136. [DS741.C3 no.5] A55
1. Huang, Ch'ao, d. 884. I. Sung, Ch'l, 998-1061. II. Levy, Howard Seymour, 1923- ed. and tr. III. Title. IV. Series: California. University. Institute of East Asiatic Studies. Chinese dynastic histories translations, no. 5

Huang, Ch'ao, d.884.

OU-YANG, Hsiu, 1007-1072. v. 12
Biography of Huang Ch'ao. (Hsin T'ang-shu 225C.1a-91) Translated and annotated by Howard S. Levy. 2d ed. revised and enlarged. Berkeley, University of California Press, 1961. 153 p. facsims. 3 fold. maps in pocket. (Chinese dynastic histories translations, no. 5) Includes bibliographies. 64-11480
1. Huang, Ch'ao, d.884. I. Levy, Howard Seymour, 1923- tr. II. Title. III. Series.

Hubbard, Barbara Marx, 1929-

HUBBARD, Barbara 973.92'092'4 B Marx, 1929-
The hunger of Eve : Barbara Marx Hubbard. Harrisburg, Pa. : Stackpole Books, c1976. 224 p. ; 24 cm. p. cm. Autobiographical. Bibliography: p. 222-224. [CT275.H662A34 1976] 76-17267 ISBN 0-8117-0861-6 : 10.00
1. Hubbard, Barbara Marx, 1929- 2. United States—Biography. I. Title.

Hubbard, Bela, 1814-1896.

BERG, Herbert 917.74'03'20924 B Andrew.
Bela Hubbard, 1814-1896; a biographical sketch East Lansing, Mich., 1967. iv, 34 l. group port. 28 cm. Cover title. Includes bibliographical references. [CT275.H663B45] 72-625537
1. Hubbard, Bela, 1814-1896.

Hubbard, Elbert, 1856-1915.

HAMILTON, Charles 808'.00924 B Franklin, 1915-
As bees in honey drown; Elbert Hubbard and the Roycrofters [by] Charles F. Hamilton. South Brunswick, A. S. Barnes [1973] 253 p. illus., facsims. 24 cm. Includes bibliographical references. [Z232.R8H35] 77-37811 ISBN 0-498-01052-X 10.00
1. Hubbard, Elbert, 1856-1915. 2. Roycroft Shop, East Aurora, N.Y. I. Title. BIP

LEVULIS, Stanley, 1924- 700'.924
The story of Elbert Hubbard and the Roycrofters of East Aurora, by Stanley and Dorothy Levulis. [Blasdell, N.Y., 1971] v, 31 p. illus. 22 cm. Cover title. [NK1149.R6L4] 79-27950 3.95
1. Hubbard, Elbert, 1856-1915. 2. Roycroft Shop, East Aurora, N.Y. I. Levulis, Dorothy, joint author. II. Title.

Hubbard, Elbert, 1856-1915—Biography.

CHAMPNEY, Freeman. 700'.924 B
Art & glory; the story of Elbert Hubbard. New York, Crown Publishers [1968] v. 248 p. illus., facsims., ports. 24 cm. Includes bibliographical references. [PS2043.C47] 68-20472
1. Hubbard, Elbert, 1856-1915—Biography. I. Title.

STOTT, Mary Roelofs, 700'.92'4 B 1918-
Elbert Hubbard, rebel with reverence : a granddaughter's tribute by Mary Roelofs Stott. Watkins Glen, N.Y. : Century House Americana Publishers, 1974 96 p. : ill. ; 26 cm. Includes index. [PS2043.S8] 74-21057 4.95
1. Hubbard, Elbert, 1856-1915—Biography. I. Title.

Hubbard, Elbert, 1856-1915—Collectibles.

HAMILTON, Charles 700'.6'574796 Franklin, 1915-
Roycroft collectibles : including collector items related to Elbert Hubbard, founder of the Roycroft shops / Charles F. Hamilton. South Brunswick, N.J. : A. S. Barnes, c1980. p. cm. Includes index. [NK1149.R6H35] 78-75308 ISBN 0-498-01919-5 : 15.00
1. Roycroft Shop, East Aurora, N.Y.—Collectibles. 2. Hubbard, Elbert, 1856-1915—Collectibles. 3. Hubbard, Elbert, 1856-1915—Biography. 4. Authors, American—19th century—Biography. 5. Printers—United States—Biography. I. Title.

Hubbard, Frank McKinney, 1868-1930.

KELLY, Fred Charters, 1882- 928.1
The life and times of Kin Hubbard, creator of Abe Martin. New York, Farrar, Straus and Young [1952] 179 p. illus. 22 cm. [PS3515.U1413Z7] 52-6982
1. Hubbard, Frank McKinney, 1868-1930. I. Title.

Hubbard, Harlan.

HUBBARD, Harlan. 917.69'04'40924
Payne Hollow : life on the fringe of society / Harlan Hubbard. New York : Eakins Press, [1974] 167 p. : ill. ; 19 cm. Autobiographical. [F456.2.H82] 73-84998 ISBN 0-87130-040-0 : 5.95
1. Hubbard, Harlan. 2. Kentucky—Description and travel—1951- I. Title. BIP

Hubbard, John Clarence, 1884-

FLEMING, Joseph Landis. 926.1
An Oklahoma rebel; the life story of Dr. John C. Hubbard.[1st ed.] Oklahoma City, Cryer Pub. Co. [1957] 182p. illus. 23cm. [R154.H7F4] 57-12875
1. Hubbard, John Clarence, 1884- I. Title.

Hubbard, Ralph

YOST, Nellie Irene 979'.00994 B Snyder.
A man as big as the West : the story of Ralph Hubbard / by Nellie Snyder Yost. Boulder, Colo. : Pruett Pub. Co., [1979] p. cm. [E76.45.H8Y67] 79-20068 ISBN 0-87108-543-7 : 11.50
1. Hubbard, Ralph 2. Indianists—The West—Biography. 3. The West—Biography. I. Title.

Hubbard, Richard Bennett, 1832-1901.

TURNER, Martha 973.8'092'4 B Anne.
Richard Bennett Hubbard : an American life / by Martha Anne Turner ; with

bibliographical assistance by Jean Sutherlin Duncan. 1st ed. Austin, Tex. : Shoal Creek Publishers, c1979. p. cm. Includes index. Bibliography: p. [F391.H875T87] 79-19049 ISBN 0-88319-043-5 : 15.00
1. Hubbard, Richard Bennett, 1832-1901. 2. Texas—Politics and government—1865-1950. 3. Texas—Politics and government—1946-1865. 4. United States—Foreign relations—Japan. 5. Japan—Foreign relations—United States. 6. Texas—Governors—Biography. 7. Ambassadors—United States—Biography. I. Duncan, Jean Sutherlin, 1930- BIP

Hubbell, Ralph, 1909-

HUBBELL, Ralph, 1909- 070.4'49'7960924
Come walk with me / Ralph Hubbell. Englewood Cliffs, N.J. : Prentice-Hall, [1975] 150 p., [6] leaves of plates : ill. ; 22 cm. [GV719.H82A33] 74-30325 ISBN 0-13-152520-4 : 7.95
1. Hubbell, Ralph, 1909- 2. Radio broadcasting of sports. 3. Television broadcasting of sports. 4. Sports—Biography. I. Title.

Hubert Walter, Abp. of Canterbury, d. 1205.

YOUNG, Charles R. 283'.0924
Hubert Walter, Lord of Canterbury and Lord of England [by] Charles R. Young. Durham, N. C., Duke University Press, 1968. viii, 196 p. 25 cm. (Duke historical publications) Includes bibliographical references. [BR754.H8Y6] 68-24438
1. Hubert Walter, Abp. of Canterbury, d. 1205. I. Series. BIP

Hubmaier, Balthasar, d. 1528.

BERGSTEN, Torsten, 1921- 284'.3
Balthasar Hubmaier : Anabaptist theologian and martyr / Torsten Bergsten ; edited by W. R. Estep, Jr. , [translated from the German by Irwin J. Barnes and William R. Estep]. Valley Forge, Pa. : Judson Press, c1978. 432 p. : ill. maps (on lining papers) ; 23 cm. Includes index. Bibliography: p. 415-416. [BX4946.H8B413] 78-2683 ISBN 0-8170-0793-8 : 19.95
1. Hubmaier, Balthasar, d. 1528. 2. Anabaptists—Biography. 3. Anabaptists. I. Estep, William Roscoe, 1920- BIP

VEDDER, Henry Clay, 1853-1935. 284'.3 B
Balthasar Hubmaier; the leader of the Anabaptists. New York, AMS Press [1971] xxiv, 333 p. illus., facsim., map, ports. 19 cm. (Heroes of the Reformation) Reprint of the 1905 ed. [BX4946.H8V4 1971] 79-149670 ISBN 0-404-06755-7
1. Hubmaier, Balthasar, d. 1528. 2. Anabaptists.

Hubner, Charles William, 1835-1929—Biography.

WALKER, Mary Hubner. 811'.4
Charles W. Hubner, poet laureate of the South / by Mary Hubner Walker. Atlanta : Cherokee Pub. Co., 1976. xi, 202 p. : ill. ; 23 cm. Includes bibliographical references and index. [PS2044.H24Z96] 76-14277 ISBN 0-87797-037-8 : 10.00
1. Hubner, Charles William, 1835-1929—Biography. 2. Poets, American—19th century—Biography. I. Title.

Hudson, George, 1800-1871.

LAMBERT, Richard Stanton, 1894- 923.342
The railway king, 1800-1871; a study of George Hudson and the business morals of his time. London, G. Allen & Unwin [dist. New Rochelle, N.Y., SportShelf, 1964, c.1949] 320p. front., illus. (incl. maps, facsim.) plates, ports. 22cm. Bibl. 6.75
1. Hudson, George, 1800-1871. 2. Railroads—Gt. Brit.—Hist. I. Title.

Hudson, Gertrude Reese,

HUDSON, Gertrude Reese, ed. 928.2
Browning to his American friends; letters between the Brownings, the Storys and James Russell Lowell, 1841-1890 edited with introd. and notes by Gertrude Reese Hudson. New York, Barnes and Noble [1965] xvi, 382 p. ports. 23 cm. Bibliography: p. 368-370. [PR4231.A3H8] 65-2653
I. Browning, Robert, 1812-1889. II. Title.

Hudson, Henry, d. 1611

SNOW, Dorothea J 1909- j92
Henry Hudson, explorer of the North. Illustrated by John C. Wonsetler. Boston, Houghton Mifflin [1962] 190 p. illus. 22 cm. (Piper books) [E129.H8S73] 62-9304
1. Hudson, Henry, d. 1611 — Juvenile literature. I. Title.

Hudson, Henry, d. 1611—Juvenile literature.

CARMER, Carl Lamson, 1893- 923.9
Henry Hudson; captain of ice-bound seas. Illustrated by John O'hara Cosgrave, II. Champaign Ill., Garrard Press [1960] 80 p. illus. 23 cm. (A Discovery book) [E129.H8C25] 60-11572
1. Hudson, Henry, d. 1611—Juvenile literature. BIP

EDUCATIONAL Research Council of America. Social Science Staff. 974.7'3'010924 B
Explorers and discoverers: Henry Hudson. Boston, Allyn and Bacon [1970] 50 p. col. illus., col. maps. 21 cm. (Concepts and inquiry: the ERC social science program) Describes the voyages of Henry Hudson as he searched for a northwest passage to China. [E129.H8E3] 70-97103
1. Hudson, Henry, d. 1611—Juvenile literature. I. Title. II. Series: Concepts and inquiry: the Educational Research Council social science program

EDUCATIONAL Research Council of America. Social Science Staff. 974.7'3'010924
Explorers and discoverers, Henry Hudson / prepared by the Social Science Staff of the Educational Research Council of America. Learner-verified ed. 2. Boston : Allyn and Bacon, [1974] 50 p. : col. ill. ; 21 cm. (Concepts and inquiry, the ERC social science program) Describes the voyages of Henry Hudson as he searched for a northwest passage to China. [E129.H8E3 1974] 92 B 73-78336 pbk. : 1.76
1. Hudson, Henry, d. 1611—Juvenile literature. I. Title. II. Series: Concepts and inquiry: the Educational Research Council social science program.

JOSEPH, Joan. 974.7'3'010924 B
Henry Hudson. New York, Watts, 1974. 57 p. illus. 26 cm. (A Visual biography) A biography of the explorer who claimed the Hudson Valley for the Dutch and the Hudson Bay area for the English. [E129.H8J67] 92 73 14704 ISBN 0-531-01276-X 4.50
1. Hudson, Henry, d. 1611—Juvenile literature. I. Title. BIP

Hudson, Hosea.

PAINTER, Nell Irvin. 335.43'092'4 B
The narrative of Hosea Hudson, his life as a Negro Communist in the South / Nell Irvin Painter. Cambridge, Mass. : Harvard University Press, 1979. xiii, 400 p. : ill. ; 25 cm. Includes index. Bibliography: p. 391-394. [HX84.H8P34] 79-4589 ISBN 0-674-60110-6 : 17.50
1. Hudson, Hosea. 2. Afro-American communists—Southern States—Biography. 3. Afro-Americans—Southern States—Biography. 4. Trade-unions—Officials and employees—Southern States—Biography. 5. Iron and steel workers—Southern States—Biography. I. Title.

Hudson, Liam.

HUDSON, Liam. 150
The cult of the fact; a psychologist's autobiographical critique of his discipline. New York, Harper & Row [1973, c1972] 189 p. illus. 23 cm. Includes bibliographical references. [BF109.H8A3 1972] 72-11872 ISBN 0-06-136115-1 7.50
1. Hudson, Liam. 2. Psychologists. 3. Psychology, Experimental. I. Title.
Pbk. 2.45.

Hudson's Bay Company.

HARGRAVE, Letitia (Mactavish) 1813-1854. 917.127'1
The letters of Letitia Hargrave; [edited with introd. and notes by Margaret Arnett MacLeod] New York, Greenwood Press, 1969. cliv, 310 p. illus., map., ports. 24 cm. (Champlain Society publication, 28) Reprint of the 1956 ed. Bibliographical footnotes. [F1060.H38 1969] 69-14502
1. Hudson's Bay Company. 2. York Factory, Can. 3. Northwest, Canadian—History—Sources. I. MacLeod, Margaret (Arnett) 1877- ed. II. Title. III. Series: Champlain Society, Toronto. Publications, 28 BIP

NUTE, Grace Lee, 1895- 971.01'6'0922
Caesars of the wilderness : Medard Chouart, Sieur des Groseilliers and Pierre Esprit Radisson, 1618-1710 / by Grace Lee Nute. Reprint ed. St. Paul : Minnesota Historical Society Press, 1978, c1943. xx, 386 p., [7] leaves of plates : ill. ; 24 cm. (Publications of the Minnesota Historical Society) Reprint of the ed. published by Appleton-Century, New York. Includes index. Bibliography: p. 359-370. [F1060.7.C483N87 1978] 78-811 ISBN 0-87351-127-1 : 12.50 ISBN 0-87351-128-X pbk. : 5.95
1 Chouart, Medard, sieur des Groseilliers, 17th century. 2. Radisson, Pierre Esprit, 1620?-1710. 3. Hudson's Bay Company. 4. New France—Discovery and exploration. 5. Explorers—France—Biography. 6. Fur trade—New France. I. Title. II. Series: Minnesota Historical Society. Publications. BIP

RADISSON, Pierre Esprit, 1620?-1710. 917.1'04'16
Voyages of Peter Esprit Radisson, being an account of his travels and experiences among the North American Indians, from 1652 to 1684. Transcribed from original manuscripts in the Bodleian Library and the British Museum. With historical illus. and an introd. by Gideon D. Scull. New York, B. Franklin [1971?] vi, 385 p. 23 cm. (Burt Franklin research and source works series, 131. American classics in history and social science, 2) Reprint of the 1885 ed., which was issued as v. 16 of the Publications of the Prince Society. [F1060.7.R12 1971] 72-184164
1. Hudson's Bay Company. 2. New France—Discovery and exploration. 3. Northwest, Canadian—History. 4. Indians of North America—Canada. 5. Iroquois Indians. I. Title. II. Series: Prince Society, Boston. Publications, v. 16. BIP

WYETH, Nathaniel Jarvis, 1802-1856. 917.95
The correspondence and journals of Captain Nathaniel J. Wyeth, 1831-6. F(rederick) G. Young, editor New York, Arno Press, 1973. xix, 262 p. 23 cm. (The Far Western frontier) Reprint of the 1899 ed., issued in series: Sources of the history of Oregon, v. 1. [F880.W98 1973] 72-9474 ISBN 0-405-05001-1 15.00
1. Hudson's Bay Company. 2. Oregon—History—To 1859—Sources. 3. Overland journeys to the Pacific. I. Young, Frederick George, 1858-1929, ed. II. Title. III. Series.

Hudson, William Henry,

HUDSON, William Henry, 1841-1922. 828'.8'09 B
Far away and long ago; a history of my early life. With a foreword by John Galsworthy. [1st AMS ed.] New York, AMS Press [1968] xx, 353 p. illus. 23 cm. (The collected works of W. H. Hudson) Reprint of the 1923 ed. [PR6015.U23Z5 1968] 72-181623
I. Title.

Hudson, William Henry, 1841-1922.

GODDARD, Harold Clarke, 1878-1950. 598.2'092'4 B
W. H. Hudson: bird-man, by Harold Goddard. New York, E. P. Dutton. [Folcroft, Pa.] Folcroft Library Editions, 1972. p. Reprint of the 1928 ed. [QL31.H85G6 1972] 72-11772 ISBN 0-8414-0915-3 (lib. bdg.)
1. Hudson, William Henry, 1841-1922.

HAMILTON, John Robert, 1908- 828'.8'09 B
W. H. Hudson; the vision of earth, by Robert Hamilton. Port Washington, N.Y., Kennikat Press [1970] x, 147 p. port. 22 cm. Reprint of the 1946 ed. Includes bibliographical references. [PR6015.U23Z65 1970] 76-113336
1. Hudson, William Henry, 1841-1922. I. Title.

HUDSON, William Henry, 1841-1922. 828'.8'09 B
Far away and long ago; a history of my early life. With a foreword by John Galsworthy. [1st AMS ed.] New York, AMS Press [1968] xx, 353 p. illus. 23 cm. (The collected works of W. H. Hudson) Reprint of the 1923 ed. [PR6015.U23Z5 1968] 72-181623
I. Title.

TOMALIN, Ruth. 928.2
W. H. Hudson. [New York] Philosophical Library [1954] 143p. illus. 21cm. Includes bibliography. [PR6015] 54-11705
1. Hudson, William Henry, 1841-1922. I. Title. BIP

TOMALIN, Ruth. 828'.8'09 B
W. H. Hudson. New York, Greenwood Press [1969, c1954] 143 p. port. 23 cm. Bibliography: p. 141-143. [PR6015.U23Z85 1969] 78-88952 ISBN 8-371-20977-
1. Hudson, William Henry, 1841-1922.

Huebner, Solomon Stephen, 1882-

STONE, Mildred F 923.373
The teacher who changed an industry; a biography of Dr. Solomon S. Huebner of the University of Pennsylvania. Homewood, Ill., R. D. Irwin, 1960. 393 p. illus. 24 cm. Includes bibliography. [HG8047.S8] 60-8390
1. Huebner, Solomon Stephen, 1882- 2. Insurance — Study and teaching. I. Title.

Huerta, Victoriano, Pres. Mexico, 1854-1916.

MEYER, Michael C. 972.08'1'0924 B
Huerta; a political portrait, by Michael C. Meyer. Lincoln, University of Nebraska Press [1972] xvi, 272 p. 24 cm. Bibliography: p. 239-255. [F1234.H87M48] 70-162343 ISBN 0-8032-0802-2 9.50
1. Huerta, Victoriano, Pres. Mexico, 1854-1916. I. Title.

Huey, Lynda.

HUEY, Lynda. 796.4'2'0924 B
A running start : an athlete, a woman / by Lynda Huey. New York : Quadrangle/New York Times Book Co., c1976. xiv, 240 p., [1] leaf of plate : ill. ; 22 cm. Autobiography. [GV697.H83A37 1976] 74-24289 ISBN 0-8129-0523-7 : 8.95
1. Huey, Lynda. 2. Track-athletics for women. I. Title. BIP

Huff, Edgar R., 1919-

JOHNSON, Jesse J., 1914- 359.9'6'0922 B
Roots of two Black Marine sergeants major, Sergeants Major Edgar R. Huff and Gilbert H. "Hashmark" Johnson : profiles in courage : a documented pictorial history / by Jesse J. Johnson. Hampton, Va. : Ebony Pub., c1978. viii, 116 p. : ill. ; 29 cm. [VE25.A1J64] 78-55171 ISBN 0-915044-14-5 pbk. : 2.25
1. Huff, Edgar R., 1919- 2. Johnson, Gilbert H., 1905-1972. 3. United States. Marine Corps—Afro-American troops—Biography. 4. Afro-American soldiers—Biography. I. Title.

Huff, James A.

HUFF, Jane. 922.573
Whom the Lord loveth; the story of James A. Hull. [1st ed.] New York, McGraw-Hill [1961] 245 p. 22 cm. [BX9225.H766H8] 61-7579
1. Huff, James A. I. Title.

Huffman, Carolyn.

HUFFMAN, Carolyn. 283'.092'4 B
Bloom where you are / Carolyn Huffman. Santa Ana, Calif. : Vision House Publishers, 1976. 152 p. ; 21 cm. Includes bibliographical references. [BX5995.H74A33] 75-42853 ISBN 0-88449-024-6 pbk. : 2.95
1. Huffman, Carolyn. 2. Protestant Episcopal Church in the U.S.A.—Biography. 3. Clergymen's wives—Pennsylvania—Pittsburgh—Biography. 4. Pittsburgh—Biography. I. Title. **BIP**

Huffman, Jasper Abraham, 1880-

HUFFMAN, Lambert. 922.8773
Not of this world. [Canton? Ohio, '1951] 159 p. illus. 20 cm. [BX8143.H8H8] 52-18156
1. Huffman, Jasper Abraham, 1880- I. Title.

Hugel, Carl Alexander Anselm, Freiherr von, 1796-1870.

HUGEL, Carl 915.4'5'0431
Alexander Anselm, Freiherr von, 1796-1870.
Travels in Kashmir & the Panjab / Baron Charles Hugel. Lahore : Qausain, 1976. xvi, 423 p., [5] leaves of plates : ill., fold. map (in pocket) ; 25 cm. Reprint of the 1845 ed. published by John Petheram, London. Includes a reproduction of the original t.p.: Travels in Kashmir and the Panjab: containing a particular account of the government and character of the Sikhs, from the German of Baron Charles Hugel; with notes by T. B. Jervis. [DS485.K2H9 1976] 76-930194 Rs108.00
1. Hugel, Carl Alexander Anselm, Freiherr von, 1796-1870. 2. Kashmir—Description and travel. 3. Punjab—Description and travel. 4. Sikhs. I. Title.

Hugel, Friedrich,

HUGEL, Friedrich, 922.242
Freiherr von, 1852-1925.
Letters from Baron Friedrich von Hugel to a niece. Edited with an introd. by Gwendolen Greene. Pref. by John B. Sheerin. Chicago, H. Regnery Co., 1955. 274p. 22cm. (A Thomas More book to live) Letters to Gwendolen Greene. [BX4705.H77A3 1955] 55-14411
I. Greene, Gwendolen Maud (Parry) 1878- II. Title.

Hugel, Friedrich, Freiherr von, 1852-1925.

DE LA BEDOYERE, Michael, 922.242
1900-
The life of Baron von Hugel. New York, Scribner [1951] xviii, 366 p. ports., facsims. 22 cm. [BX4705.H77D4 1951a] 52-8566
1. Hugel, Friedrich, Freiherr von, 1852-1925. I. Title.

HUGEL, Friedrich, 922.242
Freiherr von, 1852-1925.
Letters from Baron Friedrich von Hugel to a niece. Edited with an introd. by Gwendolen Greene. Pref. by John B. Sheerin. Chicago, H. Regnery Co., 1955. 274p. 22cm. (A Thomas More book to live) Letters to Gwendolen Greene. [BX4705.H77A3 1955] 55-14411
I. Greene, Gwendolen Maud (Parry) 1878- II. Title.

Hugenberg, Alfred, 1865-1951.

LEOPOLD, John A., 943.085'092'4 B
1937-
Alfred Hugenberg : the radical nationalist campaign against the Weimar Republic / John A. Leopold. New Haven : Yale University Press, 1977. p. cm. Includes bibliographical references and index. [DD231.H8L46] 77-4026 ISBN 0-300-02068-6 : 17.50
1. Hugenberg, Alfred, 1865-1951. 2. Deutschnationale Volkspartei—History. 3. Statesmen—Germany—Biography. 4. Germany—Politics and government—1918-1933. **BIP**

Huger, Mary Esther, 1820-1898.

HUGER, Mary Esther, 975.7'25 B
1820-1898.
The recollection of a happy childhood / by Mary Esther Huger, daughter of Francis Kinloch Huger of Long House near Pendleton, South Carolina, 1826-1848 ; edited, with notes, introd., and appendix by Mary Stevenson. Pendleton, S.C. : Research and Publication Committee, Foundation for Historic Restoration in Pendleton Area, 1976. 85 p. : ill. ; 24 x 31 cm. Includes index. Bibliography: p. 79-81. [F279.P36H83 1976] 76-4386 ISBN 0-912462-07-8
1. Huger, Mary Esther, 1820-1898. 2. Pendleton, S.C.—Biography. I. Stevenson, Mary. II. Foundation for Historic Restoration in Pendleton Area. Research and Publication Committee. III. Title.

Huggins, Molly Green,

TOO much to tell 942.084'09224
[by] Molly Huggins. London, Heinemann, [1968,c.1967] 328p. plates (incl. ports.). 23cm. [CT788.H84A3] (B) 67-106668 7.50
I. Huggins, Molly Green, Lady, 1907- Distributed by Hillary House, New York.

Hugh de Avalon, Saint, Bp. of Lincoln, 1135?-1200.

ADAM of Eynsham, fl.1196- 922.242
1232.
The life of St. Hugh of Lincoln. Edited by Decima L. Douie and Hugh Farmer. London, New York, Nelson [1961-62) 2 v. maps. 23 cm. (Medieval texts) Added t. p.: Magna vita Sancti Hugonis. English and Latin. [BX4700.H8A62] 62-6133
1. Hugh de Avalon, Saint, Bp. of Lincoln. 1135?-1200. I. Douie, Decima Langworthy, 1901- ed. II. Farmer, Hugh, ed. III. Title. IV. Title: Magna vita Sancti Hugonis. V. Series: Medieval classics (London)

ADAM OF EYNSHAM, fl. 922.242
1196-1232.
The life of St. Hugh of Lincoln. Ed. by Decima L. Douie, Hugh Farmer. [Dist. New York, Oxford, 1962,c.1961] 133p. maps. 23cm. (Medieval texts) Added t.p.: Magna vita Sancti Hugonis. English and Latin. 62-6113 8.00
1. Hugh de Avalon, Saint, Bp. of Lincoln, 1135?-1200. I. Douie, Decima Langworthy, 1901- ed. II. Farmer, Hugh. ed. III. Title. IV. Title: Magna vita Sancti Hugonis. V. Series: Medieval classics (London

ADAM OF EYNSHAM, fl. 922.242
1196-1232.
The life of St. Hugh of Lincoln. Edited by Decima L. Douie and Hugh Farmer. London, New York, Nelson [1961- v. maps. 23cm. (Medieval texts) Added t. p.: Magna vita Saneti Hugonis. English and Latin. [BX4700.H8A62] 62-6113
1. Hugh de Avalon, Saint, Bp. of Lincoln, 1135?-1200. I. Douie, Decina Langworthy, 1901- ed. II. Farmer, Hugh, ed. III. Title. IV. Title: Magna vita Saneti Hugonis. V. Series: Medieval classics (London)

[ADAM OF EYNSHAM] FL. 1196-v. 12
1232.
Magna vita Sancti Hugonis. [Edited by Decima L. Douie and Hugh Farmer] London, New York, T. Nelson [c1961- v. (Medieval texts) Added t.-p. in English: The life of St. Hugh of Lincoln. Latin and English on opposite pages.
1. Hugh de Avalon, Saint, bp. of Lincoln, 1135?-1200. I. Douie, Decima Langworthy, 1901- ed. II. Farmer, Hugh, ed. III. Title. IV. Series.

Hughes, Allison.

†HUGHES, Allison. 248'.2'0924 B
Love, honor, and obesity / Allison Hughes. Grand Rapids : Zondervan Pub. House, c1977. 167 p. ; 21 cm. Autobiographical. [BR1725.H77A35] 77-744 ISBN 0-310-26330-1 : 6.95
1. Hughes, Allison. 2. Christian biography—United States. 3. Depression, Mental. 4. Corpulence—Psychological aspects. I. Title.

Hughes, Charles Evans, 1862-1945.

GLAD, Betty. 973.910924
Charles Evans Hughes and the illusions of innocence; a study in American diplomacy. Urbana, University of Illinois Press, 1966. 365 p. 24 cm. Bibliography: p. [329]-343. [E748.H88G55] 66-11020
1. Hughes, Charles Evans, 1862-1948. 2. United States—Foreign relations—1921-1923. I. Title. **BIP**

HENDEL, Samuel, 1909- 923.473
Charles Evans Hughes and the Supreme Court. New York, King's Crown Press, 1951. xii, 337 p. 24 cm. Bibliographical references included in "Notes" (p. [297]-328) 51-9221
1. Hughes, Charles Evans, 1862-1948. I. Title. **BIP**

HENDEL, Samuel, 1909- 347.99'73 B
Charles Evans Hughes and the Supreme Court. New York, Russell & Russell [1968, c1951] xii, 337 p. 23 cm. First published in 1951 as thesis, Columbia University. Bibliographical references included in "Notes" (p. [297]-328) [KF8745.H8H4 1968] 68-10926
1. Hughes, Charles Evans, 1862-1948. I. Title.

HUGHES, Charles 973.91'092'4 B
Evans, 1862-1948.
The autobiographical notes of Charles Evans Hughes. Edited by David J. Danelski and Joseph S. Tulchin. Cambridge, Mass., Harvard University Press, 1973. xxix, 363 p. illus. 24 cm. (Studies in legal history) Includes bibliographical references. [E664.H86A32] 72-88130 ISBN 0-674-05325-7 15.00
1. Hughes, Charles Evans, 1862-1948. I. Danelski, David Joseph, 1930- ed. II. Tulchin, Joseph S., 1939- ed. III. Title. IV. Series. **BIP**

PERKINS, Dexter, 1889- 923.473
Charles Evans Hughes and American democratic statesmanship. [1st ed.] Boston, Little, Brown [1956] xxiv, 200p. 22cm. (The Library of American biography) Bibliography: p.[191]-193. [E748.H88P4] 56-6767
1. Hughes, Charles Evans, 1862-1948. I. Title. II. Series. **BIP**

PERKINS, Dexter, 973.91'092'4 B
1889-
Charles Evans Hughes and American democratic statesmanship / Dexter Perkins. Westport, Conn. : Greenwood Press, 1978,c1956. xxiv, 200 p. ; 23 cm. Reprint of the ed. published by Little, Brown, Boston, in series: The Library of American biography. Includes index. Bibliography: p. [191]-193. [E748.H88P4 1978] 78-5919 ISBN 0-313-20463-2 lib.bdg. : 17.00
1. Hughes, Charles Evans, 1862-1945. 2. United States. Supreme Court—Biography. 3. Statesmen—United States—Biography. 4. Judges—United States—Biography. 5. United States—Foreign relations—1921-1923. 6. United States—Politics and government—1901-1953. I. Title. II. Series: Library of American biography.

PUSEY, Merlo John, 1902- 923.473
Charles Evans Hughes. New York, Macmillan, 1951. 2 v. (svi, 829 p.) illus., ports. 24 cm. Bibliographical footnotes. 51-7851
1. Hughes, Charles Evans, 1862-1948. I. Title.

PUSEY, Merlo John, 1902- 923.473
Charles Evans Hughes; 2v. New York, Columbia, 1963 [c.1961] 2 v. (XVI, 829 p.) illus., ports. 24cm. Bibl. 15.00 set, bxd.
1. Hughes, Charles Evans, 1862-1948. I. Title.

WESSER, Robert F. 974.7'04'0924
Charles Evans Hughes; politics and reform in New York, 1905-1910, by Robert F. Wesser. Ithaca, N.Y., Cornell University Press [1967] xvi, 366 p. illus., ports. 24 cm. Bibliography: p. 349-359. [E748.H88W4] 67-19029
1. Hughes, Charles Evans, 1862-1948. 2. New York (State)—Politics and government—1865-1950. **BIP**

Hughes, Edmond Alexander, 1873-

WILKINS, Robert P 978.4'82'00994
Edmond A. Hughes: a memoir. Grand Forks, University of North Dakota Press, 1961. 49 p. illus. 20 cm. [F636.H8W5] 62-4987
1. Hughes, Edmond Alexander, 1873- I. Title.

***Hughes, Elmer R.**

*HUGHES, Elmer R. 220.92
Famous mothers from the Bible and history: the stories of great men and the women behind them. New York, Exposition [c.1963] 156p. 21cm. 3.00
I. Title.

Hughes, Emmy, 1863-1934.

HUGHES, Emmy, 976.8'74'050924 B
1863-1934.
Dissipations at Uffington House : the letters of Emmy Hughes, Rugby, Morgan County, Tennessee, July 5, 1881-July 15, 1887 / introd. and notes, John R. Debruyn. Memphis : Memphis State University, 1975. 87 p. : ill. ; 24 cm. (MVC bulletin ; no. 8) Letters written by the author to Lucy Taylor in England. [F444.R9H76] 75-624178
1. Hughes, Emmy, 1863-1934. 2. Rugby, Tenn.—Biography. I. Taylor, Lucy. II. Title. III. Series.

HUGHES, Emmy, 976.8'74'050924 B
1863-1934.
Dissipations at Uffington House : the letters of Emmy Hughes, Rugby, Tennessee, 1881-1887 / introd and notes by John R. DeBruyn. Memphis : Memphis State University Press, c1976. xviii, 80 p. : ill. ; 24 cm. (Memphis State University Press primary source publications) Letters written by the author to Lucy Taylor in England. Includes index. [F444.R9H76 1976] 76-18185 ISBN 0-87870-039-0 pbk. : 5.95
1. Hughes, Emmy, 1863-1934. 2. Rugby, Tenn.—Biography. I. Taylor, Lucy. II. Title. III. Series. **BIP**

Hughes, Gerard W.

HUGHES, Gerard W. 271'.53'024
In search of a way : two journeys of discovery / Gerard W. Hughes. Rome : E. J. Dwyer ; Westminster, Md. : distributed by Christian Classics, 1978. 232 p. : maps ; 20 cm. Distributor from label on t.p. [BX4705.H789A34] 78-322471 ISBN 0-85574-107-4 : 5.95
1. Hughes, Gerard W. 2. Jesuits—United States—Biography. 3. France—Description and travel—1945- 4. Italy—Description and travel—1975- I. Title. **BIP**

Hughes, Harold E.

HUGHES, Harold E. 328.73'092'4 B
The man from Ida Grove : a senator's personal story / Dick Schneider. Lincoln, Va. : Chosen Books ; Waco Tex. : distributed by Word Books, c1979. 346 p. : ill. ; 24 cm. [E840.8.H83A33] 78-31152 ISBN 0-912376-38-4 : 10.95
1. Hughes, Harold E. 2. United States. Congress. Senate—Biography. 3. Legislators—United States—Biography. 4. Christian biography—United States. I. Schneider, Richard, 1922- joint author. II. Title.

Hughes, Howard Robard,

HUGHES, Howard 670'.92'4 B
Robard, 1905-
My life and opinions [by] Howard Hughes. Edited by Robert P. Eaton. [Chicago] Best Books Press [1972] 244 p. 22 cm. [CT275.H6678A3] 70-188090 6.95

I. Eaton, Robert P., ed. II. Title.

Hughes, Howard Robard, 1905-1976.

BARTLETT, Donald L. 670'.92'4 B
Empire : the life, legend, and madness of Howard Hughes / by Donald L. Barlett and James B. Steele. 1st ed. New York : Norton, c1979. p. cm. Includes bibliographical references and index. [CT275.H6678B37 1979] 79-1331 ISBN 0-393-07513-3 : 15.95
1. Hughes, Howard Robard, 1905-1976. 2. United States—Biography. I. Steele, James B., joint author. II. Title. **BIP**

DAVENPORT, Joe. 338.7'4'0924 B
The empire of Howard Hughes / by Joe Davenport and Todd S. J. Lawson. 1st ed. San Francisco : Peace and Pieces Foundation, 1975. 81 p. : ill. ; 28 cm. [HC102.5.H8D38] 75-16010 ISBN 0-914024-22-1 : 2.95
1. Hughes, Howard Robard, 1905- I. Lawson, Todd S. J., joint author. II. Title.

DAVENPORT, Joe. 338.7'4'0924 B
The empire of Howard Hughes / by Joe Davenport and Todd S. J. Lawson. 1st ed. San Francisco : Peace and Pieces Foundation, 1975. 81 p. : ill. ; 28 cm. [HC102.5.H8D38] 75-16010 ISBN 0-914024-22-1 pbk. : 2.95
1. Hughes, Howard Robard, 1905- I. Lawson, Todd S. J., joint author. II. Title. **BIP**

DIETRICH, Noah. 670'.92'4 B
Howard, the amazing Mr. Hughes, by Noah Dietrich and Bob Thomas. Greenwich, Conn., Fawcett Publications [1972] 303 p. illus. 18 cm. (A Fawcett gold medal book) [CT275.H6678D5] 72-191817 1.50
1. Hughes, Howard Robard, 1905- I. Thomas, Bob, 1922- joint author. II. Title.

GERBER, Albert Benjamin, 1913- 338.476291300924
Bashful billionaire; the story of Howard Hughes, by Albert B. Gerber. New York, L. Stuart [1967] 384 p. 22 cm. [CT275.H6678G4] 67-15884
1. Hughes, Howard Robard, 1905-1976. I. Title.

GERBER, Albert Benjamin, 1913- 338.4'76291300924
Bashful billionaire; the story of Howard Hughes, by Albert B. Gerber. [New York, Dell, 1968, c. 1967] 352p. 18cm. (0460) [CT275.H6678G4] .95 pap.,
1. Hughes, Howard Robard, 1905- I. Title.

HUGHES, Howard Robard, 1905- 670'.92'4 B
My life and opinions [by] Howard Hughes. Edited by Robert P. Eaton. [Chicago] Best Books Press [1972] 244 p. 22 cm. [CT275.H6678A3] 70-188090 6.95
I. Eaton, Robert P., ed. II. Title.

IRVING, Clifford. 670'.92'4
Clifford Irving: what really happened; his untold story of the Hughes affair, by Clifford Irving with Richard Suskind. New York, Grove Press [1972] vi, 378 p. 18 cm. (Zebra books, Z-1106-T) [CT275.H6678I78] 72-88115 1.95 (pbk)
1. Hughes, Howard Robard, 1905- I. Suskind, Richard. II. Title: What really happened.

KEATS, John, 1920- 338.476291300924
Howard Hughes. New York, Random House [1966] x, 304 p. illus., ports. 22 cm. [HC102.5.H8K4] 65-21241
1. Hughes, Howard Robard, 1905-1976.

KEATS, John, 1920- 670'.92'4 B
Howard Hughes. [1st rev. ed.] New York, Random House [1972] x, 336 p. illus. 22 cm. [CT275.H6678K4 1972] 72-329 ISBN 0-394-48146-1 7.95
1. Hughes, Howard Robard, 1905-

MATHISON, Richard R. 670'.9'24 B
His weird and wanton ways, the secret life of Howard Hughes / by Richard Mathison. New York : Morrow, 1977. 247 p. ; 22 cm. [CT275.H6678M38] 76-51932 ISBN 0-688-03170-6 : 8.95
1. Hughes, Howard Robard, 1905-1976. 2. Millionaires—Biography.

PHELAN, James. 670'.92'4
Howard Hughes : the hidden years / James Phelan. New York : Warner Books, 1977,c1976. 301p. ; 18 cm. [CT275.H6678P47] ISBN 0-446-89521-0 pbk. : 1.95
1. Hughes, Howard Robard, 1905-1976. 2. Millionaires-United States-Biography. I. Title.
L.C. card no. for 1976 Random House ed.:76-53482. **BIP**

PHELAN, James, 1912- 670'.92'4 B
Howard Hughes, the hidden years / James Phelan. 1st ed. New York : Random House, 1977c1976 xvi, 201 p. ; 22 cm. [CT275.H6678P47] 76-53482 ISBN 0-394-41042-4 : 7.95
1. Hughes, Howard Robard, 1905-1976. 2. Millionaires—United States—Biography. I. Title.

Hughes, Jesse, 1750 (ca.)-1829.

MCWHORTER, Lucullus Virgil, 1860-1944. 975.4'02
The border settlers of northwestern Virginia from 1768-1795, embracing the life of Jesse Hughes and other noted scouts of the great woods of the trans-Allegheny, with notes and illustrative anecdotes. With pref. and additional notes by William Elsey Connelley and sketch of the author by J. P. MacLean. Published for Judge J. C. McWhorter. Baltimore, Genealogical Pub. Co., 1974. p. Reprint of the 1915 ed. published by the Republic Pub. Co., Hamilton, Ohio. [F241.M17 1974] 73-17370 ISBN 0-8063-0600-9
1. Hughes, Jesse, 1750 (ca.)-1829. 2. West Virginia—History. 3. West Virginia—Biography. I. Connelley, William Elsey, 1855-1930. II. MacLean, John Patterson, 1848-1939. III. Title.

Hughes, John, Abp., 1797-1864.

HASSARD, John Rose Greene, 1836-1888. 282'.0924 B
Life of John Hughes, first archbishop of New York. New York, Arno Press, 1969. 519 p. facsim., port. 22 cm. (Religion in America) Reprint of the 1866 ed., which was published under title: Life of the Most Reverend John Hughes, D.D. On spine: Life of Archbishop John Hughes. Includes bibliographical references. [BX4705.H79H3 1969] 74-83423
1. Hughes, John, Abp., 1797-1864.

SHAW, Richard, 1941(Oct.9)- 282'.092'4 B
Dagger John : the unquiet life and times of Archbishop John Hughes of New York / Richard Shaw. New York : Paulist Press, c1977. vi, 403 p., [2] leaves of plates : ill. ; 24 cm. Includes bibliographical references and index. [BX4705.H79S5] 77-80799 ISBN 0-8091-0224-2 : 10.95
1. Hughes, John, Abp., 1797-1864. 2. Catholic Church—Bishops—Biography. 3. Bishops—New York (City)—Biography. I. Title.

Hughes, Langston,

HUGHES, Langston, 1902- 928.1
I wonder as I wander; an autobiographical journey. New York, Rinehart [1956] 405 p. 24 cm. [PS3515.U274Z58] 56-7254
I. Title.

HUGHES, Langston, 1902 928.1
I wonder as I wander; an autobiographical journey. New York, Hill & Wang [1964 c.1956] 405 p. 21 cm (American cent. ser. ac68) pap. 2.45
I. Title. II. Series. **BIP**

HUGHES, Langston, 1902-1967. 928.1
The big sea, an autobiography. New York, Hill and Wang [1963, c1940] 335 p. 21 cm. (American century series) "AC65." [PS3515.U274Z5 1963] 63-18485
I. Title.

Hughes, Langston, 1902-1967.

DICKINSON, Donald C. 818/.5/209
A bio-bibliography of Langston Hughes, 1902-1967. by Donald C. Dickinson. Pref. by Arna Bontemps. [Hamden. Conn.] Archon, xiii, 267p. port. 22cm. An expansion of the author's dissertation. Univ. of Mich. Bibl. [PS3515.U274Z62] 67-15933 10.00
1. Hughes, Langston, 2. Hughes, Langston, 1902-1967—Bibl. I. Title.

DICKINSON, Donald C. 818'.5'209
A bio-bibliography of Langston Hughes, 1902-1967, by Donald C. Dickinson. With a pref. by Arna Bontemps. [Hamden, Conn.] Archon Books, 1967. xiii, 267 p. port. 22 cm. An expansion of the author's dissertation, University of Michigan. Bibliography: p. 257-262. 67-15933
1. Hughes, Langston, 1902-1967. 2. Hughes, Langston, 1902-1967 — Bibl. I. Title. **BIP**

DICKINSON, Donald C. 818'.5'209 B
A bio-bibliography of Langston Hughes, 1902-1967, by Donald C. Dickinson. With a pref. by Arna Bontemps. 2d ed., rev. [Hamden, Conn.] Archon Books, 1972. xiii, 273 p. port. 22 cm. An expansion of the author's dissertation, University of Michigan. Bibliography: p. 261-167. [PS3515.U274Z62 1972] 70-181877 ISBN 0-208-01269-9
1. Hughes, Langston, 1902-1967. 2. Hughes, Langston, 1902-1967—Bibliography. I. Title.

EMANUEL, James A 811'.52 (B)
Langston Hughes, by James A. Emanuel. New York, Twayne Publishers [1967] 192 p. 21 cm. (Twayne's United States authors series, TUSAS 123) Bibliography: p. 184-188. [PS3515.U274Z6] 67-24764
1. Hughes, Langston, 1902-1967. I. Title. **BIP**

HUGHES, Langston, 1902- 928.1
I wonder as I wander; an autobiographical journey. New York, Rinehart [1956] 405 p. 24 cm. [PS3515.U274Z58] 56-7254
I. Title.

HUGHES, Langston, 1902- 928.1
I wonder as I wander; an autobiographical journey. New York, Rinehart [1956] 405 p. 24 cm. [PS3515.U274Z58] 56-7254
I. Title.

HUGHES, Langston, 1902 928.1
I wonder as I wander; an autobiographical journey. New York, Hill & Wang [1964 c.1956] 405 p. 21 cm (American cent. ser. ac68) pap. 2.45
I. Title. II. Series. **BIP**

HUGHES, Langston, 1902-1967. 928.1
The big sea, an autobiography. New York, Hill and Wang [1963, c1940] 335 p. 21 cm. (American century series) "AC65." [PS3515.U274Z5 1963] 63-18485
I. Title.

LANGSTON Hughes, 811/.52
by James A. Emanuel. New York, Twayne [1967] 192p. 21cm. (Twayne's U.S. authors ser., TUSAS 123) Bibl. [PS3515.U274Z6] (B) 67-24764 3.95
1. Hughes, Langston, 1902-1967. I. Emanuel, James A.

MELTZER, Milton, 1915- 811'.5'2 B
Langston Hughes; a biography. New York, Crowell [1968] xiii, 281 p. 21 cm. Bibliography: p. 269-274. A biography of the Negro poet and playwright whose themes were based on his diverse ethnic and social experiences in Harlem and in the many places he traveled. [PS3315.U274Z68] 92 AC 68
1. Hughes, Langston, 1902-1967. I. Title.

ROLLINS, Charlemae Hill. 811'.5'2 B
Black troubadour: Langston Hughes, by Charlemae H. Rollins. Chicago, Rand McNally [1970] 143 p. illus., facsims., ports. 22 cm. Bibliography: p. 129-135. [PS3515.U274Z77] 72-117003 4.95
1. Hughes, Langston, 1902-1967. I. Title.

Hughes, Langston, 1902-1967—Biography—Juvenile literature.

HASKINS, James, 1941- 818'.5'209 B
Always movin' on : the life of Langston Hughes / by James S. Haskins. New York : Watts, 1976. x, 117 p. : ill. ; 24 cm. Includes index. Bibliography: p. [111]-112. A biography of Langston Hughes, an Afro-American poet who tried to capture in his writing the spirit and rhythms of ordinary people. [PS3515.U274Z656] 76-16107 ISBN 0-531-01211-5 lib.bdg. : 6.90
1. Hughes, Langston, 1902-1967—Biography—Juvenile literature. I. Title. **BIP**

Hughes, Langston, 1902-1967—Juvenile literature.

MYERS, Elisabeth P. 811'.5'2 B
Langston Hughes, poet of his people, by Elisabeth P. Myers. Illustrated by Russell Hoover. Champaign, Ill., Garrard Pub. Co. [1970] 144 p. illus., ports. 22 cm. ([Creative people in the arts and sciences]) A biography of the black poet whose poems were influenced greatly by jazz and blues rhythms. [PS3515.U274Z685] 92 76-94412 2.59
1. Hughes, Langston, 1902-1967—Juvenile literature. I. Hoover, Russell, illus. II. Title.

WALKER, Alice, 1944- 818'.5'209 B
Langston Hughes, American poet. Illustrated by Don Miller. New York, Crowell [1974] 33 p. illus. (part col.) 24 cm. (A Crowell biography) A biography of the American poet whose works articulated the despair of blacks over social and economic conditions. [PS3515.U274Z9] 92 73-9565 ISBN 0-690-00218-1
1. Hughes, Langston, 1902-1967—Juvenile literature. I. Miller, Don, 1923- illus. **BIP**

Hughes, Pearl W

HUGHES, Pearl W 917.4821
Scenes of my childhood, by Pearl W. Hughes. Philadelphia, Dorrance [1964] 109 p. illus. 20 cm. [CT275.H669A3] 64-21797
I. Title.

Hughes, Raymond Mollyneaux, 1873-1958.

WICKENDEN, Arthur Consaul, 1893- 378.1110924(B)
Raymond M. Hughes; leader of men, by Arthur C. Wickenden. Oxford, Ohio, Miami University Alumni association [1966] x, 115 p. illus. 22 cm. (Miami University books.) [LD3241.M517] 66-8180
1. Hughes, Raymond Mollyneaux, 1873-1958. I. Title. II. Series: Miami University, Oxford, Ohio. Alumni Association. Miami University books

Hughes, Russell Meriwether, 1898-

HUGHES, Russell Meriwether, 1898- 793.3'092'4 B
Dance out the answer : an autobiography / La Meri (Russell Meriwether Hughes) ; foreword by John Martin. New York : M. Dekker, c1977. xi, 194 p., [6] leaves of plates : ill. ; 23 cm. (The Dance program ; v. 7) Includes index. [GV1785.H77A33] 77-20139 ISBN 0-8247-6633-4 : 15.00
1. Hughes, Russell Meriwether, 1898- 2. Dancers—Biography. 3. Folk dancing. I. Title. II. Series.

Hughes, William Dudley Foulke.

HUGHES, William Dudley Foulke. 922.373
Prudently with power; William Thomas Manning, tenth Bishop of New York [by] W. D. F. Hughes. With a foreword by the Bishop of New York. West Park, N.Y., Holy Cross Publications [196-?] x, 255 p. illus., ports. 24 cm. [BX5995.M34H8]
I. Manning, William Thomas, Bp., 1806-1949. II. Title.

Hughes, William Morris, 1862-1952—Juvenile literature.

FITZHARDINGE, L. F. 994.04'1'0924 B
William Morris Hughes / L. F. Fitzhardinge. Melbourne ; New York : Oxford University Press, 1973. 30 p. : ill. ; 19 cm. (Great Australians) Bibliography: p. 30. A biography of the British emigrant and one-time umbrella mender who later served as Australia's attorney general, a member of Parliament, and prime minister

during World War I. [DU116.2.H83F57] 92 74-190663 ISBN 0-19-550421-6
1. Hughes, William Morris, 1862-1952—Juvenile literature. I. Title.

Hugo, Everett Harold, 1910-

JEFFERSON, Thomas, Pres. 923.173
U.S. 1743-1826.
Thomas Jefferson among the antiquities of southern France in 1787. A tribute to E. Harold Hugo. Princeton, N.J., 1954. 22 p. plates. 19 cm. "Four hundred copies ... printed." Two letters, one by Jefferson to the Comtesse de Tesse, the other by the comtesse in reply. [DC31.T48] 60-35423
1. Hugo, Everett Harold, 1910- 2. France — Antiq. I. Noailles de Tesse, comtesse de. II. Title.

Hugo, of Saint Victor, 1096 or 7-1141.

TAYLOR, Jerome. 921.3
The origin and early life of Hugh of St. Victor; an evaluation of the tradition. Notre Dame, Ind., Mediaeval Institute, University of Notre Dame, 1957. 70p. illus. 25cm. (Texts and studies in the history of mediaeval education, no. 5) Bibliographical footnotes. [B765.H74T3] 57-2844
1. Hugo, of Saint Victor, 1096 or 7-1141. I. Title.

TAYLOR, Jerome, 1918- 921.3
The origin and early life of Hugh of St. Victor; an evaluation of the tradition. Notre Dame, Ind., Mediaeval Institute, University of Notre Dame, 1957. 70 p. illus. 25 cm. (Texts and studies in the history of mediaeval education, no. 5) Bibliographical footnotes. [B765.H74T3] 57-2844
1. Hugo, of Saint Victor, 1096 or 7-1141. I. Title. II. Series.

Hugo, Victor Marie,

HUGO, Victor Marie, 848'.7'09 B
comte, 1802-1885.
Victor Hugo's intellectual autobiography (Postscriptum de ma vie); being the last of the unpublished works and embodying the author's ideas on literature, philosophy and religion. Translated with a study of the last phase of Hugo's genius by Lorenzo O'Rourke. New York, Haskell House Publishers, 1971. 400 p. front. 23 cm. First published in 1907. [PQ2289.P7E4 1971] 79-130260 ISBN 0-8383-1164-4
I. O'Rourke, Lorenzo.

Hugo, Victor Marie, comte, 1802-1885.

AMICIS, Edmondo de, 914.4'36'0381
1846-1908.
Studies of Paris. Translated from the Italian, by W. W. C. Freeport, N.Y., Books for Libraries Press [1972] 276 p. 22 cm. (Essay index reprint series) Translation of Ricordi di Parigi. Reprint of the 1879 ed. [DC707.A52 1972] 72-3348 ISBN 0-8369-2888-1
1. Hugo, Victor Marie, comte, 1802-1885. 2. Zola, Emile, 1840-1902. 3. Paris—Description. I. Title.

DUCLAUX, Agnes Mary 848'.7'09 B
Frances (Robinson) 1857-1944.
Victor Hugo, by Madame Duclaux. Port Washington, N.Y., Kennikat Press [1972] xii, 268 p. port. 22 cm. Reprint of the 1921 ed. Bibliography: p. 261-262. [PQ2293.D75 1972] 70-153903 ISBN 0-8046-1594-2
1. Hugo, Victor Marie, comte, 1802-1885.

EMERY, Leon. v. 12
Victor Hugo en son siecle. Lyon, Les Cahiers libres [1963] 138 p. 65-82195
1. Hugo, Victor Marie, comte, 1802-1885. I. Title.

GUYER, Foster Erwin, 1884- 928.4
The titan, Victor Hugo. New York, S. F. Vanni [1955] 238p. 23cm. [PQ2293.G8] 56-58320
1. Hugo, Victor Marie, comte, 1802-1885. I. Title.

HOUSTON, John Porter. 848'.7'09
Victor Hugo. New York, Twayne Publishing [1975, c1974] 165 p. port. 22 cm. (Twayne's world authors series, TWAS 312. France) Bibliography: p. 160-162. [PQ2293.H66 1975] 74-8729 ISBN 0-8057-2443-5
1. Hugo, Victor Marie, comte, 1802-1885.

HUDSON, William Henry, 841'.7
1862-1918.
Victor Hugo and his poetry. London, Harrap, 1918. [New York, AMS Press, 1972] 175 p. port. 19 cm. (Poetry and life series) Bibliography: p. 12. [PQ2293.H75 1972] 70-120967 ISBN 0-404-52514-8 8.00
1. Hugo, Victor Marie, comte, 1802-1885. I. Title. II. Series. **BIP**

HUGO, Victor Marie, 848'.7'09 B
comte, 1802-1885.
Victor Hugo's intellectual autobiography (Postscriptum de ma vie); being the last of the unpublished works and embodying the author's ideas on literature, philosophy and religion. Translated with a study of the last phase of Hugo's genius by Lorenzo O'Rourke. New York, Haskell House Publishers, 1971. 400 p. front. 23 cm. First published in 1907. [PQ2289.P7E4 1971] 79-130260 ISBN 0-8383-1164-4
I. O'Rourke, Lorenzo.

MAUROIS, Andre, 1885- 928.4
Olympio; the life of Victor Hugo; translated from the French by Gerard Hopkins. [1st American ed.] New York, Harper [1956] xii, 498p. illus., ports, 25cm. Bibliography: p. 447-458. [PQ2293.M353 1956a] 55-8026
1. Hugo, Victor Marie, comte, 1802-1885. I. Title.

MAUROIS, Andre, 1885-1967 928.4
Olympio; the life of Victor Hugo. Tr. from French by Gerard Hopkins. New York, Pyramid [1968,c.1956] 589p. illus., ports. 18cm. (V-1764) Bibl. [PQ2293.M353 1956a] 1.25 pap.,
1. Hugo, Victor Marie, comte, 1802-1885. I. Title.

RICHARDSON, Joanna. 848'.7'09 B
Victor Hugo / by Joanna Richardson. New York : St. Martin's Press, c1976. p. cm. Includes index. Bibliography: p. [PQ2293.R5] 76-10564 14.95
1. Hugo, Victor Marie, comte, 1802-1885. 2. Authors, French—Biography. **BIP**

Hugues Capet, King of France, d. 906.

VASILIEV, Alexander 246
Alexandrovich, 1867-
Hugh Capet of France and Byzantium. Cambridge, Mass, 1951. 30 cm. no. 6, p. [227]-251 In Dumbartrn Oaks papers. Bibliographical footnotes. [N5970.DS no. 6] 52-1149
1. Hugues Capet, King of France, d. 906. 2. France — For. rel. — Byzantine Empire. 3. Byzantine Empire — For. rel. — France. I. Title. II. Series: Dumbarton Oaks papers, no. 6, p. [227]-251

Huizenga, Lee Sjoerds, 1881-1945.

LAMBERTS, Lambertus J. 922.551
The life story of Dr. Lee S. Huizenga; an adventure in faith. Grand Rapids, Eerdmans, 1950. 194 p. ports. 21 cm. [BV3427.H38L3] 50-10807
1. Huizenga, Lee Sjoerds, 1881-1945. I. Title.

Hukbong Mapagpalaya ng Bayan (Philippine Islands)

TARUC, Luis, 1913- 364.13'1 B
He who rides the tiger; the story of an Asian guerrilla leader. Foreword by Douglas Hyde. New York, Praeger [1967] xxiii, 188 p. 22 cm. Autobiographical. [DS686.2.T3A32 1967] 67-20494
1. Hukbong Mapagpalaya ng Bayan (Philippine Islands) I. Title.

Hukov, Edward,

HUKOV, Edward, 1924- 920
The survivor; the story of Eddy Hukov, by John Ehle. [1st ed.] New York, Holt [1958] 300p. 22cm. [CT3150.H8E4] 58-6453
I. Ehle, John, 1925- II. Title.

Hull House, Chicago.

ADDAMS, Jane, 1860-1935. v. 12
Twenty years at Hull-House, with autobiographical notes. With illus. by Norah Hamilton. New York, Macmillan, 1960 [c1938] xvii, 462p. illus., plates, ports. 20cm. 'More than a third of the material in the book has appeared in the American magazine, one chapter of it in McClure's magazine.'
1. Hull House, Chicago. 2. Chicago—Soc. condit. I. Title.

UNIVERSITY of Illinois 361.4'0924
at Chicago Circle.
The Jane Addams' Hull-House. [Chicago, 1967] 1 v. (unpaged) illus., ports. 31 cm. Title from colophon. Facsim. of Jane Addams' signature on cover. [F548.8.H8U5] 67-8426
1. Hull House, Chicago. 2. Addams, Jane, 1860-1935. I. Title.

Hull, Isaac, 1773-1843.

MOLLOY, Leo Thomas, 1892- 923.573
comp.
Commodore Isaac Hull, U.S.N., his life and times. Derby, Conn., Hull Book Fund [dist. Author, 285 Hawthorne Ave., 1964] 244p. illus., ports. 24cm. 64-4940 price unreported.
1. Hull, Isaac, 1773-1843. 2. Hull family. 3. Derby, Conn.—Hist. I. Title.

Hull, Josephine (Sherwood)

CARSON, William Glasgow 927.92
Bruce, 1891-
Dear Josephine; the theatrical career of Josephine Hull. Norman, Univ. of Okla. Pr. [c.1963] 313p. illus. 23cm. Bibl. 63-9958 4.95
1. Hull, Josephine (Sherwood) 2. Hull, Shelley V. I. Title. **BIP**

Hull, Robert Marvin.

HUNT, James R. 796.3550924
Bobby Hull [by] Jim Hunt. Chicago, Follett [1966] ix, 105p. illus., ports. 21cm. [GV847.H8] 66-19135 3.95
1. Hull, Robert Marvin. I. Title.

HUNT, James R. 796.9'62'0924 B
Bobby Hull [by] Jim Hunt. Toronto, New York, McGraw-Hill Ryerson [1971] ix, 105 p. illus. 21 cm. [GV848.5.H8H8] 72-176801 ISBN 0-07-092953-X
1. Hull, Robert Marvin.

Hull, Robert Marvin—Juvenile literature.

BRAUN, Thomas, 796.9'62'0924 B
1944-
Bobby Hull / written by Thomas Braun ; illustrated by John Nelson. Mankato, Minn. : Creative Education, [1976] p. cm. A biography of hockey player Bobby Hull which stresses his concern about the increased violence and brutality in the game. [GV848.5.H8B7] 76-23411 ISBN 0-87191-264-3 lib.bdg. : 4.95
1. Hull, Robert Marvin—Juvenile literature. 2. Hockey—Juvenile literature. I. Nelson, John, 1928- II. Title.

MAY, Julian. 796.9'62'0924 B
Bobby Hull, hockey's golden jet / by Julian May. Mankato, Minn. : Crestwood House, c1974. 47 p. : ill. ; 24 cm. (Sports close-up books) Follows Bobby Hull's ice hockey career from his first pair of skates through his Stanley Cup victories to his job as a player-coach. [GV848.5.H8M39] 92 74-82741 ISBN 0-913940-06-2
1. Hull, Robert Marvin—Juvenile literature. 2. Hockey—Juvenile literature. I. Title.

YOUNG, Scott. 796.9'62'0924 B
Bobby Hull, superstar. St. Paul, EMC Corp. [1974] 38 p. illus. 24 cm. (His Hockey heroes series) A biography of the hockey star whose skating career began when he received his first pair of skates when he was not quite four years old. [GV848.5.H8Y68 1974] 92 74-8368 ISBN 0-88436-104-7 4.95
1. Hull, Robert Marvin—Juvenile literature. 2. Hockey—Juvenile literature. I. Title.
Pbk. 2.95; ISBN 0-88436-105-5.

ZALEWSKI, Ted. 796.9'62'0924 B
Bobby Hull: the Golden Jet. Illustrated by John Nelson. Mankato, Minn., Creative Education; distributed by Childrens Press, Chicago [1973] c1974. 31 p. illus. (part col.) 25 cm. (Creative's superstars.) "Prepared for the publisher by Educreative Systems, inc." A biography of the former Black Hawk, now with the Winnipeg Jets, who is sometimes called the world's greatest hockey player. [GV848.5.H8Z34] 73-10282 ISBN 0-87191-264-3 4.95
1. Hull, Robert Marvin—Juvenile literature. 2. Hockey—Juvenile literature. I. Nelson, John, 1928- illus. II. Educreative Systems, inc. III. Title.

Hulme, Kathryn Cavarly,

HULME, Kathryn Cavarly, 818.5403
1900-
Undiscovered country; a spiritual adventure, by Kathryn C. Hulme. [1st ed.] Boston, Little, Brown [1966] 306 p. 22 cm. "An Atlantic Monthly Press book." Autobiographical. [PS3515.U374U5] 66-22679
I. Title.

Hulme, Thomas Ernest, 1883-1917.

JONES, Allen Richard. 921.2
The life and opinions of T. E. Hulme. Boston, Beacon Press [1960] 233p. 21cm. 'Writings of T. E. Hulme': p. [145]-[211] Bibliography: p. [221]-226. Bibliographical footnotes. [84J6 1960] 60-11734
1. Hulme, Thomas Ernest, 1883-1917. I. Title. **BIP**

JONES, Alun Richard 921.2
The life and opinions of T. E. Hulme. Boston, Beacon Press [c.1960] 233p. 'Writings of T. E. Hulme': p.[145]-[211]. Bibl. p.[221]-226. Bibl. footnotes. 21cm. 60-11734 4.50
1. Hulme, Thomas Ernest, 1883-1917. I. Title.

ROBERTS, Michael, 1902-1948. 192
T. E. Hulme. New York, Haskell House, 1971. 310 p. 23 cm. Reprint of the 1938 ed. Includes bibliographical references. [B1646.H84R6 1971] 72-169106 ISBN 0-8383-1342-6
1. Hulme, Thomas Ernest, 1883-1917. **BIP**

Hulse, Edgar E.

HULSE, Edgar E. 813'.5'4 B
Life and love in the Ozarks; an autobiography, by Edgar Hulse. [Springfield, Mo., Printed by Midwest Litho, 1973] 229 p. illus. 21 cm. [PS3558.U4Z52] 73-92955 3.00
1. Hulse, Edgar E. I. Title.

Hulse, Helen Jo.

HULSE, Jerry. 973 B
Jody / by Jerry Hulse. New York : McGraw-Hill, c1976. 145 p. ; 21 cm. [HV875.H77] 76-16826 ISBN 0-07-031147-1 : 6.95
1. Hulse, Helen Jo.

HULSE, Jerry. 973 [B]
Jody / by Jerry Hulse. New York : Warner Books, 1977,c1976. 159p. ; 18 m. [HV875.H77] ISBN 0-446-89324-2 pbk. : 1.95
1. Hulse, Helen Jo. I. Title.
L.C. card no. for 1976 McGraw-Hill ed.: 76-16826. **BIP**

Humayun Kabir, 1906-1969.

DATTA, Dipankar, 954.04*092*4
1908-
Humayun Kabir: a political biography. Bombay, New York, Asia Pub. House [1969] viii, 80 p. illus. 22 cm. [DS481.H78D36 1969b] 71-903887 14.00
1. Humayun Kabir, 1906-1969.

Humbard, Martha Childers.

HUMBARD, Martha Childers. 269'.2'0924 B
Give me that old-time religion / Martha Childers Humbard, with Bill Armstrong. Plainfield, N.J. : Logos International, c1977. 156 p. : ill. ; 21 cm. On spine: Old-time religion. [BV3785.H76A33] 77-80161 ISBN 0-88270-227-0 : 2.95
1. Humbard, Martha Childers. 2. Evangelists—United States—Biography. I. Armstrong, Bill, 1921- joint author. II. Title. BIP

Humboldt, Alexander, Freiherr von, 1769-1859.

DE Terra, Helmut, 1900- 925
Humboldt; the life and times of Alexander von Humboldt, 1769-1859. [1st ed.] New York, Knopf, 1955. xii, 386, ix p. illus., ports., maps. 22 cm. Bibliography: p. [379]-386. [Q143.H9D4] 55-5606
1. Humboldt, Alexander, Freiherr von, 1769-1859.

DE TERRA, Helmut, 1900- 500.9'2'4 B
Humboldt : the life and times of Alexander von Humboldt, 1769-1859 / by Helmut De Terra. New York : Octagon Books, 1979, c1955. xii, 386, ix p., [7] leaves of plates : ill. ; 23 cm. Reprint of the ed. published by Knopf, New York. Includes index. Bibliography: p. 381-386. [Q143.H9D4 1979] 78-27653 ISBN 0-374-92134-2 : 21.00
1. Humboldt, Alexander, Freiherr von, 1769-1859. 2. Scientists—Germany—Biography.

GENDRON, Val. 925
The dragon tree; a life of Alexander, Baron von Humboldt. [1st ed.] New York, Longmans, Green, 1961. 214 p. illus. 21 cm. Includes bibliography. [Q143.H9G38] 61-7881
1. Humboldt, Alexander, Freiherr von, 1769-1859. I. Title.

KELLNER, Charlotte. 925
Alexander von Humboldt [by] L. Kellner. London,New York, Oxford University Press, 1963. 246 p. illus. 23 cm. Includes bibliography. [Q143.H9K4] 63-1115
1. Humboldt, Alexander, Freiherr von, 1769-1859. I. Title.

Humboldt, Wilhelm, Freiherr von, 1767-1835.

SWEET, Paul Robinson, 1907- 943'.06'0924 B
Wilhelm von Humboldt : a biography / by Paul R. Sweet. Columbus : Ohio State University Press, c1978. v. : port. ; 25 cm. Contents.Contents.—v. 1. 1767-1808. Includes bibliographical references. [DD422.H8S93] 77-26654 ISBN 0-8142-0274-8 : 18.50
1. Humboldt, Wilhelm, Freiherr von, 1767-1835. 2. Statesmen—Germany—Biography. BIP

Hume, Brit, 1943-

HUME, Brit, 1943- 070'.092'4
Inside story. [1st ed.] Garden City, N.Y., Doubleday, 1974. 304 p. 22 cm. [PN4874.H78A3] 73-83640 ISBN 0-385-06526-4 7.95
1. Hume, Brit, 1943- 2. Anderson, Jack, 1922- 3. Journalists—Correspondence, reminiscences, etc. I. Title.

Hume, David, 1711-1776.

BURTON, John Hill, 1809-1881. 192
Life and correspondence of David Hume. New York, B. Franklin [1967] 2 v. facsims., ports. 25 cm. (Burt Franklin research source works series, 186) (Philosophy monographs, 13.) Reprint of the 1846 ed. [B1497.B8 1967] 68-5777
1. Hume, David, 1711-1776. I. Title. BIP

CAVENDISH, Anthony Pike, 1916- 192
David Hume, by A. P. Cavendish. New York, Dover Publications [1968] 183 p. 22 cm. "An unabridged and unaltered republication of the work originally published ... in 1958." Bibliographical references included in "Notes" (p. 160-178) [B1498.C3 1968] 68-19552
1. Hume, David, 1711-1776.

HUXLEY, Thomas Henry, 1825-1895. 192
Hume. New York, AMS Press [1968] vi, 208 p. 22 cm. (English men of letters) "Reprinted from the edition of 1887, London." [B1497.H9 1968] 68-58382
1. Hume, David, 1711-1776.

KNIGHT, William Angus, 1836-1916. 192
Hume. Port Washington, N.Y., Kennikat Press [1970] x, 239 p. port. 20 cm. Reprint of the 1886 ed. Includes bibliographical references. [B1497.K7 1970] 72-103199 ISBN 8-04-608369-
1. Hume, David, 1711-1776. BIP

LAING, Bertram Mitchell. 192
David Hume, by B. M. Laing. New York, Russell & Russell [1968] 273 p. 23 cm. Reprint of the 1932 ed. Bibliography: p. 265-266. [B1497.L3 1968] 68-15134
1. Hume, David, 1711-1776. BIP

MOSSNER, Ernest Campbell, 1907- 921.2
The life of David Hume. Austin, University of Texas Press, 1954. xx, 683 p. illus., ports. (part col.) coats of arms, facsims., geneal. table. 25 cm. "The Humes of Ninewells; the chief authorities for the genealogical table": p. 616. Bibliography: p. 625-640. [B1497.M65] 54-7340
1. Hume, David, 1711-1776.

MOSSNER, Ernest Campbell, 1907- 192
The life of David Hume. Oxford, Clarendon Press, 1970. xviii, 683 p., fold. plate. illus., coats of arms, geneal. table, port. 24 cm. First published by Thomas Nelson and Sons ltd, in 1954. Reprinted lithographically. Bibliography: p. 625-640. [B1497 M65 1970] 75 21511 ISBN 0-19-824356-1 £5.00
1. Hume, David, 1711-1776. I. Title.

MOSSNER, Ernest Campbell, 1907- 192 B
The life of David Hume / Ernest Campbell Mossner. 2d ed. Oxford : Clarendon Press ; New York : Oxford University Press, 1979. p. cm. Includes index. Bibliography: p. [B1497.M65 1979] 78-41137 ISBN 0-19-824381-2 : 49.95
1. Hume, David, 1711-1776 2. Philosophers—Scotland Biography. I. Title. BIP

PRICE, John Valdimir. 192
David Hume. New York, Twayne Publishers [1969, c1968] 174 p. 22 cm. (Twayne's English authors series, 77) Bibliography: 167-170. [B1498.P73] 68-24287 3.95
1. Hume, David, 1711-1776. BIP

SISSON, Charles Hubert, 1914- 192
David Hume / [by] C. H. Sisson. Edinburgh : Ramsay Head Press, 1976. 93 p. ; 19 cm. (New assessments) [B1497.S45] 77-353220 ISBN 0-902859-30-7 : £2.50
1. Hume, David, 1711-1776. 2. Philosophers—Scotland—Biography.

TAYLOR, Alfred Edward, 1869-1945. 192 B
David Hume & the miraculous. [Folcroft, Pa.] Folcroft Library Editions, 1972. 54 p. 22 cm. "150 copies." Reprint of the 1927 ed., issued in series: The Leslie Stephen lectures. [B1499.M5T3 1972] 72-191241
1. Hume, David, 1711-1776. 2. Miracles. I. Title. II. Series: The Leslie Stephen lectures, 1927. BIP

Hume, David, 1711-1776—Knowledge, Theory of.

MACNABB, D. G. C. 120
David Hume: his theory of knowledge and morality, by D. G. C. MacNabb. 2d ed. Hamden, Conn., Archon Books [1966] 208 p. 19 cm. Bibliography: p. [20] [B1499.K7M27 1966a] 67-12980
1. Hume, David, 1711-1776—Knowledge, Theory of. 2. Hume, David, 1711-1776—Ethics. I. Title.

Hume, James B., 1827-1904.

DILLON, Richard H. 364.12'0924 B
Wells, Fargo detective: the biography of James B. Hume, by Richard Dillon. New York, Coward-McCann [1969] 320 p. illus., ports. 22 cm. Bibliography: p. 301-302. [HV7911.H8D5] 69-11060 7.95
1. Hume, James B., 1827-1904. 2. Wells, Fargo and Company. I. Title.

Hume, Robert Deniston, 1845-1908.

DODDS, Gordon Barlow, 1932- 926.6
The Salmon King of Oregon; R. D. Hume and the Pacific fisheries. Chapel Hill, Univ. of N. C. Pr. [1963, c.1959] 257p. illus. 23cm. 63-3158 6.00
1. Hume, Robert Deniston, 1845-1908. 2. Salmon-fisheries—Oregon. I. Title.

Hume, Walter Cunningham, 1840-1921.

HUME, Walter Cunningham, 1840-1921. 994.03'1'0924 B
A Victorian engagement : letters and journals of Walter Hume and Anna Kate Fowler during the 1860s / edited by Bertram Hume. St. Lucia, Q. : University of Queensland Press, 1975. xiii, 180 p., [6] leaves of plates : ill. ; 21 cm. [DU272.H85A4 1975] 76-371370 ISBN 0-7022-0998-8 : 12.80
1. Hume, Walter Cunningham, 1840-1921. 2. Fowler, Anna Kate, 1838-1909. 3. Statesmen—Queensland—Biography. 4. Queensland—Biography. I. Fowler, Anna Kate, 1838-1909, joint author. II. Hume, Bertram. III. Title. BIP

Hummel, Johann Nepomuk, 1778-1837.

SACHS, Joel. 786.1'092'4 B
Kapellmeister Hummel in England and France / Joel Sachs. Detroit : Information Coordinators, 1977. 153 p. : port. ; 24 cm. (Detroit monographs in musicology ; no. 6) "Biographical glossary and index": p. 117-153. Bibliography: p. 107-[115] [ML410.H93S2] 77-376975 ISBN 0-911772-82-0 : 10.50
1. Hummel, Johann Nepomuk, 1778-1837. 2. Composers—Biography. I. Title. II. Series. BIP

Humorists, American.

BENET, Laura. 928.1
Famous American humorists. New York, Dodd, Mead, 1959. 190 p. illus. 22 cm. (Famous biographies for young people) [PS433.B4] 58-9726
1. Humorists, American. I. Title.

Humphrey, Doris,

HUMPHREY, Doris, 1895-1958. 793.3'2 B
Doris Humphrey: an artist first. An autobiography, edited and completed by Selma Jeanne Cohen. Introd. by John Martin; foreword by Charles Humphrey Woodford; chronology by Christena L. Schlundt. [1st ed.] Middletown, Conn., Wesleyan University Press [1972] xiv, 305 p. illus. 23 cm. Includes bibliographical references. [GV1785.H8A3] 72-3695 ISBN 0-8195-4054-4 12.50
I. Cohen, Selma Jeanne, 1920- ed. II. Title.

HUMPHREY, Doris, 1895-1958. 793.320924
New Dance; an unfinished autobiography. With introd. by John Martin. [New York, Dance Perspectives, inc., 1966] 81 p. illus., ports. 23 cm. (Dance perspective, 25) [GV1580.D27] 66-19004
I. Martin, John Joseph, 1893- ed. II. Title. III. Series.

Humphrey, Doris, 1895-1958.

HUMPHREY, Doris, 1895-1958. 793.3'2 B
Doris Humphrey: an artist first. An autobiography, edited and completed by Selma Jeanne Cohen. Introd. by John Martin; foreword by Charles Humphrey Woodford; chronology by Christena L. Schlundt. [1st ed.] Middletown, Conn., Wesleyan University Press [1972] xiv, 305 p. illus. 23 cm. Includes bibliographical references. [GV1785.H8A3] 72-3695 ISBN 0-8195-4054-4 12.50
I. Cohen, Selma Jeanne, 1920- ed. II. Title.

HUMPHREY, Doris, 1895-1958. 793.320924
New Dance; an unfinished autobiography. With introd. by John Martin. [New York, Dance Perspectives, inc., 1966] 81 p. illus., ports. 23 cm. (Dance perspective, 25) [GV1580.D27] 66-19004
I. Martin, John Joseph, 1893- ed. II. Title. III. Series.

HUMPHREY, Doris, 1895-1958. 793.3'2 B
New Dance: an unfinished autobiography. With introd. by John Martin. [New York, Johnson Reprint Corp., 1973] p. Reprint of 1966 ed., which was issued as no. 25 of Dance perspectives. [GV1785.H8A35 1973] 73-765 ISBN 0-384-24883-7 Pap. 6.00
1. Humphrey, Doris, 1895-1958. I. Title. II. Series: Dance perspectives, no. 25.

Humphrey, Hubert Horatio, 1911-1978.

AMRINE, Michael 923.273
This is Humphrey. Foreword by Lyndon B. Johnson. New York, Popular Lib. [c.1960, 1964] 271p. 18cm. (PC1045) .75 pap.,
1. Humphrey, Hubert Horatio, 1911- I. Title.

AMRINE, Michael. 923.273
This is Humphrey; the story of the Senator. [1st ed.] Garden City, N. Y., Doubleday, 1960. 261 p. 22 cm. [E748.H945A7] 60-8678
1. Humphrey, Hubert Horatio, 1911- I. Title.

BERMAN, Edgar. 973.923'092'4 B
Hubert : the triumph and tragedy of the Humphrey I knew / Edgar Berman. New York : Putnam, c1979. 300 p., [8] leaves of plates : ill. ; 24 cm. Includes index. [E748.H945B47 1979] 79-4259 ISBN 0-399-12314-8 : 10.95
1. Humphrey, Hubert Horatio, 1911-1978. 2. United States. Congress. Senate—Biography. 3. Berman, Edgar. 4. Vice Presidents—United States—Biography. 5. Legislators—United States—Biography. I. Title. BIP

COHEN, Dan, 1936- 973.923'092'4 B
Undefeated : the life of Hubert H. Humphrey / by Dan Cohen ; foreword by Muriel Humphrey ; introd. by G. Theodore Mitau. Minneapolis : Lerner Publications, c1978. p. cm. Includes bibliographical references and index. [E748.H945C63] 78-53933 ISBN 0-8225-9953-8 : 25.00
1. Humphrey, Hubert Horatio, 1911-1978. 2. United States. Congress. Senate—Biography. 3. Legislators—United States—Biography. 4. Vice-Presidents—United States—Biography. 5. United States—Politics and government—1945- I. Title. BIP

EISELE, Albert, 1936- 973.92'092'2 B
Almost to the Presidency; a biography of two American politicians. [1st ed.] Blue Earth, Minn., Piper Co. [1972] 460 p. 24 cm. [E748.H945E5] 76-187432 ISBN 0-87832-005-9 10.95
1. Humphrey, Hubert Horatio, 1911- 2. McCarthy, Eugene J., 1916- 3. United States—Politics and government—1945- I. Title.

GRIFFITH, Winthrop. 923.273
Humphrey, a candid biography. New York, Morrow, 1965. xii, 337 p. illus., facsims., ports. 24 cm. [E748.H945G7] 65-14953
1. Humphrey, Hubert Horatio, 1911- I. Title.

HUMPHREY, Hubert, 1911-1978. 973.92'092'4
Hubert Humphrey : the man and his dream / [compiled by] Sheldon D. Engelmayer, Robert J. Wagman. New York : Methuen, c1978. xvii, 358 p., [8] leaves of plates : ill. ; 24 cm. Includes index. [E838.5.H855 1978] 78-58847 ISBN 0-458-93450-X : 12.95

1. Humphrey, Hubert, 1911-1978. 2. United States. Congress. Senate—Biography. 3. United States—Politics and government—1945- —Collected works. 4. Legislators—United States—Biography. 5. Vice-Presidents—United States—Biography. I. Engelmayer, Sheldon D. II. Wagman, Robert J.

HUMPHREY, Hubert Horatio, 1911- 973.923'092'4 B
The education of a public man : my life and politics / Hubert H. Humphrey ; edited by Norman Sherman. 1st ed. Garden City, N.Y. : Doubleday, 1976. xiii, 513 p. [12] leaves of plates : ill. ; 22 cm. Includes index. [E748.H945A34] 75-36628 ISBN 0-385-05603-6 : 12.50
1. Humphrey, Hubert Horatio, 1911- I. Title. BIP

MARTIN, Ralph G., 1920- 973.923'0924
A man for all people: Hubert H. Humphrey, by Ralph G. Martin. Captions and commentary by Hubert H. Humphrey. Introd. by Adlai E. Stevenson, III. New York, Grosset & Dunlap [1968] [175] p. illus. 28 cm. [E748.H945M3] 68-8847 7.95
1. Humphrey, Hubert Horatio, 1911- —Portraits, caricatures, etc. I. Title.

NORDSTROM, Marty 923.273
Humphrey. Photos. by Marty Nordstrom. Words by the Senator. Luce dist. New York, McKay [c.1964] 1v. (chiefly ports.) 27cm. 64-7973 1.95
1. Humphrey, Hubert Horatio, 1911- —Portraits, caricatures, etc. I. Humphrey, Hubert, Horatio, 1911- II. Title.

RYSKIND, Allan H. 973.923'0924 B
Hubert; an unauthorized biography of the Vice President, by Allan H. Ryskind. New Rochelle, N.Y., Arlington House [1968] 355 p. 24 cm. Bibliographical references included in "Notes" (p. 335-347) [E748.H945R9] 68-22456
1. Humphrey, Hubert Horatio, 1911-

SHERRILL, Robert. 973.923'0924
The drugstore liberal [by] Robert Sherrill and Harry W. Ernst. New York, Grossman Publishers, [1968] 200 p. 21 cm. [E748.H945S5] 68-31584 4.95
1. Humphrey, Hubert Horatio, 1911- I. Ernst, Harry W., joint author. II. Title.

ZEHNPFENNIG, Gladys. 973.923'0924
Hubert H. Humphrey, champion of human rights. Minneapolis, T. S. Denison [c1966] 341 p. 22 cm. (Men of achievement series) [E748.H945Z4] 66-20124
1. Humphrey, Hubert Horatio, 1911- I. Title.

Humphrey, Hubert Horatio, 1911-1978—Juvenile literature.

ERLANGER, Ellen. 973.923'092'4 B
Hubert H. Humphrey : the happy warrior / Ellen Erlanger. Minneapolis : Lerner Publications Co., c1979. p. cm. (The Achievers) Includes index. [E748.H945E74 1979] 79-1367 ISBN 0-8225-0476-6 : 5.95
1. Humphrey, Hubert Horatio, 1911-1978—Juvenile literature. 2. United States. Congress. Senate—Biography—Juvenile literature. 3. Vice-Presidents—United States—Biography—Juvenile literature. 4. Legislators—United States—Biography—Juvenile literature. I. Title. II. Series. BIP

WESTMAN, Paul. 973.923'092'4 B
Hubert H. Humphrey, the politics of joy / by Paul Westman ; illustrated by Douglas Oudekerk. Minneapolis : Dillon Press, 1979, c1978. 47 p. : ill. ; 24 cm. (Taking part books.) Traces the life of the senator from Minnesota who served as Vice President under Lyndon B. Johnson. [E748.H945W47] 92 79-9795 ISBN 0-87518-180-5 : 6.95
1. Humphrey, Hubert Horatio, 1911-1978—Juvenile literature. 2. United States. Congress. Senate—Biography—Juvenile literature. 3. Vice-Presidents—United States—Biography—Juvenile literature. 4. Legislators—United States—Biography—Juvenile literature. I. Oudekerk, Douglas. II. Title.

Humphrey, William.

LEE, James W. 813'.5/4
William Humphrey, by James W. Lee. Austin, Tex., Steck [1967] ii, 44p. 21cm. (South-west writers ser., no. 7) Bibl. [PS3558.U448Z7] 67-24560 1.00 pap.,
1. Humphrey, William. I. Title. II. Series.

Humphrey, William—Biography—Youth.

HUMPHREY, William. 813'.5'4 B
Farther off from heaven / William Humphrey. 1st ed. New York : Knopf, 1977. 241 p. ; 23 cm. [PS3558.U464Z52] 76-47936 ISBN 0-394-41188-9 : 8.95
1. Humphrey, William—Biography—Youth. 2. Authors, American—20th century—Biography. I. Title. BIP

Humphreys, Christmas, 1901-

HUMPHREYS, Christmas, 1901- 294.3'092'4 B
Both sides of the circle : the autobiography of Christmas Humphreys. London ; Boston : G. Allen & Unwin, 1978. 269 p., [8] leaves of plates : ill. ; 24 cm. Includes index. [BQ962.U527H85] 78-312354 ISBN 0-04-921023-8 : 17.95
1. Humphreys, Christmas, 1901- 2. Buddhists—England—Biography. 3. Judges—England—Biography. I. Title. BIP

Humphreys, David, 1752-1818.

HUMPHREYS, Francis Landon, 1858-1937. 973.4'0924 B
Life and times of David Humphreys; soldier—statesman—poet, "Belov'd of Washington." New York, Putnam, 1917. St. Clair Shores, Mich., Scholarly Press [1971] 2 v. illus. 21 cm. Bibliography: v. 2, p. 459-469. [E302.6.H89H9 1971] 73-145099 ISBN 0-403-01036-5
1. Humphreys, David, 1752-1818. I. Title.

Hundley, Hot Rod, 1934-

LIBBY, Bill. 796.32'3'0924 B
Clown: number 33 in your program, number 1 in your heart— Hot Rod Hundley. [1st ed.] New York, Cowles Book Co. [1970] 184 p. illus., ports. 22 cm. [GV884.H8L5 1970] 77-118891 5.95
1. Hundley, Hot Rod, 1934- I. Title.

Hundt, Ferdinand.

BEYLO, Frank, comp. 741'.0922
Of times forgotten and men remembered; nineteenth century drawings by Nepomuk Hundt [and] Ferdinand Hundt. Research compiled and text written by Frank Beylo. Discovery data offered by Santi Egitto. Johnson City, N.Y., Johnson City Pub. Co. [1968] [74] p. illus., map. 28 cm. [NC249.B48] 76-2843 2.98
1. Hundt, Ferdinand. 2. Hundt, Nepomuk. I. Title.

Huneker, James Gibbons, 1857-1921—Addresses, essays, lectures.

DE CASSERES, Benjamin, 1873-1945. 801'.95'0924
James Gibbons Huneker / by Benjamin De Casseres. Folcroft, Pa. : Folcroft Library Editions, 1977 [c1925] 62 p. ; 23 cm. Reprint of the ed. published by J. Lawren, New York. "James Gibbons Huneker, a bibliography by Joseph Lawren": p. [41]-62. [PS2044.H4Z7 1977] 77-17168 ISBN 0-8414-1895-0 : 15.00
1. Huneker, James Gibbons, 1857-1921—Addresses, essays, lectures. 2. Huneker, James Gibbons, 1857-1921—Bibliography. 3. Authors, American—19th century—Biography—Addresses, essays, lectures. BIP

Hung, Hsiu-ch'uan, 1814-1864.

HAMBERG, Theodore. 951'.03
The visions of Hung-Siu-tshuen, and origin of the Kwang-si insurrection. New York, Praeger [1969] ix, v, 63 p. 22 cm. (Praeger scholarly reprints. Source books and studies in Chinese history) Reprint of the 1854 ed. Includes bibliographical references. [DS759.H2 1969] 72-105280
1. Hung, Hsiu-ch'uan, 1814-1864. 2. Taiping Rebellion, 1850-1864. I. Title.

Hungarian Americans—Biography.

DAWSON, Glen, 1912- 937'.04'94511 B
Hungarians in the United States / by Glen Dawson. Los Angeles : B. Blau, [1972] 13 p. ; 38 mm. [E184.H95D38] 75-312368
1. Hungarian Americans—Biography. 2. United States—Biography. 3. Bibliography—Microscopic and miniature editions—Specimens. I. Title.

Hungarians in the U.S.—Biog.

*SZY, Tibor, 1908- ed. 920.04391
Hungarians in America; a biographical directory of professionals of Hungarian origin in America. New York, 10017, 441 Lexington Ave. Kossuth Found., [1966] viii, 488p. 22cm. (Eastern European biogs. & studies ser., v.2) 15.00
1. Hungarians in the U.S.—Biog. I. Title.

SZY, Tibor, 1908- ed. 920.04391
Hungarieans in America& a biographical directory of prefessionals of Hungarian origin in the Americas. New York, Hungarian Univ. Assn., [dist. Hungarians in Amer., 323 E. 66th St., c. 1963] viii, 606p. 17cm. 63-21300 15.00
1. Hungarian in the U.S.—Biog. I. Title.

Hungary

KAROLYI, Mihaly, grof, 1875-1955. 923.24391
Memoirs of Michael Karolyi; faith without illusion. Translated from the Hungarian by Catherine Karolyi. With an introd. by A. J. P. Taylor. [1st American ed.] New York, Dutton, 1957 [c1956] 392p. illus., ports., col. map (on lining papers) 24cm. [DB950.K3A38 1957] 57-5683
1. Hungary—Pol. & govt.—20th cent. I. Title.

Hungary—History.

LUKINICH, Imre, 1880-1950. 943.9'1
A history of Hungary in biographical sketches. [Translated from the Hungarian by Catherine Dallas] Freeport, N.Y., Books for Libraries Press, [1968] 224 p. illus., facsims., ports. 22 cm. (Essay index reprint series) "First published 1937." Contents.Contents.—Prince Arpad.—St. Stephen.—St. Ladislas.—King Coloman.—King Bela III.—King Bela IV.—Andrew III, the last of the Arpad line.—King Louis the Great.—John Hunyadi, Regent of Hungary.—King Matthias.—Wladislas II and Louis II.—Cardinal Martinuzzi (Friar George).—Stephen Bocskay, Prince of Hungary and Transylvania.—Gabriel Bethlen, Prince of Transylvania.—Cardinal Peter Pazmany.—Count Nicholas Zrinyi, soldier and poet.—Francis Rakoczi II, Prince of Hungary and Transylvania.—Queen Maria Theresa.—Count Stephen Szechenyi.—Louis Kossuth.—Francis Deak. [DB922.L85 1968] 68-20314
1. Hungary—History. 2. Hungary—Biography. I. Title. BIP

Hungerford, Charles Frederick Algernon Portal, Viscount Portal of, 1893-1971.

RICHARDS, Denis. 358.4'13'310924 B
Portal of Hungerford : the life of Marshal of the Royal Air Force, Viscount Portal of Hungerford, KG, GCB, OM, DSO, MC / Denis Richards. New York : Holmes & Meier, 1978 p. cm. Includes index. Bibliography: p. [UG626.2.H85R5 1977] [w] 78-14235 ISBN 0-8419-6103-4 : 24.50
1. Hungerford, Charles Frederick Algernon Portal, Viscount Portal of, 1893-1971. 2. Great Britain. Royal Air Force—Biography. 3. Marshals—Great Britain—Biography. BIP

Huning, Franz, 1827-1905.

HUNING, Franz, 1827-1905. 917.89'03'40924 B
Trader on the Santa Fe trail; memoirs of Franz Huning. With notes by his granddaughter Lina Fergusson Browne. [1st ed.] Albuquerque, N.M., University of Albuquerque [1973] xiii, 153 p. illus. 24 cm. Includes bibliographical references. [F801.H86A37 1973] 73-83963 ISBN 0-910750-29-7 8.50
1. Huning, Franz, 1827-1905. 2. New Mexico—History—1848- I. Browne, Lina Fergusson. II. Title.
Distributed by Calvin Horn Publisher Box 4204, Albuquerque, N.M. 87106

Hunley, John Bunyan,

HUNLEY, John Bunyan, 1881- 922.673
A spiritual argosy; the romance of fifty-eight years in the Christian ministry. Boston, Christopher Pub. House [1958] 313p. illus. 21cm. [BX7343.H8A3] 58-6716
I. Title.

Hunt, Alfred Ephraim, 1855-1899.

EDWARDS, Junius David, 1890- 926
A captain in industry. New York [1957] 126p. illus., ports., facsim. 27cm. 'Technical papers by Alfred E. Hunt': p. 116-118. [TA140.H8E3] 56-12914
1. Hunt, Alfred Ephraim, 1855-1899. I. Title.

Hunt, George Wylie Paul, 1859-1934.

GOFF, John S., 1931- 320.9'791'05 B
George W. P. Hunt and his Arizona, by John S. Goff. Pasadena, Calif., Socio Technical Publications [1973] 286 p. illus. 23 cm. Includes bibliographical references. [F811.G58] 72-78585 10.00
1. Hunt, George Wylie Paul, 1859-1934. 2. Arizona—Politics and government—To 1950. I. Title. BIP

Hunt, H. L.

BROWN, Stanley H. 338'.04'0924 B
H. L. Hunt / by Stanley H. Brown. 1st ed. Chicago : Playboy Press, c1976. vi, 217 p., [4] leaves of plates : ill. ; 22 cm. Includes index. Bibliography: p. 211-214. [HC102.5.H86B76] 76-12571 ISBN 0-87223-449-5 : 10.00
1. Hunt, H. L. I. Title.

Hunt, Henry Jackson, 1819-1889.

LONGACRE, Edward G., 1946- 973.7'3'0924 B
The man behind the guns : a biography of General Henry Jackson Hunt, Chief of Artillery, Army of the Potomac / by Edward G. Longacre. South Brunswick [N.J.] : A. S. Barnes, c1977. p. cm. Bibliography: p. [E467.1.H89L66] 76-10885 ISBN 0-498-01656-0 : 15.00
1. Hunt, Henry Jackson, 1819-1889. 2. United States. Army—Biography. 3. United States. Army. Army of the Potomac. 4. Generals—United States—Biography. 5. United States—History—Civil War, 1861-1865—Regimental histories—Army of the Potomac. I. Title.

Hunt, Howard, 1918—

HUNT, Howard, 1918- 327'.12'0924 B
Undercover : memoirs of an American secret agent / by E. Howard Hunt. [New York] : Berkley Pub. Corp. : distributed by Putnam, [1974] 338 p., [8] leaves of plates : ill. ; 22 cm. Includes index.

[UB271.U5H86 1974] 74-11602 ISBN 0-399-11446-7 : 8.95
1. Hunt, Howard, 1918- 2. Watergate Affair, 1972- I. Title.

SZULC, Tad. 327'.12'0924 B
Compulsive spy: the strange career of E. Howard Hunt. New York, Viking Press [1974] x, 180 p. 22 cm. [E840.8.H86S98 1974] 73-16456 ISBN 0-670-23546-6 5.95
1. Hunt, Howard, 1918- I. Title.

Hunt, James Henry Leigh, 1784-1859.

HUNT, Leigh, 1784-1859. 828.703
The autobiography of Leigh Hunt, with reminiscences of friends and contemporaries. New York, AMS Press, 1965. 2 v. port. 20 cm. Reprint of the 1850 ed. [PR4813.A3] 66-4243
I. Title.

HUNT, Leigh, 1784-1859. 928.2
Leigh Hunt's autobiography: the earliest sketches; edited with an introd. and notes by Stephen F. Fogle. Gainesville, University of Florida Press [1959] xvii, 53p. facsim. 23cm. (University of Florida monographs. Humanities, no. 2) Edited from ms. pages in the Brewer Collection of Leigh Hunt in the State University of Iowa Library. [PR4813.A3 1959] 59-63812
I. Fogle, Stephen Francis, 1912- ed. II. Title. III. Series: Florida. University, Gainesville. University of Florida monographs. Humanities, no. 2

HUNT, Leigh [James Henry Leigh Hunt] 928.2
Leigh Hunt's autobiography: the earliest sketches edited with an introd. and notes by Stephen F. Fogle. Gainesville, University of Florida Press [c.1959] xvii, 53p. facsim. 23cm. (University of Florida monographs. Humanities, no. 2) 59-63812 2.00 pap.,
I. Fogle, Stephen Francis, 1912- ed. II. Title. III. Series: Florida. University, Gainesville. University of Florida monographs. Humanities, no. 2

HUNT, Leigh [James Henry Leigh Hunt] 1784-1859 928.2
The autobiography of Leigh Hunt. Ed., introd., notes by J. E. Morpurgo. London, Cresset Pr. [dist. Chester Springs, Pa., Dufour, 1965] xxviii, 512p. 21cm. (Cresset lib.) [PR4813.A3] 49-4667 3.75 bds.,
I. Title.

JOHNSON, Reginald Brimley, 1867-1932. 824'.7 B
Leigh Hunt. [Folcroft, Pa.] Folcroft Library Editions, 1973. p. Reprint of the 1896 ed. published by S. Sonnenschein, London; Macmillan, New York, in series: The Dilettante library. [PR4813.J6 1973] 73-16134 ISBN 0-8414-5275-X (lib. bdg.)
1. Hunt, James Henry Leigh, 1784-1859. I. Series: The Dilettante library. **BIP**

Hunt, James, 1947-

WILLIAMS, Peter, 1946- 796.7'2'0924 B
The story of James Hunt / by Peter Williams. Brentwood : NPC, 1976. 3-86 p. : ill. (incl. 1 col.), port. ; 28 cm. [GV1032.H86W54] 77-357313 £0.80
1. Hunt, James, 1947- 2. Automobile racing drivers—Great Britain—Biography. 3. Grand Prix racing. I. Title.

Hunt, John Wesley, 1772-1849.

RAMAGE, James A. 338'.092'4 B
John Wesley Hunt, pioneer merchant, manufacturer, and financier / James A. Ramage. Lexington : University Press of Kentucky, c1974. 103, [1] p., [2] leaves of plates : ill. ; 21 cm. (The Kentucky bicentennial bookshelf) Bibliography: p. 101-[104] [HF3023.H85R3] 74-7881 ISBN 0-8131-0204-9 pbk. : 3.95
1. Hunt, John Wesley, 1772-1849. I. Title. II. Series.

Hunt, Leigh, 1784-1859.

BLUNDEN, Edmund Charles, 1896- 828'.7'09 B
Leigh Hunt; a biography, by Edmund Blunden. [Hamden, Conn.] Archon Books, 1970. xiii, 402 p. illus., ports. 22 cm. Reprint of the 1930 ed. "Books by Leigh Hunt": p. [352]-357. Bibliography: p. [374]-378. [PR4813.B6 1970] 74-95020
1. Hunt, Leigh, 1784-1859.

HUNT, Leigh, 1784-1859. 828.703
The autobiography of Leigh Hunt, with reminiscences of friends and contemporaries. New York, AMS Press, 1965. 2 v. port. 20 cm. Reprint of the 1850 ed. [PR4813.A3] 66-4243
I. Title.

HUNT, Leigh, 1784-1859. 928.2
Leigh Hunt's autobiography: the earliest sketches; edited with an introd. and notes by Stephen F. Fogle. Gainesville, University of Florida Press [1959] xvii, 53p. facsim. 23cm. (University of Florida monographs. Humanities, no. 2) Edited from ms. pages in the Brewer Collection of Leigh Hunt in the State University of Iowa Library. [PR4813.A3 1959] 59-63812
I. Fogle, Stephen Francis, 1912- ed. II. Title. III. Series: Florida. University, Gainesville. University of Florida monographs. Humanities, no. 2

HUNT, Leigh [James Henry Leigh Hunt] 928.2
Leigh Hunt's autobiography: the earliest sketches edited with an introd. and notes by Stephen F. Fogle. Gainesville, University of Florida Press [c.1959] xvii, 53p. facsim. 23cm. (University of Florida monographs. Humanities, no. 2) 59-63812 2.00 pap.,
I. Fogle, Stephen Francis, 1912- ed. II. Title. III. Series: Florida. University, Gainesville. University of Florida monographs. Humanities, no. 2

HUNT, Leigh [James Henry Leigh Hunt] 1784-1859 928.2
The autobiography of Leigh Hunt. Ed., introd., notes by J. E. Morpurgo. London, Cresset Pr. [dist. Chester Springs, Pa., Dufour, 1965] xxviii, 512p. 21cm. (Cresset lib.) [PR4813.A3] 49-4667 3.75 bds.,
I. Title.

Hunt, Nancy.

HUNT, Nancy. 363.1'9'66 B
Mirror image / Nancy Hunt. 1st ed. New York : Holt, Rinehart, and Winston, c1978. 263 p. ; 22 cm. Autobiographical. [RC560.C4H85] 78-4690 ISBN 0-03-040646-3 : 8.95
1. Hunt, Nancy. 2. Change of sex—United States—Biography. I. Title. **BIP**

Hunt, Reid, 1870-1948. (Series: National Academy of Sciences, Washington, D. C. Biographical memoirs, v. 26, 3d memoir)

MARSHALL, Eli Kennerly, 1889- 509'.22
Reid Hunt, 1870-1948. (In National Academy ofSciences, Washington, D. C. Biographical memoirs. Washington. 23 cm. v. 26 (1951) [3d memoir] p. 25-44. port.) Bibliography of Reid Hunt": p. 38-44. [Q141.N2 vol. 26, 3d memoir] 52-1441
1. Hunt, Reid, 1870-1948. (Series: National Academy of Sciences, Washington, D. C. Biographical memoirs, v. 26, 3d memoir) I. Title.

Hunt, Robert, 1807-1887.

PEARSON, Alan. 509'.2'4 B
Robert Hunt (1807-1887) / by A. Pearson. [St Austell] : Federation of Old Cornwall Societies, 1976. 123 p. : ill., ports. ; 21 cm. "Published works by Robert Hunt": p. 117-123. [TN140.H78P3] 77-361935 ISBN 0-902660-19-5 : £0.90
1. Hunt, Robert, 1807-1887. 2. Mineral industries—Great Britain—Biography. 3. Scientists—Great Britain—Biography.

Hunt, Rockwell Dennis,

HUNT, Rockwell Dennis, 1868- 923.773
'Mr. California'; autobiography. San Francisco, Fearon Publishers [1956] 380p. illus. 24cm. [E175.5.H87] 56-7132
I. Title.

Hunt, Violet, 1866-1942—Biography.

GOLDRING, Douglas, 1887- 820'.9'0052
South lodge : reminiscences of Violet Hunt, Ford Madox Ford, and the English review circle / by Douglas Goldring. Folcroft, Pa. : Folcroft Library Editions, 1977. xix, 239 p., [2] leaves of plates : ill. ; 26 cm. Includes bibliographical references. [PR6015.U55Z65 1977] 77-18261 ISBN 0-8414-4600-8 : 25.00
1. Hunt, Violet, 1866-1942—Biography. 2. Ford, Ford Madox, 1873-1939—Biography. 3. The English review. 4. Novelists, English—20th century—Biography. 5. Authors, English—20th century—Biography. I. Title.

Hunt, William Morris, 1824-1879.

KNOWLTON, Helen Mary, 1832-1918. 759.13
Art-life of William Morris Hunt. New York, B. Blom, 1971. xii, 219 p. illus. 21 cm. Reprint of the 1899 ed. [ND237.H9K5 1971] 75-173172
1. Hunt, William Morris, 1824-1879. I. Title. **BIP**

Hunter, Brenda.

HUNTER, Brenda. 301.42'84'0924 B
Beyond divorce : a personal journey / Brenda Hunter. Old Tappan, N.J. : F. H. Revell Co., c1978. 160 p. ; 22 cm. [HQ814.H84] 78-745 ISBN 0-8007-0903-9 : 6.95
1. Hunter, Brenda. 2. Divorcees—Biography. I. Title. **BIP**

Hunter, Frances Gardner,

HUNTER, Frances Gardner, 1916- 248'.0924 B
My love affair with Charles. Glendale, Calif., G/L Regal Books [1971] 197 p. 21 cm. Letters between the author and her husband, Charles Hunter. [BR1725.H83A4 1971] 72-150717 ISBN 0-8307-0099-4 4.95
I. Hunter, Charles, 1920- II. Title. **BIP**

Hunter, Ian, 1946-

HUNTER, Ian, 1946- 784'.092'4 B
Ian Hunter : reflections of a rock star. New York : Flash Books, c1976. 104 p. : ill. ; 26 cm. [ML420.H95A3] 75-45514 ISBN 0-8256-3905-0 pbk. : 3.95
1. Hunter, Ian, 1946- 2. Rock musicians—England—Biography.

Hunter, Jim, 1946-

LIBBY, Bill. 796.357'092'4 B
Catfish, the three million dollar pitcher / Bill Libby. New York : Coward, McCann & Geoghegan, c1976. 223 p. : ill. ; 22 cm. [GV865.H85L52 1976] 75-37643 7.95
1. Hunter, Jim, 1946- 2. Baseball. I. Title.

SULLIVAN, George, 1927- 796.357'092'4 B
The picture story of Jim Catfish Hunter / by George Sullivan. New York : J. Messner, c1977. p. cm. [GV865.H85S94] 76-52427 ISBN 0-671-32873-5 lib. bdg. : 6.64
1. Hunter, Jim, 1946- 2. Baseball players—United States—Biography—Juvenile literature. I. Title.

Hunter, Jim, 1946- —Juvenile literature.

BURCHARD, S. H. 796.357'092'4 B
Jim "Catfish" Hunter / S. H. Burchard ; illustrated with photos. and with drawings by Paul Frame. 1st ed. New York : Harcourt Brace Jovanovich, c1976. 64 p. : ill. ; 22 cm. (Sports star) An easy-to-read biography of the star pitcher of the Oakland Athletics who managed to break his contract and move to the New York Yankees. [GV865.H85B87] 92 75-35525 ISBN 0-15-278175-7 : 4.95 pbk. : 1.95
1. Hunter, Jim, 1946- —Juvenile literature. 2. Baseball—Juvenile literature. I. Frame, Paul, 1913- II. Title.

STAMBLER, Irwin. 796.357'092'4 B
Catfish Hunter : the three million dollar arm / Irwin Stambler. New York : Putnam, c1976. 127 p. : port. ; 21 cm. Includes index. A biography of Catfish Hunter, whose famous pitching arm brought him a contract with the New York Yankees for the biggest salary ever paid a ballplayer. [GV865.H85S72 1976] 92 76-10367 ISBN 0-399-61023-5 pbk. : 5.98
1. Hunter, Jim, 1946- —Juvenile literature. 2. New York (City). Baseball club (American League)—Juvenile literature. 3. Baseball—Juvenile literature. I. Title.

Hunter, Jim, 1953-

HUNTER, Jim, 1953- 796.9'3'0924 B
A man against the mountain / Jim Hunter, as told to Marshall Shelley. Elgin, Ill. : D.C. Cook Pub. Co., c1978. 191 p. : ill. ; 18 cm. [GV854.2.H86A34] 78-59283 ISBN 0-89191-143-X pbk. : 1.95
1. Hunter, Jim, 1953- 2. Skiers—Canada—Biography. I. Shelley, Marshall, joint author. II. Title. **BIP**

Hunter, John Dunn, 1798-1827.

DRINNON, Richard 970.3 B
White savage; the case of John Dunn Hunter. New York, Schocken Books [1972] xix, 282 p. illus. 24 cm. Includes bibliographical references. [E87.D77] 72-79445 12.50
1. Hunter, John Dunn, 1798-1827. 2. Indians of North America—Captivities. 3. Osage Indians. I. Title. **BIP**

Hunter, John, 1728-1793.

KOBLER, John. 926.1
The reluctant surgeon; a biography of John Hunter. [1st ed.] Garden City, N. Y., Doubleday. 1960. 359p. 25cm. [R489.H9K6] 60-6887
1. Hunter, John, 1728-1793. I. Title.

KOBLER, John [Albert John Kobler] 926.1
The reluctant surgeon; a biography of John Hunter. Garden City, N.Y., Doubleday, [c.]1960. 359p. (15p. bibl.) 25cm. 60-6887 4.95
1. Hunter, John, 1728-1793. I. Title.

KOBLER, John [Albert John Kobler] 926.1
The reluctant surgeon; a biography of John Hunter. Garden City, N. Y., Doubleday [1962, c.1960] 439p. 18cm. (Dolphin bk., C325) 1.45 pap.,
1. Hunter, John, 1728-1793. I. Title.

Hunter, John, 1728-1793—Juvenile literature.

AUCHMUTY, James Johnston. 942.07'3'0924 B
John Hunter, [by] J. J. Auchmuty. Melbourne, New York [etc.] Oxford University Press [1968] 30 p. illus., map. 19 cm. (Great Australians) Bibliography: p. 30. Brief biography of John Hunter, seaman, explorer, and governor of the Australian State of New South Wales, 1795-1801. [DU172.H94A83] 92 74-411300 unpriced
1. Hunter, John, 1738-1821—Juvenile literature. I. Title.

NOBLE, Iris. 617'.0924 B
Master surgeon: John Hunter. New York, J. Messner [1971] 191 p. 22 cm. Bibliography: p. 185. A biography of the eighteenth-century Scottish physician, biologist, and physiologist whose pioneer work in surgery greatly influenced the medical profession. [R489.H9N6] 92 72-140676 ISBN 0-671-32381-4 3.95
1. Hunter, John, 1728-1793—Juvenile literature. I. Title.

Hunter, Joseph Boone.

HUNTER, Joseph Boone. 286'.6'0924 B
Along the way. Fort Worth, Tex., Branch-Smith, 1972. xiii, 171 p. port. 22 cm. Autobiographical. [BX7343.H83A3] 71-188574 ISBN 0-87706-020-7
1. Title.

Hunter, Nora (Siens) 1873-1951.

NEAL, Hazel G 922.89
Madam President; the story of Nora Siens Hunter, founder and first president of the National Woman's Missionary Society of the Church of God, by Hazel G. Neal and Axchie A. Bolitho. Anderson, Ind., Gospel Trumpet Co. [1951] 148 p. illus. 22 cm. [BX7094.C678118] 51-30530
1. Hunter, Nora (Siens) 1873-1951. 2. Church of God (Anderson, Ind.) — Missions. I. Title.

Hunter, Samuel McFadden, 1838-1906?

HUNTER, Robbins, 1880- 923.473
The judge rode a sorrel horse. [1st ed.] New York, Dutton, 1950. 268 p. port. 23 cm. 50-9302
1. Hunter, Samuel McFadden, 1838-1906? I. Title.

Hunting.

LINCKS, Frank M 1882- 926.39
Memoirs of a Kentucky boy. [1st ed.] New York, Vantage Press [1960] 196p. illus. 21cm. [SK17.L53A3] 60-16237
1. Hunting. I. Title.

LINCKS, Frank M. (Cherokee) 926.39
Memoirs of a Kentucky boy. New York, Vantage Press [c.1960]. 196p. illus. 21cm. 60-16237 3.75 bds.,
1. Hunting. I. Title.

Hunting

CHAPMAN, Abel, 1851-1929. 639'.9'0924
On safari; big-game hunting in British West Africa, with studies in bird-life. With 170 illus. by the author and E. Caldwell. London, E. Arnold, 1908. xvi, 340. 16 p. illus., maps. 23 cm. Pages 1-16, 3d group, advertising matter. [SK255.B8C6] 64-58760
1. Hunting — Africa, British East. 2. Birds — Africa, British East. 3. Africa, British East — Descr. & trav. I. Title.

Hunting—Africa.

HARESNAPE, Geoffrey, 1939- comp. 799.2'92'2 B
The great hunters / selected with an introd., biographies and notes by Geoffrey Haresnape. Cape Town ; New York : Purnell, [1974] xv, 129 p., [4] leaves of plates : ill. ; 21 cm. (ELISA series ; v. 3) Contents.—Harris, W. C. Riding down giraffe. A lonely Christmas.—Cumming, R. G. G. A dangerous lion hunt. Antelope, innumerable and rare.—Oswell, W. C. Discovery of "The Great Inland Water". A hunter remembers.—Baldwin, W. C. Narrow escapes. Fire and water.—Chapman, J. Bushman hunters. The hippopotamus.—Selous, F. C. Buffalo hunting. Elephant.—Gillmore, P. A boer hunting party. Discomforts of the pioneer.—Pohl, V. Ready, aim, fire! The leopard stalks its prey.—Pretorius, P. J. A hunt of a different kind. Catching baby elephant.—Wolhuter, H. Mambas. Dragged off by a lion. [SK251.H36] 74-77972 ISBN 0-360-00232-3 : R4.50
1. Hunting—Africa. 2. Hunters—Biographies. I. Title.

Hunting—Burma.

GIRSHAM, Jack. 799.26'0924 B
Burma Jack, by Jack Girsham, with Lowell Thomas. [1st ed.] New York, Norton [1971] 156 p. 22 cm. Autobiographical. [CT1538.G57A3 1971] 75-155490 ISBN 0-393-08647-X 5.95
1. Hunting—Burma. I. Thomas, Lowell Jackson, 1892- II. Title.

Hunting—Pennsylvania.

TOME, Philip, 1782-1855. 917.48'04'0924 B
Pioneer life; or, Thirty years a hunter. [New York] Arno Press [1971] 238 p. 23 cm. (The First American frontier) Reprint of the 1854 ed. [E153.T65 1971] 78-146424 ISBN 0-405-02893-8
1. Hunting—Pennsylvania. 2. Frontier and pioneer life—Pennsylvania. I. Title. II. Title: Thirty years a hunter. III. Series.

Hunting with bow and arrow.

SWINEHART, Bob. 799.29'24 B
Sagittarius. [1st ed.] Covina, Calif., Gallant Pub. Co. [1970] 239 p. illus. (part col.), facsims., maps (part col.), ports. (part col.) 29 cm. Autobiographical. Includes bibliographical references. [SK36.S96] 79-132841 18.95
1. Hunting with bow and arrow. I. Title.

Huntingdon, Henry Hastings, 3rd earl of, 1535 or 6-1595.

CROSS, Claire. 942.0550924 (B)
The puritan Earl: the life of Henry Hastings, third Earl of Huntingdon, 1536-1595. London, Melbourne [etc.] Macmillan; New York, St. Martin's p 1966 [i.e.1967] xviii, 372 p. front., plates (incl. ports.) maps, tables, diagrs. 22 1/2 cm. 55 - (B67-1037) Maps on endpapers. Bibliographical references included in "Notes" (p. [283]-305) [DA317.8.H8C7 1967] 66-18871
1. Huntingdon, Henry Hastings, 3rd earl of, 1535 or 6-1595. I. Title.

Huntingdon, Selina (Shirley) Hastings, countess of, 1707-1791.

MYERS, Lucia. 920.7
Lady Huntingdon, friend of the Wesleys. Montgomery, Ala., Huntingdon College Alumnae Association [1956] 60p. illus. 24cm. [DA483.H8M9] 56-22844
1. Huntingdon, Selina (Shirley) Hastings, countess of, 1707-1791. I. Title.

Huntington, Anna Vaughn (Hyatt) 1876-

EVANS, Cerinda W. 730'.92'4
Anna Hyatt Huntington. Illustrated with photos. by William T. Radcliffe. Newport News, Va., Mariners Museum, 1965. 87 p. illus., ports. 26 cm. [NB237.H8E9] 68-7641
1. Huntington, Anna Vaughn (Hyatt) 1876-

Huntington, Archer Miltob, 1870-1955.

PROSKE, Beatrice Irene (Gilman) 1899- 811.52
Archer Milton Huntington. New York, Printed by order of the Trustess, the Hispanic Soc. of Amer. [c.]1963. 28p. illus. 22cm. 63-1745 1.25
1. Huntington, Archer Miltob, 1870-1955. I. Title. BIP

Huntington, Collis Potter, 1821-1900.

EVANS, Cerinda W 923.373
Collis Potter Huntington. Newport News, Va., Mariners' Museum, 1954. 2v. (775p.) illus., ports., maps. facsims. 24cm. ([Mariners' Museum (Warwick Co., Va.)] Museum publication no. 24) Bibliography: p[711]-747. [HE2754.H8E85] 54-913
1. Hunitington, Collis Potter, 1821-1900. I. Title. II. Series. BIP

LAVENDER, David Sievert, 1910- 385'.0924 B
The great persuader [by] David Lavender. [1st ed.] Garden City, N.Y., Doubleday, 1970. ix, 444 p. illus., maps (part col.) 25 cm. Includes bibliographical references. [HE2754.H8L3] 69-20060 7.95
1. Huntington, Collis Potter, 1821-1900. I. Title.

Huntington, Ellsworth, 1876-1947.

MARTIN, Geoffrey J. 910'.92'4 B
Ellsworth Huntington; his life and thought, by Geoffrey J. Martin. [Hamden, Conn.] Archon Books, 1973. xx, 315 p. illus. 24 cm. Bibliography: p. 276-295. [G69.H86M37] 73-5682 ISBN 0-208-01347-4
1. Huntington, Ellsworth, 1876-1947. I. Title.

Huntley, Chet,

HUNTLEY, Chet, 1911- 818
The generous years; remembrances of a frontier boyhood. New York, Random House [1968] 215 p. illus. 22 cm. Reminiscences by a well known news commentator of his boyhood experiences in Montana during and immediately following World War I. [PN1992.4.H8A3] AC 68
I. Title. BIP

Huntsman, Benjamin, 1704-1776.

BARRACLOUGH, Kenneth Charles. 338.7'66'91420924
Benjamin Huntsman, 1704-1776 / by Kenneth C. Barraclough. [Sheffield] : Sheffield City Libraries, 1976. 16 p. : ill., facsim., maps, 2 plans, port. ; 30 cm. (Local studies leaflets) "This paper is essentially the text of the commemorative lecture given ... at the Cutler's Hall, Sheffield ... 21 June 1976." Includes bibliographical references. [TN140.H79B37] 77-362650 ISBN 0-900660-30-9 : £0.50
1. Huntsman, Benjamin, 1704-1776. 2. Metallurgists—Great Britain—Biography. I. Title. II. Series.

Hurd, Peter, 1904-

HORGAN, Paul, 1903- 927.5
Peter Hurd: a portrait sketch from life. Austin, Pub. for the Amon Carter Mus. of Western Art, Fort Worth, by Univ. of Texas Pr. [c.1964, 1965] 68p. illus. (pt. col.) 29cm. Issued on the occasion of a retrospective exhibition of the artist's work at the Amon Carter Mus., Fort Worth and the Calif. Palace of the Legion of Honor in San Francisco. [ND237.H94H6] 65-13519 7.50 bds.,
1. Hurd, Peter, 1904- I. Amon Carter Museum of Western Art, Fort Worth, Tex. II. California Palace of the Legion of Honor, San Francisco. III. Title.

Hurley, Patrick Jay, 1883-1963.

LOHBECK, Don. 923.273
Patrick J. Hurley. Chicago, H. Regnery Co., 1956. 513 p. illus. 25 cm. [E748.H96L6] 56-12099
1. Hurley, Patrick Jay, 1883-1963.

Hurnscot, Loran,

HURNSCOT, Loran, pseud. 920.7
A prison, a paradise. With an introd. by Kathleen Raine. New York, Viking Press, 1959 [c1958] 320p. illus. 22cm. Excerpts from the author's diary from Nov. 3, 1922-Feb. 20, 1958. [CT788.Z9H8 1959] 59-5648
I. Title.

Hurok, Solomon, 1888-1974.

HUROK, Solomon, 1888-1974. 780'.92'4 B
Impresario : a memoir / by S. Hurok, in collaboration with Ruth Goode. Westport, Conn. : Greenwood Press, 1975, c1946. 291 p., [16] leaves of plates : ill. ; 22 cm. Reprint of the ed. published by Random House, New York. [ML429.H87A3 1975] 75-8838 ISBN 0-8371-8125-9 lib.bdg. : 17.00
1. Hurok, Solomon, 1888-1974. 2. Impresarios—Correspondence, reminiscences, etc. I. Goode, Ruth, joint author. II. Title.

Hurst, Fannie,

HURST, Fannie, 1889- 928.1
Anatomy of me; a wonderer in search of herself. [1st ed.] Garden City, N. Y., Doubleday, 1958. 367 p. 25 cm. [PS3515.U785Z5] 58-10025
I. Title.

Hurst, Gloria, 1928-

HURST, Gloria, 1928- 248'.2'0924 B
No valley too deep / Gloria Hurst. Chicago : Moody Press, c1978. 117 p. ; 22 cm. [BR1725.H855A36] 78-6505 ISBN 0-8024-5947-1 pbk. : 2.95
1. Hurst, Gloria, 1928- 2. Christian biography—United States. 3. Divorcees—United States—Biography. I. Title. BIP

Hurst, Lawrence,

HURST, Lawrence, 1883- 923.773
Sixty-one years in the school room. Boston, Meador Pub. Co. [1952] 255 p. illus. 21 cm. [LA2317.H84A3] 52-9904
I. Title.

Hurston, Zora Neale.

HEMENWAY, Robert E., 1941- 813'.5'2 B
Zora Neale Hurston : a literary biography / Robert E. Hemenway ; with a foreword by Alice Walker. Urbana : University of Illinois Press, c1977. p. cm. Includes index. Bibliography: p. [PS3515.U789Z7] 77-9605 ISBN 0-252-00652-6 : 15.00
1. Hurston, Zora Neale. 2. Novelists, American—20th century—Biography. BIP

HURSTON, Zora Neale. 813'.5'2 B
Dust tracks on a road; an autobiography. With an introd. by Larry Neal. Philadelphia, Lippincott, 1971 [c1942] xxv, 286 p. 21 cm. [PS3515.U789Z5 1971] 73-166497 5.95
I. Title. BIP

Hurtado de Mendoza, Diego, 1503-1575.

SPIVAKOVSKY, Erika, 1909- 946'.04'0924
Son of the Alhambra; Don Diego Hurtado de Mendoza, 1504-1575. Austin, University of Texas Press [1970] xvi, 450 p. illus., facsims., maps, ports. 24 cm. Bibliography: p. [417]-430. [DP175.H8S65] 78-138633 10.00
1. Hurtado de Mendoza, Diego, 1503-1575. I. Title.

Hus, Jan, 1369-1415.

BAILEY, Faith Coxe. 922.44371
John Huss; a biography for teen-agers. Grand Rapids, Zondervan Pub. House [1958] 89p. 20cm. [BX4917.B28] 58-31960
1. Hus. Jan. 1369-1415. I. Title.

GILLETT, Ezra Hall, 1823-1875. 284'.3 B
The life and times of John Huss : or, The Bohemian reformation of the fifteenth century / by E. H. Gillett. New York : AMS Press, [1978] p. cm. Reprint of the 1863 ed. published by Gould and Lincoln, Boston. [BX4917.G5 1978] 77-85271 ISBN 0-404-16150-2 : 28.50
1. Hus, Jan, 1369-1415. 2. Reformation—Czechoslovakia—Bohemia—Biography. 3. Bohemia—Church history. I. Title. BIP

LUTZOW, Franz Heinrich Hieronymus Valentin, Graf von, 1849-1916. 284'.3 B
The life & times of Master John Hus / by the Count Lutzow. 1st AMS ed. New York : AMS Press, 1978. xi, 398 p., [7] leaves of plates : ill. ; 23 cm. Reprint of the 1909 ed. published by J. M. Dent, London. Includes index. Bibliography: p. 383-386. [BX4917.L83 1978] 77-84728 ISBN 0-404-16128-6 : 28.50
1. Hus, Jan, 1369-1415. 2. Reformation—Czechoslovakia—Bohemia—Biography. 3. Bohemia—Church history. I. Title. BIP

SKODACEK, August 922.44371
Adolph, 1913-
John Hus, Biblical preacher. [Pittsburgh] Slovak Evangelical Union of America, 1952. 136 p. 22 cm. [BX4917.S57] 52-64946
1. Hus, Jan. 1309-1415. I. Title.

SPINKA, Matthew, 1890- 284.3
John Hus; a biography. Princeton, N.J., Princeton University Press, 1968. v, 344 p. illus., maps. 23 cm. Bibliography: p. 323-330. [BX4917.S69] 68-20880 10.00
1. Hus, Jan, 1369-1415. **BIP**

SPINKA, Matthew, 1890- 284'.3 B
1972.
John Hus, a biography / Matthew Spinka. Westport, Conn. : Greenwood Press, 1979, c1968. v, 344 p. ; 22 cm. Reprint of the ed. published by Princeton University Press, Princeton, N.J. Includes index. Bibliography: p. 323-330. [BX4917.S69 1979] 78-14366 ISBN 0-313-21050-0 lib. bdg. : 21.00
1. Hus, Jan, 1369-1415. 2. Reformation—Czechoslavakia—Biography.

Husband, Joseph, 1885-1938.

HUSBAND, Joseph, 338.2'7'240924 B
1885-1938.
A year in a coal-mine / Joseph Husband. New York : Arno Press, 1977, c1911. 171 p. ; 21 cm. (Work, its rewards and discontents) Reprint of the ed. published by Houghton Mifflin, Boston. [TN803.H8 1977] 77-70508 ISBN 0-405-10178-3 : 12.00
1. Husband, Joseph, 1885-1938. 2. Coal mines and mining. 3. Coal-miners—United States—Biography. I. Title. II. Series. **BIP**

Husing, Edward B.,

HUSING, Edward B., 926.21384
1901-
My eyes are in my heart, by Ted Husing, written with Cy Rice. Introd by Ralph Edwards. [New York] B. Geis Associates; distributed by Random House [1959] 287 p. illus. 22 cm. [PN1991.4H8A3] 59-13755
I. Title.

Huskisson, William, 1770-1830.

FAY, Charles Ryle, 1884- 923.242
Huskisson and his age. London, New York, Longmans, Green [1951] xv, 398 p. ports., maps, facsims. 23 cm. [DA522.H85F3] 51 13067
1. Huskisson, William, 1770-1830. 2. Gt. Brit.—Hist.—1800-1837. I. Title.

Hussein, King of Jordan, 1935-

HUSSEIN, King of 923.15695
Jordan, 1935-
Uneasy lies the head; the autobiography of His Majesty King Hussein i of the Hashemite Kingdom of Jordan. [New York] B. Geis Associates; distributed by Random House [1962] 306p. illus. 22cm. [DS154.55.H8A3] 62-11165
1. Jordan—Pol. & govt. I. Title.

SNOW, Peter 956.95'04'0924 B
John.
Hussein; a biography. Washington, R. B. Luce [1972] 256 p. illus. 23 cm. Bibliography: p. 253. [DS154.55.S62 1972b] 72-85018 7.95
1. Hussein, King of Jordan, 1935- 2. Jordan—Politics and government.

Husseini, Haj Amin, Grand Mufti of Palestine.

SCHECHTMAN, Joseph B., 923.256
1891
The Mufti and the Fuehrer; the rise and fall of Haj Amin el-Husseini. New York, Yoseloff [c.1965] 336 p. ports. 22cm. Bibl. [DS125.3.H8S3] 64-21348 6.00
1. Husseini, Haj Amin, Grand Mufti of Palestine. I. Title.

Husserl, Edmund, 1859-1938.

CAIRNS, Dorion, 1901-1973. 193 B
Conversations with Husserl and Fink / Dorion Cairns ; edited by the Husserl-Archives in Louvain ; with a foreword by Richard M. Zaner. The Hague : Nijhoff, 1976. xiv, 113 p. : diagrs. ; 25 cm. (Phaenomenologica ; 66) Bibliography of works by E. Husserl: p. 107. [B3279.H94C26 1976] 76-375023 ISBN 9-02-471531-8 : 15.00
1. Husserl, Edmund, 1859-1938. 2. Fink, Eugen. 3. Philosophers—Germany—Biography. 4. Philosophy. I. Husserl, Edmund, 1859-1938. II. Fink, Eugen. III. Title. IV. Series.
Distributed by Humanities **BIP**

NATANSON, Maurice 193 B
Alexander, 1924-
Edmund Husserl; philosopher of infinite tasks [by] Maurice Natanson. Evanston [Ill.] Northwestern University Press, 1973. xx, 227 p. port. 24 cm. (Northwestern University studies in phenomenology & existential philosophy) Bibliography: p. 209-221. [B3279.H94N3] 73-80118 ISBN 0-8101-0425-3 10.00
1. Husserl, Edmund, 1859-1938. I. Title. II. Series.

Huston, John, 1906-

BUACHE, Freddy. v. 12
John Huston [par] Freddy Buache [et al.] [Lyon, Serdoc, 1966] 130 p. illus. 18 cm. (Premier plan. no. 41) "Filmographie;" p. [126]-129; bibliographie: p. 129-130. 67-98359
1. Huston, John. I. Title.

KAMINSKY, 791.43'0233'0924 B
Stuart M.
John Huston, maker of magic / Stuart Kaminsky Boston : Houghton Mifflin, 1978. xiv, 237 p., [6] leaves of plates : ill. ; 24 cm. Includes index. "Filmography": p. [205]-222. [PN1998.A3H795] 77-17017 ISBN 0-395-25716-6 : 8.95
1. Huston, John, 1906- 2. Moving-picture producers and directors—United States—Biography. I. Title.

MADSEN, Axel. 791.43'0233'0924 B
John Huston / by Axel Madsen. Garden City, N.Y. : Doubleday, 1978. p. cm. Bibliography: p. [PN1998.A3H798] 78-55842 ISBN 0-385-11070-7 : 10.00
1 Huston, John, 1906- 2. Moving-picture producers and directors—United States—Biography. I. Title. **BIP**

NOLAN, William F 791.4302330924
1928-
John Huston, king rebel, by William F. Nolan. Los Angeles, Sherbourne Press [1965] 247 p. illus., ports. 22 cm. Bibliography: p. [245]-247. [PN1998.A3H8] 65-15790
1. Huston, John, 1906- I. Title.

Hutcheson, William Levi, 1874-1953.

RADDOCK, Maxwell C 923.273
Portrait of an American labor leader, William L. Hutcheson; saga of the United Brotherhood of Carpenters and Joiners of America, 1881-1954. [1st ed.] New York, American Institute of Social Science [c1955] 430p. illus. 24cm. [HD8073.H8R3] 56-13562
1. Hutcheson, William Levi, 1874-1953. 2. United Brotherhood of Carpenters and Joiners of America. I. Title.

Hutchins family.

HUTCHINS, Jack 929'.2'0973
Randolph, 1927-
The story of Jacob Hutchins of Athol, Massachusetts, Revolutionary soldier : and accounts of other Hutchins who served in the Revolutionary War / by Jack Randolph Hutchins. Rockville, Md. : Hutchins, c1976. xiii, 370 p. : ill. ; 24 cm. Cover title: Jacob Hutchins of Athol. Includes bibliographical references and index. [CS71.H974 1976] 76-14318 7.50
1. Hutchins family. 2. United States—Genealogy. 3. United States—History—Revolution, 1775-1783—Biography. I. Title: The story of Jacob Hutchins of Athol, Massachusetts ... II. Title: Jacob Hutchins of Athol.

Hutchins, Ross E.—Juvenile literature.

HUTCHINS, Ross E. 500.9'2'4 B
Trails to nature's mysteries : the life of a working naturalist / Ross E. Hutchins ; illustrated, with photographs by the author. New York : Dodd, Mead, c1977. 222 p. : ill. ; 24 cm. Includes index. The author describes his boyhood in the Rocky Mountains, his developing interest in plants and animals, and his experiences as a naturalist in various parts of the United States and the world. [QH31.H86A34] 92 76-50554 ISBN 0-396-07401-4 : 6.95
1. Hutchins, Ross E.—Juvenile literature. 2. Naturalists—United States—Biography—Juvenile literature. I. Title.

Hutchinson, Abijah, 1756-1843.

HUTCHINSON, K. M. 973'.04'97 S
Memoir of Abijah Hutchinson / K. M. Hutchinson. New York : Garland Pub., 1977. p. cm. (The Garland library of narratives of North American Indian captivities ; 59) Reprint of the 1843 ed. published by W. Alling, Rochester, N.Y. Issued with the reprint of the 1844 ed. of Kinzie, J. A. M. Narrative of the massacre at Chicago. New York, 1977; the reprint of the 1845 ed. of Phelps, N. A. A history of the copper mines and Newgate Prison, at Granby, Conn. New York, 1977; the reprint of the 1876 ed. of Hayes, C. W. A long journey. New York, 1977; and with the reprint of the 1845 ed. of The Bible boy taken captive by the Indians. New York, 1977. [E85.G2 vol. 59] [E263.V5] 973.3'44'3 B 77-7357 ISBN 0-8240-1683-1 : 25.00
1. Hutchinson, Abijah, 1756-1843. 2. United States. Army. Continental Army—Biography. 3. Vermont—History—Revolution, 1775-1783. 4. Indians of North America—Captivities. 5. Soldiers—United States—Biography. I. Title. II. Series.

Hutchinson, Anne (Marbury) 1591-1643.

ADAMS, Charles Francis, 277.44
1835-1915.
The Antinomian controversy : from his Three episodes in Massachusetts history / by Charles Francis Adams ; edited and with an introd. by Emery Battis. New York : DaCapo Press, 1976. lxvii, 216 p. ; 22 cm. Reprint of pt. 2. of the 1892 ed. published by Houghton Mifflin, Boston. Bibliography: p. [lxiii]-lxvii. [BR555.M4A3 1976] 74-164507 ISBN 0-306-70290-8 : 12.50
1. Hutchinson, Anne (Marbury) 1591-1643. 2. Massachusetts—Church history. 3. Antinomianism. I. Title.

CRAWFORD, Deborah. 973.2'2'0922 B
Four women in a violent time: Anne Hutchinson (1591-1643) Mary Dyer (1591?-1660) Lady Deborah Moody (1600-1659) Penelope Stout (1622-1732). New York, Crown Publishers [1970] 191 p. 22 cm. Bibliography: p. 185-186. Traces the lives of four women who struggled for civil rights and justice in seventeenth-century America. [E187.5.C7 1970] 920 74-127519 4.50
1. Hutchinson, Anne (Marbury) 1591-1643. 2. Dyer, Mary, d. 1660. 3. Moody, Deborah, Lady, 1600-1659. 4. Stout, Penelope, 1622-1732. I. Title.

RUGG, Winnifred 273'.6'0924 B
King.
Unafraid; a life of Anne Hutchinson. Freeport, N.Y., Books for Libraries Press [1970] xii, 263 p. front. 23 cm. Reprint of the 1930 ed. Bibliography: p. [255]-257. [F67.H92R8 1970] 73-114891 ISBN 0-8369-5295-2
1. Hutchinson, Anne (Marbury) 1591-1643. I. Title.

Hutchinson, Anne (Marbury) 1591-1643—Juvenile literature.

FABER, Doris, 1924- 273.6'0924 B
A colony leader: Anne Hutchinson. Illustrated by Frank Vaughn. Champaign, Ill., Garrard Pub. Co. [1970] 64 p. col. illus., col. map. 24 cm. (Colony leaders) A biography of the woman banished from the Massachusetts Bay Colony for disagreeing with the prevailing religious practices. [F67.H92F3] 92 75-111907 2.39
1. Hutchinson, Anne (Marbury) 1591-1643—Juvenile literature. I. Vaughn, Frank, 1915- illus. II. Title.

Hutchinson, John, 1615-1664.

HUTCHINSON, Lucy 942.06'2'0924 B
(Apsley) b.1620.
Memoirs of the life of Colonel Hutchinson. Edited with an introduction by James Sutherland; with the fragment of an autobiography of Mrs. Hutchinson. London, New York, Oxford University Press, 1973. xxix, 347, (12) p. illus., facsims., ports. 24 cm. (Oxford English memoirs and travels) Memoirs based on the ms. now in the Nottingham Castle Museum. Map on lining papers. Includes index. Bibliography: p. xxvi-xxvii. [DA407.H9H7 1973] 74-155348 ISBN 0-19-255403-4 14.50
1. Hutchinson, John, 1615-1664. 2. Great Britain—History—Puritan Revolution, 1642-1660. I. Title. II. Series. **BIP**

Hutchinson, Thomas, 1711-1780.

BAILYN, Bernard. 973.3'14'0924 B
The ordeal of Thomas Hutchinson. Cambridge, Mass., Belknap Press of Harvard University Press, 1974. xx, 423 p. illus. 25 cm. Includes bibliographical references. [F67.H9805] 73-76379 ISBN 0-674-64160-4 12.50
1. Hutchinson, Thomas, 1711-1780. I. Title. **BIP**

GALVIN, John R., 973.2'7'0922
1929-
Three men of Boston / John R. Galvin. New York : Crowell, c1976. 326 p. ; 23 cm. Includes index. Bibliography: p. 303-305. [E302.5.G34] 75-20331 ISBN 0-690-01018-4 : 10.00
1. Hutchinson, Thomas, 1711-1780. 2. Otis, James, 1725-1783. 3. Adams, Samuel, 1722-1803. 4. United States—History—Revolution, 1775-1783—Causes. I. Title. **BIP**

HOSMER, James 974.4'02'0924 B
Kendall, 1834-1927.
The life of Thomas Hutchinson, royal governor of the province of Massachusetts Bay. New York, Da Capo Press, 1972 [c1896] xxviii, 453 p. illus. 22 cm. (The American scene: comments and commentators) [F67.H9806 1972] 70-124926 ISBN 0-306-71038-2
1. Hutchinson, Thomas, 1711-1780. I. Massachusetts (Colony). Governor, 1770-1774 (Thomas Hutchinson). II. Massachusetts (Colony). General Court, 1773.

HUTCHINSON, Thomas, 973.31'0924
1711-1780.
The diary and letters of His Excellency Thomas Hutchinson; captain-general and governor-in-chief of his late Majesty's province of Massachusetts Bay in North America. Compiled from the original documents still remaining in the possession of his descendants, by Peter Orlando Hutchinson. New York, B. Franklin [1971] 2 v. illus., coat of arms, geneal. tables, ports. 22 cm. (Burt Franklin research and source works series, 684. American classics in history and social science, 181) "Originally published: 1884-86." Includes bibliographical references. [F67.H94 1971] 73-132679 ISBN 0-8337-1783-9
1. Hutchinson, Thomas, 1711-1780. 2. Hutchinson family. 3. Massachusetts—History—Colonial period, ca. 1600-1775—Sources. I. Hutchinson, Peter Orlando, comp.

HUTCHINSON, 974.4'02'0924 B
Thomas, 1711-1780.
The diary and letters of His Excellency Thomas Hutchinson, esq. ... Compiled from the original documents still remaining in the possession of his descendants by Peter Orlando Hutchinson. Boston, Houghton, Mifflin, 1884-86. [New York, AMS Press, 1973] 2 v. illus. 23 cm. [F67.H94 1973] 74-170056 ISBN 0-404-03464-0 30.00
1. Hutchinson, Thomas, 1711-1780. 2. Hutchinson family. 3. Massachusetts—History—Colonial period, ca. 1600-1775—

Sources. I. Hutchinson, Peter Orlando, comp. II. Title.

Hutchinson, Thomas, 1711-1780—Exhibitions.

MASSACHUSETTS 974.4'02'0924 B Historical Society, Boston.
Thomas Hutchinson and his contemporaries. Boston, 1974. [24] p. illus. 28 cm. (A Massachusetts Historical Society picture book) [F67.H98068 1974] 74-176072 2.00
1. Hutchinson, Thomas, 1711-1780—Exhibitions. 2. Massachusetts—Politics and government—Colonial period, ca. 1600-1775—Exhibitions. I. Title. II. Series.

Hutley, Walter, 1858-1931.

†HUTLEY, Walter, 266'.023'0924 B 1858-1931.
The Central African diaries of Walter Hutley, 1877 to 1881 / edited by James B. Wolf. [Brookline, Mass.] : African Studies Center, Boston University, 1976. xiv, 299 p. ; 23 cm. (African historical documents series ; no. 4) Bibliography: p. 297-299. [DT351.H87 1976] 77-152578 8.00
1. Hutley, Walter, 1858-1931. 2. London Missionary Society. 3. Africa, Central—Description and travel. 4. Missionaries—Tanzania—Ujiji—Biography. 5. Missionaries—England—Biography. 6. Missions—Tanzania—Ujiji. 7. Ujiji, Tanzania—History—Sources. I. Title. II. Series.

Hutson, Alton, 1903-

HUTSON, Alton, 976.4'847'060924 B 1903-
Alton Hutson : reminiscences of a south plains youth / by William Curry Holden. San Antonio, Tex. : Trinity University Press, [1975] 152 p. : ill. ; 29 cm. Includes bibliographical references and index. [CT275.H7956A33] 74-20118 ISBN 0-911536-54-X : 12.00
1. Hutson, Alton, 1903- I. Holden, William Curry, 1896-

Hutten, Ulrich von, 1488-1523.

HOLBORN, Hajo, 1902- 922.443
Ulrich von Hutten and the German reformation. Tr. [from German] by Roland H. Bainton. New York, Harper [c.1937, 1965] viii, 214p. front. 21cm. (Torchbk., TB1238 Acad. lib.) Bibl. [PA8535.1162] 1.60 pap.,
1. Hutten, Ulrich von, 1488-1523. 2. Reformation—Germany. I. Bainton, Roland Herbert, 1894- tr. II. Title.

HOLBORN, Hajo, 270.6'092'4 B 1902-1969.
Ulrich von Hutten and the German Reformation / by Hajo Holborn ; translated by Roland H. Bainton. Westport, Conn. : Greenwood Press, 1978, c1937. viii, 214 p., [3] leaves of plates : ill. ; 23 cm. A rev. and expanded translation of Ulrich von Hutten. Reprint of the ed. published by Yale University Press, New Haven, which was issued as no. 11 of Yale historical publications studies. Includes index. Bibliography: p. [203]-209. [BR350.H8H6413 1978] 77-25067 ISBN 0-313-20125-0 lib.bdg. : 16.50
1. Hutten, Ulrich von, 1488-1523. 2. Reformation—Germany—Biography. I. Title. II. Series: Yale historical publications : Studies ; 11. BIP

Hutton, Addison, 1834-1916.

YARNALL, Elizabeth 720'.92'4 B Biddle.
Addison Hutton: Quaker architect, 1834-1916. Introd. by George B Tatum Philadelphia, Art Alliance Press [1974] 78 p., [32] p. of illus. 29 cm. Includes bibliographical references. [NA737.H87Y37] 73-13082 ISBN 0-87982-013-6 10.00
1. Hutton, Addison, 1834-1916.

Hutton, Barbara, 1912-

JENNINGS, Dean 917.3'03'90924 B Southern, 1905-
Barbara Hutton; a candid biography. New York, F. Fell [1968] 301 p. illus., ports. 24 cm. [CT275.H796J4] 68-18140
1. Hutton, Barbara, 1912-

VAN RENSSELAER, 973.9'092'4 B Philip.
Million dollar baby : an intimate portrait of Barbara Hutton / by Philip Van Rensselaer. New York : Putnam, c1979. p. cm. Includes index. [CT275.H796V36 1979] 79-18546 ISBN 0-399-12366-0 : 10.95
1. Hutton, Barbara. 2. Millionaires—United States—Biography. I. Title.

Hutton, James, 1726-1797.

BAILEY, Edward 550.924(B) Battershy Sir 1881-
James Hutton--the founder of modern geology; with a foreword by J. E. Richey. Amsterdam, Barking (Ex.) New York, Elsevier, 1967 [i.e. 1966] xii, 161 p. 23 cm. 50/- [QE22.H9B3] (B67 66-28574
1. Hutton, James, 1726-1797. I. Title.

Hutton, William, d. 1861.

BOYCE, 917.13'585'03'20924 B Gerald Egerton, 1933-
Hutton of Hastings; the life and letters of William Hutton, 1801-61, by Gerald E. Boyce. Belleville, Ont., Hastings County Council, 1972. ix, 259 p. illus., maps (on lining papers), ports. 31 cm. Includes bibliographical references. [F1058.H85B68] 73-167016
1. Hutton, William, d. 1861. 2. Ontario—History. 3. Frontier and pioneer life—Ontario. I. Hutton, William, d. 1861. Letters. 1972. II. Title.

Huvaens, Constantijn, heer van Zuilichem, 1596-1687.

BACHRACH, Alfred Gustave 923.2492 Herbert, 1914-
Sir Constantine Huygens and Britain, 1596-1687; a pattern of cultural exchange; v.1. Leiden, Pub. for the Sir Thomas Browne Inst. at the Univ. Pr., [dist. outside the Netherlands by]Oxford [New York, 1963,c.]1962. xii, 238p. illus. (pt. fold.) ports., facsim. 22cm. (Pubns. of the Sir Thomas Browne Inst., Leiden. General ser., no. 1.) Contents.v.1. 1596-1619. Bibl. 63-2181 6.10
1. Huvaens, Constantijn, heer van Zuilichem, 1596-1687. 2. Netherlands Relations (general) with Great Britain. 3. Gt. Brit. Relations (general) with the Netherlands. I. Title. II. Series: Leyden, Rijksuniversiteit. Sir Thomas Browne Instituut. Publications. General series, no. 1

Huvelin, Henri, 1838-1910.

LOUIS-LEFEBVRE, Marie 282'.0924 B Therese.
Abbe Huvelin, Apostle of Paris, 1839-1910, by M.-Th.-Louis-Lefebvre. Translated from the French by the Earl of Wicklow. Enl. ed. with unpublished documents. Dublin, Clonmore and Reynolds [1967] 237 p. port. 22 cm. Imprint covered by label: Christian Classics, Westminster, Md. Translation of Un pretre l'abbe Huvelin. Bibliographical footnotes. [BX4705.H94L63 1967] 79-2545 25/-
1. Huvelin, Henri, 1838-1910. I. Title.

Huxley, Aldous Leonard, 1894- —Bibliography.

ESCHELBACH, Claire 016.823'9'12 John.
Aldous Huxley : a bibliography, 1916-1959 / by Claire John Eschelbach and Joyce Lee Shober ; with a foreword by Aldous Huxley. New York : Octagon Books, 1979. p. cm. Includes index. Reprint of the 1961 ed. published by University of California Press, Berkeley, in series: University of California bibliographic guides. [Z8430.2.E7 1979] [PR6015.U9] 79-9360 ISBN 0-374-92626-3 : 12.50
1. Huxley, Aldous Leonard, 1894- —Bibliography. I. Shober, Joyce Lee, joint author. II. Series: California. University. University of California bibliographies guides.

Huxley, Aldous Leonard, 1894-1963.

GHOSE, Sisirkumar. 730'.92'4
Aldous Huxley, a cynical salvationist. Bombay, New York, Asia Pub. House [1962] 205 p. 23 cm. [[PR6015]] S A
1. Huxley, Aldous Leonard, 1894- I. Title.

HENDERSON, Alexander, 828.914 1910-
Aldous Huxley [Reissue] New York, Russell & Russell, 1964. 258p. 23cm. First pub. in 1935. Bibl. 64-20668 6.50
1. Huxley, Aldous Leonard, 1994-1963. I. Title.

HUXLEY, Laura Archera. 823'.9'12
This timeless moment; a personal view of Aldous Huxley. New York, Farrar, Straus & Giroux [1968] 330 p. illus., facsims., ports. 22 cm. [PR6015.U9Z726] 68-14919
1. Huxley, Aldous Leonard, 1894-1963. I. Title. BIP

THODY, Philip Malcolm 823'.9'12 Waller, 1928-
Huxley: a biographical introduction [by] Philip Thody. New York, Scribner [1973] 144 p. 21 cm. (Leaders of modern thought) (The Scribner library. Lyceum editions: biography) Bibliography: p. [140]-141. [PR6015.U9Z89 1973b] 72-12155 ISBN 0-684-13053-X 5.95
1. Huxley, Aldous Leonard, 1894-1963.
Pbk. 2.95; ISBN 0-684-13056-4. BIP

WATTS, Harold Holliday, 823'.9'12 1906-
Aldous Huxley, by Harold H. Watts. New York, Twayne Publishers [1969] 182 p. 21 cm. (Twayne's English authors series, 79) Bibliography: p. 169-176. [PR6015.U9Z9] 68-24289
1. Huxley, Aldous Leonard, 1894-1963. BIP

Huxley, Aldous Leonard, 1894-1963—Biography.

BEDFORD, Sybille, 1911- 823'.9'12
Aldous Huxley : a biography / Sybille Bedford. 1st American ed. New York : Knopf : distributed by Random House, 1974. xxi, 769 p., xx, [13] leaves of plates : ill. ; 25 cm. Includes index. Bibliography: p. 745-746. [PR6015.U9Z562 1974] 74-7727 ISBN 0-394-46587-3 : 15.00
1. Huxley, Aldous Leonard, 1894-1963—Biography.

Huxley, Elspeth Joscelin Grant, 1907- —Biography.

HUXLEY, Elspeth 967.6'203 B Joscelin grant, 1907-
The flame trees of Thika : memories of an African childhood / Elspeth Huxley. Harmondsworth : Penguin, 1974. 281 p. ; 18 cm. [PR6015.U92Z52 1974] 75-316359 ISBN 0-14-001715-1 : £0.40
1. Huxley, Elspeth Joscelin Grant, 1907- —Biography. 2. Kenya—Social life and customs. I. Title.

HUXLEY, Elspeth 828'.9'1209 B Joscelin Grant, 1907-
Gallipot eyes : a Wiltshire diary / Elspeth Huxley. London : Weidenfeld and Nicolson, c1976. xii, 198 p. : ill. ; 24 cm. Includes index. [PR6015.U92Z523] 76-367539 ISBN 0-297-77078-0 : £4.25
1. Huxley, Elspeth Joscelin Grant, 1907- —Biography. 2. Huxley, Elspeth Joscelin Grant, 1907- —Homes and haunts. 3. Oaksey, Eng.—Description. I. Title.

Huxley, Julian Sorell, Sir, 1887-1975.

BAKER, John Randal, 574'.092'4 B 1900-
Julian Huxley, scientist and world citizen, 1887 to 1975 : a biographical memoir / by J. R. Baker ; with a bibliography compiled by Jens-Peter Green. Paris : Unesco, 1978. 184 p. : port. ; 22 cm. Bibliography: p. 57-184. [QH31.H88B34] 79-309003 ISBN 92-3-101461-7 : 6.00
1. Huxley, Julian Sorell, Sir, 1887-1975. 2. Huxley, Julian Sorell, Sir, 1887-1975—Bibliographies. 3. Biologists—England—Biography. I. Green, Jens-Peter. II. Title.
Dist. by Unipub NYC.

CLARK, Ronald William. 925.9
Sir Julian Huxley, F. R. S. London, Phoenix House; New York, Roy Publishers [1961, c1960] 109p. illus. 19cm. (The Living biographies series) [QH31.H88C5] 60-14482
1. Huxley, Julian Sorell, Sir 1887- I. Title.

HUXLEY, Julian 574'.092'4 B Sorell, Sir, 1887-
Memories [by] Julian Huxley. Harmondsworth, Penguin, 1972. 288, [16] p. illus., facsims., ports. 19 cm. [QH31.H88A3 1972] 72-305572 ISBN 0-14-003435-8 £0.45
1. Huxley, Julian Sorell, Sir, 1887- I. Title.

Huxley, Thomas Henry, 1825-1895.

AINSWORTH Davis, 574'.092'4 B James Richard, 1861-1934.
Thomas H. Huxley. London, J. M. Dent; New York, Dutton, 1907. [New York, AMS Press, 1973] xi, 288 p. port. 19 cm. Reprint of the ed. published in series: English men of science. "EMS 2." Bibliography: p. 255-279. [QH31.H9A5 1973] 70-158236 ISBN 0-404-07892-3 11.50
1. Huxley, Thomas Henry, 1825-1895. I. Series: English men of science.

BIBBY, Harold Cyril. 574'.092'4 B
Scientist extraordinary; the life and scientific work of Thomas Henry Huxley, 1825-1895, by Cyril Bibby. New York, St. Martin's Press [1972] xi, 208 p. illus. 22 cm. Bibliography: p. 183-194. [QH31.H9B48 1972b] 72-77611 8.95
1. Huxley, Thomas Henry, 1825-1895. I. Title.

BIBBY, Harold Cyril. 574'.092'4 B
Scientist extraordinary; the life and scientific works of Thomas Henry Huxley, 1825-1895, by Cyril Bibby. [1st ed.] Oxford, New York, Pergamon Press [1972] xi, 208 p. illus. 22 cm. (The Commonwealth and international library) Half title: Scientist extraordinary: T. H. Huxley. "References and bibliography": p. 183-194. [QH31.H9B48 1972] 78-147937 ISBN 0-08-016514-1
1. Huxley, Thomas Henry, 1825-1895. I. Title.

BIBBY, Harold Cyril. 925.9
T. H. Huxley: scientist, humanist, and educator. 1st American ed. New York, Horizon Press, 1960, c1959 330 p. illus. 23 cm. [QH31.H9B5 1960] 60-8165
1. Huxley, Thomas Henry, 1825-1895.

CLODD, Edward, 1840- 574'.092'4 B 1930.
Thomas Henry Huxley. [Folcroft, Pa.] Folcroft Library Editions, 1974. xiii, 226 p. 24 cm. Reprint of the 1902 ed. published by W. Blackwood, Edinburgh, in series: Modern English writers. Includes bibliographical references. [QH31.H9C6 1974] 74-2491 15.00
1. Huxley, Thomas Henry, 1825-1895 BIP

CLODD, Edward, 1840- 574'.092'4 B 1930.
Thomas Henry Huxley. [Folcroft, Pa.] Folcroft Library Editions, 1974. xiii, 226 p. 24 cm. Reprint of the 1902 ed. published by W. Blackwood, Edinburgh, in series: Modern English writers. Includes bibliographical references. [QH31.H9C6 1974] 74-2491 15.00
1. Huxley, Thomas Henry, 1825-1895 BIP

CLODD, Edward, 1840- 574'.092'4 B 1930.
Thomas Henry Huxley / by Edward Clodd. New York : AMS Press, 1976 p. cm. Reprint of the 1902 ed. published by Dodd, Mead, New York, in series: Modern English writers. Includes bibliographical references and index. [QH31.H9C6 1977] 75-30018 ISBN 0-404-14023-8 : 14.50
1. Huxley, Thomas Henry, 1825-1895. 2. Naturalists—Great Britain—Biography.

COURTNEY, Janet Elizabeth Hogarth, 1865- 192 B
Freethinkers of the nineteenth century / by Janet E. Courtney. Norwood, Pa. : Norwood Editions, 1976. p. cm. Reprint of the 1920 ed. published by Chapman & Hall, London. Contents.Contents.—Frederick Denison Maurice.—Mathew Arnold.—Charles Bradlaugh.—Thomas Henry Huxley.—Leslie Stephen.—Harriet Martineau.—Charles Kingsley. [B1569.C6 1976] 76-17266 ISBN 0-8482-0386-0 : 25.00
1. Maurice, Frederick Denison, 1805-1872. 2. Arnold, Matthew, 1822-1888—Religion and ethics. 3. Bradlaugh, Charles, 1833-1891. 4. Huxley, Thomas Henry, 1825-1895. 5. Stephen, Leslie, Sir, 1832-1904. 6. Martineau, Harriet, 1802-1876. 7. Kingsley, Charles, 1819-1875. I. Title. **BIP**

HUXLEY, Leonard, 1860-1933. 574'.0924 B
Thomas Henry Huxley, a character sketch. Freeport, N.Y., Books for Libraries Press [1969] vii, 120 p. ports. 23 cm. (Select bibliographies reprint series) Reprint of the 1920 ed. [QH31.H9H8 1969] 76-102247
1. Huxley, Thomas Henry, 1825-1895.

HUXLEY, Thomas Henry, 1825-1895. 574'.092'4
Life and letters of Thomas Henry Huxley / by his son Leonard Huxley. New York : AMS Press, [1980] c1900. p. cm. Reprint of the ed. published by D. Appleton, New York. Includes index. [QH31.H9A2 1980] 75-41152 ISBN 0-404-14980-4 : 67.50
1. Huxley, Thomas Henry, 1825-1895. 2. Naturalists—England—Biography. I. Huxley, Leonard, 1860-1933. **BIP**

PARADIS, James G., 1942- 574'.092'4 B
T. H. Huxley : man's place in nature / James G. Paradis. Lincoln : University of Nebraska Press, c1978. p. cm. Bibliogrphy: p. Includes index. [QH31.H9P35] 78-5492 ISBN 0-8032-0917-7 : 13.50.
1. Huxley, Thomas Henry, 1825-1895. 2. Science—Philosophy. 3. Biology—Philosophy. 4. Great Britain—Social life and customs—19th century. 5. Biologists—Great Britain—Biography. **BIP**

PETERSON, Houston, 1897- 574'.092'4 B
Huxley, prophet of science / by Houston Peterson. New York : AMS Press, 1977. xiii, 338 p. ; 23 cm. Reprint of the 1932 ed. published by Longmans, Green, London, New York. Includes index. Bibliography: p. 329-334. [QH31.H9P4 1977] 75-30039 ISBN 0-404-14040-8 : 21.50
1. Huxley, Thomas Henry, 1825-1895. 2. Naturalists—Great Britain—Biography. I. Title. **BIP**

Huygens, Constantijn, heer van Zullichem, 1596-1687.

BACHRACH, Alfred Gustave Herbert, 1914-- 923.2492
Sir Constantine Juygens and Britain, 1596-1687; a pattern of cultural exchange. Leiden, Published for the Sir Thomas Browne Institute at the University Press; [distributed outside the Netherlands by] Oxford University Press. London, 1962- v. illus. (part fold.) ports., facsim. 22 cm. (Publications of the Sir Thomas Browne Institute, Leiden. General series, no. 1) Contents.CONTENTS.--v. 1, 1596-1619. Bibliographical footnotes. [PT5664.Z5B3] 63-2181
1. Huygens, Constantijn, heer van Zullichem, 1596-1687. 2. Netherlands—Relations (general) with Great Britain. 3. Gt. Brit.—Relations (general) with the Netherlands. I. Title. II. Series: Leyden, Rijksunlversiteit. Sir Thomas Browne Instituut. Publications. General series, no.

Huysmans, Joris-Karl, 1848-1907.

BALDICK, Robert. 928.4
The life of J. K. Huysmans. Oxford, Clarendon Press, 1955. 425p. illus. 23 cm. Includes bibliography. [PQ2309.H4Z523] 55-3176
1. Huysmans, Joris Karl, 1848-1907. I. Title.

LAVER, James, 1899- 928.4
The first decadent, being the strange life of J. K. Huysmans. New York, Citadel Press [1955] 278 p. illus. 23 cm. Includes bibliography. [PQ2309.H4Z637 1955] 55-11864
1. Huysmans, Joris Karl, 1848-1907. I. Title.

RIDGE, George Ross. 843'.8
Joris-Karl Huysmans. New York, Twayne Publishers [1968] 123 p. 21 cm. (Twayne's world authors series, 31) Bibliography: p. 117-120. [PQ2309.I14Z68] 67-12271
1. Huysmans, Joris-Karl, 1848-1907.

Hyams, Joseph.

HYAMS, Joseph. 791.43'092'4 B
Mislaid in Hollywood [by] Joe Hyams. New York, P. H. Wyden [1973] xiv, 224 p. 22 cm. [PN1998.A2H9] 73-86178 ISBN 0-88326-064-6 6.95
1. Hyams, Joseph. 2. Moving-picture actors and actresses—United States—Correspondence, reminiscences, etc. I. Title.

HYAMS, Joseph. 070.4'49'791430924 B
Mislaid in Hollywood [by] Joe Hyams. London, New York, W. H. Allen, 1973. xiv, 225 p. ports. 23 cm. [PN1998.A2H9 1973b] 74-161865 ISBN 0-491-01140-7 £3.00
1. Hyams, Joseph. 2. Moving-picture actors and actresses—United States—Correspondence, reminiscences, etc. I. Title.

Hyde, Charles McEwen, 1832-1899.

KENT, Harold Winfield. 285'.8'0924 B
Dr. Hyde and Mr. Stevenson; the life of the Rev. Dr. Charles McEwen Hyde, including a discussion of the open letter of Robert Louis Stevenson. [1st ed.] Rutland, Vt., C. E. Tuttle [1973] 390 p. illus. 22 cm. "Father Damien, an open letter": p. 344-356. Includes bibliographical references. [BX7260.H9K46] 72-83673 ISBN 0-8048-1062-1 10.00
1. Hyde, Charles McEwen, 1832-1899. I. Stevenson, Robert Louis, 1850-1894. Father Damien. 1973. II. Title.

Hyde, Douglas, Pres. Irish Free State, 1860-1949.

DUNLEAVY, Gareth W. 941.59'092'4 B
Douglas Hyde [by] Gareth W. Dunleavy. Lewisburg [Pa.] Bucknell University Press [1974] 92 p. 21 cm. (The Irish writers series) Bibliography: p. 91-92. [DA965.H9D86 1974] 75-168805 ISBN 0-8387-7883-6 4.50
1. Hyde, Douglas, Pres. Irish Free State, 1860-1949. I. Title.
Pbk. 1.95; ISBN 0-8387-7975-1. **BIP**

Hydrocephalus—Personal narratives.

PATTERSON, Katheryn. 616.8588430926
No time for tears. Chicago, Johnson Pub. Co., 1965. 109 p. illus. 21 cm. [RJ496.H9P3] 65-23539
1. Hydrocephalus—Personal narratives. I. Title. **BIP**

Hyer, Robert Stewart, 1860-1929.

BROWN, Ray (Hyer) 923.773
Robert Stewart Hyer, the man I knew. Salado, Tex., Anson Jones Press, 1957. 206p. illus. 25cm. [LD5101.S36517 1911] 57-14800
1. Hyer, Robert Stewart, 1860-1929. I. Title.

Hymn writers.

HATFIELD, Edwin Francis, 1807-1883. 264'.2'0922 B
The poets of the church; a series of biographical sketches of hymn-writers with notes on their hymns. Boston, Milford House [1972] vii, 719 p. 22 cm. Reprint of 1884 ed. [BV325.H38 1972] 78-133349
1. Hymn writers. 2. Hymns, English—History and criticism. I. Title. **BIP**

Hymns, German—Bio-bibliography.

WINKWORTH, Catherine, 1827-1878. 264'.2
Christian singers of Germany. Freeport, N.Y., Books for Libraries Press [1972] xiii, 340 p. ports. 22 cm. (Essay index reprint series) Reprint of the 1869 ed., which was issued as v. 6 of The Sunday library for household reading. [BV480.W5 1972] 72-1295 ISBN 0-8369-2878-4
1. Hymns, German—Bio-bibliography. 2. German literature—History and criticism. I. Title. II. Series: The Sunday library for household reading, v. 6 **BIP**

Hymns writers—Biography.

HATFIELD, Edwin Francis, 1807-1883. 821'.04 B
The poets of the church : a series of biographical sketches of hymn-writers with notes on their hymns / by Edwin F. Hatfield. Detroit : Gale Research, [1978] p. cm. First published in 1884 by A. D. F. Randolph, New York. Includes index. [BV325.H38 1978] 78-19045 ISBN 0-8103-4291-X : 45.00
1. Hymns writers—Biography. 2. Hymns, English—History and criticism. I. Title.

Hyperactive children—Biography.

LIVING with our hyperactive children / edited by Marvin L. Bittinger ; foreword by John F. Zimmer. New York : BPS Books, c1977. 199 p. ; 24 cm. [RJ506.H9L58] 76-56681 ISBN 0-8467-0275-4 : 8.95 618.9'28'58
1. Hyperactive children—Biography. I. Bittinger, Marvin L.

IUr'evskaia, Ekaterina Mikhailovna (Dolgorukova) Kniaginia, 1847-1923.

TARSAIDZE, Alexandre, 1899- 947.08 B
Katia: wife before God. [New York] Macmillan [1970] 349 p. plates, ports. 22 cm. Bibliography: p. 327-336. [DK219.6.I8T37] 69-10467
1. IUr'evskaia, Ekaterina Mikhailovna (Dolgorukova) Kniaginia, 1847-1923. 2. Alexander II, Emperor of Russia, 1818-1881. I. Title.

Ibarra, Francisco de, 1538-1575.

MECHAM, John Lloyd, 1893- 972'.1'020924 B
Francisco de Ibarra and Nueva Vizcaya, by J. Lloyd Mecham. New York, Greenwood Press, 1968. ix, 265 p. fold. maps. 24 cm. Reprint of the 1927 ed. Bibliography: p. [240]-250. [F1231.I13 1968] 68-23315
1. Ibarra, Francisco de, 1538-1575. 2. Nueva Vizcaya, Mexico. 3. Mexico—History—Spanish colony, 1540-1810. I. Title. **BIP**

Ibn Abi Zimra, David ben Solomon, 1479 (ca.)-1589.

GOLDMAN, Israel M., 1904- 301.451'924'0561
The life and times of Rabbi David Ibn Abi Zimra; a social, economic and cultural study of Jewish life in the Ottoman Empire in the 15th and 16th centuries as reflected in the Responsa of the RDBZ, by Israel M. Goldman. New York, Jewish Theological Seminary of America, 1970. xxi, 256 p. facsim. 25 cm. Bibliography: p. 245-251. [BM755.I16G6] 74-141293
1. Ibn Abi Zimra, David ben Solomon, 1479 (ca.)-1589. 2. Jews in Turkey. I. Title.

Ibn Batuta, 1304-1377—Juvenile literature.

MCDONALD, Lucile Saunders, 1898- 910'.92'4 B
The Arab Marco Polo, Ibn Battuta / Lucile McDonald. 1st ed. Nashville : T. Nelson, [1975] 192 p. : maps ; 21 cm. Includes index. A biography of the fourteenth-century Muslim scholar who traveled from his native Tangier to India and China, several times through the Near East, and to black Africa. [G93.I24M32] 92 75-4651 ISBN 0-8407-6441-3 : 6.50
1. Ibn Batuta, 1304-1377—Juvenile literature. I. Title.

Ibn Sa'ud, King of Saudi Arabia, 1880-

PHILBY, Harry St. John Bridger, 1885- 923.153
Arabian jubilee. [1st American ed.] New York, Day [1953] xiv, 280p. illus., ports., map. 24cm. (An Asia book) [DS244.5.I2] 53-9562
1. Ibn Sa'ud, King of Saudi Arabia, 1880- I. Title.

Ibrahima, Abd al-Rahmen, 1762-1829.

ALFORD, Terry. 301.44'93'0924 B
Prince among slaves / by Terry Alford. New York : Harcourt Brace Jovanovich, c1977. p. cm. Includes bibliographical references. [E444.I25A78] 77-73109 ISBN 0-15-174250-2 : 10.95
1. Ibrahima, Abd al-Rahmen, 1762-1829. 2. Slavery in the United States—Mississippi. 3. Slaves—Mississippi—Biography. I. Title. **BIP**

Ibsen, Henrik, 1828-1906.

ACKER, Helen. 920.0481
Four sons of Norway. Illustrated by Nils Hogner. Freeport, N.Y., Books for Libraries Press [1970, c1948] 255 p. illus., ports. 23 cm. (Biography index reprint series) Contents.Contents.—The story of Ole Bull (1810-1880)—The story of Henrik Ibsen (1828-1906)—The story of Edvard Grieg (1843-1907)—The story of Fridtjof Nansen (1861-1930)—Bibliography (p. [256]) [DL504.A2A2] 72-117318
1. Bull, Ole Bornemann, 1810-1880. 2. Grieg, Edvard Hagerup, 1843-1907. 3. Ibsen, Henrik, 1828-1906. 4. Nansen, Fridtjof, 1861-1930. I. Title. **BIP**

BULL, Francis, 1887- 839.8'2'26
Ibsen, the man and the dramatist / by Francis Bull. Norwood, Pa. : Norwood Editions, 1975. 15 p. ; 23 cm. Reprint of the 1954 ed. published by the Clarendon Press, Oxford, issued in series: The Taylorian lecture, 1954. [PT8890.B8 1975] 75-42372 ISBN 0-88305-998-3 : 6.00
1. Ibsen, Henrik, 1828-1906. I. Title. II. Series. The Taylorian lecture, 1954.

IBSEN, Henrik, 1828-1906. 839.8'2'26 B
The correspondence of Henrik Ibsen. The translation edited by Mary Morison. New York, Haskell House, 1970. 463 p. port. 23 cm. Reprint of the 1905 ed. [PT8884.A3M6] 75-124394 ISBN 0-8383-1098-2
I. Morison, Mary, ed. II. Title. **BIP**

JAEGER, Henrik Bernhard, 1854-1895. 839.8'2'26
Henrik Ibsen; a critical biography. From the Norwegian by William Morton Payne. 2d ed., with supplementary chapter by the translator. New York, Haskell House Publishers, 1972. xii, 320 p. illus. 23 cm. Reprint of the 1901 ed. [PT8890.J313 1972] 72-567 ISBN 0-8383-1414-7 11.95
1. Ibsen, Henrik, 1828-1906.

JAEGER, Henrik Bernhard, 1854-1895. 839.8'2'26
Henrik Ibsen, 1828-1888; a critical biography. From the Norwegian by William Morton Payne. New York, B. Blom, 1972. 275 p. illus. 18 cm. Reprint of the 1890 ed. published by A. C. McClurg,

Chicago. [PT8890.J313 1972b] 70-180033 12.75
1. Ibsen, Henrik, 1828-1906. I. Payne, William Morton, 1858-1919, tr. BIP

JORGENSON, Theodore, 1894- 839.8'2'26
Henrik Ibsen : a study in art and personality / by Theodore Jorgenson. Westport, Conn. : Greenwood Press, 1978, c1945. vii, 550 p. ; 24 cm. Reprint of the ed. published by St. Olaf College Press, Northfield, Minn. Includes index. [PT8890.J6 1978] 77-28153 ISBN 0-313-20209-5 lib.bdg. : 29.75
1. Ibsen, Henrik, 1828-1906. 2. Dramatists, Norwegian—19th century—Biography. BIP

KNIGHT, George Wilson, 1897- 839.8226
Henrik Ibsen. New York, Grove [1963, c.1962] 119p. 18cm. (Evergreen pilot bks EP18) Bibl. 62-14932 .95 pap.,
1. Ibsen, Henrik, 1828-1906. I. Title.

KOHT, Halvdan, 1873-1965. 839.8'2'26 B
Life of Ibsen. Translated and edited by Einar Haugen and A. E. Santaniello. New York, B. Blom, 1971. 507 p. geneal. table, port. 26 cm. Translation of Henrik Ibsen, eit diktarliv. Bibliography: p. 482-488. [PT8890.K62 1971] 69-16322
1. Ibsen, Henrik, 1828-1906. I. Title. BIP

MEYER, Hans Georg. 839.8'2'26
Henrik Ibsen. Translated by Helen Sebba. New York, Ungar [1972] v, 201 p. illus. 21 cm. (World dramatists) Bibliography: p. 191-194. [PT8890.M4413] 72-163145 ISBN 0-8044-2616-3 6.50
1. Ibsen, Henrik, 1828-1906. BIP

MEYER, Michael Leverson. 839.8'2'26 B
Ibsen, a biography [by] Michael Meyer. [1st ed.] New York, Doubleday, 1971. xvii, 865 p. illus., facsims., ports. 25 cm. First published in London under title: Henrik Ibsen. Bibliography: p. [818]-822. [PT8890.M47] 78-150906 12.95
1. Ibsen, Henrik, 1828-1906.

ROSE, Henry, fl.1911-1913. 839.8'2'26
Henrik Ibsen: poet, mystic, and moralist. New York, Haskell House Publishers, 1973. 154 p. 23 cm. Reprint of the 1913 ed. published by A. C. Fifield, London. [PT8890.R6 1973] 72-1323 ISBN 0-8383-1428-7 9.95 (Lib. ed.)
1. Ibsen, Henrik, 1828-1906.

ZUCKER, Adolf Eduard, 1890-1971. 839.8'2'26 B
Ibsen, the master builder. New York, Octagon Books, 1973 [c1929] x, 312 p. illus. 23 cm. Reprint of the ed. published by H. Holt, New York. Bibliography: p. 291-306. [PT8890.Z8 1973] 73-4670 ISBN 0-374-98910-9 12.00 (lib. bdg.)
1. Ibsen, Henrik, 1828-1906. BIP

Icart, Louis.

SCHNESSEL, S. Michael. 760'.092'4
Icart / by S. Michael Schnessel. 1st ed. New York : Potter : distributed by Crown, 1976. p. cm. Includes index. Bibliography: p. [N6853.I22S36 1976] 76-14478 ISBN 0-517-52498-8 : 19.95
1. Icart, Louis. 2. Art deco—France.

Ickes, Harold Le Claire, 1874-1952.

ICKES, Harold Le Claire, 1874-1952. 973.917'092'4 B
The secret diary of Harold L. Ickes. New York, Da Capo Press, 1974 [c1953-54] 3 v. 22 cm. (FDR and the era of the New Deal) Reprint of the ed. published by Simon and Schuster, New York. Contents.—v. 1. The first thousand days, 1933-1936.—v. 2. The inside struggle, 1936-1939.—v. 3. The lowering clouds, 1939-1941. [E748.I28A37] 73-21721 ISBN 0-306-70626-1 28.50 (lib. bdg.).
1. Ickes, Harold Le Claire, 1874-1952. 2. United States—Politics and government—1933-1953. I. Title. BIP

Idaho—History.

SONNENKALB, Oscar, 1847-1928. 526.9'2'0924 B
Reminiscences of Oscar Sonnenkalb, Idaho surveyor and pioneer. Edited by Peter T. Harstad. Pocatello, Idaho State University Press, 1972. 66 p. illus. 24 cm. [TA533.S65A33] 72-196223
1. Idaho—History. I. Harstad, Peter T., ed. II. Title.

Idaho—Politics and government.

DUBOIS, Fred Thomas, 1851-1930. 979.6'02'0924 B
Fred T. Dubois's The making of a State. Edited by Louis J. Clements. Rexburg, Eastern Idaho Pub. Co., 1971. 207 p. illus. 24 cm. Autobiography. Bibliography: p. [201]-202. [F746.D815 1971] 75-155301 7.50
1. Idaho—Politics and government. I. Title: The making of a State.

Iddings, Andrew S., 1880-

ERWIN, Paul F. 910'.0924 B
Andrew S. Iddings, explorer; the story of his life and travels, by Paul F. Erwin. Pref. by Lowell Thomas. Cincinnati, Creative Writers & Publishers, 1967. 421 p. illus., facsims, ports. 24 cm. Bibliographical references included in "Footnotes" (p. 415-421) [G226.I3E7] 66-30736
1. Iddings, Andrew S., 1880- I. Title.

Ide, William Brown, 1796-1852.

IDE, Simeon, 1794-1889. 979.4'03'0924
A biographical sketch of the life of William B. Ide, with a minute and interesting account of one of the largest emigrating companies, 3000 miles over land, from the East to the Pacific coast, and what is claimed as the most authentic and reliable account of "the virtual conquest of California, in June, 1846, by the Bear Flag Party," as given by its leader, the late Hon. William Brown Ide. Glorieta, N.M., Rio Grande Press [1967] 239, 137, xx p. 23 cm. (A Rio Grande classic) Half title: Scraps of California history never before published. Reprint, with new prefatory matter and an index, of the 1880 editions of A biographical sketch of the life of William B. Ide, by Simeon Ide, and Who conquered California? by William B. Ide. Who conquered California? consists largely of William B. Ide's letter to Senator M. M. Wambough relating to the situation in California in 1846. The material is also included in practically the same form in A biographical sketch of the life of William BOA biographical sketch of the life of William B. I
1. Ide, William Brown, 1796-1852. 2. Bear Flag Battalion. 3. California—History—1846-1850. I. Ide, William Brown, 1796-1852. Who conquered California? II. Title. III. Title: Who conquered California? IV. Title: Scraps of California history never before published.

Iglesias, Lonnie, d. 1964.

IGLESIAS, Margaret G. 266'.023'0924 B
Messenger to the golden people; the story of Lonnie Iglesias [by] Margaret G. Iglesias. Nashville, Broadman Press [1967] 64 p. illus., group ports. 19 cm. [BV2843.P4I37] 68-12319
1. Iglesias, Lonnie, d. 1964. I. Title.

Iglesias Pantin, Santiago, 1872-1939.

SENIOR, Clarence Ollson, 1903- 328.73'092'4 B
Santiago Iglesias, labor crusader, by Clarence Senior. Foreword by Herman Badillo. Hato Rey, P. R., Inter American University Press [1972] xiii, 98 p. illus. 24 cm. Bibliography: p. 82-95. [HD6592.5.I37S45] 72-91601 ISBN 0-913480-00-2 5.00
1. Iglesias Pantin, Santiago, 1872-1939.

Ignatius Loyola, Saint, 1491-1556.

DON'T turn back! v. 12
A story of St. Ignatius Loyola. Notre Dame, Ind., Dujarie Press [c1958] 143p. illus. 22cm.
1. Ignatius Loyola, Saint, 1491-1556. I. Roberto, Brother, 1927-

Ignatius, Saint, Bp. of Antioch, 1st cent.

CORWIN, Virginia 922.1
St. Ignatius and Christianity in Antioch. New Haven, Conn., Yale University Press [c.]1960. xiv, 293p. Bibliography: p.272-281. 3 maps. 25cm. (Yale publications in religion, 1) 60-7821 5.00
1. Ignatius, Saint, Bp. of Antioch, 1st cent. 2. Antioch. I. Title. II. Title: Christianity in Antioch. III. Series.

Ihwa Yoja Taehakkyo, Seoul, Korea.

KIM, Hwal-ian, 1899- 923.7519
Grace sufficient; the story of Helen Kim by herself. Ed. by J. Manning Potts. Nashville, Upper Room [c.1964] x, 199p. facsims., port. 20cm. 64-24071 1.00
1. Ihwa Yoja Taehakkyo, Seoul, Korea. I. Title.

KIM, Hwal-lan, 1899- 923.7519
Grace sufficient; the story of Helen Kim by herself. Edited by J. Manning Potts. Nashville, Upper Room [1964] x, 199 p. facsims., port. 20 cm. [LG281.S4K5] 64-24071
1. Ihwa Yoja Taehakkyo, Seoul, Korea. I. Title.

Iles du Salut.

WILLIS, William, 1893- 365.9882
Damned and damned again. [New York] St. Martin's Press, 1959. 180 p. illus. 22 cm. Autobiographical. [HV8947.D4W5 1959] 59-10163
1. Iles du Salut. 2. French Guiana—Exiles. I. Title.

Illinois Infantry. 20th Regt., 1861-1865.

GEER, Allen Morgan, 1840-1926. 973.7'81 B
The Civil War diary of Allen Morgan Geer, Twentieth Regiment, Illinois Volunteers / edited by Mary Ann Andersen. Denver : R. C. Appleman, c1977. xxii, 306 p., [2] leaves of plates : ill. ; 22 cm. Bibliography: p. [292]-306. [E505.5 20th.G43 1977] 77-3830 15.00
1. Illinois Infantry. 20th Regt., 1861-1865. 2. United States. Army—Biography. 3. Geer, Allen Morgan, 1840-1926. 4. United States—History—Civil War, 1861-1865—Regimental histories—Illinois Infantry—20th. 5. United States—History—Civil War, 1861-1865—Personal narratives. 6. Soldiers—United States—Biography. I. Title.

Illustrators—England—Biography.

HAMMELMANN, Hanns A. 741'.092'2 B
Book illustrators in eighteenth-century England / Hanns Hammelmann ; edited and completed by T. S. R. Boase. New Haven : Published for the Paul Mellon Centre for Studies in British Art (London) by Yale University Press, 1975. xiv, 120 p., [20] leaves of plates : ill. ; 26 cm. (Studies in British art) Includes indexes. [NC978.H28] 75-2770 ISBN 0-300-01895-9 : 27.50
1. Illustrators—England—Biography. 2. Illustration of books—England. 3. Illustrated books—18th century. I. Boase, Thomas Sherrer Ross, 1898-1974. II. Title. III. Series. BIP

ROBINSON, Charles. 741'.092'4
Charles Robinson / text by Leo deFreitas. London : Academy Editions ; New York : St.Martins Press, 1976 87p. : ill.(some col.) ; 29 cm. Bibliography:p.83-87. [NC978.5.R6D43] 76-11424 ISBN 0-85670-277-3 : 12.50 ISBN 0-85670-282-X pbk. : 7.95
1. Illustrators-England-Biography. I. De Freitas, Leo. II. Robinson, Charles.

Illustrators—United States.

WATSON, Ernest William, 1884-1969. 741.6'0922
Forty illustrators and how they work, by Ernest W. Watson. With chapters by Matlack Price, Norman Kent, and Guy Rowe. Freeport, N.Y., Books for Libraries Press [1970, c1946] xv, 318 p. illus., plates (part col.), ports. 31 cm. (Essay index reprint series) [NC975.W3 1970] 76-121510 ISBN 0-8369-1899-1
1. Illustrators—United States. 2. Illustration of books—United States. I. Title. BIP

Illyes, Gyula, 1902-

GARA, Ladislas, 1905- v. 12
Az ismeretlen Illyes [irta] Gara Laszlo. Washington, Occidental Press, 1965. 178, [1], p. 20 cm. Bibliographical references included in "Jegyzetek" (p. [179]) 65-28178
1. Illyes, Gyula, 1902- I. Title.

GARA, Laszlo, 1904- v. 12
Az ismeretlen Illyes. Washington, Occidental Press, 1965. 178 p. 66-83028
1. Illyes, Gyula, 1902- I. Title. BIP

Imaginary conversations.

DOBREE, Bonamy, 1891- 820.9
As their friends saw them; biographical conversations by Bonamy Dobree. Freeport, N.Y., Books for Libraries Press [1967] 154 p. 22 cm. (Essay index reprint series) Contents.Contents.—Sir John Denham, by Bishop Henry King and Edmund Waller. —Lord Rochester, by Sir George Etherege and Mr. FitzJames.—Young Voltaire, by William Congreve and Alexander Pope.—William Congreve, by Jonathan Swift and John Gay.—The Duchess of Marlborough, by Alexander Pope and William Pulteney.—The Duke of Newcastle, by Lord Chesterfield and General Irwine.—Lord Chesterfield, by Horace Walpole and Dr. Matthew Maty. [PR6007.O354A9 1967] 67-30183
1. Imaginary conversations. 2. Biography. I. Title. BIP

Immerman, Irene.

TOULOUSE-LAUTREC MONFA, Henri Marie Raymond de, 1864-1901 759.4
Toulouse-Lautrec, by Andre Leclerc[pseud.] New York, Crown [1963] 36p. chiefly illus. 18cm. (Little bks. on great artists) First pub. in 1948? under the title: Lautrec. Biographical sketch in French, English, German. Biographical sketch in French, English, German. 63-5635 .69
1. Immerman, Irene. I. Title.

Imperato, Pascal James.

IMPERATO, Pascal James. 614.4'092'4 B
Medical detective / by Pascal James Imperato. New York : R. Marek, [1979] p. cm. Includes index. [RA424.5.I48A35] 79-15315 ISBN 0-399-90058-6 : 10.00
1. Imperato, Pascal James. 2. Epidemiologists—New York (City)—Biography. 3. Health-officers—New York (City)—Biography. I. Title. BIP

IMPERATO, Pascal James. 362.1'0966'23
A wind in Africa : a story of modern medicine in Mali / by Pascal James Imperato ; with photos. by the author. St. Louis : W. H. Green, c1975. xxi, 363 p. : ill. ; 24 cm. Includes index. Bibliography: p. 354-356. [RA390.U5I46] 73-24001 ISBN 0-87527-139-1 : 12.50
1. Imperato, Pascal James. 2. Medical assistance, American—Mali. 3. Missions, Medical—Mali. 4. Vaccination—Mali. 5. Physicians—Correspondence, reminiscences, etc. 6. Mali—Description and travel. I. Title.

Imperial federation.

CARTER, Gwendolen Margaret, 1906- 923.24
The British Commonwealth in the Asian crisis. New York, Foreign Policy Association, 1950. [106]-116 p. 27 cm. (Foreign policy "The Commonwealth and the United States": p. 115-116. Bibliographical footnotes. [D410.F65 vol. 26, no. 10] S D
1. Imperial federation. I. Title. II. Series.

Impostors and imposture.

HYND, Alan, 1908- 364.16'3
The confidence game: kings of the con. New York, Grosset & Dunlap [1970] 184 p. 18 cm. (Tempo books, 5349) "The original versions of the stories ... were first published in True—the man's magazine ... and ... in True detective magazine." Contents.Contents.—Alexander D. L. Thiel.—Sterling Clifford Weyman.—Louis Enricht.—Abraham Sykowski.—Philip Arnold.—David Morton Roll.—John Ernest Worrell Keely.—William F. Miller.—Marion Don Stanley.—Ralph Wilby. [HV6759.H89] 73-123462 0.75
1. Impostors and imposture—U.S.—Case studies. 2. Swindlers and swindling—U.S.—Case studies. I. Title.

MCBRIDE, Robert Medill, 1879- ed. 133.7
Great hoaxes of all time. Edited with notes by Robert Medill McBride and Neil Pritchie. [1st ed.] New York, R. M. McBride Co. [1956] 282p. 21cm. [CT9980.M2] 56-13433
1. Impostors and imposture. I. Pritchie, Neil, joint ed. II. Title.

MATTHEWS, Ronald, 1903- 209'.22 B
English messiahs; studies of six English religious pretenders, 1656-1927. New York, B. Blom, 1971. xvi, 230 p. illus., ports. 21 cm. Reprint of the 1936 ed. Contents.Contents.—James Nayler, "the Quakers' Jesus."—Joanna Southcott, "the bride of the Lamb."—Richard Brothers, "God Almighty's nephew."—John Nichols Tom, "the peasants' saviour."—Henry James Prince, John Hugh Smyth-Pigott and the "abode of love." [BR1718.A1M3 1971] 76-172553
1. Imposters and imposture—Great Britain. 2. Fanaticism. I. Title. **BIP**

MOSS, Norman. 001.9'5'09
The pleasures of deception / by Norman Moss. New York : Reader's Digest Press : distributed by Crowell, 1977. 208 p. ; 21 cm. Includes bibliographical references and index. [CT9980.M6] 77-131 ISBN 0-88349-131-1 : 7.95
1. Impostors and imposture—Biography. I. Title

STOKER, Bram, 1847-1912. 364.1'63 B
Famous impostors. New York, Sturgis & Walton, 1910. Detroit, Gale Research Co., 1974 p. cm. [CT9980.S85 1974] 74-19246 ISBN 0-8103-4100-X
1. Impostors and imposture. I. Title.

Impresarios.

EPSTEIN, Brian 926.5
A cellarful of noise. New York, Pyramid [1965, c.1964] 127p. illus. 18cm. (R1200) [ML429.E6A3] .50 pap.,
1. Impresarios. 2. The Beatles. 3. Musicians—Correspondence, reminscences, etc. I. Title.

EPSTEIN, Brian, 1934- 926.5
A cellarful of noise. [1st ed.] Garden City, N. Y., Doubleday, 1964. 120 p. ports. 22 cm. Autobiographical. [ML429.E6A3 1964] 64-24896
1. Impresarios. 2. The Beatles. I. Title.

Impressionism (Art)—France.

SERULLAZ, Maurice. 759.05
Phaidon encyclopedia of impressionism / [by] Maurice Serullaz ; with contributions by George Pillement ... [et al.] ; [translated from the French by E. M. A. Graham]. Oxford : Phaidon, 1978. 285 p. : ill. (some col.), ports. (some col.) ; 24 cm. Translation of Encyclopedie de l'impressionnisme. Includes index. [ND547.5.I4S4713 1978] 78-62588 ISBN 0-7148-1897-6 : 14.95 ISBN 0-7148-1911-5 pbk. : 8.95
1. Impressionism (Art)—France. 2. Painting, Modern—19th century—France. 3. Painters—France—Biography. 4. Painting—Prices. I. Title.
Distributed by E. P. Dutton, New York, NY **BIP**

Inayat Khan, 1882-1926.

INAYAT Khan, Pir Vilayat. 297'.4'0924 B
The message in our time : the life and teaching of the Sufi master, Pir-o-murshid Inayat Khan / by Pir Vilayat Inayat Khan. 1st ed. San Francisco : Harper & Row, c1978. x, 442 p. : ill. ; 24 cm. Includes bibliographical references and index. [BP80.I55I52 1979] 78-4751 ISBN 0-06-064237-8 : 14.95
1. Inayat Khan, 1882-1926. 2. Sufism—Biography. I. Title.

LONG-KEESING, Elizabeth de. 297.092 B
Inayat Khan: a biography. The Hague, East-West Publications Fonds B. V., in association with Luzac & Co. Ltd. [1974] 302 p. 20 cm. "Translated from the original Dutch edition Golven waarom komt de wind by Hayat Bouman and Penelope Goldschmidt" Includes bibliographical references. [[BP80.155]] ISBN 07189-0243-2
1. Inayat Khan, 1882-1926. I. Bouman, Hayat, tr. II. Goldschmidt, Penelope, tr. III. Title.
Distr. by Rowman and Littlefield, for 12.75 (pbk.) L.C. card no. for original edition: 73-348424

Inchbald, Elizabeth (Simpson) Mrs., 1753-1821.

LITTLEWOOD, Samuel Robinson, 1875- 828'.6'09 B
Elizabeth Inchbald and her circle; the life story of a charming woman (1753-1821), by S. R. Littlewood. [Folcroft, Pa.] Folcroft Library Editions, 1973. p. Reprint of the 1921 ed. published by D. O'Connor, London. "Mrs. Inchbald's books and plays"; p. [PR3518.L5 1973] 73-12207 17.50
1. Inchbald, Elizabeth (Simpson) Mrs., 1753-1821. I. Title.

Independence Sanitarium and Hospital. School of Nursing—History.

BUTTERWORTH, Vida E., 1905- 610.73'0922 B
The girls in white : reminiscenses of an educational director of the Independence Sanitarium and Hospital / by Vida E. Butterworth. Independence, Mo. : Herald Pub. House, c1979. 176 p. ; 20 cm. [RT80.M821522] 78-10862 ISBN 0-8309-0230-9 pbk. : 6.00
1. Independence Sanitarium and Hospital. School of Nursing—History. 2. Butterworth, Vida E., 1905- 3. Nurses—Missouri—Independence—Biography. 4. Independence, Mo.—Biography. I. Title.

India—Biography.

BROWN, Leta May. 922.654
Hira Lal of India, Diamond Precious. St. Louis, Bethany Press [1954] 224p. illus. 21cm. [BV3269.L3B7] 54-43118
I. Lal, Hira, 1875- II. Title.

EDWARDES, Michael. 954.031
Glorious Sahibs; the romantic as empire-builder, 1799-1838. New York, Taplinger Pub. Co. [1969, c1968] 248 p. illus., map, ports. 24 cm. Study based on the careers of four men: David Ochterlony, Charles Metcalfe, John Malcolm, and Mountstuart Elphinstone. Bibliography: p. [239]-241. [DS475.2.A2E3 1969] 69-18365 8.95
1. India—Biography. 2. India—History—19th century. I. Title.

NANDA, Bal Ram. 954.03'5'0922
Gokhale, Gandhi, and the Nehrus : studies in Indian nationalism / B. R. Nanda. New York : St. Martin's Press, 1974, c1973. 203 p. ; 23 cm. Includes bibliographical references and index. [DS481.A1N27 1974b] 74-76991 14.95
1. India—Biography. 2. Nationalism—India. I. Title.

RAMASWAMI AIYAR, Chetpat Pattabhirama, Sir, 1879-1966. 920.054
Biographical vistas; sketches of some eminent Indians. Bombay, New York, Asia Pub. House [1968, c1966] xii, 292 p. 23 cm. [DS434.R27 1968b] SA 68 25.00
1. India—Biography. I. Title.

RAWLINSON, Hugh George, 1880- 954'.0099 B
Makers of India. Freeport, N.Y., Books for Libraries Press [1971, c1942] 78 p. 23 cm. (Essay index reprint series) Originally published in the Living names series. Contents.Contents.—Asoka Maurya.—Sri Harsha of Kanauj.—Akbar, the great Mogul.—Sivaji the Maratha.—Maharaja Ranjit Singh.—Sir Saiyid Ahmed Khan.—Mahatma Gandhi. [DS434.R35 1971] 77-134126 ISBN 0-8369-2251-4
1. India—Biography. I. Title. **BIP**

India—Biography—Dictionaries.

BUCKLAND, Charles Edward, 1847-1941. 920.054
Dictionary of Indian biography. New York, Greenwood Press [1969] xii, 494 p. 24 cm. Reprint of the 1906 ed. Includes bibliographies. [DS434.B8 1969] 69-13845
1. India—Biography—Dictionaries. 2. Great Britain—Biography—Dictionaries. I. Title.

BUCKLAND, Charles Edward, 1847-1941. 920.054
Dictionary of Indian biography. London, S. Sonnenschein, 1906. Detroit, Gale Research Co., 1968. xii, 494 p. 22 cm. Includes bibliographies. [DS434.B8 1968] 68-23140
1. India—Biography—Dictionaries. 2. Great Britain—Biography—Dictionaries. I. Title.

BUCKLAND, Charles Edward, 1847-1941. 920.054
Dictionary of Indian biography. New York, Haskell House, 1968. xii, 494 p. 24 cm. Reprint of the 1906 ed. Bibliography: p. 471-494. [DS434.B8 1968b] 68-26350
1. India—Biography—Dictionaries. 2. Great Britain—Biography—Dictionaries. I. Title. **BIP**

India—Historiography.

SEN, Siba Pada. 954'.007'2
Historians and historiography in modern India. Edited by S. P. Sen. Calcutta, Institute of Historical Studies, 1973. xxviii, 464 p. 24 cm. "Mainly a collection of papers, read at the sixth annual conference of the Institute of Historical Studies, held at Srinagar, ... 1968." Includes bibliographical references. [DS435.S46] 73-905657
1. India—Historiography. 2. Historians—India. I. Title.
Distributed by South Asia books, 24.00 **BIP**

India—History—20th century—Biography.

SINHA, Sachchidananda, 1871-1950. 954.03'5
Some eminent Indian contemporaries / Sachchidananda Sinha. 1st ed. Patna : Janaki Prakashan, 1976. v, 257, ix p. ; 22 cm. Includes index. [DS479.1.A2S58 1976] 77-900864 Rs50.00
1. India—History—20th century—Biography. 2. India—History—19th century—Biography. 3. India—Biography. I. Title.

India—Kings and rulers.

MANKEKAR, D. R. 954.04'092'2
Accession to extinction; the story of Indian princes [by] D. R. Mankekar. Delhi, Vikas Pub. House [1974] xii, 286 p. illus. 22 cm. [DS480.45.M35] 74-900369
1. India—Kings and rulers. 2. India—Politics and government—20th century.
Distributed by International Scholarly Book Services; 10.50. **BIP**

India—Politics and government.

DIVER, Katherine Helen Maud (Marshall) 1867-1945. 954
Royal India; a descriptive and historical study of India's fifteen principal states and their rulers. Freeport, N.Y., Books for Libraries Press [1971, c1942] x, 278 p. illus., ports. 23 cm. (Essay index reprint series) [DS445.D5 1971] 76-142620 ISBN 0-8369-2152-6
1. India—Politics and government. 2. India—Kings and rulers. I. Title.

India—Social life and customs.

CHAUDHURI, Nirad C., 1897- 915.4'03'350924
The autobiography of an unknown Indian, by Nirad C. Chaudhuri. Berkeley, University of California Press, 1968 [c1951] xii, 506 p. 21 cm. [DS421.C47 1968] 68-25418
1. India—Social life and customs. I. Title. **BIP**

LANG, Monica, 1897- 915.4
Invitation to tea. [1st ed.] Cleveland, World Pub. Co. [1952] 284 p. 22 cm. Autobiographical. [DS428.L26] 52-8432
1. India—Social life and customs. I. Title.

Indiana—Biog.—Dictionaries.

HEPBURN, William Murray, 1874- ed. 920.0772
Who's who in Indiana; library of American lives. A reference edition recording the biographies of contemporary leaders in Indiana with special emphasis on their achievements in making the Hoosier State one of America's greatest. Hopkinsville, Ky., Historical Record Association [1957] 248p. ports. 27cm. [F525.H4] 59-51286
1. Indiana—Biog.—Dictionaries. I. Title.

Indiana—Biography—Collected works.

WOOLLEN, William Wesley, 1828- 977.2'00992
Biographical and historical sketches of early Indiana / William Wesley Woollen. New York : Arno Press, 1975 [c1883] p. cm. (The Mid American frontier) On spine: Sketches of early Indiana. Reprint of the ed. published by Hammond, Indianapolis. 75-131 ISBN 0-405-06896-4 : 32.00
1. Indiana—Biography—Collected works. 2. Indiana—History—Collected works. I. Title. II. Title: Sketches of early Indiana. III. Series. **BIP**

Indiana—Governors—Portraits.

PEAT, Wilbur David, 1898- 757'.3'09772074017252
Portraits and painters of the governors of Indiana, 1800-1978 / by Wilbur D. Peat ; biographies of the governors by Lana Ruegamer ; [photography, Robert Wallace]. Rev., edited, and with new entries / by Diane Gail Lazarus. Indianapolis : Indiana Historical Society, 1978. 104 p. : ill. ; 26 cm. Includes indexes. [ND1311.8.I6P42 1978] 79-107666
1. Indiana—Governors—Portraits. 2. Indiana—Governors—Biography. 3. Portraits, American. I. Lazarus, Diane Gail. II. Wallace, Robert, 1921- III. Title.

Indiana. University. Libraries.

SWISHER, Robert. 016.92'073
Black American biography, compiled by Robert Swisher, and Black American scientists, compiled by Carol Tullis, and Black Americans in public affairs, compiled by Richard Hicks. [Bloomington] Indiana

University Libraries, 1969. 52 p. 28 cm. (Focus: Black America bibliography series) [Z1361.N39S93] 73-620741
1. Indiana. University. Libraries. 2. Negroes—Biography—Bibliography—Catalogs. 3. Negro scientists—Bibliography—Catalogs. I. Indiana. University. Libraries. II. Tullis, Carol. Black American scientists. 1969. III. Hicks, Richard. Black Americans in public affairs. 1969. IV. Title. V. Title: Black American scientists. VI. Title: Black Americans in public affairs. VII. Series.

Indianapolis Speedway Race.

†BERGER, Phil. 796.7'2'0922 B
The boys of Indy / by Phil Berger and Larry Bortstein. New York : Corwin Books, c1977. 181 p. : ill. ; 24 cm. Contents.Contents.—Jerry Karl.—Al Unser.—Jan Opperman.—Bill Simpson.—John Martin.—Salt Walther.—Johnny Parsons.—Lloyd Ruby.—Wally Dallenbach.—Mark Donohue.—Dick Simon.—Johnny Rutherford. [GV1032.A1B42] 76-55144 ISBN 0-89474-002-4 : 8.95
1. Indianapolis Speedway Race. 2. Automobile racing drivers—United States—Biography. I. Bortstein, Larry, joint author. II. Title. **BIP**

DEVANEY, John. 796.7'2'0680977252
The Indianapolis 500 : a complete pictorial history / by John and Barbara Devaney Chicago : Rand McNally, c1976. p. cm. Includes index. [GV1033.5.I55D47] 76-23129 ISBN 0-528-81844-9 : 16.95
1. Indianapolis Speedway Race. 2. Automobile racing—Biography. I. Devaney, Barbara, joint author. II. Title.

LIBBY, Bill. 796.7'2'0922 B
Champions of the Indianapolis 500 the men who have won more than once / by Bill Libby. New York : Dodd, Mead, c1976. 175 p. : ill. ; 24 cm. Includes index. [GV1032.A1L5] 76-87 ISBN 0-396-07306-9 : 7.95
1. Indianapolis Speedway Race. 2. Automobile racing—United States—Biography. I. Title.

Indians of North America.

CROOK, George, 1828-1890. 923.573
General George Crook, his autobiography. Edited and annotated by Martin F. Schmitt. [new ed.] Norman, University of Oklahoma Press [1960] xx, 326 p. illus., ports., maps. 22 cm. Bibliography: p. 310-317. [E83.866.C93 1960] 60-8386
1. Indians of North America—Wars—1866-1895. 2. Pacific coast Indians, Wars with, 1847-1865.

CUSTER, George Armstrong, 1839-1876. 923.573
My life on the Plains. [Edited by Milo Milton Quaife] New York, Citadel Press [1962] 625 p. illus. 17 cm. (A Citadel pioneer book) 62-9215
1. Indians of North America — Wars — 1866-1895. 2. Great Plains — Descr. & trav. I. Title.

CUSTER, George Armstrong, 1839--1876. 923.573
My life on the plains. Edited by Milo Milton Quaife. Chicago, Lakeside Press, 1952. xiix, 626p. illus., ports., map. facsim. 17cm. (The Lakeside classics. no. 50) [F594.C97 1952] 53-1763
1. Indians of North America—Wars—1866-1895. 2. Great Plains—Descr. & trav. I. Title.

CUSTER, George Armstrong, 1893-1876. v. 12
My life on the Plains. Edited by Milo Milton Quaife. Lincoln, University of Nebraska Press [1966?] xli, 626 p. illus. (Bison books. BB328) 67-2618
1. Indians of North America — Wars — 1866-1895. 2. Great Plains — Descr. & trav. I. Title. **BIP**

DRAKE, Samuel Gardner, 1798-1875. 970.3 B
Biography and history of the Indians of North America ... Freeport, N.Y., Books for Libraries Press [1973] p. Reprint of the 1837 ed. published by the Antiquarian Institute, Boston. First ed., Boston, 1832, has title: Indian biography. [E77.D7924] 73-4433 ISBN 0-518-19028-5
1. Indians of North America. 2. Indians of North America—Biography. I. Title.

GREGG, Elinor D 610.7340924 (B)
The Indians and the nurse, by Elinor D. Gregg. [1st ed.] Norman. University of Oklahoma Press [1965] xiv, 173 p. 19 cm. (The Western frontier library, 28) Autobiographical. [R.A448.5. I 5G7] 65-24207
1. Indians of North America — Health and hygiene. 2. Public health nursing — U.S. U.S. Bureau of Indian Affairs. I. Title.

HOWARD, Oliver Otis, 1830-1909. 970.1
My life and experiences among our hostile Indians; a record of personal observations, adventures, and campaigns among the Indians of the great West, with some account of their life, habits, traits, religion, ceremonies, dress, savage instincts, and customs in peace and war. New introd. by Robert M. Utley. New York, Da Capo Press, 1972. xvii, 570 p. illus. 22 cm. Reprint of the 1907 ed. Bibliography: p. [xviii] [E83.866.H84 1972] 76-87436 ISBN 0-306-71506-6
1. Indians of North America. 2. Indians of North America—Wars—1866-1895. I. Title.

MILES, Nelson Appleton, 1839-1925. 355.3'32'0924 B
Personal recollections and observations of General Nelson A. Miles. New introd. by Robert M. Utley. New York, Da Capo Press, 1969. ix, [7], 590 p. illus., map, ports. 27 cm. (The American scene) (A Da Capo Press reprint series.) Reprint of the 1896 ed. with a new introduction and bibliography. Bibliography: p. [x] [E83.866.M64 1969] 68-23812
1. Indians of North America—Wars—1866-1895. 2. United States—History—Civil War, 1861-1865—Personal narratives. 3. Indians of North America. 4. The West—Description and travel—1860-1880. 5. Pacific coast. I. Title. **BIP**

SMET, Pierre Jean de, 1801-1873. 271'.5'0924 B
Life, letters, and travels of Father de Smet. [Edited by] Hiram Martin Chittenden and Alfred Talbot Richardson. New York, Arno Press, 1969. 4 v. (xv, 1624 p.) illus., facsims., fold. map, ports. 23 cm. (Religion in America) Reprint of the 1905, c1904 ed. Bibliography: v. 1, p. 144-146. [F591.S63 1969] 75-83418
1. Indians of North America. 2. The West—Description and travel—To 1848. 3. Northwestern States—Description and travel. 4. Northwest, Canadian—Description and travel. I. Chittenden, Hiram Martin, 1858-1917, ed. II. Richardson, Alfred Talbot, ed.

Indians of North America—Bibliography—Catalogs.

U.S. Dept. of the Interior. Library. 016.9701
Biographical and historical index of American Indians and persons involved in Indian affairs. Boston, G. K. Hall, 1966. 8 v. 36 cm. A subject index developed in the library of the Bureau of Indian Affairs under Mrs. Anita S. Tilden. In 1949, this library was consolidated with other bureau libraries to form the library of the Department of the Interior where the index is now located. From 1951 to late 1965, Mrs. Eugenia Langford continued the work of the index. [Z1209.U494] 77-5470
1. Indians of North America—Bibliography—Catalogs. I. Langford, Eugenia. II. Tilden, Anita S. III. U.S. Bureau of Indian Affairs. Library. IV. Title. **BIP**

Indians of North America—Biography.

ANDREWS, Ralph Warren, 1897- 970.3 B
Indian leaders who helped shape America, by Ralph W. Andrews. [1st ed. Seattle, Superior Pub. Co., c1971] 184 p. illus. 28 cm. Bibliography: p. 182. [E89.A82] 76-160187 12.95
1. Indians of North America—Biography. 2. Indians of North America—Portraits. I. Title.

DICTIONARY of Indians of North America / [Frank H. Gille, publisher ; Harry Waldman ... [et al.] editors]. St. Clair Shores, Mich. : Scholarly Press, c1978. 3 v. : ports. ; 21 cm. [E89.D43] 78-65222 ISBN 0-403-01799-8 : 125.00 (set) 920'.0092'97
1. Indians of North America—Biography. 2. Indians of Mexico—Biography. I. Gille, Frank H. II. Waldman, Harry.

DOCKSTADER, Frederick J. 920'.0092'97
Great North American Indians : profiles in life and leadership / Frederick J. Dockstader. New York : Van Nostrand Reinhold, [1977] p. cm. Includes index. Bibliography: p. [E89.D55] 77-23733 ISBN 0-442-02148-8 : 16.95
1. Indians of North America—Biography. I. Title. **BIP**

JOHNSTON, Charles Haven Ladd, 1877-1943. 970.4'3'0922
Famous Indian chiefs; their battles, treaties, sieges, and struggles with the whites for the possession of America. Freeport, N.Y., Books for Libraries Press [1971, c1909] xiii, 458 p. illus., ports. 23 cm. (Essay index reprint series) [E89.J72 1971] 76-152179 ISBN 0-8369-2232-8
1. Indians of North America—Biography. I. Title.

LEIPOLD, L. Edmond, 1902- 920
Famous American Indians, by L. Edmond Leipold. Minneapolis, T. S. Denison [1967] 79 p. 25 cm. (His Famous American heroes and leaders series) Short biographies of ten Americans of Indian ancestry, who made contributions to the civilization of the United States. Includes Geronimo, Jim Thorpe, Glen Curtis, and others. [E89.L48] AC 68
1. Indians of North America—Biography. I. Title.

MOYER, John William. 970.2
Famous Indian chiefs. Illustrated by James L. Vlasaty. Chicago, M. A. Donohue [1957] 81 p. illus. 31 cm. [E89.M84] 57-8406
1. Indians of North America—Biography. 2. Indians of North America—Portraits. **BIP**

STEMBER, Sol. 970.1'0922
Heroes of the American Indian. New York, Fleet Press Corp. [1971] 124 p. illus. 24 cm. Bibliography: p. 119. Traces the history of the American Indian with emphasis on the lives of notable Indian leaders from tribes throughout the United States. [E89.S82] 920 70-100088 5.00
1. Indians of North America—Biography. I. Title. **BIP**

THATCHER, Benjamin Bussey, 1809-1840. 970.1'092'2 B
Indian biography; or, An historical account of those individuals who have been distinguished among the North American natives as orators, warriors, statemen, and other remarkable characters. Glorieta, N.M., Rio Grande Press [1973] 2 v. illus. 24 cm. (A Rio Grande classic) Reprint of the 1832 ed. published by A. L. Fowle, New York; with a new pref. by W. N. Fenton. [E89.T36 1973] 73-14660 ISBN 0-87380-089-3 20.00
1. Indians of North America—Biography. 2. Indians of North America—History. I. Title. **BIP**

Indians of North America—Biography—Congresses.

AMERICAN Indian intellectuals / edited by Margot Liberty. St. Paul : West Pub. Co., c1978. viii, 248 p. : ill. ; 25 cm. (Proceedings of the American Ethnological Society ; 1976) Papers from the American Ethnological Society spring symposium, held in Atlanta, Mar. 31-Apri. 1, 1976. Includes bibliographies. [E89.A47] 78-315669 ISBN 0-8299-0223-6 pbk. : 10.95 920'.0092'97
1. Indians of North America—Biography—Congresses. 2. Anthropologists—United States—Biography—Congresses. I. Liberty, Margot. II. Series: American Ethnological Society. Proceedings of the American Ethnological Society ; 1976.

Indians of North America—Biography—Juvenile literature.

DEUR, Lynne. 970.1'0922 B
Indian chiefs. Minneapolis, Lerner Publications Co. [1972] 103 p. illus. 22 cm. (A Pull ahead book) Biographies of thirteen American Indian leaders who tried to halt the gradual destruction of their people. [E89.D39 1972] 920 75-128807 ISBN 0-8225-0461-8
1. Indians of North America—Biography—Juvenile literature. I. Title.

FRANCO, John M. 973'.04'97 B
American Indian contributors to American life / senior author, John M. Franco, writers, Katherine Logan, Suzanne Shade, Elizabeth Brown. Westchester, Ill. : Benefic Press, [1975] 192 p. : ill. ; 24 cm. Includes bibliographies and index. Sketches on three reading levels the lives and achievements of twenty North American Indians. [E89.F72] 920 74-17531 ISBN 0-8175-5611-7
1. Indians of North America—Biography—Juvenile literature. 2. Indians of North America—Biography. I. Title.

GRIDLEY, Marion Eleanor, 1906- 970.3 B
Contemporary American Indian leaders [by] Marion E. Gridley. New York, Dodd, Mead [1972] xix, 201 p. ports. 22 cm. Brief biographies of twenty-six Indians from various tribes and professions who are devoted to the advancement of their people. [E89.G74] 72-3148 ISBN 0-396-06633-X 4.95
1. Indians of North America—Biography—Juvenile literature. I. Title. **BIP**

HEUMAN, William. 970.1'092'2 B
Famous American Indians. New York, Dodd, Mead [1972] 128 p. ports. 22 cm. (Famous biographies for young people) Contents.Contents.—King Philip (1639-1676)—Pontiac (1720-1769)—Joseph Brant (1742-1807)—Sequoyah (1760-1843)—Tecumseh (1768-1813)—Osceola (1804-1838)—Chief Joseph (1840-1904)—Crazy Horse (1842-1877)—Sitting Bull (1837-1890)—A look forward. [E89.H46] 920 74-38565 ISBN 0-396-06510-4 3.50
1. Indians of North America—Biography—Juvenile literature. I. Title.

JOHNSTON, Johanna. 970.3 B
The Indians and the strangers. Illustrated with woodcuts by Rocco Negri. New York, Dodd, Mead [1972] 109 p. illus. 24 cm. [E89.J73] 920 72-1447 ISBN 0-396-06610-0 4.50
1. Indians of North America—Biography—Juvenile literature. I. Negri, Rocco, illus. II. Title.
Contents omitted. **BIP**

LEIPOLD, L. Edmond, 1902- 920 (J)
Famous American Indians, by L. Edmond Leipold. Minneapolis, T. S. Denison [1967] 79 p. 25 cm. (His Famous American heroes and leaders series) [E89.L48] 67-26345
1. Indians of North America—Biography—Juvenile literature. I. Title.

MOLLOY, Anne Stearns (Baker) 1907- 974.1'01'0922
Five kidnapped Indians; a true 17th century account of five early Americans: Tisquantum, Nahanada, Skitwarroes, Assocomoit, and Maneday, by Anne Molloy. Illustrated by Robin Jacques. New York, Hastings House [1968] xiv, 194 p. illus., map. 22 cm. Published in 1956 under title: Captain Waymouth's Indians. Bibliography: p. 190-191. Traces the travels, trials, and attempts to return to America of five Indians kidnapped off the coast of Maine in 1605 and carried to England as prime sources of information about the resources of the New World. [E89.M76 1968] 920 68-17652 3.95
1. Indians of North America—Biography—

Juvenile literature. I. Jacques, Robin, illus. II. Title.

ROLAND, Albert. 920 (J)
Great Indian chiefs. New York, Crowell-Collier Press [1966] vi, 152 p. illus., port. 22 cm. (America in the making) [E89.R6] 66-8941
1. Indians of North America—Biography—Juvenile literature. I. Title. **BIP**

SIGNIFICANT American 920'.0092'97
Indians. Chicago : Childrens Press, [1976] p. cm. Includes index. Brief biographies of 177 Indians arranged alphabetically within broad chronological periods of American history. [E89.S46] 920 75-20683 ISBN 0-516-05305-1 : 6.95
1. Indians of North America—Biography—Juvenile literature. I. Title: Indians.

WAYNE, Bennett. 973'.04'97 B
Indian patriots of the eastern woodlands / edited, with commentary by Bennett Wayne. Scarsdale, N.Y. : Garrard Pub. Co., c1976. 168 p. : ill. ; 22 cm. (A Target book) Includes index. Brief biographies of four Indian chiefs: Massasoit, Tecumseh, Black Hawk, and Osceola. [E89.W38] 920 75-20048 ISBN 0-8116-4916-4 : 4.48
1. Indians of North America—Biography—Juvenile literature. I. Title. **BIP**

Indians of North America—Canada—Biography.

MACEWAN, John Walter 970.41 B
Grant, 1902-
Portraits from the plains [by] J. W. Grant MacEwan. Toronto, New York, McGraw-Hill Co. of Canada [1971] 287 p. illus., map, ports. 22 cm. [E78.C2M213] 76-158645 ISBN 0-07-092909-2
1. Indians of North America—Canada—Biography. I. Title.

Indians of North America—Captivities.

FROST, John, 1800- 973'.04'97 S
1859.
Heroic women of the West / John Frost. New York : Garland Pub., 1976. p. cm. (The Garland library of narratives of North American Indian captivities ; v. 66) Reprint of the 1854 ed. published by A. Hart, Philadelphia. [E85.G2 vol. 66] 920.72'0978 75-7090 ISBN 0-8240-1690-4 lib.bdg. : 21.00
1. Indians of North America—Captivities. 2. Women United States—Biography. 3. Frontier and pioneer life—United States. I. Title. II. Series.

JOHNSON, John W., b.1829. 970.3
Indian John; life of John W. Johnson. Copied from the book by Edward Johnson Ladd. Fort Payne, Ala., 1962. 1 v. (unpaged) 29 cm. [E87.J68] 974.8'22'030924 71-210254
1. Indians of North America—Captivities. I. Ladd, Edward Johnson, 1906- ed. II. Title.

†MATHER, Cotton, 973'.04'97 S
1663-1728.
Good fetch'd out of evil / Cotton Mather. New York : Garland Pub., 1977. 46 p. ; 23 cm. (The Garland library of narratives of North American Indian captivities ; v. 4) Reprint of the 1706 ed. printed by B. Green, Boston. Issued with the reprint of the 1699 ed. of Dickinson, J. Gods protecting providence. New York, 1977. [E85.G2 vol. 4] 973.2'5 77-2272 25.00
1. Indians of North America—Captivities. 2. United States—History—Queen Anne's War, 1702-1713—Personal narratives. 3. United States—Biography. I. Title. II. Series.

STEELE, Zadock, 973.33'6'0924 B
1758-1845.
The Indian captive; or, A narrative of the captivity and sufferings of Zadock Steele. To which is prefixed an account of the burning of Royalton. [New York] B. Blom [1971] xiii, 166 p. map. 21 cm. (Indian captivities series) Reprint of the 1908 ed. Half-title: Captivity and sufferings of Zadock Steele. [E87.S82 1971] 71-173120
1. Indians of North America—Captivities. 2. Royalton, Vt.—Burning by the British and Indians, 1780. I. Title. II. Title: A narrative of the captivity and sufferings of Zadock Steele. III. Title: Captivity and sufferings of Zadock Steele. **BIP**

Indians of North America—Children—Juvenile literature.

EASTMAN, Charles 970.3 B
Alexander, 1858-
Indian boyhood. With illus. by E. L. Blumenschein. New York, Dover Publications [1971] viii, 247 p. illus. 22 cm. Reprint of the 1902 ed. A full-blooded Sioux Indian describes his childhood experiences and training as a warrior in the 1870's and 1880's until he was taken to live in the white man's world at age fifteen. [E99.D1E17 1971] 92 68-58282 ISBN 0-486-22037-0 2.00
1. Indians of North America—Children—Juvenile literature. 2. Dakota Indians—Juvenile literature. I. Blumenschein, Ernest Leonard, 1874-1960, illus. II. Title.

EASTMAN, Charles 970.3 B
Alexander, 1858-
Indian boyhood. With illus. by E. L. Blumenschein. New York, McClure, Philips, 1902. Ann Arbor, Mich., Gryphon Books, 1971. viii, 289 p. illus. 22 cm. A full-blooded Sioux Indian describes his childhood experiences and training as a warrior in the late nineteenth century until he was taken to live in the white man's world at age fifteen. [E99.D1E17 1971b] 92 79-170250
1. Indians of North America—Children—Juvenile literature. 2. Dakota Indians—Juvenile literature. I. Blumenschein, Ernest Leonard, 1874-1960, illus. II. Title. **BIP**

Indians of North America—Culture.

SUN Bear (Chippewa 917.3'06'97 B
Indian)
Buffalo hearts; a native American's view of Indian culture, religion and history. Healdsburg, Calif., Naturegraph Publishers, c1970. 128 p. illus., ports. 23 cm. Pages 125-128, blank for "Notes." Bibliography: p. 122-124. [E98.C9S87] 72-296573 ISBN 0-911010-86-6
1. Indians of North America—Culture. 2. Indians of North America—Biography. I. Title.

Indians of North America—History.

MCKENNEY, Thomas Loraine, 920
1785-1859.
Biographical sketches and anecdotes of ninety-five of 120 principal chiefs from the Indian tribes of North America, by Thomas L. Mckenney and James Hall. [Washington] U.S. Dept. of the Interior, Bureau of Indian Affairs [1967] xvi, 452 p. 25 cm. Reprint of History of the Indian tribes of North America, with biographical sketches and anecdotes of the principal chiefs. Embellished with one hundred and twenty portraits, from the Indian gallery in the Department of War, at Washington. By Thomas L. M'Kenney and James Hall. Vol. 1. Philadelphia, F. W. Greenough, 1838. [E77.M133 1967] 68-60299
1. Indians of North America—History. 2. Indians on North America—Biography. I. Hall, James, 1793-1868. II. Title.

MCKENNEY, Thomas Loraine, 970.3 B
1785-1859.
The Indian tribes of North America, with biographical sketches and anecdotes of the principal chiefs [by] Thomas L. McKenney and James Hall. Edited by Frederick Webb Hodge. Totowa, N.J., Rowman and Littlefield [1972- v. illus., fold. col. maps. 24 cm. Volume 3 includes an introd. by J. H. Braunholtz. Reprint of the 1933-34 ed. which was first published in 1836-44 under title: History of the Indian tribes of North America. Includes bibliographical references. [E77.M1355] 72-196021 ISBN 0-87471-119-3
1. Indians of North America—History. 2. Indians of North America—Biography. 3. Indians of North America—Portraits. I. Hall, James, 1793-1868, joint author. II. Title.

Indians of North America—Juvenile literature.

WE rode the wind : 970'.004'97
recollections of nineteenth-century tribal life / compiled and edited by Jane B. Katz. Minneapolis : Lerner Publications Co., [1975] 110 p. : ill. ; 23 cm. (Voices of the American Indian) Contents.Contents.—Eastman, C. A. Selections from Indian boyhood.—Stands in Timber, J. Selections from Cheyenne memories.—Two Leggings. Selections from Two Leggings.—Standing Bear, L. Selections from My people, the Sioux, and Land of the Spotted Eagle.—Warren, W. W. Selections from History of the Ojibway Nation.—Waheenee. Selections from Waheenee.—Whitewolf, J. Selections from Jim Whitewolf.—Black Elk. Selections from Black Elk speaks. [E77.4.W38 1975] 920 74-11909 ISBN 0-8225-0639-4 lib.bdg. : 6.95
1. Indians of North America—Juvenile literature. 2. Indians of North America—Biography—Juvenile literature. I. Katz, Jane B. II. Title. III. Series.
Contents omitted.

Indians of North America—Missions.

BRAINERD, David, 266.5'10924 B
1718-1747.
Memoirs of the Rev. David Brainerd, missionary to the Indians on the border of New York, New Jersey, and Pennsylvania; chiefly taken from his own diary, by Jonathan Edwards. Including his journal, now for the first time incorporated with the rest of his diary, in a regular chronological series, by Sereno Edwards Dwight. New Haven, S. Converse, 1822. St. Clair Shores, Mich., Scholarly Press, 1970. 504 p. 22 cm. First ed., 1749, published under title: An account of the life of the late Reverend Mr. David Brainerd. [E98.M6B7863] 70-108477
1. Indians of North America—Missions. I. Edwards, Jonathan, 1703-1758, ed. II. Dwight, Sereno Edwards, 1786-1850. III. Title.

Indians of North America—New Mexico.

ARNY, William 970.4'89'0924
Frederick Milton, 1813-1881.
Indian agent in New Mexico; the journal of special agent W. F. M. Arny, 1870. With introd. and notes by Lawrence R. Murphy. [1st ed.] Santa Fe [N.M.] Stagecoach Press [1967] 62 p. port. 18 cm. (Southwestern series, no. 5) [E78.N65A84] 67-23509
1. Indians of North America—New Mexico. 2. Indians of North America—Government relations—1869-1934. 3. New Mexico—Description and travel. I. Title.

Indians of North America—Ohio—Biography.

OHIO Historical 970.4'71 B
Society.
Indian chiefs of Ohio. Columbus [1971?] 1 portfolio (fold. map, 8 plates) 31 cm. [E78.O3O34] 73-171957
1. Indians of North America—Ohio—Biography. I. Title.

Indians of North America—The West.

RED Fox, Chief, 1870- 970.3 B
The memoirs of Chief Red Fox. With an introd. by Cash Asher. [1st ed.] New York, McGraw-Hill [1971] xii, 208 p. illus., ports. 22 cm. [E90.R4A3] 70-146473 ISBN 0-07-051362-7 6.95
1. Indians of North America—The West. I. Title.

Indians of North America—The West—Biography.

TIME-LIFE Books. 970'.004'97
The great chiefs / by the editors of Time-Life Books ; with text by Benjamin Capps. New York : Time-Life Books, c1975. 240 p. : ill. (some col.) ; 28 cm. (The Old West) Includes index. Bibliography: p. 236-237. [E78.W5T55 1975] 75-744 9.95
1. Indians of North America—The West—Biography. 2. Indians of North America—The West—Wars. 3. The West—Biography. I. Capps, Benjamin, 1922- II. Title. III. Series: The Old West (New York)

Indians of North America—The West—Biography—Juvenile literature.

SUTTON, Felix. 970.1'0922
Indian chiefs of the West. Illustrated by Russell Hoover. New York, J. Messner [1970] 96 p. illus. 23 cm. Brief biographies of five famous Indian chiefs from the western plains include Sequoyah, Crazy Horse, Chief Joseph, Sitting Bull, and Geronimo. [E89.S9] 920 B 70-107062 ISBN 0-671-32254-0 3.95
1. Indians of North America—The West—Biography—Juvenile literature. I. Hoover, Russell, illus. II. Title.

WAYNE, Bennett. 970.4'8 B
Indian patriots of the Great West. Edited, with commentary, by Bennett Wayne. Champaign, Ill., Garrard Pub. Co. [1974] 166 p. illus. (part col.) 21 cm. (A Target book) Brief biographies of four Indian chiefs: Sitting Bull, Crazy Horse, Chief Joseph, and Quanah Parker. [E78.W5W37] 920 73-17110 ISBN 0-8116-4906-7
1. Indians of North America—The West—Biography—Juvenile literature. I. Title. **BIP**

Indians of North America—Wars.

COOKE, David Coxe, 970.50922
1917-
Fighting Indians of America, by David C. Cooke. New York, Dodd, Mead [1966] xii, 226, 206 p. illus., ports. 21 cm. Fighting Indians of the West and Indians on the warpath were originally published separately. Contents.Contents.—Fighting Indians of the West.—Captain Jack and the Modoc War.—Indians on the warpath. [E81.C6] 66-31289
1. Indians of North America—Wars. 2. Indians of North America—Biography. 3. Modoc Indians—Wars, 1873. I. Cooke, David Coxe, 1917- Fighting Indians of the West. II. Cooke, David Coxe, 1917- Indians on the warpath. III. Title.

Indians of North America—Women.

GRIDLEY, Marion Eleanor, 970.1 B
1906-
American Indian women, by Marion E. Gridley. New York, Hawthorn Books [1974] vi, 178 p. illus. 22 cm. Bibliography: p. 169-170. [E98.W8G74] 73-362 5.95
1. Indians of North America—Women. 2. Indians of North America—Biography. I. Title.

Indians of North America—Women—Biography.

FOREMAN, Carolyn 970'.004'97 B
Thomas, 1875-
Indian women chiefs / by Carolyn Thomas Foreman. Washington : Zenger Pub. Co., 1975, c1954. p. cm. Reprint of the ed. published by Hoffman Print. Co., Muskogee, Okla. [E98.W8F6 1975] 75-37860 ISBN 0-89201-019-3 : 7.50
1. Indians of North America—Women—Biography. I. Title. **BIP**

Indochina, French—Description and travel.

MOUHOT, Henri, 1826-1861. 915.9
Diary: travels in the central parts of Siam, Cambodia, and Laos during the years 1858-61. Abridged and edited by Christopher Pym. Kuala Lumpur, New York, Oxford University Press, 1966. xxii, 160 p. illus., facsims., maps (part col.) ports. 23 cm. (Oxford in Asia. Historical reprints) Translation of Voyage dans les royaumes de Siam, de Cambodge, de Laos. [DS524.M7213 1966] SA 66
1. Indochina, French—Description and travel. 2. Natural history—Indochina, French. 3. Khmer language. I. Pym, Christopher, 1929- ed. II. Title.

Indonesia—Politics and government—20th century—Addresses, essays, lectures.

HATTA, Mohammad, 1902- 959.8'03'0924 B
Portrait of a patriot; selected writings. The Hague, Paris, Mouton [1972] 604 p. 25 cm. Translated in part from Indonesian or Dutch. Includes bibliographical references. [DS644.1.H38A26] 71-171098 18.50
1. Indonesia—Politics and government—20th century—Addresses, essays, lectures. I. Title.
Distributed by Humanities.

Industrial and Commercial Workers' Union of Africa.

KADALIE, Clements, 1896-1951. 331.88'0924 B
My life and the ICU; the autobiography of a Black trade unionist in South Africa. Edited, with an introd. by Stanley Trapido. New York, Humanities Press [1970] 230 p. port. 23 cm. (South African studies, no. 3) [HD8799.S73K33] 72-17283 6.00
1. Industrial and Commercial Workers' Union of Africa. 2. Trade-unions—Africa, South—Political activity. I. Title. II. Series. BIP

Industrial arts—Biography.

GLENISTER, S. H. 609'.22 B
Stories of great craftsmen, by S. H. Glenister. Freeport, N.Y., Books for Libraries Press [1970] 234 p. illus., ports. 23 cm. (Essay index reprint series) Reprint of the 1939 ed. Contents.Contents.—Gutenberg and Caxton.—Sir Christopher Wren.—Grinling Gibbons.—John Harrison.—Thomas Chippendale.—John Smeaton.—Josiah Wedgwood.—Sir Richard Arkwright.—James Watt.—George Stephenson.—William Morris.—Thomas Alva Edison. [T39.G5 1970] 75-128247
1. Industrial arts—Biography. I. Title. BIP

PARTON, James, 1822-1891. 338'.0092'2
Captains of industry; or, Men of business who did something besides making money. A book for young Americans. Freeport, N.Y., Books for Libraries Press [1972] 399 p. ports. 22 cm. (Essay index reprint series) Reprint of v. 1 of the 1884-91 ed. [T39.P283 1972] 72-2660 ISBN 0-8369-2853-9 16.50
1. Industrial arts—Biography. I. Title. BIP

SMILES, Samuel, 1812-1904 609/.22
Industrial biography: iron workers and tool makers. Reprint of the 1863 ed. with additional illus. and new introd. by L. T. C. Rolt. Newton Abbot (Devon), David & Charles [1967]. [10], iii-xiv, 342p. front., 16 plates (incl. ports., facsim., diagrs.). 23cm. [T39.S6 1967] 67-114712 11.00
1. Industrial arts—Biog. 2. Iron industry and trade—Gt. Brit. I. Title.
American distributor: Kelley, New York.

Industrial Workers of the World.

CHAPLIN, Ralph, 1887-1961. 331.88'6
Wobbly, the rough-and-tumble story of an American radical. New York, Da Capo Press, 1972 [c1948] vi, 435 p. illus. 23 cm. (Civil liberties in American history) [HX84.C55A3 1972] 70-166089 ISBN 0-306-70212-6
1. Industrial Workers of the World. I. Title. II. Series.

Indy, Vincent d', 1851-1931.

DEMUTH, Norman, 1898-1968. 780'.92'4 B
Vincent d'Indy, 1851-1931; champion of classicism, a study. Westport, Conn., Greenwood Press [1974, c1951] viii, 117 p. illus. 22 cm. Reprint of the ed. published by Rockliff, London. Bibliography: p. 109-110. [ML410.I7D4 1974] 73-6259 ISBN 0-8371-6895-3 8.00
1. Indy, Vincent d', 1851-1931.

Infeld, Leopold, 1898-1968.

INFELD, Leopold, 1898-1968. 530'.092'4 B
Why I left Canada : reflections on science and politics / Leopold Infeld ; translated by Helen Infeld ; edited with introd. and notes by Lewis Pyenson. Montreal : McGill-Queen's University Press, 1978. xii, 212 p. : ill. ; 24 cm. Translation of Szkice z przeszlosci, with chapters rearranged. Includes bibliographical references. [QC16.I6A3213] 78-392900 ISBN 0-7735-0272-6 : 16.95
1. Infeld, Leopold, 1898-1968. 2. Physicists—Poland—Biography. 3. Physics—Poland—History. 4. Physics—Canada—History. 5. Science and state—Canada. I. Title.
Distributed by McGill-Queen's University Press, Irvington, N.Y BIP

Infielders (Baseball)—United States—Biography—Juvenile literature.

SMITH, Jay H. 796.357'092'2 B
Meet the infielders / by Jay H. Smith. Mankato, Minn. : Creative Education, [c1977] 30 p. : ill. (some col.) ; 20 cm. (Creative Education early sports books) Brief profiles of five major league infielders: Joe Morgan, Brooks Robinson, Bert Campaneris, Pete Rose, and Hank Aaron. [GV865.A1S55916] 920 76-28356 ISBN 0-87191-578-2 lib.bdg. 4.95
1. Infielders (Baseball)—United States—Biography—Juvenile literature. I. Title. BIP

Ingalls family.

ANDERSON, William, 1952- 929.2'0973
The story of the Ingalls. [Mansfield, Mo., Laura Ingalls Wilder Home Association, 1967?] [14] p. illus., facsims., ports. 23 cm. Cover title. "Written ... with permission of Rose Wilder Lane." On label mounted on cover: Laura Ingalls Wilder Home and Museum, Mansfield, Mo. [CS71.I44 1967] 71-268397
1. Ingalls family. I. Laura Ingalls Wilder Home and Museum. II. Title.

Ingalls, John James, 1833-1900.

WILLIAMS, Burton J. 328.73'092'4 B
Senator John James Ingalls, Kansas' iridescent Republican, by Burton J. Williams. Lawrence, University Press of Kansas [1972] ix, 201 p. 24 cm. A revision of the author's thesis, University of Kansas. Bibliography: p. 189-194. [E664.I4W5] 72-177898 ISBN 0-7006-0086-8 7.75
1. Ingalls, John James, 1833-1900.

Inge, William Motter.

SHUMAN, Robert Baird 812.54
William Inge. New Haven, Conn., Coll. & Univ. Pr. [1966, c.1965] 190p. 21cm. (T-95) Bibl. [PS3517.N265Z87] 1.95 pap.,
1. Inge, William Motter. I. Title. BIP

Ingersoll, Charles Jared, 1782-1862.

MEIGS, William Montgomery, 1852-1929. 328.73'0924 B
The life of Charles Jared Ingersoll. New York, Da Capo Press, 1970. 351 p. port. 23 cm. (A Da Capo Press reprint series. The American scene) Includes bibliographical references. [E340.I5M5 1970] 71-127194
1. Ingersoll, Charles Jared, 1782-1862. I. Title. BIP

Ingersoll, Jared, 1722-1781.

GIPSON, Lawrence Henry, 1880- 320.9'746
Jared Ingersoll; a study of American loyalism in relation to British colonial government. New York, Russell & Russell [1969] 432 p. 23 cm. (Yale historical publications. Miscellany, 8) Reprint of the 1920 ed. Includes bibliographical references. [E302.6.I6G44 1969] 69-14216
1. Ingersoll, Jared, 1722-1781. 2. Stamp Act, 1765. 3. Connecticut—Politics and government—Colonial period, ca. 1600-1775. 4. United States—Politics and government—Colonial period, ca. 1600-1775. I. Title. II. Series.

Ingersoll, Robert Green, 1833-1899.

CRAMER, Clarence H. 922.91
Royal Bob; the life of Robert G. Ingersoll. [1st ed.] Indianapolis, Bobbs-Merrill [1952] 314 p. illus., ports. 23 cm. Bibliography: p. 296-306. [BL2790.I6C7] 52-10691
1. Ingersoll, Robert Green, 1833-1899. I. Title.

INGERSOLL, Robert Green, 1833-1899. 340'.092'4 B
The letters of Robert G. Ingersoll. Edited, with a biographical introd., by Eva Ingersoll Wakefield. Westport, Conn., Greenwood Press [1973] xii, 747 p. 22 cm. Reprint of the 1951 ed. published by Philosophical Library, New York. [BL2790.I6A4 1974] 73-14033 ISBN 0-8371-7139-3 24.50
1. Ingersoll, Robert Green, 1833-1899.

INGERSOLL, Robert Green, 1833-1899. 922.91
Letters, edited with a biographical introd. by Eva Ingersoll Wakefield. New York, Philosophical Library [1951] xii, 747 p. port. 24 cm. [BL2790.I 6A4] 51-335
I. Title.

LARSON, Orvin Prentiss. 922.91
American infidel: Robert G. Ingersoll, a biography. [1st ed.] New York, Citadel Press [1962] 316 p. illus. 22 cm. Includes bibliography. [BL2790.I6L3] 62-10223
1. Ingersoll, Robert Green, 1833-1899. I. Title.

LEWIS, Joseph, 1889- 922.91
Ingersoll the magnificent; to which has been added a special arrangement of some gems from Ingersoll for inspiration, wisdom, and courage. New York, Freethought Press Association, 1957. 576p. 20cm. [BL2728.L4] 57-44913
1. Ingersoll, Robert Green, 1833-1899. I. Ingersoll, Robert Green, 1833-1899. II. Title.

Ingersoll, Robert Sturgis,

INGERSOLL, Robert Sturgis, 1891- 917.48'11'0340924 B
Recollections of a Philadelphian at eighty [by] R. Sturgis Ingersoll. [Philadelphia, National Pub. Co.] 1971. 120 p. 23 cm. [CT275.I52A3] 74-185337
I. Title.

Ingles, Mary Draper, 1732-1815.

INGLES, John, 1766-1836. 970.3
The story of Mary Draper Ingles and son Thomas Ingles, as told by John Ingles, Sr. Edited by Roberta Ingles Steele and Andrew Lewis Ingles. [1st ed.] Radford, Va., Commonwealth Press [1969] 36 p. 19 cm. Cover title: Escape from Indian captivity. [E87.I53 1969] 73-108092
1. Ingles, Mary Draper, 1732-1815. 2. Ingles, Thomas, b. 1751? 3. Indians of North America—Captivities. I. Title. II. Title: Escape from Indian captivity.

Ingraham, Elias.

HOLLY, Forrest M. 681'.113'0924 B
For generations to come : the life story of Elias Ingraham / Forrest M. Holly. Old Tappan, N.J. : F. H. Revell Co., c1975. 224 p., [8] leaves of plates : ill. ; 24 cm. Includes index. [TS544.8.I53H64] 75-31669 ISBN 0-87653-026-9
1. Ingraham, Elias. I. Title.

Ingram, Arthur, Sir, 1565 (ca.)-1642.

UPTON, Anthony F. 929.20942
Sir Arthur Ingram, c. 1565-1642; a study of the origins of an English landed family [London] Oxford University Press, 1961. 274 p. illus. 23 cm. Includes bibliographies. [CS439.I52 1961] 61-3830
1. Ingram, Arthur, Sir, 1565 (ca.)-1642. 2. Ingram family.

Ingram, John Henry,

INGRAM, John Henry, 1842-1916. 822.3
Christopher Marlowe and his associates. New York, Cooper Square Publishers, 1970. xvi, 305 p. illus., facsims., ports. 22 cm. Reprint of the 1904 ed. Bibliography: p. 280-298. [PR2673.I5 1970] 70-116374
I. Marlowe, Christopher, 1564-1593. II. Title. BIP

Ingram, Margaret Foglesong.

INGRAM, Margaret Foglesong. 923.773
Toward an education. New York, Comet Press Books [1954] 447p. 23cm. Autobiographical. [LA2317.I55A3] 54-9550
I. Title.

Ink Spots.

WATSON, Deek. 784'.0922
The story of the "Ink Spots," by Deek Watson with Lee Stephenson. [1st ed.] New York, Vantage Press [1967] 72 p. 21 cm. [ML400.W23] 67-5817
1. Ink Spots. I. Stephenson, Lee, joint author. II. Title.

Inkanish, Mary Little Bear.

MARRIOTT, Alice Lee, 1910- 970'.004'97 B
Dance around the sun : the life of Mary Little Bear Inkanish, Cheyenne / Alice Marriott and Carol K. Rachlin. New York : Crowell, c1977. xiv, 238 p., : ill. ; 24 cm. Includes index. Bibliography: p. [227]. [E99.C53M37 1977] 77-1859 8.95
1. Inkanish, Mary Little Bear. 2. Cheyenne Indians—Biography. 3. Indians of North America—Mixed bloods—Biography. I. Rachlin, Carol K., joint author. II. Title. BIP

Inman, Samuel Guy, 1877-1965.

CASTLEMAN, William J., 1908- 286.60924
On this foundation; a historical literary biography of the early life of Samuel Guy Inman . . . covering the period, 1877-1904, by Wm. J. Castleman. St. Louis, Printed as a private ed. by Bethany Pr. [1966] 176p. 23cm. Bibl. [BX7343.I54C3] 66-8316 3.95
1. Inman, Samuel Guy, 1877-1965. I. Title.

Inmes, Jesse Woodson, 1847-1882.

JAMES, Jesse Lee, 1905- 923.4173
Jesse James and the lost cause. [1st ed.] New York, Pageant Press [1961] 183p. illus. 21cm. [F594.J2842] 61-16940
1. Inmes, Jesse Woodson, 1847-1882. I. Title.

Inness, George, 1825-1894.

CIKOVSKY, Nicolai. 759.13 B
The life and work of George Inness / Nicolai Cikovsky, Jr. New York : Garland Pub., 1977. xxv, 380 p., [65] leaves of plates : ill. ; 21 cm. (Outstanding dissertations in the fine arts) Originally presented as the author's thesis, Harvard, 1965. Bibliography: p. 371-380. [ND237.I5C55 1977] 76-23605 ISBN 0-8240-2679-9 lib.bdg. : 50.00
1. Inness, George, 1825-1894. 2. Landscape painters—United States—Biography. I. Title. II. Series. BIP

INNESS, George, 1854-1926. 759.13 B
Life, art, and letters of George Inness. Introd. by Elliott Daingerfield. New York, Kennedy Galleries [and] Da Capo Press, 1969. xxviii, 290 p. illus., ports. 24 cm. (Library of American art) Reprint of the 1917 ed. [ND237.I516 1969] 76-87444
1. Inness, George, 1825-1894. I. Title. BIP

Innis, Harold Adams, 1894-1952.

CREIGHTON, Donald Grant. 923.371
Harold Adams Innis : portrait of a sch0lar / Donald Creighton. Toronto ; Buffalo :

University of Toronto Press, c1978,c957. xiii,146p. ; 22 cm. [HB121T6C7] ISBN 0-8020-6329-2 pbk. : 4.95
1. Innis, Harold Adams,1894-1952. I. Title. L.C. card no. for 1957 hardcover ed.:58-854.

CREIGHTON, Donald Grant. 330'.092'4 B
Harold Adams Innis : portrait of a scholar / Donald Creighton. Toronto ; Buffalo : University of Toronto Press, 1978. xiii, 146 p. : port. ; 22 cm. (Canadian university paperbacks ; 202) [HB121.I6C7 1978] 78-314036 ISBN 0-8020-6329-2 : 4.95
1. Innis, Harold Adams, 1894-1952. 2. Economists—Canada—Biography. BIP

Innocentius III, Pope, 1160 or 61-1216.

ELLIOTT-BINNS, Leonard Elliott, 1885- 262'.13'0924
Innocent III, by L. Elliott Binns. [Hamden, Conn.] Archon Books, 1968. xi, 212 p. port. 19 cm. Reprint of the 1931 ed. Bibliographical footnotes. [BX1236.E5] 68-15343
1. Innocentius III, Pope, 1160 or 61-1216. I. Title.

ELLIOTT-BINNS, Leonard Elliott, 1885- 262'.13'0924
Innocent III, by L. Elliott Binns. [Hamden, Conn.] Archon Books, 1968. xi, 212 p. port. 19 cm. Reprint of the 1931 ed. Bibliographical footnotes. [BX1236.E5 1968] 68-15343
1. Innocentius III, Pope, 1160 or 61-1216.

SMITH, Charles Edward, 1905- 922.21
Innocent III, Church defender Baton Rouge, Louisiana State University Press, 1951. vi, 203 p. 23 cm. "Bibliographical note": p. 189-[192] [BX1236.S6] 51-1676
1. Innocentius III, Pope, 1160 or 61-1216 I. Title.

SMITH, Charles Edward, 1905- 262'.13'0924 B
Innocent III, church defender. Westport, Conn., Greenwood Press [1971, c1951] vi, 203 p. 23 cm. Bibliography: p. 189-[192] [BX1236.S6 1971] 79-88939 ISBN 0-8371-3145-6
1. Innocentius III, Pope, 1160 or 61-1216.

Innocentius XI, Pope, 1611-1689.

ROBERTO, Brother, 1927- 922.21
The rock cannot be moved; a story of Blessed Innocent XI. Illus. by Brother Eagan. Notre Dame, Ind., Dujarie Press1[c1957] 94p. illus. 24cm. [BX1348.R6] 57-27077
1. Innocentius XI, Pope, 1611-1689. I. Title.

Innokentii, Saint, Metropolitan of Moscow, 1797-1879.

GARRETT, Paul D., 1948- 281.9'092'4 B
St. Innocent, apostle to America / Paul D. Garrett. Crestwood, N.Y. : St. Vladimir's Seminary Press, 1979. p. cm. Includes bibliographical references. [BX597.I55G37] 79-19634 ISBN 0-913836-60-5 pbk. : 8.95
1. Innokentii, Saint, Metropolitan of Moscow, 1797-1879. 2. Christian saints—Russia—Biography. I. Title.

Inouye, Daniel K., 1924- —Juvenile literature.

GOODSELL, Jane. 328.73'092'4 B
Daniel Inouye / Jane Goodsell ; illustrated by Haru Wells. New York : Crowell, [1977] p. cm. A biography of the first Congressman from the state of Hawaii who was also the first American of Japanese descent to serve in the Congress of the United States. [E840.8.I5G66] 77-1405 ISBN 0-690-01358-2 lib.bdg. : 6.95
1. Inouye, Daniel K., 1924- —Juvenile literature. 2. Legislators—United States—Biography—Juvenile literature. I. Wells, Haru. BIP

Inquisition. Spain.

WIESENTHAL, Simon. 973.1'5'0924 B
Sails of hope; the secret mission of Christopher Columbus. Translated from the German, by Richard and Clara Winston. [1st American ed.] New York, Macmillan [1973] 248 p. illus. 22 cm. Translation of Segel der Hoffnung. Bibliography: p. 237-239. [DS135.S7W5313 1973] 73-2126 5.95
1. Inquisition. Spain. 2. Colombo, Cristoforo—Relations with the Jews. 3. Jews in Spain. I. Title.

Insanity.

HYSLOP, Theophilus Bulkeley, 1863-1933. 157'.09'22 B
The great abnormals. London, P. Allan, 1925. Ann Arbor, Mich., Gryphon Books, 1971. xxvii, 288 p. front. 22 cm. [BF423.H8 1971] 79-162514
1. Insanity. 2. Genius. I. Title. BIP

Insen, Henrik, 1828-1906.

KNIGHT, George Wilson, 1897- 839.8226
Henrik Ibsen. [Gloucester, Mass., P. Smith, 1963, c.1962] 119p. 18cm. (Evergreen pilot bk. rebound) Bibl. 3.0
1. Insen, Henrik, 1828-1906. I. Title.

Instrumental music.

*GAY, Harriet. 785.066 [B]
The Julliard string quartet. New York, Vantage Press, [1974]. 89 p. illus. 21 cm. [M452.4] ISBN 0-533-01322-4 6.95.
1. Instrumental music. 2. String quartets. I. Title.

Insull, Samuel, 1859-1938.

MCDONALD, Forrest 923.373
Insull. [Chicago] Univ. of Chic. Press. [c.1962] 350p. illus. 25cm. Bibl. 62-18110 4.95
1. Insull, Samuel, 1859-1938. I. Title. BIP

Insurance, Life—Agents—Biography.

MEYER, Ken. 658.89'368'3200922 B
The shooters : portraits, sales philosophies, and techniques of 23 of the most successful young salespeople in the nation / by Ken Meyer. Rockville Centre, N.Y. : Farnsworth Pub. Co., c1979. 248 p., [1] leaf of plates : ports. ; 24 cm. [HG8876.M39] 79-84407 ISBN 0-87863-187-9 : 9.95
1. Insurance, Life—Agents—Biography. I. Title.

Intellectuals—Japan.

ARIMA, Tatsuo. 915.2'03'320922
The failure of freedom; a portrait of modern Japanese intellectuals. Cambridge, Harvard University Press, 1969. xiii, 296 p. 22 cm. (Harvard East Asian series, 39) Thesis—Harvard University, 1961. Bibliography: p. [259]-272. [DS822.4.A7] 74-82292 ISBN 6-7429-1301- 10.00
1. Intellectuals—Japan. 2. Liberalism—Japan. I. Title. II. Series.

Intelligence service—Czechoslovak Republic.

BITTMAN, Ladislav, 1931- 327.437
The deception game; Czechoslovak intelligence in Soviet political warfare. [1st ed. Syracuse, N.Y.] Syracuse University Research Corp., 1972. xxv, 246 p. illus. 23 cm. Autobiographical. Includes bibliographical references. [DB217.B5A3] 72-682 ISBN 0-8156-8078-3
1. Intelligence service—Czechoslovak Republic. 2. Intelligence service—Europe, Eastern. I. Title.

Intercollegiate Conference of Faculty Representatives.

WILSON, Kenneth L. 796'.0922
The big ten, by Kenneth L. (Tug) Wilson and Jerry Brondfield. Englewood Cliffs, N.J., Prentice-Hall [1967] 496 p. illus., ports. 29 cm. [GV563.W53] 67-20746
1. Intercollegiate Conference of Faculty Representatives. 2. Athletes — Biog. I. Brondfield, Jerome, joint author. II. Title.

WILSON, Kenneth Leon, 1896 796'.0922
The Big Ten, by Kenneth L. (Tug) Wilson and Jerry Brondfield. Englewood Cliffs, N.J., Prentice-Hall [1967] 496 p. illus., ports. 29 cm. [GV563.W53] 67-20746
1. Intercollegiate Conference of Faculty Representatives. 2. Athletes—Biography. I. Brondfield, Terry, 1913- joint author. II. Title.

International Brotherhood of Teamsters, Chauffeurs, Warehousemen and Helpers of America.

SHERIDAN, Walter. 331.88'11'3883240924 B
The fall and rise of Jimmy Hoffa. New York, Saturday Review Press [1972] xvii, 554 p. 25 cm. [HD6515.T3S5 1972] 78-154258 ISBN 0-8415-0202-1 10.95
1. International Brotherhood of Teamsters, Chauffeurs, Warehousemen and Helpers of America. 2. Hoffa, James Riddle, 1913- I. Title.

International Business Machines Corporation.

RODGERS, William H. 338.7'61'65180924
Think; a biography of the Watsons and IBM, by William Rodgers. New York, Stein and Day [1969] 320 p. illus., ports. 25 cm. Bibliography: p. 312-313. [HD9999.B94I54] 69-19394 ISBN 8-12-812263- 7.95
1. International Business Machines Corporation. 2. Watson, Thomas John, 1874 1956. 3. Watson, Thomas J., 1914- I. Title.

International Union, United Automobile, Aerospace, and Agricultural Implement Workers of America.

HOWE, Irving. 331.88'12'920973
The UAW and Walter Reuther, by Irving Howe and B. J. Widick. New York, Da Capo Press, 1973 [c1949] x, 309 p. 22 cm. (Franklin D. Roosevelt and the era of the New Deal) Includes bibliographical references. [HD6515.A8H6 1973] 72-2375 ISBN 0-306-70485-4 10.50
1. International Union, United Automobile, Aerospace, and Agricultural Implement Workers of America. 2. Reuther, Walter Philip, 1907-1970. I. Widick, B. J., joint author. II. Title. III. Series. BIP

Interviews.

BRANDON, Henry, 1916- 920.02
Conversations with Henry Brandon. [1st American ed.] Boston, Houghton Mifflin, 1968. 288 p. 23 cm. [CT220.B7 1968] 68-13567
1. Interviews. I. Title.

Inventors.

DASSAULT, Marcel, 1892- 629.13'00924 B
The talisman; the autobiography of Marcel Dassault, creator of the mirage jet. Translated by Patricia High Painton. New Rochelle, N.Y., Arlington House [1971] 127 p. illus., ports. 22 cm. [TL540.D26A313] 75-166161 ISBN 0-87000-149-3 4.95
I. Title.

EBERLE, Irmengarde, 1898- 926
Famous inventors for young people. N.Y., Dodd, 1956 [c1941] vi, 130 p. illus. Earlier edition has title: Famous inventors for boys and girls. [T39.E304]
1. Inventors. I. Title.

EBERLE, Irmengarde, 1898- v. 12
Famous inventors for young people. New York, Dodd, Mead, 1961 [1941] 130 p. illus. 23 cm. "First published under the title "Famous inventors for boys and girls."" [608] [A 62-8677]
1. Inventors. I. Title.

EVANS, Idrisyn Oliver, 1894- 926
Inventors of the world. Illus. by Drake Brookshaw. New York, Warne [c.1962] 191p. illus. 22cm. 61-15430 2.95 bds.,
1. Inventors. I. Title.

FANNING, Leonard M. 9269328
Fathers of industries Illus by Albert Orbaan. Philadelphia, Lippincott [1962]. 256 p. illus. 22 cm 4.75
1. Inventors. I. Title.

LARSEN, Egon. 926
Men who changed the world; stories of invention and discovery. New York, Roy [1952] 224 p. illus. 22 cm. [T39.L28 1952a] 52-11610
1. Inventors. I. Title.

LEHRBURGER, Egon, 1904- 926
Men who changed the world; stories of invention and discovery, by Egon Larsen [pseud. 2d ed.] New York, Roy Publishers [1953] 224 p. illus. 22 cm. [T39.L43 1953] 52-11610
1. Inventors. I. Title.

MANCHESTER, Harland Frank, 1898- 926
Trail blazers of technology; the story of nine inventors. Illustrated by Anthony Ravielli. New York, Scribner [1962] 215p. illus. 22cm. [T39.M24] 62-17731
1. Inventors. 2. Inventions—Juvenile literature. I. Title.
Contents omitted.

PRINGLE, Patrick. v. 12
Great discoverers in modern science. Leicester, Ulverscroft [1965] 206 p. illus. 28 cm. (Ulverscroft large print series) Originally published London, Harrap, 1955. 67-58813
1. Inventors. 2. Scientists. I. Title.

PRINGLE, Patrick. 509.22
They were the first. New York, Roy Publishers [1965] 142. [2] p. illus., ports. 21 cm. Bibliography: p. [143]-[144] [CT105.P75] 65-18885
1. Inventors 2. Explorers. I. Title.

Inventors, American.

HOWARD, Robert West, 1908- 92
Eli Whitney. Illustrated by David Cunningham. Chicago, Follett Pub. Co. [c1966] 144 p. col. illus. 22 cm. (Library of American heroes) [Whitney, Eli, 1765-1825--Juvenile literature.] [TS1570.W4H6] 67-1526
I. Title.

HYLANDER, Clarence John, 1897-. 926
American inventors. New York, Macmillan, 1960 [i. e. 1963, c1934] xv, 216 p. illus., ports., diagrs. 20 cm. [T39.H9] 63-6536
1. Inventors, American. 2. Inventions — U.S. I. Title. BIP

ILES, George, 1852-1942. 608.7'22
Leading American inventors. Freeport, N.Y., Books for Libraries Press [1968] xv, 447 p. illus., ports. 23 cm. (Essay index reprint series) Reprint of the 1912 ed. Contents.Contents.—John and Robert Livingston Stevens.—Robert Fulton.—Eli Whitney.—Thomas Blanchard.—Samuel Finley Breese Morse.—Charles Goodyear.—John Ericsson.—Cyrus Hall McCormick.—Christopher Latham Sholes.—Elias Howe.—Benjamin Chew Tilghman.—Ottmar Mergenthaler. [T39.I5 1968] 68-8472
1. Inventors, American. I. Title. BIP

Inventors—Biography—Juvenile literature.

FELDMAN, Anthony. 609'.2'2 B
Scientists and inventors / by Anthony Feldman and Peter Ford. New York : Facts on File, c1979. p. cm. Includes index. Presents 160 chronologically arranged biographies of scientists and inventors with emphasis on their particular contributions to the progress of mankind. [T39.F37] 920 79-15960 ISBN 0-87196-410-4 : 17.50

1. Inventors—Biography—Juvenile literature. 2. Scientists—Biography—Juvenile literature. I. Ford, Peter. II. Title. BIP

MANCHESTER, Harland Frank, 1898- 608'.7'22 B
New trail blazers of technology / Harland Manchester ; illustrated with photos. New York : Scribner, [1976] p. cm. Includes index. Bibliography: p. Biographical sketches of ten twentieth-century inventors who have made an impact on modern life. [T39.M23] 920 76-16760 ISBN 0-684-14718-1 : 7.95
1. Inventors—Biography—Juvenile literature. I. Title. BIP

Inventors—Juvenile literature.

THARP, Edgar. 609'.22 B
Giants of invention. Illustrated by Frank Vaughn. [Rev. ed.] New York, Grosset & Dunlap [1971] 117 p. illus., ports. 28 cm. (Illustrated true books) "4494" Describes twenty-eight men whose inventions have been significant to modern science. [T39.T45 1971] 920 78-145731 ISBN 0-448-04494-3 4.95
1. Inventors—Juvenile literature. I. Vaughn, Frank, 1915- illus. II. Title.

Inventors—United States.

BURLINGAME, Roger, 1889- 926.2
Out of silence into sound; the life of Alexander Graham Bell. New York, Macmillan [c.1964] xi, 146p. illus., ports. 23cm. Bibl. 64-11033 2.95; 3.07 lib. ed.
qBell, Alexander Graham, 1847-1922.
I. Title.

THOSE inventive Americans. 609'.73
Produced by the National Geographic Special Publications Division. Foreword by Leonard Carmichael. [Washington, National Geographic Society, 1971] 231 p. illus. (part col.), ports. (part col.) 27 cm. ([National geographic special publications]) [T39.T5] 75-125340 ISBN 0-87044-089-6
1. Inventors—United States. I. National Geographic Society, Washington, D.C. Special Publications Division. BIP

WOODBURY, David Oakes, 1896- 926.2
Elihu Thomson, beloved scientist, 1853-1937; inventive genius, engineer, educator, pioneer of the electrical age. With appreciations by James R. Killian, Jr., and Owen D. Young. Boston, Museum of Science, 1960. 358 p. illus. 24 cm. First published in 1944 under title: Beloved scientist; Elihu Thomson, a guiding spirit of the electrical age. Includes bibliography. [TK140.T5W6 1960] 60-11802
I. Thomson, Elihu, 1853-1937. II. Title.

Inventors—United States—Biography—Juvenile literature.

PIZER, Vernon. 609'.2'2 B
Shortchanged by history : America's neglected innovators / by Vernon Pizer ; illustrated by Catherine Stock. New York : Putnam, c1979. 158 p. : ill. ; 24 cm. Includes index. Discusses the lives and contributions of little-known inventors in American history including Joseph Jenks who invented a more efficient scythe and James Buchanan Eads who completed and launched the first ironclad in American waters. [T39.P59 1979] 920 78-24141 ISBN 0-399-20665-5 : 7.95
1. Inventors—United States—Biography—Juvenile literature. I. Stock, Catherine. II. Title. BIP

SIGNIFICANT American inventors. 609'.2'2 B
Chicago : Childrens Press, [1976] p. cm. Includes index. Brief biographies of 145 inventors arranged in chronological-alphabetical order. [T39.S53] 920 75-20681 ISBN 0-516-05313-2 : 9.25
1. Inventors—United States—Biography—Juvenile literature. I. Title: Inventors.

Inventors—United States—Juvenile literature.

RADFORD, Ruby Lorraine, 1891- 608.7'22
Inventors in industry, by Ruby L. Radford. Illustrated by Jim Fox. New York, J. Messner [1969] 96 p. illus. 22 cm. Brief biographies of five inventors who revolutionized industry with the cotton gin, reaper, rubber, sewing machines, and electricity. [T212.R34] 920 72-85406 ISBN 0-671-32181-1 3.95
1. Inventors—United States—Juvenile literature. I. Fox, Jim, illus. II. Title.

Inzer, John Washington, 1834-1928.

†INZER, John Washington, 1834-1928. 973.7'72'0924
The diary of a Confederate soldier : John Washington Inzer, 1834-1928 / edited and annotated by Mattie Lou Teague Crow. Huntsville, Ala. : Strode Publishers, c1977. 191 p. : ill. ; 23 cm. Includes index. Bibliography: p. 184-185. [E605.158] 76-55168 ISBN 0-87397-115-9 : 7.95
1. Inzer, John Washington, 1834-1928. 2. Confederate States of America. Army—Biography. 3. United States—History—Civil War, 1861-1865—Personal narratives—Confederate ride. 4. Soldiers—Alabama—Biography. I. Crow, Mattie Lou Teague. II. Title.

Ionesco, Eugene.

COE, Richard N. 842.914
Eugene Ionesco [Gloucester, Mass., Peter Smith. c.1961] 120p. (Evergreen pilot bks., EP8, rebound) Bibl. 3.01
1. Ionesco, Eugene. I. Title. BIP

COE, Richard N 842.914
Eugene Ionesco. New York, Grove Press [1961] 120p. 18cm. (Evergreen pilot books, EP8) Includes bibliography. [PQ2617.O6Z6 1961] 61-10146
1. Ionesco, Eugene. I. Title.

COE, Richard N. 842'.9'14
Eugene Ionesco, by Richard N. Coe. [2d ed.] New York, Grove Press [1970, c1961] 129 p. 18 cm. (An Evergreen black cat book, B-235) Bibliography: p. [111]-129. [PQ2617.O6Z6 1970] 70-111004 1.50
1. Ionesco, Eugene.

Ionides, Constantine John Philip.

WYKES, Alan. 925.9
Snake Man; the story of C. J. P. Ionides. New York, Simon and Schuster, 1961 [c1960] 269 p. illus. 22 cm. [QL666.O6W9 1961] 61-7011
1. Ionides, Constantine John Philip. 2. Snakes. 3. Zoological specimens—Collection and preservation. I. Title.

Iosafat, Saint, Abp. of Polotsk, 1580 - 1623.

BORESKY, Theodosia. 922.247
Life of St. Josaphat, martyr of the Union, Archbishop of Polotsk, member, Order of St. Basil, the Great. [1st ed. New York, Comet Press Books, 1955] 381p. 23cm. [BX4700.I6B6] 55-9797
1. Iosafat, Saint, Abp. of Polotsk, 1580 - 1623. I. Title.

Iowa—Biography.

LARSEN, Beverly. 917.77'03'20922 B
The brave ones (early Iowa pioneer women). [Exira, Iowa, Pioneer Press, 1971] 87 p. illus. 17 cm. "A Pioneer publication." Bibliography: p. 81. [F620.L37] 72-171807
1. Iowa—Biography. 2. Women in Iowa—Biography. I. Title.

MILLS, George S. 920.0777
Rogues and heroes from Iowa's amazing past, by George Mills. Drawings by Frank Miller. [1st ed.] Ames, Iowa State University Press [1972] xii, 252 p. illus. 23 cm. Bibliography: p. 243-245. [F620.M5] 77-153160 ISBN 0-8138-0865-0
1. Iowa—Biography. 2. Iowa—History, Local. I. Title. II. Title: Iowa's amazing past. BIP

PURE nostalgia : 977.7'02
memories of early Iowa / edited and with introductions by Carl Hamilton. 1st ed. Ames : Iowa State University Press, 1979. viii, 212 p. : ill. ; 24 cm. [CT234.P87] 78-10810 ISBN 0-8138-0975-4 : 7.95
1. Iowa—Biography. 2. Iowa—Social life and customs. I. Hamilton, Carl, 1914- II. Title.

Ipatieff, Vladimir Nikolaevich,

IPATIEFF, Vladimir Nikolaevich, 1867-1952. 925.4
My life in the United States; the memoirs of a chemist. Evanston, Northwestern University [1959] 200p. 24cm. [QD22.I65A283] 59-13581
I. Title.

Ipswitch, Scott, 1961-1976.

IPSWITCH, Elaine. 362.1'9'642 B
Scott was here / Elaine Ipswitch. New York : Delacorte Press, c1979. xii, 210 p., [8] leaves of plates : ill. ; 22 cm. Bibliography: p. 209. [RC644.I67] 78-13969 ISBN 0-440-07665-X : 8.95
1. Ipswitch, Scott, 1961-1976. 2. Hodgkin's disease—Biography. I. Title. BIP

Iqbal, Muhammad, Sir, 1877-1938.

MCDONOUGH, Sheila. 297'.0922
The authority of the past; a study of three Muslim modernists. Chambersburg, Pa., American Academy of Religion, 1970. 56 p. 24 cm. (AAR studies in religion, 1970:1) Bibliography: p. 55-56. [BP63.I4M24] 76-141690
1. Ahmad Khan, Syed, Sir, 1817-1898. 2. Iqbal, Muhammad, Sir, 1877-1938. 3. Parwez, Ghulam Ahmad, 1903- 4. Islam—India. I. Title. II. Series: American Academy of Religion. AAR studies in religion, 1970:1

Iran—Biography—Dictionaries.

**IRAN who's who.* 920.055
Tehran, Echo of Iran 1972- v. 21 cm.
1. Iran—Biography—Dictionaries.
The first volume of a new publication is now available from International Publications Serv., New York, for 15.00, pap.

Iran—Description and travel.

VAMBERY, Armin, 1832-1913. 915.5'04'4
Arminius Vambery, his life and adventures. New York, Arno Press, 1973. p. (The Middle East collection) Reprint of the 1914 ed., published by Cassell, New York. [DS258.V35 1973] 73-6307 ISBN 0-405-05369-X 21.00
1. Iran—Description and travel. 2. Asia, Central—Description and travel. I. Title. II. Series.

Ireland—Hist—19th cent.

*ROSSA, Jeremiah O'Donovan. 941.5'8'0924
My years in English jails. Ed. by Sean Ua Cearnaigh [Tralee, Ireland] Anvil Bks. 1967. 240p. 18cm. First pub. in 1874 by Amer. News Co., New York. (B) 1.75 pap.,
1. Ireland—Hist—19th cent. I. Title.
Distributed by SportShelf, New Rochelle, N. Y.

Ireland—Biography.

BOYLAN, Henry. 920'.0415
A dictionary of Irish biography / Henry Boylan. New York : Barnes & Noble Books, 1978. xi, 385 p. ; 23 cm. Bibliography: p. 379-385. [CT862.B69] 79-102572 ISBN 0-06-490620-5 : 25.00
1. Ireland—Biography. I. Title. BIP

MCGILLION, J. 941.5'00992 B
Irish lives / J. McGillion. [Dublin] : Folens, [1973] 96 p. ; 22 cm. [DA916.M24] 75-320877
1. Ireland—Biography. I. Title.

O'KELLY, Seamus G. 941.5'8'0922 B
The bold Fenian men, by Seamus G. O'Kelly. Dublin, Irish News Service & Publicity [1967] 98 p. illus. 18 cm. (A1 books) [DA952.A1O4] 77-266356 3/6
1. Ireland—Biography. 2. Fenians. I. Title.

O'KELLY, Seamus G. 951.59'092'2 B
The glorious seven, by Seamus G. O'Kelly. [2d ed.] Dublin, Irish News Service and Publicity [1965] 48 p. ports. 19 cm. [DA965.A1O43 1965] 73-172357
1. Ireland—Biography. 2. Ireland—History—Sinn Fein Rebellion, 1916. I. Title.

Ireland—Biography—Dictionaries.

WEBB, Alfred John, 1834-1908. 920.0415
A compendium of Irish biography: comprising sketches of distinguished Irishmen and of eminent persons connected with Ireland by office or by their writings. New York, Lemma Pub. Corp., 1970. xix, 597, [1] p. 23 cm. Reprint of the 1878 ed. "Authorities": p. 590-[598] [DA916.W3 1970] 74-112680 ISBN 0-87696-007-7
1. Ireland—Biography—Dictionaries. I. Title. BIP

Ireland—Biography—Juvenile literature.

SHARE, Bernard. 920'.0415
Irish lives; biographies of fifty famous Irish men and women. Written by Bernard Share. Designed by William Bolger. Dublin, A. Figgis, 1971. 1 v. (unpaged) illus. 29 cm. [CT797.S5] 72-180792 £5.00
1. Ireland—Biography—Juvenile literature. I. Bolger, William, fl. 1965- II. Title.

Ireland—Description and travel—1951-

PLUNKETT, James, 1920- 914.15'04'9
The gems she wore; a book of Irish places. New York, Holt, Rinehart and Winston [1973, c1972] 208 p. illus. 24 cm. [DA978.P57 1973] 72-92913 ISBN 0-03-007731-1 6.95
1. Ireland—Description and travel—1951- 2. Ireland—Biography. I. Title.

Ireland, DeWitt Clinton, 1835-1913.

TETLOW, Roger T., 1924- 070.5'092'4 B
The Astorian : the personal history of DeWitt Clinton Ireland, pioneer newspaperman, printer, and publisher / by Roger T. Tetlow. 1st ed. Portland, Or. : Binford & Mort, [1976] c1975. viii, 178 p. : ill. ; 22 cm. Includes index. [PN4874.I67T4] 75-25323 ISBN 0-8323-0263-5 pbk. : 4.95
1. Ireland, DeWitt Clinton, 1835-1913. I. Title.

Ireland—History.

FALKINER, Caesar Litton, 1863-1908. 941.5
Essays relating to Ireland; biographical, historical, and topographical. With a memoir of the author by Edward Dowden. Port Washington, N.Y., Kennikat Press [1970] xx, 249 p. 22 cm. (Irish history and culture) (Kennikat Press scholarly reprints.) Contents.—Memoir.—Studies in Irish biography: Spenser in Ireland. Sir John Davis. An illustrious cavalier. Archbishop Stone. Robert Emmet.—Illustrations of Irish topography: Dublin. Youghal. Kilkenny. Drogheda. Armagh. Galway.—Studies in Irish history: Irish parliamentary antiquities.—Appendices (p. 221-240):—A. The succession of the speakers of the Irish House of Commons with biographical notices of the early speakers.—B. List of the lords spiritual and temporal in the Irish Parliament, 1568-69.—C. John Hooker's diary, or journal, Jan. 17 to Feb. 23, 1568-69. Bibliographical footnotes. [DA913.F3 1970] 74-102600
1. Ireland—History. 2. Ireland—Biography. I. Title.

Ireland—History—1910-1921.

O'BRIEN, William, 1881- 941.5'9
Forth the banners go, reminiscences of William O'Brien, as told to Edward MacLysaght. Dublin, Three Candles, 1969. viii, 314 p. ports. 20 cm. [DA965.O23A3] 79-266962
1. Ireland—History—1910-1921. I. MacLysaght, Edward. II. Title.

Ireland—Intellectual life.

MCGEE, Thomas D'Arcy, 1825-1868. 914.15'03'60922 B
Gallery of Irish writers; the Irish writers of the seventeenth century. New York, Lemma Pub. Corp., 1974. 252 p. 16 cm. Reprint of the 1846 ed. published by J. Duffy, Dublin and issued in series: Duffy's library of Ireland. Includes bibliographical references. [DA925.M325 1974] 72-87980 ISBN 0-87696-049-2 12.50
1. Ireland—Intellectual life. 2. Authors, Irish—Biography. I. Title. BIP

Ireland, John, Abp., 1838-1918.

MOYNIHAN, James H. 922.273
The life of Archbishop John Ireland. [1st ed.] New York, Harper [1953] 441 p. illus. 22 cm. [BX4705.I7M67] 53-5003
1. Ireland, John, Abp., 1838-1918. BIP

†MOYNIHAN, James H. 282'.092'4 B
The life of Archbishop John Ireland / James H. Moynihan. New York : Arno Press, 1976, c1953. xii, 441 p. : port. ; 24 cm. (The Irish-Americans) Reprint of the ed. published by Harper, New York. Includes index. Bibliography: p. 419-425. [BX4705.I7M67 1976] 76-6358 ISBN 0-405-09351-9 : 27.00
1. Ireland, John, Abp., 1838-1918. I. Title. II. Series.

SHANNON, James P. 977.6'004'9162
Catholic colonization on the western frontier / James P. Shannon. New York : Arno Press, 1976, c1957. (The Irish-Americans) Reprint of the ed. published by Yale University Press, New Haven, which was issued as no. 1 of Yale publications in American studies. Bibliography: p. [F615.I6S52 1976] 76-6365 ISBN 0-405-09357-8 : 20.00
1. Ireland, John, Abp., 1838-1918. 2. Irish Americans—Minnesota—History. 3. Agricultural colonies—Minnesota. 4. Catholics in Minnesota. 5. Minnesota—History. I. Title. II. Series. III. Series: Yale publications in American studies ; 1. BIP

Ireland—Politics and government—19th century.

SULLIVAN, Timothy Daniel, 1827-1914. 914.15'03'80922
Speeches from the dock; with introductory sketches and biographical notes, by T. D., A. M. and D. B. Sullivan. [Rev. ed.] Dublin, Gill and MacMillan [1968] 340 p. 19 cm. [DA950.S952 1968] 70-21384 25/-
1. Ireland—Politics and government—19th century. 2. Ireland—Politics and government—20th century. 3. Ireland—Biography. I. Sullivan, Alexander Martin, 1830-1884. II. Sullivan, Denis B. III. Title.

Ireland—Social life and customs—20th century.

SMITH, John Chabot. 941.5082'092'2 B
The children of Master O'Rourke : an Irish family saga / by John Chabot Smith. 1st ed. New York : Holt, Rinehart and Winston, c1977. 303 p. ; 24 cm. [DA959.1.S56] 77-23278 ISBN 0-03-016916-X : 12.95
1. Ireland—Social life and customs—20th century. 2. Ireland—Biography. I. Title.

Ireys, Henry Tillinghast, 1837-1923.

MCCAIN, William David, 1907- ed. 929'.3762'26
Memoirs of Henry Tillinghast Ireys. Papers of the Washington County Historical Society, 1910-1915. Edited by William D. McCain and Charlotte Capers. Jackson, Mississippi dept. of Archives and History, 1954. 423p. port. 23cm. Cover title: Papers of the Washington County Historical Society. Memoirs of Henry Tillinghast Ireys. [F347.W35M3] 54-63145
1. Ireys, Henry Tillinghast, 1837-1923. 2. Washington Co., Miss.—Hist.—Addresses, essays, lectures. I. Capers, Charlotte, joint ed. II. Washington County (Miss.) Historical Society. III. Title.

Irigaray, Louis—Juvenile literature.

IRIGARAY, Louis. 636.3'01'0924 B
A shepherd watches, a shepherd sings / by Louis Irigaray and Theodore Taylor. 1st ed. Garden City, N.Y. : Doubleday, c1977. x, 300 p., [6] leaves of plates : ill. ; 22 cm. Includes index. Reminiscences of the author's youth as he assists his father, a Basque immigrant to California, with their sheep business. [SF375.4.C2I74] 92 76-50772 ISBN 0-385-11652-7 : 8.95
1. Irigaray, Louis—Juvenile literature. 2. Shepherds—California—San Joaquin Valley—Biography—Juvenile literature. 3. Basque Americans—California—San Joaquin Valley—Biography—Juvenile literature. 4. San Joaquin Valley, Calif.—Biography—Juvenile literature. I. Taylor, Theodore, 1922- joint author. II. Title. BIP

Irish in California.

PRENDERGAST, Thomas F. 301.45'19'1620794
Forgotten pioneers; Irish leaders in early California. Freeport, N.Y., Books for Libraries Press [1972] iii, 278 p. ports. 22 cm. (Essay index reprint series) Reprint of the 1942 ed. Bibliography: p. 265-268. [F870.I6P7 1972] 72-1248 ISBN 0-8369-2854-7
1. Irish in California. 2. California—Biography. I. Title.

Irish in the U. S.

BREEN, George. 920
An immigrant's shenanigans; thirty-three jobs in twenty years. New York, Exposition Press [1951] 230 p. 23 cm. [E184.I 6B8] 51-14142
1. Irish in the U. S. I. Title.

Irish in the United States—Biography.

BIRMINGHAM, Stephen. 917.3'06'9162 B
Real lace: America's Irish rich. [1st ed.] New York, Harper & Row [1973] xiii, 322 p. illus. 25 cm. [E184.I6B57] 73-4061 ISBN 0-06-010336-1 10.00
1. Irish in the United States—Biography. 2. United States—Social life and customs. 3. Upper classes—United States. I. Title.

BIRMINGHAM, Stephen. 917.3069162 B
Real lace: America's Irish rich. New York, Popular Library [1974, c1973] 287 p. illus 18 cm. [E184.I6B57] 1.75 (pbk.)
1. Irish in the United States—Biography. 2. United States—Social life and customs. 3. Upper classes—United States. I. Title.
L.C. card number for original edition: 73-4061.

Irving, Henry, Sir, 1838-1905.

ARCHER, William, 1856-1924. 792'.028'0924 B
Henry Irving, actor and manager; a critical study. London, Field & Tuer. St. Clair Shores, Mich., Scholarly Press, 1970. 108 p. port. 21 cm. (The Vellum-parchment shilling series of miscellaneous literature, no. 3) Reprint of the 1883 ed. [PN2598.I7A7 1970] 76-107156 ISBN 0-403-00468-3 1/
1. Irving, Henry, Sir, 1838-1905. I. Title. II. Series.

BINGHAM, Madeleine, Baroness Clanmorris. 792'.028'0924 B
Henry Irving and the Victorian theatre / by Madeleine Bingham ; foreword by John Gielgud. London ; Boston : G. Allen & Unwin, 1978. 312 p., [5] leaves of plates : ill. ; 24 cm. American ed. published under title: Henry Irving, the greatest Victorian actor. Includes index. Bibliography: p. [302]-305. [PN2598.I7B5 1978] 78-317240 ISBN 0-04-928038-4 : 21.00
1. Irving, Henry, Sir, 1838-1905. 2. Actors—Great Britain—Biography. I. Title.

BINGHAM, Madeleine, Baroness Clanmorris. 792'.028'0924 B
Henry Irving, the greatest Victorian actor / by Madeleine Bingham. New York : Stein and Day, [1977] p. cm. Bibliography: p. [PN2598.I7B5] 76-41231 10.00
1. Irving, Henry, Sir, 1838-1905. 2. Actors—England—Biography. I. Title.

BRERETON, Austin, 1862-1922. 792'.028'0924 B
The life of Henry Irving. New York, B. Blom, 1969. 2 v. in 1. illus., facsims., ports. 24 cm. "First published 1908." Includes bibliographies. [PN2598.I7B7 1969] 74-88604
1. Irving, Henry, Sir, 1838-1905. I. Title. BIP

CRAIG, Edward Gordon, 1872-1966. 792'.028'0924 B
Henry Irving. New York, B. Blom [1969] xi, 252 p. illus., facsims., maps, ports. 21 cm. Reprint of the London, 1930, ed. [PN2598.I7C73 1969] 79-91486
1. Irving, Henry, Sir, 1838-1905. BIP

JONES, Henry Arthur, 1851-1929. 792'.028'0924
The shadow of Henry Irving. New York, B. Blom [1969] 111 p. front. 21 cm. Reprint of the 1931 ed. [PN2598.I7J6 1969] 77-91527
1. Irving, Henry, Sir, 1838-1905. I. Title. BIP

POLLOCK, Walter Herries, 1850-1926. 792'.028'0924
Impressions of Henry Irving, gathered in public and private during a friendship of many years. With a pref. by H. B. Irving. New York, B. Blom, 1971. vii, 140 p. 22 cm. Reprint of the 1908 ed. [PN2598.I7P6 1971] 70-93171
1. Irving, Henry, Sir, 1838-1905. I. Title.

STOKER, Bram, 1847-1912. 792'.028'0924
Personal reminiscences of Henry Irving. Westport, Conn., Greenwood Press [1970] 2 v. illus., facsims., ports. 23 cm. "Originally published in 1906." [PN2598.I7S7 1970] 70-98876
1. Irving, Henry, Sir, 1838-1905. 2. Actors—Correspondence, reminiscences, etc. I. Title. BIP

Irving, Washington,

IRVING, Washington, 1783-1859. 818'.2'08
Journals and notebooks. Edited by Nathalia Wright. Madison, University of Wisconsin Press, 1969- v. facsims., port. 24 cm. (The Complete works of Washington Irving) Contents.Contents.—v. 1. 1803-1806. —1819-1827, edited by W. A. Reichart. Bibliographical footnotes. [PS2081.A2 1969] 69-16115 ISBN 0-299-05320-2 (v. 1) varies
I. Wright, Nathalia, ed. II. Title.

IRVING, Washington, 1783-1859. 813'.2
Washington Irving and the House of Murray; Geoffrey Crayon charms the British, 1817-1856. Ben Harris McClary, editor. [1st ed.] Knoxville, University of Tennessee Press [1969] xlv, 242 p. illus., ports. 24 cm. Letters by Washington Irving, chiefly to John Murray II, his publisher, with the editor's commentary. Bibliography: p. 222-236. [PS2081.A3 1969] 73-77843 8.50
I. Murray, John, publisher, London. II. McClary, Ben Harris, ed. III. Title.

Irving, Washington, 1783-1859.

ADAMS, Charles, 1808-1890. 818'.2'09 B
Memoir of Washington Irving. With selections from his works and criticisms. Freeport, N.Y., Books for Libraries Press [1971] 299 p. 23 cm. Reprint of the 1870 ed. [PS2081.A6 1971] 70-148869 ISBN 0-8369-5641-9
1. Irving, Washington, 1783-1859. I. Irving, Washington, 1783-1859. Selections from his works and criticisms. 1971. II. Title.

IRVING, Pierre Munroe, 1803-1876. 818'.2'08
The life and letters of Washington Irving. Detroit, Gale Research Co., 1967. 4 v. ports. 22 cm. (The Gale library of lives and letters. American writers series) Reprint of the 1863-64 ed. [PS2081.A3 1967] 67-23893
1. Irving, Washington, 1783-1859. I. Irving, Washington, 1783-1859. II. Title.

IRVING, Pierre Munroe, 1803-1876. 818'.2'09 B
The life and letters of Washington Irving. New York, Putnam. [New York, AMS Press, 1973] 3 v. ports. 19 cm. (The works of Washington Irving, v. 12-14) At head of title: Hudson edition. Reprint of the 1889 ed. [PS2081.A3 1973] 73-8737 20.00 ea.
1. Irving, Washington, 1783-1859. I. Title. BIP

IRVING, Washington, 1783-1859. 818'.2'08
Journals and notebooks. Edited by Nathalia Wright. Madison, University of Wisconsin Press, 1969- v. facsims., port. 24 cm. (The Complete works of Washington Irving) Contents.Contents.—v. 1. 1803-1806. —1819-1827, edited by W. A. Reichart. Bibliographical footnotes. [PS2081.A2 1969] 69-16115 ISBN 0-299-05320-2 (v. 1) varies
I. Wright, Nathalia, ed. II. Title.

IRVING, Washington, 1783-1859. 914
The journals of Washington Irving (hitherto unpublished) Edited by William P. Trent and George S. Hellman. New York, Haskell House, 1970. 3 v. illus., facsims., ports. 23 cm. Reprint of the 1919 ed. [PS2081.A2 1970] 71-92970
1. Europe—Description and travel—1800-1918. 2. U.S.—Description and travel—1783-1848. I. Trent, William Peterfield, 1862-1939, ed. II. Hellman, George Sydney, 1878- joint ed. III. Bibliophile society, Boston.

IRVING, Washington, 1783-1859. 818'.2'09 B
Letters from Sunnyside and Spain. Edited by Stanley T. Williams. [Folcroft, Pa.] Folcroft Library Editions, 1973 [c1928] p. Reprint of the ed. published by Yale University Press, New Haven. [PS2081.A3 1973b] 73-15821 ISBN 0-8414-5056-0 (lib. bdg.)
1. Irving, Washington, 1783-1859. I. Title. BIP

IRVING, Washington, 1783-1859. 813'.2
Washington Irving and the House of Murray; Geoffrey Crayon charms the British, 1817 1856. Ben Harris McClary, editor. [1st ed.] Knoxville, University of Tennessee Press [1969] xlv, 242 p. illus., ports. 24 cm. Letters by Washington Irving, chiefly to John Murray II, his publisher, with the editor's commentary. Bibliography: p. 222-236. [PS2081.A3 1969] 73-77843 8.50
I. Murray, John, publisher, London. II. McClary, Ben Harris, ed. III. Title.

LEARY, Lewis Gaston, 1906- 817.2
Washington Irving. Minneapolis, University of Minnesota Press [1963] 48 p. 21 cm. (University of Minnesota. Pamphlets on American writers, no. 25) Includes bibliography. [PS2081.L4 1963] 63-62711
1. Irving, Washington, 1783-1859.

MCFARLAND, Philip James. 818'.2'09 B
Sojourners / Philip McFarland. 1st ed. New York : Atheneum, 1979. xvii, 587 p., [8] leaves of plates : ill. ; 24 cm. Includes index. Bibliography: p. [565]-572. [PS2081.M3] 79-63630 ISBN 0-689-11003-0 : 22.50
1. Irving, Washington, 1783-1859. 2. Authors, American—19th century—Biography. I. Title.

PEARE, Catherine Owens. 928.1
Washington Irving: his life. Illustrated by Margaret Ayer. [1st ed.] New York, Holt [1957] 128p. illus. 21cm. [PS2081.P4] 57-5746
1. Irving, Washington, 1783-1859. I. Title.

PEARE, Catherine Owens. 928.1
Washington Irving: his life. Illustrated by Margaret Ayer. [1st ed.] New York, Holt [1957] 128p. illus. 21cm. [PS2081.P4] 57-5746
1. Irving, Washington, I. Title.

STODDARD, Richard Henry, 1825-1903. 818'.2'09 B
The life of Washington Irving. [Folcroft, Pa.] Folcroft Library Editions, 1974 [c1879] 70 p. 23 cm. Reprint of the 1886 ed. published by J. B. Alden, New York. [PS2081.S67 1974] 74-17482 ISBN 0-8414-7816-3 (lib. bdg.)
1. Irving, Washington, 1783-1859. I. Title. BIP

WAGENKNECHT, Edward Charles, 1900- 818.2
Washington Irving: moderation displayed. New York, Oxford University Press, 1962. 223 p. illus. 21 cm. Includes bibliography. [PS2081.W2] 62-9833
1. Irving, Washington, 1783-1859.

WILLIAMS, Stanley Thomas, 1888-1956. 818'.2'09 B
The life of Washington Irving. New York, Octagon Books, 1971 [c1935] 2 v. illus. 24 cm. Includes bibliographical references. [PS2081.W45 1971] 73-154672 ISBN 0-374-98630-4
1. Irving, Washington, 1783-1859. I. Title.

WOOD, James Playsted, 1905- 92
Sunnyside; a life of Washington Irving. Illus. by Antony Saris. [New York] Pantheon Books [1967] 182 p. illus. 22 cm. Bibliography: p. [181]-182. A biography of the gentleman traveler and writer who became America's first recognized man of letters, noting the history and growth of the United States as it affected Irving's long career. [PS2081.W6] AC 67
1. Irving, Washington, 1783-1859. I. Saris, Antony, illus. II. Title.

Irving, Washington, 1783-1859—Biography.

CURTIS, George William, 1824-1892. 818'.2'09 B
Washington Irving : a sketch / by George William Curtis. Folcroft, Pa. : Folcroft Library Editions, 1976 [c1891] p. cm. Reprint of the ed. published by the Grolier Club, New York. [PS2081.C8 1976] 76-28379 ISBN 0-8414-3489-1 lib. bdg. : 20.00
1. Irving, Washington, 1783-1859—Biography. 2. Authors, American—19th century—Biography. BIP

JOHNSTON, Johanna. 818'.2'09 B
The heart that would not hold; a biography of Washington Irving. New York, M. Evans [1971] viii, 376 p. 22 cm. Bibliography: p. 363-366. [PS2081.J6] 72-122821 7.95
1. Irving, Washington, 1783-1859—Biography. I. Title. BIP

Irving, Washington, 1783-1859—Biography—Juvenile literature.

WASHINGTON Irving : 818'.2'09 B
as others saw him / by George Sanderlin. New York : Coward, McCann & Geoghegan, [1975] 128 p. : ill. ; 21 cm. Includes index. Bibliography: p. 124. A biography of one of America's earliest great literary figures with selections from his works and a collection of opinions written by critics of his day and since. [PS2081.W34 1975] 92 74-79701 ISBN 0-698-20296-1 : 5.95.
1. Irving, Washington, 1783-1859—Biography—Juvenile literature. I. Sanderlin, George William, 1915- II. Title. BIP

Irving, Washington, 1783-1859—Correspondence.

IRVING, Washington, 1783-1859. 818'.2'09 B
Letters / Washington Irving ; edited by Ralph M. Aderman, Herbert L. Kleinfield, and Jenifer S. Banks. Boston : Twayne, 1978- p. cm. (His The complete works of Washington Irving ; v. 23-) Includes index. Contents.Contents.—v. 1. 1802-1823. [PS2081.A4 1978] 78-13933 ISBN 0-8057-8522-1 lib. bdg. : 30.00
1. Irving, Washington, 1783-1859—Correspondence. 2. Authors, American—19th century—Correspondence. I. Aderman, Ralph M. II. Kleinfield, H. L. III. Banks, Jenifer S.

IRVING, Washington, 1783-1859. 818'.2'09 B
Letters from Sunnyside and Spain / by Washington Irving ; edited by Stanley T. Williams. Norwood, Pa. : Norwood Editions, 1976 [c1928] vi, 80 p. : ill. ; 24 cm. Reprint of the ed. published by Yale University Press, New Haven. [PS2081.A4 1976] 76-8537 ISBN 0-8482-1152-9 lib. bdg. : 8.50
1. Irving, Washington, 1783-1859—Correspondence. I. Title. BIP

Irving, Washington, 1783-1859—Juvenile literature.

SETON, Anya 928.1
Washington Irving. Illustrated by Harve Stein. Boston, Houghton Mifflin [c.]1960. 184p. illus. (part col.) 22cm. (North Star books [19]) 60-5216 1.95: 2.80 lib. ed.,
1. Irving, Wasington, 1783-1859—Juvenile literature. I. Title.

WOOD, James Playsted, 1905- 818'.2'08 B
Sunnyside; a life of Washington Irving. Illus. by Antony Saris. [New York] Pantheon Books [1967] 182 p. illus. 22 cm. Bibliography: p. [181]-182. [PS2081.W6] 67-20224
1. Irving, Washington, 1783-1859—Juvenile literature. I. Title.

Irwin, Henry, 1859-1902.

MERCIER, Anne. 266.3'0924 B
Father Pat; a hero of the Far West, by Mrs. Jerome Mercier. With a pref. by John Dart. Gloucester, Minchin & Gibbs, 1909; [Vernon, B.C.] Okanagan Historical Society, 1968. 109 p. illus., ports. 19 cm. [BX5620.174M4] 74-478727
1. Irwin, Henry, 1859-1902. I. Okanagan Historical Society, Vernon, B.C. II. Title.

Irwin, James Benson.

IRWIN, James Benson. 629.4'092'4 B
To rule the night; the discovery voyage of astronaut Jim Irwin, by James B. Irwin with William A. Emerson, Jr. [1st ed.] Philadelphia, A. J. Holman Co. [1973] 251 p. illus. 22 cm. [TL789.85.178A3] 73-11410 ISBN 0-87981-024-6 6.95
1. Irwin, James Benson. 2. Project Apollo. 3. Religion and astronautics. I. Emerson, William A., 1923- joint author. II. Title.

IRWIN, James Benson. 629.4'092'4 B
To rule the night; the discovery voyage of astronaut Jim Irwin, by James B. Irwin, with William A. Emerson, Jr. Boston, G. K. Hall, 1974 [c1973] 418 p. 25 cm. Large print ed. [TL789.85.I78A3 1974] 74-4364 ISBN 0-8161-6219-0 12.95 (lib. bdg.)
*1. Irwin, James Benson. 2. Project Apollo. 3. Religion and astronautics. I. Emerson, William A., 1923- joint author. II. Title.*BIP

IRWIN, James Benson. 629.4'092'4 B
To rule the night; the discovery voyage of Astronaut Jim Irwin, by James B. Irwin with William A. Emerson, Jr. New York, Ballantine Books [1974, c1973] 212 p. 18 cm. [[TL789.85.178A3]] 1.50 (pbk.)
1. Irwin, James Benson. 2. Project Apollo. Religion and astronautics. I. Emerson, William A., 1923- joint author II. Title.
L.C. card number for original edition 73-11410.

Irwin, Mary, 1938-

IRWIN, Mary, 1938- 248'.2'0924 B
The moon is not enough / Mary Irwin, with Madalene Harris. Grand Rapids : Zondervan Pub. House, c1978. 175 p., [8] leaves of plates : ill. ; 22 cm. [BR1725.178A35] 78-5395 ISBN 0-310-37050-7 : 6.95
1. Irwin, Mary, 1938- 2. Christian biography—United States. I. Harris, Madalene, 1925- joint author. II. Title. BIP

Isaac, Godfrey.

ISAAC, Godfrey. 345'.73'00924 B
I'll see you in court / Godfrey Isaac, with Richard Kleiner. Chicago : Contemporary Books, c1979. p. cm. [KF373.178A34] 79-51021 ISBN 0-8092-7399-3 : 9.95
1. Isaac, Godfrey. 2. Lawyers—United States—Biography. 3. Trials—United States. I. Kleiner, Richard, joint author. II. Title. BIP

Isaac, Stanley M., 1882-1962.

ISAACS, Edith S. 352.07471(B)
Love affair with a city; the story of Stanley M. Isaacs. by Edith S. Isaacs. New York, Random [1967] 167p. illus., ports. 22cm. [F128.5.I7818] 67-12756 4.95 bds.,
1. Isaac, Stanley M., 1882-1962. 2. New York (City)—Pol. & govt.—1898-1951. I. Title.

Isaac, the patriarch—Juvenile literature.

COHEN, Barbara. 221.9'24 B
The binding of Isaac / Barbara Cohen ; illustrated by Charles Mikolaycak. 1st ed. New York : Lothrop Lee & Shepard, c1978. [32] p. : col. ill. ; 22 cm. An aged Isaac recounts to his grandchildren the story of how God tested Abraham by asking him to sacrifice his son. [BS580.I67C63] 77-90367 ISBN 0-688-41830-9. ISBN 0-688-51830-3 lib. bdg. : 6.67
1. Isaac, the patriarch—Juvenile literature. 2. Abraham, the patriarch—Juvenile literature. 3. Bible. O.T.—Biography—Juvenile literature. 4. Patriarchs (Bible)—Biography—Juvenile literature. I. Mikolaycak, Charles. II. Title.

†GRIFFITHS, Kitty Anna. 222'.11'0924
Come, meet Isaac : the story of Genesis 25-28 / Kitty Anna Griffiths. Grand Rapids : Zondervan Pub. House, 1977. 95 p. : ill. ; 21 cm. (Come, meet series) Retells the life of Isaac, as found in Genesis. [BS580.I67G74] 76-13173 ISBN 0-310-25211-3 pbk : 1.95
1. Isaac, the patriarch—Juvenile literature. 2. Bible. O.T.—Biography—Juvenile literature. 3. Patriarchs (Bible)—Biography—Juvenile literature. I. Title.

Isaacs, Isaac Alfred, Sir, 1855-1948.

COWEN, Zelman. 354'.03'0924 B
Isaac Isaacs. Melbourne, New York, [etc.] Oxford University Press, 1967. viii, 272 p. illus., ports. 23 cm. [LAW] 68-94296 6.00 Aust.
1. Isaacs, Isaac Alfred, Sir, 1855-1948. BIP

Isaacs, Jorge, 1837-1895.

MCGRADY, Donald. 868
Jorge Isaacs. New York, Twayne Publishers [1972] 172 p. 21 cm. (Twayne's world authors series, TWAS166. Colombia) Bibliography: p. 163-165. [PQ8179.I8Z7] 75-120490
1. Isaacs, Jorge, 1837-1895. BIP

Isabel I, la Catolica, Queen of Spain, 1451-1504.

SENIOR, Ray. 946'.03
The crescent and Castile; a historical narrative on the reign of Spain's greatest queen, Isabel of Castile (1451: 1474-1504). [New York, Finch College, c1971] 124 p. port. 23 cm. "A synthesis of the reconquest": p. 81-123. Bibliography: p. 124. [DP162.S44] 76-175145
1. Isabel I, la Catolica, Queen of Spain, 1451-1504. 2. Spain—History—Ferdinand and Isabella, 1479-1516. 3. Spain—History—Arab period, 711-1492. I. Title.

Isabel I, la Catolica, Queen of Spain, 1451-1504—Juvenile literature.

NOBLE, Iris. 946'.03'0924 B
Spain's golden Queen Isabella. New York, J. Messner [1969] 191 p. 22 cm. Bibliography: p. 183. A biography of the Spanish queen who unified and strengthened her country yet brought about the infamous Spanish Inquisition. [DP163.N6] 92 70-79697 3.50
1. Isabel I, la Catolica, Queen of Spain, 1451-1504—Juvenile literature. I. Title.

Isabel II, Queen of Spain, 1830-1904.

BOETZKES, Ottilie Gertrude. 946.070924 (B)
The little queen; Isabella II of Spain, by Ottilie G. Boetzkes. [1st ed.] New York, Exposition Press [1966] 119, [1] p. illus., ports. 22 cm. Bibliography: p. [120] [DP216.B6] 66-4648
1. Isabel II, Queen of Spain, 1830-1904. I. Title.

DE POLNAY, Peter, 1906- 923.146
A queen of Spain, Isabel II. London, Hollis & Carter [dist. Chester Springs, Pa., Dufour, 1963, c.1962] 215p. illus. 23cm. 63-69 6.00
1. Isabel II, Queen of Spain, 1830-1904. I. Title.

Isabella d'Este, consort of Francis II, Marquis of Mantua, 1474-1539.

MAREK, George Richard, 1902- 945'.05'0924 B
The bed and the throne : the life of Isabella d'Este / George R. Marek. 1st ed. New York : Harper & Row, c1976. xix, 263 p. : ill. ; 25 cm. Includes index. Bibliography: p. [250]-252. [DG540.8.I7M37 1976] 76-5142 ISBN 0-06-012810-0 : 15.00
*1. Isabella d'Este, consort of Francis II, Marquis of Mantua, 1474-1539. I. Title.*BIP

MEYER, Edith Patterson. 945'.05'0924 B
First lady of the Renaissance; a biography of Isabella d'Este. [1st ed.] Boston, Little, Brown [1970] xv, 272 p. illus., map, ports. 22 cm. Bibliography: p. 266. [DG540.8.I7M46] 71-113438 5.95
1. Isabella d'Este, consort of Francis II, Marquis of Mantua, 1474-1539. I. Title.

Isackson, Maxie Bridgman, 1933-

ISACKSON, Maxie Bridgman, 1933- 973.9'092'2 B
The sandhills beckon / by Maxie Bridgman Isackson. 1st ed. Broken Bow, Neb. : Purcell's, [1977?] 156 p. : ill. ; 23 cm. [CT275.I66A37] 76-42169 10.00
1. Isackson, Maxie Bridgman, 1933- 2. Bridgman, Howard, 1906-1970. 3. United States—Biography. I. Title. BIP

Isaiah, the Prophet—Juvenile literature.

HEIFNER, Fred. 224'.1'0924 B
Isaiah, messenger for God / Fred Heifner ; illustrated by Cliff Johnston. Nashville : Broadman Press, c1978. 48 p. : col. ill. ; 24 cm. (Biblearn series) Tells how Isaiah began prophesying for God. [BS580.I7H43] 78-105150 ISBN 0-8054-4243-X pbk. : 3.95
1. Isaiah, the Prophet—Juvenile literature. 2. Bible. O.T.—Biography. 3. Prophets—Biography—Juvenile literature. I. Johnston, Cliff. II. Title.

Ise, Rose Christina (Haag) 1856-

ISE, John, 1885- 917.81215
Sod and stubble; the story of a Kansas homestead, by John Ise; illustrated by Howard Simon. New York, Wilson-Erickson, incorporated, 1936. xii p., 21., 326 p. incl. front. plates, 2 port. 23 1/2 cm. An account of the lives of the author's parents. [F686.I74] 37-10937
1. 1. Ise, Rosa Christina (Haag) 1856- 2. 2. Ise, Henry Christopher, 1841-1900. 3. Frontier and pioneer life — Kansas — Osborne Co. I. Simon, Howard, 1903- illus. II. Title. BIP

Isham, Asa Brainerd,

ISHAM, Asa Brainerd, 1844- 926.1
1912.
Autobiography of Asa Brainerd Isham, M. D., 1844-1912; condensed and rewritten by A. Chapman Isham. Published by his kin. [Ann Arbor? Mich., 1957] 107p. illus. 23cm. 'Originally titled 'An average American.' [R154. I 74A3] 58-30542
I. Title.

Isherwood. Benjamin Franklin. 1822-1915.

SLOAN, Edward 623.87220924
William, III
Benjamin Franklin Isherwood, naval engineer: the years as engineer in chief. 1861-1869. Annapolis. Md., U.S. Naval Inst. [1966, c.1965] xiii, 299p. illus., ports. 24cm. Bibl. [VM140.I8S55] 65-22011 7.50
1. Isherwood. Benjamin Franklin. 1822-1915. I. Title.

Isherwood, Christopher, 1904-

FINNEY, Brian. 823'.9'12 B
Christopher Isherwood : a critical biography / by Brian Finney. New York : Oxford University Press, 1979. p. cm. Includes index. Bibliography: p. [PR6017.S5Z65] 78-26622 ISBN 0-19-520134-5 : 12.95
1. Isherwood, Christopher, 1904- 2. Authors, English—20th century—Biography. BIP

KING, Francis Henry. 823'.9'12 B
Christopher Isherwood / by Francis King ; edited by Ian Scott-Kilvert. Harlow [Eng.] : Published for the British Council by Longman Group, 1976. 28 p. ; 22 cm. (Writers & their work ; 240) "Christopher Isherwood, a select bibliography": p. 25-26. [PR6017.S5Z75] 76-368751 ISBN 0-582-01250-3
1. Isherwood, Christopher, 1904- 2. Authors, English—20th century—Biography. I. Title. II. Series.

WILDE, Alan. 823'.9'12
Christopher Isherwood. New York, Twayne Publishers [1971] 171 p. 22 cm. (Twayne's United States authors seris, 173) Bibliography: p. 161-165. [PR6017.S5Z9] 75-120013
1. Isherwood, Christopher, 1904-

Isherwood, Christopher, 1904——Bibliography.

FUNK, Robert W., 016.823'9'12
1937-
Christopher Isherwood : a reference guide / Robert W. Funk. Boston : G. K. Hall, c1979. xviii, 196 p. ; 25 cm. (A Reference publication in literature) Includes index. [Z8441.F85] [PR6017.S5] 78-10199 ISBN 0-8161-8072-5 : 24.00
1. Isherwood, Christopher, 1904- Bibliography. I. Title. II. Series. BIP

Isherwood, Christopher, 1904- —Biography.

FRYER, Jonathan. 823'.9'12 B
Isherwood / Jonathan Fryer. 1st ed. Garden City, N.Y. : Doubleday, 1978, c1977. 304 p., [8] leaves of plates : ill. ; 22 cm. Includes index. "The major works of Christopher Isherwood": p. [293]-294. [PR6017.S5Z67 1978] 77-82941 ISBN 0-385-12608-5 : 10.00
1. Isherwood, Christopher, 1904- —Biography. 2. Authors, English—20th century—Biography. BIP

ISHERWOOD, 823'.9'12 B
Christopher, 1904-
Christopher and his kind / Christopher Isherwood. New York : Farrar, Straus and Giroux, [1976] p. cm. [PR6017.S5Z498] 76-42228 8.95
1. Isherwood, Christopher, 1904- —Biography. 2. Authors, English—20th century—Biography. I. Title. BIP

Isherwood, Christopher, 1904- —Criticism and interpretation.

PIAZZA, Paul, 1941- 823'.9'12
Christopher Isherwood : myth and anti-myth / Paul Piazza. New York : Columbia University Press, 1978. xii, 245 p. ; 22 cm. Includes index. Bibliography: p. [229]-235. [PR6017.S5Z8] 77-14271 ISBN 0-231-04118-7 : 12.50
1. Isherwood, Christopher, 1904- —Criticism and interpretation. BIP

Isherwood, Kathleen Machell Smith, 1868-1960.

ISHERWOOD, Christopher, 823'.9'12
1904-
Kathleen and Frank. New York, Curtis Bks. [1973? c.1971] 500 p. 18 cm. [PR6017.S5Z5 1972] pap., 1.25
1. Isherwood, Kathleen Machell Smith, 2. Isherwood, Francis Edward Bradshaw, I. Title. BIP

ISHERWOOD, 823'.9'12 B
Christopher, 1904-
Kathleen and Frank. New York, Simon and Schuster [1972, c1971] 510 p. illus. 23 cm. [PR6017.S5Z5 1972] 70-156155 ISBN 0-671-20991-4 10.00
1. Isherwood, Kathleen Machell Smith, 1868-1960. 2. Isherwood, Francis Edward Bradshaw, 1869-1915. I. Title.

Ishi, d. 1916.

KROEBER, Theodora. 970.3
Ishi in two worlds; a biography of the last wild Indian in North America. With a foreword by Lewis Gannett. Berkeley, University of California Press, 1961. 255 p. illus., ports., maps. 24 cm. Bibliography: p. [245]-255. [E90.I8K7] 61-7530
1. Ishi, d. 1916. 2. Yana Indians. BIP

KROEBER, Theodora. 970'.004'97 B
Ishi in two worlds : a biography of the last wild Indian in North America / Theodora Kroeber. Berkeley : University of California Press, c1976. 262 p., [12] leaves of plates : ill. ; 27 cm. Includes index. Bibliography: p. [253]-259. [E99.Y23K76 1976] 75-36501 14.95
1. Ishi, d. 1916. 2. Yana Indians. I. Title.

Ishi, d. 1916—Addresses, essays, lectures.

ISHI, the last Yahi 970'.004'97
: a documentary history / edited by Robert F. Heizer and Theodora Kroeber. Berkeley : University of California Press, c1979. viii, 242 p. : ill. ; 21 cm. [E99.Y23I8] 76-19966 ISBN 0-520-03296-9 : 17.50
1. Ishi, d. 1916—Addresses, essays, lectures. 2. Yana Indians—Biography—Addresses, essays, lectures. 3. Yana Indians—Addresses, essays, lectures. I. Heizer, Robert Fleming, 1915- II. Kroeber, Theodora.

Ishikawa, Takuboku, 1886-1912.

HIJIYA, Yukihito. 895.6'1'4 B
Ishikawa Takuboku / by Yukihito Hijiya. Boston : Twayne Publishers, c1979. 205 p. ; 21 cm. (Twayne's world authors series ; TWAS 539 : Japan) Includes index. Bibliography: p. 195-199. [PL809.S5Z656] 78-27748 ISBN 0-8057-6381-3 : 13.95
1. Ishikawa, Takuboku, 1886-1912. 2. Authors, Japanese—20th century—Biography. I. Title. BIP

Islamic Empire—Biography.

HITTI, Philip 920'.009176'7
Khuri, 1886-
Makers of Arab history, by Philip K. Hitti. New York, St. Martin's Press [1968] 268 p. maps. 22 cm. Bibliographical footnotes. [D198.3.H5] 68-20139 6.95
1. Islamic Empire—Biography. I. Title. BIP

Island Lake, Wis.

PURCELL, 917.75'13'0340924
William Gray, 1880-1965.
St. Croix Trail country; recollections of Wisconsin. Minneapolis, University of Minnesota Press [1967] ix, 123 p. illus., maps, ports. 23 cm. [F587.B3P8 1967] 67-15435
1. Island Lake, Wis. 2. St. Croix Trail. 3. Country life—Wisconsin—Bayfield Co. I. Title.

Isley, Albert E., 1871-

ISLEY, Albert E., 340'.092'4 B
1871-
A lamp in the dark; autobiography and essays, by Albert E. Isley. [Newton, Ill., Mentor-Democrat Co., 1953] 79 p. port. 22 cm. [KF373.I84A33] 74-172503
1. Isley, Albert E., 1871- I. Title.

Isma'il I, Shah of Iran, 1487-1524.

SARWAR, Ghulam, 955'.03'0924 B
historian.
History of Shah Isma'il Safawi / by Ghulam Sarwar ; with a foreword by Hadi Hasan. New York : AMS Press, 1975. xiii, 126 p. ; 23 cm. Reprint of the 1939 ed. published by the author in Aligarh. Includes index. Bibliography: p. 114-115. [DS292.3.S3 1975] 75-180376 ISBN 0-404-56322-8 : 12.50
1. Isma'il I, Shah of Iran, 1487-1524. 2. Iran—History—16th-18th centuries. I. Title.

Ismay, Hastings Lionel Ismay, Baron, 1887-1965.

ISMAY, Hastings 942.082'092'4
Lionel Ismay, Baron, 1887-1965.
The memoirs of General Lord Ismay. Westport, Conn., Greenwood Press [1974, c1960] viii, 488 p. illus. 22 cm. Reprint of the ed. published by Viking Press, New York. Includes bibliographical references. [DA69.3.I8A3 1974] 73-22504 ISBN 0-8371-6280-7
1. Ismay, Hastings Lionel Ismay, Baron, 1887-1965. 2. World War, 1939-1945—Personal narratives, English. I. Title. BIP

ISMAY, Hastings 942.082'092'4
Lionel Ismay, Baron, 1887-1965.
The memoirs of General Lord Ismay. Westport, Conn., Greenwood Press [1974, c1960] viii, 488 p. illus. 22 cm. Reprint of the ed. published by Viking Press, New York. Includes bibliographical references. [DA69.3.I8A3 1974] 73-22504 ISBN 0-8371-6280-7 19.00
1. Ismay, Hastings Lionel Ismay, Baron, 1887-1965. 2. World War, 1939-1945—Personal narratives, English. I. Title.

Ismond, Wolfe.

OGLE, Mary S., 266'.6'7510924 B
1905-
Shanghai Wolfe; the Wolfe Ismond story, by Mary S. Ogle. Nashville, Tenn., Southern Pub. Association [1972] 174 p. 22 cm. [BX6193.I74O4] 72-86322 ISBN 0-8127-0065-1
1. Ismond, Wolfe. I. Title.

Israel — hist

COMAY, Joan. 956.94'05'0924
Ben-Gurion and the birth of Israel. New York, Random House [1967] 178 p. ills., map, ports. 22 cm. (World landmark books, W-62) Ben-Gurion, David, 1886- -- Juvenile literature. [DS125.3.B37c6] 67-5329
1. Israel — hist — Juvenile literature. I. Title.

Israel-Arab War, 1967- —Biography—Juvenile literature.

BRAVERMAN, Libbie (Levin) 956
1900-
The six-day warriors; an introduction to those who gave Israel its vigor and its victories [by] Libbie L. Braverman and Samuel M. Silver. New York, Bloch Pub. Co. [1969] xi, 165 p. illus., ports. 25 cm. The events of the Six-Day War serve as background to brief biographies of Israeli soldiers and citizens who participated. [DS127.15.B7] 920 B 75-78093 4.95
1. Israel-Arab War, 1967- —Biography—Juvenile literature. I. Silver, Samuel M., joint author. II. Title. BIP

Israel—Biography.

BELONGING : 920'.05694
conversations in Israel / by James McNeish ; research by James and Helen McNeish. 1st ed. New York : Holt, Rinehart and Winston, c1980. p. cm. [CT1919.P35B44] 79-19050 ISBN 0-03-046796-9 : 9.95 9.95
1. Israel—Biography. 2. Israel—Emigration and immigration—Biography. I. McNeish, James. BIP

LITVINOFF, Barnet. 923.2564
Ben-Gurion of Israel. New York, Praeger [1954] xii, 273p. ports., maps. 22cm. [DS125.3.B37L5] 54-9526
I. Ben-Gurion, David, 1887- II. Title.

SACHAR, Howard Morley, 923.25693
1928-
Aliyah; the peoples of Israel. Cleveland, World Pub Co. [c.1961] 475p. maps. 25cm. 61-12017 7.50
1. Israel—Biog. 2. Israel—Emig. & immig. I. Title.

ST. JOHN, Robert, 1902- 922.96
They came from everywhere; twelve who helped mold modern Israel. New York, Coward [c.1962] 256p. 22cm. Bibl. 62-14743 4.95
1. Israel— Biog. I. Title.

STEIN, Sarah 956.94'05'0922 B
Kisch.
Leaders in Israel; thumb-nail sketches of the officers of the first provisional government. Edited by Sarah Kisch Stein. Freeport, N.Y., Books for Libraries Press [1971, c1948] 20 p. 23 cm. (ZOA pamphlet series, no. 10) (Biography index reprint series) [DS149.A39463 no. 10] [DS126.6.A2] 71-179743 ISBN 0-8369-8111-1
1. Israel—Biography. I. Title. II. Series: Zionist Organization of America. ZOA pamphlet series, no. 10. BIP

WHO'S who in Israel, 920.0569
1966-67 Tel-Aviv Mamut Ltd., 1966 v. illus. 25 cm. Title varies. Edit. staff: 1966-67--Z. Harkavy, others. Chief reporter: 1965-66--Moshe Virreano. 46 6380 22.50
1. Israel—Biog. I. Harkavy, Z., ed. American distributor: Heinman, New York.

WHO'S who Israel, 1963-64. 920.0569
Ed. by Peretz Dagan. Tel-Aviv, Mamut [New York, Heinman, 1964] 942p. illus., ports. 25cm. Title varies. Each v. includes a pt. 2: Public bodies and enterprises. 46-6380 15.00
1. Israel—Biog. I. Dagan, Peretz, ed.

WHO'S who Israel, 1965. 920.0569
Edit. staff: Rabbi Dr. Z. Harkavy others Chief reporter: Moshe Virreano others Tel-Aviv, Mamut Ltd. [New York, Heniman] 1965. 916p. illus., ports. 25cm. Title varies. Each v. includes a pt. 2: Public bodies and enterprises. 46-6380 20.00
1. Israel—Biog. I. Harkavy, Z., ed.

Israel. Hel ha-avir—History.

WEIZMANN, Ezer, 358.4'13'310924 B
1924-
On eagles' wings : the personal story of the leading Commander of the Israeli Air Force / Ezer Weizman. London : Weidenfeld and Nicolson, c1976. 302 p., [4] leaves of plates : ill. ; 23 cm. Includes index. [UG635.I75W46] 76-362257 ISBN 0-297-77034-9 : £5.50
1. Israel. Hel ha-avir—History. 2. Weizmann, Ezer, 1924- 3. Israel—Air defenses, Military—History. I. Title.

Issari, Mohammad Ali.

ISSARI, Mohammad 915.5'04'50924 B
Ali.
A picture of Persia / Mohammad Ali Issari and Doria A. Paul. 1st ed. Hicksville, N.Y. : Exposition Press, c1977. x, 277 p., [28] leaves of plates : ill., maps (on lining papers) ; 24 cm. (An Exposition-university book) Includes index. Bibliography: p. 273-

274. [DS318.I84] 76-678 ISBN 0-682-48410-5 : 15.00
1. Issari, Mohammad Ali. 2. Iran—Description and travel. 3. Cinematographers—Biography. I. Paul, Doris Atkinson, joint author. II. Title. **BIP**

Issiah, the prophet.

VAN ZELLER, Hubert, Father, 1905- 224.1
Isaias, man of ideas. Westminster, Md., Newman Press, 1951. 123 p. 19 cm. [BS580.I7V3] 51-13745
1. Issiah, the prophet. I. Title.

Italian Americans—Biography.

NULL, Gary. 973'.04'51 B
The Italian-Americans / by Gary Null and Carl Stone ; in cooperation with the Italian-American Civil Rights League. Harrisburg, Pa. : Stackpole Books, c1976. vii, 220 p. ; 24 cm. Includes index. Bibliography: p. 206-211. [E184.I8N84] 75-42436 ISBN 0-8117-0930-2 : 10.00
1. Italian Americans—Biography. 2. United States—Biography. I. Stone, Carl, joint author. II. Title.

Italian Americans—History.

SCHIAVO, Giovanni Ermenegildo, 1898- 973'.04'51
The Italians in America before the Revolution / by Giovanni Schiavo. New York : Vigo Press, 1976. 182 p. ; 24 cm. Bibliography: p. 139-174. [E184.I8S36] 75-36320 12.95
1. Italian Americans—History. 2. Italian Americans—Biography. I. Title. **BIP**

Italians in London.

WICKS, Margaret Campbell Walker, 1893- 325.245'09421
The Italian exiles in London, 1816-1848, by Margaret C. W. Wicks. Freeport, N.Y., Books for Libraries Press [1968] xv, 316 p. 22 cm. (Essay index reprint series) Reprint of 1937 ed. Contents.Contents.—Ugo Foscolo.—Foscolo's friends and fellow exiles.—Santa Rosa.—Antonio Panizzi.—Rossetti, the Pistrucci family, Pepoli, Gallenga, Gambardella.—Giuseppe Mazzini.—Appendix.—Documentary sources and works consulted (p. 301-306) [DG551.7.W5 1968] 68-16987
1. Italians in London. 2. Refugees, Political. I. Title.

Italians in the United States—Juvenile literature.

MARINACCI, Barbara. 920.073
They came from Italy; the stories of famous Italian-Americans. New York, Dodd, Mead [1967] viii, 246 p. illus., maps, ports. 22 cm. Contents.Contents.—Introduction: the Italians come.—An iron hand in the wilderness: Henri de Tonti.—He talked of freedom: Philip Mazzei.—The artist of the Capitol: Constantino Brumidi.—The general commands a museum: Luigi Palma di Cesnola.—A saint among the immigrants: Francesa Xavier Cabrini.—The maestro in America: Arturo Toscanini.—A banker for Americans: A. P. Giannini.—The biggest little man in the country: Fiorella H. La Guardia.—Columbus to the atomic age: Enrico Fermi.—A summing up: the Italians stay.—Bibliography (p. 231-238) [E184.I8M28] 67-12949
1. Italians in the United States—Juvenile literature. I. Title.

Italy—Biog.

HALE, J. R. 923.245
Machiavelli and Ranaissance Italy. New York, Collier [1963, c.1960] 220p. 18cm. (AS526V) Bibl. .95 pap.,
I. Title.

LA SIZERANNE, Robert de, 1866-1932. 920'.0945
Celebrities of the Italian Renaissance in Florence and in the Louvre. Translated by Jeffery E. Jeffery. Freeport, N.Y., Books for Libraries Press [1969] 363 p. illus. ports. 22 cm. (Essay index reprint series) Reprint of the 1926 ed. Translation of Les masques et les visages a Florence et au Louvre. Includes bibliographical references. [DG540.8.A1L333 1969] 73-93354
1. Italy—Biography. 2. Italy—Biography—Portraits. 3. Renaissance—Italy. I. Title. **BIP**

PHILLIPS, John, 1914- 914.50392
The Italians; face of a nation. Introd. by Cornelius Ryan. New York, McGraw 1965. 140p. illus., ports. 29cm. [CT1133.P48] 65-18616 7.95 bds.,
1. Italy—Biog. 2. National characteristics, Italian—Pictorial works. I. Title.

PLUMB, John Harold, 1911- ed. 920.045
Renaissance profiles [by] Garrett Mattingly [others] New York, Harper [1965, c.1961] 161p. 21cm. (Harper torchbks., TB1162. Acad. lib.) First pub. in The Horizon bk. of the Renaissance. [DG531.8.A1P5] 65-1493 1.65 pap.,
1. Italy—Biog. 2. Renaissance. I. Title.

VESPASIANO DA BISTICCI, Fiorentino, 1421-1498 920.045
Renaissance princes, popes, and prelates; the Vespasiano memoirs, lives of illustrious men of the XVth century. Tr. [from Italian] by William George, Emily Waters. Introd. to the Torchbk. ed. by Myron P. Gilmore [Gloucester, Mass., P. Smith, 1964, c.1963] xvi, 475p. illus., ports. 21cm. (Harper torchbks. Acad. lib., TB/1111 rebound) Bibl. 4.50
1. Italy—Biog. I. Title. II. Title: The Vespasiano memoirs.

VESPASIANO DA BISTICCI, Fiorentino, 1421-1498 920.045
Renaissance princes, popes, and prelates; the Vespasiano memoirs, lives of illustrious men of the 15th century. Tr. [from Italian] by William George, Emily Waters. Introd. to Torchbk. ed. by Myron P. Gilmore. New York, Harper [c.1963] 470p. illus. 21cm. (Harper torchbk., acad. lib., TB1111) First. pub. in tr. in England in 1926 under title; The Vespasiano memoirs. 2.45 pap.,
1. Italy—Biog. I. Title.

VESPASIANO DA BISTICCI, Fiorentino 1421-1498. 920.045
Renaissance princes, popes, and prelates; the Vespasiano memoirs, lives of illustrious men of the XVth century. Translated by William George and Emily Waters. Introd. to the Torchbook ed. by Myron P. Gilmore. New York, Harper & Row [1963] xvi, 475 p. illus., ports. 21 cm. (Harper torchbooks. The Academy library) Includes bibliographies. [DG537.8.A1V6 1963] 64-3339
1. Italy — Biog. I. Title. II. Title: The Vespasiano memoirs.

VESPASIONO da Bisticei, fiorentino, 1421-1498 920.045
Renaissance princes, popes, and prelates; the Vespasiano memoirs, lives of illustrious men of the XVth century. Tr. [from Italian] by William George, Emily Waters. Introd. to the Torchbk. ed. by Myron P. Gilmore [Gloucester, Mass., P. Smith, 1964, c.1963] xvi, 475p. illus., ports. 21cm. (Harper torchbks. Acad. lib., TB/1111 rebound) Bibl. 4.50
1. Italy—Biog. I. Title. II. Title: The Vespasiano memoirs.

Italy—Kings and rulers.

PRESCOTT, Orville. 945'.00992 B
Lords of Italy; portraits from the Middle Ages. [1st ed.] New York, Harper & Row [1972] xv, 366 p. illus. 25 cm. Bibliography: p. 347-354. [DG463.2.P74 1972] 72-79688 ISBN 0-06-013412-7 10.00
1. Italy—Kings and rulers. 2. Biography—Middle Ages, 500-1500. I. Title.

Italy—Politics and government—1914-1945.

MUSSOLINI, Benito, 1883-1945. 945,091'0924 B
My autobiography. With a foreword by Richard Washburn Child. Westport, Conn., Greenwood Press [1970] xix, 318 p. illus., ports. 23 cm. Reprint of the 1928 ed. [DG575.M8A2 1970] 78-109803 ISBN 8-371-42946-
1. Italy—Politics and government—1914-1945. I. Child, Richard Washburn, 1881-1935. **BIP**

Italy. Servizio informazione forze armate.

COLLIN, Richard. 945.092'092'4 B
The de Lorenzo gambit : the Italian coup manque of 1964 / Richard Collin. Beverly Hills, Calif. : Sage Publications, c1976. 65 p. ; 22 cm. (Sage research papers in the social sciences ; v. 5, ser. no. 90-034 : Contemporary European studies) Includes bibliographical references. [DG579.D44C64] 75-6104 pbk. : 3.00
1. De Lorenzo, Giovanni, 1907-1973. 2. Italy. Servizio informazione forze armate. 3. Italy. Servizio informazione forze armate—Officials and employees—Biography. 4. Italy—Politics and government—1945- 5. Coups d'etat. 6. Generals—Italy—Biography. 7. Fascists—Italy—Biography. I. Title. II. Series: Sage research papers in the social sciences : Contemporary European studies.

Ivan iv, the Terrible, Czar of Russia, 1530-1584.

WALISZEWSKI, Kazimierz, 1849-1935 947.04
Ivan the Terrible. Tr. from French by Lady Mary Loyd. Hamden, Conn., Archon [dist. Shoe String 1966] xiv, 431p. port. 22cm. First pub. in 1904. Bibl. [DK106.W2] 66-16088 11.50
1. Ivan iv, the Terrible, Czar of Russia, 1530-1584. 2. Russia—Hist.—Ivan iv, 1533-1584. I. Title.

Ivanov, Lev Ivanovich, 1834-1901.

SLONIMSKII, Iurii Iosifovich. 927.928
Writings on Lev Ivanov. With a biography of Ivanov in excerpts from M. Borisoglebsky.Translated and edited with annotations by Anatole Chujoy. Cover designed by Karl Leabo. [Brooklyn, Dance Perspectives, inc.] 1959. 64 p. illus. 23 cm. (Dance perspectives, 2) [GV1787.D28 no. 2] 59-2632
1. Ivanov, Lev Ivanovich, 1834-1901. I. Title. **BIP**

Ivanov, Vsevolod Viacheslavovich,

IVANOV, Vsevolod Viacheslavovich, 1895- 928.917
The adventures of a fakir, by Vsevolod Ivanov. New York, The Vanguard press [1935] viii, 300p. 22cm. Abridged translation. [PG3476.I9P583] 36-17384
I. Title.

Ives, Charles Edward, 1874-1954.

IVES, Charles Edward, 1874-1954. 780'.92'4 B
Memos. Edited by John Kirkpatrick. [1st ed.] New York, W. W. Norton [1972] 355 p. illus. 25 cm. "Memos" (Ives' own title): p. [25]-142; "Appendices": p. [143]-324. [ML410.I94A3] 76-77407 ISBN 0-393-02153-X 12.50
1. Musicians—Correspondence, reminiscences, etc. I. Kirkpatrick, John, 1905- ed. II. Title.

PERLIS, Vivian. 780'.92'4 B
Charles Ives remembered : an oral history / by Vivian Perlis. New Haven : Yale University Press, 1974. xviii, 237 p. : ill. ; 27 cm. Includes bibliographical references and index. [ML410.I94P5] 74-75288 ISBN 0-300-01758-8 : 12.50
1. Ives, Charles Edward, 1874-1954. I. Title.

PERLIS, Vivian. 780'.92'4 B
Charles Ives remembered : an oral history / by Vivian Perlis. New York : W. W. Norton, 1976, c1974. p. cm. (The Norton library) Includes bibliographical references and index. [ML410.I94P5 1976] 76-20455 ISBN 0-393-00825-8 pbk. : 3.95
1. Ives, Charles Edward, 1874-1954. **BIP**

ROSSITER, Frank R. 780'.92'4 B
Charles Ives and his America / Frank R. Rossiter. 1st ed. New York : Liveright, [1975] xv, 420 p., [4] leaves of plates : ill. ; 24 cm. Includes index. Bibliography: p. 385-395. [ML410.I94R68] 75-12663 ISBN 0-87140-610-1 : 12.50
1. Ives, Charles Edward, 1874-1954. I. Title. **BIP**

SIVE, Helen R. 780'.92'4 B
Music's Connecticut Yankee : an introduction to the life and music of Charles Ives / Helen R. Sive. 1st ed. New York : Atheneum, 1977. xii, 141 p. : ill. ; 22 cm. Includes index. Bibliography: p. 131-132. Follows the life and discusses the music of the insurance executive who composed in his spare time music of such originality and variety that he ranks today as one of this country's greatest and most thoroughly American composers. [ML3930.I94S6] 92 76-25000 ISBN 0-689-30561-3 : 6.95
1. Ives, Charles Edward, 1874-1954. I. Title. **BIP**

WOOLDRIDGE, David, 1931- 780'.92'4 B
From the steeples and mountains; a study of Charles Ives. [1st ed.] New York, Knopf, 1974. 342, x p. illus. 25 cm. [ML410.I94W7] 73-7306 ISBN 0-394-48110-0 10.00
1. Ives, Charles Edward, 1874-1954. I. Title. **BIP**

Ives. Edward Riley, 1839-1918.

HERTZ, Louis Heilbroner. 688.7
Messrs. Ives of Bridgeport; the saga of America's greatest toymakers. [1st ed.] Wethersfield, Conn., M. Haber, 1950. xv, 159 p. illus., ports. 24 cm. Bibliography: p. 118-152. [HD9999.T72 I 95] 50-10804
1. Ives. Edward Riley, 1839-1918. 2. Ives. Harry Candee, 1867-1936. 3. Ives Manufacturing Corporation. I. Title.

Iwonski, Carl G. von, 1830-1922.

MCGUIRE, James Patrick. 760'.092'4 B
Iwonski in Texas : painter and citizen / James Patrick McGuire. [San Antonio] : San Antonio Museum Association, c1976. 96 p. : ill. (some col.) ; 24 cm. "Published in conjunction with an exhibition, Iwonski in Texas: painter and citizen, held at the Witte Memorial Museum, Brackenridge Park, San Antonio, Texas, August 1, 1976, to September 30, 1976, in cooperation with the University of Texas at San Antonio Institute of Texan Cultures." Includes index. Bibliography: p. 90-92. [N6537.I75M3] 76-12295
1. Iwonski, Carl G. von, 1830-1922. 2. Artists—Texas—Biography. I. Witte Memorial Museum, San Antonio. II. Title.

Izard, Ralph, 1742-1804.

IZARD, Ralph, 1742-1804. 973.3'092'4 B
Correspondence of Mr. Ralph Izard of South Carolina : from the year 1774 to 1804, with a short memoir. Volume I. New York : AMS Press, [1976] p. cm. No more published. Reprint of the 1844 ed. published by C. S. Francis, New York. [E302.6.I92A4 1976] 79-170810 ISBN 0-404-03535-3 : 16.50
1. Izard, Ralph, 1742-1804. 2. Statesmen—United States—Correspondence. 3. United States—Foreign relations—Revolution, 1775-1783—Sources.

Jagerstatter, Franz, 1907-1943.

KENT, Bruce. 940.53'162'0924 B
Franz Jagerstatter : (the man who said "no" to Hitler) / by Bruce Kent. London : Catholic Truth Society, 1976. [2], 9 p. ; 17 cm. [CT1098.J33K46] 77-363490 £0.10
1. Jagerstatter, Franz, 1907-1943. 2. Germany—Biography.

ZAHN, Gordon Charles, 1918- 922.2436
In solitary witness: the life and death of Franz Jagerstatter [by] Gordon C. Zahn. [1st ed.] New York, Holt, Rinehart and Winston [1965, c1964] 277 p. illus., facsim., ports. 22 cm. Bibliography: p. 274-277. [BX4705.J265Z3] 64-21935
1. Jagerstatter, Franz, 1907-1943. I. Title.

Juarez, Benito Pablo, Pres. Mexico, 1806-1872.

SMART, Charles 972'.07'0924 B
Allen, 1904-1967.
Viva Juarez! : A biography / by Charles Allen Smart. Westport, Conn. : Greenwood Press, 1975, c1963. 444 p. : ill. ; 22 cm. Reprint of the ed. published by Lippincott, Philadelphia. Includes bibliographical references and index. [F1233.J9535 1975] 74-24538 ISBN 0-8371-6145-2 lib.bdg. 20.75
1. Juarez, Benito Pablo, Pres. Mexico, 1806-1872. I. Title.

Junger, Ernst, 1895—

JUNGER, Ernst, 1895- 940.4'82'43
The storm of steel : from the diary of a German storm-troop officer on the western front / Ernst Junger ; with an introd. by R. H. Mottram. New York : H. Fertig, 1975. xv, 319 p. ; 23 cm. Translation of In Stahlgewittern. Reprint of the 1929 ed. published by Chatto & Windus, London. [D640.J693 1975] 75-22372 14.00
1. Junger, Ernst, 1895- 2. European War, 1914-1918—Personal narratives, German. I. Title.

Jack, Captain, Modoc Chief, -1873.

PAYNE, Doris (Palmer) v. 12
Captain Jack, Modoc renegade. Portland, Or., Binford & Mort, 1958. 259 p. maps, ports. 67-37162
1. Jack, Captain, Modoc Chief, -1873. 2. Modoc Indians—Wars, 1873. I. Title. BIP

Jackson, Abraham Valentine Williams, 1862-1937.

JACKSON, Abraham 915.5'04'5
Valentine Williams, 1862-1937.
From Constantinople to the home of Omar Khayyam : travels in Transcaucasia and northern Persia for historic and literary research / by A. V. Williams Jackson ; with over two hundred illustrations and a map. New York : AMS Press, 1975. xxxiii, 317 p., [81] leaves of plates : ill. ; 23 cm. Reprint of the 1911 ed. published by Macmillan, New York. Includes indexes. Bibliography: p. xxvii-xxxi. [DS258.J23 1975] 74-149389 ISBN 0-404-09012-5 : 30.00.
1. Jackson, Abraham Valentine Williams, 1862-1937. 2. Iran—Description and travel. I. Title.

Jackson, Andrew, Pres. U.S., 1767-1845.

BASSETT, John 973.5'6'0924
Spencer, 1867-1928.
The life of Andrew Jackson. [Hamden, Conn.] Archon Books, 1967. xix, 766 p. illus., maps, ports. 22 cm. Reprint of the 1931 ed. Bibliographical footnotes. [E382.B35 1967] 67-26659 ISBN B
1. Jackson, Andrew, Pres. U.S., 1767-1845. I. Title. BIP

CHIDSEY, Donald 973.5'6'0924 B
Barr, 1902-
Andrew Jackson, hero / Donald Barr Chidsey. Nashville : T. Nelson, c1976. p. cm. Includes index. Bibliography: p. [E382.C47] 76-26025 ISBN 0-8407-6514-2 : 6.95
1. Jackson, Andrew, Pres. U.S., 1767-1845. 2. Presidents—United States—Biography. 3. United States—History—1815-1861. I. Title. BIP

COIT, Margaret L 923.173
Andrew Jackson [by] Margaret L. Coit. Illustrated by Milton Johnson. Boston, (Houghton Mifflin, 1965. 154 p. illus. 22 cm. Bibliography: p. [150] [E382.C67] 65-14924
1. Jackson, Andrew, Pres. U.S., 1767-1845. I. Title.

CURTIS, James C. 973.5'6'0924 B
Andrew Jackson and the search for vindication / James C. Curtis. Boston : Little, Brown, c1976. xi, 194 p. ; 20 cm. (The Library of American biography) Includes index. Bibliography: p. [185]-187. [E382.C87] 75-26427 ISBN 0-316-16554-9 : 6.95
1. Jackson, Andrew, Pres. U.S., 1767-1845. I. Title. II. Series.

CURTIS, James C. 973.5'6'0924 B
Andrew Jackson and the search for vindication / James C. Curtis ; edited by Oscar Handlin. Boston : G. K. Hall, 1976. xvi, 375 p. ; 24 cm. Large print ed. Bibliography: p. 368-375. [E382.C87 1976b] 76-10749 0-8161 10.95
1. Jackson, Andrew, Pres. U.S., 1767-1845. 2. Sight-saving books. I. Title. BIP

DAVIS, Burke. 973.5'6'0924 B
Old Hickory : a life of Andrew Jackson / Burke Davis. New York : Dial Press, c1977. viii, 438 p., [4] leaves of plates : ill. ; 24 cm. Includes index. Bibliography: p. [419]-422. [E382.D3] 77-24425 ISBN 0-8037-6548-7 : 12.95
1. Jackson, Andrew, Pres. U.S., 1767-1845. 2. Presidents—United States—Biography. 3. United States—Politics and government—1829-1837. I. Title. BIP

DE KAY, Ormonde. 92
Meet Andrew Jackson, by Ormonde De Kay, Jr. Illustrated by Isa Barnett. New York, Random House [1967] 87 p. col. illus. 22 cm. (Step-up books) An easy-to-read biography of the colorful American general whose victory over the Redcoats at the Battle of New Orleans made him a national hero and aided in helping him become America's seventh President. [E382.D4] AC 67
1. Jackson, Andrew, Pres. U.S., 1767-1845. I. Barnett, Isa, illus. II. Title. BIP

EATON, John Henry, 973.5'6'0924 B
1790-1856.
The life of Andrew Jackson. [New York] Arno Press [1971] 468 p. port. 23 cm. (The First American frontier) Reprint of the 1824 ed. "The four first chapters of this work were written by Major Reid, who was an eye witness to the events recorded by him." [E382.E12 1971] 77-146393 ISBN 0-405-02846-6
1. Jackson, Andrew, Pres. U.S., 1767 1845. 2. Creek War, 1813-1814. 3. U.S.—History—War of 1812—Campaigns and battles. 4. Southern States—History—War of 1812. I. Reid, John, d. 1816. II. Title. III. Series.

EATON, John 973.5'238'0924 B
Henry, 1790-1856.
The life of Andrew Jackson / John Reid and John Henry Eaton ; edited with introd., apparatus critica, and index by Frank Lawrence Owsley, Jr. University : University of Alabama Press, c1974. 425, cix p., [4] leaves of plates : ill. ; 23 cm. (Southern historical publications ; no. 19) Chapters 1-4 were written by J. Reid, the remainder of the work was completed by J. H. Eaton from the papers and notes of J. Reid. Reprint of the 1817 ed., published by M. Carey, Philadelphia, with additional material. Includes indexes. Bibliography: p. xlvi-lvii. [E382.E12 1974] 74-2567 ISBN 0-8173-5164-7 : 17.50
1. Jackson, Andrew, Pres. U.S., 1767-1845. 2. Creek War, 1813-1814. 3. United States—History—War of 1812—Campaigns and battles. 4. Southern States—History—War of 1812. I. Reid, John, d. 1816 II Owsley, Frank Lawrence, 1928- III. Title. IV. Series.

FOSTER, Genevieve 973.5'6'0924 B
(Stump) 1893-
Andrew Jackson. New York, Scribner [1951] 112 p. illus. 20 cm. (Her An initial biography) A biography of Andrew Jackson stressing the events that directed his path to the Presidency. [PZ7.F8138An] 92 AC 68
1. Jackson, Andrew, Pres. U.S., 1767-1845. I. Title.

JAMES, Marquis, 1891- 923.173
Andrew Jackson, portrait of a president. New York, Grosset [1961, c.1937] 627p. (Universal lib. UL94) Bibl. 1.95 pap.,
1. Jackson, Andrew, pres., U.S., 1767-1845. I. Title.

JAMES, Marquis, 1891- 923.173
1955.
Andrew Jackson, the border captain. New York, Grosset & Dunlap [c1933] 461 p. 21 cm. (The Universal library, 47) Bibliography: p. 419-424. [E382.J26 1964] 64-56683
1. Jackson, Andrew, Pres. U.S., 1767-1845. 2. New Orleans, Battle of, 1815. I. Title. BIP

JUDSON, Clara Ingram, 923.173
1879-1960.
Andrew Jackson, frontier statesman. Illus. by Lorence F. Bjorklund. Chicago, Follett [1954] 224 p. illus. 25 cm. [E382.J8 1954] 54-10101
1. Jackson, Andrew, Pres. U.S., 1767-1845.

MEADOWCROFT, Enid 973.5'6'0924 B
(La Monte) 1898-
The story of Andrew Jackson; illustrated by David Hendrickson. New York, Grosset & Dunlap [1953] 182 p. illus. 22 cm. (Signature books) A biography of the President who wasted his inheritance on horse racing and cock fights, fatally wounded a lawyer in a pistol duel, and married a divorcee in 1791. [PZ7.M506Sq] 92 AC 68
1. Jackson, Andrew, Pres. U.S., 1767-1845. I. Hendrickson, David, 1896- illus. II. Title.

PARTON, James, 1822- 973.5'6'0924 B
1891.
The Presidency of Andrew Jackson. Edited with an introd. and notes by Robert V. Remini. New York, Harper & Row [1967] xxxvii, 468 p. 21 cm. (Harper torchbooks, TB 3080) From v. 3 of the author's Life of Andrew Jackson. Bibliography: p. xxxi-xxxvii. [E381.P3] 67-21559
1. Jackson, Andrew, Pres. U.S 1767-1845. 2. United States—Politics and government—1829-1837. I. Parton, James, 1822-1891. Life of Andrew Jackson. II. Remini, Robert Vincent, 1921- ed. III. Title.

REMINI, Robert 973.5'6'0924
Vincent, 1921- comp.
The age of Jackson. Edited by Robert V. Remini. Columbia, University of South Carolina Press [1972] xxviii, 243 p. 24 cm. Includes bibliographical references. [E381.R4 1972b] 72-5337 ISBN 0-87249-274-5 9.95
1. Jackson, Andrew, Pres. U.S., 1767-1845. 2. United States—Politics and government—1829-1837—Sources. I. Title. BIP

REMINI, Robert 973.5'6'0924 B
Vincent, 1921-
Andrew Jackson, by Robert V. Remini. New York, Harper & Row [1969, c1966] 212 p. maps 18 cm. (Perennial library P132) Bibliography: p. 199-201. [E382] 76-471 1.25
1. Jackson, Andrew, Pres. U.S., 1767-1845.

REMINI, Robert 973.560924 B
Vincent, 1921-
Andrew Jackson, by Robert V. Remini. New York, Twayne Publishers [1966] 212 p. maps. 21 cm. (Twayne's rulers and statesmen of the world series, 2) Bibliography: p. 199-201. [E382.R4] 66-16124
1. Jackson, Andrew, Pres. U.S., 1767-1845.

SELLERS, Charles 973.5'6'0924
Grier, comp.
Andrew Jackson; a profile. Edited by Charles Sellers. [1st ed.] New York, Hill and Wang [1971] xxi, 231 p. 21 cm. (American profiles) Contents.Contents.—Brief biography of Andrew Jackson.—The general, by G. Dangerfield.—A dishonest and insidious intriguer, by R. R. Stenberg.—Tennessee nabob, by T. P. Abernethy.—Boom for president, by C. Sellers.—Winning the presidency, by R. V. Remini.—A remarkable man, by J. S. Bassett.—An impressive mandate and the meaning of Jacksonianism, by A. M. Schlesinger, Jr.—The assault on the Federal Bank, by B. Hammond.—Jacksonian democracy as the rise of liberal capitalism, by R. Hofstadter.—The Jacksonian persuation, by M. Meyers.—Andrew Jackson, symbol for an age, by J. W. Ward.—Bibliographical note (p. 225-227)—Contributors. [E382.S44] 75-88012 ISBN 0-8090-6051-5 6.50
1. Jackson, Andrew, Pres. U.S., 1767-1845.

STEVENSON, 973.5'6'0924 B
Augusta.
Andy Jackson, boy soldier. Illustrated by Claudine Nankivel. Indianapolis, Bobbs-Merrill [1962] 200 p. illus. 20 cm. (Childhood of famous Americans) The boyhood of the South Carolinian who fought against the British and the Indians and became seventh President of the United States. [PZ7.S8467An7] 92 AC 68
1. Jackson, Andrew, Pres. U.S., 1767-1845. I. Nankivel, Claudine, illus. II. Title.

SUMNER, William 973.5'6'0924 B
Graham, 1840-1910.
Andrew Jackson as a public man; what he was, what chances he had, and what he did with them. New York, Haskell House Publishers, 1968. 402 p. 23 cm. Reprint of the 1882 ed. Bibliography: p. [387]-392. [E382.S958] 68-24999
1. Jackson, Andrew, Pres. U.S., 1767-1845. I. Title. BIP

SUMNER, William 973.5'6'0924 B
Graham, 1840-1910.
Andrew Jackson as a public man; what he was, what chances he had, and what he did with them. Westport, Conn., Greenwood Press [1970] vi, 402 p. 23 cm. Reprint of the 1882 ed. Bibliography: p. [387]-392. [E382.S95817] 69-14103 ISBN 0-8371-4104-4
1. Jackson, Andrew, Pres. U.S., 1767-1845. I. Title.

SUMNER, William 973.5'6'0924
Graham, 1840-1910.
Andrew Jackson as a public man; what he was, what chances he had, and what he did with them. Boston, Houghton Mifflin, 1893. St. Clair Shores, Mich., Scholarly Press, 1971 [c1882] vi, 402 p. 22 cm. (American statesmen [v. 17]) Bibliography: p. [387]-392. [E382.S9582] 70-108548 ISBN 0-403-00278-8
1. Jackson, Andrew, Pres. U.S., 1767-1845. I. Title. II. Series.

WARD, John William, 1922- 973.56
Andrew Jackson, symbol for an age. New York, Oxford University Press, 1955. xii, 274 p. plates, ports, facsim. 21 cm. Based on thesis, University of Minnesota. Bibliographical references included "Notes" (p. 215-265) [E382.W24] 55-8125
1. Jackson, Andrew, Pres. U.S., 1767-1845.

WASSAM, Homer E. 973.5'6'0924 B
The avenging angel of Nashville, by Homer E. Wassam. Philadelphia, Dorrance [1969, c1968] 229 p. ports. 22 cm. [E382.W32] 68-29904 4.00
1. Jackson, Andrew, Pres. U.S., 1767-1845. I. Title.

WRIGHT, Frances v. 12
(Fitzpatrick) 1897-
Andrew Jackson, fighting frontiersman. Illustrated by Raymond Abel. New York, Abingdon Press [1958] 127 p. illus. 21 cm. (Makers of America)
1. Jackson, Andrew, Pres. U.S., 1767-1845. I. Title.

YARBROUGH, Edward, 1883- 923.173
Old Hickory, a biography of Andrew Jackson. [Tyler! Tex.] c1953. 99p. illus. 22cm. [E382.Y3] 54-16555
1. Jackson, Andrew, Pres. U. S., 1767-1845. I. Title.

Jackson, Andrew, Pres. U.S., 1767-1845—Birthplace.

REVILL, Janie. 975.6760924
President Andrew Jackson's birthplace, as found by Janie Revill. [Columbia? S.C.] 1966. 53 p. illus., facsims., maps (1 fold.) 28 cm. [E382.R48] 66-27499
1. Jackson, Andrew, Pres. U.S., 1767-1845—Birthplace. I. Title.

Jackson, Andrew, Pres. U.S., 1767-1845—Juvenile literature.

DE KAY, Ormonde. juv
Meet Andrew Jackson, by Ormonde De Kay, Jr. Illustrated by Isa Barnett. New York, Random House [1967] 87 p. col. illus. 22 cm. (Step-up books) [E382.D4] 67-19495
1. Jackson, Andrew, Pres. U.S., 1767-1845—Juvenile literature. I. Title.

DE KAY, Ormonde. juv
Meet Andrew Jackson, by Ormonde De Kay, Jr. Illustrated by Isa Barnett. New York, Random House [1967] 87 p. col. illus. 22 cm. (Step-up books) [E382.D4] 67-19495

1. Jackson, Andrew, Pres. U.S., 1767-1845—Juvenile literature. I. Title.

MYERS, Elisabeth P. 973.5'6'0924 B
Andrew Jackson [by] Elisabeth P. Myers. Chicago, Reilly & Lee Books [1970] 179 p. illus. 21 cm. (Reilly & Lee President series) Bibliography: p. 171-172. A biography of the seventh President whose election by the greatest popular margin of the nineteenth century was considered the first to truly represent the will of the people. [E382.M9] 920 74-125380 4.95
1. Jackson, Andrew, Pres. U.S., 1767-1845—Juvenile literature. I. Title.

WAYNE, Bennett. 973.5'092'2 B
Men of the wild frontier. Edited, with commentary, by Bennett Wayne. Champaign, Ill., Garrard Pub. Co. [1974] 167 p. illus. (part col.) 22 cm. (A Target book) Brief biographies of four men instrumental in opening up new American frontiers. [F454.B844] 920 73-13615 ISBN 0-8116-4905-9
1. Boone, Daniel, 1734-1820—Juvenile literature. 2. Jackson, Andrew, Pres. U.S., 1767-1845—Juvenile literature. 3. Crockett, David, 1786-1836—Juvenile literature. 4. Houston, Samuel, 1793-1863—Juvenile literature. I. Title. **BIP**

Jackson, Andrew, 1809-1865.

GALLOWAY, Linda Bennett. 973.560924
Andrew Jackson, Jr.: son of a President; a biographical study. [1st ed.] New York, Exposition Press [1966] 85 p. 21 cm. (An Exposition-Lochinvar book) Based on two articles by the author that appeared in the Tennessee historical quarterly. Bibliographical footnotes. [E382.1.J15G3] 66-31589
1. Jackson, Andrew, 1809-1865.

Jackson, Andrew, 7th pres. U.S.

NOLAN, Jeannette (Covert) 1896- v. 12
Andrew Jackson. Illustrated by Leej Ames. New York, J. Messner [1961] 178 p. illus. 21 cm. Bibliography, p. 173. 63-44934
1. Jackson, Andrew, 7th pres. U.S. I. Title.

Jackson, Anne, 1926-

JACKSON, Anne, 1926- 792'.028'0924 B
Early stages / Anne Jackson. 1st ed. Boston : Little, Brown, c1979. viii, 212 p. ; 22 cm. [PN2287.J25A34] 79-328 ISBN 0-316-45501-6 : 8.95
1. Jackson, Anne, 1926- 2. Actors and actresses—United States—Biography. I. Title. **BIP**

Jackson Co., Or.—Biography.

ATWOOD, Kay. 979.5'27
Jackson County conversations / by Kay Atwood. Medford, Or. : Jackson County Intermediate Education District, [1975] ii, 173 p. : ill. ; 23 cm. [F882.J14A88] 76-358937
1. Jackson Co., Or.—Biography. I. Title.

Jackson, Franklin C., 1917-

JACKSON, Franklin C., 1917- 978.2'783'030924 B
Echoes from the sandhills / Franklin C. Jackson. 1st ed. Lincoln, Neb. : Word Services, c1977. xviii, 124 p., [1] leaf of plates : ill. ; 23 cm. [F666.J323] 77-77333 ISBN 0-918626-00-5 : 10.00
1. Jackson, Franklin C., 1917- 2. Jackson family. 3. Frontier and pioneer life—Nebraska. 4. Pioneers—Nebraska—Biography. I. Title. **BIP**

Jackson, George, 1941-1971.

JACKSON, George, 1941-1971. 322'.42
Blood in my eye. [1st ed.] New York, Random House [1972] xix, 197 p. 22 cm. [E185.615.J28 1972] 79-37423 5.95
1. Black power—United States. 2. Revolutions—United States. 3. Fascism—United States. 4. United States—Social conditions—1960- I. Title. **BIP**

MANN, Eric. 365'.6'0924 B
Comrade George. [Cambridge, Mass., Hovey Street Press, 1972] 64 p. illus. 26 cm. [E185.615.J282M36] 72-197999 2.00
1. Jackson, George, 1941-1971. I. Title.

Jackson, Hall, 1739-1797.

ESTES, J. Worth, 1934- 610'.92'4 B
Hall Jackson and the purple foxglove : medical practice and research in Revolutionary America, 1760-1820 / J. Worth Estes. Hanover, N.H. : University Press of New England, 1979. p. cm. Includes bibliographical references and index. [R154.J27E83] 79-63083 ISBN 0-87451-173-9 : 15.00
1. Jackson, Hall, 1739-1797. 2. Withering, William, 1741-1799. 3. Physicians—New Hampshire—Portsmouth—Biography. 4. Digitalis—History—18th century. 5. Edema—History—18th century. 6. Congestive heart failure—History—18th century. 7. Portsmouth, N.H.—Statistics, Medical. 8. Medicine—United States—History—18th century. I. Title. **BIP**

Jackson, Helen Maria (Fiske) Hunt, 1831-1885—Biography.

BANNING, Evelyn I. 818'.4'09 B
Helen Hunt Jackson, by Evelyn I. Banning. New York, Vanguard Press [1973] xxi, 248 p. illus. 21 cm. "Selected books by Helen Hunt Jackson": p. [237]-238. "Selected list of Helen Hunt Jackson's publications in periodicals": p. [239]-240. Bibliography: p. [233]-236. [PS2108.B3] 73-83038 ISBN 0-8149-0735-0 5.95
1. Jackson, Helen Maria (Fiske) Hunt, 1831-1885—Biography. **BIP**

Jackson, Henry Martin, 1912-

OGNIBENE, Peter J. 328.73'092'4 B
Scoop : the life and politics of Henry M. Jackson / by Peter J. Ognibene. New York : Stein and Day, 1975. 240 p. ; 24 cm. Includes index. [E748.J22O45] 75-28238 ISBN 0-8128-1884-9 : 8.95
1. Jackson, Henry Martin, 1912- I. Title. **BIP**

PROCHNAU, William W., 1937- 328.73'0924 B
A certain Democrat: Senator Henry M. Jackson; a political biography, by William W. Prochnau and Richard W. Larsen. Englewood Cliffs, N.J., Prentice-Hall [1972] 360 p. illus. 22 cm. [E748.J22P7] 74-37158 ISBN 0-13-123158-8 6.95
1. Jackson, Henry Martin, 1912- I. Larsen, Richard W., 1928- joint author. II. Title.

Jackson, James, 1757-1806.

FOSTER, William Omer 923.273
James Jackson, duelist and militant statesman, 1757-1806. Athens, University of Georgia Press [c.1960] viii, 220p. 25cm. Bibl.: p.202-212. 60-16834 4.50
1. Jackson, James, 1757-1806. I. Title. **BIP**

Jackson, James, 1810-1834.

JACKSON, James, 1777-1867. 610'.92'4 B
A memoir of James Jackson, Jr., M.D., with extracts from his letters to his father, and medical cases, collected by him. New York, Arno Press, 1972. 444 p. 23 cm. (Medicine & society in America) Reprint of the 1835 ed. [R154.J315J2 1972] 72-180579 ISBN 0-405-03956-5
1. Jackson, James, 1810-1834. I. Title. II. Series.

Jackson, Jesse, 1941-

REYNOLDS, Barbara A. 323.4'092'4 B
Jesse Jackson, the man, the movement, the myth / Barbara A. Reynolds. Chicago : Nelson-Hall, [1975] 489 p., [8] leaves of plates : ill. ; 23 cm. Includes index. [E185.97.J25R49] 74-17813 ISBN 0-911012-80-X : 9.95
1. Jackson, Jesse, 1941- I. Title.

Jackson, Jesse, 1941- —Juvenile literature.

HALLIBURTON, Warren J. 323.4'092'4 B
The picture life of Jesse Jackson, by Warren Halliburton. New York, F. Watts, 1972. 47 p. illus. 22 cm. Photographs and easy-to-read text trace the life of the black minister who is one of the leaders in the civil rights movement. [E185.97.J25H3] 92 74-186937 ISBN 0-531-00986-6
1. Jackson, Jesse, 1941- —Juvenile literature. I. Title. **BIP**

Jackson, Joe, 1888-1951.

GROPMAN, Donald. 796.357'092'4 B
Say it ain't so, Joe! : The story of Shoeless Joe Jackson / Donald Gropman. 1st ed. Boston : Little, Brown, c1979. xvi, 232 p., [4] leaves of plates : ill. ; 22 cm. Bibliography: p. 230-232. [GV865.J29G76] 79-12477 ISBN 0-316-32925-8 : 9.95
1. Jackson, Joe, 1888-1951. 2. Baseball players—United States—Biography. I. Title. **BIP**

Jackson, John George, 1777-1825.

DAVIS, Dorothy, 1914- 973.4'6'0924 B
John George Jackson / by Dorothy Davis. Parsons, W. Va. : McClain Print. Co., 1976. xvii, 440 p., [1] fold. leaf of plates : ill. ; 22 cm. Includes index. Bibliography: p. 407-416. [E302.6.J32D38] 75-41584 ISBN 0-87012-241-X : 18.50
1. Jackson, John George, 1777-1825. 2. Legislators—United States—Biography. 3. United States—Politics and government—1803-1817. **BIP**

Jackson, Kate—Juvenile literature.

SIMPSON, Janice Claire. 791.45'028'0924 B
Kate Jackson : special kind of angel / by Janice Simpson. St. Paul : EMC Corp., 1978. p. cm. (Headliners II) A biography of Kate Jackson, one of the stars of the popular TV series "Charlie's Angels." [PN2287.J28S5] 92 78-18850 ISBN 0-88436-430-5 : 5.95 ISBN 0-88436-435-6 pbk. : 2.95
1. Jackson, Kate—Juvenile literature. 2. Television personalities—United States—Biography—Juvenile literature. I. Title. II. Series. **BIP**

Jackson, Lillie M. (Cooper)

JACKSON, Lillie M. (Cooper) 1886- 917.3039
Fanning the embers. Boston, Christopher Pub. House [c.1966] 154p. 21cm. Autobiographical [CT275.J276A3] 66-19217 3.95
I. Title.

Jackson, Madeline Manning, 1948-

JACKSON, Madeline Manning, 1948- 796.4'2'0924 B
Running for Jesus / Madeline Manning Jackson as told to Jerry B. Jenkins. Waco, Tex. : Word Books, c1977. 192 p. : ill. ; 23 cm. Autobiographical. [GV697.J3A37] 76-56483 ISBN 0-87680-460-1 : 6.95
1. Jackson, Madeline Manning, 1948- 2. Track and field athletes—United States—Biography. 3. Religion and sports. I. Jenkins, Jerry B. II. Title. **BIP**

Jackson, Madeline Manning, 1948- —Juvenile literature.

JACOBS, Linda. 796.4'26 B
Madeline Manning Jackson : running on faith / by Linda Jacobs. St. Paul, Minn. : EMC Corp., [1976] p. cm. (Black American athletes) A biography of the record-setting runner, a gold medal winner in the 1968 Olympics, whose Christian faith has helped her surmount many obstacles. [GV697.J3J32] 92 76-16 ISBN 0-88436-261-2. ISBN 0-88436-262-0 pbk.
1. Jackson, Madeline Manning, 1948- —Juvenile literature. 2. Running—Juvenile literature. I. Title. II. Series. **BIP**

Jackson, Mahalia, 1911-1972.

GOREAU, Laurraine R. 784'.092'4 B
Just Mahalia, baby / Laurraine Goreau. Waco, Tex. : Word Books, [1975] x, 611 p. : ill. ; 25 cm. [ML420.J17G67] 74-82654 12.95
1. Jackson, Mahalia, 1911-1972. I. Title.

Jackson, Mahalia, 1911-1972—Juvenile literature.

CORNELL, Jean Gay. 783.7 B
Mahalia Jackson: queen of gospel song. Illustrated by Victor Mays. Champaign, Ill., Garrard Pub. Co. [1974] 96 p. illus. (part col.) 24 cm. (Americans all) A biography of the renowned gospel singer who wanted more than anything else to "sing for the Lord." [ML3930.J2C67] 92 73-14713 ISBN 0-8116-4581-9 4.25
1. Jackson, Mahalia, 1911-1972—Juvenile literature. I. Mays, Victor, 1927- II. Title.

DUNHAM, Montrew. 783.7 B
Mahalia Jackson : young gospel singer / by Montrew Dunham ; illustrated by Robert Doremus. Indianapolis : Bobbs-Merrill, [1974] 200 p. : col. ill. ; 20 cm. (Childhood of famous Americans) Bibliography: p. 198. A biography of the gospel singer who in her desire to sing only for God rose to world fame. [ML3930.J2D8] 92 74-260
1. Jackson, Mahalia, 1911-1972—Juvenile literature. I. Doremus, Robert, ill. II. Title. **BIP**

JACKSON, Jesse. 783'.7 B
Make a joyful noise unto the Lord! the life of Mahalia Jackson, queen of gospel singers. Boston, G. K. Hall, 1974. 207 p. 24 cm. Large print ed. A biography of the famous black gospel singer who hoped, through her art, to break down some of the barriers between black and white people. [ML3930.J2J2 1974b] 92 74-18252 ISBN 0-8161-6254-9
1. Jackson, Mahalia, 1911-1972—Juvenile literature. I. Title. **BIP**

JACKSON, Jesse 783.7 B
Make a joyful noise unto the lord! The life of Mahalia Jackson, queen of gospel singers. [New York, Dell, 1975 c1974 126 p. 18 cm. (Women of America) (Laurel Leaf Library) A biography of the famous black gospel singer who hoped, through her art, to break down some of the barriers between black and white people. [ML3930J2C67] 0.95 (pbk.)
1. Jackson, Mahalia, 1911-1972—Juvenile literature I. Title.
L.C. card no. for original edition: 72-7549

JACKSON, Jesse. 783'.7 B
Make a joyful noise unto the Lord! The life of Mahalia Jackson, queen of gospel singers. Illustrated with photos. New York, T. Y. Crowell [1974] 160 p. illus. 21 cm. (Women of America) Bibliography: p. [vii]-viii. A biography of the famous black gospel singer who hoped, through her art, to break down some of the barriers between black and white people. [ML3930.J2J2] 92 72-7549 ISBN 0-690-43344-1 4.50
1. Jackson, Mahalia, 1911-1972—Juvenile literature. I. Title.

MCDEARMON, Kay. 783.7 B
Mahalia, gospel singer / Kay McDearmon ; illustrated by Nevin and Phyllis Washington. New York : Dodd, Mead, c1976. 45 p. : ill. ; 24 cm. A brief biography of the renowned gospel singer who hoped, through her art, to break down some of the barriers between black and white people. [ML3930.J2M2] 92 75-33882 ISBN 0-396-07280-1 : 4.50
1. Jackson, Mahalia, 1911-1972—Juvenile literature. I. Washington, Nevin. II. Washington, Phyllis. III. Title. **BIP**

Jackson, Rachel (Donelson) 1767-1828.

MINNIGERODE, Meade, 1887-1967. 973.4'0922
Some American ladies; seven informal biographies. Freeport, N.Y., Books for Libraries Press [1969] viii, 287 p. illus.,

ports. 23 cm. (Essay index reprint series) "First published 1926." Contents.Contents.—Martha Washington.—Abigail Adams.—Dolly Madison.—Elizabeth Monroe and Louisa Adams.—Rachel Jackson.—Peggy Eaton. [E176.M65 1969] 70-93361
1. Washington, Martha (Dandridge) Custis, 1731-1802. 2. Adams, Abigail (Smith) 1744-1818. 3. Madison, Dolley (Payne) Todd, 1768-1849. 4. Monroe, Elizabeth (Kortright) 1768-1830. 5. Adams, Louisa Catherine (Johnson) 1775-1852. 6. Jackson, Rachel (Donelson) 1767-1828. 7. Eaton, Margaret L. (O'Neale) Timberlake, 1799(?)-1879. I. Title.

Jackson, Randy.

MCMILLAN, Constance 784'.092'2 B Van Brunt.
Randy and Janet Jackson : ready and right! / By Constance Van Brunt McMillan. St. Paul : EMC Corp., 1977. p. cm. (So young, so far) A biography of the two youngest children of the performing Jackson family. [ML420.J18M2] 920 77-24073 ISBN 0-88436-404-6 lib.bdg. : 4.95 ISBN 0-88436-405-4 pbk. : 2.95
1. Jackson, Randy. 2. Jackson, Janet, 1967- 3. Singers—United States—Biography—Juvenile literature. I. Title. **BIP**

Jackson, Raymond Samuel, 1892-

MASSEY, James Earl. 289.9 B
Raymond S. Jackson: a portrait. With a foreword by Charles E. Brown. [Anderson, Ind., Warner Press, 1967] 96 p. ports. 22 cm. Bibliographical footnotes. [BX7027.Z8M3] 76-3552
1. Jackson, Raymond Samuel, 1892- I. Title.

Jackson, Reggie.

ALLEN, Maury, 796.357'092'4 B 1932-
Reggie Jackson, the three million dollar man / by Maury Allen ; photos. (except where noted) by Louis Requena. New York : Harvey House, c1978. 62 p. : ill. ; 23 cm. A biography of the New York Yankee baseball player whose batting ability has been compared with Babe Ruth's. [GV884.J34A64] 92 78-105534 ISBN 0-8178-5817-2 lib.bdg. : 4.99
1. Jackson, Reggie. 2. Baseball players—United States—Biography. I. Requena, Louis. II. Title.

JACKSON, Reggie. 796.357'092'4 B
Reggie : a season with a superstar / by Reggie Jackson, with Bill Libby. 1st ed. Chicago : Playboy Press, c1975. 272 p. ; 22 cm. [GV865.J32A37] 74-33556 ISBN 0-87223-432-0 : 9.50
1. Jackson, Reggie. 2. Baseball. I. Libby, Bill. II. Title.

Jackson, Reggie—Addresses, essays, lectures.

JACKSON, Reggie. 796.357'092'4 B
Reggie Jackson's Scrapbook / by Reggie Jackson ; edited by Robert Kraus. 1st ed. New York : Windmill Books, c1978. 120 p. : ill. ; 28 cm. [GV865.J32A56 1978] 78-2276 ISBN 0-525-615784 : 9.95. ISBN 0-525-62334-5 pbk. : 5.95
1. Jackson, Reggie—Addresses, essays, lectures. 2. Baseball players—United States—Biography—Addresses, essays, lectures. I. Kraus, Robert, 1925- II. Title. III. Title: Scrapbook.

Jackson, Reggie—Juvenile literature.

BURCHARD, S. H. 796.357'092'4 B
Reggie Jackson / S. H. Burchard. 1st ed. New York : Harcourt Brace Jovanovich, c1979. 57 p. : ill. ; 21 cm. (Sports star) Presents an account of the often stormy career of one of baseball's most powerful hitters. [GV865.J32B875] 92 78-20567 ISBN 0-15-278016-5. : 5.95
1. Jackson, Reggie—Juvenile literature. 2. New York (City). Baseball Club (American League)—Juvenile literature. 3. Baseball players—United States—Biography—Juvenile literature. I. Title.

GUTMAN, Bill. 796.357'092'4 B
The picture life of Reggie Jackson / by Bill Gutman. New York : Watts, 1978. 48 p. : ill. ; 23 cm. Photographs and brief text highlight the life of the New York Yankees' star outfielder who was chosen Most Valuable Player in the 1977 World Series. [GV865.J32G87] 92 78-1335 ISBN 0-531-01483-5 : 5.90
1. Jackson, Reggie—Juvenile literature. 2. Baseball players—United States—Biography—Juvenile literature. I. Title. **BIP**

HAHN, James. 796.357'092'4 B
Reggie Jackson : slugger supreme / by James and Lynn Hahn. St. Paul : EMC Corp., 1978. p. cm. (Their Champions and challengers 2) A biography of the baseball player who broke or tied eight World Series records in 1977. [GV865.J32H33] 92 78-12937 ISBN 0-88436-449-6 : 5.95
1. Jackson, Reggie—Juvenile literature. 2. Baseball players—United States—Biography—Juvenile literature. I. Hahn, Lynn, joint author. II. Title. III. Series. **BIP**

HALTER, Jon C. 796.357'092'4 B
Reggie Jackson, all-star in right / by Jon C. Halter. New York : Putnam, c1975. 127 p. ; 22 cm. (Putnam sports shelf) Includes index. A biography of the outstanding hitter and fielder for the Oakland Athletics. [GV865.J32H35 1975] 92 75-7860 ISBN 0-399-20472-5. ISBN 0-399-60962-8 : lib. bdg. : 5.29
1. Jackson, Reggie—Juvenile literature. 2. Baseball—Juvenile literature. I. Title.

LIBBY, Bill. 796.357'092'4 B
The Reggie Jackson story / Bill Libby. 1st ed. New York : Lothrop, Lee & Shepard, c1979. 224 p. : ill. ; 22 cm. Includes index. A biography of the controversial baseball player who has led teams to five pennants and four World Series championships and who has been Most Valuable Player in two World Series and his own league. [GV865.J32L5] 79 684 ISBN 0-688-41889-9 : 6.25 ISBN 0-688-51889-3 lib.bdg. : 6.00
1. Jackson, Reggie—Juvenile literature. 2. Baseball players—United States—Biography—Juvenile literature. I. Title. **BIP**

LIBMAN, Gary. 796.357'092'4 B
Reggie Jackson / by Gary Libman. Mankato, Minn. : Creative Education, 1979. p. cm. A biography of the baseball player famous for his powerful long-distance hitting. [GV865.J32L53] 92 79-11521 ISBN 0-87191-279-1 : 5.95 ISBN 0 89812-162-0 pbk. : 2.75
1. Jackson, Reggie—Juvenile literature. 2. Baseball players—United States—Biography—Juvenile literature. I. Title.
Publisher's Address : 123 South Broad St., Mankato, MN 56001

SULLIVAN, George, 796.357'092'4 B 1927-
The picture story of Reggie Jackson / by George Sullivan. New York : J. Messner, c1977. 63 p. : ill. ; 23 cm. A biography of the baseball player famous for his powerful long-distance hitting. [GV865.J32S94] 92 77-1660 ISBN 0-671-32913-8 lib.bdg. : 6.64
1. Jackson, Reggie—Juvenile literature. 2. Baseball players—United States—Biography—Juvenile literature. I. Title. **BIP**

VASS, George. 796.357'092'4 B
Reggie Jackson : from baseball superstar to candy bar / by George Vass. Chicago : Children's Press, [1979] p. cm. (Sports stars) A biography of the Yankee batter who broke Babe Ruth's recored by hitting three home runs in a row in the 1977 World Series. [GV865.J32V37] 92 78-21511 ISBN 0-516-04303-X lib.bdg. : 6.00
1. Jackson, Reggie—Juvenile literature. 2. Baseball players—United States—Biography—Juvenile literature. I. Title. II. Series.

Jackson, Richard,

JACKSON, Richard, 364.12'0924 Sir, 1902-
Occupied with crime. [1st ed. in the U. S. A.] Garden City, N. Y., Doubleday, 1967. 310 p. 22 cm. Autobiographical. [HV7911.J3A3] 66-17426
I. Title.

Jackson, Robert Houghwout, 1892-1954.

GERHART, Eugene C. 923.473
Supreme Court Justice Jackson, lawyer's judge. Albany 10, [N.Y.] Q Corporation [39 Sheridan Ave., c.1961] 184p. illus. (front port.) Bibl. 61-17470 4.95
1. Jackson, Robert Houghwout, 1892-1954. I. Title.

Jackson, Thomas Jonathan, 1824-1863.

CHAMBERS, Lenoir. 923.573
Stonewall Jackson. New York, W. Morrow, 1959. 2 v. ports., maps. 25 cm. Includes bibliographical references. [E467.1.J15C49] 59-14841
1. Jackson, Thomas Jonathan, 1824-1863.

COOK, Roy Bird, 1886-1961 923.573
The family and early life of Stonewall Jackson. 4th ed., rev. Charleston, W. Va., Education Found., Box 1817, 1963. ix, 206p. illus., ports. 24cm. Bibl. 63-5925 4.00
1. Jackson, Thomas Jonathan, 1824-1863. 2. Jackson family (John Jackson, 1719-1804) I. Title.

COOKE, John Esten, 973.7'3'0924 B 1830-1886.
The life of Stonewall Jackson, from official papers, contemporary narratives, and personal acquaintance, by a Virginian. Freeport, N.Y., Books for Libraries Press [1971] 305 p. ports. 23 cm. Reprint of the 1863 ed. [E467.1.J15C6 1971] 76-179511 ISBN 0-8369-6640-6
1. Jackson, Thomas Jonathan, 1824-1863. I. Title.

COOKE, John Esten, 1830- 923.573 1886.
Stonewall Jackson and the old Stonewall Brigade; edited by Richard Barksdale Harwell. Charlottesville, University of Virginia Press for the Tracy W. McGregor Library [1954] 76p. ports. 24cm. Includes bibliographies. [E467.1.J15C65] 54-6938
1. Jackson, Thomas Jonathan, 1824-1863. 2. U. S.—Hist.—Civil War—Regimental histories—Stonewall Brigade. I. Title.

DAVIS, Burke. 923.573
They called him Stonewall; a life of Lt. General T. J. Jackson, C.S.A. New York, Rinehart [1954] 470 p. illus. 22 cm. [E467.1.J15D27 1954] 54-7921
1. Jackson, Thomas Jonathan, 1824-1863. I. Title.

DOUGLAS, Henry Kyd, 1840- v. 12 1903.
I rode with Stonewall, being chiefly the war experience of the youngest member of Jackson's staff from the John Brown raid to the hanging of Mrs. Surratt. With an introd. by Philip Van Doren Stern. Greenwich, Conn., Fawcett Publications [c1961] 384 p. 18 cm. (Premier civil war classic, T-113) 65-43617
1. Jackson, Thomas Jonathan, 1824-1863. 2. U.S. — Hist. — Civil war — Personal narratives — Confederate side. I. Title.

EARLY life and letters of v. 12
General Thomas J. Jackson, 'Stonewall' Jackson, by his nephew. [Richmond, Va., Dietz Press, 1957] 379p. plates, ports., facsims. 22cm. 'Copyright, 1916, by Fleming H. Revell Company. Reprinted, 1957.' Works consulted: p. 366-367.
1. Jackson, Thomas Jonathan, 1824-1863 I. Arnold, Thomas Jackson, 1845-1933.

HAPPEL, Ralph. 973.73'0924 B
Jackson. [1st ed. Richmond, Eastern National Park and Monument Association, 1971] 63 p. illus. 23 cm. [E467.1.J15H25] 74-162789
1. Jackson, Thomas Jonathan, 1824-1863.

HENDERSON, George Francis 923.573 Robert, 1854-1903
Stonewall Jackson and the American Civil War. Modern abridgement; introd. by E. B. Long. Maps by Barbara Long. Greenwich, Conn., Fawcett [c.1962] 576p. 18cm. (Premier Civil War classic, t161) .75 pap.,
1. Jackson, Thomas Jonathan, 1824-1863. 2. U.S.—Hist. Civil War— Campaigns and battles. I. Title.

HENDERSON, George Francis 923.573 Robert, 1854-1903
Stonewall Jackson and the American Civil War. Modern abridgment. introd. by E. B. Long. Maps by Barbara Long. [Gloucester, Mass., Peter Smith, 1963, c.1962] 576p. maps. 18cm. (Premier Civil War classics, t161 rebound) 2.50
1. Jackson, Thomas Jonathan, 1824-1863. 2. U.S.— Hist.—Civil War—Campaigns and battles. I. Title.

HENDERSON, George 973.7'0924 Francis Robert, 1854-1903.
Stonewall Jackson and the American Civil War. A modern abridgment, with an introd., by E. B. Long. Maps by Barbara Long. Gloucester, Mass., P. Smith, 1968 [c1962] xiv, 576 p. maps. 21 cm. [E467.1.J15H55 1968] 68-5393
1. Jackson, Thomas Jonathan, 1824-1863. 2. United States—History—Civil War, 1861-1865—Campaigns and battles. I. Long, Everett B., 1919- ed. II. Title. **BIP**

HENDERSON, George Francis 923.573 Robert, 1854-1903.
Stonewall Jackson and the American Civil War. With an introd. by Viscount Wolseley and a pref. by Walter Bedell Smith. Authorized American ed. London, New York, Longmans, Green [c.1961] xxvi, 737p. port., maps (6 fold. in pocket) plans, tables. 'Civil War centennial edition. Bibl. footnotes. 61-324 8.95
1. Jackson, Thomas Jonathan, 1824-1863. 2. U. S.—Hist.—Civil War—Campaigns and battles. I. Title.

JACKSON, Mary Anna 973.7'3'0924 Morrison, 1831-1915.
Memoirs of Stonewall Jackson / Mary Anna Jackson ; with introductions by John B. Gordon and Henry M. Field ; and sketches by Fitzhugh Lee ... [et al.]. Dayton, Ohio : Morningside Bookshop, 1976. xxiv, 647 p., [17] leaves of plates : ill. ; 27 cm. "Facsimile 32." Reprint of the 1895 ed. published by the Prentice Press, Louisville, Ky. [E467.1.J15J16 1976] 77-153860 25.00
1. Jackson, Thomas Jonathan, 1824-1863. 2. Generals—United States—Biography. I. Title.

SELBY, John Millin. 973.7'0924
Stonewall Jackson as military commander, [by] John Selby. London, Batsford: Princeton, N. J., Van Nostrand, 1968. 251p. 27 plates (4 fold), illus., maps (some col.), plans, ports. 24cm. Bibl. [E467.1.J15S4] (B) 68-92890 8.95
1. Jackson, Thomas Jonathan, 1824-1863. I. Title.

TATE, Allen, 1899- 923.573
Stonewall Jackson, the good soldier. (Ann Arbor] University of Michigan Press [1957, c1956] 322 p. illus. 21 cm. (Ann Arbor paperbacks, AA9) Includes bibliography. [E467.1.J15T23 1957] 57-4820
1. Jackson, Thomas Jonathan, 1824-1863. I. Title. **BIP**

VANDIVER, Frank Everson, 923.573 1925-
Mighty Stonewall. New York, McGraw-Hill [1957] xi, 547 p. illus., ports., maps. 24 cm. Bibliography: p. 532-536. [E467.1.J15V3] 57-7247
1. Jackson, Thomas Jonathan, 1824-1863. I. Title. **BIP**

VANDIVER, Frank Everson, 923.573 1925-
Mighty Stonewall. New York, McGraw-Hill [1957] xi, 547 p. illus., ports., maps. 24 cm. Bibliography: p. 532-536. [E467.1.J15V3] 57-7247
1. Jackson, Thomas Jonathan, 1824-1863. I. Title.

VANDIVER, Frank 973.7'3'0924 B Everson, 1925-
Mighty Stonewall [by] Frank E. Vandiver. Westport, Conn., Greenwood Press [1974, c1957] xi, 547 p. illus. 23 cm. Reprint of the ed. published by McGraw-Hill, New York. Bibliography: p. 532-536. [E467.1.J15V3 1974] 73-20504 ISBN 0-8371-7331-0 22.50
1. Jackson, Thomas Jonathan, 1824-1863. I. Title.

WHEELER, Richard. 973.7'3'0924 B
We knew Stonewall Jackson / Richard Wheeler. New York : Crowell, c1977. 138

p. : ill. ; 24 cm. Includes index. Bibliography: p. 129-131. A biography of the great Civil War general which includes many accounts by people who knew him. [E467.1.J15W37 1977] 92 76-58009 ISBN 0-690-01218-7 : 7.95
1. Jackson, Thomas Jonathan, 1824-1863. 2. Confederate States of America. Army—Biography. 3. Generals—Confederate States of America—Biography. I. Title. **BIP**

Jackson, Thomas Jonathan, 1824-1863—Juvenile literature.

DANIELS, Jonathan, 1902- 923.573
Stonewall Jackson. Illustrated by William Moyers. New York, Random House [1959] 183 p. illus. 22 cm. (Landmark books, 86) [E467.1.J15D22] 59-5519
1. Jackson, Thomas Jonathan, 1824-1863—Juvenile literature.

SUTTON, Felix 92
The valiant Virginian, Stonewall Jackson. New York, Messner [c.1961] 192p. (Julian Messner shelf of biographies) Bibl. 61-14458 2.95
1. Jackson,Thomas Jonathan, 1824-1863—Juvenile literature. I. Title.

SUTTON, Felix 920
The valiant Virginian, Stonewall Jackson. New York, Messner [c.1961] 192p. (Julian Messner shelf of biographies) Bibl. 61-14458 2.95
1. Jackson,Thomas Jonathan, 1824-1863—Juvenile literature. I. Title.

SUTTON, Felix. j92
The valiant Virginian, Stonewall Jackson. New York, Messner [1961] 192 p. 22 cm. Includes bibliography. [E467.1.J15S8] 61-14458
1. Jackson, Thomas Jonathan, 1824-1863—Juvenile literature. I. Title.

Jackson, William Henry, 1843-1942.

JACKSON, William Henry, 1843-1942. 770'.924 B
Time exposure; the autobiography of William Henry Jackson. Profusely illustrated with photos., paintings, and drawings by the author. New York, Cooper Square Publishers, 1970 [i.e. 1971, c1940] x, 341 p. illus., facsims., ports. 22 cm. [TR140.J27A3 1971] 77-133914 ISBN 0-8154-0362-3
I. Title.

NEWHALL, Beaumont, 1908- 779'.9'9178
William H. Jackson / by Beaumont Newhall & Diana E. Edkins ; with a critical essay by William L. Broecker. Dobbs Ferry, N.Y. : Morgan & Morgan, [1974] 158 p. : ill. ; 28 cm. [TR652.N48] 73-89076 ISBN 0-87100-045-8 : 14.00
1. Jackson, William Henry, 1843-1942. 2. Photography, Artistic. 3. The West—Description and travel—Views. I. Edkins, Diana E., 1947- joint author. **BIP**

Jackson, William Henry, 1843-1942—Juvenile literature.

FORSEE, Aylesa 927.7
William Henry Jackson, pioneer photographer of the West. Drawings by Douglas Gorsline, photos. by William Henry Jackson. New York, Viking [c.1964] 205p. illus., plates, ports. 22cm. 64-13600 4.25
1. Jackson, William Henry, 1843-1942—Juvenile literature. I. Title.

FORSEE, Aylesa. 927.7
William Henry Jackson, pioneer photographer of the West. Illustrated with drawings by Douglas Gorsline, and with photos. by William Henry Jackson. New York, Viking Press [1964] 205 p. illus., plates, ports. 22 cm. [TR140.J27F6] 64-13600
1. Jackson, William Henry, 1843-1942—Juvenile literature. I. Title.

Jackson 5 (Musical group)

MANNING, Steve. 784'.092'2 B
The Jackson Five / by Steve Manning. Indianapolis : Bobbs-Merrill Co., 1976. p. cm. Traces the career of the Jackson Five from their start in Gary, Indiana, to their rise to the top of the recording industry. [ML421.J3M36] 920 76-11634 ISBN 0-672-52148-2 ISBN 0-672-52275-6 pbk. : 4.95
1. Jackson 5 (Musical group) I. Title.

Jackson 5 (Musical group)—Juvenile literature.

MORSE, Charles. 784'.092'2 B
Jackson Five. Text: Charles and Ann Morse. Illus. : John Keely. Mankato, Minn., Creative Education; [distributed by Childrens Press, Chicago, 1974, c1975] 31 p. illus. (part col.) 25 cm. (Rock 'n pop stars) Traces the Jackson Five's rise to fame, describes their family life, and gives a brief biography of each of the five stars. [ML3930.J3M67] 920 74-12248 ISBN 0-87191-389-5
1. Jackson 5 (Musical group)—Juvenile literature. I. Morse, Ann, joint author. II. Keely, John, illus. III. Title. **BIP**

Jacob, Naomi Ellington,

JACOB, Naomi Ellington, 1889- 927.92
Me--looking back. With a foreword by Bransby Williams. London, New York, Hutchinson, 1950. 244 p. illus., ports. 22 cm. [PR6019.A29Z55] 51-8583
I. Title.

Jacob, Ned.

DALLAS, Sandra. 759.13 B
Sacred paint : Ned Jacob / by Sandra Dallas. 1st ed. Kansas City, Mo. : Fenn Galleries Pub., c1979. 135 p. : ill. (some col.) ; 28 x 30 cm. [ND237.J18D34] 79-1570 ISBN 0-913504-50-5 : 35.00
1. Jacob, Ned. 2. Painters—United States—Biography. I. Title.

Jacob, the patriarch.

SANFORD, John A. 221.9'22 B
The man who wrestled with God; a study of individuation (personal growth toward wholeness) based on four Bible stories [by] John A. Sanford. King of Prussia, Pa., Religious Pub. Co. [1974] 126 p. 22 cm. Errata slip inserted. Includes bibliographical references. [BS571.S26] 74-79994 5.95
1. Jacob, the patriarch. 2. Joseph, the patriarch. 3. Moses. 4. Adam (Biblical character) 5. Eve (Biblical character) I. Title.
Publisher's address: 198 Allendale Road, King of Prussia, Pa. 19406.

Jacob, the patriarch—Juvenile literature.

GRIFFITHS, Kitty Anna. 222'.11'09505
Come, meet Jacob, God's prince : the story of Genesis 32-36 / Kitty Anna Griffiths ; illustrated by "Willy". 1st Zondervan ed. Grand Rapids : Zondervan Pub. House, 1978. 95 p. : ill. 21 cm. (Come, meet series) Tells of the journey of Jacob and his family to Hebron which Jacob had left 20 years earlier. [BS580.J3G74] 78-16593 ISBN 0-310-25281-4 pbk. : 1.95
1. Jacob, the patriarch—Juvenile literature. 2. Bible. O.T.—Biography—Juvenile literature. 3. Bible stories, English—O.T. Genesis. 4. Patriarchs (Bible)—Biography—Juvenile literature. I. Willy. II. Title.

GRIFFITHS, Kitty Anna. 222'.11'09505
Come, meet Jacob, the grabbing twin : the story of Genesis 28-31 / Kitty Anna Griffiths ; illustrated by "Willy". 1st Zondervan ed. Grand Rapids : Zondervan Pub. House, 1978. 96 p. : ill. ; 21 cm. (Come, meet series) Tells of the travels of Jacob and his marriages to Leah and Rachel. [BS580.J3G75] 78-18458 ISBN 0-310-25271-7 pbk. : 1.95
1. Jacob, the patriarch—Juvenile literature. 2. Bible. O.T.—Biography—Juvenile literature. 3. Bible stories, English—O.T. Genesis. 4. Patriarchs (Bible)—Biography—Juvenile literature. I. Willy. II. Title.

Jacobi, Abraham, 1830-1919.

TRUAX, Rhoda. 926.1
The Doctors Jacobi. [1st ed.] Boston, Little, Brown, 1952. 270 p. illus. 22 cm. [R154.J35T7] 52-5014
1. Jacobi, Abraham, 1830-1919. 2. Jacobi, Mary Putnam, 1842-1906. I. Title.

Jacobs, Dick.

JACOBS, Dick, 1916- 796.7'2
An MG experience / [by] Dick Jacobs. London : Transport Bookman Publications, 1976. 188 p. : ill., ports. ; 22 cm. Distributed in the U.S. by Motorbooks International, Minneapolis, Minn. [GV1032.J33A35] 77-354428 ISBN 0-85184-013-2 : £3.95
1. Jacobs, Dick. 2. M.G. automobile. 3. Automobile racing. 4. Automobile racing drivers—Great Britain—Biography. I. Title. **BIP**

Jacobs, Julius.

JACOBS, Julius. 974.7'275'040924 B
Bronx cheer : a memoir / by Julius Jacobs. Monroe, N.Y. : Library Research Associates, 1976. 80 p., [3] leaves of plates : ill. ; 26 cm. [F128.68.B8J35] 74-84584 ISBN 0-912526-16-5 pbk. : 3.45
1. Jacobs, Julius. 2. Bronx (Borough)—Biography. 3. Bronx (Borough)—Social life and customs. I. Title. **BIP**

Jacobs-Larkcom, Dorothy.

JACOBS-LARKCOM, Dorothy. 951.05'092'4 B
As China fell : the experiences of a British Consul's wife, 1946-1953 / [by] Dorothy Jacobs-Larkcom. Ilfracombe : Stockwell, 1976. 160 p., [8] p. of plates : ill., facsim., maps, ports. ; 22 cm. [DS777.54.J3 1976] 77-356890 ISBN 0-7223-0920-1 : £3.50
1. Jacobs-Larkcom, Dorothy. 2. China—History—Civil War, 1945-1549—Personal narratives. 3. Diplomats wives'—Biography. I. Title.

Jacobs, Michael Strauss, 1880-

DANIEL, Daniel Margowitz, 1890- 796.83
The Mike Jacobs story. [New York] Ring Book Shop [1950] 126 p. illus. ports. 22 cm. [GV1132.J3D3] 50-3769
1. Jacobs, Michael Strauss, 1880- I. Title.

Jacobs, Victoria, 1838-1861.

JACOBS, Victoria, 1838-1861. 917.94'98'0340924
Diary of a San Diego girl, 1856. Edited by Sylvia Arden. Santa Monica, Calif., N. B. Stern, 1974. 75 p. illus. 20 cm. [F869.S22J32 1974] 74-75355
1. Jacobs, Victoria, 1838-1861. 2. San Diego, Calif.—History. I. Title.

Jacobsen, Arne, 1902-

FABER, Tobias, 1915- 720.9489
Arne Jacobsen [Tr. by E. Rockwell] New York, Praeger [c.1964] xxiii, 175p. illus., plans. 26cm. English and German. 64-16676 17.50
1. Jacobsen, Arne, 1902- I. Title.

Jacobsen, Johan Adrian, 1853-1947.

JACOBSEN, Johan Adrian, 1853-1947. 979.8'004'97
Alaskan voyage, 1881-1883 : an expedition to the northwest coast of America / Johan Adrian Jacobsen; translated by Erna Gunther; from the German text of Adrian Woldt Chicago : University of Chicago Press, c1977. p. cm. Translation of Reise an der nordwestkuste Amerikas, 1881-1883. Includes index. Bibliography: p. [E78.N78J3213] 77-78066 ISBN 0-226-39032-2 : 17.50
1. Jacobsen, Johan Adrian, 1853-1947. 2. Indians of North America—Northwest coast of North America. 3. Eskimos—Alaska. 4. Alaska—Description and travel—1867-1896. 5. British Columbia—Description and travel. I. Woldt, A. II. Gunther, Erna, 1896- III. Title. **BIP**

Jacobson, Israel, 1768-1828.

MARCUS, Jacob Rader, 1896- 296.6'1 B
Israel Jacobson, the founder of the reform movement in Judaism, by Jacob R. Marcus. [2d ed., rev.] Cincinnati, Hebrew Union College Press, 1972. ix, 167 p. 22 cm. Bibliography: p. 130-134. [DS135.G5J3 1972] 74-187950 ISBN 0-87820-000-2 5.95
1. Jacobson, Israel, 1768-1828. **BIP**

Jacquemont, Victor, 1801-1832.

HAMERTON, Philip Gilbert, 1834-1894. 920'.044
Modern Frenchmen; five biographies. Freeport, N.Y., Books for Libraries Press [1972] xiv, 422 p. 22 cm. (Essay index reprint series) Reprint of the 1878 ed. Contents.Contents.—Victor Jacquemont.—Henri Perreyve.—Francois Rude.—Jean Jacques Ampere.—Henri Regnault. [CT1012.H3 1972] 72-4579 ISBN 0-8369-2947-0 14.50
1. Jacquemont, Victor, 1801-1832. 2. Perreyve, Henri, 1831-1865. 3. Rude, Francois, 1784-1855. 4. Ampere, Jean Jacques Antoine, 1800-1864. 5. Regnault, Henri, 1843-1871. I. Title. **BIP**

Jacques, Father, 1900-1945.

CARROUGES, Michel, 1910- 922.244
Pere Jacques. Translated by Salvator Attanasio. New York, Macmillan, 1961. 269p. 22cm. [BX4705.J286C33] 61-10025
1. Jacques, Father, 1900-1945. I. Title.

Jaffe, Grace Mary Spurway.

JAFFE, Grace Mary Spurway. 973.9'092'4 B
Years of Grace / by Grace M. Jaffe. Sunspot, N.M. : Iroquois House, c1979. 203 p. : ill. ; 23 cm. Includes index. Bibliography: p. 195-197. [CT275.J2778A37] 78-21186 ISBN 0-931980-02-X : 12.00. ISBN 0-931980-01-1 pbk. : 5.95
1. Jaffe, Grace Mary Spurway. 2. United States—Biography. I. Title. **BIP**

Jaffe-Richthofen, Else, 1874-

GREEN, Martin Burgess, 1927- 914 B
The von Richthofen sisters; the triumphant and the tragic modes of love: Else and Frieda von Richthofen, Otto Gross, Max Weber, and D. H. Lawrence, in the years 1870-1970 [by] Martin Green. New York, Basic Books [1974] xviii, 396 p. illus. 25 cm. Bibliography: p. [385]-388. [CS629.R514 1974] 73-81037 ISBN 0-465-09050-8 12.50
1. Richthofen family. 2. Jaffe-Richthofen, Else, 1874- 3. Lawrence, Frieda von Richthofen, 1879-1956. 4. Lawrence, David Herbert, 1885-1930. I. Title.

Jagerstatter, Franz, 1907-1943.

ZAHN, Gordon Charles, 1918- 282'.0924
In solitary witness: the life and death of Franz Jagerstatter, [by] Gordon C. Zahn. London, G. Chapman, 1966. [9], 278 p. 4 plates (incl. ports.) 22 1/2 cm. 30/- (B66-18552) Facsim. on endpapers. Bibliography: p. 274-277. [BX4705.J265Z3] 67-81115
1. Jagerstatter, Franz, 1907-1943. I. Title. BIP

Jaggard, William, 1569-1623.

WILLOUGHBY, Edwin Elliott, 1899-1959. 655'.00924
A printer of Shakespeare; the books and times of William Jaggard. New York, Haskell House, 1970. 303 p. illus., facsims., ports. 23 cm. Reprint of the 1934 ed. [Z232.J24W7 1970] 77-92993
1. Jaggard, William, 1569-1623. 2. Shakespeare, William, 1564-1616—Bibliography. I. Title.

Jaguer, Edouard.

BAJ, Enrico, 1924- 759.9493'2
Enrico Baj, by Edouard Jaguer. Milan, New York, Schettini [1956] 123p. (chiefly illus., plates (part col.) port.) 30cm. Bibliography: p. 109-115. [ND623.B17J3] 62-26168
1. Jaguer, Edouard. I. Title.

Jai, L. P., 1902-1968.

L.P. Jai : 796.358'092'4 B
memories of a great batsman / edited by Vasant Raiji. Bombay : Tyeby Press, 1976. 56 p., [4] leaves of plates : ill. ; 20 cm. [GV915.J34L26] 77-911114 Rs7.50
1. Jai, L. P., 1902-1968. 2. Cricket players—India—Biography. I. Raiji, Vasant.

Jaisohn, Philip, 1868-1951.

LIEM, Channing. 923.2519
America's finest gift to Korea: the life of Philip Jaisohn. New York, William-Frederick Press, 1952. 89 p. illus. 23 cm. [DS916.5.J3L5] 52-7537
1. Jaisohn, Philip, 1868-1951. I. Title.

Jalal al-Din Rumi, Mawlana, 1207-1273.

ARASTEH, A. Reza 297.0924
Rumi the Persian; rebirth in creativity and love. Pref. by Erich Fromm. Lahore. Sh. Muhammad Ashraf [New York, Paragon, 1965] xx, 196p. 22cm. Bibl. [BP189.7.M42C42] SA66 5.00
1. Jalal al Din Rumi, Mawlana, 1207-1273. I. Title.

FRIEDLANDER, Ira. 297'.4
The whirling dervishes, being an account of the Sufi order known as the Mevlevis and its founder the poet and mystic Mevlana Jalalu'ddin Rumi/ by Ira Friedlander; music section by Nezih Uzel. New York : Collier Books, 1975. 159 p. : ill. ; 30 cm. Bibliography: p. 158-159. [BP189.7.M42F74 1975b] 75-1299 pbk. : 4.95
1. Jalal al-Din Rumi, Mawlana, 1207-1273. 2. Mevlevi. I. Title.

Jaloux, Edmond, 1878-1949.

ROSENFELD, Marthe. 843'.9'12
Edmond Jaloux: the evolution of a novelist. With a foreword by Gabriel Marcel. New York, Philosophical Library [1972] xii, 188 p. 22 cm. Based on the author's thesis, New York University. Bibliography: p. 154-166. [PQ2619.A4Z77 1972] 72-169244 ISBN 0-8022-2064-9 7.50
1. Jaloux, Edmond, 1878-1949. BIP

Jamaica — Biog.

ROBERTS, Walter Adolphe, 1886- 920.07292
Six great Jamaicans; biographical sketches. Kingston, Pioneer Press [1952, c1951] 122 p. illus. 19 cm. [F1865.R62] 52-32400
1. Jamaica — Biog. I. Title.

James, Alice, 1848-1892.

JAMES, Alice, 1848-1892. 929'.2'0973
Alice James, her brothers, her journal / edited, with an introd., by Anna Robeson Burr. Boston : Longwood Press, 1977. p. cm. "An unabridged republication of the edition of 1934." [CT275.J29A3 1977] 77-6980 ISBN 0-89341-171-X lib.bdg. : 30.00
1. James, Alice, 1848-1892. 2. James family. 3. United States—Biography. I. Burr, Anna Robeson Brown, 1873-1941. II. Title.

James, Bruno Scott.

JAMES, Bruno Scott. 922.242
Asking for trouble. New York, Harper & Row [1963] 178 p. illus. 21 cm. Autobiographical. [BX4705.J327A3 1963] 63-12165
I. Title.

James, Ed, 1895-

JAMES, Ed, 1895- 979.6'03'0924 B
Hanging and rattling : an autobiography of W. E. "Ed" James, a told to Dulcimer Nielsen. Caldwell, Idaho : Caxton Printers, 1979. 186 p. : ill. ; 23 cm. [F746.J35] 77-78213 ISBN 0-87004-264-5 pbk. : 4.95
1. James, Ed, 1895- 2. Idaho—Biography. 3. Idaho—Social life and customs. I. Nielsen, Dulcimer. II. Title.

James family.

JAMES, Alice, 1848-1892. 929'.2'0973
Alice James, her brothers - her journal. Boston, Milford House [1972] 252 p. port. 22 cm. Reprint of the 1934 ed. [CT275.J29A3 1972] 72-165123 ISBN 0-87821-089-X
1. James family. 2. James, William, 1842-1910. 3. James, Henry, 1843-1916. 4. James, Garth Wilkinson, 1845-1883. 5. James, Robertson, 1846-1910. I. Burr, Anna Robeson (Brown) 1873-1941, ed.

James, Frank Lowber, 1841-1907.

JAMES, Frank Lowber, 1841-1907. 610'.92'4 B
Years of discontent : Doctor Frank L. James in Arkansas, 1877-1878 / edited, with an introd. by W. David Baird. Memphis, TN : Memphis State University Press, c1976. p. cm. (Memphis State University Press primary source publications) Includes index. Bibliography: p. [R154.J362A34] 76-40025 ISBN 0-87870-037-4 pbk. : 5.95
1. James, Frank Lowber, 1841-1907. 2. Physicians—Arkansas—Osceola—Biography. 3. Osceola, Ark.—History—Sources. I. Title. II. Series.

James, Frank, 1844-1915.

BREIHAN, Carl W., 1915- 364.1'55'0924
The escapades of Frank and Jesse James / by Carl W. Breihan. New York : F. Fell Publishers, [1974] 288 p. : ill. ; 22 cm. Bibliography: p. [283]-288. [F594.J24B73 1974] 73-90513 ISBN 0-8119-0228-5 : 7.95
1. James, Frank, 1844-1915. 2. James, Jesse Woodson, 1847-1882. I. Title. BIP

DACUS, Joseph A. 364.1'55'0922 B
Illustrated lives and adventures of Frank and Jesse James, and the Younger brothers, the noted western outlaws / by J. A. Dacus. New ed. Detroit : Gale Research Co., [1975] c1881. p. cm. Reprint of the ed. published by Cincinnati Pub. Co., Cincinnati. [F594.J24D32 1975] 75-16467 ISBN 0-8103-4175-1 : 18.00
1. James, Frank, 1844-1915. 2. James, Jesse Woodson, 1847-1882. 3. The Younger brothers. I. Title: Illustrated lives and adventures of Frank and Jesse James, and the Younger brothers ...

VAUGHN, Columbus. 364.15'5 B
This was Frank James, by Columbus Vaughn, Sarah Snow, and Lester Snow. Philadelphia, Dorrance [1969] xx, 180 p. illus., facsim., ports. 22 cm. "The only true story of the life of Frank James, written by himself": p. [89]-180. [F594.J29] 68-56172 3.50
1. James, Frank, 1844-1915. I. Snow, Sarah, joint author. II. Snow, Lester, joint author. III. James, Frank, 1844-1915. The only true story of the life of Frank James. IV. Title. V. Title: The only true story of the life of Frank James.

James, Garth Wilkinson, 1845-1883.

JAMES, Alice, 1848-1892. 929'.2'0973
Alice James, her brothers - her journal. Boston, Milford House [1972] 252 p. port. 22 cm. Reprint of the 1934 ed. [CT275.J29A3 1972] 72-165123 ISBN 0-87821-089-X
1. James family. 2. James, William, 1842-1910. 3. James, Henry, 1843-1916. 4. James, Garth Wilkinson, 1845-1883. 5. James, Robertson, 1846-1910. I. Burr, Anna Robeson (Brown) 1873-1941, ed.

JAMES, Alice. 1848-1892 920.7
The diary of Alice James. Ed., introd. by Leon Edel. New York [Apollo Eds., 1966. c.1934, 1964] x, 241p. 20cm. (A-125) First pub. in 1934 under title: Alice James. her brothers--her journal. Bibl. [CT275.J29A3] 64-18879 1.95 pap.,
1. James. William. 1842-1910. 2. James. Henry, 1843-1916. 3. James. Garth Wilkinson, 1845-1883. 4. James, Robertson. 1846-1910. 5. James family. I. Edel, Leon, 1907- ed. II. Title.

James, Harry Clebourne, 1896-

JAMES, Harry Clebourne, 1896- 796.54
Western campfires; reminiscences of Western camping over half a century, by Harry C. James. [1st ed.] Flagstaff, Ariz., Northland Press, 1973 [c1972] xv, 60 p. illus. 24 cm. [SK601.3.J35] 72-86326 ISBN 0-87358-103-2 7.50
1. James, Harry Clebourne, 1896- 2. Camping—North America. I. Title.

James, Henry

JAMES, Henry 928.1
Selected letters. Edited with an introd. by Leon Edel. Garden City, N.Y., Doubleday 1960 [c.1955] xxxvii, 233p. 19cm. (Anchor bk. A204) .95 pap.,
I. Title.

JAMES, Henry, 1843-1916. 928.1
Henry James: autobiography. Edited with an introd. by Frederick W. Dupee. New York, Criterion Books [1956] xiv, 622p. illus., ports. 24cm. Bibliographical references included in 'Notes' (p.601-609) [PS2123.A3] 56-6211
I. Title.
Contents omitted

JAMES, Henry, 1843-1916. 928.1
Selected letters. Edited with an introd. by Leon Edel. New York, Farrar, Straus and Cudahy [1955] xxxiv, 235 p. 22 cm. (Great letters series) [PS2123.A43] 55-11183

James, Henry, 1843-1916.

DUPEE, Frederick Wilcox, 1904- 928.1
Henry James. [2d ed.,rev., enl.] [New York, Dell] 1965. 265p. 20cm. (Delta bk. 3583) [PS2123.D8] 1.95 pap.,
1. James, Henry, 1843-1916. I. Title.

DUPEE, Frederick Wilcox, 1904- 928.1
Henry James. [New York] Sloane [1951] xiii, 301 p. port. 22 cm. (The American men of letters series) [PS2123.D8] 51-2012
1. James, Henry, 1843-1916. I. Series.

DUPEE, Frederick Wilcox, 1904- 928.1
Henry James. [2d ed., rev. and enl.] Garden City, N. Y., Doubleday, 1956. 265p. 18cm. (Doubleday anchor books, A 69) [PS2123.D8 1956] 56-5971
1. James, Henry, 1843-1916. I. Title.

DUPEE, Frederick Wilcox, 1904- 928.1
Henry James [by] F. W. Dupee. New York, Morrow, 1974 [c1956] viii, 256 p. 21 cm. (The American men of letters series) Bibliographical references in "Notes" p. vii-viii. [PS2123.D8] 73-16722 ISBN 0-688-06776-X. 2.95 (pbk.)
1. James, Henry, 1843-1916. I. Title. II. Series.

DUPEE, Frederick Wilcox, 1904- 813'.4 B
Henry James [by] F. W. Dupee. Westport, Conn., Greenwood Press, [1973, c1951] xiii, 301 p. port. 22 cm. Original ed. issued in the American men of letters series. [PS2123.D8 1973] 72-9047 ISBN 0-8371-6566-0 13.25
1. James, Henry, 1843-1916. I. Series: The American men of letters series.

EDEL, Leon, 1907- 928.1
Henry James. Minneapolis, University of Minnesota Press [1960] 47 p. 21 cm. (University of Minnesota. Pamphlets on American writers, no. 4) Includes bibliography. [PS2123.E35] 60-62855
1. James, Henry, 1843-1916.

EDEL, Leon, 1907- 813'.4 B
Henry James: the treacherous years, 1895-1901. [1st ed.] Philadelphia, Lippincott [1969] 381 p. illus. 22 cm. Includes bibliographical references. [PS2123.E38 1969] 78-31916
1. James, Henry, 1846-1916.

EDEL, Leon, 1907- 813'.4 [
Henry James: the untried years, 1843-1870. [1st ed.] Philadelphia, Lippincott [1953] 350 p. illus. 22 cm. Includes bibliographical references. [PS2123.E385 1953] 53-5421
1. James, Henry, 1843-1916.

HYDE, Harford Montgomery, 1907- 813'.4 B
Henry James at home [by] H. Montgomery Hyde. [1st American ed.] New York, Farrar, Straus & Giroux [1969] 322 p. illus. 22 cm. Includes bibliographical references. [PS2123.H9 1969] 68-14920 6.95
1. James, Henry, 1843-1916. I. Title. BIP

JAMES, Alice, 1848-1892. 929'.2'0973
Alice James, her brothers - her journal. Boston, Milford House [1972] 252 p. port. 22 cm. Reprint of the 1934 ed. [CT275.J29A3 1972] 72-165123 ISBN 0-87821-089-X
1. James family. 2. James, William, 1842-1910. 3. James, Henry, 1843-1916. 4. James, Garth Wilkinson, 1845-1883. 5. James, Robertson, 1846-1910. I. Burr, Anna Robeson (Brown) 1873-1941, ed.

JAMES, Alice. 1848-1892 920.7
The diary of Alice James. Ed., introd. by Leon Edel. New York [Apollo Eds., 1966. c.1934, 1964] x, 241p. 20cm. (A-125) First pub. in 1934 under title: Alice James. her brothers--her journal. Bibl. [CT275.J29A3] 64-18879 1.95 pap.,
1. James. William. 1842-1910. 2. James. Henry, 1843-1916. 3. James. Garth Wilkinson, 1845-1883. 4. James, Robertson. 1846-1910. 5. James family. I. Edel, Leon, 1907- ed. II. Title.

JAMES, Henry 928.1
Selected letters. Edited with an introd. by Leon Edel. Garden City, N.Y., Doubleday 1960 [c.1955] xxxvii, 233p. 19cm. (Anchor bk. A204) .95 pap.,
I. Title.

JAMES, Henry, 1843-1916. 928.1
Henry James: autobiography. Edited with an introd. by Frederick W. Dupee. New York, Criterion Books [1956] xiv, 622p. illus., ports. 24cm. Bibliographical references included in 'Notes' (p.601-609) [PS2123.A3] 56-6211
I. Title.
Contents omitted.

JAMES, Henry, 1843-1916. 928.1
Selected letters. Edited with an introd. by Leon Edel. New York, Farrar, Straus and Cudahy [1955] xxxiv, 235 p. 22 cm. (Great letters series) [PS2123.A43] 55-11183

JEFFERSON, Douglas William, 1912- 813.4
Henry James. New York, Grove Press [1961, c.1960] 120p. (Evergreen pilot books, ep2) Bibl. 61-6596 1.25 pap.,
1. James, Henry, 1843-1916. I. Title.

LE CLAIR, Robert Charles, 1908- 928.1
Young Henry James, 1843-1870. New York, Bookman Associates [1955] 469 p. illus. 23 cm. [PS2123.L4] 55-3467
1. James, Henry, 1843-1916. BIP

LE CLAIR, Robert Charles, 1908- 813'.4 B
Young Henry James, 1843-1870, by Robert C. Le Clair New York, Bookman Associates [New York, AMS Press, 1971] 469 p. port. 23 cm. Reprint of the 1955 ed. Bibliography: p. 455-462. [PS2123.L4 1971] 77-153337 ISBN 0-404-03897-2
1. James, Henry, 1843-1916. I. Title.

MCELDERRY, Bruce Robert, 1900- 818.4
Henry James. New York, Twayne [c.1965] 192p. 21cm. (Twayne's U. S. author ser. 79) Bibl. [PS2124.M26] 65-12999 3.50 bds.,
1. James, Henry, 1843-1916. I. Title.

MCELDERRY, Bruce Robert, Jr., 1900- 818.4
Henry James. New Haven, Conn., Coll. & Univ. Pr. [c.1965] 192p. 21cm. (Twayne's U. S. authors ser., T-79) Bibl. [PS2124.M26] 1.95 pap.,
1. James, Henry, 1843-1916. I. Title.

MARKOW Totevy, Georges. 813'.4
Henry James. With a pref. by Andre Maurois. Translated by John Cumming. [1st American ed. New York] Minerva Press [1969] viii, 151 p. 21 cm. Bibliography: p. 145-150. [PS2123.M313 1969] 68-22175 1.95
1. James, Henry, 1843-1916.

MOORE, Harry Thornton. 813'.4 B
Henry James [by] Harry T. Moore. New York, Viking Press [1974] 128 p. illus. 24 cm. (A Studio book) Includes bibliographical references. [PS2123.M63 1974] 73-21499 ISBN 0-670-36755-9 7.95
1. James, Henry, 1843-1916.

SWAN, Michael. 813.46
Henry James. New York, Roy [1952] 96 p. 19 cm. (The English novelists) [PS2123.S92 1952a] 53-584
1. James, Henry, 1843-1916.

James, Henry, 1843-1916—Correspondence.

JAMES, Henry, 1843-1916. 813'.4 B
Henry James and H. G. Wells : a record of their friendship, their debate on the art of fiction, and their quarrel / edited with an introd. by Leon Edel & Gordon N. Ray. Westport, Conn. : Greenwood Press, 1979, c1958. 272 p. : ports. ; 23 cm. Reprint of the ed. published by University of Illinois Press, Urbana. Includes index. [PS2123.A47 1979] 78-25756 lib. bdg. : 22.50
1. James, Henry, 1843-1916—Friends and associates. 2. James, Henry, 1843-1916—Correspondence. 3. Wells, Herbert George, 1866-1946—Friends and associates. 4. Wells, Herbert George, 1866-1946—Correspondence. 5. Fiction—Technique. 6. Novelists—Biography. I. Wells, Herbert George, 1866-1946. II. Edel, Leon, 1927- III. Ray, Gordon Norton, 1915- IV. Title. BIP

JAMES, Henry, 1843-1916. 813'.4
Henry James and Robert Louis Stevenson : a record of friendship and criticism / edited with an introd. by Janet Adam Smith. Westport, Conn. : Hyperion Press, [1979] p. cm. Reprint of the 1948 ed. published by R. Hart-Davis, London. Includes index. [PS2113.A468 1979] 78-20472 ISBN 0-88355-850-5 : 22.50
1. James, Henry, 1843-1916—Correspondence. 2. Stevenson, Robert Louis, 1850-1894—Correspondence. 3. Novelists—19th century—Correspondence. I. Stevenson, Robert Louis, 1850-1894. II. Smith, Janet Adam. III. Title. BIP

JAMES, Henry, 1843-1916. 816'.4
Henry James: letters to A. C. Benson and Auguste Monod; now first published, and edited with an introd. by E. F. Benson. New York, Haskell House Publishers, 1969. viii, 118 p. 23 cm. Half title: The Henry James correspondence. Reprint of the 1930 ed. [PS2123.A53B4 1969] 75-95433 ISBN 0-8383-0984-4
1. James, Henry, 1843-1916—Correspondence. I. Benson, Arthur Christopher, 1862-1925. II. Monod, Auguste, 1951- III. Benson, Edward Frederic, 1867-1940, ed. IV. Title: The Henry James correspondence.

JAMES, Henry, 1843-1916. 813'.4 B
Letters / Henry James ; edited by Leon Edel. Cambridge, Mass. : Belknap Press of Harvard University Press, 1974- v. : ill. ; 22 cm. Contents.Contents.—v. 1. 1843-1875.—v. 2. 1875-1883. Includes bibliographical references and index. [PS2123.A42 1974] 74-77181 ISBN 0-674-38780-5
1. James, Henry, 1843-1916—Correspondence.

JAMES, Henry, 1843-1916. 816'.4
Theatre and friendship; some Henry James letters, with a commentary by Elizabeth Robins. Freeport, N.Y., Books for Libraries Press [1969] 303 p. illus., facsim., ports. 23 cm. (Select bibliographies reprint series) Reprint of the 1932 ed. [PS2123.A53R6 1969] 73-103656 ISBN 0-8369-5156-5
1. James, Henry, 1843-1916—Correspondence. I. Robins, Elizabeth, 1862-1952, ed. II. Title.

James, Henry, 1843-1916—Friends and associates.

JAMES, Henry, 1843-1916. 813'.4 B
Henry James and H. G. Wells : a record of their friendship, their debate on the art of fiction, and their quarrel / edited with an introd. by Leon Edel & Gordon N. Ray. Westport, Conn. : Greenwood Press, 1979, c1958. 272 p. : ports. ; 23 cm. Reprint of the ed. published by University of Illinois Press, Urbana. Includes index. [PS2123.A47 1979] 78-25756 lib. bdg. : 22.50
1. James, Henry, 1843-1916—Friends and associates. 2. James, Henry, 1843-1916—Correspondence. 3. Wells, Herbert George, 1866-1946—Friends and associates. 4. Wells, Herbert George, 1866-1946—Correspondence. 5. Fiction—Technique. 6. Novelists—Biography. I. Wells, Herbert George, 1866-1946. II. Edel, Leon, 1927- III. Ray, Gordon Norton, 1915- IV. Title. BIP

James I, King of Great Britain, 1566-1625.

BINGHAM, Caroline, 1938- 942.061'0924
The making of a king; the early years of James VI and I. [1st ed. in the U.S.] Garden City, N.Y., Doubleday, 1969 [c1968] 199, [29] p. geneal. table (on lining paper), ports. 22 cm. Bibliographical references included in "Notes" (p. [201]-[207]) [DA788.B5 1969] 69-10990 5.95
1. James I, King of Great Britain, 1566-1625. I. Title.

BIRCH, Thomas, 1705-1766, comp. 942.06'1'0924 B
The court and times of James the First; illustrated by authentic and confidential letters, from various public and private collections. Compiled by Thomas Birch. Edited, with an introd. and notes, by the author of "Memoirs of Sophia Dorothea," etc. (i.e. Robert Folk[e]stone Williams) London, H. Colburn, 1849. [New York, AMS Press, 1973] 2 v. 23 cm. Includes bibliographical references. [DA391.B6 1973] 74-113558 ISBN 0-404-00906-9 32.50
1. James I, King of Great Britain, 1566-1625. 2. Great Britain—History—James I, 1603-1625. I. Williams, Robert Folkestone, 1805 (ca.)-1872, ed. II. Title. BIP

FRASER, Antonia Pakenham, Lady, 1932- 941.06'1'0924 B
King James VI of Scotland, I of England / Antonia Fraser. 1st American ed. New York : Knopf : distributed by Random House, 1975, c1974. 224 p. : ill. ; 26 cm. Includes index. Bibliography: p. 217. [DA391.F7 1975] 74-6150 ISBN 0-394-49476-8 : 12.95
1. James I, King of Great Britain, 1566-1625. 2. Great Britain—History—James I, 1603-1625.

MCELWEE, William Lloyd, 1907- 923.142
The wisest fool in Christendom; the reign of King James I and VI. [1st American ed.] New York, Harcourt [1958] 296 p. illus. 22 cm. [DA391.M23] 58-10894
1. James I, King of Great Britain, 1566-1625. I. Title.

MCELWEE, William Lloyd, 1907- 923.142
The wisest fool in Christendom; the reign of King James I and VI. London, Faber & Faber [New York, Hillary House, 1966, c.1958] 296p. illus. 22cm. [DA391.M23] 6.00
1. James I, King of Great Britain, 1566-1625. I. Title.

MCELWEE, William Lloyd, 1907- 942.06'1'0924 B
The wisest fool in Christendom; the reign of King James I and VI, by William McElwee. Westport, Conn., Greenwood Press [1974, c1958] 296 p. illus. 22 cm. Reprint of the ed. published by Harcourt, Brace, New York. Bibliography: p. 279-284. [DA391.M23 1974] 74-7449 ISBN 0-8371-7522-4 14.00
1. James I, King of Great Britain, 1566-1625. I. Title.

MATHEW, David, Abp. 1902 942.06'1'0924
James I. University, Ala., Univ. of Ala. Pr. [1968,c.1967] xi, 353p. geneal. tables, ports. 24cm. Bibl. [DA391.M32 1968] (B) 68-23459 10.00
1. James I, King of Great Britain, 1603-1625. I. Title.

MATHEW, David, Abp., 1902- 941.06'1'0924 B
James I. University, Ala., University of Alabama Press [1968, c1967] xi, 353 p. geneal. tables, ports. 24 cm. Bibliography: p. [335]-342. [DA391.M32 1968] 68-23459 10.00
1. James I, King of Great Britain, 1566-1625.

SCOTT, Otto J. 941.06'1'0924 B
James I /)Otto J. Scott. New York : Mason/Charter, 1976. 472 p. ; 25 cm. Includes index. Bibliography: p. 457-462. [DA391.S35] 75-38591 ISBN 0-88405-123-4 : 12.50
1. James I, King of Great Britain, 1566-1625.

WILLIAMS, Charles. 923.142
James I. New York, Roy [1953] 310p. illus. 22cm. Includes bibliography. [DA391.W4 1953] 53-550
1. James I, King of Great Britain, 1566-1625. I. Title.

WILLIAMS, Charles, 1886-1945. 942.06'1'0924 B
James I. Freeport, N.Y., Books for Libraries Press [1969] vii, 310 p. 22 cm. (Select bibliographies reprint series) Bibliography: p. 303-304. [DA391.W4 1969] 77-103673
1. James I, King of Great Britain, 1566-1625.

WILLSON, David Harris, 1901- 942.061
King James VI and I. New York, Holt [1956] 480 p. illus. 22 cm. [DA391.W47] 56-2623
1. James I, King of Great Britain, 1566-1625. I. Title.

WILLSON, David Harris, 1901- 942.061
King James VI and I. New York, Oxford Univ. Pr [1967, c. 1956] 480p. 21cm. (GB210) [DA391.W47 1956a] 2.75 pap.,
1. James I. King of Great Britain. 1566-1625. I. Title.

James I, King of Scotland, 1394-1437.

STEVENSON, Joseph, 1806-1895, ed. 941.04'092'4 B
The life and death of King James the First of Scotland. New York, AMS Press [1973] xxii, 82 p. 24 cm. Reprint of the 1837 ed., which was issued as no. 42 of the Maitland Club publications. [DA783.6.S75 1973] 76-144432 ISBN 0-404-53019-2
1. James I, King of Scotland, 1394-1437. I. Title. II. Series: The Maitland Club, Glasgow. Publications, no. 42. BIP

James II, King of Great Britain, 1633-1701.

†ASHLEY, Maurice Percy. 942.06'7'0924 B
James II / Maurice Ashley. Minneapolis : University of Minnesota Press, 1977. 342 p., [8] leaves of plates : ill. ; 24 cm. Includes index. Bibliography: p. 302-305. [DA450.A83 1977] 78-103953 ISBN 0-8166-0826-1 : 14.95
1. James II, King of Great Britain, 1633-1701. 2. Great Britain—History—James II, 1685-1688. 3. Great Britain—Kings and rulers—Biography.

BELLOC, Hilaire, 1870-1953. 942.06'7'0924 B
James the Second. Freeport, N.Y., Books for Libraries Press [1971, c1928] vii, 297 p. port. 23 cm. [DA450.B4 1971] 73-165615 ISBN 0-8369-5922-1
1. James II, King of Great Britain, 1633-1701. BIP

HASWELL, Chetwynd John Drake, 1919- 942.06'7'0924 B
James II; soldier and sailor [by] Jock Haswell. New York, St Martin's Press [1972] xii, 323 p. illus. 25 cm. Bibliography: p. 309-310. [DA450.H27 1972] 72-76793 10.95
1. James II, King of Great Britain, 1633-1701.

TURNER, Francis Charles 923.142
James II. London, Eyre & Spottiswoode [New York, Barnes & Noble. 1965] 544p. ports. 23cm. Bibl. [DA450] 64-9349 7.00
1. James II, King of Great Britain, 1633-1701. I. Title.

TURNER, Francis Charles 923.142
James II. London, Eyre & Spottiswoode [dist. Chester Springs, Pa., Dufour, 1965] 544p. ports. 23cm. Bibl. [DA450] 64-9349 6.95
I. James II, King of Great Britain, 1633-1701. II. Title.

James IV, King of Scotland, 1473-1513.

HANNAY, Robert Kerr, 1867-1940. 941.04
The letters of James the Fourth, 1505-1513, calendared by Robert Kerr Hannay. Edited with a biographical memoir and an introd. by R. L. Mackie, assisted by Anne Spilman. Edinburgh, Scottish History Society, 1953. lxxii, 338, 8p. port. 23cm. (Publications of the Scottish History Society. 3d ser., v.45) 'Report of the sixty-fourth annual meeting of the Scottish History Society': 8p. at end. [DA750.S25 3d ser., vol.45] 54-850
1. James IV King of Scotland, 1473-1513. I. Mackie, Robert Laird, 1885- ed. II. Title. III. Series: Scottish History Society. Publications, 3d ser., v.45

MACKIE, Robert Laird, 1885- 923.141
King James IV of Scotland, a brief survey of his life and times. Edinburgh, Oliver & boyd [dist.Chester Springs, Pa., Dufour, 1964, c.1958] 300p. illus., map. Bibl. 58-2913 6.00
1. James IV, King of Scotland, 1473-1513. I. Title.

MACKIE, Robert Laird, 1885- 941.1'04'0924 B
King James IV of Scotland : a brief survey of his life and times / by R. L. Mackie. Westport, Conn. : Greenwood Press, 1976, c1958. 300 p., [8] leaves of plates : ill. ; 23 cm. Reprint of the ed. published by Oliver and Boyd, Edinburgh. Includes index. Bibliography: p. [283]-288. [DA784.5.M25 1976] 76-9098 ISBN 0-8371-8145-3 lib.bdg. : 17.75
1. James IV, King of Scotland, 1473-1513. 2. Scotland—History—James IV, 1488-1513.

James, James Alton, 1864-1962.

LOUCKS, Vernon R 923.773
James Alton James, a short biography. [Evanston? Ill.] Published for the friends and former students of Professor James by Northwestern University Press, 1963. xiii, 120 p. illus., ports. 22 cm. [LD4046.J3L6] 63-21083
1. James, James Alton, 1864-1962. I. Title.

James, Jesse Woodson, 1847-1882.

BREIHAN, Carl W., 1915- 923.4173
The complete and authentic life of Jesse James. Introd. by Homer Croy. New York, Collier [1962, c.1953] 160p. (AS127X) .95 pap.,
1. James, Jesse Woodson, 1847-1882. I. Title.

BREIHAN, Carl W 1915- 923.4173
The complete and authentic life of Jesse James. With an introd. by Homer Croy. New York, F. Fell [1954, c1953] 287p. illus. 22cm. [F594.J26] 53-11214
1. James, Jesse Woodson, 1847-1882. I. Title.

JAMES, Jesse E., 1875- 923.4173
The facsimile edition of Jesse James, my father; the first and only true story of his adventures ever written. With a foreword by William F. Kelleher. New York, F. Fell [1957] [7] p., facsim: (198 p. ports.) 19 cm. [F594.J284 1899a] 57-14061
1. James, Jesse Woodson, 1847-1882. I. Title.

JESSEE James Bank 364.3'2'0924 Museum.
Good bye, Jesse James; a reprinting of six of the best news stories concerning the career and death of America's most famous outlaw, first printed in the Kansas City daily journal in 1882. Compiled and published by the Jesse James Bank Museum. Library, Mo. [1967] vii, 160 p. illus., port. (on cover) 22 cm. [F594.J282] 67-6403
1. James Jesse Woodson, 1847-1882. I. Kansas City journal post. II. Title.

NEWMANS, Evans. 364.1'55'0924 B
The true story of the notorious Jesse James / Evans Newmans. 1st ed. Hicksville, N.Y. : Exposition Press, c1976. 87 p. ; 21 cm. (An Exposition-Lochinvar book) [F594.N2853] 76-365656 ISBN 0-682-48534-9 : 5.00
1. James, Jesse Woodson, 1847-1882. I. Title. BIP

SETTLE, William A. 973.80922
Jesse James was his name; or, Fact and fiction concerning the careers of the notorious James brothers of Missouri, by William A. Settle, Jr. Columbia, University of Missouri Press [1966] 263 p. illus., maps, ports. 25 cm. Bibliography: p. 233-251. [F594.J2875] 65-22965
1. James, Jesse Woodson, 1847-1882. 2. James, Frank, 1844-1915. I. Title. II. Title: Fact and fiction concerning the careers of the notorious James brothers of Missouri. BIP

SETTLE, William 364.1'55'0924 B A.
Jesse James was his name : or, Fact and fiction concerning the careers of the notorious James brothers of Missouri / by William A. Settle, Jr. Lincoln : University of Nebraska Press, 1977, c1966. 263 p., [10] leaves of plates : ill. ; 23 cm. "A Bison book." Includes index. Bibliography: p. 233-251. [F594.J24S47 1977] 76-56786 pbk. : 3.50
1. James, Jesse Woodson, 1847-1882. 2. James, Frank, 1844-1915. 3. Crime and criminals—The West—Biography. 4. The West—Biography. I. Title. II. Title: Fact and fiction concerning the careers of the notorious James brothers of Missouri.

*TRIPLETT, Frank. 973.8'0924 B
The life, times and treacherous death of Jesse James / Frank Triplett. New York : Nordon Publications [1977] 176p. ; 18 cm. (A Leisure Book) [F594.J2875] pbk. : 1.25
1. James, Jesse Woodson, 1847-1882. I. Title. BIP

TRIPLETT, Frank, 364.15'5'0924 B comp.
The life, times, and treacherous death of Jesse James. With an introd. and notes by Joseph Snell. Original paintings by Jerry Vallez. Chicago, Swallow Press, 1970. xxxvii, 344 p. illus., facsims., ports. 24 cm. Cover title: Life and times of Jesse & Frank James. Reprint of the 1882 ed. Bibliography: p. [335]-338. [F594.J288 1970] 70-75734 15.00
1. James, Jesse Woodson, 1847-1882. 2. James, Frank, 1844-1915. 3. Brigands and robbers—U.S. I. Title.

TRIPLETT, Frank, 364.1'55'0924 B comp.
The life, times, and treacherous death of Jesse James / by Frank Triplett ; with an introd. and notes by Joseph Snell ; original paintings by Jerry Vallez. New York : Promontory Press, [1974?] c1970. xxxvii, 344 p., [16] leaves of plates : ill. ; 24 cm. Running title: Life and times of Jesse and Frank James. Reprint of the 1970 ed. published by Swallow Press, Chicago. Originally published in 1882 by J. H. Chambers, St. Louis. Includes index. Bibliography: p. [335]-338. [F594.J288 1974] 73-79820 ISBN 0-88394-001-9 : 15.00
1. James, Jesse Woodson, 1847-1882. 2. James, Frank, 1844-1915. 3. Brigands and robbers—United States. I. Title.

WALKER, Henry J 923.4173
Jesse James, the outlaw. [1st ed. Des Moines? 1961- v. illus. 20 cm. [F594.J295] 61-1843
1. James, Jesse Woodson, 1847-1882. I. Title.

James, Jesse Woodson, 1847-1882—Juvenile literature.

ERNST, John, 364.1'55'0924 B 1940-
Jesse James / by John Ernst. Englewood Cliffs, N.J. : Prentice-Hall, c1976. p. cm. Biography of Jesse James which examines his exploits in light of nineteenth-century society and politics. [F594.J2813] 92 76-10206 ISBN 0-13-509695-2 lib.bdg. : 4.95
1. James, Jesse Woodson, 1847-1882—Juvenile literature. I. Title. BIP

James, Joshua, 1826-1902—Juvenile literature.

BONING, Richard 623.88'87'0924 B A.
Joshua James [by] Richard A. Boning. Illustrated by Gordon Johnson. Baldwin, N.Y., Dexter & Westbrook [1972] 47 p. col. illus. 24 cm. (The Incredible series) A biography of the New England seaman who, during his long career, rescued more than 600 people from the sea. [VK1430.J3B6] 92 72-184890 4.95
1. James, Joshua, 1826-1902—Juvenile literature. I. Johnson, Gordon, illus. II. Title. BIP

James (Name)—Juvenile literature.

GLAZER, Tom. 929.4
All about your name, James, Jim, Jamie, Jimmy / by Tom Glazer ; illustrated by Demi. 1st ed. Garden City, N.Y. : Doubleday, c1978. 46 p. : ill. ; 22 cm. A collection of facts about the people, places, and things who are or have been named James. [CS2391.J3G54] 77-15153 ISBN 0-385-06436-5 : 4.95. ISBN 0-385-06449-7 lib.bdg. : 5.90
1. James (Name)—Juvenile literature. 2. Biography—Miscellanea—Juvenile literature. I. Hitz, Demi. II. Title. BIP

James, Naomi.

JAMES, Naomi, 910'.41'0924 B Dame.
Alone around the world / Naomi James. 1st American ed. New York : Coward, McCann & Geoghegan, 1979. 192 p., [16] leaves of plates : ill. ; 24 cm. [G420.J35J35 1979] 79-1403 ISBN 0-698-10986-4 : 9.95
1. James, Naomi. 2. Express Crusader (Yacht) 3. Voyages around the world—1951- 4. Travelers—England—Biography. I. Title. BIP

James, Prince of Wales, the Old Pretender, 1688-1766.

BEVAN, Bryan 942.07'0924
King James the Third of England: a study of kingship in exile. Introd. by Sir Charles Petrie. London, Hale, 1967. 192p. 8 plates (incl. ports.). 23cm. Bibl. [DA814.A3B4] (B) 67-95039 4.50 bds.,
1. James, Prince of Wales, the Old Pretender, 1688-1766. I. Title.
Distributed by Hillary House, New York.

HALLE, Marie. 923.242
James Francis Edward, the Old Chevalier, by Martin Haile [pseud.] With 11 photogravure illus. London, Dent; New York, Dutton, 1907. xii, 479 p. illus., ports. 24 cm. [DA814.A3H3] 8-15743
1. James, Prince of Wales, the Old Pretender, 1688-1766. 2. Jacobites. I. Title.

MILLER, Olive 942.07'092'4 B Peggy.
James, by Peggy Miller. New York, St. Martin's Press [1971] 344 p. illus. 24 cm. Bibliography: p. 332-334. [DA814.A3M54 1971b] 74-175028 12.95
1. James, Prince of Wales, the Old Pretender, 1688-1766. I. Title.

James V, King Of Scotland, 1512-1542.

HANNAY, Robert Kerr, 327.42'041 1867-1940.
The letters of James v, collected and calendared by the late Robert Kerr Hannay. Edited by denys Hay. Edinburgh, H. M. Stationery Off., 1954. xvi, 468p. 26cm. Bibliography: p.xiv-xvi. [DA784.7.H3] 55-3405
1. James v, King of Scotland, 1512-1542. I. Hay, Denys, ed. II. Title.

James, William,

JAMES, William, 1842-1910. 921.1
Selected letters. Edited with an introd. by Elizabeth Hardwick. New York, Farrar, Straus and Cudahy [1961] 271 p. 22 cm. (Great letters series) [B945.J24A4 1961] 61-5895
I. Hardwick, Elizabeth, ed.

James, William, 1842-1910.

ALLEN, Gay Wilson, 1903- 191 B
William James; a biography. New York, Viking Press [1967] xx, 556 p. illus., facsims., geneal. table, ports. 25 cm. Bibliographical references included in "Notes" (p. 523-545) [B945.J24A63] 67-10217
1. James, William, 1842-1910.

BRENNAN, Bernard P. 191
William James, by Bernard P. Brennan. New York, Twayne Publishers [1968] 176 p. 22 cm. (Twayne's United States authors series, 131) Bibliography: p. 170-172. [B945.J24B72] 68-24290 3.95
1. James, William, 1842-1910. I. Title.

JAMES, Alice, 1848- 929'.2'0973 1892.
Alice James, her brothers - her journal. Boston, Milford House [1972] 252 p. port. 22 cm. Reprint of the 1934 ed. [CT275.J29A3 1972] 72-165123 ISBN 0-87821-089-X
1. James family. 2. James, William, 1842-1910. 3. James, Henry, 1843-1916. 4. James, Garth Wilkinson, 1845-1883. 5. James, Robertson, 1846-1910. I. Burr, Anna Robeson (Brown) 1873-1941, ed.

JAMES, Alice. 1848-1892 920.7
The diary of Alice James. Ed., introd. by Leon Edel. New York [Apollo Eds., 1966. c.1934, 1964] x, 241p. 20cm. (A-125) First pub. in 1934 under title: Alice James. her brothers--her journal. Bibl. [CT275.J29A3] 64-18879 1.95 pap.,
1. James. William. 1842-1910. 2. James. Henry, 1843-1916. 3. James. Garth Wilkinson, 1845-1883. 4. James, Robertson. 1846-1910. 5. James family. I. Edel, Leon, 1907- ed. II. Title.

JAMES, William, 1842-1910. 921.1
Selected letters. Edited with an introd. by Elizabeth Hardwick. New York, Farrar, Straus and Cudahy [1961] 271 p. 22 cm. (Great letters series) [B945.J24A4 1961] 61-5895
I. Hardwick, Elizabeth, ed.

MOORE, Edward Carter, 1917- 101
William James. New York, Washington Sq. [c.1965] 194p. 18cm. (Great Amer. thinkers ser., W883) [B945.J24M57] 65-2183 .60 pap.,
1. James, William, 1842-1910. I. Title.

MOORE, Edward Carter, 1917- 191
William James. New York, Washington Square Press; [distributed in the U.S. by Affiliated Publishers, 1965] 194 p. 18 cm. (The Great American thinkers series) Bibliography: p. 187-188. [B945.J24M57] 65-2183
1. James, William, 1842-1910.

PERRY, Ralph Barton, 1876- 921.1
The thought and character of William James, Briefer version. New York, Harper [1964, 1935, 1948] 400p. 21cm. (Harper torchbk., Acad. lib., TB1156) Bibl. 2.25 pap.,
1. James, William, 1842-1910. I. Title.

Jameson, John Franklin, 1859-1937.

FISHER, Ruth Anna, 973.0720924 1886- ed.
J. Franklin Jameson; a tribute. Edited by Ruth Anna Fisher [and] William Lloyd Fox. Washington, D. C., Catholic University of America Press [1965] ix, 137 p. 22 cm. Contents.-- Introduction by R. A. Fisher and W. L. Fox. -- A tribute, by R. A. Fisher. -- American religious history, by J. T. Ellis. -- The List of doctoral dissertations in history, by W. L. Fox. -- The origin of the National Historical Publications Commission, by W. G. Leland. -- "Inevitably" the first incumbent, by V. W. Clapp. -- The sage and the young man, by A. Nevins. -- Hope for the young scholar, by M. R. Dearing. -- Dr. Jameson's other side, by C. W. Garrison. -- The Atlas of the historical geography of the United States, by J. K. Wright. -- The Dictionary of American biography, by D. Malone. -- The National Archives, by F. Shelley. -- Jameson as editor, by B. C. Shafer. -- J. F. H., by D. C. Mearns. -- A bibliography of J. Franklin Jameson's writings, by D. H. Mugridge (p. 103-137) Includes bibliogrOJ. Franklin Jameson; a tribute. Edited by
1. Jameson, John Franklin, 1859-1937. I. Fox, William Lloyd, joint ed. II. Title.

Jamesone, George, 1589 or 90-1644.

THOMSON, Duncan. 759.941
The life and art of George Jamesone / Duncan Thomson. Oxford : Clarendon Press, 1974. xix, 164 p., [33] leaves of plates ; ill. ; 25 cm. (Studies in the history of art and architecture) Includes bibliographical references and indexes. [ND1329.J33T48] 74-189857 ISBN 0-19-817337-7 : 41.00
1. Jamesone, George, 1589 or 90-1644. I. Title. II. Series: Oxford studies in the history of art and architecture.
Distributed by Oxford University Press, New York. BIP

Janacek, Leos, 1854-1928.

HOLLANDER, Hans. 780.92
Leos Janacek; his life and work. Translated by Paul Hamburger. New York, St Martin's Press [1963] 222 p. illus., ports., music. 21 cm. Bibliography: p. [217]-218. [ML410.J18H64] 63-11071
1. Janacek, Leos, 1854-1928.

Jan, of Nepomuk, Saint, 14th cent.

ROBERTO, Brother, 1927- 922.24371
Secrets of the silent tongue; a story of Saint John Nepomucene. Illus. by Brother Eagan. Notre Dame, Ind., Dujarie Press [1957] 95p. illus. 24cm. [BX4700.J23R58] 58-256
1. Jan, of Nepomuk, Saint, 14th cent. I. Title.

ROBERTO, Brother, 1927- 922.24371
Trial by torture; a story of St. John Nepomucene. Notre Dame, Ind., Dujarie

Press [1957] 142p. illus. 22cm. [BX4700.J23R6] 57-36872
1. Jan, of Nepomuk, Saint, 14th cent. I. Title.

Janel, Emil, 1896-

SEAL, Thomas C. 736'.4
The life and works of Emil Janel; an illustrated essay, by Thomas C. Seal. [San Francisco? 1973] viii, 81 p. illus. 32 cm. Bibliography: p. 81. [NK9798.J36S42] 73-166410
1. Janel, Emil, 1896- 2. Wood-carving, American.

Jansen, Cornelius, 1822-1894.

REIMER, Gustav Eduard. 922.8773
Exiled by the Czar; Cornelius Jansen and the great Mennonite migration, 1874, by Gustav E. Reimer and G. R. Gaeddert. Newton, Kan., Mennonite Publication Office, 1956. x, 205p. illus., ports., geneal. tables. 24cm. (Mennonite historical series, no.3) [BX8129.G4M4 vol.3] 56-25350
1. Jansen, Cornelius, 1822-1894. I. Gaeddert, Gustave Raymond. II. Title. III. Series.

Janson, Kristofer Nagel, 1841-1917—Biography.

DRAXTEN, Nina. 839.8'2'16 B
Kristofer Janson in America / by Nina Draxten. Boston : published for the Norwegian-American Historical Association by Twayne Pubishers, 1976. (Authors series ; v. 36) Includes index. Bibliography: p. [PT8902.Z5D7] 75-42198 ISBN 0-8057-9000-4 : 9.95
1. Janson, Kristofer Nagel, 1841-1917—Biography. I. Title. II. Series: Norwegian-American Historical Association. Authors series ; v. 3. BIP

Jansson, Erik, 1808-1850.

ELMEN, Paul. 284'.1'0924 B
Wheat flour messiah : Eric Jansson of Bishop Hill / Paul Elmen. Carbondale : Published for the Swedish Pioneer Historical Society by Southern Illinois University Press, c1976. p. cm. Includes index. Bibliography: p. [BX7990.J3E45] 76-28380 ISBN 0-8093-0787-1 : 7.95
1. Jansson, Erik, 1808-1850. 2. Jansonists. 3. Bishop Hill, Ill.—History. 4. Jansonists—Biography. I. Title. BIP

Janssoone, Frederic, 1838-1916.

LEGARE, Romain 922.271
An apostle of two worlds: Father Frederic Janssoone, O.F.M., of Ghyvelde. Translated [from the French] by Raphael Brown. Chicago, Franciscan Herald Press [1958,i.e.1959] 380p. illus. 22cm. Includes bibliography. 59-16743 4.50
1. Janssoone, Frederic, 1838-1916. I. Title.

Japan—History.

PERSONALITY in 952'.0099 B
Japanese history. Introduced and edited by Albert M. Craig and Donald H. Shively. Berkeley, University of California Press, 1970. x, 481 p. 24 cm. "Published under the auspices of the Center for Japanese and Korean Studies, University of California, Berkeley." Includes bibliographical references. [DS836.P46 1970] 73-111420 ISBN 0-520-01699-8 8.75
1. Japan—History. 2. National characteristics, Japanese. 3. Japan—Biography. I. Craig, Albert M., ed. II. Shively, Donald Howard, 1921- ed. III. California. University. Center for Japanese and Korean Studies.

Japan—Social life and customs.

MATSUOKA, Yoko, 1916- 915.2
Daughter of the Pacific. [1st ed.] New York, Harper [1952] 245 p. 22 cm. Autobiographical. [DS825.M23] 51-11938
1. Japan—Social life and customs. I. Title. BIP

Japanese Americans—Washington (State)—Seattle—Biography.

SONE, Monica 979.7'77'004956 B
Itoi, 1919-
Nisei daughter / by Monica Sone ; introd. by S. Frank Miyamoto. Seattle : University of Washington Press, [1979] c1953. p. cm. [F899.S49J376 1979] 79-4921 ISBN 0-295-95688-7 pbk. : 5.95
1. Sone, Monica Itoi, 1919- 2. Japanese Americans—Washington (State)—Seattle—Biography. 3. Japanese Americans—Evacuation and relocation, 1942-1945. 4. Seattle—Biography. I. Title. BIP

Japanese in the U.S.

SONE, Monica Itoi, 325.2520973
1919-
Nisei daughter. [1st ed.] Boston, Little, Brown [1953] 238 p. 22 cm. Autobiography. "An Atlantic Monthly Press book." [E184.J3S6] 52-12618
1. Japanese in the U.S. 2. Concentration camps—U. S. I. Title.

Japanese literature—Translations into English.

OMORI, Annie 895.6'8'03 B
Shepley, tr.
Diaries of court ladies of old Japan. Translated by Annie Shepley Omori and Kochi Doi. With an introd. by Amy Lowell. New York, AMS Press, [1970] xxxii, 200 p. illus. 23 cm. Reprint of the 1920 ed. Contents.Contents.—The Sarashina diary.—The diary of Murasaki Shikibu.—The diary of Izumi Shikibu. [PL782.E8O4 1970] 72-111775 ISBN 0-404-04819-6
1. Japanese literature—Translations into English. 2. English literature—Translations from Japanese. 3. Japan—Court and courtiers. I. Doi, Kochi, 1886- joint tr. II. Sugawara Takasue no musume, b. 1008. Sarashina nikki. English. 1970. III. Murasaki Shikibu, b. 978? Murasaki Shikibu nikki. English. 1970. IV. Izumi Shikibu, b. 974? Izumi Shikibu nikki. English. 1970. V. Title. BIP

Jardiel Poncela, Enrique, 1901-1952.

MCKAY, Douglas R. 862'.6'2
Enrique Jardiel Poncela, by Douglas R. McKay. New York, Twayne Publishers [1974] p. cm. (Twayne's world authors series, TWAS 333. Spain) Bibliography: p. [PQ6619.A7Z8] 74-6487 ISBN 0-8057-2462-1 6.50
1. Jardiel Poncela, Enrique, 1901-1952. BIP

Jarieot, Paciline Marie, 1799-1862.

WINDEATT, Mary Fabyan, 922.244
1910-
Pennies for Palline; the story of Marie Pauline Jaricot, foundress of the Society for the Propagation of the Faith. Illustrated by Paul A. Grout. [St. Meinrad, Ind., 1952] 245p. illus. 22cm. 'A Grail publication.' [BX4705.J37W5] 52-14492
1. Jarieot, Paciline Marie, 1799-1862. 2. Society for the Propagation of the ,faith. I. Title.

Jarnes, Benjamin, 1888—

BERNSTEIN, J. S., 1936- 863'.6'2
Benjamin Jarnes, by J. S. Bernstein. New York, Twayne Publishers [1972] 180 p. 21 cm. (Twayne's world authors series, TWAS 128. Spain) Bibliography: p. 160-173. [PQ6619.A8Z6] 78-110707
1. Jarnes, Benjamin, 1888- BIP

Jarratt, Devereux,

JARRATT, Devereux, 283'.0924 B
1733-1801.
The life of the Reverend Devereux Jarratt. New York, Arno Press, 1969. 223 p. 23 cm. (Religion in America) "A series of letters addressed to the Rev. John Coleman." Reprint of the 1806 ed. [BX5995.J27A3 1969] 79-83427
I. Coleman, John, 1758?-1816. II. Title.

Jarrell, Randall, 1914-1965.

RANDALL Jarrell, 1914- 818'.5'209
1965. Edited by Robert Lowell, Peter Taylor & Robert Penn Warren New York, Farrar, Straus & Giroux [1967] xii, 307 p. illus., ports. 21 cm. [PS3519.A86Z77] 67-13414
1. Jarrell, Randall, 1914-1965. I. Lowell, Robert, 1917- ed. II. Taylor, Peter Hillsman, 1917- ed. III. Warren, Robert Penn, 1905- ed.

Jarrett, Bede, Father, 1881-1934.

WYKEHAM-GEORGE, Kenneth.
922.242
Bede Jarrett of the Order of Preachers. by Kenneth Wykeham-George and Gervase Mathew. With a foreword by Hilary J. Carpenter. Westminster, Md., Newman Press, 1952. 168p. illus. 22cm. [BX4705.J375W9 1952a] 53-6705
1. Jarrett, Bede, Father, 1881-1934. I. Mathew, Gervase, 1905- joint author. II. Title.

Jarvis, Howard.

JARVIS, Howard. 343'.794'054 B
I'm mad as hell / Howard Jarvis with Robert Pack. New York : Times Books, 1979. p. cm. Includes index. [HJ4121.C22J37] 79-51450 ISBN 0-8129-0858-9 : 9.95
1. Jarvis, Howard. 2. Property taxes—California. 3. Businessmen—California—Biography. I. Pack, Robert, 1942- joint author. II. Title. BIP

Jascalevich, Mario.

LIFFLANDER, Matthew L. 614'.19
Final treatment : the file on "Dr. X" / Matthew L. Lifflander. 1st ed. New York : Norton, c1979. p. cm. [RA1228.L53 1979] 78-26176 ISBN 0-393-08833-2 : 11.95
1. Jascalevich, Mario. 2. Forensic toxicology—Cases, clinical reports, statistics. 3. Curare—Toxicology—Cases, clinical reports, statistics. 4. Trials (Poisoning)—New Jersey—Hackensack. 5. Surgeons—New Jersey—Biography. I. Title.

Jasny, Naum, 1883-1967.

JASNY, Naum, 1883-1967. 330.9'2'4
To live long enough : the memoirs of Naum Jasny, scientific analyst / edited, with biographical commentaries, by Betty A. Laird and Roy D. Laird. Lawrence : University Press of Kansas, c1976. vii, 190 p., [1] leaf of plates : port. ; 24 cm. Includes bibliographical references and index. [HB113.J3A35 1976] 75-33900 ISBN 0-7006-0140-6 : 11.00
1. Jasny, Naum, 1883-1967. 2. Economists—Correspondence, reminiscences, etc. 3. Agriculturists—Correspondence, reminiscences, etc. I. Laird, Betty A. II. Laird, Roy D. III. Title. BIP

Jasper, John, 1812-1901.

DAY, Richard Ellsworth, 922.673
1884-
Rhapsody in black; the life story of John Jasper. Philadelphia, Judson [1967, c.1963] 149p. illus. 20cm. [BX6455.J32D3] 53-11493 1.95 pap.,
1. Jasper, John, 1812-1901. I. Title.

HATCHER, William 286'.0924 B
Eldridge, 1834-1912.
John Jasper; the unmatched Negro philosopher and preacher. New York, Negro Universities Press [1969] 183 p. illus., port. 23 cm. Reprint of the 1908 ed. [E185.97.J36] 71-88413
1. Jasper, John, 1812-1901.

Jastremski, Leon, 1843-1907.

*PINKOWSKI, Edward. 301.451918 B
Pills, pen & politics; the story of General Leon Jastremski, 1843-1907. Wilmington, Captain Mlotkowski Memorial Brigade Society [1974] 172 p. 23 cm. Includes bibliographical references [F375] 74-29094 ISBN 0-9600814-1-0
1. Jastremski, Leon, 1843-1907. I. Title.
Publishers address: 247 Philadelphia Pike Wilmington, Del. 19809 BIP

Jastrow, Marie.

JASTROW, Marie. 974.7'1004924 B
A time to remember : growing up in New York before the Great War / Marie Jastrow. New York : Norton, c1979. 174 p. : ill. ; 24 cm. [F128.9.J5J374 1979] 79-123188 ISBN 0-393-85001-3 : 8.95
1. Jastrow, Marie. 2. Jews in New York (City)—Biography. 3. United States—Emigration and immigration—Biography. 4. New York (City)—Biography. I. Title.

Jaures, Jean Leon, 1859-1914.

GOLDBERG, Harvey, 1923- 923.244
The life of Jean Jaures. Madison, Univ. of Wis. Pr. [c.]1962. 590p. illus. 25cm. Bibl. 62-7216 12.00
1. Jaures, Jean Leon, 1859-1914. 2. Socialism in France. I. Title.

WEINSTEIN, Harold 335'.0092'4 B
Richard, 1906-
Jean Jaures; a study of patriotism in the French socialist movement, by Harold R. Weinstein. New York, Octagon Books, 1973 [c1936] 200 p. port. 23 cm. Originally presented as the author's thesis, Columbia University. Bibliography: p. [189]-195. [DC342.8.J4W4 1973] 73-3079 ISBN 0-374-98336-4 9.00 (Lib. ed.)
1. Jaures, Jean Leon, 1859-1914. 2. Socialism in France. BIP

Jaurez, Benito Pablo, Pres. Mexico, 1806-1872

STERNE, Emma 972'.07'0924(B)
(Gelders) 1894-
Benito Juarez; builder of a nation. Illus. by Ray Cruz. New York, Knopf [1967] 194p. map. 22cm. Bibl. [F1233.J9527] 67-15803 3.95 bds.,
1. Jaurez, Benito Pablo, Pres. Mexico, 1806-1872 I. Title.

Javouhey, Anne Marie, Mother, 1779-1851.

KITTLER, Glenn D 922.244
The woman God loved. [1st ed.] Garden City, N. Y., Hanover House [1959] 235p. 22cm. [BX4705.J38K5] 59-6363
1. Javouhey. Anne Marie, 1779-1851. I. Title.

MARTINDALE, Cyril 922.244
Charlie, 1879-
The life of Mere Anne-Marie Javouhey. London, New York, Longmans, Green [1953] 140p. illus. 19cm. [BX4705.J38M3] 54-1646
1. Javouhey, Anne Marie, Mother, 1779-1851. 2. Sisters of St. Joseph of Cluny. I. Title.

Jay, John, 1745-1829.

JAY, John, 1745-1829. 973.3'0924
The correspondence and public papers of John Jay. Edited by Henry P. Johnston. New York, B. Franklin [1970] 4 v. 22 cm. (Burt Franklin research and source works series, 595. American classics in history & social science, 157) Reprint of the 1890-93 ed. Contents.Contents.—v. 1. 1763-1781.—v. 2. 1781-1782.—v. 3. 1782-1793.—v. 4. 1794-1826. Includes bibliographical references. [E302.J423] 73-140983 ISBN 0-8337-1847-9
1. United States—Politics and government—1783-1809—Sources. 2. United States—Politics and government—Revolution, 1775-1783—Sources. I. Johnston, Henry Phelps, 1842-1923, ed.

JAY, John, 1745- 973.3'0924 B
1829.
The correspondence and public papers of John Jay, 1763-1826. Edited by Henry P. Johnston New York, Da Capo Press, 1971. 1 v. (various pagings) 29 cm. Reprint of the 1890-1893 ed. Includes bibliographical references. [E302.J423 1971] 69-16639 ISBN 0-306-71124-9

1. United States—Politics and government—1783-1809—Sources. 2. United States—Politics and government—Revolution, 1775-1783—Sources. I. Title. **BIP**

JAY, William, 1789-1858. 973.3'092'4 B
The life of John Jay: with selections from his correspondence and miscellaneous papers. Freeport, N.Y., Books for Libraries Press [1972] 2 v. front. 22 cm. Reprint of the 1833 ed. [E302.6.J4J42 1972] 72-2509 ISBN 0-8369-6858-1 34.50
1. Jay, John, 1745-1829.

JOHNSON, Herbert Alan. 973.3'0924 B
John Jay, 1745-1829. Albany, Office of State History, 1970. 53 p. illus., port. 22 cm. Bibliography: p. 53. [E302.6.J4J6] 72-635050
1. Jay, John, 1745-1829.

MONAGHAN, Frank, 1904-1969. 973.3'092'4 B
John Jay, defender to liberty against kings & peoples, author of the Constitution & governor of New York, president of the Continental Congress, co-author of the Federalist, negotiator of the peace of 1783 & the Jay Treaty of 1794, first chief justice of the United States. [1st AMS ed.] New York, Bobbs-Merrill, 1935. [New York, AMS Press, 1972] 497 p. illus. 24 cm. Includes bibliographical references. [E302.6.J4M6 1972] 74-153339 ISBN 0-404-04647-9 20.00
1. Jay, John, 1745-1829.

PELLEW, George, 1859-1892. 973.3'0924 B
John Jay. Boston, Houghton, Mifflin. [New York, AMS Press, 1972] ix, 350 p. illus. 19 cm. (American statesmen, v. 9) Reprint of the 1898 ed. [E302.6.J4P3 1972] 70-128973 ISBN 0-404-50859-6
1. Jay, John, 1745-1829. I. Title. II. Series. **BIP**

SMITH, Donald Lewis. 973.3'0924
John Jay; founder of a state and nation [by] Donald L. Smith. New York, Teachers College Press, Columbia University [1968] xiv, 138 p. 24 cm. (Social studies sources) Bibliography: p. 135-138. [E302.6.J4S6] 68-57156 5.25
1. Jay, John, 1745-1829. **BIP**

Jay, John, 1745-1829—Juvenile literature.

FABER, Doris, 1924- 973.30924 B
John Jay. New York, Putnam [1967, c1966] 223 p. port. 21 cm. (Lives to remember) [E302.6.J4F3] 67-599
1. Jay, John, 1745-1829—Juvenile literature.

Jay, Sarah (Livingston)

HOBART, Lois 920.7
Patriot's lady the life of Sarah Livingston Jay. New York, Funk & Wagnalls Co. [c.1960] 274p. illus. 22cm. 60-7803 3.50
1. Jay, Sarah (Livingston) 2. Jay, John, 1745-1829. I. Title.

Jay, William, 1789-1858.

TUCKERMAN, Bayard, 1855-1923. 326'.0924 B
William Jay and the constitutional movement for the abolition of slavery. With a pref. by John Jay. New York, Negro University Press [1969, c1893] xxiii, 185 p. illus., ports. 23 cm. Bibliography: p. 171-173. [E449.J4285 1969] 69-19000
1. Jay, William, 1789-1858. 2. Slavery in the United States—Anti-slavery movements. 3. United States—Politics and government—1815-1861. I. Title. **BIP**

TUCKERMAN, Bayard, 1855-1923. 326'.0924 B
William Jay and the constitutional movement for the abolition of slavery. With a pref. by John Jay. New York, B. Franklin [1969] xxiii, 185 p. illus., ports. 24 cm. (Burt Franklin research & source works series, 410.) (Sources of Negro history & culture, 4) "Originally published: 1893." Bibliography: p. 171-173. [E449.J4285 1969b] 75-108351
1. Jay, William, 1789-1858. 2. Slavery in the United States—Anti-slavery movements. 3. U.S.—Politics and government—1815-1861. I. Title. II. Series.

Jaynes, Gregory.

JAYNES, Gregory. 309.1'758'27704
Sketches from a dirt road / Gregory Jaynes ; illustrations by Richard Cuffari. 1st ed. Garden City, N.Y. : Doubleday, 1977. 209 p. : ill. ; 22 cm. [F292.W48J39] 75-36596 ISBN 0-385-11505-9 : 6.95
1. Jaynes, Gregory. 2. White Co., Ga.—Social life and customs. 3. White Co., Ga.—Biography. I. Title.

JAYNES, Gregory. 309.1'758'27704
Sketches from a dirt road / Gregory Jaynes ; illustrations by Richard Cuffari. 1st ed. Garden City, N.Y. : Doubleday, 1977. 209 p. : ill. ; 22 cm. [F292.W48J39] 75-36596 ISBN 0-385-11505-9 : 6.95
1. Jaynes, Gregory. 2. White Co., Ga.—Social life and customs. 3. White Co., Ga.—Biography. I. Title.

Jazz music.

BALLIETT, Whitney. 785.4'2'0922
Improvising : sixteen jazz musicians and their art / Whitney Balliett. New York : Oxford University Press, 1977. vi, 263 p. ; 22 cm. Includes index. [ML3561.J3B245] 76-42635 ISBN 0-19-502149-5 : 10.95
1. Jazz music. 2. Jazz musicians. I. Title. **BIP**

FEATHER, Leonard G. 785.4'2'0922 B
The pleasures of jazz : leading performers on their lives, their music, their contemporaries / Leonard Feather ; introd. by Benny Carter. New York : Horizon Press, c1976. 200 p. : ports. ; 22 cm. [ML3561.J3F425] 75-37064 ISBN 0-8180-1214-5 : 7.95
1. Jazz music. 2. Jazz musicians. I. Title.

GOODMAN, Benny [Benjamin David Goodman] 1909- 927.8
The kingdom of swing [by] Benny Goodman, Irving Kolodin. New York, Ungar [1961, c.1939]; 263p. illus. 61-17562 4.75
1. Jazz music. I. Kolodin, Irving, 1908- II. Title.

RAMSEY, Frederic, 1915- ed. 785.4'2'0922 B
Jazzmen / edited by Frederic Ramsey, Jr. and Charles Edward Smith. New York : Harcourt Brace Jovanovich, 1977, c1967. p. cm. (A Harvest/HBJ book) Reprint of the 1959 ed. published by Harcourt, Brace, New York. Includes bibliographical references and indexes. [ML3561.J3R3 1977] 77-4213 ISBN 0-15-646205-2 pbk. : 4.95
1. Jazz music. 2. Jazz musicians—Biography. I. Smith, Charles Edward, joint ed. II. Title. **BIP**

STEWART, Rex William, 1907-1967. 785.4'2'0922 B
Jazz masters of the thirties. New York, Macmillan Co. [1972] 223 p. ports. 21 cm. (The Macmillan jazz masters series) [ML3561.J3S82] 73-169239
1. Jazz music. 2. Jazz musicians. I. Title. **BIP**

WILLIAMS, Martin T. 785'.0922
Jazz masters in transition, 1957-69, by Martin Williams. [New York] Macmillan Co. [1970] 288 p. ports. 22 cm. (The Macmillan jazz masters series) [ML3561.J3W5316] 79-103687
1. Jazz music. 2. Jazz musicians. I. Title. **BIP**

Jazz music—Addresses, essays, lectures.

WILMER, Valerie. 785.4'2'0922 B
Jazz people; with photographs by the author. Indianapolis, Bobbs-Merrill Co. [1971, c1970] 167 p. ports. 23 cm. [ML3561.J3W536 1971] 70-146264
1. Jazz music—Addresses, essays, lectures. 2. Jazz musicians. I. Title. **BIP**

Jazz musicians.

BLESH, Rudi, 1899- 785.4'2'0922 B
Combo: USA; eight lives in jazz. [1st ed.] Philadelphia, Chilton Book Co. [1971] 240 p. ports. 24 cm. Louis Armstrong, Sidney Bechet, Eubie Blake, Charlie Christian, Billie Holiday, Gene Krupa, Jack Teagarden, and Lester Young. Bibliography: p. [225]-226. [ML385.B65] 78-145802 ISBN 0-8019-5250-6
1. Jazz musicians. I. Title.

GITLER, Ira. 781'.570922.
Jazz masters of the forties. New York, Collier Books [1974, c1966] 290 p. 21 cm. Includes bibliographies and discographies. [ML395.G58] 2.95 (pbk.)
1. Jazz musicians. I. Title.
L.C. card number for original ed.: 66-17874. **BIP**

GOLDBERG, Joe. 927.8
Jazz masters of the fifties. New York, Macmillan Co. [1965] 246 p. 22 cm. (The Macmillan jazz masters series) Includes a discography in connection with each musician. [ML394.G63] 65-13117
1. Jazz musicians. I. Title. **BIP**

HADLOCK, Richard. 780'.922.
Jazz masters of the twenties. New York, Collier Books [1974, c1965] 255 p. 21 cm. Includes bibliographies and descographies. [ML394.H33] 2.95 (pbk.)
1. Jazz musicians. 2. Jazz music. 3. Jazz music—Discography. I. Title.
L.C. card number for original ed.: 65-18469. **BIP**

LYDON, Michael. 785.4'2'0922 B
Boogie lightning. Photos. by Ellen Mandel. New York, Dial Press, 1974 229 p. illus. 22 cm. Includes bibliographical references. [ML394.L95] 73-18111 ISBN 0-8037-2061-0 6.95
1. Jazz musicians. 2. Phonograph. I. Title.

LYDON, Michael. 784'.0922 B
Rock folk; portraits from the rock 'n' roll pantheon. [New York] [Dell] [1973, c.1971] 199 p. illus., ports. 20 cm. (Delta Book) [ML394.L96] [B] 784 pap., 2.45
1. Jazz musicians. I. Title.

SPELLMAN, A. B., 1935- 780.922
Four lives in the bebop business, by A. B. Spellman. New York, Pantheon Books [1966] xiv, 241 p. 22 cm. [ML394.S74] 66-10410
1. Jazz musicians. 2. Afro-American musicians. I. Title.

Jazz musicians—Bio-bibliography.

CHILTON, John, 1931ot2- 785.4'2'0922 B
Who's who of jazz! Storyville to Swing Street. Foreword by Johnny Simmen. [1st American ed.] Philadelphia, Chilton Book Co. [1972] 419 p. illus. 24 cm. [ML106.U3C5 1972] 72-188159 ISBN 0-8019-5705-2
1. Jazz musicians—Bio-bibliography. 2. Musicians, American. I. Title.

Jazz musicians—Biography.

EWEN, David, 1907- 785.4'2'0922 B
Men of popular music. Freeport, N.Y., Books for Libraries Press [1972] p. (Essay index reprint series) Reprinted from the ed. of 1944, Chicago. Bibliography: p. [ML390.E84 1972] 72-6818 ISBN 0-8369-7263-5
1. Jazz musicians—Biography. 2. Music, Popular (Songs, etc.)—United States—History and criticism. I. Title. **BIP**

GITLER, Ira. 781.570922
Jazz masters of the forties. New York, Macmillan Co. [1966] 290 p. ports. 22 cm. (The Macmillan jazz masters series) Bibliography: p. 283-285. [ML395.G58] 66-17874
1. Jazz musicians—Biography. I. Title.

GOLDBERG, Joe. 927.8
Jazz masters of the fifties. New York, Macmillan Co. [1965] 246 p. 22 cm. (The Macmillan jazz masters series) Includes a discography in connection with each musician. [ML394.G63] 65-13117
1. Jazz musicians—Biography. I. Title.

HADLOCK, Richard. 780.922
Jazz masters of the twenties. New York, Macmillan [1965] 255 p. 22 cm. (The Macmillan jazz masters series) Includes bibliographies and discographies. [ML394.H33] 65-18469
1. Jazz musicians—Biography. 2. Jazz music. 3. Jazz music—Discography. I. Title.

REISNER, Robert George. 785.4'2'0924 B
The jazz titans, including "The parlance of hip" / by Robert George Reisner. New York : Da Capo Press, 1977. 168 p. : ill. ; 23 cm. (The Roots of jazz) Reprint of the 1960 ed. published by Doubleday, Garden City, N.Y. Includes discographies and bibliographies. [ML3561.J3R4 1977] 76-58559 ISBN 0-306-70866-3 : 12.95
1. Jazz musicians—Biography. 2. Jazz music—Discography. I. Title.

SHAPIRO, Nat, ed. 780'.92'2 B
The jazz makers / edited by Nat Shapiro and Nat Hentoff. Westport, Conn. : Greenwood Press, 1975. xiii, 368 p., [6] leaves of plates : ill. ; 22 cm. Reprint of the 1957 ed. published by Rinehart, New York. Includes index. [ML395.S5 1975] 73-11864 ISBN 0-8371-7098-2 lib.bdg. : 19.00
1. Jazz musicians—Biography. 2. Jazz music. I. Hentoff, Nat, joint ed. II. Title. **BIP**

SPELLMAN, A. B., 1935- 780.92'2 B
Black music, four lives, by A. B. Spellman. New York, Schocken Books [1970, c1966] xiv, 241 p. 21 cm. First ed., 1966, has title: Four lives in the bebop business. Contents.Contents.—Cecil Taylor.—Ornette Coleman.—Herbie Nichols.—Jackie McLean. [ML394.S74 1970] 76-123365 ISBN 0-8052-0281-1 1.95
1. Jazz musicians—Biography. 2. Negro musicians—Biography. I. Title.

TERKEL, Louis. 780'.92'2 B
Giants of jazz / Studs Terkel with Milly Hawk Daniel ; sketches by Robert Galster. Rev. ed. New York : Crowell, 1975. p. cm. Includes index. Discography: [ML385.T45 1975] 75-20024 ISBN 0-690-00998-4 : 6.50
1. Jazz musicians—Biography. 2. Jazz music. I. Daniel, Milly Hawk, joint author. II. Galster, Robert. III. Title.

WILLIAMS, Martin T. 781.5'7'0922
Jazz masters of New Orleans, by Martin Williams. New York, Macmillan Co. [1967] xvii, 287 p. ports. 21 cm. (The Macmillan jazz masters series) Bibliographies and discographies at ends of chapters. [ML3561.J3W5315] 67-12341
1. Jazz musicians—Biography. 2. Jazz music. 3. Jazz music—Discography. 4. Music—Louisiana—New Orleans. I. Title. **BIP**

Jazz musicians—Biography—Juvenile literature.

COLLIER, James Lincoln, 1928- 780'.42 B
The great jazz artists / by James Lincoln Collier ; ill. by Robert Andrew Parker. New York : Four Winds Press, c1977. p. cm. Includes bibliographies and index. Surveys the lives and music of such well-known jazz performers as Jelly Roll Morton, Louis Armstrong, Billie Holiday, Charlie Parker, and others. [ML3930.A2C543] 920 77-7212 ISBN 0-590-07493-8 lib.bdg. : 7.95
1. Jazz musicians—Biography—Juvenile literature. I. Parker, Robert Andrew. II. Title. **BIP**

Jazz musicians—Correspondence, reminiscences, etc.

CONDON, Eddie, 1905- 785.06'67'0973
We called it music; a generation of jazz. Narration by Thomas Sugrue. Westport, Conn., Greenwood Press [1970, c1947] 341 p. ports. 23 cm. Discography: p. 309-328. [ML419.C65A3 1970] 76-110823 ISBN 0-8371-3223-1
1. Jazz musicians—Correspondence, reminiscences, etc. 2. Jazz music. I. Sugrue, Thomas, 1907- II. Title. **BIP**

FOSTER, Pops, 787'.41'0924 B 1892-1969.
Pops Foster; the autobiography of a New Orleans jazzman as told to Tom Stoddard. Introd. by Bertram Turetzky. Interchapters by Ross Russell. Berkeley, University of California Press, 1971. xxii, 208 p. illus., ports. 24 cm. "Pops Foster discography, 1924-1940," by Brian Rust. [ML419.F68A3] 75-132414 ISBN 0-520-01826-5 8.95
1. Jazz musicians—Correspondence, reminiscences, etc. I. Stoddard, Tom. II. Russell, Ross. III. Rust, Brian A. L., 1922- IV. Title.

Jazz musicians—Interviews.

CONVERSATIONS with 785.4'2'0922 B *jazz musicians.* Detroit, Mich. : Gale Research Co., 1977. p. cm. (Conversations with ; v. 2) "All interviews by Zane Knauss." "A Bruccoli-Clark book." [ML395.C66] 77-13012 ISBN 0-8103-0944-0 : 18.00
1. Jazz musicians—Interviews. I. Knauss, Zane. II. Series.

Jazz musicians—United States—Biography.

KINGS of jazz / 785.4'2'0922 B rev. and edited by Stanley Green ; authors, Albert McCarthy ... [et al.]. South Brunswick, N.J. : A. S. Barnes, c1978. 367 p. : ill. ; 31 cm. Originally published as monographs in series: Kings of jazz. Includes bibliographies and discographies. [ML385.K56] 74-30980 ISBN 0-498-01724-9 : 20.00
1. Jazz musicians—United States—Biography. I. Green, Stanley. II. McCarthy, Albert J. **BIP**

Jeanne d'Albret, Queen of Navarre, 1528-1572.

ROELKER, Nancy 944'.028'0924 B Lyman.
Queen of Navarre; Jeanne d'Albret, 1528-1572. Cambridge, Belknap Press of Harvard University Press, 1968. xii, 503 p. geneal. table, maps, ports. 25 cm. Bibliographical references included in "Notes" (p. 441-487) [DC112.J4R6] 68-54024 10.00
1. Jeanne d'Albret, Queen of Navarre, 1528-1572. I. Title. **BIP**

Jeanne d'Arc, Saint, 1412-1431.

BEEVERS, John. 923.544
Saint Joan of Arc. Garden City, N. Y., Hanover House [1959] 190p. 22cm. [DC103.B38] 59-12615
1. Jeanne d Arc, Saint, 1412-1431. I. Title.

BEEVERS, John Leonard 923.544
Saint Joan of Arc. Garden City, N.Y., Doubleday [1962, c.1959] 152p. (Image bk., D131) .75 pap.,
1. Jeanne d'Arc, Saint, 1412-1431. I. Title.

BROWN, Mary Milbank 922.244
The secret history of Jeanne d'Arc, princess, Maid of Orleans. New York, Vantage [c.1962] 753p. illus. 21cm. 62-4579 7.50
1. Jeanne d'Arc, Saint, 1412-1431. I. Title.

CHURCHILL, Winston 944'.026'0924 Leonard Spencer, Sir, 1874-1965.
Joan of Arc; her life as told by Winston Churchill in A history of the English-speaking peoples. Pictures by Lauren Ford. New York, Dodd, Mead [1969] 46 p. col. illus. 18 cm. An extract from Winston Churchill's A History of the English-Speaking Peoples relating the life of the martyr whose divine inspiration helped Charles VII Become King of France. [DC103.C53 1969] 92 70-82623 3.50
1. Jeanne d'Arc, Saint, 1412-1431. I. Ford, Lauren, 1891- illus. II. Churchill, Winston Leonard Spencer, Sir, 1874-1965. A history of the English-speaking peoples. III. Title.

CRISTIANI, Leon, 944'.026'0924 B 1879-
St. Joan of Arc, virgin, soldier / by Leon Cristiani ; translated from the French by M. Angeline Bouchard. Boston : St. Paul Editions, c1977. 157 p. ; 22 cm. Translation of Sainte Jeanne d'Arc. A biography of the peasant girl who led the French army to victory against the English and paved the way for the coronation of King Charles VII. [DC103.C7313] 74-16747 3.95
1. Jeanne d'Arc, Saint, 1412-1431. 2. Christian Saints—France—Biography. I. Title. **BIP**

DAUGHTERS of St. 944'.026'0924 B Paul.
Wind and shadows; the story of Joan of Arc. Illustrated by the Daughters of St. Paul with the cooperation of Guy R. Pennisi. [Boston] St. Paul Editions [1968] 112 p. illus. 22 cm. A biography of Joan d'Arc as she struggled to follow the commands of her "voices" and free France from the English. [DC103.5.D35] 92 AC 68
1. Jeanne d'Arc, Saint, 1412-1431. I. Title.

DE WOHL, Louis, 1903- 923.544
St. Joan, the girl soldier. Illus. by Harvey Kidder. New York, Guild [dist. Golden, c.1956, 1962] 77p. illus. (pt. col.) 24cm. (Jr. vision bk., 30804) 2.50 bds.,
1. Jeanne d'Arc, Saint, 1412-1431. I. Title.

DE WOHL, Louis, 1903- 923.544
St. Joan, the girl soldier. Illustrated by Harry Barton. New York, Vision Books [1957] 189p. illus. 22cm. (Vision books, 22) [DC103.5.D4] 57-7698
1. Jeanne d'Arc, Saint, 1412-1431. I. Title.

ERNEST, Brother, 1897- 923.544
Flames against the sky, a story of Saint Joan of Arc. Illus. by Lucille Conroy. Notre Dame, Ind., Dujarie Press [1951] 111 p. illus. 24 cm. [DC103.5.E7] 51-3403
1. Jeanne D'Arc, Saint, 1412-1431. I. Title.

FABRE, Lucien, 1889-1952. 923.544
Joan of Arc; translated from the French by Gerard Hopkins. New York, McGraw-Hill [1954] 367 p. illus., ports., maps. 23 cm. Bibliography: p. 353-360. [DC103.F3153] 54-9709
1. Jeanne d'Arc, Saint, 1412-1431. I. Title.

FIRST biography of Joan of 922.22 *Arc* (The) with the chronicle record of a contemporary account. Tr. [from French] annotated by Daniel Rankin, Claire Qu tal. [Pittsburgh] Univ. of Pittsburgh Pr. [c.1964] xi, 155p. illus., col. coat of arms, facsims., maps, ports. 23cm. Tr. directly from MS fr. 518 in the Municipal Lib. of Orleans and from a contemporary fragment in a private collection. Bibl. 64-21449 6.00
1. Jeanne d'Arc, Saint, 1412-1431. I. Rankin, Daniel S., 1895- ed. and tr. II. Quintal, Claire, ed. and tr.

GUILLEMIN, Henri, 944'.026'0924 B 1903-
Joan, Maid of Orleans. Translated by Harold J. Salemson. [1st American ed.] New York, Saturday Review Press [1973, c1970] 280 p. illus. 22 cm. Translation of Jeanne dite Jeanne d'Arc. Includes bibliographical references. [DC103.G86713 1973] 72-88652 ISBN 0-8415-0227-7 8.95
1. Jeanne d'Arc, Saint, 1412-1431. I. Title.

HEROLD, J. Christopher. 923.544
Joan, maid of France, by J. Christophe[r] Herold. Illustratedby Frederick T. Chapman. [1st ed.] New York, Aladdin Books, 1952. 241 p. illus. 21 cm. [DC103.5.H4] 52-9327
1. Jeanne d'Arc, Saint, 1412-1431. I. Title.

HOUGHTON, Leighton. 923.544
In the steps of St. Joan of Arc. London, New York, Rich & Cowan [1951] 255 p. illus. 19 cm. [DC103.H64 1951] 51-6478
1. Jeanne d'Arc, Saint, 1412-1431. I. Title.

LIGHTBODY, Charles 923.544 Wayland
The judgements of Joan; Joan of Arc, a study in cultural history. Cambridge, Mass., Harvard [1962,c.]1961. 189p. illus. Bibl. 62-2398 5.50 bds.,
1. Jeanne d' Arc, Saint, 1412-1431. I. Title.

LOWELL, Francis 944'.026'0924 B Cabot, 1855-1911.
Joan of Arc. Freeport, N.Y., Books for Libraries Press [1973] p. Reprint of the 1896 ed. [DC103.L91 1973] 72-10643 ISBN 0-8369-7117-5
1. Jeanne d'Arc, Saint, 1412-1431.

LUCIE-SMITH, 944'.026'0924 B Edward.
Joan of Arc / Edward Lucie-Smith. London : Allen Lane, 1976. 326 p., [8] leaves of plates : maps ; 25 cm. Includes index. Bibliography: p. 284-290. [DC103.L96] 77-359073 ISBN 0-7139-0857-2 : £7.50
1. Jeanne d'Arc, Saint, 1412-1431. 2. Christian saints—France—Biography. I. Title.

LUCIE-SMITH, 944'.026'0924 B Edward.
Joan of Arc / Edward Lucie-Smith. 1st American ed. New York : Norton, 1977, c1976. xiv, 326 p., [10] leaves of plates : ill. ; 24 cm. Includes index. Bibliography: p. 284-290. [DC103.L96 1977] 77-9509 ISBN 0-393-07520-6 : 10.95
1. Jeanne d'Arc, Saint, 1412-1431. 2. Christian saints—France—Biography. I. Title.

MICHELET, Jules, 1798- 923.544 1874.
Joan of Arc; translated with an introd. by Albert Guerard. Ann Arbor, University of Michigan Press [1967] 132 p. 21 cm. [DC103.M612] 57-7746
1. Jeanne d'Arc, Saint, 1412-1431. I. Title. **BIP**

MICHELET, Jules, 1798- 923.544 1874.
Joan of Arc; translated with an introd. by Albert Guerard. Ann Arbor, University of Michigan Press [1957] 132p. 21cm. [DC103.M612] 57-7746
1. Jeanne d'Arc, Saint, 1412-1431. I. Title.

NICHOLSON, Clare Marie. 923.544
The Maid of Domremy; a portrait of Joan of Arc. [1st ed.] New York, Exposition Press [1957] 103p. 21cm. [DC103.N48] 57-10664
1. Jeanne d'Arc, Saint, 1412-1431. I. Title.

PAINE, Albert 944'.026'0924 B Bigelow, 1861-1937.
The girl in white armor; the story of Joan of Arc. Illustrated by Joe Isom. [New ed.] New York, Macmillan [1967] x, 246 p. illus., maps. 24 cm. "Abridged from the author's Joan of Arc—maid of France." [DC103.5.P3 1967] 67-19677
1. Jeanne d'Arc, Saint, 1412-1431. I. Title.

PERNOUD, Regine, 1909- 923.544
Joan of Arc. Translated by Jeanne Unger Duell. New York, Grove Press [1961] 192 p. illus. 18 cm. (Evergreen profile book, 32) Includes bibliography. [DC103.P373] 61-5532
1. Jeanne d'Arc, Saint, 1412-1431.

PERNOUD, Regine, 944.0260924 1909-
Joan of Arc by herself and her witnesses. Tr. from French by Edward Hyams. New York, Stein & Day [1966] 287p. facsims., map, plates, ports. 22cm. [DC103 P3783] 66-24807 6.95 bds.,
1. Jeanne d'Arc. Saint. 1412-1431. I. Title.

PERNOUD, Regine, 1909- 923.544
The retrial of Joan of Arc; the evidence at the trial for her rehabilitation, 1450-1456. Translated by J. M. Cohen. Foreword by Katherine Anne Porter. [1st American ed.] New York, Harcourt, Brace [1955] 264 p. 21 cm. Translation of Vie et mort de Jeanne d'Arc. [DC105.7.P412 1955a] 55-9382
1. Jeanne d'Arc, Saint, 1412-1431. 2. Jeanne D'Arc, Saint, 1412-1431—Drama. I. Title.

PURCELL, Mary. 923.544
The halo on the sword; St. Joan of Arc. With a pref. by Claude Farrere. Westminster, Md., Newman Press, 1952. 308 p. 21 cm. [DC103.P87] 52-10386
1. Jeanne d'Arc, Saint, 1412-1431. I. Title.

ROSS, Nancy Wilson, 1905- 923.544
Joan of Arc; illustrated by Valenti Angelo. New York, Random House [1953] 182 p. illus. 22 cm. (World landmark books, W-4) [DC103.R598] 53-6269
1. Jeanne d'Arc, Saint, 1412-1431.

SABATINI, Rafael, 1875- 920.02 1950.
Heroic lives; Richard I: Saint Francis of Assisi: Joan of Arc: Sir Walter Ralegh: Lord Nelson: Florence Nightingale. Freeport, N.Y., Books for Libraries Press [1971, c1934] 416 p. 23 cm. (Essay index reprint series) [D106.S28 1971] 70-99648 ISBN 0-8369-2071-6
1. Richard I, King of England, 1157-1199. 2. Francesco d'Assisi, Saint, 1182-1226. 3. Jeanne d'Arc, Saint, 1412-1431. 4. Raleigh, Walter Sir, 1552?-1618. 5. Nelson, Horatio Nelson, Viscount, 1758-1805. 6. Nightingale, Florence, 1820-1910. I. Title.

SCOTT, Walter 944'.026'0924 B Sidney, 1900-
Jeanne d'Arc, by W. S. Scott. New York, Barnes & Noble Books [1974] 239 p. illus. 23 cm. Includes bibliographical references. [DC103.S38 1974b] 73-22542 ISBN 0-06-496136-2 13.75
1. Jeanne d'Arc, Saint, 1412-1431.

SMITH, John 944'.026'0924 B Holland.
Joan of Arc. New York, Scribner [1973] 232 p. illus. 23 cm. Includes bibliographical references. [DC103.S62 1973b] 73-5176 ISBN 0-684-13515-9 8.95
1. Jeanne d'Arc, Saint, 1412-1431.

STOKES, Kathleen. 923.544
Maid of Orleans; the story of Joan of Arc. Illustrated by Marjorie Tomes. New York, Roy Publishers-[1956?] 178 p. illus. 21 cm. (Roy biographies for young readers) [DC103.4] 56-9175
1. Jeanne d'Arc, Saint, 1412-1431. I. Title.

STOLPE, Sven, 1905- 923.544
The maid of Orleans. Translated from the Swedish by Eric Lewenhaupt. [New York] Pantheon [1956] 311 p. illus. 24 cm. Translation of Jeanne d'Arc. [DC103.S832] 56-10419
1. Jeanne d'Arc, Saint, 1412-1431. I. Title.

STOLPE, Sven 1905- 923.544
The maid of Orleans. Translated from the Swedish by Eric Lewenhaupt. [New York] Pantheon [1956] 311 p. illus. 24 cm. Translation of Jeanne d'Arc. [DC103.S832] 56-10419
1. Jeanne d'Arc, Saint, 1412-1431. I. Title.

VOLTAIRE, Francois Marie 847.5 Arouet de, 1694-1778.
The virgin of Orleans; or, Joan of Arc. Translated from the French by Howard Nelson. Denver, A. Swallow [1965] 143 p. 23 cm. (A Forgotten classic) [PQ2080.P7E5 1965] 65-20155
1. Jeanne d'Arc, Saint, 1412-1431. I. Nelson, Howard, tr. II. Title. III. Title: Joan of Arc.

Jeanne d'Arc, Saint, 1412-1431—Juvenile literature.

JOHNSTON, Johanna. 920
Joan of Arc Illus. by W. T. Mars. Garden City, N.Y., Doubleday [c.]1961 88p. illus. (part col.) 32 cm. 60-6943 bds., 2.95
1. Jeanne d'Arc, Saint, 1412-1431—Juvenile literature. I. Title.

JOHNSTON, Johanna. 92
Joan of Arc. Illustrated by W. T. Mars. [1st ed.] Garden City, N. Y., Doubleday, 1961. 88p. illus. 32cm. [DC103.5.J6] 60-6943
1. Jeanne d'Arc, Saint, 1412-1431—Juvenile literature. I. Title.

Jeanne d'Arc, Saint, 1412-1431—Juvenile literature.

DAUGHTERS of St. Paul. 92 (J)
Wind and shadows; the story of Joan of Arc. Illustrated by the Daughters of St. Paul with the cooperation of Guy R. Pennisi. [Boston] St. Paul Editions [1968] 112 p. illus. 22 cm. [DC103.5.D35] 68-28106
1. Jeanne d'Arc, Saint, 1412-1431—Juvenile literature. I. Title.

FISHER, Aileen 944'.026'0924 B Lucia, 1906-
Jeanne d'Arc, by Aileen Fisher. Illustrated by Ati Forberg. New York, Crowell [1970] 52 p. illus. (part col.) 27 cm. The life of the peasant girl who led the French army to victory against the English in the fifteenth century. [DC103.5.F57 1970] 92 74-81950 4.50

1. Jeanne d'Arc, Saint, 1412-1431—Juvenile literature. I. Forberg, Ati, illus. II. Title.

STRUCHEN, Jeanette. 92 (J)
Joan of Arc, maid of Orleans. New York, F. Watts [1967] 84 p. map. 22 cm. (Immortals of history) Bibliography: p. 81-82. [DC103.5.S7] 67-12557
1. Jeanne d'Arc, Saint, 1412-1431—Juvenile literature. I. Title.

Jeanne, Saint, consort of Louis xii, King. of France, 1464-1506.

LEVIS-MIREPOIX, Antoine 923.144
Francois Joseph Pierre Marie, duc de,
Jeanne of France, princess and saint; translated by Charlotte T. Muret. [ust ed.] New York, Longmans, Green, 1950. 203 p. 21 cm. [DC108.2.L412] 50-10636
1. Jeanne, Saint, consort of Louis xii, King. of France, 1464-1506. I. Title.

Jeanneret-Gris, Charles Edouard, 1887-1965.

CHOAY, Francoise. 720.9494
Le Corbusier. New York, G. Braziller, 1960. 126 p. plates, port. 26 cm. (The Masters of world architecture series) Bibliography: p. 113-114. [NA1053.J4C5] 60-6079
1. Jeanneret-Gris, Charles Edouard, 1887- I. Title. II. Series.

CRESTI, Carlo. 720'.92'4
Le Corbusier [translated from the Italian]. London, New York, Hamlyn, 1970. 96 p. (chiefly illus. (some col.), plan, ports.). 32 cm. (Twentieth-century masters) Distributed in the U.S. by Crown Publishers. "Writings by Le Corbusier": p. 96. [NA1053.J4C713] 72-177770 ISBN 0-600-35403-2 £1.75
1. Jeanneret-Gris, Charles Edouard, 1887-1965. I. Title.

EVENSON, Norma. 711'.0924
Le Corbusier: the machine and the grand design. New York, G. Braziller [1970, c1969] 128 p. illus., maps, plans. 25 cm. (Planning and cities) Bibliography: p. 125-127. [NA9085.J4E9] 74-87063 5.95
1. Jeanneret-Gris, Charles Edouard, 1887-1965. I. Title. BIP

GARDINER, Stephen. 720'.92'4 B
Le Corbusier / Stephen Gardiner. New York : Viking Press, [1975] c1974. xxiii, 135 p. : ill. ; 19 cm. (Modern masters) Includes index. Bibliography: p. [127]-128. [NA1053.J4G26 1975] 74-6853 ISBN 0-670-42261-4 5.95
1. Jeanneret-Gris, Charles Edouard, 1887-1965.
U Pbk. 2.25; ISBN 0-670-01985-2.

JEANNERET-GRIS, Charles 720'.92'4
Edouard, 1887-1965.
Le Corbusier. Edited by Willy Boesiger. New York, Praeger [1972] 254 p. (chiefly illus.) 21 cm. Based on the author's Le Corbusier, 1910-1965 and The complete architectural works of Le Corbusier, edited by Boesiger. [NA1053.J4B5813] 79-166162 8.50
I. Boesiger, Willy, ed. II. Title.

JEANNERET-GRIS, Charles 720'.924
Edouard, 1887-1965.
Le Corbusier, 1910-65. [Edited by] W. Boesiger [and] H. Girsberger. New York, Praeger [1967] 351 p. illus. (part col.), facsims., plans (part col.), ports. 23 x 29 cm. English, French and German. Bibliography: p. 18. [NA1053.J4A49] 67-25150
I. Boesiger, Willy, ed. II. Girsberger, Hans, 1898- ed. III. Title.

JEANNERET-GRIS, Charles 720'.924
Edouard, 1887-1965.
Le Corbusier. Introd. and notes by Martin Pawley. With 75 photos. by Yukio Futagawa. New York, Simon and Schuster [1970] 136 p. illus. (part col.), plans, port. 27 cm. (Library of contemporary architects) Bibliography: p. 133. [NA1053.J4P34] 70-119716 7.50
I. Pawley, Martin. II. Futagawa, Yukio, 1932- illus.

JEANNERET-GRIS, Charles 720'.924
Edouard, 1887-1965.
Le Corbusier: last works. Edited by Willy Boesiger. [English translation by Henry A. Frey] New York, Praeger Publishers [1970] 208 p. illus. (part col.), plans (part col.) 24 x 29 cm. English, French, and German. Forms the eighth volume of Le Corbusier et P. Jeanneret, Ouvres completes. [NA1053.J4A497] 72-109665
I. Boesiger, Willy, ed. II. Title.

JENCKS, Charles. 720'.92'4
Le Corbusier and the tragic view of architecture. Cambridge, Mass., Harvard University Press, 1973. 198 p. illus. 23 cm. Includes bibliographical references. [NA1053.J4J46 1973b] 73-83422 ISBN 0-674-51860-8 13.95
1. Jeanneret-Gris, Charles Edouard, 1887-1965. I. Title. BIP

JORDAN, Robert 720'.92'4
Furneaux.
Le Corbusier. New York, L. Hill [1972] xii, 224 p. illus. 26 cm. Bibliography: p. 215-220. [NA1053.J4J67] 72-75903 10.00
1. Jeanneret-Gris, Charles Edouard, 1887-1965. BIP

Jeanneret-Gris, Charles Edouard, 1887-1965—Addresses, essays, lectures.

THE Open hand : 720'.92'4
essays on Le Corbusier / edited by Russell Walden. Cambridge : MIT Press, c1977. xiv, 484 p. : ill. ; 24 cm. Includes bibliographical references and index. [NA1053.J4O63] 76-40046 ISBN 0-262-23074-7 24.95
1. Jeanneret-Gris, Charles Edouard, 1887-1965—Addresses, essays, lectures. 2. Architecture, Modern—20th century—Addresses, essays, lectures. I. Walden, Russell. BIP

Jeans, Sir James Hopwood, 1877-1946.

MILNE, Edward Arthur, 1896- 925.3
1950.
Sir James Jeans; a biography. With a memoir by S. C. Roberts. Cambridge [Eng.] University Press, 1952. 175p. illus. 22cm. [QC16.J4M5] 53-5806
1. Jeans, Sir James Hopwood, 1877-1946. I. Title.

Jebb, Eglantyne.

WILSON, Francesca M., 362.7'0924
1888-
Rebel daughter of a country house: the life of Eglantyne Jebb, founder of the Save the Children Fund [by] Francesca M. Wilson. London, Allen 7 Unwin. 1967. 3-228p. 4 plates (ports.). diagrs. 23cm. Bibl. [HV28.J4W5] 67-93546 6.00 bds.,
1. Jebb, Eglantyne. 2. Save the Children Fund. London. I. Title.
Distributor: Hillary House, New York.

Jebb, Marjorie.

JEBB, Marjorie. 945'.5'0910924 B
Tuscan Heritage / by Marjorie Jebb ; with an introduction by Vernon Bartlett ; and illustrations by the author. London : Gollancz, 1976. 124 p., [8] p. of plates : ill., geneal. table, ports. ; 23 cm. Ill. on lining papers. [DG738.79.J4A33] 77-363185 ISBN 0-575-02160-8 : £4.95
1. Jebb, Marjorie. 2. Tuscany—Social life and customs. 3. Il Trebbio, Italy. 4. World War, 1939-1945—Personal narratives, English. 5. British in Tuscany—Biography. 6. Statesmen's wives—Italy—Biography. I. Title. BIP

Jefferaon, Thomas, Pres. U. S., 1743-1826.

RANDALL, Henry Stephens, 923.173
1811-1876.
The correspondence between Henry Stephens Randall and Hugh Blair Grigsby, 1856-1861. Edited, with an introd. and notes, by Frank J. Klingberg and Frank W. Klingberg. Berkeley, University of California Press, 1952. ix, 196p. 24cm. (University of California publications in history. v. 43) 'Appendix: Lord Macaulay on American institutions': p.185-186. Bibliographical footnotes. [E173.C15 vol. 43] A52
1. Jefferaon, Thomas, Pres. U. S., 1743-1826. 2. Randall, Henry Stephens, 1811-1876. The life of Thomas Jefferson. I. Grigaby, Hugh Blair, 1806-1881. II. Title. III. Series: California. University. University of California publications in history, v. 43

Jefferies, Richard, 1848-1887.

LOOKER, Samuel Joseph, 828.809
1888-
Richard Jefferies, man of the fields; a biography and letters, by Samuel J. Looker, Crichton Porteous. London, J. Baker [dist. Mystic, Conn., Verry, 1965, c.1964] xix, 272p. illus., facsims., port. 23cm. Bibl. [PR4823.L6] 65-8780 9.00
1. Jefferies, Richard, 1848-1887. I. Porteous, Crichton. II. Title.

SALT, Henry Stephens, 828'.8'09 B
1851-1939.
Richard Jefferies; his life and ideals. Port Washington, N.Y., Kennikat Press [1970] vi, 119 p. port. 21 cm. Reprint of the 1905 ed. Includes bibliographical references. [PR4823.S35 1970] 77-113320
1. Jefferies, Richard, 1848-1887.

THOMAS, Edward, 1878- 828'.8'09 B
1917.
Richard Jefferies / Edward Thomas ; with an introd. and bibliography by Roland Gant. London ; Boston : Faber, 1978. x, 306 p. ; 21 cm. Includes index. "A selected bibliography": p. 301-302. [PR4823.T5 1978] 78-316800 ISBN 0-571-11236-6 : 11.95 ISBN 0-571-11237-4 pbk. : 5.95
1. Jefferies, Richard, 1848-1887. 2. Authors, English—19th century—Biography. 3. Country life in literature.
Distributed by Faber & Faber, Salem, NH BIP

THOMAS, Edward, 1878- 828'.8'09 B
1917.
Richard Jefferies, his life and work. Port Washington, N.Y., Kennikat Press [1972] 340 p. illus. 23 cm. Reprint of the 1909 ed. Bibliography: p. 329-335. [PR4823.T5 1972] 78-160785 ISBN 0-8046-1617-5
1. Jefferies, Richard, 1848-1887.

Jeffers, Robinson, 1887-1962.

ADAMIC, Louis, 1899- 811'.5'2 B
1951.
Robinson Jeffers, a portrait. [Folcroft, Pa.] Folcroft Library Editions, 1973 [c1929] 35 p. 23 cm. Reprint of the ed. published by the University of Washington Book Store, Seattle, in series: University of Washington chapbooks, no. 27. [PS3519.E27Z55 1973] 73-11375 ISBN 0-8414-2881-6 (lib. bdg.)
1. Jeffers, Robinson, 1887-1962. I. Series: Washington (State). University. University of Washington chapbooks, no. 27. BIP

BENNETT, Melba Berry. 811.52 B
The stone mason of Tor House; the life and work of Robinson Jeffers. Foreword by Lawrence Clark Powell. [Los Angeles] W. Ritchie Press [1966] xvi, 264 p. illus., ports. 25 cm. Bibliography: p. 239-254. [PS3519.E27Z572] 66-17923
1. Jeffers, Robinson, 1887-1962. I. Title.

BROPHY, Robert J. 811'.5'2 B
Robinson Jeffers / by Robert J. Brophy. Boise, Idaho : Boise State University, 1976c1975 50 p. ; 21 cm. (Boise State University Western writers series ; no. 19) Bibliography: p. 47-50. [PS3519.E27Z5728] 75-29982 pbk. : 1.50
1. Jeffers, Robinson, 1887-1962. 2. Poets, American—20th century—Biography. I. Series: Boise State University. Boise State University Western writers series ; no. 19.

CARPENTER, Frederic Ives, 818.52
1903-
Robinson Jeffers. Coll. & Univ. Pr.; dist. New York, Grosset [1964, c.1962] 159p. 21cm. (Twayne's United States authors ser., 22) Bibl. 1.95 pap.,
1. Jeffers, Robinson, 1887-1962. I. Title. BIP

CARPENTER, Frederic Ives, 818.52
1903-
Robinson Jeffers. New York, Twayne Publishers [1962] 159 p. 21 cm. (Twayne's United States authors series, 22) Includes bibliography. [PS3519.E27Z575] 62-16817
1. Jeffers, Robinson, 1887-1962.

POWELL, Lawrence Clark, 811'.5'2
1906-
Robinson Jeffers: the man & his work. A foreword by Robinson Jeffers. Decorations by Rockwell Kent. Los Angeles, Primavera Press. New York, Haskell House, 1970. xviii, 215 p. illus., ports. 24 cm. Reprint of the 1934 ed. Bibliography: p. 210. [PS3519.E27Z7 1970] 68-54176
1. Jeffers, Robinson, 1887-1962.

Jeffers, Robinson, 1887-1962—Friends and associates.

RITCHIE, Ward, 1905- 811'.5'2 B
Theodore Lilienthal, Robinson Jeffers, and the Quercus Press / by Ward Ritchie ; with a Checklist of the Lilienthal Jeffers Collection by Tyrus G. Harmsen. Los Angeles, Calif. : Mary Norton Clapp Library, Occidental College, 1974. 20 p. ; 23 cm. [PS3519.E27Z74] 75-324567
1. Jeffers, Robinson, 1887-1962—Friends and associates. 2. Lilienthal, Theodore M., 1893-1972. 3. Jeffers, Robinson, 1887-1962—Bibliography. I. Harmsen, Tyrus G. II. Los Angeles. Occidental College. Mary Norton Clapp Library. Checklist of the Lilienthal Jeffers Collection. 1974. III. Title.

Jefferson Co., Ind.—Biography.

HENDRICKS, W. P. 977.2'13
1889 biographical and historical souvenir, Jefferson County, Indiana / by W.P. Hendricks. Knightstown, Ind. : The Bookmark, 1977. 216 p. in various pagings : ports. ; 23 cm. Contains several parts of the work published in 1889 under title: Biographical and historcial souvenir for the counties of Clark, Crawford, Harrison, Floyd, Jefferson, Jennings, Scott, and Washington, Indiana. Includes index. [F532.J5H46 1977] 78-103264 11.30
1. Jefferson Co., Ind.—Biography. 2. Jefferson Co., Ind.—History. I. Biographical and historical souvenir for the counties of Clark, Crawford, Harrison, Floyd, Jefferson, Jennings, Scott, and Washington, Indiana. II. Title.

Jefferson family.

JEFFERSON, Thomas, Pres. 923.173
U.s., 1743-1826.
To the girls and boys, being the delightful, little-known letters of Thomas Jefferson to and from his children and grandchildren. Selected, with historical notes, by Edward Boykin. New York, Funk & Wagnalls [1964] x, 210 p. illus., facsims., geneal. table (on lining papers) ports. 22 cm. [E332.86 1964] 64-20964
1. Jefferson family. I. Boykin, Edward Carrington, 1889- ed. II. Title.

Jefferson, Joseph,

JEFFERSON, Joseph, 1829- 927.92
1905.
"Rip Van Winkle": the autobiography of Joseph Jefferson. New York, Appleton-Century-Crofts [1950] xxxii, 375 p. plates, ports. 23 cm. First published in 1890 under title: The autobiography of Joseph Jefferson. [PN2287.J4A3 1950] 50-7350
I. Title.

Jefferson, Mark Sylvester William, 1863-1949.

MARTIN, Geoffrey J. 910'.00924 B
Mark Jefferson, geographer, by Geoffrey J. Martin. [Ypsilanti, Mich., Eastern Michigan University Press, 1968] x, 370 p. illus., port. 25 cm. "Published works of Mark Jefferson": p. 327-333. Bibliography: p. 346-347. [G69.J4M3] 68-22804 8.95
1. Jefferson, Mark Sylvester William, 1863-1949.

Jefferson. Martha (Wayles) Skelton. 1748-1782.

HALL, Gordon Langlev 973.460922
Mr. Jefferson's ladies. Boston, Beacon Pr. [c.1966] xvi. 239p. illus., ports. 21cm. Bibl. [E332.25.H3] 65-20787 4.95
1. Jefferson. Martha (Wayles) Skelton. 1748-1782. 2. Randolph. Martha (Jefferson) 1772-1836. 3. Eppes. Mary (Jefferson) 1778-1804. I. Title.

Jefferson, Ted, 1932-

JEFFERSON, Ted, 1932- 248'.24 B
One bad dude : the miraculous transformation of a four-time loser / by Ted Jefferson with Michael W. Fedo ; [original art by Dean Clark, photos. by Judy Fedo]. Kalamazoo, Mich. : Master's Press, c1978. 176 p. : ill. ; 23 cm. [BR1725.J386A34] 78-54222 ISBN 0-89251-050-1 : 6.95
1. Jefferson, Ted, 1932- 2. Christian biography—United States. I. Fedo, Michael W., joint author. II. Title.

Jefferson, Thomas,

JEFFERSON, Thomas, Pres. U. S., 1743-1826. 923.173
Autobiography. With an introd. by Dumas Malone. New York, Capricorn Books [1959] 119p. 19cm. (A Putnam Capricorn book, Cap 8) [E332.9.A8 1959] 59-9117
I. Title.

JEFFERSON, Thomas, Pres. U. S., 1743-1826. 923.173
The Jefferson-Dunglison letters. Edited by John M. Dorsey. Charlottesville, University of Virginia Press [1960] 120p. port. 26cm. [E332.88.D75] 60-16889
I. Dunglison, Robley, 1798-1869. II. Dorsey, John Morris, 1900- ed. III. Title.

JEFFERSON, Thomas, Pres.U.S., 1743-1826. 923.173
The Jefferson-Dunglison letters. Ed. by John M. Dorsey. iCharlottesville, Univ. of Virginia Press [c.1960] 120p. illus. (front. port.) 26cm. 60-16889 5.00
I. Dunglison, Robley, 1798-1869. II. Dorsey, John Morris, 1900- ed. III. Title.

JEFFERSON, Thomas, Pres. U.S., 1743-1826. 973.4'6'0924 B
Jefferson himself; the personal narrative of a many-sided American. Edited by Bernard Mayo. Charlottesville, University Press of Virginia [1970, c1942] xv, 384 p. illus., facsims., plan, ports. 23 cm. Includes bibliographical references. [E332.J464 1970] 70-87871 3.00
I. Mayo, Bernard, 1902- ed. II. Title.

JEFFERSON, Thomas, Pres. U. S., 1743-1826. 923.173
A Jefferson profile as revealed in his letters. Selected and arr. with an introd. by Saul K. Padover. New York, J. Day Co. [1956] xxiv, 359p. 22cm. Bibliography: p. 349-350. [E332.J466] 56-5981
I. Padover, Saul Kussiel, 1905- ed. II. Title.

JEFFERSON, Thomas, Pres. U.S., 1743-1826. 923.173
The Thomas Jefferson papers, by Frank Donovan. New York, Dodd, Mead [1963] ix, 304 p. ports., facsims. 22 cm. (The Papers of the Founding Fathers) [E302.J4632] 63-20410
I. Donovan, Frank Robert, 1906-

JOHNSTON, Johanna. 920
Thomas Jefferson, his many talents. Illus. by Richard Bergere. New York, Dodd [c.1961] 160p. 25 cm. Bibl. 61-13509 3.50
1. Jefferson, Thomas, Pres. U.S., 1743-1826—Juvenile literature. I. Title.

JOHNSTON, Johanna. 92
Thomas Jefferson, his many talents. Illustrated by Richard Bergere. New York, Dodd, Mead [1961] 160p. illus. 25cm. Includes bibliography. [E332.2.J6] 61-13509
1. Jefferson, Thomas, Pres. U. S., 1743-1826—Juvenile literature. I. Title.

KOMROFF, Manuel, 1890- 920
Thomas Jefferson. New York, Messner [c.1961] 191p. 61-14457 2.95
1. Jefferson, Thomas, Pres. U. S.—Juvenile literature. I. Title.

MOSCOW, Henry 920
Thomas Jefferson and his world, by the eds. of American Heritage. Narrative by Henry Moscow, with Dumas Malone. New York, Harper [c.1960,1963] 153p. illus. 27cm. (American Heritage jr. lib.) Bibl. .95;3.79 lib. ed.,
1. Jefferson, Thomas, Pres. U. S.—Juvenile literature. I. American heritage. II. Title.

MOSCOW, Henry. 92
Thomas Jefferson and his world, by the editors of American heritage. Narrative by Henry Moscow, in consultation with Dumas Malone. New York, Maerican Heritage Pub. Co.; book trade distribution by Golden Press [1960] 153 p. illus. 27 cm. (American heritage junior library) Includes bibliography. [E332.79.M6] 60-11827
1. Jefferson, Thomas, Pres. U.S. — Juvenile literature. I. American heritage. II. Title.

OLGIN, Joseph 923.173
Thomas Jefferson: champion of the people. Illus. by Eleanor Mill. Boston, Houghton Mifflin [c.1960] 192p. illus. (Piper books) 60-13065 1.95; 2.35 bds., lib. ed.,
1. Jefferson, Thomas, Pres. U.S.—Juvenile literature. I. Title.

WIBBERLEY, Leonard Patrick O'Connor, 1915- 920
A dawn in the trees; Thomas Jefferson, the years 1776 to 1789. New York, Farrar [c.1964] 188p. 22cm. (Ariel bk.) 64-17814 3.25
1. Jefferson, Thomas, Pres. U. S.—Juvenile literature. I. Title.

WIBBERLEY, Leonard Patrick O'Connor, 1915- 92
Young man from the Piedmont; the youth of Thomas Jefferson. New York, Ariel Books [1963] 184 p. 22 cm. [E332.79.W5] 63-14626
1. Jefferson, Thomas, Pres. U.S — Juvenile literature. I. Title.

Jefferson, Thomas, Pres. U.S., 1743-1826.

AMERICAN heritage. 923.173
Thomas Jefferson and his world. Narrative by Henry Moscow, in consultation with Dumas Malone. New York, American Heritage Pub. Co.; book trade distribution by Golden Press [1960] 153p. illus. 27cm. (American heritage junior library) Includes bibliography. [E332.A57] 60-11827
1. Jefferson, Thomas, Pres. U. S., 1743—1826. I. Moscow, Henry. II. Title.

AMERICAN heritage. 923.173
Thomas Jefferson and his world. Narrative by Henry Moscow, in consultation with Dumas Malone. New York, American Heritage Pub. Co.; book trade distribution by Golden Press [1960] 153p. illus. 27cm. (American heritage junior library) Includes bibliography. [E332.A57] 60-11827
1. Jefferson, Thomas, Pres. U. S., 1743—1826. I. Moscow, Henry. II. Title.

AMERICAN Heritage 923.173
Thomas Jefferson and his world, by the eds. of American Heritage. Narrative by Henry Moscow, in consultation with Dumas Malone. Amer. Heritage; bk. trade dist. by Meredith, institutional dist. by Harper & row [1962,c.1960] 153p. illus. (pt. col.) 27cm. (Amer. Heritage jr. lib.) Bibl. 3.95; 3.79 lib. ed.,
1. Jefferson, Thomas, Pres. U.S., 1743-1826. I. Moscow, Henry. II. Title.

BEAR, James Adam, comp. 917.55'48'0330924
Jefferson at Monticello, edited, with an introd., by James A. Bear, Jr. Charlottesville, University Press of Virginia [1967] xiv, 144 p. illus., ports. 22 cm. Memoirs of a Monticello slave was first published in 1951; Jefferson at Monticello, in 1862. [E332.15.B4] 67-17629
1. Jefferson, Thomas, Pres. U.S., 1743-1826. 2. Monticello, Va. I. Jefferson, Isaac, b. 1775. Memoirs of a Monticello slave. II. Pierson, Hamilton Wilcox, 1817-1888. Jefferson at Monticello. III. Title. IV. Title. V. Title: Memoirs of a Monticello slave.
Contents omitted. **BIP**

BELOFF, Max, 1913- 923.173
Thomas Jefferson and American democracy. New York, Collier Books [1962] 220p. 18cm. (Coller books, AS384V. Men and history) Includes bibliography. [E332.B43 1962] 62-18247
1. Jefferson, Thomas, Pres. U. S., 1743-1826. 2. U. S.—Hist.—1783-1865. I. Title. **BIP**

BOTTORFF, William K., 1931- 973.4'6092'4 B
Thomas Jefferson / by William K. Bottorff. Boston : Twayne Publishers, 1979. 162 p. : port. ; 21 cm. (Twayne's United States authors series ; TUSAS 327) Includes index. Bibliography: p. 141-159. [E332.2.B58] 78-12112 ISBN 0-8057-7260-X : 8.95
1. Jefferson, Thomas, Pres. U.S., 1743-1826. 2. Presidents—United States—Biography.

BRODIE, Fawn McKay 1915- 973.4'6'0924 B
Thomas Jefferson, an intimate history [by] Fawn M. Brodie. [1st ed.] New York, Norton [1974] 591 p. illus. 23 cm. Bibliography: p. 555-565. [E332.B787] 73-11348 ISBN 0-393-07480-3 14.95
1. Jefferson, Thomas, Pres. U.S., 1743-1826. **BIP**

BROWN, Stuart Gerry, 1911- 923.173
Thomas Jefferson. New York, Washington Sq. [c.1963] viii, 247p. 18cm. (Great Amer. thinkers ser.; W876) Bibl. 64-876 .60 pap.,
1. Jefferson, Thomas. Pres. U.S., 1743-1826. I. Title.

CHINARD, Gilbert, 1881- 923.173
Thomas Jefferson, the apostle of Americanism. 2d ed., rev. [Ann Arbor] University of Michigan Press [1957, c1939] 548 p. 21 cm. (Ann Arbor paperbacks, AA13) [E332.C536 1957] 57-4665
1. Jefferson, Thomas, Pres., U.S., 1743-1826. **BIP**

CONANT, James Bryant, 1893- 379.73
Thomas Jefferson and the development of American public education. Berkeley, University of California Press, 1962. x, 164 p. 24 cm. (Jefferson memorial lectures) "Bibliographic notes": p. 65. [LB695.J4C6] 61-12104
1. Jefferson, Thomas, Pres. U.S., 1743-1826. 2. Education—United States—History. I. Title. II. Series. **BIP**

DAUGHERTY, Sonia (Medvedeva) 1893- 923.173
Thomas Jefferson: fighter for freedom and human rights. Illus. by James Daugherty. New York, Ungar [c.1961] 352p. illus. Bibl. 60-53366 4.50
1. Jefferson, Thomas, Pres. U.S., 1743-1826. I. Title.

DOS PASSOS, John 1896- 923.173
The head and heart of Thomas Jefferson. [1st ed.] Garden City, N. Y., Doubleday, 1954. vi, 442p. port. 22cm. 'Notes on reading in Jefferson': p. [417]-421. [E332.D6] 53-9128
1. Jefferson, Thomas, Pres. U. S., 1743-1826. I. Title.

DOS PASSOS, John Roderigo, 1896- 923.173
The head and heart of Thomas Jefferson. Garden City, N. Y., Doubleday [1963, c.1954] vi, 442p. port. 22cm. 5.95
1. Jefferson, Thomas, Pres. U. S., 1743-1826. I. Title.

FLEMING, Thomas J. 973.4'6'0924 B
The man from Monticello; an intimate life of Thomas Jefferson, by Thomas Fleming. New York, Morrow, 1969. 409 p. illus., ports. 25 cm. Bibliography: p. 391-393. [E332.F6] 79-77220 10.00
1. Jefferson, Thomas, Pres. U.S., 1743-1826. I. Title. **BIP**

FOOTE, Henry Wilder 923.173
The religion of Thomas Jefferson. Boston, Beacon Press [1960, c.1947] ix, 86p. (bibl. footnotes) 21cm. (Beacon ser. in liberal religion, LR1) 1.25 pap.,
1. Jefferson, Thomas, Pres. U.S., 1743-1826. I. Title. **BIP**

FOOTE, Henry Wilder 923.173
The religion of Thomas Jefferson. [Gloucester, Mass, Peter Smith, 1960, c.1947] 1x, 86p. 'Copyright, 1947 . . . under the title Thomas Jefferson: champion of religious freedom, advocate of Christian morals.' 21cm. (Beacon paperback LRI rebound in cloth) 3.25
I. Title.

FRARY, Ihna Thayer, 1873- 923.173
Thomas Jefferson, architect and builder; with an introd. by Fiske Kimball. [3d ed.] Richmond, Garrett and Massie [1950] xiii, 154 p. 110 plates (incl. plans, facsim.) 29 cm. Bibliography: p. 151. [E332.F84 1950] 51-20
1. Jefferson, Thomas, Pres. U. S., 1743-1826. 2. Architecture—Virginia. I. Title.

GEORGIADY, Nicholas Peter, 1921- 92
Events in the life of Thomas Jefferson, by Nicholas P. Georgiady and Louis G. Romano. Illustrated by Buford Nixon. Milwaukee, Independents Pub. Co., c1966. [27] p. col. illus. 16 x 23 cm. (Events in American history) Recaps high points in Jefferson's life and career: his inventions, his activities as a statesman, and his contributions as America's third President. [E332.79.G4] AC 67
1. Jefferson, Thomas, Pres. U.S., 1743-1826. I. Romano, Louis G., joint author. II. Nixon, Buford, illus. III. Title.

GRAFF, Henry Franklin, 1921- 973.4'6'0924 B
Thomas Jefferson, by Henry F. Graff and the editors of Silver Burdett. Editor in charge: Sam Welles. Morristown, N.J., Silver Burdett Co. [1968] 240 p. illus. (part col.), facsims., maps, ports. (part col.) 26 cm. (Illustrious Americans) Bibliography: p. 232-234. The life of Jefferson as a child, inventor, and statesman. Excerpts from his works comprise half the volume. Includes many portraits and paintings showing colonial times. [E332.79.G68] 92 AC 68
1. Jefferson, Thomas, Pres. U.S., 1743-1826. I. Silver Burdett Company. II. Title.

GRIGGS, Edward Howard, 1868-1951. 973
American statesmen; an interpretation of our history and heritage. Freeport, N.Y., Books for Libraries Press [1970] 364 p. 24 cm. (Essay index reprint series) Reprint of the 1927 ed. Contents.Contents.—Washington: the first American.—Franklin: the practical American.—Jefferson: the democratic American.—Hamilton and the making of our government.—Lee: the American warrior.—Lincoln: the prophetic American.—Bibliography: p. 348-355. [E176.G852 1970] 76-121474
1. Washington, George, Pres. U.S., 1732-1799. 2. Franklin, Benjamin, 1706-1790. 3. Jefferson, Thomas, Pres. U.S., 1743-1826. 4. Hamilton, Alexander, 1757-1804. 5. Lee, Robert Edward, 1807-1870. 6. Lincoln, Abraham, Pres. U.S., 1809-1865. 7. Statesmen, American. I. Title. **BIP**

GUINNESS, Desmond. 720'.92'4
Mr. Jefferson, architect [by] Desmond Guinness & Julius Trousdale Sadler, Jr. New York, Viking Press [1973] 177 p. illus. 29 cm. (A Studio book) [NA737.J4G84 1973] 72-12057 ISBN 0-670-49261-2 14.95
1. Jefferson, Thomas, Pres. U.S., 1743-1826. 2. Architecture, Colonial—United States. I. Sadler, Julius Trousdale, joint author. II. Title.

JACOB, John Jeremiah, 1758?-1839. 973.2'7'0924 B
A biographical sketch of the life of the late Captain Michael Cresap. [New York] Arno

Press [1971] 158, 4-23 p. 24 cm. (The First American frontier) Reprint of the 1866 ed. A defense of Capt. Cresap, contradicting the statements made by T. Jefferson in his Notes on the State of Virginia and J. Doddridge in his Notes on the settlement and Indian wars of the western parts of Virginia and Pennsylvania from 1763 to 1783. "A journal of Wayne's campaign ... by Lieutenant Boyer": p. [1]-23 (2d group) [F517.C87J3 1971b] 73-146404 ISBN 0-405-02863-6
1. Cresap, Michael, 1742-1775. 2. Jefferson, Thomas, Pres. U.S., 1743-1826. Notes on the State of Virginia. 3. Doddridge, Joseph, 1769-1826. Notes on the settlement and Indian wars of the western parts of Virginia and Pennsylvania from 1763 to 1783. 4. Wayne's Campaign, 1794. I. Boyer, Lieutenant. A journal of Wayne's campaign. 1972. II. Title. III. Series.

JEFFERSON, Thomas, Pres. 923.173
U. S., 1743-1826.
Autobiography. With an introd. by Dumas Malone. New York, Capricorn Books [1959] 119p. 19cm. (A Putnam Capricorn book, Cap 8) [E332.9.A8 1959] 59-9117
I. Title.

JEFFERSON, 016.9734'6'0924
Thomas, Pres. U.S., 1743-1826.
Calendar of the correspondence of Thomas Jefferson. New York, B. Franklin [1970] 3 v. 24 cm. (Burt Franklin bibliography & reference series, 310) Reprint of the 1894-1903 ed. Contents.Contents.—pt. 1. Letters from Jefferson.—pt. 2. Letters to Jefferson.—pt. 3. Supplementary. [E302.J453] 74-109372
1. U.S.—Politics and government—1783-1865. I. Title. BIP

JEFFERSON, Thomas, Pres. 973.4'6
U.S., 1743-1826.
The correspondence of Jefferson and Du Pont de Nemours / with and introd. on Jefferson and the Physiocrats by Gilbert Chinard. New York : Arno Press, 1979, c1931. cxxiii, 293 p. : port. ; 24 cm. (Johns Hopkins University Press reprints) English or French. Reprint of the ed. published by Johns Hopkins Press, Baltimore, issued in series: The Johns Hopkins studies in international thought. Includes index. [E302.J457 1979] 78-19307 ISBN 0-405-10588-6 : 28.00
1. Jefferson, Thomas, Pres. U.S., 1743-1826. 2. Dupont de Nemours, Pierre Samuel, 1739-1817. 3. Presidents—United States—Correspondence. 4. Economists—France—Correspondence. 5. Political science United States—History—Sources. I. Du Pont de Nemours, Pierre Samuel, 1739-1817. II. Chinard, Gilbert, 1881-1972. III. Title. IV. Series: John Hopkins studies in international thought. V. Series: Johns Hopkins studies in international thought. BIP

JEFFERSON, Thomas, Pres. 923.173
U. S., 1743-1826.
The Jefferson-Dunglison letters. Edited by John M. Dorsey. Charlottesville, University of Virginia Press [1960] 120p. port. 26cm. [E332.88.D75] 60-16889
I. Dunglison, Robley, 1798-1869. II. Dorsey, John Morris, 1900- ed. III. Title.

JEFFERSON, Thomas, 923.173
Pres.U.S., 1743-1826.
The Jefferson-Dunglison letters. Ed. by John M. Dorsey. iCharlottesville, Univ. of Virginia Press [c.1960] 120p. illus. (front. port.) 26cm. 60-16889 5.00
I. Dunglison, Robley, 1798-1869. II. Dorsey, John Morris, 1900- ed. III. Title.

JEFFERSON, Thomas, 973.4'6'0924 B
Pres. U.S., 1743-1826.
Jefferson himself; the personal narrative of a many-sided American. Edited by Bernard Mayo. Charlottesville, University Press of Virginia [1970, c1942] xv, 384 p. illus., facsims., plan, ports. 23 cm. Includes bibliographical references. [E332.J464 1970] 70-87871 3.00
I. Mayo, Bernard, 1902- ed. II. Title.

JEFFERSON, Thomas, Pres. 923.173
U. S., 1743-1826.
A Jefferson profile as revealed in his letters. Selected and arr. with an introd. by Saul K. Padover. New York, J. Day Co. [1956] xxiv, 359p. 22cm. Bibliography: p. 349-350. [E332.J466] 56-5981
I. Padover, Saul Kussiel, 1905- ed. II. Title.

JEFFERSON, Thomas, 973.4'6'0924 B
Pres. U.S., 1743-1826.
Letters of Thomas Jefferson / selected & edited with an introd. by Frank Irwin. Tilton, N.H. : Sanbornton Bridge Press, 1975. 260 p. ; 22 cm. Bibliography: p. 251-252. [E332.86 1975] 75-12007 ISBN 0-89142-022-3 : 8.95
1. Jefferson, Thomas, Pres. U.S., 1743-1826. 2. United States—Politics and government—1783-1789—Collected works. 3. United States—Politics and government—1789-1815—Collected works. 4. Statesmen—Unites States—Correspondence, reminiscences, etc. I. Title. BIP

JEFFERSON, Thomas, 973.4'6'0924 B
Pres. U.S., 1743-1826.
Thomas Jefferson : a biography in his own words / by the editors of Newsweek books ; with an introd. by Joseph L. Gardner ; Joan Patterson Kerr, picture editor. New York : Newsweek, c1974. 2 v. (416 p.) : ill. ; 27 cm. (The Founding Fathers) "This book is based on volumes 1-19 of the papers of Thomas Jefferson, edited by Julian P. Boyd and others, published by Princeton University Press." Includes index. Bibliography: p. 408. [E332.J473 1974b] 76-351155 ISBN 0-88225-051-5. ISBN 0-88225-052-3 de luxe
1. Jefferson, Thomas, Pres. U.S., 1743-1826. I. Newsweek, inc. Book Division.

JEFFERSON, Thomas, 973.4'6'0924 B
Pres. U.S., 1743-1826.
Thomas Jefferson : a biography in his own words / by the editors of Newsweek Books ; with an introd. by Joseph L. Gardner ; Joan Patterson Kerr, picture editor. New York : Newsweek : distributed by Harper & Row, [1974] 416 p. : ill. ; 27 cm. (The Founding fathers) "This book is based on volumes 1-19 of The papers of Thomas Jefferson, edited by Julian P. Boyd and others, published by Princeton University Press." Includes index. Bibliography: p. 408. [E332.J473 1974] 72-92143 ISBN 0-06-011148-8 : 15.00
1. Jefferson, Thomas, Pres. U.S., 1743-1826. I. Newsweek, inc. Book Division. BIP

JEFFERSON, Thomas, Pres. 923.173
U.S., 1743-1826.
The Thomas Jefferson papers, by Frank Donovan. New York, Dodd, Mead [1963] ix, 304 p. ports., facsims. 22 cm. (The Papers of the Founding Fathers) [E302.J4632] 63-20410
I. Donovan, Frank Robert, 1906-

JOHNSTONE, Robert 353.03'13'0924
M., 1939-
Jefferson and the Presidency : leadership in the young Republic / Robert M. Johnstone, Jr. Ithaca : Cornell University Press, 1978, 332 p. ; 23 cm. Includes index. Bibliography: p. [315]-326. [E331.J69] 77-17460 ISBN 0-8014-1150-5 : 15.00
1. Jefferson, Thomas, Pres. U.S., 1743-1826. 2. United States—Politics and government—1801-1809. 3. Executive power United States—History. 4. Presidents—United States Biography. I. Title. BIP

JUDSON, Clara (Ingram), 923.173
1879-
Thomas Jefferson, champion of the people; illustrated by Robert Frankenberg. Chicago, Wilcox and Follett Co. [1952] 224 p. illus. 25 cm. [E332.J8] 52-3101
1. Jefferson, Thomas, Pres. U. S., 1743-1826. I. Title.

JUDSON, Clara 973.4'6'0924 B
(Ingram) 1879-1960.
Thomas Jefferson, champion of the people; illustrated by Robert Frankenberg. Chicago, Wilcox and Follett Co. [1952] 224 p. illus. 25 cm. A biography of the third President, describing his boyhood at Shadwell, his schooling and study of the law, his home at Monticello, the political progression that led to his creation of the Declaration of Independence, and the years of public office in service to his country. [E332.J8] 92 AC 68
1. Jefferson, Thomas, Pres. U.S., 1743-1826. I. Frankenberg, Robert C., illus. II. Title.

KIMBALL, Marie 973.4'6'0924 B
Goebel, 1889-1955.
Jefferson, the road to glory, 1743 to 1776 / by Marie Kimball. Westport, Conn. : Greenwood Press, [1977] c1943. ix, 358 p., [16] leaves of plates : ill. ; 23 cm. Reprint of the ed. published by Coward-McCann, New York. Includes bibliographical references and index. [E332.K5 1977] 76-52415 ISBN 0-8371-9444-X
1. Jefferson, Thomas, Pres. U.S., 1743-1826. 2. Presidents—United States—Biography. I. Title. BIP

KOCH, Adrienne, 973.4'6'0924 B
1912- comp.
Jefferson. Edited by Adrienne Koch. Englewood Cliffs, N.J., Prentice-Hall [1971] viii, 180 p. 21 cm. (Great lives observed) (A Spectrum book.) Includes bibliographical references. [E332.2.K62] 75-133052 ISBN 0-13-509810-6
1. Jefferson, Thomas, Pres. U.S., 1743-1826.

KOMROFF, Manuel, 973.4'6'0924 B
1890-
Thomas Jefferson. New York, Messner [1961] 191 p. 22 cm. A biography of the Virginian who served as member of the Virginia House of Burgesses, member of the Second Continental Congress, writer of the Declaration of Independence, Governor of Virginia, Secretary of State, and third President. [E332.79.K6] 92 AC 68
1. Jefferson, Thomas, Pres. U.S., 1743-1826. I. Title.

KUENZLI, Esther 973.5'1'0924 B
Wilcox.
The last years of Thomas Jefferson, 1809-1826 / Esther Wilcox Kuenzli 1st ed. Hicksville, N.Y. : Exposition Press, [1975] c1974. 92 p. ; 21 cm. (An Exposition-university book) Bibliography: p. 89-92. [E332.6.K83 1975] 74-21443 ISBN 0-682-48168-8 : 5.50
1. Jefferson, Thomas, Pres. U.S., 1743-1826. I. Title. BIP

KUPER, Theodore 973.4'6'0924 B
Fred.
Thomas Jefferson still lives; an outline of the life of the architect of our American heritage. With an introd. by Irving Dilliard. [New York, Patriotic Pub. Co.] c1973. 32 p. illus. 18 cm. [E332.K95] 74-170372 0.50
1. Jefferson, Thomas, Pres. U.S., 1743-1826. I. Title.

LEHMAN, Karl, 1894- v. 12
Thomas Jefferson, American humanist. Chicago, University of Chicago Press [1965] xx, 273 p. illus. (Phoenix books, P181) Bibliographical "Notes": p. 211-260. 66 87452
1. Jefferson, Thomas, Pres. U.S., 1743-1826. I. Title.

LEHMANN, Karl, 1894-1960 923.173
Thomas Jefferson, American humanist. Chicago, University of Chicago Press [1965] xx, 273 p. illus., port. 21 cm. (Phoenix books, P181) First published 1947. Bibliographical references included in "Notes" (p. 211-260) [E332.2.L4 1965] 64-66318
1. Jefferson, Thomas, Pres. U.S., 1743-1826. I. Title.

LISITZKY, Genevieve Hellen, v. 12
1899-
Thomas Jefferson, by Gene Lisitzky. New York, The Viking press [1964, c1961] 358 p. incl. front. (port.) illus. "The jacket, end papers, and illustrations for this volume have been drawn by Harrie Wood." "Books": p. 347-348. 67-40196
1. Jefferson, Thomas, Pres. U.S., 1743-1826. I. Title.

THE lost world of Thomas v. 12
Jefferson. Boston, Beacon Press [1960] 306p.
1. Jefferson, Thomas, Pres. U. S., 1743-1826. 2. Philosophy— American. 3. U. S.—Intellectual life. I. Boorstin, Daniel Joseph, 1914- BIP

MALONE, Dumas, 1892- 923.173
Jefferson and his time. Boston, Little [1966] v. 20cm. Contents.v. 1. Jefferson the Virginian. Bibl. [E332.M25] 48-5972 2.95 pap.,
1. Jefferson, Thomas, Pres. U. S., 1743-1826. I. Title.

MALONE, Dumas, 1892- 923.173
Jefferson and his time: v.3. Boston, Little [c.]1962. 545p. illus. 23cm. Contents.v.3. Jefferson and the ordeal of liberty. Bibl. 48-5972 7.50
1. Jefferson, Thomas, Pres. U.S. 1743-1826. I. Title.

MALONE, Dumas, 1892- 923.173
Jefferson and his time. Boston, Little, Brown [1968,c.1951] v. 20cm. (86) Contents.v.2. Jefferson and the rights of man. Bibl. [E332.M25] 48-5972 2.95 pap.,
1. Jefferson, Thomas, Pres. U.S., 1743-1826. I. Title.

MALONE, Dumas, 1892- 923.173
Thomas Jefferson as political leader. Berkeley, University of California Press, 1963. viii, 75 p. 23 cm. (Jefferson memorial lectures) First presented in 1962 at the University of California, Berkeley. Bibliographical footnotes. [E332.5.M3] 63-14760
1. Jefferson, Thomas, Pres. U.S., 1743-1826. 2. U. S.—Politics and government—1797-1801. I. Series. BIP

MALONE, Dumas, 973.4'6'0924 B
1892-
Thomas Jefferson as political leader / by Dumas Malone. Westport, Conn. : Greenwood Press, 1979, c1963. viii, 75 p. ; 23 cm. Reprint of the ed. published by University of California Press, Berkeley, in series: Jefferson memorial lectures. Includes bibliographical references and index. [E332.5.M3 1979] 78-21568 ISBN 0-313-20730-5 lib. bdg. : 13.50
1. Jefferson, Thomas, Pres. U.S., 1743-1829—Addresses, essays, lectures. 2. United States—Politics and government—1797 1801 Addresses, essays, lectures. 3. Presidents—United States—Biography—Addresses, essays, lectures. I. Title. II. Series: Jefferson memorial lectures.

MARTIN, Edwin Thomas. 923.173
Thomas Jefferson: scientist. New York, H Schuman [1952] x, 289 p. illus., ports. 22 cm. Bibliography: p. 261-283. [E332.M33] 52-7559
1. Jefferson, Thomas, Pres. U.S., 1743-1826. I. Title.

MORSE, John 973.4'6'0924 B
Torrey, 1840-1937.
Thomas Jefferson. Boston, Houghton, Mifflin. [New York, AMS Press, 1972] xiii, 326 p. illus. 19 cm. (American statesmen, v. 11) Reprint of the 1898 ed. [E332.M924] 77-128975 ISBN 0-404-50861-8
1. Jefferson, Thomas, Pres. U.S., 1743-1826. I. Title. II. Series.

MORSE, John Torry, 973.4'6'0924 B
1840-1937.
Thomas Jefferson. New Rochelle, N.Y., Arlington House [1970] 326 p. ports. 21 cm. (Giants of America. The Founding fathers) Originally published in 1883. [E332.M923] 72-111219 ISBN 0-87000-087-X
1. Jefferson, Thomas, Pres. U.S., 1743-1826.

NOCK, Albert Jay, 923.173
1872or3-1945.
Jefferson. Introd. by Merrill D. Peterson. New York, Hill and Wang [1960, c1956] 210 p. 20 cm. (American century series, AC34) [E332.N75 1960] 60-50800
1. Jefferson, Thomas, Pres. U.S., 1743-1826.

PANCAKE, John S. 973.4'092'2 B
Thomas Jefferson & Alexander Hamilton, by John S. Pancake. Woodbury, N.Y., Barron's Educational Series [1974] viii, 521 p. 19 cm. (The Shapers of history) Bibliography: p. 487-504. Short biographies of two members of President Washington's first cabinet emphasizing the contrast between Hamilton's concern for the public interest and Jefferson's for individual freedom. [E332.P24] 920 74-750 ISBN 0-8120-0463-9 2.95 (pbk.)
1. Jefferson, Thomas, Pres. U.S., 1743-1826. 2. Hamilton, Alexander, 1757-1804. I. Title.

PARTON, James, 973.91'1'0924 B
1822-1891.
Life of Thomas Jefferson [third President of the United States] New York, Da Capo Press, 1971. vi, 764 p. port. 23 cm. (The

American scene: comments and commentators) Reprint of the 1874 ed. Includes bibliographical references. [E332.P27 1971] 76-126604 ISBN 0-306-70049-2
1. Jefferson, Thomas, Pres. U.S., 1743-1826. I. Title.

PATTERSON, Caleb Perry, 1880- 923.173
The constitutional principles of Thomas Jefferson. Austin, University of Texas Press, 1953. xi, 211p. 24cm. Bibliography: p.191-199. [E332.P32] 53-5999
1. Jefferson, Thomas, Pres. U. S., 1743-1826. 2. U. S.—Constitutional law. I. Title.

PATTERSON, Caleb Perry, 1880- 923.173
The constitutional principles of Thomas Jefferson. Gloucester, Mass., P. Smith, 1967 [c.1953] xi, 211p. 24cm. Bibl. [E332.P32] 4.00
1. Jefferson, Thomas, Pres. U. S., 1743-1826. 2. U.S.—Constitutional law. I. Title.
Available from publisher's Magnolia, Mass. office. **BIP**

PETERSON, Merril D. 973.4'6'0924
Thomas Jefferson, a profile. Ed. by Merrill D. Peterson. New York, Hill & Wang [1968,c.1967] xx, 262p. 20cm. (Amer. century ser., AC-200) Bibl. [E332.76P4] 67-17056 1.75 pap.,
1. Jefferson, Thomas, Pres. U.S., 1743-1826—Addreeses, essays, lectures. I. Title.

PETERSON, Merrill D. 973.4'6'0924 B
Thomas Jefferson and the new nation; a biography [by] Merrill D. Peterson. New York, Oxford University Press, 1970. ix, 1072 p. illus., ports. 24 cm. Bibliography: p. [1011]-1047. [E332.P45] 70-110394 15.00
1. Jefferson, Thomas, Pres. U.S., 1743-1826. I. Title. **BIP**

PIERSON, Hamilton Wilcox, 1817-1888. 973.4'6'0924 B
Jefferson at Monticello; the private life of Thomas Jefferson. Freeport, N.Y., Books for Libraries Press [1971] 138 p. illus., facsims. 23 cm. Reprint of the 1862 ed. [E332.15.P54 1971] 71-154161 ISBN 0-8369-5777-6
1. Jefferson, Thomas, Pres. U.S., 1743-1826. I. Title. **BIP**

RANDALL, Henry Stephens, 1811-1876. 973.4'6'0924 B
The correspondence between Henry Stephens Randall and Hugh Blair Grigsby, 1856-1861. Edited with an introd. and notes by Frank J. Klingberg and Frank W. Klingberg. New York, Da Capo Press, 1972. ix, 196 p. 23 cm. (University of California publications in history, v. 43) (The American scene: comments and commentators) Reprint of the 1952 ed. [E332.R178 1972] 73-37530 ISBN 0-306-70429-3
1. Jefferson, Thomas, Pres. U.S., 1743-1826. 2. Randall, Henry Stephens, 1811-1876. The life of Thomas Jefferson. I. Grigsby, Hugh Blair, 1806-1881. II. Series: California. University. University of California publications in history, v. 43.

RANDALL, Henry Stephens, 1811-1876. 973.4'6'0924 B
The life of Thomas Jefferson. New York, Da Capo Press, 1972. 3 v. 22 cm. (The American scene) Reprint of the 1858 ed. [E332.R18 1972] 79-172011 ISBN 0-306-70250-9
1. Jefferson, Thomas, Pres. U.S., 1743-1826. I. Title.

RANDALL, Henry Stephens, 1811-1876. 973.4'6'0924 B
The life of Thomas Jefferson. Freeport, N.Y., Books for Libraries Press [1970] 3 v. illus., facsims. (part. fold.), ports. 23 cm. Reprint of the 1857 ed. Includes bibliographical references. [E332.R18 1970] 72-117890
1. Jefferson, Thomas, Pres. U.S., 1743-1826. I. Title. **BIP**

RANDOLPH, Sarah Nicholas, 1839-1892. 923.173
The domestic life of Thomas Jefferson, compiled from family letters and reminiscences by his great-granddaughter. With an introd. by Dumas Malone. New York, Ungar [1958] 432p. illus., ports., facsims. 24cm. (American classics) [E332.25.R2 1958] 58-8958
1. Jefferson, Thomas, Pres. U. S., 1743-1826. I. Title.

RANDOLPH, Sarah Nicholas, 1839-1892. 973.4'6'0924 B
The domestic life of Thomas Jefferson / compiled from family letters and reminiscences by Sarah N. Randolph. Charlottesville : Published for the Thomas Jefferson Memorial Foundation by the University Press of Virginia, 1978. 452 p. : ill. ; 24 cm. Reprint of the 1871 ed. published by Harper, New York. Includes index. [E332.25.R2 1978] 78-14312 ISBN 0-8139-0718-7 : 7.50
1. Jefferson, Thomas, Pres. U.S., 1743-1826. 2. Presidents—United States—Biography. I. Title. **BIP**

RUSSELL, Phillips, 1884- 923.173
Jefferson, champion of the free mind. Illustrated with photos. New York, Dodd, Mead, 1956. 574 p. illus. 25 cm. [E332.R93] 56-10535
1. Jefferson, Thomas, Pres. U. S., 1743-1826.

SCHACHNER, Nathan, 1895- 923.173
Thomas Jefferson, a biography. New York, Appleton Century-Crofts [1951] 2 v. (xiii, 1070 p.) illus., ports. 25 cm. Bibliography: p. 1049-1060. [E332.S32] 51-13987
1. Jefferson, Thomas, Pres. U.S., 1743-1826. I. Title.

SCHACHNER, Nathan, 1895-1955. 923.173
Thomas Jefferson, a biography. New York, T. Yoseloff [1957] xiv, 1070 p. illus., ports., facsims. 25 cm. Bibliographical references included in "notes." Bibliography: p. 1049-1060. [E332.S32 1957] 57-14046
1. Jefferson, Thomas, Pres. U.S., 1743-1826.

SHEEAN, Vincent, 1899- 923.173
Thomas Jefferson, father of democracy illustrated by Warren Chappell. New York, Random House [1953] 184p. illus. 22cm. (Landmark books, 36) [E332.S54] 53-6260
1. Jefferson, Thomas, Pres. U. S., 1743-1826. I. Title.

SMITH, Page. 973.4'6'0924 B
Jefferson : a revealing biography / by Page Smith. New York : American Heritage Pub. Co. : book trade distribution by McGraw-Hill, c1976. 310 p. : ill. ; 24 cm. Includes index. [E332.S63] 76-3593 ISBN 0-07-058461-3 : 12.50
1. Jefferson, Thomas, Pres. U.S., 1743-1826.

THREE Presidents and their books; 923.173 the reading of: Jefferson [by] Arthur Bestor; Lincoln [by] David C. Mearns; Franklin D. Roosevelt [by] Jonathan Daniels. Urbana, Univ. of Ill. Pr. [1963, c.1955] ix, 129p. 24cm. (Fifth annual Windsor lects.; Illini bks. IB-10) Bibl. .95 pap.,
1. Jefferson, Thomas, Pres. U.S., 1743-1826. 2. Lincoln, Abraham, Pres. U.S., 1809-1865. 3. Roosevelt, Franklin Delano, Pres. U.S., 1882-1945. I. Bestor, Arthur Eugene, 1908- II. Mearns, David Chambers, 1899- III. Daniels, Jonathan, 1902- IV. Series: Phineas L. Windsor lectures in librarianship, 1953

UMBREIT, Kenneth Bernard. 973.3'0922
Founding fathers; man who shaped our tradition, by Kenneth Umbreit. Port Washington, N.Y., Kennikat Press [1969, c1941] viii, 344 p. ports. 22 cm. (Essay and general literature index reprint series) Contents.Contents.—Thomas Jefferson.—John Adams.—John Hancock.—Samuel Adams.—Patrick Henry.—George Washington. [E302.5.U55 1969] 68-26228
1. Jefferson, Thomas, Pres. U.S., 1743-1826. 2. Adams, John, Pres. U.S., 1735-1826. 3. Hancock, John, 1737-1793. 4. Adams, Samuel, 1722-1803. 5. Henry, Patrick, 1736-1799. 6. Washington, George, Pres. U.S., 1732-1799. I. Title.

VAN LOON, Hendrik Willem, 1882-1944. 923.173
Fighters for freedom: Jefferson and Bolivar. Written and illustrated by Hendrik Willem van Loon. New York, Dodd, Mead [1962] 243 p. illus. 21 cm. Originally published in 1943 as two works under titles: Thomas Jefferson, and The life and times of Simon Bolivar, respectively. [E332.V28] 62-17394
1. Jefferson, Thomas, Pres. U.S. — 1743-1826. 2. Bolivar, Simon, 1783-1830. 3. South America — Hist. — Wars of Independence, 1806-1830. I. Title.

WIBBERLEY, Leonard Patrick O'Connor, 1915- 973.4'6'0924 B
Man of liberty; a life of Thomas Jefferson [by] Leonard Wibberley. New York, Farrar, Straus and Giroux [1968] vii, 404 p. 22 cm. Originally published as four separate volumes, 1963-1966. Contents.Contents.—Young man from the Piedmont.—A dawn in the trees.—The gales of spring.—Time of the harvest. [E332.W6 1968] 68-24599 5.95
1. Jefferson, Thomas, Pres. U.S., 1743-1826. I. Title. **BIP**

WILBUR, Marguerite Knowlton (Eyer) 1889- 923.173
Thomas Jefferson, apostle of liberty. New York, Liveright [c.1962] 417p. illus. 22cm. 62-19871 5.95
1. Jefferson, Thomas, Pres. U.S., 1743-1826. I. Title. **BIP**

WILBUR, Marguerite Knowlton (eyer) 1889- 923.173
Thomas Jefferson, apostle of liberty. New York, Liveright Pub. Corp. [1962] 417 p. illus. 22 cm. Includes bibliography. [E332.W63] 62-19871
1. Jefferson, Thomas, Pres. U.S., 1743-1826. I. Title.

Jefferson, Thomas, Pres. U. S., 1743-1826— Addresses, essays, lectures.

PETERSON, Merril D., 973.4'6'0924
Thomas Jefferson; a profile, ed. by Merrill D. Peterson. [1st ed.] New York, Hill & Wang [1967] xx, 262p. 21cm. (Amer. profiles) Bibl. [E332.76.P4] 67-17056 5.95
1. Jefferson, Thomas, Pres. U. S., 1743-1826— Addresses, essays, lectures. I. Title.

Jefferson, Thomas, Pres. U.S., 1743-1826—Fiction.

MIERS, Earl Schenck, 1910- 923'.1'73
The story of Thomas Jefferson; illustrated by Reynold C. Pollak. New York, Grosset & Dunlap [1955] 179 p. illus. 22 cm. (Signature books, 36) [PZ7.M59St] 55-10740
1. Jefferson, Thomas, Pres. U.S., 1743-1826—Fiction.

Jefferson, Thomas, Pres. U.S., 1743-1826—Juvenile literature.

BARRETT, Marvin. 92 (J)
Meet Thomas Jefferson. Illustrated by Angelo Torres. New York, Random House [1967] 86 p. col. illus., col. map. 21 cm. (Step-up books) [E332.79.B3] 67-19496
1. Jefferson, Thomas, Pres. U.S., 1743-1826—Juvenile literature. I. Title. **BIP**

DAVIS, Burke. 973.3'092'2 B
Three for revolution / Burke Davis ; with prints and portraits of the period. 1st ed. New York : Harcourt Brace Jovanovich, [1975] 160 p. : ill. ; 21 cm. Includes index. Bibliography: p. [154]-155. Brief biographies of the three Virginians who became "the trumpet, the pen, and the sword of the Revolution." [E302.5.D35] 920 74-24320 ISBN 0-15-286653-1 : 6.25
1. Henry, Patrick, 1736-1799—Juvenile literature. 2. Jefferson, Thomas, Pres. U.S., 1743-1826—Juvenile literature. 3. Washington, George, Pres. U.S., 1732-1799—Juvenile literature. I. Title. **BIP**

DOS PASSOS, John, 1896- j92
Thomas Jefferson, the making of a President. Illustrated by Harve Stein. Boston, Houghton Mifflin, 1964. 180 p. illus. 22 cm. (North star books [36]) Bibliography: p. [9] [E332.79.D6] 64-12275
1. Jefferson, Thomas, Pres. U.S. — Juvenile literature. I. Title.

DOUTY, Esther (Morris) 973.4'6'0924
Mr. Jefferson's Washington, by Esther M. Douty. Illustrated by Cary. Champaign, Ill., Garrard Pub. Co. [1970] 96 p. illus., plan, ports. 24 cm. ([How they lived]) Traces the history of Washington, D.C. until 1809, with emphasis on the people, schools, amusements, food, buildings, and way of life during the administration of Thomas Jefferson. [F194.3.D6] 79-92057 2.69
1. Jefferson, Thomas, Pres. U.S., 1743-1826—Juvenile literature. 2. Washington, D.C.—History—Juvenile literature. I. Cary, Louis F., 1915- illus. II. Title. **BIP**

EICHNER, James A. 973.460924
Thomas Jefferson, the complete man. New York, Watts [c.1966] xv, 157p. 22cm. (Immortals of hist.) [E332.79.E5] 65-21647 2.95; 2.21 lib. ed.,
1. Jefferson, Thomas, Pres. U.S., 1743-1826—Juvenile literature. I. Title. **BIP**

EICHNER, James A 973.460924 (B)
Thomas Jefferson, the complete man, by James A. Eichner. New York, F. Watts [1966] xv, 157 p. 22 cm. (Immortals of history) [E332.79.E5] 65-21647
1. Jefferson, Thomas, Pres. U.S., 1743-1826 — Juvenile literature. I. Title.

FLEMING, Thomas J. 973.4'6'0924
Thomas Jefferson, by Thomas J. Fleming. New York, Grosset & Dunlap [1971] 182 p. illus. 24 cm. "A W. W. Norton book." The life of America's third President, who was also a recognized architect, inventor, and lawyer. [E332.79.F56] 92 77-153921 ISBN 0-448-21413-X 4.95
1. Jefferson, Thomas, Pres. U.S., 1743-1826—Juvenile literature. I. Title.

GRAFF, Henry Franklin, 1921- 973.4'6'0924
Thomas Jefferson of Silver Burdett. Editor in charge: Sam Welles. Morristown, N. J., Silver Burdett Co. [1968] 240 p. illus. (part col.), facsims., maps, ports. (part col.) 26 cm. (Illustrious Americans) Bibliography: p. 232-234. [E332.79.G68] 67-15873
1. Jefferson, Thomas, Pres. U. S., 1743-1826—Juvenile literature. I. Silver Burdett Company. II. Title.

GRAFF, Polly Anne (Colver) 1908- 92 (J)
Thomas Jefferson, author of independence. Illustrated by Cary. Champaign, Ill., Garrard Pub. Co. [1963] 80 p. illus. 23 cm. (A Discovery book) [E332.79.G7] 63-7112
1. Jefferson, Thomas, Pres. U.S., 1743-1826—Juvenile literature.

LEE, Susan. 973.4'6'0924 B
Thomas Jefferson, by Susan & John Lee. Illustrated by Tom Dunnington. Chicago, Childrens Press [1974] 47 p. col. illus. 24 cm. (Heroes of the Revolution) A biography of the Virginian who was noted as a statesman, inventor, and author of the Declaration of Independence. [E332.79.L43] 92 73-17443 ISBN 0-516-04652-7 5.25 (lib. bdg.).
1. Jefferson, Thomas, Pres. U.S., 1743-1826—Juvenile literature. I. Lee, John, joint author. II. Dunnington, Tom, illus. III. Title.

MCMILLEN, Neil R., 1939- 973.4'6'0924 B
Thomas Jefferson: philosopher of freedom, by Neil R. McMillen. Chicago, Rand McNally [1973] 69 p. illus. (part col.) 29 cm. A biography of a statesman, lawyer, architect, inventor, scholar, and President which includes his roles as husband, father, and doting grandfather in private life. [E331.M35 1973] 92 73-12273 ISBN 0-528-82486-4 4.79 (lib. bdg.)
1. Jefferson, Thomas, Pres., U.S., 1743-1826—Juvenile literature. I. Title.

MIERS, Earl Schenck, 1910- 973.4'6'0924 B
That Jefferson boy. Illustrated by Kurt Werth. New York, World Pub. Co. [1970] 143 p. illus. 24 cm. A biography of the young Jefferson covering his career up to the signing of the Declaration of Independence in 1776. [E332.79.M5 1970] 92 74-128524 4.95
1. Jefferson, Thomas, Pres. U.S., 1743-1826—Juvenile literature. I. Werth, Kurt, illus. II. Title.

MOSCOW, Henry. v. 12
Thomas Jefferson and his world. by the editors of American heritage. Narrative by Henry Moscow, in consultation with Dumas Malone. New York, Harper & Row, 1965. 153 p. illus. 27 cm. (American heritage junior library) Includes bibliography. 67-42646
1. Jefferson, Thomas, Pres. U.S. — Juvenile literature. I. American heritage. II. Title. **BIP**

THOMAS Jefferson, j92
the making of a President. Illustrated by Harve Stein. Boston, Houghton Mifflin, 1964. 180 p. illus. 22 cm. (North star books [36]) Bibliography: p. [9] [E332.79.D6] 64-12275
1. Jefferson, Thomas, Pres. U.S. — Juvenile literature.

WIBBERLEY, Leonard Patrick O'Connor, 1915- 92
A dawn in the trees; Thomas Jefferson, the years 1776 to 1789 [by] Leonard Wibberley. New York, Ariel Books [1964] 188 p. 22 cm. [E332.79.W5] 64-17814
1. Jefferson, Thomas, Pres. U.S. — Juvenile literature. I. Title.

WIBBERLEY, Leonard Patrick O'Connor, 1915- 92
Time of the harvest; Thomas Jefferson, the years 1801-1826 [by] Leonard Wibberley. New York, Farrar [1966] 170p. 22cm. Ariel bk. Ariel bk. Bibl. [E332.79.W49] 66-8331 3.25
1. Jefferson, Thomas, Pres., U.S., 1743-1826—Juvenile literature. I. Title.

Jefferson, Thomas, Pres. U.S., 1743-1826—Law practice.

DUMBAULD, Edward, 1905- 340'.092'4
Thomas Jefferson and the law / by Edward Dumbauld. Norman : University of Oklahoma Press, [1978] c1977. p. cm. Bibliography: p. [KF363.J4D8 1978] 78-5742 ISBN 0-8061-1441-X : 25.00
1. Jefferson, Thomas, Pres. U.S., 1743-1826—Law practice. 2. Lawyers—Virginia—Biography. I. Title. **BIP**

Jefferson, Thomas, Pres. U.S., 1743-1826—Personality.

BINGER, Carl Alfred Lanning, 1889- 973.46'0924 B
Thomas Jefferson, a well-tempered mind, by Carl Binger. [1st ed.] New York, Norton [1970] 209 p. col. port. 25 cm. Bibliography: p. [197]-198. [E332.2.B55 1970] 69-14694 ISBN 0-393-01085-6 6.95
1. Jefferson, Thomas, Pres. U.S., 1743-1826—Personality.

Jefferson, Thomas, Pres. U.S., 1743-1826—Views on slavery.

MILLER, John Chester, 1907- 326
The wolf by the ears : Thomas Jefferson and slavery / John Chester Miller. New York : New American Library, 1980, c1977. p. cm. "A Meridian book." Includes index. Bibliography: p. [E332.2.M54 1980] 79-25301 ISBN 0-452-00530-2 pbk. : 5.95
1. Jefferson, Thomas, Pres. U.S., 1743-1826—Views on slavery. 2. Jefferson, Thomas, Pres. U.S., 1743-1826—Relations with Afro-Americans. 3. Presidents—United States—Biography. 4. Slavery in the United States. I. Title. **BIP**

*Jeffrey, Annie L.

*JEFFREY, Annie L. 922.673
A father's faith. New York, Vantage [1964, c.1963] 128p. 21cm. 2.75 bds.,
I. Title.

Jeffrey, Francis Jeffrey, Lord, 1773-1850.

COCKBURN, Henry Cockburn, Lord, 1779-1854. 820'.9'007 B
Life of Lord Jeffrey. With a selection from his correspondence. Philadelphia, Lippincott, 1857. [New York, AMS Press, 1973] 343, 368 p. 23 cm. [PR4825.J2Z6 1973] 70-148763 ISBN 0-404-07297-6 28.00 (2 vols.)
1. Jeffrey, Francis Jeffrey, Lord, 1773-1850. I. Title.

FLYNN, Philip. 820'.9'007 B
Francis Jeffrey / Philip Flynn. Newark : University of Delaware Press, c1977. p. cm. Includes index. Bibliography: p. [PR4825.J2Z67] 76-27915 ISBN 0-87413-123-5 : 12.00
1. Jeffrey, Francis Jeffrey, Lord, 1773-1850. 2. Critics—Scotland—Biography. 3. Judges—Scotland—Biography. **BIP**

IN search of Jeffrey, by v. 12
Blind Harry [pseud. n. p., 1957?] 1v. Arnold Prize--Harvard, 1957.
1. Jeffrey, Francis, lord, 1773-1850. I. Agnew, L R C

Jeffreys, George Jeffreys, baron, 1645-1689.

HELM, Peter J., 1916- 942.0660924 B
Jeffreys; a new portrait of England's hanging judge [by] P. J. Helm. New York, Crowell [1967, c1966] 208 p. illus., ports. 23 cm. Bibliography: p. 202. [DA447.J4H4 1967] 66-21735
1. Jeffreys, George Jeffreys, baron, 1645-1689.

Jeffries, Zay, 1888-1965.

MOGERMAN, William David, 1903- 669'.0092'4 B
Zay Jeffries; a biography, by W. D. Mogerman. Metals Park, Ohio, American Society for Metals [1973] 254 p. illus. 24 cm. Bibliography: p. 246-249. [TN140.J4M63] 73-76586
1. Jeffries, Zay, 1888-1965.

Jehovah's Witnesses—History.

HARRISON, Barbara Grizzuti. 289.9
Visions of glory : a history and a memory of Jehovah's Witnesses / Barbara Grizzuti Harrison. New York : Simon and Schuster, c1978. 413 p. ; 24 cm. Includes index. Bibliography: p. [395]-[397] [BX8525.7.H37] 77-29024 ISBN 0-671-22530-8 : 12.95
1. Jehovah's Witnesses—History. 2. Harrison, Barbara Grizzuti. 3. Jehovah's Witnesses—United States—Biography. 4. Converts, Catholic—Biography. I. Title.

Jelinek, Otto.

JELINEK, Henry, Jr. 1944- 796.910922
On thin ice [by] Henry Jelinek, Jr., Ann Pinchot [New York] New Amer. Lib. [1966, c.1965] 157p. illus. 18cm. (Signet bk., P2982) [GV850.J4J4] .60 pap.,
1. Jelinek, Otto. 2. Jelinek, Maria. I. Pinchot, Ann. II. Title.

Jemison, Mary, 1743-1833.

SEAVER, James Everett, 1787-1827. 973'.04'97 S
Life on Mary Jemison, 1856 / James Everett Seaver. Enl. ed. / edited by Lewis H. Morgan. New York : Garland Pub., 1977 [c1856] 312 p., [4] leaves of plates : ill. ; 19 cm. (The Garland library of narratives of North American Indian captivities ; v. 41) Reprint of the 4th ed. published by Miller, Orton & Mulligan, New York, of the work first published in 1824 under title: A narrative of the life of Mrs. Mary Jemison. Issued with the reprint of the 1824 ed. of the author's A narrative of the life of Mary Jemison. New York, 1977. [E85.G2] [E99.S3] 974.7'03'0924 B 75-7063 ISBN 0-8240-1665-3 lib.bdg. : 25.00
1. Jemison, Mary, 1743-1833. 2. Seneca Indians—Captivities. 3. Indians of North America—Captivities. 4. Genesee Valley, N.Y.—History. 5. New York (State)—Biography. I. Title. II. Series.

SEAVER, James Everett, 1787-1827. 973'.04'97 S
A narrative of the life of Mary Jemison, 1824 / James Everett Seaver. New York : Garland Pub., 1977. xv, 189 p. ; 19 cm. (The Garland library of narratives of North American Indian captivities ; v. 41) Reprint of the 1824 ed. printed by J. D. Bemis, Canandaigua, N.Y., under title: A narrative of the life of Mrs. Mary Jemison. Issued with the reprint of the 4th ed., 1856, of the author's Life of Mary Jemison. New York, 1977. [E85.G2 vol. 41] [E99.s3] 970'.004'97 B 76-30535 ISBN 0-8240-1665-3 lib.bdg. : 25.00
1. Jemison, Mary, 1743-1833. 2. Seneca Indians—Captivities. 3. Indians of North America—Captivities. 4. Genesee Valley, N.Y.—History. 5. New York (State)—Biography. I. Title. II. Series.

SEAVER, James Everett, 1787-1827. 920.7
A narrative of the life of Mrs. Mary Jemison. Introd. by Allen W. Trelease. New York, Corinth Books [1961] 190 p. illus. 19 cm. (The American experience series, AE3) [E87.J5295 1961] 61-8148
1. Jemison, Mary, 1743-1833. 2. Seneca Indians. **BIP**

SEAVER, James Everett, 1787-1827. 970.3
A narrative of the life of Mrs. Mary Jemison. Ann Arbor, Mich., Allegany Press [1967] 189 p. 15 cm. "This facsimilie [of the 1st ed., 1824] ... was made from an original in the collections of David Howe Public Library, Wellsville, Allegany County, New York." [E87.J5295] 67-27781
1. Jemison, Mary, 1743-1833. 2. Indians of North America—Captivities. 3. Seneca Indians. 4. Genesee Valley, N. Y. I. Title.

SEAVER, James Everett, 1787-1827. 970.3
A narrative of the life of Mrs. Mary Jemison. Ann Arbor, Mich., Allegany Press [1967] 189 p. 15 cm. "This facsimile [of the 1st ed., 1824]... was made from an original in the collections of David Howe Public Library, Wellsville, Allegany County, New York." [E87.J5295 1967] 67-27781
1. Jemison, Mary, 1743-1833. 2. Indians of North America—Captivities. 3. Seneca Indians. 4. Genesee Valley, N.Y. I. Title.

Jencken, Catherine Fox, 1836-1892.

JACKSON, Herbert G. 133.9'2'0922 B
The spirit rappers [by] Herbert G. Jackson, Jr. [1st ed.] Garden City, N.Y., Doubleday, 1972. 226 p. 22 cm. Bibliography: p. [221]-226. [BF1283.F7J33] 71-171300 6.95
1. Jencken, Catherine Fox, 1836-1892. 2. Fox, Margaret, 1833-1893. 3. Underhill, Ann Leah, 1814-1890. 4. Spiritualism—History. I. Title.

Jencken, Catherine Fox, 1836-1892—Juvenile literature.

EDMONDS, I. G. 133.9'1'0922
The girls who talked to ghosts : the story of Katie and Margaretta Fox / by I. G. Edmonds. New York : Holt, Rinehart, and Winston, c1979. 160 p. : ill. ; 22 cm. Includes index. Bibliography: p. [151]-156. A biography, with emphasis on the early years, of the Fox sisters who claimed to communicate with ghosts. Their experiences led to the founding of the Spiritualist movement. [BF1283.F7E35] 920 B 78-14089 ISBN 0-03-042691-X : 6.95
1. Jencken, Catherine Fox, 1836-1892—Juvenile literature. 2. Fox, Margaret, 1833-1893—Juvenile literature. 3. Spiritualists—United States—Biography—Juvenile literature. 4. Spiritualism—History—Juvenile literature. I. Title.

Jenghis Khan, 1162-1227.

BRENT, Peter Ludwig. 950'.2'0924 B
Genghis Khan / by Peter Brent. New York : McGraw-Hill, c1976. p. cm. Includes index. Bibliography: p. [DS22.B74 1976] 76-4896 ISBN 0-07-007650-2
1. Jenghis Khan, 1162-1227. 2. Mongols—History. I. Title.

GROUSSET, Rene, 1885-1952. 950'.2
Conqueror of the world. Translated from the French by Marian McKellar and Denis Sinor. With pref., notes, and bibliography by Denis Sinor. New York, Orion Press, 1966 [i.e. 1967] xvii, 300 p. maps (on lining papers) 24 cm. Bibliography: p. [293]-300. [DS22.G7513] 66-26535
1. Jenghis Khan, 1162-1227. I. Title.

LAMB, Harold, 1892- 951'.025
Genghis Khan, the emperor of all men. Garden City, N. Y., Doubleday, 1952. 270p. illus. 22cm. Bibliography: p. 247-257. [DS22.L] A53
1. Jenghis Kahn, 1162-1227. 2. Mongols—Hist. I. Title.

*LAMB, Harold, 1892- 951.2
Ghenghis Kahn. New York, Pinnacle Books [1976 c1927] 240 p. 18 cm. Includes index. Bibliography: p. 223-228. [DS22] ISBN 0-523-00852-X 1.50 (pbk.)
1. Jenghis Kahn, 1162-1227. 2. Mongols—History. I. Title.

LAMB, Harold Albert, 1892- 923.15
Genghis Khan, the emperor of all men. New York, Bantam [1963, c.1927] 240p. illus., map. 18cm. (Bantam pathfinder ed. FP9) Bibl. .50 pap.,
1. Jenghis Khan, 1162-1227. 2. Mongols—Hist. I. Title.

LIDDELL HART, Basil Henry, 1895- 909'.00922
Great captains unveiled. by B. H. Liddell Hart. Freeport, N.Y., Bks. for Libs. Pr. [1967] 274p. maps. 22cm. (Essay index reprint ser.) Reprint of the 1928 ed. [D106.L5 1967] 67-23240 8.50
1. Jenghis Khan, 1162-1227. 2. Saxe, Maurice, comte de, 1696-1750. 3. Gusstaf Adolf, King of Sweden, 1594-1632. 4. Wallenstein, Alberecht Wenzel Eusebius von. Herzog zu Friendland. 1583-1634. 5. Wolfe, James, 1727-1759. I. Title. Contents omitted.

LISTER, Richard Percival, 1914 950'.2 B
Genghis Khan [by] R. P. Lister. New York, Stein and Day [1969] xxii, 232 p. port. 22 cm. Bibliography: p. 223-224. [DS22.L5] 78-87955 6.95
1. Jenghis Khan, 1162-1227.

MARTIN, Henry Desmond, 1908- 951'.025'0924
The rise of Chingis Khan and his conquest of North China, by H. Desmond Martin. Introd. by Owen Lattimore. Edited by Eleanor Lattimore. New York, Octagon Books, 1971 [c1950] xvii, 360 p. 3 maps (fold. in pocket), plans, port. 24 cm. Bibliography: p. 339-344. [DS22.M3 1971] 70-120647
1. Jenghis Khan, 1162-1227. 2. China—History—Yuan dynasty, 1260-1368. I. Title.

VLADIMIRTSOV, Boris IAkovlevich, 1884-1931. 950'.2
The life of Chingis-Khan, by B. Y. Vladimirtsov. Translated from the Russian by D. S. Mirsky. New York, B. Blom [1969] xii, 172 p. 20 cm. [DS22.V6 1969] 76-82003
1. Jenghis Khan, 1162-1227. I. Title. **BIP**

Jenghis Khan, 1162-1227—Juvenile literature.

KING, Charles Nicolae Aurel, 1911- 950'.2'0924 B
The story of Genghis Khan. Written and illustrated by Charles King. New York, Roy Publishers [1971] 131 p. illus. 25 cm. Bibliography: p. 127. A biography of the twelfth-century Mongolian conqueror whose empire eventually extended from Peking to the Black Sea. Includes a section on Mongolia today. [DS22.K55 1971b] 92 70-173684 5.50
1. Jenghis Khan, 1162-1227—Juvenile literature. I. Title.

Jenkins family.

JENKINS, Jack S., 1914- 929.2'0973
Greenberry Jenkins of Cherokee County, Texas; his ancestors and descendants. With biographical sketches of families: Bailey, Evans, Harris, Hornbuckle, and Medford. Compiled by Jack S. Jenkins. Assisted by: A. C. Jenkins [and others. San Antonio,

Texas, 1968] vii, 192, A32 p. illus., geneal. table, ports. 33 cm. [CS71.J5 1968] 67-24196
1. Jenkins family. I. Title.

Jenkins, Ferguson, 1943- —Juvenile literature.

PASHKO, Stanley, 1913- 796.357'092'4 B
Ferguson Jenkins : the quiet winner / Stanley Pashko. New York : Putnam, [1975] 128 p. ; 21 cm. (Putnam sports shelf) Includes index. A biography of Ferguson Jenkins, one of only four pitchers in the past fifty years to win twenty games for six consecutive years. [GV865.J38P37 1975] 92 74-21081 ISBN 0-399-60936-9 lib. bdg. : 5.29
1. Jenkins, Ferguson, 1943- —Juvenile literature. 2. Baseball—Juvenile literature. **BIP**

Jenkins, Herbert T.

JENKINS, Herbert T. 362.2'092'4 B
Forty years on the force: 1932-1972; Herbert Jenkins reminisces on his career with the Atlanta Police Department. [Limited 1st ed. Atlanta] Center for Research in Social Change, Emory University [1974, c1973] iv, 159 p. illus. 23 cm. [HV7911.J44A3] 73-91480 4.95 (pbk.)
1. Jenkins, Herbert T. 2. Police—Correspondence, reminiscences, etc. 3. Atlanta—Police—History. I. Title.

JENKINS, Herbert T. 363.2'0924 B
Keeping the peace; a police chief looks at his job, by Herbert Jenkins. [1st ed.] New York, Harper & Row [1970] xii, 203 p. 22 cm. Autobiographical. [HV8148.A72J4] 72-95967 5.95
1. Atlanta—Police. I. Title.

Jenkins, Peter, 1951-

JENKINS, Peter, 1951- 917.3'04'9260924
A walk across America / by Peter Jenkins. 1st ed. New York : Morrow, 1979. 288 p., [8] leaves of plates : ill. ; 25 cm. [E169.02.J37] 78-10320 ISBN 0-688-03427-6 : 12.50
1. Jenkins, Peter, 1951- 2. United States—Description and travel—1960- 3. United States—Biography. 4. Walking—United States. I. Title. **BIP**

Jenkins, Warwick Hoxie, 1847-1933.

SALLEE, Annie (Jenkins) 923.473
A friend of God; highlights in the life of Judge W. H. Jenkins, outstanding Christian layman of Texas. San Antonio, Naylor Co. [1952] 127p. illus. 22cm. [BR1725.J39S2] 53-5874
1. Jenkins, Warwick Hoxie, 1847-1933. I. Title.

Jenkins, William Marshall,

JENKINS, William Marshall, 1892or3- 381'.092'4 B
And ... I'll throw in the socks; the memoirs of a Kentucky storekeeper, W. Marshall Jenkins, Sr. Written & illustrated by William M. Jenkins, Jr. Based on conversations and tape recorded interviews with his father. [Nashville, Parthenon Press [1972] 196 p. illus. 26 cm. [HF5465.U6J45] 72-189077 5.95
I. Jenkins, William M. II. Title.

Jenks, Kathleen, 1940-

JENKS, Kathleen, 1940- 135.3
Journey of a dream animal : a human search for personal identity / by Kathleen Jenks ; with a foreword by Jean Houston. New York : Julian Press, c1975. xxiv, 246 p. ; 22 cm. Autobiographical. [BF1091.J46] 75-324032 ISBN 0-87097-066-6 : 7.95
1. Jenks, Kathleen, 1940- 2. Dreams. I. Title.

Jenner, Bruce, 1949-

JENNER, Bruce, 1949- 796.4'2'0924 B
Decathlon challenge : Bruce Jenner's story / Bruce Jenner and Phillip Finch. Englewood Cliffs, N.J. : Prentice-Hall, c1977. vii, 213 p., [12] leaves of plates : ill. ; 24 cm. [GV697.J38A33] 77-4856 ISBN 0-13-197699-0 : 8.95
1. Jenner, Bruce, 1949- 2. Track and field athletes—United States—Biography. 3. Decathlon. I. Finch, Phillip. II. Title. **BIP**

Jenner, Bruce, 1949- —Juvenile literature.

AASENG, Nathan K. 796.4'2'0924 B
Bruce Jenner : decathlon winner / Nathan K. Aaseng. Minneapolis : Lerner Publications Co., c1979. p. cm. (The Achievers) Includes index. A biography of the young American whose four years of intense training enabled him to win the decathlon at the 1976 Olympics. [GV697.J38A65 1979] 92 79-4497 ISBN 0-8225-0477-4 : 5.95
1. Jenner, Bruce, 1949- —Juvenile literature. 2. Olympic Games, Montreal, Quebec, 1976—Juvenile literature. 3. Track and field athletes—United States—Biography—Juvenile literature. 4. Decathlon—Juvenile literature. I. Title. II. Series.

JENNER, Bruce, 1949- 796.4'2'0924 B
The Olympics and me / by Bruce Jenner with R. Smith Kiliper. 1st ed. New York : Doubleday, 1980. p. cm. (An I want to know about book) Includes index. The 1976 Olympics decathlon winner discusses his life, his Olympic experiences, the decathlon, and his involvement in the Special Olympics. [GV697.J38A36] 92 79-7496 ISBN 0-385-14928-X : 6.95 ISBN 0-385-14929-8 lib. bdg. : 7.90 lib. bdg. : 7.90
1. Jenner, Bruce, 1949- —Juvenile literature. 2. Track and field athletes—United States—Biography—Juvenile literature. 3. Olympic games—Juvenile literature. 4. Decathlon—Juvenile literature. I. Kiliper, R. Smith, joint author. II. Title. **BIP**

SOUCHERAY, Joe. 796.4'2'0924 B
Bruce Jenner / by Joe Soucheray. Mankato, Minn. : Creative Education, Inc., 1979. p. cm. A biographical sketch of the young American who won the decathlon at the 1976 Olympics. [GV697.J38S68] 92 79-10040 ISBN 0-87191-723-8 : 5.50
1. Jenner, Bruce, 1949- —Juvenile literature. 2. Track and field athletes—United States. 3. Decathlon—Juvenile literature. I. Title. **BIP**

Jenner, Chrystie, 1950-

JENNER, Chrystie, 1950- 792'.028'0924 B
I am Chrystie / Chrystie Jenner, with Patricia Wood. Millbrae, Calif. : Les Femmes Pub., 1977. iv, 187 p. : ill. ; 22 cm. Autobiographical. [GV697.J383A34] 77-77949 ISBN 0-89087-988-5 : 8.95. ISBN 0-89087-925-7 pbk. : 4.95
1. Jenner, Chrystie, 1950- 2. Jenner, Bruce, 1949- 3. Track and field athletes—United States—Biography. 4. Decathlon. I. Title. **BIP**

Jenner, Edward, 1749-1823.

DOLAN, Edward F. 926.1
Jenner and the miracle of vaccine. New York, Dodd, Mead [c.1960] 242p. 21cm. 60-12332 3.50
1. Jenner, Edward, 1749-1823. I. Title. **BIP**

EBERLE, Irmengarde, 1898- 926.1
Edward Jenner & smallpox vaccination. Pictures by Henry S. Gillette. New York, Watts [c.1962] 153p. illus. 22cm. (Immortals of sci., IS14) 62-10065 1.95
1. Jenner, Edward, 1749-1823. I. Title.

LEVINE, Israel E. 926.1
Conqueror of smallpox: Dr. Edward Jehner. New York, Messner [c.1960] 190p. (bibl.) 22cm. (Julian Messner shelf of biographies) 60-7817 2.95
1. Jenner, Edward, 1749-1823. I. Title.

Jennings, James S.

JENNINGS, James S. 364.1'63 B
Two shades of red [by] James S. Jennings. Nashville, Broadman Press [1974] 160 p. illus. 19 cm. Autobiographical. [HV6248.J44A33] 74-75673 ISBN 0-8054-7211-8 1.95 (pbk.)
1. Jennings, James S. 2. Forgery. I. Title.

Jennings, Waylon.

ALLEN, Bob. 784.5'2'0922 B
Waylon & Willie : the full story in words and pictures of Waylon Jennings & Willie Nelson / by Bob Allen. New York : Quick Fox, c1979. 127 p. : ports. ; 26 cm. Discography: p. 116-127. [ML400.A347] 79-90894 ISBN 0-8256-3941-7 pbk. : 4.95.
1. Jennings, Waylon. 2. Nelson, Willie, 1933- 3. Country musicians—United States—Biography. I. Title.

Jensen, Don.

ROBERTS, David, 1943- 796.5'22
Deborah: a wilderness narrative. New York, Vanguard Press [1970] 188 p. 15 illus., 3 maps. 24 cm. Personal experiences of D. Roberts and D. Jensen, while mountain climbing in Alaska, summer 1964. [F912.D6R6 1970] 76-134663 ISBN 0-8149-0677-X 6.95
1. Jensen, Don. 2. Deborah, Mount, Alaska. I. Title.

Jensen, Jackie, 1927-

HIRSHBERG, Albert, 1909- 927.963
The Jackie Jensen story. New York, J. Messner [c1961] 192p. illus. 22cm. [GV865.J4H5 1961] 61-4387
1. Jensen, Jackie, 1927- I. Title.

Jensen, Jens, 1860-1951.

EATON, Leonard K. 712.0973
Landscape artist in America; the life and work of Jens Jensen, by Leonard K. Eaton. Chicago, University of Chicago Press [1964] x, 240 p. illus., plans (1 fold.) ports. 28 cm. "Bibliographical essay": p. 237-240. [SB470.J4E2] 64-23422
1. Jensen, Jens, 1860-1951. I. Title. **BIP**

Jensen, Povl Bang, 1909-1959.

COPP, DeWitt 923.273
Betrayal at the UN, the story of Paul Bang-Jensen by DeWitt Copp and Marshall Peck. New York, Devin-Adair Co. [c.]1961. 335p. 61-6796 4.75
1. Jensen, Povl Bang, 1909-1959. 2. United Nations—Hungary. I. Peck, Marshall, joint author. II. Title.

*Jensen, Robert

*JENSEN, Robert 631.0924
My story. New York, Carlton [c.1966] 181p. 21cm. 3.75
I. Title.

Jerdan, William, 1782-1869—Biography.

JERDAN, William, 1782-1869. 828'.7'09 B
The autobiography of William Jerdan : with his literary, political, and social reminiscences and correspondence during the last fifty years. New York : AMS Press, [1976] p. cm. Reprint of the 1852-1853 ed. published by A. Hall, Virtue, London. [PR4825.J25Z5 1976] 70-170813 ISBN 0-404-07660-2 : 75.00(4vols.)
1. Jerdan, William, 1782-1869—Biography.

Jeremiah, the prophet.

DICKINSON, George T. 224'.2'06
Jeremiah, the iron prophet / by G. T. Dickinson. Nashville : Southern Pub. Association, [1978] p. cm. [BS580.J4D5] 78-15455 ISBN 0-8127-0183-6 pbk. : 4.95
1. Jeremiah, the prophet. 2. Bible. O.T.—Biography. 3. Bible. O.T. Jeremiah—Criticism, interpretation, etc. I. Title.

HOWARD, David M. 224'.2'0924 B
Words of fire, rivers of tears : the man Jeremiah / David M. Howard. Wheaton, Ill. : Tyndale House Publishers, 1976. 139 p. ; 21 cm. [BS580.J4H66] 75-37233 ISBN 0-8423-8480-4 : 2.95
1. Jeremiah, the prophet. I. Title.

Jeri z Podebrad, King of Bohemia,1420-1471.

HEYMANN, Frederick Gotthold, 1900- 943.702
George of Bohemia, King of Heretics. Princeton, N. J., Princeton [c.]1965. xvi, 671p. illus., maps., ports. 24cm. Bibl. [DB209.H4] 64-19821 15.00
1. Jeri z Podebrad, King of Bohemia,1420-1471. 2. Bohemia—Hist.—1403-1526. I. Title.

Jeritza, Maria, 1887-

JERITZA, Maria, 1887- 782.1'092'4 B
Sunlight and song ; a singer's life / Maria Jeritza ; translated by Frederick H. Martens. New York : Arno Press, 1977, [c1942] viii, 261 p., [33] leaves of plates : ill. ; 23 cm. (Opera biographies) Reprint of the 1929 ed. published by D. Appleton, New York. [ML420.J37A3 1977] 76-29942 ISBN 0-405-09684-4 : 21.00
1. Jeritza, Maria, 1887- 2. Singers—Biography. I. Title.

Jerome, Ariz.—Biography.

YOUNG, Herbert V. 979.1'57
Ghosts of Cleopatra Hill : men and legends of Old Jerome / by Herbert V. Young. Jerome, Ariz. : Jerome Historical Society, 1974. 183 p. : ill. ; 22 cm. [F819.J4Y6 1974] 74-83499
1. Jerome, Ariz.—Biography. 2. Jerome, Ariz.—History. 3. Copper mines and mining—Arizona—Jerome. I. Title.

Jerome, Jerome Klapka, 1859-1927.

FAUROT, Ruth Marie. 823'.9'12
Jerome K. Jerome. New York, Twayne Publishers [1974] 200 p. port. 22 cm. (Twayne's English authors series, TEAS 164) Bibliography: p. 189-194. [PR4825.J3F3] 73-15938 ISBN 0-8057-1291-7 5.50
1. Jerome, Jerome Klapka, 1859-1927. **BIP**

Jerome, Leonard, 1818-1891.

LESLIE, Anita. 923.373
The remarkable Mr. Jerome; illustrated with photos. [1st ed.] New York, Holt [1954] 312 p. illus. 22 cm. [CT275.J567L4] 54-10523
1. Jerome, Leonard, 1818-1891. I. Title.

Jerome, William Travers, 1859-1934.

O'CONNOR, Richard, 1915- 923.473
Courtroom warrior; the combative career of William Travers Jerome. [1st ed.] Boston, Little, Brown [1963] 342 p. illus. 22cm. Includes bibliography. [KF373.J47O26] 63-8318
1. Jerome, William Travers, 1859-1934. I. Title.

Jeron, Joy Marie.

KILL, Jim. 362.1'9'699400924 B
A life of Joy / by Jim Kill. Chicago : Franciscan Herald Press, [1975] vii, 75 p. ; 21 cm. [RC263.K54] 75-9900 ISBN 0-8199-0569-0 : 3.95
1. Jeron, Joy Marie. 2. Jeron, Robert Edward. 3. Cancer—Personal narratives. I. Title.

Jerrold, Douglas William, 1803-1857.

KELLY, Richard Michael, 1937- 822'.8
Douglas Jerrold, by Richard M. Kelly. New York, Twayne Publishers [1972] 168 p. 21 cm. (Twayne's English authors series, TEAS 146) Bibliography: p. 155-161. [PR4825.J4K43] 79-187615 5.50

*1. Jerrold, Douglas William, 1803-1857.*BIP

Jervis, John Bloomfield,

JERVIS, John 624'.0924 B
Bloomfield, 1795-1885.
The reminiscences of John B. Jervis, engineer of the Old Croton. Edited, with introd., by Neal Fitzsimons. Foreword by Robert Vogel. [1st ed. Syracuse] Syracuse University Press [1971] x, 196 p. illus., ports. 24 cm. (A York State book) [TC140.J47A3] 70-145552 ISBN 0-8156-0077-1 7.75
I. Title.

Jervis, John Bloomfield, 1795-1885.

JERVIS, John 624'.0924 B
Bloomfield, 1795-1885.
The reminiscences of John B. Jervis, engineer of the Old Croton. Edited, with introd., by Neal Fitzsimons. Foreword by Robert Vogel. [1st ed. Syracuse] Syracuse University Press [1971] x, 196 p. illus., ports. 24 cm. (A York State book) [TC140.J47A3] 70-145552 ISBN 0-8156-0077-1 7.75
I. Title.

LANKTON, Larry D. 628.1'42'0924 B
The "practicable" engineer : John B. Jervis and the old Croton Aqueduct / Larry D. Lankton. Chicago : Public Works Historical Society, 1977. ii, 30 p. : ill. ; 22 cm. (Essays in public works ; essay no. 5) Includes bibliographical references. [TC140.J47L36] 77-154107
1. Jervis, John Bloomfield, 1795-1885. I. Title. II. Series.

Jesett, Charles Coffin, 1816-1868.

BOROME, Joseph Alfred, 920.2
1919-
Charles Coffin Jewett. Chicago, American Library Association, 1951. 188 p. port. 22 cm. (American library pioneers, 7) "Selected bibliographical notes": p. 174-182. [Z720.J59B6] 51-10999
1. Jesett, Charles Coffin, 1816-1868. I. Title. II. Series.

Jesperson, Edward Christian, 1888-

HOBSON, Ina Jesperson. v. 12
The Edward Christian Jesperson-Ida Martineau book of golden memories, 1911-1916. [n.p., 1961?] 141 p. illus. 9 x 36 cm. 67-36507
1. Jesperson, Edward Christian, 1888- 2. Jesperson, Ida (Martineau) 1890- I. Title.

Jesse, Emily Tennyson, 1811-1887.

HALLAM, Arthur Henry, 824'.7 B
1811-1833.
The love story of In memoriam : letters from Arthur Hallam to Emily Tennyson / [with a foreword by] Clement Shorter. Folcroft, Pa. : Folcroft Library Editions, 1977. p. cm. Reprint of the 1916 ed. printed by C. Shorter, London. [PR4735.H4Z544 1977] 77-8199 ISBN 0-8414-7688-8 lib. bdg. : 10.00
1. Hallam, Arthur Henry, 1811-1833—Correspondence. 2. Jesse, Emily Tennyson, 1811-1887. 3. Tennyson, Alfred Tennyson, Baron, 1809-1892. In memoriam. 4. Poets, English—19th century—Correspondence. I. Jesse, Emily Tennyson, 1811-1887. II. Title.

Jesse Lee Home, Unalaska, Alaska.

WINCHELL, Mary Edna, 1878- 917.98
Home by the Bering Sea; illustrated with photos. Caldwell, Idaho, Caxton Printers, 1951. 226 p. illus. 24 cm. Autobiographical. [E78.A3W5] 51-12125
1. Jesse Lee Home, Unalaska, Alaska. 2. Aleuts. I. Title.

Jessel, George Albert,

JESSEL, George Albert, 927.92
1898-
This way, miss. With a foreword by William Saroyan. [1st ed.] New York, Holt [1955] 228 p. illus. 22 cm. Autobiographical. Sequel to So help me. [PN2287.J56A32] 55-7917
I. Title.

Jessel, George, Sir, 1824-1883.

GOODHART, Arthur 340'.57'0922 B
Lehman, Sir, 1891-
Five Jewish lawyers of the common law [by] Arthur L. Goodhart. With a new pref. to this ed. and a suppl. on Mr. Justice Felix Frankfurter. Freeport, N.Y., Books for Libraries Press [1971, c1949] vii, 81 p. 23 cm. (Biography index reprint series) Includes bibliograhical references. [KF299.J4G65 1971] 79-148212 ISBN 0-8369-8059-X
1. Benjamin, Judah Philip, 1811-1884. 2. Jessel, George, Sir, 1824-1883. 3. Brandeis, Louis Dembitz, 1856-1941. 4. Reading, Rufus Daniel Isaacs, 1st Marquis of, 1860-1935. 5. Cardozo, Benjamin Nathan, 1870-1938. I. Title. BIP

Jessop, Mary.

JESSOP, Mary. 920.7
Bubbles in my soul, the story of a woman's life. [1st ed.] New York, Exposition Press [1953] 241p. illus. 21cm. [CT275.J569A3] 53-85086
I. Title.

Jesuits.

DUHR, Joseph 922.243
Adam Schall, a Jesuit at the Court of China, 1592-1666. Adapted from the French by Rachel Attwater. Milwaukee, Bruce [c.1963] 163p. illus., map. 21cm. Bibl. 3.50
1. Attwater, Rachel, tr. I. Schall, Johann Adam von, 1591-1669. II. Title.

HASTINGS, Macdonald. 271'.53
Jesuit child. New York, St. Martin's Press [1972, c1971] 251 p. illus. 23 cm. Autobiographical. Bibliography: p. 241-242. [BX3702.2.H35 1972] 74-175001 7.95
1. Jesuits. I. Title.

O'BRIEN, John Anthony, 922.27
1893-
The first martyrs of North America; the story of the eight Jesuit martyrs, by John A. O'Brien. Notre Dame, Ind., University of Notre Dame Press [1960, c1953] x, 310 p. map (on lining papers) 21 cm. Published in 1953 under title: The American martyrs. [[BX3707]] 64-9180
1. Bibliography: p. 305-310. 2. Jesuits in North America. 3. Jesuits — Missions. 4. Martyrs — North America. I. Title.

Jesuits—Biog.

NASH, Robert, ed. 922.2
Jesuits; biographical essays. Westminster, Md., Newman Press, 1956. 230p. illus. 19cm. [BX3755.N3] 56-59194
1. Jesuits—Biog. I. Title.

Jesuits—Mexico—Baja California.

GUILLEN, Clemente, 917.2'2'042
1677-1748.
Clemente Guillen, explorer of the South : diaries of the overland expeditions to Bahia Magdalena and La Paz, 1719, 1720-1721 / translated and edited by W. Michael Mathes. Los Angeles : Dawson's Book Shop, 1979. 99 p., [1] fold. leaf of plates : map ; 22 cm. (Baja California travels series ; 42) Translation of MS 1/2.1 and MS 3/49.1 in the Biblioteca Nacional, Mexico, Archivo Franciscano. "500 copies printed." Bibliography: p. 97-99. [F1246.G83 1979] 78-73364 ISBN 0-87093-242-X : 18.00
1. Jesuits—Mexico—Baja California. 2. Guillen, Clemente, 1677-1748. 3. Baja California—Discovery and exploration. 4. Magdalena Bay, Mexico—History. 5. Indians of Mexico—Baja California. I. Mathes, W. Michael. II. Title. III. Series. BIP

Jesup, Thomas Sidney, 1788-1860.

KIEFFER, Chester 355.3'31'0924 B
L.
Maligned General : the biography of Thomas Sidney Jesup. San Rafael, Calif. : Presidio Press, c1979. xiii, 376 p. : ports. ; 24 cm. Includes index. Bibliography: p. 355-361. [U53.J47K53] 78-24028 ISBN 0-89141-027-9 : 16.95
1. Jesup, Thomas Sidney, 1788-1860. 2. United States. Quartermaster's Dept.—Biography. 3. United States. Army—History—19th century. 4. Generals—United States—Biography. I. Title.

Jesus Christ.

BERNARD, Pierre Rogatien, v. 12
1888-
The mystery of Jesus. Staten Island, N. Y., Alba House, 1966. 2 v. 24 cm. 68-28633
1. Jesus Christ—Biography. I. Title.

DANIEL-ROPS, Henry, 1901- 232.901
The life of our Lord [by] Henri Daniel-Rops. Translated from the French by J. R. Foster. Illus. by Charles Keeping. [Deluxe illustrated ed.] New York, Hawthorn Books [1965] 191 p. col. illus., maps. 24 cm. Translation of Histoire du Christ-Jesus. [BT301.2.D313 1965] 65-14642
1. Jesus Christ — Biog. I. Keeping, Charles, illus. II. Title.

DANIEL-ROPS, Henry, 1901- 232.9
The life of our Lord, by Henri Daniel-Rops. Translated from the French by J. R. Foster. [1st ed.] New York, Hawthorn Books [1964] 175 p. maps. 22 cm. (The Twentieth century encyclopedia of Catholicism, v. 68. Section 6: The word of God.) Translation of Histoire du Christ-Jesus. Bibliography: p. [174]-175. [BT301.2D313] 64-25385
1. Jesus Christ — Biog. I. Title. II. Series. III. Series: The twentieth century encyclopedia of Catholicism, v. 68

FARRAR, Frederic William, v. 12
1831-1903.
The life of Christ. Illus. by Gustave Dore and others. Portland, Oregon, Fountain Publications, 1960. 744 p. illus. 23 cm. (A Fountain publication) 65-53155
1. 1. Jesus Christ — Biog. I. Title.

FOSTER, Rupert Clinton, 220.9'2
1888-
Studies in life of Christ [2v. in 1. 3d. ed] Grand Rapids, mich, Baker [1966] (2v.in1) 505 p. illus. 23 cm Contents.An introduction to the life of christ and studies in the life of Christ. [bt301.f6] 232 5.95
1. 1. Jesus-biog. title I. Title.

FOSTER, Rupert Clinton, v. 12
1888-
Studies in the life of Christ, by R. C. Foster. [3rd ed.] Grand Rapids, Mich., Baker Book House [1966- v. illus. 23 cm. Vol. 1 is a rev. version of the first 2 vols. of the author's Studies in the life of Christ, published in 1938. Contents.Contents -- [1] Introduction and early ministry. 67 96216
1. Jesus Christ — Biog. 2. Jesus Christ — Biog. — Sources. 3. Bible. N.T. Gospels — Criticism, interpretation, etc. I. Title. BIP

GOGUEL, Maurice, 1880- v. 12
Jesus and the origins of Christianity. New York, Macmillan, 1933-1964. 3 v. Each vol. has special t.p. Translated from the French trilogy: Jesus et les origines du christianisme. Contents.Contents.-[v. 1] The life of Jesus. Trans. by Olive Wyon. 1933.-[v. 2] The birth of Christianity, Trans. by H. C. Snape. 1953.-[v. 3] The primitive church. Trans. by H. C. Snape. 1964. Bibliography: v. 1, p. [33]-35; v. 2, p. xiii-svi; v. 3, p. 587-590. 67-101449
1. Jesus Christ — Biog. 2. Church history — Primitive and early church. 3. Christianity — Early church. I. Title. II. Title: London, III. Title: The life of Jesus. IV. Title: The Birth of Christianity. V. Title: The primitive church.

GOGUEL, Maurice, 1880- v. 12
The life of Jesus: by Olive Wyon. tr. by Olive Wyon. New York, Barnes & Noble [1958] [7]-591 p. 23 cm. Imprint from label pasted on t.p. Original title: La vie de Jesus. "Bibliographical notes": p. [33]-35. 64-25391
1. Jesus Christ. Biog. I. Title.

HEINEMANN, Thea. 232.9
Stories of Jesus. Illustrated by Don Bolognese. Designed by Walter Brooks. Racine, Wis., Whitman Pub. Division, Western Pub. Co. [1968] 223 p. col. illus. 27 cm. (The Whitman library of giant books) Retellings of fifty Bible stories about Jesus from the time of His birth to His ascension. [BT302.H44 1968] AC 68
1. Jesus Crist—Biography. I. Bolognese, Don, illus. II. Title.

JONES, Mary Alice, 1898- 232.9
Tell me about Jesus. Illustrated by Dorothy Grider. A completely new ed. [Chicago] Rand McNally [1967] 71 p. illus. (part col.) 27 cm. Out of situations arising in their everyday life, parents teach their two children basic facts about Jesus, His life, and His message. [BT302.J593 1967] AC 67
1. Jesus Christ. I. Grider, Dorothy, illus. II. Title.

LOCKYEAR, Herbert 209'.22
The man who changed the world; or, conquests of Christ through the centuries. Grand Rapids. Zondervan [1966] 2v. 24cm. Bibl. [BR1700.2.L6] 66-13696 9.95
1. Christian biography. I. Title.

THE man who changed the 209'.22
world; or, Conquests of Christ, through the centuries. Grand Rapids, Zondervan Publ. House [1966] 2 v. 24 cm. Bibliography: v. 2, p. 427-428. [BR1700.2.L6] 66-13696
1. Christian biography.

MARY Eleanor, Mother, 1903- 232.9
Jesus. son of David. Illustrated by George Pollard. Milwaukee, Bruce Pub. Co. [1955] 224p. illus. 23cm. [BT301.M278] 55-7864
1. Jesus Christ—Biog. I. Title.

MESCHLER, Moritz, 1830- 232.9
1912.
The life of Our Lord Jesus Christ in meditations. translated by Sister Mary Margaret. 5th [i.e. 8th] ed. St. Louis, Herder, 1950. 2 v. maps, plan. 22 cm. [BT301.M53] 50-1304
1. Jesus Christ — Biog. I. Title.

MORGAN, Richard. 232.9
The Christ of the Cross; dare Christians follow him. New York, R. R. Smith, 1950. 285 p. 24 cm. [BT301.M73] 50-11109
1. Jesus Christ — Biog. 2. Christianity — 20th cent. I. Title.

PHIPPS, William E., 1930- 261.8'3
Was Jesus married? The distortion of sexuality in the Christian tradition [by] William E. Phipps. [1st ed.] New York, Harper & Row [1970] vii, 239 p. 22 cm. [BT708.P47 1970] 74-126282 5.95
1. Jesus Christ. 2. Paul, Saint, apostle. 3. Sex (Theology)—History of doctrines. I. Title.

SAUNDERSON, Henry Hallam, 232.9
1871-
His Word was with power. Boston, Beacon Press [1952] 248 p. 22 cm. [BT301.S336] 52-7867
1. Jesus Christ — Biog. I. Title.

TALMAGE, James Edward, v. 12
1862-1933.
Jesus the Christ; a study of the Messiah and His mission according to Holy Scriptures both ancient and modern. Published by the church. 35th ed. Salt Lake City, Deseret Book Co., 1963 804 p. 20 cm. 66-65258
1. Jesus Christ-Biog. 2. Mormons and Mormonism-Doctrinal and controversial works. I. Title.

*TAYLOR, Willard H. 232.9
The story of our Saviour. Kansas City, Mo., Beacon Hill Pr. [c.1963] 138p.19cm. Bibl. 1.25 pap.,
I. Title.

WISE, Charles C. 225.9'22 B
Picture windows on the Christ / by Charles C. Wise, Jr. ; illustrated by Thom Baker. Penn Laird, Va. : Magian Press, c1979. 354 p. : ill. ; 23 cm. Includes bibliographical references. [BS2430.W57] 78-69928 5.95
1. Bible. N.T.—Biography—Miscellanea. I. Baker, Thom. II. Title.

Jesus Christ—Art.

REMBRANDT HARMENSZOON 760.0924
VAN RIJN, 1606-1669.
Life of Christ; paintings, drawings, and etchings by Rembrandt, with quotations from the Gospels, and the Gospel stories retold by Owen S. Rachleff. New York, Abradale Press [1966] xxi, 200 p. illus., col. plates. 31 cm. [ND653.R4A5] 66-29135
1. Jesus Christ—Art. I. Bachleff, Owen S. II. Bible. N. T. English. Selections. 1966. Authorized. III. Title.

Jesus Christ—Biog.

*BARCLAY, William 232.9
The life of jesus for everyman. New York, Harper [1966,c.1965] 96p. 21cm. (Chapel bks., CB27F) .95 pap.,
1. Jesus Christ—Biog. I. Title. **BIP**

BATTENHOUSE, Henry Martin, 1885- 232.9
Christ in the Gospels; an introduction to His life and its meaning. New York, Ronald Press Co. [1952] 339 p. illus. 21 cm. (Series in religion) [BT301.B22] 52-6181
1. Jesus Christ—Biog. 2. Bible. N. T. Gospels—Introductions. I. Title.

*BAUGHMAN, Ray E. 232.9'01
The life of Christ visualized. Illus. by Bryan Lee Baughman. Chicago, Moody [1968] 256p. illus. 17cm. (Moody giants, no. 54) .89 pap.,
1. Jesus Christ—Biog. I. Title.

BIBLE. N. T. Gospels. English. 1952. Confraternity version. 232.9
A life of Christ [by] Aloys Dirksen, together with the four Gospels. New York, Dryden Press [1952] xiii, 338 p. 24 cm. "The four Gospels coustitute the upper section of the book [which is divided in a 'Dutch door arrangement']" Bibliography: p. 325-331. [BT301.D57] 52-11129
1. Jesus Christ—Biog. I. Dirksen, Aloys Herman. II. Title.

BIBLE. N. T. Gospels. English. 1962. Confraternity version. 232.9
A life of Christ, together with the four Gospels [by] Aloys Dirksen. Rev. [i. e. 2d] ed. New York, Holt [c.1952, 1962] xiv, 378p. 24cm. Gospels constitute the upper section of the bk. which is divided in a Dutch door arrangement. Bibl. 62-8479 5.75
1. Jesus Christ—Biog. I. Dirksen, Aloys Herman. II. Title.

BOUGHTON, Willis Arnold, 1885- 232.9
A complete integrated version of the four Gospels for reading and study; a unified narrative in modern English. [1st ed.] New York, Exposition Press [1959] 234p. 21cm. (A Testament book) [BT301.2.B6] 59-16012
1. Jesus Christ—Biog. I. Title.

BOWIE, Walter Russell 232.9
The Master; a life of Jesus Christ. New York Scribner [c.1928-1958] xii, 331p. 21cm. (Scribner lib. SL14) 1.45 pap.,
1. Jesus Christ—Biog. I. Title.

BOWIE, Walter Russell, 1882- 232.9
The Master; a life of Jesus Christ. [Student's ed.] New York, Scribner [1958] 331p. 21cm. [BT301.B725 1958] 58-4169
1. Jesus Christ—Biog. I. Title.

BRACKBERGER, Raymond Leopold, 1907- 232.9
The history of Jesus Christ, by R. L. Bruckberger. Pref. by Eugene Cardinal Tisserant. Translated from the French by Denver Lindley. New York, Viking Presss [1965] xiv, 462 p. 25 cm. "Reference notes": p. 461-462. [BT301.2.B6963] 64-20684
1. Jesus Christ-Biog. I. Title.

BRUCKBERGER, Raymond Leopold, 1907- 232.9
he history of Jesus Christ, Pref. by Eugene Cardinal Tisserant. Tr. from French by Denver Lindley. New York, Viking [c.1965] xiv, 462p. 25cm. Bibl. [BT301.2.B6963] 64-20684 8.50
1. Jesus Christ—Biog. I. Title.

BRUMBACK, Robert H 1892- 232.9
Where Jesus walked. Saint Louis, Mission Messenger [1959] 157p. illus. 21cm. [BT301.2.B7] 59-52475
1. Jesus Christ—Biog. I. Title.

CARRINGTON, Philip, Abp., 1892- 232.9
Our Lord and Saviour, His life and teachings. Greenwich, Conn., Seabury Press, 1958. 138p. 20cm. [BT301.C33] 58-14563
1. Jesus Christ—Biog. I. Title.

CONNICK, C. Milo 232.9
Jesus: the man the mission, and the message. Englewood Cliffs, N.J., Prentice [c.]1963. 462p. illus. 24cm. Bibl. 63-10450 9.25
1. Jesus Christ—Biog. I. Title. **BIP**

DANIEL-ROPS, Henry, 1901- 232.9
Jesus and His times. [New rev. Catholic ed.] New York, Dutton, 1956. 479p. illus. 22cm. Translated from the French by Ruby Millar. [BT301.D2213 1956] 56-8299
1. Jesus Christ—Biog. I. Title.

DOUGHERTY, Robert Lee. 232.9
Jesus the pioneer; the Christ of the Gospels. Boston, Christopher Pub. House [1952] 136 p. 21 cm. [BT301.D64] 52-11974
1. Jesus Christ—Biog. I. Title.

EDERSHEIM, Alfred, 1825-1889. 232.9
Jesus the Messiah; being an abridged edition of The life and times of Jesus the Messiah. Grand Rapids, W. B. Eerdmans Pub. Co., 1954. 645p. 23cm. [BT301] 54-1763
1. Jesus Christ—Biog. I. Title.

EIKAMP, Arthur R 220.9'2
Jesus Christ; a study of the Gospels. Anderson, Ind., Warner Press [c1963] 176 p. 22 cm. [BT301.2.E5] 63-20427
1. Jesus Christ — Biog. I. Title.

ENSLIN, Morton Scott, 1897- 232.9
The Prophet from Nazareth. New York, McGraw-Hill [c.1961] 221p. Bibl. 60-53348 4.95
1. Jesus Christ—Biog. I. Title. **BIP**

FARRAR, Frederic William, 1831-1903 232.901
The life of Christ [New] illus. ed. Cleveland, World [1965, c.1913] xvii, 427p. col. illus. 21cm. [BT301.F2] 65-23377 6.50
1. Jesus Christ—Biog. I. Title.

FERRIS, Theodore Parker, 1908- 232.9
The story of Jesus. New York, Oxford University Press, 1953. 123p. 20cm. [BT301.F33] 53-9186
1. Jesus Christ—Biog. I. Title.

FINEGAN, Jack, 1908- 232.9
Jesus, history, and you. Richmond, Va. Knox [c.1964] 144p. 21cm. Bibl. 64-15174 1.95 pap.,
1. Jesus Christ—Biog. 2. Jesus Christ—Historicity. I. Title.

FOSDICK, Harry Emerson, 1878- 232.9
The Man from Nazareth, as his contemporaries saw Him. New York, Harper [1965, c.1949] 282p. 22cm. 277p. 20cm. (Harper Chapelbks., CB8) Bibl. [BT303.F62] 1.65 pap.,
1. Jesus Christ—Biog. I. Title. **BIP**

FOSTER, Rupert Clinton, 1888- 232.9
Studies in the life of Chirst. Cincinnati, F.L. Rowe, 1938-68. 3v. 20 cm. Vol. 2-3 have imprint: Grand Rapids, Baker Book House. Contents.Early period.--The middle period. The final week. [BT301.F6] 62-13483
1. Jesus Christ—Biog. I. Title.

FOSTER, Rupert Clinton, 1888- 232.9
Studies in the life of Christ; v.3. Grand Rapids, Mich., Baker Bk. [c.]1962. 345p. 22cm. Contents.v.3. The final week. 38-15166 4.50
1. Jesus Christ—Biog. I. Title.

FOUARD, Constant Henri, 1837-1904. 232.9
The life of Christ. New York, Guild Press; distributed by Golden Press [c.1954, 1960] 415p. 17cm. (An Angelus book) 60-4875 .95 bds.,
1. Jesus Christ—Biog. I. Title.

GIORDANI, Igino, 1894- 232.9
Christ, hope of the world. Tr. by Clelia Maranzana [Boston] St. Paul Eds. [dist. Daughters of St. Paul, c.1964] 470p. col. illus. 24cm. 63-13898 7.00; 5.00 pap.,
1. Jesus Christ—Biog. I. Title.

GOGUEL, Maurice 232.9
Jesus and the origins of Christianity. Translated by Olive Wyon, with an introd. by C. Leslie Mitton. New York, Harper [c.1960] 2v.; xv, 590p. Includes bibliography. 21cm. (Harper torchbooks, TB65, 66 The Cloister library.) 60-5490 v.1, 1.35 v.2, 1.85 pap.,
1. Jesus Christ—Biog. 2. Church history—Primitive and early church. I. Title.

GOODSPEED, Edgar Johnson, 1871-1962 232.9
A life of Jesus. Large type ed. New York, Watts [1967, c.1950] 248p. 29cm. (Keith Jennison bk.) [BT301.G73] 6.95
1. Jesus Christ—Biog. I. Title.

GRAHAM, Eleanor, 1896- 232.9
The Story of Jesus, Illus. by Brian Wildsmith. Penguin [dist. New York, Atheneum, 1961, c.1959] 264 p. illus. map. (Puffin bks., PS135) 61-66128 .95, pap.
1. Jesus Christ—Biog. I. Title.

GRANDMAISON, Leonce de [Septime Leonce de Grandmaison] 1868-1927 232.9
Jesus Christ. Pref. by Jean Danielou. New York, Sheed and Ward [c.1961] 266p. 61-7286 4.50
1. Jesus Christ—Biog. I. Title.

GREEN, Doyle L 232.9
He that liveth; the story of Jesus Christ the Son of God. Salt Lake City, Deseret Book Co., 1953. 229p. illus. 22cm. [BT301.2.G7] 59-21541
1. Jesus Christ—Biog. I. Title.

GUIGNEBERT, Charles Alfred Honore, 1867- 232.9
Jesus; translated from the French by S. H. Hooke. New York, University Books [1956] xii, 563p. 22cm. Bibliography: p. 539-553. [BT301.G9472 1956] 56-7837
1. Jesus Christ—Biog. 2. Jesus Christ—Teachings. I. Title.

HENRY, Antonin Marcel, 1911- 232.9
The triumph of Christ; the Word made flesh. Notre Dame, Ind., Fides [1962, c.1958] 159p. (Fides dome bk., D14) 'Reprinted from The historical and mystical Christ, vol. V, Theology library.' Bibl. 62-1618 .95 pap.,
1. Jesus Christ—Biog. 2. Eschatology. I. Title.

HOBBS, Herschel H. 232.901
The life and times of Jesus; a contemporary approach. Grand Rapids, Mich., Zondervan [c.1966] 218p. col. map. 23cm. [BT301.2H6] 65-25953 3.50
1. Jesus Christ— Biog. I. Title.

HOBBS, Herschel H 232.901
The life and times of Jesus; a contemporary approach [by] Herschel H. Hobbs. Grand Rapids, Zondervan Pub. House [1966] 218 p. col. map. 23 cm. [BT301.2H6] 65-25953
1. Jesus Christ — Biog. I. Title.

JOHNSON, Sherman Elbridge, 1908- 232.9
Jesus in His homeland. New York, Scribner [1957] 182p. 22cm. Includes bibliography. [BT303.J63] 57-10565
1. Jesus Christ—Biog. I. Title.

KLAUSNER, Joseph Gedaliah, 1874-1958 232.9
Jesus of Nazareth; His life, times, and teaching. Tr. from Hebrew by Herbert Danby. Boston, Beacon [1964, c.1925] 434p. 21cm. (BP 185) 2.75 pap.,
1. Jesus Christ—Biog. I. Danby, Herbert, 1889- tr. II. Title.

KOMROFF, Manuel, 1890- 232.9
His great journey. New York, Pyramid Books [1961, c.1953, 1956] 160p. (G608) .35 pap.,
1. Jesus Christ—Biog. I. Title.

KOMROFF, Manuel, 1890- 232.9
His great journey; the most beautiful story in the world told anew. New York [1953] 159p. 17cm. (A Lion book, 128) [BT301.K74] 53-2405
1. Jesus Christ—Biog. I. Title.

KOMROFF, Manuel, 1890- 232.9
The story of Jesus. Drawings by Steele Savage. Philadelphia, Winston [c1955] 154p. illus. 23cm. [BT301.K75] 55-5294
1. Jesus Christ—Biog. I. Title.

LAKE, Gerard. 232.9
Our Lord; an elementary life of Christ. Westminster, Md., Newman Press, 1952. 123p. illus. 19cm. [BT301.L173] 52-8958
1. Jesus Christ—Biog. I. Title.

LAUBACH, Frank Charles, 1884- 232.9
The autobiography of Jesus, edited by Frank C. Laubach. [1st ed.] New York, Harper & Row [1962] 192 p. 22 cm. Written in the first person, following the sequence used in harmonies of the Gospels, based on Edgar J. Goodspeed's translation. Published in 1956 under title: The greatest life. [BT301.L26 1962] 62-14578
1. Jesus Christ — Biog. I. Title.

LAUBACH, Frank Charles, 1884- 232.9
The greatest life; Jesus tells his story. [Westwood, N. J.] Revell [1956] 192p. 21cm. 'Written as Jesus' autobiography, following the sequence used in harmonles of the Gospels, based on Edgar J. Goodspeed's translation. [BT301.L26] 56-7438
1. Jesus Christ—Biog. I. Title.

LAYMON, Charles M. 232.9
The life and teachings of Jesus. Rev. ed. Nashville, Abingdon [c.1955, 1962] 336p. map. 24cm. Bibl. 62-7439 4.50
1. Jesus Christ—Biog. 2. Jesus Christ—Teachings. I. Title.

LAYMON, Charles M 232.9
The life and teachings of Jesus. New York, Abingdon Press [c1955] 336p. illus. 24cm. Includes bibliographies. [BT301.L275] 55-5053
1. Jesus Christ—Biog. 2. Jesus Christ—Teachings. I. Title.

LEBRETON, Jules, 1873- v. 12
The life & teaching of Jesus Christ our Lord; translated from the French. New York, Macmillan, 1957. 2v. in l. 21cm.
1. Jesus Christ—Biog. 2. Jesus Christ-Teachings. I. Title.

LEBRETON, Jules, 1873-1956. 220.9'2
The life & teachings of Jesus Christ Our Lord. Translated from the French New York, Macmillan, 1957. 2v. in 1. 21cm. [BT301.1.] A60
1. Jesus Christ—Biog. 2. Jesus Christ — Teachings. I. Title.

A life of Jesus. v. 12
New York, Harper [1956] 248p. map. 21cm. (Harper torchlights TL1)
1. Jesus Christ—Biog. I. Goodspeed, Edgar Johnson, 1871-

LUDWIG, Emil, 1881-1948. 232.9
The Son of Man. Foreword by Charles Francis Potter. Cover painting by Max Wieczorek. Authorized rev. ed. Greenwich, Conn., Fawcett Publications [1957] 190p. 18cm. (A Premier book, d55) [BT301.L8 1957] 58-147
1. Jesus Christ—Biog. I. Title.

MAURIAC, Francois, 1885- 232.9
Life of Jesus. Tr. [from French] by Julie Kernan. New York, Avon [1961, c.1937] 224p. illus. (G1058) .50 pap.,
1. Jesus Christ—Biog. I. Title.

MAURIAC, Francois, 1885- 232.9
Life of Jesus. Translated by Julie Kernan; illustrated by George Buday. New York, D. McKay Co. [1951,c1937] 258 p. illus. 21 cm. [BT301.M342 1951] 51-12093
1. Jesus Christ—Biog I. Title. **BIP**

OURSLER, Fulton, 1893- 232.9
The greatest story ever told; a tale of the greatest life ever lived. Garden City, N. Y., Doubleday [1961, c.1949] 350p. (Image bk., 121) .95 pap.,
1. Jesus Christ—Biog. I. Title.

PAUL, Leslie Allen, 1905- 232.9
Son of Man, the life of Christ. New York, Dutton [c.]1961. 287p. illus. Bibl. 61-12484 4.00
1. Jesus Christ—Biog. 2. Jews—Hist.—586 B. C.—70 A. D. I. Title.

PAUL, Leslie Allen, 1905- 232.9
Son of Man, the life of Christ. [1st ed.] New York, Dutton, 1961. 287p. illus. 21cm. Includes bibliography. [BT301.2.P35 1961a] 61-12484
1. Jesus Christ— Biog. 2. Jews—Hist.— 586 B. C.-70 A.D. I. Title.

PEALE, Norman Vincent, 232.901
1898-
Jesus Nazareth; a dramatic interpretation of His life from Bethlehem to Calvary. Englewood Cliffs, N.J. Prentice c.1966 1v. (unpaged) 32cm. (Inspirational bk. serv. bk.) [BT301.2P4] 66-18471 3.95 bds.,
1. Jesus Christ—Biog. I. Title.

PEALE, Norman Vincent, 232.901
1898-
Jesus of Nazareth; a dramatic interpretation of His life from Bethlehem to Calvary. Englewood Cliffs, N. J., Prentice-Hall [1966] 1 v. (unpaged) 32 cm. (An Inspirational book service book) [BT301.2.P4] 66-18471
1. Jesus Christ—Biog. I. Title.

PIERCE, William Dwight, 232.9
1881-
Jesus, interpreter of the eternal; a dramatic arrangement of the Gospels and Apocryphal data as one coordinated story. [1st ed.] New York, Pageant Press [1957] ix, 565p. 24cm. Bibliographical references included in 'Footnotes.' [BT301.P633] 57-9967
1. Jesus Christ—Biog. I. Title.

PIERCE, William Dwight, 232.9
1881-
Jesus, interpreter of the eternal; a dramatic arrangement of the Gospels and Apocryphal data as one coordinated story. [1st ed.] New York, Pageant Press [1957] ix, 565p. 24cm. Bibliographical references included in 'Footnotes.' [BT301.P633] 57-9937
1. Jesus Christ—Biog. I. Title.

POLING, Daniel Alfred, 232.9
1884-
He came from Galilee, [by]Daniel A. Poling. [Rev] New York, Harper & Row [1965] viii, 246 p. 20 cm. First ed. published in 1931 under title: Between two worlds. [BT301.P68] 65-15393
1. Jesus Christ—Biog. I. Title.

PRAT, Ferdinand, 1857-1938 232.9
Jesus Christ; His life, His teaching, and His work. Translated from the 16th French ed. [by] John J. Heenan. Milwaukee, Bruce [1950] 2 v. 23 cm. (Science and culture series) Full name: Antoine Ferdinand Prat. Bibliographical footnotes. [BT301.P6852] 50-58219
1. Jesus Christ — Biog. I. Title.

PRAT, Ferdinand [Antoine 232.9
Ferdinand Prat] 1857-1938
Jesus Christ; His life, His teaching, and His work; 2v. in 1. Tr. from the 16th French ed. [by] John J. Heenan. Milwaukee, Bruce [1963, c.1950] 2v. in 1. 568p. map (pt. col. on endpapers) 23cm. Bibl. 10.00
1. Jesus Christ—Biog. I. Title.

RANKIN, John Chambers 232.9
A believer's life of Christ. Natick, Mass., W. A. Wilde Co. [c.1960] 210p. 21cm. 60-15263 3.50
1. Jesus Christ—Biog. I. Title.

RICCIOTTI, Giuseppe, 1890- 232.9
Life of]christ; translated by Alba I. Zizzamia. Abridged and edited by Aloysius Croft. Popular ed. Milwaukee, Bruce Pub. Co. [1952] 402 p. illus. 22 cm. [BT301.R4815 1952] 52-14174
1. Jesus Chirst — Biog. I. Title.

ROLLINS, Wallace Eugene, 232.9
1870-
Jesus and His ministry, by Wallace Eugene Rollins and Marion Benedict Rollins. Greenwich, Conn., Seabury Press, 1954. 299p. 22cm. [BT301.R73] 54-13076
1. Jesus Christ—Biog. I. Rollins,Marion Josephine (Benedict) 1896- joint author. II. Title.

RUFIE, Frederick Charles. 232.9
Immanuel; the story of the living Christ, the Lord of the church. Boston, Christopher Pub. House [1954] 192p. 21cm. [BT301.R8] 54-486
1. Jesus Christ— Biog. I. Title.

SHEED, Francis Joseph, 232.9
1897-
To know Christ Jesus. New York, Sheed [c.1962] 377p. 22cm. 62-15273 5.00 bds.,
1. Jesus Christ—Biog. I. Title. BIP

SHEEN, Fulton John, Bp. 232.9
Life of Christ. New York, Popular Library [1960, c.1958] xiii, 546p. 18cm. (Popular special W700) .75 pap.,
1. Jesus Christ—Biog. I. Title. BIP

SHEEN, Fulton John, 1895- 232.9
The eternal Galilean. Garden City, N.Y., Garden City Pub. Co. [1950, c1934] 280 p. 21 cm. [BT301.S418 1950] 51-1976
1. Jesus Christ—Biog. I. Title.

SHEEN, Fulton John, Bp., 232.9
1895-
The life of Christ. New York, Maca Magazine Corp., c1954 126p. illus. 24 cm [BT301.S4182] 54-1587
1. Jesus Christ—Biog. I. Title.

SINCLAIR, Upton Beall, 232.9
1878-
A personal Jesus; portrait and interpretation. New York, Evans Pub. Co. [1952] ix, 228 p. 22 cm. [BT301.S42] 52-13861
1. Jesus Christ—Biog. I. Title.

SLOYAN, Gerard Stephan, 232.9
1919-
Christ the Lord. Garden City, N. Y., Doubleday [1965, c.1962] 195p. 18cm. (Echo bk., E6) [BT301.2.S57] .75 pap.,
1. Jesus Christ—Biog. I. Title.

SLOYAN, Gerard Stephen, 232.9
1919-
Christ the Lord. [New York] Herder & Herder [c.1962] 238p. illus. 21cm. 62-17231 4.50
1. Jesus Christ—Biog. I. Title. BIP

SMYTH, John Paterson, 232.9
d.1932
A people's life of Christ. [54th ed.] Westwood, N.J., Revell [1963?] 365 p. 20 cm. [[BT301]] 63-6847 CD
1. Jesus Christ — Biog. I. Title.

STEWART, James Stuart, 232.9
1896-
The life and teaching of Jesus Christ. New York, Abingdon Press [195-?] 192p. 19cm. [BT301.S643] 57-4515
1. Jesus Christ—Biog. 2. Jesus Christ— Teachings. I. Title. BIP

STOKE, John H. 232.9
A man called Jesus. New York, Vantage Press [c.1959] 231p. illus. 21cm. 59-65453 3.50 bds.,
1. Jesus Christ—Biog. I. Title.

VOS, Howard Frederic, 1925- 232.9
The life of Our Divine Lord. Grand Rapids, Zondervan Pub. House [1956] 223 p. illus. 22 cm. Includes bibliography. [BT301.V67] 58-4624
1. Jesus Christ — Biog. I. Title.

VOS, Howard Frederic, 1925- 232.9
The life of Our Lord [orig. title: The life of Our Divine Lord] Chicago, Moody [1965, c.1958] 255p. illus. 17cm. (43) Bibl. [BT301.V67] .89 pap.,
1. Jesus Christ—Biog. I. Title.

WAND, John William Charles, 232.9
Bp. of London, 1885-
The life of Jesus Christ. New York, Morehouse- Gorham [1955] 208p. 21cm. [BT301.W24 1955a] 55-10000
1. Jesus Christ—Biog. I. Title.

WILSON, Lawrence Ray, 1896- 232.9
The triumphant Jesus. [Bartlesville? Okla., 1952] 265 p. 20 cm. [BT301.W498] 52-44004
1. Jesus Christ—Biog. I. Title.

Jesus Christ—Biog.—Devotional literature.

BEASLEY, Norman. 232.9
This is the promise. [1st ed.] New York, Duell, Sloan and Pearce [1957] 103p. illus. 21cm. [BT301.B255] 57-11056
1. Jesus Christ—Biog.—Devotional literature. I. Title.

LEVY, Rosalie Marie, 1889- 232.9
Jusus, the Divine Master. [Derby, N. Y.] Daughters of St. Paul, Apostolate of the Press [1953?] 363p. illus. 22cm. [BT301.2.L4] 59-24944
1. Jesus Christ —Biog.—Devotional literature. I. Title.

MACKAY, John Alexander. 232.9
1889-
His life and our life; the life of Christ and the life in Christ. Philadelphia, Westminster [c.1964] 80p. 19cm. 64-13757 1.45 pap.,
1. Jesus Christ—Biog.—Devotional literature. 2. Christian life. I. Title.

O'MAHONY, James Edward, 232.9
1897-
Jesus the Saviour, by Father James. Westminster, Md., Newman Press, 1956. 145p. 24cm. [BX2182O45] 56-9136
1. Jesus Christ—Biog.—Devotional literature. I. Title.

O'MAHONY, James Edward, 232.9
1897-
Jesus the Saviour, by Father James. Westminster, Md., Newman Press, 1956. 145p. 21cm. [BX2182.O45] 56-9136
1. Jesus Christ—Biog.—Devotional literature. I. Title.

VANDERLIP, George. 232.95
Jesus, teacher and Lord. Valley Forge [Pa.] Judson Press [1964] 127 p. map. 20 cm. Bibliography: p. 126-127. [BT306.5.V3] 64-15795
1. Jesus Christ — Biog. — Devotional literature. I. Title. BIP

Jesus Christ Biog.—Hist. & crit.

ANDERSON, Hugh, 1920- 232.9'009
comp.
Jesus. Englewood Cliffs, N.J., Prentice-Hall [1967] vii, 182 p. 21 cm. (Great lives observed) A Spectrum book Includes bibliographical references. [BT301.9.A5] 67-28396
1. Jesus Christ—Biog.—Hist. & crit. I. Title. BIP

EWING, Upton Clary. 232.9
The Essene Christ; a recovery of the historical Jesus and the doctrines of primitive Christianity. New York, Philosophical Lib. [c.1961] 438p. illus. 61-10608 5.75
1. Jesus Christ—Biog.—Hist. & crit. I. Title.

THEODORE, John T 232.9
Who was Jesus? A historical analysis of the misinterpretations of His life and teachings. [1st ed.] New York, Exposition Press [1961] 233 p. 21 cm (An Exposition-testament book) [BT301.9.T5] 62-16026
1. Jesus Christ — Biog. — Hist. & crit. 2. Jesus Christ — Humanity. I. Title.

Jesus Christ—Biog.—Juvenile literature.

ALLEN, Hattie Bell 232.9
(McCracken) 1896-
As Jesus passed by illustrated by Mariel Wilhoite Turner. [1st ed.] Philadelphia, Winston [1954] 32p. illus. 24cm. (A Silver shield book) [BT302.A4] 53-10715
1. Jesus Christ—Biog.—Juvenile literature. I. Title.

ARMSTRONG, April (Oursler) 232.9
Stories from the life of Jesus. Adapted from 'The greateststory ever told' by Fulton Oursler. Illustrated by Jules Gotlieb. Garden City, N. Y., Garden City Books [1955] 256p. illus., 25cm. [BT302.A7] 55-9510
1. Jesus Christ—Biog.—Juvenile literature. I. Title.

AUCLAIR, Marcelle, 1899- 232.9
The little friends of Jesus. Translated from the French. Illustrated by Mary Gehr. Chicago, H. Regnery Co. [1954] 93p. illus. 22cm. Translation of La bonne nouvelle annoncee aux enfants. [BT302] 54-4688
1. Jesus Christ—Biog.—Juvenile literature. I. Title.

BIBLE. N. T. Gospels. 232.9
English. Selections. 1956. Authorized.
The life of Christ Jesus in Bible language, from the King James Version of the Bible; arr. by Genevieve P. Olson. [San Diego, Calif.] Printed [by] Arts and Crafts Press, c1956. 52p. 19cm. [BT302.O63] 56-36567
1. Jesus Christ—Biog.—Juvenile literature. I. Olson, Genevieve P. II. Title.

BIRD, Thomas E, 1888- 232.9
A study of the Gospels. With a foreword by the Cardinal Archbishop of Westminster. Westminster, Md., Newman Press. 1950 xiv, 270 p. illus., maps. 19 cm. (Scripture textbooks for Catholicschools, v. 3) Bibliography: p. 261-270. [BT302.B43 1950] 51-5983
1. Jesus Christ—Biog.—Juvenile literature. I. Title. II. Series.

BROWN, Helen (Benjamin) 232.9
Jesus goes to the synagogue. Pictures by William M. Hutchinson. Nashville, Abingdon Press. c.1960. unpaged. illus. 22cm. 60-6811 1.25 bds.,
1. Jesus Christ—Biog.—Juvenile literature. I. Title.

BROWN, Helen (Benjamin) 232.9
1898-
Jesus goes to the synagogue. Pictures by William M. Hutchinson. New York, Abingdon Press, c1960. unpaged. illus. 22cm. [BT309.B757] 60-6811
1. Jesus Christ.—Biog.—Juvenile literature. I. Title.

BURT, Olive (Woolley) 1894- 232.9
They knew Jesus; verses and pictures about some of the people who knew Jesus. Pictures by William Heyer. Anderson, Ind., Warner Press [1959] unpaged. illus. 23cm. [BT302.B83] 59-6240
1. Jesus Chirst—Biog.—Juvenile literature. I. Title.

CHARRAT, Andre 232.901
The life of Christ for teenagers. Tr. by S. G. A. Luff. Notre Dame, Ind., Fides [1965] x, 146p. illus. 22cm. (Fides paperback textbook, 7) [BT302.C473] 65-13803 1.95
1. Jesus Christ—Biog.—Juvenile literature. I. Title.

CHUTE, Marchette Gaylord, 232.9
1909-
Jesus of Israel. [1st ed.] New York, Dutton, 1961. 116p. 21cm. [BT302.C56] 61-8429
1. Jesus Christ—Biog.—Juvenile literature. I. Title.

CRAWFORD, Mary 232.9
Who is this? A life of Jesus taken from the four Gospels. With illus. by Antony Lewis and pref. by J. B. Phillips. Westminster [London] Faith Press[dist. New York, Morehouse-Barlow, 1959, i.e. 1960] 93p. illus. (col.). map (col.) 24cm. 2.10 bds.,
1. Jesus Christ—Biog.—Juvenile literature. I. Title.

DAVIS, Sadie Holcombe. 232.9
Jesus, once a child. Nashville, Broadman Press, c1954. unpaged. illus. 25cm. (Little treasure series, 7) [BT302.D25] 54-42579
1. Jesus Christ.-Biog.—Juvenile literature. I. Title.

EGERMEIER, Elsie Emilie, 232.901
1890-
Picture-story life of Jesus. Story revisions by Arlene S. Hall. Anderson, Ind., Warner [1966,c.1965]c127p. col. illus. 25cm. Adapted from Egermeier's Bible story book. Previous eds. pub. under title: Picturestory life of Christ. [BT302.E35] 65-14972 2.95
1. Jesus Christ—Biog—Juvenile literature. 2. Bible stories, English—N. T. Gospels. I. Hall, Arlene Stevens. II. Title.

FALLON, Patrick 232.9
The life of Jesus [Staten Island, N.Y.] St. Paul Pubns. [dist. Alba, c.1963] xiv, 173p. col. illus., map. 25cm. 63-22938 4.50
1. Jesus Christ—Biog.—Juvenile literature. I. Title.

FENNER, Mabel B 232.9
Stories of Jesus; illustrated by Ralph Pallen Coleman. Philadelphia, Muhlenberg Press [1952] unpaged. illus. 23cm. [BT302.F4] 52-14242
1. Jesus Christ—Biog.—Juvenile literature. I. Title.

FILMER, Edmund. 232.9
The story of Jesus, told by Edmund Filmer, with pictures by A. W. Lacey and S. W. Donnison. Wheaton, Ill., Van Kampen Press [1954] 182p. illus. 26cm. [BT302] 54-12923
1. Jesus Christ—Biog—Juvenile literature. I. Title.

HOLLAND, Cornelius Joseph, 1873- 232.9
The divine story; a short life of Our Blessed Lord for youth. Illustrated by Gedge Harmon. St. Meinrad, Ind. [1954] 173p. illus. 22cm. 'A Grail publication.' [BT302.H7 1954] 54-11550
1. Jesus Christ—Biog.—Juvenile literature. I. Title.

HUG, Fritz. 232.9
The story of Our Lord, by Fritz and Margaret Hug. New York, Random House, 1961. unpaged. illus. 26x36cm. [BT302.H8653 1961] 61-11728
1. Jesus Christ—Biog.—Juvenile literature. I. Title.

HUNT, Marigold. 232.9
A life of Our Lord. Drawings by Rus Anderson. [Rev. ed.] New York, Sheed & Ward [1959] 191p. illus. 21cm. First published in 1939 under title: A life of Our Lord for children. [BT302.H87 1959] 59-6386
1. Jesus Christ—Biog.— Juvenile literature. I. Title.

IRVIN, Donald F. 232.9
The life of Jesus. Illus. by Ralph Pallen Coleman. Philadelphia, Muhlenberg Press [1951] 219 p. col. illus. 24 cm. [BT302.I 7] 51-11111
1. Jesus Christ—Biog.—Juvenile literature. I. Title.

JONES, Mary Alice, 1898- 232.9
His name was Jesus. Illustrated by Rafaello Busoni. Chicago, Rand McNally [1950] 208 p. illus. 24 cm. [BT302.J586] 50-10331
1. Jesus Christ—Biog.—Juvenile literature. I. Title.

JONES, Mary Alice, 1898- 232.9
My first book about Jesus; illustrated by Robert Hatch Ed. of 1953. Chicago, Rand McNally, c1953. unpaged. illus. 33cm. (A Rand McNally book-elf giant) [BT302.J589] 53-7230
1. Jesus Christ—Biog.—Juvenile literature. I. Title.

KORFKER, Dena, 1908- 232.9
The story of Jesus for boys and girls illustrated by Lou Mahacek. Grand Rapids, Zondervan Pub. House [1954] unpaged. illus. 24cm. [BT302.K6] 55-247
1. Jesus Christ— Biog.—Juvenile literature. I. Title.

*LAVIN, Pat Carey. 232.9
Jesus died for me. Notre Dame, Ind., Dujarie, 1968. 1v. (unpaged) illus. 21cm. 2.00
1. Jesus Christ—Biog.—Juvenile literature. I. Title.

THE life of Christ Jesus in Bible language, from the King James Version of the Bible; comp. by Genevieve P. Olson. 3d ed., rev. [San Diego, Calif.] Printed [by] Arts and Crafts Press [c1957] 52p. 19cm. v. 12
1. Jesus Christ—Biog. —Juvenile literature. I. Bible. N. T. Gospels. English. Selections. 1956. Authorized. II. Olson, Genevieve P.

THE life of Christ Jesus in Bible language, from the King James Version of the Bible, Compiled by Genevieve P. Olson. 3d ed., rev. Bonita, Calif., G. P. Olson [c1957] cvi, 52p. v. 12
1. Jesus Christ—Biog.—Juvenile literature. I. Bible. N. T. Gospels. English. Selections. 1957. Authorized. II. Olson, Genevieve P.

LOCKWOOD, Myna 232.9
The life of Our Lord. Pictures by Zac Zaccardi. New York, Guild. [dist. Golden] c.1963. 30p. col. illus. 29cm. 63-25079 1.95 bds.,
1. Jesus Christ—Biog.—Juvenile literature. I. Title.

MUIR, Augustus, 1892- 232.9
The story of Jesus; illustrated by Eric Winter and Eric Wade. New York, Greystone Press [1954] 128p. illus. 25cm. [BT302.M9] 54-11489
1. Jesus Christ—Biog.— Juvenile literature. I. Title.

NEELEY, Deta Petersen. 232.9
Jesus of Nazareth, by Deta Petersen Neeley and Nathan Glen Neeley. Salt Lake City, Printed by Deseret News Press, 1956. 174p. illus. 20cm. (A Child's story of the New Testament, v.1) [BT302.N35] 57-19522
1. Jesus Christ—Biog. —Juvenile literature. I. Neeley, Nathan Glen, joint author. II. Title.

RAMSAY, DeVere Maxwell. 232.9
God's Son; a book of stories about Jesus for young children, by DeVere Ramsay. Illustrated by Rita Endhoven. Grand Rapids, W. B. Eerdmans Pub. Co. [1964] 48 p. illus. 27 cm. [BT302.R17] 64-8582
1. Jesus Christ — Biog. — Juvenile literature. I. Endhoven, Rita, illus. II. Title.

*RICHARDS, Jean H. 232.901
Stories of Jesus. Racine, Wisc., Golden Press [1974] [24] p. illus. 21 cm. (A little Golden book) [BT302] 0.49
1. Jesus Christ—Biography—Juvenile literature. 2. Jesus Christ—Parables—Juvenile literature. I. Title.

ROBINSON, Ella May (White) 1882- 232.9
When Jesus was here. Nashville, Southern Pub. Association [1951] 240 p. illus. 21 cm. [BT302.R63] 52-17419
1. Jesus Christ — Biog. — Juvenile literature. I. Title.

SCRIVEN, Gerard F 1920-1949. 232.9
While angels watch; the life of Jesus our King. Illus. by Fausto Conti. St. Paul, Catechetical Guild Educational Society [1953] 192p. illus. 24cm. [BT302.S26] 54-15630
1. Jesus Christ—Biog.—Juvenile literature. I. Title.

SEBOLT, Roland H A j232.9
God's son on earth. [Text by Roland Sebolt. Illus. by Marianne Bellenhaus. St. Louis, Concordia Pub. House, 1968] 1 v. (unpaged) col. illus. 23 x 30 cm. Cover title. Translation and adaptation of Gottes Sohn auf Erden by Eleanore Beck and Gabrielle Miller. [BT302.S29] 68-13366
1. Jesus Christ—Biog.—Juvenile literature. I. Bellenhaus, Marianne, illus. II. Beck, Eleanore. Gottes Sohn auf Erden. III. Title.

SMITH, Betty 232.92
The boy Jesus. Illus. by Cicely Steed. Philadelphia, Westminster [1963, c.1962] 32p. illus. (pt. col.) 21cm. (Stories of Jesus, bk. 2) .75 bds.,
1. Jesus Christ—Biog.—Juvenile literature. I. Title.

SMITHER, Ethel Lisle. 232.9
Stories of Jesus; illustrated by Kurt Wiese. Nashville, Abingdon Press [1954] 80p. illus. 21cm. [BT302.S574] 54-8460
1. Jesus Christ— Biog.—Juvenile literature. I. Title.

TRENT, Robbie, 1894- 232.9
The life of Jesus; student's book. Nashville, Broadman [c.1965] 96p. illus. (pt. col.) maps. 21cm. (,weekday Bible study ser.) For use with 9- and 10-year-olds; may be adapted for other ages. [BT302.T69] 65-12862 pap., 1.00; teacher's ed., 2.75
1. Jesus Christ—Biog.—Juvenile literature. 2. Jesus Christ—Biog.—Study and teaching. I. Title.

TRENT, Robbie, 1894- j232.9
The life of Jesus; student's book. Nashville, Broadman Press [1965] 96 p. illus. (part. col.) maps. 21 cm. 192 p. maps 21 cm. (The Weekday Bible study series) "For use with 9 and 10-year-olds: may by adapted for other ages" Teachers book [by] Robbie Trent [and] Harriett H. Maffett, Nashville, Broadman Press[1965] [BT302.T69] 65-12862
1. Jesus Christ — Biog. — Juvenile literature. 2. Jesus Christ — Biog. — Study and teaching. I. Maffett, Harriett, H., joint author. II. Title.

TRENT, Robbie, 1894- 232.9
Stories of Jesus; illustrated by Paul Frame. Racine, Wis., Whitman Pub. Co., c1954. unpaged. illus. 21cm. (A Cozy-corner book) [BT302.T73 1954] 55-17419
1. Jesus Christ—Blog. —Juvenile literature. I. Title.

TRENT, Robbie, 1894- 232.9
They saw Jesus. Nashville, Broadman Press, c1952. unpaged. illus. 25cm. [BT302.T74] 53-5813
1. Jesus Christ —Biog.—Juvenile literature. I. Title.

Jesus Christ—Biog.—Meditations.

AMBRUZZI, Aloysius 232.9
Jesus: 'yesterday and today, and forever' (Heb. 13:8) Tr. by Gilda Dal Corso. Westminster, Md., Newman [c.]1962. 687p. 17cm. 62-21492 7.50
1. Jesus Christ—Biog.—Meditations. I. Title.

AMBRUZZI, Aloysius. 232.9
Jesus: "yesterday and today, and foreover" (Heb. 13:8) Translated by Gilda Dal Corso. Westminster, Md., Newman Press, 1962. 687 p. 17 cm. [BT306.4.A4] 62-21492
1. Jesus Christ — Biog. — Meditations. I. Title.

CROWELL, Grace (Noll) 1877- 232.9
Come see a Man. Nashville, Abingdon [1964, c.1956] 125p. 18cm. (Apex bk.) .95 pap.,
1. Jesus Christ—Biog.—Meditations. I. Title.

CROWELL, Grace (Noll) 1877- 232.9
Come see a Man. New York, Abingdon Press [1956] 125p. 18cm. Prose and poems. [BV4832.C733] 56-11409
1. Jesus Christ—Biog—Meditations. I. Title.

Jesus Christ—Biog.—Outlines, syllabi, etc.

TORREY, Reuben Archer, 1856-1928 232.90076
Studies in the life and teachings of our Lord. Grand Rapids, Mich., Baker Bk., 1966[c.1909] 346p. 21cm. [BT307] 66-3846 3.95
1. Jesus Christ—Biog.—Outlines, syllabi, etc. I. Title.

Jesus Christ—Biog.—Passion Week.

CONNIFF, James C G 232.96
The story of Easter, by James C. G. Conniff in consultation with Paul Bussard. New York, Dauntless Books [1956] unpaged. illus. 28cm. [BT430.C555] 56-6718
1. Jesus Christ—Biog.—Passion week. I. Title.

GORMAN, Ralph 232.96
The last hours of Jesus. New York, Sheed & Ward [c.1960] 277p. map 22cm. 60-7307 2.50
1. Jesus Christ—Biog.—Passion Week. I. Title. BIP

SPECTER, Ruth Rachel. 232.96
On what day did Christ die? A day-by-day account of events in Jesus Christ's last week on earth. Foreword by P. A. Gaglardi. (1st ed.) New York, Exposition Press (c1958) 86 p. illus. 21 cm. Includes bibliographies. [BT414.S6] 60-1452
1. Jesus Christ — Biog. — Passion Week. I. Title.

Jesus Christ—Biog.—Sources.

AMIOT, Francois. 232.9
The Sources for the life of Christ, by Francois Amiot [and others] Translated from the French by P. J. Hepburne-Scott. [1st ed.] New York, Hawthorn Books [1961] 128 p. 21 cm. (The Twentieth century encyclopedia of Catholicism, v. 67. Section 6: The word of God) [BT305.S613] 62-18501
1. Jesus Christ — Biog. — Sources. I. Title.

SOURCES for the life of Christ (The) by Francois Amiot [others] Tr. from French by P. J. Hepburne-Scott. New York, Hawthorn [c.1962] 128p. 21cm. (Twentieth cent. ency. of Catholicism, v.67. Section 6: The word of God) 62-18501 3.50 bds.,
1. Jesus Christ—Biog.—Sources. I. Amiot, Francois.

Jesus Christ—Biog.—Sources, Biblical.

ALLEN, Charles Livingstone, 1913- 232.9
The life of Christ. [Westwood, N. J.] Revell [c.1962] 157p. 21cm. 62-17101 2.50; 3.95 bds., deluxe ed.,
1. Jesus Christ—Biog.—Sources, Biblical. I. Bible. N. T. Gospels. English. Paraphrases. 1962. Allen. II. Title.

BIBLE. N. T. Gospels. 232.9
English. Harmonies. 1951. Authorized.
In the beginning; a history of the beginning of Christianity as translated in the language of the King James version of the Bible, from the Gospels of Matthew, Mark, Luke, and John. Selected and edited by Charles L. Wooldridge. Philadelphia, Dorrance [1951] 104 p. 20 cm. [BT299.W67] 51-7101
1. Jesus Christ—Biog.—Sources, Biblical. I. Wooldridge. Charles L. ed. II. Title.

BIBLE. N. T. Gospels. 232.9
English. Harmonies. 1951. Cary.
The life of Jesus in the words of the four Gospels. Arr. and translated from the Greek text of Wescott [i. e. Westcott] and Hort, by Edward F. Cary. [Poughkeepsie, N. Y., 1951] 224 p. 17 cm. Cover title: The Gospels life of Jesus. Map from dust Jacket Inserted. [BT299.C33] 52-18570
1. Jesus Christ—Biog.—Sources. Biblical. I. Cary, Edward F. tr. II. Title. III. Title: The Gospeis life of Jesus.

BIBLE. N. T. Gospels. 232.9
English. Harmonies. 1957. Authorized.
Jesus Christ: the way, the truth, and the life; the four Gospels combined chronologically, the text used being the King James version 1911, the New Testament of Our Lord and Saviour Jesus Christ, translated out of the original Greek, and with the former translations diligently compared and revised, by His Majesty's special command. [Edited by Sarah Norwell Craighill. Lynchburg? Va., 1957] 163p. 24cm. [BT299.C65] 57-4514
1. Jesus Christ—Biog.—Sources, Biblical. I. Craighill, Sarah Norvell., ed. II. Title.

BIBLE, N. T. Gospels. 232.9
English Harmonies. 1959. Beck.
The Christ of the Gospels; the life and work of Jesus as told by Matthew, Mark, Luke, and John, presented as one complete story in the language of today. Saint Louis, Concordia Pub. House [c.1959] xi, 227p. map 21cm. 59-11068 3.00
1. Jesus Christ—Biog.—Sources, Biblical. I. Beck, William F., tr. II. Title.

BIBLE. N.T. Gospels. 232.9
English. Harmonies. 1960. Authorized.
The Messiah; the life and ministry of Our Lord and Saviour, Jesus Christ. Compiled and arr. from events contained in the Gospel records according the accounts given by the writers, Matthew, Mark, Luke and John. [1st ed.] New York, Exposition Press [1960] 256p. illus. 21cm. (An Exposition-Testament book) [BT299.2.C55] 60-3753
1. Jesus Christ—Biog.—Sources, Sources, Biblocal. I. Cissna, William Everett. 1877- ed. II. Title.

BIBLE. N. T. Gospels. 232.9
English. Selections. 1951. Authorized.
The life of Christ; as told in selections from the New Testament, with wood engravings cut especially for this edition by Bruno Bramanti. New York, Pellegrini & Cudahy [1951] 130 p. illus. 24 cm. "Regular edition" [BT299.P37 1951a] 51-13700
1. Jesus Christ—Biog.—Sources, Biblical. I. Bramanti, Bruno. illus. II. Title.

BIBLE. N. T. Gospels. 232.9
English. Selections. 1951. Authorized.
The life of Christ; as told in selections from the New Testament, with wood engravings cut especially for this edition by Bruno Bramanti. New York, Pellegrini & Cudahy [1951] 130 p. illus. 24 cm. "This edition, signed by the artist, is limited to

150 copies ... No. 126." [BT299.P37] 52-115
1. Jesus Christ—Biog.—Sources, Biblical. I. Bramanti, Bruno. illus. II. Title.

JESUS; the four Gospels, 232.9'01
Matthew, Mark, Luke and John, combined in one narrative and rendered in modern English. [Editorial committee: Charles B. Templeton and others]. New York, Pocket Books [1975, c1974] 240 p. map. 18 cm. [BT299.2.J47] 73-20754 ISBN 0-671-78888-4
1. Jesus Christ—Biography—Sources, Biblical.

Jesus Christ—Biog.—Study.

DISCUSSIONS on the life 232.9'01
of Jesus Christ; twelve studies for students who want to know more about the person and work of Jesus Christ. [Rev. ed.] Chicago, Inter-varsity Press [1967. c1962] 54 p. 18 cm. On cover: An Inter-varsity guide for Bible discussions. [BT307.D57 1967] 67-29347
1. Jesus Christ—Biog.—Study.

LOTZ, Benjamin, 1901- 232.9
Life and work of Christ. Philadelphia, Muhlenberg Press [1957] 96p. illus. 18cm. [BT307.L6] 57-3245
1. Jesus Christ—Biog.—Study. I. Title.

MILLER, T Franklin. 232.9
Life and teachings of Jesus. [Rev. ed.] Anderson, Ind., Warner Press [1959] 124p. 19cm. [BT307.M58 1959] 59-13465
1. Jesus Christ—Biog.—Study. I. Title.

SWANK, Calvin Peter, 1880- 232.9
The Lord of Life; an account of the life and teachings of the Savior for students of high school age. [1st ed.] New York, Greenwich Book Publishers [1957] 112p. 21cm. [BT307.S89] 57-9028
1. Jesus Christ— Biog.—Study. I. Title.

SWANK, Calvin Peter, 1880- 232.9
The Lord of Life; an account of the life and teachings of the Savior for students of high school age. [1st ed.] New York, Greenwich Book Publishers [1957] 112 p. 21 cm. [BT307.S89] 57-9028
1. Jesus Christ—Biog.—Study. I. Title.

WHITEHOUSE, Elizabeth 232.9
Scott, 1895-
Jesus, friend and teacher; a cooperative weekday text for boys and girls of grades five and six. Teacher's book. [Philadelphia, Westminster Press, 1957] 192 p. 20 cm. (The Cooperative series texts for weekday religious education classes and released-time religious education instruction) [BT302.W55] 57-5977
1. Jesus Christ — Biog. — Study. I. Title.

Jesus Christ—Biog.—Study and teaching.

HEINZ, Susanna Wilder 232.907
'Who do men say that I am?' A study of Jesus. Boston, Beacon [c.1965] vii, 176p. illus., geneal. table. 24cm. (Beacon ser. in religious educ.) Bibl. [BT307.H45] 65-12240 4.95
1. Jesus Christ—Biog.—Study and teaching. I. Title.

Jesus Christ — Biog. — Early works to 1800.

THOME DE JESUS, Father, 232.9
1529?-1582.
The sufferings of Our Lord Jesus Christ. Edited by Edward Gallagher. Westminster, Md., Newman Press [1960] 584 p. 18 cm. Translation of Trabalhos de Jesus. [BT300.T412] 60-50812
1. Jesus Christ — Biog. — Early works to 1800. I. Title.

Jesus Christ—Biography.

BIBLE. N. T. Gospels. 232.9
English. 1962. Confraternity version.
A life of Christ, together with the four Gospels [by] Aloys Dirksen. Rev. [i. e. 2d] ed. New York, Holt, Rinehart and Winston [1962] xiv, 378p. 24cm. The Gospels constitute the upper section of the book which is divided in a Dutch door arrangement. Bibliography: p. [365]- 372. [BT301.D57 1962] 62-8479
1. Jusus Christ—Biog. I. Dirksen, Aloys Herman. II. Title.

*BROWN, Parker B. 232.9
He came from Galilee, [by] Parker B. Brown. New York, Hawthorne Books [1974] xii, 164 p. map on front. 22 cm. [BT301.2] 73-1935 ISBN 0-8015-3368-6 6.95
1. Jesus Christ—Biography. I. Title.

*BRUCE, F. F. BT301.2
Paul & Jesus, [by] F. F. Bruce. Grand Rapids, Baker Book House [1974] 91 p. 22 cm. (Ontario Bible College, Elmore Harris Series, no. 4) [232] ISBN 0-8010-0631-7 2.50 (pbk.)
1. Jesus Christ—Biography. 2. Paul—Saint—Apostle. I. Title.

GIORDANI, Igino, 1894- 232.9
Christ, hope of the world. Translated by Clelia Maranzana. [Boston] St. Paul Editions [1964] 470 p. col. illus. 24 cm. [BT301.2.G5] 63-13898
1. Jesus Christ — Blog. I. Title. **BIP**

GOYEN, William. 232.9'01
A book of Jesus. [New York] New American Library [1974, c1973] 128 p. 18 cm. (A Signet book) [BT301.2.G6] 1.25 (pbk.)
1. Jesus Christ—Biography. I. Title.
L.C. card for original ed.: 72-84915.

I follow Christ above v. 12
all... Nashville, Tenn., General Board of Education of the Methodist Church, Youth Department [c1956] 200p. 17cm.
1. Jesus Christ—Biography. 2. Jesus Christ—Person and offices. I. Laymon, Charles M

LAUBACH, Frank Charles, 232.9
1884-
The greatest life; Jesus tells his story. [Westwood, N. J.] Revell [1956] 192p. 21cm. Written as Jesus' autobiography, following the sequence used in harmonies of the Gospels, based on Edgar J. Goodspeed's translation. [BT301.L26] 56-7438
1. JesusChrist—Biog. I. Title.

*ROBERTSON, A. T. 232.901
Epochs in the life of Jesus; a study of development and struggle in the Messiah's work [by] A. T. Robertson. Grand Rapids, Baker Book House, [1974]. ix, 192 p. 20 cm. [BT307] ISBN 0-8010-7624-2. 2.95 (pbk.)
1. Jesus Christ—Biography. 2. Jesus Christ—Historicity. I. Title.

STAUFFER, Ethelbert, 1902- v. 12
Jesus: Gestalt und Geschichte. Bern, Francke [1957] 172 p. (Dalp-Taschenbiicher, Bd. 332)
1. Jesus Christ — Biography. I. Title.

*TAYLOR, Willard H. 232.9
The story of our Saviour. Kansas City, Mo., Beacon Hill Pr. [c.1963] 138p.19cm. Bibl. 1.25 pap.,
I. Title.

TRENT, Robbie, 1894- 232.9
Stories of Jesus; illustrated by Paul Frame. Racine, Wis., Whitman Pub. Co., c1954. unpaged. illus. 21cm. (A Cozy-corner book) [BT302.T73 1954] 55-17419
1. Jesus Christ—Blog. —Juvenile literature. I. Title.

Jesus Christ—Childhood.

ELDON, Magdalen. 232.92
The childhood of Jesus, by Magdalen Eldon and Frances Phipps. New York, D. McKay Co. [1953] 96p. illus. 26cm. [BT320.E4] 53-11366
1. Jesus Christ—Childhood. I. Phipps, Frances, joint author. II. Title.

Jesus Christ—Childhood—Juvenile literature.

DOANE, Pelagie, 1906- 232.9
The boy Jesus. New York, Oxford University Press, 1954. 54p. illus. 26cm. [Oxford books for boys and girls] Catholiced. [BT325.D6 1954] 54-4914
1. jesus Christ—Childhood—Juvenile literature. I. Title.

DOANE, Pelagie, 1906- 232.9
The boy Jesus. New York, H. Z. Walck, 1954 [i.e. 1963?] 54 p. col. illus. 26 cm. Catholic ed. [BT320.D6 1963] 63-21355
1. Jesus Christ — Childhood — Juvenile literature. I. Title.

JONES, Mary Alice, 1898- j232.92
Stories of the Christ child. Illustrated by Eleanor Corwin. Chicago, Rand McNally [1964] c1953. 1 v. (unpaged) col. illus. 33 cm. (A Rand McNally giant book) [BT302.J59 1964] 64-17038
1. Jesus Christ—Childhood—Juvenile literature. I. Corwin, Eleanor, illus. II. Title.

JONES, Mary Alice, 1898- 232.92
Stories of the Christ child; illustrated by Eleanor Corwin. Chicago, Rand McNally, c1953. unpaged. illus. 21cm. (A Rand McNally book-elf book, 484) [BT302.J59 1953] 53-34336
1. Jesus Christ—Childhood—Juvenile literature. I. Title.

Jesus Christ — Passion.

HARGROVE, Hubbard Hoyt, 225.92
1895-
Personalities around the Cross. Grand Rapids, Baker Book House, 1963. 138 p. 20 cm. [BT431.H27] 63-21468
1. Jesus Christ — Passion. 2. Bible. N.T. — Biog. I. Title.

Jesus Christ—Teachings.

MARCH, William J. 232.954
Christian belief and Christian practice. Grand Rapids, Mich., Eerdmans [c.1964] 219 p. 23 cm. 63-22535 3.50
1. Jesus Christ—Teachings. 2. Jesus Christ—Biog. Devotional literature. I. Title.

Jesus Christ—Art.

KING, Marian. 755'.52
The ageless story of Jesus. Paintings and engravings from the National Gallery of Art. Bible selections and descriptive text by Marian King. Washington, Acropolis Books [1970] 116 p. illus. (part col.) 17 x 23 cm. [N8050.K525] 73-109345 ISBN 0-87491-008-0 6.95
1. Jesus Christ—Art. 2. Jesus Christ—Biography. I. U.S. National Gallery of Art. II. Title.

Jesus Christ—Biography.

BALDWIN, Louis. 232.9'01
Jesus of Galilee : his story in everyday language / Louis Baldwin. Valley Forge, PA : Judson Press, c1979. 142 p. : map ; 22 cm. Includes index. Bibliography: p. 137-139. [BT301.2.B22] 79-11587 ISBN 0-8170-0841-1 : 4.95
1. Jesus Christ—Biography. 2. Christian biography—Palestine. I. Title.

BAN, Joseph D. 232
Jesus confronts life's issues [by] Joseph D. Ban. Valley Forge [Pa.] Judson Press [1972] 128 p. 22 cm. [BT301.2.B24] 73-182245 ISBN 0-8170-0547-1 1.95
1. Jesus Christ—Biography. I. Title. **BIP**

BARCLAY, William, 232.9'01 B
lecturer in the University of Glasgow.
Jesus of Nazareth / William Barclay ; based on the film directed by Franco Zefirelli, from the script by Anthony Burgess, Suso Cecchi d'Amico and Franco Zefirelli ; photos. by Paul Ronald. London ; Cleveland : Collins, 1977. 285 p. : col. ill. ; 26 cm. [BT301.2.B25] 77-365179 ISBN 0-00-250653-X : 14.95
1. Jesus Christ—Biography. 2. Christian biography—Palestine. I. Zefirelli, Franco. II. Burgess, Anthony, 1917- III. Cecchi d'Amico, Suso. IV. Jesus of Nazareth.

BARNETT, Walter, 1933- 232.9'01 B
Jesus, the story of His life : a modern retelling based on the Gospels / Walter Barnett. Chicago : Nelson-Hall, 1976 c1975 x, 273 p. ; 23 cm. Includes index. [BT301.2.B28] 75-28260 ISBN 0-88229-308-7 : 6.95
1. Jesus Christ—Biography. I. Title. **BIP**

BORER, Wilbur J. 232.9'01
Book of the Lord : reflections on the life of Christ / Wilbur J. Borer ; ill. by Jean Charlot. Huntington, Ind. : Our Sunday Visitor, c1978. xi, 493 p. : ill. ; 24 cm. [BT301.2.B57] 78-50696 ISBN 0-87973-852-9: 11.95
1. Jesus Christ—Biography. 2. Christian biography—Palestine. I. Title. **BIP**

BROWN, Parker B. 232.9'08
He came from Galilee / Parker B. Brown. New York : Hawthorn Books, [1974] xii, 164 p. : map ; 22 cm. Includes index. [BS2555.5.B78 1974] 73-19385 ISBN 0-8015-3368-6 : 6.95
1. Jesus Christ—Biography. 2. Bible. N.T. Gospels—History of contemporary events, etc. I. Title.

CASE, Shirley Jackson, 232.9
1872-1947.
Jesus; a new biography. New York, AMS Press, [1969] ix, 452 p. 23 cm. Reprint of the 1927 ed. Bibliographical footnotes. [BT301.C36 1969] 70-95149
1. Jesus Christ—Biography. I. Title. **BIP**

CASE, Shirley Jackson, 232.9
1872-1947.
Jesus; a new biography. New York, Greenwood Press [1968, c1927] ix, 452 p. 23 cm. Bibliographical footnotes. [BT301.C36 1968] 68-57594
1. Jesus Christ—Biography. I. Title. **BIP**

CHATHAM, Josiah George, 1914- 232
In the midst stands Jesus; a pastoral introduction to the New Testament [by] Josiah G. Chatham. Staten Island, N.Y., Alba House [1972] vi, 220 p. 22 cm. Bibliography: p. [207]-210. [BS2330.2.C49] 72-3563 ISBN 0-8189-0252-3 4.95
1. Jesus Christ—Biography. 2. Bible. N.T.—Introductions. I. Title.

COLTON, Ann Ree. 232.9'01
The Jesus story. [1st ed.] Glendale, Calif., ARC Pub. Co. [1969] 396 p. 23 cm. [BT304.93.C6] 71-1491 7.95
1. Jesus Christ—Biography. 2. Jesus Christ—Miscellanea. I. Title.

COMSTOCK, Jim F. 232.9'01 B
Good news : the life of Jesus reported in newspaper style / by Jim Comstock ; [photos. by William C. Rogers]. McLean, Va. : EPM Publications, c1974 [48] p. : ill. ; 44 cm. [BT301.2.C58] 74-22829 ISBN 0-914440-06-3 : 6.95 ($7.95 Can)
1. Jesus Christ—Biography. I. Title.

CONNICK, C. Milo. 232.9'01
Jesus: the man, the mission, and the message [by] C. Milo Connick. 2d ed. Englewood Cliffs, N.J., Prentice-Hall [1974] xiv, 464 p. illus. 24 cm. Bibliography: p. 425-439. [BT301.2.C6 1974] 74-6264 ISBN 0-13-509521-2 12.95
1. Jesus Christ—Biography. I. Title.

CONVERSE, Gordon N. 779'.9'2209
Come see the place : the Holy Land Jesus knew / photos. by Gordon N. Converse ; text by Robert J. Bull and B. Cobbey Crisler. Englewood Cliffs, N.J. : Prentice-Hall, c1978. [DS108.5.C65] 78-7054 ISBN 0-13-152538-7 : 12.95
1. Jesus Christ—Biography. 2. Palestine—Description and travel—Views. 3. Christian biography—Palestine. I. Bull, Robert J. II. Crisler, B. Cobbey, 1933- III. Title. **BIP**

COUNTS, Bill. 232.9'01 B
Once a carpenter / Bill Counts. Irvine, Calif. : Harvest House Publishers, [1975] xiii, 255 p. ; 21 cm. [BT301.2.C66] 74-32568 ISBN 0-89081-008-7 pbk. : 2.95
1. Jesus Christ—Biography. I. Title.

CRAVERI, Marcello, 1914- 232.9'01
The life of Jesus. Translated by Charles Lam Markmann. New York, Grove Press [1967] xii, 520 p. illus. 24 cm. Bibliography: p. 479-505. [BT301.2.C713] 66-30412
1. Jesus Christ—Biography. I. Title.

CULVER, Robert Duncan. 232.9'01 B
The life of Christ / Robert Duncan Culver. Grand Rapids, Mich. : Baker Book House, c1976. 304 p. : ill. ; 23 cm. Includes bibliographical references and indexes. [BT301.2.C84] 76-17967 ISBN 0-8010-2379-3 : 8.95
1. Jesus Christ—Biography. 2. Christian biography—Palestine. I. Title.

DEMERSCHMAN, Lucille. 200
New light upon old tradition, with spiritual guidelines for the new age. Los Angeles, DeVorss [1969] 279 p. 24 cm. [BL48.D385] 79-101300
1. Jesus Christ—Biography. 2. Religion. 3. Christianity. I. Title.

DRANE, John William. 232.9'01
Jesus and the four Gospels / John W. Drane. 1st U.S. ed. San Francisco : Harper & Row, c1978. p. cm. [BT301.2.D7 1978] 77-20448 ISBN 0-06-062066-8. : 7.95
1. Jesus Christ—Biography. 2. Bible. N.T. Gospels—Criticism, interpretation, etc. 3. Christian biography—Palestine. I. Title.

EMERSON, William A., 232.9'01 B
1923-
The Jesus story [by] William A. Emerson, Jr. [1st ed.] New York, Harper & Row [1971] 132 p. 21 cm. [BT301.2.E45] 70-148432 4.95
1. Jesus Christ—Biography. I. Title.

ENDO, Shusaku, 1923- 232.9'01
A life of Jesus / by Shusaku Endo ; translated from the Japanese by Richard A. Schuchert. New York : Paulist Press, c1978. v, 179 p. : ill. ; 24 cm. Translation of Iesu no shogai. [BT301.2.E5313] 78-61721 ISBN 0-8091-0269-2 : 9.95
1. Jesus Christ—Biography. 2. Christian biography—Palestine. I. Title.

ENSLIN, Morton Scott, 1897- 232.9
The prophet from Nazareth. New York, Schocken Books [1968, c1961] xiv, 221 p. 21 cm. Bibliography: p. 219-221. [BT303.E55 1968] 68-27322 5.00 (cloth)
1. Jesus Christ—Biography. I. Title.

FLOOD, Edmund. 232.9
Jesus and his contemporaries. Glen Rock, N.J., Paulist Press [1968] v, 85 p. 18 cm. (Deus books) [BT301.2.F57] 68-54403 0.95
1. Jesus Christ—Biography. I. Title. BIP

GENESIS Project, inc. 232.9'01
Jesus, his life and times. 1st ed. New York : Morrow, c1979. 224 p. : ill. (some col.) ; 29 cm. Includes indexes. [BT301.2.G38 1979] 79-66457 ISBN 0-688-03577-9 : 22.95
1. Jesus Christ—Biography. 2. Christian biography—Palestine. I. Title. BIP

GEORGE, Bill. 232.9'01 B
His story : the life of Christ / Bill George. Cleveland, Tenn. : Pathway Press, c1977. 132 p. ; 18 cm. Bibliography: p. 131-132. [BT301.2.G4] 76-53630 ISBN 0-87148-406-4 pbk. : 2.50
1. Jesus Christ—Biography. 2. Christian biography—Palestine. I. Title. BIP

GOGUEL, Maurice, 1880- 232.9'01 B
1955.
The life of Jesus / by Maurice Goguel ; translated by Olive Wyon. New York : AMS Press, [1976] p. cm. Translation of the 1st v. of a trilogy entitled Jesus et les origines du christianisme; the 2d v. has title: The birth of Christianity. Reprint of the 1933 ed. published by Macmillan, New York. Includes index. Bibliography: p. [BT301.G65 1976] 75-41114 ISBN 0-404-14546-9 : 32.50
1. Jesus Christ—Biography. 2. Bible. N.T.—Biography. I. Title.

GOODSPEED, Edgar Johnson, 232.9
1871-1962.
A life of Jesus. [1st ed.] New York, Harper [1950] 248 p. maps (on lining papers) 22 cm. [BT301.G73] 50-10789
1. Jesus Christ—Biography.

GOODSPEED, Edgar 232.9'01 B
Johnson, 1871-1962.
A life of Jesus / by Edgar J. Goodspeed. Westport, Conn. : Greenwood Press, 1979, c1950. 248 p. ; 22 cm. Reprint of the ed. published by Harper, New York. Includes bibliographical references and index. [BT301.G73 1979] 78-21540 ISBN 0-313-20728-3 lib. bdg. : 18.75
1. Jesus Christ—Biography. 2. Christian biography—Palestine. I. Title.

GOUDGE, Elizabeth, 1900- 232.9
God so loved the world. New York, Coward-McCann [1951] 311 p. 22 cm. [BT301.G77] 51-10022
1. Jesus Christ—Biography. I. Title.

GOYEN, William. 232.9'01
A book of Jesus. [1st ed.] Garden City, N.Y., Doubleday, 1973. 143 p. 18 cm. [BT301.2.G6] 72-84915 ISBN 0-385-05979-5 4.95
1. Jesus Christ—Biography. BIP

GRAHAM, Eleanor, 1896- 232.9'01
The story of Jesus; illustrated by Brian Wildsmith. Revised ed. Harmondsworth, Penguin, 1971. 206 p. illus., map. 18 cm. (Puffin books) [BT301.2.G67 1971] 72-181112 ISBN 0-14-030135-6 £0.25
1. Jesus Christ—Biography. I. Title.

GRANT, Michael, 1914- 232.9'01 B
Jesus : an historian's review of the Gospels / Michael Grant. New York : Scribner, c1977. 261 p. : maps ; 25 cm. Includes index. Bibliography: p. 251. [BT301.2.G68 1977b] 77-70218 ISBN 0-684-14889-7 : 12.50
1. Jesus Christ—Biography. 2. Christian biography—Palestine. I. Title. BIP

GUTHRIE, Donald, 1916- 232
Jesus the Messiah; an illustrated life of Christ. Grand Rapids, Zondervan Pub. House [1972] 386 p. illus. 25 cm. [BT301.2.G86] 74-189588 6.95
1. Jesus Christ—Biography. I. Title.

GUTHRIE, Donald, 1916- 232.9'01
A shorter life of Christ. Grand Rapids, Zondervan Pub. House [1970] 186 p. 21 cm. (Contemporary evangelical perspectives) Bibliography: p. 181-186. [BT301.2.G88] 71-120039
1. Jesus Christ—Biography. I. Title. BIP

HARRISON, Everett 232.9'01
Falconer, 1902-
A short life of Christ, by Everett F. Harrison. Grand Rapids, W. B. Eerdmans [1968] 288 p. 23 cm. Includes bibliographies. [BT301.2.H3] 68-30985 5.95
1. Jesus Christ—Biography. I. Title. BIP

HILL, Dave. 232.9
The most wonderful King; Luke 19:28-24:43 and John 12:12-20:31 for children. Illustrated by Betty Wind. St. Louis, Concordia Pub. House [1968] [32] p. col. illus. 21 cm. (Arch books) Briefly tells in rhyme of the death and resurrection of Jesus Christ. [BT302.H5] AC 68
1. Jesus Christ—Biography. I. Wind, Betty, illus. II. Title.

JACOBS, William J. 232.9'01 B
Jesus / by William Jacobs. N[ew] Y[ork] : Paulist Press, c1977. vii, 124 p. ; 18 cm. (Emmaus books) [BT301.2.J3] 76-24439 ISBN 0-8091-1986-2 pbk. : 1.45
1. Jesus Christ—Biography. 2. Christian biography—Palestine. I. Title.

JARVIS, Frank 232.9'01
Washington, 1939-
And still is ours today : the story of Jesus / F. Washington Jarvis. New York : Seabury Press, c1980. p. cm. Bibliography: p. [BT301.2.J36] 79-23730 ISBN 0-8164-0208-6 : 9.95 ISBN 0-8164-2005-X (pbk.) : 4.50
1. Jesus Christ—Biography. 2. Christian biography—Palestine. I. Title.

JONES, George Curtis, 225.9'2'2 B
1911-
We knew His power / G. Curtis Jones. Nashville : Abingdon, c1976. 128 p. ; 20 cm. [BS2430.J66] 75-44181 ISBN 0-687-44315-6 : 5.95
1. Jesus Christ—Biography. 2. Bible. N.T. Gospels—Biography. I. Title.

KELLER, Hippolyt. 232.9
No greater life; the story of Jesus of Nazareth. Translated by Kathryn Sullivan. New York, Catholic Book Pub. Co. [1954] 239p. illus. 20cm. Translation of Leben Jesu dem Volke erzahlt. [BT301.K433] 56-425
1. Jesus Christ—Biog. I. Title.

KELLER, Weldon 232.9'01 B
Phillip, 1920-
Rabboni ... which is to say master / W. Phillip Keller. Old Tappan, N.J. : Revell, c1977. 320 p. ; 24 cm. [BT301.2.K44] 77-24304 ISBN 0-8007-0882-2 : 8.95
1. Jesus Christ—Biography. 2. Christian biography—Palestine. I. Title.

KOSSOFF, David, 1919- 232
The book of witnesses. Boston, G. K. Hall, 1972 [c1971] 295 p. 25 cm. Large print ed. [BT301.2.K67 1972] 72-5099 ISBN 0-8161-6041-4 7.95
1. Jesus Christ—Biography. I. Title.

LAMSA, George 232.9'01
Mamishisho, 1893-
The man from Galilee; a life of Jesus [by] George M. Lamsa. [1st ed.] Garden City, N.Y., Doubleday, 1970. xv, 293 p. 22 cm. [BT301.2.L24] 73-78702 5.95
1. Jesus Christ—Biography. I. Title.

LEVIN, Simon S. 232.9'01
Jesus alias Christ; a theological detection [by] Simon S. Levin. New York, Philosophical Library [1969] 136 p. 22 cm. Bibliographical footnotes. [BT301.2.L38] 71-81814 5.50
1. Jesus Christ—Biography.

LINK, Mark J. 232.9'01
The seventh trumpet : the good news proclaimed / by Mark Link. 1st ed. Niles, Ill. : Argus Communications, c1978. iv, 208 p. : ill. ; 23 cm. Includes bibliographical references and indexes. [BT299.2.L56] 78-53943 ISBN 0-89505-014-5 : 5.95
1. Jesus Christ—Biography. 2. Christian biography—Palestine. I. Title.

LONGFORD, Frank 232.9'01 B
Pakenham, 7th Earl of, 1905-
Jesus : a life of Christ / by Lord Longford ; illustrated by Richard Cuffari. Garden City, N.Y. : Doubleday, 1975. 184, [3] p. : ill. ; 22 cm. First ed. published in 1974 under title: The life of Jesus Christ. Bibliography: p. [187] [BT301.2.L6 1975] 74-12698 ISBN 0-385-07008-X : 5.95
1. Jesus Christ—Biography. I. Title.

MANN, Christopher 232.9'012 B
Stephen.
The man for all time [by] C. S. Mann. New York, Morehouse-Barlow [1971] 126 p. maps. 19 cm. [BT301.2.M26] 75-161567 ISBN 0-8192-1127-3
1. Jesus Christ—Biography. I. Title. BIP

MORE, Paul Elmer, 1864- 232.9
1937.
The Christ of the New Testament. New York, Greenwood Press [1969, c1924] ix, 294 p. 23 cm. Bibliographical footnotes. [BT301.M6 1969] 79-88912
1. Jesus Christ—Biography. 2. Bible. N.T.—Criticism, interpretation, etc. I. Title. BIP

O'BRIEN, John Anthony, 232.9
1893-
The life of Christ. New York, J. J. Crawley [1957] 623p. illus. 22cm. [BT301.O18] 57-2585
1. Jesus Christ—Biog. I. Title.

OURSLER, Fulton, 1893- 220.9'505
1952.
Fulton Oursler's Greatest : The greatest book ever written, The greatest story ever told, The greatest faith ever known. 1st ed. Garden City, N.Y. : Doubleday, 1979. 1052 p. ; 21 cm. (A Doubleday-Galilee book) [BS1197.O79] 78-69663 ISBN 0-385-14659-0 : 8.95
1. Jesus Christ—Biography. 2. Bible. O.T.—History of Biblical events. 3. Bible. N.T.—History of Biblical events. 4. Christian biography—Palestine. 5. Apostles. I. Title. BIP

OURSLER, Fulton, 1893-1952. 232.9
The greatest story ever told; a tale of the greatest life ever lived. Paintings by Kenneth Riley. [1st illustrated ed.] Garden City, N.Y., Doubleday, 1950. xvii, 332 p. col. plates. 27 cm. [BT301.O85 1950] 50-11671
1. Jesus Christ—Biography. I. Title.

PEALE, Norman Vincent, 232.9'01
1898-
The story of Jesus / Norman Vincent Peale ; illustrated by Robert Fujitani. Norwalk, Conn. : C. R. Gibson, c1976. 88 p. : ill. ; 21 cm. [BT301.2.P43] 75-36009 ISBN 0-8378-1797-8 : 4.50
1. Jesus Christ—Biography. I. Fujitani, Robert. II. Title.

PETERSON, Edward C. 232
To find Jesus. Written by Edward C. Peterson and Barbara Nan Peterson. With illus. by Jim Padgett. Nashville, Abingdon Press [1967] 112 p. illus. (part col.) 26 cm. A biography of Jesus of Nazareth, consisting of what is conjectured scenes that may have occurred. [BT302.P45] AC 67
1. Jesus Christ—Biography. I. Peterson, Barbara Nan, joint author. II. Padgett, Jim, illus. III. Title.

PHILLIPS, Wendell, 232.9'01 B
1921-
An explorer's life of Jesus / by Wendell Phillips. New York : Two Continents Pub. Group, [1975] p. cm. Includes bibliographical references and index. [BT301.2.P476] 75-11181 ISBN 0-8467-0072-7 : 20.00
1. Jesus Christ—Biography. 2. Bible. N.T. Gospels—Criticism, interpretation, etc. I. Title.

PHILLIPS, Wendell, 232.9'01 B
1921-
A popular life of Jesus / Wendell Phillips. New York : Two Continents Pub. Group, [1975] p. cm. An abridged version of the author's An explorer's life of Jesus. Includes index. [BT301.2.P477] 75-11183 ISBN 0-8467-0073-5 : 9.95
1. Jesus Christ—Biography. 2. Bible. N.T. Gospels—Criticism, interpretation, etc. I. Title.

PHIPPS, William E., 1930- 261.8'3
The sexuality of Jesus: theological and literary perspectives [by] William E. Phipps. [1st ed.] New York, Harper & Row [1973] 172 p. 21 cm. Includes bibliographical references. [BL65.S4P5] 72-78067 ISBN 0-06-066561-0 5.95
1. Jesus Christ—Biography. 2. Sex and religion—History. I. Title.

PITTENGER, William Norman, 232.9
1905-
The life of Jesus Christ, by W. Norman Pittenger. New York, F. Watts [1968] x, 115 p. 22 cm. (Immortals of philosophy and religion) Bibliography: p. 109-111. [BT301.2.P5] 68-22144 3.95
1. Jesus Christ—Biography.

PUTNEY, Max C 1893- 232.9
The man of Galilee; a new life of Jesus. [1st ed.] New York, Exposition Press [1955] 274p. 21cm. (A Banner book) Includes bibliography. [BT301.P88] 55-10300
1. Jesus Christ—Biog. I. Title.

RADIUS, Marianne Catherine 232.9
(Vos)
God with us; a life of Jesus for young readers, by Marianne Radius. Linoleum cuts by Frederick J. Ashby. Grand Rapids, Eerdmans Pub. Co. [1966] 286 p. illus., col. map (on lining papers) 24 cm. The story of Jesus retold from the New Testament with the author's comments. [BT302.R13] AC 67
1. Jesus Christ—Biography. I. Ashby, Frederick J., illus. II. Title.

REUMANN, John Henry 232.9'01
Paul.
Jesus in the church's Gospels; modern scholarship and the earliest sources [by] John Reumann. Philadelphia, Fortress Press [1968] xviii, 539 p. 23 cm. Includes bibliographical references. [BT301.2.R4] 68-10983
1. Jesus Christ—Biography. I. Title.

ROBERTSON, Archibald 232.9'01
Thomas, 1863-1934.
Epochs in the life of Jesus : a study of development and struggle in the Messiah's work / A. T. Robertson. Nashville : Broadman Press, 1974. ix, 192 p. ; 20 cm. (A. T. Robertson library) Reprint of the 1907 ed. published by Scribner, New York. Includes index. [BT301.R59 1974] 74-193286 ISBN 0-8054-1347-2 pbk. : 2.95
1. Jesus Christ—Biography. I. Title.

ROSS, Pearl. 232
Jesus the pagan. New York, Philosophical

Library [1972] ix, 73 p. 23 cm. [BT301.2.R67] 72-82792 ISBN 0-8022-2097-5 6.00
1. Jesus Christ—Biography. I. Title. **BIP**

RUSSELL, Josiah Cox, 1900- 232.9'01
Jesus of Nazareth, by Josiah C. Russell. [1st ed. New York] Pageant Press [1967] 130 p. 21 cm. [BT301.2.R8] 67-5686
1. Jesus Christ—Biography. I. Title.

SAKLATVALA, Beram. 232.9'01 B
The rebel king : the story of Christ as seen against the historical conflict between the Roman Empire and Judaism / by Henry Marsh [i.e. B. Saklatvala]. New York : Coward, McCann & Geoghegan, [1975] xi, 222 p. ; 22 cm. Bibliography: p. 221-222. [BT301.2.S14] 74-30594 ISBN 0-698-10663-6 : 7.95
1. Jesus Christ—Biography. 2. Bible. N.T. Gospels—History of contemporary events, etc. I. Title.

SALSTRAND, George A. E., 1908- 232.9'01 B
What Jesus began : the life and ministry of Christ / George A. E. Salstrand. Nashville : Broadman Press, c1976. 180 p. : ill. ; 21 cm. [BT301.2.S163] 75-20694 ISBN 0-8054-1356-1 : 4.95
1. Jesus Christ—Biography. I. Title.

SANTUCCI, Luigi. 232
Meeting Jesus; a new way to Christ. Translated from the Italian by Bernard Wall. [New York] Herder and Herder [1971] 222 p. 24 cm. Translation of Volete andarvene anche voi? [BT301.2.S1813] 78-167865 ISBN 0-665-00020-0 7.50
1. Jesus Christ—Biography. I. Title. **BIP**

SAUNDERS, Ernest W. 232.9'01
Jesus in the Gospels [by] Ernest W. Saunders. Englewood Cliffs, N.J., Prentice-Hall [1967] xii, 324 p. illus., map (on lining papers) 22 cm. Bibliographical footnotes. [BT301.2.S2] 67-10316
1. Jesus Christ—Biography. I. Title.

SCHLEIERMACHER, Friedrich Ernst Daniel, 1768-1834. 232.9'01 B
The life of Jesus / by Friedrich Schleiermacher ; edited and with an introd. by Jack C. Verheyden ; translated by S. Maclean Gilmour. Philadelphia : Fortress Press, c1975. lxii, 481 p. ; 22 cm. (Lives of Jesus series) Translation of Das Leben Jesu. Bibliography: p. lxi-lxii. [BT301.S3613 1975] 72-87056 ISBN 0-8006-1272-8 : 14.95
1. Jesus Christ—Biography. I. Title.

SEBOLT, Roland H. A. 232.9
God's son on earth. [Text by Roland Sebolt. Illus. by Marianne Bellenhaus. St. Louis, Concordia Pub. House, 1968] [30] p. col. illus. 23 x 30 cm. Cover title. Translation and adaptation of Gottes Sohn auf Erden by Eleanore Beck and Gabrielle Miller. A brief retelling of the major events in Jesus' life, from birth to death and resurrection. [BT302.S29] AC 68
1. Jesus Christ—Biography. I. Bellenhaus, Marianne, illus. II. Beck, Eleanor. Gottes Sohn auf Erden. III. Title.

SHEEN, Fulton John, Bp., 1895- 232.9
Life of Christ. [1st ed.] New York, McGraw-Hill [1958] 559 p. 24 cm. [BT301.S4183] 58-13889
1. Jesus Christ—Biography.

SHEEN, Fulton John, Bp., 1895- 232.9
Life of Christ : complete and unabridged / Fulton J. Sheen. Garden City, N.Y. : Image Books, 1977. 476 p. ; 21 cm. Reprint of the 1958 ed. published by McGraw-Hill, New York. Includes index. [BT301.2.S464 1977] 77-81295 ISBN 0-385-13220-4 : pbk. : 3.95
1. Jesus Christ—Biography. 2. Christian biography—Palestine. I. Title.

STAUFFER, Ethelbert, 1902- 232.9
Jesus and His story. Translated from the German by Richard and Clara Winston. [1st American ed.] New York, Knopf, 1960 [c1959] 243 p. illus. 22 cm. Translation of Jesus: Gestalt und Geschicte. Includes bibliography. [BT301.2.S683] 59-15321
1. Jesus Christ—Biography. I. Title.

STEINMANN, Jean. 232.9
The life of Jesus. Translated from the French by Peter Green. [1st ed.] Boston, Little, Brown [1963] xi, 240 p. map. 21 cm. Bibliographical references included in "Notes": p. [233]-234. [BT301.2.S6913] 63-17426
1. Jesus Christ—Biography.

STORIES of Jesus. 232.9'01 B
Adapted from the Jerusalem Bible. Illustrated by Eric de Saussure. Philadelphia, Fortress Press [1973, c1968] 62 p. illus. (part col.) 23 cm. [BT301.2.S73 1973] 72-92183 ISBN 0-8006-0164-5 1.95
1. Jesus Christ—Biography. I. Saussure, Eric de, illus.

STRAUSS, David Friedrich, 1808-1874. 232.9'01
The life of Jesus, critically examined. Translated from the 4th German ed. by Marian Evans. New York, C. Blanchard, 1860. St. Clair Shores, Mich., Scholarly Press, 1970. 2 v. (901 p.) port. 23 cm. Bibliographical footnotes. [BT301.S72 1970] 74-107193
1. Jesus Christ—Biography. I. Title. **BIP**

STRAUSS, David Friedrich, 1808-1874. 232.9'01
The life of Jesus, critically examined. Edited and with an introd. by Peter C. Hodgson. Translated from the 4th German ed. by George Eliot. Philadelphia, Fortress Press [1973, c1972] lviii, 39-812 p. 22 cm. (Lives of Jesus series) Bibliography: p. 803-812. [BT301.S72 1973] 72-75655 ISBN 0-8006-1271-X 12.00
1. Jesus Christ—Biography. I. Title.

TAYLOR, Vincent, 1887- v. 12
The life and ministry of Jesus. London, Macmillan, New York, St. Martin's Press, 1961 [1954] xi, 236 p. 23 cm. A revision and enlargement of the author's The Life and ministry of Jesus, published in 1951 in the Interpreter's Bible, v. 7. 65-23976
1. Jesus Christ—Biog. I. Title.

TRAPP, Maria Augusta. 232.9'01 B
When the King was carpenter / by Maria von Trapp. Harrison, Ark. : New Leaf Press, c1976. 141 p. ; 18 cm. Includes bibliographical references. [BT301.2.T7] 75-46021 ISBN 0-89221-018-4 : 1.95
1. Jesus Christ—Biography. 2. Christian biography—Palestine. I. Title.

VAN DYK, Fay Blix, 1951- 232.9'01
His touch is love / by Fay Blix Van Dyk. Nashville : Southern Pub. Association, c1978. p. cm. [BT301.2.V35] 78-6523 ISBN 0-8127-0189-5 pbk. : 3.95
1. Jesus Christ—Biography. 2. Christian biography—Palestine. I. Title. **BIP**

VOS, Howard Frederic, 1925- 232.9'01 B
Beginnings in the life of Christ / by Howard F. Vos. Rev. ed. Chicago : Moody Press, [1975] p. cm. First ed. published in 1958 under title: The life of Our Divine Lord. Includes index. Bibliography: p. [BT301.2.V63 1975] 75-11981 ISBN 0-8024-0608-4 pbk : 2.95
1. Jesus Christ Biography. I. Title. **BIP**

YOUNG, Andrew, 1885- 232
The poetic Jesus. With six wood engravings by T. R. Williams. [1st U.S. ed.] New York, Harper & Row [1972] 88 p. illus. 22 cm. [BT301.2.Y68 1972b] 72-79467 ISBN 0-06-069731-8 3.95
1. Jesus Christ—Biography. 2. Jesus Christ—Teachings. I. Title.

Jesus Christ—Biography—Apocryphal and legendary literature.

BALLOU, Robert Oleson. 232
The other Jesus; a narrative based on apocryphal stories not included in the Bible. Arr., edited, and with comments by Robert O. Ballou. [1st ed.] Garden City, N.Y., Doubleday, 1972. xix, 213 p. 22 cm. Includes bibliographical references. [BT520.B33] 73-180058 6.95
1. Jesus Christ—Biography—Apocryphal and legendary literature. I. Title.

FABER, Andreas. 232.9'01
Jesus died in Kashmir : Jesus, Moses and the ten lost tribes of Israel / A. Faber-Kaiser. London : Gordon & Cremonesi, c1977. viii, 184 p., [8] leaves of plates : ill. ; 24 cm. Translation of Jesus vivio y murio en Cachemira. Includes index. Bibliography: p. 170-180. [BT520.F313] 78-353020 ISBN 0-86033-041-9 : 9.95
1. Jesus Christ—Biography—Apocryphal and legendary literature. 2. Kashmir—Miscellanea. I. Title.
Distributed by Atheneum Publishers

NOTOVICH, Nikolai, 1858- 232.9'01
The unknown life of Jesus Christ / by the discoverer of the manuscript, Nicholas Notovich ; translated by J. H. Connelly and L. Landsberg. New York : Gordon Press, [1974] p. cm. Translation of La vie inconnue. Reprint of the 1890 ed. published by R. F. Fenno, New York, which was issued as v. 1, no. 185, of the Globe library. [BT520.N6813 1974] 73-11500 ISBN 0-87968-073-3
1. Jesus Christ—Biography—Apocryphal and legendary literature. I. Title. II. Series: Globe library ; v. 1, no. 185. **BIP**

Jesus Christ—Biography—Collected works.

SEYMOUR, Peter S., comp. 232
Portrait of Jesus; the life of Christ in poetry and prose, edited by Peter Seymour. Illustrated with famous paintings and drawings. [Kansas City, Mo.] Hallmark Crown Editions [1973, c1972] 70 p. illus. 25 x 29 cm. [BT301.2.S44] 70-127751 ISBN 0-87529-146-5 8.50
1. Jesus Christ—Biography—Collected works. 2. Jesus Christ—Art. I. Title.

Jesus Christ—Biography—Congresses.

CENTER for Hermeneutical Studies in Hellenistic and Modern Culture. 232.9'01 B
The hero pattern and the life of Jesus : protocol of the twentyfifth colloquy, 12 December 1976 / The Center for Hermeneutical Studies in Hellenistic and Modern Culture, The Graduate Theological Union & the University of California, Berkeley, California ; Alan Dundes. Berkeley, CA : The Center, c1977. 98 p. ; 21 cm. (Protocol series of the colloquies of the Center ; no. 25 ISSN 0098-0900s) Bibliography: p. 97-98.I[BT303.C46 1977]I77-4835 ISBN 0-89242-024-3 : 3.00
1. Jesus Christ—Biography—Congresses. 2. Bible. N.T. Gospels—Criticism, interpretation, etc. Congresses. 3. Christian biography—Palestine—Congresses. 4. Folk-lore in the Bible—Congresses. 5. Heroes—Congresses. I. Dundes, Alan. II. Title. III. Series: Center for Hermeneutical Studies in Hellenistic and Modern Culture. Protocol series of the colloquies ; no. 25.

Jesus Christ—Biography—Devotional literature.

ARMSTRONG, Garner Ted. 232.9'01 B
The real Jesus / Garner Ted Armstrong. Kansas City, Mo. : Sheed Andrews and McMeel, [1977] p. cm. [BT306.5.A69] 77-20002 ISBN 0-8362-0727-0 : 9.95
1. Jesus Christ—Biography—Devotional literature. 2. Christian biography—Palestine. I. Title. **BIP**

COBURN, John B. 232.9'01 B
Christ's life, Our life / John B. Coburn. New York : Seabury Press, 1978. 101 p. ; 22 cm. "A Crossroad book." [BT306.5.C63] 77-17172 ISBN 0-8164-0384-8 : 5.95
1. Jesus Christ—Biography—Devotional literature. 2. Christian biography—Palestine. 3. Identification (Religion). I. Title. **BIP**

O'CONNELL, John P ed. 232.9
The life of Christ; Our Lord's life, with lessons in His own words for our life today. Edited by John P. O'Connell and Jex Martin. Chicago, Catholic Press [c1954] 304p. illus. 18cm. [BT301.O25] 55-1054
1. Jesus Christ—Biog.—Devotional literature. I. Martin, Jex, joint ed. II. Title.

TAYLOR, Kenneth Nathaniel. 232.9'01'08
The greatest life ever lived; selections [by] Kenneth N. Taylor. Wheaton, Ill., Tyndale House Publishers [1969] 59 p. illus. 20 cm. (Heritage edition) [BT306.5.T3] 70-75245
1. Jesus Christ—Biography—Devotional literature. I. Title.

Jesus Christ—Biography—Early life.

ARON, Robert, 1898- 232.92
The Jewish Jesus. Translated by Agnes H. Forsyth and Anne-Marie de Commaille and in collaboration with Horace T. Allen, Jr. Maryknoll, N.Y., Orbis Books [1971] viii, 183 p. 22 cm. Translation of Ainsi priait Jesus enfant. [BT310.A7313] 73-151181
1. Jesus Christ—Biography—Early life. I. Title.

Jesus Christ—Biography—Early works to 1800.

[HOLBACH, Paul Henri Thiry, baron d'] 1723-1789. 232.9'01
Ecce homo! : or, A critical inquiry into the history of Jesus of Nazareth, being a rational analysis of the Gospels / [translated by George Houston]. New York : Gordon Press, 1976. p. cm. Translation of Histoire critique de Jesus Christ. Reprint of the 1st American ed., rev. and corr., of 1827, printed for the proprietors of the Philosophical library, New York, which was issued as no. 1 of the Philosophical library. [BT300.H74 1976] 73-8281 ISBN 0-87968-077-6 lib.bdg. : 34.95
1. Jesus Christ—Biography—Early works to 1800. I. Title. II. Series: The Philosophical library ; no. 1.

MARTIN Von Cochem, Father, 1634-1712. 232.9
Life of Christ. Adapted by Bonaventure Hammer. New York, Benziger Bros., 1897. 314p. illus. 20cm. [BT7300.M34] 38-13618
1. Jesus Christ—Biog.—Early works to 1800. I. Title.

MARTIN VON COCHEM, Father, 1634?-1712. 232.9
Our Redeemer: a series of meditations drawn from the study of the life of Christ and His ever glorious mother Mary. English arrangement by Frances M. Kemp. New York, A. Eichler, c1890. x, 1148p illus. 33cm. [BT300.M35] 1-3228
1. Jesus Christ—Biog.—Early works to 1800. 2. Jesus Christ—Biog.—Meditations. 3. Mary. Virin—Meditations. 4. Devotional exercises. I. Title.

Jesus Christ—Biography—History and criticism.

CARTLEDGE, Samuel Antoine, 1903- 232.9'01
Jesus of fact and faith, studies in the life of Christ, by Samuel A. Cartledge. Grand Rapids, Eerdmands [1968] 160 p. 22 cm. Bibliographical footnotes. [BT301.9.C37] 68-56120 4.50
1. Jesus Christ—Biography—History and criticism. I. Title.

JOYCE, Donovan. 200
The Jesus scroll. [New York] Dial Press, 1973 [c1972] 216 p. 22 cm. Bibliography: p. [215]-216. [BT303.J68 1973] 73-10454 5.95
1. Jesus Christ—Biography—History and criticism. I. Title. **BIP**

Jesus Christ—Biography—Juvenile literature.

ADCOCK, Roger. 232.9'01
Stories of Jesus. Rev. by Elsiebeth McDaniel. Illustrated by Gordon King. Wheaton, Ill., Scripture Press Publications, 1971. 77 p. col. illus. 32 cm. London ed. published in 1969 under title: Story of Jesus. Retells Bible stories tracing the events of Jesus' life. [BT302.A26 1971] 70-151699 ISBN 0-361-01210-1
1. Jesus Christ—Biography—Juvenile literature. 2. Jesus Christ—Parables—Juvenile literature. I. McDaniel, Elsiebeth. II. King, Gordon, fl. 1971- illus. III. Title.

†BARCLAY, William, lecturer in the University of Glasgow. 232.9'01'0222 B
A life of Christ / text by William Barclay ;

scripted by Iain Reid ; cartoons by Eric Fraser. 1st ed. New York : Harper & Row, c1977. 94 p., [1] leaf of plates : 45 ill. ; 18 cm. (Harper jubilee books ; HJG 01) "A Harper jubilee giant." Presents the life of Jesus Christ in forty-five brief stories illustrated with cartoons. [BT302.B286] 77-94023 ISBN 0-06-060403-4 pbk. : 3.95
1. Jesus Christ—Biography—Juvenile literature. 2. Bible—Pictures, illustrations, etc. 3. Comic books, strips, etc.—Great Britain. I. Reid, Iain. II. Fraser, Eric, 1902- III. Title.

BEEBE, Catherine, 1898- 92 (J)
The story of Jesus for boys and girls. Pictured by Robb Beebe. Paterson, N.J., St. Anthony Guild Press [1967] 105 p. illus. 23 cm. [BT302.B32 1967] 67-31868
1. Jesus Christ—Biography—Juvenile literature. I. Title.

BEHNKE, John. 232.9'01 B
Stories of Jesus / words by John Behnke ; pictures by Betsy Roosen Sheppard. New York : Paulist Press, c1977. 143 p. : ill. ; 23 cm. Relates the New Testament account of the life of Jesus. [BT302.5b33] 76-24440 ISBN 0-8091-2085-2 pbk. : 1.95
1. Jesus Christ—Biography—Juvenile literature. 2. Jesus Christ—Teachings—Juvenile literature. 3. Christian biography—Palestine—Juvenile literature. I. Sheppard, Betsy Roosen. II. Title.

BIBLE. N. T. Gospels. v. 12
English. Selections. 1956.Authorized.
The life of Christ Jesus in Bible language, from the King James Version of the Bible, compiled by Genevieve P. Olson. 3d ed., rev. Bonita, Calif., G. P. Olson [1957]cvi, 52 p. 18 cm. 68-38238
1. Jesus Christ—Biog.—Juvenile literature. I. Olson, Genevieve P. II. Title.

CARRIGER, Sally A. 232.9'01 B
I-can-read-it-myself Bible stories : stories about Jesus / by Sally A. Carriger ; illustrated by Terry McBride. Washington : Review and Herald Pub. Association, c1978. 79 p. : ill. ; 20 cm. Presents seven New Testament stories about Jesus. [BT302.C34] 77-83636 pbk. : 3.50
1. Jesus Christ—Biography—Juvenile literature. 2. Christian biography—Palestine—Juvenile literature. I. McBride, Terry, 1950- II. Title.

CHAMBERLAIN, 232.9'01'024054 B
Eugene.
Jesus : God's Son, Savior, Lord / Eugene Chamberlain ; illustrated by James Padgett. Nashville : Broadman Press, c1976. 47 p. : col. ill. ; 24 cm. (Biblearn series) Discusses the life and teachings of Jesus Christ. [BT302.C45] 76-382763 ISBN 0-8054-4226-X : 3.95
1. Jesus Christ—Biography—Juvenile literature. 2. Christian biography—Palestine—Juvenile literature. I. Padgett, James. II. Title.

COLBY, Jean (Poindexter) 232.9'01
1908-
Jesus and the world. Illustrated by Jane Paton. 1st American ed. New York, Hastings House, 1968. [26] p. illus. (part col.) 26 cm. Bibliography: p. [26] Describes simply the life of Christ emphasizing His crucifixion and the importance of His teachings to civilization. [BT302.C58 1968] 68-25569 3.75
1. Jesus Christ—Biography—Juvenile literature. I. Paton, Jane, illus. II. Title.

DAUGHTERS of St. Paul. 232
I learn about Jesus. Written and illustrated by the Daughters of St. Paul. [1972 i.e. 1973] 144 p. col. illus. 25 cm. Retellings of New Testament stories with related prayers. [BV4870.D33] 72-91979 pap. 2.50
1. Jesus Christ—Biography—Juvenile literature. 2. Children—Prayer-books and devotions—English—1961- I. Title.
BIP

DILLARD, Pauline (Hargis) 92 (J)
1916-
My book about Jesus [by] Polly Hargis Dillard. Pictures by Anne R. Kasey. Nashville, Broadman Press [1968] 32 p. col. illus. 21 cm. [BT302.D55] 68-20671
1. Jesus Christ—Biography—Juvenile literature. I. Kasey, Anne R., illus. II. Title.

GODDARD, Carrie Lou. 232.9'01 B
Jesus / Carrie Lou Goddard ; illustrated by Peggy Zych. Nashville : Abingdon, c1978. 32 p. : col. ill. ; 20 x 21 cm. Seven stories demonstrate the ways Jesus reflected His Father's love for everyone. [BT302.G53] 78-51992 ISBN 0-687-19909-3 pbk. : 4.95 until Feb. 1, 1980. Thereafter, 5.95
1. Jesus Christ—Biography—Juvenile literature. 2. Christian biography—Palestine—Juvenile literature. I. Zych, Peg. II. Title.

HANSER, Richard. 232.9'01
Jesus: what manner of man is this? New York, Simon and Schuster [1972] 191 p. 22 cm. Traces the life and death of Jesus, His effect on world history, and, briefly, the reviving interest in Him found in today's "Jesus movement." [BT302.H24] 72-82219 ISBN 0-671-65200-1 4.95
1. Jesus Christ—Biography—Juvenile literature. I. Title.

HEINEMANN, Thea. 92 (J)
Stories of Jesus. Illustrated by Don Bolognese. Designed by Walter Brooks. Racine, Wis., Whitman Pub. Division, Western Pub. Co. [1968] 223 p. col. illus. 27 cm. (The Whitman library of giant books) [BT302.H44 1968] 68-11122
1. Jesus Christ—Biography—Juvenile literature. I. Bolognese, Don, illus. II. Title.

HILL, Dave. 92 (J)
The most wonderful king; Luke 19:28-24:43 and John 12:12-20:31 for children. Illustrated by Betty Wind. St. Louis, Concordia Pub. House [1968] 1 v. (unpaged) col. illus. 21 cm. (Arch books) In verse. [BT302.H5] 68-4169
1. Jesus Christ—Biography—Juvenile literature. I. Wind, Betty, illus. II. Title.

HOTH, Iva. 232.9'01
Jesus; Matthew-John. Script by Iva Hoth. Illus. by Andre Le Blanc. Bible editor: C. Elvan Olmstead. Elgin, Il., D. C. Cook Pub. Co. [1973] 158 p. illus. 18 cm. (Her The picture Bible for all ages, v. 5) [BT302.H83] 73-78172 ISBN 0-912692-17-0 0.95 (pbk.)
1. Jesus Christ—Biography—Juvenile literature. I. Title.

JESUS, our Friend. 232.9'01 B
Valley Forge, Pa. : Judson Press, c1976. 47 p. : col. ill. ; 22 cm. Traces the life of Jesus Christ through a retelling of twenty stories from the New Testament. [BS2401.J44] 75-42379 ISBN 0-8170-0713-X : 1.50
1. Jesus Christ—Biography—Juvenile literature. 2. Bible stories, English—N.T. Gospels.
BIP

JONES, Mary Alice, 1898- 92 (J)
Tell me about Jesus. Illustrated by Dorothy Grider. A completely new ed. [Chicago] Rand McNally [1967] 71 p. illus. (part col.) 27 cm. [BT302.T593 1967] 67-18282
1. Jesus Christ—Biography—Juvenile literature. I. Grider, Dorothy, illus. II. Title.

LINDSEY, Hal. 232'.12
The promise / by Hal Lindsey ; illustrated by Norm McGary. Irvine, Calif. : Harvest House, [1974] [100] p. : col. ill. ; 27 cm. Includes bibliographical references. Old Testament prophecies concerning events in the life of the promised Messiah are explained and linked with their fulfillment in the life of Jesus. [BS647.2.L53] 74-18859 ISBN 0-89081-004-4
1. Jesus Christ—Biography—Juvenile literature. 2. Bible—Prophecies—Juvenile literature. I. McGary, Norm, ill. II. Title.

MELTON, David. 232
This man—Jesus. Written and illustrated by David Melton. New York, McGraw-Hill [1972] 57 p. illus. 28 cm. Presents the adulthood of Jesus from His baptism by John to His Resurrection. [BT302.M43] 72-7240 ISBN 0-07-041442-4 3.95
1. Jesus Christ—Biography—Juvenile literature. I. Title.

MITCHELL, Curtis. 232.9
Jesus spreads His Gospel. Garden City, N. Y. [Doubleday, c1961] 64p. illus. 21cm. (Know your Bible program) [BT302.M62] 62-1009
1. Jesus Christ—Biog.— Juvenile literature. I. Title.

RADIUS, Marianne 232.9 (J)
Catherine (Vos)
God with us; a life of Jesus for young readers, by Marianne Radius. Linoleum cuts by Frederick J. Ashby. Grand Rapids, Eerdmans Pub. Co. [1966] 286 p. illus., col. map (on lining papers) 24 cm. [BT302.R13] 66-28496
1. Jesus Christ—Biography—Juvenile literature. I. Title.

SEBOLDT, Roland H. A. 232.9 (J)
God's son on earth. [Text by Roland Seboldt. Illus. by Marianne Bellenhaus. St. Louis, Concordia Pub. House, 1968] 1 v. (unpaged) col. illus. 23 x 30 cm. Cover title. Translation and adaptation of Gottes Sohn auf Erden by Eleanore Beck and Gabrielle Miller. [BT302.S29] 68-13366
1. Jesus Christ—Biography—Juvenile literature. I. Bellenhaus, Marianne, illus. II. Beck, Eleanore. Gottes Sohn auf Erden. III. Title.

SEVENTH DAY ADVENTISTS. 232.9
GENERAL CONFERENCE. DEPT. OF EDUCATION.
Day by day with Jesus; Bible stories for grades 5 and 6. Illustrated by Helen Torrey. [Teacher's ed.] Mountain View, Calif., Mountain View Pub. Assn. [1951] 269, 319 p. illus. (part col.) maps. 21 cm. "Series IIIa, even year." The main work, also issued separately, is preceded by "Teacher's guide and key for Day by day with Jesus," with special t.p. [BT302.S45 1951a] 51-8861
1. Jesus Christ — Biog. — Juvenile literature. 2. Jesus Christ — Biog. — Study. I. Title.

A Son is given. 232.9'01
Edited by Virginia Sutch. Based on God so loved the world by Adeline Hill Ostwalt. [Atlanta, John Knox Press [1974] 127 p. col. illus. 21 cm. A record of the significant events in the life of Christ as noted in the writings of Luke. [BT302.S64 1974] 73-9599 ISBN 0-8042-9507-7
1. Jesus Christ—Biography—Juvenile literature. I. Sutch, Virginia, ed. II. Ostwalt, Adeline Hill. God so loved the world.
BIP

VAN VECHTEN, Schuyler, 232.9'01
comp.
The Bethlehem star; children's newspaper reports of the life of Jesus. Created by Schuyler Van Vechten, Jr., and fifty-two children. New York, Walker [1972] [60] p. 27 cm. Reconstructs the events of Jesus' life in the form of newspaper reports, editorials, letters, and advertisements. [BT302.V36 1972] 70-183923 ISBN 0-8027-6097-X 4.95
1. Jesus Christ—Biography—Juvenile literature. I. Title.
BIP

VILLIERS, Marjorie 232.9'01
Howard, 1903-
Jesus has come / with text by Marjorie Villiers, based on the French original by Martine Douillet and Genevieve Guilhem ; illustrated by Philippe Joudiou. Valley Forge, Pa. : Judson Press, 1978, c1973. [28] p. : col. ill. ; 21 cm. Based on M. Douillet's Jesus est venu. Relates the birth and early life of Jesus Christ. [BT302.V63] 78-105555 ISBN 0-8170-0810-1 : 2.75
1. Jesus Christ—Biography—Juvenile literature. 2. Christian biography—Palestine—Juvenile literature. I. Douillet, Martine. Jesus est venu. II. Joudiou, Philippe. III. Title.

VILLIERS, Marjorie 232.9'01
Howard, 1903-
Jesus with us / with text by Marjorie Villiers ; illustrated by Philippe Joudiou ; based on the French original by Martine Douillet and Genevieve Guilhem. Valley Forge, Pa. : Judson Press, 1978, c1973. [28] p. : col. ill. ; 21 cm. Based on M. Douillet's Jesus avec nous. Describes the adult life of Jesus through His Crucifixion and Resurrection. [BT302.V64] 78-105560 pbk : 2.75
1. Jesus Christ—Biography—Juvenile literature. 2. Christian biography—Palestine—Juvenile literature. I. Douillet, Martine. Jesus avec nous. II. Joudiou, Philippe. III. Title.

Jesus Christ—Biography—Meditations.

GLICKMAN, S. Craig. 248'.4
Knowing Christ / S. Craig Glickman. Chicago : Moody Press, c1980. p. cm. Bibliography: p. [BT306.4.G57] 79-22207 ISBN 0-8024-3502-5 pbk. : 4.95
1. Jesus Christ—Biography—Meditations. 2. Christian biography—Palestine—Meditations. 3. Christian life—Meditations. I. Title.
BIP

Jesus Christ—Biography—Miscellanea.

THURMAN, Thomas D. 232
The Jesus years : a chronological study of the life of Christ / by Thomas D. Thurman ; maps, Robert Huffman ; drawings, Romilda Dilley. Cincinnati : New Life Books, c1977. 240 p. : ill. ; 22 cm. Bibliography: p. 240. [BS2556.T48] 77-80314 ISBN 0-87239-136-1 : 5.95
1. Jesus Christ—Biography—Miscellanea. 2. Bible. N.T. Gospels—Examinations, questions, etc. 3. Christian biography—Palestine—Miscellanea. I. Title.
BIP

Jesus Christ—Biography—Passion Week.

†ODENHEIMER, 915.694'4'0430924 B
William Henry, Bp., 1817-1879.
Jerusalem and its vicinity / William H. Odenheimer. New York : Arno Press, 1977, [1854]. 218 p., [6] leaves of plates : ill. ; 21 cm. (America and the Holy Land) Reprint of the 1855 ed. published by E. H. Butler, Philadelphia. [DS109.O3 1977] 77-70728 15.00
1. Jesus Christ—Biography—Passion Week. 2. Odenheimer, William Henry, Bp., 1817-1879. 3. Jerusalem—Description. 4. Christian biography—Palestine. I. Title. II. Series.

WILKINSON, John, 1929- 933
Jerusalem as Jesus knew it : archaeology as evidence / John Wilkinson. London : Thames and Husdon, c1978. 208 p. : ill. ; 20 cm. Photo. [1] leaf inserted. Includes index. Bibliography: p. 201-203. [DS109.W7] 77-20743 ISBN 0-500-05031-7 : 8.95
1. Jesus Christ—Biography—Passion Week. 2. Jerusalem—Antiquities. 3. Christian biography—Palestine. I. Title.
Distributed by W. W Norton. **BIP**

Jesus Christ—Biography—Sermons.

BISHOP, John, 1908- 232.9'01
Seeing Jesus today; a portrait of Jesus the man. Valley Forge [Pa.] Judson Press [1973, c1969] 158 p. 20 cm. [BT306.3.B56 1973] 72-6302 ISBN 0-8170-0575-7 pap 2.50
1. Jesus Christ—Biography—Sermons. 2. Methodist Church—Sermons. 3. Sermons, American. I. Title.

Jesus Christ—Biography—Sources, Biblical.

BECK, William F. 232.9
The Christ of the Gospels; the life and work of Jesus as told by Matthew, Mark, Luke, and John, presented as one complete story in the language of today, by William F. Beck. Rev. ed. St. Louis, Concordia Pub. House [1968] 231 p. 21 cm. [BT299.2.B4 1968] 68-3591
1. Jesus Christ—Biography—Sources, Biblical. I. Title.

BIBLE. N. T. Gospels. 232.9
English. Harmonies. 1956. Revised standard.
The life of Jesus; a consecutive narrative constructed from the Revised standard version New Testament, by John E. Kaltenbach. New York, T. Nelson [1956] 159p. 21cm. [BT299.K3] 56-8840
1. Jesus Christ—Biog.— Sources, Biblical. I. Kaltenbach, John E. II. Title.

CHENEY, Johnston M. 232.9'01
The life of Christ in stereo; the four gospels combined as one, by Johnston M. Cheney. Edited by Stanley A. Ellisen. Foreword by Earl D. Radmacher. Portland, Or., Western Baptist Seminary Press [1969] xviii, 273 p. 22 cm. Bibliography: p. 266. [BT299.2.C52] 74-84672 2.95
1. Jesus Christ—Biography—Sources, Biblical. I. Ellisen, Stanley A., ed. II. Title.

DELL'ISOLA, Frank. 232.9'01 B
The good news about Jesus : the New

Testament in Today's English version / edited and rearranged in a continuous narrative by Frank Dell'Isola. 3d ed. Philadelphia : A. J. Holman Co., [1975] 335 p. ; 21 cm. [BT299.2.D43 1975] 75-4579 ISBN 0-87981-043-2 : 6.95
1. Jesus Christ—Biography—Sources, Biblical. I. Title.

TAYLOR, Kenneth Nathaniel. 232.9'01
The life of Christ; a pictorial essay from The living Bible. [Photography by Alan (Wim) Auceps] Wheaton, Ill., Tyndale House Publishers [1974] 1 v. (unpaged) col. illus. 27 cm. [BT299.2.T272 1974] 73-92956 ISBN 0-8423-2215-9
1. Jesus Christ—Biography—Sources, Biblical. I. Auceps, Alan, illus. II. Title.

WHO is this man Jesus? 232.901 : the complete life of Jesus from the living Bible. New York : Bantam Books ,1976 c1966. viii, 215 p. : ill., maps ; 18 cm. Includes index. [BT299.2] ISBN 0-553-07911-5 pbk. : 1.50
1. Jesus Christ—Biography—Sources, Biblical.

Jesus Christ—Biography—Study.

FISCHER, Michael Hadwin, 1875- 232.90076
The story of Jesus, with suggestions for further study; a text for classes in Christian training schools, by M. Hadwin Fischer ... Philadelphia, Pa., The United Lutheran publication house [c1924] 174 p. incl. front., illus. (maps) diagrs. 20 1/2 cm. "For further study" at end of each chapter. [BT307.F5] 24-5834
1. Jesus Christ — Biog. — Study. I. Title.

ISAAC, F Reid. v. 12
A life of Jesus; a course for seventh and eight grades. Boston, United Church Press [1963] 128 p. illus. 26 cm. (United Church curriculum. Junior High. Teachers. 12) Bibliography: p. 126. 65-3191
1. 1. Jesus Christ — Biog. — Study. 2. Bible. N.T. — History of contemporary events, etc. 3. Religious education of adolescents. 4. United Church of Christ — Education. I. Title. II. Series.

LOTZ, Benjamin, 1901- 232.9
Life and of Christ. Philadelphia, Muhlenberg Press [1957] 96p. illus. 18cm. [BT307.L6] 57-3245
1. Jesus Christ—Biog.—Study. I. Title.

SNYDER, Russell Dewey, 1898- 232.9
Jesus: his mission and teachings. Arthur H. Getz, editor. Philadelphia, Muhlenberg Press [1959] 142 p. illus. 20 cm. Includes bibliography. [BT307.S7] 59-499
1. Jesus Christ — Biog. — Study. I. Title.

STEEVES, Paul D. 232'.07
The character and work of Jesus Christ; a Bible study for an individual and/or a group, by Paul D. Steeves. [Chicago] Inter-varsity Press [1967] 105 p. 21 cm. Bibliographical footnotes. [BT307.S78] 67-28019
1. Jesus Christ—Biography—Study. I. Title.

STEEVES, Paul D. 232'.07
The character and work of Jesus Christ; a Bible study for an individual and/or a group, by Paul D. Steeves. [Chicago] Inter-varsity Press [1967] 105 p. 21 cm. Bibliographical footnotes. [BT307.S78] 67-28019
1. Jesus Christ—Biography—Study. I. Title.

Jesus Christ—Friends and associates.

GRIFFITH, Arthur Leonard, 1920- 225.9'22 B
Gospel characters : the personalities around Jesus / by Leonard Griffith. Grand Rapids, Mich. : Eerdmans, c1976. p. cm. [BS2430.G74 1976] 76-12412 ISBN 0-8028-1646-0 pbk. : 3.95
1. Jesus Christ—Friends and associates. 2. Bible. N.T. Gospels—Biography. I. Title. BIP

KORTREY, Walter A., 1923- 225.9'22 B
People around Jesus [by] Walter A. Kortrey. Philadelphia, United Church Press [1974] 128 p. illus. 22 cm. "A Pilgrim Press book." Bibliography: p. 113. [BS2430.K65] 74-16400 ISBN 0-8298-0288-6
1. Jesus Christ—Friends and associates. I. Title.

Jesus Christ—Friends and associates—Juvenile literature.

MARQUARDT, Mervin A. 226'4'09595
Jesus' second family : Luke 10:38-42 for children / written by Mervin A. Marquardt ; illustrated by Alice Hausner. St. Louis : Concordia Publishing House, c1976. p. cm. (Arch books, series 14) Retells in verse the story of a visit Jesus made to his close friends Mary, Martha, and Lazarus who lived in Bethany. [BS2433.M37] 76-26578 ISBN 0-570-06111-3 : 0.59
1. Jesus Christ—Friends and associates—Juvenile literature. 2. Bible. N.T.—Biography—Juvenile literature. I. Hausner, Alice, illus. II. Title.

Jesus Christ—Historicity.

BARKATULLAH, Qazi Muhammad. 232.9'08
Jesus, Son of Mary: fallacy and factuality. Philadelphia, Dorrance [1973] 127 p. 22 cm. Includes bibliographical references. [BT303.2.B276] 73-77630 ISBN 0-8059-1857-4 4.95
1. Jesus Christ—Historicity. 2. Jesus Christ—Biography—History and criticism. I. Title.

KLOOSTER, Fred H. 232.9'08
Quests for the historical Jesus / Fred H. Klooster. Grand Rapids : Baker Book House, 1977. 88 p. ; 22 cm. (Baker Biblical monograph) "Originally published as Jesus Christ: history and kerygma, in Presbyterion: covenant seminary review 1 (1975): 23-50, 80-110. Includes bibliographical references and index. [BT303.2.K48] 76-51083 ISBN 0-8010-5378-1 : 3.95
1. Jesus Christ—Historicity. 2. Jesus Christ—Biography—History and criticism. I. Title. II. Series. BIP

Jesus Christ—History of doctrines—20th century.

KROPF, Richard W., 1932- 232'.092'4
Teilhard, Scripture, and revelation : a study of Teilhard de Chardin's reinterpretation of Pauline themes / Richard W. Knopf. Rutherford : Fairleigh Dickinson University Press, c1975. p. cm. Includes index. Bibliography: p. [BS500.K76 1975] 73-20907 ISBN 0-8386-1481-7 : 18.00
1. Jesus Christ—History of doctrines—20th century. 2. Teilhard de Chardin, Pierre. 3. Bible—Criticism, interpretation, etc.—History—20th century. I. Title.

Jesus Christ—Influence.

REDDING, David A. 232.9'5
Lives He touched : the relationships of Jesus / David A. Redding. 1st ed. San Francisco : Harper & Row, c1978. 119 p. ; 21 cm. [BT304.3.R43 1978] 77-20443 ISBN 0-06-066815-6 : 5.95
1. Jesus Christ—Influence. 2. Bible. N.T.—Biography. 3. Christian biography—Palestine. I. Title. BIP

Jesus Christ—Nativity—Juvenile literature.

GRIFFITHS, Kitty Anna. 232.9'21
Come, meet Jesus, the baby : the story of Matthew 1 and Luke 1-2:20 / Kitty Ann Griffiths ; illustrated by "Willy." 1st zondervan ed. Grand Rapids, Mich. : Zondervan, 1978, c1976. 111 p. : ill. ; 21 cm. (Come, meet series) Relates the events surrounding Jesus' birth including the genealogy of Joseph, the angels' announcements to Elizabeth and to Mary, the births of John the Baptist and of Jesus, and the visit of the shepherds to the stable in Bethlehem. [BT315.2.G74 1978] 78-16703 ISBN 0-310-25241-5 pbk. : 1.95
1. Jesus Christ—Nativity—Juvenile literature. 2. Bible stories, English—N.T. Gospels. 3. Christian biography—Palestine—Juvenile literature. I. Willy. II. Title.

Jesus Christ—Person and offices.

HENGEL, Martin. 232
Was Jesus a revolutionist? Translated by William Klassen. Philadelphia, Fortress Press [1971] xviii, 46 p. (p. 45-46 advertisements) 19 cm. (Facet Books. Biblical series, 28) Translation of War Jesus Recolutionar? Includes bibliographical references. [BT202.H4313] 77-157545 ISBN 0-8006-3066-1 1.00
1. Jesus Christ—Person and offices. 2. Revolution (Theology) I. Title. BIP

PIKE, Diane Kennedy. 232
The wilderness revolt; a new view of the life and death of Jesus based on ideas and notes of the late Bishop James A. Pike [by] Diane Kennedy Pike and R. Scott Kennedy. [1st ed.] Garden City, N.Y., Doubleday, 1972. xxxiii, 385 p. 22 cm. "Quotations from Bishop James A. Pike ... are excerpted and edited from transcripts of a seminar on Christian Origins given in May of 1969 for the Esalen Institute in San Francisco." Bibliography: p. [365]-375. [BT202.P53] 72-171311 7.95
1. Jesus Christ—Person and offices. 2. Qumran community. I. Kennedy, R. Scott, joint author. II. Pike, James Albert, Bp., 1913-1969. III. Title.

SHEED, Francis Joseph, 1897- 232
What difference does Jesus make? [By] F. J. Sheed. New York, Sheed and Ward [1971] xi, 242 p. 21 cm. [BT202.S5] 76-162382 ISBN 0-8362-1329-7 6.00
1. Jesus Christ—Person and offices. I. Title.

SOBRINO, Jon. 232
Christology at the crossroads : a Latin American approach / Jon Sobrino ; translated by John Drury. Maryknoll, N.Y. : Orbis Books, c1978. xxvi, 432 p. ; 21 cm. Translation of Cristologia desde America Latina. Includes bibliographical references and index. [BT202.S6213] 77-25025 ISBN 0-88344-076-8 pbk. : 12.95
1. Jesus Christ—Person and offices. 2. Liberation theology. I. Title. BIP

TROCME, Etienne. 232
Jesus as seen by his contemporaries. Philadelphia, Westminster Press [1973] x, 134 p. 22 cm. Translation of Jesus de Nazareth vu par les temoins de sa vie. Includes bibliographical references. [BT202.T7513] 72-10239 ISBN 0-664-20968-8 4.95
1. Jesus Christ—Person and offices. 2. Jesus Christ—Biography—History and criticism. I. Title.

Jesus Christ—Poetry.

JANEWAY, James, 1636?-1674. 248'.82
A token for children / James Janeway ; with a preface for the Garland ed. by Robert Miller. The Holy Bible in verse / Benjamin Harris. The history of the Holy Jesus. The school of good manners / Eleazar Moody. The prodigal daughter / with a preface for the Garland ed. by Elizabeth Williams. New York : Garland Pub., 1977. p. cm. (Classics of children's literature, 1621-1932) Reprint of 5 works published 1676-1771. Includes bibliographies. [BR1714.J3 1977] 75-32134 ISBN 0-8240-2251-3 lib.bdg. : 27.00
1. Jesus Christ—Poetry. 2. Children—Biography. 3. Children—Religious life. 4. Children—Conduct of life. 5. Theology, Puritan. I. Title. II. Series.

Jesus Christ—Spiritualistic interpretations.

CAYCE, Edgar, 1877-1945. 133.8'092'4 S
The early Christian epoch / compiled by the Readings Research Department. Virginia Beach, Va. : Association for Research and Enlightenment, c1976. xi, 593 p. : port. ; 24 cm. (The Edgar Cayce readings ; v. 6) Includes index. [BF1023.C37 vol. 6] [BT304.96] 232 77-153480 ISBN 0-87604-089-X
1. Jesus Christ—Spiritualistic interpretations. 2. Jesus Christ—Biography—Miscellanea. 3. Christian biography—Palestine—Miscellanea. 4. Church history—Primitive and early church, ca. 30-600—Miscellanea. I. Title.

Jesus Christ—Teaching.

HUNTER, Archibald Macbride. 232
The work and words of Jesus, by Archibald M. Hunter. Rev. ed. Philadelphia, Westminster Press [1973] 230 p. 22 cm. Includes bibliographical references. [BS2415.H77 1973] 73-7559 ISBN 0-664-24976-0 3.50 (pbk.)
1. Jesus Christ—Teaching. 2. Jesus Christ—Person and offices. I. Title. BIP

Jesus Crist—Biography.

BERNARD, Pierre Rogatien, 1888- v. 12
The mystery of Jesus. Staten Island, N. Y., Alba House, 1966. 2 v. 24 cm. 68-28633
1. Jesus Christ—Biography. I. Title.

DANIEL-ROPS, Henry, 1901- 232.901
The life of our Lord [by] Henri Daniel-Rops. Translated from the French by J. R. Foster. Illus. by Charles Keeping. [Deluxe illustrated ed.] New York, Hawthorn Books [1965] 191 p. col. illus., maps. 24 cm. Translation of Histoire du Christ-Jesus. [BT301.2.D313 1965] 65-14642
1. Jesus Christ — Biog. I. Keeping, Charles, illus. II Title.

DANIEL-ROPS, Henry, 1901- 232.9
The life of our Lord, by Henri Daniel-Rops. Translated from the French by J. R. Foster. [1st ed.] New York, Hawthorn Books [1964] 175 p. maps 22 cm. (The Twentieth century encyclopedia of Catholicism, v. 68. Section 6: The word of God.) Translation of Histoire du Christ-Jesus. Bibliography: p. [174]-175. [BT301.2D313] 64-25385
1. Jesus Christ — Biog I. Title. II. Series. III. Series: The twentieth century encyclopedia of Catholicism, v. 68

FARRAR, Frederic William, 1831-1903. v. 12
The life of Christ. Illus. by Gustave Dore and others. Portland, Oregon, Fountain Publications, 1960. 744 p. illus. 23 cm. (A Fountain publication) 65-53155
1. 1. Jesus Christ — Biog. I. Title.

FOSTER, Rupert Clinton, 1888- 220.9'2
Studies in life of Christ [2v. in 1. 3d. ed] Grand Rapids, mich, Baker [1966] (2v.ln1) 505 p. illus. 23 cm Contents.An introduction to the life of christ and studies in the life of Christ. [bt301.f6] 232 5.95
1. 1. Jesus-biog. title I. Title.

FOSTER, Rupert Clinton, 1888- v. 12
Studies in the life of Christ, by R. C. Foster. [3rd ed.] Grand Rapids, Mich., Baker Book House [1966- v. illus. 23 cm. Vol. 1 is a rev. version of the first 2 vols. of the author's Studies in the life of Christ, published in 1938. Contents.Contents -- [1] Introduction and early ministry. 67-96216
1. Jesus Christ — Biog. 2. Jesus Christ — Biog. — Sources. 3. Bible. N.T. Gospels — Criticism, interpretation, etc. I. Title. BIP

GOGUEL, Maurice, 1880- v. 12
Jesus and the origins of Christianity. New York, Macmillan, 1933-1964. 3 v. Each vol. has special t.p. Translated from the French trilogy: Jesus et les origines du christianisme. Contents.Contents.-[v. 1] The life of Jesus. Trans. by Olive Wyon. 1933.-[v. 2] The birth of Christianity. Trans. by H. C. Snape. 1953.-[v. 3] The primitive church. Trans. by H. C. Snape. 1964. Bibliography: v. 1, p. [33]-35; v. 2, p. xiii-svi; v. 3, p. 587-590. 67-101449
1. Jesus Christ — Biog. 2. Church history — Primitive and early church. 3. Christianity — Early church. I. Title. II. Title: London, III. Title: The life of Jesus. IV. Title: The Birth of Christianity. V. Title: The primitive church.

GOGUEL, Maurice, 1880- v. 12
The life of Jesus: by Olive Wyon. tr. by Olive Wyon. New York, Barnes & Noble [1958] [7]-591 p. 23 cm. Imprint from label pasted on t.p. Original title: La vie de Jesus. "Bibliographical notes": p. [33]-35. 64-25391
1. Jesus Christ. Biog. I. Title.

HEINEMANN, Thea. 232.9
Stories of Jesus. Illustrated by Don Bolognese. Designed by Walter Brooks. Racine, Wis., Whitman Pub. Division, Western Pub. Co. [1968] 223 p. col. illus. 27 cm. (The Whitman library of giant books) Retellings of fifty Bible stories about Jesus from the time of His birth to His ascension. [BT302.H44 1968] AC 68
1. Jesus Crist—Biography. I. Bolognese, Don, illus. II. Title.

MARY Eleanor, Mother, 1903- 232.9
Jesus. son of David. Illustrated by George Pollard. Milwaukee, Bruce Pub. Co. [1955] 224p. illus. 23cm. [BT301.M278] 55-7864
1. Jesus Christ—Biog. I. Title.

MESCHLER, Moritz, 1830-1912. 232.9
The life of Our Lord Jesus Christ in meditations. translated by Sister Mary Margaret. 5th [i.e. 8th] ed. St. Louis, Herder, 1950. 2 v. maps, plan. 22 cm. [BT301.M53] 50-1304
1. Jesus Christ — Biog. I. Title.

MORGAN, Richard. 232.9
The Christ of the Cross; dare Christians follow him. New York, R. R. Smith, 1950. 285 p. 24 cm. [BT301.M73] 50-11109
1. Jesus Christ — Biog. 2. Christianity — 20th cent. I. Title.

SAUNDERSON, Henry Hallam, 1871- 232.9
His Word was with power. Boston, Beacon Press [1952] 248 p. 22 cm. [BT301.S336] 52-7867
1. Jesus Christ — Biog. I. Title.

TALMAGE, James Edward, 1862-1933. v. 12
Jesus the Christ; a study of the Messiah and His mission according to Holy Scriptures both ancient and modern. Published by the church. 35th ed. Salt Lake City, Deseret Book Co., 1963. 804 p. 20 cm. 66-65258
1. Jesus Christ-Biog. 2. Mormons and Mormonism-Doctrinal and controversial works. I. Title.

Jevons, William Stanley, 1835-1882.

JEVONS, William Stanley, 1835-1882. 330'.08 S
Correspondence, 1850-1862. Edited by R. D. Collison Black Clifton [N.J.] A. M. Kelley, 1973. xviii, 462 p. illus. 25 cm. (Papers and correspondence of William Stanley Jevons, v. 2) (Series: Jevons, William Stanley, 1835-1882. Papers and correspondence of William Stanley Jevons, v. 2.) Includes bibliographical references. [HB103.J5A4 1972, vol. 2] 330'.08 73-157947 ISBN 0-678-07012-1 30.00
1. Jevons, William Stanley, 1835-1882. 2. Economists—Correspondence, reminiscences, etc. I. Series.
2 volume set 55.00.

Jewelers—United States—Biography.

WHO'S who in the jewelry industry / edited by Donald S. McNeil ; project coordinator, Louise Cupelli. Radnor, Pa. : Jewelers' Circular-Keystone, 1980. p. cm. [HD9747.U52W47] 79-27501 ISBN 0-931744-02-4 : 54.95 338.4'773927'0922 B
1. Jewelers—United States—Biography. 2. Clock and watch makers—United States—Biography. 3. Jewelry trade—United States. I. McNeil, Donald S., 1908- BIP

Jewett, Charles Coffin, 1816-1868.

BOROME, Joseph Alfred, 1919- 020'.92'4
Charles Coffin Jewett, by Joseph A. Borome. Boston, Gregg Press, 1972 [c1951] 188 p. port. 23 cm. (The Library reference series. Library history and biography) Reprint of the ed. published by American Library Association, Chicago, which was issued as no. 7 of American library pioneers. Includes bibliographical references. [Z720.J59B6 1972] 72-10123 ISBN 0-8398-0194-7
1. Jewett, Charles Coffin, 1816-1868. I. Series: Library history and biography. II. Series: American library pioneers, 7.

JEWETT, Charles Coffin, 1816-1868. 020'.92'4 B
The age of Jewett : Charles Coffin Jewett and American librarianship, 1841-1868 / edited by Michael H. Harris. Littleton, Colo. : Libraries Unlimited, 1975. x, 166 p. ; 24 cm. (The Heritage of librarianship series ; no. 1) Includes index. Bibliography: p. [157]-163. [Z731.J58 1975] 75-14205 ISBN 0-87287-113-4 : 11.50
1. Jewett, Charles Coffin, 1816-1868. 2. Libraries—United States—History—Sources. I. Harris, Michael H. II. Title. III. Title: Charles Coffin Jewett and American librarianship, 1841-1868. IV. Series. BIP

Jewett, Sarah Orne,

JEWETT, Sarah Orne, 1849-1909. 928.1
Letters, edited with an introd. and notes by Richard Cary. Waterville, Me., Colby College Press, 1956. 117p. illus., port., geneal. table. 26cm. 'Books by Sarah Orne Jewett': p. [16] Bibliographical footnotes. [PS2133.A3 1956] 57-181
I. Cary, Richard, 1909- ed. II. Title.

JEWETT, Sarah Orne, 1849-1909. 928.1
Letters, edited with an introd. and notes by Richard Cary. Waterville, Me., Colby College Press, 1956. 117p. illus., port., geneal. table. 26cm. 'Books by Sarah Orne Jewett': p. [16] Bibliographical footnotes. [PS2133.A3 1956] 57-181
I. Cary, Richard, 1909- ed. II. Title.

MATTHIESSEN, Francis Otto, 1902- 928.1
Sarah Orne Jewett. Gloucester, Mass., P. Smith, 1965, [c.1929] 159p. illus., ports. 21cm. First pub in 1929 by Houghton [PS2133.M3] 4.00
1. Jewett, Sarah Orne, I. Title. BIP

Jewish children.

TORDAY, Ursula. 301.451924
The children [by] Charity Blackstock. [1st ed.] Boston, Little, Brown [1966] 240 p. 21 cm. [HV640.5.J4T6] 66-20801
1. Jewish children. 2. Refugees, Jewish. I. Title.

Jewish Defense League.

KAHANE, Meir. 322.4'4'0973
The story of the Jewish Defense League / Meir Kahane. 1st ed. Radnor, Pa. : Chilton Book Co., [1975] x, 338 p. 22 cm. Includes index. [E184.J5K1165 1975] 75-5501 ISBN 0-8019-6247-1 : 7.95
1. Jewish Defense League. 2. Kahane, Meir. 3. Jews in the United States—Politics and government. I. Title.

Jewitt, John Rodgers, 1783-1821.

JEWITT, John Rodgers, 1783-1821. 970'.004'97 B
Narrative of the adventures and sufferings of John R. Jewitt : while held as a captive of the Nootka Indians of Vancouver Island, 1803 to 1805 / edited and annotated by Robert F. Heizer. Ramona, Calif. : Ballena Press, 1975. x, 111 p., [4] leaves of plates : ill. ; 28 cm. (Ballena Press publications in archaeology, ethnology, and history ; no. 5) "Written by Richard Alsop ... who interviewed Jewitt." Originally published in 1820 by T. Tegg, London. Bibliography: p. 107-111. [E99.N85J48 1975] 76-352099 ISBN 0-87919-050-7 pbk. : 4.95
1. Jewitt, John Rodgers, 1783-1821. 2. Indians of North America—Captivities. 3. Nootka Indians—Captivities. I. Alsop, Richard, 1761-1815. II. Title.

Jews as soldiers.

GUMPERTZ, Sydney Gustave, 1879- 929'.373
The Jewish legion of valor; the story of Americans of Jewish faith who distinguished themselves in the armed forces in all the wars of the Republic, and a general history of the military exploits of the Jews through the ages. New York, 1946. 449 p. illus., ports. 24 cm. Bibliographical footnotes. [E184.J5G8] 64-29718
1. Jews as soldiers. 2. Jews in the U.S. 3. U.S. Army — Medals, badges, decorations, etc. 4. U.S. Navy — Medals, badges, decorations, etc. I. Title.

RIBALOW, Harold Uriel, 1919- comp. 355.3'0922
Fighting heroes of Israel. Ed. by Harold U. Ribalow, New York, New Amer. Lib. [1967] x, 240p. ports. 18cm. (Signet bks.) [DS119.R5] 67-8835 .75 pap.,
1. Jews as soliders. 2. Israel—2. Israel—Biog. I. Title.

Jews—Bibliography.

ADLER, Bill, comp. 910.03'174'924
Growing up Jewish. Edited by Jay David. New York, W. Morrow, 1969. x, 341 p. 22 cm. [DS115.A3] 76-5084 7.50
1. Jews—Bibliography. 2. Youth, Jewish. I. Title.

Jews—Biography.

B'NAI B'rith. Dept. of Adult Jewish Education. 296'.0922
Molders of the Jewish mind. Washington [1966] viii, 245 p. 22 cm. "A B'nai B'rith book." Bibliography: p. [239]-240. [BM750.B55] 66-27649
1. Jews—Biography. I. Title.

BOLITHO, Hector. 1898-ed. 920'.009174'924
Twelve Jews. ed. by Hector Bolitho. Freeport, N.Y., Bks. for Libs. [1967] 288p. ports. 22cm. (Essay index reprint ser.) First pub. u934. [DS135.E9A12 1967] 67-23179 8.75
1. Jews—Biog. I. Title.
Contents omitted.

DAVIS, Mac, 1905- 922.96
Jews at a glance. Illustrated by Sam Nisenson. New York, Hebrew Pub. Co. [1956] 127p. illus. 27cm. [DS115.D32] 57-18547
1. Jews—Biog. I. Title.

GOLDSMITH, S. J. 920.05693
Twenty 20th century Jews. Drawings by Juliet Pannett. New York, Shengold [c.1962] 142p. illus. 24cm. 62-21948 4.50
1. Jews—Biog. I. Title.

GOLDSMITH, Samuel Joseph, 1914- 920.05693
Twenty 20th century Jews. Drawings by Juliet Pannett. New York. Shengold Publishers [1962] 142 p. illus. 24 cm. [DS125.3.A2G6] 62-21948
1. Jews-Blog. I. Title.

GOLDSMITH, Samuel Joseph, 1914- 920.009'174'924
Twenty 20th century Jews, by S.J. Goldsmith. Drawings by Juliet Pannett. Freeport, N.Y., Books for Libraries Press [1969, c1962] 142 p. ports. 23 cm. (Biography index reprint series) [DS125.3.A2G6 1969] 70-101827 ISBN 0-8369-8000-X
1. Jews—Biography. I. Title.

GREENBERG, Martin Harry. 920'.0092'924
The Jewish lists : physicists and generals, actors and writers, and hundreds of other lists of accomplished Jews / Martin H. Greenberg. New York : Schocken Books, 1979. p. cm. Includes indexes. [DS115.G67] 79-14349 ISBN 0-8052-3711-9 : 10.95
1. Jews—Biography. I. Title.

GRUNFELD, Frederic V. 943'.004'924 B
Prophets without honour : a background to Freud, Kafka, Einstein, and their world / Frederic V.Grunfeld. 1st ed. New York : Holt, Rinehart and Winston, c1979. xiii, 349 p., [6] leaves of plates : ill. ; 24 cm. Includes index. Bibliography: p. 323-334. [DS135.G33G8] 78-31645 ISBN 0-03-017871-1 : 15.00
1. Jews—Biography. 2. Jews in Germany—Intellectual life. 3. Jews in Austria—Intellecutal life. 4. Germany—Civilization—Jewish influences. 5. Austria—Civilization—Jewish influences. I. Title.

GUARDIANS of our heritage (1724-1953) New York, Bloch, 1958. viii, 728p. (Jewish library. 7) Bibliographical footnotes. v. 12
1. Jews—Biog. I. Jung, Leo, 1892- ed. II. Series.

THE Israel honorarium. 920
[Jerusalem, Israeli Pub. Institute; New York, Educational Pub. Institute, 1968] 5 v. (895 p.) illus., facsims., maps, ports. 29 cm. Cover title: The American Israel honorarium. Contents.--v. 1. One hundred and twenty famous Jews. Famous Jews in the history of the U. S. Jewish organizations in the U. S.--v. 2-5. The biographical section of American Jewry. [E184.J5I85] 68-24276
1. Jews—Biog. 2. Jews in the U. S.—Biog. I. Title: The American Israel honorarium.

JUDAIC Heritage Society. 956.94
An epic in sculpture : the medallic history of the Jewish people / conceived and directed by Robert Weber : text by Fred Bertram ; [photography, Alastair Finlay]. New York : Judaic Heritage Society, 1974. 179 p. : ill. ; 29 cm. Bibliography: p. 178-179. [CJ5793.J4J82 1974] 75-308832
1. Jews—Biography. 2. Medals, Jewish. I. Weber, Robert, 1927- II. Bertram, Fred. III. Title. IV. Title: The medallic history of the Jewish people.

JUDISCHER Plutarch : oder, Biographisches Lexicon der markantesten Manner und Frauen judischer Abkunft / hrsg. von Franz Graffer u. Simon Deutsch. Nachdr. d. Ausg. Wien 1848. Hildesheim ; New York : Olms, 1975. 2 v. in 1 : ill. ; 15 cm. Reprint of the ed. published by U. Klopf und A. Eurich. [DS115.J82 1975] 76-456162 ISBN 3-487-05631-3 : DM78.00 943.8'07'2024
1. Jews—Biography. I. Graffer, Franz, 1785-1852. II. Deutsch, Simon, 1822-1877. III. Title: Biographisches Lexicon der markantesten Manner und Frauen judischer Abkunft.

KAGAN, Henry Enoch 920.05693
Six who changed the world: Moses, Jesus, Paul, Marx, Freud, Einstein. New York, Yoseloff [c.1963] 278p. 22cm. 63-18249 6.00
1. Jews—Biog. I. Title.

MAGNUS, Katie (Emanuel) Lady, 1844-1924. 920'.0092'924
Jewish portraits. Freeport, N.Y., Books for Libraries Press [1972] 215 p. front. 22 cm. (Essay index reprint series) Reprint of the 1888 ed. Contents.Contents.—Jehudah Halevi.—The story of a street.—Heinrich Heine.—Daniel Deronda and his Jewish critics.—Manasseh ben Israel.—Charity in Talmudic times.—Moses Mendelssohn. [DS115.M18 1972] 72-3396 ISBN 0-8369-2912-8
1. Jews—Biography. 2. Jews—Charities. I. Title. BIP

MILGRIM, Shirley (Gorson) 920.05693
Stories of courage; [Ben Gurion, Freud, Brandeis, Einstein, Haym Salomon] Philadelphia, Mercury Bks., 1512 Walnut St. [c.1962] 253p. 18cm. (Mod. biog. ser., MB-103) 62-5025 .75 pap.,
1. Jews—Biog. I. Title.

NOVECK, Simon, ed. 922.96
Great Jewish personalities in ancient and medieval times. New York, Farrar, Straus and Cudahy [1959] xvi, 351p. 25cm. (The B'nal B'rith great books series [v.1]) Includes bibliographies. [BM750.N67] 59-13182
1. Jews—Biog. I. Title. BIP

NOVECK, Simon, ed. v. 12
Great Jewish personalities in ancient and medieval times. [Washington] B'nai B'rith Department of Adult Jewish Education [1962] xvi, 351 p. 25 cm. (The B'nai B'rith great books series [v. 1]) Includes bibliographies. 65-232252
1. Jews — Biog. I. Title.

NOVECK, Simon, ed. 920.05693
Great Jewish personalities in modern times. [Washington, B'nai B'rith, Dept. of Adult Jewish Education, c.1960] [dist. New York, Taplinger] xiii, 366p. 25cm. (B'nai B'rith great books series [v.2]) Bibl; Bibl. notes.: p.[345]-351. 60-16480 4.95 half cloth.
1. Jews—Biog. I. Title. II. Series.

RAISIN, Max, 1881- 922.96
Great Jews I have known; a gallery of portraits. New York, Philosophical Library [1952] 249 p. 21 cm. [DS125.3.A2R3] 52-9421
1. Jews — Biog. I. Title.

RAISIN, Max, 1881-1957. 920'.009174'924
Great Jews I have known; a gallery of portraits. Freeport, N.Y., Books for Libraries Press [1970, c1952] xiii, 249 p. 23 cm. (Biography index reprint series) [DS125.3.A2R3 1970] 71-117331 ISBN 0-8369-8023-9
1. Jews—Biography. I. Title.

RUBINSTEIN, Zvee Hirsh, 1889-1943. 922.96
The Schapiros, a page of Jewish history. [Translated by David Berger] New York, 1950. 101 p. ports. 20 cm. Appeared originally in Yiddish in serial form in "The Day" from June 28 to Aug. 2, 1924. [DS115.R8] 52-43674
1. Jews — Biog. I. Title.

ST. JOHN, Robert, 1902- 922.96
Tongue of the prophets; the life story of Eliezer Ben Yehuda. [1st ed.] Garden City, N. Y., Doubleday, 1952. 377 p. 22 cm. [DS151.B4S3] 52-5233
I. Ben-Yehudah, Eliezer, 1858-1922. II. Title.

SAUL, Shura. 920.073
The right to be different; [twenty-one sketches of those who sought a better world] Designed and illustrated by Peggy Lipschutz. Edited by Elias Picheny..Published by the friends of the family of Lionel Picheny. in the Midwest Section, National Jewish Welfare Board. [n. p.] 1961. 128p. illus. 27cm. [DS115.S3] 61-14074
1. Jews—Biog. 2. U. S.—Biog. I. Title.

SCHWARZ, Leo Walder, 1906- , ed. 920.02
Memoirs of my people; Jewish self-portraits from the 11th to the 20th centuries. New York, Schocken [1963,c.1943] 306p. 21cm. (SB51) First pub. in 1943 under title: Memoirs of my people through a thousand years. 63-11042 1.95 pap.,
1. Jews—Biog. I. Title.

WHO'S who in world 922.96
Jewry. 1955- New York. v. 28cm. Editors: 1955- H. Schnelderman and I. J. Carmin. [DS125.3.A2W5] 54-12036
1. Jews—Biog. I. Schneiderman, Harry, 1885- ed. II. Karpman, Itzhak J., ed.

WHO'S who in world 920.05693
Jewry; a biographical dictionary of outstanding Jews, 1965. Harry Schneiderman, I. J. Carmin Karpman, eds. Esther G. Karpman, managing ed. dist. New York, McKay [c.1965] xxxii, 1087p. 28cm. [DS125.3.A2W5] 54-12036 37.50
1. Jews—Biog. I. Schneiderman, Harry, 1885- ed. II. Karpman, Itzhak J. Carmin, ed.

Jews—Biography—Dictionaries.

COMAY, Joan. 920'.0092'924
Who's who in Jewish history; after the period of the Old Testament. [1st American ed.] New York, D. McKay Co. [1974] 448 p. illus. 26 cm. [DS115.C6 1974] 73-93915 ISBN 0-679-50455-9 16.95
1. Jews—Biography—Dictionaries. 2. Jews—Dictionaries and encyclopedias. I. Title.

Jews—Biography—Juvenile literature.

GROSS, David C., 1923- 920'.0092'924
Pride of our people : the stories of one hundred outstanding Jewish men and women / David C. Gross ; ports. by William D. Bramhall, Jr. 1st ed. Garden City, N.Y. : Doubleday, 1979. xviii, 424 p. : ill. ; 24 cm. Includes index. Includes biographies and portraits of notable Jewish men and women, some famous, others unknown, in both ancient and modern times. [DS115.G7] 920 77-25592 ISBN 0-385-13573-4 : 14.00
1. Jews—Biography—Juvenile literature. I. Bramhall, William D. II. Title. BIP

GUMBINER, Joseph Henry, 1906- j920
Leaders of our people. Illustrated by David Stone. New York, Union of American Hebrew Congregations [1963- v. illus. 23 cm. (Commission on Jewish Education of the Union of American Hebrew Congregations and Central Conference of American Rabbis. Union graded series) [BM750.G77] 62-22382
1. Jews — Biog. — Juvenile literature. 2. Judaism — Juvenile literature. I. Title. II. Series. BIP

KAMM, Josephine. 922.96
Leaders of the people. London, New York, Abelard-Schuman [1960, c1959] 208 p. 21 cm. [DS115.K32] 59-11276
1. Jews—Biography—Juvenile literature. I. Title.

LUCHS, Alvin Schanfarber, 1897-1949 910'.03'924
Torchbearers of the Middle Ages. Illustrated by Stanley Maxwell. Freeport, N.Y., Books for Libraries Press [1971, c1948] x, 176 p. illus. 23 cm. (Biography index reprint series) Outlines the contributions of important Jews of the Middle Ages. Includes Anan Ben David, Chasdai Ibn Shaprut, Gershom Ben Judah, and Solomon Ibn Gabirol. [BM750.L82 1971] 920 77-160924 ISBN 0-8369-8087-5
1. Jews—Biography—Juvenile literature. I. Maxwell, Stanley, illus. II. Title. BIP

Jews—Genealogy.

ROSENSTEIN, Neil, 1944- 929'.2'09174924
The unbroken chain : biographical sketches and the genealogy of illustrious Jewish families from the 15th-20th century / by Neil Rosenstein. New York : Shengold Publishers, c1976. xii, 716 p. : ill. ; 25 cm. Includes bibliographical references and index. [CS432.J4R67] 77-357470 ISBN 0-88400-043-5 : 17.50
1. Jews—Genealogy. 2. Katzenellenbogen family. I. Title.

Jews in Chicago—Biography.

BERKOW, Ira. 977.3'11'004924 B
Maxwell Street : survival in a bazaar / Ira Berkow ; special photos. by Walter Iooss, Jr. 1st ed. Garden City, N.Y. : Doubleday, 1977. xiv, 532 p., [28] leaves of plates : ill. ; 22 cm. Includes bibliographical references. [F548.9.J5B47] 76-42060 ISBN 0-385-06723-2 : 14.50
1. Jews in Chicago—Biography. 2. Chicago—Biography. 3. Chicago—Streets—Maxwell Street. I. Title. BIP

Jews in Germany.

STANLEY, Ilse (Davidsohn) 927.92
The unforgotten. [Boston] Beacon Press, 1957] 375 p. 22 cm. Autobiography. [PN2658.S75A3] 57-6527
1. Jews in Germany. I. Title.

Jews in Germany—Hist.—1096-1800.

HAMELN, Gluckel of, 1646-1724 922.96
The life of Gluckel of Hamelin, 1646-1724, written by herself. Tr. from theorig. Yiddish, ed. by Beth-Zion Abrahams. New York, Yoseloff [1963, c.1962] 190p. illus. 23cm. 63-1721 5.95
1. Jews in Germany—Hist.—1096-1800. I. Abrahams, Beth-Zion, ed. and tr. II. Title.

Jews in Great Britain—Biography.

BERMANT, Chaim 301.45'19'24042 B I.
The cousinhood [by] Chaim Bermant. [1st American ed.] New York, Macmillan [1972, c1971] xii, 466 p. illus. 24 cm. Includes bibliographical references. [DS135.E6A117 1972] 70-103682
1. Jews in Great Britain—Biography. I. Title. BIP

Jews in New York (City)

ROSKOLENKO, Harry. 917.471'06'924
The time that was then; the Lower East Side, 1900-1914, an intimate chronicle. New York, Dial Press, 1971. 218 p. map (on lining papers), plates, ports. 24 cm. [F128.9.J5R6] 76-131180 8.95
1. Jews in New York (City) I. Title.

Jews in Russia—Biography.

JEWISH 301.45'19'24073
grandmothers / Sydelle Kramer and Jenny Masur, editors. Boston : Beacon Press, [1976] p. cm. Contents.Contents.—Introduction: Breaking stereotypes.—Why they came to America: Shapiro, F. The rebel. Rothman, S. The watchmaker. Soskin, R. The hungry child.—How they came' the passage to America: Moscowitz, P. The child immigrant. Govsky, K. Getting here the hard way.—How they fared: Sharrow, A. The radical in exile.—Linker, M. The mother in the community. Pollock, B. The American par excellence. Richter, I. The entrepreneur/raconteur. Katz, R. The loneliness of old age.—Afterword: For the record.—Background notes on customs and events. [DS135.R95A13] 75-5292 ISBN 0-8070-5420-8 : 7.95
1. Jews in Russia—Biography. 2. Jews in Russia—Social conditions. 3. Jews in Chicago—Biography. 4. Jews in Chicago—Social conditions. 5. Women, Jewish. 6. Russia—Social conditions. 7. Chicago—Social conditions. I. Kramer, Sydelle. II. Masur, Jenny. BIP

SOVIET Jews : 323.1'19'24047
our motherland is the U.S.S.R. Moscow : Novosti Press Agency, c1976. 42 p. ; 21 cm. [DS135.R95A17] 77-372454
1. Jews in Russia—Biography. 2. Israel—Emigration and immigration. 3. Russia—Emigration and immigration.

Jews in Russia—Persecutions.

MATZ, Judith. 323.1'19'24047
Separated Soviet families : a collection of case histories / written and edited by Judith Matz, Margery Sanford ; coordinated by Tina Freiman, Myriam Wolf ; chief translator, Irving Dalin. Miami, Fla. : South Florida Conference on Soviet Jewry, 1976. 147 p. : ports. ; 29 cm. [DS135.R92M35] 76-26829
1. Jews in Russia—Persecutions. 2. Jews in Russia—Biography. 3. Russia—Emigration and immigration. I. Sanford, Margery, joint author. II. Title.

Jews in South Africa—Biography.

BERGER, N. 968'.004'924 B
Jewish trails through Southern Africa : a documentary / by Nathan Berger. Johannesburg : Kayor, 1976. ix, [1], 196 p. : ill. ; 22 cm. Bibliography: 11th prelim. page. [DS135.S63A13] 77-366355
1. Jews in South Africa—Biography. 2. South Africa—Biography. I. Title.

Jews in Texas—Biography.

INSTITUTE of Texan Cultures. 976.4'004'924
The Jewish Texans. [San Antonio] : University of Texas at San Antonio, Institute of Texan Cultures, [1974] 32 p. : ill. ; 22 x 28 cm. (The Texians and the Texans) Cover title. [F395.J5I57 1974] 75-621249
1. Jews in Texas—Biography. 2. Texas—Biography. I. Title. II. Series.

Jews in the United States.

MARCUS, Jacob Rader, 1896- ed. 917.3'06'924 B
Memoirs of American Jews, 1775-1865. New York, Ktav Pub. House, 1974 [i.e. 1975, c1955] 3 v. in 2. illus. 24 cm. Reprint of the 1955-56 ed. published by the Jewish Publication Society of America, Philadelphia, in series: The Jacob R. Schiff library of Jewish contributions to American democracy. [E184.J5M233 1975] 73-16218 ISBN 0-87068-232-6
1. Jews in the United States. I. Title. II. Series: Jacob R. Schiff library of Jewish contributions to American democracy.

MARSHALL, Louis, 1856-1929. 923.473
Louis Marshall: champion of liberty; selected papers and addresses. Edited by Charles Reznikoff. Introd. by Oscar Handlin. Philadelphia, Jewish Publication Society of America, 1957. 2v. illus. 24cm. (The Jacob R. Schiff library of Jewish contributions to American democracy) [E184.J5M245] 57-8138
1. Jews in the U. S. 2. Minorities—U. S. 3. Jews in Europe. 4. U. S.— Emig. &immig. I. Title

Jews in the United States—Biography.

CHYET, Stanley F., comp. 301.451'924'073 B
Lives and voices; a collection of American Jewish memoirs. Edited by Stanley F. Chyet. [1st ed.] Philadelphia, Jewish Publication Society of America, 1972. xxi, 388 p. illus. 22 cm. Contents Contents.—Prelude to America, by S. Adler.—Con brio, by N. H. Cohen.—Deep in the heart of Texas, by S. Rosinger.—A Hoosier rabbinate, by M. M. Feuerlicht.—A Philadelphia childhood, by H. L. Barroway.—The end of an era, by G. G. Fox.—Father was a rabbi, by F. R. Greenberg.—Anchors aweigh, by J. Hyman.—From Rovno to Dorchester, by J. M. Chyet. [E184.J5C5] 76-169115 6.50
1. Jews in the United States—Biography. I. Title.

EPSTEIN, Melech. 920.073
Profiles of eleven; profiles of eleven men who guided the destiny of an immigrant society and stimulated social consciousness among the American people. Detroit, Wayne State University Press, 1965. 379 p. 24 cm. Contents.Morris Winchevsky. -- Abraham Cahan. -- Joseph Barondess. -- Jacob Gordin. -- Meyer London. -- Morris Hillquit. -- Benjamin Schlesinger. -- Isaac A. Hourwich. -- Sidney Hillman. -- Chaim Zhitlowsky. -- Baruch Charney Viadeck. Bibliographical references included in "Notes" (p. 358-365) [E184.J5E62] 65-20760
1. Jews in the U.S. — Biog. I. Title.

HARRIS, Leon A. 381 B
Merchant princes : an intimate history of Jewish families who built great department stores / Leon Harris. 1st ed. New York :

Harper & Row, c1979. xx, 411 p. ; 25 cm. Includes index. Bibliography: p. 382-295. [E184.J5H34 1979] 79-1667 ISBN 0-06-011797-4 : 12.50
1. Jews in the United States—Biography. 2. Merchants, Jewish—United States—Biography. 3. Department stores—United States. 4. United States—Biography. I. Title. BIP

LEVITAN, Tina Nellie, 1922- 920.073
Jews in American life [by] Tina Levitan. New York, Hebrew Pub. Co. [1969] 253 p. illus., ports. 26 cm. [E184.J5L574] 68-31729
1. Jews in the United States—Biography. I. Title. BIP

LOTZ, Philip Henry, 1889- ed. 920.073
Distinguished American Jews. Freeport, N.Y., Books for Libraries Press [1970, c1945] viii, 107 p. 23 cm. (Essay index reprint series) Contents.Contents.—Introduction, by P. H. Lotz.—Adolph Simon Ochs, merchant of news, by E. T. Randall.—Lillian Wald, crusading nurse, by H. B. Hunting.—Charney Vladeck, a revolutionist devoid of hate, by H. B. Hunting.—Rabbi Stephen S. Wise, outstanding American rabbi, by I. G.Grimshaw.—Charles Proteus Steinmatz, wizard of Schenectady, by I. G. Grimshaw.—Fannie Hurst, celebrated author, by M. L. Grimshaw.—Paul Muni, master character actor, by M. L. Grimshaw.—Yehudi Menuhin, master of the violin, by G. C. Auten.—Joseph Goldberger, fighter of pellagra, by K. R. Stolz.—Carl Laemmle, motion picture producer, by K. R. Stolz.—Felix Adler, founder of the society for ethical culture, by K. B. Cully.—Louis Dembitz Brandeis, justice of the Supreme Court, by K. B. Cully. Includes bibliographies. [E184.J5L78 1970] 78-111842
1. Jews in the United States—Biography. I. Title. BIP

MADISON, Charles Allan. 920.073
Eminent American Jews; 1776 to the present [by] Charles A. Madison. New York, Ungar [1971, c1970] xii, 400 p. ports. 22 cm. Bibliography: p. 371-384. [E184.J5M17] 74-125967 ISBN 0-8044-1576-5
1. Jews in the United States—Biography. I. Title. BIP

MARCUS, Jacob Rader, 1896- ed. 922.96
Memoirs of American Jews, 1775-1865. Philadelphia, Jewish Publication Society of America, 1955-56 [c1955] 3v. illus., ports. 22cm. (The Jacob R. Schiff library of Jewish contributions to American democracy) [E184.J5M233] 55-8420
1. Jews in the U. S.—Biog. I. Title. II. Series. BIP

RABINOWITZ, Dorothy. 973'.004'924
New lives : survivors of the holocaust living in America / Dorothy Rabinowitz. 1st ed. New York : Knopf : distributed by Random House, 1976. viii, 242 p. ; 22 cm. [E184.J5R18 1976] 76-13709 ISBN 0-394-48573-4 : 8.95
1. Jews in the United States—Biography. 2. World War, 1939-1945—Personal narratives, Jewish. 3. United States—Emigration and immigration—Biography. 4. Refugees, Jewish—United States—Biography. 5. Holocaust, Jewish (1939-1945)—Personal narratives. I. Title. BIP

RIBALOW, Harold Uriel, 1919- comp. 920.073
Autobiographies of American Jews, comp. introd., by Harold U. Ribalow. Philadelphia, Jewish Pubn. Soc. [c.]1965. xiii, 496p. 22cm. Covers the years 1880 to 1920. [E184.J5R48] 65-17047 6.00
1. Jews in the U. S.—Biog. I. Title.

ROSENBLOOM, Joseph R. 920.05693
A biographical dictionary of early American Jews, colonial times through 1800. [Lexington] University of Kentucky Press [c.1960] xii, 175p. 25cm. Bibl.: p.ix-xii. 60-8517 10.00
1. Jews in the U. S.—Biog. I. Title.

ROSENBLOOM, Joseph R 920.05693
A biographical dictionary of early American Jews, colonial times through 1800. [Lexington] University of Kentucky Press [1960] xii, 175p. 25cm. Bibliography: p. ix-xii. [E184.J5R63] 60-8517
1. Jews in the U. S.—Biog. I. Title.

VORSPAN, Albert 922.96
Giants of justice. Illus. by Ismar David. New York, Crowell ,53c.1960]•ii, 260p. illus. 21cm. 60-9931 3.75
1. Jews in the U.S.—Biog. I. Title.

VORSPAN, Albert. 922.96
Giants of justice. Illus. by Ismar David. New York, Union of American Hebrew Congregations [1960] 280 p. illus. 21 cm. [E184J5V6] 60-9931
1. Jews in the U.S. — Biog. I. Title.

WISE, James Waterman, 1901- 920.073
Jews are like that! Freeport, N.Y., Books for Libraries Press [1969] x, 231 p. ports. 23 cm. (Essay index reprint series) Reprint of the 1928 ed. Contents.Contents.—Louis D. Brandeis.—Henry Morgenthau.—Louis Lipsky.—Stephen S. Wise.—Ludwig Lewisohn.—Felix Adler.—Aaron Sapiro.—Louis Marshall.—Nathan Straus. [E184.J5W73 1969] 70-84348
1. Jews in the United States—Biography. I. Title. BIP

Jews in the United States—History.

MARCUS, Jacob Rader, 1896- 917.3'06'0924
The colonial American Jew, 1492-1776 [by] Jacob R. Marcus. Detroit, Wayne State University Press, 1970. 3 v. (xxiv, 1650 p.) illus., ports. 24 cm. Includes bibliographical references. [E184.J5M215 1970] 69-15467 ISBN 0-8143-1403-1
1. Jews in the United States—History. 2. Jews in Latin America—History. I. Title.

Jews in the United States—Political and social conditions.

PERLMUTTER, Nathan. 917.3'06'9240924 B
A bias of reflections; confessions of an incipient old Jew. New Rochelle, N.Y., Arlington House [1972] 181 p. 22 cm. [E184.J5P36] 79-186240 ISBN 0-87000-164-7 6.95
1. Jews in the United States—Political and social conditions. 2. Right and left (Political science) I. Title.

Jews—Intellectual life.

KAHN, Lothar. 809.8'94
Mirrors of the Jewish mind; a gallery of portraits of European Jewish writers of our time. New York, T. Yoseloff [1968] 272 p. 22 cm. Bibliography: p. 259-267. [DS143.K27] 68-10317 6.00
1. Jews—Intellectual life. 2. Authors, Jewish. I. Title.

Jews—Politics and government—1948-—Addresses, essays, lectures.

HALKIN, Hillel, 1939- 956.94'001
Letters to an American Jewish friend : a Zionist's polemic / Hillel Halkin. 1st ed. Philadelphia : Jewish Publication Society of America, 1977. 246 p. ; 23 cm. [DS149.H32] 76-58650 ISBN 0-8276-0093-3 : 7.50
1. Jews—Politics and government—1948-—Addresses, essays, lectures. 2. Zionism—Addresses, essays, lectures. 3. Israel—Addresses, essays, lectures. I. Title. BIP

Jezreel, James Jershom, 1840-1885.

ROGERS, Philip George 289.9
The sixth trumpeter; the story of Jezreel and his tower. London, New York, Oxford [c.]1963. 154p. illus. 23cm. 63-2166 6.00
1. Jezreel, James Jershom, 1840-1885. I. Title.

Jiri z Podebrad, King of Bohemia, 1420-1471.

HEYMANN, Frederick Gotthold, 1900- 943.702
George of Bohemia, King of Heretics, by Frederick G. Heymann. Princeton, N. J., Princeton University Press, 1965. xvi, 671 p. illus., maps, ports. 24 cm. Bibliography: p. 621-655. [DB209.H4] 64-19821
1. Jiri z Podebrad, King of Bohemia, 1420-1471. 2. Bohemia—History—1403-1526. I. Title.

Jillson, Willard Rouse,

JILLSON, Willard Rouse, 1890- 550'.92'4 B
The memoirs of Willard Rouse Jillson. Frankfort, Ky., Roberts Print. Co., 1971. 103 p. illus. 22 cm. Bibliography: p. 98-100. [QE22.J5A3] 72-185373

Jimenez de Quesada, Gonzalo, d. 1579.

ARCINIEGAS, German, 1900- 986.1'01'0924 B
The Knight of El Dorado; the tale of Don Gonzalo Jimenez de Quesada and his conquest of New Granada, now called Colombia. Translated by Mildred Adams. New York, Greenwood Press, 1968 [c1942] 301 p. map. 23 cm. Translation of Jimenez de Quesada. Bibliography: p. [297]-301. [F2272.J553 1968] 68-23269
1. Jimenez de Quesada, Gonzaio, d. 1579. 2. Colombia—History—To 1810. I. Title.

GRAHAM, Robert Bontine Cunninghame, 1852-1936. 986.1'01'0924
The conquest of New Granada; being the life of Gonzalo Jimenez de Quesada. New York, Cooper Square Publishers, 1967. xi, 272 p. illus., maps. 22 cm. (Library of Latin American history and culture) Reprint of the 1922 ed. Bibliography: p. 264-265. [F2272.J558 1967] 66-30734
1. Jimenez de Quesada, Gonzalo, d. 1579. 2. Colombia—History—To 1810. I. Title.

GRAHAM, Robert Bontine Cunninghame, 1852-1936. 986.1'01'0924 B
The conquest of New Granada; being the life of Gonzalo Jimenez de Quesada. Boston, Milford House [1973] xi, 272 p. illus. 22 cm. Reprint of the 1922 ed. published by W. Heinemann, London. Bibliography: p. 264-265. [F2272.J558 1973] 73-5651 ISBN 0-87821-139-X 30.00 Lib. ed.,
1. Jimenez de Quesada, Gonzalo, d. 1579. 2. Colombia—History—To 1810. I. Title. BIP

GRAHAM, Robert Bontine Cunninghame, 1852-1936. 986.1'01'0924 B
The conquest of New Grenada : being the life of Gonzalo Jimenez de Quesada / by R. B. Cunninghame Graham. Boston : Longwood Press, 1977. p. cm. Reprint of the 1922 ed. published by W. Heinemann, London Bibliography: p. [F2272.J55G7 1977] 77-88572 ISBN 0-89341-279-1 lib.bdg. : 30.00
1. Jimenez de Quesada, Gonzalo, d. 1579. 2. Explorers—Colombia—Biography. 3. Colombia—Governors—Biography. 4. Colombia—History—to 1810. I. Title.

THE Knight of El Dorado; 486.1'01'0924 the tale of Don Gonzalo Jimenez de Quesada and his conquest of New Granada, now called Colombia. Tr. by Mildred Adams. New York, Greenwood Pr., 1968 [c1942] 301p. map. 23cm. Tr. of Jimenez de Quesada. Bibl. [F2272.J553 1968] (B) 68-23269 12.00
1. Jimenez de Quesada, Gonzalo, d. 1579. 2. Colombia—Hist.—To 1810. I. Arciniegas, German, 1900- BIP

Jimenez, Janey.

JIMENEZ, Janey. 365'.43'0924 B
My prisoner / by Janey Jimenez as told to Ted Berkman. Kansas City, Kan. : S. Andrews and McMeel, c1977. p. cm. [HV9468.J55A35] 77-21859 ISBN 0-8362-0739-4 : 9.95
1. Jimenez, Janey. 2. Hearst, Patricia, 1954- 3. Correctional personnel—United States—Biography. 4. Crime and criminals—California—Biography. 5. Trials (Robbery)—California. I. Berkman, Ted, joint author. II. Title.

Jimma Abba Jifar.

LEWIS, Herbert S. 321.120963
A Galla monarchy; Jimma Abba Jifar, Ethiopia, 1830-1932. Madison, Univ. of Wis. Pr. [c.]1965. xix, 148p. illus., maps. 22cm. Bibl. [DT390.G2L46] 65-24185 5.00
1. Jimma Abba Jifar. 2. Gallas. 3. Ethiopia—Hist. I. Title. BIP

Jimmy the Greek.

JIMMY the Greek. 795'.01
Jimmy the Greek / by himself ; with the editorial assistance of Mickey Herskowitz & Steve Perkins. 1st ed. Chicago : Playboy Press, c1975. 247 p., [4] leaves of plates : ill. ; 22 cm. [HV6715.J54] 74-33558 ISBN 0-87223-424-X : 8.95
1. Jimmy the Greek.

Jimulla, Viola, 1878-1966.

BARNETT, Franklin. 970.3
Viola Jimulla: the Indian chieftess; a biography. [Yuma, Ariz., Printed by Southwest Printers, 1968] viii, 43 p. illus., ports. 23 cm. "Publication sponsored by Prescott Yavapai Indians." Bibliography: p. 43. [E99.Y4J53] 68-22443
1. Jimulla, Viola, 1878-1966. 2. Yavapai Indians.

Jingoes, Stimela Jason, 1895-

JINGOES, Stimela Jason, 1895- 968'.6'020924 B
A chief is a chief by the people : the autobiography of Stimela Jason Jingoes / recorded and compiled by John and Cassandra Perry. London ; New York : Oxford University Press, 1975. xviii, 252 p., [4] leaves of plates : ill. ; 23 cm. Includes bibliographies. [DT787.2.J56A33] 75-321155 ISBN 0-19-211727-0 : 21.00 (U.S.)
1. Jingoes, Stimela Jason, 1895- 2. Lesotho—History. I. Perry, J. G. II. Perry, Cassandra. III. Title.

Jinnah, Mahomed Ali, 1876-1948.

AKHTAR, Rafique. 954.9'04'0924 B
The Quaid-e-Azam : a pictorial biography / Rafique Akhtar. Karachi : East & West Pub. Co., 1976. 200 p. (p. 199-200 blank), [1] leaf of plates : chiefly ill. ; 25 cm. [DS385.J5A737] 77-930009 Rs80.00
1. Jinnah, Mahomed Ali, 1876-1948. 2. Statesmen—Pakistan—Biography. I. Title.

BOLITHO, Hector, 1898- v. 12
Jinnah; creator of Pakistan. New York, Macmillan [1956] x, 244 p. illus. 23 cm. 68-33201
1. Jinnah, Mahomed Ali, I. Title.

BOLITHO, Hector 1898- 923.154
Jinnah, creator of Pakistan. London, Murray [Mystic, Conn., Verry, 1965] x, 244p. illus. 23cm. First pub. in Britain in 1954. Bibl. [DS481.J5B6] 54-14996 6.00
1. Jinnah, Mahomed Ali, 1876-1948. I. Title.

MCDONOUGH, Sheila, comp. 954.9'04'0924 B
Mohammed Ali Jinnah, maker of modern Pakistan. Edited with an introd by Sheila McDonough. Lexington, Mass., Heath [1970] xii, 101 p. 24 cm. (Problems in Asian civilizations) Bibliography: p. 101. [DS385.J5M24] 79-91636
1. Jinnah, Mahomed Ali, 1876-1948. 2. All India Muslim League. 3. Muslims in India. I. Title. II. Series.

TRIBUTES to Quaid-i-Azam 954'.9'04'0924 B / edited by Muhammad Hanif Shahid. 1st ed. Lahore : Sang-e-Meel Publications, 1976. 252 p. ; 22 cm. "This book is being published in connection with the Centenary celebrations of the Quaid-i-Azam." Includes index. [DS385.J5T74] 76-930257 Rs50.00
1. Jinnah, Mahomed Ali, 1876-1948. 2. Statesmen—Pakistan—Biography. I. Jinnah, Mahomed Ali, 1876-1948. II. Shahid, Muhammad Hanif.

Jinnah, Mahomed Ali, 1876-1948—Addresses, essays, lectures.

ESSAYS on Quaid-e-Azam 954.9'04'0924 B / compiled by Misbah-ul-Haque

Siddiqui, Tasneem Kausar Gilani. 1st ed. Lahore : Shahzad Publishers : can be had from Universal Books, 1976. iii, 9-185 p. ; 22 cm. [DS385.J5E77] 77-930107 Rs30.00
1. Jinnah, Mahomed Ali, 1876-1948—Addresses, essays, lectures. 2. Statesmen—Pakistan—Biography—Addresses, essays, lectures. I. Siddiqui, Misbah-ul-Haque. II. Gilani, Tasneem Kausar.

Jiri z Podebrad, King of Bohemia, 1420-1471.

ODLOZILIK, Otakar, 1899- 943.702
The Hussite King; Bohemia in European affairs. 1440-1471. New Brunswick, N.J., Rutgers [c.1965] ix, 337p. illus., maps (1 fold.) ports. 25cm. Bibl. [DB209.O3] 65-19406 10.00
1. Jiri z Podebrad, King of Bohemia, 1420-1471. 2. Europe— Hist.—476-1492. I. Title. BIP

Joachim, abbot of Fiore, 1132 (ca.)-1202.

BETT, Henry, 1876- 230'.2'0924 B
1953.
Joachim of Flora / by Henry Bett. Merrick, N.Y. : Richwood Pub. Co., 1976. vii, 184 p. : frontispiece ; 23 cm. Reprint of the 1931 ed. published by Methuen, London, in series: Great medieval churchman. Includes bibliographical references and index. [BX4705.J6B4 1976] 76-20693 ISBN 0-915172-24-0 lib.bdg. : 12.50
1. Joachim, abbot of Fiore, 1132 (ca.)-1202. I. Title. II. Series: Great medieval churchman. BIP

Joachim, Joseph, 1831-1907.

JOACHIM, Joseph, 787'.1'0924 B
1831-1907.
Letters from and to Joseph Joachim. Selected and translated by Nora Bickley. With a pref. by J. A. Fuller-Maitland. New York, Vienna House, 1972 [ie. 1973] c1914 xiii, 470 p. illus. 24 cm. [ML418.J6A43 1972] 70-183496 ISBN 0-8443-0043-8 14.50
1. Joachim, Joseph, 1831-1907. 2. Musicians—Correspondence, reminiscences, etc. BIP

Joachim Murat, King of Naples, 1767-1815.

COLE, Hubert. 944.05'092'2 B
The betrayers: Joachim and Caroline Murat. [1st American ed.] New York, Saturday Review Press [1972] 351 p. illus. 25 cm. Bibliography: p. [325]-338. [DC198.M8C65 1972] 72-79048 ISBN 0-8415-0179-3 10.00
1. Joachim Murat, King of Naples, 1767-1815. 2. Caroline Bonaparte, consort of Joachim Murat, King of Naples, 1782-1839. I. Title.

Joan, mythical female Pope.

RHOIDES, Emmanouel 262.13'0924
D., 1835-1904
Pope Joan. Translated and adapted from the Greek of Emmanuel Royidis. Baltimore, Penguin Books 1974 [158] p. 18 cm. Bibliography: p. [158] [BX958] ISBN 0-1400-3760-8 1.50 (pbk.)
1. Joan, mythical female Pope. I. Durrell, Lawrence. II. Title.

RHOIDES, Emmanouel 262'.13'0924
D., 1835-1904.
Pope Joan [by] Lawrence Durrell. Translated and adapted from the Greek of Emmanuel Royidis. [Rev. ed.] Woodstock, N.Y., Overlook Press [1972, c1960] 157 p. 22 cm. Translation of He Papissa Ioanna. Bibliography: p. 151-157. [BX958.F2R56 1972] 72-81088 ISBN 0-87951-002-1 6.50
1. Joan, mythical female Pope. I. Durrell, Lawrence. II. Title.

Joannes II Comnenus, Emperor of the East, 1088-1143.

CINNAMUS, Joannes, 949.5'03
12thcent.
Deeds of John and Manuel Comnenus / by John Kinnamos ; translated by Charles W. Brand. New York : Columbia University Press, 1976. p. cm. (Records of civilization, sources and studies ; no. 95) Translation of Epitome ton katorthomaton to makarite Vasilei kai porphyrogenneto Kyro Ioanne to Komneno kai aphegesis ton prachthenton to aoidimo hyio autou to Vasilei kai porphyrogenneto Kyro Manouel to Komneno. Includes bibliographical references and index. [DF606.C5613] 76-15317 ISBN 0-231-04080-6 : 20.00
1. Joannes II Comnenus, Emperor of the East, 1088-1143. 2. Manuel I Comnenus, Emperor of the East, 1120(ca.)-1180. 3. Byzantine Empire—History—John II Comnenus, 1118-1143. 4. Byzantine Empire—History—Manuel I Comnenus, 1143-1180. I. Title. II. Series. BIP

Joannes XXIII Pope, 1881-1963.

JOANNES, Pope XXIII 1881- 922.21
1963
Journal of a soul. Tr. [from Italian] by Dorothy White [New York] New Amer. Lib. [1966, c.1965] 509p. illus., coat of arms. facsims., ports. 18cm (Mentor-Omega bk., Y2858) Bibl. [BX1378.2.A383] 1.25 pap.,
I. Title.

JOANNES XXIII Pope, 1881- 922.21
1963.
Journal of a soul [by] Pope John XXIII. Translated by Dorothy White. New York, McGraw-Hill [1965] lvii, 453 p. illus., coat of arms, facsims., ports. 25 cm. "Bibliographical note": p. xxxi-xxxvi. Bibliographical footnotes. [BX1378.2.A383] 64-8610
I. Title.

JOANNES XXIII, 262'.13'0924 B
Pope, 1881-1963.
Pope John XXIII, letters to his family [1901-1962] Translated by Dorothy White. New York, McGraw-Hill [1970, c1969] xviii, 833 p. group port. 24 cm. Translation of Giovanni XXIII, lettere ai familiari. [BX1378.2.A3833] 70-85160 15.00
I. Title.

MACGREGOR-HASTIE, Roy 920
Pope John XXIII New York, Criterion [1962, c.1961] 126p. illus. 22cm. 62-8948 3.00
1. Joannes XXIII, Pope, 1881- —Juvenile literature. I. Title.

MACGREGOR-HASTIE, Roy. 92
Pope John xxiii. [1st American ed.] New York, Criterion Books [1962, c1961] 126p. illus. 22cm. (A Criterion book for young people) [BX1378.2.M3 1962] 62-8948
1. Joannes xxiii, Pope, 1881- —Juvenile literature. I. Title. II. Title: Pope John XXIII

ROBERTO, Brother, 1927- 922.21
Lead my sheep; a story of Pope John XXIII. Illus. by Carolyn Lee Jagodits. Notre Dame, Ind., Dujarie Press [1959] 95p. illus. 24cm. [BX1378.2.R6] 59-65328
1. Joannes XXIII, Pope, 1881- —Juvenile literature. I. Title.

Joannes XXIII, Pope, 1881-1963.

ADLER, Bill, ed. 262.130924
The Pope John album: his life, his family, his career, his words [edited by] Bill Adler and Savre Ross. [1st ed.] New York, Hawthorn [1966] 97p. illus. (pt. col.) ports. 31cm. [BX1378.2.A5] 66-16220 35.00
1. Joannes XXIII, Pope, 1881-1963. I. Ross, Sayre, joint ed. II. Title.

ALGISI, Leone. 922.21
John the Twenty-Third. Translated by Peter Ryde. Westminster, Md., Newman Press [1963] 288 p. illus. 23 cm. "Translation made from the revised French edition." [BX1378.2.A613] 63-12259
1. Joannes XXIII, Pope, 1881-1963.

ARADI, Zsolt 922.21
Pope John XXIII. Zsott Amadi, James I. Tucek, James C. O'Neill. [New York, Dell, 1961, c.1959] 384p. (Chapel b5., XI3) .75
1. Joannes Xxiii Y, Pope, 1881- I. Title.

ARADI, Zsolt. 922.21
Pope John XXIII, an authoritative biography, by Zsolt Aradi, James I. Tucek [and] James C. O'Nell. New York, Farrar, Straus and Cudahy [1959] 325p. illus. 22cm. Includes bibliography. [BX1378.2.A7] 59-9172
1. Joannes XXIII, Pope, 1881- I. Title.

BOLTON, Glorney 922.21
Living Peter; a biographical study of Pope John XXIII. London, G. Allen & Unwin. [Hollywood-by-the-Sea, Fla., Transatlantic Arts, 1962, c.1961] 6.25 bds., 62-741
1. Joannes XXIII, Pope, 1881- I. Title.

BREIG, Joseph Anthony, v. 12
1905-
Story of Pope John the twenty third St. Paul, Summit Press [c1959] 90p. illus. 20cm. A62
1. Joannes XXIII, Pope, 1881- I. Title.

CAPOVILLA, Loris. 922.21
The heart and mind of John XXIII his secretary's intimate recollection. With a foreword by Henri Daniel-Rops. Translated by Patrick Riley. Illus. by Giacomo Manzu. 1st ed.] New York, Hawthorn Books [1964] 189 p. illus., ports. 26 cm. Translation of Giovanni XXIII. Bibliography: p. 187-188. [BX1378.2.C313] 64-19206
1. Joannes XXIII, Pope, 1881-1963. I. Title.

CUSHING, Richard James, 922.21
Cardinal, 1895-
Call me John; a life of Pope John XXIII. [Boston] St. Paul Editions [1963] 157 p. illus., ports., facsims. 22 cm. [BX1378.2.C8] 63-22752
1. Joannes XXIII, Pope, 1881-1963. I. Title.

ELLIOTT, Lawrence. 262'.13'0924 B
I will be called John; a biography of Pope John XXIII. [1st ed.] New York, Reader's Digest Press, 1973. xii, 338 p. illus. 24 cm. Bibliography: p. 323-325. [BX1378.2.E44] 72-95036 ISBN 0-88349-002-1 10.00
1. Joannes XXIII, Pope, 1881-1963. I. Title.

FRANCK, Frederick, 1909- 92
"I love life!" said Pope John XXIII. Text and drawings by Frederick Franck. New York, St. Martin's Press [1967] 149 p. illus. (part col.), ports. (part col.) 24 cm. A portrait of Pope John the 23d, a great humanitarian, and leader of the Second Vatican Council. [BX1378.2.F7 1967] AC 67
1 Joannes XXIII, Pope, 1881-1963. I. Title.

GARRETT, Randall. 922.21
Pope John XXIII pastoral prince. Derby, Conn., Monarch [c.1962] 158p. (Monarch Bks., Original bidg., Monarch gaints, K59) 62-1356 .50 pap.,
1. Joahnnes XXIII, Pope, 1881- I. Title.

GROPPI, Ugo. 922.21
Above all a shepherd, Pope John XXIII, by Ugo Groppi and Julius S. Lombardi. New York, Kenedy [1959] 223p. illus. 22cm. [BX1378.2.G7] 59-8990
1. Joannes XXIII, Pope, 1881- I. Lombardi, Julius S., 1911- joint author. II. Title.

HALES, Edward Elton Young, 262.13
1908-
Pope John and his revolution. London, Eyre & Spottiswoode [Mystic, Conn., Verry, 1966, c.] 1965. xv, 222p. group port. 23cm. Bibl. [BX1378.2.H23] 65-5010 6.00 bds.,
1. Joannes XXIII, Pope, 1881-1963. I. Title.

HALES, Edward Elton 262.130924
Young, 1908-
Pope John and his revolution, by E. E. Y. Hales. [1st ed. in the U. S. A.] Garden City, N. Y., Doubleday, 1965. xv, 222 p. 22 cm. Bibliography: p. 209-213. [BX1378.2.H23 1965a] 65-23924
1. Joannes XXiII, Pope, 1881-1963. I. Title.

HATCH, Alden, 1898- 922.21
A man named John; the life of Pope John XXIII. Drawings by Allene Gaty Hatch. Garden City, N.Y., Doubleday [1965, c.1963] 237p. illus. 18cm. (Image bk. D184) [BX1378.2.H3] .95 pap.,
1. Joannes XXIII, Pope, 1881-1963. I. Title.

HATCH, Alden, 1898- 922.21
A man named John; the life of Pope John XXIII. Illustrated with drawings by Allene Gaty Hatch. [1st ed.] New York, Hawthorn Books [1963] 287 p. illus. 24 cm. [BX1378.2.H3] 63-8023
1. Joannes XXIII, Pope, 1881-1963. I. Title.

HERDER correspondence 282.0904
John XXIII; Pope Paul on his predecessor, and a documentation by the editors of Herder correspondence. [New York] Herder & Herder [c.1965] 200p. illus., ports. 21cm. Bibl. [BX1378.2.H4] 64-19731 4.50
1. Joannes XXIII, Pope, 1881-1963. I. Paulus VI, Pope, 1897- II. Title. III. Title: Pope Paul on his predecessor.

JOANNES, Pope XXIII 1881- 922.21
1963
Journal of a soul. Tr. [from Italian] by Dorothy White [New York] New Amer. Lib. [1966, c.1965] 509p. illus., coat of arms. facsims., ports. 18cm. (Mentor-Omega bk., Y2858) Bibl. [BX1378.2.A383] 1.25 pap.,
I. Title.

JOANNES XXIII, 262'.13'0924 B
Pope, 1881-1963.
Pope John XXIII, letters to his family [1901-1962] Translated by Dorothy White. New York, McGraw-Hill [1970, c1969] xviii, 833 p. group port. 24 cm. Translation of Giovanni XXIII, lettere ai familiari. [BX1378.2.A3833] 70-85160 15.00
I. Title.

JOANNES XXIII Pope, 1881- 922.21
1963.
Journal of a soul [by] Pope John XXIII. Translated by Dorothy White. New York, McGraw-Hill [1965] lvii, 453 p. illus., coat of arms, facsims., ports. 25 cm. "Bibliographical note": p. xxxi-xxxvi. Bibliographical footnotes. [BX1378.2.A383] 64-8610
I. Title.

JOHNSON, Paul, 263'.13'0924 B
1928-
Pope John XXIII. [1st ed.] Boston, Little, Brown [1974] xiii, 266 p. port. 21 cm. (The Library of world biography) Bibliography: p. [247]-250. [BX1378.2.J66] 74-12325 ISBN 0-316-46755-3 6.95
1. Joannes XXIII, Pope, 1881-1963. I. Title.

LERCARO, Giacomo, 262'.13'0924
Cardinal, 1891-
John XXIII; simpleton or saint? [By] Giacomo Lercaro and Gabriele De Rosa. Translated by Dorothy White. Chicago, Franciscan Herald Press [1967] 120 p. 23 cm. Translation of Linee per una ricerca storica. "Selected passages from the works of John XXIII": p. [53]-120. Bibliographical footnotes. [BX1378.2.L3813] 68-1884
1. Joannes XXIII, Pope, 1881-1963. I. De Rosa, Gabriele, joint author. II. Joannes XXIII, Pope, 1881-1963. III. Title.

LERCARO, Giacomo, 262'.13'0924
Cardinal, 1891-
John XXIII; simpleton or saint? (By] Giacomo Levcaro and Gabriele De Rosa. Translated by Dorothy White. Chicago, Franciscan Herald Press [1967] 120 p. 23 cm. Translation of Linee per una ricerca storica. "Selected passages from the works of John XXIII": p. [53]-120. Bibliographical footnotes. [BX1378.2.L3813 1967] 68-1884
1. Joannes XXIII, Pope, 1881-1963. I. Rosa, Gabriele de, joint author. II. Joannes XXIII, Pope, 1881-1963. III. Title.

LORIT, S. C. 262'.13'0924
Everybody's Pope; the life of John XXIII, by S. C. Lorit. [Jamaica, N.Y.] New City Pr. [1967,c.1966] 230p. 16cm. [BX1378.2.L6] (B) 67-15775 1.00
1. Joannes XXIII, Pope, 1881-1963. I. Title.

MURPHY, Francis Xavier, 1914- 922.21
Pope John XXIII comes to the Vatican. 1st ed. New York, R. M. McBride Co. [1959] 242p. illus. 21cm. [BX1378.2.M8] 59-8871
1. Joannes xxiii, Pope, 1881- I. Title.

NEVINS, Albert J., 1915- 262.130924 B
The story of Pope John XXIII, written by Albert J. Nevins. New York, Grosset & Dunlap [1966] 48 p. illus. (part col.), coats of arms, facsim., ports. (part col.) 29 cm. [BX1378.2.N4] 65-20015
1. Joannes XXIII, Pope, 1881-1963. I. Title.

PECHER, Erich, 1913- 922.21
Pope John XXIII; a pictorial biography. T New York, McGraw-Hill [1959] 143p. illus. 24cm. [BX1378.2.P363] 59-16285
1. Joannes XXIII, Pope, 1881- I. Title.

PERROTTA, Paul Christopher, 1898- 922.21
Pope John XXIII, his life and character. New York, Nelson [1959] 270 p. illus. 21 cm. [BX1378.2.P4] 59-9189
1. Joannes XXIII, Pope, 1881-1963.

SHEEHAN, Elizabeth Odell, 1919- 262.130924
Good Pope John. Illustrated by Harry Barton. New York, Vision Books [1966] 178 p. illus. 22 cm. [BX1378.2.S5] 66-14038
1. Joannes XXIII, Pope, 1881-1963. I. Title.

SHEEHAN, Elizabeth Odell, 1919- 262.130924
Good Pope John. Illus. by Harry Barton. New York, Farrar [c.1966] 178p. illus. 22cm. (Vision bk., 69) [BX1378.2.S5] 66-14038 2.25
1. Joannes XXIII, Pope, 1881-1963. I. Title.

SPINA, Tony. 262.135
The making of the Pope. Additional text by Dawson Taylor. With a foreword by John LaFarge. New York, Barnes [1962] 144 p. illus. 31 cm. [BX1378.2.S6] 62-14977
1. Joannes XXIII, Pope, 1881- I. Title.

TREVOR, Meriol. 262'.13'0924
Pope John. Garden City, N.Y., Doubleday [1968, c. 1967] 318p. 18cm. (Image bk. D249) Bibl. [BX1378.2.T7 1967b] (B) 67-19114 1.25 pap.,
1. Joannes XXIII, Pope, 1881-1963. I. Title.

TREVOR, Meriol. 262'.13'0924 (B)
Pope John. London, Melbourne [etc.] Macmillan; New York, St. Martin's P., 1967. x, 329 p. front., 15 plated (incl. ports). 22 1/2 cm. 42/- Bibliography: p. [317]-322. [BX1378.2.T7] 67-90402
1. Joanners xxiii, Pope, 1881-1963. I. Title.

TREVOR, Meriol. 262'.13'0924 (B)
Pope John. London, Melbourne [etc.] Macmillan; New York, St. Martin's P., 1967. x, 329 p. front., 15 plated (incl. ports). 22 1/2 cm. 42/- Bibliography: p. [317]-322. [BX1378.2.T7] 67-90402
1. Joanners xxiii, Pope, 1881-1963. I. Title.

Joannes XXIII, Pope, 1881-1963—Juvenile literature.

DIETHELM, Walther. 92
The story of good Pope John. [Translation by Rosalsen Brennan] Westminister, Md., Newman Press [1965] 96 p. illus. 22 cm. Translation of Was wird aus Angelo? [BX1378.2.D5] 65-26786
1. Joannes xxiii, Pope, 1881-1963 — Juvenile literature. I. Title.

RICHARDS, Norman. 262'.13'0924 B
Pope John XXIII. Chicago, Childrens Press [1969, c1968] 95 p. illus. 29 cm. (People of destiny: a humanities series) Bibliography: p. 92-93. The life of the Italian peasant who became Pope and instituted many reforms within the Catholic Church including a movement to unite Christian churches. [DX1378.2.R48] 92 68-31307
1. Joannes XXIII, Pope, 1881-1963—Juvenile literature. I. Title.

STRUCHEN, Jeanette. 262'.13'0924
Pope John XXIII; the gentle shepherd. New York, Watts [1969] xiii, 142 p. illus. 22 cm. (Immortals of philosophy and religion) Bibliography: p. 138-139. The life of the Italian priest who after his election as Pope became an internationally known figure through his efforts to update the Catholic Church. [BX1378.2.S75] 92 B 73-79671 3.95
1. Joannes XXIII, Pope, 1881-1963—Juvenile literature. I. Title.

Joao II. King of Portugal, 1455-1495.

LUCENA, Vasco Fernandes de, d. 1499. 946.9
The obedience of a king of Portugal. Translated, with commentary, by Francis M. Rogers. Minneapolis, University of Minnesota Press [1958] 120p. maps, geneal. table. 21cm. Facsimile of the University of Minnesota Library copy of the original 8 fol. edition printed about 1485 with caption title: Valasci Ferdinandi ... regis Portugallie oratoris ad Innocentium octauum ... de obedientia oratio.'Limited edition of 500 copies ... copy 166.' Includes bibliographical references. [DP600.L813 1958] 58-13520
1. Joao II. King of Portugal, 1455-1495. 2. Innocentius VIII, Pope, 1432-1492. 3. Portugal—Hist. I. Rogers, Francis Millet, ed. and tr. II. Title.

Job, the patriarch.

KAHN, Jack H. 223'.1'066
Job's illness : loss, grief, and integration : a psychological interpretation / by Jack Kahn with Hester Solomon. 1st ed. Oxford ; New York : Pergamon Press, [1975] p. cm. "The book of Job reproduced from The new English Bible": p. Bibliography: p. [BS580.J5K33 1975] 75-4834 ISBN 0-08-018087-6
1. Job, the patriarch. 2. Depression, Mental. I. Solomon, Hester, joint author. II. Bible. O.T. Job. English. New English. 1975. III. Title. BIP

KAHN, Jack H. 223'.1'066
Job's illness : loss, grief, and integration : a psychological interpretation / by Jack Kahn, with Hester Solomon. 1st ed. Oxford ; New York : Pergamon Press, 1975. lxiv, 166 p., [5] leaves of plates : ill. ; 22 cm. (Pergamon international library of science, technology, engineering, and social studies) "The book of Job reproduced from The new English Bible": p. xiv-lxiv. Includes index. Bibliography: p. 159-162. [BS580.J5K33 1975] 75-4834 ISBN 0-08-018087-6 : 14.00
1. Job, the patriarch. 2. Depression, Mental. I. Solomon, Hester, joint author. II. Bible. O.T. Job. English. New English. 1975. III. Title.

Jocelyn, Stephen Perry, 1843-1920.

JOCELYN, Stephen Perry, 1892- 923.573
Mostly alkali, a biography. Caldwell, Idaho, Caxton Printers, 1953. 436 p. illus. 24 cm. [E664.J63J6] 52-5207
1. Jocelyn, Stephen Perry, 1843-1920. I. Title.

Jockeys—Correspondence, reminiscences, etc.

PEARSON, Billy, 1920- 927.98
Never look back, the autobiography of a jockey, by Billy Pearson and Stephen Longstreet. Introd. by John Huston. New York, Simon and Schuster, 1958. 370 p. illus. 22 cm. [SF336.P4A3] 58-9043
1. Jockeys—Correspondence, reminiscences, etc. I. Longstreet, Stephen, 1907- II. Title.

SMITH,Eph, 1915- 798'.4'00924
Riding to win. London. S. Paul, 1968. 160p. 12 plates, illus., ports. 22cm. Stamped on t.p.: dist. by Sportshelf, New Rochelle, N.Y. [SF336.S6A3] (B) 68-122546 6.75 bds.,
1. Jockeys—Correspondence, reminiscences, etc. I. Title. BIP

Jogues, Isaac, Saint, 1607-1646.

†JOGUES, Isaac, Saint, 1607-1646. 973'.04'97 S
Narrative of a captivity among the Mohawk Indians / Isaac Jogues. New York : Garland Pub., 1977. 69 p. ; 23 cm. (The Garland library of narratives of North American Indian captivities ; v. 67) Reprint of the 1856 ed. published by the Press of the Historical Society, New York. Issued with the reprint of the 1856 ed. of Joseph Brown. New York, 1977. [E85.G2 vol. 67] [E99.M8] 971.4 B 75-7091 ISBN 0-8240-1691-2 : 25.00
1. Jogues, Isaac, Saint, 1607-1646. 2. Mohawk Indians—Captivities. 3. Indians of North America—Captivities. 4. Huron Indians—Missions. 5. Indians of North America—Missions. 6. Christian saints—Canada—Biography. 7. New York (State)—Description and travel. 8. Missionaries—France—Biography. 9. Missionaries—Canada—Biography. I. Title. II. Series.

KITTLER, Glenn D. v. 12
Saint in the wilderness; the story of St. Isaac Jogues and the Jesuit adventure in the New World. New York, Echo Books [1965] 197 p. (Echo E 8) 65-90402
1. Jogues, Isaac, Saint, 1607-1646. I. Title.

KITTLER, Glenn D. 922.271
Saint in the wilderness; the story of St. Isaac Jogues and the Jesuit adventure in the New World [1st ed.] Garden City N. Y., Doubleday, 1964. 216 p. 22 cm. [BX4700.J564K5] 62-15906
1. Jogues, Isaac, Saint, 1607-1646. I. Title.

KITTLER, Glenn D. 922.271
Saint in the wilderness; the story of St. Isaac Jogues and the Jesuit adventure in the New World. Garden City N. Y., Doubleday [1965 c.1964] 197p. 18cm. (Echo bk., E8) [BX4700.J564K5] .75 pap.,
1. Jogues, Isaac, Saint, 1607-1646. I. Title.

LOMASK, Milton. 922.271
Saint Isaac and the Indians. Illustrated by Leo Manso. New York, Vision Books [1956] 187 p. illus. 22 cm. (Vision books, 6) [F1030.8.J635] 56-5198
1. Jogues, Isaac, Saint, 1607-1646. I. Title.

TALBOT, Francis Xavier, 1889-1953. 922.271
Saint among savages; the life of Isaac Jogues. Garden City., N.Y., Image Books [1961, c1935] 522 p. 18 cm. (A Doubleday Image book, D112) Includes bibliography. [F1030.8.J67 1961] 61-1179
1. Jogues, Isaac, Saint, 1607-1646. 2. Jesuits in Canada. I. Title.

Johannes XXIII, Pope, 1881-1963.

BALDUCCI, Ernesto, 1922- 262.130924
John, 'the transitional Pope.' Tr. [from Italian] by Dorothy White. New York, McGraw [1965, c.1964] xiii, 318p. 23cm. [BX1378.2.B313] 65-23217 7.50 bds.,
1. Johannes XXIII, Pope, 1881-1963. I. Title.

John, Augustus Edwin,

JOHN, Augustus Edwin, 1878- 927.5
Chiaroscuro; fragments of autobiography. New York, Pellegrini & Cudahy [1952] 285 p. illus. 22 cm. [ND497.J6A2 1952a] 52-9055
I. Title.

John, Augustus Edwin, 1878-1961.

HOLROYD, Michael. 759.2 B
Augustus John : a biography / by Michael Holroyd. New York : Holt, Rinehart and Winston, [1975] xii, 676 p., [20] leaves of plates : ill. ; 24 cm. Includes index. Bibliography: p. [606]-612. [ND1329.J63H64] 74-15489 ISBN 0-03-013826-4 : 15.00
1. John, Augustus Edwin, 1878-1961.

JOHN, Augustus Edwin, 1878- 927.5
Chiaroscuro; fragments of autobiography. New York, Pellegrini & Cudahy [1952] 285 p. illus. 22 cm. [ND497.J6A2 1952a] 52-9055
I. Title.

JOHN, Augustus Edwin, 1878-1961. 759.2
Augustus John / by John Rothenstein. New York : AMS Press, [1976] p. cm. Reprint of the 1945 ed. published by Phaidon Press, Oxford, in series: British artists. [ND497.J6R6 1976] 75-41158 ISBN 0-404-14560-4 : 34.50
1. John, Augustus Edwin, 1878-1961. I. Rothenstein, John Knewstub Maurice, Sir, 1901-

John, Elton.

NEWMAN, Gerald. 784'.092'4 B
Elton John / by Gerald Newman, with Joe Bivona ; introd. by Henry Edwards. New York : New American Library, 1976. 188 p., [4] leaves of plates : ports. ; 18 cm. (A Signet book) Discography: p. 185-188. [ML410.J64N5] 76-373447 pbk. : 1.50
1. John, Elton. 2. Rock musicians—England—Biography. I. Bivona, Joe, joint author.

*STEIN, Cathi 784'.092'4 B
Elton John New York, Popular Library [1975] 159 p. illus. 18 cm. [ML420] 1.50 (pbk.)
1. John, Elton. I. Title. BIP

TATHAM, Dick. 784'.092'4 B
Elton John / [by] Dick Tatham & Tony Jasper. London : Octopus Books : Phoebus, 1976. 5-92 p. : chiefly ill. (chiefly col.), ports. (chiefly col.) ; 31 cm. Col. ill. on lining papers. Discography: p. 91. [ML410.J64T38] 76-381476 ISBN 0-7064-0548-X : £1.99
1. John, Elton. 2. Rock musicians—England—Biography. I. Jasper, Tony, joint author.

John, Elton—Interviews.

GAMBACCINI, Paul, 1949- 784'.092'4 B
A conversation with Elton John and Bernie Taupin / by Paul Gambaccini. New York : Flash Books : distributed by Quick Fox, c1975. 112 p. : ill. ; 26 cm. Discography: p. 110-111. [ML410.J64G3] 75-17446 ISBN 0-8256-3063-0 pbk. : 3.95
1. John, Elton—Interviews. 2. Taupin, Bernie—Interviews. I. Title.

John, Elton—Juvenile literature.

JACOBS, Linda. 784'.092'4 B
Elton John : Reginald Dwight & co. / by Linda Jacobs. St. Paul : EMC Corp., c1975. p. cm. (Men behind the bright lights) A biography of the English performer known for his flashy clothes and wild antics. [ML3930.J58J3] 92 75-26990 ISBN 0-88436-213-2 lib.bdg. : 4.95 ISBN 0-88436-214-0 pbk. : 2.95
1. John, Elton—Juvenile literature. I. Title.

TAYLOR, Paula. 784'.092'4 B
Elton John / text, Paula Taylor ; ill., John Keely. Mankato, Minn. : Creative Education, [1975] p. cm. A biography of the English rock star famous for his frenzied performances of his own compositions. [ML3930.J58T4] 92 75-23084 ISBN 0-87191-457-3 lib.bdg. : 4.95
1. John, Elton—Juvenile literature. I. Keely, John. II. Title. BIP

John, Elton—Portraits, etc.

NUTTER, David. 784'.092'4
Elton : it's a little bit funny / text by Bernie Taupin ; pictures by David Nutter ; dedication by Elton John. New York : Viking Press, 1977. 142 p. : ill. ; 29 cm. [ML410.J64N9 1977] 77-22114 ISBN 0-670-29244-3 : 12.95
1. John, Elton—Portraits, etc. 2. Rock musicians—England—Portraits. I. Taupin, Bernie. II. Title: It's a little bit funny.

NUTTER, David. 784'.092'4
Elton : it's a little bit funny / text by Bernie Taupin ; pictures by David Nutter ; dedication by Elton John. Harmondsworth, Eng. ; New York : Penguin Books, 1977. 142 p. : chiefly ill. ; 28 cm. [ML410.J64N9 1977b] 77-10853 ISBN 0-14-004680-1 pbk. : 6.95
1. John, Elton—Portraits, etc. 2. Rock

musicians—England—Portraits. I. Taupin, Bernie. II. Title: It's a little bit funny.

John Ena (Bark)

WILMORE, C. Ray. 910'.45
Square rigger round the horn; the making of a sailor, by C. Ray Wilmore. Camden, Me., International Marine Pub. Co. [1972] 220 p. illus. 24 cm. Based on the journal kept by the author while crew member of the bark John Ena in 1911. [G478.W5] 72-184649 ISBN 0-87742-016-5 7.95
1. John Ena (Bark) 2. Voyages and travels. I. Title.

John IV, King of Ethiopia, 1839-1889.

ZEWDE Gabre-Sellassie. 963'.04'0924
Yohannes IV of Ethiopia : a political biography / by Zewde Grabre-Sellassie. Oxford : Clarendon Press, 1975. xiii, 334 p. : ill. ; 22 cm. (Oxford studies in African affairs) Includes index. Bibliography: p. [301]-322. [DT386.7.Z48] 76-359007 ISBN 0-19-821695-5 : 24.75
1. John IV, King of Ethiopia, 1839-1889. 2. Ethiopia—History—1490-1889. 3. Ethiopia—Foreign relations. I. Title. II. Series.
Distributed by Oxford University Press N.Y., N.Y.

John, King of England, 1167?-1216.

APPLEBY, John Tate, 1907- 942.033
John, King of England. [1st ed.] New York, Knopf, 1959 [c1958] 319p. 21cm. [DA208.A7] 58-10972
1. John, King of England, 1167?-1216. I. Title.

LLOYD, Alan, 1927- 942.03'3'0924 B
The maligned monarch; a life of King John of England. [1st ed.] Garden City, N.Y., Doubleday, 1972. xxvii, 428 p. 22 cm. Bibliography: p. [396]-406. [DA208.L55] 72-76186 10.00
1. John, King of England, 1167?-1216. I. Title.

NORGATE, Kate. 942.03'3'0924 B
John Lackland. New York, AMS Press [1970] vi, 303 p. maps. 23 cm. Reprint of the 1902 ed. Includes bibliographical references. [DA208.N8 1970] 71-110740
1. John, King of England, 1167?-1216. BIP

NORGATE, Kate. 942.03'3'0924 B
John Lackland / by Kate Norgate. New York : Gordon Press, 1976. p. cm. Reprint of the 1902 ed. published by Macmillan, London. [DA208.N8 1976] 76-56784 ISBN 0-8490-0455-1 lib. bdg. : 49.95
1. John, King of England, 1167?-1216. 2. Great Britain—Kings and rulers—Biography.

PAINTER, Sidney, 1902- 942.033
The reign of King John. Baltimore, Hopkins, 1966 [c.1949] viii, 397p. 21cm. (JH-14) Bibl. [DA208.P3] 49-49221 2.45 pap.
1. John, King of England, 1167?-1216. 2. Gt. Brit.—Hist.—John, 1199-1216. I. Title.

PAINTER, Sidney, 1902-1960. 942.03'3
The reign of King John / Sidney Painter. New York : Arno Press, 1979, c1949. viii, 397 p. ; 23 cm. (Johns Hopkins University Press reprints) Reprint of the ed. published by Johns Hopkins Press, Baltimore. Includes bibliographical references and index. [DA208.P3 1979] 78-19281 ISBN 0-405-10619-X : 26.00
1. John, King of England, 1167?-1216. 2. Magna carta. 3. Great Britain—History—John, 1199-1216. 4. Great Britain—Kings and rulers—Biography. I. Title.

WARREN, Wilfred Lewis. 942.033
King John. New York, W. W. Norton [1961] 340 p. illus. 22 cm. Includes bibliographies. [DA208.W33] 61-7485
1. John, King of England, 1167?-1216. I. Title. BIP

WARREN, Wilfred Lewis. 942.03'3'0924 B
King John, [by] W. L. Warren. Harmondsworth, Penguin, 1966. 367 p. 10 maps, diagr. 20 cm. (Peregrine books, Y59) Bibliography: p. 347-353. [DA208.W33 1966] 71-353317 12/6
1. John, King of England, 1167?-1216. I. Title.

WARREN, Wilfred Lewis. 942.03'3'0924 B
King John / W. L. Warren. Berkeley : University of California Press, c1978. xi, 350 p., [5] leaves of plates : ill. ; 22 cm. (Campus ; 209) Includes index. Bibliography: p. 329-336. [DA208.W33 1978b] 77-20332 ISBN 0-520-03610-7 : 15.00 ISBN 0-520-03494-5 pbk. : 4.95
1. John, King of England, 1167?-1216. 2. Great Britain—History—John, 1199-1216. 3. Great Britain—Kings and rulers—Biography. I. Title.

John (Name)

RIVES, Hallie Erminie, 1876- 920'.02
The John book, by Hallie Erminie Rives (Mrs. Post Wheeler) and Gabrielle Elliot Forbush. Freeport, N.Y., Books for Libraries Press [1971, c1947] 304 p. illus. 23 cm. (Biography index reprint series) Bibliography: p. 295-300. [CT105.R5 1971] 76-179739 ISBN 0-8369-8107-3
1. John (Name) 2. Biography. I. Forbush, Gabrielle (Elliot) joint author. II. Title. BIP

John (Name)—Juvenile literature.

GLAZER, Tom. 929.4
All about your name, John, Johnny, Jack, Jackie / by Tom Glazer ; illustrated by Demi. 1st ed. Garden City, N.Y. : Doubleday, c1978. p. cm. Discusses the name John and people of historical, literary, and theatrical significance who have held that name. [CS2391.J6G56] 77-15154 ISBN 0-385-06424-1 : 4.95. ISBN 0-385-06428-4 lib. bdg. : 5.90
1. John (Name)—Juvenile literature. 2. Biography—Miscellanea—Juvenile literature. I. Hitz, Demi. II. Title. BIP

John of Gaunt, duke of Lancaster, 1340-1399.

ARMITAGE-SMITH, Sydney Armitage, Sir, 1876- 923.242
John of Gaunt, King of Castile and Leon, duke of Aquitaine and Lancaster, earl of Derby, Lincoln, and Leicester, seneschal of England, by Sydney Armitage-Smith. New York, Barnes & Noble [1964] xxviii, 490 p. illus., geneal. tables, 3 fold. maps, ports. 22 cm. Bibliography: p. xiii-xviii. [DA247.J6A7 1964] 64-3633
1. John of Gaunt, duke of Lancaster, 1340-1399.

John of Salisbury,

JOHN OF SALISBURY, Bp. of Chapters, d.1180. 922.242
Letters. Edited by W. J. Millor and H. E. Butler, rev. by C. N. L. Brooke. London, New York, T. Nelson [1955- v. 23cm. (53Nelson's] medieval texts) Text in Latin and English. Bibliographical footnotes. [B765.J44A4] 56-308
I. Title.

John of Salisbury, Bp. of Chartres, d. 1180.

JOHN OF SALISBURY, Bp. of Chapters, d.1180. 922.242
Letters. Edited by W. J. Millor and H. E. Butler, rev. by C. N. L. Brooke. London, New York, T. Nelson [1955- v. 23cm. (53Nelson's] medieval texts) Text in Latin and English. Bibliographical footnotes. [B765.J44A4] 56-308
I. Title.

WEBB, Clement Charles Julian, 1865-1954. 189'.4 B
John of Salisbury. New York, Russell & Russell [1971] 186 p. 20 cm. Reprint of the 1932 ed. Includes bibliographical references. [BX4705.J67W4 1971] 78-152541
1. John of Salisbury, Bp. of Chartres, d. 1180. BIP

John, Otto, 1909-

FRISCHAUER, Willi, 1906- v. 12
Berlin betrayal; the story of Otto John. New York, Belmont Books [c1958] 221 p. Earlier ed. has title: The man who came back. Bibliography: p. 219-221. 64-27200
1. John, Otto, 1909- 2. Secret service-Germany. 3. Anti-Nazi movement. I. Title.

FRISCHAUER, Willi, 1906- 343.3
The man who came back; the story of Otto John. New York, Belmont [1962, c.1958] 221p. (L524) .50 pap.,
1. John, Otto, 1909- I. Title.

JOHN, Otto, 1909- 943.086'092'4 B
Twice through the lines; the autobiography of Otto John. Translated from the German by Richard Barry. With an introd. by H. R. Trevor-Roper. [1st U.S. ed.] New York, Harper & Row [1973 c1972] xv, 340 p. illus. 22 cm. Translation of Zweimal kam ich heim. Bibliography: p. [323]-328. [DD259.7.J6A313 1972b] 72-9127 ISBN 0-06-012199-8 8.95
1. John, Otto, 1909- 2. Hitler, Adolf, 1889-1945—Assassination attempt, July 20, 1944. 3. Germany—Politics and government—1945- I. Title.

John Paul I, Pope, 1912-1978.

HEBBLETHWAITE, Peter. 262'.13'09047
The year of the three popes / Peter Hebblethwaite. London : Collins, 1978. ix, 220 p. ; 22 cm. Includes index. Bibliography: p. 213-214. [BX1389.H36] 79-307264 ISBN 0-00-215047-6 : 8.95
1. Paulus VI, Pope, 1897- 2. John Paul I, Pope, 1912-1978. 3. John Paul II, Pope, 1920- 4. Papacy History—20th century. 5. Popes—Biography. I. Title.
Distributed by Collins Publishers, Inc., Cleveland, OH 44111 BIP

John Paul II, Pope, 1920-

JOHN Paul II : 262'.13'0924 B
a pictorial biography / by Peter Hebblethwaite and Ludwig Kaufmann. 1st ed. New York : McGraw-Hill, 1979. p. cm. Includes index. [BX1378.5.J63] 79-9169 ISBN 0-07-033327-0 : 14.95 ISBN 0-07-033328-9 pbk. 7.95
1. John Paul II, Pope, 1920- 2. Popes—Biography. I. Hebblethwaithe, Peter. II. Kaufmann, Ludwig. BIP

MALINSKI, Mieczyslaw. 262'.13'0924 B
Pope John Paul II, the life of Karol Wojtyla / by Miecyslaw Malinski. New York : Seabury Press, 1979. 64 p. : ill. ; 22 cm. "A Crossroad book." Includes index. [BX1378.5.M34] 79-4906 ISBN 0-8164-0434-8 : 10.95
1. John Paul II, Pope, 1920- 2. Popes—Biography. I. Title.

ORAM, James, 1936- 262'.13'0924 B
The people's Pope : the story of Karol Wojtyla of Poland / James Oram ; [photos of contemporary Poland by Neil Duncan]. San Francisco : Chronicle Books, c1979. 244 p. : ill. ; 25 cm. Bibliography: p. 224. [BX1378.5.O7] 79-120102 ISBN 0-87701-159-1 pbk. : 7.95
1. John Paul II, Pope, 1920- 2. Popes—Biography. I. Title. BIP

John, Prester.

SILVERBERG, Robert. 915'.04'2
The realm of Prester John. [1st ed.] Garden City, N.Y., Doubleday, 1972. 344 p. illus. 24 cm. Bibliography: p. [325]-328. [G560.S55] 78-171271 8.95
1. John, Prester. I. Title.

John, Saint, apostle — Juvenile literature.

WILLETT, Franciscus. j92
The eagle of God; a story of St. John the Evangelist [by] Jeremy Premont. Illustrated by Gerald Robbins. Valatie, N.Y., Holy Cross Press, 1965. 98 p. illus. 22 cm. [BS2455.W5] 65-21803
1. John, Saint, apostle — Juvenile literature. I. Title.

John the Baptist.

JOHN the Baptist. v. 12
Westchester, Ill., Good News Pub., 1960. 63p. (A 'one evening' condensed book)
1. John the Baptist. I. Meyer, Frederick Brotherton, 1847-1929. II. Series.

MATTHEWS, Robert J. 232.9'4 B
A burning light: the life and ministry of John the Baptist [by] Robert J. Matthews. [Provo, Utah] Brigham Young University Press [1972] xviii, 125 p. map. 24 cm. Bibliography: p. 113-115. [BS2456.M34] 71-186683 ISBN 0-8425-1470-8
1. John the Baptist. I. Title.

RETIF, Andre. 225.92
John the Baptist, missionary of Christ. Westminster, Md., Newman Press, 1953. 122p. 22cm. Translated by Francis Murry. [BS2456.R413] 53-10383
1. John the Baptist. I. Title.

SCOBIE, Charles Hugh Hope 225.92
John the Baptist. Philadelphia, Fortress [c.1964] 224p. map. 23cm. Bibl. 64-55082 3.25
1. John the Baptist. I. Title.

SCOBIE, Charles Hugh Hope. v. 12
John the Baptist [by] Charles H. H. Scobie. London, SCM Press [1964] 224 p. map. 23 cm. Bibliographical footnotes. 66-49356
1. John the Baptist. I. Title.

SCOBIE, Charles Hugh Hope. 225.92
John the Baptist [by] Charles H. H. Scobie. Philadelphia, Fortress Press [1964] 224 p. map. 23 cm. Bibliographical footnotes. [BS2456.S36] 64-55082
1. John the Baptist. I. Title.

John the Baptist—Juvenile literature.

BARTON, Peggy, 1931- 225.9'2'4 B
John the Baptist / Peggy Barton. Salt Lake City : Deseret Book Co., 1978. 24 p. : ill. ; 24 cm. Presents the life and work of John the Baptist who predicted the coming of the Messiah and baptized Jesus. Explains how the Priesthood of Aaron was conferred upon Joseph Smith and Oliver Cowdery. [BS2456.B29] 78-23616 ISBN 0-87747-727-2 : 3.95
1. John the Baptist—Juvenile literature. 2. Prophets—Palestine—Biography—Juvenile literature. I. Title.

HUMAN, Johnnie. 232.9'4 B
John the Baptist, forerunner of Jesus / Johnnie Human ; illustrated by James Padgett. Nashville : Broadman Press, c1978. 47 p. : col. ill. ; 24 cm. (Biblearn series) Relates the career of John the Baptist whose preaching predicted the coming of the Messiah. [BS2456.H8] 78-105241 ISBN 0-8054-4240-5 pbk. : 3.95
1. John the Baptist—Juvenile literature. 2. Bible. N.T.—Biography—Juvenile literature. I. Padgett, James. II. Title.

John, Tommy.

JOHN, Tommy. 796.357'092'4 B
The Tommy John story / Tommy and Sally John, with Joe Musser ; foreword by Tom Lasorda. Old Tappan, N.J. : F. H. Revell Co., c1978. 175 p., [9] leaves of plates : ill. ; 22 cm. [GV865.J58A37] 78-17705 ISBN 0-8007-0923-3 : 6.95
1. John, Tommy. 2. Baseball players—United States—Biography. 3. Religion and sports. I. John, Sally, joint author. II. Musser, Joe, joint author. III. Title. BIP

Johns, Ethel.

STREET, Margaret M. 610.73'092'4 B
Watch-fires on the mountains; the life and writing of Ethel Johns [by] Margaret M. Street. [Toronto] University of Toronto Press [1973] xiv, 336 p. port. 24 cm. Bibliography: p. [307]-317. [RT37.J55S84] 72-98026 ISBN 0-8020-1987-0 12.50
1. Johns, Ethel. 2. Nurses and nursing—Canada. I. Title.

Johns, Jane (Hall), Mrs., b. 1813.

WELCH, Andrew. 970'.004'97
A narrative of the early days and remembrances of Oceola Nikkanochee, prince of Econchatti / written by his guardian. Facsim. reproductions of the 1841 ed. and of the pamphlets of 1837 and 1847 / with an introd. and indexes by Frank Laumer. Gainesville : University Presses of Florida, 1977i.e.1976 352 p. in various pagings ; 20 cm. (Bicentennial Floridiana facsimile series) "A University of Florida book." Photoreprint of the 1841 ed. published by Hatchard, London; of the 1837 ed. of A Narrative of the life and sufferings of Mrs. Jane Johns, printed by Burke & Giles, Charleston; and of the 1847 ed. of A narrative of the life of Benjamin Benson, published by the author, London. Includes bibliographical references and indexes. [E99.S28W44 1977] 76-54519 ISBN 0-8130-0411-X : 8.50
1. Osceola Nikkanochee, Seminole Indian. 2. Osceola, Seminole chief, 1804-1838. 3. Johns, Jane (Hall), Mrs., b. 1813. 4. Benson, Benjamin, b. 1818. 5. Seminole Indians—Biography. 6. United States—Biography. I. Welch, Andrew. A narrative of the life of Benjamin Benson. 1976. II. A Narrative of the life and sufferings of Mrs. Jane Johns. 1976. III. Title. IV. Title: A narrative of the early days and remembrances of Oceola Nikkanochee ... V. Series.

Johns, Jasper, 1930-

CRICHTON, Michael, 1942- 709'.2'4
Jasper Johns / by Michael Crichton. New York : Abrams, 1977. p. cm. Bibliography: p. [N6537.J6C74] 77-78150 ISBN 0-8109-1161-2 : 28.50
1. Johns, Jasper, 1930- 2. Artists—United States—Biography. I. Johns, Jasper, 1930- BIP

Johns, John, Bp., 1796-1876.

WOOD, John Sumner, 1902- 922.373
The Virginia bishop; a Yankee hero of the Confederacy. Richmond, Garrett & Massie, 1961. 187 p. illus. 24 cm. Includes bibliography. [BX5995.J55W6] 61-12694
1. Johns, John, Bp., 1796-1876. I. Title.

Johns, Orrick, 1887-1946.

JOHNS, Orrick, 1887- 811'.5'2 B 1946.
Time of our lives; the story of my father and myself. New York, Octagon Books, 1973 [c1937] 353 p. ports. 23 cm. Reprint of the ed. published by Stackpole Sons, New York. [PS3519.O135Z5 1973] 73-12706 ISBN 0-374-94215-3 12.50
1. Johns, Orrick, 1887-1946. 2. Johns, George Sibley, 1857-1941. I. Title. BIP

Johnson, Abigail Elizabeth, 1872-1958.

MEANS, Florence Crannell, 1891- 970.62666
Sunlight on the Hopi mesas; the story of Abigail E. Johnson. [1st ed.] Philadelphia, Judson Press [1960] 171 p. illus. 22 cm. [E99.H7M4] 60-9944
1. Johnson, Abigail Elizabeth, 1872-1958. 2. Hopi Indians—Missions. 3. Baptists—Missions. I. Title.

Johnson, Alexander Bryan, 1786-1867.

TODD, Charles L. 191 B
Alexander Bryan Johnson : philosophical banker / Charles L. Todd, Robert Sonkin. 1st ed. Syracuse, N.Y. : Syracuse University Press, 1977. xix, 362 p., [6] leaves of plates : ill. ; 24 cm. (A New York State study) Includes index. [CT3990.J6T63] 77-15598 ISBN 0-8156-2188-4 : 16.00
1. Johnson, Alexander Bryan, 1786-1867. 2. Scholars—United States—Biography. 3. United States—Intellectual life—1783-1865. I. Sonkin, Robert, joint author. BIP

Johnson, Alvin Saunders,

JOHNSON, Alvin Saunders, 1874- 923.773
Pioneer's progress, an autobiography. New York, Viking Press, 1952. 413 p. illus. 22 cm. [H59.J6A3] 52-12704
I. Title.

JOHNSON, Alvin Saunders, 1874- 923.773
Pioneer's progress, an autobiography. Foreword by Max Lerner. [Gloucester, Mass., P. Smith, 1963,c.1952] 413p. 21cm. (Bison bk. BB104 rebound) 3.75
I. Title.

JOHNSON, Alvin Saunders, 1874- 923.773
Pioneer's progress, an autobiography. With a foreword by Max Lerner. [Lincoln] University of Nebraska Press, [1960 [c.1952] 413p. (Bison book, BB104) 60-12940 1.85
I. Title.

Johnson, Amy, 1903-1941-Juvenile literature.

HOGG, Beth (Tootill) 1917- 629.130924
Winged victory: the story of Amy Johnson, by Elizabeth Grey. Boston, Houghton, 1966. 160, [1]p. 22cm. Bibl. [TL540.J58H6 1966a] 66-8667 3.25
1. Johnson, Amy, 1903-1941-Juvenile literature. I. Title.

Johnson, Andrew, Pres. U.S., 1808-1875.

CASTEL, Albert E. 973.8'1'0924 B
The Presidency of Andrew Johnson / by Albert Castel. Lawrence : Regents Press of Kansas, c1979. p. cm. (American Presidency series) Includes index. Bibliography: p. [E666.C23] 79-11050 ISBN 0-7006-0190-2 : 15.00
1. Johnson, Andrew, Pres. U.S., 1808-1875. 2. United States—Politics and government—1865-1869. 3. Reconstruction. 4. Presidents—United States—Biography. I. Title. II. Series. BIP

CRANE, William Dwight. 973.8'1'0924 B
Andrew Johnson, tailor from Tennessee, by William D. Crane. New York, Dodd, Mead [1968] xiv, 208 p. illus., ports. 22 cm. Bibliography: p. 203-204. A biography of the man who, although born to a poor family in North Carolina and early apprenticed to a tailor, found his forte in local politics and became mayor, State representative, Congressman, Governor, Senator, and Vice President before suceeding Lincoln in the difficult post-Civil War days. [E667.C9] 92 AC 68
1. Johnson, Andrew, Pres. U.S., 1808-1875. I. Title.

JONES, James Sawyer, 1861- 973.8'1'0924 B
Life of Andrew Johnson, seventeenth President of the United States / by James S. Jones. New York : AMS Press, [1975] p. cm. Reprint of the 1901 ed. published by East Tennessee Pub. Co., Greeneville. [E667.J75 1975] 70-170824 ISBN 0-404-04606-1 : 24.50
1. Johnson, Andrew, Pres. U.S., 1808-1875. BIP

MCKITRICK, Eric L., comp. 973.8'1'0924 B
Andrew Johnson; a profile. Edited by Eric L. McKitrick. [1st ed.] New York, Hill and Wang [1969] xxvi, 224 p. 22 cm. (American profiles) Includes bibliographical references. [E667.M3] 73-80429 5.95
1. Johnson, Andrew, Pres. U.S., 1808-1875.

REECE, Brazilla Carroll, 1889-1961. 923.173
The courageous commoner; a biography of Andrew Johnson. Charleston, W. Va., Education Foundation, 1962. 168 p. illus. 24 cm. Includes bibliography. [E667.R4] 63-27394
1. Johnson, Andrew, Pres. U.S., 1808-1875. I. Title.

ROYALL, Margaret Shaw. 923.173
Andrew Johnson—presidential scapegoat; a biographical re-evaluation. [1st ed.] New York, Exposition Press [1958] 175 p. 21 cm. Includes bibliography. [E667.R6] 58-4400
1. Johnson, Andrew, Pres. U.S., 1808-1875.

STEELE, Robert V. P. 973.8'1'0924 B
The first President Johnson; the three lives of the seventeenth President of the United States of America, by Lately Thomas. New York, Morrow, 1968. x, 676 p. illus., ports. 25 cm. Bibliography: p. 639-652. [E667.S7 1968] 68-25487 12.50
1. Johnson, Andrew, Pres. U.S., 1808-1875. I. Title.

STRYKER, Lloyd Paul, 1885- 973.8'1'0924 B
Andrew Johnson; a study in courage. New York, Macmillan Co., 1929. St. Clair Shores, Mich., Scholarly Press, 1971. xvi, 881 p. illus., ports. 22 cm. Bibliography: p. 838-844. [E667.S92 1971] 74-145320 ISBN 0-403-01231-7
1. Johnson, Andrew, Pres. U.S., 1808-1875. 2. U.S.—Politics and government—1865-1869. BIP

WINSTON, Robert Watson, 1860-1944. 973.8'1'0924
Andrew Johnson, plebeian and patriot. New York, AMS Press [1970] xvi, 549 p. illus., facsims., map, ports. 23 cm. Reprint of the 1928 ed. Bibliography: p. 529-540. [E667.W78 1970] 76-124772
1. Johnson, Andrew, Pres. U.S., 1808-1875. I. Title.

WINSTON, Robert Watson, 1860-1944. 973.8'1'0924
Andrew Johnson; plebeian and patriot, by Robert W. Winston. New York, Barnes & Noble [1969, c1928] xvi, 549 p. illus., facsims., map, ports. 24 cm. Bibliography: p. 529-540. [E667.W78 1969] 77-7684 10.00
1. Johnson, Andrew, Pres. U.S., 1808-1875.

Johnson, Andrew, Pres. U.S., 1808-1875—Impeachment.

HOROWITZ, Robert F. 973.8'092'4 B
The great impeacher : a political biography of James M. Ashley / by Robert F. Horowitz. New York : Brooklyn College Press ; distributed by Columbia University Press, 1979. xii, 227 p. ; 23 cm. (Studies on society in change ; no. 9) Includes index. Bibliography: p. [207]-219. [E415.9.A77H67] 78-62276 ISBN 0-930888-03-0 : 15.00
1. Ashley, James Monroe, 1824-1896. 2. Johnson, Andrew, Pres. U.S., 1808-1875—Impeachment. 3. United States. Congress. House—Biography. 4. Reconstruction. 5. Legislators—United States—Biography. I. Title.

Johnson, Andrew, Pres. U. S., 1808-1875—Juvenile literature.

GREEN, Margaret 920
Defender of the Constitution: Andrew Johnson. New York, Messner [c.1962] 192p. Bibl. 62-10193 2.95; 2.99 lib. ed.,
1. Johnson, Andrew, Pres. U. S., 1808-1875—Juvenile literature. I. Title.

HOYT, Edwin Palmer 923.173
Andrew Johnson. Chicago, Reilly & Lee [c.]1965. 145p. illus. 21cm. Bibl. [E667.H6] 64-66130 3.95
1. Johnson, Andrew, Pres. U.S., 1808-1875—Juvenile literature. I. Title.

LOMASK, Milton. 092
Andy Johnson: the tailor who became President. New York, Ariel Books [1962] 181 p. 22 cm. [E667.L82] 62-9221
1. Johnson, Andrew, Pres. U.S., 1808-1875—Juvenile literature.

PALEY, Alan L. 973.8'1'0924 B
Andrew Johnson: the President impeached, by Alan L. Paley. Charlotteville, N.Y., SamHar Press, 1972. 31 p. 22 cm. (Outstanding personalities, no. 31) Bibliography: p. 31. A biography of the man who became President upon the assassination of Lincoln emphasizing his turbulent White House years. [E667.P34] 92 74-190248
1. Johnson, Andrew, Pres. U.S., 1808-1875—Juvenile literature. I. Title.

SEVERN, William 92
In Lincoln's footsteps; the life of Andrew Johnson, by Bill Severn. New York, Washburn [c.1966] 215p. 21cm. [E667.S48] 66-10677 3.95
1. Johnson, Andrew, Pres. U. S., 1808-1875—Juvenile literature. I. Title.

***Johnson, Anna**

*JOHNSON, Anna 917.74'03'40924
Anna--the story of an immigrant. New York, Carlton [1967] 77p. 21cm. 2.00
I. Title.

Johnson, Barbara E.

JOHNSON, Barbara E. 301.42'7
Where does a mother go to resign? / Barbara Johnson. Minneapolis : Bethany Fellowship, c1979. 154 p. ; 21 cm. [HQ759.J62] 79-12686 ISBN 0-87123-606-0 pbk. : 3.50
1. Johnson, Barbara E. 2. Mothers—United States—Biography. 3. Housewives—United States—Biography. 4. Homosexuals, Male—United States—Family relationships. I. Title. BIP

Johnson, Blaine, 1944-

JOHNSON, Blaine, 1944- 796.32'3'0924 B
What's happenin'? : A revealing journey through the world of professional basketball / by Blaine Johnson. Englewood Cliffs, N.J. : Prentice-Hall, c1978. p. cm. [GV885.7.J63A35] 78-16719 ISBN 0-13-955120-4 : 9.95
1. Johnson, Blaine, 1944- 2. Basketball—United States. 3. Sportswriters—United States—Biography. I. Title.

Johnson, Bob, 1893-

SMITH, Steve, 1941- 629.13'092'4 B
Fly the biggest piece back / Steve Smith. Missoula, Mont. : Mountain Press Pub. Co., c1979. p. cm. Includes index. [TL726.3.M9S64] 79-13586 ISBN 0-87842-108-4 : 18.95
1. Johnson, Bob, 1893- 2. Johnson Flying Service, Missoula, Mont. 3. Air pilots—Montana—Biography. I. Title. BIP

Johnson, Bushrod Rust, 1817-1880.

CUMMINGS, Charles M. 973.73'0924
Yankee Quaker, Confederate general; the curious career of Bushrod Rust Johnson [by] Charles M. Cummings. Rutherford [N.J.] Fairleigh Dickinson University Press [1971] 417 p. illus., facsims., maps, ports. 22 cm. Bibliography: p. 385-394. [E467.1.J6C8] 76-118805 ISBN 0-8386-7706-1 15.00
1. Johnson, Bushrod Rust, 1817-1880. I. Title. BIP

Johnson, Carole, 1939-1962.

JOHNSON, L. D., 1916- 242'.4
The morning after death / L. D. Johnson. Nashville : Broadman Press, c1978. 150 p. ; 20 cm. Includes bibliographical references. [BX6495.J49J63] 77-99255 ISBN 0-8054-2412-1 : 5.95
1. Johnson, Carole, 1939-1962. 2. Baptists—United States—Biography. 3. Grief. 4. Theodicy. I. Title. BIP

Johnson, Charles Oscar, 1886-

NYGAARD, Normal Eugene, 1897- 286.1778
Where cross the crowded ways; the story of the Third Baptist Church of St. Louis,

Missouri, and its minister, Dr. C. Oscar Johnson. New York, Greenberg [1950] viii, 240 p. illus., ports. 21 cm. "Where cross the crowded ways of life" (words and music): verse of frontispiece. [BX6480.S27T47] 50-4729
1. Johnosn, Charles Oscar, 1886- 2. St. Louis. Third Baptist Church. I. Title.

Johnson, Claudia Alta (Taylor) 1912-

BANNETT, Carole. 973.9230922
Partners to the President. [1st ed.] New York, Citadel Press [1966] 92 p. ports. 21 cm. [E848.B3] 66-16485
1. Johnson, Claudia Alta (Taylor) 1912- 2. Johnson, Lynda Bird, 1944- 3. Johnson, Luci Baines, 1947- I. Title.

HALL, Gordon Langley. 973.923'0922
Lady Bird and her daughters. Philadelphia, M. Smith Co. [1967] 254 p. ports. 22 cm. "Selected bibliography": p. [253]-254. [E848.H3] 66-26497
1. Johnson, Claudia Alta (Taylor) 1912- 2. Johnson, Lynda Bird, 1944- 3. Nugent, Luci Baines (Johnson) 1947- I. Title.

LEIGHTON, Frances Spatz 920.7
They call her Lady Bird [by] Frances Spatz Leighton, Helen Baldwin. [New York] Macfadden [1965] 224p. illus. 19cm. (75-139) [E848.J6L4] 65-3582 .75 pap.,
1. Johnson, Claudia Alta (Taylor) 1912- I. Baldwin, Helen (Pool) 1903- joint author. II. Title.

LEIGHTON, Frances Spatz. 920.7
They call her Lady Bird [by] Frances Spatz Leighton and Helen Baldwin. [New York] Macfadden-Bartel [Corp., 1964] 224 p. illus. 19 cm. (A Macfadden-Bartell book, 75-139) [E848.J6L4] 65-3582
1. Johnson, Claudia Alta (Taylor) 1912- I. Baldwin, Helen (Pool) 1903- joint author. II. Title.

*MONTGOMERY, Ruth Shiche 1912- 920.7
Mrs. L.B.J. [New York] Avon [c.1964] 192p. 19cm. (S155) .60 pap.,
1. Johnson, Claudia Alta (Taylor) 1912- I. Title.

MONTGOMERY, Ruth (Shick) 1912- 920.7
Mrs. L. B. L. [1st ed.] New York, Holt, Rinehart and Winston [1964] 212 p. 22 cm. [E848.J6M6] 64-15307
1. Johnson, Claudia Alta (Taylor) 1912- I. Title.

MONTGOMERY, Ruth (Shick) 1912- v. 12
Mrs. LBJ. [New York, Avon Books, c1964] 192 p. 18 cm. (An Avon book) "S155." 65-71192
1. Johnson, Claudia Alta (Taylor) 1912- I. Title.

SIMMONS, Dawn Langley. 973.923'0922
Lady Bird and her daughters, by Gordon Langley Hall. Philadelphia, M. Smith Co. [1967] 254 p. ports. 22 cm. "Selected bibliography": p. [253]-254. [E848.S5] 66-26497
1. Johnson, Claudia Alta (Taylor) 1912- 2. Robb, Lynda Bird, 1944- 3. Nugent, Luci Baines (Johnson) 1947- I. Title.

SMITH, Marie D. 920.7
The President's lady; an intimate biography of Mrs. Lyndon B. Johnson. Foreword by Harry S. Truman. New York, Random [c.1964] vi, 243p. illus., ports. 22cm. 64-17940 4.95
1. Johnson, Claudia Alta (Taylor) 1912- I. Title.

Johnson, Edith E

JOHNSON, Edith E 926.1
Leaves from a doctor's diary. With a foreword by Alvin Johnson. Palo Alto, Calif., Pacific Books [1954] 279p. illus. 22cm. [R154.J634A3] 54-12719
I. Title.

Johnson, Edward, 1881-1959.

MERCER, Ruby. 782.1'092'4 B
The tenor of his time : Edward Johnson of the Met / Ruby Mercer ; with discography by J. B. McPherson and W. R. Moran. Toronto : Clarke, Irwin, c1976. xv, 336 p., [8] leaves of plates : ill. ; 24 cm. Includes index. [ML420.J73M5] 76-380967 ISBN 0-7720-0736-5 : 13.95
1. Johnson, Edward, 1881-1959. 2. Singers—Biography. I. Title.

Johnson, Emily Pauline, 1861-1913—Biography—Juvenile literature.

HARTLEY, Lucie. 811'.4 B
Pauline Johnson / by Lucie K. Hartley. Minneapolis : Dillon Press, c1978. p. cm. A biography of the nineteenth-century Canadian poet who gained fame through her one-woman shows which brought directly to the people her verses of her Mohawk heritage and of her country. [PR9199.2.J64Z7] 92 78-8040 ISBN 0-87518-156-2 : 5.95
1. Johnson, Emily Pauline, 1861-1913—Biography—Juvenile literature. 2. Poets, Canadian—19th century—Biography—Juvenile literature. 3. Mohawk Indians—Biography—Juvenile literature. I. Title. BIP

Johnson, Esther, 1681-1728.

LEBROCQUY, Sybil 928.2
Cadenus; a reassessment in the light of new evidence of the relationships between Swift, Stella and Vanessa. Dublin, Dolmen Pr. [dist. Chester Springs, Pa., Dufour, 1964, c.1962] 160p. illus. 21cm. Bibl. [PR3726.L37] 63-453 3.95 bds.,
1. Swift, Jonathan, 1667-1745. 2. Johnson, Esther, 1681-1728. 3. Vanhomrigh, Esther, 1690-1723. I. Title.

Johnson, Eyvind, 1900-

ORTON, Gavin, 1943- 839.7'3'72
Eyvind Johnson. New York, Twayne Publishers [1972] 160 p. 21 cm. (Twayne's world authors series, TWAS 150. Sweden) Bibliography: p. 154-158. [PT9875.J6Z8] 79-120396
1. Johnson, Eyvind, 1900- BIP

Johnson family.

ORMSBEE, Mary Chalfant, 1912- comp. 929'.2'0973
Letters to Sarah Ann Olds Johnson, written to her by her relatives and friends between 1857 and 1887. [Boulder, Colo., c1972] 222 p. illus. 24 cm. [CS71.J7 1972d] 74-151343
1. Johnson family. 2. Old family. 3. Johnson, Sarah Ann Olds, 1834-1901. I. Johnson, Sarah Ann Olds, 1834-1901. II. Title.

Johnson, Frank Minis, 1918-

KENNEDY, Robert Francis, 1954- 347'.73'2034 B
Judge Frank M. Johnson, Jr. : a biography / by Robert Francis Kennedy, Jr. New York : Putnam, c1978. 288 p., [4] leaves of plates : ill. ; 23 cm. Includes bibliographical references and index. [KF373.J55K46] 77-27540 ISBN 0-399-12123-4 : 8.95
1. Johnson, Frank Minis, 1918- 2. Judges—Alabama—Biography. 3. Civil rights—Alabama. BIP

Johnson, Franklin Winslow, 1870-1956.

MARRINER, Ernest Cummings, 1891- 370'.924 B
The man of Mayflower Hill; a biography of Franklin W. Johnson [by] Ernest C. Marriner. Waterville, Me., Colby College Press, 1967. ix, 137 p. illus., ports. 24 cm. [LD1061.C717 1967] 67-9602
1. Johnson, Franklin Winslow, 1870-1956. 2. Colby College, Waterville, Me. I. Title. BIP

Johnson, Frederick, 1932-

JOHNSON, Frederick, 1932- 301.45'16'8729507471
The tumbleweeds, somersaulting up and out of the city streets / Frederick Johnson. 1st ed. New York : Harper & Row, c1977. 246 p., [4] leaves of plates : ill. ; 22 cm. [F128.9.P85J6 1977] 76-26236 ISBN 0-06-012216-1 : 10.00
1. Johnson, Frederick, 1932- 2. Puerto Ricans in New York (City) 3. Acrobats and acrobatism. 4. Social workers—New York (City)—Biography. 5. Social work with youth—New York (City) 6. New York (City)—Biography. I. Title.

Johnson, Gilbert H., 1905-1972.

JOHNSON, Jesse J., 1914- 359.9'6'0922 B
Roots of two Black Marine sergeants major, Sergeants Major Edgar R. Huff and Gilbert H. "Hashmark" Johnson : profiles in courage : a documented pictorial history / by Jesse J. Johnson. Hampton, Va. : Ebony Pub., c1978. viii, 116 p. : ill. ; 29 cm. [VE25.A1J64] 78-55171 ISBN 0-915044-14-5 pbk. : 2.25
1. Huff, Edgar R., 1919- 2. Johnson, Gilbert H., 1905-1972. 3. United States. Marine Corps—Afro-American troops—Biography. 4. Afro-American soldiers—Biography. I. Title.

Johnson, James.

JOHNSON, James. 973'.04'97 S
Narrative of James Johnson. New York : Garland Pub., 1976. p. cm. (The Garland library of narratives of North American Indian captivities ; v. 104) Issued with the reprint of the 1900 ed. of Janney, A. Narrative of the capture of Abel Janney. New York, 1976. Reprint of the 1902 ed. privately printed in Manchester, N.H. under title: Scout journals, 1757. Narrative of James Johnson, a captive during the French and Indian Wars. [E85.G2 vol. 104] [E199.J65] 973.2'6'0924 75-40150 ISBN 0-8240-1728-5 lib.bdg. : 21.00
1. Johnson, James. 2. Indians of North America—Captivities. 3. United States—History—French and Indian War, 1755-1763—Personal narratives. I. Title. II. Series.

Johnson, James E., 1926-

JOHNSON, James E., 1926- 973.92'092'4 B
Beyond defeat / by James E. Johnson, with David W. Balsiger ; introd. by Charles W. Colson. 1st ed. Garden City, N.Y. : Doubleday, 1978. ix, 274 p., [6] leavs of plates : ill. ; 22 cm. "A Doubleday-Galilee original." [E185.97.J685A33] 77-16849 ISBN 0-385-13486-X : 7.95
1. Johnson, James E., 1926- 2. Afro-Americans—Biography. 3. Christian biography—United States. I. Balsiger, Dave, joint author. II. Title. BIP

Johnson, James Weldon, 1871-1938.

JOHNSON, James Weldon, 1871-1938. v. 12
Along this way; the autobiography of James Weldon Johnson. New York, Viking Press [1965, c1961] 418 p. illus. 25 cm. 66-38958
1. Johnson, James Weldon, 1871-1938. I. Title.

JOHNSON, James Weldon, 1871-1938. 818'.5'209
Along this way; the autobiography of James Weldon Johnson. New York, Da Capo Press, 1973 [c1933] 418 p. illus. 23 cm. [E185.97.J692A3 1973] 72-8404 ISBN 0-306-70539-7 15.00
I. Title. BIP

TARRY, Ellen, 1906- 92
Young Jim; the early years of James Weldon Johnson. New York, Dodd, Mead [1967] xii, 230 p. facsims., ports. 22 cm. A recreation of the childhood and youth of the great Negro poet and executive director of the N.A.A.C.P. [PS3519.O2625Z89] AC 67
1. Johnson, James Weldon, 1871-1938. I. Title. BIP

Johnson, James Weldon, 1871-1938—Biography.

LEVY, Eugene D. 818'.5'209 B
James Weldon Johnson, Black leader, Black voice [by] Eugene Levy. Chicago, University of Chicago Press [1973] xiii, 380 p. port. 23 cm. (Negro American bibliographies and autobiographies) Bibliography: p. 351-368. [PS3519.O2625Z7] 72-95134 ISBN 0-226-47603-0 14.50
1. Johnson, James Weldon, 1871-1938—Biography. I. Title. II. Series.

Johnson, James Weldon, 1871-1938—Juvenile literature.

EGYPT, Ophelia Settle. 818'.5'209 B
James Weldon Johnson. Illustrated by Moneta Barnett. New York, Crowell [1974] 40 p. illus. (part col.) 24 cm. (A Crowell biography) Brief biography of the turn-of-the-century black author, educator, lawyer, and diplomat who started the first Negro daily newspaper in the United States. [PS3519.O2625Z65] 92 73-9521 ISBN 0-690-00214-9
1. Johnson, James Weldon, 1871-1938—Juvenile literature. I. Barnett, Moneta, illus. II. Title.

FELTON, Harold W., 1902- 818'.5'209 B
James Weldon Johnson [by] Harold W. Felton. Illustrated by Charles Shaw. New York, Dodd, Mead [1971] 91 p. illus. 24 cm. A biography of the lawyer, poet, editor, and musician who helped found the NAACP. [E185.97.J692F4] 92 72-132625 ISBN 0-396-06274-1 3.75
1. Johnson, James Weldon, 1871-1938—Juvenile literature. I. Shaw, Charles, 1941- illus. II. Title.

TARRY, Ellen, 1906- juv
Young Jim; the early years of James Weldon Johnson. New York, Dodd, Mead [1967] xii, 230 p. facsims., ports. 22 cm. [PS3519.O2625Z89] 67-22194
1. Johnson, James Weldon, 1871-1938—Juvenile literature. I. Title.

Johnson, James, 1835 or 6-1917.

AYANDELE, Emmanuel Ayankanmi. 320.1'59'24
Holy Johnson: pioneer of African nationalism, 1836-1917, by E. A. Ayandele. New York, Humanities Press [1970] 417 p. maps, ports. 23 cm. (Africana modern library, no. 13) Bibliography: p. 391-396. [DT504.J64A9 1970] 72-18063 11.00
1. Johnson, James, 1835 or 6-1917. I. Title. II. Series: Cass library of African studies. Africana modern library, no. 13. BIP

Johnson, John A.

LARSON, Agnes Mathilda, 1892-1967. 917.3'03 B
John A. Johnson; an uncommon American, by Agnes M. Larson. Northfield, Minn., Norwegian-American Historical Association, 1969. viii, 312 p. illus., facsims., ports. 24 cm. Bibliographical footnotes. [CT275.J677L3] 74-11269
1. Johnson, John A.

Johnson, John Arthur, 1878-1946.

DECOY, Robert H. 796.8'30924 B
The big black fire, by Robert H. DeCoy. Los Angeles, Holloway House Pub. Co. [1969] 312 p. 18 cm. [GV1132.J7D4] 70-76391 0.95
1. Johnson, John Arthur, 1878-1946. I. Title. BIP

FARR, Finis. 927.9683
Black champion; the life and times of Jack Johnson. New York, Scribner [1964] 245 p. ports. 22 cm. [GV1132.J73F3] 64-13631

1. Johnson, John Arthur, 1878-1946. I. Title.

FARR, Finis. 796.8'3'0924 B
Black champion; the life and times of Jack Johnson. Greenwich, Conn., Fawcett Publications [1969] 192 p. ports. 18 cm. (A Fawcett gold medal book) [GV1132.J7F3 1969] 78-7679 0.75
1. Johnson, John Arthur, 1878-1946. I. Title.

GILMORE, Al-Tony. 796.8'3'0924 B
Bad Nigger! The national impact of Jack Johnson. Port Washington, N.Y., Kennikat Press, 1975. 162 p. illus. 23 cm. (Kennikat Press national university publications. Series in American studies) Bibliography: p. 155-159. [GV1132.J7G54] 74-80590 ISBN 0-8046-9061-8
1. Johnson, John Arthur, 1878-1946. 2. Boxing. I. Title. **BIP**

JOHNSON, John Arthur, 1878-1946. 796.8'3'0924 B
Jack Johnson in the ring and out. With introductory articles by "Tad," Ed. W. Smith, Damon Runyon, and Mrs. Jack Johnson; special drawings by Edwin William Krauter. Chicago, National Sports Pub. Co., 1927. Detroit, Gale Research Co., 1975. 259 p. illus. 22 cm. [GV1132.J7A18 1975] 72-162515 ISBN 0-8103-4047-X 9.00
1. Johnson, John Arthur, 1878-1946. 2. Boxing. I. Title. **BIP**

JOHNSON, John Arthur, 1878-1946. 796.8'30924 B
Jack Johnson is a dandy; an autobiography. Introductory essays by Dick Schaap and the Lampman. New York, Chelsea House [1969] 262 p. illus., ports. 29 cm. [GV1132.J7A3] 78-79537 8.95
1. Boxing—Biography. I. Title.

Johnson, John Lipscomb.

JOHNSON, John Lipscomb. 922.673
Autobiographical notes. [Boulder? Colo.] 1958. 387p. illus. 25cm. [BX6495.J5A3] 58-37264
I. Title.

Johnson, John W., b. 1829.

†JOHNSON, John W., b.1829. 973'.04'97 S
Life of John W. Johnson / John W. Johnson. New York : Arno Press Co., 1977 [c1861] 152 p. ; 23 cm. (The Garland library of narratives of North American Indian captivities ; v. 111) Reprint of the ed. published by Johnson, Biddeford, Me. Issued with the reprint of the 1940 ed. of Knowles, N. The torture of captives by the Indians of eastern North America. New York, 1977. [E85.G2 vol. 111] [E99.M6] 970'.004'97 75-7139 ISBN 0-8240-1735-8 : 25.00 (set)
1. Johnson, John W., b. 1829. 2. Micmac Indians—Captivities. 3. Indians of North America—Captivities. 4. Maine—Biography. I. Title. II. Series.

Johnson, John W., 1892-1976.

JOHNSON, John W., 1892-1976. 634.9'092'4 B
Reminiscences of a forest ranger, 1914-1944 / by John W. Johnson ; with an introd. by Daniel L. Johnson. Dayton, Ohio : J. C. Robinette, c1976. 122 p. : ill. ; 24 cm. [SD129.J64A33] 76-18451 5.95
1. Johnson, John W., 1892-1976. 2. Forest rangers—Arizona—Biography. 3. Forest rangers—New Mexico—Biography. I. Title.

JOHNSON, John W., 1892-1976. 634.9'092'4 B
Reminiscences of a forest ranger, 1914-1944 / by John W. Johnson ; with an introd. by Daniel L. Johnson. Dayton, Ohio : J. C. Robinette, c1976. 122 p. : ill. ; 24 cm. [SD129.J64A33] 76-18451 5.95
1. Johnson, John W., 1892-1976. 2. Forest rangers—Arizona—Biography. 3. Forest rangers—New Mexico—Biography. I. Title.

Johnson, Joseph Ellis, 1817-1882.

JOHNSON, Rufus David, 1882- v. 12
J. E. J.: trail to sundown, Casadaga to Casa Grande, 1817-1882, the story of a pioneer: Joseph Ellis Johnson. (Salt Lake City? Printed by Deseret News Press, c1961] 514 p. illus., ports. 24 cm. 64-14148
1. Johnson, Joseph Ellis, 1817-1882. I. Title.

Johnson, Joseph, 1738-1809.

HAYWOOD, Peter. 020'.8 S
Joseph Johnson, publisher, 1738-1809 / [by] Peter Haywood. [Aberystwyth] : College of Librarianship, Wales, 1976. [5], 62 [i.e. 63] p. : facsims. ; 30 cm. (Student project - College of Librarianship, Wales ; no. 6) Includes bibliographical references. [Z671.C625 no. 6] [Z325.J72] 070.5'0924 77-372257 ISBN 0-904020-01-0 : £0.75
1. Johnson, Joseph, 1738-1809. 2. Publishers and publishing—England—History. 3. Authors, English—18th century. I. Title. II. Series: College of Librarianship, Wales. Students projects ; no. 6.

Johnson, Josephine Winslow, 1910-

JOHNSON, Josephine Winslow, 1910- 813'.5'2 B
Seven houses; a memoir of time and places [by] Josephine W. Johnson. With illus. by Peter Parnall. New York, Simon and Schuster [1973] 157 p. illus. 22 cm. [PS3519.O2633Z52] 72-86987 ISBN 0-671-21454-3 5.95
1. Johnson, Josephine Winslow, 1910- I. Title. **BIP**

Johnson, Lois Walfrid.

JOHNSON, Lois Walfrid. 248'.2 B
Either way, I win : a guide for growth in the power of prayer / Lois Walfrid Johnson. Minneapolis : Augsburg Pub. House, c1979. 192 p. ; 18 cm. [BR1725.J59A34] 79-50078 ISBN 0-8066-1706-3 pbk. : 2.50
1. Johnson, Lois Walfrid. 2. Christian biography—United States. 3. Cancer—Biography. I. Title. **BIP**

Johnson, Lynda Bird, 1944-

BANNETT, Carole. 973.9230922
Partners to the President. [1st ed.] New York, Citadel Press [1966] 92 p. ports. 21 cm. [E848.B3] 66-16485
1. Johnson, Claudia Alta (Taylor) 1912- 2. Johnson, Lynda Bird, 1944- 3. Johnson, Luci Baines, 1947- I. Title.

SULLIVAN, George Edward, 1927- 973.9230922
The personal story of Lynda & Luci Johnson. NewYork, Popular Lib. [c.1966] 144p. 18cm. [E848.S8] 66-5692 .50 pap.,
1. Johnson, Lynda Bird, 1944- 2. Johnson, Luci Baines, 1947- I. Title.

Johnson, Lyndon Baines, Pres. U.S., 1908-1973.

CARPENTER, Liz. 973.923'0924
Ruffles and flourishes; the warm and tender story of a simple girl who found adventure in the White House. [1st ed.] Garden City, N.Y., Doubleday, 1970. xv, 341 p. illus., ports. 25 cm. [E847.C35] 74-97707 6.95
1. Johnson, Lyndon Baines, Pres. U.S., 1908- 2. Johnson, Claudia Alta (Taylor) 1912- I. Title.

CHRISTIAN, George, 1927- 973.923'0924 B
The President steps down: a personal memoir of the transfer of power. [New York] Macmillan [1970] 282 p. 21 cm. [E846.C53] 75-110985
1. Johnson, Lyndon Baines Pres. U.S. 1908- 2. U.S.—Politics and government—1963-1969. I. Title.

CORMIER, Frank. 973.923'092'4 B
LBJ the way he was / Frank Cormier. 1st ed. Garden City, N.Y. : Doubleday, 1977. 276 p., [4] leaves of plates : ill. ; 22 cm. Includes index. [E847.C57] 76-18338 ISBN 0-385-04825-4 : 8.95
1. Johnson, Lyndon Baines, Pres. U.S., 1908-1973. 2. Cormier, Frank. 3. Presidents—United States—Biography. 4. Journalists—United States—Biography. 5. United States—Politics and government—1963-1969. I. Title.

DAVIE, Michael 973.9230924
LBJ: a foreign Observer's viewpoint. New York, Duell, [dist.Meredith, c.1966] 83p. 20cm. [E847.D3] 66-17040 2.95 bds.,
1. Johnson, Lyndon Baines, Pres. U. S., 1908- I. Title.

DAVIE, Michael 973.9230924
LBJ: a foreign observer's viewpoint. New York, Ballantine [1967,c.1966] 123p. 18cm. (U5062) [E847.D3] .60 pap.,
1. Johnson, Lyndon Baines, Pres. U.S.,1908- I. Title.

ELLIOTT, Bruce, ed. 082
The Johnson story. Jack Podell, editorial director; Bruce Elliott, editor/writer; David Burke, art director [and] Edith Conner Smith, copy editor. New York, Macfadden-Bartell Corp. [1964] 78 p. illus., ports. 28 cm. [E847.J6] 64-57866
1. Johnson, Lyndon Baines, Pres. U.S., 1908- I. Podell, Jack J., ed. II. Title.

OLDS, Helen (Diehl) 1895- j92
Lyndon Baines Johnson, by Helen D. Olds. Illus. by Paul Frame. New York, Putnam [1965] 64 p. col. illus., col. ports. 23 cm. (A See and read beginning to read biography) [E847.O4] 65-20714
1. Johnson, Lyndon Baines, Pres. U.S., 1908 — Juvenile literature. I. Frame, Paul, illus. II. Title. **BIP**

THOMPSON, Pat 923.73
Ladybird's man. Los Angeles, Holloway House [c.1964] 1 v. (chiefly illus.) 14x18cm. (HH-111) 64-4956 .75 pap.,
1. Johnson, Lyndon Baines, Pres. N. S., 1908- —Portraits, caricatures, etc. 2. Johnson, Claudia Alta (Taylor) 1912- —Portraits, caricatures, etc. I. Title.
1. Johnson, Lyndon Baines, Pres. U. S., 1908- —Juvenile literature. I. Title.

WHITNEY, David C. 92
Let's find out about Lyndon Baines Johnson, by David C. Whitney. New York, Watts [1967] 53p. illus., ports. 22cm. [E847.W542] 67-820 2.62; 1.95 lib. ed.,

FRANTZ, Joe Bertram, 1917- comp. 973.923'092'4 B
37 years of public service; the honorable Lyndon B. Johnson, by Joe B. Frantz. Austin, Tex., Shoal Creek Publishers [1974] 1 v. (unpaged) illus. 29 cm. [E847.F72] 73-91025
1. Johnson, Lyndon Baines, Pres. U.S., 1908-1973. I. Title.

HALEY, James Evetts, 1901- 923.173
A Texan looks at Lyndon; a study in illegitimate power. Canyon, Tex., Duro Pr., Box 390 [c.1964] 256p. 17cm. 64-56794 1.00 pap.,
1. Johnson, Lyndon Baines, Pres. U.S., 1908- I. Title.

HARWOOD, Richard. 973.923'092'4 B
Lyndon [by] Richard Harwood and Haynes Johnson. New York, Praeger Publishers [1973] 187 p. illus. 26 cm. "A Washington post book." [E847.H34] 73-5226 6.95
1. Johnson, Lyndon Baines, Pres. U.S., 1908-1973. I. Johnson, Haynes Bonner, 1931- joint author. II. Title.

JOHNSON, Claudia Alta (Taylor) 1912- 973.923'0924
A White House diary [by] Lady Bird Johnson. [1st ed.] New York, Holt, Rinehart and Winston [1970] ix, 806 p. illus., ports. 24 cm. [E848.J6] 78-124088 ISBN 0-03-085254-4 10.95
1. Johnson, Lyndon Baines, Pres. U.S., 1908- 2. Washington, D.C.—Social life and customs—1951- I. Title.

JOHNSON, Sam Houston. 973.923'0924 B
My brother, Lyndon. Edited by Enrique Hank Lopez. [1st ed.] New York, Cowles Book Co. [1970] 278 p. ports. 22 cm. [E847.J65 1970] 78-90068 6.95
1. Johnson, Lyndon Baines, Pres. U.S., 1908- I. Title.

JOHNSON story (The) 923.273
Jack Podell, edit. direct.;Bruce Elliott, ed. writer; David Burke, art direct.; Edith Conner Smith, copy ed. New York, Macfadden [1964] 78p. illus., ports. 28cm. [E847.J6] 64-57866 .50 pap.,
1. Johnson, Lyndon Baines, Pres. U.S., 1908- I. Elliott, Bruce, ed. II. Podell, Jack J., ed.

KEARNS, Doris. 973.923'092'4 B
Lyndon Johnson and the American dream / Doris Kearns. 1st ed. New York : Harper & Row, c1976. xii, 432 p. ; 24 cm. Includes bibliographical references and index. [E847.K42 1976] 75-42831 ISBN 0-06-012284-6 : 12.50
1. Johnson, Lyndon Baines, Pres. U.S., 1908-1973. 2. Presidents—United States—Biography. 3. United States—Politics and government—1963-1969. I. Title.

KEARNS, Doris. 973.923'092
Lyndon Johnson and the American dream / Doris Kearns. New York : New American Library, 1977,c1976. 463p. ; 18 cm. Includes bibliographical references and index. [E847.K42 1976] ISBN 0-451-07609-5 pbk. : 2.50
1. Johnson, Lyndon Baines, Pres. U.S., 1908-1973. 2. Presidents-United States-Biography. 3. United States-Politics and government-1963-1969. I. Title.
L.C. card no. for 1976 Harper & Row ed.: 75-42831. **BIP**

MOONEY, Booth, 1912- 973.923'092'4 B
LBJ : an irreverent chronicle / Booth Mooney. New York : Crowell, c1976. vii, 290 p. ; 24 cm. Includes index. [E847.M58] 75-33693 ISBN 0-690-01089-3
1. Johnson, Lyndon Baines, Pres. U.S., 1908-1973. I. Title. **BIP**

MOONEY, Booth, 1912- 923.273
The Lyndon Johnson story. New York, Farrar, Straus and Cudahy [1956] 178p. illus. 22cm. [E748.J74M6 1956] 56-10521
1. Johnson, Lyndon Baines, 1908- I. Title.

MOONEY, Booth, 1912- v. 12
The Lyndon Johnson story. [New York, Avon Books, c1964] 191 p. ports. 18 cm. (An Avon book) "S148." 65-71175
1. Johnson, Lyndon Baines, Pres. U.S., 1908- I. Title.

MOONEY, Booth, 1912- 923.173
The Lyndon Johnson story. New York, Farrar, Straus [1964] xxii, 198 p. ports. 22 cm. "Revised and expanded edition." [E847.M6] 64-15366
1. Johnson, Lyndon Baines, Pres. U.S., 1908- I. Title.

NEWLON, Clarke. 923.173
L. B. J., the man from Johnson City. New York, Dodd, Mead [1964] x, 213 p. illus., ports., geneal. table. 21 cm. [E847.N4] 64-20010
1. Johnson, Lyndon Baines, Pres. U.S., 1908- I. Title. **BIP**

NEWLON, Clarke. 973.9230924
L. B. J., the man from Johnson City. Rev. and enl. ed. New York, Dodd, Mead [1966] x, 244 p. illus., geneal. table, ports. 21 cm. [E847.N4 1966] 66-20511
1. Johnson, Lyndon Baines, Pres. U.S., 1908- I. Title.

NEWLON, Clarke. 973.9230924
L. B. J., the man from Johnson City. Rev. and enl. ed. New York, Dodd, Mead [1966] x, 244 p. illus., geneal. table, ports. 21 cm. [E847.N4 1966] 66-20511
1. Johnson, Lyndon Baines, Pres. U.S., 1908- I. Title.

NEWLON, Clarke. 973.923'0924 B
L. B. J., the man from Johnson City. Rev. and enl. ed. New York, Dodd, Mead [1970] x, 244 p. illus., geneal. table, ports. 21 cm. [E847.N4 1970] 72-135209 ISBN 0-396-04983-4 5.00
1. Johnson, Lyndon Baines, Pres. U.S., 1908- I. Title.

NEWLON, Clarke. 973.923'0924 B
L. B. J., the man from Johnson City. Rev. and enl. ed. New York, Dodd, Mead [1970] x, 244 p. illus., geneal. table, ports. 21 cm. [E847.N4 1970] 72-135209 ISBN 0-396-04983-4 5.00
1. Johnson, Lyndon Baines, Pres. U.S., 1908- I. Title.

NEWLON, Clarke. 973.923'092'4 B
L. B. J., the man from Johnson City / Clarke Newlon. Rev. and updated ed. New York : Dodd, Mead, 1976. p. cm. Includes index. A biography of Lyndon Johnson, the Texas senator who become the thirty-sixth President. [E847.N4 1976] 76-12156 ISBN 0-396-07340-9 : 5.95
1. Johnson, Lyndon Baines, Pres. U.S., 1908-1973. I. Title.

POOL, William C. 973.9230924
Lyndon Baines Johnson: the formative years [by] William C. Pool, Emmie Craddock, David E. Conrad. Illus. by Boyd Saunders. San Marcos, Tex., 78666 Southwest Texas State Coll. Pr. [1966, c.] 1965. 185p. illus., ports. 24cm. Bibl. [E847.P6] 66-398 5.25
1. Johnson, Lyndon Baines, Pres U. S., 1908- I. Craddock, Emmie, joint author. II. Conrad, David Eugene, joint author. III. Title.

PROVENCE, Harry 923.173
Lyndon B. Johnson, a biography. New York, Paperback Lib. [1965, c.1964] 174p. 18cm. (52-822) [E847.P7] .50 pap.,
1. Johnson, Lyndon Baines, Pres. U.S., 1908- I. Johnson, Lyndon Baines, Pres. U.S., 1908- II. Title.

PROVENCE, Harry 923.173
Lyndon B. Johnson, a biography. New York, Fleet [c.1964] 192p. 21cm. Appendix (p.[171]-184) contains addresses delivered by L.B. Johnson on May 30, Nov.27, and Nov 28,1963. 64-15704 4.50
1. Johnson, Lyndon Baines, Pres. U.S., 1908- I. Johnson, Lyndon Baines, Pres.U.S., 1908- II. Title.

SHERRILL, Robert. 973.923
The accidental President. New York, Pyramid Books [1968] 251 p. 19 cm. [E847.S47 1968b] 68-4857
1. Johnson, Lyndon Baines, Pres. U.S., 1908- 2. United States—Politics and government—1963-1969. I. Title.

SHERRILL, Robert. 973.923
The accidental President. New York, Pyramid Books [1968] 251 p. 19 cm. [E847.S47 1968b] 68-4857
1. Johnson, Lyndon Baines, Pres. U.S., 1908- 2. United States—Politics and government—1963-1969. I. Title.

SIDEY, Hugh. 973.923'0924
A very personal Presidency; Lyndon Johnson in the White House. [1st ed.] New York, Atheneum, 1968. ix, 305 p. 22 cm. [E847.S48 1968] 68-12545
1. Johnson, Lyndon Baines, Pres. U.S., 1908- I. Title.

SIDEY, Hugh. 973.923'0924
A very personal Presidency; Lyndon Johnson in the White House. [1st ed.] New York, Atheneum, 1968. ix, 305 p. 22 cm. [E847.S48 1968] 68-12545
1. Johnson, Lyndon Baines, Pres. U.S., 1908- I. Title.

SINGER, Kurt D., 1911- 923.173
Lyndon Baines Johnson, man of reason, by Kurt Singer, Jane Sherrod. Minneapolis, Denison [c.1964] 384p. ports. 22cm. 64-17743 3.95
1. Johnson, Lyndon Baines, Pres. U.S., 1908- I. Sherrod, Jane, joint author. II. Title.

SINGER, Kurt D 1911- 923.173
Lyndon Baines Johnson, man of reason, by Kurt Singer and Jane Sherrod. Minneapolis, T. S. Denison [1964] 384 p. ports. 22 cm. [E847.S5] 64-17743
1. Johnson, Lyndon Baines, Pres. U.S., 1908- I. Sherrod, Jane, joint author. II. Title.

STEINBERG, Alfred, 973.923'0924 B
1917- ,
Sam Johnson's boy; a close-up of the President from Texas. New York, Macmillan [1968] 871 p. 24 cm. [E847.S7] 68-21306
1. Johnson, Lyndon Baines, Pres. U.S., 1908- I. Title.

VALENTI, Jack. 973.923'092'4 B
A very human President / by Jack Valenti. 1st ed. New York : Norton, [1975] xii, 402 p. ; 21 cm. Includes index. [E847.V34 1975] 75-17701 ISBN 0-393-05552-3 : 9.95
1. Johnson, Lyndon Baines, Pres. U.S., 1908-1973. 2. Valenti, Jack. I. Title.

VALENTI, Jack 973.9230924
A very human president / Jack Valenti New York : Pocket Books ,1977 c1975 xi, 321 p. : ill. ; 18 cm. Includes index [E847.V34] ISBN 0-671-80834-6 pbk. : 1.95
1. Johnson, Lyndon Baines, Pres. U.S., 1908-1973 2. Valenti, Jack I. Title.
L.C. card no. for 1975 Norton edition: 75-17701. **BIP**

WHITE, William Smith 923.173
The professional: Lyndon B. Johnson. Boston, Houghton [c.]1964. 273p. 22cm. 64-21165 5.00
1. Johnson, Lyndon Baines, Pres. U.S., 1908- I. Title.

WHITE, William Smith 923.173
The professional: Lyndon B. Johnson. Boston, Houghton [c.]1964. 273p. 22cm. 64-21165 5.00
1. Johnson, Lyndon Baines, Pres. U.S., 1908- I. Title.

WHITE, William Smith 923.173
The professional: Lyndon B. Johnson. Greenwich, Conn., Fawcett [c.1964] 176p. 18cm. (Crest bk. R738) .60 pap.,
1. Johnson, Lyndon Baines, Pres. U.S 1908- I. Title.

ZEIGER, Henry A 923.173
Lyndon B. Johnson: man and President. With a foreword by James Tracy Crown. New York, Popular Library [1963] 143 p. 18 cm. "PC1033." [E847.Z4] 64-450
1. Johnson, Lyndon Baines, Pres. U.S., 1908- I. Title.

Johnson, Lyndon Baines, Pres. U.S., 1908-1973—Juvenile literature.

BARD, Bernard. 973.923'0924 B
LBJ; the picture story of Lyndon Baines Johnson. [New York] Lion Press [1966] 90 p. illus., ports 29 cm. Photographs and brief text trace the life and career of America's thirty-sixth President. [E847.B35] 92 70-2993
1. Johnson, Lyndon Baines, Pres. U.S., 1908- —Juvenile literature. I. Title.

KURLAND, Gerald, 973.924'092'4 B
1942-
Lyndon Baines Johnson, President caught in an ordeal of power. Charlotteville, N.Y., SamHar Press, 1972. 32 p. 22 cm. (Outstanding personalities, no. 25) Bibliography: p. 32. A biography of the Texas Senator who became thirty-sixth President of the United States. [E847.K87] 92 76-190243 ISBN 0-87157-525-6 1.98
1. Johnson, Lyndon Baines, Pres. U.S., 1908- —Juvenile literature. I. Title. Pap. $0.98 ISBN 0-87157-025-4

LYNCH, Dudley M., 973.923'092'4 B
1940-
The President from Texas, Lyndon Baines Johnson / by Dudley Lynch ; illustrated with photographs. New York : Crowell, [1975] 169 p., [8] leaves of plates : ill. ; 21 cm. Includes index. Bibliography: p. 160-164. A biography of the Texas Senator who became thirty-sixth President of the United States. [E847.L96 1975] 92 74-26817 ISBN 0-690-00627-6 : 5.95
1. Johnson, Lyndon Baines, Pres. U.S., 1908-1973—Juvenile literature. I. Title.

NEWMAN, Shirlee 973.923 (J)
Petkin.
The story of Lyndon B. Johnson, by Shirlee P. Newman. Philadelphia, Westminster Press [1967] 95 p. ports. 24 cm. Bibliography: p. 87-89. [E847.N43] 67-10662
1. Johnson, Lyndon Baines, Pres. U.S., 1908- Juvenile literature. I. Title.

Johnson, Lyndon Baines, Pres. U.S. 1908-

BELL, Jack, 1904- 923.173
The Johnson treatment; how Lyndon B. Johnson took over the Presidency and make it his own. [1st ed.] New York, Harper & Row [1965] 305 p. 22 cm. [E846.B4] 64-25107
1. Johnson, Lyndon Baines, Pres. U.S., 1908- 2. U.S. — Pol. & govt. — 1963- I. Title.

HALEY, James Evetts, 923.173
1901-
A Texan looks at Lyndon; a study in illegitimate power, by J. Evetts Haley. Canyon, Tex., Palo Duro Press [1964] 256 p. 17 cm. [E847.H3] 64-56794
1. Johnson, Lyndon Baines, Pres. U.S 1908- I. Title.

KLUCKHOHN, Frank L 923.173
The inside on LBJ [by] Frank L. Kluckhohn. Derby, Conn., Monarch Books [1964] 191 p. 19 cm. (Monarch select books, 457) [E847.K55] 64-4220
1. Johnson, Lyndon Baines, Pres. U.S., 1908- I. Title.

Johnson, Montford T., 1843-1896.

JOHNSON, Neil R 917.66
The Chickasaw rancher. Stillwater, Okla., Realands Press, 1961. 242p. illus. 24cm. [F697.J6J62 1961] 61-13159
1. Johnson, Montford T., 1843-1896. 2. Frontier and pioneer life— Oklahoma. 3. Ranch life. I. Title.

Johnson, Nunnally —Biography.

JOHNSON, Nora. 791.43'0232'0924 B
Flashback : Nora Johnson on Nunnally Johnson / Nora Johnson. 1st ed. Garden City, N.Y. : Doubleday, 1979. 369 p., [12] leaves of plates : ill. ; 22 cm Includes index. [PS3519.O2834Z73] 78-18137 ISBN 0-385-13406-1 : 11.95
1. Johnson, Nunnally—Biography. 2. Johnson, Nora—Biography. 3. Screen writers—United States—Biography. 4. Moving-picture producers and directors—United States—Biography. 5. Authors, American—20th century—Biography. I. Title. **BIP**

STEMPEL, Tom, 1941- 812'.5'2 B
Screenwriter, the life and times of Nunnally Johnson / Tom Stempel. South Brunswick [N.J.] : A. S. Barnes, 1979, c1980. p. cm. Includes index. Filmography: p. [PS3519.O2834Z86] 78-75339 ISBN 0-498-02382-6 : 8.95
1. Johnson, Nunnally—Biography. 2. Screen writers—United States—Biography. 3. Authors, American—20th century—Biography. I. Title.

Johnson, Oliver, 1821-1907.

JOHNSON, 977.2'52'030924 B
Oliver, 1821-1907.
A home in the woods : pioneer life in Indiana / as related by Howard Johnson. Bloomington : Indiana University Press, [1977] p. cm. Reprint of the 1951 ed. published by Indiana Historical Society, Indianapolis, as v. 16, no. 2, of its Publications. Original ed. has subtitle: Oliver Johnson's reminiscences of early Marion County. [F532.M4J6 1977] 77-74426 ISBN 0-253-32842-X : 9.95
1. Johnson, Oliver, 1821-1907. 2. Frontier and pioneer life—Indiana—Marion Co. 3. Pioneers—Indiana—Marion Co.—Biography. 4. Marion Co., Ind.—Biography. I. Johnson, Howard, 1873- II. Title. III. Series: Indiana Historical Society. Publications ; v. 16, no. 2. **BIP**

Johnson, Pamela Hansford, 1912- — Biography.

JOHNSON, Pamela 823'.9'12 B
Hansford, 1912-
Important to me / Pamela Hansford Johnson. New York : Scribner, [1975] c1974. 254 p. ; 24 cm. [PR6019.O3938Z52 1975] 74-24704 ISBN 0-684-13993-6 : 7.95
1. Johnson, Pamela Hansford, 1912- — Biography. I. Title.

Johnson, Philip Cortelyou, 1906-

JACOBUS, John M 720.973
Philip Johnson. New York, G. Braziller, 1962. 127p. illus., port. 26cm. (Makers of contemporary architecture) Bibliography: p. [123]-124. [NA737.J6J3] 62-16264
1. Johnson, Philip Cortelyou, 1906- I. Title. II. Series.

Johnson, Reginald Brimley,

JOHNSON, Reginald 828'.7'09 B
Brimley, 1867-1932.
Leigh Hunt. New York, Haskell House [1970]. vi, 152 p. port. 23 cm. Reprint of the 1896 ed. Includes bibliographical references. [PR4813.J6 1970] 73-115182 ISBN 8-383-10109-
I. Hunt, Leigh, 1784-1859. **BIP**

Johnson, Reverdy, 1796-1876.

STEINER, Bernard 973.8'1'0924 B
Christian, 1867-1926.
Life of Reverdy Johnson. New York, Russell & Russell [1970] 284 p. port. 23 cm. Reprint of the 1914 ed. Includes bibliographical references. [E415.9.J56S7 1970] 76-81475
1. Johnson, Reverdy, 1796-1876. 2. U.S.—Politics and government—1849-1877. I. Title. **BIP**

Johnson, Richard Mentor, 1781-1850.

MEYER, Leland 973.5'7'0924 B
Winfield, 1892-
The life and times of Colonel Richard M. Johnson of Kentucky. New York, AMS Press, 1967. 508 p. illus. 23 cm. (Studies in history, economics and public law, no. 359) Reprint of the 1932 ed.; also issued as the author's thesis, Columbia University, 1932. Bibliography: p. 479-493. [E340.J69M4 1967] 72-29893
1. Johnson, Richard Mentor, 1781-1850. 2. Kentucky—Politics and government—1792-1865. 3. U.S.—Politics and government—19th century. I. Title. II. Series: Columbia studies in the social sciences, 359 **BIP**

Johnson, Samuel,

JOHNSON, Samuel, 828'.6'09 B
1709-1784.
Letters of Samuel Johnson, LL.D. Collected and edited by George Birkbeck Hill. Freeport, N.Y., Books for Libraries Press [1973] p. Reprint of the 1892 ed. Contents.Contents.—v. 1. Oct. 30, 1731-Dec. 21, 1776.—v. 2. Jan 15, 1777 Dec. 18, 1784. [PR3533.A44 1973] 72-13658 ISBN 0-8369-8187-1
I. Hill, George Birkbeck Norman, 1835-1903, ed.

JOHNSON, Samuel, 1709-1784. 928.2
The Letters of Samuel Johnson, with Mrs. Thrale's geniuine letters to him. Collected edited by R. W. Chapman. Oxford, Clarnendon Press, 1952. 3v. facsims. 23cm. Contents.v. 1. 1719-1774.--v. 2. 1775-1782.--v. 3. 1783-1784. [PR3533.A2 1952] 53-6169
I. Piozzi, Hester, Lyuch (Salusbury) Thrale, 1741-1821. II. Title.

Johnson, Samuel, 1696-1772.

CARROLL, Peter N. 283'.092'4 B
The other Samuel Johnson : a psychohistory of early New England / Peter N. Carroll. Rutherford [N.J.] : Fairleigh Dickinson University Press, c1978. p. cm. Includes index. Bibliography: p. [BX5995.J59C37] 77-74413 ISBN 0-8386-2059-0 : 15.00
1. Johnson, Samuel, 1696-1772. 2. Church of England—Clergy—Biography. 3. Clergy—New England—Biography. 4. New England—Biography. I. Title. **BIP**

JOHNSON, Samuel, 378.1'12'0924 B
1696-1772.
Samuel Johnson, president of King's College, his career and writings. Edited by Herbert and Carol Schneider, with a foreword by Nicholas Murray Butler. New York, Columbia University Press, 1929. [New York, AMS Press, 1972] 4 v. fronts.

24 cm. Contents.Contents.—v. 1. Autobiography and letters.—v. 2. The philosopher.—v. 3. The churchman.—v. 4. Founding King's College. "Bibliography and chronological index": v. 4, p. [283]-361. [LD1245 1754.A53] 72-153333 95.00
1. Johnson, Samuel, 1696-1772. 2. Columbia University—History—Sources. I. Title.

Johnson, Samuel, 1709-1784.

ANDERSON, Robert, 1750-1830. 828'.6'09 S
The life of Samuel Johnson, LL.D. New York, Garland Pub., 1974. p. cm. (The Life & times of seven major British writers. Johnsoniana, 25) Reprint of the 1815 ed. printed for Doig and Stirling, London. [PR3533.J59 vol. 25] 828'.6'09 B 74-14889 ISBN 0-8240-1303-4 22.00
1. Johnson, Samuel, 1709-1784. I. Series: Johnsoniana, 25.

BAILEY, John Cann, 1864-1931. 828'.6'09 B
Dr. Johnson and his circle / by John Bailey . Darby, Pa. : Arden Library, 1978. p. cm. Reprint of the 1913 ed. published by H. Holt, New York, which was issued as no. 57 of Home university library of modern knowledge. Includes index. Bibliography: p. [PR3533.B2 1978] 78-17750 ISBN 0-8495-0414-7 lib. bdg. : 20.00
1. Johnson, Samuel, 1709-1784. 2. Boswell, James, 1740-1795. 3. Authors, English—18th century—Biography. I. Title. **BIP**

BATE, Walter Jackson, 1918- 828'.6'09 B
Samuel Johnson / by W. Jackson Bate. New York : Harcourt Brace Jovanovich, c1977. p. cm. Includes index. Bibliography: p. [PR3533.B334] 77-73044 19.95
1. Johnson, Samuel, 1709-1784. 2. Authors, English—18th century—Biography.

BOSWELL, James, 1740-1795 928.2
Bosewell's life of Samuel Johnson. Abridged, introd. by Anne H. and Irvin Ehrenpreis. New York, Washington Sq. [c.1965] 524p. 18cm. (W1083) [PR3533.B6] .90 pap.,
1. Johnson, Samuel, 1709-1784. I. Title.

BOSWELL, James, 1740-1795. v. 12
Boswell's Johnson sampler; selections from the life of Samuel Johnson. Edited by Archibald Marshall. Greenwich, Conn., Fawcett Publications [c1957] 240 p. (Sampler series) Also published under titles Boswell's Johnson and Everybody's Boswell. 66-3428
1. Johnson, Samuel, 1709-1784. I. Marshall, Archibald 1866-1934. II. Title.

BOSWELL, James, 1740-1795 928.2
Boswell's Life of Johnson, abridged, ed., with an introd. by Charles Grosvenor Osgood. New York, Scribners [1963, c.1917] xix, 574p. 17cm. (Modern Student's Lib.) 1.50 pap.,
1. Johnson, Samuel, 1709-1784. I. Osgood, Charles Grosvenor, 1871- ed. II. Title.

BOSWELL, James, 1740-1795 928.2
Life of Johnson. New York, Oxford Univ. Press [1961] xxiv, 1491p. (Oxford standard authors) 3.75 pap.,
*1. Johnson, Samuel, 1709-1784. I. Title.***BIP**

BOSWELL, James, 1740-1795. 928.2
Life of Johnson. [Oxford standard authors ed.] London, New York, Oxford University Press [1953] xxiv, 1491p. 19cm. [PR3533.B6 1953] 54-4092
1. Johnson, Samuel, 1709-1784. I. Titlc.

BOSWELL, James, 1740-1795. 928.1
Life of Johnson. Edited, with an introd., by Charles Norman. [1st ed.] New York, Collier Books [1961] 637p. 18cm. (Collier books, BS35) An abridgment. [PR3533.B62 1961] 61-18127
1. Johnson, Samuel, 1709-1784. I. Title.

BOSWELL, James, 1740-1795. 823'.5
Life of Johnson, together with Journal of a tour to the Hebrides and Johnson's Diary of a journey into North Wales. Edited by George Birkbeck Hill. Rev. and enl. ed. by L. F. Powell. Oxford, Clarendon Press, 1934-64. 6 v. illus., facsims., fold. map. ports. 23 cm. Vols. 5-6, with revisions by L. F. Powell, first published in 1950; republished in 1964 as 2d ed., with further revisions. Errata slips inserted. Contents.CONTENTS. -- v. 1-4. The life. -- v. 5. The tour to the Hebrides, and The journey into North Wales. 2d ed. -- v. 6. Index, table of anonymous persons, bibliography, errata. 2d ed. [PR3533.B6] 34-32393
1. Johnson, Samuel, 1700-1784. 2. Hebrides — Descr. & trav. I. Boswell, James, 1740-1795. Journal of a tour to the Hebrides. II. Johnson, Samuel, 1709-1784. Diary of a journey into North Wales. III. Hill, George Birkbeck Norman, 1835-1903, ed. IV. Powell, Lawrence Fitzroy, 1881- ed. V. Title.

BOSWELL, James, 1740-1795 824'.6
The life of Samuel Johnson. Ed. & abridged, with introd., by Frank Brady. New York, New Amer. Lib. [1968] 664p. 18cm. (Signet classic, CY378) Bibl. [PR3533.B62 1968] 68-18400 1.25 pap.,
1. Johnson, Samuel, 1709-1784. I. Brady, Frank. ed. II. Title.

BOSWELL, James, 1740-1795. 928.2
Life of Samuel Johnson. Abridged and with an introd. by Anne H. Ehrenpreis and Irvin Ehrenpreis. New York, Washington Square Press [1965] xviii, 524 p. 18 cm. [PR3533.B62] 65-4451
1. Johnson, Samuel, 1709-1784. I. Ehrenpreis, Anne Henry, ed. II. Ehrenpreis, Irvin, 1920- ed. III. Title. **BIP**

BOSWELL, James, 1740-1795. 928.2
The life of Samuel Johnson; abridged, with an introd. by Bergen Evans. [1st ed.] New York, Modern Library [1952] xv, [1], 559 p. 19 cm. (The Modern Library of the world's best books [282]) Bibliography: p [xvi] [PR3533.B62 1952] 52-5875
1. Johnson, Samuel, 1709-1784. I. Evans, Bergen, 1904- II. Title.

BOSWELL, James, 1740-1795. 823'.5
The life of Samuel Johnson, LL.D. With marginal comments and markings from two copies annotated by Hester Lynch Thrale Piozzi. Prepared for publication with an introd. by Edward G. Fletcher. New York, Heritage Press [1963] 3 v. col. ports. 24 cm. "A chronological catalogue of the prose works of Samuel Johnson, LL.D": v. 1, p. [xiix]-iviii. [PR3533.B62] 63-23806
1. Johnson, Samuel, 1709-1784. I. Piozzi, Hester Lynch (Salusbury) Thrale, 1741-1821. II. Fletcher, Edward Garland, 1903- ed. III. Title.

BOSWELL, James, 1740-1795. 928.2
Vie de Samuel Johnson. (The life of Samuel Johnson) Traduction de J. P. Le Hoc. Paris, Gallimard [1954] 421p. 23cm. (Les Classiques anglais) [PR3533.B613] 54-29877
1. Johnson, Samuel, 1709-1784. I. Title.

BRACK, O. M., comp. 828'.6'09
The early biographies of Samuel Johnson / edited by O. M. Brack, Jr., Robert E. Kelley. Iowa City : University of Iowa Press, [1974] ix, 367 p. ; 23 cm. Includes index. Bibliography: p. [293]-337. [PR3533.B75] 73-77385 ISBN 0-87745-038-2 : 15.00
1. Johnson, Samuel, 1709-1784. I. Kelley, Robert E., joint comp. II. Title. **BIP**

CHRISTIANI, Sigyn. 928'.2
Samuel Johnson als kritiker im lichte von pseudo-klassizismus und romantik, von Sigyn Christiani. Leipzig, B. Tauchnitz, 1931. New York, Johnson. Reprint, 1968. 6p. 1., 120p. 24cm. (Added t.-p.: Beitrage zur englischen philologie, 18. hft.) The author's inaugural dissertation, Munich, 1930, Vorwort signed: Ellen Sigyn Christiani. Literatur-verzeichnis: 6th prelim. leaf. [PR3534.C48] 32-7763 6.00 pap.,
*1. Johnson, Samuel, 1709-1784. I. Title.***BIP**

CLIFFORD, James Lowry, 1901- 928.2
Young Sam Johnson. New York, McGraw-Hill [1955] 377 p. illus. 21 cm. [PR3533.C6] 54-12672
1. Johnson, Samuel, 1709-1784. I. Title.

CLIFFORD, James Lowry, 1901- v. 12
Young Sam Johnson. New York, Oxford University Press 1961. 377 p. illus. 21 cm. (Hesperides Books, HS5) 63-3884
1. Johnson, Samuel, 1709-1784. I. Title.

CLIFFORD, James Lowry, 1901- 928.2
Young Samuel Johnson. New York, Oxford, 1961 [c.1955] 377p. (Hesperides bk., HS5) Bibl. 2.95 pap.,
1. Johnson, Samuel, 1709-1784. II. Title.

COOK, William, d.1824. 828'.6'09 S
The life of Samuel Johnson, LL.D., 1785 [by] William Cooke. New York, Garland Pub., 1974. p. cm. (The Life & times of seven major British writers. Johnsoniana, 15) Reprint of the 1785 ed. printed for G. Kearsley, London. [PR3533.J59 vol. 15] 828'.6'09 B 74-14887 ISBN 0-8240-1293-3 22.00
1. Johnson, Samuel, 1709-1784. I. Johnson, Samuel, 1709-1784. II. Series: Johnsoniana, 15.

DAVIS, Bertram Hylton 928.2
Johnson before Boswell; a study of Sir John Hawkins' Life of Samuel Johnson. New Haven, Conn., Yale University Press, 1960 [c.1957] xi, 222p. Includes bibliography. 23cm. 60-6603 4.50
1. Johnson, Samuel, 1709-1784. 2. Hawkins, John, Sir 1719-1789. The life of Samuel Johnson, LL. D. I. Title.

DRAKE, Nathan, 1766-1836. 824'.5'09
Essays, biographical, critical and historical illustrative of the Rambler, Adventurer & Idler. With a new introd. by Robert Donald Spector. New York, Johnson Reprint Corp., 1968. 2 v. 16 cm. (Belles lettres in English) Cover title: Essays illustrative of the Rambler, Adventurer, and Idler. Reprint of the 1809-1810 ed. [PR925.D7 1968] 68-29512
1. Johnson, Samuel, 1709-1784. 2. Hawkesworth, John, 1715?-1773. 3. English essays—History and criticism. 4. English periodicals. 5. English literature—18th century—History and criticism. I. Title. II. Title: Essays illustrative of the Rambler, Adventurer and Idler.

FOUR biographies, 1786-1805. 828'.6'09 B
New York : Garland Pub. Co., 1975[i.e.1976] 335 p. in various pagings ; 23 cm. (The Life & times of seven major British writers) (Johnsoniana ; 19) Reprint of An essay on the life, character, and writings of Dr. Samuel Johnson, by J. Towers, first printed in 1786 for C. Dilly, London; of The character of Dr. Johnson, by W. Temple, first printed in 1792 for C. Dilly, London; of The life of Dr. Samuel Johnson, by F. Thomas, first printed in 1792 for the author, London; and of Dialogue between Mrs. Knowles and Dr. Johnson, first printed in 1805 by C. Stower, London. [PR3533.J59 vol. 19] 75-26710 ISBN 0-8240-1297-6 lib.bdg. : 28.00
1. Johnson, Samuel, 1709-1784. I. Title. II. Series.

HAWKINS, John, Sir, 1719-1789. 928.1
The life of Samuel Johnson, LL. D. Edited, abridged, and with an introd., by Bertram H. Davis. New York, Macmillan, 1961. 341 p. illus. 22 cm. [PR3533.H3 1961] 61-10764
1. Johnson, Samuel, 1709-1784.

HAYLEY, William, 1745-1820. 828'.6'09 S
Two dialogues. New York, Garland Pub., 1974. p. cm. (The Life and times of seven major British writers. Johnsoniana, 22) Reprint of the 1787 ed. printed for T. Cadell, London. [PR3533.J59 vol. 22] 820'.9'005 74-16270 ISBN 0-8240-1300-X 22.00
1. Johnson, Samuel, 1709-1784. 2. Chesterfield, Philip Dormer Stanhope, 4th Earl of, 1694-1773. I. Title. II. Series: Johnsoniana, 22.

HAYLEY, William, 1745-1820. 820.9'005
Two dialogues: containing a comparative view of the lives, characters, and writings of Philip, the late Earl of Chesterfield, and Samuel Johnson (1787). Gainesville, Fla., Scholars' Facsimiles & Reprints, 1970. xviii, xxiv, 240 p. 23 cm. A facsim. reproduction from a copy in Yale University Library with a new introd. by Robert E. Kelley. Original t.p. reads: Two dialogues; containing a comparative view of the lives, characters, and writings of Philip, the late Earl of Chesterfield, and Dr. Samuel Johnson. London: Printed for T. Cadell, in the Strand. 1787. [PR3533.H35 1970] 71-122486
1. Johnson, Samuel, 1709-1784. 2. Chesterfield, Philip Dormer Stanhope, 4th Earl of, 1694-1773. I. Title. **BIP**

HOLLIS, Christopher, 1902- 828'.6'09 B
Dr. Johnson / Christopher Hollis. New York : Haskell House Publishers, [1976,i.e.1977] p. cm. Reprint of the 1928 ed. published by V. Gollancz, London. [PR3533.H5 1976] 76-27 ISBN 0-8383-1863-0 lib.bdg. : 12.95
1. Johnson, Samuel, 1709-1784. **BIP**

HUDSON, William Henry, 1862-1918. 821'.6'09
Johnson & Goldsmith & their poetry. London, G. G. Harrap, 1918. [New York, AMS Press, 1972] 175, [1] p. port. 19 cm. (Poetry and life series) Bibliography: p. 175-[176] [PR3533.H8 1972] 75-120963 ISBN 0-404-52515-6 8.00
1. Johnson, Samuel, 1709-1784. 2. Goldsmith, Oliver, 1728-1774. I. Title. II. Series.

HUDSON, William Henry, 1862-1918. 821'.6'09
Johnson & Goldsmith & their poetry. [Folcroft, Pa.] Folcroft Press, 1970. 175 p. front. 23 cm. "Limited to 150 copies." Reprint of the 1922 ed., issued in series: Poetry & life. Includes bibliographical references. [PR3533.H8 1970] 72-194976
1. Johnson, Samuel 1709-1784. 2. Goldsmith, Oliver, 1728-1774. I. Title. II. Series: Poetry and life series. **BIP**

JOYCE, Michael. 928.2
Samuel Johnson. London, New York, Longmans, Green [1955] 171p. illus. 19cm. (Men and books) [PR3533.J68] 55-12627
1. Johnson, Samuel, 1709-1784. I. Title.

KELLEY, Robert E. 828'.6'09
Samuel Johnson's early biographers [by] Robert E. Kelley and O. M. Brack, Jr. Iowa City, University of Iowa Press [1971] xvi, 159 p. illus., ports. 23 cm. [PR3533.K4] 74-151649 ISBN 0-87745-021-8
1. Johnson, Samuel, 1709-1784. I. Brack, O. M., joint author. II. Title. **BIP**

KRUTCH, Joseph Wood, 1893- 982.2
Samuel Johnson. New York, Harcourt, Brace & World [1963] 697 p. 21 cm. (A Harbinger book) Includes bibliography. [PR3533.K7] 63-12157
1. Johnson, Samuel, 1700-1784. I. Title.

KRUTCH, Joseph Wood, 1893- 928.2
Samuel Johnson. New York, Harcourt, Brace & World [1963] 597 p. 21 cm. (A Harbinger book) Includes bibliography. [PR3533.K7 1963] 63-12157
1. Johnson, Samuel, 1709-1784.

LIFE of Johnson. v. 12
Introd. by Sir Sydney Roberts; index by Alan Dent. London, Dent; New York, Dutton [1930] 2v. 19cm. (Everyman's library, 1- 2.Biography)
1. Johnson, Samuel, 1709-1784. I. Boswell, James, 1740-1795.

LUNN, Hugh Kingsmill, 1889-1949. 828'.6'09
Samuel Johnson / by Hugh Kingsmill. New York : Haskell House, 1975. 249 p. ; 21 cm. Reprint of the 1934 ed. published by Viking Press, New York. Includes index. [PR3533.L75 1976] 75-42205 ISBN 0-8383-2061-9 ; 15.95
1. Johnson, Samuel, 1709-1784.

MILLER, Clarence Altha, 1890- 828'.6'09
Sir John Hawkins, Dr. Johnson's friend-attorney-executor-biographer; a reorientation of the knight, the lady, and Boswell, by C. A. Miller. [Folcroft, Pa.] Folcroft Library Editions, 1972. 39 p. 34 cm. Reprint of the 1951 ed. Includes bibliographical references. [PR3533.M5 1972] 72-10377 ISBN 0-8414-0450-X
1. Johnson, Samuel, 1709-1784. 2. Hawkins, John, Sir, 1719-1789. I. Title.

MURPHY, Arthur, 1727- 828'.6'09 B 1805.
An essay on the life and genius of Samuel Johnson, LL.D New York, Garland Pub., 1970. 187 p. 22 cm. Facsim. from a copy loaned by Stephen Weissman of Ximenes; Rare Books, inc. with imprint: London, T. Longman [etc.] 1792. [PR3533.M8 1792a] 74-112191
1. Johnson, Samuel, 1709-1784. I. Title.

NORMAN, Charles, 1904- 928.2
Mr. Oddity, Samuel Johnson. LL. D. Drexel Hill, Pa., Bell Pub. Co. [1951] xi, 348 p. 22 cm. [PR3533.N6] 51-12372
1. Johnson, Samuel, 1709-1784. I. Title.

NOSWELL, James, 1740-1795. 823'.5
The life of Samuel Johnson, L. L. D.; complete and unabridged, with notes. With an introd. by Herbert Askwith. New York, Modern Library [195-] xv, 1200p. 21cm. (The Modern library of the world's best books) 'The present text follows that of Malone's sixth edition.' [PR3533.B] A55
1. Johnson, Samuel, 1709-1784. I. Malone, Edmond, 1741-1812. II. Title.

PEARSON, Hesketh, 1887- 928.2
Johnson and Boswell; the story of their lives. New York, Harper [1959, c1958] 390p. illus. 22cm. Includes bibliography. [PR3533.P34] 58-8862
1. Johnson, Samuel, 1709-1784. 2. Boswell, James, 1740-1795. I. Title.

PIOZZI, Hester Lynch 828'.6'09 B (Salusbury) Thrale, 1741-1821.
Anecdotes of Samuel Johnson, by Hester Lynch Piozzi. Edited and with an introd. by S. C. Roberts. Freeport, N.Y., Books for Libraries Press [1969] xxx, 196 p. 23 cm. (Select bibliographies reprint series) Reprint of the 1925 ed. [PR3533.P4 1969] 75-99668
1. Johnson, Samuel, 1709-1784. I. Title **BIP**

PIOZZI, Hester Lynch 828'.6'09 B (Salusbury) Thrale, 1741-1821.
Anecdotes of the late Samuel Johnson, LL.D., during the last twenty years of his life. Edited, with an introd. by S. C. Roberts. Westport, Conn., Greenwood Press [1971] xlix, 205 p. front. 23 cm. Reprint of the 1925 ed. Bibliography: p. [ix]-xii. [PR3533.P4 1971] 70-95109 ISBN 0-8371-3138-3
1. Johnson, Samuel, 1709-1784. I. Title.

PIOZZI, Hester Lynch 828'.6'09 B Salusbury Thrale, 1741-1821.
Anecdotes of the late Samuel Johnson, LL.D., 1786. New York, Garland Pub., 1974. p. cm. (The Life & times of seven major British writers: Johnsoniana, 18) Reprint of the 1786 ed. printed for Messers. Moncrieffe and others, Dublin. [PR3533.J59 vol. 18] 74-14883 22.00
1. Johnson, Samuel, 1709-1784. I. Title. II. Series: Johnsoniana, 18.

ROBERTS, Sydney 828'.6'09 B Castle, 1887-1966.
Doctor Johnson. [Folcroft, Pa.] Folcroft Library Editions, 1973. p. Reprint of the 1935 ed. published by Duckworth, London, in series: Great lives. [PR3533.R54 1973] 73-16388 10.00
1. Johnson, Samuel, 1709-1784. I. Title.

ROBERTS, Sydney 828'.6'09 B Castle, Sir, 1887-1966.
The story of Doctor Johnson; being an introduction to Boswell's Life. Folcroft, Pa.] Folcroft Library Editions, 1973. p. Reprint of the 1919 ed. published by the University Press, Cambridge. Bibliography: p. [PR3533.R6 1973] 73-12614 20.00
1. Johnson, Samuel, 1709-1784. I. Boswell, James, 1740-1795. The life of Samuel Johnson. II. Title.

ROSCOE, Edward Stanley, 828'.6'09 1849-1932.
Aspects of Doctor Johnson. [Folcroft, Pa.] Folcroft Library Editions, 1973. p. Reprint of the 1928 ed. published by the University Press, Cambridge, Eng. [PR3533.R65 1973] 73-6688 ISBN 0-8414-2575-2 (lib. bdg.)
1. Johnson, Samuel, 1709-1784. I. Title. **BIP**

SCHWARTZ, Richard B. 509'.24
Samuel Johnson and the new science [by] Richard B. Schwartz. Madison, University of Wisconsin Press [1971] x, 188 p. port. 23 cm. Includes bibliographical references. [Q143.J64S3] 76-161089 ISBN 0-299-06010-1 10.00
1. Johnson, Samuel, 1709-1784. 2. Science—Philosophy. I. Title. **BIP**

SHAW, William, 1749- 828'.6'09 S 1831.
Memoirs of the life and writings of the late Dr. Samuel Johnson. New York, Garland Pub., 1974. p. cm. (The Life & times of seven major British writers. Johnsoniana, 16) Reprint of the 1785 ed. printed for J. Walker, London. [PR3533.J59 vol. 16] 828'.6'09 B 74-14888 ISBN 0-8240-1294-1 22.00
1. Johnson, Samuel, 1709-1784. I. Series: Johnsoniana, 16.

SHAW, William, 1749- 828'.6'09 B 1831.
Memoirs of the life and writings of the late Dr. Samuel Johnson [by] William Shaw. Anecdotes of the late Samuel Johnson, LL.D., during the last twenty years of his life [by] Hesther Lynch Piozzi. Edited with an introd. by Arthur Sherbo. London, New York, Oxford University Press, 1974. xxii, 201 p. illus. 25 cm. (Oxford English memoirs and travels) Half title: Memoirs and anecdotes of Dr. Johnson. On spine: Memoirs of Dr. Johnson. Bibliography: p. xvii-xviii. [PR3533.S5 1974] 74-177118 ISBN 0-19-255416-6 13.00
1. Johnson, Samuel, 1709-1784. I. Piozzi, Hester Lynch Salusbury Thrale, 1741-1821. Anecdotes of the late Samuel Johnson. 1974. II. Title. III. Title: Anecdotes of the late Samuel Johnson. IV. Title: Memoirs and anecdotes of Dr. Johnson. V. Title: Memoirs of Dr. Johnson. VI. Series. **BIP**

STEPHEN, Leslie, Sir, 828'.6'09 1832-1904.
Samuel Johnson. New York, AMS Press [1968] 195 p. 22 cm. (English men of letters) Reprint of the 1887 ed. [PR3533.S7 1968] 68-58398
1. Johnson, Samuel, 1709-1784.

VULLIAMY, Colwyn 828'.6'09 B Edward, 1886-
Ursa Major; a study of Dr. Johnson and his friends [by] C. E. Vulliamy. [Folcroft, Pa.] Folcroft Library Editions, 1973. p. Reprint of the 1946 ed. published by M. Joseph, London. [PR3533.V84 1973] 73-16143 25.00
1. Johnson, Samuel, 1709-1784. I. Title. **BIP**

WAIN, John. 828'.6'09 B
Samuel Johnson / John Wain. New York : Viking Press, 1975, c1974. 388 p., [8] leaves of plates ; ill. ; 25 cm. Includes index. Bibliography: p. [380] [PR3533.W33 1975] 74-6851 ISBN 0-670-61671-0 : 10.00.
1. Johnson, Samuel, 1709-1784. **BIP**

WAIN, John. 828'.6'09 B
Samuel Johnson : a biography / by John Wain. New York : McGraw-Hill, [1976] c1974. p. cm. Includes index. Bibliography: p. [PR3533.W33 1976] 76-2369 ISBN 0-07-067715-8 pbk. : 4.95
1. Johnson, Samuel, 1709-1784. **BIP**

Johnson, Samuel, 1709-1784—Biography.

BOSWELL, James, 1740- 828'.6'09 B 1795.
The conversations of Dr. Johnson; extracted from the Life by James Boswell and edited with a pref. by Raymond Postgate. New York, Taplinger Pub. Co. [1970, c1930] 326 p. 23 cm. [PR3533.B62 1970] 70-121337 ISBN 0-8008-4735-0 6.95
1. Johnson, Samuel, 1709-1784—Biography. I. Postgate, Raymond William, 1896- ed. II. Title.

BOSWELL, James, 1740- 828'.6'09 B 1795.
Life of Johnson; edited by R. W. Chapman; a new edition corrected by J. D. Fleeman. New ed. London, New York, Oxford U.P., 1970. xxiv, 1492 p. 21 cm. (Oxford paperbacks, 204) Includes bibliographical references. [PR3533.B6 1970] 78-515717 30/-
1. Johnson, Samuel, 1700-1784—Biography. I. Chapman, Robert William, 1881-1960, ed.

BOSWELL, James, 1740- 828'.6'09 B 1795.
Life of Johnson; edited by R. W. Chapman; a new edition corrected by J. D. Fleeman. New ed. London, New York, Oxford U.P., 1970. xxiv, 1492 p. 21 cm. (Oxford paperbacks, 204) Includes bibliographical references. [PR3533.B6 1970] 78-515717 30/-
1. Johnson, Samuel, 1700-1784—Biography. I. Chapman, Robert William, 1881-1960, ed.

BOSWELL, James, 1740- 828'.6'09 B 1795.
The life of Samuel Johnson. Edited and abridged, with an introd., by Frank Brady. New York, New American Library [1968] 664 p. 18 cm. (A Signet classic, CY378) Bibliography: p. 664. [PR3533.B62 1968] 68-18400
1. Johnson, Samuel, 1709-1784—Biography. I. Brady, Frank, ed. II. Title.

BOSWELL, James, 1740- 828'.6'09 B 1795.
The life of Samuel Johnson; abridged, with an introd. by Bergen Evans. [1st ed.] New York, Modern Library [1952] xv, [1], 559 p. 19 cm. (The Modern library of the world's best books [282]) Bibliography: p. [xvi] [PR3533.B62 1952] 52-5875
1. Johnson, Samuel, 1709-1784—Biography. I. Evans, Bergen, 1904-

BOSWELL, James, 1740- 828'.6'09 B 1795.
Life of Samuel Johnson, LL.D. Chicago, Encyclopadia Britannica [1955, c1952] xvii, 618 p. 25 cm. (Great books of the Western World, v. 44) "A chronological catalogue of the prose works of Samuel Johnson, LLD.": p. xiv-xvii. Bibliographical footnotes. [AC1.G72 vol. 44] 55-10350
1. Johnson, Samuel, 1709-1784—Biography.

CLIFFORD, James 828'.6'09 B Lowry, 1901-
Dictionary Johnson : the middle years of Samuel Johnson / by James L. Clifford. New York : McGraw-Hill, c1979. p. cm. Includes bibliographical references and index. [PR3533.C58] 79-13497 ISBN 0-07-011378-5 : 15.00
1. Johnson, Samuel, 1709-1784—Biography. 2. Authors, English—18th century—Biography. 3. Lexicographers—England—Biography. I. Title. **BIP**

GRANT, Francis 828'.6'09 B Richard Charles.
Life of Samuel Johnson. Port Washington, N.Y., Kennikat Press [1972] 173, xxviii p. 21 cm. Reprint of the 1887 ed. "Bibliography by John P. Anderson": p. [i]-xxviii. [PR3533.G7 1972] 70-160756 ISBN 0-8046-1574-8
1. Johnson, Samuel, 1709-1784—Biography. I. Anderson, John Parker, 1841- **BIP**

HAWKINS, John, Sir, 828'.6'09 S 1719-1789.
The life of Samuel Johnson, L.L.D. (1787) New York, Garland Pub., 1974. 605 p. 22 cm. (The Life & times of seven major British writers, Johnsoniana 20) Reprint of the ed. printed for J. Buckland, London. [PR3533.J59 vol. 20] 828'.6'09 B 74-16102 ISBN 0-8240-1298-4
1. Johnson, Samuel, 1709-1784—Biography. I. Title. II. Series: Johnsoniana 20.

HAY, James, 1838- 828'.6'09 B 1904.
Johnson : his characteristics and aphorisms / by James Hay. Folcroft, Pa. : Folcroft Library Editions, 1976. p. cm. Reprint of the 1884 ed. published by A. Gardner, London. Includes index. [PR3533.H33 1976] 76-16036 ISBN 0-8414-4806-X : 25.00
1. Johnson, Samuel, 1709-1784—Biography. I. Title. **BIP**

JOHNSON, Samuel, 828'.6'09 B 1709-1784.
Johnson on Johnson : a selection of the personal and autobiographical writings of Samuel Johnson (1709-1784) / selected with an introd. and commentary by John Wain. 1st ed. New York : E. P. Dutton, 1976. xxiii, 247 p. ; 23 cm. [PR3533.A24 1976] 75-42757 ISBN 0-525-13725-4 : 10.00
1. Johnson, Samuel, 1709-1784—Biography. 2. Johnson, Samuel, 1709-1784—Correspondence. I. Wain, John. II. Title.

JOHNSON, Samuel, 828'.6'09 B 1709-1784.
Johnson on Johnson : a selection of the personal and autobiographical writings of Samuel Johnson (1709-1784) / selected, with an introduction and commentary, by John Wain. London : Dent, 1976. xxiii, 247 p. ; 23 cm. Bibliography: p. xvii. [PR3533.A24 1976b] 76-371466 ISBN 0-460-00003-9 : £4.50
1. Johnson, Samuel, 1709-1784—Biography. 2. Authors, English—18th century—Biography. I. Wain, John. II. Title.

JOHNSON, Samuel, 828'.6'09 B 1709-1784.
Letters of Samuel Johnson, LL.D. Collected and edited by George Birkbeck Hill. Freeport, N.Y., Books for Libraries Press [1973] p. Reprint of the 1892 ed. Contents.Contents.—v. 1. Oct. 30, 1731-Dec. 21, 1776.—v. 2. Jan. 15, 1777-Dec. 18, 1784. [PR3533.A44 1973] 72-13658 ISBN 0-8369-8187-1
I. Hill, George Birkbeck Norman, 1835-1903, ed.

JOHNSON, Samuel, 1709-1784. 928.2
The Letters of Samuel Johnson, with Mrs. Thrale's geniuine letters to him. Collected edited by R. W. Chapman. Oxford, Clarnendon Press, 1952. 3v. facsims. 23cm. Contents.v. 1. 1719-1774.--v. 2. 1775-1782.--v. 3. 1783-1784. [PR3533.A2 1952] 53-6169
I. Piozzi, Hester, Lyuch (Salusbury) Thrale, 1741-1821. II. Title.

LUNN, Hugh Kingsmill, 828'.6'09 B 1889-1949, ed.
Johnson without Boswell; a contemporary portrait of Samuel Johnson, edited by Hugh Kingsmill. St. Clair Shores, Mich., Scholarly Press [1974, c1940] p. cm. Reprint of the ed. published by Knopf, New York. Bibliography: p. [PR3533.L73 1974] 74-3134 ISBN 0-403-03060-9
1. Johnson, Samuel, 1709-1784—Biography. I. Title.

MACAULAY, James, 828'.6'09 B 1817-1902.
Doctor Johnson : his life, works & table talk / by James Macaulay. Folcroft, Pa. : Folcroft Library Editions, 1977. p. cm. Reprint of the 1884 ed. published by T. F. Unwin, London. [PR3533.M25 1977] 77-21841 ISBN 0-8414-6215-1 lib. bdg. : 17.50
1. Johnson, Samuel, 1709-1784—Biography. 2. Authors, English—18th century—Biography. I. Title. **BIP**

PEARSON, Hesketh, 828'.6'09 B 1887-1964.
Johnson and Boswell; the story of their lives. Westport, Conn., Greenwood Press [1972, c1958] 390 p. illus. 23 cm. Includes bibliographies. [PR3533.P34 1972] 73-138124 ISBN 0-8371-1834 4
1. Johnson, Samuel, 1709-1784—Biography. 2. Boswell, James, 1740-1795—Biography.

ROBERTS, Sydney 828'.6'09 B Castle, Sir, 1887-1966.
The story of Doctor Johnson; being an introduction to Boswell's Life. [Folcroft, Pa.] Folcroft Library Editions, 1974. xi, 157 p. illus. 24 cm. Reprint of the 1919 ed. published by the University Press, Cambridge. Bibliography: p. 156-157. [PR3533.R6 1974] 73-14816 ISBN 0-8414-7205-X (lib. bdg.)
1. Johnson, Samuel, 1709-1784—Biography. I. Boswell, James, 1740-1795. The life of Samuel Johnson. II. Title.

ROBERTS, Sydney 828'.6'09 B Castle, Sir., 1887-1966.
The story of Doctor Johnson, being an introduction to Boswell's Life / by S. C. Roberts. Norwood, Pa. : Norwood Editions, 1975. p. cm. Reprint of the 1919 ed. published at the University Press, Cambridge. Bibliography: p. [PR3533.R6 1975] 75-33264 ISBN 0-88305-571-6 : 20.00
1. Johnson, Samuel, 1709-1784—Biography. I. Boswell, James, 1740-1795. Life of Samuel Johnson. II. Title.

SALPETER, Harry. 828'.6'09 B
Dr. Johnson & Mr. Boswell / by Harry Salpeter. Folcroft, Pa. : Folcroft Library Editions, 1977, c1929. p. cm. Reprint of the ed. published by Coward-McCann, New York. [PR3533.S25 1977] 77-9392 ISBN 0-8414-7669-1 lib. bdg. : 30.00
1. Johnson, Samuel, 1709-1784—Biography. 2. Boswell, James, 1740-1795—Biography. 3. Boswell, James, 1740-1795. The life of Samuel Johnson. 4. Authors, English—18th century—Biography. I. Title. BIP

Johnson, Samuel, 1709-1784—Correspondence.

HENDERSON, Andrew, 828'.6'09 S fl.1734-1775.
A letter to Samuel Johnson (1775) and A second letter to Johnson (1775) / by Andrew Henderson. New York : Garland Pub., 1975. 48, 24 p. ; 22 cm. (The Life & times of seven major British writers) (Johnsoniana ; 7) Reprint of 2 works, the 1st printed for the author and sold by J. Henderson; the 2d printed for J. Henderson, London. [PR3533.J59 vol. 7] 808 B 75-4823 ISBN 0-8240-1285-2 lib.bdg. : 28.00
1. Johnson, Samuel, 1709-1784—Correspondence. 2. Henderson, Andrew, fl. 1734-1775. I. Title. II. Series.

Johnson, Samuel, 1709-1784—Criticism and interpretation.

FOLKENFLIK, Robert, 828'.6'09 1939-
Samuel Johnson, biographer / Robert Folkenflik. Ithaca : Cornell University Press, 1978. 237 p. ; 23 cm. Includes index. Bibliography: p. 221-228. [PR3537.B54F64] 78-58050 ISBN 0-8014-0968-3 : 12.50
1. Johnson, Samuel, 1709-1784—Criticism and interpretation. 2. Biography (as a literary form) I. Title. BIP

Johnson, Samuel, 1709-1784—Friends and associates.

CRAIG, William Henry, 828'.6'09 B 1835-
Doctor Johnson and the fair sex : a study of contrasts / by W. H. Craig. Folcroft, Pa. : Folcroft Library Editions, 1977. p. cm. Reprint of the 1895 ed. published by S. Low, Marston, London. [PR3533.C7 1977] 77-10656 ISBN 0-8414-1836-5 lib. bdg. : 30.00
1. Johnson, Samuel, 1709-1784—Friends and associates. 2. Authors, English—18th century—Biography. I. Title. BIP

QUENNELL, Peter, 828'.6'09 B 1905-
Samuel Johnson; his friends and enemies. New York, American Heritage Press [1973, c1972] 272 p. illus. 25 cm. Bibliography: p. [265]-[266] [PR3533.Q4 1973] 72-3470 ISBN 0-07-051040-7 12.95
1. Johnson, Samuel, 1709-1784—Friends and associates.

Johnson, Samuel, 1709-1784—Journeys—Addresses, essays, lectures.

†ELIAS, C. F. 910'.92'4 B
Dr. Samuel Johnson as traveller : an address read before the Liverpool Philomathic Society at the opening of the one hundred and third session, October 5th, 1927 / by C. F. Elias. Folcroft, Pa. : Folcroft Library Editions, 1976. 34 p. ; 22 cm. Reprint of the 1927 ed. published by D. Marples, Liverpool. [PR3533.E4 1976] 76-28301 ISBN 0-8414-3909-5 lib. bdg. : 6.00
1. Johnson, Samuel, 1709-1784—Journeys—Addresses, essays, lectures. 2. Travelers—Great Britain—Biography—Addresses, essays, lectures. I. Title.

Johnson, Samuel, 1709-1784—Journeys—England—Cambridge.

ROBERTS, Sydney 828'.6'09 B Castle, Sir, 1887-1966.
Doctor Johnson in Cambridge : essays in Boswellian imitation / by S. C. Roberts. Folcroft, Pa. : Folcroft Library Editions, 1977. p. cm. Reprint of the 1922 ed. published by Putnam, London. [PR3533.R55 1977] 77-23775 ISBN 0-8414-7393-5 lib. bdg. : 8.50
1. Johnson, Samuel, 1709-1784—Journeys—England—Cambridge. 2. Boswell, James, 1740-1795—Biography. 3. Cambridge. University. 4. Authors, English—18th century—Biography. I. Title.

Johnson, Samuel, 1709-1784—Journeys—Scotland.

HILL, George Birkbeck 914.11'04'7 Norman, 1835-1903.
Footsteps of Dr. Johnson (Scotland) / by George Birkbeck Hill ; with ill. by Lancelot Speed. Folcroft, Pa. : Folcroft Library Editions, 1977. p. cm. Reprint of the 1890 ed. published by S. Low, Marston, Searle & Rivington, London. Includes index. Bibliography: p. [DA865.H6 1977] 77-23040 ISBN 0-8414-4855-8 lib. bdg. : 50.00
1. Johnson, Samuel, 1709-1784—Journeys—Scotland. 2. Hill, George Birkbeck Norman, 1835-1903. 3. Scotland—Description and travel—1801-1900. 4. Hebrides—Description and travel. I. Title. BIP

Johnson, Samuel, 1709-1784—Knowledge—Geography.

CURLEY, Thomas M. 828'.6'09 B
Samuel Johnson and the age of travel / by Thomas M. Curley. Athens : University of Georgia Press, c1976. 285 p. : ill. ; 24 cm. Includes bibliographical references and index. [PR3537.G44C8] 74-30677 ISBN 0-8203-0380-1 : 12.50
1. Johnson, Samuel, 1709-1784—Knowledge—Geography. 2. Johnson, Samuel, 1709-1784—Journeys. 3. Travel in literature. 4. English literature—18th century—History and criticism. 5. Voyages and travels. I. Title. BIP

Johnson, Vernon Cecil,

JOHNSON, Vernon Cecil, 922.244 1886-
Spiritual childhood- a study of St. Teresa's teaching. New York, Sheed and Ward, 1954. 216p. 22cm. [BX4700.T5J6] 54-8061
1. Therese, Saint, 1873-1897. II. Title.

Johnson, Wallace E., 1901-

JOHNSON, 338.7'61'647940924 B Wallace E., 1901-
Together we build : the life and faith of Wallace E. Johnson / by Wallace E. Johnson , with Eldon Roark. New York : Hawthorn Books, c1978. xii, 209 p., [8] leaves of plates : ill. ; 21 cm. Originally published in 1973 under title: Work is my play. [TX910.5.J58A38 1978] 77-90091 ISBN 0-8015-8851-0 : pbk. : 4.95
1. Johnson, Wallace E., 1901- 2. Hotel management—Biography. I. Roark, Eldon, 1897- joint author. II. Title.

Johnson, William, Bart., Sir, 1715-1774.

HAMILTON, Milton 973.2'6'0924 B Wheaton, 1901-
Sir William Johnson, Colonial American, 1715-1763 / Milton W. Hamilton. Port Washington, N.Y. : Kennikat Press, 1976. xiv, 402 p., [8] leaves of plates : ill. ; 24 cm. (Series in American studies) (National university publications) Includes bibliographical references and index. [E195.J664] 76-10657 ISBN 0-8046-9134-7 : 17.50
1. Johnson, William, Bart., Sir, 1715-1774. 2. United States—History—French and Indian War, 1755-1763. 3. Indians of North America—Government relations—To 1789. I. Title. BIP

Johnson, William Bullein, 1782-1862.

WOODSON, Hortense. 922.673
Giant in the land; a biography of William Bullein Johnson, first president of the Southern Baptist Convention. Nashville, Broadman Press [1950] xii, 164 p. illus., ports. 23 cm. Bibliography: p. 163-164. [BX6495.J53W6] 50-84126
1. Johnson, William Bullein, 1782-1862. 2. Southern Baptist Convention — Hist. I. Title.

Johnson, William Geary, 1880-1949.

SONNIER, Austin M. 785.4'2'0924 B
Willie Geary "Bunk" Johnson : the New Iberia years / Austin M. Sonnier, Jr. New York : Crescendo Pub., c1977. 81 p., [3] leaves of plates ; ill. ; 23 cm. Discography: p. 27-37. [ML419.J65S6] 76-16330 ISBN 0-87597-102-4 : 5.00
1. Johnson, William Geary, 1880-1949. 2. Jazz musicians—United States—Biography. BIP

Johnson, William Samuel, 1727-1819.

BEARDSLEY, Eben 327.73'.092'4 B Edwards, 1808-1891.
Life and times of William Samuel Johnson, first Senator in Congress from Connecticut, and president of Columbia College, New York. Freeport, N.Y., Books for Libraries Press [1972] xii, 218 p. port. 22 cm. Reprint of the 1876 ed. [E302.6.J7B3 1972] 72-4207 ISBN 0-8369-6872-7
1. Johnson, William Samuel, 1727-1819.

GROCE, George Cuthbert, v. 12 1899-
William Samuel Johnson, a maker of the Constitution. New York, AMS Press, 1967. x, 227 p. front. (port.) double plan. Includes bibliography. 68-95929
1. Johnson, William Samuel, 1727-1819. I. Title. BIP

MCCAUGHEY, 973.3'092'4 B Elizabeth P., 1948-
From Loyalist to Founding Father : the political odyssey of William Samuel Johnson / Elizabeth P. McCaughey. New York : Columbia University Press, 1979. p. cm. Includes index. Bibliography: p. [E302.6.J7M3] 79-17042 ISBN 0-231-04506-9 : 22.50
1. Johnson, William Samuel, 1727-1819. 2. United States. Congress. Senate—Biography. 3. Columbia University—Presidents—Biography. 4. Connecticut—Politics and government—Colonial period, ca. 1600-1775. 5. United States—Politics and government—1783-1789. 6. Legislators—United States—Biography. 7. College presidents—United States—Biography. I. Title. BIP

Johnson, William, Sir, bart., 1715-1774.

FLEXNER, James 973.2'6'0924 B Thomas, 1908-
Lord of the Mohawks : a biography of Sir William Johnson / James Thomas Flexner ; newly illustrated and with a new foreword. Boston : Little, Brown, c1979. xviii, 400 p., [15] leaves of plates : ill. ; 24 cm. On dust jacket: "A revised edition." First ed. published in 1959 under title: Mohawk baronet. Includes index. Bibliography: p. 361-368. [E195.J63F57 1979] 79-14843 ISBN 0-316-28609-5 : 12.95
1. Johnson, William, Sir, bart., 1715-1774. 2. United States—History—French and Indian War, 1755-1763. 3. Indians of North America—Government relations—To 1789. 4. Indians of North America—Wars—1750-1815. 5. Soldiers—Great Britain—Biography. 6. Colonial administrators—Great Britain—Biography. 7. Colonial administrators—United States—Biography. I. Title. BIP

POUND, Arthur, 1884- 950.5'0924 B 1966.
Johnson of the Mohawks; a biography of Sir William Johnson, Irish immigrant, Mohawk war chief, American soldier, empire builder, by Arthur Pound in collaboration with Richard E. Day. Freeport, N.Y., Books for Libraries Press [1971] xvii, 556 p. illus., facsims., maps (2 fold.), ports. 23 cm. Reprint of the 1930 ed. Bibliography: p. 537-538. [E195.J675 1971] 75-164621 ISBN 0-8369-5904-3
1. Johnson, William, Sir, bart., 1715-1774. I. Day, Richard Edwin, 1852-1936, joint author. II. Title.

Johnson, William, 1771-1834.

MORGAN, Donald Grant. 923.773
Justice William Johnson, the first dissenter; the career and constitutional philosophy of a Jeffersonian judge. Columbia, University of South Carolina Press, 1954. xiv, 326p.port. 25cm. Bibliography: p. 301-305. Bibliographical footnotes. 54-14788
1. Johnson, William, 1771-1834. I. Title. BIP

Johnson, William, 1809-1851.

DAVIS, Edwin 917.62'26'0350924 B Adams, 1904-
The barber of Natchez; wherein a slave is freed and rises to a very high standing; wherein the former slave writes a two-thousand-page journal about his town and himself; wherein the free Negro diarist is appraised in terms of his friends, his code, and his community's reaction to his wanton murder, by Edwin Adams Davis and William Ransom Hogan. Port Washington, N.Y., Kennikat Press [1972, c1954] 272 p. illus. 23 cm. [E185.97.J697D3 1972] 77-159069 ISBN 0-8046-1663-9
1. Johnson, William, 1809-1851. 2. Natchez, Miss.—Social life and customs. I. Hogan, William Ransom, 1908- joint author. II. Title.

DAVIS, Edwin 917.62'26'0350924 B Adams, 1904-
The barber of Natchez; wherein a slave is freed and rises to a very high standing; wherein the former slave writes a two-thousand-page journal about his town and himself; wherein the free Negro diarist is appraised in terms of his friends, his code, and community's reaction to his wanton murder, by Edwin Adams Davis and William Ransom Hogan. Baton Rouge, Louisiana State University Press [1973] 278 p. port. 22 cm. [E185.97.J697D3 1973] 74-159049 ISBN 0-8071-0212-1
1. Johnson, William, 1809-1851. 2. Natchez, Miss.—Social life and customs. I. Hogan, William Ransom, 1908-1971, joint author. II. Title.

Johnston, Albert Chandler, 1900-

WHITE, William Lindsay, 325.26 1900-
Lost boundaries. New York, Harcourt [1967, c.1948] 83p. 18cm. (Harbrace paperback lib. HPL24) [E185.97.J76W4] 48-6112 .50 pap.,
1. Johnston, Albert Chandler, 1900- 2. Johnston, Albert Chandler, 1925- 3. Negroes. I. Title. BIP

Johnston, Albert Sidney, 1803-1862.

ROLAND, Charles Pierce, 923.573 1918-
Albert Sidney Johnston, soldier of three republics, by Charles P. Roland. Austin, University of Texas Press 1964 xi, 384 p. illus., plans, ports. 24 cm. Bibliography: p. 355 -365. [E467.1.J73R6] 64-10319
1. Johnston, Albert Sidney, 1803-1862.

Johnston, Brian, 1912-

JOHNSTON, Brian, 791.44'092'4 B 1912-
It's been a lot of fun : an autobiography / Brian Johnston. London ; New York : W. H. Allen, 1974. 310 p., [24] p. of plates : ill., ports. ; 23 cm. Includes index. [GV719.J63A34] 75-325164 ISBN 0-491-01471-6 : £3.50
1. Johnston, Brian, 1912- 2. Radio broadcasting of sports. 3. Television broadcasting of sports. 4. Cricket. I. Title.

Johnston, Edward, 1872-1944.

JOHNSTON, 745.6'1'0924 B Priscilla, 1910-
Edward Johnston / by Priscilla Johnston. 2nd ed. London : Barrie and Jenkins, 1976. 316 p., [20] p. of plates : ill., facsims., ports. ; 23 cm. Text on lining papers.

Includes index. Bibliography: p. [14] [NK3631.J63J63 1976] 76-377127 ISBN 0-214-20253-4 : £5.25. ISBN 0-214-20295-X pbk.
1. Johnston, Edward, 1872-1944. 2. Calligraphers—Great Britain—Biography. BIP

Johnston family.

JOHNSTON, 917.58'03'30924 B Elizabeth (Lichtenstein) 1764-1848.
Recollections of a Georgia loyalist. Written in 1836. Edited by Arthur Wentworth Eaton. London, De La More Press. [Spartanburg, S.C., Reprint Co., 1972, c1901] 224 p. ports. 23 cm. [E278.J7J72 1972] 76-187388 ISBN 0-87152-083-4
1. Johnston family. I. Title. BIP

Johnston, Fran.

JOHNSTON, Fran. 248
Please don't strike that match; a young mother in today's world faces the fires of adversity. Grand Rapids, Mich., Zondervan Pub. House [1970] 133 p. 21 cm. Autobiographical. [BR1725.J64A33] 79-120049 3.50
I. Title.

Johnston, Harry Hamilton, Sir, 1858-1927—Juvenile literature.

SCHLEIN, Miriam. 599'.7357
On the track of the mystery animal : the story of the discovery of the okapi / by Miriam Schlein ; illustrated by Ruth Sanderson. New York : Four Winds Press, c1978. 58 p. : ill. ; 26 cm. Includes index. Bibliography: p. 57. Describes Sir Harry Johnston's efforts to locate and identify the okapi, a member of the giraffe family found deep in Central Africa's rain forest. [QL737.U56S35] 78-5387 ISBN 0-590-07488-1 : 6.95
1. Johnston, Harry Hamilton, Sir, 1858-1927—Juvenile literature. 2. Okapi—Juvenile literature. 3. Zoologists—Great Britain—Biography—Juvenile literature. I. Sanderson, Ruth. II. Title. BIP

Johnston, James, 1738-1808.

LAWRENCE, Alexander A 655.4758 1906-
James Johnston, Georgia's first printer. With decorations & remarks on Johnston's work by Ray Dilley. Savannah, Pigeonhole Press, 1956. 54p. illus. facsims. 24cm. Bibliographical references included in 'Notes' (p. [45]-54) [Z232.J7L3] 57-18403
1. Johnston, James, 1738-1808. I. Title.

Johnston, John Young, 1857-1931.

JOHNSTON, Faith, 269'.2'0924 B 1902-
Anchor post / by Faith Johnston. [Mount Pleasant] : Clarke Historical Library, Central Michigan University, c1975. 354 p., [9] leaves of plates : ill., ports. ; 24 cm. [BX7990.H62J634] 75-329981
1. Johnston, John Young, 1857-1931. I. Title.

Johnston, John, 1822 (ca.)-1900.

THORP, Raymond W 1896- 923.973
Crow Killer; the saga of Liver-Eating Johnson [by] Raymond W. Thorp [and] Robert Bunker. Bloomington, Indiana University Press [1958] 190 p. illus. 21 cm. [CT275.J689T45] 58-8120
1. Johnston, John, 1822 (ca.)-1900. I. Bunker, Robert Manson, 1918- joint author. II. Title.

THORP, Raymond W., 1896- 923.973
Crow Killer; the saga of Liver-Eating Johnson [by] Raymond W. Thorp [and] Robert Bunker. New York, New Amer. Lib. [1972] 127 p. illus. 18 cm. A Signet Book, T4889 [CT275.J689T45] 58-8120 Pap. .75
1. Johnston, John, 1822 (ca.)-1900. BIP

THORP, Raymond W., 978'.02'0924 B 1896-
Crow Killer; the saga of Liver-Eating Johnson [by] Raymond W. Thorp [and] Robert Bunker. Foreword by Richard M. Dorson. Bloomington, Indiana University Press [1969] 190 p. illus., map (on lining papers), port. 22 cm. Bibliographical footnotes. [CT275.J689T45 1969] 77-92323 5.00
1. Johnston, John, 1822 (ca.)-1900. I. Bunker, Robert Manson, 1918- joint author.

Johnston, Joseph Eggleston, 1807-1891.

GOVAN, Gilbert 973.7'3'0924 B Eaton, 1892-
A different valor; the story of General Joseph E. Johnston, C.S.A., by Gilbert E. Govan and James W. Livingood. Westport, Conn., Greenwood Press [1973, c1956] 470 p. illus. 22 cm. Reprint of the ed. published by Bobbs-Merrill, Indianapolis. Bibliography: p. 448-456. [E467.1.J74G6 1973] 73-9372 ISBN 0-8371-7012-5 17.50
1. Johnston, Joseph Eggleston, 1807-1891. 2. Davis, Jefferson, 1808-1889. I. Livingood, James Weston, joint author. II. Title.

GOVAN, Gilbert Eaton, 923.573 1892-
A different valor, the story of General Joseph E. Johnston, C.S.A., by Gilbert E. Govan and James W. Livingood. Indianapolis, Bobbs-Merrill [1956] 470 p. illus., maps, port, 24 cm. Bibliography: p. 448-456. [E467.1.J74G6] 56-13278
1. Johnston, Joseph Eggleston, 1807-1891. 2. Davis, Jefferson, 1808-1889. I. Livingood, James Weston, joint author. II. Title. BIP

Johnston, Olin Dewitt, 1896-

HUSS, John Ervin, 1910- 923.273
Senator for the South; a biography of Olin D. Johnston. Introd. by Stuart Symington. [1st ed.] Garden City, N. Y., Doubleday, 1961. 238p. illus. 22cm. [F748.J75H8] 61-9518
1. Johnston, Olin Dewitt, 1896- I. Title.

Johnston, Percy Hampton, 1881-

NYE, Frank Wilson, 1887- 923.373
Knowledge is power; the life story of Percy Hampton Johnston, banker. New York, Random House [c1956] 347p. illus. 24cm. [HG2463.J6N9] 56-6545
1. Johnston, Percy Hampton, 1881- 2. Chemical Corn Exchange Bank, New York. I. Title.

Johnston, Randolph Wardell, 1904-

JOHNSTON, Randolph 730'.92'4 B Wardell, 1904-
Artist on his island : a study in self-reliance / by Randolph W. Johnston ; with notes by Denny Johnston. Park Ridge, N.J. : Noyes Press, [1976] c1975. 186 p. : ill. ; 23 cm. [N6537.J66A22] 75-34929 ISBN 0-8155-5042-1 : 8.95
1. Johnston, Randolph Wardell, 1904- 2. Artists—United States. 3. Artists—Bahamas—Great Abaco Island. I. Title.

Johnston, Richard Malcolm, 1822-1898.

HITCHCOCK, Bert. 813'.4
Richard Malcolm Johnston / Bert Hitchcock. Boston : Twayne Publishers, 1978. p. cm. (Twayne's United States authors series ; TUSAS 314) Includes index. Bibliography: p. [PS2148.H5] 78-19049 ISBN 0-8057-7238-3 lib. bdg. : 9.95
1. Johnston, Richard Malcolm, 1822-1898. 2. Authors, American—19th century—Biography. BIP

Johnston, William Cameron.

JOHNSTON, William Cameron. 817.5
Bathroom's down the hall. New York, Exposition Press [1951] 178 p. 23 cm. (A Banner book) Autobiographical. [CT275.J695A3] 51-21194
I. Title.

Johnstone, Mildred T.

JOHNSTONE, Mildred T. 248'.2 B
Brother wolf / Mildred T. Johnstone. Los Angeles : Center Publications, [1979] p. cm. [BR1725.J643A33] 79-20422 ISBN 0-916820-13-0 : 6.95
1. Johnstone, Mildred T. 2. Johnstone, Tommy. 3. Christian biography—United States. I. Title. BIP

Johnstone, Rae,

JOHNSTONE, Rae, 1905- 927.98
The Rae Johnstone story. London, St. Paul [stamped: distributed by Sportshelf, New Rochelle, N. Y.] 1959, c1958; 202p. illus. 22cm. [SF336.J6A3] 59-4056
I. Title.

Joliet, Louis, 1645-1700.

EIFERT, Virginia Louise 923.944 (Snider) 1911-1966.
Louis Jolliet, explorer of rivers. With maps by James Macdonald. New York, Dodd, Mead, 1961. 242 p. illus. 22 cm. Includes bibliography. [F1030.3.E35] 61-14787
1. Joliet, Louis, 1645-1700.

Joliot, Frederic, 1900-1958.

BIQUARD, Pierre. 539.70924
Frederic Joliot-Curie; the man and his theories. Translated by Geoffrey Strachan [1st American ed.] New York, P. S. Eriksson [1966, c1965] 192 p. illus., ports. 24 cm. (A Profile in science) Translation of Joliot-Curie. Bibliography: p. [187] [QC16.J65B513] 65-24212
1. Joliot, Frederic, 1900-1958. I. Title.

Jolson, Al, d. 1950.

FREEDLAND, Michael, 784'.092'4 B 1934-
Al Jolson. London, New York, W. H. Allen, 1972. 318 p. illus. 22 cm. American ed. published under title: Jolson. [ML420.J74F7] 72-170972 ISBN 0-491-00633-0 £3.00
1. Jolson, Al, d. 1950.

FREEDLAND, Michael, 784'.092'4 B 1934-
Jolson. New York, Stein and Day [1972] 256 p. illus. 24 cm. London ed. published under title: Al Jolson. [ML420.J74F7 1972b] 72-83094 ISBN 0-8128-1523-8 8.95
1. Jolson, Al, d. 1950.

JOLSON, Harry, 1882- 927.8
Mistah Jolson; as told to Alban Emley by Harry Jolson. Hollywood [Calif.] House-Warven ['1951] 257 p. illus. 24 cm. [ML420.J74A33] 52-6670
1. Jolson, Al, d. 1950. I. Emley, Alban Maurice, 1890- II. Title.

SIEBEN, Pearl 927.8
The immortal Jolson; his life and times. New York, Fell [1963, c.1962] 231p. 22cm. 62-20865 4.95 bds.,
1. Jolson, Al, d. 1950. I. Title.

Joly, Robert de.

JOLY, Robert de. 551.4'4 B
Memoirs of a speleologist : the adventurous life of a famous French cave explorer / Robert de Joly ; edited by Pierre Boulanger ; translated from the French by Peter Kurz. Teaneck, N.J. : Zephyrus Press, c1975. p. cm. (Speleologia) Translation of Ma vie aventureuse d'explorateur d'abimes. [GB601.6.J6A313] 75-31836 ISBN 0-914264-08-7. ISBN 0-914264-09-5 pbk.
1. Joly, Robert de. 2. Speleology—France. I. Title. BIP

JOLY, Robert de. 551.4'4 B
Memoirs of a speleologist : the adventurous life of a famous French cave explorer / Robert de Joly ; edited by Pierre Boulanger ; translated from the French by Peter Kurz. Teaneck, N.J. : Zephyrus Press, c1975. p. cm. (Speleologia) Translation of Ma vie aventureuse d'explorateur d'abimes. [GB601.6.J6A313] 75-31836 ISBN 0-914264-08-7 : 9.00 ISBN 0-914264-09-5 pbk. : 5.00
1. Joly, Robert de. 2. Speleology—France. I. Title.

Jonah, the prophet.

ELLUL, Jacques. 224'.92'077
The judgment of Jonah. Translated by Geoffrey W. Bromiley. Grand Rapids, Mich., Eerdmans [1971] 103 p. 22 cm. Translation of Le livre de Jonas. [BS580.J55E4413] 70-142901 1.95
1. Jonah, the prophet. I. Title. BIP

FAIRBAIRN, Patrick, 1805- 221.92 1874
Jonah: his life. character and mission. Foreword by Joseph C. Holbrook. Jr. Grand Rapids, Mich., Kregel 1964. 237p. 19cm. 64-16635 3.50
1. Jonah. the prophet. I. Title.

OVERDUIN, Jacobus, 1902- 248
Adventures of a deserter, by Jan Overduin. [Tr. by Harry Van Dyke from the Dutch ed.] Grand Rapids, Mich., Eerdmans [c.1964, 1965] 153p. 23cm. [BS580.J55O93] 65-18098 3.50
1. Jonah, the prophet. I. Title.

Jonah, the prophet—Juvenile literature.

BULLA, Clyde 224'.92'09505 Robert.
Jonah and the great fish. Illustrated by Helga Aichinger. New York, Crowell [1970] [39] p. col. illus. 27 cm. More than once stubborn Jonah had to be taught not to question the will of the Lord. [BS580.J55B8] 69-13636 4.50
1. Jonah, the prophet—Juvenile literature. I. Aichinger, Helga, illus. II. Title. BIP

CHRISTIAN, Mary 224'.92'09505 Blount.
Jonah, go to Nineveh! : Jonah and the whale for beginning readers : the Book of Jonah for children / by Mary Blount Christian ; illustrated by Aline Cunningham. St. Louis : Concordia Pub. House, c1976. [48] p. : col. ill. ; 23 cm. (I can read a Bible story) An easy-to-read retelling of the trials of Jonah, who has trouble understanding the essence of God's love. [BS580.J55C48] 76-15286 ISBN 0-570-07307-3 : 3.95
1. Jonah, the prophet—Juvenile literature. I. Cunningham, Aline. II. Title.

DOSS, Helen (Grigsby) 221.6'6
Jonah. Illustrated by Norman Kohn. New York, Abingdon Press [1964] 111 p. illus., map (on lining papers) 25 cm. [BS580.J55D6] 64-14791
1. Jonah, the prophet — Juvenile literature. I. Title.

LEMKE, Stefan. 224'.92'0924 B
Jonah / [art by Stefan Lemke and Marie-Luise Lemke-Pricken]. Philadelphia : Fortress Press, 1976. [20] p. : col. ill. ; 19 cm. "A Sunshine book." Retells the story of Jonah who was sent by God to warn the people of Nineveh about their evil ways. [BS580.J55L45] 76-11275 ISBN 0-8006-1577-8 pbk. : 1.75
1. Jonah, the prophet—Juvenile literature. 2. Bible. O.T.—Biography—Juvenile literature. I. Lemke-Pricken, Marie-Luise, joint author. II. Title.

Jonas, Justus, 1493-1555.

LEHMANN, Martin Ernest. 922.443
Justus Jonas, loyal reformer. Minneapolis, Augsburg Pub. House [1963] viii, 208 p. 22 cm. Based on thesis, Princeton Theological Seminary. Bibliography: p. 196-200. [BR350.J6L4] 63-16601
1. Jonas, Justus, 1493-1555.

Jones, Alfred Lewis, Sir, 1845-1909.

DAVIES, P. N. 387.5'092'4 B
Sir Alfred Jones : shipping entrepreneur par excellence / P. N. Davies. London : Europa Publications, c1978. lxii, 162 p. : ill. ; 23 cm. (The Europa library of business biography) Includes index. Bibliography: p. 147-154. [HE569.J66D38] 78-312287 ISBN 0-905118-17-0 : 15.00

1. Jones, Alfred Lewis, Sir, 1845-1909. 2. Merchant marine—Great Britain—Biography.
Distributed by International Publication Services

Jones, Anson, 1798-1858.

GAMBRELL, Herbert Pickens, 1898- 923.273
Anson Jones, the last President of Texas. Foreword by William Ransom Hogan [2d ed. With annotation, enl. bibl.] Austin, Univ. of Tex. Pr. [c.1947-1964] xiv, 530p. maps (on lining papers) port. 23cm. Bibl. 64-19412 6.00
1. Jones, Anson, 1798-1858. 2. Texas—Pol. & govt.—Republic, 1836-1846. I. Title.

GAMBRELL, Herbert Pickens, 1898- 923.273
Anson Jones, the last President of Texas, by Herbert Gambrell. Foreword by William Ransom Hogan. [2d ed. With annotation and enl. bibliography] Austin, University of Texas Press, [1964] xiv, 530 p. maps (on lining papers) port. 23 cm. Bibliography: p. [505]-520. [F389.J6G3 1964] 64-19412
1. Jones, Anson, 1798-1858. 2. Texas — Pol. & govt. — Republic, 1836-1846. I. Title.

Jones, Benjamin Allyn, 1882-1961.

HIRSCH, Joe. 798'.43'0922 B
In the winner's circle: the Jones boys of Calumet Farm [by] Joe Hirsch and Gene Plowden. [1st ed.] New York, Mason & Lipscomb Publishers [1974] xii, 172 p. illus. 25 cm. [SF336.A2H57] 74-11021 ISBN 0-88405-087-4 7.95
1. Jones, Benjamin Allyn, 1882-1961. 2. Jones, Horace Allyn, 1906- 3. Horse-racing—United States. I. Plowden, Gene, joint author. II. Title.

Jones, Bert, 1951-

FOX, Larry. 796.33'2'0924 B
Bert Jones and the battling Colts / Larr Fox ; introd. by John Unitas. New York : Dodd Mead, c1977. xiv, 237 p., [8] leaves of plates : ill. ; 22 cm. [GV939.J62F69] 77-10112 ISBN 0-396-07503-7 : 7.95
1. Jones, Bert, 1951- 2. Baltimore. Football club (National League) 3. Football players—United States—Biography. I. Title. BIP

Jones, Bert, 1951- —Juvenile literature.

SULLIVAN, George, 1927- 796.33'2'0924 B
Bert Jones : born to play football / by George Sullivan. New York : Putnam, c1977. 158 p. : ill. ; 21 cm. (Putnam sports shelf) Includes index. A biography of the star quarterback for the Baltimore Colts. [GV939.J62S84] 92 77-24906 ISBN 0-399-61103-7 : 5.29
1. Jones, Bert, 1951- —Juvenile literature. 2. Baltimore. Football club (National League)—Juvenile literature. 3. Football players—United States—Biography—Juvenile literature. I. Title. BIP

Jones, Charles,

JONES, Charles, 1925- 920.5
Double trouble; the autobiography of the Jones twins, by Charles and Eugene Jones, with Dale Kramer. [1st ed.] Boston, Little, Brown [1952] 317 p. illus., ports. 21 cm. [PN4874.J63A3] 52-9067
I. Jones, Eugene Simons, 1925- joint author. II. Title.

Jones, Charles Jesse, 1844-1919.

EASTON, Robert Olney. 923.973
Lord of beasts; the saga of Buffalo Jones [by] Robert Easton and Mackenzie Brown. Foreword by Jack Schaefer. Illus. by Mac Schweitzer. Tucson, University of Arizona Press [1961] 287 p. illus. 24 cm. Includes bibliography. [SK17.J6E3] 61-14501
1. Jones, Charles Jesse, 1844-1919. I. Brown, Donald Mackenzie, 1908- joint author. II. Title. BIP

KERSEY, Ralph T 923.973
Buffalo Jones, a true biography. [Garden City, Kan., Elliott Printers, 1958] 184p. illus. 20cm. [SK45.K4] 58-35851
1. Jones, Charles Jesse, 1844-1919. I. Title.

Jones, Christopher, 1570 (ca.)-1622.

DEGERING, Etta. 974.48 (B)
Christopher Jones, captain of the Mayflower. Illustrated by William Ferguson. New York, D. McKay Co. [1965] xii, 112 p. illus., geneal. table, maps. 21 cm. Bibliography: p. 107-112. [F68.J6D4] 65-22963
1. Jones, Christopher, 1570 (ca.)-1622. 2. Mayflower (Ship) 3. Pilgrim Fathers. I. Title.

Jones, Cleon, 1942-

JONES, Cleon, 1942- 796.357'0924 B
Cleon, by Cleon Jones with Ed Hershey. New York, Coward-McCann [1970] 191 p. plates, ports. 22 cm. [GV865.J64A3 1970] 78-113524 5.95
1. Baseball—Biography. I. Hershey, Ed, joint author. II. Title. BIP

YOUNG, Andrew Sturgeon Nash, 1919- 796.357'0922 B
The Mets from Mobile: Cleon Jones and Tommie Agee, by A. S. "Doc" Young. [1st ed.] New York, Harcourt, Brace & World [1970] 145 p. illus., ports. 24 cm. Traces the careers of the two black athletes who began playing baseball as boyhood friends in Mobile and eventually came together again to lead the New York Mets to victory in the 1969 World Series. [GV865.J64Y6] 920 70-103832 4.25
1. Jones, Cleon, 1942- 2. Agee, Tommie, 1942- I. Title.

Jones, David James Gwenallt.

MORGAN, Dyfnallt. 891.6'6'12
D. Gwenallt Jones. [Cardiff], University of Wales Press for the Welsh Arts Council, 1972. [3], 84 p. leaf, port. 25 cm. (Writers of Wales) Bibliography: p. 77-80. [PB2298.J46Z75] 73-330643
1. Jones, David James Gwenallt. I. Welsh Arts Council.
Distributed by Verry; 4.00 (pbk.) BIP

Jones, David Michael, 1895-

BLAMIRES, David Malcolm. 760'.092'4
David Jones: artist and writer [by] David Blamires. [Toronto] University of Toronto Press, 1972. viii, 220 p. illus. 23 cm. Bibliography: p. 207-213. [PR6019.O53Z6 1972] 77-190341 ISBN 0-8020-1877-7 10.00
1. Jones, David Michael, 1895-

RAINE, Kathleen Jessie, 1908- 821'.9'12 B
David Jones : solitary perfectionist / Kathleen Raine. Ipswich : Golgonooza Press, 1974. [4], 11 p. : facsim. ; 23 cm. Limited ed. of 350 copies, no. 276. Includes bibliographical references. [PR6019.O53Z85] 75-305195 ISBN 0-903880-02-4 : £1.00
1. Jones, David Michael, 1895-

Jones, David Michael, 1895-1974—Correspondence.

JONES, David Michael, 1895-1974. 821'.9'12
David Jones, letters to Vernon Watkins / edited with notes by Ruth Pryor ; foreword by Gwen Watkins. Cardiff : University of Wales Press, 1976. 79 p., plate : facsim. ; 23 cm. Includes bibliographical references. [PR6019.O53Z548 1976] 76-379252 ISBN 0-7083-0616-0 : 8.50
1. Jones, David Michael, 1895-1974—Correspondence. 2. Watkins, Vernon Phillips, 1906-1967—Correspondence. 3. Authors, Welsh—20th century—Correspondence. I. Watkins, Vernon Phillips, 1906-1967. II. Title.
Distributed by Verry. BIP

Jones, Deacon, 1939-

LIBBY, Bill. 796.332'0924
Life in the pit; the Deacon Jones story. [1st ed.] Garden City, N.Y., Doubleday, 1970. 208 p. illus., ports. 22 cm. [GV939.J63L5] 70-129891 5.95
1. Jones, Deacon, 1939- I. Title. BIP

Jones, Eli Stanley,

JONES, Eli Stanley, 1884- 287'.1'0924
A song of ascents; a spiritual autobiography [by] E. Stanley Jones. Nashville, Abingdon Press [1968] 400 p. 23 cm. [BX8495.J58A3] 68-17451
I. Title. BIP

Jones, Ernest,

JONES, Ernest, 1879-1958. 926.1
Free associations; memories of a psychoanalyst. New York, Basic Books [1959] 263p. illus. 22cm. [R489.J64A3] 59-13027
I. Title.

Jones, Frederick Lafayette,

JONES, Frederick Lafayette, 1901- 928.2
The Shelley legend in White, Newman Ivey, 1892-1948. An examination of The Shelley legend. Philadelphia, Univ. of Pennsylvania Press, 1951. [PR5431.S76W5] 51-12162
I. Title.

Jones, Frederick McKinley, 1893-1961—Juvenile literature.

OTT, Virginia. 609'.2'4 B
Man with a million ideas : Fred Jones, genius/inventor / Virginia Ott & Gloria Swanson. Minneapolis : Lerner Publications Co., c1977. 109 p. : ill. ; 23 cm. A biography of Frederick McKinley Jones, the black engineer and inventor who is credited with many inventions, including refrigeration units for trucks and railroad cars, portable x-ray unit, and ticket dispenser. [T40.J59O87 1977] 92 76-22444 ISBN 0-8225-0761-7 lib.bdg. : 6.95
1. Jones, Frederick McKinley, 1893-1961—Juvenile literature. 2. Inventors—United States—Biography—Juvenile literature. I. Swanson, Gloria Borseth, joint author. II. Title. BIP

Jones, Henry Arthur, 1851-1929.

JONES, Doris Arthur, 1888- 822'.9'12 B
The life and letters of Henry Arthur Jones. London, V. Gollancz, 1930. St. Clair Shores, Mich., Scholarly Press, 1971. 448 p. illus., facsims., geneal. table, ports. 22 cm. Bibliography: p. 425-431. [PR4828.J6 1971] 79-145115 ISBN 0-403-01053-5
1. Jones, Henry Arthur, 1851-1929. I. Jones, Henry Arthur, 1851-1929. Life and letters of Henry Arthur Jones. 1971. II. Title. BIP

Jones, Howard Mumford, 1892- —Biography.

JONES, Howard Mumford, 1892- 809 B
Howard Mumford Jones : an autobiography. Madison : University of Wisconsin Press, 1979. xiii, 292 p., [1] leaf of plates : port. ; 24 cm. Includes bibliographical references and index. [PS3519.O425Z465] 78-65013 ISBN 0-299-07770-5 : 17.50
1. Jones, Howard Mumford, 1892- —Biography. 2. Authors, American—20th century—Biography. 3. Educators—United States—Biography. BIP

Jones, Inigo, 1573-1652.

GOTCH, John Alfred, 1882-1942. 720'.924 B
Inigo Jones. New York, B. Blom, 1968. xi, 271 p. illus., port. 24 cm. Reprint of the 1928 ed. "References and notes": p. 237-245. [NA997.J7G6 1968] 68-20224
1. Jones, Inigo, 1573-1652.

Jones, James, 1921-

JONES, James, 1921- 915.97'03'430924 B
Viet journal. New York, Delacorte Press [1974] 257 p. 22 cm. [DS557.A692J66] 73-21922 ISBN 0-440-08764-3 7.95
1. Jones, James, 1921- 2. Vietnamese Conflict, 1961- —Armistices. I. Title. BIP

Jones, James, 1921-1977—Biography.

MORRIS, Willie. 813'.5'4 B
James Jones : a friendship / by Willie Morris. 1st ed. Garden City, N.Y. : Doubleday, 1978. 259 p., [12] leaves of plates : ill. ; 22 cm. [PS3560.O49Z79] 78-4709 ISBN 0-385-14432-6 : 8.95
1. Jones, James, 1921-1977—Biography. 2. Morris, Willie—Friends and associates. 3. Authors, American—20th century—Biography. BIP

Jones, Jesse Holman, 1874-1956.

TIMMONS, Bascom Nolly, 1890- 923.273
Jesse H. Jones, the man and the statesman. Illustrated with photos. [1st ed.] New York, Holt [1956] 414p. illus. 25cm. [E748.J764T5] 56-10519
1. Jones, Jesse Holman, 1874-1956. I. Title.

TIMMONS, Bascom Nolly, 1890- 923.273
Jesse H. Jones, the man and the statesman. Illustrated with photos. [1st ed.] New York, Holt [1956] 414 p. illus. 25 cm. [E748.J764T5] 56-10519
1. Jones, Jesse Holman, 1874-1956 I. Title.

TIMMONS, Bascom Nolly, 1890- 973.917'092'4 B
Jesse H. Jones, the man and the statesman / by Bascom N. Timmons. Westport, Conn. : Greenwood Press, 1975, c1956. 414 p., [17] leaves of plates : ill. ; 23 cm. Reprint of the ed. published by Holt, New York. Includes bibliographical references and index. [E748.J764T5 1975] 74-31366 ISBN 0-8371-7925-4 lib.bdg. : 23.25
1. Jones, Jesse Holman, 1874-1956. I. Title.

Jones, Jim, 1931-1978.

NUGENT, John Peer. 289.9 B
White night / John Peer Nugent. 1st ed. New York : Rawson, Wade Publishers, c1979. p. cm. Includes index. Bibliography: p. [BP605.P46N83 1979] 79-64720 ISBN 0-89256-116-5 : 10.95
1. Jones, Jim, 1931-1978. 2. Peoples Temple—Biography. 3. Peoples Temple. I. Title.

Jones, John Coffin.

GAST, Ross H. 382'.092'4 B
Contentious consul : a biography of John Coffin Jones, first United States consular agent at Hawaii / by Ross H. Gast. Los Angeles : Dawson's Book Shop, 1976. 212 p. : ill. ; 24 cm. Includes bibliographical references and index. [HF3023.J66G37] 76-28141 10.00
1. Jones, John Coffin. 2. Commercial attaches—Hawaii—Biography. I. Title. BIP

Jones, John Paul, 1747-1792.

LORENZ, Lincoln, 1895- 923.573
The admiral and the Empress: John Paul Jones and Catherine the Great. New York, Bookman Associates [1954] 194 p. illus. 22 cm. Includes bibliography. [E207.J7L77] 54-12218
1. Jones, John Paul, 1747-1792. 2. Catharine II, Empress of Russia, 1729-1796. I. Title.

SPERRY, Armstrong, 1897- 923.573
John Paul Jones: fighting sailor; written and illustrated by Armstrong Sperry. New York, Random House [1953] 180 p. illus. 22 cm. (Landmark books, 39) [E207.J7S77] 53-6261
1. Jones, John Paul, 1747-1792.

Jones, John Paul, 1747-1792.

ABBAZIA, Patrick. 973.3'5'0924 B
John Paul Jones, America's first naval hero / by Patrick Abbazia. Charlotteville, N.Y. : SamHar Press, 1976. p. cm. (Outstanding personalities of the American Revolution) (Outstanding personalities ; no. 86) Bibliography: p. [E207.J7A64] 76-40970 lib.bdg. : 2.45 pbk. : 1.25
1. Jones, John Paul, 1747-1792. 2. United States. Navy—Biography. 3. Seamen—United States—Biography. 4. United States—History—Revolution, 1775-1783—Naval operations. I. Title. BIP

BUELL, Augustus C., 1847-1904. 973.35'0924 B
Paul Jones, Founder of the American Navy; a history. Freeport, N.Y., Books for Libraries Press [1971] 2 v. illus., facsim., map, plan, ports. 23 cm. Reprint of the 1900 ed. Bibliography: v. 2, p. 355-359. [E207.J7B92 1971] 70-157326 ISBN 0-8369-5786-5
1. Jones, John Paul, 1747-1792.

JONES, John Paul, 1747-1792. 973.35'0924 B
Memoirs of Rear-Admiral Paul Jones, compiled from his original journals and correspondence. New York, Da Capo Press, 1972. 2 v. in 1. port. 23 cm. (The Era of the American Revolution) Reprint of the 1830 ed. [E207.J7A3 1972] 77-166333 ISBN 0-306-70247-9
1. United States—History—Revolution, 1775-1783—Naval operations.

LA CROIX, Robert de 923.573
John Paul Jones. Tr. from French by Edward Fitzgerald. London, F. Muller [New Rochelle, N.Y., SportShelf, 1963, c.1962] 222p. port. 21cm. 63-6138 5.00 bds.,
1. Jones, John Paul, 1747-1792. I. Title.

MACKENZIE, Alexander Slidell, 1803-1848. 973.35'0924 B
The life of Paul Jones, by Edward Hamilton. Freeport, N.Y., Books for Libraries Press [1971] 304 p. 23 cm. Reprint of the 1848 ed. [E207.J7M16 1971] 70-160981 ISBN 0-8369-5849-7
1. Jones, John Paul, 1747-1792. I. Title. BIP

MORISON, Samuel Eliot, 1887- 923.573
John Paul Jones, a sailor's biography. Charts, diagrs. by Erwin Raisz and with photos. Boston, AtlanticLittle [1963, c.1959] xxii, 453p. illus., ports., maps. 20cm. (27) Bibl. 2.45 pap.,
1. Jones, John Paul, 1747-1792. I. Title.

MORISON, Samuel Eliot, 1887- v. 12
John Paul Jones, a sailor's biography. With a new introd. by Daniel V. Gallery. New York, Time [1964] 456 p. illus., ports., maps. (Time Reading Program special edition) Includes bibliography. 66-85779
1. Jones, John Paul, 1747-1792. I. Title. BIP

MORISON, Samuel Eliot, 1887- 923.573
John Paul Jones, a sailor's biography. With charts and diagrs. by Erwin Raisz and with photos. [1st ed.] Boston, Little, Brown [1959] xxii, 453 p. illus., ports., maps. 22 cm. Bibliography: p. [431]-443. [E207.J7M6] 59-5285
1. Jones, John Paul, 1747-1792.

MUNRO, Donald John, 1869- 923.573
Commodore John Paul Jones, U. S. Navy; a biography of our first great naval hero. New York, William-Frederick Press, 1954. 108p. illus. 23cm. [E207.J7M8] 53-11943
1. Jones, John Paul, 1747-1792. I. Title.

STEWART, Charles West, 1859-1929, comp. 359.3'32'0924
John Paul Jones; commemoration at Annapolis, April 24, 1906. Compiled under the direction of the Joint Committee on Printing by Charles W. Stewart. Washington, Govt. Print. Off., [for sale by the Supt. of Docs.] 1966. 210 p. illus., ports. 26 cm. Reprint of 1907 edition. Contents.Contents.—Introduction.—Addresses at Annapolis.—Papers and reports. Discovery, identification, and transfer of remains of John Paul Jones.—Letters of John Paul Jones.—Chronology.—Appendix. Includes bibliographies. [E207.J7S83 1966] 66-62679
1. Jones, John Paul, 1747-1792. I. United States. Congress. Joint Committee on Printing. II. Title.

SYME, Ronald, 1910- 973.35'0924 B
Captain John Paul Jones, America's fighting seaman. Illustrated by William Stobbs. New York, Morrow [1968] 94, [2] p. illus., maps 22 cm. Bibliography: p. [95] As John Paul his career was undistinguished except that he was charged twice for murder; as John Paul Jones he became the founder of the American Navy and won recognition as a maritime hero. [E207.J7S9] 92 AC 68
1. Jones, John Paul, 1747-1792. I. Stobbs, William, illus. II. Title.

WEIR, Ruth Cromer, 1912- 923.573
John Paul Jones of the U.S. Navy. Illustrated by Edward Shenton. New York, Abingdon Press [1958] 128 p. illus. 21 cm. [E207.J7W4] 58-3113
1. Jones, John Paul, 1747-1792.

Jones, John Paul, 1747-1792—Juvenile literature

GRAFF, Stewart 920.9
John Paul Jones, sailor hero. Illus. by William Hutchinson. Champaign, Ill., Garrard Press [c.1961] 80p. col. illus. (Discovery book) 61-5486 2.25
1. Jones, John Paul, 1747-1792—Juvenile literature. I. Title.

GRANT, Matthew G. 973.3'5'0924 B
John Paul Jones, naval hero [by] Matthew G. Grant. Illustrated by John Keely. [Mankato, Minn., Creative Education; distributed by Childrens Press, Chicago, 1974] 31 p. illus. (part col.) 25 cm. (His Gallery of great Americans series. War heroes of America) A brief biography of John Paul Jones stressing his naval career. [E207.J7G73] 92 73-18212 ISBN 0-87191-300-3 3.95 (lib. bdg.)
1. Jones, John Paul, 1747-1792—Juvenile literature. I. Keely, John, illus. II. Title.

LEE, Susan. 973.3'5'0924 B
John Paul Jones, by Susan & John Lee. Illustrated by Tom Dunnington. Chicago, Children's Press [1974] 47 p. col. illus. 24 cm. (Heroes of the Revolution) Easy-to-read biography of John Paul Jones, naval hero during the American Revolution. [E207.J7L43] 92 74-8938 ISBN 0-516-04655-1
1. Jones, John Paul, 1747-1792—Juvenile literature. I. Lee, John, joint author. II. Dunnington, Tom, illus. III. Title.

RINK, Paul, 1912- 92 (J)
John Paul Jones: conquer or die. Illustrated by Tran Mawicke. New York, Putnam [1968] 95 p. illus. 24 cm. (An American pioneer biography) [E207.J7R5 1968] 68-22545
1. Jones, John Paul, 1747-1792—Juvenile literature.

SYME, Ronald, 1910- 92 (J)
Captain John Paul Jones, America's fighting seaman. Illustrated by William Stobbs. New York, Morrow [1968] 94, [2] p. illus., maps. 22 cm. Bibliography: p. [95] [E207.J7S9] 68-14230
1. Jones, John Paul, 1747-1792—Juvenile literature. I. Stobbs, William, illus. II. Title.

WORCESTER, Donald Emmet, 1915- 920
John Paul Jones: soldier of the sea. Illus. by Forest Orr. New York, Houghton [c.1961] 190p. col. illus. (Piper bks.) 61-8754 2.24; 1.76 piper ed.,
1. Jones, John Paul, 1747-1792—Juvenile literature I. Title.

Jones Joseph Russell, 1823-1909.

JONES, George Roberts, 1883- 923.273
Joseph Russell Jones, by George R. Jones. With the editorial assistance of Richard Penn Hartung. Chicago, 1964. x. 93 p. illus., port. 23 cm. Bibliographical references included in "Footnotes" (p. 87-93) [E664.J765J6] 64-66445
1. Jones Joseph Russell, 1823-1909. I. Title.

Jones, Joseph, 1833-1896.

BREEDEN, James O. 610'.92'4 B
Joseph Jones, M.D. : scientist of the Old South / James O. Breeden. Lexington : University Press of Kentucky, [1975] xiii, 293 p., [4] leaves of plates : ill. ; 25 cm. Includes index. Bibliography: p. 277-283. [R154.J66B73] 73-80462 ISBN 0-8131-1296-6 : 13.25
1. Jones, Joseph, 1833-1896. 2. United States—History—Civil War, 1861-1865—Medical and sanitary affairs. BIP

Jones, Ken [John Kenneth Jones]

JONES, Ken [John Kenneth Jones] 923.573
Admiral Arleigh (31-knot) Burke; the story of a fighting sailor. by Ken Jones, Hubert Kelley, Jr. Philadelphia, Chilton [c.1962] 203p. illus. 25cm. 62-18614 7.50
I. Title.

Jones, Laurence Clifton, 1884-

DAY, Beth Feagles, 1924- 923.773
The little professor of Piney Woods; the story of Professor Laurence Jones. New York, Messner [1955] 192 p. illus. 22 cm. [LC2852.B713J63] 55-10543
1. Jones, Laurence Clifton, 1884- 2. Piney Woods Country Life School, Braxton, Miss. I. Title.

Jones, Lawrence Evelyn,

JONES, Lawrence Evelyn, 1885- 828.9
A Victorian boyhood. London, Macmillan; New York, St. Martin's Press, 1955. 244p. illus. 22cm. Reminiscences. [CT788.J65A3] 55-969
I. Title.

Jones, Lawrence Evelyn, bart.,

JONES, Lawrence Evelyn, bart., Sir 1885- 828.91
Georgian afternoon. New York, St. Martin's Press, 1958. 269p. 22cm. Autobiographical. [CT788.J65A33] 58-14607
I. Title.

Jones, Lehi Willard, 1854-1947.

JONES, York F., 1925- 289.3'3 B
Lehi Willard Jones; biography, by York and Evelyn Jones. [Salt Lake City, Woodruff Print. Co., 1972] xiii, 258 p. illus. 24 cm. [F834.C4J6] 72-181634
1. Jones, Lehi Willard, 1854-1947. 2. Cedar City, Utah—History. 3. Mormons and Mormonism in Utah. I. Jones, Evelyn, joint author.

Jones, Margaret Jean.

JONES, Margaret Jean. 248'.2 B
The world in my mirror / Margaret Jean Jones. Nashville : Abingdon, c1979. 160 p. ; 21 cm. [BR1725.J645A38] 79-17730 ISBN 0-687-45880-3 : 7.95
1. Jones, Margaret Jean. 2. Christian biography—United States. 3. Paraplegia—Biography. I. Title. BIP

Jones, Mary (Harris) 1830-1930.

ATKINSON, Linda. 331.88'092'4 B
Mother Jones, the most dangerous woman in America / by Linda Atkinson. New York : Crown Publishers, c1978. viii, 246 p. : ill. ; 24 cm. Includes index. Bibliography: p. 238-240. Traces the life and career of an Irish-born labor leader whose work began in the 1870's before the advent of strong unions and labor laws and continued for more than 50 years. [HD8073.J6A74 1978] 92 77-15863 ISBN 0-517-53201-8 : 7.95
1. Jones, Mary Harris, 1830-1930. 2. Women in trade-unions—United States—Biography. I. Title.

FETHERLING, Dale, 1941- 331.88'092'4 B
Mother Jones the miners' angel; a portrait. Carbondale, Southern Illinois University Press [1974] viii, 263 p. illus. 24 cm. Bibliography: p. 219-227. [HD8073.J6F48] 73-12444 ISBN 0-8093-0643-3 11.85
1. Jones, Mary (Harris) 1830-1930. I. Title. BIP

FETHERLING, Dale, 1941- 331.88'092'4 [B]
Mother Jones, the miners' angel: a portrait / by Dale Fetherling. Carbondale : Southern Illinois University Press, 1979, c1974. p. cm. (Arcturus books ; 145) Includes index. Bibliography: p. [HD8073.J6F48 1979] 78-16328 ISBN 0-8093-0896-7 pbk. : 4.95
1. Jones, Mary (Harris) 1830-1930. 2. United Mine Workers of America—History. 3. Labor and laboring classes—United States—Biography. I. Title.

JONES, Mary (Harris) 1830-1930. 331.88'092'4 B
Autobiography of Mother Jones. New York, Arno, 1969. 242 p. ports. 23 cm. (American labor: from conspiracy to collective bargaining) Reprint of the 1925 ed. [HD8073.J6A3 1969] 71-89741
I. Title. II. Series.

JONES, Mary (Harris) 1830-1930. 331.88'092'4 B
The autobiography of Mother Jones. Edited by Mary Field Parton. Foreward [sic] by Clarence Darrow. Introd. and bibliography by Fred Thompson. Chicago, Published by C. H. Kerr for the Illinois Labor History Society, 1972. xxiii, 242 p. illus. 20 cm. Bibliography: p. xvi-xx. [HD8073.J6A3 1972] 71-185477 2.95
I. Title. BIP

Jones, Mary (Harris) 1830-1930—Juvenile literature.

WERSTEIN, Irving. 331.88'092'4 B
Labor's defiant lady; the story of Mother Jones. New York, Crowell [1969] 146 p. 21 cm. (Women of America) Bibliography: p. 137-138. A biography of a union organizer who became known as "the patron saint of the picket lines." [HD8073.J6W47] 69-18667 3.95
1. Jones, Mary (Harris) 1830-1930—Juvenile literature. I. Title.

Jones, Melvin, 1885-1973.

*TRUE, Leslie. 920'.9
Glass eyes can see / by Leslie True. 1st ed. St. Petersburg, Fla, : Freedom Press, 1977. 78p. : ill. ; 22 cm. [HV1792] 3.50
1. Jones, Melvin, 1885-1973. 2. Blind-Biography. I. Title.
Publisher's address: 2139 1st Avenue South, St. Petersburg, Florida 33712. BIP

Jones, Morgan, 1839-1926.

SPENCE, Vernon Gladden, 1924- 385'.0924 B
Colonel Morgan Jones: grand old man of Texas railroading. [1st ed.] Norman, University of Oklahoma Press [1971] xix, 240 p. illus. 23 cm. Bibliography: p. 220-

231. [TF140.J64S6] 73-160505 ISBN 0-8061-0977-7
1. Jones, Morgan, 1839-1926. I. Title.

Jones, Robert Tyre, 1902-

JONES, Robert Tyre, 1902- 927.96352
Golf is my game. [1st ed.] Garden City, N.Y., Doubleday, 1960. 255 p. illus. 25 cm. Autobiographical. [GV965.J63] 60-13386
1. Golf. I. Title.

KEELER, Oscar Bane, 1882-1950. 927.96352
The Bobby Jones story, from the writings of O. B. Keeler, by Grantland Rice. Atlanta, Tupper & Love [1953] 304 p. illus. 22 cm. [GV964.J6K4] 53-13159
1. Jones, Robert Tyre, 1902- I. Rice, Grantland, 1880-1954. ed.

Jones, Rufus Matthew, 1863-1948.

HAVERFORD College. 922.8673
Rufus M. Jones, January 25, 1863-June 16, 1948; in memoriam. Haverford, Pa., 1950. 57 p. port. 22 cm. [BX7795.J55H3] 51-22839
1. Jones, Rufus Matthew, 1863-1948. I. Title.

HINSHAW, David, 1882- 922.8673
Rufus Jones, master Quaker. New York, Putnam [1951] xi, 306 p. illus., ports. 22 cm. Bibliography: p. 295-298. [BX7795.J55H5] 51-9891
1. Jones, Rurus Mattbew, 1863-1948. I. Title. BIP

HINSHAW, David, 1882- 289.6'0924 B
Rufus Jones, master Quaker. Freeport, N.Y., Books for Libraries Press [1970, c1951] xi, 306 p. illus., ports. 23 cm. Bibliography: p. 295-298. [BX7795.J55H5 1970] 74-133522
1. Jones, Rufus Matthew, 1863-1948.

VINING, Elizabeth (Gray) 1902- 922.8673
Friend of life; the biography of Rufus M. Jones. [1st ed.] Philadelphia, Lippincott [1958] 347 p. illus. 24 cm. [BX7795.J55V5] 58-11131
1. Jones, Rufus Matthew, 1863-1948. I. Title.

VINING, Elizabeth (Gray) 1902- 922.8673
Friend of life; the biography of Rufus M. Jones [Reissue] London, Michael Joseph.) [dist. Berkeley, Calif. Peacock Pr., Box 875, 1962, c.1958] L London, Michael Joseph [dist. Berkeley, Calif. Peacock Pr., Box 875, 1962, c.1958] 350p. illus. 24cm. 3.00
1. Jones, Rufus Matthew, 1863-1948. I. Title.

Jones, Sir William, 1746-1794.

CANNON, Garland Hampton, 1924- 320.9'54
Oriental Jones, a biography of Sir William Jones, 1746-1794. Bombay, New York, Asia Pub. House [for] Indian Council for Cultural Relations [1964] x, 215 p. port. 25 cm. Bibliography: p. [196]-206. [PK109.J6C3] SA63
1. Jones, Sir William, 1746-1794. I. Title.

Jones, Thomas Elsa, 1888-

JONES, Thomas Elsa, 1888- 289.6'092'4 B
Light on the horizon; the Quaker pilgrimage of Tom Jones, by Thomas E. Jones. Richmond, Ind., Friends United Press [1973] vii, 225 p. illus. 22 cm. [BX7795.J58A34] 73-12707 ISBN 0-913408-08-5 4.95
1. Jones, Thomas Elsa, 1888- 2. Fisk University, Nashville. 3. Earlham College, Richmond, Ind. I. Title. BIP

Jones, Thomas H.

JONES, Thomas H. 301.44'93'0973
The experience of Thomas H. Jones, who was a slave for forty-three years / written by a friend, as related to him by Brother Jones. New York : AMS Press, [1975] p. cm. Reprint of the 1871 ed. printed by E. Anthony, New Bedford, Mass. [E444.J793 1975] 74-170825 ISBN 0-404-00267-6 : 6.50
1. Jones, Thomas H. 2. Slavery in the United States—Personal narratives. 3. Slavery in the United States—North Carolina. I. Title.

Jones, Thomas Henry, 1921-1965.

CROFT, Julian, 1941- 821'.9'14
T. H. Jones / [by] Julian Croft. [Cardiff] : University of Wales Press [for] the Welsh Arts Council, 1976. [3], 124 p., plate : port. ; 25 cm. (Writers of Wales) Bibliography: p. 117-119. [PR6019.O685Z6] 76-375912 £1.00
1. Jones, Thomas Henry, 1921-1965. 2. Authors, Welsh—Biography. BIP

Jones, Tom.

JONES, Peter, 1930- 784'.0924 B
Tom Jones. Chicago, Regnery [1970] 161 p. illus., ports. 22 cm. [ML420.J76J6] 78-126153 4.95
1. Jones, Tom. BIP

Jones, William,

JONES, William, Sir, 1746-1794. 826'.6
The letters of Sir William Jones; edited by Garland Cannon. Oxford, Clarendon P., 1970. 2 v. (xlix, 452 p., 6 plates; 453-977 p., 6 plates). illus., facsims., ports. 23 cm. Bibliography: p. 939-948. [PK109.J6A4 1970] 71-141315 12/10/-
I. Cannon, Garland Hampton, 1924- ed. BIP

JONES, William, Sir, 1746-1794. 826'.6
The letters of Sir William Jones; edited by Garland Cannon. Oxford, Clarendon P., 1970. 2 v. (xlix, 452 p., 6 plates; 453-977 p., 6 plates). illus., facsims., ports. 23 cm. Bibliography: p. 939-948. [PK109.J6A4 1970] 71-141315 12/10/-
I. Cannon, Garland Hampton, 1924- ed. BIP

Jones, William Sir 1746-1794.

CANNON, Garland Hampton, 1924- 923.442
Oriental Jones, a biography of Sir William Jones. 1746-1794. New York, Asia Pub. [for] Indian Council for Cultural Relations [dist. Taplinger, c.1964] x, 215p. port. 25cm. Bibl. SA63 13.50
1. Jones, William Sir 1746-1794. I. Title.

JONES, William, Sir, 1746-1794. 826'.6
The letters of Sir William Jones; edited by Garland Cannon. Oxford, Clarendon P., 1970. 2 v. (xlix, 452 p., 6 plates; 453-977 p., 6 plates). illus., facsims., ports. 23 cm. Bibliography: p. 939-948. [PK109.J6A4 1970] 71-141315 12/10/-
I. Cannon, Garland Hampton, 1924- ed. BIP

JONES, William, Sir, 1746-1794. 826'.6
The letters of Sir William Jones; edited by Garland Cannon. Oxford, Clarendon P., 1970. 2 v. (xlix, 452 p., 6 plates; 453-977 p., 6 plates). illus., facsims., ports. 23 cm. Bibliography: p. 939-948. [PK109.J6A4 1970] 71-141315 12/10/-
I. Cannon, Garland Hampton, 1924- ed. BIP

Jonson, Ben, 1573?-1637.

BEN Jonson of Westminster. v. 12
New York, Dutton, 1960. 380p. (Dutton Everyman paperbacks. D60) Bibliography: p.351-360.
1. Jonson, Ben, 1573?-1637. I. Chute, Marchette Gaylord, 1909-

BOUGHNER, Daniel Cliness, 1909- 822'.3
The devil's disciple; Ben Jonson's debt to Machiavelli, by Daniel C. Boughner. New York, Philosophical Library [1968] 264 p. 21 cm. Bibliographical references included in "Notes" (p. 227-261) [PR2636.B6] 67-24571
1. Jonson, Ben, 1573?-1637. 2. Machiavelli, Niccolo, 1469-1527—Influence—Jonson. I. Title. BIP

CHETWOOD, William Rufus, d.1766, ed. 828'.3'09 B
Memoirs of the life and writings of Ben Johnson Esq. New York, Garland, 1970. 72, 126 p. 22 cm. Includes "Two comedies, (wrote by Ben. Jonson, etc. and not printed in his works) called The widow, and Eastward hoe." Facsimile of a copy in the Yale University Library, published in 1756. [PR2631.C5 1756a] 77-112094
1. Jonson, Ben, 1573?-1637. I. Chapman, George, 1559?-1634. Eastward hoe. 1970. II. Middleton, Thomas, d. 1627. The widow. 1970. III. Title: The widow. IV. Title: Eastward hoe.

CHUTE, Marchette Gaylord, 1909- 928.2
Ben Jonson of Westminster. [1st ed.] New York, Dutton, 1953. 380 p. illus. 23 cm. Includes bibliography. [PR2631.C53] 53-10335
1. Jonson, Ben, 1573?-1637.

HENDERSON, Philip, 1906- v. 12
Christopher Marlowe. Lincoln, Univ. of Nebraska Press [1966] 182 p. illus. 67-101088
1. Marlowe, Christopher, 1564-1593. 2. Jonson, Ben, 1572-1637. 3. Webster, John, 1580?-1625? 4. Ford, John, 1586-ca. 1640. I. Title. II. Title: Ben Jonson III. Title: John Webster IV. Title: John Ford

LINKLATER, Eric, 1899- 822.3 B
Ben Jonson and King James; biography and portrait. Port Washington, N.Y., Kennikat Press [1972] 328 p. illus. 21 cm. Reprint of the 1931 ed. [PR2631.L5 1972] 74-168250 ISBN 0-8046-1689-2
1. Jonson, Ben, 1573?-1637. 2. James I, King of Great Britain, 1566-1625. 3. Gt. Brit.—Court and courtiers. I. Title. BIP

PALMER, John Leslie, 1885-1944. 828.309
Ben Jonson. Port Washington, N.Y., Kennikat Press [1967] 330 p. illus., facsim., ports 22 cm. Reprint of 1934 ed. [PR2631.P3 1967] 66-25935
1. Jonson, Ben, 1573?-1637.

SYMONDS, John Addington, 1840-1893. 828'.3'09 B
Ben Jonson. New York, AMS Press [1970] 202 p. 19 cm. Reprint of the 1886 ed. [PR2631.S8 1970] 75-128937
1. Jonson, Ben, 1573?-1637. BIP

Jonson, Ben, 1573?-1637—Miscellanea.

DRUMMOND, William, 1585-1649. 822'.3
Ben Jonson's conversations with William Drummond of Hawthornden. Edited with introd. and notes by R. F. Patterson. [Folcroft, Pa.] Folcroft Library Editions, 1974. p. cm. Reprint of the 1923 ed. published by Blackie, London. Includes bibliographical references. [PR2262.B4 1974b] 74-11330 10.00
1. Jonson, Ben, 1573?-1637—Miscellanea. I. Jonson, Ben, 1573?-1637. II. Patterson, Richard Ferrar, 1888- ed. III. Title.

Joplin, Janis.

*CAREY, Gary 784.0924
Lenny, Janis, and Jimi. New York, Pocket Books, [1975] 299 p. 18 cm. [ML420] ISBN 0-671-78969-4 1.75 (pbk.)
1. Bruce, Lenny 2. Joplin, Janis 3. Hendrix, Jimi I. Title. BIP

DALTON, David. 784.0924 [B]
Janis. Written and edited by David Dalton. New York, Popular Library [1973 c.1971] 317 p. illus., ports. 18 cm. "Songs," p. [273]-317. [ML420.J77D3] 1.50 (pbk.)
1. Joplin, Janis. I. Title.
L.C. card no. for hardbound edition: 72-159128. BIP

FRIEDMAN, Myra. 784'.092'4 B
Buried alive; the biography of Janis Joplin. New York, W. Morrow, 1973. 333 p. ports. 22 cm. [ML420.J77F7] 78-189274 ISBN 0-688-00160-2 7.95
1. Joplin, Janis. I. Title. BIP

FRIEDMAN, Myra. 784'.092'4 B
Buried alive; the biography of Janis Joplin. New York, Bantam Books [1974] 398 p. illus. 18 cm. [ML420.J77F7] 1.95 (pbk.)
1. Joplin, Janis. I. Title.
L.C. card number for hardbound ed.: 78-189274. BIP

LANDAU, Deborah. 784'.0924 B
Janis Joplin, her life and times. New York, Paperback Library [1971] 160 p. ports. 18 cm. Discography: p. 158-160. [ML420.J77L3] 71-24058 0.75
1. Joplin, Janis.

Joplin, Scott, 1868-1917.

HASKINS, James, 1941- 780'.92'4 B
Scott Joplin / James Haskins, with Kathleen Benson. 1st ed. Garden City, N.Y. : Doubleday, 1978. xiii, 248 p., leaves of plates : ill. ; 22 cm. Includes index. Bibliography: p. 229-235. [ML410.J75H34] 76-50768 ISBN 0-385-11155-X : 8.95
1. Joplin, Scott, 1868-1917. 2. Composers—United States—Biography. I. Benson, Kathleen, joint author. BIP

Joplin, Scott, 1868-1917—Juvenile literature.

EVANS, Mark. 780'.92'4 B
Scott Joplin and the ragtime years / Mark Evans. New York : Dodd, Mead, c1976. vii, 120 p. : ill. ; 22 cm. Includes index. A biography of Scott Joplin, king of the ragtime writers. [ML3930.J66E9] 92 75-38362 ISBN 0-396-07308-5 : 4.95
1. Joplin, Scott, 1868-1917—Juvenile literature. I. Title. BIP

Jordan—Pol. & govt.

HUSSEIN, King of Jordan, 1935- 923.15695
Uneasy lies the head; the autobiography of His Majesty King Hussein i of the Hashemite Kingdom of Jordan. [New York] B. Geis Associates; distributed by Random House [1962] 306p. illus. 22cm. [DS154.55.H8A3] 62-11165
1. Jordan—Pol. & govt. I. Title.

Jordan. al-Jaysh al-'Arabi.

GLUBB, John Bagot, Sir, 1897- 355.3'095695
The story of the Arab Legion / by John Bagot Glubb (Glubb Pasha). New York : Da Capo Press, 1976. p. cm. (The Middle East in the 20th century) Reprint of the 1948 ed. published by Hodder & Stoughton, London. [UA853.J6G55 1976] 76-7060 25.00
1. Jordan. al-Jaysh al-'Arabi. 2. Glubb, John Bagot, Sir, 1897- I. Title. BIP

Jordan, Barbara, 1936-

BRYANT, Ira Babington, 1908- 328.73'092'4 B
Barbara Charline Jordan : from the ghetto to the Capitol / by Ira B. Bryant. Houston : D. Armstrong Co., c1977. iii, 105 p. : ill. ; 24 cm. [E840.8.J62B78] 77-153691 7.50
1. Jordan, Barbara, 1936- 2. United States. Congress. House—Biography. 3. Legislators—United States—Biography.
Available from the author: 3319 Holman Ave. Houston, Tex. 77004

JORDAN, Barbara, 1936- 328.73'092'4 B
Barbara Jordan, a self-portrait / Barbara Jordan and Shelby Hearon. 1st ed. Garden City, N.Y. : Doubleday, 1979. viii, 269 p., [4] leaves of plates : ill. ; 22 cm. [E840.8.J62A33] 78-2049 ISBN 0-385-13599-8 : 9.95
1. Jordan, Barbara, 1936- 2. United States. Congress. House—Biography. 3. Legislators—United States—Biography. I. Hearon, Shelby, 1931- joint author. II. Title.

Jordan, Barbara, 1936- —Juvenile literature.

HASKINS, James, 1941- 328.73'092'4 B
Barbara Jordan / by James Haskins. New York : Dial Press, c1977. p. cm. Includes index. Bibliography: p. A biography of the Congresswoman from Texas, the first black woman ever to be elected to that office from the South. [E840.8.J62H36] 92 77-71522 ISBN 0-8037-0452-6 : 7.95
1. Jordan, Barbara, 1936- —Juvenile literature. 2. Legislators—United States—Biography—Juvenile literature. I. Title. BIP

JACOBS, Linda. 328.73'092'4 B
Barbara Jordan : keeping faith / by Linda Jacobs. St. Paul : EMC Corp., 1978. p. cm. (Headliners II) A biography of the Afro-American who after serving in the Texas legislature became a representative to the United States Congress. [E840.8.J62J33] 78-9550 ISBN 0-88436-432-1 : 5.95 ISBN 0-88436-433-X pbk. : 2.95
1. Jordan, Barbara, 1936- —Juvenile literature. 2. United States. Congress. House—Biography—Juvenile literature. 3. Legislators—United States—Biography—Juvenile literature. I. Title. II. Series. BIP

Jordan, Clarence.

LEE, Dallas. 335'.9'758913 B
The cotton patch evidence. [1st ed.] New York, Harper & Row [1971] x, 240 p. 22 cm. (A Koinonia publication) [BX6495.J65L4] 70-150593 5.95
1. Jordan, Clarence. 2. Koinonia Farm. I. Title.

Jordan, Crystal Lee, 1940-

LEIFERMANN, Henry P. 331.88'17'700924 B
Crystal Lee, a woman of inheritance / Henry P. Leifermann. New York : Macmillan, 1975. 190 p. ; 21 cm. [HD8073.J65L44] 75-14118 ISBN 0-02-570220-3 8.95
1. Jordan, Crystal Lee, 1940- 2. Textile workers—North Carolina. 3. Trade-unions—North Carolina. 4. Cotton trade—North Carolina. I. Title.

Jordan, David Starr, 1851-1931.

BURNS, Edward McNall, 1897- 923.773
David Starr Jordan: prophet of freedom. Stanford, Calif., Stanford University Press [1953] 243 p. illus. 24 cm. [LD3025 1891.B87] 53-5525
1. Jordan, David Starr, 1851-1931.

MORAN, Hugh Anderson, 1881- 378.1'11'0924
David Starr Jordan, his spirit and decision of character [by] Hugh A. Moran. [Palo Alto, Calif., Daily Press, 1969] 70 p. illus., ports. 26 cm. [LD3019.J6M6] 78-8086
1. Jordan, David Starr, 1851-1931.

Jordan, Dorothy (Bland) 1761-1816.

JERROLD, Clare Armstrong (Bridgman) 1861- 792'.028'0924 B
The story of Dorothy Jordan, by Clare Jerrold. With illus. from the collections of A. M. Broadley and others. New York, B. Blom [1969] 429 p. illus., ports. 24 cm. Reprint of the 1914 ed. [PN2598.J6J5 1969] 70-82555
1. Jordan, Dorothy (Bland) 1761-1816. I. Title. BIP

Jordan family.

JORDAN, Gilbert John, 1902- 929'.2'0973
Ernst and Lisette Jordan: German pioneers in Texas, by Gilbert J. Jordan and Terry G. Jordan. [Austin, Tex., Printed by Von Boeckmann-Jones Co., 1971. viii, 126 p. illus. 24 cm. Bibliography: p. 42-45. [CS71.J82 1971b] 72-188896
1. Jordan family. 2. German Americans—Texas. I. Jordan, Terry G., joint author. II. Title.

JORDAN, Gilbert John, 1902- 976.4'62'00431
Yesterday in the Texas hill country / by Gilbert J. Jordan ; foreword by Terry G. Jordan. 1st ed. College Station : Texas A & M University Press, c1979. xiv, 171 p., [8] leaves of plates : ill. ; 24 cm. Includes index. Bibliography: p. [163]-166. [F392.M36J67] 78-21774 ISBN 0-89096-067-4 : 12.95
1. Jordan family. 2. Jordan, Gilbert John, 1902- 3. Methodists in Mason Co., Tex. 4. German Americans—Texas—Mason Co.—Social life and customs. 5. German Americans—Texas—Mason Co.—Biography. I. Title. BIP

Jordan, Gilbert John, 1902-

JORDAN, Gilbert John, 1902- 976.4'62'00431
Yesterday in the Texas hill country / by Gilbert J. Jordan ; foreword by Terry G. Jordan. 1st ed. College Station : Texas A & M University Press, c1979. xiv, 171 p., [8] leaves of plates : ill. ; 24 cm. Includes index. Bibliography: p. [163]-166. [F392.M36J67] 78-21774 ISBN 0-89096-067-4 : 12.95
1. Jordan family. 2. Jordan, Gilbert John, 1902- 3. Methodists in Mason Co., Tex. 4. German Americans—Texas—Mason Co.—Social life and customs. 5. German Americans—Texas—Mason Co.—Biography. I. Title. BIP

Jordan, Len B., 1899-

JORDAN, Grace (Edgington) 328.73'092'4 B
The unintentional senator, by Grace E. Jordan. [Boise, Syms-York Co., 1972] xii, 318 p. illus. 23 cm. [E840.8.J63J67] 72-95050 7.00
1. Jordan, Len B., 1899- I. Title.

Jordan, Mickey.

JORDAN, Mickey. 248'.2'0924 B
Someday I'll be somebody. Foreword by Rosalind Rinker. Atlanta, Forum House [1974] 200 p. 23 cm. Autobiographical. [BR1725.J67A34] 72-97822 ISBN 0-913618-09-8 5.95
1. Jordan, Mickey. I. Title.

Jordan of Saxony, d.1237.

ARON, Marguerite. 922.244
Saint Dominic's successor the life of Blessed Jordan of Saxony, master-general of the Dominican Order, 1222-1237. Introd. by P. Mandonnet. St. Louis, Herder [1955] 203p. illus. 23cm. Translation of Un animateur de la jeunesse au xiii siecle. [BX4705.J7A715] 55-3759
1. Jordan of Saxony, d.1237. 2. Dominicans. I. Title.

JORDAN of Saxony d.1237. 922.245
To heaven with Diana! A study of Jordan of Saxony and Diana d'Andalo, with a translation of the letters of Jordan, by Gerald Vann. [New York] Pantheon Books [1960] 160p. 22cm. [BX4705.J7A43] 60-11759
I. Diana de Andalc, 1201 (ca.)- 1236. II. Vann, Gerald, 1906- III. Title.

JORDAN of Saxony d.1237. 922.245
To heaven with Diana! A study of Jordan of Saxony and Diana d'Andalo, with a translation of the letters of Jordan, by Gerald Vann. [New York] Pantheon Books [c.1960] 160p. (Bibl. footnotes) 22cm. 60-11759 3.50
I. Diana de Andalo, 1201 (ca.)—1236. II. Vann, Gerald. III. Title.

Jordan, Pat.

JORDAN, Pat. 796.357'092'4 B
A false spring / by Pat Jordan. New York : Dodd, Mead, [1975] 277 p. ; 22 cm. [GV865.J67A34] 74-31082 ISBN 0-396-07078-7 : 7.95
1. Jordan, Pat. 2. Baseball. 3. Pitching (Baseball) I. Title.

JORDAN, Pat. 796.357'092'4
A false spring. New York, Bantam Books [1976 c1975] 245 p. 18 cm. [GV865.J67A34] 1.75 (pbk.)
1. Jordan, Pat. 2. Baseball. 3. Pitching (Baseball) I. Title.
L.C. card no. of 1975 Dodd, Mead edition: 74-31082. BIP

JORDAN, Pat. 796.357'092'2
The suitors of spring. New York, Dodd, Mead [1973] xi, 211 p. illus. 22 cm. [GV865.A1J67 1973] 72-9933 ISBN 0-396-06711-5 6.95
1. Baseball—Biography. 2. Pitchers (Baseball)—Biography. I. Title. BIP

Jordan, Patricia, 1922-

JORDAN, Patricia, 1922- 610.73'092'4 B
District nurse / Patricia Jordan. New York : St. Martin's Press, c1977. 176 p. ; 22 cm. [RT37.J57A33 1977] 77-17785 ISBN 0-312-21358-1 : 7.95
1. Jordan, Patricia, 1922- 2. Nurses—England—Biography. 3. Public health nursing—England. I. Title. BIP

Jorden, Paul J.

JORDEN, Paul J. 617'.3'00924 B
Surgeon on safari / Paul J. Jorden, with James R. Adair. New York : Hawthorn Books, c1976. xiv, 173 p., [8] leaves of plates : ill. ; 22 cm. Bibliography: p. 173. [R722.32.J67A37] 75-41806 ISBN 0-8015-2147-5 : 6.95
1. Jorden, Paul J. 2. Missionaries, Medical—Kenya—Biography. 3. Orthopedists—Illinois—Biography. 4. Africa, East—Description and travel—1951- I. Adair, James R., 1923- joint author. II. Title.

Jorgen, Eriksson, 1535-1604.

QUAM, John Elliott. 284'.1'0924
Jorgen Eriksson; a study in the Norwegian reformation, 1571-1604. [New Haven, Conn.] 1968. xii, 272 l. port. 28 cm. Thesis—Yale University. Bibliography: leaves 259-272. [BR403.Q3] 77-2688
1. Jorgen Eriksson, 1535-1604. 2. Reformation—Norway.

Jorgensen, Christine.

JORGENSEN, Christine. 616.85'83
Christine Jorgensen; personal autobiography. With an introd. by Harry Benjamin. New York, P. S. Eriksson [1967] xvii, 332 p. ports. 22 cm. [RC560.C4J6] 67-21524

Jorgensen, Johannes, 1866-1956.

JONES, W. Glyn. 839.8'1'172
Johannes Jorgensen, by W. Glyn Jones. New York, Twayne Publishers [1969] 183 p. 21 cm. (Twayne's world authors series, TWAS 70. Denmark) Bibliography: p. 175-177. [PT8175.J73Z79] 67-25192
1. Jorgensen, Johannes, 1866-1956.

Josephine, Consort of Napoleon I, 1763-1814.

CARTLAND, Barbara, 1902- 944.05'092'4 [B]
Josephine, Empress of France. New York, Pyramid Books [1974, c1961] 206 p. 18 cm. [DC216.1.C3] ISBN 0-515-03326-X. 1.25 (pbk.)
1. Josephine, consort of Napoleon I, 1763-1814. I. Title.
L.C. card number for original ed.: 61-66119

CASTELOT, Andre 944.05'0924 B
Josephine. Translated by Denise Folliot. [1st American ed.] New York, Harper & Row [1967] vi, 506 p. port. 22 cm. Bibliography: p. 489-496. [DC216.1.C3413 1967] 66-20728
1. Josephine, consort of Napoleon I, 1763-1814.

COLE, Hubert 923.144
Josephine. New York, Viking [1963, c.1962] 308p. illus. 22cm. 63-7927 6.00
1. Josephine, consort of Napoleon I, 1763-1814. I. Title. BIP

EPTON, Nina Consuelo. 944.05'092'4 B
Josephine : the Empress and her children / Nina Epton. 1st American ed. New York : Norton, 1976, c1975. 230 p., [6] leaves of plates : ill. ; 22 cm. Includes index. Bibliography: p. 221-222. [DC216.1.E7 1976] 75-37549 ISBN 0-393-07500-1 : 10.95
1. Josephine, Consort of Napoleon I, 1763-1814. BIP

KUNSTLER, Chalres, 1887- 923.144
The private life of the Empress Josephine. Adapted from the French by Herma Briffault. New York, D. McKay Co. [1957] 242p. 21cm. [DC216.1.K82] 57-11082
1. Josephine, consort of Napoleon I, 1763-1814. I. Title.

KUNSTLER, Charles, 1887- 923.144
The private life of the Empress Josephine. Adapted from the French by Herma Briffault. New York, D. McKay Co. [1957] 242p. 21cm. [DC216.1.K82] 57-11082
1. Josephine, consort of Napoleon I, 1763-1814. I. Title.

LAING, Margaret Irene. 944.05'092'4 B
Josephine & Napoleon [by] Margaret Laing. New York, Mason/Charter, 1974 [c1973] 196 p. illus. 25 cm. [DC216.1.L3 1974] 74-14700 ISBN 0-88405-091-2
1. Josephine, consort of Napoleon I, 1763-1814. 2. Napoleon I, Emperor of the French, 1769-1821. I. Title.

VANCE, Marguerite. 923.144
The empress Josephine; from Martinique to Malmaison. Illustrated by Nedda Walker. [1st ed.] New York, Dutton, 1956. 160 p. illus. 21 cm. [D216.1V3] 56-8307
1. Josephine, Consort of Napoleon I, 1763-1814.

Josephine, Consort of Napoleon I, 1763-1814—Juvenile literature.

MOSSIKER, Frances. 944.05'0924 B
More than a queen; the story of Josephine Bonaparte. Drawings by Michael Eagle. New York, Knopf [1971] 150 p. illus. 24 cm. A biography of the Creole girl from the island of Martinique who became Empress of France. [DC216.1.M63 1971] 92 74-131386 ISBN 0-394-92049-X
1. Josephine, Consort of Napoleon I, 1763-1814—Juvenile literature. I. Eagle, Michael, illus. II. Title.

Josel, of Rosheim, 1480 (ca.)-1554.

STERN, Selma, 1890- 943.031009174924
Josel of Rosheim, commander of Jewry in the Holy Roman Empire of the German nation. Tr. from German by Gertrude Hirschler [Philadelphia] Jewish Pubn. Soc. [c.]1965. xx,327p. 22cm. Bibl. [DS135.G5J653] 65-17044 4.50
1. Josel, of Rosheim, 1480 (ca.)-1554. I. Title.

Joseph Bonaparte, King of Spain, 1768-1844.

CONNELLY, Owen. 946'.06'0924
The gentle Bonaparte; a biography of Joseph, Napoleon's elder brother. New York, Macmillan [1968] xiv, 335 p. maps, ports. 22 cm. Bibliography: p. [301]-322. [DC216.5.C6] 68-11854
1. Joseph Bonaparte, King of Spain, 1766-1844. I. Title.

ROSS, Michael, 1905- 946'.06'0924 B
The reluctant king : Joseph Bonaparte, King of the two Sicilies and Spain / by Michael Ross. New York : Mason/Charter, 1977, c1976. 302 p., [4] leaves of plates : ill. ; 24 cm. Includes index. Bibliography: p. 290-291. [DC216.5.R67 1977] 76-51395 ISBN 0-88405-493-4 : 12.50
1. Joseph Bonaparte, King of Spain, 1768-1844. 2. Statesmen—France—Biography. I. Title.

Joseph, Emily,

JOSEPH, Emily, Sister, comp. 232.932
Joseph son of David. Paterson, N.J., St. Anthony's Guild, c.1961. 97p. 1.50; .75 pap.,
I. Title.

Joseph I, Emperor of Germany, 1678-1711.

INGRAO, Charles W. 943'.044'0924 B
In quest and crisis : Emperor Joseph I and the Habsburg monarchy / by Charles W. Ingrao. West Lafayette, Ind. : Purdue University Press, 1979. xi, 278 p. : maps ; 24 cm. Includes bibliographical references and index. [DB68.I53] 77-88358 ISBN 0-911198-53-9 : 12.95
1. Joseph I, Emperor of Germany, 1678-1711. 2. Holy Roman Empire—Kings and rulers—Biography. 3. Rakozi, Ferenc II, Prince of Transylvania, 1676-1735. 4. Austria—History—Joseph I, 1705-1711. 5. Hungary—History—1683-1848. I. Title. BIP

Joseph II, Emperor of Germany, 1741-1790.

BERNARD, Paul P. 943'.057'0924 B
Joseph II, by Paul P. Bernard. New York, Twayne Publishers [1968] 155 p. 21 cm. (Twayne's rulers and statesmen of the world series, 5) Bibliography: p. 149-151. [DB74.B43] 67-25205
1. Joseph II, Emperor of Germany, 1741-1790.

BRIGHT, James Franck, 1832-1920. 943'.057'0924
Joseph II. Port Washington, N.Y., Kennikat Press [1970] xi, 222 p. 21 cm. Reprint of the 1897 ed. [DB74.B85 1970] 78-112795
1. Joseph II, Emperor of Germany, 1741-1790. 2. Austria—History—Joseph II, 1780-1790.

GOOCH, George Peabody, 1873-1968, 923.1436
Maria Theresa, and other studies. London, New York, Longmans, Green [1951] viii, 432 p. ports. 23 cm. [DB71.G63] 51-14318
1. Joseph II, Emperor of Germany, 1741-1790. 2. Marie Antoinette, consort of Louis XVI, King of France, 1755-1793. 3. Maria Theresa, Empress of Austria, 1717-1780. 4. Historiography. 5. History—Study and teaching.

PADOVER, Saul Kussiel, 1905- 943'.057'0924 B
The revolutionary Emperor, Joseph II of Austria [by] Saul K. Padover. [Rev. ed. Hamden, Conn.] Archon Books, 1967. 316 p. maps, ports. 23 cm. Bibliography: p. [295]-307. [DB74.P3 1967] 67-25159
1. Joseph II, Emperor of Germany, 1741-1790. 2. Austria—History—Joseph II, 1780-1790. I. Title.

Joseph (Name)—Juvenile literature.

GLAZER, Tom. 929.4
All about your name, Joseph, Joe, Joey, Jo-Jo / by Tom Glazer ; illustrated by Demi. 1st ed. Garden City, N.Y. : Doubleday, c1978. p. cm. Discusses the name Joseph and identifies people of significance with that name. [CS2391.J65G54] 920 77-15155 ISBN 0-385-06554-X : 4.95. ISBN 0-385-06558-2 lib. bdg.,
1. Joseph (Name)—Juvenile literature. 2. Biography—Miscellanea—Juvenile literature. I. Hitz, Demi. II. Title. BIP

Joseph, Nez Perce chief, 1840-1904.

BEAL, Merrill D., 1898- 970.3
'I will fight no more forever' Chief Joseph and the Nez Perce War. Seattle, Univ. of Wash. Pr. [c.]1963. xvii, 366p. illus., ports., maps. 24cm. Bibl. 62-13278 6.00
1. Joseph, Nez Perce chief, 1840-1904. 2. Nez Perce Indians—Wars, 1877- I. Title.

BURT, Olive (Woolley) 1894- 92
Chief Joseph, boy of the Nez Perce, by Olive W. Burt. Illustrated by William Moyers. Indianapolis, Bobbs-Merrill [1967] 200 p. col. illus. 20 cm. (Childhood of famous Americans) Bibliography: p. 198. A biography of the Nez Perce chief who led his people on a great military retreat in 1877. Concentrates on Joseph's childhood and youth. [E83.877.B8] AC 67
1. Joseph, Nez Perce chief, 1840-1904. I. Moyers, William, illus. II. Title.

GARST, Doris Shannon, 1899- 970.1
Chief Joseph of the Nez Perces; illustrated by Douglas Gorsline. New York, J. Messner [1953] 184p. illus. 22cm. Includes bibliography. [E83.877.G3] [E83.877.G3] 970.2 53-8046 53-8046
1. Joseph, Nez Perce chief, 1840-1904. I. Title.

GARST, Doris Shannon, 1899- 970.3 B
Chief Joseph of the Nez Perces; illustrated by Douglas Gorsline. New York, J. Messner [1953] 184 p. illus. 22 cm. Includes bibliography. Fighting the government's efforts to force the Nez Perce Indians onto a reservation, Chief Joseph led his people on a one-thousand-mile retreat from the military troops whom he could outwit but not overpower. Only forty miles from his goal—Canada—he was forced to surrender. [E83.877.G3] 92 AC 68
1. Joseph, Nez Perce chief, 1840-1904. 2. Nez Perce Indians. I. Gorsline, Douglas W., 1913- illus. II. Title.

HOWARD, Helen Addison 970.30924
Saga of Chief Joseph. Maps, illus. by George D. McGrath. Caldwell, Idaho, Caxton, 1965[c.1941, 1965] 395p. illus. (pt. col.) col. maps, ports. 24cm. Pub. in 1941 under title; War Chief Joseph. Bibl. [E90.J8H6] 65-18666 4.95
1. Joseph. Nez Perce chief, 1840-1904. 2. Nez Perce Indians—Wars, 1877. I. Title.

HOWARD, Helen Addison. 970'.004'97 B
Saga of Chief Joseph / by Helen Addison Howard ; maps and ill. by George D. McGrath. Lincoln : University of Nebraska Press, 1978, c1965. p. cm. Reprint of the 1971 ed. published by Caxton Printers, Caldwell, Idaho; first published in 1941 under title: War Chief Joseph. Bibliography: p. [E99.N5J584 1978] 78-16138 ISBN 0-8032-7202-2 pbk. : 4.95
1. Joseph, Nez Perce chief, 1840-1904. 2. Nez Perce Indians—Wars, 1877. 3. Nez Perce Indians—Biography. I. Title. BIP

HOWARD, Helen Addison. v. 12
War chief Joseph, by Helen Addison Howard, assisted in the research by Dan L. McGrath; maps and illus. by George D. McGrath. Caldwell, Idaho, Caxton Printers, 1958. 368 p. illus. 24 cm. 63-233887
1. Joseph, Nez Perce chief, 1840-1904. 2. Nez Perce Indians—Wars—1877. I. Title.

HOWARD, Oliver Otis, 1830-1909. 970.3 B
Nez Perce Joseph; an account of his ancestors, his lands, his confederates, his enemies, his murders, his war, his pursuit and capture. New York, Da Capo Press, 1972. xii, 274 p. illus. 22 cm. Reprint of the 1881 ed. [E83.877.J83 1972] 70-39379 ISBN 0-306-70461-7
1. Joseph, Nez Perce Chief, 1840-1904. 2. Nez Perce Indians—Wars, 1877.

MILLER, Helen Markley. 970.2
Thunder Rolling; the story of Chief Joseph. Illustrated by Albert Orbaan. New York, Putnam [1959] 190 p. illus. 21 cm. (A Westerners book) [E90.J8M54] 59-6502
1. Joseph, Nez Perce chief, 1840-1904. I. Title.

POLLOCK, Dean, 1897- 970.2
Joseph, chief of the Nez Perce. Pictures and text by Dean Pollock. [Portland, Or.] Binfords & Mort, c1950. 62 p. illus. 28 cm. Text ends on p. [3] of cover. [E83.877.J87] 50-13177
1. Joseph, Nez Perce chief, 1840-1904. 2. Nez Perce Indians—Wars, 1877. BIP

WOOD, Erskine. 970.3 B
Days with Chief Joseph; diary, recollections, and photos. [Portland] Oregon Historical Society, 1970. 1 v. (unpaged) illus., facsim., ports. 23 cm. [E90.J8W6] 79-634517 ISBN 0-87595-026-4
1. Joseph, Nez Perce chief, 1840-1904. I. Title.

Joseph, Nez Perce chief, 1840-1904—Juvenile literature.

BURT, Olive (Woolley) 1894- 973.8'1'0924
Chief Joseph, boy of the Nez Perce, by Olive W. Burt. Illustrated by William Moyers, Indianapolis, Bobbs-Merrill [1967] 200 p. col. illus. 20 cm. (Childhood of famous Americans) Bibliography: p. 198. [E83.877.B8] 67-26335
1. Joseph, Nez Perce chief, 1840-1904—Juvenile literature. I. Title.

BURT, Olive (Woolley) 1894- 970.1
Chief Joseph, boy of the Nez Perce, by Olive W. Burt. Illustrated by William Moyers. Indianapolis, Bobbs-Merrill [1967] 200 p. col. illus. 20 cm. (Childhood of famous Americans) Bibliography: p. 198. [E83.877.B8] 67-26335
1. Joseph, Nez Perce chief, 1840-1904—Juvenile literature. I. Title.

GRANT, Matthew G. 970.3 B
Chief Joseph of the Nez Perce [by] Matthew G. Grant. Illustrated by John Keely. [Mankato, Minn., Creative Education; distributed by Children Press, Chicago, 1974] 30 p. illus. (part col.) 25 cm. (His Gallery of great Americans series. Indians of America) Biography of the Nez Perce Chief who in a dispute with the United States Army successfully led his outnumbered tribe on a one-thousand mile retreat. [E99.N5J583] 92 73-9816 ISBN 0-87191-251-1
1. Joseph, Nez Perce chief, Juvenile literature. I. Keely, John, illus. II. Title.

GRANT, Matthew G. 970.3 B
Chief Joseph of the Nez Perce [by] Matthew G. Grant. Illustrated by John Keely. [Mankato, Minn., Creative Education; distributed by Children Press, Chicago, 1974] 30 p. illus. (part col.) 25 cm. (His Gallery of great Americans series. Indians of America) Biography of the Nez Perce Chief who in a dispute with the United States Army successfully led his outnumbered tribe on a one-thousand mile retreat. [E99.N5J583] 92 73-9816 ISBN 0-87191-251-1 4.95
1. Joseph, Nez Perce chief, Juvenile literature. I. Keely, John, illus. II. Title.

JOHNSON, Robert Proctor, 1924- 970.3 B
Chief Joseph, by R. P. Johnson. Minneapolis, Dillon Press [1974] 74 p. illus. 23 cm. (The Story of an American Indian) A biography of the nineteenth-century Nez Perce chief concentrating on his unending struggle to win peace and equality for his people. [E99.N5J585] 92 74-11467 ISBN 0-87518-062-0 4.95
1. Joseph, Nez Perce chief, 1840-1904—Juvenile literature. I. Title. BIP

MONTGOMERY, Elizabeth Rider. 970.3 B
Chief Joseph, guardian of his people. Illustrated by Frank Vaughn. Champaign, Ill., Garrard Pub. Co. [1969] 80 p. col. illus. 24 cm. (Garrard Indian books) An easy-to-read biography of the nineteenth-century Nez Perce chief who suffered many wrongs and much humiliation in his attempts to achieve peace and equality for his people. [E90.J8M67] 92 69-12424 2.39
1. Joseph, Nez Perce chief, 1840-1904—Juvenile literature. I. Vaughn, Frank, 1915- illus. II. Title.

Joseph, Nez Perce chief, 1840-1904. Nez Perce Indians— Wars, 1877.

HOWARD, Helen Addison 970.2
War chief Joseph, by Helen Addison Howard, assisted by Dan L. McGrath; maps & illus. by George D. McGrath. Lincoln, Univ. of Neb. Pr. [1964, c.1941] 368p. illus., ports., maps. 21cm. (Bison bk. BB178) Bibl. 1.65
1. Joseph, Nez Perce chief, 1840-1904. Nez Perce Indians— Wars, 1877. I. McGrath, Dan L. II. Title.

Joseph of the Sacred Heart, Mother, 1823-1902.

MCCROSSON, Mary of the Blessed Sacrament. 922.273
The bell and the river. In collaboration with Sister Mary Leopoldine and Sister Maria Theresa. Palo Alto, Calif., Pacific Books [1957] 268p. illus. 24cm. [BX4705.J7145M2] 57-7385
1. Joseph of the Sacred Heart, Mother, 1823-1902. I. Title.

Joseph, Saint.

ERNEST, Brother, 1897- 232.932
A story of Saint Joseph. Pictures by Carolyn Lee Jagodits. Notre Dame, Ind., Dujarie Press [1957] unpaged. illus. 21cm. [BS2458.E7] 57-4988
1. Joseph, Saint. I. Title.

FLECK, Raymond, 1927- 232.932
Good Saint Joseph. Illus. by Carolyn Lee Jagodits. Notre Dame, Ind., Dujarie Press [1957] 95p. illus. 24cm. [BS2458.F5] 57-59235
1. Joseph, Saint. I. Title.

LEVY, Rosalie Marie, 1889- 232.932
Joseph, the just man. [Derby, N. Y., Daughters of St. Paul, Apostolate of the Press [c1955] 285p. 22cm. [BS2458.L46] 59-23942
1. Joseph, Saint. I. Title.

LLAMERA, Boniface 232.932
Saint Joseph. Tr. [from Spanish] by Sister Mary Elizabeth. St. Louis, B. Herder [c.1962] 316p. Bibl. 62-10506 5.50
1. Joseph, Saint. I. Title.

RONDET, Henri, 1898- 232.932
Saint Joseph. Translated and edited by Donald Attwater. New York, P. J. Kenedy [1956] 243p. illus. 21cm. [BS2458.R63] 56-6430
1. Joseph, Saint. I. Title.

ZELLER, Renee C T 232.932
The book of Joseph. Translated from the French by Salvator Attanasio. [1st ed.] New York, Hawthorn Books [1963] 224 p. illus. 24 cm. Translation of Joseph le charpentier. Includes bibliography. [BS2458.Z413] 63-8018
1. Joseph, Saint. I. Title.

Joseph, the patriarch.

HAYNES, Carlyle Boynton, 1882- 221.92
God sent a man. Washington, D.C., 6856 Eastern Ave., N.W. Review and Herald Pub. Assn., [1962] 192p. 22cm. 62-9140 3.00
1. Joseph, the patriarch. I. Title.

SANFORD, John A. 221.9'22 B
The man who wrestled with God; a study of individuation (personal growth toward wholeness) based on four Bible stories [by] John A. Sanford. King of Prussia, Pa., Religious Pub. Co. [1974] 126 p. 22 cm. Errata slip inserted. Includes bibliographical references. [BS571.S26] 74-79994 5.95
1. Jacob, the patriarch. 2. Joseph, the patriarch. 3. Moses. 4. Adam (Biblical

character) 5. Eve (Biblical character) I. Title.
Publisher's address: 198 Allendale Road, King of Prussia, Pa. 19406.

Joseph, the patriarch — Juvenile literature.

BULLA, Clyde Robert. 222'.11'0924
Joseph, the dreamer. Illustrated by Gordon Laite. New York, Crowell [1971] [64] p. illus. (part col.) 27 cm. A retelling of the Bible story in which Joseph is reunited with his family many years after being sold into slavery in Egypt. [BS580.J6B8 1971] 75-94791 ISBN 0-690-46554-8 4.95
1. Joseph, the patriarch—Juvenile literature. I. Laite, Gordon, illus. II. Title.

COHEN, Barbara. 222'.11'0924 B
I am Joseph / by Barbara Cohen ; illustrated by Charles Mikolaycak. New York : Lothrop, Lee, & Shepard Books, c1980. p. cm. Retells the Biblical story of Joseph, from his viewpoint, relating how he was sold into slavery and became the Egyptian Pharaoh's adviser. [BS580.J6C64] 79-20001 ISBN 0-688-41933-X : 9.95 ISBN 0-688-51933-4 lib. bdg. : 9.55
1. Joseph, the patriarch—Juvenile literature. 2. Bible. O.T.—Biography—Juvenile literature. 3. Patriarchs (Bible)—Biography—Juvenile literature. I. Mikolaycak, Charles. II. Title. **BIP**

JONES, Mary Alice, 1898- 221.95
The story of Joseph, Illus. by Manning de V. Lee. Chicago, Rand McNally [1966] c.1965. 1 v. (unpaged) col. illus. 33cm. (Rand McNally giant bk.) [BS580.J6J55] 66-14816 1.00 bds.,
1. Joseph, the patriarch — Juvenile literature. I. Lee, Manning de Villeneuve, 1894- illus. II. Title.

MOORE, Doraine. j220.9
A dream and a promise. Saint Louis, Concordia Pub. House [1964] 151 p. 21 cm. [BS580.J6M6] 63-23490
1. Joseph, the patriarch — Juvenile literature. I. Title.

SUMMERS, Jester. 222'.11'0924 B
Joseph the forgiver / Jester Summers ; illustrated by Michael Sloan. Nashville : Broadman Press, c1976. 48 p. : col. ill. ; 24 cm. (Biblearn series) Discusses the events of Joseph's life that enabled him to provide for his family during a famine and forgive his brothers for their cruelties. [BS580.J6S95] 76-383002 ISBN 0-8054-4224-3 : 3.95
1. Joseph, the patriarch—Juvenile literature. 2. Bible. O.T.—Biography—Juvenile literature. I. Sloan, Michael. II. Title.

WIEMER, Rudolf Otto, 1905- 92
Joseph in Egypt. Illus. by Reinhard Herrmann. Translation by Paul T. Martinsen. Minneapolis, Augsburg Pub. House [c1967] 1 v. (unpaged) col. illus. 27 cm. Translation of Joseph in Agypten. [BS580.J6.W523] 67-8396
1. Joseph, the patriarch — Juvenile literature. I. Title.

Josephine, consort of Napoleon I, 1763-1814.

KNAPTON, Ernest John. 923.144
Empress Josephine. Cambridge, Mass., Harvard University Press, 1963. xiii, 359 p. illus., ports. 25 cm. "Bibliographical essay": p. 333-343. Bibliographical references included in "Notes" (p. 344-350) [DC216.1K55] 63-17203
1. Josephine, consort of Napoleon I, 1763-1814. I. Title.

VANCE, Marguerite. 923.144
The empress Josephine; from Martinique to Malmaison. Illustrated by Nedda Walker. [1st ed.] New York, Dutton, 1956. 160 p. illus. 21 cm. [DC216.1.V3] 56-8307
1. Josephine, consort of Napoleon I, 1763-1814. I. Title.

Josephtal, Giora Georg,

JOSEPHTAL, Giora 956.94'04'0924 Georg, 1912-1962.
The responsible attitude; life and opinions of Giora Josephthal. Edited by Ben Halpern and Shalom Wurm. With a biographical sketch by Senta Josephthal. New York, Schocken Books [1967, c1966] xi, 269 p. ports. 24 cm. [DS126.6.J6A254] 66-26006
I. Halpern, Ben, ed. II. Wurm, Shalom, ed. III. Title.

Josephus, Flavius.

BENTWICH, Norman 933'.007'2024 B De Mattos, 1883-1971.
Josephus / by Norman Bentwich. Folcroft, Pa. : Folcroft Library Editions, 1976. 266 p. ; 23 cm. Reprint of the 1914 ed. published by The Jewish Publication Society of America, Philadelphia. Includes index. Bibliography: p. [261]-263. [DS115.9.J6B4 1976] 76-49584 ISBN 0-8414-1760-1 lib bdg. : 25.00
1. Josephus, Flavius. 2. Historians, Jewish—Biography. **BIP**

CHARLESWORTH, Martin 920.037 Percival, 1895-1950.
Five men; character studies from the Roman Empire. Freeport, N.Y., Books for Libraries Press [1967] viii, 170 p. 22 cm. (Essay index reprint series) Martin classical lectures, v.6. Reprint of the 1936 ed. Includes bibliographical references. [PA25.M3 vol. 6 1967] 67-30202
1. Agrippa I, King of Judea, B. C. 10 (ca.)-A. D. 44. 2. Musonius Rufus, C. 3. Josephus, Flavius. 4. Agricola, Cn. Julius, 37-93. 5. Rome—Civilization. I. Title. II. Series: Martin classical lectures, v. 6 **BIP**

THACKERAY, Henry St. 933'.072'024 John, 1869-1930
Josephus, the man and the historian. Pref. by George Foot Moore. Introd. by Samuel Sandmel. New York, Ktav [1968, c1967] xxi, 160p. 24cm. (Hilda Stich Stroock lects. at the Jewish Inst. of Religon, 1928) [DS115.9.J6T5 1968] 67-18816 6.95
1. Josephus, Flavius. I. Title. II. Series: Jewish Institute of Religion, New York. The Hilda Stich Stroock lectures, 1928

Joshua.

*MACVEAGH, Rogers 221.92
Joshua, by Rogers MacVeagh, Thomas B. Costain. Introd. by Norman Vincent Peale. New York, Popular Lib. [1964, c.1943, 1948] 190p. map. 18cm. (M2067) 60 pap.,
1. Joshua. I. Costain, Thomas Bertram, 1885- II. Title.

Joshua, son of Nun.

PETERSEN, Mark E. 222'.2'0924
Joshua, man of faith / Mark E. Petersen. Salt Lake City, Utah : Deseret Book Co., 1978. 95 p. ; 24 cm. Includes index. [BS580.J7P47] 78-10143 ISBN 0-87747-720-5 : 4.95
1. Joshua, son of Nun. 2. Bible. O.T.—Biography. I. Title.

WEYNE, Arthur. 221.92
Joshua, the redeemer; illustrated by Dan Samuels. New York, Behrman House [1952] 116p. illus. 21cm. [BS580.J7W47] 53-50
1. Joshua, son of Nun. I. Title.

Joslin, Elliott Proctor, 1869-1962.

HOLT, Anna C. 610'.924 B
Elliott Proctor Joslin; a memoir, 1869-1962, by Anna C. Holt. Worcester, Mass., ASA Bartlett Press, 1969. ix, 68 p. illus., port. 23 cm. [R154.J67H6] 70-275938
1. Joslin, Elliott Proctor, 1869-1962.

Josselin, Ralph, 1617-1683.

JOSSELIN, Ralph, 1617- 309.1'41 S 1683.
The diary of Ralph Josselin 1616-1683 / edited by Alan MacFarlane. London : Oxford University Press for the British Academy, 1976. xxvi, 727 p., [1] leaf of plates : ill. ; 26 cm. (Records of social and economic history ; new ser., 3) Includes bibliographical references and indexes. [HC251.B7 n.s., no. 3] [BX5199.J66] 283'.092'4 B 76-379883 ISBN 0-19-725955-3 : 52.00
1. Josselin, Ralph, 1617-1683. 2. Church of England—Clergy—Biography. 3. Clergy—England—Essex—Biography. I. MacFarlane, Alan. II. Title. III. Series. **BIP**

Josselyn, Amos Piatt, 1820-1885.

JOSSELYN, Amos Piatt, 1820- 917.8 1885.
The overland journal of Amos Piatt Josselyn : Zanesville, Ohio, to the Sacramento Valley, April 2, 1849, to September 11, 1849 : together with letters, financial accounts, a guide, and related documentary materials concerning his life before, during, and after the California gold rush / edited by J. William Barrett, II. Baltimore : Gateway Press, 1978. 129 p. : ill. ; 24 cm. Includes index. Bibliography: p. 124-126. [F593.J67A33] 78-63322 8.50
1. Josselyn, Amos Piatt, 1820-1885. 2. Overland journeys to the Pacific. 3. Pioneers—The West—Biography. 4. California—Gold discoveries. I. Barrett, J. William. II. Title.
Available from J. William Barrett II: 1942-Euclid Ave Zanes Ville, Ohio 43701

Joudry, Patricia, 1921- —Biography.

JOUDRY, Patricia, 812'.5'4 B 1921-
Spirit River to Angels' Roost : religions I have loved and left / Patricia Joudry. Montreal ; Plattsburgh, N.Y. : Tundra Books, c1977. 196 p. ; 24 cm. [PR9199.3.J66S6] 76-22996 ISBN 0-912766-46-8 (Plattsburgh) : 8.95
1. Joudry, Patricia, 1921- —Biography. 2. Authors, Canadian—20th century—Biography. I. Title. **BIP**

Jouett, John, 1754-1822—Juvenile literature.

HALEY, Gail E. 973.3'8 B
Jack Jouett's ride, written and illustrated by Gail E. Haley. [1st ed.] New York, Viking Press [1973] [31] p. col. illus. 23 x 29 cm. Recaptures the incident during the American Revolution when Jack Jouett rode to warn Thomas Jefferson and others of the coming of Tarleton's raiders. [E237.J6H34] 73-5137 ISBN 0-670-40466-7 5.95
1. Jouett, John, 1754-1822—Juvenile literature. I. Title. **BIP**

Jouett, Matthew Harris, 1787-1827.

STRODE-JACKSON, Arnold N S 927.5
Kentucky heyday 1787-1827 the life and times of Kentucky's foremost portrait painter. [1st ed.] New York, Vantage Press [1956] 387p. illus. 21cm. 'A bibliographical novel. [ND237.J8S75] [ND237.J8S75] 759 56-7510
1. Jouett, Matthew Harris, 1787-1827. I. Title.

Journalism, Agricultural—United States—Biography.

OGILVIE, 070.4'49'630922 B William Edward.
Pioneer agricultural journalists. New York, Beekman Publishers, 1974. viii, 128 p. illus. 23 cm. (American newspapermen, 1790-1933) Reprint of the 1927 ed. published by A. G. Leonard, Chicago. [S415.O34 1974] 74-3267 ISBN 0-8464-0010-3 9.00
1. Journalism, Agricultural—United States—Biography. 2. United States—Biography. I. Title.

Journalism—Great Britain—History.

ESCOTT, Thomas Hay 070'.922 Sweet, 1844-1924.
Masters of English journalism; a study of personal forces. Westport, Conn., Greenwood Press [1970] 368 p. illus. 23 cm. Reprint of the 1911 ed. Includes bibliographical references. [PN5114.E7 1970] 74-98834 ISBN 0-8371-3020-4
1. Journalism—Great Britain—History. 2. Journalists—Great Britain—Biography. I. Title.

ESCOTT, Thomas Hay 070'.92'2 Sweet, 1844-1924.
Masters of English journalism; a study of personal forces. [Folcroft, Pa.] Folcroft Library Editions, 1970. 368 p. illus. 24 cm. "Limited to 150 copies." Reprint of the 1911 ed. Includes bibliographical references. [PN5114.E7 1970b] 72-192044 6.50
1. Journalism—Great Britain—History. 2. Journalists, English—Biography. I. Title. **BIP**

Journalists, American.

LEWIS, Mildred. 920.5
Famous modern newspaper writers, by Mildred and Milton Lewis. New York, Dodd, Mead, 1962. 153 p. 22 cm. (Famous biographies for young people) [PN4871.L4] 62-7756
1. Journalists, American. I. Lewis, Milton, joint author. II. Title.

Journalists, American—Biography.

CHALMERS, David Mark. 301.153
The social and political ideas of the muckrakers. [1st ed.] New York, Citadel Press [1964] 127 p. 21 cm. "References": p. 117-127. [E743.C45] 64-15960
1. Journalists, American—Biography. 2. Journalism—Social aspects. 3. Journalism—Political aspects. I. Title. **BIP**

Journalists, American—Correspondence, reminiscences, etc.

BUTCHER, Fanny. 070.4'092'4 B
Many lives—one love, [1st ed.] New York, Harper & Row [1972] x, 463 p. illus. 22 cm. (A Cass Canfield book) Autobiographical. [PN4874.B855A3] 70-156511 ISBN 0-06-010402-3 10.00
1. Journalists, American—Correspondence, reminiscences, etc. 2. Authors—Correspondence, reminiscences, etc. I. Title.

HENRY, William 070.4'4'0924 Mellors, 1890-1970.
Behind the headlines with Bill Henry, 1903-1970. Edited by Patricia Henry Yeomans. Los Angeles, Ward Ritchie Press [1972] xi, 304 p. illus. 24 cm. [PN4874.H46A3] 74-164941
1. Journalists, American—Correspondence, reminiscences, etc. I. Yeomans, Patricia Henry, ed. II. Title.

Journalists—Australia—Correspondence, reminiscences, etc.

COURTNEY, Victor. v. 12
All I may tell; a journalist's story. London, New York, Shakespeare Head Press [1956] x, 246 p. 22 cm. [PN5586.C6A3] 77-21403 25/-
1. Journalists—Australia—Correspondence, reminiscences, etc. I. Title.

Journalists—Biography—Indexes.

JOURNALISTS 016.070'92'2 B
biographical master index : a guide to more than 82,000 sketches of and references to historical and modern journalists in over 200 biographical directories and other sources / Alan E. Abrams, editor. 1st ed. Detroit : Gale Research Co., c1979. p. cm. (Gale biographical index series ; no. 4) [Z6940.J58] [PN4820] 77-9144 ISBN 0-8103-1086-4 : 40.00
1. Journalists—Biography—Indexes. I. Abrams, Alan E. II. Gale Research Company.

Journalists—Correspondence, reminiscences, etc.

ANDREWS, Robert Douglas, 927.92 1903-
A corner of Chicago. [1st ed.] Boston, Little, Brown [1963] 365 p. 22 cm. Full name: Charles Robert Douglas Hardy

Andrews. Autobiographical. [PN4874.A54A3] 63-8954
1. Journalists — Correspondence, reminiscences, etc. I. Title.

ANDREWS, Robert Douglas 927.92 [Charles Robert Douglas Hardy Andrews] 1903-
A corner of Chicago. Boston, Little [c.1963] 365p. 22cm. 63-8954 5.95
1. Journalists—Correspondence, reminiscences, etc. I. Title.

BAILLIE, Hugh, 1890- 920.5
High tension; the recollections of Hugh Baillie. [1st ed.] New York, Harper [1959] 300p. illus. 22cm. [PN4874.B24A3] 59-6299
1. Journalists—Correspondence, reminiscences, etc. 2. World politics. I. Title.

BAILLIE, Hugh, 1890- 070'.924 1966.
High tension; the recollections of Hugh Baillie. Freeport, N.Y., Books for Libraries Press [1970, c1959] x, 300 p. illus., ports. 23 cm. (Essay index reprint series) [PN4874.B24A3 1970] 79-90604
1. Journalists—Correspondence, reminiscences, etc. 2. World politics—20th cent. I. Title.

CANNON, James J. 920.5
Nobody asked me. New York, Dial Press, 1951. 339 p. 21 cm. [PN4874.C24A3] 51-10245
1. Journalists—Correspondence, reminiscences, etc. 2. Sports—U. S. I. Title.

CARTER, Hodding. 920.5
Where Main Street meets the river. New York, Rinehart [1953] 339p. 22cm. Autobiographical. [PN4874.C27A3 1953] 53-6133
1. Journalists—Correspondence, reminiscences, etc. I. Title.

CARTER, Hodding, 1907-. 920.5
First person rural. [1st ed.] Garden City, N. Y., Doubleday, 1963. viii, 249 p. 22 cm. Autobiographical. Full name: William Hodding Carter. [PN4874.C27A32] 63-18226
1. Journalists — Correspondents, reminiscences, etc. I. Title. **BIP**

CARTER, Hodding, 1907- 920.5
Where Main Street meets the river. New York, Rinehart [1953] 339p. 22cm. Autobiographical. [PN4874.C27A3 1953] 53-6133
1. Journalists—Correspondence, reminiscences, etc. I. Title.

CARTER, Hodding [William Hodding Carter] 1907- 920.5
First person rural. Garden City, N.Y., Doubleday [c.]1963. viii, 249p. 22cm. 63-18226 4.50
1. Journalists—Correspondence, reminiscences, etc. I. Title.

CATLING, Patrick Skene. 920.5
Better than working. New York, Macmillan, 1960. 212p. 22cm. [PN4874.C33A35] 60-12171
1. Journalists—Correspondence, reminisciences, etc. I. Title.

CHAMBERLIN, William Henry, 1897- 920.5
The evolution of a conservative. Chicago, Regnery, 1959. 295p. 21cm. [PN4874.C37A32] 59-8885
1. Journalists—Correspondence, reminiscences, etc. 2. World politics. 3. Conservatism. 4. U. S.—Civilization. I. Title.

CHAPIN, Earl V. 920.5
Long Wednesdays. New York, Abelard Press [1953] 268 p. 22 cm. Autobiographical. [PN4874.C46A3] 53-8363
1. Tamarack sentinel. 2. Journalists—Correspondence, reminiscences, etc. I. Title.

CHASE, Edna Woolman, 1877- 920.5
Always in Vogue, by Edna Woolman Chase and Ilka Chase. [1st ed.] Garden City, N. Y., Doubleday, 1954. 381 p. illus. 22 cm. Memoirs of Edna Woolman Chase, editor of Vogue. [PN4874.C464A3] 54-10774
1. Journalists—Correspondence, reminiscences, etc. 2. Vogue. I. Chase, Ilka, 1905- joint author. II. Title.

CLARKE, Donald Henderson, 1887- 920.5
Man of the world; recollections of an irreverent reporter. New York, Vanguard Press [1951] 304 p. 22 cm. [PS3505.L3878M3] 51-10053
1. Journalists—Correspondence, reminiscences, etc. I. Title.

COCKBURN, Claud, 1904- v. 12
Autobiography. New York, Simon and Schuster [c1956- v. Vol. 2 has imprint: New York, Monthly Review Press; v. 3: London, MacGibbon & Kee. Contents.-- [v. 1] a discord of trumpets. -- v. 2. Crossing the line. -- 3. View from the West. 63-3983
1. Journalists — Correspondence, reminiscences, etc. I. Title. II. Title: A discord of trumpets. III. Title: Crossing the line. IV. Title: View from the West.

CORUM, Bill, 1894-1958. 920.5
Off and running. Edited by Arthur Mann. [1st ed.] New York, Holt [1959] 303 p. illus. 22 cm. [PN4874.C73A3] 59-14012
1. Journalists—Correspondence, reminiscences, etc. 2. Sports—U.S. I. Title.

DIEHL, Joe 920.5
West of Broadway: dedicated to the losers of the world. Illustrated by Jean Diehl. Chicago, Sheldon Organization [c.1960] [dist. New York, Taplinger] 158p. illus. 21cm. 60-9505 3.75
1. Journalists—Correspondence, reminiscences, etc. 2. Sports—U.S. 3. Entertainers—U.S. I. Title.

DIXON, George Hall, 1900- 920.5
Leaning on a column. Philadelphia, Lippincott [c.1961] 215p. 61-8686 3.95 bds.,
1. Journalists—Correspondence, reminiscences, etc. 2. Washington, D. C.—Soc. life & cust. 3. U. S.—Pol. & govt.—1945- I. Title.

DRAWBELL, James Wedgwood, 1899- 920.5
James Drawbell, an autobiography. New York, Pantheon Books [1964, c1963] 383 p. 22 cm. [PN5123.D7A28 1964] 63-13704
1. Journalists—Correspondence, reminiscences, etc.

DUMAS, Lloyd, Sir, 1891- 070.4'0924 B
The story of a full life. Melbourne, Sun Books [1969] vii, 226 p. illus., ports. 23 cm. [PN5510.D8] 70-558305 4.95
1. Journalists—Correspondence, reminiscences, etc. I. Title.

FOWLER, Gene, 1890-1960. 818.52
Skyline; a reporter's reminiscence of the 1920s. New York, Viking Press, 1961. 314 p. 22 cm. [PN4874.F58A3] 61-5860
1. Journalists—Correspondence, reminiscences, etc. I. Title.

FRISCHAUER, Willi, 1906- 920.5
European commuter. New York, Macmillan [1964] v. 311 p. 22 cm. Autobiographical. [PN5123.F67A3] 64-15838
1. Journalists—Correspondence, reminiscences, etc. I. Title.

GARDNER, Hy, 1904- 920.5
Champagne before breakfast. [1st ed.] New York, Holt [1954] 303p. 22cm. Reminiscences. [PN4874.G32A3] 54-10521
1. Journalists— Correspondence, reminiscences, etc. I. Title.

GILMORE, Eddy, 1907- 920.5
Me and my Russian wife. [1st ed.] Garden City, N. Y., Doubleday, 1954. 313p. 22cm. [PN4874.G39A3] 54-7312
1. Journalists—Correspondence, reminiscences, etc. 2. Russia—Soc. life & cust. I. Title.

GILMORE, Eddy, 1907-1967. 920.5
Me and my Russian wife. [1st ed.] Garden City, N. Y., Doubleday, 1954. 313 p. 22 cm. [PN4874.G39A3] 54-7312
1. Journalists—Correspondence, reminiscences, etc. I. Title. **BIP**

GILMORE, Eddy, 1907- 070.924 B 1967.
Me and my Russian wife. New York, Greenwood Press, 1968 [c1954] 313 p. 22 cm. [PN4874.G39A3 1968] 69-10098
1. Journalists—Correspondence, reminiscences, etc. 2. Russia—Social life and customs. I. Title.

GUNTHER, John, 1901-1970. 928.1
A fragment of autobiography; the fun of writing the inside books. [1st ed.] New York, Harper & Row [1962] 116 p. illus. 22 cm. [PN4874.G8A3] 62-16423
1. Journalists—Correspondence, reminiscences, etc. I. Title.

HECHT, Ben, 1893- 818.52
Gaily, gaily. [1st ed.] Garden City, N.Y., Doubleday, 1963. 227 p. 22 cm. Autobiographical. [PS3515.E18Z52] 63-11233
1. Journalists—Correspondence, reminiscences, etc. I. Title.

INGERSOLL, Ralph McAllister, 1900- 920.5
Point of departure, an adventure in autobiography. [1st ed.] New York, Harcourt, Brace & World [1961] 217p. 21cm. [PN1871.I5A3] 61-15811
1. Journalists Correspondence, reminiscences, etc. I. Title.

LYONS, Eugene, 1898- 914.7'03'842
Assignment in Utopia. Westport, Conn., Greenwood Press [1971, c1937] xiii, 658 p. 23 cm. Autobiography. [D413.L9A3 1971] 76-110271
1. Journalists—Correspondence, reminiscences, etc. 2. Communism—Russia. 3. Russia—Description and travel—1917- I. Title. **BIP**

MCBRIDE, Mary Margaret, 1899- 927.92
A long way from Missouri. New York, Putnam [1959] 254p. illus. 21cm. The author's experiences as a news reporter during the 1920's and early 1930's. [PN4874.M33A3] 59-6172
1. Journalists—Correspondence, reminiscences, etc. I. Title.

MCCLURE, Samuel Sidney, 1857-1949 920.5
My autobiography. Introd. by Louis Filler. New York, Ungar Pub. Co. [c.1963] 266p. illus. 21cm. (Amer. classics) 63-11334 4.75
1. Journalists— Correspondence, reminiscences, etc. I. Title.

MILLER, Alexander Quintella, 1874- 920.5
Jayhawk editor; a biography of A. Q. Miller, Sr., compiled and edited by James D. Callahan from the recollections, writings, and papers of A. Q. Miller, Sr. [1st ed. Los Angeles, Sterling Press, 1955] 256p. illus. 22cm. [PN4874.M489A3] 56-71
1. Journalists—Correspondence, reminiscences, etc. 2. Kansas—Hist. I. Callahan, James D., ed. II. Title.

MOTT, Frank Luther, 1886-1964. 070'.92'4 B
Time enough; essays in autobiography. Westport, Conn., Greenwood Press [1972, c1962] 248 p. 24 cm. [PN4874.M59A3 1972] 72-5654 ISBN 0-8371-6445-1
1. Journalists—Correspondence, reminiscences, etc. I. Title. **BIP**

MYDANS, Carl. 920.5
More than meets the eye. [1st ed.] New York, Harper [1959] 310p. 23cm. [PN4874.M9A3] 59-10589
1. Journalists —Correspondence, reminiscences, etc. 2. War correspondents, American— Correspondence, reminiscences, etc. 3. War correspondents, American— Correspondence, reminiscences, etc. I. Title.

PANCOAST, Chalmers Lowell, 1880- 070'.92'4
Saga of a roving reporter; the Chalmers Pancoast story, by Kathleen Brown. [Limited, 1st ed.] Frankfort, Ind., G. Y. Fowler's Sons, c1960. 211p. illus. 20cm. [PN4874.P33A33] 60-50360
1. Journalists—Correspondence, reminiscences, etc. I. Brown, Kathleen. II. Title.

PATTERSON, Grove, 1881- 920.5
I like people; the autobiography of Grove Patterson. New York, Random House [1954] 300 p. 22 cm. [PN4874.P353A3] 54-7813
1. Journalists—Correspondence, reminiscences, etc. I. Title.

PEELE, Herbert, 1882-1946. 920.5
Mr. Albemarle; some quotations from Herbert Peele's editorials and Peelings, compiled by his wife, Kate. With introd. by Bill Sharpe. Winston-Salem, N. C., Collins Co. [1955] 205p. illus. 24cm. [PN4874.P4A3] 55-12955
1. Journalists—Correspondence, reminiscences, etc. I. Title.

PHILLIPS, John, 1914- 920.5
Odd world; a photo-reporter's story. New York, Simon and Schuster, 1959. 307 p. 22 cm. [PN5123.P5O3] 59-11199
1. Journalists—Correspondence, reminiscences, etc. I. Title. **BIP**

PRAGER, Theodore. 920.5
Police reporter, by Theodore Prager in collaboration with Donald D. McLennan. [1st ed.] New York, Duell, Sloan and Pearce [c1957] 212p. 21cm. [PN4874.P67A3] 57-11061
1. Journalists— Correspondence, reminiscences, etc. 2. Reporters and reporting. I. Title.

REYNOLDS, Quentin James, 1902- 920.7
By Quentin Reynolds. New York, Pyramid [1964, c.1963] 350p. 21cm. (T-1000) .75 pap.,
1. Journalists—Correspondence, reminiscences, etc. I. Title.

REYNOLDS, Quentin James, 1902-1965. 920.7
By Quentin Reynolds. [1st ed.] London, New York, McGraw-Hill [1963] 356 p. 22 cm. "52035." Autobiography. [PN4874.R45A29 1963] 63-14258
1. Journalists—Correspondence, reminiscences, etc. I. Title.

RICHARDSON, James Hugh, 1894- 920.5
For the life of me; memoirs of a city editor. New York, Putnam [1954] 312 p. 22 cm. [PN4874.R49A3] 54-10503
1. Journalists—Correspondence, reminiscences, etc. I. Title.

ROGERS, Ernest, 1897- 920.5
Peachtree parade. Illustrated by Lou Erickson. Atlanta, Tupper and Love [1956] 221p. illus. 21cm. [PN4874.R55A3] 56-1803
1. Journalists—Correspondence, reminiscences, etc. 2. The Atlanta journal. I. Title.

ROMERO, Jose, 1911- 920.5
Mexican jumping bean. New York, Putnam [1953] 282p. 21cm. Autobiographical. [PN4973.R6A3] 53-8162
1. Journalists—Correspondence, reminiscences, etc. I. Title.

ROOSEVELT, Nicholas, 1893- 920.5
A front row seat. [1st ed.] Norman, University of Oklahoma Press [1953] 304 p. illus. 24 cm. Autobiographical. [PN4874.R57A3] 53-8809
1. Journalists—Correspondence, reminiscences, etc. 2. Europe—Politics—20th century. 3. U.S.—Politics and government—20th century. I. Title.

ST. John, Robert, 1902- 920.5
This was my world. [1st ed.] Garden City, N. Y., Doubleday, 1953. 380 p. 22 cm. [PN4874.S26A3] 53-6937
1. Journalists—Correspondence, reminiscences, etc. I. Title.

SCRIPPS, Edward Wyllis, 1854-1926. 070'.924
Damned old crank; a self-portrait of E. W. Scripps drawn from his unpublished writings. Edited by Charles R. McCabe. Westport, Conn., Greenwood Press [1971, c1951] xvii, 259 p. port. 23 cm. [PN4874.S37A3 1971] 77-156209 ISBN 0-8371-6159-2
1. Journalists—Correspondence, reminiscences, etc. I. Title.

SCRIPPS, Edward Wyllis, 920.5
1854-1926.
Damned old crank, a self-portrait of E. W. Scripps drawn from his unpublished writings; edited by Charles R. McCabe. [1st ed.] New York, Harper [1951] xvii, 259 p. port. 22 cm. [PN4874.S37A3] 51-10365
1. Journalists—Correspondence, reminiscences, etc. I. McCabe, Charles R., ed. II. Title. BIP

SMITH, Harry Allen, 917'.303917
1907-
3 Smiths in the wind [by H. Allen Smith Westport, Conn., Greenwood Press [1971, c1946] xv, 205, v, 218, 223 p. 23 cm. Contents.Contents.—Low man on a totem pole.—Life in a putty knife factory.—Lost in the horse latitudes. [PN4874.S56A35 1971] 73-112330 ISBN 0-8371-4719-0
1. Journalists—Correspondence, reminiscences, etc. I. Title.

SMITH, Harry Allen, 1907- 920.5
To hell in a handbasket. [1st ed.] Garden City, N. Y., Doubleday, 1962. 341 p. illus. 22 cm. Autobiography. [PN4874.S56A26] 62-7680
1. Journalists—Correspondence, reminiscences, etc. I. Title.

SMITH, Paul Clifford, 1908- 920.5
Personal file, by Paul C. Smith. [1st ed.] New York, Appleton-Century [1964] 476 p. 24 cm. [PN4874.S564A3] 61-17699
1. Journalists—Correspondence, reminiscences, etc. I. Title.

SPALDING, William Andrew, 920.5
1852-1941
William Andrew Spalding, Los Angeles newspaperman; an autobiography account. Ed., introd. by Robert V. Hine. San Marino, Calif., Huntington Lib. [c.]1961. 156p. illus. (Huntington Lib. pubns.) Bibl. 61-11264 5.00
1. Journalists—Correspondence, reminiscences, etc. I. Title.

SPAYTH, George W 920.5
It was fun the hard way, by George W. Spayth. 1st ed. Dunellen, N.J., Spayth Press, 1964. 237 p. illus., ports. 24 cm. Autobiographical. [PN4874.S59A3] 64-8092
1. Journalists — Correspondence, reminiscences, etc. I. Title.

SPAYTH, George W. 920.5
It was fun the hard way, by George W. Spayth. 1st ed. Dunellen, N.J., Spayth Press, 1964. 237 p. illus., ports. 24 cm. Autobiographical. [PN4874.S59A3] 64-8092
1. Journalists—Correspondence, reminiscences, etc. I. Title.

STEFFENS, Joseph Lincoln, 920.5
1866-1936.
The autobiography of Lincoln Steffens. New York, Grosset & Dunlap [1957, c1931] 884p. illus. 22cm. (Biographies of distinction) [PN4874] 57-652
1. Journalists—Correspondence, reminiscences, etc. I. Title.

STEFFENS, Joseph 070'.92'4
Lincoln, 1866-1936.
The autobiography of Lincoln Steffens. New York, Harcourt, Brace & World [1968, c1958] 2 v. (x, 884 p.) illus., facsims. 21 cm. "A Harvest book." [PN4874.S68A3 1968] 68-5917
1. Journalists—Correspondence, reminiscences, etc.

STEFFENS, Joseph Lincoln, 071.3
1866-1936
The autobiography of Lincoln Steffens. New York, Harcourt, [1968, c1958] 2v. (x, 884p.) illus., facsims. 21cm. Harvest bk. [PN4874.S68A3 1968] (B) 68-5917 2.25; pap., v. 1, 2.95 v. 2,
1. Journalists—Correspondence, reminiscences, etc. I. Title. BIP

STERN, Julius David, 1886- 920.5
Memoirs of a maverick publisher. New York, S. & S. [c.]1962. 320p. 24cm. 62-9610 5.00
1. Journalists—Correspondence, reminiscences, etc. 2. Journalism— U.S. I. Title.

SULLIVAN, Mark, 1874- 070'.924 B
1952.
The education of an American. [1st ed.] New York, Doubleday, Doran, 1938. New York, Johnson Reprint Corp. [1970] 320 p. illus., ports. 23 cm. (Series in American studies) [PN4874.S78A3 1970] 74-18803
1. Journalists—Correspondence, reminiscences, etc. I. Title. BIP

SULZBERGER, Cyrus Leo, 070'.924
1912-
A long row of candles; memoirs and diaries, 1934-1954 [by] C. L. Sulzberger. [New York] Macmillan [1969] xvi, 1061 p. illus., facsims., ports. 24 cm. Sequel: The last of the giants. [PN4874.S786A3] 69-10642
1. Journalists—Correspondence, reminiscences, etc. I. Title.

SWING, Raymond, 1887- 920.5
"Good evening!" A professional memoir. [1st ed.] New York, Harcourt, Brace & World [1964] 311 p. 22 cm. [PN4874.S794A3] 64-11541
1. Journalists—Correspondence, reminiscences, etc. I. Title.

THOMAS, Christy, 1887- 920.5
Bylines and bygones. New York, Exposition [c.1964] 269p. 22cm. (EP42138) An autobiography [PN4874.T42A3] 64-57958 5.00
1. Journalists—Correspondence, reminiscences, etc. I. Title.

THOMAS, Christy, 1887-. 920.5
Bylines and bygones. [1st ed.] New York, Exposition Press [1964] 269 p. 22 cm. An autobiography. [PN4874.T42A3] 64-57958
1. Journalists — Correspondence, reminiscences, etc. I. Title.

WOODWARD, Stanley. 920.5
Paper tiger. [1st ed.] New York, Atheneum, 1964 [c1963] 294 p. 22 cm. Autobiographical. [PN4874.W695A3] 63-22037
1. Journalists—Correspondence, reminiscences, etc. I. Title.

Journalists, English—Correspondence, reminiscences, etc.

CHURCHILL, Randolph 920.5
Spencer, 1911-1968.
Twenty-one years [by] Randolph S. Churchill. Boston, Houghton Mifflin, 1965, c. 1964, 1965. 152 p. illus., ports. 23 cm. Autobiographical. [PN5123.C42A3] 65-15161
1. Journalists, English—Correspondence, reminiscences, etc. I. Title.

Journalists—United States—Biography.

BEHRENS, John C. 070'.92'2 B
The typewriter guerillas : close-ups of 20 top investigative reporters / by John Behrens. Chicago : Nelson-Hall, c1977. p. cm. Includes index. Bibliography: p. [PN4871.B35] 77-3439 ISBN 0-88229-266-8 : 9.95
1. Journalists—United States—Biography. I. Title.

FANG, Irving E. 070'.92'2 B
Those radio commentators! / Irving E. Fang. 1st ed. Ames : Iowa State University Press, 1977. p. cm. Bibliography: p. [PN4871.F3] 77-8871 ISBN 0-8138-1500-2 : 12.45
1. Journalists—United States—Biography. 2. Radio journalism—United States—History. I. Title. BIP

Journalists—United States—Biography—Juvenile

SQUIRE, Elizabeth 070'.92'2 B
Daniels.
Heroes of journalism. New York, Fleet Press Corp. [1974] 141 p. illus. 24 cm. Bibliography: p. 137-138. Brief biographies of twenty-five American pioneers in journalism from pre-Revolutionary War days to the present. [PN4871.S63] 920 76-161377 ISBN 0-8303-0114-3 5.95
1. Journalists—United States—Biography—Juvenile I. Title. BIP

Journalists—United States—Directories.

WHO was who in 070'.025'73
journalism, 1925-1928 : a consolidation of all material appearing in the 1928 edition of Who's who in journalism, with unduplicated biographical entries from the 1925 edition of Who's who in journalism / originally compiled by M. N. Ask and S. Gershanek. Detroit : Gale Research Co., c1978. p. cm. (Gale composite biographical dictionary series ; no. 4) "A Firenze book." [PN4871.W65] 78-13580 ISBN 0-8103-0401-5 : 42.00
1. Journalists—United States—Directories. 2. Journalists—Canada—Directories. I. Ask, Mihran Nicholas. II. Gershanek, Sinai, 1880- III. Who's who in journalism.

Journeycake, Charles, Chief of the Delaware Indians, 1817-1894.

ROARK, Harry M. 970.3
Charles Journeycake: Indian statesman and Christian leader, by Harry M. Roark. [Dallas, Printed by Taylor Pub. Co., 1970] xiii, 133 p. geneal. table, ports. (part col.) 22 cm. Originally presented as the author's thesis, Central Baptist Theological Seminary, 1948. This ed. includes a genealogy of the Journeycake family, by J. S. Merritt (p. 96-131) Bibliography: p. 132-133. [E90.J9R6] 70-115831 7.00
1. Journeycake, Charles, Chief of the Delaware Indians, 1817-1894. I. Merritt, James Scott, 1915-

Joyce, James, 1882-1941.

COLUM, Mary Maguire. 928.2
Our friend James Joyce, by Mary and Padraic Colum. [1st ed.] Garden City, N. Y., Doubleday, 1958. 239 p. 22 cm. [PR6019.O9Z527] 58-8086
1. Joyce, James, 1882-1941. I. Colum, Padraic, 1881-1972. II. Title. BIP

SULLIVAN, Kevin. 928.2
Joyce among the Jesuits. New York, Columbia University Press, 1958. 259 p. 21 cm. Includes bibliography. [PR6019.O9Z82] 58-12373
1. Joyce, James, 1882-1941. I. Title.

Joyce, James, 1882-1941.

ALLT, Peter. 823'.9'12
Some aspects of the life and works of James Augustine Joyce; inaugural lecture. [Folcroft, Pa.] Folcroft Library Editions, 1974. 15 p. 26 cm. Reprint of the 1952 ed. published by J. B. Wolters, Groningen. [PR6019.O9Z525 1974] 74-2083 ISBN 0-8414-2962-6 (lib. bdg.)
1. Joyce, James, 1882-1941. I. Title.

ANDERSON, Chester G 823'.9'12 B
James Joyce and his world / by Chester G. Anderson. New York : Scribner, [1978] 144 p. : ill. ; 24 cm. Includes index. Bibliography: p. 133. [PR6019.O9Z5252 1978] 77-83678 ISBN 0-684-15510-9 : 9.95
1. Joyce, James, 1882-1941. 2. Authors, Irish—20th century—Biography. I. Title. BIP

ARNOLD, Armin. 828
James Joyce. [Translated and completely rev. by Armin Arnold with Judy Young] New York, Ungar [1969] v, 126 p. 21 cm. (Modern literature monographs) Bibliography: p. 121-126. [PR6019.O9Z52563] 68-31445 4.50
1. Joyce, James, 1882-1941.

BROWN, Richard K 823
Joyce's A portrait of the artist as a young man, by Richard K. Brown, New York, Barrister Pub. Co. [c1966] 100 p. 22 cm. (Bar notes literature study and examination guides) Bibliography: p. 98-100. [PR6019.O9P6434] 66-30256
1. Joyce, James, I. Title.

BYRNE, John Francis, 1880- 920.5
Silent years; an autobiography with memoirs of James Joyce and our Ireland. New York, Farrar, Straus and Young [1953] 307p. illus. 22cm. [CT808.B9A3] 53-9680
1. Joyce, James, 1882-1941. I. Title.

CIXOUS, Helene, 1937- 823'.9'12
The exile of James Joyce / Helene Cixous ; translated from the French by Sally A. J. Purcell. London : John Calder (Publishers) Ltd, 1976. xv, 765 p. : ports. ; 24 cm. Translation of L'Exil de James Joyce. Originally presented as the author's thesis, Paris, 1968. Includes index. Bibliography: p. [746]-751. [PR6019.O9Z526613 1976] 76-371491 ISBN 0-7145-3507-9 : £15.00
1. Joyce, James, 1882-1941. 2. Novelists, Irish—Biography. I. Title.

COLUM, Mary (Maguire) 928.2
Our friend James Joyce, by Mary and Padraic Colum. New York, Doubleday [1960, c.1958] 154p. 19cm. (Dolphin bk. C27) .95 pap.,
1. Joyce, James, 1882-1941. I. Colum, Padraic. II. Title.

CURRAN, C. P. 823
James Joyce remembered :[by] C. P. Curran. London, New York, Oxford Univ. Pr., 1968. xii, 129p. 4 plates, ports. 23cm. Bibl. [PR6019.O9Z528 1968b] 68-101783 5.75
1. Joyce, James, 1882-1941. I. Title.

CURRAN, C. P. 823
James Joyce remembered [by] C. P. Curran. New York, Oxford University Press, 1968. 129 p. ports. 22 cm. Includes bibliographical footnotes. [PR6019.O9Z528] 68-20359
1. Joyce, James, 1882-1941. I. Title.

FREUND, Gisele 823.912
James Joyce in Paris: his final years, by Gisele Freund, V. B. Carleton. Pref. by Simone de Beauvoir. New York, Harcourt [c.1965] ix, 117p. illus., ports. 29cm. [PR6019.O9Z5334] 65-21029 8.50
1. Joyce, James, 1882-1941. I. Carleton, Verna B. II. Title.

GOLDBERG, Samuel Louis 823.912
James Joyce. New York, Grove [1963, c.1962] 120p. 19cm. (Evergreen pilot bks.) Bibl. 62-15844 .95 pap.,
1. Joyce, James, 1882-1941. I. Title.

GOLDBERG, Samuel Louis 823.912
James Joyce [Gloucester, Mass., P. Smith, 1963, c.1962] 120p. 19cm. (Evergreen pilot bk. rebound) Bibl. 3.00
1. Joyce, James, 1882-1941. I. Title.

GOLDBERG, Samuel Louis 823.912
Joyce. New York, Barnes & Noble [1966, c.1962] 120p. 20cm. (Writers & critics) Bibl. 2.50 bds.,
1. Joyce, James. 1882-1941 I. Title. II. Series.
Previously published by Grove under the title 'James Joyce.' Published in Britian by Oliver & Boyd.

GORMAN, Herbert 823'.9'12
Sherman, 1893-1954
James Joyce, his first forty years / by Herbert S. Gorman. New York : Haskell House Publishers, 1974. 238 p. : port. ; 22 cm. Reprint of the ed. published by B. W. Huebsch, New York. Bibliography: p. 235-238. [PR6019.O9Z55 1974b] 74-30368 ISBN 0-8383-2015-5 : 12.95
1. Joyce, James, 1882-1941.

JOYCE, James, 1882-1941. 928.2
Letters, edited by Stuart Gilbert. New York, Viking Press, 1957-[66] 3 v. facsims., ports 25 cm. Vols. 2-3 edited by Richard Ellmann. "A chronology of the life of James Joyce, by Richard Ellmann": v. 1, p. 43-50. [PR6019.O9Z52] 57-5129
1. Authors — Correspondence, reminiscences, etc. I. Gilbert, Stuart, ed. II. Ellmann, Richard, 1918- ed. III. Title.

JOYCE, Stanislaus. 928.2
Dublin diary. Edited by George Harris Healey. Ithaca, N. Y., Cornell University Press [1962] 119p. 23cm. [PR6019.O9Z648] 62-51465
1. Joyce. James, 1882-1941. I. Title.

JOYCE, Stanislaus. 928.2
My brother's keeper; James Joyce's early years. Edited with an introd. and notes by Richard Ellmann. Pref. by T. S. Eliot. [1st ed.] New York, Viking Press, 1958. 266p. illus. 22cm. [PR6019.O9Z649] 58-5403
1. Joyce, James, 1882-1941. I. Title.

JOYCE, Stanislaus. v. 12
My brother's keeper; James Joyce's early

years. Edited with an introd. and notes by Richard Ellmann. Pref. by T. S. Eliot. New York, McGraw-Hill Book Co. [1964] xxii, 266 p. 21 cm. (McGraw-Hill paperbacks) 65-86980
1. Joyce, James, 1882-1941. I. Title. II. Series.

JOYCE, Stanislaus [John Stanislaus Joyce] 928.2
My brother's keeper; James Joyce's early years. Ed., introd., notes by Richard Ellmann. Pref. by T. S. Eliot. New York, McGraw [1964, c.1958] 266p. 21cm. (33055) 2.85 pap.,
1. Joyce, James, 1882-1941. I. Title.

KENNER, Hugh 823.912
Dublin's Joyce. Boston, Beacon [1962] 372p. front. port. 21cm. (BP 144) 2.25 pap.,
1. Joyce, James, 1882-1941. I. Title. **BIP**

KENNER, Hugh. 823.91
Dublin's Joyce. Bloomington, Indiana University Press, 1956. xi, 372 p. port. 23 cm. Bibliographical footnotes. [PR6019.O9Z67] 56-5486
1. Joyce, James, 1882-1941. I. Title.

KENNER, Hugh. 828
Dublin's Joyce. Gloucester, Mass., P. Smith, 1969. xi, 372 p. port. 21 cm. Reprint of the 1956 ed. Includes bibliographical references. [PR6019.O9Z67 1969] 76-10721
1. Joyce, James, 1882-1941. I. Title.

LITZ, A. Walton. 821
James Joyce by A. Walton Litz. New York, Twayne Publishers [1966] 141 p. 21 cm. (Twayne's English author series, 31) "Selected bibliography": p. 129-137. [PR6019.O9Z715] 66-16113
1. Joyce, James, 1882-1941.

MAGALANER, Marvin 928.2
Joyce; the man, the work, the reputation [by] Marvin Magalaner. Richard M. Kain. New York, Collier [1962, c.1956] 383p. (BS54) Bibl. 1.50 pap.,
1. Joyce, James Augustine Aloysius, 1882-1941. I. Title.

MAGALANER, Marvin, 1920- 823.91
Joyce, the man, the work, the reputation [by] Marvin Magalaner and Richard M. Kain. New York, New York University Press, 1956. xi, 377p. port. 24cm. Bibliography: p. 351-364. Bibliographical references included in 'Notes' (p. 315-349) [PR6019.O9Z72] 56-6292
1. Joyce, James, 1882-1941. I. Kain, Richard Morgan, 1908- joint author. II. Title.

*PORTRAIT of the artist 823.912
as a young man (The) by James Joyce; notes including chapter summaries and commentaries, glossary of persons, places and terms, questions for review, by Katherine A. Lilly. Lincoln, Neb., Cliff's Notes [c.1964] 50p. 22cm. 1.00 pap.,
1. Joyce, James, 1882-1941. I. Lilly, Katherine A.

POUND, Ezra Loomis, 1885- 816'.5'2
Pound/Joyce; the letters of Ezra Pound to James Joyce, with Pound's essays on Joyce. Edited and with commentary by Forrest Read. [New York, New Directions Pub. Corp., 1967] vi, 314 p. 25 cm. (A New Directions book) Bibliographical footnotes. [PS3531.O82Z533] 66-27616
1. Joyce, James, 1882-1941. I. Joyce, James, 1882-1941. II. Read, Forrest, ed. III. Title.

RYF, Robert Stanley, 1918- 823.912
A new approach to Joyce, the Portrait of the artist as a guidebook. Berkeley, University of California Press, 1962. 211 p. 23 cm. (Perspectives in criticism, 8) [PR6019.O9P648 1962] 61-7522
1. Joyce, James, 1882-1941. A portrait of the artist as a young man. 2. Joyce, James, 1882-1941. I. Title.

TINDALL, William York, 1903- 928.2
The Joyce country. [University Park?] Pennsylvania State University Press [1960] 162 p. (chiefly illus.) 22 cm. [PR6019.O9Z832] 60-14467
1. Joyce, James, 1882-1941. 2. Literary landmarks—Dublin. 3. Dublin—Descr.—Views. I. Title. **BIP**

[WILSON JOHN ANTHONY BURGESS] 1917- 823.912
Re Joyce [by] Anthony Burgess. New York, Ballantine [1966, c.1965] 349p. 18cm. (U7053) London ed. (Faber) has title: Here comes everybody. [PR6019.O9Z96 1965] .95 pap.,
1. Joyce, James, 1882-1941. I. Title.

Joyce, James, 1882-1941—Biography.

BARGER, James. 823'.9'12 B
James Joyce, modern Irish writer. Compiled with the assistance of the research staff of SamHar Press. Charlotteville, N.Y., SamHar Press, 1974. p. cm. (Outstanding personalities, no. 77) Bibliography: p. [PR6019.O9Z52568] 74-14701 2.29; 0.98 (pbk.)
1. Joyce, James, 1882-1941—Biography. **BIP**

DAVIES, Stan Gebler. 823'.9'12 B
James Joyce : a portrait of the artist / Stan Gebler Davies. New York : Stein and Day, 1975. 328 p., [3] leaves of plates : ill. ; 24 cm. Includes index. Bibliography: p. 316-318. [PR6019.O9Z5286] 75-11940 ISBN 0-8128-1828-8
1. Joyce, James, 1882-1941—Biography. **BIP**

GORMAN, Herbert Sherman, 1893-1954. 823'.9'12 B
James Joyce. New York, Octagon Books, 1974 [c1948] viii, 358 p. illus. 23 cm. Reprint of the ed. published by Rinehart, New York. [PR6019.O9Z547 1974] 74-12172 ISBN 0-374-93219-0
1. Joyce, James, 1882-1941—Biography.

Joyce, James, 1882-1941—Biography—Addresses, essays, lectures.

PORTRAITS of the artist 823'.9'12
in exile : recollections of James Joyce by Europeans / edited by Willard Potts. Seattle : University of Washington Press, c1979. xvi, 304 p. : ill. ; 25 cm. Translated from various languages. Includes bibliographical references and index. [PR6019.O9Z7823] 78-4367 ISBN 0-295-95614-3 : 12.95
1. Joyce, James, 1882-1941—Biography—Addresses, essays, lectures. 2. Authors, Irish—20th century—Biography—Addresses, essays, lectures. I. Potts, Willard, 1929- **BIP**

Joyce, James, 1882-1941—Biography—Character.

SHECHNER, Mark. 823'.9'12
Joyce in Nighttown; a psychoanalytic inquiry into Ulysses. Berkeley, University of California Press [1974] xiv, 271 p. 21 cm. Bibliography: p. 253-264. [PR6019.O9Z795] 72-95308 ISBN 0-520-02398-6 10.00
1. Joyce, James, 1882-1941—Biography—Character. 2. Joyce, James, 1882-1941. Ulysses. I. Title. **BIP**

Joyce, James, 1882-1941—Biography—Last years and death.

EDEL, Leon, 1907- 823'.9'12 B
James Joyce : the last journey / by Leon Edel. Brooklyn, N.Y. : Haskell House, [1977] c1947. p. cm. Reprint of the ed. published by Gotham Book Mart, New York. [PR6019.O9Z533 1977] 77-10505 ISBN 0-8383-2214-X lib.bdg. : 9.95
1. Joyce, James, 1882-1941—Biography—Last years and death. 2. Joyce, James, 1882-1941—Homes and haunts—Switzerland—Zurich. 3. Authors, Irish—20th century—Biography. 4. Zurich—History. **BIP**

Joyce, James, 1882-1941—Correspondence.

JOYCE, James, 1882-1941. 823'.9'12
Selected letters of James Joyce / edited by Richard Ellmann. New York : Viking Press, 1975. xxix, 440 p. ; 24 cm. Includes bibliographical references and indexes. [PR6019.O9Z52 1975] 71-83240 ISBN 0-670-63190-6 : 10.95 ISBN 0-670-00276-3 pbk. : 6.95
1. Joyce, James, 1882-1941—Correspondence.

Joyce, James, 1882-1941—Criticism and interpretation.

GORMAN, Herbert Sherman, 1893-1954. 823'.9'12
James Joyce, his first forty years. [Folcroft, Pa.] Folcroft Library Editions, 1974. p. cm. Reprint of the 1926 ed. published by G. Bles, London. Bibliography: p. [PR6019.O9Z55 1974] 74-11431 20.00
1. Joyce, James, 1882-1941—Criticism and interpretation.

PEAKE, Charles. 823'.9'12
James Joyce, the citizen and the artist / C. H. Peake. Stanford, Calif. : Stanford University Press, 1977. x, 369 p. ; 24 cm. Includes bibliographical references and index. [PR6019.O9Z7815] 76-47985 ISBN 0-8047-0914-9 : 16.95
1. Joyce, James, 1882-1941—Criticism and interpretation. I. Title.

Joyeuse, Henri, duc de, 1567-1608.

BROUSSE, Jacques, 1590-1673. 923.544
The lives of Ange de Joyeuse and Benet Canfield. Edited from Robert Rookwood's translation of 1623, by T. A. Birrell. London, New York, Sheed and Ward [1959] 183p. 23cm. (The Makers of Christendom) Translation of La vie du Reverend Pere Angel de Joyeuse, predicateur capucin, autrefols duc, pair, et marechal de France, et eouverneur pour le rol en Languedoc, ensemble les vies des RR. PP. P. Benolst et P. Archange Escossois, du meme ordre. [DC122.9.J6B713 1959] 59-3362
1. Joyeuse, Henri, duc de, 1567-1608. 2. Benoit de Canfield, Father, 1562-1610. I. Title.

Juarez, Benito Pablo, Pres. Mexico, 1806-1872.

BLANCKE, W. Wendell. 972'.07'0924 B
Juarez of Mexico [by] W. Wendell Blancke. New York, Praeger [1971] 152 p. illus. 23 cm. (Praeger pathfinder biographies) Bibliography: p. 147. A biography of the Zapotec Indian who instituted many reforms during his fourteen years as President of Mexico. [F1233.J932] 92 75-143964 5.50
1. Juarez, Benito Pablo, Pres. Mexico, 1806-1872. I. Title.

ROEDER, Ralph, 1890- 972'.07'0924 B
Juarez and his Mexico; a biographical history. New York, Greenwood Press, 1968 [c1947] 2 v. (763 p.) ports. 24 cm. Bibliography: p. [741]-750. [F1233.J949 1968] 68-23322
1. Juarez, Benito Pablo, Pres. Mexico, 1806-1872. 2. Mexico—History—European intervention, 1861-1867. I. Title. **BIP**

SMART, Charles Allen, 1904-1967. 923.172
Viva Juarez! A biography. [1st ed.] Philadelphia, Lippincott [1963] 444 p. illus. 22 cm. Includes bibliography. [F1233.J9535] 63-13180
1. Juarez, Benito Pablo, Pres. Mexico, 1806-1872. I. Title.

Juarez, Benito Pablo, Pres. Mexico, 1806-1872—Juvenile literature.

TREVINO, Elizabeth Borton, 1904- 972'.07'0924 B
Juarez, man of law [by] Elizabeth Borton de Trevino. New York, Farrar, Straus and Giroux [1974] xv, 142 p. 21 cm. Bibliography: p. [135] A biography of a Zapotec Indian who, as a civil leader and as president, championed equal rights for the poor of Mexico and whose memory is honored annually by a national holiday. [F1233.J95463 1974] 92 74-12012 ISBN 0-374-33950-3 5.95
1. Juarez, Benito Pablo, Pres. Mexico, 1806-1872—Juvenile literature. I. Title. **BIP**

Juan, Chi, 210-263.

HOLZMAN, Donald. 895.1'1'2 B
Poetry and politics : the life and works of Juan Chi (A.D. 210-263) / by Donald Holzman. Cambridge ; New York : Cambridge University Press, 1976. p. cm. (Cambridge studies in Chinese history, literature and institutions) Includes index. Bibliography: p. [PL2664.J8Z69] 75-27798 ISBN 0-521-20855-6 : 28.00
1. Juan, Chi, 210-263. I. Juan, Chi, 210-263. II. Title. **BIP**

Juan de Austria, 1547-1578.

PETRIE, Charles Alexander, Sir, bart., 1895- 946'.04'0924 B
Don John of Austria [by] Sir Charles Petrie. New York, Norton [1967] 335 p. illus., maps, ports. 22 cm. Bibliographical footnotes. [DH193.P4 1967b] 67-12447
1. Juan de Austria, 1547-1578. I. Title.

Juan de Dios, Saint, 1495-1550.

GREENE, Gerard, 1921- 922.246
The runaway saint; a story of Saint John of God. Illus. by Brother Bernard Howard. Notre Dame, Ind., Dujarie Press [1953] 86p. illus. 24cm. [BX4700.J65G7] 53-3997
1. Juan de Dios, Saint, 1495-1550. I. Title.

MCMAHON, Norbert. 922.246
St. John of God, Heavenly patron of the sick and dying, nurses and hospitals. New York, McMullen Books [1953?] 205p. 21cm. [BX4700.J65M2] 53-11801
1. Juan de Dios, Saint, 1495-1550. I. Title.

NEWCOMB, Covelle 922.246
Brother Zero; a story of the life of Saint John of God. With a foreword by Richard Cardinal Cushing. Abp. of Boston. Decorations by Addison Burbank. New York, Dodd, Mead, [c.]1959. ix, 305p. illus. (2p. bibl.) 21cm. 59-10568 3.50
1. Juan de Dios, Saint, 1495-1550. I. Title.

NEWCOMB, Covelle, 1908- 922.246
Brother Zero; a story of the life of Saint John of God. With a foreword by Richard Cardinal Cushing, Abp. of Boston. Decorations by Addison Burbank. New York, Dodd, Mead, 1959. 005p. illus. 11cm. Includes bibliography. [BX4700.J65N4] 59-10568
1. Juan de Dois, Saint, 1495-1550. I. Title.

Juan de la Cruz, Saint, 1542-1591.

BRENAN, Gerald. 271'.73'024 B
St John of the Cross; his life and poetry. With a translation of his poetry by Lynda Nicholson. Cambridge [Eng.] University Press, 1973. xii, 232 p. illus. 23 cm. Includes the poems of Juan de la Cruz in the original Spanish with parallel English translations. Bibliography: p. 224-227. [BX4700.J7B64] 72-83577 ISBN 0-521-20006-7
1. Juan de la Cruz, Saint, 1542-1591. I. Nicholson, Lynda, tr. II. Juan de la Cruz, Saint, 1542-1591. Poems. English & Spanish. 1973.
Distributed by Cambridge University Press N.Y; 11.95. **BIP**

BRUND DE JESUS-MARIE, Father. 922.246
St. John of the Cross. Edited by Benedict Zimmerman. With an introd. by Jacques Maritain. New York, Sheed & Ward [1957] 495p. 22cm. [BX4700.J7B72 1957] 57-14030
1. Juan de la Cruz, Saint, 1542-1591. I. Title.

BRUNO DE JESUS-MARIE, Father. 922.246
St. John of the Cross. Edited by Benedict Zimmerman. With an introd. by Jacques Maritain. New York, Sheed & Ward [1957] 495p. 22cm. [BX4700.J7B72 1957] 57-14030
1. Juan de la Cruz, Saint, 1542-1591. I. Title.

CRISTIANI, Leon [Augustin Louis Leon Pierre Cristiani] 1879- 922.246
St. John of the Cross, prince of mystical theology. Tr. from French. Garden City, N. Y., Doubleday [c.] 1962. 298p. 22cm. 62-7617 4.50
1. Juan de la Cruz, Saint, 1542-1591. I. Title.

PEERS, Edgar Allison. 920.046
St. John of the Cross, and other lectures and addresses, 1920-1945. Freeport, N.Y., Books for Libraries Press [1970] 231 p. 23 cm. (Biography index reprint series) Reprint of the 1946 ed. Contents.Contents.—St. John of the Cross ... the Rede lecture for 1932.—Some centenary lectures: Ramon Lull: doctor illuminate. Columbus, America, and the future. Juan Luis Vives and England. Lope de Vega: two portraits. A forgotten mystic: Fra Josep of Montserrat.—Aspects of the Catalan Renaissance: Beginnings of the Renaissance: Aribau, Cabanyes. Rubio i Ors and the Jocs Florals. Jacinto Verdaguer. Joan Maragall.—Modern Spain: Angel Ganivet. The real Blasco Ibanez. Francesc Macia. Antonio Machado. Alfonso XIII and Spain's future. Includes bibliographical references. [DP58.P35 1970] 70-136650 ISBN 0-8369-8045-X
1. Juan de la Cruz, Saint, 1542-1591. 2. Spain—Biography. 3. Spanish literature—History and criticism. I. Title.

PEERS, Edgar Allison. 271'.73'024 B
Spirit of flame : a study of St. John of the Cross / by E. Allison Peers. Folcroft, Pa. : Folcroft Library Editions, 1976. p. cm. Reprint of the 1943 ed. published by Student Christian Movement Press, London. Includes bibliographical references and index. [BX4700.J7P43 1976] 76-40107 ISBN 0-8414-6784-6 lib. bdg. : 17.50
1. Juan de la Cruz, Saint, 1542-1591. 2. Christian saints—Spain—Biography. I. Title. BIP

Juana Ines de la Cruz, Sister, 1651-1695.

FLYNN, Gerard C. 868 B
Sor Juana Ines de la Cruz, by Gerard Flynn. New York, Twayne Publishers [1971] 123 p. 22 cm. (Twayne's world authors series, TWAS 144: Mexico) Bibliography: p. 117-120. [PQ7296.J6Z662] 75-120482
1. Juana Ines de la Cruz, Sister, 1651-1695. BIP

Juarez, Benito Pablo, Pres. Mexico, 1806-1872—Juvenile literature.

SYME, Ronald, 1910- 972'.07'0924 B
Juarez, the founder of modern Mexico. Illustrated by William Stobbs. New York, Morrow, 1972. 191 p. illus. 21 cm. Bibliography: p. 191. A biography of the Mexican Indian, a president of his country, who instituted many reforms and overthrew Maximilian. [F1233.J9545] 92 72-1544 ISBN 0-688-20031-1 4.50
1. Juarez, Benito Pablo, Pres. Mexico, 1806-1872—Juvenile literature. 2. Mexico—History—Juvenile literature. I. Cuffari, Richard, 1925- illus. II. Title. BIP

Jubilee Singers.

MARSH, J. B. T. 784'.0922 B
The story of the Jubilee Singers; with their songs [by J. B. T. Marsh] New York, AMS Press [1971] viii, 243 p. group port. 19 cm. Reprint of the 1880 ed. "Jubilee songs": p. 125-243. [ML400.M34 1971] [M1670] 72-165509 ISBN 0-404-04189-2
1. Jubilee Singers. 2. Negro musicians. 3. Negro songs.

Judah, Theodore Dehone, 1828-1863.

JONES, Helen Hinckley, 1903- 385'.0924
Rails from the West; a biography of Theodore D. Judah, by Helen Hinckley. San Marino, Calif., Golden West Books [1969] vii, 207 p. illus., maps, ports. 23 cm. Bibliography: p. 201-203. [HE2754.J8J6] 69-20448 6.95
1. Judah, Theodore Dehone, 1828-1863. 2. Central Pacific Railroad. I. Title.

Judaism—Addresses, essays, lectures.

MY life and my message. v. 12 [Beaumont, Texas, 1958] 4p. l., 536p. 24cm.
1. Judaism—Addresses, essays, lectures. I. Rosinger, Samuel, 1877-

Judaism—Controversial literature.

URIEL Acosta: 211'.4'0924
A specimen of human life. New York, Bargman [1967] 127 p. illus. 22 cm. Contents.Contents.—Uriel Acosta's Account of his own life.—Uriel Acosta's Eleven theses against the tradition.—Excommunication of Uriel Acosta.—Limborch's defense of Christianity in answer to Acosta's objections.—Bibliography (p. 126—27) [BL2790.A2U7] 66-28486
1. Judaism—Controversial literature. I. Acosta, Uriel, 1585 (ca.)-1640. Account of his own life. II. Acosta, Uriel, 1585 (ca.)-1640. Eleven theses against the tradition. III. Limborch, Philippus van, 1663-1712. The remarkable life of Uriel Acosta. IV. Title: A specimen of human life.

Judas Iscariot.

FLETCHER, Howard A. 232.961
Saint Judas Iscariot. Introd. by Ananda Bhavanani. New York, Vantage Press [c.1961] 144p. 61-4041 3.00
I. Title.

HUFFMAN, Jasper Abraham, 1880- 225.92
Judas; the biography of a soul. Marion, Ind., Wesley Press [1958] 166p. 20cm. [BS2460.J8H8] 58-48847
1. Judas Iscariot. I. Title.

Judd, Gerrit Parmele, 1803-1873.

JODD, Gerrit Parmele, 1915- 923.2969
Dr. Judd, Hawaii's friend; a biography of Gerrit Parmele Judd, 1803-1873. [1st ed.] Honolulu, University of Hawaii Press, 1960. 300p. illus. 24cm. [DU627.17.J8J8] 60-10394
1. Judd, Gerrit Parmele, 1803-1873. 2. Hawaiian Islands— Hist. I. Title.

JUDD, Gerrit Parmele 923.2969
Dr. Judd, Hawaii's friend; a biography of Gerrit Parmele Judd, 1803-1873. Honolulu, University of Hawaii Press [c.]1960. 300p. Bibl. and bibl. notes: p.243-291. illus. 24cm. 60-10394 7.00
1. Judd, Gerrit Parmele, 1803-1873. 2. Hawaiian Islands—Hist. I. Title.

Judd, Lawrence M.

JUDD, Lawrence M. 996.9'03'0924 B
Lawrence M. Judd & Hawaii: an autobiography, by Lawrence M. Judd as told to Hugh W. Lytle. Rutland, Vt., C. E. Tuttle Co. [1971] 296 p. port. 22 cm. [DU627.7.J8A3] 71-147177 ISBN 0-8048-0910-0 8.00
I. Lytle, Hugh W., 1902- II. Title. BIP

Judd, Sylvester, 1813-1853.

HALL, Arethusa, 1802-1891. 818'.4'09 B
Life and character of the Rev. Sylvester Judd. Port Washington, N.Y., Kennikat Press [1971] x, 531 p. port. 21 cm. (Kennikat Press scholarly reprints. Series on literary America in the nineteenth century) Reprint of the 1854 ed. [BX9869.J8H3 1971] 72-122655
1. Judd, Sylvester, 1813-1853. I. Title. BIP

Judges

GORE, Ralph Thomas 347.999530924
Justice versus sorcery [Brisbane] Jacaranda Pr.; San Francisco, Tri-Ocean [1965] v, 218p. illus., ports. 22cm. 66-915 6.45 bds.,
1. Judges—Australia—Correspondence, reminiscences, etc. 2. Australia—Native races. I. Title.

ALLEN, Florence Ellinwood, 1884- 347.90924
To do justly. Cleveland, Press of Western Reserve University [1965] ix, 201 p. ports. 23cm. Autobiography. [KF373.A4A3] 65-18872
1. Judges—United States—Correspondence, reminiscences, etc. I. Title. BIP

BOTEIN, Bernard. 923.473
Trial judge; the candid, behind-the-bench story of Justice Bernard Botein. New York, Simon and Schuster, 1952. 337 p. 24 cm. 52-9188
1. Judges—New York (State)—Correspondence, reminiscences, etc. 2. Trial practice—New York (State) I. Title. BIP

GALSTON, Clarence G., 1876- 923.473
Behind the judicial curtain. [1st ed.] Chicago, Barrington House, 1959. 150 p. illus. 24cm. [KF373.G27A3] 60-28931
1. Judges—United States—Correspondence, reminiscences, etc. I. Title.

HARRELL, Allen W., 1922- 347'.73'2234
Splinters from my gavel; confessions of a judge, by Allen W. Harrell. Grand Rapids, Zondervan Pub. House [1970] 93 p. 21 cm. (A Zondervan paperback) [KF373.H37A3] 70-133352 0.95
1. Judges—U.S.—Correspondence, reminiscences, etc. I. Title.

MAHAJAN, Mehr Chand, 1889- 923.454
Looking back; the autobiography of Mehr Chand Mahajan, former chief justice of India. New York, Asia Pub. [dist. Taplinger, c.1963] vi, 299p. port. 23cm. 63-24927 10.75
1. Judges— India—Correspondence, reminiscences, etc. I. Title.

MOORE, Ben, 1891- 923.473
Heritage of freedom, an autobiography. With an introd. by Bolitha J. Laws. Minneapolis, T. S. Denison [1957] 273p. 22cm. 57-10766
1. Judges—U.S.—Correspondence, reminiscences, etc. I. Title.

OLIVER, L. Stauffer, 1879- 340.0924
The bench is a hard seat. an autobiography. Philadelphia, Dorrance [c.1965] 177p. illus. 21cm. 65-14556 4.50
1. Judges—U. S.—Correspondence, reminiscences, etc. I. Title.

SHEEHY, Eugene. 923.415
May it please the court. Dublin, C.J. Fallon [1951] 154 p. illus. 22 cm. 52-28995
1. Judges—Ireland—Correspondence, reminiscences, etc. I. Title.

TAYLOR, Charles William, 1896- ed. 923.473
Eminent judges and lawyers of the Northwest, 1843-1955. Palo Alto, Calif. [1954] 505p. ports. 28cm. 54-43870
1. Judges—Northwest, Pacific. 2. Lawyers—Northwest, Pacific. I. Title.

THOMASON, Robert Ewing, 1879- 347'.7322'034 B
Thomason; the autobiography of a Federal judge. Edited and annotated by Joseph M. Ray. El Paso, Texas Western Press, 1971. xii, 131 p. illus., map (on lining papers), ports. 25 cm. Edited, cut, and revised from an autobiography written in 1952: The saga of Era. Bibliography: p. 125-126. [KF373.T52R3] 76-150750 ISBN 0-87404-030-2 6.00
1. Judges—U.S.—Correspondence, reminiscences, etc. I. Ray, Joseph Malchus, 1907- ed.

Judges—Arizona—Biography.

GOFF, John S., 1931- 347'.73'2634 B
The Supreme Court justices, 1863-1912 / by John S. Goff. Cave Creek, Ariz. : Black Mountain Press, c1975. 200 p. : ill. ; 24 cm. (Arizona territorial officials ; 1) Bibliography: p. 196-199. [KF354.A7G6] 75-322221
1. Judges—Arizona—Biography. I. Title. II. Series.

Judges—California—Correspondence, reminiscences, etc.

GIBSON, Lilburn I., 1892- 340'.0924
Some reminiscences of my seventy-four years in Mendocino County as a youngster, cowboy, lawyer, district attorney, judge of the Superior Court, and now retired, 1892-1966, by Lilburn Gibson. 2d ed. [Ukiah? Calif., 1967] 203 p. illus., facsims., ports. 23 cm. [KF373.G5A3 1967] 67-2126
1. Judges—California—Correspondence, reminiscences, etc. I. Title.

Judges—Colorado—Correspondence, reminiscences, etc.

JOHNSON, Frank Thomas, 1860- 923.473
Autobiography of a centenarian. Denver, Big Mountain Press [1961] 296 p. illus. 24cm. [KF373.J57A33] 61-16290
1. Judges—Colorado—Correspondence, reminiscences, etc. I. Title.

JOHNSON, Samuel Wallace, 1872- 923.473
Autobiography. Denver, Big Mountain Press [1960] 232 p. illus. 24cm. [KF373.J58A3] 60-2127
1. Judges—Colorado—Correspondence, reminiscences, etc. 2. Colorado—Politics and government—1876-1950.

Judges—Great Britain.

FOSS, Edward, 1787-1870. 347'.42'014
The judges of England; with sketches of their lives, and miscellaneous notices connected with the courts at Westminster, from the time of the conquest. London, Longman, Brown, Green and Longmans, 1848-64. New York, AMS Press, 1966. 9 v. 22 cm. [LAW] 128'.3 76-168126
1. Judges—Great Britain. 2. Great Britain—Biography. 3. Courts—Great Britain. I. Title.

HEUSTON, R. F. V. 923.442
Lives of the Lord Chancellors, 1885-1940 [New York] Oxford [c.]1964. xxiii, 632p. 24 ports. 25cm. Bibl. 64-4531 10:10
1. Judges—Gt. Brit. I. Title.

HEUSTON, R. F. V. 923.442
Lives of the Lord Chancellors, 1885-1940, by R. F. V. Heuston. Oxford, Clarendon Press, 1964. xxiii, 632 p. 24 ports. 25 cm. Bibliographical footnotes. 64-4531
1. Judges — Gt. Brit. I. Title.

Judges—Gt. Brit.—Biography.

CAMPBELL, John Campbell, Baron, 1779-1861. 347'.42'0350922
The lives of the Chief Justices of England, from the Norman conquest till the death of Lord Tenterden, by John Lord Campbell. Freeport, N.Y., Books for Libraries Press [1971] 3 v. 23 cm. Reprint of the 1849-57 ed. [LAW] 70-152976 ISBN 0-8369-5728-8
1. Judges—Gt. Brit.—Biography. I. Title. BIP

Judges—Louisiana—Biography.

LOUISIANA District 347'.73'2234 B
Judges Association.
Biographies of Louisiana judges. 1971 ed. [J. Cleveland Fruge, editor. Lake Charles, La.; for sale by Claitor's Publishing Division, Baton Rouge, 1971] vi, 208 p. ports. 28 cm. [KF354.L6L63] 72-180973
1. Judges—Louisiana—Biography. I. Fruge, J. Cleveland, 1900- ed. II. Title.

MILLER, Minos D., 347'.763'014 B
1920-
Biographies of judges of Louisiana. [Gathered and supervised by M. D. Miller, Jr.] Baton Rouge, Claitor's Pub. Division, 1971. 78 l. 29 cm. Cover title. [KF354.L6M5 1971] 72-179421
1. Judges—Louisiana—Biography. I. Title.
BIP

Judges—Nevada—Biography.

BIOGRAPHY of 347'.793'0234 B
district court judges, beginning 1861. [Reno? 196-] 28 l. 28 cm. Cover title. [KF354.N38B5] 75-627627
1. Judges—Nevada—Biography.

Judges—Ohio—Correspondence, reminiscences, etc.

LAMNECK, John Howard, 923.473
1891-
From lamplight to satellite, an autobiography. Boston, Christopher Pub. House [1961] 390 p. illus. 21cm. [KF373.L3A3] 61-15197
1. Judges—Ohio—Correspondence, reminiscences, etc. I. Title.

SILBERT, Samuel H., 1883- 923.473
Judge Sam. With Sidney A. Eisenberg. Manhasset, N.Y., Channel Press [1963] 192 p. 21cm. Autobiographical. [KF373.S54A3] 63-19919
1. Judges—Ohio—Correspondence, reminiscences, etc. I. Eisenberg, Sidney A., joint author. II. Title.

Judges—Oklahoma—Correspondence, reminiscences, etc.

KING, Hiram Burris, 345'.766'01 B
1890-
Memoirs of an Oklahoma jurist. San Antonio, Naylor Co. [1973] xi, 123 p. 22 cm. [KF373.K5A34] 73-9958 ISBN 0-8111-0495-8 5.95
1. Judges—Oklahoma—Correspondence, reminiscences, etc. I. Title.

Judges—United States.

BIOGRAPHICAL 347'.73'14 B
dictionary of the Federal judiciary / compiled by Harold Chase ... [et al.]. Detroit : Gale Research Co., c1976. xxvi, 381 p. ; 29 cm. Bibliography: p. xxv-xxvi. [KF353.B5] 76-18787 ISBN 0-8103-1125-9 : 38.00
1. Judges—United States. I. Chase, Harold William, 1922-
BIP

DAMON, Ethel Moseley, 923.273
1883-
Sanford Ballard Dole and his Hawaii. With an analysis of Justice Dole's legal opinions by Samuel B. Kemp. Palo Alto, Calif., Published for the Hawaiian Historical Society by Pacific Books [1957] 394 p. illus. 24 cm. [DU627.7.D3] 56-12362
I. Dole, Sanford Ballard, 1844-1926. II. Title.

HAMMOND, Harold Earl, 923.473
1922-
A commoner's judge; the life and times of Charles Patrick Daly. With an introd. by Allan Nevins. Boston, Christopher Pub. House [1954] 456p. illus. 21cm. Issued also as thesis, Columbia University, in microfilm form. 54-10958
I. Daly, Charles Patrick, 1816-1899. II. Title.

HEATON, Ronald H., 347'.73'2634
1898-
Justices of the Supreme Court identified as Masons by Ronald E. Heaton. Washington, Masonic Service Association [1968] ix, 41 p. ports. 28 cm. [KF8744.H4] 75-308321
1. Judges—United States. 2. Freemasons—Biography. I. Title.

Judson, Adoniram, 1788-1850.

ANDERSON, Courtney. 922.654
To the Golden Shore; the life of Adoniram Judson. [1st ed.] Boston, Little, Brown [1956] 530 p. illus. 22 cm. [BV3271.J7A5] 56-6766
1. Judson, Adoniram, 1788-1850. I. Title.

*BADCOCK, D. I. 266.00954
Burma prisoner; the story of Adoniram Judson. Chicago, Moody [1967,c.1962] 63p. 19cm. (Moody arrow: missionary, no. 22) .50 pap.,
1. Judson, Adoniram, d. 1849. 2. Missions—India. I. Title.

BAILEY, Faith Coxe. 922.654
Adoniram Judson, Missionary to Burma, 1813 to 1850. Chicago, Moody Press [1955] 128p. 18cm. (Colportage library, 287) [BV3271.J7B3] 56-16597
1. Judson, Adoniram, 1788-1850. I. Title.

MCELRATH WILLIAM 266'.6'10924 B
N.
To be the first : adventures of Adoniram Judson, America's first foreign missionary / William N. McElrath. Nashville : Broadman Press, c1976. 189 p. : ill. ; 21 cm. [BV3271.J7M3] 75-14893 ISBN 0-8054-4318-5 pbk. : 4.95
1. Judson, Adoniram, 1788-1850. 2. Missionaries—United States—Biography. 3. Missionaries—Burma—Biography. I. Title.

TO the golden shore, v. 12
the life of Adoniram Judson. Garden City, N. Y., Doubleday [1961, c1956] 520p. 18cm. (Dolphin books, C192)
1. Judson, Adoniram, 1788-1850. I. Anderson, Courtney.

Judson, Clara (Ingram)

JUDSON, Clara (Ingram) 1879- 920
Abraham Lincoln, friend of the people. Pen drawings by Robert Frankenberg; kodachromes of the Chicago Historical Society Lincoln dioramas. Chicago, Follett Pub. Co. [1961, c.1950] 206p. illus. (part. col.) 3.50 bds.,
I. Title.

Judson, Edward Zane Carroll, 1823-1886.

MONAGHAN, James, 1891- 928.1
The Great Rascal; the life and adventures of Ned Bunttine. [1st ed.] Boston, Little, Brown, 1952 [c1951] xi, 353 p. illus., ports. 22 cm. Bibliography: p. 312-333. [PS2156.J2Z75] 52-5003
1. Judson, Edward Zane Carroll, 1823-1886. I. Title.

Judson, Eli, 1770-1821.

JUDSON, Marguerite M 923.873
The Judson papers. [1st ed.] New York, Vantage Press [c1955] 89p. illus. 21cm. 'Based on letters exchanged from 1800 to 1830 between two Judson brothers.' [CT275.J95J8] 55-10854
1. Judson, Eii, 1770-1821. 2. Judson, David, 1757-1831. I. Title.

Jugan, Jeanne, 1792?-1879.

TROCHU, Francis, 1877- 922.244
Jeanne Jugan, Sister Marie of the Cross, foundress of the Institute of the Little Sisters of the Poor, 1792-1879. Translated by Hugh Montgomery. Westminster, Md., Newman Press, 1950. xii, 288 p. 23 cm. Translation of La servante de Dieu, Jeanne Jugan, Sarur Marie de la Croix. [BX4705.J79T72] 51-5570
1. 1. Jugan, Jeanne, 1792?-1879. 2. Little Sisters of the Poor. I. Title.

Juh (Apache chief) d. 1883.

THRAPP, Dan L. 970.3 B
Juh: an incredible Indian, by Dan L. Thrapp. El Paso, Texas Western Press [1973] 44 p. illus. 23 cm. (Southwestern studies, monograph no. 39) Includes bibliographical references. [E99.A6J847] 74-155433 3.00 (pbk.).
1. Juh (Apache chief) d. 1883. I. Title. I'. Series: Southwestern studies (El Paso, Tex.) monograph no. 39.

Juilliard String Quartet.

GAY, Harriet. 785.7'0092'2
The Juilliard String Quartet / by Harriet Gay. 1st ed. New York : Vantage Press, [1974] 89 p., [26] leaves of plates : ill. ; 22 cm. [ML398.J84] 74-182386 ISBN 0-533-01322-4 : 6.95
1. Juilliard String Quartet.

Julian, George Washington. 1817-1899.

RIDDLEBERGER, Patrick 973.0924(B)
W.
George Washington Julian, radical Republican; a study in nineteenth- century politics and reform, by Patrick W. Riddleberget. [Indianapolis] Indiana Hist. Bureau, 1966. xiii, 344p. ports. 24cm. (Indiana hist. collections, v. 45) Bibl. [E415.6.J964R5] 66-65504 5.00
1. Julian, George Washington. 1817-1899. 2. U.S.—Pol. & govt.—1849-1877. I. Title. II. Series.
Publisher's address: 140 N. Senate Ave., Indianapolis, Ind. 46204.

Julian, Hubert Fauntleroy, 1897-

NUGENT, John Peer. 629.13'0924 B
The Black Eagle. New York, Stein and Day [1971] 191 p. 22 cm. [CT275.J97N83] 73-149808 ISBN 0-8128-1370-7 6.95
1. Julian, Hubert Fauntleroy, 1897- I. Title.

Julian, Joseph.

JULIAN, Joseph. 791.44'028'0924 B
This was radio : a personal memoir / Joseph Julian ; introd. by Harold Clurman. New York : Viking Press, 1975. xiii, 238 p., : ill. ; 22 cm. "A Richard Seaver book." [PN1991.4.J84A37] 74-4805 ISBN 0-670-70299-4 : 8.95
1. Julian, Joseph. 2. Radio broadcasting—History. I. Title.

Juliana, Queen of the Netherlands, 1909-

HOFFMAN, William, 949.2'07'0924 B
1937-
Queen Juliana : the story of the richest woman in the world / William Hoffman. 1st ed. New York : Harcourt Brace Jovanovich, c1979. p. cm. Includes index. [DJ288.H647] 79-1827 ISBN 0-15-146531-2 : 11.95
1. Juliana, Queen of the Netherlands, 1909- 2. Netherlands—Biography, Kings and rulers.

Julianus, Apostata, Emperor of Rome, 331-363.

BOWERSOCK, Glen 937'.08'0924 B
Warren.
Julian the Apostate / by G. W. Bowersock. Cambridge : Harvard University Press, [1977] p. cm. Includes index. Bibliography: p. [DG317.B68] 77-22769 ISBN 0-674-48881-4 : 12.50
1. Julianus, Apostata, Emperor of Rome, 331-363. 2. Roman emperors—Biography. I. Title.
BIP

BROWNING, Robert, 937'.08'0924 B
1914-
The Emperor Julian / Robert Browning. Berkeley : University of California Press, c1976. xii, 256 p., [4] leaves of plates : ill. ; 25 cm. Includes index. Bibliography: p. [238]-240. [DG317.B76 1976] 75-13159 ISBN 0-520-03034-6 : 12.50
1. Julianus, Apostata, Emperor of Rome, 331-363. I. Title.

BROWNING, 937'.08'0924 [B]
Robert, 1914-
The Emperor Julian / Robert Browning. Berkeley : University of California Press, 1978, c1976. xii, 256p. [4] leaves of plates : ill. ; 24 c. Includes index. Bibliography: p. [238]-240. [DG317.B76] pbk. : 4.95
1. Julianus, Apostata, Emperor of Rome, 331-363. I. Title.
L.C. card no. for 1976 hardcover ed.: 73-13159.
BIP

GARDNER, Alice, 937'.08'0924 B
1854-1927.
Julian, philosopher and emperor, and the last struggle of paganism against Christianity / by Alice Gardner. New York : AMS Press, 1978. xx, 364 p., [21] leaves of plates (3 fold.) : ill. ; 19 cm. Reprint of the 1895 ed. published by Putnam, New York, which was issued in series: Heroes of the nations. Includes bibliographical references and index. [DG317.G33 1978] 73-14444 ISBN 0-404-58262-1 : 30.00
1. Julianus, Apostata, Emperor of Rome, 331-363. 2. Roman emperors—Biography. 3. Philosophers—Rome—Biography. 4. Rome—History—Empire, 284-476. I. Title. II. Series: Heroes of the nations.

HEAD, Constance. 937'.08'0924 B
The Emperor Julian / by Constance Head. Boston : Twayne Publishers, c1976. 229 p. : ill. ; 22 cm. (Twayne's world leaders series ; TWLS 53) Includes index. Bibliography: p. 219-222. [DG317.H5] 75-15724 ISBN 0-8057-7650-8 lib.bdg. : 8.95
1. Julianus, Apostata, Emperor of Rome, 331-363. 2. Roman emperors—Biography. I. Title.
BIP

Julius II, Pope, 1443-1513.

ERASMUS, 262'.13'0924 B
Desiderius, d.1536, supposed author.
The Julius exclusus. Translated by Paul Pascal. Introd. and critical notes by J. Kelly Sowards. Bloomington, Indiana University Press [1968] 141 p. 21 cm. Translation of Julius Secundus. Bibliographical references included in "Notes" (p. 93-141) [BX1314.E713] 68-14600
1. Julius II, Pope, 1443-1513. I. Pascal, Paul, tr. II. Sowards, Jesse Kelley, 1924- III. Title.

Jumel, Eliza (Bowen) 1775?-1865.

FALKNER, Leonard 920.7
Painted lady, Eliza Jumel: her life and times. New York, Dutton [c.]1962. 252p. 21cm. 62-7819 4.75 bds.,
1. Jumel, Eliza (Bowen) 1775?-1865. I. Title.

Jumel, Stephen, 1755-1832.

MINNIGERODE, Meade, 1887- 920.073
1967.
Lives and times; four informal American biographies. Freeport, N.Y., Books for Libraries Press [1970] viii, 215 p. illus., ports. 23 cm. (Essay index reprint series) Reprint of the 1925 ed. Contents.Contents.—Stephen Jumel, merchant.—William Eaton, hero.—Theodosia Burr, prodigy.—Edmond Charles Genet, citizen. [E302.5.M66 1970] 76-121490
1. Jumel, Stephen, 1755-1832. 2. Eaton, William, 1764-1811. 3. Alston, Theodosia (Burr) 1783-1813. 4. Genet, Edmond Charles, 1763-1834. I. Title.

Juneau. Solomon Laurent, 1793-1856—Juvenile literature.

LAWSON, Marion. 923.971
Solomon Juneau, voyageur. Illus. by Robert Hallock. New York, Crowell [1960] 226p. illus. 21cm. [F589.M6J96] 60-11542
1. Juneau. Solomon Laurent, 1793-1856—Juvenile literature. I. Title.

Jung, Carl Gustav,

JUNG, Carl Gustav, 1875-1961 921
Memories, dreams, reflections. Recorded, ed. by Aniet Jaffe. Tr. from German by Richard and Clara Winston. New York, Pantheon [1963] 698p. illus. 24cm. 62-14264 7.50
I. Title.

JUNG, Carl Gustav, 1875-1961 921
Memories, dreams, reflections. Recorded,

ed. by Aniela Jaffe. Tr. from German by Richard and Clara Winston. New York, Random [1965, c.1961-1963] xiii, 418p. 20cm. (Vintage bk. V-268) [BF109.J8A33] 2.45 pap.,
I. Title.

FRANZ, Marie Luise von, 1915- 150'.19'54
C. G. Jung, his myth in our time / Marie-Louise von Franz ; translated from the German by William H. Kennedy. Boston : Little, Brown, [1977] c1975. viii, 355 p. ; 20 cm. Includes index. Bibliography: p. 288-319. [BF173.J85F6913 1977] 77-1442 ISBN 0-316-90530-5 pbk. : 4.95
1. Jung, Carl Gustav, 1875-1961. 2. Psychoanalysts—Switzerland—Biography. I. Title.

HANNAH, Barbara. 150'.19'54 B
Jung, his life and work : a biographical memoir / by Barbara Hannah. New York : Putnam, c1976. 376 p., [1] leaf of plates : ill. ; 24 cm. Includes index. Bibliography: p. 361-365. [BF173.J85H33 1976] 76-13365 ISBN 0-399-11441-6 : 12.95
1. Jung, Carl Gustav, 1875-1961. 2. Psychoanalysts—Switzerland—Biography. I. Title.

JAFFE, Aniela. 150.19'54 B
C. G. Jung, word and image / edited by Aniela Jaffe. Princeton, N.J. : Princeton University Press, c1979. 238 p. : ill. ; 29 cm. (Bollingen series ; 97:2) Translation of C. G. Jung, Bild und Wort. "The collected works of C. G. Jung": p. [231] Includes index. [BF173.J85J44313] 78-17319 ISBN 0-691-09942-1 : 25.00
1. Jung, Carl Gustav, 1875-1961. 2. Psychoanalysts—Switzerland—Biography. 3. Psychoanalysis. I. Title. II. Series.

JAFFE, Aniela. 150.19'54
From the life and work of C. G. Jung. Translated by R. F. C. Hull. New York, Harper & Row [1971] ix, 137 p. 22 cm. (A Torchbook library edition, 44) Translation of Aus Leben und Werkstatt von C. G. Jung: Parapsychologie, Alchemie, Nationalsozialismus, Erinnerungen aus den letzten Jahren. Includes bibliographical references. [BF173.J85J4413 1971b] 78-29952 ISBN 0-06-136044-9 8.50
1. Jung, Carl Gustav, 1875-1961. I. Title.

JUNG, Carl Gustav, 1875-1961. 150'.19'5408
Letters. Selected and edited by Gerhard Adler, in collaboration with Aniela Jaffe. Translations from the German by R. F. C. Hull [Princeton, N.J.] Princeton University Press [1973- v. illus. 25 cm. (Bollingen series, 95: 1-) Contents.Contents.—v. 1. 1906-1950. Includes bibliographical references. [BF175.J8513 1973] 74-166378 17.50 (v. 1)
1. Jung, Carl Gustav, 1875-1961. 2. Psychoanalysts—Correspondence, reminiscences, etc. I. Title. II. Series.

JUNG, Carl Gustav, 1875-1961 921
Memories, dreams, reflections. Recorded, ed. by Aniet Jaffe. Tr. from German by Richard and Clara Winston. New York, Pantheon [1963] 698p. illus. 24cm. 62-14264 7.50
I. Title.

JUNG, Carl Gustav, 1875-1961 921
Memories, dreams, reflections. Recorded, ed. by Aniela Jaffe. Tr. from German by Richard and Clara Winston. New York, Random [1965, c.1961-1963] xiii, 418p. 20cm. (Vintage bk. V-268) [BF109.J8A33] 2.45 pap.,
I. Title.

STERN, Paul J. 150'.19'54
C.G. Jung : the haunted prophet / by Paul J. Stern. New York : Dell Pub. Co., 1977. 267p. ; 21 cm. (A Del ta Book) Includes index. [RC339.52.J84S73] ISBN 0-440-54744-X pbk. : 3.95
1. Jung, Carl Gustav, 2. Psychoanalysis. I. Title.
L.C. card no. for 1976 G. Braziller ed.:75-37827. BIP

STERN, Paul J. 150'.19'54
C. G. Jung—the haunted prophet / by Paul J. Stern. New York : G. Braziller, c1976. 267 p. ; 22 cm. Includes index. Bibliography: p. 259-262. [RC339.52.J84S73] 75-37827 ISBN 0-8076-0811-4 : 9.95
1. Jung, Carl Gustav, 1875-1961. 2. Psychoanalysis. I. Title.

WEHR, Gerhard. 150.19'54 B
Portrait of Jung; an illustrated biography. Translated by W. A. Hargreaves. [New York] Herder and Herder [1971] 173 p. illus., facsims., ports. 21 cm. Translation of C. G. Jung in Selbstzeugnissen und Bilddokumenten. Bibliography: p. 171-173. [BF173.J85W4213] 73-150141 6.95
1. Jung, Carl Gustav, 1875-1961. I. Title.

Juniperus, of Assisi, Brother, 13th cent.

FRANCESCO D'ASSISI, Saint. Legend. Fioretti. 922.22
La vita di Frate Ginepro (testo latino e volgarizzamento) a cura di Giorgio Petrocchi. Bologna, Commissione per i testi di lingua, 1960. xxxvi, 99 p. 18 cm. (Scelta di curiosita letterarie inedite o rare dal secolo xiii al xix in appendice alla Collesione di opere inedite o rare. Dispensa 256) Includes bibliographical references. [BX4700.F63A1] 65-35836
1. Juniperus, of Assisi, Brother, 13th cent. I. Patrocchi, Giorgio, 1921- ed. II. Title. III. Series. IV. Series: Scelta di curiosita letterarie inedite o rare dal secolo xiii al xix. Dispensa 256

PETROCCHI, Giorgio, 1921- ed. 922.22
La vita di Frate Ginepro (testo latino e volgarizzamento) a cura di Giorgio Petrocchi. (Scelta di curiosita letterarie inedite o rare dal secolo xiii al xix in appendice alla Collesione di opere inedite o rare. Dispensa 256) Includes bibliographical references. [BX4700.F63A1] 65-35836
1. Juniperus, of Assisi, Brother, 13th cent. I. Patrocchi, Giorgio, 1921- ed. II. Title. III. Series. IV. Series: Scelta di curiosita letterarie inedite o rare dal secolo xiii al xix. Dispensa 256

Jureidini, Said M., 1866-1952.

MCRAE, Jane Carroll. 266.6'1'0924 B
Photographer in Lebanon; the story of Said Jureidini. Nashville, Broadman Press [1969] 64 p. illus., ports. 19 cm. [BX6495.J95M3] 69-19024
1. Jureidini, Said M., 1866-1952. 2. Baptists—Lebanon. I. Title.

Justice, Charlie, 1924-

QUINCY, Bob. 927.9633
Choo Choo, the Charlie Justice story, by Bob Quincy and Julian Scheer. Illus. by Lee Kolbe. Foreword by W.D. Carmichael, Jr. [1st ed.] Chapel Hill, N. C., Bentley Pub. Co., 1958. 132 p. illus., ports. 31 cm. [GV939.J8Q5] 58-59827
1. Justice, Charlie, 1924- I. Scheer, Julian, joint author. II. Title.

Justinianus I, Emperor of the East, 483?-565.

BROWNING, Robert, 1914- 949.5'01'0922 B
Justinian and Theodora. New York, Praeger [1971] 272 p. illus., facsims. (1 col.), geneal. table, maps, plates (part col.), ports. (part col.) 26 cm. Bibliography: p. 265-266. [DF572.B76 1971b] 72-100907 15.00
1. Justinianus I, Emperor of the East, 483?-565. 2. Theodora, consort of Justinianus I, Emperor of the East, d. 548. I. Title.

FITZGERALD, Thomas. 949.5'01'0924 B
Justinian the Great; Roman Emperor of the East. New York, F. Watts [1970] 122 p. illus., map. 22 cm. (Immortals of history) [DF572.F57] 70-93766
1. Justinianus I, Emperor of the East, 483?-565. I. Title.

Justinus Martyr, Saint.

BARNARD, Leslie William. 230'.13
Justin Martyr: his life and thought, by L. W. Barnard. London, Cambridge U.P., 1967. viii, 193 p. 22 1/2 cm. Bibliography: p. 180-183. [BR65.J86B3] 66-16665
1. Justinus Martyr, Saint.

Jusus Christ—Biog.

BIBLE. N. T. Gospels. English. 1962. Confraternity version. 232.9
A life of Christ, together with the four Gospels [by] Aloys Dirksen. Rev. [i. e. 2d] ed. New York, Holt, Rinehart and Winston [1962] xiv, 378p. 24cm. The Gospels constitute the upper section of the book which is divided in a Dutch door arrangement. Bibliography: p. [365]- 372. [BT301.D57 1962] 62-8479
1. Jusus Christ—Biog. I. Dirksen, Aloys Herman. II. Title.

Juvenalis, Patriarch of Jerusalem, d. 458?

HONIGMANN, Ernst, 1892- 270.2
Juvenal of Jerusalem. (In Dumbarten Oaks papers. Cambridge, Mass., 1950. 30 cm. no. 5, p. [209]-279) Includes bibliographies. [N5970.D8 no. 5] 51-4862
1. Juvenalis, Patriarch of Jerusalem, d. 458? I. Title. II. Series: Dumbarton Oaks papers, no. 5, p. [209]-279

Kadar, Janos, 1912—

SHAWCROSS, William. 320.9'439'05 B
Crime and compromise; Janos Kadar and the politics of Hungary since revolution. [1st ed.] New York, Dutton, 1974. 311 p. 22 cm. Includes bibliographical references. [DB950.K23S5 1974] 73-15503 10.00
1. Kadar, Janos, 1912- 2. Hungary—Politics and government—1945- I. Title.

K'ang, Yu-wei, 1858-1927.

K'ANG Yu-wei; 951'.03'0924 B
a biography and a symposium. Edited, with translation by Jung-pang Lo. Tucson, Published for the Association for Asian Studies by University of Arizona Press [1967] 541 p. illus., map (on lining papers) ports. 24 cm. (Association for Asian Studies. Monographs and papers no. 23) Bibliography: p. 410-480. [DS763.K3K33] 66-20911
1. K'ang, Yu-wei, 1858-1927. I. Lo, Jung-pang, 1912- ed. II. Association for Asian Studies. III. Title. IV. Series. BIP

Kotoku, Denjiro, 1871-1911.

NOTEHELFER, F. G. 952'.03'10924
Kotoku Shusui, portrait of a Japanese radical [by] F. G. Notehelfer. Cambridge [Eng.] University Press, 1971. x, 227 p. ports. 24 cm. Based on the author's thesis, Princeton, 1968. Bibliography: p. 209-217. [DS884.K65N68] 76-134620 ISBN 0-521-07989-6
1. Kotoku, Denjiro, 1871-1911. I. Title.

Krshnadasa Kaviraja, b. 1518 or 19.

BHAKTIVEDANTA, A.C. Swami 1896- 294.5'6'3 B
Lord Caitanya in five features : chapter 7, Adi-lila of Krsnadasa Kaviraja Gosvami's Sri-Caitanya-caritamrta / A. C. Bhaktivedanta Swami. New York : Bhaktivedanta Book Trust, 1973. 156 p., [2] leaves of plates : ill. ; 21 cm. Bengali and English. [BL1245.V36K7733] 75-322016 ISBN 0-912776-52-8
1. Krshnadasa Kaviraja, b. 1518 or 19. Srisricaitanyacaritamrta. 2. Chaitanya, 1486-1534. I. Krshnadasa Kaviraja, b. 1518 or 19. Srisricaitanyacaritamrta. 1973. II. Title.

Kaahumanu, consort of Kamehameha I, the Great, King of the Hawaiian Islands, 1772-1832.

MELLEN, Kathleen Dickenson. 923.1969
The magnificent matriarch, Kaahumanu, Queen of Hawaii. New York, Hastings House [1952] 291 p. illus. 21 cm. Sequel to The lonely warrior. [DU627.11.M4] 52-8221
1. Kaahumanu, consort of Kamehameha I, the Great, King of the Hawaiian Islands, 1772-1832. I. Title. BIP

Kaapu, Myrtle King, 1898-

KAAPU, Myrtle King, 1898- 996.9'03'0924 B
I married a prince : a Cinderella story from Hawaii / Myrtle King Kaapu. 1st ed. Hicksville, N.Y. : Exposition Press, c1977. 271 p., [10] leaves of plates : ill. ; 22 cm. [DU627.7.K32A34] 76-40773 ISBN 0-682-48649-3 : 10.00
1. Kaapu, Myrtle King, 1898- 2. David, Prince of Punaluu. 3. Hawaii—Princes and princesses—Biography. I. Title. BIP

Kabaphes, Konstantinos Petrou, 1863-1933.

LIDDELL, Robert, 1908- 889'.1'32 B
Cavafy : a biography / Robert Liddell. New York : Schocken Books, 1976, c1974. 220 p., [4] leaves of plates : ill. ; 23 cm. Includes index. Bibliography: p. [212]-214. [PA5610.K2Z74 1976] 76-9135 ISBN 0-8052-3634-1 : 8.95
1. Kabaphes, Konstantinos Petrou, 1863-1933.

Kabiro, Ngugi, 1929-

KABIRO, Ngugi, 1929- 967.6'2'030924 B
The man in the middle : the story of Ngugi Kabiro / taped and edited by Don Barnett ; illustrated by Selma Waldman. Richmond, B. C. : LSM Information Center, c1973. 75 p. : ill., map, port. ; 22 cm. (Life histories from the Revolution : Kenya, Mau Mau ; 2) [DT433.576.K3A34] 75-313393 1.50
1. Kabiro, Ngugi, 1929- 2. Mau Mau. I. Barnett, Donald L. II. Title. III. Series.

Kabongo, Kikuyu chief.

BAKER, Richard St. Barbe, 1889- 572.9676
Kabongo; the story of a Kikuyu chief. With engravings by Yvonne Skargon. [1st ed.] New York, Barnes [1955] 126p. illus. 21cm. [DT433] 56-5565
1. Kabongo, Kikuyu chief. 2. Kikuyu tribe. I. Title.

Kabotie, Fred.

KABOTIE, Fred. 759.13 B
Fred Kabotie, Hopi Indian artist : an autobiography told with Bill Belknap. 1st ed. Flagstaff : Museum of Northern Arizona, c1977. xv, 149 p. : ill. (some col.) ; 24 x 27 cm. Includes index. [E99.H7K32] 77-79071 ISBN 0-87358-164-4 : 35.00
1. Kabotie, Fred. 2. Hopi Indians—Biography. 3. Artists—Arizona—Biography. I. Belknap, Bill, 1920- joint author. II. Title.

Kafka, Franz,

KAFKA, Franz, 1883-1924 928.3
The diaries of Franz Kafka [2v.] Ed. by Max Brod. New York, Schocken [1965, c.1948, 1949] 2v. (345; 343p.) 21cm. [PT2621j.A26Z625] 48-6432 1.95 pap., ea.,
I. Brod, Max, 1884- ed. II. Kresh, Joseph, 1909- tr. III. Title.
Contents omitted.

Kafka, Franz, 1883-1924.

BAUER, Johann. 833'.9'12 B
Kafka and Prague. Text by Johann Bauer. Photos. by Isidor Pollak. Design by Jaroslav Schneider. Translated by P. S. Falla. New York, Praeger [1971] 191 p. illus. 34 cm. Bibliography: p. 188. [PT2621.A26Z582613] 73-153833 14.95
1. Kafka, Franz, 1883-1924. I. Pollak, Isidor, illus. II. Title.

BROD, Max, 1884- 928.3
Franz Kafka, a biography. 2d. enl., ed. [Translated from the German by G. Humphreys Robert and by Richard Winston] New York, Schocken Books [67 Park Ave., c.1937-1960] 267p. illus. 21cm. 60-14601 4.50
1. Kafka, Franz, 1883-1924. I. Title.

CRAWFORD, Deborah. 833'.9'12 B
Franz Kafka: man out of step. [1st ed.] New York, Crown Publishers [1973] 183 p. illus. 22 cm. Bibliography: p. 179-180. [PT2621.A26Z67 1973] 72-79793 ISBN 0-517-50075-2 4.95
1. Kafka, Franz, 1883-1924.

FLORES, Angel, 1900- ed. 833'.922
Franz Kafka today. Edited by Angel Flores and Homer Swander. Madison, University of Wisconsin Press, 1958. viii, 290 p. 24 cm. Bibliography: p. 251-285. [PT2621.A26Z69] 57-9818
1. Kafka, Franz, 1883-1924. I. Swander, Homer D., 1921- joint ed. **BIP**

†GOODMAN, Paul, 1911-1972. 833'.9'12 B
Kafka's prayer / by Paul Goodman ; introd. by Raymond Rosenthal. New York : Hillstone : [distributed by G. Braziller], c1976. xix, 265 p. ; 21 cm. [PT2621.A26Z74 1976] 76-152185 ISBN 0-88373-047-2 : 3.95
1. Kafka, Franz, 1883-1924. 2. Authors, Austrian—20th century—Biography. I. Title. **BIP**

JANOUCH, Gustav. 928.3
Conversations with Kafka; notes and reminiscences. With an introd. by Max Brod. Translated by Goronwy Rees. New York, F. A. Praeger [1953] 108p. 23cm. (Books that matter) [PT2621.A26Z748] 53-5320
1. Kafka, Franz, 1883-1924. I. Title.

KAFKA, Franz, 1883-1924 928.3
The diaries of Franz Kafka [2v.] Ed. by Max Brod. New York, Schocken [1965, c.1948, 1949] 2v. (345; 343p.) 21cm. [PT2621j.A26Z625] 48-6432 1.95 pap., ea.,
I. Brod, Max, 1884- ed. II. Kresh, Joseph, 1909- tr. III. Title.
Contents omitted.

KAFKA, Franz, 1883-1924 928.3
Letters to Milena. Ed. by Willi Haas; tr. by Tania and James Stern. New York, Schocken [1962, c.1953] 238p. 21cm. (SB24) 62-13139 1.75 pap.,
1. Authors—Correspondence, reminiscences, etc. I. Jesenska, Milena, 1896-1944. II. Title.

KAFKA, Franz, 1883-1924. 928.3
Letters to Milena. Edited by Willy Haas; translated by Tania and James Stern. [New York] Schocken Books [1954, c 1953] 238 p. 21 cm. [PT2621.A26Z553 1954] 54-1529
1. Authors, German—Correspondence, reminiscences, etc. I. Jesenska, Milena, 1896-1944. II. Haas, Willy, 1891- ed. III. Title. **BIP**

POLITZER, Heinrich, 1910- 838.912
Franz Kafka, parable and paradox. Ithaca, N.Y., Cornell University Press [1962] xxi, 376 p. facsim. 25 cm. Bibliographical references included in "Notes" (p. 359-365) Bibliography: p. 367-371. [PT2621.A26Z817 1962] 62-20733
1. Kafka, Franz, 1883-1924.

SOKEL, Walter Herbert, 1917- 838.91209
Franz Kafka, by Walter H. Sokel. New York, Columbia University Press, 1966. 48 p. 21 cm. (Columbia essays on modern writers no. 19) Bibliography: p. 45-48. [PT2621.A26Z868] 66-26005
1. Kafka, Franz, 1883-1924. I. Title. II. Series. **BIP**

SPANN, Meno, 1903- 833'.9'12 B
Franz Kafka / by Meno Spann. Boston : Twayne Publishers, 1976. 205 p. : port. ; 21 cm. (Twayne's world authors series ; TWAS 381 : Germany) Includes index. Bibliography: p. 195-200. [PT2621.A26Z877] 75-26548 ISBN 0-8057-6182-9 lib. bdg. : 7.95
1. Kafka, Franz, 1883-1924.

Kafka, Franz, 1883-1924 — Bibl.

BENSON, Ann. v. 12
Franz Kafka: An American bibliography. Boston, 1958. 112-114 p. 26 cm. Pub. with: Cohen, L. O., Shalom Asch . . . Excerpt: Bulletin of bibliography, v. 22. [NUC66-43251]
1. Kafka, Franz, 1883-1924 — Bibl. I. Title.

Kafka, Franz, 1883-1924—Biography.

BROD, Max, 1884-1968. 928.3
Franz Karka, a biography. 2d, enl., ed. [Translated from the German by G. Humphreys Roberts and by Richard Winston] New York, Schocken Books [1960] 267 p. illus. 21 cm. [PT2621.A26Z62 1960] 60-14601
1. Kafka, Franz, 1883-1924—Biography.

JANOUCH, Gustav. 833'.9'12 B
Conversations with Kafka. Translated by Goronwy Rees. 2d ed., rev. and enl. [New York] New Directions [1971] 219 p. 21 cm. Translation of Gesprache mit Kafka. Includes bibliographical references. [PT2621.A26Z748 1971] 74-156976 8.50
1. Kafka, Franz, 1883-1924—Biography. I. Title. **BIP**

KAFKA, Franz, 1883-1924. 833'.9'12 B
I am a memory come alive; autobiographical writings. Edited by Nahum N. Glatzer. New York, Schocken Books [1974] xvi, 264 p. 21 cm. Includes bibliographical references. [PT2621.A26Z5] 74-8781 ISBN 0-8052-3556-6 10.00
1. Kafka, Franz, 1883-1924—Biography. I. Glatzer, Nahum Norbert, 1903- ed. II. Title. **BIP**

Kafka, Franz, 1883-1924—Correspondence.

CANETTI, Elias, 1905- 833'.9'12 B
Kafka's other trial; the letters to Felice. Translated by Christopher Middleton. New York, Schocken Books [1974] 121 p. 21 cm. Translation of Der andere Prozess. Includes bibliographical references. [PT2621.A26Z64813] 74-3048 ISBN 0-8052-3553-1 6.50
1. Kafka, Franz, 1883-1924—Correspondence. 2. Bauer, Felice, 1887-1960—Correspondence. I. Title.

KAFKA, Franz, 1883-1924. 833'.9'12 B
Letters to Felice / [by] Franz Kafka ; edited by Erich Heller and Jurgen Born ; translated [from the German] by James Stern and Elisabeth Duckworth ; with, Kafka's other trial / by Elias Canetti ; translated [from the German] by Christopher Middleton. Harmondsworth ; New York : Penguin, 1978. 697 p. ; 19 cm. (Penguin modern classics) Translation of Briefe an Felice und andere Korrespondenz aus der Verlobungszeit. Includes bibliographical references and index. [PT2621.A26Z53813 1978] 78-388468 ISBN 0-14-004440-X pbk. : 2.00
1. Kafka, Franz, 1883-1924—Correspondence. 2. Bauer, Felice, 1887-1960—Correspondence. 3. Authors, Austrian—20th century—Correspondence. I. Bauer, Felice, 1887-1960. II. Heller, Erich, 1911- III. Born, Jurgen. IV. Canetti, Elias, 1905- Der andere Prozess. English. 1978. V. Title. **BIP**

Kagawa, Toyohiko, 1888-

BRADSHAW, Emerson Otho, 1881- 922
Unconquerable Kagawa, by Emerson O. Bradshaw for the Kagawa National Committee. [1st ed.] St. Paul, Macalester Park Pub. Co. [1952] 157p. illus. 21cm. [BV3457.K3B7] 53-2123
1. Kagawa, Toyohiko, 1888- I. Kagawa National Committee. II. Title.

SIMON, Charlie May Hogue, 1897- 922
A seed shall serve; the story of Toyohiko Kagawa, spiritual leader of modern Japan. Illustrated with photos. [1st ed.] New York, Dutton, 1958. 158 p. illus. 21 cm. Includes bibliography. [BV3457.K3S5] 58-9579
1. Kagawa, Toyohiko, 1888- I. Title.

Kagwa, Apolo, Sir, 1864?-1927.

MUKASA, Ham. 914.2'03'83
Uganda's Katikiro in England. Translated and edited by Ernest Millar. Freeport, N.Y., Books for Libraries Press, 1971. xxv, 278 p. illus., ports. 23 cm. (The Black heritage library collection) Reprint of the 1904 ed. [DA630.M76 1971] 74-152926 ISBN 0-8369-8770-5
1. Kagwa, Apolo, Sir, 1864?-1927. 2. Gt. Brit.—Description and travel—1901-1945. I. Title. II. Series. **BIP**

Kagwa, Benjamin N. H.

KAGWA, Benjamin N. H. 616.8'9'00924 B
A Ugandan, defiant and triumphant : an autobiography / by Benjamin N. H. Kagwa. 1st ed. Hicksville, N.Y. : Exposition Press, c1978. 252 p., [4] leaves of plates : ill. ; 22 cm. Includes bibliographies. [RC339.52.K34A34] 77-90186 ISBN 0-682-49032-6 : 10.00
1. Kagwa, Benjamin N. H. 2. Psychiatrists—Uganda—Biography. I. Title.

Kahan, Israel Meir, 1838-1933.

ECKMAN, Lester Samuel. 296.6'1 B
Revered by all; the life and works of Rabbi Israel Meir Kagan—Hafets hayyim (1838-1933). New York, Shengold Publishers [1974] 214 p. 25 cm. Bibliography: p. 205-211. [BM755.K25E26] 73-89418 ISBN 0-88400-002-8 10.00
1. Kahan, Israel Meir, 1838-1933. I. Title.

Kahbe nagwi wens, ca. 1790-1922.

ZAPFFE, Carl Andrew. 970'.004'97 B
The man who lived in 3 centuries : a biographic reconstruction of the life of Kahbe nagwi wens, a native Minnesotan / by Carl A. Zapffe. Brainerd, Minn. : Historic Heartland Association, c1975. 96 p. : ill. ; 28 cm. Includes bibliographical references and index. [E99.C6K349] 74-33871
1. Kahbe nagwi wens, ca. 1790-1922. 2. Indians of North America—Minnesota. 3. Chippewa Indians. I. Title.

Kahn, Edgar A.

KAHN, Edgar A. 617'.48'0924 B
Journal of a neurosurgeon, by Edgar A. Kahn. With a foreword by Bronson S. Ray. Springfield, Ill., Thomas [1972] ix, 172 p. illus. 24 cm. [R154.K23A34] 78-187663 ISBN 0-398-02325-5
I. Title. **BIP**

Kahn, Ely Jacques, 1916-

KAHN, Ely Jacques, 1916- 070'.92'4 B
About the New Yorker and me : a sentimental journal / E. J. Kahn, Jr. New York : Putnam, c1979. 453 p. ; 24 cm. Includes index. [PN4874.K25A32 1979] 78-11497 ISBN 0-399-12300-8 : 12.95
1. Kahn, Ely Jacques, 1916- 2. The New Yorker (New York, 1925-) 3. Journalists—United States—Biography. I. Title. **BIP**

KAHN, Ely Jacques, 1916- 818'.5'403 B
Who, me? By E. J. Kahn, Jr. Freeport, N.Y., Books for Libraries Press [1971, c1949] xi, 238 p. 23 cm. (Biography index reprint series) [PS3521.A23W5 1971] 77-179731 ISBN 0-8369-8099-9
I. Title. **BIP**

Kahn, Erich Itor.

KAHN, Frida, 1905- 927.8
Generation in turmoil. Introd. by Joseph Machlis; sketches by Jo Mullen. Great Neck, N. Y., Channel Press [1960] 224p. illus. 21cm. Autobiographical. [ML423.K15A3] 60-10270
1. Kahn, Erich Itor. 2. Musicians—Correspondence, reminiscences, etc. 3. Refugees, Jewish—Personal narratives. I. Title.

Kahn, Louis I., 1901-1974.

GIURGOLA, Romaldo. 720'.92'4
Louis I. Kahn / by Romaldo Giurgola, Jaimini Mehta. Boulder, Colo. : Westview Press, [1975] p. cm. Includes index. [NA737.K32G58] 75-19210 ISBN 0-89158-502-8 : 39.50
1. Kahn, Louis I., 1901-1974. I. Mehta, Jaimini, joint author.

KOMENDANT, August E. 720'.92'4 B
18 years with architect Louis I. Kahn / August E. Komendant Englewood, N.J. : Aloray, [1975] xiii, 192 p. : ill. ; 24 cm. [NA737.K32K65] 75-14437 ISBN 0-913690-06-6 : 15.00
1. Kahn, Louis I., 1901- 2. Komendant, August E. I. Title.

RONNER, Heinz. 720'.92'4
Louis I. Kahn : complete works, 1935-74 / Heinz Ronner, Sharad Jhaveri, Alessandro Vasella. Boulder, Colo. : Westview Press, [1977] p. cm. Bibliography: p. [NA737.K32R66] 76-41392 ISBN 0-89158-648-2 : 39.50
1. Kahn, Louis I., 1901-1974. I. Jhaveri, Sharad, joint author. II. Vasella, Alessandro, joint author. **BIP**

Kahtahah—Juvenile literature.

PAUL, Frances Lackey, 1889-1970. 970'.004'97 B
Kahtahah / Frances Lackey Paul ; illustrated by Rie Munoz. Anchorage : Alaska Northwest Pub. Co., c1976. ix, 109 p. : ill. ; 27 cm. Draws on the experiences of a real person to recreate the life of a Tlingit Indian girl of nineteenth-century Alaska. [E99.T6P38] 76-17804 ISBN 0-88240-058-4 pbk. : 5.95
1. Kahtahah—Juvenile literature. 2. Tlingit Indians—Juvenile literature. I. Munoz, Rie. II. Title. **BIP**

Kain, Karen.

STREET, David, 1947- 792.8'092'4 B
Karen Kain : lady of dance / David Street ; text by David Mason. Toronto ; New York : McGraw-Hill Ryerson, c1978. 127 p. : ill. (some col.) ; 29 cm. [GV1785.K25S77] 78-323362 ISBN 0-07-082705-2 : 14.95
1. Kain, Karen. 2. Dancers—Canada—Biography. I. Mason, David, 1938-

Kaiser, Henry J., 1882-1967.

KAISER Industries Corporation. v. 12
The Kaiser story. [Oakland, Calif., 1968] 72 p. illus., ports. Cover title. 68-94481
1. Kaiser, Henry J., 1882-1967. I. Title.

Kaisher Badadur K. C., 1907-

KAISHER Bahadur K. C., 1907- 954.9'6
Nepal after the revolution of 1950 / by Kaisher Bahadur K. C. Kathmandu : Sharada Prakashan Griha, 1976- v. ; 23

cm. [DS495.5K34] 76-904322 Rs75.00 ($7.50 U.S.) (v. 1)
1. Kaisher Badadur K. C., 1907- 2. Nepal—History—1951- 3. Historians—Nepal—Biography. I. Title.

Kaiulani, Princess of Hawaii, 1875-1899.

WEBB, Nancy. 920.7
Kaiulani: Crown Princess of Hawaii, by Nancy Webb and Jean Francis Webb. New York, Viking Press [1962] 218 p. 24 cm. [DU627.17.K3W4] 62-9630
1. Kaiulani, Princess of Hawaii, 1875-1899. I. Webb, Jean Francis, joint author.

Kakianak, Nathan.

KAKIANAK, Nathan. 970.4'98 B
Eskimo boyhood; an autobiography in psychosocial perspective. [Edited by] Charles C. Hughes. [Lexington] University Press of Kentucky [1974] 429 p. 24 cm. (Studies in anthropology, no. 8) Bibliography: p. 427-429. [E99.E7.K125] 73-80465 ISBN 0-8131-1301-6 12.75
1. Kakianak, Nathan. 2. Eskimos—Alaska—St. Lawrence Island. I. Hughes, Charles Campbell, ed. II. Title. III. Series: Studies in anthropology (Lexington, Ky.) no. 8.

Kalakaua, David, King of Hawaii, 1886-1891.

BURNS, Eugene. 923.1969
The last king of Paradise. New York, Pellegrini & Cudahy [1952] 345 p. 22 cm. [DU627.16.B8] 52-5050
1. Kalakaua, David, King of Hawaii, 1886-1891. I. Title. **BIP**

BURNS, Eugene. 996.9'02 B
The last king of Paradise. Freeport, N.Y., Books for Libraries Press [1973, c1952] p. [DU627.16.B8 1973] 72-10607 ISBN 0-8369-7102-7
1. Kalakaua, David, King of Hawaii, 1836-1891. I. Title.

Kalb. Jean. baron de., originally Johann Kalb, 1721-1780.

ZUCKER, Adolf Eduard. 973.3470924
1890-
General de Kalb. Lafayette's mentor. Chapel Hill. Univ. of N.C. Pr. [1966] ix, 251p. port. 23cm. (Univ. of N.C. Studies in the Germanic langs. and lits., no. 53) Bibl. [PD25.N6 no. 53] 66-3536 7.00
1. Kalb. Jean. baron de., originally Johann Kalb, 1721-1780. I. Title.
(Series: North Carolina. University. Studies in the Germanic languages and literatures, no. 53) **BIP**

Kaline, Albert William, 1934

HIRSHBERG, Albert, 927.96357
1909-
The Al Kaline story. New York, Messner [c.1964] 191p. ports. 22cm. 64-11368 3.25; 3.19 lib. ed.,
1. Kaline, Albert William, 1934- I. Title.

Kalish, Max, 1891-1945.

KALISH, Alice. 730'.924
Max Kalish as I knew him. Los Angeles, 1969. 91 l. illus., ports. 28 cm. [NB237.K3K3] 75-285206
1. Kalish, Max, 1891-1945. I. Title.

Kalleel, George.

KALLEEL, John G 1925- 920
Mount Lebanon trembled; a true story of one man's pilgrimage and proud return. [1st ed.] New York, Greenwich Book Publishers [1960] 72p. 22cm. [CT275.K3215A3] 60-8814
1. Kalleel, George. I. Title.

Kaluiani, Princess of Hawaii, 1875-1899.

WEBB, Nancy (Bukeley) 1915- 920.7
Kaiulani: Crown Princess of Hawaii, by Nancy Webb and Jean Francis Webb. New York, Viking Press [1962] 218 p. 24 cm. [DU627.17.K3W4] 62-9630
1. Kaluiani, Princess of Hawaii, 1875-1899. I. Webb, Jean Francis, joint author. II. Title.

Kamala, the wolf girl, 1912-1929.

MACLEAN, Charles. 155.4'5'67
The wolf children / Charles Maclean. 1st American ed. New York : Hill and Wang, 1978, c1977. 319 p., [9] leaves of plates : ill. ; 22 cm. Bibliography: p. [305]-[312] [GN372.M32 1978] 78-6778 ISBN 0-8090-9776-1 : 10.00
1. Kamala, the wolf girl, 1912-1929. 2. Amala, the wolf girl, 1919?-1921. 3. Feral children—India—Biography. I. Title. **BIP**

Kamehameha I, the Great, King of the Hawaiian Islands, d. 1819.

GOWEN, Herbert 966.9'02'0924 B
Henry, 1864-
The Napoleon of the Pacific : Kamehameha the Great / by Herbert H. Gowen. New York : AMS Press, 1977. p. cm. Reprint of the 1919 ed. published by Revell, New York. Includes index. [DU627.1.G6 1977] 75-35193 ISBN 0-404-14221-4 : 26.00
1. Kamehameha I, the Great, King of the Hawiian Islands, d. 1819. 2. Hawaii—Kings and rulers—Biography. 3. Hawaii—History—To 1893. I. Title.

GOWEN, Herbert 966.9'02'0924 B
Henry, 1864-
The Napoleon of the Pacific : Kamehameha the Great / by Herbert H. Gowen. New York : AMS Press, 1977. p. cm. Reprint of the 1919 ed. published by Revell, New York. Includes index. [DU627.1.G6 1977] 75-35193 ISBN 0-404-14221-4 : 26.00
1. Kamehameha I, the Great, King of the Hawiian Islands, d. 1819. 2. Hawaii—Kings and rulers—Biography. 3. Hawaii—History—To 1893. I. Title.

KING Kamehameha I and 920.0969
Father Damien; Hawaii's presentation to the National statuary collection. [Compiled under the direction of the Joint Committee on Printing. Washington, U.S. Govt. Print. Off., 1970] viii, 40 p. illus., facsim., ports. 27 cm. (91st Congress, 1st session. Senate document no. 91-54) "Proceedings in the Rotunda, United States Capitol, Apr. 15, 1969." Bibliography: p. 39. [DU627.1.K54] 77-609419
1. Kamehameha I, the Great, King of the Hawaiian Islands, d. 1819. 2. Damien, Father, 1840-1889. I. U.S. Congress. Joint Committee on Printing. II. Series: U.S. 91st Congress, 1st session, 1969. Senate. Document no. 91-54

MINER, Lewis S. 920
King of the Hawaiian Islands, Kamehameha I. New York, Messner [c.1963] 191p. map. 22cm. Bibl. 63-16786 3.25
1. Kamehamcha I, the Great, King of the Hawaiian Islands, d. 1819 Juvenile literature I. Title.

POLE, James T 996.902
Hawaii's first king. [1st ed.] Indianapolis, Bobbs-Merrill [1959] 191p. illus. 22cm. [DU627.1.P6] 59-14297
1. Kamehameha I, the Great, King of the Hawaiian Islands, d. 1819. I. Title.

Kaminska, Ida.

KAMINSKA, Ida. 792'.028'0924 B
My life, my theater. Edited and translated by Curt Leviant. New York, Macmillan [1973] ix, 310 p. illus. 22 cm. [PN3035.K32A34] 73-2747 7.95
1. Kaminska, Ida. I. Title. **BIP**

Kampen, Irene—Biography.

KAMPEN, Irene. 818'.5'409 B
Nobody calls at this hour just to say hello / Irene Kampen. 1st ed. Garden City, N.Y. : Doubleday, 1975. 135 p. ; 22 cm. [PS3561.A44Z52] 71-175385 ISBN 0-385-04566-2 : 5.95
1. Kampen, Irene—Biography. I. Title.

Kano, Eitoku, 1543-1590.

KANO, Eitoku, 1543-1590. 759.952
Kano Eitoku / Tsuneo Takeda ; translated and adapted by H. Mack Horton and Catherine Kaputa. 1st ed. Tokyo ; New York : Kodansha International, 1977. 178 p. : ill. (some col.) ; 27 cm. (Japanese arts library ; v. 3) Includes index. Bibliography: p. [169]-174. [ND1059.K17T3413] 76-44155 ISBN 0-87011-295-3 : 15.00
1. Kano, Eitoku, 1543-1590. 2. Painters—Japan—Biography. I. Takeda, Tsuneo, 1925- II. Title. III. Series.

Kanamuzeyi, Yona, 1918-1964.

CHURCH, John 266'.00967'571
Edward.
Forgive them; the story of an African martyr, by J. E. Church, and colleagues of the Rwanda Mission (C.M.S.) Chicago, Moody Press [1967, c1966] 126 p. map. 20 cm. [BX5700] 67-4600
1. Kanamuzeyi, Yona, 1918-1964. I. Church Missionary Society. Ruanda Mission. II. Title.

Kandinsky, Wassily, 1866-1944.

CONIL-LACOSTE, Michel. 759.7 B
Kandinsky / by Michel Conil-Lacoste ; [translated from the French by Alice Sachs]. New York : Crown Publishers, c1978. p. cm. [ND699.K3C6613] 78-11609 ISBN 0-517-53708-7 pbk. : 5.95
1. Kandinsky, Wassily, 1866-1944. 2. Painters—Russian Republic—Biography. **BIP**

GROHMANN, Will, 1887-1968. 759.7
Wassily Kandinsky: life and work. [Translated from the German by Norbert Guterman] New York, H. N. Abrams [1958] 428 p. illus. (part mounted col.) ports. 30 cm. Bibliography: p. 413-425. [ND699.K3G693] 58-13479
1. Kandinsky, Wassily, 1866-1944.

LASSAIGNE, Jacques, 1910- 759.7
Kandinsky; biographical and critical study. Tr. from French by H. S. B. Harrison [Geneva] Skira [dist. Cleveland, World, c.1964] 131p. mounted col. illus. 19cm. (Taste of our time, v.41) Bibl. 63-23078 6.75
1. Kandinsky, Wassily, 1866-1944. I. Title.

Kane, Elisha Kent, 1820-1857.

MIRSKY, Jeannette, 1903- 923.973
Elisha Kent Kane and the seafaring frontier. [1st ed.] Boston, Little, Brown [1954] 201 p. illus. 21 cm. (The Library of American biography) [G635.K2M5] 54-6886
1. Kane, Elisha Kent, 1820-1857. 2. Arctic regions. **BIP**

MIRSKY, 919.8'04'0924 B
Jeannette, 1903-
Elisha Kent Kane and the seafaring frontier. Edited by Oscar Handlin. Westport, Conn., Greenwood Press [1971, c1954] viii, 201 p. map. 23 cm. Bibliography: p. [191]-193. [G635.K2M5 1971] 71-148639 ISBN 0-8371-6004-9
1. Kane, Elisha Kent, 1820-1857. 2. Arctic regions. I. Title.

Kane, Elisha Kent, 1820-1857—Juvenile literature.

STOUTENBURG, Adrien. 92 (J)
Elisha Kent Kane, Arctic challenger, by Lace Kendall [pseud.] Philadelphia, Macrae Smith Co. [1963] 189 p. 22 cm. [G635.K2S8] 63-10716
1. Kane, Elisha Kent, 1820-1857—Juvenile literature.

*Kane, Joseph Nathan

*KANE, Joseph Nathan 923.1
Facts about the Presidents from Washington to Johnson, rev & enl. New York, Pocket Bks. [1964, c.1959, 1964] 504p. 19cm. (75001) .75 pap.,
I. Title.

Kane, Margaret (Fox) 1836-1893.

FORNELL, Earl Wesley 920.913391
The unhappy medium; spiritualism and the life of Margaret Fox. Drawings by Lowell Collins. Austin, Univ. of Tex. Pr. [c.1964] x, 204p. illus., ports. 24cm. Bibl. [BF1283.F7F6] 64-10317 5.00
1. Kane, Margaret (Fox) 1836-1893. 2. Spiritualism. 3. Fox family. I. Title.

Kang, Younghill,

KANG, 917.3'03'910924 B
Younghill, 1903-
East goes West. Chicago, Follett Pub. Co. [1968, c1937] 401 p. 24 cm. Autobiography. [CT275.K325A3 1968] 68-17743
I. Title.

Kanhoji Angri, d. 1731.

KANHOJI Angrey, Maratha v. 12
Admiral; an account of his life and his battles with the English. Bombay. New York, Asia Pub. House [c1959] 303p. maps. Bibliography: p.294.
1. Kanhoji Angri, d. 1731. 2. India—Hist.—1500-1765 (European settlements) I. Malgonkar, Manohar, 1913-

Kano, Aminu, 1920-

FEINSTEIN, Alan. 966.9'03'0924 B
African revolutionary; the life and times of Nigeria's Aminu Kano. [New York] Quadrangle [1973] xvi, 299 p. illus. 22 cm. Includes bibliographical references. [DT515.76.K36F44 1973] 72-91378 ISBN 0-8129-0321-8 9.95
1. Kano, Aminu, 1920- I. Title.

Kansas—Biography.

MILLER, Nyle H. 978.103
Great gunfighters of the Kansas cowtowns, 1867-1886, by Nyle H. Miller and Joseph W. Snell Lincoln, University of Nebraska Press [1967, c1963] 476 p. illus., map. 21 cm. "A Bison book." "Consists of selections from [the author's Why the West was wild] ... comprising in all about two-thirds of the original." Includes bibliographies. [F680.M52] 929'.2'0973 67-65946
1. Kansas—Biography. 2. Peace officers—Kansas. 3. Crime and criminals—Kansas. I. Snell, Joseph W., joint author. II. Title. **BIP**

Kant, Immanuel, 1724-1804.

KANT. v. 12
[Harmondsworth, Middlesex Baltimore, Penguin Books [1960] 230p. 18cm. (Pelican book, A338)
1. Kant, Immanuel, 1724-1804. I. Korner, Stephan., 1913- **BIP**

WALLACE, William, 1844- 193 B
1897.
Kant. Freeport, N.Y., Books for Libraries Press [1972] vi, 219 p. port. 22 cm. Reprint of the 1882 ed., which was issued as v. 5 of the Philosophical classics for English readers. [B2797.W3 1972] 72-4162 ISBN 0-8369-6894-8
1. Kant, Immanuel, 1724-1804. I. Series: Philosophical classics for English readers, v. 5. **BIP**

Kantrowitz, Arnie, 1940-

KANTROWITZ, Arnie, 301.41'57'0924
1940-
Under the rainbow : growing up gay / by Arnie Kantrowitz. New York : Morrow, 1977. 255 p. : ill. ; 22 cm. [HQ75.8.K36A37] 76-30442 ISBN 0-688-03191-9 : 8.95
1. Kantrowitz, Arnie, 1940- 2. Homosexuals, Male—United States—Biography. I. Title. **BIP**

KANTROWITZ, Arnie, 1940- 301.41'57'0924
Under the rainbow : growing up gay / Arnie Kantrowitz. New York : Pocket Books, 1978,c1977. 239 p. ; 18 cm. (A Kangaroo Book) [HQ75.8.K36A37] ISBN 0-671-81965-8 pbk. : 2.25
1. Kantrowitz, Arnie, 1940- 2. Homosexuals, Male—United States—Biography. I. Title.
L.C. card no. for 1977 Morrow edition: 76-30442.

Kao, Ch'i, 1336-1374.

MOTE, Frederick W 1922- 895.11
The poet Kao Ch'i, 1336-1374. Princeton, N. J., Princeton University Press, 1962. 261p. illus. 23cm. [PL2694.K3Z65] 62-7411
1. Kao, Ch'i, 1336-1374. I. Title.

Kapaun, Emil Joseph, 1916-1951.

TONNE, Arthur, 1904- 922.273
The story of Chaplain Kapaun, patriot priest of the Korean conflict. Emporia, Kan., Didde Publishers [1954] 255p. illus. 22cm. [BX4705.K32T6] 54-13151
1. Kapaun, Emil Joseph, 1916-1951. 2. Korean War, 1950-1953—Religious aspects. I. Title.

Kaplan, Chaim Aron, 1880-ca. 1942.

KAPLAN, Chaim Aron, 1880-ca.1942. 940.54'05
The Warsaw diary of Chaim A. Kaplan. Translated and edited by Abraham I. Katsh. Rev. ed. New York, Collier Books [1973] 410 p. maps. 21 cm. Translation of Megilat yisurin. [DS135.P62W27713 1973] 72-90277 2.95
1. Kaplan, Chaim Aron, 1880-ca. 1942. 2. Jews in Warsaw. 3. Holocaust, Jewish (1939-1945)—Warsaw. I. Title.

Kaplan, Gabriel—Juvenile literature.

JACOBS, Linda. 791.45'028'0924 B
Gabriel Kaplan, a spirit of laughter / by Linda Jacobs. St. Paul : EMC Corp., 1978. 39 p. : ill. ; 23 cm. (Headliners I) A biography of the comedian who gained fame with the television program, "Welcome Back Kotter." [PN2287.K24J3] 92 77-28232 ISBN 0-88436-428-3 lib. bdg. : 4.95. ISBN 0-88436-429-1 pbk. : 2.95
1. Kaplan, Gabriel—Juvenile literature. 2. Comedians—United States—Biography—Juvenile literature. I. Title. II. Series.

Kaplan, Mordecai Menahem, 1881-

EISENSTEIN, Ira, 1906- ed. 922.96
Morceaux choisis des ouvres de corneille [et al.] c6 New York, Jewish Reconstructionist Foundation, 1952. ix, 324 p. port. 21 cm. Includes bibliographical references. [BM40.E35] 52-2178
1. Kaplan, Mordecai Menahem, 1881- 2. Judaism—Addresses, essays, lectures. I. Kohn, Eugene, 1887- joint ed. II. Title. III. Title: M IV. Title: Morderai M. Kaplan
Contents Omitted.

Kaplun, Morris J.

ZALESKY, Moses, 1905- 361'.02'0924 B
Profile of purposeful living; the life story of Morris J. Kaplun. New York, Shengold Publishers [1968] 71 p. illus., ports. 23 cm. [CT275.K328Z3] 68-20083
1. Kaplun, Morris J. I. Title.

Kapodistrias, Ioannes Antoniou, Governor of Greece, 1776-1831.

WOODHOUSE, Christopher Montague, 1917- 949.5'05'0924 B
Capodistria: the founder of Greek independence [by] C. M. Woodhouse. London, New York, Oxford University Press, 1973. xi, 544 p., leaf. map, port. 25 cm. Bibliography: p. [514]-528. [DF815.K3W66 1973] 73-162273 ISBN 0-19-211196-5
1. Kapodistrias, Ioannes Antoniou, Governor of Greece, 1776-1831. I. Title.
Distributed by Oxford University Press N.Y; 32.00.

Kapp, Ardeth Greene, 1931-

KAPP, Ardeth Greene, 1931- 971.23'4
Echoes from my prairie / Ardeth Greene Kapp ; illustrated by Kathleen Pulsipher. Salt Lake City, Utah : Bookcraft, c1979. x, 112 p., [1] leaf of plates : ill. ; 23 cm. [F1079.5.G56K36] 79-53128 ISBN 0-88494-384-4 : 5.50
1. Kapp, Ardeth Greene, 1931- 2. Glenwood, Alta.—Biography. I. Title.

KAPP, Ardeth Greene, 1931- 289.3'3 B
Miracles in pinafores & bluejeans / Ardeth Greene Kapp. Salt Lake City : Deseret Book Co., 1977. 81 p. ; 24 cm. A woman shares the experiences of herself and others which exemplify the principles of living a spiritually enriched life. [BX8695.K35A35] 92 77-4268 ISBN 0-87747-644-6 : 3.95
1. Kapp, Ardeth Greene, 1931- 2. Mormons and Mormonism in Utah—Biography. I. Title.
BIP

Kaqawa, Toyohiko, 1888-1960.

DAVEY, Cyril James 922
Kagawa of Japan. Nashville, Abingdon Press [1961, c.1960] 150p. front. port. 61-16084 2.50 bds.,
1. Kaqawa, Toyohiko, 1888-1960. I. Title.

Karadja, Kyra.

KARADJA, Kyra. 947.08'092'4 B
Kyra's story : reminiscences of a girlhood in revolutionary Russia / by Kyra Karadja ; with a pref. by Margaret Mead. New York : Morrow, 1975. 283 p. ; 22 cm. [CT1218.K333A34] 75-14314 ISBN 0-688-02939-6
1. Karadja, Kyra. 2. Russia—History—Revolution, 1917-1921—Personal narratives. I. Title.

Kardiner, Abram, 1891-

KARDINER, Abram, 1891- 616.8'917'0924 B
My analysis with Freud : reminiscences / A. Kardiner. 1st ed. New York : Norton, c1977. 123 p. : port. ; 22 cm. [RC506.K37 1977] 76-55343 ISBN 0-393-01135-6 : 6.95
1. Kardiner, Abram, 1891- 2. Freud, Sigmund, 1856-1939. 3. Psychoanalysis—Biography. I. Title.

KARDINER, Abram, 1891- 616.8'917'0924 B
My analysis with Freud : reminiscences / A. Kardiner. 1st ed. New York : Norton, c1977. 123 p. : port. ; 22 cm. [RC506.K37 1977] 76-55343 ISBN 0-393-01135-6 : 6.95
1. Kardiner, Abram, 1891- 2. Freud, Sigmund, 1856-1939. 3. Psychoanalysis—Biography. I. Title.
BIP

Karelitz, Abraham Isaiah.

KAHANA, Kalman, 1910- v. 12
Rabbi Abraham Isaiah Karelitz, Hazon Ish. [New York, 1965?] 1 v. (unpaged) illus., port. 35 cm. Reprinted from Men of spirit, edited by Leo Jung, N.Y. Kymson, 1964. 68-58244
1. Karelitz, Abraham Isaiah. I. Title.

Karl I, Emperor of Austria, 1887-1922.

BROOK-SHEPHERD, Gordon, 1918- 943.6'04'0924 B
The last Habsburg [by] Gordon Brook-Shepherd. New York, Weybright and Talley [1969, c1968] xiii, 358 p. illus. 25 cm. Bibliography: p. 345-349. [DB92.B76 1969] 69-15585 10.00
1. Karl I, Emperor of Austria, 1887-1922. I. Title.

Karl v. Emperor of Germany, 1500-1558.

ARMSTRONG, Edward, 1846-1928. 943'.031'0924 B
The Emperor Charles V. Freeport, N.Y., Books for Libraries Press [1973] p. Reprint of the 1902 ed. published by Macmillan, London. Bibliography: [DD180.5.A73 1973] 73-4613 ISBN 0-518-19012-9
1. Karl V, Emperor of Germany, 1500-1558. 2. Germany—History—1519-1556. 3. Holy Roman Empire—History—Charles V, 1519-1556. I. Title.
BIP

FERNANDEZ Alvarez, Manuel, 1921- 943'.031'0924 B
Charles V : elected emperor and hereditary ruler / Manuel Fernandez Alvarez ; translated from the Spanish by J.A. Lalguna. London : Thames and Hudson, c1975. 220 p., [8] leaves of plates : ill. ; 23 cm. (Men in office) Includes index. Bibliography: p. [205]-208. [DD179.F4713] 76-359886 ISBN 0-500-87001-2 : 15.00
1. Karl V, Emperor of Germany, 1500-1558. 2. Germany—History—Charles V, 1519-1556. 3. Spain—History—Charles I, 1516-1556.
Distributed by Transatlantic Arts. BIP

OTTO, Archduke of Austria, 1912- 943'.031'0924
Charles V [by] Otto von Hapsburg. Translated from the French by Michael Ross. New York, Praeger [1970, c1969] xiv, 258 p. illus., ports. 23 cm. Translation of Charles Quint. Bibliography: p. 243-246. [DD179.O813 1970b] 76-100916 8.95
1. Karl V, Emperor of Germany, 1500-1558. I. Title.

ROBERTSON, William, 1721-1793. 943'.031'0924 B
The history of the reign of the Emperor Charles the Fifth. With an account of the Emporor's life after his abdication by William H. Prescott. Edited by Wilfred Harold Munro. Montezuma ed. New York, AMS Press [1968] 4 v. illus. 22 cm. (The Works of William H. Prescott, v. 12-15) Reprint of the 1904 ed. Includes bibliographical references. [DD179.R6 1968] 72-186525
1. Karl V, Emperor of Germany, 1500-1558. 2. Holy Roman Empire—History—Charles V, 1519-1556. 3. Europe—History—1492-1643. I. Prescott, William Hickling, 1796-1859. II. Title.

SCHWARZENFELD, Gertrude von. 923.143
Charles V, father of Europe [Translation from the original German by Ruth Mary Bethell.] Chicago, H. Regnery Co., 1957. 306p. illus. 23cm. [DP172.S36] 57-4864
1. Karl v. Emperor of Germany, 1500-1558. I. Title.

TYLER, Royall, 1884-1953. 923.143
The Emperor Charles the Fifth. Foreword by Carl J. Burckhardt. Fair Lawn, N. J., Essential Books, 1956. 375p. illus., ports. (1 col.) maps (on lining papers (1 fol.)) facsim., geneal. tables. 25cm. 'Sources and bibliography': p. 351-369. [DD180.5.T9] 56-14317
1. Karl v, Emperor of Germany, 1500-1558. I. Title.

Karl V, Emperor of Germany, 1500-1558—Juvenile literature.

GRANT, Neil. 943'.031'0924 B
Charles V, Holy Roman Emperor. New York, F. Watts [1970] 217 p. maps, geneal. table. 22 cm. (Immortals of history) Includes bibliographical references. A biography of the Holy Roman Emperor whose reign influenced almost every important event in Western history between 1516 and 1556. [DD180.5.G7] 92 79-104187
1. Karl V, Emperor of Germany, 1500-1558—Juvenile literature. I. Title.

Karl XII, King of Sweden, 1682-1718.

BAIN, Robert Nisbet, 1854-1909. 948'.503'0924 B
Charles XII and the collapse of the Swedish Empire, 1682-1719. Freeport, N.Y., Books for Libraries Press [1969] xviii, 320 p. illus., map, plans, ports. 23 cm. (Select bibliographies reprint series) Reprint of the 1895 ed. "Original documents": p. vi-vii. [DL732.B16 1969] 70-95062
1. Karl XII, King of Sweden, 1682-1718. 2. Sweden—History—Charles XII, 1697-1718. I. Title.

BENGTSSON, Frans Gunnar, 1894-1954. 923.1485
The sword does not jest; the heroic life of King Charles XII of Sweden. Translated from the Swedish by Naomi Walford. With an introd. by Eric Linklater. New York, St. Martin's Press, 1960. 495 p. illus. 23 cm. Translation of Karl XII:s levnad. [DL732.B413] 60-13877
1. Karl XII, King of Sweden, 1682-1718. I. Title.

HATTON, Ragnhild Marie. 948.5'03'0924 B
Charles XII of Sweden [by] R. M. Hatton. New York, Weybright and Talley [1969, c1968] xvii, 656 p. illus., maps, plan, ports. 25 cm. Bibliography: p. [531]-542. [DL732.H35 1969] 69-10605 15.00
1. Karl XII, King of Sweden, 1682-1718.

LIFE of Charles the twelfth King of Sweden, 1697-1718. v. 12
Translated from the Swedish by Naomi Walford. With an introduction by Eric Linklater. London, Macmillan; New York, St. Martin's Press, 1960. xiv, 495p. illus., plates, ports., maps. Translation of Karl XII, slevnad.
1. Karl XII, king of Sweden, 1682-1718. I. Bengtsson, Frans Gunnar, 1894-1954.

Karloff, Boris, 1887-1969.

JENSEN, Paul M. 791.43'028'0924 B
Boris Karloff and his films, by Paul M. Jensen. South Brunswick, A. S. Barnes [1974] 194 p. illus. 27 cm. Bibliography: p. 173-176. [PN2287.K25J4] 72-9940 ISBN 0-498-01324-3
1. Karloff, Boris, 1887-1969. I. Title. BIP

LINDSAY, Cynthia Hobart. 791.43'028'0924 B
Dear Boris : the life of William Henry Pratt / Cynthia Lindsay. 1st ed. New York : Knopf, 1975. p. cm. Filmography: p. [PN2287.K25L5] 74-21295 ISBN 0-394-47579-8 : 12.50
1. Karloff, Boris, 1887-1969. I. Title.

UNDERWOOD, Peter, 1923- 791.43'028'0924 B
Karloff; the life of Boris Karloff, with an appendix of the films in which he appeared. [New York] Drake Publishers [1972] 238 p. illus. 23 cm. Bibliography: p. 168-169. [PN2287.K25U5] 72-192923 ISBN 0-87749-258-1 5.95
1. Karloff, Boris, 1887-1969.

Karo, Lindon.

KARO, Nancy. 242'.4
Adventure in dying / by Nancy Karo, with Alvera Mickelsen. Chicago : Moody Press, c1976. 223 p. ; 22 cm. [BT993.2.K37] 76-809 ISBN 0-8024-0141-4 pbk. : 3.50
1. Karo, Lindon. 2. Apostles' Creed—Sermons. 3. Baptists—Sermons. 4. Sermons, American. 5. Cancer patients—Biography. 6. Baptists—Clergy—Biography. 7. Clergy—United States—Biography. I. Mickelsen, Alvera, joint author. II. Title.
BIP

Karpis, Alvin.

KARPIS, Alvin. 364.1'0924 B
The Alvin Karpis story, by Alvin Karpis, with Bill Trent. New York, Coward, McCann & Geoghegan [1971] 256 p. illus., ports. 22 cm. [HV6248.K36A3] 78-136446 6.95
I. Trent, Bill. II. Title.

Karpov, Anatolii Evgen'evich.

KARPOV, Anatolii Evgen'evich. 794.1'092'4 B
Anatoly Karpov : chess is my life / by Anatoly Karpov and Alexandr Roshal ; translated by Kenneth P. Neat. Oxford ; New York : Pergamon Press, 1979. p. cm. (Pergamon chess series) (Pergamon international library of science, technology,

engineering, and social studies) Translation of Shakhmaty—moia zhizn'. Includes index. [GV1439.K37A3713 1979] 78-41215 ISBN 0-08-023118-7 : 30.00 ISBN 0-08-023119-5 pbk. : 14.00
1. Karpov, Anatolii Evgen'evich. 2. Chess players—Russia—Biography. I. Roshal', Aleksandr, joint author. II. Title: Chess is my life. **BIP**

Karras, Alex.

KARRAS, Alex. 796.33'2'0924 B
Even big guys cry / Alex Karras with Herb Gluck. 1st ed. New York : Holt, Rinehart and Winston, c1977. p. cm. [GV939.K3A34] 77-71376 ISBN 0-03-017371-X : 8.95
1. Karras, Alex. 2. Football players—United States—Biography. I. Gluck, Herb. II. Title. **BIP**

Karras, Alex—Juvenile literature.

KARRAS, Alex. 796.33'2'092 B
Alex Karras : my life in football, television, and movies / Alex Karras ; conceived and produced by Whitehall, Hadlyme & Smith, inc. 1st ed. Garden City, N.Y. : Doubleday, c1979. 86 p. : ill. ; 22 cm. (An I want to know about book) Includes index. The author describes his experiences growing up in Gary, Indiana, and his careers as a football player, actor, and television personality. [GV939.K3A33] 92 78-18138 ISBN 0-385-12529-1 : 5.95. ISBN 0-385-12530-5 lib.bdg. : 6.90
1. Karras, Alex—Juvenile literature. 2. Football players—United States—Biography—Juvenile literature. I. Whitehall, Hadlyme & Smith. II. Title. **BIP**

Karsavina, Tamara.

KARSAVINA, Tamara 927.93
Theatre Street; the reminiscences of Tamara Karsavina. Rev. ed. New York, Dutton, 1961 [c.1931, 1950] 301p. illus., (Everyman paperback D71) 1.45 pap.,
1. Ballet. I. Title.

KARSAVINA, Tamara. 927.93
Theatre Street; the reminiscences of Tamara Karsavina. New ed., rev. and enl. New York, Dutton [1950] xi, 301 p. illus., ports. 22 cm. [GV1785.K3A3 1950] 50-241
1. Ballet. I. Title.

KARSAVINA, Tamara. 792.8'092'4 B
Theatre Street; the reminiscences of Tamara Karsavina. [Brooklyn, N.Y.] Dance Horizons [1973? c1950] xi, 301 p. illus. 21 cm. (A Dance horizons republication 43) Reprint of the ed. published by Dutton, New York. [GV1785.K3A3 1973] 73-77506 ISBN 0-87127-043-9 4.95
1. Karsavina, Tamara. 2. Ballet. I. Title.

KARSAVINA, Tamara. 792.8'092'4 B
Theatre Street; the reminiscences of Tamara Karsavina. [Brooklyn, N.Y.] Dance Horizons [1973? c1950] xi, 301 p. illus 21 cm. (A Dance horizons republication 43) Reprint of the ed. published by Dutton, New York. [GV1785.K3A3 1973] 73-77506 ISBN 0-87127-043-9 4.95 (pbk.)
1. Karsavina, Tamara 2. Ballet. I. Title.

Karsh, Yousuf,

KARSH, Yousuf, 1908- 927.7
In search of greatness; reflections of Yousuf Karsh. New York, Knopf, 1962. 210 p. illus. 23 cm. [TR140.K3A3] 62-52117
I. Title.

Karsh, Yousuf, 1908-

KARSH, Yousuf, 1908- 927.7
In search of greatness; reflections of Yousuf Karsh. New York, Knopf, 1962. 210 p. illus. 23 cm. [TR140.K3A3] 62-52117
I. Title.

KARSH, Yousuf, 1908- 779'.2'0924
Karsh Canadians / Yousuf Karsh. Toronto ; Buffalo : University of Toronto Press, c1978. 203 p. : ports. ; 31 cm. [TR681.T3K375] 79-302029 ISBN 0-8020-2317-7 :
1. Karsh, Yousuf, 1908- 2. Photography—Portraits. 3. Canada—Biography—Portraits. I. Title.

Kartsonakis, Dino.

KARTSONAKIS, Dino. 786.2'1'0924 B
The Dino story / Dino Kartsonakis ; with Jeanette Lockerbie. Old Tappan, N.J. : F. H. Revell Co., [1975] 128 p. : ill. ; 21 cm. [ML417.K3A3] 75-4518 ISBN 0-8007-0733-8 : 4.95
1. Kartsonakis, Dino. I. Lockerbie, Jeanette W. II. Title. **BIP**

Kashishian, Pearl, 1888-1977.

DYER, Donita. 973'.04'91992 B
Pearl, her love touched two worlds / Donita Dyer. Wheaton, Ill. : Tyndale House, 1977. 254 p. ; 21 cm. [CT275.K356D9] 77-72445 ISBN 0-8423-4813-1 pbk. : 4.95
1. Kashishian, Pearl, 1888-1977. 2. United States—Biography. 3. Armenian Americans—Biography. I. Title.

Kasper, Maria, 1820-1898.

MEAGHER, George T 922.243
With attentive ear and courageous heart; a biography of Mother Mary Kasper, foundress of the Poor Handmaids of Jesus Christ. Milwaukee, Bruce Press [c1957] xii, 258p. illus., port. 23cm. (Catholic life publications) [BX4705.K3M38] 58-562
1. Kasper, Maria, 1820-1898. 2. Poor Handmaids of Jesus Christ. I. Title.

Kataev, Valentin Petrovich, 1897- — Biography.

KATAEV, Valentin Petrovich, 1897- 891.7'3'42 B
A mosaic of life : or, The magic horn of Oberon : memoirs of a Russian childhood / Valentin Katayev ; translated by Moira Budberg and Gordon Latta. Chicago : J. P. O'Hara, c1976. 447 p. ; 24 cm. Translation of Razbitaia zhizn', ili Volshebnyi rog Oberona. [PG3476.K4Z5213] 75-10698 15.00
1. Kataev, Valentin Petrovich, 1897- — Biography. I. Title.

KATAEV, Valentin Petrovich, 1897- 891.7'3'42 B
A mosaic of life : or, The magic horn of Oberon : memoirs of a Russian childhood / [by] Valentin Katayev ; translated [from the Russian] by Moira Budberg and Gordon Latta. London : Angus and Robertson, 1976. 447 p. ; 24 cm. Translation of Razbitaia zhizn', ili Volshebnyi rog Oberona. [PG3476.K4Z5213 1976b] 77-472306 ISBN 0-207-95644-8 : £7.50
1. Kataev, Valentin Petrovich, 1897- — Biography. 2. Authors, Russian—20th century—Biography. I. Title.

Katayama, Sen, 1859-1983.

KUBLIN, Hyman. 923.252
Asian revolutionary; the life of Sen Katayama. Princeton, N. J., Princeton University Press, 1964. xiii, 370 p. ports. 23 cm. Bibliography: p.241-362. [HX412.K33Ks] 63-7156
1. Katayama, Sen, 1859-1983. 2. Socialism in Japan. I. Title.

Katherine (Name)—Juvenile literature.

GLAZER, Tom. 929.4
All about your name, Katherine : Catherine, Cathy, Kate, Katie, Kathy / by Tom Glazer ; illustrated by Demi. 1st ed. Garden City, N.Y. : Doubleday, c1978. 46 p. : ill. ; 22 cm. Discusses the name Katherine and people of historical significance who have held that name. [CS2391.K37G57] 77-15151 ISBN 0-385-06536-1 : 4.95. ISBN 0-385-06476-4 lib.bdg. : 5.90
1. Katherine (Name)—Juvenile literature. 2. Biography—Miscellanea—Juvenile literature. I. Hitz, Demi. II. Title.

Katselas, Tasso,

KATSELAS, Tasso, 1927- 720'.924
Tasso Katselas: architect, planner. [Edited by Edith Wile and Jules Ehrman. Pittsburgh, Geyer Print. Co.; distributed by Stricker Associates, c1969] [58] p. illus. (part col. (1 fold.)), plans, col. port. 30 cm. Cover title. [NA737.K36A55] 77-248134
I. Title.

Katsushika, Hokusai, 1760-1849.

RIPLEY, Elizabeth. 760'.0924 B
Hokusai, a biography. [1st ed.] Philadelphia, Lippincott [1968] 71 p. illus. 27 cm. Bibliography: p. 70. The life of the eighteenth-century Japanese artist whose many sketches, prints, and paintings of flowers, animals, and landscapes brought him lasting fame and popularity. [ND1059.K23R5] 92 AC 68
1. Katsushika, Hokusai, 1760-1849. I. Title.

STRANGE, Edward Fairbrother, 1862-1929. 760'.092'4 B
Hokusai, the old man mad with painting / by Edward F. Strange. Folcroft, Pa. : Folcroft Library Editions, 1977. 71 p., [9] leaves of plates : ill. ; 22 cm. Reprint of the 1906 ed. published by Siegel, Hill, London, which was issued as v. 17 of the Langham series. [NE1325.K3S77 1977] 77-357 ISBN 0-8414-7753-1 lib. bdg. : 10.00
1. Katsushika, Hokusai, 1760-1849. 2. Printmakers—Japan—Biography. I. Title. II. Series: The Langham series ; v. 17. **BIP**

Katz, Alex, 1927-

KATZ, Alex, 1927- 709'.2'4
Alex Katz / by Irving Sandler. New York : H. N. Abrams, 1979. 222 p. : ill. (some col.) ; 28 x 30 cm. Bibliography: p. 216-219. [N6537.K32A4 1979] 78-12470 ISBN 0-8109-1202-3 : 55.00
1. Katz, Alex, 1927- 2. Artists—United States—Biography. I. Sandler, Irving, 1925- **BIP**

Katz, Arthur,

KATZ, Arthur, 1929- 301.451'924'024 B
Ben Israel; the odyssey of a modern Jew, by Arthur Katz, with Jamie Buckingham. Plainfield, N.J., Logos International [1970] 207 p. 22 cm. Autobiographical. [E184.J5K24] 79-95765 ISBN 0-912106-05-0 4.95
I. Buckingham, Jamie. II. Title.

Katz, Josef, 1918-

KATZ, Josef, 1918- 940.54'05 B
One who came back; the diary of a Jewish survivor. Translated from the German by Hilda Reach. New York, Herzl Press [1973] x, 277 p. 22 cm. [D810.J4K286] 73-75616 6.95
1. Katz, Josef, 1918- 2. World War, 1939-1945—Personal narratives, Jewish. I. Title.

Katz, Myron.

KATZ, Myron. 790.2'092'4 B
Papa, play for me : the hilarious, heartwarming autobiography of comedian and bandleader Mickey Katz / by Mickey Katz, as told to Hannibal Coons ; introd. by Joel Grey. New York : Simon and Schuster, c1977. 223 p. : ill. ; 23 cm. [PN2287.K27A36] 77-9951 ISBN 0-671-22543-X : 7.95
1. Katz, Myron. 2. Entertainers—United States—Biography. I. Coons, Hannibal. II. Title.

Katzer, Friedrich Xaver, Abp., 1844-1903.

BLIED, Benjamin Joseph, 1908- 922.273
Three archbishops of Milwaukee: Michael Heiss (1818-1890) Frederick Katzer (1844-1903) Sebastian Messmer (1847-1930) Milwaukee, 1955. 160p. 23cm. [BX1417.M5B5] 55-30113
1. Heiss, Michael, Abp., 1818-1890. 2. Katzer, Friedrich Xaver, Abp., 1844-1903. 3. Messmer, Sebastian Gebhard, Abp., 1847-1930. 4. Bishops—U. S.—Milwaukee. I. Title.

Kauffman, Daniel, Bp.

GINEGRICH, Alice (Kauffman) 922.8773
Life and times of Daniel Kauffman. Scottdale, Pa., Herald Press [1954] 160p. illus. 21cm. [BX8143.K3G5] 54-11502
1. Kauffman, Daniel, Bp. I. Title.

Kauffmann, Maria Anna Angelica Catharina, 1741-1807.

MANNERS, Victoria Alexandra Elizabeth Dorothy, Lady, 1876-1933. 759.9494 B
Angelica Kauffmann, R. A., her life and her works / by Lady Victoria Manners and G. C. Williamson. New York : Hacker Art Books, 1976. xiii, 268 p., [32] leaves of plates : ill. ; 28 cm. Reprint of the 1924 ed. published by Bodley Head, London. Includes index. Bibliography: p. 247. [ND853.K29M36 1976] 75-10527 ISBN 0-87817-183-5 lib.bdg. : 40.00
1. Kauffmann, Maria Anna Angelica Catharina, 1741-1807. 2. Painters—Switzerland—Biography. I. Williamson, George Charles, 1858-1942, joint author.

Kaufman, George Simon, 1889-1961.

GOLDSTEIN, Malcolm. 812'.5'2
George S. Kaufman : his life, his theater / Malcolm Goldstein. New York : Oxford University Press, 1979. p. cm. [PS3521.A727Z67] 79-12819 ISBN 0-19-502623-3 : 20.00
1. Kaufman, George Simon, 1889-1961. 2. Dramatists, American—20th century—Biography. I. Title. **BIP**

TEICHMANN, Howard. 812.5'2 B
George S. Kaufman; an intimate portrait. [New York] [Dell Publishing Co.] [1973, c1972] 332 p. illus. 18 cm. Bibliography: p. [308]-315. [[PS3521.A727Z9]] 1.95 (pbk)
1. Kaufman, George Simon 1889-1961. I. Title.

TEICHMANN, Howard 812'.5'2 B
George S. Kaufman; an intimate portrait. [1st ed.] New York, Atheneum, 1972. xiv, 371 p. illus. 24 cm. Bibliography: p. 355-361. [PS3521.A727Z9] 72-75262 ISBN 0-689-10508-8 10.00
1. Kaufman, George Simon, 1889-1961.

Kaufman, George Simon, 1889-1961—Biography.

MEREDITH, Scott. 812'.5'2 B
George S. Kaufman and his friends. [1st ed.] Garden City, N.Y., Doubleday, 1974. xvi, 723 p. illus. 24 cm. Bibliography: p. 681-704. [PS3521.A727Z75] 73-22632 ISBN 0-385-01566-6
1. Kaufman, George Simon, 1889-1961—Biography. I. Title.

Kaufman, Murray

KAUFMAN, Murray 791.450924
Murray the K tells it like it is, baby Forewords by Tony Bennett [others 1st ed] New York Holt [1966] 127 p. illus. (pt.col.) ports. 26 cm. Includes the unacc. melodies "It's what's happening, Baby" (p.[74]) and "You're what's happening, Baby" (p.[87]) [ML429.K38A3] 66-216115 bds 3.95
I. Title.

***Kaufmann, Helen L.**

*KAUFMANN, Helen L. 927
Anvil chorus: the story of Guiseppe Verdi. Illus. by Vivian Berger. New York, Hawthorn [c.1964] 185p. 22cm. (Credo bk.) 64-21459 2.95
I. Title.

Kaunda, Kenneth David, Pres. Zambia, 1924-

HATCH, John Charles. 967.8'04'0924 B
Two African statesmen : Kaunda of Zambia and Nyerere of Tanzania / John Hatch. Chicago : Regnery, 1976. xv, 268 p., [4] leaves of plates : ill. ; 25 cm. [DT963.82.K39H37 1976b] 76-6268 ISBN 0-8092-8405-7 : 15.00. ISBN 0-8092-7979-7 pbk. : 5.95
1. Kaunda, Kenneth David, Pres. Zambia, 1921- 2. Nyerere, Julius Kambage, Pres. Tanzania, 1922- 3. Zambia—Presidents—Biography. 4. Tanzania—Presidents—Biography. I. Title. **BIP**

HATCH, John Charles. 968.9'4'04'0924 B
Two African statesmen : Kaunda of Zambia and Nyerere of Tanzania / John Hatch. London : Secker & Warburg, 1976. xv, 268 p., [4] leaves of plates : ill. ; 24 cm. Includes index. [DT963.82.K39H37] 76-369276 ISBN 0-436-19127-X : £6.00
1. Kaunda, Kenneth David, Pres. Zambia, 1924- 2. Nyerere, Julius Kambarage, Pres. Tanzania, 1922- 3. Zambia—Presidents—Biography. 4. Tanzania—Presidents—Biography. I. Kaunda, Kenneth David, Pres. Zambia, 1924- II. Nyerere, Julius Kambarage, Pres. Tanzania, 1922- III. Title.

MACPHERSON, Fergus. 968.9'4'040924 B
Kenneth Kaunda of Zambia : the times and the man / Fergus Macpherson. Lusaka ; New York : Oxford University Press, 1974, [i.e.1975] xviii, 478 p., [9] leaves of plates : ill. ; 22 cm. Includes index. Bibliography: p. [466]-469. [DT963.82.K39M3 1974] 75-312699 ISBN 0-19-572338-4 : 10.75
1. Kaunda, Kenneth David, Pres. Zambia, 1924- I. Title. **BIP**

Kaunda, Kenneth David, Pres. Zambia, 1924- —Juvenile literature.

POLATNICK, Florence T. 968.9'4'00994 B
Zambia's president, Kenneth Kaunda, by Florence T. Polatnick and Alberta L. Saletan. New York, J. Messner [1972] 188 p. 22 cm. Bibliography: p. 181-182. A biography of the African leader, Kenneth Kaunda, who practiced non-violence in the long struggle to bring progress to Zambia. [DT963.6.K3P64] 92 76-176378 ISBN 0-671-32498-5 4.50
1. Kaunda, Kenneth David, Pres. Zambia, 1924- —Juvenile literature. I. Saletan, Alberta L., joint author. II. Title.

Kause, Selma.

KAUSE, Selma. 917.3039
Mahalo. Illus. by Chuck Winter. Tucson, Ariz., Rutz Press [1965] 373 p. illus. 21 cm. Autobiographical. [CT275.K39A3] 65-26658
I. Title.

KAUSE, Selma. 917.3039
Mahalo, nui, nui aloha. Illus. by Chuck Winter. Tucson, Ariz., Post Printing, inc. [c1966] 341 p. illus. 21 cm. Autobiographical. [CT275.K39A32] 66-29638
I. Title.

Kautsky, Karl, 1854-1938.

STEENSON, Gary P., 1944- 335.4'092'4 B
Karl Kautsky, 1854-1938 : Marxism in the classical years / Gary P. Steenson. Pittsburgh : University of Pittsburgh Press, c1978. p. cm. Bibliography: p. [HX273.K34S7] 78-3701 ISBN 0-8229-3377-2 : 15.95
1. Kautsky, Karl, 1854-1938. 2. Socialism. 3. Socialists—Biography.

Kavanagh, Arthur Macmurrough, 1831-1889.

MCCORMICK, Donald 1911- 923.2415
The incredible Mr. Kavanagh. New York, Devin-Adair Co., 1961 [c.1960] 205p. illus. Bibl. 61-4428 5.00
1. Kavanagh, Arthur Macmurrough, 1831-1889. I. Title.

Kavanagh, Patrick,

KAVANAGH, Patrick, 1905- 928.2
The green fool. New York, Harper, 1939. 350 p. 22 cm. [PR6021.A74G7] 39-27139
I. Title.

Kavanagh, Peter.

KAVANAGH, Peter. 821
Lapped furrows; correspondence, 1933-1967, between Patrick and Peter Kavanagh, with other documents. Edited by Peter Kavanagh. New York, P. Kavanagh Hand Press [1969] 307 p. 24 cm. [PR6021.A747Z54] 70-12971
I. Kavanagh, Patrick, 1904-1967. II. Title.

Kavanagh, Peter—Biography.

KAVANAGH, Peter. 821'.9'14 B
Beyond affection : an autobiography / Peter Kavanagh. 1st ed. New York : P. Kavanagh Hand Press, 1978,c1977 v, 201 p. ; 24 cm. [PR6021.A747Z514] 76-57462 20.00
1. Kavanagh, Peter—Biography. 2. Kavanagh, Patrick, 1904-1967—Biography. 3. Authors, Irish—20th century—Biography. I. Title.

Kawakami, Hajime, 1879-1946.

BERNSTEIN, Gail. 335.43'092'4 B
Japanese Marxist : a portrait of Kawakami Hajime, 1879-1946 / Gail Lee Bernstein. Cambridge, Mass. : Harvard University Press, 1976. p. cm. (Harvard East Asian series ; 86) Includes index. Bibliography: p. [HX412.K345B47] 76-20516 ISBN 0-674-47193-8 : 13.00
1. Kawakami, Hajime, 1879-1946. I. Title. II. Series.

Kay Co., Okla.—History.

DAUGHTERS of the American Revolution. Oklahoma. Ponoa City Chapter. 917.66'24'0340922 B
The last run, Kay County, Oklahoma, 1893; stories. [3d ed.] Ponoa City, Okla., Courier Print. Co., 1939. [Ponoa City, Okla., Skinner & Son Print. Co., 1970] 352 p. illus. 28 cm. [F702.K23D3 1970] 72-169899
1. Kay Co., Okla.—History. I. Title.

Kay, John, 1742-1826.

*EVANS, Hilary. 709.2
John Kay of Edinburgh; barber, miniaturist and soccial commentator 1742-1826, [by] Hilary and Mary Evans. Aberdeen, Impulse, 1973. 53 p. illus. 26 cm. [N44]
1. Kay, John, 1742-1826. 2. Artists—Biography and works. I. Evans, Mary, joint author. II. Title.
Distributed by International Publications Service, N.Y., for 22.50.

Kaye, Danny, 1913-

SINGER, Kurt D., 1911- 927.92
The Danny Kaye story. New York, T. Nelson [1958] 241 p. 22 cm. [PN2287.K3S5] 58-13652
1. Kaye, Danny, 1913-

Kaye, Morris, 1901- —Juvenile literature.

SOBOL, Harriet Langsam. 301.42'7
Grandpa, a young man grown old / by Harriet Langsam Sobol ; photos. by Patricia Agre. New York : Coward, McCann & Geoghegan, [1980] p. cm. A 17-year-old's views of her grandfather are juxtaposed with his descriptions of his life. [HQ1061.K39S6] 92 79-20133 ISBN 0-698-20508-1 : 8.95
1. Kaye, Morris, 1901- —Juvenile literature. 2. Aged—Biography—Juvenile literature. 3. Jews in the United States—Juvenile literature. 4. Grandfathers—Juvenile literature. I. Agre, Patricia. II. Title.

Kayira, Legson.

KAYIRA, Legson. 920
I will try. [1st ed.] Garden City, N.Y., Doubleday, 1965. 251 p. 22 cm. Autobiographical. [CT2750.K3A3] 65-13099
I. Title.

Kaytor, Lyn Maureen.

KAYTOR, Evelyn. 362.4'3'0924 B
Born to live; the inspiring story of Lyn Kaytor. Mountain View, Calif., Pacific Press Pub. Association [1974] 109 p. ports. 22 cm. (A Destiny book, D-146) [RD796.K38K36] 74-78781 2.95 (pbk.).
1. Kaytor, Lyn Maureen. 2. Handicapped—Personal narratives. I. Title.

Kazan, Elia.

KAZAN, Elia. 791.43'0233'0924 B
Kazan on Kazan [by] Michel Ciment. New York, Viking Press [1974] 199 p. illus. 20 cm. (Cinema one, 26) A series of taped interviews conducted by M. Ciment, chiefly in Aug. 1971. "Biofilmography, by Michel Ciment and Olivier Eyquem": p. 180-199. [PN1998.A3K345 1974] 73-11978 ISBN 0-670-41187-6 7.50
1. Kazan, Elia. I. Ciment, Michel, 1938- II. Title. **BIP**

Kazantzakes, Nikos, 1883-1957.

KAZANTZAKE, Helene. 889'.8'3209 B
Nikos Kazantzakis; a biography based on his letters, by Helen Kazantzakis. Translated by Amy Mims. New York, Simon and Schuster [1968] 589 p. ports. 25 cm. Translation of Le dissident. [PA5610.K39Z77] 68-14840 12.00
1. Kazantzakes, Nikos, 1883-1957.

Kazimierz, Saint, 1458-1484.

UMINSKI, Sigmund H. 282'.0924 B
The royal prince; the story of Saint Casimir, by Sigmund H. Uminski. With a foreword by Alfred L. Abramowicz. New York, Polish Publication Society of America [1971] xiii, 146 p. illus., ports. 22 cm. Bibliography: p. 136-141. [BX4700.K3U55] 76-147844 4.00
1. Kazimierz, Saint, 1458-1484. I. Title.

Kazin, Alfred, 1915-

KAZIN, Alfred, 1915- 810.9 B
New York Jew / Alfred Kazin. 1st ed. New York : Knopf : distributed by Random House, 1978. 307 p. ; 25 cm. Includes index. [PS29.K38A36] 78-1932 ISBN 0-394-49567-5 : 12.50
1. Kazin, Alfred, 1915- 2. Critics—United States—Biography. 3. American literature—20th century—History and criticism. I. Title. **BIP**

KAZIN, Alfred, 1915- 810'.9 B
New York Jew / Alfred Kazin. 1st Vintage Books edition. New York : Vintage Books, 1979. 464 p. ; 18 cm. Includes index. [PS29.K38A36 1979] 78-23501 ISBN 0-394-72867-X pbk. : 4.95
1. Kazin, Alfred, 1915- 2. Critics—United States—Biography. 3. American literature—20th century—History and criticism. 4. New York (City)—Intellectual life. I. Title.

Kean, Edmund, 1787-1833.

DISHER, Maurice Willson, 1893- 927.92
Mad genius; a biography of Edmund Kean with particular reference to the women who made and unmade him. London, New York, Hutchinson, 1950. 196 p. plates. 24 cm. [PN2598.K3D5] 51-7620
1. Kean, Edmund, 1787-1833. I. Title.

FITZSIMONS, Raymund. 792'.028'0924 B
Edmund Kean : fire from heaven / by Raymund Fitzsimons. London : Hamilton, 1976. xiii, 255 p., 8 p. of plates : ill., ports. ; 23 cm. Includes index. Bibliography: p. [240]-244. [PN2598.K3F44 1976b] 76-371409 ISBN 0-241-89337-2 : £5.25
1. Kean, Edmund, 1787-1833. 2. Actors—Great Britain—Biography. **BIP**

FITZSIMONS, Raymund. 792'.028'0924 B
Edmund Kean, fire from heaven / by Raymund Fitzsimons. New York : Dial Press, 1976. xiii, 255 p., [4] leaves of plates : ill. ; 22 cm. Includes index. Bibliography: p. [240]-244. [PN2598.K3F44] 76-176 ISBN 0-8037-4533-8 : 8.95
1. Kean, Edmund, 1787-1833. I. Title.

HAWKINS, Frederick William, 1849-1900. 792'.028'0924 B
The life of Edmund Kean. London, 1869. New York, B. Blom, 1969. 2 v. 21 cm. [PN2598.K3H3 1969] 76-82831
1. Kean, Edmund, 1787-1833. **BIP**

HILLEBRAND, Harold Newcomb, 1887-1953. 792'.028'0924 B
Edmund Kean. New York, AMS Press, 1966 [c1933] viii, 387 p. illus. 23 cm. [PN2598.K3H5 1966] 77-181904
1. Kean, Edmund, 1787-1833. **BIP**

PLAYFAIR, Giles, 1910- 792'.028'0924
Kean. Westport, Conn., Greenwood Press [1973, c1939] viii, 347 p. illus. 23 cm. Reprint of the ed. published by E. P. Dutton, New York. Includes bibliographical references. [PN2598.K3P5 1973] 73-10878 ISBN 0-8371-7047-8 15.00
1. Kean, Edmund, 1787-1833. **BIP**

PROCTER, Bryan Waller, 1787-1874. 792'.028'0924 B
The life of Edmund Kean [by] B. W. Procter (Barry Cornwall) New York, B. Blom, 1969. 2 v. in 1. port. 21 cm. Reprint of the 1835 ed. [PN2598.K3P7 1969] 70-82840
1. Kean, Edmund, 1787-1833. I. Title. **BIP**

Kearl family.

TAYLOR, Alley Vernon Johnson, 1895- 929'.2'0973
Kearl family history; biographies of James Kearl, 1833-1902, his wives and posterity. Editor: Alley V. Johnson Taylor. 1st ed. Provo, Utah, Printed by J. G. Stevenson [1963?- v. 25 cm. [CS71.K226] 65-67224
1. Kearl family. I. Title.

Kearney, Peadar, 1883-1942.

KEARNEY, Peadar, 1883-1942. 365'.6'0924 B
My dear Eva : letters written from Ballykinlar Internment Camp (1921) / by Peadar Kearney ; introduced by Seamus de Burca. Dublin : P. J. Bourke, 1976. 43 p. : ill. ; 23 cm. [HV9647.K4A45 1976] 77-358929 ISBN 0-85163-032-4 : £1.00 ($3.00 U.S.)
1. Kearney, Peadar, 1883-1942. 2. Political prisoners—Great Britain—Biography. I. Title.

Kearny, Philip, 1815-1862.

WERSTEIN, Irving. 923.5
Kearny, the magnificent; the story of General Philip Kearny, 1815-1862. New York, John Day Co. [1962] 248 p. illus. 21 cm. Includes bibliography. [E467.1.K24W4] 62-10957
1. Kearny, Philip, 1815-1862. I. Title.

Kearny's Expedition, 1846—Juvenile literature.

SCHMIDT, James Norman, 1912- 973.6'23'0924
Kearny rode west, by James Norman. New York, Putnam [1971] 190 p. 22 cm. (American battles and campaigns) Traces the events of the 1846 expedition, led by Army officer Stephen Watts Kearny, which helped to expand the United States frontier to the California coast. [E405.2.S35 1971] 79-133928 4.29
1. Kearny's Expedition, 1846—Juvenile literature. 2. Kearny's Expedition, 1846. I. Title.

Kearny, Stephen Watts, 1794-1848.

CLARKE, Dwight Lancelot, 1885- 923.573
Stephen Watts Kearny, soldier of the West. 1st ed. Norman, University of Oklahoma Press 1961 xv, 448 p. illus., ports, fold. map. 24 cm. "Notes on sources": p. 401-426. [E403.1.K2C5] 61-15148
1. Kearny, Stephen Watts, 1794-1848. I. Title.

Keaton, Buster,

KEATON, Buster, 1895-1966. 927.92
My wonderful world of slapstick [by] Buster Keaton with Charles Samuels. [1st ed.] Garden City, N. Y., Doubleday, 1960. 282 p. illus. 22 cm. [PN2287.K4A3] 60-5934
I. Title.

Keaton, Buster, 1895-1966.

BLECH, Rudi, 1899- 791.430924 (B)
Keaton. New York, Macmillan [1966] xii, 395 p. illus., ports. 24 cm. [PN2287.K4B5] 66-13563
1. Keaton, Buster, 1895-1966. I. Title. BIP

DARDIS, Tom. 791.43'028'0924 B
Keaton, the man who wouldn't lie down / Tom Dardis. New York : Scribner, c1979. xi, 340 p. : ill. ; 24 cm. Includes index. Filmography: p. 285-317. [PN2287.K4D3] 79-857 ISBN 0-684-16150-8 : 12.50
1. Keaton, Buster, 1895-1966. 2. Moving-picture actors and actresses—United States—Biography. 3. Comedians—United States—Biography. I. Title.

KEATON, Buster, 1895-1966. 927.92
My wonderful world of slapstick [by] Buster Keaton with Charles Samuels. [1st ed.] Garden City, N. Y., Doubleday, 1960. 282 p. illus. 22 cm. [PN2287.K4A3] 60-5934
I. Title.

LEBEL, Jean Patrick, 1942- 791 43'0924
Buster Keaton, by J.-P. Lebel;tr. [from French] by P. D. Stovin. London, Zwemmer New York, A. S. Barnes, 1967. 179p. plates (incl. ports.) 16cm. (Intl. film guide ser.) [PN2287.K4L413 1967] 67-89803 2.25 pap.,
1. Keaton, Buster, 1895-1966. I. Title.

LEBEL, Jean Patrick, 1942- 792.0924 (B)
Buster Keaton, by J.-P. Lebel; translated from the French by P. D. Stovin. London, Zwemmer; New York, Barnes, 1967. Seattle [Argus Press, c1964] 179 p. plates (incl. ports.). 16 cm. 120 p. (International film guide series) 12/6 (B 67-8680) [PN2287.K4L413 1967] 67-89803 66-86924
1. Keaton, Buster, 1895-1966. I. Leber, Francis. II. Title. III. Title: Gravitation and radiation; misconceptions in physics.

MOEWS, Daniel. 791.43'028'0924
Keaton : the silent features close up / Daniel Moews. Berkeley : University of California Press, c1977. ix, 337 p. ; 21 cm. Includes index. Bibliography: p. 313-322. [PN2287.KM6] 75-27930 ISBN 0-520-03126-1 : 11.95 ISBN 0-520-03155-5 pbk. : 4.50
1. Keaton, Buster, 1895-1966. BIP

ROBINSON, David. 791.43'028'0924 B
Buster Keaton. Bloomington, Indiana University Press [1969] 198 p. illus. 20 cm. (Cinema one, 10) Title on spine: Keaton. [PN2287.K4R6 1969] 68-66394 5.95
1. Keaton, Buster, 1895-1966. BIP

Keaton, Diane.

MUNSHOWER, Suzanne L. 791.43'028'0924 B
The Diane Keaton scrapbook / by Suzanne Munshower. New York : Grosset & Dunlap, c1979. 95 p. : ill. ; 28 cm. [PN2287.K44M8] 78-67808 ISBN 0-448-16380-2 : 5.95
1. Keaton, Diane. 2. Moving-picture actors and actresses—United States—Biography. I. Title. BIP

Keats, John,

KEATS, John, 1795-1821. 928.2
Letters, edited by Maurice Buxton Forman. 4th ed., with revisions and additional letters. London, New York, Oxford University Press, 1952. ixx, 570 p. ports. 23 cm. "Bibliographical memoranda concerning Keats's correspondents by the late H. Buxton Forman, C B., revised by the editor": p. xxxiii-ixv. [PR4836.A56 1952] 52-11497
I. Title.

KEATS, John, 1795-1821. 928.2
The letters of John Keats, 1814-1821. Edited by Hyder Edward0Rollins. Cambridge, Harvard University Press, 1958. 2 v. illus., ports., maps (on lining papers) facsims. 24cm. Includes bibliographical references. [PR4836.A5776] 58-5597
I. Rollins, Hyder Edward, 1889- ed. II. Title.

KEATS, John, 1795-1821. 928.2
Life and letters of John Keats, by Lord Houghton. London, New York, Oxford University Press [1951] 282 p. 16 cm. [The World's classics, 364) [[PR4836]] 63-22989
I. Houghton, Richard Monckton Milnes, baron, 1809-1885, ed. II. Title. BIP

KEATS, John, 1795-1821. 928.2
Selected letters; edited with an introd. by Lionel Trilling. New York, Farrar, Straus and Young [1951] 282 p. 22 cm. (Great letters series) [PR4836.A58] 51-10786
I. Title.

Keats, John, 1795-1821.

BUSH, Douglas, 1896- 821.7
John Keats, his life and writings. New York, Collier [1967,c.1966] 224p. 20cm. (Masters of world lit. ser.) Bibl. [PR4836.B79] 1.95 pap.,
1. Keats, John, 1795-1821. I. Title.

BUSH, Douglas, 1896- 821.7 B
John Keats, his life and writings. New York, Macmillan [1966] 224 p. 21 cm. (Masters of world literature series) "Some suggestions for further reading": p. 213-215. [PR4836.B79] 66-11583
1. Keats, John, 1795-1821. I. Title.

COLVIN, Sidney, Sir, 1845-1927. 821'.7 B
John Keats; his life and poetry, his friends, critics and after-fame. New York, Octagon Books, 1970 [c1917] xviii, 598 p. illus., facsims., ports. 24 cm. Includes bibliographical references. [PR4836.C5 1970] 73-96155
1. Keats, John, 1795-1821.

COLVIN, Sidney, Sir, 1845-1927. 821'.7 B
Keats. [Folcroft, Pa.] Folcroft Library Editions, 1973. p. Reprint of the 1902 ed. published by Macmillan, London, in series: English men of letters. [PR4836.C6 1973] 73-11378 ISBN 0-8414-3388-7 (lib. bdg.)
1. Keats, John, 1795-1821.

EVANS, Benjamin Ifor, Sir, 1899- 821'.7 B
Keats, by B. Ifor Evans. London, Duckworth [1934] St. Clair Shores, Mich., Scholarly Press, 1971. 143 p. 22 cm. (Great lives, 32) "A note on books": p. 143. [PR4836.E8 1971] 77-131699 ISBN 0-403-00586-8
1. Keats, John, 1795-1821.

EVANS, Benjamin Ifor, Sir, 1899- 821'.7 B
Keats, by B. Ifor Evans. New York, Haskell House Publishers, 1974. 143 p. 20 cm. Reprint of the 1934 ed. published by Duckworth, London, which was issued as no. 32 of Great lives. [PR4836.E8 1974] 74-6371 ISBN 0-8383-1858-4
1. Keats, John, 1795-1821.

EVANS, Benjamin Ifor, Sir, 1899- 821'.7 B
Keats, by B. Ifor Evans. [Folcroft, Pa.] Folcroft Library Editions, 1974. p. cm. Reprint of the 1934 ed. published by Duckworth, London, which was issued as no. 32 of Great lives. Bibliography: p. [PR4836.E8 1974b] 74-16285 9.45
1. Keats, John, 1795-1821.

GARROD, Heathcote William, 1878- v. 12
Keats. 2d ed. Oxford, Clarendon Press [1962] 155 p. 63-11576
1. Keats, John, 1795-1821. I. Title. BIP

GITTINGS, Robert. 821'.7 B
John Keats : the living year, 21 September 1818 to 21 September 1819 / by Robert Gittings. Westport, Conn. : Greenwood Press, 1979. xv, 247 p. ; 23 cm. Reprint of the 1968 ed. published by Barnes & Noble, New York. Includes index. Bibliography: p. 239-240. [PR4836.G5 1978] 78-6098 ISBN 0-313-20390-3 lib. bdg. : 21.00
1. Keats, John, 1795-1821. 2. Poets, English—19th century—Biography.

GITTINGS, Robert 821.7
The Keats inheritance. New York, Barnes & Noble [1965, c.1964] xi, 82p. general. table. 22cm. Bibl. [PR4836.G515] 65-5187 3.75
1. Keats, John, 1795-1821—Estate. I. Title.

GITTINGS, Robert 920
The story of John Keats. by Robert Gittings. Jo Manton. Illus. by Susan Einzig. New York, Dutton [1963, c.1962] 192p. 21cm. 63-5889 3.25
1. Keats, John. 1795-1821—Juvenile literature. I. Manton, Jo, 1919- joint author. II. Title.

HALE-WHITE, William, Sir, 1857-1949. 821'.7 B
Keats as doctor and patient. [Folcroft, Pa.] Folcroft Press [1970] 96 p. illus. 23 cm. Reprint of the 1938 ed. Includes bibliographical references. [PR4836.H27 1970] 72-193726
1. Keats, John, 1795-1821. 2. Medicine—Great Britain—London. I. Title. BIP

HEWLETT, Dorothy. 928.2
A life of John Keats. 2d ed., rev. and enl. New York, Barnes & Noble, 1950. 408 p. illus., ports., map (on lining papers) facsims. 23 cm. First published in 1937 under title: Adonais, a life of John Keats. Bibliography: p. 385-386. [PR4836.H] A51
1. Keats, John, 1795-1821. I. Title.

HILTON, Timothy, 1941- 821'.7 B
Keats and his world. New York, Viking Press [1971] 144 p. illus., facsims., ports. 24 cm. (A Studio book) Bibliography: p. 131. [PR4836.H58 1971] 78-146972 ISBN 0-670-41196-5 7.95
1. Keats, John, 1795-1821. I. Title.

KEATS, John, 1795-1821. 928.2
The letters of John Keats, 1814-1821. Edited by Hyder Edward0Rollins. Cambridge, Harvard University Press, 1958. 2 v. illus., ports., maps (on lining papers) facsims. 24cm. Includes bibliographical references. [PR4836.A5776] 58-5597
I. Rollins, Hyder Edward, 1889- ed. II. Title.

KEATS, John, 1795-1821. 928.2
Life and letters of John Keats, by Lord Houghton. London, New York, Oxford University Press [1951] 282 p. 16 cm. [The World's classics, 364) [[PR4836]] 63-22989
I. Houghton, Richard Monckton Milnes, baron, 1809-1885, ed. II. Title. BIP

KEATS, John, 1795-1821. 928.2
Selected letters; edited with an introd. by Lionel Trilling. New York, Farrar, Straus and Young [1951] 282 p. 22 cm. (Great letters series) [PR4836.A58] 51-10786
I. Title.

MURRY, John Middleton, 1889-1957. 821'.7
Keats and Shakespeare : a study of Keats' poetic life from 1816 to 1820 / by John Middleton Murry. Westport, Conn. : Greenwood Press, [1978] c1925. p. cm. Reprint of the ed. published by Oxford University Press, London. [PR4836.M8 1978] 78-15430 ISBN 0-313-20581-7 lib.bdg. : 18.75
1. Keats, John, 1795-1821. 2. Shakespeare, William, 1564-1616—Influence—Keats. 3. Poets, English—19th century—Biography. I. Title. BIP

RICHARDSON, Joanna 928.2
The everlasting spell; a study of Keats and his friends. London, J. Cape [Mystic, Conn., Verry, 1964, c.1963] 255p. illus., ports. 23cm. Bibl. 64-35812 7.00
1. Keats, John, 1795-1821—Friends and associates. I. Title.

ROGERS, Neville, comp. 821.7
Keats, Shelley & Rome; an illustrated miscellany. Postscript by Earl Wavell. Pub. on behalf of the Keats-Shelley Memorial Assn. [2d ed.] New York, Ungar [1961] 76p. illus. 62-351 2.75
1. Keats, John, 1795-1821. 2. Shelley, Percy Bysshe, 1792-1822. 3. Literary landmarks—Rome (City) I. Keats-Shelley Memorial, Rome. II. Title.

ROLLINS, Hyder Edward, 1889-1958, ed. 821.7 (B)
The Keats circle; letters and papers, and more letters and poems of the Keats circle. 2d ed. Cambridge, Harvard University Press, 1965. 2 v. illus. facsims., ports. 24 cm. Selected principally from the Keats Collection in the Houghton Library of Harvard University. [PR4836.R54] 65-13632
1. Keats, John, 1795-1821—Friends and associates. I. Harvard University. Library. Houghton Library. II. Title.

ROLLINS, Hyder Edward, 1889-1958, ed. 821.7
The Keats circle; letters and papers, and more letters and poems of the Keats circle; 2v. 2d ed. Cambridge, Mass., Harvard 1965. [c.1948-1965] 2v. (various p.) illus., facsims., ports. 24cm. Selected principally from the Keats Collection in the Houghton Lib. of Harvard [PR4836.R54] 65-4647 20.00, set, bxd.
1. Keats, John, 1795-1821—Friends and associates. I. Harvard University. Library. Houghton Library. II. Title.

WARD, Aileen 928.2
John Keats: the making of a poet. New York, Viking [1967, c.1963] xii, 450p. illus. 20cm. (Compass bks., C203) Bibl. 1.85 pap.,
1. Keats, John, 1795-1821. I. Title.

WARD, Aileen. 928.2
John Keats; the making of a poet. New York, Viking Press [1963] 450 p. illus. 24 cm. Includes bibliography. [PR4836.W3] 63-15218
1. Keats, John, 1795-1821.

WELLS, Walter Augustine, 1870- 928.2
A doctor's life of John Keats. [1st ed.] New York, Vantage Press [1959] 247 p. illus. 22 cm. [PR4836.W4] 59-11248
1. Keats, John, 1795-1821. I. Title.

Keats, John, 1795-1821—Addresses, essays, lectures.

ROGERS, Neville, comp. 821'.7'09 B
Keats, Shelley & Rome : an illustrated miscellany / compiled by Neville Rogers ; postscript by Earl Wavell. New York : Haskell House Publishers, [1976, i.e.1975] p. cm. Reprint of the 1949 ed. publshed by C. Johnson, London. [PR4836.R53 1976] 75-22076 ISBN 0-8383-2080-5 lib.bdg. : 9.95
1. Keats, John, 1795-1821—Addresses, essays, lectures. 2. Shelley, Percy Bysshe, 1792-1822—Addresses, essays, lectures. 3. Keats Shelley Memorial Association. 4. Literary landmarks—Rome (City) I. Title. Contents omitted.

Keats, John, 1795-1821—Biography.

ASKWITH, Betty, Hon., 1909- 821'.7 B
Keats / by Betty Askwith. Folcroft, Pa. : Folcroft Library Editions, 1976 [c1941] 288 p. : port. ; 26 cm. Reprint of the ed. published by Collins, London. Includes index. [PR4836.A8 1976] 76-43959 ISBN 0-8414-2892-1 lib. bdg. : 25.00

1. Keats, John, 1795-1821—Biography. 2. Poets, English—19th century—Biography.

BROWN, Charles Armitage, 1786-1842. 821'.7 B
Life of John Keats. Edited with an introd. and notes by Dorothy Hyde Bodurtha and Willard Bissell Pope. [Folcroft, Pa.] Folcroft Library Editions, 1974. 129 p. 26 cm. Reprint of the 1937 ed. published by Oxford University Press, London. Includes bibliographical references. [PR4836.B76 1974] 74-3172 ISBN 0-8414-3116-7 (lib. bdg.)
1. Keats, John, 1795-1821—Biography. I. Bodurtha, Dorothy Hyde, ed. II. Pope, Willard Bissell, ed.

HEWLETT, Dorothy. 821'.7 B
A life of John Keats. [3d rev. ed.] New York, Barnes & Noble [1970] 408 p. illus., ports. 24 cm. First published in 1937 under title: Adonais, a life of John Keats. Bibliography: p. 385-386. [PR4836.H5 1970b] 75-17691 ISBN 0-389-02041-9 7.50
1. Keats, John, 1795-1821—Biography. I. Title. BIP

MURCHIE, Guy, 1872- 821'.7 B
The spirit of place in Keats, sketches of personns and places known by him, and his reaction to them / Guy Murchie ; with a foreword by the assistant curator and librarian of the Keats Memorial House, Hampstead. Folcroft, Pa. : Folcroft Library Editions, 1978. p. cm. Reprint of the 1955 ed. published by N. Neame, London. Includes bibliographical references and index. [PR4836.M7 1978] 78-11851 ISBN 0-8414-6327-1 lib. bdg. : 30.00
1. Keats, John, 1795-1821—Biography. 2. Poets, English—19th century—Biography. I. Title.

ROSSETTI, William Michael, 1829-1919. 821'.7 B
Life of John Keats. New York, AMS Press [1971] 217, xi p. 18 cm. Reprint of the 1887 ed. "Bibliography, by John P. Anderson": p. [i]-xi. [PR4836.R6 1971] 75-126695 ISBN 0-404-05428-5
1. Keats, John, 1795-1821—Biography. BIP

Keats, John, 1795-1821-Correspondence, reminiscences, etc.

*PACK, Robert, comp. 821'.7
Selected letters of John Keats, edited and with an introduction by Robert Pack. New York, New American Library [1974] 242 p. 18 cm. (A Signet classic) Bibliography: [p. 239-242] [PR4836] 73-83712 1.95 (pbk.)
1. Keats, John, 1795-1821-Correspondence, reminiscences, etc. I. Title.

Keats, John, 1795-1821—Homes and haunts—Rome (City)

CACCIATORE, Vera, 1911- 821'.7'09
A room in Rome. New York, Keats-Shelley Association of America [1970] 56 p. illus., facsim., ports. 21 cm. Includes bibliographical references. [PR4836.C27] 70-298912
1. Keats, John, 1795-1821—Homes and haunts—Rome (City) 2. Shelley, Percy Bysshe, 1792-1822—Homes and haunts—Rome (City) I. Title.

Keats, John, 1920-

KEATS, John, 1920- 917.13'7'00924
Of time and an island. New York, Charterhouse [1974] vii, 245 p. map (on lining papers) 22 cm. [CT275.K397A36] 73-91123 ISBN 0-88327-033-1 7.95
1. Keats, John, 1920- I. Title.

Keayne, Robert,

KEAYNE, Robert, 1595-1656. 347.6'5
The apologia of Robert Keayne; the last will and testament of me, Robert Keayne, all of it written with my own hands and began by me, mo: 6:1:1653, commonly called August; the self-portrait of a Puritan merchant. Edited by Bernard Bailyn. Gloucester, Mass., P. Smith, 1970 [c1964] xii, 93 p. 21 cm. "Originally published as a chapter in Publications of the Colonial Society of Massachusetts, volume XLII, Transactions 1952-1956, published in 1964." [HF3023.K35A3 1970] 78-17046
I. Bailyn, Bernard, ed. II. Title.

Keble, John, 1792-1866.

BATTISCOMBE, Georgina. 922.342
John Keble; a study in limitations. New York, Knopf, 1964 [c1963] xix, 395 p. illus., facsims., ports. 24 cm. Includes bibliographies. [BX5199.K3B3 1964] 64-12222
1. Keble, John, 1792-1866. 2. Oxford movement.

COLERIDGE, John Taylor, Sir, 1790-1876. 821'.7 B
A memoir of the Rev. John Keble, M.A., late Vicar of Hursley / by the Right Hon. Sir John Taylor Coleridge. New York : AMS Press, 1977. xvi, 620 p. ; 19 cm. Reprint of the 2d ed. published in 1869 by J. Parker, Oxford. Includes bibliographical references and index. [BX5199.K3C7 1977] 75-30019 ISBN 0-404-07374-3 : 38.50
1. Keble, John, 1792-1866. 2. Church of England—Clergy—Biography. 3. Clergy—England—Biography. I. Title.

Kechik bin Syed Mohamed, Syed, 1928-

ROSS-LARSON, Bruce Clifford, 1942- 320.9'595'305
The politics of federalism : Syed Kechik in East Malaysia / Bruce Ross-Larson. Singapore : Ross-Larson, 1976. x, 240 p., [1] leaf of plates : maps ; 23 cm. Includes index. [DS597.337.K43R67] 77-940579 15.00 ($8.00 U.S.)
1. Kechik bin Syed Mohamed, Syed, 1928- 2. Sabah—Politics and government. 3. Sarawak—Politics and government. 4. Politicians—Malaysia—Biography. I. Title.

Keck, L. Robert, 1935-

KECK, L. Robert, 1935- 615'.852 B
The spirit of synergy : God's power and you / L. Robert Keck. Nashville : Abingdon, c1978. 159 p. ; 21 cm. Bibliography: p. 157-159. [BV4813.K42] 78-732 ISBN 0-687-01693-2 : 6.95
1. Keck, L. Robert, 1935- 2. Methodist Church—Clergy—Biography. 3. Meditation. 4. Clergy—United States—Biography. 5. Faith-cure. I. Title. BIP

Keely, John Ernest Worrell, 1827-1898.

CROSSEN, Joseph B. 609'.2'4 B
Keely: quack or visionary? by Joseph B. Crossen. [York, Pa., Maple Press Co., 1972] 16 p. illus., ports. 23 cm. (The Printed page, no. 25) Cover title. [T40.K38C76] 73-171816
1. Keely, John Ernest Worrell, 1827-1898. I. Title.

Keely, Patrick Charles, 1816-1896.

KERVICK, Francis William Wynn. 927.2
Patrick Charles Keely, architect; a record of his life and work. [South Bend, Ind., Priv. print., 1953] 63p. illus. 26cm. [NA737.K43K4] 53-26750
1. Keely, Patrick Charles, 1816-1896. I. Title.

Keene, N.H. First Congregational Church.

PROPER, David R. 285'.8742'9
History of the First Congregational Church, Keene, New Hampshire, by David R. Proper. Keene, N.H., 1973. xvi, 232 p. illus. 24 cm. [BX7255.K43F576] 73-172822
1. Keene, N.H. First Congregational Church. 2. Keene, N.H.—Biography.

Kefauver, Estes, 1903-1963.

ANDERSON, Jack. 923.273
The Kefauver story, by Jack Anderson and Fred Blumenthal. New York, Dial Press [1956] 240p. 20cm. [F436.K4A6] 56-8111
1. Kefauver, Estes, 1903- I. Blumenthal, Frederick G., joint author. II. Title.

GORMAN, Joseph Bruce. 973.9'0924 B
Kefauver: a political biography. New York, Oxford University Press, 1971. viii, 434 p. ports. 22 cm. Includes bibliographical references. [E748.K314G6] 77-159645 ISBN 0-19-501481-2 10.00
1. Kefauver, Estes, 1903-1963. I. Title.

SWADOS, Harvey. 973.9'092'4 B
Standing up for the people; the life and work of Estes Kefauver. [1st ed.] New York, E. P. Dutton [1972] xiv, 189 p. illus. 24 cm. Bibliography: p. 183. A biography of the Tennessee Senator of populist persuasion who championed many unpopular causes during his term in office. [E748.K314S9 1972] 92 79-179055 ISBN 0-525-39872-4 6.50
1. Kefauver, Estes, 1903-1963. I. Title.

Keim, De Benneville Randolph, 1841-1914.

KEIM, De Benneville Randolph, 1841-1914. 973.8'1
Sheridan's troopers on the borders : a winter campaign on the Plains / by De B. Randolph Keim. Glorieta, N.M. : Rio Grande Press, c1977. 320 p., [13] leaves of plates : ill. ; 24 cm. (A Rio Grande classic) Reprint of the ed. published by Claxton, Remsen & Haffelfinger, Philadelphia. Includes index. [E83.869.K44 1977] 77-878 ISBN 0-87380-124-5 lib.bdg. : 12.00
1. Keim, De Benneville Randolph, 1841-1914. 2. Indians of North America—Wars—1868-1869—Personal narratives. 3. Indians of North America—Great Plains—Social life and customs. 4. Frontier and pioneer life—The West. 5. War correspondents—United States—Biography. I. Title. BIP

Keiser, Albert,

KEISER, Albert, 1887-1959 923.773
The way up; an autobiography Peterborough, N. H., R. R. Smith [1962, c.1961] 223p. illus. 61-17913 4.00
I. Title.

Keiser, Bea.

KEISER, Bea. 362.1'9'612300926 B
All our hearts are trump / Bea Keiser, with Janice Booker. Durham, N.C. : Moore Pub. Co., c1976. 103 p. ; 23 cm. [RC685.I6K44] 76-1455 ISBN 0-87716-066-X : 6.95
1. Keiser, Bea. 2. Heart—Infarction—Biography. I. Booker, Janice, joint author. II. Title. BIP

Keister, William Hampton, 1865-

THE beloved schoolmaster; v. 12
a biography of William Hampton Koister. Foreword by Dr. Francis P. Gaines. [Boyce, Va., Carr Pub. Co., 1956] 81p. illus., ports. 23cm.
1. Keister, William Hampton, 1865- 2. Harrison-burg, Va.—Public schools. I. Wright, Melton.

WRIGHT, Melton. v. 12
The beloved schoolmaster; a biography of William Hampton Keister. Foreword by Dr. Francis P. Gaines. [Boyce, Va., Carr Pub. Co., 1956] 81 p. illus., ports. 23 cm.
1. Keister, William Hampton, 1865- 2. Harrisonburg, Va. — Public schools I. Title.

Keitel, Wilhelm, 1882-1946.

KEITEL, Wilhelm, 1882-1946. 355.3'31'0924 B
In the service of the Reich / edited with an introd. and epilogue by Walter Gorlitz ; translated by David Irving. New York : Stein and Day, 1979. p. cm. Translation of Generalfeldmarschall Keitel. Originally published as The memoirs of Field-Marshal Keitel. Includes index. [DD247.K42A313 1979] 66-14952 ISBN 0-8128-2613-2 : 11.95. ISBN 0-8128-6029-2 pbk. : 5.95
1. Keitel, Wilhelm, 1882-1946. 2. Germany. Wehrmacht. Oberkommando—Biography. 3. Generals—Germany—Biography. I. Gorlitz, Walter, 1913- II. Title. BIP

Keith, Arthur,

KEITH, Arthur, Sir 1866- 925.7
An autobiography. New York, Philosophical Library [1950] vi, 721 p. illus., ports. 22 cm. [QH31.K44A3 1950a] 50-10836
I. Title.

Keith, Charles A.

KEITH, Charles A. 920
Fast balls and college halls; an autobiography. New York, Vantage Press [c.1959] 146p. 22cm. 2.95 bds.,
I. Title.

Keith, Charles Alexander,

KEITH, Charles Alexander, 1883- 923.773
Fast balls and college halls, an autobiography. [1st ed.] New York, Vantage Press [1960, c1959] 146p. 21cm. [LA2317.K33A3] 60-431
I. Title.

Keith, Elmer, 1899-

KEITH, Elmer, 1899- 799.2'092'4 B
Keith : an autobiography / Elmer Keith. New York : Winchester Press, [1974] x, 381 p., [18] leaves of plates : ill. ; 25 cm. Includes index. [SK17.K45A33] 73-78837 ISBN 0-87691-137-8 : 10.00
1. Keith, Elmer, 1899- 2. Hunting. I. Title.

Keith, Gladys, 1905-

WAGNON, Marilyn Simpson. 266.6'0924 B
Light on the riverfront; the story of Gladys Keith [by] Marilyn S. Wagnon. Nashville, Broadman Press [1967] 64 p. illus., ports. 19 cm. [BX6495.K355W3] 68-12322
1. Keith, Gladys, 1905- I. Title.

Keith, Minor Cooper, 1848-1929.

HATCH, John Keith. v. 12
Minor C. Keith, pioneer of the American tropics. [McLean, Va.] 1962 [c1963] iii, 82 l. 23 cm. Cover title. Bibliography: p. 80-82. [HE2823.H3] 64-39316
1. Keith, Minor Cooper, 1848-1929. 2. Railroads — Central America — Hist. 3. United Fruit Company. I. Title.

STEWART, Watt, 1892- 926.5
Keith and Costa Rica; a biographical study of Minor Cooper Keith. [1st ed.] Albuquerque, University of New Mexico Press [1964] xiii, 210 p. illus., map (on lining papers) ports. 24 cm. Bibliography: p. 201-204. [CT275.K426S8] 63-21373
1. Keith, Minor Cooper, 1848-1929. 2. Cyprus (Brig) 3. Convict labor—Gt. Brit. 4. Pirates. 5. Costa Rica—Industries. I. Stephensen, Percy Reginald, 1901- joint author. II. Title.

Kelkar, Narsinha Chintaman, 1872-1947—Biography.

GOLE, R. M. 891'.46'8509 B
N. C. Kelkar / by R. M. Gole. New Delhi : Sahitya Akademi, 1976. 90 p. ; 23 cm. (Makers of Indian literature) Includes bibliographical references and index. [PK2418.K414Z67] 76-905002 Rs2.50
1. Kelkar, Narsinha Chintaman, 1872-1947—Biography. 2. Authors, Marathi—20th century—Biography.

Kell, John McIntosh, 1823-1900.

DELANEY, Norman C. 973.7'57'0924 B
John McIntosh Kell of the raider Alabama, by Norman C. Delaney. University, University of Alabama Press [1973] 270 p. illus. 24 cm. Bibliography: p. [257]-266.

[E596.K292D44] 72-7349 ISBN 0-8173-5106-X 8.50
1. Kell, John McIntosh, 1823-1900. 2. Alabama (Confederate cruiser) 3. Sumter (Confederate cruiser) 4. United States—History—Civil War—Naval operations—Confederate States. I. Title. **BIP**

Keller, George W., 1842-1935.

RANSOM, David F. 720'.92'4
George Keller, architect / David F. Ransom ; introd. by Barry Hannegan. Hartford, Conn. : Stowe-Day Foundation, c1978. xxxiii, 218 p. : ill. (some col.) ; 28 cm. Includes index. Bibliography: p. 208-210. [NA737.K44R36] 77-14060 ISBN 0-917482-14-X pbk. : 9.95
1. Keller, George W., 1842-1935. 2. Architects—United States—Biography. I. Title. **BIP**

Keller, Gottfried, 1819-1890.

LINDSAY, James Martin. 838'.8'09
Gottfried Keller; life and works [by] J. M. Lindsay. [Chester Springs, Pa.] Dufour, 1969. 258 p. illus. 23 cm. Bibliography: p. [248]-254. [PT2374.Z4L5 1969] 69-14390 7.95
1. Keller, Gottfried, 1819-1890.

Keller, Helen Adams, 1880-1968.

BIGLAND, Eileen. 92
Helen Keller. Illustrated by Lili Cassel Wronker. [Rev. and enl.] New York, S. G. Phillips [1967] 192 p. illus. 22 cm. A biography of Helen Keller containing a detailed account of her progress under the patient tutoring of Anne Sullivan. [HV1624.K4B45 1967] AC 67
1. Keller, Helen Adams, 1880- 2. Blind-deaf—Education. I. Wronker, Lili Cassel, illus. II. Title.

BROOKS, Van Wyck, 1886- 920.7
Helen Keller; sketch for a portrait. [1st ed.] New York, Dutton, 1956. 166p. 20cm. 'Abridged form published in Harper's magazine, March, 1954. [HV1624.K4B7] 55-11080
1. Keller, Helen Adams, 1880- I. Title.

GREENE, Jay Elihu, 1914- 920.02 ed.
Four complete biographies. New York, Globe Book Co. [1962] 750p. illus. 22cm. [CT106.G652] 62-5357
1. Churchill, Winston Leonard Spencer, Sir 1874- 2. Keller, Helen Adams, 1880- 3. Schweitzer, Albert, 1875- 4. Barnum, Phineas Taylor, 1810-1891 I. Title.
Contents omitted.

HARRITY, Richard. 920.7
The three lives of Helen Keller [by] Richard Harrity and Ralph G. Martin. [1st ed.] Garden City, N.Y., Doubleday, 1962. 189 p. illus. 27 cm. [HV1624 K4H37] 62-7644
1. Keller, Helen Adams, 1880-1968. I. Martin, Ralph G., 1920- joint author. II. Title.

KELLER, Helen Adams 1880- 920.7
The story of my life. Foreword by Eleanor Roosevelt. [New York] Dell [1961, c.1902-1961] 416p. (F111) .50 pap.,
I. Title.

KELLER, Helen Adams, 362.4'0924 B 1880-1968.
Midstream: my later life. New York, Greenwood Press, 1968 [c1929] xxiii, 362 p. port. 22 cm. [HV1624.K4A17 1968] 68-8063
I. Title.

PEARE, Catherine Owens. 920.7
The Helen Keller story. New York, Crowell [1959] 183 p. illus. 21 cm. [HV1624.K4P4] 59-10979
1. Keller, Helen Adams, 1880-1968. **BIP**

TIBBLE, John William, 1901- 920.7
Helen Keller, By J. W. & Anne Tibble. Illustrated by Harper Johnson. [1st American ed.] New York, Putnam [1958] 125 p. illus. 21 cm. (Lives to remember) [HV1624.K4T5 1958] 58-7458
1. Keller, Helen Adams, 1880- I. Tibble, Anne (Northgrave) joint author. II. Title.

TIBBLE, John William, 1901- 920.7
Helen Keller, by J. W. & Anne Tibble. Illustrated by Harper Johnson. [1st American ed.] New York, Putnam [1958] 125 p. illus. 21 cm. (Lives to remember) [HV1624.K4T5 1958] 58-7458
1. Keller, Helen Adams, 1880-1968. I. Tibble, Anne Northgrave, joint author.

WAITE, Helen Elmira 920.7
Valiant companions, Helen Keller and her 'miracle worker.' New York. Scholastic [1964, c.1959] 279p. 17cm. (T537) .45 pap.,
1. Keller, Helen Adams, 1880- 2. Macy, Anne (Sullivan) 1866-1936. I. Title.

WAITE, Helen Elmira. 920.7
Valiant companions, Helen Keller and Anne Sullivan Macy. Philadelphia, Macrae Smith [1959] 223 p. 22 cm. [HV1624.K4W3] 59-8243
1. Keller, Helen Adams, 1880-1968. 2. Macy, Anne (Sullivan) 1866-1936. I. Title.

Keller, Helen Adams, 1880-1968—Juvenile literature.

BIGLAND, Eileen. 92 (J)
Helen Keller. Illustrated by Lili Cassel Wronker. [Rev. and enl.] New York, S. G. Phillips [1967] 192 p. illus. 22 cm. [HV1624.K4B45 1967] 67-22810
1. Keller, Helen Adams, 1880- —Juvenile literature.

DAVIDSON, 362.7'8'410924 B Mickie.
Helen Keller, by Margaret Davidson. Illus. by Vicki Fox. New York, Hastings House [1971, c1969] 94 p. illus., ports. 22 cm. A biography stressing the childhood of the woman who overcame the handicaps of being blind and deaf. [HV1624.K4D36] 92 71-150016 ISBN 0-8038-3015-7 3.96
1. Keller, Helen Adams, 1880-1968—Juvenile literature. I. Fox, Vicki, illus. II. Title.

GRAFF, Stewart 92
Helen Keller; toward the light, by Stewart and Polly Anne Graff. Illus. by Paul Frame. Champaign, Ill., Garrard [c.1965] 80p. col. illus. 24cm. [Discovery bk.) [HV1624K4G7] 65-14550 1.98 lib. ed.,
1. Keller, Helen Adams, 1880- —Juvenile literature. I. Graff, Polly Anne (Colver) 1908- joint author. II. Title.

GRAFF, Stewart 92
Helen Keller: toward the light, by Stewart and Polly. Anne Graff. Illus. by Paul Frame [New York, Dell, 1966, c.1965] 80p illus. 20cm. (Discovery bk., Yearling bk., 3655) [HV1624.K4G7] .50 pap.,
1. Keller, Helen Adams, 1880- —Juvenile literature. I. Graff, Polly Anne (Colver) 1908- II. Title.

GRAFF, Stewart. 92 (J)
Helen Keller; toward the light, by Stewart and Polly Anne Graff. Illustrated by Paul Frame. Champaign, Ill., Garrard Pub. Co. [1965] 80 p. col. illus. 23 cm. (A Discovery book) [HV1624.K4G7] 65-14550
1. Keller, Helen Adams, 1880-—Juvenile literature. I. Graff, Polly Anne (Colver) 1908- joint author.

JOHNSON, Ann 362.4'092'4 B Donegan.
The value of determination : the story of Helen Keller / by Ann Donegan Johnson ; illustrated by Pileggi. 2d ed. Jolla, Calif. : Value Communications, c1976. 62 p. : col. ill. ; 29 cm. (ValueTales) First ed. published in 1975 under title: The ValueTale of Helen Keller. Focuses on Helen Keller's determination to hear, see, and speak and her equal determination to help others with handicaps similar to her own. [HV1624.K4J63 1976] 92 76-54762 ISBN 0-916392-07-4 : 4.95
1. Keller, Helen Adams, 1880-1968—Juvenile literature. 2. Blind-deaf—Juvenile literature. I. Pileggi, Steve. II. Title. **BIP**

KELTON, Nancy. 362.4'092'4 B
The finger game miracle / author, Nancy Kelton ; illustrator, Ron Recchio. Milwaukee : Raintree Editions ; Chicago : distributed by Childrens Press, c1977. 31 p. : ill. ; 23 cm. A biography of Helen Keller who overcame her handicap with the help of teacher Anne Sullivan. [HV1624.K4K45] 76-46408 ISBN 0-8172-0452-0 lib. bdg. : 4.95
1. Keller, Helen Adams, 1880-1968—Juvenile literature. 2. Blind-deaf—Biography—Juvenile literature. 3. Blind—United States—Biography—Juvenile literature. I. Recchio, Ron. II. Title. **BIP**

WAYNE, Bennett. 920.72
Four women of courage, edited with commentary by Bennett Wayne. Champaign, Ill., Garrard Pub. Co. [1975] 167 p. illus. 22 cm. (A Target book) Brief biographies of four women who achieved their ambitions against great odds. [HQ1412.W39] 920 74-13482 ISBN 0-8116-4911-3 3.98 (lib. bdg.)
1. Cochran, Jacqueline—Juvenile literature. 2. Dix, Dorothea Lynde, 1802-1887—Juvenile literature. 3. Keller, Helen Adams, 1880-1968—Juvenile literature. 4. Richards, Linda Ann Judson, 1841-1930—Juvenile literature. I. Title. **BIP**

WILKIE, Katharine 362.4'0924 B Elliot, 1904-
Helen Keller; handicapped girl, by Katharine E. Wilkie. [Illustrated by Robert Doremus] Indianapolis, Bobbs-Merrill [1969] 200 p. col. illus., col. port. 20 cm. (Childhood of famous Americans) A biography of Helen Keller concentrating on her childhood and the important years spent with her first teacher, Anne Sullivan. [HV1624.K4W53] 92 70-77818
1. Keller, Helen Adams, 1880-1968—Juvenile literature. 2. Macy, Anne (Sullivan) 1866-1936—Juvenile literature. I. Doremus, Robert, illus. II. Title.

WYMER, Norma 92
The young Helen Keller. Illus. by William Randell. New York, Roy [1966, c.1965] 141p. illus. 21cm. [HV1624.K4W9] 66-13352 3.25 bds.,
1. Keller, Helen Adams, 1880- —Juvenile literature. I. Title.

Keller, May Lansfield.

KELLER, May 370'.92'4 B Lansfield.
May Lansfield Keller, life and letters, 1877-1964 / Pauline Turnbull, author and editor. Verona, Va. : McClure Press, 1975. 399 p. : ill. ; 24 cm. [LA2317.K35A33] 75-20968 8.95
1. Keller, May Lansfield. I. Turnbull, Pauline.

Kelley, Ada Campbell.

KELLEY, Ada Campbell. 920 (B)
The brighter half. [1st ed.] New York, Greenwich Book Publishers [1965] 248 p. 22 cm. [CT275.K439A3] 65-11659
I. Title.

Kelley family.

KELLY, Mary Ann. 976.9'35
My old Kentucky home, good-night / by Mary Ann Kelly. 1st ed. Hicksville, N.Y. : Exposition Press, c1978. xiii, 310 p., [16] leaves of plates : ill. ; 24 cm. [F459.L9K44] 78-71897 ISBN 0-682-49143-8 : 15.00
1. Kelley family. 2. Kelly, Mary Ann. 3. Ludlow, Ky.—Biography. 4. Ludlow, Ky.—History—Miscellanea. 5. Irish Americans—Kentucky—Ludlow—Biography. I. Title. **BIP**

LEWIS, Arthur H., 929'.2'0973 1906-
Those Philadelphia Kellys, with a touch of Grace / by Arthur H. Lewis. New York : Morrow, 1977. 288 p. : ill. ; 22 cm. Includes index. [CS71.K29 1977] 77-5724 ISBN 0-688-03226-5 : 8.95
1. Kelley family. 2. Grace, Princess of Monaco, 1929- 3. Monaco—Princes and princesses—Biography. I. Title. **BIP**

Kelley, Florence, 1859-1932.

BLUMBERG, Dorothy Rose 360.0924
Florence Kelley; the making of a social pioneer. New York, Kelley, 1966. xii, 194p. illus., ports. 24cm. Bibl. [HN57.B55] 65-16982 5.00
1. Kelley, Florence, 1859-1932. I. Title. **BIP**

BLUMBERG, Dorothy Rose. 360.0924
Florence Kelley; the making of a social pioneer. New York, A. M. Kelley, 1966. xii, 194 p. illus., ports. 23 cm. Bibliography: p. 181-188. [HN57.B55] 65-16982
1. Kelley, Florence, 1859-1932. I. Title.

GOLDMARK, Josephine 923.673 Clara, 1877-1950.
Impatient crusader; Florence Kelley's life story. Urbana, University of Illinois Press, 1953. 217p. 24cm. [HN57.K4G6] 52-12408
1. Kelley, Florence, 1859-1982. I. Title. **BIP**

Kelley, Frances.

KELLEY, Frances. 248'.2 B
Better than I was / Frances Kelley with Helen Kooiman Hosier. Nashville : T. Nelson, c1979. 154 p. ; 20 cm. [BR1725.K43A34] 79-1095 ISBN 0-8407-5671-2 pbk. : 3.95
1. Kelley, Frances. 2. Christian biography—United States. 3. Faith-cure. I. Hosier, Helen Kooiman, joint author. II. Title. **BIP**

Kelley, Shirley Dyckes, 1933-

KELLEY, Shirley 973.92'092'4 B Dyckes, 1933-
Love is not for cowards : the autobiography of Shirley Dyckes Kelley / as told to Elizabeth Gullander. Englewood Cliffs, N.J. : Prentice-Hall, c1978. 281 p., [8] leaves of plates : ill. ; 24 cm. [CT275.K4393A35 1978] 77-26211 ISBN 0-13-541029-0 : 9.95
1. Kelley, Shirley Dyckes, 1933- 2. United States—Biography. 3. Ex nuns—United States—Biography. I. Gullander, Elizabeth, joint author. II. Title. **BIP**

Kelley, William Dennis, 1825-1888.

McCULLOUGH, William 926.1 Wallace, 1887-
Doctor William Dennis Kelley, 1825-1888, Texas physician and surgeon; a biography, by William Wallace McCullough, Jr., with notes on related families: Agnew, Baldridge, Donnell, Hodge [and] Vinson. Galveston, Tex, 1961. 122p. illus. 29cm. Includes bibliography. [R154.K26M3] 61-46828
1. Kelley, William Dennis, 1825-1888. I. Title.

Kellogg, Clara Louise, 1842-1916.

KELLOGG, Clara 782.1'092'4 B Louise, 1842-1916.
Memoirs of an American prima donna / by Clara Louise Kellogg (Mme. Strakosch). New York : Da Capo Press, 1978, [c1913] xiii, 382 p., [38] leaves of plates : ill. ; 24 cm. (Da Capo Press music reprint series) Reprint of the ed. published by Putnam, New York. Includes index. [ML420.K27A3 1978] 77-16534 ISBN 0-306-77527-1 : 25.00
1. Kellogg, Clara Louise, 1842-1916. 2. Singers—United States—Biography. **BIP**

Kellogg, Frank Billings, 1856-1937.

ELLIS, Lewis Ethan, 1898- 327.73
Frank B. Kellogg and American foreign relations, 1925-1929, by L. Ethan Ellis. Westport, Conn., Greenwood Press [1974, c1961] ix, 303 p. 23 cm. Reprint of the ed. published by Rutgers University Press, New Brunswick, N.J. Bibliography: p.

[286]-291. [E791.E5 1974] 74-10636 ISBN 0-8371-7651-4
1. Kellogg, Frank Billings, 1856-1937. 2. United States—Foreign relations—1923-1929. I. Title. **BIP**

Kellough, Ethel Booth.

KELLOUGH, Ethel Booth. 917.81'93'033
When drawers were long. Wichita, Kan., McCormick-Armstrong Co., Publishing Division [1967] 61 p. illus., ports. 24 cm. Autobiographical. [CT275.K4395A3] 67-7633
I. Title.

Kelly, Edward, 1854-1880.

CARROLL, Brian, 1930- 364.1'55'0924 B
Ned Kelly, bushranger / Brian Carroll. Dee Why West, Australia : Lansdowne Press, 1976. 264 p. : ill. ; 24 cm. Includes index. Bibliography: p. 262-263. [DU222.K4C37] 77-375562
1. Kelly, Edward, 1854-1880. 2. Bushrangers—Biography. I. Title.

FARWELL, George, 1911- 364.1'55'0924 B
Ned Kelly; the life & adventures of Australia's notorious bushranger. [Melbourne] Cheshire [1970] 207 p. illus. (part col.) 22 cm. At head of title: What a life! Bibliography: p. 206-207. [DU222.K4F37] 73-173755 ISBN 0-7015-1319-5 4.50
1. Kelly, Edward, 1854-1880. I. Title: What a life!

JENNINGS, Margaret Jean. 364.1'0924 B
Ned Kelly, the legend and the man [by] M. J. Jennings. [Melbourne] Hill of Content [1968] 144 p. illus., map, ports. 18 cm. Bibliography: p. 144. [DU222.K4J4] 76-363106 1.15
1. Kelly, Edward, 1854-1880. I. Title.

NED Kelly in pictures; the man who became an Australian legend. Over 50 original photographs and line drawings. Melbourne, Southdown Press [1968] 15 p. illus., port. 43 cm. Cover title. [DU222.K4N4] 77-466087 0.50 364.1'0924 B
1. Kelly, Edward, 1854-1880.

Kelly, Emmett, 1898- —Juvenile literature.

QUACKENBUSH, Robert M. 791.3'3'0924
The man on the flying trapeze : the circus life of Emmett Kelly, Sr. told with pictures & song! / Robert Quackenbush. 1st ed. Philadelphia : Lippincott, [1975] [33] p. : col. ill. ; 19 x 26 cm. The circus experiences of Emmett Kelly, Sr., "America's favorite clown," are related in verse to be sung to the tune of the familiar song "The Man on the Flying Trapeze." [GV1811.K4Q32] 92 75-5614 ISBN 0-397-31643-7 : 5.95
1. Kelly, Emmett, 1898- —Juvenile literature. 2. Clowns—Juvenile literature. I. Title. **BIP**

Kelly, Fanny Wiggins, b. 1845. 1845.

KELLY, Fanny Wiggins, b.1845. 973'.04'97 S
Narrative of my captivity among the Sioux Indians / Fanny Kelly. New York : Garland Pub., 1976, [c1871] 285 p., [11] leaves of plates : ill. ; 19 cm. (The Garland library of narratives of North American Indian captivities ; v. 85) Reprint of the ed. published by Mutual Pub. Co., Hartford, Conn. [E85.G2 vol. 85] [E99.D1] 977.1'45'030924 75-7111 ISBN 0-8240-1709-9 lib.bdg. : 21.00
I. Kelly, Fanny Wiggins, b. 1845. 1845. 2. Dakota Indians—Captivities. 3. Indians of North America—Captivities. 4. Dakota Indians—Wars, 1862-1865. I. Title. II. Series.

Kelly, Frances Maria, 1790-1882.

HOLMAN, L. E. 792'.028'0924 B
Lamb's 'Barbara S—'; the life of Frances Maria Kelly, actress, by L. E. Holman. [Folcroft, Pa.] Folcroft Library Editions, 1973. p. Reprint of the 1935 ed. published by Methuen, London. [PN2598.K37H6 1973] 73-12897 ISBN 0-8414-4746-2 (lib. bdg.)
1. Kelly, Frances Maria, 1790-1882. 2. Lamb, Charles, 1775-1834. I. Title.

Kelly, Gene, 1912-

HIRSCHHORN, Clive. 791.43'028'0924 B
Gene Kelly : a biography / Clive Hirschhorn. Chicago : Regnery, 1975, c1974. 335 p., [20] leaves of plates : ill. ; 23 cm. Includes index. Filmography: p. 313-319. [PN2287.K64H5] 74-27811 ISBN 0-8092-8260-7 : 11.95
1. Kelly, Gene, 1912-

Kelly, Harold Osman, 1884-1956.

JOHNSON, William Weber, 1909- 927.5
Kelly blue. Foreword by Tom Lea. [1st ed.] Garden City, N. Y., Doubleday, 1960. 263 p. illus. 22 cm. [ND237.K445J6] 60-8875
1. Kelly, Harold Osman, 1884-1956. I. Title. **BIP**

JOHNSON, William Weber, 1909- 927.5
Kelly Blue. Foreword by Tom Lea. Lincoln, University of Nebraska Press [1974, c1960] 263 p. 21 cm. (A Bison book) [ND237.K445J6] ISBN 0-8032-5795-3. 2.95 (pbk.)
1. Kelly, Harold Osman, 1884-1956. I. Title.
L.C. card number for original ed.: 60-8875.

JOHNSON, William Weber, 1909- 759.13 B
Kelly blue / William Weber Johnson ; foreword by Tom Lea. College Station : Texas A&M University Press, c1979. xii, 175 p., [8] leaves of plates : ill. (some col.) ; 24 cm. Reprint of the 1960 ed. published by Doubleday, Garden City, N.Y. [ND237.K445J6 1979] 78-21773 ISBN 0-89096-073-9 : 14.95
1. Kelly, Harold Osman, 1884-1955. 2. Painters—United States—Biography. I. Title.

Kelly, James, 1791-1859.

BOWDEN, Keith Macrae. 639.28
Captain James Kelley of Hobart Town [by] K. M. Bowden. [Parkville] Melbourne University Press; New York, Cambridge University Press [1965] vi. 126 p. illus., maps. 22 cm. Bibliography: p. 124-126. [SH381.B68] 65-24883
1. Kelly, James, 1791-1859. I. Title.

BOWDEN, Keith Macrae 639.28
Captain James Kelly of Hobart Town [Parkville] Melbourne Univ. Pr; New York, Cambridge [1965] vi, 126p. illus., maps. 22cm. Bibl. [SH381.B68] 65-24883 6.50
1. Kelly, James, I. Title.

Kelly, Michael, 1764?-1826.

KELLY, Michael, 1764?-1826. 782.1'092'4 B
Reminiscences / Michael Kelly ; edited with an introd. by Roger Fiske. London ; New York : Oxford University Press, 1975. xx, 396 p., [8] leaves of plates : ill. ; 25 cm. (Oxford English memoirs and travels) Includes index. [ML420.K292A3 1975] 75-324124 ISBN 0-19-255417-4 : £7.50
1. Kelly, Michael, 1764?-1826. 2. London. King's Theatre. 3. Singers—Correspondence, reminiscences, etc. I. Fiske, Roger. II. Title. III. Series.

Kelly, Orville E., 1930-

KELLY, Orville E., 1930- 362.1'9'699400924 B
Make today count / Orville E. Kelly with Randall Becker ; foreword by Elisabeth Kubler-Ross. New York : Delacorte Press, [1975] xi, 203 p. ; 22 cm. [RC263.K43] 75-17813 ISBN 0-440-05256-4 : 7.95
1. Kelly, Orville E., 1930- 2. Cancer—Personal narratives. I. Becker, Randall, joint author. II. Title. **BIP**

KELLY, Orville E., 1930- 362.1'9'699409 B
Until tomorrow comes / Orville E. Kelly. 1st ed. New York : Everest House, c1979. p. cm. [RC280.L9K44 1979] 78-74582 ISBN 0-89696-031-5 : 8.95
1. Kelly, Orville E., 1930- 2. Lymphoma—Biography. 3. Cancer patients—Rehabilitation. I. Title. **BIP**

Kelly, Plympton J.

KELLY, Plympton J. 979'.004'97
We were not summer soldiers : the Indian war diary of Plympton J. Kelly, 1855-1856 / with introductory essay and annotations by William N. Bischoff. Tacoma : Washington State Historical Society. 1976. 191 p., [1] fold. leaf of plates : ill. ; 24 cm. Includes index. Bibliography: p. 178-187. [E83.84.K44] 76-11999 ISBN 0-917048-00-8 : 8.75
1. Kelly, Plympton J. 2. Pacific coast Indians, War with, 1847-1865. 3. Yakima Indians—Wars. I. Bischoff, William Norbert. II. Washington State Historical Society. III. Title. IV. Title: The Indian war diary of Plymton J. Kelly, 1855-1856.

***Kelly, Regina (Zimmerman)**

*KELLY, Regina (Zimmerman) 1898- 920
The picture story and biography of Marquette and Joliet, Illus. by W. T. Mars. Chicago, Follett [c.1965] 144p. illus. (pt. col.) 22cm. (Lib. of Amer heroes) 65-14479 1.95 bds.,
I. Title.

Kelly, Walt.

LEVIN, Martin, ed. 818.082
Five boyhoods: Howard Lindsay, Harry Golden, Walt Kelly, William K. Zinsser and John Updike. [1st ed.] New York, Doubleday, 1962. 198 p. illus. 22 cm. [PS221.L4] 61-9527
1. Lindsay, Howard, 1889- 2. Golden, Harry Lewis, 1902- 3. Kelly, Walt. 4. Zinsser, William Knowlton. 5. Updike, John. I. Title.

Kelty, Matthew.

KELTY, Matthew. 271'.125'024 B
Flute solo : reflections of a Trappist hermit / Matthew Kelty. Kansas City, Kan. : Andrews and McMeel, c1979. 128 p. ; 23 cm. [BX4705.K375A34] 79-13335 ISBN 0-8362-3912-1 : 7.95
1. Kelty, Matthew. 2. Trappist in the United States—Biography. 3. Monastic and religious life. I. Title. **BIP**

Kelvin, William Thomson, baron, 1824-1907.

SHARLIN, Harold I. 530'.092'4 B
Lord Kelvin, the dynamic Victorian / Harold Issadore Sharlin, in collaboration with Tiby Sharlin. University Park : Pennsylvania State University Press, c1978. p. cm. Includes bibliographical references. [QC16.K3S53] 78-50771 ISBN 0-271-00203-4 : 16.00
1. Kelvin, William Thomson, Baron, 1824-1907. 2. Physicists—Great Britain—Biography. 3. Science—Great Britain—History. I. Sharlin, Tiby. II. Title.

THOMPSON, Silvanus Phillips, 1851-1916. 530'.092'4
The life of Lord Kelvin / by Silvanus P. Thompson. 2d ed. Bronx, N.Y. : Chelsea Pub. Co., [1976] p. cm. Originally published in 1910 under title: The life of William Thomson, Baron Kelvin of Largs. Bibliography: v. 2, p. [QC16.K3T7 1976] 75-45133 ISBN 0-8284-0292-2 : 39.50 (set)
1. Kelvin, William Thomson, baron, 1824-1907. I. Title. **BIP**

Kemble, Charles, 1775-1854.

WILLIAMSON, Jane. 792'.0924 B
Charles Kemble, man of the theatre. Lincoln, University of Nebraska Press [1970] x, 267 p. port. 23 cm. Bibliography: p. 241-254. [PN2598.K375W5 1970] 69-19105 7.95
1. Kemble, Charles, 1775-1854.

Kemble, Frances Anne, 1809-1893.

DRIVER, Leota Stultz. 792'.028'0924 B
Fanny Kemble, by Leota S. Driver. New York, Negro Universities Press [1969] xiv, 271 p. illus., ports. 23 cm. Reprint of the 1933 ed. Bibliography: p. [243]-255. [PN2598.K4D7 1969] 76-97449
1. Kemble, Frances Anne, 1809-1893. **BIP**

KEMBLE, Frances Anne, 1809-1893. 792'.092'4 B
Fanny, the American Kemble: her journals and unpublished letters. Edited with annotations by Fanny Kemble Wister. Tallahassee [South Pass Press] 1972. xv, 227 p. illus. 24 cm. [PN2598.K4A25 1972] 72-80474
I. Stokes, Frances K. (Wister) II. Title.

MARSHALL, Dorothy. 792'.028'0924 B
Fanny Kemble / Dorothy Marshall. New York : St. Martin's Press, 1978, c1977. 280 p., [4] leaves of plates : ill. ; 23 cm. Includes index. [PN2598.K4M3 1978] 77-3854 ISBN 0-312-28162-5 : 8.95
1. Kemble, Frances Anne, 1809-1893. 2. Actors—Great Britain—Biography. **BIP**

WISE, Winifred Esther, 1906- 792.0924 (B)
Fanny Kemble: actress, author, abolitionist [by] Winifred E. Wise. New York, Putnam [1967, c1966] 222 p. port. 21 cm. Bibliography: p. 217-218. [PN2598.K4W5] 67-276
1. Kemble, Frances Anne, 1800-1893. I. Title.

Kemble, Frances Anne, 1809-1893—Juvenile literature.

KERR, Laura (Nowak) 1904- 927.92
Footlights to fame; the life of Fanny Kemble. New York, Funk & Wagnalls [1962] 217p. 22cm. 62-16173 3.50
1. Kemble, Frances Anne, 1809-1893—Juvenile literature. I. Title.

SCOTT, John Anthony, 1916- 917.58'03'30924 B
Fanny Kemble's America. Illustrated with photos. New York, Crowell [1973] x, 146 p. illus. 21 cm. (Women of America) Bibliography: p. 138-140. Biography of a famous English actress who wrote Journal of a Residence on a Georgian Plantation, which recorded her observations of slavery on her husband's estates. [PN2598.K4S3] 72-7557 ISBN 0-690-28911-1 4.50
1. Kemble, Frances Anne, 1809-1893—Juvenile literature. I. Title.

SCOTT, John Anthony, 1916- 917.58'03'30924 B
Fanny Kemble's America. [New York, Dell, 1975, c1973] 144 p. 18 cm. (Laurel-leaf library) (Women of America) Bibliography: p. 137-139 Biography of a famous English actress who wrote Journal of a Residence on a Georgian Plantation, which recorded her observations of slavery on her husband's estates. [PN2598.K4S3] 0.95 (pbk.)
1. Kemble, Frances Anne, 1809-1893—Juvenile literature. I. Title.
L.C. card number for the original ed.: 72-7557 **BIP**

Kemble, John Mitchell, 1807-1857—Biography—Addresses, essays, lectures.

DICKINS, Bruce, 1889- 410'.92'4 B
Two Kembles, John and Henry / [by] Bruce Dickins. Cambridge ([Corpus Christi College, Cambridge]) : The author, 1974. 34 p., plate : ports. ; 26 cm. Contents.Contents.—John Mitchell Kemble and old English scholarship.—The story of "Washington Square." [PE64.K4D53 1974] 74-190131 ISBN 0-9503285-0-2 : £0.50
1. Kemble, John Mitchell, 1807-1857—Biography—Addresses, essays, lectures. 2. Kemble, Henry Stephen, 1789-1836. I. Title.

Kemble, John Philip, 1757-1823.

BOADEN, James, 1762-1839. 792'.028'0924 B
Memoirs of the life of John Philip Kemble. New York, B. Blom, 1969. 2 v. port. 21 cm. Reprint of the 1825 ed. [PN2598.K5B6 1969] 77-89713
1. Kemble, John Philip, 1757-1823. 2. Theater—England—History. I. Title. BIP

FITZGERALD, Percy Hetherington, 1834-1925. 792'.028'0922 B
The Kembles; an account of the Kemble family, including the lives of Mrs. Siddons, and her brother, John Philip Kemble. New York, B. Blom, 1969- v. ports. 21 cm. Reprint of the 1871 ed. [PN2598.K38F5 1969] 73-89712
1. Kemble, John Philip, 1757-1823. 2. Siddons, Sarah (Kemble) 1755-1831. 3. Kemble family. I. Title.

Kemmerer, John—Chronology.

KEMMERER, John. 818'.5'209 B
A biographical note / John Kemmerer. 1st ed. New York : Kemmerer, 1975. 19 p. ; 21 cm. "Seventy copies." [PS3521.E448B55] 76-355732
1. Kemmerer, John—Chronology I. Title.

Kemp, Ben E., 1860-1932.

KEMP, Ben W., 1890- 917.64'03'5
Cow dust and saddle leather, by Ben W. Kemp with J. C. Dykes. [1st ed.] Norman, University of Okalahoma Press [1968] xvii, 300 p. illus., ports. 24 cm. [F786.K4] 67-24617
1. Kemp, Ben E., 1860-1932. 2. Frontier and pioneer life—Southwest, New. I. Dykes, Jefferson Chenowth, 1900- II. Title.

Kemp, Clarence E.

KEMP, Clarence E. 266'.023'0924
It's a long trip from Shinglehouse to Angmagsalik, by Clarence E. Kemp, Jr. Forward by J. F. Rodriguez. Editings by Freda Hark, Betty Kemp [and] Mary Anne Measer. 1st ed. Lancaster, N.Y., [1969] 114 p. illus., facsims., ports. 24 cm. Title on spine: Shinglehouse to Angmagsalik. Autobiographical. [BX6495.K357A3] 79-10955
I. Title. II. Title: Shinglehouse to Angmagsalik.

Kemp, Harry Curtis.

KEMP, Harry Curtis. 926.3
Kemp's life story. New York, Carlton Press, 1960. 100p. 21cm. (A Comet reflection book) [CT275.K449A3] 61-795
I. Title.

Kemp, Mary (Lockwood).

THURSTON, Katherine (Kemp) 920.7
The winds of doctrine; the story of the life of Mary Lockwood Kemp in Mormon Utah during the last half of the nineteenth century. [1st ed.] New York, Exposition Press [1952] 259 p. illus. 23 cm. [BX8695.K4T45] 52-7662
1. Kemp, Mary (Lockwood). I. Title.

Kemp-Welch, Lucy, 1869-1958.

MESSUM, David. 759.2 B
The life and work of Lucy Kemp-Welch / by David Messum ; edited by Laura Wortley. [Woodbridge] : Antique Collectors' Club, 1976. 111 p. : ill. (some col.), ports. ; 29 cm. Includes catalogue of the L. Kemp-Welch Studio Collection exhibited at the David Messum Gallery, Spring 1976. Ill. on lining papers. [ND497.K446M47] 77-360045 ISBN 0-902028-43-X : 30.00
1. Kemp-Welch, Lucy, 1869-1958. 2. Painters—Great Britain—Biography. 3. Animals in art. I. Kemp-Welch, Lucy, 1869-1958. II. David Messum Gallery. The Lucy Kemp-Welch studio collection. 1976. III. Title.
Distributed by Antique Collectors' Club 1515 Broadway, New York

Kempe, Margery (Burnham) b. ca. 1373.

CHOLMELEY, Katharine. 248'.2'0924 B
Margery Kempe, genius and mystic / by Katherine Cholmeley. Folcroft, Pa. : Folcroft Library Editions, 1978. p. cm. Reprint of the 1947 ed. published by Longmans, Green, London. [PR2007.K4Z7 1978] 78-7811 ISBN 0-8414-0296-5 lib. bdg. : 17.50
1. Kempe, Margery Burnham, b. ca. 1373. 2. Authors, English—Middle English, 1100-1500—Biography. 3. Mystics—England—Biography. I. Title. BIP

COLLIS, Louise. 922.242
Memoirs of a medieval woman; the life and times of Margery Kempe. New York, Crowell [1964] 269 p. illus. 22 cm. First published in London in 1964 under title: The apprentice saint. Bibliography: p. 261-263. [PR2007.K4Z72] 64-23138
1. Kempe, Margery (Burnham) b. ca. 1373. I. Title.

Kemper, Edmund Emil, 1948

CHENEY, Margaret. 364.1'523'0924 B
The coed killer / by Margaret Cheney. New York : Walker, 1976. xv, 222 p. ; 24 cm. [HV6248.K415C46 1976] 75-25196 ISBN 0-8027-0514-6 : 8.95
1. Kemper, Edmund Emil, 1948- I. Title. BIP

Kemper, Robert G.

KEMPER, Robert G. 285'.8'0924 B
An elephant's ballet / Robert G. Kemper. New York : Seabury Press, c1977. p. cm. "A Crossroad book." [BX7260.K38A34 1977] 77-22165 ISBN 0-8164-0373-2 : 6.95
1. Kemper, Robert G. 2. Congregationalists—United States—Biography. 3. Clergy—United States—Biography. 4. Blind—United States—Biography. I. Title. BIP

Kenaga, R. F., 1898-

KENAGA, R. F., 1898- 979.5 B
Impact : a generation of changes : [autobiography] / by R. F. Kenaga. Portland, Or. : Metropolitan Press, 1974. vi, 140 p., [7] leaves of plates : ill. ; 22 cm. [CT275.K4518A34] 75-307274 4.50
1. Kenaga, R. F., 1898- 2. Kenaga family. I. Title.

Kendon, Frank,

KENDON, Frank, 1893- 928.2
The small years. With an introd. by Walter De La Mare. [2d ed.] Cambridge [Eng.] University Press, 1950. xvii, 208 p. map (on lining papers) 20 cm. Memories of the first few years of the author's childhood. [PR6021.E63Z5 1950] 51-7618
I. Title.

Kendrick, Charles, 1876-1970.

KENDRICK, Charles, 1876-1970. 338.7'67 B
Memoirs of Charles Kendrick. Edited and annotated with an introd. by David Warren Ryder. A foreword by Ben C. Duniway, and pref. by Timothy McDonnell. Decorations by Dan Adair. [San Francisco, 1972] xvii, 203 p. illus. 27 cm. [CT275.K4546A3] 73-157149
1. Kendrick, Charles, 1876-1970.

Kenmore, Carolyn.

KENMORE, Carolyn. 659.15'2
Mannequin; my life as a model. [New York] Bartholomew House [1969] 313 p. 22 cm. [HD6073.M72U54] 79-79434 5.95
I. Title.

Kennan, George Frost,

KENNAN, George Frost, 1904- 327'.73
Memoirs [by] George F. Kennan. [1st ed.] Boston, Little, Brown [1967-72] 2 v. 24 cm. "An Atlantic Monthly Press book." Contents.—[1] 1925-1950.—[2] 1950-1963. [E748.K374A3] 67-23834

Kennedy, Caroline.

*MARTINIS, Gloria K. 920.72
The two Carolines, by Gloria K. Martinis. New York, Leisure Books [1976] 204 p. illus. 18 cm. [HQ1420] 1.50 (pbk.)
1. Kennedy, Caroline. 2. Grimaldi, Caroline. I. Title. BIP

Kennedy, Edward Moore, 1932-

DAVID, Lester. 973.92'0924 B
Ted Kennedy; triumphs and tragedies. New York, Award Books [1975] 351 p. illus. 18 cm. [E840.8.K35D3] 1.95 (pbk.)
1. Kennedy, Edward Moore, 1932- I. Title. L.C. no. of original edition: 70-183019.

DAVID, Lester. 973.92'0924 B
Ted Kennedy, triumphs and tragedies. New York, Grosset & Dunlap [1972] 274 p. illus. 22 cm. [E840.8.K35D3] 70-183019 ISBN 0-448-01767-9 7.95
1. Kennedy, Edward Moore, 1932-

HERSH, Burton. 973.92'092'4 B
The education of Edward Kennedy; a family biography. New York, Morrow, 1972. xiii, 510 p. illus. 25 cm. Bibliography: p. [497]-500. [E840.8.K35H4] 72-182451 10.95
1. Kennedy, Edward Moore, 1932- I. Title. BIP

HONAN, William Holmes. 973.924'092'4 B
Ted Kennedy, profile of a survivor; Edward M. Kennedy after Bobby, after Chappaquiddick, and after three years of Nixon, by William H. Honan. [New York] Quadrangle Books [1972] vii, 180 p. ports. 21 cm. [E840.8.K35H6 1972] 71-187325 6.95
1. Kennedy, Edward Moore, 1932- I. Title.

LIPPMAN, Theo. 328.73'092'4 B
Senator Ted Kennedy / Theo Lippman, Jr. 1st ed. New York : Norton, c1976. xi, 296 p., [4] leaves of plates : ill. ; 24 cm. Includes index. [E840.8.K35L56 1976] 75-28347 ISBN 0-393-05568-X : 8.95
1. Kennedy, Edward Moore, 1932- I. Title.

RUST, Zad. 973.923'0924
Teddy bare, the last of the Kennedy clan. Boston, Western Islands [1971] x, 275 p. illus., ports. 22 cm. [E840.8.K35R8] 79-25329 7.00
1. Kennedy, Edward Moore, 1932- 2. Kopechne, Mary Jo, 1941-1969. I. Title.

SHERRILL, Robert. 973.92'092'4 B
The last Kennedy / Robert Sherrill. New York : Dial Press, 1976. ix, 239 p. ; 24 cm. Includes index. Bibliography: p. 229-230. [E840.8.K35S55] 76-2212 ISBN 0-8037-4419-6 : 8.95
1. Kennedy, Edward Moore, 1932- 2. Kopechne, Mary Jo, 1941-1969. I. Title.

TED Kennedy, heir to greatness. 973.923'0924 [Editor: Gene Wright. New York, Universal Pub. and Distributing Corp., 1968] 64 p. (chiefly illus., ports.) 28 cm. "An Award special-events edition." [E840.8.K35T4] 68-7739 1.00
1. Kennedy, Edward Moore, 1932- I. Wright, Gene, 1939- ed.

Kennedy, Ethel Skakel.

DAVID, Lester. 973.922'0924 B
Ethel; the story of Mrs. Robert F. Kennedy. New York, World Pub. Co. [1971] xi, 274 p. 22 cm. [CT275.K4574D38] 73-145833 7.95
1. Kennedy, Ethel Skakel. I. Title.

Kennedy family.

†ADLER, Bill. 973.92'0922 B
The Kennedy kids / [by Bill Adler]. 1st ed. Chicago : Playboy Press, c1976. 191 p. : ports. ; 18 cm. Includes bibliographical references. [E843.A34] 76-9586 pbk. 1.75
1. Kennedy family. I. Title.

BUCK, Pearl (Sydenstricker) 1892- 973.92'0922
The Kennedy women; a personal appraisal [by] Pearl S. Buck. [1st ed.] New York, Cowles Book Co. [1970] 218 p. ports. 22 cm. [E843.B78 1970] 74-90067 5.95
1. Kennedy family. I. Title.

CARR, William A. H. 929.2
Those fabulous Kennedy women. New York, Wisdom House, 520 Fifth Ave. [c.1961] 157p. (W103) 61-65117 .50 pap.,
1. Kennedy family. I. Title.

CARR, William H A 929.2
Those fabulous Kennedy women. New York, Wisdom House [1961] 157 p. 19 cm. [E843.K4C3] 61-65117
1. Kennedy family. I. Title.

*DUNLEAVY, Stephen 973.92'092'2 B
Those wild, wild Kennedy boys. Reported by Stephen Dunleavy and Peter Brennan. New York, Pinnacle Books [1976] 211 p. illus. 18 cm. [E843] ISBN 0-523-00968-2 1.75 (pbk.)
1. Kennedy family. I. Brennan, Peter, joint author. II. Title. BIP

FRIEDMAN, Stanley P., 1925- 920.7
The magnificent Kennedy women. Derby, Conn., Monarch [c.1964] 157p. ports. 19cm. (Select bks., MS25) 64-1266 .75 pap.,
1. Kennedy family. I. Title.

HIRSCH, Phi, ed. 923.573
The Kennedy war heroes. New York, Pyramid [c.1960-1962] 159p. 19cm. (F-748) 62-5781 .40 pap.,
1. World War, 1939-1945—Biog. I. Title.

*HIRSCH, Phil, ed. 920.073
The Kennedy courage, ed. by Phil Hirsch, Edward Hymoff. New York, Pyramid [c.1965] 128p. 18cm. (X-1238) .60 pap.,
I. Title.

HIRSCH, Phil, ed. 929.2
The Kennedy courage, edited by Phil Hirsch and Edward Hymoff. New York, Pyramid Books [1965] 128 p. illus., ports. 18 cm. [E843.K4H5] 66-3914
1. Kennedy family. 2. Courage. I. Hymoff, Edward, joint ed. II. Title.

HIRSCH, Phil, ed. 923.573
The Kennedy war heroes. New York, Pyramid Books [1962] 159p. 19cm. (Pyramid books, F-748) Accounts of World War II combat experiences of members of President Kennedy's administration. [D736.H5] 62-5781
1. World War, 1939-1945—Biog. I. Title.

SHAW, Maud 973.9220922
White House nannie; my years with Caroline and John Kennedy, Jr. [New York] New Amer. Lib. [1966, c.1965] 127p. 18cm. (Signet bk., P3063) .60 pap.,
1. Kennedy family. 2. Kennedy, John Fitzgerald, 1960- 3. Kennedy, Caroline, 1957- I. Title.

SHAW, Maud. 973.9220922
White House nannie; my years with Caroline and John Kennedy, Jr. [New York] New American Library [1966] 205 p. ports. 21 cm. [E843.S53 1966] 66-17883
1. Kennedy family. 2. Kennedy, John Fitzgerald, 1960- 3. Kennedy, Caroline, 1957- I. Title.

THOMPSON, Nelson. 973.922'092'2 B
The dark side of Camelot / by Nelson Thompson. 1st ed. Chicago : Playboy Press, c1976. 172 p. ; 18 cm. Includes bibliographical references. [E483.T48] 76-2163 pbk. : 1.75
1. Kennedy family. I. Title.

Kennedy family—Portraits, caricatures, etc.

SHAW, Mark. 923.173
The John F. Kennedys; a family album. [New York] Farrar, Straus [1964] 159 p. (chiefly illus., ports.) 28 cm. [E843.S5 1964] 64-16278
1. Kennedy family—Portraits, caricatures, etc. 2. Kennedy, John Fitzgerald, Pres. U.S., 1917-1963—Portraits, caricatures, etc. I. Title.

Kennedy, Florynce, 1916-

KENNEDY, Florynce, 1916- 340'.092'4
Color me Flo : my hard life and good times / by Flo Kennedy. Englewood Cliff, N.J. : Prentice-Hall, c1976. 168 p. : ill. ; 25 cm. [KF373.K45A3] 76-17893 ISBN 0-13-152371-6 : 7.95 ISBN 0-13-152363-5 pbk. : 4.95
1. Kennedy, Florynce, 1916- 2. Lawyers—United States—Correspondence, reminiscences, etc. I. Title.

Kennedy, Hannah (Baker)—Juvenile literature.

HEATH, May A. (Van Dyn) 920.7
Iowa Hannah. Illus. by Charles Walker. New York, Hastings House [c.1961] 117p. 60-14619 2.75
1. Kennedy, Hannah (Baker)—Juvenile literature. 2. Frontier and pioneer life—Iowa—Waterloo—Juvenile literature. I. Title.

Kennedy, Harold J.

KENNEDY, Harold J. 792'.0233'0924 B
No pickel, no performance : an irrevelent theatrical excursion from Tallulah to Travolta / Harold J. Kennedy. New York : Berkley Pub. Corp., 1979, c1978. viii, 262p. : ill. ; 18 cm. (A Berkley book) [PN2287.K652A35] ISBN 0-425-04148-4 pbk. : 2.25
1. Kennedy, Harold J. 2. Theatrical producers and directors — United States — Biography. I. Title.
L.C. card no. for 1978 Doubleday ed.: 77-11767.

KENNEDY, Harold J. 792'.0233'0924 B
No pickle, no performance : an irreverent theatrical excursion from Tallulah to Travolta / Harold J. Kennedy. 1st ed. Garden City, N.Y. : Doubleday, 1978. 237 p., [16] leaves of plates : ill. ; 22 cm. [PN2287.K652A35] 77-11767 8.95
1. Kennedy, Harold J. 2. Theatrical producers and directors—United States—Biography. I. Title. **BIP**

Kennedy, Jacqueline (Bouvier) 1929-

CURTIS, Charlotte 920.7
First Lady. New York, Pyramid [c.1962] 158p. illus. 18cm. (R-767) 62-52325 .50 pap.,
1. Kennedy, Jacqueline (Bouvier) 1929- I. Title.

DAREFF, Hal 917.3
Jacqueline Kennedy, a portrait in courage. Illustrated by Tom Quinn. New York, Parents' Magazine Press [1965] 192 p. illus. 22 cm. [E843.K4D3] 65-26386
1. Kennedy, Jacqueline (Bouvier) 1929- — Juvenile literature. I. Title.

HALL, Gordon Langley 920.7
Jacqueline Kennedy, a biography, by Gordon Langley Hall, Ann Pinchot. New York, Fell [c.1964] 275p. ports. 22cm. 62-8518 4.95
1. Kennedy, Jacqueline (Bouvier) 1929- I. Pinchot, Ann, joint author. II. Title.

HALL, Gordon Langley 920.7
Jacqueline Kennedy, a biography by Gordon Langlev Hall, Ann Pinchot [New York] New Amer. Lib. [1966, c.1964] 192p. ports. 18cm. (Signet bk., P2819) [E843.K4113] .60 pap.,
1. Kennedy, Jacqueline (Bouvier) 1929- I. Pinchot, Ann, joint author. II. Title.

HALL, Gordon Langley. 920.7
Jacqueline Kennedy, a biography, by Gordon Langley Hall and Ann Pinchot. New York, F. Fell [1964] 275 p. ports. 22 cm. [E843.K4113] 64-8518
1. Kennedy, Jacqueline (Bouvier) 1929- I. Pinchot, Ann, joint author. II. Title.

HARDING, Robert T. 973.9220924
Jacqueline Kennedy, a woman for the world, by Robert T. Harding, A. L. Holmes. New York, Encyclopedia Enterprises; dist. by Vanguard [c.1966] 128p. illus., ports. (pt. col.) 32cm. [E843.K4I33] 66-4408 5.95 bds.,
1. Kennedy, Jacqueline (Bouvier) 1929- I. Holmes, A. L., joint author. II. Title.

HARDING, Robert T 973.9220924
Jacqueline Kennedy, a woman for the world, by Robert T. Harding and A. L. Holmes. New York, Encyclopedia Enterprises; distributed by Vanguard Press [1966] 128 p. illus., ports. (part col.) 32 cm. [E843.K4H33] 66-4408
1. Kennedy, Jacqueline (Bouvier) 1929- I. I. Holmes, A. L., joint author. II. Title. **BIP**

HELLER, Deane, 1924- 920.7
Jacqueline Kennedy [New enlarged ed. by] Deane and David Heller. Derby, Conn., Monarch [c.1959, 1963] 222p. illus. 18cm. (Select bk., MS23) .75 pap.,
1. Kennedy, Jacqueline (Bouvier) 1929- I. Heller, David, 1922- joint author. II. Title.

HELLER, Deane, 1924- 920.7
Jacqueline Kennedy: the complete story of America's glamorous first lady [by] Deane and David Heller. Derby, Conn., Monarch Books [1961] 139p. 19cm. (Monarch books, K54) [E843.K4H4] 61-851
1. Kennedy, Jacqueline (Bouvier) 1929- I. Heller, David, 1922- joint author. II. Title.

HELLER, Deane, 1924- 741.5973
Jacqueline Kennedy; the warmly human life story of the woman all Americans have taken to their heart [by] Deane and David Heller. [New., enl. ed.] Derby, Conn., Monarch Books [1963] 222 p. ports. 19 cm. (Monarch select books, MS23) "Special memorial edition." [E843.K4114 1963] 64-1497
1. Kennedy, Jacqueline (Bouvier) 1929- I. Title.

PODELL, Jack J., ed. v. 12
Jacqueline Kennedy, woman of valor. Jack J. Podell, editorial director; Claire Safran, editor; Kenneth Cunningham, art direction [and] Marion Will, assistant art director. New York, Macfadden-Bartell, 1964. 80 p. illus., ports. 28 cm.
1. Kennedy, Jacqueline (Bouvier) 1929- I. Afran, Claire, ed. II. Title.

THAYER, Mary Van Rensselaer. 920.7
Jacqueline Bouvier Kennedy, [1st ed.] Garden City, N.Y., Doubleday, 1961. 127 p. illus. 27 cm. [E843.K4T5] 61-17432
1. Kennedy, Jacqueline (Bouvier) 1929- I. Title.

Kennedy, Jacqueline (Bouvier) 1929- —Juvenile Literature.

DAREFF, Hal 917.3
Jacaueline Kennedy, a portrait in courage. Illus. by Tom Quinn. New York, Parents' Mag. Pr. [c.1965] 192p. illus. 22cm. [E843.K4D3] 66-26386 2.95; 3.03 lib. ed.,
1. Kennedy, Jacqueline (Bouvier) 1929- — Juvenile Literature. I. Title.

Kennedy, Jacqueline Lee (Bouvier) 1929- Iconography.

TATLER Pub. Co., Washington, D.C. v. 12
One dozen red roses, the life story of Jacqueline Kennedy. Washington, D.C., Tatler Pub. Co., 1964. 72 p. illus., ports. 28 cm. Photographs by United Press International and Chase Studios, Ltd., Washington, D.C. 66-185
1. Kennedy, Jacqueline Lee (Bouvier) 1929- Iconography. I. Title.

Kennedy, Joan Bennett.

DAVID, Lester. 973.92'092'4 B
Joan—the reluctant Kennedy; a biographical profile. New York, Funk & Wagnalls [1974] 264 p. illus. 21 cm. [CT275.K4575D38] 74-7243 ISBN 0-308-10122-7 6.95
1. Kennedy, Joan Bennett. I. Title.

DAVID, Lester. 973.91'092'4 B
Joan—the reluctant Kennedy : a biographical profile / by Lester David. New York : Warner Paperback Library, 1975. 255 p. : ill. ; 18 cm. Includes index. [CT275.K4575D38 1975] 75-324332 ISBN 0-446-59761-9 pbk. 1.75
1. Kennedy, Joan Bennett. I. Title.

Kennedy, John Fitzgerald, Pres. U.S., 1917-1963.

BERGQUIST, Lauara 973.9220924
A very special President. Photos. by Stanley Tretick. Designed by Leonard Jossel. New York, McGraw [c.1965] 203p. illus., ports. 27cm. [E842.B37] 65-26163 9.95
1. Kennedy, John Fitzgerald, Pres. U. S., 1917-1963. I. Tretick, Stanley, illus. II. Title.

BISHOP, James Alonzo, 1907- 923.173
A day in the life of President Kennedy. New York, Bantam [c.1964] 145p. illus. 18cm. (F2867) .50 pap.,
1. Kennedy, John Fitzgerald, Pres., U.S., 1917-1963. I. Title.

BRADLEE, Benjamin. 923.173
That special grace. [1st ed.] Philadelphia, Lippincott [1964] 1 v. (unpaged) ports. 22 cm. "Test ... originally appeared in Newsweek [under the title: He had that special grace]" [E842.B7] 64-18629
1. Kennedy, John Fitzgerald, Pres., U.S., 1917-1963.

BURNS, James MacGregor. 923.173
John Kennedy: a political profile. New York, Harcourt, Brace & World [1961] xxiii, 309p. ports. 21cm. 'Bibliographical note': p. 283-284. Bibliographical references included in 'Chapter notes' (p. 285-298) [E842.B8 1961] 61-65170
1. Kennedy, John Fitzgerald, Pres. U. S., 1917- I. Title.

DONOVAN, Robert J. 940.545973
PT109, John F. Kennedy in World War II. Introd. letter by President Kennedy: Greenwich, Conn., Fawcett [1963, c.1961] 160p. 18cm. (Crest bk. d523) .50 pap.,
1. Kennedy, John Fitzgerald, Pres. U.S., 1917- 2. World War, 1939-1945—Pacific Ocean. 3. World War, 1939-1945—Naval operations, American. I. Title.

THE First Family photo album, by Earle Doud, Bob Booker [and] George Foster. Greenwich, Conn., Fawcett Publications, 1963. unpaged. illus. 16 x 21 cm. (A Fawcett special, no. 5) [E843.D6] 63-4909 741.5973
1. Kennedy, John Fitzgerald, Pres. U.S., 1917- 2. Kennedy family.

FITZGERALD, Gordon. v. 12
A Catholic rebels. Dallas, Distributed by Teacher Pub. Co. [c1962] 95 p. 20 cm. Bibliography and bibliographical notes: p. 91-95. 64-67281
1. Kennedy, John Fitzgerald, Pres. U.S. 1917-1963. 2. U.S. Pol. & govt. 1961- I. Title.

GARIANO, Carmelo. v. 12
Saga de Kennedy. Dibujos de Michael Grotzki. [Hollywood, Calif., Orbe Publications, inc., 1966] 94 p. illus. 21 cm. (Coleccion actualidades liricas) Poem. 68-89216
1. Kennedy, John Fitzgerald, Pres., U.S., 1917-1963. I. Title.

GROMYKO, Anatolii Andreevich. 301.15'43'973922
Through Russian eyes: President Kennedy's 1036 days [by] Anatolii Andreievich Gromyko. [Edited by Philip A. Garon.] Washington, International Library, 1973. xx, 227 p. 21 cm. Cover title. Translation of Tysiacha tridtsat' shest' dnei prezidenta Kennedi. [E841.G713] 73-75637 9.95
1. Kennedy, John Fitzgerald, Pres., U.S., 1917-1963. I. Title.
Publisher's address: 2425 Wilson Blvd., Arlington, Va. 22201

HANFF, Helene. v. 12
John F. Kennedy; young man of destiny. Garden City, N.Y., Nelson Doubleday [c1965] 64 p. illus. 21 cm. (Know your America program [no. 29]) 67-100295
1. Kennedy, John Fitsgerald, Pres. U.S., 1917-1963. I. Title. II. Series.

HOOPES, Roy Harry, 1922- JUV
What the President does all day; a typical office day in the Presidency, presented through photographs and brief text. New York, John Day, c.1962. 64p. illus. 26cm. 62-12615 2.50; 2.68 lib. ed.,
1. Kennedy, John Fitzgerald, Pres. U.S., 1917- I. Title.

KENNEDY, John Fitzgerald, Pres. U.S., 1917-1963. 817'.5'4
The complete Kennedy wit. Edited by Bill Adler. [1st ed.] New York, Citadel Press [1967] 203 p. port. 22 cm. Includes most of the material from The Kennedy wit and More Kennedy wit, and new material. [E842.A25A34] 67-25653
I. Adler, Bill, ed. II. Title.

LASKY, Victor. 923.173
J.F.K. : the man and the myth / Victor Lasky. New York : Dell Pub. Co., 1977,c1966. 883p. ; 18 cm. (A Dell Book) Includes bibliographical references and index. [E842.L3] ISBN 0-440-14407-8 pbk. : 2.75
1. Kennedy, John Fitzgerald, Pres. U.S.,1917- 2. United States-Politics and government-1961- I. Title.
L.C. card for c1963 Macmillian ed.:63-16367. **BIP**

LINCOLN, Anne H. 394'.4'0973
The Kennedy White House Parties [by] Anne H. Lincoln. New York, Viking [1967] 181p. illus. (pt. col.), facsims., ports. (pt. col.) 29cm. (Studio bk.) [E842.1.L5] 67-26085 12.50
1. Kennedy, John Fitzgerald, Pres. U. S., 1917-1963. 2. Kennedy, Jacqueline (Bouvier) 1929- 3. Washington, D. C. — Amusements. 4. Washington, D. C.—White House. I. Title.

MCCARTHY, Joe. 923.273
The remarkable Kennedys. New York, Popular Library [c.1960] 143p. 18cm. (Popular Giant PC850) .50 pap.,
1. Kennedy, John Fitzgerald, 1917. 2. Kennedy family. I. Title.

MCCARTHY, Joe, 1915- 923.273
The remarkable Kennedys. New York, Dial Press, 1960. 190p. 22cm. [E747.M25] 60-8394
1. Kennedy, John Fitzgerald. 1917- 2. Kennedy family. I. Title.

MCCARTHY, Joe, 1915- 923.273
The remarkable Kennedys. New York, Dial Press, 1960. 190p. 22cm. [E747.M25] 60-8394
1. Kennedy, John Fitzgerald. 1917- 2. Kennedy family. I. Title.

MCCARTHY, Joe [Joseph Weston McCarthy] 923.273
The remarkable Kennedys. New York, Dial Press, [c.]1960 190p. 22cm. 60-8394 3.50; 1.95 pap.,
1. Kennedy, John Fitzgerald, 1917- 2. Kennedy family. I. Title.

MCCARTHY, Joe [Joseph Weston McCarthy] 923.273
The remarkable Kennedys. New York,

Dial Press, [c.]1960 190p. 22cm. 60-8394 3.50; 1.95 pap.,
1. Kennedy, John Fitzgerald, 1917- 2. Kennedy family. I. Title.

MARKMANN, Charles Lam 973.922
John F. Kennedy: a sense of purpose [by] Charles Lam Markmann, Mark Sherwin. New York, St. Martin's [c.1961] 346p. 61-13380 4.95
1. Kennedy, John Fitzgerald, Pres. U. S., 1917- 2. U. S.—Pol. & govt.—1961- I. Sherwin, Mark, joint author. II. Title.

MARKMANN, Charles Lam. 973.922
John F. Kennedy: a sense of purpose [by] Charles Lam Markmann and Mark Sherwin. New York, St. Martin's Press [1961] 346p. 22cm. [E841.M3] 61-13380
1. Kennedy, John Fitzgerald, Pres. U. S., 1917- 2. U. S.—Pol. & govt.—1961- I. Sherwin, Mark, joint author. II. Title.

MEYERS, Joan Simpson, 973.9220924 ed.
John Fitzgerald Kennedy; as we remember him. Ed., produced under the direction of Goddard Lieberson. Ed., Joan Meyers; art director, Ira Teichberg. New York, Macmillan [1967, c.1965] ix, 241p. illus., facsim., group ports. 23x24cm. [E842.M46] 2.95 pap.,
1. Kennedy, John Fitzgerald, Pres. U.S. 1917-1963. I. Lieberson, Goddard, 1911- ed. II. Teichberg, Ira, Illus. III. Title.

PLIMPTON, George. 973.922'0924
Go Caroline! [Newport? R.I., 1963] [14] p. illus. 28 cm. [E843.P6] 77-11492
1. Kennedy, John Fitzgerald, President, 1917-1963. 2. Kennedy, Caroline, 1957- I. Title.

SALINGER, Pierre 973.9220924
With Kennedy. [New York] Avon [1967,c.1966] xvi, 476p. ports. 18cm. (N164) [E841.S2] .95 pap.,
1. Kennedy, John Fitzgerald, Pres. U. S., 1917-1963. 2. U. S.—Hist.—1945- I. Title.

*SCHOOR, Gene 923.273
Young John Kennedy. Illus. with photogs. [New York] Macfadden [1964, c.1963] 192p. illus. 18cm. (75-132) .75 pap.,
1. Kennedy, John Fitzgerald, Pres. U.S., 1917- I. Title.

SHEPARD, Tazewell Taylor, 973.922 1921-
John F. Kennedy, man of the sea, by Tazewell Shepard, Jr. Introd. by Edward M. Kennedy. New York, W. Morrow, 1965. 161 p. illus. (part col.) ports. (part col.) 32 cm. [E842.S44] 65-26256
1. Kennedy, John Fitzgerald, Pres. U. S., 1917-1963. I. Title.

SIDEY, Hugh 923.173
John F. Kennedy, President. New York, Atheneum, [c.1963] 400p. 24cm. 63-7800 6.95
1. Kennedy, John Fitzgerald, Pres U. S., 1917 2. U. S.—Pol. & govt.—1961- I. Title.

STEWART, Charles J ed. 923.173
A man named John F. Kennedy; sermons on his assassination. Edited by Charles J. Stewart and Bruce Kendall. Glen Rock, N.J., Paulist Press [1964] 208 p. 19 cm. (Deus books) [E842.9.S7] 64-66061
1. Kennedy, John Fitzgerald, Pres. U.S.,1917-1963 — Funeral and memorial services. I. Kendall, Bruce, joint ed. II. Title.

STEWART, Charles J ed. 923.173
A man named John F. Kennedy; sermons on his assassination. Edited by Charles J. Stewart and Bruce Kendall. Glen Rock, N.J., Paulist Press [1964] 208 p. 19 cm. (Deus books) [E842.9.S7] 64-66061
1. Kennedy, John Fitzgerald, Pres. U.S.,1917-1963 — Funeral and memorial services. I. Kendall, Bruce, joint ed. II. Title.

TREGASKIS, Richard 940.545973 William, 1916-
John F. Kennedy: war hero. [New York, Dell, c.1962] 223p. illus. (Dell bk., F194) An expanded ed. of John F. Kennedy and PT-log pub. by Random. 62-2846 .50 pap.,
1. Kennedy, John Fitzgerald, Pres. U.S., 1917- 2. Pt-109 (Boat) I. Title.

Kennedy, John Fitzgerald, Pres. U.S., 1917-1963.

MANCHESTER, William 973.922'0924 Raymond, 1922-
Portrait of a President: John F. Kennedy in profile. Rev. ed. with a new introd. and epilouge. Large type ed., complete and unabridged. New York, F. Watts [1967] xxii, 266 p. 29 cm. "A Keith Jennison Book." [E842.M3 1967]
1. Kennedy, John Fitzgerald, Pres. U.S., 1917-1963. 2. Sight-saving books. I. Title.

SAMMIS, Edward R 364.152
John Fitzgerald Kennedy, youngest President. New York, Scholastic Book Services [1961] 62p. illus. 21cm. [E842.S3] 62-1738
1. Kennedy, John Fitzgerald, Pres. U. S., 1917- I. Title.

Kennedy, John Fitzgerald, Pres. U.S., 1917-1963.

BISHOP, James Alonzo, 923.173 1907-
A day in the life of President Kennedy. New York, Random [c.1964] xi, 108p. 22cm. 64-15303 3.95 bds.,
1. Kennedy, John Fitzgerald. Pres. U.S., 1917-1963. I. Title.

BLAIR, Joan, 973.922'092'4 B 1929-
The search for JFK / by Joan and Clay Blair, Jr. New York : Berkley Pub. Corp. : distributed by Putnam, c1976. 608 p., [16] leaves of plates : ill. ; 24 cm. Includes index. [E842.B58 1976] 76-8257 ISBN 0-399-11418-1 : 12.95
1. Kennedy, John Fitzgerald, Pres. U.S., 1917-1963. I. Blair, Clay, 1925- joint author. II. Title. BIP

BRADLEE, 973.922'092'4 B Benjamin.
Conversations with Kennedy / Benjamin C. Bradlee. New York : Norton, [1975] 251 p. : ill. ; 22 cm. [E842.B69] 75-4956 ISBN 0-393-08722-0 7.95
1. Kennedy, John Fitzgerald, Pres. U.S., 1917-1963. 2. Bradlee, Benjamin. I. Kennedy, John Fitzgerald, Pres. U.S., 1917-1963. II. Title.

BRADLEE, Benjamin. 973.922'092'4
Conversations with Kennedy [by] Benjamin C. Bradlee. New York, Pocket Books [1976 c1975] 254 p. illus. 18 cm. [E842.B69] ISBN 0-671-80432-4 1.95 (pbk.)
1. Kennedy, John Fitzgerald, Pres. U.S., 1917-1963. 2. Bradlee, Benjamin. I. Title. L.C. card no. of 1975 Norton edition: 75-4956. BIP

BURNS, James 973.922'0924 B MacGregor.
John Fitzgerald Kennedy; a profile. [Abridged ed. San Rafael, Calif., Published by J. V. Lund for the U.S. Information Service, 1960] 41 p. 23 cm. (American civilization series, no. 6) [E842.B82] 68-49017
1. Kennedy, John Fitzgerald, Pres. U.S., 1917-1963. I. Title. II. Series.

BURNS, James MacGregor. 923.273
John Kennedy: a political profile. [1st ed.] New York, Harcourt, Brace [1960] 309 p. illus. 21 cm. [E842.B8 1960] 60-5440
1. Kennedy, John Fitzgerald, Pres. U.S., 1917-1963.

CHRISTOPHERSON, Edmund. 923.173
"Westward I go free"; the story of J. F. K. in Montana. [1st ed. Missoula, Mont., Earthquake Press, 1964] 88 p. illus. 23 cm. [E842.C5] 64-6640
1. Kennedy, John Fitzgerald, Pres. U.S., 1917-1963. I. Title.

DAMORE, Leo. 973.922'0924 B
The Cape Cod years of John Fitzgerald Kennedy. Englewood Cliffs, N.J., Prentice-Hall [1967] vii, 262 p. illus. 24 cm. Bibliographical references included in "Notes" (p. 246-262) [E842.D3] 67-24024
1. Kennedy, John Fitzgerald, Pres. U.S., 1917-1963. 2. Cape Cod. I. Title.

DINNEEN, Joseph Francis, 929.2 1897-
The Kennedy family. [1st ed.] Boston, Little, Brown [1960, c1959] 238 p. illus. 22 cm. [E747.D5] 59-11100
1. Kennedy, Joseph Patrick, 1888-1969. 2. Kennedy, John Fitzgerald, Pres. U.S., 1917-1963. 3. Kennedy family.

DOLLEN, Charles. 923.173
John F. Kennedy, American. [Boston, St. Paul Editions 1965] 244 p. illus., ports. 22 cm. [E842.D58] 64-66105
1. Kennedy, John Fitzgerald, Pres. U.S., 1917-1963. I. Title.

DOLLEN, Charles 923.173
John F. Kennedy, American [Boston] St. Paul Eds. [dist. Daughters of St. Paul, c.1965] 244p. illus., ports. 21cm. [E842.D58] 64-66105 5.00; 4.00 pap.,
1. Kennedy, John Fitzgerald, Pres. U.S., 1917-1963. I. Title. BIP

*FEDOSIUK, Polly Curren 973.922
To light a torch; the John F. Kennedy story. Illus. by Hal MacIntosh. New York, Guild [1966] 160p. illus. 17cm. (Crusader bk. for young people, 31416) .50 pap.,
1. Kennedy, John Fitzgerald, Pres. U.S., 1917-1963. I. Title.

FLAVIUS, Brother, 973.922'0924 B 1927-
In virtue's cause; a story of John F. Kennedy, by Brother Flavius. With illus. by Carolyn Lee Jagodits. [Notre Dame, Ind.] Dujarie Press [1967] 96 p. illus., ports. 24 cm. Biography of John Fitzgerald Kennedy, his childhood and boyhood years, his spectacular stint in the Navy, his Senate career and brief term as thirty-fifth President. [E842.F55] 92 AC 68
1. Kennedy, John Fitzgerald, Pres. U.S., 1917-1963. I. Jagodits, Carolyn Lee, illus. II. Title.

GRAVES, Charles Parlin, v. 12 1911-
John F. Kennedy, new frontiersman Illustrated by Paul Frame. [New York, Dell Pub. Co., 1966, c1965] 80 p. illus. 20 cm. (A Discovery book) "A Dell Yearling book, 4242." 68-33285
1. Kennedy, John Fitzgerald, Pres. U.S., 1917-1963. I. Title. BIP

GROMYKO, Anatolii 973.922'092'4 Andreevich.
Through Russian eyes: President Kennedy's 1036 days, by Anatolii Andreievich Gromyko. [Authorized translation edited by Philip A. Garon]. Washington, International Library, 1973. xviii, 239 p. 23 cm. Translation of Tysiacha tridtsat' shest' dnei prezidenta Kennedi. [E841.G713 1973b] 74-156772 9.95
1. Kennedy, John Fitzgerald, Pres. U.S., 1917-1963. I. Title.

*KENNEDY, John F., 923.273
Profiles in courage Teen age abridged ed. Foreword by Robert F. Kennedy New York, Scholastic [c.1955-1964] xix, 133p. 16cm. (T597) .45 pap.,
I. Title.

KENNEDY, John 817'.5'4 Fitzgerald, Pres. U.S., 1917-1963.
The complete Kennedy wit Edited by Bill Adler. [1st ed.] New York, Citadel Press [1967] 203 p. port. 22 cm. Includes most of the material from The Kennedy wit and More Kennedy wit, and new material. [E842.A25A34] 67-25653
I. Adler, Bill, ed. II. Title.

KOCH, Thilo. 973.922'0922
Fighters for a new world: John F. Kennedy, Martin Luther King, Robert F. Kennedy. New York, Putnam [1969] 204 p. illus., ports. 25 cm. Translation of Kampfer fur eine nee Welt. [E840.6.K613] 69-18183 6.95
1. Kennedy, John Fitzgerald, Pres. U.S., 1917-1963. 2. King, Martin Luther. 3. Kennedy, Robert F., 1925-1968. I. Title.

LASKY, Victor. 923.173
J. F. K.: the man and the myth. New York, Macmillan [1963] 653 p. 24 cm. Includes bibliography. [E842.L3] 63-16367
1. Kennedy, John Fitzgerald, Pres. U.S., 1917-1963. 2. United States—Politics & government—1961-1963. I. Title.

LEVINE, Israel E. 923.173
Young man in the White House: John Fitzgerald Kennedy, by I. E. Levine. New York, Messner [1964] 192 p. 22 cm. Bibliography: p. 189. [E842.L46] 64-20160
1. Kennedy, John Fitzgerald, Pres. U.S., 1917-1963. I. Title.

LINCOLN, Evelyn. 973.9220924
My twelve years with John F. Kennedy. New York, D. McKay Co. [1965] x, 371 p. 23 cm. [E842.L54] 65-24490
1. Kennedy, John Fitzgerald, Pres. U.S., 1917-1963. I. Title.

LONGFORD, Frank 973.922'092'4 B Pakenham, 7th Earl of, 1905-
Kennedy / [by] Lord Longford. London : Weidenfeld and Nicolson, 1976. x, 223 p., [8] p. of plates : ill., ports. ; 23 cm. Includes index. Bibliography: p. 211-213. [E842.L58] 77-353529 ISBN 0-297-77244-9 : £5.95
1. Kennedy, John Fitzgerald, Pres. U.S., 1917-1963. 2. Presidents—United States—Biography. 3. United States—Politics and government—1961-1963.

LOOK. v. 12
JFK memorial book. A permanent keepsake prepared by the editors of Look. [Des Moines? 1964] 1 v. ports. illus. (part col.) 35 cm. 68-78419
1. Kennedy, John Fitzgerald, Pres. U.S., 1917-1963. I. Title.

MCEVOY, Kevin, comp. 973.922'0922
Two Kennedys. Glen Rock, N.J., Paulist Press [1969] v, 90 p. 19 cm. (Deus books) Bibliographical footnotes. [E842.M35] 68-55581 1.25
1. Kennedy, John Fitzgerald, Pres. U.S., 1917-1963. 2. Kennedy, Robert F., 1925-1968. I. Title.

MANCHESTER, William 973.922'0924 Raymond, 1922-
Portrait of a President; John F. Kennedy in profile. Rev. ed., with a new introd. and an epilogue (Large type ed.) New York, Watts [1967, c1962] xxi, 266p. 29cm. (Keith Jennison Bk.) Bibl. [E842.M3 1967] 7.95
1. Kennedy, John Fitzgerald, Pres. U.S., 1917-1963. I. Title.

MANCHESTER, William 973.922'0924 Raymond, 1922-
Portrait of a President; John F. Kennedy in profile [by] William Manchester. Rev. ed., with a new introd. and epilogue. Boston, Little, Brown [1967] xxii, 266 p. 21 cm. Bibliography: p. xii-xiv. [E842.M3 1967] 67-12910
1. Kennedy, John Fitzgerald, Pres. U.S., 1917-1963. I. Title.

MEYERS, Joan Simpson, 973,9220924 ed.
John Fitzgerald Kennedy; as we remember him. Edited and produced under the direction of Goddard Lieberson. Editor, Joan Meyers; art director, Ira Teichberg. [1st ed.] New York, Atheneum, 1965. ix, 241 p. illus. facsims., group ports. 33 cm. (A Columbia records legacy collection book) [E842.M46] 65-27334
1. Kennedy, John Fitzgerald, Pres. U.S., 1917-1963. I. Lieberson, Goddard, 1911- ed. II. Teichberg, Ira, illus. III. Title.

MEYERS, Joan Simpson, 973.9220924 ed.
John Fitzgerald Kennedy; as we remember him. Edited and produced under the direction of Goddard Lieberson. Editor, Joan Meyers; art director, Ira Teichberg. [1st ed.] New York, Atheneum, 1965. ix, 241 p. illus., facsims., group ports. 33 cm. (A Columbia records legacy collection book) Issued also with phonodisc: John Fitzgerald Kennedy; as we remember him. [E842.M46] 65-27334
1. Kennedy, John Fitzgerald, Pres. U.S., 1917-1963. I. Lieberson, Goddard, 1911- ed. II. Teichberg, Ira, illus. III. Title.

MIROFF, Bruce. 973.922'092'4
Pragmatic illusions : the Presidential politics of John F. Kennedy / Bruce Miroff. New York : McKay, c1976. p. cm. Includes bibliographical references and index. [E841.M54] 76-7554 ISBN 0-679-30298-0 : 8.95. ISBN 0-679-30299-9 college.
1. Kennedy, John Fitzgerald, Pres. U.S., 1917-1963. 2. United States—Politics and government—1961-1963. 3. United States—Foreign relations—1961-1963. I. Title. BIP

O'DONNELL, Kenneth P. 973.922'092'4 B
Johnny, we hardly knew ye; memories of John Fitzgerald Kennedy, by Kenneth P. O'Donnell and David F. Powers, with Joseph McCarthy. [1st ed.] Boston, Little, Brown [1972] p. [E842.O3] 72-5693 ISBN 0-316-71625-1
1. Kennedy, John Fitzgerald, Pres. U.S., 1917-1963. I. Powers, David F., joint author. II. Title. BIP

O'DONNELL, Kenneth P. 973.922'092'4 [B]
Johnny, we hardly knew ye; memories of John Fitzgerald Kennedy, by Kenneth P. O'Donnell and David F. Powers, with Joe McCarthy. New York, Pocket Books [1973, c.1972] xv, 508 p. 18 cm. [E842.O3] ISBN 0-671-78640-7 1.95 (pbk.)
1. Kennedy, John Fitzgerald, Pres. U.S., 1917-1963. I. Powers, David F., joint author. II. Title.
L.C. card no. for the hardbound edition: 72-5693.

PAPER, Lewis J. 973.922'092'4
The promise and the performance : the leadership of John F. Kennedy / by Lewis J. Paper. New York : Crown Publishers, [1975] xi, 408 p. ; 24 cm. Includes bibliographical references and index. [E841.P35 1975] 75-19456 ISBN 0-517-52342-6 : 9.95
1. Kennedy, John Fitzgerald, Pres. U.S., 1917-1963. 2. United States—Politics and government—1961-1963. I. Title.

SALINGER, Pierre. 973.9220924
With Kennedy. [1st ed.] Garden City, N.Y., Doubleday, 1966. xvi, 391 p. ports. 24 cm. [E841.S2] 66-17423
1. Kennedy, John Fitzgerald, Pres. U.S., 1917-1963. 2. United States—History—1945- I. Title.

SCHWAB, Peter, 1940- 973.922'092'4 B
John F. Kennedy [by] Peter Schwab and J. Lee Shneidman. New York, Twayne Publishers [1974] 173 p. port. 21 cm. (Twayne's world leaders series) Bibliography: p. 164-166. [E842.S36] 73-14874 ISBN 0-8057-3696-4 5.95
1. Kennedy, John Fitzgerald, Pres. U.S., 1917-1963. I. Shneidman, Jerome Lee, 1929- joint author. BIP

SORENSEN, Theodore C v. 12
Kennedy. New York, Bantam Books [1966, c1965] xii, 881 p. 18 cm. (A Bantam book, D3257) 68-62473
1. Kennedy, John Fitzgerald, Pres. U.S., 1917-1963. I. Title. BIP

SORENSEN, Theodore C. 973.922
Kennedy. New York, Harper [c.1965] viii, 783p. port. 25cm. [E841.S6] 65-14660 10.00
1. Kennedy, John Fitzgerald, Pres. U.S., 1917-1963. 2. U.S.—Hist.—1945- I. Title.

SORENSEN, Theodore C. 973.922'0922 B
The Kennedy legacy [by] Theodore C. Sorensen. [New York] Macmillan [1969] 414 p. 22 cm. [E842.S57] 75-95303
1. Kennedy, John Fitzgerald, Pres. U.S., 1917-1963. 2. Kennedy, Robert F., 1925-1968. I. Title.

STAFFORD, Jean, 1915- v. 12
A mother in history. New York, Bantam Books [1966] 119 p. 18 cm. (Bantam books, s3344) 67-62594
1. Kennedy, John Fitzgerald, Pres. U.S., 1917-1963. I. Oswald, Marguerite. II. Title.

THOUSAND days (The); 923.173
John Fitzgerald Kennedy as President. Book designed by John Raymond. Edit. by Paul Ballot [New York, Citadel., 1964] 124p. illus. (pt. col.) ports. (pt. col.) 29cm. [E841.T53] 64-25947 4.95
1. Kennedy, John Fitzgerald, Pres. U.S., 1917-1963. I. Ballot, Paul.

•VILNIS, Aija 923.173
The bearer of the star-spangled banner; in memory of President John Fitzgerald Kennedy. Tr. [from Latvian] by Lilija Pavars. New York, Speller [c.1964] unpaged. illus. 15cm. 1.00 bds.,
1. Kennedy, John Fitzgerald, Pres. U.S., 1917-1963. I. Pavars, Lilija, tr. II. Title.

WICKER, Tom. 923.173
Kennedy without tears, the man beneath the myth. Foreword by Arthur Krock. Illus. by Bill Berry. New York, Morrow, 1964. 61 p. 22 cm. [E842.W55] 64-24638
1. Kennedy, John Fitzgerald, Pres. U.S., 1917-1963. I. Title. BIP

WOOD, James Playsted, 1905- 973.922'0924 B
The life and words of John F. Kennedy, by James Playsted Wood and the editors of Country beautiful magazine. Elm Grove, Wis., Country Beautiful Foundation; distributed by Doubleday, Garden City, N.Y. [1964] 80 p. illus. (part col.) ports. (part col.) 32 cm. Celebrates the life of the thirty-fifth President, describing his childhood, education, family, and political development. Includes many photographs and excerpts from Kennedy's speeches and writings. [E842.W6] 92 AC 68
1. Kennedy, John Fitzgerald, Pres. U.S., 1917-1963. I. Title. BIP

Kennedy, John Fitzgerald, Pres. U.S., 1917-1963

FROLICK, S. J. 920
Once there was a President. [New York, Kanrom, c.1964] [56]p. illus., ports. 32cm. 64-18687 3.00 bds.,
1. Kennedy, John Fitzgerald, Pres, U.S., 1917-1963—Juvenile literature. 2. Kennedy, John Fitzgerald, Pres. U. S., 1917-1963 —Portraits, caricatures, etc. I. Title.

KENNEDY, John Fitzgerald, 1917-1963 200.8
Religious views of President John F. Kennedy in his own words. Comp. by Nicholas A. Schneider. St. Louis, B. Herder [c.]1965. xv, 125p. 23cm. [E842.1.A6S3] 65-26875 price unreported
1. Kennedy, John Fitzgerald, Pres. U.S., 1917-1963—Religion. I. Schneider, Nicholas A., comp. II. Title.

KENNEDY, John Fitzgerald, Pres. U.S., 1917-1963. 200.8
Religious views of President John F. Kennedy in his own words. Compiled by Nicholas A. Schneider. St. Louis, Herder, 1965. xv, 125 p. 23 cm. [E842.1.A6S3] 65-26875
1. Kennedy, John Fitzgerald, Pres. U.S., 1917-1963 — Religion. I. Schneider, Nicholas A., comp. II. Title.

LEE, Bruce 920
Boy's life of John F. Kennedy. New York, Bold Face Bks., dist. Sterling [c.1961] 189p. illus. 61-15730 2.95 bds.,
1. Kennedy, John Fitzgerald, Pres. U. S., 1917-Juvenile literature. I. Title.

LEE, Bruce 923.273
Boys' life of John F. Kennedy. Memorial ed. New York, Bold Face Bks.; dist. Sterling [c.1961, 1964] 196p. illus., ports. 22cm. 64-452 2.95
1. Kennedy, John Fitzgerald, Pres. U.S., 1917-1963—Juvenile literature. I. Title.

LEE, Bruce 920
The life of John F. Kennedy [Sch. ed.] New York, Globe [c.1961, 1964] 117p. illus., ports. 22cm. Previous eds. pub. under title: Boys' life of John F. Kennedy. 64-3092 2.80
1. Kennedy, John Fitzgerald, Pres. U.S., 1917-1963—Juvenile literature. I. Title.

SCHOOR, Gene 920
Young John Kennedy. New York, Harcourt [c.1963] 253p. illus. 22cm. 63-9092 3.95
1. Kennedy, John Fitzgerald, Pres. U.S., 1917- —Juvenile literature. I. Title.

SPINA, Tony. 923.173
This was the President. Text and photos. by Tony Spina. New York, A.S. Barnes [1964] 190 p. (chiefly illus., ports.) 29 cm. [E842.S6] 64-21355
1. Kennedy, John Fitzgerald, Pres. U.S., 1917-1963 — Portraits, caricatures, etc. I. Title.

STROUSSE, Flora, 1897- 920
John Fitzgerald Kennedy, man of courage. Illus. with photos. New York, Kenedy [c.1964] 189p. ports. 22cm. (Amer. background bks., 28) Bibl. 64-21854 2.50
1. Kennedy, John Fitzgerald, Pres. U. S., 1917-1963—Juvenile literature. I. Title. II. Series.

WHITE, Nancy Bean. j92
Meet John F. Kennedy. New York, Random House [1965] 85 p. illus., ports. 22 cm. (Step-Up books) [E842.W52] 65-10947
1. Kennedy, John Fitzgerald, Pres. U.S., 1917-1963 — Juvenile literature. I. Title. BIP

Kennedy, John Fitzgerald, Pres. U.S., 1917-1963—Art collections.

BARNES, Clare. 736'.6
John F. Kennedy: scrimshaw collector. Photos. by Alan Fontaine. [1st ed.] Boston, Little, Brown [1969] 129 p. col. illus. 29 cm. Bibliography: p. 127-129. [NK6022.B37] 70-83737 15.00
1. Kennedy, John Fitzgerald, Pres. U.S., 1917-1963—Art collections. 2. Scrimshaws.

Kennedy, John Fitzgerald, Pres. U.S., 1917-1963—Assassination.

KANTOR, Seth. 364.1'523'0924
Who was Jack Ruby? / By Seth Kantor. [New York] : Everest House, c1978. xi, 242 p. ; 24 cm. Includes bibliographical references and index. [E842.9.K29] 78-54078 ISBN 0-89696-004-8 : 10.95
1. Kennedy, John Fitzgerald, Pres. U.S., 1917-1963—Assassination. 2. Ruby, Jack. 3. Oswald, Lee Harvey. 4. Crime and criminal—Texas—Dallas—Biography. 5. Dallas—Biography. I. Title. BIP

OGLESBY, Carl. 364.1'31'0973
The yankee and cowboy war : conspiracies from Dallas to Watergate / by Carl Oglesby. Mission, Kan. : Sheed Andrews and McMeel, c1976. p. cm. Includes bibliographical references and index. [E842.9.O34] 76-23321 ISBN 0-8362-0680-0 : 12.00 ISBN 0-8362-0688-6 pbk. :
1. Kennedy, John Fitzgerald, Pres. U.S., 1917-1963—Assassination. 2. Watergate Affair, 1972- 3. Corruption (in politics)—United States. I. Title.

ROBERTS, Charles, 1916- 973.922'0924
The truth about the assassination, by Charles Roberts. Foreword by Pierre Salinger. New York, Grosset & Dunlap [1967] 128 p. illus. (on cover) 21 cm. [E842.9.R57] 67-20840
1. Kennedy, John Fitzgerald, Pres. U.S., 1917-1963—Assassination. I. Title.

ROFFMAN, Howard, 1953- 973.922'092'4
Presumed guilty / Howard Roffman. South Brunswick [N.J.] : A. S. Barnes, c1976. 299 p., [5] leaves of plates : ill. ; 22 cm. Includes index. Bibliography: p. 290-294. [E842.9.R58 1976] 75-42961 ISBN 0-498-01933-0 : 8.95
1. Kennedy, John Fitzgerald, Pres. U.S., 1917-1963—Assassination. 2. Oswald, Lee Harvey. I. Title.

ROFFMAN, Howard, 1953- 973.922'092'4
Presumed guilty: Lee Harvey Oswald in the assassination of President Kennedy. Rutherford [N.J.] Fairleigh Dickinson University Press [1975] 297 p. illus. 22 cm. Bibliography: p. 288-292. [E842.9.R58] 74-1119 ISBN 0-8386-1526-0 10.00
1. Kennedy, John Fitzgerald, Pres. U.S., 1917-1963—Assassination. 2. Oswald, Lee Harvey. I. Title.

Kennedy, John Fitzgerald, Pres. U.S., 1917-1963—Juvenile literature.

FLAVIUS, Brother, 1927- j92
In virtue's cause; a story of John F. Kennedy, by Brother Flavius. With illus. by Carolyn Lee Jagodits. [Notre Dame, Ind.] Dujarie Press [1967] 96 p. illus., ports. 24 cm. [E842.F55] 66-22268
1. Kennedy, John Fitzgerald, Pres. U. S., 1917-1963—Juvenile literature. I. Title.

GRAVES, Charles Parlin, 1911- 92
John F. Kennedy: new frontiersman, by Charles P. Graves. Illus. by Paul Frame. Champaign, Ill., Garrard [c.1965] 80p. col. illus. 23cm. (Discovery bk.) [E842.G7] 65-10509 1.98
1. Kennedy, John Fitzgerald, Pres. U.S., 1917-1963—Juvenile literature. I. Title.

GRAVES, Charles Parlin, 1911- 92
John F. Kennedy: new frontiersman. Illus. by Paul Frame [New York, Dell, 1966, c.1965] 80p. illus. 20cm. (Discovery bk., Yearling bk., 4242) [E842.G7] .50 pap.,
1. Kennedy, John Fitzgerald, Pres., U.S., 1917-1963—Juvenile literature. I. Title.

GRAVES, Charles Parlin, 1911- 92 (J)
John F. Kennedy: new frontiersman, by Charles P. Graves. Illustrated by Paul Frame. Champaign, Ill., Garrard Pub. Co. [1965] 80 p. col. illus. 23 cm. (A Discovery book) [E842.G7] 65-10509
1. Kennedy, John Fitzgerald, Pres. U.S., 1917-1963—Juvenile literature.

KELLY, Regina (Zimmerman) 1898- 973.922'0924 B
John F. Kennedy, by Regina Z. Kelly. Chicago, Follett Pub. Co. [1969] 157, [3] p. illus., ports. 23 cm. (Library of American heroes) Bibliography: p. [158] A biography of the thirty-fifth and youngest President of the United States stressing his private as well as public achievements. [E842.Z9K4] 92 75-13187 1.95
1. Kennedy, John Fitzgerald, Pres. U.S., 1917-1963—Juvenile literature. I. Title.

LEE. BRUCE. 364.152
Boys' life of John F. Kennedy. Memorial ed. New York, Bold Face Books, distributed by Sterling Pub. Co. [1964] 196 p. illus., ports. 22 cm. [E842.L4 1964] 64-452
1. Kennedy, John Fitzgerald, Press, U.S., 1917-1963 — Juvenile literature. I. Title.

MARTIN, Patricia Miles. 92
John Fitzgerald Kennedy. Illustrated by Paul Frame. New York, G. P. Putnam's Sons [1964] 64 p. col. illus. 23 cm. (A See and read beginning to read biography) [E842.M34] 64-18022
1. Kennedy, John Fitzgerald, Pres. U.S., 1917-1963—Juvenile literature. BIP

MIERS, Earl Schenck, 1910- 923
The story of John F. Kennedy. Editorial production: Donald D. Wolf. Design and layout by Margot L. Wolf. Edited under the supervision of Paul E. Blackwood. New York, Wonder Books [1964] 48 p. illus. (part col.), ports. (part col.) 28 cm. (A Spotlight wonder book) [E842.M5 1964a] 66-4728
1. Kennedy, John Fitzgerald, Pres. U.S., 1917-1963—Juvenile literature. I. Title.

REIDY, John P. 92
John F. Kennedy, by John P. Reidy, Norman Richards. Chicago, Childrens Pr. [c1967] 95p. illus., map, ports. 29cm. (People of destiny: a humanities ser.) Bibl. [E842.R39] 68-1551 4.50
1. Kennedy, John Fitzgerald, Pres. U.S., 1917-1963—Juvenile literature. I. Richards, Norman. joint author. II. Title.

REIDY, John P. 973.922'0924
The true story of John Fitzgerald Kennedy, U.S. President, by John P. Reidy. Chicago, Childrens Press [1967] 144 p. illus. 23 cm. [E842.R4] 67-20107
1. Kennedy, John Fitzgerald, Pres. U.S., 1917-1963—Juvenile literature. I. Title.

SCHOOR, Gene. 92
Young John Kennedy. [1st ed.] New York, Harcourt, Brace & World [1963] 253 p. illus. 22 cm. [E842.S35] 63-9092
1. Kennedy, John Fitzgerald, Pres. U. S., 1917—Juvenile literature. I. Title. BIP

SHAPP, Martha 92
Let's find out about John Fitzgerald Kennedy, by Martha and Charles Shapp [Rev. ed.] Illus. with photographs. New York, Watts, c.1965, 1966. 53p. illus.

22cm. [PE1127.H5S465] 65-11581 2.50; 1.98 lib. ed.,
1. Kennedy, John Fitzerald, Pres. U.S., 1917-1963—Juvenile literature. 2. Readers-Biography. I. Shapp, Charles, joint author. II. Title.

SHAPP, Martha. 923'.1'73
Let's find out about John Fitzgerald Kennedy, by Martha and Charles Shapp. Pictures by Leonard Everett Fisher. New York, F. Watts [1965] 60 p. col. illus. 22 cm. [PE1127.H5S465] 65-11581
1. Kennedy, John Fitzgerald, Pres. U.S., 1917-1963—Juvenile literature. 2. Readers—Biography. I. Shapp, Charles, joint author. II. Fisher, Leonard Everett, illus. III. Title.

STEINBERG, Alfred, 973.92'0922 E
1917-
The Kennedy brothers. New York, Putnam [1969] 223 p. 22 cm. (Lives to remember) Brief biographies of four American brothers who were groomed from an early age to serve their country. [E843.S7 1969] 920 74-75596 3.64
1. Kennedy, John Fitzgerald, Pres. U.S., 1917-1963—Juvenile literature. 2. Kennedy, Joseph Patrick, 1915-1944—Juvenile literature. 3. Kennedy, Robert F., 1925-1968—Juvenile literature. 4. Kennedy, Edward Moore, 1932- —Juvenile literature. I. Title. BIP

STROUSSE, Flora, 1897- 92
John Fitzgerald Kennedy, man of courage. Illustrated with photos. New York, P. J. Kenedy [1964] 189 p. ports. 22 cm. (American background books, 28) Bibliography: p. [183] [E842.S83] 64-21854
1. Kennedy, John Fitzgerald, Pres. U.S 1917-1963 — Juvenile literature. I. Title. II. Series.

TREGASKIS, Richard 940.54
William, 1916-
John F. Kennnedy and PT-109 New York, Random [c.1962] 192p. illus. (Landmark bks., 99) 62-9009 1.95
1. Kennedy, John Fitzgerald, Pres. U.S., 1917- —Juvenile literature. 2. PT-199 (Boa—Juvenile literature. I. Title.

VINTON, Iris. 92 (J)
The story of President Kennedy. Illustrated by Carl Cassler. Cover port. by Earl Mayan. New York, Grosset & Dunlap [1966] viii, 180 p. illus. 22 cm. (Signature books) [E842.V55] 67-1047
1. Kennedy, John Fitzgerald, Pres. U.S., 1917-1963—Juvenile literature. I. Title.

WOOD, James Playsted, 923 173
1905
The life and words of John F. Kennedy, by James Playsted Wood and the editors of Country beautiful magazine. Elm Grove, Wis., Country Beautiful Foundation; distributed by Doubleday, Garden City, N. Y. [1964] 80 p. illus. (part col.) ports. (part col.) 32 cm. [E842.W6] 64-24582
1. Kennedy, Edward Fitzgerald, Pres. U.S., 1917-1963—Juvenile literature. I. Title.

Kennedy, John Fitzgerald, Pres. U.S., 1917-1963—Naval career.

DONOVAN, Robert J 940.545973
PT109, John F. Kennedy in World War II. [1st ed] New York, McGraw-Hill [1961] 247 p. illus. 22 cm. [E842.D6] 61-18168
1. Kennedy, John Fitzgerald, Pres. U.S., 1917-1963—Naval career. 2. World War, 1939-1945—Pacific Ocean. 3. World War, 1939-1945—Naval operations, American. I. Title.

Kennedy, John Fitzgerald, 1960-

SHAW, Maud 973.9220922
White House nannie; my years with Caroline and John Kennedy, Jr. [New York] New Amer. Lib. [1966, c.1965] 127p. 18cm. (Signet bk., P3063) .60 pap.,
1. Kennedy family. 2. Kennedy, John Fitzgerald, 1960- 3. Kennedy, Caroline, 1957- I. Title.

SHAW, Maud. 973.9220922
White House nannie; my years with Caroline and John Kennedy, Jr. [New York] New American Library [1966] 205 p. ports. 21 cm. [E843.S53 1966] 66-17883
1. Kennedy family. 2. Kennedy, John Fitzgerald, 1960- 3. Kennedy, Caroline, 1957- I. Title.

Kennedy, John Pendleton, 1795-1870.

BOHNER, Charles H. 928.1
John Pendleton Kennedy, gentleman from Baltimore. Baltimore, Johns Hopkins Press [c.1961] 266p. front. por. Bibl. 61-10735 5.50
1. Kennedy, John Pendleton, 1795-1870. I. Title. BIP

BOHNER, Charles H 928.1
John Pendleton Kennedy, gentleman from Baltimore. Baltimore, Johns Hopkins Press [1961] 266p. illus. 22cm. Includes bibliography. [E415.9.K35B6] 61-10735
1. Kennedy, John Pendleton, 1795-1870. I. Title.

Kennedy, Joseph Patrick, 1888-1969.

DALLAS, Rita. 973.9'092'4 B
The Kennedy case, by Rita Dallas and Jeanira Ratcliffe. New York, Putnam [1973] 352 p. illus. 22 cm. [E748.K376D3 1973] 72-87611 ISBN 0-399-11057-7 7.95
1. Kennedy, Joseph Patrick, 1888-1969. 2. Kennedy family. I. Ratcliffe, Jeanira, joint author. II. Title. BIP

DINNEEN, Joseph Francis, 929.2
1897-
The Kennedy family. [1st ed.] Boston, Little, Brown [1960, c1959] 238 p. illus. 22 cm. [E747.D5] 59-11100
1. Kennedy, Joseph Patrick, 1888-1969. 2. Kennedy, John Fitzgerald, Pres. U.S., 1917-1963. 3. Kennedy family.

DUNCLIFFE, William J 923.273
The life and times of Joseph P. Kennedy [by] William J. Duncliffe. [New York, Macfadden-Bartell, 1965] 158 p. ports. 18 cm. "75-115." [E843.K43D8] 65-1392
1. Kennedy, Joseph Patrick, 1888- I. Title.

KENNEDY, John 741.5973
Fitzgerald, Pres. U.S., 1917- ed.
As we remember Joe. Cambridge, Mass., Privately printed, University Press, 1945. xi, 75 p. col. illus., ports., facsims. 24 cm. xi, 75 p. on [73] leaves. 28 cm. E843.K4K4 1945a Photocopy. [E843.K4K4 1945] 63-25548
1. Kennedy, Joseph Patrick, 1915-1944. I. Title.

KOSKOFF, David E., 973.9'092'4 B
1939-
Joseph P. Kennedy: a life and times [by] David E. Koskoff. Englewood Cliffs, N.J., Prentice-Hall [1974] x, 643 p. illus. 24 cm. Bibliography: p. 616-629. [E748.K376K67] 73-21578 ISBN 0-13-511154-4 10.00
1. Kennedy, Joseph Patrick, 1888-1969. I. Title.

WHALEN, Richard J., 1935- 923.273
The founding father; the story of Joseph P. Kennedy, by Richard J. Whalen. [New York] New American Library [1964] xiv, 541 p. ports. 25 cm. (An NAL-World book) Bibliographical references included in "Notes" (p. 489-[526]) [E843.K43W5] 64-16872
1. Kennedy, Joseph Patrick, 1888- I. Title.

Kennedy, Joseph Patrick, 1915-1944.

SEARLS, Henry. 940.542'1
The lost prince : young Joe, the forgotten Kennedy / Hank Searles. New York : Ballantine Books, 1977,c1969. 304 [16]p. : ill. ; 18 cm. Includes index. Bibliography: p. 286-287. [E843.K44S4] ISBN 0-345-27395-8 pbk. : 2.25
1. Kennedy, Joseph Patrick, 1915-1944. I. Title.
L.C. card no. for 1969 World Pub. Co. ed.: 73-93468.

SEARLS, Henry. 940.542'1'0924 B
The lost prince: young Joe, the forgotten Kennedy; the story of the oldest brother, by Hank Searls. New York, World Pub. Co. [1969] 334 p. illus., maps, ports. 22 cm. "An NAL book." Bibliography: p. [321]-322. [E843.K44S4] 73-93468 6.95
1. Kennedy, Joseph Patrick, 1915-1944. I. Title.

Kennedy, Joseph Patrick, 1915-1944—Juvenile literature.

STEINBERG, Alfred, 973.92'0922 E
1917-
The Kennedy brothers. New York, Putnam [1969] 223 p. 22 cm. (Lives to remember) Brief biographies of four American brothers who were groomed from an early age to serve their country. [E843.S7 1969] 920 74-75596 3.64
1. Kennedy, John Fitzgerald, Pres. U.S., 1917-1963—Juvenile literature. 2. Kennedy, Joseph Patrick, 1915-1944—Juvenile literature. 3. Kennedy, Robert F., 1925-1968—Juvenile literature. 4. Kennedy, Edward Moore, 1932- —Juvenile literature. I. Title. BIP

Kennedy, Richard, 1910-

KENNEDY, 338.7'61'0705092 B
Richard, 1910-
A boy at the Hogarth Press / [by] Richard Kennedy ; illustrated by the author ; with an introduction by Bevis Hillier. Harmondsworth ; New York [etc.] : Penguin, 1978. 104 p. : ill. ; 20 cm. [PR6021.E712Z463 1978] 79-306749 ISBN 0-14-004862-6 pbk. : 1.95
1. Kennedy, Richard, 1910- 2. Hogarth Press. 3. Woolf, Virginia Stephen, 1882-1941—Biography. 4. Woolf, Leonard Sidney, 1880-1969—Biography. 5. Authors, English—20th century—Biography. I. Title. BIP

Kennedy, Robert F., 1925-

THOMPSON, Robert E 923.273
Robert F. Kennedy; the brother within, by Robert E. Thompson and Hortense Myers. New York, Macmillan [1962] 224 p. illus. 22 cm. [E748.K377T5 1962] 62-20598
1. Kennedy, Robert F., 1925- I. Myers. Hortense, joint author. II. Title.

Kennedy, Robert F., 1925-1968.

BROWN, Stuart 329'.023'730923
Gerry, 1912-
The presidency on trial, Robert Kennedy's 1968 campaign and afterwards. Honolulu, University Press of Hawaii, 1972. viii, 155 p. 24 cm. Includes bibliographical references. [E851.B7] 70-175162 ISBN 0-8248-0202-0 6.95
1. Kennedy, Robert F., 1925-1968. 2. Presidents—United States—Election—1968. 3. United States—Politics and government—1969-1974. 4. United States—Politics and government—20th century. I. Title. BIP

†CASSIDAY, Bruce. 973.922'092'4 B
RFK : a special kind of man / by Bruce Cassiday and Bill Adler. 1st ed. Chicago : Playboy Press, c1977. 270 p. ; 18 cm. Bibliography: p. 267-270. [E840.8.K4C37] 76-51630 pbk. : 2.25
1. Kennedy, Robert F., 1925-1968. 2. United States. Congress. Senate—Biography. 3. Legislators—United States—Biography. I. Adler, Bill, joint author. II. Title.

DE TOLEDANO, Ralph, 973.92'0924
1916-
R. F. K., the man who would be President. New York, Putnam [1967] 381 p. 24 cm. [E840.8.K4D4] 67-15195
1. Kennedy, Robert F., 1925- I. Title.

DE TOLEDANO, Ralph, 973.92'0924
1916-
R. F. K., the man who would be President. New York, Putnam [1967] 381 p. 24 cm. [E840.8.K4D4] 67-15195
1. Kennedy, Robert F., 1925-1968. I. Title.

GUTHMAN, Edwin, 973.922'0924 B
1919-
We band of brothers. [1st ed.] New York, Harper & Row [1971] x, 339 p. 22 cm. [E840.8.K4G8] 72-123932 ISBN 0-06-011716-8 7.95
1. Kennedy, Robert F., 1925-1968. I. Title.

HALBERSTAM, David. 329.3'023'0924
The unfinished odyssey of Robert Kennedy. New York, Random House [1969, c1968] 211 p. 22 cm. [E840.8.K4H3] 69-14435 4.95
1. Kennedy, Robert F., 1925-1968. I. Title. BIP

KENNEDY, Robert F., 1925- 300'.8
1968.
Bobby Kennedy off-guard. Compiled by Sue G. Hall. New York, Grosset & Dunlap [1968] 111 p. 21 cm. "Portions of this book were published previously in The quotable Robert F. Kennedy." [E840.8.K4A252] 68-15284
I. Hall, Sue G., comp. II. Title.

KENNEDY, Robert F., 1925- 300'.8
1968.
A new day: Robert F. Kennedy. Edited by Bill Adler. Picture editor: Michael O'Keefe. [New York] New American Library [1968] 157 p. illus., ports. 18 cm. (A Signet book) [E840.8.K4A5] 68-6703 0.75
I. Adler, Bill, ed. II. Title.

MACFADDEN-BARTELL 973.92'0924 B
Corporation, New York.
The Robert F Kennedy story; the man & his dream, Bobby. [New York, 1968] 79 p. illus., ports. 28 cm. Cover title. [E840.8.K4M3] 68-6430
1. Kennedy, Robert F., 1925-1968. I. Title.

NEWFIELD, Jack. 973.923'0924
Robert Kennedy; a memoir. [1st ed.] New York, Dutton, 1969. 318 p. 24 cm. [E840.8.K4N4] 72-83381 6.95
1. Kennedy, Robert F., 1925-1968.

NEWFIELD, Jack. 973.923'0924
Robert Kennedy; a memoir. [Large print ed.] Lancaster, N.Y., Associated Reprinting Co. [1970, c1969] 351 p. 34 cm. [E840.8] 74-141628
1. Kennedy, Robert F., 1925-1968. I. Title.

NICHOLAS, William. 973.922'0924
The Bobby Kennedy nobody knows. Greenwich, Conn., Fawcett [1967] 1 v. (unpaged) illus., ports. 18cm. (Fawcett gold medal bk., 5) [E840.8.K4N5] 68-4619 .60
1. Kennedy, Robert F., 1925-1968. I. Title.

NICHOLAS, William. 973.922
The Bobby Kennedy nobody knows. Greenwich, Conn., Fawcett [1967] 1v. (unpaged) illus., ports. 18cm. (Fawcett gold medal bk., 5) [E840.8.K4N5] 68-4619 .60 pap.,
1. Kennedy, Robert F., 1925-1968. I. Title.

NICHOLAS, William. 328.73'092'4
The Bobby Kennedy nobody knows. Greenwich, Conn., Fawcett Publications [1967] 1 v. (unpaged) illus., ports. 18 cm. (A Fawcett gold medal book, 5) [E840.8.K4N5] 68-4619
1. Kennedy, Robert F., 1925-1968. I. Title.

QUIRK, Lawrence 973.923'0924 (B)
J
Robert Francis Kennedy; the man and the politician, by Lawrence J. Quirk. Los Angeles, Holloway House Pub. Co.; [distributed by: All America Distributors Corp., 1968] 316 p. 18 cm. [E840.8.K4Q5] 68-28298
1. Kennedy, Robert F., 1925-1968. I. Title.

ROSS, Douglas. 973.92'0924
Robert F. Kennedy, apostle of change. New York, Trident Press [1968] xxi, 600 p. 23 cm. Bibliography: p. [594] [E840.8.K4R59] 68-56909 7.95
1. Kennedy, Robert F., 1925-1968. 2. United States—Politics and government—

1963-1969. 3. World politics—1955-1965. I. Title. BIP

SCHAAP, Richard, 1934- 973.922'0924
R.F.K. Picture editor: Michael O'Keefe. [New York] The New American Library [1967] 201 p. illus. (part col.) ports. (part col.) 32 cm. [E840.8.K4S3] 67-28481
1. Kennedy, Robert F., 1925-1968. I. Title.

SCHLESINGER, Arthur Meier, 1917- 973.922'092'4 B
Robert Kennedy and his times / Arthur M. Schlesinger, Jr. Boston : Houghton Mifflin, 1978. xvii, 1066 p., [8] leaves of plates : ill. ; 24 cm. Includes bibliographical references and index. [E840.8.K4S33] 78-8469 ISBN 0-395-24897-3 : 19.95
1. Kennedy, Robert F., 1925-1968. 2. United States. Congress. Senate—Biography. 3. Legislators—United States—Biography. 4. United States—Politics and government—1945- I. Title. BIP

STEIN, Jean. 973.923'0924
American journey; the times of Robert Kennedy. Interviews by Jean Stein. Edited by George Plimpton. [1st ed.] New York, Harcourt Brace Jovanovich [1970] xii, 372 p. 24 cm. [E840.8.K4S77] 73-78867 8.95
1. Kennedy, Robert F., 1925-1968. I. Plimpton, George, ed. II. Title.

SWINBURNE, Laurence. 973.923'0924 B
RFK, the last knight. New York, Pyramid Books [1969] 158 p. 18 cm. (A Pyramid hi-lo original, H-704) [E840.8.K4S9] 73-7482 0.60
1. Kennedy, Robert F., 1925-1968. I. Title.

THOMPSON, Robert E. 923.273
Robert F. Kennedy; the brother within, by Robert E. Thompson, Hortense Myers. [New York, Dell, c.1962] 224p. illus. 17cm. (7468) .50 pap.,
1. Kennedy, Robert F., 1925 I. Myers, Hortense, joint author. II. Title.

VANDEN Heuvel, William J. 973.923'0924
On his own: Robert F. Kennedy, 1964-1968 [by] William Vanden Heuvel and Milton Gwirtzman. [1st ed.] Garden City, N.Y., Doubleday, 1970. xii, 393 p. illus., facsim., map, ports. 25 cm. Bibliographical footnotes. [E840.8.K4V3] 79-98105 7.95
1. Kennedy, Robert F., 1925-1968. I. Gwirtzman, Milton, 1933- joint author. II. Title.

Kennedy, Robert F., 1925-1968—Addresses, essays, lectures.

"AN Honorable profession"; a tribute to Robert F. Kennedy. Edited by Pierre Salinger [and others. 1st ed.] Garden City, N.Y., Doubleday, 1968. 182 p. illus., facsims., ports. 24 cm. [E840.8.K4H6] 68-55381 973.923'0924
1. Kennedy, Robert F., 1925-1968—Addresses, essays, lectures. I. Kennedy, Robert F., 1925-1968. II. Salinger, Pierre.

Kennedy, Robert F., 1925-1968—Juvenile literature.

GRAVES, Charles Parlin, 1911- 973.922'0924 B
Robert F. Kennedy; man who dared to dream, by Charles P. Graves. Illustrated by Victor Mays. Champaign, Ill., Garrard Pub. Co. [1970] 96 p. illus. (part col.), ports. 24 cm. (Americans all) A biography of the senator who served as attorney general under his brother's administration and was assassinated during his own Presidential Campaign in 1968. [E840.8.K4G7] 92 76-101302 2.49
1. Kennedy, Robert F., 1925-1968—Juvenile literature. I. Mays, Victor, 1927- illus. II. Title. BIP

SCHOOR, Gene. 973.923'0924 B
Young Robert Kennedy. New York, McGraw-Hill [1969] 191 p. ports. 21 cm. Bibliography: p. 189. A biography of the New York Senator who was shot and killed as he campaigned for presidential office in 1968. [E840.8.K4S35] 92 75-91686 4.95
1. Kennedy, Robert F., 1925-1968—Juvenile literature. I. Title.

STEINBERG, Alfred, 1917- 973.92'0922 E
The Kennedy brothers. New York, Putnam [1969] 223 p. 22 cm. (Lives to remember) Brief biographies of four American brothers who were groomed from an early age to serve their country. [E843.S7 1969] 920 74-75596 3.64
1. Kennedy, John Fitzgerald, Pres. U.S., 1917-1963—Juvenile literature. 2. Kennedy, Joseph Patrick, 1915-1944—Juvenile literature. 3. Kennedy, Robert F., 1925-1968—Juvenile literature. 4. Kennedy, Edward Moore, 1932- —Juvenile literature. I. Title. BIP

ZEIGER, Henry A. 973.923'0924 B
Robert F. Kennedy; a biography, by Henry A. Zeiger [1st ed.] New York, Meredith Press [1969, c1968] vii, 152 p. 21 cm. A biography of the prominent politician who, during his campaign to become Democratic nominee for the Presidency, suffered a fate similar to that of his assassinated brother. [E840.8.K4Z4] 92 68-9519 4.95
1. Kennedy, Robert F., 1925-1968—Juvenile literature. I. Title.

Kennedy, Rose Fitzgerald, 1890-

CAMERON, Gail. 973.9'0924 [B]
Rose; a biography of Rose Fitzgerald Kennedy. [New York] Berkley Pub. Co. [1974, c1971] 320 p. illus. 18 cm. (A Berkley medallion book) [E748.K378C3] ISBN 0-425-02109-2 1.50 (pbk.)
1. Kennedy, Rose Fitzgerald, 1890- I. Title.
L.C. card number for original ed.: 72-105595.

KENNEDY, Rose Fitzgerald, 1890- 973.9'092'4 B
Times to remember. New York, Bantam Books, [1975] 588 p. illus., 18 cm. [E748.K378A37] 2.50 (pbk.)
1. Kennedy, Rose Fitzgerald, 1890- I. Title.
L.C. card no for original edition: 73-79682. BIP

Kennedy, Rose Fitzgerald, 1890- —Juvenile literature.

HAWKES, Ann 973.90924
Rose Kennedy / by Anne Hawkes [sic] ; ill. by Reisie Lonette. New York : Putnam, [1975] 60 p. : ill. ; 23 cm. (A See and read biography) An easy-to-read biography of the woman who along with her family has gained fame through political and social activities. [E748.K378H38 1975] [92] 74-83015 ISBN 0-399-60921-0 lib.bdg. : 3.96
1. Kennedy, Rose Fitzgerald, 1890- —Juvenile literature. I. Lonette, Reisie. II. Title. BIP

Kennerly, David Hume, 1947-

KENNERLY, David Hume, 1947- 770'.92'4 B
Shooter / David Hume Kennerly. 1st ed. New York : Newsweek Books, 1979. 269 p. : ill. ; 24 cm. Includes index. [TR820.K44] 79-2138 ISBN 0-88225-265-8 : 9.95
1. Kennerly, David Hume, 1947- 2. Photography, Journalistic. 3. Photographers—United States—Biography. I. Title. BIP

Kennett Square, Pa. Longwood Gardens.

THOMPSON, George E. 974.8'13
A man and his garden : the story of Pierre S. du Pont's development of Longwood Gardens / by George E. Thompson, Sr., with the assistance of Richard G. Taylor. Kennett Square, Pa. : Longwood Gardens, 1976. x, 203 p. : ill. ; 24 cm. "Originally published as weekly installments in the Kennett news and advertiser." [SB466.U7L68] 75-32847
1. Kennett Square, Pa. Longwood Gardens. 2. DuPont, Pierre Samuel, 1870-1954. I. Taylor, Richard G., joint author. II. Title.

Kenny, Elizabeth.

BIGLAND, Eileen 926.1
The true book about Sister Kenny. Illus., F. Stocks May. [2d, rev. ed.] [dist. Sportshelf, New Rochelle, N.Y., 1961, c.1956, 1960] 142p. (True bks.) 61-1532 2.75 bds.,
1. Kenny, Elizabeth. I. Title.

COHN, Victor. 616.8'35'0620924 B
Sister Kenny : the woman who challenged the doctors / by Victor Cohn. Minneapolis : University of Minnesota Press, c1975. 302 p., [8] leaves of plates : ill., map ; 24 cm. Includes index. Bibliography: p. 265-270. [RT37.K39C63 1975] 75-15401 ISBN 0-8166-0755-9 : 16.50
1. Kenny, Elizabeth. 2. Poliomyelitis—History. I. Title. BIP

LEVINE, Herbert Jerome, 1906- 616.9
I knew Sister Kenny; a story of a great lady and little people. Boston, Christopher Pub. House [1954] 234p. illus. 21cm. [RC180.5.K4L4] [RC180.5.K4L4] 616.83 54-9072 54-9072
1. Kenny, Elizabeth. I. Title.

THOMAS, Henry, 1886- 926.1
Sister Elizabeth Kenny. Illustrated by Polly Bolian. New York, Putnam [1958] 126 p. illus. 21 cm. (Lives to remember) [RC180.5.K4T45 1958] 58-7456
1. Kenny, Elizabeth. I. Title.

Kenny, Robert Walker, 1901-

STEVENSON, Janet. 979.4'05'0924 B
The undiminished man / by Janet Stevenson. Novato, Calif. : Chandler & Sharp Publishers, 1980. p. cm. Includes index. [F866.K35S75] 80-10889 ISBN 0-88316-538-4 : 11.95 ISBN 0-88316-539-2 pbk. : 5.95
1. Kenny, Robert Walker, 1901- 2. California. Legislature. Senate—Biography. 3. California—Politics and government—1846-1950. 4. Law—California—History and criticism. 5. Legislators—California—Biography. 6. Judges—California—Biography. I. Title.

Kenschaft, Patricia C.

KENSCHAFT, Patricia C. 618.4'5
Childbirth, cooperative style : family experience with prepared childbirth and prenatal classes / Pat Kenschaft. 1st ed. Hicksville, N.Y. : Exposition Press, c1977. 95 p. : ill. ; 22 cm. (An Exposition-banner book) Bibliography: p. 95. [RG661.K46] 76-58205 ISBN 0-682-48785-6 : 6.00
1. Kenschaft, Patricia C. 2. Natural childbirth. 3. Mothers—Biography. I. Title. BIP

Kent, James, 1763-1847.

KENT, William, 1858-1910. 347.9924 B
Memoirs and letters of James Kent. New York, Da Capo Press, 1970. x, 341 p. port. 23 cm. "Chancellor Kent's memoirs of Alexander Hamilton": p. [279]-331. Reprint of the 1898 ed. [KF213.K4K4 1970] 78-99481
1. Kent, James, 1763-1847. 2. Hamilton, Alexander, 1757-1804. I. Title. BIP

Kent, N.Y. (Putnam Co.)—History.

AN Historic biographical profile of the town of Kent, Putnam County, New York / [editors, Margaret Brutting, Betty M. Light Behr, Nancy Sorel]. Bicentennial ed. [Kent, N.Y. : Town of Kent Bicentennial Committee], 1976. viii, 175 p. : ill. ; 28 cm. Cover title. Includes index. [F129.K37H57] 76-371350 974.7'32
1. Kent, N.Y. (Putnam Co.)—History. 2. Kent, N.Y. (Putnam Co.)—Biography. 3. Kent, N.Y. (Putnam Co.)—Genealogy. I. Brutting, Margaret. II. Behr, Betty M. Light. III. Sorel, Nancy Caldwell. IV. Town of Kent Bicentennial Committee.

Kent, Rockwell, 1882-1971.

KENT, Rockwell, 1882- 927
It's me, O Lord; the autobiography of Rockwell Kent. New York, Dodd, Mead [1955] x, 617 p. illus. (part col.) 25 cm. [NC139.K4A3] 55-6470
1. Artists—Correspondence, reminiscences, etc. I. Title. BIP

KENT, Rockwell, 1882-1971. 741.9'73 B
It's me, O Lord : the autobiography of Rockwell Kent. New York : Da Capo Press, 1977, c1955. x, 617 p., [23] leaves of plates : ill. ; 24 cm. (Da Capo Press series in graphic art) Reprint of the ed. published by Dodd, Mead, New York. [NC975.5.K46A25 1977] 77-5590 ISBN 0-306-77412-7 : 39.50
1. Kent, Rockwell, 1882-1971. 2. Illustrators—United States—Biography. I. Title.

Kent, Tyler Gatewood, 1911-

SNOW, John Howland. 923.273
The case of Tyler Kent. New Canaan, Conn., Long House [1962] 59 p. 23 cm. [D810.S8K4 1962] 62-19461
1. Kent, Tyler Gatewood, 1911- I. Title. BIP

Kenton, Simon, 1755-1836.

JAHNS, Patricia. 923.973
The violent years; Simon Kenton and the Ohio-Kentucky frontier. New York, Hastings House [1962] 309p. 21cm. Includes bibliography. [F517.K367] 62-10090
1. Kenton, Simon, 1755-1836. I. Title.

KENTON, Edna, 1876-1954. 976.8'02'0924 B
Simon Kenton, his life and period, 1755-1836. [New York] Arno Press [1971, c1930] xxiii, 352 p. illus. 23 cm. (The First American frontier) Bibliography: p. 337-340. [F517.K37 1971] 70-146406 ISBN 0-405-02865-2
1. Kenton, Simon, 1755-1836. I. Title. II. Series. BIP

Kenton, Simon, 1755-1836—Juvenile literature.

GARST, Doris Shannon, 1899- 920
Frontier hero: Simon Kenton. New York, Messner [c.1963] 191p. 22cm. Bibl. 63-8643 3.25; 3.19 lib. ed.,
1. Kenton, Simon, 1755-1836—Juvenile literature. I. Title.

Kenton, Stan.

EASTON, Carol. 785.4'1'0924 B
Straight ahead: the story of Stan Kenton. New York, Morrow, 1973. xiv, 252 p. illus. 22 cm. [ML422.K35E3] 73-9840 ISBN 0-688-00196-3 7.95
1. Kenton, Stan. I. Title.

Kentucky—Biography.

PERRIN, William Henry, d.1892? 920.0769
Kentucky genealogy and biography [by] Battle—Perrin—Kniffin. Editor: Thomas W. Westerfield. Owensboro, Ky., Genealogical Reference Co., 1970- v. ports. 28 cm. Reprinted from various editions of Kentucky: a history of the state, by W. H. Perrin, J. H. Battle, and G. K. Kniffin. Contents.Contents.—v. 1. Sketches from Hancock, La Rue, Hardin, Edmonson, Hart, Breckinridge, Grayson, and Meade Counties.—v. 2. Sketches from Allen, Monroe, Metcalfe, Barren, and Warren Counties.—v. 3. Sketches from Butler, McLean, Muhlenburgh, and Ohio counties.—v. 4. Sketches from Caldwell, Crittenden, Hopkins, Livingston, Logan, Lyon, Simpson, Union, and Webster counties.—v. 5. Sketches from Adair, Boyle, Casey, Cumberland, Garrard, Green, Lincoln, Madison, Marion, Mercer, Nelson, Taylor, Washington counties. [F450.P46] 77-24519
1. Kentucky—Biography. I. Battle, J. H., joint author. II. Kniffin, G. C., joint author. III. Title.

TAPP, Hambleton, ed. 920.0769
Kentucky lives: the Blue Grass State who's who; a reference edition recording the biographies of contemporary leaders in Kentucky ... Hopkinsville, Ky., Historical

Record Association, 1966. 617 p. ports. 27 cm. [F450.T3] 66-13966
1. Kentucky—Biog. I. Title.

Kentucky—Biography—Dictionaries.

WHO'S who in 920'.0769
Kentucky; a compilation of biographical information on outstanding citizens of the State of Kentucky. 1st ed. Atlanta, United States Public Relations Service [1974] xiv, 526 p. ports. 24 cm. [CT236.W46] 74-76962
1. Kentucky—Biography—Dictionaries. I. United States Public Relations Service.

Kentucky—Governors—Biography.

POWELL, Robert A. 976.9'00992 B
Kentucky governors / drawings and text by Robert A. Powell ; J. Winston Coleman, Jr., historical advisor ; Harry Lee Waterfield, political advisor ; Charles Manning, editorial advisor. 1st ed. Frankfort : Kentucky Images, 1976. 136 p. : ill. ; 29 cm. Includes index. Includes one-page profiles of fifty governors of Kentucky and other related historical data. [F450.P68] 76-150686 15.00
1. Kentucky—Governors—Biography. I. Title.

Kentucky. University—Football.

RICE, Russell. 796.33'263'0976947
The Wildcats : a story of Kentucky football / by Russell Rice. Huntsville, Ala. : Strode Publishers, c1975. 387 p. : ill. ; 24 cm. Includes index. [GV958.K4R52] 75-26071 ISBN 0-87397-075-6 : 7.95
1. Kentucky. University—Football. 2. Football—Biography. I. Title.

Kenward, James,

KENWARD, James, 1908- 942.3'74
The suburban child. Illustrated by Edward Ardizzone. Cambridge [Eng.] University Press, 1955. 141p. illus. 21cm. Autobiographical. [CT788.K45A3] 55-13644
I. Title.

Kenworthy, Leonard Stout, 1912-

KENWORTHY, Leonard 300'.92'4 B
Stout, 1912-
Worldview : the autobiography of a social studies teacher and Quaker / by Leonard S. Kenworthy. Richmond, Ind. : Friends United Press, c1977. ix, 262 p. : ill. ; 21 cm. [H59.K45A38] 77-70183 ISBN 0-913408-27-1 pbk. : 4.95
1. Kenworthy, Leonard Stout, 1912- 2. Social scientists—United States—Biography. 3. Educators—United States—Biography. 4. Friends in the United States—Biography. I. Title.

Kenya—Politics and government.

ODINGA, Ajuma 967.6'2'040924
Oginga, 1911-
Not yet uhuru; the autobiography of Oginga Odinga. [1st American ed.] New York, Hill and Wang, [1967] xiv, 323 p. illus., map (on lining papers). ports. 21 cm. [DT434.E26O3 1967b] 67-26850
1. Kenya — Pol. & govt. I. Title.

ODINGA, Ajuma 967.6'2'040924
Oginga, 1911-
Not yet uhuru; the autobiography of Oginga Odinga. [1st American ed.] New York, Hill and Wang [1967] xiv, 323 p. illus., map (on lining papers), ports. 21 cm. [DT434.E26O3 1967b] 67-26850
1. Kenya—Politics and government. I. Title.

Kenyatta, Jomo.

DELF, George. 967.6'2'030924 B
Jomo Kenyatta : towards truth about "the light of Kenya" / by George Delf. Westport, Conn. : Greenwood Press, 1975, c1961. p. cm. Reprint of the ed. published by Doubleday, New York. Bibliography: p. [DT433.576.K46D44 1975] 75-17469 ISBN 0-8371-8307-3 lib.bdg. : 13.25
1. Kenyatta, Jomo. BIP

DELF, George. 967.62
Jomo Kenyatta: towards truth about "The Light of Kenya." [1st ed. in the U. S. A.] Garden City, N. Y., Doubleday, 1961. 215 p. 26 cm. Includes bibliography. [DT434.E26K43 1961a] 61-10348
1. Kenyatta, Jomo.

MURRAY-BROWN, 967.6'2'030924 B
Jeremy, 1932- MurrayBrown Jeremy 1932
Kenyatta. [1st ed.] New York, E. P. Dutton, 1973 [c1972] 445 p. illus. 25 cm. Includes bibliographical references. [DT433.576.K46M87 1972] 72-94703 ISBN 0-525-13855-2 12.50
1. Kenyatta, Jomo. BIP

MURRAY-BROWN, 967.6'204'0924 B
Jeremy, 1932-
Kenyatta / by Jeremy Murray-Brown. 2d ed. London ; Boston : Allen & Unwin, 1979. 381 p., [8] leaves of plates : ill. ; 24 cm. Includes bibliographical references and index. [DT433.576.K46M87 1979] 79-316123 ISBN 0-04-920059-3 : 22.50 22.50
1. Kenyatta, Jomo. 2. Kenya—Presidents—Biography. 3. Statesmen—Kenya—Biography.

Kenyatta, Jomo—Juvenile literature.

ARCHER, Jules. 967.6'2'040924 B
African firebrand; Kenyatta of Kenya. New York, J. Messner [1969] 192 p. 22 cm. Bibliography: p. 186. A biography of the African shepherd boy who rose to international prominence as the leader of Kenya, the country whose independence and racial peace he helped win. [DT434.E26K415] 92 69-12103 3.50
1. Kenyatta, Jomo—Juvenile literature. I. Title.

Kenyon, Mel, 1933-

KENYON, Mel, 1933- 796.7'2'0924 B
Burned to life / by Mel Kenyon ; as told to Bruce A. Darnall and Mike Christopulos. Harrison, Ark. : New Leaf Press, c1976. 128 p. : ill. ; 23 cm. [GV1032.K46A33] 76-1060 ISBN 0-89221-013-3 : 5.95
1. Kenyon, Mel, 1933- 2. Automobile racing drivers—United States—Biography. 3. Religion and sports. I. Darnall, Bruce A. II. Christopulos, Mike. III. Title. BIP

Keogh, Myles Walter, 1840-1876.

LUCE, Edward Smith. 973.8'1'0922
Keogh, Comanche, and Custer / by Edward S. Luce ; foreword by Robert M. Utley. 2d ed. Ashland, Or. : L. Osborne, 1974. 148 p., [4] leaves of plates : ill. ; 28 cm. [E83.866.L83 1974] 74-81372
1. Keogh, Myles Walter, 1840-1876. 2. Custer, George Armstrong, 1839-1876. 3. Indians of North America—Wars—1866-1895. 4. Little Big Horn, Battle of the, 1876. I. Title.

Kephart, George S.

KEPHART, George S. 634.9'092'4 B
Campfires rekindled : a forester recalls life in the Maine woods of the twenties / by George S. Kephart. Marion, Mass. : Channing Books, c1977. xii, 146 p. : ill. ; 23 cm. [GV191.42.M2K46] 77-85453 ISBN 0-9600496-7-3 pbk. : 6.95
1. Kephart, George S. 2. Outdoor life—Maine—History. 3. Maine—Social life and customs—History. 4. Foresters—Maine—Biography. 5. Lumbering—Maine. I. Title.

Kepler, Johann,

KEPLER, Johann, 1571-1630. 925.2
Johannes Kepler: life and letters, by Carola Baumgardt. With an introd. by Albert Einstein. New York, Philosophical Library [1951] 209 p. illus., port. 24 cm. Bibliography: p. 199-202. [QB36.K4A3] 51-3157
I. Baumgardt, Carola, ed. and tr.

Kepler, Johann, 1571-1630.

ARMITAGE, Angus, 1902- 520'.924 B
John Kepler. New York, Roy Publishers [1966] 194 p. illus., ports. 21 cm. Bibliographical footnotes. [QB36] 67-12680
1. Kepler, Johann, 1571-1630.

CASPAR, Max 925.2
Kepler, Tr., ed. by C. Doris Hellman. New York, Collier [1962, c.1959] 416p. 18cm. (BS55) Bibl. 1.50 pap.,
1. Kepler, Johann, 1571-1630. I. Title.

CASPAR, Max, 1880-1956. 925.2
Kepler. Translated and edited by C. Doris Hellman. London, New York, Abelard-Schuman [c1959] 401p. 23cm. (The Life of science library, 36) Includes bibliography. [QB36.K4C33] 59-5797
1. Kepler, Johann, 1571-1630. I. Title.

CASPER, Max 925.2
kepler. Translated [from the German] and edited by C. Doris Hellman. New York, Abelard-Schuman [c.1959] 401p. Includes bibliography. 23cm. (The Life of science library, 36) 59-5797 7.50
1. Kepler, Johann, 1571-160)030. I. Title.

KEPLER, Johann, 1571-1630. 925.2
Johannes Kepler: life and letters, by Carola Baumgardt. With an introd. by Albert Einstein. New York, Philosophical Library [1951] 209 p. illus., port. 24 cm. Bibliography: p. 199-202. [QB36.K4A3] 51-3157
I. Baumgardt, Carola, ed. and tr.

KOESTLER, Arthur, 1905- 925.2
The watershed; a biography of Johannes Kepler. Foreword by John Durston. Illustrated by R. Paul Larkin. Garden City, N.Y., Anchor Books, 1960. 280 p. illus. 18 cm. (Science study series, S16) "From The sleepwalkers." [QB36.K4K6] 60-13537
1. Kepler, Johann, 1571-1630. I. Title.

LEAR, John. 523.3
Kepler's Dream. With the full text and notes of Somnium. sive Astronomia lunaris Joannis Keplew. Translated by Patricia Frueh Kirkwood. Berkeley, University of California Press, 1965. 182 p. illus. 23 cm. Bibliographical footnotes. [QB41.K422L4] 64-21775
1. Kepler, Johann. 1571-1630. Somnium. I. Kepler, Johann 1571-1630. The dream. II. Title. BIP

ROSEN, Sidney. 92
The harmonious world of Johann Kepler. Illustrated by Rafaello Busoni. [1st ed.] Boston, Little, Brown [1962] 212 p. illus. 22 cm. Includes bibliography [QB36.K4R57] 62-12389
1. Kepler, Johannes, 1571-1630. I. Title.

Kepler, Johann, 1571 1630—Juvenile literature.

LAND, Barbara 523
The quest of Johannes Kepler, astronomer. Illus. by Sam Wisnom. Garden City, N.Y., Doubleday [c.1963] 128p. col. illus. 62-7097 2.95
1. Kepler, Johann, 1571-1630—Juvenile literature. I. Title.

TINER, John Hudson, 520'.92'4 B
1944-
Johannes Kepler, giant of faith and science / by John Hudson Tiner ; illustrated by Rod Burke ; edited by Norma Cournow Camp. Milford, Mich. : Mott Media, c1977. 200 p. : ill. ; 21 cm. (The sowers) Includes index. Bibliography: p. [198]. A biography of the German astronomer who discovered three laws of planetary motion. [QB36.K4T56 1977] 92 77-558 ISBN 0-915134-10-1 : 5.95. ISBN 0-915134-11-X pbk. : 3.50
1. Kepler, Johann, 1571-1630—Juvenile literature. 2. Astronomers—Germany—Biography—Juvenile literature. I. Burke, Rod. II. Title.

Kepler, Johann, 1571-1630. Somnium.

LEAR, John 523.3
Kepler's Dream. With the full text and notes of Somnium, sive Astronomia lunaris Joannis Kepleri. Tr. [from Latin] by Patricia Frueh Kirkwood. Berkeley, Univ. of Calif. Pr. [c.]1965. 182p. illus. 23cm. Bibl. [QB41.K422L4] 64-21775 5.00
1. Kepler, Johann, 1571-1630. Somnium. I. Kepler, Johann, 1571-1630. The dream. II. Title.

Keppel, Frederick Paul, 1875-1943.

KEPPEL, David, 1877- 920
FPK, an intimate biography of Frederick Paul Keppel. Washington, Priv. print. [1951, '1950] 116 p. illus., ports. 24 cm. [CT275.K4586K4] 51-22045
1. Keppel, Frederick Paul, 1875-1943. I. Title.

Kerkorian, Kirk, 1917—

TORGERSON, Dial, 338'.0092'4 B
1928-
Kerkorian: an American success story. New York, Dial Press, 1974. 306 p. 24 cm. [HC102.5.K47T65] 74-4287 ISBN 0-8037-4421-8 8.95
1. Kerkorian, Kirk, 1917- I. Title.

Kern, Janet,

KERN, Janet, 1924- 818.64
Yesterday's child. [1st ed.] Philadelphia, Lippincott [1962] 239 p. 21 cm. Autobiographical. [CT275.K45863A3] 62-15199
I. Title.

Kern, Jerome, 1885-1945.

EWEN, David, 1907- 927.8
The story of Jerome Kern. [1st ed.] New York, Holt [1953] 148 p. illus. 22 cm. [ML410.K385E9] 52-13066
1. Kern, Jerome, 1885-1945. 2. Kern, Jerome, 1885-1945—Discography.

EWEN, David, 1907- 927.8
The world of Jerome Kern, a biography. [1st ed.] New York, Holt [1960] 178 p. illus. 22 cm. [ML410.K385E93] 60-5302
1. Kern, Jerome, 1885-1945.

Kern River Valley—Biography.

WALKER, Ardis 917.94'88'0340922
Manly, 1901-
The rough and the righteous of the Kern River diggins, by Ardis M. Walker. Illustrated by Katherine F. Clarke. [Balboa Island, Calif., Paisano Press, 1971] xvi, 175 p. illus., map (on lining paper) 25 cm. [F868.K33W3] 76-24149
1. Kern River Valley—Biography. I. Title.

Kerouac, John, 1922-1969.

CHARTERS, Ann. 813'.5'4 B
Kerouac, a biography. [San Francisco, Straight Arrow Books, 1973] 419 p. illus. 24 cm. Includes bibliographical references. [PS3521.E735Z6] 72-95055 ISBN 0-87932-055-9 7.95
1. Kerouac, John, 1922-1969.

CHARTERS, Ann. 813'.5'4 B
Kerouac; a biography. [New York] Warner Paperback Library [1974, c1973] 416 p. illus. 18 cm. Includes bibliographical references. [PS3521.E73526] 1.95 (pbk.)
1. Kerouac, John, 1922-1969. I. Title.
L.C. card number for original ed.: 72-95055.

*GIFFORD, Barry. 818'.5'4
Kerovac's town; on the second anniversary of his death. With photos by Marshall Clements. Santa Barbara [Calif.] Capra Press, 1973. 30 p. illus. 18 cm. (Yes! Capra chapbook series, no. 12) ISBN 0-912264-78-0 2.50 (pbk.)
1. Kerovac, John, 1922-1969. 2. Lowell, Mass.—Description and travel. I. Title. II. Series.

Kerouac, John, 1922-1969 -

CASSADY, Carolyn. 813'.5'4 B
Heart beat : my life with jack & neal / by Carolyn Cassady. New York : Pocket Books, 1978. 125p. : ill. ; 18 cm.

[PS3521.E735Z59] ISBN 0-671-81713-2 pbk. : 1.95
1. Kerouac, John, 1922-1969 — Relationship with women — Carolyn Cassady. 2. Cassady, Carolyn. 3. Cassady, Ned. 4. Authors, American — 20th Century — Biography. 5. Wives — United States — Biography. I. Title.
L.C. card no. for 1976 Creative Arts ed.: 76-12732.

Kerouac, John, 1922-1969—Biography.

GIFFORD, Barry, 1946- 813'.5'4 B
Jack's book : an oral biography of Jack Kerouac / by Barry Gifford & Lawrence Lee. New York : St. Martin's Press, c1978. 339 p. : ill. ; 24 cm. Includes index. Bibliography: p. 333-334. [PS3521.E735Z635] 77-15824 ISBN 0-312-43942-3 : 10.95
1. Kerouac, John, 1922-1969—Biography. 2. Authors, American—20th century—Biography. 3. Bohemianism—United States—Biography. I. Lee, Lawrence, 1941- II. Title.

GIFFORD, Barry, 1946- 813'.5'4 B
Jack's book : an oral biography of Jack Kerouac / by Barry Gifford & Lawrence Lee. New York : Penguin Books, [1978] p. cm. Includes index. Bibliography: p. [PS3521.E735Z635 1978b] 79-9139 ISBN 0-14-005269-0 pbk. : 3.95
1. Kerouac, John, 1922-1969—Biography. 2. Authors, American—20th century—Biography. 3. Bohemianism—United States—Biography. I. Lee, Lawrence, 1941- joint author. II. Title. **BIP**

GINSBERG, Allen, 810'.9'0054 B 1926-
The visions of the great rememberer / by Allen Ginsberg ; with letters by Neal Cassady ; & drawings by Basil King. Amherst, Mass. : Mulch Press, c1974. 71 p., [3] leaves of plates : ill. ; 22 cm. (A Haystack book) [PS3521.E735Z65] 74-77758 ISBN 0-913142-03-4 : 2.50
1. Kerouac, John, 1922-1969—Biography. 2. Cassady, Neal. 3. Ginsberg, Allen, 1926- —Correspondence. 4. Authors—Correspondence, reminiscences, etc. I. Title.

JARVIS, Charles E. 813'.5'4 B
Visions of Kerouac / by Charles E. Jarvis. Lowell, Mass. : Ithaca Press, c1973, 1974 printing. x, 220 p. : ill. ; 22 cm. Bibliography: p. 219-220. [PS3521.E735Z73 1974] 75-322475
1. Kerouac, John, 1922-1969—Biography. I. Title.

MCNALLY, Dennis. 813'.5'4 B
Desolate angel : Jack Kerouace, the Beat generation, and America / Dennis McNally. 1st ed. New York : Random House, c1979. xi, 400 p., [8] leaves of plates : ill. ; 24 cm. Includes index. [PS3521.E735Z775] 78-23786 ISBN 0-394-50011-3 : 15.00
1. Kerouac, John, 1922-1969—Biography. 2. Authors, American—20th century—Biography. 3. Bohemianism—United States—Biography. I. Title.

Kerouac, John, 1922-1969—Friends and associates.

MONTGOMERY, John, 813'.5'4 B 1919-
Kerouac West Coast : a Bohemian pilot detailed navigational instructions / by John Montgomery. 1st ed. Palo Alto, Calif. : Fels & Firn Press, c1976. [24] p. : ill. ; 24 cm. [PS3521.E735Z78] 76-40359 1.50
1. Kerouac, John, 1922-1969—Friends and associates. 2. Authors, American—20th century—Biography. I. Title. **BIP**

Kerouac, John, 1922-1969—Homes and haunts.

GIFFORD, Barry, 1946- 813'.5'4 B
Kerouac's town / by Barry Gifford ; with photos. by Marshall Clements. Rev., expanded ed. Berkeley, CA : Creative Arts Book Co. : distributed by Book People, 1977. 60 p. : ill. ; 18 cm. (Modern authors monograph series ; no. 2) [PS3521.E735Z64] 76-50838 ISBN 0-916870-07-3 pbk. : 2.50
1. Kerouac, John, 1922-1969—Homes and haunts. 2. Lowell, Mass.—Description. 3. Authors, American—20th century—Biography. I. Title. II. Series. **BIP**

Kerouac, John, 1922-1969—Relationship with women—Carolyn Cassady.

CASSADY, Carolyn. 813'.5'4 B
Heart beat : my life with Jack & Neal / by Carolyn Cassady. Berkeley, CA : Creative Arts Book Co. : distributed by Book People, 1976. 93 p. : ill. ; 23 cm. [PS3521.E735Z59] 76-12732 ISBN 0-916870-03-0 pbk. : 4.00
1. Kerouac, John, 1922-1969—Relationship with women—Carolyn Cassady. 2. Cassady, Carolyn. 3. Cassady, Neal. 4. Authors, American—20th century—Biography. 5. Wives—United States—Biography. I. Title. **BIP**

Kerr, Deborah, 1921-

BRAUN, Eric. 791.43'028'0924 B
Deborah Kerr / Eric Braun. New York : St. Martin's Press, 1978, c1977. 264 p., [16] leaves of plates : ill. ; 25 cm. Includes index. Bibliography: p. 236. [PN2598.K627B7 1978] 78-3971 ISBN 0-312-18895-1 : 8.95
1. Kerr, Deborah, 1921- 2. Actors—Great Britain—Biography. I. Title. **BIP**

Kerr, John Robert, Sir, 1914-

KERR, John Robert, 994.06'092'4 B Sir, 1914-
Matters for judgment : an autobiography of Sir John Kerr / foreword by Lord Hailsham of St. Marylebone ; epilogue by Eugene Forsey. New York : St. Martin's Press, 1979, c1978. p. cm. Includes index. Bibliography: p. [DU117.2.K47A35 1979] 79-17249 ISBN 0-312-52305-X : 25.00
1. Kerr, John Robert, Sir, 1914- 2. Australia—Politics and government—1945- 3. Australia—Constitutional history. 4. Australia—Governors—Biography. 5. Judges—Australia—Biography. I. Title.

Kerr, Robert Samuel, 1896-1963.

MORGAN, Anne 328.73'092'4 B Hodges, 1940-
Robert S. Kerr : the Senate years / by Anne Hodges Morgan. 1st ed. [Norman] : University of Oklahoma Press, c1977. xiv, 337 p., [12] leaves of plates : ill. ; 24 cm. Includes index. Bibliography: p. 319-326. [E748.K42M67] 76-62514 ISBN 0-8061-1402-9 : 12.50
1. Kerr, Robert Samuel, 1896-1963. 2. Legislators—United States—Biography. 3. Oklahoma—Governors—Biography. 4. United States—Politics and government—20th century. 5. Oklahoma—Politics and government—1907- **BIP**

Kerrison, Raymond.

KERRISON, Raymond. 922.273
Bishop Walsh of Maryknoll, a biography. New York, Putnam [1962] 314p. 22cm. [BX4705.W2573K40] SS61
I. Walsh, James Edward, Bp., 1891- II. Title.

Kerry, Stephen Seamus.

KERRY, Stephen 610'.92'4 B Seamus.
Ship's doctor [by] Stephen Kerry. New York, Taplinger Pub. Co. [1972, c1971] 181 p. 22 cm. London ed. published in 1971 under title: Doctor's cabin. [R489.K37A3 1972] 74-164018 ISBN 0-8008-7179-0 6.50
I. Title. **BIP**

Kersten, Felix, 1898-1960.

KESSEL, Joseph, 1898- 926.1
The man with the miraculous hands. Introd. by H. R. Trevor-Roper. Translated from the French by Helen Weaver and Leo Raditsa. New York, Farrar, Straus and Cudahy [1961] 235p. 22cm. Translation of Les mains du miracle. [RM699.7.K4K413] 61-6988
1. Kersten, Felix, 1898-1960. I. Title.

KESSEL, Joseph, 615'.822'0924 B 1898-
The man with the miraculous hands. Translated from the French by Helen Weaver and Leo Raditsa. Introd. by H. R. Trevor-Roper. Freeport, N.Y., Books for Libraries Press [1971, c1961] xiii, 235 p. 23 cm. (Biography index reprint series) Translation of Les mains du miracle. [RM699.7.K4K413 1971] 70-160922 ISBN 0-8369-8085-9
1. Kersten, Felix, 1898-1960. I. Title. **BIP**

Kertzer, Morris Norman, 1910-

KERTZER, Morris 296'.092'4 B Norman, 1910-
Tell me, rabbi / Morris N. Kertzer. New York : Bloch Pub. Co., 1977,c1976 xii, 196 p. ; 22 cm. [BM755.K37A35] 76-8324 ISBN 0-8197-0395-8 : 7.95
1. Kertzer, Morris Norman, 1910- 2. Rabbis—United States—Biography. 3. Jews in the United States—Anecdotes, facetiae, satire, etc. I. Title.

KERTZER, Morris 296'.092'4 B Norman, 1910-
Tell me, rabbi / Morris N. Kertzer. New York : Bloch Pub. Co., 1977,c1976 xii, 196 p. ; 22 cm. [BM755.K37A35] 76-8324 ISBN 0-8197-0395-8 : 7.95
1. Kertzer, Morris Norman, 1910- 2. Rabbis—United States—Biography. 3. Jews in the United States—Anecdotes, facetiae, satire, etc. I. Title. **BIP**

Kessel, Joseph,

KESSEL, Joseph, 1898- 926.1
The man with the miraculous hands. Introd. by H. R. Trevor-Roper. Tr. [from French] by Helen Weaver, Leo Raditsa. [New York] Dell [1962, c.1961] 256p. (F182) .50 pap.,
I. Kersten, Felix, 1898-1960. II. Title.

Kesselring, Albert,

KESSELRING, Albert, 1885- 923.543
Kesselring: a soldier's record. [Translated by Lynton Hudson] With an introd. by S.L.A. Marshall. New York, Morrow, 1954. 381p. illus. 22cm. Translation of Soldat bis zum letzten Tag. [DD247.K45A33 1954] 54-6795
I. Title.

KESSELRING, 355.3'31'0924 B Albert, 1885-1960.
Kesselring: a soldier's record. With an introd. by S. L. A. Marshall. Westport, Conn., Greenwood Press [1970, c1954] xvi, 381 p. illus., maps. 23 cm. Translation of Soldat bis zum letzten Tag. [DD247.K45A33 1970] 70-100164
I. Title.

Kessler, Henry Howard,

KESSLER, Henry 617'.00924 B Howard, 1896-
The knife is not enough, by Henry H. Kessler. [1st ed.] New York, W. W. Norton [1968] 295 p. illus., ports. 22 cm. Autobiographical. [R154.K28A3] 68-20822 5.95
I. Title. **BIP**

Ketchum, Carlton G., 1892-

KETCHUM, Carlton 940.54'49'73 B G., 1892-
The recollections of Colonel Retread, USAAF 1942-1945 / by Carlton G. Ketchum. 1st ed. Pittsburgh : Hart Books, c1976. 296 p. : ill. ; 24 cm. Autobiographical. [D790.K47] 76-29524 9.00
1. United States. Army Air Forces. 9th Air Force. 2. Ketchum, Carlton G., 1892- 3. United States. Army Air Forces—Biography. 4. World War, 1939-1945—Aerial operations, American. 5. World War, 1939-1945—Personal narratives, American. I. Title.

Ketchum, Creston Donald.

KETCHUM, Creston Donald. 922
His path is in the waters. New York, Prentice-Hall [1955] 183 p. illus. 21 cm. Autobiographical. [BV3705.K47A3] 55-6313
I. Title.

Ketchum, Thomas Edward, 1865 or 6-1901.

BARTHOLOMEW, Ed 923.4173 Ellsworth.
Black Jack Ketchum, last of the hold-up kings; an authentic biography of the Old West. Houston, Frontier Press of Texas, 1955. 116 p. illus. 22 cm. [F595.K4B3] 55-4448
1. Ketchum, Thomas Edward, 1865 or 6-1901. 2. Outlaws. 3. Crime and criminals—The West. I. Title.

Ketchum, Zophar, 1746-1814.

MEARS, Neal F 920
Zophar Ketchum of Orange County, New York. [Chicago? 1950] 7 l. 28 cm. [CT275.K4587M4] 51-17428
1. Ketchum, Zophar, 1746-1814. I. Title.

Kettering, Charles Franklin, 1876-1958.

BOYD, Thomas Alvin, 1888- 926.29
Professional amateur; the biography of Charles Franklin Kettering. With a foreword by Alfred P. Sloan, Jr. [1st ed.] New York, Dutton, 1957. 242 p. illus. 22 cm. [TL140.K4B6] 57-5336
1. Kettering, Charles Franklin, 1876-1958. I. Title. **BIP**

BOYD, Thomas Alvin, 620'.0092'4 B 1888-
Professional amateur; the biography of Charles Franklin Kettering. New York, Arno Press, 1972 [c1957] xii, 242 p. illus. 23 cm. (Technology and society) [T40.K4B6 1972] 72-5036 ISBN 0-405-04689-8
1. Kettering, Charles Franklin, 1876-1958. I. Title. II. Series.

JEFFRIES, Zay, 1888- 509'.22
Charles Franklin Kettering, August 29, 1876-November 25, 1958. (In National Academy of Sciences, Washington, D. C. Biographical memoirs. New York. 24cm. v. 34 (1960) [5th memoir] p. [106]-122. port.) (National Academy of Sciences, Washington, D. C. Biographical memoirs, v. 34, 5th memoir) Bibliography: p. 117-121. Patents: p. 122. [Q141.N2 vol. 34, 5th memoir] 61-148
1. Kettering, Charles Franklin, 1876-1958. I. Title. II. Series.

LAVINE, Sigmund A. 926.29
Kettering: master inventor. New York, Dodd. Mead, [c.]1960. xii, 173p. illus. 21cm. 60-7033 3.00
1. Kettering, Charles Franklin, 1876-1958. I. Title.

LAVINE, Sigmund A 926.29
Kettering: master inventor. New York, Dodd, Mead, 1960. 173p. illus. 21cm. [T40.K4L3] 60-7033
1. Kettering, Charles Franklin, 1876-1958. I. Title.

YOUNG, Rosamond McPherson. 926.29
Boss Ket; a life of Charles F. Kettering. Decorations by Allan Thomas. New York, Longmans, Green, 1961. 210 p. 21 cm. Includes bibliography. [T40.K4Y6] 61-12659
1. Kettering, Charles Franklin, 1876-1958. I. Title.

Kettering, Charles Franklin, 1876-1958—Juvenile literature.

ZEHNPFENNIG, Gladys 920
Charles F. Kettering: inventor and idealist; a biographical sketch of a man who refused to recognize the impossible. Minneapolis, Denison [c.1962] 199p. 22cm. (Men of achievement ser.) 62-21654 3.00
1. Kettering, Charles Franklin, 1876-1958—Juvenile literature. I. Title.

Kevin, Mother, O.S.F., 1875-1957.

LOUIS, Sister, O.S.F. 266.2'0924 B
Love is the answer; the story of Mother Kevin, by Sister M. Louis. [Dublin, Fallon's Educational Supply Co.]; Distributor in the U.S. and Canada: St. Anthony's Guild, Paterson, N.J. [1964] xiv, 254 p. plates, ports. 22 cm. [BX4705.K46L68] 79-250999
1. Kevin, Mother, O.S.F., 1875-1957. I. Title.

Kevin, Saint, Abbot of Glendalough, d. 618—Juvenile literature.

PETERS, Caroline 920
The story of Saint Kevin. Illus. by Henrietta Milstead. Paterson, N.J., St. Anthony Guild [c.1962] 27p. col. illus. 23cm. 62-20769 1.39 bds.,
1. Kevin, Saint, Abbot of Glendalough, d. 618—Juvenile literature. I. Title.

Key, David McKendree, 1824-1900.

ABSHIRE, David M. 973.8'0924
The South rejects a prophet; the life of Senator D. M. Key, 1824-1900 [by] David M. Abshire. Foreword by Ralph McGill. New York, F. A. Praeger [1967] xii, 250 p. illus., ports. 22 cm. Bibliographical references included in "Notes" (p. 225-241) [E664.K47A7] 67-24671
1. Key, David McKendree, 1824-1900. I. Title.

Keyes, Evelyn, 1917—

KEYES, Evelyn, 1917- 791.43'028'0924 B
Scarlett O'Hara's younger sister : my lively life in and out of Hollywood / Evelyn Keyes. 1st ed. Secaucus, N.J. : L. Stuart, c1977. 318 p., [8] leaves of plates : ill. ; 24 cm. Includes index. [PN2287.K655A38] 77-5607 ISBN 0-8184-0243-1 : 10.00
1. Keyes, Evelyn, 1917- 2. Moving-picture actors and actresses—United States—Biography. I. Title. BIP

Keyes, Roger John Brownlow Keyes, Baron, 1872-1945.

KEYES, Roger John Brownlow Keyes, Baron, 1872-1945. 359.3'3'10924 B
Adventures ashore and afloat / [by] Roger Keyes ; with a foreword by Winston S. Churchill. London ; New York : White Lion Publishers, 1973. [2], 373 p., 25 leaves : ill., maps, plan, ports. : 23 cm. Reprint of the 1939 ed. published by G. G. Harrap, London. Includes index. [DA89.1.K4A3 1973] 74-189000 ISBN 0-85617-140-9 : £3.25
1. Keyes, Roger John Brownlow Keyes, Baron, 1872-1945. 2. Great Britain. Navy—Sea life. I. Title

Keynes, John Maynard, 1883-1946.

HARRIS, Seymour Edwin, 1897- 923.342
John Maynard Keynes, economist and policy maker. New York, Scribner, 1955. 234 p. 22 cm. (Twentieth century library) [HB103.K47H27] 54-7274
1. Keynes, John Maynard, 1883-1946.

HARROD, Sir Roy Forbes, 1900- v. 12
The life of John Maynard Keynes, by R. F. Harrod. London, Macmillan; New York, St. Martin's Press, 1966. xvi, 674 p. facsim., ports. 22 cm. (Papermac 44) "First edition 1951. Reprinted...1966." 68-16277
1. Keynes, John Maynard, 1883-1946. I. Title.

HARROD, Roy Forbes, Sir 1900- 923.342
The life of John Maynard Keynes. New York, St. Martin's [1964] xvi, 674p. facsim., ports. 22cm. (Papermac 44) 63-15863 7.25 pap.,
1. Keynes, John Maynard, 1883-1946. I. Title. BIP

HARROD, Roy Forbes, Sir, 1900- 330.15'6 B
The life of John Maynard Keynes, [by] R. F. Harrod. Harmondsworth, Penguin, 1972. xx, 807 p. 19 cm. (Pelican biographies) Includes bibliographical references. [HB103.K47H28 1972] 72-193074 ISBN 0-14-021440-2 £1.00
1. Keynes, John Maynard, 1883-1946. 2. Keynesian economics. I. Title.

HARROD, Roy Forbes, Sir, 1900- 330.15'6'0924 B
The life of John Maynard Keynes, by R. F. Harrod. New York, A. M. Kelley, 1969. xvi, 674 p. illus., ports. 23 cm. (Reprints of economic classics) Reprint of the 1951 ed. Bibliographical footnotes. [HB103.K47H28 1969] 68-30524
1. Keynes, John Maynard, 1883-1946. 2. Keynesian economics. I. Title.

KEYNES Seminar, 1st, University of Kent at Canterbury, 1972. 330.15'6
Keynes : aspects of the man and his work : the first Keynes Seminar held at the University of Kent at Canterbury, 1972 / edited by D. E. Moggridge. New York : St. Martin's Press, 1974. viii, 107 p. : port. ; 23 cm. Includes bibliographical references and index. [HB103.K47K4 1974] 74-78897 10.95
1. Keynes, John Maynard, 1883-1946. 2. Keynesian economics—Congresses. I. Moggridge, Donald Edward.

MOGGRIDGE, Donald Edward. 330.15'6 B
John Maynard Keynes / D. E. Moggridge. New York : Viking Press, [1976] p. cm. (Modern masters) Includes index. Bibliography: p. [HB103.K47M55] 76-21630 ISBN 0-14-004319-5 pbk. : 2.50
1. Keynes, John Maynard, 1883-1946. 2. Keynesian economics. BIP

MOGGRIDGE, Donald Edward. 330.15'6 B
Keynes / D. E. Moggridge. [London] : Fontana/Collins, 1976. 189 p. ; 18 cm. (Modern masters) American ed. published under title: John Maynard Keynes. Bibliography: p. [182] 189. [HB103.K47M55 1976b] 76-369331 ISBN 0-00-634193-4 : £0.95
1. Keynes, John Maynard, 1883-1946. 2. Keynesian economics. 3. Economists—England—Biography.

VICTOR, R. F. 330.15'6 B
John Maynard Keynes, father of modern economics, by R. F. Victor. Charlotteville, N.Y., SamHar Press, 1972. 31 p. 22 cm. (Outstanding personalities, no. 17) Bibliography: p. 29-30. [HB103.K47V5] 76-190235 ISBN 0-87157 517-5 1.98
1. Keynes, John Maynard, 1883-1946. I. Title.
pap. $0.98, ISBN0-87157-017-3

Keynes, John Maynard, 1883-1946—Addresses, essays, lectures.

ROBINSON, Edward Austin Gossage. 330.15'6
John Maynard Keynes: economist, author, statesman: inaugural Keynes lecture, 22 April 1971 [by] Austin Robinson. London, New York, Oxford University Press for the British Academy, 1971. 20 p. 25 cm. (Keynes lecture, 1971) [HB99.7.K38R6] 72-182177 ISBN 0-19-725665-1 £0.30
1. Keynes, John Maynard, 1883-1946—Addresses, essays, lectures. I. Title. II. Series.

Keynes, John Maynard, 1883-1946—Library.

FRACCHIA, Charles A. 020'.75
John Maynard Keynes, book collector, by Charles A. Fracchia. San Francisco, Champion Press, 1968. 20, [2] p. illus., port. 26 cm. (The Series of great book collectors, no. 1) Bibliographical references included in "Notes" (p. [21]-[22]) [Z989.K4F7] 68-5182
1. Keynes, John Maynard, 1883-1946—Library.

Keys, Brady—Juvenile literature.

ROBERTS, Eric B. 796.332'0924 B
From football to finance; the story of Brady Keys, Jr., by Eric B. Roberts. [1st ed.] New York, Harcourt Brace Jovanovich [1971] 103 p. illus., ports. 22 cm. (Curriculum-related books) [GV939.K4R6] 70-151026 ISBN 0-15-230265-4 3.95
1. Keys, Brady—Juvenile literature. I. Title. BIP

Keystone View Company.

GARAI, Bernhard, 1891- 770'.924 (B)
The man from Keystone, by Bert Garai. New York, Living Books [1966] 247 p. illus., ports. 23 cm. Autobiographical. [TR140.G3A3 1966] 66-26818
1. Keystone View Company. I. Title.

Khan, Sajid,

KHAN, Sajid, 1951- 791'.0924
Sajid Khan: this is my story, as told to Floyd Ackerman. New York, Grosset & Dunlap [1969] 85 p. illus., ports. 21 cm. [PN2287.K66A3] 69-17271 1.00
I. Ackerman, Floyd. II. Title: This is my story.

Khan, Zarak.

BEVAN, A J. 954.2
The story of Zarak Khan. London, New York, Jarrolds [1950] 176p. port. 22cm. [DS485.N7B4] 51-18295
1. Khan, Zarak. I. Title.

BEVAN, A J 954.2
Zarak; the story of Zarak Khan. New York, Avon Publications [c1956] 192p. illus. 17cm. (Avon, T-150) First published in 1950 under title: The story of Zarak Khan. [DS485.N7B4 1956] 57-1283
1. Khan, Zarak. I. Title.

BEVAN, Anthony J 954.2
The story of Zarak Khan. London, New York, Jarrolds [1950] 176p. port. 22cm. [DS485.N7B4] 51-18295
1. Khan, Zarak. I. Title.

BEVAN, Anthony J 954.2
Zarak; the story of Zarak Khan. New York, Avon Publications [c1956] 192p. illus. 17cm. (Avon, T-150) First published in 1950 under title: The story of Zarak Khan. [DS485.N7B4 1956] 57-1283
1. Khan, Zarak. I. Title.

Kherdian, Veron, 1907——Juvenile literature.

KHERDIAN, David. 949.6'1'01
The road from home : the story of an Armenian girl / by David Kherdian. 1st ed. New York : Greenwillow Books, c1979. xi, 238 p. : map ; 22 cm. A biography of the author's mother concentrating on her childhood in Turkey before the Turkish government deported its Armenian population. [DR435.A7K47] 92 78-72511 ISBN 0-688-80205-2 : 8.95 ISBN 0-688-84205-4 lib. bdg. : 7.63
1. Kherdian, Veron, 1907——Juvenile literature. 2. Armenians in Turkey—Biography—Juvenile literature. 3. Children in Turkey—Juvenile literature. 4. Armenian massacres, 1915-1923—Juvenile literature. I. Title.

Khrushchev, Nikita Sergeevich, 1894-1971.

ALEXANDROV, Victor, 1908- 923.247
Khrushchev of the Ukraine, a biography. [Translated from the French by Paul Selver and Wade Baskin] New York, Philosophical Library [1957] 216p. 22cm. [DK275.K5A4] 57-14072
1. Khrushchev, Nikita Sergeevich, 1894- I. Title.

CRANKSHAW, Edward. v. 12
Khruschev: a biography. New York, Viking Press [1966] 316 p. 16 plates (ports.) 24 cm. NUC67
1. Khruschev, Nikita Sergeevich, 1894- I. Title.

CRANKSHAW, Edward 947.085(B)
Khrushchev; a career. [New York] Avon [1967, c.1966] 320p. 18cm. (Discuss bks., NS15) Bibl. [DX275.K5C7] .95 pap.,
1. Khrushchev, Nikita Sergeevich, 1894- I. Title. BIP

CRANKSHAW, Edward. 947.085 B
Khrushchev; a career. New York, Viking Press [1966] 311 p. ports. 24 cm. Bibliographical references included in "Notes" (p. 293-302) [DK275.K5C7] 66-15880
1. Khrushchev, Nikita Sergeevich, 1894- I. Title.

FRANKLAND, Mark, 1934- 947.085 (B)
Khruschev. Harmondsworth, Penguin, 1966. 213 p. 18 1/2 cm. (Political leaders of the twentieth century) 5/- Pelican books A858. [DK275.K5F7] 66-77536
1. Khrushchev, Nikita Sergeevich, 1894- I. Title.

HEARST, William Randolph, 1908- 923.247
Ask me anything; our adventures with Khrushchev [by] William Randolph Hearst, Jr., Frank Conniff [and] Bob Considine. [1st ed.] New York, McGraw-Hill [1960] 271 p. 22 cm. [DK275.K5H4] 60-12772
1. Khrushchev, Nikita Sergeevich, 1894-1971. I. Title.

HEARST, William Randolph, 1908- 923.247
Khurshchev and the Russian challenge. Original title 'Ask me anything--our adventures with Khurschev.' With new chapters added. [By] William Randolph Hearst, Jr., Frank Conniff [and] Bob Considine. New York, Avon Book Division [c1961] 255p. 18cm. [DK275.K5H4 1961] 62-51119
1. Khurshchev, Nikita Sergeevich, 1894- I. Title.

HIRSCHFELD, Burt, 1923- 947.085'0924 B
Khrushchev. [1st ed.] New York, Hawthorn Books [1968] 192 p. illus., ports. 22 cm. Bibliography: p. 185-186. [DK275.K5H5] 68-27644 4.95
1. Khrushchev, Nikita Sergeevich, 1894- I. Title.

HYLAND, William, 1929- 947.085'0924
The fall of Khrushchev [by] William Hyland and Richard Wallace Shryock. New York, Funk & Wagnalls [1968] xi, 209 p. 21 cm. Includes bibliographical references. [DK275.K5H87] 68-23419 4.95
1. Khrushchev, Nikita Sergeevich, 1894- 2. Russia—Politics and government 1953- I. Shryock, Richard Wallace, joint author. II. Title.

KELLEN, Konrad. 923.247
Khrushchev, a political portrait. New York, Praeger [1961] 271 p. 21 cm. (Praeger publications in Russian history and world communism, no. 98) Books that matter. Includes bibliography. [DK275.K5K4] 61-10511
1. Khrushchev, Nikita Sergeevich, 1894-1971.

KHRUSCHEV. 947.085 (B)
Harmondsworth, Penguin, 1966. 213 p. 18 1/2 cm. (Political leaders of the twentieth century) 5/- Pelican books A858. [DK275.K5F7] 66-77536
1. Khrushchev, Nikita Sergeevich, 1894-

KHRUSHCHEV, Nikita Sergeevich, 1894-1971. 947.085'092'4 B
Khrushchev remembers; the last testament. Translated and edited by Strobe Talbott. With a foreword by Edward Crankshaw and an introd. by Jerrold L. Schecter. [1st ed.] Boston, Little, Brown [1974] xxxi, 602 p. illus. 24 cm. The second and concluding volume of the author's oral memoirs, begun in Khrushchev remembers, 1970. [DK275.K5A326] 74-4095 12.95
1. Khrushchev, Nikita Sergeevich, 1894-1971. 2. Russia—Politics and government—1953- I. Talbott, Strobe, ed. II. Title.

KURLAND, Gerald, 1942- 947.085'0924 B
Nikita Sergeievich Khrushchev, modern dictator of the USSR. Charlotteville, N.Y., SamHar Press, 1971. 32 p. 22 cm. (Outstanding personalities, no. 12) Bibliography: p. 32. [DK275.K5K87] 74-185668
1. Khrushchev, Nikita Sergeevich, 1894-1971. 2. Russia—History—20th century.

MACGREGOR-HASTIE, Roy. 923.247
The man from nowhere. [1st American ed.] New York, Coward-McCann [1961] 224p. 21cm. [DK275.K5M25 1961] 61-15069
1. Khrushchev, Nikita Sergeevich, 1894- I. Title.

MEDVEDEV, Roi 947.085'092'4
Aleksandrovich, 1925-
Khrushchev : the years in power / Roy A. Medvedev and Zhores A. Medvedev. New York : Columbia University Press, 1976. p. cm. Translation of N. S. Khrushchev, gody u vlasti. Includes index. [DK275.K5M413] ISBN 0-231-03939-5 : 8.95
1. Khrushchev, Nikita Sergeevich, 1894-1971. 2. Russia—Politics and government—1953- I. Medvedev, Zhores Aleksandrovich, joint author. II. Title. BIP

PALOCZI HORVATH, Gyorgy. 923.247
Khrushehev the making of a dictator, [1st ed.] Boston, Little, Brown [1960] 311p. illus. 22cm. [DK275.KP29] 60-6528
1. Khrushehev, Nikita Sergeevich, I. Title.

PALOCZI HORVATH, Gyorgy 923.247
[George Paloczi-Horvath]
Khrushchev: the making of a dictator. Boston, Little, Brown [c.1960] 314p. illus. port. 22cm. 60-6528 4.95
1. Khrushchev, Nikita Sergeevich I. Title.

Khvajah Mir, 1719?-1785?—Religion and ethics.

SCHIMMEL, 297.4'092'2 B
Annemarie.
Pain and grace : a study of two mystical writers of eighteenth-century Muslim India / by Annemarie Schimmel. Leiden : E. J. Brill, 1976. xiv, 310 p. ; 25 cm. (Studies in the history of religions, supplements to Numen ; 36) Includes indexes. Bibliography: p. [291]-296. [BP80.K54S34] 77-351051 ISBN 9-00-404771-9
1. Khvajah Mir, 1719?-1785?—Religion and ethics. 2. 'Abd al-Latif, Shah, ca. 1689-ca. 1752—Religion and ethics. 3. Sufism—India—Biography. I. Title. II. Series.

Khwaja Asim 1672-1738

•MALIK, Zahiruddin. 915.4'03'2
A mughal statesman of the eighteenth century; Khan-I-Dauran, MirBakshi of Muhammad Shah 1719-1739 [Delhi, India] , Asia Pub. House [1973] vi, 120 p., 25 cm. Published for the Centre of advanced study, Dept. of history, Aligarh Muslim University. Bibliography: 111-115. [DS461] ISBN 0-210-40544-9
1. Khwaja Asim 1672-1738 I. Title.
Distributed by Asia Pub. House, New York, 2.25 (pbk.)

Kickham, Charles Joseph, 1826 (ca.)-1882.

MURPHY, William. 821'.8
Charles Joseph Kickham : patriot, novelist and poet / William Murphy. Facsimile ed. Blackrock : Carraig Books, 1976. [35] p. ; 21 cm. (Carraig chapbooks ; 4) Originally published in 1903. Includes poems by C. J. Kickham. [PR4839.K365Z8 1976] 76-382965 £0.50
1. Kickham, Charles Joseph, 1826 (ca.)-1882. 2. Authors, Irish—19th century—Biography. I. Kickham, Charles Joseph, 1826 (ca.)-1882.

Kid, Z-D

KID, Z-D 920
The poor millionaire of Tookany Frankford-Rama. New York Vantage [c.1962] 54p.,21cm. 2.00;bds.,
I. Title.

Kidder, Alfred Vincent, 1885-1963.

WOODBURY, 917.2'03'50924 B
Richard Benjamin, 1917-
Alfred V. Kidder, by Richard B. Woodbury. New York, Columbia University Press, 1973. viii, 199 [1] p. illus. 23 cm. (Leaders of modern anthropology series) Part II contains excerpts from Kidder's professional writings, 1910-1961. Bibliography: p. 195-[200] [GN21.K5W66] 72-10082 ISBN 0-231-03484-9 2.95 (pbk.)
1. Kidder, Alfred Vincent, 1885-1963. I. Title. II. Series.
Cloth 8.00 ISBN 0-231-03485-7. BIP

Kidneys—Addresses, essays, lectures.

SMITH, Homer William, 612.4630924
1895-1962
Homer William Smith, SC. D.: his scientific & literary achievements. Ed. by Herbert Chasis, William Goldring. [New York] N. Y. U. [c.]1965. x, 282p. illus., ports. 23cm. Bibl. [QP26.S6A25] 65-10765 4.50
1. Kidneys—Addresses, essays, lectures. 2. Biology—Philosophy—Addresses, essays, lectures. I. Chasis, Herbert, 1905- ed. II. Goldring, William, 1898- ed. III. Title.

SMITH, Homer William, 612.4630924
1895-1962.
Homer William Smith, S.C.D.: his scientific & literary achievements. edited by Herbert Chasis and William Goldring. [New York] New York University Press, 1965. x, 282 p. illus., ports. 23 cm. Excerpts from the author's writings. "Bibliography of the writings of Homer W. Smith from 1918 to 1962": p. 259-268. [QP26.S6A25 1965] 65-10765
1. Kidneys — Addresses, essays, lectures. 2. Biology — Philosophy — Addresses, essays, lectures. I. Chasis, Herbert, 1905-ed. II. Goldring, William, 1898- ed. III. Title.

Kidwai, Rafi Ahmad, 1894-1954.

JAIN, Ajit Prasad, 954.0350924
1902-
Rafi Ahmad Kidwai; a memoir of his life and times New York, Asia Pub. [dist. Taplinger, c.1965] ix, 130p. illus., ports. 23cm. [DS481.K5J3] 65-16044 6.00
1. Kidwai, Rafi Ahmad, 1894-1954. I. Title.

Kiely, Benedict.

ECKLEY, Grace. 828'.9'1409
Benedict Kiely. New York, Twayne Publishers [1972] 184 p. 21 cm. (Twayne's English authors series, TEAS 145) Bibliography: p. 175-178. [PR6009.K5Z65] 72-187616 5.50
1. Kiely, Benedict. BIP

Kiemel, Ann—United States.

KIEMEL, Ann. 248'.2 B
Yes / Ann Kiemel. Wheaton, Ill. : Tyndale House Publishers, c1978. 127 p. : ill. ; 23 cm. [BX8699.N38K534] 78-58743 ISBN 0-8423-4653-8 pbk. : 5.95
1. Kiemel, Ann—United States. 2. Church of the Nazarene—Biography. I. Title. BIP

Kieninger, Clara Louise, 1883-1970.

KIENINGER, Clara 362.1'092'4 B
Louise, 1883-1970.
Ich dien : the compelling memoirs of Clara Louise Kieninger, a woman whose life-style made her a true humanitarian, edited and compiled by Elizabeth Clare Prophet. Colorado Springs : Summit University Press, 1975. 234 p., [8] leaves of plates : col. ill. ; 21 cm. In English. Includes bibliographical references. [BP605.G68K53 1970] 74-20377 3.95
1. Kieninger, Clara Louise, 1883-1970. 2. Great White Brotherhood. I. Prophet, Elizabeth. II. Title.

Kiep, Otto, 1886-1944.

CLEMENTS, Bruce. 327'.2'0924 B
From ice set free; the story of Otto Kiep. New York, Farrar, Straus and Giroux [1972] 215 p. illus. 22 cm. [DD247.K5C55 1972] 70-184703 ISBN 0-374-32468-9 5.50
1. Kiep, Otto, 1886-1944. I. Title.

Kierkegaard, Soren Aabye, 1813-1855.

ATTWATER, Donald, 270.8'1'0922
1892- ed.
Modern Christian revolutionaries; an introduction to the lives and thought of: Kierkegaard, Eric Gill, G. K. Chesterton, C. F. Andrews [and] Berdyaev. Edited by Donald Attwater. Freeport, N.Y., Books for Libraries Press [1971, c1947] xiii, 390 p. illus., ports. 23 cm. (Essay index reprint series) Contents.—Soren Kierkegaard, by M. Chaning-Pearce.—G. K. Chesterton, by F. A. Lea.—Eric Gill, by D. Attwater.—C. F. Andrews, by N. MacNichol.—Nicolas Berdyaev, by E. Lampert.—Bibliography (p. [383]-390) [BR1700.A8 1971] 76-156608 ISBN 0-8369-2304-9
1. Kierkegaard, Soren Aabye, 1813-1855. 2. Chesterton, Gilbert Keith, 1874-1936. 3. Gill, Eric, 1882-1940. 4. Andrews, Charles Freer, 1871-1940. 5. Berdiaev, Nikolai Aleksandrovich, 1874-1948. I. Title.

GATES, John Alexander, 921.8489
1898-
The life and thought of Kierkegaard for everyman. Philadelphia, Westminster Press [1960] 172 p. 21 cm. Includes bibliography. [B4376.G3] 60-7326
1. Kierkegaard, Sooren Aabye, 1813-1855. I. Title.

GRIMSLEY, Ronald. 198'.9
Kierkegaard; a biographical introduction. New York, Scribner [1973] 127 p. 21 cm. (The Scribner library. Lyceum editions) Bibliography: p. [122]-125. [B4376.G73 1973b] 72-12154 ISBN 0-684-13054-8 5.95
1. Kierkegaard, Soren Aabye, 1813-1855.
Pbk., 2.95, ISBN 0-684-13055-6.

HAMILTON, Kenneth. 230'.0924
The promise of Kierkegaard. [1st ed.] Philadelphia, Lippincott [1969] 116 p. 21 cm. (The Promise of theology) Bibliography: p. 112-116. [B4377.H34] 69-14495 1.50
1. Kierkegaard, Soren Aabye, 1813-1855. 2. Christianity—Philosophy. I. Title.

HOHLENBERG, Johannes 198'.9
Edouard, 1881-
Soren Kierkegaard / by Johannes Hohlenberg ; translated by T. H. Croxall. New York : Octagon Books, 1978, c1954. x, 321 p. : ill. ; 24 cm. Reprint of the ed. published by Pantheon Books, New York. Includes bibliographies and index. [B4376.H612 1978] 78-946 ISBN 0-374-93923-3 lib.bdg. : 15.00
1. Kierkegaard, Soren Aabye, 1813-1855. 2. Philosophers—Denmark—Biography. I. Title.

KIERKEGAARD, Soren 921.8489
Aabye, 1813-1855.
Diary. Translated from the Danish by Gerda M. Andersen. Edited by Peter P. Rohde. New York, Philosophical Library [1960] 255p. 19cm. Bibliography: p. 254-255. [B4376.K5A33] 60-13649
I. Rohde, Peter Preisler, 1902- ed. II. Title.

KIERKEGAARD, Soren Aabye, 201
1813-1855.
The difficulty of being Christian. Texts edited and introduced by Jacques Colette. English version by Ralph M. McInerny and Leo Turcotte. Notre Dame, University of Notre Dame Press [1968] xx, 311 p. 21 cm. Translation of La difficulte d'etre chretien. Bibliography: p. 5-9. [BX4827.K5A253] 68-17063
1. Kierkegaard, Soren Aabye, 1813-1855. I. Colette, Jacques, ed. II. Title. BIP

KIERKEGAARD, Soren 921.8489
Aabye, 1813-1855.
Journals. Translated, selected, and with an introd. by Alexander Dru. New York, Harper [1959] 254 p. 21 cm. (Harper torchbooks, TB52) [BX4827.K5A4 1959] 59-6650

KIERKEGAARD, Soren 198'.9 B
Aabye, 1813-1855.
Letters and documents / Kierkegaard ; translated by Henrik Rosenmeier, with introd. and notes. Princeton, N.J. : Princeton University Press, c1978. xxviii, 518 p. : maps ; 23 cm. (His Kierkegaard's writings ; 25) (Series: Kierkegaard, Soren Aabye, 1813-1855. Works. English. 1977 ; 25.) Translation of Breve og aktstykker. Includes index. Bibliography: p. [507] [B4376.A413 1978] 77-85897 ISBN 0-691-07228-0 : 22.50
1. Kierkegaard, Soren Aabye, 1813-1855. 2. Philosophers—Denmark—Correspondence. 3. Philosophers—Denmark—Biography. I. Rosenmeier, Henrik, 1931- II. Series.

LOWRIE 921.8489
A short life of Kierkegaard. Garden City, N.Y., Doubleday 1961 [c.1942] 226p. (Anchor bk., A273) Bibl. .95 pap.,
I. Title.

LOWRIE, Walter, 1868- 921.8489
1959.
Kierkegaard. 2v. [Gloucester, Mass., Peter Smith, c.1962] 2v. xviii, 640p. illus. 21cm. (Harper torchbks. Cloister lib. TB89-90 rebound) v.1, 3.75; v.2, 4.00
1. Kierkegaard, Soren Aabye, 1813-1855. I. Title.

LOWRIE, Walter, 1868- 921.8489
1959.
Kierkegaard. New York, Harper [1962] 2 v. (xviii, 640 p.) ports. 21 cm. (Harper torchbooks. The Cloister library, TB89-90) Includes translations of many extracts from Kierkegaard's works. "Synopsis of Kierkegaard's works": v. 2, p. [605]-618. "Selected bibliography, by Lee M. Capel": v. 2, p. [619]-625. [B4377.L6 1962] 62-853
1. Kierkegaard, Soren Aabye, 1813-1855.

LOWRIE, Walter, 1868-1959. v. 12
A short life of Kierkegaard. Princeton, N.J., Princeton University Press [1965] xi, 271 p. 20 cm. Bibliography: p. 261-264. 67-101837
1. Kierkegaard, Soren Aabye, 1813-1855. I. Title. BIP

PALEY, Alan L. 198'.9 B
Soren Kierkegaard, philospher [sic] and existentialist, by Alan L. Paley. Charlottesville, N.Y., SamHar Press, 1972. 32 p. 22 cm. (Outstanding personalities, no. 40) Bibliography: p. 31-32. A biography of the nineteenth-century Danish philosopher who created an intellectual universe though he spent his life in a limited environment. [B4376.P26] 92 72-81903
1. Kierkegaard, Soren Aabye, 1813-1855. I. Title.

PERKINS, Robert L., 230'.0924
1930-
Soren Kierkegaard, by Robert L. Perkins. Richmond, John Knox Press [1969] ix, 46 p. 19 cm. (Makers of contemporary theology) [B4377.P36] 69-14337 1.25
1. Kierkegaard, Soren Aabye, 1813-1855.

ROHDE, Peter Preisler, 921.8489
1902-
Soren Kierkegaard: an introduction to his life and philosophy. Tr. [from Danish] foreword by Alan Moray Williams. New York, Humanities [1964, c.1963] 164p. illus., ports. 64-1591 5.00 bds.,
1. Kierkegaard, Soren Aabye, 1813-1855. I. Title.

SIKES, Walter W. 230.0924
On becoming the truth; an introduction to the life and thought of Soren Kierkegaard. St. Louis, Bethany Press, 1968. 190 p. 20 cm. (The Library of contemporary theology) Bibliography: p. 181-184. [BX4827.K5S55] 68-26112 2.95
1. Kierkegaard, Soren Aabye, 1813-1855. I. Title.

THOMPSON, Josiah. 198'.9
Kierkegaard. [1st ed.] New York, Knopf; [distributed by Random House] 1973. xviii, 286, viii p. illus. 22 cm. Bibliography: p. [281]-286. [B4376.T46 1973] 72-11043 ISBN 0-394-47092-3 8.95

1. Kierkegaard, Soren Aabye, 1813-1855. BIP

Kierkegaard, Soren Aabye, 1813-1855.

HOHLENBERG, Johannes Edouard, 1881- 921.8489
Soren Kierkegaard; translated by T. H. Croxall. New York, Pantheon Books [1954] x, 321 p. illus., ports. 24 cm. Includes bibliographies. [B4376.H612] 53-8941
1. Kierkegaard, Soren Aabye, 1813-1855. BIP

Kiesinger, Kurt Georg, 1904-

KLARSFELD, Beate, 1939- 940.53'1503'924
Wherever they may be! / Beate Klarsfeld ; translated from the French by Monroe Stearns and Natalie Gerardi. New York : Vanguard Press, c1975. vi, 344 p., [6] leaves of plates : ill. ; 24 cm. Translation of Partout ou ils seront. Includes bibliographical references and index. [DD259.4.K5413 1975] 74-81809 ISBN 0-8149-0748-2 : 10.00
1. Kiesinger, Kurt Georg, 1904- 2. Klarsfeld, Beate, 1939- 3. Germany, West Politics and government. 4. Holocaust, Jewish (1939-1945) I. Title.

Kiick, Jim.

CSONKA, Larry. 796.33'2'0922
Always on the run, by Larry Csonka and Jim Kiick, with Dave Anderson. [1st ed.] New York, Random House [1973] xi, 223 p. 22 cm. Two stars of the Miami Dolphins exchange their thoughts about their lives, football, Coach Shula, and other topics. [GV939.A1C78] 73-5052 6.95
1. Csonka, Larry. 2. Kiick, Jim. 3. Miami Dolphins (Football club) 4. Backfield play (Football) I. Kiick, Jim. II. Anderson, Dave. III. Title.

Kiki, Albert Maori,

KIKI, Albert Maori, 1931- 995 B
Kiki; ten thousand years in a lifetime, a New Guinea autobiography. New York, F. A. Praeger [1968] 190 p. illus., map. 23 cm. [DU746.K5A3] 68-30943 4.95
I. Title.

KIKI, Albert Maori, 1931- 995 B
Kiki, ten thousand years in a lifetime; a New Guinea autobiography. Melbourne, Canberra [etc.] Cheshire [1968] 190 p. illus., map, ports. 23 cm. [DU746.K5A3 1968] 74-363833 3.50
I. Title.

Kilbracken, John Raymond Godley,

KILBRACKEN, John Raymond Godley, baron, 1920- 920
Living like a lord. Boston, Houghton Mifflin, 1956 [c1955] 243 p. 22 cm. Autobiography. [CT788.K49A3 1956] 56-5056
I. Title.

Kilburn, Sam, b. 1877.

MACFIE, Harry, 1879- 917.1
Wasa-wasa, a tale of trails and treasure in the far North, by Harry Macfie, with Hans G. Westerlund. Translated from the Swedish by F. H. Lyon. New York, Norton [1951] 288 p. 22 cm. [F1015.M213 1951a] 51-12479
1. Kilburn, Sam, b. 1877. 2. Frontier and pioneer life—Canada. 3. Frontier and pioneer life—Alaska. I. Title.

Kilgallen, Dorothy.

ISRAEL, Lee. 070'.92'4 B
Kilgallen / Lee Israel. New York : Delacorte Press, c1979. x, 485 p., [8] leaves of plates : ill. ; 24 cm. Includes bibliographical references and index. [PN4874.K5318] 79-19738 ISBN 0-440-04297-6 : 12.95
1. Kilgallen, Dorothy. 2. Journalists—United States—Biography. I. Title.

Kilgore, Hermina Gertrude.

KILGORE, Hermina Gertrude. 920
Rough road in the Rockies. Denver, Big Mountain Press [1961] 135p. illus. 23cm. Autobiographical. [CT275.K48A3] 61-16173
I. Title.

Killam, Izaak Walton, 1885-1955.

HOW, Douglas. 338'.092'2 B
A very private person : the story of Izaak Walton Killam, and his wife Dorothy / by Douglas How. [s.l. : s.n.], c1976 ([s.l. : Dalhousie Graphics) 123 p. : ill. ; 26 cm. [HC112.5.K54H68] 77-374069
1. Killam, Izaak Walton, 1885-1955. 2. Killam, Dorothy Johnston. 3. Businessmen—Canada—Biography. I. Title.

Killebrew, Harmon Clayton, 1936-

ANDERSON, Wayne J. 796.357'0924 B
Harmon Killebrew, baseball's superstar [by] Wayne J. Anderson. Salt Lake City, Deseret Book Co., 1971. 500 p. illus., ports. 24 cm. [GV865.K49A5] 77-159034 ISBN 0-87747-405-2 6.95
1. Killebrew, Harmon Clayton, 1936-

BUTLER, Hal 796.3570924
The Harmon Killebrew story. New York, Messner [c.1966] 191p. ports. 22cm. [GV865.K49B8] 66-14005 3.25; 3.19 lib. ed.,
1. Killebrew, Harmon Clayton, 1936- I. Title.

Killian, James Rhyne, 1904-

KILLIAN, James Rhyne, 1904- 353.008'55'0924
Sputnik, scientists, and Eisenhower : a memoir of the first special assistant to the President for science and technology / James R. Killian, Jr Cambridge, Mass. : MIT Press, c1977. xix, 315 p. : ill. ; 24 cm. Includes index. Bibliography: p. [303]-305. [Q143.K42A37] 77-21560 ISBN 0-262-11066-0 : 14.95
1. Killian, James Rhyne, 1904- 2. Eisenhower, Dwight David, Pres. United States, 1890-1969. 3. Science and state—United States. 4. Technology and state—United States. 5. United States—History—Sources. I. Title. BIP

Killigrew, Sir Henry, 1525(ca.)-1603.

MILLER, Amos C. 923.242
Sir Henry Killigrew, Elizabethan soldier and diplomat. Foreword by A. L. Rowse [Leicester, Eng.] Leicester Univ. Pr. [dist. New York, Humanities, 1964, c.1963] xi, 279p. 22cm. Bibl. 64-1690 6.00
1. Killigrew, Sir Henry, 1525(ca.)-1603. I. Title.

Killigrew, Thomas, 1612-1683.

HARBAGE, Alfred, 1901- 822'.4 B
Thomas Killigrew, cavalier dramatist, 1612-83 New York, B. Blom [1967] viii, 247 p. port. 20 cm. Reprint of the 1930 ed. Bibliography: p. 232-239. [PR3539.K5H3 1967] 67-23854
1. Killigrew, Thomas, 1612-1683. BIP

Killilea, Karen, 1940-

KILLILEA, Marie Lyons. v. 12
With love from Karen. [New York, Dell Pub. Co., c1963, 1965] 320 p. (Dell 9615) Sequel to Karen. 68-47129
1. Killilea, Karen, 1940- 2. Cerebral palsy. I. Title. BIP

Killy, Jean Claude.

KILLY, Jean Claude. 796.9'3'0924 B
Comeback: [by] Jean-Claude Killy, with Al Greenberg. New York, Macmillan [1974] xi, 189 p. ports. 22 cm. [GV854.2.K5A32] 73-18515 ISBN 0-02-563040-7 5.95
1. Killy, Jean Claude. 2. Ski racing. I. Greenberg, Al, joint author. II. Title.

KILLY, Jean Claude. 796.9'3'0924 B
Comeback: an autobiography [by] Jean-Claude Killy, with Al Greenberg. New York, Macmillan [1974] p. [GV854.2.K5A32] 73-19524 ISBN 0-02-563040-7 6.95
1. Killy, Jean Claude. 2. Ski racing. I. Greenberg, Al. II. Title.

Killy, Jean-Claude—Juvenile literature.

MORSE, Charles. 796.9'3'0924 B
Jean-Claude Killy, by Charles and Ann Morse. Illustrated by Harold Henriksen. Mankato, Minn., Amecus Street; [distributed by Childrens Press, Chicago, 1974] 31 p. col. illus. 25 cm. (Superstars) Brief biography emphasizing the career of the French skier who won three gold medals at the 1968 Olympics. [GV854.2.K5M67] 92 74-4489 ISBN 0-87191-343-7 4.95 (lib. bdg.)
1. Killy, Jean-Claude—Juvenile literature. 2. Skis and skiing—Juvenile literature. I. Morse, Ann, joint author. II. Henriksen, Harold, illus. III. Title. BIP

Kilmer, Joyce, 1886-1918.

CARGAS, Harry J 92
I lay down my life; biography of Joyce Kilmer, by Harry J. Cargas. [Boston] St. Paul Editions [1964] 122 p. 21 cm. [PS3521.I38Z66] 64-21604
1. Kilmer, Joyce, 1886-1918. I. Title.

Kilmer, Joyce, 1886-1918 — Juvenile literature.

ROBERTO, Brother, 1927- 92
Death beneath the trees; a story of Joyce Kilmer. Illus. Carolyn Lee Jagodits. Notre Dame, Ind., Djuarie Press, 1964. 144 p. port. 22 cm. [PS3521.I38Z78] 65-809
1. Kilmer, Joyce, 1886-1918 — Juvenile literature. I. Title.

Kilpatrick, William Heard, 1871-

TENENBAUM, Samuel, 1902- 923.773
William Heard Kilpatrick, trail blazer in education; with an introd. by John Dewey. [1st ed.] New York, Harper [1951] xiii, 318 p. port., 25 cm. Bibliographical footnotes. [LB875.K53T4] 51-6825
1. Kilpatrick, William Heard, 1871- 2. Project method in teaching. I. Title.

Kilvert, Robert Francis, 1840-1879.

LE QUESNE, A. Laurence. 941.08
After Kilvert / A. L. Le Quesne. Oxford [Eng.] ; New York : Oxford University Press, 1978. ix, 233 p. : ill. ; 23 cm. Includes index. [BX5199.K49A32] 78-40173 ISBN 0-19-211748-3 : 15.95
1. Kilvert, Robert Francis, 1840-1879. Kilvert's diary. 2. Kilvert, Robert Francis, 1840-1879. 3. Church of England—Clergy—Biography. 4. Le Quesne, A. Laurence. 5. Clergy—England—Biography. 6. Clyro, Wales—Description. I. Title. BIP

LE QUESNE, A. Laurence. 941.08
After Kilvert / A. L. Le Quesne. Oxford [Eng.] ; New York : Oxford University Press, 1978. ix, 233 p. : ill. ; 23 cm. Includes index. [BX5199.K49A32] 78-40173 ISBN 0-19-211748-3 : 15.95
1. Kilvert, Robert Francis, 1840-1879. Kilvert's diary. 2. Kilvert, Robert Francis, 1840-1879. 3. Church of England—Clergy—Biography. 4. Le Quesne, A. Laurence. 5. Clergy—England—Biography. 6. Clyro, Wales—Description. I. Title. BIP

Kimhi, David, 1160?-1235?

TALMAGE, Frank. 221.6'092'4 B
David Kimhi, the man and the commentaries / Frank Ephraim Talmage. Cambridge, Mass. : Harvard University Press, 1975. viii, 236 p. : map ; 24 cm. (Harvard Judaic monographs ; 1) Includes indexes. Bibliography: p. 189-193. [BS1161.K55T34] 75-1747 ISBN 0-674-19340-7 : 10.00
1. Kimhi, David, 1160?-1235? 2. Bible. O.T.—Criticism, interpretation, etc., Jewish. I. Title. II. Series.

Kim, Richard E.,

KIM, Richard E., 1932- 813'.5'4 B
Lost names; scenes from a Korean boyhood [by] Richard E. Kim. New York, Praeger [1970] vii, 195 p. 22 cm. [PS3561.I415Z5] 71-83338 5.95
I. Title.

Kimama—History.

RIEDESEL, Gerhard A., 1904- 917.96'33
Arid acres; a history of the Kimama-Minidoka homesteaders, 1912 to 1932, by people who were there, compiled and edited by Gerhard Riedesel. Pullman, Wash. [1969] 79 p. illus., map. ports. 28 cm. [F754.K5R5] 72-176360
1. Kimama—History. 2. Minidoka—History. 3. Kimama—Biography. 4. Minidoka—Biography. I. Title. BIP

Kimball, Dexter Simpson,

KIMBALL, Dexter Simpson, 1865-1952. 926.2
I remember. 1st ed. New York, McGraw-Hill, 1953. 259 p. illus. 21 cm. [TJ140.K5A3] 52-9445
I. Title.

Kimball, Gussie

KIMBALL, Gussie 920.9
Gitele. New York, Vantage Press [c.1960] 355p. 3.75 bds.,
I. Title.

Kimball, James Floyd, 1853-1918.

LUDEMAN, Annette Martin. 286'.1'0924 B
Pioneering in the faith, James Floyd Kimball, Baptist minister and missionary, 1853-1918. [Quanah, Tex., Nortex Offset Publications, c1973] 84 p. illus. 28 cm. [BX6495.K49L82] 73-80111
1. Kimball, James Floyd, 1853-1918. I. Title.

Kimball, James P., b. ca. 1829.

KIMBALL, James P., b.ca.1829. 973'.04'97 S
Short narrative of James Kimball. New York : Garland Pub., 1977. 15 p., [1] fold. leaf of plates : facsim. ; 23 cm. (The Garland library of narratives of North American Indian captivities ; v. 76) Issued with the reprint of the 1860 ed. of Bone, J. H. A the Indian captive. New York, 1977. Reprint of the 1930 ed. printed for friends of C. E. Heartman, Metuchen, N.J., which was originally published in the Cleveland weekly plain dealer, Jan. 30, 1861. [E85.G2 vol. 76] [E99.S4] 970'.004'97 B 76-54520 ISBN 0-8240-1700-5 : part of a 7 vol. set : 29.50 (set)
1. Kimball, James P., b. ca. 1829. 2. Shoshoni Indians—Captivities. 3. Indians of North America—Captivities. 4. United States—Biography. I. Title. II. Series.

Kimball, Spencer W., 1895-

KIMBALL, Edward L., 1930- 289.3'3 B
Spencer W. Kimball, twelfth president of the Church of Jesus Christ of Latter-day Saints / Edward L. Kimball, Andrew E. Kimball, Jr. Salt Lake City : Bookcraft, 1977. x, 438 p. : ill. ; 24 cm. Includes index. [BX8695.K53K55] 77-14714 ISBN 0-88494-330-5 : 8.50
1. Kimball, Spencer W., 1895- 2. Mormons and Mormonism—Biography. I. Kimball, Andrew E., joint author. II. Title.

Kimbangu, Simon, 1889?-1951.

MARTIN, Marie-Louise. 289.9 B
Kimbangu : an African prophet and his church / Marie-Louise Martin ; with a foreword by Bryan R. Wilson ; translated by D. M. Moore. 1st American ed. Grand Rapids : Eerdmans, 1976. xxiv, 198 p. ; 23 cm. Translation of Kirche ohne Weisse. Includes indexes. Bibliography: p. 185-188.

[BX7435.E44M3713 1976] 75-45371 ISBN 0-8028-3483-3 : 8.95
1. Kimbangu, Simon, 1889?-1951. 2. Eglise de Jesus-Christ sur la terre par le prophete Simon Kimbangu.

Kimbolton, Australia—History.

RANDELL, John Ormond, 1926- 994.5 B
Kimbolton / [by] John Ormond Randell. Carlton, Vic. : Queensberry Hill, 1976. 115 p., [13] leaves of plates : ill. ; 25 cm. Includes index. Bibliography: p. 110. [DU230.K56R36] 77-360476 ISBN 0-909174-02-4
1. Kimbolton, Australia—History. 2. Kimboltan, Australia—Biography. 3. Sheep ranches—Australia—Kimbolton—History. 4. Sheep ranches—Australia—Kimbolton—Biography.

Kimbrough, Emily,

KIMBROUGH, Emily, 1899- 818'.5'207
Now and then. Drawings by Mircea Vasiliu. [1st ed.] New York, Harper & Row [1972] 176 p. illus. 22 cm. Autobiographical. [PS3521.I457Z52] 72-79678 ISBN 0-06-012366-4 5.95
I. Title.

Kincaid, Trevor, 1872-1970.

GUBERLET, Muriel Lewin. 595.7'0092'4 B
The windows to his world : the story of Trevor Kincaid / Muriel L. Guberlet. Palo Alto, Calif. : Pacific Books, c1975. 287 p. : ill. ; 23 cm. "Publications of Trevor Kincaid": [274]-276. Includes index. Bibliography: p. [277]-278. [QH31.K56G8] 73-91594 ISBN 0-87015-210-6 : 9.95
1. Kincaid, Trevor, 1872-1970. I. Title. BIP

Kincheloe, Iven Carl, 1928-1958.

HAGGERTY, James J., Jr. 926.294
First of the spacemen, Iven C. Kincheloe, Jr. New York, Duell, Sloan and Pearce [c.1960] ix, 148p. illus. 21cm. 60-12828 3.50
1. Kincheloe, Iven Carl, 1928-1958. I. Title.

HAGGERTY, James J 1920- 926.294
First of the spacemen, Iven C. Kincheloe, Jr. [1st ed.] New York, Duell, Sloan and Pearce [1960] 148p. illus. 21cm. [TL540.K48H3] 60-12828
1. Kincheloe, Iven Carl, 1928-1958. I. Title.

Kind, Z-D

KIND, Z-D 920
The poor millionaire of Tookany Frankford-Rama. New York Vantage [c.1962] 54p.,21cm. 2.00;bds.,
I. Title.

King, Alexander,

KING, Alexander, 1900- 818.5
Mine enemy grows older. New York, Simon and Schuster, 1958. 374 p. 22 cm. Autobiography. [CT275.K49A3] 58-13170
I. Title. BIP

King, Anna Josepha (Coombe)

THE Governor's lady, Mrs., v. 12
Philip Gidley King; an Australian narrative. 2d ed. London, New York, Oxfor University Press, 1956. xii, 131p. illus. 22cm.
1. King, Anna Josepha (Coombe) 2. New South Wales—Hist. 3. Norfolk Island. I. Bassett, Marnie (Masson) 1889-

King, Billie Jean.

KING, Billie Jean. 796.34'2'0924
Billie Jean, by Billie Jean King with Kim Chapin. [1st ed.] New York, Harper & Row [1974] xi, 208 p. illus. 22 cm. [GV994.K56A32 1974] 73-4099 ISBN 0-06-012392-3 5.95
1. King, Billie Jean. 2. Tennis. I. Chapin, Kim, joint author. BIP

King, Billie Jean—Juvenile literature.

BAKER, Jim, 1941- 796.34'2'0924 B
Billie Jean King / by Jim Baker. New York : Grosset & Dunlap, c1974. 90 p. : ill. ; 21 cm. (Tempo books) A biography of the tennis champion who has been a leader in making an equal place for women in athletics. [GV994.K56B34] 92 74-7690 ISBN 0-448-07436-2 : 1.50
1. King, Billie Jean—Juvenile literature. 2. Tennis—Juvenile literature. I. Title.

BRAUN, Thomas, 1944- 796.34'2'0924 B
Billie Jean King / written by Thomas Braun ; illustrated by John Nelson. Mankato, Minn. : Creative Education, [1976] p. cm. Biography of Billie Jean King, whose career in tennis has included work for women's equality. [GV994.K56B72] 92 76-12090 ISBN 0-87191-275-9
1. King, Billie Jean—Juvenile literature. 2. Tennis—Juvenile literature. I. Nelson, John, 1928- II. Title.

BURCHARD, Marshall. 796.34'2'0924 B
Sports hero, Billie Jean King / by Marshall and Sue Burchard. New York : Putnam, [1975] 93 p. : ill. ; 22 cm. (The Sports hero biographies) An easy-to-read biography of the tennis player who has won every major tennis title open to women and has fought to get recognition and equal prize money for women's matches. [GV994.K56B87 1975] 92 74-16623 ISBN 0-399-60907-5 lib. bdg. : 4.69
1. King, Billie Jean—Juvenile literature. 2. Tennis—Juvenile literature. I. Burchard, Sue, joint author. II. Title.

MAY, Julian. 796.34'2'0924 B
Billie Jean King, tennis champion / by Julian May ; designed by William Dichtl. Mankato, Minn. : Crestwood House, c1974. 46 p. : ill. ; 24 cm. (Sports close-up books) A biography of Billie Jean King, American tennis champion who has helped popularize women's tennis. [GV994.K56M38 1974] 92 74-82744 ISBN 0-913940-09-7
1. King, Billie Jean—Juvenile literature. 2. Tennis—Juvenile literature. I. Title.

OLSEN, James T. 796.34'2'0924 B
Billie Jean King; the lady of the court, by James T. Olsen. Mankato, Minn., Creative Education; distributed by Childrens Press, Chicago [1974] 31 p. illus. (part col.) 25 cm. (Creative's Superstars) A biography of a champion, winner of almost every amateur tennis title in the world, whose present interests include bringing tennis to ghetto children and Women's Lib to the tennis court. [GV994.K56047] 92 73-12438 ISBN 0-87191-275-9 4.95
1. King, Billie Jean—Juvenile literature. I. Nelson, John, illus. II. Title.

King, Carole—Juvenile literature.

TAYLOR, Paula. 784'.092'4 B
Carole King / text, Paula Taylor ; ill., John Keely. Mankato, Minn. : Creative Education, [1975] p. cm. [ML3930.K47T4] 75-23185 ISBN 0-87191-465-4 lib.bdg. : 4.95
1. King, Carole—Juvenile literature. I. Keely, John. II. Title. BIP

King, Charles C.

KING, Charles C. 923.573
Life has been interesting. Boston, Forum [c.1962] 148p. 20cm. 2.00 pap.,
I. Title.

King, Clarence, 1842-1901.

SHEBL, James M. 551'.092'4 B
King, of the mountains / James M. Shebl ; original drawings by L. F. Bjorklund. 1st ed. Stockton, Calif. : Pacific Center for Western Historical Studies, University of the Pacific, c1974. i, 76 p., [3] leaves of plates : ill. ; 23 cm. (Monograph - Pacific Center for Western Historical Studies ; no. 5) Includes index. "The printed works of Clarence King": p. 64-66. [PS2174.K3Z86] 75-309627 4.50
1. King, Clarence, 1842-1901. I. Title. II. Series: Pacific Center for Western Historical Studies. Monograph ; no. 5. BIP

WILKINS, Thurman. 925.5
Clarence King, a biography. New York, Macmillan, 1958. 441 p. illus. 22 cm. Includes bibliography. [QE22.K5W5] 58-6965
1. King, Clarence, 1842-1901.

YOUNG, Bob, 1916- 551'.0924B
Frontier scientist: Clarence King, by Bob and Jan Young. New York, J. Meesner [1968] 190 p. 22 cm. $3.50 Bibliography: p. 183. [QE22.K5Y6] 68-25092
1. King, Clarence, 1842-1901. I. Young, Jan 1919- joint author II. Title.

King, Clarence, 1842-1901—Juvenile literature.

YOUNG, Bob, 1916- 551'.0924 B
Frontier scientist: Clarence King, by Bob and Jan Young. New York, J. Messner [1968] 190 p. 22 cm. Bibliography: p. 183. A biography of the geologist who first organized and directed the United States Geological Survey and explored and mapped many isolated areas of the United States. [QE22.K5Y6] 92 68-25092 3.50
1. King, Clarence, 1842-1901—Juvenile literature. I. Young, Jan, 1919- joint author. II. Title.

King, Coretta Scott, 1927-

VIVIAN, Octavia. 323.4'0924 B
Coretta; the story of Mrs. Martin Luther King, Jr. Philadelphia, Fortress Press [1970] x, 111 p. ports. 18 cm. [E185.97.K47V5] 72-119765 1.95
1. King, Coretta Scott, 1927- I. Title.

King, Coretta Scott, 1927- —Juvenile literature.

PATTERSON, Lillie. 323.4'092'4 B
Coretta Scott King / by Lillie Patterson. Champaign, Ill. : Garrard Pub. Co., [1977] 96 p. : ill. ; 24 cm. (Americans all) Includes index. A biography of the wife of the slain civil rights leader, Martin Luther King, Jr. [E185.97.K47P37] 92 76-19077 ISBN 0-8116-4585-1 lib.bdg. : 3.84
1. King, Coretta Scott, 1927- —Juvenile literature. 2. Afro-Americans—Biography—Juvenile literature. I. Title. BIP

TAYLOR, Paula. 323.4'092'4 B
Coretta Scott King. Illustrated by Harold Henriksen. Mankato, Minn., Creative Education [1974] p. cm. A brief biography of the wife of the slain civil rights leader, Martin Luther King, Jr. [E185.97.K47T39] 92 74-17360 ISBN 0-87191-410-7 4.95 (lib. bdg.).
1. King, Coretta Scott, 1927- —Juvenile literature. I. Henriksen, Harold, illus. II. Title. BIP

TAYLOR, Paula. 323.4'092'4 B
Coretta Scott King, a woman of peace. Illustrated by Harold Henriksen. Mankato, Minn., Creative Education; [distributed by Childrens Press, Chicago, 1974] 31 p. col. illus. 25 cm. (Creative Education close-ups) A brief biography of the wife of the slain civil rights leader, Martin Luther King, Jr. [E185.97.K47T39] 92 74-17360 ISBN 0-87191-410-7
1. King, Coretta Scott, 1927- —Juvenile literature. I. Henriksen, Harold, illus. II. Title.

King, Edward, Bp. of Lincoln, 1829-1910.

CHADWICK, Owen. 283'.092'4 B
Edward King: Bishop of Lincoln, 1885-1910. [Lincoln, Eng.] Friends of Lincoln Cathedral, 1968. 31 p. port. 22 cm. (Lincoln Minster pamphlets. Second series, no. 4) Includes bibliographical references. [BX5199.K5C4] 75-303738
1. King, Edward, Bp. of Lincoln, 1829-1910.

King, Eleanor.

KING, Eleanor. 793.3'2'0924 B
Transformations : the Humphrey-Weidman era : a memoir / by Eleanor King. Brooklyn, N.Y. : Dance Horizons, c1978. xii, 324 p. : ill. ; 24 cm. Includes bibliographical references and index. [GV1785.K48A37] 76-44682 ISBN 0-87127-100-1 : 22.50
1. King, Eleanor. 2. Dancers—United States—Biography. I. Title.

King, Ernest Joseph, 1878-1956.

KING, Ernest Joseph, 1878-1956. 940.54'59'730924 B
Fleet Admiral King : a naval record / by Ernest J. King and Walter Muir Whitehill. New York : Da Capo Press, 1976, c1952. xv, 674 p. [12] leaves of plates : ill. ; 24 cm. (The Politics and strategy of World War II) Reprint of the 1st ed. published by Norton, New York. [E182.K53 1976] 76-14889 ISBN 0-306-70772-1 : 39.50
1. King, Ernest Joseph, 1878-1956. I. Whitehill, Walter Muir, 1905- joint author. II. Title.

King, Eusebio Francisco, 1644-1711—Juvenile literature.

STEFFAN, Alice Jacqueline (Kennedy) 922.273
Padre Kino and the trail to the Pacific by Jack Steffan [pseud.] Illustrated by Anthony D'Adamo. New York, P. J. Kenedy [c. 1960] 188p. illus., map 22cm. (American background books, 14) 60-8385 2.50
1. King, Eusebio Francisco, 1644-1711—Juvenile literature. I. Title.

King, Harriet Lethbridge,

KING, Harriet Lethbridge, 1796-1874. 994'.02'0924
The admiral's wife; Mrs. Phillip Parker King, a selection of letters 1817-56. Edited and with an introduction by Dorothy Walsh. Melbourne, Hawthorn [1967] 147 p. illus., geneal. tables (on lining papers) ports. 25 cm. Bibliographical footnotes. [DU114.K47A4] 70-455662 7.50
I. Walsh, Dorothy, ed. II. Title.

King, Harry.

KING, Harry. 364.1'62'0924 B
Box man; a professional thief's journey, by Harry King. As told to and edited by Bill Chambliss. With commentary by Bill Chambliss. New York, Harper & Row [1972] xi, 179 p. 21 cm. (Harper torchbooks, TB 1667) [HV6248.K52A3] 72-76245 ISBN 0-06-131667-9 2.95
I. Chambliss, William J. II. Title.

King, Henry, Bp. of Chichester, 1592-1669.

BERMAN, Ronald 828.4
Henry King & the seventeenth century. London, Chatto & Windus [dist. New York, Oxford, c.]1964. 160p. 23cm. Bibl. 64-2554 3.40
1. King, Henry, Bp. of Chichester, 1592-1669. I. Title.

King, Henry Churchill, 1858-1934.

LOVE, Donald M 923.773
Henry Churchill King, of Oberlin. New Haven, Published for Oberlin College by Yale University Press, 1956. xi, 300p. illus., ports. 25cm. Bibliography: p. 288-291. [LD4166 1902.L6] 56-10871
1. King, Henry Churchill, 1858-1934. I. Title.

King, Julina Boone.

DUNCAN, Kunigunde, 1886- 380.1'41'6100924 B
Half a million wild horses; an informal biography of Julina Boone King. Boston, Branden Press [1969] 204 p. 23 cm. [CT275.K564D8] 68-16220 6.95
1. King, Julina Boone. I. Title.

King, Karl C., 1897-

KING, Karl C., 328.73'092'4 B 1897-
Prairie dogs and postulates; an autobiography, by Karl C. King. [Limited ed. Trenton, N.J., Priv. print. by Parker Print. Co., 1974] viii, 251 p. illus. 21 cm. [CT275.K5645A36] 74-166472
1. King, Karl C., 1897- I. Title.

King, Karl, 1891-1971.

HATTON, Thomas J., 785'.092'4 B 1935-
Karl L. King : an American bandmaster / by Thomas J. Hatton. Evanston, Ill. : Instrumentalist Co., c1975. 214 p. : ill. ; 22 cm. "Complete works of Karl King": p. 197-200. [ML410.K4363H4] 75-322039
1. King, Karl, 1891-1971.

King, Martin Luther.

BENNETT, Lerone, 1928- 922.673
What manner of man; a biography of Martin Luther King, Jr. With an introd. by Benjamin E. Mays. Chicago, Johnson Pub. Co., 1964. 227 p. illus., ports. 25 cm. [E185.97.K5B4] 64-66315
1. King, Martin Luther. I. Title.

BENNETT, Lerone, 1928- 323.40924
What manner of man; a biography of Martin Luther King, Jr., with an introd. by Benjamin F. Mays. [2d ed., rev. and enl.] Chicago, Johnson Pub. Co., 1964 [i.e. 1965, c1964] 245 p. illus., ports. 25 cm. [E185.97.K5B4] 66-7898
1. King, Martin Luther. I. Title.

BENNETT, Lerone, 323.4'0924 B 1928-
What manner of man; a biography of Martin Luther King, Jr. With an introd. by Benjamin E. Mays. [3d rev. ed.] Chicago, Johnson Pub. Co., 1968. 251 p. illus., ports. 21 cm. [E185.97.K5B4 1968] 68-5925 5.95
1. King, Martin Luther. I. Title.

BENNETT, Lerone, 1928- v. 12
What manner of man; a biography of Martin Luther King, Jr., With an introd. by Benjamin E. Mays. Abridged. New York, Pocket Books, 1965. 156 p. 22 cm. [A Pocket Book special] Epilogue: Acceptance statement by Martin Luther King, Jr., Nobel Peace Prize Ceremony, Dec. 10, 1964.
1. King, Martin Luther. I. Title. **BIP**

BENNETT, Lerone, Jr. 922.673
What manner of man; a biography of Martin Luther Ki g, Jr. Introd. by Benjamin E. Mays. Chicago, Johnson [c.] 1964. 227p. illus., ports. 25cm. [E185.97.K5B4] 64-66315 4.95
1. King, Martin Luther. I. Title.

BISHOP, James Alonzo, 323.4'0924 1907-
The days of Martin Luther King, Jr., by Jim Bishop. New York, Putnam [1971] xii, 516 p. 23 cm. Bibliography: p. [497]-499. [E185.97.K5B5 1971] 70-161607 8.95
1. King, Martin Luther. I. Title.

BLEIWEISS, Robert M. 323.4'0924 B
Marching to freedom; the life of Martin Luther King, Jr. Robert M. Bleiweiss, editor, with Jacqueline L. Harris and Joseph R. Marfuggi. Middletown, Conn., American Education Publications [1968] vii, 152 p. illus., ports. 18 cm. [E185.97.K5B55] 68-9356 0.75
1. King, Martin Luther. I. Harris, Jacqueline L., joint author. II. Marfuggi, Joseph R., joint author. III. Title. **BIP**

FEUERLICHT, Roberta v. 12 Strauss.
Martin Luther King, Jr.; a concise biography. New York, American R.D.M Corp. [1966] 73 p. port. (A study master publication. 940) Bibliography: p. 73. 67-92011
1. King, Martin Luther. I. Title.

FIVE dark days in 323.4'092'4 *history;* biography of a non-violent warrior: Dr. Martin Luther King, Jr. (Dr. Ralph Abernathy carries on) [Editor: Jim Matthews. Los Angeles, Creative Advertising Media, 1968] 1 v. (unpaged) illus., ports. 28 cm. [E185.97.K5F5] 301.5'92 78-241152 2.00
1. King, Martin Luther. I. Matthews, James P., ed.

GOODWIN, Bennie. 286'.132'0924 B
Martin Luther King, Jr. : God's messenger of love, justice and hope / by Bennie Goodwin. Jersey City : Goodpatrick, c1976. 89 p. ; 22 cm. [BX6455.K56G66] 76-382764 2.00
1. King, Martin Luther. 2. Baptists—Clergy—Biography. 3. Clergy—United States—Biography.

HOYT, Robert G. 323.4'0924 B
Martin Luther King, Jr. Text by Robert G. Hoyt. Waukesha, Wisc., Country Beautiful Foundation; distributed by Rand McNally [Chicago, c1970] 96 p. illus., ports. 31 cm. [E185.97.K5H6] 70-124086 6.95
1. King, Martin Luther. **BIP**

HUIE, William 364.1'524'0924 B Bradford, 1910-
Did the F.B.I. kill Martin Luther King? / By William Bradford Huie. Nashville : T. Nelson, c1977. p. cm. Contains the author's He slew the dreamer, with a new prologue and epilogue. [HV6248.R39H82 1977] 77-11881 ISBN 0-8407-4062-X pbk. : 3.95
1. Ray, James Earl, 1928- 2. King, Martin Luther. 3. United States. Federal Bureau of Investigation. 4. Crime and criminals—Biography. I. Title. **BIP**

HUIE, William 364.15'24'0924 B Bradford, 1910-
He slew the dreamer; my search, with James Earl Ray, for the truth about the murder of Martin Luther King. New York, Delacorte Press [1970] 212 p. 22 cm. [HV6248.R39H82] 76-110606 5.95
1. King, Martin Luther. I. Ray, James Earl, 1928- II. Title.

KING, Coretta Scott, 323.4'0924 1927-
My life with Martin Luther King, Jr. [1st ed.] New York, Holt, Rinehart and Winston [1969] ix, 372 p. illus., ports. 24 cm. [E185.97.K5K5] 69-11805 6.95
1. King, Martin Luther. I. Title. **BIP**

KOCH, Thilo. 973.922'0922
Fighters for a new world: John F. Kennedy, Martin Luther King, Robert F. Kennedy. New York, Putnam [1969] 204 p. illus., ports. 25 cm. Translation of Kampfer fur eine nee Welt. [E840.6.K613] 69-18183 6.95
1. Kennedy, John Fitzgerald, Pres. U.S., 1917-1963. 2. King, Martin Luther. 3. Kennedy, Robert F., 1925-1968. I. Title.

LEWIS, David L. 323.4'0924 B
King; a critical biography [by] David L. Lewis. New York, Praeger [1970] xii, 460 p. illus., ports. 22 cm. Bibliography: p. 417-438. [E185.97.K5L45 1970] 79-95678 7.95
1. King, Martin Luther. I. Title.

LEWIS, David L. 323.4'092'4 B
King : a biography / David L. Lewis. 2d ed. Urbana : University of Illinois Press, c1978. 468 p. ; 21 cm. (Blacks in the New World) First published 1970 under title: King : a critical biography. Includes index. Bibliography: p. 425-446. [E185.97.K5L45 1978] 78-5261 ISBN 0-252-00679-8 : 17.50 ISBN 0-252-00680-1 pbk. : 5.95
1. King, Martin Luther. 2. Afro-Americans—Biography. 3. Baptists—Clergy—Biography. 4. Clergy—United States—Biography. I. Title. II. Series. **BIP**

LINCOLN, Charles 323.4'0924 B Eric, comp.
Martin Luther King, Jr.; a profile, edited by C. Eric Lincoln. [1st ed.] New York, Hill and Wang [1970] xix, 232 p. 21 cm. (American profiles) (American century series.) Bibliography: p. 229-230. [E185.97.K5L5] 69-16828 1.95
1. King, Martin Luther. **BIP**

LOKOS, Lionel. 323.4'0924
House divided; the life and legacy of Martin Luther King. New Rochelle, N.Y., Arlington House [1968] 567 p. 22 cm. Bibliographical references included in "Notes" (p. [505]-555) [E185.97.K5L6] 68-26830 6.95
1. King, Martin Luther. I. Title.

MARTIN Luther King, 323.4'0924 *Jr.* 1929-1968 Chicago, Johnson Pub. Co., 1968. 76 p. (chiefly illus., ports.) 28 cm. "An Ebony picture biography." [E185.97.K5M3] 68-29476
1. King, Martin Luther.

MARTIN Luther King, 323.4'092'4 B *Jr. :* a documentary, Montgomery to Memphis / with an introd. by Coretta Scott King ; editor, Flip Schulke ; associate editor, Bob Fitch ; text by Penelope McPhee. 1st ed. New York : Norton, c1976. 224 p. : ill. ; 29 cm. [E185.97.K5M29 1976] 76-358943 ISBN 0-393-07487-0 : 10.00. ISBN 0-393-07492-7 pbk. : 5.95
1. King, Martin Luther. I. Schulke, Flip. **BIP**

MARTIN Luther King, 323.4'0924 *Jr., 1929-1968.* Chicago, Johnson Pub. Co., 1968. 76 p. (chiefly illus., ports.) 28 cm. "An Ebony picture biography." [E185.97.K5M3] 68-29476
1. King, Martin Luther.

MILLER, William 323.4'0924 B Robert.
Martin Luther King, Jr.; his life, martyrdom, and meaning for the world. New York, Weybright and Talley [1968] ix, 319 p. illus., maps, ports. 22 cm. Bibliography: p. 302-308. [E185.97.K5M5] 68-31241 7.95
1. King, Martin Luther.

MULLER, Gerald 323.4'0924 B Francis, 1927-
Martin Luther King, Jr., civil rights leader, by Gerald F. Muller. Minneapolis, Denison [1971] 311 p. 23 cm. (Men of achievement series) The life of the Baptist minister from Georgia whose demonstrations for "human rights" changed the course of the civil rights movement in the 1960's. [E185.97.K5M85] 92 78-165765 ISBN 0-513-01105-6 5.58
1. King, Martin Luther.

PRESTON, Edward, 323.4'0924 B 1925-
Martin Luther King: fighter for freedom. [1st ed.] Garden City, N.Y., Doubleday [1968] 142 p. illus., ports. 22 cm. (Doubleday signal books) A biography of the Negro minister who dedicated his life to helping American Negroes gain equal rights through new legislation and non-violent boycotts, sit-ins, marches, and demonstrations. [E185.97.K5P7] 92 AC 68
1. King, Martin Luther. I. Title.

TIME-LIFE Books. 323.4'0924 B
I have a dream; the story of Martin Luther King in text and pictures. New York, [1968] 96 p. illus., ports. 28 cm. "Parts of this book appeared originally in Time and Life magazines." [E185.97.K5T5] 68-29113
1. King, Martin Luther. I. Title.

TIME-LIFE Books. 323.4'0924
I HAVE a dream; the story of Martin Luther King in text and pictures. New York, Time-Life [1968] 96p. illus., ports. 28cm. Pts. of this bk., appeared orig. in Time and Life magazines. [E185.97.K512] (B) 68-29113 1.50 pap.,
1. King, Martin Luther. I. Title.

WILLIAMS, John Alfred, 323.4'0924 1925-
The King God didn't save; reflections on the life and death of Martin Luther King, Jr., by John A. Williams. New York, Coward-McCann [1970] 221 p. 22 cm. [E185.97.K5W5 1970] 72-104693 5.95
1. King, Martin Luther. I. Title.

King, Martin Luther—Iconography.

MARTIN Luther King, 323.4'0924 *Jr.;* man and teacher. [Baltimore, Printed by Vinmar Lithographing Co., 1968] 1 v. (unpaged) illus., ports. 26 cm. Title covers 3 pages. [E185.97.K5M34] 68-8609
1. King, Martin Luther—Iconography.

King, Martin Luther—Juvenile literature.

BOONE-JONES, 323.4'0924 B Margaret.
Martin Luther King, Jr.; a picture story. Illus. by Roszel Scott. Chicago, Childrens Press [1968] [32] p. illus., ports. 25 cm. A picture biography of Martin Luther King stressing the childhood that influenced him to help Negroes gain equal rights. [E185.97.K5B6] 92 68-9483
1. King, Martin Luther—Juvenile literature. I. Scott, Roszel, illus. II. Title.

DE KAY, James T. 323.4'0924 B
Meet Martin Luther King, Jr., by James T. de Kay. Illustrated with photos., and drawings by Ted Burwell. New York, Random House [1969] 89 p. illus., ports. 22 cm. (Step-up books, SU 19) A biography of the man largely responsible for uniting American Negroes in the fight for civil rights. [E185.97.K5D43] 92 78-79789
1. King, Martin Luther—Juvenile literature. I. Burwell, Ted, illus. II. Title. **BIP**

FABER, Doris, 1924- 323.4'092'4 B
The assassination of Martin Luther King, Jr. / by Doris and Harold Faber. New York : Watts, 1978. 85 p. : ill. ; 23 cm. (A Focus book) Includes index. Bibliography: p. 77. A biography of Dr. Martin Luther King, Jr., focusing on his involvement in the civil rights movement. Discusses the investigations of his assassination. [E185.97.K5F3] 92 78-1726 ISBN 0-531-02465-2 lib. bdg. : 4.90
1. King, Martin Luther—Juvenile literature. 2. King, Martin Luther—Assassination—Juvenile literature. 3. Baptists—Clergy—Biography—Juvenile literature. 4. Clergy—United States—Biography—Juvenile literature. 5. Afro-Americans—Biography—Juvenile literature. I. Faber, Harold, joint author. II. Title. **BIP**

FEUERLICHT, Roberta 001.4'4'0922 Strauss.
In search of peace; the story of four Americans who won the Nobel Peace Prize. New York, J. Messner [1970] 96 p. illus., ports. 22 cm. Bibliography: p. 91. A brief history of the Nobel Prizes and a biography of the man who founded them accompanies biographies of four Americans who received the Nobel Peace Prize. [E176.8.F45 1970] 920 70-123165 3.95
1. Addams, Jane, 1860-1935—Juvenile literature. 2. Bunche, Ralph Johnson, 1904-—Juvenile literature. 3. King, Martin Luther—Juvenile literature. 4. Roosevelt, Theodore, Pres. U.S., 1858-1919—Juvenile literature. 5. Nobel prizes—Juvenile literature. I. Title.

HASKINS, James, 323.4'092'4 B 1941-
The life and death of Martin Luther King, Jr. / by James Haskins. New York : Lothrop, Lee & Shepard, 1977. p. cm. A biography of a man who dedicated his life to the cause of civil rights, which also reexamines unanswered questions concerning his assassination. [E185.97.K5H33] 77-3157 ISBN 0-688-41802-3 : 6.95 ISBN 0-688-51802-8 lib.bdg. : 5.94
1. King, Martin Luther—Juvenile literature. 2. King, Martin Luther—Assassination—Juvenile literature. 3. Afro-Americans— Civil rights—Juvenile literature. 4. Afro-Americans— Biography—Juvenile literature. I. Title. **BIP**

MILLENDER, 323.4'0924 B Dharathula H.
Martin Luther King, Jr., boy with a dream, by Dharathula H. Millender. Illustrated by Al Fiorentino. Indianapolis, Bobbs-Merrill [1969] 200 p. col. illus. 20 cm. (Childhood of famous Americans) A biography of the civil rights leader whose philosophy and practice of nonviolent civil disobedience helped American Negroes win many battles for equal rights. [E185.97.K5M48] 92 73-77819
1. King, Martin Luther—Juvenile literature. I. Fiorentino, Al, illus. II. Title.

PATTERSON, Lillie. 323.4'0924 B
Martin Luther King, Jr.; man of peace. Illustrated by Victor Mays. Champaign, Ill., Garrard Pub. Co. [1969] 96 p. illus. (part col.), ports. 24 cm. (Americans all) A biography of the minister, orator, and crusader for equal civil rights who was awarded the Nobel Peace Prize in 1964. [E185.97.K5P3] 92 69-19152 2.39
1. King, Martin Luther—Juvenile literature. I. Mays, Victor, 1927- illus. II. Title. **BIP**

WILSON, Beth P. 323.4'0924
Martin Luther King, Jr. Written by Beth P. Wilson. Illustrated by Floyd Sowell. New York, Putnam [1971] 64 p. illus. 23 cm. (A See and read beginning to read biography) An easy-to-read biography of the slain black leader whose activities from 1955 to 1968 chronicle the advances in civil rights for that period. [E185.97.K5W53] 92 79-142460 2.97
1. King, Martin Luther—Juvenile literature. I. Sowell, Floyd, illus. II. Title. BIP

King, Paul Henry, 1853-

KING, Paul Henry, 1853- 951'.03'0924 B
In the Chinese customs service : a personal record of forthy-seven years / Paul King. New York : Garland Pub., 1980. p. cm. (The Modern Chinese economy) Reprint of the 1924 ed. published by T. F. Unwin, London. Includes index. [DS763.K5A3 1980] 78-74327 ISBN 0-8240-4254-9 lib. bdg. : 30.00
1. King, Paul Henry, 1853- 2. China. Hai kuan tsung shui wu ssu shu. 3. China—Officials and employees—Biography. 4. China—Description and travel. I. Title. II. Series: Modern Chinese economy.

King, Rufus, 1755-1827.

ERNST, Robert, 1915- 973.4'0924 B
Rufus King, American federalist. Chapel Hill, Published for the Institute of Early American History and Culture at Williamsburg, Va., by University of North Carolina Press [1968] ix, 446 p. ports. 24 cm. Bibliographical footnotes. [E302.6.K5E7] 68-15747
1. King, Rufus, 1755-1827. I. Institute of Early American History and Culture, Williamsburg, Va. BIP

KING, Rufus, 1755-1827. 973.4'0924 B
The life and correspondence of Rufus King; comprising his letters, private and official, his public documents, and his speeches. Edited by Charles R. King. New York, Da Capo Press, 1971. 6 v. ports. 23 cm. Reprint of the 1894-1900 ed. Contents.Contents.—v. 1. 1755-1794.—v. 2. 1795-1799.—v. 3. 1799-1801.—v. 4. 1801-1806.—v. 5. 1807-1816.—v. 6. 1816-1827. [E302.K542] 69-16653 ISBN 0-306-71125-7
1. King, Rufus, 1755-1827.

King, Stanley, 1883-1951.

FUESS, Claude Moore, 1885- 923.773
Stanley King of Amherst. New York, Columbia University Press, 1955. 374p. illus. 24cm. [LD152.71932.F8] 55-6617
1. King, Stanley, 1883-1951. I. Title.

King, Thomas Butler, 1800-1864.

STEEL, Edward M 923.273
Butler King of Georgia, by Edward M. Steel, Jr. Athens, University of Georgia Press [1964] viii, 204 p. port. 25 cm. [E415.9.K57S8] 64-17061
1. "Bibliographical note": p. 194-199. 2. King, Thomas Butler, 1800-1864. I. Title.

STEEL, Edward M., Jr. 923.273
T. Butler King of Georgia. Athens Univ. of Ga. Pr. [c.1964] viii, 204p. port. 25cm. Bibl. 64-17061 5.00
1. King, Thomas Butler, 1800-1864. I. Title. BIP

King, Thomas Starr, 1824-1864.

CROMPTON, Arnold. 922.8173
Apostle of liberty: Starr King in California. Boston, Beacon Press, 1950. xii. 74 p. port. 22 cm. [BX9869.K5C7] 50-12447
1. King, Thomas Starr, 1824-1864. I. Title.

King, Titus, 1729?-1791.

KING, Titus, 1729?-1791. 973'.04'97 S
Narrative of Titus King / Titus King. New York : Garland Pub., 1977. 21 p. ; 23 cm. (The Garland library of narratives of North American Indian captivities ; v. 109) Issued with the reprint of the 1927 ed. of Meredith, G. E. Girl captives of the Cheyennes. New York, 1977. Reprint of the 1938 ed. published by Connecticut Historical Society, Hartford under title: Narrative of Titus King of Northampton, Mass., a prisoner of the Indians in Canada, 1755-1758. [E85.G2 vol. 109] [E199] 973.2'6 76-51252 ISBN 0-8240-1733-1 lib.bdg. : 25.00 (set)
1. King, Titus, 1729?-1791. 2. United States—History—French and Indian War, 1755-1763—Personal narratives. 3. Indians of North America—Captivities. 4. Soldiers—Massachusetts—Biography. I. Title. II. Series.

King, William Lyon Mackenzie, 1874-1950.

DAWSON, Robert MacGregor, 1895- 923.271
William Lyon Mackenzie King, a political biography; v.2 [Toronto] Univ. of Toronto Pr. [c.1963] 452p. illus. 24cm. Contents.v.2, 1924-1932: the lonely heights [by] H. Blair Neatby. Bibl. 54-347 7.95
1. King, William Lyon Mackenzie, 1874-1950. I. Neatby, H. Blair. II. Title.

FERNS, Henry Stanley, 1913- 971.06'22'0924
The age of Mackenzie King / Henry Ferns and Bernard Ostry ; introd. by John Meisel. Toronto : J. Lorimer, 1976. xviii, 356 p., [8] leaves of plates : ill. ; 21 cm. Originally published in 1955. Includes bibliographical references and index. [F1033.K53F4 1976] 77-374270 ISBN 0-88862-115-9. ISBN 0-88862-114-0 pbk.
1. King, William Lyon Mackenzie, 1874-1950. 2. Liberal Party (Canada)—History. 3. Canada—Politics and government—1867-1914. 4. Canada—Politics and government—1914-1945. 5. Politicians—Canada—Biography. I. Ostry, Bernard, 1927- joint author. II. Title.

HARDY, Henry Reginald, 1903- 971.06'0924 B
Mackenzie King of Canada; a biography, by H. Reginald Hardy. Westport, Conn., Greenwood Press [1970, c1949] xii, 390 p. illus., ports. 23 cm. [F1033.K53H36] 77-135245 ISBN 0-8371-5164-3
1. King, William Lyon Mackenzie, 1874-1950. BIP

HUTCHISON, Bruce, 1901- 923.271
The incredible Canadian; a candid portrait of Mackenzie King, his works, his times, and his nation. [1st ed.] Toronto, New York, Longmans, Green, 1952. 454 p. illus. 23 cm. [F1033.K53H8 1952] 53-44
1. King, William Lyon Mackenzie, 1874-1950. 2. Canada—History—1914- I. Title.

STACEY, Charles Perry, 1906- 971.06'22'0924 B
A very double life : the private world of Mackenzie King / C. P. Stacey. Toronto : Macmillan of Canada, c1976. 256 p., [8] leaves of plates : ill. ; 24 cm. Includes bibliographical references and index. [F1033.K53S72] 76-366908 ISBN 0-7705-1390-5
1. King, William Lyon Mackenzie, 1874-1950. I. Title.

King, William, 1685-1763.

GREENWOOD, David Charles. 942.07'2'0924 B
William King: Tory and Jacobite. Oxford, Clarendon P., 1969. xi, 386 p., plate. port. 23 cm. Includes bibliographical references. [PR3539.K73Z65] 77-458332 ISBN 0-19-811683-7 75/-
1. King, William, 1685-1763.

King, William, 1812-1895.

JAMIESON, Annie Straith. 971.3'54 B
William King, friend and champion of slaves. New York, Negro Universities Press [1969] 209 p. illus., ports. 23 cm. Reprint of the 1925 ed. [F1058.K56J3 1969] 76-91662
1. King, William, 1812-1895. 2. Negroes in Ontario. BIP

ULLMAN, Victor. 971.3'54 B
Look to the North Star; a life of William King. Boston, Beacon Press [1969] xii, 337 p. illus., map. 22 cm. [F1058.K56U4] 7.50
1. King, William, 1812-1895. 2. Negroes in Buxton, Ont. I. Title.

Kingdon-Ward, Francis, 1885-1958.

KINGDON-WARD, Francis, 1885-1958. 581.9'54'162
Plant hunting on the edge of the world / by F. Kingdon Ward. Sakonnet [R.I.] : Theophrastus, 1977. p. cm. Reprint of the 1930 ed. published by V. Gollancz, London. Includes index. [QK358.K56 1977] 76-30428 ISBN 0-913728-21-7 : 12.50
1. Kingdon-Ward, Francis, 1885-1958. 2. Botany—India—Assam. 3. Botany—Burma. 4. Assam—Description and travel. 5. Burma—Description and travel. 6. Botanists—Great Britain—Biography. I. Title.

Kinglake, Alexander William, 1809-1891.

DE GAURY, Gerald. 947'.07'072024 B
Travelling gent: the life of Alexander Kinglake (1809-1891). London, Boston, Routledge and K. Paul, 1972. xi, 211, 8 p. illus., map, ports. 23 cm. Bibliography: p. 205-208. [CT788.K493D43 1972] 73-150433 ISBN 0-7100-7310-0 10.95
1. Kinglake, Alexander William, 1809-1891. I. Title. BIP

Kings and rulers.

EGAN, E. W. 909 B
Kings, rulers, and statesmen / compiled and edited by Edward W. Egan, Constance B. Hintz, and L. F. Wise. Rev. ed. New York : Sterling Pub. Co., c1976. 512 p. : ill. ; 25 cm. Previous ed. by L. F. Wise and E. W. Egan. [D107.W5 1976] 76-151225 ISBN 0-8069-0050-4 : 20.00. lib.bdg. : 16.79
1. Kings and rulers. 2. Statesmen. I. Hintz, Constance B., joint author. II. Wise, Leonard F., joint author. III. Title. BIP

HAYWARD, Arthur Lawrence, 1885- 923.1
A book kings and queens. New York, Roy Publishers [1956?] 228p. illus. 19cm. [D107] 56-8350
1. Kings and rulers. I. Title.

HAYWARD, Arthur Lawrence, 1885- 923.1
A book of kings and queens. New York, Roy Publishers [1956?] 228p. illus. 19cm. [D107] 56-8350
1. Kings and rulers. I. Title.

NICOLSON, Harold George, Sir 1886- 929.7
Kings Courts and monarchy. New York, Simon and Schuster, 1962. 335p. illus. (part col.) ports. (part col.) facsims. 26cm. Bibliography: p. 327-330. [JC375.N5] 62-17896
1. Kings and rulers. I. Title.

SANDFORD, Christine (Lush) 963'.05'0924 B
The Lion of Judah hath prevailed, being the biography of His Imperial Majesty Haile Selassie I, by Christine Sandford. Illustrated with 16 pages of photos. Westport, Conn., Greenwood Press [1972] xi, 192 p. illus. 22 cm. Reprint of the 1955 ed. [DT387.7.S38 1972] 73-135611 ISBN 0-8371-5198-8
I. Haile Selassie I, Emperor of Ethiopia, 1891- II. Title.

*WEDGWOOD, Cicely Veronica, 1910- 949.2'03'0924
William the Silent, William of Nassau, Prince of Orange, 1533-1584 by C. V. Wegwood. New York, Norton [1968] 256p. 20cm. (N185) (B) 1.95 pap.,
I. Title.

WISE, Leonard F. 920.02
Kings, rulers. and statesmen, comp. & ed. by L. F. Wise, E. W. Egan. New York, Sterling [1967] 446p. illus. ports. 22cm. [D107.W5] 67-16020 4.95;4.89 bds., lib. ed.,
1. Kings and rulers. 2. Statesmen. I. Egan, E. W., joint author. II. Title.

Kings and rulers—Biography.

CANNING, John, 1920- 909'.00922
100 great kings, queens, and rulers of the world. Edited by john Canning. New York, Taplinger Pub. Co. [1968, c1967] 671 p. illus., ports. 23 cm. [D107.C25 1968] 68-23429 6.95
1. Kings and rulers—Biography. 2. Queens—Biography. I. Title.

DAHMUS, Joseph Henry, 1909- 940.1'0922
Seven medieval kings [by] Joseph Dahmus. [1st ed.] Garden City, N.Y., Doubleday, 1967. 332 p. map (on lining-papers) 25 cm. [D107.D27] 67-11188
1. Kings and rulers—Biography. I. Title.

KLONSKY, Milton, comp. 909 B
The fabulous ego; absolute power in history. [New York] Quadrangle [1974] xii, 436 p. illus. 25 cm. Contents.Contents.—Sardanapalus (c. 800 B.C.).—Shih Huang Ti (259-210 B.C.).—Elagabalus (204-222).—Justinian (483-565) and Theodora (508-548).—Harun al-Rashid (764-809).—The once and future King of Cambodia (c. 1300).—Tamerlane (1336-1405).—Pope Alexander VI (1431-1503).—Ivan the Terrible (1530-1584).—Akbar the Great (1542-1605).—The Grand Signor (c. 1605).—Charles I (1600-1649).—Louis XV (1710-1774).—Catherine the Great (1729-1796).—Napoleon I (1769-1821). [D107.K55 1974] 74-77951 ISBN 0-8129-0490-7 15.00
1. Kings and rulers—Biography. 2. Despotism. I. Title. BIP

RIBADEAU Dumas, Francois. 616.89'0922
Madness in power. Translated from the French by Frances Frenaye. [1st American ed.] Philadelphia, Chilton Book Co. [1969] x, 259 p. 21 cm. Translation of La folie au pouvoir. [D107.R513 1969] 69-18332
1. Kings and rulers—Biography. 2. Authoritarianism. I. Title.

RITTER, Gerhard, 1888- 943'.053'0924
Frederick the Great; a historical profile. Tr. introd., by Peter Paret. Berkeley, Univ. of Calif. Pr. 1968. xiv, 207p. port. 23cm. [DD404.R513] (B) 68-15815 7.50
I. Frederick. II. der Grosse, King of Prussia, 1712-1786. III. Title.
Translation of the third edition of "Friedrich der Grosse: Ein Historisches Profil" published by Quelle & Meyer, Heidelberg, 1954.

THOMAS, Henry, 1886- 909 B
Living biographies of famous rulers, by Henry Thomas and Dana Lee Thomas (Henry T. Schnittkind and Dana A. Schnittkind). Illus. by Gordon Ross. Freeport, N.Y., Books for Libraries Press [1972, c1940] viii, 310 p. ports. 23 cm. (Essay index reprint series) [D107.T55 1972] 72-38752 ISBN 0-8369-2671-4
1. Kings and rulers—Biography. I. Thomas, Dana Lee, 1918- joint author. II. Title.

WILSON, Lawrence Patrick Roy 943.0840924
The incredible Kaiser; a portrait of William II. New York, A. S. Barnes [1965, c.1963] 196p. illus., geneal. table ports. 22cm. Bibl. [DD229.W55] 65-24580 5.00
I. Title.

Kings and rulers—Chronology.

ROSS, Martha. 920.02
Rulers and governments of the world. London ; New York : Bowker, 19 v. ; 23 cm. Vols. 2 and 3 are translated with revisions from v. 3 and 4 of B. Spuler's Regenten und Regierungen der Welt. Includes index. Contents.Contents.— —v. 2. Spuler, B. 1492 to 1929. [D11.5.R67 1977] 77-70294 ISBN 0-85935-051-7 : 45.00
1. Kings and rulers—Chronology. 2. Heads of state—Chronology. 3. Cabinet officers—Chronology. I. Spuler, Bertold, 1911- joint author. II. Title.

Kings and rulers—Juvenile literature.

NEWTON, Douglas 1920- 923.1
The first book of kings. Pictures by John Griffin. New York, F. Watts [c.1961] 66p. illus. (First books, 130) 60-5574 1.95
1. Kings and rulers—Juvenile literature. I. Title.

UNSTEAD, R. J. 350'.003'0922
Royal adventurers [by] R. J. Unstead. Illustrated by William Stobbs. Chicago, Follett Pub. Co. [1967, c1963] 144 p. illus. 23 cm. Contents.Contents.—Akhnaten of Egypt.—Julius Caesar.—Charlemagne.—Genghis Kahn and Kublai Khan.—Mary, Queen of Scots.—Queen Christina.—Charles II.—Frederick the Great.—Marie Antoinette. [D107.U52 1967] 67-3570
1. Kings and rulers—Juvenile literature. I. Stobbs, William, illus. II. Title.

UNSTEAD, R. J. 350'.003'0922
Some kings and queens [by] R. J. Unstead. Illustrated by William Stobbs. Chicago, Follett Pub. Co. [1967, c1962] 128 p. illus. 23 cm. Contents.Contents.—Alexander the Great.—Alfred the Great.—Harold, the last of the English.—Montezuma, King of the Aztecs.—William the Silent.—Elizabeth of England.—Louis the Fourteenth.—Peter the Great.—Napoleon Bonaparte.—The Princess Victoria. [D107.U53 1967] 67-3571
1. Kings and rulers—Juvenile literature. I. Stobbs, William, illus. II. Title.

Kingsford-Smith, Charles Edward, Sir, 1897-1935.

MCNALLY, Ward. 621.13'092'4 B
The man on the twenty dollar note : Sir Charles Kingsford-Smith / [by] Ward McNally. Terrey Hills, N.S.W. : Reed, 1976. 216 p. : ill. ; 22 cm. Includes index. [TL540.K5M29] 77-361929 ISBN 0-589-07211-0
1. Kingsford-Smith, Charles Edward, Sir, 1897-1935. 2. Air pilots—Australia—Biography. I. Title.

Kingsford-Smith, Sir Charles Edward, 1897-1935.

STANNAGE, John. 926.29
Smithy. [London] Oxford University Press [1950] viii, 120 p. plates, ports., maps. 19 cm. [TL540.K5S8] 50-36769
1. Kingsford-Smith, Sir Charles Edward, 1897-1935. I. Title.

Kingsley, Charles, 1819-1875.

BROWN, William Henry, 1868- 823'.8 B
Charles Kingsley, the work and influence of Parson Lot. [Folcroft, Pa.] Folcroft Library Editions, 1973. p. Reprint of the 1924 ed. published by T. F. Unwin, London. [PR4843.B7 1973] 73-12770 17.50
1. Kingsley, Charles, 1819-1875. 2. Cooperation—Great Britain.

KAUFMAN, Moritz, 1839-1920. 823'.8 B
Charles Kingsley, Christian socialist and social reformer / by M. Kaufmann. Folcroft, Pa. : Folcroft Library Editions, 1974. p. cm. Reprint of the 1892 ed. published by Methuen, London. [PR4843.K3 1974] 74-32173 ISBN 0-8414-5515-5 : 30.00
1. Kingsley, Charles, 1819-1875.

KAUFMAN, Moritz, 1839-1920. 823'.8 B
Charles Kingsley, Christian socialist and social reformer / by M. Kaufmann. Folcroft, Pa. : Folcroft Library Editions, 1974[i.e.1975] p. cm. Reprint of the 1892 ed. published by Methuen, London. [PR4843.K3 1974] 74-32173 ISBN 0-8414-5515-5 : 30.00
1. Kingsley, Charles, 1819-1875.

KENDALL, Guy, 1876- 823'.8 B
Charles Kingsley and his ideas. New York, Haskell House Publishers 1973. 190 p. illus. 23 cm. Reprint of the 1947 ed. Includes bibliographical references. [PR4843.K4 1973] 72-6679 ISBN 0-8383-1639-5 10.95
1. Kingsley, Charles, 1819-1875. I. Title. BIP

KINGSLEY, Charles, 1819-1875. 823'.8 B
Charles Kingsley: his letters and memories of his life. Edited by his wife. London, H. S. King, 1877. [New York, AMS Press, 1973] 2 v. illus. 23 cm. [PR4843.A5 1973] 74-148803 ISBN 0-404-08869-4 13.00
1. Kingsley, Charles, 1819-1875. I. Kingsley, Frances Eliza Grenfell, 1814-1891, ed. II. Title.
25.00 (2 vols.) BIP

MARTIN, Robert Bernard. 928.2
The dust of combat, a life of Charles Kingsley. [1st American ed.] New York, Norton [1960] 308 p. illus. 23 cm. [PR4843.M3 1960] 60-2623
1. Kingsley, Charles, 1819-1875. I. Title.

POPE-HENNESSY, Una (Birch) Dame, 1876-1949. 823'.8 B
Canon Charles Kingsley; a biography. New York, Macmillan. Millwood, N.Y., Kraus Reprint Co., 1973. 294 p. illus. 24 cm. Reprint of the 1949 ed. Includes bibliographical references. [PR4843.P6 1973] 73-9669 ISBN 0-527-71900-5 15.00
1. Kingsley, Charles, 1819-1875.

STUBBS, Charles William, Bp. of Truro, 1845-1912. 823'.8 B
Charles Kingsley and the Christian social movement. London, Blackie, 1899. [New York, AMS Press, 1974] 199 p. 19 cm. Original ed. issued in The Victorian era series. Includes bibliographical references. [PR4843.S7 1974] 70-148310 ISBN 0-404-08914-3
1. Kingsley, Charles, 1819-1875. 2. Church and social problems—Great Britain. I. Title. II. Series: The Victorian era series. BIP

THORP, Margaret (Farrand) 1891- 823'.8 B
Charles Kingsley, 1819-1875. New York, Octagon Books, 1969 [c1937] vii, 212 p. illus., ports. 24 cm. "Bibliography of Charles Kingsley's works": p. [191]-204. [PR4843.T5 1969] 70-96170
1. Kingsley, Charles, 1819-1875. BIP

Kingsley, Charles, 1819-1875—Biography.

CHITTY, Susan, Lady. 823'.8 B
The beast and the monk : a life of Charles Kingsley / Susan Chitty. New York : Mason/Charter, 1975, c1974. 317 p., [8] leaves of plates : ill. ; 24 cm. Includes index. "Supposititious works of Charles Kingsley": p. [302] [PR4843.C5 1975] 75-15680 ISBN 0-88405-121-8 : 11.95
1. Kingsley, Charles, 1819-1875—Biography. I. Title.

Kingsley, Charles, 1819-1875—Criticism and interpretation.

UFFELMAN, Larry K. 823'.8
Charles Kingsley / by Larry K. Uffelman. Boston : Twayne Publishers, 1979. p. cm. (Twayne's English authors series ; TEAS 273) Includes index. Bibliography: p. [PR4844.U3] 79-13295 ISBN 0-8057-6752-5 : 11.95
1. Kingsley, Charles, 1819-1875—Criticism and interpretation. BIP

Kingsley, Charles, 1819-1875—Homes and haunts—England—Devon.

CHITTY, Susan, Lady. 823'.8 B
Charles Kingsley's landscape / Susan Chitty. Newton Abbot ; North Pomfret, Vt. : David and Charles, 1976. 148 p. : ill., map ; 23 cm. Includes index. Bibliography: p. 141. [PR4843.C53 1976] 76-8619 ISBN 0-7153-7215-7 : 10.95
1. Kingsley, Charles, 1819-1875—Homes and haunts—England—Devon. 2. Devon, Eng.—Description and travel. 3. Novelists, English—19th century—Biography. I. Title.

Kingsley, Henry, 1830-1876.

ELLIS, Stewart Marsh. 823'.8 B
Henry Kingsley, 1830-1876 : towards a vindication / by S. M. Ellis. Folcroft, Pa. : Folcroft Library Editions, 1979. p. cm. Reprint of the 1931 ed. published by G. Richards, London. Includes index. Letters of H. Kingsley: p. Bibliography: p. [PR4845.K5Z6 1979] 79-24172 ISBN 0-8414-4000-X (lib. bdg.) : 30.00
1. Kingsley, Henry, 1830-1876. 2. Kingsley, Henry, 1830-1876—Congresses. 3. Novelists, English—19th century—Biography. I. Kingsley, Henry, 1830-1876.

SCHEUERLE, William H. 823'.8 B
The neglected brother; a study of Henry Kingsley [by] William H. Scheuerle. Tallahassee, Florida State University Press, 1971. ix, 185 p. 24 cm. Bibliography: p. 173-179. [PR4845.K5Z83] 77-149955 10.00
1. Kingsley, Henry, 1830-1876. I. Title. BIP

Kingsley, Mary Henrietta, 1862-1900—Juvenile literature.

SYME, Ronald, 1910- 923.942
African traveler; the story of Mary Kingsley. Illustrated by Jacqueline Tomes. New York, Morrow, 1962. 191 p. illus. 21 cm. Includes bibliography. [DT504.K5S9] 62-10657
1. Kingsley, Mary Henrietta, 1862-1900—Juvenile literature. I. Title.

Kingston, Kenny.

KINGSTON, Kenny. 133.8
Sweet spirits / Kenny Kingston and Brenda Marshall. Chicago : Contemporary Books, c1978. p. cm. Includes index. [BF1027.K53A35 1978] 78-57439 ISBN 0-8092-7625-9 : 9.95
1. Kingston, Kenny. 2. Psychical research—Biography. 3. Psychical research. I. Marshall, Brenda, joint author. II. Title. BIP

Kingston, Maxine Hong.

KINGSTON, Maxine Hong. 979.4'61'050924 B
The woman warrior : memoirs of a girlhood among ghosts / Maxine Hong Kingston. New York : Vintage Books, 1977, c1976. 243 p. ; 18 cm. [CT275.K5764A33 1977] 77-3246 ISBN 0-394-72392-9 pbk. : 2.45
1. Kingston, Maxine Hong. 2. United States—Biography. I. Title. BIP

KINGSTON, Maxine Hong. 979.4'61'050924 B
The woman warrior / Maxine Hong Kingston. South Yarmouth, Ma. : J. Curley, 1978. p. cm. Large print ed. [CT275.K5764A33 1978] 78-2521 ISBN 0-89340-130-7 pbk. : 9.95
1. Kingston, Maxine Hong. 2. United States—Biography. 3. Large type books. I. Title. BIP

Kingston, Ont. Queen's University—Biography.

WALLACE, Robert Charles, 1881-1955, ed. 378.713'72 B
Some great men of Queen's: Grant, Watson, Dupuis, Cappon, Jordan, Shortt. Freeport, N.Y., Books for Libraries Press [1969] 133 p. 23 cm. (Essay index reprint series) A series of lectures honoring the occasion of the centerary celebration of Queen's University. Reprint of the 1941 ed. "Some works of Professor John Watson": p. 50. Contents.Contents.—George Monro Grant (1835-1902) by J. R. Watts.—John Watson (1847-1939) by J. M. MacEachran.—Nathan Fellowes Dupuis (1836-1917) by J. Matheson.—James Cappon (1854-1939) by W. E. McNeill.—William George Jordon (1852-1939) by W. T. McCree.—Adam Shortt (1859-1931) by W. A. Mackintosh. [LE3.Q31W3 1969] 79-86792 ISBN 8-369-12004-
1. Kingston, Ont. Queen's University—Biography. I. Title. BIP

Kingston, Reba.

KINGSTON, Reba. 917.14
Living in Clover. Philadelphia, Dorrance [1965] 142 p. 21 cm. Autobiographical. [CT310.K5A3] 64-7622
I. Title.

Kinnan, Mary Lewis, 1763-1848.

KINNAN, Mary Lewis, 1763-1848. 973'.04'97 S
A true narrative of the sufferings of Mary Kinnan / Mary Kinnan. New York : Garland Pub., 1977. p. cm. (The Garland library of narratives of North American Indian captivities ; v. 21) Reprint of the 1794 ed. printed by S. Kollock, Elizabethtown. Issued with the reprint of the 1792 ed. of Rogers, John. Letter to Henry Lee. New York, 1977. [E85.G2 vol. 21] [E99.S35] 970'.004'97 B 77-4820 ISBN 0-8240-1645-9 lib.bdg. : 25.00
1. Kinnan, Mary Lewis, 1763-1848. 2. Shawnee Indians—Captivities. 3. Indians of North America—Captivities. 4. Virginia—Biography. I. Title. II. Series.

Kinnersley, Ebenezer, 1771-1778.

LEMAY, Joseph A. Leo, 1935- 923.773
Ebenezer Kinnersley, Franklin's friend. Philadelphia, University of Pa. Pr. [c.1964] 143p. illus., facsim. 22cm. Bibl. 64-10894 4.00
1. Kinnersley, Ebenezer, 1771-1778. 2. Franklin, Benjamin, 1706-1790. I. Title.

Kinney, Richard, 1923-

CRIST, Lyle M. 362.4'1'0924 B
Through the rain and rainbow: the remarkable life of Richard Kinney [by] Lyle M. Crist. Nashville, Abingdon Press [1974] 224 p. ports. 22 cm. [HV1792.K55C7] 73-22386 ISBN 0-687-42036-9 5.95
1. Kinney, Richard, 1923- 2. Blind-deaf—Biography. I. Title.

Kinney, Troy,

KINNEY, Troy, 1871-1938. 927.6
Selected letters of Troy Kinney to Doris Niles. Pref. Written by Meg Villars. This work includes a portrait of Mr. Kinney and 8 reproductions of Adeline Genee, Anna Pavlova, Alexandra Volinine, and Doris Niles. Los Angeles, S. Leslie, 1952. 81p. ports. 31cm. The letters are reproduced from ms. copy. [NE539.K53N5] 53-27131
1. Niles, Doris. II. Title.

Kino, Eusebio Francisco, 1644-1711.

ARIZONA Pioneers' Historical Society. 917.3'04'16
Kino; a commemoration. A short assessment [by] Patricia P. Paylore. Kino sketches [by] Ted De Grazia. Bibliography [by] Donald M. Powell. Tucson, 1961. unpaged. illus. 23cm. Includes bibliography [F799.K57] 61-3243
1. Kino, Eusebio Francisco, 1644-1711. I. Paylore, Patricia P. II. Title.

BOLTON, Herbert Eugene, 1870-1953. 922.273
The Padre on horseback. Chicago, Loyola University Press [1963] xvi, 90 p. illus., port. 24 cm. (The American West, a Loyola University Press reprint series) Reprint of the 1st ed. published in 1932 by the Sonora Press, San Francisco, under title: The Padre on horseback, a sketch of Eusebio Francisco Kino, S. J., apostle to the Plums. Bibliographical references included in "Notes" (p. 86-90) [F799.K58 1963] 63-13248
1. Kino, Eusebio Francisco, 1644-1711. I. Title. II. Series. BIP

BOLTON, Herbert Eugene, 1870-1953. 922.273
Rim of Christendom; a biography of Eusebio Francisco Kino, Pacific coast pioneer. New York, Russell & Russell, 1960 [c.1936] xiv, 644p. illus., fold. maps, facsims. 25cm. Bibl. 60-10705 10.00
1. Kino, Eusebio Francisco, 1644-1711. I. Title.

LOS Angeles. Southwest Museum. 701
Padre Kino, memorable events in the life and times of the immortal priest-colonizer of the Southwest depicted in drawings by DeGrazia. With commentaries on the artist and his work by noted authorities on southwestern history and art. Los Angeles,

1962. 54 p. illus., map. 27 cm. [NC139.D4L6] 62-53443
1. Kino, Eusebio Francisco, 1644-1711. 2. DeGrazia, Ted Ettore, 1909- I. Title.

SMITH, Fay Jackson 979.102
Father Kino in Arizona, by Fay Jackson Smith, John L. Kessel, Francis J. Fox. Maps by Don Bufkin. Phoenix, Ariz. Hist. Found. 1966. xvii, 142p. illus., facsims., col. maps (1 fold.) 29cm. Contents.pt. 1. The Relacion diaria of Father Kino, by F. J. Smith.--pt. 2. Peaceful conquest in southern Arizona, by J. L. Kessell.--pt. 3. Bibliography, compiled and edited by F. J. Fox. [F799.K633] 66-25525 7.50
1. Kino, Eusebio Francisco, 1644-1711. 2. Missions—Arizona. 3. Jesuits in Pimeria Alta. I. Kessell, John L. II. Fox, Francis J. III. Title.

Kino, Eusebio Francisco, 1644-1711 — Juvenile literature.

THAYER, John. 922.273
Desert padre, Eusebio Francisco Kino. Illustrated by Anne Merriman Peck. Milwaukee, Bruce Pub. Co. [1959] 153 p. illus. 22 cm. (Catholic treasury books) [F799.K635] 59-13232
1. Kino, Eusebio Francisco, 1644-1711 — Juvenile literature. I. Title.

Kinsey, Alfred Charles, 1894-1956.

CHRISTENSON, Cornelia V. 155.3'0924 B
Kinsey, a biography [by] Cornelia V. Christenson. Bloomington, Indiana University Press [1971] xii, 241 p. illus., ports. 25 cm. Includes bibliographical references. [BF109.K53C47 1971] 72-154897 ISBN 0-253-14625-9 6.95
1. Kinsey, Alfred Charles, 1894-1956. 2. Sex (Psychology) 3. Sex (Biology) I. Title.

ROBINSON, Paul A., 1940- 301.41'792'2
The modernization of sex : Havelock Ellis, Alfred Kinsey, William Masters, and Virginia Johnson / Paul Robinson. 1st ed. New York : Harper & Row, c1976. viii, 200 p. ; 22 cm. Includes bibliographical references and index. [HQ18.3.R6] 75-24500 ISBN 0-06-013583-2 : 8.95
1. Ellis, Havelock, 1859-1939. 2. Kinsey, Alfred Charles, 1894-1956. 3. Masters, William H. 4. Johnson, Virginia E. 5. Sexologists. I. Title.

Kinzie, Juliette Augusta Magill, 1806-1870.

KINZIE, Juliette Augusta Magill, 1806-1870. 977'.02
Wau-bun, the "early day" in the North-west / Juliette Kinzie. New York : Garland Pub., 1976. 498 p., [4] leaves of plates : ill. ; 23 cm. (The Garland library of narratives of North American Indian captivities ; v. 70) Reprint of the 1856 ed. published by Derby & Jackson, New York. [E85.G2 vol. 70] [F484.3] 75-7095 ISBN 0-8240-1694-7 lib.bdg. : 21.00
1. Kinzie, Juliette Augusta Magill, 1806-1870. 2. Northwest, Old—History—1775-1865. 3. Indians of North America—Northwest, Old. I. Title. II. Series.

Kiowa Apache Indians.

WHITEWOLF, Jim. 970.3'0924 B
Jim Whitewolf: the life of a Kiowa Apache Indian. Edited, and with an introd. and epilogue, by Charles S. Brant. New York, Dover Publications [1969] xi, 144 p. map. 22 cm. Bibliographical footnotes. [E90.W55A3] 67-25596 1.75
1. Kiowa Apache Indians. I. Brant, Charles S., ed. II. Title.

Kiowa Indians.

BATTEY, Thomas C. 970.5'0924
The life and adventures of a Quaker among the Indians, by Thomas C. Battey. With an introd. by Alice Marriott. Norman, University of Oklahoma Press [1968] xxvi, 355 p. illus., ports. 20 cm. (The Western frontier library, no. 36) [E99.K5B3 1968] 67-64445
1. Kiowa Indians. I. Title.

Kipling, Rudyard,

KIPLING, Rudyard, 1865-1936. 820.9
The man who was. Philadelphia, H. Altemus [n. d.] 69 p. 17 cm. [PR4854.M14] 51-38453
I. Title.

Kipling, Rudyard, 1865-1936.

AMIS, Kingsley. 828'.9'09 B
Rudyard Kipling and his world / Kingsley Amis. New York : Scribner, c1975. 128 p. : ill. ; 24 cm. Includes indexes. Bibliography: p. 116-117. [PR4856.A54 1975b] 75-29827 ISBN 0-684-14550-2 : 8.95
1. Kipling, Rudyard, 1865-1936. I. Title.

BROWN, Hilton, 1890- 828'.8'09 B
Rudyard Kipling, a new appreciation. With a foreword by Frank Swinnerton. [Folcroft, Pa.] Folcroft Library Editions, 1974. p. Reprint of the 1945 ed. published by H. Hamilton, London. Bibliography: p. [PR4856.B7 1974b] 74-12167 14.75 (lib. bdg.).
1. Kipling, Rudyard, 1865-1936.

CARRINGTON, Charles Edmund, 1897- 928.2
The life of Rudyard Kipling. [1st ed.] Garden City, N. Y., Doubleday, 1955. xxi, 433 p. ports., geneal. table. 22 cm. "Chronology of Kipling's life and work": p. xiii-xiv. "Sources": p. 404-406. [PR4856.C35] 55-11329
1. Kipling, Rudyard, 1865-1936.

CHARLES, Cecil. 828'.8'09
Rudyard Kipling, his life and works. [Folcroft, Pa.] Folcroft Library Editions, 1972. 49 p. front. 23 cm. Reprint of the 1911 ed. [PR4856.C4 1972] 72-11585 ISBN 0-8414-0903-X (lib. bdg.)
1. Kipling, Rudyard, 1865-1936. BIP

CHARLES, Cecil. 828'.8'09 B
Rudyard Kipling, his life and works / by Cecil Charles. Norwood, Pa. : Norwood Editions, 1975. 49 p., [1] leaf of plates : ill. ; 23 cm. Reprint of the 1911 ed. published by J. Hewetson, Hampstead, London. [PR4856.C4 1975] 75-42092 ISBN 0-88305-124-9 : 8.00
1. Kipling, Rudyard, 1865-1936.

CROFT-COOKE, Rupert, 1903- 828'.8'09 B
Rudyard Kipling. New York, Haskell House, 1974. 107 p. 20 cm. Reprint of the 1948 ed. published by Home & Van Thal, London, in series: the English novelists. [PR4856.C7 1974] 74-7100 ISBN 0-8383-1856-8
1. Kipling, Rudyard, 1865-1936. I. Series: The English novelists (London)

DOBREE, Bonamy, 1891- 928.2
Rudyard Kipling. London, New York, Published for the British Council by Longmans, Green [1951] 55p. port. 22cm. (Bibliographical series of supplements to British book news) 'Rudyard Kipling: a select bibliography': p. 33-42. 'Index to prose [of Kipling]' : p. 43-55. [PR4856.D57] A 53
1. Kipling, Rudyard, 1865-1936. I. Title. II. Series.

FIDO, Martin. 828'.8'09
Rudyard Kipling / Martin Fido. New York : Viking Press, 1974. 144 p. : ill. ; 31 cm. (A Studio book) Includes index. [PR4856.F5] 73-22500 ISBN 0-670-61026-7 : 14.95
1. Kipling, Rudyard, 1865-1936.

GROSS, John J., comp. 828'.8'09 B
The age of Kipling. Edited by John Gross. New York, Simon and Schuster [1972] xii, 178 p. illus. 26 cm. London ed. (Weidenfeld & Nicolson) published under title: Rudyard Kipling: the man, his work and his world. [PR4856.G7 1972b] 72-83900 ISBN 0-671-21405-5 12.95
1. Kipling, Rudyard, 1865-1936. I. Title.
Contents Omitted. BIP

HOPKINS, Robert Thurston, 1884- 828'.8'09 B
Rudyard Kipling : the story of a genius / by R. Thurston Hopkins. Folcroft, Pa. : Folcroft Library Editions, 1977 [c1930] p. cm. Reprint of the 1st ed. published by C. Palmer, London. Includes index. [PR4856.H733 1977] 77-10659 ISBN 0-8414-4956-2 lib. bdg. : 25.00
1. Kipling, Rudyard, 1865-1936. 2. Authors, English—19th century—Biography. BIP

HOPKINS, Robert Thurston, 1884- 828'.8'09
Rudyard Kipling, a literary appreciation / by R. Thurston Hopkins. Folcroft, Pa. : Folcroft Library Editions, 1978 [c1916] p. cm. Reprint of the 2d ed. published by Simpkin, Marshall, Hamilton, Kent, London. Includes index. Bibliography: p. [PR4856.H73 1978] 78-13606 ISBN 0-8414-4871-X lib. bdg. : 35.00
1. Kipling, Rudyard, 1865-1936. 2. Authors, English—19th century—Biography. I. Title.

KIPLING, Rudyard, 1865-1936. 820.9
The man who was. Philadelphia, H. Altemus [n. d.] 69 p. 17 cm. [PR4854.M14] 51-38453
I. Title.

MASON, Philip. 828'.8'09 B
Kipling : the glass, the shadow and the fire / Philip Mason. New York : Harper & Row, [1975] p. cm. Includes index. Bibliography: p. [PR4856.M36] 74-29175 ISBN 0-06-012833-X : 8.95
1. Kipling, Rudyard, 1865-1936. I. Title. BIP

STEWART, John Innes MacKintosh, 1906- 828.809 B
Rudyard Kipling, by J. I. M. Stewart. New York, Dodd, Mead [1966] vi, 245 p. illus. 21 cm. "Published works of Rudyard Kipling referred to in this work": p. 240. [PR4856.S7] 66-22906
1. Kipling, Rudyard, 1865-1936.

SUTCLIFF, Rosemary. 928.2
Rudyard Kipling. [1st American ed.] New York, H. Z. Walck [1961, c1960] 61 p. illus. 19 cm. Includes bibliography. [PR4856.S8 1961] 61-8580
1. Kipling, Rudyard, 1865-1936.

WILSON, Angus. 828'.8'09
The strange ride of Rudyard Kipling : his life and work / Angus Wilson. Harmondsworth, Eng. ; New York : Penquin Books, 1979, c1977. xvi, 370 p., [28] leaves of plates : ill. ; 20 cm. Includes bibliographical references and index. [PR4856.W54 1979] 78-27541 ISBN 0-14-005122-8 pbk. : 3.95
1. Kipling, Rudyard, 1865-1936. 2. Authors, English—19th century—Biography. I. Title.

Kipling, Rudyard, 1865-1936—Biography.

BIRKENHEAD, Frederick Winston Furneaux Smith, 2d Earl of, 1907-1975. 828'.8'09 B
Rudyard Kipling / Lord Birkenhead. New York : Random House, 1978. p. cm. Includes index. Bibliography: p. [PR4856.B57 1978] 78-57110 15.00
1. Kipling, Rudyard, 1865-1936—Biography. 2. Authors, English—19th century—Biography.

Kipling, Rudyard, 1865-1936—Juvenile literature.

MANLEY, Seon 928.2
Rudyard Kipling, creative adventurer. New York, Vanguard [c.1965] 256p. illus., facsims., ports. 25cm. Bibl. [PR4856.M26] 65-10230 4.95
1. Kipling, Rudyard, 1865-1936—Juvenile literature. I. Title. BIP

Kipling, Rudyard, 1865-1936—Homes and haunts—Vermont.

VAN DE WATER, Frederic Franklyn, 1890- 828'.809 B
Rudyard Kipling's Vermont feud [by] Frederic F. Van de Water. Drawings by Bernadine Custer. New York, Reynal & Hitchcock. New York, Haskell House Publishers [1974, c1937] p. cm. "A John Day book." [PR4856.V3 1974] 74-1100 ISBN 0-8383-2024-4 9.95
1. Kipling, Rudyard, 1865-1936—Homes and haunts—Vermont. 2. Balestier, Beatty. I. Title. BIP

Kirby, John Henry, 1860-1940.

LASSWELL, Mary, 1905- 338.7'63'497510924
John Henry Kirby: prince of the pines. Pref. by Edmunds Travis. Austin, Encino Press, 1967. xv, 203 p. ports. 24 cm. Bibliography: p. 203. [HD9760.K65L35] 68-3428
1. Kirby, John Henry, 1860-1940. I. Title.

LASSWELL, Mary, 1905- 338.7'63'497510924 B
John Henry Kirby: prince of the pines. Pref. by Edmunds Travis. Austin, Encino Press, 1967. xv, 203 p. ports. 24 cm. Bibliography: p. 203. [HD9760.K65L35] 68-3428
1. Kirby, John Henry, 1860-1940. I. Title.

Kirby, Louis Paul,

KIRBY, Louis Paul, 1870- 920.5
Fourscore breathless years. Boston, Meador Pub. Co. [1951] 429 p. 21 cm. Autobiography. [PN4874.K55A3] 51-5729
I. Title.

Kirby-Smith, Edmund, 1824-1893.

PARKS, Joseph Howard. 923.573
General Edmund Kirby Smith, C.S.A. Baton Rouge, Louisiana State University Press [1954] viii, 537 p. illus., maps, ports. 22 cm. (Southern biography series) "Critical essay on authorities": p. [510]-515. Bibliographical footnotes. [E467.1.K35P3] 54-3764
1. Kirby-Smith, Edmund, 1824-1893. I. Title. II. Series.

Kircher, Athanasius, 1602-1680.

GODWIN, Joscelyn. 907'.202'4 B
Athanasius Kircher : Renaissance man and the quest for lost knowledge / Joscelyn Godwin. Boulder, Colo. : Shambhala ; New York : distributed by Random House, 1979. p. cm. Bibliography: p. [CT1098.K46G62] 79-2107 ISBN 0-394-73737-7 pbk. : 6.95
1. Kircher, Athanasius, 1602-1680. 2. Germany—Biography. BIP

Kirchner, Ernst Ludwig, 1880-1938.

GORDON, Donald E. 759.3
Ernst Ludwig Kirchner [by] Donald E. Gordon. Cambridge, Mass., Harvard University Press, 1968. 475 p. illus., plates (part col.) 30 cm. Bibliography: p. [441]-447. [ND588.K47G62] 68-25610 40.00
1. Kirchner, Ernst Ludwig, 1880-1938. BIP

Kirk, Claude R., 1926-

DE TOLEDANO, Ralph, 1916- 975.9'06'0924
Claude Kirk—man and myth [by] Ralph de Toledano & Philip V. Brennan, Jr. [Moonachie, N.J., Produced for the authors by Pyramid Publications, 1970] 124 p. 18 cm. (An Anthem book) [F316.2.K54D4] 72-15270 0.95
1. Kirk, Claude R., 1926- I. Brennan, Philip Vincent, 1926- joint author.

Kirk, Donald, 1938-

KIRK, Donald, 1938- 959.704'38
Tell it to the dead : memories of a war / Donald Kirk. Chicago : Nelson-Hall, c1975. p. cm. [DS559.5.K57] 75-29137 ISBN 0-88229-287-0 : 6.95
1. Kirk, Donald, 1938- 2. Vietnamese Conflict, 1961-1975—Personal narratives, American. I. Title. BIP

Kirker, James, 1793-1852 or 3.

MCGAW, William Cochran. 917.8'03'20924 B
Savage scene; the life and times of James Kirker, frontier king. New York, Hastings House [1972] xi, 242 p. illus. 22 cm.

Bibliography: p. 223-234. [F800.K52M3] 76-38962 ISBN 0-8038-6712-3
1. Kirker, James, 1793-1852 or 3. 2. Indians of North America—Southwest, New—History. 3. Southwest, New—History. I. Title. **BIP**

Kirkham, James Mercer, 1872-1957.

KIRKHAM, Arne, ed. 922.8373
James Mercer Kirkham: highlights of his successful life. [Salt Lake City? c1961. 80p. illus. 29cm. [BX8695.K55K5] 62-2434
1. Kirkham, James Mercer, 1872-1957. I. Title.

KIRKHAM, ElMoine W. v. 12
James Mercer Kirkham. Salt Lake City, 1961. 79 p. illus., ports. 28 cm. 65-5010
1. Kirkham, James Mercer, 1872-1957. I. Title.

Kirkwood, Kenneth Porter, 1899-1968.

KIRKWOOD, Kenneth Porter, 1899-1968. 395'.3
The diplomat at table; a social and anecdotal history through the looking-glass. Metuchen, N.J., Scarecrow Press, 1974. xv, 282 p. port. 22 cm. [D413.K57A3 1974] 74-2416 ISBN 0-8108-0714-9 10.00
1. Kirkwood, Kenneth Porter, 1899-1968. 2. Dinners and dining. 3. Diplomatic etiquette. I. Title.

Kirley, Joseph, 1847-1933?

MCALLISTER, Laura (Kirley) 1882 920
Gumbo trails. [n.p., 1957] 202p. illus. 24cm. [CT275.K5935M3] 57-58316
1. Kirley, Joseph, 1847-1933? I. Title.

Kirpal Singh, 1894-1974.

KIRPAL Singh, 1894-1974. 294.6'6'3 B
Kirpal Singh : a visual biography / compiled by Robert Leverant ; [photos., Malcolm Tillis et al.]. [Berkeley, Calif. : Images Press, c1974] 47 p. : ill. ; 17 cm. "Text from talks in San Jose, San Francisco & Dallas by Kirpal Singh in November 1972 & Morning talks." Bibliography: p. 47. [BL624.K57] 74-24723 ISBN 0-9600374-3-8 : 2.95
1. Kirpal Singh, 1894-1974. 2. Meditations.

Kirpal Singh, 1894-1974—Juvenile literature.

SCOTTI, Juliet. 294.6'8'30924 B
Kirpal Singh : the story of a saint / compiled and adapted for children by Juliet Scotti and Ricki Linksman ; ill. by Valerie Tarrant. 1st ed. [Bowling Green, Va.] : Sawan Kirpal Publications, 1977. xi, 92, [2] p. : ill. ; 28 cm. (Children's series ; no. 1) Bibliography: p. [94] Relates episodes from the life of Kirpal Singh, a spiritual leader who became president of the World Fellowship of Religions. [BL2017.9.S53S35] 92 77-79840 ISBN 0-918224-05-5 pbk. : 3.95
1. Kirpal Singh, 1894-1974—Juvenile literature. 2. Sikhs in India—Biography—Juvenile literature. I. Linksman, Ricki, 1952- joint author. II. Tarrant, Valerie, 1951- III. Title. **BIP**

Kishi, Nobusuke.

KURZMAN, Dan 923.252
Kishi and Japan; the search for the sun. Foreword by James A. Michener. New York, Ivan Obolensky [c.1960] xviii, 394p. 25cm. 60-9041 5.95
1. Kishi, Nobusuke. 2. Japan—Pol. & govt.—1945- I. Title.

Kissinger, Henry Alfred.

*ASHMAN, Charles. 973.924'092'4 B
Kissinger; the adventures of Super-Kraut. [New York, Dell, 1975, c1972] 272 p. 18 cm. [E840.8] 1.50 (pbk.)
1. Kissinger, Henry Alfred. I. Title.

ASHMAN, Charles R. 973.924'092'4 B
Kissinger; the adventures of super-kraut [by] Charles R. Ashman. Secaucus, N.J., Lyle Stuart [1972] 240 p. 25 cm. [E840.8.K58A83] 72-76847 7.95
1. Kissinger, Henry Alfred. **BIP**

BROWN, William R. 327.56'073
The last crusade : a negotiator's Middle East handbook / William R. Brown. Chicago : Nelson-Hall, [1980] p. cm. Includes index. [DS63.2.U5B76] 79-18462 ISBN 0-88229-554-3 : 22.95 ISBN 0-88229-738-4 pbk. : 11.95
1. Kissinger, Henry Alfred. 2. Near East—Foreign relations—United States. 3. United States—Foreign relations—Near East. 4. Jewish-Arab relations—1973- 5. Near East—Politics and government—1945- 6. Statesmen—United States—Biography. 7. United States—Foreign relations—1969-1974. I. Title. **BIP**

DICKSON, Peter W. 973.924'092'4 B
Kissinger and the meaning of history / Peter W. Dickson. Cambridge [Eng.] ; New York : Cambridge University Press, 1978. x, 197 p. ; 24 cm. Includes index. Bibliography: p. [183]-191. [E840.8.K58D53] 78-5633 ISBN 0-521-22113-7 : 14.95
1. Kissinger, Henry Alfred. 2. Statesmen—United States—Biography. 3. United States—Foreign relations—1969-1974. 4. United States—Foreign relations—1974-1977. I. Title. **BIP**

*GRAUBARD, Stephen R. 923.2
Kissinger; portrait of a mind, [by] Stephen R. Graubard. New York, W. W. Norton, [1974, c1973]. xix, 312 p. 21 cm. [E181] ISBN 0-393-09278-X. 3.45 (pbk.)
1. Kissinger, Henry Alfred. 2. U.S.—Biography. I. Title.

GRAUBARD, Stephen Richards. 973.924'092'4 B
Kissinger: portrait of a mind [by] Stephen R. Graubard. [1st ed.] New York, Norton [1973] xix, 288 p. 24 cm. Bibliography: p. 279-280. [E840.8.K58G72] 73-1888 ISBN 0-393-05481-0 7.95
1. Kissinger, Henry Alfred. I. Title.

GRAUBARD, Stephen Richards. 973.924'092'4 B
Kissinger: portrait of a mind [by] Stephen R. Graubard. New York, Norton [1974] xix, 312 p. 21 cm. "Bibliography of Henry Kissinger's works": p. 299-300. [E840.8.K58G72 1974] 74-5296 ISBN 0-393-09278-X 6.95
1. Kissinger, Henry Alfred. I. Title.

KALB, Marvin L. 973.924'092'4 B
Kissinger, by Marvin Kalb and Bernard Kalb. [1st ed.] Boston, Little, Brown [1974] xiii, 577 p. illus. 25 cm. Includes bibliographical references. [E840.8.K58K34] 74-5892 12.50
1. Kissinger, Henry Alfred. 2. United States—Foreign relations—1969- I. Kalb, Bernard, joint author. **BIP**

LANDAU, David. 973.924'092'4
Kissinger: the uses of power. Boston, Houghton Mifflin, 1972. ix, 279 p. 23 cm. Bibliography: [265]-267. [E855.L36] 72-4128 ISBN 0-395-14366-7 5.95
1. Kissinger, Henry Alfred. 2. United States—Foreign relations—1969- 3. United States—Foreign relations—Vietnam. 4. Vietnam—Foreign relations—United States. I. Title: The uses of power. **BIP**

LANDAU, David. 973.924'092'4 B
Kissinger: the uses of power. New York, Crowell [1974] xiii, 274 p. 20 cm. (Apollo editions, A-354) Bibliography: p. [269]-271. [E855.L36 1974] 73-17190 ISBN 0-8152-0354-3 2.95 (pbk.)
1. Kissinger, Henry Alfred. 2. United States—Foreign relations—1969- 3. United States—Foreign relations—Vietnam. 4. Vietnam—Foreign relations—United States. I. Title.

MAZLISH, Bruce, 1923- 973.924'092'4 B
Kissinger : the European mind in American policy / Bruce Mazlish. New York : Basic Books, c1976. xiii, 330 p., [4] leaves of plates : ill. ; 22 cm. Includes bibliographical references and index. [E840.8.K58M38] 76-18120 ISBN 0-465-03727-5 : 10.95
1. Kissinger, Henry Alfred. 2. Statesmen—United States—Biography. 3. United States—Foreign relations—1969-1974. 4. United States—Foreign relations—1974- I. Title. **BIP**

MORRIS, Roger. 327.73
Uncertain greatness : Henry Kissinger and American foreign policy / Roger Morris. 1st ed. New York : Harper & Row, c1977. viii, 312 p. ; 25 cm. Includes index. [E855.M67 1977] 75-30339 ISBN 0 06-013097-0 : 10.00
1. Kissinger, Henry Alfred. 2. United States—Foreign relations—1969-1974. 3. United States—Foreign relations—1974-1977. 4. Statesmen—United States—Biography. I. Title. **BIP**

PAOLUCCI, Henry. 973.924'092'4 B
Who is Kissinger? New York [Griffon-House Publications] 1972. 40 p. 22 cm. (A Griffon torch-bearer, no. 1) [E855.P3] 72-181635 1.00
1. Kissinger, Henry Alfred. 2. United States—Foreign relations—1969- 3. United States—Politics and government—1969-1974. I. Title.

SHAWCROSS, William. 959.704'342'09596
The sideshow : Nixon, Kissinger, and the destruction of Cambodia / William Shawcross. New York : Simon and Schuster, c1979. p. cm. Includes index. Bibliography: p. [DS557.8.C3S5] 78-31826 ISBN 0-671-23070-0 : 10.95
1. Kissinger, Henry Alfred. 2. Nixon, Richard Milhous, 1913- 3. Vietnamese Conflict, 1961-1975—Campaigns—Cambodia. 4. Cambodia—History—Civil War, 1970-1975. 5. United States—Politics and government—1969-1974. 6. Cabinet officers—United States—Biography. I. Title.

SHEEHAN, Edward R. F. 327.73'056
The Arabs, Israelis, and Kissinger : a secret history of American diplomacy in the Middle East / Edward R. F. Sheehan. New York : Readers Digest Press : distributed by Crowell, 1976. xii, 287 p. : maps ; 24 cm. Includes bibliographical references and index. [DS63.2.U5S387 1976] 76-21811 ISBN 0-88349-100-1 : 8.95
1. Kissinger, Henry Alfred. 2. United States—Foreign relations—Near East. 3. Near East—Foreign relations—United States. 4. Jewish-Arab relations—1967-1973. 5. Jewish-Arab relations—1973- I. Title.

Kistiakowsky, George Bogdan.

KISTIAKOWSKY, George Bogdan. 353.008'55'0924 B
A scientist at the White House : the private diary of President Eisenhower's Special Assistant for Science and Technology / George B. Kistiakowsky ; with an introd. by Charles S. Maier. Cambridge : Harvard University Press, 1976. lxvii, 448 p. : port. ; 24 cm. Includes index. [Q127.U6K53] 76-19013 ISBN 0-674-79496-6 : 15.00
1. Kistiakowsky, George Bogdan. 2. Science and state—United States. 3. Technology and state—United States. 4. Scientists—United States Biography. I. Title.

Kitchener, Horatio Herbert Kitchener, 1st Earl, 1850-1916.

MAGNUS, Philip Montefiore, Sir, Bart., 1906- 942.08'0924 B
Kitchener: portrait of an imperialist [by] Philip Magnus. Harmondsworth, Penguin, 1968. 485 p. 16 plates, illus., 2 maps, ports. 18 cm. Bibliographical footnotes. [DA68.32.K6M3 1968] 72-366576 12/6
1. Kitchener, Horatio Herbert Kitchener, 1st Earl, 1850-1916.

Kitchin, Claude, 1869-1923.

ARNETT, Alex Mathews, 1888- 973.91'3'0924
Claude Kitchin and the Wilson war policies. New York, Russell & Russell [1971, c1937] xii, 341 p. illus., ports. 23 cm. Bibliography: p. 331-337. [E748.K57A8 1971] 73-139897
1. Kitchin, Claude, 1869-1923. 2. Wilson, Woodrow, Pres. U.S., 1856-1924. 3. European War, 1914-1918—U.S. I. Title. **BIP**

Kitchner, Horatlo Herbert Kitchner, 1st earl, 1850-1916.

MAGNUS, Philip Montefiore, Sir Bart., 1906- 923.542
Kitchner; portrait of an imperialist. [1st American ed.] New York, Dutton, 1959 [c1958] 410p. illus. 22cm. [DA68.32.K6M3 1959] 58-5246
1. Kitchner, Horatlo Herbert Kitchner, 1st earl, 1850-1916. I. Title.

Kitman, Marvin,

KITMAN, Marvin, 1929- 817.54
The number one best seller; the true adventures of Marvin Kitman. New York, Dial Press, 1966. xiv, 134 p. 21 cm. [CT275.K596A3] 66-12827
1. Title.

Kitt, Eartha.

KITT, Eartha. 784'.092'4 B
Alone with me / Eartha Kitt. Chicago : H. Regnery Co., 1975 [i.e.,1976] p. cm. [ML420.K5A32] 75-13229 ISBN 0-8092-8351-4 : 8.95
1. Kitt, Eartha. 2. Musicians—Correspondence, reminiscences, etc. I. Title.

Kittler, Glenn D.

KITTLER, Glenn D. 282.0922
The wings of eagles. Garden City, N.Y., Doubleday [1967, c.1966] 197p. 19cm. (Echo bks., E37) [BX4651.2K5] .85 pap.,
I. Catholic Church—Biog. II. Title.

Kittredge, George Lyman, 1860-1941.

HYDER, Clyde Kenneth, 1902- 923.773
George Lyman Kittredge: teacher and scholar. Lawrence, University of Kansas Press, 1962. 216p. illus. 22cm. [PE64.K5H9] 62-14233
1. Kittredge, George Lyman, 1860-1941. I. Title.

Kivengere, Festo.

KIVENGERE, Festo. 283'.092'4 B
I love Idi Amin : the story of triumph under fire in the midst of suffering and persecution in Uganda / Festo Kivengere, with Dorothy Smoker. Old Tappan, N.J. : F. H. Revell Co., c1977. 63 p. : ill. ; 18 cm. (New Life ventures) [BX5700.8.Z8K58] 77-79929 ISBN 0-8007-9004-9 : 0.95
1. Kivengere, Festo. 2. Church of Uganda, Rwanda, Burundi, and Boga—Zaire—Bishops—Biography. 3. Amin, Idi, 1925- 4. Bishops—Uganda—Biography. I. Smoker, Dorothy, joint author. II. Title.

Klaasen, Ruth.

KLAASEN, Ruth. 289.7'3 B
How green is my mountain / Ruth Klaasen. Downers Grove, Ill. : InterVarsity Press, c1979. 162 p. ; 21 cm. [BX8143.K47A33] 79-1646 ISBN 0-87784-561-1 : 3.95
1. Klaasen, Ruth. 2. Mennonites in the Philippine Islands—Biography. I. Title. **BIP**

Klah, Hasteen.

NEWCOMB, Franc (Johnson) 970.2
Hosteen Klah, Navaho medicine man and sand painter, [1st ed.] Norman, University of Oklahoma Press [1964] xxxiii, 27 p. illus., maps (1 fold.) ports. 23 cm. (The Civilization of the American Indian series) Bibliography: p. 221. [E99.N3N37] 64-20759
1. Klah, Hasteen. 2. Navaho Indians. I. Title. II. Series.

Klausner, Joseph, 1874-1958.

KLING, Simcha. 956.94'001'0924 B
Joseph Klausner. New York, T. Yoseloff [1970] 161 p. ports. 22 cm. Bibliography: p. 151-158. [DS115.9.K5K54] 72-88274 6.00

1. Klausner, Joseph, 1874-1958.

Klee, Paul, 1879-1940.

GROHMANN, Will, 1887-1968. 927.5
Paul Klee. New York, H. N. Abrams [1954?] 448 p. illus., plates (part col.), ports, facsim. 31 cm. Bibliography: p. 432-445. [ND588.K5G75] [ND588] 759.9494 55-3209

1. Klee, Paul, 1879-1940.

HAFTMANN, Werner. 927.5
The mind and work of Paul Klee. New York, Praeger [1954] 213 p. illus. (part col.) 22 cm. (Books that matter) Translation of Paul Klee; Wege bildnerischen Denkens. Bibliography: p. 207-208. [ND588.K5H314 1954a] 759.9494 54-11543

1. Klee, Paul, 1879-1940. I. Title. **BIP**

KLEE, Felix, 1907- 927.5
Paul Klee, his life and work in documents, selected from posthumous writings and unpublished letters. With 121 reproductions of paintings, drawings, photos, and other documents. Tr. from German by Richard and Clara Winston. New York, Braziller, [c.]1962. x, 212p. illus. 25cm. 62-16271 7.50 bds.,
1. Klee, Paul, 1879-1940. I. Klee, Paul, 1879-1940. II. Title.

KLEE, Paul, 1879-1940 927.5
The diaries of Paul Klee. 1898-1918. Ed., introd., by Felix Klee. Berkeley, Univ. of Calif. Pr., 1964. xx, 424p. illus., facsims., ports. 25cm. First complete English-language version based upon the text of the German hardcover ed., pub. in 1957. 64-20693 10.00
1. Artists—Correspondence, reminiscences, etc. I. Klee, Felix, 1907- ed. II. Title.

KLEE, Paul, 1879-1940 927.5
The diaries of Paul Klee, 1898-1918. Ed., introd., by Felix Klee. Berkeley, Univ. of Calif. Pr., 1968. [c.1964] xx, 434p. illus., facsims., ports. 25cm. (Cal 158) First complete English-language version based upon the text of the German hardcover ed., pub. in 1957. [ND588.K5A252] 64-20993 3.45 pap.,
1. Artists—Correspondance, reminiscences, etc. I. Klee, Felix, 1907- ed. II. Title.

KLEE, Paul, 1879-1940. 709'.494
The diaries of Paul Klee, 1898-1918. Edited, with an introd. by Felix Klee. Berkeley, University of California Press, 1968 [c1964] xx, 434 p. illus. 21 cm. "First California paper-bound printing." Translation of Tagebucher. [ND588.K5A252 1968] 68-6958 3.45
1. Artists—Correspondence, reminiscences, etc. I. Klee, Felix, 1907- ed. **BIP**

KLEE, Paul, 1879-1940. 927.5
The diaries of Paul Klee, 1898-1918. Edited, with an introd., by Felix Klee. Berkeley, University of California Press, 1964. xx, 424 p. illus., facsims., ports. 25 cm. "First complete English-language version ... based upon the text of the German hardcover edition, published ... in 1957." [ND588.K5A252] 64-20993
1. Artists — Correspondence, reminiscences, etc. I. Klee, Felix, 1907- ed. II. Title.

KLEE, Paul, 1879-1940. 759.9494
Klee. Text by Robert Fisher. Edited by Theodore Reff. New York, Tudor Pub. Co. [1966] 36 p. 91 col. plates. 18 cm. [ND588.K5R43] 66-10559
I. Fisher, Robert, 1931- II. Reff, Theodore, ed.

PAUL Klee. v. 12
New York, Abrams [1960] 447p. illus. (part col.) 30cm. Gruppenkatalog (p. 385-408) in German, English and French. Bibliography comp. by Hannah Muller.
1. Klee, Paul, 1879-1940. I. Grohmann, Will, 1887-

PAUL Klee. 759.9494
Translated by Alexander Gode. [A Lee Ault ed.] New York, Viking Press, 1952. 156 p. illus., port. 28 cm. Bibliography: p. 151-156. [ND588.K5G5] 927.5 52-13848
1. Klee, Paul, 1879-1940. I. Giedion-Welcker, Carola.

PONENTE, Nello. 759.3
Klee: biographical and critical study. Translated from the Italian by James Emmons. [Lausanne] Skira; [distributed by World Pub. Co., Cleveland, 1960] 140 p. mounted col. illus. 19 cm. (The Taste of our time, v. 31) Bibliography: p. 123-[129] [ND588.K5P63] 60-8729
1. Klee, Paul, 1879-1940.

SAN Lazzaro, Gualtieri 759.9494
di.
Klee; a study of his life and work. Translated from the Italian by Stuart Hood. New York, Praeger [1957] 304p. illus. (part col.) 22cm. 'Klee's writings, [books illustrated by Him, and principal exhibitions of his works]': p. 281-284. Bibliography: p. 284-286. [ND588.K5S26] 927.5 57-11232
1. Klee, Paul, 1879-1940. I. Title.

SAN Lazzaro, Gualtieri di. 927.5
Klee; a study of his life and work. Translated from the Italian by Stuart Hood. New York, Praeger [1957] 304 p. illus. (part col.) 22 cm. "Klee's writings [books illustrated by him, and principal exhibitions of his works]": p. 281-284. Bibliography: p. 284-286. [ND588.K5S26] 759.9494 57-11232
1. Klee, Paul, 1879-1940.

SAN LAZZARO, Gualtieri di. v. 12
Klee; a study of his life and work. [Translated from the Italian by Stuart Hood. 2d ed.] New York, Praeger [1964] 304 p. illus. (part col.) 22 cm. "Klee's writings, [books illustrated by him, and principal exhibitions of his works]": p. 281-284. Bibliography: p. 284-286. 68-78797
1. Klee, Paul, 1879-1940. I. Title.

Klee, Paul, 1879-1940—Juvenile literature.

RABOFF, Ernest 760'.0924 (J)
Lloyd.
Paul Klee, by Ernest Raboff. Garden City, N.Y., Doubleday, 1968. 1 v. (unpaged) illus. (part col.) 29 cm. (Art for children) (A Gemini-Smith book.) [ND588.K5R3] 68-26550 3.95
1. Klee, Paul, 1879-1940—Juvenile literature. **BIP**

Kleiber, Hans, 1887-1967.

FORREST, James Taylor, 760'.0924
1921-
Hans Kleiber; artist of the Big Horns [by James T. Forrest] Big Horn, Wyo., Bradford Brinton Memorial, 1968. 14 p. illus., group port. 23 cm. [N6537.K55F6] 73-243389
1. Kleiber, Hans, 1887-1967. I. Title.

Klein, Henry, 1951-

KLEIN, Henry, 1951- 963'.06
Through ferrengi eyes : the diary of a Peace Corps volunteer in Ethiopia, 1974-1976 / Henry Klein. 1st ed. Hicksville, N.Y. : Exposition Press, c1979. 220 p., [4] leaves of plates : ill. ; 21 cm. [DT387.95.K53] 79-115082 ISBN 0-682-49303-1 : 9.00
1. Klein, Henry, 1951- 2. Ethiopia—History—Revolution, 1974—Personal narratives. 3. Ethiopia—Politics and government—1974- —Sources. 4. Americans in Ethiopia—Biography. I. Title. **BIP**

Klein, Hermann, 1856-1934.

KLEIN, Hermann, 1856- 782.1'09421
1934.
The golden age of opera. New York : Arno Press, 1977. p. cm. (Opera biographies) Reprint of the 1933 ed. published by G. Routledge, London. [ML1731.8.L7K4 1977] 76-29943 ISBN 0-405-09685-2 : 32.00
1. Klein, Hermann, 1856-1934. 2. Opera—London. 3. London—Social life and customs. 4. Singers. 5. Music critics—Biography. 6. London—Biography. I. Title.

Klein, Michel, dr.

KLEIN, Michel, 636.089'092'4 B
dr.
For the love of animals : the autobiography of a veterinary surgeon / by Michel Klein ; translated from the French by J. Maxwell Brownjohn. 1st U.S. ed. New York : Morrow, 1979. 316 p., [8] leaves of plates : ill. ; 25 cm. Translation of Ces betes qui m'ont fait homme. [SF613.K55A3213 1979] 78-73972 ISBN 0-688-03341-5 : 10.95
1. Klein, Michel, dr. 2. Veterinarians—France—Biography. 3. Zoo animals—Diseases. I. Title.

Klein, Rochelle,

KLEIN, Rochelle, 1899- 920.7
The girl who never played. New York, Comet Press Books [1957] 54p. 21cm. (A Reflection book) Autobiographical. [CT275.K598A3] 57-7256
I. Title.

Kleinhans, Theodore J

KLEINHANS, Theodore J 927.8
The music master; the story of Johann Sebastian Bach. Philadelphia, Muhlenberg Press [1962] 156p. 21cm. [ML410.B13K6] 62-8199
I. Bach, Johann Sebastian, 1685-1750. II. Title. **BIP**

***Kleinholz, Frank,**

*KLEINHOLZ, Frank, 1901- 759.1747
Frank Kleinholz: a self portrait. Introd. by Philip Evergood. New York. Garland Pr., 63 E. 57 [c.1964] 95p. illus. (pt. col.) 27cm. 12.50, lim. ed., bxd.
I. Title.

KLEINHOLZ, Frank, 1901- 759.13
Frank Kleinholz: a self portrait. Introd. by Philip Evergood. New York, Shorewood Publishers [1964] 95 p. plates (part col.) 27 cm. [ND237.K555A2] 64-14859
I. Title.

Kleist, Heinrich von,

KLEIST, Heinrich von, 838'.6'09 B
1777-1811.
An abyss deep enough : the life of Heinrich von Kleist in his parables, essays, and letter / Heinrich von Kleist ; edited, translated, and introduced by Philip B. Miller. 1st ed. New York : Dutton, c1979. p. cm. Includes bibliographical references. [PT2378.A2E5 1979] 78-16900 ISBN 0-525-05479-0 : 12.95
I. Miller, Philip B. II. Title. **BIP**

Kliewer, Bruce, 1963-

KLIEWER, Evelyn. 362.7'8'19687 B
Please, God, help me get well in your spare time / Evelyn Kliewer. Minneapolis : Bethany Fellowship, c1979. p. cm. [RJ496.P64K55] 79-17683 ISBN 0-87123-027-5 pbk. : 3.50
1. Kliewer, Bruce, 1963- 2. Kliewer, Evelyn. 3. Polyradiculoneuritis in children—Biography. 4. Mothers—California—Biography. I. Title. **BIP**

Klimsch, Karl, 1812-1890.

KLIMSCH, Karl, 1812- 745.4'49'24
1890.
Florid Victorian ornament / Karl Klimsch. New York : Dover Publications, 1977. [52] leaves of plates : all ill. ; 29 cm. (Dover pictorial archive series) Reprint of the 1877? ed. published by Asher, London, under title: Ornaments invented & designed by Charles Klimsch. [NK1535.K55A52 1977] 76-58573 ISBN 0-486-23490-8 pbk. : 3.50
1. Klimsch, Karl, 1812-1890. 2. Design, Decorative—Plant forms. 3. Decoration and ornament—Victorian style. I. Title. **BIP**

Klimt, Gustav, 1862-1918.

HOFMANN, Werner, 1928- 759.36
Gustav Klimt. [Translated by Inge Goodwin] Greenwich, Conn., New York Graphic Society [1972, c1971] 60 p. illus. (part col.) 28 x 31 cm. Translation of Gustav Klimt und die Wiener Jahrhundertwende. Bibliography: p. 56-57. [M6811.5.K55H613 1972b] 70-186455 ISBN 0-8212-0452-1 27.50
1. Klimt, Gustav, 1862-1918. **BIP**

KLIMT, Gustav, 1862-1918. 759.36
Gustav Klimt / Alessandra Comini. New York : G. Braziller, 1975. 29, 80 p. : ill. (some col.) ; 28 cm. Includes bibliographical references. [ND511.5.K55C65] 75-10965 ISBN 0-8076-0805-X : 15.00 ISBN 0-8076-0806-8 pbk. : 8.95
1. Klimt, Gustav, 1862-1918. I. Comini, Alessandra.

Kline, Franz. 1910-1962.

DAWSON, Fielding, 1930- 759.13
An emotional memoir of Franz Kline. New York, Pantheon [1967] 147p. 22cm. [ND237.K56D3] 67-23964 4.95
1. Kline, Franz. 1910-1962. I. Title.

Kline, John, 1797-1864.

KLINE, John, 1797-1864. 922.673
Life and labors of Elder John Kline, the martyr missionary; collated from his diary by Benjamin Funk. Elgin, Ill., Brethren Pub. House, 1900. 480 p. illus. 24 cm. [BX7843.K55A3] 44-26497
I. Funk, Benjamin. II. Title.

SAPPINGTON, Roger Edwin, 922.673
1929-
Courageous prophet, chapters from the life of John Kline. Elgin, Ill., Brethren [c.1964] 128p. illus. 21cm. Bibl. 64-4948 2.25 pap.,
1. Kline, John, 1797-1864. I. Title.

SAPPINGTON, Roger Edwin, 922.673
1929-
Courageous prophet, chapters from the life of John Kline [by] Roger E. Sappington. Book design by Paul Dailey. Elgin, Ill., Brethren Press [1964] 128 p. illus. 21 cm. Bibliographical references included in "Notes" (p. [118]-124) [BX7843.K55S2] 64-4948
1. Kline, John, 1797-1864. I. Title.

Kloh, Hasteen.

NEWCOMB, Franc (Johnson) 970.2
Hosteen Klah, Navaho medicine man and sand painter. Norman, Univ. of Okla. Pr. [c.1964] xxxii, 227p. illus., maps (1 fold.) ports. 23cm. (Civilization of the Amer. Indian ser.) Bibl. 64-20759 5.95
1. Kloh, Hasteen. 2. Navaho Indians. I. Title. II. Series. **BIP**

Klose, Virginia Taylor,

KLOSE, Virginia Taylor, 920.7
1911-
Call me mother illustrated by Mircea Vasiliu. New York, Dodd, Mead [1956] 243p. illus. 21cm. [CT275.K62A3] 56-9874
I. Title.

Knapp, Bliss, 1877-

HOUPT, Charles 289.5'092'4 B
Theodore, 1912-
Bliss Knapp, Christian Scientist / Charles Theodore Houpt. [s.l.] : Houpt, 1976. iv, 619, [2] p., [6] leaves of plates : ill. ; 28

cm. "References to and articles by Bliss Knapp in the Christian Science periodicals": p. [621]. [BX6996.K49H68] 76-369136
1. Knapp, Bliss, 1877- 2. Christian Science—Biography. I. Title.

Knapp, Seaman Asahel, 1833-1911.

BAILEY, Joseph Cannon, 1899- 630'.924 B
Seaman A. Knapp: schoolmaster of American agriculture. New York, Arno Press, 1971 [c1945] 307 p. port. 24 cm. (American education: its men, ideas, and institutions. Series II) Originally presented as the author's thesis, Columbia, 1944, which was issued as no. 10 of Columbia University studies in the history of American agriculture. Bibliography: p. [281]-290. [S417.K6B3 1971] 73-165702 ISBN 0-405-03691-4
1. Knapp, Seaman Asahel, 1833-1911. 2. Agriculture—United States. 3. Agricultural extension work—United States. I. Title. II. Series. III. Series: Columbia University studies in the history of American agriculture, no. 10

Knapp, William Ireland,

KNAPP, William Ireland, 1835-1908. 828'.8'09 B
Life, writings and correspondence of George Borrow, 1803-1881; based on official and other authentic sources, by William I. Knapp. Detroit, Gale Research Co., 1967. 2 v. illus., facsims, map, plans, port. 22 cm. (The Gale library of lives and letters. British writers series) Title page includes original imprint: New York, Putnam, 1899. "Chronological bibliography (1823-1874)": (v. 2, p. 341-375) [PR4156.K5 1967] 67-23870
I. Borrow, George Henry, 1803-1881. II. Title.

Knaths, Karl, 1891-

MOESANYI, Paul. 759.13
Karl Knaths. Introd. by Duncan Phillips. An appreciation by Emanuel Benson. Commentary by Karl Knaths. Washington, Phillips Gallery, 1957. 101p. illus. (part col.) port. 27cm. [ND237.K59M6] 927.5 57-13428
1. Knaths, Karl, 1891- I. Title.

Knauff, Ellen Raphael, 1915-

KNAUFF, Ellen Raphael, 1915- 342'.73'082
The Ellen Knauff story. New York, Da Capo Press, 1974 [c1952] xvi, 242, 18, 2 p. 22 cm. (Civil liberties in American history) Reprint of the ed. published by Norton, New York. Bibliography: p. 237-238. [JV6507.K56 1974] 73-21679 ISBN 0-306-70230-X 12.95
1. Knauff, Ellen Raphael, 1915- 2. Jacobson, Gunther. 3. Emigration and immigration law—United States. I. Title. II. Series. **BIP**

Knievel, Evel, 1938- —Juvenile literature.

BATSON, Larry, 1930- 796.7'5'0924 B
Evel Knievel. Illustrated by John Keely. Mankato, Minn., Creative Education ; [distributed by Childrens Press, Chicago, 1974] 31 p. col. illus. 25 cm. (Superstars) A brief biography of the professional motorcycle daredevil. [GV1060.2.K58B37] 92 74-18302 ISBN 0-87191-385-2 4.95
1. Knievel, Evel, 1938- —Juvenile literature. 2. Motorcycling—Juvenile literature. I. Keely, John, illus. II. Title.

KRASKE, Robert. 791'.092'2 B
Daredevils do amazing things / by Robert Kraske ; illustrated by Ivan Powell. New York : Random House, c9178. 69 p. : ill. ; 22 cm. (Step-up books ; 26) Describes the daring feats of adventures Blondin, Harry Houdini, Annie Oakley, Harry Rieseberg, and Evel Knievel. [GV1811.A1K7] 920 77-90194 ISBN 0-394-83623-5 : 2.95. ISBN 0-394-93623-X lib. bdg. : 3.99
1. Houdini, Harry, 1874-1926—Juvenile literature. 2. Oakley, Annie, 1860-1926—Juvenile literature. 3. Rieseberg, Harry Earl—Juvenile literature. 4. Knievel, Evel, 1938- —Juvenile literature. 5. Blondin, Jean Francois Gravelet, known as, 1824-1897—Juvenile literature. 6. Entertainers—United States—Biography—Juvenile literature. I. Powell, Ivan. II. Title. **BIP**

Knight, Bobby—Juvenile literature.

BATSON, Larry, 1930- 796.32'3'0924 B
An interview with Bobby Knight / by Larry Batson ; photographs by Rich Clarkson. Mankato, Minn. : Creative Education, c1977. 31 p. : col. ill. ; 25 cm. A biography of the basketball coach at the University of Indiana, whose undefeated team won the NCAA tournament in 1976. [GV884.K58B37] 92 76-42271 ISBN 0-87191-574-X lib.bdg. 5.95
1. Knight, Bobby—Juvenile literature. 2. Basketball coaches—United States—Biography—Juvenile literature. I. Clarkson, Rich. II. Title. **BIP**

Knight, Cornelia, 1758-1837.

LUTTRELL, Barbara 920.72
The prim romantic; a biography of Ellis Cornelia Knight, 1758-1837. Introd. by Roger Fulford. London, Chatto & Windus, 1965. 240p. illus., port. 23cm. Bibl. [DA538.K65L8] 66-35044 6.00
1. Knight, Cornelia, 1758-1837. I. Title.
American distributor: Verry Mystic, Conn.

Knight, David C

KNIGHT, David C 926.1
Robert Koch, father of bacteriology. Pictures by Gustav Schrotter. New York, F. Watts [1961] 165p. illus. 22cm. (A First biography) [QR31.K6K57] 61-7501
I. Koch, Robert, 1843-1910. II. Title.

Knight, Richard Payne, 1750-1824.

MESSMANN, Frank J. 914.2'03'73 B
Richard Payne Knight; the twilight of virtuosity, by Frank J. Messmann. The Hague, Mouton, 1974 [c1973] 178 p. 22 cm. (Studies in English literature, v. 89) Bibliography: p. [168]-175. [PR3539.K8M4 1974] 73-79281
1. Knight, Richard Payne, 1750-1824.
Distributed by Humanities Press, 13.75 **BIP**

Knights of Labor.

POWDERLY, Terence Vincent, 1849-1924. 331.88'092'4 B
The path I trod; the autobiography of Terence V. Powderly. Edited by Harry J. Carman, Henry David and Paul N. Guthrie. New York, AMS Press [1968] xiv, 460 p. illus. 23 cm. Reprint of the 1940 ed., which was issued as no. 6 of Columbia studies in American culture. [HD8073.P69A3 1968] 77-181971
1. Knights of Labor. 2. Labor and laboring classes—United States. I. Title. II. Series: Columbia studies in American culture, no. 6.

Knights of Malta.

PEYREFITTE, Roger. 929.71
Knights of Malta. Translated from the French by Edward Hyams. New York, Criterion Books [1959] 317 p. 21 cm. [CR4723.P413] 59-12194
1. Knights of Malta. **BIP**

Knights of Malta—Biog.

ENGEL, Claire Eliane. 923.5
Knights of Malta; a gallery of portraits. New York, Roy Publishers [1963, i.e. 1964] 204 p. illus. ports. 23 cm. Bibliography: p. 194-200. [CR4729.K55E5] 64-13619
1. Knights of Malta — Biog. I. Title.

ENGEL, Claire Eliane 923.5
Kinghts of Malta; a gallery of portraits. New York, Roy [1964, c.1963] 204p. illus., ports. 23cm. Bibl 64-13619 5.95 bds.,
1. Knights of Malta—Biog. I. Title.

Knives.

HUGHES, B. R. 621.9'3
The Gun digest book of knives, by B. R. Hughes and Jack Lewis. Chicago, Follett Pub. Co. [1973] 287 p. illus. 28 cm. [TS380.H85] 73-83465 ISBN 0-695-80429-4 5.95
1. Knives. 2. Knifesmiths—United States. I. Lewis, Jack P., 1924- joint author. II. Title. III. Title: Book of knives.

Knollys, Hanserd, 1599?-1691.

DUNCAN, Pope A. 922.642
Hanserd Knollys: seventeenth-century Baptist. Nashville, Broadman [c.1965] 61p. 21cm. Bibl. [BX6495.K63D8] 65-12865 .95 pap.,
1. Knollys, Hanserd, 1599?-1691. I. Title.

DUNCAN, Pope A v. 12
Hanserd Knollys; seventeenth-century Baptist [by] Pope A. Duncan. Nashville, Broadman Press [1965] 61 p. 21 cm. Bibliography: p. 52-60.
1. Knollys, Hanserd, 1599?-1691. I. Title.

DUNCAN, Pope A 922.642
Hanserd Knollys; seventeenth-century Baptist [by] Pope A. Duncan. Nashville, Broadman Press [1965] 61 p. 21 cm. Bibliography: p. 52-60. [BX6495.K63D8] 65-12865
1. Knollys, Hanserd, 1599?-1691. I. Title.

Knopf, Alfred A., 1892-

ALFRED A. Knopf at 60, September 12, 1952 [Norwood Mass.] Priv. print. [1952] 59 p. port. 20 cm. "Edition ... of 250 copies for presentation only." [Z473.K72A38] 52-4457 926.55
1. Knopf, Alfred A., 1892-
Contents Omitted.

Knott, Walter.

KOOIMAN, Helen W. 791'.068'24 B
Walter Knott, keeper of the flame, by Helen Kooiman. Fullerton, Calif., Plycon Press [1973] xii, 236 p. illus. 24 cm. [TX910.5.K6K66] 73-83770 7.95
1. Knott, Walter. I. Title. **BIP**

NYGAARD, Norman Eugene, 1897- 926.3
Walter Knott, twentieth century pioneer; the story of the man behind Knott's Berry Farm, internationally-known tourist attraction, by Norman E. Nygaard. Grand Rapids, Mich., Zondervan [1965] 118p. illus., ports. 21cm. [TX910.5.K6N9] 64-7640 2.50
1. Knott, Walter. I. Title.

Knowles, Paul John.

FAWKES, Sandy. 364.1'523'0924 B
Killing time / Sandy Fawkes. 1st American ed. New York : Taplinger Pub. Co., 1979, c1977. 167 p. ; 22 cm. [HV6248.K59F38 1979] 78-27405 ISBN 0-8008-4463-7 : 8.95
1. Knowles, Paul John. 2. Crime and criminals—United States—Biography. I. Title.

Knox, Edmund George Valpy, 1881-1971.

FITZGERALD, Penelope. 920'.042
The Knox brothers / Penelope Fitzgerald. 1st American ed. New York : Coward, McCann & Geoghegan, c1977. p. cm. [BX4705.K6F57 1977] 77-22621 ISBN 0-698-10860-4 : 10.95
1. Knox, Ronald Arbuthnott, 1888-1957. 2. Knox, Edmund George Valpy, 1881-1971. 3. Knox, Wilfred Lawrence, 1886-1950. 4. Knox, Dillwyn, 1883-1943. 5. England—Biography. I. Title. **BIP**

Knox, Henry, 1750-1806.

BROOKS, Noah, 1830-1903. 973.3'092'4 B
Henry Knox, a soldier of the Revolution. New York, Da Capo Press, 1974 [c1900] xv, 286 p. illus. 22 cm. (The Era of the American Revolution) Reprint of the ed. published by Putnam, New York. [E207.K74B8 1974] 74-8496 ISBN 0-306-70617-2 15.00
1. Knox, Henry, 1750-1806. I. Title. **BIP**

CALLAHAN, North. 923.573
Henry Knox, General Washington's general. New York, Rinehart [1958] 404 p. illus. 24 cm. Includes bibliography. [E207.K74C18] 58-10699
1. Knox, Henry, 1750-1806.

GRIFFITHS, Thomas Morgan. 929.2
Major General Henry Knox and the last heirs to Montpelier. Edited by Arthur Morgan Griffiths. Monmouth, Me., Monmouth Press, 1965. 130 p. illus. (part col.) maps, ports. (part col.) 24 cm. [E207.K74G7] 66-4264
1. Knox, Henry, 1750-1806. 2. Thomaston, Me. Montpelier. 3. Knox family. I. Title.

Knox, Henry, 1750-1806—Juvenile literature.

DENZEL, Justin F. 973.4'1'0924 B
Champion of liberty, Henry Knox, by Justin F. Denzel. New York, J. Messner [1969] 188 p. 22 cm. Bibliography: p. 183-184. A biography of the man who was the first Secretary of War of the United States and one of the founders of the State of Maine. [E207.K74D4] 92 69-13046 3.50
1. Knox, Henry, 1750-1806—Juvenile literature. I. Title.

Knox, John, 1505-1572.

COWAN, Henry, 1844-1932. 285'.2'0924 B
John Knox, the hero of the Scottish Reformation. New York, AMS Press [1970] xxxiii, 404 p. illus., port. 19 cm. Reprint of the 1905 ed. Bibliography: p. xxiii-xxxiii. [BX9223.C68 1970] 70-133817
1. Knox, John, 1505-1572.

MACGREGOR, Geddes. 922.541
The thundering Scot; a portrait of John Knox. Philadelphia, Westminster Press [1957] 240p. 21cm. [BX9223.M35] 57-6850
1. Knox, John, 1505-1572. I. Title.

MUIR, Edwin, 1887-1959. 285'.2'0924 B
John Knox: portrait of a Calvinist. Freeport, N.Y., Books for Libraries Press [1971] 316 p. ports. 23 cm. Reprint of the 1929 ed. [BX9223.M8 1971] 76-148892 ISBN 0-8369-5656-7
1. Knox, John, 1505-1572.

MUIR, Edwin, 1887-1959. 285'.2'0924 B
John Knox: portrait of a Calvinist. Port Washington, N.Y., Kennikat Press [1972] 316 p. ports. 22 cm. Reprint of the 1929 ed. [BX9223.M8 1972] 78-159096 ISBN 0-8046-1639-6
1. Knox, John, 1505-1572. **BIP**

PERCY of Newcastle, Eustace Percy, baron, 1887-1958. 922.541
John Knox by Lord Eustace Percy. Foreword by the Duke of Hamilton. [American ed.] Richmond, John Knox Press [1965] 343 p. port. 21 cm. [BX9223.P45] 65-11937
1. Knox, John, 1505-1572. I. Title.

PERCY of Newcastle, Eustace Percy, baron, 1887-1958. 922.541
John Knox [by] Lord Eustace Percy. Foreword by the Duke of Hamilton. [American ed.] Richmond, John Knox Press [1965] 343 p. port. 21 cm. [BX9223.P45 1965] 65-11937
1. Knox, John, 1505-1572.

REID, William Stanford, 1913- 285'.2'0924 B
Trumpeter of God; a biography of John Knox [by] W. Stanford Reid. New York, Scribner [1974] xvi, 353 p. illus. 24 cm. Bibliography: p. [328]-340. [BX9223.R4] 73-1356 ISBN 0-684-13782-8 12.50
1. Knox, John, 1505-1572. I. Title.

RIDLEY, Jasper Godwin. 285'.2'0924 B
John Knox [by] Jasper Ridley. New York, Oxford University Press [1968] vi, 596 p. ports. 22 cm. Bibliography: p. [552]-574. [BX9223.R5] 68-55648 9.50

1. Knox, John, 1505-1572.

Knox, Robert, 1791-1862.

RAE, Isobel, 1902- 926.1
Knox, the anatomist [Edinburgh, Oliver &Boyd] Springfield, Ill., Thomas [1965, c.1964] v, 164p. illus., ports. 23cm. Bibl. [QM16.K6R3] 64-55371 6.50
1. Knox, Robert, 1791-1862. I. Title.

Knox, Ronald Arbuthnott, 1888-1957.

FITZGERALD, Penelope. 920'.042
The Knox brothers / Penelope Fitzgerald. 1st American ed. New York : Coward, McCann & Geoghegan, c1977. p. cm. [BX4705.K6F57 1977] 77-22621 ISBN 0-698-10860-4 : 10.95
1. Knox, Ronald Arbuthnott, 1888-1957. 2. Knox, Edmund George Valpy, 1881-1971. 3. Knox, Wilfred Lawrence, 1886-1950. 4. Knox, Dillwyn, 1883-1943. 5. England—Biography. I. Title. BIP

WAUGH, Evelyn, 1903- 922.242
Monsignor Ronald Knox, fellow of Trinity College, Oxford, and Protonotary Apostolic to His Holiness Pope Pius XII. Compiled from the original sources. [1st American ed.] Boston, Little, Brown [1959] 357 p. illus. 22 cm. London ed. (Chapman & Hall) has title: The life of the Right Reverend Ronald Knox ... [BX4705.K6W3 1959a] 59-11891
1. Knox, Ronald Arbuthnott, 1888-1957. I. Title.

Knox, Wilfred Lawrence, 1886-1950.

FITZGERALD, Penelope. 920'.042
The Knox brothers / Penelope Fitzgerald. 1st American ed. New York : Coward, McCann & Geoghegan, c1977. p. cm. [BX4705.K6F57 1977] 77-22621 ISBN 0-698-10860-4 : 10.95
1. Knox, Ronald Arbuthnott, 1888-1957. 2. Knox, Edmund George Valpy, 1881-1971. 3. Knox, Wilfred Lawrence, 1886-1950. 4. Knox, Dillwyn, 1883-1943. 5. England—Biography. I. Title. BIP

Knox, William, 1732-1810.

BELLOT, Leland J., 1936- 973.3'1'0924 B
William Knox : the life & thought of an eighteenth-century imperialists / by Leland J. Bellot. Austin : University of Texas Press, c1977. xii, 264 p. : port. ; 24 cm. Includes index. Bibliography: p. 249-257. [DA506.K58B44] 76-44006 ISBN 0-292-79007-4 : 12.95
1. Knox, William, 1732-1810. 2. Statesmen—Great Britain—Biography. BIP

Knudson, K. O., 1894-

HARVEY, James Monroe. 370'.92'4 B
K. O. Knudson: a true life story. Narrated by James Monroe Harvey. [Las Vegas, Nev., 1972] 286 p. 23 cm. "With the exception of K. O. Knudson, his father, mother, and brothers, the characters in this true life story are entirely the product of the author's imagination." [LA2317.K57H37] 74-186125 9.95
1. Knudson, K. O., 1894- I. Title.

Kosciuszko, Tadeusz Andrzej Bonawentura, 1746-1817.

ABODAHER, David J. 943.8'02'0924 B
Warrior on two continents: Thaddeus Kosciuszko [by] David J. Abodaher. New York, J. Messner [1968] 192 p. 22 cm. Bibliography: p. [185] A biography of the Polish patriot and champion of freedom who fought in the American Revolution and then spent the rest of his life fighting for Polish independence. [DK434.8.K8A63] 92 AC 68
1. Kosciuszko, Tadeusz Andrzej Bonawentura, 1746-1817. I. Title.

HAIMAN, Miecislaus, 1888-1949. 973.3'3'0924 B
Kosciuszko in the American Revolution. With a new introd. and pref. by George Athan Billias. Boston, Gregg Press, 1972 [c1943] xi, vii, 198 p. illus. 24 cm. (The American Revolutionary series. American and French accounts of the American Revolution) Reprint of the ed. published by Polish Institute of Arts and Sciences in America, New York, which was issued as no. 4 of Polish Institute series. Bibliography: p. 168-174. [E207.K8H3 1972] 72-10782 ISBN 0-8398-0807-0
1. Kosciuszko, Tadeusz Andrzej Bonawentura, 1746-1817. 2. United States—History—Revolution, 1775-1783. I. Title. II. Series: Polish Institute of Arts and Sciences in America. Polish Institute series, no. 4. III. Series: American and French accounts of the American Revolution. BIP

HAIMAN, Miecislaus, 1888-1949. 943.8'02'0924
Kosciuszko, leader and exile / by Miecislaus Haiman. New York : Kosciuszko Foundation, 1977. 183 p., [1] leaf of plates : ill. ; 24 cm. (The Library of Polish studies ; v. 5) Continues Kosciuszko in the American Revolution. Reprint of the 1946 ed. published by Polish Institute of Arts & Sciences in America, New York as no. 9 of Polish Institute series. Includes index. Bibliography: p. 157-167. [E207.K8H32 1977] 76-17926 ISBN 0-917004-10-8 : 7.50
1. Kosciuszko, Tadeusz Andrzej Bonawentura, 1746-1817. 2. Generals—Poland—Biography. I. Title. II. Series. III. Series: Polish Institute of Arts and Sciences in America. Polish Institute series ; no. 9.
Publisher's address : 15 E. 65th St., New York, NY 10021

Kobayashi, Issa, 1763-1827, in fiction, drama, poetry, etc.

KOBAYASHI, Issa, 1763-1827. 895.6'8'307
The year of my life. A translation of Issa's Oraga haru by Nobuyuki Yuasa. 2d ed. Berkeley, University of California Press [1972] 140 p. illus. 19 cm. On cover: An autobiography in haibun - a mixed form of haiku and prose. [PL797.2.O7E5 1972] 73-161158 ISBN 0-520-02328-5 2.45
1. Kobayashi, Issa, 1763-1827, in fiction, drama, poetry, etc. I. Title.

Kobayashi, Issa, 1763-1827—Juvenile literature.

FUKUDA, Hanako. [92]
Wind in my hand. With the editorial assistance of Mark Taylor. Haiku translations by Hanako Fukuda. Illustrated by Lydia Cooley. San Carlos, Calif., Golden Gate Junior Books [1970] 61 p. illus. (part col.) 27 cm. The life of the eighteenth-century Japanese haiku poet. Includes translations of some of the poems. [PL797.2.Z5F83] 70-84698 4.95
1. Kobayashi, Issa, 1763-1827—Juvenile literature. I. Cooley, Lydia, illus. II. Title.

Kobayashi, Kokei,

KOBAYASHI, Kokei, 1883-1957. 759.952
Kobayashi Kokei; 1883-1957. Text by Michiaki Lawakita. English adaptation by Ray andrew Miller. 51st Engliah ed.*Kobayashi Kokei eighteen eighty-three-nineteen fifty-seven Rutland, Vt., C. E. Tuttle Co. [1957] 1v. (unpaged) 47 plates (incl. cover, part fold., part col.) 18cm. e(Kodansha library of Japanese art, no. 11) Bibliography on last page. [ND1059.K6K3] 927.5 57-12495
I. Kawakita, Michiaki, 1914- II. Miller, Roy Andrew. III. Title.

Koch, Frederick Henry. 1877-1944.

SELDEN, Samuel, 1899- 792.0924 (B)
Frederick Henry Koch, pioneer playmaker; a brief biography, by Samuel Selden and Mary Tom Sphangos. With notes by Jonathan Daniels [and others] Chapel Hill, University of North Carolina Library, 1954. viii, 92p. illus., port. 23cm. (The University of North Carolins. Library extension publication, v. 19, no. 4) (Series. North Carolina. University. Library. Extension Dept. Library extension publication, v. 19, no. 4) 'Folk playmaking, by Frederick H. Koch': p. [59]-68. [PN2287.K68S4] 54-62896
1. Koch, Frederick Henry. 1877-1944. 2. Carolina playmakers, Chapel Hill, N. C. I. Sphangos, Mary Tom, joint author. II. Title. III. Series.

Koch, Howard—Biography.

KOCH, Howard. 812'.5'2 B
As time goes by : memoirs of a writer / by Howard Koch. 1st ed. New York : Harcourt Brace Jovanovich, c1979. xvii, 220 p., [4] leaves of plates : ill. ; 22 cm. [PS3521.O25Z463] 78-22260 ISBN 0-15-109769-0 : 10.95
1. Koch, Howard—Biography. 2. Screen writers—United States—Biography. I. Title.

Koch, Robert, 1843-1910.

DOLAN, Edward F 1924- 926.1
Adventure with a microscope; a story of Robert Koch, by Edward F. Dolan, Jr. New York, Dodd, Mead [1964] x, 240 p. 21 cm. [QR31.K6D6] 64-18743
1. Koch, Robert, 1843-1910. I. Title.

KNIGHT, David C. 926.1
Robert Koch, father of bacteriology. Pictures by Gustav Schrotter. New York, Watts [c. 1961] 165p. (First biography) 61-7501 1.95
1. Koch, Robert, 1843-1910. I. Title.

Koch, Rudolf, 1876-1934.

A B C Hook. v. 12
[Meriden, Conn., Printed by the Meriden Gravure Company for the Department of Printing and Graphic Arts of the Harvard College Library, 1956] unpaged. illus. 14cm. '600 copies printed.' 'A note about this reproduction', by Philip Hofer: [2]p.] at end.
1. Koch, Rudolf, 1876-1934. 2. Primers. I. Harwerth, Willi, 1894- II. Hofer, Philip, 1898-

Koch, William Frederick,

WAHL, Albert Leopold, 1906-1948. 926.1
The birth of a science, by Albert L. Wahl, Bessie L. Rehwinkel [and] Lawrence Reilly. [3d ed., rev,] Detroit, Lutheran Research Society [c1950] 315 p. illus., facsims. 20 cm. [R154.K42W3] 51-1151
1. Koch, William Frederick, 1885- I. Title.

Kochtitzky, Oscar, 1830-1891.

HESS, Caroline. 920
An adventurous career, by Caroline Hess and Isabella Hess. [n. p., 1958] 138p. illus. 22cm. [CT275.K75H4] 58-40471
1. Kochtitzky, Oscar, 1830-1891. I. Hess, Isabella, joint author. II. Title.

Kochtitzky, Otto.

KOCHTITZKY, Otto. 926.2
Otto Kochtitzky; the story of a busy life. Cape Girardeau, Mo., Ramfre Press [1957] 172p. illus. 23cm. [TC140.K55A3] 57-38194
I. Title.

Kodaly, Zoltan, 1882-

YOUNG, Percy Marshall, 1912- 780.92
Zoltan Kadaly. a Hungariam musician. london, E. Benn [dist. New York, Grove, c.1964] xvi, 231p. music. plates (incl. facsims.) 23cm. Bibl. 64-54500 6.50
1. Kodaly, Zoltan, 1882- I. Title.

Koenigsberg, Moses.

KOENIGSBERG, Moses. 070'.924 B
King news, an autobiography. Freeport, N.Y., Books for Libraries Press [1972] 511 p. 23 cm. (BCL/select bibliographies index reprint series) Reprint of the 1941 ed. [PN4874.K63A3 1972] 73-39377 ISBN 0-8369-9917-7
I. Title.

Koerner, William Henry Dethlef.

HUTCHINSON, William Henry, 1910- 741'.092'4 B
The world, the work, and the West of W. H. D. Koerner / W. H. Hutchinson. 1st ed. Norman : University of Oklahoma Press, c1978. xii, 243 p. : ill. (some col.) ; 29 cm. Includes index. Bibliography: p. 234-238. [NC975.5.K63H87] 78-58125 ISBN 0-8061-1471-1 : 35.00
1. Koerner, William Henry Dethlef. 2. Illustrators—United States—Biography. 3. The West in art. I. Title. BIP

Koestler, Arthur, 1905-

ATKINS, John Alfred, 1916- 928.2
Arthur Koestler. New York, Roy Publishers [1956] 224p. 22cm. [PR6021] 57-10084
1. Koestler, Arthur, 1905- I. Title.

KOESTLER, Arthur, 1905- 928.2
Arrow in the blue, an autobiography. New York, Macmillan, 1961 [c.1962] 353p. (Macmillan paperback, 40) 1.75 pap.,
I. Title.

KOESTLER, Arthur, 1905- 928.2
Arrow in the blue, an autobiography. New York, Macmillan, 1952-54. 2v. illus., ports. 22cm. Vol. 2 has also special title: The invisible writing. [PR6021.O4Z5] 52-3443
I. Title. II. Title: The invisible writing.

KOESTLER, Arthur, 1905- 823'.9'12 B
Arrow in the blue. [1st American Danube ed. New York] Macmillan [1970, c1969] 414 p. illus., ports. 21 cm. (The Danube edition) The first volume of an autobiography: 1905-31; v. 2 has title The invisible writing. Originally published in 1952, reprinted with a new pref. by the author. [PR6021.O4Z5 1970] 77-85781 7.95

KOESTLER, Arthur, 1905- 928.2
The invisible writing; an autobiography. Boston, Beacon Press [1955, c1954] 431p. illus. 21cm. (Beacon paperbacks, 18) Beacon contemporary affairs series.

Published in 1954 as v. 2 of the author's Arrow in the blue. [PR6021] 55-13803
I. Title.

KOESTLER, Arthur, 1905- 823'.9'12 B
The invisible writing. [1st American Danube ed. New York] Macmillan [1970, c1969] 526 p. illus., ports. 21 cm. (The Danube edition) The second volume of an autobiography, 1932-40; v. 1 has title Arrow in the blue. Originally published in 1954, reprinted with author's Note to the Danube ed. [PR6021.O4Z53 1970] 70-85782 8.95
I. Title. BIP

MAYS, Wolfe. 828'.9'1209 B
Arthur Koestler. Valley Forge, Pa., Judson Press [1973] 57 p. 19 cm. (Makers of modern thought) Bibliography: p. 56-57. [B1646.K774M38 1973] 72-7723 ISBN 0-8170-0594-3 1.50 (pbk.)
1. Koestler, Arthur, 1905-

Koffend, John B.

KOFFEND, John B. 301.42'8
A letter to my wife [by] John B. Koffend. New York, Saturday Review Press [1972] xxxv, 218 p. 22 cm. [PN4874.K635A3] 74-154273 ISBN 0-8415-0127-0 6.95
I. Title.

Kogan, David S 1929-1951.

KOGAN, David S 1929-1951. 920
Diary. Edited, with an introd., by Meyer Levin. New York, Beechhurst Press [1955] 255p. illus. 22cm. [CT275.K82A3] 55-14472
I. Title.

Koht, Halvdan,

KOHT, Halvdan, 1873- 928.3982
Education of an historian. With an introd. by WaldemarWestergaard. Translated and with notes by Erik Wahlgren. [1st ed.] New York, R. Speller, 1957. xv, 237p. illus., ports. 22cm. (Makers of history) Translation of Historikar i laere. [DL445.7.K65A33] 57-10591
I. Title.

Kohut, Rebekah (Bettelheim),

KOHUT, Rebekah (Bettelheim), 1864- 922.96
More yesterdays, an autobiography (1925-49) A sequel to My portion. Foreword by Fannie Hurst. New York, Bloch Pub. Co., 1950. xii, 209 p. 20 cm. [HQ1413.K6A32] 50-7290
I. Title.

Kohut, Rebekah Bettelheim, 1864-1951.

KOHUT, Rebekah (Bettelheim), 1864- 922.96
More yesterdays, an autobiography (1925-49) A sequel to My portion. Foreword by Fannie Hurst. New York, Bloch Pub. Co., 1950. xii, 209 p. 20 cm. [HQ1413.K6A32] 50-7290
I. Title.

KOHUT, Rebekah Bettelheim, 1864-1951. 296'.092'4 B
My portion : (an autobiography) / Rebekah Kohut. New York : Arno Press, 1975 [c1925] xvi, 301 p. ; 23 cm. (The Modern Jewish experience) Reprint of the ed. published by T. Seltzer, New York. Includes index. [HQ1413.K6A37 1975] 74-27995 ISBN 0-405-06722-4 : 19.00
1. Kohut, Rebekah Bettelheim, 1864-1951. I. Title. II. Series.

Kokoschka, Oskar, 1886-

HODIN, Josef Paul 759.2 (B)
Oskar Kokoschka; the artist and his time; a biographical study by J. P. Hodin. [Greenwich, Conn.] N.Y. Graphic [1966] xii, 251p. illus. (pt. col.) ports. 25cm. Bibl. [ND538.K62H583] 66-15797 12.50
1. Kokoschka, Oskar, 1886- I. Title.

HODIN, Josef Paul. 759.2 (B)
Oskar Kokoschka; the artist and his time; a biographical study by J. P. Hodin. [Greenwich, Conn.] New York, Graphic Society [1966] xii, 251 p. illus. (part col.) ports. 25 cm. Bibliography: p. 235-245. [ND538.K62H583] 66-15797
1. Kokoschka, Oskar, 1886- I. Title.

KOKOSCHKA, Oskar, 1886- 759.2 B
My life / Oskar Kokoschka ; translated by David Britt. 1st American ed. New York : Macmillan, 1974. 240 p., [8] leaves of plates : ill. ; 24 cm. Translation of Mein Leben. Includes index. [ND511.5.K6A213 1974] 74-2645 10.00
1. Kokoschka, Oskar, 1886- 2. Painters—Austria—Correspondence, reminiscences, etc. I. Title.

Kolbe, Emma Eliza (Coe) 1850-1913.

ROBSON, Robert William, 1885- 995
Queen Emma, the Samoan-American girl who cfounded an empire in 19th century New Guinea. Sydney, Pacific Pubns.; San Francisco, Tri-Ocean [1966, c.1965] 239p illus., map, ports. 21cm. [DU746.K6R6] 66-522 4.75
1. Kolbe, Emma Eliza (Coe) 1850-1913. I. Title.

Kolbe, Maximilian, Father, 1894-1941.

ROBERTO, Brother, 1927- 922.2438
Music from the hunger pit; a story of Father Maximilian Kolbe. Illus. by Anthony Joyce. Notre Dame, Ind., Dujarie Press [1954] 96p. illus. 24cm. [BX4705.K64R6] 54-41986
1. Kolbe, Maximilian, Father, 1894-1941. I. Title.

ROBERTO, Brother, 1927- 922.2438
A tomb for the living; a story of Father Maximilian Kolbe. Notre Dame, Ind., Dujarie Press [1957] 139p. illus. 22cm. [BX4705.K64R62] 57-37127
1. Kolbe, Maximilian, Father, 1894-1941. I. Title.

Kollek, Teddy, 1911-

KOLLEK, Teddy, 1911- 956.94'4'050924
For Jerusalem : a life / by Teddy Kollek, with his son, Amos Kollek. 1st American ed. New York : Random House, c1978. xii, 269 p., [8] leaves of plates : ill. ; 24 cm. Includes index. [DS109.86.K64A33 1978] limited ed. : 25.00
1. Kollek, Teddy, 1911- 2. Jerusalem—Mayors—Biography. I. Kollek, Amos, joint author. II. Title.

Kollontai, Aleksandra Mikhailovna, 1872-1952.

CLEMENTS, Barbara Evans, 1945- 335.43'092'4 B
Bolshevik feminist : the life of Aleksandra Kollontai / Barbara Evans Clements. Bloomington : Indiana University Press, 1979, c1978 xiii, 352 p., [5] leaves of plates : ill. ; 24 cm. Includes index. Bibliography: p. 315-344. [HQ1662.K6C55] 78-3240 ISBN 0-253-31209-4 15.00
1. Kollontai, Aleksandra Mikhailovna, 1872-1952. 2. Socialists—Russia—Biography. I. Title. BIP

Kollwitz, Kathe Schmidt, 1867-1945.

KEARNS, Martha. 769'.92'4 B
Kaethe Kollwitz / by Martha Kearns. Old Westbury, N.Y. : Feminist Press, 1974. p. cm. (Feminist Press biography ; no. 5) Bibliography: p. [NE654.K6K42] 74-26743 ISBN 0-912670-15-0
1. Kollwitz, Kathe Schmidt, 1867-1945.

KLEIN, Mina C. 709'.2'4 B
Kathe Kollwitz, life in art / Mina C. Klein, H. Arthur Klein. New York : Schocken Books, 1975, c1972. xvi, 183 p. : ill. ; 26 cm. Reprint of the ed. published by Holt, Rinehart and Winston. Includes index. Bibliography: p. 171-172. [NC251.K6K55 1975] 75-10858 ISBN 0-8052-0504-7 pbk. : 6.95
1. Kollwitz, Kathe Schmidt, 1867-1945. I. Klein, H. Arthur, joint author. II. Title.

Koningsberger, Hans.

KONINGSBERGER, Hans. 813'.5'4 B
The almost world [by] Hans Koning. New York, Dial Press, 1972. 213 p. 23 cm. Autobiographical. [PS3561.O46Z5] 72-3632
I. Title. BIP

Konsag, Ferdinand, 1703-1759.

ZEVALLOS, Francisco. 972'.2'020924 B
The apostolic life of Fernando Consag, explorer of Lower California. Translated and annotated, with an introd., by Manuel P. Servin. Los Angeles, Dawson's Book Shop, 1968. 93 p. illus., facsims., map. 22 cm. (Baja California travels series, 15) 500 copies printed. Translation of Carta del Padre Provincial, Francisco Zevallos sobre la apostolica vida, y virtudes del P. Fernando Konsag. Bibliographical footnotes. [F864.K7Z413] 68-31888
1. Konsag, Ferdinand, 1703-1759. 2. Jesuits in Baja California. 3. Missions—Baja California. I. Servin, Manuel P., 1920- tr. II. Title. III. Series.

Kook, Abraham Isaac, 1865-1935.

AGUS, Jacob Bernard, 1911- 296.6'1'0924 B
High priest of rebirth; the life, times, and thought of Abraham Isaac Kuk, by Jacob B. Agus. [2d ed.] New York, Bloch Pub. Co. [1972] xvii, 243 p. 22 cm. First ed. published in 1946 under title: Banner of Jerusalem. Includes bibliographical references. [BM755.K66A5 1972] 79-189017 ISBN 0-8197-0281-1 6.95
1. Kook, Abraham Isaac, 1865-1935. I. Title. BIP

Koolau, fl. 1864.

TEXEIRA, John D. 920.8
Koolau, leper king of Kalalau Ke Ana. New York, Vantage [1963, c.1962] 93p. 21cm. 63-4421 2.50 bds.,
1. Koolau, fl. 1864. I. Title.

Koontz, Bessie B.,

KOONTZ, Bessie B., 1893- 209'.24 B
Trails through God's back pastures, by Bessie B. Koontz. Philadelphia, Dorrance [1968] 171 p. 22 cm. Autobiographical. [BR1725.K66A3] 68-22807 4.00
I. Title.

Kooper, Al.

KOOPER, Al. 784'.092'4 B
Nothing personal : a godfather of rock remembers the sixties / by Al Kooper, with Ben Edmonds. New York : Stein and Day, [1975] p. cm. [ML420.K8A3] 75-11758 ISBN 0-8128-1840-7 . 8.95
1. Kooper, Al. 2. Rock musicians—Correspondence, reminiscences, etc. I. Edmonds, Ben, joint author. II. Title.

Kootenay, B.C. (District)—History.

AFFLECK, Edward Lloyd. 971.1'45 S
Kootenay pathfinders : settlement in the Kootenay District, 1885-1920 / by Edward L. Affleck. [Vancouver, B.C. : A. Nicolls Press, c1976] iv, 222 p. : ill. ; 28 cm. (His Kootenays in retrospect ; v. 2) Includes index. Bibliography: p. 21-22. [F1089.K7A36 vol. 2] 971.1'45 77-367249 ISBN 0-920034-02-0
1. Kootenay, B.C. (District)—History. 2. Pioneers—British Columbia—Kootenay District—Biography. 3. Frontier and pioneer life—British Columbia—Kootenay (District) I. Title.

Kopay, David.

KOPAY, David. 796.33'2'0924 B
The David Kopay story : an extraordinary self-revelation / by David Kopay and Perry Deane Young. New York : Arbor House, c1977. xii, 247 p. : ill. ; 22 cm. [GV939.K6A34 1977] 76-29229 ISBN 0-87795-145-4 : 8.95
1. Kopay, David. 2. Football players—United States—Biography. 3. Homosexuals, Male—Biography. I. Young, Perry Deane, joint author. II. Title.

Kopelev, Lev Zalmanovich.

KOPELEV, Lev Zalmanovich. 365'.45'0924 B
To be preserved forever / Lev Kopelev ; translated and edited by Anthony Austin ; published and translated under the auspices of Ardis. Philadelphia : Lippincott, c1977. 268 p., [4] leaves of plates : ill. ; 25 cm. Abridged translation of Khranit' vechno. [HV8959.R9K6613 1977] 77-1926 ISBN 0-397-01140-7 : 12.50
1. Kopelev, Lev Zalmanovich. 2. Political prisoners—Russia—Biography. I. Austin, Anthony. II. Title.

Kopf, Carl Heath, 1902-1958.

ALLDREDGE, Margarete J 922.573
Carl Heath Kopf, a man of God. Nashville, Parthenon Press [1959] 109p. illus. 23cm. [BX7260.K65A5] 59-3096
1. Kopf, Carl Heath, 1902-1958. I. Title.

Kopf, Maxim,

KOPF, Maxim, 1892- 759.371
Maxim Kopf. New York, Praeger [1960] 92p. plates (part col.) 31cm. (Books that matter) [ND538.K66A5] 60-16694
I. Title
Contents omitted.

Kopp, Sheldon B., 1929-

KOPP, Sheldon B., 1929 616.8'914
An end to innocence : facing life without illustions / Sheldon Kopp. New York : Macmillan, c1978. p. cm. Includes bibliographical references. [BF575.I48K66] 78-12450 ISBN 0-02-566470-0 : 7.95
1. Kopp, Sheldon B., 1929- 2. Innocence (Psychology) 3. Psychotherapy patients—Cases, clinical reports, statistics. 4. Psychologists—United States—Biography. I. Title.

Kopperl, Bert.

KOPPERL, Bert. 770'.92'4 B
With two wheels and a camera / Bert Kopperl. 1st ed. Hicksville, N.Y. : Exposition Press, c1979. ix, 242 p., [32] leaves of plates : ill. ; 24 cm. (An Exposition-banner book) [TR140.K66A34] 79-52360 ISBN 0-682-49352-X : 12.50
1. Kopperl, Bert. 2. Photographers—United States—Biography. I. Title. BIP

Korbut, Olga, 1955-

BEECHAM, Justin. 796.4'1'0924 B
Olga. With photos. by Alan Baker and others, and illus. by Paul Buckle of the Diagram Group. New York, Paddington Press [1974] 128 p. illus. 24 cm. [GV460.2.K67B43] 73-15022 ISBN 0-8467-0018-2 2.95
1. Korbut, Olga, 1955- 2. Gymnastics.

Korbut, Olga, 1955- —Juvenile literature.

JACOBS, Linda. 796.4'1'0924 B
Olga Korbut, tears and triumph. St. Paul, EMC Corp. [1974] 38 p. illus. 24 cm. (Her Women who win) A biography of the tiny Russian gymnast who at the age of seventeen won three gold medals in the 1972 Olympics. [GV460.2.K67J32 1974] 92 74-2384 ISBN 0-88436-124-1 3.95 (lib. bdg.)
1. Korbut, Olga, 1955- —Juvenile literature. 2. Gymnastics for women—Juvenile literature.
Pbk. 1.75; ISBN 0-88436-125-X

SMITH, Jay H. 796.4'1'0924 B
Olga Korbut, by Jay H. Smith. Illustrated by Harold Henriksen. Mankato, Minn., Creative Education [1974] p. cm. A brief

biography of the Russian gymnast who captured the attention of the American public during the 1972 Olympics. [GV460.2.K67S58] 92 74-19169 ISBN 0-87191-384-4 4.95
1. Korbut, Olga, 1955- —Juvenile literature. I. Henriksen, Harold, illus. II. Title. BIP

SUPONEV, Michael. 796.4'1'0924 B
Olga Korbut : a biographical portrait / by Michael Suponev. 1st ed. Garden City, N.Y. : Doubleday, 1975. 87 p., [16] leaves of plates : ill. ; 21 cm. Translation of Olga Korbut. A biography of the famous Soviet gymnast stressing her career and including her suggested exercises for making the body supple in preparation for real gymnastics. [GV460.2.K67S9613] 92 73-11636 ISBN 0-385-09498-1 : 6.95
1. Korbut, Olga, 1955- —Juvenile literature. 2. Gymnastics for women—Juvenile literature. I. Title.

SUPONEV, Michael. 796.4'1'0924 B
Olga Korbut: a biographical portrait. [New York] Warner Books [1976 c1975] 78 p., [16] leaves of plates ill. 18 cm. Translation of Olga Korbut. A biography of the famous Soviet gymnast stressing her career and including her suggested exercises for making the body supple in preparation for real gymnastics. [GV460.2K67S9613] 1.25 (pbk.)
1. Kobut, Olga, 1955-—Juvenile literature. 2. Gymnastics for women—Juvenile literature. I. Title.
L.C. card no. of 1975 Doubleday edition: 73-11636. BIP

TAYLOR, Paula. 796.4'1'0924 B
Gymnastics' happy superstar, Olga Korbut / by Paula Taylor. [Mankato, MN] : Creative Education, [c1977] 30 p. : ill. ; 19 cm. (The Allstars) A biography of the young Russian gymnast who stunned Olympic spectators by performing maneuvers not thought possible such as a back somersault from the balance beam. [GV460.2.K67T39] 92 76-28451 ISBN 0-87191-581-2 lib.bdg. 4.95
1. Korbut, Olga, 1955- —Juvenile literature. 2. Gymnasts—Russia—Biography—Juvenile literature. I. Title.

Korchnoi, Viktor, 1931—

KORCHNOI, Viktor, 1931- 794.1'092'4 B
Chess is my life : autobiography and games / Victor Korchnoi ; translated by Ken Neat. New York : Arco Pub. Co., 1978. 167 p. ; 22 cm. Includes indexes. [GV1439.K637A34] 77-17659 ISBN 0-668-04528-0 : 8.95
1. Korchnoi, Viktor, 1931- 2. Chess Mayers—Russia—Biography. 3. Chess—Collections of games. I. Title. BIP

Korda, Alexander, Sir, 1893-1956.

KORDA, Michael, 1933- 791.43'0232'0924 B
Charmed lives : a family romance / Michael Korda. 1st ed. New York : Random House, c1979. 498 p., [16] leaves of plates : ill. ; 24 cm. Includes index. [PN1998.A3K587] 79-4762 ISBN 0-394-41954-5 : 15.00
1. Korda, Alexander, Sir, 1893-1956. 2. Moving-picture producers and directors – Great Britain—Biography. 3. Moving-picture producers and directors—United States—Biography. I. Title. BIP

Korea—History.

IM, Yong-sin, 1899- 923.2519
My forty year fight for Korea, by Louise Yim, with the editorial assistance of Emanuel H. Demby. New York, A. A. Wyn [1951] 313 p. 22 cm. [DS916.5.I5A3] 51-14062
1. Korea—History. I. Title.

Korean War, 1950-1953—Personal narratives, American.

*WILKINSON, Allen Byron, 1930- 951.9'042 [B]
Up front Korea. [First ed.] New York, Pilot Books [1974] 440 p. 18 cm. Autobiographical. [DS921.6] 1.98 (pbk.)
1. Korean War, 1950-1953—Personal narratives, American. I. Title.

Korean War, 1950-1953—Prisoners and prisons.

DEAN, William Frishe, 1899- 951.9'042'0924 B
General Dean's story, as told to William L. Worden by William F. Dean. Westport, Conn., Greenwood Press [1973, c1954] x, 305 p. illus. 22 cm. [DS921.D4 1973] 72-12310 ISBN 0-8371-6690-X 14.00
1. Korean War, 1950-1953—Prisoners and prisons. I. Worden, William L. II. Title. BIP

WILLS, Morris R., 1933- 301.453'73'051
Turncoat; an American's 12 years in Communist China; the story of Morris R. Wills as told to J. Robert Moskin Englewood Cliffs, N.J., Prentice-Hall [1968] 186 p. ports. 22 cm. [DS921.2.W5] 68-13217
1. Korean War, 1950-1953—Prisoners and prisons. 2. Americans in China. I. Moskin, J. Robert. II. Title.

Koren, Else Elisabeth Hysing, 1832-1918.

KOREN, Else Elisabeth Hysing, 1832-1918. 977.7'32 B
The diary of Elisabeth Koren, 1853-1855 / translated and edited by David T. Nelson. New York : Arno Press, 1979, c1955. p. cm. (Scandinavians in America) Translation of Dagbog. Reprint of the ed. published by the Norwegian-American Historical Association, Northfield, Minn. [F629.D29K67413 1979] 78-15199 ISBN 0-405-11653-5 : 26.00
1. Koren, Else Elisabeth Hysing, 1832-1918. 2. Norwegian Americans—Iowa—Decorah—Biography. 3. Decorah, Iowa—Biography. I. Title. II. Series. BIP

Korn, Arthur, 1870-1945.

KORN, Terry. 926.2138
Trailblazer to television; the story of Arthur Korn, by Terry and Elizabeth P. Korn. Illustrated by Elizabeth P. Korn. New York, Scribner, 1950. 144 p. illus. 21 cm. [TK6635.K6K6] 50-10142
1. Korn, Arthur, 1870-1945. I. Korn, Elizabeth P. joint author. II. Title.

Kosciuszko, Tadeusz Andrzej Bonawentura, 1746-1817—Juv. lit.

I fight for freedom; v. 12
a story of Thaddeus Kosciuszko. Illus. by Carolyn Lee Jagodits. Notre Dame, Ind., Dujarie Press [1961] 95p. illus. 24cm.
1. Kosciuszko, Tadeusz Andrzej Bonawentura, 1746-1817—Juv. lit. I. Roberto, Brother, 1927-

JOHNS, Joseph P. 923.5438
Koscuiuszko; a biographical study with a historical background of the times. Detroit, Endurance [c.] 1965. x, 99p. illus., maps. 21cm. [DK434.8.K8J6] 64-15908 3.00
1. Kosciuszko, Tadeusz Andrzej Bonawentura, 1746-1817—Juvenile literature. I. Title.

Kosmas ho Aitolos, Saint, 1714-1779.

CAVARNOS, Constantine, comp. 281.9'0924 B
St. Cosmas Aitolos: great missionary, illuminator, and martyr of Greece; an account of his life, character, and message, together with selections from his teachings. Belmont, Mass., Institute for Byzantine and Modern Greek Studies [1971] 71 p. port. 21 cm. (Modern Orthodox Saints, 1) The introduction is a revision of an article by the compiler originally published in St. Vladimir's Seminary Quarterly in 1966. The biography of the Saint is by Saphiros Christodoulidis. [BX395.K67C38] 73-157457 1.50
1. Kosmas ho Aitolos, Saint, 1714-1779.

KOSMAS ho Aitolos, Saint, 1714-1779. 281.9'092'4 B
Father Kosmas, the apostle of the poor : the life of St. Kosmas Aitolos, together with an English translation of his teaching and letters / by Nomikos Michael Vaporis ; illustrated by Vasilia Laskaris. Brookline, Mass. : Holy Cross Orthodox Press, c1977. ix, 164 p. : ill. ; 22 cm. (The Archbishop Iakovos library of ecclesiastical and historical sources ; no. 4) Includes index. [BX395.K67A2513 1977] 77-77664 ISBN 0-916586-10-3 pbk. : 4.95 ISBN 0-916586-17-0 : 7.95
1. Kosmas ho Aitolos, Saint, 1714-1779. 2. Christian saints—Greece—Biography. I. Vaporis, Nomikos Michael. II. Title. III. Series.

Kossuth, Lajos, 1802-1894.

DEAK, Istvan. 943.9'04'0924 B
The lawful revolution : Louis Kossuth and the Hungarians, 1848-1849 / Istvan Deak. New York : Columbia University Press, 1979. xxi, 415 p., [8] leaves of plates : ill. ; 24 cm. Includes index. Bibliography: p. [385]-399. [DB937.D42] 78-22063 ISBN 0-231-04602-2 : 16.95
1. Kossuth, Lajos, 1802-1894. 2. Statesmen—Hungary—Biography. 3. Hungary—History—Uprising of 1848-1849. I. Title.

HEADLEY, Phineas Camp, 1819-1903. 943.9'04'0924 B
The life of Louis Kossuth, governor of Hungary, including notices of the men and scenes of the Hungarian revolution; to which is added an appendix containing his principal speeches, &c. With an introd. by Horace Greeley. Freeport, N.Y., Books for Libraries Press [1971] xvi, 461 p. port. 23 cm. [DB937.H43 1971] 78-154152 ISBN 0-8369-5768-7
1. Kossuth, Lajos, 1802-1894. 2. Hungary—History—Uprising of 1848-1849. I. Title.

LENGYEL, Emil, 1895- 943.9'1'040924 B
Lajos Kossuth, Hungary's great patriot. New York, F. Watts [1969] viii, 145 p. illus. 22 cm. (Immortals of history) [DB937.L4] 69-12097
1. Kossuth, Lajos, 1802-1894.

SEBESTYEN, Endre, 1885- 923.24391
Kossuth, a Magyar apostle of world democracy. Pittsburgh, Expert Print. Co., 1950. 218 p. illus. 24 cm. [DB937.8S4] 51-34935
1. Kossuth, Lajos, 1802-1894. I. Title.

SPENCER, Donald S., 1945- 301.29'73'0439
Louis Kossuth and young America : a study of sectionalism and foreign policy 1848-1852 / Donald S. Spencer. Columbia : University of Missouri Press, 1977. vii, 203 p. : ill. ; 23 cm. Includes index. Bibliography: p. 185-196. [DB937.3.S66] 77-2123 ISBN 0-8262-0223-3 : 12.50
1. Kossuth, Lajos, 1802-1894. 2. Heads of state—Hungary—Biography. 3. United States—Politics and government—1849-1861. 4. United States—Foreign relations—1849-1853. I. Title. BIP

ZAREK, Otto, 1898-1958. 943.9'104'0924 B
Kossuth. Translated from the German by Lynton Hudson. Port Washington, N.Y., Kennikat Press [1970] 295 p. illus., map, ports. 23 cm. Reprint of the 1937 ed. [DB937.Z32 1970] 78-112823
1. Kossuth, Lajos, 1802-1894. 2. Hungary—Politics and government—19th century. 3. Hungary—History—Uprising of 1848-1849.

Kossuth, Lajos, 1802-1894—Bibliography.

SZEPLAKI, Joseph. 016.9173'04'640924
Louis Kossuth, "the Nation's guest" :/ a bibliography on his trip in the United States, December 4, 1851-July 14, 1852 / compiled and edited by Joseph Szeplaki. Ligonier, Pa. : Bethlen Press, 1976. 160 p. : ill. ; 22 cm. Includes index. [Z8467.55.S949] [DB937.3] 73-88884 ISBN 0-87934-009-6 pbk. : 5.00
1. Kossuth, Lajos, 1802-1894—Bibliography. I. Title.

Kostelanetz, Richard.

KOSTELANETZ, Richard. 810'.9'0054
"The end" appendix : "Intelligent writing" reconsidered / Richard Kostelanetz. Metuchen, N.J. : Scarecrow Press, 1979. p. cm. "Addendum to The end of intelligent writing." Includes index. [PS221.K642] 79-51580 ISBN 0-8108-1246-0 : 11.50
1. Kostelanetz, Richard. The end of intelligent writing—Addresses, essays, lectures. 2. American literature—20th century—History and criticism—Addresses, essays, lectures. 3. Publishers and publishing—United States—Addresses, essays, lectures. 4. Authors and publishers—United States—Addresses, essays, lectures. I. Kostelanetz, Richard. End of intelligent writing. II. Title.

Kosterina, Nina Alekseevna,

KOSTERINA, Nina Alekseevna, 1921-1941. 914.7'03'8420924 B
The diary of Nina Kosterina. Translated from the Russian with an introd. by Mirra Ginsburg. New York, Crown Publishers [1968] 192 p. 22 cm. (Young adult books from Crown) Translation of Dnevnik (romanized form) [DK268.K62A313 1968] 68-9057 3.95
I. Ginsburg, Mirra, tr. II. Title.

Kosterlitzky, Emilio, 1853-1928.

SMITH, Cornelius Cole, 1913- 972'.1'0810924 B
Emilio Kosterlitzky, eagle of Sonora and the Southwest border, by Cornelius C. Smith, Jr., with pen and ink sketches by the author. Glendale, Calif., A. H. Clark Co., 1970. 344 p. illus., facsims., maps, ports. 25 cm. (Frontier military series, 7) Bibliography: p. [327]-333. [F1233.5.K6S6] 72-130052 ISBN 0-87062-074-6
1. Kosterlitzky, Emilio, 1853-1928. I. Title. II. Series.

Kottler, Moses, 1896-

SCHOLTZ, Johannes Du Plessis. 730'.92'4 B
Moses Kottler : his Cape years / J. du P. Scholtz. 1st ed. Cape Town : Tafelberg, 1976. 134 p. : ill. ; 29 cm. Includes catalogue illustrations and catalogue of paintings and sculptures. Includes bibliographical references and index. [N7396.K67S36] 77-355339 ISBN 0-624-00956-4
1. Kottler, Moses, 1896- 2. Artists—South Africa—Biography. I. Kottler, Moses, 1896-

Koufax, Sanford, 1935-

HANO, Arnold, 1922- 796.35722
Sandy Koufax, strikeout king. New York, Putnam [c.1964] 219p. port. 21cm. 64-19920 3.50
1. Koufax, Sanford, 1935- I. Title.

MITCHELL, Jerry. 796.3570924 B
Sandy Koufax. New York, Grosset & Dunlap [1966] 186 p. 20 cm. (Grosset sports library) [GV865.K67M5] 66-14281
1. Koufax, Sanford, 1935-

Koufax, Sanford, 1935- —Juvenile literature.

KOUFAX, Sanford, 1935- 796.3570924 B
Koufax, by Sandy Koufax with Ed Linn.

New York, Viking Press [1966] 294 p. port. 22 cm. [GV865.K67A9] 66-19162
1. Baseball. I. Linn, Edward. II. Title. BIP

LISS, Howard 796.357220924
The Sandy Koufax album [1st ed.] New York, Hawthorn [1966] 63p. illus, ports. 27cm. [GV865.K67L5] 66-7477 2.95
1. Koufax, Sanford, 1935- —Juvenile literature. I. Title.

Kourdakov, Sergei, 1951-

KOURDAKOV, Sergei, 1951-1973. 914.7'03'850924 B
The persecutor. Old Tappan, N.J., F. H. Revell Co. [1973] 254 p. illus. 21 cm. [BV4935.K68A3] 73-15681 ISBN 0-8007-0631-5 5.95
1. Kourdakov, Sergei, 1951- I. Title. BIP

Koussevitzky, Serge, 1874-1951.

LOURIE, Arthur, 1884?- 785'.0924 B
Sergei Koussevitzky and his epoch; a biographical chronicle. Translated from the Russian by S. W. Pring. Freeport, N.Y., Books for Libraries Press [1969] xiv, 253, v p. illus., ports. 23 cm. (Select bibliographies reprint series) "First published 1931." [ML422.K7L7 1969] 78-94276
1. Koussevitzky, Scrge, 1874-1951. I. Pring, S. W., tr. II. Title.

Kovach, Nora, 1931-

MIKES, George. 927.933
Leap through the Curtain; the story of Nora Kovach & Istvan Rabovsky. Illustrated with photos. [1st American ed.] New York, Dutton, 1956 [c1955] 223 p. illus. 21 cm. [GV1785.K6M5 1956] 56-5267
1. Kovach, Nora, 1931- 2. Rabovsky, Istvan, 1930- I. Title.

Kovacs, Ernie, 1919-1962.

WALEY, David. 791'.092'4 B
The Ernie Kovaks phile / by David G. Walley. New York : Bolder : [distributed by Farrar, Straus & Giroux, 1979?] c1975. 244 p., [2] leaves of plates : ill. ; 23 cm. First published in 1975 under title: Nothing in moderation. Filmography: p. 241. [PN2287.K7W3 1979] 78-64637 ISBN 0-918282-06-3 pbk. : 5.95 5.95
1. Kovacs, Ernie, 1919-1962. 2. Comedians—United States—Biography. I. Title.

WALLEY, David. 791'.092'4 B
Nothing in moderation : a biography of Ernie Kovacs / by David G. Walley. New York : Drake Publishers, 1975. 246 p. : ill ; 24 cm. [PN2287.K7W3] 74-22609 ISBN 0-87749-738-9 : 9.95
1. Kovacs, Ernie, 1919-1962. I. Title.

Kovalevskaia, Sof'ia Vasil'evna Korvin-Krukovskaia, 1850-1891.

KOVALEVSKAIA, Sof'ia Vasil'evna Korvin-Krukovskaia, 1850-1891. 510'.92'4 B
A Russian childhood / Sofya Kovalevskaya ; translated, edited, an introduced by Beatrice Stillman ; with an analysis of Kovalevskaya's Mathematics by P. Y. Kochina. New York : Springer-Verlag, c1978. xiii, 250 p., [2] leaves of plates : ill. ; 24 cm. Translation of Vospominaniia detstva. Includes bibliographical references. [QA29.K67A3513] 78-12955 ISBN 0-387-90348-8 : 14.80
1. Kovalevskaia, Sof'ia Vasil'evna Korvin-Krukovskaia, 1850-1891. 2. Mathematicians—Russia—Biography. I. Title. BIP

Kovanov, Vladimir Vasil'evich, 1909-

KOVANOV, Vladimir Vasil'evich, 1909- 617'.092'4 B
In the name of life : reflections of a Soviet surgeon / V. V. Kovanov ; [translated from the Russian by Raissa Bobrova and Yuri Sviridov]. Moscow : Progress Publishers, 1976. 326 p. : ill. ; 21 cm. Translation of Prizvanie. Includes bibliographical references. [R534.K67A313] 77-357490
1. Kovanov, Vladimir Vasil'evich, 1909- 2. Surgeons—Russian Republic—Biography. I. Title.

Kovic, Ron.

KOVIC, Ron. 959.704'38
Born on the fourth of july / Ron Kovic. New York : Pocket Books, 1977c1976. 224p. ; 18 cm. (A Kangaroo Book) [DS559.5.K68] ISBN 0-671-81185-1 pbk. : 1.95
1. Kovic, Ron. 2. Vietnamese Conflict, 1961-1975-Personal narratives, American. I. Title.
L.C. card no. for 1976 McGraw-Hill.:76-7508. BIP

Kovner, Abraham Uri, 1842-1909.

GROSSMAN, Leonid Petrovich, 1888-1965. 947.08'092'4 B
Confession of a Jew / Leonid Grossman ; translated by Ranne Moab. New York : Arno Press, 1975. 189 p. ; 24 cm. (The Modern Jewish experience) Translation of Ispoved' odnogo evreia. Includes bibliographical references. [DS135.R95K647313 1975] 74-27990 ISBN 0-405-06717-8 : 12.00
1. Kovner, Abraham Uri, 1842-1909. 2. Dostoevskii, Fedor Mikhailovich, 1821-1881—Political and social views. 3. Jews in Russia. 4. Russia—Politics and government—19th century. I. Title. II. Series. BIP

Kowalska, Faustyna, Sister, 1905-1938.

CEGIELKA, Francis A 922.244
Siostra Faustyna, szafarka milosierdzia Bozego. North Tonawanda, N. Y., Pallottinum, 1954. 396p. illus. 20cm. [BX4705.K687C4] 57-22210
1. Kowalska, Faustyna, Sister, 1905-1938. I. Title.

Koxinga, 1624-1662.

CROIZIER, Ralph C. 951'.249'030924 B
Koxinga and Chinese nationalism : history, myth, and the hero / by Ralph C. Croizier. Cambridge : East Asian Research Center, Harvard University : distributed by Harvard University Press, 1977. 116 p., [2] leaves of plates : ill. ; 23 cm. (Harvard East Asian monographs ; 67) Includes index. Bibliography: p. [99]-109. [DS753.6.K6C76] 76-30404 ISBN 0-674-50566-2 pbk. : 6.00
1. Koxinga, 1624-1662. 2. Generals—China—Biography. 3. Taiwan—History. 4. Nationalism—China. I. Title. II. Series. BIP

Kozacik family.

KOZACIK, Mary, 1896- 929.2
John and Susan Kozacik; a biography. East Chicago, Ind., 1965. 16 p. geneal. table, map, port. 24 cm. Additions and corrections in ms. [CS71.K88 1965] 77-3476
1. Kozacik family. I. Title.

Kraft, Barbara, 1939-

KRAFT, Barbara, 1939- 301.41'2'0924
The restless spirit : journal of a Gemini / Barbara Kraft ; pref. by Anais Nin. Millbrae, Calif. : Les Femmes Pub., c1976. 201 p. ; 22 cm. [HQ1413.K63A35] 76-11372 ISBN 0-89087-917-6 pbk. : 4.95
1. Kraft, Barbara, 1939- 2. Women—United States—Biography. I. Title. BIP

Krakel, Dean Fenton, 1923-

KRAKEL, Dean Fenton, 1923- 069'.9'70924 B
Adventures in Western art / by Dean Krakel. Kansas City, Mo. : Lowell Press, [1977] p. cm. Bibliography: p. [N654.K7] 76-21136 ISBN 0-913504-35-1 : 11.95
1. Krakel, Dean Fenton, 1923- 2. National Cowboy Hall of Fame and Western Heritage Center. 3. Museum directors—United States—Biography. 4. The West in art. I. Title. BIP

Kramer, Daniel.

KRAMER, Daniel. 780'.924
Bob Dylan. New York, Pocket Bks. [1968, c1967] 210p. ports. 18cm. (77029) [ML420.D98K7] .95 pap.,
I. Dylan, Bob, 1941- II. Title.

Kramer, Jack, 1940-

KRAMER, Jack, 1940- 813'.5'4
Travels with the celestial dog : a documentary / Jack Kramer. London : Wildwood House, 1976. [8], 177 p. ; 23 cm. "Parts of this book have appeared in Evergreen in the U.S.A." [PN4874.K72A38] 77-354189 ISBN 0-7045-0146-5 : £4.95
1. Kramer, Jack, 1940- 2. Journalists—United States—Biography. I. Title.

Kramer, Jerry,

KRAMER, Jerry, 1936- 796.332'0924 B
Farewell to football. Edited by Dick Schaap. With a foreword by Rod McKuen. New York, World Pub. Co. [1969] xx, 202 p. illus., ports. 22 cm. Autobiographical. [GV939.K7A3] 75-92537 5.95
I. Title.

Kramer, John Albert, 1921-

KRAMER, John Albert, 1921- 796.34'2'0924 B
The game : my 40 years in tennis / by Jack Kramer, with Frank Deford. New York : Putnam, c1979. 318 p., [8] leaves of plates : ill. ; 24 cm. Includes index. [GV994.K7A34 1979] 78-31299 ISBN 0-399-12336-9 : 10.95
1. Kramer, John Albert, 1921- 2. Tennis players—United States—Biography. I. Deford, Frank, joint author. II. Title.

Kramer, Norbert A., 1910-1959.

KRAMER, Herbert George. 271'.7 B
Brother Norbert's masterpiece : biography of Brother Norbert A. Kramer, S.M., 1910-1959 / by Herbert George Kramer. St. Louis : Marianist Provincialate, 1975. vi, 172 p. ; 22 cm. [BX4705.K692K7] 75 25179
1. Kramer, Norbert A., 1910-1959. I. Title.

Kramer, Stanley.

SPOTO, Donald, 1941- 791.43'023'0924 B
Stanley Kramer, film maker / by Donald Spoto. New York . Putnam, c1978. 367 p. : ill. ; 24 cm. Includes index. Filmography: p. [327]-361. [PN1998.A3K725 1978] 78-18834 12.95
1. Kramer, Stanley. 2. Moving-picture producers and directors—United States—Biography. I. Title.

Krans, Olof, 1838-1916.

SWANK, George. 759.13
Painter Krans of Bishop Hill Colony / by George Swank. Galva, Ill. : Galvaland Press, 1976. 176 p. : ill. (some col.) ; 29 cm. [ND237.K67S9] 76-375114
1. Krans, Olof, 1838-1916. 2. Painters—United States—Bishop Hill, Ill.—Biography. 3. Bishop Hill, Ill.—History. I. Title.

Kranz, Kurt.

KRANZ, Kurt. 709'.2'4
Kurt Kranz : early form sequences, 1927-1932 = Kurt Kranz : fruhe form-reihen, 1927-1932 / Hans Richter, Werner Haftmann, Werner Hofmann. Hamburg : H. Christians, c1975. 228 p. : ill. (some col.) ; 27 cm. English and German. Includes indexes. Bibliography: p. 220-221. [N6888.K74R52 1975b] 76-358047 ISBN 0-262-11060-1 (U.S.A.)
1. Kranz, Kurt. I. Richter, Hans, 1888- II. Haftmann, Werner. III. Hofmann, Werner, 1928-

Kratz, Clayton, b. 1896—Juvenile literature.

HARDER, Geraldine Gross. 289.7'092'4 B
When apples are ripe; the story of Clayton Kratz. Drawings by Allan Eitzen. Scottdale, Pa., Herald Press [1972, c1971] 223 p. illus. 21 cm. Chronicles the life of a young American Mennonite who vanished into a Russian prison in the early 1920's. [BX8128.W4H37] 92 73-160722 ISBN 0-8361-1656-9 4.95
1. Kratz, Clayton, b. 1896—Juvenile literature. 2. Mennonites in Russia—Juvenile literature. 3. Russia—History—Revolution, 1917-1921—Civilian relief. I. Title.

Kraus, Hans Peter, 1907-

KRAUS, Hans Peter, 1907- 658.8'09'0705730924 B
A rare book saga : the autobiography of H. P. Kraus. New York : Putnam, c1978. xvii, 386 p., [8] leaves of plates : ill. ; 24 cm. Includes index. [Z473.K74K7] 77-28643 15.00
1. Kraus, Hans Peter, 1907- 2. Antiquarian booksellers—United States—Biography. I. Title. BIP

Krauth, Charles Porterfield, 1823-1883.

SPAETH, Adolph, 1839-1910. 284'.1'0924 B
Charles Porterfield Krauth. New York, Arno Press, 1969. 2 v. in 1. port. 23 cm. (Religion in America) Reprint of the 1898-1909 ed. Contents Contents.—v. 1. 1823-1859.—v. 2. 1859-1883. Includes bibliographical references. [BX8080.K68S62] 78-83440
1. Krauth, Charles Porterfield, 1823-1883. BIP

Kray, Charles, 1927-

KRAY, Charles, 1927- 364.1'092'4 B
Me and my brothers / [by] Charles Kray, with Jonathan Sykes. London : Everest, 1976. 256 p., [12] p. of plates : ill., ports. ; 23 cm. Includes index. [HV6248.K63A35] 77-358909 ISBN 0-905018-14-1 : £3.95
1. Kray, Charles, 1927- 2. Kray, Reginald, 1933- 3. Kray, Ronald, 1933- 4. Crime and criminals—Great Britain—Biography. I. Sykes, Jonathan, joint author. II Title.

Kray, Reginald, 1933-

KRAY, Charles, 1927- 364.1'092'4 B
Me and my brothers / [by] Charles Kray, with Jonathan Sykes. London : Everest, 1976. 256 p., [12] p. of plates : ill., ports. ; 23 cm. Includes index. [HV6248.K63A35] 77-358909 ISBN 0-905018-14-1 : £3.95
1. Kray, Charles, 1927- 2. Kray, Reginald, 1933- 3. Kray, Ronald, 1933- 4. Crime and criminals—Great Britain—Biography. I. Sykes, Jonathan, joint author. II. Title.

Krebs, Albert, 1899-

KREBS, Albert, 1899- 943.085'092'4
The infancy of Nazism : the memoirs of ex-Gauleiter Albert Krebs, 1923-1933 / edited and translated by William Sheridan Allen. New York : New Viewpoints, 1976. xiii, 328 p. ; 21 cm. Translation of Tendenzen und Gestalten der NSDAP. Includes index. Bibliography: p. [316]-320. [DD247.K73A3713] 75-29153 ISBN 0-531-05376-8 : 12.50 pbk. : 5.95
1. Krebs, Albert, 1899- 2. Nationalsozialistische Deutsche Arbeiter-Partei. 3. Germany—Politics and government—1918-1933. I. Allen, William Sheridan. II. Title.

Krehbiel, Christian,

KREHBIEL, Christian, 1832-1909. 922.8773
Prairie Pioneer; the Christian Krehbiel story. Newton, Kan., Faith and Life Press [1961] 160p. illus. 24cm. (Mennonite historical series) [BX8143.K68A3] 61-66125
I. Title.

Krents, Harold.

KRENTS, Harold. 362.4'1'0924 B
To race the wind; an autobiography. New York, Putnam [1972] 282 p. illus. 22 cm. [HV1792.K7A3] 72-75957 ISBN 0-399-10924-2 6.95
I. Title.

KRENTS, Harold. 362.4'1'0924 B
To race the wind; an autobiography. Boston, G. K. Hall, 1974 [c1972] 506 p. 24 cm. Large print ed. [HV1792.K7A3 1974] 73-20333 ISBN 0-8161-6172-0 11.95
1. Krents, Harold. 2. Blind—Biography. I. Title.

Kreskin, 1935-

KRESKIN, 1935- 133.8'092'4 B
The amazing world of Kreskin. [1st ed.] New York, Random House [1973] xi, 209 p. 22 cm. Bibliography: 203-209. [BF1027.K75A3] 72-11411 ISBN 0-394-48440-1 5.95
1. Kreskin, 1935- 2. Psychical research. 3. Occult sciences. I. Title. **BIP**

Kreuger, Ivar, 1880-1932.

SHAPLEN, Robert, 1917- 923.3485
Kreuger, genius and swindler. With an introd. by John Kenneth Galbraith. [1st ed.] New York, Knopf, 1960. 251 p. illus. 22 cm. [HD9999.M23S872] 60-10700
1. Kreuger, Ivar, 1880-1932.

Kreutzer, William Richard, 1877-1956.

SHOEMAKER, Len. 1881- 926.349
Saga of a forest ranger, a biography of William R. Kreutzer, forest ranger no. 1, and a historical account of the U.S. Forest Service in Colorado. Boulder, University of Colorado Press, 1958. 216 p. illus. 24 cm. [SD129.K7S5] 58-35137
1. Kreutzer, William Richard, 1877-1956. 2. U.S. Forest Service. I. Title.

Kreymborg, Alfred,

KREYMBORG, Alfred, 1883- 928.1
Troubadour, an American autobiography. New York, Sagamore Press, 1957. 333p. 21cm. (American century series, S-22) [PS3521.R55Z5 1957] 57-12442
I. Title.

KREYMBORG, Alfred, 1883- 928.1
Troubadour, an American autobiography. New York, Sagamore Press, 1957. 333p. 21cm. (American century series, S-22) [PS3521.R55Z5 1957] 57-12442
I. Title.

Krizanic, Juraj, 1618-1683—Addresses, essays, lectures.

JURAJ Krizanic 947'.007'2024 B
(1618-1683), russophile and ecumenic visionary : a symposium / edited by Thomas Eckman and Ante Kadic. The Hague : Mouton, 1976. viii, 360 p., [1] leaf of plates : ill. ; 25 cm. (Slavistic printings and reprintings ; 292) English, French or German. Includes indexes. Bibliography: p. [329]-352. [DB378.K68J87] 76-476043 ISBN 9-02-793034-1 : 43.25
1. Krizanic, Juraj, 1618-1683—Addresses, essays, lectures. I. Eekman, Tom. II. Kadic, Ante. III. Title. IV. Series.
Distributed by Humanities press.

Krieghoff, Cornelius, 1815-1872.

HARPER, J. Russell. 759.11 B
Krieghoff / J. Russell Harper. Toronto ; Buffalo : University of Toronto Press, 1979. xvi, 204 p. : ill. (some col.) ; 26 cm. Includes index. Bibliography: p. [187]-188. [ND249.K7H37] 80-452634 ISBN 0-8020-2348-7 : 29.95
1. Krieghoff, Cornelius, 1815-1872. 2. Painters—Canada—Biography. I. Krieghoff, Cornelius, 1815-1872. **BIP**

Krishna Menon, Kizhekkepat, 1894-

GEORGE, Thayil Jacob Sony 954.040924
Krishna Menon, a biography. New York, Taplinger [1965, c.1964] 272p. port. 23cm. Bibl. [DS481.K73G4] 65-17329 5.00
1. Krishna Menon, Kizhekkepat, 1894- I. Title.

Krishna Menon, Vengalil Krishnan.

GUPTA, Ratanlal N., 1931- 954.04'092'4
V. K. Krishna Menon : an appraisal of the man and his rhetoric / Ratanlal N. Gupta. Fort Valley, Ga. : R. N. Gupta, 1973. 168 p. ; 22 cm. [DS481.K73G86] 75-310438 Rs30.00
1. Krishna Menon, Vengalil Krishnan. I. Title.

LENGYEL, Emil, 1895- 923.254
Krishna Menon. New York, Walker [c.1962] 253p. 21cm. 62-19497 5.00
1. Krishna Menon, Vengalil Krishnan. I. Title.

Krishnamurti, Jiddu, 1895-

KRISHNAMURTI, Jiddu, 1895- 181'.4 B
Krishnamurti's notebook / by J. Krishnamurti ; with a foreword by Mary Lutyens. 1st U.S. ed. New York : Harper & Row, c1976. 252 p. ; 21 cm. [B5134.K76A34 1976b] 76-9952 10.00
1. Krishnamurti, Jiddu, 1895- 2. Philosophers—India—Biography. 3. Philosophy. I. Title. **BIP**

LUTYENS, Mary, 1908- 181'.4 B
Krishnamurti : the years of awakening / Mary Lutyens. New York : Farrar, Straus and Giroux, 1975. xi, 325 p., [8] leaves of plates : ill. ; 22 cm. Includes bibliographical references and index. [B5134.K76L87 1975] 75-17840 ISBN 0-374-18222-1 : 8.95
1. Krishnamurti, Jiddu, 1895- **BIP**

Krist, Gary Steven.

KRIST, Gary Steven. 364.1'54'0924 B
Life: the man who kidnapped Barbara Mackle. [New York] Olympia Press [1972] xii, 370 p. illus. 24 cm. Autobiography. [HV6248.K7A3] 70-190768 ISBN 0-7004-0100-8 6.95
I. Title.

Kristina, Queen of Sweden, 1626-1689.

GERSON, Noel Bertram, 1914-. 923.1485
Queen of caprice, a biography of Kristina of Sweden, by Paul Lewis [pseud. 1st ed.] New York, Holt, Rinehart, and Winston [1062] 307 p. 22 cm. [DL719.G42] 62-7703
1. Kristina, Queen of Sweden, 1626-1689. I. Title.

LEWIS, Paul. 923.1485
Queen of caprice, a biography of Kristina of Sweden. [1st ed.] New York, Holt, Rinehart, and Winston [1962] 307 p. 22 cm. [DL719.L4] 62-7703
1. Kristina, Queen of Sweden, 1626-1689. I. Title.

MASSON, Georgina. 948.5'02'0924 B
Queen Christina. [1st American ed.] New York, Farrar, Straus & Giroux [1969, c1968] 405 p. illus., ports. 23 cm. Bibliography: p. [393]-396. [DL719.M35 1969] 67-13412 7.95
1. Kristina, Queen of Sweden, 1626-1689. I. Title.

STOLPE, Sven, 1905- 948.5020924 B
Christina of Sweden. Edited by Sir Alec Randall. [Translation by Sir Alec Randall and Ruth Mary Bethell] New York, Macmillan, 1966. xii, 360 p. illus., facsim., ports (part col.) 23 cm. Translated from the abridged German version, Konigin Christine von Schweden, of the Swedish original, Drottning Kristina. [DL719.S8132] 66-15496
1. Kristina, Queen of Sweden, 1626-1689. I. Title.

Kristofferson, Kris.

KALET, Beth. 784'.092'4 B
Kris Kristofferson / by Beth Kalet. New York : Quick Fox, c1979. 96 p. : ill. ; 26 cm. Discography: p. 94-96. A biography of the successful songwriter, singer, and actor. [ML420.K93K3] 92 79-63528 ISBN 0-8256-3932-8 pbk. : 4.95
1. Kristofferson, Kris. 2. Singers—United States—Biography. 3. Composers—United States—Biography. 4. Moving-picture actors and actresses—United States—Biography. I. Title. **BIP**

Krivitsky, Walter G., 1899-1941.

KRIVITSKY, Walter G., 1899-1941. 327'.12'0924 B
In Stalin's secret service : an expose of Russia's secret policies by the former chief of the Soviet intelligence in Western Europe / W. G. Krivitsky. Westport, Conn. : Hyperion Press, [1979] p. cm. Reprint of the 1939 ed. published by Harper, New York. [DK268.K75A3 1979] 78-20477 ISBN 0-88355-854-8 : 22.50
1. Krivitsky, Walter G., 1899-1941. 2. Russia (1923- U.S.S.R.). Ob"edinennoe gosudarstvennoe politicheskoe upravlenie. 3. Russia—Politics and government—1917- 4. Spies—Russia—Biography. I. Title.

Kriyananda, Swami.

KRIYANANDA, Swami. 181'.45'0924 B
The path : autobiography of a Western yogi / by Swami Kriyananda (Donald Walters) ; with a preface by John W. White. Nevada City, Calif. : Ananda Publications, 1977. xviii, 640 p. : ill. ; 22 cm. Includes index. [BP605.S43K744] 77-7287 ISBN 0-916124-11-8 : 15.00
1. Kriyananda, Swami. 2. Self-Realization Fellowship—Biography. I. Title. **BIP**

Krmpotic, Vesna, 1932- —Biography.

KRMPOTIC, Vesna, 1932- 891.8'2'15 B
Eyes of eternity : a spiritual autobiography / Vesna Krmpotic translated by Lovett F. Edwards. 1st ed. New York : Harcourt Brace Jovanovich, c1979. viii, 204 p. ; 22 cm. Translation of Dijamantni faraon. [PG1619.21.R63Z51413] 78-23591 10.95
1. Krmpotic, Vesna, 1932- —Biography. 2. Krmpotic, Vesna, 1932- —Journeys. 3. Authors, Croatian—20th century—Biography. I. Title. **BIP**

Kroc, Ray, 1902-

KROC, Ray, 1902- 647'.9573 [B]
Grinding it out : the making of McDonald's / Ray Kroc, with Robert Anderson. New York : Berkley Pub. Corp., 1978, c1977. 218p. : ill. ; 18 cm. (A Berkley Book) Includes index. [TX910.5.K76A34] ISBN 0-425-03842-4 pbk. : 1.95
1. Kroc, Ray, 1902- 2. McDonald's Corporation. 3. Restauranteurs — United States — Biography. I. Anderson, Robert, 1930- joint author. II. Title.
L.C. card no. for 1977 H. Regnery ed.: 76-56878. **BIP**

Kroc, Ray, 1902- —Juvenile literature.

SIMPSON, Janice Claire. 338.4'7'64795 B
Ray Kroc : Big Mac man / by Janice Simpson. St. Paul : EMC Corp., 1978. p. cm. (Headliners II) A biography of Ray Kroc, founder of the McDonald's hamburger chain. [TX910.5.K76S55] 92 78-18752 ISBN 0-88436-434-8 : 5.95
1. Kroc, Ray, 1902- —Juvenile literature. 2. McDonald's Corporation—Juvenile literature. 3. Restaurateurs—United States—Biography—Juvenile literature. I. Title. II. Series. **BIP**

WESTMAN, Paul. 338.7'61'64795 B
Ray Kroc, mayor of McDonaldland / by Paul Westman. Minneapolis : Dillon Press, 1979. p. cm. (Taking part ; 3) A biography of the man whose assembly line methods of preparing food revolutionized the restaurant business and gave birth to the McDonald restaurant chain. [TX910.5.K76W47] 92 79-19913 ISBN 0-87518-185-6 lib. bdg. : 6.95 6.95
1. Kroc, Ray, 1902- —Juvenile literature. 2. McDonald's Corporation—Juvenile literature. 3. Restaurateurs—United States—Biography—Juvenile literature. I. Title. **BIP**

Krock, Arthur,

KROCK, Arthur, 1886- 070'.92'4 B
Myself when young; growing up in the 1890's. [1st ed.] Boston, Little, Brown [1973] xi, 237 p. 21 cm. [PN4874.K73A3] 72-8830 ISBN 0-316-50441-6 12.50
I. Title.

Kroeber, Alfred Louis, 1876-1960.

KROEBER, Theodora. 301.2'092'4 B
Alfred Kroeber; a personal configuration. Berkeley, University of California Press, 1970. xi, 292 p. illus., ports. 24 cm. Bibliography: p. 289-292. [GN21.K7A3] 71-94983 7.95
1. Kroeber, Alfred Louis, 1876-1960. I. Title.

STEWARD, Julian Haynes, 1902-1972. 301.2'092'4 B
Alfred Kroeber. New York, Columbia University Press, 1973. xii, 137 p. 23 cm. (Leaders of modern anthropology series) Includes selections from Kroeber's writings (p. 63-131) and a select bibliography of his works (p. 133-137) [GN21.K7S84] 72-8973 ISBN 0-231-03489-X 8.00
1. Kroeber, Alfred Louis, 1876-1960. I. Kroeber, Alfred Louis, 1876-1960. Selections. 1973. II. Title. III. Series.
pap. 2.95 ISBN 0-231-03490-3. **BIP**

Kropotkin, Petr Alekseevich, kniaz', 1842-1921.

KROPOTKIN, Petr Alekseevich, kniaz, 1842-1921. 923.347
Memoirs of a revolutionist. Edited by James Allen Rogers. .garden City, N. Y., Doubleday, 1962. 338p. 19cm. (Anchor books, A287) [HX915.K92 1962] 62-16035
1. Russia—Pol. & govt. 2. Anarchism and anarchists. I. Title.

KROPOTKIN, Petr Alekseevich, kniaz', 1842-1921. 947.08'0924 B
Memoirs of a revolutionist, by Peter Kropotkin. With a new introd. and notes by Nicolas Walter. New York, Dover Publications [1971] xxxiv, 557 p., port. 22 cm. [HX915.K92 1971] 75-121700 ISBN 0-486-22485-6 4.00
1. Russia—Politics and government. 2. Anarchism and anarchists. I. Walter, Nicolas. II. Title.

KROPOTKIN, Petr Alekseevich, kniaz, 1842-1921. 947'.08'0924 (B)
Memoirs of a revolutionist, Edited by James Allen Rogers. Gloucester, Mass., P. Smith, 1967 [c1962] xviii, 338 p. 21 cm. "Bibliography (of major works of Kropotkin in English)": p. [316] Bibliographical references included in "Notes" (p. [317]-332) [HX915.K92] 67-2480
1. Russian — Pol. & govt. 2. Anarchism and anarchists. I. Rogers, James Allen, 1929- ed. II. Title.

KROPOTKIN, Petr 947.08'0924 B
Alekseevich, Kniaz, 1842-1921.
Memoirs of a revolutionist. New York, Horizon Press [1968] xxxviii, 519 p. 2 ports. 24 cm. The 1899 ed., with Georg Brandes' introd., reprinted with a new foreword by Barnett Newman, a pref. by Paul Goodman, and an index. "[First] published in 'The Atlantic monthly' (September 1898, to September 1899), under the title, 'The autobiography of a revolutionist.'" [HX915.K92 1968] 68-54186 10.00
1. Russia—Politics and government. 2. Anarchism and anarchists. I. Title. **BIP**

KROPOTKIN, Petr 923.347
Alekseevich, kniaz, 1842-1921.
Memoirs of a revolutionist. Ed. by James Allen Rogers. Garden City, N. Y., Doubleday [c.]1962. 338p. (Anchor bks., A287) Bibl. 62-16035 1.45 pap.,
1. Russia—Pol. & govt. 2. Anarchism and anarchists. I. Title.

WOODCOCK, George, 1912- 923.347
The anarchist prince; a biographical study of Peter Kropotkin, by George Woodcock and Ivan Avakumovic. London, New York, T. V. Boardman [1950] 463 p. ports., map (on lining paper) 22 cm. Bibliography: p. 455-458. [HX914.K7W6] 51-5772
1. Kropotkin, Petr Alekseevich, Kniaz', 1842-1921. I. Avakumovic, Ivan, joint author. II. Title.

WOODCOCK, George, 947.08'0924 B
1912-
The anarchist prince; a biographical study of Peter Kropotkin, by George Woodcock and Ivan Avakumovic. New York, Schocken Books [1971] 465 p. ports. 21 cm. (Studies in the libertarian and utopian tradition) Bibliography: p. 455-459. [HX914.K7W6 1971] 70-152571 ISBN 0-8052-0305-2 3.95
1. Kropotkin, Petr Alekseevich, kniaz', 1842-1921. I. Avakumovic, Ivan, joint author. II. Title.

Krueger, Max, 1851-1927.

KRUEGER, Max, 976.4'004'31 B
1851-1927.
Second Fatherland : the life and fortunes of a German immigrant / by Max Amadeus Paulus Krueger ; edited with an introd. by Marilyn McAdams Sibley. Rev. ed. College Station : Texas A & M University Press, c1976. xix, 161 p., [5] leaves of plates : ill. ; 24 cm. (The Centennial series of the Association of Former Students, Texas A & M University ; no. 4) Published in 1930 under title: Pioneer life in Texas. Includes index. [F391.K94 1976] 76-17539 ISBN 0-89096-017-8 : 10.00
1. Krueger, Max, 1851-1927. 2. Frontier and pioneer life—Texas. 3. Ranch life—Texas. 4. German Americans—Texas. 5. Texas—Biography. I. Title. II. Series: Texas. A & M University, College Station. Association of Former Students. The centennial series of the Association of Former Students, Texas A & M University ; no. 4. **BIP**

Kruk, Zofia.

KRUK, Zofia. 941.085'092'4 B
The taste of hope / Zofia Kruk. Richmond, Vic. : Hutchinson of Australia, 1977, i.e. 1978. 197 p. ; 22 cm. Continues: The taste of fear. [CT1232.K76A37 1977b] 78-305206 ISBN 0-09-130230-7 : 8.95
1. Kruk, Zofia. 2. Refugees—Poland—Biography. 3. World War, 1939-1945—Refugees. 4. Melbourne—Biography. I. Title.
Distributed by Hutchinson, Salem, NH **BIP**

Krulewitch, Melvin L., 1895-

KRULEWITCH, Melvin 359.9'6'0924 B
L., 1895-
Now that you mention it [by] Melvin L. Krulewitch. [New York, Quadrangle, 1973] xiv, 257 p. illus. 22 cm. [E182.K946 1973] 72-90462 ISBN 0-8129-0325-0 6.95
1. Krulewitch, Melvin L., 1895- I. Title.

Krupp family.

BATTY, Peter, 1931- 338.7'6'72
The House of Krupp. New York, Stein and Day [1967, c1966] 333 p. illus., ports. 25 cm. [HD9523.9.K7B3 1966a] 67-14093
1. Krupp family. 2. Krupp'sche Gussstahlfabrik, Essen. I. Title. **BIP**

MANCHESTER, William 338.7'672
Raymond, 1922-
The arms of Krupp, 1587-1968, by William Manchester. [1st. ed.] Boston, Little, Brown [1968] xvi, 976 p. illus., facsims., geneal. table, ports. 25 cm. Bibliography: p. [915]-931. [HD9523.9.K7M35] 68-24450 12.50
1. Krupp von Bohlen und Halbach, Alfried, 1907-1967. 2. Krupp family. 3. Krupp'sche Gusstahlfabrik, Essen. I. Title. **BIP**

MUHLEN, Norbert. 338.476691
The incredible Krupps; the rise, fall, and comeback of Germany's industrial family. [1st ed.] New York, Holt [1959] 308 p. illus. 22 cm. Includes bibliography. [HD9523.9.K7M8] 59-14013
1. Krupp family. 2. Krupp'sche Gussstahlfabrik, Essen. I. Title.

Krupp von Bohlen und Halbach, Alfried, 1907-1967.

MANCHESTER, William 338.7'672
Raymond, 1922-
The arms of Krupp, 1587-1968, by William Manchester. [1st. ed.] Boston, Little, Brown [1968] xvi, 976 p. illus., facsims., geneal. table, ports. 25 cm. Bibliography: p. [915]-931. [HD9523.9.K7M35] 68-24450 12.50
1. Krupp von Bohlen und Halbach, Alfried, 1907-1967. 2. Krupp family. 3. Krupp'sche Gusstahlfabrik, Essen. I. Title. **BIP**

Krupskaia, Nadezhda Konstantinovna, 1869-1939.

MCNEAL, Robert 947.084'1'0924 B
Hatch, 1930-
Bride of the revolution; Krupskaya and Lenin, by Robert H. McNeal. Ann Arbor, University of Michigan Press [1972] 326 p. illus. 24 cm. Bibliography: p. 298-301. [DK254.K77M3 1972] 75-185155 ISBN 0-472-61600-5 10.00
1. Krupskaia, Nadezhda Konstantinovna, 1869-1939. 2. Lenin, Vladimir Il'ich, 1870-1924. 3. Communism—Russia. I. Title. **BIP**

Krusen, Frank Hammond, 1898-

ROBISON, Mabel Otis 926.1
Frank H. Krusen, M.D., pioneer in physical medicine and rehabilitation. Introd. by Charles Mayo. Minneapolis, Denison [c.1963] 249p. 22cm. (Men of achievement ser.) 63-17356 3.00
1. Krusen, Frank Hammond, 1898- I. Title.

ROBISON, Mabel Otis. 926.1
Frank H. Krusen, M.D., pioneer in physical medicine and rehabilitation. With an introd. by Charles Mayo. Minneapolis, T. S. Denison [1963] 240 p. 22 cm. (Men of achievement series) [RM699.7.K7R6] 63-17356
1. Krusen, Frank Hammond, 1898- I. Title.

Kshesinskaia, Matil'da Feliksovna,

KSHESINSKAIA, Matil'da 927.928
Feliksovna, 1872-
Dancing in Petersburgh; the memoirs of Kschessinska, H. S. H. the Princess Romanovsky-Krassinsky. Translated by Arnold Haskell. [1st American ed.] Garden City, N. Y., Doubleday, 1961 [c1960] 272 p. illus. 22 cm. "Originally published ... under the title: Souvenirs de la Kschessinska." [GV1785.K75A33 1961] 60-16442
I. Title.

Kshesinskaia, Matil'da Feliksovna, 1872-1971.

KSHESINSKAIA, Matil'da 927.928
Feliksovna, 1872-
Dancing in Petersburgh; the memoirs of Kschessinska, H. S. H. the Princess Romanovsky-Krassinsky. Translated by Arnold Haskell. [1st American ed.] Garden City, N. Y., Doubleday, 1961 [c1960] 272 p. illus. 22 cm. "Originally published ... under the title: Souvenirs de la Kschessinska." [GV1785.K75A33 1961] 60-16442
I. Title.

KSHESINSKAIA, 792.8'092'4 B
Matil'da Feliksovna, 1872-1971.
Dancing in Petersburg : the memoirs of Kschessinska / H. S. H. the Princess Romanovsky-Krassinsky ; translated by Arnold Haskell. New York : Da Capo Press, 1977, c1960. 272 p., [24] leaves of plates : ill. ; 23 cm. (Da Capo series in dance) Reprint of the 1961 ed. published by Doubleday, Garden City, N.Y. Translation of Souvenirs de la Kschessinska. [GV1785.K75A33 1977] 77-7799 ISBN 0-306-77433-X lib.bdg. : 25.00
1. Kshesinskaia, Matil'da Feliksovna, 1872-1971. 2. Dancers—Biography. I. Title. **BIP**

Ku Klux Klan (1915-)

MARS, 301.45'19'60730762685
Florence, 1923-
Witness in Philadelphia : a Mississippi WASP's account of the 1964 civil rights murders / Florence Mars. Baton Rouge : Louisiana State University Press, c1977. p. cm. Includes bibliographical references and index. [F349.P47M37] 76-50660 ISBN 0-8071-0265-2 : 15.00
1. Ku Klux Klan (1915-) 2. Mars, Florence, 1923- 3. Afro-Americans—Mississippi—Philadelphia. 4. Civil rights workers—Mississippi—Philadelphia. 5. Philadelphia, Miss.—Biography. 6. Murder—Mississippi—Philadelphia. 7. Philadelphia, Miss.—Race question. I. Title.

MIKELL, Robert Mosley. v. 12
They say-blood on my hands; the story of Robert M. Shelton, Imperial Wizard of the United Klans of America. [Huntsville, Ala., Publishers Enterprise, 1966] 184 p. illus., ports. 68-59502
1. Ku Klux Klan (1915-) 2. Shelton, Robert M., 1929- I. Title.

Kuac, Moses.

VANDEVORT, Eleanor. 266.5'1629'3
A leopard tamed; the story of an African pastor, his people, and his problems. Drawings by James Howard. [1st ed.] New York, Harper & Row [1968] xii, 218 p. illus. 22 cm. [BV3625.S83K8] 68-17585
1. Kuac, Moses. 2. Missions—Sudan. 3. Nuer (African tribe) I. Title.

Kubin, Alfred, 1877-

ALFRED Kubin: Leben, Werk, Wirkung. v. 12 Zusammengestellt von Paul Raabe. Hamburg, Rowohlt, 1957. 295p. illus. 24cm.
1. Kubin, Alfred, 1877- I. Otte, Kurt, ed.

RAABE, Paul, ed. 704.9425
Alfred Kubin: Leben, Werk, Wirkung. Im Auftrage von Kurt Otte, Kubin-Archiv in Hamburg, zusammengestellt. Hamburg, Rowohlt, 1957. 295p. illus., plates (4 col.) ports., facsim. 25cm. 'Chronologisches Werkverzeichnis : p. 68-189. 'Bibliographischer Lebensbericht': p. 190-249. [NC1145.K825R2] A57
1. Kubin, Alfred, 1877- 2. Kubin, Alfred, 1877- -Bibl. I. Title.

Kubitschek, Juscelino, Pres. Brazil, 1902-

MEDAGLIA, Francisco. 923.181
Juscelino Kubitschek, President of Brazil, the life of a self-made man. [New York? 1959] 128p. illus. 21cm. [F2538.2.K8M4] 59-3153
1. Kubitschek, Juscelino, Pres. Brazil, 1902- I. Title.

Kublai Khan, 1216-1294—Juvenile literature.

SILVERBERG, Robert 950.20924
Kublai Khan, lord of Xanadu [by] Walker Chapman. [1st ed.] Indianapolis, Bobbs [1966] 214p. map. 22cm. Bibl. [DS752.S44] 66-18602 3.95
1. Kublai Khan, 1216-1294—Juvenile literature. I. Title.

Kubrick, Stanley.

WALKER, 791.43'0233'0924
Alexander, film critic.
Stanley Kubrick directs. [1st ed.] New York, Harcourt Brace Jovanovich [1971] 272 p. illus., ports. 23 cm. "A creation of Halcyon Enterprises." Includes bibliographical references. [PN1998.A3K75] 77-153692 ISBN 0-15-184885-8
1. Kubrick, Stanley. I. Title. **BIP**

WALKER, 791.43'0233'0924
Alexander, film critic.
Stanley Kubrick directs. Expanded ed. New York, Harcourt Brace Jovanovich [1972] 304 p. illus. 25 cm. "A creation of Halcyon Enterprises." Filmography: p. 300-304. [PN1998.A3K75 1972] 72-192870 ISBN 0-15-684892-9
1. Kubrick, Stanley. I. Title.

Kudirka, Simas.

KUDIRKA, Simas. 323.6'4'0924 B
For those still at sea : Simas Kudirka & Larry Eichel. New York : Dial Press, c1978. viii, 226 p., [4] leaves of plates : ill. ; 22 cm. [DK511.L28K874] 78-5699 ISBN 0-8037-2684-8 : 7.95
1. Kudirka, Simas. 2. Defectors—Russia—Biography. 3. Political prisoners—Russia—Biography. I. Eichel, Lawrence E., joint author. II. Title.

Kudo, Naotaro, 1895-

KUDO, Naotaro, 914.26'0485'7
1895-
A stranger in East Anglia / by Naotaro Kudo. Ipswich : East Anglian Magazine Ltd, 1976. [1], 110 p., [8] p. of plates : ill., port. ; 22 cm. [DA670.E14K8] 76-362307 ISBN 0-900227-19-2 : £2.00
1. Kudo, Naotaro, 1895- 2. East Anglia—Description and travel. I. Title.

Kuhaulua, Jesse, 1944-

KUHAULUA, Jesse, 1944- 796.8'125
Takamiyama; the world of Sumo, with John Wheeler; photographs by D. Turner Givens. [Tokyo, New York] Kodansha International [1973] 171 p. illus. 27 cm. [GV1197.K83] 72-96129 ISBN 0-87011-195-7 10.00 (U.S.)
1. Kuhaulua, Jesse, 1944- 2. Sumo. I. Wheeler, John Krepps. II. Title.

Kuhler, Otto.

KUHLER, Otto. 625.2'0924
My iron journey; an autobiography of a life with steam and steel. Denver, Intermountain Chapter. National Railway Historical Society [1967] 244 p. illus. (port col.) ports. 29 cm. [TJ149.K75A3] 67-18268
I. Title.

Kuhlman, Kathryn.

BUCKINGHAM, Jamie. 269'.2'0924 B
Daughter of destiny : Kathryn Kuhlman, her story / by Jamie Buckingham. Plainfield, N.J. : Logos International, c1976. ix, 309 p., [8] leaves of plates : ill. ; 22 cm. [BV3785.K84B8] 76-12034 ISBN 0-88270-078-2 : 6.95
1. Kuhlman, Kathryn. 2. Evangelists—Pennsylvania—Pittsburgh—Biography. 3. Healers—Pennsylvania—Pittsburgh—Biography. 4. Pittsburgh—Biography. I. Title.

BUCKINGHAM, 269'.2'0924 [B]
Jamie.
Daughter of destiny : Kathryn Kuhlman, her story / by Jamie Buckingham. New York : Pocket Books, 1978,c1976. 253p. : ill. ; 18 cm. (A Kangaroo Book) [BV3785.K84B8] ISBN 0-671-82005-2 pbk. : 1.95
1. Kuhlman, Kathryn. 2. Evangelists — Pennsylvania — Pittsburgh — Biography.

3. Healers — Pennsylvania — Pittsburgh — Biography. 4. Pittsburgh — Biography. I. Title.
L.C. card no. for 1977 Logos International ed.: 76-12034

HOSIER, Helen Kooiman. 269'.2'0924 B
Kathryn Kuhlman : the life she led, the legacy she left / Helen Kooiman Hosier. Boston : G. K. Hall, 1976. p. cm. Large print ed. Includes bibliographical references. [BV3785.K84H67 1976] 76-41341 ISBN 0-8161-6411-8 : 10.95
1. Kuhlman, Kathryn. 2. Evangelists—United States—Biography. 3. Sight-saving books.

SPRAGGETT, Allen. 615'.852'0924 B
Kathryn Kuhlman: the woman who believes in miracles. New York, World Pub. Co. [1970] xiv, 177 p. 22 cm. Bibliography: p. 175-177. [RZ405.S75] 71-103843 5.95
1. Kuhlman, Kathryn. 2. Faith-cure.

Kuhn, Isaac,

KUHN, Isaac, ed. 923.173
Abraham Lincoln. [E457.8.K95] 53-30532
I. Title.

Kuhn, Isobel.

CANFIELD, Carolyn L. 922
One vision only. [Biography of Isobel Kuhn] Chicago, Moody [1967, c.1959] 191p. 18cm. (Pocket bks., 97) [BV3427.K8C3] .59 pap.,
1. Kuhn, Isobel. I. Title.

KUHN, Isobel. 922
In the arena. Chicago, Moody Press [1958] 222p. 22cm. Autobiographical. [BV3427.K8A3] 58-932
I. Title. BIP

Kuhn, Walt, 1877-1949.

ADAMS, Philip Rhys, 1908- 759.13
Walt Kuhn, painter : his life and work / by Philip Rhys Adams. Columbus : Ohio State University Press, [1978] p. cm. Includes index. [ND237.K8A84] 78-3502 ISBN 0-8142-0258-6 : 10.00
1. Kuhn, Walt, 1877-1949. 2. Painters—United States—Biography. I. Title. BIP

Kulp, Harold Stover, 1894-1964.

KULP, Mary Ann Moyer. 266.6'5 B
No longer strangers; a biography of H. Stover Kulp. Elgin, Ill., Brethren Press [1968] 188 p. illus., maps, ports. 21 cm. [BV3625.N6K84] 68-4439
1. Kulp, Harold Stover, 1894-1964. 2. Missions—Nigeria. I. Title.

Kulski, Julian Eugene, 1929-

KULSKI, Julian Eugene, 1929- 940.53'438'4 B
Dying, we live : the personal chronicle of a young freedom fighter, Warsaw, 1939-1945 / by Julian Eugeniusz Kulski. 1st ed. New York : Holt, Rinehart and Winston, c1979. 304 p. : ill. ; 25 cm. [D802.P62W36] 78-31656 16.95
1. Kulski, Julian Eugene, 1929- 2. Poland. Polskie Sily Zbrojne. Armia Krajowa—Biography. 3. World War, 1939-1945—Underground movements—Poland—Warsaw—Biography. 4. World War, 1939-1945—Personal narrative, Polish. 5. Warsaw—Biography. 6. Soldiers—Poland—Biography. I. Title.

Kundek, Joseph, 1810-1857.

MCANDREWS, Dunstan. 922.273
Father Joseph Kundek, 1810-1857; a missionary priest of the Diocese of Vincennes. St. Meinrad, Ind. [1954] 74p. illus. 22cm. (A Grail publication) [BX4705.K78M3] 55-42633
1. Kundek, Joseph, 1810-1857. I. Title.

Kung, Ai-ling (Sung) 1888-

HAHN, Emily, 1905- 951.04'2'0922
The Soong sisters. Westport, Conn., Greenwood Press [1970, c1941] xxi, 349 p. ports. 23 cm. [DS778.A1H3 1970] 78-110041
1. Kung, Ai-ling (Sung) 1888- 2. Sun, Ch'ing-ling (Sung) 1890- 3. Chiang, Mei-ling (Sung) 1897- I. Title. BIP

Kung, Ai-ling Sung, 1888- —Juvenile literature.

EUNSON, Roby. 951.04'092'2
The Soong sisters / by Roby Eunson. New York : Franklin Watts, 1975. 136 p. : ill. ; 24 cm. Includes index. Bibliography: p. 131-132. A biography of the three sisters who as Mrs. H. H. Kung, Mme Sun Yat-sen, and Mme Chiang Kai-shek exerted more influence upon United States policy toward China than almost "any other person or persons in this century." [DS778.K778E9] 920 75-5952 ISBN 0-531-02835-6 lib.bdg. : 5.90
1. Kung, Ai-ling Sung, 1888- —Juvenile literature. 2. Sun, Ch'ing-ling Sung, 1890- —Juvenile literature. 3. Chiang, Mei-ling Sung, 1897- —Juvenile literature. I. Title.

Kunhardt, Philip B.

KUNHARDT, Philip B. 818'.5'409
My father's house [by] Philip B. Kunhardt, Jr. [1st ed.] New York, Random House [1970] 239 p. 22 cm. Autobiographical. [PN4874.K83A3] 72-103976 5.95
I. Title.

Kuniyoshi, Yasuo, 1893-1953.

YASUO Kuniyoshi, 1889-1953 : 760'.092'4
a retrospective exhibition, February 9-March 23, 1975, University Art Museum, the University of Texas at Austin, U.S.A.... Austin : University of Texas Art Museum, [1975] 71 p. : ill. (some col.) ; 22 cm. [N6537.K83Y37] 74-620196
1. Kuniyoshi, Yasuo, 1893-1953. I. Texas. University at Austin. Art Museum.

Kuo, Mo-jo, 1892-

ROY, David Tod, 1933- 915.1'03'40924 B
Kuo Mo-jo: the early years. Cambridge, Mass., Harvard University Press, 1971. 244 p. 2 ports. 22 cm. (Harvard East Asian series, 55) Bibliography: p. 202-214. [CT1828.K87R68] 77-123569 ISBN 0-674-50570-0 7.50
1. Kuo, Mo-jo, 1892- I. Title. II. Series. BIP

Kuprin, Aleksandr Ivanovich, 1870-1938.

LUKER, N. J. L. 891.7'3'3 B
Alexander Kuprin / by Nicholas Luker. Boston : Twayne Publishers, c1978. 171 p. : port. ; 21 cm. (Twayne's world authors series ; TWAS 481 : Russia) Includes index. Bibliography: p. 163-165. [PG3467.K8Z84] 78-1535 ISBN 0-8057-6322-8 : 10.95
1. Kuprin, Aleksandr Ivanovich, 1870-1938. 2. Authors, Russian—20th century—Biography. 3. Journalists—Russia—Biography. I. Title. BIP

Kutuzov, Mikhail Illarionovich svetleishii kniaz' Smolenskii, 1745-1813.

PARKINSON, Roger. 355.3'31'0924 B
The fox of the north : the life of Kutuzov, General of War and Peace / Roger Parkinson. London : P. Davies, 1976. 253 p., [2] leaves of plates : ill. ; 23 cm. Includes index. Bibliography: p. 245-247. [DK169.K8P37] 77-352208 ISBN 0-432-11601-X : £6.50
1. Kutuzov, Mikhail Illarionovich svetleishii kniaz' Smolenskii, 1745-1813. 2. Russia. Armiia—Biography. 3. Generals—Russia—Biography. I. Title. BIP

Kuyper, Abraham, 1837-1920.

VANDENBERG, Frank. 923.2492
Abraham Kuyper. Grand Rapids, Mich. Eerdmans [c.1960] 307p. illus. 23cm. 59-14580 4.00 bds.,
1. Kuyper, Abraham, 1837-1920. I. Title.

Kwak, Pyong-gyu.

KWAK, Pyong-gyu. 365'.45'0957
The land of eternal darkness : memories of Siberian labor camps / by Kwak Byong Kyu [i.e. Kwak Pyong-gyu] ; co-translated by Paul J. White, Michael P. Regan, Lim H. Suop. 1st ed. New York : Vantage Press, c1978. 384 p. ; 21 cm. Translation of Nat kwa pam i omnun taeji. [HV8964.R8K813] 78-108066 ISBN 0-533-03149-4 : 10.00
1. Kwak, Pyong-gyu. 2. Concentration camps—Siberia. 3. Political prisoners—Russia. 4. Political prisoners—Korea. 5. Korea—Biography. I. Title. BIP

Kwakiutl Indians.

NOWELL, Charles James, 1870- 970.3
Smoke from their fires; the life of a Kwakiutl chief, by Clellan S. Ford. [Hamden, Conn.] Archon Books, 1968 [c1941] 248 p. col. illus., map, port. 23 cm. The life story of Charles James Nowell (Tlalis), a Kwakiutl chief, as told to C. S. Ford. "An introduction to Kwakiutl society [by C. S. Ford]": p. 1-40. [E90.K85N6 1968] 68-15344
1. Kwakiutl Indians. I. Ford, Clellan Stearns, 1909- ed. II. Title.

Kyasht, Lydia.

KYASHT, Lydia. 792.8'092'4 B
Romantic recollections / by Lydia Kyasht ; edited by Erica Beale. New York : Da Capo Press, 1978. 247 p., [15] leaves of plates : ill. ; 23 cm. (Da Capo series in dance) Reprint of the 1929 ed. published by Brentano, London, New York. [GV1785.K93A35 1978] 77-27057 ISBN 0-306-77572-7 lib.bdg. : 19.50
1. Kyasht, Lydia. 2. Dancers—Biography. I. Title. BIP

Kyemba, Henry.

†KYEMBA, Henry. 967.6'104'0924 B
A state of blood : the inside story of Idi Amin / by Henry Kyemba ; with a foreword by Godfrey Lule. New York : Grosset & Dunlap, 1977. 288 p. : ill. ; 22 cm. Includes index. [DT433.282.K92A34] 77-87111 10.00
1. Kyemba, Henry. 2. Amin, Idi, 1925- 3. Uganda—Politics and government—1962- 4. Political crimes and offenses—Uganda. 5. Cabinet officers—Uganda—Biography. 6. Refugees, Political—Uganda—Biography. 7. Refugees, Political—Great Britain—Biography. I. Title. BIP

Leautaud, Paul, 1872-1956—Biography.

HARDING, James. 848'.9'1209 B
Lost illusions : Paul Leautaud and his world / James Harding. 1st American ed. Rutherford, [N.J.] : Fairleigh Dickinson University Press, [1975] c1974 230 p., [7] leaves of plates : ill. ; 22 cm. Includes index. Bibliography: p. [221]-224. [PQ2623.E14Z7 1974b] 75-4066 ISBN 0-8386-1744-1 : 10.00
1. Leautaud, Paul, 1872-1956—Biography. I. Title. BIP

L'Enfant, Pierre Charles, 1755-1825.

CAEMMERER, Hans Paul, 1884- 975.3
The life of Pierre Charles L'Enfant, planner of the city beautiful, the city of Washington. Based on original sources. Washington, National Republic Pub. Co., 1950. xxvi, 480 p. illus., ports., maps, 24 cm. Bibliography: p. 472-473. [F195.L53] 51-8048
1. L'Enfant, Pierre Charles, 1755-1825. 2. Washington, D. C.—L'Enfant plan. I. Title.

CAEMMERER, Hans Paul, 1884-1962. 711'.0924 B
The life of Pierre Charles L'Enfant. New York, Da Capo Press, 1970 [c1950] xxvi, 480 p. illus., facsims., maps, plans, ports. 24 cm. (Da Capo press series in architecture and decorative art, v. 33) Bibliography: p. 472-473. [F195.L53 1970] 71-87546
1. L'Enfant, Pierre Charles, 1755-1825. 2. Washington, D.C.—L'Enfant plan. BIP

L'Engle, Madeleine.

L'ENGLE, Madeleine. 818'.5'403 B
A circle of quiet. [1st ed.] New York, Farrar, Straus and Giroux [1972] 245 p. 22 cm. Autobiographical. [PS3523.E55Z5] 75-164542 ISBN 0-374-12374-8 6.95
I. Title. BIP

L'Engle, Madeleine—Biography.

L'ENGLE, Madeleine. 813'.5'4 B
The summer of the great-grandmother. New York, Farrar, Straus and Giroux [1974] 245 p. ports. 22 cm. [PS3523.E55Z52 1974] 74-13157 ISBN 0-374-27174-7 8.95
1. L'Engle, Madeleine—Biography. 2. Camp, Madeleine Barnett. I. Title. BIP

Leon, Luis Ponce de, 1528?-1591.

DURAN, Manuel, 1925- 868'.3'09 B
Luis de Leon. New York, Twayne Publishers [1971] 182 p. 21 cm. (Twayne's world authors series, TWAS 136: Spain) Bibliography: p. 171-175. [PQ6410.L3D8] 79-120491
1. Leon, Luis Ponce de, 1528?-1591. BIP

L'Estoile, Claude de, 1597-1652.

PARKER, Richard Alexander, 1898- 841'.4
Claude de L'Estoille, poet and dramatist, 1597-1652. Baltimore, Johns Hopkins Press, 1930. [New York, Johnson Reprint Corp., 1973] x, 111 p. 22 cm. Original ed. issued as v. 16 of the Johns Hopkins studies in Romance literatures and languages. Bibliography: p. 103-107. [PQ1817.L66Z8 1973] 72-11864 ISBN 0-384-44862-3
1. L'Estoile, Claude de, 1597-1652. I. Series: The Johns Hopkins studies in Romance literatures and languages, v. 16. BIP

Levesque, Rene, 1922—

DESBARATS, Peter. 971.4'04'0924 B
Rene : a Canadian in search of a country / Peter Desbarats. Toronto : McClelland and Stewart, c1976. 223 p. ; 24 cm. [F1053.2.L582D47] 77-369925 ISBN 0-7710-2691-9 : 10.00
1. Levesque, Rene, 1922- 2. Parti Quebecois. 3. Prime ministers—Quebec (Province)—Biography. 4. Quebec (Province)—History—Autonomy and independence movements. I. Title.

Levi-Strauss, Claude.

LEACH, Edmund Ronald. 301.29'24
Claude Levi-Strauss [by] Edmund Leach. New York, Viking Press [1970] xi, 142 p. illus. 20 cm. (Modern masters) Bibliography: p. [133]-137. [GN21.L4L38 1970] 71-104142
1. Levi-Strauss, Claude. BIP

LEACH, Edmund Ronald. 301.2'092'4
Claude Levi-Strauss / Edmund Leach. Rev. ed. New York : Viking Press, 1974. xi, 146 p. : ill. ; 20 cm. (Modern masters) Original and rev. British ed. published under title: Levi-Strauss. Includes index. Bibliography: p. [137]-142. [GN21.L4L38 1974] 74-1122 ISBN 0-670-22515-0. ISBN 0-670-01980-1 pbk. : 7.50
1. Levi-Strauss, Claude.

Loben Sels, Pieter Justus van.

LOBEN Sels, 914.92'03'60924
Pieter Justus van.
The memoirs of Pieter Justus van Ioben Sels. [Menlo Park, Calif., c1966] 89 p. illus., facsims., ports. 24 cm. No. 144 of 200 copies. "Footnotes": p. 82-83. [DJ219.L6A3] 67-8444
I. Title.

Lopez, Luis Carlos, 1883-1950.

BAZIK, Martha S. 861
The life and works of Luis Carlos Lopez / by Martha S. Bazik. Chapel Hill : U.N.C. Dept. of Romance Languages : [distributed by University of North Carolina Press] 1977. 147 p. ; 24 cm. (North Carolina studies in the Romance languages and literatures ; no. 182) Bibliography: p. [111]-115. [PQ8179.L57Z58] 77-550 ISBN 0-8078-9183-5 : 7.95
1. Lopez, Luis Carlos, 1883-1950. 2. Poets, Colombian—20th century—Biography. I. Title. II. Series. **BIP**

Lopez, Martin.

GARDINER, Clinton 972'.02'0924
Harvey.
Martin Lopez, conquistador citizen of Mexico, by C. Harvey Gardiner. Westport, Conn., Greenwood Press [1974, c1958] ix, 193 p. illus. 22 cm. Reprint of the ed. published by the University of Kentucky Press, Lexington. Bibliography: p. [179]-184. [F1230.L84G3 1974] 73-19307 ISBN 0-8371-7322-1 10.00
1. Lopez, Martin. 2. Mexico—History—Conquest, 1519-1540. **BIP**

La Farge, John, 1835-1910.

CORTISSOZ, Royal, 1869- 759.13 B
1948.
John La Farge; a memoir and a study. New York, Kennedy Graphics, 1971 [c1911] xii, 268 p. illus., ports. 24 cm. (Library of American art) [ND237.L2C6 1971] 70-87508
1. La Farge, John, 1835-1910.

La Farge, John, 1880-1963.

LA FARGE, John, 1880- 922.273
The manner is ordinary. [1st ed.] New York, Harcourt, Brace [1954] 408 p. illus. 22 cm. Autobiography. [BX4705.L237A3] 54-5250
1. Catholic Church—Clergy—Correspondence, reminiscences, etc. I. Title.

LA FARGE, John, 1880- 922.273
The manner is ordinary. Garden City, N, Y., Image Books [1957] 352p. 19cm. (A Doubleday image book, D52) Autobiography. [BX4705.L237A3 1957] 57-3403
1. Catholic Church—Clergy—Correspondence, reminiscences, etc. I. Title.

STROUSSE, Flora, 271'.5'0924 (B)
1897-
John La Farge, gentle Jesuit. Illustrated by Salem Tamer. New York, P.J. Kenedy [1968, c1967] 188 p. illus., ports. 22 cm. (American background books, 33) [BX4705.L237S7] 67-26801 2.50
1. La Farge, John, 1880-1963. I. Title. II. Series.

STROUSSE, Flora, 282'.0924 B
1897-
John La Farge, gentle Jesuit. Illustrated by Salem Tamer. New York, P. J. Kenedy [1968, c1967] 188 p. illus., ports. 22 cm. (American background books, 33) A biography of the American Jesuit who devoted himself to fighting prejudice of all sorts, especially during his term as editor of a major journal of Catholic opinion. [BX4705.L237S7] 92 AC 68
1. La Farge, John, 1880-1963. I. Tamer, Salem, illus. II. Title. III. Series.

La Farge, Oliver, 1901-1963.

MCNICKLE, D'Arcy, 301.2'0924 B
1904-
Indian man; a life of Oliver La Farge. Bloomington, Indiana University Press [1971] xiii, 242 p. port. 22 cm. Bibliography: p. xii-xiii. [GN21.L24M3] 70-135010 ISBN 0-253-14000-5 7.95
1. La Farge, Oliver, 1901-1963. I. Title. **BIP**

La Farge, Phyllis.

LA FARGE, Phyllis. 814'.5'4
Keeping going. [1st ed.] New York, Harcourt Brace Jovanovich [1971] ix, 180 p. 21 cm. Personal reminiscences. "Sponsored by the Boston Children's Hospital Medical Center." [PS3562.A27Z5 1971] 72-142086 ISBN 0-15-146875-3
I. Title.

La Fayette, Marie Joseph Paul Yves Roch Gilbert du Motier, marquis de, 1757-1834—Juvenile literature.

GRANT, Matthew G. 944.04'092'4 B
Lafayette; freedom's general [by] Matthew G. Grant. Illustrated by John Keely and Dick Brude. [Mankato, Minn., Creative Education; distributed by Childrens Press, Chicago, 1974] 31 p. illus. (part col.) 25 cm. (His Gallery of great American series. War heroes of America) An easy-to-read biography of the French nobleman who was a leader in both the American and French revolutions. [DC146.L2G72] 92 73-18155 ISBN 0-87191-301-1 3.95 (lib. bdg.)
1. La Fayette, Marie Joseph Paul Yves Roch Gilbert du Motier, marqius de, 1757-1834—Juvenile literature, I. Keely, John, illus. II. Brude, Dick, illus. III. Title.

La Flesche, Francis, d. 1932.

LA FLESCHE, Francis, 970'.004'97
d.1932.
The Middle Five : Indian schoolboys of the Omaha Tribe / Francis La Flesche ; foreword by David A. Baerreis. Lincoln : University of Nebraska Press, [1978] c1963. p. cm. Reprint of the ed. published by the University of Wisconsin Press, Madison. [E99.O4L165 1978] 78-17409 ISBN 0-8032-2852-X : 10.95 ISBN 0-8032-7901-9 pbk. : 2.95
1. La Flesche, Francis, d. 1932. 2. Omaha Indians—Children. 3. Omaha Indians—Education. 4. Omaha Indians—Biography. 5. Indians of North America—Nebraska—Children. 6. Indians of North America—Nebraska—Education. I. Title. **BIP**

La Flesche, Susette, 1854-1903.

WILSON, Dorothy Clarke. 970.3 B
Bright Eyes; the story of Susette La Flesche, an Omaha Indian. New York, McGraw-Hill [1974] 396 p. 24 cm. Bibliography: p. [379]-385. [E99.O4W54] 73-15636 ISBN 0-07-070752-9 8.95
1. La Flesche, Susette, 1854-1903. I. Title. **BIP**

La Flesche, Susette, 1854-1903—Juvenile literature.

CRARY, Margaret. 970.3 B
Susette La Flesche: voice of the Omaha Indians. New York, Hawthorn Books [1973] 178 p. illus. 22 cm. Bibliography: p. 173. Traces Susette La Flesche's lifetime campaign to better conditions for her people in spite of the nineteenth-century handicaps of being both a woman and an Indian. [E99.O4C72 1973] 92 72-7773 5.95
1. La Flesche, Susette, 1854-1903—Juvenile literature. 2. Omaha Indians—Juvenile literature. I. Title.

La Follette, Robert Marion, 1855-1925.

MAXWELL, Robert S., 973.91'5'0924
comp.
La Follette. Edited by Robert S. Maxwell. Englewood Cliffs, N.J., Prentice Hall [1969] vii, 182 p. 21 cm. (Great lives observed) (A Spectrum book, S-713.) "Bibliographical note": p. 178-179. [E664.L16M28] 69-15341 1.95
1. La Follette, Robert Marion, 1855-1925. **BIP**

MAXWELL, Robert S. 923.273
La Follette and the rise of the Progressives in Wisconsin. [Madison] State Historical Society of Wisconsin [1956] vii, 271 p. illus., ports. 24 cm. Bibliography: p. 245-255. [E664.L16M3] 56-58553
1. La Follette, Robert Marion, 1855-1925. 2. Wisconsin—Politics and government—1848-1950. 3. Progressivism (U. S. politics) I. Title. **BIP**

MAXWELL, Robert S. 973.91'092'4 B
La Follette and the rise of the Progressives in Wisconsin [by] Robert S. Maxwell. New York, Russell & Russell [1973, c1956] viii, 271 p. illus. 23 cm. Reprint of the ed. published by the State Historical Society of Wisconsin, Madison. Bibliography: p. 245-255. [E664.L16M3 1973] 72-85000 ISBN 0-8462-1696-5 18.00
1. La Follette, Robert Marion, 1855-1925. 2. Wisconsin—Politics and government—1848-1950. 3. Progressivism (United States politics) I. Title.

THELEN, David Paul 977.5040924
The early life of Robert M. La Follete. 1855-1884. Chicago. Loyola [c.] 1966. x, 147p. 24cm. Bibl. [E664.L16T5] 66-11931 3.50
1. La Follette, Robert Marion. 1855-1925. I. Title.

THELEN, David Paul. 977.5040924
The early life of Robert M. LaFollette, 1855-1884. Chicago, Loyola University Press, 1966. x, 147 p. port. 24 cm. "William P. Lyons master's essay award, 1965." Bibliographical references included in "Notes" (p. 109-130) [E664.L16T5] 66-11931
1. La Follette, Robert Marion, 1855-1925. I. Title.

La Follette, Robert Marion, 1895-1953.

MANEY, Patrick J., 973.91'092'4 B
1946-
"Young Bob" La Follette : a biography of Robert M. La Follette, Jr., 1895-1953 / Patrick J. Maney. Columbia : University of Missouri Press, 1978. 338 p. ; 24 cm. Includes index. Bibliography: p. [315]-324. [E748.L22M36] 77-24991 ISBN 0-8262-0230-6 : 18.00
1. La Follette, Robert Marion, 1895-1953. 2. Legislators—United States—Biography. 3. Social reformers—United States—Biography. 4. Progressivism (United States politics) I. Title.

La Fontaine, Jean de, 1621-1695.

KING, Ethel M. 841'.4 B
Jean de La Fontaine, by Ethel King. Brooklyn, N.Y., Gaus [1970] 76 p. port. 23 cm. Bibliography: p. 76. [PQ1812.K5] 75-122444 3.00
1. La Fontaine, Jean de, 1621-1695.

MACKAY, Agnes Ethel. 841'.4 B
La Fontaine and his friends; a biography. New York, G. Braziller [1973, c1972] 227 p. illus. 22 cm. Bibliography: p. 217-220. [PQ1812.M26 1973] 73-79049 ISBN 0-8076-0694-4 8.95
1. La Fontaine, Jean de, 1621-1695. I. Title.

SUTHERLAND, Monica La 841'.4 B
Fontaine.
La Fontaine, by Monica Sutherland. [Folcroft, Pa.] Folcroft Library Editions, 1974. p. cm. Reprint of the 1953 ed. published by J. Cape. London. Bibliography: p. [PQ1812.S8 1974] 74-7095 20.00 (lib. bdg.).
1. La Fontaine, Jean de, 1621-1695. I. Title.

WADSWORTH, Philip Adrian, 841'.4
1913-
Young La Fontaine; a study of his artistic growth in his early poetry and first fables, by Philip A. Wadsworth. New York, AMS Press [1970, c1952] ix, 236 p. 24 cm. (Northwestern University humanities series, v. 29) Bibliography: p. 221-229. [PQ1812.W3 1970] 78-128943 ISBN 0-404-50729-8
1. La Fontaine, Jean de, 1621-1695. I. Title. II. Series: Northwestern University studies. Humanities series, v. 29.

La Forge, Margaret Swain (Getchell) 1841-1880.

JOHNSON, Curtiss 658.916588710924
S.
America's first lady boss; a wisp of a girl, Macy's, and romance [by] Curtiss S. Johnson. Norwalk, Conn., Silvermine Publishers [1965] 164 p. illus., facsims., ports. 22 cm. [HF3023.L3J6] 65-20595
1. La Forge, Margaret Swain (Getchell) 1841-1880. 2. Macy (R. H.) and Company, New York. I. Title.

La France, Marston.

THE Stoic strain in 810'.9
American literature : essays in honour of Marston LaFrance, 1927-75 / edited by Duane J. MacMillan. Toronto : University of Toronto Press, c1979. xiii, 224 p. ; 24 cm. Contents.Contents.—Johnston, G. For Marston LaFrance.—Buitenhuis, P. The Stoic strain in American literature.—Stern, M. R. Towards Bartleby the scrivener.—Allen, G. W. Walt Whitman and Stoicism.—Beattie, M. Henry James: the voice of Stoicism.—Davison, R. A. A reading of Frank Norris's The pit.—Salomon, R. B. The mock-heroics of desire.—Backman, M. Death and birth in Hemingway.—MacMillan, D. J. His "Magnun O": Stoic Humanism in Faulkner's A fable.—Fuchs, D. Saul Bellow and the example of Dostoevsky.—Lawson, L. A. The moviegoer and the Stoic heritage.—Middlebro's, T. Marston LaFrance: a tribute and memorial bibliography. Includes bibliographical references. [PS121.S76] 79-523 ISBN 0-8020-5441-2 : 17.50
1. La France, Marston. 2. American literature—History and criticism—Addresses, essays, lectures. 3. Stoics in literature. 4. Authors, American—20th century—Biography. I. La France, Marston. II. MacMillan, Duane J., 1937- Contents omitted.

La Guardia, Fiorello Henry,

LA GUARDIA, Fiorello 923.273
Henry, 1882-1947
The making of an insurgent, an autobiography: 1882-1919. Introds. by H. M. Christman, M. R. Werner. New York [Putnam, 1961, c.1948, 1961] 222p. (Capricorn bk. CAP54) 1.25 pap.,
I. Title.

LA GUARDIA, Fiorello 923.273
Henry, 1882-1947
The making of an insurgent, an autobiography; 1882-1919. Introds by H. M. Christman, M. R. Werner [Gloucester, Mass., Peter Smith, c.1948, 1961] 222p. (Capricorn bk., CAP54 rebound) 3.25
I. Title.

La Guardia, Fiorello Henry, 1882-1947.

CUNEO, Ernest, 1905- 923.273
Life with Fiorello; a memoir. New York, Macmillan, 1955. 209 p. illus. 22 cm. [E748.L23C8] 55-13723
1. La Guardia, Fiorello Henry, 1882-1947. I. Title.

HECKSCHER, 974.7'1'040924 B
August, 1913-
Mayor LaGuardia and New York's legendary years / by August Heckscher, with Phyllis Robinson. 1st ed. New York : Norton, c1978. p. cm. Includes index. Bibliography: p. [F128.5.H44 1978] 78-18203 ISBN 0-393-07534-6 : 15.00
1. La Guardia, Fiorello Henry, 1882-1947. 2. New York (City)—Politics and government—1898-1951. 3. New York (City)—Mayors—Biography. I. Robinson, Phyllis, joint author. II. Title.

LA GUARDIA, Fiorello 923.273
Henry, 1882-1947
The making of an insurgent, an autobiography: 1882-1919. Introds. by H. M. Christman, M. R. Werner. New York

[Putnam, 1961, c.1948, 1961] 222p. (Capricorn bk. CAP54) 1.25 pap.,
I. Title.

LA GUARDIA, Fiorello 923.273
Henry, 1882-1947
The making of an insurgent, an autobiography; 1882-1919. Introds. by H. M. Christman, M. R. Werner [Gloucester, Mass., Peter Smith, c.1948, 1961] 222p. (Capricorn bk., CAP54 rebound) 3.25
I. Title.

MANN, Arthur. 923.273
La Guardia, a fighter against his times. [1st ed.] Philadelphia, Lippincott [1959- v. illus. 22 cm. Contents.Contents.--[1] 1882-1933. Includes bibliography. [E748.L23M3] 59-13077
1. La Guardia, Fiorello Henry, 1882-1947. BIP

MANN, Arthur. 320.974710924
La Guardia comes to power: 1933. 1st ed.] Philadelphia, Lippincott [1965] 199 p. maps. 22 cm. Bibliographical references included in "Notes" (p. 176-192) [E748.L23M32] 65-24920
1. La Guardia, Fiorello Henry, 1882-1947. 2. New York (City)—Politics and government—1898-1961. 3. Politics, Practical—Case studies. I. Title.

MANNERS, 974.7'1'040924 B
William, 1907-
Patience and fortitude : Fiorello La Guardia : a biography / by William Manners. 1st ed. New York : Harcourt Brace Jovanovich, c1976. 290 p., [4] leaves of plates : ill. ; 24 cm. Includes index. Bibliography: p. 279-281. [E748.L23M33] 76-895 ISBN 0-15-171290-5 : 12.95
1. La Guardia, Fiorello Henry, 1882-1947. I. Title.

WESTON, Paul B. 923.273
A hammer in the city. Evanston, [Ill.] Regency Books [1962] 158 p. 16 cm. Includes bibliography. [E748.L23W4] 62-53066
1. La Guardia, Fiorello Henry, 1882-1947. I. Title.

ZINN, Howard, 328.73'092'4 B
1922-
LaGuardia in Congress. Westport, Conn., Greenwood Press [1972, c1959] xi, 288 p. 23 cm. Originally presented as the author's thesis, Columbia. Bibliography: p. 275-284. [E748.L23Z5 1972] 72-4007 ISBN 0-8371-6434-6 13.25
1. La Guardia, Fiorello Henry, 1882-1947. I. Title. BIP

La Guardia, Fiorello Henry, 1882-1947—Juvenile literature.

KAUFMAN, Mervyn 974.7'1'040924 B
D.
Fiorello La Guardia, by Mervyn Kaufman. Illustrated by Gene Szafran. New York, Crowell [1972] 32 p. illus. (part col.) 24 cm. (A Crowell biography) A biography of the first Italian-American mayor of New York, a man noted for his honesty and dynamism. [E748.L23K3 1972] 92 75-171005 ISBN 0-690-29817-X 3.75
1. La Guardia, Fiorello, Henry, 1882-1947—Juvenile literature. I. Szafran, Gene, illus. II. Title.

KURLAND, Gerald, 974.7'1'040924
1942-
Fiorello La Guardia, the people's mayor of New York. Charlotteville, N.Y., SamHar Press, 1972. 32 p. 22 cm. (Outstanding personalities, no. 20) Includes bibliographical references. A biography of the man considered by some to be the best mayor New York City ever had. [E748.L23K87] 92 77-190238
1. La Guardia, Fiorello Henry, 1882-1947—Juvenile literature. I. Title.

La Motta, Jake.

LA MOTTA, Jake. 796.8'3'0924 B
Raging bull; my story, by Jake La Motta with Joseph Carter and Peter Savage. Englewood Cliffs, N.J., Prentice-Hall [1970] 218 p. illus., ports. 24 cm. [GV1132.L3A3] 73-124514 ISBN 0-13-752527-3 6.95
I. Carter, Joseph. II. Savage, Peter. III. Title.

La Motte-Fouque, Karoline Auguste (von Briest) frilin de, 1773-1831.

WILDE, Jean T 1898- 928.3
The romantic realist: Caroline de la Motte Fouque. New York, Bookman Associates [1955] 474p. port. 25cm. Thesis--Columbia University. Theis statement on label mounted on t. p. Bibliography: p. 445-462. [PT2390.L13Z95 1955] 55-2599
1. La Motte-Fouque, Karoline Auguste (von Briest) frilin de, 1773-1831. I. Title.

La Oe, Else Kienle,

LA OE, Else Kienle, 1900- 926.1
Woman surgeon, the autobiography of Else K. La Roe. New York, Dial Oress, 1957. 373p. 21cm. [R)154.L28.A3] 56-12133
I. Title.

La Revelliere de Lepeaux, Louis Marie de, 1753-1824.

ROBISON, Georgia, 944.04'092'4 B
1905-
Revelliere-Lepeaux, citizen director, 1753-1824. New York, Octagon Books, 1972 [c1938] 307 p. illus. 24 cm. Original ed. issued as no. 438 of the Studies in history, economics, and public law. Originally presented as the author's thesis, Columbia. Bibliography: p. 278-288. [DC146.L27R6 1972] 72-8923 ISBN 0-374-96893-4 10.75
1. La Revelliere de Lepeaux, Louis Marie de, 1753-1824. 2. France—History—Revolution, 1795-1799. I. Title. II. Series: Columbia studies in the social sciences, no. 348. BIP

La Roe, Else K.,

LA ROE, Else K., M.D. 926.17
Woman surgeon, autobiography. New York, Popular Lib. [1966, c.1957] 317p. 18cm. (75-1186) .75 pap.,
I. Title.

La Roe, Else Kienle,

LA ROE, Else Kienle, 1900- 926.1
Woman surgeon; the autobiography of Else K. La Roe. New York, Dial Press, 1957. 373 p. 21 cm. [R154.L28A3] 56-12133
I. Title.

LA ROE, Else Kienle, 1900- 926.1
Woman surgeon; the autobiography of Else K. La Roe. New York, Popular Library [1961, c.1957] 317p. (Popular special SP 79) .50 pap.,
I. Title.

La Salle, Jean Baptiste de, Saint, 1651-1719.

BURKHARD, Leo Charles. 922.244
Master of mischief makers, Saint John Baptist de la Salle; the life story of a teacher saint of France. Illustrated by Gilbert Titus. St. Meinrad, Ind. [1952] 211 p. illus. 22 cm. "Grail publication." [LB475.L2B8] 52-44149
1. La Salle, Jean Baptiste de, Saint, 1651-1719. I. Title.

FARNUM, Mabel Adelaide 922.44
St. John Baptist de La Salle, the schoolmaster. New York, St. Paul Pubns. [dist. Alba House, c.1962] 154p. 19cm. 62-21596 2.50;.95 pap.,
1. La Salle, Jean Baptiste de, Saint, 1651-1719. I. Title.

FARNUM, Mabel Adelaide, 922.244
1887-
St. John Baptist de La Salle, the schoolmaster. New York, St. Paul Publications [1962] 154 p. 20 cm. [LB475.I.22F3] 62-21596
1. La Salle, Jean Baptiste de, Saint, 1651-1719. I. Title.

FITZPATRICK, Edward 922.244
Augustus, 1884-
La Salle, patron of all teachers. Milwaukee, Bruce Pub. Co. [1951] xvii, 428 p. port. 23 cm. Includes bibliographies. [BX4700.L3F5] 51-14473
1. La Salle, Jean Baptiste de, Saint, 1651-1719. I. Title.

LA SALLE, Jean Baptiste 922.244
de, Saint, 1651-1719.
Letters and documents edited by W. J. Battersby. London, New York, Longmans, Green [1952] xxxix, 270p. port., facsims. 23cm. French and English. [LB475.L22A4] 52-12332
1. Brothers of the Christian Schools. I. Title.

MAILLEFER, Elie 922.244
The life of John Baptist de La Salle, priest, doctor, former canon of the Cathedral of Rheims, and founder of the Brothers of the Christian Schools. Tr. by Didymus John. Illus. by James Francis Heinlen. Winona, Minn., St. Mary's College Pr. [c.]1963. 179p. illus. 22cm. 63-5419 3.75
1. La Salle, Jean Baptiste de, Saint, 1651-1719. 2. Brothers of the Christian Schools I. Title.

ST. John Baptist de la v. 12
Salle; with a foreword by H. O. Evennett. New York, Macmillan [1957] 346p. illus.
1. La Salle, Jean Baptiste de, Saint, 1651-1719. I. Battersby, William John.

La. Salle, Jean Baptiste de, Saint, 1651-1719—Juvenile literature.

ROBERTO, Brother, 271.780924
1927-
Boys and Brothers; a life of Saint John Baptist de la Salle, Illus. by Carolyn Lee Jagodits. Notre Dame, Ind., 46556, Dujarie Pr. [1965] 95p. illus. 24cm. [LB475.L22R6] 65-27762 2.25
1. La. Salle, Jean Baptiste de, Saint, 1651-1719—Juvenile literature. I. Title.

La Salle, Robert Cavelier, sieur de, 1643-1687.

COX, Isaac Joslin, 970'.02'0924
1873-1956, ed.
The journeys of Rene Robert Cavelier, sieur de La Salle; as related by his faithful lieutenent, Henri de Tonty; his missionary colleagues, Fathers Zenobius Membre, Louis Hennepin, and Anastasius Douay; his early biographer, Father Christian Le Clercq; his trusted subordinate, Henri Joutel; and his brother, Jean Cavelier: together with memoirs, commissions, etc. Edited with an introd. by Isaac Joslin Cox. Austin [Tex.] Pemberton Press, 1968- v. port. 23 cm. (Brasada reprint series, 6) Reprint of the 1905 ed. Includes bibliographical references. [F1030.5.C88] 72-27245 12.50
1. La Salle, Robert Cavelier, sieur de, 1643-1687. I. Title. II. Series.

COX, Isaac 917.3'04'240924
Joslin, 1873-1956, ed.
The journeys of Rene Robert Cavelier, sieur de LaSalle, as related by his faithful lieutenant, Henri de Tonty; his missionary colleagues, Fathers Zenobius Membre, Louis Hennepin, and Anastasius Douay; his early biographer, Father Christian LeClercq; his trusted subordinate, Henri Joutel; and his brother, Jean Cavelier; together with memoirs, commissions, etc. Edited with an introd. New York, Allerton Book Co., 1922. [New York, AMS Press, 1973] 2 v. illus. 19 cm. Original ed. issued in series: American explorers. Bibliography: v. 2, p. 246-250. [F1030.5.C883] 72-2828 ISBN 0-404-54917-9 26.00
1. La Salle, Robert Cavelier, sieur de, 1643-1687. I. Title. II. Series: American explorers.

MACLEAN, Harrison 917.7'04'10924
John.
The fate of the Griffon / by Harrison John MacLean. Chicago : Sage Books, [1975] c1974. [10], 118 p. : ill. ; 23 cm. Bibliography: 8th prelim. page. [F1030.5.M32 1975] 74-14399 ISBN 0-8040-0674-1 : 8.95
1. La Salle, Robert Cavelier, sieur de, 1643-1687. 2. Griffon (Ship) 3. MacLean, Harrison John. 4. Great Lakes—Discovery and exploration. I. Title. BIP

PARKMAN, Francis, 1823- 136.76
1893.
La Salle and the discovery of the Great West. Introd. by Allan Nevins. New York, F. Ungar Pub. Co. [1965] xxv, 483 p. illus., maps. 22 cm. (His France and England in North America, v. 3) American classics. First ed. published in 1869 under title: The discovery of the Great West. Reprint of the 11th ed., published in 1879. Bibliographical footnotes. [F1030.P24v] [l.3] 922.271 973 66-1670
1. La Salle, Robert Cavelier, sieur de, 1643-1687. 2. New France—Disc. & explor. 3. Mississippi River—Disc & explor. I. Title. BIP

TERRELL, John 970'.02'0924 B
Upton, 1900-
La Salle: the life and times of an explorer. New York, Weybright and Talley [1968] 282 p. 22 cm. "Bibliographical notes": p. 267-271. [F1030.5.T4] 68-28272 5.95
1. La Salle, Robert Cavelier, sieur de, 1643-1687. I. Title.

WEDDLE, Robert S. 973.1'6
Wilderness manhunt: the Spanish search for La Salle [by] Robert S. Weddle. Austin, University of Texas Press [1973] xiv, 291 p. illus. 23 cm. Bibliography: p. [267]-276. [F352.W42] 72-1579 ISBN 0-292-79000-7 8.50
1. La Salle, Robert Cavelier, sieur de, 1643-1687. 2. Mississippi Valley—Discovery and exploration. 3. Spaniards in North America. 4. French in the United States. 5. Texas—History—To 1856. I. Title. BIP

La Salle, Robert Cavelier, sieur de, 1643-1687—Juvenile literature.

JACOBS, William 970'.02'0924 B
Jay.
Robert Cavelier de La Salle / W. J. Jacobs ; illustrated with authentic prints, documents, and maps. New York : F. Watts, 1975. 57 p. : ill. ; 26 cm. (A Visual biography) Includes index. Bibliography: p. 54. A brief biography of the seventeenth-century French explorer who traveled the entire length of the Mississippi and took possession of all its surrounding territory for France. [F1030.5.J33] 92 75-8598 ISBN 0-531-02843-7 lib.bdg. : 4.90
1. La Salle, Robert Cavelier, sieur de, 1643-1687—Juvenile literature. I. Title. BIP

La Verendrye, Pierre Gaultier de Varennes, sieur de, 1685-1749—Juvenile literature.

SYME, Ronald, 970.03'092'4 B
1910-
Fur trader of the North; the story of Pierre de la Verendrye. Illustrated by Richard Cuffari. New York, Morrow, 1973. 191 p. illus. 21 cm. Bibliography: p. 191. Biography of an eighteenth-century fur trader from New France who, while searching for a river leading to the Pacific, discovered instead areas in western North America. [F1060.7.L43 1973] 92 72-13603 ISBN 0-688-20076-1 4.75
1. La Verendrye, Pierre Gaultier de Varennes, sieur de, 1685-1749—Juvenile literature. 2. New France—Discovery and exploration—Juvenile literature. I. Title. Library binding; 4.32, ISBN 0-688-30076-6. BIP

La Valliere, Louise Francoise de La Baume Le Blanc, duchesse de, 1644-1710.

SANDERS, Joan. 920.7
La petite; the life of Louise de la Valliere. Boston, Houghton Mifflin, 1959. 280 p. illus. 22 cm. [DC130.L4S3] 59-8863
1. La Valliere, Louise Francoise de La Baume Le Blanc, duchesse de, 1644-1710. I. Title.

La Verendrye, Pierre Gaultier de Varennes, sieur de, 1685-1749.

CROUSE, Nellis Maynard, 923.971
1884-
La Verendrye, fur trader and explorer. Ithaca, N. Y., Cornell University Press [1956] ix, 247p. port., maps (part fold.) 24cm. Bibliography: p. 237-241. [F1060.7.L3914] 56-13891
1. La Verendrye, Pierre Gaultier de Varennes, sieur de, 1685-1749. 2. New France—Disc. & explor. I. Title.

CROUSE, Nellis Maynard, 1884- 970'.03'0924 B
La Verendrye, fur trader and explorer [by] Nellis M. Crouse. Port Washington, N.Y., Kennikat Press [1972, c1956] ix, 247 p. illus., maps (part fold.) 23 cm. Bibliography: p. 237-241. [F1060.7.L3914 1972] 79-153210 ISBN 0-8046-1520-9
1. La Verendrye, Pierre Gaultier de Varennes, sieur de, 1685-1749. 2. New France—Discovery and exploration. I. Title.

Laban, Rudolf von, 1879-1958.

LABAN, Rudolf von, 1879-1958. 793.3'2'0924 B
A life for dance : reminiscences / Rudolf Laban ; with drawings by the author ; translated and annotated by Lisa Ullmann. New York : Theatre Arts Books, 1975. 193 p. : ill. ; 23 cm. Translation of Ein Leben fur den Tanz. Includes index. [GV1785.L2A3313] 74-32538 ISBN 0-87830-073-2 : 10.45
1. Laban, Rudolf von, 1879-1958. 2. Dancing. 3. Movement notation. I. Title.

LaBastille, Anne.

LABASTILLE, Anne. 500.9'747'53
Woodswoman / Anne LaBastille. 1st ed. New York : E. P. Dutton, c1976. vi, 277 p. : ill. ; 22 cm. [QH31.L15A34 1976] 75-34071
1. LaBastille, Anne. 2. Natural history—New York (State)—Adirondack mountains. I. Title. BIP

Labor and laboring classes—Biography.

SELVIN, David F. 331.88
Champions of Labor, by David F. Selvin. London, New York [etc.] Abelard-Schuman [1967] 256 p. ports. 22 cm. "Some notes on further reading": p. 244-247. A history of the labor union movement in the United States traced through the influence and activities of William H. Sylvis, Terence V. Powderly, Samuel Gompers, Eugene V. Debs, William D. Haywood, William Green, John L. Lewis, Sidney Hillman, David Dublinsky, Philip Murray, Walter Reuther, George Meany, and A. Philip Randolph. [HD8073.A1S4] AC 68
1. Labor and laboring classes—Biography. 2. Labor unions—History. I. Title.

Labor and laboring classes—Great Britain—Biography.

BURNETT, John, fl.1966- comp. 301.44'42'0942
The annals of labour, autobiographies of British working-class people, 1820-1920. Edited by John Burnett Bloomington, Indiana University Press [1974] 364 p. 23 cm. Includes bibliographical references. [HD8393.A1B8 1974] 73-19584 12.50
1. Labor and laboring classes—Great Britain—Biography. I. Title. BIP

EVANS, J. N. 331'.0922
Great figures in the labour movement, by J. N. Evans. [1st ed.] Oxford, New York, Pergamon Press [1966] viii, 176 p. ports. 20 cm. (The Commonwealth and international library. History division) Includes bibliographies. [HD8393.A1E9 1966] 66-28417
1. Labor and laboring classes—Great Britain—Biography. 2. Trade-unions—Great Britain—History. 3. Great Britain—Biography. I. Title.

Labor and laboring classes—Great Britain—Biography—Collections.

BELLAMY, Joyce M. 331'.092'2 B
Dictionary of labour biography [by] Joyce M. Bellamy and John Saville. [Clifton] N.J., A. M. Kelley, 1972- v. 25 cm. Includes bibliographical references. [HD8393.A1B44] 78-185417 ISBN 0-678-07008-3
1. Labor and laboring classes—Great Britain—Biography—Collections. I. Saville, John, joint author. II. Title. BIP

Labor and laboring classes—U.S.

BUCHANAN, Joseph Ray, 1851-1924. 331.88'0924 B
The story of a labor agitator. Westport, Conn., Greenwood Press [1970] xi, 460 p. illus., port. 23 cm. Reprint of the 1903 ed. [HD8073.B8A3 1970] 70-88521 ISBN 0-8371-4973-8
1. Labor and laboring classes—U.S. 2. Strikes and lockouts—U.S. I. Title. BIP

Labor and laboring classes—U.S.—Biography.

BRANSTEN, Richard, 1906-1955. 331.88'0922 B
Men who lead labor, by Bruce Minton and John Stuart. With drawings by Scott Johnston. Freeport, N.Y., Books for Libraries Press [1969] 270 p. ports. 23 cm. (Essay index reprint series) Reprint of the 1937 ed. Contents.Contents.—William Green.—William Hutcheson.—Edward F. McGrady.—John L. Lewis.—Heywood Broun.—A. Philip Randolph.—Harry Bridges.—Giant killers.—A few labor terms.—Bibliography (p. [250]-264) [HD6509.A2B7 1969] 73-93362
1. Labor and laboring classes—U.S.—Biography. 2. Trade-unions—U.S. I. Stuart, John, 1912- joint author. II. Title. BIP

COOK, Roy Anthony Paul 331.0922
Leaders of labor [by] Roy Cook. [1st ed.] Philadelphia, Lippincott [1966] 152p. ports. 22cm. [HD8073.A1C65] 66-7604 3.75
1. Labor and laboring classes—U. S.—Biog. I. Title.

FINK, Gary M. 331.88'092'2 B
Biographical dictionary of American labor leaders. Editor in chief: Gary M. Fink. Advisory editor: Milton Cantor. Contributing editors: John Hevener [and others] Westport, Conn., Greenwood Press [1974] xiv, 559 p. 24 cm. [HD8073.A1F56] 74-9322 ISBN 0-8371-7643-3 19.95
1. Labor and laboring classes—United States—Biography. I. Title. BIP

Labor and laboring classes—U.S.—Biography—Juvenile literature.

DANIELS, Patricia. 331'.0922 B
Famous labor leaders. New York, Dodd, Mead [1970] 172 p. ports. 22 cm. (Famous biographies for young people) Contents.Contents.—William H. Sylvis.—Terence V. Powderly.—Samuel Gompers.—William D. Haywood.—William Green.—John L. Lewis.—Philip Murray.—Sidney Hillman.—A. Philip Randolph.—David Dubinsky.—George Meany.—Walter Reuther.—Some heroes, some villains, some others. [HD8073.A1D3] 920 70-105293 3.50
1. Labor and laboring classes U.S.—Biography—Juvenile literature. I. Title. BIP

LEIPOLD, L. Edmond, 1902- 331.88'092'2 B
Famous American labor leaders, by L. E. Leipold. Minneapolis, T. S. Denison [1972] 91 p. 25 cm. (His Famous American heroes and leaders series) Brief biographies of ten leaders in the American labor movement including Samuel Gompers, John L. Lewis, and David Dubinsky. [HD8073.A1L44] 920 76-178991 ISBN 0-513-01200-1 3.99
1. Labor and laboring classes—United States—Biography—Juvenile literature. I. Title.

SELVIN, David F 331.88'0922
Champions of Labor, by David F. Selvin. London, New York [etc.] Abelard-Schuman [1967] 256 p. ports. 22 cm. "Some notes on further reading": p. 244-247. [HD8073.A1S4] 67-16836 unpriced
1. Laboring and laboring classes—U.S.—Biog.—Juvenile literature. I. Title. BIP

Labor and laboring classes—United States—History.

GINZBERG, Eli, 1911- 331.0973
The American worker in the twentieth century, a history through autobiographies [by] Eli Ginzberg [and] Hyman Berman. [New York] Free Press of Glencoe [1963] 368 p. 24 cm. Includes bibliography. [HD8072.G46] 63-10649
1. Labor and laboring classes—United States—History. 2. Trade-unions—United States—History. I. Berman, Hyman, joint author. II. Title.

Laboure Catherine, Saint, 1806-1876.

ERNEST, Brother, 1897- 922.244
Our Lady comes to Paris; the story of St. Catherine Laboure and the Miraculous Medal. Illus. by Brother Bernard Howard. Notre Dame, Ind., Dujarie Press [1953] 95p. illus. 24cm. [BX4700.L2E7] 53-2907
1. Laboure Catherine, Saint, 1806-1876. 2. Miraculous Medal. I. Title.

Laboure, Catherine, Saint, 1806-1876.

WINDEATT, Mary Fabyan, 1910- 922.244
The medal; the story of Saint Catherine Laboure. Illustrated by Gedge Harmon. St. Meinrad, Ind. [1950] 107 p. illus. 22 cm. "A Grail publication." [BX4700.L2W53] 50-7062
1. Laboure, Catherine, Saint, 1806-1876. 2. Miraculous Medal. I. Title.

Laboure, Catherine, Saint, 1806-1876—Juvenile literature.

POWER-WATERS, Alma (Shelley) 1896- 920
St. Catherine Laboure and the Miraculous Medal. Illus. by James Fox. New York [dist.] Farrar [c.1962] 192p. illus. (Vision bks., 54) 62-8842 2.25
1. Laboure, Catherine, Saint, 1806-1876—Juvenile literature. 2. Miraculous Medal. I. Title.

Lacenaire, Pierre Francois,

LACENAIRE, Pierre Francois, 1800-1836. 923.4144
Memoirs. Translated and edited by Philip John Stead. London, New York, Staples Press [1952] 239 p. illus. 19 cm. [HV6248.L15A42] 52-2317
I. Title.

LACENAIRE, Pierre Francois, 1800-1836. 923.4144
Memoirs. Translated and edited by Philip JohnStead. New York, Roy Publishers [1955] 239p. illus., port. 19cm. Bibliography: p. 233. [HV6248] 55-6009
I. Title.

Lackington, James, 1746-1815.

LACKINGTON, James, 1746-1815. 686.2'092'4
Memoirs of the first forty-five years of James Lackington. New York : Garland Pub., 1974. 328 p. ; 18 cm. (The English book trade, 1660-1853) Reprint of the 1794 ed. printed for the author, London under title: Memoirs of the forty-five first years of the life of James Lackington, with new pref. Includes index. [Z325.L23A35 1974b] 74-23631 ISBN 0-8240-0979-7 : 22.00
1. Lackington, James, 1746-1815. 2. Booksellers and bookselling—London—Correspondence, reminiscences, etc. I. Title. II. Series.

LACKINGTON, James, 1746-1815. 686.2'092'4
Memoirs of the forty-five first years of the life of James Lackington, written by himself. Clifton, N.J., A. M. Kelley, 1974. p. cm. (The English book trade, 17) Half title: Memoirs of James Lackington. Reprint of the 1794 ed., London. [Z325.L23A3 1974] 70-146462 ISBN 0-678-00843-4 15.00
1. Lackington, James, 1746-1815. 2. Booksellers and bookselling—London—Correspondence, reminiscences, etc. BIP

LaCloche, James, b. 1647.

WASHINGTON, George Sydney Horace Lee, 1910- 942.06'6'0924
King Charles II's Jesuit son, by George S. H. L. Washington. Revised ed. Cambridge, privately printed for the author, 15 Clare St., 1968. vi, 19 p. 3 plates, 1 illus., 2 facsims. 23 cm. Includes bibliographical references. [DA445.W3 1968] 70-474960 21/-
1. LaCloche, James, b. 1647. 2. Charles II, King of Great Britain, 1630-1685. I. Title.

Lacombe, Albert, 1827?-1916.

PHELAN, Josephine. 922.271
The bold heart; the story of Father Lacombe. Illustrated by Jerry Lazare. New York, St. Martin's Press, 1956. 182p. illus. 22cm. (Great stories of Canada) [F1060.9.L144] 56-4604
1. Lacombe, Albert, 1827?-1916. I. Title.

Lacordaire, Jean Baptiste Henri Dominique de. 1802-1861.

SHEPPARD, Lancelot Capel, 1906- 922.244
Lacordaire, a biographical essay. New York, Macmillan [c.]1964. xi, 184p. illus., ports. 23cm. 63-16130 6.95
1. Lacordaire, Jean Baptiste Henri Dominique de. 1802-1861. I. Title.

Lacy, Leslie Alexander.

LACY, Leslie Alexander. 301.45'19'6073 B
Native daughter [by] Leslie Lacy. New York, Macmillan [1974] 205 p. 22 cm. Autobiographical. [E185.97.L23A28] 73-10785 6.95
1. Lacy, Leslie Alexander. I. Title. BIP

LACY, Leslie Alexander. 323.2'0924 B
The rise and fall of a proper Negro; an autobiography. [New York] Macmillan [1970] viii, 244 p. 21 cm. [E185.97.L23A3] 71-95302
1. U.S.—Race question. I. Title. BIP

Ladd, Alan.

LINET, Beverly. 791.43'028'0924 B
Ladd, the life, the legend, the legacy of Alan Ladd : a biography / by Beverly Linet. New York : Arbor House, c1979. xxi, 294 p., [16] leaves of plates : ill. ; 24 cm. Includes index. [PN2287.L13L54] 78-57334 ISBN 0-87795-203-5 : 10.95
1. Ladd, Alan. 2. Moving-picture actors and actresses—United States—Biography. I. Title.

LINET, Beverly. 791.43'028'0924
Ladd : the life, the legend, the legacy of Alan Ladd / Beverly Linet. New York : Berkley Pub. Corp. 1980. c1979 291 : ill ; 18 cm. Includes index and bibliographical references. [PN2287.Li3L54] ISBN 0-425-04531-5 pbk. ; 2.75
1. Ladd, Alan 2. Moving-pictures actor and actresses — United States — Biography I. Title.
L.C card no. for 1979 Arbor House ed.:78-57334 BIP

Ladd, Daniel, 1817-1872.

SHOFNER, Jerrell H., 1929- 338'.04'0924 B
Daniel Ladd, merchant prince of frontier Florida / Jerrell H. Shofner. Gainesville : University Presses of Florida, 1977. p. cm. Includes index. Bibliography: p. [HC107.F6L337] 77-21789 ISBN 0-8130-0546-9
1. Ladd, Daniel, 1817-1872. 2. Businessmen—Florida—Biography. 3. Merchants—Florida—Biography. I. Title.

SHOFNER, Jerrell H., 1929- 333'.04'0924 B
Daniel Ladd, merchant prince of frontier Florida / Jerrell H. Shofner. Gainesville : University Presses of Florida, 1977. ix, 180 p. : ill. ; 24 cm. "A University of Florida book". Includes index. Bibliography: p. 167-172. [HC107.F6L337] 77-21789 ISBN 0-8130-0546-9 : 8.50
1. Ladd, Daniel, 1817-1872. 2. Businessmen—Florida—Biography. 3. Merchants—Florida—Biography. I. Title.

Ladd, George Trumbull, 1842-1921.

MILLS, Eugene S., 1924- 150'.924 B
George Trumbull Ladd: pioneer American psychologist [by] Eugene S. Mills. Cleveland, Press of Case Western Reserve University, 1969. xi, 299 p. 24 cm. Includes bibliographical references. [BF109.L3M5] 69-17683 8.95
1. Ladd, George Trumbull, 1842-1921.

Ladd, William, 1778-1841.

HEMMENWAY, John. 327'.172'0924 B
The apostle of peace: memoir of William Ladd. With an introd. by Elihu Burritt. Boston, American Peace Society, 1872. [New York, J. S. Ozer, 1972] 272 p. port. 22 cm. (The Peace movement in America) [JX1962.L2H5 1972] 70-137544 11.95 (Lib. Ed.)
1. Ladd, William, 1778-1841. I. Title. II. Series.

Laemmle, Carl, 1867-1939.

DRINKWATER, John, 1882-1937. 791.43'023'0924 B
The life and adventures of Carl Laemmle / John Drinkwater. New York : Arno Press, 1978. p. cm. (Aspects of film) Reprint of the 1931 ed. published by W. Heinemann, London. [PN1998.A3L34 1978] 77-11374 ISBN 0-405-11130-4 : 28.00
1. Laemmle, Carl, 1867-1939. 2. Moving-picture producers and directors—United States—Biography. I. Title. II. Series. **BIP**

Laennec, Rene Theophile Hyacinthe, 1781-1826.

KERVAN, Roger, 1911- 926.1
Laennec: his life and times. Tr. from French by D. C. Abrahams-Curiel New York, Pergamon Press [c.]1960. 213p. Bibl. 59-14491 3.50
1. Laennec, Rene Theophile Hyacinthe, 1781-1826. I. Title.

LAENNEC; his life and times. Translated from the French by D. C. Abrahams-Curiel. New York, Pergamon Press, 1960. x, 213p. 23cm. Bibliography, p. 211-213. v. 12
1. Laennec, Rene Theophile Hyacinthe, 1781-1826. I. Kervran, Roger, 1911-

LaFarge, Marie Fortunee Cappelle Pouch, 1816-1852.

SAUNDERS, Edith. 928.4
The mystery of Marie Lafarge. New York, Morrow, 1952. 256 p. 23 cm. [PQ2323.L5S3 1952] 52-6974
1. LaFarge, Marie Fortunee Cappelle Pouch, 1816-1852. I. Title.

Lafayette, Marie Adrienne (de Noailles) marquise de, 1759-1807.

MAUROIS, Andre, 1885- 920.7
Adrienne; the life of the Marquise de La Fayette. Translated by Gerard Hopkins. New York, McGraw-Hill [1961] 482p. illus. 24cm. Includes bibliography. [DC146.L21M213] 61-10135
1. Lafayette, Marie Adrienne (de Noailles) marquise de, 1759-1807. I. Title.

Lafayette, Marie Joseph Paul Yves Roch Gilbert du Motier, marquis de, 1757-1834.

BRANDON, Edgar Ewing, 1865- ed. 923.544
Lafayette, guest of the Nation; a contemporary account of the triumphal tour of General Lafayette through the United States in 1824-1825, as reported by the local newspapers. Oxford, Ohio, Oxford Historical Press, 1950- v. port. 24 cm. Bibliography: v. 1. p. 273-275. [E207.L2B68] 51-14813
1. Lafayette. Marie Joseph Paul Yves Roch Gilbert du Motier, marquis de, 1757-1834. I. Title.

BUCKMAN, Peter. 944.04'092'4 B
Lafayette : a biography / by Peter Buckman. New York : Paddington Press : distributed by Grosset & Dunlap, c1977. 288 p. : port. ; 24 cm. Includes index. Bibliography: p. 280-284. [DC146.L2B78] 76-53319 ISBN 0-448-22060-1 : 10.00
1. Lafayette, Marie Joseph Paul Yves Roch Gilbert du Motier, marquis de, 1757-1834. 2. Statesmen—France—Biography. I. Title.

CRISS, Mildred, 1890- 923.544
La Fayette: on the heights of freedom. New York, Dodd, Mead, 1954. 264 p. illus. 21 cm. Includes bibliography. [DC146.L2C8] 54-10999
1. Lafayette, Marie Joseph Paul Yves Roch Gilbert du Motier, marquis de, 1757-1834.

GERSON, Noel Bertram, 1914- 944.04'092'4 B
Statue in search of a pedestal : a biography of the Marquis de Lafayette / Noel B. Gerson. New York : Dodd, Mead, c1976. ix, 244 p. ; 22 cm. Includes index. Bibliography: p. 237. [DC146.L2G47] 76-18118 ISBN 0-396-07341-7 : 7.95
1. Lafayette, Marie Joseph Paul Yves Roch Gilbert du Motier, Marquis de, 1757-1834. I. Title.

GOTTSCHALK, Louis Reichenthal, 1899- 923.544
Lafayette between the American and the French Revolution (1783-1789) Chicago, University of Chicago Press [1950] xi, 461 p. 24 cm. "The fourth of a series of studies [by the author] on the life andtimes of Lafayette." Includes bibliographical notes. [DC146.L2G59] 50-5286
1. Lafayette, Marie Joseph Paul Yves Roch Gilbert Du Motier, marquis de, 1757-1834. I. Title. **BIP**

GOTTSCHALK, Louis Reichenthal, 1899- v. 12
Lafayette comes to America. Chicago, Ill., University of Chicago Press [1965] xiii, 184 p. 24 cm. "Published 1935. Second impression (with corrections) 1965." 66-37682
1. Lafayette, Marie Joseph Paul Yves Roch Gilbert du Motier, marquis de, 1757-1834. I. Title. **BIP**

GRAHAM, Alberta (Powell). 923.544
Lafayette, friend of America; illustrated by Ralph Ray. New York, Abingdon-Cokesbury Press [1952] 127 p. illus. 21 cm. [Makers of America] [E207.L2G75] 52-11650
1. Lafayette, Marie Joseph Paul Yves Roch Gilbert du Motier, marquis de, 1757-1834. I. Title.

KLAMKIN, Marian. 973.5'4'0924 B
The return of Lafayette, 1824-1825. New York, Scribner [1975] viii, 212 p. illus. 24 cm. Bibliography: p. 203-206. [E207.L2K55] 74-8956 ISBN 0-684-13887-5
1. Lafayette, Marie Joseph Paul Yves Roch Gilbert du Motier, Marquis de, 1757-1834. I. Title.

LA FUYE, Maurice de, 1886- 923.544
The apostle of liberty: life of La Fayette, by Maurice de La Fuye and Emile Babean. [Translated by Edward Hyams] New York, T. Yoseloff [1956] 344p. 23cm. Translation of La Fayette, Soldat de deux patries. Bibliography: p. 334-335. [DC116.L2L3572] 56-3815
1. Lafaytte, Marie Joseph Paul Yves Roch Gilbert du Motier, Marquis de, 1753-1831. I. Babeau, Emile Albert, 1881- joint author. II. Title.

LOTH, David Goldsmith, 1899- 923.544
The people's general; the personal story of Lafayette. New York, Scribner, 1951. vi, 346 p. port. 22 cm. Bibliography: p. 323-326. [DC146.L2L6] 51-1338
1. Lafayette, Marie Joseph Paul Yves Roch Gilbert du Motier, marquis de, 1757-1834. I. Title.

MACINTIRE, Jane Bacon. 917.3'04'540924 B
Lafayette, the guest of the Nation; the tracing of the route of Lafayette's tour of the United States in 1824-25. [Newton, Mass., A. J. Simone Press, 1967] ix, 260 p. illus. 23 cm. Bibliography: p. 258-260. [E207.L2M28] 73-172414
1. Lafayette, Marie Joseph Paul Yves Roch Gilbert du Motier, marquis de, 1757-1834. 2. United States—Description and travel—1783-1848. I. Title.

TUCKERMAN, Bayard, 1855-1923. 944'.035'0924 B
Life of General Lafayette, with a critical estimate of his character and public acts. London, S. Low, Marston, Searle, & Rivington, 1889. [New York, AMS Press, 1973] 2 v. illus. 19 cm. [DC146.L2T8 1973] 72-177575 ISBN 0-404-07187-2 10.00
1. Lafayette, Marie Joseph Paul Yves Roch Gilbert du Motier, marquis de, 1757-1834. 2. France—History—Revolution, 1789-1799. 3. France—History—1789-1900. 4. United States—History—Revolution, 1775-1783. I. Title.
Two volume set, 19.00.

Lafayette, Marie Joseph Paul Yves Roch Gilbert du Motier, marquis de, 1757-1834—Juvenile literature.

BEAHRS, Virginia Oakley, 1911- 973.3'092'4 B
The fire and the glory : Lafayette and America's fight for freedom / Virginia Oakley Beahrs. Philadelphia : Westminster Press, c1976. 191 p. : ill. ; 21 cm. Includes index. Bibliography: p. 179-183. A biography of the teen-age general from France who plunged into America's fight for freedom, contributing his own money as well as his leadership. [E207.L2B4] 92 76-5848 ISBN 0-664-32592-0 8.95
1. Lafayette, Marie Joseph Paul Yves Roch Gilbert du Motier, marquis de, 1757-1834—Juvenile literature. I. Title. **BIP**

BISHOP, Claire (Huchet) 923.544
Lafayette: French-American hero. Illustrated by Maurice Brevannes. Champaign, Ill., Garrard Press [1960] 80 p. illus. 23 cm. (A Discovery book) [E207.L2B52] 60-6467
1. Lafayette, Marie Joseph Paul Yves Roch Gilbert du Motier, Marquis de, 1757-1834—Juvenile literature. I. Title.

CARTER, Hodding, 1907- 923.544
The Marquis de Lafayette; bright sword for freedom. Illustrated by Mimi Korach. New York, Random House [1958] 182p. illus. 22cm. (World landmark books [W-34] [DC146.L2C28] 58-6186
1. Lafayette, Marie Joseph Paul Yves Roch Gilbert du Motier, marquis de, 1757-1834—Juvenile literature. I. Title.

HOLBROOK, Sabra. 944.04'092'4 B
Lafayette, man in the middle / by Sabra Holbrook. New York : Atheneum, 1977. p. cm. Includes index. Bibliography: p. A biography of the Frenchman whose belief in democracy led him to participate in the American and French Revolutions. [DC146.L2H563] 77-2553 ISBN 0-689-30585-0 : 7.95
1. Lafayette, Marie Joseph Paul Yves Roch Gilbert du Motier, marquis de, 1757-1834—Juvenile literature. 2. Statesmen—France—Biography—Juvenile literature. I. Title.

MAUROIS, Andre, 1885-1967. 923.544
Lafayette in America. Illustrated by Frank Nicholas. [Boston] Houghton Mifflin. c1960. 184 p. illus. 22 cm. (North Star books, 15) [E207.L2M3] 59-9730
1. Lafayette, Marie Joseph Paul Yves Roch Gilbert du Motier, marquis de, 1757-1834—Juvenile literature. I. Nicholas, Frank, illus. II. Title.

Lafayette, Marie Joseph Paul Yves Roch Gilbert du Motier, marquis de, 1757-1834—Manuscripts—Indexes.

GOTTSCHALK, Louis Reichenthal, 1899- 016.944'035'0924 B
Lafayette : a guide to the letters, documents, and manuscripts in the United States / edited by Louis Gottschalk, Phyllis S. Pestieau, Linda J. Pike. Ithaca, N.Y. : Cornell University Press, 1975. p. cm. [Z6616.L35G68] [DC146.L2] 75-18724 ISBN 0-8014-0953-5 : 37.50
1. Lafayette, Marie Joseph Paul Yves Roch Gilbert du Motier, marquis de, 1757-1834—Manuscripts—Indexes. I. Pestieau, Phyllis S., joint author. II. Pike, Linda J., joint author.

GOTTSCHALK, Louis Reichenthal, 1899- 016.944'035'0924 B
Lafayette : a guide to the letters, documents, and manuscripts in the United States / edited by Louis Gottschalk, Phyllis S. Pestieau, Linda J. Pike. Ithaca, N.Y. : Cornell University Press, 1975. p. cm. [Z6616.L35G68] [DC146.L2] 75-18724 ISBN 0-8014-0953-5
1. Lafayette, Marie Joseph Paul Yves Roch Gilbert du Motier, marquis de, 1757-1834—Manuscripts—Indexes. I. Pestieau, Phyllis S., joint author. II. Pike, Linda J., joint author. **BIP**

Lafferty, L. D., b. 1800.

ABNEY, A. H. 973'.04'97 S
Life and adventures of L. D. Lafferty / A. H. Abney. New York : Garland Pub., c1976. 219 p. : ill. ; 19 cm. (The Garland library of narratives of North American Indian captivities ; v. 89) Reprint of the 1875 ed. published by H. S. Goodspeed, New York. [E85.G2 vol. 89] [F389] 976.4'004'97 75-7116 ISBN 0-8240-1713-7 lib.bdg. : 21.00
1. Lafferty, L. D., b. 1800. 2. Frontier and pioneer life—Texas. 3. Indians of North America—Texas. 4. Texas—History—To 1846. I. Title. II. Series.

Laffite, Jean, 1782-1854.

DE GRUMMOND, Jane Lucas, 1905- 973.5'239
The Baratarians and the Battle of New Orleans / by Jane Lucas de Grummond, with Biographical sketches of the veterans of the Battalion of Orleans, 1814-1815 / by Ronald R. Morazan. Baton, Rouge, La. : Legacy Pub. Co., [1979] xi, 180, xiii, 300 p. : ill. ; 23 cm. De Grummond's work is a reprint of the 1961 ed. published by the Louisiana State University Press, Baton Rouge. Includes bibliographical references and indexes. [E356.N5D4 1979] 79-65176 ISBN 0-918784-23-9 : 15.00
1. Laffite, Jean, 1782-1854. 2. Louisiana. Militia. Uniformed Battalion of Orleans Volunteers—Biography. 3. New Orleans, Battle of, 1815. 4. New Orleans, Battle of, 1815—Biography. 5. Soldiers—Louisiana—New Orleans—Biography. I. Morazan, Ronald R. Biographical sketches of the veterans of the Battalion of Orleans, 1814-1815. 1979. II. Title.
Publisher's address: 2008 Perkins Rd., Baton Rouge, LA 70808

LAFFITE, Jean, 1782-1854. 923.4144
The journal of Jean Laffite; the privateer-patriot's own story. [1st ed.] New York, Vantage Press [1958] 153p. 21cm. [F374.L123] 58-10660
I. Title.

TALLANT, Robert, 1909- 923.4144
The pirate Lafitte and the Battle of New Orleans; illustrated by John Chase. New

York, Random House [1951] 186 p. illus. 22 cm. (Landmark books, 19) [F374.L2] 51-13894
1. Lafitte, Jean, 1780?-1826? 2. New Orleans, Battle of, 1815. I. Title. **BIP**

Laforgue, Jules, 1860-1887.

COLLIE, Michael. 848'.8'09 B
Jules Laforgue / by Michael Collie. London : Athlone Press, 1977. [10], 134 p. ; 21 cm. (Athlone French poets) Distributed in the U.S.A. and Canada by Humanities Press, New Jersey. Includes index. Bibliography: p. [129]-132. [PQ2323.L8Z59] 77-378629 ISBN 0-485-14606-1 : 11.50 ISBN 0-485-12206-5 pbk. : 5.50
1. Laforgue, Jules, 1860-1887. 2. Poets, French—19th century—Biography. I. Title. **BIP**

RAMSEY, Warren, 1914- 841'.8
Jules Laforgue, essays on a poet's life and work, edited by Warren Ramsey. With a pref. by Harry T. Moore. Carbondale, Southern Illinois University Press [1969] xxx, 194 p. 22 cm. (Crosscurrents: modern critiques) Includes bibliographical references. [PQ2323.L8Z873] 69-11503 4.95
1. Laforgue, Jules, 1860-1887. I. Title.

Laforgue, Jules, 1860-1887—Biography.

ARKELL, David. 841'.8 B
Looking for Laforgue : an informal biography / by David Arkell. Manchester : Carcanet New Press, 1979. 248 p., [8] leaves of plates : ill. ; 24 cm. Includes bibliographical references and index. [PQ2323.L8Z57] 80-451554 ISBN 0-85635-285-3 : 20.00
1. Laforgue, Jules, 1860-1887—Biography. 2. Poets, French—19th century—Biography. I. Title.
Distributed by Persea Books, 225 Lafayette St., New York, NY 10012

Lagarde, Paul Anton de, 1827-1891.

LOUGEE, Robert W. 923.743
Paul de Lagarde, 1827-1891; a study of radical conservatism in Germany. Cambridge, Mass., Harvard [c.]1962. viii, 357p. port. 22cm. Bibl. 62-17221 7.50
1. Lagarde, Paul Anton de, 1827-1891. I. Title.

LOUGEE, Robert W 923.743
Paul de Lagarde, 1827-1891; a study of racial conservation in Germany Cambridge, Harvard University Press, 1962. viii, 357 p. port. 22 cm. "A bibliographical note" (p. [321]-326) Bibliographical references included in "Notes" (p. [327]-351) [DD205.L3L6] 62-17221
1. Lagarde, Paul Anton de, 1827-1891. I. Title.

Lagerlof, Selma Ottiliana Louisa, 1858-1940—Biography.

BERENDSOHN, Walter Arthur, 1884- 839.7'3'72
Selma Lagerlof; her life and work, by Walter A. Berendsohn. Adapted from the German by George F. Timpson, with a pref. by V. Sackville-West. Port Washington, N.Y., Kennikat Press [1968] xx, 136 p. illus., ports. 22 cm. Reprint of the abridged translation of Selma Legerlof; Heimat und Leben ... which was first published in 1931. [PT9770.B42 1968] 67-27576
1. Lagerlof, Selma Ottiliana Lovisa, 1858-1940. I. Timpson, George Frederick, tr. **BIP**

LAGERLOF, Selma Ottiliana Lovisa, 1858-1940. 839.7'3'72 B
Memories of my childhood : further years at Marbacka / Selma Lagerlof ; translated by Velma Swanston Howard. Millwood, N.Y. : Kraus Reprint Co., 1975, [c1934] p. cm. Translation of Ett barns memoarer. Reprint of the ed. published by Doubleday, Garden City, N.Y. [PT9770.A25 1975] 75-5996 ISBN 0-527-54010-2 : 17.00
1. Lagerlof, Selma Ottiliana Lovisa, 1858-1940—Biography. I. Title. **BIP**

Lagrange, Albert, 1855-1938.

BRAUN, Francois Marie, 1893- 922.244
The work of Pere Lagrange. Adapted from French by Richard T. A. Murphy. Milwaukee, Bruce [1963] 306p. illus. 23cm. Bibl. 63-15632 7.00
1. Lagrange, Albert, 1855-1938. I. Title.

Lahr, Bert, 1895-1967.

LAHR, John, 1941- 791'.0924 B
Notes on a cowardly lion; the biography of Bert Lahr. [1st ed.] New York, Knopf, 1969. x, 394 p. illus., ports. 25 cm. [PN2287.L15L3 1969] 78-79344 8.95
1. Lahr, Bert, 1895-1967. I. Title.

Laine, Cleo.

CLEO and John : 784'.092'4 B
a biography of the Dankworths / [compiled and edited] by Graham Collier. London : Quartet Books, 1976. [9], 187 p., [34] p. of plates : ports. ; 23 cm. Includes index. [ML421.D14C6] 77-351584 ISBN 0-7043-2113-0 : £4.95
1. Laine, Cleo. 2. Dankworth, John. 3. Jazz musicians—England—Biography. I. Collier, Graham, 1937-

Laing, Ronald David.

BOYERS, Robert, comp. 616.89'00924
R. D. Laing & anti-psychiatry. New York, Harper & Row [1971] viii, 304 p. 18 cm. (Perennial library, P 229) On cover: Edited by Robert Boyers and Robert Orrill. Contents.Contents.—Preface, by R. Boyers.—R. D. Laing: self, symptom & society, by P. Sedgwick.—The meta-journey of R. D. Laing, by J. B. Gordon.—Schizophrenia & the mad psychotherapist, by L. H. Farber.—Laings models of madness, by M. Siegler, H. Osmond & H. Mann. An interview with Dr. T. Lidz.—An R. D. Laing symposium with R. Coles, L. Farber, E. Friedenberg, K. Lux.—Madness and morals, by M. Schatzman.—An interview with Dr. Joseph Berke.—Flection, by M. Barnes.—Reflection, by M. Barnes.—Afterword: a medium with a message: R. D. Laing, by B. Nelson. Includes bibliographical references. [RC454.B68 1971] 74-168940 ISBN 0-06-080229-4 1.50
1. Laing, Ronald David. 2. Psychiatry. I. Title.

BOYERS, Robert, comp. 616.8'9'00924
R. D. Laing & anti-psychiatry. New York, Octagon Books, 1974 [c1971] viii, 304 p. 21 cm. Reprint of the ed. published by Harper & Row, New York, which was issued as no. P229 of Perennial library. Contents.Contents.—Sedgwick, P. R. D. Laing: self, symptom & society.—Gordon, J. B. The meta-journey of R. D. Laing.—Farber, L. H. Schizophrenia & the mad psychotherapist.—Siegler, M., Osmond, H., and Mann, H. Laings models of madness.—An interview with Dr. Theodore Lidz.—An R. D. Laing symposium with R. Coles, L. Farber, E. Friedenberg, K. Lux.—Schatzman, M. Madness and morals.—An interview with Dr. Joseph Berke.—Barnes, M. Flection.—Barnes, M. Reflection.—Nelson, B. Afterword: a medium with a message: R. D. Laing. Includes bibliographical references. [RC454.B68 1974] 73-20294 ISBN 0-374-90906-7 11.50
1. Laing, Ronald David. 2. Psychiatry. I. Title.
Contents omitted. **BIP**

COLLIER, Andrew, 1944- 150'.19'50924
R. D. Laing : the philosophy and politics and psychotherapy / Andrew Collier. 1st American ed. New York : Pantheon Books, c1977. x, 214 p. ; 22 cm. Includes index. Bibliography: p. 204-211. [RC437.5.C64 1977] 76-62705 ISBN 0-394-41130-7 : 10.00. ISBN 0-394-73353-3 pbk. : 3.95
1. Laing, Ronald David. 2. Psychiatry—Philosophy. 3. Antipsychiatry. **BIP**

EVANS, Richard Isadore, 1922- 616.8'9'00924
R. D. Laing : the man and his ideas / Richard I. Evans. 1st ed. New York : Dutton, 1976. lxxv, 170 p. ; 21 cm. (Dialogues with notable contributors to personality theory ; v. 10) Includes index. Bibliography: p. [160]-163. [RC339.52.L34E9 1976] 75-14294 ISBN 0-525-18765-0 : 12.95 ISBN 0-525-47411-0 pbk. : 3.95
1. Laing, Ronald David. 2. Psychiatry. 3. Psychology.

FRIEDENBERG, Edgar Zodiag, 1921- 616.8'9'00924
R. D. Laing [by] Edgar Z. Friedenberg. New York, Viking Press [1974, c1973] 118 p. 19 cm. (Modern masters) Bibliography: p. [109]-111. [RC339.52.L34F74 1974] 73-9586 5.95
1. Laing, Ronald David. **BIP**

LAING, Ronald David. 616.8'00924
The facts of life / R. D. Laing. London : Allen Lane, 1976. 143 p. ; 23 cm. Includes bibliographical references. [RC437.5.L34 1976] 77-361330 ISBN 0-7139-1015-1 : £3.25
1. Laing, Ronald David. 2. Psychiatry—Philosophy. 3. Psychiatrists—Great Britain—Biography. I. Title. **BIP**

LAING, Ronald David. 616.8'9'00924
The facts of life : an essay in feelings, facts, and fantasy / R. D. Laing. 1st ed. New York : Pantheon Books, c1976. xi, 153 p. ; 24 cm. [RC437.5.L34] 75-38852 ISBN 0-394-49666-3 : 7.95
1. Laing, Ronald David. 2. Psychiatry—Philosophy. 3. Psychiatrists—Correspondance, reminiscenses, etc. I. Title. **BIP**

Laird, Carobeth, 1895-

LAIRD, Carobeth, 1895- 362.6'11'60926 B
Limbo / Carobeth Laird. Novato, Calif. : Chandler & Sharp, c1979. x, 178 p. ; 23 cm. [RA997.5.A7L34] 79-10937 ISBN 0-88316-535-X : 7.95 ISBN 0-88316-536-8 pbk. : 5.95 4.50
1. Laird, Carobeth, 1895- 2. Nursing home patients—Arizona—Biography. I. Title. **BIP**

Laird, Margaret Nicholl.

LAIRD, Margaret Nicholl. 266'.023'0924 B
They called me Mama / by Margaret Nicholl Laird, with Phil Landrum. Chicago : Moody Press, [1975] 185 p. ; 22 cm. [BV3625.C42L345] 75-15885 ISBN 0-8024-8683-5 pbk. 2.95
1. Laird, Margaret Nicholl. 2. Missions—Central African Republic. I. Landrum, Phil joint author. II. Title. **BIP**

Lajoie, Napoleon, 1875-1959—Juvenile literature.

EPSTEIN, Samuel, 1909 796.357'092'2
More stories of baseball champions: in the Hall of Fame, by Sam and Beryl Epstein. Illustrated by Victor Mays. Champaign, Ill., Garrard Pub. Co. [1973] 96 p. illus. (part col.) 24 cm. Traces the careers of three baseball stars elected to the Baseball Hall of Fame in 1937. [GV865.A1E59] 920 73-2941 2.98
1. Young, Denton True, 1867-1955—Juvenile literature. 2. Lajoie, Napoleon, 1875-1959—Juvenile literature. 3. Speaker, Tris—Juvenile literature. 4. Cooperstown, N.Y. National Baseball Hall of Fame and Museum—Juvenile literature. 5. Baseball—Biography—Juvenile literature. I. Epstein, Beryl (Williams) 1910- joint author. II. Mays, Victor, 1927- illus. III. Title.

Lajpat Rai, Lala, 1865-1928.

DHANPAT Rai, Lala. 954.3'5'0924 B
Life story of Lala Lajpat Rai / written in Urdu by his brother, Lala Dhanpat Rai ; translated, edited, and enl. by Ishwar Das Puri and R. C. Puri ; with a foreword by S. N. Prasad. New Delhi : Metropolitan Book Co., 1976. xi, 119 p., [2] leaves of plates : ports. ; 23 cm. Includes index. "Lists of Lalaji's works": p. 93-96. [DS479.1.L27D4713] 76-903625 ISBN 0-88386-312-X : 9.00
1. Lajpat Rai, Lala, 1865-1928. 2. Statesmen—India—Biography. 3. India—Politics and government—1765-1947. I. Puri, Ishwar Das, 1898- II. Puri, R. C., 1939. III. Title.
Distributed by South Asia Bks. **BIP**

Lakanal, Joseph, 1762-1845.

DAWSON, John Charles, 1876- 370'.924 B
Lakanal, the regicide; a biographical and historical study of the career of Joseph Lakanal. Freeport, N.Y., Books for Libraries Press [1970, c1948] xvii, 213 p. port. 24 cm. Bibliography: p. [203]-209. [CT275.L25D32 1970] 74-130547
1. Lakanal, Joseph, 1762-1845.

Lake District, Eng.—Biography.

BELL, David, 1924- 920.0428
Curious characters of Lakeland; evoked by David Bell & Edwin Patterson. Newcastle upon Tyne, Oriel, 1970. [1], 32 p. illus., map, ports. 22 cm. [DA670.L1B49] 73-511477 6/-
1. Lake District, Eng.—Biography. I. Patterson, Edwin, joint author. II. Title.

Lake George region, N.Y.—Biography.

O'BRIEN, Kathryn E. 974.7'51
The great and the gracious on Millionaires' Row / by Kathryn E. O'Brien ; special photography by John R. Lustyik. 1st ed. Sylvan Beach, N.Y. : North County Books, 1978. xiv, 278 p. : ill. ; 26 cm. Bibliography: p. 276-278. [F127.G3O27] 79-115586 ISBN 0-932052-17-7 : 14.95
1. Lake George region, N.Y.—Biography. 2. Upper classes—New York (State)—Lake George region. 3. Lake George region, N.Y.—Social life and customs. I. Title.

Lake, Jimmy,

LAKE, Jimmy, 1879- 927.91
Footlights, fistfights, and femmes; the Jimmy Lake story as told to Helen Giblo. [1st ed.] New York, Vantage Press [1957] 252p. 21cm. [PN2287.L2A3] 57-59302
I. Giblo, Helen. II. Title.

Lake of the Hills, Fla.—Biography.

KAUCHER, Mildred. 975.9'67
Lake of the Hills, its history / as told to Mildred Kaucher. [s.l. : s.n., c1976] (Tampa, Fla : Bay Center Corp.) 92 p., [7] leaves of plates : ill. ; 25 cm. [F319.L18K38] 77-152836
1. Lake of the Hills, Fla.—Biography. 2. Lake of the Hills, Fla.—History. 3. Lake of the Hills, Fla.—Description—Tours. I. Title.

KAUCHER, Mildred. 975.9'67
Lake of the Hills, its history / as told to Mildred Kaucher. [s.l. : s.n., c1976] (Tampa, Fla : Bay Center Corp.) 92 p., [7] leaves of plates : ill. ; 25 cm. [F319.L18K38] 77-152836
1. Lake of the Hills, Fla.—Biography. 2. Lake of the Hills, Fla.—History. 3. Lake of the Hills, Fla.—Description—Tours. I. Title.

Laklan, Carli.

LAKLAN, Carli. 796.4
Olympic champions: why they win. New York, Funk & Wagnalls [1968] 168 p. illus., ports. 25 cm. Analyzes the will to win of famous Olympic champions, citing the discipline and training of various athletes, their stamina, sportsmanship, and determination to overcome odds. [GV721.5.L3] AC 68
I. Title.

Lalor, Peter, 1827-1889—Juvenile literature.

TURNER, Ian. 328.94'092'4 B
Peter Lalor / [by] Ian Turner. Melbourne ;

New York : Oxford University Press, 1974. 30 p. : ill. ; 19 cm. (Great Australians) Bibliography: p. 30. [DU222.L3T83] 75-328829 ISBN 0-19-550422-4 : 0.80
1. Lalor, Peter, 1827-1889—Juvenile literature. 2. Eureka stockade—Juvenile literature.

Lam, Wifredo.

LAM, Wifredo. 759.97291 B
Wifredo Lam / Max-Pol Fouchet. New York : Rizzoli, 1976. 266 p. : chiefly ill. (some col.) ; 30 cm. Includes index. Bibliography: p. 261-266. [ND305.L3F6813] 76-11245 ISBN 0-8478-0032-6 : 50.00
1. Lam, Wifredo. 2. Painters—Cuba—Biography. I. Fouchet, Max Pol.

Lamaism.

THUBTEN, Jigme 1922- 922.943
Tibet is my country; the autobiography of Thubten Jigme Norbu, brother of the Dalai Lama, as told to Heinrich Harrer. Translated from the German by Edward Fitzgerald. [1st ed.] New York, Dutton, 1961. 264 p. illus. 23 cm. Translation of Tibet, verlorene Heimat. [BL1489.T5A33 1961] 61-5040
1. Lamaism. 2. Tibet—Soc. life & cust. I. Harrer, Heinrich 1912- II. Title.

Lamar Co., Tex.—Social life and customs.

OWENS, William A., 1905- 917.64'263'0360924
This stubborn soil [by] William A. Owens. New York, Scribner [1966] 307 p. col. map (on lining papers) 22 cm. Autobiography. [F392.L36O9] 66-23604
1. Lamar Co., Tex.—Social life and customs. I. Title. **BIP**

Lamar, Eugenia Dorothy (Blount),

LAMAR, Eugenia Dorothy (Blount), 1867- 920.7
When all is said and done. Athens, University of Georgia Press, 1952. 286 p. illus. 22 cm. Autobiographical. [CT275.L2528A3] 52-10106
I. Title.

Lamar, Lucius Quintus Cincinnatus, 1825-1893.

MAYES, Edward, 1846-1917. 973.8'092'4 B
Lucius Q. C. Lamar: his life, times, and speeches, 1825-1893. 2d ed. Nashville, Tenn., Publishing House of the Methodist Episcopal Church, South, 1896. [New York, AMS Press, 1974] 820 p. illus. 24 cm. [E664.L2M4 1974] 70-173065 ISBN 0-404-04613-4
1. Lamar, Lucius Quintus Cincinnatus, 1825-1893.

MURPHY, James B. 328.73'092'4 B
L. Q. C. Lamar: pragmatic patriot [by] James B. Murphy. Baton Rouge, Louisiana State University Press [1973] 294 p. port. 24 cm. (Southern biography series) Bibliography: p. 275-289. [E664.L2M85] 72-94150 ISBN 0-8071-0217-2 11.95
1. Lamar, Lucius Quintus Cincinnatus, 1825-1893. I. Title. II. Series.

Lamarr, Hedy,

LAMARR, Hedy, 1915- 791.430924
Ecstasy and me; my life as a woman. Greenwich, Conn., Fawcett [1967, c.1966] 256p. illus. 18cm. (Crest bk., t1035) [PN2287.L24A3] .75 pap.,
I. Title.

LAMARR, Hedy, 1915- 791.430924
Ecstasy and me; my life as a woman, by Hedy Lamarr. [New York] Bartholomew House [1966] 318p. illus., ports. 22cm. [PN2287.L24A3] 66-25426 5.95 bds.,
I. Title.
Available from Taplinger.

Lamartine, Alphonse Marie Louis de, 1790-1869.

WHITEHOUSE, Henry Remsen, 1857- 841'.7 B
The life of Lamartine. Freeport, N.Y., Books for Libraries Press [1969] 2 v. illus., ports. 23 cm. (Select bibliographies reprint series) Reprint of the 1918 ed. Bibliographical footnotes. [PQ2326.W5 1969] 73-103672
1. Lamartine, Alphonse Marie Louis de, 1790-1869. I. Title. **BIP**

Lamartine, Alphonse Marie Louis de, 1790-1869—Journeys—Near East.

LAMARTINE, Alphonse Marie Louis de, 1790-1869. 956'.01
A pilgrimage to the Holy Land / by Alphonse de Lamartine ; a facsim. reproduction with an introd. by Charles M. Lombard. Delmar, N.Y. : Scholars' Facsimiles & Reprints, 1978. p. cm. Translation of Voyage en Orient. Reprint of the 1838 ed. published by Carey, Lea, and Blanchard, Philadelphia. [DS48.L2313 1978] 78-14368 ISBN 0-8201-1323-9 : 40.00
1. Lamartine, Alphonse Marie Louis de, 1790-1869—Journeys—Near East. 2. Near East—Description and travel. 3. Palestine—Description and travel. 4. Poets, French—19th century—Biography. I. Title.

Lamas.

SNELLGROVE, David L. 294.3'0922
Four lamas of Dolpo; Tibetan biographies, ed. & tr. by David L. Snellgrove. Cambridge, Harvard, 1967- v. illus., 2 fold. maps, ports. 23cm. Contents.v.1. Introduction & translations. Bibl. [BL1490.A1S62] 67-7913 14.50
1. Lamas. I. Title.

Lamb, Burley Frank, 1886-

SANDERSON, Ross Warren, 1884- 922.89
B. F. Lamb, ecumenical pioneer; a biography of Rev. B. F. Lamb, D. D., LL. D.; including the development of church cooperation in Ohio, the growth of the Ohio Council of Churches, and progress toward the Temple of Good Will, by Ross W. Sanderson. [Nashville] Printed by the Parthenon Press Manufacturing Division of the Methodist Pub. House [1964] 250 p. illus., ports. 23 cm. [BX6.8,L3S3] 65-1310
1. Lamb, Burley Frank, 1886- 2. Ohio Council of Churches. I. Title.

Lamb, Caroline (Ponsonby) Lady, 1785-1828.

BLYTH, Henry. 823'.7 B
Caro: the fatal passion; the life of Lady Caroline Lamb. [1st American ed.] New York, Coward, McCann & Geoghegan [1973, c1972] 260 p. illus. 24 cm. Bibliography: p. 252-254. [PR4859.L9B5 1973] 72-87583 ISBN 0-698-10498-6 8.95
1. Lamb, Caroline (Ponsonby) Lady, 1785-1828. 2. Byron, George Gordon Noel Byron, Baron, 1788-1824. I. Title.

CECIL, David, Lord, 1902- 942.07'3'0924 B
Melbourne. Westport, Conn., Greenwood Press [1971, c1954] 450 p. ports. 23 cm. Parts 1 and 2 were published in 1939 under the title of The young Melbourne. [DA536.M5C48 1971] 76-138583 ISBN 0-8371-5782-X
1. Melbourne, William Lamb, 2d Viscount, 1779-1848. 2. Lamb, Caroline (Ponsonby) Lady, 1785-1828. 3. Victoria, Queen of Great Britain, 1819-1901.

Lamb, Charles,

LAMB, Charles, 1775-1834. 824'.7 B
The letters of Charles Lamb, to which are added those of his sister, Mary Lamb. Edited by E. V. Lucas. [1st AMS ed. London] J. M. Dent. New York, AMS Press [1968] 3 v. illus. 24 cm. Reprint of the 1935 (London) ed. [PR4863.A33 1968] 68-59268
I. Lamb, Mary Ann, 1764-1847. II. Lucas, Edward Verrall, 1868-1938, ed. III. Title.

LAMB, Charles, 1775-1834. 824'.7 B
The life, letters, and writings of Charles Lamb. Edited by Percy Fitzgerald. Freeport, N.Y., Books for Libraries Press [1971] 6 v. 19 ports. 23 cm. "Preface to Sketch of life, &c." (v. 1, p. xix-xxiv) is lacking in this reprint ed. Contents.Contents.—v. 1. [A sketch of the life of Charles Lamb with final memorials, by T. N. Talfourd] Correspondence.—v. 2. Correspondence.—v. 3. Miscellaneous correspondence. Elia. The last essays of Elia.—v. 4. The last essays of Elia. Miscellaneous essays. Letters. Tales.—v. 5. Tales from Shakspeare. Stories contributed to Mrs. Leicester's school. Dramatic works. Sketches, ephemeral papers, &c.—v. 6. Sketches, ephemeral writings, &c. Contributions to Hone's Every day book. Criticisms. Reviews. Letters to the editor. Poems. Sonnets. Blank verse. Album verses and acrostics. Commendatory verses. Translations. Miscellaneous poems. Prologues &c. Satirical and humourous pieces. Additional pieces. Includes bibliographical references. [PR4860.A2 19OThe life, letters, and writings of
I. Fitzgerald, Percy Hetherington, 1834-1925, ed. **BIP**

LAMB, Charles, 1775-1834. 928.2
Selected letters; edited with an introd. by T. S. Matthews. New York, Farrar, Straus and Cudahy [1956] xxvi, 291 p. 22 cm. (Great letters series) [PR4863.A34] 56-7818

Lamb, Charles, 1775-1834.

ANTHONY, Katharine Susan, 1877-1965. 824'.7 B
The Lambs; a study of pre-Victorian England, by Katharine Anthony. Westport, Conn., Greenwood Press [1973, c1948] 256 p. illus. 22 cm. "The writings of Mary and Charles Lamb": p. 252. [PR4863.A6 1973] 72-7815 ISBN 0-8371-6523-7 12.50
1. Lamb, Charles, 1775-1834. 2. Lamb, Mary Ann, 1764-1847. **BIP**

BARNETT, George Leonard. 824'.7 B
Charles Lamb / by George L. Barnett. Boston : Twayne Publishers, c1976. 172 p. : port. ; 21 cm. (Twayne's English authors series ; TEAS 195) Includes index. Bibliography: p. 159-165. [PR4863.B327] 76-47526 ISBN 0-8057-6668-5 : 7.95
1. Lamb, Charles, 1775-1834. 2. Authors, English—19th century—Biography. I. Title.

BARNETT, George Leonard. 824'.7
Charles Lamb: the evolution of Elia [by] George L. Barnett. New York, Haskell House, 1973 [c1964] xi, 286 p. ports. 23 cm. (Indiana. University Indiana University humanities. Series, no. 53.) Original ed. issued as no. 53 of Indiana University humanities series. Bibliography: p. 270-271. [PR4863.B33 1972] 72-6858 ISBN 0-8383-1652-2 11.95
1. Lamb, Charles, 1775-1834. I. Title. II. Title: The evolution of Elia. III. Series.

HAZLITT, William Carew, 1834-1913. 824'.7 B
The Lambs: their lives, their friends, and their correspondence; new particulars and new material. London, E. Mathews; New York, Scribner, 1897. [New York, AMS Press, 1973] 244 p. 19 cm. [PR4863.H35 1973] 70-168955 ISBN 0-404-07369-7 10.00
1. Lamb, Charles, 1775-1834. 2. Lamb, Mary Ann, 1764-1847. **BIP**

HINE, Reginald Leslie, 1883- 928.2
Charles Lamb and his Hertfordshire. New York, Macmillan, 1950. xxv, 374 p. illus., ports., maps. 23 cm. Bibliography: p. 345-354. [PR4863.H5 1950] 50-7053
1. Lamb, Charles, 1775-1834. 2. Hertfordshire, Eng.—Descr. & trav. I. Title. **BIP**

LAKE, Bernard, 1877- 824'.7
A general introduction to Charles Lamb : together with a special study of his relation to Robert Burton, the author of the "Anatomy of melancholy" / by Bernard Lake. Folcroft, Pa. : Folcroft Library Editions, 1977. 91 p. ; 23 cm. Reprint of the 1903 ed. published by Dr. Seele, Leipzig. Originally presented as the author's thesis, Universitat Leipzig. Includes bibliographical references and index. [PR4864.L3 1977] 77-7515 ISBN 0-8414-5815-4 lib. bdg. : 20.00
1. Lamb, Charles, 1775-1834. 2. Burton, Robert, 1577-1640—Influence—Lamb. 3. Burton, Robert, 1577-1640. The anatomy of melancholy. 4. Authors, English—18th century—Biography. I. Title.

MARTIN, Benjamin Ellis, d.1909. 824'.7
In the footprints of Charles Lamb. Illustrated by Herbert Railton and John Fulleylove; with a bibliography by E. D. North. [Folcroft, Pa.] Folcroft Library Editions, 1973. p. Reprint of the 1891 ed. published by R. Bentley, London. Bibliography: p. [PR4863.M3 1973] 73-15755 ISBN 0-8414-6052-3 (lib. bdg.)
1. Lamb, Charles, 1775-1834. 2. Lamb, Charles, 1775-1834—Bibliography. I. Title. **BIP**

MORLEY, Frank Vigor, 1899- 824'.7 B
Lamb before Elia [by] F. V. Morley. [Folcroft, Pa.] Folcroft Library Editions, 1973. p. Reprint of the 1932 ed. published by J. Cape, London, which was issued as no. 66 of The life and letters series. [PR4863.M54 1973] 73-12357 ISBN 0-8414-5995-9 (lib. bdg.)
1. Lamb, Charles, 1775-1834. I. Title. II. Series: The Life and letters series (London), no. 66. **BIP**

PROCTER, Bryan Waller, 1787-1874. 824'.7 B
Charles Lamb: a memoir, by Barry Cornwall. [Folcroft, Pa.] Folcroft Library Editions, 1973. p. Reprint of the new ed., 1869, published by E. Moxon, London. [PR4863.P7 1973] 73-12285 ISBN 0-8414-3429-8 (lib. bdg.)
1. Lamb, Charles, 1775-1834. I. Title. **BIP**

ROSS, Ernest Carson. 824'.7 B
Charles Lamb and Emma Isola; a survey of the evidence relevant to their personal relationship. [Folcroft, Pa.] Folcroft Library Editions, 1973. 38 p. 23 cm. Reprint of the 1950 ed. published by the Charles Lamb society, London. Includes bibliographical references. [PR4863.R6 1973] 73-8833 10.00 (lib. bdg.)
1. Lamb, Charles, 1775-1834. 2. Moxon, Emma Isola, 1809-1891. I. Title.

WARD, Alfred Charles, 1891- 824'.7 B
The frolic and the gentle; a centenary study of Charles Lamb, by A. C. Ward. Port Washington, N.Y., Kennikat Press [1970] viii, 230 p. port. 19 cm. Reprint of the 1934 ed. Bibliography: p. 223-224. [PR4863.W3 1970] 78-103215 ISBN 8-04-608520-
1. Lamb, Charles, 1775-1834. I. Title. **BIP**

WEST, Trudy 92
The young Charles Lamb. Illus. by Susan E. Sims. New York, Roy [1965, c.1964] 119p. illus. 21cm. [PR4863.W4] 65-18881 3.25 bds.,
1. Lamb, Charles, 1775-1834—Juvenile literature. I. Title.

Lamb, Charles, 1775-1834—Biography.

AINGER, Alfred, 1837-1904. 824'.7 B
Charles Lamb. New York, AMS Press [1968] x, 186 p. 22 cm. (English men of letters) "Reprinted from the edition of 1888, London." Bibliography: p. [vii] [PR4863.A5 1968] 68-58369
1. Lamb, Charles, 1775-1834—Biography. **BIP**

BLUNDEN, Edmund Charles, 1896-1974, comp. 824'.7 B
Charles Lamb : his life recorded by his contemporaries / compiled by Edmund Blunden. Folcroft, Pa. : Folcroft Library Editions, 1975. p. cm. Reprint of the 1934 ed. published by L. and V. Woolf at the Hogarth Press, London, which was issued

as v. 1 of Biographies through the eyes of contemporaries. [PR4863.B63 1975] 75-26549 ISBN 0-8414-3303-8 lib. bdg. : 27.50
1. Lamb, Charles, 1775-1834—Biography. I. Series: Biographies through the eyes of contemporaries ; [v. 1] **BIP**

DANIEL, George, 1789-1864. 824'.7 B
Recollections of Charles Lamb / by George Daniel. Norwood, Pa. : Norwood Editions, 1975. 66 p. ; 18 cm. Reprint of the 1927 ed. published by E. Mathews & Marrot, London, in series: The Baskerville series. [PR4863.D3 1975] 75-43970 ISBN 0-88305-170-2 lib. bdg. . 8.50
1. Lamb, Charles, 1775-1834—Biography. I. Title. II. Series: The Baskerville series. **BIP**

FITZGERALD, Percy Hetherington, 1834-1925. 824'.7
Charles Lamb : his friends, his haunts, and his books / by Percy Fitzgerald. 2d ed. Folcroft, Pa. : Folcroft Library Editions, 1978. vii, 229 p., [3] leaves of plates : ill. ; 23 cm. Reprint of the 1866 ed. published by R. Bentley, London. [PR4863.F5 1978] 78-2784 ISBN 0-8414-4359-9 lib. bdg. : 30.00
1. Lamb, Charles, 1775-1834—Biography. 2. Authors, English—19th century—Biography. **BIP**

LUCAS, Edward Verrall, 1868-1938. 824'.7
The life of Charles Lamb. London, Methuen. New York, AMS Press [1968] 2 v. in 1 (xv, 963 p.) ports. 21 cm. "Reprinted ... from the fifth and revised edition of 1921." [PR4863.L8 1968] 68-59324
1. Lamb, Charles, 1775-1834—Biography. 2. Lamb, Mary Ann, 1764-1847—Biography.

†STODDARD, Richard Henry, 1825-1903, ed. 828'.7'09 B
Personal recollections of Lamb, Hazlitt, and others / edited by Richard Henry Stoddard. Folcroft, Pa. : Folcroft Library Editions, 1976 [c1875] xxii, 322 p. [4] leaves of plates : ill. ; 24 cm. Selections from My friends and acquaintance, by P. G. Patmore. Reprint of the ed. published by Scribner, Armstrong, New York, which was issued as no. 9 of the Bric-a-brac series. Includes index. [PR105.S74 1976] 76-17557 ISBN 0-8414-7623-3 lib. bdg : 27.50
1. Lamb, Charles, 1775-1834—Biography. 2. Haylett, William, 1778-1830—Biography. 3. Campbell, Thomas, 1777-1844—Biography. 4. Blessington, Marguerite Power Farmer Gardiner, Countess of, 1789-1849—Biography. 5. Authors, English—19th century—Correspondence, reminiscences, etc. I. Patmore, Peter George, 1786-1855. My friends and acquaintance. Selections. 1976. II. Title. III Series: Bric-a-brac series ; no. 9. **BIP**

Lamb, Charles, 1775-1834—Correspondence.

LAMB, Charles, 1775-1834. 824'.7'09 B
Lamb and Hazlitt: further letters and records hitherto unpublished. Edited by William Carew Hazlitt. New York, Dodd, Mead, 1899. [New York, AMS Press, 1973] liv, 161 p. 19 cm. [PR4863.A27 1973] 76-168954 9.00
1. Lamb, Charles, 1775-1834—Correspondence. 2. Hazlitt, William, 1778-1830. I. Hazlitt, William, 1778-1830. II. Hazlitt, William Carew, 1834-1913, ed.

LAMB, Charles, 1775-1834. 824'.7'09 B
The letters of Charles and Mary Anne Lamb / edited by Edwin W. Marrs, Jr. Ithaca, N.Y. : Cornell University Press, 1975- v. : ill. ; 25 cm. Includes indexes. Contents.Contents.—v. 1. Letters of Charles Lamb, 1796-1801.—v. 2. 1801-1809. [PR4863.A2 1975] 75-8436 ISBN 0-8014-0930-6 : 25.00 (v. 1)
1. Lamb, Charles, 1775-1834—Correspondence. 2. Lamb, Mary Anne, 1764-1847—Correspondence. I. Lamb, Mary Anne, 1764-1847, joint author. II. Marrs, Edwin W. **BIP**

LAMB, Charles, 1775-1834. 824'.7 B
The letters of Charles Lamb, to which are added those of his sister, Mary Lamb. Edited by E. V. Lucas. [1st AMS ed. London] J. M. Dent. New York, AMS Press [1968] 3 v. illus. 24 cm. Reprint of the 1935 (London) ed. [PR4863.A33 1968] 68-59268
1. Lamb, Mary Ann, 1764-1847. II. Lucas, Edward Verrall, 1868-1938, ed. III. Title.

LAMB, Charles, 1775-1834. 824'.7 B
The life, letters, and writings of Charles Lamb. Edited by Percy Fitzgerald. Freeport, N.Y., Books for Libraries Press [1971] 6 v. 19 ports. 23 cm. "Preface to Sketch of life, &c." (v. 1, p. xix-xxiv) is lacking in this reprint ed. Contents.Contents.—v. 1. [A sketch of the life of Charles Lamb with final memorials, by T. N. Talfourd] Correspondence.—v. 2. Correspondence.—v. 3. Miscellaneous correspondence. Elia. The last essays of Elia.—v. 4. The last essays of Elia. Miscellaneous essays. Letters. Tales.—v. 5. Tales from Shakspeare. Stories contributed to Mrs. Leicester's school. Dramatic works. Sketches, ephemeral papers, &c.—v. 6. Sketches, ephemeral writings, &c. Contributions to Hone's Every day book. Criticisms. Reviews. Letters to the editor. Poems. Sonnets. Blank verse. Album verses and acrostics. Commendatory verses. Translations. Miscellaneous poems. Prologues &c. Satirical and humourous pieces. Additional pieces. Includes bibliographical references. [PR4860.A2 19OThe life, letters, and writings of
I. Fitzgerald, Percy Hetherington, 1834-1925, ed. **BIP**

LAMB, Charles, 1775-1834. 928.2
Selected letters; edited with an introd. by T. S. Matthews. New York, Farrar, Straus and Cudahy [1956] xxvi, 291 p. 22 cm. (Great letters series) [PR4863.A34] 56-7818

Lamb, Charles, 1775-1834—Friends and associates.

BLUNDEN, Edmund Charles, 1896- 824'.7
Charles Lamb and his contemporaries, by Edmund Blunden. [Hamden, Conn.] Archon Books, 1967. ix, 215 p. 19 cm. (The Clark lectures, Trinity College, Cambridge, 1932) First published 1933. [PR4863.B6 1967] 67-19516
1. Lamb, Charles, 1775-1834—Friends and associates. I. Title. II. Series: The Clark lectures, Trinity College, Cambridge University, 1932. **BIP**

HOWE, Will David, 1873-1946. 824'.7 B
Charles Lamb and his friends. Westport, Conn., Greenwood Press [1972, c1944] 364 p. illus., ports. 22 cm. Bibliography: p. 345-347. [PR4863.H6 1972] 72-6196 ISBN 0-8371-6454-0 15.75
1. Lamb, Charles, 1775-1834—Friends and associates. I. Title. **BIP**

Lamb, Charles, 1775-1834—Homes and haunts.

BENSUSAN, Samuel Levy, 1872-1958. 824'.7 B
Charles Lamb, his homes and haunts / by S. L. Bensusan. Folcroft, Pa. : Folcroft Library Editions, 1979. p. cm. Reprint of the 1910? ed. published by Dodge Pub. Co., New York, as no. 2 of the Pilgrim books. Includes index. [PR4863.B38 1979] 79-14593 ISBN 0-8414-9834-2 lib. bdg. : 10.00
1. Lamb, Charles, 1775-1834—Homes and haunts. 2. Authors, English—19th century—Biography. I. Title.

Lamb, Charles, 1775-1834—Homes and haunts—Hertfordshire, Eng.

HINE, Reginald Leslie, 1883-1949. 824'.7 B
Charles Lamb and his Hertfordshire. Westport, Conn., Greenwood Press [1973] xxv, 374 p. illus. 22 cm. Reprint of the 1949 ed. published by Dent, London. Bibliography: p. 345-354. [PR4863.H5 1973] 73-13023 ISBN 0-8371-7111-3 16.00
1. Lamb, Charles, 1775-1834—Homes and haunts—Hertfordshire, Eng. I. Title.

Lamb County—History.

SCOTT, Evalyn Parrott, 1922- 976.4'843
A history of Lamb County [featuring biographies of pioneers. 1st ed. Sudan? Tex. c1968] v, 281 p. illus., map (on lining papers), ports. 28 cm. Cover title. Bibliography: p. 281. [F392.L37S34] 68-57943
1. Lamb County—History. 2. Lamb County—Biography. I. Title.

Lamb, Edward.

LAMB, Edward. 923.873
No lamb for slaughter; an autobiography. Foreword by Estes Kefauver. [1st ed.] New York, Harcourt, Brace & World [1963] 248 p. illus. 22 cm. Full name: Edward Oliver Lamb. [CT275.L2529A3] 63-8100
I. Title.

LAMB, Edward. 332'.092'4 B
The sharing society / by Edward Lamb. 1st ed. Secaucus, N.J. : Lyle Stuart, inc., 1979. 272 p. ; 24 cm. [HC102.5.L28A37] 79-18669 ISBN 0-8184-0284-9 : 12.00
1. Lamb, Edward. 2. Businessmen—United States—Biography. 3. Lawyers United States—Biography. I. Title. **BIP**

Lamb, George Robert.

LAMB, George Robert. 920
Roman road. New York, Sheed and Ward, 1951. 125p. 20cm. Autobiography. [CT788.L28A3 1951] 51-2287
I. Title.

Lamb, Harold,

LAMB, Harold, 1892- 923.247
Chief of the Cossacks. Illustrated by Robert Frankenberg. New York, Random House [1959] 184p. illus. 22cm. (World landmark books, W-39) [DK118.5.L3] 59-5521
I. Razin, Stepan Timofeevich, d. 1671. II. Title.

Lamb, John, 1735-1800.

LEAKE, Isaac Q. 973.3'0924 B
Memoir of the life and times of General John Lamb, an officer of the Revolution, who commanded the post at West Point at the time of Arnold's defection, and his correspondence with Washington, Clinton, Patrick Henry, and other distinguished men of his time, by Isaac Q. Leake. Glendale, N.Y., Benchmark Pub. Co., 1970. x, 431 p. maps, port. 23 cm. Reprint of the 1857 ed. Includes bibliographical references. [E207.L22L4 1970] 75-22578 9.50
1. Lamb, John, 1735-1800. 2. United States—History—Revolution, 1775-1783. I. Title.

LEAKE, Isaac Q. 973.3'0924 B
Memoir of the life and times of General John Lamb; an officer of the Revolution who commanded the post at West Point at the time of Arnold's defection, with his correspondence with Washington, Clinton, Patrick Henry, and other distinguished men of his time, by Isaac Q. Leake. New York, Da Capo Press, 1971 [c1850] x, 431 p. plans, port. 23 cm. (The Era of the American Revolution) Includes bibliographical references. [E207.L22L3 1971] 72-152230 ISBN 0-306-70122-7
1. Lamb, John, 1735-1800. 2. United States—History—Revolution, 1775-1783.

Lamb, Mary Ann, 1764-1847.

GILCHRIST, Anne (Burrows) 1828-1885. 824'.7 B
Mary Lamb. Boston, Roberts Bros., 1883. [New York, AMS Press, 1972] xii, 336 p. 19 cm. Original ed. issued in series: Famous women. Bibliography: p. [xi]-xii. [PR4865.L2G5 1972] 78-148784 ISBN 0-404-07348-4 13.50
1. Lamb, Mary Ann, 1764-1847. I. Series: Famous women **BIP**

Lamb, Richard Ernest, 1887-1973.

ELLIOTT, Errol T. 289.6'092'4 B
R. Ernest Lamb, Irish-American Quaker : the life, work, and wit of a world Friend / by Errol T. Elliott. Richmond, IN : Friends United Press, c1977. xiv, 140 p. : ill. ; 22 cm. [BX7795.L28E44] 77-70184 ISBN 0-913408-29-8 : 4.95
1. Lamb, Richard Ernest, 1887-1973. 2. Friends, Society of—United States—Biography. 3. Friends, Society of—Clergy—Biography. I. Title.

Lamballe, Marie Therese Louise de Savoie-Carignan, princesse de, 1749-1792.

DOBSON, Austin, 1840-1921. 944.04'092'2 B
Four Frenchwomen. Freeport, N.Y., Books for Libraries Press [1972] p. (Essay index reprint series) Reprint of the 1923 ed., which was issued as no. 248 of The World's classics. Contents.Contents.—Mademoiselle de Corday.—Madame Roland.—The Princess de Lamballe.—Madame de Genlis. [DC145.D7 1972] 72-6853 ISBN 0-8369-7269-4
1. Corday d'Armont, Marie Anne Charlotte de, 1768-1793. 2. Roland de la Platiere, Marie Jeanne (Phlipon) 1754-1793. 3. Lamballe, Marie Therese Louise de Savoie-Carignan, princesse de, 1749-1792. 4. Genlis, Stephanie Felicite Ducrest de Saint-Aubin, comtesse de, afterwards marquise de Sillery, 1746-1830. I. Title. **BIP**

Lambarde, William, 1536-1601.

DUNKEL, Wilbur Dwight 340.0924
William Lambarde, Elizabethan jurist, 1536-1601 New Brunswick, N. J. Rutgers [c.1965] xxiv, 210p. 22cm. Bibl. 65-23236 7.50
1. Lambarde, William, 1536-1601. I. Title.

DUNKEL, Wilbur Dwight. 340.0924
William Lambarde, Elizabethan jurist, 1536-1601 [by] Wilbur Dunkel. New Brunswick, N.J., Rutgers University Press [1965] xxiv, 210 p. 22 cm. Bibliography: p. 197-206. 65-23236
1. Lambarde, William, 1536-1601. I. Title.

Lambert, Charles James.

LAMBERT, Charles James. 983
Sweet Waters : a Chilean farm / C. J. Lambert. Westport, Conn. : Greenwood Press, 1975, c1952. 212 p., [7] leaves of plates : ill. ; 22 cm. Reprint of the ed. published by Chatto & Windus, London. [F3060.L3 1975] 75-14091 ISBN 0-8371-8201-8 lib.bdg. : 12.75
1. Lambert, Charles James. 2. Chile—Social life and customs. 3. Ranch life—Chile. I. Title.

Lambert, Gerard Barnes,

LAMBERT, Gerard Barnes, 1886- 926.5
All out of step, a personal chronicle. [1st ed.] New York, Doubleday, 1956. 316 p. illus. 22 cm. [HC102.5.L3A3] 56-11502
I. Title.

Lambertini, Imelda, 1321-1333.

DAUGHTERS of St. Paul. 92 (J)
Her dream came true; the life of Blessed Imelda Lambertini, written and illustrated by the Daughters of St. Paul. [Boston] St. Paul Editions [1967] 66 p. illus. 22 cm. (Their Encounter books) [BX4705.L258D35] 67-20461
1. Lambertini, Imelda, 1321-1333. I. Title.

ERNEST, Brother, 1897- 922.245
A story of Blessed Imelda. Pictures by Sister M. John Vianney. Notre Dame, Ind., Dujarie Press [1956] unpaged. illus. 22cm. [BX4705.L258E7] 56-42849
1. Lambertini, Imelda, 1321-1333. I. Title.

Lamennais, Hugues Felicite Robert de, 1782-1854

ROE, William Gordon 320.924
Lamennais and England; the reception of Lamennais's religious ideas in England in the nineteenth century, by W. G. Roe, Oxford, Oxford Univ Pr., 1966. viii, 241p. 23cm. (Oxford mod. lang. & lit. monographs) Bibl. [BX4705.L26R6] 66-75625 6.10
1. Lamennais, Hugues Felicite Robert de, 1782-1854 2. Gt. Brit.—Church history—19th cent. I. Title.
Available from publisher's New York office.

Lamneck, Philip, 1845-

LAMNECK, John Howard 920
The country squire; the romance of a law-abiding citizen. Boston, Christopher Pub. House [c.1960] 289p. illus. 21cm. 60-9028 4.00
1. Lamneck, Philip. 1845- I. Title.

LAMNECK, John Howard, 1891- 920
The country squire; the romance of a law-abiding citizen. Boston. Christopher Pub. House [1960] 289p. illus. 21cm. [CT275.L257L3] 60-9028
1. Lamneck, Philip, 1845- I. Title.

Lamont, Corliss,

LAMONT, Corliss, 1902- ed. 921.1
Dialogue on George Santayana [by] James Gutmann [and others] Edited by Corliss Lamont with the assistance of Mary Redmer. New York, Horizon Press, 1959. 115p. 21cm. [B945.S24L3] 59-14696
1. Santayana, George, 1863-1952. II. Gutmann, James, 1897- III. Title.

LAMONT, Corliss, 1902- ed. 921.1
Dialogue on John Dewey [by] James T. Farrell [and others] Edited by Corliss Lamont, with the assistance of Mary Redmer. New York, Horizon Press, 1959. 155p. 21cm. [B945.D44L3] 59-14697
I. Dewey, John, 1859-1952. II. Farrell, James Thomas, 1904- III. Title.

Lamont, Thomas William,

LAMONT, Thomas William, 1870-1948. 923.373
Across world frontiers. [1st regular ed.] New York, Harcourt, Brace [1951] vii, 278 p. port. 22 cm. Autobiographical. [HG2463.L3A27 1951] 51-12158
I. Title.

Lampkin-Asam, Julia McCain, 1931-

LAMPKIN-ASAM, Julia McCain, 1931- 616.9'94'00924
Malignant intrigue / by Julia McCain Lampkin-Asam. 3d ed. Miami, Fla. : Acme Press, c1975. xv, 769 p. : ill. ; 23 cm. [RC267.L35 1975] 75-328423
1. Lampkin-Asam, Julia McCain, 1931- 2. Cancer research—United States. 3. Physiologists—Correspondence, reminiscences, etc. I. Title.

Lamy, Jean Edouard, 1853-1931.

ROBERTO, Brother, 1927- 922.244
Angel of the ragpickers; a story of Father Jean Lamy Illus. by Brother Eagan. Notre Dame, Ind., Dujarie Press [1956] 96p. illus. 24cm. [BX4705.L264R6] 56-1600
1. Lamy, Jean Edouard, 1853-1931. I. Title.

Lamy, John Baptist, Abp., 1814-1888.

HORGAN, Paul, 1903- 282'.092'4 B
Lamy of Santa Fe, his life and times / Paul Horgan. New York : Farrar, Straus and Giroux, 1975. 523 p., [8] leaves of plates : ill. ; 24 cm. Includes bibliographical references and index. [BX4705.L265H67 1975] 75-5870 ISBN 0-374-18300-7 : 15.00
1. Lamy, John Baptist, Abp., 1814-1888. I. Title.

Lancaster Co., Pa.—Biography.

HARRIS, Alexander, 1827- 917.48'15'030922 B
A biographical history of Lancaster County: being a history of early settlers and eminent men of the county; as also much other unpublished historical information, chiefly of a local character. Baltimore, Genealogical Pub. Co., 1974. 638 p. 23 cm. Reprint of the 1872 ed. published by E. Barr, Lancaster, Pa. [F157.L2H2 1974] 73-16336 ISBN 0-8063-0590-8
1. Lancaster Co., Pa.—Biography. I. Title.

Lancaster, Osbert,

LANCASTER, Osbert, 1908- 741*.092*4
The Penguin Osbert Lancaster. [Harmondsworth, Middlesex, Eng.] Penguin Books [1964] 114 p. 20 cm. [NC1479.L282A55] 72-206517
I. Title.

Lancaster, William Newton, 1898-1933.

BARKER, Ralph, 1917- 629.13'0924 B
Verdict on a lost flyer; the story of Bill Lancaster. New York, St. Martin's Press [1971, c1969] 238 p. illus., facsims., maps, ports. 24 cm. [TL540.L29B3 1971] 70-135523 6.95
1. Lancaster, William Newton, 1898-1933. I. Title.

Lance, LaBelle.

LANCE, LaBelle. 353.007'1'0924 B
This, too, shall pass / by LaBelle Lance, with Gary Sledge. 1st ed. Chappaqua, NY : Christian Herald Books, c1978. 150 p., [4] leaves of plates : ill. ; 23 cm. [CT275.L263A35] 77-90114 ISBN 0-915684-30-6 : 7.95
1. Lance, LaBelle. 2. Lance, Bert, 1931- 3. Wives—United States—Biogrphy. 4. Bankers—Georgia—Biography. 5. Cabinet officers—United States—Biography. I. Sledge, Gary, joint author. II. Title. BIP

Lanchaise, Gaston, 1882-

*NORDLAND, Gerald. 730.92
Gaston Lanchaise; the man and his work. New York, George Braziller, [1974] viii, 184 p. illus. 26 cm. Bibliography: p. 183-184 [NA549] 74-80661 ISBN 0-8076-0761-4 15.00
1. Lanchaise, Gaston, 1882- 2. Artists—Biography. 3. Sculptors—Biography. I. Title.

Lanchester, Frederick William, 1868-1946.

KINGSFORD, Peter Wilfred 926.2
F. W. Lanchester: a life of an engineer. [dist. New York, St. Martin's Press, 1961, c.1960] 246p. illus. Bibl. 6.75
1. Lanchester, Frederick William, 1868-1946. I. Title.

Lancia, Vincenzo.

FROSTICK, Michael. 629.22'2
Lancia / Michael Frostick. London : D. Watson ; Osceola, Wis. : distributed in the U.S.A. by Motorbooks International, 1976. 208 p. : ill. ; 26 cm. [TL215.L35F76] 77-369956 ISBN 0-901564-22-2 : 19.95
1. Lancia, Vincenzo. 2. Lancia automobile. I. Title. BIP

Lande, Alfred, 1888—

PERSPECTIVES in quantum theory / edited by Wolfgang Yourgrau and Alwyn van der Merwe. New York : Dover Publications, 1979, c1971. xxxvii, 283 p. : graphs ; 21 cm. "Essays in honor of Alfred Lande." Reprint of the ed. published by MIT Press, Cambridge, Mass. Includes bibliographical references and index. [QC174.125.P47 1979] 78-74119 ISBN 0-486-63778-6 pbk. : 5.00 530.1'2
1. Lande, Alfred, 1888- 2. Quantum theory—Addresses, essays, lectures. 3. Physicists—United States—Biography. I. Yourgrau, Wolfgang. II. Van der Merwe, Alwyn. III. Lande, Alfred, 1888- BIP

Landau, Lev Davidovich, 1908-

DOROZYNSKI, Alexander. 925.3
The man they wouldn't let die. New York, Macmillan [1965] xiii, 207 p. illus., ports. 22 cm. [QC16.L25D6] 65-15181
1. Landau, Lev Davidovich, 1908- I. Title.

Landauer, Gustav, 1870-1919.

HYMAN, Ruth Link-Salinger, 1926- 335'.0092'4
Gustav Landauer, philosopher of Utopia / by Ruth Link-Salinger Hyman : with a scholarly bibliography, "Oeuvres Gustav Landauer" edited by Arthur Hyman. Indianapolis : Hackett Pub. Co., c1977. x, 171 p. ; 24 cm. Includes index. "'Oeuvres Gustav Landauer', edited by Arthur Hyman": p. 123-141. [HX273.L26H9] 76-49585 ISBN 0-915144-27-1 : 17.50
1. Landauer, Gustav, 1870-1919. 2. Landauer, Gustav, 1870-1919—Bibliography. I. Title.

LUNN, Eugene. 335'.83'0924
Prophet of community; the romantic Socialism of Gustav Landauer. Berkeley, University of California Press, 1973. x, 434 p. port. 22 cm. Bibliography: p. 405-425. [HX273.L26L85] 70-186105 ISBN 0-520-02207-6 13.75
1. Landauer, Gustav, 1870-1919. I. Title. BIP

MAURER, Charles B., 1933- 335'.83'0924 B
Call to revolution; the mystical anarchism of Gustav Landauer [by] Charles B. Maurer. Detroit, Wayne State University Press, 1971. 218 p. 24 cm. Bibliography: p. 207-211. [HX708.L3M37 1971] 75-148270 ISBN 0-8143-1441-4 9.50
1. Landauer, Gustav, 1870-1919. I. Title. BIP

Landeen, William M.

HAUSSLER, Doris Holt. 378'.00924 B
From immigrant to emissary. Nashville, Southern Pub. Association [1969] 192 p. 22 cm. [LD2935.L85A6] 71-92039
1. Landeen, William M. I. Title.

Landero, Victor.

LANDERO, Victor. 269'.2'0924 B
The victor : the Victor Landero story / as told to Bob Owen, with David M. Howard. Old Tappan, N.J. : F. H. Revell, c1979. 157 p. ; 21 cm. [BV3785.L27A38] 78-26841 ISBN 0-8007-0974-8 : 3.95
1. Landero, Victor. 2. Evangelists—Colombia—Biography. I. Owen, Bob. II. Howard, David M. III. Title. BIP

Landon, Alfred Mossman, 1887-

MCCOY, Donald R. 329.6'00924
Landon of Kansas [by] Donald R. McCoy. Lincoln, University of Nebraska Press [1966] x, 607 p. illus., ports. 24 cm. Includes bibliographical references. [F686.L26] 65-16190
1. Landon, Alfred Mossman, 1887- I. Title. BIP

Landon, Letitia Elizabeth, 1802-1838.

ASHTON, Helen, 1891-1958. 928.2
Letty Landon. New York, Dodd, Mead, 1951. 306 p. 21 cm. [PR4865.L5A9] 51-12416
1. Landon, Letitia Elizabeth, 1802-1838.

Landor, Robert Eyres, 1781-1869.

PARTRIDGE, Eric, 1894- 828'.7'09
Robert Eyres Landor. Freeport, N.Y., Books for Libraries Press [1970] 2 v. in 1. 23 cm. Reprint of the 1927 editions of the author's Robert Eyres Landor: A biographical and critical sketch, and his compilation of Selections from Robert Landor. [PR4865.L8Z7 1970] 78-117909 ISBN 8-369-53622-
1. Landor, Robert Eyres, 1781-1869. I. Landor, Robert Eyres, 1781-1869. Selections from Robert Landor.

Landor, Walter Savage, 1775-1864.

COLVIN, Sidney, Sir, 1845-1927. 821'.7 B
Landor. New York, AMS Press [1968] viii, 224 p. 22 cm. (English men of letters) [PR4873.C6 1968] 68-58374
1. Landor, Walter Savage, 1775-1864. BIP

ELWIN, Malcolm, 1902- 821'.7 B
Landor, a replevin. [Hamden, Conn.] Archon Books, 1970 [c1958] 502 p. illus., ports. 24 cm. Bibliography: p. 471-477. "List of Landor's publications": p. 478-480. [PR4873.E54 1970] 75-122401 ISBN 0-208-00990-6 15.00
1. Landor, Walter Savage, 1775-1864.

FORSTER, John, 1812-1876. 821'.7 B
Walter Savage Landor; a biography. [Author's ed.] Boston, Fields, Osgood, 1869. St. Clair Shores, Mich., Scholarly Press, 1972. v, 693 p. illus. 22 cm. [PR4873.F6 1972] 79-115241 ISBN 0-403-00407-1
1. Landor, Walter Savage, 1775-1864.

SUPER, Robert Henry, 1914- 928.2
Walter Savage Landor: a biography. New York, New York University Press, 1954. xv, 654 p. ports., facsim. 25 cm. Bibliographical references included in "Notes" (p. 511-614) [PR4873.S83] 54-7237
1. Landor, Walter Savage, 1775-1864.

Landor, Walter Savage, 1775-1864—Biography.

SUPER, Robert Henry, 1914- 821'.7 B
Walter Savage Landor : a biography / by R. H. Super. Westport, Conn. : Greenwood Press, [1977] p. cm. Reprint of the 1954 ed. published by New York University Press, New York. Includes index. Bibliography: p. [PR4873.S83 1977] 77-10142 ISBN 0-8371-9783-X lib.bdg. : 35.00
1. Landor, Walter Savage, 1775-1864—Biography. 2. Authors, English—19th century—Biography. I. Title. BIP

Landscape painters—Great Britain—Biography—Dictionaries.

BEREA, T. B. 758'.1'0942
Handbook of 17th, 18th, and 19th century British landscape painters & watercolorists [by] T. B. Berea. [Chattanooga? Tenn., 1970] 72 p. 22 cm. [ND496.B4] 78-13623
1. Landscape painters—Great Britain—Biography—Dictionaries. I. Title.

Landseer, Edwin Henry, Sir, 1802-1873.

LENNIE, Campbell, 1926- 759.2 B
Landseer : the Victorian paragon / [by] Campbell Lennie. London : Hamilton, 1976. [10], 259 p., 16 p. of plates : ill., ports. ; 24 cm. Includes index. Bibliography: p. 250-252. [ND497.L2L46 1976] 76-375309 ISBN 0-241-89432-8 : £6.95
1. Landseer, Edwin Henry, Sir, 1802-1873. 2. Painters—Great Britain—Biography. BIP

Landvater, David.

LANDVATER, Dorothy, 1927- 362.7'8'30926 B
David : a mother's story of her son's recovery from a coma and brain damage / by Dorothy Landvater. Englewood Cliffs, N.J. : Prentice-Hall, c1976. p. cm. [RJ486.L32] 76-10139
1. Landvater, David. 2. Brain-damaged children—Personal narratives. I. Title. BIP

Lane, Arthur Bliss, 1894-1956.

PETROV, Vladimir, 1915- 327.73 B
A study in diplomacy; the story of Arthur Bliss Lane. Chicago, H. Regnery Co. [1971] 302 p. 24 cm. (Foundation for Foreign Affairs series, no. 14) Includes bibliographical references. [D413.L35P48] 70-143846 12.00
1. Lane, Arthur Bliss, 1894-1956. 2. U.S.—Foreign relations—20th century. I. Title. II. Series.

Lane, Elizabeth

LANE, Elizabeth 827.914
Our Uncle Charlie; 'and that's the way she goes.' Adelaide, Rigby [San Francisco, Tri-Ocean, 1965, c.1964] 189p. illus. 23cm. [CT2858.L3A3] 64-8738 3.50 bds.,
I. Title.

Lane, Franklin Knight, 1864-1921.

OLSON, Keith W. 973.8'092'4 B
Biography of a progressive, Franklin K. Lane, 1864-1921 / Keith W. Olson. Westport, Conn. : Greenwood Press, 1979. x, 233 p. ; 22 cm. (Contributions in American history ; no. 78 ISSN 0084-9219s) Includes index.IBibliography: p. [221]-223. [E664.L23O57] 78-57766 ISBN 0-313-20613-9 : 17.95
1. Lane, Franklin Knight, 1864-1921. 2. Politicians—United States—Biography. 3. Social reformers—United States—Biography. 4. Progressivism (United States politics) 5. United States—Politics and government—1865-1933. I. Title.

Lane, Homer Tyrrell, 1876-1925.

WILLS, William David, 1903- 923.742
Homer Lane, a biography. London, Allen & Unwin. [New York, Hillary, c.1964] 275p. ports. 23cm. [LB875.L34W5] 65-398 7.50
1. Lane, Homer Tyrrell, 1876-1925. I. Title.

Lane, Hugh Perry, Sir, 1875-1915.

GREGORY, Isabella Augusta (Persse), Lady, 1852-1932. 704'.7 B
Sir Hugh Lane: his life and legacy. With a foreword by James White. New York, Oxford University Press, 1973. 324 p. illus. 23 cm. (Coole edition, 10) [N5247.L3G73 1973] 73-164508 19.25
1. Lane, Hugh Perry, Sir, 1875-1915. 2. Dublin. Municipal Gallery of Modern Art. 3. Dublin. National Gallery of Ireland.

Lane, Isaac, Bp., 1834-1937.

SAVAGE, Horac C 922.773
Life and time of Bishop Isaac Lane. Nashville, National Publication Co., 1958. 240p. illus. 29cm. [BX8473.L3S3] 58-30008
1. Lane, Isaac, Bp., 1834-1937. I. Title.

Lane, James Henry, 1814-1866.

BAILES, Kndall E 081
Rider on the wind: Jim Lane and Kansas. [1st ed.] Shawnee Mission,Kan., Wheel Press, 1962. 228p. illus. 22cm. Includes bibliography. [F685.L26] 62-20088
1. Lane, James Henry, 1814-1866. I. Title.

Lane, Lunsford, 1803-

HAWKINS, William George, 1823-1909. 301.45'22'0924 B
Lunsford Lane, or, Another helper from North Carolina. New York, Negro Universities Press [1969] xii, 305 p. port. 23 cm. Reprint of the 1863 ed. [E444.L26H3 1969b] 76-91260
1. Lane, Lunsford, 1803- BIP

Lane, Rose (Wilder) 1887-1968.

LANE, Rose (Wilder) 1887-1968. 813'.5'2 B
The lady and the tycoon; letters of Rose Wilder Lane and Jasper Crane. Edited by Roger Lea MacBride. Caldwell, Idaho, Caxton Printers, 1973. xiv, 401 p. ports. 24 cm. [PS3523.A553Z544 1973] 72-78366 ISBN 0-87004-234-3 5.95
1. Lane, Rose (Wilder) 1887-1968. 2. Crane, Jasper, 1881-1969. I. Crane, Jasper, 1881-1969. II. Title.

Lane, Rose Wilder, 1887-1968—Biography—Youth.

LANE, Rose Wilder, 1887-1968. 813'.5'2 B
Rose Wilder Lane : her story / Rose Wilder Lane and Roger Lea MacBride. New York : Stein and Day, 1977. p. cm. [PS3523.A553Z524 1977] 77-12072 ISBN 0-8128-2161-0 : 8.95
1. Lane, Rose Wilder, 1887-1968—Biography—Youth. 2. Authors, American—20th century—Biography. I. MacBride, Roger Lea, 1929- joint author.

Lane, William Arbuthnot, Sir Bart., 1856-1943.

LAYTON, Thomas Bramley, 1882- 926.1
Sir William Arbuthnot Lane, Bt., C. B., M. S.; an enquiry into the mind and influence of a surgeon. Edinburgh, E. & S. Livingstone, 1956. 127p. illus. 23cm. [R489.L3L3] 56-14574
1. Lane, William Arbuthnot, Sir Bart., 1856-1943. I. Title.

Lane, William Guerrant,

LANE, William Guerrant, 1919- 828'.7'09
Richard Harris Barham, by William G. Lane. Columbia, Univ. of Mo. Pr. [1968, c.1967] xv, 271p. 23cm. Bibl. [PR4059.L3] (B) 67-15811 7.00
I. Barham, Richard Harris, 1788-1845. II. Title.

Lanfranc, Abp. of Canterbury, 1005?-1089.

GIBSON, Margaret T. 271'.1'024 B
Lanfranc of Bec / Margaret Gibson. Oxford [Eng.] : Clarendon Press, 1978. xii, 266 p., [1] leaf of plates : ill. ; 23 cm. Includes bibliographical references and indexes. [DA199.L2G53] 77-30168 ISBN 0-19-822462-1 : 22.00
1. Lanfranc, Abp. of Canterbury, 1005?-1089. 2. Bishops—England—Biography. 3. Statesmen—Great Britain—Biography. Distributed by Oxford University Press, NY BIP

Lang, Andrew, 1844-1912.

GREEN, Roger Lancelyn. 928.2
Andrew Lang. [1st American ed.] New York, H. Z. Walck [1962] 84p. illus. 19cm. (A Walck monograph) [PR4877.G66] 62-18333
1. Lang, Andrew, 1844-1912. I. Title.

GREEN, Roger Lancelyn. 828'.8'09 B
Andrew Lang, a critical biography with a short-title bibliography of the works of Andrew Lang. [Folcroft, Pa.] Folcroft Library Editions, 1973. p. Reprint of the 1946 ed. published by E. Ward, Leicester, Eng. [PR4877.G68 1973] 73-16259 ISBN 0-8414-4485-4 (lib. bdg.)
1. Lang, Andrew, 1844-1912.

Lang, John Dunmore, 1799-1878.

LANG, John Dunmore, 1799-1878. 285'.2'0924 B
Reminiscences of my life and times both in church and state in Australia for upwards of fifty years. Edited with an introduction and notes by D. W. A. Baker. Melbourne, Heinemann, 1972. viii, 240 p. port. 22 cm. [BX9225.L26A3 1972] 72-165750 ISBN 0-85561-015-8 8.75
1. Lang, John Dunmore, 1799-1878. I. Baker, David William Archdall, ed. II. Title.

MACMILLAN, David S. 285'.2'0924 B
John Dunmore Lang, [by] David S. Macmillan. Melbourne, New York Oxford University Press [1962] 30 p. illus., ports. 19 cm. (Great Australians) Bibliography: p. 30. [BX9225.L26M3 1962] 79-17546
1. Lang, John Dunmore, 1799-1878.

Langdon, John, 1741-1819.

MAYO, Lawrence Shaw, 1888-1947. 974.2'3'0924 B
John Langdon of New Hampshire. Port Washington, N.Y., Kennikat Press [1970] 303 p. illus., ports. 22 cm. (Kennikat American bicentennial series) Reprint of the 1937 ed. [E302.6.L26M3 1970] 75-120884
1. Langdon, John, 1741-1819. BIP

Lange, Dorothea.

MELTZER, Milton, 1915- 770'.92'4 B
Dorothea Lange : a photographer's life / Milton Meltzer. New York : Farrar Straus Giroux, c1978. xii, 399 p. : ill. ; 24 cm. Includes index. Bibliography: p. 385-391. [TR140.L3M44 1978] 78-5509 ISBN 0-374-14323-4 : 15.00
1. Lange, Dorothea 2. Photographers—United States—Biography. BIP

Langer, William Leonard, 1896-

LANGER, William Leonard, 1896- 378.1'2'0924 B
In and out of the ivory tower : the autobiography of William L. Langer / by William L. Langer. New York : N. Watson Academic Publications, [1977] p. cm. [LD2137.L33] 77-20035 ISBN 0-88202-177-X : 15.00
1. Langer, William Leonard, 1896- 2. Harvard University—Faculty. 3. College teachers—Massachusetts—Biography. I. Title. BIP

Langer, William, 1886-1959.

GEELAN, Agnes. 328.73'092'4 B
The Dakota Maverick : the political life of William Langer, also known as "Wild Bill" Langer / by Agnes Geelan. [Fargo? N.D.] : Geelan, c1975. 166 p., [6] leaves of plates : ill. ; 24 cm. Includes index. Bibliography: p. 155-158. [E748.L27G43] 75-32629 7.95
1. Langer, William, 1886-1959. I. Title.

SMITH, Glenn H., 1922- 327.73
Langer of North Dakota : a study in isolationism, 1940-1959 / Glenn H. Smith New York ; Garland Pub., 1979. viii, 238 p. ; 21 cm. (Modern American history) Includes index. Bibliography: p. 228-234. [E806.S685] 78-62502 ISBN 0-8240-3639-5 : 24.00
1. Langer, William, 1886-1959. 2. United States. Congress. Senate—Biography. 3. United States—Foreign relations—1933-1945. 4. United States—Foreign relations—1945- 5. United States—Neutrality. 6. Legislators—United States—Biography. I. Title. II. Series.

Langley, Francis, 1548-1602.

INGRAM, William. 338.7'61'7920924 B
A London life in the brazen Age : Francis Langley, 1548-1602 / William Ingram. Cambridge, Mass. : Harvard University Press, 1978. ix, 335 p. ; 24 cm. Includes bibliographical references and index. [PN2598.L2215] 77-28573 ISBN 0-674-53842-0 : 17.50
1. Langley, Francis, 1548-1602. 2. London. Swan theatre. 3. Theatrical managers—England—London—Biography. I. Title. BIP

Langley, Samuel Pierpont, 1834-1906.

VAETH, Joseph Gordon, 1921- 629.13'00924 B
Langley, man of science and flight [by] J. Gordon Vaeth. New York, Ronald Press Co. [1966] vii, 117 p. illus., ports. 22 cm. Bibliography: p. 113-114. [TL540.L3V3] 66-29472
1. Langley, Samuel Pierpont, 1834-1906. I. Title.

Langmuir, Irving, 1881-1957.

WESTERVELT, Virginia Veeder. 540'.924 B
Incredible man of science. New York, Messner [1968] 192 p. 22 cm. Bibliography: p. [183]-184. Biography of the pioneer researcher of the atom, first man to work on weather control, and Nobel Prize winner. [Q143.L34W4] 68-25093 3.50
1. Langmuir, Irving, 1881-1957. I. Title.

Langston, John Mercer,

LANGSTON, John Mercer, 1829-1897. 973.8'0924 B
From the Virginia plantation to the National Capitol; an autobiography. New York, Bergman Publishers [1969] 540 p. illus., ports. 24 cm. Reprint of the 1894 ed. [E185.97.L27 1969b] 70-77329
I. Title.

LANGSTON, John Mercer, 1829-1897. 973.8'0924 B
From the Virginia plantation to the National Capitol. New York, Arno Press, 1969. 534 p. illus., ports. 23 cm. (The American Negro, his history and literature) Reprint of the 1894 ed. [E185.97.L27 1969] 69-18567
I. Title. II. Series. BIP

Langstroth, Lorenzo Lorraine, 1810-1895.

NAILE, Florence. 638'.1'0924 B
America's master of bee culture : the life of L. L. Langstroth / by Florence Naile ; edited, with a foreword and an introd., by Everett Franklin Phillips ; and a new foreword by Roger A. Morse. Ithaca, N.Y. : Cornell University Press, c1976. 215 p. : ill. ; 23 cm. First published in 1942 under title: The life of Langstroth. "Langstroth's collection of books about bees and beekeeping": p. [SF523.L3N34 1976] 76-12817 9.95
1. Langstroth, Lorenzo Lorraine, 1810-1895. 2. Bee culture—United States—History. 3. Beekeepers—United States—Biography. I. Title. BIP

Langton, Stephen, Cardinal, d. 1228.

POWICKE, Sir Frederick Maurice, 1879-1963. 922.242
Stephen Langton; being the Ford lectures delivered in the University of Oxford in Hilary term, 1927. New York, Barnes & Noble [1965] viii, 227 p. front. 23 cm. Includes bibliographies. [DA228.L3P6] 65-3087
1. Langton, Stephen, Cardinal, d. 1228. I. Title. II. Series: Oxford University. Ford lectures, 1927

POWICKE, Frederick Maurice, Sir 1879-1963 922.242
Stephen Langton; being the Ford lectures delivered in the University of Oxford in Hilary term, 1927. New York, Barnes & Noble [c.1965] viii, 227p. front. 23cm. Bibl. [DA228.L3P6] 65-3087 7.00
1. Langton, Stephen, Cardinal, d. 1228. I. Title. II. Series: Oxford University. Ford lectures, 1927

Langtry, Lillie, 1852-1929.

BROUGH, James, 1918- 792'.028'0924 B
The Prince & the Lily / James Brough. 1st American ed. New York : Coward, McCann & Geoghegan, 1975. 352 p., [16] leaves of plates : ill. ; 24 cm. Includes index. Includes bibliographical references. [PN2598.L23B7 1975] 74-79684 ISBN 0-698-10610-5 : 10.95

1. Langtry, Lillie, 1852-1929. 2. Edward VII, King of Great Britain, 1841-1910. I. Title.

SICHEL, Pierre. 927.92
The Jersey Lily; the story of the fabulous Mrs. Langtry. Englewood Cliffs, N. J., Prentice-Hall [1958] 456 p. illus. 22 cm. Includes bibliographies. [PN2598.L23S5] 58-11744
1. Langtry, Lillie, 1852-1929. I. Title.

Lanham, Maude (Nation)

BROWN, Pearl E 1887- 920.5
'Marian': modern pionner woman. [Springfield? Ill., 1957] 207p. illus. 22cm. [PN4874.L25B7] 57-860
1. Lanham, Maude (Nation) I. Title.

Lanier family.

CLEMENT, Maud Carter. 929'.2'0973
Lanier, her name, in memoriam, Elizabeth Lanier Clement, May 19, 1904-December 24, 1927. [Danville, Va., 1954] 55p. illus. 23cm. [CS71.L276 1954] 56-52177
1. Lanier family. I. Title.

Lanier, Sidney,

LANIER, Sidney, 1842-1881. 811'.4
Letters of Sidney Lanier; selections from his correspondence, 1866-1881. Edited by Henry Wysham Lanier. Freeport, N.Y., Books for Libraries Press [1972] ix, 245 p. illus. 23 cm. Reprint of the 1899 ed. [PS2213.A3 1972] 71-37890 ISBN 0-8369-6727-5
I. Title.

LANIER, Sidney, 1842-1881. 811'.4
Letters of Sidney Lanier; selections from his correspondence, 1866-1881. Edited by Henry Wysham Lanier. Freeport, N.Y., Books for Libraries Press [1972] ix, 245 p. illus. 23 cm. Reprint of the 1899 ed. [PS2213.A3 1972] 71-37890 ISBN 0-8369-6727-5
I. Title.

Lanier, Sidney, 1842-1881.

LANIER, Sidney, 1842-1881. 811'.4
Letters of Sidney Lanier; selections from his correspondence, 1866-1881. Edited by Henry Wysham Lanier. Freeport, N.Y., Books for Libraries Press [1972] ix, 245 p. illus. 23 cm. Reprint of the 1899 ed. [PS2213.A3 1972] 71-37890 ISBN 0-8369-6727-5
I. Title.

MIMS, Edwin, 1872-1959. 811'.4 B
Sidney Lanier. Port Washington, N.Y., Kennikat Press [1968, c1905] vii, 386 p. 19 cm. Bibliographical footnotes. [PS2213.M5 1968] 68-16281
1. Lanier, Sidney, 1842-1881. BIP

Lanier, Sidney, 1842-1881—Addresses, essays, lectures.

GATES, Merrill Edwards, 1848-1922. 811'.4
Sidney Lanier : a paper / by Merrill E. Gates. Folcroft, Pa. : Folcroft Library Editions, 1977. p. cm. Reprint of a paper which first appeared in the Presbyterian review, Oct. 1887. [PS2213.G3 1977] 77-14263 ISBN 0-8414-2001-7 lib. bdg. : 8.50
1. Lanier, Sidney, 1842-1881—Addresses, essays, lectures. 2. Poets, American—19th century—Biography—Addresses, essays, lectures.

GATES, Merrill Edwards, 1848-1922. 811'.4
Sidney Lanier : a paper / by Merrill E. Gates. Folcroft, Pa. : Folcroft Library Editions, 1977. p. cm. Reprint of a paper which first appeared in the Presbyterian review, Oct. 1887. [PS2213.G3 1977] 77-14263 ISBN 0-8414-2001-7 lib. bdg. : 8.50
1. Lanier, Sidney, 1842-1881—Addresses, essays, lectures. 2. Poets, American—19th century—Biography—Addresses, essays, lectures. BIP

Lansburg, George, 1859-1940.

POSTGATE, Raymond William, 1896- 923.242
The life of George Lansbury. London, New York, Longmans, Green [1951] 331 p. illus. 22 cm. [DA566.9L33P6] 52-1652
1. Lansburg, George, 1859-1940. 2. Gt. Brit. — Pol. & govt. — 20th cent. I. Title.

Lansdowne, Henry Charles Keith Petty-Fitzmaurice, 5th marquis of, 1845-1927.

BARKER, Dudley. 942.082'0922 B
Prominent Edwardians. [1st American ed.] New York, Atheneum, 1969. 254 p. ports. 22 cm. Contents.Contents.—Fisher of Kilverstone.—An episode in the life of William Butler Yeats.—The Marquess of Lansdowne.—Mrs. Emmeline Pankhurst. Bibliography: p. 247-248. [DA568.A1B34 1969] 68-27658 6.50
1. Fisher, John Arbuthnot Fisher, baron, 1841-1920. 2. Yeats, William Butler, 1865-1939. 3. Lansdowne, Henry Charles Keith Petty-Fitzmaurice, 5th marquis of, 1845-1927. 4. Pankhurst, Emmeline (Goulden) 1858-1928. I. Title.

Lansky, Meyer, 1902-

EISENBERG, Dennis, 1929- 364.1'092'4 B
Meyer Lansky : mogul of the mob / Dennis Eisenberg, Uri Dan, Eli Landau. New York : Paddington Press : distributed Grosset & Dunlap, c1979. 346 p., [14] leaves of plates : ill. ; 25 cm. Includes index. [HV6248.L25E57] 79-15979 ISBN 0-448-22206-X : 11.95
1. Lansky, Meyer, 1902- 2. Crime and criminals—United States—Biography. 3. Mafia. I. Dan, Uri, joint author. II. Landau, Eli, 1939- joint author. BIP

MESSICK, Hank. 364.1'06'0924 B
Lansky. New York, Putnam [1971] 286 p. 22 cm. [HV6248.L25M46] 76-136798 6.95
1. Lansky, Meyer, 1902-

Lanza, Mario, 1921-1959.

BERNARD, Matt. 784'.0924 B
Mario Lanza. [New York, Macfadden-Bartell Corp., 1971] 224 p. 18 cm. [ML420.L24B5] 71-31452 1.25
1. Lanza, Mario, 1921-1959. BIP

CALLINICOS, Constantine, musician. 927.8
The Mario Lanza story, by Constantine Callinicos with Ray Robinson. New York, Coward-McCann [1960] 256 p. illus., ports 21 cm. "The Mario Lanza discography": p. 251-256. [ML420.L24C3] 60-12480
1. Lanza, Mario, 1921-1959.

Lao-tzu.

SIMS, Bennett B. 299'.5146'3 B
Lao-Tzu and the Tao te Ching, by Bennett B. Sims. New York, F. Watts [1971] 122 p. 22 cm. (Immortals of philosophy and religion) A brief introduction to and commentary on the life of the Chinese philosopher Lao-tzu is followed by an interpretative text of his teachings. [BL1900.L35S47] 92 73-142996 ISBN 0-531-00961-0
1. Lao-tzu. Tao te ching.—Juvenile literature. I. Title.

Laperouse, Jean Francois deGamp comte de, 1741-1788.

DONDO, Mathurin Marius 923.944
LaPerouse in Maui Waivuku, Maui, Hawaii, Printed by Maui Pub Co., [dist. Honolulu 16, Old Island books, p.o. box 7025) 1959 62 p. front (por.) 21 cm Includes biblioggraphy. 60-779 pap. 2.00
1. Laperouse, Jean Francois deGamp comte de, 1741-1788. 2. mavi. I. Title.

Lapham, Roger Dearborn, 1883-1966.

LAPHAM, Helen Abbot. 910'.92'4 B
Roving with Roger. [San Francisco, Cameron, 1971] xiii, 472 p. illus. 24 cm. [E748.L33L36] 73-154446 10.95
1. Lapham, Roger Dearborn, 1883-1966. I. Title.

Lapidus, Morris.

LAPIDUS, Morris. 720'.92'4 B
An architecture of joy / Morris Lapidus. Miami, Fla. : E. A. Seemann, [1977] p. cm. Includes index. [NA737.L32A42] 77-9090 ISBN 0-912458-96-8 : 14.95
1. Lapidus, Morris. 2. Architects—United States—Biography. I. Title. BIP

Larcom, Lucy, 1824-1893.

ADDISON, Daniel Dulany, 1863-1936. 818'.4'09
Lucy Larcom; life, letters, and diary. Freeport, N.Y., Books for Libraries Press [1971] viii, 295 p. port. 23 cm. Reprint of the 1894 ed. [PS2223.A4 1971] 74-154143 ISBN 0-8369-5759-8
1. Larcom, Lucy, 1824-1893. BIP

ADDISON, Daniel Dulany, 1863-1936. 818'.4'09
Lucy Larcom: life, letters, and diary. Detroit, Gale Research Co., 1970. viii, 295 p. 22 cm. Reprint of the 1894 ed. [PS2223.A4 1970] 75-99065
1. Larcom, Lucy, 1824-1893.

lardner, Ring Wilmer, 1885-1933.

ELDER, Donald. 928.1
Ring Lardner; a biography. [1st ed.] Garden City, N. Y., Doubleday, 1956. 409 p. illus. 22 cm. [PS3523.A7Z65] 56-7656
1. lardner, Ring Wilmer, 1885-1933.

Lardner, Ring Wilmer, 1885-1933—Biography.

LARDNER, Ring Wilmer, 1885-1933. FIC
The story of a wonder man : being the autobiography of Ring Lardner / illustrated by Margaret Freeman. Westport, Conn. : Greenwood Press, 1975. p. cm. Reprint of the 1927 ed. published by Scribner, New York. [PS3523.A7Z52 1975] 818'.5'209 B 75-26216 ISBN 0-8371-8414-2 lib.bdg. : 10.75
1. Lardner, Ring Wilmer, 1885-1933—Biography. I. Title. BIP

YARDLEY, Jonathan. 818'.5'209
Ring : a biography of Ring Lardner / by Jonathan Yardley. 1st ed. New York : Random House, c1977. 415 p., [8] leaves of plates : ill. ; 25 cm. Includes index. Bibliography: p. [399]-405. [PS3523.A7Z9] 77-1661 ISBN 0-394-49811-9 : 12.95
1. Lardner, Ring Wilmer, 1885-1933—Biography. 2. Authors, American—20th century—Biography. BIP

Lardner, Ring Wilmer, 1885-1933—Biography—Journalistic career—Addresses, essays, lectures.

LARDNER, Ring Wilmer, 1885-1933. 818'.5'209 B
Some champions : sketches & fiction / by Ring Lardner ; edited by Matthew J. Bruccoli & Richard Layman ; with a foreword by Ring Lardner, Jr. New York : Scribner, c1976. xv, 205 p. ; 24 cm. Previously uncollected sketches and stories. [PS3523.A7Z518 1976] 75-38544 ISBN 0-684-14582-0 : 8.95
1. Lardner, Ring Wilmer, 1885-1933—Biography—Journalistic career—Addresses, essays, lectures. I. Title.

Larison, Cornelius Wilson,

LARISON, Cornelius Wilson, 1837-1910. 301.45'22 B
Silvia Dubois (now 116 yers old); a biografy of the slav who whipt her mistres and gand her fredom. New York, Negro Universities Press [1969] 124 p. illus., port. 23 cm. Reprint of the 1883 ed. Text in phonetic type. [PE1152.L48 1969] 78-90120
I. Dubois, Silvia, b. 1768.

Larkin, James, 1876-1947.

LARKIN, Emmet J., 1927- 923.31415
James Larkin, Iris labour leader, 1876-1947. Cambridge, Mass., M.I.T. [1964, c.1965] xviii, 334p. illus., ports. 23cm. Bibl. [HD8393.L3L3] 64-22134 7.50
1. Larkin, James, 1876-1947. 2. Trade-unions—Ireland. 3. Labor and laboring classes—Ireland. I. Title.

Larkin, Philip.

TIMMS, David. 821'.9'14 B
Philip Larkin. New York, Barnes & Noble, [1973] 138 p. 20 cm. (Modern writers) Bibliography: p. 132-138. [PR6023.A66Z9 1973b] 74-164388 ISBN 0-06-496915-0 5.75
1. Larkin, Philip.

Larra, Mariano Jose de, 1809-1837.

ULLMAN, Pierre L., 1929- 070.4'49'320924 B
Mariano de Larra and Spanish political rhetoric [by] Pierre L. Ullman. Madison, University of Wisconsin Press [1971] xi, 428 p. port. 24 cm. Bibliography: p. 403-413. [PQ6533.Z5U35] 72-133239 ISBN 0-299-05750-X
1. Larra, Mariano Jose de, 1809-1837. 2. Spain—Politics and government—1833-1868. I. Title. BIP

Larrey, Dominique Jean, baron, 1766-1842.

RICHARDSON, Robert G. 940.2'7'0924 B
Larrey: surgeon to Napoleon's Imperial Guard [by] Robert G. Richardson. [London] Murray [1974, i.e.1975] x, 266 p. illus. 22 cm. Bibliography: p. [255]-258. [UH347.L3R52] 74-173703 ISBN 0-7195-3103-9 15.50
1. Larrey, Dominique Jean, baron, 1766-1842. 2. France. Armee. Garde imperiale (1804-1815) 3. Medicine, Military—France—History. I. Title.
Distributed by Transatlantic Arts, Levittown, N.Y.

Larsen, Lawrence Harold, 1931-

RECTOR, James Ward. 378.1'12'0924 B
Analysis of a biography. Madison, State Historical Society of Wisconsin, 1968. vii, 43 p. 23 cm. [LD6125 1925.L33R4] 68-66245
1. Larsen, Lawrence Harold, 1931- The president wore spats. 2. Frank, Glenn, 1887-1940. I. Title.

Larson, Melvin Gunnard, 1916-1972.

GROENHOFF, Edwin L. 285'.7'0924 B
The quiet prince; a biography of Dr. Melvin G. Larson, Christian journalist [by] Edwin L. Groenhoff. Minneapolis, His International Service [1974] 127 p. illus. 22 cm. [BX7548.Z8L373] 74-79531 ISBN 0-911802-36-3 5.95
1. Larson, Melvin Gunnard, 1916-1972. I. Title.

Larsson, Carl Olof, 1853-1919—Juvenile literature.

LARSSON, Carl Olof, 1853-1919. 759.85 B
A family / Carl Larsson ; with paintings by Carl Larsson and a text by Lennart Rudstrom. New York : Putnam, [1979] p. cm. Translation of En malare och hans familj. Reproductions of several of Larsson's paintings of his large family are accompanied by commentary on the paintings, the life, and the career of this noted Swedish artist. [ND793.L27A4 1979] 79-14291 ISBN 0-399-20700-7 : 7.95
1. Larsson, Carl Olof, 1853-1919—Juvenile literature. 2. Painters—Sweden—Biography—Juvenile literature. I. Rudstrom, Lennart. II. Title.

Larteguy, Jean, 1920- —Biography.

LARTEGUY, Jean, 1920- 843'.9'14 B
The face of war : reflections on men and combat / by Jean Larteguy ; translated by Beth de Bilio. Indianapolis : Bobbs-Merrill, c1979. p. cm. Translation of La guerre nue. [PQ2672.A73Z46413] 79-2049 ISBN 0-672-52350-7 : 13.95
1. Larteguy, Jean, 1920- —Biography. 2. War—History—20th century. 3. Authors, French—20th century—Biography. I. Title. BIP

Lasker, Albert Davis, 1876-1952.

GUNTHER, John, 1901- 926.591
Taken at the flood; the story of Albert D. Lasker. New York, Popular Lib. [1961, c.1960] 320p. illus. (Popular special, SP108) Bibl. .50 pap.,
1. Lasker, Albert Davis, 1876-1952. I. Title.

GUNTHER, John, 1901-1970. 926.591
Taken at the flood; the story of Albert D. Lasker. [1st ed.] New York, Harper [1960] 368 p. illus. 22 cm. Includes bibliography. [HF5810.L3G9] 59-6309
1. Lasker, Albert Davis, 1876-1952. I. Title.

Lasker, Emanuel, 1868-1941.

HANNAK, Jacques. 794.1
Emanuel Lasker, the life of a chess master, with annotations of more than 100 of his greatest games. Foreword by Albert Einstein. Translated by Heinrich Fraenkel. New York, Simon and Schuster [1959] 320 p. illus. 23 cm. [GV1439.L3H33] 59-1462
1. Lasker, Emanuel, 1868-1941.

Laski, Harold Joseph, 1896-1960.

MARTIN, Kingsley, 1897- 923.242
Harold Laski, 1893-1950, a biographical memoir. New York, Viking Press, 1953 278p. illus. 22cm. [JC257.L4M3 1953a] 52-14034
1. Laski, Harold Joseph, 1896-1960. I. Title.

Lasky, Bessie Mona (Gainess)

LASKY, Bessie Mona (Gainess) 1890- 759.13
Candle in the sun. Los Angeles, De Vorss [1957] 316p. illus. 21cm. Autobiographical. [CT275.L2765A3] 927.5 57-4714
I. Title.

Lasky, Jesse Lenard, 1910- —Biography.

LASKY, Jesse Lenard, 1910- 791.43'092'4
Whatever happened to Hollywood? / by Jesse L. Lasky, Jr. London ; New York : W. H. Allen, 1973. [9], 308 p., [32] p. of plates : ill., ports. ; 23 cm. Includes index. [PS3523.A735Z52 1973] 75-301001 ISBN 0-491-01172-5 : £3.50
1. Lasky, Jesse Lenard, 1910- —Biography. 2. Hollywood, Calif. Social life and customs. I. Title.

Lasky, William R., 1921-

LASKY, William., 1921- 248
Tell it on the mountain / by William R. Lasky, with James F. Scheer. 1st ed. Garden City, N.Y. : Doubleday, 1976. viii, 271 p., [4] leaves of plates : ill. ; 22 cm. Autobiography. [BV4935.L32A34] 76-2998 ISBN 0-385-11366-8 : 7.95
1. Lasky, William R., 1921- 2. Conversion. I. Scheer, James F., joint author. II. Title. BIP

Lassalle, Ferdinand Johann Gottlieb, 1825-1864.

BERNSTEIN, Eduard, 1850-1932. 335.4'0924
Ferdinand Lassalle as a social reformer. Translated by Eleanor Marx Aveling. New York, Greenwood Press [1969] xiv, 192 p. 23 cm. Reprint of the 1893 ed. "With some slight alterations, a translation of my introduction to the complete edition of Lassalle's Speeches and works." [HX276.L3B5 1969] 69-13824
1. Lassalle, Ferdinand Johann Gottlieb, 1825-1864. BIP

BRANDES, Georg Morris Cohen, 1842-1927. 335.4'0924
Ferdinand Lassalle [by] George Brandes. Westport, Conn., Greenwood Press [1970] xi, 230 p. 23 cm. First published in the Danish periodical Det 19. aarhundrede in 1874 and 1875. Reprint of the 1911 ed. Includes bibliographical references. [HX276.L3B812 1970] 76-97832
1. Lassalle, Ferdinand Johann Gottlieb, 1825-1864. BIP

FOOTMAN, David, 1895- 335.4'0924
Ferdinand Lassalle, romantic revolutionary. New York, Greenwood Press [1969] xx, 251 p. 23 cm. Reprint of the 1947 ed. "Bibliographical note": p. 245-246. [HX273.L3F6 1969] 70-90145
1. Lassalle, Ferdinand Johann Gottlieb, 1825-1864. BIP

Lassen Co., Calif.—History.

GARATE, Donald T., 1950- 979.4'26'00922
Red Rock to Ravendale : memories of a northern California community / by Donald T. Garate. Ravendale, Calif. : Garate, c1975. xvi, 288 p. : ill. ; 23 cm. Includes index. Bibliography: p. [280]-[281] [F868.L33G37] 75-19928 Pbk. : 8.50
1. Lassen Co., Calif.—History. 2. Lassen Co., Calif.—Biography. I. Title.

Lassen, Peter, 1800-1859.

SWARTZLOW, Ruby Johnson. 923.973
Lassen: his life and legacy. Mineral, Calif., Loomis Museum Association, 1964. 90 p. illus., facsims., maps (1 fold., 1 col.) ports. 28 cm. "Sources and selected readings": p. 84-86. [F864.L328] 64-55270
1. Lassen, Peter, 1800-1859. I. Title.

Last, Clifford, 1918-

DIMAACK, Max 730'.92'4
Clifford Last. Melbourne, Hawthorn Press, 1972. 90 p. plates. 25 cm. Bibliography: p. 88-89. [NB1105.L37D55] 73-151182 ISBN 0-7256-0052-7 7.50
1. Last, Clifford, 1918-

Last, James.

LAST, James. 785'.0924
James Last Story. Hamburg : R. Gloss, [1975] 303, [1] p. : ill. ; 21 cm. Discography: p. 302-[304] [ML422.L34A3] 75-315985 ISBN 3-87261-005-8
1. Last, James. 2. Jazz musicians—Correspondence, reminiscences, etc. I. Title.

WILLOX, Bob, 1954- 785'.092'4 B
James Last / [by] Bob Willox. London : Everest, 1976. 207 p., [16] p. of plates : ill., ports. ; 23 cm. Discography: p. [5]-[6] [ML422.L34W5] 77-361210 ISBN 0-905018-12-5 : £3.95
1. Last, James. 2. Conductors (Music)—Germany—Biography.

Last words.

MARVIN, Frederic Rowland, 1847-1918. 920.02
The last words (real and traditional) of distinguished men and women. collected from various sources. Detroit, Gale Research Co., 1970 [c1901] 354 p. 23 cm. "Facsimile reprint of the 1901 edition." [PN6328L3M3 1901ab] 72-140424 8.50
1. Last words. I. Title.

MYERS, John, 1925- comp. 920.02
Voices from the edge of eternity. Northridge, Calif., Voice Publications [1968] 246 p. 23 cm. [BR1702.M9] 68-7043 3.95
1. Last words. I. Title.

Lasuen, Fermin Francisco de, 1736-1803.

GUEST, Francis F. 271.3'024 B
Fermin Francisco de Lasuen (1736-1803); a biography, by Francis F. Guest. Washington, Academy of American Franciscan History, 1973. xx, 374 p. illus. 27 cm. (Publications of the Academy of American Franciscan History. Monograph series, v. 9) Bibliography: p. 359-366. [F864.G93] 73-159539
1. Lasuen, Fermin Francisco de, 1736-1803. 2. California—History—To 1846. 3. Missions—California—History. 4. Franciscans in California—History. I. Title. II. Series: Academy of American Franciscan History. Monograph series, v. 9. BIP

Latham, Edward H.

GIDLEY, Mick. 970'.004'97
With one sky above us : life on an Indian reservation at the turn of the century / M. Gidley ; photos. by Edward H. Latham. New York : Putnam, 1979. 159 p. : ill. ; 26 cm. "A Webb & Bower book." Inludes index. Bibliography: p. 154-156. [E78.W3G52] 79-63443 ISBN 0-399-12420-9 : 14.95
1. Latham, Edward H. 2. Colville Indian Reservation, Washington (State) 3. Nez Perce Indians—Social life and customs. 4. Indians of North America—Washington (State)—Social life and customs. 5. Photographers—Washington (State)—Colville Indian Reservation—Biography. 6. Physicians—Washington (State)—Colville Indian Reservation—Biography. I. Latham, Edward H. II. Title. BIP

Latham, John R.

LATHAM, John, 1908- 914'.04'55
Adventures of Hebe / John Latham. Chicago : H. Regnery, c1976. 200 p., [8] leaves of plates : ill. ; 24 cm. [D923.L37 1976] 75-32973 ISBN 0-8092-8190-2 : 9.95
1. Latham, John R. 2. Europe—Description and travel—1971- 3. Yachts and yachting—Europe. I. Title.

Lathrop, Julia Clifford, 1858-1932.

ADDAMS, Jane, 1860-1935. 362.7'092'4 B
My friend, Julia Lathrop New York, Arno Press, 1974 [c1935] ix, 228 p. port. 21 cm. (Children and youth: social problems and social policy) Reprint of the ed. published by Macmillan, New York. [HV28.L35A5 1974] 74-1660 ISBN 0-405-05942-6 14.00
1. Lathrop, Julia Clifford, 1858-1932. I. Title. II. Series. BIP

Lathrop, Rose (Hawthorne) 1851-1926.

BURTON, Katherine (Kurz) 1890- 922.273
Sorrow built a bridge, the life of Mother Alphonsa, daughter of Nathaniel Hawthorne. Garden City, N. Y., Image Books [1956, c1937] 274p. 19cm. (A Doubleday image book, D43) [PS2231] 923.673 56-4954
1. Lathrop, Rose (Hawthorne) 1851-1926. I. Title.

SHEEHAN, Arthur T. 923.673
Rose Hawthorne; the pilgrimage of Nathaniel's daughter, by Arthur and Elizabeth Odell Sheehan. Illustrated by Norman Sasowsky. New York, Vision Books [1959] 190 p. illus. 22 cm. (Vision books, 41) [BX4705.L35S5] 59-5468
1. Lathrop, Rose (Hawthorne) 1851-1926. I. Sheehan, Elizabeth Odell, 1919- joint author. II. Title.

VANCE, Marguerite. 922.273
On wings of fire; the story of Nathaniel Hawthorne's daughter, Rose (Mother Alphona)0sa) Illustrated by Nedda Walker. [1st ed.] -new York, Dutton, 1955. 160p. illus. 21cm. [BX4705.L35V3] [bX4705.L35V3] 923.673 55-5365 55-5365
1. Lathrop, Rose (Hawthorne) 1851-1926. I. Title.

Latimer, Hugh, Bp. of Worcester, 1485?-1555.

CHESTER, Allan Griffith, 1900- 922.342
Hugh Latimer, apostle to the English. Philadelphia, University of Pennsylvania Press, 1954. x, 261p. port. 24cm. Bibliography: p. 244-250. [BX5199.L2C5] 54-5010
1. Latimer, Hugh, Bp. of Worcester, 1485?-1555. I. Title.

CHESTER, Allan Griffith, 1900- 283'.092'4 B
Hugh Latimer, apostle to the English / Allan G. Chester. New York : Octagon Books, 1978, c1954. x, 261 p. : port. ; 24 cm. Reprint of the ed. published by University of Pennsylvania Press, Philadelphia. Includes index. Bibliography: p. 244-250. [BX5199.L2C5 1978] 78-18798 lib.bdg. : 13.50
1. Latimer, Hugh, Bp. of Worcester, 1485?-1555. 2. Church of England—Bishops—Biography. 3. Bishops—England—Biography. I. Title. BIP

GRAY, Charles Montgomery. 922.342
Hugh Latimer and the sixteenth century; an essay in interpretation. Cambridge, Harvard University Press, 1950. 62 p. 18 cm. (The Harvard Phi Beta Kappa prize essays, 1949) "Originally written as an undergraduate thesis in history and literature at Harvard College." Bibliography: p. 59-62. [BX5199.L2G7 1950] 50-5187
1. Latimer, Hugh, Bp. of Worcester, 1485?-1555. I. Title.

Latin America—Biography.

ALEXANDER, Robert Jackson, 1918- 923.28
Prophets of the revolution, profiles of Latin American leaders. New York, Macmillan, 1962. 322 p. 22 cm. Includes bibliography. [F1407.A38] 62-7363
1. Latin America—Biography. 2. Latin America—Politics and government.

DAVIS, Harold Eugene, 1902- 920.08
Latin American leaders, by Harold E. Davis. New York, Cooper Square Publishers, 1968 [c1949] 170 p. 24 cm. (Library of Latin American history and culture) With a new preface by the author. Includes bibliographical references. [F1407.D29 1968] 68-56189
1. Latin America—Biography. I. Title.

DAVIS, Harold Eugene, 1902- 980.00922
Makers of democracy in Latin America, by Harold E. Davis. New York, Cooper Square Publishers, 1968. 124 p. 24 cm. (Library of Latin American history and culture.) (Inter-American Bibliographical and Library Association. Publications, ser. 1, v. 9) Reprint of the 1945 ed. with a new introd. Includes bibliographies. [F1407.D3 1968] 68-56190
1. Latin America—Biography. 2. Latin America—Politics and government. 3. Democracy. I. Title. II. Series. BIP

DAVIS, Harold Eugene, 1902- 920'.08
Revolutionaries, traditionalists, and dictators in Latin America, by Harold Eugene Davis. With contributions by Donald J. Mabry [and others] New York, Cooper Square Publishers, 1973. ix, 210 p. 24 cm. (Library of Latin American history and culture) Includes bibliographies. [F1407.D32] 72-77988 ISBN 0-8154-0420-4 7.50
1. Latin America—Biography. I. Title. BIP

LATIN American government leaders. 980*.04*092 Edited by Lewis A. Tambs [and others] Tempe, Center for Latin American Studies of Arizona State University, 1970. 60 p. 23 cm. [F1407.L37] 73-631271
1. Latin America—Biography. 2. Statesmen, Latin American. I. Tambs, Lewis A., 1927- ed. II. Arizona. State University, Tempe. Center for Latin American Studies. BIP

STEWART, Watt, 1892- 920.08
Builders of Latin America [by] Watt Stewart and Harold F. Peterson. Freeport,

N.Y., Books for Libraries Press [1972] xiii, 343 p. illus. 23 cm. (Essay index reprint series) Reprint of the 1942 ed. [F1407.S8 1972] 76-167425 ISBN 0-8369-2724-9
1. Latin America—Biography. 2. Latin America—History. I. Peterson, Harold F., joint author. II. Title. BIP

WORCESTER, Donald Emmet, 1915- 980.00922 (B)
Makers of Latin America, by Donald E. Worcester. [1st ed.] New York, Dutton [1966] 222 p. maps, ports. 24 cm. [F1407.W6] 65-12188
1. Latin America — Biog. 2. Latin America — Hist. I. Title.

WORCESTER, Donald Emmet, 1915- 980.00922
Makers of Latin America. New York, Dutton [c.1966] 222p. maps, ports. 24cm. [F1407.W6] 65-12188 4.95
1. Latin America—Biog. 2. Latin America—Hist. I. Title.

Latin America—Biography—Dictionaries.

WHO'S who in Latin America; a biographical dictionary of notable living men and women of Latin America. Edited by Ronald Hilton. 3d ed. Stanford, Calif., Stanford University Press. Detroit, B. Ethridge, 1971 [c1945] 2 v. 24 cm. Contents.Contents.—Mexico, Central America, and Panama; Cuba, Dominican Republic, and Haiti; Colombia, Ecuador, and Venezuela.—2. Brazil, Bolivia, Chile, and Peru; Argentina, Paraguay, and Uruquay. [CT506.W48 1971] 76-165656 ISBN 0-87917-021-2 920.08
1. Latin America—Biography—Dictionaries. I. Hilton, Ronald, 1911- ed.

Latin America—Biography—Juvenile literature.

BAILEY, Helen Miller. 920.08
Fifteen famous Latin Americans [by] Helen Miller Bailey [and] Maria Celia Grijalva. Englewood Cliffs, N.J., Prentice-Hall [1971] xxii, 190 p. illus. (part col.), col. maps, col. plates, ports. 24 cm. Bibliography: p. 176-181. Brief biographies of fifteen Latin Americans who, as political leaders, artists, writers, musicians, and soldiers, contributed to the development of their respective countries. [F1407.B32] 920 76-22258 ISBN 0-13-314609-X
1. Latin America—Biography—Juvenile literature. I. Grijalva, Maria Celia, joint author. II. Title. BIP

BAUM, Patricia. 980'.00992 B
Dictators of Latin America. New York, Putnam [1972] 191 p. ports. 22 cm. Bibliography: p. 187. Brief biographies of seven Latin American dictators emphasizing the events which brought them to power and the relationship of their countries to the United States. Included are Diaz, Trujillo, Vargas, Stroessner, Peron, Papa Doc, and Castro. [F1407.B36 1972] 920 76-166984 4.29
1. Latin America—Biography—Juvenile literature. 2. Dictators—Biography—Juvenile literature. I. Title. BIP

YOUNG, Bob, 1916-1969. 980'.02'0922 B
Liberators of Latin America [by] Bob and Jan Young. New York, Lothrop, Lee & Shepard Co. [1970] 224 p. illus., maps, ports. 22 cm. Bibliography: p. [220] Concentrates on nine Latin Americans who worked for the freedom of the Spanish dominated colonies. [F1407.Y6 1970] 920 70-120166 4.95
1. Latin America—Biography—Juvenile literature. I. Young, Jan, 1919- joint author. II. Title. BIP

Latin America—Politics and government—1948-

BOURNE, Richard, 1940- 980'.03'0922 B
Political leaders of Latin America. [1st American ed.] New York, Knopf, 1970. 310, x p. 22 cm. Contents.Contents.—Che Guevara.—Alfredo Stroessner.—Eduardo Frei Montalva.—Juscelino Kubitschek.—Carlos Lacerda.—Eva Peron.—Bibliography (p. [307]-310) [F1414.2.B6 1970] 79-127090 ISBN 0-394-44119-2 8.95
1. Latin America—Politics and government—1948- 2. Statesmen—Latin America. I. Title.

BOURNE, Richard, 1940- 980'.03'0922 B
Political leaders of Latin America: Che Guevara; Alfredo Stroessner; Eduardo Frei Montalva; Juscelino Kubitschek; Carlos Lacerda; Eva Peron. Harmondsworth, Penguin, 1969. 306 p. 18 cm. (Political leaders of the twentieth century) Bibliography: p. [293]-296. [F1414.2.B6] 74-437851 ISBN 0-14-021091-1 7/-
1. Latin America—Politics and government—1948- 2. Statesmen—Latin America. I. Title.

Latrobe, Benjamin Henry, 1764-1820.

CARTER, Edward Carlos, 1928- 362.5'092'4 B
Benjamin Henry Latrobe and public works : professionalism, private interest, and public policy in the age of Jefferson / Edward C. Carter II, with the assistance of Darwin H. Stapleton and Lee W. Formwalt. Washington : Public Works Historical Society, c1976. 29 p. : ill. ; 22 cm. (Essays in public works history ; no. 3) "An expanded version of the Bicentennial lecture in public works history which was delivered at the second annual meeting of the Public Works Historical Society in Las Vegas, Nevada, on September 27, 1976." Includes bibliographical references. [HD3885.C37] 77-363020
1. Latrobe, Benjamin Henry, 1764-1820. 2. United States—Public works—History. I. Stapleton, Darwin H., joint author. II. Formwalt, Lee W., joint author. III. Public Works Historical Society. IV. Title. V. Series.

HAMLIN, Talbot Faulkner, 1889- 927.2
Benjamin Henry Latrobe. New York, Oxford University Press, 1955. xxxvi, 633p. illus., ports., facsims., plans. 24cm. Bibliography: p. 605. Bibliographical footnotes. [NA737.L34H3] 55-8117
1. Latrobe, Benjamin Henry, 1764-1820. I. Title.

LATROBE, Benjamin Henry, 1764-1820. 720'.92'4 B
The Virginia journals of Benjamin Henry Latrobe, 1795-1798 / Edward C. Carter II, editor, Angeline Polites, associate editor ; Lee W. Formwalt and John C. Van Horne, editorial assistants. New Haven : Published for the Maryland Historical Society by Yale University Press, 1977. p. cm. (The papers of Benjamin Henry Latrobe : Series I, Journals) Includes index. Contents.Contents.—v. 1. 1795-1797.—v. 2. 1797-1798. [NA737.L34C37] 77-12101 ISBN 0-300-02198-4 : 60.00
1. Latrobe, Benjamin Henry, 1764-1820. 2. Architects—United States—Biography. 3. Virginia—Social life and customs—Colonial period. I. Carter, Edward Carlos, 1928- II. Maryland Historical Society. III. Title. IV. Series. BIP

REGIONAL Conference in Economic History, Eleutherian Mills Historical Library, 1974. 624'.092'2
Benjamin Henry Latrobe & Moncure Robinson : the engineer as agent of technological transfer / Regional Conference in Economic History, May 17, 1974 ; edited by Barbara E. Benson. [Greenville, Del.] : Eleutherian Mills Historical Library, [1975] 71 p. : ill. ; 23 cm. Includes bibliographical references. [TA139.R35 1974] 75-314515 ISBN 0-914650-07-6 pbk. : 1.25
1. Latrobe, Benjamin Henry, 1764-1820. 2. Robinson, Moncure, 1802-1891. 3. Technology transfer—Congresses. I. Benson, Barbara Ellen, 1943- II. Eleutherian Mills Historical Library, Greenville, Del. III. Title.

Latrobe, Benjamin Henry, 1764-1820—Bibliography.

GROPIUS, Wren, Latrobe, Wright. Charlottesville, Published for the American Association of Architectural Bibliographers [by the] University Press of Virginia [1972] 132 p. 24 cm. (American Association of Architectural Bibliographers. Papers, v. 9) [Z5941.A5 vol. 9] [Z8369.43] 016.72'092'2 72-195645 ISBN 0-8139-0391-2 7.50 016.72 S
1. Gropius, Walter, 1883-1969—Bibliography. 2. Wren, Christopher, Sir, 1632-1723—Bibliography. 3. Latrobe, Benjamin Henry, 1764-1820—Bibliography. 4. Wright, Frank Lloyd, 1867-1959—Bibliography. I. American Association of Architectural Bibliographers. II. Title. III. Series.

Latrobe, Charles Joseph, 1801-1875—Juvenile literature.

EASTWOOD, Jennifer Jill. 994.5'03'10924 B
Charles Joseph La Trobe [by] Jill Eastwood. Melbourne, New York; Oxford University Press [1972] 30 p. illus. 19 cm. (Great Australians) Bibliography: p. 30. Brief biography of the nineteenth-century English civil servant who as Lieutenant-Governor of the newly established colony of Victoria did much to foster its early development. [DU222.L34E23] 92 74-169315 ISBN 0-19-550423-2
1. Latrobe, Charles Joseph, 1801-1875—Juvenile literature. I. Title.

Lattimore, Owen, 1900-

BOAS, George, 1891- ed. 928.1
Lattimore the scholar, edited by George Boas and Harvey Wheeler, with a pref. by Gerald W. Johnson. Baltimore, 1953. 61p. 23cm. [DS510.5.L3B6] 53-595
1. Lattimore, Owen, 1900- I. Wheeler, Harvey, joint ed. II. Title.

Latting, Thyrl.

SCOTT, Roszel. 791.8 B
Big city rodeo rider; a true story. Written and illustrated by Roszel Scott; prepared under the direction of Margaret Friskey. Chicago, Childrens Press [1968] 29 p. illus., port. 21 cm. (An Open-door book) A brief biography of a horse-lover who didn't let city living prevent him from becoming one of the best known names on the rodeo circuit. [GV1834.S35] 92 AC 68
1. Latting, Thyrl. I. Title.

Lattre de Tassigny, Jean Joseph Marie Gabriel de, 1889-1952.

SALISBURY-JONES, Guy, Sir 1896- 923.544
So full a glory; a biography of Marshal de Lattre de Tassigny. With a foreword by Viscount Norwich. New York, Praeger [1955] 288p. illus. 23cm. [DC373.L33S3 1955] 55-9488
1. Lattre de Tassigny, Jean Joseph Marie Gabriel de, 1889-1952. I. Title.

Laubach, Frank Charles, 1884-

MASON, David E. 92
Frank C. Laubach, teacher of millions, by David E. Mason. Minneapolis, T. S. Denison [1967] 334 p. plates (incl. ports.) 22 cm. (Men of achievement series) Biography of the Christian educator whose philosophy of "each one teach one" has brought knowledge to millions of illiterates around the world. [LA2317.L3M3] AC 67
1. Laubach, Frank Charles, 1884- 2. Educators.

MEDARY, Marjorie. 379.2
Each one teach one; Frank Laubach, friend to millions. [1st ed.] New York, Longmans, Green, 1954. 227 p. illus. 21 cm. [LC149.M4] 54-5550
1. Laubach, Frank Charles, 1884- 2. Illiteracy. I. Title.

Laud, William, Abp. of Canterbury, 1573-1645.

TREVOR-ROPER, Hugh Redwald 922.342
Archbishop Laud. 1573-1645. 2d ed. Hamden, Conn., Archon Bks. [dist. Shoe String, c.]1962. 464p. illus. 23cm. 62-6426 6.50
1. Laud, William, Abp. of Canterbury, 1573-1645. I. Title.

Lauda, Niki, 1949-

LAUDA, Niki, 1949- 796.7'2'0924 B
My years with Ferrari / Niki Lauda. Osceola, Wis. : Motorbooks International, c1978. 237 p. ; ill. ; 21 cm. Translation of Protokoll. British ed. published under title: For the record. [GV1032.L38A3613] 78-7559 ISBN 0-87938-059-4 : 12.95
1. Lauda, Niki, 1949- 2. Automobile racing drivers—Biography. 3. Ferrari automobile. I. Title. BIP

Laughton, Charles, 1899-1962.

HIGHAM, Charles, 1931- 791'.092'4 B
Charles Laughton : an intimate biography / by Charles Higham ; introd. by Elsa Lanchester. 1st ed. Garden City, N.Y. : Doubleday, 1976. xviii, 239 p., [8] leaves of plates : ill. ; 22 cm. Includes index. [PN2598.L27H5] 75-21228 ISBN 0-385-09403-5 : 8.95
1. Laughton, Charles, 1899-1962.

HIGHAM, Charles, 1931- 791'.092'4 B
Charles Laughton : an intimate biography / by Charles Higham ; introd. by Elsa Lanchester. 1st British ed. London : W. H. Allen, 1976. xiii, 239 p., [8] leaves of plates : ill. ; 22 cm. Includes index. [PN2598.L27H5 1976b] 76-379526 ISBN 0-491-01696-4 : £4.95
1. Laughton, Charles, 1899-1962. 2. Actors—Great Britain—Biography.

Laughton, Tom.

LAUGHTON, Tom. 338.7'61'647940924 B
Pavilions by the sea : the memoirs of an hotel-keeper / by Tom Laughton. London : Chatto and Windus, 1977. xi, 216 p., leaf of plate, 4 p. of plates : ill., ports. ; 23 cm. Includes index. [TX910.5.L37A36] 77-363341 ISBN 0-7011-2205-6 : 12.50
1. Laughton, Tom. 2. Hotel management—Biography. I. Title.
Distributed by Transatlantic Arts, N. Village Green, Levittown, NY 11756

Laune, Seigniora Russell.

LAUNE, Seigniora Russell. 917.6'03'40924 B
Sand in my eyes / by Seigniora Russell Laune ; illustrated by Paul Laune. New ed. Flagstaff [Ariz.] : Northland Press, 1974. 256 p. : ill. ; 21 cm. [F786.L33 1974] 74-82365 ISBN 0-87358-130-X : 7.50
1. Laune, Seigniora Russell. 2. Frontier and pioneer life—Southwest, New. 3. Southwest, New—History—1848- I. Title. BIP

Laure, Augustin, 1857-1892.

GARRAND, Victor. 266'.2'797
Augustine Laure, S. J., missionary to the Yakimas / by Victor Garrand ; Edward J. Kowrach, editor. Fairfield, Wash. : Galleon Press, 1977. 35 p. : ill. ; 29 cm. Translation of Le pere Augustin Laure, de la Compagnie de Jesus, missionaire aux montagnes Rocheuses. [E99.Y2G3513] 77-8126 ISBN 0-87770-176-8 : 6.95 pbk. : 3.95
1. Laure, Augustin, 1857-1892. 2. Yakima Indians—Missions. 3. Missionaries—Washington (State)—Biography. 4. Missionaries—France—Biography. 5. Indians of North America—Washington (State)—Missions. I. Title.
Publisher's address : P.O. Box 400, Fairfield, WN 99012 BIP

Laurel, Stan.

†*THE History of Laurel and Hardy* / [editor, Ron Haydock] . Sherman Oaks, CA : E-Go Enterprises, c1976. 66 p. : ill. ; 28 cm. (E-GO collectors series ; 2) [PN2287.L285H5] 76-377119 1.00 791.43'028'0922 B
1. Laurel, Stan. 2. Hardy, Oliver Norvell, 1892-1957. 3. Comedians—United States—Biography. I. Haydock, Ron.
Publisher's address: 13510 Ventura Blvd., Sherman Oaks, Calif.

MCCABE, John 927.92
Mr. Laurel and Mr. Hardy Doubleday [c.] 1961. 240p. illus. 61-7658 4.50 half cloth,
1. Laurel, Stan. 2. Hardy, Oliver Norvell. 1892-1957. I. Title.

MCCABE, John, 1920- 791'.092'4 B
The comedy world of Stan Laurel. [1st ed.] Garden City, N.Y., Doubleday, 1974. xv, 221 p. illus. 22 cm. [PN2287.L285M28] 73-22789 ISBN 0-385-06645-7 7.95
1. Laurel, Stan. I. Title.

MCCABE, John, 1920- 927.92
Mr. Laurel and Mr. Hardy. [1st ed.] Garden City, N. Y., Doubleday, 1961. 240 p. illus. 22 cm. [PN2287.L285M3] 61-7658
1. Laurel, Stan. 2. Hardy, Oliver Norvell, 1892-1957. I. Title.

Laurence, Margaret—Journeys.

LAURENCE, Margaret. 814'.5'4
Heart of a stranger / Margaret Laurence. Toronto : McClelland and Stewart, 1976. 221 p. ; 22 cm. [PR9199.3.L33Z52] 77-352512 ISBN 0-7710-4710-X : 8.95
1. Laurence, Margaret—Journeys. 2. Voyages and travels. 3. Authors, Canadian—Biography. I. Title.
Distributed by Lippincott,N.Y. Contents omitted

Laurens, Henry, 1724-1792.

WALLACE, David Duncan, 1874-1951. 973.3'0924 B
The life of Henry Laurens, with a sketch of the life of Lieutenant-Colonel John Laurens. New York, Russell & Russell [1967] xi, 539 p. illus., ports. 22 cm. Reprint of the 1915 ed. Bibliography: p. 511-515. [E302.6.L3W2 1967] 66-27173
1. Laurens, Henry, 1724-1792. 2. Laurens, John, 1754-1782. I. Title.

WALLACE, David Duncan, 1874-1951. 973.3'0924 (B)
The life of Henry Laurens, with a sketch of the life of Lieutenant-Colonel John Laurens. New York, Russell & Russell [1967] xi, 539 p. illus., ports. 22 cm. Reprint of the 1915 ed. Bibliography: p. 511-515. [E302.6.L3W2] 66-27173
1. Laurens, Henry, 1724-1792. 2. Laurens, John, 1754-1782. I. Title.

Laurens, John, 1754-1782.

TOWNSEND, Sara Bertha. 923.573
An American soldier; the life of John Laurens drawn largely from correspondence between his father and himself. Raleigh, N.C., Edwards & Broughton Co. [c1958] xiii, 266 p. illus., ports., map (on lining papers) facsims. 24 cm. Bibliography: p. 265-266. [E207.L28T6] 58-11883
1. Laurens, John, 1754-1782. I. Laurens, John, 1754-1782. II. Laurens, Henry, 1724-1792. III. Title.

Laurie, James Woodin, 1903-1970.

BRACKENRIDGE, R. Douglas 378.1'12'0924 B
Beckoning frontiers : a biography of James Woodin Laurie / by R. Douglas Brackenridge. San Antonio : Trinity University Press, c1976. xii, 198 p. : ill. ; 24 cm. Includes bibliographical references and index. [LD5361.T617 1951.B7] 75-27591 ISBN 0-911536-61-2 : 10.00
1. Laurie, James Woodin, 1903-1970. 2. College presidents—Texas—Biography. I. Title. BIP

Laurier, Wilfrid, Sir, 1841-1919.

CLIPPINGDALE, Richard, 1941- 971.05'6'0924 B
Laurier, his life and world / Richard Clippingdale. Toronto ; New York : McGraw-Hill Ryerson, c1979. 224 p. : ill. (some col.) ; 26 cm. ([Prime Ministers of Canada]) Includes index. Bibliography: p. 219-220. [F1033.L37C58] 79-319343 ISBN 0-07-082302-2 : 17.95
1. Laurier, Wilfrid, Sir, 1841-1919. 2. Canada—Politics and government—1867-1914. 3. Prime ministers—Canada—Biography. I. Title. II. Series.

ROBERTSON, Barbara. 354'.71'03130924 B
Wilfrid Laurier: the great conciliator. Toronto, Oxford University Press, 1971. 160 p. illus. 20 cm. (Canadian lives) Bibliography: p. 155-157. [F1033.L376] 72-185029 ISBN 0-19-540192-1
1. Laurier, Wilfrid, Sir, 1841-1919. 2. Canada—Politics and government—1867- I. Title.

Lauro, Joseph,

LAURO, Joseph, 1912- 282'.0924 B
Action priest; the story of Father Joe Lauro. By Joseph Lauro and Arthur Orrmont. With a foreword by Richard Cardinal Cushing. New York, Morrow, 1971 [c1970] 357 p. port. 22 cm. [BX4705.L3684A3] 75-118269 8.95
I. Orrmont, Arthur, joint author. II. Title. BIP

Lausmann, Anton Albert, 1889-

WEBBER, Bert. 634.9'82'0924 B
Swivel-chair logger : the life and work of Anton A. "Tony" Lausmann / by Bert Webber. Fairfield, Wash. : Ye Galleon Press, 1976. p. cm. Includes index. Bibliography: p. [SD537.52.L38W4] 76-28404 ISBN 0-87770-163-6 pbk. : 5.50
1. Lausmann, Anton Albert, 1889- 2. Loggers—Oregon—Biography. I. Title.

Laussat, Pierre Clement de, 1756-1835.

LAUSSAT, Pierre Clement de, 1756-1835 976.3'04'0924 B
Memoirs of my life to my son during the years 1803 and after, which I spent in public service in Louisiana as Commissioner of the French Government for the retrocession to France of that colony and for its transfer to the United States / by Pierre Clement de Laussat ; translated from the French, with an introd. by Agnes-Josephine Pastwa ; edited with a foreword, by Robert D. Bush. Baton Rouge : Published for the Historic New Orleans Collection by the Louisiana State University Press, c1978. xxiii, 137 p.; [5] leaves of plates : ill. ; 24 cm. (The Historic New Orleans Collection monograph series) Translation of Memoires sur ma vie. Includes index. Bibliography: p. [131]-132. [F374.L26 1977] 77-12113 12.50
1. Laussat, Pierre Clement de, 1756-1835. 2. Colonial administrators—France—Biography. 3. Colonial administrators—Louisiana—Biography. 4. Louisiana—History—1803-1865—Sources. I. Title: Memoirs of my life to my son ... II. Series: Historic New Orleans Collection. The Historic New Orleans Collection monograph series.

Lauterer, Arch, 1904-1957.

ARCH Lauterer- v. 12
poet in the theatre. [San Francisco, Impulse Publications, 1959] 64p. illus., ports., diagrs. 28cm. (Impulse 1959; the annual of contemporary dance) Includes bibliographies.
1. Lauterer, Arch, 1904-1957. I. Impulse.

Lauzun, Antonin Nompar de Caumont, duc de, 1633-1723.

WILLIAMS, Adair G. 923.544
The heat of the sun; the life of the Duke de Lauzun (1633-1723) favorite of Louis XIV. New York, Pageant [1964, c.1963] 295p. port., map. 24cm. Bibl. 63-22454 5.00
1. Lauzun, Antonin Nompar de Caumont, duc de, 1633-1723. I. Title.

Laval, Pierre, 1883-1945.

COLE, Hubert. 923.244
Laval, a biography. [1st American ed.] New York, Putnam [1963] 314 p. illus. 23 cm. [DC373.L35C6] 63-9657
1. Laval, Pierre, 1883-1945.

LAVAL, Pierre, 1883-1945. 944'.081'0924
The diary of Pierre Laval / with a pref. by Josee Laval. New York : AMS Press, 1978. xv, 240 p., [2] leaves of plates : ill. ; 23 cm. Reprint of the 1948 ed. published by Scribner, New York. [DC373.L35A3 1978] 72-6725 ISBN 0-404-10644-7 : 16.50
1. Laval, Pierre, 1883-1945. 2. Statesmen—France—Biography. 3. France—Politics and government—1940-1945. I. Title. BIP

THOMSON, David, 1912- 944.081'092'2 B
Two Frenchmen, Pierre Laval and Charles de Gaulle / by David Thomson. Westport, Conn. : Greenwood Press, 1975. p. cm. Reprint of the 1951 ed. published by Cresset Press, London. Includes bibliographical references and index. [DC373.L35T47 1975] 75-8806 ISBN 0-8371-8115-1
1. Laval, Pierre, 1883-1945. 2. Gaulle, Charles de, Pres., France, 1890-1970. I. Title.

WARNER, Geoffrey, 1937- 944.081'6'0924 B
Pierre Laval and the eclipse of France. [1st American ed.] New York, Macmillan [1969, c1968] xvii, 461 p. illus., maps, ports. 22 cm. Bibliography: p. 431-445. [DC373.L35W3 1969] 68-54475 8.95
1. Laval, Pierre, 1883-1945. 2. France—Politics and government—1914-1940. 3. France—Politics and government—1940-1945. I. Title.

Laveau, Marie, 1794-1881.

MYSTERIOUS Marie Laveau, v. 12
voodoo queen, and folk tales along the Mississippi. New Orleans, Harmanson [1956] 96p. illus. 22cm. Bibliography: p. 96.
1. Laveau, Marie, 1794-1881 2. Voodoism. 3. Folk-lore—Louisiana—New Orleans. I. Martineq, Raymond Joseph.

Lavender, David Sievert, 1910-

LAVENDER, David Sievert, 1910- 917.88'04'3
David Lavender's Colorado / by David Lavender ; with 105 photos. in color by the author and Lee Boltin. 1st ed. Garden City, N.Y. : Doubleday, 1976. xii, 227 p., [40] leaves of plates : ill. ; 32 cm. Includes index. Bibliography: p. 221-222. [F781.2.L38] 75-32013 ISBN 0-385-06337-7 : 24.95
1. Lavender, David Sievert, 1910- 2. Colorado—Description and travel—1951- I. Boltin, Lee. II. Title. BIP

LAVENDER, David Sievert, 1910- 978.8 B
One man's West / by David Lavender ; line drawings by William Arthur Smith. Lincoln : University of Nebraska Press, 1977, c1956. 316 p. : ill. ; 21 cm. Reprint of the ed. published by Doubleday, Garden City, N.Y. "A Bison book." [F781.L3 1977] 76-45450 ISBN 0-8032-0908-8 : 13.50 ISBN 0-8032-5855-0 pbk. : 3.95
1. Lavender, David Sievert, 1910- 2. Ranch life—Colorado. 3. Cowboys—Colorado—Biography. 4. Colorado—Biography. I. Title. BIP

Lavender, Lucille.

LAVENDER, Lucille. 286'.1'0924
Up the staircase backwards / Lucille Lavender ; illustrated by Dean McElhattan. Denver : Accent Books, c1978. 127 p. : ill. ; 21 cm. [BX6495.L33A36] 77-93248 ISBN 0-916406-96-2 pbk. : 2.95
1. Lavender, Lucille. 2. Baptists—United States—Biography. 3. Leg—Fractures—Biography. 4. Christian life—Baptist authors. I. Title. BIP

Laver, James,

LAVER, James, 1899- 928.2
Museum piece; os, The education of an iconographer. 1st American Ed. Boston, Houghton Mifflin, 1964 [c1963] 255 p. illus., ports. 22 cm. Autobiography. [N8375.L36A2 1964] 62-11482
I. Title. II. Title: The education of an iconographer.

LAVER, James, 1899- 928.2
Museum piece; or, The education of an iconographer. [1st American ed.] Boston, Houghton Mifflin, 1964 [c1963] 255 p. illus., ports. 22 cm. Autobiography. [N8375.L36A2 1964] 62-11482
I. Title. II. Title: The education of an iconographer.

Laves, Georg Ludwig Friedrich, 1788-1864.

HOELTJE, Georg, 1906- v. 12
Georg Ludwig Friedrich Laves, mit einem Beitrag uber Georg Ludwig Friedrich Laves als Bauingenieur von Helmut Weber. Hannover, Steinback, 1964. 255 p. illus. (part mounted col.) plans, ports., geneal. table, facsims. 35 cm. Bibliography: p. 196-197. 65-94672
1. Laves, Georg Ludwig Friedrich, 1788-1864. I. Weber, Helmut, 1923- II. Title.

Lavoisier, Antoine Laurent, 1743-1794.

DAVIS, Kenneth Sydney, 1912- 540.922
The cautionary scientists: Priestley, Lavoisier, and the founding of modern chemistry. New York, Putnam [c.1966] 256p. 22cm. Bibl. [QD22.L4D32] 66-15580 5.75
1. Lavoisier, Antoine Laurent, 1743-1794. 2. Priestley, Joseph, 1733-1804. I. Title.

DAVIS, Kenneth Sydney, 1912- 540.922
The cautionary scientists: Priestley, Lavaisier, and the founding of modern chemistry [by] Kenneth S. Davis. New York, Putnam [1966] 256 p. 22 cm. Bibliography: p 245 247. [QD22.L4D32] 66-15580
1. Lavoisier, Antoine Laurent, 1743-1794. 2. Priestley, Joseph, 1733-1804. I. Title.

GUERLAC, Henry. 540'.92'4 B
Antoine-Laurent Lavoisier, chemist and revolutionary / Henry Guerlac. New York : Scribner, c1975. 174 p. : ill. ; 21 cm. (DSB editions) A rev. and expanded version of the article which originally appeared in the Dictionary of scientific biography. Includes index. Bibliography: p. 143-163. [QD22.L4G82] 75-7596 ISBN 0-684-14221-X : 7.95. ISBN 0-684-14222-8 pbk. : 2.95
1. Lavoisier, Antoine Laurent, 1743-1794. I. Title.

MCKIE, Douglas 925.4
Antoine Lavisier: scientist, economist, social reformer. New York, Collier [1962, c.1952] 317p. (Men of sci. lib., AS106X) Bibl. .95 pap.,
1. Lavoisier, Antoine Laurent, 1743-1794. I. Title.

MCKIE, Douglas. 925.4
Antoine Lavoisier: scientist, economist, social reformer. New York, H. Schuman [1952] 440 p. illus. 22 cm. (The Life of science library, no. 25) [QD22.L4M32 1952] 52-13428
1. Lavoisier, Antoine Laurent, 1743-1794. I. Title.

RIEDMAN, Sarah Regal, 1902- 925.4
Antoine Lavoisier, scientist and citizen. New York, Nelson [1957] 192 p. illus. 21 cm. Includes bibliography. [QD22.L4R5] 57-10023
1. Lavoisier, Antoine Laurent, 1743-1794.

RIEDMAN, Sarah Regal, 1902- 92
Antoine Lavoisier, scientist and citizen, by Sarah R. Riedman. Reissue with over thirty new photographs. London, New

York [etc.] Abelard-Schuman, 1967. 192 p. illus. 22 cm. Bibliography: p. 187-188. A biography of the eighteenth century French scientist who is known as the father of chemistry for his work on combustion, oxygen and respiration. [QD22.L4R5 1967] AC 67
1. Lavoisier, Antoine Laurent, 1743-1794. I. Title.

Lavoisier, Antoine Laurent, 1743-1794—Juvenile literature.

RIEDMAN, Sarah Regal, 1902- 540'.924
Antoine Lavoisier, scientist and citizen, by Sarah R. Riedman. Reissue with over thirty new photographs. London, New York, Abelard-Schuman, 1967. 192 p. illus. 22 cm. Bibliography: p. 187-188. [QD22.L4R5 1967] 67-21485 unpriced
1. Lavoisier, Antoine Laurent, 1743-1794—Juvenile literature.

Law

HOLDSWORTH, William Searle, Sir 1871-1944 340.0922
The historians of Anglo-American law. Hamden, Conn., Archon [dist., Shoe String, 1966[c.1928] 175p. 20cm. (Columbia Univ. lects., 1927. James S. Carpentier Found.) Title. (Series: James S. Carpentier lectures, 1927) 66-16777 4.25
1. Law—Gt. Brit.—Hist. & crit. 2. Law—U.S.—Hist. & crit. 3. Lawyers—Gt. Brit.—Biog. 4. Lawyers—U.S.—Biog. I. Title. II. Series.

LEE, William Little, 1821-1857. 923.4969
William L. Lee: his address at the opening of the first term of the Superior Court held in the new courthouse, Honolulu, July 5, 1852; to which is added a biographical note by Meiric K. Dutton. Honolulu, Loomis House Press, 1953. unpaged. illus. 16cm. 54-27027
1. Law—Addresses, essays, lectures. I. Dutton, Meiric Keeler, 1900- II. Title.

Law, Andrew Bonar, 1858-1923.

BLAKE, Robert, 1916- 923.242
Unrepentant Tory; the life and times of Andrew Bonar Law, 1858-1923, Prime Minister of the United Kingdom. New York, St. Martin's Press, 1956 [c1955] 556p. illus., ports. 23cm. Bibliographical reference included in 'Notes' (p. 535-541) [DA566.9] 56-1452
1. Law, Andrew Bonar, 1858-1923. 2. Gt. Brit. —Pol. & govt.—20th cent. I. Title.

Law—Biography.

SEAGLE, William, 1898- 340'.922 B
Men of law, from Hammurabi to Holmes. New York, Hafner Pub. Co., 1971 [c1947] 391 p. 23 cm. [LAW] 78-159979
1. Law—Biography. I. Title.

Law, John, 1671-1729.

MINTON, Robert, 1918- 332'.092'4 B
John Law, the father of paper money / Robert W. Minton. New York : Association Press, [1975] p. cm. Includes index. Bibliography: p. [HG172.L3M55] 75-15734 ISBN 0-8096-1904-0 : 10.00
1. Law, John, 1671-1729. 2. Capitalists and financiers—Biography. 3. Paper money—France—History. I. Title.

Law libraries — Direct.

AMERICAN Association of Law Libraries. 020'.92'2
Biographical directory of law librarians in the United States and Canada. St. Paul, West Pub. Co., 1964. 57 p. 25 cm. "Printed for private distribution." [Z720.A4U373] 64-5056
1. Law libraries — Direct. I. Title.

Law reporters—Virginia—Biography.

THE Virginia law reporters before 1880 / edited by W. Hamilton Bryson. 348'.755'0430922 B Charlottesville : University Press of Virginia, 1978. 130 p. ; 23 cm. Includes bibliographical references. [KFV2926.C68V57] 77-21451 ISBN 0-8139-0747-0 : 9.75
1. Law reporters—Virginia—Biography. 2. Virginia—History. I. Bryson, William Hamilton, 1941- **BIP**

Law—United States—History and criticism.

BLOOMFIELD, Maxwell H. 340'.0973
American lawyers in a changing society, 1776-1876 / Maxwell Bloomfield. Cambridge, Mass. : Harvard University Press, 1976. ix, 397 p. ; 24 cm. (Studies in legal history) Includes bibliographical references and index. [KF366.B5] 75-14172 ISBN 0-674-02910-0 : 15.00
1. Law—United States—History and criticism. 2. Lawyers—United States—Biography. I. Title.

Law, Virginia W.

LAW, Virginia W. 287.6'0924
As far as I can step [by] Virginia Law. Waco, Tex., Word Books [1970] 157 p. 23 cm. Autobiographical. [BX8495.L36A3 1970] 74-111963 3.95
I. Title. **BIP**

Law, William, 1686-1761.

HOBHOUSE, Stephen Henry, 1881-1961. 283'.092'4
William Law and eighteenth century Quakerism; including some unpublished letters and fragments of William Law and John Byrom. New York, B. Blom, 1972. 342 p. illus. 21 cm. Reprint of the 1927 ed. published by G. Allen & Unwin, London. Includes bibliographical references. [BX5199.L3H62 1972] 77-175870 14.50
1. Law, William, 1686-1761. 2. Byrom, John, 1692-1763. 3. Dodshon, Frances (Henshaw) Paxton, 1714-1793. 4. Friends, Society of. I. Title.

Lawes, Henry, 1596-1662.

EVANS, Willa McClung, 1899- v. 12
Henry Lawes, musician and friend of poets. New York, Modern Language Association of America, 1941; New York, Kraus Reprint Corp., 1966. xvi, 250 p. ports., facsims. 23 cm. (Modern Language Association of America. Revolving fund series, 11) 68-64841
1. Lawes, Henry, 1596-1662. 2. Music—England—Hist. & crit. 3. Music—Hist. & crit.—16th-17th cent. I. Title. II. Series.

Lawford, Valentine.

LAWFORD, Valentine. 923.242
Bound for diplomacy. [1st American ed.] Boston, Little, Brown [1963- v. illus. 22 cm. Autobiographical. [DA585.L3A32] 63-12098
I. Title.

Lawick-Goodall, Jane, Barones van—Juvenile literature.

COERR, Eleanor. 591'.092'4 B
Jane Goodall / by Eleanor Coerr ; drawings by Kees de Kiefte. New York : Putnam, c1976. 61 p. : ill. ; 22 cm. (A See and read book) A biography of the woman whose childhood love of wildlife led her into the African bush to study chimpanzees and into later becoming a world-famous ethologist. [QL31.L38C63 1976] 92 75-32503 ISBN 0-399-60994-6 lib.bdg. : 4.29
1. Lawick-Goodall, Jane, Barones van—Juvenile literature. I. De Kiefte, Kees. II. Title. **BIP**

Lawrence, Amos Adams, 1814-1886.

LAWRENCE, William, Bp., 1850-1941. 974.4'03'0924 B
Life of Amos A. Lawrence, with extracts from his diary and correspondence. Freeport, N.Y., Books for Libraries Press [1971] x, 289 p. illus., ports. 23 cm. Reprint of the 1888 ed. [E415.9.L38L4 1971] 70-154158 ISBN 0-8369-5774-1
1. Lawrence, Amos Adams, 1814-1886. 2. Massachusetts—Politics and government—1775-1865. 3. Kansas—Politics and government—1854-1861. I. Title.

Lawrence, David Herbert, 1885-1930.

ALDINGTON, Richard, 1892-1962. 823'.9'12
D. H. Lawrence. [Folcroft, Pa.] Folcroft Library Editions, 1973. p. Reprint of the 1930 ed. published by Chatto & Windus, London. [PR6023.A93Z55 1973] 73-10098 5.00 (Lib. bdg)
1. Lawrence, David Herbert, 1885-1930.

ALDINGTON, Richard, 1892-1962. 928.2
D. H. Lawrence, portrait of a genius but. [1st American ed.] New York, Duell, Sloan and Pearce [1950] x, 432 p. illus., ports. 22 cm. Bibliography included in "Acknowledgements" (p. 416-419) [PR6023.A93Z553] 50-7701
1. Lawrence, David Herbert, 1885-1930. I. Title. **BIP**

ALDINGTON, Richard, 1892-1962. 823'.9'12 B
D. H. Lawrence / by Richard Aldington. Philadelphia : R. West, 1976. p. cm. Reprint of the 1930 ed. published by Chatto & Windus, London. [PR6023.A93Z55 1976] 76-46279 ISBN 0-8492-0007-5 : 8.50
1. Lawrence, David Herbert, 1885-1930.

ALDINGTON, Richard, 1892-1962. v. 12
D. H. Lawrence, portrait of a genius but ... New York, Collier Books [1961] 350 p. (Collier books: biography. BS19X) NUC64
1. Lawrence, David Herbert, 1885-1930. I. Title.

BYNNER, Witter, 1881- 928.2
Journey with genius; recollections and reflections concerning the D. H. Lawrences. New York, J. Day Co. [1951] xv, 361 p. illus., ports. 22 cm. [PR6023.A93Z58] 51-11710
1. Lawrence, David Herbert, 1885-1930. 2. Lawrence, Frieda (von Richthofen) 1879- I. Title. **BIP**

BYNNER, Witter, 1881-1968. 823'.9'12 B
Journey with genius; recollections and reflections concerning the D. H. Lawrences. New York, Octagon Books, 1974 [c1951] xv, 361 p. illus. 23 cm. Reprint of the ed. published by the John Day Co., New York. [PR6023.A93Z58 1974] 73-21674 ISBN 0-374-91137-1 13.50
1. Lawrence, David Herbert, 1885-1930. 2. Lawrence, Frieda (von Richthofen) 1879-1956. I. Title.

CARSWELL, Catherine MacFarlane, 1879-1946. 823'.9'12 B
The savage pilgrimage; a narrative of D. H. Lawrence. St. Clair Shores, Mich., Scholarly Press, 1972. xii, 307 p. 22 cm. Reprint of the 1951 ed. [PR6023.A93Z6 1972] 75-144937 ISBN 0-403-00899-9
1. Lawrence, David Herbert, 1885-1930. I. Title. **BIP**

CHAMBERS, Jessie 928.2
D. H. Lawrence: a personal record, by E. T. (Jessie Chambers) 2d ed., ed. by J. D. Chambers. New York, Barnes & Noble [1965] xli, 242p. facsim. ports. 20cm. [PR6023.A93Z6213] 65-3809 5.00
1. Lawrence, David Herbert, 1885-1930. I. Title.

CORKE, Helen, 1882- 823'.9'12 B
D. H. Lawrence's "Princess"; a memory of Jessie Chambers. [Folcroft, Pa.] Folcroft Library Editions, 1973. 47 p. ports. 24 cm. Reprint of the 1951 ed. published by the Merle Press, Thames Ditton, Surrey, Eng. [PR6023.A93Z622 1973] 73-18344 ISBN 0-8414-3528-6 (lib. bdg.)
1. Lawrence, David Herbert, 1885-1930. 2. Chambers, Jessie. 3. Corke, Helen, 1882- I. Title.

D. H. Lawrence. v. 12
New York, Edinburgh, Oliver and Boyd [1961] 128p. 18cm. (Writers and critics) Includes bibliography.
1. Lawrence, David Herbert, 1885-1930. I. Beal, Anthony. II. Series.

DELANY, Paul. 823'.9'12 B
D. H. Lawrence's nightmare : the writer and his circle in the years of the Great War / by Paul Delany. New York : Basic Books, c1978. p. cm. Includes bibliographical references and index. [PR6023.A93Z623547] 78-54998 ISBN 0-465-01641-3 : 15.95
1. Lawrence, David Herbert, 1885-1930. 2. Authors, English—20th century—Biography. 3. European war, 1914-1918—Literature and the war. 4. European war, 1914-1918—Great Britain. 5. Great Britain—Intellectual life—20th century. I. Title. **BIP**

DRAPER, Ronald P., 1928- 823'.9'12 B
D. H. Lawrence / by Ronald P. Draper. New York : St. Martin's Press, [1975] c1964. 194 p. ; 21 cm. (The Griffin authors series) Includes index. Bibliography: p. 183-189. [PR6023.A93Z624 1975] 74-80241 pbk. : 3.95
1. Lawrence, David Herbert, 1885-1930.

FAY, Eliot Gilbert, 1902- 928.2
Lorenzo in search of the sun; D. H. Lawrence in Italy, Mexico, and the American Southwest. New York, Bookman Associates [1953] 147p. 23cm. [PR6023.A93Z628] 53-7763
1. Lawrence, David Herbert, 1885-1930. I. Title. **BIP**

FAY, Eliot Gilbert, 1902- 823'.9'12 B
Lorenzo in search of the sun; D. H. Lawrence in Italy, Mexico, and the American Southwest, by Eliot Fay. New York, Bookman Associates [1953. New York, AMS Press, 1972] 147 p. 23 cm. Bibliography: p. 136-137. [PR6023.A93Z628 1972] 76-168012 ISBN 0-404-02373-8 8.00
1. Lawrence, David Herbert, 1885-1930. I. Title.

THE intelligent heart; v. 12
the story of D. H. Lawrence, [Rev. ed. Harmondsworth, Middlesex] Penguin Books [1960] 560p. plates, ports., facsims., map. 18cm. (Penguin biography 1514) 'Books by D.H. Lawrence': p. [543]-544.
1. Lawrence, David Herbert, 1885-1930. I. Moore, Harry Thornton.

LAWRENCE, Ada 823.912
Young Lorenzo; early life of D. H. Lawrence, containing hitherto unpublished letters, articles, and reproductions of pictures, by Ada Lawrence, G. Stuart Gelder. New York, Russell & Russell, 1966. xii, 275p. illus., ports. 23cm. First pub. in 1931. [PR6023.A93Z64] 66-11880 7.50
1. Lawrence, David Herbert, 1885-1930. I. Gelder, George Stuart, joint author. II. Title.

LAWRENCE, David Herbert, 1885-1930 928.2
Collected letters; 2v. Ed. introd. by Harry T. Moore. NewYork, Viking [c.1962] 2v. (ivi, 1307p.) 62-9685 17.50 set, bxd.
1. Authors—Correspondence, reminiscences, etc. I. Title.

LAWRENCE, David Herbert, 1885-1930. 928.2
Selected letters. Edited with an introd. by Diana Trilling. New York, Farrar, Straus, and Cudahy [1958] xiiii, 322p. 22cm. (Great letters series) [PR6023.A93Z532] 57-11489
1. Authors—Correspondence, reminiscences, etc. I. Title.

LAWRENCE, David Herbert, 1885-1930. 928.2
Selected letters. Edited with an introd. by Diana Trilling. Garden City, N. Y., Anchor books [dist. by Doubleday] 1961 [c.1958, 1961] 352p. 18cm. (Anchor books, A236) Bibl. footnotes. 60-52285 1.45 pap.,
1. Authors—Correspondence, reminiscences, etc. I. Title.

LAWRENCE, Frieda (von Richthofen) 1879-1956 828.912
Frieda Lawrence; the memoirs and

correspondence. Ed. by E. W. Tedlock, Jr. [1st Amer. ed.] New York, Knopf [c.1961, 1964] xix, 481p. ports. 22cm. 64-12307 7.50
1. Lawrence, David Herbert, 1885-1930. I. Title.

LAWRENCE, Frieda (von Richthofen) 1879-1956. v. 12
The memoirs and correspondence. Edited by E. W. Tedlock. New York, A. Knopf, 1964. 481 p. 22 cm. 65-40035
1. Lawrence, David Herbert, 1885-1930. I. Title.

MERRILD, Knud, 1894- 928.2
With D. H. Lawrence in New Mexico; a memoir of D. H. Lawrence. New York, Barnes & Noble [1965] xx, 369p. illus., ports. 23cm. First pub. in 1938 under title: A poet and two painters [PR6023.A93Z68] 65-3107 6.00
1. Lawrence, David Herbert, 1885-1930. I. Title.

MOORE, Harry Thornton. 928.2
The intelligent heart; the story of D.H. Lawrence. New York, Farrar, Straus, and Young [1954] 468 p. illus. 22 cm. [PR6023.A93Z685] 54-12704
1. Lawrence, David Herbert, 1885-1930. I. Title.

MURRY, John Middleton, 1889-1957. 823'.9'12 B
Reminiscences of D. H. Lawrence. Freeport, N.Y., Books for Libraries Press [1971] 279 p. 23 cm. Reprint of the 1933 ed. [PR6023.A93Z69 1971] 75-157349 ISBN 0-8369-5810-1
1. Lawrence, David Herbert, 1885-1930. BIP

NEHLS, Edward, ed. 928.2
D. H. Lawrence: a composite biography, gathered, arranged, and edited by Edward Nehls. Madison, University of Wisconsin Press, 1957-59. 3v. illus., ports. 24cm. Contents.v. 1. 1885-1919.--v. 2. 1919-1925.-- v. 3. 1925-1930. Includes bibliographies. [PR6023.A93Z73] 57-9817
1. Lawrence, David Herbert, 1885-1930. I. Title

PINION, F. B. 823'.9'12
A D. H. Lawrence companion : life, thought, and works / F. B. Pinion. New York : Barnes & Noble Books, 1979, c1978. xi, 316 p., [8] leaves plates : ill. ; 22 cm. Includes index. Bibliography: p. 303-305. [PR6023.A93Z7695 1979] 78-12348 ISBN 0-06-495574-5 : 23.50
1. Lawrence, David Herbert, 1885-1930. 2. Authors, English—20th century—Biography. I. Title. BIP

SPENDER, Stephen, 1909- comp. 823'.9'12 B
D. H. Lawrence: novelist, poet, prophet. [1st U.S. ed.] New York, Harper & Row [1973] 250 p. illus. 26 cm. Includes bibliographical references. [PR6023.A93Z9175 1973b] 73-2000 ISBN 0-06-013956-0 12.95
1. Lawrence, David Herbert, 1885-1930. Contents omitted.

TINDALL, William York, 1903- 823'.9'12
D. H. Lawrence & Susan his cow. New York, Cooper Square Publishers, 1972 [c1939] xiv, 231 p. 22 cm. Reprint of the ed. published by Columbia University Press, New York. Bibliography: p. [213]-219. [PR6023.A93Z93 1972] 72-85664 ISBN 0-8154-0436-0 6.50
1. Lawrence, David Herbert, 1885-1930. I. Title. BIP

TREASE, Geoffrey, 1909- 823'.9'12 B
The phoenix and the flame: D. H. Lawrence; a biography. [1st ed.] New York, Viking Press [1973] xii, 177 p. illus. 24 cm. Bibliography: p. 169-171. [PR6023.A93Z934 1973] 73-11418 ISBN 0-670-55228-3
1. Lawrence, David Herbert, 1885-1930. I. Title.

WEST, Anthony, 1914- 823'.9'12 B
D. H. Lawrence. London, A. Barker. [Folcroft, Pa.] Folcroft Library Editions, 1973. p. "First published 1950; first published in ... [the Novelists series] 1957." [PR6023.A93Z947 1973] 73-477 ISBN 0-8414-1422-X
1. Lawrence, David Herbert, 1885-1930. BIP

WEST, Anthony, 1914- 823'.9'12 B
D. H. Lawrence / by Anthony West. Norwood, Pa. : Norwood Editions, 1975. 152 p. ; 23 cm. Reprint of the 1950? ed. published by A. Swallow, Denver. Includes index. "The principal works of D. H. Lawrence": p. 147-148. [PR6023.A93Z947 1975] 75-34084 ISBN 0-88305-782-4 lib. bdg. : 12.50
1. Lawrence, David Herbert, 1885-1930.

Lawrence, David Herbert, 1885-1930—Addresses, essays, lectures.

PINTO, Vivian de Sola, 1895- 823'.9'12
D. H. Lawrence, prophet of the Midlands / by Vivian de Sola Pinto. Folcroft, Pa. : Folcroft Library Editions, 1975. 24 p. ; 24 cm. Lecture delivered at the University of Nottingham on Oct. 26, 1951. Reprint of the 1951 ed. Includes bibliographical references. [PR6023.A93Z77 1975] 75-17879 ISBN 0-8414-3677-0 lib. bdg. : 5.00
1. Lawrence, David Herbert, 1885-1930—Addresses, essays, lectures. I. Title

Lawrence, David Herbert, 1885-1930—Bibliography.

STOLL, John E. 016.823'9'12
D. H. Lawrence : a bibliography, 1911-1975 / compiled by John E. Stoll. Troy, N.Y. : Whitston Pub. Co., 1977. 216 p. ; 24 cm. Includes index. [Z8490.5.S86] [PR6023.A93] 73-78073 ISBN 0-87875-042-8 : 15.00
1. Lawrence, David Herbert, 1885-1930—Bibliography. BIP

Lawrence, David Herbert, 1885-1930—Biography.

CALLOW, Philip. 823'.9'12 B
Son and love, the young D. H. Lawrence / by Philip Callow. New York : Stein and Day, [1975] p. cm. [PR6023.A93Z59] 75-9615 ISBN 0-8128-1819-9 : 10.00
1. Lawrence, David Herbert, 1885-1930—Biography. I. Title.

LAWRENCE, Frieda von Richthofen, 1879-1956. 823'.9'12 B
"Not I, but the wind ..." Afterword by Harry T. Moore. Carbondale, Southern Illinois University Press [1974, c1934] ix, 306 p. illus. 21 cm. Reprint of the ed. published by Viking Press, New York. [PR6023.A934Z5 1974] 74-8660 ISBN 0-8093-0690-5 10.00
1. Lawrence, Frieda von Richthofen, 1879-1956. 2. Lawrence, David Herbert, 1885-1930—Biography. 3. Lawrence, David Herbert, 1885-1930—Correspondence. I. Title.

MOORE, Harry Thornton. 823'.9'12 B
The priest of love; a life of D. H. Lawrence [by] Harry T. Moore. Rev. ed. New York, Farrar, Straus and Giroux [1974] ix, 550 p. illus. 24 cm. Earlier eds. published under title: The intelligent heart. [PR6023.A93Z685 1974] 72-97082 ISBN 0-374-23718-2 15.00
1. Lawrence, David Herbert, 1885-1930—Biography. I. Title. BIP

Lawrence, David Herbert, 1885-1930—Correspondence.

LAWRENCE, David Herbert, 1885-1930. 823'.9'12 B
Letters to Thomas and Adele Seltzer / D. H. Lawrence ; edited by Gerald M. Lacy. Santa Barbara, CA: Black Sparrow Press, 1976. xiv, 284 p. : ill. ; 24 cm. Bibliography: p. 283-284. [PR6023.A93Z5354 1976] 76-10782 ISBN 0-87685-224-X : 14.00. ISBN 0-87685-225-8 pbk. : 4.00
1. Lawrence, David Herbert, 1885-1930—Correspondence. 2. Seltzer, Thomas. 3. Seltzer, Adele Szold, 1876- 4. Authors, English—20th century—Correspondence. I. Seltzer, Thomas. II. Seltzer, Adele Szold, 1876- III. Lacy, Gerald M. IV. Title. BIP

Lawrence, David Herbert, 1885-1930—Criticism and interpretation.

NIVEN, Alastair. 823'.9'12
D. H. Lawrence : the novels / Alastair Niven. Cambridge [Eng.] ; New York : Cambridge University Press, c1978. 188 p. : ill. ; 23 cm. (British authors, introductory critical studies) Bibliography: p. 187-188. [PR6023.A93Z7557] 77-8475 ISBN 0-521-21744-X : 16.95
1. Lawrence, David Herbert, 1885-1930—Criticism and interpretation. BIP

SKLAR, Sylvia. 822'.9'12
The plays of D. H. Lawrence : a biographical and critical study / Sylvia Sklar. New York : Barnes & Noble Books, 1975. 271 p. ; 23 cm. (Barnes & Noble critical studies) Includes index. Bibliography: p. 263-265. [PR6023.A93Z915 1975b] 74-10003 ISBN 0-06-496333-0 : 14.75
1. Lawrence, David Herbert, 1885-1930—Criticism and interpretation. I. Title.

Lawrence, David Herbert, 1885-1930—Exhibitions.

†NOTTINGHAM, Eng. University. 016.823'9'12 B
D. H. Lawrence after thirty years, 1930-1960 : catalogue of an exhibition held in the Art Gallery of the University of Nottingham, 17 June-30 July, 1960 / edited by V. de S. Pinto. [Folcroft, Pa.] : Folcroft Library Editions, 1977. 55 p., [5] leaves of plates : ill. ; 29 cm. Reprint of the 1960 ed. published by the University of Nottingham. Includes bibliographical references and index. [PR6023.A93Z756] 77-22536 ISBN 0-8414-3824-2 lib. bdg. : 12.50
1. Lawrence, David Herbert, 1885-1930—Exhibitions. I. Pinto, Vivian de Sola, 1895- II. Title.

Lawrence, David Herbert, 1885-1930—Relationship with women.

HAHN, Emily, 1905- 823'.9'12 B
Lorenzo : D. H. Lawrence and the women who loved him / by Emily Hahn. 1st ed. Philadelphia : Lippincott, [1975] 367 p. ; 24 cm. Includes index. Bibliography: p. 354-356. [PR6023.A93Z63117] 75-11865 ISBN 0-397-00772-8 : 12.95
1. Lawrence, David Herbert, 1885-1930—Relationship with women. I. Title. BIP

Lawrence, Ernest Orlando, 1901-1958.

CHILDS, Herbert, 1904- 539.7'0924 B
An American genius; the life of Ernest Orlando Lawrence. New York, Dutton, 1968. 576 p. illus., ports. 24 cm. Bibliography: p. 540-548. [QC16.L36C5] 68-12456
1. Lawrence, Ernest Orlando, 1901-1958. I. Title.

DAVIS, Nuel Pharr, 1915- 539.7'0922
Lawrence and Oppenheimer. New York, Simon and Schuster [1968] 384 p. illus. 24 cm. Bibliography: p. 365-371. [QC16.L36D38] 68-19940 7.50
1. Lawrence, Ernest Orlando, 1901-1958. 2. Oppenheimer, J. Robert, 1904-1967. I. Title. BIP

Lawrence, Frieda (von Richthofen)

LAWRENCE, Frieda (von Richthofen) 1879-1956. 823'.9'12 B
"Not I, but the wind ..." New York, Viking Press, 1934. St. Clair Shores, Mich., Scholarly Press, 1972. xi, 297 p. illus. 22 cm. The author's memoirs together with letters and some material written by her husband, D. H. Lawrence. [PR6023.A934Z5 1972] 77-145136 ISBN 0-403-00764-X
1. Lawrence, David Herbert, 1885-1930. II. Title.

Lawrence, Frieda von Richthofen, 1879-1956.

GREEN, Martin Burgess, 1927- 914 B
The von Richthofen sisters; the triumphant and the tragic modes of love: Else and Frieda von Richthofen, Otto Gross, Max Weber, and D. H. Lawrence, in the years 1870-1970 [by] Martin Green. New York, Basic Books [1974] xviii, 396 p. illus. 25 cm. Bibliography: p. [385]-388. [CS629.R514 1974] 73-81037 ISBN 0-465-09050-8 12.50
1. Richthofen family. 2. Jaffe-Richthofen, Else, 1874- 3. Lawrence, Frieda von Richthofen, 1879-1956. 4. Lawrence, David Herbert, 1885-1930. I. Title.

LAWRENCE, Frieda (von Richthofen) 1879-1956. 823'.9'12 B
"Not I, but the wind ..." New York, Viking Press, 1934. St. Clair Shores, Mich., Scholarly Press, 1972. xi, 297 p. illus. 22 cm. The author's memoirs together with letters and some material written by her husband, D. H. Lawrence. [PR6023.A934Z5 1972] 77-145136 ISBN 0-403-00764-X
I. Lawrence, David Herbert, 1885-1930. II. Title.

LAWRENCE, Frieda von Richthofen, 1879-1956. 823'.9'12 B
"Not I, but the wind ..." Afterword by Harry T. Moore. Carbondale, Southern Illinois University Press [1974, c1934] ix, 306 p. illus. 21 cm. Reprint of the ed. published by Viking Press, New York. [PR6023.A934Z5 1974] 74-8660 ISBN 0-8093-0690-5 10.00
1. Lawrence, Frieda von Richthofen, 1879-1956. 2. Lawrence, David Herbert, 1885-1930—Biography. 3. Lawrence, David Herbert, 1885-1930—Correspondence. I. Title.

Lawrence, Gertrude.

ALDRICH, Richard Stoddard. 927.92
Gertrude as Mrs. A. Introd. and teaching aids byLilian M. Popp. New York, Globe Book Co. [1961] 441p. illus. 22cm. [PN2598.L28A7 1961] 61-534
1. Lawrence, Gertrude. I. Title.

ALDRICH, Richard Stoddard 927.92
Gertrude Lawrence as Mrs. A. Introd. and teaching aids by Lilian M. Popp. New York, Globe Book Co. [c.1961] 441p. front. 61-534 3.00
1. Lawrence, Gertrude. I. Title.

ALDRICH, Richard Stoddard. 792'.028'0924
Gertrude Lawrence as Mrs. A, an intimate biography of the great star. New York, Greenwood Press [1969, c1954] 414 p. illus., ports. 23 cm. [PN2598.L28A7 1969] 78-94600
1. Lawrence, Gertrude. I. Title.

ALDRICH, Richard Stoddard. 927.92
Gertrude Lawrence as Mrs. A; an intimate biography of the great star. New York, Bantam [1968,c.1954] 377p. 18cm. (N3948) Orig. pub. by Greystone Pr. [PN2598.L28A7] .95 pap.,
1. Lawrence, Gertrude. I. Title. BIP

Lawrence, Henry Montgomery, Sir, 1806-1857.

ABDULLAH, Achmed, 1881-1945. 909'.09'712420810922
Dreamers of empire, by Achmed Abdullah [and] T. Compton Pakenham. Illustrated by B. K. Morris. Freeport, N.Y. Books for Libraries Press [1968] xiv, 368 p. ports. 23 cm. (Essay index reprint series) Reprint of the 1929 ed. Contents.Contents.—Cecil John Rhodes.—Richard Francis Burton.—John Nicholson.—Henry Montgomery Lawrence.—William Walker.—Charles George Gordon. [DA531.1.A2 1968] 68-57300
1. Rhodes, Cecil John, 1853-1902. 2. Burton, Richard Francis, Sir, 1821-1890. 3. Nicholson, John, 1822-1857. 4. Lawrence, Henry Montgomery, Sir, 1806-1857. 5. Walker, William, 1824-1860. 6. Gordon, Charles George, 1833-1885. I. Pakenham, Thomas Compton, joint author. II. Title. BIP

Lawrence, Thomas Edward, 1888-1935.

ALDINGTON, Richard, 1892- 923.542
Lawrence of Arabia; a biographical enquiry. Chicago, H. Regnery Co., 1955. 448p. illus. 22cm. [D568.4] 55-13505
1. Lawrence, Thomas Edward, 1888-1935. I. Title.

ALDINGTON, Richard, 1892-1962. 941.083'092'4 B
Lawrence of Arabia : a biographical enquiry / by Richard Aldington. Westport, Conn. : Greenwood Press, 1976. 448 p., [9] leaves of plates : ill. ; 22 cm. Reprint of the 1955 ed. published by Collins, London. Includes index. Bibliography: p. 421-425. [D568.4.L45A6 1976] 75-36506 ISBN 0-8371-8634-X lib.bdg. : 25.00
1. Lawrence, Thomas Edward, 1888-1935.

ARMITAGE, Flora. 923.542
The desert and the stars; a biography of Lawrence of Arabia. Illustrated with photos. [1st ed.] New York, Holt [1955] 318 p. illus. 22 cm. [D568.4.L45A68] 55-9223
1. Lawrence, Thomas Edward, 1888-1935. I. Title.

BERAUD-VILLARS, Jean Marcel Eugene. 923.542
T. E. Lawrence; or, The search for the absolute. Translated from the French by Peter Dawnay. New York, Duell, Sloan [1959] 358 p. illus. 23 cm. Translation of Le colonel Lawrence. [D568.4.L45B43] 59-16200
1. Lawrence, Thomas Edward, 1888-1935.

BRENT, Peter Ludwig. 940.4'15'0924 B
T. E. Lawrence / Peter Brent ; introd. by Elizabeth Longford. 1st American ed. New York : Putnam, 1975. 232 p. : ill. ; 26 cm. Includes index. Bibliography: p. 225. [D568.4.L45B7 1975] 74-32436 ISBN 0-399-11584-6 : 12.95
1. Lawrence, Thomas Edward, 1888-1935.

CARRINGTON, Charles Edmund, 1897- 940.4'15'0924 B
T. E. Lawrence / by Charles Edmonds [i.e. C. E. Carrington]. Brooklyn : Haskell House Publishers, 1977. 191 p. ; 21 cm. Reprint of the 1935 ed. published by P. Davies, London. Includes index. Bibliography: p. 190. [D568.4.L45C3 1977] 76-52954 ISBN 0-8383-2177-1 lib.bdg. : 11.95
1. Lawrence, Thomas Edward, 1888-1935. 2. Soldiers—England—Biography. 3. European War, 1914-1918—Campaigns—Turkey and the Near East.

*GRAVES, Richard Perceval. 940.4150924
Lawrence of Arabia and his world. / Richard Perceval Graves. New York, : Scribner's, c1976. 126 p. : ill. ; 24 cm. Includes index. Bibliography: p. 117-118. [D568.L45M8] 76-7183 ISBN 0-684-14726-2 : 8.95
1. Lawrence, Thomas Edward, 1888-1935. I. Title. **BIP**

GRAVES, Richard Perceval. 940.4'15'0924 B
Lawrence of Arabia and his world / Richard Perceval Graves. London : Thames and Hudson, c1976. 127 p. : ill. ; 24 cm. Includes index. Bibliography: p. 117-118. [D568.4.L45G68 1976b] 77-358241 ISBN 0-500-13054-X : £3.50
1. Lawrence, Thomas Edward, 1888-1935. 2. Soldiers—England—Biography. 3. European War, 1914-1918—Campaigns—Turkey and the Near East. I. Title.

HYDE, Harford Montgomery, 1907- 940.4'15'0924
Solitary in the ranks : Lawrence of Arabia as airman and private soldier / by H. Montgomery Hyde. 1st American ed. New York : Atheneum, 1978, c1977. p. cm. Includes index. Bibliography: p. [D568.4.L45H92 1978] 77-88903 ISBN 0-689-10848-6 : 11.95
1. Lawrence, Thomas Edward, 1888-1935. 2. Great Britain. Royal Air Force—Biography. 3. Air pilots—Great Britain—Biography. 4. European War, 1914-1918—Biography. I. Title. **BIP**

KIERNAN, Reginald Hugh, 1900- 940.4'15'0924
Lawrence of Arabia / by R. H. Kiernan. Folcroft, Pa. : Folcroft Library Editions, 1977. p. cm. Reprint of the 1935 ed. published by G. G. Harrap, London. Bibliography: p. [D568.4.L45K5 1977] 77-17428 ISBN 0-8414-5451-5 lib. bdg. : 25.00
1. Lawrence, Thomas Edward, 1888-1935. 2. Soldiers—England—Biography. 3. European War, 1914-1918—Campaigns—Turkey and the Near East. I. Title.

KNIGHTLEY, Phillip. 940.4'15'0924 B
The secret lives of Lawrence of Arabia [by] Phillip Knightley and Colin Simpson. [1st U.S. ed.] New York, McGraw-Hill [1970] xiv, 333 p. illus., ports. 24 cm. Bibliography: p. 317-318. [D568.4.L45K55 1970] 71-105951
1. Lawrence, Thomas Edward, 1888-1935. I. Simpson, Colin, 1908- joint author. II. Title.

LAWRENCE, Arnold Walter, 1900- ed. 923.542
Letters to T. E. Lawrence. London, Cape [dist. Chester Springs, Pa., Dufour, 1964, c.1962] 216p. facsims. 24cm. 63-5213 6.95
1. Authors—Correspondence, reminiscences, etc. I. Lawrence, Thomas Edward, 1888-1935. II. Title.

LAWRENCE, Thomas Edward, 1888-1935 923.542
T. E. Lawrence to his biographers, Robert Graves, Liddell Hart. Garden City, N.Y., Doubleday, 1963[c.1938] viii, 187 iv, 260p. 22cm. Pub. in 1938 as two separate works under titles: T. E. Lawrence to his biographer, Robert Graves, and T. E. Lawrence to his biographer, Liddell Hart. 63-11220 6.50
I. Graves, Robert, 1895- II. Liddell Hart, Basil Henry, 1895- III. Title.

MACK, John E., 1929- 941.083'092'4 B
A prince of our disorder : the life of T. E. Lawrence / John E. Mack. 1st ed. Boston : Little, Brown, [1975] p. cm. Includes index. Bibliography: p. [D568.4.L45M28] 75-22481 ISBN 0-316-54232-6 : 15.00
1. Lawrence, Thomas Edward, 1888-1935. I. Title. **BIP**

MACLEAN, Alistair, 1922or3- 923.542
Lawrence of Arabia. Illustrated by Gil Walker. New York, Random House [1962] 177p. illus. 22cm. (World landmark books [W-52]) [D568.4.L45M3] 62-7878
1. Lawrence, Thomas Edward, 1888-1935. I. Title.

MACLEAN, Alistair Stuart, 1922or3- 923.542
Lawrence of Arabia. Illus. by Gil Walker. New York, Random [c.1962] 177p. illus. (pt. col.) col. maps. 22cm. (World landmark bks. [W-52]) 62-7878 1.95
1. Lawrence, Thomas Edward, 1888-1935. I. Title.

MUSA, Sulayman 940.4150924
T. E. Lawrence; an Arab view [by] Suleiman Mousa; tr. [from Arabic] by Albert Butros. London, New York[etc.] Oxford Univ. Pr., 1966. x. 301p. 3 maps. 23cm. Bibl. [D568.4.L45M8] 66-73739 6.50
1. Lawrence, Thomas Edward, 1888-1935. 2. European War, 1914-1918—Campaigns—Turkey and the Near East. I. Title.

NUTTING, Anthony 923.542
Lawrence of Arabia; the man and the motive. New York, New Amer. Lib. [1962, c.1961] 252p. illus. 18cm. (Signet bk., T2106) Bibl. .75 pap.,
1. Lawrence, Thomas Edward, 1888-1935. I. Title.

NUTTING, Anthony. 923.542
Lawrence of Arabia: the man and the motive. New York, C. N. Potter [c1961] 256p. illus. 22cm. [D568.4.L45N8 1961a] 61-15108
1. Lawrence, Thomas Edward, 1888-1935. I. Title.

OCAMPO, Victoria [Victoria Ocampo de Estrada] 923.452
338171 T. E. (Lawrence of Arabia) Tr. [from French] by David Garnett New York, Dutton, 1963 [c.1947, 1963] 128p. 20cm. 63-20844 3.00
1. Lawrence, Thomas Edward, 1888-1935. I. Title.

ORGILL, Douglas, 1922- 940.4'15'0924 B
Lawrence. [New York, Ballantine Books, 1973] 159, [1] p. illus. 21 cm. (Ballantine's illustrated history of the violent century. War leader book no. 18) Bibliography: p. [160] [D568.4.L45O74] 73-164603 1.00
1. Lawrence, Thomas Edward, 1888-1935. 2. European War, 1914-1918—Campaigns—Turkey and the Near East. 3. European War, 1914-1918—Arabia.

PAYNE, Robert 1911- 923.2
Lawrence of Arbia, a triumph. New York, Pyramid [c.1962] 190p. map (R-685) .50 pap.,
1. Lawrence, Thomas Edward, 1888-1935. I. Title.

PHILLIPS, Jill M. 940.4'15'0924 B
T. E. Lawrence : portrait of the artist as hero : controversy and caricature in the biographies of "Lawrence of Arabia" / by Jill M. Phillips. New York : Gordon Press, 1976. p. cm. Bibliography: p. [D568.4.L45P45] 76-47008 ISBN 0-87968-336-8 : 35.00
1. Lawrence, Thomas Edward, 1888-1935. 2. Soldiers—England—Biography. 3. European War, 1914-1918—Campaigns—Turkey and the Near East.

RICHARDS, Vyvyan 923.542
Portrait of T. E. Lawrence. New York, Scholastic [1964] map. 148p. 17cm. (T543) Bibl. .35 pap.,
1. Lawrence, Thomas Edward, 1888-1935. I. Title. **BIP**

RICHARDS, Vyvyan. 941.083'092'4 B
Portrait of T. E. Lawrence / by Vyvyan Richards. New York : Haskell House Publishers, [1976] c1939. p. cm. "The title of this book has been transposed from another book by the same author." Reprint of the 1964 ed. published by Scholastic Book Services, New York, which was first published by Duckworth, London, under title: T. E. Lawrence. Bibliography: p. [D568.4.L45R53 1976] 75-22043 ISBN 0-8383-2093-7 lib.bdg. : 10.95
1. Lawrence, Thomas Edward, 1888-1935.

ROBINSON, Edward, 1897- 940.4'15'0924 B
Lawrence, the story of his life / by Edward Robinson ; with an introductory note by A. W. Lawrence. Folcroft, Pa. : Folcroft Library Editions, 1979. p. cm. Reprint of the 1935 ed. published by Oxford University Press, London, New York. [D568.4.L45R58 1979] 79-23393 ISBN 0-8414-7442-7 (lib. bdg.) : 25.00
1. Lawrence, Thomas Edward, 1888-1935. 2. Soldiers—Great Britain—Biography. 3. Soldiers—Near East—Biography. 4. European War, 1914-1918—Campaigns—Turkey and the Near East. **BIP**

STEWART, Desmond Stirling. 940.4'15'0924 B
T. E. Lawrence / by Desmond Stewart. 1st U.S. ed. New York : Harper & Row, c1977. xii, 352 p., [6] leaves of plates : ill. ; 24 cm. Includes bibliographical references and index. [D568.4.L45S75 1977] 76-57916 ISBN 0-06-014123-9 : 15.00
1. Lawrence, Thomas Edward, 1888-1935. 2. Soldiers—England—Biography. 3. European War, 1914-1918—Campaigns—Turkey and the Near East.

THOMAS, Lowell Jackson, 1892- 923.542
With Lawrence in Arabia. New York, Grosset & Dunlap [1961, c1924] 316 p. 22 cm. (Great adventure library) [[D568.4]] CD62
1. Lawrence, Thomas Edward, 1888-1935. 2. European War, 1914-1918 — Arabia. I. Title.

THOMAS, Lowell Jackson, 1892- 940.4'15
With Lawrence in Arabia, by Lowell Thomas. Original photos. taken by H. A. Chase and by the author. New enl. ed. Garden City, N.Y., Doubleday, 1967. xxx, 320 p. illus., map, ports. 22 cm. [D568.4.L45T53 1967] 66-24339
1. Lawrence, Thomas Edward, 1888-1935. 2. European War, 1914-1918—Arabia. I. Title.

WEINTRAUB, Stanley, 1929- 923.542
Private Shaw and public Shaw, a dual portrait of Lawrence of Arabia and G.B.S. New York, Braziller [c.]1963. 302p. illus. 22cm. Bibl. 62-19925 5.00
1. Lawrence, Thomas Edward, 1888-1935. 2. Shaw, George Bernard, 1856-1950. I. Title.

WEINTRAUB, Stanley, 1929- 923.542
Private Shaw and public Shaw, a dual portrait of Lawrence of Arabia and G. B. S. New York, G. Braziller, 1963. 302 p. illus. 22 cm. Includes bibliography. [D568.4.L45W4] 62-19925
1. Lawrence, Thomas Edward, 1888-1935. 2. Shaw, George Bernard, 1856-1950. I. Title.

Lawrence, Thomas Edward, 1888-1935—Bibliography.

DUVAL, Elizabeth W. 012
T. E. Lawrence, a bibliography, by Elizabeth W. Duval. New York, Haskell House Publishers, 1972. 95 p. 23 cm. Reprint of the 1938 ed. [Z8491.5.D95 1972] 74-185877 ISBN 0-8383-1385-X
1. Lawrence, Thomas Edward, 1888-1935—Bibliography. **BIP**

Lawrence, Thomas Edward, 1888-1935—Juvenile literature.

DAVIS, Paxton, 1925- 940.4'15'0924 B
Ned / by Paxton Davis ; drawings by Harold Little. 1st ed. New York : Atheneum, 1978. 140 p. : ill. ; 22 cm. A biography of T. E. Lawrence based on the premise that the contradictory aspects of his life could be reconciled by his "lifelong determination to live out the ideals of chivalry." [D568.4.L45D38 1978] 92 78-4187 ISBN 0-689-30650-4 : 7.95
1. Lawrence, Thomas Edward, 1888-1935—Juvenile literature. 2. Soldiers—England—Biography—Juvenile literature. 3. European War, 1914-1918—Campaigns—Turkey and the Near East—Juvenile literature. I. Little, Harold. II. Title. **BIP**

EBERT, Richard. 940.4'15'0924 B
Lawrence of Arabia / by Richard Ebert ; ill. by Roy Schofield. Milwaukee : Raintree Publishers, c1979. p. cm. Recounts the adventures of the British soldier who helped the Arabs gain freedom from the Turks during World War I. [D568.4.L45E23] 92 78-31450 ISBN 0-8393-0150-2 lib. bdg. : 7.32
1. Lawrence, Thomas Edward, 1888-1935—Juvenile literature. 2. Soldiers—England—Biography—Juvenile literature. 3. European War, 1914-1918—Campaigns—Turkey and the Near East—Juvenile literature. I. Schofield, Roy Malcolm. II. Title.

KNIGHTLEY, Phillip. 940.41'5'0924 B
Lawrence of Arabia / by Phillip Knightley. 1st U.S. ed. Nashville : T. Nelson, c1976. p. cm. Includes index. A biography of the English soldier and adventurer who fought with the Arabs during their conflict with the Turks. [D568.4.L45K545 1976b] 92 76-42226 ISBN 0-8407-6507-X : 5.95
1. Lawrence, Thomas Edward, 1888-1935—Juvenile literature. 2. Soldiers—England—Biography—Juvenile literature. 3. European War, 1914-1918—Campaigns—Turkey and the Near East—

Juvenile literature. I. Title.

THOMAS, John, 1914- 920
The true story of Lawrence of Arabia. Chicago, Childrens [c.1953, 1964] 141p. col. illus. 23cm. First pub. in London in 1953 under title: The true book about Lawrence of Arabia. 64-12903 3.50; 2.63 lib.ed.,
1. Lawrence, Thomas Edward, 1888-1935— Juvenile literature. I. Title.

THOMAS, Lowell Jackson, 1892- 923.542
The boys' life of Colonel Lawrence. New York, Roy Publishers [1959?] 160 p. illus. 20 cm. [D568.4.L45T5 1959] 59-9895
1. Lawrence, Thomas Edward, 1883-1935 — Juvenile literature. 2. European War, 1914-1918 — Arabia. I. Title.

THOMAS, Ronald Wills, 1910- 923.542
The young Lawrence of Arabia [by] James Cadell (pseud.) Illustrated by William Randell. New York, Roy Publishers [1961, c1960] 139 p. illus. 21 cm. [D568.4.L45T45] 60-14480
1. Lawrence, Thomas Edward, 1888-1935 — Juvenile literature. I. Title.

Lawrence, Thomas, Sir, 1796-1830.

ARMSTRONG, Walter, Sir, 1850-1918. 759.2 B
Lawrence. New York, AMS Press [1969] xi, 199 p. ports. 23 cm. Reprint of the 1913 ed. "Catalogue of pictures": p. 107-193. [ND497.L4A7 1969] 70-100531
1. Lawrence, Thomas, Sir, 1796-1830. **BIP**

Lawrenson, Helen.

LAWRENSON, Helen. 070.40924
Stranger at the party / Helen Lawrenson. New York : Popular Library, 1977c1972. 255p. : ill. ; 18 cm. [PN4874 L28A37] ISBN 0 445-08366-5 pbk. : 1.95
1. Lawrenson, Helen. 2. Journalists-United States-Correspondence, reminiscences, etc. I. Title.
L.C. card no. for 1975 Random House edition: 74-23421 **BIP**

LAWRENSON, Helen. 070.4'092'4 B
Stranger at the party : a memoir / Helen Lawrenson. 1st ed. New York : Random House, [1975] 244 p., [4] leaves of plates : ill. ; 22 cm. [PN4874.L28A37] 74-23421 ISBN 0-394-48900-4 : 6.95
1. Lawrenson, Helen. 2. Journalists— United States—Correspondence, reminiscences, etc. I. Title. **BIP**

LAWRENSON, Helen. 070.4'092'4 B
Whistling girl / Helen Lawrenson. lst ed. Garden City, N.Y. : Doubleday, 1978. 182 p. ; 22 cm. [PN4874.L28A30] 77-89682 ISBN 0-385-11573-3 : 6.95
1. Lawrenson, Helen. 2. Journalists— United States—Biography. I. Title. **BIP**

Lawson, Andrew Cowper, 1861-1952

VAUGHAN, Francis Edward, 1889- 550'.924 B
Andrew C. Lawson: scientist, teacher, philosopher [by] Francis E. Vaughan. Glendale, Calif., A. H. Clark, 1970. 474 p. ports. 25 cm. [QE22.L28V38] 77-134587 ISBN 0-87062-097-5
1. Lawson, Andrew Cowper, 1861-1952.

Lawson, Harry Sutherland Wightman, Sir, 1875-1952.

LAWSON, Robert Sutherland. 994.5'041'0924 B
Sir Harry Lawson : premier and senator / [by] Robert S. Lawson. Canterbury, Vic. : Mullaya, 1976. 93 p., [8] p. of plates : ill. ; 23 cm. Includes bibliographical references and index. [DU172.L33L38] 77-352184 ISBN 0-85914-016-4 : 4.95
1. Lawson, Harry Sutherland Wightman, Sir, 1875-1952. 2. Statesmen—Australia—Biography. I. Title.

Lawson, Thomas William, 1857-1925.

FALES, William E S v. 12
The life of Lawson; his birth and parentage, together with a history of his career and the financial operations he has engaged in. New York City, Dixie Book Shop [n.d.] 67 p. illus., port. 19 cm. 68-42552
1. Lawson, Thomas William, 1857-1925. I. Title.

Lawson, Victor Fremont, 1850-1925.

DENNIS, Charles Henry, 1860-1943. 070.924
Victor Lawson; his time and his work. New York, Greenwood Press [1968, c1935] xi, 470 p. facsims., ports. 23 cm. [PN4874.L3D4 1968] 68-57598
1. Lawson, Victor Fremont, 1850-1925.

Lawson, William A., 1927-

LAWSON, Jo, 1928- 248'.86
Healed of Cancer / by Jo Lawson. Plainfield, N.J. : Logos International, c1978 120 p. ; 18 cm. [RC263.L36] 77-20586 ISBN 0-582-79721-7 pbk. : 1.95
1. Lawson, William A., 1927- 2. Cancer—Biography. 3. Christian life—1960- I. Title. **BIP**

Lawyers.

BROWN, Clinton Giddings. 923.473
You may take the witness. Drawings by Doug Anderson. Austin, University of Texas Press, 1955. 223p. illus. 22cm. Autobiographical. 55-8471
1. Lawyers—Texas— Correspondence, reminiscences, etc. I. Title.

CAMPBELL, James, 1813-1892. 923.473
Journal. San Antonio, Naylor Co. [c1955] ix, 334p. port. 23cm. 'Limited to 100 copies, of which this is no. 100.' 56-23076
1. Lawyers— Pennsylvania— Correspondence, reminiscences, etc. I. Title.

DARROW, Clarence Seward, 1857-1938. 923.473
The story of my life. New York, Scribners [1965, c.1932, 1960] viii, 495p. illus. 21cm. (SL109) [CT275.D2374A3] 1.95 pap.,
1. Lawyers Correspondence, reminiscences, etc. I. Title.

EARLE, Walter Keese, 1886- v. 12
Mr. Shearman and Mr. Sterling and how they grew; being annals of their law firm, with biographical and historical highlights, by Walter K. Earle. [New Haven, Conn., Yale university press, 1963] [iii]-xxi, 443 p. front., illus., ports. 21 cm. 64-33972
1. Lawyers—New York (City) I. Shearman & Sterling, New York. II. Title.

GRANT, William West, 1881- 923.473
Such is life. [Denver, 1952] 234 p. illus. 24 cm. Autobiography. 52-25156
1. Lawyers—Colorado—Correspondence, reminiscences, etc. I. Title.

KARCHER, Joseph T 1903- 923.473
Main Street lawyer. Illustrated by Bill Canfield. Boston, Meador Pub. Co. [1959] 189p. illus. 21cm. 59-10392
1. Lawyers—New Jersey—Correspondence, reminiscences, etc. I. Title.

KENTUCKY State Bar Association: 340'.0922 portraits and biographical sketches of the members, 1967. 1st ed. Louisville, Lawyers Pub. House [1967] 479 p. ports. 26 cm. [KF332.K44K4] 67-4306
1. Lawyers — Kentucky — Biog.

MACDONELL, John, Sir, 1846-1921, ed. 340'.0922 B
Great jurists of the world, edited by Sir John Macdonell and Edward Manson. With an introd. by Van Vechten Veeder. South Hackensack, N.J., Rothman Reprints, 1968. xxxii, 607 p. ports. 23 cm. (The Continental legal history series, v. 2) Reprint of the 1914 ed. Bibliographical footnotes. [LAW] 68-54739
1. Lawyers. 2. Law—History and criticism. I. Manson, Edward William Donoghue, 1849-1919, joint ed. II. Title. III. Series. **BIP**

MEREDITH, Vincent Robert Sissions, Sir 1877-1965 340.0924
A long brief; recollections of a crown solicitor. Auckland [N.Z] Collins. 1966. 213p. port. 22cm. 66-9394 5.45 bds.,
1. Lawyers—New Zealand—Correspondence, reminiscences, etc. I. Title.
Available from Tri-Ocean, San Francisco.

MULLEN, James Morfit, 1877- 923.473
Let justice be done. Philadelphia, Dorrance [1952] 371 p. 20 cm. Autobiographical. 52-8366
1. Lawyers — Maryland — Correspondence, reminiscences, etc. 2. Law — Maryland — Hist. & crit. I. Title.

TAYLOR, Charles William, 1896- 923.473
Bench and bar of Alameda County, 1953. Published by C. W. Taylor, Jr. and Theodore N. Chapin. [Palo Alto? Calif, 1953] 207p. ports. 28cm. 'History of bench and bar of Alameda County, 1850- 1953.' 53-39583
1. Lawyers—Alameda Co., Calif. 2. Judges—Alameda Co., Calif. I. Chapin, Theodore N., joint author. II. Title.

Lawyers — American

ARNOLD, Thurman Wesley, 1891- 923.473
Fair fights and foul; a dissenting lawyer's life. New York, Harcourt [c.1951, 1960, 1965] xi, 292p. illus. 22cm. Bibl. 65-14716 5.95
1. Lawyers—U.S.—Correspondence, reminiscences, etc. I. Title.

ARNOLD, Thurman Wesley, 1891-1969. 923.473
Fair fights and foul; a dissenting lawyer's life [by] Thurman Arnold. [1st ed.] New York, Harcourt, Brace & World [1965] 292 p. illus. 22cm. Bibliographical footnotes. [KF373.A7A3] 65-14716
1. Lawyers—United States—Correspondence, reminiscences, etc. I. Title.

BIDDLE, Francis Beverley, 1886-1968. 923.473
A casual past. [1st ed.] Garden City, N.Y., Doubleday, 1961. 408 p. illus. 22cm. Autobiographical. [KF373.B5A3] 61-9480
1. Lawyers—United States—Correspondence, reminiscences, etc. I. Title.

BIDDLE, Francis Beverley, 1886-1968. 923.473
In brief authority. [1st ed.] Garden City,N.Y., Doubleday, 1962. 494 p. illus. 22cm. A continuation of the author's A casual past. Autobiographical. [KF373.B5A32] 62-16744
1. Lawyers—United States—Correspondence, reminiscences, etc. I. Title. **BIP**

EHRLICH, Jacob W., 1900- 923.473
A life in my hands; an autobiography [by] J. W. Ehrlich. NewYork, Putnam [1965] 379 p. 22cm. [KF373.E35A32] 65-10851
1. Lawyers—United States—Correspondence, reminiscences, etc. I. Title.

ELDREDGE, Laurence Howard, 1902- 340'.0924 B
Trials of a Philadelphia lawyer, by Laurence H. Eldredge. [1st ed.] Philadelphia, Lippincott [1968] viii, 257 p. 22 cm. "A Philadelphia bulletin book." [KF373.E4A3] 68-12483
1. Lawyers—United States—Correspondence, reminiscences, etc. I. Title.

ERNST, Morris Leopold, 1888- 347.99'73 B
A love affair with the law; a legal sampler, by Morris L. Ernst. New York, Macmillan [1968] 181 p. 22 cm. Autobiographical. [KF373.E7A3] 68-14438
1. Lawyers—United States—Correspondence, reminiscences, etc. I. Title.

ERNST, Morris Leopold, 1888- 923.473
Touch wood, a year's diary. [1st ed.] New York, Atheneum, 1960. 370 p. 22cm. [KF373.E7A363] 60-7776
1. Lawyers—United States—Correspondence, reminiscences, etc. I. Title.

ERNST, Morris Leopold, 1888- 923.473
Untitled: the diary of my 72nd year. New York, R.B. Luce [1962] 272 p. 21cm. [KF373.E7A364] 62-21200
1. Lawyers—United States—Correspondence, reminiscences, etc. I. Title.

FARROW, Tiera. 923.473
Lawyer in petticoats. New York, Vantage Press [1953] 214p. illus. 23cm. Autobiography. 53-10291
1. Lawyers—U. S.—Correspondence, reminiscences, etc. I. Title.

FRANCE, Royal Wilbur. 923.473
My native grounds. [1st ed.] New York, Cameron Associates, 1957. 255p. 21cm. Autobiography. 57-13899
1. Lawyers—U.S.—Correspondence, reminiscences, etc. I. Title.

FRANKFURTER, Felix, 1882- v. 12
Felix Frankfurter reminisces, recorded in talks with Harlan B. Phillips. Garden City, N.Y., Doubleday, 1962, [c1960] 358 p. 19 cm. (Anchor books, A310) 63-17142
1. Lawyers — U.S. — Correspondence, reminiscences, etc. 2. Judges — U.S. — Correspondence, reminiscences, etc. I. Phillips, Harlan Buddington, 1920- II. Title. III. Series.

GIESLER, Jerry, 1886-1962. 923.473
The Jerry Giesler story, by Jerry Giesler as told to Pete Martin. New York, Simon and Schuster, 1960. 341 p. illus. 22cm. [KF373.G53A3] 60-8011
1. Lawyers—United States—Correspondence, reminiscences, etc. I. Martin, Thornton, 1901-

GIESLER, Jerry [Harold Lee Giesler] 923.473
The Jerry Giesler story, by Jerry Giesler as told by Pete Martin. New York, Simon and Schuster [c.1960] vii 341 p. illus. 22 cm 60-8011 4.50
1. lawyer—U.S.—Correspondence,

reminiscenses, ect. Martin Thornton. I. Title.

HALLINAN, Vincent. 923.473
A lion in court. New York, Putnam [1963] 319 p. 22cm. Autobiography. [KF373.H27A3] 62-18278
1. Lawyers—United States—Correspondence, reminiscences, etc. I. Title.

HOLMAN, Frank Ezekial, 923.473 1886-
The life and career of a western lawyer, 1886-1961. [n.p. 1963] 788 p. illus. 24 cm. 63-19303
1. Lawyers — U.S. — Correspondence, reminiscences, etc. I. Title.

HOPKINS, Albert L., 340.0924 1886-
Autobiography of a lawyer [by] Albert L. Hopkins. Chicago, 1966. lx, 236 p. port. 23cm. [KF373.H635A3] 66-2736
1. Lawyers—United States—Correspondence, reminiscences, etc. I. Title.

HOPKINS, William Foster. 343.0924
Murder is my business. New York, World Pub. Co. [1970] 344 p. 22 cm. [KF373.H64A4] 74-115796 7.95
1. Lawyers—U.S.—Correspondence, reminiscences, etc. I. Title. **BIP**

JOSEPH, Daniel 340'.092'4 Coblens, 1888-
Send me up a blanket! A lawyer's recollection, by Daniel C. Joseph. Edited by Earl Arnett. Baltimore, Peregrine Press [1972] 95 p. illus. 24 cm. [KF373.J66A3] 72-80248 3.95
1. Lawyers—United States—Correspondence, reminiscences, etc. I. Title.

MUSMANNO, Michael Angelo. 923.473
Verdict! The adventures of the young lawyer in the brown suit. [1st ed.] Garden City, N. Y., Doubleday, 1958. 384p. 22cm. Autobiographical. 58-5951
1. Lawyers—U. S.— Correspondence, reminiscences, etc. I. Title.

QUILICI, George L. 340'.0977311
The Italian American lawyers of Chicago, by George L. Quilici. Rev. [4th ed. Chicago, Justinian Society of Lawyers, 1968] 36 p. ports. 26 cm. [KF355.C5Q54 1968] 75-304427
1. Lawyers—Chicago. 2. Italians in Chicago. I. Justinian Society of Lawyers. II. Title.

SCHOENRICH, Otto, 1876- 340'.0924
Reminiscences of an itinerant lawyer. Baltimore [Printed by J. H. Furst Co.] 1967. 664 p. illus., ports. 24 cm. [KF373.S34A35] 66-29686
1. Lawyers—United States—Correspondence, reminiscences, etc. I. Title.

SWANNER, Charles 340.0924 Douglas, 1894-
50 years a barrister in Orange County, by Charles D. Swanner. [1st ed.] Claremont, Calif., Fraser Press [1965] 165 p. illus., ports. 24cm. [KF373.S9A3] 65-4993
1. Lawyers—United States—Correspondence, reminiscences, etc. I. Title.

TRIALS of a 340'.0924
Philadelphia lawyer, by Laurence H. Eldredge. [1st ed.] Philadelphia. Lippincott [1968] viii, 257p. 22cm. Philadelphia bulletin bk. [KF373.E4] (B) 68-12483 5.95
1. Lawyers—U. S.—Correspondence, reminiscences, etc. I. Eldredge, Laurence Howard, 1902-

Lawyers—Correspondence, reminiscences, etc.

BELL, Landon Covington, 923.473 1880-
Southsider, a lawyer's life; law, lumber, and coal. Richmond, Richmond Press, 1954. 403p. illus. 24cm. 54-43365
1. Lawyers—Virginia—Correspondence. reminiscences, etc. I. Title.

CAMPBELL, Litta Belle 818.54 (Hibben) 1886-
Here I raise mine Ebenezer. New York, Simon and Schuster, 1963 [c1962] 256 p. 21cm. Autobiographical. [KF373.C33A28] 63-7315
1. Lawyers—California—Correspondence, reminiscences, etc. I. Title.

FERNALD, Charles, 1830- 923.473 1892.
A county judge in Arcady; selected private papers of Charles Fernald, pioneer California jurist. With an introd. and notes by Cameron Rogers. Glendale, Calif., A. H. Clark Co., 1954. 268p. ports., facsim. 25cm. 54-36577
1. Lawyers—California—Correspondence, reminiscences, etc. I. Rogers, Cameron, 1900- II. Title.

Lawyers—Great Britain.

BIRKETT, Norman 340'.0922 B Birkett, Baron, 1883-1962.
Six great advocates. Freeport, N.Y., Books for Libraries Press [1972, c1961] 109 p. 23 cm. (Biography index reprint series) Original ed. issued as no. 1702 of the Penguin books series. Contents.Contents.—Sir Edward Marshall Hall.—Sir Patrick Hastings.—Sir Edward Clarke.—Sir Rufus Isaacs.—Sir Charles Russell.—Thomas Erskine.—The art of advocacy. [LAW] 75-38517 ISBN 0-8369-8132-4
1. Lawyers—Great Britain. I. Title.

BIRKETT, Norman Birkett, 923.442 baron [William Norman Birkett, baron Birkett] 1883-
Six great advocates. Baltimore, Penguin [dist. Boston, Houghton, 1962, c.1961] 109p. illus. (Penguin bks. 1702) 62-2238 .95 pap.,
1. Lawyers—Gt. Brit. I. Title. **BIP**

Lawyers—Gt. Brit.—Correspondence, reminiscences, etc.

ARMSTRONG, John Warneford 923.442 Scobell, 1877-
Yesterday. London, Hutchinson [1955] 191p. illus. 22 cm. 56-20209
1. Lawyers—Gt. Brit.—Correspondence, reminiscences, etc. I. Title.

CROCKER, William 340'.0924 Charles, Sir, 1886-
Far from humdrum; a lawyer's life. New York, World Pub. Co. [1970, c1967] 264 p. illus., facsim., ports. 22 cm. [LAW] 70-120092
1. Lawyers—Gt. Brit.—Correspondence, reminiscences, etc. I. Title.

HASTINGS, Patrick, Sir 923.442 1800-1952.
Autobiography. New York, Roy Publishers [1954?] 302p. illus. 23cm. 54-10474
1. Lawyers—Gt. Brit.—Correspondence, reminiscences, etc. I. Title.

MORTLOCK, Bill, Pseud. 923.442
Lawyer, heal thyself! New York, Macmillan, 1960 [c.1959] 211p. 22cm. 60-6165 3.95
1. Lawyers.—Gr. Brit.—Correspondence, reminiscences, etc. I. Title.

Lawyers—Massachusetts.

DAVIS, William Thomas, 340'.092'2 1822-1907.
Bench and bar of the Commonwealth of Massachusetts. New York, Da Capo Press, 1974. 2 v. ports. 23 cm. (Da Capo Press reprints in American constitutional and legal history) Reprint of the 1895 ed. published by Boston History Co., Boston. [KF354.M3D38 1974] 74-9765 ISBN 0-306-70612-1 65.00 (2 vol.)
1. Lawyers—Massachusetts. 2. Massachusetts—Biography. I. Title. **BIP**

Lawyers—Mohave Co., Ariz.—Biography.

MORROW, Robert E., 328.791'0922 1894-
Mohave County lawmakers; a biographical summary, compiled by Robert E. Morrow. Kingman, Ariz., Mohave County Miner, 1968. 35 p. illus., ports. 30 cm. [KF355.M6M6] 73-2636
1. Lawyers—Mohave Co., Ariz.—Biography. I. Title.

Lawyers—New Mexico—Correspondence, reminiscences, etc.

HANNETT, Arthur Thomas, 923.473 1884-
Sagebrush lawyer. [1st ed.] New York, Pageant Press [1964] 321 p. ports., map. facsim. 21cm. Autobiography. [KF373.H3A3] 63-23471
1. Lawyers—New Mexico—Correspondence, reminiscences, etc. I. Title.

Lawyers—Oklahoma—Correspondence, reminiscences, etc.

DALE, Fred Hiner, 1881- 340.069 1969.
An Oklahoma lawyer. Guymon, Okla., Printed by Guymon Pub. Co., c1961. 233 p. illus. 24cm. Autobiography. [KF373.D25A3] 62-625
1. Lawyers—Oklahoma—Correspondence, reminiscences, etc. I. Title.

MATHERS, James H 1877- 923.473
From gun to gavel; the courtroom recollections of James Mathers of Oklahoma, as told to Marshall Houts. New York, Morrow, 1954. 246p. 22cm. 54-10301
1. Lawyers—Oklahoma—Correspondence, reminiscences, etc. 2. Trials— Oklahoma. I. Houts, Marshall. II. Title.

Lawyers—South Carolina.

O'NEALL, John 340'.092'2 B Belton, 1793-1863.
Biographical sketches of the bench and bar of South Carolina / by John Belton O'Neall. Spartanburg, S.C. : Reprint Co., 1975. 2 v. ; 22 cm. Reprint of the 1859 ed. published by S. G. Courtenay, Charleston. [KF354.S6O58 1975] 75-1159 ISBN 0-87152-198-9 : 21.00(vol.1); 24.00(vol.2) ISBN 0-87152-199-7
1. Lawyers—South Carolina. 2. South Carolina—Biography. I. Title. **BIP**

Lawyers—Texas—McLennan Co.—Biography.

THE Bench and bar of 340'.092'2 B
Waco and McLennan County, 1849-1976 / edited by Betty Ann McCartney McSwain ; compiled by the Waco-McLennan County Bar Auxiliary for the Bicentennial. 1st ed. Waco, Tex. : Texian Press, c1976. xvi, 386 p., [10] leaves of plates : ill. ; 29 cm. "Including a reprint of Waco bar and incidents of Waco history, by William M. Sleeper and Allan D. Sanford." Includes bibliographical references and index. [KF355.M23B46] 76-43570
1. Lawyers—Texas—McLennan Co.—Biography. 2. Lawyers—Texas—Waco—Biography. 3. McLennan Co., Tex.—Biography. 4. Waco, Tex.—Biography. I. McSwain, Betty Ann McCartney. II. Waco-McLennan County Bar Auxiliary. III. Sleeper, William M., 1859-1944. Waco bar and incidents of Waco history. 1976.

Lawyers—U.S.—Biography.

LEWIS, William 340'.0922 B Draper, 1867-1949, ed.
Great American lawyers: the lives and influence of judges and lawyers who have acquired permanent national reputation, and have developed the jurisprudence of the United States; a history of the legal profession in America. Philadelphia, J. C. Winston Co., 1907-09. South Hackensack, N.J., Rothman Reprints, inc., 1971. 8 v. ports. 23 cm. [KF367.L45 1971] 75-157105
1. Lawyers—U.S.—Biography. 2. Judges—U.S.—Biography.

Lawyers—United States—Juvenile literature.

LEVY, Elizabeth. 340'.092'2 B
Lawyers for the people; a new breed of defenders and their work. New York, A. A. Knopf; [distributed by Random House, 1974] 120 p. front. 22 cm. Biographies of nine public interest lawyers who have been involved in cases such as stopping the use of DDT, justice for juveniles, equal rights for women, the defense of radicals, and prison reform. [KF372.L48] 920 74-4490 ISBN 0-394-82659-0
1. Lawyers—United States—Juvenile literature. I. Title. **BIP**

Lax, David, 1910-

LAX, David, 1910- 759.13 B
One man show / David Lax. New York : Washington Irving Gallery, c1976. xiv, 353 p. : ill. ; 24 cm. Includes index. Bibliography: p. 333-334. [ND237.L35A447] 76-47850
1. Lax, David, 1910- 2. Painters—United States—Biography. I. Title.

Laxalt, Dominique.

LAXALT, Robert, 1921- 920
Sweet promised land. [1st ed.] New York, Harper [1957] 176p. 22cm. [E184.B15L3] 56-11077
1. Laxalt, Dominique. I. Title.

LAXALT, Robert, 1921- 920
Sweet promised land. [Large type ed.] New York, Harper [1967, c.1957] 176p. 29cm. [E184.B15L3] 5.11
1. Laxalt, Dominique. I. Title.

LAXALT, Robert, 917.93'03'30924 1921-
Sweet promised land. Large type ed. New York, Harper & Row [196-? c1957] 176 p. 22 cm. [[E184.B15]] 68-2367
1. Laxalt, Dominique. I. Title.

LAXALT, Robert, 917.93'03'30924 B 1921-
Sweet promised land. Large type ed. New York, Harper & Row [196-? c1957] 176 p. 22 cm. A large print edition of the account a son writes of his father, an old Basque sheepherder who lived and worked in the American West for most of his life, who, in fulfilling his dream of returning to the Pyrenees, came to a new realization of what America meant to him. [E184.B15] 92 AC 68
1. Laxalt, Dominique. 2. Basques in the United States. 3. Sight-saving books. I. Title.

*Laxalt, Robert,

*LAXALT, Robert, 1921- 920.9
Sweet promised land. New York, Harper [1964, c.1957] 176p. 21cm. (Perennial Lib., 17) .60 pap.,
I. Title. **BIP**

Layard, Austin Henry, Sir, 1817-1894.

BRACKMAN, Arnold C. 935'.03 B
The luck of Nineveh : the greatest adventure in modern archaeology / by Arnold C. Brackman. New York : McGraw-Hill, c1978. p. cm. [DS70.88.L3B7] 78-1893 ISBN 0-07-007030-X : 12.95
1. Layard, Austin Henry, Sir, 1817-1894. 2. Nineveh. 3. Archaeologists—Great Britain—Biography. 4. Archaeologists—Iraq—Biography. I. Title.

Layard, Sir Austen Henry, 1817-1894—Juvenile literature.

SILVERBERG, Robert. 925.71
The man who found Nineveh; the story of Austen Henry Layard. [1st ed.] New York, Holt, Rinehart and Winston [1964] 207 p. map. 21 cm. Bibliography: p. 201-202. [DS70.88.L3S5] 64-18257

1. Layard, Sir Austen Henry, 1817-1894—Juvenile literature. 2. Nineveh—Juvenile literature. I. Title.

SLVERBERG, Robert 925.71
The man who found Nineveh the story of Austen Henry Layard. New York, Holt [c.1964] 206p. map. 21cm. Bibl. 64-18257 3.95; 3.59 bds., lib. ed.,
1. Layard, Sir Austen Henry, 1817-1894—Juvenile literature. 2. Nineveh—Juvenile literature. I. Title.

Layden, Elmer.

LAYDEN, Elmer. 796.332'0924
It was a different game; the Elmer Layden story [by] Elmer Layden with Ed Snyder. Englewood Cliffs, N.J., Prentice-Hall [1969] ix, 175 p. illus., ports. 22 cm. [GV939.L315A3] 74-81969 ISBN 0-13-507517-3 5.95
I. Snyder, Ed. II. Title.

Laye, Camara,

LAYE, Camara, 916.6'52'0330924 B
1928-
The dark child. With an introd. by Philippe Thoby-Marcellin. [Translated from the French by James Kirkup and Ernest Jones] New York, Farrar, Straus and Giroux [1969, c1954] 188 p. 21 cm. Translation of L'enfant noir. Autobiographical. [DT543.4.L313 1969] 73-5733 5.95
I. Title. BIP

Layton, Del, 1906-

MCLENDON, 975.9'381'060924 B
James.
Pioneer in the Florida Keys : the life and times of Del Layton / James McLendon ; with a foreword by Ted Williams. Miami, Fla. : E. A. Seemann Pub., 1977, c1976 148 p. : ill., map (on lining papers) ; 25 cm. Includes indexes. Bibliography: p. 143. [F319.M6L395] 76-55891 ISBN 0-912458-79-8 : 9.95
1. Layton, Del, 1906- 2. Miami, Fla.—Biography. 3. Florida Keys—Biography. I. Title. BIP

Lazare, Bernard, 1865-1903.

WILSON, Nelly. 301.45'19'24044 B
Bernard-Lazare : antisemitism and the problem of Jewish identity in late nineteenth-century France / Nelly Wilson. Cambridge ; New York : Cambridge University Press, 1978. x, 348 p., [3] leaves of plates : ill. ; 22 cm. Includes index. Bibliography: p. [326]-339. [DS135.F9L398] 77-82524 ISBN 0-521-21802-0 : 28.50
1. Lazare, Bernard, 1865-1903. 2. Dreyfus, Alfred, 1859-1935. 3. Jews in France—Biography. 4. Antisemitism—France. 5. Journalists—France—Biography. 6. France—Biography.

Lazarillo de Tormes.

LAZARILLO de Tormes. v. 12
The life of Lazarillo de Tormes: his fortunes and adversities. Translated by W. S. Merwin. With an introd. by Leonardo C. de Morelos. Gloucester, Mass., Peter Smith, 1970 [c1962] 152 p. 21 cm. Reprint of 1962 edition. [PQ6408.E5 1962b] 62-15925
I. Merwin, William S., 1927- tr. BIP

LAZARILLO de Tormes. v. 12
The life of Lazarillo de Tormes: his fortunes and adversities. Translated by W. S. Merwin. With an introd. by Leonardo C. de Morelos. Gloucester, Mass., Peter Smith, 1970 [c1962] 152 p. 21 cm. Reprint of 1962 edition. [PQ6408.E5 1962b] 62-15925
I. Merwin, William S., 1927- tr. BIP

LIFE of Lazarillo de 863.3
Tormes, his fortunes and adversities (The). A mod. tr. [from Spanish] notes by James Parsons. Introd. by Glen Willbern. New York, Amer. R.D.M. [1966] 96p. 21cm. (Study master pubn., T47) Bibl. 1.25 pap.,
1. Lazarillo de Tormes. 2. La vida de Lazarillo de Tormes. I. Parsons, James, tr.

Lazaro, Joe.

LAZARO, Joe. 796.352'3
The right touch / by Joe Lazaro ; introd. by Bob Hope; ill. by Elmer Wexler. 1st ed. Weston, Mass. : J. Mahoney, c1978. 142 p. : ill. ; 24 cm. [GV965.L36] 78-108832 7.95
1. Lazaro, Joe. 2. Golf. 3. Golfers—United States—Biography. I. Title.

Lazarus, Emma, 1849-1887.

MERRIAM, Eve, 1916- 928.1
Emma Lazarus, woman with a torch. [1st ed.] New York, Citadel Press [1956] 160p. 21cm. [PS2234.M4] 56-10276
1. Lazarus, Emma, 1849-1887. I. Title.

MERRIAM, Eve, 1916- 928.1
Emma Lazarus, woman with a torch. [1st ed.] New York, Citadel Press [1956] 160 p. 21 cm. [PS2234.M4] 56-10276
1. Lazarus, Emma, 1849-1887.

MERRIAM, Eve, 1916- 928.1
The voice of liberty; the story of Emma Lazarus. Illustrated by Charles W. Walker. [New York] Farrar, Straus and Cudahy [1959] 179p. illus. 22cm. (Covenant books [6]) [PS2234.M42] 59-6067
1. Lazarus, Emma, 1849-1887. I. Title.

LaZebnik, Edith.

LAZEBNIK, Edith. 947'.004'924 B
Such a life / by Edith LaZebnik. 1st ed. New York : Morrow, 1978. 287 p. ; 22 cm. [DS135.R95L265] 78-759 ISBN 0-688-03280-X : 8.95
1. LaZebnik, Edith. 2. Jews in Russia—Biography. 3. Russia—Biography. I. Title. BIP

LAZEBNIK, Edith. 947'.004'924 B
Such a life / by Edith LaZebnik. 1st ed. New York : Pocket Books, 1979, c1978. 293p. : 18 cm. [DS135.R95L265] ISBN 0-671-82282-9 pbk. : 2.50
1. LaZebnik, Edith. 2. Jews in Russia — Biography. 3. Russia — Biography. I. Title. L.C. card no. for 1978 Morrow ed: 78-759

Laziosi, Pellegrino, Saint, 1265-1345—Juvenile literature.

BALSKUS, Pat. 282'.092'4 B
Mary's pilgrim; life of St. Peregrine. Illustrated by the Daughters of St. Paul. [Boston] St. Paul Editions [1972] 92 p. illus. 22 cm. (Encounter books) The life of the thirteenth-century Italian priest who became the patron against cancer after being miraculously cured of that disease. [BX4700.L43B34] 92 68-58160 1.50
1. Laziosi, Pellegrino, Saint, 1265-1345—Juvenile literature. I. Daughters of St. Paul. II. Title.

Le Clerc du Tremblay, Francois, 1577-1638.

HUXLEY, Aldous Leonard, 922.244
1894-
Grey eminence. New York, Meridian Books [1959, c1941] 342p. 19cm. (Meridian books, M70) [DC123.9.L5H8 1959] 59-12139
1. Le Clerc du Tremblay, Francois, 1577-1638. I. Title. BIP

Le Corbusier-Galerie Heidi Weber—Juvenile literature.

HOAG, Edwin. 720'.922 B
Masters of modern architecture : Frank Lloyd Wright, Le Corbusier, Mies van der Rohe, and Walter Gropius / by Edwin and Joy Hoag. Indianapolis : Bobbs-Merrill, c1977. xiii, 209 p., [8] leaves of plates : ill. ; 23 cm. Includes index. Bibliography: p. 193-197. Discusses the founding of modern architecture through the lives and works of four important architects. [NA680.H54] 920 77-76888 ISBN 0-672-52365-5 pbk. : 10.00
1. Wright, Frank Lloyd, 1867-1959—Juvenile literature. 2. Le Corbusier-Galerie Heidi Weber—Juvenile literature. 3. Mies van der Rohe, Ludwig, 1886-1969—Juvenile literature. 4. Gropius, Walter, 1883-1969—Juvenile literature. 5. Architecture, Modern—20th century—Juvenile literature. 6. Architects—Biography—Juvenile literature. I. Hoag, Joy, joint author. II. Title.

Le Gallienne, Eva, 1899-

LE GALLIENNE, 792'.028'0924 B
Eva, 1899-
With a quiet heart; an autobiography. Westport, Conn., Greenwood Press [1974, c1953] viii, 311 p. illus. 22 cm. Reprint of the ed. published by Viking Press, New York. [PN2287.L3A35 1974] 74-3745 ISBN 0-8371-7470-8 15.00
1. Le Gallienne, Eva, 1899- 2. Actresses—Correspondence, reminiscences, etc. I. Title.

LE GALLIENNE, Eva, 1899- 927.92
With a quiet heart, an autobiography. New York, Viking Press, 1953. 311p. illus. 22cm. [PN2287.L3A35] 53-5201
1. Actors—Correspondence, reminiscences, etc. I. Title.

Le Gallienne, Richard, 1866-1947.

WHITTINGTON-EGAN, Richard, 928.2
1924-
The quest of the golden boy; the life and letters of Richard Le Gallienne, by Richard Whittington-Egan & Geoffrey Smerdon. [1st American ed.] Barre, Mass., Barre Pub. Co., 1962 [c1960] 580 p. illus. 26 cm. [PR4882.W45 1962] 62-16849
1. Le Gallienne, Richard, 1866-1947. I. Smerdon, Geoffrey, joint author. II. Title.

Le Gras, Louise de Marillac, Saint, 1591-1660.

MEYERS, Bertrande. 922.244
A woman named Louise; biography. [1st ed.] [Normandy, Mo.] [Marillac College Press] [1956] 222 p. 17 cm. [BX4700.L5M4] 56-10153
1. Le Gras, Louise de Marillac, Saint, 1591-1660. I. Title.

Le Marchant, John Gaspard, 1766-1812.

SCIENTIFIC 355'.0071'14229
soldier: a life of General Le Marchant 1766-1812 [by] R. H. Thoumine. London; New York, Oxford Univ. Pr., 1968. xi, 212p. 7 plates, illus., facsims., 3 maps port. 23cm. Bibl. [DA506.L44T5] (B) 68-10414 6.00
1. Le Marchant, John Gaspard, 1766-1812. I. Thoumine, R. H.

THOUMINE, R H 355'.0071'14229 (B)
Scientific soldier: a life of General Le Marchant 1766-1812 [by] R. H. Thoumine. London, New York [etc.] Oxford U. P., 1968. xi, 212 p. 7 plates, illus., facsims., 3 maps, port. 23 cm. Bibliography: p. [199]-202. [DA506.L44T5] 68-104414
1. Le Marchant, John Gaspard, 1766-1812. I. Title.

Le Moyne d'Iberville, Pierre, 1661-1706.

CROUSE, Nellis 359.3'31'0924 B
Maynard, 1884-
Lamoyne d'Iberville: soldier of New France, by Nellis M. Crouse. Port Washington, N.Y., Kennikat Press [1972, c1954] 280 p. illus. 24 cm. Bibliography: p. 270-274. [F1030.L468 1972] 71-159054 ISBN 0-8046-1677-9
1. Le Moyne d'Iberville, Pierre, 1661-1706.

REED, Charles 359.33'1'0924 B
Bert, 1866-1940.
The first great Canadian, the story of Pierre Le Moyne, sieur d'Iberville. Freeport, N.Y., Books for Libraries Press [1972] p. Reprint of the 1910 ed. Bibliography: p. [F1030.L48 1972] 72-8430 ISBN 0-8369-6987-1
1. Le Moyne d'Iberville, Pierre, 1661-1706. I. Title.

Le Notre, Andre, 1613-1700.

ANDRE Le Notre, 712.5
garden architect to kings. New York, Crown Publishers [1962] 176 p. illus., port., plans (part col.) 26 cm. Bibliography: p. 170-176. [SB470.L4F6] 62-17518
1. Le Notre, Andre, 1613-1700.

Le Sueur, Arthur, 1867-1950.

LE SUEUR, Meridel. 923.373
Crusaders. New York, Blue Heron Press [1955] 94p. illus. 20cm. [HX84.L4L4] 55-13869
1. Le Sueur, Arthur, 1867-1950. 2. Le Sueur, Marian, 1877-1954. I. Title.

Le Vay, David.

LE VAY, David. 617'.092'4 B
Scenes from surgical life / [by] David Le Vay. London : Owen, 1976. 200 p. ; 22 cm. Includes bibliographical references. [RD728.L4A3] 77-366461 ISBN 0-7206-0384-6 : £4.95
1. Le Vay, David. 2. Orthopedists—England—Biography. 3. Medicine—Philosophy. I. Title. BIP

Le Vier, Anthony William,

LE VIER, Anthony 926.2913
William, 1913-
Pilot, by Tony Le Vier, as told to John Guenther. Foreword by Arthur Godfrey. [1st ed.] New York, Harper [1954] 263 p. illus. 22 cm. Autobiography. [TL540.L44A3] 54-6018
I. Guenther, John, 1911- II. Title.

Leach, Bernard Howell, 1887-

LEACH, Bernard 738'.092'4 B
Howell, 1887-
Beyond East and West : memoirs, portraits, and essays / Bernard Leach. London ; Boston : Faber, 1978. 320 p., [12] leaves of plates : ill. ; 26 cm. Includes index. [NK4210.L35A2 1978] 78-315916 ISBN 0-571-11138-6 : 15.95
1. Leach, Bernard Howell, 1887- 2. Potters—England—Biography. I. Title. Distributed by Watson Publishing Co., 6608 Hesperia Ave. Reseda, CA 91335

Leach, Frank Aleamon, 1846-

LEACH, Frank 070.5'092'4 B
Aleamon, 1846-
Recollections of a newspaperman (a record of life and events in California) New York, Beekman Publishers, 1974. 416 p. illus. 23 cm. (American newspapermen, 1790-1933) Reprint of the 1917 ed. published by S. Levinson, San Francisco. [PN4874.L34A326 1974] 74-752 ISBN 0-8464-0016-7 18.50
1. Leach, Frank Aleamon, 1846- 2. California—Politics and government—1850-1950. 3. Frontier and pioneer life—California. I. Title. BIP

Leacock, Stephen Butler, 1869-1944.

CURRY, Ralph L. 928.1
Stephen Leacock, humorist and humanist. [1st ed.] Garden City, N.Y., Doubleday, 1959. 383 p. 22 cm. [PR6023.E15Z7] 59-11587
1. Leacock, Stephen Butler, 1869-1944.

Leadership.

MACMUNN, George Fletcher, 920.02
Sir, 1869-1952.
Leadership through the ages. Freeport, N.Y., Books for Libraries Press [1968] viii, 354 p. 22 cm. (Essay index reprint series) Reprint of the 1935 ed. Contents.Contents.—Concerning leaders.—Moses.—Alexander of Macedon.—Queen Elizabeth.—Oliver Cromwell in the making.—Oliver Cromwell the dictator.—Some thumbnail sketches.—Tseu-hi (1835-1908): the Dowager Empress of China.—Abraham Lincoln.—Some Victorians and after.—Benito Mussolini.—Adolf Hitler. [CT104.M26 1968] 68-16951
1. Leadership. 2. Biography. I. Title. BIP

League of Nations.

BARROS, James. 341.22'092'4 B
Office without power : Secretary General Sir Eric Drummond, 1919-1933 / by James Barros. Oxford : Clarendon Press ; New York : Oxford University Press, 1979. xii, 4213 p. ; 23 cm. Includes bibliographical references and index. [D413.P45B37] 78-40312 ISBN 0-19-822551-2 : 41.00
1. Perth, James Eric Drummond, 16th Earl of, 1876- 2. League of Nations. 3. League of Nations—Biography. 4. Europe—Politics and government—1918-1945. 5. Diplomats—Great Britain—Biography. I. Title.
Distributed by Oxford University Press, New York, NY **BIP**

Leahy, Frank William, 1908-1973.

TWOMBLY, Wells. 796.33'2'0924 B
Shake down the thunder! The official biography of Notre Dame's Frank Leahy. [1st ed.] Radnor, Pa., Chilton [1974] xvii, 328 p. illus. 22 cm. [GV939.L35T92 1974] 74-17348 ISBN 0-8019-5943-8 8.95
1. Leahy, Frank William, 1908-1973. 2. Notre Dame, Ind. University—Football. 3. Football. 4. Football coaching. I. Title.

WILLIAMS, Bernard J. 796.33'2'0924 B
The Frank Leahy legend; an unauthorized biography, by B. J. Williams. [Torrance, Calif., JCL Services, 1974] 340 p. illus. 21 cm. [GV939.L35W54] 74-163535
1. Leahy, Frank William, 1908-1973. 2. Football. I. Title.

Leake, Robert Rowland, 1811-1860.

YELLAND, E. M. 338.1'7'6368099423 B
The baron of the frontiers: South Australia-Victoria, Robert Rowland Leake (1811-1860), by E. M. Yelland. Melbourne, Hawthorn Press, 1973. 206 p. plates. 23 cm. Index. Bibliography: p. 187-193. [SF375.5.A8Y43] 74-178174 ISBN 0-7256-0105-1 8.50
1. Leake, Robert Rowland, 1811-1860. 2. Sheep—South Australia. 3. Frontier and pioneer life—South Australia. 4. Frontier and pioneer life—Victoria, Australia. 5. Saxon merino sheep. I. Title.

Leakey, Louis Seymour Bazett, 1903-1972.

COLE, Sonia Mary. 301.2'092'4 B
Leakey's luck : the life of Louis Seymour Bazett Leakey, 1903-1972 / Sonia Cole. 1st American ed. New York : Harcourt Brace Jovanovich, c1975. 448 p., [15] leaves of plates : maps (on lining papers), ports ; 22 cm. Includes bibliographical references and index. [GN21.L37C64 1975b] 75-327272 ISBN 0-15-149456-8 : 14.95
1. Leakey, Louis Seymour Bazett, 1903-1972. I. Title. **BIP**

LEAKEY, Louis Seymour Bazett, 1903- 916.7 [B]
White African; an early autobiography, by L. S. B. Leakey. With a foreword by Kirtley F. Mather and a new pref. by the author. New York, Ballantine [1973 c.1966] 274 p. 18 cm. (Ballantine Walden Edition) [DT433.L4A3 1973] 67-7042 1.50 (pbk.)
1. Africa, East—Descr. & trav. 2. Stone age—Africa, East. I. Title. **BIP**

LEAKEY, Louis Seymour Bazett, 1903-1972. 569'.9'0924 B
By the evidence : memoirs, 1932-1951 / L. S. B. Leakey. New York : Harcourt Brace Jovanovich, [1976] c1974. p. cm. (A Harvest book ; HB 344) Includes index. [GN21.L37A32 1976] 76-14846 ISBN 0-15-615000-X pbk. : 3.95
1. Leakey, Louis Seymour Bazett, 1903-1972. I. Title.

Leakey, Louis Seymour Bazett, 1903-1972—Juvenile literature.

MALATESTA, Anne. 570'.92'4 B
The white Kikuyu, Louis S. B. Leakey / by Anne Malatesta and Ronald Friedland ; illustrated with photos. New York : McGraw-Hill, [1977] p. cm. A biography of the anthropologist who made important discoveries in eastern Africa concerning man's origins. [GN21.L37M34] 77-78765 ISBN 0-07-039750-3 lib.bdg. : 5.72
1. Leakey, Louis Seymour Bazett, 1903-1972—Juvenile literature. 2. Anthropologists—Great Britain—Juvenile literature. I. Friedland, Ronald, 1937- joint author. II. Title.

Lear, Edward, 1812-1888.

†BYROM, Thomas. 760'.092'4 B
Nonsense and wonder : the poems and cartoons of Edward Lear / by Thomas Byrom. 1st ed. New York : Dutton, c1977. 244 p. : ill. ; 24 cm. "A Brandywine Press book." Includes index. Bibliography: p. 239-242. [PR4879.L2Z59] 77-14560 ISBN 0-525-16835-4 : 12.95
1. Lear, Edward, 1812-1888. 2. Poets, English—19th century—Biography. 3. Artists—England—Biography. I. Lear, Edward, 1812-1888. Nonsense and wonder. 1977. II. Title. **BIP**

DAVIDSON, Angus, 1898- 759.2 B
Edward Lear; landscape painter and nonsense poet, 1812-1888. New York, Barnes & Noble [1968] xv, 280 p. illus. 23 cm. Bibliography: p. 273. [ND497.L48D3 1968c] 75-3497 6.00
1. Lear, Edward, 1812-1888.

GARVEY, Eleanor M. 760'.092'4 B
Edward Lear, painter, poet, and draughtsman; an exhibition of drawings, watercolors, oils, nonsense and travel books, Worcester Art Museum [April 18-June 2, 1968. Prepared by Eleanor M. Garvey. Worcester, Mass., Worcester Art Museum] 1968. 88 p. illus. 16 x 23 cm. Includes bibliographical references. [N6797.L42G37] 74-151308
1. Lear, Edward, 1812-1888. I. Worcester, Mass. Art Museum. II. Title.

LEAR, Edward, 1812-1888. 821'.8
Letters of Edward Lear to Chichester Fortescue, Lord Carlingford and Frances, Countess Waldegrave. Edited by Lady Strachey. Freeport, N.Y., Books for Libraries Press [1970] xl, 327 p. illus., plates, ports. 23 cm. Reprint of the 1907 ed. [NC242.L4A3 1970] 70-107812
I. Strachie, Constance (Braham) Strachey, Baroness, d. 1936, ed.

LEHMANN, John, 1907- 760'.092'4 B
Edward Lear and his world / John Lehmann. New York : Scribner, c1977. 128 p. : ill. ; 25 cm. Includes index. Bibliography: p. 118. [ND497.L48L44 1977] 77-73133 ISBN 0-684-15173-1 : 9.95
1. Lear, Edward, 1812-1888. 2. Painters—England—Biography. 3. Authors, English—19th century—Biography. I. Title. **BIP**

NOAKES, Vivien, 1937- 760'.0924 B
Edward Lear; the life of a wanderer. [1st American ed.] Boston, Houghton Mifflin, 1969 [c1968] 359 p. illus., facsims., map, ports. 23 cm. Bibliography: p. 343-346. [ND497.L48N6 1969] 69-15024 8.95
1. Lear, Edward, 1812-1888. I. Title.

Lear, Edward, 1812-1888—Juvenile literature.

KELEN, Emery, 1896- 760'.092'4 B
Mr. Nonsense: a life of Edward Lear. With illus. by Edward Lear. [1st. ed.] Nashville, T. Nelson [1973] 128 p. illus. 22 cm. Bibliography: p. [121] Biography of a nineteenth-century Englishman known for his nonsense verse and limericks. [PR4879.L2Z67] 92 73-2672 ISBN 0-8407-6278-X 4.95
1. Lear, Edward, 1812-1888—Juvenile literature. I. Title.

Lear, Harold Alexander, 1920-1978.

LEAR, Martha Weinman. 362.1'9'61209 B
Heartsounds / Martha Weinman Lear. New York : Simon and Schuster, c1979. p. cm. [RC685.I6L397] 79-23100 ISBN 0-671-24329-2 : 9.95
1. Lear, Harold Alexander, 1920-1978. 2. Heart—Infarction—Biography. I. Title. **BIP**

Lear Heap, Winifred, 1907- —Biography—Youth.

LEAR Heap, Winifred, 1907- 942.083'092'4 B
Down the rabbit hole / Winifred Lear. New York : St. Martin's Press, 1975. 224 p. ; 23 cm. [PR6023.E2Z52 1975b] 74-18734 7.95
1. Lear Heap, Winifred, 1907- —Biography—Youth. I. Title.

Lear, William Powell, 1902-

BOESEN, Victor. 629.13'00924 B
They said it couldn't be done: the incredible story of Bill Lear. [1st ed.] Garden City, N.Y., Doubleday, 1971. 204 p. illus., ports. 22 cm. [TL540.L364B64] 71-111153 6.95
1. Lear, William Powell, 1902- I. Title.

Lear, William Powell, 1902 —Juvenile literature.

BOESEN, Victor. 629.04 B
William P. Lear : from high school dropout to space age inventor / Victor Boesen. New York : Hawthorn Books, [1974] 109, [8] p. : ill. ; 22 cm. Includes index. A biography of the inventive genius of radio and jet fame whose recent development of the steam automobile may be the answer to automobile pollution. [TL540.L364B65 1974] 92 73-21312 ISBN 0-8015-4528-5 : 5.95
1. Lear, William Powell, 1902 —Juvenile literature. I. Title.

Leary, Timothy Francis, 1920-

SLACK, Charles W. 301.2'2 B
Timothy Leary, the madness of the sixties and me, by Charles W. Slack. New York, P. H. Wyden [1974] xvi, 264 p. 21 cm. Bibliography: p. [263]-264. [HV5825.S55] 74-76237 ISBN 0-88326-051-4 7.95
1. Leary, Timothy Francis, 1920-

Lease, Mary Elizabeth (Clyens) 1853-1933—Juvenile literature.

STILLER, Richard. 329.8 B
Queen of Populists; the story of Mary Elizabeth Lease. New York, T. Y. Crowell Co. [1970] viii, 245 p. illus. 21 cm. (Women of America) Bibliography: p. 234-236. Biography of the first important female politician in America who did much to further the cause of farmers and the Populist Party of the 1890's. [F686.L4S7] 92 78-94801 4.50
1. Lease, Mary Elizabeth (Clyens) 1853-1933—Juvenile literature. 2. People's Party of the United States—Juvenile literature. I. Title. **BIP**

Leautaud, Paul,

LEAUTAUD, Paul, 1872-1956. 928.4
Journal of a man of letters, 1898-1907. Tr. from French by Geoffrey Sainsbury, Pref. by Alan Pryce Jones [dist. New York, Humanities Pr. [1961, c.1960] 258p. front. port. 61-665 5.00
1. Title.

Leavell, Frank Hartwell, 1884-1949.

BROACH, Claude U. 922.673
Dr. Frank; an informal biography of Frank H. Leavell, leader of Baptist youth. Nashville, Broadman Press [1950] xv, 137 p. illus., ports. 21 cm. [BX6495.L36B7] 50-58225
1. Leavell, Frank Hartwell, 1884-1949. I. Title.

Leavenworth, Thaddeus, 1802-1893.

RIDOUT, Lionel Utley. 283'.092'2 B
Renegade, outcast, and maverick: three Episcopal clergymen in the California gold rush, by Lionel U. Ridout. San Diego, University Press, San Diego State University, c1973. iii, 127 p. 24 cm. On spine: Pioneer clergy. Includes bibliographical references. [BX5990.R52] 74-180275
1. Leavenworth, Thaddeus, 1802-1893. 2. Ver Mehr, John Leonard, ca. 1809-1886. 3. Ewer, Ferdinand Cartwright, 1826-1883. I. Title. II. Title: Pioneer clergy.

Leavis, Frank Raymond, 1895-

HAYMAN, Ronald, 1932- 801'.95'0924
Leavis / Ronald Hayman. London : Heinemann ; Totowa, N.J. : Rowman and Littlefield, 1976. xiv, 161 p. ; 23 cm. Includes index. Bibliography: p. [147]-153. [PR29.L4H39 1976] 77-357285 ISBN 0-87471-917-8 (Rowman & Littlefield) : 10.00
1. Leavis, Frank Raymond, 1895- **BIP**

Leavitt, Dudley, 1830-1908.

BROOKS, Juanita, 1898- 917.92'03'20924
On the ragged edge; the life and times of Dudley Leavitt. [Salt Lake City] Utah State Historical Society, 1973. x, 175 p. illus. 23 cm. Expansion of the author's work published in 1942 under title: Dudley Leavitt, pioneer to southern Utah. [F826.B872 1973] 73-620222 ISBN 0-913738-24-7 5.00
1. Leavitt, Dudley, 1830-1908. 2. Frontier and pioneer life—Utah. 3. Mormons and Mormonism in Utah. 4. Utah—History. I. Title.

Lebanon—Biog.

WHO'S who in Lebanon, 920.05692
2ed.; 1965-1966 Beyrouth Edns. Publictec. v. 21cm. biennial. In French. [DS80.75.W5] [PL480:UAR-D-147] NE 65 35.00
1. Lebanon—Biog.
American distributor: Intl. Pubns. Serv., New York.

Lebbe, Vincent, 1877-1940.

LECLERCQ, Jacques, 1891- 922.251
Thunder in the distance; the life of Pere Lebbe. Translated by George Lamb. New York, Sheed & Ward [1958] 322 p. 22 cm. [BV3427.L39L4] 58-5884
1. Lebbe, Vincent, 1877-1940. I. Title.

Lebby family.

ELLIS, Edmund Detreville, 1890- 929.2'0973
Nathaniel Lebby, patriot, and some of his descendants, by E. Detreville Ellis. [Chevy Chase? Md.] 1967. xi, 553 p. illus., map (on p. [2]-[3] of cover), ports. 28 cm. "Footnotes": p. 506-510. Bibliography: p. 511-519. [CS71.L443 1967] 76-4359
1. Lebby family. I. Title.

Lebec, Peter, d. 1837.

WOOD, Raymund Francis, 1911- 923.973
The life and death of Peter Lebec. Fresno, Calif., Academy Library Guild, 1954. 78p. illus. 21cm. [F868.K3L4] 56-39540
1. Lebec, Peter, d. 1837. I. Title.

LeBlanc, Claude, 1669-1728.

STURGILL, Claude C., 1933- 944'.034'0924 B
Claude Le Blanc : civil servant of the king / Claude C. Sturgill. Gainesville : University Presses of Florida, 1976. 202 p., [1] leaf of plates : ill. ; 23 cm. "A

University of Florida book." Includes index. Bibliography: p. 191-198. [DC135.L4S88] 75-40269 ISBN 0-8130-0393-8 : 8.50
1. LeBlanc, Claude, 1669-1728.

LeBlanc, Dudley J.

CLAY, Floyd Martin. 976.3'06'0924 B
Coozan Dudley LeBlanc: from Huey Long to Hadacol. Gretna [La.] Pelican Pub. Co., 1973. xii, 264 p. illus. 23 cm. Bibliography: p. [245]-259. [F375.L422C55] 73-14609 ISBN 0-911116-69-9 10.00
1. LeBlanc, Dudley J. 2. Louisiana—Politics and government—1865-1950. I. Title.

Leblanc, Georgette, 1869-1941.

LEBLANC, Georgette, 1869-1941. 848'.9'1209 B
Souvenirs : my life with Maeterlinck / by Georgette Leblanc ; translated from the French by Janet Flanner. New York : Da Capo Press, 1976, c1932. p. cm. (The Lyric stage) Reprint of the 1st ed. published by Dutton, New York. [PQ2625.A6L42 1976] 76-22154 ISBN 0-306-70841-8 : 22.50
1. Leblanc, Georgette, 1869-1941. 2. Maeterlinck, Maurice, 1862- —Biography. I. Title.

Lechner, Franziska, 1832 or 3-1894.

BURTON, Katherine (Kurz) 1890- 922.243
One thing needful; the biography of Mother Franziska Lechner, F. D. C., foundress of the Daughters of Divine Charity. New York, Kenedy [1960] 210p. illus. 22cm. [BX4333.1.Z8L4] 60-9053
1. Lechner, Franziska, 1832 or 3-1894. 2. Daughters of Divine Charity. I. Title.

Lechner, Walter W., 1890-

CLARK, James Anthony, 1907- 622'.3382'0924 B
An oilman's oilman : a biographical treatment of Walter W. Lechner / by James A. Clark ; edited by Judith King. Houston, Tex. : Gulf Pub. Co., Book Division, c1979. vii, 143 p., [8] leaves of plates : ill. ; 24 cm. Includes index. [TN140.L42C57] 75-5318 ISBN 0-88415-633-8 : 8.95
1. Lechner, Walter W., 1890- 2. Petroleum workers United States—Biography. I. King, Judith. II. Title.

Lecomte du Nouy, Pierre, 1883-1947.

LECOMTE du Nouy, Mary Bishop Harriman. 925
The road to Human destiny; a life of Pierre Lecomte du Nouy. [1st ed.] New York, Longmans, Green, 1955. 344 p. 21 cm. [Q143.L44L4] 55-9823
1. Lecomte du Nouy, Pierre, 1883-1947. 2. Lecomte du Nouy, Pierre, 1883-1947. Human destiny. I. Title.

Lecouvreur, Adrienne, 1692-1730.

RICHTMAN, Jack, 1927- 792'.028'0924 B
Adrienne Lecouvreur: the actress and the age; a biography. Englewood Cliffs, N.J., Prentice-Hall [1971] 240 p. illus. 22 cm. Bibliography: p. 225-230. [PN2638.L35R5] 76-164920 ISBN 0-13-008698-3 7.95
1. Lecouvreur, Adrienne, 1692-1730. I. Title.

Lederer, William J.,

LEDERER, William J., 1912- 923.573
All the ships at sea. New York, Sloane [1950] 292 p. 22 cm. Autobiography. [V63.L4A3] 50-59952
I. Title.

LEDERER, William J., 1912- 359.3'3'20924
All the ship's at sea [by] William J. Lederer. New York, Norton [1970, c1950] 292 p. 22 cm. [V63.L4A3 1970] 70-95882 6.95
I. Title.

Ledivelec, Madeleine.

MANET, Edouard, 1832-1883 759.4
Manet, by Madeleine Ledivelec. New York, Crown [1963] 36p. chiefly illus. 18cm. (Little bks. on great artists) Biographical sketch in French, English, German. 63-5630 .69
1. Ledivelec, Madeleine. I. Title.

Ledoux, Claude Nicolas, 1736-1806.

LEMAGNY, J. C. 720'.922
Visionary architects: Boulee, Ledoux, Lequeu. [Houston, Tex., Printed by Gulf Print. Co., 1968] 240 p. illus. 23 cm. Catalogue of an exhibition held at the University of St. Thomas, Houston, Tex., Oct. 19, 1967-Jan. 3, 1968, and at four other American museums, Jan. 22-Oct. 29, 1968. Bibliography: p. 235-240. [NA1052.L4] 68-24454
1. Boulee, Etienne Louis, 1728-1799. 2. Ledoux, Claude Nicolas, 1736-1806. 3. Lequeu, Jean Jacques, 1757-ca. 1825. I. Houston, Tex. University of St. Thomas. II. Title.

Ledyard, John, 1751-1789—Juvenile literature.

MANTEL, S. G. 910'.924 B
Explorer with a dream: John Ledyard, by S. G. Mantel. New York, J. Messner [1969] 190 p. 22 cm. Bibliography: p. 183. A biography of the eighteenth-century sailor and explorer who recruited Indian students for Dartmouth, sailed with Captain Cook, developed an Alaskan fur trade, and journeyed on the main continents of the world. [G226.L5M3] 92 69-17429 3.50
1. Ledyard, John, 1751-1789—Juvenile literature. I. Title.

Lee, Andrew Daulton, 1953-

LINDSEY, Robert. 327'.12'0922 B
The Falcon and the Snowman : a true story of friendship and espionage / Robert Lindsey. New York : Simon and Schuster, c1979. 359 p., [8] leaves of plates : ill. ; 24 cm. [UB271.R92L425] 79-9234 ISBN 0-671-24560-0 : 11.95
1. Lee, Andrew Daulton, 1953- 2. Boyce, Christopher John. 3. Spies—United States—Biography. 4. Espionage, Russian—United States. I. Title. BIP

Lee, Ann, 1736-1784.

CAMPION, Nardi Reeder. 289.8'092'4 B
Ann the Word : the life of Mother Ann Lee, founder of the Shakers / Nardi Reeder Campion. 1st ed. Boston : Little, Brown, c1976. xiv, 208 p. : ill. ; 21 cm. Includes index. Bibliography: p. 197-200. [BX9793.L4C35] 76-6568 ISBN 0-316-12767-1 lib.bdg. : 6.95
1. Lee, Ann, 1736-1784. 2. Shakers—History. I. Title. BIP

EVANS, Frederick William, 1808-1893. 289.8
Shakers : compendium of the origin, history, principles, rules and regulations, government, and doctrines of the United Society of Believers in Christ's Second Appearing ... / by F. W. Evans. 4th ed. New York : AMS Press, 1975. 190 p. ; 19 cm. (Communal societies in America) Reprint of the 1867 ed. published in New Lebanon, N.Y. Bibliography: p. [188]-190. [BX9771.E85 1975] 72-2985 ISBN 0-404-10747-8
1. Shakers. 2. Shakers—Biography. 3. Lee, Ann, 1736-1784. 4. Lee, William, 1740-1784. 5. Whittaker, James, 1751-1787. 6. Hocknell, John, 1723?-1799. 7. Meacham, Joseph, 1742-1796. 8. Wright, Lucy, 1760-1821. I. Title: Compendium of the origin, history, principles, rules and regulations, government, and doctrines of the United Society of Believers in Christ's Second Appearing. BIP

JOY, Arthur F 1910- 922.8873
The queen of the Shakers. Minneapolis, T. S. Denison [1960] 272p. 22cm. Includes bibliography. [BX9793.L4J6] 60-12060
1. Lee, Ann, 1736-1784. I. Title.

MARSHALL, Mary, b.1780. 289.8
A portraiture of Shakerism. New York, AMS Press [1972] xvi, 446 p. 22 cm. Reprint of the 1822 ed. [BX9773.M3A3 1972] 70-134420 ISBN 0-404-08461-3 17.50
1. Lee, Ann, 1736-1784. 2. Shakers. I. Title. BIP

SHAKERS. 289.8'092'2 B
Testimonies of the life, character, revelations, and doctrines of Mother Ann Lee, and the elders with her, through whom the word of eternal life was opened in this day, of Christ's second appearing, collected from living witnesses, in union with the church. 2d ed. New York : AMS Press, 1975. 302 p. ; 19 cm. (Communal societies in America) Reprint of the 1888 ed. printed by Weed, Parsons, Albany, N.Y. [BX9793.L4S5 1975] 72-2994 ISBN 0-404-10756-7 : 16.00
1. Lee, Ann, 1736-1784. 2. Lee, William, 1740-1784. 3. Whittaker, James, 1751-1787. 4. Shakers. I. Title: Testimonies of the life, character, revelations, and doctrines of Mother Ann Lee ... BIP

Lee, Archy.

LAPP, Rudolph M. 343'.5
Archy Lee; a California fugitive slave case, by Rudolph M. Lapp. [San Francisco] Book Club of California, 1969. xii, 67 p. col. illus., facsims., ports. 24 cm. (The Book Club of California publication no. 131) "500 copies." "Sources": p. xii. [E450.L4L3] 77-7763
1. Lee, Archy. I. Series: Book Club of California, San Francisco. Publication no. 131

Lee, Arthur, 1740-1792.

LEE, Richard Henry, 1794-1865. 973.32'0924 B
Life of Arthur Lee, LL.D., joint commissioner of the United States to the court of France, and sole commissioner to the courts of Spain and Prussia, during the Revolutionary War; with his political and literary correspondence and his papers on diplomatic and political subjects, and the affairs of the United States during the same period. Boston, Wells and Lilly, 1829. Freeport, N.Y., Books for Libraries Press [1969] 2 v. 23 cm. (Select bibliographies reprint series) [E249.L49 1969] 69-18528
1. Lee, Arthur, 1740-1792. 2. United States—History—Revolution, 1775-1783—Sources. 3. United States—Foreign relations—Revolution, 1775-1783. I. Lee, Arthur, 1740-1792.

Lee Boo, d. 1784.

THE History of Prince Lee Boo, to which is added, The life of Paul Cuffee, a man of colour, also, Some account of John Sackhouse, the Esquimaux. Dublin, Printed by C. Crooks, 1820. Miami, Fla., Mnemosyne Pub. Co. [1969] 180 p. illus. 23 cm. [G525.H58 1969] 72-89405 910.4'53
1. Lee Boo, d. 1784. 2. Cuffe, Paul, 1759-1817. 3. Sackhouse, John, 1797-1819.

Lee, Bruce, 1940-1973.

*BLOCK, Alex Ben. 791.43'028'0924 [B]
The legend of Bruce Lee [by] Alex Ben Block. [New York, Dell, 1974] 171 p. photos 18 cm. Bibliography: p. 170-171. [PN2287] 1.25 (pbk.)
1. Lee, Bruce, 1940-1973. I. Title.

LEE, Linda. 791.43'028'0924 B
Bruce Lee : the man only I knew / by Linda Lee. New York : Warner Paperback Library, 1975. 207 p. : ill. ; 18 cm. [PN2878.L4L4] 75-312238 ISBN 0-446-78774-4 pbk. : 1.50
1. Lee, Bruce, 1940-1973. BIP

UYEHARA, M. 791.43'028'0924 B
Bruce Lee—farewell, my friend / by M. Uyehara. Burbank, Calif. : Ohara Publications, c1976. [77] p. : ill. ; 28 cm. (A collectors series) [PN2878.L4U9] 76-25359 3.95
1. Lee, Bruce, 1940-1973. 2. Actors—Hongkong—Biography. I. Title. BIP

Lee, Charles, 1731-1782.

PATTERSON, Samuel White, 1883- 923.573
Knight errant of liberty; the triumph and tragedy of General Charles Lee. New York, Lantern Press [1958] 287p. illus. 22cm. Includes bibliography. [E207.L47P35] 58-5874
1. Lee, Charles, 1731-1782. I. Title.

THAYER, Theodore George, 1904- 973.3'34'0924 B
The making of a scapegoat : Washington and Lee at Monmouth / Theodore Thayer. Port Washington, N.Y. : Kennikat Press, 1976. viii, 124 p. : ports. ; 23 cm. (Series in American studies) (Kennikat Press national university publications) On spine: Washington and Lee at Monmouth. Includes index. Bibliography: p. 115-120. [E207.L47T46] 76-7477 ISBN 0-8046-9139-8 : 9.95
1. Lee, Charles, 1731-1782. 2. Monmouth, Battle of, 1778. I. Title. II. Title: Washington and Lee at Monmouth.

Lee, Daniel.

COULTER, Ellis Merton, 1890- 630'.92'4 B
Daniel Lee, agriculturist; his life North and South, by E. Merton Coulter. Athens, University of Georgia Press [1972] ix, 165 p. illus. 25 cm. Bibliography: p. 154-157. [S417.L4C68] 79-188568 ISBN 0-8203-0285-6 6.00
1. Lee, Daniel. BIP

Lee, Ettie.

STEWART, Ora (Pate) 1910- 353.008'5
Tender apples; a biography of Ettie Lee. Illus. by Adell Reese Palmer. Salt Lake City, Deseret Book Co., 1965. xiii, 337 p. illus., port. 24 cm. [LA2317.L44S8] 65-27490
1. Lee, Ettie. I. Title.
distributed by longman, new york

Lee family.

ORR, Lucinda Lee. 975.5'2'030924 B
Journal of a young lady of Virginia : Lucinda Lee, 1787. [s.l. ; s.n.] c1976 (Richmond : Whittet and Shepperson) 57 p. : ill. ; 19 cm. Includes index. [F230.O75 1976] 76-150866
1. Lee family. 2. Orr, Lucinda Lee. 3. Virginia—Social life and customs. 4. Virginia—Biography. I. Title.

Lee, Gypsy Rose,

LEE, Gypsy Rose, 1914- 927.91
Gypsy, a memoir. [New York, Dell, 1962, c.1957] 319p. 16cm. (3340) .60 pap.,
I. Title.

LEE, Gypsy Rose, 1914- 927.91
Gypsy, a memoir. [1st ed.] New York, Harper [1957] 337 p. illus. 22 cm. [PN2287.L29A3] 57-6129
I. Title.

LEE, Gypsy Rose, 1914- 927.91
Gypsy, a memoir. [1st ed.] New York, Harper [1957] 337p. illus. 22cm. [PN2287.L29.A3] 57-6129
I. Title.

Lee, Harper Baylor, 1884-1941.

HAIL, Marshall. 927.9182
Knight in the sun; Harper B. Lee, first Yankee matador. With illus. by Tom Lea. [1st ed.] Boston, Little, Brown [1962] 234 p. illus. 22 cm. [GV1108.L4H3] 62-13910
1. Lee, Harper Baylor, 1884-1941. I. Title.

Lee, Helen Jackson.

LEE, Helen Jackson. 974.9'66'040924 B
Nigger in the window / Helen Jackson Lee. 1st ed. Garden City, N.Y. : Doubleday, 1978. 239 p. ; 22 cm. [F144.T79N44] 76-54016 ISBN 0-385-07142-6 : 7.95
1. Lee, Helen Jackson. 2. Afro-American women—Employment—New Jersey—Trenton. 3. Discrimination in employment—New Jersey—Trenton. 4. Trenton—Social conditions. 5. Afro-Americans—New Jersey—Trenton—Biography. I. Title. BIP

Lee, Henry, 1756-1818.

GERSON, Noel Bertram, 1914- 357.10924
Light-Horse Harry; a biography of Washington's great cavalryman, General Henry Lee, by Noel B. Gerson. Garden City, N. Y., Doubleday, 1966. 257 p. port. 22 cm. Bibliography: p. [245]-248. [E207.L5G4] 66-17424
1. Lee, Henry, 1756-1818. I. Title.

GERSON, Noel Bertram, 1914- 357.10924 [B]
Light-Horse Harry, a biography of Washington's great cavalryman, General Henry Lee [by] Noel B. Gerson. New York, Ballantine Books [1974, c1966] 241 p. 18 cm. (A Mockingbird book) [E207.L5G4] ISBN 0-345-24073-1. 1.50 (pbk.)
1. Lee, Henry, 1756-1818. I. Title.
L.C. card number for original ed.: 66-17424.

Lee, Howard Burton, 1879-

LEE, Howard Burton, 1879- 340'.092'4 B
Lost tales of Appalachia / by Howard B. Lee. Parsons, W. Va. : McClain Print. Co., 1977. xi, 206 p. : ports. ; 23 cm. Includes index. [KF373.L4A3] 74-84256 ISBN 0-87012-193-6 : 8.00
1. Lee, Howard Burton, 1879- 2. Attorneys-general—West Virginia—Biography. I. Title. BIP

lee, Ivy Ledbetter, 1877-1934.

HIEBERT, Ray Eldon 659.20924
Courtier to the crowd; the story of Ivy Lee and the development of public relations. Ames, Iowa State Univ. Pr. [c.1966] xvi, 351p. ports. 24cm. Bibl. [HM263.H48] 66-12838 6.95
1. lee, Ivy Ledbetter, 1877-1934. I. Title.

Lee, Jesse,

LEE, Jesse, 1758-1816. 287'.6'0924 B
Memoir of the Rev. Jesse Lee. With extracts from his journals. New York, Arno Press, 1969. viii, 360 p. 23 cm. (Religion in America) Reprint of the 1823 ed. [BX8495.L4A3 1969] 72-83428

Lee, John Alexander, 1891-

OLSSEN, Erik. 993.103'092'4 B
John A. Lee / Erik Olssen. Dunedin : University of Otago Press, 1977. xii, 223 p., [16] p. of plates : ill., facsim., ports. ; 25 cm. Includes index. Bibliography: p. [213]-216. [DU422.L4O45] 78-302192 ISBN 0-908569-04-1 : 20.00
1. Lee, John Alexander, 1891- 2. New Zealand—Politics and government. 3. Statesmen—New Zealand—Biography.
Distributed by International Pubns. Service, New York, NY 10016 BIP

Lee, John Doyle, 1812-1877.

BROOKS, Juanita, 1898- 922.8373
John Doyle Lee: zealot, pioneer, builder, scapegoat. Glendale, Calif., A. H. Clark Co., 1962[c1961] 404p. illus. 25cm. (Western frontiersmen series, 9) Includes bibliography. [F826.L4753] 61-11284
1. Lee, John Doyle, 1812-1877. I. Title.

Lee, John Theophilus, Sir, 1787- — Juvenile literature.

GARFIELD, Leon. 359'.0092'4 B
Child o'war; the true story of a boy sailor in Nelson's navy. Recreated by Leon Garfield in consultation with David Proctor. Decorations by Antony Maitland. [1st American ed.] New York, Holt, Rinehart and Winston [1972] 128 p. illus. 22 cm. Based on the memoirs of Sir John Theophilus Lee. An account of an early nineteenth-century British naval officer's experiences as a boy sailor serving under Nelson. [DA88.1.L4G37 1972] 92 73-189822 ISBN 0-03-091607-0 4.59
1. Lee, John Theophilus, Sir, 1787- — Juvenile literature. 2. Great Britain—History, Naval—18th century—Juvenile literature. 3. Great Britain—History, Naval—19th century—Juvenile literature. I. Proctor, David. II. Maitland, Antony, 1935- illus. III. Title.

Lee, Johnnie.

EDWARDS, Josephine Cunnington. 248.2'4
"And I John saw." Nashville, Southern Pub. Association [1969] 96 p. 22 cm. [BX6193.L4E3] 79-76850
1. Lee, Johnnie. I. Title.

Lee, Joseph Bracken, 1890-

RUSSELL, George B 923.273
J. Bracken Lee; the taxpayer's champion. [1st ed.] New York, R. Speller [1961] x, 284p. illus., ports. 22cm. Bibliography: p. 280. [F826.L48R8] 61-11075
1. Lee, Joseph Bracken, 1890- 2. Utah—Pol. & govt. I. Title.

Lee, Laurel.

LEE, Laurel. 362.1'9'642
Signs of spring / by Laurel Lee ; illustrated with drawings by the author. New York : Dutton, 1980. p. cm. "A Henry Robbins book." [RC644.L4] 79-20224 ISBN 0-525-20428-8 : 7.95
1. Lee, Laurel. 2. Hodgkin's disease—Biography. 3. Christian life—1960- I. Title. BIP

LEE, Laurel. 616.4'2 B
Walking through the fire : a hospital journal / Laurel Lee. 1st ed. New York : E. P. Dutton, c1977. 113 p. : ill. ; 22 cm. "A Henry Robbins book." [RC644.L42] 76-58416 ISBN 0-525-22955-8 : 6.95
1. Lee, Laurel. 2. Hodgkin's disease—Biography. 3. Pregnancy, Complications of—Biography. I. Title. BIP

Lee, Laurie.

LEE, Laurie. 828.914
The edge of day; a boyhood in the west of England. With drawings by John Ward. New York, Morrow, 1960 [c1959] 275 p. illus. 22 cm. Autobiographical. First published in 1959 under title: Cider with Rosie. [CT788.L415A3 1960] 60-6513
I. Title.

Lee, Mabel, 1886-

LEE, Mabel, 1886- 613.7'045
Memories beyond bloomers, 1924-1954 / Mabel Lee. Washington : American Alliance for Health, Physical Education, and Recreation, 1979, c1978. xvi, 458 p. : ports. ; 24 cm. (AAHPER leaders speak series) Continues Memories of a bloomer girl, 1894-1924. Includes bibliographical references and index. [GV439.L388] 79-110434 16.95
1. Lee, Mabel, 1886- 2. Nebraska. University. 3. Physical education of women—United States—History. 4. Physical education teachers—United States—Biography. I. Title. II. Series: American Alliance for Health, Physical Education, and Recreation. AAHPER leaders speak series. BIP

LEE, Mabel, 1886- 613.7'045
Memories of a bloomer girl, 1894-1924 / Mabel Lee. Washington : American Alliance for Health, Physical Education, and Recreation, c1977. 384 p. : ill. ; 24 cm. (AAHPER leaders speak series) Includes bibliographical references. [GV439.L39] 77-151528 12.50
1. Lee, Mabel, 1886- 2. Physical education for women—United States—History. 3. Physical education teachers—United States—Biography. I. Title. II. Series: American Alliance for Health, Physical Education, and Recreation. AAHPER leaders speak series.
Publisher's address 1201 16th st. N. W. Wash. DC 20036 BIP

Lee, Nelson, b., 1807.

LEE, Nelson, b.,1807. 973'.04'97 S
Three years among the Camanches / Nelson Lee. New York : Garland Pub., 1976. p. cm. (The Garland library of narratives of North American Indian captivities ; v. 75) Reprint of the 1859 ed. published by B. Taylor, Albany. [E85.G2 vol. 75] [E99.C85] 970'.004'97 75-7100 ISBN 0-8240-1699-8 lib.bdg. : 21.00
1. Lee, Nelson, b., 1807. 2. Comanche Indians—Captivities. 3. Indians of North America—Captivities. I. Title. II. Series.

Lee, Patsy (Li) 1936-

GEHRING, Frederic P. 920.7
A child of miracles; the story of Patsy Li, by Frederic P. Gehring, Martin Abramson. New York, Funk & Wagnalls [c.1962] 305p. illus. 22cm. 62-18325 5.00 bds.,
1. Lee, Patsy (Li) 1936- I. Title.

GEHRING, Rev. Frederic P. 920.7
A child of miracles; the story of Patsy Li [by] Frederic P. Gehring, Martin Abramson. Garden City, N.Y., Doubleday [1965, c.1962] 236p. 18cm. (Echo bks., E13) .85 pap.,
1. Lee, Patsy (Li) 1936- I. Title.

Lee, Robert Edward, 1807-1870.

ALEXANDER, Holmes Moss, 1906- FIC
The equivocal men; tales of the establishment, by Holmes M. Alexander. Boxton, Western Islands [1964] xi, 237 p. 21 cm. [PZ3.A37713Eq] [E312.17.A4] 973.00922 64-25260 65-28197
1. Lee, Robert Edward, 1807-1870. I. Title. BIP

BROOKS, William Elizabeth, 1875- 973.7'3'0924 B
Lee of Virginia : a biography / by William E. Brooks. Westport, Conn. : Greenwood Press, 1975, c1932. p. cm. Reprint of the ed. published by Bobbs-Merrill, Indianapolis. Includes index. Bibliography: p. [E467.1.L4B852 1975] 75-16842 ISBN 0-8371-8270 lib.bdg. : 18.50
1. Lee, Robert Edward, 1807-1870. I. Title. BIP

CARTER, Hodding, 1907- 923.573
Robert E. Lee and the road of honor; illustrated by William Hutchinson. New York, Random House [1955] 186 p. illus. 22 cm. (Landmark books [54]) [E467.1.L4C3] 55-5819
1. Lee, Robert Edward, 1807-1870.

COMMAGER, Henry Steele, 1902- 923.573
America's Robert E. Lee [by] Henry Steele Commager and Lynd Ward. Boston, Houghton Mifflin, 1951. 111 p. illus. 25 cm. [E467.1.L4C65] 51-6327
1. Lee, Robert Edward, 1807-1870. I. Ward, Lynd Kendall, 1905- illus. II. Title. BIP

CONNELLY, Thomas Lawrence. 973.7'3'0924 B
The marble man : Robert E. Lee and his image in American society / Thomas L. Connelly. Louisiana pbk. ed. Baton Rouge : Louisiana State University Press, 1978, c1977. p. cm. Includes bibliographical references and index. [E467.1.L4C67 1978] 78-18749 ISBN 0-8071-0474-4 pbk. : 5.95
1. Lee, Robert Edward, 1807-1870. 2. Generals—United States—Biography. I. Title. BIP

CONNELLY, Thomas Lawrence. 973.7'3'0924 B
The marble man, Robert E. Lee and his image in American society / Thomas L. Connelly. 1st ed. New York : Knopf, 1977. xv, 249 p., [4] leaves of plates : ill. ; 25 cm. Includes bibliographical references and index. [E467.1.L4C67 1977] 76-41778 ISBN 0-394-47179-2 : 10.00
1. Lee, Robert Edward, 1807-1870. I. Title.

DAVIS, Jefferson, 1808-1889. 973.730924
Robert E. Lee. Edited and with an introd. and notes by Harold B. Simpson. [1st ed. Hillsboro, Tex.] Hill Junior College Press [1966] xiii, 81 p. ports. 24 cm. Originally published in the January, 1890 issue of The North American review. Bibliography: p. 73-74. [E467.1.L4D34] 66-29652
1. Lee, Robert Edward, 1807-1870. I. Simpson, Harold B., ed.

DOWDEY, Clifford, 1904- 973.730924
Lee. With photos. and with maps by Samuel H. Bryant. [1st ed.] Boston, Little, Brown [1965] xiv, 781 p. illus., maps, ports. 24 cm. Includes bibliographies. [E467.1L4D6] 65-20743
1. Lee, Robert Edward, 1807-1870.

EARLE, Peter, 1937- 973.7'3'0924 B
Robert E. Lee. New York, Saturday Review Press [1974, c1973] 224 p. illus. 26 cm. Bibliography: p. 218-219. [E467.1.L4E12 1974] 73-75722 ISBN 0-8415-0256-0 12.50
1. Lee, Robert Edward, 1807-1870.

EATON, Jeanette. 923.573
Lee, the gallant general; illustrated by Harry Daugherty. New York, Morrow, 1953. 72 p. illus. 22 cm. (Morrow junior books) [E467.1.L4E23] 53-6658
1. Lee, Robert Edward, 1807-1870.

EMERY, Russell Guy, 1908- 923.573
Robert E. Lee. New York, Messner [1951] 176 p. 22 cm. [E467.1.L4E5] 51-9830
1. Lee, Robert Edward, 1807-1870.

FISHWICK, Marshall William 923.573
Lee after the war. New York, Dodd [c.1963] 242p. illus. 22cm. Bibl. 63-10239 4.00
1. Lee, Robert Edward, 1807-1870. I. Title. BIP

FISHWICK, Marshall William. 973.8'092'4 B
Lee after the war [by] Marshall W. Fishwick. Westport, Conn., Greenwood Press [1973, c1963] xi, 242 p. illus. 22 cm. Reprint of the ed. published by Dodd, Mead, New York. Bibliography: p. 231-233. [E467.1.L4F5 1973] 73-7102 ISBN 0-8371-6911-9 12.00
1. Lee, Robert Edward, 1807-1870. I. Title.

FREEMAN, Douglas Southall, 1886-1953. 923.573
Lee. New York, Scribner [1961] xvii, 601 p. illus., ports., maps. 24 cm. "An abridgement in one volume, by Richard Harwell, of the four-volume R. E. Lee." [E467.1.L4F85] 61-11585
1. Lee, Robert Edward, 1807-1870. I. Harwell, Richard Barksdale, ed.

FREEMAN, Douglas Southall, 1886-1953. 973.573
Lee of Virginia. New York, Scribner [1958] xi, 243 p. illus. 24 cm. [E467.1.L4F825] 58-11643
1. Lee, Robert Edward, 1807-1870. I. Title.

GRIGGS, Edward Howard, 1868-1951. 973
American statesmen; an interpretation of our history and heritage. Freeport, N.Y., Books for Libraries Press [1970] 364 p. 24 cm. (Essay index reprint series) Reprint of the 1927 ed. Contents.Contents.—Washington: the first American.—Franklin: the practical American.—Jefferson: the democratic American.—Hamilton and the making of our government.—Lee: the American warrior.—Lincoln: the prophetic American.—Bibliography: p. 348-355. [E176.G852 1970] 76-121474
1. Washington, George, Pres. U.S., 1732-1799. 2. Franklin, Benjamin, 1706-1790. 3. Jefferson, Thomas, Pres. U.S., 1743-1826. 4. Hamilton, Alexander, 1757-1804. 5. Lee, Robert Edward, 1807-1870. 6. Lincoln, Abraham, Pres. U.S., 1809-1865. 7. Statesmen, American. I. Title. BIP

LEE, Fitzhugh, 1835-1905. 923.573
General Lee. With an introd. by Philip Van Doren Stern. Greenwich, Conn., Fawcett Publications [1961] 416p. illus. 18cm. (Premier Civil War classics) [E467.1.L4L4 1961] 61-685
1. Lee, Robert Edward, 1807-1870. I. Title.

LEE, Robert Edward, 1807-1870 923.173
The story of Robert E. Lee, as told in his own words and those of his contemporaries. Ed. by Ralston B. Lattimore [Philadelphia, Eastern Natl. Park & Monument Assn.] 1964. viii, 96p. illus. (pt. col.) facsims., ports. (pt. col.) 30cm. (Source bk. ser., no. 1) Bibl. 64-19183 price unreported
1. Lee, Robert Edward, 1807-1870. I. Lattimore, Ralston B., ed. II. Title.

LEE, Robert Edward, 1807-1870. 923.273
The story of Robert E. Lee, as told in his own words and those of his contemporaries. Edited by Ralston B. Lattimore. [1st ed. Washington, Colortone Press] 1964. viii, 96 p. illus. (part col.) facsims., ports (part col.) 30 cm. [Eastern National Park and Monument Association] Source book series, no. 1) Published also in Philadelphia in 1964 by Eastern National Park and Monument Association. Bibliography: p. 94-95. [E467.1.L4L435] 67-7376
1. Lee, Robert Edward, 1807-1870. I. Lattimore, Ralston B., ed. II. Title. III. Series.

LEE, Robert Edward, 1843-1914. 923.573
My father, General Lee. A new ed. of Recollections and letters of General Robert E. Lee, by his son Robert E. Lee, Jr. With a new introd. and Lee chronology by Philip Van Doren Stern. Garden City, N. Y., Doubleday, 1960. xxv, 453 p. illus., ports., facsims. 22 cm. [E467.1.L4L433] 60-11384
1. Lee, Robert Edward, 1807-1870.

MCDOWELL, David. 923.573
Robert E. Lee; illustrated by William Hutchinson. New York, Random House [1953] unpaged. illus. 29cm. [E467.1.I4M13] 53-6289
1. Lee, Robert Edward, 1807-1870. I. Title.

MCMEEKIN, Isabel (McLennan) 1895- 923.573
Robert E. Lee, knight of the South. New York, Dodd, Mead, 1950. viii, 238p. illus., ports. 21cm. Bibliography: p. 233-234. [E467.1.L4M18] 50-10886
1. Lee, Robert Edward, 1807-1870. I. Title.

MCMEEKIN, Isabella (McLennan) 1895- 923.573
Robert E. Lee, knight of the South. New York, Dodd, Mead, 1950. viii. 238 p. illus. ports. 21 cm. Bibliography: p. 233-234. [E467.1.L4M18] 50-10886
1. Lee, Robert Edward, 1807-1870. I. Title.

MAURICE, Frederick Barton, Sir, 1871- 973.7'3'0924 B
Robert E. Lee, the soldier. Freeport, N.Y., Books for Libraries Press [1972] vii, 313 p. maps (part fold.), port. 23 cm. Reprint of the 1925 ed. Bibliography: p. [303] [E467.1.L4M45 1972] 70-37898 ISBN 0-8369-6736-4
1. Lee, Robert Edward, 1807-1870.

MIERS, Earl Schenck, 1910- 923.573
Robert E. Lee; a great life in brief. New York, Random [1961, c.1956] 203p. (Vintage bk., V189) Bibl. .95 pap.,
1. Lee, Robert Edward, 1807-1870. I. Title.

MIERS, Earl Schenck, 1910- 923.573
Robert E. Lee, a great life in brief. [1st ed.] New York, Knopf, 1956. 203p. 19cm. (Great lives in brief, a new series of biographies) --Another issue. Arlington ed. Autographed by the author for the members of the Civil War Book Club.' Includes bibliography. [E467.1.L4M6 1956] 55-9295
1. Lee, Robert Edward, 1807-1870. I. Title.

PORTER, George Alexander, 1942- 923.573
General Robert E. Lee of the Confederacy; a condensation of the life of Robert E. Lee. Illustrated by Dale Lynch. [Pembroke, Mass., 1961] 72p. illus. 23cm. Includes bibliography. [E467.1.L4P6] 61-36533
1. Lee, Robert Edward, 1807-1870. I. Title.

RIKHOFF, Jean. 973.73'0924 B
Robert E. Lee, soldier of the South. Illustrated by Tran Mawicke. New York, Putnam [1968] 96 p. col. illus. 24 cm. (An American pioneer biography) A biography of the general who turned down command of the Union armies because he felt he could not fight against his own state, and became leader of the Confederate forces. [E467.1.L4R55] 92 AC 68
1. Lee, Robert Edward, 1807-1870. I. Mawicke, Tran, illus. II. Title.

RILEY, Franklin Lafayette, 1868-1929, ed. 378.1'12'0924
General Robert E. Lee after Appomattox. Freeport, N.Y., Books for Libraries Press [1971] xiv, 250 p. illus. 23 cm. Reprint of the 1922 ed. [E467.1.L4R57 1971] 72-37353 ISBN 0-8369-6700-3
1. Lee, Robert Edward, 1807-1870. 2. Washington and Lee University, Lexington, Va. I. Title.

SANBORN, Margaret. 973.730924 B
Robert E. Lee. [1st ed.] Philadelphia, Lippincott [1966-67] 2 v. illus., ports. 25 cm. Contents.Contents.—v. 1. A portrait, 1807-1861.—v. 2. The complete man, 1861-1870. Bibliography: v. 2, p. 399-412. [E467.1.L4S26] 66-19989
1. Lee, Robert Edward, 1807-1870.

STERN, Philip Van Doren, 1900- v. 12
Robert E. Lee; the man and the soldier. A pictorial biography by Philip Van Doren Stern. New York, Bonanza Books [c1963] 256 p. illus. 29 cm. 67-1987
1. Lee, Robert Edward, 1807-1870. I. Title.

STERN, Philip Van Doren, 1900- 923.573
Robert E. Lee, the man and the soldier; a pictorial biography. [1st ed.] New York, McGraw Hill [1963] 256 p. illus., ports., maps. 29 cm. [E467.1.L4S83] 63-18544
1. Lee, Robert Edward, 1807-1870.

WAYLAND, John Walter, 1872- 923.573
Robert E. Lee and his family. Staunton, Va., McClure Print, Co., 1951. 104 p. illus. 24 cm. [E467.1.L4W29] 52-21916
1. Lee, Robert Edward, 1807-1870. 2. Lee family. I. Title.

WELLS, Rosa Lee. 923.573
General Lee, a great friend of youth. New York, Vantage Press [c1950] 356 p. illus., ports. 23 cm. Bibliography: p. 352-256. [E467.1.L4W34] 51-1613
1. Lee, Robert Edward, 1807-1870. I. Title.

WHITE, Henry Alexander, 1861-1926. 973.73'0924 B
Robert E. Lee. New York, Greenwood Press [1969] xi, 467 p. illus., ports. 23 cm. (Famous epoch-makers) On spine: Lee and the Southern Confederacy. Reprint of the 1897 ed. published under title: Robert E. Lee and the Southern Confederacy, 1807-1870. Includes bibliographical references. [E467.1.L4W5 1969] 69-14148 ISBN 0-8371-1864-6
1. Lee, Robert Edward, 1807-1870. 2. United States—History—Civil War, 1861-1865—Campaigns and battles. I. Title: Lee and the Southern confederacy. BIP

Lee, Robert Edward, 1807-1870—Juvenile literature.

DANIELS, Jonathan, 1902- 923.573
Robert E. Lee. Illustrated by Robert Frankenburg. Boston. Houghton Mifflin, 1960. 184 p. illus. 22 cm. (North Star books [21]) Includes bibliography. [E467.1.L4D185] 60-5215
1. Lee, Robert Edward, 1807-1870—Juvenile literature.

GRANT, Matthew G. 973.7'3'0924 B
Robert E. Lee; the South's great general [by] Matthew G. Grant. Illustrated by John Keely. [Mankato, Minn., Creative Education; distributed by Childrens Press, Chicago, 1974] 31 p. illus. (part col.) 25 cm. (His Gallery of great Americans series. War heroes of America) An easy-to-read biography of the leader of the Confederate forces in the Civil War. [E467.1.L4G58] 92 73-18078 ISBN 0-87191-302-X 3.95
1. Lee, Robert Edward, 1807-1870—Juvenile literature. I. Keely, John, illus. II. Title.

GRAVES, Charles Parlin, 1911-1972. 92 (J)
Robert E. Lee, hero of the South. Illustrated by Nathan Goldstein. Champaign, Ill., Garrard Pub. Co. [1964] 96 p. col. illus. 28 cm. (A Discovery Book) [E467 1.L4G64] 64-10125
1. Lee, Robert Edward, 1807-1870—Juvenile literature. I. Title.

RADFORD, Ruby Lorraine, 1891- 973.7'3'0924 B
Robert E. Lee, by Ruby L. Radford. Illustrated by Tran Mawicke. New York, Putnam [1973] 64 p. illus. 23 cm. (A See and read beginning to read biography) A portrait of the Confederate leader for beginning readers. [E467.1.L4R3 1973] 92 73-75829 ISBN 0-399-20329-X 3.39
1. Lee, Robert Edward, 1807-1870—Juvenile literature. I. Mawicke, Tran, illus.

RIKHOFF, Jean. 92 (J)
Robert E. Lee, soldier of the South. Illustrated by Tran Mawicke. New York, Putnam [1968] 96 p. col. illus. 24 cm. (An American pioneer biography) [E467.1.L4R55] 68-15076
1. Lee, Robert Edward, 1807-1870—Juvenile literature.

RODDY, Lee, 1921- 973.7'3'0924 B
Robert E. Lee, Christian general and gentleman / Lee Roddy ; edited by Norma Cournow Camp ; illustrated by A. G. Smith. Milford, Mich. : Mott Media, c1977. p. cm. (The Sowers) Includes index. Bibliography: p. A biography of the leader of the Confederate forces during the Civil War. [E467.1.L4R63] 77-7520 ISBN 0-915134-40-3 pbk. : 3.50
1. Lee, Robert Edward, 1807-1870—Juvenile literature. 2. Confederate States of America. Army—Biography—Juvenile literature. 3. Generals—Confederate States of America—Biography—Juvenile literature. I. Smith, Albert Gray, 1945- II. Title.

TROW, George Swift. 973.73'0924 B
Meet Robert E. Lee. Illustrated by Ted Lewin. New York, Random House [1969] 64 p. col. illus., col. map. 22 cm. A simple biography of the general who led the Confederate Army in the Civil War. [E467.1.L4T77] 92 69-18097
1. Lee, Robert Edward, 1807-1870—Juvenile literature. I. Lewin, Ted, illus. II. Title. BIP

Lee, Robert Greene, 1886

HUSS, John Ervin, 1910- 286'.0924 B
Robert G. Lee; the authorized biography, by John E. Huss. Grand Rapids, Zondervan Pub. House [1967] 252 p. illus., ports. 23 cm. Bibliography: p. 245. [BX6495.L39H8] 67-24828
1. Lee, Robert Greene, 1886-

LEE, Robert Greene, 1886- 286.'1'0924 B
Payday everyday / Robert G. Lee. Nashville : Broadman Press, [1975] c1974. 146 p. : ill. ; 21 cm. [BX6495.L39A36 1975] 74-80721 ISBN 0-8054-5548-5 : 3.95
1. Lee, Robert Greene, 1886- I. Title. BIP

Lee, Roger Irving,

LEE, Roger Irving, 1881- 926.1
The happy life of a doctor. [1st ed.] Boston, Little, Brown [1956] 278 p. illus. 22 cm. [R154.L36A3] 56-10644
I. Title.

Lee, Rossie.

SAMS, Jessie (Bennett) 920.7
White mother. [1st ed.] New York, McGraw-Hill [1957] 241p. 21cm. Autobiographical. [CT275.L344S3] 57-12911
1. Lee, Rossie. I. Title.

Lee, Russell, 1903-

LEE, Russel, 1903- 779'.92'4
Russell Lee, photographer / F. Jack Hurley ; introd. by Robert Coles. Dobbs Ferry, N.Y. : Morgan & Morgan, c1978. 206 p. : ill. ; 24 x 30 cm. Bibliography: p. 204-206. [TR820.5.L42] 78-61494 ISBN 0-87100-151-9 : 25.00
1. Lee, Russell, 1903- 2. Photography, Documentary. 3. Photographers—United States—Biography. I. Hurley, Forrest Jack. II. Title.

Lee, Samuel E.

LEE, Samuel E. 976.3 B
Recollections of Country Joe / by S. E. Lee. Gretna, La. : Pelican Pub. Co., 1976. 104 p. ; 21 cm. [CT275.L346A33] 75-31650 ISBN 0-88289-040-9 : 5.95
1. Lee, Samuel E. I. Title. BIP

Lee, William, d. 1610?

GRASS, Milton N. 677'.661'0924 B
Stockings for a queen; the life of the Rev. William Lee, the Elizabethan inventor [by] Milton and Anna Grass. [1st American ed.] South Brunswick, A. S. Barnes [1969, c1967] xvi, 188 p. illus., facsims., ports. 22 cm. Bibliography: p. 173-180. [TS1440.L4G7 1969] 69-14886 5.95
1. Lee, William, d. 1610? I. Grass, Anna, joint author. II. Title.

GRASS, Milton N. 677'.661'0924 (B)
Stockings for a queen: the life of the Rev. William Lee, the Elizabethan inventor [by] Milton and Anna Grass. London, Heinemann, 1967. xvi, 188p. illus., 16 plates (incl. ports., map, facsims.), diagrs. 23cm. Illus. on endpapers. Bibl. [TS1440.L4G7] 67-105059 7.00
1. Lee, William, d. 1610? I. Grass, Anna, joint author. II. Title.
American distributor: Verry, Mystic, Conn.

Lee, William, 1740-1784.

EVANS, Frederick William, 1808-1893. 289.8
Shakers : compendium of the origin, history, principles, rules and regulations, government, and doctrines of the United Society of Believers in Christ's Second Appearing ... / by F. W. Evans. 4th ed. New York : AMS Press, 1975. 190 p. ; 19 cm. (Communal societies in America) Reprint of the 1867 ed. published in New Lebanon, N.Y. Bibliography: p. [188]-190. [BX9771.E85 1975] 72-2985 ISBN 0-404-10747-8
1. Shakers. 2. Shakers—Biography. 3. Lee, Ann, 1736-1784. 4 Lee, William, 1740-1784. 5. Whittaker, James, 1751-1787. 6. Hocknell, John, 1723?-1799. 7. Meacham, Joseph, 1742-1796. 8. Wright, Lucy, 1760-1821. I. Title: Compendium of the origin, history, principles, rules and regulations, government, and doctrines of the United Society of Believers in Christ's Second Appearing. BIP

SHAKERS. 289.8'092'2 B
Testimonies of the life, character, revelations, and doctrines of Mother Ann Lee, and the elders with her, through whom the word of eternal life was opened in this day, of Christ's second appearing, collected from living witnesses, in union with the church. 2d ed. New York : AMS Press, 1975. 302 p. ; 19 cm. (Communal societies in America) Reprint of the 1888 ed. printed by Weed, Parsons, Albany, N.Y. [BX9793.L4S5 1975] 72-2994 ISBN 0-404-10756-7 : 16.00
1. Lee, Ann, 1736-1784. 2. Lee, William, 1740-1784. 3. Whittaker, James, 1751-1787. 4. Shakers. I. Title: Testimonies of the life, character, revelations, and doctrines of Mother Ann Lee ... BIP

Lee, Y. M., 1871-1951.

JUAN, Ellen (Li) 922.351
Intangible inheritance, a lyrical memoir. New York, Pageant Press [c.1960] 100p. 21cm. 60-4268 2.50
1. Lee, Y. M., 1871-1951. I. Title.

JUAN, Ellen (Li) 1915- 922.351
Intangible inheritance, a lyrical memoir. [1st ed.] New York, Pageant Press [1960] 100p. 21cm. [BX5680.3.Z8L43] 60-4268
1. Lee, Y. M., 1871-1951. I. Title.

Leeds, Paul, 1869-1958.

JOHNSON, Kathryn S. 922.573
Patteran; the life and works of Paul Leeds, by Kathryn S. Johnson and Paul Leeds. San Antonio, Naylor Co. [1964] xi, 162 p. illus., fold. map (on lining papers) ports. 22 cm. Book 2 (p. 89-152) consists of memoirs written by Paul Leeds and edited by the author. [BX7260.L42] 64-25607
1. Leeds, Paul, 1869-1958. 2. Koasati Indians — Missions. I. Leeds, Paul, 1869-1958. II. Title.

JOHNSON, Kathryn S. 922.573
Patteran; the life and works of Paul Leeds, by Kathryn S. Johnson, Paul Leeds. San Antonio, Naylor [c.1964] xi, 162p. illus., fold map (on lining paps.) ports. 22cm. Bk. 2 (p.89-152) consists of memoirs written by Paul Leeds, ed. by the author. 64-25607 4.95 bds.,
1. Leeds, Paul, 1869-1958. 2. Koasati Indians—Missions. I. Leeds, Paul, 1869-1958. II. Title.

Leen, Edward, 1885-1944.

O'CARROLL, Michael. 922.2415
Edward Leen, c. s. sp. Wesminster, Md., Newman Press, 1953. 278p. illus. 22cm. [BX4705.L464O3 1953] 53-7494
1. Leen, Edward, 1885-1944. I. Title.

Lees-Milne, James.

LEES-MILNE, James. 720'.924 B
Another self. With a wood engraving by Reynolds Stone. [1st American ed.] New York, Coward-McCann [1970] vii, 157 p. illus., ports. 22 cm. Autobiographical. [N7483.L4A3] 70-129177 4.95
I. Title.

LEESMILNE, James 828'.9'1403 B
Ancestral voices / James Lees-Milne. New York : Scribner, 1978. x, 301 p. ; 23 cm. Autobiographical. Continued by: Prophesying peace. Includes bibliographical references and index. [NA2599.8.L43A2 1975] 77-92997 ISBN 0-684-15647-4 : 10.95
1. Lees-Milne, James. 2. Architectural historians—Great Britain—Biography. I. Title. BIP

LEES-MILNE james. 828'.9'1403 B
Prophesying peace / James Lees-Milne. New York : Scribner, 1978. 253 p. : port. ; 23 cm. Includes index. [NA2599.8.L43A2 1977b] 77-92996 ISBN 0-684-15646-6 : 10.95
1. Lees-Milne, James. 2. Architectural historians—Great Britain—Biography. I. Title.

Leeth, John, 1755-1832.

LEETH, John, 1755- 973'.04'97 S
1832.
A short biography of John Leeth. New York : Garland Pub., 1977. 90 p. ; 19 cm. (The Garland library of narratives of North American Indian captivities ; v. 47) Reprint of the 1883 ed. published by R. Clarke, Cincinnati. Issued with the reprint of the 1830 ed. of The contrast. New York, 1977. [E85.G2 vol. 47] [E87] 978'.004'97 B 77-1139 25.00
1. Leeth, John, 1755-1832. 2. Indians of North America—Captivities. 3. Northwest, Old—History—To 1775—Sources. 4. Indians of North America—Northwest, Old. 5. United States—Biography. I. Title. II. Series.

LEETH, John, 1755-1832. 970.4'8 B
A short biography of John Leeth, with an account of his life among the Indians. Reprinted from the original ed. of 1831 with introd. by Reuben Gold Thwaites. New York, B. Blom, 1972. 70 p. 18 cm. Half-title: Leeth's narrative. Reprint of the 1904 ed., issued in series: Narratives of captivities. Includes reproduction of original t.p.: A short biography of John Leeth, giving a brief account of his travels and sufferings among the Indians for eighteen years. Together with his religious exercises, from his own relation, by Ewel Jeffries. Lancaster, Ohio, Printed at the Gazette office, 1831. [E87.L49 1972] 74-180034 12.50
1. Leeth, John, 1755-1832. 2. Indians of North America—Captivities. 3. Northwest, Old—History. 4. Indians of North America—Northwest, Old. I. Jeffries, Ewel. II. Series: Narratives of captivities.

Leeuwenhoek, Anthony van, 1632-1723.

PAYNE, Alma Smith. 92 (J)
Discoverer of the unseen world; a biography of Antoni van Leeuwenhoek. Illustrated by Donn Albright. Cleveland, World Pub. Co. [1966] 159 p. illus. 21 cm. [QH31.L55P3] 66-31252
1. Leeuwenhoek, Anthony van, 1632-1723. I. Title.

SCHIERBEEK, Abraham 925.9
Measuring the invisible world; the life and works of Antoni van Leeuwenhoek. With a biographical chapter by Maria Rooseboom. London, New York, Abelard-Schuman [c.1959] 223p. (bibl.) illus. 23cm. (The Life of science library, 37) 59-13233 5.00
1. Leeuwenhoek, Anthony van, 1632-1723. I. Title.

Lefevre, Edwin, 1871-1943.

LEFEVRE, Edwin, 332.6'092'4 B
1871-1943.
The making of a stockbroker / Edwin Lefevre. New York : Arno Press, 1975, c1925. 341 p. ; 22 cm. (Wall Street and the security markets) Reprint of the 1930 ed. published by Doubleday, Doran, Garden City, N.Y. [HG172.L43A32 1975] 75-2645 ISBN 0-405-06970-7 : 19.00
1. Lefevre, Edwin, 1871-1943. 2. Capitalists and financiers—United States—Correspondence, reminiscences, etc. I. Title. II. Series. BIP

Leffman, Lewis, 1798?-1885.

LOKER, Donald E. 917.47'98'008 S
Lewis Leffman, ordnance sergeant, United States Army, by Donald E. Loker. [Lockport, N.Y., Niagara County Historical Society] 1974. xvi, 64 p. illus. 23 cm. (Occasional contributions of the Niagara County Historical Society, no. 22) Includes bibliographical references. [F127.N5N5 no. 22] [U53.L4] 917.47'98'0330924 B 74-170457
1. Leffman, Lewis, 1798?-1885. 2. Niagara Co., N.Y.—Biography. I. Series: Niagara County Historical Society. Occasional contributions, no. 22.

LeFlore, Ron.

LEFLORE, Ron. 796.352'092'4 B
Breakout : from prison to the big leagues / by Ron LeFlore with Jim Hawkins. 1st ed. New York : Harper & Row, c1978. viii, 180 p., [4] leaves of plates : ill. ; 24 cm. "An Associated Features book." Includes index. [GV865.L37A33 1978] 77-3759 ISBN 0-06-012552-7 : 8.95
1. LeFlore, Ron. 2. Baseball players—United States—Biography. 3. Prisoners—United States—Biography. I. Hawkins, Jim, joint author. II. Title.

LeFlore, Ron—Juvenile literature.

BURCHARD, 796.357'092'4 B
Marshall.
Sports hero Ron LeFlore / by Marshall Burchard. New York : Putnam, 1979. p. cm. (Sports hero biography) A biography of the Detroit Tiger whose baseball career began on a team for a state prison. [GV865.L37B87] 78-31111 ISBN 0-399-61134-7 lib.bdg. : 5.49
1. LeFlore, Ron—Juvenile literature. 2. Detroit. Baseball Club (American League)—Juvenile literature. 3. Baseball players—United States—Biography—Juvenile literature. 4. Prisoners—United States—Biography—Juvenile literature.

Leforge, Thomas H., 1850-1931.

LEFORGE, Thomas H., 1850- 970.3 B
1931.
Memoirs of a White Crow Indian (Thomas H. Leforge) as told by Thomas B. Marquis. With an introd. by Joseph Medicine Crow and Herman J. Viola. Lincoln, University of Nebraska Press [1974, c1928] xx, 356 p. 21 cm. "A Bison book." Reprint of the ed. published by Century Co., New York. [E99.C92L49 1974] 74-6222 ISBN 0-8032-5800-3 3.95 (pbk.).
1. Leforge, Thomas H., 1850-1931. 2. Crow Indians. 3. Indians of North America—Wars—1866-1895. I. Marquis, Thomas Bailey, 1869-1935, ed. II. Title.

Legare, James Matthews, 1823-1859.

DAVIS, Curtis Carroll, 811'.3 B
1916-
That ambitious Mr. Legare; the life of James M. Legare of South Carolina, including a collected edition of his verse. [1st ed.] Columbia, University of South Carolina Press [1971] xvii, 338 p. illus., port. 23 cm. [PS2239.L14Z6] 76-86191 ISBN 0-87249-166-8 9.95
1. Legare, James Matthews, 1823-1859. I. Title.

Legat, Nikolai Gustavovich, 1869-1937.

†HERITAGE of a 792.8'092'4 B
ballet master, Nicolas Legat / compiled and edited by John Gregory, in collaboration with Andre Eglevsky. New York : Dance Horizons, 1977. ix, 114 p. : ill. ; 29 cm. "Exercises at the bar (explanatory notes and music by Nicolas Legat)": p. 100-104; "Exercises in the Centre (explanatory notes and music by Nicolas Legat)": p. 105-110. Includes index. [GV1785.L38H47] 76-49253 ISBN 0-87127-094-3 : 18.50
1. Legat, Nikolai Gustavovich, 1869-1937. 2. Dancers—Biography. 3. Dance teachers—England—Biography. 4. Ballet dancing. I. Gregory, John, 1914- II. Eglevsky, Andre. III. Legat, Nikolai Gustavovich, 1869-1937.

Legends—China.

GILES, Lionel, 1875- 398.2'2'0951
1958, tr.
A gallery of Chinese immortals / selected biographies translated from Chinese sources by Lionel Giles. New York : AMS Press, [1979] p. cm. Reprint of the 1948 ed. published by J. Murray, London, issued in series: The Wisdom of the East series. Includes index. [GR335.G5 1979] 75-36229 ISBN 0-404-14478-0 : 10.50
1. Legends—China. 2. China—Biography. I. Title. II. Series: The Wisdom of the East series.

Legere, J. Roy, 1922-

LEGERE, J. Roy, 282'.092'4 B
1922-
Be my son / J. Roy Legere. Notre Dame, Ind. : Ave Maria Press, c1976. 191 p. : ill. ; 21 cm. Autobiographical. [BX4705.L515A33] 76-41592 ISBN 0-87793-121-6 pbk. : 2.95
1. Legere, J. Roy, 1922- 2. Catholics in New Brunswick—Biography. 3. Catholics in Connecticut—Biography. I. Title. BIP

Legett, Kirvin Kade, 1857-1926.

SPENCE, Vernon 347'.73'14 B
Gladden, 1924-
Judge Legett of Abilene : a Texas frontier profile / by Vernon Gladden Spence ; introd. by Rupert Norval Richardson. 1st ed. College Station : Texas A & M University Press, c1977. xviii, 264 p., [8] leaves of plates : ill. ; 24 cm. (The centennial series of the Association of Former Students, Texas A & M University ; no. 5) Includes index. Bibliography: p. [243]-251. [KF373.L43S66] 77-89508 ISBN 0-89096-041-0 : 11.75
1. Legett, Kirvin Kade, 1857-1926. 2. Judges—Texas—Biography. I. Title. II. Series: Texas. A & M University, College Station. Association of Former Students. The centennial series of the Association of Former Students, Texas A & M University ; no. 5. BIP

Legislative bodies—United States—Biography.

*DOUTH, George. 328.73092
Leaders in profile; the United States Senate. 1975 edition. New York, Sperr and Douth [1975] xx, 923 p. ill. 21 cm. Includes index. The ninety-fourth Congress. [JK1154] 75-1131 ISBN 0-912902-76-0 24.95
1. Legislative bodies—United States—Biography. I. Title.
Pbk. 10.00; ISBN: 0-912902-75-2. Distributed by International Scholarly Book Services.

Legislators.

*HARVEY, Ralph 328.730924.
Autobiography of Hoosier Congressman [Knightstown, Ind, Tri-state Trader, 1975] 163p. 22 cm. [JK1030.] 74-31662 6.00
1. Legislators. I. Title.

Legislators—Alaska—Biography.

ATWOOD, Evangeline. 320.9'2'2
Who's who in Alaskan politics : a biographical dictionary of Alaskan political personalities, 1884-1974 / compiled by Evangeline Atwood and Robert N. DeArmond. 1st ed. Portland, Or. : Published by Binford & Mort for the Alaska Historical Commission, 1977. xiii, 109 p. ; 28 cm. [F903.A88] 77-76025 ISBN 0-8323-0287-2 : 10.00
1. Legislators—Alaska—Biography. 2. Politicians—Alaska—Biography. 3. Alaska—Biography. I. DeArmond, R. N., joint author. II. Alaska Historical Commission. III. Title. BIP

Legislators—Georgia—Biography.

MELLICHAMP, 328'.758'0922 B
Josephine.
Senators from Georgia / by Josephine Mellichamp. Huntsville, Ala. : Strode Publishers, c1976. 304 p. : ill. ; 24 cm. Includes index. Bibliography: p. 300-302. [F285.M44] 75-32113 ISBN 0-87397-082-9 : 12.95
1. Legislators—Georgia—Biography. 2. Georgia—Biography. I. Title. BIP

Legislators—U.S.

CHRISTOPHER, Maurine. 328.73'0922
America's Black congressmen. New York, Crowell [1971] xvi, 283 p. illus., ports. 24 cm. Bibliography: p. 270-273. [E185.96.C5 1971] 70-146280 ISBN 0-690-08585-0 8.95
1. Legislators—U.S. 2. Negroes—Biography. I. Title.

MOSELEY, J. H. 923.273
Sixty years in Congress and twenty-eight out. New York, Vantage Press [c.1960] 99p. illus. 21cm. 60-3728 2.95
1. Legislators—U.S. 2. Negroes—Biog. I. Title.

MOSELEY, J H 1882- 923.273
Sixty years in Congress and twenty-eight out. [1st ed.] New York, Vantage Press [1960] 99p. illus. 22cm. [JK1021.M75] 60-3728
1. Legislators—U. S. 2. Negroes—Biog. I. Title.

Legislators—United States—Biography—Juvenile literature.

LEE, Essie E. 328.73'092'2 B
Women in Congress / Essie E. Lee. New York : J. Messner, c1979. 224 p. : ports. : 22 cm. Includes index. Presents biographies of prominent women in politics, including Bella Abzug, Shirley Chisholm, Millicent Fenwick, Elizabeth Holtzman, Barbara A. Mikulski, and Cardiss Collins. [JK1013.L43] 920 78-31947 ISBN 0-671-32896-4 Lib. bdg. : 8.29
1. Legislators—United States—Biography—Juvenile literature. 2. Women legislators—

United States—Biography—Juvenile literature. I. Title.

Lehar, Ferenc, 1870-1948.

GRUN, Bernard, 1901- 782.8'1'0924 B
Gold and silver; the life and times of Franz Lehar. New York, D. McKay Co. [1970] 300 p. illus., music, ports. 23 cm. Includes bibliographical references. [ML410.L42G85 1970b] 75-16635 8.95
1. Lehar, Ferenc, 1870-1948. I. Title.

Lehi (Book of Mormon character)

HILTON, Lynn M. 289.3'22
In search of Lehi's trail / Lynn M. Hilton, Hope Hilton ; photography by Gerald W. Silver. Salt Lake City : Deseret Book Co., 1977 148 p. : col. ill. ; 29 cm. Includes bibliographical references and index. [BX8627.H53] 76-54478 ISBN 0-87747-620-9 : 9.95
1. Lehi (Book of Mormon character) 2. Book of Mormon—Biography. I. Hilton, Hope A., joint author. II. Title. BIP

Lehmann, Andrew George.

LEHMANN, Andrew George. 928.4
Sainte-Beuve: a portrait of the critic, 1804-1842. Oxford, Clarendon Press, 1962. xvi, 430p. plates, ports. 23cm. 'Select biographical appendix': p.[401]-410. Bibliographical references included in 'Notes' Charles Augustin, 1804-1869. [PQ2391.Z5L25] 62-2346
I. Title.

Lehmann, Herman, 1859-1932.

GREENE, A. C., 1923- 970.3
The last captive, by A. C. Greene. [1st ed.] Austin, Encino Press [1972] xxi, 161 p. illus. 26 cm. "The lives of Herman Lehmann, who was taken by the Indians as a boy from his Texas home & adopted by them; his career as an authentic wild warrior with the Apache & Comanche tribes; his subsequent restoration to the bosom of his family & the difficulties & confusions faced in adjusting his savage training to a civilized society; his experiences carrying him from the time of the scalping knife to the very threshold of our atomic age; together with verifying accounts by members of his family and others who shared some of those extraordinary & historical events." "A combination of Herman's story in his own words and the author's commentary."—dust jacket. Bibliography. p. 161. [E99.A6L443] 72-184838 8.95
1. Lehmann, Herman, 1859-1932. 2. Apache Indians. 3. Comanche Indians. I. Lehmann, Herman, 1859-1932. II. Title. BIP

Lehmann, John,

LEHMANN, John, 1907- 821'.9'12 B
In my own time; memoirs of a literary life. [1st ed.] Boston, Little, Brown [1969] xv, 558 p. illus., ports. 25 cm. "An Atlantic Monthly Press book." Originally published separately. Contents.Contents.—The whispering gallery.—I am my brother.—The ample proposition. [PR6023.E4Z5] 69-16967 15.00
I. Title.

LEHMANN, John, 1907- 928.2
The whispering gallery: autobiography I [1st American ed.] New York, Harcourt, Brace [1955] 342p. illus. 22cm. [PR6023.FAZ52] 55-10813
I. Title.

LEHMANN, John, 1907- 928.2
The whispering gallery: autobiography: I- London, New York, Longmans, Green [1955- v. illus. 22cm. 'The first volume of [the author's]... autobiography, In my own time.'--Dust Jacket. [PR6023.E4Z52 1955a] 55-4541
I. Title.

Lehmann, John, 1907- —Biography.

LEHMANN, John, 1907- 928.2
I am my brother. New York, Reynal [1960] 326p. illus. 22cm. 'The continuation of the autobiography...[begun] in The whispering gallery. [PR6023.FAZ518] 59-13418
1. Authors—Correspondence, reminiscences, etc. 2. World War, 1939-1945—Gt. Brit.— London. I. Title.

LEHMANN, John, 1907- 821'.9'12 B
In my own time; memoirs of a literary life. [1st ed.] Boston, Little, Brown [1969] xv, 558 p. illus., ports. 25 cm. "An Atlantic Monthly Press book." Originally published separately. Contents.Contents.—The whispering gallery.—I am my brother.—The ample proposition. [PR6023.E4Z5] 69-16967 15.00
I. Title.

LEHMANN, John, 1907- 821'.9'12 B
Thrown to the Woolfs / John Lehmann. 1st American ed. New York : Holt, Rinehart, and Winston, 1979, c1978. xx, 164 p., [4] leaves of plates : ill. ; 22 cm. Includes index. [PR6023.E4Z519 1979] 79-1925 ISBN 0-03-052191-2 : 10.95
1. Lehmann, John, 1907- —Biography. 2. Woolf, Leonard Sidney, 1880-1969—Friends and associates. 3. Woolf, Virginia Stephen, 1882-1941—Friends and associates. 4. Hogarth Press. 5. Authors, English—20th century—Biography. I. Title. BIP

LEHMANN, John, 1907- 928.2
The whispering gallery: autobiography I [1st American ed.] New York, Harcourt, Brace [1955] 342p. illus. 22cm. [PR6023.FAZ52] 55-10813
I. Title.

LEHMANN, John, 1907- 928.2
The whispering gallery: autobiography: I- London, New York, Longmans, Green [1955- v. illus. 22cm. 'The first volume of [the author's]... autobiography, In my own time.'--Dust Jacket. [PR6023.E4Z52 1955a] 55-4541
I. Title.

Lehmann, Lotte.

LEHMANN, Lotte. 782.1'092'4 B
My many lives, translated by Frances Holden. Westport, Conn., Greenwood Press [1974, c1948] p. cm. Reprint of the ed. published by Boosey & Hawkes, New York. [ML420.L33A37 1974] 74 3689 ISBN 0-8371-7361-2 13.75
1. Lehmann, Lotte. I. Holden, Frances, tr. II. Title. BIP

Lehmbruck, Wilhelm, 1881-1919.

HOFF, August, 1892- 730'.924
Wilhelm Lehmbruck; life and work. New York, Praeger [1969] 160 p. plates (part col.) 29 cm. [NB588.L45H613] 71-89603 16.00
1. Lehmbruck, Wilhelm, 1881-1919. I. Title.

Lehr, Harry Symes, 1869-1929.

DECIES, Elizabeth Wharton Drexel Beresford, Baroness. 974.7'1'040924 B
"King Lehr" and the gilded age / Elizabeth Drexel Lehr. New York : Arno Press, 1975, c1935. p. cm. (The Leisure class in America) Reprint of the ed. published by Lippincott, Philadelphia. [CT275.L355D4 1975] 75-1852 20.00
1. Lehr, Harry Symes, 1869-1929. 2. New York (City)—Social life and customs. I. Title. II. Series.

Leibniz, Gottfried Wilhelm, Freiherr von, 1646-1716.

CALINGER, Ronald. 193 B
Gottfried Wilhelm Leibniz / Ronald Calinger ; with an essay by Leibniz on the German language translated by Caryn and Bernhard Wunderlich. Troy, N.Y. : Edwin B. Allen Mathematics Memorial, Rensselaer Polytechnic Institute, 1976. 102 p., [1] leaf of plates : port. ; 22 cm. On spine: Leibniz. Includes index. Bibliography: p. [93]-97. [B2597.C27] 76-55039
1. Leibniz, Gottfried Wilhelm, Freiherr von, 1646-1716. 2. Philosophers—Germany—Biography. 3. German language—Idioms, corrections, errors—Addresses, essays, lectures. BIP

CARR, Herbert Wildon, 1857-1931. 193.1
Leibniz. New York, Dover Publications [1960] 222 p. 21 cm. [B2597.C3 1960] 60-3073
1. Leibniz, Gottfried Wilhelm, Freiherr von, 1646-1716.

Leibowitz, Samuel Simon, 1893-

HARRIS, Robin. 345'.0092'4 B
This is Leibowitz! The true-inside story, as reported exclusively by Robin Harris. [Special ed. New York, National News Dealers, 1953] 46 p. illus. 22 cm. [KF373.L45H3] 75-304099
1. Leibowitz, Samuel Simon, 1893- I. Title.

REYNOLDS, Quentin James, 1902-1965. 343'.0924
Courtroom, the story of Samuel S. Leibowitz. Freeport, N.Y., Books for Libraries Press [1970, c1950] xiv, 419 p. 23 cm. [KF373.L45R4 1970] 77-119943
1. Leibowitz, Samuel Simon, 1893- 2. Trials (Murder)—U.S. 3. Crime and criminals—U.S. I. Title.

Leicester, Robert Dudley, earl of, 1532?-1588..

JENKINS, Elizabeth [Margaret Elizabeth Heald Jenkins] 942.055
Elizabeth and Leicester. New York, Coward [1962, c.1961] 384p. illus. Bibl. 62-7360 5.75
1. Leicester, Robert Dudley, earl of, 1532?-1588.. 2. Elizabeth, Queen of England, 1533-1603. I. Title.

Leider, Frida, 1888-

LEIDER, Frida, 1888- 782.1'092'4 B
Playing my part / Frida Leider ; translated by Charles Osborne. New York : Da Capo Press, 1978, c1966. 217 p., [7] leaves of plates : ill. ; 22 cm. (Da Capo Press music reprint series) Translation of Das war mein Teil. Reprint of the ed. published by Calder & Boyars, London. Includes index. Discography: p. 211-214. [ML420.L34A33 1978] 77-26171 ISBN 0-306-77535-2 : 19.50
1. Leider, Frida, 1888- 2. Singers—Germany—Biography. I. Title.

Leigh, Elizabeth Medora, 1814-1849

TURNEY, Catherine 821.7
Byron's daughter : a biography of Elizabeth Medora Leigh / Catherine Turney New York : Avon ,1977 c1972 xvi, 302 p. ; 18 cm. Includes index Bibliography: pp. 289-291 [PR4382.T85] ISBN 0-380-00880 7 pbk. : 1.75
1. Leigh, Elizabeth Medora, 1814-1849 2. Byron, George Gordon Noel Byron, Baron, 1788-1824 I. Title.
L.C. card no. for 1972 Scribner edition: 79-37206

Leigh-Mallory, George Herbert, 1886-1924.

STYLES, Showell, 1908- 796.5'22'0924
Mallory of Everest. New York, Macmillan [c1967] 174p. illus., maps. 22cm. [DS486.E8S77 1967b] 68-20610 4.95
1. Leigh-Mallory, George Herbert, 1886-1924. 2. Everest, Mount I. Title. BIP

Leigh, Vivien, 1913-1967.

EDWARDS, Anne, 1927- 791'.092'4 B
Vivien Leigh : a biography / by Anne Edwards. New York : Simon and Schuster, c1977. 319 p., [16] leaves of plates : ill. ; 25 cm. Includes index. [PN2598.L46E3] 76-58432 ISBN 0-671-22496-4 : 9.95
1. Leigh, Vivien, 1913-1967. 2. Actors—Great Britain—Biography. BIP

Leigh, William Robinson, 1866-1955.

DUBOIS, June, 1927- 709'.2'4 B
William R. Leigh, artist of frontiers / by June DuBois. Kansas City, Mo. : Lowell Press, [1977] p. cm. [N6537.L423D8] 77-15343 ISBN 0-913504-42-4 : 40.00
1. Leigh, William Robinson, 1866-1955. 2. Artists—United States—Biography. 3. The West in the art. I. Title.

Leighton, Frederic Leighton, Baron, 1830-1896.

BARRINGTON, Emilie Isabel (Wilson) d.1933. 759.2 B
The life, letters and work of Frederic Leighton, by Mrs. Russell Barrington. New York, Macmillan, 1906. [New York, AMS Press, 1973] 2 v. illus. 24 cm. Bibliography: v. 2, p. 381-392. [ND497.L6B3 1973] 70-140032 ISBN 0-404-00659-0 95.00
1. Leighton, Frederic Leighton, baron, 1830-1896.
Two volumes 47.50 ea.

BAYLISS, Wyke, Sir, 1835-1906. 759.2
Five great painters of the Victorian era: Leighton, Millais, Burne-Jones, Watts, Holman Hunt. New York, AMS Press [1971] vii, 159 p. illus., ports. 19 cm. Reprint of the 1902 ed. [ND467.B4 1971] 72-129384 ISBN 0-404-00696-5
1. Leighton, Frederic Leighton, Baron, 1830-1896. 2. Millais, John Everett, Sir, bart., 1829-1896. 3. Burne-Jones, Edward Coley, Sir, bart., 1833-1898. 4. Watts, George Frederick, 1817-1904. 5. Hunt, William Holman, 1827-1910.

Leininger, Regina, b. 1746?

WEISER, Reuben, 1807-1885. 973'.04'97 S
Regina, the German captive / Reuben Weiser. New York : Garland Pub. Co., 1977. 252 p., [5] leaves of plates ; 19 cm. (The Garland library of narratives of North American Indian captivities ; v. 69) Reprint of the 1860 ed. published by T. N. Kurtz, Baltimore. [E85.G2 no. 69] [E90.L45] 973.2'6 B 75-7093 ISBN 0-8240-1693-9 : 25.00
1. Leininger, Regina, b. 1746? 2. Indians of North America—Captivities. 3. United States—Biography. 4. United States—History—French and Indian War, 1775-1763. I. Title. II. Series.

Leinsdorf, Erich, 1912-

LEINSDORF, Erich, 1912- 785'.092'4 B
Cadenza : a musical career / Erich Leinsdorf. Boston ; Houghton Mifflin, 1976. x, 321 p., [8] leaves of plates : ill. ; 24 cm. Includes index. [ML422.L38A3] 76-3553 ISBN 0-395-24401-3 : 10.00
1. Leinsdorf, Erich, 1912- 2. Conductors (Music)—Correspondence, reminiscences, etc. I. Title. BIP

Leinster, Rafaelle Fitzgerald, Duchess of.

LEINSTER, Rafaelle Fitzgerald, Duchess of. 914.2'03'820924 B
The Duchess from Brooklyn [by] Rafaelle, Duchess of Leinster. Foreword by Beverley Nichols. New York, John Day Co. [1973] 198 p. illus. 22 cm. [CT275.L3567A29] 73-177610 6.95
1. Leinster, Rafaelle Fitzgerald, Duchess of. I. Title.

LEINSTER, Rafaelle Fitzgerald, Duchess of. 914.2'03'820924 B
So brief a dream [by] Rafaelle, Duchess of Leinster. Foreword by Beverley Nichols. London, New York, W. H. Allen, 1973. 198 p. illus. 23 cm. [CT275.L3567A3 1973] 74-155260 ISBN 0-491-01290-X
1. Leinster, Rafaelle Fitzgerald, Duchess of. I. Title.

Leiserson, William Morris, 1883-1957.

EISNER, J. Michael 331.15'0924
William Morris Leiserson: a biography [by] J. Michael Eisner. Madison. Univ. of Wis

Pr., 1967. 144p. ports. 25cm. Bibl. [HD8073.L37E35] 67-13557 6.75
1. Leiserson, William Morris, 1883-1957. I. Title.

Leisner, Karl, 1915-1945.

PIES, Otto. 922.243
The victory of Father Karl. Translated from the German by Salvator Attanasio. New York, Farrar, Straus, and Cudahy [1957] 210p. illus. 22cm. Translation of Stephanus heute Karl Leinser, Priester und Opfer. [BX4705.L526P52] 57-7127
1. Leisner, Karl, 1915-1945. I. Title.

Leissner, Cleo Winslett Schiewitz, 1898-

LEISSNER, Cleo 371.1'0092'4 B
Winslett Schiewitz, 1898-
Chalk dust dreams. San Antonio, Naylor Co. [1974] viii, 123 p. 22 cm. [LA2317.L56A33] 74-7492 ISBN 0-8111-0531-8 5.95
1. Leissner, Cleo Winslett Schiewitz, 1898- I. Title.

Leith, Charles Kenneth, 1875-1956.

MCGRATH, Sylvia 550'.924 B
Wallace.
Charles Kenneth Leith; scientific adviser. Madison, University of Wisconsin Press [1971] xii, 255 p. illus., map, ports. 25 cm. Includes bibliographical references. [QE22.L515M3] 73-157394 ISBN 0-299-05970-7 15.00
1. Leith, Charles Kenneth, 1875-1956.

Leiv Eiriksson, d. ca. 1020.

AULAIRE, Ingri 973.1'3 B
(Mortenson) d', 1904-
Leif the lucky, by Ingri & Edgar Parin d'Aulaire. Garden City, N.Y., Doubleday [1965, c1941] 61 p. illus. (part col.) 32 cm. Tells how Leif sailed with his father, Eric the Red, from Iceland to Greenland where he grew up; describes his journeys back to Norway, where he became a Christian and then to the land he called Vinland; and tells how his kinsmen settled in Vinland and met the Indians. [PZ8.1.A86Le5] 92 AC 68
1. Leiv Eiriksson, d. ca. 1020. I. Aulaire, Edgar Parin d', 1898- joint author. II. Title.

WEIR, Ruth Cromer, 1912- 923.9
Leif Ericson, explorer; illustrated by Harve Stein. New York, Abingdon-Cokesbury Press [1951] 127 p. illus. 21 cm. [E105.W4] 51-12750
1. Leiv Eiriksson, d. ca. 1020.

Leiv Eiriksson, d. ca.1020—Juvenile literature.

GRANT, Matthew G. 973.1'3'0924 B
Leif Ericson; explorer of Vinland, [by] Matthew G. Grant. Illustrated by Dick Brude. [Mankato, Minn., Creative Education; distributed by Childrens Press, Chicago, 1974] 29 p. illus. (part col.) 25 cm. (His Gallery of Great Americans series. Explores in America) A brief account of the life and discoveries of the Norse explorer who became one of the first white men to visit America. [E105.G76] 92 73-14531 ISBN 0-87191-278-3 3.95
1. Leiv Eiriksson, d. ca.1020—Juvenile literature. I. Brude, Dick, illus. II. Title.

Leland, Charles Godfrey,

LELAND, Charles 070.9'24 B
Godfrey, 1824-1903.
Memoirs, by Charles Godfrey Leland (Hans Breitmann) New York, Appleton, 1893. Detroit, Gale Research Co., 1968. x, 439 p. port. 23 cm. (Library of lives & letters) [PS2243.A4 1968] 68-22036

Leland, Charles Godfrey, 1824-1903.

LELAND, Charles 070.9'24 B
Godfrey, 1824-1903.
Memoirs, by Charles Godfrey Leland (Hans Breitmann) New York, Appleton, 1893. Detroit, Gale Research Co., 1968. x, 439 p. port. 23 cm. (Library of lives & letters) [PS2243.A4 1968] 68-22036

PENNELL, Elizabeth 070'.924 B
(Robins) 1855-1936.
Charles Godfrey Leland; a biography. Freeport, N.Y., Books for Libraries Press [1970] 2 v. illus., facsims., ports. 23 cm. Reprint of the 1906 ed. Bibliography: v. 2, p. [429]-433. [PS2243.P4 1970] 76-140370 ISBN 0-8369-5613-3
1. Leland, Charles Godfrey, 1824-1903. BIP

Leland, Henry M., b. 1843.

LELAND, Ottilie 629.22'22'0924 B
M.
Master of precision : Henry M. Leland / Mrs. Wilfred C. Leland, with Minnie Dubbs Millbrook ; with an introd. by Allan Nevins and Frank E. Hill. Westport, Conn. : Greenwood Press, 1975, c1966. 296 p., [8] leaves of plates : ill. ; 22 cm. Reprint of the ed. published by Wayne State University Press, Detroit. Includes bibliographical references and index. [TL140.L4L4 1975] 73-15315 ISBN 0-8371-7192-X lib.bdg. : 16.25
1. Leland, Henry M., b. 1843. I. Millbrook, Minnie Dubbs, joint author. II. Title. BIP

Leland, John, 1 54-1841.

FEARHEILEY, Don M. 922.673
The John Leland story. Nashville, Broadman [c.1964] 123p. 20cm. (Broadman inner circle bk.) 64-15097 1.50 bds.,
1. Leland, John, 1 54-1841. I. Title.

Lelooska, 1934-

FALK, Randolph, 1939- 970'.004'97
Lelooska / by Randolph Falk. Millbrae, Calif. : Celestial Arts, c1976. p. cm. [E99.K9F34] 76-11348 ISBN 0-89087-126-4 pbk. : 7.95
1. Lelooska, 1934- 2. Indians of North America—Northwest coast of North America—Art. 3. Kwakiutl Indians—Biography. 4. Artists—Biography. BIP

Lemay, Harding.

LEMAY, Harding. 812'.5'4 B
Inside, looking out; a personal memoir. [1st ed.] New York, Harper's Magazine Press Book [1971] 273 p. 22 cm. [PS3562.E466Z5] 74-144181 6.95
I. Title. BIP

Lemieux, Jean Paul, 1904-

ROBERT, Guy, 1933- 759.11
Lemieux / Guy Robert ; translated by Jean David Allan. Toronto : Gage Pub., 1978. 303 p. : ill. (some col.) ; 32 cm. Translation of Lemieux. Bibliography: p. 296-301. [ND249.L394R613] 79-309710 ISBN 0-7715-9352-X : 39.50
1. Lemieux, Jean Paul, 1904- I. Lemieux, Jean Paul, 1904- II. Title.
Distributed by Vanguard Press. NYC BIP

Lemke, William, 1878-1950.

BLACKORBY, Edward C. 923.273
Prairie rebel; the public life of William Lemke. Lincoln, Univ. of Neb. Pr. [1964, c.1963] ix, 339p. illus., maps. 24cm. Bibl. 63-14690 6.50
1. Lemke, William, 1878-1950. I. Title.

Lemmon, Jack.

HOLTZMAN, Will. 791.43'028'0924
Jack Lemmon / by Will Holtzman. New York : Pyramid Publications, 1977. 159 p. : ill. ; 20 cm. (A Pyramid illustrated history of the movies) Includes index. Filmography: p. 151-154. [PN2287.L42H6] 77-73159 ISBN 0-515-04291-9 pbk. : 1.95
1. Lemmon, Jack. 2. Moving-picture actors and actresses—United States—Biography. BIP

WIDENER, Don. 791.43'028'0924 B
Lemmon : a biography / Don Widener. New York : Macmillan, 1975. vi, 247 p., [16] leaves of plates : ill. ; 24 cm. Includes index. [PN2287.L42W5] 75-25712 ISBN 0-02-628200-3 : 9.95
1. Lemmon, Jack.

Lemon, Bob, 1920-

MCAULEY, Ed. 927.96357
Bob Lemon, the Work Horse. New York, A. S. Barnes [1951] 25 p. illus. 21 cm. (The Barnes all-star library) [GV865.L4M3] 51-12688
1. Lemon, Bob, 1920-

Lena Pope Home, Fort Worth, Tex.

POPE, Lena 362.7'32'0976453
(Holston) 1881-
A hand on my shoulder; the story of Lena Pope and the home that evolved from her dreams. Fort Worth, Tex., Branch-Smith, 1966. 218 p. illus., ports. 24 cm. [HV885.F6P6] 67-8127
1. Lena Pope Home, Fort Worth, Tex. I. Title.

Lenclos, Anne, called Ninon de, 1620-1705.

COHEN, Edgar H. 944'.033'0924 B
Mademoiselle Libertine; a portrait of Ninon de Lanclos, by Edgar H. Cohen. Boston, Houghton-Mifflin, 1970. xx, 329 p. port. 22 cm. Bibliography: p. [309]-313. [DC130.L5C6] 71-120824 6.95
1. Lenclos, Anne, called Ninon de, 1620-1705. I. Title.

DAY, Lillian, 1893- 920.7
Ninon, a courtesan of quality. [1st ed.] Garden City, N. Y., Doubleday, 1957. 290p. illus. 22cm. [DC130.L5D3] 57-10451
1. Lenclos, Anne, called Ninon de, 1620-1705. I. Title.

Lenin, Vladimir Il'ich, 1870-1924.

ADAMS, Paul. 947.084'1'0924 B
V. I. Lenin / [by] Paul Adams. London : Workers Fight, [1976] [1], 18 p. : ill., ports. ; 21 cm. (A Workers' fight pamphlet) Cover title. [HX314.Z7A33] 76-372589 ISBN 0-9504710-3-8 : £0.05
1. Lenin, Vladimir Il'ich, 1870-1924. 2. Communism—Russia—History.

BOX, Pelham Horton, 909.82 B
1898-1937.
Three master builders and another; studies in modern revolutionary and liberal statesmanship. With an introd. by Ernest Barker. Freeport, N.Y., Books for Libraries Press [1968] 395 p. ports. 22 cm. (Essay index reprint series) Reprint of the 1925 ed. Contents.Contents.—Nikolai Lenin.—Benito Mussolini.—Eleutherios Venizelos.—Woodrow Wilson. Includes bibliographies. [D412.6.B6 1968] 68-22904
1. Lenin, Vladimir Il'ich, 1870-1924. 2. Mussolini, Benito, 1883-1945. 3. Venizelos, Eleutherios, 1864-1936. 4. Wilson, Woodrow, Pres. U.S., 1856-1924. I. Title. BIP

BRADFORD, Gamaliel, 1863- 920.02
1932.
The quick and the dead. Port Washington, N.Y., Kennikat Press [1969, c1931] x, 282 p. ports. 22 cm. (Essay and general literature index reprint series) Contents.Contents.—Theodore Roosevelt.—Woodrow Wilson.—Thomas Alva Edison.—Henry Ford.—Nikolai Lenin.—Benito Mussolini.—Calvin Coolidge. Bibliographical references included in "Notes" (p. [259]-[274]) [CT120.B65 1969] 70-85991
1. Roosevelt, Theodore, Pres. U.S., 1858-1919. 2. Wilson, Woodrow, Pres. U.S., 1856-1924. 3. Edison, Thomas Alva, 1847-1931. 4. Ford, Henry, 1863-1947. 5. Lenin, Vladimir Il'ich, 1870-1924. 6. Mussolini, Benito, 1883-1945. 7. Coolidge, Calvin, Pres. U.S., 1872-1933. I. Title.

CONQUEST, 947.084'1'0924 B
Robert.
V. I. Lenin. New York, Viking Press [1972] 152 p. 20 cm. (Modern masters) Bibliography: p. [145]-146. [DK254.L4C665 1972b] 70-181980 ISBN 0-670-74220-1 6.95
1. Lenin, Vladimir Il'ich, 1870-1924. 2. Russia—History—Nicholas II, 1894-1917. 3. Russia—History—1917-

DEUTSCHER, 947.084'1'0924 B
Isaac, 1907-1967.
Lenin's childhood. London, New York, Oxford University Press, 1970. vii, 67 p. 23 cm. [DK254.L44D48 1970] 79-18168 ($4.95 U.S.)
1. Lenin, Vladimir Il'ich, 1870-1924. I. Title. BIP

FISCHER, Louis, 1896- 923.247
1970.
The life of Lenin. [1st ed.] New York, Harper & Row [1964] viii, 703 p. ports. 24 cm. Bibliographical footnotes. [DK254.L4F53] 64-14385
1. Lenin, Vladimir Il'ich, 1870-1924. I. Title.

FULOP-MILLER, Rene, 1891- 335
1963.
Lenin and Gandhi. Translated from the German by F. S. Flint and D. F. Tait. Freeport, N.Y., Books for Libraries Press [1972] p. Reprint of the 1927 ed. Bibliography: p. [DK254.L46F813 1972] 72-7057 ISBN 0-8369-6932-4
1. Lenin, Vladimir Il'ich, 1870-1924. 2. Gandhi, Mohandas Karamchand, 1869-1948. I. Title. BIP

FULOP-MILLER, Rene, 1891- 320.5
1963.
Lenin and Gandhi. Translated from the German by F. S. Flint and D. F. Tait. With a new introd. for the Garland ed. by Margaret W. Fisher. New York, Garland Pub., 1972. 29, xi, 343 p. 22 cm. (The Garland library of war and peace) Reprint of the 1927 ed. Bibliography: p. [321]-329. [DK254.L4F83 1972] 79-147617 ISBN 0-8240-0374-8
1. Lenin, Vladimir Il'ich, 1870-1924. 2. Gandhi, Mohandas Karamchand, 1869-1948. I. Title. II. Series.

GOURFINKEL, 947.084'1'0924 B
Nina, 1898-
Lenin / Nina Gourfinkel ; translated by Maurice Thornton. Westport, Conn. : Greenwood Press, 1975. p. cm. Reprint of the 1961 ed. published by Grove Press, N.Y. which was issued as Evergreen profile book 29. Translation of Lenine. Bibliography: p. [DK254.L4G683 1975] 75-11424 ISBN 0-8371-8191-7
1. Lenin, Vladimir Il'ich, 1870-1924. I. Title. BIP

GOURFINKEL, 947.084'1'0924 B
Nina, 1898-
Lenin / Nina Gourfinkel ; translated by Maurice Thornton. Westport, Conn. : Greenwood Press, 1975. p. cm. Reprint of the 1961 ed. published by Grove Press, N.Y. which was issued as Evergreen profile book 29. Translation of Lenine. Bibliography: p. [DK254.L4G683 1975] 75-11424 ISBN 0-8371-8191-7 lib.bdg. : 15.75
1. Lenin, Vladimir Il'ich, 1870-1924. I. Title.

GOURFINKEL, 947.084'1'0924 B
Nina, 1898-
Portrait of Lenin; an illustrated biography. Translated by Maurice Thornton. [New York] Herder and Herder [1972] 175, [1] p. illus. 21 cm. Translation of Lenine; this translation was first published in 1961 under title: Lenin. Bibliography: p. 175-[176] [DK254.L4G683 1972] 70-181014 6.95
1. Lenin, Vladimir Il'ich, 1870-1924. I. Title.

KRUPSKAIA, 947.84'1'0924 B
Nadezhda Konstantinovna, 1869-1939.
Reminiscences of Lenin, by N. K. Krupskaya. [Translated by Bernard Isaacs. 1st U.S. ed.] New York, International Publishers [1970, c1960] 552 p. ports. 21 cm. Translation of Vospominaniia o Lenine (romanized form) [DK254.L42K7213 1970] 67-27253 6.95
1. Lenin, Vladimir Il'ich, 1870-1924. I. Title. BIP

LENIN: the man, the theorist, the leader; a reappraisal. 947.084'1'0924 B
Editors: Leonard Schapiro and Peter Reddaway. Assistant editor: Paul Rosta.

New York, F. A. Praeger [1967] x, 317 p. 23 cm. (Hoover Institution publications) "Published in association with the Hoover Institution on War, Revolution, and Peace." "A series of papers to our graduate seminar ... at the London School of Economics and Political Science." Includes bibliographies. [DK254.L4A153] 67-28181
1. Lenin, Vladimir Il'ich, 1870-1924. I. Schapiro, Leonard Bertram, 1908- ed. II. Reddaway, Peter, ed. III. Stanford University. Hoover Institution on War, Revolution, and Peace. IV. London School of Economics and Political Science. V. Series: Stanford University. Hoover Institution on War, Revolution, and Peace. Publications.

LENIN, Vladimir Il'ich, 1870-1924. 947.084'1'0924 B
The letters of Lenin. Translated and edited by Elizabeth Hill and Doris Mudie. Westport, Conn., Hyperion Press [1973, c1937] vi, 499 p. illus. 23 cm. Translation of Pis'ma. Reprint of the ed. published by Harcourt, Brace, New York. [DK254.L4A36 1973] 73-848 ISBN 0-88355-045-8 22.00
1. Lenin, Vladimir Il'ich, 1870-1924. 2. Russia—Politics and government—1894-1917. 3. Russia—Politics and government—1917-1936. 4. Communism—Russia. I. Title. BIP

MAILLOUX, Kenneth F., 1926- 947.084'1'0924 B
Lenin; the exile returns [by] Kenneth F. and Heloise P. Mailloux. Princeton, Auerbach Publishers [1971] ix, 150 p. illus. 22 cm. Bibliography: p. 144-146. [DK254.L4M217 1971] 74-163108 ISBN 0-87769-091-X
1. Lenin, Vladimir Il'ich, 1870-1924. 2. Russia—History—Revolution, 1917-1921. I. Mailloux, Heloise P., joint author II. Title.

MORGAN, Michael Croke. 947.084'1'0924 B
Lenin, by M. C. Morgan. [Athens] Ohio University Press, 1971. xii, 236 p. ports. 23 cm. Bibliography: p. [223]-229. [DK254.L4M625 1971b] 74-158177 ISBN 0-8214-0094-0 8.75
1. Lenin, Vladimir Il'ich, 1870-1924.

PAGE, Stanley W. 947.084'1'0924
Lenin and world revolution [by] Stanley W. Page. Gloucester, Mass., P. Smith, 1968 [c1959] xviii, 252 p. 21 cm. Bibliography: p. 245-248. [HX40.P3 1968] 68-3456
1. Lenin, Vladimir Il'ich, 1870-1924. 2. Communism—History. 3. Communism—Russia. 4. Social conflict. I. Title. BIP

PAYNE, Pierre Stephen Robert, 1911- 923.247
The life and death of Lenin, by Robert Payne. New York, Simon and Schuster [1964] 672 p. illus., facsims., col. maps (on lining papers) ports. 25 cm. Bibliography: p. 641-644. [DK254.L4P35] 64-11190
1. Lenin, Vladimir Il'ich, 1870-1924. I. Title.

POSSONY, Stefan Thomas, 1913- 923.247
Lenin: the compulsive revolutionary. Chicago, Regnery [1964] xvi, 418 p. illus., facsims., geneal. tables., ports. 25 cm. (The Hoover Institution series) Bibliography: p. 401-408. [DK254.L4P647] 63-12887
1. Lenin, Vladimir Il'ich, 1870-1924. I. Title.

SHUB, David, 1887-1973. 335.43'092'4
Lenin: a biography. Revised ed. Harmondsworth, Penguin, 1966. 496 p. 18 1/2 cm. (Political leaders of the twentieth century) Pelican book A809. Bibliographical reference included in "Notes" (p. [452]-478) [DK254.L4S48 1966] 66-78539
1. Lenin, Vladimir Il'ich, 1870-1924. BIP

THEEN, Rolf H. W., 1937- 947.084'1'0924 B
Lenin: genesis and development of a revolutionary [by] Rolf H. W. Theen. [1st ed.] Philadelphia, Lippincott [1973] 194 p. 22 cm. (Portraits) Bibliography: p. [183]-188. [DK254.L4T47] 73-1802 ISBN 0-397-00830-9 6.95
1. Lenin, Vladimir Il'ich, 1870-1924. I. Title.

TROTSKII, Lev, 1879-1940. 947.084'1'0924 B
The young Lenin, by Leon Trotsky. Translated from the Russian by Max Eastman. Edited and annotated by Maurice Friedberg. Garden City, N.Y., Doubleday, 1972. xiii, 224 p. front. 22 cm. [DK254.L44T79 1972] 69-20101 7.95
1. Lenin, Vladimir Il'ich, 1870-1924. I. Title.

VERNADSKY, George, 1887- 947.084'1'0924 B
Lenin, red dictator. Translated from the Russian by Malcolm Waters Davis. New York, AMS Press [1970] 351 p. illus., ports. 23 cm. Reprint of the 1931 ed. Bibliography: p. [331]-335. [DK254.L4V4 1970] 76-119660
1. Lenin, Vladimir Il'ich, 1870-1924. 2. Russia—Politics and government—1894-1917. 3. Russia—Politics and government—1917-1936. I. Title. BIP

WOLFE, Bertram David, 1896- 947.08
Three who made a revolution; a biographical history. [4th rev. ed.] New York, Dial Press, 1964. viii, 659 p. ports. 22 cm. [DK254.L4W6 1964] 64-3227
1. Lenin, Vladimir Il'ich, 1870-1924. 2. Trotskii, Lev, 1879-1940. 3. Stalin, Iosif, 1879-1953. I. Title.

WOLFE, Bertram David, 1896-1977. 947.084'1'0924 B
Lenin / Bertram D. Wolfe. New York : Stein and Day, 1978. p. cm. [DK254.L4W59] 78-7263 ISBN 0-8128-2519-5 : 12.95
1. Lenin, Vladimir Il'ich, 1870-1924. 2. Heads of state—Russia—Biography. 3. Revolutionists—Russia—Biography. BIP

WOLFENSTEIN, E. Victor. 335.43
The revolutionary personality: Lenin, Trotsky, Gandhi, by E. Victor Wolfenstein. Princeton, N. J., [Published for the Princeton Center of International Studies by] Princeton University Press, 1967. x, 330 p. 33 cm. Bibliography: p. 319-325. [HX312.L36W6] 67-11035
1. Lenin, Vladimir Il'ich, 1870-1924. 2. Trotskii, Lev, 1879-1940. 3. Gandhi, Mohandas Karamchand, 1869-1948. 4. Revolutionists. I. Princeton University. Center of International Studies. II. Title.

Lenin, Vladimir Il'ich, 1870-1924—Addresses, essays, lectures.

LENIN, Vladimir Il'ich, 1870-1924. 947.084'1'0924 B
Lenin. Edited by Saul N. Silverman. Englewood Cliffs, N.J., Prentice-Hall [1972] vii, 213 p. 21 cm. (Great lives observed) (A Spectrum book, S-730) Includes views on Lenin written by his contemporaries and other historians. Bibliography: p. 205-208 [DK254.L3A5785] 72-2034 ISBN 0-13-529271-9 2.45 ($2.75 Can.)
1. Lenin, Vladimir Il'ich, 1870-1924—Addresses, essays, lectures. I. Silverman, Saul N., ed. II. Title.

Lenin, Vladimir Il'ich, 1870-1924—Iconography.

CASH, Anthony, 1933- comp. 947.084'1'0924
Lenin. London, Jackdaw Publications, in association with Grossman, New York [1972] 1 v. illus., facsims., col. maps, ports. 23 x 35 cm. (Jackdaw no. 113) Introductory booklet (8 p.), 9 reproductions of contemporary documents with 1 translation, map, and 6 explanatory broadsheets in portfolio. [DK254.L45C37 1972] 70-167820 ISBN 0-670-42343-2 (Grossman) £0.80
1. Lenin, Vladimir Il'ich, 1870-1924—Iconography. I. Title. II. Series.

Lenin, Vladimir Il'ich, 1870-1924—Journey to Russia, 1917.

PEARSON, Michael. 947.084'1'0924
The sealed train / by Michael Pearson. New York : Putnam, [1975] 320 p., [4] leaves of plates : ill. ; 22 cm. Includes index. Bibliography: p. 308-313. [DK254.L443P4] 73-88527 ISBN 0-399-11262-6 : 8.95
1. Lenin, Vladimir Il'ich, 1870-1924—Journey to Russia, 1917. 2. Revolutionists—Russia. 3. Russia—History—Revolution, 1917-1921. I. Title.

Lenin, Vladimir Il'ich, 1870-1924—Juvenile literature.

CHARNOCK, Joan (Thomson) 947.084'1'0924 B
Red revolutionary; a life of Lenin [by] Joan Charnock. [1st U.S. ed.] New York, Hawthorn Books [1970] 138 p. 21 cm. Bibliography: p. 133. A biography of the man who led the Russian Revolution of 1917 and became the first Communist leader of that country. [DK254.L455C5 1970] 92 78-102419 4.95
1. Lenin, Vladimir Il'ich, 1870-1924—Juvenile literature. I. Title.

LEVINE, Israel E. 947.084'1'0924 B
Lenin, the man who made a revolution, by I. E. Levine. New York, Messner [1969] 189 p. 22 cm. A biography of the Communist leader who shaped the course of the Russian Revolution of 1917. Bibliography: p. 183-184. [DK254.L4L42] 92 69-12112 3.50
1. Lenin, Vladimir Il'ich, 1870-1924—Juvenile literature. I. Title.

LIVERSIDGE, Douglas, 1913- 947.084'1'0924 B
Lenin: genius of revolution. London, New York, Franklin Watts Ltd., 1969. [5], 186 p., 8 plates. illus., maps, ports. 23 cm. (Immortals of history) [DK254.L455L58 1969] 77-598692 ISBN 0-85166-293-5 £1.25
1. Lenin, Vladimir Il'ich, 1870-1924—Juvenile literature. I. Title.

Leningrad. Gosudarstvennoe Khoreograficheskoe uchilische.

BARNES, Patricia. 792.8'07'104745
The children of Theatre Street / text by Patricia Barnes ; introd. by Earle Mack. New York : Penguin Books, 1978. p. cm. Includes index. Bibliography: p. [GV1788.6.L46B37] 78-13492 ISBN 0-14-005019-1 pbk. : 6.95
1. Leningrad. Gosudarstvennoe Khoreograficheskoe uchilische. I. Title. BIP

Lennhoff, F. G.

LENNHOFF, F. G. 369.4'092'4 B
The first thirty years / by F. G. Lennhoff. Shrewsbury : Shotton Hall Publications, [1976] 162 p. ; 22 cm. [HV763.L45] 76-374601 ISBN 0-904902-03-X : £1.85
1. Lennhoff, F. G. 2. Social workers—Biography. 3. Social work with children—Germany. I. Title.

Lennon, Dianne Barbara, 1939-

PARR, Adolph Henry, 1900- 927.8
The Lennon sisters, sweethearts of song. Introd. by Lawrence Welk. [1st ed.] Garden City, N. Y., Doubleday, 1960. 188p. illus. 22cm. [ML400.P17] 60-7880
1. Lennon, Dianne Barbara, 1939- 2. Lennon, Margaret Anne, 1941- 3. Lennon, Kathleen Mary, 1943- 4. Lennon, Janet Elizabeth, 1946- I. Title.

Lennon, Glenda—Juvenile literature.

MCREYNOLDS, Ginny. 797.2'1'0924 B
Woman overboard / Ginny McReynolds ; ill., Mark Gray. Milwaukee : Raintree, 1980. p. cm. Relates the events that turn a young woman's leisurely swim off the Florida coast into a struggle to remain alive. [GV838.L46M32] 79-21834 ISBN 0-8172-1569-7 (lib. bdg.) : 7.99
1. Lennon, Glenda—Juvenile literature. 2. Swimmers—United States—Biography—Juvenile literature. I. Gray, Mark. II. Title. BIP

Lennon, John,

LENNON, John, 1940- 784'.0924 B
Lennon remembers. [1st ed.] San Francisco, Straight Arrow Books [1971] 189 p. illus. 22 cm. "Interview ... conducted by Jann Wenner." [ML420.L38L4] 79-158521 ISBN 0-87932-009-5 4.95
I. Wenner, Jann. II. Title. BIP

Lennon, John, 1940-

FAWCETT, Anthony, 1948- 784'.092'4 B
John Lennon : one day at a time : a personal biography of the seventies / by Anthony Fawcett. New York : Grove Press, 1976. 192 p. : ill. ; 26 cm. (An Evergreen book) Chronology: p. [184]-187. [ML420.L38F4] 76-14557 ISBN 0-394-17920-X : 6.95
1. Lennon, John, 1940- 2. Singers—England—Biography. I. Title. BIP

LENNON, John, 1940- 784'.0924 B
Lennon remembers. [1st ed.] San Francisco, Straight Arrow Books [1971] 189 p. illus. 22 cm. "Interview ... conducted by Jann Wenner." [ML420.L38L4] 79-158521 ISBN 0-87932-009-5 4.95
I. Wenner, Jann. II. Title. BIP

Lennon, Kathleen Mary, 1943-

PARR, Adolph Henry, 1900- 927.8
The Lennon sisters, sweethearts of song. Introd. by Lawrence Welk. [1st ed.] Garden City, N. Y., Doubleday, 1960. 188p. illus. 22cm. [ML400.P17] 60-7880
1. Lennon, Dianne Barbara, 1939- 2. Lennon, Margaret Anne, 1941- 3. Lennon, Kathleen Mary, 1943- 4. Lennon, Janet Elizabeth, 1946- I. Title.

Lennon, Margaret Anne, 1941-

PARR, Adolph Henry, 1900- 927.8
The Lennon sisters, sweethearts of song. Introd. by Lawrence Welk [1st ed.] Garden City, N. Y., Doubleday, 1960. 188p. illus. 22cm. [ML400.P17] 60-7880
1. Lennon, Dianne Barbara, 1939- 2. Lennon, Margaret Anne, 1941- 3. Lennon, Kathleen Mary, 1943- 4. Lennon, Janet Elizabeth, 1946- I. Title.

Lenox, James, 1800-1880.

STEVENS, Henry, 1819-1886. 923.673
Recollections of James Lenox and the formation of his library; revised and elucidated by Victor Hugo Paltsite. New York, New York Public Library, 1951. xxxvi, 187 p. ports., map, facsims. 24 cm. Includes bibliographical references. [Z989.L45S8] 51-12041
1. Lenox, James, 1800-1880. 2. Lenox Library, New York. I. Paltaits, Victor Hugo, 1867- ed. II. Title.

Lenski, Lois,

LENSKI, Lois, 1893- 813'.5'2 B
Journey into childhood. The autobiography of Lois Lenski. [1st ed.] Philadelphia, Lippincott [1972] 208 p. illus. 21 cm. Autobiography. [PS3523.E575Z5] 74-141451 ISBN 0-397-31177-X
I. Title.

Leo IIII, Pope, 1810-1903.

BURTON, Katherine (Kurz) 1890- 922.21
Leo the Thirteenth, the first modern pope. [1st ed.] New York, D. MqKay Co. [1962] 213p. 21cm. Includes bibliography. [BX1374.B8] 62-17443
1. Leo IIII, Pope, 1810-1903. I. Title.

Leo X, Pope, 1475-1521.

ROSCOE, William, 1753-1831. 262'.13'0924 B
The life and pontificate of Leo the Tenth, by William Roscoe. 6th ed. Rev. by Thomas Roscoe. London, H. G. Bohn, 1853. [New York, AMS Press, 1973] 2 v. ports. 19 cm. Original ed. issued in series: Bohn's standard library. Includes bibliographical references. [BX1315.R7 1973] 75-174965 ISBN 0-404-05430-7 40.00

1. Leo X, Pope, 1475-1521. I. Roscoe, Thomas, 1791-1871, ed. II. Title. **BIP**

VAUGHAN, Herbert Millingchamp, 1870-1948. 945'.05
The Medici Popes (Leo X and Clement VII.). Port Washington, N.Y., Kennikat Press [1971] xxii, 359 p. illus., geneal. table, ports. 22 cm. Reprint of the 1908 ed. Bibliography: p. xxi-xxii. [DG540.V3 1971] 74-118554 ISBN 0-8046-1179-3
1. Leo X, Pope, 1475-1521. 2. Clemens VII, Pope, 1478-1534. 3. Medici, House of. 4. Italy—History—1492-1559. I. Title.

Leo XII, Pope, 1760-1829.

WISEMAN, Nicholas Patrick Stephen, Cardinal, 1802-1865. 262'.13'0922
Recollections of the last four popes and of Rome in their times. New and rev. ed. Freeport, N.Y., Books for Libraries Press [1973] p. (Essay index reprint series) "First published 1858." [BX1386.W5 1973] 72-14111 ISBN 0-518-10032-4
1. Pius VII, Pope, 1742-1823. 2. Leo XII, Pope, 1760-1829. 3. Pius VIII, Pope, 1761-1830. 4. Gregorius XVI, Pope, 1765-1846. I. Title. II. Title: The last four popes.

Leo XIII, Pope, 1810-1903.

GARGAN, Edward T., 1922-, ed. 922.21
Leo XIII and the modern world. New York, Sheed and Ward [c.1961] 246p. Bibl. 61-7288 4.50
1. Leo XIII, Pope, 1810-1903. I. Title.

KIEFER, William J 922.21
Leo XIII, a light from heaven. Milwaukee, Bruce Pub. Co. [1961] 222p. illus. 23cm. Includes bibliography. [BX1374.K5] 61-17582
1. Leo XIII, Pope, 1810-1903. I. Title.

QUARDT, Robert, 1893- 922.21
The master diplomat, from the life of Leo XIII, by Robert Quardt [Tr. from German by Ilya Wolston] Staten Island, N.Y., Alba [c.1964] 112p. 20cm. 64-15371 2.50
1. Leo XIII, Pope, 1810-1903. I. Title.

Leon, Martin de, 1765-1833.

HAMMETT, Arthur B. J. 917.64'125'0330922 B
The empresario Don Martin de Leon, by A. B. J. Hammett. Waco, Tex., Texian Press, 1973. xiii, 197 p. illus. 24 cm. [F394.V6H35] 73-83276 ISBN 0-87244-035-4 10.00
1. Leon, Martin de, 1765-1833. 2. Leon family. 3. Victoria, Tex.—History. I. Title.

Leonardo da Vinci, 1452-1519.

ACKER, Helen. 920.045
Five sons of Italy. New York, Nelson [1950] 191 p. 21 cm. Bibliography: p. 190-191. [DG463.A28] 50-8995
1. Leonardo da Vinci, 1452-1519. 2. Buonarroti, Michel Angelo, 1475-1564. 3. Galilei, Galileo, 1564-1642. 4. Paganini, Nicolo, 1782-1840. 5. Verdi, Giuseppe, 1813-1901. I. Title.

FREUD, Sigmund, 1856-1939. 927.5
Leonardo da Vinci; a study in psychosexuality. Authorized translation by A. A. Brill. New York, Random House [1955, c1947] 122p. illus. 19cm. (Modern library paperbacks, P11) [ND623] 55-8302
1. Leonardo da Vinci, 1452-1519. I. Title.

FREUD, Sigmund, 1856-1939 927.5
Leonardo da Vinci and a memory of his childhood. Tr. by Alan Tyson. Standard ed., tr. from German under the general editorship of James Strachey with Anna Freud. Assisted by Alix Strachey, Alan Tyson [1st Amer. ed.] New York, Norton [1964] 101p. illus. 22cm. Bibl. 64-17514 3.50
1. Leonardo da Vinci, 1452-1519. I. Title.

FRIEDENTHAL, Richard 759.5
Leonardo da Vinci; a pictorial biography. [Translated from the German by Margaret Shenfield] New York, Viking Press [1959] 143p. illus. (part col.) facsims. 24cm. (A Studio book) 60-1258 6.50
1. Leonardo da Vinci, 1452-1519. I. Title.

FUSERO, Clemente. 759.5 B
Leonardo / Clemente Fusero. New York : Praeger Publishers, 1975. p. cm. Includes index. Bibliography: p. [ND553.L827F8713] 73-17776 ISBN 0-275-10180-0 : 12.50
1. Leonardo da Vinci, 1452-1519. I. Title.

GILLETTE, Henry S. 927.5
Leonardo da Vinci, pathfinder of science. Pictures by the author. New York, Watts [c.1962] 168p. illus. 22cm. (Immortals of sci.) 62-8426 1.95
1. Leonardo da Vinci, 1452-1519. I. Title.

GOULD, Cecil Hilton Monk, 1918- 759.5 B
Leonardo : the artist and the non-artist / by Cecil Gould. Boston : New York Graphic Society, 1975. p. cm. Includes index. Bibliography: p. [ND623.L5G68] 74-21495 ISBN 0-316-52100-0 : 22.50
1. Leonardo da Vinci, 1452-1519.

HAHN, Emily, 1905- 927.5
Leonardo da Vinci; illustrated by Mimi Korach. New York, Random House [1956] 181 p. illus. 22 cm. (World landmark books [W-27]) [ND623.L5H3] 759.5 56-5461
1. Leonardo da Vinci, 1452-1519.

HART, Ivor Blashka, 1889- 927.5
The world of Leonardo da Vinci, man of science, engineer and dreamer of flight New York, Viking Press [1962, c1961] 374 p. illus. 24 cm. Includes bibliography. [Q143.L5H33 1962] 62-17389
1. Leonardo da Vinci, 1452-1519. I. Title.

LEONARDO da Vinci. v. 12
New York, Reynal [c1956] 518p. illus.
1. Leonardo da Vinci, 1452-1519. I. Howard, Elizabeth Jane.

LEONARDO da Vinci; 759.5
illustrated by Mimi Korach. New York, Random House [1956] 181p. illus. 22cm. (World landmark books [W-27]) [ND623.L5H3] 927.5 56-5461
1. Leonardo da Vinci, 1452-1519. I. Hahn, Emily, 1905-

LEONARDO da Vinci, 1452-1519. 759.5
Leonardo / by Mina Bacci. 1st U.S. ed. New York : Avenel Books : distributed by Crown, c1978. 15 lxiii p. : chiefly col. ill. ; 31 cm. [ND623.L5A4 1978] 78-18879 ISBN 0-517-24952-9 pbk. : 4.98
1. Leonardo da Vinci, 1452-1519. I. Bacci, Mina. II. Title.

LEVINGER, Elma (Ehrlich) 1887- 759.5
Leonardo da Vinci, Who followed the sinking star. Illustrated with photos. and with sketches from da Vinci's notebooks. New York, J. Messner [1954] 192p. illus. 22cm. [ND623.L5L46] [ND623.L5L46] 927.5 54-10591 54-10591
1. Leonardo da Vinci, 1452-1519. I. Title.

LOS Angeles Co., Calif. Museum, Los Angeles. 759.5
Leonardo da Vinci loan exhibition, June 3 to July 1, 1949. [Catalogue prepared by W. R. Valentiner in collaboration with William E. Suida and others] Los Angeles [1949] xvi, 144 p. 67 plates (part col.) 26 cm. Contents.Partial Contents. -- Two sixteenth-century biographies of Leonardo. -- Leonardo's early life, by W. R. Valentiner. -- Selected list of books and articles (p. 65-67) [ND623.L5L6] 49-49132
1. Leonardo da Vinci, 1452-1519. 2. Art, Italian — Exhibitions. I. Title.

MCLANATHAN, Richard B K 741.0924
Images of the universe; Leonardo da Vinci: the artist as scientist. by Richard McLanathan. [1st ed. in the U.S.A.] Garden City, N.Y., Doubleday, 1966. 192 p. facsims. 29 cm. "List of books": p. 187-188. [NC1055.L5M25] 66-8249
1. Leonardo da Vinci, 1452-1519. I. Title.

MONTI, Raffaele. 759.5
Leonardo da Vinci. [Translated from the Italian by Pearl Sanders. 1st American ed.] New York, Grosset & Dunlap [1967] 39, [81] p. illus. (part col.) 18 cm. (The New Grosset art library, 1) On cover: Leonardo da Vinci; the life and work of the artist. [ND623.V63M63] 67-24227
1. Leonardo da Vinci, 1452-1519.

PAYNE, Pierre Stephen Robert, 1911- 759.5 B
Leonardo / Robert Payne. 1st ed. Garden City, N.Y. : Doubleday, 1978. xix, 344 p., [36] leaves of plates : ill. ; 24 cm. Includes index. Bibliography: p. [321]-326. [ND623.L5P37] 78-869 ISBN 0-385-04154-3 : 12.95
1. Leonardo da Vinci, 1452-1519. 2. Painters—Italy—Biography. I. Title. **BIP**

RIPLEY, Elizabeth. [759.5] 927.5
Leonardo da Vinci, a biography. With drawings and paintings by Leonardo. New York, Oxford University Press, 1952. 67 p. illus. 26 cm. [Oxford books for boys and girls] [ND623.L5H56] 52-9432
1. Leonardo da Vinci, 1452-1519. I. Title.

RIPLEY, Elizabeth, 1906- 759.5
Leonardo da Vinci, a biography. With drawings and paintings by Leonardo. New York, Oxford University Press, 1952. 67 p. illus. 26 cm. [Oxford books for boys and girls] [ND623.L5R56] 52-9432
1. Leonardo da Vinci, 1452-1519.

RITCHIE-CALDER, Peter Ritchie, Baron Ritchie Calder, 1906- 759.5 B
Leonardo & the age of the eye [by] Ritchie Calder. New York, Simon and Schuster [1970] 288 p. illus. (part col.) 27 cm. Bibliography: p. 278. [ND623.L5R62] 71-124472 12.95
1. Leonardo da Vinci, 1452-1519. I. Title.

VINCI, Leonardo da 1452-1519. 759.5
Leonardo da Vinci. New York, Reynal [1956] 518p. illus., plates (part col.) ports., facsims. 38cm. 'This memorial edition arose out of the great Leonardo Exposition beld at Milan [1938] ... Authors of the sections of this work have labored to assemble the documents that show how deeply Leonardo penetrated into the most varied fields of human knowledge.' Bibliography: p. 511-518. [ND623.L5A45 1956] 927.5 57-8078
I. Title.

ZUBOV, Vasilii Pavlovich. 709'.45 B
Leonardo da Vinci [by] V. P. Zubov. Translated from the Russian by David H. Kraus. Cambridge, Harvard University Press, 1968. xviii, 335 p. illus., facsims., port. 25 cm. Translation of Leonardo da Vinchi (romanized form) Includes bibliographical references. [ND623.L5Z83] 67-27096
1. Leonardo da Vinci, 1452-1519. **BIP**

Leonardo da Vinci, 1452-1519—Juvenile literature.

ALMEDINGEN, Martha Edith, 1898- 92
The young Leonardo da Vinci [by] E. M. Almedingen. Illus. by Azpelicueta. New York, Roy [1964, c.1963] 143p. illus. 21cm. 64-1024 3.25 bds.,
1. Leonardo da Vinci, 1452-1519—Juvenile literature. I. Title.

NOBLE, Iris 927.5
Leonardo da Vinci: the universal genius. New York, Norton [c.1965] 224p. illus., port. 21cm. [ND623.L5N6] 64-17534 3.50; 3.28 bds., lid. ed.,
1. Leonardo da Vinci, 1452-1519—Juvenile literature. I. Title.

Leonardo de Vinci, 1452-1519—Knowledge—Science.

HART, Ivor Blashka, 1889- 509'.2'4 B
The world of Leonardo da Vinci; man of science, engineer, and dreamer of flight [by] Ivor B. Hart. Clifton [N.J.] A. M. Kelly, 1974 [c1961] p. cm. (Viking reprint editions) Reprint of the ed. published by Viking Press, New York. Bibliography: p. [Q143.L5H33 1974] 74-122058 ISBN 0-678-03162-2 22.50
1. Leonardo de Vinci, 1452-1519—Knowledge—Science. I. Title.

Leonhard, Thomas S.

WALLER, Leslie, 1923- 364.1'06'073
Hide in plain sight : the true story of how the United States Government and organized crime kept a man from his own children / Leslie Waller. New York : Delacorte Press, c1976. 275 p. ; 24 cm. [HV6245.W35] 76-10287 ISBN 0-440-03666-6 : 8.95
1. Leonhard, Thomas S. 2. Calabrese, Pascal. 3. Informers—United States—Biography. 4. Organized crime—United States. I. Title.

WALLER, Leslie, 1923- 364.1'06'073
Hide in plain sight : the true story of how the United States Government and organized crime kept a man from his own children / Leslie Waller. New York : Dell Pub. Co., 1978,c1976. 287p. ; 18 cm. (A Dell Book) [HV6245.W35] ISBN 0-440-13603-2 pbk. : 1.95
1. Leonhard, Thomas S. 2. Calabrese, Pascal. 3. Informers — United States — Biography. 4. Organized crime — United States. I. Title.
L.C. card no. for 1976 Delacorte Press ed.: 76-10287.

Leonid, 1896-

LEONID, 1896- 759.13 B
The three worlds of Leonid / Leonid Berman ; with a pref. by Virgil Thomson ; [translated from the French by Olivier Bernier]. New York : Basic Books, c1978. xii, 275 p., [8] leaves of plates : ill. ; 22 cm. Includes index. [ND237.L56A2 1978] 78-54503 ISBN 0-465-08618-7 : 15.00
1. Leonid, 1896- 2. Painters—United States—Biography. I. Title.

Leonie, Mother, 1840-1912.

ERNEST, Brother, 1897- 922.271
Just for today a story of Mother Leonie, P. S. S. F. Illus. by Carolyn Lee Jagodits. Notre Dame, Ind., Dujarie Press [1955] 96p. illus. 24cm. [BX4705.L545E7] 55-38582
1. Leonie, Mother, 1840-1912. I. Title.

Leonowens, Louis, ca. 1855-1919.

BRISTOWE, William Syer. 959.3'03'0922
Louis and the King of Siam / by W. S. Bristowe. London : Chatto & Windus, 1976. 156 p., [2] leaves of plates : ill. ; 23 cm. [DS578.32.L46B74 1976b] 77-358245 ISBN 0-7011-2164-5 : £4.50
1. Leonowens, Louis, ca. 1855-1919. 2. Chulalong Korn, King of Thailand, 1853-1910. 3. Mongkut, King of Thailand, 1804-1868. 4. Thailand—Biography. 5. Thailand—History. I. Title. **BIP**

BRISTOWE, William Syer. 959.3'03'0924 B
Louis and the King of Siam / by W. S. Bristowe. New York : Thai-American Publishers, c1976. 156 p., [2] leaves of plates : ill. ; 23 cm. Includes bibliographical references. [DS578.32.L46B74] 76-24045 ISBN 0-915806-03-7 : 8.95
1. Leonowens, Louis, ca. 1855-1919. 2. Chulalong Korn, King of Thailand, 1853-1910. 3. Mongkut, King of Thailand, 1804-1868. 4. Thailand—Biography. 5. Thailand—History. I. Title.

Leont'ev, Konstantin Nikolaevich, 1831-1891.

BERDIAEV, Nikolai 197'.2 B
Aleksandrovich, 1874-1948.
Leontiev [by] Nicolas Berdyaev. [Translated from the Russian by George Reavey. Folcroft, Pa.] Folcroft Library Editions, 1973. xii, 229 p. 23 cm. Reprint of the 1940 ed., published by G. Bles, The Centenary Press, London. [B4249.L44B42 1973] 73-9622 17.50
1. Leont'ev, Konstantin Nikolaevich, 1831-1891. BIP

Leopold, Aldo, 1886-1948.

FLADER, Susan L. 574.5'092'4 B
Thinking like a mountain : Aldo Leopold and the evolution of an ecological attitude toward deer, wolves, and forests / Susan L. Flader. Lincoln : University of Nebraska Press, 1978, c1974. p. cm. "Bison book edition." Reprint of the ed. published by the University of Missouri Press, Columbia. Includes index. Bibliography: p. [QH31.L618F57 1978] 78-17667 ISBN 0-8032-6850-5 pbk. : 4.25
1. Leopold, Aldo, 1886-1948. 2. Ecology—United States—History. 3. Wildlife management United States—History. 4. Ecologists—Biography—United States. 5. Deer. I. Title. BIP

THE Sand country of 500.9'775'5
Aldo Leopold; a photographic interpretation by Charles Steinhacker. Essay by Susan Flader. Selections from the writings of Aldo Leopold. Edited with an introd. by Anthony Wolff. Designed by Charles Curtis. San Francisco, Sierra Club [1973] 94 p. col. illus. 24 cm. [QH31.L618S36] 73-85045 ISBN 0-87156-075-5 14.95
1. Leopold, Aldo, 1886-1948. 2. Naturalists—Biography. 3. Wisconsin—Description and travel. I. Steinhacker, Charles, illus. II. Flader, Susan. III. Leopold, Aldo, 1886-1948.

Leopold I, King of the Belgians, 1790-1865.

RICHARDSON, Joanna 923.1493
My dearest uncle; a life of Leopold, first King of the Belgians. London, J. Cape[Mystic, Conn.,Verry, 1964, c.1961] 232p. illus. 23cm. Bibl. 62-5785 5.00
1. Leopold I, King of the Belgians, 1790-1865. I. Title.

Leopold II, King of the Belgians, 1835-1909.

ASCHERSON, Neal 923.1493
The King incorporated; Leopold II in the age of trusts. Garden City, N.Y., Doubleday, 1964 [c.1963] 310p. illus., maps. 22cm. Bibl. 64-13100 4.95
1. Leopold II, King of the Belgians, 1835-1909. I. Title.

Leopold, Nathan Freudenthal,

LEOPOLD, Nathan 923.4173
Freudenthal, 1904or5-
Life plus 99 years. Garden City, N. Y., Doubleday, 1958. 381p. 25cm. [HV6248.L43A3] 58-5947
I. Title. II. Title: Introd. by Erle Stanley Gardner. [1st ed.]

Leopold, Nathan Freudenthal, Jr.,

LEOPOLD, Nathan 923.4173
Freudenthal, Jr., 1904or5-
Life plus 99 years. Introd. by Erle Stanley Gardner New York, Popular Lib. [1965, c.1957, 1958] 415p. 18cm. (W1166) [HV6248.L43A3] .75 pap.,
I. Title.

Leopold, Nathan Freudenthal, 1904 or 5-1971.

LEOPOLD, Nathan 923.4173
Freudenthal, 1904or5-
Life plus 99 years. Garden City, N. Y., Doubleday, 1958. 381p. 25cm. [HV6248.L43A3] 58-5947
I. Title. II. Title: Introd. by Erle Stanley Gardner. [1st ed.]

LEOPOLD, Nathan 364.1'523'0924 B
Freudenthal, 1904or5-1971.
Life plus 99 years. Introd. by Erle Stanley Gardner. Westport, Conn., Greenwood Press [1974, c1958] 381 p. 23 cm. Reprint of the ed. published by Doubleday, Garden City, N.Y. [HV6248.L43A3 1974] 73-16644 ISBN 0-8371-7207-1
1. Leopold, Nathan Freudenthal, 1904 or 5-1971. I. Title.

LEOPOLD, Nathan 923.4173
Freudenthal, Jr., 1904or5-
Life plus 99 years. Introd. by Erle Stanley Gardner New York, Popular Lib. [1965, c.1957, 1958] 415p. 18cm. (W1166) [HV6248.L43A3] .75 pap.,
I. Title.

LePan, Douglas Valentine, 1914- — Bibliography.

LEPAN, Douglas 811'.5'4 B
Valentine, 1914-
Bright glass of memory : a set of four memoirs / by Douglas LePan. Toronto ; New York : McGraw-Hill Ryerson, c1979. 245 p. ; 23 cm. Includes bibliographical references. [PR9199.3.L45Z464] 79-320208 ISBN 0-07-082945-4 : 15.95
1. LePan, Douglas Valentine, 1914- — Bibliography. 2. Authors, Canadian—20th century—Biography. 3. Diplomats—Canada—Biography. I. Title.

Leprosy.

BURGESS, Perry, 1886- 616.998
Born of those years, an autobiography. [1st ed.] New York, Holt [1951] 307 p. illus. 22 cm. [RC154.B867] 51-14409
1. Leprosy. I. Title.

Lerdo de Tejada, Sebastian, Pres. Mexico, 1820-1889.

KNAPP, Frank 972.08'1'0924 B
Averill, 1922-
The life of Sebastian Lerdo de Teja [i.e. Tejada] 1823-1889: a study of influence and obscurity. New York, Greenwood Press, 1968. ix, 292 p. port. 24 cm. Reprint of the 1951 ed. Bibliography: p. [269]-280. [F1233.5.L4K57 1968] 68-23305
1. Lerdo de Tejada, Sebastian, Pres. Mexico, 1820-1889. I. Title.

Lermontov, Mikhail IUrevich, 1814-1841—Biography.

KELLY, Laurence, 891.7'1'3 B
1933-
Lermontov : tragedy in the Caucasus / Laurence Kelly. 1st ed. New York : G. Braziller, 1978, c1977. 259 p., [9] leaves of plates : ill. ; 22 cm. "Poems": p. [194]-219. Includes index. Bibliography: p. [243]-250. [PG3337.L42K4 1978] 77-77560 ISBN 0-8076-0874-2 : 8.95
1. Lermontov, Mikhail IUrevich, 1814-1841—Biography. 2. Authors, Russian—19th century—Biography. BIP

Lerner, Gerda, 1920-

LERNER, Gerda, 616.9'94'810926 B
1920-
A death of one's own : fragments from my life / by Gerda Lerner. New York : Simon and Schuster, c1978. p. cm. [RC280.B7L48] 78-45 ISBN 0-671-24008-0 : 8.95
1. Lerner, Gerda, 1920- 2. Brain—Tumors—Biography. I. Title.

Leroux, Joaquin Antoine, 1801 (ca.)-1861.

PARKHILL, Forbes, 917.80320924
1892-
The blazed trail of Antoine Leroux. Los Angeles, Westernlore Pr. [c.] 1965. 235p. 21cm. (Westernlore Great West and Indian ser., 30) Bibl. [F592.L38] 65-28473 7.50
1. Leroux, Joaquin Antoine, 1801 (ca.)-1861. I. Title.

Leroux, Pierre, 1797-1871.

BAKUNIN, Jack. 335'.2 B
Pierre Leroux and the birth of democratic socialism, 1797-1848 / by Jack Bakunin. New York : Revisionist Press, 1976. p. cm. Includes index. Bibliography: p. [HX263.L35B34] 75-44403 ISBN 0-87700-221-5 lib.dg. : 39.95
1. Leroux, Pierre, 1797-1871. I. Title. BIP

Les Canadiens.

RICHARD, Maurice, 1921- 796.9'62
The flying Frenchmen; hockey's greatest dynasty, by Maurice "Rocket" Richard and Stan Fischler. New York, Hawthorn Books [1971] ix, 340 p. illus., ports. 22 cm. "A Stuart L. Daniels book." Contents.Contents.—A history and critique of the Canadiens, by S. Fischler.—My life with the Canadiens, by M. Richard.—Records of the Canadiens. [GV848.C3R5 1971] 72-130726 6.95
1. Les Canadiens. I. Fischler, Stan. II. Title.

Lesbians—France—Biography.

PERRIN, Elula. 301.41'57'0922
So long as there are women / Elula Perrin ; translated from the French by Harold J. Salemson. New York : Morrow, 1980. p. cm. Translation of Tant qu'il y aura des femmes. [HQ75.3.P4713] 79-26502 ISBN 0-688-03596-5 : 9.95
1. Lesbians—France—Biography. I. Title. BIP

Leschetitzki, Theodor, 1830-1915.

NEWCOMB, Ethel, 786.1'0924 B
1879-
Leschetizky as I knew him. With a new introd. by Edwine Behre. New York, Da Capo Press, 1967. xxiii, viii, 320 p. ports. 23 cm. Bibliography (p. 301-308) compiled by Frederick Freedman and Philip Solomita. [ML417.L62N3 1967] 65-27355
1. Leschetitzki, Theodor, 1830-1915. I. Title.

Leshenotsky Family.

MARKELL, Jan, 1944- 248'.246
Gone the golden dream / Jan Markell. Minneapolis : Bethany Fellowship, c1979. 171 p. ; 21 cm. [BV2623.A1M37] 79-16718 ISBN 0-87123-049-6 pbk. : 3.50
1. Leshenotsky Family. 2. Lessin Family. 3. Converts from Judaism—Biography. I. Title. BIP

Leskov, Nikolai Semenovich, 1831-1895.

MCLEAN, Hugh, 1925- 891.7'3'3 B
Nikolai Leskov : the man and his art / Hugh McLean. Cambridge, Mass. : Harvard University Press, 1977. p. cm. Includes index. Bibliography: p. [PG3337.L5Z77] 77-647 30.00
1. Leskov, Nikolai Semenovich, 1831-1895. 2. Authors, Russian—19th century—Biography. BIP

Leslie, Miriam Florence Folline Squier, d. 1914.

STERN, Madeleine Bettina, 920.4
1912-
Purple passage; the life of Mrs. Frank Leslie. [1st ed.] Norman, University of Oklahoma Press [1953] 281 p. illus. 23 cm. Includes bibliography. [Z473.L54S8] 53-8811
1. Leslie, Miriam Florence Folline Squier, d. 1914. I. Title. BIP

Lespinasse, Julie Jeanne Eleonore de, 1732-1778.

BOUISSOUNOUSE, Janine 928.4
Julie; the life of Mademoiselle de Lespinasse: her salon, her friends, her loves. Tr. by Pierre de Fontnouvelle. New York, Appleton [dist. Meredith, c.1962] 309p. 21cm. Bibl. 62-8507 5.95
1. Lespinasse, Julie Jeanne Eleonore de, 1732-1778. I. Title.

Lesseps, Ferdinand Marie, comte de, 1805-1894.

BEATTY, Charles Robert 926.2
Longfield.
De Lesseps of Suez; the man and his times. New York, Harper [1956] 334p. illus. 22cm. Published in England under the title of Ferdinand de Lesseps.' Includes bibliography. [TA140.L6B35 1956a] 56-12440
1. Lesseps, Ferdinand Marie, comte de, 1805-1894. I. Title.

BEATTY, Charles Robert 926.2
Longfield.
De Lesseps of Suez; the man and his times. New York, Harper [1956] 334 p. illus. 22 cm. "Published in England under the title of Ferdinand de Lesseps." Includes bibliography. [TA140.L6B35 1956a] 56-12440
1. Lesseps, Ferdinand Marie, comte de, 1805-1894.

LONG, Laura. 926.2
De Lesseps, builder of Suez. Decorations by Clotilde Embree Funk. [1st ed.] New York, Longmans, Green [1958] 154 p. illus. 21 cm. [TA140.L6L7] 58-7328
1. Lesseps, Ferdinand Marie, comte de, 1805-1894. 2. Suez Canal.

Lessing, Doris May, 1919-

BREWSTER, Dorothy, 1883- 823.914
Doris Lessing. New York, Twayne Publishers [1965] 173 p. 21 cm. (Twayne's English authors series, 21) Bibliography: p. 165-170. [PR6023.E833Z58] 65-18222
1. Lessing, Doris May, 1919-

Lessing, Doris May, 1919- — Biography.

LESSING, Doris May, 828'.9'1408
1919-
Particularly cats / Doris Lessing ; ill. by Tudor Banus. New York : Simon and Schuster, [1978] c1967. 128 p. : ill. ; 20 cm. (A Fireside book) [PR6023.E833P3 1978] 78-16028 ISBN 0-671-24414-0 pbk. : 3.95
1. Lessing, Doris May, 1919- —Biography. 2. Novelists, English—20th century—Biography. 3. Cats. I. Title. BIP

Lessing, Gotthold Ephraim, 1729-1781.

GARLAND, Henry Burnand. 838'.6'09
Lessing, by H. B. Garland. [Folcroft, Pa.] Folcroft Library Editions, 1973. 209 p. 24 cm. Reprint of the 1949 ed. published by Bowes & Bowes, Cambridge, Eng. Bibliography: p. 205. [PT2406.G3 1973] 73-95
1. Lessing, Gotthold Ephraim, 1729-1781.

GARLAND, Henry Burnand. 838'.6'09
Lessing, by H. B. Garland. [Folcroft, Pa.] Folcroft Library Editions, 1973. 209 p. 24 cm. Reprint of the 1949 ed. published by Bowes & Bowes, Cambridge, Eng. Bibliography: p. 205 [PT2406.G3 1973] 73-95 ISBN 0-8414-1375-4 (lib. bdg.)
1. Lessing, Gotthold Ephraim, 1729-1781.

ROLLESTON, Thomas 838'.6'09 B
William Hazen, 1857-1920.
Life of Gotthold Ephraim Lessing. Port Washington, N.Y., Kennikat Press [1972] 218, xv p. 22 cm. Reprint of the 1889 ed. "Bibliography, by John P. Anderson": p. [i]-xv. [PT2406.R6 1972] 78-160777 ISBN 0-8046-1609-4
1. Lessing, Gotthold Ephraim, 1729-1781. I. Title. BIP

Lester, Julius—Biography.

LESTER, Julius. 813'.5'4 B
All is well / by Julius Lester. New York : Morrow, 1976. 319 p. ; 24 cm. [PS3562.E853Z515] 75-40219 ISBN 0-688-03045-9 : 9.95
1. Lester, Julius—Biography. I. Title. BIP

Letcher, John, 1813-1884.

BONEY, F. N. 975.5'03'0924
John Letcher of Virginia; the story of Virginia's Civil War Governor, by F. N.

Boney. University, Ala., University of Alabama Press [1966] 319 p. port. 21 cm. (Southern historical publications, no. 11) Bibliographical references included in "Notes": p. 248-303. [F230.L6B6] 66-25023
1. Letcher, John, 1813-1884. 2. Virginia — Pol. & govt. — 1775-1865. 3. Virginia — Hist. — Civil War. 4. U.S. — Pol. & govt. — 1849-1861. I. Title. II. Series. BIP

Letchworth, William Pryor, 1823-1910.

LARNED, Josephus Nelson, 1836-1913. 361'.92'4 B
The life and work of William Pryor Letchworth, student and minister of public benevolence. Montclair, N.J., Patterson Smith, 1974. viii, 470 p. illus. 22 cm. (Patterson Smith series in criminology, law enforcement & social problems, publication no. 182) Reprint of the 1912 ed. published by Houghton Mifflin, Boston. "List of writings": p. [447]-460. [HV28.L43L34 1974] 71-172592 ISBN 0-87585-182-7
1. Letchworth, William Pryor, 1823-1910. I. Title. BIP

Lethbridge, Alice.

LETHBRIDGE, Alice. 977.4'37
Well do I remember / by Alice Lethbridge. [s.l.] : Berwyn-London Publishers, 1976. x, 98 p. : ill. ; 24 cm. Includes index. [F574.F62L47] 75-44529 ISBN 0-916536-01-7
1. Lethbridge, Alice. 2. Flint, Mich.—History. 3. Flint, Mich.—Biography. I. Title. BIP

LeTourneau, Robert Gilmour,

LETOURNEAU, Robert Gilmour, 1888- 926
Mover of men and mountains; autobiography. Englewood Cliffs, N. J., Prentice-Hall [1960] 282 p. illus. 21 cm. [TA140.L63A3] 60-8319
I. Title.

LETOURNEAU, Robert Gilmour, 1888- 624'.0924 B
Mover of men and mountains; the autobiography of R. G. LeTourneau. Chicago, Moody Press [1967] 290 p. illus. 17 cm. (Moody diamonds, no. 18) [TA140.L63A3 1967] 68-3053
I. Title. BIP

Leuci, Robert, 1940-

DALEY, Robert. 363.2'09747'1
Prince of the city : the true story of a cop who knew too much / by Robert Daley. Boston : Houghton Mifflin, 1978. p. cm. [HV7911.L44D34] 78-15137 ISBN 0-395-27096-0 : 10.95
1. Leuci, Robert, 1940- 2. New York (City)—Police—Biography. 3. Police corruption—New York (City) 4. New York (City)—Police. I. Title. BIP

Leukemia—Personal narratives.

SANDERLIN, Johnny, 1947-1963. 616.1'55'00924 B
Johnny. [Edited by] Owenita Sanderlin. South Brunswick [N.J.] A. S. Barnes [1969, c1968] 154 p. ports. 22 cm. "Taken from the diary and weekly newspaper of Johnny Sanderlin." [RJ416.L4S2] 68-27234 5.95
1. Leukemia—Personal narratives. I. Sanderlin, Owenita, ed. II. Title. BIP

Leusse, Claude de.

LEUSSE, Claude de. 616.9'9 B
For love of Anne; the poignant story of a mother's struggle to save her dying daughter. Translated by Robert Bullen and Rosette Letellier. [1st American ed.] New York, McKay [1973] viii, 180 p. 22 cm. Translation of Le dernier jour de Juillet. [PQ2672.E867D413 1973] 73-84067 ISBN 0-679-50423-0 5.95
I. Title.

Levenson, Samuel,

LEVENSON, Samuel, 1911- 818.5403
Everything but money, by Sam Levenson. New York, Simon and Schuster [1966] 285 p. 22 cm. Autobiographical. [PN2287.L433A3] 66-20257
I. Title. BIP

Levenson, Samuel, 1911-

LEVENSON, Samuel, 1911- 818.5403
Everything but money, by Sam Levenson. New York, Simon and Schuster [1966] 285 p. 22 cm. Autobiographical. [PN2287.L433A3] 66-20257
I. Title. BIP

LEVENSON, Samuel, 1911- 791'.092'4 B
Everything but money / by Sam Levenson. New York : Simon and Schuster, [1978] c1966. 285 p. ; 21 cm. (A Fireside book) [PN2287.L433A3 1978] 77-28155 ISBN 0-671-24216-4 pbk. : 3.95
1. Levenson, Samuel, 1911- 2. Comedians—United States—Biography. I. Title.

Lever, Charles James, 1806-1872.

STEVENSON, Lionel, 1902- 823 B
Dr. Quicksilver; the life of Charles Lever. New York, Russell & Russell [1969] vii, 308 p. port. 23 cm. Reprint of the 1939 ed. Bibliography: p. 297-301. [PR4885.S8 1969] 68-27089
1. Lever, Charles James, 1806-1872. I. Title. BIP

Leverhulme, William Hesketh Lever, 1st Viscount, 1851-1925.

JOLLY, W. P. 338.7'66'8120924 B
Lord Leverhulme : a biography / [by] W. P. Jolly. London : Constable, 1976. viii, 246 p., leaf of plate, [16] p. of plates : ill., ports. ; 23 cm. Includes bibliographical references and index. [HC257.H4J64 1976] 76-372926 ISBN 0-09-461070-3 : £5.50
1. Leverhulme, William Hesketh Lever, 1st Viscount, 1851-1925.

Leveridge family.

TIVY, Louis, 1902-1972. 929'.2'0971
Your loving Anna; letters from the Ontario frontier. [Toronto] University of Toronto Press [1972] 120 p. 23 cm. [CS90.L48 1972] 72-86392 ISBN 0-8020-1927-7 7.50
1. Leveridge family. 2. Hastings Co., Ont.—History. I. Leveridge, Anna Maria Godbolt, 1846-1928. Letters. 1972. II. Title.

TIVY, Louis, 1902-1972. 929'.2'0971
Your loving Anna; letters from the Ontario frontier. Toronto University of Toronto Press [1974, c1972] 120 p. 23 cm. [CS90.L48 1972] ISBN 0-8020 ISBN 0-8020-6166-4. 2.95 (pbk.)
1. Leveridge family. 2. Hastings Co., Ont—History. I. Leveridge, Anna Maria Godbolt, 1846-1928 Letters. 1972. II. Title.
L.C. card no. for hardcover edition: 72-86392. BIP

Leverone, Nathaniel.

ZEHNPFENNIG, Gladys 926.5
Nathaniel Leverone, pioneer in automatic merchandising. Minneapolis, Denison [c.1963] 281p. 22cm. (Men of achievement ser.) 63-19060 3.50
1. Leverone, Nathaniel. 2. Vending machines. I. Title.

ZEHNPFENNIG, Gladys. 926.5
Nathaniel Leverone, pioneer in automatic merchandising. Minneapolis, T. S. Denison [1963] 281 p. 22 cm. (Men of achievement series) [HF5483.Z4] 63-19060
1. Leverone, Nathaniel. 2. Vending machines. I. Title.

Leverson, Ada.

WYNDHAM, Violet. 928.2
The sphinx and her circle; a biographical sketch of Ada Leverson, 1862-1933. New York, Vanguard Press [1964, c1963] 128 p. ports. 22 cm. [PR6023.E875Z95 1964] 64-16261
1. Leverson, Ada. I. Title.

Levi Isaac ben Meir, of Berdichev, 1740-1809.

DRESNER, Samuel H. 296.6'1 B
Levi Yitzhak of Berditchev; portrait of a Hasidic master, by Samuel H. Dresner. New York, Hartmore House [1974] 224 p. map. 25 cm. Bibliography: p. 223-224. [BM755.L44D73] 73-91739 ISBN 0-87677-144-4 10.00
1. Levi Isaac ben Meir, of Berdichev, 1740-1809. I. Title. BIP

Levin, Arieh, 1885-1969.

RAZ, Simhah. 296.6'1'0924 B
A tzaddik in our time : the life of Rabbi Aryeh Levin / Simcha Raz ; translated from the Hebrew, rev., and expanded by Charles Wengrov ; foreword by Isser Judah Unterman ; introd. by Chaim Herzog ; [edited by Isaiah Dvorkas]. 1st ed. Jerusalem ; New York : Feldheim Publishers, c1976. 468 p. : ill. ; 25 cm. Translation of Ish tsadik hayah. [BM755.L446R3813] 77-371079 ISBN 0-87306-130-6 : 12.50
1. Levin, Arieh, 1885-1969. 2. Rabbis—Jerusalem—Biography. 3. Chaplains, Prison—Jerusalem—Biography. 4. Jews in Jerusalem—Social life and customs. I. Title.

Levine, Eugen.

MEYER-LEVINE, Rosa, 1890- 335'.0092'4 B
Levine, the Spartacist / Rosa Levine-Meyer ; with an introd. by E. J. Hobsbawm. London ; New York : Gordon & Cremonesi, 1978. x, 225 p. ; 24 cm. (Gordon & Cremonesi : paper editions) Includes bibliographical references and index. [DD248.L4M494] 78-325667 ISBN 0-86033-062-1 pbk. : 6.95
1. Levine, Eugen. 2. Revolutionists—Germany—Biography. 3. Germany—History—Revolution, 1918. 4. Communism—Bavaria. I. Title.
Distributed by Atheneum, New York BIP

Levin, Louis Hiram, 1866-1923.

LEVIN, Alexandra Lee, 1912- 361'.92'4 B
Dare to be different; a biography of Louis H. Levin of Baltimore, a pioneer in Jewish social service. New York, Bloch Pub. Co. [1972] xvi, 319 p. illus. 22 cm. Bibliography: p. [301]-306. [HV28.L45L4] 73-184073 ISBN 0-8197-0280-3 7.50
1. Levin, Louis Hiram, 1866-1923. I. Title.

Levin, Shmarya,

LEVIN, Shmarya, 1867-1935 956.94/001/0924
Forward from exile; the autobiography of Shmarya Levin. Tr., ed. by Maurice Samuel. [1st ed.] Philadelphia, Jewish Pubn. Soc. of Amer., 1967. xxiii, 419p. 22cm. Issued previously in three separate vs. with titles: Childhood in exile; Youth in revolt; The arena. [DS135.R95L358] (B) 67-16188 7.50
I. Title. II. Title: Childhood in exile. III. Title: Youth in revolt. IV. Title: The arena.

LEVIN, Shmarya, 1867-1935. 956.94'001'0924 (B)
Forward from exile; the autobiography of Shmarya Levin. Translated and edited by Maurice Samuel. [1st ed.] Philadelphia, Jewish Publication Society of America, 1967. xxiii, 419 p. 22 cm. Issued previously in three separate volumes with titles: Childhood in exile: Youth in revolt; The arena. [DS135.R95L358] 67-16188
I. Title. II. Title: Childhood in exile. III. Title: Youth in revolt. IV. Title: The arena.

Levin, Shmarya, 1867-1935.

LEVIN, Shmarya, 1867-1935. 956.94'001'0924 B
The arena / by Shmarya Levin. New York : Arno Press, 1975 [c1932] v, 305 p. ; 23 cm. (The Modern Jewish experience) Reprint of the ed. published by Harcourt, Brace, New York. The third part of the author's autobiography; the first of which has title: Childhood in exile, and the second: Youth in revolt. [DS151.L44A333 1975] 74-27999 ISBN 0-405-06726-7 : 19.00
1. Levin, Shmarya, 1867-1935. 2. Zionists—Correspondence, reminiscences, etc. 3. Jews in Russia—Politics and government. I. Title. II. Series.

LEVIN, Shmarya, 1867-1935 956.94/001/0924
Forward from exile; the autobiography of Shmarya Levin. Tr., ed. by Maurice Samuel. [1st ed.] Philadelphia, Jewish Pubn. Soc. of Amer., 1967. xxiii, 419p. 22cm. Issued previously in three separate vs. with titles: Childhood in exile; Youth in revolt; The arena. [DS135.R95L358] (B) 67-16188 7.50
I. Title. II. Title: Childhood in exile. III. Title: Youth in revolt. IV. Title: The arena.

LEVIN, Shmarya, 1867-1935. 956.94'001'0924 (B)
Forward from exile; the autobiography of Shmarya Levin. Translated and edited by Maurice Samuel. [1st ed.] Philadelphia, Jewish Publication Society of America, 1967. xxiii, 419 p. 22 cm. Issued previously in three separate volumes with titles: Childhood in exile: Youth in revolt; The arena. [DS135.R95L358] 67-16188
I. Title. II. Title: Childhood in exile. III. Title: Youth in revolt. IV. Title: The arena.

Levine, Isaac Don, 1892-

LEVINE, Isaac Don, 1892- 070.4'1'0924
Eyewitness to history; memoirs and reflections of a foreign correspondent for half a century. New York, Hawthorn Books [1973] xii, 305 p. illus. 25 cm. "A Martin Dale book." Includes bibliographical references. [PN4874.L39A34] 72-4919 10.00
1. Levine, Isaac Don, 1892- 2. Foreign correspondents—Correspondence, reminiscences, etc. I. Title.

Levine, Lawrence W.

LEVINE, Lawrence W. 923.273
Defender of the faith: William Jennings Bryan; the last decade, 1915-1925. New York, Oxford Univ. Pr. [1968, c.1965] ix, 386p. port. 20cm. (GB 254) Bibl. [E664,B87L4] 65-12465 2.25 pap.,
I. Bryan, William Jennings, 1860-1925. II. Title.

Levitt, Zola.

LEVITT, Zola. 248'.246 B
Christ in the country club / Zola Levitt and Daniel M. McGann. Scottdale, Pa. : Herald Press, c1976. 120 p. ; 18 cm. [BV2623.L45A32] 76-5299 ISBN 0-8361-1315-2 pbk. : 1.75
1. Levitt, Zola. 2. McGann, D. 3. Converts—United States—Biography. I. McGann, D., joint author. II. Title. BIP

LEVITT, Zola. 248'.246'0924 B
Corned beef, knishes and Christ : the story of a 20th-century Levite / Zola Levitt. Wheaton, Ill. : Tyndale House Publishers, 1975. 145 p. ; 18 cm. Autobiographical. [BV2623.L45A33] 74-19647 ISBN 0-8423-0440-1 pbk. : 1.45
1. Levitt, Zola. I. Title.

LEVITT, Zola. 248'.246'0924 B
The underground church of Jerusalem / by Zola Levitt. Nashville : T. Nelson, c1978. 166 p. ; 21 cm. [DS107.4.L45] 77-14970 pbk. : 2.95
1. Levitt, Zola. 2. Israel—Description and travel. 3. Converts from Judaism—Biography. 4. Missions to Jews—Israel. I. Title. BIP

Levski, Vasil Ivanov, 1837-1873.

MACDERMOTT, Mercia. 949.7'701'0924 B
Apostle of freedom; a portrait of Vasil Levsky against a background of nineteenth century Bulgaria. [1st American ed.] South Brunswick [N.J.] A. S. Barnes [1969, c1967] 407 p. illus., map, ports. 22 cm. Bibliography: p. 395-400. [DR83.2.L4M3 1969] 68-29859 7.50
1. Levski, Vasil Ivanov, 1837-1873. I. Title.

Levy, Aaron, 1742-1815.

FISH, Sidney Meshulam, 1908- 923.273
Aaron Levy, founder of Aaronsburg; with a foreword by Lee M. Friedman. New York, American Jewish Historical Society, 1951. ix, 81 p. illus., ports. 24 cm. (Studies in American Jewish history, no. 1) Bibliographical footnotes. [F153.L5F5] 51-2554
1. Levy, Aaron, 1742-1815. I. Title. II. Series.

Levy, George Morton.

LITTLETON, Martin Wilie, 1872- 923.473
My partner-in- law; the life of George Morton Levy, by Martin W. Littleton as told to Kyle Crichton. New York, Farrar, Straus & Cudahy [1957] 256p. 22cm. 57-10318
1. Levy, George Morton. I. Crichton, Kyle Samuel, 1896- II. Title.

LITTLETON, Martin Wilson, 1897- 923.473
My partner-in-law, the life of George Morton Levy, by Martin W. Littleton as told to Kyle Crichton. New York, Farrar, Straus & Cudahy [1957] 256 p. 22 cm. 57-10318
1. Levy, George Morton. I. Crichton, Kyle Smauel, 1896-1960. II. Title.

LITTLETON, Martin Wilson, 1897- 923.473
My partner-in-law; the life of George Morton Levy, by Martin W. Littleton as told to Kyle Crichton. New York, Farrar, Straus & Cudahy [1957] 256 p. 22cm. [KF373.L48L58] 57-10318
1. Levy, George Morton. I. Crichton, Kyle Samuel, 1896-1960. II. Title.

Levy, Harriet Lane.

LEVY, Harriet Lane. 301.45'19'24024 B
920 O'Farrell Street / Harriet Lane Levy. New York : Arno Press, 1975, c1947. vi, 273 p. : ill. ; 22 cm. (The Modern Jewish experience) Autobiographical. Reprint of the ed. published by Doubleday, Garden City, N.Y. [CT275.L378A3 1975] 74-29501 ISBN 0-405-06728-3 : 17.00
1. Levy, Harriet Lane. 2. San Francisco—Social life and customs. I. Title. II. Series.

Levy, Uriah Phillips, 1792-1862.

EISEMAN, Alberta. 973'.04'924 B
Rebels and reformers : biographies of four Jewish Americans : Uriah Phillips Levy, Ernestine L. Rose, Louis D. Brandeis, Lillian D. Wald / by Alberta Eiseman ; illustrated by Herb Steinberg. 1st ed. Garden City, N.Y. : Zenith Books, 1976. 131 p. : ill. ; 22 cm. Includes index. Biographies of four Jewish Americans whose activities in women's rights, abolition, law, nursing, and the military contributed to the growth, development, and needed reform of the country. [E184.J5E34] 920 75-21224 ISBN 0-385-01588-7 : 4.95. ISBN 0-385-09662-3 pbk. : 2.50
1. Levy, Uriah Phillips, 1792-1862. 2. Rose, Ernestine Louise, 1810-1892. 3. Brandeis, Louis Dembitz, 1856-1941. 4. Wald, Lillian D., 1867-1940. 5. Jews in the United States. I. Steinberg, Herbert, 1928- II. Title.

FITZPATRICK, Donovan. 923.573
Navy maverick: Uriah Phillips Levy [by] Donovan Fitzpatrick and Saul Saphire. [1st ed.] Garden City, N.Y., Doubleday, 1963. 273 p. illus. 22 cm. Includes bibliography. [E182.L55F5] 63-12985
1. Levy, Uriah Phillips, 1792-1862. I. Saphire, Saul, 1893- joint author. II. Title.

STERNLICHT, Sanford V 359.32
Uriah Phillips Levy, the Blue Star Commodore, by Sanford V. Sternlicht. Together with an account of the relationship between the Commodore Levy Chapel, United States Naval Station, Norfolk, and the Norfolk Jewish community. Foreword by Arych Lev. Compiled and edited by Malcolm H. Stern. Norfolk, Va., Norfolk Jewish Community Council [1961] 64 p. illus. 24 cm. [E182.L55S8] 61-18250
1. Levy, Uriah Phillips, 1792-1862. 2. U.S. Naval Station, Norfolk, Va. Commodore Levy Chapel. I. Title.

Levy, Uriah Phillips, 1792-1862—Juvenile literature.

FELTON, Harold W., 1902- 973.60924 B
Uriah Phillips Levy / Harold W. Felton. New York : Dodd, Mead, [1978] p. cm. Includes index. Bibliography: p. A biography of the Jewish American who fought anti-semitism within the United States Navy and was instrumental in preserving Thomas Jefferson's home, Monticello. [E182.L55F38] 78-7726 ISBN 0-396-07604-1 : 5.25
1. Levy, Uriah Phillips, 1792-1862—Juvenile literature. 2. United States. Navy—Biography—Juvenile literature. 3. Jews in the United States—Biography—Juvenile literature. I. Title. BIP

Lewes, George Henry, 1817-1878.

TJOA, Hock Guan, 1943- 192
George Henry Lewes : a Victorian mind / Hock Guan Tjoa. Cambridge, Mass. : Harvard University Press, 1977. vii, 172 p, , 21 cm. (Harvard historical monographs ; 70) Includes index. Bibliography: p. 149-151. [B1593.Z7T59] 77-8610 10.00
1. Lewes, George Henry, 1817-1878. 2. Philosophers—England—Biography. I. Title. II. Series. BIP

Lewin, Kurt, 1890-1947.

MARROW, Alfred Jay, 1905- 150.19'82'0924
The practical theorist; the life and work of Kurt Lewin, by Alfred J. Marrow. New York, Basic Books [1969] xxii, 290 p. illus., ports. 24 cm. "A bibliography of the works of Kurt Lewin": p. 238-243. Bibliography: p. 267-284. [HM251.M286] 73-93693 8.50
1. Lewin, Kurt, 1890-1947. I. Title. BIP

MARROW, Alfred Jay, 1905- 150'.1'9820924
The practical theorist : the life and work of Kurt Lewin / by Alfred J. Marrow. New York : Teachers College Press, 1977, c1969. xxii, 290 p., [3] leaves of plates : ill. ; 24 cm. Reprint of the ed. published by Basic Books, New York. Includes index. "A bibliography of the wrks of Kurt Lewin": p. 238-243. [HM251.M286 1977] 77-1400 ISBN 0-8077-2525-0 pbk. : 5.95
1. Lewin, Kurt, 1890-1947. 2. Psychologists—Biography. I. Title.

Lewis, Alfred Baker, 1897-

LEWIS, Alfred Baker, 1897- 362'.924 B
A political odyssey, alone and together : memoirs / by Alfred Baker Lewis. 1st ed. Hicksville, N.Y. : Exposition Press, c1979. 200 p. ; 22 cm. [H59.L46A36] 79-50692 ISBN 0-682-49343-0 : 8.00
1. Lewis, Alfred Baker, 1897- 2. Social reformers—United States—Biography. I. Title.

Lewis, Alfred Henry, 1857-1914.

RAVITZ, Abe C. 813'.4
Alfred Henry Lewis / by Abe C. Ravitz. Boise, Idaho : Boise State University, c1978. 46 p. ; 21 cm. (Boise State University Western writers series ; no. 32) Bibliography: p. 45-46. [PS3523.E8468Z85] 78-52560 ISBN 0-88430-056-0 pbk. : 2.00
1. Lewis, Alfred Henry, 1857-1914. 2. Novelists, American—19th century—Biography. I. Series: Boise State University. Boise State University Western writers series ; no. 32. BIP

Lewis and Clark Expedition—Juvenile literature.

GRANT, Matthew G. 917.8'04'2
Lewis and Clark, western trailblazers, by Matthew G. Grant. Illustrated by John Kelly and Don Pulver. [Mankato, Minn., Creative Education; distributed by Childrens Press, Chicago, 1974] 29 p. illus. (part col.) 25 cm. (His Gallery of great Americans series. Explorers of America) An easy-to-read account of the expedition to explore the Louisiana Territory and the two men who led it. [F592.7.G72] 920 73-14582 ISBN 0-87191-277-5 3.95
1. Lewis and Clark Expedition—Juvenile literature. 2. Lewis, Meriwether, 1774-1809—Juvenile literature. 3. Clark, William, 1770-1838—Juvenile literature. I. Keely, John, illus. II. Pulver, Don, illus. III. Title.

Lewis and Clark Expedition—Sources.

JACKSON, Donald Dean, 1919- ed. 978'.02'0924
Letters of the Lewis and Clark Expedition, with related documents, 1783-1854 / edited by Donald Jackson. 2d ed., with additional documents and notes. Urbana : University of Illinois Press, c1978. 2 v. (xxxi, 806 p., [12] leaves of plates : ill. ; 25 cm. Includes index. Bibliography: v. 2, p. 750-769. [F592.7.J14 1978] 78-15288 ISBN 0-252-00697-6 : 35.00 ISBN 0-252-00705-0 : 75.00 (deluxe)
1. Lewis and Clark Expedition—Sources. 2. Lewis, Meriwether, 1774-1809. 3. Clark, William, 1770-1838. 4. The West—History—To 1848—Sources. 5. Explorers—The West—Correspondence. BIP

Lewis, Carola Regester.

LEWIS, Carola Regester. 917.3'03'920924
Ramblings. Parsons, W. Va., McClain Print, Co., 1974 194 p. illus. 23 cm. [CT275.L3833A34] 73-91452 ISBN 0-87012-161-8 6.50
1. Lewis, Carola Regester. 2. Lewis, Allen L. I. Title. BIP

Lewis Cass Expedition, 1820.

DOUGLASS, David Bates, 1790-1849. 917.74'8'043
American voyageur; the journal of David Bates Douglass. Edited by Sydney W. Jackman and John F. Freeman. Assisted by Donald S. Rickard and James L. Carter. [1st ed.] Marquette, Northern Michigan University Press, 1969. xxii, 128 p. illus., maps, port. 24 cm. Bibliography: p. 122-124. [F484.3.D67] 77-95246 4.25
1. Lewis Cass Expedition, 1820. I. Jackman, Sydney Wayne, 1925- ed. II. Freeman. John F., ed. III. Title. BIP

Lewis, Cecil Day

LEWIS, Cecil Day 928.2
The buried day. New York, Harper [c.1960] 243p. illus. port. 22cm. 60-10402 3.95half cloth,
I. Title.

Lewis, Clive Staples, 1898-1963.

GREEN, Roger Lancelyn. 828'.9'1209 B
C. S. Lewis; a biography [by] Roger Lancelyn Green & Walter Hooper. [1st American ed.] New York, Harcourt, Brace, Jovanovich [1974] 320 p. 22 cm. [BX5199.L53G73] 74-11360 ISBN 0-15-123190-7 6.95
1. Lewis, Clive Staples, 1898-1963. I. Hooper, Walter, joint author. II. Title. BIP

GREEN, Roger Lancelyn. 828'.9'1209 B
C. S. Lewis : a biography / Roger Lancelyn Green & Walter Hooper. New York : Harcourt Brace Jovanovich, c1974. 320 p. ; 21 cm. (A Harvest book ; HB 331) Includes index. [BX5199.L53G73 1974c] 75-29425 ISBN 0-15-623205-7 pbk. : 3.95
1. Lewis, Clive Staples, 1898-1963. I. Hooper, Walter, joint author. II. Title.

Lewis, Clive Staples, 1898-1963—Addresses, essays, lectures.

C. S. Lewis at the breakfast table, and other reminiscences / edited by James T. Como. New York : Macmillan, c1979. p. cm. "A bibliography of the writing of C. S. Lewis, revised and enlarged [by] Walter Hooper": p. [PR6023.E926Z598] 79-9778 ISBN 0-02-570620-9 : 9.95 828'.9'1209 B
1. Lewis, Clive Staples, 1898-1963—Addresses, essays, lectures. 2. Authors, English—20the century—Biography—Addresses, essays, lectures. I. Lewis, Clive Staples, 1898-1963. II. Como, James T.

Lewis, Clive Staples, 1898-1963—Biography.

GILBERT, Douglas, 1942- 828'.9'1209 B
C. S. Lewis: images of his world. [Photography by] Douglas Gilbert. [Text by] Clyde S. Kilby. Grand Rapids, Mich., W. B. Eerdmans Pub. Co. [1973] 192 p. illus. 24 x 29 cm. Includes bibliographical references. [PR6023.E926Z66] 73-8697 ISBN 0-8028-1545-6 12.95
1. Lewis, Clive Staples, 1898-1963—Biography. I. Kilby, Clyde S. II. Title.

Lewis, Clive Staples, 1898-1963—Biography—Juvenile literature.

ARNOTT, Anne. 828'.9'1209 B
The secret country of C. S. Lewis. Illus. by Patricia Frost. Grand Rapids, Eerdmans [1975] 127 p. illus. 21 cm Bibliography: 125-127. A biography of C. S. Lewis emphasizing his growth from boyhood into an author famed for both adult and children's books and his zeal in the Christian faith which he adopted as an adult. [PR6023.E926Z58 1974] 92 74-13191 4.95
1. Lewis, Clive Staples, 1898-1963—Biography—Juvenile literature. I. Frost, Patricia, illus. II. Title. BIP

Lewis, Clive Staples, 1898-1963—Correspondence.

LEWIS, Clive Staples, 1898-1963. 826.912
Letters. Edited, with a memoir, by W. H. Lewis. [1st American ed.] New York, Harcourt, Brace & World [1966] 308 p. 8 plates (incl. ports.) 22 cm. [PR6023.E926Z535 1966a] 66-22280
I. Lewis, Warren Hamilton.

LEWIS, Clive Staples, 1898-1963. 828'.9'1209 B
Letters of C. S. Lewis. Edited, with a memoir, by W. H. Lewis. New York, Harcourt Brace Jovanovich [1975, c1966] 308 p. 21 cm. (A Harvest book, HB 300) [PR6023.E926Z535 1975] 74-13416 4.25 (pbk.)
1. Lewis, Clive Staples, 1898-1963—Correspondence. I. Lewis, Warren Hamilton. BIP

Lewis, Clive Staples, 1898-1963— Friends and associates.

CARPENTER, Humphrey. 823'.9'12 B
The inklings : C. S. Lewis, J. R. R. Tolkien, Charles Williams, and their friends / by Humphrey Carpenter. 1st American ed. Boston : Houghton Mifflin, 1978, c1979. xiv, 287 p., [8] leaves of : ill. ; 25 cm. Includes index. Bibliography: p. 260-265. [PR6023.E926Z613 1979] 78-26042 ISBN 0-395-27628-4 : 9.95
1. Lewis, Clive Staples, 1898-1963—Friends and associates. 2. Tolkien, John Ronald Reuel, 1892-1973—Friends and associates. 3. Williams, Charles, 1886-1945—Friends and associates. 4. Authors, English—20th century—Biography. 5. Oxford—Biography. 6. England—Intellectual life—20th century. I. Title.

Lewis, David, 1814-1895, tr.

TERESA, Saint, 1515-1582 922.246
The life of St. Teresa of Avila, including the relations of her spiritual state, written by herself. Tr. from Spanish by David Lewis. Introd. by David Knowles. Westminster, Md., Newman [c.1962] 432p. 20cm. (Orchard bks.) 62-51605 4.50
1. Lewis, David, 1814-1895, tr. I. Title.

Lewis, Fulton.

HERNDON, Booton. 920.5
Praised and damned; the story of Fulton Lewis, Jr. Edited by Gordon Carroll. [1st ed.] New York, Duell, Sloan and Pearce [1954] 147 p. 20 cm. [PN4874.L4H4] 54-8290
1. Lewis, Fulton. I. Title.

Lewis, George, 1900-1968.

BETHELL, Tom. 788'.62'0924 B
George Lewis : a jazzman from New Orleans / Tom Bethell. Berkeley : University of California Press, c1977. 387 p. : ill. ; 23 cm. Discography: p. [291]-363; bibliography: p. [371]-379; includes index. [ML419.L45B5] 76-3872 12.50
1. Lewis, George, 1900-1968. 2. Jazz musicians—Louisiana—New Orleans—Biography. 3. Jazz music—Louisiana—New Orleans. BIP

TAIT, Dorothy. 788'.62 B
Call him George [by] Ann Fairbairn. New York, Crown Publishers [1969] 303 p. illus. 22 cm. [ML419.L45T3 1969] 73-93389 5.95
1. Lewis, George, 1900-1968.

Lewis, Gilbert Newton, 1875-1946.

LACHMAN, Arthur, 1873- 925.4
Borderland of the unknown; the life story of Gilbert Newton Lewis, one of the world's great scientists. [1st ed. New York] Pageant Press, 1955. 184p. 21cm. [QD22.L57L3] 55-8382
1. Lewis, Gilbert Newton, 1875-1946. I. Title.

[Lewis, Gladys Adelina]

[LEWIS, Gladys Adelina] 920.7
call house madam',; the story of the career of Beverly Davis, as told by Serge G. Wolsey [pseud.] New York, Paperback Lib. [193)063, c.1942, 1954] 320p. 18cm. (Gold ed., 54-187) .75 pap.,
I. Title.

Lewis, Graceanna, 1821-1912.

WARNER, Deborah Jean. 500.9'092'4 B
Graceanna Lewis, scientist and humanitarian / Deborah Jean Warner. Washington : Smithsonian Institution Press, 1979. p. cm. Includes index. Bibliography: p. [QH31.L65W37] 79-14366 ISBN 0-87474-955-7 pbk. : 3.95
1. Lewis, Graceanna, 1821-1912. 2. Naturalists—United States—Biography. 3. Philanthropists—United States—Biography. I. Title.

Lewis, Gwilym Hugh.

LEWIS, Gwilym Hugh. 940.4'49'410924 B
Wings over the Somme, 1916-1918 / by Gwilym H. Lewis; edited by Chaz Bowyer] London : Kimber, 1976. 205 p. : ill., facsims., map, ports. ; 24 cm. Includes index. [D640.L454] 77-351194 ISBN 0-7183-0324-5 : £4.95
1. Lewis, Gwilym Hugh. 2. Great Britain. Royal Flying Corps—Biography. 3. European War, 1914-1918—Personal narratives, English. 4. European War, 1914-1918—Aerial operations, British. 5. Air pilots—Great Britain—Biography. I. Title.

Lewis, Henry Clay.

ANDERSON, John Q 817.3
Louisiana swamp doctor. Baton Rouge, Louisiana State University Press [1962] xi, 296p. illus., facsims. 23cm. [PS2246.L363Z56] 62-10480
1. Lewis, Henry Clay. I. Lewis, Henry Clay. Dod leves from the life of a Louisiana Swamp doctor' II. Title. Contents omitted.

Lewis, Isham, d. 1815(?)

MERRILL, Boynton, 1925- 976.9'03
Jefferson's nephews : a frontier tragedy / Boynton Merrill, Jr. Princeton, N.J. : Princeton University Press, c1976. p. cm. Includes index. Bibliography: p. [F455.M47] 76-3267 ISBN 0-691-04640-9 : 16.50
1. Lewis, Isham, d. 1815(?) 2. Lewis, Lilburn, d. 1812. 3. Lewis family. 4. Kentucky—History—1792-1865. I. Title. BIP

Lewis, Jerry, 1926-

GEHMAN, Richard. 927.92
That kid: the story of Jerry Lewis. [New York, Avon Books, 1964] 192 p. 18 cm. "S145." [PN2287.L435G4] 64-1492
1. Lewis, Jerry, 1926- I. Title.

Lewis, Joe E.

COHN, Art, 1909-1958. 927.92
The joker is wild; the story of Joe E. Lewis. New York, Random House [1955] 368 p. illus. 21 cm. [PN2287.L44C6] 55-10633
1. Lewis, Joe E. I. Title.

Lewis, John,

LEWIS, John, 1889- 335.40924 (B)
The life and teaching of Karl Marx. [1st U.S. ed.] New York, International Publishers [1965] 286 p. 21 cm. Bibliographical footnotes. [HX39.5.L45218] 65-9169
I. Marx, Karl, 1818-1883. II. Title.

Lewis, John Llewellyn, 1880-1969.

ALINSKY, Saul David, 1909-1972. 331.88'33'0924 B
John L. Lewis, an unauthorized biography. New York, Vintage Books [1970] xvii, 389 p. 19 cm. Includes bibliographical references. [HD8073.L4A5 1970] 77-128443 ISBN 0-394-70882-2
1. Lewis, John Llewellyn, 1880-1969.

DUBOFSKY, Melvyn, 1934- 331.88'33'0924 B
John L. Lewis : a biography / Melvyn Dubofsky and Warren Van Tine. New York : Quadrangle/New York Times Book Co., c1977. xvii, 619 p. : ill. ; 24 cm. Includes index. Bibliography: p. 593-600. [HD6509.L4D8 1977] 76-50819 ISBN 0-8129-0673-X : 17.50
1. Lewis, John Llewellyn, 1880-1969. 2. United Mine Workers of America—History. 3. Trade-unions—United States—Officials and employees—Biography. I. Van Time, Warren R., joint author.

WECHSLER, James Arthur, 1915- 331.88'33'0924 B
Labor baron: a portrait of John L. Lewis, by James A. Wechsler. Westport, Conn., Greenwood Press [1972, c1944] viii, 278 p. 22 cm. Bibliography: p. 269-271. [HD8073.L4W4 1972] 72-143312 ISBN 0-8371-5968-7
1. Lewis, John Llewellyn, 1880-1969. I. Title.

Lewis, John Llewellyn, 1880-1969— Juvenile literature.

KORSON, George Gershon, 1899-1967. 331.881'2'2330924 B
John L. Lewis, young militant labor leader. Illustrated by Fred M. Irvin. Indianapolis, Bobbs-Merrill [1970] 200 p. col. illus. 20 cm. (Childhood of famous Americans) Bibliography: p. 198. A biography concentrating on the childhood of the former President of the United Mine Workers. [HD6509.L4K6] 92 71-127588
1. Lewis, John Llewellyn, 1880-1969—Juvenile literature. I. Irvin, Fred M., illus. II. Title.

KURLAND, Gerald, 1942- 331.88'33'0924 B
John L. Lewis, strong willed organizer. Charlotteville, N.Y., SamHar Press, 1973. 32 p. 22 cm. (Outstanding personalities, no. 56) Bibliography: p. 32. A brief biography of the leader of industrial unionism and the founder of the Congress of Industrial Organizations (CIO). [HD8073.L4K87] 73-77597 0.98 (pbk.)
1. Lewis, John Llewellyn, 1880-1969—Juvenile literature. I. Title. Library binding; 1.98.

Lewis, Joseph Cephus, 1885-

TOWLER, Juby Earl, 1913- 923.573
The evil we seek; a biography of Detective Capt'n Joe Lewis of the Danville, Va., Police Department. Illus. by Fred Cousins. [1st ed. Danville, Va., 1952] 120 p. illus. 23 cm. [HV7911.L45T6] 52-43260
1. Lewis, Joseph Cephus, 1885- 2. Crime and criminals — Virginia — Danville. I. Title.

Lewis, Lilburn, d. 1812.

MERRILL, Boynton, 1925- 976.9'03
Jefferson's nephews : a frontier tragedy / Boynton Merrill, Jr. Princeton, N.J. : Princeton University Press, c1976. p. cm. Includes index. Bibliography: p. [F455.M47] 76-3267 ISBN 0-691-04640-9 : 16.50
1. Lewis, Isham, d. 1815(?) 2. Lewis, Lilburn, d. 1812. 3. Lewis family. 4. Kentucky—History—1792-1865. I. Title. BIP

Lewis, Matthew Gregory, 1775-1818.

PECK, Louis F 1904- 928.2
A life of Matthew G. Lewis. Cambridge, Harvard University Press, 1961. ix, 331p. ports., facsims. 25cm. 'Selected letters': p. [181]-272. 'Lewis' principal works': p. [275]-276. Bibliography: p.[277]-288. [PR4888.P4] 61-11027
1. Lewis, Matthew Gregory, 1775-1818. I. Title. BIP

Lewis, Meriwether, 1774-1809.

BEBENROTH, Charlotta M., 1890- 973.4'6'0924 B
Meriwether Lewis, boy explorer. Illustrated by Edward Caswell. Indianapolis, Bobbs-Merrill [1953] 182 p. illus. 20 cm. (The Childhood of famous Americans series) A childhood spent roaming the woods at night and in all weather, caring for lost animals, and running his mother's plantation prepared Meriwether Lewis for leadership of the expedition across the Louisiana Territory. [PZ7.B3806Me2] 92 AC 68
1. Lewis, Meriwether, 1774-1809. I. Caswell, Edward C., illus. II. Title.

DILLON, Richard H. 923.973065-10888
Meriwether Lewis; a biography. New York, Coward [c.]1965. xvii, 364p. illus. 22cm. Bibl. [F592.7.L678] 6.95
1. Lewis, Meriwether, 1774-1809. I. Title.

DILLON, Richard H. 923.973
Meriwether Lewis; a biography [by] Richard Dillon. New York, Coward-McCann, 1965. xvii, 364 p. illus. 22 cm. [F592.7.L678] 65-10888
1. Lewis, Meriwether, 1774-1809.

FISHER, Vardis, 1895-1968. 923.973
Suicide or murder? The strange death of Governor Meriwether Lewis. Denver, A. Swallow [1962] 288 p. illus., ports., facsims. 23 cm. Bibliographical references included in "Acknowledgments and notes" (p. [276]-285) [F592.7.L68] 62-12402
1. Lewis, Meriwether, 1774-1809. I. Title.

JACKSON, Donald Dean, 1919- ed. 978'.02'0924
Letters of the Lewis and Clark Expedition, with related documents, 1783-1854 / edited by Donald Jackson. 2d ed., with additional documents and notes. Urbana : University of Illinois Press, c1978. 2 v. (xxxi, 806 p., [12] leaves of plates : ill. ; 25 cm. Includes index. Bibliography: v. 2, p. 750-769. [F592.7.J14 1978] 78-15288 ISBN 0-252-00697-6 : 35.00 ISBN 0-252-00705-0 : 75.00 (deluxe)
1. Lewis and Clark Expedition—Sources. 2. Lewis, Meriwether, 1774-1809. 3. Clark, William, 1770-1838. 4. The West—History—To 1848—Sources. 5. Explorers—The West—Correspondence. BIP

Lewis, Meriwether, 1774-1809— Juvenile literature.

GRANT, Matthew G. 917.8'04'2
Lewis and Clark, western trailblazers, by Matthew G. Grant. Illustrated by John Kelly and Don Pulver. [Mankato, Minn., Creative Education; distributed by Childrens Press, Chicago, 1974] 29 p. illus. (part col.) 25 cm. (His Gallery of great Americans series. Explorers of America) An easy-to-read account of the expedition to explore the Louisiana Territory and the two men who led it. [F592.7.G72] 920 73-14582 ISBN 0-87191-277-5 3.95
1. Lewis and Clark Expedition—Juvenile literature. 2. Lewis, Meriwether, 1774-1809—Juvenile literature. 3. Clark, William, 1770-1838—Juvenile literature. I. Keely, John, illus. II. Pulver, Don, illus. III. Title.

HAYS, Wilma Pitchford. 973.4'6'0924
The Meriwether Lewis mystery. Philadelphia, Westminster Press [1971] 128 p. illus., map, ports. 24 cm. Bibliography: p. [125] A biography of the man who commanded the 1804-1806 expedition to the Pacific to explore and map the newly-acquired northwestern territories. [F592.7.H34] 92 70-141194 ISBN 0-664-32493-2 4.95
1. Lewis, Meriwether, 1774-1809—Juvenile literature. I. Title.

Lewis, Norman.

LEWIS, Norman. 940.54'81'41
Naples '44 / Norman Lewis. 1st American ed. New York : Pantheon Books, c1978. 206 p. ; 22 cm. [D811.L432A36 1978b] 78-13060 ISBN 0-394-50354-6 : 8.95
1. Lewis, Norman. 2. Great Britain. Army. Field Security Personnel—Biography. 3. World War, 1939-1945—Personal narratives, English. 4. World War, 1939-1945—Italy—Naples. 5. Naples—History. 6. Soldiers—Great Britain—Biography. I. Title. BIP

Lewis, Rosa (Ovendon)

FIELDING, Daphne (Vivian) 1904- 926.4
The Duchess of Jermyn Street; the life and good times of Rosa Lewis of the Cavendish Hotel, by Daphne Fielding. [Pref. by Evelyn Waugh. 1st American ed.] Boston, Little, Brown [1964] 208 p. illus., ports. 22 cm. [DA566.9.L4F5] 64-12100
1. Lewis, Rosa (Ovendon) I. Title. BIP

Lewis, Rosa Ovendon.

FIELDING, Daphne 641.5'092'4 B
Vivian, 1904-
The Duchess of Jermyn Street : the life and good times of Rosa Lewis of the Cavendish Hotel / by Daphne Fielding. Harmondsworth, Eng. ; New York : Penguin Books, 1978, c1964. 208 p., [17] leaves of plates : ill. ; 19 cm. Reprint of the ed. published by Little, Brown. Includes index. [TX910.5.L48F53 1978] 78-9804 ISBN 0-14-004909-6 pbk. : 1.95
1. Lewis, Rosa Ovendon. 2. Cavendish hotel, London. 3. Hotel management—England—Biography. 4. London—Social life and customs. I. Title.

MASTERS, Anthony, 642'.47'0924' B
1940-
Rosa Lewis, an exceptional Edwardian / Anthony Masters. New York : St. Martin's Press, 1978, c1977. xi, 210 p., [4] leaves of plates : ill. ; 23 cm. Includes index. Bibliography: p. 202-204. [TX910.5.L48M37 1978] 78-3126 ISBN 0-312-69317-6 : 8.95
1. Lewis, Rosa Ovendon. 2. Cavendish hotel, London. 3. Hotel management—Biography. 4. London—Social life and customs. I. Title.

Lewis, Sinclair, 1885-1951.

DERLETH, August William, 818.52
1909-
Three literary men; a memoir of Sinclair Lewis, Sherwood Anderson, Edgar Lee Masters. New York, Candlelight Press, 1963. 56 p. ports. 22 cm. 63-23595
1. Lewis, Sinclair, 1885-1951. 2. Anderson, Sherwood, 1876-1941. 3. Masters, Edgar Lee, 1969-1950. I. Title. **BIP**

GREBSTEIN, Sheldon Norman. v. 12
Sinclair Lewis, by ... New Haven, Conn., College & University Press, 1962. 192 p. 21 cm. 67-95342
1. Lewis, Sinclair, 1885-1951. I. Title. **BIP**

LEWIS, Grace (Hegger) 928.1
With love from Gracie. Sinclair Lewis: 1912-1925. [1st ed.] New York, Harcourt, Brace [c1956, 1955] 335p. illus. 22cm. [PS3523.E94Z62] 55-5325
1. Lewis, Sinclair, 1885-1951. I. Title.

LEWIS, Grace (Hegger) 928.1
With love from Gracie. Sinclair Lewis: 1912-1925. [1st ed.] New York, Harcourt, Brace [c1956, 1955] 335p. illus. 22cm. [PS3523.E94Z62] 55 5325
1. Lewis, Sinclair, 1885-1951. I. Title.

LEWIS, Sinclair, 1885-1951. 928.1
From Main Street to Stockholm; letters of Sinclair Lewis, 1919-1930. Edited and with an introd. by Harrison Smith. [1st ed.] New York, Harcourt, Brace [1952] xii, 307 p. port. 24 cm. [PS3523.E94Z53] 52-6449
1. Harcourt, Brace and Company. I. Harcourt, Alfred, 1881- II. Smith, Harrison, 1888- ed. III. Title.

O'CONNOR, Richard, 813'.5'2 B
1915-
Sinclair Lewis. New York, McGraw-Hill [1971] 144 p. 21 cm. (American writers) Bibliography: p. 140. [PS3523.E94Z66] 72-140258
1. Lewis, Sinclair, 1885-1951.

SCHORER, Mark, 1908- 928.1
Sinclair Lewis, an American life. [1st ed.] New York, McGraw-Hill [1961] 867 p. illus. 25 cm. Includes bibliography. [PS3523.E94Z78] 61-12961
1. Lewis, Sinclair, 1885-1951.

VAN DOREN, Carl 813'.5'2 B
Clinton, 1885-1950.
Sinclair Lewis, a biographical sketch. With a bibliography by Harvey Taylor. Port Washington, N.Y., Kennikat Press [1969, c1933] 205 p. port. 21 cm. Bibliography: p. [77]-187. [PS3523.E94Z9 1969] 77-93075
1. Lewis, Sinclair, 1885-1951. 2. Lewis, Sinclair, 1885-1951—Bibliography. I. Taylor, Harvey. II. Title.

Lewis, Sinclair, 1885-1951—Interviews.

DERLETH, August 810'.9'0052
William, 1909-1971.
Three literary men : a memoir of Sinclair Lewis, Sherwood Anderson, Edgar Lee Masters / by August Derleth. Folcroft, Pa. : Folcroft Library Editions, 1978 [c1963] p. cm. Reprint of the ed. published by Candlelight Press, New York. [PS3507.E69Z475 1978] 78-11518 ISBN 0-8414-3686-X lib. bdg. : 10.00
1. Derleth, August William, 1909-1971—Friends and associates. 2. Lewis, Sinclair, 1885-1951—Interviews. 3. Anderson, Sherwood, 1876-1941—Interviews. 4. Masters, Edgar Lee, 1869-1950—Interviews. 5. Authors, American—20th century—Biography. I. Title.

Lewis, Sir Samuel, 1843-1903.

HARGREAVES, J D 923.2664
A life of Sir Samuel Lewis. London, Oxford University Press, 1958. 111p. illus. 21cm. (West African history series) Includes bibliography. [DT516.H28] 58-1131
1. Lewis, Sir Samuel, 1843-1903. 2. Sierra Leone—Hist. I. Title.

HARGREAVES, John D 923.2664
A life of Sir Samuel Lewis. London, Oxford University Press, 1958. 111 p. illus. 21 cm. (West African history series) Includes bibliography. [DT516.H28] 58-1131
1. Lewis, Sir Samuel, 1843-1903. 2. Sierra Leone — Hist. I. Title.

Lewis, Spencer, 1854-

LEWIS, Eleanor Frances, 1882- 922
Beads of jade [1st ed.] New York, Vantage Press [1958] 258p. illus. 21cm. [BV3427.L46L4] 59-109
1. Lewis, Spencer, 1854- 2. Lewis, Esther M, (Bilble) I. Title.

Lewis, William Bryant.

ASHMORE, Ann Lewis. 922.7675
The call of the Congo. Nashville, Parthenon Press [c1957] 178p. illus. 20cm. [BV3625.C63L4] 58-897
1. Lewis, William Bryant. 2. Lewis, Zaidee Nelson. I. Title.

THE *call of the Congo.* v. 12
Nashville, Parthenon Press [c1957, c1958] 173p. illus. 20cm.
1. Lewis, William Bryant. 2. Lewis, Zaidee Nelson. I. Ashmore, Ann Lewis.

Lewis, William J., 1870-1960.

LEWIS, Willie Newbury. 917.64'8 B
Tapadero: the making of a cowboy. Foreword by Victor White. Austin, University of Texas Press [1972] xvi, 189 p. illus. 23 cm. (The M. K. Brown range life series, no. 11) [F391.L482L4] 76-185237 ISBN 0-292-78001-X 7.50
1. Lewis, William J., 1870-1960. 2. Ranch life—Texas. 3. Cattle trade—Texas. I. Title. **BIP**

Lewis, Wilmarth Sheldon,

LEWIS, Wilmarth 818'.5'203
Sheldon, 1895-
One man's education. [1st ed.] New York, Knopf, 1967. xii, 488, xx p. illus., ports. 25 cm. Autobiography. [CT275.L386A3] 67-18624
I. Title.

Lewis, Wyndham,

LEWIS, Wyndham, 1886- 928.2
Rude assignment; a narrative of my career up-to-date. Illustrated with works by the author. London, New York, Hutchinson [1950] 231 p. illus., ports. 24 cm. "A list of books [by the author] with approximate dates": p. 223. [PR6023.E97Z53] 51-5220
I. Title.

Lewis, Wyndham, 1882-1957.

LEWIS, Wyndham, 1886- 928.2
Rude assignment; a narrative of my career up-to-date. Illustrated with works by the author. London, New York, Hutchinson [1950] 231 p. illus., ports. 24 cm. "A list of books [by the author] with approximate dates": p. 223. [PR6023.E97Z53] 51-5220
I. Title.

PRITCHARD, William H. 823'.9'12
Wyndham Lewis, by William H. Pritchard. New York, Twayne Publishers [1968] 180 p. 21 cm. (Twayne's English authors series, 65) Bibliography: p. 170-175. [PR6023.E97Z84] 68-17244
1. Lewis, Wyndham, 1882-1957.

WAGNER, Geoffrey 828'.9'1209 B
Atheling.
Wyndham Lewis: a portrait of the artist as the enemy, by Geoffrey Wagner. Westport, Conn., Greenwood Press [1973, c1957] xvi, 363 p. 22 cm. Bibliography: p. [315]-348. [PR6023.E97Z95 1973] 72-12320 ISBN 0-8371-6692-6 14.75
1. Lewis, Wyndham, 1882-1957.

Lewis, Wyndham, 1886-1957.

WAGNER, Geoffrey Atheling. 928.2
Wyndlham Lewis, a portrait of the artist as the enemy. New Haven, Yale University Press, 1957. xvi, 363 p. 24 cm. "Checklist of the writings of Wyndham Lewis": p. [315]-336. Bibliography: p. 336-348. [PR6023.E97Z95] 57-6347
1. Lewis, Wyndham, 1886-1957. I. Title.

Lewisohn, Ludwig, 1882-1955—Biography.

LEWISOHN, Ludwig, 813'.5'2 B
1882-1955.
Mid-channel / by Ludwig Lewisohn. New York : Arno Press, 1975, c1929. vi, 310 p. ; 22 cm. (The Modern Jewish experience) Reprint of the ed. published by Harper, New York. The second part of the author's autobiography; the first of which has title: Up stream. The third part, by Ludwig and Edna Lewisohn, has title: Haven. [PS3523.E96Z55 1975] 74-29502 ISBN 0-405-06729-1 : 19.00
1. Lewisohn, Ludwig, 1882-1955—Biography. I. Title. II. Series. **BIP**

Lewton, Val.

SIEGEL, Joel E. 791.43'0233'0924
Val Lewton. the reality of terror [by] Joel E. Siegel. New York, Viking Press [1973] 176 p. illus. 21 cm. (Cinema one, 22) Includes bibliographical references. [PN1998.A3L487] 72-75340 ISBN 0-670-74231-7 6.95
1. Lewton, Val. I. Title.

Leyda, Jay,

LEYDA, Jay, 1910- 928.1
The years and hours of Emily Dickinson. New Haven, Conn., Yale University Press [c.]1960. 2 v. 'The sources': p. 485-488. 'Locations of manuscripts, illustrations, memorabilia'. p.489-503. illus., posed, facsims. 24cm. 'Variety of juxtaposed documents(transcribed and extracted from manuscript and printed sources, ordered and dominated by a single chronology. 60-11132 25.00, back., bxd.
I. Title.

Leyendecker, J. C., 1874-1951.

LEYENDECKER, J. C., 741.9'73
1874-1951.
J. C. Leyendecker, by Michael Schau. New York, Watson-Guptill Publications [1974] 207 p. illus. (part col.) 32 cm. [NC975.5.L4S32] 74-7125 ISBN 0-8230-2757-0 27.50
1. Leyendecker, J. C., 1874-1951. I. Schau, Michael, 1945-

Leyva, Marianna de, known as Signora di Monza, 1575-1650.

MAZZUCCHELLI, Mario, 922.245
1896-
The nun of Monza. Translated by Evelyn Gendel. New York, Simon and Schuster, 1963. 253 p. 22 cm. [BX4705.L619M383] 63-15363
1. Leyva, Marianna de, known as Signora di Monza, 1575-1650. I. Title. **BIP**

Lhevinne, Josef, 1874-1944.

WALLACE, Robert K., 786.1'092'2 B
1944-
A century of music-making : the lives of Josef & Rosina Lhevinne / Robert K. Wallace. Bloomington : Indiana University Press, c1976. xi, 350 p., [9] leaves of plates : ill. ; 24 cm. Includes index. Bibliography: p. 333-335. [ML417.L65W3] 75-28908 ISBN 0-253-31330-9 : 17.50
1. Lhevinne, Josef, 1874-1944. 2. Lhevinne, Rosina, 1880- I. Title. **BIP**

Li, Fei-kan, 1905- —Biography.

†MUNOZ, Vladimiro, 335'.83'0924
1920-
Li Pei Kan and Chinese anarchism / by V. Munoz. New York : Revisionist Press, 1976. p. cm. (Men and movements in the history and philosophy of anarchism) Bibliography: p. [PL2780.F4Z83] 76-21308 ISBN 0-87700-242-8 lib.bdg. : 39.95
1. Li, Fei-kan, 1905- —Biography. 2. Anarchism and anarchists—China—History. I. Title. II. Series.

Li, Hsiu-ch'eng,

LI, Hsiu-ch'eng, 951'.03'0924 B
1823-1864.
The autobiography of the Chung-Wang translated from the Chinese, by W. T. Lay. New York, Praeger Publishers [1970] ix, 104 p. 22 cm. (Praeger scholarly reprints. Source books and studies in Chinese history) Translation of Li Hsiu-ch'eng kung (romanized form) Reprint of the 1865 ed. [DS760.9.L48A3713] 70-104919
I. Title.

Li, Hung-chang, 1823-1901.

BLAND, John Otway 951'.03'0924 B
Percy, 1863-1945.
Li Hung-chang. Freeport, N.Y., Books for Libraries Press [1971] vi, 327 p. 23 cm. Reprint of the 1917 ed. "Bibliographical note": p. [313]-314. [DS763.L6B6 1971] 77 175688 ISBN 0 8369 6603 1
1. Li, Hung-chang, 1823-1901. 2. China—Politics and government.

Li, Khai Fai, 1875-1954.

LI, Ling-ai. 610'.92'2 B
Life is for a long time; a Chinese Hawaiian memoir. New York, Hastings House [1972] v, 343 p. 22 cm. [R604.L46L5] 72-5796 ISBN 0-8038-4284-8 7.95
1. Li, Khai Fai, 1875-1954. 2. Li, Tai Heong Kong, 1875-1950. I. Title. **BIP**

Li Po, 705?-762.

WALEY, Arthur. 928.951
The poetry and career of Li Po, 701-762 A.D. London, G. Allen and Unwin; New York, Macmillan Co. [1950] x, 123 p. 19 cm. (Ethical and religious classics of East and West, no. 3) [PL2997.L5W23] 51-13161
1. Li Po, 705?-762. I. Title.

Li, Tsung-jen, 1890-1969.

LI, Tsung-jen, 951.04'2'0924 B
1890-1969.
The memoirs of Li Tsung-jen / Te-kong Tong and Li Tsung-jen. Boulder, Colo. : Westview Press, [1978] p. cm. (Studies of the East Asian Institute of Columbia University) Includes index. [DS778.L416A35] 78-60155 ISBN 0-89158-343-2 lib. bdg. : 25.00
1. Li, Tsung-jen, 1890-1969. 2. Heads of state—China—Biography. 3. China—

History—Republic, 1912-1949. I. Tong, Te-Kong, 1920- II. Title. III. Series: Columbia University. East Asian Institute. Studies. BIP

Liang, Shu-ming, 1893-

ALITTO, Guy. 181'.09'512 B
The last Confucian : Liang Shu-ming and the Chinese dilemma of modernity / Guy S. Alitto. Berkeley : University of California Press, c1979. xvii, 396 p. : ill. ; 24 cm. "Sponsored by the Center for Chinese Studies, University of California, Berkeley." Includes index. Bibliography: p. [341]-386. [B5234.L52A44] 75-27920 ISBN 0-520-03123-7 : 17.50
1. Liang, Shu-ming, 1893- 2. Philosophers—China—Biography. I. California. University. Center for Chinese Studies. II. Title. BIP

Libanius.

LIEBESCHUETZ, John Hugo Wolfgang Gideon. 320.9'37'06
Antioch: city and imperial administration in the later Roman Empire, [by] J. H. W. G. Liebeschuetz. Oxford, Clarendon Press, 1972. xiv, 303 p., fold. leaf. maps. 23 cm. Based on the author's thesis, London University. Bibliography: p. [281]-288. [DS99.A6L54] 72-177640 ISBN 0-19-814295-1 £5.00
1. Libanius. 2. Antioch—History. I. Title.

Libby, Mont.—History—Miscellanea.

TIMES we remember in and around Libby, Montana 917.86'81 [by Libby Writers Group] Libby, Libby Montana Institute of the Arts Writers Group, 1974. 104 p. illus. 22 cm. [F739.L5T55] 74-180344
1. Libby, Mont.—History—Miscellanea. 2. Libby, Mont.—Biography. I. Libby Writers Group.

Liber, Benzion,

LIBER, Benzion, 1875- 926.1
A doctor's apprenticeship; autobiographical sketches. New York, Rational Living [c1956] 611p. illus. 20cm. [R154.L45A3] 56-493
I. Title.

LIBER, Benzion, 1875- 926.1
A doctor's apprenticeship; autbiographical sketches. 2d ed. New York, Rational living [1957] 627p. illus. 20cm. [R154.L45A3 1957] 57-28570
I. Title.

Liberace, 1919-

LIBERACE, 1919- 786.1'0924
Liberace an autoibiography. New York : Popular Library, 1976 c1973. xii, 316 p. : ill. ; 17 cm. [ML417.L67A3] ISBN 0-445-08493-6 pbk. : 1.95
1. Liberace, 1919- 2. Musicians—Correspondence, reminiscenses, etc. I. Title.
L.C. card no. for original ed.: 73-8203.

LIBERACE, 1919- 786.1'092'4 B
The things I love / Liberace ; edited by Tony Palmer. New York : Grosset & Dunlap, c1976. 222 p. : ill. (some col.) ; 28 cm. [ML417.L67A34] 76-21150 ISBN 0-448-12718-0 : 17.95.
1. Liberace, 1919- 2. Pianists—United States—Biography. I. Title. BIP

Liberation News Service.

MUNGO, Raymond, 1946- 070'.924 B
Famous long ago; my life and hard times with Liberation News Service. Boston, Beacon Press [1970] 202 p. illus. 22 cm. [CT275.M755A3 1970] 77-103937
1. Liberation News Service. I. Title.

Libermann, Francoise Marie Paul, 1802-1852.

VAN KAAM, Adrian L., 922.244
A light to the Gentiles; the life story of the venerable Francis Libermann. Milwaukee, Bruce [1962,c.1959] 311p. illus. 22cm. Bibl. 62-19998 5.25
1. Libermann, Francoise Marie Paul, 1802-1852. I. 2 1920- Vankaam adrian l 1920 II. Title.

VAN KAAM, Adrian L., 1920- 922.244
A light to the Gentiles; the life story of the venerable Francis Libermann. Milwaukee, Bruce [1962,c.1959] 311p. illus. 22cm. Bibl. 62-19998 5.25
1. Libermann, Francoise Marie Paul, 1802-1852. I. Title.

Libersat, Henry.

LIBERSAT, Henry. 282'.092'4 B
Ragin' Cajun. Liguori, Mo., Liguori Publications [1974] 192 p. 18 cm. Autobiography. [BX4705.L622A37] 74-77996 1.95 (pbk.).
1. Libersat, Henry. I. Title.

Liberty.

CARMER, Carl Lamson, 1893- 323.44'0922 B
For the rights of men, by Carl Carmer. Freeport, N.Y., Books for Libraries Press [1969, c1947] 64 p. illus., ports. 24 cm. (Essay index reprint series) Brief biographies of six men who upheld and fought for equal application of the rights cited in the Bill of Rights. Included are J. P. Zenger, Matthew Lyon, W. L. Garrison, Elijah Lovejoy, Bill Prendergast, and John Peter Altgeld. [JC599.U5C3 1969] 920 75-86740
1. Liberty. 2. U.S.—Biography. I. Title. BIP

Liberty of conscience.

UPHAUS, Willard Edwin. 923.673
Commitment. [1st ed.] New York, McGraw-Hill [1963] 266 p. 22 cm. Autobiographical. [E743.5.U6] 63-13167
1. Liberty of conscience. 2. Communism — U.S. — 1917- I. Title.

Librarians

WHO'S who in library service; 020.922 a biographical directory of professional librarians in the United States and Canada. Ed.: Lee Ash; assoc. ed.: B. A. Uhlendorf; asst. ed.: Martha J. Sullivan. 4th ed. [Hamden, Conn.] Shoe String, 1966. 776p. 26cm. Sponsored by the Council of Natl. Lib. Assns. [Z720.A4U58 1966] 66-24910 25.00
1. Librarians — U.S. I. Ash. Lee, 1917- ed. II. Council of National Library Associations.

WHO'S who in library service; 920.2 a biographical directory of professional librarians of the United States and Canade. 3d ed. Dorothy Ethlyn Cole, editor. Prepared under the direction of the Council on Who's Who in Library Service for the School of Library Service, Columbia University. New York, Grolier Society, 1955. xxiii, 546 p. 26 cm. [Z720.A4U58 1955] 55-7959
1. Librarians—U.S. I. Cole, Dorothy Ethlyn, 1907- ed. II. Columbia University. School of Library Service.

WHO'S who in library service; 020.922 a biographical directory of professional librarians in the United States and Canada. Editor: Lee Ash; associate editor: B. A. Uhlendorf; assistant editor: Martha J. Sullivan. 4th ed. [Hamden, Conn.] Shoe String Press, 1966. 776 p. 26 cm. "Sponsored by the Council of National Library Associations." Beginning with 5th ed. (1970) published under title: A biographical directory of librarians in the United States and Canada. [Z720.A4U58 1966] 66-24910
1. Librarians—United States. 2. Librarians—Canada. I. Ash, Lee, 1917- ed. II. Council of National Library Associations. BIP

Librarians. American.

PIONEERING leaders in librarianship. 920.2 Edited by Emily Miller Danton. Chicago, American Library Association, 1953- v. ports. 23 cm. (American library pioneers, 8) Bibliographical footnotes. [Z720.A4U47] 53-10258
1. Librarians, American. I. Danton, Emily Miller, 1888- ed. II. American Library Association. III. Series.

THORNTON, Eileen, comp. 920.2
Library masterpieces. compiled by Eileen Thornton and Dorothy Ethlyn Cole. Photography by William F. Stickle. New York, Grolier Society, 1956. 30 p. of ports. 21 cm. [Z720.A1T5] 56-58906
1. Librarians. American. I. Cole, Dorothy Ethlyn, 1907- joint comp. II. Title.

Librarians—Correspondence, reminiscences, etc.

COMPTON, Charles Herrick, 1880- 020'.92'2
Memories of a librarian. [St. Louis] St. Louis Public Library, 1954. 212p. illus. 20cm. [Z720.C73A3] 55-503
1. Librarians—Correspondence, reminiscences, etc. I. Title.

MITCHELL, Sydney Bancroft, 1878-1951. 920.2
Mitchell of California; the memoirs of Sydney B. Mitchell, librarian, teacher, gardener, Pref. by Lawrence Clark Powell. Berkeley 7, California Library Association, 829 Coventry Rd. [1961] 263p. illus Bibl. 61-541 5.00
1. Librarians—Correspondence, reminiscences, etc. I. Title.

MOHBERG, Nora Fladeboe, 1903- 020'.8
After you, Andrew. Grafton, N.D., Record Printers [1970] 84 p. 23 cm. [Z720.M67A3] 72-197552
1. Librarians—Correspondence, reminiscences, etc. 2. Bookmobiles—North Dakota. I. Title.

Librarians—Great Britain—Biography.

LANDAU, Thomas, ed. 920.2
Who's who in librarianship. With a foreword by Robert L. Collison. [Cambridge, Eng.] Bowes & Bowes [1954] 269 p. 26 cm. Later ed. published in 1972 under title: Who's who in librarianship and information science. [Z720.A4G7] 55-543
1. Librarians—Great Britain—Biography. I. Title.

LANDAU, Thomas. 020'.92'2
Who's who in librarianship and information science; edited by T. Landau. 2nd ed. London, New York, Abelard-Schuman, 1972. v, 311 p. 26 cm. Previous ed. published as Who's who in librarianship. Cambridge: Bowes, 1954. [Z720.A46G75 1972] 70-184398 ISBN 0-200-71871-1
1. Librarians—Great Britain—Biography. I. Title.
Distributed by International Publishers Service, 17.50 BIP

Librarians—U.S.—Directories.

A Biographical directory of librarians in the United States and Canada. 020'.922 B Lee Ash, editor. B. A. Uhlendorf, associate editor. 5th ed. Chicago, American Library Association, 1970. xviii, 1250 p. 27 cm. "Sponsored by the Council of National Library Associations." First-4th ed. published under title: Who's who in library service. [Z720.A4W47 1970] 79-118854 ISBN 8-389-00844-
1. Librarians—U.S.—Directories. 2. Librarians—Canada—Directories. I. Ash, Lee, 1917- ed. II. Uhlendorf, Bernhard Alexander, 1893- ed. III. Council of National Library Associations. BIP

Librarians—United States—Biography.

DICTIONARY of American library biography 020'92'2 B / editorial board, George S. Bobinski, Jesse Hauk Shera, Bohdan S. Wynar ; edited by Bohdan S. Wynar. Littleton, Colo. : Libraries Unlimited, 1978. xxxix, 596 p. ; 29 cm. p. cm. Includes bibliographies and index. [Z720.A4D5] 77-28791 ISBN 0-87287-180-0 lib.bdg. : 65.00
1. Librarians—United States—Biography. I. Bobinski, George Sylvan. II. Shera, Jesse Hauk, 1903- III. Wynar, Bohdan S.

PIONEERING leaders in librarianship. 020'.92'2 Edited by Emily Miller Danton. Boston, Gregg Press, 1972 [c1953] 202 p. ports. 23 cm. (The Library reference series. Library history and biography) Reprint of the ed. published by the American Library Association, Chicago, as v. 8 of American Library pioneers. Includes bibliographical references. [Z720.A4P55 1972] 72-10164 ISBN 0-8398-0379-6
1. Librarians—United States—Biography. I. Danton, Emily (Miller) 1888- ed. II. Series: Library history and biography. III. Series: American library pioneers, 8.

TREJO, Arnulfo D. 020'.92'2 B
Quien es quien : a who's who of Spanish-heritage librarians in the United States / edited by Arnulfo D. Trejo, with the assistance of Kathleen L. Lodwick. Tucson : University of Arizona, College of Education, Bureau of School Services, c1976. x, 29 p. ; 23 cm. (Graduate Library School monograph ; no. 5) [Z720.A4T73] 77-621461
1. Librarians—United States—Biography. 2. Spanish Americans in the United States—Biography. I. Lodwick, Kathleen L., joint author. II. Title. III. Series: Arizona. University. Graduate Library School. Graduate Library School monograph ; no. 5.

Lichnowsky, Karl Max, Furst von, 1860-1928.

YOUNG, Harry F. 940.3'24'43 B
Prince Lichnowsky and the Great War / Harry F. Young. Athens : University of Georgia Press, c1977. xii, 281 p., [4] leaves of plates : ill. ; 25 cm. Includes index. Bibliography: p. [251]-267. [DD231.L5Y68] 75-11448 ISBN 0-8203-0385-2 : 11.00
1. Lichnowsky, Karl Max, Furst von, 1860-1928. 2. Ambassadors—Germany—Biography. 3. European War, 1914-1918—Causes. 4. Germany—Foreign relations—Great Britain. 5. Great Britain—Foreign relations—Germany. I. Title. BIP

Lichtenstein, Grace.

LICHTENSTEIN, Grace. 070'.92'4 [B]
Desperado / by Grace Lichtenstein. New York : Dial Press, c1977. vi, 213 p. ; 24 cm. [PN4874.L43A33] 77-11160 ISBN 0-8037-1898-5 : 8.95
1. Lichtenstein, Grace. 2. Journalists—United States—Biography. I. Title. BIP

LICHTENSTEIN, Grace. 796.34'2
A long way, baby; behind the scenes in women's pro tennis. Photography by Nancy Moran. New York, Morrow, 1974. 239 p. illus. 22 cm. [GV999.L52] 74-1166 ISBN 0-688-00263-3 6.95
1. Tennis. 2. Tennis—Biography. I. Title. BIP

LICHTENSTEIN, Grace. 796.34'2
A long way, baby; behind the scenes in women's pro tennis. Photography by Nancy Moran. New York, Morrow, 1974. 239 p. illus. 22 cm. [GV999.L52] 74-1166 ISBN 0-688-00263-3 6.95
1. Tennis. 2. Tennis—Biography. I. Title. BIP

Lichtenstein, Roy,

LICHTENSTEIN, Roy, 1923- 709'.24
Roy Lichtenstein [by] Diane Waldman. New York, H. N. Abrams [1971] 248 p. 183 illus. (part col.) 31 cm. Bibliography: p. [240]-241. [N6537.L5W32] 74-146825 ISBN 0-8109-0256-7
I. Waldman, Diane.

LICHTENSTEIN, Roy, 1923- 709'.24
Roy Lichtenstein, by Diane Waldman. [Exhibition, the Solomon R. Guggenheim Museum, New York. New York, Solomon R. Guggenheim Foundation, 1969] 112 p. illus. (part col.), port. 26 cm. Bibliography: p. 104-112. [N6537.L5W3] 70-95575
I. Waldman, Diane. II. Solomon R. Guggenheim Museum, New York.

of New Mexico Press, 1958. 256 p. illus. 24 cm. Includes bibliography. [F594.L73] 58-6870
1. Lillie, Gordon William, 1860-1942.

Lilly, Benjamin Vernon, 1856-1936.

DOBIE, James Frank, 1888-1964. 923.973
The Ben Lilly legend. [1st ed.] Boston, Little, Brown, 1950. xv, 237 p. illus., ports. 21 cm. Bibliography: p. 225-229. [SK17.L5D6 1950] 50-7737
1. Lilly, Benjamin Vernon, 1856-1936. 2. Bears. I. Title. **BIP**

Lilly, Gene, 1939-

HUNTER, Charles, 1920- 248'.2
Don't limit God! : The story of Gene Lilly / by Charles [and] Frances Hunter. Houston, Tex. : Hunter Ministries Pub. Co., c1976. 101 p. ; 21 cm. [RC660.H88] 77-352045 1.95
1. Lilly, Gene, 1939- 2. Diabetes—Biography. 3. Multiple sclerosis—Biography. I. Hunter, Frances Gardner, 1916- joint author. II. Title.

Lilly, William, 1602-1618

LILLY, William, 1602-1681 133.5'092'4 B
The last of the astrologers; Mr. William Lilly's history of his life and times from the year 1602 to 1681; reprinted from the second edition of 1715 with notes and introduction by Katherine M. Briggs. [London] [The Folklore Society] [1975 c1974] xvii, 108 p. 1 ill. 23 cm. (Mistletoe books, no. 1) First published in 1715 under title: Mr. William Lilly's history of his life and times from the year 1602 to 1681. Bibliography: p. xvii. [BF1598.L5A33] 74-181741
1. Lilly, William, 1602-1618 2. Astrology. I. Briggs, Katherine Mary, ed. II. Title. III. Series.
Distributed by Rowman and Littlefield for 9.00.

Limanowski, Boleslaw, 1835-1935.

COTTAM, K. Jean. 943.8'03'0924
Boleslaw Limanowski, 1835-1935 : a study in socialism and nationalism / by Kazimiera Janina Cottam. Boulder, [Colo.] : East European quarterly ; New York : distributed by Columbia University Press, 1978. xvi, 365 p. ; 23 cm. (East European monographs ; no. 41) A revision of the author's thesis, University of Toronto, 1970. Includes index. Bibliography: p. [331]-349. [DK4395.L55C67 1978] 77-82395 ISBN 0-914710-34-6 : 18.50
1. Limanowski, Boleslaw, 1835-1935. 2. Statesmen—Poland—Biography. 3. Socialists—Poland—Biography. 4. Historians—Poland—Biography. 5. Socialism—Poland—History. I. Title. II. Series.

Lin, Piao, 1908-

EBON, Martin. 951.05'0924 B
Lin Piao; the life and writings of China's new ruler. New York, Stein and Day [1970] 378 p. illus., ports. 25 cm. Bibliography: p. 359-362. [DS778.L4725E24] 70-104636 10.00
1. Lin, Piao, 1908-

Linacre, Thomas, 1460-1524—Addresses, essays, lectures.

ESSAYS on the life 610'.92'4 B *and work of Thomas Linacre, c. 1460-1524* / edited by Francis Maddison, Margaret Pelling, and Charles Webster. Oxford [Eng.] : Clarendon Press, 1977. liii, 416 p., [10] leaves of plates : ill. ; 23 cm. (Linacre studies) "The life of Thomas Linacre: a brief chronology": p. [xlix]-liii. Includes bibliographical references and index. [R489.L7E87] 77-359094 ISBN 0-19-858150-5 : 26.50
1. Linacre, Thomas, 1460-1524—Addresses, essays, lectures. 2. Physicians—England—Biography—Addresses, essays, lectures. 3. Humanists—England—Biography—Addresses, essays, lectures. 4. Medicine—15th-18th centuries—Addresses, essays, lectures. I. Linacre, Thomas, 1460-1524. II. Maddison, Francis Romeril. III. Pelling, Margaret. IV. Webster, Charles. V. Series.
Distributed by Oxford University Press, New York.

ESSAYS on the life 610'.92'4 B *and work of Thomas Linacre, c. 1460-1524* / edited by Francis Maddison, Margaret Pelling, and Charles Webster. Oxford [Eng.] : Clarendon Press, 1977. liii, 416 p., [10] leaves of plates : ill. ; 23 cm. (Linacre studies) "The life of Thomas Linacre: a brief chronology": p. [xlix]-liii. Includes bibliographical references and index. [R489.L7E87] 77-359094 ISBN 0-19-858150-5 : 26.50
1. Linacre, Thomas, 1460-1524—Addresses, essays, lectures. 2. Physicians—England—Biography—Addresses, essays, lectures. 3. Humanists—England—Biography—Addresses, essays, lectures. 4. Medicine—15th-18th centuries—Addresses, essays, lectures. I. Linacre, Thomas, 1460-1524. II. Maddison, Francis Romeril. III. Pelling, Margaret. IV. Webster, Charles. V. Series.
Distributed by Oxford University Press, New York.

Lincoln, Abraham, Pres. U.S., 1809-1865.

ABBOTT, John Stevens Cabot, 1805-1877. 973'.074'016971
Life of Abraham Lincoln; a biographical sketch of President Lincoln taken from Abbott's "Lives of the Presidents." Chicago, Illustrated Booklet Co. [n. d.] 159 p. illus., ports. 13 cm. [E457.A13] 52-52864
1. Lincoln, Abraham, Pres. U. S., 1809-1865. I. Title.

ABRAHAM Lincoln; v. 12
The prairie years, and the war years. Laurel ed. New York, TM, Dell Pub. Co., 1959. 3v. illus. 17cm.
1. Lincoln, Abraham, Pres. U. S., 1809-1865. 2. U. S.— Hist.—Civil War. I. Sandburg, Carl, 1878-

ABRAHAM Lincoln, v. 12
and the times that tried his soul. Translated by Eden and Cedar Paul. Authorized abridgment. New York, Fawcett Publications [1956] 284p. 18cm. (Premier book, D34) 'First Premier printing, September 1956.'
1. Lincoln, Abraham, Pres. U. S., 1809-1865. I. Ludwig, Emil, 1881-1948.

ABRAHAM Lincoln, and the v. 12
times that tried his soul, Translated by Eden and Cedar Paul. Authorized abridgment. New York, Fawcett Publications [1956] 284p. 18cm. (Premier book, D34) 'First Premier printing, September 1956.'
1. Lincoln, Abraham, Pres. U. S., 1809-1865. I. Ludwig, Emil, 1881-1948.

AGAR, Herbert, 1897- 923.173
Abraham Lincoln. Hamden, Conn., Archon [dist. Shoe String] 1965[c.1952, 1965] 141 [1]p. illus., maps, ports. 21cm. (Makers of hist.) Bibl. [E457.A25] 65-4283 4.00
1. Lincoln, Abraham. Pres. U.S., 1809-1865. I. Title.

AGAR, Herbert. 1897- 923.173
Abraham Lincoln. New York, Macmillan [1952] 143p. port., maps. 20cm. (Brief lives, no. 6) Bibliography: p.143. [E457.A25] 53-209
1. Lincoln, Abraham, Pres, U. S., 1809-1865. I. Title. II. Series.

ANGLE, Paul McClelland, 1900- ed. 923.173
The Lincoln reader. New York, Pocket Books [1955, c1947] xii, 626p. 17cm. (A Cardinal giant, GC23. Biography. 3) 'A biography written by sixty-five authors.' Bibliography: p. 597-601. [E457.A58 1955] 56-27707
1. Lincoln, Abraham, Pres. U. S., 1809-1865. I. Title.

BARRETT, Joseph Hartwell, 1824-1910. 973'.074'016971
Life of Abraham Lincoln, presenting his early history, political career and speeches in and out of Congress; also, a general view of his policy as President of the United States, with his messages, proclamations, letters, etc., and a history of his eventful administration, and of the scenes attendant upon his tragic and lamented demise. [Arundel ed.] New York, W.L.Allison, 1889. 842p. illus. 19cm. [E457.B2752] 52-57545
1. Lincoln. Abraham, Pres. U.S., 1809-1865. I. Title.

BARRETT, Joseph Hartwell, 1824-1910. 973'.074'016971
Life of Abraham Lincoln; his early history, political career, speeches in and out of Congress, together with many characteristic stories and yarns by and concerning Lincoln which has earned for him the sobriquet, 'The Story Telling President.' By Joseph H. Barrett and Charles Walter Brown. Chicago, M.A. Donohue [c1902] 842p. illus., ports. 23cm. [E457.B2754] 55-55799
1. Lincoln, Abraham, Pres. U. S., 1809-1865. I. Brown, Charles Walter, 1866-1934, joint author. II. Title.

BARTON, William Eleazar, 1861-1930. 923.173
The life of Abraham Lincoln. Boston, Books, inc. [1943] 1925] xvi, 517, 516p. illus., ports., facsims. 22cm. [E457.B3 1943] 54-49291
1. Lincoln, Abraham, Press. U. S., 1809-1865. I. Title.

BARZUN, Jacques, 1907- 923.173
Lincoln, the literary genius. Evanston, Ill., Schori Private Press, 1960 [c1959] 49p. port. 22cm. 'Printing ... limited to five hundred numbered and signed copies of which this is nunber 110. [Signed] Ward K. Schori.' [E457.2.B295] 61-3287
1. Lincoln, Abraham, Press). U S.—Literary art. I. Title.

BASLER, Roy Prentice, 1906- 923.173
Linclon [Gloucester, Mass., Peter Smith, 1963] 192p. illus. 18cm. (Evergreen profile bk., 37, rebound) Bibl. 3.00
1. Lincoln, Abraham, Pres. U.S., 1809-1865. I. Title.

BASLER, Roy Prentice, 1906- 923.173
Lincoln. New York, Grove [1962] 192p. illus. 18cm. (Evergreen profile, 37) 61-14022 .95 pap.,
1. Lincoln, Abraham, Pres. U.S., 1809-1865. I. Title.

BASLER, Roy Prentice, 1906- 973.7'092'4 B
Lincoln / Roy P. Basler. New York : Octagon Books, 1975. p. cm. Reprint of the 1961 ed. published by Grove Press, New York, which was issued as Evergreen profile book, 37. Bibliography: p. [E457.B34 1975] 75-29365 ISBN 0-374-90454-5 lib.bdg. : 10.50
1. Lincoln, Abraham, Pres. U.S., 1809-1865.

BASSETT, Margaret Byrd, 1902- 973.7'092'4 B
Abraham & Mary Todd Lincoln [by] Margaret Bassett. New York, Crowell [1973] 58 p. illus. 24 cm. The biographies of President and Mrs. Lincoln were previously published in the author's Profiles & portraits of American Presidents & their wives; the biography of President Lincoln was also published earlier, in her Profiles and portraits of American Presidents. "A Bond Wheelwright book." Bibliography: p. 57-58. [E457.B352] 73-525 ISBN 0-690-05177-8 4.95
1. Lincoln, Abraham, Pres. U.S., 1809-1865. 2. Lincoln, Mary (Todd) 1818-1882. I. Title. **BIP**

BEVERIDGE, Albert Jeremiah, 1862-1927. 973.7'0924 B
Abraham Lincoln, 1809-1858. Boston, Houghton Mifflin, 1928 St. Clair Shores, Mich., Scholarly Press, 1971. 2 v. illus., ports. 22 cm. Bibliography: v. 1, p. [xvii]-xxviii. [E457.3.B576 1971] 73-144879 ISBN 0-403-00865-4
1. Lincoln, Abraham, Pres. U.S., 1809-1865.

BROGAN, Denis William, Sir, 1900- 923.173
Abraham Lincoln. New York, Schocken Books 1963 143 p. 21 cm. "SB48." Includes bibliography. [E457.B865 1963] 63-11068
1. Lincoln, Abraham, Pres. U.S., 1809-1865.

BROOKS, Noah, 1830-1903. 973.7'092'4
Abraham Lincoln and the downfall of American slavery / by Noah Brooks. New York : AMS Press, 1978. xv, 471 p., [19] leaves of plates : ill. ; 19 cm. Reprint of the 1894 ed. published by Putnam, New York, which was issued in series: Heroes of the nations. Includes index. [E457.B876 1978] 73-14436 ISBN 0-404-58254-0 : 30.00
1. Lincoln, Abraham, Pres. U.S., 1809-1865. 2. Presidents—United States—Biography. I. Title. II. Series: Heroes of the nations. **BIP**

BROWN, Virginia Stuart. 923.173
Through Lincoln's door. Illus. by the author. [Ed. 1. Springfield? Ill., 1952] 84 p. illus. 18 cm. [F549.S7B7] 52-2943
1. Lincoln, Abraham, Pres. U. S., 1809-1865. 2. Springfield. Ill. Lincoln Home. I. Title.

CARABELLI, Angelina Jacqueline. 630'.973
Abraham Lincoln: his legacy to American agriculture. Edited by Angelina J. Carabelli. [Beltsville, Md., Associates of the National Agricultural Library, 1972] 20 p. illus. 23 cm. Bibliography: p. 18-20. [S441.C26] 72-191252
1. Lincoln, Abraham, Pres. U.S., 1809-1865. 2. Agriculture—United States. I. United States. National Agricultural Library. Associates.

CARNEGIE, Dale, 188-1955. 923.173
The unknown Lincoln. Originally titled: Lincoln, the unknown. New York, Pocket Books [1952, c1932] x, 234p0), [3]p. 17cm. (Pocket book 391) Bibliography: p. [235]-3237] [E457.C28 1952] 56-18133
1. Lincoln, Abraham, Pres. U S., 1809-1865. I. Title.

CAVANAH, Frances. 973.7'0924 B
Abe Lincoln gets his chance. Illustrated by Paula Hutchison. Chicago, Rand McNally [1959] 92 p. illus. 24 cm. A short biography of Lincoln that concentrates on his boyhood years and his relationship with his family. [PZ7.C28Ab] 92 AC 68
1. Lincoln, Abraham, Pres. U.S., 1809-1865. I. Hutchison, Paula A., illus. II. Title. **BIP**

CURRENT, Richard Nelson 923.173
The Lincoln nobody knows. New York, Hill & Wang [1963, c.1958] 314p. 21cm. (Amer. Century Ser., AC59) Bibl. 1.95 pap.,
1. Lincoln, Abraham, Pres. U. S., 1809-1865. I. Title.

CURRENT, Richard Nelson. 923.173
The Lincoln nobody knows. [1st ed.] New York, McGraw-Hill [1958] 314 p. 22 cm. Includes bibliography. [E457.C96] 58-12994
1. Lincoln, Abraham, Pres. U.S., 1809-1865. I. Title. **BIP**

DAUGHERTY, James Henry, 1889- v. 12
Abraham Lincoln, by James Daugherty, illustrated with lithographs in two colors by the author. New York, The Viking press [1966, 1943] 216 p. col. illus. (incl. ports.) 28 cm. "First published November 1943." 67-88697
1. Lincoln, Abraham, Pres. U.S., 1809-1865. I. Title.

DODGE, Grenville Mellen, Maj.-Gen. 1831-1916 923.73
Personal recollections of President Abraham Lincoln, General Ulysses S. Grant, and General William T. Sherman. Denver. Sage [dist. Swallow, 1966] 237p. illus., ports. 23cm. Reprinted from a private ed. (Western Sage paperbk.) [E467.D64] 65-14621 1.85 pap.,
1. Lincoln. Abraham. Pres. U.S., 1809-1865. 2. Grant, Ulysses Simpson, Pres. U.S., 1822-1885. 3. Sherman, William Tecumseh, 1820-1891. I. Title.

DODGE, Grenville Mellen, 923.173
1931-1916
Personal recollections of President Abrahm Lincoln, General Ulysses S. Grant, and General William T. Sherman. Denver, Sage [dist. Swallow, 1965] 237p. illus., ports. 23cm. Reprinted from a private ed. with the imprint: Council Bluffs, Iowa, The Monarch Printing Company, 1914. [E467.D64] 65-14621 6.00
1. Lincoln, Abraham, Pres. U.S., 1809-1865. 2. Grant, Ulysses Simpson, Pres. U.S., 1822-1885. 3. Sherman, William Tecumseh, 1820-1891. I. Title.

FEHRENBACHER, Don 973.7'0924 B
Edward, 1920- comp.
The leadership of Abraham Lincoln [by] Don E. Fehrenbacher. New York, Wiley [1970] 194 p. 22 cm. (Problems in American history) Includes bibliographical references. [E457.F4] 77-114013
1. Lincoln, Abraham, Pres. U.S., 1809-1865. I. Title. **BIP**

FEHRENBACHER, Don Edward, 923.173
1920-
Prelude to greatness; Lincoln in the 1850's. New York, McGraw [1964, c.1962] 205p. 20cm. Bibl. 2.65 pap.,
1. Lincoln, Abraham, Pres. U. S., 1809-1865. I. Title. **BIP**

FISHER, Aileen 973.7'0924 B
Lucia, 1906-
My Cousin Abe. Drawings by Leonard Vosburgh. New York, Nelson [1962] 285 p. illus. 22 cm. Includes bibliography. A view of Lincoln drawn from a biography by his law partner, William Herndon; based largely on Herndon's interviews and correspondence with the first cousin of Lincoln's mother, Nancy Hanks. [PZ7.F4989My] 92 AC 68
1. Lincoln, Abraham, Pres. U.S., 1809-1865. I. Vosburgh, Leonard, illus. II. Title.

FOSTER, Genevieve 973.7'0924 B
(Stump) 1893-
Abraham Lincoln. New York, Scribner [1950] 111 p. col. illus. 20 cm. (Her An initial biography) A biography of Lincoln that concentrates chiefly, but briefly, on events that led to the Presidency. [E457.905.F67] 92 AC 68
1. Lincoln, Abraham, Pres. U.S., 1809-1865. I. Title.

FREEMAN, Andrew A. 923.173
Abraham Lincoln goes to New York. New York, Coward-McCann [c.1960] 160p. (bibl. notes: p. 145-153) 21cm. 60-6873 3.95
1. Lincoln, Abraham, Pres. U S. Cooper Institute speech. 2. New York, (City)—Descr. I. Title.

FULLER, Edmund Maybank, 920.073
1914- ed.
4 American biographies [by] Edmund Fuller, O. B. Davis. New York, Harcourt, [c.1961] 779p. illus. (Adventures in good bks.) 61-19640 3.75
1. Lincoln, Abraham, Pres. U. S., 1809-1865. 2. Holmes, Oliver Wendell, 1841-1935. 3. Clemens, Samuel Langhorne, 1835-1910. 4. Keller, Helen Adams, 1880- I. Davis, O. B., joint ed. II. Title.
Content omitted.

GAMMANS, Harold Winsor, 923.173
1885-
Lincoln names and epithets. Boston, Bruce Humphries [1955] 38p. 21cm. [E457.2.G35] 55-7624
1. Lincoln, Abraham, Pres, U. S., 1809-1865. I. Title.

GILBERT, C. E. 973.7'092'2 B
Two presidents: Abraham Lincoln [and] Jefferson Davis, by C. E. Gilbert. Introductions, highlights, and explanations by Tom Hudson, editor. San Antonio, Tex., Naylor Co. [1973] xxiii, 85 p. ports. 21 cm. Reprint of the 1927 ed. [E459.G53 1973] 73-6581 ISBN 0-8111-0484-2 6.95
1. Lincoln, Abraham, Pres. U.S., 1809-1865. 2. Davis, Jefferson, 1808-1889. 3. United States—History—Civil War—Causes. I. Title.

GRUBER, Michael. 973'.074'016971
Abraham Lincoln; a concise biography, by Michael Gruber. New York, American R. D. M. Corp. [c1965] 72 p. illus., port. 21 cm. (A Study master publication, 904) Bibliography: p. 72. [E457.G89] 67-2011
1. Lincoln, Abraham, Pres. U.S., 1809-1865. I. Title.

HAMILTON, Holman. 973'.0992 B
The three Kentucky presidents—Lincoln, Taylor, Davis / Holman Hamilton. Lexington : University Press of Kentucky, c1978. xv, 69 , [1] p., [4] leaves of plates : ill. ; 21 cm. (The Kentucky Bicentennial bookshelf) Bibliography: p. 67-[70]. [E176.H248] 77-92922 ISBN 0-8131-0246-4 : 4.95
1. Lincoln, Abraham, Pres. U.S., 1809-1865. 2. Taylor, Zachary, Pres. U.S., 1784-1850. 3. Davis, Jefferson, 1808-1889. 4. Presidents—United States—Biography. 5. Kentucky—Biography. I. Title. II. Series.

HERNDON, William Henry, 923.173
1818-1891.
Herndon's life of Lincoln; the history and personal recollections of Abraham Lincoln, as originally written by William H. Herndon and Jesse W. Weik. With a newly rev. introd. and notes by Paul M. Angle. Greenwich, Conn., Fawcett Publications [1961] 496p. 18cm. (Premier Civil War classics) First published in 1889 under title: Herndon's Lincoln. [E457.H576 1961] 61-682
1. Lincoln, Abraham, Pres. U. S., 1809-1865. I. Weik, Jesse William, 1857-1930, joint author. II. Title.

HERNDON, William Henry, 923.173
1818-1891.
Life of Lincoln; the history and personal recollections of Abraham Lincoln, as originally written by William H. Herndon and Jesse W. Weik. With an introd. and notes by Paul M. Angle. New York, A. & C. Boni, 1936 [c1930] xivi, 511p. 20cm. (Bonibooks [48] First published in 1889 under title: Herndon's Lincoln. [E457.H575 1936] 55-55797
1. Lincoln, Abraham, Pres. U. S., 1809-1865. I. Weik, Jesse William, 1857-1930, joint author. II. Title.

HERTZ, Emanuel, 973.7'092'4 B
1870-1940, ed.
Abraham Lincoln; the tribute of the synagogue. Foreword by J. H. Hertz. Pref. by Nicholas Murray Butler. Easton [Pa.] Hive Pub. Co., 1973. p. (Responsa series, no. 3) Reprint of the 1927 ed. published by Bloch Pub. Co., New York. [E457.8.H57 1973] 73-10471 ISBN 0-87960-100-0 23.50
1. Lincoln, Abraham, Pres. U.S., 1809-1865. 2. Lincoln, Abraham, Pres. U.S., 1809-1865—Addresses, sermons, etc.

HOLLAND, Josiah Gilbert, v. 12
1819-1881.
Life of Abraham Lincoln. New York, Paperback Library, Inc. [1961] 447 p. 18 cm. (Paperback Library, GB109) "First printing, August 1961." 63-23006
1. Lincoln, Abraham, Pres. U.S., 1809-1865. I. Title.

HORGAN, Paul, 1903- 923.173
Citizen of New Salem. Greenwich, Conn., Fawcett [1962, c.1961] 160p. illus. (Crest bk., d503) .50 pap.,
1. Lincoln, Abraham, Pres. U.S., 1809-1865. 2. New Salem, Ill. I. Title. **BIP**

HORGAN, Paul, 1903- 923.173
Citizen of New Salem. Illus. by Douglas Gorsline. New York, Farrar, Straus and Cudahy [1961] 89 p. illus. 24 cm. [E457.35.H65] 61-9893
1. Lincoln, Abraham, Pres. U.S., 1809-1865. 2. New Salem, Ill. I. Title.

HORGAN, Paul, 1930- 923.173
Citizen of New Salem. New York, Avon [1968, c1961] 121p. illus., cover art by Douglas Gorshine. 18cm. (ZS134) .60 pap.,
1. Lincoln, Abraham, Pres. U.S., 1809-1865. 2. New Salem, Ill. I. Title.

HOWELLS, William Dean, 923.173
1837-1920.
Life of Abraham Lincoln. Bloomington, Indiana University Press, 1960. xxxii p., facsim. (xi-xii, 17-94 p. port.), [5] p. 21 cm. "This campaign biography corrected by the hand of Abraham Lincoln in the summer of 1860 is reproduced here with careful attention to the appearance of the original volume." Reproduction of a part of Samuel C. Parks' copy of a work, with t. p. reading: Lives and speeches of Abraham Lincoln and Hannibal Hamlin.—Columbus, O., Follett, Foster, 1860. [E457.H86 1860c] 60-8917
1. Lincoln, Abraham, Pres. U.S., 1809-1865.

HUNT, Eugenia (Jones) 973.70922
1846-1947.
My personal recollections of Abraham and Mary Todd Lincoln. [Peoria, Ill., H. A. Moser, 1966] 76 p. 22 cm. [E457.15.H93] 66-9591
1. Lincoln, Abraham, Pres. U.S., 1809-1865. 2. Lincoln, Mary (Todd) 1818-1882. I. Title.

JUDSON, Clara 973.7'0924 B
(Ingram) 1879-1960.
Abraham Lincoln, friend of the people. Pen drawings by Robert Frankenberg; kodachromes of the Chicago Historical Society Lincoln dioramas. Chicago, Wilcox and Follett Co. [1950] 206 p. illus. (part col.) 25 cm. A biography of Lincoln whose success story became the symbol of the American dream—the backwoods boy who by honesty, dignity, and kindness won the highest office in the country. [E457.905.J8] 92 AC 68
1. Lincoln, Abraham, Pres. U.S., 1809-1865. I. Frankenberg, Robert C., illus. II. Title.

KECKLEY, Elizabeth 973.7'0922
(Hobbs) 1824-1907.
Behind the scenes; thirty years a slave and four years in the White House. New York, Arno Press, 1968. xvi, 371 p. port. 18 cm. (The American Negro, his history and literature) Reprint of the 1868 ed. [E457.15.K26 1968] 68-29006
1. Lincoln, Abraham, Pres. U.S., 1809-1865. 2. Lincoln, Mary (Todd) 1818-1882. I. Title. II. Series. **BIP**

KEMPF, Edward John, 1885- 923.173
Abraham Lincoln's philosophy of common sense; an analytical biography of a great mind [3v.] [New York, N. Y. Acad. of Scis., c.1965] 3v. (xxiv, 1443p.) facsims., fold. map, ports. 24cm. (Special pubns. of the N. Y. Acad. of Scis., v.6) Bibl. Title. (Series: New York Academy of Sciences. Special publications, v.6) [E457.K4] 65-3503 30.00 set,
1. Lincoln, Abraham, Pres. U. S., 1809-1865. I. Title. II. Series.

KOMROFF, Manuel, 973.7'0924 B
1890-
Abraham Lincoln. Illustrated by Charles Beck. New York, Putnam [1959] 127 p. illus. 21 cm. (Lives to remember) Biography of the backwoods boy whose dedication to education, honesty, and equality, made him yesterday's hero, today's legend. [E457.905.K59] 92 AC 68
1. Lincoln, Abraham, Pres. U.S., 1809-1865. I. Beck, Charles, illus. II. Title

KUHN, Isaac, ed. 923.173
Abraham Lincoln. [E457.8.K95] 53-30532
I. Title.

†LINCOLN, Abraham, 973.7'092'4
Pres. U.S., 1809-1865.
Abraham Lincoln, a documentary portrait through his speeches and writings / edited and with an introd. by Don E. Fehrenbacher. Stanford, Calif. : Stanford University Press, 1977, c1964. xxix, 288 p. : 19 cm. Bibliography: p. 286-288. [E457.92 1977] 76-53865 ISBN 0-8047-0942-4 : 10.00 ISBN 0-8047-0946-7 pbk. : 2.95
1. Lincoln, Abraham, Pres. U.S., 1809-1865. 2. Presidents—United States—Biography—Collected works. 3. United States—Politics and government—1815-1861—Collected works. I. Fehrenbacher, Don Edward, 1920- II. Title.

LINCOLN, Abraham, Pres. 923.173
U.S., 1809-1865.
Abraham Lincoln: a decomentary portrait through his speeches and writings. Edited and with an introd. by Don E. Fehrenbacher. [New York] New American Library [1964] 288 p. 18 cm. (A Signet classic) "CT265." Bibliography: p. 286-288. [E457.92] 64-55382
I. Fehrenbacher, Don Edward, 1920- ed. II. Title.

LINCOLN, Abraham, 973.7'0924 B
Pres. U.S., 1809-1865.
Abraham Lincoln; an autobiographical narrative. Written and edited by Ralph Geoffrey Newman. Illustrated with 24 original drawings by Lloyd Ostendorf. Chicago, Lincoln Mint, 1970. 77 p. illus., ports. 27 cm. At head of title: The life of Lincoln. An amalgamation of 2 autobiographical sketches written in 1859 and 1860, supplemented by autobiographical excerpts from Lincoln's letters and speeches. [E457.L734] 79-20050
I. Newman, Ralph G., 1911- ed. II. Title: The life of Lincoln.

LINCOLN, Abraham, 973.7'0924 B
Pres. U.S., 1809-1865.
Abraham Lincoln; an autobiographical narrative. Written and edited by Ralph Geoffrey Newman. Illustrated with 24 original drawings by Lloyd Ostendorf. Lincoln, Ill., Lincoln College, 1971. 77 p. illus., ports. 27 cm. Two sketches by Lincoln combined into a single narrative, with minor changes, supplemented by autobiographical excerpts from Lincoln's letters and speeches, and editorial comments. The 1st sketch was originally prepared by him fro J. W. Fell in 1859 and the 2d, written in the 3d person, for J. L. Scripps in 1860. "This special edition, limited to three hundred numbered and signed copies, is issued in honor of Miss Helen B. McKinstry, of Delavan, Illinois ... Number 284." [E457.L734 1971] 70-274484
I. Newman, Ralph Geoffrey, 1911- ed. II. Ostendorf, Lloyd, illus.

LINCOLN, Abraham, 973.7'092'4 B
Pres. U.S., 1809-1865.
Abraham Lincoln, his story in his own words / edited and with notes by Ralph Geoffrey Newman. Garden City, N.Y. : Doubleday, 1975, c1970. 117 p. : port. ; 22 cm. An amalgamation of 2 autobiographical sketches written in 1859 and 1860, supplemented by autobiographical excerpts from Lincoln's letters and speeches. Includes index. [E457.L734 1975] 73-81989 ISBN 0-385-08410-2 : 6.95
1. Lincoln, Abraham, Pres. U.S., 1809-1865. I. Newman, Ralph Geoffrey, 1911- ed.

LINCOLN, Abraham, Pres. 923.173
U. S., 1809-1865.
The Lincoln ideals-his personality and principles as reflected in his own words. Washington, Lincoln Sesquicentennial Commission [1959] 49p. port. 22cm. [E457.2.L74] 59-61353
1. Lincoln, Abraham, Pres. U. S.—Personality. I. Title.

LONGFORD, Frank 973.7'092'4 B
Pakenham, 7th Earl of, 1905-
Abraham Lincoln / Lord Longford ; introd. by Elizabeth Longford. 1st American ed. New York : Putnam, 1975. 231 p. : ill. ; 26 cm. Includes index. Bibliography: p. 227. [E457.L843 1975] 74-19870 12.95
1. Lincoln, Abraham, Pres. U.S., 1809-1865.

LORANT, Stefan, 973'.074'016971
1901-
La vie d'Abraham Lincoln. Ed. facile. [New York Distributed by Boarts International, 1962] 136 p. 16 cm. "Translation of the abridged and simplified Ladder Edition published by New American Library, New York." [E457.L884] 64-42005
1. Lincoln, Abraham, Pres. U.S., 1809-1865. I. Title.

LORANT, Stefan, 1901- 923.173
The life of Abraham Lincoln, a short, illustrated biography. New York, McGraw-Hill [1954] 256 p. illus., ports., facsims. 21 cm. [E457.L87] 54-7674
1. Lincoln, Abraham, Pres. U.S., 1809-1865.

LORANT, Stefan, 1901- v. 12
The life of Abraham Lincoln; a short, illustrated biography. [New York] New American Library [1961, c1954] 256 p. illus., ports., facsims. 18 cm. (A Mentor book, MT 323) 67-103164

1. Lincoln, Abraham, Pres. U.S., 1809-1865. I. Title.

LINCOLN, Abraham, Pres. U.S., 1809-1865. 923.173
The living Lincoln; the man, his mind, his times, and the war he fought, reconstructed from his own writings. Edited by Paul M. Angle and Earl Schenck Miers. New Brunswick, N.J., Rutgers University Press, 1955. viii, 673 p. 24 cm. [E457.92 1955] 55-9955
1. Angle, Paul McClelland, 1900- ed. II. Miers, Earl Schenck, 1910- ed. III. Title.

LINCOLN, Abraham, Pres. U.S., 1809-1865. 973.7'0924
The political thought of Abraham Lincoln. Edited by Richard N. Current. Indianapolis, Bobbs-Merrill [1967] xl, 340 p. 21 cm. (The American heritage series, 46) Bibliography: p. 35-37. [E457.92 1967b] 67-30069
I. Current, Richard Nelson, ed. II. Title.

LINCOLN, Abraham, Pres. U. S., 1809-1865. 923.173
Speeches and letters, 1832-1865, selected and edited by Paul M. Angle. [Rev. ed.] London, Dent; New York, Dutton [1957] xiii, 300p. 19cm. (Everyman's library, 206. Oratory) Bibliography: p. x-xi. [E457.92 1957b] 59-3398
I. Title.

LINCOLN, Abraham, Pres. U.S., 1809-1865. 973'.074'016971
The wit and wisdom of Abraham Lincoln. New York, Pyramid Books [1967, c1965] 63 p. 14 cm. (A Little paperback classic, LP6) Contents.Contents.—Speeches.—Autobiographical.—Letters to his stepbrother.—Letters to ladies.—Letters to generals.—Wit and wisdom. [E457.92 1967c] 68-3326
I. Title.

LORANT, Stefan 1901- 923.173
The life of Abraham Lincoln; a short illustrated biography. New York, Bantam Books [1976 c1954] 256 p. illus., ports. facsims. 18 cm. [E457.L87] 1.95 (pbk.)
1. Lincoln, Abraham, Pres. U.S., 1809-1865. I. Title.
L.C. card no. of 1954 McGraw Hill edition: 54-7674.

LORANT, Stefan, 1901- 923.173
The life of Abraham Lincoln. Adapted by Adolph Myers. [New York] New American Library [1959] 127p. illus. 19cm. (The Ladder series) 'A simplified English edition ... condensed in length and the vocabulary has been reduced to 3,000 words.' [E457.L88] 60-601
1. Lincoln, Abraham, Pres. U.S., 1809-1865. I. Title.

LOWITZ, Sadyebeth. 973.7'0924 B
Barefoot Abe; a really truly story by Sadyebeth and Anson Lowitz, with illus. by the latter. [Rev. ed.] Minneapolis, Lerner Publications Co. [1967] [56] p. illus. 19 x 22 cm. A simple biography of Lincoln which concentrates on his experiences as a child and young man. [E457.905.L69 1967] 92 AC 68
1. Lincoln, Abraham, Pres. U.S., 1809-1865. I. Lowitz, Anson, joint author. II. Title.

LUTHIN, Reinhard Henry, 1905- 923.173
The real Abraham Lincoln; a complete one volume history of his life and times. Englewood Cliffs, N. J., Prentice-Hall [1960] 778 p. 24 cm. [E456.L8] 60-13048
1. Lincoln, Abraham, Pres, U. S., 1809-1865. I. Title.

MARTIN, Patricia Miles. 92
Abraham Lincoln. Illustrated by Gustav Schrotter. New York, Putnam [1964] 64 p. col. illus. 23 cm. (A See and read beginning to read biography) [E457.905.M33] 63-15573

MCCLURE, Alexander Kelly, 1828-1909. 973.7'092'2 B
Abraham Lincoln and men of war-times; some personal recollections of war and politics during the Lincoln administration. With introd. by A. C. Lambdin. Freeport, N.Y., Books for Libraries Press [1973] p. Reprint of the 1892 ed. published by The Times Pub. Co., Philadelphia. [E467.M143] 73-6544 ISBN 0-518-19060-9
1. Lincoln, Abraham, Pres. U.S., 1809-1865. 2. United States—History—Civil War—Biography. I. Title.

MEREDITH, Roy, 1908- 973.7
Mr. Lincoln's contemporaries; an album of portraits by Mathew B. Brady. New York, Scribner, 1951. xii, 233 p. illus., ports. 29 cm. [E415.8.M4] 51-12294
1. Lincoln, Abraham, Pres. U.S., 1809-1865. 2. U.S.—Biography—Portraits. 3. U.S.—History—Civil War, 1861-1865—Portraits. I. Brady, Mathew B., 1823 (ca.)-1896. II. Title.

MILLER, Francis Trevelyan, 1877-1959. 973.7'0924 B
Portrait life of Lincoln; life of Abraham Lincoln, the greatest American, told from original photographs taken with his authority during the great crisis through which he led his country—treasured among the 7000 Secret Service war negatives in the Brady-Gardner Collection at Springfield, Massachusetts, and in private collections, valued at $150,000, collected by Edward Bailey Eaton. Freeport, New York, Books for Libraries Press [1970] 164 p. illus., ports. 27 cm. Reprint of the 1910 ed. "Hundred greatest books on Abraham Lincoln": p. 161-164. [E457.6.M64 1970] 76-133528
1. Lincoln, Abraham, Pres. U.S., 1809-1865. 2. Lincoln, Abraham, Pres. U.S., 1809-1865—Portraits. I. Title.

MITGANG, Herbert, comp. 973.7'0924 B
Abraham Lincoln, a press portrait; his life and times from the original newspaper documents of the Union, the Confederacy, and Europe. Chicago, Quadrangle Books, 1971. xix, 519 p. illus., ports. 23 cm. [E457.M69] 72-143572 ISBN 0-8129-0170-3 9.00
1. Lincoln, Abraham, Pres. U.S., 1809-1865. I. Title.

MORSE, John Torrey, 1840-1937. 973.7'0924 B
Abraham Lincoln. Boston, Houghton, Mifflin. [New York, AMS press, 1972] 2 v. illus. 19 cm. (American statesmen, v. 25-26) Reprint of the 1899 ed. [E457.M884 1972] 73-128958 ISBN 0-404-50892-8
1. Lincoln, Abraham, Pres. U.S., 1809-1865. I. Title. II. Series.

MOSES, Elbert Raymond, 1879- 923.173
Abraham Lincoln: from cabin to Capitol. Prefatory note by Waldo H. Dunn. Daytona Beach, Fla., College Pub. Co. [1955] 139p. illus. 22cm. Includes bibliography. [E457.M885] 55-25898
1. Lincoln, Abraham, Pres. U. S., 1809-1865. I. Title.

NICOLAY, John George, 1832-1901. 973.70924
Abraham Lincoln, a history, by John G. Nicolay and John Hay. Abridged and edited by Paul M. Angle. [Abridged ed.] Chicago, University of Chicago Press [1966] xix, 394 p. group port., map. 21 cm. (Classic American historians) "First published in book form in ten volumes by the Century Company [in] 1890." [E457.N658] 66-20590
1. Lincoln, Abraham, Pres. U.S., 1809-1865. 2. United States—History—Civil War, 1861-1865. I. Hay, John, 1838-1905, joint author. II. Angle, Paul McClelland, 1900- ed. **BIP**

NOLAN, Jeanette (Covert) 1896- v. 12
Abraham Lincoln; illustrated by Lee Ames. New York, J. Messner [1965] 182 p. illus. 22 cm. (Archway books) "Sixth printing." Bibliography: p. 178. 68-58450
1. Lincoln, Abraham, Pres. U. S.—Fiction. I. Title.

NORTH, Sterling, 1906- 923.173
Abe Lincoln, log cabin to White House. Illustrated by Lee Ames. New York, Random House [c1956] 184p. illus. 22cm. (Landmark Books [61]) [E457.N659] 56-5450
1. Lincoln, Abraham, Pres. U. S., 1809-1865. I. Title.

OATES, Stephen B. 973.7'092'4 B
With malice toward none : the life of Abraham Lincoln / Stephen B. Oates. 1st ed. New York : Harper & Row, c1977. xvii, 492 p., [16] leaves of plates : ill. ; 24 cm. Includes bibliographical references and index. [E457.O17 1977] 76-12058 ISBN 0-06-013283-3 : 15.00
1. Lincoln, Abraham, Pres. U.S., 1809-1865. I. Title. **BIP**

OATES, Stephen B. 973.7'092'4
With malice toward none : the life of Abraham Lincoln / Stephen B. Oates. New York : New American Library, 1978,c1977. xvii, 542p., 8 p. of plates : ill. ; 18 cm. (A Mentor Book) Includes bibliographical references and index. [E457.O17] ISBN 0-451-61627-8 pbk. : 2.95
1. Lincoln, Abraham, Pres. U.S., 1809-1865. I. Title.
L.C. card no. for 1977 Harper & Row ed.: 76-12058.

RANDALL, James Garfield, 1881-1953 923.173
Mr. Lincoln. Ed. by Richard N. Current. New York, [Apollo Eds., 1968, c.1967] xl, 392p. 20cm. (A-178) Incorporates those parts [the four-volume study, Lincoln, the President] which deal primarily with Lincoln the man and with his personal relationships. [E457.R215] 2.25 pap.,
1. Lincoln, Abraham, Pres. U.S., 1809-1865. I. Title.

RANDALL, James Garfield, 1881-1953. 923.173
Mr. Lincoln. Edited by Richard N. Current. New York, Dodd, Mead, 1957. xiii, 392 p. illus., ports., facsims. 22 cm. "Incorporates those parts of...[the four-volume study, Lincoln, the President] which deal primarily with Lincoln the man and with his personal relationships." [E457.R215] 57-5873
1. Lincoln, Abraham, Pres. U.S., 1809-1865. I. Title. **BIP**

RANDELL, James Garfield, 1881-1953 923.173
Lincoln, the president. 2.v. New York [Apollo Eds. 1966, c.1945] (395; 381p.) 20cm. (A-126 & A-127) Contents.v.1-2. Springfield to Gettysburg. Cover title: v.1. Springfield to Bull Run--v.2. Bull Run to Gettysburg. Bibl. [E437.R2] 2.95 pap., ea.,
1. Lincoln, Abraham, Pres. U.S., 1809-1865. I. Title. II. Series.

RANDALL, Ruth (Painter) 923.173
The courtship of Mr. Lincoln. [1st ed.] Boston, Little, Brown [c1957] 219p. illus. 21cm. Includes bibliography. [E457.25.R24] 57-5515
1. Lincoln, Abraham, Pres. U. S., 1809-1865. 2. Lincoln, Mary (Todd) 1818-1882. I. Title.

ROBINSON, Luther Emerson, 1867- 973.7'092'4 B
Abraham Lincoln as a man of letters. [Folcroft, Pa.] Folcroft Library Editions, 1974 [c1918] p. cm. Reprint of the ed. published by Reilly & Britton, Chicago. "Selections from Lincoln's works": p. [E457.2.R65 1974] 74-11355 22.50 (lib. bdg.)
1. Lincoln, Abraham, Pres. U.S., 1809-1865. I. Lincoln, Abraham, Pres. U.S., 1809-1865. Selected works. 1974. II. Title. **BIP**

RUBINGER, Naphtali J. 973'.074'016971
Abraham Lincoln and the Jews. New York, J. David [1962] 75 p. 23 cm. [E457.2.R89] 62-13693
1. Lincoln, Abraham, Pres. U.S. — Relations with Jews. I. Title.

RUSSELL, G. Darrell. 973'.0992
Lincoln and Kennedy: looked at kindly together, by G. Darrell Russell, Jr. New York, Carlton Press [1973] 75 p. 21 cm. (A Hearthstone book) Bibliography: p. 73-75. [E457.R956] 73-176477 3.50
1. Lincoln, Abraham, Pres. U.S., 1809-1865. 2. Kennedy, John Fitzgerald, Pres. U.S., 1917-1963. I. Title.

SAGE, Harold Kenneth, 1890- 973.7'092'4
Jesse W. Fell and the Lincoln autobiography, by Harold K. Sage. Normal, Ill., 1971. 17 p. illus. 23 cm. Includes bibliographical references. [E457.S16] 72-187787
1. Lincoln, Abraham, Pres. U.S., 1809-1865. 2. Fell, Jesse W., 1808-1887. I. Title.

SANCHEZ-TORRENTO, Eugenio. 973.7'092'4 B
A modern biography of Abraham Lincoln. [Miami, Impreso Editorial A.I.P., 1970] 50 p. 18 cm. Bibliography: p. 47-50. [E457.S19] 74-151289
1. Lincoln, Abraham, Pres. U.S., 1809-1865. I. Title.

SANDBURG, Carl 923.173
Abraham Lincoln; the prairie years and the war years. In 3 v. New York, Dell [1959, c.1925-1954] v. 1, 320p.; v. 2-3, 928p. 'Sources and acknowledgements': p.986-903 illus., ports. 17cm. (Laurel eds. LX113, LX114, LX15) .75 pap., ea.,
1. Lincoln, Abraham, Pres. U.S., 1809-1865. I. Title.

SANDBURG, Carl, 1878-1967. 973.7'092'4 B
Abe Lincoln grows up. With illus. by James Daugherty. New York, Harcourt Brace Jovanovich [1975, c1928] p. cm. (A Voyager book, AVB 92) Reprint of the ed. published by Harcourt Brace & World, New York. [E457.3.S23 1975] 74-17180 1.95 (pbk.)
1. Lincoln, Abraham, Pres. U.S., 1809-1865. I. Title. **BIP**

SANDBURG, Carl, 1878- 923.173
Abraham Lincoln; the prairie years and the war years. [1st ed.] New York, Harcourt, Brace [1954] xiv, 762p. illus., ports., maps. 25cm. 'Sources and acknowledgments':p. 743-747. [E457.S215] 54-9720
1. Lincoln, Abraham, Pres. U. S., 1809-1865. I. Title.

SANDBURG, Carl, 1878-1967. 973.7'092'4 B
Abraham Lincoln; the prairie years and the war years. One-volume ed. New York, Harcourt Brace Jovanovich [1974, c1966] xiv, 762 p. illus. 21 cm. (A Harvest book, HB 297) Abridged by the author. Bibliography: p. 743-747. [E457.S215 1974] 74-8388 ISBN 0-15-602611-2
1. Lincoln, Abraham, Pres. U.S., 1809-1865.

SCHULTE, Nordholt, J. W., 1920- 973'.074'016971
Abraham Lincoln. Arnhem, Van Loghum Slaterus, 1959. 266p. illus., ports., map. 23cm. Bibliography: p. 259-266. [E457.S38] A60
1. Lincoln, Abraham, Pres. U. S., 1809-1865. I. Title.

SCRIPPS, John Locke, 1818-1866. 973.6'0924 B
Life of Abraham Lincoln. Edited with introd. and notes by Roy P. Basler and Lloyd A. Dunlap. New York, Greenwood Press, 1968 [c1961] 192 p. facsims. 23 cm. Bibliographical footnotes. [E457.3.S423 1968] 68-56041
1. Lincoln, Abraham, Pres. U.S., 1809-1865.

SEARCHER, Victor. 923.173
Lincoln's journey to greatness; a factual account of the twelve-day inaugural trip. [1st ed.] Philadelphia, Winston [1960] 279p. illus. 22cm. [E457.4.S4] 60-6057
1. Lincoln. Abraham, Pres. U.S.—Journey to Washington, Feb. 1861. I. Title.

SHUTES, Milton Henry, 1883- 923.173
Lincoln's emotional life. Philadelphia, Dorrance [1957] 222p. illus. 20cm. Includes bibliography. [E457.2.S55] 57-8482
1. Lincoln, Abraham, Press. U. S.—Personality. I. Title.

STEVENSON, Augusta. 973.7'0924 B
Abe Lincoln, frontier boy. Illustrated by Jerry Robinson. Indianapolis, Bobbs-Merrill [1959] 192 p. illus. 20 cm. (Childhood of famous Americans) Tells of the childhood of the man who was President during the Civil War. [PZ7.S8467Ab5] 92 AC 68

Lincoln, Abraham, Pres. U.S., 1809-1865—Addresses, essays, lectures.

Lincoln, Abraham, Pres. U.S., 1809-1865—Anecdotes.

Lincoln, Abraham, Pres. U.S., 1809-1865—Assassination.

1. Lincoln, Abraham, Pres. U.S., 1809-1865—Assassination. 2. Booth, John Wilkes, 1838-1865. 3. United States. Army. Military Commission. Lincoln's assassins. 1865. 4. Weichmann, Louis J. I. Richards, A. C., d. 1907. II. Title.

WEICHMANN, Louis J. 973.7'092'4 B
A true history of the assassination of Abraham Lincoln and of the conspiracy of 1865 / Louis J. Weichmann ; edited by Floyd E. Risvold. New York : Vintage Books, 1977, c1975. xxx, 492, xvi p. ; 24 cm. Includes 23 letters written by A. C. Richards to L. J. Weichmann from Apr. 1898 to Nov. 1901. Includes index. Bibliography: p. 461-463. [E475.5.W44 1977] 76-41211 ISBN 0-394-72260-4 pbk. 5.95
1. Lincoln, Abraham, Pres. U.S., 1809-1865—Assassination. 2. Booth, John Wilkes, 1838-1865. 3. United States. Army. Military Commission. Lincoln's assassins. 1865. 4. Weichmann, Louis J. I. Richards, A. C., d. 1907. II. Title. BIP

Lincoln, Abraham, Pres. U.S., 1809-1865—Books and reading.

BARTON, William Eleazer, 1861-1930. 973.7'092'4
Abraham Lincoln and his books : with selections from the writings of Lincoln and a bibliography of books in print relating to Abraham Lincoln / by William E. Barton. Folcroft, Pa. : Folcroft Library Editions, 1976, [c1920] 108 p., [1] leaf of plates : ports. ; 24 cm. Reprint of the ed. published by the Book Section of M. Field, Chicago. [E457.2.B28 1976] 76-5911 ISBN 0-8414-3346-1 lib. bdg. : 10.00
1. Lincoln, Abraham, Pres. U.S., 1809-1865—Books and reading. 2. Lincoln, Abraham, Pres. U.S., 1809-1865—Bibliography. I. Lincoln, Abraham, Pres. U.S., 1809-1865. Selections. 1976. II. Title.

Lincoln, Abraham, Pres. U.S., 1809-1865—Childhood.

VAN NATTER, Francis Marion 923.173
Lincoln's boyhood; a chronicle of his Indiana years. Foreword by Karl Detzer. Washington, D.C., Public Affairs [c.1963] 224p. illus. 24cm. Bibl. 63-10816 4.50
1. Lincoln, Abraham, Pres. U.S.—Childhood. I. Title.

WARREN, Louis Austin, 1885- 923.173
Lincoln's youth: Indiana years, seven to twenty-one, 1816-1830. New York, Appleton, Century, Crofts [1959] xxii, 298 p. illus., ports., maps, facsims. 24 cm. Bibliography: p. 271-281. [E457.32.W284] 59-14644
1. Lincoln, Abraham, Pres. U.S., 1809-1865—Childhood. I. Title.

Lincoln, Abraham, Pres. U.S., 1809-1865—Childhood and youth.

WARREN, Louis Austin, 1885- 973.7'092'4 B
Lincoln's youth : Indiana years, seven to twenty-one, 1816-1830 / by Louis A. Warren. Westport, Conn. : Greenwood Press, 1976, c1959. p. cm. Reprint of the ed. published by Indiana Historical Society, Indianapolis. Includes index. Bibliography: p. [E457.32.W284 1976] 75-26223 lib.bdg. : 21.00
1. Lincoln, Abraham, Pres. U.S., 1809-1865—Childhood and youth. I. Title.

Lincoln, Abraham, Pres. U.S., 1809-1865—Childhood and youth—Juvenile literature.

BABER, Adin. 973.7'0924
Sarah and Abe in Indiana. Durham, N.C., Moore Pub. Co. [1970] 240 p. illus. 23 cm. Illustrated by L. Ostendorf. An account of the childhood and teen-age years of Sarah and Abe Lincoln in Indiana. Includes detailed descriptions of the pioneer way of life. [E457.32.B18] 920 73-99295 5.95
1. Lincoln, Abraham, Pres. U.S., 1809-1865—Childhood and youth—Juvenile literature. 2. Lincoln Sarah, 1807-1828—Juvenile literature. I. Ostendorf, Lloyd, illus. II. Title. BIP

Lincoln, Abraham, Pres. U.S., 1809-1865—Family.

RANDALL, Ruth (Painter) 923.173
Lincoln's sons. [1st ed.] Boston, Little, Brown [1955] 373p. illus. 23cm. [E457.25.R26] 56-5046
1. Lincoln, Abraham, Pres. U. S.—Family. I. Title.

SEMONES, Hattie, 1891-1969. 813'.5'4
Duel with destiny / by Hattie Semones. Radford, Va. : Commonwealth Press, c1976. viii, 131 p. ; 23 cm. [E457.32.S45 1976] 75-37226 ISBN 0-89227-001-2 : 6.95
1. Lincoln, Abraham, Pres. U.S., 1809-1865—Family. I. Title. BIP

Lincoln, Abraham, Pres. U.S., 1809-1865—Homes.

COLEMAN, Charles Hubert, 1900- 973.1
Abraham Lincoln and Coles County, Illinois. New Brunswick, N. J., Scarecrow Press, 1955. xii, 268 p. illus., ports., maps. 23 cm. Bibliography: p. 248-253. Bibliographical footnotes. [E457.64.C6] 55-14236
1. Lincoln, Abraham, Pres. U.S., 1809-1865—Homes. 2. Coles Co., Ill.

Lincoln, Abraham, Pres. U.S., 1809-1865—Iconography.

HANSER, Richard. 923.173
Meet Mr. Lincoln, by Richard Hanser and Donald B. Hyatt. New York, Golden Press [1960] 131 p. illus. 28 cm. Adapted from the motion picture, Meet Mr. Lincoln, televised by the National Braodcasting Company as a Project twenty event on the 150th anniversary of Lincoln's birth. Producer and director: Donald B. Hyatt. Script: Richard Hanser. [E457.6.H3] 59-15868
1. Lincoln, Abraham, Pres. U.S., 1809-1865—Iconography. I. Hyatt, Donald B.

LINCOLN, Abraham, Pres. U.S., 1809-1865. 973.7'0924
Lincoln and the Lincoln country; a souvenir guidebook. [Springfield, Ill., Octavo Press, 1968] [31] p. incl. cover. illus., facsims., maps, ports. 31 cm. Cover title. Includes Abraham Lincoln autobiography, published in 1860 and written in the third person; facsims. of Lincoln manuscripts and letters; typical Lincoln humor. [E457.64.L5 1968] 74-12152 0.95
1. Lincoln, Abraham, Pres. U.S., 1809-1865—Iconography. I. Title.

LORANT, Stefan, 1901- 923.173
Lincoln, a picture story of his life. New York, Harper [1952] 256 p. illus. ports., facsims. 33 cm. "Contents and bibliography": p. 251-256. [E457.6.L78] 52-8481
1. Lincoln, Abraham, Press. U. S. 1809-1865—Inconography. I. Title.

LORANT, Stefan, 1901- 923.173
Lincoln, a picture story of his life. Rev. and enl. ed. New York, Harper [1957] 304 p. illus., ports., facsims. 33 cm. "Contents and bibiliography": p. 299-304. [E457.6.L78 1957] 57-11110
1. Lincoln, Abraham, Pres. U.S., 1809-1865—Iconography.

LORANT, Stefan, 1901- 973.7'0924
Lincoln; a picture story of his life. Rev. and enl. ed. New York, Norton [1969] 336 p. illus., facsims., ports. 33 cm. "Contents and bibliography": p. 329-334. [E457.6.L78 1969] 69-11484 7.95
1. Lincoln, Abraham, Pres. U.S., 1809-1865—Iconography. I. Title.

Lincoln, Abraham, Pres. U.S., 1809-1865—Journey to Washington, Feb, 1861—Fiction.

HYND, Alan, 1908- fic
Arrival: 12:30, the Baltimore plot against Lincoln. [Camden, N.J.] Nelson [1967] 127 p. illus. 21 cm. Bibliography: p. 127. [PZ4.H998Ar] 67-24667
1. Lincoln, Abraham, Pres. U.S., 1809-1865—Journey to Washington, Feb, 1861—Fiction. I. Title.

Lincoln, Abraham, Pres. U.S., 1809-1865—Journey to Washington, Feb. 1861—Juvenile literature.

PHELAN, Mary Kay. 973.7'092'4 B
Mr. Lincoln's inaugural journey. Drawings by Richard Cuffari. New York, Crowell [1972] 211 p. illus. 21 cm. Bibliography: p. [199]-203. A day-by-day account of Lincoln's roundabout journey to Washington, D.C., for his first inauguration, a journey plagued by rumors of a planned assassination attempt. [E457.4.P46 1972] 76-175110 4.50
1. Lincoln, Abraham, Pres. U.S., 1809-1865—Journey to Washington, Feb. 1861—Juvenile literature. I. Cuffair, Richard, 1925- illus. II. Title. BIP

Lincoln, Abraham, Pres. U.S., 1809-1865—Juvenile literature.

ABRAHAM Lincoln, the children's story. 923.173 Based on a story by Helen van Hoogendyk. Illustrated by George Avison. Kenosha, Wis., S. Lowe Co. [1953] unpaged. illus. 20cm. (A Bonnie book, 4275) [E457.905.A3] 54-32488
1. Lincoln, Abraham, Pres. U. S.—Juvenile literature. I. Avison, George, 1885- illus.

ARMSTRONG, William Howard, 1914- 973.7'092'4 B
The education of Abraham Lincoln, by William H. Armstrong. New York, Coward, McCann & Geoghegan [1974] 127 p. illus. 23 cm. Bibliography: p. 125-127. Discusses Abe's "developing years" and the schools, teachers, and early nineteenth-century environment which helped shape the man to come. [E457.905.A76 1974] 74-76235 ISBN 0-698-20273-2. 4.64 (lib. bdg.)
1. Lincoln, Abraham, Pres. U.S., 1809-1865—Juvenile literature. I. Title. BIP

AULAIRE, Ingri (Mortenson) d;, 1904- 923.173
Abraham Lincoln. by Ingri Edgar Parin's Aulaire. Garden City, N. Y., Doubleday, c1957. unpaged. illus. 32cm. [E457.905.A86 1957] 57-2502
1. Lincoln, Abraham, Pres. U. S.—Juvenile literature. I. Aulaire, Edgar Parin d', 1898- joint author. II. Title.

BAILEY, Bernadine (Freeman) 1901- 923.173
Abraham Lincoln: man of courage. Illustrated by Nathan Goldstein. Boston, Houghton Mifflin [c.1960] 191p. illus., map 22cm. (Piper books) 60-13064 1.95; 2.35 lib. ed.,
1. Lincoln, Abraham, Pres. U. S.—Juvenile literature. I. Title.

BAILEY, Bernadine (Freeman) 1901- 923.173
Abraham Lincoln: man of courage. Illustrated by Nathan Goldstein. Boston, Houghton Mifflin [1960] 191p. illus. 22cm. (Piper books) [E457.905.B18] 60-13064
1. Lincoln, Abraham, Pres. U.S.—Juvenile literature. I. Title.

BRAGDON, Lillian J. 923.173
Abraham Lincoln, courageous leader. Illustrated by Edward Shenton. Nashville, Abingdon Press [c.1960] 125p. illus. 22cm. (Makers of America) 60-6806 1.75
1. Lincoln, Abraham, Pres. U.S.—Juvenile literature. I. Title.

CAVANAH, Frances. 923.173
They knew Abe Lincoln, a boy in Indiana: illustrated by Harve Stein. Chicago, Rand McNally [1952] 255 p. illus. 21 cm. [E457.905.C3] 52-7106
1. Lincoln, Abraham, Pres. U. S.—Juvenile literature. I. Title.

COLLINS, David R. 973.7'092'4 B
Abraham Lincoln / by David R. Collins ; illustrated by Myron Quinton ; edited by Norma Cournow Camp. Milford, Mich. : Mott Media, c1976. 150 p. : ill. (some col.) ; 23 cm. (The Sowers) Includes index. Bibliography: p. [147] Abraham Lincoln recounts the story of his life. [E457.905.C64] 92 76-2456 ISBN 0-915134-09-8 : 5.95
1. Lincoln, Abraham, Pres. U.S., 1809-1865—Juvenile literature. I. Title.

COLLINS, David R. 973.7'092'4 B
I, Abraham Lincoln / by David R. Collins. Milford, Mich. : Mott Media, [1976] p. cm. (The Sowers) Includes index. Bibliography: p. Abraham Lincoln recounts the story of his life. [E457.905.C64] 92 76-2456 ISBN 0-915134-09-8 : 5.95
1. Lincoln, Abraham, Pres. U.S., 1809-1865—Juvenile literature. I. Title.

COLVER, Anne, 1908- 923.173
Abraham Lincoln; for the people. Illus. by Irv Docktor. New York, Scholastic Bk. Servs. [1962, c.1960] 64p. 21cm. (TW 359) .35 pap.,
1. Lincoln, Abraham, Pres. U.S.—Juvenile literature. I. Title.

COLVER, Anne, 1908- 923.173
Abraham Lincoln; for the people. Illustrated by William Moyers. Champaign, Ill., Garrard Press [c.1960] 78p. illus. (part col.) 23cm. (A Discovery book) 60-7079 2.25
1. Lincoln, Abraham, Pres. U. S.—Juvenile literature. I. Title.

COOLIDGE, Olivia E. 973.7'092'4 B
The apprenticeship of Abraham Lincoln / Olivia Coolidge. New York : Scribner, [1974] viii, 242 p., [3] leaves of plates : ill. ; 24 cm. Includes index. A biography concentrating on the first fifty years in the life of Abraham Lincoln who became President at the age of fifty-two. [E457.3.C66] a2 74-11713 ISBN 0-684-14003-9 : 6.95
1. Lincoln, Abraham, Pres. U.S., 1809-1865—Juvenile literature. I. Title. BIP

ELTING, Mary, 1909- 923.173
The real book about Abraham Lincoln, by Michael Gorham [pseud.] illustrated by Elinore Blaisdell. Garden City, N. Y., Garden City Books [1951] llus. 21cm. 186p. illus. 21cm. (Real books) (Real books) [E457.905.E4] 51-12212
1. Lincoln, Abraham, Pres. U. S.—Juvenile literature. I. Title.

FOSTER, GNevieve (Stump) 1893- v. 12
Abraham Lincoln. New York, Scribner [1966, c1950] 111 p. col. illus. 20 cm. (Her An initial biography) On cover: Scribners library binding. 68-32758
1. Lincoln, Abraham, Pres. U.S., 1809-1865—Juvenile literature. I. Title.

GRAFF, Polly Anne (Colver) 1908- 92
Abraham Lincoln; for the people. Illustrated by William Moyers. New York, Grosset & Dunlap [1962]c1960. 78 p. illus. 23 cm. (A Discovery book) [E457.905] A 62
1. Lincoln, Abraham, Pres. U.S., 1809-1865 — Juvenile literature. I. Title.

JOHNSON, Ann Donegan. 973.7'092'4 B
The value of respect : the story of Abraham Lincoln / by Ann Donegan Johnson. La Jolla, Calif. : Value Communications, c1977. p. cm. (ValueTales) A brief biography of Abraham Lincoln emphasizing the importance of respect of his life. [E457.905.J63] 92 77-12455 ISBN 0-916392-14-7 : 4.95
1. Lincoln, Abraham, Pres. U.S., 1809-1865—Juvenile literature. 2. Presidents—United States—Biography—Juvenile literature. 3. Respect—Juvenile literature. I. Title. BIP

JUDSON, Clara (Ingram), 1879- 923.173
Abraham Lincoln, friend of the people. Pen drawings by Robert Frankenberg; kodachromes of the Chicago Historical Society Lincoln dioramas. Chicago, Wilcox and Follett Co. [1950] 206 p. illus. (part col.) 25 cm. [E457.905.J8] 50-10859
1. Lincoln, Abraham, Pres. U. S.—Juvenile literature. I. Title.

LATHAM, Frank Brown, 1910- 973.7'092'4 B
Abraham Lincoln, by Frank B. Latham. New York, F. Watts [1968] vi, 163 p. illus., map, ports. 22 cm. (Immortals of history) A biography of the sixteenth President with emphasis on the Civil War years. [E457.905.L3] 92 68-22141

1. Lincoln, Abraham, Pres. U.S., 1809-1865—Juvenile literature.

LEE, Susan. 973.7'092'4 B
Abraham Lincoln / by Susan Dye Lee ; illustrated by Ralph Canaday. Chicago : Children's Press, c1978. 47 p. : col. ill. ; 24 cm. (Heroes of the Civil War) A brief biography of Abraham Lincoln who was President during the Civil War. [E457.905.L4] 77-20125 ISBN 0-516-04701-9 lib.bdg. : 6.60
1. Lincoln, Abraham, Pres. U.S., 1809-1865—Juvenile literature. 2. Presidents—United States—Biography—Juvenile literature. 3. United States—History—Civil War, 1861-1865—Juvenile literature. I. Canaday, Ralph. II. Title. III. Series.

LINCOLN. 973.7'0924 B
[Maplewood, N.J., Hammond Incorporated, c1970] 1 v. col. illus. 27 cm. (A Hammond temporama, no. 5) Cover title. Folding book; illus. on continuous strip, 27 x 141 cm. Parallel outlines trace the events of Abraham Lincoln's life and the political, military, and cultural events taking place in the world at the same time. [E457.905.L54] 92 68-54492
1. Lincoln, Abraham, Pres. U.S., 1809-1865—Juvenile literature. I. Hammond Incorporated. II. Title. III. Series.

LOWITZ, Sadyebeth. 92 (J)
Barefoot Abe; a really truly story by Sadyebeth and Anson Lowitz, with illus. by the latter. [Rev. ed.] Minneapolis, Lerner Publications Co. [1967] 1 v. (unpaged) illus. 19 x 22 cm. [E457.905.L69 1967] 67-29824
1. Lincoln, Abraham, Pres. U.S., 1809-1865—Juvenile literature. I. Lowitz, Anson, joint author. II. Title. BIP

MCNEER, May Yonge, 1902- 923.173
America's Abraham Lincoln. Illustrated by Lynd Ward. Boston, Houghton Mifflin, 1957. 119p. illus. 25cm. [E457.905.M25] 57-5882
1. Lincoln, Abraham, Pres. U. S.—Juvenile literature. I. Title.

MEET Abe Lincoln, 973.7'092'4 B
President of the people. Greenfield, Mass., C. L. Bete Co., 1973, c1972. 15 p. illus. 21 cm. (A Scriptographic booklet) Cover title. [E457.M484] 73-174911
1. Lincoln, Abraham, Pres. U.S., 1809 1865—Juvenile literature. I. Title.

MIERS, Earl Schenck, 1910- 92 (J)
That Lincoln boy. Illustrated by Kurt Werth. Cleveland, World Pub. Co. [1968] 141 p. illus. 24 cm. [E457.905.M53] 68-14693
1. Lincoln, Abraham, Pres. U.S., 1809-1865—Juvenile literature. I. Title.

MITGANG, Herbert. 973.7'092'4 B
The fiery trial; a life of Lincoln. [1st ed.] New York, Viking Press [1974] 207 p. illus. 25 cm. Bibliography: p. [192]-196. A biography of the sixteenth President from his early years in Springfield through the Civil War to his assassination in 1865. [E457.M7] 92 73-23089 ISBN 0-670-31182-0 6.95
1. Lincoln, Abraham, Pres. U.S., 1809-1865—Juvenile literature. I. Title. BIP

MONJO, F. N. 973.7'092'2 B
Me and Willie and Pa; the story of Abraham Lincoln and his son Tad, by F. N. Monjo. Illustrated by Douglas Gorsline. New York, Simon and Schuster [1973] 94 p. illus. 27 cm. Bibliography: p. 93-94. President Lincoln's youngest son recounts his own and his family's experience during their four years in the White House. [E457.905.M58] 73-11464 ISBN 0-671-65211-7 5.95
1. Lincoln, Abraham, Pres. U.S., 1809-1865—Juvenile literature. 2. Lincoln, Thomas, 1853-1871—Juvenile literature. 3. Lincoln, William Wallace, 1850-1862—Juvenile literature. 4. United States—History—Civil War, 1861-1865—Juvenile literature. I. Gorsline, Douglas W., 1913- illus. II. Title.

NORMAN, Gertrude. 923.173
A man named Lincoln. Illustrated by Joseph Cellini. New York, Putnam [1960] unpaged. illus. 23cm. [E457.905.N6] 60-5639
1. Lincoln. Abraham, Pres. U. S.—Juvenile literature. I. Title.

OSTENDORF, Lloyd 920
A picture story of Abraham Lincoln Illus. by the author. [New York] Lothrop [c.1962] 159p. 26cm. 62-11065 3.50
1. Lincoln, Abraham, Pres. .S.—Juvenile literature. I. Title.

OSTENDORF, Lloyd. 92
A picture story of Abraham Lincoln. Illustrated by the author. [New York] Lothrop, Lee and Shepard [1962] 159p. illus. 26cm. [E457.905.O8] 62-11065
1. Lincoln, Abraham, Press. U. S.—Juvenile literature. I. Title.

WABER, Bernard 920
Just like Abraham Lincoln. Boston, Houghton [c.]1964. 40p. col. illus. 28cm. 64-19981 3.25; 3.07 lib. ed.,
1. Lincoln, Abraham, Pres. U. S.—Juvenile literature. I. Title. BIP

Lincoln, Abraham, Pres. U.S., 1809-1865—Law practice.

DUFF, John J v. 12
A. Lincoln: prairie lawyer. [1st ed.] New York, Bramhall House, 1960. 433 p. illus. 24 cm. Includes bibliography. 68-37045
1. Lincoln, Abraham, Pres. U.S.—Law practice. I. Title.

DUFF, John J. 923.173
A. Lincoln: prairie lawyer. [1st ed.] New York, Rinehart [1960] 433 p. illus. 24 cm. Includes bibliography. [E457.2.D8] 60-5228
1. Lincoln, Abraham, Pres. U.S., 1809-1865—Law Practice.

FRIEND, Henry C., 973.7'092'4
1909-
Abraham Lincoln's commercial practice; a series of articles by Henry C. Friend. [Chicago] Commercial Law Foundation, 1970. 28 p. ports. 23 cm. [E457.2.F79] 75-304308
1. Lincoln, Abraham, Pres U.S., 1809-1865—Law practice. I. Lincoln, Abraham, Pres. U.S., 1809-1865. II. Title.

KYLE, Otto R 923.173
Abraham Lincoln in Decatur. [1st ed.] New York, Vantage Press [1957] 176p. illus. 21cm. Includes bibliography. [E457.3.K9] 56-12770
1. Lincoln, Abraham, Pres. U. S.—Law practice. 2. Lincoln, Abraham, Pres. U. S.—Political career before 1861. I. Title.

Lincoln, Abraham, Pres. U.S., 1809-1865—Oratory.

LINCOLN, Abraham, Pres 923.173
U.S., 1809-1865.
Abraham Lincoln: a docementary portrait through his speeches and writings. Edited and with an introd. by Don E. Fehrenbacher. [New York] New American Library [1964] 288 p. 18 cm. (A Signet classic) "CT265." Bibliography: p. 286-288. [E457.92] 64-55382
I. Fehrenbacher, Don Edward, 1920- ed. II. Title.

LINCOLN, Abraham, Pres. 923.173
U. S., 1809-1865.
Speeches and letters, 1832-1865, selected and edited by Paul M. Angle. [Rev. ed.] London, Dent; New York, Dutton [1957] xiii, 300p. 19cm. (Everyman's library, 206. Oratory) Bibliography: p. x-xi. [E457.92 1957b] 59-3398
I. Title.

WILEY, Earl 973.7'0924
Wellington.
Abraham Lincoln: portrait of a speaker. [1st ed.] New York, Vantage Press [1970] 573 p. ports. 22 cm. Bibliography: p. 564-573. [E457.2.W68] 70-16509 7.50
1. Lincoln, Abraham, Pres. U.S., 1809-1865—Oratory.

Lincoln, Abraham, Pres. U.S., 1809-1865—Political career before 1861.

FINDLEY, Paul, 973.7'092'4 B
1921-
A. Lincoln, the crucible of Congress / by Paul Findley. New York : Crown Publishers, c1979. xvii, 270 p. : ill. ; 27 cm. Includes index. Bibliography: p. 263-266. [E457.4.F5 1979] 79-4256 ISBN 0-517-53436-3 : 14.95
1. Lincoln, Abraham, Pres. U.S., 1809-1865—Political career before 1861. 2. United States. Congress. House—Biography. 3. United States—Politics and government—1845-1861. 4. Presidents—United States—Biography. 5. Legislators—United States—Biography. I. Title.

HAYES, Melvin L 923.173
Mr. Lincoln runs for President. [1st ed.] New York, Citadel Press [1960] 352p. illus. 22cm. Includes bibliography. [E440.H33] 60-15448
1. Lincoln, Abraham,Pres. U. S.—Political career before 1861. 2. Presidents—U. S.—Election—1860. I. Title.

RIDDLE, Donald Wayne, 923.173
1894-
Congressman Abraham Lincoln. Urbana, University of Illinois Press, 1957. vii, 280p. 24cm. Bibliography: p. [253]-266. [E457.4.R5] 57-6956
1. Lincoln, Abraham, Pres. U. S.—Political career before 1861. I. Title. BIP

Lincoln, Abraham, Pres. U.S., 1809-1865—Portraits—Addresses, essays, lectures.

OSTENDORF, Lloyd. 770'.92'2
Lincoln and his photographers; address at annual meeting, Lincoln Fellowship of Wisconsin, Madison, 1971. [Madison] 1972. 14 p. ports. 26 cm. ([Historical Fellowship of Wisconsin] Historical bulletin no. 27) Cover title. [TR681.F3O8] 73-151399
1. Lincoln, Abraham, Pres. U.S., 1809-1865—Portraits—Addresses, essays, lectures. 2. Photographers, American—Addresses, essays, lectures. I. Title. II. Series.

Lincoln, Abraham, Pres. U.S., 1809-1865—Quotations.

LINCOLN, Abraham, 973.7'092'4
Pres. U.S., 1809-1865.
Lincoln, his words and his world. Fort Atkinson, Wis. : Home Library Pub. Co., c1976. 96 p. : ill. (some col.) ; 32 cm. [E457.98.L552 1976] 76-374927 ISBN 0-87294-088-8 : 4.98
1. Lincoln, Abraham, Pres. U.S., 1809-1865—Quotations. I. Home Library Publishing Company. II. Title. BIP

Lincoln, Abraham, Pres. U.S., 1809-1865—Religion.

SMITH, Thomas Vernor, 923.173
1890-
Abraham Lincoln and the, spiritual life. Boston, Beacon Press, 1951. viii, 95 p. 17 cm. [E457.2.S63] 51-3983
1. Lincoln, Abraham, Pres. U.S.—Religion. I. Title.

THUROW, Glen E. 320.5'092'4
Abraham Lincoln and American political religion / Glen E. Thurow. Albany : State University of New York Press, [1976] p. cm. Includes bibliographical references. [E457.2.T44] 76-12596 ISBN 0-87395-334-7 : 10.00
1. Lincoln, Abraham, Pres. U.S., 1809-1865—Religion. I. Title. BIP

TRUEBLOOD, David 973.7'092'4 B
Elton, 1900-
Abraham Lincoln; theologian of American anguish [by] Elton Trueblood. [1st ed.] New York, Harper & Row [1973] ix, 149 p. 22 cm. Includes bibliographical references. [E457.2.T78 1973] 72-79955 ISBN 0-06-063801-X 4.95
1. Lincoln, Abraham, Pres. U.S., 1809-1865—Religion. I. Title.

WOLF, William J. 923.173
The almost chosen people; a study of the religion of Abraham Lincoln. [1st ed.] Garden City, N. Y., Doubleday, 1959. 215 p. 22 cm. [E457.2.W853] 59-12662
1. Lincoln, Abraham, Pres. U.S., 1809-1865—Religion. I. Title.

WOLF, William J. 248'.0924
Lincoln's religion [by] William J. Wolf. Philadelphia, Pilgrim Press [1970] 219 p. 18 cm. First ed. published in 1959 under title: The almost chosen people. Includes bibliographical references. [E457.2.W853 1970] 70-123035 1.95
1. Lincoln, Abraham, Pres. U.S., 1809-1865—Religion. I. Title. BIP

WOLF, William J. 923.173
The religion of Abraham Lincoln. [Rev. ed.] New York, Seabury, 1963[c.1959, 1963] 219p. 21cm. First ed. pub. in 1959 under title: The almost chosen people. Bibl. 63-18697 3.95
1. Lincoln, Abraham, Pres. U.S.—Religion. I. Title.

Lincoln, Abraham, Pres. U.S., 1809-1865—Surveying career.

BABER, Adin. 526.9'0924
A. Lincoln with compass and chain; surveying career as seen in his notes and maps, and with an account of the Hanks family cousins, makers of fine surveying and mathematical instruments. Kansas, Ill., Priv. print. by the author, 1968. xx, 180 p. illus., maps, ports. 29 cm. (His Hanks family historical series, 5) Includes bibliographies. [E457.35.B22] 73-832
1. Lincoln, Abraham, Pres. U.S., 1809-1865—Surveying career. I. Title.

Lincoln Co., N. M.—Hist.

TUNSTALL, John 917.89640340924
Henry, 1853-1878
The life & death of John Henry Tunstall; the letters, diaries & adventures of an itinerant Englishman supplemented with other documents & annotations. [Albuquerque] Univ. of N. M. Pr. [c.1965] xvi, 480p. illus., facsims., ports. 24cm. Bibl. [F802.L7T8] 64-17809 6.00
1. Lincoln Co., N. M.—Hist. 2. U. S.—Descr. & trav.—1865-1900. I. Nolan, Frederick W., 1931- ed. II. Title. BIP

Lincoln Co., N.M.—History.

KLASNER, 917.89'64'0340924 B
Lily, 1862-1946.
My girlhood among outlaws. Edited by Eve Ball. Tucson, University of Arizona Press [1972] vi, 336 p. illus. 23 cm. Excerpts from J. S. Chisum's personal diary, Jan., 1878 (p. 261-287) [F802.L7K55 1972] 77-165206 ISBN 0-8165-0328-1
1. Lincoln Co., N.M.—History. 2. Frontier and pioneer life—New Mexico. 3. Frontier and pioneer life—Texas. I. Chisum, John Simpson, 1824-1884. II. Title. BIP

Lincoln, Mary (Todd) 1818-1882.

CASHMAN, Dorothy 973.7'0924
Moline.
Lincoln's only love, by Dorothy M. Cashman. [Springfield, Ill., 1969] 19 p. ports. 22 cm. Cover title. [E457.25.C3] 75-8284
1. Lincoln, Mary (Todd) 1818-1882. I. Title.

ELLETSON, D. H. 920.7
Maryannery; Mary Ann Lincoln and Mary Anne Disraeli. London, J. Murray [dist.]: Hollywood-by-the-Sea, Fla., Transatlantic Arts [1959, i.e., 1960] 164p. Bibl. p.156-159 illus. 22cm. 60-4841 4.50
1. Lincoln, Mary (Todd) 1818-1882. 2. Beaconsfield, Mary Anne (Evans) Disraeli, viscountess, 1792-1872. I. Title.

MARY Lincoln; v. 12
biography of a marriage. [New York, Dell Pub. Co., 1961] 480p. 17cm. (Dell book, X3)
1. Lincoln, Mary (Todd) 1818-1882. I. Randall, Ruth (Painter) II. Series.

RANDALL, Ruth Painter 920.7
Mary ,lincoln; biography of a marriage. [New York] Dell [1961, c.1953] 480p. (X) .75 pap.,
1. Lincoln, Mary (Todd) 1818-1882. I. Title. BIP

RANDALL, Ruth (Painter) 920.7
Mary Lincoln; biography of a marriage. [1st ed.] Boston, Little, Brown [c1953] xiv, 555p. illus., ports. 23cm. Bibliographical references included in Notes (p.[445]-516)

Bibliography: p.[517]-529. [E457.25.R3] 52-12621
1. Lincoln, Mary (Todd) 1818-1882. I. Title.

ROSS, Ishbel, 1897- 973.7'092'4 B
The President's wife: Mary Todd Lincoln; a biography. New York, Putnam [1973] 378 p. illus. 23 cm. Bibliography: p. 361-366. [E457.25.R67 1973] 72-97309 ISBN 0-399-11132-8 8.95
1. Lincoln, Mary (Todd) 1818-1882. I. Title.

SANDBURG, Carl, 1878-1967. v. 12
Mary Lincoln, wife and widow; part I, by Carl Sandburg; part II, letters, documents & appendix, by Paul M. Angle. New York, Harcourt, Brace & World [c1960] 357 p. illus. Includes bibliography. 67-80860
1. Lincoln, Mary (Todd) 1818-1882. I. Angle, Paul McClelland, 1900- II. Title.

SIMMONS, Dawn Langley. 973.7'0924 B
A rose for Mrs. Lincoln; a biography of Mary Todd Lincoln. Boston, Beacon Press [1970] x, 197 p. illus., ports. 24 cm. Bibliography: p. [195]-197. [E457.25.S5 1970] 68-24369 ISBN 0-8070-5448-8 8.50
1. Lincoln, Mary (Todd) 1818-1882. I. Title.

TURNER, Justin G. 973.7'092'4 B
Mary Todd Lincoln: her life and letters [by] Justin G. Turner [and] Linda Lovitt Turner. With an introd. by Fawn M. Brodie. [1st ed.] New York, Knopf, 1972. xxv, 750, xxxvi p. illus. 25 cm. Bibliography: p. [745]-750. [E457.25.T87 1972] 69-10700 ISBN 0-394-46643-8 15.00
1. Lincoln, Mary (Todd) 1818-1882. I. Turner, Linda Lovitt, joint author. II. Lincoln, Mary (Todd) 1818-1882. Mary Todd Lincoln: her life and letters. 1972. III. Title.

Lincoln, Mary (Todd) 1818-1882—Juvenile literature.

RANDALL, Ruth (Painter) 920.7
I Mary; a biography of the girl who married Abraham Lincoln. [1st ed.] Boston, Little, Brown [1959] 242p. illus. 21cm. [E457.25.R25] 59-7358
1. Lincoln, Mary (Todd) 1818-1882—Juvenile literature. I. Title.

Lincoln, Mary Todd, 1818-1882—Juvenile literature.

ANDERSON, LaVere. 973.7'092'4 B
Mary Todd Lincoln: President's wife. Illustrated by Cary. Champaign, Ill., Garrard Pub. Co. [1975] 80 p. col. illus. 23 cm. (A Discovery book) An easy-to-read biography of Mary Todd Lincoln, wife of the sixteenth President of the United States. [E457.25.A77] 92 74-18303 ISBN 0-8116-6316-7 3.12 (lib. bdg.)
1. Lincoln, Mary Todd, 1818-1882—Juvenile literature. I. Cary, Louis F., 1915- illus.

Lincoln, Nancy (Hanks) 1784-1818

BABER, Adin 920.7
Nancy Hanks, the destined mother of a President; the factual story of a pioneer family as revealed in an exhaustive study of ancestral history. Glendale, Calif., Arthur H. Clark Co., Box 230, 1963. xx, 174p. col. port., facsim. 24cm. (His Hanks family hist. ser. 3) Bibl. 63-21514 15.00
1. Lincoln, Nancy (Hanks) 1784-1818 2. Lincoln, Abraham, Pres. U. S.—Family. 3. Hanks family. I. Title.

PETERSON, James Andrew, 1897- 929.2'0973
In re Lucey Hanks / compiled and written by James A. Peterson. 1st ed. Yorkville, Ill. : Peterson, 1973. 42 [i.e. 71] leaves : ill. ; 24 cm. No. 91 of 150 copies printed. Includes bibliographical references. [E457.32.P44] 75-324177
1. Hanks, Lucey, d. 1825. 2. Lincoln, Nancy Hanks, 1784-1818. 3. Lincoln, Abraham, Pres. U.S., 1809-1865—Family. I. Title.

Lincoln, Nancy (Hanks) 1784-1818.

BRIGGS, Harold Edward, 1896- 920.7
Nancy Hanks Lincoln, a frontier portrait, by Harold E. Briggs and Ernestine B. Briggs. New York, Bookman Associates, 1952 [i. e. 1953] 135p. map. 22cm. [E457.32.B8] 53-6827
1. Lincoln, Nancy (Hanks) 1784-1818. I. Briggs, Ernestine Bennett, joint author. II. Title.

LUDWIG, Charles, 1918- 92
Nancy Hanks, mother of Lincoln. Grand Rapids, Mich., Baker Bk. [c.]1965. 88p. illus. 21cm. (Valor ser., no. 13) [E457.32.L83] 65-25475 1.95
1. Lincoln, Nancy (Hanks) 1784-1818—Juvenile literature. I. Title.

Lincoln, Robert Todd, 1843-1926.

ANDERSON, LaVere. JUV
Robert Todd Lincoln, President's boy. Illustrated by Al Fiorentino. Indianapolis, Bobbs-Merrill [1967] 200 p. col. illus., col. ports. 20 cm. (Childhood of famous Americans) Bibliography: p. 198. Biography of Lincoln's precocious son, Robert, and his childhood escapades in Illinois and the White House. [PZ7.A5439Ro] 92 AC 67
1. Lincoln, Robert Todd, 1843-1926. I. Fiorentino, Al, illus. II. Title.

GOFF, John S., 1931- 973.8'0924 B
Robert Todd Lincoln: a man in his own right, by John S. Goff. [1st ed.] Norman, University of Oklahoma Press [1968, c1969] xv, 286 p. illus., ports. 23 cm. Bibliography: p. 266-278. [E664.L63G6] 68-15686
1. Lincoln, Robert Todd, 1843-1926.

Lincoln, Robert Todd, 1843-1926.—Juvenile fiction.

ANDERSON, La Vere. JUV
Robert Todd Lincoln, President's boy. Illus. by Al Fiorentino. Indianapolis, Bobbs [1967] 200p. col. illus., col. ports. 20cm. (Childhood of famous Americans) Bibl. [PZ7.A5439Ro] 923'.173 67-26337 2.50
1. Lincoln, Robert Todd, 1843-1926.—Juvenile fiction. I. Title.

Lincoln, Robert Todd, 1843-1926—Juvenile literature.

ANDERSON, LaVere. juv
Robert Todd Lincoln, President's boy. Illustrated by Al Fiorentino. Indianapolis, Bobbs-Merrill [1967] 200 p. col. illus., col. ports. 20 cm. (Childhood of famous Americans) Bibliography: p. 198. [PZ7.A5439Ro] 67-26337
1. Lincoln, Robert Todd, 1843-1926—Juvenile literature.

Lincoln, Thomas, 1853-1871.

WEAVER, John Downing, 1912- 920
Tad Lincoln, michief-maker in the White House. Illus. by Robert Handville. New York, Dodd [c.1963] vii, 145p. illus. 24cm. 63-18782 3.50
1. Lincoln, Thomas, 1853-1871. 2. Lincoln, Abraham, Pres. U. S., 1809-1865. I. Title.

WEAVER, John Downing, 1912- j92
Tad Lincoln, mischief-maker in the White House. Illustrated by Robert Handville. New York, Dodd, Meade [1963] viii, 145 p. illus. 24 cm. [E457.25.W4] 63-18782
1. Lincoln, Thomas, 1853-1871. 2. Lincoln, Abraham, Pres. U.S., 1809-1865. I. Title.

WHIPPLE, Wayne, 1856-1942. 973'.074'016971
Tad Lincoln. New York, G. Sully [c1926] 60p. port. 19cm. [E457.25.W56 1926a] 55-53727
1. Lincoln, Thomas, 1853-1871. I. Title.

Lincoln, Thomas, 1853-1871—Juvenile literature.

ANDERSON, LaVere. 973.7'0924 B
Tad Lincoln, Abe's son. Illustrated by William Hutchinson. Champaign, Ill., Garrard Pub. Co. [1971] 80 p. col. illus. 24 cm. (A Discovery book) Relates the activities of Abraham Lincoln's youngest son during the years he lived in the White House. [E457.25.A78] 92 70-151987 ISBN 0-8116-6307-8
1. Lincoln, Thomas, 1853-1871—Juvenile literature. I. Hutchinson, William M., illus. II. Title.

MONJO, F. N. 973.7'092'2 B
Me and Willie and Pa; the story of Abraham Lincoln and his son Tad, by F. N. Monjo. Illustrated by Douglas Gorsline. New York, Simon and Schuster [1973] 94 p. illus. 27 cm. Bibliography: p. 93-94. President Lincoln's youngest son recounts his own and his family's experience during their four years in the White House. [E457.905.M58] 73-11464 ISBN 0-671-65211-7 5.95
1. Lincoln, Abraham, Pres. U.S., 1809-1865—Juvenile literature. 2. Lincoln, Thomas, 1853-1871—Juvenile literature. 3. Lincoln, William Wallace, 1850-1862—Juvenile literature. 4. United States—History—Civil War, 1861-1865—Juvenile literature. I. Gorsline, Douglas W., 1913- illus. II. Title.

Lind, Bruno, 1909-

SANTAYANA, George, 1863-1952. 921.1
Vagabond scholar, a venture into the privacy of George Santayana, by Bruno Lind. New York, Bridgehead Bks., 458 Bway. [c.]1962. 191p. illus. 62-10792 5.95
1. Lind, Bruno, 1909- I. Title.

Lind-Goldschmidt, Jenny Maria, 1820-1887.

[DUNLOP, Agnes Mary Robertson] 784.092
The Swedish nightingale: Jenny Lind, by Elisabeth Kyle. New York, Holt [1965, c.1964] 223, [1]p. 22cm. Bibl. [ML420.L7D8] 65.21539 3.75; 3.45 bds., lib. ed.,
1. Lind-Goldschmidt, Jenny Maria, 1820-1887. I. Title.

DUNLOP, Agnes Mary Robertson. juv
The Swedish nightingale: Jenny Lind, by Elisabeth Kyle. [1st ed.] New York, Holt, Rinehart and Winston [1966, c1964] 223, [1] p. 22 cm. Bibliography: p. [224] [ML420.L7D8] 65-21539
1. Lind-Goldschmidt, Jenny Maria, 1820-1887. I. Title.

HOLLAND, Henry Scott, 1847-1918. 782.1'092'4 B
Memoir of Madame Jenny Lind-Goldschmidt : her early art-life and dramatic career, 1820-1851 / Henry Scott Holland and W. S. Rockstro. Boston : Longwood Press, 1978. p. cm. Reprint of the 1891 ed. published by J. Murray, London. [ML420.L7H6 1978] 77-90799 ISBN 0-89341-416-6 lib.bdg. : 60.00
1. Lind-Goldschmidt, Jenny Maria, 1820-1887. 2. Singers—Sweden—Biography. I. Rockstro, William Smyth, 1823-1895, joint author. BIP

MAUDE, Jenny Maria Catherine Goldschmidt. 782.1'092'4 B
The life of Jenny Lind / Jenny Maria Catherine Goldschmidt Maude. New York : Arno Press, 1977. 222 p., [15] leaves of plates : ill. ; 23 cm. (Opera biographies) Reprint of the 1926 ed. published by Cassell, London. Includes index. [ML420.L7M2 1977] 76-29953 ISBN 0-405-09694-1 : 25.00
1. Lind-Goldschmidt, Jenny Maria, 1820-1887. 2. Singers—Sweden—Biography. I. Title.

MAUDE, Jenny Maria Catherine Goldschmidt. 782.1'092'4 B
The life of Jenny Lind / briefly told by her daughter, Mrs. Raymond Maude. 1st AMS ed. New York : AMS Press, 1978. 222 p., [16] leaves of plates : ill. ; 19 cm. Reprint of the 1926 ed. published by Cassell, London. Includes index. [ML420.L7M2 1978] 74-24149 ISBN 0-404-13041-0 : 17.50
1. Lind-Goldschmidt, Jenny Maria, 1820-1887. 2. Singers—Sweden—Biography. BIP

MYERS, Elisabeth P. 784'.0924 B
Jenny Lind; songbird from Sweden, by Elisabeth P. Myers. Illustrated by Frank Vaughn. Champaign, Ill., Garrard Pub. Co. [1968] 143 p. illus., ports. 22 cm. (Creative arts biographies) The biography of the nineteenth-century Swedish singer whose vocal range and tone quality made her one of the leading opera stars of her day. [ML3930.L55M9] 92 AC 68
1. Lind-Goldschmidt, Jenny Maria, 1820-1887. I. Vaughn, Frank E., illus. II. Title.

SHULTZ, Gladys Denny 927.84
Jenny Lind: the Swedish nightingale. Philadelphia, Lippincott [c.1962] 345p. 22cm. 62-10537 6.50 bds.,
I. Title.

SHULTZ, Gladys (Denny) 927.8
Jenny Lind: the Swedish nightingale. [1st ed.] Philadelphia, Lippincott [1962] 845 p. illus. 22 cm. [ML420.L7S5] 62-10537
1. Lind-Goldschmidt, Jenny Maria, 1820-1887. I. Title.

Lind, Jakov,

LIND, Jakov, 1927- 838'.9'1409 B
Counting my steps; an autobiography. [New York] Macmillan [1969] 223 p. 21 cm. [PT2672.I48Z5] 70-80794
I. Title.

LIND, Jakov, 1927- 838'.9'1409 B
Numbers; a further autobiography. [1st ed.] New York, Harper & Row [1972] xi, 140 p. 22 cm. [PR6062.I45Z5] 79-138790 ISBN 0-06-012628-0 5.95
I. Title.

Lind, James, 1716-1794.

RODDIS, Louis Harry, 1886- 926.1
James Lind, founder of nautical medicine. New York, H. Schuman [c1950] xi, 177 p. illus., ports., facsims. 22 cm. [The Life of science library] "Bibliography of James Lind": p. 157-163. "Sources of information": p. 164-168. [VG228.L5R6] 51-1222
1. Lind, James, 1716-1794. 2. Medicine, Naval — Hist. I. Title.

Lind, John, 1854-1930.

STEPHENSON, George Malcolm, 1883-1958. 398.73'0924 B
John Lind of Minnesota. Port Washington, N.Y., Kennikat Press [1971] 398 p. illus., ports. 22 cm. (Kennikat Press scholarly reprints. Series in Latin-American history and culture) Reprint of the 1935 ed. Bibliography: p. 369-372. [E748.L72S7 1971] 73-130335
1. Lind, John, 1854-1930. 2. U.S.—Foreign relations—Mexico. 3. Mexico—Foreign relations—U.S. BIP

Linda Marie, 1943-

LINDA Marie, 1943- 364.36'4'0924 B
I must not rock / Linda Marie. 1st ed. New York : Daughters Pub. Co., c1977. 207 p. ; 21 cm. [HV742.C2L56] 77-80960 ISBN 0-913780-19-7 : 5.00
1. Linda Marie, 1943- 2. Child abuse—California—Case studies. 3. Juvenile delinquency—California—Case studies. 4. Delinquent girls—California—Biography. I. Title. BIP

Lindberg, Charles Augustus, 1902-1974.

MOSLEY, Leonard, 1913- 629.13'092'4B
Lindbergh : a biography / Leonard Mosley. New York : Dell Pub. Co., 1977. 544p. : ill. ; 18 cm. (A Dell Book) Includes index. [TL540.L5M63] ISBN 0-440-15057-4 pbk. : 2.25
1. Lindberg, Charles Augustus, 1902-1974. I. Title.
L.C. crd no. 1976 Doubleday ed.:75-40736.

Lindbergh, Anne Morrow, 1906-

LINDBERGH, Anne 818'.5'209 B
Morrow, 1906-
Hour of gold, hour of lead; diaries and letters of Anne Morrow Lindbergh, 1929-1932. Boston, G. K. Hall, 1974 [c1973] 576 p. 24 cm. Large print ed. Continuation of the author's Bring me a unicorn. [TL540.L49A4 1974] 73-22114 ISBN 0-8161-6184-4 11.95
1. Lindbergh, Anne Morrow, 1906- 2. Air pilots—Correspondence, reminiscences, etc. I. Title.

LINDBERGH, Anne 818'.5'209 B
Morrow, 1906-
Locked rooms and open doors: diaries and letters of Anne Morrow Lindbergh, 1933-1935. [1st ed.] New York, Harcourt Brace Jovanovich [1974] xxvi, 352 p. illus. 22 cm. "A Helen and Kurt Wolff book." [PS3523.I516Z52] 73-16152 ISBN 0-15-152958-2 7.95
1. Lindbergh, Anne Morrow, 1906- I. Title.

LINDBERGH, Anne 818'.5'209 B
Morrow, 1906-
Locked rooms and open doors; diaries and letters of Anne Morrow Lindbergh, 1933-1935. Boston, G. K. Hall, 1974. xxxii, 616 p. 25 cm. Continuation of the author's Hour of gold, hour of lead. Continued by the author's The flower and the nettle. Large print ed. [TL540.L49A285] 74-10546 ISBN 0-8161-6231-X
1. Lindbergh, Anne Morrow, 1906- I. Title.

Lindbergh, Anne Morrow, 1906- — Diaries.

LINDBERGH, Anne 818'.5'209 B
Morrow, 1906-
The flower and the nettle : diaries and letters of Anne Morrow Lindbergh, 1936-1939. 1st ed. New York : Harcourt Brace Jovanovich, c1976. xxix, 605 p., [16] leaves of plates : ill. ; 22 cm. Continuation of the author's Locked rooms and open doors. "A Helen and Kurt Wolff book." Includes index. [PS3523.I516Z516] 75-25708 12.95
1. Lindbergh, Anne Morrow, 1906- — Diaries. 2. Lindbergh, Anne Morrow, 1906- —Correspondence. I. Title.

Lindbergh, Charles August, 1859-1924.

LARSON, Bruce L. 328.73'092'4 B
Lindbergh of Minnesota; a political biography [by] Bruce L. Larson. Foreword by Charles A. Lindbergh, Jr. [1st ed.] New York, Harcourt Brace Jovanovich [1973] xix, 363 p. illus. 22 cm. Based on the author's thesis, University of Kansas. Bibliography: p. 343-351. [E748.L74L37] 73-6596 ISBN 0-15-152400-9 14.50
1. Lindbergh, Charles August, 1859-1924. 2. United States—Politics and government—1901-1953. 3. Minnesota—Politics and government. I. Title. **BIP**

LINDBERGH, Charles 629.13'092'4 B
Augustus, 1902-
Boyhood on the upper Mississippi; a reminiscent letter, by Charles A. Lindbergh. St. Paul, Minnesota Historical Society, 1972. xiii, 50 p. illus. 28 cm. (Publications of the Minnesota Historical Society) [TL540.L5A28] 72-75804 ISBN 0-87351-069-0 4.50
I. Title. II. Series: Minnesota Historical Society. Publications. **BIP**

LINDBERGH, Charles 629.13'0924 B
Augustus, 1902-
The wartime journals of Charles A. Lindbergh. [1st ed.] New York, Harcourt, Brace, Jovanovich [1970] xx, 1038 p. illus., ports., col. maps (on lining papers) 24 cm. [TL540.L5A3 1970] 78-124830
I. Title. **BIP**

Lindbergh, Charles Augustus, 1902-1974.

GILL, Brendan, 629.13'092'4 B
1914-
Lindbergh alone / by Brendan Gill. 1st ed. New York : Harcourt Brace Jovanovich, c1977. 216 p. : ill. ; 26 cm. Errata slip inserted. [TL540.L5G54] 76-54288 ISBN 0-15-152401-7 : 11.95
1. Lindbergh, Charles Augustus, 1902-1974. 2. Air pilots—United States—Biography. I. Title. **BIP**

LINDBERGH, Charles 629.13'092'4 B
Augustus, 1902-
Boyhood on the upper Mississippi; a reminiscent letter, by Charles A. Lindbergh. St. Paul, Minnesota Historical Society, 1972. xiii, 50 p. illus. 28 cm. (Publications of the Minnesota Historical Society) [TL540.L5A28] 72-75804 ISBN 0-87351-069-0 4.50
I. Title. II. Series: Minnesota Historical Society. Publications. **BIP**

LINDBERGH, Charles 629.13'0924 B
Augustus, 1902-
The wartime journals of Charles A. Lindbergh. [1st ed.] New York, Harcourt, Brace, Jovanovich [1970] xx, 1038 p. illus., ports., col. maps (on lining papers) 24 cm. [TL540.L5A3 1970] 78-124830
I. Title. **BIP**

LINDBERGH, Charles 629.13'092'4 B
Augustus, 1902-1974.
Autobiography of values / Charles A. Lindbergh ; editor, William Jovanovich, coeditor, Judith A. Schiff. 1st ed. New York : Harcourt Brace Jovanovich, c1978. xxi, 423 p., [20] leaves of plates : ill. ; 24 cm. Includes index. Bibliography: p. 407-411. [TL540.L5A27 1978] 77-7873 ISBN 0-15-110202-3 : 12.95
1. Lindbergh, Charles Augustus, 1902-1974. 2. Air—Pilots—United States—Biography I. Title.

MOSLEY, Leonard, 629.13'092'4 B
1913-
Lindbergh : a biography / Leonard Mosley. 1st ed. Garden City, N.Y. : Doubleday, 1976. xxx, 446 p., [12] leaves of plates : ill. ; 24 cm. Includes index. Bibliography: p. [394]-428. [TL540.L5M63] 75-40736 ISBN 0-385-09578-3 : 12.50
1. Lindbergh, Charles Augustus, 1902-1974. I. Title. **BIP**

MOSLEY, Leonard, 629.13'092'4 B
1913-
Lindbergh : a biography / [by] Leonard Mosley. London : Hodder and Stoughton, 1976. xxxi, 446 p., [24] p. of plates : ill., ports. ; 24 cm. Includes index. Bibliography: p. [394]-428. [TL540.L5M63 1976b] 77-357410 ISBN 0-340-20117-7 : £6.50
1. Lindbergh, Charles Augustus, 1902-1974. 2. Air pilots—United States—Biography.

ROSS, Walter 629.13'092'4 B
Sanford, 1916-
The last hero, Charles A. Lindbergh / by Walter S. Ross. Rev. ed. New York : Harper & Row, c1976. xv, 400 p., [8] leaves of plates : ill. ; 22 cm. Includes bibliographical references and index. [TL540.L5R67 1976] 76-359745 ISBN 0-06-013666-9 : 12.50
1. Lindbergh, Charles Augustus, 1902 1974. I. Title.

Lindbergh, Charles Augustus, 1902-1974—Juvenile literature.

COLLINS, David R. 629.13'092'4 B
Charles Lindbergh, hero pilot / by David R. Collins ; illustrated by Victor Mays. Champaign, Ill. : Garrard Pub. Co., c1978. 80 p. : ill. ; 23 cm. (A Discovery book) A biography concentrating on the early years of the aviator who made the first solo flight across the Atlantic Ocean. [TL540.L5C56] 92 77-13956 ISBN 0-8116-6322-1 lib.bdg. : 3.96
1. Lindbergh, Charles Augustus, 1902-1974—Juvenile literature. 2. Air pilots—United States—Biography—Juvenile literature. I. Mays, Victor, 1927- II. Title.

DE LEEUW, Adele 629.13'0924 B
Louise, 1899-
Lindbergh, lone eagle, by Adele DeLeeuw. Philadelphia, Westminster Press [1969] 192 p. port. 24 cm. Bibliography: p. 181. A biography of "Lucky Lindy," the pilot who made the first solo non-stop flight from New York to Paris in 1927. [TL540.L5D45] 92 70-80979 4.75
1. Lindbergh, Charles Augustus, 1902- — Juvenile literature. I. Title.

FOSTER, John T. 629.13'092'4 B
The flight of the Lone Eagle; Charles Lindbergh flies nonstop from New York to Paris, by John T. Foster. New York, Watts, 1974. 61 p. illus. 22 cm. (A Focus book) Bibliography: p. 57. An account of the first solo nonstop transatlantic flight, made by Charles Lindbergh in 1927 in The Spirit of St. Louis, an event which marked the beginning of the Air Age. [TL540.L5F65] 92 74-898 ISBN 0-531-02723-6 3.45 (lib. bdg.)
1. Lindbergh, Charles Augustus, 1902- — Juvenile literature. 2. Transatlantic flights—Juvenile literature. I. Title. **BIP**

GRIERSON, John, 629.13'092'4 B
1909-
I remember Lindbergh / John Grierson ; with an introd. by Anne Morrow Lindbergh. New York : Harcourt Brace Jovanovich, c1977. p. cm. Includes index. Flier John Grierson's personal recollections of his friend Charles A. Lindbergh. [TL540.L5G68] 92 77-76436 ISBN 0-15-238895-8 : 8.95
1. Lindbergh, Charles Augustus, 1902-1974—Juvenile literature. I. Title.

GRIERSON, John, 629.13'092'4 B
1909-
I remember Lindbergh / John Grierson ; with an introd. by Anne Morrow Lindbergh. New York : Harcourt Brace Jovanovich, c1977. p. cm. Includes index. Flier John Grierson's personal recollections of his friend Charles A. Lindbergh. [TL540.L5G68] 92 77-76436 ISBN 0-15-238895-8 : 8.95
1. Lindbergh, Charles Augustus, 1902-1974—Juvenile literature. I. Title. **BIP**

LEIPOLD, L. 629.13'092'4 B
Edmond, 1902-
Charles A. Lindbergh, aviation pioneer, by L. E. Leipold. Minneapolis, Denison [1972] 189 p. illus. 22 cm. (Men of achievement series) A biography of one of the world's best known aviators—the first man to fly alone non-stop across the Atlantic. [TL540.L5L38] 92 70-151420 ISBN 0-513-01104-8
1. Lindbergh, Charles Augustus, 1902-— Juvenile literature.

WISE, William. 629.13'0924 B
Charles A. Lindbergh; aviation pioneer. Illustrated by Paul Sagsoorian. New York, Putnam [1970] 95 p. illus. 24 cm. (American hero and pioneer biography series) (An American hero biography.) The life of the man who in 1927 performed one of the most daring feats of the twentieth century - first non-stop solo flight across the Atlantic. [TL540.L5W5 1970] 92 79-110324
1. Lindbergh, Charles Augustus, 1902- — Juvenile literature. I. Sagsoorian, Paul, illus. II. Title.

Lindbergh family.

EUBANK, Nancy. 929.2'0973
The Lindberghs : three generations / by Nancy Eubank. St. Paul : Minnesota Historical Society, 1975. 14 p. : ill. ; 27 cm. (Publications of the Minnesota Historical Society) (Minnesota historic sites pamphlet series ; no. 12) Bibliography: p. 14. [CS71.L7424 1975] 75-12517 ISBN 0-87351-094-1
1. Lindbergh family. 2. Lindbergh, Charles Augustus, 1902- I. Title. II. Series. III. Series: Minnesota Historical Society. Publications.

Lindley, Daniel, 1801-1880.

SMITH, Edwin William, 922.568
1876-
The life and times of Daniel Lindley, 1801-80; missionary to the Zulus, pastor of the Voortrekkers, Ubebe Omhlope. New York, Library Publishers [1952] 456p. illus. 23cm. [BV3625.Z8S55 1952] 52-8100
1. Lindley, Daniel, 1801-1880. I. Title.

Lindner, Richard,

LINDNER, Richard, 1901- 759.3
Richard Lindner. [Text by] Dore Ashton. New York, H. N. Abrams [1970] 217 p. (chiefly illus., part col.) 28 x 30 cm. Bibliography: p. 215-217. [N6537.L55A9] 69-12799 ISBN 0-8109-0246-X
I. Ashton, Dore.

Lindon, Frances (Brawne) 1800-1865.

RICHARDSON, Joanna. 920.7
Fanny Brawne; a biography. [New York] Vanguard Press [1952] ix, 190 p. ports., facsims., geneal. table. 22 cm. Bibliography: p. 179-182. [PR4836.R5] 52-13206
1. Lindon, Frances (Brawne) 1800-1865. 2. Keats, John, 1795-1821. I. Title.

Lindsay, Catherine

NELSON, Kathryn Luella 361.5'0924
(Jensen) 1891-
Kate Lindsay, M. D., nurse physician educator, author, 1842-1923. Illustrated by Jim Padgett. Nashville, Southern Pub. Association [c1963] 192 p. illus. ports. 21 cm. [RT37.L54N4] 63-17059
1. Lindsay, Catherine 1942-1923. I. Title.

Lindsay, Elizabeth Sherman (Hoyt)

LINDSAY, Elizabeth Sherman 920.7
(Hoyt) 1885-1954.
Letters, 1911-1954. Edited by Olivia James New York, 1960. 246 p. illus. 27 cm. [CT275.L4684A4] 63-28365
I. Title.

Lindsay, Howard, 1889-

LEVIN, Martin, ed. 818.082
Five boyhoods: Howard Lindsay, Harry Golden, Walt Kelly, William K. Zinsser and John Updike. [1st ed.] New York, Doubleday, 1962. 198 p. illus. 22 cm. [PS221.L4] 61-9527
1. Lindsay, Howard, 1889- 2. Golden, Harry Lewis, 1902- 3. Kelly, Walt. 4. Zinsser, William Knowlton. 5. Updike, John. I. Title.

Lindsay, Howard, 1889-1968—Biography.

SKINNER, Cornelia 790.2'092'2 B
Otis, 1901-
Life with Lindsay & Crouse / Cornelia Otis Skinner. Boston : Houghton Mifflin, 1976. xiv, 242 p., [8] leaves of plates : ill. ; 23 cm. Includes index. [PS3523.I575Z86] 76-22571 ISBN 0-395-24511-7 : 10.00
1. Lindsay, Howard, 1889-1968—Biography. 2. Crouse, Russel, 1893-1966—Biography. I. Title. **BIP**

Lindsay, John Vliet.

BUTTON, Daniel E 328.320924
Lindsay; a man for tomorrow, by Daniel E. Button. Pref. By Bennett Cerf. New York, Random ouse [1965] 239 p. illus., ports. 22 cm. [E840.8.L5B8] 65-26991
1. Lindsay, John Vliet. I. Title.

KLEIN, Woody, 1929- 328.73'0924
Lindsay's promise: the dream that failed; a personal account. [New York] Macmillan [1970] xv, 349 p. 21 cm. [F128.52.K55] 73-114327
1. Lindsay, John Vliet. 2. New York (City)—Politics and government—1951- I. Title.

Lindsay, Nicholas Vachel, 1879-1931.

FLANAGAN, John 811'.5'2 B
Theodore, 1906- comp.
Profile of Vachel Lindsay. Compiled by John T. Flanagan. Columbus, Ohio, Merrill [1970] vi, 122 p. 23 cm. (Charles E. Merrill profiles) (Charles E. Merrill program in American literature.) [PS3523.I58Z58] 79-130279
1. Lindsay, Nicholas Vachel, 1879-1931. I. Title. **BIP**

HARRIS, Mark, 1922- 928.1
City of discontent; an interpretive biography of Vachel Lindsay, being also the story of Springfield, Illinois, USA, and of the love of the poet for that city, that

State and that Nation. [1st ed.] Indianapolis, Bobbs-Merrill [1952] 403 p. 23 cm. [PS3523.I 58Z6] 52-5806
1. Lindsay, Nicholas Vachel, 1879-1931. I. Title. BIP

MASTERS, Edgar Lee, 1869-1950. 811'.5'2 B
Vachel Lindsay; a poet in America. New York, Biblo and Tannen, 1969 [c1935] ix, 392 p. illus., ports. 24 cm. [PS3523.I58Z73 1969] 68-56452
1. Lindsay, Nicholas Vachel, 1879-1931.

RUGGLES, Eleanor, 1916- 928.1
The west-going heart; a life of Vachel Lindsay. [1st ed.] New York, Norton [1959] 448p. illus. 22cm. Includes bibliography. [PS3523.I58Z76] 59-11337
1. Lindsay, Nicholas Vachel, 1879-1931. I. Title.

Lindsay, Nicholas Vachel, 1879-1931—Biography.

HARRIS, Mark, 1922- 811'.5'2 B
City of discontent : an interpretive biography of Vachel Lindsay, being also the story of Springfield, Illinois, USA, and of the love of the poet for that city, that state, and that nation / Mark Harris. New York : Octagon Books, 1975, c1952. 403 p. ; 23 cm. Reprint of the ed. published by Bobbs-Merrill, Indianapolis. [PS3523.I58Z6 1975] 75-5950 ISBN 0-374-93676-5 : 15.00
1. Lindsay, Nicholas Vachel, 1879-1931—Biography. I. Title.

Lindsay, Norman, 1879-1969.

HETHERINGTON, John Aikman, 1907- 709'.2'4 B
Norman Lindsay: the embattled olympian [by] John Hetherington. Melbourne, New York, Oxford University Press, 1973. xiv, 272 p. ill., plates (1 col.) 25 cm. Aus Index. Bibliography: p. 259-262. [N7405.L5H47] 74-160531 ISBN 0-19-550388-0 14.00
1. Lindsay, Norman, 1879-1969. BIP

Lindsay, Pearl.

MAXSON, Eva. 286'.73 B
A mountain to climb / by Eva Maxson. Mountain View, Calif. : Pacific Press Pub. Association, c1976. 122 p. : ill. ; 22 cm. (A destiny book ; D-158) [BX6193.L56M38] 775 pbk. : 2.95
1. Lindsay, Pearl. 2. Seventh-Day Adventists—Caribbean area—Biography. I. Title. BIP

Lindsey, Benjamin Barr, 1869-1943.

LARSEN, Charles Edward. 347'.79493'0234 B
The good fight; the life and times of Ben B. Lindsey [by] Charles Larsen. Chicago, Quadrangle Books, 1972. xi, 307 p. 22 cm. Bibliography: p. 270-289. [HV28.L54L34] 78-152095 ISBN 0-8129-0237-8 10.00
1. Lindsey, Benjamin Barr, 1869-1943. I. Title. BIP

Lindsey, Hubert.

LINDSEY, Hubert. 266'.022 B
Bless your dirty heart. Edited by Howard G. Earl. Plainfield, N.J., Logos International, 1973 [c1972] xi, 205 p. 21 cm. [BV3785.L47A33] 72-93081 1.95
1. Lindsey, Hubert. 2. Church work with students. 3. Evangelistic work—Berkeley, Calif. I. Title.

Linehan, Kevin, 1948-

LINEHAN, Kevin, 1948- 248'.2 B
Such were some of you : the spiritual odyssey of an ex-gay Christian / Kevin Linehan. Scottdale, Pa. : Herald Press, 1979. 231 p. ; 20 cm. [BR1725.L446A35] 79-12178 ISBN 0-8361-1890-1 : 5.95
1. Linehan, Kevin, 1948- 2. Christian biography—United States. 3. Homosexuals—United States—Biography. 4. Homosexuality and Christianity. I. Title.

Lingo, William Bernard.

LINGO, William Bernard. 926.1
The man who traveled alone with God. New York, Comet Press Books, 1958. 150p. 24cm. (A Reflection book) Autobiography. [R154.L52A3] 58-3587
1. Title.

Linguists.

SEBEOK, Thomas A., 1920- ed. 410.922
Portraits of linguists; a biographical source book for the history of western linguistics, 1746-1963. Edited by Thomas A. Sebeok. Bloomington, Indiana University Press [1966] 2 v. 24 cm. (Indiana University studies in the history and theory of linguistics) English, French, or German. Contents.Contents.—v. 1. From Sir William Jones to Karl Brugmann.—v. 2. From Eduard Sievers to Benjamin Lee Whorf. Bibliography: v. 1, p. xiv. Bibliographical footnotes. [P83.S4] 64-64663
1. Linguists. I. Title. II. Series: Indiana. University. Indiana University studies in the history and theory of linguistics

Linguists—Biography.

SEBEOK, Thomas Albert, 1920- ed. 410'.92'2 B
Portraits of linguists : a biographical source book for the history of western linguistics, 1746-1963 / edited by Thomas A. Sebeok. Westport, Conn. : Greenwood Press, 1976, c1966. p. cm. Reprint of the ed. published by Indiana University Press, Bloomington, issued in series: Indiana University studies in the history and theory of linguistics. English, French, or German. Includes index. Contents.Contents.—v. 1. From Sir William Jones to Karl Brugmann.—v. 2. From Eduard Sievers to Benjamin Lee Whorf. Bibliography: v. 1, p. [P83.S4 1976] 75-45352 ISBN 0-8371-8731-1 lib.bdg. : 60.00
1. Linguists—Biography. I. Title. II. Series: Indiana. University. Indiana University studies in the history and theory of linguistics.

Linke, Maria Zeitner.

HUNT, Ruth. 940.54'72'430924 B
East wind : the story of Maria Zeitner Linke / as written by Ruth Hunt. Grand Rapids, Mich. : Zondervan Pub. House, c1976. 240 p. : ill. ; 23 cm. [BR1725.L447H86] 76-21288 6.95
1. Linke, Maria Zeitner. 2. World War, 1939-1945—Prisoners and prisons, Russian. 3. Prisoners of war—Russia—Biography. 4. Christian biography—Germany, West. I. Title.

Linne, Carl von, 1707-1778.

BLUNT, Wilfrid, 1901- 581'.092'4 B
The compleat naturalist; a life of Linnaeus [by] Wilfrid Blunt, with the assistance of William T. Stearn. New York, Viking Press [1971] 256 p. illus. (part col.) 26 cm. (A Studio book) Includes bibliographies. [QH44.B54 1971] 78-147393 ISBN 0-670-23396-X 14.95
1. Linne, Carl von, 1707-1778. I. Stearn, William Thomas, 1911- II. Title.

DICKINSON, Alice. 581'.0924 B
Carl Linnaeus; pioneer of modern botany. New York, F. Watts [1967] ix, 209 p. illus., facsims., ports. 22 cm. (Immortals of science) [QH44.D5] 67-18897
1. Linne, Carl von, 1707-1778.

DICKINSON, Alice. 581'.0924 B
Carl Linnaeus; pioneer of modern botany. New York, F. Watts [1967] ix, 209 p. illus., facsims., ports. 22 cm. (Immortals of science) A biography of the eighteenth century Swedish botanist whose system of classifying and naming plants brought uniformity and consistency to the science of taxonomy. [QH44.D5] 92 AC 68
1. Linne, Carl von, 1707-1778. I. Title.

STOUTENBURG, Adrien. 925.8
Beloved botanist; the story of Carl Linnaeus, by Adrien Stoutenburg and Laura Nelson Baker. New York, Scribner [1961] 192 p. illus. 21 cm. [QH44.S8715] 61-13376
1. Linne, Carl von, 1707-1778. I. Baker, Laura Nelson, 1911- joint author. II. Title.

Linne, Carl von, 1707-1778—Juvenile literature.

SILVERSTEIN, Alvin. 574'.0924 B
Carl Linnaeus; the man who put the world of life in order [by] Alvin and Virginia Silverstein. Illustrated by Lee J. Ames. New York, John Day Co. [1969] 80 p. illus. 22 cm. (Great men of science) A biography of the eighteenth-century Swedish naturalist whose scientific naming of plants and animals provided an international language of nature. [QH44.S56] 92 69-15732 3.49
1. Linne, Carl von, 1707-1778—Juvenile literature. I. Silverstein, Virginia B., joint author. II. Ames, Lee J., illus. III. Title.

Linschoten, Jan Huygen van, 1563-1611.

PARR, Charles McKew 923.9492
Jan van Linschoten: the Dutch Marco Polo. New York, Crowell [1964] x1vii, 312p. illus., ports. (map on lining papers) 24cm. Bibl. 64-12116 8.95
1. Linschoten, Jan Huygen van, 1563-1611. I. Title.

Linsley, Kenneth Williams.

LINSLEY, Kenneth W. 248'.5'0924 B
Advocate for God : a lawyer's experience in personal evangelism / Kenneth Williams Linsley. Valley Forge, Pa. : Judson Press, c1977. 80 p. ; 22 cm. Includes bibliographical references. [BV4520.L47] 76-48749 ISBN 0-8170-0723-7 pbk. : 2.50
1. Linsley, Kenneth Williams. 2. Witness bearing (Christianity) 3. Baptists—United States—Biography. I. Title. BIP

Linton, Ralph, 1893-1953.

LINTON, Adelin Sumner (Briggs) 1899- 301.2'0924 B
Ralph Linton, by Adelin Linton and Charles Wagley. New York, Columbia University Press, 1971. 196 p. port. 23 cm. "The writings of Ralph Linton": p. 193-196. [GN21.L485L5] 76-174708 ISBN 0-231-03355-9 7.50
1. Linton, Ralph, 1893-1953. 2. Ethnology. I. Wagley, Charles, 1913- joint author. BIP

Lionel of Antwerp, Duke of Clarence, 1338-1368.

COOK, Albert Stanburrough, 1853-1927. 821'.1 B
The last months of Chaucer's earliest patron. New Haven, 1916. [New York, AMS Press, 1973] 144 p. illus. 23 cm. Reprint of the ed. published by Tuttle, Morehouse & Taylor Co., which was issued as v. 21, p. 1-144 of Transactions of the Connecticut Academy of Arts and Sciences. Includes bibliographical references. [PR1906.C6 1973] 72-1000 ISBN 0-404-01698-7 6.50
1. Chaucer, Geoffrey, d. 1400—Friends and associates. 2. Lionel of Antwerp, Duke of Clarence, 1338-1368. 3. Visconti family. 4. Alan (Hound) I. Title. II. Series: Connecticut Academy of Arts and Sciences, New Haven. Transactions, v. 21, p. 1-144. BIP

Lipchitz, Jacques, 1891-

LIPCHITZ, Jacques, 1891- 730'.92'4 B
Jacques Lipchitz. Text by A. M. Hammacher. New York, Abrams [1975] p. Bibliography: p. [NB553.L55H297] 74-11331 ISBN 0-8109-0238-9 35.00
1. Lipchitz, Jacques, 1891- I. Hammacher, Abraham Marie, 1897-

PATAI, Irene. 730.944
Encounters; the life of Jacques Lipchiz. Foreword by Andrew C. Ritchie. New York, Funk & Wagnalls Co. [1961] 438 p. illus. 24 cm. Includes bibliography. [NB553.L55P3] 61-16858
1. Lipchitz, Jacques, 1891- I. Title.

Lipman, David.

LIPMAN, David. 796.3570924
Ken Boyer. New York, Putnam [1967] 221 p. 22 cm. (Putnam sports shelf) [GV865.B7L5] 67-14792
I. Title.

Lipman, Jacob Goodale, 1874-1939.

WAKSMAN, Selman Abraham, 1888- 631.460924
Jacob G. Lipman: agricultural scientist, humanitarian, by Selman A. Waksman. New Brunswick, N.J., Rutgers [1966] 148p. ports. 22cm. Bibl. [S417.L48 W3] 66-18879 5.00
1. Lipman, Jacob Goodale, 1874-1939. I. Title.

Lippmann, Walter, 1889-

CHILDS, Marquis William, 1903- ed. 920.5
Walter Lippmann and his times, edited by Marquis Childs and James Reston. [1st ed.] New York, Harcourt, Brace [1959] x, 246 p. 22 cm. Contents.Contents.—Notes on contributors.—Introduction: The conscience of the critic, by M. Childs.—A child of the enlightenment, by C. Binger.—Walter Lippmann, the New republic, and the Russian Revolution, by G. F. Kennan.—W. L. and the world, by A. Nevins.—The early personal journalists, by A. Krock.—The columnist as teacher and historian, by R. Aron.—The logic of Allies unity, by I. McDonald.—Interpreter of East and West, by F. Moraes.—Apostle of excellence: the view from afar, by H. S. Ashmore.—The democratic elite and American foreign policy, by R. Niebuhr.—Walter Lippmann: the intellectual v. politics, by A. M. Schlesinger, Jr.—Conclusion: The mockingbird and the taxicab, by J. Reston. Bibliographical footnotes. [PN4874.L45C5] 59-10255
1. Lippmann, Walter, 1889- I. Reston, James Barrett, 1909- joint ed.

CHILDS, Marquis William, 1903- ed. 070'.924
Walter Lippmann and his times, edited by Marquis Childs and James Reston. Freeport, N.Y., Books for Libraries Press [1968, c1959] x, 246 p. 23 cm. (Essay index reprint series) Contents.Contents.—Introduction: The conscience of the critic, by M. Childs.—A child of the enlightenment, by C. Binger.—Walter Lippmann, the New republic, and the Russian Revolution, by G. F. Kennan.—W. L. and the world, by A. Nevins.—The early personal journalists, by A. Krock.—The columnist as teacher and historian, by R. Aron.—The logic of Allied unity, by I. McDonald.—Interpreter of East and West, by F. Moraes.—Apostle of excellance: the view from afar, by H. S. Ashmore.—The Democratic elite and American foreign policy, by R. Niebuhr.—Walter Lippmann: the intellectual v. politics, by A. M. Schlesinger, Jr.—Conclusion: The mockingbird and the taxicab, by J. Reston. Bibliographical footnotes. [PN4874.L45C5 1968] 68-58778
1. Lippmann, Walter, 1889- I. Lippmann, Walter, 1889- II. Reston, James Barrett, 1909- joint ed. III. Title.

DAM, Hari N. 320.5'092'4
The intellecutal odyssey of Walter Lippmann; a study of his protean thought, 1910-1960, by Hari N. Dam. New York, Gordon Press, 1973. xi, 177 p. 24 cm. Includes bibliographical references. [JC251.L55D35] 73-7049 ISBN 0-87968-057-1 16.50
1. Lippmann, Walter, 1889- I. Title.

LUSKIN, John. 070'.92'4
Lippmann, liberty, and the press. University, University of Alabama Press [1972] vi, 273 p. 25 cm. Includes bibliographical references. [PN4874.L45L8] 72-4060 ISBN 0-8173-4722-4 7.95
1. Lippmann, Walter, 1889- I. Title. BIP

SCHAPSMEIER, Edward L. 070.9'24 B
Walter Lippmann: philosopher-journalist

[by] Edward L. Schapsmeier and Frederick H. Schapsmeier. Washington, Public Affairs Press [1969] 188 p. 22 cm. Includes bibliographical references. [PN4874.L45S3] 70-96032 5.00
1. Lippmann, Walter, 1889- I. Schapsmeier, Frederick H., joint author. II. Title.

WEINGAST, David Elliott, 1912- 070'.924 B
Walter Lippmann; a study in personal journalism. With an introd. by Harold L. Ickes. Westport, Conn., Greenwood Press [1970, c1949] xx, 155 p. port. 23 cm. Originally presented as the author's thesis, Columbia. Bibliography: p. 145-150. [PN4874.L45W4 1970] 75-97383
1. Lippmann, Walter, 1889-

Lipton, Dean, 1919-

LIPTON, Dean, 1919- 346'.73'033
Malpractice : autobiography of a victim / Dean Lipton. South Brunswick : A. S. Barnes, c1978. p. cm. [KF2905.3.L56] 77-84574 ISBN 0-498-02185-8 : 9.95
1. Lipton, Dean, 1919- 2. Medical personnel—Malpractice—United States. I. Title. BIP

Lipton, Sir Thomas Johnstone, bart., 1850-1931.

WAUGH, Alec, 1898- 923.842
The Lipton story, a centennial biography. [1st ed.] Garden City, N. Y., Doubleday, 1950. c277 p.port. 22 cm. [CT828.L5W3] 50-5444
1. Lipton, Sir Thomas Johnstone, bart., 1850-1931. I. Title.

Liquori, Marty.

LIQUORI, Marty 796.4'26 B
On the run : in search of the perfect race / by Marty Liquori and Skip Myslenski. 1st ed. New York : Morrow, 1979. 288 p. : ill. ; 22 cm. [GV697.L57A34] 78-10409 9.95
1. Liquori, Marty. 2. Runners (Sports)—United States—Biography. 3. Running. I. Myslenski, Skip, joint author. II. Title. BIP

Lisa, Manuel, 1772-1820.

DOUGLAS, Walter Bond, 1851- 917.8'04'2
Manuel Lisa. With hitherto unpublished material annotated and edited by Abraham P. Nasatir. New York, Argosy-Antiquarian, 1964. 207 p. illus., facsims., ports. 23 cm. "First published in the Missouri historical collections, volume three, numbers three and four, 1911." Includes bibliographical references. [F598.D6] 63-21496
1. Lisa, Manuel, 1772-1820. 2. Fur trade — Missouri Valley. I. Nasatir, Abraham Phineas, 1904- ed. II. Title. BIP

KELSEY, Vera. 978
Young men so daring; fur traders who carried the frontier west. [1st ed.] Indianapolis, Bobbs-Merrill [1956] 288 p. illus. 22 cm. [F592.K38] 56-7606
1. Pond, Peter, 1740-1807? 2. Lisa, Manuel, 1772-1820. 3. Astor, John Jacob, 1763-1848. 4. Bridger, James, 1804-1881. I. Title.

OGLESBY, Richard Edward. 978
Manuel Lisa and the opening of the Missouri fur trade. [1st ed.] Norman, University of Oklahoma Press [1963] 246 p. illus. 24 cm. Includes bibliography. [F598.O3] 63-9956
1. Lisa, Manuel, 1772-1820. 2. Fur trade—Missouri Valley.

Lisitskii, Lazar' Markovich,

LISITSKII, Lazar' Markovich, 1890-1941. 709'.47
El Lissitzky; life, letters, texts [edited by] Sophie Lissitzky-Kuppers. Introd. by Herbert Read. Translated from the German by Helene Aldwinckle and Mary Whittall Greenwich, Conn., New York Graphic Society [1968] 407 p. illus. (part col.), ports. 28 cm. Includes bibliographical references. [N6999.L5K813] 68-12366 30.00
I. Kuppers-Lissitzky, Sophie, 1891- ed.

Lisovy, Vasyl Semenovich, 1937-

THREE philosophers- 364.1'3'0922
political prisoners in the Soviet Union / translated and edited by Taras Zakydalsky. Baltimore : Smoloskyp Publishers, 1976. 18 p. : ill. ; 18 cm. (Smoloskyp samvydav series ; no. 4) (Documents of Ukrainian samvydav) [DK508.8.T45] 77-375724
1. Lisovy, Vasyl Semenovich, 1937- 2. Pronyuk, Yevhen, 1936- 3. Bondar, Mykola Vasylevich, 1939- 4. Political prisoners—Russia—Ukraine. 5. Ukraine—History—1917- I. Zakydalsky, Taras. II. Title. III. Series.

Lister, Joseph Lister, baron, 1827-1912.

FARMER, Laurence, 1895- 926.1
Master surgeon; a biography of Joseph Lister. New York, Harper & Row [c.1962] 141p. illus. 22cm. Bibl. 61-12083 2.95
1. Lister, Joseph Lister, baron, 1827-1912. I. Title.

FISHER, Richard B. 617'.092'4 B
Joseph Lister / Richard Fisher. New York : Stein and Day, [1977] p. cm. Includes index. Bibliography: p. [R489.L75F5] 76-50614 ISBN 0-8128-1929-2 : 15.00
1. Lister, Joseph Lister, Baron, 1827-1912. 2. Surgeons—Great Britain—Biography. 3. Surgery, Aseptic and antiseptic—History. BIP

MECHNIKOV, il'ia Il'ich, 1845-1916. 610'.922 B
The founders of modern medicine: Pasteur, Koch, Lister, by Elie Metchnikoff. Including Etiology of wound infections, by Robert Koch, The antiseptic system, by Sir Joseph Lister, and Prevention of rabies, by Louis Pasteur. Freeport, N.Y., Books for Libraries Press [1971] 387 p. 23 cm. (Essay index reprint series) Reprint of 1939 ed. Translation of Trois foundateurs de la medecine moderne. [R134.M42 1971] 78-142669 ISBN 0-8369-2111-9
1. Pasteur, Louis, 1822-1895. 2. Lister, Joseph Lister, Baron, 1827-1912. 3. Koch, Robert, 1843-1910. I. Pasteur, Louis, 1822-1895. II. Lister, Joseph Lister, Baron, 1827-1912. III. Koch, Robert, 1843-1910. IV. Title.

NOBLE, Iris. 926.1
The courage of Dr. Lister. New York, Messner [1960] 191 p. 22 cm. [R489.L75N6] 60 13267
1. Lister, Joseph Lister, baron, 1827-1912. I. Title.

Lister, Joseph Lister, baron, 1827-1912—Juvenile literature.

CARTWRIGHT, Frederick Fox 926.1
Joseph Lister, the man who made surgery safe. London, Weidenfeld & Nicolson [dist. New Rochelle, N.Y., SportShelf, 1964, c.1963] 128p. illus. 19cm. (Pathfinder biogs., 15) 64-5672 3.50 bds.,
1. Lister, Joseph Lister, baron, 1827-1912—Juvenile literature. I. Title.

Liston, Sonny.

YOUNG, Andrew Sturgeon Nash, 1919- 927.9683
Sonny Liston, the champ nobody wanted, by A. S. "Doc" Young. Chicago, Johnson Pub. Co. [1963] 224 p. illus. 21 cm. [GV1132.L5Y6] 63-15652
1. Liston, Sonny.

Liszt, Franz,

LISZT, Franz, 1811-1886. 780'.924
Letters of Franz Liszt. Collected and edited by La Mara. Translated by Constance Bache. New York, Haskell House Publishers, 1968. 2 v. facsim., music, port. 23 cm. Contents.Contents.—v. 1. Years of travel as virtuoso. Weimar.—v. 2. Rome. Weimar.-Pest.-Rome. [ML410.L7A31 1968] 68-25294
I. Lipsius, Ida Maria, 1837-1927, ed. II. Bache, Constance, 1846-1903, tr.

LISZT, Franz, 1811-1886. 780'.924
Letters of Franz Liszt. Collected and edited by La Mara. Translated by Constance Bache. New York, Greenwood Press [1969] 2 v. facsim., music, port. 23 cm. "Originally published in 1894." Contents.Contents.—v. 1. Years of travel as virtuoso. Weimar.—v. 2. Rome. Weimar.-Pest.-Rome. [ML410.L7A31 1969] 69-13973
I. Lipsius, Ida Maria, 1837-1927, ed. II. Bache, Constance, 1846-1903, tr.

LISZT, Franz, 1811-1886. 780'.92'4 B
Letters of Franz Liszt. Collected and edited by La Mara. Translated by Constance Bache. St. Clair Shores, Mich., Scholarly Press, 1972. p. "First published 1894." Contents.Contents.—v. 1. From Paris to Rome.—v. 2. From Rome to the end. [ML410.L7A31 1972] 74-115256 ISBN 0-403-00360-1
I. Lipsius, Ida Maria, 1837-1927, ed. II. Bache, Constance, 1846-1903, tr. BIP

LISZT, Franz, 1811-1886. 780'.924 B
The letters of Franz Liszt to Marie zu Sayn-Wittgenstein. Translated and edited by Howard E. Hugo. Westport, Conn., Greenwood Press [1971, c1953] x, 376 p. 23 cm. Bibliography: p. 356-361. [ML410.L7A365 1971] 71-142931 ISBN 0-8371-5933-4
I. Hohenlohe-Schillingsfurst, Marie (Sayn-Wittgenstein) Prinzessin zu, 1837-1920. BIP

Liszt, Franz, 1811-1886.

CORDER, Frederick, 1852-1932. 780'.92'4 B
Ferencz (Francois) Liszt / by Frederick Corder. New York : AMS Press, 1979. p. cm. Reprint of the 1925 ed. published by Harper, New York. Includes index. Bibliography: [ML410.L7C78 1979] 74-24062 ISBN 0-404-12888-2 : 18.50
1. Liszt, Franz, 1811-1886. 2. Composers—Biography. BIP

FRIEDHEIM, Arthur, 1859-1932. 927.8
Life and Liszt; the recollections of a concert pianist. Edited by Theodore L. Bullock. New York, Taplinger Pub. Co. [1961] 335 p. illus. 22 cm. [ML417.F75A3] 61-15656
1. Liszt, Franz, 1811-1886. 2. Musicians—Correspondence, reminiscences, etc. I. Title.

HUNEKER, James Gibbons, 1857-1921. 780'.924 B
Franz Liszt. New York, AMS Press [1971] 458 p. illus., ports. 18 cm. Reprint of the 1911 ed. [ML410.L7H9 1971] 79-137245 ISBN 0-404-03387-3
1. Liszt, Franz, 1811-1886. BIP

LENZ, Wilhelm von, 1808-1883. 786.1'092'2 B
The great piano virtuosos of our time, by W. von Lenz; this revised translation [from the German] edited by Philip Reder. London, New York, Regency Press, 1971. [7], 91 p. ports. 20 cm. Revised translation of Die grossen piano-virtuosen unserer zeit aus persönlicher bekanntschaft. [ML397.L57 1971] 72-190224 ISBN 0-7212-0138-5 £1.20
1. Liszt, Franz, 1811-1886. 2. Chopin, Fryderyk Franciszek, 1810-1849. 3. Tausig, Karl, 1841-1871. 4. Henselt, Adolf von, 1814-1889. I. Title. BIP

LINGG, Ann M. 927.8
Mephisto waltz, the story of Franz Liszt. [1st ed.] New York, Holt [1951] 307 p. 22 cm. [ML410.L7L47] 51-14005
1. Liszt, Franz, 1811-1886. 2. Liszt, Franz, 1811-1886—Discography. I. Title.

LISZT, Franz, 1811-1886. 780'.924
Letters of Franz Liszt. Collected and edited by La Mara. Translated by Constance Bache. New York, Haskell House Publishers, 1968. 2 v. facsim., music, port. 23 cm. Contents.Contents.—v. 1. Years of travel as virtuoso. Weimar.—v. 2. Rome. Weimar.-Pest.-Rome. [ML410.L7A31 1968] 68-25294
I. Lipsius, Ida Maria, 1837-1927, ed. II. Bache, Constance, 1846-1903, tr.

LISZT, Franz, 1811-1886. 780'.924
Letters of Franz Liszt. Collected and edited by La Mara. Translated by Constance Bache. New York, Greenwood Press [1969] 2 v. facsim., music, port. 23 cm. "Originally published in 1894." Contents.Contents.—v. 1. Years of travel as virtuoso. Weimar.—v. 2. Rome. Weimar.-Pest.-Rome. [ML410.L7A31 1969] 69-13973
I. Lipsius, Ida Maria, 1837-1927, ed. II. Bache, Constance, 1846-1903, tr.

LISZT, Franz, 1811-1886. 780'.92'4 B
Letters of Franz Liszt. Collected and edited by La Mara. Translated by Constance Bache. St. Clair Shores, Mich., Scholarly Press, 1972. p. "First published 1894." Contents.Contents.—v. 1. From Paris to Rome.—v. 2. From Rome to the end. [ML410.L7A31 1972] 74-115256 ISBN 0-403-00360-1
I. Lipsius, Ida Maria, 1837-1927, ed. II. Bache, Constance, 1846-1903, tr. BIP

LISZT, Franz, 1811-1886. 780'.924 B
The letters of Franz Liszt to Marie zu Sayn-Wittgenstein. Translated and edited by Howard E. Hugo. Westport, Conn., Greenwood Press [1971, c1953] x, 376 p. 23 cm. Bibliography: p. 356-361. [ML410.L7A365 1971] 71-142931 ISBN 0-8371-5933-4
I. Hohenlohe-Schillingsfurst, Marie (Sayn-Wittgenstein) Prinzessin zu, 1837-1920. BIP

LISZT, Franz, 1811-1886. 780'.92'4 B
The letters of Franz Liszt to Olga von Meyendorff, 1871-1886, in the Mildred Bliss Collection at Dumbarton Oaks / translated by William R. Tyler ; introd. and notes by Edward N. Waters. Washington : Dumbarton Oaks, Trustees for Harvard University ; Cambridge, Mass. : distributed by Harvard University Press, 1979. xxi, 532 p. ; 25 cm. Includes bibliographical references and index. [ML410.L7A363] 77-82381 ISBN 0-88402-078-9 : 30.00
1. Composers—Correspondence. I. Meyendorff, Olga von, Baroness, 1838-1926. II. Title. BIP

NEWMAN, Ernest, 1868-1959. 780'.924 B
The man Liszt; a study of the tragicomedy of a soul divided against itself. New York, Taplinger Pub. Co. [1970, c1935] xxii, 313 p. ports. 23 cm. Bibliography: p. [xviii]-xxii. [ML410.L7N4 1970] 74-119622 7.50
1. Liszt, Franz, 1811-1886. I. Title.

NOHL, Ludwig, 1831-1885. 785'.0924 B
Life of Liszt, by Louis Nohl. Translated from the German by George P. Upton. Detroit, Gale Research Co., 1970. 198 p. port. 22 cm. Reprint of the 1889 ed. [ML410.L7N85 1970] 70-140402
1. Liszt, Franz, 1811-1886. BIP

PERENYI, Eleanor Spencer Stone, 1918- 780'.92'4 B
Liszt: the artist as romantic hero [by] Eleanor Perenyi. [1st ed.] Boston, Little, Brown [1974] x, 466 p. illus. 24 cm. "An Atlantic-Monthly Press book." Bibliography: p. 423-429. [ML410.L7P3] 74-8916 ISBN 0-316-69910-1 15.00
1. Liszt, Franz, 1811-1886. I. Title.

ROSTAND, Claude. 780'.92'4 B
Liszt. Translated by John Victor. New York, Grossman Publishers, 1972. 192 p. illus. 22 cm. ([Library of composers, 5]) Bibliography: p. 191-192. [ML410.L7R723 1972b] 77-143541 ISBN 0-670-43022-6 7.95
1. Liszt, Franz, 1811-1886. I. Title. II. Series.

SEROFF, Victor Ilyitch, 1902- 780.924
Franz Liszt, by Victor Seroff. New York, Macmillan Co. [1966] 152 p. illus., ports. 23 cm. Discography: p. [147]-149. [ML410.L7S45] 66-16106
1. Liszt, Franz, 1811-1886. I. Title. BIP

SEROFF, Victor Ilyitch, 1902- 780'.924 B
Franz Liszt, by Victor Seroff. Freeport, N.Y., Books for Libraries Press [1970, c1966] 152 p. illus., ports. 23 cm.

(Biography index reprint series) Discography: p. [147]-149. [ML410.L7S45 1970] 77-136652
1. Liszt, Franz, 1811-1886.

SITWELL, Sacheverell, 1897- 927.8
Liszt. [Rev. ed.] New York, Philosophical Library [1956] xxx, 400p. illus., ports., facsims. 23cm. 'Catalogue of works by Liszt': p. 338-357. Bibliography: p. 362-366. [ML410] 56-58019
1. Liszt, Franz, 1811-1886. I. Title.

SITWELL, Sacheverell, 1897- 780.924 (B)
Liszt. New York, Dover Publications [1967] xxxvi, 400 p. illus., ports. 22 cm. "This Dover edition is an unabridged republication, with minor corrections, of the revised edition published in 1965." "Catalogue of works by Liszt": p. 338-357. Bibliography: p. 356-366. [ML410.L7S62 1967] 66-26822
1. Liszt, Franz, 1811-1886. I. Title. BIP

SZABOLCSI, Bence, 1899- 780'.92'4 B
The twilight of Ferenc Liszt. [Translated by Andras Deak] Boston, Crescendo Pub. Co. [1973, c1959] 134 p. music. 21 cm. Translation of Liszt Ferenc esteje. Reprint of the ed. published by Akademiai Kiado, Budapest. Appendix (p. [81]-134) contains lesser-known works principally for piano composed by Liszt after 1880. [ML410.L7S983 1973] 73-179156 5.00
1. Liszt, Franz, 1811-1886. 2. Piano music. I. Liszt, Franz, 1811-1886. Works, piano. Selections. 1973. II. Title. BIP

WALKER, Alan, writer on music, comp. 780'.924
Franz Liszt; the man and his music. Edited by Alan Walker. New York, Taplinger Pub. Co. [1970] xiv, 471 p. illus., facsims., music, ports. 24 cm. Contents.Contents.—Liszt; a character study, by S. Sitwell.—Liszt; the pianist and teacher, by A. Hedley.—Liszt's musical background, by A. Walker.—Solo piano music (1827-61), by L. Kentner.—Solo piano music (1861-86), by J. Ogdon.—Transcriptions for piano, by D. Wilde.—The interpretation of Liszt's piano music, by L. Kentner.—The songs, by C. Headington.—Works for piano and orchestra, by R. Collet.—The orchestral works, by H. Searle.—Choral and organ music, by R. Collet.—Liszt and the twentieth century, by A. Walker. Bibliography: p. 387-389. [ML410.L7W28] 72-108274 12.00
1. Liszt, Franz, 1811-1886. BIP

Liszt, Franz, 1811-1886—Juvenile literature.

WALKER, Alan, writer on music. 780'.92'4 B
Liszt. New York, T. Y. Crowell Co. [1973, c1971] 108 p. illus. 25 cm. (The Great composers) Bibliography: p. 99. A biography of the Hungarian pianist and composer who began his career with a piano recital at age nine. Includes examples and analyses of his work. [ML410.L7W29 1973] 92 78-155097 ISBN 0-690-49698-2 4.95
1. Liszt, Franz, 1811-1886—Juvenile literature. I. Title.

Literary agents—Correspondence, reminiscences, etc.

REYNOLDS, Paul Revere, 1904- 070.5'2'0924 B
The middle man; the adventures of a literary agent [by] Paul R. Reynolds. New York, Morrow, 1972 [c1971] 223 p. 22 cm. [PN163.R4 1972] 76-151932 6.95
1. Literary agents—Correspondence, reminiscences, etc. I. Title. BIP

Literary landmarks—Durham, Eng. (County)

POPE-HENNESSY, Una (Birch) Dame, 1876-1949. 820.9'007 B
Durham Company. Freeport, N.Y., Books for Libraries Press [1972] 223 p. illus. 23 cm. (Essay index reprint series) Reprint of the 1941 ed. Contents.Contents.—The Byrons at Seaham.—Wordsworth at Sockburn.—Sequel to Sockburn.—Robert Surtees of Mainsforth.—Rokeby and Sir Walter Scott.—Hamsterley and Jorrocks. [PR110.D8P6 1972] 70-39167 ISBN 0-8369-2714-1
1. Literary landmarks—Durham, Eng. (County) 2. Authors, English—Biography. I. Title. BIP

Literary landmarks—United States.

POETS' homes; pen and 811'.3'09
pencil sketches of American poets and their homes, by Richard H. Stoddard and others. Freeport, N.Y., Books for Libraries Press [1972] p. (Essay index reprint series) Reprint of the 1879 ed. [PS141.P59 1972] 72-3491 ISBN 0-8369-2926-8
1. Literary landmarks—United States. 2. Poets, American—19th century—Biography. I. Stoddard, Richard Henry, 1825-1903.

Literature—Dictionaries.

CONCISE dictionary of 016.8
literature [ed. by] I. A. Langnas, J. S. List. New York, Philosophical [c.1963] 526p. 22cm. 60-15958 6.00
1. Literature—Dictionaries. 2. Literature—Bio-bibl. I. Langnas, Isaac A., ed. II. List, Jacob Samuel, ed. III. Title: Dictionary of literature.

LANGNAS, Isaac A., ed. 016.8
Concise dictionary of literature [edited by] I. A. Langnas and J. S. List. New York, Philosophical Library [1963] 526 p. 22 cm. [PN41.C63] 60-15958
1. Literature — Dictionaries. 2. Literature — Bio-bibl. I. List, Jacob Samuel, ed. II. Title. III. Title: Dictionary of literature. BIP

MAGILL, Frank Northen, 1907- ed. 803
Cyclopedia of world authors. Associate editor, Dayton Kohler. New York, Harper [1958] xii, 1198, ii p. 24 cm. "Also appears under the title of Masterplots cyclopedia of world authors." Includes bibliographies. [PN41.M26 1958a] 58-12461
1. Literature—Dictionaries. 2. Literature—Bio-bibliography. I. Title. BIP

MAGILL, Frank Northen, 1907- ed. 803
Masterplots cyclopedia of world authors. Associate editor: Dayton Kohler. New York, Salem Press [1958] 2 v. (xii, 1198 p.) 24 cm. Vol. 2: 1st ed. "Also appears under the title of Cyclopedia of world authors." Includes bibliographies. [PN41.M26 1958] 58-2821
1. Literature—Dictionaries. 2. Literature—Bio-bibliography. I. Title.

MAJOR writers of the 928.03
world [by] I. A. Langnas, J. S. List. Paterson, N.J., Littlefield, Adams [c.]1963. 526p. 21cm. (New students outline ser., no. 148) Issued also under title: Concise dictionary of literature. 63-6177 2.25 pap.,
1. Literature —Dictionaries. 2. Literature—Bio-bibl. I. Langas, Isaac A., ed. II. List, Jacob Samuel(ed. III. Series.

Literature—Bio-bibliography.

KUNITZ, Stanley Jasspon, 1905- ed. 920.04
European authors, 1000-1900; a biographical dictionary of European literature, ed. by Stanley J. Kunitz, Vineta Colby. New York, Wilson, 1967. ix, 1016p. ports. 26cm. (Authors ser.) [PN451.K8] 67-13870 18.00
1. Literature, Modern—Bio-bible. 2. Authors, European. I. Colby, Vineta, joint ed. II. Title. III. Series.

MAGILL, Frank Northen, 1907- ed. 803
Cyclopedia of world authors. Edited by Frank N. Magill. Associate editors: Dayton Kohler [and] Tench Francis Tilghman. Rev. ed. Englewood Cliffs, N.J., Salem Press [1974] 3 v. (vii, 1973, xi p.) 24 cm. "An earlier edition ... appears under the title of 'Masterplots cyclopedia of world authors." Contents.Contents.—v. 1. A-GAB.—v. 2. GAL-OCO.—v. 3. ODE-Z. Includes bibliographies. [PN451.M36 1974] 74-174980
1. Literature—Bio-bibliography. I. Kohler, Dayton, joint ed. II. Tilghman, Tench Francis, joint ed. III. Title.

TOD, Thomas Miller. 820'.9 B
A necrology of literary celebrities, 1321-1943, by T. M. Tod. [Folcroft, Pa.] Folcroft Press [1969] 67, xiii p. 29 cm. "First published 1947." [PN41.T6 1969] 72-195326
1. Literature—Bio-bibliography. I. Title.

Literature—History and criticism—Indexes.

LITERARY criticism and 016.809
authors' biographies : an annotated index / compiled by Alison P. Seidel, under the auspices of the Millbrae Branch, San Mateo County Library, California. Metuchen, N.J. : Scarecrow Press, 1978. vi, 209 p. ; 23 cm. [Z6511.L56] [PN501] 78-11857 ISBN 0-8108-1172-3 : 9.00
1. Literature—History and criticism—Indexes. 2. Authors—Biography—Indexes. I. Seidel, Alison P. II. San Mateo County Library. Millbrae Branch. BIP

Literature, Modern—20th century—Bio-bibliography.

THE Concise 809'.04 B
encyclopedia of modern world literature. Edited by Geoffrey Grigson. [2d ed.] New York, Hawthorn Books [1971, c1963] 430 p. 26 cm. [PN771.C58 1971] 76-29851 12.95
1. Literature, Modern—20th century—Bio-bibliography. 2. Literature, Modern—20th century—Dictionaries. I. Grigson, Geoffrey, 1905- ed. II. Title: Modern world literature.

THE Concise encyclopedia of 803
modern world literature. Edited by Geoffrey Grigson. [1st ed.] New York, Hawthorn Books [1963] 512 p. ports. (part col.) 26 cm. [PN41.C64] 62-8388
1. Literature, Modern—20th century—Bio-bibliography. 2. Literature, Modern—20th century—Dictionaries. I. Grifson, Geoffrey, 1905- ed. II. Title: Encyclopedia of modern world literature. III. Title: Modern world literature.

KUNITZ, Stanley Jasspon, 1905- ed. 928
Twentieth century authors, a biographical dictionary of modern literature, edited by Stanley J. Kunitz and Howard Haycraft. With 1850 biographies and 1700 ports. New York, Wilson, 1942. New York, Wilson, 1955. vii, 1577p. ports. (2mounted) 26cm. vii, 1123p. ports. 26cm. (The Authors series) (The Authors series) PN771.K86s 'Supersedes ... Living authors (1931) and Authors today and yesterday (1933) [PN771.K86] 43-51003
1. Literature, Modern—20th cent.—Bio-bibl. I. Haycraft, Howard, 1905- joint ed. II. Title. III. Title: — — First supplement. Assistant editor: Vineta Colby.

SEYMOUR-SMITH, Martin. 809'.04
Who's who in twentieth-century literature / by Martin Seymour-Smith. New York : Holt, Rinehart and Winston, c1976. p. cm. [PN451.S4] 75-21470 ISBN 0-03-013926-0 : 12.95
1. Literature, Modern—20th century—Bio-bibliography. I. Title. BIP

SEYMOUR-SMITH, Martin. 809'.04
Who's who in twentieth century literature / Martin Seymour-Smith. London : Weidenfeld & Nicolson, 1976. 414 p. ; 24 cm. Includes index. [PN451.S4 1976b] 76-371976 ISBN 0-297-77085-3 : £6.50
1. Literature, Modern—20th century—Bio-bibliography. I. Title.

SEYMOUR-SMITH, Martin. 809'.04
Who's who in twentieth-century literature / Martin Seymour-Smith. New York : McGraw-Hill, 1977, c1976. 414 p. ; 21 cm. Includes index. [PN451.S4 1976c] 77-15611 ISBN 0-07-056350-0 pbk. : 4.95
1. Literature, Modern—20th century—Bio-bibliography. I. Title.

WAKEMAN, John. 809'.04 B
World authors, 1950-1970; a companion volume to Twentieth century authors, edited by John Wakeman Editorial consultant Stanley J. Kunitz New York, Wilson, 1975. 1594 p. illus. 27 cm. (The Authors series) "Continues the work done by Stanley J. Kunitz and Howard Haycraft in Twentieth century authors [and its first suppl.]" [PN451.W3] 75-172140 ISBN 0-8242-0419-0 60.00
1. Literature, Modern—20th century—Bio-bibliography. I. Kunitz, Stanley Jasspon, 1905- Twentieth century authors. II. Title. III. Series.

Litman, Ray (Frank) 1864 or 5-1948.

LITMAN, Simon 1873- 920.7
Ray Frank Litman: a memoir. New York, American Jewish Historical Society, 1957. 202p. illus. 24cm. (Studies in American Jewish history, no. 3) [CT275.L478L5] 57-7833
1. Litman, Ray (Frank) 1864 or 5-1948. I. Title.

LITMAN, Simon, 1873- 920.7
Ray Frank Litman: a memoir. New York, American Jewish Historical Society, 1957. 202p. illus. 24cm. (Studies in American Jewish history, no. 3) [CT275.L478L5] 57-7833
1. Litman, Ray (Frank) 1864 or 5-1948. I. Title.

Little Crow, Dakota Chief, d. 1863.

SMITH, George H v. 12
Sixteen Indians. [n.p., c1961] 96 p. 23 cm.
1. Little Crow, Dakota Chief, d. 1863. 2. Indians of North America — Biog. I. Title.

Little Dipper (Cutter)

BAUM, Richard, 1913- 797.1'24
By the wind. New York, Van Nostrand Reinhold Co. [1973] xiii, 200 p. illus. 24 cm. [GV822.L5B3 1973] 73-177613 ISBN 0-442-20608-9 8.95
1. Little Dipper (Cutter) 2. Baum, Richard, 1913- 3. Atlantic Ocean. I. Title.

Little, Karl St. Clair, 1898-

LEATHAM, Louis Salisbury, 1902- 334.209792
Karl S. Little, Utah's Mr. Credit Union; a biography of Karl S. Little, together with a brief account of the beginnings of the world credit union movement and a more detailed history of its inception and growth in the State of Utah. outlining the important part Mr. Little played in its development. Salt Lake City, Utah Credit Union League, 1963. 333p. illus. 24cm. Bibl. 63-13544 apply
1. Little, Karl St. Clair, 1898- 2. Banks and banking, Cooperative—U. S. I. Title.

Little League Baseball, inc.

RALBOVSKY, Marty. 796.357'092'2 B
Destiny's darlings; a world championship Little League team twenty years later. New York, Hawthorn Books [1974] 255 p. illus. 22 cm. [GV865.A1R34 1974] 73-9308 7.95
1. Little League Baseball, inc. 2. Baseball—Biography. I. Title.

Little, Malcolm, 1925-1965.

CLARKE, John Henrik, 1915- comp. 301.451'96'073
Malcolm X; the man and his times. Edited, with an introd. and commentary, by John Henrik Clarke. Assisted by A. Peter Bailey and Earl Grant. [New York] Macmillan [1969] xxiv, 360 p. 22 cm. "A selected bibliography of books and articles relating to the life of Malcolm X, compiled by A. Peter Bailey": p. 352-356. [E185.97.L75C55] 77-75902
1. Little, Malcolm, 1925-1965. I. Bailey, A. Peter, joint comp. II. Grant, Earl, joint comp. III. Title.

CURTIS, Richard. 301.451'96'073024 B
The life of Malcolm X. Philadelphia, Macrae Smith Co. [1971] 160 p. illus., ports. 24 cm. A biography of the controversial black leader who became a Muslim while serving a prison term and turned against that group two years before his assassination at age thirty-nine.

[E185.97.L5C8 1971] 92 70-150675 ISBN 0-8255-2786-4 4.95
1. Little, Malcolm, 1925-1965. I. Title. **BIP**

*GOLDMAN, Peter. 301.45196073
The death and life of Malcolm X. New York, Harper & Row [1974] 482 p. illus. 18 cm. (Perennial library) [E185.97] 1.95 (pbk.)
1. Little, Malcolm, 1925-1965. 2. Black Muslims. I. Title. **BIP**

GOLDMAN, Peter 320.5'4'0924 B
Louis, 1933-
The death and life of Malcolm X [by] Peter Goldman. [1st ed.] New York, Harper & Row [1973] xx, 438 p. illus. 22 cm. Includes bibliographical references. [E185.97.L5G64 1973] 70-138726 ISBN 0-06-011582-3 8.95
1. Little, Malcolm, 1925-1965. I. Title.

GOLDMAN, Peter 320.5'4'0924 B
Louis, 1933-
The death and life of Malcolm X / Peter Goldman. 2d ed. Urbana : University of Illinois Press, c1979. p. cm. (Blacks in the New World) Includes index. Bibliography: p. [BP223.Z8L5735 1979] 79-18105 ISBN 0-252-00774-3 pbk. : 7.95
1. Little, Malcolm, 1925-1965. 2. Black Muslims—Biography. I. Title. II. Series.

[LITTLE, 301.451960730924
Malcolm,] 1925-1965
The autobiography of Malcolm X. WithAlex Haley. Introd. by M. S. Handler. Epilogue by Alex Haley. New York, Grove [c.1964, 1965] xvi, 455p. illus., ports. 24cm. [E185.97.L5A3] 65-27331 7.50
1. Black Muslims. I. Haley, Alex. II. Title.

*SHEPARD, 301.451'96'073'0924
Ray.
Autobiography of Malcolm X: notes, including life of the author, list of characters, critical commentaries, assessments of Malcolm, character analyses, review questions. Consulting editor: James L. Roberts. Lincoln, Neb., Cliff's Notes [1973] 69 p. 21 cm. Bibliography: p. 68-69. [E185.97] ISBN 0-8220-0802-5 1.25 (pbk.)
1. Little, Malcolm, 1925-1965. I. Roberts, James L., ed. II. Title.

Little, Malcolm, 1925-1965—Assassination.

BREITMAN, 364.1'524'0924 B
George.
The assassination of Malcolm X / George Breitman, Herman Porter, and Baxter Smith ; edited with an introd. by Malik Miah. New York : Pathfinder Press, 1977 190 p. : ill. ; 19 cm. [BP223.Z8L572] 76-47347 ISBN 0-87348-472-X : 8.00. ISBN 0-87348-473-8 pbk. : 1.95
1. Little, Malcolm, 1925-1965—Assassination. 2. Black Muslims—Biography. 3. Afro-Americans—Biography. I. Porter, Herman, joint author. II. Smith, Baxter, joint author. III. Miah, Malik. IV. Title. **BIP**

Little, Malcolm, 1925-1965—Juvenile literature.

ADOFF, Arnold. 301.451'96'073 B
Malcolm X. Illustrated by John Wilson. New York, Crowell [1970] 41 p. illus. (part col.) 24 cm. (Crowell biographies) Relates briefly the rise of a convict through self-education and love of his black brothers to become a leader of the black people of the United States. [E185.97.L5A6] 92 70-94787 3.75
1. Little, Malcolm, 1925-1965—Juvenile literature. I. Wilson, John, 1922 (Apr. 14)- illus. II. Title. **BIP**

HASKINS, 301.45'19'6073024 B
James, 1941-
The picture life of Malcolm X, by James S. Haskins. New York, F. Watts, 1975. 43 p. illus. 22 cm. (Picture lives) Brief text and photographs present the life of the controversial black Muslim leader who was assassinated in 1965. [BP223.Z8L574] 92 74-7441 ISBN 0-531-02771-6 3.90 (lib. bdg.)
1. Little, Malcolm, 1925-1965—Juvenile literature. I. Title. **BIP**

WHITE, 301.45'19'6073024 B
Florence Meiman, 1910-
Malcolm X: Black and proud, by Florence M. White. Illustrated by Victor Mays. Champaign, Ill., Garrard Pub. Co. [1975] 95 p. illus. (part col.) 24 cm. (Americans all) A biography of the black man who, as leader of the Black Muslims and later of the Organization of Afro-American Unity, sought a better life for his people. [BP223.Z8L578] 92 74-16264 ISBN 0-8116-4582-7 3.28 (lib. bdg.)
1. Little, Malcolm, 1925-1965—Juvenile literature. I. Mays, Victor, 1927- illus. II. Title.

Little, Royal, 1896-

LITTLE, Royal, 1896- 332'.092'4 B
How to lose $100,000,000 and other valuable advice / Royal Little. 1st ed. Boston : Little, Brown, c1979. xvii, 334 p. : ill. ; 34 cm. Includes index. [HG172.L54A34] 79-11628 ISBN 0-316-52786-6 : 9.95
1. Little, Royal, 1896- 2. Textron, inc. 3. Capitalists and financiers—United States—Biography. 4. Conglomerate corporations—United States. I. Title.

Little Turtle, Miami chief, d. 1812—Juvenile literature.

CUNNINGHAM, 970'.004'97 B
Margaret, 1916-
Little Turtle / by Maggi Cunningham. Minneapolis : Dillon Press, c1978. p. cm. (The Story of an American Indian) A biography of the Miami Indian chief who formed a confederation of Miami, Shawnee, and Potawatomi Indians that unsuccessfully attempted to drive white settlers from tribal lands. [E99.M48L485] 77-16764 ISBN 0-87518-158-9 : 5.95
1. Little Turtle, Miami chief, d. 1812—Juvenile literature. 2. Miami Indians—Biography—Juvenile literature. 3. Indians of North America—Wars—1790-1794—Juvenile literature. I. Title. **BIP**

Littlefield, Milton Smith, 1830-1899.

DANIELS, Jonathan, 973.8'092'4
1902-
Prince of carpetbaggers. Westport, Conn., Greenwood Press [1974, c1958] 319 p. port. 22 cm. Reprint of the ed. published by Lippincott, Philadelphia. Bibliography: p. 306-311. [E664.L673D36 1974] 74-3742 ISBN 0-8371-7466-X
1. Littlefield, Milton Smith, 1830-1899. 2. Reconstruction. I. Title. **BIP**

Littlejohn, Bruce, 1913-

LITTLEJOHN, Bruce, 340'.02'07
1913-
Laugh with the judge : humorous anecdotes from a career on the bench / by Bruce Littlejohn. 1st ed. Lexington, S.C. : Sandlapper Store, 1974. xiii, 146 p. : ill. ; 24 cm. [KF373.L536A3] 74-22868 ISBN 0-87844-025-9 : 6.95
1. Littlejohn, Bruce, 1913- 2. Judges—South Carolina—Correspondence, reminiscences, etc. 3. Law—South Carolina—Anecdotes, facetiae, satire, etc. I. Title.

Littlepage, Lewis, 1762-1802.

BOAND, Nell 943.8'02'0924 B
Holladay.
Lewis Littlepage. Richmond, Va., Whittet & Shepperson, 1970. x, 290 p. ports. 25 cm. [E302.6.L65B6] 75-139608
1. Littlepage, Lewis, 1762-1802. 2. Poland—History—Partition period, 1763-1796.

DAVIS 1916- 920
The king's chevalier; a biography of Lewis Littlepage. Indianapolis, Bobbs-Merrill [c.1961] 442p. illus. Bibl. 61-13150 7.50 bds.,
1. Littlepage, Lewis, 1762-1802. I. Title.

Littlepage, Lewis, 1762-1802.

DAVIS, Curtis Carroll, 1916- 920
The king's chevalier; a biography of Lewis Littlepage. [1st ed.] New York, Bobbs-Merrill [1961] 442 p. illus. 24 cm. Includes bibliography. [E302.6.L65D3] 61-13150
1. Littlepage, Lewis, 1762-1802. I. Title.

Littler, Gene.

LITTLER, Gene. 796.352'092'4 B
The real score / Gene Littler, with Jack Tobin. Waco, Tex. : Word Books, c1976. 199 p. : ports. ; 23 cm. A biography of golfer Gene Littler who has won several major tournaments after recovering from cancer. [GV964.L58A33] 92 75-36185 ISBN 0-87680-425-3 : 7.95
1. Littler, Gene. 2. Golf. 3. Cancer—Personal narratives. I. Tobin, Jack, joint author. II. Title.

Litvinoff, Barnet.

LITVINOFF, Barnet. 923.2564
Ben-Gurion of Israel. New York, Praeger [1954] xii, 273p. ports., maps. 22cm. [DS125.3.B37L5] 54-9526
1. Ben-Gurion, David, 1887- II. Title.

Liu, Aimee.

LIU, Aimee. 362.7'8'19685 B
Solitaire : a narrative / by Aimee Liu. 1st ed. New York : Harper & Row, c1979. viii, 215 p. ; 22 cm. [RC552.A5L58 1979] 78-20174 ISBN 0-06-012652-3 : 10.00
1. Liu, Aimee. 2. Anorexis nervosa—United States—Biography. I. Title.

Liu, Shao-ch'i, 1900-1974.

DITTMER, Lowell. 951.05'092'4
Liu Shao ch'i and the Chinese cultural revolution : the politics of mass criticism / Lowell Dittmer. Berkeley : University of California Press, [1974] xiv, 386 p. : graphs ; 24 cm. Includes index. Bibliography: p. 359-373. [DS778.L49D57] 73-85786 ISBN 0-520-02574-1 : 12.95 pbk. : 4.95
1. Liu, Shao-ch'i, 1900-1974. 2. China—Politics and government—1949- 3. Communist self-criticism. I. Title. **BIP**

Liu. Yung-yung.

HUNTER, Edward, 1902- 922
The story of Mary Liu. New York, Farrar, Straus and Cudahy [1957] 248p. 21cm. [BV3427.L58H8 1957] 57-5919
1. Liu. Yung-yung. I. Title.

Liu, Yung-yung.

HUNTER, Edward, journalist 922
The story of Mary Liu. New York, Farrar, Straus and Cudahy [1957] 248 p. 21 cm. [BV3427.L58H8 1957] 57-59190
1. Liu, Yung-yung.

Liveright, Horace Brisbin, 1886-1933.

GILMER, Walker. 655.4'24 B
Horace Liveright, publisher of the twenties. New York, D. Lewis [1970] xi, 287 p. port. 23 cm. Includes bibliographical references. [Z473.L56G5] 75-125880 8.95
1. Liveright, Horace Brisbin, 1886-1933.

Livermore, Jesse Lauriston, 1877-1940.

SARNOFF, Paul. 332.6'45'0924 (B)
Jesse Livermore: speculator-king. [Palisades Park, N.J.] Investors' Press, 1967. 136 p. ports. 23 cm. Bibliography: p. 129. [CT275.L497S36] 66-12752
1. Livermore, Jesse Lauriston, 1877-1940. I. Title.

SARNOFF, Paul. 332.6'45'0924
Jesse Livermore: speculator-king. [Palisades Park, N.J.] Investors' Pr., 1967. 136p. ports. 23cm. Bibl. [CT275.L497S36] (B) 66-12752 3.95
1. Livermore, Jesse Lauriston, 1877-1940. I. Title.

Livermore, Mary Ashton Rice, 1820-1905.

LIVERMORE, Mary 973.7'75'0924 B
Ashton Rice, 1820-1905.
The story of my life. New York, Arno Press, 1974 [c1897] 730 p. illus. 23 cm. (Women in America: from colonial times to the 20th century) Reprint of the 1899 ed. published by A. D. Worthington, Hartford, Conn. [CT275.L5A3 1974] 74-3960 ISBN 0-405-06108-0
1. Livermore, Mary Ashton Rice, 1820-1905. I. Title. II. Series.

Livermore, Robert, 1799-1858.

NEWTON, Janet. 979.4'6'030924 B
Las Positas; the story of Robert and Josefa Livermore. Livermore, Calif., R. and J. Newton, 1969. x, 195 p. illus., facsims., maps, ports. 24 cm. Includes bibliographical references. [F864.L75N4] 74-97695
1. Livermore, Robert, 1799-1858. 2. California—History—To 1846. I. Title.

Liverpool, Robert Banks Jenkinson, 2d Earl of, 1770-1828.

BROCK, William 942.07'4'0924
Ranulf.
Lord Liverpool and Liberal Toryism, 1820 to 1827, by W. R. Brock. [2d ed. Hamden, Conn.] Archon Books, 1967. 300 p. ports. 20 cm. Bibliography: p. [293]-296. [DA522.L7B7 1967a] 67-4292
1. Liverpool, Robert Banks Jenkinson, 2d Earl of, 1770-1828. 2. Great Britain—Politics and government—1820-1830. I. Title. **BIP**

COOKSON, J. E. 942.07'4'0924
Lord Liverpool's administration, 1815-1822 / J. E. Cookson. Hamden, Conn. : Archon Books, 1975. p. cm. Includes bibliographical references. [DA535.C66] 74-22080 ISBN 0-208-01495-0 : 15.00
1. Liverpool, Robert Banks Jenkinson, 2d Earl of, 1770-1828. 2. Great Britain—Politics and government—1800-1837. I. Title.

Livingston, Edward, 1764-1836.

HATCHER, William B. 973.4'0924 B
Edward Livingston: Jeffersonian Republican and Jacksonian Democrat. Gloucester, Mass., P. Smith, 1970 [c1940] xiv, 518 p. illus., facsim., map, ports. 21 cm. (Southern biography series) Includes bibliographical references. [E302.6.L68H3 1970] 70-21735
1. Livingston, Edward, 1764-1836. I. Title. II. Series.

Livingston, Robert R., 1746-1813.

DANGERFIELD, George 923.273
[Bubb] 1904-
Chancellor Robert R. Livingston of New York, 1746-1813. New York, Harcourt, Brace [c.1960] viii, 532p. 'A bibl. note': p.441-450. port., foldout geneal. table. 24cm. 60-10924 10.00
1. Livingston, Robert R., 1746-1813. I. Title.

Livingstone, Belle,

LIVINGSTONE, Belle. 920.7
Belle out of order. Pref. by Cleveland Amory. [1st ed.] New York, Holt [1959] 341 p. illus. 22 cm. [CT275.L56A33] 59-9856

LIVINGSTONE, Belle, 1875- 920.7
1957
Belle out of order. Preface by Cleveland Amory. New York, Avon [1961, c.1959] 256p. illus. (G-1077) .50 pap.,
I. Title.

Livingstone, David,

LIVINGSTONE, David, 1813- 923.942
1873.
Livingstone's missionary correspondence, 1841-1856. Ed., Introd. by I. Schapera. Berkeley, Univ. of Calif. Pr. [c.]1961. xxvi, 342p. illus., maps. Bibl. 62-1597 7.00

I. Title. II. Title: Missionary correspondence. 1841-1856.

LIVINGSTONE, David, 1813- 1873. 923.942
Livingstone's missionary correspondence, 1841-1856. Edited with an introd. by I. Schapera. Berkeley, University of California Press, 1961. xxvi, 312p. plates, ports., maps. 23cm. Bibliography: p. 327-329. [DT731.L736 1961] 62-1597
I. Title. II. Title: Missionary correspondence, 1841-1856.

Livingstone, David, 1813-1873.

BIRKINSHAW, Philip. 916'.04'20924 B
The Livingstone touch. Cape Town, New York, Purnell [1973] x, 182 p. illus. 26 cm. Bibliography: p. x. [DT731.L8B38] 72-82954 ISBN 0-360-00163-7 R5.75
1. Livingstone, David, 1813-1873. I. Livingstone, David, 1813-1873. II. Title.

BLAIKIE, William Garden, 1820-1899. 916 B
The personal life of David Livingstone, chiefly from his unpublished journals and correspondence in the possession of his family. New York, Negro Universities Press [1969] 508 p. map, port. 23 cm. Reprint of the 1880 ed. [DT731.L8B4 1969] 69-19353
1. Livingstone, David, 1813-1873. I. Title.

CAMPBELL, Reginald John, 1867-1956. 916'.04'20924 B
Livingstone. Westport, Conn., Greenwood Press [1972, c1929] x, 295 p. illus. 22 cm. Bibliography: p. 283-286. [DT731.L8C3 1972] 77-138212 ISBN 0-8371-5567-3
1. Livingstone, David, 1813-1873.

CHAMBLISS, J. E. 916.7 B
The life and labors of David Livingstone ... covering his entire career in Southern and Central Africa, by J. E. Chambliss. Westport, Conn., Negro Universities Press [1970] 805 p. illus., facsims., ports. 23 cm. Reprint of the 1875 ed. Issued also in 1881 under title: The lives and travels of Livingstone and Stanley. [DT731.L8C4 1971] 76-132642 ISBN 0-8371-3636-9
1. Livingstone, David, 1813-1873. 2. Africa, Southern—Description and travel. 3. Africa, Central—Description and travel. I. Title.

DAVID Livingstone: 922.342
his life and letters. New York, Harper [1957] 650p. ports., maps. 22cm. Bibliography: p. 631-635. [DT731.L8S4] 923.942 57-9884
1. Livingstone, David, 1813-1873. I. Seaver, George, 1890-

HUXLEY, Elspeth Joscelin Grant, 1907- 916'.04'20924 B
Livingstone and his African journeys [by] Elspeth Huxley. New York, Saturday Review Press [1974] 224 p. illus. (part col.) 26 cm. Bibliography: p. 218. [DT731.L8H88 1974b] 73-87557 ISBN 0-8415-0289-7 12.50
1. Livingstone, David, 1813-1873. I. Title.

JEAL, Tim. 916.7'04 B
Livingstone. [1st American ed.] New York, Putnam [1973] xiv, 427 p. illus. 24 cm. Bibliography: p. [391]-394. [DT731.L8J47 1973] 73-82030 ISBN 0-399-11215-4 10.00
1. Livingstone, David, 1813-1873.

LATHAM, Robert O 922.342
Trail maker; the story of David Livingstone. New York, Roy Publishers [1957?] 95p. illus. 19cm. (Stories of faith and fame) [DT731.L3] 923.942 57-10701
1. Livingstone, David, 1813-1873. I. Title.

LISTOWEL, Judith Marffy-Mantuano Hare, Countess of, 1904- 916.7'04'0924 B
The other Livingstone / Judith Listowel. New York : Scribner, [1975] c1974. 292 p. : ill. ; 23 cm. Includes index. Bibliography: p. [284]-286. [DT731.L8L54 1974c] 74-14007 ISBN 0-684-14130-2 : 8.95
1. Livingstone, David, 1813-1873. 2. Africa, Southern—Discovery and exploration. 3. Africa, Central—Discovery and exploration. I. Title.

LIVINGSTONE, David, 1813- 1873. 916.7 B
The last journals [of] David Livingstone in Central Africa, from 1865 to his death; continued by a narrative of his last moments and sufferings, obtained from his faithful servants, Chuma and Susi, by Horace Waller. Westport, Conn., Greenwood Press [1970] 2 v. illus., facsims., fold. maps, port. 23 cm. Reprint of the 1874 ed. [DT731.L735 1970] 68-55201 ISBN 0-8371-3899-X
1. Africa, Central—Description and travel. I. Waller, Horace, 1833-1896, ed. II. Title. BIP

LIVINGSTONE, David, 1813- 1873. 923.942
Livingstone's missionary correspondence, 1841-1856. Ed., Introd. by I. Schapera. Berkeley, Univ. of Calif. Pr. [c.]1961. xxvi, 342p. illus., maps. Bibl. 62-1597 7.00
I. Title. II. Title: Missionary correspondence. 1841-1856.

LIVINGSTONE, David, 1813- 1873. 923.942
Livingstone's missionary correspondence, 1841-1856. Edited with an introd. by I. Schapera. Berkeley, University of California Press, 1961. xxvi, 312p. plates, ports., maps. 23cm. Bibliography: p. 327-329. [DT731.L736 1961] 62-1597
I. Title. II. Title: Missionary correspondence, 1841-1856.

LIVINGSTONE in Africa. 922.342
New York, Association Press [1957] 92p. illus. 20cm. (World Christian books) [DT731.L8N6 1957a] 923.942 57-11613
1. Livingstone, David, 1813-1873. I. Northcott, William Cecil, 1902-

LIVINGSTONE the pathfinder. 922.342
Illustrated by Kurt Wiese. New ed. New York, Friendship Press [c1954] 166p. illus. 21cm. [DT731.L8M3 1954] [DT731.L8M3 1954] 923.942 54-11981 54-11981
1. Livingstone, David, 1813-1873. I. Mathews, Basil Joseph, 1879-1951.

LLOYD, Brendan W., 1904- 916.7'04 B
Livingstone 1873-1973, edited by B. W. Lloyd. Cape Town, C. Struik, 1973. 99 p. illus. (part col.) 22 cm. Includes bibliographies. [DT731.L8L63] 73-170070 ISBN 0-86977-027-6
1. Livingstone, David, 1813-1873.
Distributed by Verry, 7.85

MORRILL, Leslie. 923.942
Livingstone, trail blazer for God by Leslie and Madge Morrill. Mountain View Calif., Pacific Press Pub. Association [1959] 155p. illus. 23cm. (An Authors awards book) [DT731.L8M6] 59-12527
1. Livingstone, David, 1813-1873. I. Morrill, Madge (Haines) joint author. II. Title.

NORTHCOTT, William Cecil, 1902- 916.8'03'40924 B
David Livingstone: his triumph, decline, and fall, by Cecil Northcott. Philadelphia, Westminster Press [1973] 140 p. illus. 23 cm. Bibliography: p. 131-133. [DT731.L8N59] 73-5834 ISBN 0-664-20980-7 6.95
1. Livingstone, David, 1813-1873. I. Title.

PACHAI, Bridglal. 916.7'04 B
Livingstone: man of Africa: memorial essays, 1875-1973; edited by Bridglal Pachai. [London], Longman, 1973. [8], 245, [8] p. illus., maps, ports. 23 cm. Bibliography: p. 235-239. [DT731.L8P26] 73-164050 ISBN 0-582-64135-7 9.00
1. Livingstone, David, 1813-1873. I. Title.

PRINGLE, Patrick. 922.342
Lion of Africa; the story of David Livingstone. New York, Roy Publishers [1953] 144p. illus., ports., maps. 19cm. [DT731.L8] [DT731.L8] 923.942 53-10357 53-10357
1. Livingstone, David, 1813-1873. I. Title.

RANKIN, Arthur Edward, 1879- 923.942
Livingstone returned; the story of a measureless labor of love. With an introd. by G. Lake Imes. [1st ed.] New York, Exposition Press [1955] 131p. 21cm. [DT731.L8R3] 55-9409
1. Livingstone, David, 1813-1873. I. Title.

RANSFORD, Oliver, 1914- 916.7'04'0924 B
David Livingstone, the dark interior / Oliver Ransford. New York : St. Martin's, 1978. x, 332 p. : [6] leaves of plates ; ill. ; 24 cm. Includes index. Bibliography: p. 320-321. [DT731.L8R33 1978] 78-50673 ISBN 0-312-18379-8 : 18.95
1. Livingstone, David, 1813-1873. 2. Explorers—Africa, Southern—Biography. 3. Explorers—Scotland—Biography. 4. Missionaries, Medical—Africa, Southern—Biography. 5. Missionaries, Medical—Scotland—Biography. I. Title.

ROBERTS, John S., fl.1868-1882. 916'.042'0924 B
The life and explorations of David Livingstone, LL. D., by John S. Roberts, including extracts from Dr. Livingstone's last journal, by E. A. Manning. Boston, B. B. Russell, 1875. Detroit, Negro History Press, 1971. 384 p. illus., map, port. 21 cm. [DT731.L8R7 1971] 71-116318 ISBN 0-403-00314-8
1. Livingstone, David, 1813-1873. 2. Africa, South—Description and travel—1801-1900. I. Title.

SEAVER, George, 1890- 922.342
David Livingstone: his life and letters. New York, Harper [1957] 650p. ports., maps. 22cm. Bibliography: p. 634-635. [DT731.S8S4] [DT731.L8S4] 923.942 57-9884 57-9884
1. Livingstone, David, 1813-1873. I. Title.

SIMMONS, Jack, 1915- 923.942
Livingstone and Africa. New York, Collier [c.1962] 160p. 18cm. (AS460V) Bibl. .95 pap.,
1. Livingstone, David, 1813-1873. I. Title.

STANLEY, Henry Morton, Sir, 1841-1904. 916.7
How I found Livingstone. [New York] Arno [1970, c1872] xxiii, 736 p. illus., maps (part fold.), ports. 24 cm. (The American journalists) [DT351.S78 1970] 71-125717 ISBN 0-405-01698-0
1. Livingstone, David, 1813-1873. 2. Africa, Central—Description and travel. I. Title. BIP

THE way to Ilala; 922.342
David Livingstone's pilgrimage. London, New York, Longmans, Green [1955] 336p. illus., ports., maps (part fold.) 23cm. [DT731.L8D4] [DT731.L8D4] 923.942 55-3783 55-3783
1. Livingstone, David, 1813-1873. I. Debenham, Frank, 1883-

Livingstone, David, 1813-1873— Juvenile literature.

ARNOLD, Richard, 1912- 92
The true story of David Livingstone, Explorer. Chicago, Childrens [c.1957, 1964] 139p. col. illus. 23cm. First pub. in London in 1957 under title: The true book about David Livingstone. 64-12909 3.50; 2.63 lib.ed.,
1. Livingstone, David, 1813-1873—Juvenile literature. I. Title.

ARNOLD, Richard, 1912- j92
The true story of David Livingstone, Explorer. [American ed.] Chicago, Childrens Press [1964] 139 p. col. illus. 23 cm. First published in London in 1957 under title: The true book about David Livingstone. [DT731.L8A7] 64-12909
1. Livingstone, David, 1813-1873 — Juvenile literature. I. Title.

PRINGLE, Patrick 920
The young Livingstone. Illus. by William Randell. New York, Roy [1962] 136p. illus. 21cm. 62-9030 3.00
1. Livingstone, David, 1813-1873—Juvenile literature. I. Title.

Livius, Titus.

STORONI Mazzolani, Lidia. 937'.007'2022
Empire without end / Lidia Storoni Mazzolani ; with a foreword by Mario Pei ; translated by Joan McConnell and Mario Pei. New York : Harcourt Brace Jovanovich, c1976. p. cm. "A Helen and Kurt Wolff book." Translation of L'impero senza fine. Includes index. Bibliography: p. [DG206.S3S7613] 76-20672 ISBN 0-15-128780-5 : 10.95
1. Sallustius Crispus, C. 2. Livius, Titus. 3. Tacitus, Cornelius. 4. Rome—Historiography. I. Title.

Llerena, Mario.

LLERENA, Mario. 972.91'063
The unsuspected revolution : the birth and rise of Castroism / Mario Llerena. Ithaca, N.Y. : Cornell University Press, 1978. 324 p. : ill. ; 24 cm. Includes bibliographical references and index. [F1787.5.L55 1978] 77-3119 ISBN 0-8014-1094-0 : 12.50
1. Llerena, Mario. 2. Cuba—History—1933-1959. 3. Cuba—History—1959- 4. Revolutionists—Cuba—Biography. I. Title. BIP

Lloyd, Cecil Francis, 1884-1938— Correspondence.

LLOYD, Cecil Francis, 1884-1938. 811'.5'2 B
Rest, perturbed spirit : being the life of Cecil Francis Lloyd 1884-1938 : presented in a cento of excerpts from his letters / edited by Watson Kirkconnell ; with a critical epilogue and quotations from his work. Windsor, N.S. : Lancelot Press, 1974. 60 p. ; 21 cm. Includes bibliographical references. [PR9199.3.L57Z53 1974] 75-326205
1. Lloyd, Cecil Francis, 1884-1938—Correspondence. I. Kirkconnell, Watson, 1895- II. Title.

Lloyd. David, 1656-1731.

LOKKEN, Roy Norman, 1917- 923.273
David Lloyd, colonial lawmaker. Seattle, University of Washington Press, 1959. xiii, 305p. illus., map. 23cm. (University of Washington publications in history) Bibliography: p. 281-296. [F152.L77] 59-13419
1. Lloyd. David, 1656-1731. 2. Pennsylvania—Pol. & govt.—Colonial period. I. Title. II. Series: Washington (State) University. University of Washington publications in history BIP

Lloyd George, David Lloyd George, 1st Earl, 1863-1945.

BEAVERBROOK, William Maxwell Aitken, Baron, 1879-1964. 923.242
The decline and fall of Lloyd George. [1st ed.] New York, Duell, Sloan and Pearce [1963] 320 p. illus. 24 cm. [DA566.9.L5B4] 63-14328
1. Lloyd George, David Lloyd George, 1st earl, 1863-1945. I. Title.

BEAVERBROOK, William Maxwell Aitken, Baron, 1879-1964. 942.083'0924
The decline and fall of Lloyd George: and great was the fall thereof [by] Lord Beaverbrook. [New ed.] London, Collins, 1966. 320 p. front., 11 plates (incl. facsims., ports.) 23 cm. 36/- (B66-22376) [DA566.9.L5B4] 67-84899
1. Lloyd George, David Lloyd George, 1st Earl, 1863-1945. I. Title.

BEAVERBROOK, William Maxwell Aitken, baron. 1879- 923.242
The decline and fall of Lloyd George. New York, Duell [dist. Meredith, c.1963] 320p. illus. 24cm. 63-14328 4.95
1. Lloyd George, David Lloyd George, 1st earl, 1863-1945. I. Title.

CREGIER, Don M., 1930- 941.083'092'4 B
Bounder from Wales : Lloyd George's career before the First World War / Don M. Cregier. Columbia : University of Missouri Press, c1976. vi, 292 p. ; 24 cm. Includes index. Bibliography: p.[266]-281. [DA566.9.L5C73] 76-4894 ISBN 0-8262-0203-9 : 12.50
1. Lloyd George, David Lloyd George, 1st Earl, 1863-1945. 2. Great Britain—Politics and government—1837-1901. 3. Great Britain—Politics and government—1901-1936. 4. Statesmen—Great Britain—Biography. I. Title. BIP

FRY, Michael G. 941.083'092'4
Lloyd George and foreign policy / Michael G. Fry. Montreal : McGill-Queen's

University Press, 1977- v. : ports. ; 24 cm. Includes index. Contents.Contents.—v. 1. The education of a statesman, 1890-1916. Bibliography: v. 1, p. [299]-306. [DA566.9.L5F75] 77-377211 ISBN 0-7735-0274-2 (v. 1) : 18.50
1. Lloyd George, David Lloyd George, 1st Earl, 1863-1945. 2. Great Britain—Foreign relations—1837-1901. 3. Great Britain—Foreign relations—20th century. 4. Prime ministers—Great Britain—Biography. I. Title.
Distributed by McGill-Queen's University Press, Irvington, NY

GEORGE, William Richard Philip. 941.093'092'4 B
The making of Lloyd George / W. R. P. George. Hamden, Conn. : Archon Books, 1976. 184 p., [4] leaves of plates : ill. ; 23 cm. Includes index. [DA566.9.L5G46 1976] 76-22843 ISBN 0-208-01627-9 : 12.50
1. Lloyd George, David Lloyd George, 1st Earl, 1863-1945. 2. Statesmen—Great Britain—Biography. 3. Great Britain—Politics and government—1837-1901. I. Title. BIP

GILBERT, Martin, 1936- comp. 942.083'0924 B
Lloyd George. Englewood Cliffs, N.J., Prentice-Hall [1968] ix, 182 p. 21 cm. (Great lives observed) (A Spectrum book.) "Bibliographical note": p. 177-179. Bibliographical footnotes. [DA566.9.L5G6] 68-17825 4.95
1. Lloyd George, David Lloyd George, 1st Earl, 1863-1945.

GRIGG, John, 1924- 941.083'092'4 B
Lloyd George, the people's champion, 1902-1911 / John Grigg. Berkeley : University of California Press, c1978. 391 p., [5] leaves of plates : ill. ; 24 cm. Continues The young Lloyd George. Includes index. Bibliography : p. [371]-376. [DA566.9.L5G78 1978b] 77-91762 ISBN 0-520-03634-4 : 25.00
1. Lloyd George, David Lloyd George, 1st Earl, 1863-1945. 2. Great Britain—Politics and government—1901-1936. 3. Statesmen—Great Britain—Biography. I. Title.

GRIGG, John, 1924- 942.081'092'4 B
The young Lloyd George. Berkeley, University of California Press [1974, c1973] 320 p. illus. 24 cm. Bibliography: p. [301]-307. [DA566.9.L5G8 1974] 73-91067 ISBN 0-520-02677-2 12.00
1. Lloyd George, David Lloyd George, 1st Earl, 1863-1945. I. Title.

JONES, Thomas, 1870-1955. 923.242
Lloyd George. Cambridge, Harvard University Press, 1951. x, 330 p. illus., map, ports. 23 cm. (Makers of modern Europe) Bibliography: p. 291-303. [DA566.9.L5J6] 51-12384
1. Lloyd George, David Lloyd George, 1st earl, 1863-1945. I. Series.

LLOYD George, David Lloyd George, 1st Earl, 1863-1945. 942.083'092'4 B
Lloyd George family letters, 1885-1936, edited by Kenneth O. Morgan. Cardiff, University of Wales P., 1973. x, 227 p. ports. 22 cm. [DA566.9.L5A4 1973] 73-160011 ISBN 0-19-211717-3
1. Lloyd George, David Lloyd George, 1st Earl, 1863-1945. I. Morgan, Kenneth O., ed. II. Title.
Distributed by Oxford University Press; 14.50.

LLOYD George, Frances Louise (Stevenson) Lloyd George, Countess, 1888- 942.083'0924 B
Lloyd George: a diary, by Frances Stevenson. Edited by A. J. P. Taylor. [1st U.S. ed.] New York, Harper & Row [1971] xiii, 338 p. illus. 25 cm. [DA566.9.L5L475 1971b] 77-160652 ISBN 0-06-014116-6 10.00
1. Lloyd George, David Lloyd George, 1st Earl, 1863-1945.

LLOYD George, Richard Lloyd George, 2d earl, 1889- 923.242
My father, Lloyd George. New York, Crown Publishers [1961, c1960] 248 p. illus. 22 cm. First published in 1960 under title: Lloyd George. [DA566.9.L5L52 1961] 61-10305
1. Lloyd George, David Lloyd George, 1st earl, 1863-1945. I. Title.

MCCORMICK, Donald, 1911- 923.242
The mask of Merlin; a critical biography of David Lloyd George. [1st ed.] New York, Holt, Rinehart and Winston [1964, c1963] 343 p. illus., ports. 24 cm. Bibliography: p. 317-334. [DA566.9.L5M25 1964] 64-20102
1. Lloyd George, David Lloyd George, 1st earl, 1863-1945. I. Title.

MOWAT, Charles Loch, 1911- 923.242
Lloyd George [dist. New York, Oxford, 1965, c.]1964. 64p. illus., facsim., maps, ports, 21cm. (Clarendon biog., 1) Bibl. [DA566.9.L5M6] 65-2225 1.40 bds.,
1. Lloyd George, David Lloyd George, 1st earl, 1863-1945. I. Title.

OWEN, Frank, 1905- 923.242
Tempestuous journey Lloyd George, his life and times. New York, McGraw- Hill [1955] 784p. illus., ports., facsims. 24cm. Bibliography: p. 759-762. [DA566.9] 55-6979
1. Lloyd George, David Lloyd George, 1st earl, 1863-1945. I. Title.

ROWLAND, Peter, 1938- 941.083'092'4 B
David Lloyd George : a biography / Peter Rowland. 1st American ed. New York : Macmillan 1976, c1975. xix, 872 p., [8] leaves of plates : ill. ; 24 cm. First published in 1975 under title: Lloyd George. Includes index. Bibliography. p. 829-831. [DA566.9.L5R69 1976] 75-44300 ISBN 0-02-605590-2 : 20.00
1. Lloyd George, David Lloyd George, 1st Earl, 1863-1945. BIP

Lloyd, Harold Clayton, 1894-1971.

REILLY, Adam. 791.43'028'0924
Harold Lloyd : the king of daredevil comedy / Adam Reilly. New York : Collier Books, 1977. xv, 240 p. : ill. ; 28 cm. Includes index. Bibliography: p. 229. [PN2287.L5R4] ISBN 0-02-036350-8 pbk. :
1. Lloyd, Harold Clayton, 1894-1971. BIP

Lloyd-Jones, William Llewellyn.

LLOYD-JONES, William Llewellyn. 636.0890924 (B)
The animals came in one by one; an autobiography [by] Buster Lloyd-Jones. With drawings by Duffy Ayers. [1st American ed.] New York, John Day Co, [1967, c1966] 221 p. illus. 21 cm. [SF613.L55A3 1967] 67-10828
I. Title.

LLOYD-JONES, william Llewellyn. 636.0890924 B
The animals came in one by one; an autobiography [by] Buster Lloyd-Jones. With drawings by Duffy Ayers. [1st American ed.] New York, John Day Co. [1967, c1966] 221 p. illus. 21 cm. [SF613.L55A3 1967] 67-10828
I. Title.

LoBagola, Bata Kindai Amgoza ibn.

LOBAGOLA, Bata Kindai Amgoza ibn. 916.6'8'0330924 B
LoBagola; and African savage's own story. New York, Negro Universities Press [1970] xxiii, 402 p. facsims., ports. 23 cm. Reprint of the 1930 ed. [CT2750.L6A3 1970] 71-109331

Lobbying—United States.

LIPSEN, Charles B. 328.73'07'8
Vested interest / by Charles B. Lipsen, with Stephan Lesher. 1st ed. Garden City, N.Y. : Doubleday, 1977. viii, 184 p. ; 22 cm. [JK1118.L56] 76-18359 ISBN 0-385-11470-2 : 7.95
1. Lobbying—United States. 2. Lobbyists—United States—Biography. I. Lesher, Stephan, joint author. II. Title.

Loben Sels, Pieter Justus van.

LOBEN SELS, Pieter Justus van. 914.92'03'60924
The memoirs of Pieter Justus van Loben Sels. [Menlo Park, Calif., c1966] 89 p. illus., facsims., ports. 24 cm. No. 144 of 200 copies. "Footnotes": p. 82-83. [DJ219.L6A3] 67-8444
I. Title.

Lobsang, Rampa T.,

LOBSANG, Rampa T., pseud. 922.94
The third eye; the autobiography of a Tibetan lama. Illus. by Tessa Theobald. New York, Ballantine [1964 c.1956, 1958] 221p. illus. 21cm. (U5026) .60 pap.,
I. Title.

LOBSANG RAMPA, T., pseud. 922.94
Doctor from Lhasa. [1st U. S. ed] Clarksburg, W. Va, Saucerian Books [c1959] 239p. illus. 23cm. 'Continuation of ... [The author's] autobiography [The third eye]' [BL1490.L6A32 1959a] 60-8079
I. Title.

LOBSANG RAMPA, T., pseud. 922.94
The third eye; the autobiography of a Tibetan lama. Illustrated by Tessa Theobald. Garden City, N. Y., Doubleday [c1958] 256p. illus. 22cm. [BL1490.L6A3 1958] 58-11100
I. Title.

LOBSANG RAMPA, T., pseud. 922.94
The third eye; the autobiography of a Tibetan lama. Illustrated by Tessa Theobald. [1st ed.] Garden City, N. Y., Doubleday. 1957 [c1956] 256p. illus. 22cm. [BL1490.L6A3] 57-6296
I. Title.

Lobster fisheries—New Zealand—Fiordland.

POWELL, Paul Sidney, 1917- 639'.54'1
Fishermen of Fiordland / Paul Powell. Wellington : Reed, 1976. xi, 118 p. : ill. (some col.), map (on lining paper) ; 25 cm. [SH380.2.N45P68] 76-382755 ISBN 0-589-00938-9
1. Lobster fisheries—New Zealand—Fiordland. 2. Fishermen New Zealand Fiordland—Biography. 3. Fiordland, N.Z. 4. Jasus edwardsii. I. Title.

Locke, David Ross, 1833-1888.

HARRISON, John M. 070'.924 B
The man who made Nasby: David Ross Locke, by John M. Harrison. Chapel Hill, University of North Carolina Press [1968, c1969] ix, 335 p. port. 24 cm. Includes bibliographical references. [PS2248.L8Z7] 69-15864 3.75
1. Locke, David Ross, 1833-1888. I. Title.

Locke, Elizabeth N

LOCKE, Elizabeth N 917.430340924 (B)
A good heritage, by Elizabeth N. Locke. [1st ed.] New York, Greenwich Book Publishers [1965] 270 p. 21 cm. Autobiographical. [CT275.L595A3] 65-17178
I. Title.

Locke, John, 1632-1704.

AARON, Richard Ithamar, 1901- 192
John Locke, by Richard I. Aaron. 3rd ed. Oxford, Clarendon Press, 1971. xiv, 383 p. 23 cm. Bibliography: p. 367-376. [B1296.A62 1971] 79-586664 ISBN 0-19-824355-3 £3.00
1. Locke, John, 1632-1704. BIP

COLLINS, James Daniel. 146'.4
The British empiricists: Locke, Berkeley, Hume, by James Collins. Milwaukee, Bruce Pub. Co. [1967] viii, 152 p. 22 cm. Includes bibliographical references. [B1297.C6] 67-26506
1. Locke, John, 1632-1704. 2. Berkeley, George, Bp. of Cloyne, 1685-1753. 3. Hume, David, 1711-1776. 4. Empiricism. I. Title.

CRANSTON, Maurice William, 1920- 921.2
John Locke, a biography [London] Longmans [dist. Mystic, Conn., Verry, 1965] 496p. illus. 23cm. [B1297.C7] 57-2958 10.00
1. Locke, John, 1632-1704. I. Title.

CRANSTON, Maurice William, 1920- 192 B
John Locke / Maurice Cranston. New York : Arno Press, 1979, c1957. p. cm. (European political thought) Reprint of the ed. published by Macmillan, New York, under title: John Locke, a biography. Includes index. [B1296.C7 1979] 78-67349 ISBN 0-405-11690-X : 30.00
1. Locke, John, 1632-1704. 2. Philosophers—England—Biography. I. Title. II. Series.

CRANSTON, Maurice William, 1920- 921.2
John Locke, a biography. London, New York, Longmans, Green [1957] 496p. illus. 23cm. [B1297.C7 1957] 57-2958
1. Locke, John, 1632-1704. I. Title.

FRASER, Alexander Campbell, 1819-1914. 192 B
Locke. Port Washington, N.Y., Kennikat Press [1970] x, 299 p. port. 20 cm. Reprint of the 1890 ed. Includes bibliographical references. [B1296.F8 1970] 71-103188
1. Locke, John, 1632-1704. BIP

JAMES, David Gwilym, 1905-1968. 192
The life of reason; Hobbes, Locke, Bolingbroke. Freeport, N.Y., Books for Libraries Press [1972] xiii, 272 p. 24 cm. (Biography index reprint series) Reprint of the 1949 ed., which was issued as v. 1 of the author's The English Augustans. [B1131.J3 1972] 76-38378 ISBN 0-8369-8122-7
1. Hobbes, Thomas, 1588-1679. 2. Locke, John, 1632-1704. 3. Bolingbroke, Henry Saint-John, 1st viscount, 1678-1751. I. Title. BIP

JOHN Locke, v. 12
a biography. New York, Macmillan [1957] xvi, 496p. 23cm.
1. Locke, John, 1632-1704. I. Cranston, Maurice William, 1920- BIP

KING, Peter King, Baron, 1776-1833. 192 B
The life and letters of John Locke, with extracts from his journals and common-place books. With a general index. New York, B. Franklin [1972, i.e. 1973] viii, 503 p. 23 cm. (Philosophy and religious history monographs, 93) (Burt Franklin research and source works series) Reprint of the 1884 ed. published by G. Bell, London. [B1296.K5 1972] 75-159702 ISBN 0-8337-2148-8 22.50
1. Locke, John, 1632-1704. I. Title.

LOCKE, John, 1632-1704. 192
The correspondence of John Locke / edited by E. S. De Beer. Oxford [Eng.] : Clarendon Press, 1976- v. ; 23 cm. (The Clarendon edition of the works of John Locke) Includes index. Contents.Contents.—v. 1. Introduction; letters nos. 1-461. Bibliography: v. 1, p. lxxx-xcv. [B1296.A4 1976] 76-381096 ISBN 0-19-824396-0 : 65.00ea.(2vols.)
1. Locke, John, 1632-1704. 2. Philosophers—England—Correspondence. I. Title.
Distributed by Oxford University Press N.Y. N.Y. BIP

LOCKE, John, 1632-1704. 192
The correspondence of John Locke and Edward Clarke. Edited, with a biographical study by Benjamin Rand. Freeport, N.Y., Books for Libraries Press [1973] p. Reprint of the 1927 ed. [B1296.A4 1973] 72-10623 ISBN 0-8369-7116-7
1. Philosophers, British—Correspondence, reminiscences, etc. I. Clarke, Edward, 1649?-1710. II. Rand, Benjamin, 1856-1934, ed. III. Title.

Lockhart, Howard M.

LOCKHART, Howard M. 791.44'092'4
On my wavelength [by] Howard Lockhart. Aberdeen, Impulse Books, 1973. [5], 140, [16] p. illus., ports. 23 cm. Bibliography: p. 140. [PN1991.4.L6A3] 73-163657 ISBN 0-901311-33-2 £2.80
1. Lockhart, Howard M. 2. Radio broadcasting—Scotland. I. Title.

Lockhart, John Gibson, 1794-1854.

THE Ballantyne- 828'.7'09 B
Lockhart controversy, 1838-1839. New York, Garland Pub. Inc., 1974. 88, 122, 125, 97 p. 22 cm. (The English book trade, 1660-1853) Reprint of Refutation of the mistatements and calumnies contained in Mr Lockhart's Life of Sir Walter Scott, bart., respecting the Messrs Ballantyne, by the trustees and son of the late Mr James Ballantyne, first published in 1838 by Longman, Orme, Brown, Green, and Longmans, London; of The Ballantyne-humbug handled, in a letter to Sir Adam Fergusson, by J. G. Lockhart, first published in 1839 by R. Cadell, Edinburgh; and of Reply to Mr Lockhart's pamphlet, entitled, "The Ballantyne-humbug handled," by the authors of a Refutation of the mistatements and calumnies contained in Mr Lockhart's Life of Sir Walter Scott, bart., respecting the Messrs Ballantyne, first published in 1839 by Longman, Orme, Brown, Green, and Longmans, London. [PR5338.B35 1974] 74-13211 ISBN 0-8240-0986-X
1. Scott, Walter, Sir, bart., 1771-1832—Friends and associates. 2. Ballantyne, James, 1772-1833. 3. Ballantyne, John, 1774-1821. 4. Lockhart, John Gibson, 1794-1854. Life of Sir Walter Scott. 5. Lockhart, John Gibson, 1794-1854. The Ballantyne-humbug handled. I. Lockhart, John Gibson, 1794-1854. The Ballantyne-humbug handled. 1974. II. Refutation of the mistatements and calumnies contained in Mr Lockhart's Life of Sir Walter Scott, bart., respecting the Messrs. Ballantyne. 1974. III. Reply to Mr. Lockhart's pamphlet, entitled, "The Ballantyne-humbug handled." 1974. IV. Title. V. Series.

LANG, Andrew, 1844-1912. 823'.7
The life and letters of John Gibson Lockhart. New York, AMS Press [1970] 2 v. illus., ports. 23 cm. Reprint of the 1897 ed. [PR4891.L4L3 1970] 79-110131
1. Lockhart, John Gibson, 1794-1854. I. Lockhart, John Gibson, 1794-1854. BIP

Lockhart, John Gibson, 1794-1854—Biography.

CARSWELL, Donald, 828'.7'09 B
1882-1940.
Sir Walter: a four-part study in biography (Scott, Hogg, Lockhart, Joanna Baillie) [Folcroft, Pa.] Folcroft Library Editions, 1973. p. cm. Reprint of the 1930 ed. published by J. Murray, London; American ed. originally published in 1930 under: Scott and his circle. Bibliography: p. [PR5332.C3 1973] 73-20091 ISBN 0-8414-3532-4 (lib. bdg.)
1. Scott, Walter, Sir, Bart., 1771-1832—Biography. 2. Hogg, James, 1770-1835—Biography. 3. Lockhart, John Gibson, 1794-1854—Biography. 4. Baillie, Joanna, 1762-1851—Biography. I. Title.

Lockhart, Robert Hamilton Bruce, Sir, 1887-1970.

LOCKHART, Robert 940.54'81'42
Hamilton Bruce, Sir, 1887-1970.
Comes the reckoning. New York, Arno Press, 1972. 384 p. 23 cm. (International propaganda and communications) Reprint of the 1947 ed. [D810.P7G758 1972] 72-4672 ISBN 0-405-04756-8 19.00
1. World War, 1939-1945—Propaganda. 2. World War, 1939-1945—Diplomatic history. 3. World War, 1939-1945—Personal narratives, English. I. Title. II. Series. BIP

LOCKHART, Robert 070.4'3'0924 B
Hamilton Bruce, Sir, 1887-1970.
The diaries of Sir Robert Bruce Lockhart / edited by Kenneth Young. New York : St. Martin's Press, 1974 [i.e. 1975] c1973- v. : ill. ; 25 cm. Contents.Contents.—v. 1. 1915-1938. Includes bibliographical references and index. [DA566.9.L54A3 1975] 73-92618 15.00 (v. 1)
1. Lockhart, Robert Hamilton Bruce, Sir, 1887-1970. I. Young, Kenneth, 1916- II. Title.

Locklear, Ormer Leslie, 1891-1920.

RONNIE, Art. 797.5'4'0924 B
Locklear: the man who walked on wings. South Brunswick, A. S. Barnes [1973] 333 p. illus. 27 cm. Bibliography: p. 313-317. [TL540.L62R65] 75-37816 ISBN 0-498-01073-2 12.00
1. Locklear, Ormer Leslie, 1891-1920. I. Title.

Lockridge, Ross Franklin, 1914-1948—Biography.

LEGGETT, John, 1917- 812'.5'409 B
Ross and Tom; two American tragedies. New York, Simon and Schuster [1974] 447 p. illus. 25 cm. [PS3562.O274Z78] 74-118 ISBN 0-671-21733-X 10.95
1. Lockridge, Ross Franklin, 1914-1948—Biography. 2. Heggen, Thomas, 1919-1949—Biography. I. Title.

LEGGETT, John, 1917- 812'.5'409 B
Ross and Tom; two American tragedies. New York, Penguin [1975, c1974] 447 p. illus. 19 cm. [PS3562.O274Z78] ISBN 0-14-004051-X 2.95 (pbk.)
1. Lockridge, Ross Franklin, 1914-1948—Biography. 2. Heggen, Thomas, 1919-1949—Biography. I. Title.
L.C. card number for original ed.: 74-118.

Lockwood, Belva Ann Bennett, 1830-1917—Juvenile literature.

DUNNAHOO, Terry. 340'.092'4 B
Before the Supreme Court; the story of Belva Ann Lockwood. Illustrated by Bea Holmes. Boston, Houghton Mifflin Co., 1974. 186 p. illus. 22 cm. A biography of Belva Ann Lockwood, fighter for women's rights, who became the first woman to practice law before the Supreme Court and to plead the first case for a Negro there. [KF368.L58D8] 92 73-22057 ISBN 0-395-18520-3 4.95
1. Lockwood, Belva Ann Bennett, 1830-1917—Juvenile literature. I. Holmes, Bea, illus. II. Title. BIP

FOX, Mary Virginia. 340'.092'4 B
Lady for the defense : a biography of Belva Lockwood / Mary Virginia Fox. 1st ed. New York : Harcourt Brace Jovanovich, [1975] 158 p. : port. ; 24 cm. Bibliography: p. 157-158. A biography of the first woman lawyer to practice before the United States Supreme Court who also was the first woman candidate for President. [KF368.L58F69] 92 74-27460 ISBN 0-15-243400-3 : 6.50
1. Lockwood, Belva Ann Bennett, 1830-1917—Juvenile literature. I. Title.

Lodge family.

HATCH, Alden, 1898- 973'.0992
The Lodges of Massachusetts. New York, Hawthorn Books [1973] viii, 360 p. illus. 25 cm. Includes bibliographical references. [CS71.L818 1973] 72-4922 10.95
1. Lodge family. I. Title.

Lodge, George Cabot, 1873-1909.

ADAMS, Henry, 1838-1918. 811'.4
The life of George Cabot Lodge / by Henry Adams ; a facsim. reproduction with an introd. by John W. Crowley. Delmar, N.Y. : Scholars' Facsims. & Reprints, 1978. p. cm. Reprint of the 1911 ed. published by Houghton Mifflin, Boston. [PS3523.O27Z6 1978] 78-16619 ISBN 0-8201-1316-6 : 22.00
1. Lodge, George Cabot, 1873-1909. 2. Poets, American—20th century—Biography. I. Title. BIP

CROWLEY, John William, 811'.4 B
1945-
George Cabot Lodge / by John W. Crowley. Boston : Twayne Publishers, c1976. 148 p. : port. ; 21 cm. (Twayne's United States authors series ; TUSAS 264) Includes index. Bibliography: p. 139-143. [PS2249.L34Z6] 75-44429 ISBN 0-8057-7165-4 lib.bdg. : 7.50
1. Lodge, George Cabot, 1873-1909. BIP

Lodge, Henry Cabot, 1850-1924.

GARRATY, John Arthur, 923.273
1920-
Henry Cabot Lodge, a biography. [1st ed.] New York, Knopf, 1953. xiii, 433, xvi p. ports. 25 cm. Bibliography: p. 425-433. [E664.L7G3] 53-6852
1. Lodge, Henry Cabot, 1850-1924.

GARRATY, John Arthur, 973.90924
1920-
Henry Cabot Lodge, a biography. New York, Knopf, 1965 [c1953] xiii, 433, xvi p. ports. 25 cm. Bibliography: p. 425-433. 68-102130
1. Lodge, Henry Cabot, 1850-1924. I. Title.

LODGE, Henry 328.73'092'4 B
Cabot, 1850-1924.
Early memories / Henry Cabot Lodge. New York : Arno Press, 1975, c1913. p. cm. (The Leisure class in America) Reprint of the ed. published by Scribner, New York. [E664.L7A33 1975] 75-1853 ISBN 0-405-06919-7 : 22.00
1. Lodge, Henry Cabot, 1850-1924. I. Title. II. Series. BIP

Lodge, Henry Cabot, 1902-

MILLER, William 973.9'0924 B
Johnson.
Henry Cabot Lodge; a biography by William J. Miller. New York, Heineman [1967] 449 p. illus., ports. 25 cm. Bibliography: p. 427. [E748.L8M5] 64-23625
1. Lodge, Henry Cabot, 1902- BIP

ZEIGER, Henry A. 923.273
The remarkable Henry Cabot Lodge. New York, Popular Lib. (c.1964) 144p. 18cm. (PC1036) 64-4529 .50 pap.,
1. Lodge, Henry Cabot, 1902- I. Title.

ZEIGER, Henry A 923.273
The remarkable Henry Cabot Lodge. New York, Popular Library [1964] 144 p. 18 cm. "PC1036." [E748.L8Z4] 64-4529
1. Lodge, Henry Cabot, 1902- I. Title.

Lodge, Oliver Joseph

LODGE, Oliver Joseph Sir 925.2
1851-1940
Pioneers of science and the development of their scientific theories. New York, Dover Pubns. [1960] (Gloucester, Mass., P. 404p. illus., diagrs., maps (Dover Newton ISSN a biography, 1942-1727)
I. Title.

Lodge, Oliver Joseph, Sir, 1851-1940.

JOLLY, W. P. 530'.092'4 B
Sir Oliver Lodge / W. P. Jolly. 1st American ed. Rutherford : Fairleigh Dickinson University Press, 1975, c1974. 255 p., [2] leaves of plates : ill. ; 22 cm. Includes bibliographical references and index. [QC16.L6J64 1975] 74-24803 ISBN 0-8386-1703-4 : 10.00
1. Lodge, Oliver Joseph, Sir, 1851-1940.

LODGE, Oliver Joseph Sir 925.2
1851-1940
Pioneers of science and the development of their scientific theories. New York, Dover Pubns. [1960] (Gloucester, Mass., P. 404p. illus., diagrs., maps (Dover Newton ISSN a biography, 1942-1727)
I. Title.

Lodge, Thomas, 1558?-1625.

RYAN, Pat M 928.2
Thomas Lodge, gentleman. Hamden, Conn., Shoe String Press, 1958 [i. e. 1959] 121p. 22cm. Includes bibliography. [PR2298.R9] 59-8792
1. Lodge, Thomas, 1558?-1625. I. Title.

SISSON, Charles Jasper, 820.9003
1885- ed.
Thomas Lodge and other Elizabethans, edited by Charles J. Sisson. New York, Octagon Books, 1966 [c1933] xii, 526 p. illus., maps, geneal. tables. 24 cm. Contents.Contents.—Thomas Lodge and his family, by C. J. Sisson.—Barnabe Barnes, by M. Eccles.—Lodowick Bryskett and his family, by D. Jones.—John Lyly at St. Bartholomew's, or Much ado about washing, by D. Jones.—Sir George Buc, master of the revels, by M. Eccles. [PR2298.S5 1966] 66-18029
1. Lodge, Thomas, 1558?-1625. 2. Barnes, Barnabe, 1569?-1609. 3. Bryskett, Lodowick, ca. 1545-ca. 1612. 4. Lyly, John, 1554?-1606. 5. Buck, George, Sir, d. 1623. I. Eccles, Mark. II. Jones, Deborah. III. Title. BIP

TENNEY, Edward Andrews, 821'.3
1899-
Thomas Lodge. New York, Russell & Russell [1969] ix, 202 p. 23 cm. (Cornell studies in English, v. 26) Bibliography: p. 192-195. [PR2298.T43 1969] 68-25680
1. Lodge, Thomas, 1558?-1625. I. Series: Cornell University. Cornell studies in English, v. 26 BIP

WALKER, Alice, 1900- 828'.3'09 B
The life of Thomas Lodge. [Folcroft, Pa.] Folcroft Library Editions, 1974. 23 p. 26 cm. Reprint of the 1933 ed. published by Sidgwick & Jackson, London. Includes bibliographical references. [PR2298.W3 1974] 74-16101 ISBN 0-8414-9552-1 (lib. bdg.)
1. Lodge, Thomas, 1558?-1625? I. Title. BIP

Loeb, Gerald M.

MARTIN RALPH G., 1920- 332.620924
The wizard of Wall Street; the story of Gerald M. Loeb. New York, Morrow [c.] 1965. 192p. 25cm. [HG4521.M33] 65-20938 4.95 bds.,
1. Loeb, Gerald M. 2. Investments. I. Title.

Loeb, William, 1905-

CASH, Kevin, 1926- 070.5'092'4 B
Who the hell is William Loeb? / Kevin Cash. 1st ed. Manchester, N.H. ; Amoskeag Press, c1975. xii, 472, [xiii]-xxxii p. ; 22 cm. Bibliography: p. [xxx]-xxxii. [PN4874.L59C3] 75-33630 8.95 pbk. : 5.95
1. Loeb, William, 1905- 2. Knox, Franklin, 1874-1944. 3. Manchester union leader. I. Title.

CASH, Kevin 070.5'092'4 B
Richard, 1926-
Who the hell is William Loeb? / Kevin Richard Cash ; introd. by Jimmy Breslin. Hooksett, N.H. : Amoskeag Press, [1975] p. cm. Bibliography: p. [PN4874.L59C3] 75-33630
1. Loeb, William, 1905- 2. Knox, Franklin, 1874-1944. 3. Manchester union leader. I. Title. BIP

Loebl, Eugen.

†LOEBL, Eugen, 1907- 364.1'3
My mind on trial / Eugen Loebl. New York : Harcourt Brace Jovanovich, 1977, c1976 p. cm. (A Harvest/HBJ book) "A Helen and Kurt Wolff book." [DB217.L63A35 1976 b] 77-16098 ISBN 0-15-663800-2 : 8.95
1. Loebl, Eugen. 2. Political prisoners—Czechoslovakia—Biography. I. Title. BIP

Loewenberg, Jacob.

LOEWENBERG, Jacob. 191 B
Thrice-born; selected memories of an immigrant, by J. Loewenberg. New York, Hobbs, Dorman [1968] viii, 202 p. 22 cm. [B945.L484A3] 68-19635
I. Title.

Loewi, Otto.

LEMBECK, Fred. 615'.0924
Otto Loewi, Ein Lebensbild in Dokumenten. Biographische Dokumentation und Bibliographie. [Von] Fred Lembeck und Wolfgang Giere. Berlin. Heidelberg, New York, Springer-Verlag. 1968. xii, 241p. with illus. front. 25cm. Die Sammlung der biographischen Daten, das Anlegen der Dokumentation und der Bibliographie sind has Werk von Herrn W. Giere in Form einer medisinischen Doktorarbeit an der Universitat Tubingen. [R502.L57L4 1968] (B) 67-21938 9.00
1. Loewi, Otto. I. Giere, Wolfgang. II. Loewi, Otto. III. Title.

Loewy, Raymond Fernand, 1893-

LOEWY, Raymond Fernand, 1893- 745.2'092'4 B
Industrial design / Raymond Loewy. Woodstock, N.Y. : Overlook Press, 1979. p. cm. Includes index. [TS140.L63A34] 79-15104 ISBN 0-87951-098-6 : 45.00 ISBN 0-87951-102-8 deluxe ed. : 175.00
1. Loewy, Raymond Fernand, 1893- 2. Industrial designers—Biography. I. Title. BIP

Lofland, Luther, 1959-

†LOFLAND, Sandra Jean. 618.9'28'5300924 B
The sharing of my love / by Sandra Jean Lofland. St. Petersburg, Fla. : Johnny Reads, inc., c1977. 87 p. : ill. ; 23 cm. [RJ496.E6L63] 76-27966 5.95 ISBN 0-910812-23-3 pbk. : 2.95
1. Lofland, Luther, 1959- 2. Lofland, Sandra Jean. 3. Epilepsy in children—Biography. 4. Learning disabilities—Biography. 5. Mothers—Biography. I. Title. BIP

Logan. Benjamin, 1743-1802.

TALBERT, Charles Gano, 1912- 923.973
Benjamin Logan, Kentucky frontiersman. [Lexington] University of Kentucky Press [1962] ix, 332 p. 24 cm. Includes bibliographical references. [F454.L7813] 62-13458
1. Logan. Benjamin, 1743-1802. 2. Kentucky — Hist. — To 1792. I. Title.

Logan, Daniel,

LOGAN, Daniel, 1936- 133'.0924
The reluctant prophet. [1st ed.] Garden City, N.Y., Doubleday, 1968. 283 p. 22 cm. [BF1027.L6A3] 68-18087
I. Title.

Logan, George, 1753-1821.

TOLLES, Frederick Barnes, 1915- 923.273
George Logan of Philadelphia. New York, Oxford University Press, 1953. xix, 362p. illus., ports. 24cm. Bibliographical references included in 'Notes' (p. 320-350) [E302.6.L8T6] 53-9192
1. Logan, George, 1753-1821. I. Title. BIP

TOLLES, Frederick Barnes, 1915- 973.4'092'4 B
George Logan of Philadelphia [by] Frederick B. Tolles. New York, Arno Press, 1972 [c1953] xix, 362 p. illus. 23 cm. (The Right wing individualist tradition in America) Includes bibliographical references. [E302.6.L8T6 1972] 78-172236 ISBN 0-405-00444-3
1. Logan, George, 1753-1821. I. Title. II. Series.

Logan, Harvey, ca. 1867-ca. 1910.

WALLER, Brown. 364.1'0924 B
Last of the great Western train robbers. South Brunswick [N. J.] A. S. Barnes [1968] 272 p. illus., facsims., ports. 22 cm. Bibliography: p. 265-267. [F594.L8W3 1968] 67-18983
1. Logan, Harvey, ca. 1867-ca. 1910. I. Title.

Logan, James, 1674-1751.

TOLLES, Frederick Barnes, 1915- 974.8'02'0924 B
James Logan and the culture of provincial America / Frederick B. Tolles. Westport, Conn. : Greenwood Press, 1978, c1957. x, 228 p. ; 23 cm. Reprint of the ed. published by Little, Brown, Boston, in series: The library of American biography. Includes index. Bibliography: p. [215]-219. [F152.L82T64 1978] 77-27832 ISBN 0-313-20197-8 lib.bdg. : 18.00
1. Logan, James, 1674-1751. 2. Merchants—Pennsylvania—Biography. 3. Pioneers—Pennsylvania—Biography. 4. Pennsylvania—History—Colonial period, ca. 1600-1775. I. Title. BIP

Logan, John Alexander, 1826-1886.

JONES, James Pickett. 973.73 B
Black Jack: John A. Logan and southern Illinois in the Civil War era, by James P. Jones. Tallahassee, Florida State University, 1967. xvii, 314 p. maps, ports. 24 cm. (Florida State University studies, no. 51) Bibliography: p. [287]-294. [E664.L83J6] 67-64458
1. Logan, John Alexander, 1826-1886. I. Title. II. Series: Florida. State University, Tallahassee. Research Council. Florida State University studies, no. 51 BIP

JONES, James Pickett, 1931- v. 12
Black Jack; John A. Logan and southern Illinois in the Civil War era, by James P. Jones. Tallahassee, Florida State University, 1967. xvii, 314 p. illus. (Florida State University studies, 51) 68-94691
1. Logan, James Alexander, 1826-1886. I. Title.

JONES, James Pickett, 1931- v. 12
Black Jack; John A. Logan and southern Illinois in the Civil War era, by James P. Jones. Tallahassee, Florida State University, 1967. xvii, 314 p. illus. (Florida State University studies, 51) 68-94691
1. Logan, James Alexander, 1826-1886. I. Title.

LOGAN, Mary Simmerson (Cunningham) 1838-1923. 973.7'0924
Reminiscences of the Civil War and Reconstruction. Edited with an introd. by George Worthington Adams. Carbondale, Southern Illinois University Press [1970] xi, 324 p. illus., ports. 23 cm. An abridgement of the author's Reminiscences of a soldier's wife published in 1913. Includes bibliographical references. [E661.L84] 73-93878 ISBN 0-8093-0425-2 10.00
1. Logan, John Alexander, 1826-1886. 2. United States—History—Civil War, 1861-1865—Personal narratives. 3. United States—Politics and government—1865-1900. I. Adams, George Worthington, ed. II. Title. BIP

Logan, Joshua.

LOGAN, Joshua. 791'.092'4 B
Josh, my up and down, in and out life / by Joshua Logan. New York : Delacorte Press, c1976. 408 p. : ill. ; 24 cm. Includes index. [PN2287.L59A34] 75-44171 ISBN 0-440-04235-6 : 10.00
1. Logan, Joshua. I. Title.

LOGAN, Joshua. 791'.092'4 B
Movie stars, real people, and me / Joshua Logan. New York : Dell Pub. Co. Inc., 1979, c1978. 573 p. : ill. ; 18 cm. [PN2287.L59A36] pbk. : 2.75
1. Logan, Joshua. 2. Theatrical producers and directors — United States — Biography, 3. Moving-picture producers and directors -United States — Biographies. I. Title.
L.C. card no. for 1978 Delacorte Press ed.: 78-5657

LOGAN, Joshua. 791'.092'4 B
Movie stars, real people, and me / Joshua Logan. New York : Delacorte Press, c1978. xii, 368 p. : ill. ; 24 cm. Includes index. Chronology of plays and films written, produced, and/or directed by J. Logan: p. 351-358. [PN2287.L59A36] 78-5657 10.00
1. Logan, Joshua. 2. Theatrical producers and directors—United States—Biography. 3. Moving-picture producers and directors—United States—Biography. I. Title. BIP

Loginov, IUrii Nikolaevich.

CARR, Barbara Comyns. 327'.12'0924
Spy in the sun [by] Barbara Carr. London, New York, Allan Wingate-Baker Ltd., 1970. 255 p. 23 cm. [UB271.R92L54 1970] 75-513923 35/-
1. Loginov, IUrii Nikolaevich. I. Title.

Logue, Jeanne.

LOGUE, Jeanne. 636.089'092'4 B
The wonder of it all / Jeanne Logue. 1st ed. New York : Harper & Row, c1979. 207 p. : ill. ; 22 cm. [SF613.L6A33 1979] 78-20175 ISBN 0-06-012654-X : 8.95
1. Logue, Jeanne. 2. Veterinarians—New York (State)—Biography. 3. Veterinary medicine—New York (State) I. Title. BIP

Loher, George T.

LOHER, George T. 796.6 B
The wonderful ride : being the true journal of Mr. George T. Loher who in 1895 cycled from coast to coast on his Yellow Fellow wheel / with introd. and commentary by Mr. Loher's granddaughter Ellen Smith. 1st ed. San Francisco : Harper & Row, c1978. p. cm. "A Westword book." [GV1051.L63A38 1978] 78-3358 ISBN 0-06-250540-8 : 7.95
1. Loher, George T. 2. Cyclists—United States—Biography. 3. United States—Description and travel—1960- I. Title.

Loisy, Alfred Firmin,

RATTE, John,(1936- 282'.0922
Three modernists; Alfred Loisy, George Tyrrell, William L. Sullivan. New York, Sheed [1967] viii. 370p. 22cm. Bibl. [BX1396.R3] 67-13763 6.95
1. Loisy, Alfred Firmin, 2. Sullivan, William Laurence, 1872-1935. 3. Tyrell, George, 1861-1909. 4. Modernism—Catholic Church. I. Title.

Loman, Mini.

LOMAN, Mini. 248'.2'0924 B
Train of terror / Mini Loman. Old Tappan, N.J. : F. H. Revell Co., c1978. 63 p. ; 18 cm. (New life ventures) Autobiographical. [BR1725.L64A36] 77-26160 ISBN 0-8007-9005-7 pbk. : 0.95
1. Loman, Mini. 2. Christian biography—Netherlands. 3. Hijacking of trains—Netherlands. I. Title. BIP

Lombard, Carole, 1908-1942.

*MALTIN, Leonard. 791.43'028'0924
Carole Lombard / by Leonard Maltin. New York : Pyramid Publications, 1976. 159p. : ill., ports. ; 20 cm. (A Pyramid illustrated history of the movies.) Includes index. Bibliography: p. 143-144. [PN2287] ISBN 0-515-04085-1 pbk. : 1.75
1. Lombard, Carole, 1908-1942. I. Title. BIP

MORELLA, Joe. 791.43'028'0922 B
Cable & Lombard & Powell & Harlow / [by] Joe Morella & Edward Z. Epstein. 1st British ed. London : W. H. Allen, 1976. 204 p., [8] p. of plates : ill., ports. ; 23 cm. [PN1998.A2M56 1976] 76-383446 ISBN 0-491-01975-0 : £3.50
1. Gable, Clark, 1901-1960. 2. Lombard, Carole, 1908-1942. 3. Powell, William, 1892- 4. Harlow, Jean, 1911-1937. 5. Moving-picture actors and actresses—United States—Biography. I. Epstein, Edward Z., joint author. II. Title.

SWINDELL, Larry. 791.43'028'0924 B
Screwball : the life of Carole Lombard / by Larry Swindell. New York : Morrow, 1975. 324 p., [14] leaves of plates : ill. ; 24 cm. Includes index. Filobraphy: p. [305]-314. [PN2287.L625S9] 75-12536 ISBN 0-688-00287-0 : 8.95
1. Lombard, Carole, 1908-1942. I. Title.

Lombardi, Vince.

FLYNN, George L. 796.33'2'0924 B
The Vince Lombardi scrapbook / by George L. Flynn. New York : Grosset & Dunlap, c1976. 224 p. : ill. ; 28 cm. Includes index. [GV939.L6F55] 76-556 ISBN 0-448-12401-7. 6.95
1. Lombardi, Vince. 2. Football coaches—United States—Biography. I. Title.

KLEIN, Dave. 796.332'0924 B
The Vince Lombardi story. New York, Lion Books, 1971. xix, 154 p. ports. 22 cm. [GV939.L6K55 1971] 74-170971 ISBN 0-87460-256-4 5.67
1. Lombardi, Vince. I. Title. BIP

KRAMER, Jerry, 1936- 796.332'0924 B
Lombardi: winning is the only thing, edited by Jerry Kramer. New York [Maddick Manuscripts Inc.; distributed by] World Pub. Co. [1970] 173 p. illus., ports. 22 cm. "Consists of some two dozen interviews [mostly conducted by J. Kramer] with people who knew Vince." [GV939.L6K7] 74-128488 6.95
1. Lombardi, Vince. I. Title.

WELLS, Robert W. 796.33'2'0924 B
Lombardi: his life and times, by Robert W. Wells. [1st ed.] Madison, Wis., Wisconsin House [1971] 207 p. illus. 24 cm. [GV939.L6W4] 75-178223 7.95
1. Lombardi, Vince.

Lombardi, Vince—Juvenile literature.

ETTER, Les. 796.33'2'0924 B
Vince Lombardi: football legend. Illustrated by Herman Vestal. Champaign, Ill., Garrard Pub. Co. [1975] 96 p. illus. (part col.) 24 cm. A brief biography of the football coach who turned Wisconsin's Green Bay Packers into a virtually unbeatable team. [GV939.L6E88] 92 74-18076 ISBN 0-8116-6670-0 3.28 (lib. bdg.)
1. Lombardi, Vince—Juvenile literature. 2. Football—Juvenile literature. 3. Football coaching—Juvenile literature. I. Vestal, Herman B., illus. II. Title.

SCHOOR, Gene. 796.33'2'0924 B
Football's greatest coach: Vince Lombardi. New York, Pocket Books [1975, c1974] 229 p. illus. 18 cm. A biography of the head coach whose molding of the Green Bay Packer's from a losing Squad into a championship team made his name a football legend. [GV939.L6S36 1975] 92 74-1506 ISBN 0-671-80130-9. 1.50 (pbk.)
1. Lombardi, Vince—Juvenile literature. 2. Football—Juvenile literature. I. Title. BIP

SCHOOR, Gene. 796.33'2'0924 B
Football's greatest coach: Vince Lombardi. [1st ed.] Garden City, N.Y., Doubleday [1974] 204 p. illus. 22 cm. A biography of the head coach whose molding of the Green Bay Packers from a losing squad into a championship team made his name a football legend. [GV939.L6S36 1974] 92 74-1506 ISBN 0-385-08513-3. 4.95; 5.70 (lib. bdg.)
1. Lombardi, Vince—Juvenile literature. 2. Football—Juvenile literature. I. Title.

ZALEWSKI, Ted. 796.33'2'0924 B
Vince Lombardi—he is still with us. Illustrated by John Nelson. [Mankato, Minn., Creative Education; distributed by Childrens Press, Chicago, 1973, c1974] 30 p. illus. (part col.) 25 cm. (Creative's Superstars) "Prepared for the publisher by Educreative Systems, inc." A brief biography of the football coach who turned Wisconsin's Green Bay Packers into a virtually unbeatable team. [GV939.L6Z34] 92 73-10289 ISBN 0-87191-261-9 4.95
1. Lombardi, Vince—Juvenile literature. I. Nelson, John, 1928- illus. II. Educreative Systems, inc. III. Title.

Lombardo, Guy, 1902-

HERNDON, Booton. 927.8
The sweetest music this side of heaven; the Guy Lombardo story. [1st ed.] New York, McGraw-Hill [1964] 234 p. 22 cm. [ML422.L76H47] 64-25172
1. Lombardo, Guy, 1902- I. Title.

LOMBARDO, Guy, 1902- 785'.092'4 B
Auld acquaintance / by Guy Lombardo

with Jack Altshul ; introd. by Jules Stein. 1st ed. Garden City, N.Y. : Doubleday, 1975. xii, 295 p., [18] leaves of plates : ill. ; 22 cm. [ML422.L76A3] 73-15353 ISBN 0-385-02863-6 : 8.95
1. Lombardo, Guy, 1902- 2. Musicians—Correspondence, reminiscences, etc. I. Altshul, Jack, joint author. II. Title.

Lombardo Toledano, Vicente 1894-

MILLON, Robert Paul 972.0820924
Vicente Lombardo Toledano, Mexican Marxist. Chapel Hill, Univ. of N. C. Pr. [1966] 222p. port. 24cm. Bibl. [F1234.L84M5] 66-19276 6.00
1. Lombardo Toledano, Vicente 1894- I. Title.

Lomonosov, Mikhail Vasil'evich, 1711-1765.

MENSHUTKIN, Boris 928.917
Nikolaevich, 1874-1938.
Russia's Lomonosov, chemist, courtier, physicist, poet. [Translated from the Russian by Jeanette Eyre Thal and Edward J. Webster under the direction of W. Chapin Huntington] Princeton, Princeton University Press, 1952. viii, 208 p. illus., port., facsims. 23 cm. "Published for the Russian Translation Project of the American Council of Learned Societies." Translation of Zhizneopisanie Mikhaila Vasil'evicha Lomonosova. [PG3316.Z6M43] 52-5826
1. Lomonosov, Mikhail Vasil'evich, 1711-1765. I. Title. BIP

London

STONE, William, 1857- 920
The squire of Piccadilly; memories of William Stone in conversation with Henry Baerlein. London, New York, Jarrolds [1951] 184 p. illus. 22 cm. [CT788.S795A3] 52-35079
1. London — Soc. life & cust. I. Title.

London—Biography—Addresses, essays, lectures.

WHERE I was young 942.1'082'0922
: memories of London childhoods / [edited by] Valerie Jenkins ; with line drawings by George Murray. London : Hart-Davis MacGibbon, 1976. vi, 161 p. : ill. ; 25 cm. Based on a series of interviews published in the Evening standard. Ill. on lining papers. [DA676.8.A1W47 1976] 77-364079 ISBN 0-246-10873-8 : £4.95
1. London—Biography—Addresses, essays, lectures. I. Title.

London—Dwellings.

RICKARDS, Maurice, 914.21'04
1919-
Where they lived in London. New York, Taplinger [1972] 104 p. illus. 22 cm. [DA689.H48R5 1972b] 72-145542 ISBN 0-8008-8245-8 7.95
1. London—Dwellings. 2. Biography. I. Title.

London. East End.

FISHMAN, William J. 914.21'06'924
Jewish radicals : from Czarist stetl to London ghetto / by William J. Freeman. 1st American ed. New York : Pantheon Books, [1975] c1974. xvi, 336 p., [8] leaves of plates : ill. ; 22 cm. Includes index. Bibliography: p. [325]-327. [DS135.E5F5 1975] 74-26194 ISBN 0-394-49764-3 : 12.95
1. London. East End. 2. Liebermann, Aaron Samuel, 1844-1880. 3. Rocker, Rudolf, 1873-1958. 4. Jews in London. 5. Radicalism—Jews. I. Title.

London—Intellectual life.

BELL, Quentin. 820.9'009'12
Bloomsbury. New York, Basic Books [1969, c1968] 126 p. illus., ports. 23 cm. Includes bibliographical references. [PR471.B4 1969] 69-16313
1. London—Intellectual life. 2. Authors, English—20th century—Biography. I. Title.

EDEL, Leon, 1907- 942.1'082
Bloomsbury : a house of lions / Leon Edel. 1st ed. Philadelphia : Lippincott, c1979. 288 p., [4] leaves of plates : ill. ; 24 cm. Includes index. Bibliography: p. 275-278. [DA688.E3] 79-4341 ISBN 0-397-01043-5 : 12.95
1. London—Intellectual life. 2. London—Biography. 3. Bloomsbury group. I. Title. BIP

GADD, David. 914.21'03'820922
The loving friends : a portrait of Bloomsbury / David Gadd. New York : Harcourt Brace Jovanovich, [1975] c1974. xii, 210 p., [8] leaves of plates : ill. ; 21 cm. Includes index. Bibliography: p. 201-203. [DA688.G23 1975] 74-26596 ISBN 0-15-154740-8 : 6.95
1. London—Intellectual life. 2. Authors, English—20th century—Biography. I. Title.

London, Jack, 1876-1916.

BAMFORD, Georgia 818'.5'209 B
(Loring)
The mystery of Jack London, some of his friends, also a few letters, a reminiscence. With illus. by the author and also from photos. [Folcroft, Pa.] Folcroft Library Editions, 1973 [c1931] p. [PS3523.O46Z6 1973] 73-15997 10.00
1. London, Jack, 1876-1916. I. Title.

DAY, Arthur Grove, 818'.5'209 B
1904-
Jack London in the South Seas, by A. Grove Day. New York, Four Winds Press [1971] xi, 167 p. illus., map, ports. 24 cm. A biography of the well-known author that concentrates on his 1907-1909 South Sea voyage. [PS3523.O46Z622] 92 70-142529
1. London, Jack, 1876-1916. I. Title.

FONER, Philip Sheldon, 928.1
1910-
Jack London, American rebel. [rev. ed.] New York, Citadel Press [1964] iv, 155 p. 21 cm. First ed., 1947, included selections from London's social writings. Bibliography: p. [152]-155. [PS3523.O46Z624 1964] 64-2837
1. London, Jack, 1876-1916. I. Title.

FRANCHERE, Ruth. FIC
Jack London; the pursuit of a dream. New York, Crowell [1962] 264 p. 21 cm. [PS3523.O46Z625] 813.5 62-16542
1. London, Jack, 1876-1916.

*FREEMAN, A. W., 1921- 813'.5 [B]
A search for Jack London. Chicago, Ill., Adams Press, 1973. 81 p. 22 cm. [PS3523]
1. London, Jack, 1876-1916. I. Title.

LONDON, Joan. 813'.5'2
Jack London and his times; an unconventional biography. Seattle, University of Washington Press [1968] xvii, 385 p. port. 23 cm. (Americana library) Reprint of the 1939 ed., with a new introd. by the author. [PS3523.O46Z75 1968] 68-5816 6.95
1. London, Jack, 1876-1916. 2. United States—History—1898- I. Title. BIP

O'CONNOR, Richard, 1915- 928.1
Jack London, a biography. [1st ed.] Boston, Little, Brown [1964] x, 430 p. ports. 22 cm. Bibliography: p. [411]-414. [PS3523.O46Z84] 64-21486
1. London, Jack, 1876-1916.

London, Jack, 1876-1916—Biography.

BARLTROP, Robert. 818'.5'209 B
Jack London : the man, the writer, the rebel / Robert Barltrop. London : Pluto Press ; [New York : available from Urizen Books], 1976[i.e.1977] 206 p., [7] leaves of plates : ill. ; 23 cm. Includes bibliographical references and index. [PS3523.O46Z6116] 77-357097 ISBN 0-904383-18-0 : 10.00
1. London, Jack, 1876-1916—Biography. 2. Authors, American—20th century—Biography.

RATHER, Lois, 1905- 818'.5'209 B
Jack London, 1905 / Lois Rather. Oakland, Calif. : Rather Press, 1974. 132 p. ; 24 cm. "One hundred and fifty copies, of which this is no. 149." Includes bibliographical references and index. [PS3523.O46Z864] 75-307502
1. London, Jack, 1876-1916—Biography. 2. London, Jack, 1876-1916—Relationship with women—Charmian (Kittredge) London. 3. London, Charmian (Kittredge) I. Title.

SINCLAIR, Andrew. 818'.5'209 B
Jack : a biography of Jack London / Andrew Sinclair. 1st ed. New York : Harper & Row, c1977. xv, 297 p. : ill. ; 25 cm. Includes index. Bibliography: p. 281-283. [PS3523.O46Z876] 76-57899 ISBN 0-06-013899-8 : 12.95
1. London, Jack, 1876-1916—Biography. 2. Novelists, American—20th century—Biography. I. Title. BIP

STONE, Irving, 1903- 818'.5'209 B
Irving Stone's Jack London, his life, Sailor on horseback (a biography), and twenty-eight selected Jack London stories. 1st ed. Garden City, N.Y. : Doubleday, 1977. xi, 777 p. ; 22 cm. Irving Stone's Jack London originally published in 1938 under title: Sailor on horseback; the biography of Jack London. [PS3523.O46Z9 1977] 76-53418 ISBN 0-385-12797-9 : 12.95
1. London, Jack, 1876-1916—Biography. 2. Novelists, American—20th century—Biography. I. London, Jack, 1876-1916. Selected works. 1977. II. Title. III. Title: Jack London, his life (a biography), and selected Jack London stories.

London, Jack, 1876-1916—Iconography.

KINGMAN, Russ. 818'.5'209 B
A pictorial life of Jack London / Russ Kingman ; foreword by Irving Stone. New York : Crown Publishers, 1980, c1979. p. cm. Includes index. [PS3523.O46Z665 1979] 79-17998 ISBN 0-517-53163-1 : 14.95
1. London, Jack, 1876-1916—Iconography. 2. Authors, American—20th century—Biography. I. Title.

London, Jack, 1876-1916—Relationship with women—Charmian (Kittredge) London.

RATHER, Lois, 1905- 818'.5'209 B
Jack London, 1905 / Lois Rather. Oakland, Calif. : Rather Press, 1974. 132 p. ; 24 cm. "One hundred and fifty copies, of which this is no. 149." Includes bibliographical references and index. [PS3523.O46Z864] 75-307502
1. London, Jack, 1876-1916—Biography. 2. London, Jack, 1876-1916—Relationship with women—Charmian (Kittredge) London. 3. London, Charmian (Kittredge) I. Title.

London, Ont. University of Western Ontario. — Hist.

FOX, William Sherwood, 378.7127'3
1878-
Sherwood Fox of Western, reminiscences. Toronto, Burns and MacEachern, 1964. xvii, 250 p. illus., ports. 24 cm. [LE3.W42F68] 65-66419
1. London, Ont. University of Western Ontario. — Hist. I. Title.

London—Social life and customs.

BYRD, William, 1674-1744. 923.273
The London diary, 1717-1721, and other writings. Edited by Louis B. Wright and Marion Tinling. New York, Oxford University Press, 1958. vi, 647 p. illus., port. 24 cm. "The diary ... is transcribed from a shorthand notebook (Mss 5:1B 9964:1) in the library of the Virginia Historical Society." Contents.Contents.—The life of William Byrd of Virginia, 1674-1744.—The secret diary of William Byrd of Westover from December 13, 1717 to May 19, 1721.—History of the dividing line.—A journey to the land of Eden.—A progress to the mines. Bibliographical footnotes. [F229.B9685] 57-10389
1. London—Social life and customs. 2. Virginia—Social life and customs. I. Wright, Louis Booker, 1899- ed. II. Tinling, Marion Rose Goble, 1904- ed. III. Title.

London Township, Ont.—Biography.

ROSSER, Frederick T. 971.3'26
London Township pioneers, including a few families from adjoining areas / by Frederick T. Rosser. Belleville, Ont. : Mika Pub. Co., 1975. 237 p. : ill. ; 24 cm. Includes index. [F1059.5.L6R67] 75-328685 ISBN 0-919302-95-5
1. London Township, Ont.—Biography. 2. London Township, Ont.—Genealogy. 3. London Township, Ont.—History. I. Title.

Londonberry, probert Stewart, 2d marquis of, 1769-1822.

BARTLETT, 942.0730924 (B)
Christopher John.
Castlereagh [by] C. J. Bartlett. New York, Scribner [1967, c1966] ix. 292 p. illus. ports. 22 cm. "Bibliographical note": p. 281-285. [DA522.L8B3 1967] 67-16525
1. Londonberry, probert Stewart, 2d marquis of, 1769-1822. I. Title. BIP

DERRY, John 941.07'3'0924 B
Wesley.
Castlereagh / John W. Derry. London : A. Lane, 1976. 247 p. ; 23 cm. (British political biography) Includes index. Bibliography: p. [239]-241. [DA522.L8D47 1976b] 76-362048 ISBN 0-7139-0838-6 : £7.50. ISBN 0-7139-0839-4 pbk.
1. Londonderry, Robert Stewart, 2d Marquis of, 1769-1822. I. Title. BIP

DERRY, John 941.07'3'0924 B
Wesley.
Castlereagh / John W. Derry. New York : St. Martin's Press, 1976. viii, 247 p. ; 23 cm. (British political biography) Includes index. Bibliography: p. [239]-241. [DA522.L8D47 1976] 75-29820 15.00
1. Londonderry, Robert Stewart, 2d Marquis of, 1769-1822. 2. Great Britain—Politics and government—1789-1820. 3. Ireland—Politics and government—1760-1820. I. Title.

Londonerry, Frances Anne Emily (Vane-Tempest) Vane, marchioness of, 1800-1865.

FRANCES Anne: v. 12
the life and times of Frances Anne, marchioness of Londonderry, and her husband, Charles, third marques of Londonderry. London, Macmillan. New York, St. Martin's Press, 1958. 315p. illus. 23cm.
1. Londonerry, Frances Anne Emily (Vane-Tempest) Vane, marchioness of, 1800-1865. 2. Londonderry, Charles William Vane, 3d marquis of, 1778-1854. I. Londonderry, Edith Helen (Chaplin) Vane-Tempest—Stewart, marchioness of, 1878-

Lonergan, Bernard J. F.

TRACY, David. 230.2'0924
The achievement of Bernard Lonergan. [New York] Herder and Herder [1970] xv, 302 p. 22 cm. Bibliography: p. 270-287. [BX4705.L7133T7] 79-87773 9.50
1. Lonergan, Bernard J. F. I. Title. BIP

Long, Crawford Williamson, 1815-1878.

RADFORD, Ruby 617'.0924 B
Lorraine, 1891-
Prelude to fame; Crawford Long's discovery of anaesthesia, by Ruby L. Radford. Los Altos, Calif., Geron-X [1969] 175 p. ports. 22 cm. Bibliography: p. [173]-175. [R154.L72R3] 74-81776 4.95
1. Long, Crawford Williamson, 1815-1878. I. Title. BIP

Long, Huey Pierce, 1893-1935.

BEALS, Carleton, 976.306'0924 B
1893-
The story of Huey P. Long. Westport, Conn., Greenwood Press [1971, c1935] 414 p. 23 cm. [E748.L86B4 1971] 75-136054 ISBN 0-8371-5204-6
1. Long, Huey Pierce, 1893-1935. 2.

Louisiana—Politics and government—1865-1950. I. Title. **BIP**

DETHLOFF, Henry C., comp. 976.3'06'0924
Huey P. Long: Southern demagogue or American democrat? Edited with an introd. by Henry C. Dethloff. Boston, Heath [1967] viii, 115 p. 24 cm. (Problems in American civilization) Bibliography: p. [113]-115. [E748.L86D4] 67-8164
1. Long, Huey Pierce, 1893 1935. I. Title. II. Series.

GRAHAM, Hugh Davis, comp. 976.3'06'0924 B
Huey Long. Englewood Cliffs, N.J., Prentice-Hall [1970] vii, 184 p. 21 cm. (Great lives observed) (A Spectrum book.) Includes bibliographical references. [E748.L86G7] 77-96968
1. Long, Huey Pierce, 1893-1935. **BIP**

LONG, Huey Pierce, 1893-1935 923.273
Every man a king; the autobiography of Huey P. Long. Introd. by T. Harry Williams. Chicago, Quadrangle [c.1933-1964] xxviii, 348p. illus. 22cm. (QP8) Bibl. 64-2488 2.25 pap.,
1. Louisiana—Pol. & govt.—1865- I. Title.

LONG, Huey Pierce, 1893-1935 923.273
Every man a king; the autobiography of Huey P. Long. Introd. by T. Harry Williams [Gloucester, Mass., P. Smith, 1966, c.1933-1964] xxviii, 348p. illus. 22cm. (Quandrangle paperbacks, QP8 rebound) Bibl. [E748.L86L8 1964] 4.25
1. Louisiana—Pol. & govt.—1865- I. Title.

OPOTOWSKY, Stan. 923.273
The Longs of Louisiana. [1st ed.] New York, Dutton, 1960. 271 p. ports. 21 cm. [E748.L86O6] 60-6001
1. Long, Huey Pierce, 1893-1935. 2. Long family. I. Title.

WILLIAMS, Thomas Harry, 1909- 976.3'06'0924 B
Huey Long [by] T. Harry Williams. [1st ed.] New York, Knopf, 1969. xiv, 884, xxii p. illus., facsims., ports. 25 cm. Includes bibliographical references. [E748.L86W48 1969] 69-10692 12.50
1. Long, Huey Pierce, 1893-1935. **BIP**

Long Island—Biography.

DYSON, Verne, 1879- 920.0747'21
The human story of Long Island. Port Washington, N.Y., I. J. Friedman, 1969. 139 p. 22 cm. (Empire State historical publications series, no. 78) [F127.L8D92] 76-8295
1. Long Island—Biography. I. Title. II. Series: Empire State historical publication, no. 78 **BIP**

Long, Jane Herbert (Wilkinson) 1798-1880.

TURNER, Martha Anne. 917.64'03 B
The life and times of Jane Long. [Waco, Tex., Texian Press, 1969] xiv, 193 p. illus., map, ports. (1 col.) 24 cm. Bibliography: p. [176]-184. [CT275.L656T8] 69-20090 7.50
1. Long, Jane Herbert (Wilkinson) 1798-1880. I. Title.

Long, John Davis,

LONG, John Davis, 1838-1915. 923.273
Journal. Edited by Margaret Long. Rindge, N. H., R. R. Smith, 1956. ix, 363p. ports., facsims., geneal. table. 25cm. Bibliography: p. 350-351. [E664.L84A3] 56-11747
I. Title.

Long, Mary Ann, 1946-1959.

ATLANTA. Our Lady of Perpetual Help Free Cancer Home. 001.2
A memoir of Mary Ann, by the Dominican nuns of Our Lady of Perpetual Help Home, Atlanta, Georgia. Introd. by Flannery O Connor. New York, Farrar, Straus and Cudahy [1961] 134p. 21cm. [CT275.L663A8] 61-13682
1. Long, Mary Ann, 1946-1959. I. O'Connor, Flannery, ed. II. Title.

ATLANTA. Our lady of Perpetual Help Home. 920.7
A memoir of Mary Ann, by the Dominican nuns of Our Lady of Perpetual Help Home, Atlanta, Georgia. Introd. by Flannery O'Connor. New York, Dell [1962, c.1961] 128p. 17cm. (Chapel Bk. 5551) .40 pap.,
1. Long, Mary Ann, 1946-1959. I. O'Connor, Flannery, ed. II. Title.

Long, Mason,

LONG, Mason, 1842-1903. 248'.2'0924
The life of Mason Long, the converted gambler. Being a record of his experience as a white slave; a soldier in the Union Army; a professional gambler; a patron of the turf; a variety theater and minstrel manager; and, finally, a convert to the Murphy cause and to the Gospel of Christ. 4th ed. Fort Wayne, Ind., 1883. 280p. illus., ports. 18cm. [BV4935.L6A3 1883] 59-58984
I. Title.

Long, Stephen Harriman, 1784-1864.

LONG, Stephen Harriman, 1784-1864. 917.7'04'2
The northern expeditions of Stephen H. Long : the journals of 1817 and 1823 and related documents / edited by Lucile M. Kane, June D. Holmquist, and Carolyn Gilman. St. Paul : Minnesota Historical Society Press, 1978. xii, 407 p. : ill. ; 24 cm. (Publications of the Minnesota Historical Society) "The journal of James E. Colhoun, 1823": p. [269]-327. Includes bibliographical references and index. [F597.L83 1978] 78-5166 ISBN 0-87351-129-8 : 17.50
1. Long, Stephen Harriman, 1784-1864. 2. Mississippi River—Description and travel. 3. Northwest, Old—Description and travel. 4. Minnesota—Description and travel—To 1858. 5. Great Lakes—Description and travel. 6. Explorers—United States—Biography. I. Kane, Lucile M. II. Holmquist, June Drenning. III. Gilman, Carolyn, 1954- IV. Colhoun, James Edward. The journal of James E. Colhoun. 1978. V. Title. **BIP**

Longacre, Charles Smull, 1871-1958.

KRUM, Nathaniel. 922.673
Charles S. Longacre, champion of religious liberty. Washington, Review and Herald Pub. Association [1959] 123p. illus. 21cm. [BX6193.L63K7] 59-4296
1. Longacre, Charles Smull, 1871-1958. I. Title.

Longden, Johnny, 1910-

BECKWITH, Brainerd Kellogg, 1903- 798'.43'0924 B
The Longden legend [by] B. K. Beckwith. South Brunswick, A. S. Barnes [1973] 235 p. illus. 27 cm. [SF336.L56B43] 72-5185 ISBN 0-498-01242-5 9.95
1. Longden, Johnny, 1910- I. Title. **BIP**

Longfellow, Henry Wadsworth,

LONGFELLOW, Henry Wadsworth, 1807-1882. 816'.3
The letters of Henry Wadsworth Longfellow. Edited by Andrew Hilen. Cambridge, Belknap Press of Harvard University Press, 1966 [i.e. 1967]- v. illus., facsims., ports. 24 cm. Contents.Contents.—v. 1. 1814-1836.—v. 2. 1837-1843.—v. 3. 1844-1856.—v. 4. 1857-1865. Includes bibliographies. [PS2281.A3H5] 66-18248
I. Hilen, Andrew R., 1913- ed. II. Title. **BIP**

Longfellow, Henry Wadsworth — Juvenile literature.

HOLBERG, Ruth (Langland) 1891- 920
An American bard; the story of Henry Wadsworth Longfellow. Illus. by Aldren A. Watson, New York, Crowell [c.1963] 168p. illus. 21cm. 63-15090 3.00
1. Longfellow, Henry Wadsworth—Juvenile literature. I. Title.

HOLBERG, Ruth (Langland) 1891- j 92
An American bard; the story of Henry Wadsworth Longfellow. Illustrated by Aldren A. Watson. New York Crowell [1963] 168 p. illus. 21 cm. [PS2281.H6] 63-15090
1. Longfellow, Henry Wadsworth — Juvenile literature. I. Title. **BIP**

Longfellow, Henry Wadsworth, 1807-1882.

ARVIN, Newton, 1900-1963. 811'.3
Longfellow, his life and work / Newton Arvin. Westport, Conn. : Greenwood Press, 1977. 338 p. : port. ; 23 cm. Reprint of the 1963 ed. published by Little, Brown, Boston. Includes index. [PS2281.A6 1977] 77-1342 ISBN 0-8371-9505-5 lib.bdg. : 20.00
1. Longfellow, Henry Wadsworth, 1807-1882. 2. Poets, American—19th century—Biography. I. Title.

AUSTIN, George Lowell, 1849-1893. 811'3 B
Henry Wadsworth Longfellow; his life, his works, his friendships. [Folcroft, Pa.] Folcroft Library Editions, 1973. p. Reprint of the 1883 ed. published by Lee and Shepard, Boston. "Longfellow bibliography": p. [PS2281.A7 1973] 73-12138 ISBN 0-8414-2889-1 (lib. bdg.)
1. Longfellow, Henry Wadsworth, 1807-1882.

AUSTIN, George Lowell, 1849-1893. 811'.3 B
Henry Wadsworth Longfellow, his life, his works, his friendships / by George Lowell Austin. New ed. Folcroft, Pa. : Folcroft Library Editions, 1974. p. cm. Reprint of the 1888 ed. published by Lee and Shepard, Boston. Includes index. Bibliography: p. [PS2281.A7 1974] 74-32205 ISBN 0-8414-2859-X lib. bdg. : 40.00
1. Longfellow, Henry Wadsworth, 1807-1882. I. Title.

HIGGINSON, Thomas Wentworth, 1823-1911. 811'.3 B
Henry Wadsworth Longfellow. [Folcroft, Pa.] Folcroft Library Editions, 1973 [c1902] p. Reprint of the ed. published by Houghton Mifflin, Boston, in series: Riverside popular biographies, and in series: Great American authors. Bibliography: p. [PS2281.H5 1973b] 73-12598 ISBN 0-8414-4740-3 (lib. bdg.)
1. Longfellow, Henry Wadsworth, 1807-1882.

IANNETTA, Sabatino. 811'.3
Henry W. Longfellow and Montecassino, his Rhode Island friendship, his birthplace. New York, Haskell House Publishers, 1973. 136 p. illus. 23 cm. Reprint of the 1938 ed. Includes bibliographical references. [PS2284.I3 1973] 72-10002 ISBN 0-8383-1678-6 8.95
1. Longfellow, Henry Wadsworth, 1807-1882. 2. Monte Cassino (Benedictine monastery) I. Title. **BIP**

JONES, Herbert Granville, 1883- 928.1
The amazing Mr. Longfellow: little known facts about a well-known poet. Pen sketches by the author. [150th Longfellow anniversary ed.] Portland, Me., Longfellow Press [1957] 133p. illus. 21cm. [PS2281.J64] 57-4143
1. Longfellow, Henry Wadsworth, 1807-1882. I. Title.

KENNEDY, William Sloane, 1850-1929. 811'.3
Henry W. Longfellow: biography, anecdote, letters, criticism. [Folcroft, Pa.] Folcroft Library Editions, 1973. 368 p. illus. 20 cm. Reprint of the 1882 ed. published by M. King, Cambridge, Mass. Bibliography: p. 353-362. [PS2281.K4 1973] 73-12452 12.75
1. Longfellow, Henry Wadsworth, 1807-1882.

LONGFELLOW, Fanny (Appleton) 1817-1861. 928.1
Mrs. Longfellow: selected letters and journals, edited by Edward Wagenknecht. [1st ed.] New York, Longmans, Green, 1956. xi. 235p. illus., ports. 22cm. [PS2281.L54] 56-12080
1. Longfellow, Henry Wadsworth, 1807-1882. I. Wagenknecht, Edward Charles, 1900- ed. II. Title.

PEARE, Catherine Owens. 928.1
Henry Wadsworth Longfellow, his life; illustrated by Margaret Ayer. [1st ed.] New York, Holt [1953] 116 p. illus. 21 cm. [PS2281.P4] 53-8972
1. Longfellow, Henry Wadsworth, 1807-1882.

PEARE, Catherine Owens. 811'.3 B
Henry Wadsworth Longfellow, his life; illustrated by Margaret Ayer. [1st ed.] New York, Holt [1953] 116 p. illus. 21 cm. A biography of the poet whose poems Hiawatha, Miles Standish, The Children's Hour, Evangeline, and the Village Blacksmith have remained favorites for Americans of all ages. [PS2281.P4] 92 AC 68
1. Longfellow, Henry Wadsworth, 1807-1882. I. Ayer, Margaret, illus. II. Title.

ROBERTSON, Eric Sutherland. 811'.3 B
Life of Henry Wadsworth Longfellow, by Eric S. Robertson. Port Washington, N.Y., Kennikat Press [1972] 177, xii p. 21 cm. Reprint of the 1887 ed. "Bibliography by John P. Anderson": p. [i]-xii. [PS2281.R6 1972] 70-160775 ISBN 0-8046-1607-8
1. Longfellow, Henry Wadsworth, 1807-1882. I. Title.

ROBERTSON, Eric Sutherland. 811'.3 B
Life of Henry Wadsworth Longfellow, by Eric S. Robertson. [Folcroft, Pa.] Folcroft Library Editions, 1973. p. Reprint of the 1887 ed. published by W. Scott, London, in the Great writers series. "Bibliography, by John P. Anderson": p. [PS2281.R6 1973] 73-12139 7.75
1. Longfellow, Henry Wadsworth, 1807-1882. I. Title. **BIP**

SMEATON, William Henry Oliphant, 1856-1914. 811'.3
Longfellow & his poetry. London, G. G. Harrap, 1913. [New York, AMS Press, 1972] 143 p. front. 19 cm. (Poetry and life series) Bibliography: p. [144] [PS2281.S6 1972] 76-120966 ISBN 0-404-52533-4 8.00
1. Longfellow, Henry Wadsworth, 1807-1882. I. Title. II. Series. **BIP**

THOMPSON, Lawrance Roger, 1906- 811'.3 B
Young Longfellow (1807-1843) by Lawrence Thompson New York, Octagon Books [1969, c1938] xxiv, 443 p. illus., facsim., ports. 25 cm. Bibliographical references included in "Notes" (p. 343-423) [PS2282.T5 1969] 78-76011
1. Longfellow, Henry Wadsworth, 1807-1882. I. Title. **BIP**

UNDERWOOD, Francis Henry, 1825-1894. 811'.3 B
Henry Wadsworth Longfellow; a biographical sketch. [Folcroft, Pa.] Folcroft Library Editions, 1973 [c1882] p. Reprint of the ed. published by J. R. Osgood, Boston. [PS2281.U5 1973b] 73-12589 9.75
1. Longfellow, Henry Wadsworth, 1807-1882. 2. Wadsworth, Peleg, 1748-1829. **BIP**

UNDERWOOD, Francis Henry, 1825-1894. 811'.3 B
Henry Wadsworth Longfellow; a biographical sketch. New York, Haskell House Publishers, 1973. xvi, 303 p. illus. 23 cm. Reprint of the 1882 ed. Bibliography: p. 287-302. [PS2281.U5 1973] 72-1974 ISBN 0-8383-1449-X 12.95
1. Longfellow, Henry Wadsworth, 1807-1882. 2. Wadsworth, Peleg, 1748-1829.

WAGENKNECHT, Edward Charles, 1900- 811.3
Henry Wadsworth Longfellow: portrait of an American humanist [by] Edward Wagenknecht. New York, Oxford University Press, 1966. xi, 252 p. port. 22 cm. Bibliography: p. 237-241. [PS2281.W16 1966] 66-13267
1. Longfellow, Henry Wadsworth, 1807-1882.

WILLIAMS, Cecil Brown, 1901- 928.1
Henry Wadsworth Longfellow. New York, Twayne [1965, c.1964] 221p. 21cm.

(Twayne's U.S. authors ser., 68) Bibl. [PS2281.W47] 64-20718 3.50 bds.,
1. Longfellow, Henry Wadsworth, 1807-1882. I. Title. BIP

Longfellow, Henry Wadsworth, 1807-1882—Biography.

NORTON, Charles Eliot, 811'.3 B 1827-1908.
Henry Wadsworth Longfellow : a sketch of his life / by Charles Eliot Norton ; together with Longfellow's chief autobiographical poems. Norwood, Pa. : Norwood Editions, 1975 [c1906] vii, 120 p., [2] leaves of plates : ports ; 23 cm. Reprint of the 1907 ed. published by Houghton, Mifflin, Boston. [PS2281.N6 1975] 75-33888 ISBN 0-88305-453-1 lib. bdg. : 15.00
1. Longfellow, Henry Wadsworth, 1807-1882—Biography. I. Longfellow, Henry Wadsworth, 1807-1882.

Longfellow, Henry Wadsworth, 1807-1882—Biography—Juvenile literature.

CODY, Sherwin, 1868- 811'.3'09 1959.
Four American poets : William Cullen Bryant, Henry Wadsworth Longfellow, John Greenleaf Whittier, Oliver Wendell Holmes : a book for young Americans / by Sherwin Cody. Folcroft, Pa. : Folcroft Library Editions, 1977. p. cm. Reprint of the 1899 ed. published by American Book Co., New York, which was issued as v. 4 of The Four great Americans series. Essays discussing the life and work of four major American poets of the nineteenth century. [PS96.C57 1977] 920 77-24729 ISBN 0-8414-1811-X lib. bdg. : 25.00
1. Bryant, William Cullen, 1794-1878—Biography—Juvenile literature. 2. Longfellow, Henry Wadsworth, 1807-1882—Biography—Juvenile literature. 3. Whittier, John Greenleaf, 1807-1892—Biography—Juvenile literature. 4. Holmes, Oliver Wendell, 1809-1894—Biography—Juvenile literature. 5. Poets, American—19th century—Biography—Juvenile literature. I. Title. II. Series: The Four great Americans series ; v. 4.

Longfellow, Henry Wadsworth, 1807-1882—Biography—Last years and death.

MACCHETTA, Blanche 811'.3 B Roosevelt Tucker, 1853-1898.
The home life of Henry W. Longfellow; reminiscences of many visits at Cambridge and Nahant, during the years 1880, 1881, and 1882. [Folcroft, Pa.] Folcroft Library Editions, 1974. p. cm. Reprint of the 1882 ed. published by G. W. Carleton, New York. [PS2282.M3 1974] 74-19094 ISBN 0-8414-8604-2 (lib. bdg.)
1. Longfellow, Henry Wadsworth, 1807-1882—Biography—Last years and death. I. Title.

MURPHY, Patrick, 1862?- 811'.3 B
Henry Wadsworth Longfellow : a memory / by P. Murphy. Folcroft, Pa. : Folcroft Library Editions, 1976. p. cm. Reprint of the 1882 ed. published by Routledge, London. [PS2282.M8 1976] 76-44808 ISBN 0-8414-6055-8 : 10.00
1. Longfellow, Henry Wadsworth, 1807-1882—Biography—Last years and death. 2. Poets, American—19th century—Biography.

Longfellow, Henry Wadsworth, 1807-1882—Correspondence, reminiscences, etc.

LONGFELLOW, Henry 816'.3 Wadsworth, 1807-1882.
The letters of Henry Wadsworth Longfellow. Edited by Andrew Hilen. Cambridge, Belknap Press of Harvard University Press, 1966 [i.e. 1967]- v. illus., facsims., ports. 24 cm. Contents.Contents.—v. 1. 1814-1836.—v. 2. 1837-1843.—v. 3. 1844-1856.—v. 4. 1857-1865. Includes bibliographies. [PS2281.A3H5] 66-18248
I. Hilen, Andrew R., 1913- ed. II. Title. BIP

LONGFELLOW, Samuel, 811'.3 B 1819-1892.
Life of Henry Wadsworth Longfellow, with extracts from his journals and correspondence. New York, Greenwood Press [1969] 3 v. illus., facsims., ports. 23 cm. Reprinted from the 1891 ed. Bibliography: v. 3, p. 427-437. [PS2281.L6 1969] 68-57619 ISBN 0-8371-1048-3
1. Longfellow, Henry Wadsworth, 1807-1882—Correspondence, reminiscences, etc. I. Title.

Longfellow, Henry Wadsworth, 1807-1882—Juvenile fiction.

MELIN, Grace Hathaway. JUV
Henry Wadsworth Longfellow, gifted young poet. Illustrated by William K. Plummer. Indianapolis, Bobbs-Merril Co. [1968] 200 p. col. illus. 20 cm. (Childhood of famous Americans) A biography concentrating on the boyhood of one of the major American poets of the nineteenth century whose works include "Hiawatha" and "The Village Blacksmith." [PZ7.M51595He] 811'.3 B 68-55146
1. Longfellow, Henry Wadsworth, 1807-1882—Juvenile fiction. I. Plummer, William K., illus. II. Title.

Longfield, Mountifort, 1802-1884.

MOSS, Laurence S., 330'.15'3'0924 1944-
Mountifort Longfield, Ireland's first professor of political economy / Laurence S. Moss. Ottawa, Ill. : Green Hill Publishers, [1975] p. cm. Includes index. Bibliography: p. [HB103.L65M67] 75-34003 ISBN 0-916054-02-0 : 14.95
1. Longfield, Mountifort, 1802-1884. I. Title.

Longley, Charles Thomas, Abp. of Canterbury, 1794-1868—Manuscripts—Catalogs.

LAMBETH Palace. 016.262'12'0924 Library.
Calendar of the papers of Charles Thomas Longley, Archbishop of Canterbury, 1862-1868, in Lambeth Palace Library / [compiled] by J. E. Sayers and E. G. W. Bill. London : Mansell Information Publishing, 1976. viii, 79 p. : port. ; 28 cm. (Calendars and indexes to the letters and papers of the Archbishops of Canterbury in Lambeth Palace Library ; v. 2) Label mounted on t.p.: Distributed by International Scholarly Book Services, Inc., Forest Grove, Oregon. Includes index. [Z6616.L825L3 1976] [BX5199.L78] 76-375027 ISBN 0-7201-0551-X : 32.50
1. Longley, Charles Thomas, Abp. of Canterbury, 1794-1868—Manuscripts—Catalogs. I. Sayers, Jane E. II. Bill, Edward Geoffrey Watson. III. Title: Calendar of the papers of Charles Thomas Longley, Archbishop of Canterbury, 1862-1868, ... IV. Series: Lambeth Palace. Library. Calendars and indexes to the letters and papers of the Archbishops of Canterbury in Lambeth Palace Library ; v. 2.

Longley, James B.

JOHNSON, Willis, 974.1'04'0924 1938-
The year of the Longley / by Willis Johnson. Stonington, Me. : Penobscot Bay Press, 1978. 148 p. ; 22 cm. [F26.32.L66J63] 78-70046 pbk. : 4.75
1. Longley, James B. 2. Governors—Maine—Biography. 3. Maine—Politics and government—1951- I. Title. BIP

Longley, Lydia, 1674-1758.

MCCARTHY, Helen A 922.273
Lydia Longley, the first American nun. Illustrated by John Lawn. New York, Vision Books [1958] 190p. illus. 22cm. (Vision books, 29) [BX4705.L714M25] 58-5114
1. Longley, Lydia, 1674-1758. I. Title.

Longley. William Preston. 1851-1878.

BARTHOLOMEW, Ed 933.4173 Ellsworth.
Wild Bill Longley, a Texas hard-case illustrated from the famous Rose Collection Houston, Frontier Press of Texas, 1953. 117p. illus. 23cm. [CT275.L668B3] 53-1761
1. Longley. William Preston. 1851-1878. I. Title.

Longstreet, Augustus Baldwin, 1790-1870.

WADE, John 917.5'03'30924 B Donald, 1892-
Augustus Baldwin Longstreet; a study of the development of culture in the South. Edited with an introd. and a Wade bibliography, by M. Thomas Inge. Athens, University of Georgia Press [1969] xxxvi, 392 p. port. 25 cm. Bibliography: p. 373-383. [F213.L85 1969] 70-83729
1. Longstreet, Augustus Baldwin, 1790-1870. I. Inge, M. Thomas, ed. BIP

Longstreet, James, 1821-1904.

SANGER, Donald Bridgman, 923.573 1889-1947.
James Longstreet: Soldier, by Donald Bridgman Sanger. Politician, officeholder, and writer, by Thomas Robson Hay. Baton Rouge, Louisiana State University Press [1952] vii, 460 p. ports., maps, facsim, 25 cm. Includes bibliographies. [E467.1.L55S32] 52-13435
1. Longstreet, James, 1821-1904. 2. U.S. — Hist. — Civil War — Campaigns and battles. I. Hay, Thomas Robson, 1888- II. Title.

SANGER, Donald 973.73'0924 B Bridgman, 1889-1947.
James Longstreet: I. Soldier, by Donald Bridgman Sanger; II. Politician, officeholder, and writer, by Thomas Robson Hay. Gloucester, Mass., P. Smith, 1968 [c1952] viii, 460 p. illus., maps, ports. 24 cm. Title on spine: James Longstreet: soldier, politician, officeholder, and writer. Includes bibliographical references. [E467.1.L55S32 1968] 70-2958 7.50
1. Longstreet, James, 1821-1904. 2. United States—History—Civil War, 1861-1865—Campaigns and battles. I. Hay, Thomas Robson, 1888- II. Title: James Longstreet: soldier, politician, officeholder, and writer.

Longworth, Alice Roosevelt, 1884-

BROUGH, James, 973.9'092'4 B 1918-
Princess Alice : a biography of Alice Roosevelt Longworth / by James Brough. 1st ed. Boston : Little, Brown, [1975] 335 p. : ill. ; 25 cm. Includes index. [E748.L87B76] 74-22016 ISBN 0-316-10989-4 : 10.00
1. Longworth, Alice Roosevelt, 1884-

TEICHMANN, Howard. 973.9'092'4 B
Alice, the life and times of Alice Roosevelt Longworth / by Howard Teichmann. Englewood Cliffs, N.J. : Prentice-Hall, c1979. xvi, 286 p., [8] leaves of plates : ill. ; 24 cm. Includes index. Bibliography: p. 269-277. [E757.3.T44] 79-12512 ISBN 0-13-022210-0 : 12.95
1. Longworth, Alice Roosevelt, 1884- 2. Roosevelt, Theodore, Pres. U.S., 1858-1919—Family. 3. Presidents—United States—Children—Biography. I. Title.

Longworth, Nicholas, 1869-1931.

CHAMBRUN, Clara 328.73'0924 B (Longworth) comtesse de, 1873-1954.
The making of Nicholas Longworth; annals of an American family. Freeport, N.Y., Books for Libraries Press [1971] 322 p. illus., ports. 23 cm. Reprint of the 1933 ed. [E748.L88C4 1971] 73-164598 ISBN 0-8369-5882-9
1. Longworth, Nicholas, 1869-1931. 2. Longworth family. I. Title. BIP

Longyear, Edmund Joseph,

LONGYEAR, Edmund Joseph, 926.2234 1864-
Mesabi pioneer; reminiscences of Edmund J. Longyear, edited by Grace Lee Nute in collaboration with the author. St. Paul, Minnesota Historical Society, 1951. 116 p. illus. 24 cm. (Publications of the Minnesota Historical Society) [TN140.L65A3] 51-61905
I. Title.

Lonsdale. Frederick, 1881-1954.

DONALDSON, Frances 928.2 (Lonsdale)
Freddy. Philadelphia, Lippincott [1957] 257 p. illus. 22 cm. London ed. (Heinemann) has title: Freddy Lonsdale. [PR6023.O53Z64 1957a] 57-10270
1. Lonsdale. Frederick, 1881-1954. I. Title.

Lonsdale, Gordon Arnold,

LONSDALE, Gordon 327.120924 Arnold, 1924-
Spy; twenty years in Soviet secret service: the memoirs of Gordon Lonsdale. [1st Amer. ed.] New York, Hawthorn [c.1965] 220p. illus. 22cm. [UB271.R92L6] 65-23634 4.95
I. Title.

Lonsdale, Hugh Cecil Lowther, 5th earl of, 1857-1944.

SUTHERLAND, Douglas 914.20380924
The yellow earl, the life of Hugh Lowther, 5th earl of Lonsdale, K. G., G. C. V. O., 1857-1944. Pref. by the present earl [1st Amer. ed.] New York, Coward [1966, c.1965] 272p. illus., coat of arms, geneal. tables, ports. 22cm. Bibl. [DA566.9.L65S9] 66-10422 6.00
1. Lonsdale, Hugh Cecil Lowther, 5th earl of, 1857-1944. I. Title.

Loomis, Mahlon, 1826-1886.

APPLEBY, Thomas, 621.38'0924 B 1886-
Mahlon Loomis, inventor of radio. [Washington? 1967] 145 p. illus., facsims., map, ports. 20 cm. Includes bibliographies. [TK5739.L7A6] 67-8875
1. Loomis, Mahlon, 1826-1886. I. Title.

Loos, Adolf, 1870-1933.

MUNZ, Ludwig. 1889-1957. 720.924
Adolf Loos, pioneer of modern architecture [by] Ludwig Munz and Gustav Kunstler. With an introd. by Nikolaus Pevsner and an appreciation by Oskar Kokoschka. [Translated from the German by Harold Meek] New York, Praeger [1966] 234 p. illus., plans. port. 24 cm. Translation of Der Architekt Adolf Loos. Bibliography: p. 215. [NA1038.L6M83] 66-12528
1. Loos, Adolf, 1870-1933. I. Kunstler, Gustav, joint author. II. Title.

Loos, Anita, 1894- —Biography.

LOOS, Anita, 1894- 791.43'092'4 B
Cast of thousands / Anita Loos. New York : Grosset & Dunlap, c1977. 280 p. : ill. ; 28 cm. Includes index. Bibliography: p. 242-275. [PS3523.O557Z49] 76-43243 ISBN 0-448-12264-2 : 19.95
1. Loos, Anita, 1894- —Biography. 2. Authors, American—20th century—Biography. I. Title. BIP

LOOS, Anita, 1894- 812'.5'2 B
Kiss Hollywood good-by. New York, Viking Press [1974] 213 p. illus. 22 cm. Autobiographical. [PS3523.O557K5] 73-16942 ISBN 0-670-41374-7 7.95
1. Loos, Anita, 1894- —Biography. I. Title. BIP

LOOS, Anita, 1894- 812'.5'2 B
Kiss Hollywood good-by / Anita Loos. Boston : G. K. Hall, 1975, c1974. 360 p. ; 25 cm. Large print ed. Filmography: p. 340-360. [PS3523.O557Z52 1975] 74-32240 ISBN 0-8161-6263-8 lib.bdg. : 10.95

1. Loos, Anita, 1894- —Biography. 2. Sight-saving books. I. Title.

Lopate, Phillip, 1943-

LOPATE, Phillip, 1943- 372.6'2
Being with children / Phillip Lopate. 1st ed. Garden City, N.Y. : Doubleday, 1975. viii, 392 p. ; 22 cm. [LB1576.L64] 74-25117 ISBN 0-385-00362-5 : 7.95
1. Lopate, Phillip, 1943- 2. Creative writing (Elementary education) 3. Teachers—Correspondence, reminiscences, etc. I. Title.

Lopes, Francisco Solano, Pres. Paraguay, 1827-1870.

BARRETT, William Edmund, 1900- 923.189
Woman on horseback; the story of Francisco Lopez and Elisa Lynch. Garden City, N. Y., Doubleday, 1952. xi, 362 p. 22 cm. Bibliographical references included in "Notes" (p. 333-358) [F2687.L83 1952] 52-11723
1. Lopes, Francisco Solano, Pres. Paraguay, 1827-1870. 2. Lynch, Eliza Alicia, 1835?-1886. 3. Paraguayan War, 1865-1870. 4. Paraguay—Hist—1811-1870. I. Title.

Lopez, Aaron, 1731-1782.

CHYET, Stanley F. 380'.0924 B
Lopez of Newport; colonial American merchant prince, by Stanley F. Chyet. Detroit, Wayne State University Press, 1970. 246 p. illus., ports. 24 cm. Bibliography: p. [226]-230. [F82.L66C5 1970] 78-93898 ISBN 0-8143-1407-4 8.95
1. Lopez, Aaron, 1731-1782. I. Title. BIP

Lopez, Arthur,

LOPEZ, Arthur, 1934- 361'.0023
El rancho de muchachos, by Arthur Lopez, with Kenneth G. Richards. [Chicago, Childrens Press, 1970] 64 p. illus., ports. 19 cm. (An Open door book) Autobiographical. The son of a California migrant worker relates how he worked his way up from farm hand to director of a boys' ranch. Briefly discusses opportunities and qualifications for a job in social work. [HV7428.L6] 92 72-101738
I. Richards, Kenneth G., 1926- joint author. II. Title.

Lopez, Jose Jesus, 1852-1939.

LATTA, Frank Forrest, 1892- 979.4'8'050924 B
Saga of Rancho El Tejon / by Frank F. Latta. Bicentennial ed. Santa Cruz, Calif. : Bear State Books, c1976. xv, 293 p. : ill. ; 27 cm. Based on the narrative statements of Jose Jesus Lopez set down in his own words. Includes index. [F868.S173L664 1976] 76-9620
1. Lopez, Jose Jesus, 1852-1939. 2. Lopez family. 3. Sheep ranchers—California—San Joaquin Valley—Biography. 4. Rancho El Tejon, Calif. 5. San Joaquin Valley, Calif.—History. I. Lopez, Jose Jesus, 1852-1939. II. Title.

Lopez, Nancy—Juvenile literature.

ROBISON, Nancy. 796.352'092'4 B
Nancy Lopez : wonder woman of golf / by Nancy Robison. Chicago : Childrens Press, [1979] p. cm. (Sports stars) A biography of the young golfer named the 1978 Ladies Professional Golf Association's Rookie-of-the-Year and Player-of-the-Year. [GV964.L67R6] 92 78-23931 ISBN 0-516-04302-1 : 6.00
1. Lopez, Nancy—Juvenile literature. 2. Golfers—United States—Biography—Juvenile literature. I. Title. II. Series. BIP

SCHUMACHER, Craig. 796.352'092'4 B
Nancy Lopez / by Craig Schumacher. Mankato, MN : Creative Education, [1979] p. cm. A biography of a young woman whose unorthodox form has helped her become a top money-winner during her first year on the professional gold circuit. [GV964.L67S38] 92 79-10370 ISBN 0-87191-694-0 : 5.95 ISBN 0-89812-164-7 pbk. : 2.75
1. Lopez, Nancy—Juvenile literature. 2. Golfers—United States—Biography—Juvenile literature. I. Title.
Publisher's Address : 123 South Broad St., Mankato, MN 56001 BIP

Lopez, Nancy, 1957-

LOPEZ, Nancy, 1957- 796.352'092'4 B
The education of a woman golfer / Nancy Lopez, with Peter Schwed. New York : Simon and Schuster, c1979. 191 p. : ill. ; 25 cm. [GV964.L67A33] 79-9149 ISBN 0-671-24756-5 : 8.95
1. Lopez, Nancy, 1957- 2. Golfers—United States—Biography. 3. Golf. I. Schwed, Peter, joint author. II. Title. BIP

Lopez, Trini—Juvenile literature.

WHEELOCK, Warren. 973'.04'68 S
Henry B. Gonzales, greater justice for all ; Trini Lopez, the Latin sound ; Edward Roybal, awaken the sleeping giant / written by Warren H. Wheelock and J. O. "Rocky" Maynes, Jr. ; consultants, Jorge Valdivieso, Amalia Perez, Fabiola Franco. St. Paul : EMC Corp., 1976. 48 p. : ill. ; 23 cm. (Their Hispanic heroes of U.S.A. ; 2) Brief biographies of three Spanish Americans: two United States Congressmen and a popular singer. [E184.S75W5 vol. 2] 920'.0092'68 920 75-40232 ISBN 0-88436-242-6. pbk. : 2.95 lib.bdg. : 4.95
1. Gonzales, Henry Barbosa, 1916- —Juvenile literature. 2. Lopez, Trini—Juvenile literature. 3. Roybal, Edward Ross, 1916- —Juvenile literature. I. Maynes, J. O., joint author. II. Title. III. Title: Trini Lopez, the latin sound. IV. Title: Edward Roybal, awaken the sleeping giant.

WHEELOCK, Warren H. 973'.04'68 S
Henry B. Gonzalez, mas justicia para todos. Trini Lopez, et ritmo latino. Edward Roybal, despierten al gigante dormido / Warren H. Wheelock ; adaptacion, J. O. "Rocky" Maynes ; consultantes, Jorge Valdivieso, Amalia Perez, Ruben A. Soruco B. St. Paul, Minn. : EMC, 1976. p. cm. (His Ilustres hispanos de los EE. UU. ; 2) Translation of Henry B. Gonzalez, greater justice for all. Brief biographies of three Spanish Americans: two United States Congressmen and a popular singer. [E184.S75W517 vol. 2] 920'.0092'6873 920 76-2418 ISBN 0-88436-250-7. ISBN 0-88436-251-5 pbk.
1. Gonzalez, Henry Barbosa, 1916- —Juvenile literature. 2. Lopez, Trini—Juvenile literature. 3. Roybal, Edward Ross, 1916- —Juvenile literature. I. Maynes, J. O. II. Title. III. Title. Trini Lopez, el ritmo latino. IV. Title: Edward Roybal, despierten al gigante dormido.

Lord, Daniel Aloysius, 1888-1955.

†GAVIN, Thomas F. 271'.53'024 B
Champion of youth : biography of Father Daniel A. Lord, S. J. / by Thomas F. Gavin. Boston : St. Paul Editions, c1977. p. cm. Bibliography: p. [BX4705.L742G38] 77-70827 6.50 pbk. : 5.00
1. Lord, Daniel Aloysius, 1888-1955. 2. Jesuits—United States—Biography. I. Title.

†GAVIN, Thomas F. 271'.53'024 B
Champion of youth : biography of Father Daniel A. Lord, S. J. / by Thomas F. Gavin. Boston : St. Paul Editions, c1977. p. cm. Bibliography: p. [BX4705.L742G38] 77-70827 6.50 pbk. : 5.00
1. Lord, Daniel Aloysius, 1888-1955. 2. Jesuits—United States—Biography. I. Title.

LORD, Daniel Aloysius, 1888-1955. 922.273
Played by ear. With an introd. by R. Bakewell Morrison. Chicago, Loyol University Press, 1956. 383p. illus. 24cm. Autobiography. [BX4705.L742A4] 56-7099
1. Catholic Church—Clergy—Correspondence, reminiscences, etc. I. Title.

LORD, Daniel Aloysius, 1888-1955. 922.273
Played by ear; the autobiography of Daniel A. Lord, S.J. Introd. by R. Bakewell Morrison. Chicago, Loyola University Press; Hanover House, distributor, Garden City, N.Y., [1956] 398p. 22cm. [BX4705.L742A4 1956a] 56-7800
1. Catholic Church—Clergy—Correspondence, reminiscences, etc. I. Title.

MCGLOIN, Joseph T 922.273
Backstage missionary: Father Dan Lord, S. J. [1st ed.] New York, Pageant Press [1958] 134p. 21cm. [BX4705.L742M2] 58-14138
1. Lord, Daniel Aloysius, 1888-1955. I. Title.

Lord family.

LETTERS eighteen eleven to eighteen fifty-six Tidd, Lord, Henchman, Carret / [compiled by Margaret Garrison Phoutrides]. [Berkeley, Calif. : Phoutrides, 1955] 146 p. ; 28 cm. [CS71.T556 1955] 75-319464 929'.2'0973
1. Tidd family. 2. Lord family. 3. Carret family. I. Phoutrides, Margaret Garrison.

Lord, Simeon, 1771-1840.

HAINSWORTH, David Roger. 382'.0924 B
Simeon Lord [By] D. R. Hainsworth. Melbourne, New York [etc] Oxford University Press [1968] 30 p. illus. 19 cm. (Great Australians) Bibliography: p. 30. [HC602.5.L6H34] 70-414794 0.60
1. Lord, Simeon, 1771-1840.

HAINSWORTH, David Roger. 382'.09944
The Sydney traders: Simeon Lord and his contemporaries, 1788-1821 [by] D. R. Hainsworth. [Melbourne] Cassell Australia [1971] xiii, 264 p. illus. 24 cm. Bibliography: p. 247-255. [HF3960.S9H35] 72-183984 ISBN 0-304-93900-5
1. Lord, Simeon, 1771-1840. 2. Sydney—Commerce—History. 3. Entrepreneur. I. Title.

Loren, Sophia, 1934-

HOTCHNER, A. E. 791.43'028'0924 B
Sophia, living and loving : her own story / by A. E. Hotchner. New York : Morrow, 1979. 256 p. : ill. ; 24 cm. Filmography: p. [245]-249. [PN2688.L65H6] 78-23858 ISBN 0-688-03428-4 : 9.95
1. Loren, Sophia, 1934- 2. Moving-picture actors and actresses—Italy—Biography. I. Title. BIP

ZEC, Donald. 791.43'028'0924 B
Sophia / Donald Zec. New York : McKay, [1975] xix, 263 p., [16] leaves of plates : ill. ; 22 cm. Includes index. [PN2688.L65Z4] 75-4567 ISBN 0-679-50547-4 : 8.95
1. Loren, Sophia, 1934- I. Title.

ZEC, Donald. 791.43'028'0924 B
Sophia. New York, Pinnacle Books [1976 c1975] 263 p. illus. 18 cm. Includes index. [PN26888.L65Z4] ISBN 0-523-00863-5 1.75 (pbk.)
1. Loren, Sophia, 1934- I. Title.
L.C. card no. of 1975 McKay edition: 75-4567.

ZEC, Donald. 791.43'028'0924 B
Sophia / Donald Zec. Boston : G. K. Hall, 1976, c1975. xxvii, 463 p. ; 24 cm. Large print ed. Filmography: p. 454-463. [PN2688.L65Z4 1976] 76-10840 ISBN 0-8161-6379-0 lib.bdg. : 12.95
1. Loren, Sophia, 1934- 2. Sight-saving books. I. Title.

Lorenz, Konrad.

NISBETT, Alec. 591.5'092'4 B
Konrad Lorenz / [by] Alec Nisbett. London : Dent, 1976. xiv, 240 p., [16] p. of plates : ill., ports. ; 24 cm. Includes index. Bibliography: p. 225-230. [QL31.L76N57 1976] 77-365296 ISBN 0-460-04215-7 : £5.95
1. Lorenz, Konrad. 2. Zoologists—Austria—Biography.

Lorenz, Lovis Hans, 1898- —Biography.

LORENZ, Lovis Hans, 1898- 438
Leicht geschminkt : ein Oevelgonner Selbstbildnis / Lovis H. Lorenz ; [Zeichn. im Text von Hildegard Hudemann]. Hamburg : Christians, 1975. 127 p. : ill. ; 20 cm. [PT2623.O715Z52] 75-521970 ISBN 3-7672-0364-2 : DM16.00
1. Lorenz, Lovis Hans, 1898- —Biography. I. Title.

Lorenzo da Brindisi, Saint, 1559-1619.

ARTURO DA CARMIGNANO, Father 922.245
St. Lawrence of Brindisi. Tr. [from Italian] by Paul Barrett. Westminster, Md., Newman [c.]1963. 165p. illus. 22cm. 63-12237 3.50
1. Lorenzo da Brindisi, Saint, 1559-1619. I. Title.

CAPUCHIN Educational Conference. 922.245
Saint Lawrence of Brindisi, doctor of the Universal Church; report of the commemorative ceremonies in honor of St. Lawrence of Brindisi, of the Order of Friars Minor Capuchin, as doctor of the Universal Church, sponsored by the Capuchin Friars of North America on Tuesday, October 11, 1960, at Washington, D. C. Washington, 1961. 128p. illus., ports., maps. 23cm. (Its [Report] v. 2) Bibliographical footnotes. [BX4700.L64C3] 61-35102
1. Lorenzo da Brindisi, Saint, 1559-1619. I. Title.

Loring, William Wing, 1818-1886.

WESSELS, William L. 355.3'31'0924 B
Born to be a soldier; the military career of William Wing Loring of St. Augustine, Florida, by William L. Wessels. Fort Worth, Texas Christian University Press, 1971. 122 p. port. 23 cm. (Texas Christian University monographs in history and culture, no. 8) [U53.L67W48] 71-143789
1. Loring, William Wing, 1818-1886. I. Title. II. Series.

Los Angeles Co., Calif.—Biog.

ARMSTRONG, Alice Catt, ed. 920.0794
Who's who in Los Angeles County. Los Angeles, Who's Who Historical Society. 1950/51. v. ports. 28 cm. Editor: 1950/51- A.C. Amstrong. [F868.L8W56] 51-31641
1. Los Angeles Co., Calif.—Biog. I. Title.

Los Angeles. Hollenbeck Home for the Aged.

YOUNG, Nellie May. 917.94'94'0340924
William Stewart Young, 1859-1937: builder of California institutions; an intimate biography Glendale, Calif., A. H. Clark, 1967. 196 p. illus., ports. 25 cm. [F869.L8Y68] 67-18217
1. Young, William Stewart, 1859-1937. 2. Presbyterian Church in Los Angeles. 3. Los Angeles. Hollenbeck Home for the Aged. 4. Los Angeles. Occidental College. I. Title: Builder of California institutions.

Los Angeles. University of Southern California—Football.

MCKAY, John H. 796.33'2'0924 B
McKay : a coach's story / John McKay with Jim Perry. 1st ed. New York : Atheneum, 1974. xviii, 333 p. : ill. ; 22 cm. [GV939.M33A35 1974] 74-81267 ISBN 0-689-10624-6 : 10.00
1. Los Angeles. University of Southern California—Football. 2. McKay, John H. 3. Football. 4. Football coaching. I. Perry, Jim.

Lose, M. Phyllis.

LOSE, M. Phyllis. 630.1'08'90924 B
No job for a lady : the autobiography of M. Phyllis Lose, V. M. D. / as told to

Daniel Mannix. New York : Macmillan, c1979. 217 p. ; 24 cm. [SF613.L67A36] 79-14790 12.95
1. Lose, M. Phyllis. 2. Veterinarians—Pennsylvania—Biography. I. Mannix, Daniel Pratt, 1911- II. Title.

Losey, Joseph.

LOSEY, Joseph. 791.43'0233'0924
Losey on Losey. Edited and introduced by Tom Milne. Garden City, N.Y., Doubleday, 1968. 192 p. illus., ports. 20 cm. (Cinema world, 2) [PN1998.A3L56 1968] 68-12993
I. Milne, Tom, ed. II. Title.

Lothian, Philip Henry Kerr, 11th marquis of, 1882-1940.

BUTLER, James Ramsay Montagu 923.242
Lord lothtan, Philip Kerr, 1882-1940. New York, St. Martin's Press, [1960] xiii, 384p. illus. 23cm. 60-2023 10.00
1. Lothian, Philip Henry Kerr, 11th marquis of, 1882-1940. I. Title.

Lotto, Lorenzo, 1480 -1556

BERENSON, Bernhard, 1865- v. 12
Lorenzo Lotto; complete ed. with 400 illus. New York, Phaidon Publishers distributed by Garden City Books [1556] xiv, 477p. plates (part col.) 27cm. A 56
1. Lotto, Lorenzo, 1480 -1556 I. Title.

Lotz, Wolfgang.

LOTZ, Wolfgang. 327'.12
The champagne spy; Israel's master spy tells his story. New York, St. Martin's Press [1972] 240 p. illus. 23 cm. [DS119.8.E3L68 1972] 72-84761 6.95
1. Lotz, Wolfgang. 2. Espionage, Israeli—Egypt. 3. Spies. I. Title.

Louys, Pierre, 1870-1925—Biography.

CLIVE, H. P. 848'.9'1409 B
Pierre Louys (1870-1925) : a biography / H. P. Clive. Oxford [Eng.] : Clarendon Press, 1978. vi, 264 p. : port. ; 23 cm. Includes index. Bibliography: p. [241]-256. [PQ2623.O8Z5536 1978] 77-30282 ISBN 0-19-815751-7 : 24.00
1. Louys, Pierre, 1870-1925—Biography. 2. Authors, French—20th century—Biography.
Distributed by Oxford University Press, New York, NY

Loucks, Jennie (Erickson)

LOUCKS, Jennie (Erickson) 920 1893-
Oklahoma was young and so was I. San Antonio, Naylor Co. [1964] vii, 166 p. 22 cm. [CT275.L6924A3] 64-20851
I. Title.

LOUCKS, Jennie (Erickson) 920 1893-
Oklahoma was young and so was I. San Antonio, Naylor Co. [1964] vii, 166 p. 22 cm. [CT275.L6924A3] 64-20851
I. Title.

Loud, Pat, 1926-

LOUD, Pat, 1926- 917.3'03'924
Pat Loud: a woman's story [by] Pat Loud with Nora Johnson. New York, Bantam Books [1974] 213 p. 18 cm. [CT275.L69244A36] 1.75 (pbk.)
1. Loud, Pat, 1926- 2. An American family. [Motion picture] I. Johnson, Nora, joint author. II. Title.
L.C. card no. for original ed.: 73-88543.

LOUD, Pat, 1926- 917.3'03'924
Pat Loud: a woman's story, by Pat Loud with Nora Johnson. New York, Coward, McCann & Geoghegan [1974] 223 p. 22 cm. Autobiographical. [CT275.L69244A36] 73-88543 ISBN 0-698-10578-8 6.95
1. Loud, Pat, 1926- 2. An American family. [Motion picture] I. Johnson, Nora, joint author. II. Title.

Loudon, Jane (Webb) 1807-1858.

HOWE, Bea 926.3
Lady with green fingers; the life of Jane Loudon [Dist. Hollywood-by-the-Sea, Fla., Transatlantic, 1962, c.1961] 184p. illus. Bibl. 62-2648 7.50
1. Loudon, Jane (Webb) 1807-1858. I. Title.

Loudon, John Claudius, 1783-1843.

GLOAG, John, 1896- 720'.924 B
Mr. Loudon's England: the life and work of John Claudius Loudon, and his influence on architecture and furniture design. Newcastle upon Tyne, Oriel P., 1970. 224 p., 8 plates. illus., facsims., maps, plans, ports. 25 cm. Includes bibliographical references. [NA997.L63G55] 68-55974 ISBN 8-536-20423- 50/-
1. Loudon, John Claudius, 1783-1843. I. Title.

Loughborough Technical College—Biography.

HARVEY, Joan M. 378.1'1'0924 B
Herbert Schofield and Loughborough College / by Joan M. Harvey. Diseworth : The author, [1976] [3], 92 p. : ill., coat of arms, map, ports. ; 22 cm. Bibliography: p. 92. [T173.L9513S374] 77-369141 £1.50
1. Loughborough Technical College—Biography. 2. Schofield, Herbert, 1883-1963. 3. Educators—England—Biography. I. Title.

Louis Ferdinand,

LOUIS FERDINAND, Prince 926.2913 of Prussia, 1907-
The rebel prince memoirs. Introd. by Louis P. Lochner. Chicago, H. Regnery, 1952. xv, 356 p. ports. 22 cm. [DD229.8L68A3] 52-13202
I. Title.

Louis I, le Pieux, Emperor, King of the Franks, 778-840.

SON of Charlemagne; 923.144
a contemporary life of Louis the Pious. Translated, with introd. and notes, by Allen Cabaniss. [Syracuse, N.Y.] Syracuse University Press [1961] 182 p. 22 cm. Translation based on the MGH (Monumenta Germaniae historica) and MPL (Migne's Patrologiae cursus completus ... series Latina) editions of Vita Hludowici imperatoris, ascribed to the so-called Astronomus, a member of the court. Cf. M. Manitius. Geschichte der latein. Lit. des Mittelalters. Munchen, 1911. t. 1, p. 655-657. [DC74.V513] 61-13987
1. Louis I, le Pieux, Emperor, King of the Franks, 778-840. 2. France—History—To 987. I. Astronomus, fl. 814-840, supposed author. II. Cabaniss, James Allen, 1911- ed. and tr.

Louis IX, Saint, King of France, 1214-1270.

GAZAGNE, Louis, 1885- 923.144
The Saint on horseback; a story of St. Louis IX, King of France. Illus. by Brother Bernard Howard. Notre Dame, Ind., Dujarie Press [1953] 88p. illus. 24cm. [DC91.G35] 53-29794
1. Louis IX, Saint, King of France, 1214-1270. I. Title.

JOINVILLE, Jean, sire de, 923.144 1224?-1317?
The life of St. Louis; translated by Rene Hague from the text edited by Natalis de Wailly. New York, Sheed and Ward, 1955. 306p. illus. 22cm. (The Makers of Christendom) Translation of L'histoire et chronique du ... roy S. Loys. [DC91.J7 1955] 55-10924
1. Louis IX, Saint, King of France, 1214-1270. 2. Crusades—Seventh, 1248-1250. I. Title.

LABARGE, Margaret 944'.023'0924 B Wade.
Saint Louis: Louis IX, most Christian King of France. [1st] American ed. Boston, Little, Brown [1968] 303 p. illus., facsims., geneal. table, maps, ports. 24 cm. Bibliography: p. [281]-291. [DC91.L24 1968] 68-17271
1. Louis IX, Saint, King of France, 1214-1270.

Louis, Joe,

LOUIS, Joe, 1914- 927.9383
The Joe Louis story. [Written with the editorial aid of Chester L. Washington and Haskell Cohen] New York, Grosset & Dunlap [1953] 197p. illus. 21cm. First ed. published in 1947 under title: My life story. [GV1132.L6A3 1953] 53-11991
I. Title.

Louis, Joe, 1914-

DIAMOND, Wilfrid. 927.9683
How great was Joe Louis? New York, Paebar Co. ['1950] 85 p. illus. 22 cm. [GV1132.L6D5] 52-1467
1. Louis, Joe, 1914- I. Title.

EDMONDS, Anthony 796.8'3'0924 B O.
Joe Louis, by Anthony O. Edmonds. [Grand Rapids] Erdmans [1973] 112 p. port. 22 cm. (A Great men of Michigan book) Bibliography: p. 111-112. [GV1132.L6E35] 72-77186 ISBN 0-8028-7026-0 pap. 2.45
1. Louis, Joe, 1914-

FLEISCHER, Nathaniel S. 927.9683
The Louis legend; the amazing story of the Brown Bomber's rise to the heavyweight championship of the world and his retirement from boxing. [n.p., c1956] 181p. illus. 22cm. [GV1132.L6F5] 57-3410
1. Louis, Joe, 1914- I. Title.

LOUIS, Joe, 1914- 796.8'3'0924 B
Joe Louis, my life / by Joe Louis, with Edna and Art Rust, Jr. 1st ed. New York : Harcourt Brace Jovanovich, c1978. 277 p., [16] leaves of plates : ill. ; 22 cm. [GV1132.L6A29] 77-91341 ISBN 0-15-146375-1 : 10.95
1. Louis, Joe, 1914- 2. Boxers (Sports)—United States—Biography. 3. Boxing. I. Rust, Edna, joint author. II. Rust, Art, 1927- joint author. III. Title.

LOUIS, Joe, 1914- 927.9383
The Joe Louis story. [Written with the editorial aid of Chester L. Washington and Haskell Cohen] New York, Grosset & Dunlap [1953] 197p. illus. 21cm. First ed. published in 1947 under title: My life story. [GV1132.L6A3 1953] 53-11991
I. Title.

NAGLER, Barney. 796.8'3'0924 B
Brown bomber. New York, World Pub. [1972] 236 p. illus. 24 cm. [GV1132.L6N3 1972] 71-183089 ISBN 0-529-04522-2 7.95
1. Louis, Joe, 1914- I. Title.

Louis Philippe, King of the French, 1773-1850.

HOWARTH, Thomas 944.06'3'0924 B Edward Brodie.
Citizen-king : the life of Louis Philippe / T. E. B. Howarth. London ; New York : White Lion Publisher, 1975. 358 p., [8] p. of plates : ill., facsim., geneal. table, map, ports. ; 23 cm. Bibliography: p. 341-344. [DC268.H6 1975] 76-355061 ISBN 0-7274-0058-4 : £4.25
1. Louis Philippe, King of the French, 1773-1850. I. Title.

LOUIS Philippe, 944.06'3'0924 B King of the French, 1773-1850.
Memoirs, 1773-1793 / Louis-Philippe ; translated and with an introd. by John Hardman ; foreword by Henri Comte de Paris. 1st ed. New York : Harcourt Brace Jovanovich, c1977. xxxiii, 476 p., [8] leave of plates : ill. ; 24 cm. Translation of Memoires de Louis Philippe. "A Helen and Kurt Wolff book." Includes index. [DC268.A3413] 76-44441 ISBN 0-15-158855-4 : 19.95
1. Louis Philippe, King of the French, 1773-1850. 2. France—Kings and rulers—Biography.

STOECKL, Agnes Barron, 923.144 baroness de.
King of the French; a portrait of Louis Philippe, 1773-1850. [1st American ed.] New York, Putnam [1958, c1957] 308 p. illus. 22 cm. [DC268.S78 1958] 58-10759
1. Louis Phillippe, King of the French, 1773-1850.

Louis XI, King of France, 1423-1483.

CHAMPION, Pierre 944'.027'0924 B Honore Jean Baptiste, 1880-1942.
Louis XI. Translated and adapted by Winifred Stephens Whalel. Freeport, N.Y., Books for Libraries Press [1970] ix, 316 p. illus., ports. 23 cm. "First published 1929." [DC106.C53 1970] 73-109617
1. Louis XI, King of France, 1423-1483.

CLEUGH, James. 944'.027 B
Chant royal; the life of King Louis XI of France (1423-1483) [1st ed.] Garden City, N.Y., Doubleday [1970] 312 p. illus. 25 cm. Bibliography: p. [303]-304. [DC106.C56] 71-89078 6.95
1. Louis XI, King of France, 1423-1483. I. Title.

Louis XIII. King of France, 1601-1643.

CHAPMAN, Hester W., 1899- 920.02
Privileged persons; four seventeenth-century studies [by]Hester W. Chapman. New York, Revnal [1966 ie 1967] 319p. plates (ports.) general.tables 23 cm Bibl. [CT117.C5 1966a] 66-24558
1. Louis XIII. King of France, 1601-1643. 2. Sophie, consort of Ernest Augustus, Elector of Hanover. 1630-1714. 3. Mararin. Hortense (Mancini) de La Porte, duchess de. 1649-1699. 4. Ailesbury, Thomas Bruce, 2d earl of, 1656-1741. I. Title.
Contents omitted. BIP

Louis XIV, King of France, 1638-1715.

APSLER, Alfred 944.0330924
The Sun King: Louis XIV of France. New York. Messner [c.1965] 191p. 22cm. Bibl. [DC125.A6] 65-12953 3.25: 3.19 lib. ed.,
1. Louis XIV, King of France, 1638-1715. I. Title.

APSLER, Alfred. 944.0330924 (B)
The Sun King; Louis XIV of France. New York, J. Messner, [1965] 191 p. 22 cm. Bibliography: p. 185-186. [DC125.A6] 65-12953
1. Louis XIV, King of France, 1638-1715. I. Title.

CHURCH, William 944'.033'0924 Farr, 1912- ed.
The greatness of Louis XIV, edited and with an introd. by William F. Church. 2d ed. Lexington, Mass., Heath [1972] xix, 200 p. 21 cm. (Problems in European civilization) Bibliography: p. 193-200. [DC129.C5 1972] 72-5149 ISBN 0-669-82016-4 2.50
1. Louis XIV, King of France, 1638-1715. I. Title. II. Series.

CRONIN, Vincent. 923.144
Louis XIV. [1st American ed.] Boston, Houghton Mifflin, 1965 [c1964] 384 p. illus., geneal. table, maps, plans, ports. 24 cm. "Sources and notes": p. 355-371. [DC129.C7 1965] 65-11779
1. Louis XIV, King of France, 1638-1715.

ERLANGER, 944'.033'0924 B Philippe, 1903-
Louis XIV. Translated from the French by Stephen Cox. New York, Praeger [1970] 412 p. illus., geneal. tables, ports. 25 cm. Bibliography: p. 391-392. [DC129.E713 1970] 79-109471 10.00
1. Louis XIV, King of France, 1638-1715.

HALL, Geoffrey 944'.033'0922 B Fowler, 1888-
Moths round the flame; studies of charmers and intriguers. Freeport, N.Y., Books for Libraries Press [1969] xv, 364 p. illus., geneal. tables, map (on lining paper), ports. 23 cm. (Essay index reprint series) Reprint of the 1935 ed. Bibliography: p.

xiii-xiv. [DC130.A2H3 1969] 72-93343 ISBN 8-369-14139-
1. Louis XIV, King of France, 1638-1715. 2. France—Court and courtiers. 3. France—History—Louis XIV, 1643-1715. 4. Women in France—Biography. I. Title.

HATTON, Ragnhild 944'.033'0924 B Marie.
Louis XIV and his world [by] Ragnhild Hatton. New York, Putnam [1972] 128 p. illus. 24 cm. Bibliography: p. 121-122. [DC129.H34 1972b] 79-189991 6.95
1. Louis XIV, King of France, 1638-1715. I. Title.

LEWIS, Warren Hamilton. 923.144
Louis XIV, an informal portrait. [1st American ed.] New York, Harcourt, Brace [1959] 224 p. illus. 23 cm. [DC125.L48 1959] 59-7424
1. Louis XIV, King of France, 1638-1715.

MITFORD, Nancy, 1904- 944.0330924
The Sun King. New York, Harper [1966] 255p. 2 col. fronts., 131 illus. (incl. ports.) 54 col. plates, maps. facsim., tables. diagrs. 26cm. Illus. on endpapers. Bibl. [DC125.M5] 66-74868 15.00
1. Louis XIV. King of France. 1638-1715. I. Title.

OGG. DAVID, 1887- 944'.03'3'0924 1965
Louis XIV. 2nd ed. London, New York, Oxford Univ. Pr., 1967. [5], 152p. 21cm. (Oxford paperbacks univ. ser., no. 21) Bibl. [DC129.O4 1967] (B) 67-92115 1.20 pap.,
1. Louis XIV, King of France, 1638-1715. I. Title.

RULE, John C., 944'.033'0924 B comp.
Louis XIV, edited by John C. Rule. Englewood Cliffs, N.J., Prentice Hall [1973, c1974] vii, 181 p. 21 cm. (Great lives observed) (A Spectrum book) Bibliography: p. 174-178. [DC129.R8] 73-16430 ISBN 0-13-540773-7 6.95
1. Louis XIV, King of France, 1638-1715. Pbk. 2.95; ISBN 0-13-540765-6.

STEARNS, Monroe. 944'.033'0924 B
Louis XIV. London, New York, F. Watts, 1971. viii, 183 p. illus., geneal. table, maps, ports. 22 cm. Bibliography: p. 177-178. [DC129.S79 1971b] 72-169554 ISBN 0-85166-329-X £1.25
1. Louis XIV, King of France, 1638-1715.

STEARNS, Monroe. 944'.033'0924 B
Louis XIV of France, pattern of majesty. New York, Watts [1971] viii, 183 p. illus., maps, ports. 22 cm. (Immortals of history) Bibliography: p. 177-178. A biography of "the Sun King" who strengthened France in many ways but at the same time planted the seeds for the French Revolution through his neglect and persecution of peasants and Huguenots. [DC129.S79] 92 77-137152 ISBN 0-531-00962-9
1. Louis XIV, King of France, 1638-1715. I. Title.

SUTHERLAND, Monica (La 923.144 Fontaine)
Louis XIV and Marie Mancini. New York, Roy Publishers [1957?] 213 p. illus. 24 cm. [(DC130)] 57-10088
1. Louis XIV, King of France, 1638-1715. 2. Colonna, Maria (Mancini) principessa di Paliano, 1639-1715. I. Title.

WOLF, John 944'.033'0924 B Baptist, 1907- comp.
Louis XIV; a profile. Edited by John B. Wolf. [1st ed.] New York, Hill and Wang [1972] xxii, 265 p. 21 cm. (World profiles) [DC129.W62 1972] 73-163574 ISBN 0-8090-6683-1 6.50
1. Louis XIV, King of France, 1638-1715. Contents omitted. Paperback ed. 2.45.

WOLF, John 944'.033'0924 B Baptist, 1907-
Louis XIV, by John B. Wolf. [1st ed.] Louis the Fourteenth New York, Norton [1968] xix, 678 p. illus., coat of arms, maps, port. 25 cm. Bibliographical references included in "Notes" (p. [621]-662) [DC129.W6 1968] 67-20618
1. Louis XIV, King of France, 1638-1715.

Louis XIV, King of France, 1638-1715—Juvenile literature.

WILKINSON, Burke, 944'.033'0924 B 1913-
Young Louis XIV; the early years of the Sun King. Illustrated by Doreen Roberts [New York] Macmillan [1970] 148 p. illus. 22 cm. Bibliography: p. [143]-144. Traces the years from birth to early manhood of the seventeenth-century French monarch known as the "Sun King." [DC125.W54] 92 70-89596
1. Louis XIV, King of France, 1638-1715—Juvenile literature. I. Roberts, Doreen, illus. II. Title.

Louis XV, king of France. 1710-1774.

DU HAUSSET, Mme, b-ca1720 v. 12
The private memoirs of Louis XV, from the memoirs of Madame du Hasset, Lady's maide to Madame de Pompadour. Philadelphia, Rittenhouse Press [n.d.] xii, 282 p. front. 21 cm. At head of title: Secret and historic memoirs of the courts of France. 68-39926
1. Louis XV, king of France. 1710-1774. 2. France—History—Louis XV, 1715-1774. 3. France—Court and courtiers. I. Title.

GOOCH, George Peabody, 923.144 1873-
Louis XV; the monarchy in decline. London, New York, Longmans, Green [1956] 285p. illus. 23cm. [DC133.3.G6] 56-59058
1. Louis xv, King of France, 1710-1774. I. Title.

GOOCH, George 944'.034'0924 Peabody, 1873-1968.
Louis XV : the monarchy in decline / G.P. Gooch. Westport, Conn. : Greenwood Press, 1976. p. cm. Reprint of the 1956 ed. published by Longmans, Green, London. Includes index. Bibliography: p. [DC133.3.G6 1976] 75-36361 ISBN 0-8371-8632-3
1. Louis XV, King of France, 1710-1774. 2. France—History—Louis XV, 1715-1774.

Louis XVI, King of France, 1754-1793.

CRONIN, Vincent. 944'.035'0924 B
Louis and Antoinette / by Vincent Cronin. New York : Morrow, 1975, c1974. 445 p., [9] leaves of plates : ill. ; 24 cm. Includes bibliographical references and index. [DC137.C76 1975] 74-15762 ISBN 0-688-00331-1 : 12.50
1. Louis XVI, King of France, 1754-1793. 2. Marie Antoinette, consort of Louis XVI, King of France, 1755-1793. I. Title. BIP

FAY, Bernard, 944'.035'0924 B 1893-
Louis XVI; or, The end of a world. translated by Patrick o'Brian from the French Chicago, H. Regnery Co. [1968, c1967] 414 p. illus., geneal. table, ports. 22 cm. Translation of Louis XVI; ou, la Fin d'un monde. [DC136.F313 1968b] 68-18268
1. Louis XVI, King of France, 1754-1793. 2. France—History—Louis XVI, 1774-1793.

JORDAN, David P., 944'.035'0924 B 1939-
The king's trial : the French Revolution vs. Louis XVI / David P. Jordan. Berkeley : University of California Press, c1979. xx, 275 p., [7] leaves of plates : ports. ; 24 cm. Includes index. Bibliography: p. 249-268. [DC137.08.J68] 78-54797 ISBN 0-520-03684-0 : 14.95
1. Louis XVI, King of France, 1754-1793. 2. France—History—Revolution, 1792-1793. 3. France—Kings and rulers—Biography. I. Title.

PADOVA, Saul Kussiel, 923.114 1905-
The life and death of Louis XVI. New York, Pyramid [1964, c.1939, 1963] x, 323p. illus., plans. 19cm. (T-1078) Bibl. 64-57024 .75 pap.,
1. Louis XVI, King of France, 1754-1793. I. Title.

PADOVER, Saul Kussiel, 923.144 1905-
The life and death of Louis XVI. New ed. New York, Taplinger 1953[c.1939,1963] xiv, 373p. illus., port., map. 23cm. Bibl. 63-18335 7.50
1. Louis XVI, King of France, 1754-1793. I. Title.

PADOVER, Saul Kussiel, 923.144 1905-
The life and death of Louis XVI, by Saul K. Padover. New York, Pyramid Books [1963] x. 323 p. illus., plans. 19 cm. Bibliography: p. 297-310. [[DC137.P12] 64-57024
1. Louis XVI, King of France, 1754-1793. I. Title. BIP

WEBSTER, Nesta 944'.035'0924 B Helen.
Louis XVI and Marie Antoinette during the Revolution / by Nesta H. Webster. New York : Gordon Press, [1976] c1938. p. cm. Continues the author's Louis XVI and Marie Antoinette before the Revolution. Reprint of the ed. published by Putnam, New York. Bibliography: p. [DC137.W42 1976] 75-36680 ISBN 0-87968-364-3 lib.bdg. : 44.95
1. Louis XVI, King of France, 1754-1793. 2. Marie Antoinette, consort of Louis XVI, King of France, 1755-1793. I. Title.

Louis XVII, of France, 1785-1795.

BEAUCHESNE, Alcide 944.04'092'4 B Hyacinthe du Bois de, 1804-1873.
Louis XVII : his life, his suffering, his death, the captivity of the royal family in the Temple / by A. de Beuchesne; translated and edited by W. Hazlitt. New York : AMS Press, [1976] p. cm. Reprint of the 1855 ed. published by Harper, New York. [DC137.3.B38 1976] 78-161731 ISBN 0-404-07546-0 : 55.00(2 vols)
1. Louis XVII, of France, 1785-1795. 2. France—History—Revolution, 1789-1795.

Louise, Chris.

LOUISE, Frances D. 362.1'97375
Malpractice : the doctor's delinquency / by Frances D. Louise. 1st ed. Port Washington, N.Y. : Ashley Books, c1978. 232 p. ; 22 cm. [RD594.3.L68] 77-88484 ISBN 0-87949-090-X : 8.95
1. Louise, Chris. 2. Spinal cord—Wounds and injuries—Biography. 3. Paralysis—Biography. 4. Surgeons Malpractice California. 5. Trials (Malpractice)—California. I. Title.

Louise de Marillac, Saint, 1591-1660.

DIRVIN, Joseph I. 282'.0924 B
Louise de Marillac [by] Joseph I. Dirvin. New York, Farrar, Straus & Giroux [1970] xi, 468 p. 22 cm. Bibliography: p. [415]-418. [BX4700.L66D57] 73-115750 10.00
1. Louise de Marillac, Saint, 1591-1660.

LOUISE de Marillac, 282'.092'4 B Saint, 1591-1660.
Letters of St. Louise de Marillac. Translated from the French by Sister Helen Marie Law [and] Daughters of Charity. [Emmitsburg, Md., Saint Joseph's Provincial House Press] 1972. 629 p. 26 cm. [BX4700.L66A413 1972] 72-97031
1. Louise de Marillac, Saint, 1591-1660.

Louisiana

LONG, Huey Pierce, 1893- 923.273 1935
Every man a king; the autobiography of Huey P. Long. Introd. by T. Harry Williams. Chicago, Quadrangle [c.1933-1964] xxviii, 348p. illus. 22cm. (QP8) Bibl. 64-2488 2.25 pap.,
1. Louisiana—Pol. & govt.—1865- I. Title.

LONG, Huey Pierce, 1893- 923.273 1935
Every man a king; the autobiography of Huey P. Long. Introd. by T. Harry Williams [Gloucester, Mass., P. Smith, 1966, c.1933-1964] xxviii, 348p. illus. 22cm. (Quandrangle paperbacks, QP8 rebound) Bibl. [E748.L86L8 1964] 4.25
1. Louisiana—Pol. & govt.—1865- I. Title.

Louisiana

ZIMMER, Maude Files 920.7
A time to remember. New York, Speller [c.1963] 152p. 23cm. 63-22673 3.95
1. Louisiana—Soc. life & cust. I. Title. BIP

Louisiana—Emigration and immigration.

VILLERE, Sidney Louis. 929'.3763
The Canary Islands migration to Louisiana, 1778-1783; the history and passenger lists of the Islenos volunteer recruits and their families. New Orleans, Genealogical Research Society of New Orleans [1971] xxiii, 94 l. maps. 28 cm. [F368.V54] 77-28404
1. Louisiana—Emigration and immigration. 2. Canary Islands—Emigration and immigration. 3. Louisiana—Genealogy. I. Title.

Louisiana. Militia. Uniformed Battalion of Orleans Volunteers—Biography.

MORAZAN, Ronald 973.5'2463'0922 B R.
Biographical sketches of the veterans of the Battalion of Orleans, 1814-1815 / by Ronald R. Morazan. [Baton Rouge, La.] : Legacy Pub. Co., 1979. xiii, 300 p. : ill. ; 23 cm. Includes index. Bibliography: p. 289-300. [E356.N5M6] 79-65180 ISBN 0-918784-51-4 : 12.50
1. Louisiana. Militia. Uniformed Battalion of Orleans Volunteers—Biography. 2. New Orleans, Battle of, 1815—Biography. 3. Soldiers—Louisiana—New Orleans—Biography. I. Title.
Publisher's address: 2008 Perkins Rd., Baton Rouge, LA 70808 BIP

Loukaris, Kurillos, Patriarch of Constantinople, 1572-1638.

CHATZEANTONIOU, Georgios 922.1496 A.
Protestant patriarch; the life of Cyril Lucarius, 1572-1638. Patriarch of Constantinople [by] George A. Hadjiantoniou. Richmond, Va., John Knox Press [c.1961] 160p. illus. (front port) Bibl. 61-7594 3.50
1. Loukaris, Kurillos, Patriarch of Constantinople, 1572-1638. I. Title.

Lovasik, Leo Edward, 1921-1943.

LOVASIK, Lawrence George, 922.273 1913-
Our Lady's knight; the true story of Technical Sergeant Leo E. Lovasik, 1921-1943. [Boston] St. Paul Editions [1960] 203p. illus. 22cm. [BX4705.L77L6] 60-50067
1. Lovasik, Leo Edward, 1921-1943. I. Title.

Lovat, Simon Christopher Joseph Fraser, Baron, 1911-

LOVAT, Simon 940.54'81'411 Christopher Joseph Fraser, Baron, 1911-
March past : a memoir / by Lord Lovat ; with an introd. by Sir Iain Moncreiffe. New York : Holmes & Meier, c1979. p. cm. Includes index. [D811.L69 1979] 79-17915 ISBN 0-8419-6302-9 : 20.00
1. Lovat, Simon Christopher Joseph Fraser, Baron, 1911- 2. Great Britain. Combined Operations Command—Biography. 3. World War, 1939-1945—Personal narratives, Scottish. 4. World War, 1939-1945—Campaigns—Western. 5. Soldiers—Great Britain—Biography. 6. Scotland—Nobility—Biography. I. Title.

Love.

CRAIGIN, Elisabeth. 176
Either is love / Elisabeth Craigin. New York : Arno Press, 1975, c1937. p. cm. (Homosexuality) Reprint of the ed. published by Harcourt, Brace, New York. [HQ76.C7 1975] 75-12311 ISBN 0-405-07379-8 : 9.00
1. Love. 2. Lesbianism—United States. 3. Homosexuality—Personal narratives. I. Title. II. Series. BIP

EWART, Andrew. 301.41'4
The great lovers. Picture research: Marion Geisinger. New York, Hart Pub. Co. [1968] 412 p. illus. 24 cm. First published under title: The world's greatest love affairs. Contents.Contents.—Antony and Cleopatra.—Justinian and Theodora.—Charles II and Nell Gwynne.—Napoleon and Josephine.—Lord Nelson and Emma Hamilton.—Robert Browning and Elizabeth Barrett.—Prince Albert and Queen Victoria.—George Henry Lewes and George Eliot.—Dostoevsky and Apollinaria.—Bernard Shaw and Ellen Terry.—Woodrow Wilson and Edith Bolling.—William Randolph Hearst and Marion Davies.—King Carol and Madame Lupescu.—Lord Mountbatten and Edwina.—The Duke of Windsor and Wallis Simpson. [HQ801.A2E9 1968b] 68-24730 7.95
1. Love. 2. Courtship. I. Title.

MANDEL, Morris, 1911- 301.41'092'2
Secret love affairs / by Morris Mandel. Middle Village, N.Y. : J. David Publishers, [1975] p. cm. [HQ801.A2M25] 75-14242 ISBN 0-8246-0201-3 : 9.95
1. Love. 2. Biography. I. Title. **BIP**

Love, Nat,

LOVE, Nat, 1854-1921. 978'.02'0924 B
The life and adventures of Nat Love. New York, Arno Press, 1968. iv, 162 p. illus., ports. 25 cm. (The American Negro, his history and literature) Reprint of the 1907 ed.; with new introd. by W. L. Katz. [F594.L89 1968] 68-29007
I. Title. II. Series.

Love, Nat, 1854-1921—Juvenile literature.

CLARK, Charlotte R. 978'.02'0924 B
Black cowboy; the story of Nat Love, by Charlotte R. Clark. Illustrated by Leighton Fossum. Eau Claire, Wis., E. M. Hale [1970] [47] p. col. illus. 23 cm. An easy-to-read biography of one of the first black cowboys, renowned for his riding, roping, and sharpshooting. [F594.L892C55] 70-93092 ISBN 0-8382-1051-1
1. Love, Nat, 1854-1921—Juvenile literature. I. Fossum, Leighton, illus. II. Title.

FELTON, Harold W., 1902- 917.8'03'20924 B
Nat Love, Negro cowboy [by] Harold W. Felton. Illustrated by David Hodges. New York, Dodd, Mead [1969] 93 p. illus. (part col.) 24 cm. A biography of a boy freed from slavery during the Civil War who, at age fifteen, went West to become a cowpuncher, champion roper, sharpshooter, and bronco rider, and finally a Pullman porter. [F594.L892F4] 92 69-13730 3.25
1. Love, Nat, 1854-1921—Juvenile literature. I. Hodges, David, illus. II. Title.

Love, Stan.

LOVE, Stan. 796.32'3'0924 B
Love in the NBA : a player's uninhibited diary / Stan Love and Ron Rapoport. 1st ed. New York : Saturday Review Press, [1975] 184 p. ; 22 cm. [GV884.L68A34 1975] 75-23499 ISBN 0-8415-0398-2 : 7.95
1. Love, Stan. 2. National Basketball Association. 3. Basketball. I. Rapoport, Ron, joint author. II. Title.

Lovecraft, Howard Phillips, 1890-1937.

COOK, W. Paul, 1881-1948. 818'.5'209
H. P. Lovecraft; a portrait, by W. Paul Cook. Baltimore, Mirage, 1968. iii, 66 p. 21 cm. (The Anthem series) [PS3523.O833Z58] 68-7900
1. Lovecraft, Howard Phillips, 1890-1937.

Lovecraft, Howard Phillips, 1890-1937—Biography.

DE CAMP, Lyon Sprague, 1907- 813'.5'2 B
Lovecraft; a biography, by L. Sprague de Camp. [1st ed.] Garden City, N.Y., Doubleday, 1975. xvi, 510 p. illus. 22 cm. Bibliography: p. [477]-498. [PS3523.O833Z59] 74-9483 ISBN 0-385-00578-4 5.95
1. Lovecraft, Howard Phillips, 1890-1937—Biography. **BIP**

LONG, Frank Belknap, 1903- 813'.5'2 B
Howard Phillips Lovecraft : dreamer on the nightside / by Frank Belknap Long. Sauk City, Wis. : Arkham House, 1975. xiv, 237 p., [6] leaves of plates : ill. ; 20 cm. On spine: Dreamer on the nightside. [PS3523.O833Z75] 74-18652 ISBN 0-87054-068-8 : 8.50
1. Lovecraft, Howard Phillips, 1890-1937—Biography. I. Title: Dreamer on the nightside. **BIP**

Lovecraft, Howard Phillips, 1890-1937—Correspondence.

LOVECRAFT, Howard Phillips, 1890-1937. 813'.5'2 B
Lovecraft at last / by H. P. Lovecraft and Willis Conover ; foreword by Harold Taylor. Arlington, Va. : Carrollton, Clark, c1975. xxii, 272 p. : ill. ; 29 cm. (Miskatonic university classics ; v. 1) Includes index. Bibliography: p. 261-263. [PS3523.O833Z543 1975] 74-29658 ISBN 0-915490-02-1 : 19.75
1. Lovecraft, Howard Phillips, 1890-1937—Correspondence. 2. Conover, Willis. I. Conover, Willis, joint author. II. Title.

Lovecraft, Howard Phillips, 1890-1937—Criticism and interpretation.

SCHWEITZER, Darrell, 1952- 813'.5'2
The dream quest of H. P. Lovecraft / Darrell Schweitzer. 1st ed. San Bernardino, Calif. : Borgo Press, 1978. 63 p. ; 21 cm. (The Milford series) (Popular writers of today ; v. 12) Bibliography: p. 62-63. [PS3523.O833Z857] 78-891 pbk. : 2.45
1. Lovecraft, Howard Phillips, 1890-1937—Criticism and interpretation. I. Title. **BIP**

Lovejoy, Elijah Parish, 1802-1837.

LOVEJOY, Joseph Cammet, 1805-1871. 973.5'0924 B
Memoir of the Rev. Elijah P. Lovejoy; who was murdered in defence of the liberty of the press, at Alton, Illinois, Nov. 7, 1837, by Joseph C. and Owen Lovejoy. With an introd. by John Quincy Adams. Freeport, N.Y., Books for Libraries Press [1970] 382 p. 23 cm. Title on spine: Memoir of E. P. Lovejoy. Reprint of the 1838 ed. [F549.A4L7 1970] 72-117882
1. Lovejoy, Elijah Parish, 1802-1837. 2. Alton, Ill.—Riot, 1837. I. Lovejoy, Owen, 1811-1864, joint author. II. Title.

SIMON, Paul, 1928- 923.673
Lovejoy, martyr to freedom. St. Louis, Concordia [1964] 150 p. 21 cm. Bibliography: p. 145-150. [E449.L889S5] 64-19896
1. Lovejoy, Elijah Parish, 1802-1837. I. Title.

TANNER, Henry. 326'.0924 B
The martyrdom of Lovejoy; an account of the life, trials, and perils of Rev. Elijah P. Lovejoy, who was killed by a pro-slavery mob at Alton, Illinois, the night of November 7, 1837. By an eye-witness. New York, A. M. Kelley, 1971 [c1880] 233 p. facsims., port. 22 cm. (Reprints of economic classics) [F549.A4T2 1971] 68-18603 ISBN 0-678-00744-6
1. Lovejoy, Elijah Parish, 1802-1837. 2. Alton, Ill.—Riot, 1837. I. Title. **BIP**

Lovejoy, Esther (Clayson) Pohl, 1870-1967.

BURT, Olive (Woolley) 1894- 610'.92'4 B
Physician to the world Esther Pohl Lovejoy, by Olive W. Burt. New York, J. Messner [1973] 189 p. 21 cm. Bibliography: p. 185-186. [R154.L59B87] 72-13147 ISBN 0-671-32587-6 4.79
1. Lovejoy, Esther (Clayson) Pohl, 1870-1967. I. Title.

Lovell, Jimmie, 1896-

YOUNGS, Bill. 9173'03'9
The man of action; the story of Jimmie Lovell. Austin, Tex., Sweet Pub. Co. [1969] 136 p. illus., ports. 22 cm. [BX7077.Z8L65] 78-87920
1. Lovell, Jimmie, 1896- I. Title.

Loving, Albert L., 1891-

LOVING, Albert L., 1891- 266'.9'33 B
When I put out to sea : autobiography of Albert L. Loving. Independence, Mo. : Herald Pub. House, c1975. 216 p. ; 21 cm. [BX8678.L68A33] 74-82510 ISBN 0-8309-0124-8
1. Loving, Albert L., 1891- I. Title.

Low, David,

LOW, David, 1891- 927.415
Autobiography. New York, Simon and Schuster, 1957 [c1956] 387p. illus. 24cm. [NC1479. 65A2 1957] 57-7304
I. Title.

Low, James, d. 1852.

LOW, James, d.1852. 915.95'1
The British settlement of Penang. With an introd. by James Jackson. Singapore, New York, Oxford University Press, 1972, [i.e. 1973] xxiv, v, 321 p. illus. 23 cm. (Oxford in Asia historical reprints) Reprint of the 1836 ed. printed at Singapore Free Press Office, Singapore, under title: A dissertation on the soil & agriculture of the British settlement of Penang. [S471.M272P564 1972] 73-180268 15.50
1. Low, James, d. 1852. 2. Agriculture—Pinang. 3. Pinang. I. Title. **BIP**

Low, Juliette (Gordon) 1860-1927.

SHULTZ, Gladys (Denny) 923.673
Lady from Svannah; the life of Juliette Low, by Gladys Denny Shultz and Daisy Gordon Lawrence. [1st ed] Philadelphia, Lippincott [1959] 383 p. illus. 22 cm. [HS3353.G5L88] 58-5844
1. Low, Juliette (Gordon) 1860-1927. 2. Girl Scouts. I. Lawrence, Daisy (Gordon) joint author. II. Title.

Low, Seth, 1850-1916.

LOW, Benjamin Robbins Curtis, 1880-1941. 320.97471'08'0924 B
Seth Low. [1st AMS ed.] New York, AMS Press [1971] xi, 92, xix p. port. 19 cm. Reprint of the 1925 ed. [F128.5.L9 1971] 70-137256 ISBN 0-404-04037-3
1. Low, Seth, 1850-1916. **BIP**

Lowden, Frank Orren, 1861-1943.

HUTCHINSON, William Thomas, 1895- 923.273
Lowden of Illinois; the life of Frank O. Lowden. [Chicago] University of Chicago Press [1957] 2 v. illus. 25cm. Contents.v. 1. City and State.--v. 2. Nation and countryside. [F546.L92] 57-6274
1. Lowden, Frank Orren, 1861-1943. I. Title.

Lowe, Charles John, Sir, 1880-

ROSENTHAL, Newman Hirsch. 347.99'24 B
Sir Charles Lowe; a biographical memoir [by] Newman Rosenthal. Melbourne, Robertson and Mullens [1968] 214 p. ports. 23 cm. [LAW] 68-132629 5.25 Aust.
1. Lowe, Charles John, Sir, 1880-

Lowe, Frank Gordon, 1921-

LOWE, Frank Gordon, 1921- 070.4'092'4
I beg to differ / by Frank Lowe. Toronto : Totem Books, 1976. 224 p. ; 18 cm. [PN4913.L6A52 1976] 77-369241
1. Lowe, Frank Gordon, 1921- 2. Journalists—Canada—Biography. I. Title.

Lowe, Thaddeus S. C., 1832-1913—Juvenile literature.

SIMS, Lydel 92
Thaddeus Lowe: Uncle Sam's first airman New York, Putnam [c.1964] 223p. 21cm. (Lives to remember) Bibl. 64-14406 3.50
1. Lowe, Thaddeus S. C., 1832-1913—Juvenile literature. I. Title.

Lowell, Abbott Lawrence, 1856-1943.

YEOMANS, Henry Aaron, 1877- 378.1'12'0924
Abbott Lawrence Lowell, 1856-1943 / Henry aaron Yeomans New York : Arno Press, 1977, c1948. p. cm. (The Academic profession) Reprint of the ed. published by Harvard University Press, Cambridge, Mass. Includes index. [LD2175 1909c] 76-55181 ISBN 0-405-10009-4 lib.bdg. : 33.00
1. Lowell, Abbott Lawrence, 1856-1943. 2. College teachers—United States—Biography. I. Title. II. Series. **BIP**

Lowell, Amy, 1874-1925.

GREGORY, Horace, 1898- 928.1
Amy Lowell; portrait of the poet in her time. Edinburgh, New York, T. Nelson [1958] 213p. illus. 22cm. [PS3523.O88Z67] 58-11247
1. Lowell, Amy, 1874-1925. 2. Poets, American. I. Title.

GREGORY, Horace, 1898- 811'.5'2 B
Amy Lowell; portrait of the poet in her time. Freeport, N.Y., Books for Libraries Press [1969, c1958] ix, 213 p. illus., ports. 23 cm. (Select bibliographies reprint series) [PS3523.O88Z67 1969] 69-16855
1. Lowell, Amy, 1874-1925. 2. Poets, American.

WOOD, Clement, 1888-1950. 811'.5'2 B
Amy Lowell. [Folcroft, Pa.] Folcroft Library Editions, 1973 [c1926] 185 p. 24 cm. [PS3523.O88Z8 1973] 73-3300 15.00
1. Lowell, Amy, 1874-1925.

Lowell, Amy, 1874-1925—Biography.

GOULD, Jean, 1909- 811'.5'2 B
Amy : the world of Amy Lowell and the Imagist movement / by Jean Gould. New York : Dodd, Mead, [1975] xii, 372 p., [8] leaves of plates : ill. ; 24 cm. Includes index. Bibliography: p. 359-362. [PS3523.O88Z66] 75-11563 ISBN 0-396-07022-1 : 12.50
1. Lowell, Amy, 1874-1925—Biography. 2. Imagist poetry—History and criticism. I. Title. **BIP**

HEYMANN, Clemens David, 1945- 811'.5'209 B
American aristocracy : the lives and times of James Russell, Amy, and Robert Lowell / by C. David Heymann. New York : Dodd, Mead, [1979] i.e. 1980. p. cm. Includes bibliographical references and index. [PS129.H44] 79-9351 ISBN 0-396-07608-4 : 17.95
1. Lowell family. 2. Lowell, James Russell, 1819-1891—Biography. 3. Lowell, Amy, 1874-1925—Biography. 4. Lowell, Robert, 1917-1977—Biography. 5. Poets, American—Biography. 6. New England—Intellectual life. I. Title. **BIP**

Lowell, Charles Russell, 1835-1864.

EMERSON, Edward Waldo, 1844-1930. 973.78'1'0924
Life and letters of Charles Russell Lowell, captain Sixth United States Cavalry, colonel Second Massachusetts Cavalry, brigadier-general United States Volunteers. Port Washington, N.Y., Kennikat Press [1971] viii, 499 p. illus., map, ports. 21 cm.

(Kennikat Press scholarly reprints. Series in American history and culture in the nineteenth century) Reprint of the 1907 ed. [E467.1.L6E5 1971] 71-137909 ISBN 0-8046-1477-6
1. Lowell, Charles Russell, 1835-1864. 2. United States—History—Civil War, 1861-1865—Personal narratives.

Lowell family.

HEYMANN, Clemens David, 1945- 811'.5'209 B
American aristocracy : the lives and times of James Russell, Amy, and Robert Lowell / by C. David Heymann. New York : Dodd, Mead, [1979] i.e. 1980. p. cm. Includes bibliographical references and index. [PS129.H44] 79-9351 ISBN 0-396-07608-4 : 17.95
1. Lowell family. 2. Lowell, James Russell, 1819-1891—Biography. 3. Lowell, Amy, 1874-1925—Biography. 4. Lowell, Robert, 1917-1977—Biography. 5. Poets, American—Biography. 6. New England—Intellectual life. I. Title. BIP

Lowell, James Russell.

LOWELL, James Russell, 1819-1891. 816'.3
Letters of James Russell Lowell. Edited by Charles Eliot Norton. New York, AMS Press, 1966. 3 v. illus. 23 cm. (The Complete writings of James Russell Lowell. Elmwood ed., v. 14-16) Reprint of the 1904 ed. [PS2331.A3N6 1966] 811.3 76-172754
I. Norton, Charles Eliot, 1827-1908, ed.

Lowell, James Russell, 1819-1891.

BEATTY, Richmond Croom, 1905- 811'.3 B
James Russell Lowell. [Hamden, Conn.] Archon Books, 1969 [c1942] xviii, 316 p. illus., ports. 23 cm. Bibliographical references included in "Notes" (p. 298-309) [PS2331.B4 1969] 69-13623
1. Lowell, James Russell, 1819-1891.

CHILD, Francis James, 1825-1896. 928.1
The scholar-friends; letters of Francis James Child and James Russell Lowell, edited by M. A. De Wolfe Howe and G. W. Cottrell, Jr. Cambridge, Harvard University Press, 1952. 84 p. illus., ports. 25 cm. "Reprinted from the ... Harvard Library bulletin, vol. v, nos. 2, 3 ... vol. vi, nos. 1, 2." [PS1292.C85Z53] 52-9390
I. Lowell, James Russell, 1819-1891. II. Howe, Mark Antony De Wolfe, 1864- ed. III. Cottrell, George William. ed. IV. Title. BIP

DUBERMAN, Martin B. 811.3 B
James Russell Lowell [by] Martin Duberman. Boston, Houghton Mifflin, 1966. xxii, 516 p. illus., facsims., ports. 22 cm. Bibliography: p. [373]-386. [PS2331.D8] 66-19835
1. Lowell, James Russell, 1819-1891

GREENSLET, Ferris, 1875-1959. 811'.3 B
James Russell Lowell: his life and work. Boston, Houghton, Mifflin, 1905. Detroit, Gale Research Co., 1969. x, 309 p. illus., facsim., ports. 22 cm. [PS2331.G7 1969] 77-77162
1. Lowell, James Russell, 1819-1891.

HALE, Edward Everett, 1863-1932. 811'.3 B
James Russell Lowell. [Folcroft, Pa.] Folcroft Library Editions, 1973 [c1899] p. Reprint of the ed. published by Kegan Paul, Trench, Trubner, London, in series: The Beacon biographies of eminent Americans. [PS2331.H33 1973] 73-14571 15.00
1. Lowell, James Russell, 1819-1891. I. Series: The Beacon biographies of eminent Americans (London)

HALE, Edward Everett, 1863-1932. 811'.3 B
James Russell Lowell. [Folcroft, Pa.] Folcroft Library Editions, 1973 [c1899] xviii, 128 p. port. 23 cm. Reprint of the ed. published by Kegan Paul, Trench, Trubner, London, in series: The Beacon biographies of eminent Americans. Bibliography: p. [124] [PS2331.H33 1973] 73-14571 ISBN 0-8414-4764-0 (lib. bdg.)
1. Lowell, James Russell, 1819-1891. I. Series: The Beacon biographies of eminent Americans (London)

HOWARD, Leon. 928.1
Victorian knight-errant; a study of the early literary career of James Russell Lowell. Berkeley, University of California Press, 1952. x, 388 p. 25 cm. Bibliographical references included in "Notes" (p. [363]-373) [PS2331.H6] 52-11395
1. Lowell, James Russell, 1819-1891. I. Title. BIP

HOWARD, Leon. 811'.3 B
Victorian knight-errant; a study of the early literary career of James Russell Lowell. Westport, Conn., Greenwood Press [1971, c1952] x, 388 p. 23 cm. Includes bibliographical references. [PS2331.H6 1971] 72-136072 ISBN 0-8371-5222-4
1. Lowell, James Russell, 1819-1891. I. Title.

HUDSON, William Henry, 1862-1918. 811'.3
Lowell & his poetry. London, G. G. Harrap, 1914. [New York, AMS Press, 1972] 136 p. port. 19 cm. (Poetry and life series) Includes bibliographical references. [PS2331.H8 1972] 78-120988 ISBN 0-404-52517-2 8.00
1. Lowell, James Russell, 1819-1891. I. Title. II. Series. BIP

LOWELL, James Russell, 1819-1891. 816'.3
Letters of James Russell Lowell. Edited by Charles Eliot Norton. New York, AMS Press, 1966. 3 v. illus. 23 cm. (The Complete writings of James Russell Lowell. Elmwood ed., v. 14-16) Reprint of the 1904 ed. [PS2331.A3N6 1966] 811.3 76-172754
I. Norton, Charles Eliot, 1827-1908, ed.

SCUDDER, Horace Elisha, 1838-1902. 811'.3 B
James Russell Lowell; a biography. Boston, Houghton Mifflin, 1901. Grosse Pointe, Mich., Scholarly Press, 1968. 2 v. illus., ports. 22 cm. "A list of the writings of James Russell Lowell ... ": v. 2., p. [421]-447. [PS2331.S4 1968] 79-2947
1. Lowell, James Russell, 1819-1891.

WAGENKNECHT, Edward Charles, 1900- 811'.3 B
James Russell Lowell; portrait of a many-sided man [by] Edward Wagenknecht. New York, Oxford University Press, 1971. ix, 276 p. port. 21 cm. Includes bibliographical references. [PS2331.W3] 76-135975 7.50
1. Lowell, James Russell, 1819-1891.

Lowell, James Russell, 1819-1891—Biography.

HEYMANN, Clemens David, 1945- 811'.5'209 B
American aristocracy : the lives and times of James Russell, Amy, and Robert Lowell / by C. David Heymann. New York : Dodd, Mead, [1979] i.e. 1980. p. cm. Includes bibliographical references and index. [PS129.H44] 79-9351 ISBN 0-396-07608-4 : 17.95
1. Lowell family. 2. Lowell, James Russell, 1819-1891—Biography. 3. Lowell, Amy, 1874-1925—Biography. 4. Lowell, Robert, 1917-1977—Biography. 5. Poets, American—Biography. 6. New England—Intellectual life. I. Title. BIP

SCUDDER, Horace Elisha, 1838-1902. 811'.3 B
James Russell Lowell; a biography. Boston, Houghton, Mifflin, 1901. [New York, AMS Press, 1974] 2 v. illus. 19 cm. "A List of the writings of James Russell Lowell": v. 2, p. [421]-447. [PS2331.S4 1974] 73-126665 ISBN 0-404-05664-4
1. Lowell, James Russell, 1819-1891—Biography. BIP

Lowell, Josephine Shaw, 1843-1905.

STEWART, William Rhinelander, 1852-1929. 361'.92'4 B
The philanthropic work of Josephine Shaw Lowell, containing a biographical sketch of her life, together with a selection of her public papers and private letters. Collected and arranged for publication by William Rhinelander Stewart. Montclair, N.J., Patterson Smith, 1974. xiv, 584 p. illus. 22 cm. (Patterson Smith series in criminology, law enforcement & social problems. Publication no. 163) Reprint of the 1911 ed. published by Macmillan, New York. Bibliography: p. 551-561. [HV28.L66S83 1974] 71 172576 ISBN 0 87585 163 0
1. Lowell, Josephine Shaw, 1843-1905. 2. Social service—New York (City) I. Title. BIP

Lowell, Robert, 1917-1977.

AXELROD, Steven Gould, 1944- 811'.5'2
Robert Lowell : life and art / Steven Gould Axelrod. Princeton, N.J. : Princeton University Press, c1978. p. cm. Includes bibliographical references and index. [PS3523.O89Z56] 78-51155 ISBN 0-691-06363-X : 15.00
1. Lowell, Robert, 1917-1977. 2. Poets, American—20th century—Biography. BIP

Lowell, Robert, 1917- -Bibliog.

STAPLES, Hugh B v. 12
Robert Lowell; bibliography 1939-1959, with an illustrative critique. [Cambridge, Mass. 1959] 292-318 p. 26 cm. "Offprint from Harvard Library Bulletin, volume XIII, number 2, Spring 1959." 66-57282
1. Lowell, Robert, 1917- -Bibliog. I. Title.

Lowenstein (M.) and Sons, inc.

THE Lowenstein story. v. 12
[n. p., 1956] 89p. illus. 28cm.
1. Lowenstein (M.) and Sons, inc.

Lower, Arthur Reginald Marsden, 1889-

HIS own man : 971
essays in honour of Arthur Reginald Marsden Lower / edited by W. H. Heick and Roger Graham. Montreal : McGill-Queen's University Press, 1974. xi, 187 p. : ill., port. ; 26 cm. Includes bibliographical references. [F1026.H48] 75-309541 10.00
1. Lower, Arthur Reginald Marsden, 1889- 2. Canada—History—Addresses, essays, lectures. I. Lower, Arthur Reginald Marsden, 1889- II. Heick, W. H. III. Graham, Roger.
Contents omitted. Distributed by McGill Queens University Press, Irvington, New York.

Lowie, Robert Harry,

LOWIE, Robert Harry, 1883-1957. 925.72
Robert H. Lowie, ethnologist; a personal record. Berkeley, University of California Press, 1959. 198p. illus. 25cm. [GN21.L73A3] 59-8762
I. Title. BIP

Lowie, Robert Harry, 1883-1957.

LOWIE, Robert Harry, 1883-1957. 925.72
Robert H. Lowie, ethnologist; a personal record. Berkeley, University of California Press, 1959. 198p. illus. 25cm. [GN21.L73A3] 59-8762
I. Title. BIP

MURPHY, Robert Francis, 1924- 309.2'092'4 B
Robert H. Lowie, by Robert F. Murphy. New York, Columbia University Press, 1972. viii, 179 p. 23 cm. (Leaders of modern anthropology series) "Selected writings of Robert H. Lowie": p. 77-175. [GN21.L73M8] 72-1969 ISBN 0-231-03375-3 7.50 2.95 (pbk)
1. Lowie, Robert Harry, 1883-1957. 2. Ethnology. I. Lowie, Robert Harry, 1883-1957. II. Title. III. Series.

Lowndes, Rawlins, 1721-1800.

VIPPERMAN, Carl J., 1928- 975.7'03'0924 B
The rise of Rawlins Lowndes, 1721-1800 / by Carl J. Vipperman 1st ed. Columbia : Published for the South Carolina Tricentennial Commission by the University of South Carolina Press, 1978. p. cm. (Tricentennial studies ; no. 12) Includes bibliographical references and index. [F272.L87V56] 78-17353 ISBN 0-87249-259-1 lib.bdg. : 14.95
1. Lowndes, Rawlins, 1721-1800. 2. Legislators—South Carolina—Biography. 3. South Carolina—History—Colonial period, ca. 1600-1775. 4. South Carolina—History—Revolution, 1775-1783. I. Title. II. Series: South Carolina Tricentennial Commission. Tricentennial studies ; no. 12. BIP

Lowrie

LOWRIE 921.8489
A short life of Kierkegaard. Garden City, N.Y., Doubleday 1961 [c.1942] 226p. (Anchor bk., A273) Bibl. .95 pap.,
I. Title.

Lowry, Laurence Stephen, 1887-1976.

SPALDING, Julian. 759.2 B
Lowry / Julian Spalding. Oxford : Phaidon ; New York : Dutton, 1979. 16 p., 48 leaves of plates : col. ill. ; 31 cm. Bibliography: p. 15. [ND497.L83S66 1979] 79-50324 ISBN 0-7148-1996-4 : 12.50
1. Lowry, Laurence Stephen, 1887-1976. 2. Painters—Great Britain—Biography. I. Lowry, Laurence Stephen, 1887-1976.

Lowry, Malcolm, 1909-1957.

BRADBROOK, Muriel Clara. 813'.5'4
Malcolm Lowry: his art & early life; a study in transformation [by] M. C. Bradbrook. [London] Cambridge University Press [1974] xiii, 170 p. maps. 21 cm. Bibliography: p. 164-166. [PR6023.O96Z57] 74-76945 ISBN 0-521-20473-9
1. Lowry, Malcolm, 1909-1957. I. Title.
Distributed by Cambridge University Press, New York; 6.95

DAY, Douglas. 813'.5'4 B
Malcolm Lowry; a biography. New York, Oxford University Press, 1973. xiii, 483 p. illus. 24 cm. Bibliography: p. 473-478. [PR6023.O96Z598] 73-82665 ISBN 0-19-501711-0 10.00
1. Lowry, Malcolm, 1909-1957. BIP

Lowry, Thomas, 1843-1909.

LOWRY, Goodrich. 388.4'6'0924 B
Streetcar man : Tom Lowry and the Twin City Rapid Transit Company / Goodrich Lowry. Minneapolis : Lerner Publications, Co., c1979. p. cm. Includes index. Bibliography: p. [HE2754.L63L68 1979] 79-2584 ISBN 0-8225-0764-1 : 7.95
1. Lowry, Thomas, 1843-1909. 2. Twin City Rapid Transit Company—History. 3. Street-railroads—Employees—Biography. I. Title. BIP

Loy, Myrna, 1905-

KAY, Karyn. 791.43'028'0924 B
Myrna Loy / by Karyn Kay. New York : Pyramid Publications, 1977. 160 p. : ill. ; 20 cm. (A Pyramid illustrated history of the movies) Includes index. Bibliography: p. 141. [PN2287.L67K3] 77-73158 ISBN 0-515-04290-0 pbk. : 1.95
1. Loy, Myrna, 1905- 2. Moving-picture actors and actresses—United States—Biography.

KAY, Karyn. 791.43'028'0924 B
Myrna Loy / by Karyn Kay. New York : Pyramid Publications, 1977. 160 p. : ill. ; 20 cm. (A Pyramid illustrated history of the movies) Includes index. Bibliography: p. 141. [PN2287.L67K3] 77-73158 ISBN 0-515-04290-0 pbk. : 1.95
1. Loy, Myrna, 1905- 2. Moving-picture actors and actresses—United States—Biography. BIP

Loyola, Ignacio de,

LOYOLA, Ignacio de, Saint 1491-1556. 922.246
Letters of St. Ignatius of Loyola, selected and translated by William J. Young. Chicago, Loyola University Press, 1959. xlii, 450p. 24cm. Bibliographical footnotes. [BX4700.L7A38] 59-13459
I. Young, William John, 1885- ed. and tr. II. Title.

LOYOLA, Ignacio de, Saint 1491-1556. 922.246
Letters to women. [Collected by] Hugo Rahner. [New York] Herder and Herder [1960] xxiii, 564p. ports., facsims. 23cm. 'This English translation by Kathleen Pond and S. A. H. Weetman is based on the first German edition of 'Ignatius von Loyola, Briefwechsel mit Frauen,' published by Herder, Freiburg, 1956.' Bibliographical references included in 'Notes' (p. 481-540) [BX4700.L7A376 1960a] 59-14554
I. Rahner, Hugo, 1900- ed. II. Title.

LOYOLA, Ignacio de, Saint 1491-1556. 922.246
St. Ignatius' own story, as told to luis Gonzalez de Camera; with a sampling of his letters. Translated by William J. Young. Chicago, H. Regnery Co., 1956. 138p. 22cm. (Library of living Catholic thought) [BX4700.L7A322] 56-10674
I. Gonzalez de Camara, Luis, 16th cent. II. Title.

Loyola, Ignacio de, Saint, 1491-1556.

CHARMOT, Francois. 230.0922
Ignatius Loyola and Francis de Sales: two masters, one spirituality [by] F. Charmot. Translated by Sister M. Renelle. St. Louis, B. Herder Book Co. [1966] x, 251 p. 21 cm. (Cross and crown series of spirituality, no. 32) Translation of Deux maitres, une spiritualite: Ignace de Loyola, Francois de Sales. Bibliography: p. 250-251. [BX4700.L7C53] 66-17096
1. Loyola, Ignacio de. Saint, 1491-1556. 2. Francois de Sales, Saint, Bp. of Geneva, 1567-1622. 3. Spiritual life — History of doctrines. I. Title. II. Series.

DERLETH, August William, 1909- 922.246
St. Ignatius and the Company of Jesus. Illustrated by John Lawn. New York, Vision Books [1956] 184p. illus. 22cm. (Vision books, 9) [BX4700.L7D4] 56-7278
1. Loyola, Ignacio de, Saint, 1491-1556. I. Title.

FULOP-MILLER, Rene, 1891- 922
The saints that moved the world; Anthony, Augustine, Francis, Ignatius, Theresa. Tr(by Alexander Gode, Erika Fulop-Miller. New York, Collier [1962, c.1945] 511p. 18cm. (AS268 9) Bibl. .95 pap.,
1. Augustinus, Aurelius, Saint, bp. of Hippo. 2. Francesco d'Assisi, Saint, 1182-1226. 3. Loyola, Ignacio de, saint, 1491-1556. 4. Teresa, Saint, 1515-1582. 5. Antonius, Saint, 'the Great.' I. Gode, Alexander, tr. II. Eulop-Miller, Erika, joint tr. III. Title. BIP

JOLY, Henri, 1839-1925. 271'.53'024 B
Saint Ignatius of Loyola / by Henri Joly ; translated by Mildred Partridge ; with a pref. by George Tyrrell. New York : AMS Press, [1976] p. cm. Translation of Saint Ignace de Loyola. Reprint of the 1899 ed. published by Duckworth, London, which was issued in series: The Saints. [BX4700.L7J6 1976] 70-170821 ISBN 0-404-03597-3
1. Loyola, Ignacio de, Saint, 1491-1556. I. Title. II. Series: The Saints.

LOYOLA, Ignacio de, Saint, 1491-1556. 282'.092'4 B
The autobiography of St. Ignatius Loyola, with related documents. Edited with introd. and notes by John C. Olin. Translated by Joseph F. O'Callaghan. New York, Harper & Row [1974] vii, 112 p. illus. 21 cm. (Harper torchbooks) Bibliography: p. 111-112. [BX4700.L7A313 1974] 73-7468 ISBN 0-06-139170-0 2.95 (pbk.)
1. Loyola, Ignacio de, Saint, 1491-1556. I. Title.

LOYOLA, Ignacio de, Saint 1491-1556. 922.246
Letters of St. Ignatius of Loyola, selected and translated by William J. Young. Chicago, Loyola University Press, 1959. xlii, 450p. 24cm. Bibliographical footnotes. [BX4700.L7A38] 59-13459
I. Young, William John, 1885- ed. and tr. II. Title.

LOYOLA, Ignacio de, Saint 1491-1556. 922.246
Letters to women. [Collected by] Hugo Rahner. [New York] Herder and Herder [1960] xxiii, 564p. ports., facsims. 23cm. 'This English translation by Kathleen Pond and S. A. H. Weetman is based on the first German edition of 'Ignatius von Loyola, Briefwechsel mit Frauen,' published by Herder, Freiburg, 1956.' Bibliographical references included in 'Notes' (p. 481-540) [BX4700.L7A376 1960a] 59-14554
I. Rahner, Hugo, 1900- ed. II. Title.

LOYOLA, Ignacio de, Saint 1491-1556. 922.246
St. Ignatius' own story, as told to luis Gonzalez de Camera; with a sampling of his letters. Translated by William J. Young. Chicago, H. Regnery Co., 1956. 138p. 22cm. (Library of living Catholic thought) [BX4700.L7A322] 56-10674
I. Gonzalez de Camara, Luis, 16th cent. II. Title.

MARCUSE, Ludwig, 1894- 271'.53'0924 B
Soldier of the church; the life of Ignatius Loyola. Translated from the German and edited by Christopher Lazare. New York, Simon and Schuster, 1939. [New York, AMS Press, 1972] vi, 352 p. 23 cm. Translation of Ignatius von Loyola. [BX4700.L7M37 1972] 70-172842 ISBN 0-404-04187-6 12.50
1. Loyola, Ignacio de, Saint, 1491-1556. I. Title. BIP

MATT, Leonard von 922.246
St. Ignatius of Loyola [by] Leonard von Matt, Hugo Rahner [-Tr. from German] New York, Universe [c.1963] 48p. 72 illus. (incl. ports., facsims.) 18cm. (Orbis bks., 2) Summary of St. Ignatius of Loyola, a pictorial biography, orig. pub. in German under title: Ignatius von Loyola. 63-18343 1.75 pap.,
1. Loyola, Ignacio de, Saint, 1491-1556. I. Rahner, Hugo, 1900- II. Title.

PAIASOGLI. GIORGIO. 922.246
Saint Ignatius of Loyola. Translated from the Italian by Paul Garvin. New York, Society of St. Paul [c1959] 351p. illus. 22cm. Includes bibliography. [BX4700.L7P313] 58-12224
1. Loyola. Ignacio de. Saint, 1491-1556. I. Title.

PAPASOGLI, Giorgio. 922.246
Saint Ignatius of Loyola. Translated from the Italian by Paul Garvin. New York, Society of St. Paul [c.1959] 351p. bibl. illus. 22cm. 58-12224 4.00
1. Loyola, Ignacio de, Saint, 1491-1556. I. Title.

PENNING de Vries, Piet. 271'.5'024
Discernment of spirits, according to the life and teachings of St. Ignatius of Loyola. Translated by W. Dudok Van Heel. [1st ed.] New York, Exposition Press [1973] 252 p. 22 cm. (An Exposition-Testament book) Bibliography: p. 247-248. [BX2350.2.P4193] 72-90063 ISBN 0-682-47592-0 8.00
1. Loyola, Ignacio de, Saint, 1491-1556. 2. Spiritual life—History of doctrines. I. Title.

RAHNER, Hugo, 1900- 230.2'0924
Ignatius the theologian. Translated by Michael Barry. [New York] Herder and Herder [1968] viii, 238 p. 22 cm. Translation of Ignatius von Loyola als Mensch und Theologe, chapters 11-16. Bibliographical footnotes. [BX4700] 68-22567 6.95
1. Loyola, Ignacio de, Saint, 1491-1556. I. Title.

RAHNER, Hugo, 1900- 922.246
The spirituality of St. Ignatius Loyola, an account of its historical development; translated by Francis John Smith. Westminster, Md., Newman Press, 1953. 142p. 21cm. Translation of Ignatius von Loyola und das geschichtliche Werden seiner Frommigkeit. [BX4700.L7R313] 53-5586
1. Loyola, ignacio de, Saint, 1491-1556. I. Title. BIP

RICHTER, Friedrich, priest 922.443
Martin Luther and Ignatius Loyola, spokesman for two worlds of belief. Translated from the German by Leonard F. Zwinger. Westminster, Md., Newman Press [c.]1960. 248p. (Bibl.) 21cm. 60-10728 3.75
1. Luther, Martin, 1483-1546. 2. Loyola, Ignacio de, Saint, 1491-1556. 3. Lutheran Church—Relations— Catholic Church. 4. Lutheran Church—Relations—Catholic Church. 5. Catholic Church—Relations—Lutheran Church. I. Title.

RIVADENEIRA, Pedro de, 1527-1611. 230'.2 S
The life of B. Father Ignatius of Loyola, 1616 / Pedro de Ribadeneira. Ilkley [Eng.] : Scolar Press, 1976. 358 p. ; 19 cm. (English recusant literature 1558-1640 ; v. 300) (Series: Rogers, David Morrison, comp. English recusant literature, 1558-1640 ; v. 300.) Translation of Vita Ignatii Loiolae. Reprint of the 1616 ed. STC 20967 [BX1750.A1E5 Vol. 300] [BX4700.L7] 271'.53'024 B 76-378334 ISBN 0-85967-301-4
1. Loyola, Ignacio de, Saint, 1491-1556. 2. Christian saints—Biography. I. Title. II. Series.

ROBERTO, Brother, 1927- 922.246
The man who limped to heaven; a story of St. Ignatius Loyola. Illus. by Anthony Joyce. Notre Dame, Ind., Dujarie Press [1954] 92p. illus. 24cm. [BX4700.L7R55] 54-7749
1. Loyola, Ignacio de, Saint, 1491-1556. I. Title.

THOMPSON, Francis, 1859-1907. 922.246
Saint Ignatius Loyola, edited by John H. Pollen. With an appreciation by Hugh Kelly. Baltimore, Carroll Press [1951, c1950] 192 p. port. 22 cm. [BX4700.L7T5] 51-6271
1. Loyola, Ignacio de, Saint, 1491-1556. I. Title.

THOMPSON, Francis, 1859-1907 922.246
Saint Ignatius Loyola, ed. by John J. Pollen. Introd. by James Brodrick. London, Burns & Oates [dist. Fresno, Calif., Academy Lib. Guild, c.1962] 190p. 18cm. (Universe bk.) 1.25 pap.,
1. Loyola, Ignacio de, Saint, 1491-1556. I. Title.

VAN DYKE, Paul, 1859-1933. 271'.5'0924
Ignatius Loyola, the founder of the Jesuits. Port Washington, N.Y., Kennikat Press [1968, c1926] vi, 381 p. 21 cm. Bibliography: p. 364-368. [BX4700.L7V3 1968] 67-27659
1. Loyola, Ignacio de, Saint, 1491-1556.

Loyola, Ignacio de, Saint, 1491-1556—Juvenile literature.

LIVERSIDGE, Douglas, 1913- 271.5'0924 B
Ignatius of Loyola; the soldier-saint. New York, F. Watts [1970] 150 p. map. 22 cm. (Immortals of philosophy and religion) A biography of the man who turned from a military life to God's service, becoming famous for writing Spiritual Exercises and founding the Society of Jesus. [BX4700.L7L55] 92 70-103098
1. Loyola, Ignacio de, Saint, 1491-1556—Juvenile literature. I. Title.

Lu, Pan.

HITZ, Demi. 694'.092'4 B
Lu Pan, the carpenter's apprentice / adapted and illustrated by Demi Hitz. Englewood Cliffs, N.J. : Prentice-Hall, c1978. 48 p. : ill. ; 22 cm. A brief biography of a young apprentice, living during the fifth century, B.C., who became a master carpenter and one of China's greatest artisans. [HD8039.C32C644] 92 77-26838 ISBN 0-13-541284-6 : 5.95
1. Lu, Pan. 2. Carpenters—China—Biography—Juvenile literature. I. Title.

Lubchenco, Portia (McKnight)

LUBCHENCO, Portia (McKnight) 926.1
Doctor Portia, her first fifty years in medicine, as told to Anna C. Petteys. Denver, Golden Bell Press, 1964. 315 p. illus., ports. 23 cm. [R154.L8A3] 64-8450
I. Petteys, Anna C. II. Title.

Lubin, David, 1849-1919.

EISENBERG, Azriel Louis, 1903- 338.10924
Feeding the world; a biography of David Lubin, by Azriel Eisenberg. Illustrated with drawings by Laszlo Matulay and with photos. London, New York, Abelard-Schuman [1965] 191 p. illus., ports. 21 cm. [HD1430.L9E52] 65-12934
1. Lubin, David, 1849-1919. I. Title.

Lubitsch, Ernst, 1892-1947.

CARRINGER, Robert. 791.43'0233'0924
Ernst Lubitsch : a guide to references and resources / Robert Carringer, Barry Sabath. Boston : G. K. Hall, [1978] xx, 262 p. ; 25 cm. (A Reference publication in film) Includes indexes. [PN1998.A3L832] 78-1639 ISBN 0-8161-7895-X : 20.00
1. Lubitsch, Ernst, 1892-1947. I. Sabath, Barry, joint author. II. Title. III. Series. BIP

Luby, James,

LUBY, James, 1856-1925. 070.4'092'4
James Luby, journalist. New York, Beekman Publishers, 1974. 135 p. port. 23 cm. (American newspaperman, 1790-1933) Reprint of the 1930 ed. published by Ransdell, Washington. [AC8.L85 1974] 74-2065 ISBN 0-8464-0014-6 10.00

Lucas, Edward Verrall,

LUCAS, Edward Verrall, 1868-1938. 828'.9'1209 B
What a life! : An autobiography / by E. V. Lucas and George Morrow ; illustrated by Whiteley's ; with a new introd. by John Ashbery. New York : Dover Publications, 1975. xii, 128 p. : ill. ; 21 cm. Illustrations taken from Whiteley's general catalogue. Reprint of the 1911 ed. published by Methuen, London. [PR6023.U24W5 1975] 74-16979 ISBN 0-486-23133-X pbk. : 2.50
I. Morrow, George, 1869-1955. II. Whiteley's Ltd. Whiteley's general catalogue. III. Title.

Lucas, Fielding, 1781-1854.

FOSTER, James William, 1890- 920.4
Fielding Lucas Jr., Jr. early 19th century publisher of fine books and maps. Worcester, Mass., American Antiquarian Society, 1956. 162-212p. illus. 25cm. 'Reprinted from the Proceedings of the American Antiquarian Society for October 1955.' [Z473.L88F6] 56-4846
1. Lucas, Fielding, 1781-1854. I. Title.

Lucas, George A., 1824-1909.

LUCAS, George A., 1824-1909. 706'.5 B
The diary of George A. Lucas, 1857-1909 / transcribed and with introd. by Lilian M.C. Randall Princeton, N.J. : Princeton University Press, c1979. p. cm. Includes bibliographical references and index. [N8660.L8A2 1979] 77-85561 ISBN 0-691-03933-X : 50.00
1. Lucas, George A., 1824-1909. 2. Art dealers—United States—Biography. I. Randall, Lilian M. C. II. Title.

Lucas, Sharalee.

LUCAS, Sharalee. 783.7'092'4 B
Always becoming / Sharalee. Nashville : Impact Books, c1978. 104 p. ; 22 cm. [ML420.L928A3] 78-58204 ISBN 0-914850-32-6 : 4.95
1. Lucas, Sharalee. 2. Gospel musicians—United States—Biography. I. Title. BIP

Luce, Clare (Boothe) 1906-

HATCH, Alden, 1898- 923.273
Ambassador Extraordinary Clare Boothe Luce. Illustrated with photos. [1st ed.] New York, Holt [c1956] 254p. illus. 22cm. [E748.L894H3] 55-10640
1. Luce, Clare (Boothe) 1906- I. Title.

Luce, Henry Robinson, 1898-1967.

KOBLER, John. 655.4'24
Luce; his time, life, and fortune. [1st ed.] Garden City, N.Y., Doubleday, 1968. ix, 296 p. 22 cm. Bibliography: p. 294-296. [PN4874.L76K6] 68-11033
1. Luce, Henry Robinson, 1898-1967. I. Title.

SWANBERG, W. A. 070.5'092'4 [B]
Luce and his empire. [New York, Dell, 1973, c.1972] 734 p. 18 cm. Includes bibliographical references. [PN4874.L76S9] 1.95 (pbk.)
1. Luce, Henry Robinson, 1898-1967. I. Title.
L.C. card no. for the hardbound edition: 73-162778.

Lucia Filippini, Saint, 1672-1732.

BASILE, Giacinta. 271'.97 B
Forever yes : the story of Lucy Filippini / by Giacinta Basile and Geraldine Calabrese. Philadelphia : Dorrance, c1979. xvi, 139 p. ; 22 cm. Bibliography: p. 139. [BX4700.L73B37] 78-72582 ISBN 0-8059-2602-X : 5.95
1. Lucia Filippini, Saint, 1672-1732. 2. Christian saints—Italy—Biography. I. Calabrese, Geraldine, joint author. II. Title.

Luciano, Charles.

GOSCH, Martin A. 364.1'092'4 B
The last testament of Lucky Luciano [by] Martin A. Gosch [and] Richard Hammer. [1st ed.] Boston, Little, Brown [1975] viii, 461 p. ports. 25 cm. [HV6248.L92G67 1975] 74-12296 ISBN 0-316-32140-0
1. Luciano, Charles. I. Hammer, Richard, joint author. II. Luciano, Charles. III. Title.

GOSCH, Martin A. 364.1'092'4 B
The last testament of Lucky Luciano [by] Martin A. Gosch and Richard Hammer. [New York] Dell [1976 c1975] 460 p. 18 cm. Includes index. [HV6248.L92G67] 1.95 (pbk.)
1. Luciano, Charles. I. Hammer, Richard, joint author. II. Title.
L.C. card no. of 1974 Little, Brown edition: 74-12296. BIP

POWELL, Hickman. 345'.73'0253
Lucky Luciano, his amazing trial and wild witnesses / by Hickman Powell ; introd. by Charles Grutzner. Secaucus, N.J. : Citadel Press, 1975. xxvi, 338 p. ; 22 cm. Reprint of the 1939 ed. published by Harcourt, Brace, New York, under title: Ninety times guilty. An Arno Press book. [HQ316.N6P6 1975b] 75-4467 ISBN 0-8065-0493-5 : 7.95
1. Luciano, Charles. 2. Prostitution—New York (City) I. Title.

Luckey, Henry Carl.

LUCKEY, Henry Carl. 923.273
85 American years; memoirs of a Nebraska congressman [1st ed.] New York, Exposition Press [1955] 230p. illus. 21cm. [E748.L896A3] 55-8684
I. Title.

Luckhardt, Mildred Madeleine (Corell)

LUCKHARDT, Mildred 922.1
Madeleine (Corell)
The story of Saint Nicholas. Illustrated by Gordon Laite. New York, Abingdon Press [c.1960] 112p. illus. (part col.) 23cm. 60-6815 2.75
I. Title.

Luckner, Felix, Graf von, 1881-1966.

HOYT, Edwin 940.4'59'430924
Palmer.
Count von Luckner; knight of the sea, by Edwin P. Hoyt. New York, McKay [1969] xi, 176 p. illus. 21 cm. Bibliographical references included in "Notes" (p. 175-176) [D581.L87H6] 74-94504 5.95
1. Luckner, Felix, Graf von, 1881-1966. 2. European War, 1914-1918—Naval operations, German.

HOYT, Edwin 940.4'59'430924
Palmer.
Sea Eagle [by] Edwin P. Hoyt. London, New York, Allan Wingate, 1970. 192 p. 21 cm. [D581.L87H63] 75-546551 ISBN 0-85523-016-9 25/-
1. Luckner, Felix, Graf von, 1881-1966. 2. European War, 1914-1918—Naval operations, German. I. Title.

Lucretius Carus, Titus.

SIKES, Edward Ernest, 871'.01 B
1867-1940.
Lucretius, poet & philosopher. New York, Russell & Russell [1971] ix, 186 p. 22 cm. Reprint of the 1936 ed. Includes bibliographical references. [PA6484.S5 1971] 76-139477
1. Lucretius Carus, Titus. I. Title. BIP

Lucy, Saint, d. 304?

ERNEST, Brother, 1897- 922.1
A story of Saint Lucy. Pictures by Sister Mary Manus. iNotre Dame, Ind., Dujarie Press [1957] unpaged. illus. 21cm. [BR1720.L8E7] 57-30285
1. Lucy, Saint, d. 304? I. Title.

Ludendorff, Erich, 1865-1937.

GIES, Joseph. 940.4'0943
Crisis, 1918; the leading actors, strategies, and events in the German gamble for total victory on the Western Front. [1st ed.] New York, Norton [1974] 288 p. illus. 21 cm. Bibliography: p. 270-275. [D531.G5 1974] 73-14861 ISBN 0-393-05493-4 7.95
1. Ludendorff, Erich, 1865-1937. 2. European War, 1914-1918—Germany. 3. European War, 1914-1918—Campaigns—Western. I. Title.

GOODSPEED, Donald 943.0840924
James, 1919-
Ludendorff; genius of World War I [by] D. J. Goodspeed. Boston, Houghton Mifflin, 1966. xii, 335 p. illus., maps, ports. 22 cm. Bibliography: p. [313]-326. [DD231.L8G6] 66-17175
1. Ludendorff, Erich, 1865-1937.

PARKINSON, Roger. 355.3'31'0924 B
Tormented warrior : Ludendorff and the Supreme Command / Roger Parkinson. New York : Stein and Day, 1979, c1978. p. cm. Includes index. Bibliography: p. [DD231.L8P37 1979] 78-24691 ISBN 0-8128-2597-7 : 12.95
1. Ludendorff, Erich, 1865-1937. 2. Generals—Germany—Biography. I. Title.

TSCHUPPIK, Karl, 355.3'31'0924 B
1878-1937.
Ludendorff, the tragedy of a military mind / by Karl Tschuppik ; translated by W. H. Johnston. Westport, Conn. : Greenwood Press, 1975. vi, 282 p. : ill. ; 22 cm. Translation of Ludendorff, die Tragodie des Fachmanns. Reprint of the 1932 ed. published by Houghton, Mifflin, New York. Includes index. Bibliography: p. 277-278. [DD231.L8T7 1975] 74-14118 ISBN 0-8371-7788-X
1. Ludendorff, Erich, 1865-1937. 2. European War, 1914-1918—Germany. 3. European War, 1914-1918—Campaigns. I. Title.

Ludibheid, Colm.

LUDIBHEID, 914.15'03'59024 B
Colm.
All the green gold; an Irish boyhood. New York, Praeger [1970] vi, 194 p. map. 22 cm. [CT808.L8A3] 73-123639 5.95
I. Title.

Ludington, Sybil, b. 1761—Juvenile literature.

GRANT, Anne. 973.3'33
Danbury's burning : the story of Sybil Ludington / by Anne Grant. New York : McKay, c1976. p. cm. A retelling if the events surrounding Sybil Ludington's ride to warn the townspeople about the burning of Danbury during the Revolutionary War. [E241.D2G7] 92 75-37483 ISBN 0-8098-5007-9 : 6.95
1. Ludington, Sybil, b. 1761—Juvenile literature. 2. Danbury, Conn.—Burning by the British, 1777—Biography—Juvenile literature. I. Title.

Ludlow family.

SEVERSMITH, Herbert Furman, v. 12
1904-
Roger Ludlow (1590-1665/1666) [Washington] National Genealogical Society, 1963. 150-234 p. 26 cm. Reprinted from National Genealogical Society Quarterly, v. 51, September and December 1963. Presented in advance of the publication of the author's The ancestry of Roger Ludlow (volume v of Colonial familes of Long Island, New York, Connecticut) Cover title. 68-14969
1. Ludlow family. I. Title.

Ludlow, John Malcolm Forbes, 1821-1911.

MASTERMAN, Neville 923.642
Charles
John Malcolm Ludlow, the builder of Christian socialism. New York, Cambridge [c.]1963. 299p. illus. 23cm. Bibl. 63-5469 5.50
1. Ludlow, John Malcolm Forbes, 1821-1911. I. Title.

Ludwick, Christopher, 1720-1801.

RUSH, Benjamin, 1745- 917.3'03 B
1813.
An account of the life and character of Christopher Ludwick. New York, MSS Information Corp. [1972] p. Reprint of the 1831 ed. [CT275.L835R7 1972] 72-8082 ISBN 0-8422-8133-9
1. Ludwick, Christopher, 1720-1801. I. Title.

Ludwig, Charles,

LUDWIG, Charles, 267'.15'0924
1918-
The lady general. Grand Rapids, Baker Book House, 1962. 93p. illus. 20cm. (Valor series, sBooth, Evangeline Cory, 1865-1950--Juvenile literature:. [BX9743.B63L8] 62-18416
I. Title.

Ludwig II, King of Bavaria, 1845-1886.

BLUNT, Wilfrid, 943'.3'080924 B
1901-
The dream king; Ludwig II of Bavaria. With a chapter on Ludwig and the arts by Michael Petzet. [Harmondsworth, Eng., Baltimore] Penguin Books [1973, c1970] 264 p. illus. 25 cm. Bibliography: p. 257-258. [DD801.B387B55 1973] 73-165426 ISBN 0-14-003606-7 4.95 (U.S.)
1. Ludwig II, King of Bavaria, 1845-1886. I. Title.

Ludwig, Twyla I., 1890-1960.

LUDWIG, Charles, 266'.023'0924 B
1918-
Mama was a missionary. Grand Rapids, Zondervan Pub. House [1970, c1963] 192 p. illus., ports. 21 cm. (A Zondervan paperback) [BV3625.K42L8 1970] 77-133354 0.95
1. Ludwig, Twyla I., 1890-1960. 2. Missions—Kenya. I. Title.

Lue, Gim Gong, 1858 or 9-1925—Juvenile literature.

MURRAY, Marian. 635'.0924 B
Plant wizard; the life of Lue Gim Gong. Illus. by Eros Keith. [New York] Crowell-Collier Press [1970] 118 p. illus. 22 cm. Bibliography: p. [113]-114. A biography of the Chinese immigrant who became a horticulturist renowned for his work with citrus fruits. [QK31.L82M87] 92 77-119131
1. Lue, Gim Gong, 1858 or 9-1925—Juvenile literature. I. Keith, Eros, illus. II. Title. BIP

Lugard, Frederick John Dealtry, Baron, 1858-1945.

PERHAM, Margery 966.9'03'0924 B
Freda, Dame, 1895-
Lugard, by Margery Perham. Hamden, Conn., Archon Books, 1968. 2 v. illus., maps, ports. 23 cm. Reprint of the 1956 ed. Contents.Contents.—pt. 1. The years of adventure, 1858-1898.—pt. 2. The years of authority, 1898-1945. Includes bibliographies. [DA566.9.L82P42] 68-6290
1. Lugard, Frederick John Dealtry, Baron, 1858-1945. BIP

Lugosi, Bela, 1882-1956.

CREMER, Robert. 791.43'028'0924 B
Lugosi : the man behind the cape / Robert Cremer ; introd. by Bela Lugosi, Jr. Chicago : H. Regnery Co., c1976. xvii, 307 p., [8] leaves of plates : ill. ; 24 cm. Includes index. Stageography: p. 241-274. [PN2859.I186L833] 76-6901 ISBN 0-8092-8137-6 : 9.95
1. Lugosi, Bela, 1882-1956.

LENNIG, Arthur. 791.43'028'0924 B
The Count : the life and films of Bela "Dracula" Lugosi / Arthur Lennig. New York : Putnam, [1974] 347 p. : ill. ; 24 cm. Includes index. Filmography: p. [319]-338. [PN2859.H86L835] 73-93735 ISBN 0-399-11340-1 : 10.00
1. Lugosi, Bela, 1882-1956. I. Title.

Luhan, Mabel Ganson Dodge, 1879-1962.

HAHN, Emily, 1905- 973.9'092'4 B
Mabel : a biography of Mabel Dodge Luhan / by Emily Hahn ; illustrated with photographs. Boston : Houghton Mifflin, 1977. 228 p., [8] leaves of plates : ill. ; 24 cm. Includes bibliographical references and index. [CT275.L838H34] 76-58905 ISBN 0-395-25349-7 : 10.00
1. Luhan, Mabel Ganson Dodge, 1879-1962. 2. United States—Biography. BIP

Luhn, Hans Peter, 1896-1964.

LUHN, Hans Peter, 1896- 029.7
1964.
H. P. Luhn: pioneer of information science; selected works. Edited by Claire K. Schultz. New York, Spartan Books [1968] 320 p. illus., ports. 29 cm. "Bibliography of H. P. Luhn's publications": p. 287-289. [Z699.L78] 67-30872
1. Luhn, Hans Peter, 1896-1964. 2. Information science—Addresses, essays, lectures. I. Schultz, Claire K., ed. II. Title.

Luigi Gonzaga, Saint, 1568-1591.

ERNEST, Brother, 1897- 922.245
A story of St. Aloysius Gonzaga. Pictures by Carolyn Lee Jagodits. Notre Dame, Ind., Dujarie Press [1957] unpaged. illus. 21cm. [BX4700.L75E68] 57-59266
1. Luigi Gonzaga, Saint, 1568-1591. I. Title.

O'BRIEN, Bartholomew J 922.245
The heroic Aloysius, a story of the patron saint of youth; soldier, student, statesman, seminarian, saint, star. Illustrated by Paul A. Grout. St. Meinrad, Ind. [1954] 83p.

illus. 22cm. 'A Grall publication.' [BX4700.L75O2] 54-11551
1. Luigi Gonzaga, Saint, 1568-1591. I. Title.

Luis Bunuel, 1900—

HIGGINBOTHAM, Virginia, 1935- 791.43'0233'0924 B
Luis Bunuel / Virginia Higginbotham. Boston : Twayne Publishers, 1979. 222 p. : ill. ; 21 cm. (Twayne's theatrical arts series) Includes index. Bibliography: p. 205-205. [PN1998.A3L86] 78-24229 ISBN 0-8057-9261-9 : 10.95
1. Luis Bunuel, 1900- 2. Moving-picture producers and directors—Spain—Biography. 3. Moving-pictures—Spain—Catalogs. BIP

Lujack, Larry.

LUJACK, Larry. 791.44'5 B
Superjock : the loud, frantic, nonstop world of a rock radio DJ / Larry Lujack, with Daniel A. Jedlicka. Chicago : H. Regnery Co., [1975] 200 p., [4] leaves of plates : ports. ; 22 cm. Autobiographical. [ML429.L9A3] 75-16226 ISBN 0-8092-8302-6 : 7.95
1. Lujack, Larry. 2. Disc jockeys—Correspondence, reminiscences, etc. I. Jedlicka, Daniel A. II. Title.

Luke, Frank, 1897-1918.

HALL, Norman Shannon. 940.4'49'730924 B
The balloon buster, Frank Luke of Arizona, by Norman S. Hall. [New York] Arno Press [1972, c1928] 191 p. illus. 22 cm. (Literature and history of aviation) [D606.H25 1972] 70-169420 ISBN 0-405-03765-1
1. Luke, Frank, 1897-1918. 2. European War, 1914-1918—Aerial operations, American. I. Title. II. Series.

Luke, Frank, 1897-1918—Juvenile fiction.

COOMBS, Charles Ira, 1914- juv
Frank Luke, Balloon buster, by Charles I. Coombs. Editor: Emmett A. Betts. Illus. by Raymon Naylor. Maps by Paul Hazelrigg. New York, Harper & Row [1967] 256 p. illus., maps. 20 cm. (The American adventures series) [PZ7.C7785Fr] 67-6277
1. Luke, Frank, 1897-1918—Juvenile fiction.

Lukens, Theodore Parker, 1848-1918.

SARGENT, Shirley. 634.9'0924 B
Theodore Parker Lukens: father of forestry. Los Angeles, Dawson's Book Shop, 1969. x, 91 p. illus., ports. 24 cm. 500 copies printed. Bibliographical footnotes. [SD129.L8S3] 77-81226
1. Lukens, Theodore Parker, 1848-1918.

Lull, Ramon, d. 1315.

PEERS, Edgar Allison. 189'.4 B
Fool of love; the life of Ramon Lull [by] E. Allison Peers. [Folcroft, Pa.] Folcroft Library Editions, 1974. p. cm. Reprint of the 1946 ed. published by S.C.M. Press, London. [BX4705.L93P4 1974] 74-10835 15.00
1. Lull, Ramon, d. 1315. I. Title. BIP

PEERS, Edgar Allison. 189'.4 B
Ramon Lull; a biography, by E. Allison Peers. New York, B. Franklin, 1969. xviii, 454 p. 22 cm. (Selected essays in history, economic & social science, #84) (Burt Franklin bibliography & reference series, #266.) Reprint of the 1929 ed. Bibliography: p. [421]-434. [B765.L84P38 1969] 77-76019
1. Lull, Ramon, d. 1315. BIP

Lum, Ray, 1891-

FERRIS, Bill. 381'.41'6100924 B
Ray Lum, mule trader : an essay / by Bill Ferris ; booklet edited by Jack Friedman ; graphics by George Walker. Memphis : Center for Southern Folklore, c1976. p. cm. Bibliography: p. [HD9434.U6L854] 76-53834 ISBN 0-89267-003-7 ; 3.50
1. Lum, Ray, 1891- 2. Horses—Southern States. 3. Mules—Southern States. 4. Auctioneers—Southern States—Biography. I. Center for Southern Folklore. II. Title.

RAY Lum, mule trader 381'.41'6100924 B
: record transcript / booklet transcribed and edited by Jack Friedman ; record edited by Judy Peiser, Barbara Moore ; record recorded by Bill Ferris, Judy Peiser ; liner notes by Bill Ferris ; graphics by George Walker. Memphis : Center for Southern Folklore, c1976. p. cm. [HD9434.U6L857] 76-53836 ISBN 0-89267-002-9 : 3.50
1. Lum, Ray, 1891- 2. Horses—Southern States. 3. Mules—Southern States. 4. Auctioneers—Southern States—Biography. I. Friedman, Jack. II. Center for Southern Folklore.

Lumbermen—Wisconsin.

BLANCHARD, Louie, 1872-1959. 331.7'63'49820924
The lumberjack frontier; the life of a logger in the early days on the Chippeway. Retold from the recollections of Louie Blanchard by Walker D. Wyman, with the assistance of Lee Prentice. Lincoln, University of Nebraska Press [1969] xi, 88 p. illus., facsim., map (on lining papers) 21 cm. (The Pioneer heritage series) [HD8039.L92U53] 78-76168 3.95
1. Lumbermen—Wisconsin. I. Wyman, Walker Demarquis, 1907- II. Prentice, Lee. III. Title. IV. Series.

Lumley, Benjamin, 1812-1875.

LUMLEY, Benjamin, 1812-1875. 782.1'092'4 B
Reminiscences of the opera / by Benjamin Lumley. New York : Da Capo Press, 1976. xx, 448 p. : port. ; 23 cm. (The Lyric stage) Reprint of the 1864 ed. published by Hurst and Blackett, London. [ML429.L95A3 1976] 76-15185 ISBN 0-306-70842-6 : 25.00
1. Lumley, Benjamin, 1812-1875. 2. London. King's Theatre. 3. Opera—London.

LUNDY, Benjamin, 1789-1839. 973.7114'0924 B
The life, travels, and opinions of Benjamin Lundy; including his journeys to Texas and Mexico, with a sketch of contemporary events, and a notice of the revolution in Hayti. Compiled under the direction and on behalf of his children [by Thomas Earle] New York, Negro Universities Press [1969] 316 p. map, port. 23 cm. Reprint of the 1847 ed. [E446.L955 1969] 70-92750
1. Texas—Description and travel. 2. Mexico—Description and travel. 3. Slavery in the United States—Anti-slavery movement. I. Earle, Thomas, 1796-1849, comp. II. Title. BIP

LUNDY, Benjamin, 1789-1839. 973.71'14'0924 B
The life, travels and opinions of Benjamin Lundy, compiled by Thomas Earle, 1847. With the addition of his pamphlet The war in Texas [by a citizen of the United States] 1836. New York, A. M. Kelley, 1971. 316, 56 p. fold. map, port. 22 cm. (America through European eyes) [E446.L956 1971] 76-136302 ISBN 0-678-00809-4
1. Texas—Description and travel. 2. Mexico—Description and travel. 3. Slavery in the United States—Anti-slavery movements. 4. Texas—History—Revolution, 1835-1836. I. Earle, Thomas, 1796-1849, comp. II. A citizen of the United States. III. Title: The war in Texas. BIP

Lummis, Charles Fletcher, 1859-1928.

BINGHAM, Edwin R 920.5
Charles F. Lummis, editor of the Southwest. San Marino, Huntington Library, 1955. x, 218p. plates, ports. 24cm. (Huntington Library Publications) Bibliography: p.192-201. [PN4874.L84B5] 55-42204
1. Lummis, Charles Fletcher, 1859-1928. 2. Out West magazine. I. Title. II. Series: Henry E. Huntington Library and Art Gallery, San Marine, Calif. Huntington Library Publications BIP

BINGHAM, Edwin R. 070.4'092'4
Charles F. Lummis, editor of the Southwest, by Edwin R. Bingham. Westport, Conn., Greenwood Press [1974, c1955] x, 218 p. illus. 22 cm. Reprint of the ed. published by Huntington Library, San Marino, Calif., in series: Huntington Library publications. Bibliography: p. 192-201. [PN4874.L84B5 1973] 73-15058 ISBN 0-8371-7149-0 10.75
1. Lummis, Charles Fletcher, 1859-1928. 2. Out West magazine. I. Title. II. Series: Henry E. Huntington Library and Art Gallery, San Marino, Calif. Huntington Library publications.

GORDON, Dudley Chadwick. 917.94'03'40924 B
Charles F. Lummis: crusader in corduroy, by Dudley Gordon. Foreword by Lawrence Clark Powell. [Los Angeles] Cultural Assets Press [1972] xix, 344 p. illus. 24 cm. Bibliography: p. 327-330. [PS3523.U49Z67] 72-84194 12.50
1. Lummis, Charles Fletcher, 1859-1928.

Lummis, Charles Fletcher, 1859-1928—Biography.

FISKE, Turbese Lummis. 917.94'03'40924 B
Charles F. Lummis: the man and his West, by Turbese Lummis Fiske and Keith Lummis. [1st ed.] Norman, University of Oklahoma Press [1975] x, 230 p. illus. 29 cm. Bibliography: p. 225-226. [PS3523.U49Z65] 74-15910 ISBN 0-8061-1228-X
1. Lummis, Charles Fletcher, 1859-1928—Biography. I. Lummis, Keith, 1904- joint author. II. Title.

Lumumba, Patrice, 1925-1961.

HEINZ, G. 967.5'03'0924 B
Lumumba: the last fifty days, by G. Heinz and H. Donnay. Translated from the French by Jane Clark Seitz. New York, Grove Press [1970, c1969] xi, 210 p. illus., facsim., map, ports. 21 cm. Translation of Lumumba Patrice: les cinquante derniers jours de sa vie. "Patrice Lumumba speaks," translated by H. R. Lane: p. 159-169. [DT663.L8H4313] 70-99428 6.95
1. Lumumba, Patrice, 1925-1961. I. Donnay, H., joint author. II. Title.

KANZA, Thomas R. 967.51'03'0924
Conflict in the Congo: the rise and fall of Lumumba [by] Thomas Kanza. Translated from the French. Harmondsworth, Penguin, 1972. 346 p. 18 cm. (Penguin African library) [DT658.K257] 72-190318 ISBN 0-14-041030-9 £0.65 ($3.25 U.S.)
1. Lumumba, Patrice, 1925-1961. 2. Zaire—Politics and government—1960- I. Title.

MCKOWN, Robin. 967.5'03'0924 B
Lumumba; a biography. Introd. by Herbert F. Weiss. [1st ed.] Garden City, N.Y., Doubleday [1969] xi, 202 p. illus., maps, ports. 22 cm. Bibliography: p. [196]-198. The life of the African leader who became the first Prime Minister of the Congo after it gained independence from Belgium. [DT663.L8M3] 92 79-78717 3.95
1. Lumumba, Patrice, 1925-1961. I. Title.

Lundborg, Louis B.

LUNDBORG, Louis B. 973.9'092'4 B
Up to now / Louis B. Lundborg. 1st ed. New York : Norton, c1978. 241 p. : ill. ; 22 cm. Autobiographical. [CT275.L842A35 1978] 77-16628 ISBN 0-393-07525-7 : 8.95
1. Lundborg, Louis B. 2. United States—Biography. I. Title.

Lundy, Benjamin, 1789-1839.

DILLON, Merton Lynn, 1924- 973.71140924 B
Benjamin Lundy and the struggle for Negro freedom [by] Merton L. Dillon. Urbana, University of Illinois Press, 1966. vi, 285 p. port. 24 cm. Bibliography: p. [263]-267. [E446.D54] 66-15473
1. Lundy, Benjamin, 1789-1839. 2. Slavery in the United States—Anti-slavery movements. I. Title. BIP

LUNDY, Benjamin, 1789-1839. 973.7114'0924 B
The life, travels, and opinions of Benjamin Lundy; including his journeys to Texas and Mexico, with a sketch of contemporary events, and a notice of the revolution in Hayti. Compiled under the direction and on behalf of his children [by Thomas Earle] New York, Negro Universities Press [1969] 316 p. map, port. 23 cm. Reprint of the 1847 ed. [E446.L955 1969] 70-92750
1. Texas—Description and travel. 2. Mexico—Description and travel. 3. Slavery in the United States—Anti-slavery movement. I. Earle, Thomas, 1796-1849, comp. II. Title. BIP

LUNDY, Benjamin, 1789-1839. 973.71'14'0924 B
The life, travels and opinions of Benjamin Lundy, compiled by Thomas Earle, 1847. With the addition of his pamphlet The war in Texas [by a citizen of the United States] 1836. New York, A. M. Kelley, 1971. 316, 56 p. fold. map, port. 22 cm. (America through European eyes) [E446.L956 1971] 76-136302 ISBN 0-678-00809-4
1. Texas—Description and travel. 2. Mexico—Description and travel. 3. Slavery in the United States—Anti-slavery movements. 4. Texas—History—Revolution, 1835-1836. I. Earle, Thomas, 1796-1849, comp. II. A citizen of the United States. III. Title: The war in Texas. BIP

Lundy, George, 1882-

MARTS, Arnaud C. 361.7'3'0924 B
George Lundy of Iowa; one of the pioneers of the new 20th century careers of fund-raising counsellors to private institutions which serve the public good, by Arnaud C. Marts. New York, 1967. 116 p. ports. 24 cm. [HG172.L8M3] 68-1108
1. Lundy, George, 1882- 2. Fund raising—United States. I. Title.

Lunin, Mikhail Sergeevich, 1787-1845.

BARRATT, G. R. V. 947'.04'0924 B
M. S. Lunin : Catholic Decembrist / by Glynn Barratt. The Hague : Mouton, 1976. xi, 137 p. : ports. ; 24 cm. (Slavistic printings and reprintings ; 272) Includes index. Bibliography: p. [129]-132. [DK209.6.L8B37] 76-474540 ISBN 9-02-793444-4 pbk. : 17.00
1. Lunin, Mikhail Sergeevich, 1787-1845. 2. Decembrists—Biography. I. Title. II. Series.
Distributed by Humanities. BIP

Lunt, Alfred.

FREEDLEY, George, 1904- 927.92
The Lunts: an illustrated study of their work, with a list of their appearances on stage and screen. New York, Macmillan, 1958 [c1957] 134 p. illus. 23 cm. (Theatre world monograph, no. 10) [PN2287.L8F7 1958] 58-14756
1. Lunt, Alfred. 2. Fontanne, Lynn. I. Title.

ZOLOTOW, Maurice, 1913- 927.92
Stagestruck; the romance of Alfred Lunt and Lynn Fontanne. [1st ed.] New York, Harcourt, Brace & World [1965] x, 278 p. illus., ports. 22 cm. [PN2287.L8Z6] 65-11995
1. Lunt, Alfred. 2. Fontanne, Lynn. I. Title.

ZOLOTOW MAURICE 1913- 927.92
Stagestruck; the romance of Alfred Lunt and Lynn Fontanne. Greenwich, Conn., Fawcett [1968,c.1965] viii, 320p. illus. ports. 18cm. (Crest bk., m 1092) [PN2287.L8Z6] .95 pap.,
1. Lunt, Alfred. 2. Fontanne, Lynn. I. Title.

Lunt, Richard D

LUNT, Richard D 923.273
The high ministry of government: the political career of Frank Murphy, by Richard D. Lunt. Detroit, Wayne State

University Press, 1965. 263 p. illus. ports. 24 cm. Bibliographical references included in "Notes" (p. 223-250) Bibliography: p. 251-258. [E748.M868L8] 65-10195
I. Title. BIP

Luparelli, Joseph.

MESKIL, Paul, 1923- 364.1'523'0924 B
The Luparelli tapes : the true story of the Mafia hitman who contracted to kill both Joey Gallo and his own wife / Paul S. Meskil. 1st ed. Chicago : Playboy Press, c1976. p. cm. [HV6248.L97M48] 76-15256 ISBN 0-87223-450-9 : 8.95
1. Luparelli, Joseph. 2. Crime and criminals—United States—Biography. I. Title.

Lupescu, Magda.

MOATS, Alice Leone. 920.7
Lupescu. [1st ed.] New York, Holt [1955] 220p. illus. 22cm. [DR266.M6] 55-10645
1. Lupescu, Magda. 2. Carol II, King of Rumania, 1898-1953. I. Title.

Lupino, Ida, 1918-

VERMILYE, Jerry. 791.4'092'4 B
Ida Lupino / by Jerry Vermilye. New York : Pyramid Publications, 1977. 160 p. : ill. ; 20 cm. (A Pyramid illustrated history of the movies) Includes index. Bibliography: p. 143-145. [PN2287.L84V4] 77-77592 ISBN 0-515-04306-0 pbk. : 1.95
1. Lupino, Ida, 1918- 2. Moving-picture actors and actresses—United States—Biography. BIP

Lurana Mary Francis, Mother, 1870-1935.

MARY Celine, Sister, S.A. 922.273
A woman of unity; a biography of a remarkable woman, Mother Lurana of Graymoor. Garrison, N. Y., Franciscan Sisters of the Atonement [c1956] 357p. illus. 22cm. [BX4705.L94M3] 56-9206
1. Lurana Mary Francis, Mother, 1870-1935. 2. ,franciscan Sisters of the Atonement. I. Title.

Lurtsema, Bob.

GIFFORD, Thomas. 796.33'2'0924 B
Benchwarmer Bob : the story of Bob Lurtsema / Thomas Gifford. 1st ed. Blue Earth, Minn. : Piper Pub., c1974. 115 p., [4] leaves of plates : ill. ; 22 cm. [GV939.L87G54] 74-13550 ISBN 0-87832-015-6 : 6.95 pbk. : 3.95
1. Lurtsema, Bob. 2. Football. I. Title.

Luster, Gertrude.

LUSTER, Gertrude. 817.54
Well, for the love of Greg! Illustrated by Al Luster. San Antonio, Naylor Co. [1962] 102p. illus. 20cm. Autobiographical. [CT275.L843A3] 62-14625
I. Title.

Lustig, Victor, 1890-1947.

JOHNSON, James Francis, 1898- 923.41
The man who sold the Eiffel Tower, by James F. Johnson as told to Floyd Miller. New York, Pocket Bks. [1963, c.1961] 181p. 17cm. (7030) .50 pap.,
1. Lustig, Victor, 1890-1947. I. Miller, Floyd. II. Title.

JOHNSON, James Francis, 1898- 923.41
The man who sold the Eiffel Tower, by James F. Johnson as told to Floyd Miller. [1st ed.] Garden City, N. Y., Doubleday, 1961. 216p. 22cm. [HV6248.L98J6] 61-9522
1. Lustig, Victor, 1890-1947. I. Miller, Floyd. II. Title.

Luther, Katharina (von Bora) 1499-1552.

MALL, E Jane, 1920- 922.443
Kitty, my rib. Saint Louis, Concordia Pub. House [1959] 173p. 21cm. [BR328.M25] 59-10977
1. Luther, Katharina (von Bora) 1499-1552. I. Title. BIP

SCHREIBER, Clara Seuel. 922.443
Katherine, wife of Luther. Philadelphia, Muhlenberg Press [1954] 232p. 20cm. [BR328.S35] 54-9178
1. Luther, Katharina (von Bora) 1499-1552. I. Title.

Luther, Martin, 1483-1546.

ALAND, Kurt. 280'.4 B
Four reformers : Luther, Melanchthon, Calvin, Zwingli / Kurt Aland ; translated by James L. Schaff. Minneapolis : Augsburg Pub. House, c1979. 174 p. ; 20 cm. Translation of Die Reformatoren. Bibliography: p. 159-174. [BR315.A4513] 79-50091 ISBN 0-8066-1709-8 pbk. : 4.95
1. Luther, Martin, 1483-1546. 2. Melanchthon, Philipp, 1497-1560. 3. Calvin, Jean, 1509-1564. 4. Zwingli, Ulrich, 1484-1531. 5. Reformation—Biography. 6. Reformation. I. Title.

ATKINSON, James, 1914- 270.6'0924
Martin Luther and the birth of Protestantism. Harmondsworth, Penguin, 1968. 352 p. 2 maps. 19 cm. (Pelican books, A865) 7/6 Bibliography: p. [337]-340. [BR325.A8] 68-115719
1. Luther, Martin, 1483-1546. I. Title.

ATKINSON, James, 1914- 284'.1'0924 B
Martin Luther and the birth of Protestantism. Baltimore, Penguin Books [1968] 352 p. maps. 19 cm. "Select bibliography of books in English": p. [337]-340. [BR325.A8 1968b] 75-2378 1.95
1. Luther, Martin, 1483-1546. I. Title.

BAINTON, Roland Herbert, 1894- v. 12
Here I stand; a life of Martin Luther. [New York] The New American Library [1961] 336 p. illus., facsims. (Mentor book, 310) First pub. 1950. NUC63
1. Luther, Martin, 1483-1546. I. Title.

BAINTON, Roland Herbert, 1894- 922.443
Here I stand; a life of Martin Luther. New York, Abingdon-Cokesbury Press [1950] 422 p. illus., ports., music. 24 cm. Bibliography: p. 387-395. [BR325.B26] 50-9795
1. Luther, Martin, 1483-1546. I. Title.

BOOTH, Edwin Prince 922.443
Martin Luther, oak of Saxony [New note by author] Nashville, Abingdon [1966, c.1961] vii, 271p. incl. front. (port.) 21cm. (Apex bks., Y-1) [BR325.B66] 2.75 pap.,
1. Luther, Martin, 1483-1546. I. Title.

COWIE, Leonard W. 284'.1'0924 B
Martin Luther, leader of the Reformation [by] Leonard W. Cowie. New York, Praeger [1969] vi, 122 p. illus., maps, ports. 23 cm. (Praeger pathfinder biographies) Bibliography: p. 120. [BR325.C68] 69-12703 4.25
1. Luther, Martin, 1483-1546.

EDWARDS, Mark U. 270.6'092'4
Luther and the false brethren / Mark U. Edwards, Jr. Stanford, Calif. : Stanford University Press, 1975. viii, 242 p. ; 23 cm. Includes bibliographical references and index. [BR325.E34] 75-181 ISBN 0-8047-0883-5 : 10.00
1. Luther, Martin, 1483-1546. I. Title. BIP

ERIKSON, Erik Homburger, 1902- 922.443
Young man Luther; a study in psychoanalysis and history. New York, Norton [c.1958, 1962] 288p. 20cm. (Norton lib., N170) Bibl. 1.75 pap.,
1. Luther, Martin, 1483-1546. I. Title.

ERIKSON, Erik Homburger, 1902- 922.443
Young man Luther; a study in psychoanalysis and history. New York, Norton [1962] 288 p. 20 cm. (Austen Riggs monograph no. 4) The Norton library, N170. [BR325.E7] 63-3546
1. Luther, Martin, 1483-1546. I. Title.

ERIKSON, Erik Homburger, 1902- 922.443
Young man Luther; a study in psychoanalysis and history. [1st ed.] New York, Norton [1958] 288 p. 22 cm. (Austen Riggs monograph no. 4) Bibliography: p. 269-277. [BR325.E7] 58-11113
1. Luther, Martin, 1483-1546. I. Title. II. Series: Austen Riggs Center For the Study and Treatment of Neuroses, Stockbridge, Mass. Monograph no. 4.

FIFE, Robert Herndon, 1871- 922.443
The revolt of Martin Luther. New York, Columbia University Press, 1957. 726p. 24cm. Includes bibliography. [BR325.F53 1957] 56-11910
1. Luther, Martin, 1483-1546. I. Title.

FIFE, Robert Herndon, 1871-1958. 270.6'0924 B
Young Luther; the intellectual and religious development of Martin Luther to 1518. New York, AMS Press [1970] 232 p. 19 cm. Reprint of the 1928 ed. Includes bibliographical references. [BR325.F54 1970] 79-131040
1. Luther, Martin, 1483-1546. I. Title.

*FISCHER, Robert H. 922.443
Luther. Frank W. Klos, ed. Gustav Rehberger, illustrator. Philadelphia. Lutheran Church Pr. [1966] 192p. illus. 21cm. (LCA sch. of religion ser.) Bibl. 1.25 pap. 1.50
1. Luther, Martin, 1483 1546. 2. Reformation—Europe. I. Title. II. Series.

FISCHER, Robert H 284'.1'0924
Luther, by Robert H. Fischer. Frank W. Klos, editor. Gustav Rehberger, illustrator. Philadelphia, Lutheran church Press [c1966] 192 p. illus. 21 cm. (LCA School of religion series) Includes 5 German chorales with English translations in close score. Bibliography: p. 191-192. [BR325.F58] 67-1178
1. Luther, Martin, 1483-1546. I. Title.

FOSDICK, Harry Emerson, 1878-1969. 922.443
Martin Luther; illustrated by Steele Savage. New York, Random House [1956] 184 p. illus. 22 cm. (World landmark books [W-23]) [BR325.F67] 56-5462
1. Luther, Martin, 1483-1546.

FREYTAG, Gustav, 1816-1895. 270.6'092'4 B
Martin Luther. Translated by Henry E. O. Heinemann. Chicago, Open Court Pub. Co., 1897. [New York, AMS Press, 1972] vi, 130 p. illus. 23 cm. Translation of Doktor Luther. [BR325.F73 1972] 78-144612 ISBN 0-404-02577-3 10.00
1. Luther, Martin, 1483-1546. BIP

FRIEDENTHAL, Richard, 1896- 270.6'0924
Luther; his life and times. Translated from the German by John Nowell. [1st American ed.] New York, Harcourt, Brace, Jovanovich [1970] viii, 566 p. illus., ports. 24 cm. "A Helen and Kurt Wolff book." Includes bibliographical references. [BR325.F7713 1970] 72-124834 ISBN 1-515-47858-
1. Luther, Martin, 1483-1546.

GAHL, Lois. 922.443
Luther, young man of God. Rock Island, Ill., Augustana Press [1956] 90p. illus. 20cm. [BR325.G3] 56-23819
1. Luther, Martin, 1483-1546. I. Title.

GREEN, Vivian Hubert Howard. 922.443
Luther and the Reformation. London, B. T. Batsford; New York, Putnam [1964] 208 p. illus., ports., facsims. 23 cm. "Books for further reading": p. 200-201. [BR325.G68] 64-13032
1. Luther, Martin, 1483-1546. 2. Reformation. I. Title.

GRISAR, Hartmann, 1845-1932. 922.443
Martin Luther, his life and work; adapted from the 2d German ed. by Frank J. Eble, edited by Arthur Preuss. Westminster, Md., Newman Press, 1950. x, 609 p. 23 cm. Bibliography: p. 586-600. [BR325.G75 1950] 50-10519
1. Luther, Martin, 1483-1546. 2. Reformation—Germany. I. Title.

GRISAR, Hartmann, 1845-1932. 230'.4'10924 B
Martin Luther: his life and work. Adapted from the 2d German ed. by Frank J. Eble. New York, AMS Press [1971] x, 609 p. 23 cm. Reprint of the 1930 ed. Bibliography: p. 586-600. [BR325.G75 1971] 71-137235 ISBN 0-404-02935-3
1. Luther, Martin, 1483-1546. 2. Reformation—Germany.

HERE I stand; v. 12
a life of Martin Luther. New York, Abingdon Press, [1957?] 422p. illus., ports., music. 24cm. Bibliography: p. 387-395.
1. Luther, Martin, 1483-1546. I. Bainton, Roland Herbert, 1894- BIP

HYMA, Albert, 1893- 922.443
New light on Martin Luther, with an authentic account of the Luther film of 1953. Grand Rapids, Eerdmans, 1958 [c1957] 287p. illus. 24cm. [BR325.H86] 58-14744
1. Luther, Martin, 1483-1546. 2. Martin Luther (Motion pictures) I. Title.

ILGENSTEIN, Anna (Katterfeld) 1880- 922.443
The story of Martin Luther for young people. Translated from the German by Lydia Regehr. [1st ed.] Grand Rapids, Eerdmans, 1955. 90p. 20cm. [BR325.I38] 55-1820
1. Luther, Martin, 1483-1546. I. Title.

JACOBS, Henry Eyster, 1844-1932. 284'.1'0924 B
Martin Luther, the hero of the Reformation, 1483-1546. New York, Putnam. [New York, AMS Press, 1973] xv, 454 p. illus. 19 cm. Reprint of the 1898 ed. which was issued as v. 1 of Heroes of the Reformation. Includes bibliographical references. [BR325.J2 1973] 72-170838 ISBN 0-404-03544-2 18.00
1. Luther, Martin, 1483-1546. I. Title. BIP

JENSEN, De Lamar, 1925- 230'.4'10924 B
Confrontation at Worms: Martin Luther and the Diet of Worms. With a complete English translation of the Edict of Worms. [Provo, Utah, Brigham Young University Press, 1973] 119 p. illus. 29 cm. The Edict is translated from the copy in the J. Reuben Clark, Jr., Library at Brigham Young University, "a French version published in Paris, apparently by the printer Pierre Gromors." Includes bibliographical references. [BR326.6.J45] 73-5906 ISBN 0-8425-1524-0 10.50
1. Luther, Martin, 1483-1546. 2. Worms, Diet of, 1521. I. Holy Roman Empire. Laws, statutes, etc., 1519-1556 (Charles V). Edict of Worms. English. 1973. II. Title.

KOOIMAN, W. J., 1903- 922.443
By faith alone; the life of Martin Luther. Translated by Bertram Lee Woolf. New York, Philosophical Library [1955] 218 p. 22 cm. Translation of Maarten Luther, doctor der Heilige Schrift, reformator der kerk. [BR325.K7853] 56-13585
1. Luther, Martin, 1483-1546. I. Title.

THE last days of Luther, 270.6'0924 B
by Justus Jonas, Michael Coelius, and others. Translated and annotated by Martin Ebon. With an introd. by Theodore G. Tappert. [1st ed.] Garden City, N.Y., Doubleday, 1970. 120 p. 3 fold. maps. 22 cm. Translation of Vom christlichen Abschied aus diesem todlichen Leben des Ehrwerdigen Herrn D. M. Lutheri, originally published in Wittenberg in 1546. Facsim. of the German text and English translation on opposite pages (p. 45-103). Contents.Contents.—Luther and death, by T. G. Tappert.—Only thirty-one days, by M. Ebon.—Biographical notes.—Concerning the Christian departure from this mortal life of the Reverend Dr. Martin Luther, by J. Jonas, M. Coelius, and others who were present.—Martin Luther-life chronology.—Chronology: January 23 to February 22, 1546.—Bibliography (p. 117-120) [BR325.V57] 74-120743 5.00
1. Luther, Martin, 1483-1546. I. Jonas, Justus, 1493-1555. II. Caelius, Michael, 1492-1559. III. Ebon, Martin, tr.

LAU, Franz. 922.443
Luther. Translated by Robert H. Fischer. Philadelphia, Westminster Press [1963] 178 p. 21 cm. [BR325.L373] 62-17812
1. Luther, Martin, 1483-1546.

LEE, Robert E. A. 284'1'0924
Martin Luther: the Reformation years. Based on the film 'Martin Luther.' Ed. by Robert E. A. Lee. Minneapolis, Augsburg [1967] 96p. illus. 28cm. [BR325.L46] 67-25369 2.50 pap.,
1. Luther, Martin, 1483-1546. I. Martin, Luther (Motion picture) II. Title.

LILJE, Hanns, Bp., 270.6'0924
1899-
Luther and the Reformation; an illustrated review, by Hanns Lilje in collaboration with Karl F. Reinking. American ed. Translated and eidted by Martin O. Dietrich. Philadelphia, Fortress Press,[1967] 223 p. illus., facsims., ports. 23 cm. Translation of Martin Luther; eine Bildmonographie. [BR325.L4743] 67-24339
1. Luther, Martin, 1483-1546. I. Reinking, Karl Frans. II. Title.

LINDSAY, Thomas 270.6'0924 B
Martin, 1843-1914.
Luther and the German Reformation. Freeport, N.Y., Books for Libraries Press [1970] xii, 300 p. 23 cm. Reprint of the 1900 ed. "Chronological summary of the history of the Reformation": p. 267-291. Bibliography: p. 293-296. [BR325.L48 1970] 71-133524
1. Luther, Martin, 1483-1546. 2. Reformation—Germany. I. Title. BIP

LUTHER, Martin, 284'.1'0924 B
1483-1546.
Luther. Edited by Ian D. Kingston Siggins. New York, Barnes & Noble Books [1972] x, 209 p. 23 cm. (Evidence and commentary) Bibliography: p. 190-203. [BR331.E5S53 1972b] 73-166414 ISBN 0-06-496246-6 10.50
1. Luther, Martin, 1483-1546. I. Siggins, Ian D. Kingston, ed.
Pbk. 5.50; ISBN 0-06-496247-4.

MACKINNON, James, 1860- 922.443
1945.
Luther and the Reformation. New York, Russell & Russell, 1962. 4v. 22cm. Contents.v.1. Early life and religious development to 1517.--v.2. The breach with Rome (1517-21)--v.3. Progress of the movement (1521-29)--v.4. Vindication of the movement (1531-46) Bibliographical footnotes. [BR325.M27 1962] 62-10691
1. Luther, Martin, 1483-1546. 2. Reformation. I. Title.

MCNEER, May Yonge, 1902- 922.443
Martin Luther, by May McNeer and Lynd Ward. Nashville, Abingdon-Cokesbury Press [1953] 95 p. illus. 25 cm. [BR325.M28] 53-8955
1. Luther, Martin, 1483-1546. I. Ward, Lynd Kendall, 1905- illus.

MEE, Charles L. 270.6'092'4 B
White robe, black robe [by] Charles L. Mee, Jr. New York, Putnam [1972] 316 p. 22 cm. Bibliography: p. 301-303. [BR325.M4125 1972] 76-183547 7.95
1. Luther, Martin, 1483-1546. 2. Leo X, Pope, 1475-1521. 3. Reformation. I. Title.

MERLE d'Aubigne, Jean 922.443
Henri, 1794-1872.
The life and times of Martin Luther. Selections from D'Aubigne's famed History of the Reformation of the sixteenth century. Translated from the French by H. White and rev. by the author. Chicago, Moody Press, 1950. 559 p. 21 cm. (The Tyndale series of great biographies) [BR305.M52] 51-5666
1. Luther, Martin, 1483-1546. 2. Reformation. I. Series. BIP

MORE about Luther v. 12
[by] Jaroslav J. Pelikan, Regin Prenter [and] Herman A. Preus. Decorah, Iowa, Luther College Press [1958] vii, 214p. 23cm. (Martin Luther lectures, v. 2, 1958)
1. Luther, Martin, 1483-1546. I. Pelikan, Jaroslav, 1923-

O'NEILL, Judith, 230'.4'10924 B
1930-
Martin Luther / Judith O'Neill. Minneapolis : Lerner Publications Co., 1978, c1975. p. cm. (A Cambridge topic book) (The Cambridge history library) Includes index. [BR325.O64 1978] 78-56804 ISBN 0-8225-1215-7 lib bdg. : 4.95
1. Luther, Martin, 1483-1546. 2. Reformation—Germany—Biography. I. Title. II. Series.

PELIKAN, Jaroslav Jan, v. 12
1923-
Luther and the liturgy by Jaroslav J. Pelikan, Regin Prenter and Herman A. Preus. Decorah, Iowa, Luther College Press [1958 vii, 214 p. 23 cm. (Martin Luther lectures, v. 2) Bibliographical footnotes. 68-15369
1. Luther, Martin, 1483-1546. I. Prenter, Regin, 1907- II. Preus, Herman Amberg, 1896- III. Title.

PELIKAN, Jaroslav Jan, 270.6'0924
1923-
Spirit versus structure; Luther and the institutions of the church [by] Jaroslav Pelikan. [1st ed.] New York, Harper & Row [1968] x, 149 p. 21 cm. Bibliographical references included in "Notes" (p. 140-149) [BR325.P45] 68-29557
1. Luther, Martin, 1483-1546. 2. Reformation. I. Title.

PITTENGER, William 270.6'0924
Norman, 1905-
Martin Luther: the great reformer, by W. Norman Pittenger. [1st ed.] New York, Watts [1969] ix, 182 p. 22 cm. (Immortals of philosophy and religion) Bibliography: p. 175-176. [BR325.P53] 69-11189
1. Luther, Martin, 1483-1546.

RICHTER, Friedrich, 922.443
priest
Martin Luther and Ignatius Loyola, spokesman for two worlds of belief. Translated from the German by Leonard F. Zwinger. Westminster, Md., Newman Press [c.]1960. 248p. (Bibl.) 21cm. 60-10728 3.75
1. Luther, Martin, 1483-1546. 2. Loyola, Ignacio de, Saint, 1491-1556. 3. Lutheran Church—Relations— Catholic Church. 4. Lutheran Church—Relations—Catholic Church. 5. Catholic Church—Relations—Lutheran Church. I. Title.

RITTER, Gerhard, 1888- 922.443
Luther, his life and work. Tr. from German by John Riches. New York, Harper [1964, c.1963] 256p. 21cm. 64-10753 4.00
1. Luther, Martin, 1483-1546. I. Title.

RITTER, Gerhard, 230'.4'10924 B
1888-1967.
Luther, his life and work / by Gerhard Ritter ; translated from the German by John Riches. Westport, Conn. : Greenwood Press, 1978, c1963. 256 p. ; 23 cm. Translation of Luther, Gestalt und Tat. Reprint of the ed. published by Harper & Row, New York. [BR325.R633 1978] 78-2717 ISBN 0-313-20347-4 lib. bdg. : 18.50
1. Luther, Martin, 1483-1546. 2. Reformation—Biography. I. Title.

RUPP, Ernest Gordon 922.443
Luther's progress to the Diet of Worms. New York, Harper [c.1964] 109p. 21cm. (Harper torchbks., TB120, Cloister lib.) Bibl. 64-7447 .95 pap.,
1. Luther, Martin, 1483-1546. I. Title.

SCHWIEBERT, Ernest 922.443
George.
Luther and his times; the Reformation from a new perspective. St. Louis, Concordia Pub. House [1950] xxii, 892 p. illus., ports., maps. 26 cm. Bibliographical references included in "Notes" (p. 765-878) [BR325.S335] 50-11670
1. Luther, Martin, 1483-1546. 2. Reformation. I. Title. BIP

SHORT, Ruth Gordon. v. 12
Martin Luther, the man. Westchester, Ill., Good News Publishers, 1960. 63 p. (A "one evening" condensed book) 63-58451
1. Luther, Martin, 1483-1546. I. Title. II. Series.

SHORT, Ruth Gordon. 922.443
Meet Martin Luther: His life and teachings. Grand Rapids, Zoadervan Pub. House [1959] 194 p. 22 cm. Includes bibliography. [BR325.S47] 59-65409
1. Luther, Martin, 1483-1546. I. Title.

SHORT, Ruth Gordon 922.443
Meet Martin Luther: his life and teachings. Grand Rapids, Mich., Zondervan Pub. House [c.1959] 194p. Includes bibliography. 22cm. 50-65409 2.95 bds.,
1. Luther, Martin, 1483-1546. I. Title.

SMITH, Preserved, 270.6'0924
1880-1941.
The life and letters of Martin Luther. New York, Barnes & Noble [1968] xvi, 490 p. illus., facsim., ports. 23 cm. Reprint of the 1911 ed. Bibliography: p. [433]-470. [BR325.S6 1968] 68-20697
1. Luther, Martin, 1483-1546. I. Title.

THIEL, Rudolph, 1899- 922.443
Luther. Translated by Gustav K. Wiencke. Philadelphia, Muchlenberg Press [1955] 492p. 24cm. [BR325.T455] 55-11781
1. Luther, Martin, 1483-1546. I. Title.

THULIN, Oskar, ed. 284.10924
A life of Luther, told in pictures and narrative by the reformer and his contemporaries. Translated by Marten O. Dietrick. Philadelphia, Fortress Press [1966] 210 p. illus., facsims., ports. (part col.) 26 cm. Translation of Martin Luther. "References": p. 206-209. [BR325.T4713] [B] 66-24281
1. Luther, Martin, 1483-1546. I. Title.

TODD, john Murray 922.443
Martin Luther, a biographical study. Glen Rock, N.J., Paulist [1967, c.1964] xix, 290p. 21cm illus. Bibl. [BR325.T6] 2.75 pap.,
1. Luther, Martin, 1483-1546. I. Title.

TODD, John Murray. 922.443
Martin Luther, a biographical study, by John M. Todd. Westminister, Md., Newman Press [1964] xix, 290 p. illus., facsims., ports. 23 cm. Bibliographical footnotes. [BR325.T6] 64-56136
1. Luther, Martin, 1483-1546.

TOWNSEND, Allan W. 284'.1'0924 B
A short life of Luther [by] Allan W. Townsend. Philadelphia, Fortress Press [1967] iv, 76 p. illus. 18 cm. Bibliographical references included in "Notes" (p. 76) [BR325.T67] 67-21532
1. Luther, Martin, 1483-1546. I. Title.

Luther, Martin, 1483-1546—Addresses, essays, lectures.

KOENIGSBERGER, 230'.4'10924 B
Helmut Georg, comp.
Luther; a profile. Edited by H. G. Koenigsberger. [1st ed.] New York, Hill and Wang [1973] xxi, 234 p. 21 cm. (World profiles) Contents.Contents.—Brief biography of Martin Luther.—Ranke, L. von. The beginning of the Reformation.—Febvre, L. The crisis of 1521-1525.—Ritter, G. The founder of the Evangelical churches.—Engels, F. The Marxist interpretation of Luther.—Erikson, E. H. The search for identity.—Rupp, G. Luther and government.—Hagglund, B. The doctrine of justification.—Ebeling, G. Luther's words.—Pinomaa, L. The doctrine of predestination.—Gerrish, B. A. Luther's belief in reason.—Bornkamm, H. Luther's translation of the New Testament.—Blume, F. Luther the musician.—Bibliography (p. 227-229) [BR326.K575 1973] 76-184946 ISBN 0-8090-6702-1 7.95
1. Luther, Martin, 1483-1546—Addresses, essays, lectures. I. Title.

Luther, Martin, 1483-1546—Criticism and interpretation—History.

DALLMANN, William, 1862- 922.443
Martin Luther: his life and his labor. [Rev. ed.] Saint Louis, Concordia Pub. House ['1951] 262 p. illus. 22 cm. [BR325.D3 1951] 52-7234
I. Luther, Martin, 1483-1546. II. Title.

INTERPRETERS of 230.4'1'0924
Luther; essays in honor of Wilhelm Pauck. Edited by Jaroslav Pelikan. Philadelphia, Fortress Press [1968] viii, 374 p. port. 23 cm. Contents.Contents.—Wilhelm Pauck: a tribute, by J. Pelikan.—Martin Luther on Luther, by K. Holl.—Robert Barnes on Luther, by C. S. Anderson.—John Calvin on Luther, by B. A. Gerrish.—The Elizabethans on Luther, by W. A. Clebsch.—Joseph Priestly on Luther, by G. H. Williams.—N. F. S. Grundtvig on Luther, by E. D. Nielsen.—Walther, Schaff, and Krauth on Luther, by E. T. Bachmann.—Soren Kierkegaard on Luther, by E. B. Koenker.—Adolf von Harnack on Luther, by J. Pelikan.—Ernst Troeltsch on Luther, by K. Penzel.—Paul Tillich on Luther, by J. L. Adams.—Wilhelm Pauck: a biographical essay, by M. H. Pauck.—Bibliography of the published writings of Wilhelm Pauck, by M. H. Pauck (p. 362-366) Includes bibliographical references. [BR333.2.I58] 68-23992 8.25
1. Luther, Martin, 1483-1546—Criticism and interpretation—History. 2. Pauck, Wilhelm, 1901- I. Pauck, Wilhelm, 1901- II. Pelikan, Jaroslav Jan, 1923- ed.

REU, Johann Michael, 284'.4'0924
1869-1943.
Thirty-five years of Luther research. New York, AMS Press [1970] 155 p. facsims. (part fold.), ports. 18 cm. Reprint of the 1917 ed. Includes bibliographical references. [BR325.R52 1970] 79-131505 ISBN 0-404-05284-3
1. Luther, Martin, 1483-1546—Criticism and interpretation—History. I. Title. BIP

STAUFFER, Richard 284'.1'0924
Luther as seen by Catholics. [Tr. by Mary Parker, T. H. L. Parker] Richmond, Knox [1967] 83p. 22cm. (Ecumenical studies in hist., no. 7) Tr. of Luther vu par les catholiques. Bibl. [BR333. 2. S713] 67-21482 1.95 pap.,
1. Luther, Martin, 1483-1546—Criticism and interpretation—Hist. 2. Theology, Doctrinal—Hist.—20th cent. I. Title. II. Series.

Luther, Martin, 1483-1546—Juvenile literature.

ELDER, Michael 284.10924
The young Martin Luther [by] Michael Elder. Illus. by Lewis Davies. New York, Roy [1966] 126p. illus. 21cm. [BR325.E4 1966a] 66-22228 3.25 bds.,
1. Luther, Martin, 1483-1546—Juvenile literature. I. Title.

NOHL, Frederick 920
Martin Luther, hero of faith. Illus. by Richard Hook. St. Louis, Concordia [c.1962] 150p. 24cm. 62-14146 2.75
1. Luther, Martin, 1483-1546—Juvenile literature. I. Title.

Luther, Martin. 1483-1546—Music.

NETTL, Paul, 1889- 783'.0924
Luther and music. Translated by Frida Best and Ralph Wood. New York, Russell & Russell [1967] 174 p. 20 cm. "Reprinted from a copy [of the 1948 ed.] in the collections of the New York Public Library." Bibliography: p. 165-167. [ML410.L964N42] 66-27133
1. Luther, Martin, 1483-1546—Music. I. Title. BIP

Luther, Martin, 1483-1546—Mysticism.

HOFFMAN, Bengt Runo, 230'.4'10924
1913-
Luther and the mystics : a re-examination of Luther's spiritual experience and his relationship to the mystics / Bengt R. Hoffman. Minneapolis : Augsburg Pub. House, c1976. 285 p. ; 23 cm. Includes indexes. Bibliography: p. 273-278. [BR333.5.M9H63] 75-22724 ISBN 0-8066-1514-1 : 9.95
1. Luther, Martin, 1483-1546—Mysticism. 2. Luther, Martin, 1483-1546—Theology. I. Title. BIP

Luther, Martin, 1483-1546—Theology.

EBELING, Gerhard, 230.4'1'0924
1912-
Luther; an introduction to his thought. Translated by R. A. Wilson. Philadelphia, Fortress Press [1970] 287 p. 22 cm. Includes bibliographical references. [BR333.2.E313 1970] 77-99612 5.95
1. Luther, Martin, 1483-1546—Theology. BIP

WICKS, Jared, 1929- 230.4'1'0924
Man yearning for grace; Luther's early spiritual teaching. Foreword by George A. Lindbeck. Washington, Corpus Books [1968] xvi, 410 p. 21 cm. Bibliography: p. 399-405. [BR333.2.W5] 68-25762 12.50
1. Luther, Martin, 1483-1546—Theology. I. Title.

Lutheran Church—Clergy—Biography.

ADAMS, James Edward, 1941- 284'.1'0924 B
Preus of Missouri and the great Lutheran civil war / James E. Adams. 1st ed. New York : Harper & Row, c1977. x, 242 p. ; 21 cm. Includes index. [BX8080.P73A65 1977] 76-62931 ISBN 0-06-060071-3 : 10.00
1. Preus, Jacob Aall Ottesen, 1920- 2. Lutheran Church—Clergy—Biography. 3. Lutheran Church—Missouri Synod—Doctrinal and controversial works. 4. Clergy—United States—Biography. I. Title.

Lutheran Church—Collected works.

RUPP, Ernest Gordon, comp. 270.6'0924 B
Martin Luther. Edited by E. G. Rupp and Benjamin Drewery. New York, St. Martin's Press [1970] xii, 179, [1] p. 21 cm. (Documents of modern history) Bibliography: p. [180] [BR331.E5R86 1970b] 79-124955 6.00
1. Lutheran Church—Collected works. 2. Theology—Collected works—16th century. I. Drewery, Benjamin, joint comp. II. Luther, Martin, 1483-1546.

Lutheran Church in America.

MR. Protestant: v. 12
an informal biography of Franklin Clark Fry. [Philadelphia] The Board of Publication of the United Lutheran Church in America [c1960] 76 p. illus., ports. 21 cm. 67-9761
1. Lutheran Church in America.

Lutheran Church in New York (Colony)—History—Sources.

BERKENMEYER, Wilhelm Christoph, 1686-1751. 284'.1747
The Albany protocol; Wilhelm Christoph Berkenmeyer's chronicle of Lutheran affairs in New York Colony, 1731-1750. Translated by Simon Hart and Sibrandina Geertruid Hart-Runeman. Translation initiated by Harry J. Kreider. Edited by John P. Dern. Ann Arbor, Mich., 1971. lx, 643 p. illus., facsims., geneal. tables, maps 23 cm. Translated from a photostatic copy of the Dutch MS. in the library of the Lutheran Theological Seminary at Gettysburg. The bound photostatic copy has title on spine: Berkenmeyer chronicle. Bibliography: p. 592-600. [BX8080.B447A313] 74-27484
1. Lutheran Church in New York (Colony)—History—Sources. I. Title. II. Title: Berkenmeyer chronicle.

Lutherans, Negro.

YOUNG, Rosa, 1890- 922.473
Light in the Dark Belt; the story of Rosa Young as told by herself. [Rev. ed.] Saint Louis, Concordia Pub. House, 1950. 200 p. illus. 19 cm. [BX8060.N5Y6] 51-8460
1. Lutherans, Negro. 2. Lutheran Church in Alabama. I. Title.

Luthuli, Albert John, 1898-

HARCOURT, Melville 248.0922
Portraits of destiny. Illus. by Giles Harcourt. New York, Sheed [1966] 239p. ports. 22cm. [BR1700.2.H3] 66-22014 5.50
1. Dolci, Danilo. 2. Luthuli, Albert John, 1898- 3. Munk, Kaj Harold-Leininger, 1898-1944. 4. Szabo, Violette (Bushnell) 1921-1945. I. Title.

Lutyens, Sir Edwin Landseer, 1869-1944.

HUSSEY, Christopher, 1899- 927.2
The life of Sir Edwin Lutyens. London, Country Life; New York, Scribner, 1950. xxii, 602p. illus., ports., map, plans. 26cm. (The Lutyens memorial) [NA997.L8H8 1950] 57-22239
1. Lutyens, Sir Edwin Landseer, 1869-1944. I. Title. II. Series.

Lutz, Frank Eugene, 1879-1943.

PALLISTER, John. 92
In the steps of the great American entomologist: Frank Eugene Lutz. Illus. by Kathleen Elgin. New York, Published by M. Evans and distributed in association with Lippincott, Philadelphia [1966] 127 p. illus. 21 cm. ([In the steps of the great American naturalists]) Biography of Frank Lutz, researcher in genetics, who conducted a lengthy and unusual study on the common fruit fly. [PZ10.P248] AC 67
1. Lutz, Frank Eugene, 1879-1943. 2. Entomologists. I. Elgin, Kathleen, 1923- illus. II. Title.
BIP

Luxemburg, Rosa, 1870-1919.

BASSO, Lelio. 335.43'092'4
Rosa Luxemburg, a reappraisal / Lelio Basso ; translated from the Italian by D. Parmee. New York : Praeger, 1975. p. cm. Includes index. [HX273.L83B29] 72-93288 ISBN 0-275-19790-5 10.00
1. Luxemburg, Rosa, 1870-1919.

FLORENCE, Ronald. 335.4'0922 B
Marx's daughters : Eleanor Marx, Rosa Luxemburg, Angelica Balabanoff / Ronald Florence. New York : Dial Press, 1975. 258 p., [4] leaves of plates : ill. ; 24 cm. Includes index. Bibliography: p. 237-243. [HX23.F55] 75-9576 ISBN 0-8037-5432-9 : 10.00
1. Aveling, Eleanor Marx, 1855-1898. 2. Luxemburg, Rosa, 1870-1919. 3. Balabanoff, Angelica, 1878-1965. 4. Marx, Karl, 1818-1883. I. Title.
BIP

FROLICH, Paul, 1884-1953. 335.43'092'4 B
Rosa Luxemburg; her life and work. Translated by Edward Fitzgerald. With a new pref. by Sebastian Franck. New York, H. Fertig, 1969. xii, [9]-339 p. 20 cm. "First published in English in 1940." [HX276.L86F7 1969] 68-9668
1. Luxemburg, Rosa, 1870-1919.

FROLICH, Paul, 1884-1953. 335.4'092'4 B
Rosa Luxemburg: her life and work. Newly translated by Johanna Hoornweg. New York, Monthly Review Press [1972] xx, 329 p. 21 cm. (Modern reader, PB-260) Translation based on the 3rd rev. German ed. Bibliography: p. [319]-324. [HX276.L86F7 1972] 72-81776 3.95 (pbk)
1. Luxemburg, Rosa, 1870-1919.

LUXEMBURG, Rosa, 1870-1919. 335.4'0924 B
Rosa Luxemburg speaks. Edited with an introd. by Mary-Alice Waters. New York, Pathfinder Press, 1970. 473 p. port. 23 cm. "A Merit book." [HX276.L8433] 76-119530 10.00
1. Socialism—Addresses, essays, lectures. 2. Socialism—Collected works. I. Title.
BIP

NETTL, J. P. 335.40924
Rosa Luxemburg. 2v. New York, Oxford [c.]1966. 2v. (xvi, xi, 984p.) 2 fronts, 24 plates (incl. facsims., ports.) 23cm. Bibl. [HX273.L83N4] 66-2563 20.20 set,
1. Luxemburg, Rosa, 1870-1919. I. Title.

NETTL, J. P. 335.4'0924 B
Rosa Luxemburg [by] J. P. Nettl. Abridged ed. London, New York, Oxford U.P., 1969. xvii, 557 p. 21 cm. (Oxford paperbacks, no. 67) Bibliography: p. [520]-523. [HX273.L83N4 1969] 76-463973 25/-
1. Luxemburg, Rosa, 1870-1919.

Luzan, Ignacio, 1702-1754.

MCCLELLAND, Ivy Lilian 808.1'092'4
Ignacio de Luzan, by Ivy L. McClelland. New York, Twayne Publishers [1973] 198 p. 22 cm. (Twayne's world authors series, TWAS 221. Spain) Bibliography: p. 191-194. [PQ6536.L9Z8] 75-185269 5.95
1. Luzan, Ignacio, 1702-1754.
BIP

Luzinski, Greg.

*GUTMAN, Bill. 796.357'092'2 [B]
Grand slammers : Rice, Luzinski, Foster, Hisle / by Bill Gutman. New York : Tempo Books, 1979. 182p. ; 18 cm. [GV865] ISBN 0-448-17344-1 pbk. : 1.50
1. Rice, Jim. 2. Luzinski, Greg. 3. Hisle, Larry. 4. Foster, George. 5. Baseball players — United States — Biography. I. Title.

Luzzatto, Moses Hayyim, 1707-1747.

GINZBURG, Simon, 1890-1944. 892.4'1'3 B
The life and works of Moses Hayyim Luzzatto ; founder of modern Hebrew literature / by Simon Ginzburg. Westport, Conn. : Greenwood Press, 1975. p. cm. Originally presented as the author's thesis, Dropsie College for Hebrew and Cognate Learning, 1923. Reprint of the 1931 ed. published by the Dropsie College for Hebrew and Cognate Learning, Philadelphia. Includes index. Bibliography: p. [PJ5051.L876 1975] 73-97282 ISBN 0-8371-2604-5 : 11.00
1. Luzzatto, Moses Hayyim, 1707-1747. I. Title.

Lwanga, Charles, d. 1866—Juvenile literature.

DOLLEN, Charles. 92 (J)
African triumph; life of Charles Lwanga. Illustrated by the Daughters of St. Paul under the direction of Guy R. Pennisi. [Boston] St. Paul Editions [1967] 70 p. illus., map. 22 cm. [BX4705.L8D6] 67-29693
1. Lwanga, Charles, d. 1866—Juvenile literature. 2. Christian martyrs—Uganda—Juvenile literature.

*Lyall, Leslie T.

*LYALL, Leslie T. 922.8
John Sung, flame for God in the Far East. 5th ed. Chicago, Moody [1964] 159p. 18cm. (China Inland mission bk., MP59) .59 pap.,
I. Title.

Lyall, William—Juvenile literature.

O'NEILL, Judith, 1930- 994.6'02
Transported to Van Diemen's Land / Judith O'Neill. Cambridge; New York Cambridge University Press 1976 p. cm. (Cambridge introduction to the history of mankind : topic book) The true story of two nineteenth-century British convicts who were sent to a penal colony in Tasmania, met, married, and eventually moved to Australia where as respected citizens they raised a family of seven children. [HV8950.T3O53] 76-20614 ISBN 0-521-21231-6 pbk. : 2.75
1. Lyall, William—Juvenile literature. 2. Battersby, Ann—Juvenile literature. 3. Tasmania—Exiles—Juvenile literature. 4. Penal colonies, British—Juvenile literature. I. Title.
BIP

Lycan, Dixie (Cline)—Juvenile literature.

MCDONNELL, Virginia B. 92
Dixie Cline, animal doctor; the complete life story of a girl who fought to make her way in the 'man's world' of veterinary medicine. New York, Nelson [c.1966] 127p. illus., ports. 22cm. (Champion bks. A Rutledge bk.) [SF613.L9M2] 66-15984 2.95
1. Lycan, Dixie (Cline)—Juvenile literature. I. Title.

Lyell, Charles, Sir, bart., 1797-1875.

BAILEY, Edward Battersby, Sir, 1881- 925
Charles Lyell. [1st ed.] Garden City, N.Y., Doubleday, 1963 [c1962] 214 p. illus. 21 cm. (British men of science) [QE22.L8B3 1963] 62-18878
1. Lyell, Charles, Sir, bart., 1797-1875.

Lyle family.

LYLE, Daniel, 1869- 929'.2'0973
Daniel Lyle, immigrant; one of the Lyle family who emigrated from Ireland to America and settled in the valley of Virginia in 1840 [i.e.1740] Peck, Idaho, 1946. 60 p. illus. 23 cm. [CS71.L985 1946] 65-48677
1. Lyle family. I. Title.

Lyle, Judge Matthew,

LYLE, Judge Matthew, 1896- 926.1
Life of Judge M. Lyle, M.D., an autobiography. Fort Worth, Tex., H. L. Geddie Co. [1964] 157 p. illus., facsims., geneal. table, ports. 21 cm. [R154.L95A3] 64-54718
I. Title.

Lyles Baptist Church, Fluvanna Co., Va.

THOMPSON, Archie Paul, 1921- 286'.1755'47
Lyles Baptist Church, 1774-1974, Fluvanna County, Virginia / A. Paul Thompson. 1st ed. [s.l. : s.n., 1974] (Charlottesville, Va. : King Lindsay Print. Corp.) v, 124 p. : ill. ; 23 cm. [BX6480.L9T47] 74-193283
1. Lyles Baptist Church, Fluvanna Co., Va. 2. Fluvanna Co., Va.—Biography.

Lyly, John, 1554?-1606.

SISSON, Charles Jasper, 1885- ed. 820.9003
Thomas Lodge and other Elizabethans, edited by Charles J. Sisson. New York, Octagon Books, 1966 [c1933] xii, 526 p. illus., maps, geneal. tables. 24 cm. Contents.Contents.—Thomas Lodge and his family, by C. J. Sisson.—Barnabe Barnes, by M. Eccles.—Lodowick Bryskett and his family, by D. Jones.—John Lyly at St. Bartholomew's, or Much ado about washing, by D. Jones.—Sir George Buc, master of the revels, by M. Eccles. [PR2298.S5 1966] 66-18029
1. Lodge, Thomas, 1558?-1625. 2. Barnes, Barnabe, 1569?-1609. 3. Bryskett, Lodowick, ca. 1545-ca. 1612. 4. Lyly, John, 1554?-1606. 5. Buck, George, Sir, d. 1623. I. Eccles, Mark. II. Jones, Deborah. III. Title.
BIP

WILSON, John Dover, 1881-1969. 828'.3'09
John Lyly. New York, Haskell House, 1970. vii, 148 p. 23 cm. Reprint of the 1905 ed. Bibliography: p. [141]-142. [PR2303.W5 1970] 68-24926
1. Lyly, John, 1554?-1606
BIP

Lyman, Francis Marion, 1840-1916.

LYMAN, Albert R 1880- 922.8373
Biography [of] Francis Marion Lyman, 1840-1916; apostle, 1880-1916. Edited, printed, and published by Melvin A. Lyman. Delta, Utah, 1958. 218p. illus. 24cm. [BX8695.L93L9] 59-28510
1. Lyman, Francis Marion, 1840-1916. I. Title.

Lyman, Isaac, 1759-1827.

LYMAN, Robert Ray. 974.8'55'030924 B
The life and times of Major Isaac Lyman, founder of Potter County, Pennsylvania. Researched and compiled, 1959 through 1964, by Robert R. Lyman. Coudersport, Pa., Potter County Historical Society, 1969. 129, [6] p. illus., coat of arms, facsim., ports. 22 cm. Bibliography: p. [131] [F153.L9L93] 77-251162
1. Lyman, Isaac, 1759-1827. I. Potter County (Pa.). Historical Society. II. Title.

Lyman, Mel.

LYMAN, Mel. 780'.924 B
Mirror at the end of the road. [Illustrated by Ebon Given. Photos. by Link Devereaux and others. New York, Ballantine Books, 1971] 1 v. (unpaged) illus. 21 cm. "An American Avatar publication." Autobiographical. [ML419.L88A3] 77-30652 3.95

I. Title.

Lynch, Eliza Alicia, 1835?-1886.

BRODSKY, Alyn. 989.2'05'0924 B
Madame Lynch & friend : a true account of an Irish adventuress and the dictator of Paraguay, who destroyed that American nation / Alyn Brodsky. 1st ed. New York : Harper & Row, [1975] xx, 312 p. ; 22 cm. Includes index. Bibliography: p. 297-301. [F2686.L9826 1975] 74-15813 ISBN 0-06-010487-2 : 10.00
1. Lynch, Eliza Alicia, 1835?-1886. 2. Lopez, Francisco Solano, Pres. Paraguay, 1827-1870. 3. Paraguayan War, 1865-1870. I. Title.

Lynch, Mary Fran.

LYNCH, Maureen. 362.3'092'6 B
Mary Fran and Mo / Maureen Lynch. New York : St. Martin's Press, c1979. 169 p. ; 22 cm. [HV3006.A4L954] 79-16493 ISBN 0-312-51864-1 : 8.95
1. Lynch, Mary Fran. 2. Mentally handicapped—Biography. 3. Helping behavior. 4. Mentally handicapped—United States—Family relationships. I. Title. **BIP**

Lynedoch, Thomas Graham, baron, 1748-1843.

BRETT-JAMES, Antony, 1920- 923.241
General Graham, Lord Lynedoch. New York, St. Martin's Press, 1959. 368p. illus. 23cm. [DA68.12.L9B7] 59-15723
1. Lynedoch, Thomas Graham, baron, 1748-1843. I. Title.

GENERAL Graham, Lord v. 12
Lynedoch. London, Macmillan; New York, St. Martin's Press, 1959. 368p. illus. 23cm. Bibliography: p.342-355.
1. Lynedoch, Thomas Graham, baron, 1748-1843. I. Brett-James, Antony, 1920-

Lynk, Miles Vandahurst,

LYNK, Miles Vandahurst, 1871- 926.1
Sixty years of medicine; or, The life and times of Dr. Miles V. Lynk, and autobiography. Memphis, Twentieth Century Press, c1951. 125 p. ports. 23 cm. [R154.L96A3] 51-2703
I. Title.

Lynn, Conrad J.

LYNN, Conrad J. 342'.73'085 B
There is a fountain : the autobiography of a civil rights lawyer / by Conrad Lynn. 1st ed. Westport, Conn. : L. Hill, 1979. xv, 240 p. ; 22 cm. Includes index. [KF373.L96A35] 78-19854 ISBN 0-88208-098-9 : 10.00
1. Lynn, Conrad J. 2. Lawyers—United States—Biography. I. Title. **BIP**

Lynn, Fred—Juvenile literature.

DOLAN, Edward F., 1924- 796.357'092'4 B
Fred Lynn : the hero from Boston / Edward F. Dolan, Jr., and Richard B. Lyttle. 1st ed. Garden City, N.Y. : Doubleday, c1978. 87 p., [12] leaves of plates : ill. ; 22 cm. Includes index. A biography of the Boston Red Sox player who was the first man in baseball to win the double honor of Rookie of the Year and Most Valuable Player in one season. [GV865.L94D64] 92 77-12846 ISBN 0-385-12528-3 : 5.95
1. Lynn, Fred—Juvenile literature. 2. Boston. Baseball club (American League)—Juvenile literature. 3. Baseball players—United States—Biography—Juvenile literature. I. Lyttle, Richard B., joint author. **BIP**

LIBBY, Bill. 796.357'092'4 B
Fred Lynn, young star / by Bill Libby. New York : Putnam, c1977. 160 p. : ill. ; 22 cm. (Putnam sports shelf) Includes index. A biography of the baseball player who became the first "Rookie of the Year" to also win the "Most Valuable Player" award in the major leagues. [GV865.L94L5 1977] 92 77-4278 ISBN 0-399-61102-9 lib.bdg. 5.29
1. Lynn, Fred—Juvenile literature. 2. Baseball players—United States—Biography—Juvenile literature. I. Title.

SOUCHERAY, Joe. 796.357'092'2 B
Fred Lynn / by Joe Soucheray ; photos. by Ronald Modra. Mankato, Minn. : Creative Education, c1977. 31 p. : ill. (some col.) ; 25 cm. (Creative Education sports superstars) A career biography of the Red Sox hitter who in 1975 became the only rookie in history to win Rookie of the Year and Most Valuable Player honors in the same year. [GV865.L94S68] 92 76-28377 ISBN 0-87191-528-6 lib.bdg. 4.95
1. Lynn, Fred—Juvenile literature. 2. Baseball players—United States—Biography—Juvenile literature. I. Modra, Ronald. II. Title. **BIP**

Lynn, Janet—Juvenile literature.

JACOBS, Linda. 796.9'62'0924 B
Janet Lynn, sunshine on ice. St. Paul, EMC Corp. [1974] 40 p. illus. 24 cm. (Her Women who win) A biography of a professional ice skater who at age twenty signed a three-year contract with the Ice Follies for almost a million and a half dollars. [GV850.L96J32 1974] 92 74-2133 ISBN 0-88436-122-5 3.95 (lib. bdg.)
1. Lynn, Janet—Juvenile literature. I. Title. Pbk. 1.75; ISBN 0-88436-123-3 **BIP**

MORSE, Ann. 796.9'1'0924 B
Janet Lynn / by Ann Morse ; illustrated by John Keely. Mankato, Minn. : Creative Education, [1975] p. cm. A biography of the figure skater whose lack of desire to "skate to win" made her decide to turn professional. [GV850.L96M67] 92 75-20355 ISBN 0-87191-456-5 lib.bdg. : 4.95
1. Lynn, Janet—Juvenile literature. 2. Skating—Juvenile literature. I. Keely, John. II. Title. **BIP**

Lynn, Loretta.

KRISHEF, Robert K. 784'.092'4
Loretta Lynn / Robert K. Krishef. Minneapolis : Lerner Publications Co., c1978. 62, [1] p. : ill. ; 21 cm. (Country music library) Includes index. Discography: [63] A biography of the singer recently recognized as country music "Entertainer of the year." [ML420.L947K7] 77-90155 ISBN 0-8225-1401-X : 4.95
1. Lynn, Loretta. 2. Country musicians—United States—Biography. I. Title. II. Series.

LYNN, Loretta. 784'.092'4 B
Loretta Lynn : Coal miner's daughter / Loretta Lynn, with George Vecsey. Chicago : Regnery, c1976. xiv, 204 p., [8] leaves of plates : ill. ; 24 cm. "A Bernard Seis Associates book." Includes index. [ML420.L947A3] 75-32976 ISBN 0-8092-8122-8 : 7.95
1. Lynn, Loretta. 2. Country musicians—Correspondence, reminiscences, etc. I. Vecsey, George.

Lyon. Carolyn Hamilton (Talcott) 1860-1936.

REMINGTON, Carolyn Sibyl (Lyon) 1902- 371.9120922
Vibrant silence; a biography [Ed. by Elizabeth C. Whalen. Rochester, N.Y., Lawyers Co-operative, c.1965] 336p. illus., coats of arms. facsims., gencal. tables, ports. 27cm. Bibl. [HV2426.L9R4] 66-878 3.95
1. Lyon. Carolyn Hamilton (Talcott) 1860-1936. 2. Lyon. Edmund. 3. Deaf—Education— U.S. I. Title.

Lyon, John,

LYON, John, d.1814. 925.8
John Lyon, nurseryman and plant hunter, and his Journal, 1799-1814. [By] Joseph and Nesta Ewan. Philadelphia, American Philosophical Society, 1963. 69 p. maps, facsims. 30 cm. (Transactions of the American Philosophical Society, new ser., v. 53, pt. 2) Bibliography: p. 60-61. [Q11.P6 n.s., vol. 53, pt. 2] 63-16191
I. Ewan, Joseph Andorfer, 1909- II. Ewan, Nesta. (American Philosophical Society, Philadelphia. Transactions, new ser., v. 53, pt. 2) III. Title. IV. Series.

Lyon, Mary, 1797-1849

BANNING, Evelyn I 378.744230924(B)
Mary Lyon of Putnam's Hill; a biography, by Evelyn I. Banning. New York, Vanguard Press [1965] 189 p. 22 cm. Bibliography: p. [187]-189. [LA2317.93B3] 66-10683
1. Lyon, Mary, 1797-1849 I. Title.

Lyon, Matthew, 1750-1822.

WILLIAMS, Robert Percy, 1906- 328.73'092'4 B
By the bulls that redamed me; the odyssey of Matthew Lyon [by] Robert P. Williams. [1st ed.] New York, Exposition Press [1972] 204 p. 22 cm. [E302.6.L9W55] 72-75485 ISBN 0-682-47464-9 6.50
1. Lyon, Matthew, 1750-1822. I. Title.

Lyons, B. J.

LYONS, B. J. 923.973
Thrills and spills of a cowboy rancher. 1st ed. New York, Vantage Press [1959] 172 p. illus. 21 cm. Autobiographical. [CT275.L9A3] 59-2028
I. Title.

Lyons, Barbara—Biography—Youth.

LYONS, Barbara. 398'.092'4 B
The brook / by Barbara Lyons. Honolulu : Topgallant Pub. Co., 1976. 248 p. : ill. ; 21 cm. [PS3562.Y448Z52] 75-42444 ISBN 0-914916-10-6 : 10.00 ISBN 0-914916-15-7 pbk. : 3.50
1. Lyons, Barbara—Biography—Youth. 2. Authors, American—20th century—Biography. I. Title. **BIP**

Lyons, Daniel.

MCCALLUM, John Dennis, 1924- 282'.092'4 B
The story of Dan Lyons, S.J., by John D. McCallum. New York, Guild Books [1973] xviii, 443 p. illus. 22 cm. [BX4705.L97M3] 72-94967 7.95
1. Lyons, Daniel. I. Title.

Lysaght, Sidney Royse, d. 1941.

MACLYSAGHT, Edward. 823'.9'12
S. R. Lysaght : the author and the man / by Edward MacLysaght. [Dublin] : MacLysaght, 1974. Folder ([6] p.) : ports. ; 23 cm. Bibliography: p. [6] [PR6023.Y5Z82] 75-321118 ISBN 0-9504079-0-9
1. Lysaght, Sidney Royse, d. 1941.

Lysenko, Trofim Denisovich, 1898-1976.

LECOURT, Dominique. 575'.0092'4 B
Proletarian science? : The case of Lysenko / Dominique Lecourt ; introd. by Louis Althusser ; translated by Ben Brewster. London : NLB ; Atlantic Highlands, N.J. : Humanities Press, 1977. 165 p. ; 22 cm. Translation of Lyssenko. Includes bibliographical references and index. [QH31.L95L413] 77-23002 ISBN 0-391-00738-6 : 11.50
1. Lysenko, Trofim Denisovich, 1898-1976. 2. Geneticists—Russia—Biography. 3. Agriculturists—Russia—Biography. 4. Biology—History. I. Title. **BIP**

Lysippus, sculptor.

SJOQVIST, Erik, 1903- 730'.924
Lysippus. [Cincinnati] University of Cincinnati, 1966. 31 p. illus., ports. 24 cm. (Lectures in memory of Louise Taft Semple, 2d ser.) Lectures delivered Apr. 11-12, 1966 at the request of the University of Cincinnati and its Dept. of Classics. Includes bibliographical references. [NB98.S55] 70-268864
1. Lysippus, sculptor. I. Series: Cincinnati. University. Lectures in memory of Louise Taft Semple

Lytle, Andrew Nelson, 1902- — Biography.

LYTLE, Andrew Nelson, 1902- 813'.5'2 B
A wake for the living : a family chronicle / by Andrew Lytle. New York : Crown Publishers, [1975] 270 p. : ill. ; 24 cm. [PS3523.Y88Z52] 75-4616 ISBN 0-517-51901-1 : 8.95
1. Lytle, Andrew Nelson, 1902- — Biography. 2. Lytle, Andrew Nelson, 1902- —Biography—Ancestry. I. Title.

Lytton, Edward George Earle Lytton Bulwer-Lytton, 1st Baron, 1803-1873.

ESCOTT, Thomas Hay Sweet, 1844-1924. 823'.8 B
Edward Bulwer, first Baron Lytton of Knebworth; a social, personal, and political monograph. Port Washington, N.Y., Kennikat Press [1970] viii, 348 p. port. 22 cm. Reprint of the 1910 ed. [PR4931.E7 1970] 75-113309
1. Lytton, Edward George Earle Lytton Bulwer-Lytton, 1st Baron, 1803-1873. **BIP**

LYTTON, Victor Alexander George Robert Bulwer-Lytton, 2d Earl of, 1876-1947. 823'.8 B
Bulwer-Lytton, by the Earl of Lytton. [Folcroft, Pa.] Folcroft Library Editions, 1973. p. Reprint of the 1948 ed. published by Home & Van Thal, London, in series: The English novelists. [PR4931.L76 1973] 73-15670 ISBN 0-8414-8552-6 (lib. bdg.)
1. Lytton, Edward George Earle Lytton Bulwer-Lytton, 1st Baron, 1803-1873. I. Series: The English novelists (London). **BIP**

LYTTON, Victor Alexander George Robert Bulwer-Lytton, 2d Earl 823'.8 B

of, 1876-1947.
The life of Edward Bulwer, first Lord Lytton, by his grandson, the Earl of Lytton. Freeport, N.Y., Books for Libraries Press [1973] p. Reprint of the 1913 ed. published by Macmillan, London. Bibliography: v. 2, p. [PR4931.L8 1973] 73-4395 ISBN 0-518-19034-X
1. Lytton, Edward George Earle Lytton Bulwer-Lytton, 1st baron, 1803-1873. I. Title.

Lytton, Edward George Earle Lytton Bulwer-Lytton, 1st Baron, 1803-1873—Correspondence.

LYTTON, Edward George Earle Lytton Bulwer-Lytton, 1st Baron, 1803-1873. 823'.8 B
Letters of the late Edward Bulwer, Lord Lytton, to his wife : with extracts from her MSS. "Autobiography" and other documents / published in vindication of her memory by Louisa Devey. New York : AMS Press, 1976. 451 p. ; 19 cm. Reprint of the 1889 ed. published by G. W. Dillingham, New York. [PR4931.A45 1976] 79-148815 24.50
1. Lytton, Edward George Earle Lytton Bulwer-Lytton, 1st Baron, 1803-1873—Correspondence. 2. Lytton, Rosina Doyle Wheeler Bulwer-Lytton, Baroness, 1802-1882. I. Devey, Louisa. II. Title.

M

*ROUECHE, Berton, 1911- 616.092
A man named Hoffman and other narratives of medical detection. [New York] Berkley [1966, c.1958-1965] 190p. 18cm. (Medallion bk., S1259) .75 pap.,
1. M 2. Medicine—Cases, clinical reports, statistics. I. Title.

Mammanmappila, K. C., 1873-1953.

KOSHY, M. J., 1931- 954'.83'0350924 B
K. C. Mammen Mappilai : the man and his vision / by M. J. Koshy ; foreword by K. P. S. Menon. Trivandrum : Kerala Historical Society, 1976. xxiv, 673 p. ; 23 cm. Appendix (p. [274]-641) comprises selected articles, correspondence, and other documents. Includes index. Bibliography: p. [643]-655. [DS485.K4K65] 76-902119 Rs120.00
1. Mammanmappila, K. C., 1873-1953. 2. Kerala—Biography. 3. Kerala—History.

M'Connel, Alexander.

THE Escape of Alexander M'Connel. 973'.04'97 S
Alexander M'Connel. New York : Garland Pub., 1977. p. 7-9 ; 23 cm. (The Garland library of narratives of North American Indian captivities ; v. 37) Originally published in Hunt's family almanac, for 1855, by U. Hunt, Philadelphia. Issued with the reprint of the 1820 ed. of Alexander M'Connell's escape and Adventure with the Indians. New York, 1977, the reprint of the 1820 ed. of A tale of other times. New York, 1977, the reprint of the 1822 ed. of Cornelius, E. The little Osage captive. New York, 1977, the reprint of the 1824 ed. of Jamison, A. An interesting narrative. New York, 1977, the reprint of the 1825 ed. of Segar, N. A brief narrative. New York, 1977, and the reprint of the 1825 ed. of Biggs, W. Narrative of William Biggs. New York, 1977. [E85.G2 vol. 37] [E87.M3] 976.9'53'0924 77-626 ISBN 0-8240-1661-0 lib.bdg. : 25.00
1. M'Connel, Alexander. 2. Indians of North America—Captivities. 3. Kentucky—Biography. I. Series.

M'Culloch, John, 1754?-1824.

SPIESEKE, Alice Winifred, 1899- 973'.07'2024
The first textbooks in American history and their compiler, John M'Culloch. New York, Bureau of Publications, Teachers College, Columbia University, 1938. [New York, AMS Press, 1972, ie 1973] vi, 135 p. facsims. 22 cm. Reprint of the 1938 ed., issued in series: Teachers College, Columbia University. Contributions to education, no. 744. Originally presented as the author's thesis, Columbia. Bibliography: p. [122]-131. [E175.85.S72 1972] 71-177749 ISBN 0-404-55744-9 10.00
1. M'Culloch, John, 1754?-1824. 2. United States—Historiography. I. Title. II. Series: Columbia University. Teachers College. Contributions to education, no. 744. BIP

M'Toy, Ida.

WELTY, Eudora, 1909- 976.2'12 B
Ida M'Toy / by Eudora Welty. Urbana : University of Illinois Press, c1979. [40] p. : ill. ; 26 cm. First published in 1942 in Accent. [F349.J13M788] 79-63771 ISBN 0-252-00760-3 : 25.00
1. M'Toy, Ida. 2. Afro-Americans—Mississippi—Jackson—Biography. 3. Jackson, Miss.—Biography. BIP

Maiakovskii, Vladimir Vladimirovich, 1894-1930—Relationship with women—Lili Brik.

CHARTERS, Ann. 891.7'1'42 B
I love : the story of Vladimir Mayakovsky and Lili Brik / Ann & Samuel Charters. New York : Farrar Straus Giroux, 1979. xiv, 398 p. : ill. ; 24 cm. Includes index. Bibliography: p. 389-392. [PG3476.M312C45 1979] 79-92 ISBN 0-374-17406-7. : 15.00
1. Maiakovskii, Vladimir Vladimirovich, 1894-1930 Relationship with women—Lili Brik. 2. Brik, Lili IUr'evna. 3. Poets, Russian—20th century—Biography. 4. Mistresses—Russia—Biography. I. Charters, Samuel Barclay, joint author. II. Title. BIP

Maass, Clara Louise, 1876-1901—Juvenile literature.

TENGBOM, Mildred. 610.73'092'4 B
No greater love : the gripping story of Nurse Clara Maass / written by Mildred Tengbom. St. Louis : Concordia Pub. House, c1978. 159 p. : ill. ; 24 cm. (Greatness with faith) Bibliography: p. 157-159. [RT37.M17T46] 77-28588 ISBN 0-570-07878-4 : 4.95. ISBN 0-570-07883-0 pbk. : 2.95
1. Maass, Clara Louise, 1876-1901—Juvenile literature. 2. Nurses—United States—Biography—Juvenile literature. 3. Lutherans—United States—Biography—Juvenile literature. 4. Yellow fever—History—Juvenile literature. I. Title. II. Series.

Macapagal, Diosdado, Pres. Philippines, 1910-

REYNOLDS, Quentin James, 1902- 991.4040924
Macapagal, the incorruptible, by Quentin Reynolds and Geoffrey Bocca. New York, D. McKay Co. [1965] vii, 215 p. 20 cm. Bibliography: p. 209-210. [DS686.6.M24R4] 65-25142
1. Macapagal, Diosdado, Pres. Philippines, 1910- I. Bocca, Geoffrey, joint author. II. Title.

Macari, Lou.

MACARI, Lou. 796.33'4'0924 B
United we shall not be moved / Lou Macari. London : Souvenir Press, 1976. 187 p., [4] leaves of plates : ill. ; 23 cm. [GV942.7.M25A38 1976] 77-354725 ISBN 0-285-62260-9 : £3.50
1. Macari, Lou. 2. Manchester United Football Club. 3. Soccer players—Great Britain—Biography. I. Title.

Macarius III, Patriarch of Antioch, fl. 1636-1666.

PAUL, of Aleppo, Archdeacon, fl.1654-1666. 914.7'03'4
The travels of Macarius, 1652-1660. Selected and arranged by Lady Laura Ridding. New York, Arno Press, 1971. xi, 125 p. 23 cm. (Russia observed) Reprint of the 1936 ed. "Extracts from the diary of the travels of Macarius ... written in Arabic." [BX395.M3P3 1971] 77-115577 ISBN 0-405-03089-4
1. Macarius III, Patriarch of Antioch, fl. 1636-1666. 2. Orthodox Eastern Church. 3. Russia—Description and travel. 4. Balkan Peninsula—Description and travel. I. Title.

MacArthur, Charles, 1895-1956.

HECHT, Ben, 1893- 928.1
Charlie; the improbable life and times of Charles MacArthur. [1st ed.] New York, Harper [1957] 242 p. illus. 22 cm. [PS3525.A1147Z7] 57-7976
1. MacArthur, Charles, 1895-1956.

MacArthur, Douglas,

MACARTHUR, Douglas, 1880-1964 355.3320924
Courage was the rule; General Douglas MacArthur's own story. New York, Whittlesey-McGraw [c.1964, 1965] 296p. illus., maps, ports. (1 col.) 21cm. An abridged ed. of the author's Reminiscences [E745.M3A35] 65-23558 3.75; 3.26 lib. ed.,
I. Title.

MACARTHUR, Douglas, 1880-1964. 355.3320924
Duty, honor, country; a pictorial autobiography. New York, McGraw [1965] 218p. illus., ports. 29cm. [E745.M3A36] 65-25518 7.95
I. Title.

MACARTHUR, Douglas, 1880-1964 923.573
Reminiscences. Greenwich, Conn., Fawcett [1965, c.1964] 496p. illus. 18cm. (Crest bk., m850) [E745.M3A34] .95 pap.,
I. Title.

MACARTHUR, Douglas, 1880-1964. 923.573
Reminiscences. [1st ed.] New York, McGraw-Hill [1964] viii, 438 p. illus., maps. 24 cm. [E745.M3A34] 64-22955
I. Title.

MacArthur, Douglas, 1880-1964.

ARCHER, Jules. 923.573
Front-line general: Douglas MacArthur. New York, Messner [1963] 191 p. 22 cm. [E745.M3A8] 63-16791
1. MacArthur, Douglas, 1880-1964. I. Title.

ARMY times, Washington, D.C. 923.573
The banners and the glory; the story of General Douglas MacArthur, by eds. of the Army times. New York, Putnam [c.1965] 189p. illus., facsims., ports. 26cm. Bibl. [E745.M3A82] 65-10847 6.95
1. MacArthur, Douglas, 1880-1964. I. Title.

CONSIDINE, Robert Bernard, 1906- 923.573
General Douglas MacArthur. Greenwich, Conn., Fawcett [c.1964] 126p. illus., ports. 18cm. (Gold Medal d1408) 64-3602 .50 pap.,
1. MacArthur, Douglas, 1880-1964. I. Title. II. Title: The long and illustrious career of General Douglas MacArthur.

FREDRICKS, Edgar J. 327.73
MacArthur: his mission and meaning, by Edgar J. Fredricks. With a foreword by Guy Vander Jagt. Philadelphia, Whitmore Pub. Co. [1968] 91 p. 22 cm. Thesis (M.A.)—Western Michigan University. Bibliography: p. 89-91. [E745.M3F7] 68-28061 3.50
1. MacArthur, Douglas, 1880-1964. 2. United States—Foreign relations—1945- I. Title.

GUNTHER, John, 1901-1970. 923.573
The riddle of MacArthur; Japan, Korea, and the Far East. [1st ed.] New York, Harper [1951] xiv, 240 p. 22 cm. [E745.M3G8] 51-548
1. MacArthur, Douglas, 1880-1964. 2. Japan—History—Allied occupation, 1945-1952. I. Title. BIP

HUFF, Sidney L. 923.573
My fifteen years with General MacArthur [by] Sid Huff with Joe Alex Morris. New York, Paperback Lib. [1964, c.1951] 142p. 18cm. (52-288) 64-3913 .50 pap.,
1. MacArthur, Douglas, 1880-1964. I. Morris, Joe Alex, 1904- II. Title.

HUNT, Frazier, 1885- v. 12
The untold story of Douglas MacArthur.

New York, New American Library, 1964. 478 p. maps. 18 cm. 66-4655
1. MacArthur, Douglas, 1880-1964. I. Title. BIP

HUNT, Frazier, 1885- 923.573
The untold story of Douglas MacArthur. New York, Devin-Adair Co., 1954. 533 p. illus. 22 cm. [E745.M3H8] 54-10811
1. MacArthur, Douglas, 1880-1964. I. Title.

JAMES, Dorris Clayton, 1931- 355.3'31'0924 B
The years of MacArthur [by] D. Clayton James. Boston, Houghton Mifflin, 1970- v. maps, ports. 22 cm. Contents.Contents.—v. 1. 1880-1941.—v. 2. 1941-1945. Includes bibliographical references. [E745.M3J3] 76-108685 12.50 (v. 1)
1. MacArthur, Douglas, 1880-1964. I. Title. BIP

MACARTHUR, Douglas, 1880-1964 355.3320924
Courage was the rule; General Douglas MacArthur's own story. New York, Whittlesey-McGraw [c.1964, 1965] 296p. illus., maps, ports. (1 col.) 21cm. An abridged ed. of the author's Reminiscences [E745.M3A35] 65-23558 3.75; 3.26 lib. ed.,
I. Title.

MACARTHUR, Douglas, 1880-1964. 355.3320924
Duty, honor, country; a pictorial autobiography. New York, McGraw [1965] 218p. illus., ports. 29cm. [E745.M3A36] 65-25518 7.95
I. Title.

MACARTHUR, Douglas, 1880-1964 923.573
Reminiscences. Greenwich, Conn., Fawcett [1965, c.1964] 496p. illus. 18cm. (Crest bk., m850) [E745.M3A34] .95 pap.,
I. Title.

MACARTHUR, Douglas, 1880-1964. 923.573
Reminiscences. [1st ed.] New York, McGraw-Hill [1964] viii, 438 p. illus., maps. 24 cm. [E745.M3A34] 64-22955
I. Title.

MANCHESTER, William Raymond, 1922- 355.3'31'0924 B
American Caesar, Douglas MacArthur, 1880-1964 / William Manchester. 1st ed. Boston : Little, Brown, c1978. xvii, 793 p., [4] leaves of plates : ill. ; 24 cm. Includes index. Bibliography: p. [745]-762. [E745.M3M27] 78-8004 ISBN 0-316-54498-1 : 15.00
1. MacArthur, Douglas, 1880-1964. 2. United States. Army—Biography. 3. Generals—United States—Biography. 4. United States—History, Military—20th century. I. Title.

MAYER, Sydney L., 1937- 355.3'31'0924 B
MacArthur [by] Sydney L. Mayer. [New York, Ballantine Books, 1971] 160 p. illus., ports. 21 cm. (Ballantine's illustrated history of the violent century. War leader book no. 2) Cover title. Bibliography: p. 160. [E745.M3M3] 70-24607 1.00
1. MacArthur, Douglas, 1880-1964.

MAYER, Sydney L., 1937- 327.73'092'4
MacArthur in Japan [by] Sydney L. Mayer. [New York, Ballantine Books, 1973] 160 p. illus. 21 cm. (Ballantine's illustrated history of the violent century. War leader book no. 19) Bibliography: p. 160. [E745.M3M32] 73-164540 1.00
1. MacArthur, Douglas, 1880-1964. 2. Japan—History—Allied occupation, 1945-1952. I. Title.

NEWLON, Clarke. 923.573
The fighting Douglas MacArthur. New York, Dodd, Mead, [1965] vii, 211 p. illus., maps, ports. 21 cm. Bibliography: p. 205-206. [E745.M3N4] 65-16300
1. MacArthur, Douglas, 1880-1964. I. Title. BIP

RICHARDS, Norman. 355.3'31'0924 B
Douglas MacArthur. Chicago, Children's Press [1967] 94 p. illus. (part col.), col. map, ports. 29 cm. (People of destiny: a humanities series) Bibliography: p. 91. A biography of the controversial military leader remembered for his defense of the Philippines during World War II, administration of occupied Japan after the war, and leadership of United Nations troops in Korea until his recall by President Truman. [E745.M3R52] 92 AC 68
1. MacArthur, Douglas, 1880-1964. I. Title.

ROVERE, Richard Halworth, 1915- 327.730924
The MacArthur controversy and American foreign policy [by] Richard H. Rovere, Arthur Schlesinger, Jr. New York, Farrar [c.1951, 1965] xv, 366p. illus., map. 21cm. First pub. in 1951 under title. The general and the President. Bibl. [E745.M3R6] 65-6284 5.75
1. MacArthur, Douglas, 1880-1964. 2. Korean War, 1950-1953. 3. U.S.—For. rel.—1945-1953. I. Schlesinger, Arthur Meier, 1917- joint author. II. Title.

WHITNEY, Courtney. 973.91'092'4 B
MacArthur : his rendezvous with history / by Courtney Whitney. Westport, Conn. : Greenwood Press, 1977, c1955. xi, 547, xii p. : maps ; 24 cm. Reprint of the 1956 ed. published by Knopf, New York. Includes index. [E745.M3W48 1977] 77-2965 ISBN 0-8371-9564-0 lib.bdg. : 29.75
1. MacArthur, Douglas, 1880-1964. 2. Generals—United States—Biography.

WITTNER, Lawrence S., comp. 355.3'31'0924
MacArthur. Edited by Lawrence S. Wittner. Englewood Cliffs, N.J., Prentice-Hall [1971] vi, 186 p. 21 cm. (Great lives observed) Bibliography: p. 182-183. [E745.M3W55] 77-160530 ISBN 0-13-541425-3 2.45
1. MacArthur, Douglas, 1880-1964. I. Title.

MacArthur, Douglas, 1880-1964—Juvenile literature.

ALTMAN, Frances. 355.3'31'0924 B
General Douglas MacArthur, military genius. Minneapolis, Denison [1973] 158 p. 23 cm. (Men of achievement series) A biography of a famous general from his boyhood in the New Mexico Territory, through his controversial military career, to his later years when many honors were conferred upon him. [E745.M3A68] 92 72-85654 ISBN 0-513-01109-9 4.98 (Lib. ed.)
1. MacArthur, Douglas, 1880-1964—Juvenile literature. I. Title.

DEVANEY, John. 355.3'31'0924
Douglas MacArthur, something of a hero / by John Devaney. New York : Putnam, c1979. p. cm. Includes index. A biography of the controversial general with emphasis on his service during the two World Wars and the Korean War. [U53.M25D48] 92 B 78-10820 ISBN 0-399-20660-4 : 8.95
1. MacArthur, Douglas, 1880-1964—Juvenile literature. 2. Generals—United States—Biography—Juvenile literature. I. Title.

JULIAN, Allen Phelps 920
MacArthur, the life of a general. By Allen Phelps Julian for the eds., the Army times. New York, Deuel [dist. Meredith, c.1963] xi, 179p. illus., ports. 21cm. Bibl. 63-20603 3.95
1. MacArthur, Douglas, 1880- —Juvenile literature. I. Army times, Washington, D.C. II. Title.

RICHARDS, Norman. 973.91'0924 (B)
Douglas MacArthur. Chicago, Children's Press [1967] 94 p. illus. (part col.), col. map. ports. 29 cm. (People of destiny: a humanities series) Bibliography: p. 91. [E745.M3R52] 67-20102
1. MacArthur, Douglas, 1880-1964.—Juvenile literature. I. Title.

STEINBERG, Alfred, 1917- 923.573
Douglas MacArthur. New York, Putnam [1961] 192 p. illus. 21 cm. (Lives to remember) Includes bibliography. [E745.M3S8] 60-12537
1. MacArthur, Douglas, 1880- Juvenile literature. I. Title.

Macarthur, Mary Reid, 1880-1921.

HAMILTON, Mary Agnes Adamson, 1883- 331.88'092'4 B
Mary Macarthur : a biographical sketch / by Mary Agnes Hamilton. Westport, Conn. : Hyperion Press, 1976. 209 p. : port. ; 23 cm. (Pioneers of the woman's movement) Reprint of the 1926 ed. published by T. Seltzer, New York. [HD8393.M2H3 1976] 74-33945 ISBN 0-88355-266-3 : 16.50
1. Macarthur, Mary Reid, 1880-1921. 2. Women in trade-unions—Great Britain—Biography.

Macartney, Clarence Edward Nobel,

MACARTNEY, Clarence Edward Nobel, 1879-1957. 922.573
The making of a minister; the autobiography of Clarence E. Macartney. Edited and with an introd. by J. Clyde Henry. Foreword by Frank E. Gaebelein. Great Neck, N. Y., Channel Press [1961] 224p. 21cm. [BX9225.M14A3] 61-7571
I. Title.

Macaulay, Rose,

MACAULAY, Rose, Dame. 928.2
Letter to a sister. Edited by Constance Babington-Smith. [1st American ed.] New York, Atheneum, 1964. 352 p. geneal. table., ports. 22 cm. Letters written to the author's sister, Jean Macaulay, from 1926 to 1958. [PR6025.A16Z52] 64-18730
I. Macaulay, Jean Babington, 1882- II. Title.

Macaulay, Thomas Babington Macaulay, Baron, 1800-1859.

BEATTY, Richmond Croom, 1905-1961. 942.081'0924
Lord Macaulay, Victorian liberal. [Hamden, Conn.] Archon Books, 1971 [c1938] xvi, 387 p. port. 23 cm. "Bibliographical note": p. 381. [DA3.M3B4 1971] 72-116905 ISBN 0-208-01037-8
1. Macaulay, Thomas Babington Macaulay, Baron, 1800-1859. I. Title. BIP

BRYANT, Arthur, Sir, 1899- 828'.8'09 B
Macaulay / Arthur Sryant. New York : Barnes & Noble, 1979, c1932. xxvi, 145 p., [2] leaves of plates : ill. ; 22 cm. Reprint of the ed. published by P. Davies, London. Includes index. Bibliography: p. 131-140. [DA3.M3B72 1979] 78-27536 ISBN 0-06-490761-9 : 23.50
1. Macaulay, Thomas Babington Macaulay, Baron, 1800-1859. 2. Historians—Great Britain—Biography. 3. Authors, English—19th century—Biography. 4. Statesmen—Great Britain—Biography. BIP

CLIVE, John. 907'.2'024 B
Macaulay—the shaping of the historian / by John Clive. New York : Vintage Books, 1975, c1973. xii, 499, xxxvi p. ; 21 cm. Includes bibliographical references and index. [DA3.M3C5 1975] 74-23999 ISBN 0-394-71507-1 pbk. : 4.95
1. Macaulay, Thomas Babington Macaulay, Baron, 1800-1859. I. Title.

GAY, Peter, 1923- 907'.2'022
Style in history. New York, Basic Books [1974] xiii, 242 p. illus. 22 cm. Bibliography: p. 219-238. [D14.G39] 73-91076 ISBN 0-465-08304-8 8.95
1. Gibbon, Edward, 1737-1794. 2. Ranke, Leopold von, 1795-1886. 3. Macaulay, Thomas Babington Macaulay, Baron, 1800-1859. 4. Burckhardt, Jakob Christoph, 1818-1897. 5. Historiography. I. Title. BIP

MACAULAY, Thomas Babington Macaulay, Baron, 1800-1859. 828'.8'09 B
The letters of Thomas Babington Macaulay, edited by Thomas Pinney. [London] Cambridge University Press, 1974- v. 24 cm. On spine: The letters of Macaulay. Contents.Contents.— —v. 2. March 1831-December 1833. [DA3.M3A4 1974] 73-75860 ISBN 0-521-20202-7
1. Macaulay, Thomas Babington Macaulay, Baron, 1800-1859. I. Pinney, Thomas, ed. II. Title. III. Title: The letters of Macaulay. Distributed by Cambridge University Press; New York 31.50 ea.

*MACAULAY, Thomas Bobington Macaulay baron, 1800-1859. 828.'8'9
The letters of Thomas Babington Macaulay. New York : Cambridge University Press.
Vol. III, edited by Thomas Pinney and covering the period Jan. 1834-Aug. 1841 is available for 42.50.ISBN 0-521-21125-2.L.C. card no.: 73-75860.

TREVELYAN, George Otto, Sir, bart., 1838-1928. 941.081'092'4 B
The life and letters of Lord Macaulay / by his nephew George Otto Trevelyan ; with a pref. by G. M. Trevelyan. Oxford ; New York : Oxford University Press, 1978. 2 v. in 1 ; 19 cm. Includes bibliographical references and index. [DA3.M3T5 1978] 79-302140 ISBN 0-19-822487-7 pbk. : 10.50
1. Macaulay, Thomas Babington Macaulay, Baron, 1800-1859. 2. Historians—Great Britain—Biography. 3. Authors, English—19th century—Biography. 4. Statesmen—Great Britain—Biography. I. Title. BIP

TREVELYAN, Sir George Otto, bart., 1838-1928. 928.2
The life and letters of Lord Macaulay. With a pref. by G. M. Trevelyan. [London] Oxford University Press, 1961. 2 v. 16 cm. [DA3.M3T5] 62-156
1. Macaulay, Thomas Babington Macaulay, 1st baron, 1800-1850. I. Title.

MacBride, Maud Gonne.

CARDOZO, Nancy. 941.5'082'10924 B
Lucky eyes and a high heart : the biography of Maud Gonne / Nancy Cardozo. New York : Bobbs-Merrill, [1978] p. cm. [DA958.M25C37] 76-44665 ISBN 0-672-52080-X : 15.00
1. MacBride, Maud Gonne. 2. Irish question. 3. Politicians—Ireland—Biography. I. Title.

LEVENSON, Samuel. 941.5082'1'0924 B
Maud Gonne / Samuel Levenson. [New York] : Reader's Digest Press : distributed by Crowell, 1976. p. cm. [DA958.M25L48] 76-32 ISBN 0-88349-089-7 : 15.00
1. MacBride, Maud Gonne. I. Title.

MacCallum, Frank Lyman, 1893-1955.

PADWICK, Constance Evelyn, 1886- 922
Call to Istanbul. London, New York, Longmans, Green [1958] 209p. illus. 21cm. [BV2372.M2P2 1958] 58-3885
1. MacCallum, Frank Lyman, 1893-1955. 2. Bible. Turkish—Hist. I. Title.

MacCurdy, Edward,

MACCURDY, Edward, 1871- 927.5
The mind of Leonardo da Vinci. London, J. Cape [dist. Chester Springs, Pa., Dufour, 1964] 360p. 21cm. 4.50
I. Title.

MacDonagh, Thomas, 1878-1916.

NORSTEDT, Johann A. 821'.8 B
Thomas MacDonagh, a critical biography / Johann A. Norstedt. Charlottesville : University Press of Virginia, 1979. p. cm. Includes index. Bibliography: p. [PR6025.A22Z8] 78-31320 ISBN 0-8139-0786-1 : 12.95
1. MacDonagh, Thomas, 1878-1916. 2.

Poets, Irish—20th century—Biography. I. Title.

PARKS, Edd Winfield, 1906- 828 (B)
Thomas MacDonagh; the man, the patriot, the writer, by Edd Winfield Parks, Aileen Wells Parks. Athens, Univ. of Ga. Pr. [1967] xiv, 151p. group port. 24cm. Bibl. [PR6025.A22Z82] 67-17404 5.00
1. MacDonagh, Thomas, 1878-1916. I. Parks, Aileen Wells, joint author. II. Title.

MacDonald, Angus,

MACDONALD, Angus, 1926- 322'.0924 B
Middle ground. Cambridge, Mass., MIT Press [1971] 375 p. 21 cm. Autobiographical. [TL540.M24A3] 70-148845 ISBN 0-262-13073-4 7.95
I. Title. BIP

MacDonald, Betty (Bard)

MACDONALD, Betty (Bard) 920.7
Anybody can do anything. [1st ed.] Philadelphia, Lippincott [1950] 236 p. 21 cm. Autobiographical. [CT275.M43A27] 50-8800
I. Title.

MACDONALD, Betty (Bard) 920.7
Who, me? The autobiography of Betty MacDonald. [1st ed.] Philadelphia, Lippincott [1959] 352p. 21cm. 'Contains portions of The egg and I, The plague and I, Anybody can do anything ... and Onlons in the stew.' [CT275.M43A43] 59-13252
I. Title.

MacDonald, Eleanor Davenport.

MACDONALD, Eleanor Davenport. 978.9'82 B
I remember old MacDonald's Farmington / Eleanor Davenport MacDonald ; illustrated by Eve and Enid. Santa Fe, N.M. : Sleeping Fox Enterprises, c1975. 127 p. : ill. ; 24 cm. [F804.F37M32] 76-358073 6.95
1. MacDonald, Eleanor Davenport. 2. Farmington, N.M.—Biography. I. Title.

MacDonald, Flora Isabel, 1926-

ARMSTONG, Alvin. 971.064'4'0924 B
Flora MacDonald / by Alvin Armstrong. Don Mills, Ont. : J. M. Dent & Sons (Canada), 1976. vi, 217 p. : ill. ; 24 cm. Includes index. Bibliography: p. 209-210. [HQ1455.M32A75] 77-363885 ISBN 0-460-91698-X : 9.95
1. MacDonald, Flora Isabel, 1926- 2. Canada Politics and government—1945- 3. Politicians—Canada—Biography.

Macdonald, Flora (Macdonald) 1722-1790.

VINING, Elizabeth (Gray) 1902- 941.070924 (B)
Flora; a biography. [1st ed.] Philadelphia, Lippincott [1966] 208 p. maps, ports. 22 cm. Bibliographical references included in "Notes" (p. 199-208) [DA814.M14V5] 66-12343
1. Macdonald, Flora (Macdonald) 1722-1790. I. Title. BIP

Macdonald, George, 1824-1905.

JOHNSON, Joseph. 823'.8
George MacDonald; a biographical and critical appreciation. New York, Haskell House Publishers, 1973. viii, 302 p. port. 23 cm. Reprint of the 1906 ed. "The books of George MacDonald": p. 286-289. [PR4968.J6 1973] 72-4090 ISBN 0-8383-1609-3 12.95 (Lib. ed.)
1. Macdonald, George, 1824-1905.

MACDONALD, Greville, 1856-1944. 823'.8 B
George Macdonald and his wife. With an introd. by G. K. Chesterton. London, G. Allen & Unwin. New York, Johnson Reprint Corp., 1971. 575 p. illus. 24 cm. Reprint of the 1924 ed. Bibliography: p. 563-565. [PR4968.M3 1971] 74-177274
1. Macdonald, George, 1824-1905. 2. Macdonald, Louisa (Powell) 1822-1902. I. Title. BIP

Macdonald, James A., 1874-

LIEBLING, Abbott Joseph, 1904- 818.5
The honest rainmaker; the life and times of Colonel John R. Stingo. [1st ed.] Garden City, N. Y., Doubleday, 1953. 317 p. 22 cm. [CT275.M432L5] 52-13568
1. Macdonald, James A., 1874-

MacDonald, James Ramsay, 1866-1937.

HAMILTON, Mary Agnes (Adamson) 1883- 942.083'0924 B
J. Ramsay MacDonald, by Mary Agnes Hamilton. Freeport, N.Y., Books for Libraries Press [1971] 305 p. port. 23 cm. Revised and adapted from [the author's] The man of to-morrow, 1923, and James Ramsay MacDonald, 1925. [DA566.9.M25H28 1971] 79-165638 ISBN 0-8369-5947-7
1. MacDonald, James Ramsay, 1866-1937. BIP

MacDonald, Jeanette, 1907-1965.

PARISH, James Robert. 791.43'02'80924 B
The Jeanette MacDonald story / James Robert Parish. New York : Mason/Charter, 1976. x, 181 p. ;[14] leaves of plates : ill. ; 24 cm. [ML420.M135P4] 76-16553 ISBN 0-88405-360-1 : 10.00
1. MacDonald, Jeanette, 1907-1965. I. Title.

STERN, Lee Edward. 791.43'028'0924 B
Jeanette MacDonald / by Lee Edward Stern. New York : Jove Publications, 1977. p. cm. (An Illustrated history of the movies) (A Harvest/HBJ book) Includes index. Bibliography: p. [ML420.M135S7] 77-76449 ISBN 0-15-646215-X : 2.50
1. MacDonald, Jeanette, 1907-1965. 2. Singers—United States—Biography. 3. Moving-pictures, Musical—Pictorial works. I. Title. BIP

Macdonald, John Alexander, Sir, 1815-1891.

POPE, Joseph, Sir, 1854-1926. 971.05'0924 B
Memoirs of the Right Honourable Sir John Alexander Macdonald, G.C.B., first Prime Minister of the Dominion of Canada. London, Edward Arnold, 1894. [New York, AMS Press, 1971] 2 v. port. 23 cm. [F1033.M13 1971] 76-137271 ISBN 0-404-05086-7 (v. 1)
1. Macdonald, John Alexander, Sir, 1815-1891. 2. Canada—Politics and government—19th century. I. Title.

WAITE, Peter B. 971.05'4'0924
Macdonald : his life and world / P. B. Waite. Toronto ; New York : McGraw-Hill Ryerson, c1975. 224 p. : ill. ; 26 cm. Includes index. Bibliography: p. 221-222. [F1033.M135] 76-355909 ISBN 0-07-082301-4
1. Macdonald, John Alexander, Sir, 1815-1891. 2. Canada—Politics and government—19th century.

Macdonald, John Sandfield, 1812-1872.

HODGINS, Bruce Willard, 1931- 971.3'02'0924 B
John Sandfield Macdonald, 1812-1872, [by] Bruce W. Hodgins. [Toronto] University of Toronto Press [1971] 131 p. 21 cm. (Canadian biographical studies) Includes bibliographical references. [F1032.M116H6] 76-21991 ISBN 0-8020-3248-6 4.50
1. Macdonald, John Sandfield, 1812-1872. BIP

MacDonald, Susanne (Rike)

MACDONALD, Susanne (Rike) 920.7
The backward look, memoirs. [1st ed.] New York, Exposition Press [1957] 62p. 21cm. [CT275.M4328A3] 56-12372
I. Title.

MACDONALD, Susanne (Rike) 920.7
Three score years and then . . . Memoirs of Anne MacFarland [pseud. 1st ed.] New York, Exposition Press [1955] 105p. 21cm. [CT275.M433A3] 55-11123
I. Title.

MacDonald, Willard Scott, 1931-

MACDONALD, Willard Scott, 1931- 362.3
Moose, the story of a very special person / by W. Scott MacDonald and Chester W. Oden, Jr. Minneapolis : Winston Press, c1978. 200 p., [9] leaves of plates : ill. ; 22 cm. [RJ506.D68M32] 78-50413 ISBN 0-03-043936-1 pbk. : 3.95
1. MacDonald, Willard Scott, 1931- 2. Down's syndrome—United States—Biography. I. Oden, Chester W., joint author. II. Title.

Macdonell, Alastair Ruadh, 1725?-1761.

LANG, Andrew, 1844-1912. 942.07'2
Pickle the Spy; or, The incognito of Prince Charles. [1st AMS ed.] New York, AMS Press [1970] xxi, 344 p. ports. 23 cm. Reprint of the 1897 ed. Includes bibliographical references. [DA814.5.L28 1970] 72-110132
1. Macdonell, Alastair Ruadh, 1725?-1761. 2. Charles Edward, the Young Pretender, 1720-1788. 3. Jacobite Rebellion, 1745-1746. I. Title.

Macdonough, Thomas. 1783-1825.

MULLER, Charles G., 1897- 359.3'32 B
Hero of two seas; the story of midshipman Thomas Macdonough, by Charles G. Muller. Illustrated by John Flynn. New York, McKay [1968] 179 p. maps. 21 cm. A biography concentrating on the early career of the man who became a prominent officer in the U.S. Navy in the early nineteenth century. [V63.M28M8] 92 68-26822 4.25
1. Macdonough, Thomas. 1783-1825. I. Flynn, John, illus. II. Title.

MacDowell. Charles Henry, 1867-

MACDOWELL, Claire Leavitt. 926.6
Two ears of corn, by way of the chemical kettle; the life story of Charles H. MacDowell. [1st ed.] Stonington, Conn., Pequot. Press [c1954] 242p. illus. 22cm. [TP140.M15M15] 54-12625
1. MacDowell. Charles Henry, 1867- 2. Fertilizers and manures. I. Title.

MacDowell, Marian Griswold (Nevins) 1857-1956.

MCKEE, Nancy 920.7
Valiant woman. San Antonio, Naylor [c.1962] 79p. illus. 20cm. Bibl. 62-18515 3.95 bds.,
1. MacDowell, Marian Griswold (Nevins) 1857-1956. 2. MacDowell, Esward Alexander, 1861-1908. I. Title.

MCKEE, Nancy. 784'.092'4
Valiant woman. San Antonio. Naylor Co. [1962] 79p. illus. 20cm. Includes bibliography. [ML410.M121M3] 62-18515
1. MacDowell, Marian Griswold (Nevins) 1857-1956. 2. MacDowell, Edward Alexander, 1861-1908. I. Title.

Macedonia—Queens—Biography.

MACURDY, Grace Harriet. 938'.08'0922
Hellenistic queens : a study of woman-power in Macedonia, Seleucid Syria, and Ptolemaic Egypt / by Grace Harriet Macurdy. New York : AMS Press, [1976 p. cm. Reprint of the 1932 ed. published by the Johns Hopkins Press, Baltimore, which was issued as no. 14 of the Johns Hopkins University studies in archaeology. Includes index. Bibliography: p. [DF235.3.M3 1977] 75-41184 ISBN 0-404-14683-X : 17.50
1. Macedonia—Queens—Biography. 2. Syria—Queens—Biography. 3. Egypt—Queens—Biography. I. Title. II. Series: Johns Hopkins University studies in archaeology ; no. 14. BIP

Macedonian authors—20th century—Biography.

DRUGOVAC, Miodrag. 891.8'19'09
Contemporary Macedonian writers / Miodrag Drugovats ; [translated by Militsa Moyich Rekalich]. Skopje : Macedonian review, 1976. 195 p. : ports. ; 24 cm. Includes bibliographical references. [PG1182.D78] 77-376057
1. Macedonian authors—20th century—Biography. 2. Macedonian literature—20th century—Bio-bibliography. I. Title.

Maceo, Antonio, 1845-1896.

FONER, Philip Sheldon, 1910- 972.91'05'0924
Antonio Maceo : The "bronze titan" for Cuba's struggle for independence / by Philip S. Foner. New York : Monthly Review Press, [1977] p. cm. Bibliography: p. [F1783.M125F66] 77-76163 ISBN 0-85345-423-X : 15.00
1. Maceo, Antonio, 1845-1896. 2. Revolutionists—Cuba—Biography. BIP

Macfadden, Bernarr Adolphus, 1888-

MACFADDEN, Mary (Williamson) 926.137
Dumbbells and carrot strips; the story of Bernarr Macfadden, by Mary Macfadden & Emile Gauvreau. New York, Holt [1953] 405p. illus. 22cm. [GV333.M3M2] 52-11046
1. Macfadden, Bernarr Adolphus, 1888- I. Gauvreau, Emile Henry, 1891- joint author. II. Title.

Macfall, Haldane,

MACFALL, Haldane, 1860-1928. 741.6'092'4 B
Aubrey Beardsley, the man and his work. [Folcroft, Pa.] Folcroft Library Editions, 1971. xiv, 109 p. plates. 29 cm. "Limited to 150 copies." Reprint of the 1928 ed. [NC242.B3M32 1972b] 72-194767 15.00

MACFALL, Haldane, 1860-1928. 741.6'092'4 B
Aubrey Beardsley, the man and his work. [Folcroft, Pa.] Folcroft Library Editions, 1971. xiv, 109 p. plates. 29 cm. "Limited to 150 copies." Reprint of the 1928 ed. [NC242.B3M32 1972b] 72-194767 15.00

MacGregor, Francis, b. 1882.

MACGREGOR, Francis, b.1882. 971.6'13 B
Days that I remember : stories with a Scottish accent / by Francis MacGregor. Windsor, N.S. : Lancelot Press, 1976. 44 p. ; 22 cm. [F1039.5.B18M325] 77-369873 ISBN 0-88999-052-2
1. MacGregor, Francis, b. 1882. 2. Baddeck, N.S.—Biography. 3. Baddeck, N.S.—History. I. Title.

MacGregor, William, Sir, 1847-1919.

JOYCE, R. B. 325'.31'0924 B
Sir William MacGregor [by] R. B. Joyce. Melbourne, New York, Oxford University Press, 1971. xvi, 484 p. illus. 23 cm. Bibliography: p. 450-466. [JV1009.M34J68] 72-180267 ISBN 0-19-550367-8
1. MacGregor, William, Sir, 1847-1919. 2. Great Britain—Colonies—Administration. I. Title. BIP

Mach, Ernst, 1838-1916.

BLACKMORE, John T. 530'.092'4 B
Ernst Mach; his work, life, and influence

[by] John T. Blackmore. Berkeley, University of California Press, 1972. xx, 414 p. illus. 25 cm. Bibliography: p. 361-375. [B3303.B5] 79-138514 ISBN 0-520-01849-4 16.95
1. Mach, Ernst, 1838-1916.

Machado de Assis, Joaquim Maria, 1839-1908.

BETTENCOURT Machado, Jose. 928.69
Machado of Brazil, the life and times of Machado de Assis. New York, Bramerica, 1953. 246 p. illus. 22 cm. Includes bibliography. [PQ9697.M18Z5678] 53-4205
1. Machado de Assis, Joaquim Maria, 1839-1908. I. Title.

BETTENCOURT, Machado, Jose. v. 12
Machado of Brazil, the life and times of Machado de Assis, Brasil's greatest novelist. New York, C. Frank, 1962. 246 p. port. 21 cm. Includes bibliography. NUC64
1. Machado de Assis, Joaquim Maria, 1839-1908. I. Title.

Machen, Arthur,

MACHEN, Arthur, 1863-1947 828.91203
The autobiography of Arthur Machen. Introd. by Morchard Bishop. London, Richards Press [Mystic, Conn., Verry, 1965] 307p. ports. 21cm. [PR6025] 65-29920 3.50
I. Title. II. Title: Far off things. III. Title: Things near and far.
Contents omitted.

Machen, Arthur, 1863-1947.

MACHEN, Arthur, 1863-1947 828.91203
The autobiography of Arthur Machen. Introd. by Morchard Bishop. London, Richards Press [Mystic, Conn., Verry, 1965] 307p. ports. 21cm. [PR6025] 65-29920 3.50
I. Title. II. Title: Far off things. III. Title: Things near and far.
Contents omitted.

REYNOLDS, Aidan 828.912
Arthur Machen, a short account of his life and work [by] Aidan Reynolds, William Charlton. Introd. by D. B. Wyndham Lewis [Chester Springs, Pa.] Dufour, 1964[c.1963] xiv, 202p. illus., ports. 23cm. Bibl. [PR6025] 64-25454 6.00
1. Machen, Arthur, 1863-1947. I. Charlton, William E., joint author. II. Title.

SWEETSER, Wesley D. 828.912
Arthur Machen, by Wesley D. Sweetser. New York, Twayne Publishers [1964] 175 p. 21 cm. (Twayne's English authors series, 8) Bibliography: p. 157-165. [PR6025.A245Z915] 64-19033
1. Machen, Arthur, 1863-1947.

Machen, Arthur, 1863-1947—Bibliography.

DANIELSON, Henry. 016.823'9'12
Arthur Machen, a bibliography. With notes, biographical and critical, by Arthur Machen and an introd. by Henry Savage. [Folcroft, Pa.] Folcroft Library Editions, 1973. x, 59 p. port. 26 cm. Reprint of the 1923 ed. published by H. Danielson, London. [Z8533.75.D18 1973] 73-13506 ISBN 0-8414-3683-5 (lib. bdg.)
1. Machen, Arthur, 1863-1947—Bibliography. I. Machen, Arthur, 1863-1947. BIP

Machen, John Gresham, 1881-1937.

STONEHOUSE, Ned Bernard, 1902- 922.573
J. Gresham Machen, a biographical memoir. [1st ed.] Grand Rapids, Eerdmans, 1954. 520 p. illus. 23 cm. [BX9225.M24S8] 54-6236
1. Machen, John Gresham, 1881-1937.

Machiavelli, Niccolo, 1469-1527.

BARINCOU, Edmond. 945'.06'0924 B
Machiavelli / Edmond Barincou ; translated by Helen R. Lane. Westport, Conn. : Greenwood Press, 1975. 192 p. : ill. ; 21 cm. Translation of Machiavel, par lui-meme. Reprint of the 1961 ed. published by Grove Press, New York, which was issued as Evergreen profile book 23. Bibliography: p. 191-192. [DG738.14.M2B3713 1975] 75-11427 ISBN 0-8371-8185-2 lib.bdg. : 14.00
1. Machiavelli, Niccolo, 1469-1527.

BONDANELLA, Peter E., 1943- 914.5'03'60924 B
Machiavelli and the art of Renaissance history [by] Peter E. Bondanella. Detroit, Wayne State University Press, 1973 [i.e. 1974] 186 p. port. 24 cm. Includes bibliographical references. [DG738.14.M2B66 1974] 73-9729 ISBN 0-8143-1499-6 10.95
1. Machiavelli, Niccolo, 1469-1527. I. Title. BIP

JENSEN, De Lamar, 1925- ed. 923.245
Machiavelli: cynic, patriot, or political scientist? Boston, Heath [1960] 111 p. 24 cm. (Problems in European civilization) [DG738.14.M2J4] 60-11574
1. Machiavelli, Niccolo, 1469-1527.

MACHIAVELLI, Niccolo, 1469-1527 923.245
The letters of Machiavelli, a selection of his letters. Tr. [from Italian] ed. with introd. by Allan Gilbert. New York, [Putnam, c.1961] 252p. (Capricorn original, Cap 40) 60-15111 1.65 pap.,
I. Gilbert, Allan H., 1888- ed. and tr. II. Title.

MACHIAVELLI, Niccolo, 1469-1527. 923.245
The letters of Machiavelli, a selection of his letters. Translated and edited with an introd. by Allan Gilbert. New York, Capricorn Books [1961] 252p. 19cm. (A Capricorn original, Cap 40) [DG738.14.M2A413] 60-15111
I. Gilbert, Allan H., 1888- ed. and tr. II. Title.

MACHIAVELLI, Niccolo, 1469-1527 923.245
The letters of Machiavelli, a selection of his letters. Tr. [from Italian] ed. with introd. by Allan Gilbert. New York, [Putnam, c.1961] 252p. (Capricorn original, Cap 40) 60-15111 1.65 pap.,
I. Gilbert, Allan H., 1888- ed. and tr. II. Title.

MACHIAVELLI, Niccolo, 1469-1527. 923.245
The letters of Machiavelli, a selection of his letters. Translated and edited with an introd. by Allan Gilbert. New York, Capricorn Books [1961] 252p. 19cm. (A Capricorn original, Cap 40) [DG738.14.M2A413] 60-15111
I. Gilbert, Allan H., 1888- ed. and tr. II. Title.

MACHIAVELLI, Niccolo, 1469-1527 923.245
Machiavelli [by] Edmond Barincou. Tr. by Helen R. Lane [Gloucester, Mass., Peter Smith, 1963] 192p. illus. 18cm. (Evergreen profile bk. 23 rebound) Bibl. 3.00
I. Barincou, Edmond. II. Title.

MACHIAVELLI, Niccolo, 1469-1527. 923.245
Machiavelli [by] Edmond Barincou. Translated by Helen R. Lane. New York, Grove Press [1962] 192p. illus. 18cm. (Evergreen profile book 23) Includes bibliography. [DG738.14.M2A53 1962] 61-11371
I. Barincou, Edmond. II. Title.

MACHIAVELLI, Niccolo, 1469-1527 923.245
Machiavelli [by] Edmond Barincou. Tr. by Helen R. Lane [Gloucester, Mass., Peter Smith, 1963] 192p. illus. 18cm. (Evergreen profile bk. 23 rebound) Bibl. 3.00
I. Barincou, Edmond. II. Title.

MACHIAVELLI, Niccolo, 1469-1527. 923.245
Machiavelli [by] Edmond Barincou. Translated by Helen R. Lane. New York, Grove Press [1962] 192p. illus. 18cm. (Evergreen profile book 23) Includes bibliography. [DG738.14.M2A53 1962] 61-11371
I. Barincou, Edmond. II. Title.

MACHIAVELLI, Noccolo, 1469-1527. 914.5'03'60924 B
Machiavelli. With an introd. by Henry Cust. New York, AMS Press, 1967. 2 v. illus. 23 cm. Reprint of the 1905 ed., which was issued as no. 39-40 of the Tudor translations, 1st series. Contents.Contents.—v. 1. The art of war, translated by P. Whitehorne, 1560. The prince, translated by E. Dacres, 1640.—v. 2. The Florentine history, translated by T. Bedingfeld, 1595. [DG731.5.M325 1967] 73-153695
1. Florence—History. 2. Military art and science—Early works to 1800. 3. Political science—Early works to 1700. 4. Political ethics. I. Cust, Henry John Cockayne, 1861-1917. II. Series: The Tudor translations, no. 39-40.

MORLEY, John Morley, Viscount, 1838-1923. 945'.06'0924
Machiavelli. [Folcroft, Pa.] Folcroft Press [1969] 63 p. 26 cm. Reprint of the 1897 ed., issued in series: The Romanes lecture, 1897. [DG738.14.M2M6 1969] 72-195763
1. Machiavelli, Niccolo, 1469-1527. I. Series: The Romanes lecture, 1897.

MUIR, Dorothy Erskine Sheepshanks, 1889- 945'.06'0924 B
Machiavelli and his times / by D. Erskine Muir. Westport, Conn. : Greenwood Press, 1976 [c1936] p. cm. Reprint of the 1st ed., published by Dutton, New York. Bibliography: p. [DG738.14.M2M75 1976] 74-30928 ISBN 0-8371-7889-4 lib.bdg. : 18.25
1. Machiavelli, Niccolo, 1469-1527. 2. Italy—History—1492-1559. I. Title.

PREZZOLINI, Giuseppe, 1882- 320.10924
Machiavelli. [Translated by Gioconda Savine. 1st ed.] New York, Farrar, Straus & Giroux [1967] 372 p. 22 cm. Bibliography: p. [353]-363. [DG738.14.M2P5913] 67-10921
1. Machiavelli, Niccolo, 1469-1527.

ROEDER, Ralph, 1890- 920.045
The man of the Renaissance; four lawgivers: Savonarola, Machiavelli, Castiglione, Aretino. New York, Meridian Books [1958] 504 p. illus. 21 cm. (Meridian books, MG17) [DG533.R6 1958] 58-11929
1. Savonarola, Girolamo Maria Francesco Matteo, 1452-1498. 2. Machiavelli, Niccolo, 1469-1527. 3. Castiglione, Baldassare, conte, 1478-1529. 4. Aretino, Pietro, 1492-1556. 5. Renaissance—Italy. I. Title.

ROEDER, Ralph, 1890-1970. 945'.05'0922
The man of the Renaissance : four lawgivers, Savonarola, Machiavelli, Castiglione, Aretino / by Ralph Roeder. Clifton, N.J. : A. M. Kelley, 1975, c1933. p. cm. (Viking reprint editions) Reprint of the ed. published by Viking Press, New York. Bibliography: p. [DG533.R6 1975] 78-122059 ISBN 0-678-03171-1
1. Savonaroldа, Girolamo Maria Francesco Matteo, 1452-1498. 2. Machiavelli, Niccolo, 1469-1527. 3. Castiglione, Baldassare, conte, 1478-1529. 4. Aretino, Pietro, 1492-1556. 5. Renaissance—Italy. I. Title. BIP

TARLTON, Charles D. 914.5'03'60924 B
Fortune's circle; a biographical interpretation of Niccolo Machiavelli, by Charles D. Tarlton. Chicago, Quadrangle Books, 1970. 159 p. 22 cm. Includes bibliographical references. [DG738.14.M2T37] 74-106058 6.95
1. Machiavelli, Niccolo, 1469-1527. I. Title.

VILLARI, Pasquale, 1827-1917. 914.5'03'60924
The life and times of Niccolo Machiavelli. Translated by Linda Villari. New York, Haskell House Publishers, 1969. 2 v. port. 23 cm. Reprint of the 1892 ed. Translation of Niccolo Machiavelli e i suoi tempi. Bibliographical footnotes. [DG738.14.M2V613 1969] 68-25275
1. Machiavelli, Niccolo, 1469-1527. 2. Italy—History—1492-1559. I. Title. BIP

VILLARI, Pasquale, 1827-1917. 914.50360924 B
The life and times of Niccolo Machiavelli. Translated by Linda Villari. [New ed.] London, E. Benn [1929] St. Clair Shores, Mich., Scholarly Press [1969?] 2 v. in 1. port. 22 cm. "First published 1891." Translation of Niccolo Machiavelli e i suoi tempi. Bibliographical footnotes. [DG738.14.M2V613 1969b] 77-8543
1. Machiavelli, Niccolo, 1469-1527. 2. Italy—History—1492-1559. I. Title.

VILLARI, Pasquale, 1827-1917. 914.5'03'60924 B
The life and times of Niccolo Machiavelli. Translated by Linda Villari. New ed., augmented by the author, rev. by the translator. New York, Greenwood Press [1968] 2 v. illus. (part fold), facsims., ports. 23 cm. Reprint of the 1892 ed. Translation of Niccolo Machiavelli e i suoi tempi. Bibliographical footnotes. [DG738.14.M2V613 1968] 68-31007
1. Machiavelli, Niccolo, 1469-1527. 2. Italy—History—1492-1559. I. Villari, Linda (White) Mazini, 1836-1915, tr. II. Title.

Machinery.

MASCHINENFABRIK Augsburg-Nurnberg A. G. v. 12
M. A. N. Forschugsheft, 1951. [Augsburg, E. Kieser , 1951] 95p. illus. diagrs. 30cm.gSummary in German, English and French at head of most articles. Includes bibliographies. A53
1. Machinery. 2. Motors. I. Title.
Contents omitted.

Machlup, Fritz, 1902-

BREADTH and depth in economics : Fritz Machlup—the man and his ideas / edited by Jacob S. Dreyer. 330'.092'4 B Lexington, Mass. : Lexington Books, c1978. xiii, 316 p. : ill. ; 24 cm. Bibliography: p. 313-316. [HB119.M25B73] 77-238 ISBN 0-669-01430-3 : write for information
1. Machlup, Fritz, 1902- 2. Economists—United States—Biography—Addresses, essays, lectures. 3. Economics—Addresses, essays, lectures. I. Dreyer, Jacob S.

Maciel, Antonio Vicente Mendes, 1828 (ca.)-1897.

GRAHAM, Robert Bontine Cunninghame, 1852-1936. 981'.05'0924 B
A Brazilian mystic; being the life and miracles of Antonio Conselheiro. Freeport, N.Y., Books for Libraries Press [1971] xii, 238 p. fold. map. 23 cm. Reprint of the 1920 ed. Includes bibliographical references. [F2537.C74 1971] 70-146856 ISBN 0-8369-5623-0
1. Maciel, Antonio Vicente Mendes, 1828 (ca.)-1897. 2. Brazil—History—Conselheiro Insurrection, 1897. I. Title.

Macintyre, Donald, G. F. W.

MACINTYRE, Donald, G. F. W. 940.54'51
U-Boat killer / Donald Macintyre ; foreword by Robert B. Carney. Annapolis : Naval Institute Press, c1976. 175 p. ; 23 cm. [D780.M32 1976] 76-27163 ISBN 0-87021-964-2 : 8.95
1. Macintyre, Donald, G. F. W. 2. Great Britain. Navy—Biography. 3. World War, 1939-1945—Naval operations—Submarine. 4. World War, 1939-1945—Naval operations, British. 5. World War, 1939-1945—Atlantic Ocean. 6. World War, 1939-1945—Personal narratives, Scottish. 7. Seamen—Great Britain—Biography. I. Title. BIP

MacIver, Robert Morrison,

MACIVER, Robert Morrison, 1882- 301'.0924 B
As a tale that is told; the autobiography of

R. M. MacIver. Chicago, University of Chicago Press [1968] ix, 269 p. illus., ports. 21 cm. [HM22.U52M3] 68-15632
I. Title.

Mack, Isaac Foster, 1837-1912.

FROHMAN, Charles E. 070.4'1'0924 B
Sandusky's editor; Isaac Foster Mack's blazing forty years as editor of the Sandusky Register, by Charles E. Frohman. Columbus, Ohio Historical Society [1972] iv, 110 p. port. 24 cm. [PN4874.M376F7] 72-79071
1. Mack, Isaac Foster, 1837-1912. 2. Sandusky, Ohio—Biography. I. Title.

Mack, Julian William, 1866-1943.

BARNARD, Harry, 1906- 347'.73'2434 B
The forging of an American Jew : the life and times of Judge Julian W. Mack / by Harry Barnard. New York : Herzl Press, [1974] xxi, 346 p. : port. ; 22 cm. Includes index. Bibliography: p. 324-333. [KF373.M219B3] 74-78908 7.95
1. Mack, Julian William, 1866-1943. I. Title. **BIP**

Mack, Maynard, 1909-

THE Author in his work : 820'.9
essays on a problem in criticism / edited by Louis L. Martz and Aubrey Williams ; introd. by Patricia Meyer Spacks. New Haven : Yale University Press, 1978. xix, 407 p. ; 24 cm. Includes index. "Bibliography of writings and editions by Maynard Mack": p. 391-395. [PR151.A95A9] 77-16309 ISBN 0-300-02179-8 : 22.50
1. Mack, Maynard, 1909- 2. English literature—History and criticism—Addresses, essays, lectures. 3. Authors in literature—Addresses, essays, lectures. 4. Autobiography—Addresses, essays, lectures. I. Martz, Louis Lohr. II. Williams, Aubrey L.

Mackay, John William.

MANTER, Ethel H (Van Vick) 1907- 923.373
Rocket of the Comstock; the story of John William Mackay. Caldwell, Idaho, Caxton Printers, 1950. 256 p. illus., ports. 24cm. Bibliographical references included in "Footnotes" (p. [253]-256) [F841.M15] 50-6702
1. Mackay, John William. 2. Comstock lode, Nev. I. Title.

MacKaye, Steele, 1842-1894.

MACKAYE, Percy, 1875-1956. 792'.028'0924 B
Epoch; the life of Steele MacKaye, genius of the theatre, in relation to his times & contemporaries, a memoir by his son. New York, Boni & Liveright [c1927] Grosse Pointe, Mich., Scholarly Press, 1968. 2 v. illus., facsims., ports. 23 cm. "A chronological list of the dramatic works of Steele MacKaye": v. 2, p. [xvi]-[xviii] Bibliography: v. 2, p. civ-cvii. [PS2359.M42Z8 1968] 71-5100
1. MacKaye, Steele, 1842-1894. 2. Theater—U.S. I. Title. **BIP**

Mackenzie, Alexander, Sir, 1763-1820.

LAUT, Agnes Christina, 1871-1936. 971.2'01
Pathfinders of the West; being the thrilling story of the adventures of the men who discovered the great Northwest, Radisson, La Verendrye, Lewis, and Clark. Illus. by Remington, Goodwin, Marchand and others. Freeport, N.Y., Books for Libraries Press [1969] xxv, 380 p. illus., maps, ports. 23 cm. (Essay index reprint series) "First published 1904." [F1060.7.L38 1969] 74-90651
1. Radisson, Pierre Esprit, 1620?-1710. 2. La Verendrye, Pierre Gaultier de Varennes, sieur de, 1685-1749. 3. Hearne, Samuel, 1745-1792. 4. Mackenzie, Alexander, Sir, 1763-1820. 5. Lewis and Clark Expedition. 6. Northwest, Canadian—Discovery and exploration. I. Title.

SMITH, James K. 971.9'01'0924 B
Alexander Mackenzie, explorer; the hero who failed [by] James K. Smith. Toronto, New York; McGraw-Hill Ryerson [1973] 190 p. illus. 23 cm. Bibliography: p. 183-186. [F1060.7.M252] 73-2359 ISBN 0-07-077619-9
1. Mackenzie, Alexander, Sir, 1763-1820. I. Title.

Mackenzie, Alexander, Sir, 1763-1820—Juvenile literature.

SMITH, James K. 971.9'01'0924 B
Alexander Mackenzie / James K. Smith. Don Mills, Ont. : Fitzhenry & Whiteside, c1976. 60, [2] p. : ill. ; 22 cm. (The Canadians) Bibliography: p. [62] [F1060.7.S63] 77-367417 ISBN 0-88902-225-9
1. Mackenzie, Alexander, Sir, 1763-1820—Juvenile literature. 2. Explorers—Canada—Biography—Juvenile literature. 3. Fur trade—Canada—History—Juvenile literature. 4. Northwest, Canadian Discovery and exploration—Juvenile literature. I. Title. II. Series.

SYME, Ronald, 1910- 92 (J)
Alexander Mackenzie, Canadian explorer. Illustrated by William Stobbs. New York, Morrow, 1964. 96 p. illus. 22 cm. [F1060.S9] 64-10133
1. Mackenzie, Alexander, Sir, 1763-1820—Juvenile literature. I. Title. **BIP**

Mackenzie, Alexander, 1822-1892.

BUCKINGHAM, William, 1832-1915. 971.05'0924 B
The Hon. Alexander Mackenzie: his life and times, by William Buckingham and Geo. W. Ross. New York, Haskell House, 1969. 678 p. illus., facsims., ports. 24 cm. Reprint of the 1892 ed. [F1033.M14B8 1969b] 68-25225
1. Mackenzie, Alexander, 1822-1892. 2. Canada—History—19th century. I. Ross, George William, Sir, 1841-1914, joint author.

BUCKINGHAM, William, 1832-1915. 971.05'0924 B
The Hon. Alexander Mackenzie: his life and times, by William Buckingham and Geo. W. Ross. New York, Greenwood Press Publishers [1969] 678 p. illus., facsims., ports. 23 cm. Reprint of the 5th ed., 1892. [F1033.M14B8 1969] 69-13844 ISBN 8-371-10742-
1. Mackenzie, Alexander, 1822-1892. 2. Canada—History—19th century. I. Ross, George Williams, Sir, 1841-1914, joint author.

Mackenzie, Gregor.

MACKENZIE, Gregor. 799.1'1'0924 B
Memoirs of a ghillie / Gregor Mackenzie ; ill. by Jean Weeks. Newton Abbot [Eng.] ; North Pomfret, Vt. : David & Charles, c1978. 159 p. : ill. ; 22 cm. [SH605.M27] 78-52177 ISBN 0-7153-7584-9 : 15.95
1. Mackenzie, Gregor. 2. Atlantic salmon fishing—Great Britain. 3. Trout fishing—Great Britain. 4. Guides for hunters, fishermen, etc.—Great Britain—Biography. 5. Riverkeepers—Great Britain—Biography. I. Title. II. Title: Ghillie. **BIP**

Mackenzie, James, Sir, 1853-1925.

MAIR, Alexander. 610'.92'4 B
Sir James Mackenzie, M.D., 1853-1925; general practitioner, by Alex Mair. Edinburgh, Churchill Livingstone, 1973. xii, 366 p. illus. 24 cm. Includes bibliographical references. [R489.M197M34] 74-156801 ISBN 0-443-01001-3
1. Mackenzie, James, Sir, 1853-1925.
Distributed by Longman, 14.00

Mackenzie, John, 1835-1899.

MACKENZIE, William Douglas, 1859-1936. 968'.101'0924 B
John Mackenzie, South African missionary and statesman. New York, Negro Universities Press [1969] xii, 564 p. port. 23 cm. Reprint of the 1902 ed. [DT776.M2M2 1969] 78-97373 ISBN 0-8371-2443-3
1. Mackenzie, John, 1835-1899. 2. Africa, South—Politics and government—1836-1909. **BIP**

SILLERY, Anthony. 968'.101'0924 B
John Mackenzie of Bechuanaland, 1835-1899; a study in humanitarian imperialism. Cape Town, A. A. Balkema, 1971. xii, 236 p. illus. 26 cm. (South African biographical & historical studies, 8) Bibliography: p. 189-194. [DT776.M2S53] 72-175774
1. Mackenzie, John, 1835-1899. I. Title. II. Series.
Distributed by Verry 15.00.

Mackenzie, Ranald Slidell. 1840-1889.

CARTER, Robert Goldthwaite, 1845-1936. 974'.06'0924
On the border with Mackenzie; or, Winning west Texas from the Comanches. New York Antiquarian Press, 1961. 580 p. illus. 23 cm. [F391.C] A 62
1. Mackenzie, Ranald Slidell. 1840-1889. 2. Texas — Hist. — 1846- . 3. Frontier and pioneer life — Texas. 4. Frontier and pioneer life — Southwest, New. 5. Indians of North America — Wars — 1866-1895. 6. U. S. Army. 4th Cavalry. 7. Comanche Indians — Wars. I. Title. II. Title: Winning west Texas from the Comanches.

Mackintosh, Charles Rennie, 1868-1928.

HOWARTH, Thomas, 1914- 927.2
Charles Rennie Mackintosh and the modern movement. [New York] Wittenborn Publications [1953] xxviii, 329p. illus., 96 plates (incl. ports.) 26cm. Bibliography: p. 309-314. [NA997.M3H6 1953] 53-13143
1. Mackintosh, Charles Rennie, 1868-1928. I. Title. **BIP**

HOWARTH, Thomas, 1914- 720'.92'4
Charles Rennie Mackintosh and the modern movement / Thomas Howarth. 2d ed. London : Routledge & Kegan Paul, 1977. 1, 335 p., [48] leaves of plates : ill. ; 26 cm. Includes index. Bibliography: p. 311-320. [N6797.M23H68 1977b] 77-72348 ISBN 0-7100-8538-9 : 26.50
1. Mackintosh, Charles Rennie, 1868-1928. 2. Art nouveau—Great Britain. I. Title.
Distributed by Routledge & Kegan Paul, Boston

Macklin, Charles, 1697?-1797.

COOK, William, d.1824. 792'.028'0924
Memoirs of Charles Macklin, comedian, with the dramatic characters, manners, anecdotes, &c., of the age in which he lived; forming an history of the stage during almost the whole of the last century, and a chronological list of all the parts played by him [by] William Cooke. London, Printed for J. Asperne by T. Maiden, 1804. New York, B. Blom, 1972, ie 1973] 444 p. illus. 21 cm. [PN2598.M2C6 1972] 72-82822 15.75
1. Macklin, Charles, 1697?-1797. 2. Theater—London. I. Title.

MacLean, Donald Murdo.

MACLEAN, Donald Murdo. 387.50924
The captain's bridge; Queens' company [by] Donald MacLean. Garden City, N.Y., Doubleday, 1965. 228 p. illus., ports. 22 cm. Autobiography. London ed. (Hutchinson) has title: Queens' company. [V65.M22A3] 65-23782
I. Title.

MACLEAN, Donald Murdo 387.50924
The Captain's bridge (Queen's company) Garden City, N.Y., Doubleday [c.]1965. 228p. illus., ports. 22cm. First pub. in England by Hutchinson under the title: Queen's company; the autobiography of Commodore Donald MacLean [V65.M22A3] 65-6192 4.95
I. Title.

Maclean, Fitzroy, Sir, bart., 1911-

MACLEAN, Fitzroy, Sir, bart., 1911- 914.7'9'0485
To Caucasus, the end of all the earth : an illustrated companion to the Caucasus and Transcaucasia / Fitzroy Maclean. London : J. Cape, 1976. 203 p., [49] leaves of plates : ill. (some col.) ; 26 cm. Continues the author's To the back of beyond. Includes index. [DK511.C1M25] 76-383743 £6.50
1. Maclean, Fitzroy, Sir, bart., 1911- 2. Causasus—Description and travel. 3. Caucasus—History. I. Title.

Maclean, George, 1801-1847.

METCALFE, George Edgar 923.8
Maclean of the Gold Coast; the life and times of George Maclean, 1801-1847. [Dist. New York] Oxford, 1962. 344p. illus. 23cm. (West African hist. ser.) 62-6639 5.60
1. Maclean, George, 1801-1847. 2. Ghana—Hist. 3. British in Ghana—Hist. I. Title.

Macleod, James Alexander Farquharson, 1836-1894.

WOOD, Kerry 923.571
The Queen's cowboy, Colonel Macleod of the Mounties. Illustrated by Joseph Rosenthal. [New York, St. Martin's Press] 1960[ ] 157p. illus. (part col.) (Great stories of Canada. 22) 60-52037 2.95 bds.,
1. Macleod, James Alexander Farquharson, 1836-1894. 2. Canada. Royal Canadian Mounted Police. I. Title.

MacLysaght, Edward.

MACLYSAGHT, Edward. 941.5082'092'4 B
Changing times : Ireland since 1898 / as seen by Edward MacLysaght. Gerrards Cross [Eng.] : Smythe ; Atlantic Highlands, N.J. : distributed by Humanities Press, 1978. 248 p., [4] leaves of plates : ill. ; 23 cm. Includes bibliographical references and index. [CT868.M3A33] 79-300981 ISBN 0-901072-88-5 : 14.50
1. MacLysaght, Edward. 2. Ireland—Biography. 3. Ireland—History—20th century. I. Title.

MacMillan, Carleton Lamont, 1903-

MACMILLAN, Carleton Lamont, 1903- 610'.92'4 B
Memoirs of a Cape Breton doctor / C. Lamont MacMillan. Toronto ; New York : McGraw-Hill Ryerson, [1975] xiv, 177 p. : map ; 23 cm. [R464.M28A35] 75-319175 ISBN 0-07-077759-4 ; 7.95
1. MacMillan, Carleton Lamont, 1903- 2. Physicians (General practice)—Nova Scotia—Cape Breton—Correspondence, reminiscences, etc. 3. Medicine, Rural—Nova Scotia—Cape Breton. 4. Cape Breton—History. I. Title.

MacMillan, Donald Baxter, 1874-

ALLEN, Everett S. 923.973
Arctic odyssey; the life of Rear Admiral Donald B. MacMillan. New York, Dodd, Mead, 1962. 340 p. illus. 22 cm. [G635.M33A6] 62-14447
1. MacMillan, Donald Baxter, 1874- I. Title.

Macmillan, Harold, 1894—

MACMILLAN, Harold, 1894- 354'.41'000922 B
The past masters : politics and politicians, 1906-1939 / Harold Macmillan. 1st U.S. ed. New York : Harper & Row, c1975. 240 p. : ill. ; 25 cm. (A Cass Canfield book) Bibliography: p. [239]-240. [DA574.A1M33 1975b] 75-29880 ISBN 0-06-012814-3 : 15.00
1. Macmillan, Harold, 1894- 2. Statesmen—Great Britain—Biography. 3. Great Britain—Politics and government—1901-1936. I. Title. **BIP**

SAMPSON, Anthony. 942.082'0924
Macmillan; a study in ambiguity. New York, Simon and Schuster [1967] 256 p.

22 cm. Bibliographical references included in "Notes" (p. [242]-248) [DA566.9.M33S3 1967b] 67-22940
1. Macmillan, Harold, 1894- BIP

Macmillan, William John.

MACMILLAN, William John. 926.158
The reluctant healer, a remarkable autobiography. New York, Crowell [1953, c1952] 243p. 21cm. [RZ999.M3 1953] 53-10707
I. Title.

MacNeil, Malcolm F.

MACNEIL, Malcolm F. 923.8
The rewarding path; an autobiography. Boston, Christopher Pub. House [c.1961] 177p. illus. 61-9667 3.75
I. Title.

MacNeill, Norman Merle, 1888-1965.

BAUER, Edward Louis, 1890- 610'.924 B
Profile of a gentle man; the life story of Norman M. MacNeill. Boston, Christopher Pub. House [1967] 193 p. illus., ports. 21 cm. [R154.M2913B3] 67-23752
1. MacNeill, Norman Merle, 1888-1965. I. Title.

MacNeish, Richard Stockton.

MACNEISH, Richard Stockton. 930'.1'0924 B
The science of archaeology? / Richard S. MacNeish. North Scituate, Mass. : Duxbury Press, c1978. xiii, 253 p. : ill. ; 24 cm. Includes bibliographical references and index. [CC115.M23A37] 77-26805 ISBN 0-87872-153-3 pbk. : 7.95
1. MacNeish, Richard Stockton. 2. Archaeologists—United States—Biography. 3. Archaeology. I. Title.

MacNicol, Roy,

MACNICOL, Roy, 1889- 759.13
Paintbrush ambassador. [1st ed.] New York, Vantage Press [c1957] 255p. illus. 21cm. Autobiography. [ND237.M217A3] 927.5 56-1272
I. Title.

Macon, David, 1870-1952.

RINZLER, Ralph. 784'.092'4 B
Uncle Dave Macon; a bio-discography, by Ralph Rinzler and Norm Cohen. Los Angeles, Calif., John Edwards Memorial Foundation, c1970. 50 p. illus. 23 cm. (JEMF special series, no. 3) [ML156.7.M25R5] 74-156530
1. Macon, David, 1870-1952. 2. Macon, David, 1870-1952—Discography. I. Cohen, Norm, joint author. II. Title. III. Series: John Edwards Memorial Foundation. JEMF special series, no. 3.

Macon, Nathaniel, 1757-1837.

DODD, William Edward, 1869-1940. 973.4'6'0924 B
The life of Nathaniel Macon. New York, B. Franklin [1970] xvi, 443 p. 19 cm. (American classics in history and social science 143) (Burt Franklin research and source works series 537.) Reprint of the 1908 ed. Bibliography: p. xvi. [E302.6.M17D6 1970] 78-130600
1. Macon, Nathaniel, 1757-1837. I. Title. BIP

MacPhail, Margaret, 1887- —Biography.

PILLAR, Mabel MacPhail, 1919- 813'.5'4 B
Aunt Peggy from Loch Bras d'Or / by Mabel (MacPhail) Pillar. Windsor, N.S. : Lancelot Press, 1976. 131 p., [2] leaves of plates : ill. ; 21 cm. [PR9199.3.M3368Z8] 77-354175 ISBN 0-88999-057-3
1. MacPhail, Margaret, 1887- —Biography. 2. Authors, Canadian—20th century—Biography. I. Title.

Macpherson, James, 1736-1796.

SAUNDERS, Thomas Bailey, 1860-1928. 821'.6 B
The life and letters of James Macpherson, containing a particular account of his famous quarrel with Dr. Johnson, and a sketch of the origin and influence of the Ossianic poems. New York, Haskell House, 1968. xi, 327 p. ports. 22 cm. Reprint of the 1894 ed. Bibliographical footnotes. [PR3544.S2 1968] 68-24916
1. Macpherson, James, 1736-1796. I. Title.

SAUNDERS, Thomas Bailey, 1860-1928. 821'.6
The life and letters of James Macpherson; containing a particular account of his famous quarrel with Dr. Johnson, and a sketch of the origin and influence of the Ossianic poems, by Bailey Saunders. New York, Greenwood Press [1969] xi, 327 p. port. 23 cm. Reprint of the 1894 ed. Bibliographical footnotes. [PR3544.S2 1969] 69-14071
1. Macpherson, James, 1736-1796. I. Title.

Macready, William Charles, 1793-1873.

ARCHER, William, 1856-1924. 792'.028'0924 B
William Charles Macready. New York, B. Blom, 1971. vii, 224 p. 22 cm. Reprint of the 1890 ed. [PN2598.M3A8 1971] 74-91892
1. Macready, William Charles, 1793-1873.

MACREADY, William Charles, 1793-1873. 792'.028'0924
The diaries of William Charles Macready, 1833-1851. Edited by William Toynbee. New York, B. Blom [1969] 2 v. ports. 24 cm. Reprint of the 1912 ed. [PN2598.M3A3 1969] 78-84519
1. Actors—Correspondence, reminiscences, etc. I. Toynbee, William, 1849- ed. BIP

MacVane, John.

MACVANE, John. 940.54'21
On the air in World War II / by John MacVane. New York : Morrow, 1979. p. cm. [D756.3.M32] 79-18973 ISBN 0-688-03558-2 : 12.50
1. MacVane, John. 2. World War, 1939-1945—Europe. 3. World War, 1939-1945—Personal narratives, American. 4. World War, 1939-1945—Africa, North. 5. World War, 1939-1945—Journalists. 6. War correspondents—United States—Biography. I. Title. BIP

MacVeagh, Lincoln, 1890-1972.

MACVEAGH, Lincoln, 1890-1972. 916'.03'08 S
"Dear Franklin ... " letters to President Roosevelt from Lincoln MacVeagh, U.S. Minister to South Africa, 1942-1943. [Pasadena, Munger Africana Library] 1972. 43 p. illus. 28 cm. (Munger Africana Library notes, no. 12) [Z733.M9175 no. 12] [E183.8.A4] 327.73'068 74-154397 3.00
1. MacVeagh, Lincoln, 1890-1972. 2. Roosevelt, Franklin Delano, Pres. U.S., 1882-1945. 3. United States—Foreign relations—Africa, South. 4. Africa, South—Foreign relations—United States. 5. Africa, South—Politics and government—1909- I. Roosevelt, Franklin Delano, Pres. U.S., 1882-1945. II. Title. III. Series: Munger Africana Library. Notes, no. 12.

MacVicar, Angus, 1908- —Biography.

MACVICAR, Angus, 1908- 823'.9'12 B
Rocks in my scotch : still more confessions of a minister's son / [by] Angus MacVicar. London : Hutchinson, 1977, i.e.1978 [9], 182 p., [8] p. of plates : ill., map (on lining paper), ports. ; 23 cm. Includes index. [PR6025.A34Z498] 77-365384 ISBN 0-09-128380-9 : 8.95
1. MacVicar, Angus, 1908- —Biography. 2. Authors, Scottish—20th century—Biography. I. Title.
Distributed by Hutchinson, Salem, NH

Macy, Anne (Sullivan) 1866-1936.

HICKOK, Lorena A 920.7
The touch of magic; the story of Helen Keller's great teacher, Anne Sullivan Macy. New York, Dodd, Mead, 1961. 184p. illus. 21cm. [HV1624.M3H5] 61-15996
1. Macy, Anne (Sullivan) 1866-1936. 2. Keller, Helen Adams, 1880- I. Title.

KELLER, Helen Adams, 1880-1968. 920.7
The story of my life [by] Helen Keller, with her letters (1887-1901) and a supplementary account of her education, including passages from the reports and letters of her teacher, Anne Mansfield Sullivan, by John Albert Macy. Introd. by Ralph Barton Perry. Garden City, N.Y., Doubleday, 1954. 382 p. illus., ports. 22 cm. [HV1624.K4A15 1954] 54-11951
1. Macy, Anne (Sullivan) 1866-1936. I. Title.

KELLER, Helen Adams, 1880-1968. 920.7
Teacher: Anne Sullivan Macy; a tribute by the fosterchild of her mind. Introd. by Nella Braddy Henney. [1st ed.] Garden City, N.Y., Doubleday, 1955. 247 p. illus. 22 cm. [HV1624.M3K4] 55-9986
1. Macy, Anne Sullivan, 1866-1936. I. Title.

Macy, Annie Sullivan, 1866-1936—Juvenile literature.

*DAVIDSON, Mickie 92
Helen Keller's teacher. Illus, by Wayne Bickerstaff. New York, Scholastic [c.1965] 154p. illus. 20cm. (TX784) .50 pap.,
1. Macy, Annie Sullivan, 1866-1936—Juvenile literature. 2. Keller, Helen Adams, 1880- —Juvenile literature. I. Title.

Macy, Robert W.

MACY, Robert W. 978'.03'0924 B
Few clothes and plenty horse / by Robert W. Macy. Moorcroft, Wyo. : Warbonnet Ranch, 1975. x, 125 p., [9] leaves of plates : ill. ; 23 cm. Includes indexes. [F769.M66M3] 74-33543
1. Macy, Robert W. 2. Moorcroft, Wyo. I. Title.

Macy, Rowland Hussey, 1822-1877.

JOHNSON, Curtiss S. 926.5887
The indomitable R. H. Macy. New York, Vantage [c.1964] 215p. illus., ports. Bibl. 64-55074 3.95 bds.,
1. Macy, Rowland Hussey, 1822-1877. I. Title.

JOHNSON, Curtiss S. 926.5887
The indomitable R. H. Macy, by Curtiss S. Johnson [1st ed.] New York, Vantage Press [1964] 215 p. illus., ports. 21 cm. Bibliography: p. 209. [HF3023.M3J6] 64-55074
1. Macy, Rowland Hussey, 1822-1877. I. Title.

JOHNSON, Curtiss S. 926.5887
The indomitable R. H. Macy, by Curtiss S. Johnson [1st ed.] New York, Vantage Press [1964] 215 p. illus., ports. 21 cm. Bibliography: p. 209. [HF3023.M3J6] 64-55074
1. Macy, Rowland Hussey, 1822-1877. I. Title.

Madagascar—Description and travel.

ELLIS, William, 1794-1872. 916.91'03'1
Three visits to Madagascar during the years 1853-1854-1856; including a journey to the capital, with notices of the natural history of the country and of the present civilization of the people. New York, Harper, 1859. Detroit, Negro History Press, 1971. 514 p. illus., map, ports. 22 cm. [DT469.M26E5 1971] 74-116288 ISBN 0-403-00412-8
1. Madagascar—Description and travel. I. Title.

Madariaga, Salvador de, 1886-

MADARIAGA, Salvador de, 1886- 946.08'092'4 B
Morning without noon: memoirs. [Farnborough, Eng.] Saxon House [1974, c1973] xiii, 441 p. illus. 25 cm. [D413.M25A33 1974] 73-10625 ISBN 0-347-00014-2 14.75
1. Madariaga, Salvador de, 1886- I. Title.
Distributed by Atheneum, New York.

Maddocks, Margaret Kathleen Avern—Biography—Youth.

MADDOCKS, Margaret Kathleen Avern. 823'.9'12 B
An unlessoned girl / [by] Margaret Maddocks ; with drawings by Margaret Wetherbee. London : Hutchinson, 1977. 142 p. : ill. ; 23 cm. Ill. on lining papers. [PR6025.A355Z475] 78-302985 ISBN 0-09-128520-8 : 8.95
1. Maddocks, Margaret Kathleen Avern—Biography—Youth. 2. Novelists, English—20th century—Biography. I. Title.
Distributed by Hutchinson, Salem, NH

Maddox, Lester, 1915-

MADDOX, Lester, 1915- 975.8'04'0924 B
Speaking out : the autobiography of Lester Garfield Maddox. 1st ed. Garden City, N.Y. : Doubleday, 1975. 183 p., [12] leaves of plates : ill. ; 22 cm. Includes index. [F291.3.M3A33] 74-2521 ISBN 0-385-08956-2 : 6.95
1. Maddox, Lester, 1915- I. Title.

Maddy, Joseph Edgar, 1891-

BROWNING, Norma Lee. 780.729774
Joe Maddy of Interlochen. Foreword by Van Cliburn. Chicago, H. Regnery Co., 1963. 297 p. illus. 21 cm. [ML422.M13B8] 63-12894
1. Maddy, Joseph Edgar, 1891- I. Title.

Madeleine Sophie, Saint, 1779-1865.

BROU, Alexandre, 1862- 922.22
Saint Madeleine Sophie Barat: her life of prayer and her teaching, based on unpublished documents. Translated by Jane Wynne Saul. New York, Desclee Co. [1963] ix, 189 p. port. 22 cm. "An abridgement of the original publication." [BX4700.M2B733] 64-12766
1. Madeleine Sophie, Saint, 1779-1865. 2. Society of the Sacred Heart. I. Title.

MAGUIRE, C E 922.244
Saint Madelein Sophie Barat. New York, Sheed and Ward [1960] 214p. 21cm. [BX4700.M2M25] 60-12875
1. Madeleine Sophie, Saint, 1779-1865. I. Title.

MAGUIRE, C. E. 922.244
Saint Madeleine Sophie Barat. New York, Sheed and Ward [c.1960] 214p. 21cm. 60-12875 3.75 half cloth,
1. Madeleine Sophie, Saint, 1779-1865. I. Title.

Maderno, Carlo, 1556-1629.

HIBBARD, Howard, 1928- 720'.92'4
Carlo Maderno and Roman architecture, 1580-1630. London, Zwemmer, 1971. xvi, 404 p. illus., geneal. tables, plans. 31 cm. (Studies in architecture, v. 10) Sole distributor in the U.S.A.; Pennsylvania State University Press, University Park, Pa. English or Italian. "Catalogue": p. 107-234. Bibliography: p. 380-390. [NA1123.M3H5 1971] 72-195351 ISBN 0-302-02161-2
1. Maderno, Carlo, 1556-1629. 2. Architecture—Rome (City) I. Title.
39.50 BIP

Madero, Francisco Indalecio, Pres. Mexico. 1873-1913.

ROSS, Stanley Robert, 1921- 923.172
Francisco I. Madero, apostle of Mexican democracy. New York, Columbia University Press, 1955. xii, 378p. port., maps (1fold.) 22cm. Issued also in

microfilm form as thesis, Columbia University, under title: Mexican apostle: the life of Francisco I. Madero. Bibliography: p. [343]-357. [F1234.M244 1955] 54-10744
1. Madero, Francisco Indalecio, Pres. Mexico. 1873-1913. 2. Diaz, Porfirio, Pres. Mexico, 1830-1915. 3. Mexico—Pol. & govt.—1910-1946. I. Title. BIP

Madison, Dolley (Payne) Todd, 1768-1849.

ARNETT, Ethel 973.5'1'0924 B
Stephens.
Mrs. James Madison; the incomparable Dolley. [1st ed.] Greensboro, N.C., Piedmont Press; [distributed by Straughan's Book Shop] 1972. xiii, 520 p. illus. 24 cm. Bibliography: p. 489-498. [E342.1.A76] 78-183987 10.95
1. Madison, Dolley (Payne) Todd, 1768-1849. I. Title. BIP

GERSON, Noel 973.5'1'0924 B
Bertram, 1914-
The velvet glove : a life of Dolly Madison / Noel B. Gerson. 1st ed. Nashville : T. Nelson, [1975] p. cm. Includes index. Bibliography: p. [E342.1.G47] 75-23124 ISBN 0-8407-6472-3 : 6.95
1. Madison, Dolley Payne Todd, 1768-1849. I. Title. BIP

GOODWIN, Maud(Wilder), 973.51
1856-1935
Dolly Madison, by Maud Wilder Godwin New York, Scribner's 1911 [Spartonburg, S.C., Reprint Co., 1967] xiv, p., 1 l., 287p. front. (port.) 18cm. (Women of colonial & revolutionary times, Virginia Heritage ser., no. 5) [E342.1.G66] (B) 67-30157 12.50
1. Madison, Dorothy (Payne) Todd, 1768-1849. I. Title.

MADISON, Dolley 973.5'1'0924
(Payne) Todd, 1768-1849.
Memoirs and letters of Dolly Madison, wife of James Madison, President of the United States. Edited by her grand-niece. Port Washington, N.Y., Kennikat Press [1971] 210 p. 18 cm. (Kennikat Press scholarly reprints. Series in American history and culture in the nineteenth century.) First published in 1886. [E342.1.M18 1971] 70-137922
1. Washington, D.C.—Social life and customs. I. Cutts, Lucia Beverly, 1851- ed.

MAYER, Jane (Rothschild) 920.7
1903-
Dolly Madison; illustrated by Walter Buehr. New York, Random House [1954] 184p. illus. 22cm. (Landmark books, 47) [E342.1.M3 1954] 54-6266
1. Madison, Dorothy (Payne) Todd, 1768-1849. I. Title.

MINNIGERODE, Meade, 973.4'0922
1887-1967.
Some American ladies; seven informal biographies. Freeport, N.Y., Books for Libraries Press [1969] viii, 287 p. illus., ports. 23 cm. (Essay index reprint series) "First published 1926." Contents.Contents.—Martha Washington.—Abigail Adams.—Dolly Madison.—Elizabeth Monroe and Louisa Adams.—Rachel Jackson.—Peggy Eaton. [E176.M65 1969] 70-93361
1. Washington, Martha (Dandridge) Custis, 1731-1802. 2. Adams, Abigail (Smith) 1744-1818. 3. Madison, Dolley (Payne) Todd, 1768-1849. 4. Monroe, Elizabeth (Kortright) 1768-1830. 5. Adams, Louisa Catherine (Johnson) 1775-1852. 6. Jackson, Rachel (Donelson) 1767-1828. 7. Eaton, Margaret L. (O'Neale) Timberlake, 1799(?)-1879. I. Title.

THANE, Elswyth, 973.5'1'0924 B
1900-
Dolley Madison, her life and times. [New York] Crowell-Collier Press [1970] viii, 184 p. illus., facsim., ports. 21 cm. Bibliography: p. [179]-180. [E342.1.T5] 77-108148
1. Madison, Dolley (Payne) Todd, 1768-1849. I. Title.

Madison, Dolley (Payne) Todd, 1768-1849—Juvenile literature.

DAVIDSON, Mary Richmond. juv
Dolly Madison, famous first lady, by Mary R. Davidson. Illustrated by Erica Merkling. Champaign, Ill., Garrard Pub. Co. [1966] 80 p. col. illus. 23 cm. (A Discovery book) [E342.1.D25] 66-13702
1. Madison, Dolley (Payne) Todd, 1768-1849—Juvenile literature.

GRANT, Matthew G. 973.5'1'0924 B
Dolley Madison; First Lady of the land [by] Matthew G. Grant. Illustrated by Nancy Inderieden. [Mankato, Minn., Creative Education; distributed by Childrens Press, Chicago, 1974] 31 p. illus. (part col.) 25 cm. (His Gallery of great Americans series. Women of America) A biography of the First Lady noted for the graciousness and unprecedented elegance she brought to early nineteenth-century Washington. [E342.1.G72] 92 73-15848 ISBN 0-87191-308-9 3.95
1. Madison, Dolley (Payne) Todd, 1768-1849—Juvenile literature. I. Inderieden, Nancy, illus. II. Title.

MARTIN, Patricia Miles. 92 (J)
Dolley Madison. Illustrated by Unada. New York, Putnam [1967] 62 p. col. illus. 23 cm. (A See and read beginning to read biography) [E342.1.M26] 67-24163
1. Madison, Dolley (Payne) Todd, 1768-1849—Juvenile literature. I. Unada, illus.

MELICK, Arden 973.5'1'0924 B
Davis.
Dolley Madison, First Lady. Illustrated by Ronald Dorfman. New York, Putnam [1970] 78 p. illus. 24 cm. (An American heroine biography) (American pioneer biography.) A brief biography of the First Lady who fled the Capital before the invading British but still managed to save many state papers and a portrait of George Washington. [E342.1.M4] 92 71-92816 3.29
1. Madison, Dolley (Payne) Todd, 1768-1849—Juvenile literature. I. Dorfman, Ronald, illus. II. Title.

WAYNE, Bennett. 973'.0992 B
Women in the White House : four first ladies / edited, with commentary by Bennett Wayne. Champaign, Ill. : Garrard Pub. Co., c1976. 168 p. : ill. ; 23 cm. (A Target book) Includes indexes. Brief biographies of Martha Washington, Abigail Adams, Dolly Madison, and Mary Lincoln. [E176.2.W38] 920 75-20388 ISBN 0-8116-4915-6 : 4.48
1. Washington, Martha Dandridge Custis, 1731-1802—Juvenile literature. 2. Adams, Abigail Smith, 1744-1818—Juvenile literature. 3. Madison, Dolley (Payne) Todd, 1768-1849—Juvenile literature. 4. Lincoln, Mary Todd, 1818-1882—Juvenile literature. I. Title. BIP

Madison, James, Pres. U.S., 1751-1836.

BURNS, Edward McNall, 1897- 320.5
James Madison: philosopher of the Constitution. With a new pref. and a new chapter (IV) by the author. New York, Octagon Books, 1968. x, 240 p. 22 cm. (Rutgers University studies in history, v. 1) Bibliography: p. 229-234. [E342.B87 1968] 67-18757
1. Madison, James, Pres. U.S., 1751-1836. 2. United States—Constitutional history. BIP

FREDMAN, Lionel E. 973.5'1'0924 B
James Madison, American president and constitutional author, by Lionel E. Fredman. Compiled with the assistance of the research staff of SamHar Press. Charlotteville, N.Y., SamHar Press, 1974. p. cm. (Outstanding personalities of the American Revolution, no. 8) (Outstanding personalities, no. 78) Bibliography: p. [E342.F74] 74-14592 2.29; 0.98 (pbk.)
1. Madison, James, Pres. U.S., 1751-1836. BIP

GAY, Sydney 973.5'1'0924 B
Howard, 1814-1888.
James Madison. Boston, Houghton, Mifflin. [New York, AMS Press, 1972] vii, 346 p. illus. 19 cm. (American statesmen, v. 12) Reprint of the 1898 ed. [E342.G28 1972] 70-128976 ISBN 0-404-50862-6
1. Madison, James, Pres. U.S., 1751-1836. I. Title. II. Series.

GAY, Sydney 973.5'1'0924 B
Howard, 1814-1888.
James Madison. New Rochelle, N.Y., Arlington House [1970] 346 p. illus., ports. 21 cm. (Giants of America. The Founding Fathers) Originally published in 1884. Includes bibliographical references. [E342.G28 1970] 78-111223 ISBN 0-87000-084-5
1. Madison, James, Pres. U.S., 1751-1836.

HUNT, Gaillard, 973.5'1'0924 B
1862-1924.
The life of James Madison. New York, Russell & Russell [1968] viii, 402 p. port. 23 cm. Reprint of the 1902 ed. Bibliographical footnotes. [E342.H943 1968] 66-27105
1. Madison, James, Pres. U.S., 1751-1836. I. Title. BIP

KETCHAM, Ralph 973.5'1'0924 B
Louis, 1927-
James Madison; a biography, by Ralph Ketcham. New York, N.Y., Macmillan [1971] xiv, 753 p. map (on lining papers) plates, ports. 24 cm. Bibliography: p. 673-678. [E342.K46 1971] 79-85779
1. Madison, James, Pres. U.S., 1751-1836. BIP

MADISON, James, 016.9735'1'0924
Pres. U.S., 1751-1836.
Calendar of the correspondence of James Madison. New York, B. Franklin [1970] vii, 739, 70 p. 24 cm. (American classics in history & social sciences, 120) (Burt Franklin bibliography & reference series, 328.) Reprint of the 1894 ed., and index originally published in 1895. [E302.M16 1970] 73-119768
1. U.S.—History—1783-1865—Sources. I. Title. BIP

MADISON, James, 973.5'1'0924 B
Pres. U.S., 1751-1836.
James Madison, a biography in his own words. Edited by Merrill D. Peterson, with an introd. by Robert A. Rutland. Joan Paterson Kerr, picture editor. New York, Newsweek; distributed by Harper & Row [1974] 416 p. illus. 27 cm. (The Founding Fathers) Based on the Papers of James Madison, edited by W. T. Hutchinson and W. M. E. Rachal (v. 1-7) and by R. A. Rutland and W. M. E. Rachal (v. 8) Bibliography: p. 408-409. [E342.A34 1974b] 74-161791 ISBN 0-06-013332-5 15.00
1. Madison, James, Pres. U.S., 1751-1836. I. Peterson, Merrill D., ed. II. Madison, James, Pres. U.S., 1751-1836. Papers. BIP

MOORE, Virginia, 973.5'1'0922 B
1903-
The Madisons / Virginia Moore. New York : McGraw-Hill, c1979. p. cm. Includes index. Bibliography: p. [E342.M6] 78-17958 ISBN 0-07-042903-0 : 17.50
1. Madison, James, Pres. U.S., 1751-1836. 2. Madison, Dolley Payne Todd, 1768-1849. 3. Presidents—United States—Biography. 4. Presidents—United States—Wives—Biography. I. Title.

RIEMER, Neal, 1922- 321.8'0924
James Madison. New York, Washington Square Press [1968] 238 p. 18 cm. (The Great American thinkers series) "Bibliographical essay": p. 200-208. [JC211.M35R52] 79-106 0.75
1. Madison, James, Pres. U.S., 1751-1836.

RIVES, William 973.5'1'0924 B
Cabell, 1793-1868.
History of the life and times of James Madison. Freeport, N.Y., Books for Libraries Press [1970] 3 v. port. 23 cm. Reprint of the 1859-1868 ed. Includes bibliographical references. [E342.R623] 76-126253
1. Madison, James, Pres. U.S., 1751-1836. 2. U.S.—Politics and government—1783-1809. I. Title. BIP

Madison, James, Pres. U.S., 1751-1836—Juvenile literature.

KELLY, Regina (Zimmerman) j92
1898-
James Madison, statesman and President [by] Regina Z. Kelly. Illustrated by Carolyn Cather. Boston, Houghton Mifflin [1966] 192 p. col. illus. 22 cm. (Piper books) [E342.K4] 66-10882
1. Madison, James, Pres. U.S. 1751-1836 — Juvenile literature. I. Title.

MARTIN, Patricia 973.5'1'0924 B
Miles.
James Madison, Illustrated by Richard Cuffari. New York, Putnam [1970] 63 p. illus. (part col.), ports. (part col.) 22 cm. (A See and read beginning to read biography) An easy-to-read biography of the man who served the United States as an expert on law, a delegate to the Continental Congress, and third President. [E342.M3] 92 70-92813 2.68
1. Madison, James, Pres. U.S., 1751-1836—Juvenile literature. I. Cuffari, Richard, 1925- illus. II. Title.

STEINBERG, Alfred, 973.510924 B
1917-
James Madison. New York, Putnam [1965] 224 p. 21 cm. (Lives to remember) Bibliography: p. 219-220. [E342.S7] 65-20699
1. Madison, James, Pres. U.S., 1751-1836—Juvenile literature.

WILKIE, Katharine Elliott, j92
1904-
Father of the Constitution: James Madison, by Katharine E. Wilkie and Elizabeth R. Moseley. New York, Messner [1963] 191 p. 22 cm. "Books about James Madison and his times": p. 186. [E342.W5] 63-16789
1. Madison, James, Pres. U.S., 1751-1836 — Juvenile literature. I. Moseley, Elizabeth Robards. joint author. II. Title.

Madison, N.J. Giralda Farms.

BARNES, Valerie. 974.9'74
Behind the scenes at Giralda Farms : [Geraldine Rockefeller Dodge's fabled estate] / Valerie Barnes. Bernardsville, N.J. : Bernardsville Book Co., 1976. 119 p. ; 18 cm. [F144.M18B37] 76-9518 ISBN 0-916600-01-7 pbk. : 2.95
1. Madison, N.J. Giralda Farms. 2. Dodge, Geraldine Rockefeller, 1882-1973. 3. Dodge family. 4. Rockefeller family. I. Title.

Madixxa, Donna.

PARKHILL, Forbes, 1892- 347.6
Donna Madixxa goes West; the biography of a witch. Boulder, Colo., Pruett Press [1968] 141 p. illus., ports. 23 cm. [CT275.M4466P3] 68-58183 6.00
1. Madixxa, Donna. I. Title.

Madog ab Owain Gwynedd, 1150-1180?

KNIGHT, Bernard. 973.1'4'0924 B
Madoc, prince of America / Bernard Knight. New York : St. Martin's Press, 1977. 189 p. ; 21 cm. [E109.W4M334 1977] 76-4653 7.95
1. Madog ab Owain Gwynedd, 1150-1180? 2. America—Discovery and exploration—Welsh. 3. Explorers—Wales—Biography. I. Title.

Madsen, Christian, 1852-1944.

CROY, Homer, 1883- 923.573
Trigger marshal; the story of Chris Madsen. [1st ed.] New York, Duell, Sloan and Pearce [1958] 267 p. illus. 21 cm. Includes bibliography. [F595.M24C7] 58-10436
1. Madsen, Christian, 1852-1944. 2. Crime and criminals—The West. I. Title.

Maekawa, Kunio, 1905-

ALTHERR, Alfred, 1911- 720.922
Three Japanese architects. Drei japanische Architekten; Mayekawa, Tange, Sakakura. [English version by D. Q. Stephenson] New York, Architectural Book Pub. Co. [1968] 179 p. illus., plans. 23 x 29 cm. English and German. [NA1559.M3A78 1968] 68-5228
1. Maekawa, Kunio, 1905- 2. Tange, Kenzo, 1913- 3. Sakakura, Junzo. 4. Architecture, Modern—20th century—Japan. I. Title. II. Title: Drei japanische Architekten.

Maeser, Karl Gottfried, 1828-1901.

BURTON, Alma P 1913- 922.8373
Karl G. Maeser, Mormon educator. Salt Lake City, Deseret Book Co., 1953. 79p. illus. 23cm. 'Condensation of a thesis . . . for the degree of master of science . . . Brigham Young University.' [BX8695.M3B8] 53-35200
1. Maeser, Karl Gottfried, 1828-1901. 2. Mormons and Mormonism—Education. I. Title.

Maeterlinck, Maurice, 1862-1949.

BITHELL, Jethro, 1878- 848'.8'09 B
Life and writings of Maurice Maeterlinck. Port Washington, N.Y., Kennikat Press [1972] xvi, 199, [1] p. 19 cm. Reprint of the 1913 ed. Bibliography: p. 175-[200] [PQ2625.A6B5 1972] 71-160743 ISBN 0-8046-1556-X
1. Maeterlinck, Maurice, 1862-1949. BIP

HALLS, W. D. 928.4
Maurice Maeterlinck; a study of his life and thought. [New York, Oxford Univ. Press c.]1960[i.e. 1961] 189p. illus. port. Bibl. 61-603 5.60
1. Maeterlinck, Maurice, 1862-1949. I. Title. BIP

HALLS, W. D. 848'.8'09 B
Maurice Maeterlinck : a study of his life and thought / by W. D. Halls. Westport, Conn. : Greenwood Press, [1978] c1960. p. cm. Reprint of the ed. published at the Clarendon Press, Oxford. Bibliography: p. [PQ2625.A6H25 1978] 78-16379 ISBN 0-313-20574-4 lib.bdg. : 16.50
1. Maeterlinck, Maurice, 1862-1949. 2. Authors, Belgian—20th century—Biography.

MAHONEY, Patrick, 1911- 928.4
The magic of Maeterlinck. Hollywood, Calif., House-Warven [c1951] 175 p. 22 cm. [PQ2625.A6M3] 52-489
1. Maeterlinck, Maurice, I. Title. BIP

SLOSSON, Edwin Emery, 1865-1929. 920.04
Major prophets of to-day, by Edwin E. Slosson. Freeport, N.Y., Books for Libraries Press [1968] xii, 299 p. ports. 23 cm. (Essay index reprint series) Reprint of the 1914 ed. "The chapters of this volume have appeared in the Independent ... in a series under the general title of Twelve major prophets of to-day." Contents.Contents.—Maurice Maeterlinck.—Henri Bergson.—Henri Poincare.—Elie Metchnikoff.—Wilhelm Ostwald.—Ernst Haeckel. [CT119.S6 1968] 68-8493
1. Maeterlinck, Maurice, 1862-1949. 2. Bergson, Henri Louis, 1859-1941. 3. Poincare, Henri, 1854-1912. 4. Mechnikov, Il'ia Il'ich, 1845-1916. 5. Ostwald, Wilhelm, 1853-1932. 6. Haeckel, Ernst Heinrich Philipp August, 1834-1919. I. Title. BIP

Maeztu, Ramiro de, 1875-1936.

LANDEIRA, Ricardo L. 070'.92'4 B
Ramiro de Maeztu / by Ricardo Landeira. Boston : Twayne, c1978. 155 p. : port. ; 21 cm. (Twayne's world authors series ; TWAS 484 : Spain) Includes index. Bibliography: p. 147-151. [PN5316.M3L3 1978] 77-15591 ISBN 0-8057-6325-2 : 10.95
1. Maeztu, Ramiro de, 1875-1936. 2. Journalists—Spain—Biography. BIP

Mafia.

*HANNA, David. 364.10924 [B]
Bugsy Siegel. New York, Belmont Tower Books [1974] 189 p. 18 cm. (The Godfather series) [HV6248] 1.25 (pbk.)
1. Mafia. I. Title.

*HANNA, David. 364'.10924[B]
Carlo Gambino: King of the Mafia. New York, Belmont Tower Books [1974] 170 p. illus. 18 cm. (The Godfather series) [HV6248] 1.25 (pbk.)
1. Mafia. I. Title.

*HANNA, David. 364.10924 [B]
Vito Genovese. New York, Belmont Tower Books [1974] 185 p. illus. 18 cm. (The Godfather series) [HV6248] 1.25 (pbk.)
1. Mafia. I. Title.

Magalhaes, Fernao de, d. 1521.

GUILLEMARD, Francis Henry Hill, 1852-1933. 910.924 B
The life of Ferdinand Magellan and the first circumnavigation of the globe, 1480-1521. New York, AMS Press [1971] viii, 353 p. illus., coat of arms, geneal. table, maps (part fold.), ports. 19 cm. (The World's great explorers and explorations) Reprint of the 1890 ed. Includes bibliographical references. [G286.M2G9 1971] 70-127901 ISBN 0-404-02947-7
1. Magalhaes, Fernao de, d. 1521. 2. Voyages around the world. I. Title. BIP

PARR, Charles McKew. 923.9469
Ferdinand Magellan, circumnavigator. Introd. by Edward P. Beach. [2d ed.] New York, Crowell [1964] xx, 123 p. illus., maps, ports. 24 cm. First ed. published in 1953 under title: So noble a captain. "List of transcriptions from records in the Archivo General de Indias, Seville": p. 398-401. Bibliography: p. 402-414. [G286.M2P3 1964] 64-19817
1. Magalhaes, Fernao de, d. 1521. I. Title.

PARR, Charles McKew. 923.9469
Ferdinand Magellan, circumnavigator. Introd. by Edward L. Beach [12nd ed.] New York, Crowell [1964] xx, 423 p. illus., maps, ports. 24 cm. First ed. published in 1953 under title: So noble a captain. "List of transcriptions from records in the Archivo General de Indias, Seville": p. 398-401. Bibliography: p. 402-414. [G286.M2P3] 64-19817
1. Magalhaes, Fernao de, d. 1521. I. Title.

PARR, Charles McKew. 923.9469
So noble a captain; the life and times of Ferdinand Magellan. New York, Crowell [1953] xv, 423 p. illus., ports., maps. 24 cm. "List of transcriptions from records in the Archivo General de Indias, Seville": p. 398-401. Bibliography: p. 402-414. [G286.M2P3] 53-7525
1. Magalhaes, Fernao de, d. 1521. I. Title. BIP

PARR, Charles McKew. 910'.92'4 B
So noble a captain : the life and times of Ferdinand Magellan / Charles McKew Parr. Westport, Conn. : Greenwood Press, 1975, c1953. xv, 423 p. : ill. ; 24 cm. Reprint of the ed. published by Crowell, New York. Includes index. "List of transcriptions from records in the Archivo General de Indias, Seville": p. 398-401. Bibliography: p. 402-414. [G286.M2P3 1975] 75-31439 ISBN 0-8371-8521-1 lib.bdg. : 23.75
1. Magalhaes, Fernao de, d. 1521. I. Title.

PODITI, Edouard. 910'.92'4 B
Magellan of the Pacific. [1st American ed.] New York, McGraw-Hill Book Co. [1973, c1972] 271 p. illus. 22 cm. Bibliography: p. 260-264. [G286.M2B62 1973] 72-12759 ISBN 0-07-073754-1 6.95
1. Magalhaes, Fernao de, d. 1521. I. Title.

POND, Seymour Gates, 1896- 923.9469
Ferdinand Magellan, master mariner. Illustrated by Jack Coggins. New York, Random House [1957] 180 p. illus. 22 cm. (World landmark books, W-31) [G286.M2P6] 57-7515
1. Magalhaes, Fernao de, d. 1521.

WELCH, Ronald. 923.9469
Ferdinand Magellan. Illustrated by William Stobbs. New York, Criterion Books [1956] 178p. illus. 22cm. [G286.M2W4] 56-9963
1. Magalhaes, Fernad de, d. 1521 I. Title.

Magalhaes, Fernao de, d. 1521—Juvenile literature.

EDUCATIONAL Research Council of America. Social Science Staff. 910'.924 B
Explorers and discoverers: Magellan. Boston, Allyn and Bacon [1970] 49 p. col. illus., col. maps. 21 cm. (Concepts and inquiry: the ERC social science program) An easy-to-read account of the first trip around the world begun by Magellan and completed by his men after he was killed in the Spice Islands. [G286.M2E33] 92 79-97108
1. Magalhaes, Fernao de, d. 1521—Juvenile literature. I. Title. II. Series: Concepts and inquiry: the Educational Research Council social science program

ROBERTO, Brother, 1927- 923.9469
Cry mutiny! A story of Ferdinand Magellan. Notre Dame, Ind., Dujarie Press [1959] 143p. 22cm. [G286.M2R6] 59-65504
1. Magalihaes, Fernao de, d. 1521—Juvenile literature. I. Title.

ROBERTO, Brother, 1927- 923.9469
We sail at dawn! A story of Ferdinand Magellan. Illus. by Carolyn Lee Jagodits. Notre Dame, Ind., Dujarie Press [c1960] 94p. illus. 24cm. [G286.M2R63] 59-65505
1. Magalihaes, Fernao de, d. 1521—Juvenile literature. I. Title.

WILKIE, Katharine Elliott, 1904- j92
Ferdinand Magellan: noble captain. Illustrated by Phillip M. Coyle. Boston, Houghton Mifflin [1963] 190 p. col. illus., col. maps. 22 cm. (Piper books) [G286.M2W5] 63-15657
1. Magalhaes, Ferniio de, d. 1521 — Juvenile literature. I. Title. BIP

WILKIE, Katharine Elliott, 1904- 920
Ferdinand Magellan: noble captain. Illus. by Philip M. Coyle. Boston, Houghton [c.1963] 190p. col. illus., col. maps. 22cm. (Piper bks.) 63-15657 1.95
1. Magalhaes, Fernao de, d. 1521—Juvenile literature. I. Title.

Magalhues, Fernio de, d. 1521.

FELTON, Ronald Oliver, 1909- 923.9469
Ferdinand Magellan [by] Ronald Welch [pseud.] Illustrated by William Stobbs. New York, Criterion Books [1956] 178 p. illus. 22 cm. [G286.M2F4] 56-9963
1. Magalhues, Fernio de, d. 1521. I. Title.

Magan, Percy Tilson, 1867-1947.

NEFF, Merlin L 922.6773
For God and C. M. E.; a biography of Percy Tilson Magan upon the historical background of the educational and medical work of Seventh-Day Adventists. Mountain View, Calif., Pacific Press Pub. Association [1964] 341 p. port. 23 cm. Includes bibliographies. [BX6193.M26N4] 64-16798
1. Magan, Percy Tilson, 1867-1947. 2. Los Angeles. College of Medical Evangelists. I. Title.

Magee, David Bickersteth, 1905-

MAGEE, David Bickersteth, 1905- 381'.45'0705730924
Infinite riches; the adventures of a rare book dealer, by David Magee. Introd. by Lawrence Clark Powell. New York, P. S. Eriksson [1973] xiii, 274 p. illus. 22 cm. [Z473.M22A3] 73-75235 ISBN 0-8397-3553-7 8.95
1. Magee, David Bickersteth, 1905- 2. Antiquarian booksellers—Correspondence, reminiscences, etc. I. Title. BIP

Magee, James H.,

MAGEE, James H., 1839- 286'.0924 B
The night of affliction and morning of recovery; an autobiography, by J. H. Magee. Cincinnati, 1873. Miami, Fla., Mnemosyne Pub. Co. [1969] 173 p. port. 23 cm. [E185.97.M2 1969] 77-89397
I. Title.

Magic—Biography.

GODWIN, William, 1756-1836. 133.4'092'2 B
Lives of the necromancers : or, An account of the most eminent persons in successive ages who have claimed for themselves, or to whom has been imputed by others, the exercise of magical power / by William Godwin. New York : Gordon Press, [1975] p. cm. Reprint of the 1876 ed. published by Chatto and Windus, London. [BF1597.G7 1975] 75-31779 ISBN 0-87968-281-7 lib.bdg. : 39.95
1. Magic—Biography. 2. Witchcraft—Biography. 3. Magic—History. 4. Witchcraft—History. I. Title.

Magic — Ghana.

NEAL, James H. 133.470924
Jungle magic; my life among the witch doctors of West Africa [by] James H. Neal. [1st Amer. ed.] New York, McKay [1966] 190p. illus., ports. 21cm. Autobiographical. London ed. (Harrap) has title: Ju-ju in my life. [BF1622.G5N4 1966] 66-25146 4.50 bds.,
1. Magic — Ghana. I. Title.

Magicians.

FROST, Thomas, 1821-1908. 793.8'0922
The lives of the conjurors. A new ed. Ann Arbor, Mich., Plutarch Press, 1971. viii, 360 p. 22 cm. "Facsimile reprint of the 1881 edition." [BF1597.F76 1881a] 78-84902
1. Magicians. 2. Magic—History. I. Title.

Magicians—Biography—Juvenile literature.

FORTMAN, Janis L., 1949- 793.8'092'2 B
Houdini and other masters of magic / by Jan Fortman. New York : Contemporary Perspectives, [1977] p. cm. Highlights the lives and careers of magicians Doug Henning, Robert-Houdin, John Henry Anderson, Alexander Herrmann, and Houdini. [GV1545.A2F67] 920 77-12638 ISBN 0-8172-1032-6 lib. bdg. : 4.95
1. Magicians—Biography—Juvenile literature. 2. Conjuring—Juvenile literature. I. Title. BIP

Maglie, Salvatore Anthony, 1917-

SHAPIRO, Milton J 927.96357
The Sal Maglie story. New York, J. Messner [1957] 192p. illus. 22cm. [GV865.M32S5] 57-6839
1. Maglie, Salvatore Anthony, 1917- I. Title.

SHAPIRO, Milton J. 796.3570924
The Sal Maglie story. New York, J. Messner [1957] 192 p. illus. 22 cm. [GV865.M32S5] 927 57-6839
1. Maglie, Salvatore Anthony, 1917- I. Title.

Magnes, Judah Leon, 1877-1948.

BENTWICH, Norman De Mattos, 1883- 922.96
For Zion's sake; a biography of Judah L. Magnes, first chancellor and first president of the hebreW University of Jerusalem. Philadelphia, Jewish Publication Society of America, 1954. 329p. illus. 22cm. (The Jacob R. Schiff library of Jewish contributions to American democracy) [LG341.J45M35] 54-7440
1. Magnes, Judah Leon, 1877-1948. I. Title.

Magnuson, Paul Budd,

MAGNUSON, Paul Budd, 1884- 926.1
Ring the night bell; the autobiography of a surgeon. Edited by Finley Peter Dunne, Jr. [1st ed.] Boston, Little, Brown [1960] 376 p. illus. 22 cm. [R154.M2915A3] 60-6031
I. Title.

MAGNUSON, Paul Budd, 1884- 926.1
Ring the night bell; the autobiography of a surgeon, by Paul B. Magnuson, ed. by Finley Peter Dunne, Jr. New York, Popular Lib. [1967, c.1960] 319p. 18cm. (75-1233) [R154.M2915 A3] .75 pap.,
I. Title.

Magone, Michael.

LAPPIN, Peter. 922.245
General Mickey, a true story. New Rochelle, N. Y., Salesiana Publishers [1952] 166 p. 23 cm. [BX4705.M2585L3] 52-32347
1. Magone, Michael. I. Title.

Magruder, Jeb Stuart, 1934-

MAGRUDER, Jeb 364.1'32'0924 B
Stuart, 1934-
From power to peace / Jeb Stuart Magruder ; foreword by Mark O. Hatfield. Waco, Tex. : Word Books, c1978. 224 p. : ill. ; 22 cm. [E860.M393] 77-92464 ISBN 0-8499-0074-3 : 7.95
1. Magruder, Jeb Stuart, 1934- 2. Watergate Affair, 1972- —Personal narratives. 3. Christian biography—United States. I. Title. **BIP**

Magsaysay, Ramon, Pres. Philippines, 1907-1957.

GRAY, Marvin M 991.4040924 (B)
1921-
Island hero; the story of Ramon Magsaysay, by Marvin M. Gray. Illustrated by Alan Moyler. New York, Hawthorn Books [1965] 188 p. illus. 22 cm. Bibliography: p. [183] [DS686.6.M3G7] 65-12736
1. Magsaysay, Ramon, Pres. Philippines, 1907-1957. I. Title.

PANLILIO, Benjamin L v. 12
Ramon Magsaysay, ideal citizen, by Benjamin L. Panlilio and Maximo Ramos. Illustrated by Florante M. Hernando. Quezon City, Phoenix Pub. House [1959] 109 p. illus. 21 cm. 65-80622
1. Magsaysay, Ramon, Pres. Philippines, 1907-1957. I. Ramos, Maximo, 1910- II. Title.

ROMULO, Carlos Pena, 923.1914
1899-
The Magsaysay story, by Carlos P. Romulo and Marvin M. Gray. New York, J. Day Co. [1956] 316 p. illus. 22 cm. [DS686.6.M3R6] 56-11935
1. Magsaysay, Ramon, Pres. Philippines, 1907- I. Gray, Marvin M., 1921- joint author.

Magubane, Peter.

MANDELA, Zindzi, 1960- 821
Black as I am / Zindzi Mandela and Peter Magubane ; foreword, Andrew Young. Los Angeles : Guild of Tutors Press, c1978. 120 p. : ill. ; 28 cm. Includes index. [PR9369.3.M346B57] 77-87417 ISBN 0-89615-001-1 : 5.95
1. Magubane, Peter. I. Title.
Publisher's address : 1019 Gavley Ave., Los Angeles, CA 90024 **BIP**

Mahan, Alfred Thayer, 1840-1914.

MAHAN, Alfred 359.3'32'0924
Thayer, 1840-1914.
Letters and papers of Alfred Thayer Mahan / edited by Robert Seager II and Doris D. Maguire. Annapolis : Naval Institute Press, c1975. 3 v. : ports ; 26 cm. (Naval letters series ; 4) Contents.Contents.—v. 1. 1847-1889.—v. 2. 1890-1901.—v. 3. 1902-1914. Includes bibliographical references and indexes. [E182.M24] 73-91863 ISBN 0-87021-339-3 : 95.00
1. Mahan, Alfred Thayer, 1840-1914. 2. United States—History, Naval—Sources. I. Title. II. Series.

SEAGER, Robert, 907'.2'024 B
1924-
Alfred Thayer Mahan : the man and his letters / by Robert Seager II. Annapolis, Md. : Naval Institute Press, c1977. xvii, 713 p. : ill. ; 27 cm. Includes bibliographical references and index. [E182.M242S4] 77-74158 ISBN 0-87021-182-X : 24.95
1. Mahan, Alfred Thayer, 1840-1914. 2. United States. Navy—Biography. 3. Historians—United States—Biography. 4. United States—History, Naval—To 1900. **BIP**

WEST, Richard 359'.00922 B
Sedgewick, 1902-
Admirals of American empire; the combined story of George Dewey, Alfred Thayer Mahan, Winfield Scott Schley, and William Thomas Sampson, by Richard S. West, Jr. Westport, Conn., Greenwood Press [1971, c1948] 354 p. illus. 23 cm. Includes bibliographical references. [E182.W45 1971] 73-156216 ISBN 0-8371-6167-3
1. Dewey, George, 1837-1917. 2. Mahan, Alfred Thayer, 1840-1914. 3. Schley, Winfield Scott, 1839-1911. 4. Sampson, William Thomas, 1840-1902. 5. U.S.—History, Naval—To 1900. I. Title. **BIP**

Mahan, Asa, 1800-1889.

MAHAN, Asa, 1800- 285'.8'0924 B
1889.
Autobiography : intellectual, moral, and spiritual / Asa Mahan. 1st AMS ed. New York : AMS Press, 1979. x, 458 p. ; 19 cm. (Philosophy in America) Reprint of the 1882 ed. published by T. Woolmer, London. [BX7260.M3A3 1979] 75-3269 ISBN 0-404-59257-0 : 24.50
1. Mahan, Asa, 1800-1889. 2. Congregational churches—Clergy—Biography. 3. Clergy—England—Biography.

Maharaj, Rabindranath R.

MAHARAJ, Rabindranath 248'.246 B
R.
Death of a guru / Rabindranath R. Maharaj, with Dave Hunt. 1st ed. Philadelphia : A. J. Holman Co., c1977. 224 p. ; 22 cm. [BV4935.M25A32] 77-5701 ISBN 0-87981-083-1 : 3.95
1. Maharaj, Rabindranath R. 2. Converts from Hinduism—Biography. I. Hunt, Dave, joint author. II. Title. **BIP**

Maharashtra, India (State)—Biog.

KARVE, Dinakar Dhondo, 920.05479
1899- ed. and tr.
The new Brahmans: five Maharashtrian families. Selected, tr. by D. D. Karve with the ed. assistance of Ellen E. McDonald. Berkeley, Univ. of California Pr. [c.] 1963. 303p. map. 24cm. 63-11389 5.50
1. Maharashtra, India (State)—Biog. I. Title.

KARVE, Dinakar Dhondo, 920.05479
1899- ed. and tr.
The new Brahmans; five Maharashtrian families. Selected and translated by D. D. Karve with the editorial assistance of Ellen E. McDonald. Berkeley, University of California Press, 1963. 803 p. 24 cm. [DS481.A1K3] 63-11389
1. Maharashtra, India (State) — Biog. I. Title. **BIP**

Maher, John, 1940-

SALES, Grover. 362.2'93'0924 B
John Maher of Delancey Street : a guide to peaceful revolution in America / by Grover Sales. 1st ed. New York : Norton, c1976. 176 p. : ill. ; 22 cm. [HV9306.S42D47] 75-35880 ISBN 0-393-07499-4 : 7.95
1. Maher, John, 1940- 2. Delancey Street Foundation. 3. Halfway houses—San Francisco. I. Title. **BIP**

Mahesh Yogi, Maharishi.

*JEFFERSON, William. 294
The story of the Maharishi. New York, Pocket Books [1976] 128 p. 18 cm. Bibliography: p. 125-128. [BL627] ISBN 0-671-80526-6 1.50 (pbk.)
1. Mahesh Yogi, Maharishi. 2. Transcendental meditation. I. Title. **BIP**

OATES, Bob. 294 B
Celebrating the dawn : Maharishi Mahesh Yogi and the TM technique / epilogue by Maharishi Mahesh Yogi ; written by Robert Oates, Jr. New York : Putnam, c1976. 227 p. : ill. ; 24 cm. [BF637.T68017 1976] 76-14884 ISBN 0-399-11815-2 : 12.95
1. Mahesh Yogi, Maharishi. 2. Transcendental Meditation. 3. Yogis—Biography. I. Title.

Mahesh Yogi, Maharishi—Addresses, essays, lectures.

EBON, Martin, comp. 294 B
Maharishi : the founder of Transcendental Meditation / edited by Martin Ebon. New York : New American Library, 1968, 1975 printing. xvii, 149 p. ; 18 cm. (A Signet book) Contents.Contents.—Ebon, M. Twentieth century guru.—Newhouse, J. C. New York is ready!—Ballantine, M. The road to bliss consciousness.—Singh, K. How does meditation work?—Lefferts, B. Chief guru of the western world.—Butterworth, C. The Beatles without mask.—The Beatles talk about Maharishi.—White, P. The case of Mia Farrow.—Read, E. Why Efrem Zimbalist is silent. Crenshaw, J. Maharishi's man in L.A.—McNeill, D. He turned us on!—Crenshaw, J. The hippies: beyond pot and LSD.—Crenshaw, J. His global man Friday.—Zielinski, L. Yoga, meditation, mantras.—Winters, R. America's love affair with yoga.—Maynard, A. From Gurdjieff to Maharishi.—Fleming, G. The house on 78th Street.—Otani, J.-P. Springtime on the Ganges.—Mahesh Yogi, M. Toward world peace.—Ebon, M. What next for the TM movement? [BL1175.M29E2 1975] 75OMaharishi :
1. Mahesh Yogi, Maharishi—Addresses, essays, lectures. I. Title.

Mahler, Gustav, 1860-1911.

BLAUKOPF, Kurt. 780'.92'4 B
Gustav Mahler. Translated by Inge Goodwin. New York, Praeger [1973] 279 p. illus. 23 cm. Bibliography: p. 265-266. [ML410.M23B63] 73-109467 10.00
1. Mahler, Gustav, 1860-1911.

ENGEL, Gabriel. 780'.92'4 B
Gustav Mahler, song-symphonist. Pref. by Jack Diether. New York, D. Lewis [1970?] 132 p. port. 21 cm. Reprint of the 1932 ed. Bibliography: p. [127]-[128] [ML410.M23E7 1970] 70-114842
1. Mahler, Gustav, 1860-1911.

GARTENBERG, Egon. 780'.92'4 B
Mahler : the man and his music / Egon Gartenberg. New York : Schirmer Books, c1977. p. cm. Includes index. Bibliography: p. [ML410.M23G37] 77-70274 ISBN 0-02-870840-7 : 15.00
1. Mahler, Gustav, 1860-1911. 2. Composers—Austria—Biography. **BIP**

GUSTAV Mahler in 780'.92'4 B
Vienna / contributors, Pierre Boulez ... [et al.] ; edited by Sigrid Wiesmann ; translated by Anne Shelley ; designed by Jaroslav Krejci. New York : Rizzoli International Publications, 1976. 160 p. : ill. ; 28 x 31 cm. Translation of Gustav Mahler und Wien. [ML410.M23G933] 76-11243 ISBN 0-8478-0039-3 : 25.00
1. Mahler, Gustav, 1860-1911. 2. Composers—Austria—Vienna—Biography. I. Boulez, Pierre, 1925- II. Wiesmann, Sigrid.
Contents omitted

LA GRANGE, Henry 780'.92'4 B
Louis de.
Mahler. [1st ed.] Garden City, N.Y., Doubleday, 1973- v. illus. 25 cm. Includes bibliographical references. [ML410.M23L32] 72-76147 ISBN 0-385-00524-5 17.50 (v. 1)
1. Mahler, Gustav, 1860-1911. I. Title. **BIP**

MAHLER : 780'.92'4 B
a documentary study / compiled and edited by Kurt Blaukopf ; with contributions by Zoltan Roman ; [translated from the German by Paul Baker ... et al.]. New York : Oxford University Press, 1976. 280 p. : ill. (some col.) ; 31 cm. Translation of Mahler : sein Leben, sein Werk und seine Welt in zeitgenossischen Bildern und Texten. Includes index. [ML410.M23M173] 76-9218 ISBN 0-19-519877-8 : 37.50
1. Mahler, Gustav, 1860-1911. 2. Composers—Austria—Biography. I. Blaukopf, Kurt.

WALTER, Bruno, 1876- 927.8
Gustav Mahler. Translation from the German supervised by Lotte Walter Lindt. New York, Knopf, 1958 [c1957] 175 p. illus. 20 cm. [ML410.M23W25 1958] 57-7551
1. Mahler, Gustav, 1860-1911. I. Title. **BIP**

WALTER, Bruno, 1876-1962. 927.8
Gustav Mahler. Translation from the German supervised by Lotte Walter Lindt. New York, Schocken Books [1974, c1957] xvii [176 p.] [vi], 21 cm. [ML410.M23W25] 57-7551 ISBN 0-8052-0446-6. 2.75 (pbk.)
1. Mahler, Gustav, 1860-1911. I. Title.

WALTER, Bruno, 1876- 780'.92'4 B
1962.
Gustav Mahler. Translated by James Galston. With a biographical essay by Ernst Krenek. New York, Da Capo Press, 1970 [c1941] xi, 236 p. illus. 23 cm. (Da Capo Press music reprint series) "Gustav Mahler, by Ernst Krenek": p. 157-220. [ML410.M23W25 1970] 78-87691 ISBN 0-306-71701-8
1. Mahler, Gustav, 1860-1911. 2. Krenek, Ernst, 1900-

WALTER, Bruno, 1876- 780'.92'4 B
1962.
Gustav Mahler. Translated by James Galston. With a biographical essay by Ernst Krenek. New York, Vienna House [1973, c1941] xi, 236 p. illus. 22 cm. Reprint of the ed. published by Greystone Press, New York. Includes bibliographical references. [ML410.M23W25 1973] 73-89928 ISBN 0-8443-0035-7 2.95 (pbk.)
1. Mahler, Gustav, 1860-1911. I. Krenek, Ernst, 1900-

WERFEL, Alma (Schindler) 927.8
Mahler.
Gustav Mahler; memories and letters, by Alma Mahleg, tr. by Basil Creighton Seattle, Univ. of Wash. Pr. [1968, c. 1946] vi p., 2 l., 277p. front., plates, ports., facsim. (music) 20cm. (WP-34) [ML410M23W53 1946] rev 2.95 pap.,
1. Mahler, Gustav, 1860-1911. I. Title.

WERFEL, Alma 780'.92'4 B
Schindler Mahler.
Gustav Mahler : memories and letters / by Alma Mahler ; edited by Donald Mitchell ; translated by Basil Creighton. 3d ed. further enl. with a new appendix and chronology / by Knud Martner and Donald Mitchell, and a new appendix for the 1975 American ed. by Donald Mitchell. Seattle : University of Washington Press, 1975, c1946. xlii, 399 p., [8] leaves of plates : ill. ; 21 cm. Translation of Gustav Mahler: Erinnerungen und Briefe. Includes index. [ML410.M23W53 1975] 74-26502 ISBN 0-295-95378-0 pbk. : 3.95
1. Mahler, Gustav, 1860-1911. I. Mahler, Gustav, 1860-1911. II. Mitchell, Donald, 1925- ed.

WERFEL, Alma (Schindler) 780'.924
Mahler.
Gustav Mahler; memories and letters, by Alma Mahler. Enl. ed., rev. and edited with an introd. by Donald Mitchell. Translated by Basil Creighton. New York, Viking Press [1969] xl, 369 p. facsims. (incl. music), ports. 25 cm. [ML410.M23W532 1969] 69-18800 ISBN 6-7035-8096- 10.00
1. Mahler, Gustav, 1860-1911.

Mahler, Gustav, 1860-1911. Symphonies.

CARDUS, Neville, 1889- 785.110924
Gustav Mahler: his mind and his music

[v.1] With music examples copied. written. ed. by Rudolf Schwarz. New York, St. Martin's [1966, c.1965] 191p. music. port. 24cm. Bibl. [MT130.M25C43] 66-15822 10.00
1. Mahler, Gustav, 1860-1911. Symphonies. I. Title.
Contents omitted.

Mahmud, Sultan of Ghazni, 971-1030.

HABIB, Mohammad 954'.02'0924
Sultan Mahmud of Ghaznin. 2d ed. Delhi, S. Chand, 1967 xi, 128p. 19cm. Bibl. [DS458.3.H3 1967] 67-6760 3.00
1. Mahmud, Sultan of Ghazni, 971-1030. I. Title.
American distributor: Verry, Mystic, Conn.

Mahon, John Lincoln.

ARNOT, Robert Page, 1890- 335'.0092'4
William Morris, the man and the myth : including letters of William Morris to J. L. Mahon and Dr. John Glasse / by R. Page Arnot. Westport, Conn. : Greenwood Press, 1976, c1964. 131 p. ; 23 cm. Reprint of the ed. published by Monthly Review Press, New York. Includes bibliographical references and index. [HX243.A8 1976] 76-107 ISBN 0-8371-8652-8 lib.bdg. : 10.25
1. Morris, William, 1834-1896. 2. Mahon, John Lincoln. 3. Glasse, John. 4. Socialists—Great Britain. I. Morris, William, 1834-1896. II. Mahon, John Lincoln. III. Glasse, John. IV. Title.

Mahovlich, Frank—Juvenile literature.

YOUNG, Scott. 796.9'62'0924 B
Frank Mahovlich, the Big M. St. Paul, EMC Corp. [1974] 38 p. illus. 24 cm. (His Hockey heroes series) A brief biography tracing the professional career of Canadian hockey player Frank Mahovlich, one of the highest scorers in pro hockey history. [GV848.5.M34Y68] 92 74-8436 ISBN 0-88436-102-0 4.95
1. Mahovlich, Frank—Juvenile literature. 2. Hockey—Juvenile literature. I. Title.
Pbk. 2.95; ISBN 0-88436-103-9.

Mahta, Ved Parkash.

MEHTA, Ved Parkash. 362.4'1'0924 B
Face to face / Ved Mehta. Oxford ; New York : Oxford University Press, 1978, c1957. p. cm. [HV1792.M4A33 1978] 77-12984 ISBN 0-19-520014-4 pbk. : 3.50
1. Mahta, Ved Parkash. 2. Blind—United States—Biography. 3. Blind—India—Biography. I. Title. BIP

Maiakovskii, Vladimir Vladimirovich, 1894-1930.

BAROOSHIAN, Vahan D. 891.7'1'42 B
Brik and Mayakovsky / Vahan D. Barooshian. [2514 GC] The Hague, [Noordeinde 41] ; New York : Mouton, 1979. ix, 159 p. ; 24 cm. (Slavistic printings and reprintings ; 301) Bibliography of works by O. Brik: p. [149]-154. [PG3476.B74Z59] 79-348013 ISBN 90-279-7826-3 : 28.25
1. Brik, Osip Maksimovich, 1888-1945. 2. Maiakovskii, Vladimir Vladimirovich, 1894-1930. 3. Brik, Osip Maksimovich, 1888-1945—Relationship with men—Vladimir Maiakovskii. 4. Brik, Lili IUr'evna. 5. Brik, Osip Maksimovich, 1888-1945—Relationship with women—Lili Brik. 6. Maiakovskii, Vladimir Vladimirovich, 1894-1930—Relationship with women—Lili Brik. 7. Poets, Russian—20th century—Biography. 8. Futurism. I. Title. II. Series. BIP

SHKLOVSKII, Viktor Borisovich, 1893- 891.7'1'42 B
Mayakovsky and his circle, by Viktor Shklovsky. Edited and translated by Lily Feiler. New York, Dodd, Mead [1972] xxiv, 259 p. illus. 22 cm. Translation of O Maiakovskom. Includes bibliographical references. [PG3476.M312S5413] 72-5649 ISBN 0-396-06701-8 8.95
1. Maiakovskii, Vladimir Vladimirovich, 1894-1930. 2. Authors, Russian—Biography. I. Title.

WOROSZYLSKI, Wiktor. 891.7'1'42 B
The life of Mayakovsky. Translated from the Polish by Boleslaw Taborski. New York, Orion Press, 1970 [c1971] x, 559 p. illus., ports. 24 cm. Translation of Zycie Majakowskiego. Includes bibliographical references. [PG3476.M312W613] 68-31899 ISBN 0-670-46351-5 15.00
1. Maiakovskii, Vladimir Vladimirovich, 1894-1930. I. Title.

Maier, Walter Arthur, 1893-1950.

MAIER, Paul L. 922.473
A man spoke, a world listened; the story of Walter A. Maier and the Lutheran hour. New York, McGraw-Hill [1963] 411 p. illus. 22 cm. [BX8080.M17M3] 63-12129
1. Maier, Walter Arthur, 1893-1950. 2. Lutheran hour (Radio program) I. Title.

Maigumeri, Charles.

HENNESSY, Maurice N. 923.5669
Soldier of Africa, by Maurice N. Hennessy, Edwin Sauter, Jr. New York, Washburn [dist.] McKay [c.1965] viii, 150p. 21cm. (Men of Africa, 3) [U55.M32H4] 65-12983 3.50
1. Maigumeri, Charles. I. Sauter, Edwin, joint author. II. Title.

Mailer, Norman

MAILER, Norman 928.1
Advertisements for myself. [New York] New Amer. Lib. [1960, c.1959] 477p. (Signet bk. T1889) .75 pap.,
I. Title. BIP

MAILER, Norman. 928.1
Advertisements for myself. New York, Putnam [1959] 532p. 22cm. A collection of the author's short stories, articles, and essays, connected by an autobiographical narrative. [PS3525.A4152Z52] 59-11020
I. Title.

Mailer, Norman—Biography.

MAILER, Norman 928.1
Advertisements for myself. [New York] New Amer. Lib. [1960, c.1959] 477p. (Signet bk. T1889) .75 pap.,
I. Title. BIP

MAILER, Norman. 928.1
Advertisements for myself. New York, Putnam [1959] 532p. 22cm. A collection of the author's short stories, articles, and essays, connected by an autobiographical narrative. [PS3525.A4152Z52] 59-11020
I. Title.

WEATHERBY, William J. 813'.5'4 B
Squaring off : Mailer vs Baldwin / by W. J. Weatherby. New York : Mason/Charter, 1977. 217 p. ; 24 cm. [PS3525.A4152Z95] 76-53559 ISBN 0-88405-449-7 : 8.95
1. Mailer, Norman—Biography. 2. Baldwin, James, 1924- —Biography. 3. Authors, American—20th century—Biography. I. Title. BIP

Mailliard, Anne Eliza (Ward) 1824-1895.

THARP, Louise (Hall) 1898- 929'.2'0973
Three saints and a sinner; Julia Ward Howe, Louisa, Annie, and Sam Ward. [1st ed.] Boston, Little, Brown [1956] 406 p. illus. 23 cm. Includes bibliography. [CS71.W26 1956] 56-10638
1. Howe, Julia (Ward) 1849-1910. 2. Terry, Louisa (Ward), 1823-1897. 3. Mailliard, Anne Eliza (Ward) 1824-1895. 4. Ward, Samuel, 1814-1884. I. Title.

Maillol, Aristide Joseph Bonaventure, 1861-1944.

WALDEMAR-GEORGE, pseud. 730.944
Aristide Maillol. Biography by Dina Vierny. [Tr. from French by Diana Imber] Greenwich, Conn., N. Y. Graphic [1965] 235p. illus. (pt. mounted col.) 29cm. Bibl. [NB553.M3W313] 65-14124 25.00
1. Maillol, Aristide Joseph Bonaventure, 1861-1944. I. Title.

Maine—Biography.

FRANKLIN, Lynn. 920'.0741
Profiles of Maine / by Lynn Franklin. 1st ed. Waldoboro : Maine Antique Digest, c1976. 160 p. : ill. ; 28 cm. [CT238.F7] 76-19858 ISBN 0-917312-00-7 pbk. : 6.95
1. Maine—Biography. I. Title. BIP

Maine—Social life and customs.

GOULD, John, 1908- 818.5203
Last one in; tales of a New England boyhood, a gently pleasing dip into a cool soothing pool of the not-so-long-ago, so to speak, With illus by F. Wenderoth Saunders. [1st ed.] Boston, Little, Brown [1966] 248 p. illus. 20 cm. Autobiographical. [F25.G69] 66-22675
1. Maine—Social life and customs. I. Title.

MACKENZIE, Gertrude. 917.41
My love affair with the State of Maine, by Gertrude Mackenzie, with Ruth Goode. New York, Simon and Schuster [1955] 311 p. 22 cm. [CT275.M4357A3] 55-7132
1. Maine—Social life and customs. I. Goode, Ruth. II. Title. BIP

MAINSE, David. 289.9'4'0924
100 Huntley Street : the exciting success story from the host of Canada's popular television program / by David Mainse with David Manuel Plainfield, NJ : Logos International, c1979. xi, 158 p., [7] leaves of plates : ill. ; 21 cm. [BX8762.Z8M374] ISBN 0-88270-383-8 pbk. : 3.95 3.95
1. Mainse, David. 2. 100 Huntley Street (Television program) 3. Pentecostals—Clergy—Biography. 4. Clergy—Canada—Biography. I. Manuel, David, joint author. II. 100 Huntley Street (Television program)

Maintenon, Francoise d'Aubigne, marquise de, 1635-1719.

HALDANE, Charlotte (Franken) 1894-1969. 944'.033'0924 B
Madame de Maintenon; uncrowned Queen of France. Indianapolis, Bobbs-Merrill [1970] 310 p. illus., geneal. tables, ports. 23 cm. Bibliography: p. [287]-288. [DC130.M2H35 1970] 75-98285 7.50
1. Maintenon, Francoise d'Aubigne, marquise de, 1635-1719. I. Title.

Mairaux, Andre,1901-

BLEND, Charles Daniels, 1918- 848.912
Andre Malraux: tragic humanist. [Columbus, Ohio State University Press [1963] viii, 255 p. 21 cm. Based on thesis, Ohio State University. Bibliography: p. [247]-255. [PQ2625.A716Z58] 62-19865
1. Mairaux, Andre,1901- I. Title.

Maisse, Andre Hurault, sieur de, 1539-1607.

MAISSE, Andre Hurault, sieur de, 1539-1607. 942.05'5
De Maisse : a journal of all that was accomplished by Monsieur de Maisse, ambassador in England from King Henry IV to Queen Elizabeth, anno Domini 1597 / translated from the French and edited with an introd. by G. B. Harrison and R. A. Jones Folcroft, Pa. : Folcroft Library Editions, 1976. p. cm. Reprint of the 1931 ed. published by Nonesuch Press, London. [DA350.M33 1976] 76-15982 ISBN 0-8414-4822-1 lib. bdg. : 20.00
1. Maisse, Andre Hurault, sieur de, 1539-1607. 2. Great Britain—Foreign relations—1558-1603—Sources. 3. France—Foreign relations—1589-1610—Sources. 4. Great Britain—Foreign relations—France—Sources. 5. France—Foreign relations—Great Britain—Sources.

Maistre, Joseph Marie, conte de, 1753-1821.

LOMBARD, Charles M. 808 B
Joseph de Maistre / by Charles M. Lombard. Boston : Twayne, c1976. p. cm. (Twayne's world authors series ; TWAS 407 : France) Includes index. Bibliography: p. [PQ2342.M28Z69] 76-13846 ISBN 0-8057-6247-7 lib. bdg. : 8.50
1. Maistre, Joseph Marie, conte de, 1753-1821. BIP

Maitland, Frederic William, 1850-1906.

FIFOOT, Cecil Herbert Stuart, 1899- 342'.42'00924 B
Frederic William Maitland; a life [by] C. H. S. Fifoot. Cambridge, Mass., Harvard University Press, 1971. x, 313 p. port. 24 cm. (Studies in legal history) Bibliography: p. v-vi. [LAW] 73-145892 ISBN 0-674-31825-0 10.00
1. Maitland, Frederic William, 1850-1906. I. Title. II. Series. BIP

MAITLAND, Frederic William, 1850-1906 923.442
Letters. Ed. by C. H. S. Fifoot. Cambridge, Mass., Harvard [c.]1965. xxiv, 397p. facsims., port. 26cm. (Selden Soc., London, Suppl. ser., v.1) Bibl. 65-2542 12.50
I. Fifoot, Cecil Herbert Stuart, 1899- ed. (Series) II. Title.

SMITH, Arthur Lionel, 1850-1924. 342'.42'00924 B
Frederic William Maitland; two lectures and a bibliography, by A. L. Smith. New York, B. Franklin [1971] 71 p. 21 cm. (Burt Franklin research and source works series, 804. Selected essays in history, economics & social science, 290) Reprint of the 1908 ed. Bibliography: p. [59]-71. [LAW] 73-170960 ISBN 0-8337-4396-1
1. Maitland, Frederic William, 1850-1906.

Majors, Alexander, 1814-1900—Juvenile literature.

BAILEY, Ralph Edgar, 1893- 978'.02'0924
Wagons Westward! The story of Alexander Majors. Map by James MacDonald. Frontispiece by Richard Cuffari. New York, Morrow [1969] 188 p. illus., map. 22 cm. Bibliography: p. [177]-179. [F591.M24B3] 92 69-20036 4.25
1. Majors, Alexander, 1814-1900—Juvenile literature. I. Title.

Makarios III, Archbishop of Cyprus, 1913-

VANEZIS, P. N. 956.4'504'0924
Makarios : pragmatism v. idealism / P. N. Vanezis ; foreword by Lord Caradon. London : Abelard-Schuman, 1974. xix, 203 p., [2] leaves of plates : ill. ; 23 cm. Label mounted on t.p.: Transatlantic Arts, Inc., Levittown, N.Y., [DS54.9.V363] 75-305487 ISBN 0-200-72207-7 : 8.25
1. Makarios III, Archbishop of Cyprus, 1913- 2. Cyprus—Politics and government. BIP

Makarios, Saint, Metropolitan of Corinth, d. 1805.

CAVARNOS, Constantine. 281.9'092'4 B
St. Macarios of Corinth, Archbishop of Corinth ... an account of his life, character, and message, together with selections three of his publications. Belmont, Mass., Institute for Byzantine and Modern Greek Studies [1972] 118 p. port. 21 cm. (His Modern Orthodox saints, 2) Includes bibliographical references. [BX619.M26C38] 72-85116 2.75
1. Makarios, Saint, Metropolitan of Corinth, d. 1805.

Makarova, Natalia, 1940-

AUSTIN, Richard. 792.8'092'4 B
Natalia Makarova, ballerina / Richard Austin. Brooklyn : Dance Horizons, 1978. 139 p., [9] leaves of plates : ill. ; 25 cm. Includes indexes. [GV1785.M26A96] 77-94038 ISBN 0-87127-103-6 : 15.95
1. Makarova, Natalia, 1940- 2. Dancers—Russia—Biography. I. Title. BIP

MAKAROVA, Dina. 792.8'092'4
Natalia Makarova / photos. and text by Dina Makarova. [Brooklyn, N.Y. : Dance Horizons, 1975] 22 p., [1] leaf of plates : ill. ; 23 cm. (Dance Horizons spotlight series) [GV1785.M26M34] 75-9152
1. Makarova, Natalia, 1940- 2. Ballet. BIP

MAKAROVA, Natalia, 1940- 792.8'092'4 B
A dance autobiography / by Natalia Makarova ; introduced and edited by Gennady Shmakov ; photos. by Dina Makarova and others. 1st ed. New York : Knopf, 1979. p. cm. Includes index.

[GV1785.M26A35 1979] 78-20621 ISBN 0-394-50141-1 : 22.50
1. Makarova, Natalia, 1940- 2. Dances—Russia—Biography. I. Shmakov, Gennadii Grigor'evich. II. Makarova, Dina. III. Title. BIP

Makdougall-Brisbane, Thomas, Sir, bart., 1773-1860.

TEALE, Ruth. 994'.02'0924 B
Thomas Brisbane. Melbourne, New York, Oxford University Press [1971] 30 p. illus., port. 19 cm. (Great Australians) Bibliography: p. 30. [DU172.M34T4] 70-865580 ISBN 0-19-550334-1
1. Makdougall-Brisbane, Thomas, Sir, bart., 1773-1860.

Makemie, Francis,

MAKEMIE, Francis, 1658-1708. 285'.2'0924 B
The life and writings of Francis Makemie. Edited with an introd. by Boyd S. Schlenther. Philadelphia, Presbyterian Historical Society, 1971. 287 p. 24 cm. (Presbyterian Historical Society publications, 11) Includes bibliographical references. [BX9225.M34A3 1971] 76-30771 6.00
I. Schlenter, Boyd S., 1936- ed. II. Series: Presbyterian Historical Society. Publications, 11.

Makhluf, Sharbal, Father, 1828-1896.

EID, Joseph, 1896- 922.2569
The hermit of Lebanon, Father Sharbel; a first essay on the servant of God ... New York, Printed by the Paulist Press [1952] 110 p. illus. 22 cm. [BX4705.M2635E4] 52-4049
1. Makhluf, Sharbal, Father, 1828-1896. I. Title.

Makhno, Nestor Ivanovich, 1884-1934.

†PALIJ, Michael. 947'.71'08410924 B
The anarchism of Nestor Makhno, 1918-1921 : an aspect of the Ukrainian revolution / Michael Palij. Seattle : University of Washington Press, c1976. xii, 428 p. : ill., map (on lining paper) ; 24 cm. (Publications on Russia and Eastern Europe of the Institute for Comparative and Foreign Area Studies ; no. 7) Includes index. Bibliography: p. 313-416 [DK265.8.U4P23] 76-7796 ISBN 0-295-95511-2 : 14.50
1. Makhno, Nestor Ivanovich, 1884-1934. 2. Ukraine—History—Revolution, 1917-1921. I. Title. II. Series: Washington (State). University. Institute for Comparative and Foreign Area Studies. Publications on Russia and Eastern Europe ; no. 7.

Makiguchi, Tsunesaburo, 1871-1944.

BETHEL, Dayle M., 1923- 370.1'92'4 B
Makiguchi the value creator, revolutionary Japanese educator and founder of Soka Gakkai, by Dayle M. Bethel. [1st ed.] New York, Weatherhill [1973] 174 p. illus. 21 cm. Bibliography: p. 163-167. [LB775.M3414B47] 72-92097 ISBN 0-8348-0077-2 7.95
1. Makiguchi, Tsunesaburo, 1871-1944. 2. Education—Philosophy. I. Title.

Makino, Frederick Kinzaburo, 1877-1953.

COMPILATION Committee for the Publication of Kinzaburo Makino's Biography. v. 12
Life of Kinzaburo Makino Edited by the Compilation Committee for the Publication of Kinzaburo's Biography. [Honolulu, 1965] 160 p., 143 p. illus., ports. English and Japanese. 68-34839
1. Makino, Frederick Kinzaburo, 1877-1953. 2. Hawaii Hochi. 3. Hawaii—Hist.—Territory, 1900-1959. I. Title.

Maklakov, Vasilii Alekseevich, 1870-1957.

ADAMOVICH, Georgii Viktorovich 923.247
Title transliterated: Vasilii Alekseevich Maklakov. in Russian. New York, Gregory Lounz, 1959, i.e., 1960] 260p. ports. 23cm. 60-12987 3.50 pap.,
1. Maklakov, Vasilii Alekseevich, 1870-1957. I. Title.

Makowski, Tadeusz, 1882-1932.

JAWORSKA, Wladyslawa. 759.71
Tadeusz Makowski : e. poln. Maler in Paris / Wladyslawa Jaworska ; [Ubers. d. poln. Ms. von Anna Jankowska]. Dresden : Verlag der Kunst, 1975. 276 p. : ill. (some col.) ; 28 cm. Includes indexes. Bibliography: p. [274] [ND955.P63M3124] 75-522494 54.00M
1. Makowski, Tadeusz, 1882-1932.

Malachy O'Morgair, Saint, 1094?-1148.

SCOTT, A. Brian. 282'.092'4 B
Malachy / A. Brian Scott. Dublin : Veritas Publications, 1976. 119 p. ; 19 cm. Bibliography: p. 118-119. [BX4700.M23S28] 77-463451 ISBN 0-905092-10-4 : £1.00
1. Malachy O'Morgair, Saint, 1094?-1148. 2. Bernard de Clairvaux, Saint, 1091?-1153. Vita Sancti Malachiae. 3. Christian saints—Ireland—Biography.

SCOTT, A. Brian. 282'.092'4 B
Malachy / A. Brian Scott. Dublin : Veritas Publications, 1976. 119 p. ; 19 cm. Bibliography: p. 118-119. [BX4700.M23S28] 77 463451 ISBN 0 905092-10-4 : £1.00
1. Malachy O'Morgair, Saint, 1094?-1148. 2. Bernard de Clairvaux, Saint, 1091?-1153. Vita Sancti Malachiae. 3. Christian saints—Ireland—Biography.

Malaysia—Biog.

WHO'S who in Malaysia (The), 1965. Ed., pub. by J. Victor Morais [New York, Intl. Pubns. Serv., 1966] lxxiv, 489p. ports. 27cm. (KDN 1334) (KDN 1334) Title varies. 59-54082 15.00 920.0595
1. Malaysia—Biog. I. Morais, John Victor, 1910- ed.

WHO'S who in Malaysia (The) 1963 [4th ed.] Ed. by J. Victor Morais, Kuala Lumpar, J. Victor Morais [dist. S. Pasadena, Calif., Hutchins, 1963] 342p. ports. 27cm. Title varies: 1956-1960. The leaders of Malaya and who's who. 59-54082 10.00 920.0595
1. Malaysia—Biog. I. Morais, John Victor, 1910- ed.

WHO'S Who in Malaysia (The) 1967 Kuala Lumpur. v. ports. 27cm. Ed.: 1956- J. V. Morais. Title varies: 1956-1959/60, The Leaders of Malaya and who's who. [DS595.5.L4] 59-54082 15.00 920.0595
1. Malaysia—Biog. I. Morais, John Victor, 1910- ed.
Distributed by Intl. Pubns. Serv., New York. BIP

Malbone, Edward Greene, 1777-1807.

TOLMAN, Ruel Pardee, 1878- [759.13] 927.5
The life and works of Edward Greene Malbone, 1777-1807. With an introd. by Theodore Bolton, and a foreword by John Davis Hatch, Jr. New York, New-York Historical Society, 1958. xxiii, 322 p. illus., col. ports., facsims. 25 cm. (The John Divine Jones Fund series of histories and memoirs, 13) Bibliography: p. 280-288. [ND1337.U6M32] 58-2879
1. Malbone, Edward Greene, 1777-1807. 2. U.S. — Biog. — Portraits. I. Title. II. Series: New York Historical Society. The John Divine Jones Fund series of histories and memoirs, 13 BIP

Malenkov, Georgil Maksimilianovich, 1901-

FRAZIER, Robert, 1915- 923.247
Malenkov. New York, Lion Books [1953] 150p. 17cm. (A Lion book, 145) [DK268.M33F7] 54-157386
1. Malenkov, Georgil Maksimilianovich, 1901- I. Title.

Malibran, Maria Felicita, 1808-1836.

BUSHNELL, Howard. 782.1'092'4 B
Maria Malibran : a biography of the singer / Howard Bushnell. University Park : Pennsylvania State University Press, 1979. p. cm. Includes index. Bibliography: p. [ML420.M2B87] 79-14880 ISBN 0-271-00222-0 : 17.95
1. Malibran, Maria Felicita, 1808-1836. 2. Singers—Biography. BIP

Malinki, Morrison.

EDWARDS, Josephine Cunnington. 266'.673
Malinki of Malawi / Josephine Cunnington Edwards. Mountain View, Calif. : Pacific Press Pub. Association, c1978. 128 p. ; 22 cm. (A Destiny book ; D-168) [BV3625.N82M343] 78-55903 pbk. : 3.50
1. Malinki, Morrison. 2. Missionaries—Malawi—Biography. I. Title. BIP

Mall, E. Jane, 1920-

MALL, E. Jane, 1920- 248'.843'0924 B
How am I doing, God? By E. Jane Mall. St. Louis, Concordia Pub. House [1973] 160 p. 18 cm. Autobiographical. [BX8080.M22A33 1973] 72-97343 ISBN 0 570 03150 8 pap. 1.75
1. Mall, E. Jane, 1920- I. Title. BIP

Mallarme, Stephane, 1842-1898.

MICHAUD, Guy. 928.4
Mallarme. Translated by Marie Collins and Bertha Humez. [New York] New York University Press, 1965. viii, 180 p. 22 cm. "Bibliographical note": p. 169-172. [PQ2344.Z5M483] 65-10766
1. Mallarme, Stephane, 1842-1898. I. Title. BIP

Mallea, Eduardo, 1903-

LEWALD, Herald Ernest. 863 B
Eduardo Mallea / by H. Ernest Lewald. Boston : Twayne Publishers, c1977. 118 p. : ill. ; 21 cm. (Twayne's world authors series ; TWAS 433 : Argentina) Includes index. Bibliography: p. 113-115. [PQ7797.M225Z73] 76-44804 ISBN 0-8057-6273-6 lib.bdg. : 9.50
1. Mallea, Eduardo, 1903- 2. Authors, Argentine—20th century—Biography.

Mallea, Eduardo, 1903- —Criticism and interpretation.

PINTOR Genaro, Mercedes. 863 B
Eduardo Mallea, novelista / Mercedes Pintor Genaro. 1. ed. [Rio Piedras] : Editorial Universitaria, Universidad de Puerto Rico, 1976. p. cm. (Coleccion Mente y palabra) Originally presented as the author's thesis, Madrid, 1964. Bibliography: [PQ7797.M225Z77 1976] 76-6545 ISBN 0-8477-0524-2 : 5.00. ISBN 0-8477-0525-0 pbk. : 4.00
1. Mallea, Eduardo, 1903- —Criticism and interpretation. I. Title. BIP

Mallet du Pan, Jacques, 1749-1800.

ACOMB, Frances Dorothy, 1907- 070'.92'4 B
Mallet du Pan (1749-1800); a career in political journalism [by] Frances Acomb. Durham, N.C., Duke University Press, 1973. xii, 304 p. 25 cm. Bibliography: p. [283]-291. [DC146.M25A64] 72-96985 ISBN 0-8223-0295-0
1. Mallet du Pan, Jacques, 1749-1800.

Mallet-Joris, Francoise,

MALLET-JORIS, Francoise, 1930- 843'.9'14 B
The paper house; translated [from the French] by Derek Coltman. London, New York, W. H. Allen, 1971. [5], 250 p. 22 cm. Translation of La maison de papier. [PQ2625.A7124Z523 1971b] 72-179708 £2.50
I. Title. BIP

Mallinckrodt, Pauline von, 1817-1881.

BURTON, Katherine (Kurz) 1890- 922.243
Whom love impels; the life of Pauline von Mallinckrodt, foundress of the Congregation of the Sisters of Christian Charity. New York, P. J. Kenedy [1952] 234p. illus. 21cm. [BX4705.M27B85] 53-5827
1. Mallinckrodt, Pauline von, 1817-1881. I. Title.

ERNEST, Brother, 1897- 922.243
A happy heart; a story of Mother Pauline von Mallinckrodt. Illus. by Hilarion Brezik. Notre Dame, Ind., Dujarie Press [1956] 96p. illus. 24cm. [BX4705.M27E7] 56-59253
1. Mallinckrodt, Pauline von, 1817-1881. I. Title.

Mallory, Kathleen Moore, 1879-1954.

USSERY, Annie (Wright) 922.673
The story of Kathleen Mallory. Nashville, Broadman Press [c1956] 199p. illus. 22cm. [BX6495.M29U8] 57 6324
1. Mallory, Kathleen Moore, 1879-1954. 2. Southern Baptist Convewtion. Woman's Missionary Union. I. Title.

USSERY, Annie (Wright) 922.673
The story of Kathleen Mallory. Nashville, Broadman Press [c1956] 199 p. illus. 22 cm. [BX6495.M29U8] 57-6324
1. Mallory, Kathleen Moore, 1879-1964. 2. Southern Baptist Convention, Woman's Missionary Union. I. Title.

Mallory, Stephen Russell, 1813-1873.

DURKIN, Joseph Thomas, 1903- 923.273
Stephen R. Mallory: Confederate Navy chief. Chapel Hill, University of North Carolina Press, 1954. xi, 446 p. 25 cm. "Critical bibliography": p. 417-434. [E596.M3D8] 54-12567
1. Mallory, Stephen Russell, 1813-1873. I. Title.

PENSACOLA Home & Savings Association. 973.71'3'0924 B
Stephen R. Mallory, Secretary of the Navy, Confederate States of America. [Pensacola, Fla., 1969] [24] p. illus., ports. 23 cm. Cover title. [E596.M3P4] 70-28062
1. Mallory, Stephen Russell, 1813-1873.

Mallowan, Max Edgar Lucien.

MALLOWAN, Max Edgar Lucien. 930'.1'0924 B
Mallowan's memoirs / by Max Mallowan. New York : Dodd, Mead, [1977] p. cm. [CC115.M27A35] 77-3658 ISBN 0-396-07467-7 : 10.95 10.95
1. Mallowan, Max Edgar Lucien. 2. Christie, Agatha Miller, 1891-1976—Biography—Marriage. 3. Archaeologists—England—Biography. 4. Novelists, English—20th century—Biography. I. Title. BIP

Malory, Thomas, Sir, 15th century.

HICKS, Edward, 1878- 813.2
Sir Thomas Malory, his turbulent career; a biography. New York, Octagon Books, 1970 [c1928] ix, 118 p. illus., facsim., port. 23 cm. Includes bibliographical references. [PR2045.H5 1970] 78-120630
1. Malory, Thomas, Sir, 15th century.

Malory, Thomas, Sir, 15th cent.—Juvenile literature.

HODGES, Margaret. 823'.2 B
Knight prisoner : the tale of Sir Thomas Malory and his King Arthur / Margaret Hodges ; decorations by Don Bolognese and Elaine Raphael. New York : Farrar, Straus and Giroux, c1976. xi, 195 p. : ill. ; 21 cm. Includes index. Bibliography: p. 185-189. A biography of the 15th century knight who collected stories about King Arthur and his knights and rewrote them into a work that was to influence poets and writers throughout the ages. [PR2045.H6] 92 76-26693 ISBN 0-374-34269-5 : 6.95
1. Malory, Thomas, Sir, 15th cent.—Juvenile literature. 2. Authors, English—Middle English, 1100-1500—Biography—Juvenile literature. I. Bolognese, Don. II. Raphael, Elaine. III. Title. BIP

Malraux, Andre, 1901-1976.

GALANTE, Pierre. 914.4'03'810924 B
Malraux. Translated by Haakon Chevalier. [1st ed.] New York, Cowles Book Co. [1971] xv, 271 p. illus., map, ports. 24 cm. Bibliography: p. 260-262. [PQ2625.A716Z665] 79-102821 ISBN 0-402-12441-3 8.95
1. Malraux, Andre, 1901-

HEWITT, James Robert. 843'.9'12 B
Andre Malraux / James Robert Hewitt. New York : F. Ungar Pub. Co., [1978] p. cm. (Modern literature monographs) Includes index. Bibliography: p. [PQ2625.A716Z6813] 70-15661 ISBN 0-8044-2379-2 : 8.00
1. Malraux, Andre, 1901-1976. 2. Authors, French—20th century—Biography. BIP

MALRAUX : 843.9'12 B
life and work / edited by Martine de Courcel. London : Weidenfeld and Nicolson, 1976. x, 284 p., [16] p. of plates : ill., facsims., ports. ; 24 cm. Includes index. Bibliography: p. [275]-278. [PQ2625.A716Z6994] 76-381331 ISBN 0-297-77177-9 : £6.95
1. Malraux, Andre, 1901- —Addresses, essays, lectures. 2. Novelists, French—20th century—Biography—Addresses, essays, lectures. I. Courcel, Martine de.

PAYNE, Pierre Stephen Robert, 1911- 914.4'03'810924 B
A portrait of Andre Malraux [by] Robert Payne. Englewood Cliffs, N.J., Prentice-Hall [1970] viii, 481 p. illus., facsims., ports. 24 cm. Bibliography: p. 441-446. [PQ2625.A716Z79] 72-118697 10.00
1. Malraux, Andre, 1901- I. Title.

Malraux, Andre, 1901-1976—Biography.

LACOUTURE, Jean. 843'.9'12
Andre Malraux / Jean Lacouture ; translated from the French by Alan Sheridan. 1st American ed. New York : Pantheon Books, c1975. 510 p., [4] leaves of plates : ill. ; 25 cm. Includes bibliographical references and index. [PQ2625.A716Z686813 1975] 75-10361 ISBN 0-394-48367-7 : 12.95
1. Malraux, Andre, 1901- —Biography. BIP

MADSEN, Axel. 843'.9'12 B
Malraux : a biography / by Axel Madsen. New York : Morrow, 1976. p. cm. Includes index. "Books by Andre Malraux.": p. [PQ2625.A716Z698] 76-7558 ISBN 0-688-03075-0 : 11.95
1. Malraux, Andre, 1901- —Biography.

MALRAUX, Andre, 1901-1976. 843'.9'12 B
Lazarus / Andre Malraux ; translated by Terence Kilmartin. New York : Holt, Rinehart and Winston, 1977. 149 p. ; 22 cm. (His The mirror of limbo) (Series: Malraux, Andre, 1901-1976. Le miroir des limbes. English.) Translation of Lazare. [PQ2625.A716Z51713] 76-58426 ISBN 0-03-015351-4 : 7.95
1. Malraux, Andre, 1901-1976—Biography. 2. Authors, French—20th century—Biography. I. Title. II. Series.

MALRAUX, Andre, 1901-1976. 843'.9'12 B
Lazarus / Andre Malraux ; translated from the French by Terence Kilmartin. 1st ed. New York : Grove Press, 1978, c1977. 149 p. ; 20 cm. (His The mirror of limbo) (Series: Malraux, Andre, 1901-1976. Le miroir des limbes. English.) Translation of Lazare. [PQ2625.A716Z51713 1978] 78-8377 ISBN 0-394-17068-7 pbk. : 2.95
1. Malraux, Andre, 1901-1976—Biography. 2. Authors, French—20th century—Biography. I. Title. II. Series. BIP

Malraux, Andre, 1901- —Interviews.

SUARES, Guy. 843'.9'12 B
Malraux, past, present, future : conversations with Guy Suares / translated from the French by Derek Coltman. 1st American ed. Boston : Little, Brown, [1974] 196 p. : ill. ; 32 cm. Translation of Malraux, celui qui vient. "Andre Malraux/bibliography": p. 193-194. [PQ2625.A716Z9413] 74-6557 15.00
1. Malraux, Andre, 1901- —Interviews. 2. Bergamin, Jose, 1895- I. Malraux, Andre, 1901- II. Title.

Malthus, Thomas Robert, 1766-1834.

BONAR, James, 1852-1941 301.320924
Malthus and his work, by James Bonar. New York, Kelley, 1966. vi, p., 21., 438p. front. (port.) 23cm. In this reprint the biog has been expanded, notes added and some mistakes corrected. Otherwise the book remains as it was in 1885. cf. Introd. [HB863.B7 1924] 12.50
1. Malthus, Thomas Robert, 1766-1834. 2. Malthusianism. I. Title.

JAMES, Patricia D. 304.6'092'4 B
Population Malthus, his life and times / Patricia James. London ; Boston : Routledge & Kegan Paul, 1979. xv, 524 p., [4] leaves of plates : ill. ; 24 cm. Includes bibliographical references and index. [HB863.M23J35 1979] 79-40584 ISBN 0-7100-0266-1 : 43.50
1. Malthus, Thomas Robert, 1766-1834. 2. Demographers—Great Britain—Biography. 3. Economists—Great Britain—Biography. I. Title.

PETERSEN, William. 301.32'092'4 B
Malthus / William Petersen. Cambridge, Mass. : Harvard University Press, 1979. p. cm. Includes index. Bibliography: p. [HB863.P47] 78-31479 ISBN 0-674-54425-0 : 17.50
1. Malthus, Thomas Robert, 1766-1834. 2. Demographers—Great Britain—Biography. 3. Economists—Great Britain—Biography. BIP

Malvern, Godfrey Martin Huggins, 1st viscount, 1883-

GANN, Lewis H., 1924- 923.2689
Huggins of Rhodesia; the man and his country, by L. H. Gann, M. Gelfand. London, Allen & Unwin [dist. New Rochelle, N.Y., SportShelf, 1965, c.1964] 285p. illus., ports. 23cm. Bibl. [DT960.M3G3] 65-2537 11.00
1. Malvern, Godfrey Martin Huggins, 1st viscount, 1883- 2. Rhodesia—Hist. I. Gelfand, Michael, joint author. II. Title.

Malz, Betty.

MALZ, Betty. 248'.2'0924 B
My glimpse of eternity / Betty Malz. Waco, Tex. : Chosen Books : distributed by Word Books, c1977. 125 p. ; 23 cm. [BR1725.M3166A33] 77-22671 5.95
1. Malz, Betty. 2. Christian biography—United States. 3. Future life. 4. Death, Apparent. I. Title. BIP

Mamoulian, Rouben.

MILNE, Tom. 791.43'0233'0924
Rouben Mamoulian. Bloomington, Indiana University Press [1970, c1969] 176 p. illus., ports. 20 cm. (Cinema one, 13) [PN1998.A3M319 1970] 75-97237 5.95
1. Mamoulian, Rouben.

Manasseh ben Joseph ben Israel, 1604-1657.

ROTH, Cecil, 1899-1970. 296.6'1 B
A life of Menasseh ben Israel, rabbi, printer, and diplomat / by Cecil Roth. New York : Arno Press, 1975 [c1934] xii, 373 p., [9] leaves of plates : ill. ; 21 cm. (The Modern Jewish experience) Reprint of the ed. published by the Jewish Publication Society of America, Philadelphia. Includes index. Bibliography: p. 291-307. [BM755.M25R6 1975] 74-29518 ISBN 0-405-06743-7 : 24.00
1. Manasseh ben Joseph ben Israel, 1604-1657. 2. Jews in Amsterdam. 3. Jews in Great Britain. I. Title. II. Series.

Manby, Arthur Rochford, 1859?-1929?

WATERS, Frank, 1902- 978.9'53'04'0924 B
To possess the land; a biography of Arthur Rochford Manby. [1st ed.] Chicago, Sage Books [1974, c1973] viii, 287 p. illus. 24 cm. Bibliography: p. 275-278. [F802.T2W37 1974] 73-13210 ISBN 0-8040-0647-4 8.95
1. Manby, Arthur Rochford, 1859?-1929? 2. Taos Co., N.M.—History. 3. Land grants—New Mexico—Taos Co. I. Title. BIP

Mancham, James R., 1939-

LEE, Christopher. 969'.6 B
Seychelles : political castaways / [by] Christopher Lee. London : Elm Tree Books, 1976. [5], 169 p., [8] p. of plates : ill. (some col.), ports. ; 23 cm. Includes index. [DT469.S4L43 1976] 76-378321 ISBN 0-241-89440-9 : £4.50
1. Mancham, James R., 1939- 2. Seychelles. 3. Prime ministers—Seychelles—Biography. I. Title.

Mandel, Georges, 1885-1944.

SHERWOOD, John M. 944.081'0924
Georges Mandel and the Third Republic [by] John M. Sherwood. Stanford, Calif., Stanford University Press, 1970. ix, 393 p. illus., ports. 24 cm. Bibliography: p. [365]-375. [DC373.M23S53] 74-97916 12.95
1. Mandel, Georges, 1885-1944.

Mandel, Ursula Greenshaw, M.D.,

MANDEL, Ursula Greenshaw, M.D., 1898- 610.924
I live my life; the autobiography of Ursula Greenshaw Mandel. New York, Exposition [c.1965] 647p. illus., facsims., ports. 21cm. [R154.M2925A3] 65-8545 7.50
I. Title.

Mandel'shtam, Osip Emil'evich, 1891-1938—Journeys—Armenia.

MANDEL'SHTAM, Osip Emil'evich, 1891-1938. 915.66'2'042
Journey to Armenia / Osip Mandelstam ; translated by Sidney Monas. Mandelstam and the Journey / Henry Gifford. San Francisco : G. F. Ritchie, 1979. 77 p. ; 25 cm. Journey to Armenia, originally published in Osip Mandelstam, selected essays. [PG3476.M355Z46513 1979] 78-68632 32.00
1. Mandel'shtam, Osip Emil'evich, 1891-1938—Journeys—Armenia. 2. Mandel'shtam, Osip Emil'evich, 1891-1938—Biography. 3. Armenia—Description and travel. 4. Poets, Russian—20th century—Biography. I. Gifford, Henry. Mandelstam and the Journey. 1979. II. Title.
Publishers' address: 665 Time st., 503 Sanfrancisco CA 94108 BIP

Manderson, Rita,

MANDERSON, Rita, 1916- 248.2'4
The awakening. [Baltimore, Printed by Reese Press, 1968] 213 p. ports. 22 cm. [BV4935.M28A3] 68-6922
I. Title.

Manely, Frank H.

MANLEY, Frank H. 636.089'092'4 B
A veterinary odyssey / Frank H. Manley. 1st ed. Hicksville, N.Y. : Exposition Press, c1978. 143 p., [8] leaves of plates : ill. ; 22 cm. [SF613.M34A34] 78-108497 ISBN 0-682-49115-2 : 7.50
1. Manely, Frank H. 2. Veterinarians—Biography. I. Title. BIP

Manessier, Alfred, 1911-

HODIN, Josef Paul. 759.4
Manessier, by J. P. Hodin. New York, Praeger [1972] 243 p. illus. (part col.) 32 cm. Bibliography: p. 242-243. [ND553.M29H6 1972b] 71-172994 35.00
1. Manessier, Alfred, 1911-

Manet, Edouard, 1832-1883.

BATAILLE, Georges, 1897- 927.5
Manet; [biographical and critical study. Translated by Austryn Wainhouse and James Emmons. New York] Skira [1955?] 135 p. 53 mounted col. illus. 19 cm. (The Taste of our time, v. 14) Bibliography: p. 125-[127] [ND553.M3B275] 759.4 55-10593
1. Manet, Edouard, 1832-1883.

ORIENTI, Sandra. 759.4
Manet. [1st American ed. Translated from the Italian by Caroline Beamish] New York, Grosset & Dunlap [1967] 39, [80] p. col. illus. 18 cm. (The New Grosset ar library, 12) On cover: Manet; the life and work of the artist. Bibliography: p. 35-36. [ND553.M3O713 1967] 68-12746
1. Manet, Edouard, 1832-1883.

PERRUCHOT, Henri, 1917- 927.5
Manet. Tr. [from French] by Humphrey Hare. Ed. by Jean Ellsmoor. Cleveland, World [1963, c.1962] 296p. illus. 23cm. (His Art and destiny, v.3) Bibl. 63-8776 6.50
1. Manet, Edouard, 1832-1883. I. Title.

REFF, Theodore. 759.4
Manet, Olympia / Theodore Reff. New York : Viking Press, 1977, c1976. 132 p. : ill. ; 23 cm. Includes index. [ND553.M3R23] 75-42149 ISBN 0-670-45408-7 : 14.95
1. Manet, Edouard, 1832-1883. Olympia. I. Title. BIP

REY, Robert, 1888- 759.4
Manet. [Tr. from French by Edward Lucie Smith] New York, Crown [1962] 94, [2]p. illus. (pt. col.) 29cm. Bibl. 62-51030 3.50
1. Manet, Edouard, 1832-1883. I. Title.

Manfred, Frederick Feikema, 1912- —Interviews.

MANFRED, Frederick Feikema, 1912- 813'.5'4 B
Conversations with Frederick Manfred. Moderated by John R. Milton. With a foreword by Wallace Stegner. Drawings by Arnold John Dyson. Salt Lake City, University of Utah Press [1974] xviii, 169 p. illus. 23 cm. An interview taped for KVSD-TV. Portions were previously published in South Dakota review. Bibliography: p. [vi] [PS3525.A52233C6] 73-93300 ISBN 0-87480-091-9 6.50

1. Manfred, Frederick Feikema, 1912- — Interviews. I. Milton, John R. II. Title. BIP

Manfred, Frederick Feikema, 1912- — Journeys—The West.

MANFRED, Frederick Feikema, 1912- 813'.5'4 B
The wind blows free : a reminiscence / by Frederick Manfred ; [ill. by Elsie Thorson]. 1st ed. Sioux Falls, S.D. : Center for Western Studies, Augustana College, 1979. vi, 255 p., [2] leaves of plates : ill. ; 22 cm. [PS3525.A52233Z478] 79-53217 ISBN 0-931170-09-5 : 9.95
1. Manfred, Frederick Feikema, 1912- — Journeys—The West. 2. The West—Description and travel—1880-1950. 3. Authors, American—20th century—Biography. I. Title.

Mangan, James Clarence, 1803-1849.

MANGAN, James Clarence, 1803-1849. 821 B
Autobiography; edited from the manuscript by James Kilroy. Dublin, Dolmen P., 1968. 36 p. 21 cm. (The New Dolmen chapbooks, 9) Bibliographical footnotes. [PR4973.Z5A3 1968] 76-427694 10/6
I. Kilroy, James, ed.

O'DONOGHUE, David James, 1866-1917. 821'.8
The life and writings of James Clarence Mangan. Edinburgh, P. Geddes & Colleagues; Chicago, P. V. Fitzpatrick, 1897. [New York, Johnson Reprint Corp., 1972] xxiv, 250 p. illus. 21 cm. (Belles lettres in English) [PR4973.Z5O4 1972] 78-38696
*1. Mangan, James Clarence, 1803-1849.*BIP

Mangas Coloradas, Apache chief, d. 1863?

COOKE, David Coxe, 1917- 970.3 B
Apache warrior. [1st ed.] New York, Norton [1963] 212 p. illus. 21 cm. Includes bibliography. A biography of one of the great leaders of the Apache Nation, whose vengeance on Mexicans and whites sprang from their responsibility for the massacre of his tribe at Santa Rita Fort in New Mexico territory. [E99.A6C6] 92 AC 68
1. Mangas Coloradas, Apache chief, d. 1863? 2. Apache Indians. I. Title.

Mangione, Jerre Gerlando, 1909- — Biography.

MANGIONE, Jerre Gerlando, 1909- 813'.5'2 B
An ethnic at large a memoir of America in the thirties and forties / by Jerre Mangione. New York : Putnam, c1978. 378 p., [8] leaves of plates : ill. ; 23 cm. Includes index. [PS3563.A47A47] 77-27447 ISBN 0-399-11774-1 : 10.95
1. Mangione, Jerre Gerlando, 1909- — Biography. 2. Authors, American—20th century—Biography. I. Title. BIP

Manguin, Henri, 1874-1949.

ARIZONA. University. Museum of Art. 759.4 B
Manguin in America : Henri Manguin, 1874-1949 : [catalogue of the exhibition]. Tucson : University of Arizona Museum of Art, 1974. 214 p. : ill. (some col.) ; 32 cm. English and French. Bibliography: p. 209-212. [ND553.M312A89 1974] 74-620113
1. Manguin, Henri, 1874-1949. I. Manguin, Henri, 1874-1949. II. Title.

Mangum, Willie Person,

MANGUM, Willie Person, 1792-1861. 923.273
Papers; edited by Henry Thomas Shanks. Raleigh, State Dept. of Archives and History, 1950- v. illus., ports., fold. maps. 24 cm. (Publications of the State Dept. of Archives and History) "Willie Person Mangum, a biographical sketch": v. 1, p. xv-xiiii. Contents.CONTENTS v. 1. 1807 1832. [E340.M3A33] 51-62481
I. Title. II. Series: North Carolina. State Dept. of Archives and History. Publications

Manifold family

MANIFOLD, Jesse Benjamin, 1881- 920
My first seventy-five years; memoirs of a very common man. [Ann Arbor? 1957] 73p. illus. 28cm. [CT275.M4556A3] 57-37146
1. Manifold family I. Title.

Manilow, Barry.

BEGO, Mark. 784'.092'4 B
Barry Manilow : an unauthorized biography / by Mark Bego. New York : Grosset & Dunlap, c1977. 139 p., [5] leaves of plates : ill. ; 18 cm. Discography: p. 131-139. [ML410.M283B4] 78-110484 ISBN 0-448-14550-2 : 1.25
1. Manilow, Barry. 2. Rock musicians—United States—Biography.

BEGO, Mark. 784'.092'4 B
Barry Manilow / by Mark Bego ; edited by Barbara Williams Prabhu. New York : Grosset & Dunlap, c1979. 88 p. : ill. ; 21 cm. (Tempo books) Abridged. [ML410.M283B4 1979] 79-320729 ISBN 0-448-17035-3 (pbk.) : 1.95
1. Manilow, Barry. 2. Rock musicians—United States—Biography. I. Prabhu, Barbara Williams. II. Title. BIP

Manilow, Barry—Juvenile literature.

MORSE, Ann 784'.092'4 B
Barry Manilow / by Ann Morse ; designed by Mark Landkamer. Mankato, Minn. : Creative Education, c1978. 31 p. : ill. ; 25 cm. (Rock 'n pop stars) A brief biography emphasizing the career of the popular musician and singer. [ML3930.M3M7] 92 77-24653 ISBN 0-87191-617-7 : 4.95
1. Manilow, Barry—Juvenile literature. 2. Rock musicians—United States—Biography—Juvenile literature. I. Title. BIP

Mankiewicz, Herman Jacob, 1897-1953.

MERYMAN, Richard, 1926- 812'.5'2
Mank : the wit, world, and life of Herman Mankiewicz / by Richard Meryman. 1st ed. New York : Morrow, 1978. 351 p. : ill. ; 22 cm. Includes index. Bibliography: p. [339]-341. [PN1998.A3M31955] 78-8276 ISBN 0-688-03356-3 : 10.95
1. Mankiewicz, Herman Jacob, 1897-1953. 2. Screen writers—United States—Biography. I. Title. BIP

Mankiewicz, Joseph L.

GEIST, Kenneth L. 791.43'023'0924 B
Pictures will talk : the life and films of Joseph L. Mankiewicz / by Kenneth L. Geist. New York : Scribner, c1978. xiii, 443 p. : ill. ; 24 cm. "The films of Joseph L. Mankiewicz": p. [401]-429. Includes bibliographical references and index. [PN1998.A3M3198] 78-1104 ISBN 0-684-15500-1 : 12.50
1. Mankiewicz, Joseph L. 2. Moving-picture producers and directors—United States—Biography. I. Title. BIP

Mankles, Giannes.

HIONIDES, Harry. 889'.3'32 B
Yannis Manglis / Harry T. Hionides. Boston : Twayne Publishers, [1975] 162 p. : port. ; 21 cm. (Twayne's world authors series ; TWAS 350 : Greece) Includes index. Bibliography: p. 159-160. [PA5610.M26Z7] 74-31099 ISBN 0-8057-2578-4 lib.bdg. : 7.50
1. Mankles, Giannes. BIP

Manley, Seon.

MANLEY, Seon. 814'.5'4
My heart's in the heather. New York, Funk & Wagnalls [1968] 188 p. 21 cm. Autobiographical. [PS3563.A53Z5] 68-15422
I. Title.

Mann, Ambrose Dudley.

MANN, Ambrose Dudley. 923.273
'My ever dearest friend,' the letters of A. Dudley Mann to Jefferson Davis, 1869-1889. Edited with an introd. by John Preston Moore. [Limited ed.] Tuscaloosa, Ala., Confederate Pub. Co., 1960. 114p. 22cm. (Confederate centennial studies, no. 14) 'Only four hundred and fifty copies of this book have been printed.' Bibliography: p. [103]-107. [E664.M27A43] 60-4725
I. Davis, Jefferson, 1808-1889. II. Title. III. Series.

Mann, Dick,

MANN, Dick, 1934- 796.6
Motorcycle ace; the Dick Mann story [by] Dick Mann with Joe Scalzo. Chicago, Regnery [1972] 198 p. illus. 22 cm. [GV1060.2.M27A35] 72-80930 5.95
I. Scalzo, Joe, joint author. II. Title.

Mann, Horace, 1796-1859.

DOWNS, Robert Bingham, 1903- 370'.92'4 B
Horace Mann: champion of public schools [by] Robert B. Downs. New York, Twayne Publishers [1974] 163 p. port. 21 cm. (Twayne's great educators series, 2) Bibliography: p. 159. [LB695.M35D68] 73-14831 ISBN 0-8057-3544-5 5.95
1. Mann, Horace, 1796-1859. 2. Education—Massachusetts—History. I. Title.

MANN, Mary Tyler (Peabody) 1806-1887. 370'.924 B
Life of Horace Mann. New ed. Boston, W. Small, 1888. Miami, Fla., Mnemosyne Pub. Co. [1969] xi, 9-609 p. port. 23 cm. [LB695.M35M3 1969] 73-89396
1. Mann, Horace, 1796-1859. BIP

MESSERLI, Jonathan, 1926- 370'.92'4 B
Horace Mann; a biography. [1st ed.] New York, Knopf, 1972 [c1971] xviii, 604, xxxvii p. illus. 25 cm. Bibliography: p. [591]-595. [LB695.M35M4] 78-154905 ISBN 0-394-42920-6 15.00
1. Mann, Horace, 1796-1859.

THARP, Louise (Hall) 1898- 923.773
Until victory: Horace Mann and Mary Peabody. [1st ed.] Boston, Little, Brown [1953] xii, 367p. illus., ports. 23cm. Bibliographical references included in 'Chapter notes' (p. [321]-345) [LB695.M35T5] 53-7321
1. Mann, Horace, 1796-1859. 2. Mann, Mary Tyler (Peabody) 1806-1887. I. Title.

THARP, Louise Hall, 1898- 370'.92'2 B
Until victory : Horace Mann and Mary Peabody / Louise Hall Tharp. Westport, Conn. : Greenwood Press, 1977. p. cm. Reprint of the 1953 ed. published by Little, Brown of Boston. Includes bibliographical references and index. [LB695.M35T5 1977] 77-6360 ISBN 0-8371-9653-1 lib.bdg. : 23.00
1. Mann, Horace, 1796-1859. 2. Mann, Mary Tyler Peabody, 1806-1887. 3. Educators—United States—Biography. I. Title. BIP

Mann, Horace, 1796-1859—Bibliography.

KING, Clyde S. 016.370924
Horace Mann, 1796-1859; a bibliography, by Clyde S. King. Dobbs Ferry, N.Y., Oceana Publications, 1966. 453 p. 22 cm. [Z8547.4.K5] 66-11926
1. Mann, Horace, 1796-1859—Bibliography.

Mann, Horace, 1796-1859—Juvenile literature.

PIERCE, Edith Gray. 370'.924 B
Horace Mann: our Nation's first educator. Minneapolis, Lerner Publications Co. [1972] 55 p. illus. 23 cm. (The Real life books) A biography of the nineteenth-century lawyer who dedicated himself to reforming education in the United States. [LB695.M35P57] 92 78-128805 ISBN 0-8225-0703-X
1. Mann, Horace, 1796-1859—Juvenile literature. I. Title.

TREICHLER, Jessie 923.773
Horace Mann; educating for democracy. Illus. by Robert Boehmer. Chicago, Ency. Britannica [1963, c.1962] 192p. col. illus. 22cm. (Britannica bkshelf; great lives for young Amer.) 62-10426 2.36 lib. ed.,
1. Mann, Horace, 1796-1859—Juvenile literature. I. Title.

Mann, Klaus, 1906-1949.

HOFFER, Peter T., 1942- 833'.9'12
Klaus Mann / by Peter T. Hoffer. Boston : Twayne Publishers, c1976. 149 p. : port. ; 21 cm. (Twayne's world authors series ; TWAS 435 : Germany) Includes index. Bibliography: p. 143-146. [PT2625.A435Z7] 77-22472 ISBN 0-8057-6309-0 : 9.50
1. Mann, Klaus, 1906-1949. 2. Authors, German—20th century—Biography. BIP

Mann, Myrtle,

MANN, Myrtle, ed. 920.7
Eliza one, Eliza two; a family correspondence, 1849-1959, collected and with commentaries by Myrtle Mann. New York, Carlton Press, 1961. 147p. illus. 21cm. (A Reflection book) [CT275.P883M3] 61-4152
I. Puroue, Eliza, 1800-1878. II. Mann, Eliza (Barker) 1864-1958. III. Title.

Mann, Thomas, 1875-1955.

BAUER, Arnold. 833'.9'12
Thomas Mann. Translated by Alexander and Elizabeth Henderson. New York, Ungar [1971] v, 117 p. 20 cm. (Modern literature monographs) Bibliography: p. 105-109. [PT2625.A44Z54183] 71-139221 ISBN 0-8044-2023-8
1. Mann, Thomas, 1875-1955.

BURGIN, Hans. 833'.9'12 B
Thomas Mann, a chronicle of his life [by] Hans Burgin and Hans-Otto Mayer. English translation by Eugene Dobson. University, University of Alabama Press [1969] xi, 290 p. facsims., ports. 23 cm. Includes bibliographical references. [PT2625.A44Z54373] 68-10989 12.50
1. Mann, Thomas, 1875-1955. I. Mayer, Hans Otto, 1903- joint author.

CLEUGH, James. 838'.9'1209
Thomas Mann; a study. New York, Russell & Russell [1968] 208 p. port. 20 cm.

Reprint of the 1933 ed. Bibliography: p. 207-208. [PT2625.A44Z544 1968] 66-27054
1. Mann, Thomas, 1875-1955.

GRONICKA, Andre von, 1912- 833'.9'12
Thomas Mann: profile and perspectives, with two unpublished letters and a chronological list of important events. [1st ed.] New York, Random House [1970] xiv, 237 p. 21 cm. (Studies in language and literature, SLL 27) Bibliography: p. [225]-232. [PT2625.A44Z576] 70-104296 ISBN 0-394-30843-3
1. Mann, Thomas, 1875-1955. I. Title.

MANN, Erika, 1905- 928.3
The last year of Thomas Mann; a revealing memoir by his daughter. Translated by Richard Graves. New York, Farrar, Straus and Cudahy, 1958. 119 p. illus. 21 cm. London ed. (Secker & Warburg) has title: The last year, a memoir of my father. [PT2625.A44Z74613 1958a] 58-6460
1. Mann, Thomas, 1875-1955. I. Title.

MANN, Erika, 1905- 833'.9'12 B
The last year of Thomas Mann; a revealing memoir by his daughter. Translated by Richard Graves. Freeport, N.Y., Books for Libraries Press [1970, c1958] 119 p. illus., facsim., ports. 23 cm. (Biography index reprint series) Translation of Das letzte Jahr. [PT2625.A44Z74613 1970] 72-126323 ISBN 8-369-80299-
1. Mann, Thomas, 1875-1955. I. Title.

MANN, Thomas, 1875-1955. 833'.9'12 B
The letters of Thomas Mann to Caroline Newton. With a foreword by Robert F. Goheen. [Princeton, N.J.] 1971. 112 p. 25 cm. [PT2625.A44Z5383] 73-167636
I. Newton, Caroline, 1893-

MANN, Thomas, 1875-1955. 928.3
A sketch of my life. Translated from the German by H. T. Lowe-Porter. [1st American ed.] New York, Knopf, 1960. 87 p. 22 cm. "Originally published in German as 'Lebensabriss' in Die neue Rundschau, S. Fischer, Berlin, July 7, 1930." "The principal works of Thomas Mann": p. 79-87. [PT2625.A44Z5 1960] 60-11424

THIRLWALL, John Connop, 1904- 833.912
In another language; a record of the thirty-yearrelationship between Thomas Mann and his English translator, Helen Tracy Lowe-Porter, by John C. Thirlwall. [1st ed.] New York, Knopf, 1966. xx, 208, vii p. 22cm. [PT2625.A44Z87] 66-12394 5.95
1. Mann, Thomas, 1875-1955. 2. Lowe, Helen Tracy Porter) 1876-1963. I. Title.

Mann, Thomas, 1875-1955—Biography.

HAMILTON, Nigel. 833'.03 B
The brothers Mann : the lives of Heinrich and Thomas Mann, 1871-1950 and 1875-1955 / Nigel Hamilton. New Haven : Yale University Press, 1979, c1978. 422 p. ; 24 cm. Includes bibliographical reference and index. [PT2625.A43Z647 1979] 78-15114 ISBN 0-300-02348-0 : 16.90
1. Mann, Thomas, 1875-1955—Biography. 2. Mann, Heinrich, 1871-1950—Biography. 3. Novelists, German—20th century—Biography. I. Title.

MANN, Katia, 1883- 833'.9'12' B
Unwritten memories / Katia Mann ; edited by Elisabeth Plessen and Michael Mann ; translated from the German by Hunter and Hildegarde Hannum. 1st American ed. New York : Knopf : distributed by Random House, 1975. ix, 165 p., [8] leaves of plates : ill. ; 22 cm. Translation of Meine ungeschriebenen Memoiren. [PT2625.A44Z74619513 1975] 74-21317 ISBN 0-394-49403-2 : 7.95
1. Mann, Thomas, 1875-1955—Biography. 2. Mann, Katia, 1883- —Biography. I. Title.

Mann, Thomas, 1875-1955—Correspondence.

MANN, Thomas, 1875-1955. 833'.9'12 B
Letters of thomas mann eighteen eighty-nine-nineteen fifty-five Selected and translated from the German by Richard and Clara Winston. New York, Vintage Books [1975] xlv, 482, xviii, [3] p. 21 cm. Bibliography: p. [1]-[3] (4th group) [PT2625.A44Z5233 1975] 74-13415 ISBN 0-394-71327-3 6.95 (pbk.)
1. Mann, Thomas, 1875-1955—Correspondence. I. Winston, Richard. II. Winston, Clara. III. Title.

Mann, William d'Alton,

LOGAN, Andy. 364.163
The man who robbed the robbed barons. [1st ed.] New York W. W. Norton [1965] 260 p. illus. 22 cm. [PN4874.M477L6] 65-13031
1. Mann, William d'Alton, 1839-1920. I. Title.

Mannerheim, Carl Gustaf Emil,

MANNERHEIM, Carl Gustaf Emil, freiherr, 1867-1951. 923.5471
Memoirs; translated by Count Eric Lewenhaupt. [1st American ed.] New York, Dutton, 1954. 540 p. port., maps. 22 cm. [DK461.M32A33 1954a] 54-5060

Mannes, David, 1866-1959.

MANNES, David, 1866-1959. 787'.1'0924 B
Music is my faith : an autobiography / by David Mannes. New York : Da Capo Press, 1978. p. cm. (Da Capo Press music reprint series) Reprint of the 1938 ed. published by Norton, New York. [ML418.M16A2 1978] 78-9601 ISBN 0-306-77595-6 lib.bdg. : 22.50
1. Mannes, David, 1866-1959. 2. Violinists, violoncellists, etc.—United States—Biography. I. Title. **BIP**

Mannes, Marya.

MANNES, Marya. 813'.5'4
Out of my time. [1st ed. in the U.S.A.] Garden City, N.Y., Doubleday, 1971. x, 251 p. illus. 22 cm. Autobiographical. [PS3525.A542Z5 1971] 70-168284 7.95
I. Title.

Mannin, Ethel Edith, 1900- —Biography.

MANNIN, Ethel Edith, 1900- 823'.9'12
Sunset over Dartmoor / [by] Ethel Mannin ; photographs by F. W. Ziemsen. London : Hutchinson, 1977. 200 p., [8] p. of plates : ill. ; 23 cm. Includes index. [PR6025.A477Z527] 77-375065 ISBN 0-09-128010-9 : 10.95
1. Mannin, Ethel Edith, 1900- —Biography. 2. Authors, English—20th century—Biography. I. Title.
Distributed by Hutchinson, Salem, NH **BIP**

Manning, Henry Edward, Cardinal, 1808-1892.

DONALD, Gertrude. 283'.43
Men who left the movement: John Henry Newman, Thomas W. Allies, Henry Edward Manning, Basil William Maturin. Freeport, N.Y., Books for Libraries Press [1967] viii, 422 p. 21 cm. (Essay index reprint series) Reprint of the 1933 ed. [BX5100.D6 1967] 67-23207
1. Newman, John Henry, Cardinal, 1801-1890. 2. Allies, Thomas William, 1813-1903. 3. Manning, Henry Edward, Cardinal, 1808-1892. 4. Maturin, Basil William, 1847-1915. 5. Oxford movement. I. Title.

FITZSIMONS, John, 1913- ed. 262'.135'0924 B
Manning, Anglican and Catholic / edited by John Fitzsimons. Westport, Conn. : Greenwood Press, 1979. vii, 160 p. ; 23 cm. Reprint of the 1951 ed. published by Burns, Oates, London. [BX4705.M3F5 1979] 78-11571 ISBN 0-313-21005-5 lib. bdg. : 15.00
1. Manning, Henry Edward, Cardinal, 1808-1892. 2. Cardinals—England—Biography. I. Title.

LESLIE, Shane, bart., Sir 1885- 922.342
Cardinal Manning, his life and labours. With a pref. by Sir Henry Slesser. New York, P. J. Kenedy [1954] 226p. 22cm. An abstract, with new material, of the author's Henry Edward Manning, published in 1921. [BX4705.M3L42] 54-9458
1. Manning, Henry Edward, Cardinal, 1808-1892. I. Title.

LESLIE, Shane, Sir, bart., 1885- 262'.135'0924 B
Henry Edward Manning, his life and labours. Westport, Conn., Greenwood Press [1970] xxiii, 515 p. ports. 23 cm. Reprint of the 1921 ed. [BX4705.M3L4 1970] 78-109767 ISBN 0-8371-4257-1
1. Manning, Henry Edward, Cardinal, 1808-1892. **BIP**

MCCLELLAND, Vincent Alan 922.342
Cardinal Manning. his public life and influence, 1865-1892. New York, Oxford [c.]1962. 256p. 23cm. 62-51804 5.60
1. Manning, Henry Edward, Cardinal, 1808-1892. I. Title.

PURCELL, Edmund Sheridan, 1824(?)-1899. 262'.135'0924 B
Life of Cardinal Manning, Archbishop of Westminster. New York, Da Capo Press, 1973. 2 v. ports. 22 cm. (Europe 1815-1945) Reprint of the 1895-96 ed. Includes bibliographical references. [BX4705.M3P872] 70-126605 ISBN 0-306-70050-6 45.00 (set)
1. Manning, Henry Edward, Cardinal, 1808-1892. I. Title. II. Series. **BIP**

STRACHEY, Giles Lyton, 1880-1932 920.042
Eminent Victorians: Cardinal Manning, Florence Nightingale, Dr. Arnold, General Gordon. New York [Putnam, 1963] vii, 338p. (Capricorn bk., 83) Bibl. 1.65 pap.,
1. Manning, Henry Edward, cardinal, 1808-1892. 2. Nightingale, Florence, 1820-1910. 3. Arnold, Thomas, 1795-1842. 4. Gordon, Charles George, 1833-1885. I. Title.

STRACHEY, Giles Lytton, 1880-1932 920.042
Eminent Victorians: Cardinal Manning, Florence Nightingale, Dr. Arnold, General Gordon. [Gloucester, Mass., P. Smith, 1964] vii, 338p. 18cm. (Capricorn ed. rebound) Bibl. 3.65
1. Manning, Henry Edward, Cardinal, 1808-1892. 2. Nightingale Florence, 1820-1910. 3. Arnold, Thomas, 1795-1842. 4. Gordon, Charles George, 1833-1885. I. Title.

Manningham, John, d. 1622.

MANNINGHAM, John, d.1622. 942.05'5
The diary of John Manningham of the Middle Temple, 1602-1603 : newly edited in complete and unexpurgated form from the original manuscript in the British Museum : with introd., notes, and life of the author / by Robert Parker Sorlien. Hanover, N.H. : Published for the University of Rhode Island by the University Press of New England, 1976. xi, 467 p. ; 24 cm. Includes bibliographical references and index. [KD621.M28A33 1976] 74-22553 ISBN 0-87451-113-5 : 20.00
1. Manningham, John, d. 1622. 2. Lawyers—Great Britain—Biography. 3. Great Britain—History—Elizabeth, 1558-1603—Sources. 4. Great Britain—History—James I, 1603-1625—Sources. I. Title.

Mannix, Daniel, Abp., 1864-1963.

BRENNAN, Niall. 922.244
Dr. Mannix. Adelaide, Rigby [1964] 336 p. illus., facisms., ports. (2 col.) 25 cm. Bibliography: p. 329-331. [BX4705.M314B7] 64-8739
1. Mannix, Daniel, Abp., 1864-1963. I. Title.

BRENNAN, Niall 922.294
Dr. Mannix [Australia] Rigby [dist. San Francisco, Tri-Ocean Bks., 1965 c.1964] 336p. illus., facsism., ports. (2 col.) 25cm. Bibl. [BX4705.M314B7] 64-8739 6.65
1. Mannix, Daniel, Abp., 1864-1963. I. Title.

MURPHY, Frank. 282'.092'4 B
Daniel Mannix: Archbishop of Melbourne 1917-1963. [New, i.e., 2d ed.] Melbourne, Polding Press, 1972. 288 p. illus. 19 cm. Includes bibliographical references. [BX4705.M314M87 1972] 73-154985 ISBN 0-85884-001-4 2.95
1. Mannix, Daniel, Abp., 1864-1963.

Manolescu, Georges, 1871-1911.

LYNX, J. J. 923.41498
The prince of thieves. New York, Pyramid [1965, c.1963] 205p. 18cm. (R1160) [HV6248.M279L9] .50 pap.,
1. Manolescu, Georges, 1871-1911. I. Title.

LYNX, J. J. 923.41498
The prince of thieves; a biography of George Manolesco, alias H. H. Prince Lahovary, alias the Duke of Otranto. [1st American ed.] New York, Atheneum, 1964 [c1963] 236 p. port. 22 cm. [HV6248.M279L9 1964] 64-14547
1. Manolescu, Georges, 1871-1911. I. Title.

Manolescu, John.

MANOLESCU, John. 920
Permitted to land; an autobiography. London, New York, Staples Press [1950] 212 p. 23 cm. [CT1438.M3A3] 51-3055
I. Title.

Manouche.

PEYREFITTE, Roger. 301.41'5'0924
Manouche / Roger Peyrefitte ; translated by Sam Flores. New York : Grove Press : distributed by Random House, [1974] vi, 262 p. : ports. ; 25 cm. [CT1018.M324P4913 1974] 73-21041 ISBN 0-8021-0046-5 : 8.95
1. Manouche.

Mansfield, Edward Deering, 1801-1880.

MANSFIELD, Edward Deering, 1801-1880. 973.5'092'4
Personal memories, social, political, and literary, 1803-1843. [New York] Arno [1970, c1879] viii, 348 p. 23 cm. (The American journalists) Reprint of the ed. published by R. Clarke, Cincinnati. Includes bibliographical references. [E338.M28 1970b] 74-125707 ISBN 0-405-01688-3
1. Mansfield, Edward Deering, 1801-1880. 2. United States—Politics and government—1815-1861. 3. Cincinnati—History. I. Title. **BIP**

Mansfield, Jayne.

MANN, May. 791.43'028'0924 B
Jayne Mansfield; a biography. New York, Drake Publishers [1973] xiv, 277 p. illus. 24 cm. [PN2287.M37M3] 72-10488 ISBN 0-87749-415-0 7.95
1. Mansfield, Jayne.

*MANSFIELD, Jayne 927.914
Jayne Mansfield s wild, wild world, by Jayne Mansfield, Mike Hargitay. Los Angeles, Holloway House [c.1963] 128p. illus. 18cm. (HH110) .75 pap.,
I. Hargitay, Mike, joint author. II. Title.

SAXTON, Martha. 791.43'023'0924 B
Jayne Mansfield and the American fifties / Martha Saxton. Boston : Houghton Mifflin, 1975. 223 p., [6] leaves of plates : ill. ; 24 cm. [PN2287.M37S2] 74-28209 ISBN 0-395-20289-2 : 8.95 8.95
1. Mansfield, Jayne. I. Title.

SAXTON, Martha. 791.43'023'0924 B
Jayne Mansfield and the American fifties.

New York, Bantam Books [1976 c1975] 202 p. [8] leaves of plates, illus. 18 cm. [PN2287.M37S2] ISBN 0-553-02556-2 1.75 (pbk.)
1. Mansfield, Jayne. I. Title.
L.C. card no. of 1975 Houghton Mifflin edition: 74-28209.

STRAIT, Raymond. 791.43'028'0924 B
The tragic secret life of Jayne Mansfield. Chicago, Regnery [1974] xlv, 207 p. illus. 24 cm. [PN2287.M37S8] 74-6913 ISBN 0-8092-8400-6 7.95
1. Mansfield, Jayne. I. Title.

Mansfield, Katherine, 1888-1923.

ALPERS, Antony, 1919- 928.2
Katherine Mansfield, a biography. [1st American ed.] New York, Knopf, 1953. xvi, 376, xvi p. illus., ports. 22 cm. Bibliography: p. 367-376. [PR6025.A57Z557] 52-12181
1. Mansfield, Katherine, 1888-1923.

BERKMAN, Sylvia. 928.2
Katherine Mansfield, a critical study. New Haven, Published for Wellesley College by Yale University Press, 1951. 246 p. ports. 21 cm. Bibliography: p. 231-236. [PR6025.A57Z567] 51-3206
1. Mansfield, Katherine, 1888-1923. I. Title.

CARSWELL, John. 820'.9'00912
Lives and letters : A. R. Orage, Beatrice Hastings, Katherine Mansfield, John Middleton Murry, S. S. Koteliansky : 1906-1957 / by John Carswell. New York : New Directions Pub. Corp., 1978. p. cm. Includes index. Bibliography: p. [PR106.C37] 77-15986 ISBN 0-8112-0681-5 : 15.00
1. Orage, Alfred Richard, 1873-1934. 2. Hastings, Beatrice. 3. Mansfield, Katherine, 1888-1923. 4. Murry, John Middleton, 1889-1957. 5. Koteliansky, Samuel Solomonovitch, 1880-1955. 6. Authors, English—20th century—Biography. I. Title. BIP

CARSWELL, John. 820'.9'00912
Lives and letters : A. R. Orage, Beatrice Hastings, Katherine Mansfield, John Middleton Murry, S. S. Koteliansky, 1906-1957 / by John Carswell. London ; Boston : Faber and Faber, 1978. 306 p., [4] leaves of plates : ill. ; 23 cm. Includes index. Bibliography: p. 294-297. [PR106.C37 1978] 78-313376 ISBN 0-571-10596-3 : 15.00
1. Orage, Alfred Richard, 1873-1934. 2. Hastings, Beatrice. 3. Mansfield, Katherine, 1888-1923. 4. Murry, John Middleton, 1889-1957. 5. Koteliansky, Samuel Solomonovitch, 1880-1955. 6. Authors, English—20th century—Biography I. Title Distributed by New Directions Publishing Corp., 333 Ave of the Americas, New York, NY 10014

FRIIS, Anne. 828 B
Katherine Mansfield: life and stories. [Folcroft, Pa.] Folcroft Library Editions, 1974 [c1946] 182, [1] p. port. 23 cm. Reprint of the ed. published by E. Munksgaard, Copenhagen. Bibliography: p. 182-[183] [PR6025.A57Z7 1974] 74-4423 20.00
1. Mansfield, Katherine, 1888-1923.

MANSFIELD, Katherine, 1888-1923 928.2
Journal of Katherine Mansfield. Ed., introd., notes, by John Middletown Murry. New York, McGraw [1965, c.1927] xvi, 255p. ports. 21cm. [PR6025.A57Z5] 65-488 2.95 pap.,
I. Murry, John Middletown, 1889-1957, ed. II. Title.

MANSFIELD, Katherine, 1888-1923. 828 B
Journal of Katherine Mansfield. Edited by J. Middleton Murry. New York, H. Fertig, 1974 [c1927] xvi, 255 p. illus. 21 cm. Reprint of the 1959 ed. published by Knopf, New York. [PR6025.A57Z5 1974] 74-14981 13.00
1. Mansfield, Katherine, 1888-1923. I. Title. BIP

MOORE, Leslie, 1888- 828 B
Katherine Mansfield; the memories of LM. New York, Taplinger Pub. Co. [1972, c1971] 242 p. illus. 22 cm. [PR6025.A57Z826 1972] 76-183598 ISBN 0-8008-4447-5 7.95
1. Mansfield, Katherine, 1888-1923. I. L. M. II. M., L. III. Title. BIP

Mansfield, Katherine, 1888-1923—Biography.

ALPERS, Antony, 1919- 823'.9'12
The life of Katherine Mansfield / Antony Alpers. New York : Viking Press, [1980] p. cm. Includes index. Bibliography: p. [PR9639.3.M258Z58] 79-12088 ISBN 0-670-42805-1 : 16.95
1. Mansfield, Katherine, 1888-1923—Biography. 2. Authors, New Zealand—20th century—Biography. I. Title. BIP

CLARKE, Isabel Constance. 828 B
Katherine Mansfield; a biography by Isabel C. Clarke. Introd. by P. A. Lawlor. [Folcroft, Pa.] Folcroft Library Editions, 1974. p. cm. Reprint of the 1944 ed. published by Beltane Book Bureau, Wellington, N.Z., in series: The Beltane Book Bureau's New Zealand literary memoirs. [PR6025.A57Z57 1974] 74-7387 5.50 (lib. bdg.).
1. Mansfield, Katherine, 1888-1923—Biography.

MANTZ, Ruth Elvish. 828 B
The life of Katherine Mansfield, by Ruth Elvish Mantz and J. Middleton Murry. [Folcroft, Pa.] Folcroft Library Editions, 1974. vii, 349 p. illus. 23 cm. Reprint of the 1933 ed. published by Constable, London. [PR6025.A57Z8 1974] 74-11453 ISBN 0-8414-6160-0 (lib. bdg.)
1. Mansfield, Katherine, 1880-1923—Biography. I. Murry, John Middleton, 1889-1957, joint author. II. Title.

MANTZ, Ruth Elvish. 828 B
The life of Katherine Mansfield / by Ruth Elvish Mantz and J. Middleton Murry. New York : Haskell House Publishers, 1976 v, 349 p. ; 21 cm. Reprint of the 1933 ed. published by Constable, London. [PR6025.A57Z8 1975b] 75 42109 ISBN 0-8383-1882-7 lib.bdg. : 18.95
1. Mansfield, Katherine, 1888-1923—Biography. I. Murry, John Middleton, 1889-1957, joint author. BIP

MEYERS, Jeffrey. 823'.9'12 B
Katherine Mansfield : a biography / Jeffrey Meyers. New York : New Directions Pub. Corp., 1979, c1978. p. cm. Includes index. Bibliography: p. [PR9639.3.M258Z8 1979] 79-18885 ISBN 0-8112-0751-X . 17.50
1. Mansfield, Katherine, 1888-1923—Biography. 2. Authors, English—20th century—Biography. BIP

Mansfield, Katherine, 1888-1923—Correspondence.

MANSFIELD, Katherine, 1888-1923. 828 B
The letters of Katherine Mansfield. Edited by J. Middleton Murry. New York, H. Fertig, 1974 [c1929] vii, 517 p. 23 cm. Reprint of the ed. published by Knopf, New York. [PR6025.A57Z55 1974] 74-16016
1. Mansfield, Katherine, 1888-1923—Correspondence. 2. Authors, English—Correspondence, reminiscences, etc. BIP

MANSFIELD, Katherine, 1888-1923. 826'.9'12
Passionate pilgrimage : a love affair in letters : Katherine Mansfield's letters to John Middleton Murry from the South of France, 1915-1920 / in an edition by Helen McMeish ; [photographs by Helen McNeish]. London : Joseph, 1976. 143 p. : ill., facsims., ports. ; 23 cm. Facsims on lining papers. [PR6025.A57Z556 1976] 76-380171 ISBN 0-7181-1479-5 : £4.50
1. Mansfield, Katherine, 1880-1923—Correspondence. 2. Murry, John Middleton, 1889-1957—Correspondence. 3. Authors, English—20th century—Correspondence. I. Murry, John Middleton, 1889-1957. II. Title.

Mansfield, Richard, 1857-1907.

WILSTACH, Paul, 1870-1952. 792'.028'0924 B
Richard Mansfield; the man and the actor. Freeport, N.Y., Books for Libraries Press [1970] xvii, 500 p. illus., ports. 23 cm. Reprint of the 1908 ed. Bibliography: p. 485-490. [PN2287.M4W5 1970] 79-107836
1. Mansfield, Richard, 1857-1907.

WINTER, William, 1836-1917. 792'.028'0924 B
Life and art of Richard Mansfield, with selections from his letters. Westport, Conn., Greenwood Press [1970] 2 v. illus., ports. 23 cm. Reprint of the 1910 ed. [PN2287.M4W6 1970b] 70-100211 ISBN 0-8371-4084-6
1. Mansfield, Richard, 1857-1907. I. Title.

WINTER, William, 1836-1917. 792'.028'0924 B
Life and art of Richard Mansfield, with selections from his letters. Freeport, N.Y., Books for Libraries Press [1970] 2 v. illus., facsims., ports. 23 cm. Reprint of the 1910 ed. [PN2287.M4W6 1970] 77-126264
1. Mansfield, Richard, 1857-1907. I. Title.

Manson, Charles, 1934-

SANDERS, Ed. 301.44'94
The family; the story of Charles Manson's dune buggy attack battalion. [1st ed.] New York, Dutton, 1971. 412 p. maps. 22 cm. [HV6248.M2797S25] 77-125906 ISBN 0-525-10300-7 6.95
1. Manson, Charles, 1934- I. Title.

WATKINS, Paul, 1950- 364.1'523'0924 B
My life with Charles Manson / Paul Watkins, with Guillermo Soledad. New York : Bantam Books, 1979. 278 p. ; 18 cm. [HV6248.M2797W37] 79-118250 ISBN 0-553-12788-8 pbk. : 2.25
1. Manson, Charles, 1934- 2. Watkins, Paul, 1950 3. Crime and criminals—California—Biography. I. Soledad, Guillermo, joint author. II. Title. BIP

WATSON, Charles, 1945- 364.1'523'0924 B
Will you die for me? / Tex Watson as told to Chaplain Ray. Old Tappan, N.J. : F. H. Revell, c1978. 223 p., [8] leaves of plates : ill. ; 24 cm. Includes index. [HV6248.M2797W38] 77-18539 ISBN 0-8007-0912-8 : 7.95
1. Manson, Charles, 1934- 2. Watson, Charles, 1945- 3. Crime and criminals—Biography. 4. Murder—California—Case studies. I. Hoekstra, Ray. II. Title.

WIZINSKI, Sy. 364.1'523'0924 B
Charles Manson : love letters to a secret disciple : a psychoanalytical search / by Sy Wizinski. Terre Haute, Ind. : Moonmad Press, 1977,c1976 iv, 219 p. : ill. ; 22 cm. [HV6248.M2797W59] 76-28869 ISBN 0-917918-01-0 : 9.95
1. Manson, Charles, 1934- 2. Crime and criminals—California—Biography. I. Manson, Charles, 1934-

Manson, Sir Patrick, 1844-1922.

MANSON-BAHR, Philip Henry, Sir 1881- 610'.92'4
Patrick Manson, the father of tropical medicine [by] Sir Philip Manson-Bahr. London, New York, T. Nelson [1962] viii, 192 p. illus., ports. 21 cm. (British men of science) Bibliographical footnotes. [R489.M35M32] 68-6448
1. Manson, Sir Patrick, 1844-1922. 2. Tropics—Diseases and hygiene. I. Title.

MANSON-BAHR, Philip Henry, Sir, 1881- 610'.92'4
Patrick Manson, the father of tropical medicine [by] Sir Philip Manson-Bahr. London, New York, T. Nelson [1962] viii, 192 p. illus., ports. 21 cm. (British men of science) Bibliographical footnotes. [R489.M35M32] 68-6448
1. Manson, Patrick, Sir, 1844-1922. 2. Tropics—Diseases and hygiene.

Mantle, Mickey, 1931-

SCHAAP, Dick. 927.96357
Mickey Mantle, the indispensable Yankee. New York, Bartholomew House [1961] 157p. 18cm. (Sport magazine library, no.5) [GV865.M33S28] 61-4386
1. Mantie, Mickey, 1931- I. Title.

SCHOOR, Gene. 927.96357
Mickey Mantle of the Yankees. New York, Putnam [1959, c1958] 190 p. 21 cm. [GV865.M33S3] 58-13314
1. Mantle, Mickey, 1931-

SHAPIRO, Milton J. 796.3570924
Mickey Mantle, Yankee slugger. New York, J. Messner [1962] 192 p. illus. 22 cm. [GV865.M33S29] 927 62-10196
1. Mantle, Mickey, 1931- I. Title.

SILVERMAN, Al. 927.96357
Mickey Mantle, Mister Yankee. New York, Putnam [1963] 224 p. illus. 21 cm. [GV865.M33S5] 63-13994
1. Mantle, Mickey, 1931-

SILVERMAN, Al. 927.96357
Mickey Mantle, Mister Yankee. New York, Putnam [1963] 224 p. illus. 21 cm. [GV865.M33S5] 63-13994
1. Mantle, Mickey, 1931-

Mantle, Mickey, 1931- —Juvenile literature.

HASEGAWA, Sam. 796.357'092'4 B
Mickey Mantle. Illustrated by Harold Henriksen. Mankato, Minn., Creative Education; [distributed by Childrens Press, Chicago, 1974] 31 p. col. illus. 25 cm. (Superstars) A biography of the New York Yankee famed for his legendary hitting ability. [GV865.M33H37] 74-9807 ISBN 0-87191-375-5
1. Mantle, Mickey, 1931- —Juvenile literature. 2. Baseball—Juvenile literature. I. Henriksen, Harold, illus. II. Title. BIP

LISS, Howard 796.3576
The Mickey Mantle album. [1st ed.] New York, Hawthorn [1966] 62p. illus., ports. 27cm. [GV865.M33L5] 66-7937 2.95
1. Mantle, Mickey, 1931- —Juvenile literature. I. Title.

Manuel II, King of Portugal, 1889-1932.

BENTON, Russell E. 946.9'03'0924 B
The downfall of a king : Dom Manuel II of Portugal / Russell E. Benton. Washington : University Press of America, c1977. vi, 230 p. : ill. ; 22 cm. [DP673.B46] 78-303902 ISBN 0-8191-0168-0 pbk. : 8.25
1. Manuel II, King of Portugal, 1889-1932. 2. Portugal—Kings and rulers—Biography. 3. Portugal—History—Manuel II, 1908-1910 I. Title. BIP

Manuel II Palaeologus, Emperor of the East, 1350-1425.

BARKER, John W. 949.5'04'0924 B
Manuel II Palaeologus (1391-1425); a study in late Byzantine statesmanship [by] John W. Barker. New Brunswick, N.J., Rutgers University Press [1969] liii, 614 p. illus., maps. 25 cm. (Rutgers Byzantine series) Bibliography: p. 552-578. [DF639.B3] 68-63074 ISBN 0-8135-0582-8 25.00
1. Manuel II Palaeologus, Emperor of the East, 1350-1425. 2. Byzantine Empire—History—Manuel II Palaeologus, 1350-1425. BIP

Manuscripts—Great Britain—Catalogs.

DEE, John, 1527-1608. 192 B
The private diary of Dr. John Dee, and the catalogue of his library of manuscripts, from the original manuscripts in the Ashmolean Museum at Oxford, and Trinity College Library, Cambridge. Edited by James Orchard Halliwell. [1st AMS ed.] Printed for the Camden Society, 1842. New York, AMS Press [1968] viii, 102, 35 p. 24 cm. Original ed. issued as no. 19 of Publications of the Camden Society. Camden Society's reports, lists of members, etc.: p. [1]-35 at end. [BF1598.D5A36 1968] 71-163690
1. Manuscripts—Great Britain—Catalogs. I. Title. II. Series: Camden Society, London. Publications, no. 19. BIP

Manuzio, Aldo Pio, 1449 or 50-1515.

LOWRY, Martin. 070.5'092'4 B
The world of Aldus Manutius : business and scholarship in Renaissance Venice / Martin Lowry. [Ithaca, N.Y.] : Cornell University Press, 1979. 350 p., [4] leaves of plates : ill. ; 25 cm. Includes index. Bibliography: p. 309-331. [Z232.M3L68 1979] 78-58631 ISBN 0-8014-1214-5 : 28.50
1. Manuzio, Aldo Pio, 1449 or 50-1515. 2. Printers—Italy—Venice—Biography. 3. Venice—Biography. 4. Venice—Intellectual life. I. Title. BIP

Manyanet, Joseph, 1833-1901.

MOREA, Dominic, 1907- 922.246
Among the stars; the life of Father Joseph Manyanet. [1st ed.] New York, Exposition Press [1957] 70p. illus. 21cm. [BX4705.M3234M6] 58-14504
1. Manyanet, Joseph, 1833-1901. I. Title.

Manzoni, Alessandro, 1785-1873—Biography.

COLQUHOUN, Archibald. 853'.7 B
Manzoni and his times : a biography of the author of The betrothed (I promessi sposi) / by Archibald Colquhoun. Westport, Conn. : Hyperion Press, 1979. x, 281 p., [15] leaves of plates : ill. ; 22 cm. Reprint of the 1954 ed. published by Dent, London. Includes index. Bibliography: p. 261-269. [PQ4715.C58 1979] 78-59013 ISBN 0-88355-688-X : lib.bdg. : 23.50
1. Manzoni, Alessandro, 1785-1873—Biography. 2. Authors, Italian—19th century—Biography. I. Title. BIP

Mao, Tse-tung, 1893-1976.

ARCHER, Jules. 951.05'092'4 B
Mao Tse-Tung. New York, Hawthorn Books [1972] x, 211 p. 22 cm. Bibliography: [201]-204. [DS778.M3A76 1972] 70-179129 5.95
1. Mao, Tse-tung, 1893- BIP

ARCHER, Jules. 951.05'092'4 [B]
Mao Tse-tung. New York, Washington Sq. Pr. [1973, c.1972] 205 p. 18 cm. Bibliography: p. 195-197. [DS778.M3A76] ISBN 0-671-47910-5 0.95 (pbk.)
1. Mao, Tse-tung, 1893- I. Title.
L.C. card no. for the hardbound edition: 70-179429.

BOUC, Alain. 951.05'092'4
Mao Tse-tung : a guide to his thought / Alain Bouc ; translated by Paul Auster and Lydia Davis. New York : St. Martin's Press, c1977. p. cm. Includes texts by Mao Tse-tung. Bibliography: p. [DS778.M3B6813] 76-62749 ISBN 0-312-51397-6 : 10.00
1. Mao, Tse-tung, 1893-1876. 2. Heads of state—China—Biography. I. Mao, Tse-tung, 1893-1976. BIP

CH'EN, Jerome, 951.05'0924 B
1919- comp.
Mao. Englewood Cliffs, N.J., Prentice-Hall [1969] x, 176 p. 22 cm. (Great lives observed) Includes bibliographical references. [DS778.M3C473] 69-15346
1. Mao, Tse-tung, 1893-

DEVILLERS, 951.05'0924 B
Philippe, 1920-
Mao. Translated by Tony White. New York, Schocken Books [1969] 317 p. 22 cm. (What they really said series) Translation of Ce que Mao a vraiment dit. Bibliography: p. 295-309. [DS778.M3D413 1969] 79-85141 5.95
1. Mao Tse-tung, 1893- I. Mao Tse-tung, 1893-

FITZGERALD, Charles 320.951
Patrick, 1902-
Mao Tsetung and China / C. P. Fitzerald. New York : Holmes & Meier Publishers, 1976. vi, 166 p. [4] leaves of plates : ill. ; 23 cm. Includes index. Bibliography: p. [161]. [DS778.M3F57] 76-3700 ISBN 0-8419-0268-2 : 9.50
1. Mao, Tse-tung, 1893- 2. China—Politics and government—1949- I. Title. BIP

GRAY, Jack, M.A. 951.05'0924 B
Mao Tse-tung. Valley Forge, Pa., Judson Press [1974] 88 p. 19 cm. (Makers of modern thought) Bibliography: p. 87-88. [DS778.M3G68 1974] 73-12789 ISBN 0-8170-0596-X 1.95 (pbk.)
1. Mao, Tse-tung, 1893-

HAN, Suyin, pseud. 951.05'092'4 B
The morning deluge; Mao Tsetung and the Chinese revolution, 1893-1954. [1st ed.] Boston, Little, Brown [1972] xiv, 571 p. illus. 23 cm. Includes bibliographical references. [DS778.M3H35] 72-4816 ISBN 0-316-34289-0
1. Mao, Tse-tung, 1893- 2. Communism—China. I. Title. BIP

HSIAO, Yu, 1894- 923.551
Mao Tse-tung and I were beggars. Illustrated by the author, Siao-yu. With a foreword by Lin Yutang, pref. by Raymond F. Piper, and historical commentary and notes by Robert C. North. [Syracuse, N. Y.] Syracuse University Press [1959] 266 p. illus. 24 cm. [DS778.M3H75] 59-15411
1. Mao, Tse-tung, 1893-1976. BIP

MACGREGOR-HASTIE, Roy. 923.151
The red barbarians; the life and times of Mao Tse-tung. [1st American ed.] Philadelphia, Chilton Co., Book Division [1962, c1961] 224p. illus. 21cm. [DS778.M3M23 1962] 62-16021
1. Mao-Tse-tung, 1893- 2. Communism—China. I. Title.

PALOCZI Horvath, 923.151
Gyorgy.
Mao Tse-tung, emperor of the blue ants. [1st ed. in the U.S.A.] Garden City, N. Y., Doubleday, 1963 [c1962] 393 p. 24 cm. [DS778.M3P28 1963] 63-11223
1. Mao, Tse-tung, 1893-1976. BIP

PALOCZI 951.05'092'4 B
Horvath, Gyorgy.
Mao Tse-tung, emperor of the blue ants [by] George Paloczi-Horvath. Westport, Conn., Greenwood Press [1973, c1962] x, 393 p. 23 cm. Reprint of the ed. published by Doubleday, Garden City, N.Y. Bibliography: p. [382]-389. [DS778.M3P28 1973] 73-434 ISBN 0-8371-6775-2 16.75
1. Mao, Tse-tung, 1893- I. Title.

PAYNE, Pierre 951.05'0924 B
Stephen Robert, 1911-
Mao Tse-tung [by] Robert Payne. New York, Weybright and Talley [1969] vi, 343 p. illus., facsim., maps, ports 25 cm. 1950 and 1951 editions published under title: Mao Tse-tung, ruler of Red China. The new and rev. ed. was published in 1961 under title: Portrait of a revolutionary: Mao Tse-tung. Bibliography: p. 333-336. [DS778.M3P32 1969] 68-17753 10.00
1. Mao, Tse-tung, 1893-

PAYNE, Pierre Stephen 923.551
Robert, 1911-
Mao Tse-tung, ruler of Red China. New York, Schuman [1950] xvii, 303 p. ports., maps. 24 cm. Bibliography: p. [289]-293. [DS778.M3P32] 50-10288
1. Mao, Tse-tung, 1893-1976.

PAYNE, Pierre Stephen 923.551
Robert, 1911-
Portrait of a revolutionary; Mao Tse-tung. [New and rev. ed.] New York, Abelard [1962, c.1950, 1961] 311p. illus. Previous eds. pub. under title: Mao Tse-tung, ruler of Red China. Bibl. 61-15322 5.00
1. Mao, Tse-tung, 1893- I. Title.

PYE, Lucian W., 951.05'092'4 B
1921-
Mao Tse-tung : the man in the leader / Lucian W. Pye. New York : Basic Books, c1976. xviii, 346 p., [7] leaves of plates : ill. ; 22 cm. Includes bibliographical references and index. [DS778.M3P93] 75-31832 ISBN 0-465-04396-8
1. Mao, Tse-tung, 1893- BIP

THE red barbarians: v. 12
the life and times of Mao Tse-tung. London, New York, Boardman [1961] 224p. 8 plates (incl. ports.) map. 21cm.
1. Mao, Tse-Tung, 1893- 2. Bolshevism—China. I. MacGregor—Hastie, Roy.

SCHRAM, Stuart R. 951.05/0924
Mao Tse-tung [by] Stuart Schram. Baltimore, Penguin [1967] 372p. 29 plates (incl. ports.) maps. 18cm. (Pol. leaders of the 20th cent.; Pelican bk., A840) Bibl. [DS778.M3S3 1967b] 67-105785 1.65 pap.,
1. Mao, Tse-tung, 1893- I. Title.

SCHRAM, Stuart R. 951'.05'0924 B
Mao Tse-tung [by] Stuart Schram. New York, Simon and Schuster [1967, c1966] 351 p. illus., ports. 22 cm. Bibliographical footnotes. Bibliographical references included in "Notes" (p. 327-336) [DS778.M3S3 1967] 67-12918
1. Mao, Tse-tung, 1893- BIP

SCHRAM, Stuart R. 951.90430924 B
Mao Tse-tung [by] Stuart Schram. Harmondsworth, Penguin, 1966. 352 p. 16 plates (incl. ports.), maps. 18 1/2 cm. (Political leaders of the twentieth century) (Pelican book A840) Facsim. on endpapers. Includes bibliographical references. [DS778.M3S3] 67-76482
1. Mao, Tse-tung, 1893-

SHIH, Bernadette 951.05'092'4 B
P. N.
Mao—a young man from the Yangtze Valley / by Bernadette P. N. Shih. 1st ed. Port Washington, N.Y. : Ashley Books, c1974. 320 p. ; 24 cm. Bibliography: p. 315-320. [DS778.M3S52 1974] 74-76433 ISBN 0-87949-026-8 : 12.95
1. Mao, Tse-tung, 1893- I. Title.

UHALLEY, Stephen. 951.05'092'4 B
Mao Tse-tung, a critical biography, by Stephen Uhalley, Jr. New York, New Viewpoints [1975] p. cm. Bibliography: p. [DS778.M3U35] 74-13441 ISBN 0-531-05363-6 12.50
1. Mao, Tse-tung, 1893- 2. China—History—1949-

Mao, Tse-tung, 1893- —Bibliography.

MAO, Tse-tung, 016.95105'0924
1893-
Mao papers, anthology and bibliography edited by Jerome Ch'en. London, New York, Oxford University Press, 1970. xxxiii, 221 p. ports. 23 cm. A chronological bibliography in English and Chinese: p. 163-221. [DS778.M3A4295] 76-147091 10.00 (U.S.)
1. Mao, Tse-tung, 1893- —Bibliography. I. Ch'en, Jerome, 1919- ed. II. Title.

SHU, Austin C. W. 016.95105'092'4
On Mao Tse-tung; a bibliographic guide [by] Austin C. W. Shu. East Lansing, Asian Studies Center, Michigan State University, 1972. x, 78 p. 28 cm. (East Asia series, no. 2) [Z8548.3.S55] 72-619503
1. Mao, Tse-tung, 1893- —Bibliography. I. Title. II. Series.

Mao, Tse-tung, 1893- —Juvenile literature.

EUNSON, Roby. 951.05'092'4 B
Mao Tse-tung; the man who conquered China. New York, Watts, 1973. 151 p. illus. 24 cm. "An Associated Press book." Bibliography: p. [141]-144. A biography of the Chinese Communist leader stressing his influence on the history and culture of modern China. [DS778.M3E94] 92 72-10420 ISBN 0-531-02617-5 5.95
1. Mao, Tse-tung, 1893- —Juvenile literature. 2. China (People's Republic of China, 1949-)—Politics and government—Juvenile literature. I. Title.

KURLAND, Gerald, 951.05'092'4 B
1942-
Mao Tse-tung, founder of Communist China. Charlotteville, N.Y., SamHar Press, 1972. 32 p. 23 cm. (Outstanding personalities, no. 14) Bibliography: p. 32. A biography of the Chinese peasant who became the leader of the People's Republic of China in 1949. [DS778.M3K87] 92 75-190232
1. Mao, Tse-tung, 1893- —Juvenile literature. I. Title.

PURCELL, Hugh. 951.05'092'4 B
Mao Tse-tung / by Hugh Purcell. New York : St. Martin's Press, [1977] p. cm. (History makers series) Includes index. Bibliography: p. A biography of a modern Chinese leader emphasizing his character and leadership qualities. [DS778.M3P86] 77-188 ISBN 0-312-51399-2 : 10.00
1. Mao, Tse-tung, 1893-1976—Juvenile literature. 2. Heads of state—China—Biography—Juvenile literautre. I. Title.

Maoris—Education.

ASHTON-WARNER, Sylvia. 371.9893
Teacher. New York, Simon and Schuster, 1963. 224 p. illus. 24 cm. Autobiographical. [LC3501.M3A8] 63-8659
1. Maoris—Education. 2. Education—Experimental methods. I. Title.

Maranos.

KAYSERLING, Meyer, 970'.01'504924
1829-1905.
Christopher Columbus and the participation of the Jews in the Spanish and Portuguese discoveries / by M. Kayserling ; translated from the author's manuscript with his sanction and revision by Charles Gross. Folcroft, Pa. : Folcroft Library Editions, 1978, c1894. xv, 189 p. ; 24 cm. Reprint of the ed. published by Longmans, Green, New York. English, Spanish, and Latin. Includes bibliographical references and index. [E111.K23 1978] 78-26172 ISBN 0-8414-5478-7 lib. bdg. : 25.00
1. Colombo, Cristoforo—Relations with Jews. 2. Maranos. 3. Santangel, Luis de, d. 1505. 4. Santangel family. 5. America—Discovery and exploration—Spanish. 6. Jews in Spain—History. 7. Spain—History—Ferdinand Isabella, 1479-1516. I. Title. BIP

Mararin. Hortense (Mancini) de La Porte, duchess de. 1649-1699.

CHAPMAN, Hester W., 1899- 920.02
Privileged persons; four seventeenth-century studies [by]Hester W. Chapman. New York, Revnal [1966 ie 1967] 319p. plates (ports.) general.tables 23 cm Bibl. [CT117.C5 1966a] 66-24558
1. Louis XIII. King of France, 1601-1643. 2. Sophie, consort of Ernest Augustus, Elector of Hanover. 1630-1714. 3. Mararin. Hortense (Mancini) de La Porte, duchess de. 1649-1699. 4. Ailesbury, Thomas Bruce, 2d earl of, 1656-1741. I. Title.
Contents omitted. BIP

Marat, Jean Paul, 1743-1793.

GOTTSCHALK, Louis 944.04'0924
Reichenthal, 1899-
Jean Paul Marat; a study in radicalism, by

Louis R. Gottschalk. Chicago, University of Chicago Press [1967] xiii, 225 p. port. 21 cm. Bibliography: p. 197-214. [DC146.M3G6 1967] 67-16987
1. Marat, Jean Paul, 1743-1793. 2. France—History—Revolution, 1789-1793.

GOTTSCHALK, Louis Reichenthal, 1899- 944.040924
Jean Paul Marat; a study in radicalism, by Louis R. Gottschalk. New York, B. Blom [1966] xv, 221 p. port. 23 cm. "First published 1927." Bibliography: p. 197-212. [DC146.M3G6 1966] 66-29542
1. Marat, Jean Paul, 1743-1793. 2. France—History—Revolution, 1789-1793. BIP

SCHERR, Marie. 944.04'0924
Charlotte Corday and certain men of the revolutionary torment. New York, AMS Press [1970] 237 p. port. 22 cm. Reprint of the 1929 ed. [DC146.C8S3 1970] 79-100512 ISBN 0-404-05588-5
1. Corday D'Armont, Marie Anne Charlotte de, 1768-1793. 2. Danton, Georges Jacques, 1759-1794. 3. Marat, Jean Paul, 1743-1793. 4. Robespierre, Maximilien Marie Isidore de, 1758-1794. 5. France—History—Revolution, 1789-1799. 6. Girondists. I. Title. BIP

Marathon running.

HENDERSON, Joe, 1943- 796.4'26
Road racers and their training. Los Altos, Calif., Tafnews Press [1970] 96 p. illus., ports. 22 cm. [GV1065.H38] 72-113473
1. Marathon running. 2. Marathon running—Biography. I. Title.

Maravich, Pete, 1948-

SALADINO, Tom. 796.32'3'0924 B
Pistol Pete Maravich / the Louisiana purchase / by Tom Saladino. Huntsville, Ala. : Strode Publishers, c1974. 140 p. : ill. ; 24 cm. [GV884.M3S24] 74-15507 ISBN 0-87397-056-X : 5.95
1. Maravich, Pete, 1948- 2. Basketball. I. Title. BIP

Maravich, Pete, 1948- —Juvenile literature.

ARMSTRONG, Robert, 1938- 796.32'3'0924 B
Pete Maravich / by Robert Armstrong. Mankato, Minn. : Creative Education ; Chicago : distributed by Children Press, c1978. Mankato, Minn. : Creative Education, 1978. 31 p. : col. ill. ; 25 cm. (Creative Education sports superstars) Presents highlights in the career of Pistol Pete Maravich, New Orleans Jazz guard. [GV884.M3A85] 92 77-18054 ISBN 0-87191-669-X : 4.95
1. Maravich, Pete, 1948- —Juvenile literature. 2. Basketball players—United States—Biography—Juvenile literature. I. Title. BIP

Marble, Manton, 1834-1917.

MCJIMSEY, George T. 070.4'0924 B
Genteel partisan: Manton Marble, 1834-1917 [by] George T. McJimsey. [1st ed.] Ames, Iowa State University Press [1971] xi, 333 p. 24 cm. Bibliography: p. 319-322. [PN4874.M483M3] 79-126164 ISBN 0-8138-1105-8
1. Marble, Manton, 1834-1917. I. Title.

Marburg, Theodore, 1862-1946.

ATKINSON, Henry Avery, 1877- v. 12
Theodore Marburg, the man and his work. [New York? c1951] viii, 221p. ports. 22cm. Bibliography: p. 220-221. A 53
1. Marburg, Theodore, 1862-1946. I. Title.

Marc, Franz, 1888-1916.

LEVINE, Frederick S. 759.3 B
The apocalyptic vision : the art of Franz Marc as German expressionism / by Frederick S. Levine. 1st ed. New York : Harper & Row, c1979. 200 p. : ill. ; 24 cm. (Icon editions) Includes index. Bibliography: p. [186]-192. [ND588.M194L46 1979] 78-4736 ISBN 0-06-435275-7 : 17.50
1. Marc, Franz, 1888-1916. 2. Painters—Germany—Biography. 3. Expressionism (Art)—Germany. I. Title. BIP

Marca-Relli, Conrad, 1913-

MARCA-RELLI, Conrad, 1913- 709'.24
Marca-Relli. [Catalog] Marlborough-Gerson Gallery Inc., New York. Associated galleries: Marlborough Fine Art (London) Ltd. [and] Marlborough Galleria d'Arte, Rome. New York, Marlborough-Gerson Gallery, 1970. 38 p. illus. 31 cm. "Cat. no. 267." [N6537.M36M37] 73-170845
1. Marca-Relli, Conrad, 1913- I. Marlborough-Gerson Gallery. II. Marlborough Fine Art, ltd., London. III. Marlborough galleria d'arte.

Marcantonio, Vito, 1902-1954.

LAGUMINA, Salvatore John, 1928- 973.91'0924
Vito Marcantonio, the people's politician. Dubuque, Iowa, Kendall/Hunt Pub. Co. [1969] ix, 171 p. 23 cm. Bibliographical references included in "Footnotes" (p. 143-166) [E748.M33L3] 77-95613
1. Marcantonio, Vito, 1902-1954.

SCHAFFER, Alan. 973.910924 B
Vito Marcantonio, radical in Congress. [1st ed. Syracuse, N.Y.] Syracuse University Press [1966] ix, 256 p. group ports. 21 cm. (Men and movements) Bibliography: p. 217-242. [E748.M33S3] 66-29201
1. Marcantonio, Vito, 1902-1954. I. Title. BIP

March, Gladys.

RIVERA, Diego [Diego Maria 759.972
My art, my life; an autobiography [by] Diego Rivera, with Gladys March. New York, Citadel Press [c.1960] oncepcion Juan Nepomuceno Estanislao de la Rivera y Barrientos Acosta y Rodriguez] 1886-1957. 318p. illus., ports. 22cm. 60-15451 6.00
1. March, Gladys. I. Title.

Marchesi, Blanche, 1864-1940.

MARCHESI, Blanche, 1864-1940. 782.1'092'4 B
Singer's pilgrimage / by Blance Marchesi. New York : Da Capo Press, 1977. p. cm. (Da Capo Press music reprint series) Reprint of the 1923 ed. published by Small, Maynard, Boston [ML420.M315A3 1977b] 77-1941 ISBN 0-306-70878-7 : 22.50
1. Marchesi, Blanche, 1864-1940. 2. Singers—Biography. I. Title. BIP

MARCHESI, Blanche, 1864-1940. 782.1'092'4 B
Singer's pilgrimage / Blanche Marchesi ; with a discography by W. R. Moran. New York : Arno Press, 1977. 304, [3] p., [16] leaves of plates : ill. ; 23 cm. (Opera biographies) Reprint of the 1923 ed. published by G. Richards, London. Discography: p. [1-3] [ML420.M315A3 1977] 76-29951 ISBN 0-405-09692-5 : 20.00
1. Marchesi, Blanche, 1864-1940. 2. Singers—Biography. I. Title.

Marchesi, Mathilde Graumann, 1822-1913.

MARCHESI, Mathilde Graumann, 1822-1913. 784.9'32'0924 B
Marchesi and music : passages from the life of a famous singing-teacher / by Mathilde Marchesi ; with an introd. by Massenet. New York : Da Capo Press, 1978, [c1897]. xiv, 301 p., [8] leaves of plates : ill. ; 23 cm. (Da Capo Press music reprint series) Reprint of the 1898 ed. published by Harper, New York. [ML420.M322A3 1978] 77-27354 ISBN 0-306-77577-8 lib.bdg. : 22.50
1. Marchesi, Mathilde Graumann, 1822-1913. 2. Singers—Biography. I. Title. BIP

Marciano, Rocky, 1923-1969.

LIBBY, Bill. 796.8'3'0924 B
Rocky: the story of a champion. New York, Messner [1971] 192 p. illus., ports. 22 cm. [GV1132.M3L5] 70-139084 ISBN 0-671-32371-7 3.95
1. Marciano, Rocky, 1923-1969. I. Title.

SKEHAN, Everett M. 796.8'3'0924 B
Rocky Marciano : the biography of a first son / by Everett M. Skehan, with family assistance by Peter, Louis, and Mary Anne Marciano. Boston : Houghton Mifflin, 1977. 369 p., [4] leaves of plates : ill. ; 24 cm. [GV1132.M3S54] 77-409 ISBN 0-395-25356-X : 10.95
1. Marciano, Rocky, 1923-1969. 2. Boxers (Sports)—United States—Biography. I. Title.

Marciano. Rocky, 1924—

CUTTER, Bob, 1930-- 927.9683
The Rocky Marciano story; illustrated by Lennie Hollreiser. New York, W. Allen Pub. Co. [1954] 79p. illus. 23cm. [GV1132.M3C8] 54-9567
1. Marciano, Rocky, 1924— I. Title.

Marconi, Guglielmo, marchese, 1874-1937.

COE, Douglas, pseud. v. 12
Marconi, pioneer of radio, by Douglas Coe, illustrated by Kreigh Collins. New York, J. Messner, inc. [1963] 256 p. illus., diagrs. 23 cm. Map on lining-papers. Bibliography: p. 257-259. 68-87360
1. Marconi, Guglielmo, marchese, 1874-1937. 2. Telegraph, Wireless—Hist. I. Title.

GUNSTON, David 621.384'0924(B)
Marconi, father of radio. Drawings by Eric J. Woodley. New York, Crowell-Collier [1967, c.1965] 128p illus., ports 21cm. Bibl. [TK5739.M3G8] 67-25612 3.50
1. Marconi, Guglielmo, marchese, 1874-1937. 2. Telegraph, Wireless — Hist. I. Title.

HINSHAW, John V. 621.3841'092'4 B
Marconi and his South Wellfleet wireless [by] John V. Hinshaw. Chatham, Mass., Chatham Press, c1969] 30 p. illus., plans, ports. 24 cm. (Cape Cod history guide, v. 1) [TK6545.M4H56] 72-187671
1. Marconi, Guglielmo, Marchese, 1874-1937. I. Title.

JOLLY, W. P. 621.3841'092'4 B
Marconi [by] W. P. Jolly. New York, Stein and Day [1972] 291 p. illus. 25 cm. Bibliography: p. 274. [TK140.M35J64 1972b] 72-79746 ISBN 0-8128-1507-6 7.95
1. Marconi, Guglielmo, marchese, 1874-1937.

MARCONI, Degna, 1908- 926.2
My father, Marconi, [1st ed.] New York, McGraw-Hill [1962] 320 p. illus. 22 cm. [TK5739.M3M28] 62-11199
1. Marconi, Guglielmo, marchese, 1874-1937. I. Title.

Marcos, Ferdinand Edralin, Pres. Philippines.

SPENCE, Hartzell, 1908- 991'.404'0924
Marcos of the Philippines; a biography. New York, World Pub. Co. [1969] 365 p. illus. 22 cm. 1964 ed. published under title: For every tear a victory. 79-84747 6.95
1. Marcos, Ferdinand Edralin, Pres. Philippines. I. Title.

Marcus, David, 1901-1948.

BERKMAN, Ted 923.573
Cast a giant shadow; the story of Mickey Marcus who died to save Jerusalem. New York, Pocket Bks. [1963, c.1962] 326p. illus. 17cm. (Permabk. ed., M.5075) .50 pap.,
1. Marcus, David, 1901-1948. I. Title.

BERKMAN, Ted. 923.573
Cast a giant shadow; the story of Mickey Marcus who died to save Jerusalem. [1st ed.] Garden City, N. Y., Doubleday, 1962. 321 p. illus. 22 cm. [E745.M35B4] 62-12495
1. Marcus, David, 1901-1948. I. Title.

BERKMAN, Ted 956.94'04'0924
Cast a giant shadow; the story of Mickey Marcus; a soldier for all humanity. Philadelphia. Jewish Pubn. Soc., 1967. 185p. illus., maps (on lining papers) ports. 22cm. (Covenant bks., 20) Abridgement of the author s work pub. in 1962 under the same title. [E745.M35B42] 67-16184 2.95
1. Marcus, David, 1901-1948. I. Title. BIP

Marcus, Stanley, 1905-

MARCUS, Stanley, 1905- 381'.092'4 B
Minding the store; a memoir. [1st ed.] Boston, Little, Brown [1974] xii, 383 p. illus. 24 cm. Autobiographical. [HF5429.5.D2M37] 74-10833 ISBN 0-316-54623-2
1. Marcus, Stanley, 1905- 2. Businessmen—Correspondence, reminiscences, etc. I. Title.

MARCUS, Stanley, 1905- 381'.092'4 B
Quest for the best / Stanley Marcus. New York : Viking Press, 1979. ix, 227 p. : ill. ; 25 cm. Includes index. [HF5429.5.D2M373] 78-26864 ISBN 0-670-58470-3 : 14.95
1. Marcus, Stanley, 1905- 2. Businessman—Biography. 3. Commercial products. 4. Quality of products. I. Title. BIP

Marcy, Randolph Barnes, 1812-1887.

HOLLON, William Eugene, 1913- 923.573
Beyond the cross timbers; the travels of Randolph B. Marcy, 1812-1887. [1st ed.] Norman, University of Oklahoma Press [1955] 270p. illus. 22cm. Includes bibliography. [F593.M34H6] 55-6357
1. Marcy, Randolph Barnes, 1812-1887. I. Title.

Marcy, William Learned, 1786-1857.

SPENCER, Ivor Debenham. 923.273
The victor and the spoils; a life of William L. Marcy. Providence, Brown University Press, 1959. 438 p. illus. 24 cm. Includes bibliography. [E415.9.M18S6] 59-6898
1. Marcy, William Learned, 1786-1857. I. Title. BIP

Margaret of Anjou, consort of Henry VI, King of England, 1430-1482.

ERLANGER, Philippe, 1903- 942.04'3'0924 B
Margaret of Anjou, Queen of England. Coral Gables, Fla., University of Miami Press [1971, c1970] 251 p. illus. 23 cm. Translation of Marguerite d'Anjou et la Guerre des deux roses. Bibliography: p. 250-251. [DA247.M3E613 1971] 79-161438 ISBN 0-87024-214-8 7.95
1. Margaret of Anjou, Consort of Henry VI, King of England, 1430-1482. I. Title.

HASWELL, Chetwynd John Drake, 1919- 942.04'3'0924 B
The ardent queen : Margaret of Anjou and the Lancastrian heritage / Jock Haswell. London : Peter Davies, 1976. 224 p., [2] leaves of plates : ill., geneal. tables (on lining papers) ; 23 cm. Includes index. Bibliography: p. [217]-218. [DA247.M3H37] 76-383138 ISBN 0-432-06580-6 : £4.50
1. Margaret of Anjou, consort of Henry VI, King of England, 1430-1482. 2. Great Britain—History—Lancaster and York,

1399-1485. 3. Great Britain—Queens—Biography. I. Title.

Margaret, Princess of Great Britain, 1930-

BARDENS, Dennis 920.7
Princess Margaret. New York, Abelard [c.1965] 224p. ports. 23cm. [DA585.A5M29] 65-19987 4.50
1. Margaret, Princess of Great Britain, 1930- I. Title.

BARDENS, Dennis 923.142
Princess Margaret. New York, Scholastic [1965, c.1964] 310p. illus. 17cm. (T816) [DA585.A5M29] .50 pap.,
1. Margaret, Princess of Gt. Brit., 1930- I. Title.

BARDENS, Dennis. 920.7
Princess Margaret. London, New York, Abelard-Schuman [1965] 224 p. ports. 23 cm. [DA585.A5M29 1965] 65-19987
1. Margaret, Princess of Great Britain, 1930- I. Title.

BROUGH, James, 941.085'092'4 B 1918-
Margaret, the tragic princess / James Brough. New York : Putnam, c1977. 323 p., [4] leaves of plates : ill. ; 22 cm. Includes index. [DA585.A5M32 1978] 77-21635 9.95
1. Margaret, Princess of Great Britain, 1930- 2. Great Britain—Princes and princesses—Biography. I. Title.

BROUGH, James, 941.085'092'4 B 1918-
Margaret, the tragic princess * by James Brough. New York : Avon Books, 1979, c1978. 281p., [4] leaves of plates : ill. ; 18 cm. Includes index. [DA2585.A5M32 1978] ISBN 0-380-44206-X pbk. : 2.25
1. Margaret, Princess of Great Britain, 1930- 2. Great Britian — Princes and princesses — Biography. I. Title.
LC card no. for 1977 Putnam ed.: 77-21635

CRAWFORD, Marion, 1909- 920.7
Margaret; the story of a modern princess. [1st American ed.] New York, Prentice-Hall [1954] 190 p. illus. 21 cm. [DA585.A5M33 1954] 54-6352
1. Margaret, Princess of Great Britain, 1930-

FRISCHAUER, 941'.085'0924 B Willi, 1906-
Margaret : princess without a cause / [by] Willi Frischauer. London : Joseph, 1977, i.e.1978 220 p., [8] of plates : ports. ; 23 cm. Includes index. [DA585.A5M334 1977] 77-377104 ISBN 0-7181-1611-9 : 11.95
1. Margaret, Princess of Great Britain, 1930- 2. Great Britain—Princes and princesses—Biography. I. Title.
Distributed by Michael Joseph, 22 S. Broadway, Salem, NH 03079

GLENTON, William. 920
Tony's room; the secret love story of Princess Margaret. [New York] B. Geis Associates [1965] 183 p. illus., ports. 18 cm. [DA585.A5M336] 65-9217
1. Margaret, Princess of Great Britain, 1960- 2. Snowdon, Antony Armstrong-Jones, 1st earl of, 1930- I. Title.

HALL, Gordon Langley. 920.7
Princess Margaret, an informal biography. Philadelphia, Macrae Smith Co. [1958] 253 p. illus. 21 cm. [DA585.A5M34] 58-12167
1. Margaret, Princess of Great Britain, 1930-

HOPE, Alice. 920.7
Princess Margaret; the story of a royal romance. [Rev. ed.] Indianapolis, Bobbs-Merrill [1961] 217p. illus. 22cm. [DA585.A4H6 1961] 61-15138
1. Margaret, Princess of Great Britain, 1930- I. Title.

HUTCHINSON, 941.085'092'2 B Roger.
A family affair : the British royal family, its scandals, its crises and what really happened when Margaret and Tony's marriage broke up / by Roger Hutchinson and Gary Kahn. New York : Two Continents/Bunch Books, c1977. p. cm. [DA585.A5M338] 77-83854 ISBN 0-8467-0389-0 : 8.95
1. Margaret, Princess of Great Britain, 1930- 2. Snowdon, Anthony Armstrong-Jones, 1st Earl of, 1930- 3. Windsor, House of. 4. Great Britain—Princes and princesses—Biography. I. Kahn, Gary, joint author. II. Title.

PAYNE, David John 920.7
My life with Princess Margaret. Greenwich, Conn., Fawcett [c.1961, 1962] 208p. illus. 18cm. (Gold medal bks., d1222) 62-5536 .50 pap.,
1. Margaret, Princess of Great Britain, 1930- I. Title.

Margaret Tudor, consort of James IV, King of Scotland, 1489-1541.

CHAPMAN, Hester 942.05'2'0922 B W., 1899-
The thistle and the rose [by] Hester W. Chapman. [1st American ed.] New York, Coward, McCann & Geoghegan [1971, c1969] 223 p. geneal. table (on lining papers), ports. 23 cm. First published in London under title: The sisters of Henry VIII. Bibliography: p. 217-218. [DA784.3.M3C5 1971] 79-159754 6.95
1. Margaret Tudor, consort of James IV, King of Scotland, 1489-1541. 2. Mary, consort of Louis XII, King of France, 1496-1533. I. Title.

GLENNE, Michael. 923.141
King Harry's sister, Margaret Tudor, Queen of Scotland. New York, Roy Publishers [1953] 224p. illus. 22cm. [DA784.3] 53-10352
1. Margaret Tudor, consort of James IV, King of Scotland, 1489-1541. I. Title.

GLENNE, Michael. 923.141
King Harry's sister, Margaret Tudor, Queen of Scotland. London, New York, J. Long [1952] 224p. illus. 22cm. [DA784.3.M3G55] 53-1267
1. Margaret Tudor, consort of James IV, King of Scotland, 1489-1541. I. Title.

HARVEY, Nancy 941.1'04'0924 B Lenz.
The rose and the thorn : the lives of Mary and Margaret Tudor / by Nancy Lenz Harvey. New York : Macmillan, 1975. p. cm. Includes index. Bibliography: p. [DA784.3.M3H37] 75-22442 ISBN 0-02-548550-4 : 7.95
1. Margaret Tudor, consort of James IV, King of Scotland, 1489-1541. 2. Mary, consort of Louis XII, King of France, 1496-1533. 3. Henry VIII, King of England, 1491-1547. I. Mary, consort of Louis XII, King of France, 1496-1533. II. Margaret Tudor, consort of James IV, King of Scotland, 1489-1541. III. Title.

Margaretha, of Austria, regent of the Netherlands, 1480-1530.

IONGH, Jane de. 923.1492
Margaret of Austria, regent of the Netherlands; translated by M. D. Herter Norton. New York, Norton [1953] 256 p. illus. 22 cm. Includes bibliography. [DH183.I55] 53-13087
1. Margaretha, of Austria, regent of the Netherlands, 1480-1530.

Margherita da Citta di Castello, 1287-1320.

BONNIWELL, William 922.245 Raymond, 1888-
The story of Margaret of Metola. Drawings by Sister Mary of the Compassion. New York, Kenedy [1952] 177 p. illus. 20 cm. [BX4705.M32515B6] 52-13327
1. Margherita da Citta di Castello, 1287-1320. I. Title.

Margherita da Cortona, Saint, 1247-1297.

ROBERTO, Brother, 1927- 922.245
The flame still burns; a story of St. Margaret of Cortona. Illus. by William Pero. Notre Dame, Ind., Dujarie Press [1956] 94p. illus. 24cm. [BX4700.M36R6] 56-1572
1. Margherita da Cortona, Saint, 1247-1297. I. Title.

ROBERTO, Brother, 1927- 922.245
The flame still burns; a story of St. Margaret of Cortona. Illus. by William Pero. Notre Dame, Ind., Dujarie Press [1956] 94p. illus. 24cm. [BX4700.M3CR6] 56-1572
1. Margherita da Cortona, Saint, 1247-1297. I. Title.

Margherita di Savola, consort of Theodore

MARY Estelle, Sister, O. 922.245 P.
Wheat and cockle; the life and times of Blessed Margaret of Savoy. New York, St. Paul Publications [1960] 282p. illus. 21cm. [BX4705.M32517M34] 60-14929
1. Margherita di Savola, consort of Theodore I. marquis of Montferrat, 1382?-1464. II. Title.

Marguerite de Valois, consort of Henry IV, King of France, 1553-1615.

CHAMBERLIN, Eric 944'.031'0924 B Russell.
Marguerite of Navarre [by] E. R. Chamberlin. New York, Dial Press, 1974. v, 296 p. 23 cm. Bibliography: p. 285-286. [DC122.9.M2C45] 74-6095 ISBN 0-8037-5207-5 10.00
1. Marguerite de Valois, consort of Henry IV, King of France, 1553-1615. I. Title. BIP

HALDANE, 944'.031'0924 B Charlotte (Franken) 1894-1969.
Queen of hearts; Marguerite of Valois, 'La reine Margot', 1553-1615, by Charlotte Haldane. Indianapolis, Bobbs-Merrill [1968] 307 p. facsims., map, ports. 22 cm. [DC122.9.M2H3 1968b] 68-11148
1. Marguerite de Valois, consort of Henry IV, King of France, 1553-1615. I. Title.

Maria,

MARIA, consort of 949.8'02'0924 B Ferdinand I, King of Romania, 1875-1938.
The story of my life. New York, Arno Press, 1971 [c1934-35] 2 v. illus., ports. 24 cm. (The Eastern Europe collection) Vol. 2 previously published in 1935 under title: Ordeal; the story of my life. [DR262.A2A3 1970] 79-135819 ISBN 0-405-02793-1
I. Title.

Maria Antonia,

MARIA ANTONIA, Sister, 922.281 1900-1939.
Under angel wings; the autobiography of Sister Maria Antonia, religious of the Sisters of St. Francis of Penance and Christian Charity. Translated by Conall O'Leary from the original Portuguese edited by J. Batista Reus. Paterson, N. J., St. Anthony Guild Press, 1953. 214p. illus. 20cm. [BX4705.M32528A3] 54-90981
I. Title.

Maria Assunta, Sister, 1878-1905.

THE theme song of 922.245
Assunta, compiled by one of her sisters. [North Providence, R. I.] Franciscan Missionaries of Mary, St. Francis of Assisi 45 Province, 1956. 166p. illus. 23cm. [BX4705.M3254T5] 57-32587
1. Maria Assunta, Sister, 1878-1905.

Maria, consort of Louis II, King of Hungary, 1505-1558.

IDNGH, Jane de. 923.14391
Mary of Hungary, second regent of the Netherlands. Translated by M. D. Herter Norton. [1st ed.] New York, Norton [1958] 304p. illus. 22cm. Includes bibliographies. [DB932.2.M3 I 613 1958] 58-7389
1. Maria, consort of Louis II, King of Hungary, 1505-1558. 2. Netherlands—Hist.—Charles v. 1506-1555. I. Title.

Maria Crocifissa di Gesu, madre, 1713-1787.

MEAD, Jude. 271'.979 B
Dove in the cleft; the life of Mother Mary Crucified of Jesus, C.P., the first Passionist nun, 1713-1787. [1st ed.] New York, Exposition Press [1971] 248 p. port. 21 cm. (An Exposition-testament book) Bibliography: p. [235]-241. [BX4705.M32545143M4] 78-156078 ISBN 0-682-47263-8 6.00
1. Maria Crocifissa di Gesu, madre, 1713-1787. I. Title.

Maria, de Jesus de Agreda, Mother, 1602-1665.

KENDRICK, Thomas 271'.973 Downing. Sir
Mary of Agreda: the life and legend of a Spanish nun [by] T. D. Kendrick. London, Routledge & K. Paul, 1967. xii, 178p. 8 plates (incl. ports., facsims.), diagrs. 22cm. Bibl. [BX4705.M3255K4] (B) 67-109481 4.50
1. Maria, de Jesus de Agreda, Mother, 1602-1665. I. Title.
Distributed by Fernhill House, 162 E. 23 St., New York, N. Y. 10010.

Maria de Passione, Mere, 1839-1904.

WILLMANN, Agnes. 271'.973'024 B
Everywhere people waiting; the life of Helen de Chappotin de Neuville (Mother Mary of the Passion) 1839-1904, foundress of the Franciscan Missionaries of Mary. North Quincy, Mass., Christopher Pub. House [1973] 376 p. port. 23 cm. Bibliography: p. 375-376. [BX4351.Z8W44] 72-94708 ISBN 0-8158-0294-3 5.95
1. Maria de Passione, Mere, 1839-1904. I. Title.

Maria Goretti, Saint, 1890-1902.

BUEHRLE, Marie Cecilia, 922.245 1887-
Saint Maria Goretti. Milwaukee, Bruce Pub. Co. [1950] x, 164 p. illus., ports. 21 cm. [BX4700.M368B8] 50-9799
1. Maria Goretti, Saint, 1890-1902. I. Title.

DI DONATO, Pietro, 1911- 922.245
The penitent. New York, Hawthorn [c.1962] 190p. 62-9038 3.95
1. Maria Goretti, Saint, 1890-1902. 2. Serenelli, Alessandro. I. Title.

MACCONASTAIR, Alfred, 922.245 1908-
Lily of the marshes, the story of Maria Goretti. New York, Macmillan, 1951. xi, 200 p. illus., ports. 21 cm. [BX4700.M368M2] 51-9964
1. Maria Goretti, Saint, 1890-1902. I. Title.

MAGUIRE, C E 922.245
Saint Maria Goretti, martyr of purity,

1890-1902. Foreword by Isidore L. Smith. New York, Catholic Book Pub. Co. [1950] 95 p. illus., ports. 16 cm. [BX4700.M368M3] 51-2822
1. Maria Gorretti, Saint. I. Title.

MORELLI, James. 922.245
Teen-ager's saint; Saint Maria Goretti. Edited by William Peil; illus. by Gertryd Januszewski. St. Meinrad, Ind., Grail [1954] 84p. illus. 22cm. [BX4700.M368M6] 54-11421
1. Maria Goretti, Saint, 1890-1902. I. Title.

POAGE, Godfrey Robert, 922.245
1920-
In garments all red. [1st ed.] [Chicago] Paluch Publications [1950] 118 p. illus., ports., map. 19 cm. (Lumen books) [BX4700.M368P6] 50-56874
1. Maria Goretti, Saint, 1890-1902. I. Title.
BIP

POAGE, Godfrey 282'.092'4 B
Robert, 1920-
In garments all red : the life story of St. Maria Goretti / by Godfrey Poage. Boston : St. Paul Editions, c1977. 118 p. : ill. ; 18 cm. [BX4700.M368P6 1977] 77-4485 pbk. : 1.50
1. Maria Goretti, Saint, 1890-1902. 2. Christian saints—Italy—Biography. I. Title.

RYAN, William Dennis. 922.245
The Red Lily, St. Maria Gorett, by "Uncle Jeff," William Dennis Bryan. [1st ed.] Chicago, Paluch Publications [1950] 85 p. illus. map. 19 cm. (Lumen books: junior series) Includes "Maria's cradle song" (words and music) [BX4700.M368R8] 50-56875
1. Maria Goretti, Saint, 1890-1902. I. Title.

SABINUS, Brother, 1917- 922.245
The maid of Corinaldo; a story of Saint Maria Goretti. Illus. by Brother Bernard Howard. Notre Dame, Ind., Dujarie Press [1953] 92p. illus. 24cm. [BX4700.M368S3] 53-3996
1. Maria Goretti, Saint, 1890-1902. I. Title.

Maria Luisa Josefa of the Most Blessed Sacrament, Mother, 1866-1937.

QUEEN, William M 1893- 922.272
The doctor's widow; the story of a good neighbor. Fresno, Calif., Academy Library Guild, 1956. 127p. illus. 22cm. [BX4705.M334Q4] 56-14291
1. Maria Luisa Josefa of the Most Blessed Sacrament, Mother, 1866-1937. I. Title.

Maria Maddalena de' Pazzi, Saint 1566-1607.

MARY Minima, Sister 922.245
Seraph among angels; the life of St. Mary Magdalene de' Pazzi, Carmelite and mystic. Translated from the Italian and edited by Gabriel N. Pausback. Chicago, Carmelite Press, 1958. 363p. 22 cm. [BX4700.M37M33] 59-20257
1. Maria Maddalena de Pazzi, Saint, 1566-1607. I. Title.

VAN DER KLEY, Francesca. 922.245
Marian mystic; a short life of St. Mary Magdalen de' Pazzi. [Special limited 1st ed.] Chicago, Carmelite Third Order Press, 1957. 96 p. illus. 17 cm. [BX4700.M3V3] 57-35446
1. Maria Maddalena de' Pazzi, Saint 1566-1607. I. Title.

Maria Theresa, Empress of Austria, 1717-1780.

BRIGHT, James 943'.053'0924
Franck, 1832-1920.
Maria Theresa. Freeport, N.Y., Books for Libraries Press [1971] 224 p. 23 cm. "First published 1897." [DB70.B85 1971] 71-154145 ISBN 0-8369-5761-X
1. Maria Theresia, Empress, of Austria, 1717-1780. 2. Austria—History—Maria Theresa, 1740-1780.
BIP

CRANKSHAW, 943'.053'0924 B
Edward.
Maria Theresa. New York, Viking Press [1970, c1969] 366 p. illus., geneal. table, fold. map, ports. 22 cm. Bibliography: p. 339-344. [DB71.C7 1970] 70-94850 ISBN 0-670-45631-4 6.95
1. Maria Theresa, Empress of Austria, 1717-1780. 2. Austria—History—Maria Theresa, 1740-1780.

PICK, Robert, 1898- 943.6030924
Empress Maria Theresa; the earlier years, 1717-1757. New York, Harper [c.1966] xii, 335p. illus., map, ports. 25cm. Bibl. [DB71.P55] 66-15736 8.95
1. Maria Theresia, Empress of Austria, 1717-1780 I. Title.

ROIDER, Karl A., 943'.053'0924 B
comp.
Maria Theresa. Edited by Karl A. Roider, Jr. Englewood Cliffs, N.J., Prentice-Hall [1973] vi, 186 p. 21 cm. (Great lives observed) (A Spectrum book) [DB71.R6] 72-10940 ISBN 0-13-556191-4 2.45
1. Maria Theresa, Empress of Austria, 1717-1780. 2. Austria—History—Maria Theresa, 1740-1780.
Contents Omitted. BIP

Mariategui, Jose Carlos, 1894-1930.

CHAVARRIA, 335.43'092'4 B
Jesus, 1935-
Jose Carlos Mariategui and the rise of modern Peru, 1890-1930 / Jesus Chavarria. 1st ed. Albuquerque : University of New Mexico Press, c1979. xi, 247 p., [4] leaves of plates : ill. ; 25 cm. Includes index. Bibliography: p. 221-240. [HX222.M38C45] 78-21426 ISBN 0-8263-0507-5 : 16.50
1. Mariategui, Jose Carlos, 1894-1930. 2. Communists—Peru—Biography. 3. Peru—History. 4. Journalists—Peru—Biography. I. Title.
BIP

Marichal, Juan—Juvenile literature.

DEVANEY, John. 796.357'0924 B
Juan Marichal, Mister Strike. New York, Putnam [1970] 190 p. ports. 21 cm. A biography stressing the baseball career of the boy from the Dominican Republic who became "the keystone of the pitching corps of the San Francisco Giants." [GV865.M335D4 1970] 92 74-113515 3.86
1. Marichal, Juan—Juvenile literature. I. Title.

MARICHAL, Juan. 796.3572'2'0924
A pitcher's story, by Juan Marichal with Charles Einstein. [1st ed.] Garden City, N.Y., Doubleday, 1967. 215 p. illus. 22 cm. [GV865.M335A3] 67-19069
I. Einstein, Charles, joint author. II. Title.
BIP

Marie Adelaide de Savole, Duchess of Burgundy, Dauphine of France, 1685-1712.

NORTON, Lucy. 944'.033'0924 B
First lady of Versailles : Marie, Adelaide of Savoy, Dauphine of France / Lucy Norton. Philadelphia : Lippincott, c1978. 402 p., [4] leaves of plates : ill. ; 23 cm. Includes index. [DC130.M35N67] 78-17534 ISBN 0-397-01051-6 15.00
1. Marie Adelaide de Savoie, Duchess of Burgundy, Dauphine of France, 1685-1712. 2. France—Court and courtiers—Bibography. 3. France—Princes and princesses—Biography. I. Title.

Marie Antoinette, consort of Louis xvi, King of France, 1755-1793.

ASQUITH, 944.035'092'4
Annunziata.
Marie Antoinette. Annunziata Asquith. New York : Taplinger, 1976 c1974. 232 p. : ill. (part col.), facsims., geneal. table, maps, ports. (some col.) ; 26 cm. Includes index. Bibliography: p. 224. [DC137.1.A75] 76-5195 ISBN 0-8008-5119-6 : 13.95
1. Marie Antoinette, consort of Louis XVI, King of France, 1755-1793. I. Title.

BELLOC, Hilaire, 944'.035'0924 B
1870-1953.
Marie Antoinette. Freeport, N.Y., Books for Libraries Press [1972, c1909] x, 559 p. illus. 23 cm. [DC137.1.B46 1972] 70-37871 ISBN 0-8369-6708-9
1. Marie Antoinette, consort of Louis XVI, King of France, 1755-1793. 2. France—History—Revolution, 1789-1799.

CASTELOT, Andre. 923.144
Queen of France; a biography of Marie Antoinette. Translated from the French by Denise Folliot. [1st ed.] New York, Harper [1957] 434 p. illus. 22 cm. Translation of Marie Antoinette d'apres des documents inedits. [DC137.1.C313 1957a] 56-6021
1. Marie Antoinette, consort of Louis XVI, King of France, 1755-1793. I. Title.

GOOCH, George Peabody, 923.1436
1873-1968,
Maria Theresa, and other studies. London, New York, Longmans, Green [1951] viii, 432 p. ports. 23 cm. [DB71.G63] 51-14318
1. Joseph II, Emperor of Germany, 1741-1790. 2. Marie Antoinette, consort of Louis XVI, King of France, 1755-1793. 3. Maria Theresa, Empress of Austria, 1717-1780. 4. Historiography. 5. History—Study and teaching.

GOSSELIN, Louis 944'.035'0924 B
Leon Theodore, 1857-1935.
The flight of Marie Antoinette, from the French of G. Lenotre (pseud.) by Mrs. Rodolph Stawell. London, W. Heinemann; Philadelphia, Lippincott, 1906. [New York, AMS Press, 1973] xi, 340 p. illus. 23 cm. Includes bibliographical references. [DC137.05.G8 1973] 73-168160 ISBN 0-404-07128-7
1. Marie Antoinette, consort of Louis XVI, King of France, 1755-1793. 2. France—History—Revolution, 1789-1799. I. Title.
BIP

GOWER, Ronald 944'.035'0924 B
Charles Sutherland, Lord, 1845-1916.
Last days of Marie Antoinette; an historical sketch. Boston, Roberts Bros., 1886. [New York, AMS Press, 1973] 154 p. illus. 19 cm. [DC137.17.G72 1973] 74-168163 ISBN 0-404-07129-5 6.50
1. Marie Antoinette, consort of Louis XVI, King of France, 1755-1793. I. Title. BIP

*HEARSEY, John E. N. 944.035 [B]
Marie Antoinette [by] John E. N. Hearsey. [First ed.] New York, Dutton, 1973. [296 p.] 22 cm. [DC137] 72-90785 ISBN 0-525-15290-3 7.95
1. Marie Antoinette, Queen Consort of Louis VI, King of France, 1755-1793. I. Title.

HUISMAN, 944'.035'0924 B
Philippe.
Marie Antoinette [by] Philippe Huisman [and] Marguerite Jallut. New York, Viking Press [1971] 249 p. illus. (part col.), facsims., maps, ports. (part col.) 27 cm. (A Studio book) [DC137.1.H8413] 70-162666 ISBN 0-670-45697-7 25.00
1. Marie Antoinette, consort of Louis XVI, King of France, 1755-1793. I. Jallut, Marguerite, joint author.

KOMROFF, Manuel, 1890- 92
Marie Antoinette, by Manuel Komroff and Odette Komroff. New York, J. Messner [1967] 191 p. 22 cm. Bibliography: p. [186] -189. A biography of the beautiful but spoiled Austrian princess whose frivolous reign as Queen of France helped provoke the Revolution and her own death on the guillotine. [DC137.1.K6] AC 67
1. Marie Antoinette, consort of Louis XVI, King of France, 1755-1793. I. Komroff, Odette, joint author. II. Title.

LOOMIS, Stanley. 944'.035'0924 B
The fatal friendship; Marie Antoinette, Count Fersen and the flight to Varennes. [1st ed.] Garden City, N.Y., Doubleday, 1972. 341 p. illus. 25 cm. Bibliography: p. 339-341. [DC137.19.L66] 72-175388 9.95
1. Marie Antoinette, consort of Louis XVI, King of France, 1755-1793. 2. Fersen, Hans Axel von, greve, 1755-1810. 3. France—History—Revolution, 1789-1799. I. Title.

MAYER, Dorothy 944'.035'0924 B
Moulton (Piper) Lady.
Marie Antoinette; the tragic queen. [1st American ed.] New York, Coward-McCann [1969, c1968] 385 p. illus., facsims., geneal. tables, ports. 22 cm. Published in 1968 under title: The tragic queen. Bibliography: p. 367-370. [DC137.1.M38 1969] 77-79786 6.95
1. Marie Antoinette, consort of Louis XVI, King of France, 1755-1793.

SCHERMAN, Bernardine 923.144
(Kielty)
Marie Antoinette, by Bernardine Kielty. Illustrated by Douglas Gorsline. New York, Random House [1955] 184 p. illus. 22 cm. (World landmark books, W-20) [DC137.1.S3] 55-10011
1. Marie Antoinette, consort of Louis xvi, King of France, 1755-1793. I. Title.

VANCE, Marguerite. 923.144
Marie Antoinette, daughter of an empress. Illustrated by Nedda Walker. [1st ed.] New York, Dutton [1950] 159 p. illus. 21 cm. [DC137.1.V3] 50-9930
1. Marie Antoinette, consort of Louis XVI, King of France, 1755-1793.

Marie Antoinette, consort of Louis xvi, King of France, 1755-1793 — Juvenile literature.

KOMROFF, Manuel, 1890- j92
Marie Antoinette, by Manuel Komroff and Odette Komroff. New York, J. Messner [1967] 191 p. 22 cm. Bibliography: p. [186] -189. [DC137.1.K6] 67-2943
1. Marie Antoinette, consort of Louis xvi, King of France, 1755-1793 — Juvenile literature. I. Komroff, Odette, joint author. II. Title.

Marie de Jesus, Mother. 1876-1931.

NAPOLI PRARIO, Lucy. 922.245
Three white veils for Sandra. [New York, Dell, 1963,c.1956] 224p. 16 cm. (8865) pap.,0.40
1. Marie de Jesus, Mother, 1876-1931 I. Title.

NAPOLI PRARIO, Lucy. 922.245
Three white veils for Sandra, by Lucy Prarie. New York, Farrar, Straus and Cudahy [1956] 243p. 22cm. [BX4705.M356N33] 56-6159
1. Marie de Jesus, Mother. 1876-1931. I. Title.

Marie de l Incarnation, Mother, 1566-1618.

SHEPPARD, Lancelot Capel, v. 12
1906-
Barbe Acarie, with and mystic a biography. New York, McKay, 1953. xi, 210p. plates. 23cm. A53
1. Marie de l Incarnation, Mother, 1566-1618. I. Title.

Marie de l'Incarnation, Mother, 1599-1672.

MAHONEY, Denis, Mother. 922.244
Marie of the Incarnation, mystic and missionary. [1st ed.] Garden City, N.Y., Doubleday, 1964. ix, 421 p. 22 cm. Bibliography: p. 409-412. [BX4705.M36M3] 64-19285
1. Marie de l'Incarnation, Mother, 1599-1672.

MARIE de l'Incarnation, 922.271
Mother
The autobiography of Venerable Marie of the Incarnation, O.S.U., mystic and missionary. Tr. [from French] by John J. Sullivan. Pref. by James Brodrick. Chicago, Loyola Univ. Pr. [c.]1964. xxi, 218p. 24cm. 64-3038 6.00
I. Title.

Marie de Medicis, Consort of Henry IV, King of France, 1573-1642.

BATIFFOL, Louis, 944'.031'0924
1865-1946.
Marie de Medicis and the French court in the XVIIth century: translated from the French of Louis Batiffol by Mary King,

edited by H. W. Carless Davis. Freeport, N.Y., Books for Libraries Press [1970] xi, 314 p. port. 23 cm. Translation of La vie intime d'une reine de France au XVIIe siecle. Reprint of the 1908 ed. [DC122.9.M3B3 1970] 72-137368
1. Marie de Medicis, Consort of Henry IV, King of France, 1573-1642. 2. France—Court and courtiers. I. Davis, Henry William Carless, 1874-1928, ed. II. Title.

Marie Louise,

MARIE Louise, Princess, 942.08
1872-1956.
My memories of six reigns. [1st American ed.] New York, Dutton, 1957. 256 p. illus. 22 cm. [DA574.A45M3 1957] 57-8958
I. Title. BIP

Marie Louise, consort of Napoleon I, 1791-1847.

MARIE Louise, Princess, 942.08
1872-1956.
My memories of six reigns. [1st American ed.] New York, Dutton, 1957. 256 p. illus. 22 cm. [DA574.A45M3 1957] 57-8958
I. Title. BIP

STOECKL, Agnes(Barron) 923.144
Baroness de
Four years an empress; Marie-Louise, second wife of Napoleon. London, J. Murray [dist. Hollywood-By-The-Sea, Fla., Transatlantic, 1963, c.1962] 304p. illus. 23cm. Bibl. 63-53513 7.00
1. Marie Louise, consort of Napoleon I, 1791-1847. I. Title.

TURNBULL, Patrick. 944.05'092'4 B
Napoleon's second empress. New York, Walker [1972, c1971] 304 p. illus. 24 cm. Bibliography: p. 294-295. [DC216.2.T87 1972] 77-183925 ISBN 0-8027-0376-3 7.95
1. Marie Louise, consort of Napoleon I, 1791-1847. 2. Napoleon I, Emperor of the French, 1769-1821. I. Title. BIP

TURNBULL, 944'.05'0924 [B]
Patrick.
Napoleon's second empress; a life of passion. [New York] Manor Books [1974, c1971] 304 p. illus. 18 cm. Bibliography: p. 294-295. [DC216.2T87] 1.95 (pbk.)
1. Marie Louise, consort of Napoleon I, 1791-1847. 2. Napoleon I, Emperor of the French, 1769-1821. I. Title.
L.C. card no. for original ed. is 77-183925.

Marie Rose, Mother, 1811-1849.

EULALIA TERESA, Sister, 922.271
1898-
So short a day; the life of Mother Marie-Rose, foundress of the Congregation of the Sisters of the Holy Names of Jesus and Mary, 1811-1849. New York, McMullen Books [c1954] 281p. illus. 21cm. [BX4705.M395E8] 55-14158
1. Marie Rose, Mother, 1811-1849. 2. Sisters of the Holy Names of Jesus and Mary. I. Title.

Marie Rose, Mother, 1811-1849—Juvenile literature.

MARY Michaeline, Sister. 922.271
The rose tree; life of Mother Marie Rose Durocher (1811-1849) foundress of the Sisters of the Holy Names of Jesus and Mary. Milwaukee, Bruce Pub. Co. [1961] 125p. illus. 23cm. [BX4499.Z8M34] 61-17408
1. Marie Rose, Mother, 1811-1849—Juvenile literature. I. Title.

Mariia Feodorovna, consort of Alexander III, Emperor of Russia, 1847-1928.

TISDALL, Evelyn Ernest 923.147
Percy, 1907-
Marie Fedorovna, Empress of Russia. New York, J. Day Co. [1958] 319 p. illus. 21 cm. "Published in England [1957] in a slightly different version, as The dowager Empress." [DK236.A2T5 1958] 57-14520
1. Mariia Feodorovna, consort of Alexander III, Emperor of Russia, 1847-1928. I. Title.

Marin, Francisco de Paula, 1774?-1837.

GAST, Ross H. 919.69'1'0320924 B
Don Francisco de Paula Marin; a biography, by Ross H. Gast. The letters and journal of Francisco de Paula Marin, edited by Agnes C. Conrad. Honolulu, University Press of Hawaii for the Hawaiian Historical Society [1973] 344 p. illus. 24 cm. Bibliography: p. [332]-334. [DU627.17.M37G37] 77-188980 ISBN 0-8248-0220-9 8.50
1. Marin, Francisco de Paula, 1774?-1837. I. Marin, Francisco de Paula, 1774?-1837.

Marin, John, 1870-1953.

MARIN, John, 1870-1953. 759.13
John Marin. Edited by Cleve Gray. [1st ed.] New York, Holt, Rinehart and Winston [1970] 176 p. illus. (part col.), facsims., ports. 29 cm. [ND237.M24G7] 77-102144 22.95

MARIN, John, 1870-1953. 759.13
John Marin. Edited by Cleve Gray. [1st ed.] New York, Holt, Rinehart and Winston [1970] 176 p. illus. (part col.), facsims., ports. 29 cm. [ND237.M24G7] 77-102144 22.95

MARIN, John, 1870-1953. 759.13
Letters of John Marin. Edited, with an introd. by Herbert J. Seligmann. Westport, Conn., Greenwood Press [1970] 1 v. (unpaged) facsims. 23 cm. Reprint of the 1931 ed. [ND1839.M35A3 1970] 77-109780 ISBN 0-8371-4270-9 202

MARIN, John, 1870-1953. 759.13
Letters of John Marin. Edited, with an introd. by Herbert J. Seligmann. Westport, Conn., Greenwood Press [1970] 1 v. (unpaged) facsims. 23 cm. Reprint of the 1931 ed. [ND1839.M35A3 1970] 77-109780 ISBN 0-8371-4270-9 201

WILLIAMS, William Carlos, 759.13
1883-
John Marin: tributes by William Carlos Williams, Duncan Phillips [and] Dorothy Norman. Conclusion to a biography, by Mackinley Helm. John Marin, frontiersman, by Frederick S. Wight. Berkeley, University of California Press, 1956. [78]p. illus. (part col.) 28cm. Bibliography: p. [77]-[78] [ND237.M24J6] 927.5 56-6988
1. Marin, John, 1870-1953. I. Wight, Frederick Stallknecht, 1902- II. Title.

WILLIAMS, William Carlos, 759.13
1883-
John Marin: tributed by William Carlos Williams, Duncan Phillips [and] Dorothy Norman. Conclusion to a biography, by Mackinley Helm. John Marin, frontiersman, by Frederick S. Wight. Berkeley, University of California Press, 1956. [78]p. illus. (part col.) 28cm. Bibliography: p. [77]-[78] [ND237.M24J6] 927.5 56-6988
1. Marin, John, 1870-1953. I. Wieght, Frederick Stallknecht 1902- II. Title.

Marini, Marino,

MARINI, Marino, 1901- 709.24
Complete works. Introd. by Herbert Read. General text by Patrick Waldberg. Catalogues and notes by G. di San Lazzaro. New York, Tudor Pub. Co. [1970] 506 p. illus., plates (part col.), ports. 36 cm. Bibliography: p. 493-[494] [N6923.M27W3] 72-20429
1. Waldberg, Patrick. II. San Lazzaro, Gualtieri di.

Mario, Giuseppe, conte di Candia, 1810-1883.

PEARSE, Cecilia 782.1'092'4 B
Maria de Candia.
The romance of a great singer : a memoir of Mario / Cecilia Maria de Candia Pearse and Frank Hird. New York : Arno Press, 1977. ix, 309 p., [7] leaves of plates ; 22 cm. (Opera biographies) Reprint of the 1910 ed. published by Smith, Elder, London. Includes index. [ML420.M33P3 1977] 76-29961 ISBN 0-405-09701-8 : 19.00
1. Mario, Giuseppe, conte di Candia, 1810-1883. 2. Singers—Biography. I. Title. BIP

Marion, Francis, 1732-1795.

BASS, Robert Duncan. 973.33
Swamp Fox; the life and campaigns of General Francis Marion. [1st ed.] New York, Holt [1959] 275 p. illus. 22 cm. [E207.M3B3] 59-5368
1. Marion, Francis, 1732-1795. I. Title.

EPSTEIN, Beryl (Williams) 923.573
1910-
Francis Marion, Swamp Fox of the Revolution, by Beryl Williams and Samuel Epstein. New York, J. Messner [1956] 192 p. illus. 22 cm. [E207.M3E6] 56-10442
1. Marion, Francis, 1732-1795. I. Epstein, Samuel, 1909- joint author. II. Title.

RANKIN, Hugh F. 973.3'092'4 B
Francis Marion: the Swamp Fox [by] Hugh F. Rankin. New York, Crowell [1973] xv, 346 p. illus. 24 cm. (Leaders of the American Revolution series) Bibliography: p. 328-334. [E207.M3R36] 73-10062 ISBN 0-690-00097-9 10.00
1. Marion, Francis, 1732-1792.

SIMMS, William 975.7'02'0924
Gilmore, 1806-1870.
The life of Francis Marion. Freeport, N.Y., Books for Libraries Press [1971] 347 p. illus., ports. 23 cm. Reprint of the 1844 ed. [E207.M3S54] 75-153130 ISBN 0-8369-5740-7
1. Marion, Francis, 1732-1795. BIP

WEEMS, Mason 973.3'3'0924 B
Locke, 1759-1825.
The life of Gen. Francis Marion, a celebrated partisan officer in the Revolutionary War, against the British and Tories in South Carolina and Georgia / by P. Horry and M. L. Weems. Charleston, S.C. : Tradd Street Press, [1976] viii, 252 p. : ill., map (on lining papers) ; 24 cm. Rewritten by M. L. Weems from material provided by P. Horry. On spine: Francis Marion. Reprint of the 1824? ed. [E207.M3W3 1976] 76-21439
1. Marion, Francis, 1732-1795. 2. South Carolina—Militia—Biography. 3. Generals—United States—Biography. 4. South Carolina—History—Revolution, 1775-1783. 5. Georgia—History—Revolution, 1775-1783. I. Horry, Peter, joint author. II. Title: The life of Gen. Francis Marion, a celebrated partisan officer in the Revolutionary War ...

Marion, Francis, 1732-1795—Juvenile literature.

GRANT, Matthew G. 973.3'092'4 B
Francis Marion, Swamp Fox [by] Matthew G. Grant. Illustrated by John Keely and Dick Brude. [Mankato, Minn., Creative Education; distributed by Childrens Press, Chicago, [1973, c1974] 29 p. illus. (part col.) 25 cm. (His Gallery of great Americans series. Frontiersmen of America) A brief biography of the southern plantation owner whose knowledge of the swamps helped keep the Revolution alive in the South. [E207.M3G72] 92 73-10061 ISBN 0-87191-257-0 3.95
1. Marion, Francis, 1732-1795—Juvenile literature. I. Keely, John, illus. II. Brude, Dick, illus. III. Title.

Marion, Francis, literature.

HOLBROOK, Stewart Hall, 923.573
1893-
The Swamp Fox of the Revolution. Illustrated by Ernest Richardson. New York, Random House [1959] 180p. illus. 22cm. (Landmark books [90]) Includes bibliography. [E207.M3H6] 59-12369
1. Marion, Francis, literature. I. Title.

Maritain, Jacques, 1882-1973.

EVANS, Joseph William, ed. 194
Jacques Maritain: the man and his achievement. New York, Sheed & Ward [c.1963] xii, 258p. 22cm. Bibl. 63-17143 5.00
1. Maritain, Jacques, 1882- I. Title.

KERNAN, Julie, 1901- 194 B
Our friend, Jacques Maritain : a personal memoir / by Julie Kernan. 1st ed. Garden City, N.Y. : Doubleday, 1975. 192 p., [2] leaves of plates : ill. ; 22 cm. Includes bibliographical references. [B2430.M34K47] 74-3696 ISBN 0-385-09659-3 : 6.95
1. Maritain, Jacques, 1882-1973. I. Title.

Maritain, Raissa.

MARITAIN, Raissa. 282'.092'4 B
Raissa's Journal / presented by Jacques Maritain ; pref. by Rene Voillaume. Enl. with new matter for this translation. Albany : Magi Books, [1975] c1974. xxii, 404 p., [4] leaves of plates : ports. ; 19 cm. [BX4705.M3994A3313 1975] 72-95648 ISBN 0-87343-041-7 : 12.95
1. Maritain, Raissa. I. Title. BIP

Maritime Provinces, Canada—Biog.

KERR, J Ernest. 920.0715
Imprint of the Maritimes; highlights in the lives of 100 interesting Americans whose roots are in Canada's Atlantic Provinces. Boston, Christopher Pub. House [1959] 229p. illus. 21cm. [F1035.8.K39] 59-8807
1. Maritime Provinces, Canada—Biog. I. Title.

Marius, C.

KILDAHL, Phillip 937'.05'0924 (B)
Andrew.
Caius Marius, by Phillip A. Kildahl. New York, Twayne Publishers [1968] 191 p. map. 21 cm. (Twayne's rulers and statesmen of the world series, 7) Includes bibliographical references. [DG256.5.K5] 67-28862
1. Marius, C. I. Title.

KILDAHL, Phillip 937'.05'0924 B
Andrew.
Caius Marius, by Phillip A. Kildahl. New York, Twayne Publishers [1968] 191 p. map. 21 cm. (Twayne's rulers and statesmen of the world series, 7) Includes bibliographical references. [DG256.5.K5] 67-28862
1. Marius, C.

Mark, Saint—Juvenile literature.

HAUGHTON, Rosemary 225.924
The young Saint Mark. Illus. by the author. New York, Roy [1965, c.1964] 136p. illus. 21cm. (Young biographies) [BS2475.H3] 65-18879 3.25 bds.,
1. Mark, Saint—Juvenile literature. I. Title.

Markel, Bart, 1935-

SCALZO, Joe. 796.7'5 B
The Bart Markel story. [Newport Beach, Calif.] Bond/Parkhurst Books [1972] 125 p. illus. 23 cm. [GV1060.2.M3S28] 76-189019 ISBN 0-87880-010-7 5.95
1. Markel, Bart, 1935- I. Title. BIP

Markel, Robert.

CANIZIO, Frank 923.4173
A man against fate, [by] Frank Canizio as told to Robert Markel. New York, Permabooks [dist. Pocket Books] [1959, c.1958] 200p. 17cm. (Permabk. M4133) .35 pap.,
1. Markel, Robert. I. Title.

Marketing—United States—Biography.

WRIGHT, John 380.1'092'2 B
Sherman, 1920- comp.
Pioneers in marketing; a collection of twenty-five biographies of men who contributed to the growth of marketing thought and action. Edited by John S.

Wright and Parks B. Dimsdale, Jr. Atlanta, Publishing Services Division, School of Business Administration, Georgia State University, 1974. 162 p. 22 cm. [HF5415.1.W74] 73-620235 ISBN 0-88406-016-0 1.95 (pbk.).
1. Marketing—United States—Biography. I. Dimsdale, Parks B., joint comp. II. Title. Contents omitted.

Markham family.

MARKHAM, Robert S., 1892- 929'.2'0973
Heritage and biography / by Robert S. Markham. [Soldier, Kan. : Markham], c1975. 83 p. : ill. ; 28 cm. [CS71.M3445 1975] 75-326384
1. Markham family. I. Title.

Markham, Violet Rosa.

MARKHAM, Violet Rosa. 923.242
Return passage; the autobiography of Violet R. Markham, C. H. London, New York, Oxford University Press, 1953. 260p. illus. 23cm. [HV28.M33A3] 54-8156
I. Title.

Markievicz, Constance Georgina Gore-Booth de, 1868-1927.

MARRECO, Anne Acland-Troyte, 1912- 941.5'9'0924
The Rebel Countess; the life and times of Constance Markievicz [by] Anne Marreco. [1st ed.] Philadelphia, Chilton Books [1967] xii, 330 p. illus., ports. 23 cm. Bibliography: p. 307-309. [DA965.M35M3 1967a] 67-16674
1. Markievicz, Constance Georgina Gore-Booth de, 1868-1927. I. Title.

VAN VORIS, Jacqueline. 941.59'092'4 B
Constance de Markievicz. [1st ed.] [Old Westbury, Long Island, N.Y.] Feminist Press, 1972. 143 p. ports. 19 cm. (Feminist Press biography series) "The material ... was originally included in a full-length biography of Constance de Markievicz published in 1967." Bibliography: p. 142-143. [DA965.M35V32] 72-7000 ISBN 0-912670-04-5
1. Markievicz, Constance Georgina (Gore-Booth) de, 1868-1927.

VAN VORIS, Jacqueline 941.5'9'0924 (B)
Constance de Markievicz in the cause of Ireland. [Amherst] Univ. of Mass. Pr., 1967. 384p. ports. 24cm. Bibl. [DA965.M35V3] 67-11245 7.50
1. Markievicz, Constance Georgina (GoreBooth) de, 1868-1927. I. Title.

Markish, Peretz, 1895-1952—Biography.

MARKISH, Esther, 1912- 839'.09'13
The long return / Esther Markish ; with a foreword by David Roskies. 1st ed. New York : Ballantine Books, c1978. xii, 307 p., [4] leaves of plates : ill. ; 18 cm. "Originally published in France as Le long retour." Includes index. [PJ5129.M34Z713] 77-6137 ISBN 0-345-24803-1 pbk. : 2.25
1. Markish, Peretz, 1895-1952—Biography. 2. Markish, Esther, 1912- 3. Authors, Yiddish—Biography. 4. Wives—Russia—Biography. 5. Jews in Russia—Biography. I. Title. BIP

Markova, Alicia, 1910-

ANTHONY, Gordon. 927.93
Alicia Markova. With an appreciation by Dame Adeline Gence-Isitt. London, Phoenix House; New York, British Book Center [1951] 111 p. illus. 25 cm. [GV1785.M3A48] 51-14746
1. Markova, Alicia, 1910- I. Title.

Marks, Jeannette Augustus, 1875-1964.

WELLS, Anna Mary. 378.1'12'0974423
Miss Marks and Miss Woolley / by Anna Mary Wells. Boston : Houghton Mifflin, 1978. xviii, 268 p., [8] leaves of plates : ill. ; 24 cm. Bibliography: p. [267]-268. [LD7092.7 1901.W44] 78-1391 ISBN 0-395-25724-7 : 10.95
1. Woolley, Mary Emma, 1863-1947. 2. Mount Holyoke College. 3. Marks, Jeannette Augustus, 1875-1964. 4. Wellesley College. 5. Lesbians—United States—Biography. I. Title.

Marland, Ernest Whitworth,

MATHEWS, John Joseph. 923.273
Life and death of an oilman; the career of E. W. Marland. With drawings by J. Craig Sheppard. [1st ed.] Norman, University of Oklahoma Press [1951] 259 p. illus. 22 cm. [HD9570.M3M3] 51-13242
1. Marland, Ernest Whitworth, 2. Petroleum industry and trade—U. S. I. Title.

Marlborough, John Churchill, 1st Duke of, 1650-1722.

BARNETT, Correlli. 941.06'9'0924 B
The first Churchill : Marlborough, soldier and statesman / Correlli Barnett. 1st American ed. New York : Putnam, 1974. 288 p. : ill. ; 26 cm. Includes index. Bibliography: p. 279. [DA462.M3B23 1974] 73-88531 ISBN 0-399-11297-9 : 14.95
1. Marlborough, John Churchill, 1st Duke of, 1650-1722. I. Title.

CHANDLER, David G. 335.3'31'0924 B
Marlborough as military commander [by] David Chandler. New York, Scribner [1973] 368 p. illus. 23 cm. Bibliography: p. [353]-356. [DA462.M3C37 1973b] 72-12160 ISBN 0-684-13314-8 14.95
1. Marlborough, John Churchill, 1st Duke of, 1650-1722. I. Title. BIP

CHANDLER, David G. 940.2'526'0924
Marlborough as military commander / [by] David Chandler ; with a foreword by the eleventh Duke of Marlborough. 2nd ed. London : Batsford, 1979. xvi, 368 p., [24] p. of plates : ill., facsims., maps, plans, ports. ; 24 cm. Includes index. Bibliography: p. [353]-356. [DA462.M3C37 1979] 79-315991 ISBN 0-7134-2075-8 : 14.95 14.95
1. Marlborough, John Churchill, 1st Duke of, 1650-1722. 2. Great Britain—History, Military—Stuarts, 1603-1714. 3. Generals—Great Britain—Biography. I. Title.
Distributed By Hippocrene Books, Inc., 171 Madison Ave., New York, NY 10016

CHURCHILL, Winston Leonard Spencer, Sir, 1874-1965. 942.06'9'0924 B
Marlborough; his life and times. Abridged and with an introd. by Henry Steele Commager. New York, Scribner [1968] xxxiii, 983 p. illus., maps, ports. 25 cm. Bibliography: p. 927-931. [DA462.M3C45 1968] 68-12353
1. Marlborough, John Churchill, 1st Duke of, 1650-1722. 2. Great Britain—History—1660-1714. I. Commager, Henry Steele, 1902- BIP

DEFOE, Daniel, 1661?-1731. 941.06'9'0924 B
A short narrative of the life and actions of His Grace John, D. of Marlborough / Daniel Defoe ; introd. by Paula R. Backscheider. [Los Angeles] : William Andrews Clark Memorial Library, University of California, Los Angeles, 1974. xv, 51 p. ; 22 cm. (Publication - The Augustan Reprint Society ; no. 168) Reprint of the 1711 ed. printed for J. Baker, London. Includes bibliographical references. [DA462.M3D4 1974] 75-622507
1. Marlborough, John Churchill, 1st Duke of, 1650-1722. I. Title: A short narrative of the life and actions of His Grace John ... II. Series: Augustan Reprint Society. Publication ; no. 168.

MARLBOROUGH, v. 12
by Maurice Ashley. New York, Macmillan [c1939, 1956] 144p. 19cm. (Great lives. 81) Bibliography: p. 144.
1. Marlborough, John Churchill, 1st duke of, 1650-1722. I. Ashley, Maurice Percy.

SAINTSBURY, George Edward Bateman, 1845-1933. 941.06'9'0924 B
Marlborough / by George Saintsbury. Folcroft, Pa. : Folcroft Library Editions, 1976. p. cm. Reprint of the 1888 ed. published by Longmans, Green, London, in series: English worthies. Includes bibliographical references and index. [DA462.M3S2 1976] 76-22738 ISBN 0-8414-7733-7 lib. bdg. : 25.00
1. Marlborough, John Churchill, 1st Duke of, 1650-1722. I. Series: English worthies. BIP

THOMSON, George Malcolm, 1899- 941.06'9'0924 B
The first Churchill : the life of John, 1st Duke of Marlborough / George Malcolm Thomson. 1st U.S. ed. New York : Morrrow, 1980, c1979. xi, 338 p., [8] leaves of plates : ill. ; 25 cm. Includes index. Bibliography: p. 318-324. [DA462.M3T53 1980] 79-66008 ISBN 0-688-03556-6 : 12.95
1. Marlborough, John Churchill, 1st Duke of, 1650-1722. 2. Great Britain—History—1660-1714. 3. Great Britain—History—George I, 1714-1727. 4. Statesmen—Great Britain—Biography. I. Title.

Marlborough, John Churchill, 1st Duke of, 1650-1722—Bibliography.

HORN, Robert Dewey. 016.94206'9'0924
Marlborough: a survey; panegyrics, satires, and biographical writings, 1688-1788, by Robert D. Horn. New York, Garland Pub., 1974. p. cm. [Z8550.38.H67] 74-14647 ISBN 0-8240-1054-X 50.00
1. Marlborough, John Churchill, 1st Duke of, 1650-1722—Bibliography.

Marlborough, Sarah (Jennings) Churchill, Duchess of, 1660-1744.

BUTLER, Iris. 942.06'9'0924
The great duchess; the life of Sarah Churchill. New York, Funk & Wagnalls [1968, c1967] 379 p. illus., ports. 22 cm. First published in 1967 under title: Rule of three. Bibliography: p. [363]-365. [DA462.M4B8 1968] 68-13267
1. Marlborough, Sarah (Jennings) Churchill, Duchess of, 1660-1744. I. Title.

DOBREE, Bonamy, 1891- 920.02
Three eighteenth century figures: Sarah Churchill, John Wealy, Giacomo Casanova New York, Oxford, 1962[ ] 248p. Bibl. 62-1635 4.80
1. Marlborough, Sarah (Jennings) duchess of, 1660-1744. 2. Wesley, Hohn, 1703-1791. 3. Casanova de Scingalt, Giacomo Girolamo, 1725-1798. I. Title.

GREEN, David Bronte, 1910- 942.06'9'0924 B
Sarah, Duchess of Marlborough. New York, Scribner [1967] 351 p. illus., ports. 24 cm. Bibliography: p. 326-329. [DA462.M4G7 1967b] 67-24061
1. Marlborough, Sarah (Jennings) Churchill, Duchess of, 1660-1744. I. Title.

KRONENBERGER, Louis, 1904- 920.7
Marlborough's duchess; a study in worldiness. [1st ed.] New York, Knopf, 1958. 314 p. illus. 22 cm. [DA462.M4K7] 58-9667
1. Marlborough, Sarah Jennings Churchill, duchess of, 1660-1774. I. Title.

MARLBOROUGH, Sarah (Jennings) Churchill, Duchess of, 1660-1744. 942.06'9'0924 B
Letters of Sarah, Duchess of Marlborough. Now first published from the original manuscripts at Madresfield Court. With an introd. London, Murray, 1875. [New York, AMS Press, 1973] xl, 174 p. 19 cm. On spine: WOL. [DA462.M4A25 1973] 77-37708 ISBN 0-404-56766-5 12.00
1. Marlborough, Sarah (Jennings) Churchill, Duchess of, 1660-1744. BIP

Marlowe, Christopher, 1564-1593.

BAKELESS, John Edwin, 1894- v. 12
Christopher Marlowe; the man in his time. New York, Washington Square Press [1964] xii, 335 p. 18 cm. (A Washington Square Press book, W-1082) "Check list of early extant editions": p. 281 283. Bibliography: P. 285-293. NUC65
1. Marlowe, Christopher, 1564-1593. I. Title. II. Series.

BAKELESS, John Edwin, 1894- 822'.3
Christopher Marlowe / by John Bakeless. New York : Haskell House Publishers, 1976 357 p. ; 21 cm. Reprint of the 1938 ed. published by J. Cape, London. Includes bibliographical references and index. [PR2673.B3 1975] 75-42103 ISBN 0-8383-1881-9 lib.bdg. : 17.95
1. Marlowe, Christopher, 1564-1593.

BAKELESS, John Edwin, 1894- 822.3
The tragicall history of Christopher Marlowe, by John Bakeless. Hamden, Conn., Archon Books, 1964- v. facsims., illus. 23 cm. [PR2673.B32 1964] 64-19943
1. Marlowe, Christopher, 1564-1593. I. Title. BIP

BOAS, Frederick Samuel, 1862-1957. 822'.3 B
Marlowe and his circle; a biographical survey. New York, Russell & Russell [1968] 159 p. facsims. 17 cm. Reprint of the 1929 ed. Bibliography: p. 143-154. [PR2673.B6 1968] 68-15102
1. Marlowe, Christopher, 1564-1593. I. Title. BIP

CHRISTOPHER Marlowe: v. 12
a biographical and critical study, by Frederick S. Boas... Oxford, The Clarendon press, [1960] xvi, 336p. illus., double map, facsims. (part double) 22cm. 'A list of principal documents and early editions': p. [315]-328.
1. Marlowe, Christopher, 1564-1593. I. Boas, Frederick Samuel, 1862-

ECCLES, Mark. 822'.3
Christopher Marlowe in London. New York, Octagon Books, 1967 [c1934] vi, 185 p. 21 cm. (Harvard studies in English v. 10) Bibliographical footnotes. [PR2673.E4 1967] 67-18761
1. Marlowe, Christopher, 1564-1593. 2. Watson, Thomas, 1557?-1592. I. Title. II. Series. BIP

HENDERSON, Philip, 1906- 822'.3 B
And morning in his eyes; a book about Christopher Marlowe. New York, Haskell House Publishers, 1972. 352 p. illus. 23 cm. Reprint of the 1937 ed. Bibliography: p. 343-345. [PR2673.H4 1972] 75-39861 ISBN 0-8383-1406-6 15.95
1. Marlowe, Christopher, 1564-1593. I. Title.

HENDERSON, Philip, 1906- 822'.3 B
Christopher Marlowe / by Philip Henderson. 2d ed. New York : Barnes & Noble Books, 1974. xxii, 162 p., [2] leaves of plates : ill. ; 19 cm. Bibliography: p. 158-160. [PR2673.H43 1974b] 75-306225 ISBN 0-06-492811-X : 8.00
1. Marlowe, Christopher, 1564-1593.

HENDERSON, Philip, 1906- v. 12
Christopher Marlowe. Lincoln, Univ. of Nebraska Press [1966] 182 p. illus. 67-101088
1. Marlowe, Christopher, 1564-1593. 2. Jonson, Ben, 1572-1637. 3. Webster, John, 1580?-1625? 4. Ford, John, 1586-ca. 1640. I. Title. II. Title: Ben Jonson III. Title: John Webster IV. Title: John Ford

HOFFMAN, Calvin. 822.33
The murder of the man who was 'Shakespeare.' New York, Grosset & Dunlap [c1960] 264p. illus. 21cm. (The Universal library) [PR2947.M3H6 1960] 61-3653
1. Marlowe, Christopher, 1564-1593. 2. Shakespeare, William— Authorship. I. Title.

HOTSON, Leslie, 1897- 822'.3
The death of Christopher Marlowe, by J. Leslie Hotson. New York, Haskell House, 1965. 76 p. illus., facsims., maps. 24 cm. Reprint of the 1925 ed. Bibliographical references included in "The notes" (p. 75-76) [PR2673.H6] 65-26464
1. Marlowe, Christopher, 1564-1593. I. Title. BIP

HOTSON, Leslie, 1897- 821'.3
The death of Christopher Marlowe, by J. Leslie Hotson. New York, Russell & Russell [1967] 76 p. facsims., maps. 22 cm.

Reprint of the 1925 ed. Bibliographical references included in "Notes" (p. 75-76) [PR2673.H6 1967] 67-18292
1. Marlowe, Christopher, 1564-1593. I. Title. BIP

INGRAM, John Henry, 1842-1916. 821'.3
Marlowe & his poetry. London, G. G. Harrap, 1914. [New York, AMS Press, 1972] 151 p. front. 19 cm. (Poetry and life series) Bibliography: p. 151. [PR2673.I6 1972] 72-120965 ISBN 0-404-52522-9 8.00
1. Marlowe, Christopher, 1564-1593. I. Title. II. Series. BIP

NORMAN, Charles, 1904- 822'.3 B
Christopher Marlowe; the muse's darling. Indianapolis, Bobbs-Merrill [1971] xvi, 273 p. illus., facsims., maps. 22 cm. First published in 1946 under title: The muses' darling. Bibliography: p. 267. [PR2673.N6 1971] 70-142471 7.50
1. Marlowe, Christopher, 1564-1593. BIP

NORMAN, Charles, 1904- 928.2
The muses' darling, Christopher Marlowe. New York, Macmillan, 1960[c.1946, 1950] 272p. illus., maps, facsims. (Macmillan paperbacks, 34) Bibl.: p.265 and bibl. notes 1.85 pap.,
1. Marlowe, Christopher, 1564-1593. I. Title.

POIRIER, Michel. 828'.3'09
Christopher Marlowe. [Hamden, Conn.] Archon Books, 1968 [c1952] 215 p. 21 cm. Bibliography: p. 213-214. [PR2673.P6 1968] 68-5689
1. Marlowe, Christopher, 1564-1593.

ROSS Williamson, Hugh, 1901- 822'.3 B
Kind Kit; an informal biography of Christopher Marlowe. New York, St. Martin's Press [1973, c1972] 269 p. 23 cm. [PR2673.R66 1973] 72-90758 6.95
1. Marlowe, Christopher, 1564-1593. I. Title.

ROWSE, Alfred Leslie, 1903- v. 12
Christopher Marlowe, a biography. New York, Harper & Row [c1964] xi, 219 [1] p. illus., ports. 23 cm. Includes bibliography. 67-61359
1. Marlowe, Christopher, 1564-1593. I. Title.

ROWSE, Alfred Leslie, 1903- 828.3
Christopher Marlowe, his life and work, by A. L. Rowse. New York, Harper [1965, c.1964] viii, 219p. illus., facsim., plan, ports. 24cm. Bibl. [PR2673.R69] 64-25120 5.95
1. Marlowe, Christopher, 1564-1593. I. Title.

ROWSE, Alfred Leslie, 1903- 828.3
Christopher Marlowe, his life and work. by A. L. Rowse. New York, Grosset [1966, c.1964] viii, 219p. illus., facsim., plan. ports. 21cm. (Univ. lib., UL198) Bibl. [PR2673.R69] 2.65 pap.,
1. Marlowe, Christopher, 1564-1593. I. Title.

ROWSE, Alfred Leslie, 1903- 928.2
Christopher Marlowe, a biography, by A. L. Rowse. London, Macmillan, 1964. xi, 219 p. illus., ports. 23 cm. Bibliographical references includes in "Notes" (p. 209-215) [PR2673.R68] 65-7479
1. Marlowe, Christopher, 1564-1593. I. Title.

Marlowe, Christopher, 1564-1593—Biography.

HILTON, Della. 822'.3 B
Who was Kit Marlowe? : The story of the poet and playwright / Della Hilton. New York : Taplinger Pub. Co., 1977. xi, 163 p., [4] leaves of plates : ill. ; 23 cm. Includes index. Bibliography: p. 159-160. [PR2673.H54 1977b] 76-53911 ISBN 0-8008-8291-1 : 8.50
1. Marlowe, Christopher, 1564-1593—Biography. 2. Dramatists, English—Early modern, 1500-1700—Biography. I. Title.

Marlowe, Julia, 1865-1950.

MARLOWE, Julia, 1865-1950. 927.92
Julia Marlowe's story, by E. H. Sothern [as she told it to him] Edited by Fairfax Downey. New York, Rinehart [c1954] 237p. illus. 22cm. [PN2287.M5A3] 53-10923
1. Marlowe, Julia, 1865-1950. 2. Actors—Correspondence, reminiscences, etc. I. Sothern, Edward Hugh, 1859-1933. II. Title.

OVINGTON, Adelaide (Alexander) 927.92
The star that didn't twinkle. New York, Vantage Press [c.1961] 145p. illus. (front. port.) 61-3197 3.50 bds.,
1. Marlowe, Julia, 1865-1950. I. Title.

Marmion, Columba, Abbot, 1858-1923.

PHILIPON, Marie Michel, 1898- 922.2415
The spiritual doctrine of Dom Marmion. Translated by Matthew Dillon. Westminster, Md., Newman Press [1956] 221p. 23cm. [BX4705.M411P52] 56-10000
1. Marmion, Columba, Abbot, 1858-1923. 2. Spiritual life—Catholic authors. I. Title.

Marquand, John Phillips, 1893-1960.

BIRMINGHAM, Stephen. 818'.5'209 B
The late John Marquand; a biography. [1st ed.] Philadelphia, Lippincott [1972] xiii, 322 p. illus. 25 cm. "A John P. Marquand check list": p. 301-310. [PS3525.A6695Z59] 76-39182 ISBN 0-397-00886-4
1. Marquand, John Phillips, 1893-1960. I. Title.

HAMBURGER, Philip Paul, 1914- 818'.5'209 B
J. P. Marquand, Esquire; a portrait in the form of a novel. Freeport, N.Y., Books for Libraries Press [1973] p. (Biography index reprint series) Reprint of the 1952 ed. [PS3525.A6695Z7 1973] 72-13303 ISBN 0-8369-8144-8
1. Marquand, John Phillips, 1893-1960. I. Title. BIP

HAMBURGER, Philip Paul, 1914- v. 12
J. P. Marquand, Esquire, a portrait in the form of a novel. New York, Charter Books [1952, 1963] 114 p. 20 cm. 65-69921
1. Marquand, John Phillips, 1896- I. Title.

Marquand, John Phillips, 1893-1960—Biography.

BELL, Millicent. 818'.5'209 B
Marquand : an American life / Millicent Bell. 1st ed. Boston : Little, Brown, c1979. p. cm. "An Atlantic Monthly Press book." Includes bibliographical references and index. [PS3525.A6695Z57] 79-12818 ISBN 0-316-08828-5 : 17.95
1. Marquand, John Phillips, 1893-1960—Biography. 2. Authors, American—20th century—Biography. BIP

Marquette, Jacques, 1637-1675.

DONNELLY, Joseph P. 973.1'8'0924 B
Jacques Marquette, S. J., 1637-1675, by Joseph P Donnelly Chicago, Loyola University Press, 1968. xii, 395 p. facsims., geneal. table, map. 24 cm. Bibliography: p. 341-357. [F1030.2.D6] 68-9498 8.00
1. Marquette, Jacques, 1637-1675.

Marquette, Jacques, 1637-1675—Juvenile literature.

SYME, Ronald, 1910- 977'.01'0922 B
Marquette and Joliet: voyagers on the Mississippi. Illustrated by William Stobbs. New York, Morrow, 1974. 95, [1] p. illus. 22 cm. Bibliography: p. [96] A biography of the two seventeenth-century French explorers who were the first to chart the course of the Mississippi River. [F352.S95 1974] 920 73-14504 ISBN 0-688-20105-9 3.95
1. Marquette, Jacques, 1637-1675—Juvenile literature. 2. Joliet, Louis, 1645-1700—Juvenile literature. 3. Mississippi River—Discovery and exploration—Juvenile literature. I. Stobbs, William, illus. II. Title.
Library binding 3.78; ISBN 0-688-30105-3.

Marquis, Don, 1878-1937.

ANTHONY, Edward, 1895- 928.1 B
O rare Don Marquis, a biography. [1st ed.] Garden City, N. Y., Doubleday, 1962. 670 p. illus. 22 cm. [PS3525.A67Z57] 62-7596
1. Marquis, Don, 1878-1937. I. Title.

Marrant, John, b. 1755.

MARRANT, John, b. 1755. 973'.04'97 S
A narrative of the Lord's wonderful dealings with John Marrant, a Black / John Marrant. New York : Garland Pub., 1978. v, 38 p. ; 23 cm. (The Garland library of narratives of North American Indian captivities ; v. 17) "Taken down from his own relation, arranged, corrected, and published by the Rev. Mr. Aldridge."—1785 ed. t.p. Reprint of the 1785 ed. printed by Gilbert and Plummer, London. Issued with the reprints of the 1785 and 1875 editions of Swetland, L. A very remarkable narrative. New York, 1978. The reprint of the 1915 ed. of Merrifield, E. The story of the captivity and rescue from the Indians of Luke Swetland. New York, 1978. The reprints of the 1786 and 1794 editions of M'Donald, P. A surprising account of a captivity and escape. New York, 1978. The reprints of the 1788 and 1794 editions of a Very surprising narrative of a young woman discovered in a rocky-cave, by A. Panther. New York, 1978. [E85.G2 vol. 17] [E99.C5] 970'.004'97 B 77-27409 ISBN 0-8240-1641-6 : OA narrat
1. Marrant, John, b. 1755. 2. Cherokee Indians—Captivities. 3. Indians of North America—Captivities. 4. Converts—United States—Biography. I. Aldridge, William, 1737-1797. II. Title. III. Series.

Marriage—Biblical teaching.

HARBOUR, Brian L. 301.42'7
Famous couples of the Bible / Brian L. Harbour. Nashville : Broadman Press, c1979. 132 p. ; 18 cm. Includes bibliographical references. [BS680.M35H29] 78-60053 ISBN 0-8054-5630-9 pbk. : 2.25
1. Bible—Biography. 2. Marriage—Biblical teaching. I. Title. BIP

SEAGREN, Daniel. 220.9'2 B
Couples in the Bible; a discussion guide [by] Daniel R. Seagren. Grand Rapids, Baker Book House [1972] 162 p. 18 cm. (Contemporary discussion series) Includes bibliographical references. [BS579.H8S4] 72-90330 ISBN 0-8010-7971-3 1.25
1. Bible—Biography. 2. Marriage—Biblical teaching. I. Title.

STRAUSS, Richard L. 248'.4
Living in love : secrets from Bible marriages / Richard L. Strauss. Wheaton, Ill. : Tyndale House Publishers, c1978. 141 p. ; 21 cm. [BS680.M35S8] 77-93752 ISBN 0-8423-2488-7 pbk. : 3.95
1. Bible—Biography. 2. Marriage—Biblical teaching. I. Title.

Marriott, John Willard, 1900-

O'BRIEN, Robert, journalist. 642'.5'0924 B
Marriott : the J. Willard Marriott story / Robert O'Brien. Salt Lake City : Deseret Book Co., 1977. 336 p., [8] leaves of plates : ill. ; 24 cm. Includes index. [TX910.5.M333O27] 77-17123 ISBN 0-87747-683-7 : 6.95. ISBN 0-87747-682-9 pbk. : 1.95
1. Marriott, John Willard, 1900- 2. Hotels, taverns, etc.—United States—Biography. 3. Food service—United States—Biography.

Marryat, Frederick, 1792-1848.

HANNAY, David, 1853-1934. 823'.7 B
Life of Frederick Marryat. New York, Haskell House, 1973. 163, [9] p. 23 cm. Reprint of the 1889 ed. published by W. Scott, London, and W. J. Cage, New York, in series: Great writers. Bibliography: p. [165]-[171] [PR4978.H3 1973] 73-6945 ISBN 0-8383-1695-6 9.95
1. Marryat, Frederick, 1792-1848. I. Title. BIP

WARNER, Oliver, 1903- 823'.7 B
Captain Marryat : a rediscovery / Oliver Warner. Westport, Conn. : Hyperion Press, 1979. 210 p., [9] leaves of plates : ill. ; 22 cm. Reprint of the 1953 ed. published by Constable, London. Includes index. Bibliography: p. 195-197. [PR4978.W3 1979] 78-59050 ISBN 0-88355-721-5 : 19.50
1. Marryat, Frederick, 1792-1848. 2. Novelists, English—19th century—Biography. BIP

Mars Hill Presbyterian Church, Athens, Tenn.

BOYER, Reba Bayless. 285'.1768'865
A history of Mars Hill Presbyterian Church, by Reba B. Boyer and Budd L. Duncan. [Athens, Tenn., 1973] 126 p. 24 cm. [BX9211.A77M373] 73-92011
1. Mars Hill Presbyterian Church, Athens, Tenn. 2. Athens, Tenn.—Biography. I. Duncan, Budd L., joint author. II. Title.

Mars, Stanl,

MARS, Stanl, 1902- 926.467
Half brother of Zhukov. New York, Brady Books; distributed by Merlin Press, 1957. 155p. 21cm. Autobiographical. [TT955.M3A3] 57-59469
I. Title.

Marsden, Edward, 1869-1932.

BEATTIE, William Gilbert. 922.573
Marsden of Alaska, a modern Indian, minister, missionary, musician, engineer, pilot, boat builder, and church builder. New York, Vantage Press [1955] 246 p. illus. 23 cm. [BV2803.A4B4] 54-12648
1. Marsden, Edward, 1869-1932.

Marsden, Samuel, 1764-1838.

WANNAN, Bill. 994.4'02
Early colonial scandals: the turbulent times of Samuel Marsden. Melbourne, Lansdowne, 1972. 223, [6] p. 22 cm. First ed. published in 1962 under title Very strange tales; the turbulent times of Samuel Marsden. Bibliography: p. [226-228] [DU172.M37W28 1972] 73-158389 ISBN 0-7018-0006-2 4.95
1. Marsden, Samuel, 1765-1838. 2. New South Wales—History. I. Title.

YARWOOD, A. T. 283'.092'4 B
Samuel Marsden : the great survivor / [by] A. T. Yarwood. Carlton, Vic. : Melbourne University Press, 1977. xv, 341 p., [11] leaves of plates : ill. ; 25 cm. Distributed in the U.S.A. by International Scholarly Book Services, Forest Grove, Ore. Includes index. Bibliography: p. 323-332. [BV3667.M3Y37] 77-380002 ISBN 0-522-84120--1 : 26.00
1. Marsden, Samuel, 1765-1838. 2. Missionaries—England—Biography. 3. Missionaries—Australia—New South Wales—Biography. 4. Missionaries—New Zealand—Biography. BIP

Marsden, Samuel, 1764-1838—Juvenile literature.

YARWOOD, Alexander Turnbull. 994'.4'020924 B
Samuel Marsden [by] A. T. Yarwood. Melbourne, New York [etc.] Oxford University Press [1968] 30 p. illus., ports. 19 cm. (Great Australians) Bibliography: p. 30. [DU172.M37Y3] 78-374958 0.55
1. Marsden, Samuel, 1764-1838—Juvenile literature.

Marsh, Edward Howard, Sir, 1872-1953.

HASSALL, Christopher Vernon, 1912-1963. 923.242
A biography of Edward Marsh. [1st American ed.] New York, Harcourt, Brace [1959] 732 p. illus. 22 cm. [PR6025.A642Z6] 59-11654
1. Marsh, Edward Howard, Sir, 1872-1953. BIP

Marsh, Floyd R., 1898-

MARSH, Floyd R., 1898- 979.8'04'0924
20 years a soldier of fortune / by Floyd R. Marsh. 1st ed. Portland, Or. : Binford & Mort, c1976. p. cm. Autobiography. Includes index. [F909.M36] 76-864 ISBN 0-8323-0270-8 : 6.50. ISBN 0-8323-0269-4 pbk. : 4.50
1. Marsh, Floyd R., 1898- 2. Gold mines and mining—Alaska—Personal narratives. 3. Gold mines and mining—The West—Personal narratives. 4. Alaska—History 1896-1959. 5. The West—History—1848-1950. I. Title.

Marsh, Othniel Charles, 1831-1899.

PLATE, Robert. 925.6
The dinosaur hunters: Othniel C. Marsh and Edward D. Cope. New York, D. McKay Co., 1964. vi, 281 p. 21 cm. Bibliography: p. 267-272. [QE707.M4P53] 64-17627
1. Marsh, Othniel Charles, 1831-1899. 2. Cope, Edward Drinker, 1840-1897. I. Title.

SCHUCHERT, Charles, 1858-1942. 560'.9 B
O. C. Marsh : pioneer in paleontology / Charles Schuchert and Clara Mae LeVene. New York : Arno Press, 1978, c1940. p. cm. (Biologists and their world) Reprint of the ed. published by Yale University Press, New Haven. Includes index. Bibliography: p. [QE707.M4S32 1978] 77-81133 ISBN 0-405-10733-1 lib. bdg. : 35.00
1. Marsh, Othniel Charles, 1831-1899. 2. Paleontologists—United States—Biography. I. LeVene, Clara Mae, joint author. II. Title. III. Series. BIP

Marsh, Robert Lee.

MARSH, Robert Lee. 266'.6'70924 B
Surgeon in the South Pacific / Robert Lee Marsh. Washington : Review and Herald Pub. Association, c1975. 63 p. ; 19 cm. [R722.32.M37A33] 74-28752
1. Marsh, Robert Lee. 2. Missionaries, Medical—Papua, New Guinea—Correspondence, reminiscences, etc. 3. Oceanica—Description and travel—1951- I. Title.

Marshak, Samuil Iakovlevich,

MARSHAK, Samuil Iakovlevich, 1887- 928.917
At life's beginning; some pages of reminiscence, by Samuel Marshak. Tr. [from Russian] by Katherine Hunter Blair. Foreword by Moura Budberg. Illus. by G. Philippovsky. New York, Dutton [c.1964] 208p. illus. 22cm. 64-19544 4.00
I. Title.

Marshall, Catherine (Wood)

MARSHALL, Catherine (Wood) 1914- 922.573
To live again. [1st ed.] New York, McGraw Hill [1957] 335 p. illus. 22 cm. [BX9225.M3515A3] 57-13338
I. Title. BIP

Marshall, Edison,

MARSHALL, Edison, 1894- FIC
Dian of the lost land. Philadelphia, Chilton Books [1966] 148 p. 23 cm. [PZ3.M3565Di5] fic 66-14787
I. Title.

Marshall, Frank Hamilton, 1868-

MYERS, Oma Lou, 1909- 922.673
This one thing I do; a biography of Frank Hamilton Marshall, pioneer Christian educator. [Portland? Or., 1953] 153p. illus. 23cm. [BX7343.M29M9] 53-31319
1. Marshall, Frank Hamilton, 1868- I. Title.

Marshall, George Catlett, 1880-1959.

MCCARTHY, Joseph Raymond, 1909- 923.573
The story of General George C. Marshall. [n.p.] c1952. 187p. 23cm. Published in 1931 under title: America's retreat from victory; the story of George Catlett Marshall. [E745.M37M2 1952] 54-1340
1. Marshall, George Catlett, 1880- 2. U.S.—For. rel.—1945- I. Title.

MCCARTHY, Joseph Raymond, 1909- 923.573
The story of General George C. Marshall. [n.p.] c1952. 187p. 23cm. Published in 1931 under title: America's retreat from victory; the story of George Catlett Marshall. [E745.M37M2 1952] 54-1340
1. Marshall, George Catlett, 1880- 2. U.S.—For. rel.—1945- I. Title.

PAYNE, Pierre Stephen Robert, 1911- 923.573
The Marshall story: a biography of General George C. Marshall. [1st ed.] New York, Prentice-Hall [1951] xii, 344 p. ports. 24 cm. Bibliography: p. 334-337. [E745.M37P3] 52-6159
1. Marshall, George Catlett, 1880- I. Title.

PAYNE, Pierre Stephen Robert, 1911- 923.573
The Marshall story: a biography of General George C. Marshall. [1st ed.] New York, Prentice-Hall [1951] xii, 344 p. ports. 24 cm. Bibliography: p. 334-337. [E745.M37P3] 52-6159
1. Marshall, George Catlett, 1880- I. Title.

POGUE, Forrest C. 923.573
George C. Marshall. With the editorial assistance of Gordon Harrison. Foreword by Omar N. Bradley. New York, Viking Press [1963- v. port., maps. 24 cm. Includes bibliographies. Contents.Contents.—[1] Education of a general, 1880-1939.—2. Ordeal and hope, 1939-1942. [E745.M37P6] 63-18373
1. Marshall, George Catlett, 1880-1959.

POGUE, Forrest C. 355.3'31'0924
George C. Marshall: global commander [by] Forrest C. Pogue. [Colorado Springs, Colo.] U.S. Air Force Academy, 1968. 20 p. port. 21 cm. (The Harmon memorial lectures in military history, no. 10) [U53.M37P6] 68-67265
1. Marshall, George Catlett, 1880-1959. I. Title. II. Series.

WILSON, Rose Page, 1911- 973.917'0924 B
General Marshall remembered. Englewood Cliffs, N.J., Prentice-Hall [1968] 399 p. illus., ports. 24 cm. [E745.M37W5] 68-19612
1. Marshall, George Catlett, 1880-1959. I. Title.

Marshall, George Catlett, 1880-1959—Juvenile literature.

FABER, Harold. 923.573
Soldier and statesman; General George C. Marshall. New York, Ariel Books [1964] 227 p. port. 22 cm. Bibliography: p. [223]-224. [E745.M37F3] 64-17812
1. Marshall, George Catlett, 1880-1959—Juvenile literature. I. Title.

Marshall, James.

MARSHALL, James. 373.1'1'00924 B
A school in Uganda / by James Marshall ; with a foreword by Leonard Barnes. London : Gollancz, 1976. 224 p. ; 23 cm. [LA1567.M37] 76-378248 ISBN 0-575-02050-4 : 13.00
1. Marshall, James. 2. Education, Secondary—Uganda. 3. Teachers—Biography. I. Title.
Distributed by Verry BIP

Marshall, James Wilson, 1810-1885.

GAY, Theressa. 979.4/03/0924
James W. Marshall, the discoverer of California gold; a biography. Georgetown, Calif., Talisman Pr., 1967. 558p. illus., facsims., maps, ports. (pt. col.) 24cm. Bibl. [F865.M355] (B) 67-26262 10.00
1. Marshall, James Wilson, 1810-1885. I. Title.
Publisher's address: P. O. Box 455, Georgetown, Calif. 95634.

GAY, Theressa. 917.94
James W. Marshall, the discoverer of California gold; a biography. Georgetown, Calif., Talisman Press, 1967. 558 p. illus., facsims., maps. ports. (part col.) 24 cm. Bibliographical references in "Notes" (p. 436-517) [F865.M355] [979.4'03'924 (B)] 976.3355 67-26262
1. Marshall, James Wilson, 1810-1885. I. Title.

Marshall, John, 1755-1835.

BAKER, Leonard. 347'.73'2634 B
John Marshall: a life in law. New York, Macmillan [1974] x, 845 p. illus. 24 cm. Bibliography: p. 771-785. [KF8745.M3B3] 73-2751 ISBN 0-02-506360-X 14.95
1. Marshall, John, 1755-1835. I. Title.

CUNEO, John R. 347'.73'2634 B
John Marshall, judicial statesman [by] John R. Cuneo. New York, McGraw-Hill [1974, c1975] 164 p. port. 24 cm. Bibliography: p. 153-155. A biography of the Supreme Court justice who strengthened the Supreme Court and made it a fully equal third branch of the government. [KF8745.M3C85] 74-9717
1. Marshall, John, 1755-1835. I. Title. BIP

KUTLER, Stanley I., comp. 347'.73'2634 B
John Marshall. Edited by Stanley I. Kutler. Englewood Cliffs, N.J., Prentice-Hall [1972] xi, 179 p. 21 cm. (Great lives observed) (A Spectrum book) Bibliography: p. 174-176. [KF8745.M3K85] 72-6101 ISBN 0-13-510271-5 2.45 ($2.75 Can)
1. Marshall, John, 1755-1835.

MAGRUDER, Allan Bowie. 347'.73'2634 B
John Marshall. Boston, Houghton, Mifflin. [New York, AMS Press, 1972] viii, 296 p. illus. 19 cm. (American statesmen, v. 10) Reprint of the 1898 ed. [KF8745.M3M33 1972] 73-128974 ISBN 0-404-50860-X
1. Marshall, John, 1755-1835. I. Title. II. Series.

MARSHALL, John, 1755-1835. 347'.73'2634 B
An autobiographical sketch by John Marshall, edited by John Stokes Adams. New York, Da Capo Press, 1973 [c1937] xxiii, 48 p. 26 cm. Includes bibliographical references. [E302.6.M1A32 1973] 71-160849 ISBN 0-306-70216-9 8.50 (Lib. ed.)
1. Marshall, John, 1755-1835. 2. Story, Joseph, 1779-1845.

MARSHALL, John, 1755-1835. 347'.73'2634
The papers of John Marshall. Herbert A. Johnson, editor. Charles T. Cullen, associate editor. Nancy G. Harris, assistant editor. Chapel Hill, N.C., University of North Carolina Press [1974- v. illus. 24 cm. "Sponsored by the College of William and Mary and the Institute of Early American History and Culture under the auspices of the National Historical Publications Commission." Contents.Contents.—v. 1. Correspondence and papers, November 10, 1775-June 23, 1788. Account book, September 1783-June 1788. Includes bibliographical references. [E302.M365] 74-9575 ISBN 0-8078-1233-1 17.95
1. Marshall, John, 1755-1835. I. Johnson, Herbert Alan, ed. II. Institute of Early American History and Culture, Williamsburg, Va.

MASON, Frances Norton. 923.473
My dearest Polly; letters of Chief Justice John Marshall to his wife, with their background, political and domestic, 1779-1831. Richmond, Garrett & Massie, 1961. xiv, 386p. illus., ports., facsims., geneal. tables: 24cm. 'Basic sources': p. 353-354. Bibliographical references included in 'Notes' (p. 355-367) 61-15099
1. Marshall, John, 1755-1835. 2. Marshall, Mary Willis (Amber) 1766-1831. I. Title.

SEVERN, William. 347.9924 B
John Marshall, the man who made the Court supreme, by Bill Severn. New York, D. McKay Co. [1969] 248 p. 21 cm. Bibliography: p. 241. [KF8745.M3S4] 69-13784 4.95
1. Marshall, John, 1755-1835.

SURRENCY, Erwin C ed. 923.473
The Marshall reader; the life and contributions of Chief Justice John Marshall. Bicentenary ed. New York, Oceana Publications, 1955. 256p. 21cm. (Docket series, v. 3) 55-11500
1. Marshall, John, 1755-1835. I. Title.

THAYER, James Bradley, 1831-1902. 347'.73'2634 B
John Marshall. New introd. by Wallace Mendelsohn. New York, Da Capo Press, 1974. xliv, 157 p. port. 21 cm. (Da Capo Press reprints in American constitutional and legal history) Reprint of the 1901 ed. published by Houghton, Mifflin, Boston, which was issued as no. 7 in the Riverside biographical series. Bibliography: p. xliii-xliv. [E302.6.M4T3 1974] 76-155923 ISBN 0-306-70287-8 12.95 (lib. bdg.)
1. Marshall, John, 1755-1835. I. Series: The Riverside biographical series, no. 7. BIP

Marshall, John, 1755-1835—Juvenile literature.

BROWN, Richard Carl, 1919- 347.99'73 B
John Marshall, by Richard C. Brown and the editors of Silver Burdett. Morristown, N.J., Silver Burdett Co. [1968] 240 p. illus. (part col.), facsims., ports. (part col.) 27 cm. (Illustrious Americans) "Annotated bibliography": p. 232-234. A biography of the fourth Chief Justice of the United States whose decisions during his thirty-four years on the Supreme Court established the Court as a third and equal branch of government. [E302.6.M4B87] 92 67-15874
1. Marshall, John, 1755-1835 Juvenile literature. I. Silver Burdett Company. II. Title.

COOK, Fred J. 92
John Marshall; fighting for justice. Ilus. by Richard Mlodock. Chicago, Britannica Bks., Div. of Ency: Britannical0pa [1963, c.1961] 192p. col. illus. 22cm. (Britannica bkshelf.: Great lives for young Amers.) 2.36 lib. ed.,
1. Marshall, John, 1755 1835 Juvenile literature. I. Title.

MARTIN, Patricia Miles. 92
John Marshall. Illustrated by Salem Tamer. New York, Putnam [1967] 63 p. col. illus., col. ports. 23 cm. (A See and read beginning to read biography) [E302.6.M4M35] 67-4519
1. Marshall, John, 1755-1835—Juvenile literature.

MARTINI, Teri. 347'.73'2634 B
John Marshall. Illustrated by Alex Stein. Philadelphia, Westminster Press [1974] 124, [1] p. illus. 21 cm. Bibliography: p. [125] A biography of the Chief Justice of the Supreme Court, first appointed by James Madison, who strengthened the court and made it a power that could balance the executive and legislative branches. [E302.6.M4M36] 92 73-11430 ISBN 0-664-32540-8 5.25
1. Marshall, John, 1755-1835—Juvenile literature. I. Stein, Alex, illus. II. Title.

STEINBERG, Alfred, 1917- 920
John Marshall. New York, Putnam [c.1962] 192p. 21cm. (Lives to remember) Bibl. 62-14408 2.95
1. Marshall, John, 1755-1835— Juvenile literature. I. Title.

TUCKER, Caroline, pseud. 923.473
John Marshall, the great Chief Justice. New York, Ariel [dist. Farrar, c.1962] 209p. 22cm. Bibl. 62-13071 3.25
1. Marshall, John, 1755-1835—Juvenile literature. I. Title.

TUCKER, Caroline, pseud. 923.473
John Marshall, the great Chief Justice. New York, Ariel Books [1962] 209 p. 22 cm. 62-13071
1. Marshall, John, 1755-1835 — Juvenile literature. I. Title.

Marshall, Peter, 1902-1949.

MARSHALL, Catherine Wood, 1914- v. 12
A man called Peter; the story of Peter Marshall. Greenwich, Conn., Fawcett Publications. [1951, 1962] 342 p. 68-66732
1. Marshall, Peter, 1902-1949. I. Title.

MARSHALL, Catherine (Wood) 1914- 922.573
A man called Peter; the story of Peter Marshall. Greenwich, Conn., Fawcett [1964, c.1951] 351p. 18cm. (Crest t729) .75 pap.,
1. Marshall, Peter, 1902-1949. I. Title.

MARSHALL, Catherine (Wood) 1914- 922.573
A man called Peter; the story of Peter Marshall. New York, McGraw-Hill [1951] 354 p. illus. 24 cm. [BX9225.M352M3] 51-13266
1. Marshall, Peter, 1902-1949. I. Title.

Marshall, Samuel Lyman Atwood, 1900-

MARSHALL, Samuel Lyman Atwood, 1900- 355'.0092'4 B
Bringing up the rear : a memoir / by S. L. A. Marshall ; edited by Cate Marshall. San Rafael, Calif. : Presidio Press, c1979. p. cm. Includes index. [D15.M34A32] 79-14949 ISBN 0-89141-084-8 : 12.95
1. Marshall, Samuel Lyman Atwood, 1900- 2. Historians—United States—Biography. I. Marshall, Cate. II. Title.

Marshall, Thurgood, 1908-

BLACK Americans in government. 973.92'0922
[Text and exercises by Sheila Hobson and Harvey D. Goldenberg. General editor: Saunders Redding]. Produced by Buckingham Learning Corporation. [Jamaica, N.Y., Buckingham Learning Corp., 1969] 5 v. illus., ports. 28 cm. Cover title. Contents.Contents.—[1] The three wars of Edward Brooke; the story of the first black U.S. Senator since Reconstruction.—[2] Fighting Shirley Chisholm; the story of the first black U.S. Congresswoman.—[3] Ambassador for progress; the story of Patricia Harris, former U.S. Ambassador to Luxembourg.—[4] Equal under the law; the story of Supreme Court Justice Thurgood Marshall.—[5] Robert Weaver sees a new city; the story of the first Secretary of Housing and Urban Development. [E185.96.B53] 79-20085
1. Brooke, Edward William, 1919- 2. Chisholm, Shirley, 1924- 3. Harris, Patricia Roberts, 1924- 4. Marshall, Thurgood, 1908- 5. Weaver, Robert Clifton, 1907- I. Hobson, Sheila. II. Goldenberg, Harvey D.

Marshall, Thurgood, 1908—Juvenile literature.

FENDERSON, Lewis H. 347.99'24 B
Thurgood Marshall: fighter for justice, by Lewis H. Fenderson. Illustrated by Dave Hodges. New York, McGraw-Hill [1969] 127 p. illus. 22 cm. (McGraw-Hill Black legacy) "A Rutledge book." A biography of the lawyer who in 1967 became the first Negro Justice appointed to the Supreme Court. [KF8745.M34F4] 92 76-77099
1. Marshall, Thurgood, 1908—Juvenile literature. I. Hodges, David, illus. II. Title. III. Series.

YOUNG, Margaret B. 347'.7326'34 B
The picture life of Thurgood Marshall, by Margaret B. Young. New York, Watts [1971] 46 p. illus., ports. 23 cm. Photographs and easy-to-read text trace the life of the first black man to be appointed an associate justice of the highest court in the country. [KF8745.M34Y6] 92 79-131154 ISBN 0-531-00984-X
1. Marshall, Thurgood, 1908- —Juvenile literature. I. Title. BIP

Marshals—France.

YOUNG, Peter. 940.2'7
Napoleon's marshals. Color plates by Michael Youens. [New York] Hippocrene Books [1973] 203 p. illus. 25 cm. Bibliography: p. 203. [DC198.A1Y68 1973] 73-83138 ISBN 0-88254-175-7 12.50
1. Marshals—France. 2. France--History—Consulate and Empire, 1799-1815. I. Title.

YOUNG, Peter. 940.2'7
Napoleon's marshals; colour plates by Michael Youens. Reading, Osprey Publishing, 1973. 2-203, [16] p. illus. (some col.), ports. 24 cm. Bibliography: p. 203. [DC198.A1Y68] 73-165854 ISBN 0-85045-112-4 £3.95
1. Marshals—France. 2. France—History—Consulate and Empire, 1799-1815. I. Title.

Marston, Isaac, 1840-1891.

SHEARER, James, 1884- comp. 347'.774'03534 B
In chambers; aspects of the life of Justice Isaac Marston, Michigan Supreme Court, 1875-1883. Edited by James Shearer, II. [Ann Arbor] University of Michigan Law School, 1973. ix, 81 p. ports. 23 cm. Includes bibliographical references. [KF368.M28S46] 73-174003
1. Marston, Isaac, 1840-1891. I. Title.

Marten, Ethel Sexton.

MARTEN, Ethel Sexton. 380.1'45'66400924 B
For my grandchildren, some reminiscences. Chicago, Franciscan Herald Press [1973, i.e.1974] p. [HD9009.S47M36] 73-21588 ISBN 0-8199-0488-0 5.00
1. Marten, Ethel Sexton. 2. Sexton, John & co. 3. Food industry and trade—United States. I. Title.

Marti, Jose, 1853-1895.

GONZALEZ, Manuel Pedro, 1893- 928.6
Jose Marti, epic chronicler of the United States in the eighties; with an introd. by Sturgis E. Leavitt. Chapel Hill, University of North Carolina Press [1953] 79p. 25cm. [F1783.M38G643] 53-6783
1. Marti, Jose, 1853-1895. 2. United States in literature. 3. U. S.—Hist.—Historiography. I. Title.

GRAY, Richard Butler, 1922- 928.6
Jose Marti, Cuban patriot. Gainesville, University of Florida Press, 1962. 307 p. 24 cm. Includes bibliography. [F1783.M38G67] 62-20772
1. Marti, Jose, 1853-1895.

LIZASO, Felix, 1891- 928.6
Martf, martyr of Cuban independence; translated by Esther Elise Shuler. 53Albuquerque] University of New Mexico Press [1953] vii, 260p. mounted port. 24cm. Translation of Marti, Mistico del deber. [F1783.M38L492] 53-12559
1. Martf, Jose, 1853-1895. I. Title.

LIZASO, Felix, 1891- 972.91'05'0924 B
Marti, martyr of Cuban independence. Translated by Esther Elise Shuler. Westport, Conn., Greenwood Press [1974, c1953] vii, 260 p. port. 22 cm. Reprint of the ed. published by University of New Mexico Press, Albuquerque. Translation of Marti, mistico del deber. [F1783.M38L492 1974] 73-20502 ISBN 0-8371-7329-9 12.00
1. Marti, Jose, 1853-1895. BIP

MANACH, Jorge 928.6
Marti, el apostol. Prologo de Gabriela Mistral. New York, Las Americas [1964, c.1963] 292p. 21cm. 63-24137 5.00; 3.00 pap.,
1. Marti, Jose, 1853-1895. 2. Cuba—Hist.—1878-1895. I. Title.

MANACH, Jorge, 1898- 928.6
Marti: apostle of freedom; translated from the Spanish by Coley Taylor. With a pref. by Gabriela Mistral. New York, Devin-Adair, 1950. xvi, 363 p. illus., ports., map. 22 cm. Full name: Jorge Manach y Robato. [F1783.M38M2413] 50-7768
1. Marti, Jose, 1853-1895. 2. Cuba—Hist.—1878-1895. I. Title.

MARQUEZ STERLING, Carlos, 1899- 972.9105924
Marti, ciudadano de America. New York, Las Americas [c.]1965. 419p. 21cm. [F1783.M38M266] 65-5290 3.50 pap.,
1. Marti, Jose, 1853-1895. I. Title.

Martin, Alfred Manuel, 1928-

ARCHIBALD, Joseph, 1898- 927.96357
The Billy Martin story. New York, J. Messner [1959] 192 p. illus. 22 cm. [GV865.M35A7] 59-7007
1. Martin, Alfred Manuel, 1928-

SMITH, Norman Lewis. 796.357'092'4 B
The return of Billy the Kid / Norman Lewis Smith. New York : Coward, McCann & Geoghegan, c1977. 213 p., [5] leaves of plates : ill. ; 22 cm. [GV865.M35S58 1977] 77-7541 ISBN 0-698-10834-5 : 8.95
1. Martin, Alfred Manuel, 1928- 2. Baseball players—United States—Biography. I. Title. BIP

Martin de Porres, Saint, 1579-1639.

BENZIGER, Marieli G. 271'.2'024 B
Saint Martin de Porres: many sided Martin; the first Negro saint of the Western Hemisphere, by Marieli and Rita Benziger. Altadena, Calif., Benziger Sisters [1973] 134 p. port. 21 cm. [BX4700.M397B38] 73-86681
1. Martin de Porres, Saint, 1579-1639. I. Benziger, Rita, joint author. II. Title.

BISHOP, Claire (Huchet) 922.285
Martin de Porres, hero; illustrated by Jean Charlot. Boston, Houghton Mifflin, 1954. 120p. illus. 24cm. [BX4705.M4124B5] 53-10992
1. Martin de Porres, 1579-1639. I. Title.

CAVALLINI, Giuliana 922.285
St. Martin de Porres; apostle of charity. Tr. [from Italian] by Caroline Holland [St.Louis] B. Herder [c.1963] ix, 254p. 21cm. (Cross & crown ser. of spirituality, no. 26) Bibl. 63-21560 3.95
1. Martin de Porres, Saint, 1579-1639. I. Title.

CAVALLINI, Giuliana. 922.285
St. Martin de Porres, apostle of charity. Translated by Caroline Holland. [St. Louis] B. Herder Book Co. [1963] ix, 254 p. 21 cm. (Cross and crown series of spirituality, no. 26) Translation of I fioretti del beato Martino. Bibliography: p. 243-245. [BX4700.M397C33] 63-21560
I. Martin de Porres, Saint, 1579-1639. II. Title. III. Series.

CUSHING, Richard James, Cardinal, 1895- 922.285
St. Martin de Porres. [Boston] St. Paul Eds. [dist. Daughters of St. Paul, c.1962] 74p. illus. 22cm. 62-20203 1.00; .75 pap.,
1. Martin de Porres, Saint, 1579-1639. I. Title.

ERNEST, Brother, 1897- 922.285
A story of Blessed Martin de Porres. Pictures by Carolyn Lee Jagodits. Notre Dame, Ind., Dujarie Press [1957] unpaged. illus. 21cm. [BX4705.M4124E7] 57-30277
1. Martin de Porres, 1579-1639. I. Title.

FLECK, Raymond, 1927- 922.285
An angel in the streets, a story of Blessed Martin de Porres. Illus. by Brother Bernard Howard. Notre Dame, Ind., Dujarie Press [1952] 96 p. illus. 24 cm. [BX4705.M4124F6] 52-3970
1. Martin de Porres, 1579-1639. I. Title.

FUMET, Stanislas. 922.22
Life of St. Martin de Porres, patron saint of interracial justice. Translated from the French by Una Morrissy. [1st ed.] Garden City, N. Y., Doubleday, 1964. 119 p. 22 cm. [BX4700.M397F8] 64-19281
1. Martin de Porres, Saint, 1579-1639. I. Title.

HUMPHREYS, Nicholas, 1890- v. 12
Blessed Martin de Porres, pioneer social worker. New York, The Blessed Martin guild [1960] 68 p. port. 18 cm. 64-72678
1. Martin de Porres, Saint, 1579-1639. I. Title.

TARRY, Ellen, 1906- 920
Martin de Porres, saint of the New World. Illus. by James Fox. London, Burns and Oates; New York, Farrar [c.1963] 173p. illus. 22cm. (Vision bks., 57) 63-9924 2.25
1. Martin de Porres, Saint, 1579-1639. I. Title.

TARRY, Ellen, 1906- 92
Martin de Porres, saint of the New World. Illustrated by James Fox. London, Burns and Oates; New York, Vision Books [1963] 173 p. illus. 22 cm. (Vision books, 57) [BX4700.M397T3] 63-9924
1. Martin de Porres, Saint, 1579-1639. I. Title.

THREE studies in simplicity, 282'.092'2 B
by Malachy Carroll and Pol de Leon Albaret. [Pol de Leon Albaret's Sainte Benedict l'Africain translated from the French by Malachy Carroll] Chicago, Franciscan Herald Press [1974] vii, 201 p. 21 cm. [BX4655.2.T45] 74-8284 ISBN 0-8199-0533-X 5.95
1. Pio da Pietrelcina, Father. 2. Martin de Porres, Saint, 1579-1639. 3. Benedetto da San Filadelfo, Saint, 1526-1589. I. Carroll, Malachy Gerard, 1918- Padre Pio. 1974. II. Carroll, Malachy Gerard, 1918- St. Martin de Porres. 1974. III. Albaret, Pol de Leon, Father, 1906- Benedict l'Africain. English. 1974.
Contents omitted.

Martin Descalzo, Jose Luis,

MARTIN DESCALZO, Jose Luis, 1930- 922.246
A priest confesses. Translated by Rita Goldberg. [1st American ed. Fresno, Calif.] Academy Guild Press [1960] 218p. 22cm. Autobiography. [BX4705.M41242A33] 60-14624
I. Title.

Martin, Edward,

MARTIN, Edward, 1879- 923.273
Always be on time; an autobiography. Limited ed. Harrisburg. Pa., Telegraph Press [1959] 183p. illus. 23cm. [E748.M365.A3] 60-246
I. Title.

Martin, Elta Jay,

MARTIN, Elta Jay, 1863- 923.773
After glow; autobiography. [Fremont? Mich., 1952] 189 p. 20 cm. [CT275.M4592A3] 52-28217
I. Title.

Martin family.

MCFARLAND, Drucilla H., 1891- 929.2'0973
Mormon John Martin; Utah pioneer family history, by Drucilla H. McFarland and Ruth M. White. [Bountiful, Utah., Printed by Carr Print. Co., 1969] 356 p. illus., facsims., geneal. table, maps, ports. 24 cm. Bibliography: p. 353-356. [CS71.M38 1969] 78-11113
1. Martin family. I. White, Ruth McFarland, 1915- joint author. II. Title.

Martin, Fletcher, 1904-

EBERSOLE, Barbara (Warren3 1915- 927.5
Fletcher Martin. Foreword [by] William Saroyan. Gainesville, University of Florida Press, 1954. xvii, 51p. illus., port. 29cm. [ND237.M247E2] 54-7231
1. Martin, Fletcher, 1904- I. Title.

Martin, Frederick Townsend, 1849-1914.

MARTIN, Frederick 301.44'1 B
Townsend, 1849-1914.
Things I remember / Frederick Townsend Martin. New York : Arno Press, 1975. p. cm. (The Leisure class in America) Reprint of the 1913 ed. published by E. Nash, London. [CT275.M45924A34 1975] 75-1859 ISBN 0-405-06925-1 : 17.00
1. Martin, Frederick Townsend, 1849-1914. I. Title. II. Series. **BIP**

Martin, Glenn Luther, 1886-1955.

HARLEY, Ruth. 92
Glenn L. Martin: boy conqueror of the air, by Ruth W. Harley. Illustrated by Bob Doremus. Indianapolis, Bobbs-Merrill [1967] 200 p. illus., 20 cm. (Childhood of famous Americans) A biography stressing the childhood and youth of a man whose interest in kites, birds, bicycles, and automobiles spurred his achievement in aeronautical experiment and engineering. [TL540.M366H3] AC 67
1. Martin, Glenn Luther, 1886-1955. I. Doremus, Robert, illus. II. Title.

STILL, Henry. 926.2913
To ride the wind; a biography of Glenn L. Martin. New York, Messner [1964] 256 p. illus., ports. 22 cm. [TL540.M366S7] 64-12578
1. Martin, Glenn Luther, 1886-1955. I. Title.

Martin, Glenn Luther, 1886-1955—Juvenile literature.

HARLEY, Ruth W., 1919- 92
Glenn L. Martin: boy conqueror of the air, by Ruth W. Harley. Illus. by Bob Doremus. Indianapolis, Bobbs [1967] 200p. illus., 20cm. (Childhood of famous Americans) [TL540.M366H3] 67-17739 2.50
1. Martin, Glenn Luther, 1886-1955—Juvenile literature. I. Title.

Martin, Greg.

MARTIN, Greg. 362.2'92'0926 B
Spiritus contra spiritum : the struggle of an alcoholic pastor / by Greg Martin. Philadelphia : Westminster Press, c1977. 192 p. ; 21 cm. [RC565.M32] 76-46355 ISBN 0-664-24131-X pbk. : 5.65
1. Martin, Greg. 2. Alcoholics—United States—Biography. 3. Clergy—United States—Biography. I. Title. **BIP**

Martin, Harold H.

MARTIN, Harold H. 975.8'0094'3
Harold Martin remembers a place in the mountains / illustrated by Bill Drath. Atlanta : Peachtree Publishers, c1979. x, 166 p. : ill. ; 24 cm. [F291.2.M37] 79-67094 ISBN 0-931948-03-7 : 10.95
1. Martin, Harold H. 2. Mountain life—Georgia. 3. Georgia—Description and travel—1951- 4. Journalists—Georgia—Atlanta—Biography. 5. Atlanta—Biography. I. Title. II. Title: Place in the mountains. **BIP**

Martin, John Bartlow.

MARTIN, John 973.921'0921'4 [B]
Bartlow.
Adlai Stevenson and the world : the life of Adlai E. Stevenson / John Bartlow Martin. Garden City, N.Y. : Anchor Books, 1978, c1977. 946p. : ill. ; 24 cm. Includes bibliographical references and index. [E748.S84M36] ISBN 0-385-12649-2 pbk. : 7.95
I. Title.
L.C. card no. for 1977 Doubleday ed.: 76-23781. **BIP**

Martin, Joseph William, 1884-1968.

MARTIN, Joseph William 923.273
My first fifty years in politics, as told to Robert J. Donovan. New York. McGraw-Hill [c.1960] 261p. illus. 22cm. 60-15002 4.95 bds.,
1. U.S.—Pol. & govt.—20th cent. I. Donovan, Robert J. II. Title.

MARTIN, Joseph William, 923.273
1884-
My first fifty years in politics, as told to Robert J. Donovan. New York, McGraw-Hill [1960] 261p. illus. 22cm. [E748.M375A3] 60-15002
1. U. S.—Pol. & govt.—20th cent. I. Donovan, Robert J. II. Title.

MARTIN, Joseph 328.73'092'4 B
William, 1884-1968.
My first fifty years in politics / Joe Martin ; as told to Robert J. Donovan. Westport, Conn. : Greenwood Press, 1975, c1960. 261 p., [4] leaves of plates : ill. ; 22 cm. Reprint of the ed. published by McGraw-Hill, New York. Includes index. [E748.M375A3 1975] 74-28530 ISBN 0-8371-7919-X
1. Martin, Joseph William, 1884-1968. 2. United States—Politics and government—20th century. I. Donovan, Robert J. II. Title. **BIP**

Martin, Kingsley, 1897-1969.

HEWITT, Cecil Ralph 070.4'092'4 B
1901-
Kingsley: the life, letters, and diaries of Kingsley Martin, by C. H. Ralph. London, Gollancz, [1974, c1973] 413, [12] p. illus., parts. 22 cm. Includes bibliographical references. [PN5123.M35H4]
1. Martin, Kingsley, 1897-1969. I. Title.
Distributed by International Publications Service, for 14.00. L.C. card number for original ed.: 73-164111.

MARTIN, Kingsley, 070.4'0924 B
1897-1969.
Editor: New statesman years, 1931-1945. Chicago, H. Regnery Co. [1970, c1968] 340 p. illus. 22 cm. Subtitle varies slightly. The second of a two-volume autobiography. Includes bibliographical references. [PN5123.M35A32 1970] 78-125889 7.50
I. Title.

Martin, Louis Joseph Aloys Stanislaus, 1823-1894.

BULGER, James E 1889- 922.244
Louis Martin's daughter. Milwaukee, Bruce Pub. Co. [1952] 161p. 21cm. [BX4700.T5B8] 53-181
1. Therese, Saint, 1873-1897. 2. Martin, Louis Joseph Aloys Stanislaus, 1823-1894. 3. Martin, Zelie Marie (Guerin) 1831-1877. I. Title.

SAINTE FACE, Genevieve de 922.244
la Sister, 1869-
The father of the Little Flower (Saint Therese of the Child Jesus) 1823-1894. The sister of St. Therese tells us about her father. Translated from the French by Michael Collins. Westminster, Md., Newman Press, 1955. 153p. 17cm. [BX4705.M41233G45] 55-4603
1. Martin, Louis Joseph Aloys Stanislaus, 1823-1894. I. Title.

WUST, Louis. 922.244
Louis Martin, an ideal father, by Louis and Marjorie Wust. With an introd. by Edwin V. Byrne. [Boston] St. Paul Editions [c1957] 371 p. illus. 22 cm. [BX4705.M41233W8 1957] 59-24941
1. Martin, Louis Joseph Aloys Stanislaus, 1823-1894. 2. Martin, Zelie Marie (Guerin) 1837-1877. 3. Therese, Saint, 1873-1897. I. Wust, Marjorie, joint author. II. Title.

Martin, Louis Joseph Aloys Stanislaus, 1823-1894—Juvenile literature.

ROBERTO, Brother, 1927- 922.244
The merry watch maker; a story of Louis Martin. Illus. by Carolyn Lee Jagodits. Notre Dame, Ind., Dujarie Press [1959] 94p. illus. 24cm. [TS544.8.M3R6] 59-65365
1. Martin, Louis Joseph Aloys Stanislaus, 1823-1894—Juvenile literature. I. Title.

Martin, Luther, 1748-1826.

CLARKSON, Paul 340.0924 B
Stephen.
Luther Martin of Maryland [by] Paul S. Clarkson and R. Samuel Jett. Baltimore, Johns Hopkins Press [1970] ix, 336 p. port. 24 cm. Bibliography: p. 319-329. [KF368.M3C5] 76-94392 12.00
1. Martin, Luther, 1748-1826. I. Jett, R. Samuel, 1901- joint author. II. Title. **BIP**

Martin, Mary, 1913-

MARTIN, Mary, 792'.028'0924 B
1913-
My heart belongs / by Mary Martin. New York : Morrow, 1976. 320 p. : ill. ; 24 cm. Includes index. [ML420.M332A3] 75-31857 ISBN 0-688-03009-2 : 8.95
1. Martin, Mary, 1913- I. Title. **BIP**

Martin, Patricia Miles.

MARTIN, Patricia Miles. 92
Abraham Lincoln. Illustrated by Gustav Schrotter. New York, Putnam [1964] 64 p. col. illus. 23 cm. (A See and read beginning to read biography) [E457.905.M33] 63-15573

MARTIN, Patricia Miles. 92
Pocahontas. Illustrated by Portia Takakjian. New York, Putnam [1964] 63 p. col. illus. 23 cm. (A See and read beginning to read biography) [E90.P6M3] 64-13037

Martin, Paul, 1864-1944.

FLUKINGER, Roy, 1947- 770'.92'4 B
Paul Martin : Victorian photographer / by Roy Flukinger, Larry Schaaf, and Standish Meacham. Austin : University of Texas Press, c1977. p. cm. Includes index. Bibliography: p. [TR140.M35F59] 77-4764 ISBN 0-292-76436-7 : 24.95
1. Martin, Paul, 1864-1944. 2. Photographers—England—Biography. I. Schaaf, Larry, 1947- joint author. II. Meacham, Standish, joint author.

Martin, Paul Elliott, 1897-

VERNON, Walter N. 287'.6'0924 B
Forever building; the life and ministry of Paul E. Martin [by] Walter N. Vernon. Foreword by Joseph D. Quillian, Jr. Dallas, Southern Methodist University Press [1973] x, 146 p. illus. 24 cm. Includes bibliographical references. [BX8495.M324V47] 73-88016 ISBN 0-87074-142-X 6.95
1. Martin, Paul Elliott, 1897- I. Title. **BIP**

Martin, Robert Hugh, 1858-1939.

MARTIN, Robert 973.7'82'0924 B
Hugh, 1858-1939.
A boy of old Shenandoah / by Robert Hugh Martin ; edited by Carolyn Martin Rutherford. Parsons, W. Va. : McClain Print. Co., 1977. viii, 125 p. : ill. ; 23 cm. [E487.M38 1977] 76-45041 ISBN 0-87012-265-7 : 7.50
1. Martin, Robert Hugh, 1858-1939. 2. Martin, Albion, 1822-1894. 3. United States—History—Civil War, 1861-1865—Personal narratives—Confederate side. 4. Shenandoah Co., Va.—Biography. I. Title. **BIP**

Martin, Saint, Bp. of Tours. 4th cent.

CULLEN, Franklin, 1917- 922.1
The song of the sword, a story of Saint Martin of Tours. Illus. by Brother Eagan. Notre Dame, Ind., Dujarie Press [1952] 93 p. illus. 24 cm. [BX4700.M39C8] 52-41237
1. Martin, Saint, Bp. of Tours. 4th cent. I. Title.

DE LA MARE, Edith 922.244
Saint Martin. Tr. by Rosemary Sheed. New York, Macmillan, 1962[c.1960, 1962] 116p. 18cm. (Your name--your saint ser.) Bibl. 62-12423 2.50
1. Martin, Saint, Bp. of Tours, 4th cent. I. Title.

Martin, Saint, Bp. of Tours, 4th cent.—Juvenile literature.

SMITH, Verena 92
The life of St. Martin; pictures by Emile Probst. London, Burns & Oates; New York, Herder &Herder [1966, i.e. 1967] 26p. col. front., col. illus. 19x21cm. [BX4700.M39S6] 67-82363 1.75 bds.,
1. Martin, Saint, Bp. of Tours, 4th cent.—Juvenile literature. I. Probst, Emile, illus. II. Title.

Martin, Thornton,

MARTIN, Thornton, 1901- 927.92
Pete Martin calls on ... by Pete Martin. New York, Simon and Schuster, 1962. 510p. 22cm. [PN2285.M35] 62-14279
I. Title.

Martin, Tony.

MARTIN, Tony. 784'.092'4 B
The two of us / Tony Martin & Cyd Charisse, as told to Dick Kleiner. New York : Mason/Charter, 1976. 286 p., [147] leaves of plates : ill. ; 24 cm. [ML420.M3325A3] 76-20713 ISBN 0-88405-363-6 : 12.50
1. Martin, Tony. 2. Charisse, Cyd. 3. Musicians—Correspondence, reminiscences, etc. I. Charisse, Cyd, joint author. II. Kleiner, Dick, 1921- III. Title.

Martin, Victoria (Claflin) Woodhull, 1838-1927.

ARLING, Emanie 301.41'2'0924 B
(Nahm)
"The terrible siren." Victoria Woodhull [by] Emanie Sachs <Arling> New York, Arno Press, 1972 [c1928] xiv, 423 p. illus. 23 cm. (American women: images and realities) Bibliography: p. 416-422. [JK1899.M3A7 1972] 72-2587 ISBN 0-405-04474-7 20.00
1. Martin, Victoria (Claflin) Woodhull, 1838-1927. I. Title. II. Series.

JOHNSTON, 301.41'29'0924(B)
Johanna
Mrs. Satan the incredible saga of Victoria C. Woodhull. New York, Putnam [1967] 319p. illus., ports. 23cm. Bibl. [JK1899.M3J6] 67-15111 5.95
1. Martin, Victoria (Claflin) Woodhull, 1838-1927. I. Title.

JOHNSTON, 301.41'29'0924 [B]
Johanna.
Mrs. Satan; the incredible saga of Victoria C. Woodhull. New York, Popular Lib. [1973? c.1967] 288 p. 18 cm. Bibliography: p. 274-277. [JK1899.M3J6] pap., 0.95
1. Martin, Victoria (Claflin) Woodhull, 1838-1927. I. Title.

Martin, Victoria Claflin Woodhull, 1838-1927—Juvenile literature.

MEADE, Marion, 301.41'2'0924 B
1934-
Free woman : the life and times of Victoria W. Woodhull / Marion Meade. New York : Knopf, c1976. xiii, 174 p. : port. ; 22 cm. Bibliography: p. 173-174. A biography of the spiritualist, stock broker, publisher, lecturer, advocate of women's rights, and Presidential candidate who shocked nineteenth-century America with her revolutionary ideas and behavior. [HQ1413.M35M4 1976] 92 75-30905 ISBN 0-394-83035-0 : 6.95 lib. bdg.
1. Martin, Victoria Claflin Woodhull, 1838-1927—Juvenile literature. 2. Feminism—United States—History—Juvenile literature. 3. United States—Social conditions—1865-1918—Juvenile literature. I. Title.

Martin, William Alexander Parsons, 1827-1916.

COVELL, Ralph R. 266'.023'0924 B
W. A. P. Martin : pioneer of progress in China / by Ralph Covell. Grand Rapids : Eerdmans, c1977. p. cm. Bibliography: p. [BV3427.M295C68] 77-13321 ISBN 0-8028-1715-7 pbk. : 4.95
1. Martin, William Alexander Parsons,

1827-1916. 2. Missionaries—China—Biography. 3. Missionaries—United States—Biography. 4. Missions—China. I. Title. BIP

Martin, Zelie Marie (Guerin) 1831-1877.

FOLEY, Barbara 922.244
Zelie Martin, mother of Saint Therese of Lisieux. Boston, the Daughters of St. Paul [c.1960] 58p. illus. 19cm. (St. Paul Editions) 60-54164 1.00;.50 pap.,
1. Martin, Zelie Marie (Guerin) 1831-1877. 2. Therese, Saint, 1873-1897. I. Title.

WUST, Louis. 922.244
Louis Martin, an ideal father, by Louis and Marjorie Wust. With an introd. by Edwin V. Byrne. [Boston] St. Paul Editions [c1957] 371 p. illus. 22 cm. [BX4705.M41233W8 1957] 59-24941
1. Martin, Louis Joseph Aloys Stanislaus, 1823-1894. 2. Martin, Zelie Marie (Guerin) 1837-1877. 3. Therese, Saint, 1873-1897. I. Wust, Marjorie, joint author. II. Title.

WUST, Louis. 271'.971'0924 B
Zelie Martin, mother of St. Therese, by Louis and Marjorie Wust. With an introd. by Martin J. O'Connor. [Boston?] St. Paul Editions [1969] 336 p. 22 cm. Bibliography: p. 331-336. [BX4705.M41235W8] 68-28103 4.00
1. Martin, Zelie Marie (Guerin) 1831-1877. 2. Therese, Saint, 1873-1897. I. Wust, Marjorie, joint author. II. Title.

Martin, Zelle Marie (Guerin) 1831-1877-Juvenile literature.

ROBERTO, Brother, 1927- 922.244
No wings for nine angels; a story of Zelie Martin. Illus. by Carolyn Lee Jagodits. Notre Dame, Ind., Dujarie Press [1959] 94p. illus. 24cm. [BX4705.M41235R6] 60-19254
1. Martin, Zelle Marie (Guerin) 1831-1877-Juvenile literature. I. Title.

Martineau, Harriet, 1802-1876.

COLSON, Percy, 1873-1952. 920.042
Victorian portraits. Freeport, N.Y., Books for Libraries Press [1968] 256 p. ports. 22 cm. (Essay index reprint series) Reprint of the 1932 ed. Contents.Contents.—The unhappy prince and Baron Stockmar.—The best of both worlds [Bishop Samuel Wilberforce]—Virtue is its own reward [Harriet Martineau]—A fallen idol [Felix Mendelssohn-Bartholdy] Bibliography: p. 255-256. [DA562.C7 1968] 68-16921
1. Albert, Consort of Queen Victoria, 1819-1861. 2. Wilberforce, Samuel, Bp. of Winchester, 1805-1873. 3. Martineau, Harriet, 1802-1876. 4. Mendelssohn-Bartholdy, Felix, 1809-1847. I. Title. BIP

COURTNEY, Janet Elizabeth Hogarth, 1865- 192 B
Freethinkers of the nineteenth century / by Janet E. Courtney. Norwood, Pa. : Norwood Editions, 1976. p. cm. Reprint of the 1920 ed. published by Chapman & Hall, London. Contents.Contents.—Frederick Denison Maurice.—Mathew Arnold.—Charles Bradlaugh.—Thomas Henry Huxley.—Leslie Stephen.—Harriet Martineau.—Charles Kingsley. [B1569.C6 1976] 76-17266 ISBN 0-8482-0386-0 : 25.00
1. Maurice, Frederick Denison, 1805-1872. 2. Arnold, Matthew, 1822-1888—Religion and ethics. 3. Bradlaugh, Charles, 1833-1891. 4. Huxley, Thomas Henry, 1825-1895. 5. Stephen, Leslie, Sir, 1832-1904. 6. Martineau, Harriet, 1802-1876. 7. Kingsley, Charles, 1819-1875. I. Title. BIP

MILLER, Florence Fenwick, 1854-1935. 823'.8 B
Harriet Martineau. Port Washington, N.Y., Kennikat Press [1972] ix, 224 p. 21 cm. Reprint of the 1884 ed. [PR4984.M5Z7 1972] 70-160772 ISBN 0-8046-1604-3
1. Martineau, Harriet, 1802-1876. BIP

NEVILL, John Cranstoun, 1893- 823'.8 B
Harriet Martineau. [Folcroft, Pa.] Folcroft Library Editions, 1973 [i.e. 1974] 128 p. port. 24 cm. Reprint of the 1943 ed. published by F. Muller, London. Bibliography: p. 124. [PR4984.M5Z75 1974] 73-11354 ISBN 0-8414-2368-7 (lib. bdg.)
1. Martineau, Harriet, 1802-1876.

WEBB, Robert Kiefer. 928.2
Harriet Martineau; a radical Victorian. New York, Columbia University Press, 1960. xiii, 385 p. illus., ports., facsims. 23 cm. Bibliography: p. 368-377. [PR4984.M5Z93 1960a] 59-11698
1. Martineau, Harriet, 1802-1876. I. Title.

WEBB, Robert Kiefer 928.2
Harriet Matineau, a radical Victorian New York, Columbia University Press [c]1960. xiii, 385 p. Bibliography 59-11698 5.00
1. Martineau, Harriet, 1802-1876. I. Title.

WHEATLEY, Vera. 928.2
The life and work of Harriet Martineau. Fair Lawn, N.J., Essential Books, 1957. 421 p. illus. 23 cm. Includes bibliography. [PR4984.M5Z95] 57-4263
1. Martineau, Harriet, 1802-1876. I. Title. BIP

Martineau, Harriet, 1802-1876—Biography.

BOSANQUET, Theodora. 823'.8 B
Harriet Martineau; an essay in comprehension. [Folcroft, Pa.] Folcroft Library Editions, 1974. p. cm. Reprint of the 1927 ed. published by F. Etchells & H. Macdonald, London, in series: The Haslewood books. Bibliography: p. [PR4984.M5Z56 1974] 74-16320 25.00 (lib. bdg.).
1. Martineau, Harriet, 1802-1876—Biography. I. Series: The Haslewood books. BIP

Martinez Alonso, Eduardo.

MARTINEZ Alonso, Eduardo. 926.1
Memoirs of a medico. 1st ed. Garden City, N. Y., Doubleday, 1961. 335p. 22cm. [R558.M35A3] 61-9536
I. Title.

Martinez, Antonio Jose, 1793-1867.

DE ARAGON, Ray John. 282'.092'3 B
Padre Martinez and Bishop Lamy / by Ray John de Aragon. Las Vegas, N.M. : Pan-American Pub. Co., c1978. vi, 141 p. : ill. ; 22 cm. Includes bibliographies. [BX4705.M412553D4] 78-70565 ISBN 0-932906-00-1 pbk. : 6.95
1. Martinez, Antonio Jose, 1793-1867. 2. Catholic Church—Clergy—Biography. 3. Lamy, John Baptist, Abp., 1814-1888. 4. Clergy—New Mexico—Biography. I. Title. BIP

SANCHEZ, Pedro, b.1831. 282'.092'4 B
Recollections of the life of the priest Don Antonio Jose Martinez = Memorias sobre la vida del presbitero Don Antonio Jose Martinez / by Pedro Sanchez ; translated by Ray John de Aragon. Santa Fe, N.M. : Lightning Tree, c1978. 85 p. ; 18 cm. English and Spanish. [BX4705.M412553S2713] 78-51362 ISBN 0-89016-044-9 : 9.95 ISBN 0-89016-045-7 (pbk.) : 4.95
1. Martinez, Antonio Jose, 1793-1867. 2. Catholic Church—Clergy—Biography. 3. Clergy—New Mexico—Biography. 4. Statesmen—New Mexico—Biography. 5. New Mexico—Biography. I. Title.

Martinez, Antonio Jose, 1793-1867—Juvenile literature.

BERNARD, Jacqueline. 978.9'0092'2 B
Voices from the Southwest: Antonio Jose Martinez, Elfego Baca, Reies Lopez Tijerina. New York, Scholastic Book Services [1972] 128 p. illus. 22 cm. (Firebird books) Discusses the struggles of three Mexican Americans in various historical periods to redress the wrongs that their people suffered at the hands of the English-speaking majority. [F805.M5B47] 920 72-77478 ISBN 0-590-024655. 2.97
1. Martinez, Antonio Jose, 1793-1867—Juvenile literature. 2. Baca, Elfego, 1864-1945—Juvenile literature. 3. Tijerina, Reies—Juvenile literature. 4. Mexican Americans—New Mexico—Juvenile literature. I. Title.
pap. 1.24; ISBN 0-590-024477.

Martinez, Luis Maria, Abp., 1881-1956.

TREVINO, Jose Guadalupe, 1889- 282'.0924 B
The spiritual life of Archbishop Martinez [by] Joseph G. Trevino. Translated by Sister Mary St. Daniel Tarrant. St. Louis, B. Herder Book Co. [1966] xiii, 219 p. 21 cm. (Cross and crown series of spirituality, no. 33) Translation of Monsenor Martinez, semblanza de su vida interior. [BX4705.M41256T73] 66-29272
1. Martinez, Luis Maria, Abp., 1881-1956. I. Title.

Martinez, Maria Montoya.

PETERSON, Susan. 738.3'092'4 B
The living tradition of Maria Martinez / Susan Peterson. 1st ed. Tokyo : Kodansha International ; New York : distributed through Harper & Row, 1977. 300 p. : ill. (some col.) ; 31 cm. Includes index. Bibliography: p. 289-296. [E99.S213M377] 77-75373 ISBN 0-87011-319-4 : 35.00
1. Martinez, Maria Montoya. 2. San Ildefonso, N.M.—Biography. 3. Pottery—New Mexico—San Ildefonso. 4. Indians of North America—New Mexico—Pottery. I. Title. BIP

SPIVEY, Richard L. 738.3'092'2
Maria / Richard L. Spivey. 1st ed. Flagstaff, Ariz. : Northland Press, 1979. xxi, 136 p. : ill. (some col.) ; 32 cm. Includes index. Bibliography: p. 129-131. [E99.S213M3785] 78-71373 ISBN 0-87358-181-4 : 27.50
1. Martinez, Maria Montoya. 2. San Ildefonso, N.M.—Biography. 3. Potters—New Mexico—San Ildefonso—Biography. 4. Pottery—New Mexico—San Ildefonso. 5. Pueblo Indians—Pottery. 6. Indians of North America—New Mexico—San Ildefonso—Pottery.

Martinez, Maria Montoya—Juvenile literature.

NELSON, Mary Carroll. 738.3'092'4 B
Maria Martinez. Minneapolis, Dillon Press [1972] 77 p. illus. 24 cm. (The Story of an American Indian) A biography of the Pueblo Indian woman who became renowned for her skill in pottery. [E99.S213N44] 92 78-172871 ISBN 0-87518-038-8
1. Martinez, Maria (Montoya)—Juvenile literature. I. Title. BIP

NELSON, Mary Carroll. 738.3'092'4 B
Maria Martinez. Minneapolis, Dillon Press [1974, c1972] 74 p. illus. 24 cm. (The Story of an American Indian) A biography of the Pueblo Indian woman who became renowned for her skill in pottery. [E99.S213N44 1974] 92 74-12323 ISBN 0-87518-098-1
1. Martinez, Maria Montoya—Juvenile literature. I. Title.

Martinez Montanes, Juan, 1568-1648.

PROSKE, Beatrice Irene (Gilman) 1899- 730'.924 B
Juan Martinez Montanes; Sevillian sculptor, by Beatrice Gilman Proske. New York, Hispanic Society of America, 1967. ix, 190 p. 212 plates. 26 cm. (Hispanic notes & monographs; essays, studies, and brief biographies. Peninsular series) [NB813.M36P7] 67-66244
1. Martinez Montanes, Juan, 1568-1648. I. Title. II. Series. BIP

Martino, Mario.

MARTINO, Mario. 616.6
Emergence : a transsexual autobiography / by Mario Martino ; with Harriett. New York : New American Library, 1979. 242p. : photos ; 18 cm. (A Signet book) [RC560.C4M37 1977] ISBN 0-451-08520-5 pbk. : 2.50
1. Martino, Mario. 2. Transsexuals — United States — Biography. I. Title.
L.C. card no. for 1977 Crown ed.: 77-3329.

Martinson, Martin H.,

MARTINSON, Martin H., 1882- 917.74'81
Hendrik's diary, by Martin H. Martinson. [Alpena? Mich., 1969] xii, 300 p. illus., ports. 23 cm. Autobiographical. [CT275.M4596A3] 70-12751
I. Title.

Martinu, Bohuslav, 1890-1959.

LARGE, Brian. 780'.92'4 B
Martinu / Brian Large. New York : Holmes & Meier, 1976, c1975. xiv, 198 p., [13] leaves of plates : ill. ; 24 cm. Includes index. "Catalogue of works": 157-186. [ML410.M382L3 1976] 75-45082 ISBN 0-8419-0256-9 : 18.50
1. Martinu, Bohuslav, 1890-1959. BIP

Marto, Francisco, 1908-1919.

DAUGHTERS of St. Paul. 92
Boy with a mission; the life of Francis Marto of Fatima. Written and illustrated by the Daughters of St. Paul. [Boston] St. Paul Editions [1967] 98 p. illus. 22 cm. (Their Encounter books) A biography of one of the three Portuguese children who saw the vision of Our Lady of Fatima in the early twentieth century. [BX4705.M4133D3] AC 67
1. Marto, Francisco, 1908-1919. I. Title.

Marto, Francisco, 1908-1919—Juvenile literature.

DAUGHTERS OF ST. PAUL. 92
Boy with a mission; the life of Francis Marto of Fatima. Written, illus. by the Daughters of St. Paul. [Boston]0St. Paul Eds. [1967] 98p. illus. 22cm. (Their Encounter bks.) [BX4705.M4133D3] 65-24081 1.50
1. Marto, Francisco, 1908-1919—Juvenile literature. I. Title.

Marto, Francisco, 1908-1919 — Juvenile literature.

DAUGHTERS of St. Paul. 92
Boy with a mission; the life of Francis Marto of Fatima. Written and illustrated by the Daughters of St. Paul. [Boston] St. Paul Editions [1967] 98 p. illus. 22 cm. (Their Encounter books) [BX4705.M4133D3] 65-24081
1. Marto, Francisco, 1908-1919 — Juvenile literature. I. Title.

Marto, Jacintha, 1910-1920.

OLIVEIRA, Jose Galamba de, 1903- 922.2469
A flower of Fatima. Translated by a Daughter of St. Paul. [Boston] St. Paul Editions [c1957] 179p. illus. 22cm. [BX4705.M4134O53 1957] 59-23936
1. Marto, Jacintha, 1910-1920. 2. Fatima, Nossa Senhora da. I. Title.

Martov, IUlli Osipovich, 1873-1923.

GETZLER, Israel. 947.08'0924 (B)
Martov; a political biography of a Russian social democrat. Cambridge, Cambridge U. P.; Melbourne, Melbourne U. P., 1967. 246 p. front., illus., 4 plates (incl. ports., facsims.) 24 1/2 cm. 70/- . (B 67-13662) Bibliography: p. 227-238. [HX312.M27G4] 67-10778
1. Martov, IUlli Osipovich, 1873-1923. I. Title.

GETZLER, Israel. 947.08'0924 (B)
Martov: a political biography of a Russian social democrat. [Melbourne] Melbourne University Press; London, New York, Cambridge U. P. [1967] viii, 246 p. illus., ports. 26 cm. $8.50 Aust. (Aus 67-521) Bibliography: p. 227-238. [HX312.M27G4 1967b] 67-103767
1. Martov, IUlli Osipovich, 1873-1923. I. Title. BIP

Marts, Arnaud C.

CARTER, Paul C. 361'.924 B
Arnaud Cartwright Marts; a winner in the American tradition [by] Paul C. Carter. New York, Algonquin Press, 1970. xiv, 377 p. illus., facsims., ports. 22 cm. "The early years of Arnaud C. Marts; autobiography": p. 1-45. [HV28.M34C3] 76-16792 7.50
1. Marts, Arnaud C. I. Marts, Arnaud C.

Marty, Sid, 1944-—Homes and haunts—Canada—Rocky Mountains.

MARTY, Sid, 1944- 813'.5'4 B
Men for the mountains / Sid Marty. 1st U.S. ed. New York : Vanguard Press, 1979, c1978. 270 p. : maps (on lining papers) ; 24 cm. [PR9199.3.M39Z473 1979] 78-71651 ISBN 0-8149-0812-8 : 12.95
1. Marty, Sid, 1944-—Homes and haunts—Canada—Rocky Mountains. 2. National parks and reserves—Canada 3. Authors, Canadian—20th century—Biography. I. Title. BIP

Martyrs.

FOXE, John, 1516-1587. 272
The acts and monuments of John Foxe; with a life of the martyrologist, and vindication of the work, by George Townsend. New York, AMS Press, 1965. 8 v. illus. 24 cm. Reprint of the 1843-49? ed. First complete English ed. published in 1563 under title: Actes and monuments of these latter and perillous dayes, touching matters of the church. [BR1600.F6 1965] 72-185708
1. Martyrs. 2. Persecution. 3. Church history. I. Townsend, George, 1788-1857. II. Title.

MUSURILLO, Herbert 272'.1'0922 B
Anthony, comp.
The acts of the Christian martyrs; introduction, texts and translations by Herbert Musurillo. Oxford, Clarendon Press, 1972. lxxiii, 379 p. 21 cm. (Oxford early Christian texts) Parallel Greek or Latin texts with English translations. Includes bibliographical references. [BR1603.A1M87] 72-177389 ISBN 0-19-826806-8 £6.00
1. Martyrs. 2. Persecution—Early church, ca. 30-1600. I. Title. II. Series.

Marvell, Andrew, 1621-1678.

BIRRELL, Augustine, 821'.4 B
1850-1933.
Andrew Marvell. Freeport, N.Y., Books for Libraries Press [1972] vii, 242 p. 23 cm. Reprint of the 1905 ed., issued in the series: English men of letters. [PR3546.B4 1972] 77-39666 ISBN 0-8369-9929-0
1. Marvell, Andrew, 1621-1678. BIP

BIRRELL, Augustine, 821'.4 B
1850-1933.
Andrew Marvell / by Augustine Birrell. Folcroft, Pa. : Folcroft Library Editions, 1978 [c1905] p. cm. Reprint of the ed. published by Macmillan, New York, issued in series: English men of letters. Includes bibliographical references and index. [PR3546.B4 1978] 78-14755 ISBN 0-8414-1730-X : 25.00
1. Marvel, Andrew, 1621-1678—Biography. 2. Authors, English—Early modern, 1500-1700—Biography.

HUNT, John Dixon. 821'.4
Andrew Marvell : his life and writings / John Dixon Hunt. Ithaca, N.Y. : Cornell University Press, 1978. 206 p. : ill. ; 25 cm. Includes bibliographical references and index. [PR3546.H8 1978] 78-57689 ISBN 0-8014-1202-1 : 17.50
1. Marvell, Andrew, 1621-1678. 2. Poets, English—Early modern, 1500-1700—Biography. BIP

LEGOUIS, Pierre, 1891- 821'.4 B
Andrew Marvell: poet, puritan, patriot. 2nd ed. Oxford, Clarendon P., 1968. iii-xv, 262 p. 23 cm. Abridged version of a French book published in 1928 under title: Andre Marvell, poete, puritain, patriote, 1621-1678. Bibliography: p. [249]-254. [PR3546.L423 1968] 70-374771 30/-
1. Marvell, Andrew, 1621-1678.

SACKVILLE-WEST, Victoria 821'.4
Mary, Hon., 1892-1962.
Andrew Marvell. New York, Russell & Russell [1971] 63 p. 20 cm. Reprint of the 1929 ed. Includes bibliographical references. [PR3546.S3 1971] 70-102539
1. Marvell, Andrew, 1621-1678. BIP

Marx, Arthur,

MARX, Arthur, 1921- 928.1
Not as a crocodile; illustrated by Gil Walker. [1st ed.] New York, Harper [1958] 207p. illus. 22cm. Autobiographical. [PS3525.A7737Z55] 58-6153
I. Title.

Marx Brothers.

ADAMSON, Joseph. 790.2'092'2
Groucho, Harpo, Chico, and sometimes Zeppo; a history of the Marx Brothers and a satire on the rest of the world, by Joe Adamson. New York, Simon and Schuster [1973] 464 p. illus. 23 cm. Bibliography: p. 447-451. [PN2297.M3A4] 72-87944 ISBN 0-671-21458-6 10.00
1. Marx Brothers. I. Title.

ADAMSON, Joseph. 790.2'092'2
Groucho, Harpo, Chico, and sometimes Zeppo; a history of the Marx Brothers and a satire on the rest of the world, by Joe Adamson. New York, Pocket Books [1976 c1973] 484 p. illus. 18 cm. Includes index. Bibliography, p. 467-471. [PN2297.M3A4] ISBN 0-671-80365-4 2.50 (pbk.)
1. Marx Brothers. I. Title.
L.C. card no. for original edition: 72-87944.

CRICHTON, Kyle Samuel, 927.92
1896-
The Marx Brothers. [1st ed.] Garden City, N. Y., Doubleday, 1950. viii, 310 p. ports. 22 cm. [PN2297.M3C7] 50-8052
1. Marx Brothers.

*WOLF, William. 791.43'028'0924 B
The Marx brothers. New York, Pyramid, [1975] 157 p. ill. 20 cm. (Pyramid illustrated history of the movies.) Includes index. "The major films of the Marx Brothers" p. 149-151. Bibliography: p. 147-148. [PN2287] 75-29948 ISBN 0-515-03754-0 1.75 (pbk.)
1. Marx Brothers. 2. Moving-pictures—Biography. 3. Moving picture actors and actresses. I. Sennett, Ted. ed. II. Title.

Marx, Groucho, 1891-

ACRE, Hector. 790.2'092'4 B
Groucho : the biography of Groucho Marx / by Hector Arce. New York : Putnam, c1978. p. cm. Includes index. Bibliography: p. [PN2287.M53A7 1978] 78-16019 10.00
1. Marx, Groucho, 1891-1977. 2. Comedians—United States—Biography. I. Title.

CHANDLER, 790.2'092'4 B
Charlotte.
Hello, I must be going : Groucho and his friends / by Charlotte Chandler. 1st ed. Garden City, N.Y. : Doubleday, 1978. vi, 568 p., [12] leaves of plates : ill. ; 22 cm. [PN2287.M53C5] 77-89877 ISBN 0-385-12444-9 : 10.95
1. Marx, Groucho, 1891- 2. Comedians—United States—Biography. I. Title. BIP

CHANDLER, 790.2'092'4 B
Charlotte.
Hello, I must be going : Groucho and his friends / by Charlotte Chandler. Harmondsworth, Eng. ; New York : Penguin Books, 1979, c1978. viii, 568 p., [12] leaves of plates : ill. ; 20 cm. Reprint of the 1978 ed. published by Doubleday, Garden City, N.Y. [PN2287.M53C5 1979] 79-15631 ISBN 0-14-005222-4 pbk. : 4.95
1. Marx, Groucho, 1891-1977. 2. Comedians—United States—Biography. I. Title.

MARX, Arthur 927.92
Life with Groucho. New York, Popular Library [1960, c.1954] 255p. 18cm. (Popular giant PC600) .35 pap.,
1. Marx, Groucho, 1891— I. Title.

MARX, Arthur, 1921- 927.92
Life with Groucho. New York, Simon and Schuster, 1954. 310 p. 22 cm. [PN2287.M53M3] 54-9802
1. Marx, Groucho, 1891- I. Title.

MARX, Arthur, 1921- 791'.092'4
Son of Groucho. New York, D. McKay Co. [1972] xii, 357 p. ports. 24 cm. Autobiographical. [PN2287.M525A3] 72-86964 7.95
1. Marx, Groucho, 1891- 2. Marx, Arthur, 1921- I. Title.

MARX, Groucho, 1891 927.92
Groucho and me. [New York] B. Geis Associates; distributed by Random House [1959] 344 p. illus. 22 cm. [PN2287.M53A3] 59-13753
I. Title. BIP

MARX, Groucho, 1891- 816'.5'2
The Groucho letters; letters from and to Groucho Marx. New York, Simon and Schuster [1967] 319 p. 22 cm. [PN2287.M53A4] 67-12921
I. Title.

MARX, Groucho, 790.2'092'4 B
1891-
The Groucho/phile : a illustrated life ; introd. by Hector Arce. Indianapolis : Bobbs-Merrill, [1976] p. cm. Includes index. [PN2287.M53A34] 76-11630 ISBN 0-672-52239-X : 17.50
1. Marx, Groucho, 1891- I. Title.

MARX, Harpo 927.92
Harpo speaks! [By] Harpo Marx, Rowland Barber. Illus. by Susan Marx. New York, Avon [1962, c.1961] 384p. (V-2050) .75 pap.,
1 Actors—Correspondence, reminiscences, etc. I. Title.

Marx, Karl, 1818-1883.

ALEXANDER, Albert. 335.4'0924 B
Karl Marx, the father of modern socialism. New York, F. Watts [1969] 147 p. illus., ports. 22 cm. (Immortals of history) Bibliography: p. 139-141. [HX39.5.A553] 69-13451
1. Marx, Karl, 1818-1883. I. Title.

APSLER, Alfred. 335.4
Prophet of revolution: Karl Marx. New York, J. Messner [1967] 191 p. 22 cm. Bibliography: p. [186]-187. Biography of the writer and philosopher whose doctrine of socialism influenced workers as well as leaders throughout the world. [HX39.5.A56] AC 67
1. Marx, Karl, 1818-1883. I. Title.

BERLIN, Isaiah, Sir. 923.343
Karl Marx; his life and environment. 3d ed. London, New York, Oxford University Press, 1963. 295 p. 17 cm. (The Home university library of modern knowledge, 189) Bibliography: p. [285]-289. [HX39.5.B4 1963] 64-1146
1. Marx, Karl, 1818-1883. I. Title.

BERLIN, Isaiah, Sir ed. 923.343
Karl Marx, his life and environment. New York, Oxford University Press, 1959. 280p. 21cm. (A Galaxy book GB25) [HX39.5.B4 1959] 59-3993
1. Marx, Karl, 1818-1883. I. Title.

BERLIN, Isaiah. Sir v. 12
Karl Marx; his life and environment. 2d ed. [with corrections] New York, Oxford University Press [1948, 1960] 286 p. (The Home University Library of modern knowledge) Bibliography: p. [275]-280. 64-54701
1. Marx, Karl, 1818-1883. I. Title.

BERLIN, Isaiah. Sir v. 12
Karl Marx, his life and environment, With a new introduction by Robert Heilbroner. [3d ed.] New York, Time [c1963] xix, 246 p.21 cm. "Time reading program special edition." Bibliography: p. [237]-240. NUC64
1. Marx, Karl, 1818-1883. I. Title.

BERLIN, Isaiah, 335.4'092'4 B
Sir.
Karl Marx : his life and environment / Isaiah Berlin. 4th ed. London ; New York : Oxford University Press, 1978. p. cm. Includes index. Bibliography: p. [HX39.5.B4 1978b] 77-26943 ISBN 0-19-520052-7 : 11.95
1. Marx, Karl, 1818-1883. 2. Communists—Biography. I. Title. BIP

BERLIN, Isaiah, 335.4'092'4 B
Sir.
Karl Marx, his life and environment / Isaiah Berlin. 4th ed. Oxford [Eng.] ; New York : Oxford University Press, 1978. xii, 228 p. ; 21 cm. (Oxford paperbacks university series) Includes index. Bibliography: p. [209]-222. [HX39.5.B4 1978] 77-30374 pbk. : 3.95
1. Marx, Karl, 1818-1883. 2. Communists—Biography. I. Title.

BLUMENBERG, Werner. 335.4'092'4 B
Portrait of Marx; an illustrated biography. Translated by Douglas Scott. [New York] Herder and Herder [1972] 196 p. illus. 21 cm. Translation of Karl Marx in Selbstzeugnissen und Bilddokumenten. Bibliography: p. [187]-191. [HX39.5.B5813] 74-178874 6.95
1. Marx, Karl, 1818-1883. I. Title.

CARMICHAEL, Joel. 335.4'0924 B
Karl Marx, the passionate logician. New York, Scribner [1967] viii, 262 p. ports. 22 cm. Bibliography: p. [251] A biography examining the events that tampered Karl Marx's intellectual growth, his personal life struggle, and his creation of Marxism. [HX39.5.C28] 92 AC 68
1. Marx, Karl, 1818-1883. I. Title.

CARMICHAEL, Joel. 335.4'0924
Karl Marx, the passionate logician. New York, Scribner [1967] viii, 262 p. ports. 22 cm. Bibliography: p. [251] [HX39.5.C28] 67-24047
1. Marx, Karl 1818-1883. I. Title.

CARROLL, L Ray, 1879- 923.343
The pixylated prophet; the life and adventures of Karl Marx, a crack pot philosopher. [Billings? Mont., 1953] 141p. illus. 19cm. [HX39.5.C3 1953] 53-30739
1. Marx, Karl, 1818-1883. I. Title.

DELFGAAUW, Bernardus 335.4'0924
Maria Ignatius.
The young Marx [by] Bernard Delfgaauw. Translated [from the Dutch] by Franklin Schutz and Martin Redfern; with a letter from Karl Marx to his father translated [from the German] by William Glen-Doepel. Westminster, Md., Newman Press [1967] x, 117 p. 21 cm. Translation of De jonge Marx. Bibliography: p. 113-117. Bibliographical footnotes. [HX39.5.D413 1967b] 67-23611
1. Marx, Karl, 1818-1883. I. Title.

EVANS, Michael, 320.5'32'0924 B
1936-
Karl Marx. Bloomington, Indiana University Press [1975] 215 p. 23 cm. Bibliography: p. 201-209. [HX39.5.E9 1975] 74-15712 ISBN 0-253-33172-2
1. Marx, Karl, 1818-1883.

FETSCHER, Iring. 335.4'0924
Marx and Marxism. [New York] Herder and Herder [1971] xii, 354 p. 22 cm. Translation of Karl Marx und der Marxismus. Includes bibliographical references. [HX39.5.F4713] 77-150299 12.50
1. Marx, Karl, 1818-1883. 2. Socialism. 3. Communism. I. Title. BIP

GEMKOW, Heinrich. 335.4'0924 B
Karl Marx. A biography. In collaboration with Oskar Hoffmann [and others] Edited by the Institute of Marxism-Leninism of the Central Committee of the Socialist Unity Party of Germany. Dresden, Verlag Zeit im Bild, 1968. 426 p., several l. of illus. 21 cm. Translation of Karl Marx-eine Biographie. Bibliography: p. [399]-416. [HX39.5.G413] 74-463805 17.00
1. Marx, Karl, 1818-1883. I. Berlin. Institut fur Marxismus-Leninismus.

GOLDENDACH, David 335.4'092'2 B
Borisovich, 1870-1942.
Karl Marx and Friedrich Engels; an introduction to their lives and work, by David Riazanov. Translated by Joshua Kunitz. With an introd. by Dirk J. Struik. New York, Monthly Review Press [1974, c1927] vi, 231 p. 21 cm. Reprint of the ed. published by International Publishers, New York, which was issued as v. 2 of the Marxist library. [HX39.5.G613 1973] 73-8055 ISBN 0-85345-297-0 8.95
1. Marx, Karl, 1818-1883. 2. Engels, Friedrich, 1820-1895. I. Series: Marxist library, v. 2.

KARL Marx, v. 12
his life and environment. 2d. ed. London, New York, Oxford Univ. Press [1956] 280p. 17cm. (The Home university library of modern knowledge, 189) Bibliography: p. [269]-273.
1. Marx, Karl, 1818-1883. I. Berlin, Isaiah, Sir II. Series.

**KARL Marx;* 335.40924
a concise biography, by Helene Lecar. Foreword by Ellsworth Raymond. Series ed.: Roberta Strauss Feuerlicht. New York, Amer. R.D.M. [c.1966] 77p. front port. 21cm. (Study master pubn., 919) Bibl. 1.00 pap.,
1. Marx, Karl, 1818-1883. I. Lecar, Helene.

KARL Marx his life and v. 12
development. . . 2d ed. London, Oxford university press [1960] 286p. 17cm. (Home university library of modern knowledge. 189) 'Second edition 1948; reprinted. . . (With corrections) 1960.' Bibliography: p. [275]-280.
1. Marx, Karl. 1818-1883. I. Berlin, Isaiah. Sir

LECAR, Helene. v. 12
Karl Marx, a concise biography. Foreword by Ellsworth Raymond. New York, American R.D.M. Corporation [1966] 77 p. ports. 21 cm. (A study-master publication, 919) Bibliography: p. 77. 67-102301
1. Marx, Karl, 1818-1883. I. Title.

LIEBKNECHT, Wilhelm 335.4'0924 B
Philipp Christian Martin Ludwig, 1826-1900.
Karl Marx; biographical memoirs. Translated by Ernest Untermann. New York, Greenwood Press [1968] 181 p. 18 cm. Reprint of the 1901 edition. [HX39.5.L47 1968] 69-10119
1. Marx, Karl, 1818-1883. I. Title.

LIEBKNECHT, Wilhelm 335.4'0924 B
Philipp Christian Martin Ludwig, 1826-1900.
Karl Marx; biographical memoirs. Translated by Ernest Untermann. Chicago, C. H. Kerr [1901] Michigan, Scholarly Press [1969?] 181 p. 19 cm. [HX39.5L463 1969] 77-106904
1. Marx, Karl, 1818-1883. I. Title. BIP

LORIA, Achille, 335.4'092'4 B
1857-1943.
Karl Marx / by Achille Loria ; authorized translation from the Italian with a foreword by Eden & Cedar Paul. New York : Gordon Press, [1976] c1920. p. cm. Reprint of the ed. published by T. Seltzer, New York. [HB501.M5L83 1976] 75-44280 ISBN 0-87968-304-X lib.bdg. : 34.95
1. Marx, Karl, 1818-1883. 2. Socialism. 3. Capitalism.

MCLELLAN, David. 335.4'092'4 B
Karl Marx / David McLellan. New York : Penguin Books, 1976, c1975. p. cm. (Penguin modern masters) Includes index. Bibliography: p. [HX39.5.M257 1976] 76-22700 ISBN 0-14-004320-9 pbk. : 4.95
1. Marx, Karl, 1818-1883.

MCLELLAN, David. 335.4'092'4 B
Karl Marx / David McLellan. New York : Viking Press, 1975. xiv, 110 p. ; 19 cm. (Modern masters) Includes index. Bibliography: p. [97]-103. [HX39.5.M257] 75-4633 ISBN 0-670-41172-8 : 7.95 ISBN 0-670-01989-5 pbk. : 2.95
1. Marx, Karl, 1818-1883.

MCLELLAN, David. 335.4'092'4 B
Karl Marx: his life and thought. [1st U.S. ed.] New York, Harper & Row [1974, c1973] xii, 498 p. illus. 24 cm. Bibliography: p. [469]-489. [HX39.5.M26 1974] 73-4104 ISBN 0-06-012829-1 12.50
1. Marx, Karl, 1818-1883.

MCLELLAN, David. 335.4'0924 B
Marx before Marxism. [1st U.S. ed.] New York, Harper & Row [1970] viii, 233 p. map. 22 cm. Bibliography: p. 223-229. [HX39.5.M27 1970b] 70-105231 6.50
1. Marx, Karl, 1818-1883. I. Marx, Karl, 1818-1883. II. Title.

MCLELLAN, David. 335.4'092'4
Karl Marx : his life and thought. New York : Harper and Row, 1977. xii, 498p. : ill. ; 21 cm. (Harper Colophon Books) Bibliography:p.[469]-489. [HX39.5.M26] ISBN 0-06-090585-9 pbk. : 5.95
1. Marx, Karl,1818-1883. I. Title.
L.C. card no. for 1973 Harper and Row ed.:73-4104. BIP

MCLELLAN, David 335.430924
The Thought of Karl Marx; an introduction [by] David McLellan New York, Harper Torchbooks [1974, c1971] x, 237, 21 cm. [HX39.5M28] ISBN 0-06-131835-3 2.95 (pbk.)
1. Marx, Karl, 1818-1883 I. Marx, Karl, 1818-1883 Selections. English. 1972. II. Title.
L.C. card number for original ed.: 74-181634

MCLELLAN, David. 335.43'092'4
The thought of Karl Marx; an introduction [by] David McLellan. [1st U.S. ed.] New York, Harper & Row [1972, c1971] x, 237 p. 22 cm. Bibliography: p. [229]-233. [HX39.5.M28 1972] 74-181634 ISBN 0-06-012904-2 6.95
1. Marx, Karl, 1818-1883. I. Marx, Karl, 1818-1883. Selections. English. 1972. II. Title.

MARX comes to India 335.4'092'4 B
: earliest Indian biographies of Karl Marx, by Lala Hardayal and Swadeshabhimani Ramakrishna Pillai, with critical introductions / P. C. Joshi, K. Damodaran. Delhi : Manohar Book Service, 1975. 133 p., [3] leaves of plates : ill. ; 22 cm. Includes bibliographical references and index. [HX39.5.M372] 75-905019 9.50
1. Marx, Karl, 1818-1883. I. Dayal, Har, 1884-1939. II. Ramakrishna Pillai, K., 1878- III. Joshi, Puran Chandra, 1907- IV. Damodaran, K., 1912-
Distributed by South Asia Books.

MARX, Karl, 1818- 335.4'092'4
1883.
The letters of Karl Marx / selected and translated with explanatory notes and an introd. by Saul K. Padover. Englewood Cliffs, N.J. : Prentice-Hall, c1979. xxvii, 576 p. ; 24 cm. Includes indexes. Bibliography: p. 532-534. [HX39.5.A4 1979] 79-10894 ISBN 0-13-531533-6 : 19.95
1. Communists—Correspondence. 2. Communists—Biography. I. Padover, Saul Kussiel, 1905- BIP

MARX, Karl, 1818-1883. 335.4'0924
The unknown Karl Marx; documents concerning Karl Marx. Edited with an introd. by Robert Payne. New York, New York University Press, 1971. viii, 339 p. illus. 24 cm. Contents.Contents.—The unknown Karl Marx, by R. Payne.—Three essays.—Oulanem, a tragedy.—A letter from Heinrich Heine.—A report sent to Lord Palmerston.—A short sketch of an eventful life, by J. Marx.—The story of the life of Lord Palmerston.—Secret diplomatic history of the eighteenth century.—The letters of Eleanor Marx to Frederick Demuth.—Bibliography (p. 339) [HX39.5.A224 1971c] 78-179986 ISBN 0-8147-6554-8
I. Payne, Pierre Stephen Robert, 1911- ed. II. Title.

MARX, Karl, 1818-1883. 335.4'0924
The unknown Karl Marx; documents concerning Karl Marx. Edited with an introd. by Robert Payne. New York, New York University Press, 1971. viii, 339 p. illus. 24 cm. Contents.Contents.—The unknown Karl Marx, by R. Payne.—Three essays.—Oulanem, a tragedy.—A letter from Heinrich Heine.—A report sent to Lord Palmerston.—A short sketch of an eventful life, by J. Marx.—The story of the life of Lord Palmerston.—Secret diplomatic history of the eighteenth century.—The letters of Eleanor Marx to Frederick Demuth.—Bibliography (p. 339) [HX39.5.A224 1971c] 78-179986 ISBN 0-8147-6554-8
I. Payne, Pierre Stephen Robert, 1911- ed. II. Title.

MEHRING, Franz, 1846-1919 923.343
Karl Marx, the story of his life. Tr. by Edward Fitzgerald. New introd. by Max Shachtman. [Ann Arbor] Univ. of Mich. Pr. [c.1962] 575p. 21cm. (Ann Arbor paperbacks for the study of communism and Marxism, AA73) Bibl. 62-53142 2.95 pap.,
1. Marx, Karl, 1818-1883. I. Title.

MEHRING, Franz, 1846- 923.343
1919.
Karl Marx, the story of his life. Translated by Edward Fitzgerald. New introd. by Max Shachtman. [Ann Arbor] University of Michigan Press [1962] 575p. 21cm. (Ann Arbor paperbacks for the study of communism and Marxism, AA73) Includes bibliography. [HX39.5.M4163 1962] 62-53142
1. Marx, Karl, 1818-1883. I. Title.

NIKOLAEVSKII, 335.4'092'4 B
Boris Ivanovich, 1887-1966.
Karl Marx : man and fighter / [by] Boris Nicolaievsky and Otto Maenchen-Helfen ; translated from the German [MS.] by Gwenda David and Eric Mosbacher. Revised and extended ed. / [edited by Louis Evrard]. Harmondsworth [etc.] : Penguin, 1976. xii, 492 p. ; 19 cm. (Pelican biographies) Translation of Karl Marx. Includes index. Bibliography: p. [423]-443. [HX39.5.N483 1976] 76-375385 ISBN 0-14-021594-8 pbk. : 4.95
1. Marx, Karl, 1818-1883. 2. Communists—Biography. I. Manchen-Helfen, Otto, joint author.
Distributed by Penguin, Baltimore, Md. BIP

PADOVER, Saul 335.4'092'4 B
Kussiel, 1905-
The man Marx : an intimate biography / by Saul K. Padover. New York : McGraw-Hill, c1978. p. cm. Includes index. Bibliography: p. [HX39.5.P23] 77-17449 ISBN 0-07-048072-9 : 15.00
1. Marx, Karl, 1818-1883. 2. Communists—Biography. I. Title.

PALEY, Alan L. 335.4'092'4 B
Karl Marx, philosophical father of communism / Alan L. Paley. Charlotteville, N.Y. : SamHar Press, 1975. p. cm. (Outstanding personalities ; 79) Bibliography: p. [HX39.5.P25] 75-33692 lib.bdg. : 2.29 pbk. : 0.98
1. Marx, Karl, 1818-1883. I. Title.

PAYNE, Pierre 335.4'0924 B
Stephen Robert, 1911-
Marx [by] Robert Payne. New York, Simon and Schuster [1968] 582 p. illus., facsims., ports. 25 cm. Bibliography: p. 553-556. [HX39.5.P3] 68-11014
1. Marx, Karl, 1818-1883.

RADDATZ, Fritz Joachim. 330.1
Karl Marx : eine polit. Biographie / Fritz J. Raddatz. 1.-30. Tsd. Hamburg : Hoffmann und Campe, 1975. 539 p., [1] leaf of plates : port. ; 23 cm. Includes index. Bibliography: p. 485-495. [HX39.5.R263] 75-510581 ISBN 3-455-06010-2 : DM38.00
1. Marx, Karl, 1818-1883.

RADDATZ, Fritz 335.4'092'4 B
Joachim.
Karl Marx : a political biography / by Fritz J. Raddatz ; translated from the German by Richard Barry. 1st English language ed. Boston : Little, Brown, c1978. ix, 335 p. ; 24 cm. Includes index. Bibliography: p. [315]-325. [HX39.5.R26313 1978] 78-23341 ISBN 0-316-73210-9 : 16.95
1. Marx, Karl, 1818-1883. 2. Communists—Biography. BIP

RIUS. 335.4'092'4
Marx for beginners / by Rius. 1st Pantheon ed. New York : Pantheon Books, [1979] c1976. 156 p. : ill. ; 21 cm. Translation of Marx para principiantes. Bibliography: p. 155-156. [HX39.5.R54313 1979] 78-20422 ISBN 0-394-73716-4 pbk. : 2.95
1. Marx, Karl, 1818-1883. 2. Marx, Karl, 1818-1883—Political science. 3. Communists—Biography. I. Title. BIP

RUBEL, Maximilien. 335.4'092'4 B
Marx without myth : a chronological study of his life and work / Maximilien Rubel and Margaret Manale. New York : Harper & Row, c1975. xv, 368 p. ; 23 cm. Includes index. "Selected bibliography of Marx's writings": p. [333]-340. [HX39.5.R7964 1975b] 74-33107 ISBN 0-06-136173-9 : 20.00
1. Marx, Karl, 1818-1883. I. Manale, Margaret, joint author. II. Title.

SEIGEL, Jerrold E. 335.4'092'4 B
Marx's fate : the shape of a life / by Jerrold Seigel. Princeton, N.J. : Princeton University Press, c1978. ix, 451 p. ; 24 cm. Includes bibliographical references and index. [HX39.5.S36] 77-85563 ISBN 0-691-05259-X : 16.50
1. Marx, Karl, 1818-1883. 2. Communists—Biography. 3. Socialism. I. Title. BIP

SPRIGGE, Cecil Jackson 923.343
Squire, 1896-
Karl Marx. New York, Collier [1962] 125p. 18cm. (AS185Y) .95 pap.,
1. Marx, Karl, 1818-1883. I. Title. BIP

SPRIGGE, Cecil Jackson v. 12
Squire, 1896-
Karl Marx. New York, Macmillan [1957] 144 p. port. (Great lives) Bibliography: p. 143-144.
1. Marx, Karl, 1818-1883. I. Title.

TONNIES, 335.4'092'4 B
Ferdinand, 1855-1936.
Karl Marx, his life and teachings (Leben und Lehre) / by Ferdinand Tonnies ; translated from the German by Charles P. Loomis and Ingeborg Paulus. [East Lansing] : Michigan State University Press, 1974. xvi, 169 p. ; 24 cm. Translation of Karl Marx, Leben und Lehre. Includes bibliographical references and index. [HX39.5.T5613 1974] 73-91768 ISBN 0-87013-181-8 : 8.50
1. Marx, Karl, 1818-1883. I. Title.

Marx, Karl, 1818-1883—Addresses, essays, lectures.

BOTTOMORE, T. B., 335.4'092'4 B
comp.
Karl Marx, edited by Tom Bottomore. Englewood Cliffs, N.J., Prentice-Hall [1973] iii, 188 p. 21 cm. (A Spectrum book) (Makers of modern social science) [HX39.5.B62] 73-5887 ISBN 0-13-559708-0 2.45 (pbk.)

1. Marx, Karl, 1818-1883—Addresses, essays, lectures. 2. Dialectical materialism—Addresses, essays, lectures. I. Title. II. Series.
Cloth ed. 6.95; ISBN 0-13-559716-1
Contents omitted.

VARDYS, Vytas Stanley, 335.4'0924
1924- comp.
Karl Marx: scientist? revolutionary? humanist? Edited and with an introd. by V. Stanley Vardys. Lexington, Mass., Heath [1971] xviii, 94 p. 24 cm. (Problems in political science) Bibliography: p. 90-94. [HX39.5.V29] 75-92013
1. Marx, Karl, 1818-1883—Addresses, essays, lectures.

Marx, Karl, 1818-1883—Juvenile literature.

APSLER, Alfred. 335.4'0924
Prophet of revolution: Karl Marx. New York, J. Messner [1967] 191 p. 22 cm. Bibliography: p. [186]-187. [HX39.5.A56] 67-2768
1. Marx, Karl, 1818-1883—Juvenile literature. I. Title.

KETTLE, Arnold 923.343
Karl Marx, founder of modern communism. New York, Roy [1964, c.1963] 120p. illus., ports. 19cm. (Roy's pathfinder biogs.) Bibl. 64-10671 3.50 bds.,
1. Marx, Karl, 1818-1883—Juvenile literature. I. Title. II. Title: Founder of modern communism.

RICE, Edward E., 335.4'092'4 B
1918-
Marx, Engels, and the workers of the world / by Edward Rice. New York : Four Winds Press, c1977. vii, 184 p. : ill. ; 24 cm. Includes index. Biographies of the theoreticians whose interpretations of socialism and communism have been adopted by much of the world's population. [HX39.5.R48] 76-56183 ISBN 0-590-07407-5 : 7.95
1. Marx, Karl, 1818-1883—Juvenile literature. 2. Engels, Friedrich, 1820-1895—Juvenile literature. 3. Communists—Biography—Juvenile literature. 4. Communism—Juvenile literature. I. Title.
BIP

Mary Adelaide, Mother, 1874-

MARY Florence, Sister, O. 922.273
S. F.
Our mother; a portrait of Venerable Mother Mary Adelaide, foundress of the Sisters of St. Francis of the Congregation of Our Lady of Lourdes, whose motherhouse is in Sylvania, Ohio. with a foreword by Karl J. Alter. [Sylvania'] 1959. 55p. illus. 23cm. [BX4320.3.Z8M25] 60-44
1. Mary Adelaide, Mother, 1874- 2. Sisters of the Third Order Regular of St. Francis of the Congregation of Our Lady of Lourdes, Sylvania, Ohio. I. Title.

Mary Cleophas, Mother,

MARY Christina, Mother. 922.273
Mother Mary Cleophas of the Society of the Holy Child Jesus, president of Rosemont College, 1939-1916. With a foreword by Fulton J. Sheen. Philadelphia, Reilly [1950] xiii, 156 p. ports 20 cm. [BX4705.M32546M3] 50-12389
1. Mary Cleophas, Mother, I. Title.

Mary, Consort of George V, King of Great Britain, 1867-1953.

BLOOM, Ursula. 941.083'092'4 B
The great Queen Consort / Ursula Bloom. London : Hale, 1976. 168 p., [6] leaves of plates : ports. ; 23 cm. [DA574.A2B55 1976] 77-367798 ISBN 0-7091-5659-6 : £4.25
1. Mary, consort of George V, King of Great Britain, 1867-1953. 2. Great Britain—Queens—Biography. I. Title.

CRAWFORD, Marion, 1909- 923.142
Mother and queen; the story of Queen Mary. [1st American ed.] New York, Prentice-Hall [1951] 232 p. illus. 21 cm. [DA574.A2C7] 51-13997
1. Mary, Consort of George V, King of Great Britain, 1867-1953. I. Title.

POPE-HENNESSY, James. 923.142
Queen Mary, 1867-1953. [1st American ed.] New York, Knopf, 1960. 654p. illus. 25cm. [DA574.A2P6 1960] 60-5256
1. Mary, consort of George v, King of Great Britain, 1867-1953. I. Title.

Mary, consort of Louis XII, King of France, 1496-1533.

HARVEY, Nancy 941.1'04'0924 B
Lenz.
The rose and the thorn : the lives of Mary and Margaret Tudor / by Nancy Lenz Harvey. New York : Macmillan, 1975. p. cm. Includes index. Bibliography: p. [DA784.3.M3H37] 75-22442 ISBN 0-02-548550-4 : 7.95
1. Margaret Tudor, consort of James IV, King of Scotland, 1489-1541. 2. Mary, consort of Louis XII, King of France, 1496-1533. 3. Henry VIII, King of England, 1491-1547. I. Mary, consort of Louis XII, King of France, 1496-1533. II. Margaret Tudor, consort of James IV, King of Scotland, 1489-1541. III. Title.

RICHARDSON, 942.05'2'0924 B
Walter Cecil, 1902-
Mary Tudor, the white queen [by] Walter C. Richardson. Seattle, University of Washington Press [1970] xvi, 328 p. illus., facsims., geneal. tables, ports. 23 cm. Bibliography: p. 287-307. [DC108.R5 1970b] 68-11050 10.00
1. Mary, consort of Louis XII, King of France, 1496-1533.
BIP

Mary Euthymia, Sister, 1914-1955.

MEYER, Wendelin 922.243
To the least; a biography of Sister Mary Euthymia. Translated by Herman J. Fister. Chicago, Franciscan Herald Press [1960] 85p. 18cm. 60 9292 .95 pap.,
1. Mary Euthymia, Sister, 1914-1955. I. Title.

Mary Faustina, Sister, 1905-1938.

ZAREMBA, Theodore 922.2438
Anthony.
Mercy is forever: the story of the devotion to the mercy of God. Pulaski, Wis., Franciscan Publishers, 1957. 159p. 22cm. [BX4705.M417Z3] 57-13889
1. Mary Faustina, Sister, 1905-1938. 2. God—Mercy. I. Title.

Mary I, Queen of England, 1516-1558.

ERICKSON, 942.05'4'0924 B
Carolly, 1943-
Bloody Mary / Carolly Erickson. 1st ed. Garden City, N.Y. : Doubleday, 1978. xii, 533 p., [9] leaves of plates : ill. ; 24 cm. Includes index. Bibliography: p. [511]-517. [DA347.E74] 77-75868 ISBN 0-385-11663-2 : 14.95
1. Mary I, Queen of England, 1516 1558. 2. Great Britain—History—Mary I, 1553-1558. 3. Great Britain—Kings and rulers—Biography. I. Title.

LUKE, Mary M. 942.05'2
A crown for Elizabeth [by] Mary M. Luke. New York, Coward-McCann [1970] 573 p. illus., ports. 24 cm. Sequel to Catherine, the queen. Sequel: Gloriana; the years of Elizabeth I. Bibliography: p. [541]-542. [DA317.1.L8] 70-113530 10.00
1. Mary I, Queen of England, 1516-1558. 2. Elizabeth, Queen of England, 1533-1603. 3. Edward VI, King of England, 1537-1553. I. Title.

MAYNARD, Thedore, 1890- 923.142
Bloody Mary. Milwaukee, Bruce Pub. Co. [1955] 297p. 23cm. [DA347.M29] 55-7865
1. Mary Queen of England, 1516-1558. I. Title.

MORRISON, Nancy 942.05'092'2 B
Brysson.
King's quiver: the last three Tudors [by] N. Brysson Morrison. New York, St. Martin's Press [1973, c1972] vii, 212 p. illus. 23 cm. Bibliography: p. 203-204. [DA317.1.M67 1973] 73-80311 6.95
1. Mary I, Queen of England, 1516-1558. 2. Elizabeth, Queen of England, 1533-1603. 3. Edward VI, King of England, 1537-1553. I. Title.

PRESCOTT, Hilda Frances 923.142
Margaret, 1896-
Mary Tudor. [Rev.] New York, Macmillan, 1962[c.1953] xiii, 439p. illus. (Macmillan paperbacks, 91) Pub. in England, 1940, under title: Spanish Tudor. Bibl. 1.95 pap.,
1. Mary I, Queen of England, 1516-1558. I. Title.

PRESCOTT, Hilda Frances 923.142
Margaret, 1896-
Mary Tudor. [Rev.] New York, Macmillan, 1953. xiii, 439p. ports. 22cm. Published in England, 1940, under title: Spanish Tudor. Bibliography: p. 396-399. [DA347.P7 1953a] 53-12739
1. Mary I, Queen of England, 1516-1558. I. Title.

PRESCOTT, Hilda 942.05'4'0924 B
Frances Margaret, 1896-
A Spanish Tudor; the life of "Bloody Mary." by H. F. M. Prescott. New York, AMS Press [1970] xv, 562 p. illus., port. 23 cm. Reprint of the New York, 1940 ed. "List of authorities": p. 505-541. [DA347.P7 1970] 77-112942 ISBN 4-04-051332-
1. Mary I Queen of England, 1516-1558. I. Title.
BIP

WALDMAN, Milton, 942.05'4'0924 B
1895-
The Lady Mary; a biography of Mary Tudor, 1516-1558. New York, Scribner [1972] 224 p. illus. 22 cm. [DA347.W34 1972b] 72-3802 ISBN 0-684-13095-5 7.95
1. Mary I, Queen of England, 1516-1558. I. Title.

Mary I, Queen of England, 1516-1558—Juvenile literature.

ROLL, Winifred, 942.5'4'0924 B
Lady.
Mary I : the history of an unhappy Tudor Queen / by Winifred Roll. Englewood Cliffs, N.J. : Prentice-Hall, c1979. p. cm. Includes index. Bibliography: p. A biography of the daughter of Henry VIII and Catherine of Aragon who, during a brief reign, tried to bring Protestant England back to the Roman Catholic Church. [DA347.R62] 78-16779 ISBN 0-13-559096-5 : 8.95
1. Mary I, Queen of England, 1516-1558—Juvenile literature. 2. Great Britain—History—Mary I, 1553-1558—Juvenile literature. 3. Great Britain—Kings and rulers—Biography—Juvenile literature. I. Title.
BIP

Mary II, Queen of Great Britain, 1662-1694.

CHAPMAN, Hester 942.06'8'0924 B
W., 1899-
Mary II, Queen of England / by Hester W. Chapman. Westport, Conn. : Greenwood Press, 1976. p. cm. Reprint of the 1953 ed. published by Cape, London. Includes index. Bibliography: p. [DA462.A3C47 1976] 75-17197 ISBN 0-8371-8302-2 lib.bdg. : 18.00
1. Mary II, Queen of Great Britain, 1662-1694. 2. Great Britain—Queens—Biography. 3. Great Britain—History—William and Mary, 1689-1702.

HAMILTON, 942.06'8'0924 B
Elizabeth, Lady, 1928-
William's Mary; a biography of Mary II. New York, Taplinger Pub. Co. [1972] xii, 369 p. illus. 25 cm. Bibliography: p. 338-343. [DA462.A3H35 1972] 78-164583 ISBN 0-8008-8248-2 12.95
1. Mary II, Queen of Great Britain, 1662-1694. I. Title.

Mary Jeremy,

MARY Jeremy, Sister, 1907- 922.273

All the days of my life. [1st ed.] Indianapolis, Bobbs-Merrill [1959] 191 p. 22 cm. [BX4705.M4217A3] 59-14295
I. Title.

Mary Magdalene, Saint.

BRUCKBERGER, Raymond 225.92
Leopold, 1907-
Mary Magdalene. Translated by H. L. Binsse. New York, Pantheon [1953] 192p. illus. 22cm. [BS2485.B753] 53-6127
1. Mary Magdalene, Saint. I. Title.

BRUCKBERGER, Raymond 225.92
Leopold, 1907
Mary Magdalene; translated by H. L. Binsse. Annotated ed. New York, Pantheon [1953] 263p. illus. 22cm. [BS2485.B753 1953a] 53-7153
1. Mary Magdalene, Saint. I. Title.

EMMERICH, Anna Katharina, 225.92
1774-1824
And she was called Magdalen; the life of Saint Mary Magdalen, as revealed in the visions of the most outstanding stigmatist-mystic of the last century, Sister Anna Catharina Emmerick. Ed. by Robert Emmet Curtiss. New York, Vantage [c.1962] 47p. illus. 21cm. 62-5295 2.00
1. Mary Magdalene, Saint. I. Title.

Mary Mercy, Sister, 1903-

MARIA DEL REY, Sister. 951.9
Her name is Mercy. New York, Scribner [1957] 184p. illus. 25cm. [R154M2987M] 951.9 57-6074 57-6074
1. Mary Mercy, Sister, 1903- 2. Missions, Medical—Korea. I. Title.

Mary Odilia, Mother, 1823-1880.

MARY Gabriel, Sister, S. 922.273
S. M.
But what is greatness; an account of the life of Mother Mary Odilia, foundress of the Sisters of St. Mary, by Sister Mary Gabriel and Jane L. Berdes. St. Louis, Sisters of St. Mary, 1959. 131p. illus. 24cm. [BX4491.3.Z8M3] 59-15707
1. Mary Odilia, Mother, 1823-1880. 2. Sisters of St. Mary of the Third Order of St. Francis, St. Louis. I. Berdes, Jane L., joint author. II. Title.

Mary of Bethany.

MARSHALL, Effie Lawrence, 225.92
1873-
Mary of Bethany. Manchester, Me., Falmouth Pub. House [1954] 197p. 21cm. [BS2490.M2M3] 54-7446
1. Mary of Bethany. I. Title.

Mary of Modena, consort of James II, King of Great Britain, 1658-1718.

HOPKIRK, Mary 923.142
Queen over the water, Mary Beatrice of Modena, Queen of James II. London, Murray [Mystic, Conn., Verry, 1965] 320p. illus. 22cm. Bibl. [DA450.H6] 5.00
1. Mary of Modena, consort of James II, King of Great Britain, 1658-1718. I. Title.

Mary, of Modena, consort of James II, King of Great Britain, 1658-1718.

LENANTON, Carola Mary 923.142
Anima (Aman) 1897-
Mary of Modena [London] Hodder & staughton [dist.Mystic, Conn.,Verry, 1964,c.1962] 270p. illus. 23cm. Bibl. 63-5539 7.50
1. Mary, of Modena, consort of James II, King of Great Britain, 1658-1718. I. Title.

Mary Stuart, Queen of the Scots, 1542-1587.

BREGY, Katherine Marie Cornelia, 1888- 923.141
Queen of paradox, a Stuart tragedy. Milwaukee, Bruce [1950] xiv, 221 p. port. 22 cm. Bibliography: p. 217-218. [DA787.A1B7] 50-9940
1. Mary Stuart, Queen of the Scots, 1542-1587. I. Title.

BUCHANAN, George, 1506-1582. 941.105
The tyrannous reign of Mary Stewart : George Buchanan's account / translated and edited by W. A. Gatherer. Westport, Conn. : Greenwood Press, [1978] c1958. x, 228 p., [3] leaves of plates : ill. ; 23 cm. Reprint of the ed. published by the University Press, Edinburgh, which was issued as no. 10 of Edinburgh University publications, history, philosophy, and economics. Includes index. Bibliography: p. 215-218. [DA787.A1B8 1978] 78-3556 ISBN 0-313-20343-1 lib.bdg. : 18.25
1. Mary Stuart, Queen of the Scots, 1542-1587. 2. Scotland—History—Mary Stuart, 1542-1567. 3. Scotland—Kings and rulers—Biography. I. Gatherer, W. A. II. Title. III. Series: Edinburgh. University. Edinburgh University publication : History, philosophy, and economics ; 10.

CARRUTH, James Aloysius. 941.05'092'4 B
Mary Queen of Scots, text by J. A. Carruth. Norwich, Jarrold & Sons [1973] [34] p. illus. (chiefly col.), facsims., geneal. table, col. ports. 25 cm. [DA787.A2C37] 74-164037 ISBN 0-85306-395-8 £0.30
1. Mary Stuart, Queen of the Scots, 1542-1587. I. Title.

DAVISON, Meredith Henry Armstrong. 941.050924
The casket letters; a solution to the mystery of Mary, Queen of Scots, and the murder of Lord Darnley, by M. H. Armstrong Davison. [Washington] University Press of Washington, D. C. [1965] xviii, 352 p. illus., facsims., plans. 24 cm. Bibliography: p. 326-340. [DA787.A36D39] 65-176370
1. Mary Stuart, Queen of the Scots, 1542-1587. 2. Darnley, Henry Stewart, lord, 1545-1567. I. Title.

DONALDSON, Gordon. 941.05'092'4 B
Mary, Queen of Scots / [by] Gordon Donaldson ; with a foreword by A. L. Rowse. London : English Universities Press, 1974. 200 p., [8] p. of plates : ill., ports. ; 23 cm. (Men and their times) Includes index. Bibliography: p. [193]-194. [DA787.A1D59] 74-186753 ISBN 0-340-12383-4 : 7.50
1. Mary Stuart, Queen of the Scots, 1542-1587.
Distributed by Lawrence Verry.

EDWARDS, Francis 942.054
The dangerous queen. London, G. Chapman. [New York, Hillary House, 1966, c.1964] 432p. illus., port. 23cm. Bibl. [DA787.A1E3] 66-33122 8.00 bds.,
1. Mary Stuart, Queen of the Scots, 1542-1587. I. Title.

FRASER, Antonia (Pakenham) Lady, 1932- 941'.05 B
Mary, Queen of Scots, by Antonia Fraser. New York, Delacorte Press [1969] xv, 613 p. illus., geneal. tables, facsim., ports. 25 cm. Bibliography: p. [585]-594. [DA787.A1F74 1969b] 74-89707 10.00
1. Mary Stuart, Queen of the Scots, 1542-1587. I. Title.

FRASER, Antonia Pakenham, Lady, 1932- 941.105'092'4 B
Mary Queen of Scots / Antonia Fraser. Illustrated abridged ed. New York : Delacorte Press, c1978. 208 p. : ill. ; 28 cm. Includes index. Bibliography: p. 203-204. [DA787.A1F742 1978] 78-703 ISBN 0-440-05261-0 : 17.95
1. Mary Stuart, Queen of the Scots, 1542-1587. 2. Scotland—History—Mary Stuart, 1542-1567. 3. Scotland—History—James VI, 1567-1625. 4. Great Britain—History—Elizabeth, 1558-1603. 5. Scotland—Kings and rulers—Biography. I. Title.

HAHN, Emily, 1905- 923.142
Mary, Queen of Scots; illustrated by Walter Buehr. New York, Random House [1953] 184 p. illus. 22 cm. (World landmark books, W-6) [DA787.A1H2] 53-6265
1. Mary Stuart, Queen of the Scots, 1542-1587.

HENDERSON, Thomas Finlayson, 1844-1923. 941'.05'0924 B
Mary, Queen of Scots; her environment and tragedy, a biography. New York, Haskell House, 1969. 2 v. (x, 690 p.) illus., ports. 24 cm. Reprint of the 1905 ed. Bibliographical footnotes. [DA787.A1H4 1969] 68-25241
1. Mary Stuart, Queen of the Scots, 1542-1587.

HIBBERT, Eleanor, 1906- 941.105'092'4 B
Mary Queen of Scots : the fair devil of Scotland / Jean Plaidy [i.e. E. Hibbert]. New York : Putnam, [1975] p. cm. [DA787.A1H5] 75-7904 ISBN 0-399-11581-1 : 15.95
1. Mary Stuart, Queen of the Scots, 1542-1587. I. Title.

KING, Marian. 923.141
Young Mary Stuart, Queen of Scots. [1st ed.] Philadelphia, Lippincott [1954] 158 p. 21 cm. Includes bibliography. [DA787.A1K5] 54-7298
1. Mary Stuart, Queen of the Scots, 1542-1587.

LANG, Andrew, 1844-1912. 941'.05'0924
The mystery of Mary Stuart. New York, AMS Press [1970] xxii, 452 p. illus., facsims., ports. 23 cm. Reprint of the 1901 ed. Includes bibliographical references. [DA787.A1L2 1970] 78-111771 ISBN 4-04-038581-
1. Mary Stuart, Queen of the Scots, 1542-1587. I. Title. BIP

LINKLATER, Eric, 1899- 923.141
Mary, Queen of Scots. London, D. Dobson [ChesterSprings, Pa., Dufour, 1964] 160p. illus. 20cm. (20th century classics) [DA787.A1L65] 53-24658 2.50 bds.,
1. Mary Stuart, Queen of the Scots, 1542-1587. I. Title.

MACNALTY, Arthur Salisbury, Sir 1880- 923.141
Mary, Queen of Scots, the daughter of debate. New York, Ungar [1961, c.1960] 247p. illus. Bibl. 61-2503 4.50
1. Mary Stuart, Queen of the Scots., 1542-1587. I. Title.

MARY, v. 12
Queen of Scots, the daughter of debate. New York, Ungar [1961, c1960] 247p. port., geneal. table. 22cm. (Medical viewpoint series) Bibliography, p. 241-243.
1. Mary Stuart, Queen of the Scots, 1542-1587. I. MacNalty, Arthur Sallsbury, Sir 1880-

MARY Stuart, Queen of the Scots, 1542-1587, supposed author. 923.141
The casket letters of Mary Stuart, a study in fraud and forgery. A vindication of the Queen by H. F. Diggle. [Harrogate? 1960] 139p. 22cm. Letters allegedly written by Mary Stuart to Bothwell. [DA787.A36M3] 61-1507
I. Bothwell, James Hepburn, 4th earl of, 1536?-1578. II. Diggle, Henry Frederick. III. Title.

MORRISON, Nancy Agnes Brysson 923.171
Mary, Queen of Scots. New York, Vanguard Press [c.1960] 286p. illus. 60-9723 4.50
1. Mary Stuart, Queen of the Scots, 1542-1587. I. Title.

MORRISON, Nancy Brysson. 923.141
Mary, Queen of Scots. New York, Vanguard Press [1960] 286p. illus. 23cm. [DA787.A1M72] 60-9723
1. Mary Stuart, Queen of the Scots, 1542-1587. I. Title.

STRONG, Roy C. 941.05'092'4 B
Mary Queen of Scots. Evocation: Roy Strong. Spectacle: Julia Travelyan Oman. New York, Stein and Day [1972] 80 p. illus. 22 cm. [DA787.A3S86 1972b] 72-90026 ISBN 0-8128-1533-5 4.95
1. Mary Stuart, Queen of the Scots, 1542-1587. I. Oman, Julia Trevelyan, illus. II. Title.

THOMSON, George Malcolm, 1899- 941'.05'0924
The crime of Mary Stuart, [1st ed.] New York, Dutton, 1967. 175 p. geneal, table, col, map (on lining papers), ports. 22 cm. Bibliography: p. 167-169. [DA787.A1T5] 67-26602
1. Mary Stuart, Queen of the Scots, 1542-1587. 2. Darnley, Henry Stewart, Lord, 1545-1567. 3. Bothwell, James Hepburn, 4th Earl of, 1536?-1578. I. Title.

THOMSON, George Malcolm, 1899- 941'.05'0924
The crime of Mary Stuart. [1st ed.] New York, Dutton, 1967. 175 p. geneal. table, col. map (on lining papers), ports. 22 cm. Bibliography: p. 167-169. [DA787.A1T5 1967b] 67-26602
1. Mary Stuart, Queen of the Scots, 1542-1587. 2. Darnley, Henry Stewart, Lord, 1545-1567. 3. Bothwell, James Hepburn, 4th Earl of, 1536?-1578. I. Title.

Mary Stuart, Queen of the Scots, 1542-1587—Juvenile literature.

HIBBERT, Eleanor, 1906- j92
The young Mary, Queen of Scots [by] Jean Plaidy [pseud.] Illustrated by William Randell. New York, Roy Publishers [1963] 144 p. illus. 21 cm. Includes bibliography. [DA787.A5H5] 62-18440
1. Mary Stuart, Queen of the Scots, 1542-1587 — Juvenile literature. I. Title.

VANCE, Marguerite 920
Scotland's Queen; the story of Mary Stuart. Illus. by J. Luis Pellicer. New York, Dutton [c.1962] 158p. 21cm. 62-14705 3.50
1. Mary Stuart, Queen of the Scots, 1542-1587—Juvenile literature. I. Title.

Mary Veronica, Mother, 1838-1904.

MARY Teresa, Sister 922.273
The fruit of His compassion; the life of Mother Mary Veronica, foundress of the Sisters of the Divine Compassion. Foreword by Francis Cardinal Spellman. New York, Pageant [c.1962] 563p. illus. 24cm. Bibl. 62-16331 5.95
1. Mary Veronica, Mother, 1838-1904. I. Title.

MARY Teresa, Sister. 922.273
The fruit of His compassion; the life of Mother Mary Veronica, foundress of the Sisters of the Divine Compassion. Foreword by Francis Cardinal Spellman. [1st ed.] New York, Pageant Press [1962] 563p. illus. 24cm. Includes bibliography. [BX4493.5.Z8M3] 62-16331
1. Mary Veronica, Mother, 1838-1904. I. Title.

Mary, Virgin.

ALBERIONE. GIACOMO GIUSEPPE, 1884- 232.931
Mary, Queen of the Apostles, by James Alberione. Translated by a Daughter of St. Paul. [Derby? N. Y.] Apostolate of the Press [c1956] 346p. illus. 22cm. [BT638.A413] 59-28488
1. Mary, Virgin. I. Title.

BAIRD, Mary Julian. 922.2
The court of the Queen. St. Meinrad, Ind., Grail Publications [1956] 73p. 22cm. [BX4652.B27] 55-11578
1. Catholic Church—Biog. 2. Mary, Virgin—Apparitions and miracies (Modern) I. Title.

BEEBE, Catherine, 1898- 232.931
The story of Mary, the mother of Jesus. Illustrated by Robb Beebe. Milwaukee, Bruce [1950] ix, 147 p. illus. 23 cm. [BT607.B36] 50-13526
1. Mary, Virgin. I. Title.

GIORDANI, Igino, 1894- v. 12
Mary of Nazareth Translated by Clelia Muranzana and Mary Paula Williamson. Boston, St. Paul Editions [1965] xix, 181 p. plates. 24 cm.
1. Mary, Virgin. I. Title. BIP

GIORDANI, Igino, 1894- 232.91
Mary of Nazareth. Tr. by Clelia Maranzana and Mary PaulaWilliamson. [Boston] St. Paul Eds. [dist. Daughters of St. Paul, c.1965] xix, 181p. plates 24cm. [BT601.G47] 65-24079 5.00; 4.00 pap.,
1. Mary, Virgin. I. Title.

GUITTON, Jean. 232.931
The Virgin Mary; translated by A. Gordon Smith. New York, Kenedy [1952] 190 p. 21 cm. London ed. (Burns, Oates) has title: The Blessed Virgin. [BT601.G813 1952a] 52-9718
1. Mary, Virgin. I. Title.

HOPHAN, Otto. 232.931
Mary, Our Most Blessed Lady. Translated by Berchmans Bittle. Milwaukee, Bruce Pub. Co. [1959] 374p. 24cm. Includes bibliography. [BT602.H613] 59-10217
1. Mary, Virgin. I. Title.

Mary, Virgin—Biog.

ALBERIONE, Giacomo Giuseppe, 1884- 232.931
Mary, hope of the world, by James Alberione. Translation by Hilda Calabro. [Boston?] St. Paul Editions [c1958] 218p. illus. 22cm. [BT605.2.A113] 59-28503
1. Mary, Virgin—Biog. I. Title.

EMMERICH ANNA KATHARINA, 1774-1824. v. 12
The life of the Blessed Virgin Mary, from the visions of Anne Catherine Emmerich. Translated by Sir Michael Palairet, with supplementary notes by Sebastian Bullough. Springfield, Ill., Templegate [1954] xiv, 383p. 21cm. 'I have omitted some of Clemens Brentano's notes altogether and have translated only extracts of some of the others.'-- Translator s note. Translation of Leben der Heil. Jungfrau Maria, first published in 1852. A55
1. Mary, Virgin—Biog. I. Title.

ERNEST, Brother, 1897- 232.931
Your mother and mine; a story of the Blessed Virgin. Illus. by Albert Kern. Notre Dame, Ind., Dujarie Press [1954] 85p. illus. 24cm. [BT605.E7] 54-3701
1. Mary, Virgin—Biog. I. Title.

GAROFALO, Salvatore 232.931
Mary in the Bible. Tr. [from Italian] by Thomas J. Tobin. Milwaukee, Bruce [c.1961] 106p. 61-17436 3.00
1. Mary, Virgin—Biog. I. Title.

RESCH, Peter Anthony, 1895- 232.931
A life of Mary, co-redemptrix. Milwaukee, Bruce Pub. Co. [1954] 96p. 20cm. [BT605.R4] 54-2419
1. Mary, Virgin—Biog. I. Title.

SPEYR, Adrienne von. 232.931
The Handmaid of the Lord. Translated by Alexander Dry. New York, D. McKay Co. [1955] 186p. 21cm. [BT605.S615] 55-14892
1. Mary, Virgin—Biog. I. Title.

Mary, Virgin—Juvenile literature.

BRUCE, Janet 232.93
The life of the Blessed Virgin Mary. Pictures by Emile Probst. New York, Herder & Herder [1965] iv. (unpaged) col. illus. 19cm. (Men of God, 2) [BT607.B7] 65-13485 1.50 bds.,
1. Mary, Virgin—Juvenile literature. I. Probst, Emile, illus. II. Title. III. Series.

Mary Zita. Mother. 1844-1917.

SISTERS of Reparation of the Congregation of Mary. 922.273
'Blessed are the merciful'; the life of Mother Mary Zita, foundress. New York [1953] 112p. illus. 22cm. [BX4705.M4243S5] 54-17456
1. Mary Zita. Mother. 1844-1917. I. Title.

Maryland—Biography.

AGNUS, Felix, 1839-1925, ed. 929.5
The book of Maryland: men and

institutions, a work for press reference. Editors: Felix Agnus, editor-in-chief [and others] Baltimore, Maryland Biographical Association, 1920. 350 p. illus., ports. 31 cm. Includes advertisements. [F180.A3] 65-78463
1. Maryland—Biog. 2. Maryland—History, Local. I. Title.

BELL, Eric Temple 1883- 925.1
Men of mathematics, by E. T. Bell. New York S. & S. [1961, c.1937] xxi, 592p. illus. (Essandess paperback) 2.25 pap., sMathematicizns.
1. Mathematics—Hist. I. Title.

THE Biographical cyclopedia of representative men of Maryland and District of Columbia. 929.5 Baltimore, National Biographical Pub. Co., 1879 [c1878] viii, [5]-716. 97 ports. 28 cm. Binder's title: Biographical cyclopedia of Maryland and District of Columbia. [F180.B61] 3-28904
1. Maryland—Biog. 2. District of Columbia—Biog.

NOTABLE Maryland women 920.72'09752 / edited by Winifred G. Helmes. Cambridge, Md. : Tidewater Publishers, 1977. xiii, 418 p. ; 24 cm. Includes bibliographies. [CT239.N67] 77-966 ISBN 0-87033-236-8 : 12.50 pbk. : 8.00
1. Maryland—Biography. 2. Women—Maryland—Biography. I. Helmes, Winifred Gertrude, 1913-

NOTABLE Maryland women 920.72'09752 / edited by Winifred G. Helmes. Cambridge, Md. : Tidewater Publishers, 1977. xiii, 418 p. ; 24 cm. Includes bibliographies. [CT239.N67] 77-966 ISBN 0-87033-236-8 : 12.50 pbk. : 8.00
1. Maryland—Biography. 2. Women—Maryland—Biography. I. Helmes, Winifred Gertrude, 1913- BIP

ROLLO, Vera A Foster. 920.0752
Maryland personality parade, by Vera F. Rollo. Lanham, Maryland Historical Press [1967-] v. illus., map. ports. 23 cm. Bibliogrpahy: p. 96. [F180.R57] 67-25959
1. Maryland—Biog. I. Title.

Maryland. General Assembly—Biography.

A Biographical dictionary of the Maryland Legislature, 1635-1789 328.752'092'2 B / Edward C. Papenfuse ... [et al.]. Baltimore : Johns Hopkins University Press, c1979- v. : maps ; 27 cm. (Studies in Maryland history and culture) [JK3866.B56] 78-18042 ISBN 0-8018-1995-4 : 19.50
1. Maryland. General Assembly—Biography. 2. Maryland. General Assembly—History. 3. Legislators—Maryland—Biography. I. Papenfuse, Edward C. II. Title. III. Series.

Masamune, Hakucho, 1879-1962.

ROLF, Robert. 895.6'8'409
Masamune Hakucho / by Robert Rolf. Boston : Twayne Publishers, 1979. 171 p., [1] leaf of plates : port. ; 21 cm. (Twayne's world authors series ; TWAS 533 : Japan) Includes index. "Titles of Hakucho's works cited": p. 156-157. [PL811.A8Z85] 78-27532 ISBN 0-8057-6375-9 : 13.95
1. Masamune, Hakucho, 1879-1962. 2. Authors, Japanese—20th century—Biography. BIP

Masaryk, Jan Garrigue, 1886-1948.

LOCKHART, Robert 923.2437 Hamilton Bruce, Sir 1887-
Jan Masaryk, a personal memoir [London] Putnam [dist. Chester Springs, Pa., Dufour, 1964] 80p. illus. 20cm. 57-3132 2.95
1. Masaryk, Jan Garrigue, 1886-1948. I. Title.

Masaryk, Tomas Garrigue, Pres. Czechoslovak Republic, 1850-1937.

MACHOTKA, Otakar, 1899- 923.1437
T. G. Masaryk. Washington, Published on the occasion of T. G. Masaryk's centenary by Council of Free Czechoslovakia, 1950. 31 p. 22 cm. "Chief works of T. G. Masaryk": p. 30. Bibliography: p. 31. [DB217.M3M25] 50-14276
1. Masaryk, Tomas Garrigue, Pres. Czechoslovak Republic, I. Title.

MASARYK, Tomas 943.7'03'0924 B Garrigue, Pres. Czechoslovak Republic, 1850-1937.
President Masaryk tells his story [by] Karel Capek. New York, Arno Press, 1971. 302 p. 23 cm. (The Eastern Europe collection) Reprint of the 1935 ed. Translation of Hovory s T. G. Masarykem. [DB217.M3A55 1971] 71-135797
I. Capek, Karel, 1890-1938. II. Title.

SELVER, Paul, 943.7'03'0924 B 1888-
Masaryk : a biography / by Paul Selver ; introd. by Jan Masaryk. Westport, Conn. : Greenwood Press, 1975. 326 p., [15] leaves of plates : ill. ; 22 cm. Reprint of the 1940 ed. published by M. Joseph, London. Includes index. [DB217.M3S4 1975] 74-33506 ISBN 0-8371-7972-6 lib.bdg. : 18.25
1. Masaryk, Tomas Garrigue, Pres. Czechoslovak Republic, 1850-1937.

SELVER, Paul, 943.7'03'0924 B 1888-
Masaryk : a biography / by Paul Selver ; introd. by Jan Masaryk. Westport, Conn. : Greenwood Press, 1975. 326 p., [15] leaves of plates : ill. ; 22 cm. Reprint of the 1940 ed. published by M. Joseph, London. Includes index. [DB217.M3S4 1975] 74-33506 ISBN 0-8371-7972-6 lib.bdg. : 18.25
1. Masaryk, Tomas Garrigue, Pres. Czechoslovak Republic, 1850-1937.

STREET, Cecil John 973.7'02'0924 Charles, 1884-
President Masaryk, by Cecil J. C. Street. Freeport, N.Y., Books for Libraries Press [1970] 256 p. ports. 23 cm. Reprint of the 1930 ed. [DB217.M3S7 1970] 74-119945
1. Masaryk, Tomas Garrigue, Pres. Czechoslovak Republic, 1850-1937. BIP

STREET, Cecil John 973.7'02'0924 Charles, 1884-
President Masaryk, by Cecil J. C. Street. Freeport, N.Y., Books for Libraries Press [1970] 256 p. ports. 23 cm. Reprint of the 1930 ed. [DB217.M3S7 1970] 74-119945
1. Masaryk, Tomas Garrigue, Pres. Czechoslovak Republic, 1850-1937. BIP

Mascarenhas, Telo de.

MASCARENHAS, Telo de. 954'.799 B
When the mango-trees blossomed : quasi-memoirs / Telo de Mascarenhas. Bombay : Orient Longman, 1976. xii, 291 p., [4] leaves of plates : ill. ; 23 cm. Includes index. [DS498.8.M34A38] 76-901528 10.00
1. Mascarenhas, Telo de. 2. Goa—Politics and government. 3. Goa—Biography. I. Title.
Distributed by Longman, New York

Masefield, John, 1878-1967.

FISHER, Margery (Turner) 828.912 1913-
John Masefiled. New York, Walck [1963] 67p. port. 19cm. Bibl. 63-14498 2.50
1. Masefield, John, 1878- I. Title.

LAMONT, Corliss, 822'.9'1209 1902-
Remembering John Masefield. Introd. by Judith Masefield. Rutherford, Fairleigh Dickinson University Press [1971] 119 p. illus., facsims., ports. 22 cm. Includes bibliographical references. [PR6025.A77Z75] 73-139992 ISBN 0-8386-7836-X 6.00
1. Masefield, John, 1878-1967. 2. Masefield, 1878-1967—Correspondence. 3. Lamont, Corliss, 1902- I. Title. BIP

MASEFIELD. JOHN. 1878 828.91203
Grace before ploughing; fragments of autobiography. New York. Macmillan [1966] vi, 90p. 21cm. [PR6025.A77Z52 1966] 66-21163 3.95
I. Title.

MASEFIELD, John, 1878- 828.91203 1967.
Grace before ploughing; fragments of autobiography. New York, Macmillan [1966] vi, 90 p. 21 cm. [PR6025.A77Z52 1966] 66-21163
I. Title.

MASEFIELD, John 1878-1967. 928.2
So long to learn. New York, Macmillan, 1952. 181 p. 22 cm. Autobiographical. [PR6025.A77Z54] 52-7822
I. Title.

Masefield, John, 1878-1967—Biography.

BABINGTON-SMITH, 821'.9'12 B Constance.
John Masefield : a biography / Constance Babington-Smith. New York : Macmillan, c1978. p. cm. [PR6025.A77Z553] 78-8648 ISBN 0-02-504600-4 : 14.95
1. Masefield, John, 1878-1967—Biography. 2. Poets, English—20th century—Biography.

Masefield, John, 1878-1967—Correspondence.

LAMONT, Corliss, 822'.9'1209 1902-
Remembering John Masefield. Introd. by Judith Masefield. Rutherford, Fairleigh Dickinson University Press [1971] 119 p. illus., facsims., ports. 22 cm. Includes bibliographical references. [PR6025.A77Z75] 73-139992 ISBN 0-8386-7836-X 6.00
1. Masefield, John, 1878-1967. 2. Masefield, 1878-1967—Correspondence. 3. Lamont, Corliss, 1902- I. Title. BIP

MASEFIELD, John, 828'.9'1209 B 1878-1967.
Letters of John Masefield to Florence Lamont / edited by Corliss Lamont and Lansing Lamont. New York : Columbia University Press, 1979. p. cm. [PR6025.A77Z546 1979] 78-27134 ISBN 0-231-04706-1 : 20.00
1. Masefield, John, 1878-1967—Correspondence. 2. Lamont, Florence Haskell Corliss, 1873-1952. 3. Poets, English—20th century—Correspondence. I. Lamont, Florence Haskell Corliss, 1873-1952. II. Lamont, Corliss, 1902- III. Lamont, Lansing. IV. Title. BIP

Masepa, Ivan Stepanovich, hetman of the Cossacks, d. 1709.

MANNING, Calrence 923.247 Augustus, 1893-
Hetman of Ukraine: Ivan Mazeppa. New York, Bookman Associates [1957] 234p. 23cm. [DK508.6.M3M3] 57-2869
1. Masepa, Ivan Stepanovich, hetman of the Cossacks, d. 1709. I. Title.

Maslow, Abraham Harold.

ABRAHAM H. Maslow: 150'.92'4 B a memorial volume. International Study Project, inc., Menlo Park, California. Compiled with the assistance of Bertha G. Maslow. Monterey, Calif., Brooks/Cole Pub. Co. [1972] 133 p. illus. 26 cm. ([The A. H. Maslow series]) In a case. Bibliography: p. 115-133. [BF109.M33A63] 74-178890 ISBN 0-8185-0033-6
1. Maslow, Abraham Harold. 2. Humanistic psychology. I. Maslow, Bertha G., comp. II. International Study Project. III. Title. IV. Series. BIP

GOBLE, Frank G. 150'.924
The third force; the psychology of Abraham Maslow [by] Frank G. Goble. Foreword by Abraham Maslow. New York, Grossman, 1970. xii, 201 p. 24 cm. Bibliography: p. [185]-192. [BF698.G56 1970] 71-114940 7.95
1. Maslow, Abraham Harold. 2. Personality. 3. Social psychology. I. Title.

LOWRY, Richard, 1940- 150'.92'4
A. H. Maslow: an intellectual portrait. Written for the International Study Project, inc., by Richard J. Lowry. Monterey, Calif., Brooks/Cole Pub. Co. [1973] xi, 110 p. port. 25 cm. (The A. H. Maslow series) Includes bibliographical references. [BF109.M33L68] 72-95177 ISBN 0-8185-0083-2
1. Maslow, Abraham Harold. 2. Humanistic psychology. I. International Study Project. II. Title. III. Series. BIP

Mason, Alexander James, 1857 or 8-1942.

TREVELYAN, Raleigh 920.8
A hermit disclosed. New York, St. Martin's Press [1961, c.1960] 308p. illus. 60-16807 4.75 bds.,
1. Mason, Alexander James, 1857 or 8-1942. I. Title.

Mason family.

ALLYN, James H., 1908- 974.6'5
Major John Mason's Great Island / by James H. Allyn. Mystic, Conn. : R. N. Bohlander, c1976. xii, 97 p., [2] fold. leaves of plates : ill. ; 26 cm. Errata slip inserted. [F102.N7A44] 76-49716
1. Mason family. 2. Mason Island, Conn.—History. 3. Mason Island, Conn.—Biography. I. Title.

Mason, Gabriel Richard.

MASON, Gabriel 370'.92'4 B Richard.
Gabriel blows his horn: the evolution of a rebel. Philadelphia, Dorrance [1973, c1972] 200 p. 22 cm. [LA2317.M29A34] 72-87524 ISBN 0-8059-1747-0 4.95
1. Mason, Gabriel Richard. I. Title.

Mason, George, 1725-1792.

COPELAND, Pamela 973.3'092'4 B C., 1906-
The five George Masons : patriots and planters of Virginia and Maryland / Pamela C. Copeland and Richard K. MacMaster. Charlottesville : Published for the Board of Regents of Gunston Hall by the University Press of Virginia, 1975. viii, 341 p., [2] leaves of plates (1 fold.) : ill. ; 27 cm. Includes index. Bibliography: p. [313]-319. [E302.6.M45C58] 75-8565 ISBN 0-8139-0550-8
1. Mason, George, 1725-1792. 2. Mason family. I. MacMaster, Richard Kerwin, 1935- joint author. II. Board of Regents of Gunston Hall. III. Title. BIP

MILLER, Helen Day 320.50924 (Hill) 1899-
George Mason, constitutionalist, by Helen Hill. Gloucester, Mass., P. Smith, 1966 [c1938] xxii, 300 p. illus., fold. map. ports. 21 cm. Bibliography: p. [259]-262. [E302.6.M45] 67-833
1. Mason, George, 1725-1792. I. Title.

MILLER, Helen Day 973.3'092'4 B Hill, 1899-
George Mason, gentleman revolutionary / by Helen Hill Miller. Chapel Hill :

University of North Carolina Press, [1975] xi, 388 p. : ill. ; 26 m. Includes bibliographical references and index. [E302.6.M45M53] 75-1377 ISBN 0-8078-1250-1 : 16.95
1. Mason, George, 1725-1792. I. Title.

ROWLAND, Kate Mason, d. 1916. 923.273
The life of George Mason, 1725-1792; including his speeches, public papers, and correspondence. v.1&2. [Reissue] Introd. by Fitzhugh Lee. New York, Russell Russell, 1964. 2v. (454) 527p.) facsims., ports. 22cm. Orig. pub. in 1892. Bibl. 64-23460 20.00 set, lim. ed.
1. Mason, George, 1725-1792. I. Title.

*RUTLAND, Robert Allen, 1922- 923.273
George Mason, reluctant statesman. Foreword by Dumas Malone. Charlottesville, Univ. of Va. Pr. [1963, c.1961] 123p. illus. 19cm. (Dominion bks.) Bibl. 1.45 pap.,
1. Mason, George, 1725-1792. I. Title.

RUTLAND, Robert Allen, 1922- 923.273
George Mason, reluctant statesman Foreword by Dumas Malone. Williamsburg, Va., Colonial Williamsburg; distributed by Holt, Rinehart and Winston, New York [1961] 123 p. illus. 21 cm. (Williamsburg in America series, 4) Includes bibliography. [F234.W7W7 vol. 4] [E302.6.M45R808] 61-11480
1. Mason, George, 1725-1792.

Mason, George, 1725-1792—Juvenile literature.

HENRI, Florette. 973.2'0924 B
George Mason of Virginia. New York, Crowell-Collier Press [1971] 182 p. port. 21 cm. A biography of the influential eighteenth-century Virginia statesman whose Declaration of Rights for that colony served as the basis for the Bill of Rights incorporated into the Constitution. [E302.6.M45H4] 92 70-127460
1. Mason, George, 1725-1792—Juvenile literature. I. Title. BIP

Mason, John, 1586-1635.

DEAN, John Ward, 1815-1902. 917.42'03'3
Capt. John Mason, the founder of New Hampshire including his tract on Newfoundland, 1620; the American charters in which he was a grantee; with letters and other historical documents together with a memoir by Charles Wesley Tuttle. Edited with historical illus. by John Ward Dean. New York, B. Franklin [1967] xii, 492 p. illus. 23 cm. (Burt Franklin research and source works series, 131. American classics in history and social science. 2) Reprint of the 1887 ed. which was issued as v. 17 of the Publications of the Prince Society. Includes bibliographical references. [F37.M4 1967] 72-184504
1. Mason, John, 1586-1635. 2. Mason family. 3. New Hampshire—History—Colonial period, ca. 1600-1775. 4. Newfoundland—History. 5. Newfoundland—Bibliography. I. Series: Prince Society, Boston. Publications, v. 17

Mason, Joseph—Juvenile literature.

BRENNER, Barbara. 598.2'092'4
On the frontier with Mr. Audubon / by Barbara Brenner. New York : Coward, McCann & Geoghegan, [1976] p. cm. Audubon's young apprentice describes the experiences he shared with his master during their eighteen month trip down the Mississippi studying and drawing the birds they found along the way. [QH31.M28B73] 920 76-41601 ISBN 0-698-20385-2 : 6.95.
1. Mason, Joseph—Juvenile literature. 2. Audubon, John James, 1785-1851—Juvenile literature. 3. Naturalists—United States—Biography—Juvenile literature. 4. Artists—United States—Biography—Juvenile literature. I. Title. BIP

Mason, M.

MASON, M. 973'.04'97 S
Captivity and sufferings of Mrs. Mason. New York : Garland Pub., 1977. 1 fold. leaf : ill. ; 23 cm. (The Garland library of narratives of North American Indian captivities ; v. 52) Issued with the reprint of the 1833 ed. of Priest, J. The captivity and sufferings of Gen. Freegift Patchin. New York, 1977. Reprint of an undated broadside, lacking imprint. [E85.G2 vol. 52] [E83.835] 973.5'7 76-51391 ISBN 0-8240-1676-9 : lib.bdg. : 25.00(set)
1. Mason, M. 2. Seminole War, 2d, 1835-1842. 3. Seminole Indians—Captivities. 4. Indians of North America—Captivities. 5. Florida—Biography. I. Title. II. Series.

Mason, Miles, 1752-1822.

HAGGAR, Reginald George, 1905- 338.7'61'7380922
Mason porcelain and ironstone 1796-1853 : Miles Mason and the Mason manufactories / by Reginald Haggar and Elizabeth Adams. London : Faber, 1977. 2-135 p., A-H, [80] p. of plates : ill. (some col.), facsim., plan ; 26 cm. (Faber monographs on pottery and porcelain) Includes index. Bibliography: p. 125-126. [NK4210.M3H27] 77-372940 ISBN 0-571-10945-4 : 34.95
1. Mason, Miles, 1752-1822. 2. Mason, Charles James, 1791-1856. 3. Potters—England—Biography. 4. Porcelain, English. I. Adams, B. Elizabeth, joint author. II. Title.
Distributed by Faber and Faber, Salem, Mass.

Mason, Philip.

MASON, Philip. 354'.54'060924 B
A shaft of sunlight / by Philip Mason. New York : Scribner, [1978] p. cm. Includes index. [CT788.M253A37 1978b] 78-13718 ISBN 0-684-15920-1 : 12.50
1. Mason, Philip. 2. England—Biography. 3. India—Biography. I. Title. BIP

Massachusetts—Biography.

FLAGG, Charles Allcott, 1870-1920, comp. 929'.3744
An index of pioneers from Massachusetts to the West especially the State of Michigan : this list includes many sons and daughters of old Bay State families who removed to New York and states of the Middle West / compiled by Charles A. Flagg. Baltimore : Genealogical Pub. Co., 1975. iii. 86 p. ; 23 cm. Reprint of the 1915 ed. published by Salem Press, Salem, Mass. Bibliography: p. [1]-5. [F63.F53 1975] 72-29148 ISBN 0-8063-0660-2 : 7.50
1. Massachusetts—Biography. 2. Michigan—Biography. I. Title. BIP

Massachusetts—History—Colonial period, ca. 1600-1775.

JAMES, Sydney V ed. 923.273
Three visitors to early Plymouth; letters about the pilgrim settlement in New England during its first seven years, by John Pory Emmanuel Altham, and Isaack de Rasiere. Edited by Sydney V. James Jr., with an introd. by Samuel Eliot Morison. [Plymouth, Mass.] Plimoth Plantation [c1963] xiii, 84 p. map. 24 cm. "Bibliographical note": p. 81-82. [F68.J27] 66-8244
1. Massachusetts—Hist.—Colonial period (New Plymouth) I. Pory, John, 1570?-1635. II. Altham, Emmanuel, 1600-1635 or 6. III. Rasieres, Isaack de, b. 1595. IV. Title.

MORISON, Samuel Eliot, 1887-1976. 974.4'02 B
Builders of the Bay colony / by Samuel Eliot Morison. New York : AMS Press, 1978. xiv, 365 p., [39] leaves of plates : ill. ; 23 cm. Reprint of the 1930 ed. published by Houghton Mifflin, Boston. Includes index. Bibliography: p. [347]-355. [F67.M86 1978] 75-41198 ISBN 0-404-14741-0 : 23.50
1. Massachusetts—History—Colonial period, ca. 1600-1775. 2. Massachusetts—Biography. 3. Puritans. I. Title. BIP

Massachusetts—History—Colonial period, ca. 1600-1775—Sources.

MATHER, Cotton, 1663-1728. 974.4
Diary of Cotton Mather. New York, F. Ungar Pub. Co. [1957?] 2 v. fold. map. 25 cm. (American classics) Contents.Contents.—v. 1. 1681-1709 [i.e. 1708]—v. 2. 1709-1724. [F67.M4213] 57-8651
1. Massachusetts—History—Colonial period, ca. 1600-1775—Sources.

Massachusetts—History—New Plymouth, 1620-1691—Sources.

YOUNG, Alexander, 1800-1854. 974.4'02
Chronicles of the Pilgrim fathers of the colony of Plymouth, from 1602 to 1625. Now first collected from original records and contemporaneous printed documents, and illustrated with notes. Baltimore, Genealogical Pub. Co., 1974. xvi, 502 p. illus. 22 cm. Reprint of the 2d ed. published in 1844 by C. C. Little and J. Brown, Boston. Contents.Contents.—Gov. Bradford's History of Plymouth colony.—Bradford's and Winslow's journal.—Cushman's discourse.—Winslow's relation.—Winslow's brief narration.—Gov. Bradford's dialogue.—Gov. Bradford's memoir of Elder Brewster.—Letters. Includes bibliographical references. [F68.Y68 1974] 74-830 ISBN 0-8063-0611-4
1. Massachusetts—History—New Plymouth, 1620-1691—Sources. 2. Pilgrim Fathers. I. Title. BIP

Massachusetts—Politics and government—Revolution, 1775-1783.

DE BERDT, Dennys, 1694?-1770. 973.2'7'0924
Letters of Dennys De Berdt, 1757-1770. Edited by Albert Matthews. Freeport, N.Y., Books for Libraries Press [1971] [293]-461 p. illus. 23 cm. Reprint of the 1911 ed. "Originally reprinted from the Publications of the Colonial Society of Massachusetts, v. XIII." [E263.M4D28 1971] 77-165624 ISBN 0-8369-5931-0
1. Massachusetts—Politics and government—Revolution, 1775-1783. 2. United States—Politics and government—Revolution, 1775-1783. I. Matthews, Albert, 1860-1946, ed. II. Title. BIP

Massari, Angelo

MASSARI, Angelo 332.120924
The wonderful life of Angelo Massari; an autobiography. Tr. [from Italian] by Arthur D. Massolo. New York, Exposition [c.1965] 314p. illus., facsims., ports. 21cm. (EP 43069) [CT275.M4627A33] 65-4438 5.00
I. Title.

Massasoit, Indian chief, 1580-1661.

PEIRCE, Ebenezer Weaver, 1822-1903. 970.3
Indian history, biography, and genealogy: pertaining to the good sachem Massasoit of the Wampanoag tribe, and his descendants. With an appendix. Freeport, N.Y., Books for Libraries Press [1972] xiv, 261 p. illus. 22 cm. Reprint of the 1878 ed. [E83.67.P37 1972] 72-4336 ISBN 0-8369-6890-5
1. Massasoit, Indian chief, 1580-1661. 2. King Philip's War, 1675-1676. 3. Indians of North America—New England—History. I. Title.

Massasoit, Indian chief, 1580-1661—Juvenile literature.

VOIGHT, Virginia Frances. 970.3 B
Massasoit, friend of the Pilgrims, by Virginia Voight. Illustrated by Cary. Champaign, Ill., Garrard Pub. Co. [1971] 80 p. illus. (part col.), map, ports. 23 cm. (Gerrard Indian books) A biography of the Wampanoag Indian chief whose friendship with the pilgrims helped them survive in a strange land. [E99.W2V6] 92 76-133552 ISBN 0-8116-6609-3 2.39
1. Massasoit, Indian chief, 1580-1661—Juvenile literature. I. Cary, Louis F., illus. II. Title.

Massena, Andre, Prince d'Essling, 1758-1817.

MARSHALL-CORNWALL, James Handyside, 1887- 923.544
Marshall Massena. New York, Oxford [c.] 1965. xi, 319p. illus., maps, ports. 23cm. Bibl. [DC146.M34M3] 65-3088 6.75
1. Massena, Andre, Prince d'Essling, 1758-1817. I. Title.

Massenet, Jules Emile Frederic, 1842-1912.

FINCK, Henry Theophilus, 1854-1926. 782.1'092'4
Massenet and his operas / by Henry T. Finck. New York : AMS Press, 1976. 245 p., [18] leaves of plates : ill. ; 18 cm. Reprint of the 1910 ed. published by John Lane, New York. Includes index. Bibliography: p. 237-239. [ML410.M42F4 1976] 74-24085 ISBN 0-404-12912-9 : 17.00
1. Massenet, Jules Emile Frederic, 1842-1912. Operas. I. Title. BIP

HARDING, James. 782.1'0924 B
Massenet. New York, St. Martin's Press [1971, c1970] 229 p. illus., music, ports. 25 cm. "The works of Massenet": p. 203-218. [ML410.M41H4 1971] 70-132189 8.95
1. Massenet, Jules Emile Frederic, 1842-1912. BIP

IRVINE, Demar Buel. 782.1'092'4 B
Massenet; a chronicle of his life and times, by Demar Irvine. [Seattle, 1974] x, 483 p. 29 cm. Bibliography: p. 409-412. [ML410.M41I8] 74-157950
1. Massenet, Jules Emile Frederic, 1842-1912.

MASSENET, Jules Emile Frederic, 1842-1912. 782.1'0924
My recollections. The authorized translation done at the master's express desire by his friend H. Villiers Barnett. Freeport, N.Y., Books for Libraries Press [1970] 304 p. illus., ports. 23 cm. "First published 1919." [ML410.M41A33 1970] 75-107819
1. Musicians—Correspondence, reminiscences, etc. BIP

MASSENET, Jules Emile Frederic, 1842-1912. 780'.92'2 B
My recollections, by Jules Massenet. The authorized translation done at the master's express desire by his friend H. Villiers Barnett. Westport, Conn., Greenwood Press [1970] 304 p. illus., ports. 23 cm. "Originally published in 1919." [ML410.M41A33 1970b] 79-109786 ISBN 0-8371-4276-8
1. Musicians—Correspondence, reminiscences, etc.

MASSENET, Jules Emile Frederic, 1842-1912. 782.1'0924 B
My recollections (1848-1912). [1st a M S New York, AMS Press, 1971] 304 p. illus., facsim., ports. 19 cm. Reprint of the 1919 ed. Translation of Mes souvenirs. [ML410.M41A33 1971] 70-137259 ISBN 0-404-04229-5
1. Musicians—Correspondence, reminiscences, etc. I. Title.

Massey, Raymond.

MASSEY, Raymond. 791.43'028'0924 B
A hundred different lives, an autobiography / by Raymond Massey ; foreword by Christopher Plummer. 1st American ed. Boston : Little, Brown, c1979. 447 p. : ill. ; 24 cm. [PN2287.M545A34 1979] 79-64864 ISBN 0-316-54971-1 : 13.95
1. Massey,Raymond. 2. Actors—United States—Biography. I. Title.

MASSEY, Raymond. 791.43'028'0924 B
When I was young / by Raymond Massey. Toronto : McClelland and Stewart, c1976. 269 p., [16] leaves of plates : ill. ; 24 cm. [PN2308.M3A37] 76-371105 ISBN 0-7710-5854-3 : 13.95
1. Massey, Raymond. I. Title. BIP

MASSEY, Raymond. 791.43'028'0924 B
When I was young / Raymond Massey. 1st American ed. Boston : Little, Brown, 1976. 271 p. : ill. ; 24 cm. [PN2308.M3A37 1976b] 76-21929 ISBN 0-316-54977-0 : 10.00
1. Massey, Raymond. 2. Actors—Canada—Biography. I. Title.

Massey, Vincent,

MASSEY, Vincent, 1887- 923.271
What's past is prologue; the memoirs of the Right Honourable Vincent Massey, C.H. New York, St Martin's Press, 1964 [c1963] 540 p. illus., ports. 23 cm. [F1034.M34] 64-163969
I. Title.

Massinger, Philip, 1583-1640.

BALL, Robert Hamilton, 1902- 822'.3
The amazing career of Sir Giles Overreach; being the life and adventures of a nefarious scoundrel who for three centuries pursued his sinister designs in almost all the theatres of the British Isles and America, the whole comprising a history of the stage. New York, Octagon Books, 1968 [c1939] ix, 467 p. illus. 24 cm. Bibliography: p. [425]-438. [PR2704.N4B3 1968] 68-15300
1. Massinger, Philip, 1583-1640. A new way to pay old debts. 2. Theater—Great Britain—History. 3. Theater—United States—History. I. Title. II. Title: Sir Giles Overreach.

Massingham, Henry William, 1860-1924.

HAVIGHURST, Alfred F. 070.4'092'4
Radical journalist: H. W. Massingham (1860-1924) [by] Alfred F. Havighurst. [London, New York] Cambridge University Press [1974] xv, 350 p. 23 cm. (Conference on British studies. Biographical series) Bibliography: p. 327-333. [PN5123.M355H3] 73-83106 ISBN 0-521-20355-4 19.50
1. Massingham, Henry William, 1860-1924. I. Title. II. Series.

Masson, Andre, 1896—

RUBIN, William Stanley. 759.4 B
Andre Masson / by William Rubin and Carolyn Lanchner. New York : Museum of Modern Art, c1976. 232 p. : ill. (some col.) ; 25 cm. "Bibliography, compiled by Inga Forslund": p. 225-232. [ND553.M36R82] 76-1492 ISBN 0-87070-465-6 : 20.00.
1. Masson, Andre, 1896- 2. Painters—France—Biography. I. Lanchner, Carolyn, joint author.
Contents omitted. BIP

Masson, David,

MASSON, David, 1822-1907. 821'.3
Drummond of Hawthornden: the story of his life and writings. New York, Greenwood Press [1969] xv, 490 p. port. 23 cm. Reprint of the 1873 ed. [PR2263.M3 1969] 69-13991
1. Drummond, William, 1585-1649. II. Title.

Masson, Flora.

MASSON, Flora. 820.9'008
Victorians all. Port Washington, N.Y., Kennikat Press [1970] 128 p. 21 cm. Reprint of the 1931 ed. Contents.Contents.—Mainly about Dickens and Thackeray.—Holman Hunt and Sir Atalanta.—A London childhood.—A philosopher at play.—Evenings at Avenue Road.—Mainly about the Carlyles and Mazzini.—Edinburgh and the Highlands.—Giants of those days.—Mainly about Stevenson and Browning.—Florence Nightingale and later friendships. [PR6025.A7955V5 1970] 75-105806
I. Title. BIP

Masson, Paul, 1859-1940.

BALZER, Robert Lawrence. 641
This uncommon heritage; the Paul Masson story. Los Angeles, Ward Ritchie Press [1970] 118 p. illus. (part col.), facsims., ports. 29 cm. [TP547.M35B34] 76-111969
1. Masson, Paul, 1859-1940. 2. Masson (Paul) Vineyards, Saratoga, Calif. I. Title.

Massoud, Muhammad Said, 1893-

MASSOUD, Muhammad Said, 1893- 971'.004'927 B
I fought as I believed : an Arab Canadian speaks out on the Arab-Israeli conflict / Muhammad Said Massoud. [s.l. : s.n.], c1976 (Montreal : Ateliers des Sourds) xiv, 724 p. : ill. ; 26 cm. [DS119.7.M316] 77-353288
1. Massoud, Muhammad Said, 1893- 2. Jewish-Arab relations—1917—Addresses, essays, lectures. 3. Arabs in Canada—Biography. 4. Canada—Biography. I. Title.

Masterman, Charles Frederick Gurney, 1873-1927.

MASTERMAN, Lucy Blanche (Lyttelton), 1884- 328.42'0924
C. F. G. Masterman: a biography [by] Lucy Masterman. 1st ed., new impression. London, Cass, 1968. 400p. 8 plates, illus., ports. 23cm. Bibl. [DA566.9.M38M3 1968] (B) 68-88329 15.00
1. Masterman, Charles Frederick Gurney, 1873-1927. 2. Gt. Brit.—Pol. & govt.—1901-1936. I. Title.
Distributed by Kelley, New York.

Masters, Edgar Lee,

MASTERS, Edgar Lee, 1869-1950. 811'.5'2 B
Across Spoon River; an autobiography. New York, Octagon Books, 1969 [c1936] 426 p. illus., ports. 24 cm. [PS3525.A83Z5 1969] 70-96162
I. Title.

Masters, George.

MASTERS, George. 646.7'2'0924 B
The Masters way to beauty / by George Masters and Norma Lee Browing. 1st ed. New York : E. P. Dutton, c1977. p. cm. "A Sunrise book." [TT955.M33A34] 76-54959 ISBN 0-87690-232-8 : 9.95
1. Masters, George. 2. Beauty operators—California—Biography. 3. Beauty, Personnal. 4. Entertainers—Anecdotes, facetiae, satire, etc. I. Browing, Norma Lee, joint author. II. Title. BIP

MASTERS, George. 646.7'2'0924 [B]
The masters way to beauty / by George Masters and Norma Lee Browning. New York : New American Library, 1978,c1977. 254p. ; 18 cm. (A Signet Book) Includes index. [TT955.M33A34] pbk. : 2.25
1. Masters, George. 2. Beauty operators — California — Biography. 3. Beauty, Personnal. 4. Entertainers — Anecdotes, facetiae, satire, etc. I. Browning, Norma Lee, joint author. II. Title.
L.C. card no. for 1977 Dutton ed.: 76-54959.

Masters, John,

MASTERS, John, 1914- 928.1
Bugles and a tiger; a volume of autobiography. New York, Viking Press, 1956. 312 p. illus. 23 cm. [PS3525.A8314Z5] 55-10471
I. Title.

MASTERS, John, 1914- 928.1
Bugles and a tiger; a volume of autobiography. New York, Ballantine [1968,c.1956] 317p. illus. 18cm. (U6044) [PS3525.A8314Z5] .75 pap.,
I. Title.

MASTERS, John, 1914- 813'.5'4 B
Pilgrim son; a personal odyssey. New York, Putnam [1971] 383 p. 22 cm. [PS3525.A8314Z52] 78-151213 6.95
I. Title.

Masters, William H.

ROBINSON, Paul A., 1940- 301.41'792'2
The modernization of sex : Havelock Ellis, Alfred Kinsey, William Masters, and Virginia Johnson / Paul Robinson. 1st ed. New York : Harper & Row, c1976. viii, 200 p. ; 22 cm. Includes bibliographical references and index. [HQ18.3.R6] 75-24500 ISBN 0-06-013583-2 : 8.95
1. Ellis, Havelock, 1859-1939. 2. Kinsey, Alfred Charles, 1894-1956. 3. Masters, William H. 4. Johnson, Virginia E. 5. Sexologists. I. Title.

Masterson, Tom, 1905-

MASTERSON, Tom, 1905- 385'.092'4 B
Mountain enginemen. Auckland, Collins [1973] 207 p. illus. 22 cm. [TF140.M33A35] 74-157436
1. Masterson, Tom, 1905- 2. Railroads—New Zealand—History. I. Title.
Distributed by International Publications Service, N.Y. for 10.40.

Masterson, William Barclay, 1853-1921.

DEARMENT, Robert K., 1925 978'.02'0924 B
Bat Masterson, the man and the legend / by Robert K. DeArment. 1st ed. Norman : University of Oklahoma Press, c1979. p. cm. Includes index. Bibliography: p. [F594.M33D4] 78-21383 ISBN 0-8061-1522-X : 14.95
1. Masterson, William Barclay, 1853-1921. 2. Frontier and pioneer life—The West. 3. The West—History—1848-1950. 4. Pioneers—The West—Biography. I. Title.

O'CONNOR, Richard, 1915- 923.573
Bat Masterson. [1st ed.] Garden City, N.Y., Doubleday, 1957. 263 p. 22 cm. Includes bibliography. [F594.M33O3] 57-9508
1. Masterson, William Barclay, 1853-1921.

Masterson, William Barclay, 1853-1921—Juvenile literature.

PLACE, Marian (Templeton) 923.573
Bat Masterson, by Dale White [pseud.] J. Messner [c.1960] 191p. Bibl.: p.185-186 22cm. (Julian Messner shelf of biographies) 60-12451 2.95
1. Masterson, William Barclay, 1853-1921—Juvenile literature. I. Title.

Masterton, Elsie.

MASTERTON, Elsie. 647.94
Nothing whatever to do, by Elsie and John Masterton. Drawings by Elsie Masterton. New York, Crown, 1956. 277 p. illus. 22 cm. Autobiographical. [TX910.5.M34A3] 56-11361
I. Masterton, John, joint author. II. Title.

MASTERTON, Elsie. 818.54
Off my toes. [1st ed.] Boston, Little, Brown [1961] 298 p. 21 cm. Autobiographical. [CT275.M4637A3] 61-12806
I. Title.

Maston, Thomas Bufford, 1897- — Addresses, essays, lectures.

AN Approach to 286'.1'0924
Christian ethics : the life, contribution, and thought of T. B. Maston / William M. Pinson, Jr., compiler/contributor. Nashville : Broadman Press, c1979. 204 p. ; 21 cm. Includes bibliographical references. [BX6495.M362A66] 78-71465 ISBN 0-8054-6120-5 : 5.95
1. Maston, Thomas Bufford, 1897- — Addresses, essays, lectures. 2. Baptists—Clergy—Biography—Addresses, essays, lectures. 3. Clergy—United States—Biography—Addresses, essays, lectures. I. Pinson, William M. BIP

Matas, Rudolph, 1860-1957.

COHN, Isidore, 1885- 926.1
Rudolph Matas; a biography of one of the great pioneers in surgery [by] Isidore Cohn with Hermann B. Deutsch. [1st ed.] Garden City, N. Y., Doubleday, 1960. 431 p. illus. 25 cm. [R154.M29875C6] 60-9471
1. Matas, Rudolph, 1860-1957.

Materia medica, Vegetable—Addresses, essays, lectures.

MESSEGUE, Maurice. 615'.351'0924 B
Of men and plants; the autobiography of the world's most famous plant healer. [1st American ed.] New York, Macmillan [1973] vi, 327 p. 21 cm. Translation of Des hommes et des plantes. [RS164.M39513 1973] 72-81079 7.95
1. Materia medica, Vegetable—Addresses, essays, lectures. I. Title.

MESSEGUE, Maurice. 615'.351'0924 B
Of men and plants; the autobiography of the world's most famous plant healer. New York, Bantam Books [1974, c1973] vi, 345 p. 18 cm. Translation of Des hommes et des plantes. [RS164.M39513 1974] 1.75 (pbk.)
1. Materia medica, Vegetable—Addresses, essays, lectures. I. Title.
L.C. card number for original ed.: 72-81079.

Mathematicians.

MUIR, Jane. 925.1
Of men and numbers; the story of the great mathematicians. New York, Dodd, Mead, 1961. 249 p. illus. 21 cm. Includes bibliography. [QA28.M8] 60-14795
1. Mathematicians. I. Title.

TURNBULL, Herbert Westren, 1885-1961. v. 12
The great mathematicians. New York, Simon and Schuster, 1962 [c1961] 141 p. illus. 21 cm. 68-72967
1. Mathematicians. 2. Mathematics—Hist. I. Title. BIP

Mathematicians—Biography.

FANG, Joong. 510'.92'2 B
Mathematicans from antiquity to today [by] J. Fang, in collaboration with U. Dudley. A prelim. ed. [Hauppauge, N.Y.] Paideia [1972- v. 24 cm. (Studies in the nature of modern mathematics) Includes bibliographical references. [QA28.F3] 70 131575 ISBN 0-912490-07-1 12.80 (v. 1)
1. Mathematicians—Biography. I. Title.

TURNBULL, Herbert Westren, 1885-1961. 925.1
The great mathematicians. New York, New York University Press, 1961. 141 p. illus. 22 cm. 61-16934
1. Mathematicians—Biography. 2. Mathematics—History.

Mathematics—Early works to 1800.

BRADWARDINE, Thomas, Abp. of Canterbury, 1290?-1349. 510
Thomas of Bradwardine, his Tractatus de proportionibus; its significance for the development of mathematical physics. Edited and translated by H. Lamar Crosby, Jr. Madison, University of Wisconsin Press, 1955. xi,203 p. 24 cm. Latin and English. Bibliography: p. 195-197. [QA32.B7 1955] 54-6740
1. Mathematics—Early works to 1800. 2. Proportion. I. Crosby, Henry Lamar, 1880- ed. II. Title: Tractatus de proportionibus.

Mathematics—History.

HOOPER, Alfred. 510.9
Makers of mathematics. New York, Random House [1958, c1948] 402 p. illus. 19 cm. (Modern library paperbacks, P38) Includes bibliography. [QA21.H76 1958] 58-6370

1. Mathematics—History. 2. Mathematicians—Biography. I. Title.

MORGAN, Brian Stanford. 510'.92'2
Men and discoveries in mathematics [by] Bryan Morgan. [London] J. Murray [1972] xii, 235 p. illus. 19 cm. Bibliography: p. [xi]-xii. [QA21.M827] 72-171094 ISBN 0-7195-2587-X
1. Mathematics—History. 2. Mathematicians—Biography. I. Title.
Distributed by Transatlantic 8.75. BIP

Mather, Cotton, 1663-1728.

BEALL, Otho T. 610'.92'4
Cotton Mather / Otho T. Beall, Jr. and Richard H. Shryock. New York : Arno Press, 1979, c1954. ix, 241 p., [1] leaf of plates : ill. ; 21 cm. (Johns Hopkins University Press reprints) (Reprint of the ed. published by Johns Hopkins Press, Baltimore issued in series: Publications of the Institute of the History of Medicine, 1st ser., Monographs, v. 5.) Includes bibliographical references and index. [F67.M43B42 1979] 78-19290 ISBN 0-405-10580-0 : 18.00
1. Mather, Cotton, 1663-1728. 2. Puritans—Massachusetts—Biography. 3. Medicine—United States—History—18th century. I. Shryock, Richard Harrison, 1893-1972. II. Title. III. Series: Johns Hopkins University. Institute of the History of Medicine. Publications ; 1st ser. : Monographs ; v. 5.

BEALL, Otho T 922.573
Cotton Mather, first significant figure in American medicine by Otho T. Beall, Jr., and Richard H. Shryock Baltimore, Johns Hopkins Press [1954 ix, 241p. port., facsim. 24cm. (Publications of the Institute of the History of Medicine. 1st ser.: Monographs, v. 5) Reprinted from volume 63 of the Proceedings of American Antiquarian Society.' Bibliographical footnotes. [F67.M4218] 54-8009
1. Mather, Cotton, 1663-1728. 2. Medicine—15th-18th cent. I. Shryock, Richard Harrison, 1893- joint author. II. Title. III. Series: Johns Hopkins University. Institute of the History of Medicine. Publications. 1st ser.: Monographs, v. 5

BOAS, Ralph Philip, 1887- 922.573
Cotton Mather, keeper of the Puritan conscience, by Ralph and Louise Boas. Hamden, Conn., Archon [dist. Shoe String] 1964 [c.1928] ix, 271p. 21cm. 64-15910 7.50
1. Mather, Cotton, 1663-1728. I. Boas, Louise (Schutz) joint author. II. Title.

LEVIN, David, 1924- 973.2'092'4 B
Cotton Mather : the young life of the Lord's Remembrancer, 1663-1703 / David Levin. Cambridge, Mass. : Harvard University Press, 1978. xvi, 360 p. : ill. ; 24 cm. Includes bibliographical references and index. [F67.M43L48] 78-2355 ISBN 0-674-17507-7. : 16.50
1. Mather, Cotton, 1663-1728. 2. Congregational Churches—Clergy—Biography. 3. Clergy—Massachusetts—Biography. 4. Massachusetts—Biography. BIP

MARVIN, Abijah Perkins. 973.2'092'4 B
The life and times of Cotton Mather, D.D., F.R.S.; or, A Boston minister of two centuries ago, 1663-1728. New York, Haskell House Publishers, 1973. v, 582 p. illus. 23 cm. Reprint of the 1892 ed. published by the Congregational Sunday-School and Publishing Society, Boston. [F67.M426 1973] 72-1979 ISBN 0-8383-1454-6 18.95
1. Mather, Cotton, 1663-1728. I. Title.

MATHER, Cotton, 1663-1728. 974.4
Diary of Cotton Mather. New York, F. Ungar Pub. Co. [1957?] 2 v. fold. map. 25 cm. (American classics) Contents.Contents.—v. 1. 1681-1709 [i.e. 1708]—v. 2. 1709-1724. [F67.M4213] 57-8651
1. Massachusetts—History—Colonial period, ca. 1600-1775—Sources.

MATHER, Cotton, 1663-1728. 973.2'092'4 B
Paterna : the autobiography of Cotton Mather / edited by Ronald A. Bosco. Delmar, N.Y. : Scholars' Facsimiles & Reprints, 1976. p. cm. Includes inde. Bibliography: p. [F67.M42145] 76-10595 ISBN 0-8201-1273-9 lib.bdg. : 40.00
1. Mather, Cotton, 1663-1728. I. Title. BIP

MATHER, Cotton, 1663-1728. 917.3'03'25
Selected letters of Cotton Mather. Compiled with commentary by Kenneth Silverman. Baton Rouge, Louisiana State University Press [1971] xxvi, 446 p. port. 24 cm. [F67.M4215] 78-142338 ISBN 0-8071-0920-7 15.00
I. Silverman, Kenneth. II. Title. BIP

WENDELL, Barrett, 1855-1921 922.573
Cotton Mather, the Puritan priest. New introd. by Alan Heimert. New York, Harcourt [1963] 248p. 21cm. (Harbinger bk.; H022) Bibl. 63-12740 2.25 pap.,
1. Mather, Cotton, 1663-1728. I. Title.

Mather, Cotton, 1663-1728—Juvenile literature.

WOOD, James Playsted, 1905- 973.2'0924 B
The admirable Cotton Mather. New York, Seabury Press [1971] ix, 164 p. 22 cm. Bibliography: p. [155]-158. A biography of the colonial minister who was one of the most influential men of his time in politics, education, foreign affairs, literature, and the church. [F67.M455] 92 76-129212 5.95
1. Mather, Cotton, 1663-1728—Juvenile literature. I. Title.

Mather, Increase, 1639-1723.

MURDOCK, Kenneth Ballard, 1895- 974.4'02'0924
Increase Mather, the foremost American Puritan. New York, Russell & Russell, 1966 [c1953] xv, 442 p. illus., facsims., maps, ports. 22 cm. "Appendix C; list of books referred to": p. [407]-415. Appendix D: check list of Mather's writings": p. [416]-422. [F67.M477 1966] 66-24736
1. Mather, Increase, 1639-1723. I. Title. BIP

MURDOCK, Kenneth Ballard, 1895- 974.4'02'0924
Increase Mather, the foremost American Puritan. New York, Russell & Russell, 1966 [c1953] xv, 442 p. illus., facsims., maps, ports. 22 cm. "Appendix C; list of books referred to": p. [407]-415. "Appendix D; check list of Mather's writing": p. [416]-422. [F67.M477 1966] 66-24736
1. Mather, Increase, 1639-1723. I. Title.

Mather, Richard, 1596-1669.

BURG, Barry Richard, 1938- 285'.8'0924 B
Richard Mather of Dorchester / B. R. Burg. [Lexington, Ky.] : University Press of Kentucky, c1976. xiii, 207 p. ; 23 cm. Includes index. Bibliography: p. [191]-200. [BX7260.M368B87] 75-41987 ISBN 0-8131-1343-1 : 15.95
1. Mathcr, Richard, 1596-1669. 2. Congregational churches—Clergy—Biography. 3. Clergy—Massachusetts—Biography. I. Title. BIP

Mather, Stephen Tyng, 1867-1930.

SHANKLAND, Robert, 1916- 923.273
Steve Mather of the National parks. Introd. by Gilbert Grosvenor. 2d ed., rev. and enl. New York, Knopf, 1954. 346p. illus. 22cm. Includes bibliography. [SB482.A479 1954] 54-4899
1. Mather, Stephen Tyng, 1867-1930. 2. U. S. National Park Service. 3. National parks and reserves—U. S. I. Title.

SHANKLAND, Robert, 1916- 333.7'8'0924 B
Steve Mather of the national parks. 3d ed., rev. and enl. New York, Knopf, 1970. xii, 370, xxiii p. illus., map, ports. 22 cm. Bibliography: p. 365-370. [SB482.A4S48 1970] 69-10702 8.95
1. Mather, Stephen Tyng, 1867-1930. 2. U.S. National Park Service. 3. National parks and reserves—U.S. I. Title.

SHANKLAND, Robert, 1916- 926.349
Steve Mather of the National parks. Introd. by Gilbert Grosvenor. [1st ed.] New York, Knopf, 1951. xii, 326, xxii p. illus., ports., fold. map. 22 cm. Bibliography: p. 323-326. [SB482.A479] 51-10310
1. Mather, Stephen Tyng, 1867-1930. 2. U.S. National Park Service. 3. National parks and reserves—U.S. I. Title.

Mathers, Moina MacGregor, 1865-1928.

COLQUHOUN, Ithell, 1906- 135.4'3'0924
Sword of wisdom : MacGregor Mathers and the Golden Dawn / Ithell Colquhoun. 1st. American ed. New York : Putnam, 1975. 307 p., [6] leaves of plates : ill. ; 23 cm. Includes index. [BF1623.R7C784 1975] 76-351557 8.95
1. Hermetic Order of the Golden Dawn. 2. Mathers, S. Liddell MacGregor. 3. Mathers, Moina MacGregor, 1865-1928. 4. Colquhoun, Ithell, 1906- I. Title.

Mathers, S. Liddell MacGregor.

COLQUHOUN, Ithell, 1906- 135.4'3'0924
Sword of wisdom : MacGregor Mathers and the Golden Dawn / Ithell Colquhoun. 1st. American ed. New York : Putnam, 1975. 307 p., [6] leaves of plates : ill. ; 23 cm. Includes index. [BF1623.R7C784 1975] 76-351557 8.95
1. Hermetic Order of the Golden Dawn. 2. Mathers, S. Liddell MacGregor. 3. Mathers, Moina MacGregor, 1865-1928. 4. Colquhoun, Ithell, 1906- I. Title.

Matheson, George, 1812-1906.

TYLER, John Crew, 1923- 922.541
The blind seer: George Matheson. New York, Philosophical Library [1959] 175 p. 23 cm. [BX9225.M36T9] 59-16371
1. Matheson, George, 1812-1906. I. Title.

Mathews, Alfred Edward, 1831-1874.

MUMEY, Nolie, 1891- 927.6
Alfred Edward Mathews, 1831-1874: Union soldier, illustrator of Civil War battles, author, traveler, map maker, and delineator of Western scenes, especially those of the Territories of Colorado and Montana [biography] Boulder, Colo., Johnson Pub. Co., 1961. xiv, 78p. port., fold. map. 26cm. 350copies. Bibliographical footnotes. [NC139.M3M8] 61-41483
1. Mathews, Alfred Edward, 1831-1874. I. Title.

Mathews, Eddie, 1931-

HIRSHBERG, Albert 927.96357
The Eddie Mathews story. New York, J. Messner [c.1960] 192p. illus. 22cm. (Favorite sports biographies) 60-12452 2.95
1. Mathews, Eddie. I. Title.

HIRSHBERG, Albert, 1909- 927.96357
The Eddie Mathews story. New York, J. Messner [1960] 192p. illus. 22cm. [GV865.M36H5] 60-12452
1. Mathews, Eddie, 1931- I. Title.

Mathews, Loulie (Albee)

MATHEWS, Loulie (Albee) 922.97
Not every sea hath pearls. [Portsmouth N. H., 1951] 173 p. 20 cm. Autobiographical. [BP395.M3A3] 52-16005
I. Title.

MATHEWS, Loulie (Albee) 922.97
So early in the morning. [Milford? N. H., 1953] 78p. illus. 20cm. Autobiographical. [CT275.M46443A3] 53-27377
I. Title.

Mathewson, Christopher, 1880-1925.

MATHEWSON, Christopher, 1880-1925. 796.357'092'4 B
Pitching in a pinch : or, Baseball from the inside / Christy Mathewson ; introduction by Red Smith, with a foreword by John N. Wheeler ; edited by Ziegel and Neil Offen. New York : Stein and Day, c1977. xv, 306 p., [13] leaves of plates : ill. ; 22 cm. Originally published in 1912 by Putnam, New York. [GV865.M37A34 1977] 76-55835 ISBN 0-8128-2196-3 : 10.00 ISBN 0-8128-2207-2 pbk. : 3.95
1. Mathewson, Christopher, 1880-1925. 2. Baseball players—United States—Biography. I. Title.

SCHOOR, Gene. 927.96357
Christy Mathewson, baseball's greatest pitcher, by Gene Schoor with Henry Gilfond. New York, J. Messner [1953] 180 p. illus. 22 cm. [GV865.M37S3] 53-9033
1. Mathewson, Christopher, 1880-1925.

Mathias, Robert Bruce, 1930-

SCOTT, Jim, 1912- 927.96
Bob Mathias, champion of champions. New York, Prentice-Hall [1952] 247 p. illus. 21 cm. [GV697.M3S35] 52-12998
1. Mathias, Robert Bruce, 1930-

SCOTT, Jim, 1912- 920
Bob Mathias, champion of champions. [Rev. ed.] Minneapolis, Denison [c.1952, 1960] 210p. 22cm. (Men of achievement ser.) 63-19061 3.00
1. Mathias, Robert Bruce, 1930- I. Title.

SCOTT, Jim, 1912- 927.96
Bob Mathias, Champion of champions. New York, Prentice-Hall [1952] 247p. illus. 21cm. [GV697.M3S35] 52-12998
1. Mathias, Robert Bruce, 1930- I. Title.

SCOTT, Jim, 1912- 92
Bob Mathias, champion of champions. [Rev. ed.] Minneapolis, T.S. Denison [1963] 210 p. 22 cm. (Men of achievement series) [GV697.M3S35] 63-19061
1. Mathias, Robert Bruce, 1930- I. Title.

Mathieu, Edward F

MATHIEU, Edward F 926.4794
The life of a chef. [1st ed.] New York, Comet Press Books, 1958. 276p. 21cm. (A Reflection book) Autobiographical. [TX140.M3A3] 58-14962
I. Title.

Mathieu, Georges, 1921-

MATHIEU, Georges, 1921- 759.4
Mathieu / by Dominique Quignon-Fleuret. New York : Crown Publishers, 1977, c1973. p. cm. Bibliography: p. [ND553.M368Q5413 1977] 77-5886 ISBN 0-517-53086-4 pbk. : 4.95
1. Mathieu, Georges, 1921- 2. Painters—France—Biography. I. Quignon-Fleuret, Dominique, 1943- BIP

Mathilde Bonaparte, Princess, 1820-1904.

RICHARDSON, Joanna. 944.07'0924 B
Princess Mathilde. New York, Scribner [1969] 356 p. illus., ports. 23 cm. Bibliography: p. [342]-347. [DC255.M3R5 1969b] 70-75880 7.95
1. Mathilde Bonaparte, Princess, 1820-1904. I. Title.

Mathius, Robert Bruce, 1930- —Juvenile literature.

FINLAYSON, Ann. 796.4
Decathlon men; greatest athletes in the world. Illustrated by Gray Morrow. Champaign, Ill., Garrard Pub. Co. [1966] 95 p. illus. (part col.) 24 cm. ([Garrard sports library]) [GV1060.7.F5] 66-11897
1. Mathius, Robert Bruce, 1930- —Juvenile literature. 2. Johnson, Rafer Lewis, 1935-

—Juvenile literature. 3. Decathlon—Juvenile literature. I. Title. **BIP**

Mathu, Eliud.

ROELKER, Jack R. 967.6'203'0924 B
Mathu of Kenya : a political study / Jack R. Roelker. Stanford, Calif. : Hoover Institution Press, Stanford University, c1976. xviii, 202 p., [1] leaf of plates : port. ; 24 cm. (Hoover Institution publications ; 157) (Hoover colonial studies) Includes index. Bibliography: p. [181]-193. [DT433.576.M36R63] 76-20294 ISBN 0-8179-6571-8 : 8.85
1. Mathu, Eliud. 2. Kenya—Politics and government—To 1963. 3. Legislators—Kenya—Biography. I. Title. II. Series. III. Series: Stanford University. Hoover Institution on War, Revolution, and Peace. Publications ; 157. **BIP**

Matisse, Henri, 1869-1954.

BARR, Alfred Hamilton, 1902- 759.4 B
Matisse, his art and his public, by Alfred H. Barr, Jr. Reprint ed. [New York] Published for the Museum of Modern Art by Arno Press, 1966 [c1951] 591 p. illus., ports. 27 cm. Bibliography: p. 564-574. [ND553.M37B34 1966] 66-26118
1. Matisse, Henri, 1869-1954. I. New York (City) Museum of Modern Art.

ESCHOLIER, Raymond, 1882- 759.4
Matisse: a portrait of the artist and the man. Translated [from the French] by Geraldine and H. M. Colvile. With introd. and notes on the illus. by R. H. Wilenski. New York, Praeger [1960] 226p. Bibl. notes. illus., plates (part col.) 26cm. 60-8715 12.50
1. Matisse, Henri, 1869-1954. I. Title.

GOWING, Lawrence. 759.4 B
Matisse / Lawrence Gowing. New York : Oxford University Press, 1979. p. cm. (World of art) Includes index. Bibliography: p. [ND553.M37G59 1979] 79-87876 ISBN 0-19-520157-4 : 13.95 ISBN 0-19-520158-2 pbk. : 7.95
1. Matisse, Henri, 1869-1954. 2. Painters—France—Biography. I. Title. II. Series.

MARCHIORI, Giuseppe. 759.4 B
Matisse. New York, Reynal [1967] 134 p. 119 illus. (part col., incl. ports.) 28 cm. Bibliography: p. 131-132. [ND553.M37M37] 67-31965
1. Matisse, Henri, 1869-1954.

MATISSE, Henri, 1869- 759.4
Henri Matisse (1869-) Text by Clement Greenberg. New York, H. N. Abrams in association with Pocket Books [1953] [74] p. 39 illus. (part col.) 18cm. (The Pocket library of great art, A10) An Abrams art book. Bibliography: p. [74] [ND553.M37G65] [ND553.M37G65] 927.5 54-16485 54-16485
I. Greenberg, Clement, 1909- II. Title.

MATISSE, Henri, 1896-1954. 759.4
Henri Matisse. Text by John Jacobus. New York, H. N. Abrams [1973] 184 p. illus. (part col.) 34 cm. (The Library of great painters) Bibliography: p. 183-184. [ND553.M37J32] 72-6633 ISBN 0-8109-0277-X 22.50
1. Matisse, Henri, 1869-1954. I. Jacobus, John M.

SELZ, Jean. 759.4
Matisse. [Translated from the French by A. P. H. Hamilton] New York, Crown Publishers [1964] 94 p. illus. (part mounted, part col.) ports. (part mounted, part col.) 29 cm. Bibliography: p. 94. [ND553.M37S383] 64-54749
1. Matisse, Henri, 1869-1954. **BIP**

Matson, Louise Klassen.

MATSON, Louise Klassen. 289.7'092'4 B
Louise : Louise Klassen Matson's flight to freedom as told to Margaret J. Anderson. Wheaton, Ill. : H. Shaw Publishers, c1977. 134 p. : map ; 18 cm. [BX8143.M37A35] 77-71626 ISBN 0-87788-517-6 pbk. : 1.95
1. Matson, Louise Klassen. 2. Mennonites—Russia—Biography. 3. Mennonites—United States—Biography. I. Anderson, Margaret J.

Matson, Peter H.

MATSON, Peter H. 974.4'1'040924 B
A place in the country : a narrative on the imperfect art of homesteading and the value of ignorance / Peter H. Matson. 1st ed. New York : Random House, c1977. ix, 235 p. : ill. ; 22 cm. [CT275.M46445A35] 76-53470 ISBN 0-394-49591-8 : 8.95
1. Matson, Peter H. 2. United States—Biography. I. Title. **BIP**

MATSON, Peter H. 974.4'1'040924 B
A place in the country : a narrative on the imperfect art of homesteading and the value of ignorance / Peter H. Matson. 1st Harvest/HBJ ed. New York : Harcourt Brace Jovanovich, 1978, c1977. p. cm. (A Harvest/HBJ book) [CT275.M46445A35 1978] 78-6074 ISBN 0-15-672008-6 : 3.95
1. Matson, Peter H. 2. United States—Biography. I. Title.

Matson, Randy.

STOWERS, Carlton. 796.435 B
The Randy Matson story. [Los Altos, Calif.] Tafnews Press [1971] iv, 186 p. illus. 23 cm. [GV1094.M3S85] 70-179433 ISBN 0-911520-30-9 5.95
1. Matson, Randy. I. Title. **BIP**

Matsuda, Kiyoko.

DANKER, William J. 248'.2'0924 B
More than healing, the story of Kiyoko Matsuda [by] William J. Danker and Kiyoko Matsuda. St. Louis, Concordia Pub. House [1973] 135 p. illus. 21 cm. [BR1317.M37D36] 73-78105 ISBN 0-570-03161-3 2.25
1. Matsuda, Kiyoko. I. Matsuda, Kiyoko, joint author. II. Title.

Matsudaira, Sadanobu, 1759-1829.

OOMS, Herman. 952'.025'0924 B
Charismatic bureaucrat; a political biography of Matsudaira Sadanobu, 1758-1829. Chicago, The University of Chicago Press, 1975. xiii, 225 p. 24 cm. Bibliography: p. 192-208. [DS872.M32O65] 74-10342 ISBN 0-226-63031-5 12.50
1. Matsudaira, Sadanobu, 1759-1829. I. Title. **BIP**

Matsuo, Basho, 1644-1694.

UEDA, Makoto, 1931- 895.6'1'3 B
Matsuo Basho. New York, Twayne Publishers [1970] 202 p. map. 21 cm. (Twayne's world authors series, TWAS 102) Bibliography: p. 189-195. [PL794.4.Z5U4] 73-110703
1. Matsuo, Basho, 1644-1694.

Matsuoka, Yoko, 1916—

MATSUOKA, Yoko, 1916- 915.2 B
Daughter of the Pacific. Westport, Conn., Greenwood Press [1973, c1952] 245 p. 22 cm. Reprint of the ed. published by Harper, New York. Autobiographical. [CT1838.M32A33 1973] 72-12634 ISBN 0-8371-6683-7 11.25
1. Matsuoka, Yoko, 1916- I. Title.

Matthew, Saint, apostle—Juvenile literature.

ULMER, Louise. 226'.4'09505
The man who learned to give : Luke 5:27-32 for children / written by Louise Ulmer ; illustrated by John D. Firestone & Associates. St. Louis : Concordia Pub. House, 1977,c1976. p. cm. (Arch books ; ser. 14) Retells in verse the story of Matthew's conversion from tax collector to a disciple of Jesus. [BS2495.U45] 76-27272 ISBN 0-570-06109-1 pbk. : 0.59
1. Matthew, Saint, apostle—Juvenile literature. 2. Bible. N.T.—Biography—Juvenile literature. I. John D. Firestone & Associates. II. Title.

Matthews, Daniel, 1837-1902.

CATO, Nancy. 266'.023'0924 B
Mister Maloga : Daniel Matthews and his mission, Murray River, 1864-1902 / [by] Nancy Cato. St. Lucia, Q. : University of Queensland Press, 1976. xiv, 422 p. : ill. ; 23 cm. Includes index. Bibliography: p. [403]-408. [BV3667.M34C37] 77-359982 ISBN 0-7022-1110-9 : 22.80
1. Matthews, Daniel, 1837-1902. 2. Missionaries—Australia—New South Wales—Biography. 3. New South Wales—Biography. 4. Missions to Australian aborigines—Australia—New South Wales. I. Title.
Available from P.Warren 1136 Fifth Ave.,New York,N.Y.10028 **BIP**

Matthews, Mary Lathrop (Wright) 1891-1955.

MATTHEWS, Alexander, 1888- 926.1
A nurse named Mary; a biography. [1st ed.] New York, Pageant Press [1957] 155p. illus. 21cm. [RT37.M32M3] 57-8307
1. Matthews, Mary Lathrop (Wright) 1891-1955. I. Title.

Matthews, Thomas Stanley, 1901-

MATTHEWS, Thomas Stanley 920.5
Name and address, an autobiography. New York, Simon and Schuster, [c.] 1960. 309p. 22cm. 60-6724 4.50 half cloth,
I. Title.

MATTHEWS, Thomas Stanley, 1901- 070.4'092'4 B
Jacks or better : a narrative / by T. S. Matthews. 1st ed. New York : Harper & Row, c1977. vii, 354 p. : ill. ; 24 cm. Includes index. [PN4874.M4837A29] 76-57874 ISBN 0-06-012842-9 : 12.50
1. Matthews, Thomas Stanley, 1901- 2. Journalists—United States—Biography. 3. Authors—20th century—Biography. I. Title. **BIP**

MATTHEWS, Thomas Stanley, 1901- 920.5
Name and address, an autobiography. New York, Simon and Schuster, 1960. 309p. 22cm. [PN4874.M4837A3] 60-6724
I. Title.

Matthews, Vincent, 1947-

MATTHEWS, Vincent, 1947- 796.4'26 B
My race be won [by] Vincent Matthews, with Neil Amdur. New York, Charterhouse [1974] 396 p. 22 cm. Autobiographical. [GV697.M34A35] 73-93025 ISBN 0-88327-023-4 10.00
1. Matthews, Vincent, 1947- 2. Running. I. Amdur, Neil, joint author. II. Title.

Matthews William, 1770-1854.

DURKIN, Joseph Thomas, 1903- 922.273
William Matthews, priest and citizen. Foreword by John W. McCormack. New York, Benziger [1964, c.1963] vii, 162p. illus., ports. 22cm. Bibl. 64-1710 4.95
1. Matthews William, 1770-1854. I. Title.

Matthiessen, Francis Otto,

SWEEZY, Paul Marlor, 1910- ed. 928.1
F. O. Matthiessen, 1902-1950; a collective portrait. Edited by Paul M. Sweezy and Leo Huberman New York, Schuman [1950] xii, 154 p. ports. 22 cm. "Originally published as the October, 1950, issue of ... Monthly review." Contents.Contents. -- The education of a socialist, by F. O. Matthiessen. -- Of crime and punishment, by F. O. Matthiessen. -- The teacher, by L. Marx. -- The making of an American scholar, by B. Bowron. -- American Renaissance, by H. N. Smith. -- Labor and political activities by P. M. Sweezy. -- Notes for a character study, by J. Rackliffe. -- Statements by H. Baker [and others] -- A preliminary bibliography of F. O. Matthiessen (p. 148-154) [PN75.M3S9] 50-58262
1. Matthiessen, Francis Otto, 1902-1950. I. Huberman, Leo, 1903- joint author II. Title.

Mattias, Maria de, 1805-1866.

MASTERSON, Mary Adrian. 271'.979 B
Smiling Maria: Blessed Maria de Mattias; the girl who gave everything for love. Illustrator: Margaret Holt Griffith. Ruma, Ill., Sisters Adorers of the Most Precious Blood [1966] 74 p. illus. (part col.) 21 cm. A brief biography of Maria de Mattias whose schools in nineteenth-century Italy made many friends for the Catholic Church. [BX4700.M3984M37] 92 70-20344
1. Mattias, Maria de, 1805-1866. I. Griffith, Margaret Holt, illus. II. Title.

Mattingly, Edward Raymond, 1919-1942.

RAABE, Evelyn Marie, 1903- 922.273
The white robe. [The biography of Edward Raymond Mattingly. San Francisco? 1951] 194 p. illus., ports. 23 cm. [BX4705.M429R3] 51-3573
1. Mattingly, Edward Raymond, 1919-1942. I. Title.

Mattix, Velva.

†MATTIX, Velva. 286'.1'0924 B
I cried ... and He answered / Velva Mattix. Denver : Accent Books, c1976. 160 p. : ill. ; 21 cm. [BX6495.M363A35] 76-42815 ISBN 0-916406-59-8 pbk. : 2.95
1. Mattix, Velva. 2. Baptists—Wyoming—Midwest—Biography. 3. Midwest, Wyo.—Biography. 4. Friedreich's ataxia—Biography. I. Title.

Mattson, Hans, 1832-1893.

MATTSON, Hans, 1832-1893. 973'.04'397
Reminiscences : the story of an emigrant / Hans Mattson. New York : Arno Press, 1979, c1891. p. cm. (Scandinavians in America) Translation of Minnen. Reprint of the ed. published by D. D. Merrill Co., St. Paul. [E184.S23M413 1979] 78-15201 ISBN 0-405-11651-9 : 22.00
1. Mattson, Hans, 1832-1893. 2. Swedish Americans—Biography. 3. India—Description and travel—1859-1900. I. Title. II. Title: The story of an emigrant. **BIP**

Maua, Irineo Evangelista de Souza, visconde de, 1813-1889.

MARCHANT, Anyda, 1911- 380.0924
Viscount Maua and the empire of Brazil; a biography of Irineu Evangelista de Sousa, 1813-1889. Berkeley, Univ. of Calif. Pr. [c.]1965. xx, 291p. port. 23cm. Bibl. [F2536.M2675] 65-10773 6.50
1. Maua, Irineo Evangelista de Souza, visconde de, 1813-1889. 2. Brazil—Hist.—1822-1889. 3. Brazil—Econ. condit. I. Title. **BIP**

Maud United Methodist Church.

CLOUSE, Joe V. 287'.6764'197
The history of Maud United Methodist Church, 1874-1974. Written by Joe V. Clouse and F. E. Cooley. [Maud, Tex., 1974] 1 v. (unpaged) illus. 28 cm. [BX8481.M3M38] 74-83517
1. Maud United Methodist Church. 2. Maud, Tex.—Biography. I. Cooley, Floyd E., joint author. II. Title.

Maugham, Frederic Herbert Maugham, 1st Viscount, 1866-1958.

MAUGHAM, Robin, 1916- 823'.9'14 B
Somerset and all the Maughams / Robin Maugham. Westport, Conn. : Greenwood Press, 1977, c1966. xiv, 270 p., [12] leaves of plates : ill. ; 23 cm. Reprint of the ed. published by New American Library, New York. Includes bibliographical references and index. [PR6025.A858Z517 1977] 75-22759 lib. bdg.: 18.75
1. Maugham, Robin, 1916- —Biography. 2. Maugham, William Somerset, 1874-1965—Biography. 3. Maugham, Frederic Herbert Maugham, 1st Viscount, 1866-1958. 4. Maugham family. I. Title.

Maugham, Robin,

MAUGHAM, Robin, 1916- 823'.9'14 B
Escape from the shadows; an autobiography. New York, McGraw-Hill [1973, c1972] xii, 273 p. illus. 24 cm. Bibliography: p. 239-245. [PR6025.A858Z5 1973] 72-7418 ISBN 0-07-040969-2 8.95
I. Title.

Maugham, Robin, 1916- —Biography.

MAUGHAM, Robin, 1916- 823'.9'14 B
Escape from the shadows; an autobiography. New York, McGraw-Hill [1973, c1972] xii, 273 p. illus. 24 cm. Bibliography: p. 239-245. [PR6025.A858Z5 1973] 72-7418 ISBN 0-07-040969-2 8.95
I. Title.

MAUGHAM, Robin, 1916- 823'.9'14 B
Somerset and all the Maughams / Robin Maugham. Westport, Conn. : Greenwood Press, 1977, c1966. xiv, 270 p., [12] leaves of plates : ill. ; 23 cm. Reprint of the ed. published by New American Library, New York. Includes bibliographical references and index. [PR6025.A858Z517 1977] 75-22759 lib. bdg.: 18.75
1. Maugham, Robin, 1916- —Biography. 2. Maugham, William Somerset, 1874-1965—Biography. 3. Maugham, Frederic Herbert Maugham, 1st Viscount, 1866-1958. 4. Maugham family. I. Title.

Maugham, Syrie, 1879-1955.

FISHER, Richard B. 747'.22 B
Syrie Maugham / Richard B. Fisher. London : Duckworth, 1979. 78 p., [4] leaves of plates : ill. (some col.) ; 29 cm. Bibliography: p. 77-78. [NK2047.6.M38F57] 79-313010 ISBN 0-7156-1307-3 : 13.95
1. Maugham, Syrie, 1879-1955. 2. Interior decorators—England—Biography. I. Title. Distributed by Biblio Distribution Centre, Totowa, NJ 07511 **BIP**

Maugham, William Somerset, 1874-1965.

CORDELL, Richard Albert. 823'.9'12 B
Somerset Maugham, a writer for all seasons; a biographical and critical study, by Richard A. Cordell. [2d ed.] Bloomington, Indiana University Press [1969] 308 p. illus., ports. 22 cm. Bibliography: p. 295-299. [PR6025.A86Z56 1969] 78-3602 6.95
1. Maugham, William Somerset, 1874-1965.

KANIN, Garson, 1912- 823.912
Remembering Mr. Maugham. Foreword by Noel Coward. [1st ed.] New York, Atheneum, 1966. vi, 313p. 22cm. [PR6025.A86Z65] 66-23574 5.95
1. Maugham, William Somerset, 1874-1965. I. Title.

MAUGHAM, Robin, 1916- 928.91209
Somerset and all the Maughams [New York] New Amer. Lib. [1967, c.1966] 280p. illus. 18cm. (Signet bk., Q3166) Bibl. [PR6025.A858S6] .95 pap.,
1. Maugham, William Somerset, 1874-1965. 2. Maugham, Frederic Herbert Maugham, 1st viscount, 1866-1958. I. Title. **BIP**

MAUGHAM, William Somerset, 1874-1965. 940.54'81
Strictly personal / by W. Somerset Maugham. New York : Arno Press, 1977 p. cm. (The works of W. Somerset Maugham) (Series: Maugham, William Somerset, 1874-1965. Works. 1976.) Reprint of the 1st ed. published in 1941 by Doubleday, Doran, Garden City, N.Y. [D811.5.M2957 1976] 75-25376 ISBN 0-405-07829-3 : 15.00
1. Maugham, William Somerset, 1874-1965. 2. World War, 1939-1945—Personal narratives, English. I. Title. II. Series. **BIP**

MENARD, Wilmon. 823.912
The two worlds of Somerset Maugham. [1st ed.] Los Angeles, Sherbourne Press [1965] x, 374 p. illus., ports. 24 cm. "The writings of W. Somerset Maugham": p. 371-374. [PR6025.A86Z76] 65-27855
1. Maugham, William Somerset, 1874-1965. I. Title.

NAIK, M. K. 828.91208
W. Somerset Maugham, by M. K. Naik. [1st ed.] Norman. Univ. of Okla. Pr. [1966] ix, 221p. 22cm. Bibl. [PR6025.A86Z77] 66-13430 4.95
1. Maugham. William Somerset. 1874-1965. I. Title.

PFEIFFER, Karl G 928.2
W. Somerset Maugham; a candid portrait. Introd. by Jerome Weidman. [1st ed.] New York, W. W. Norton [1959] 222p. illus. 22cm. [PR6025.A86Z83] 59-5622
1. Maugham, William Somerset, 1874- I. Title.

RAPHAEL, Frederic, 1931- 823'.9'12 B
W. Somerset Maugham and his world / Frederic Raphael. New York : Scribner, [1977] 128 p. : ill. ; 24 cm. Includes index. Bibliography: p. 120-121. [PR6025.A86Z85] 76-19742 ISBN 0-684-14839-0 : 8.95
1. Maugham, William Somerset, 1874-1965. 2. Authors, English—20th century—Biography. I. Title. **BIP**

RAPHAEL, Frederic, 1931- 823'.9'12 B
W. Somerset Maugham and his world / Frederic Raphael. London : Thames and Hudson, 1976. 128 p. : ill. ; 24 cm. Title on spine: Somerset Maugham and his world. Includes index. Bibliography: p. 120-121. [PR6025.A86Z85 1976] 77-359502 ISBN 0-500-13059-0 : £3.95
1. Maugham, William Somerset, 1874-1965. 2. Authors, English—20th century—Biography. I. Title. II. Title: Somerset Maugham and his world.

Maugham, William Somerset, 1874-1965—Addresses, essays, lectures.

W. Somerset Maugham, 823'.9'12 B
novelist, essayist, dramatist / by Charles Hanson Towne ... [et al.] ; with a note on novel writing by Mr. Maugham. Folcroft, Pa. : Folcroft Library Editions, 1976. 64 p. ; 20 cm. Reprint of the 1925 ed. published by G. H. Doran Co., New York. Contents.Contents.—Farrar, J. Introduction.—Towne, C. H. Mr. W. Somerset Maugham at home.—Van Doren, C. and Van Doren, M. W. Somerset Maugham.—Mann, D. L. Somerset Maugham in his mantle of mystery.—Goodrich, M. A. After ten years "Of human bondage."—Maugham, W. S. To a young novelist.—Appreciations of his work. [PR6025.A86Z89 1976] 76-13210 ISBN 0-8414-8551-8 lib. bdg. : 7.50
1. Maugham, William Somerset, 1874-1965—Addresses, essays, lectures. I. Towne, Charles Hanson, 1877-1949. Contents omitted

Maugham, William Somerset, 1874-1965—Biography.

CURTIS, Anthony. 823'.9'12
Somerset Maugham / Anthony Curtis. 1st American ed. New York : Macmillan, 1977. 216 p. : ill. ; 26 cm. Includes index. Bibliography: p. [208] [PR6025.A86Z5718 1977] 77-6618 ISBN 0-02-529280-3 : 12.95
1. Maugham, William Somerset, 1874-1965—Biography. 2. Authors, English—20th century—Biography.

CURTIS, Anthony. 823'.9'12
Somerset Maugham / Anthony Curtis. 1st American ed. New York : Macmillan, 1977. 216 p. : ill. ; 26 cm. Includes index. Bibliography: p. [208] [PR6025.A86Z5718 1977] 77-6618 ISBN 0-02-529280-3 : 12.95
1. Maugham, William Somerset, 1874-1965—Biography. 2. Authors, English—20th century—Biography. **BIP**

MAUGHAM, Robin, 1916- 823'.9'12 B
Conversations with Willie : recollections of W. Somerset Maugham / by Robin Maugham. New York : Simon and Schuster, c1978. 188 p., [8] leaves of plates : ill. ; 22 cm. [PR6025.A86Z755] 78-2641 ISBN 0-671-24046-3 : 8.95
1. Maugham, William Somerset, 1874-1965—Biography. 2. Authors, English—20th century—Biography. I. Title. **BIP**

MAUGHAM, Robin, 1916- 823'.9'14 B
Somerset and all the Maughams / Robin Maugham. Westport, Conn. : Greenwood Press, 1977, c1966. xiv, 270 p., [12] leaves of plates : ill. ; 23 cm. Reprint of the ed. published by New American Library, New York. Includes bibliographical references and index. [PR6025.A858Z517 1977] 75-22759 lib. bdg.: 18.75
1. Maugham, Robin, 1916- —Biography. 2. Maugham, William Somerset, 1874-1965—Biography. 3. Maugham, Frederic Herbert Maugham, 1st Viscount, 1866-1958. 4. Maugham family. I. Title.

MAUGHAM, William Somerset, 1874-1965. 823'.9'12 B
The summing up / W. Somerset Maugham. New York : Arno Press, 1976, c1938. p. cm. (The works of W. Somerset Maugham) (Series: Maugham, William Somerset, 1874-1965. Works. 1976.) Reprint of the ed. published by Doubleday, Doran, Garden City, N.Y. [PR6025.A86Z525 1976] 75-25377 ISBN 0-405-07830-7 : 15.00
1. Maugham, William Somerset, 1874-1965—Biography. I. Title. II. Series.

MORGAN, Ted, 1932- 823'.9'12 B
Maugham / Ted Morgan. New York : Simon and Schuster, 1979, c1980. p. cm. Includes index. Bibliography: p. [PR6025.A86Z765 1979] 79-21905 ISBN 0-671-24077-3 : 16.95
1. Maugham, William Somerset, 1874-1965—Biography. 2. Authors, English—20th century—Biography. **BIP**

Maugham, William Somerset, 1874-1965—Journeys—Andalusia.

MAUGHAM, William Somerset, 1864-1965. 914.6'8'04
Andalusia, "the land of the Blessed Virgin" / by W. Somerset Maugham. New York : Arno Press, 1977. p. cm. (The works of W. Somerset Maugham) (Series: Maugham, William Somerset, 1874-1965. Works. 1976.) First ed. published in 1920 under title: The land of the Blessed Virgin. Reprint of the 1935 ed. published by Knopf, New York. [DP302.A46M3 1976] 75-25381 ISBN 0-405-07833-1 : 15.00
1. Maugham, William Somerset, 1874-1965—Journeys—Andalusia. 2. Andalusia—Description and travel. I. Title. II. Series.

Maukar, Daniel.

DOWARD, Jan S. 629.132'52'0924 B
Last tiger out; the true story of Dan Maukar, ace pilot in the Indonesian Air Force, by Jan S. Doward. Mountain View, Calif., Pacific Press Pub. Association [1973] 127 p. illus. 23 cm. [TL540.M372D68] 72-92689
1. Maukar, Daniel. I. Title.

Mauldin, William Henry,

MAULDIN, William Henry, 1921- 741'.0924 B
The brass ring [by] Bill Mauldin. [1st ed.] New York, Norton [1971] 275 p. illus. 25 cm. [NC1429.M428A2 1971] 78-152671 ISBN 0-393-07463-3 7.95
I. Title.

Maunoir, Julien, 1606-1683.

HARNEY, Martin Patrick, 1896- 922.2441
Good father in Britiany; the life of Blessed Julien Maunoir, by Martin P. Harney. [Boston, St. Paul Editions [1964] 322 p. illus., map (on lining papers) ports. 22 cm. Bibliography: p. 321-322. [BX4700.M399H3] 64-19478
1. Maunoir, Julien, 1606-1683. I. Title.

HARNEY, Martin Patrick, 1896- 922.2441
Good father in Brittany; the life of Blessed Julien Maunoir [Boston] St. Paul Eds. [dist. Daughters of St. Paul, c.1964] 322p. illus., map (on lining papers) ports. 22cm. Bibl. 64-19478 5.00;4.00 pap.,
1. Maunoir, Julien, 1606-1683. I. Title.

Maupassant, Guy de, 1850-1893.

LERNER, Michael G. 843'.8 B
Maupassant / Michael G. Lerner. New York : G. Braziller, 1975. 301 p., [4] leaves of plates : ports. ; 22 cm. Includes index. Bibliography: p. [291]-293. [PQ2353.L44 1975] 75-10912 ISBN 0-8076-0803-3 : 12.50
1. Maupassant, Guy de, 1850-1893. **BIP**

SHERARD, Robert Harborough, 1861-1943. 843'.8 B
The life, work, and evil fate of Guy de Maupassant (gentilhomme de lettres) / by Robert Harborough Sherard. Folcroft, Pa. : Folcroft Library Editions, 1976. p. cm. Reprint of the 1926 ed. published by T. Werner Laurie, London. [PQ2353.S5 1976] 76-15985 ISBN 0-8414-7621-7 lib. bdg. : 20.00
1. Maupassant, Guy de, 1850-1893. I. Title.

STEEGMULLER, Francis, 1906- 843'.8 B
Maupassant, a lion in the path. Freeport, N.Y., Books for Libraries Press [1972, c1949] viii, 430 p. 23 cm. Includes bibliographical references. [PQ2353.S8 1972] 76-39210 ISBN 0-8369-6812-3
1. Maupassant, Guy de, 1850-1893. I. Title.

Maurelian, Brother.

BATTERSBY, William John. 378.1'011'0924 B
Brother Maurelian: founder of Christian Brothers College, Memphis, visitor of the district of St. Louis, by W. J. Battersby. Winona, Minn., St. Mary's College Press [1968] xv, 174 p. illus., ports. 23 cm. Bibliography: p. 169. [LD961.C317 1880.B3] 76-289066
1. Maurelian, Brother. 2. Christian Brothers' College, Memphis, Tenn.—History. I. Title.

Mauriac, Francois,

MAURIAC, Francois, 1885- 928.4
Proust's way; translated from the original French "Du cote de chez Proust" by Elsie Pell. New York, Philosophical Library [1950] 105 p. port. 23 cm. [PQ2631.R63Z772] 50-6681
I. Proust,Marcel, 1871-1922. II. Title.

Maurice, Frederick Denison, 1805-1872.

BROSE, Olive J. 283'.0924 B
Frederick Denison Maurice, rebellious conformist [by] Olive J. Brose. [Athens] Ohio University Press [1972, c1971] xxiii, 308 p. illus. 22 cm. Bibliography: p. 294-301. [BX5199.M3B76] 74-141380 ISBN 0-8214-0092-4 12.50
1. Maurice, Frederick Denison, 1805-1872.

COURTNEY, Janet Elizabeth 192 B Hogarth, 1865-
Freethinkers of the nineteenth century / by Janet E. Courtney. Norwood, Pa. : Norwood Editions, 1976. p. cm. Reprint of the 1920 ed. published by Chapman & Hall, London. Contents.Contents.—Frederick Denison Maurice.—Mathew Arnold.—Charles Bradlaugh.—Thomas Henry Huxley.—Leslie Stephen.—Harriet Martineau.—Charles Kingsley. [B1569.C6 1976] 76-17266 ISBN 0-8482-0386-0 : 25.00
1. Maurice, Frederick Denison, 1805-1872. 2. Arnold, Matthew, 1822-1888—Religion and ethics. 3. Bradlaugh, Charles, 1833-1891. 4. Huxley, Thomas Henry, 1825-1895. 5. Stephen, Leslie, Sir, 1832-1904. 6. Martineau, Harriet, 1802-1876. 7. Kingsley, Charles, 1819-1875. I. Title. BIP

Maurin, Peter.

SHEEHAN, Arthur T. 922.273
Peter Maurin: gay believer. [1st ed.] Garden City, H.Y. Hanover House [1959] 217 p. 22 cm. [BX4705.M4563S5] 59-12644
1. Maurin, Peter. I. Title.

Mauritius—Biog.

HOLLINGWORTH, Derek 969.820922
They came to Mauritius; portraits of the eighteenth and nineteenth centuries. [New York] Oxford [c.]1965. xv, 175p. illus., maps. ports. 19cm. (Three crowns bk.) Bibl. [DT469.M46A14] 66-535 1.40 pap.,
1. Mauritius—Biog. I. Title.

Maurois, Andre,

MAUROIS, Andre, 848'.9'1208 B 1885-1967.
Memoirs, 1885-1967. Translated from the French by Denver Lindley [1st ed.] New York, Harper & Row [1970] 439 p. port. 25 cm. (A Cass Canfield book) The first part of this work was published in 1942, in French under title: Memoires; in English translation under title: I remember, I remember. [PQ2625.A95Z5213 1970b] 76-83611 10.00

Maury, Matthew Fontaine, 1806-1873.

JAHNS, Patricia. 925
Matthew Fontaine Maury & Joseph Henry, scientists of the Civil War. New York, Hastings House [1961] 308 p. 22 cm. [GC30.M4J3] 61-7201
1. Maury, Matthew Fontaine, 1806-1873. 2. Henry, Joseph, 1797-1878. 3. U.S.—History—Civil War, 1861-1865.

LEWIS, Charles 359.3'31'0924 B Lee, 1886-
Matthew Fontaine Maury, the pathfinder of the seas. New York, AMS Press [1969] xvii, 264 p. illus., ports. 23 cm. Reprint of the 1927 ed. [GC30.M4L4 1969] 72-98638
1. Maury, Matthew Fontaine, 1806-1873. BIP

WILLIAMS, Frances Leigh. 925.5
Matthew Fontaine Maury, scientist of the sea. New Brunswick, Rutgers University Press [1963] xx, 720 p. illus., ports., charts, forms. 25 cm. Bibliography: p. 659-692. "Bibliography of the published works of Matthew Fontaine Maury": p. 693-710. [GC30.M4W5] 63-10564
1. Maury, Matthew Fontaine, 1806-1873. I. Title.

WILLIAMS, Frances 551.4600924 Leigh
Ocean pathfinder; a biography of Matthew Fontaine Maury. New York, Harcourt [c.1966] 192p. illus., maps. port. 20cm. Bibl. [V63.M3W5] 66-4869 3.95
1. Maury, Matthew Fontaine, 1806-1873. I. Title.

WILLIAMS, Frances 551.4600924 (B) Leigh.
Ocean pathfinder; a biography of Matthew Fontaine Maury. [1st ed.] New York, Harcourt, Brace & World [1966] 192 p. illus., maps, ports. 20 cm. Bibliography: p. 185-186. [V63.M3W5] 66-4869
1. Maury, Matthew Fontaine, 1806-1873. I. Title.

Maury, Matthew Fontaine, 1806-1873—Juvenile literature.

BEATY, Janice J. 92
Seeker of seaways; a life of Matthew Fontaine Maury, pioneer oceanographer, by Janice J. Beaty. Illus. by Joseph Cellini. [New York] Pantheon [1966] 162, [3] p. illus. 22cm. (Pantheon portrait) Bibl. [GC30.M4B45] 66-12460 3.95
1. Maury, Matthew Fontaine, 1806-1873—Juvenile literature. I. Title.

*PARRIOTT, Virginia 910.45 [B] Patterson.
Maury, master mariner; a biography of Matthew Fontaine Maury, pathfinder of the seas. New York, Vantage [1973] 45 p. illus. 21 cm. ISBN 0-533-00540-X 3.95
1. Maury, Matthew Fontaine, 1806-1873—Juvenile literature. I. Title.

Maus, Cynthia Pearl,

MAUS, Cynthia Pearl, 1880- 922.6
Time to remember; the memoirs of Cynthia Pearl Maus. New York, Exposition [c.1964] 278p. illus., ports. 24cm. 64-25103 5.00
I. Title.

Maverick, Maury, 1895-1954.

HENDERSON, Richard 973.9'0924 B B., 1921-
Maury Maverick, a political biography, by Richard B. Henderson. Foreword by Joe B. Frantz. Austin, University of Texas Press [1970] xxiii, 386 p. illus., ports. 24 cm. Bibliography: p. [355]-370. [E748.M415H4] 75-134494 8.50
1. Maverick, Maury, 1895-1954.

Maverick, Samuel Augustus, 1803-1870.

SEXTON, Irwin, 1921- 923.973
Samuel A. Maverick, by Irwin and Kathryn Sexton. San Antonio, Tex., Naylor [c.1964] viii, 68p. illus., port. 20cm. Bibl. 63-21360 2.95
1. Maverick, Samuel Augustus, 1803-1870. I. Sexton, Kathryn, joint author. II. Title.

Mavor, Osborne Henry, 1888-1951.

LUYBEN, Helen L v. 12
James Bridie: clown and philospher, by Helen L. Luyben. Philadelphia, University of Pen[n]sylvania Press [1965] 180 p. 22 cm. Bibilography: p. 177-178. [PR6025.A885Z77 1965] 64-24508
1. Mavor, Osborne Henry, 1888-1951. I. Title.

Maweja Apollo.

KEIDEL, Levi O. 248'.246'0924 B
Black Samson : an African's astounding pilgrimage to personhood / by Levi Keidel. Carol Stream, Ill. : Creation House, c1975. 144 p. ; 21 cm. Includes bibliographical references. [BV4935.M36K44 1975] 75-22577 ISBN 0-88419-116-8 : 3.50
1. Maweja Apollo. 2. Conversion. I. Title.

Mawson, Douglas, Sir, 1882-1958.

BICKEL, Lennard. 919.89
Mawson's will : the greatest survival story ever written / Lennard Hillary. New York : Stein and Day, 1977. 237 p., [8] leaves of plates : ill. ; 24 cm. [G875.B5A34 1977] 76-50125 8.95
1. Mawson, Douglas, Sir, 1882-1958. 2. Australasian Antarctic Expedition, 1911-1914. 3. Antarctic regions. 4. Explorers—Australia—Biography. I. Title. BIP

Maxey, Samuel Bell, 1825-1895.

HORTON, Louise, 976.4'06'0924 B 1916-
Samuel Bell Maxey; a biography. Austin, University of Texas Press [1974] xii, 222 p. illus. 23 cm. Bibliography: p. [197]-211. [F391.M478H67] 73-17406 ISBN 0-292-77509-1 10.00
1. Maxey, Samuel Bell, 1825-1895. BIP

Maximilian, Emperor of Mexico, 1832-1867.

CORTI, Egon 972'.07'0924 B Caesar, conte, 1886-1953.
Maximilian and Charlotte of Mexico. Translated from the German by Catherine Alison Phillips. [Hamden, Conn.] Archon Books 1968. xii, 976 p. illus., facsims., map, ports. 24 cm. Reprint of the 1928 ed. Bibliography: p. 949-962. [F1233.M4542 1968] 68-20375 20.00
1. Maximilian, Emperor of Mexico, 1832-1867. 2. Charlotte, consort of Maximilian, Emperor of Mexico, 1840-1927. 3. Mexico—History—European intervention, 1861-1867. BIP

HARDING, Bertita 923.172 (Leonarz)
Phantom crown; the story of Maximilian & Carlota of Mexico. [2d ed. Dist. New York, Heinman, 1961, c.]1960[ ] 443p. illus. Bibl. 8.00
1. Maximilian, emperor of Mexico, 1832-1867. 2. Charlotte, consort of Maximilian, emperor of Mexico, 1840-1927. 3. Mexico—Hist.—European intervention, 1861-1867. I. Title.

HASLIP, Joan, 972'.07'0924 B 1911-
The crown of Mexico; Maximilian and his Empress Carlota. New York, Holt, Rinehart and Winston [1972, c1971] viii, 531 p. illus. 22 cm. First published in 1971 under title: Imperial adventurer: Emperor Maximilian of Mexico. Bibliography: p. 512-516. [F1233.M457 1972] 76-155513 ISBN 0-03-086572-7 10.00
1. Maximilian, Emperor of Mexico, 1832-1867. 2. Charlotte, Consort of Maximilian, Emperor of Mexico, 1840-1927. 3. Mexico—History—European intervention, 1861-1867. I. Title.

O'CONNOR, Richard, 972'.07'0924 B 1915-
The cactus throne; the tragedy of Maximilian and Carlotta. [New York] Avon [1976 c1971] 344 p. 18 cm. Includes index. Bibliography: p. 335-336. [F1233.o36] ISBN 0-380-00641-3
1. Maximilian, Emperor of Mexico, 1832-1867. 2. Charlotte, consort of Maximilian, Emperor of Mexico, 1840-1927. 3. Mexico—History—European intervention, 1861-1867. I. Title.
L.C. no. of original edition: 72-136797.

SMITH, Gene. 972'.07'0924 B
Maximilian and Carlota; a tale of romance and tragedy. New York, Morrow, 1973. 318 p. illus. 25 cm. Bibliography: p. 295-300. [F1233.S66] 70-182969 ISBN 0-688-00173-4 8.95
1. Maximilian, Emperor of Mexico, 1832-1867. 2. Charlotte, consort of Maximilian, Emperor of Mexico, 1840-1927. I. Title.

Maximilian, Emperor of Mexico, 1832-1867—Juvenile literature.

MCKOWN, Robin 972'.07'0924 B
The execution of Maximilian, June 19, 1867; a Hapsburg emperor meets disaster in the New World. New York, Watts, 1973. 65 p. illus. 22 cm. (A World focus book) Bibliography: p. 64. A biography of Maximilian emphasizing the political events leading to his assumption of power in Mexico and eventual execution. [F1233.M4587] 92 73-3427 ISBN 0-531-02165-3 3.95 (pbk.)
1. Maximilian, Emperor of Mexico, 1832-1867—Juvenile literature. 2. Mexico—History—European intervention, 1861-1867—Juvenile literature. I. Title.

VANCE, Marguerite. 923.172
Ashes of empire; Carlota and Maximilian of Mexico. Illustrated by J. Luis Pellicer. [1st ed.] New York, Dutton, 1959. 159 p. illus. 21 cm. Includes bibliography. [F1233.M547] 59-11502
1. Maximilian, Emperor of Mexico, 1832-1867—Juvenile literature. 2. Charlotte, consort of Maximilian, Emperor of Mexico, 1840-1927—Juvenile literature. I. Title.

Maxwell, Elsa.

MAXWELL, Elsa. 920.7
R.S.V.P.; Elsa Maxwell's own story. [1st ed.] Boston, Little, Brown [1954] 326 p. illus. 22 cm. [CT275.M464718A3] 54-8315
I. Title.

Maxwell family.

MAXWELL, William, 929.2'0973 1908-
Ancestors. [1st ed.] New York, Knopf, 1971. 311 p. 23 cm. Autobiographical. [CS71.M465 1971] 75-136342 ISBN 0-394-43522-2 6.95
1. Maxwell family. I. Title.

Maxwell, Gavin, 1914-1969.

FRERE, Richard, 1922- 500.9'2'4 B
Maxwell's ghost : an epilogue to Gavin Maxwell's Camusfearna / by Richard Frere ; with decorations by Robin McEwan. London : Gollancz, 1976. 253 p., [12] p. of plates : ill., maps, ports. ; 23 cm. [QH31.M35F73] 76-377062 ISBN 0-575-02044-X : £5.50
1. Maxwell, Gavin, 1914-1969. 2. Naturalists—Scotland—Biography. I. Title. BIP

MAXWELL, Gavin. 828.91403
The House of Elrig. [1st ed.] New York, Dutton, 1965. 211 p. illus., ports. 22 cm. Autobiographical. [CT828.M34A3] 65-25604
I. Title.

Maxwell, James Clerk, 1831-1879.

CAMPBELL, Lewis, 530'.0924 B 1830-1908.
The life of James Clerk Maxwell, by Lewis Campbell and William Garnett. With a new pref. and appendix with letters, by Robert H. Kargon. New York, Johnson Reprint Corp., 1969. xxv, xvi, 662 p. illus. (part col.), ports. 22 cm. (The Sources of science no. 85) Reprint of the 1882 ed., with a selection of letters from the 1884 ed. [QC16.M4C2 1969] 69-20272
1. Maxwell, James Clerk, 1831-1879. I. Garnett, William, 1850-1932, joint author. II. Title. BIP

EVERITT, C. W. 530'.092'4 B Francis, 1934-
James Clerk Maxwell : physicist and natural philosopher / C. W. F. Everitt. New York : Scribner, c1975. 205 p. : ill. ; 21 cm. (DBS editions) Includes index. Bibliography: p. 189-193. [QC16.M4E8 1975] 76-354009 7.95. ISBN 0-684-14253-8 pbk. : 2.95
1. Maxwell, James Clerk, 1831-1879. BIP

EVERITT, C. W. 530'.092'4 B Francis, 1934-
James Clerk Maxwell : physicist and natural philosopher / C. W. F. Everitt. New York : Scribner, c1975. 205 p. : ill. ; 21 cm. (DBS editions) Includes index. Bibliography: p. 189-193. [QC16.M4E8 1975] 76-35400 ISBN 0-684-14254-6 : 7.95. ISBN 0-684-14253-8 pbk. : 2.95
1. Maxwell, James Clerk, 1831-1879.

MACDONALD, David Keith 925.3 Chalmers, 1920-
Faraday, Maxwell, and Kelvin. [1st ed.] Garden City, N.Y., Anchor Books, 1964. xvi, 143 p. illus., ports., facsims. 19 cm. (Science study series, S33) [QC15.M27] 64-11313
1. Faraday, Michael, 1791-1867. 2. Maxwell, James Clerk, 1831-1879. 3. Kelvin, William Thomson, baron, 1824-1907. I. Title. II. Series.

Maxwell, John, 1905-1962.

MCCLURE, David. 759.9411 B
John Maxwell / by David McClure. Edinburgh : Edinburgh University Press, c1976. 69 p. : ill. (some col.) ; 16 x 22 cm. (Modern Scottish painters ; no. 4)

Bibliography: p. 66. [ND497.M48M33] 77-362553 ISBN 0-85224-300-6 : 5.00
1. Maxwell, John, 1905-1962. 2. Painters—Scotland—Biography.
Distributed by Edinburgh University Press, Totowa, N.J.

Maxwell, Mary Elizabeth Braddon, 1837-1915.

WOLFF, Robert Lee. 823'.8
Sensational Victorian : the life and fiction of Mary Elizabeth Braddon / Robert Lee Wolff. New York : Garland Publishing, 1978. p. cm. Includes bibliographical references and index. [PR4989.M4Z96] 76-52717 ISBN 0-8240-1618-1 : lib.bdg. : 20.00
1. Maxwell, Mary Elizabeth Braddon, 1837-1915. 2. Novelists, English—19th century—Biography. I. Title.

Maxwell, Patricia, 1935-

MAXWELL, Patricia, 1935- 248'.4
How to become a Christian and stay one / by Patricia Maxwell. Nashville : Southern Pub. Association, c1979. 62 p. ; 21 cm. [BX6193.M33A34] 79-4603 ISBN 0-8127-0221-2 pbk. : 0.95
1. Maxwell, Patricia, 1935- 2. Seventh Day Adventists—Biography. I. Title. BIP

May, Earl.

BEAVER, Ninette. 384.54'092'4 B
Behind the mike with Earl May : the story of a broadcasting pioneer / by Ninette Beaver and Bill Tombrink. [Shenandoah, Iowa : May Seed and Nursery Co.], c1976. 64 p., [2] leaves of plates : ill. ; 22 cm. [HE8689.8.B4] 76-376136
1. May, Earl. 2. May Seed and Nursery Company. 3. May Broadcasting Company. 4. Broadcasters—United States—Biography. I. Tombrink, Bill, joint author. II. Title.

May, Ellis Connell,

MAY, Ellis Connell, 1868- 923.473
Recollections of a pioneer Florida judge. New York, Vantage Press [1952-55; v. 1, c1953] 2v. 23cm. Vol. 2 published by the author, Inverness, Fla. Contents.[v.1] 'Gatars, skeeters, and malary.--v.2. From dawa to sunset. 52-13300
I. Title.

May, Karl Friedrich, 1842-1912—Biography.

MAY, Karl Friedrich, 1842-1912. 438
Mein Leben und Streben / Karl May ; Vorwort, Anmerkungen, Nachwort, Sach-, Personen- und geographisches Namenregister von Hainer Plaul. Hildesheim ; New York : Olms, 1975. xiii, 570 p. ; 19 cm. Reprint of the ed. published by F. E. Fehsenfeld, Freiburg i. B., 1910. Includes bibliographical references and indexes. [PT2625.A848Z52 1975] 75-522125 ISBN 3-487-08084-2
1. May, Karl Friedrich, 1842-1912—Biography. I. Plaul, Hainer. II. Title.

May, Mortimer, 1892-

SHANKMAN, Samuel, 1890- 923.673
Mortimer May, foot soldier in Zion. New York, Pub. for Southeastern Region, Zionist Organization of America by Bloch [c.1963] 224p. illus., ports. 20cm. 63-18690 4.50
1. May, Mortimer, 1892- I. Title.

SHANKMAN, Samuel, 1890- 923.673
Mortimer May, foot soldier in Zion. New York, Published for Southeastern Region, Zionist Organization of America by Bloch Pub. Co. [1963] 224 p. illus., ports. 20 cm. [DS151.M3S5] 63-18690
1. May, Mortimer, 1892- I. Title.

May, Scott, 1954- —Juvenile literature.

DOLAN, Edward F., 1924- 796.32'3'0924 B
Scott May, basketball champion / Edward F. Dolan, Jr. and Richard B. Lyttle. 1st ed. Garden City, N.Y. : Doubleday, c1978. x, 85 p., [12] leaves of plates : ill. ; 22 cm. (A Doubleday signal book) Includes index. A biography emphasizing the career of the champion player who was a member of the gold medal winning United States team in the 1976 Olympics. [GV884.M36D64] 92 77-12849 ISBN 0-385-12527-5 : 5.95
1. May, Scott, 1954- —Juvenile literature. 2. Olympic Games, Montreal, Quebec, 1976—Juvenile literature. 3. Basketball players—United States—Biography—Juvenile literature. I. Lyttle, Richard B., joint author. II. Title.

May Seed and Nursery Company.

BEAVER, Ninette. 384.54'092'4 B
Behind the mike with Earl May : the story of a broadcasting pioneer / by Ninette Beaver and Bill Tombrink. [Shenandoah, Iowa : May Seed and Nursery Co.], c1976. 64 p., [2] leaves of plates : ill. ; 22 cm. [HE8689.8.B4] 76-376136
1. May, Earl. 2. May Seed and Nursery Company. 3. May Broadcasting Company. 4. Broadcasters—United States—Biography. I. Tombrink, Bill, joint author. II. Title.

Mayas—Antiquities.

BRUNHOUSE, Robert Levere, 1908- 913'.031'0922
In search of the Maya; the first archaeologists [by] Robert L. Brunhouse. Albuquerque, University of New Mexico Press [1973] vii, 243 p. illus. 22 cm. Bibliography: p. 215-232. [F1435.B874] 73-75904 ISBN 0-8263-0276-9 7.95
1. Mayas—Antiquities. 2. Archaeologists—Biography. 3. Mexico—Antiquities. 4. Central America—Antiquities. I. Title. BIP

BRUNHOUSE, Robert Levere, 1908- 930'.1'0922
Pursuit of the ancient Maya : some archaeologists of yesterday / Robert L. Brunhouse. 1st ed. Albuquerque : University of New Mexico Press, [1975] viii, 252 p., [8] leaves of plates : ill. ; 24 cm. Includes index. Bibliography: p. 221-243. [F1435.B875] 74-27443 ISBN 0-8263-0363-3 : 8.95
1. Mayas—Antiquities. 2. Archaeologists—Biography. 3. Mexico—Antiquities. 4. Central America—Antiquities. I. Title. BIP

Maybeck, Bernard R.

CARDWELL, Kenneth H., 1920- 720'.92'4 B
Bernard Maybeck : artisan, architect, artist / Kenneth H. Cardwell. Santa Barbara : Peregrine Smith, 1977. p. cm. Includes index. Bibliography: p. [NA737.M435C37] 77-13773 ISBN 0-87905-022-5 : 24.95
1. Maybeck, Bernard R. 2. Architects—California—Biography. BIP

Mayer, Francis Blackwell, 1827-1899.

MAYER, Francis Blackwell, 1827-1899. 977.6'04
With pen and pencil on the frontier in 1851 : the diary and sketches of Frank Blackwell Mayer / Bertha L. Heilbron, editor. New York : Arno Press, 1975 [c1932] p. cm. (Reprint of the ed. published by the Minnesota Historical Society, Saint Paul, issued in series: Publications of the Minnesota Historical Society and as v. 1 of the Society's Narratives and documents.) (The Mid-American frontier) [F606.M387 1975] 75-103 ISBN 0-405-06871-9 : 13.00
1. Mayer, Francis Blackwell, 1827-1899. 2. Minnesota—Description and travel—To 1858. 3. Indians of North America—Minnesota. 4. Indians of North America—Social life and customs. I. Heilbron, Bertha Lion, 1895- ed. II. Title. III. Series. IV. Series: Minnesota Historical Society. Publications. V. Series: Minnesota Historical Society. Narratives and documents ; v. 1. BIP

Mayer, Joseph, 1887-

MAYER, Joseph, 1887- 917.3'03 B
The making of a rebel. San Antonio, Naylor [1973] vii, 114 p. 22 cm. [CT275.M46516A33] 73-7988 ISBN 0-8111-0497-4 4.95
1. Mayer, Joseph, 1887- I. Title.

Mayer, Louis Burt, 1885-1957.

CROWTHER, Bosley 927.9143
Hollywood rajah; the life and times of Louis B. Mayer. [New York] Dell [1961, c.1960] 382p. illus. (S13) .60 pap.,
1. Mayer, Louis Burt, 1885-1957. I. Title.

CROWTHER, Bosley. 927.9143
Hollywood rajah; the life and times of Louis B. Mayer. [1st ed.] New York, Holt [1960] 339 p. illus. 22 cm. [PN1998.A3M33] 60-6435
1. Mayer, Louis Burt, 1885-1957. I. Title.

MARX, Samuel, 1902- 791.43'0233'0922 B
Mayer and Thalberg : the make-believe saints / by Samuel Marx. 1st ed. New York : Random House, [1975] xiv, 273 p., [8] leaves of plates : ill. ; 25 cm. Includes index. [PN1998.A3M34] 74-29600 ISBN 0-394-48842-3 : 10.00
1. Mayer, Louis Burt, 1885-1957. 2. Thalberg, Irving, 1899-1936. I. Title.

MARX, Samuel, 1902- 791.43'0232'0922 B
Mayer and Thalberg : the makebelieve saints / by Samuel Marx. London : W. H. Allen, 1976. xiv, 273 p., [16] p. of plates : ill., ports. ; 24 cm. Includes index. [PN1998.A3M34 1976] 76-374951 ISBN 0-491-01755-3 : £5.50
1. Mayer, Louis Burt, 1885-1957. 2. Thalberg, Irving, 1899-1936. 3. Moving-picture producers and directors—United States—Biography. I. Title.

Mayer, Tom.

MAYER, Tom. 629.13'092'4 B
Climb for the evening star. Boston, Houghton, Mifflin, 1974. 115 p. illus. 22 cm. [TL540.M373A33] 73-21811 ISBN 0-395-18483-5 5.95
1. Mayer, Tom. 2. Air pilots—Correspondence, reminiscences, etc. I. Title.

Mayhew, Jonathan, 1720-1766.

AKERS, Charles W. 922.8173
Called unto liberty; a life of Jonathan Mayhew, 1720-1766 [by] Charles W. Akers. Cambridge, Harvard University Press, 1964. xii, 285 p. illus., facsims., ports. 22 cm. "Bibliography of Jonathan Mayhew, with short titles used in the "Notes": p. [238]-241. Bibliographical references included in "Notes" (p. [243]-272) [BX9869.M45A7] 64-21783
1. Mayhew, Jonathan, 1720-1766. I. Title.

Mayhew, Thomas, 1593?-1682.

HARE, Lloyd Custer Mayhew, 1893- 974.4'94'0924 B
Thomas Mayhew, patriarch to the Indians (1593-1682); the life of the worshipful governor and chief magistrate of the Island of Martha's Vineyard; Proprietary of Martha's Vineyard, Nantucket and the Elizabeth Islands, and lord of the Manor of Tisbury in North America, by Lloyd C. M. Hare. New York, AMS Press [1969] xii, 231 p. illus., geneal. table, maps. 23 cm. Reprint of the 1932 ed. [F67.M526 1969] 76-104347
1. Mayhew, Thomas, 1593?-1682. 2. Martha's Vineyard, Mass.—History. 3. Nantucket, Mass.—History. 4. Indians of North America—Massachusetts. 5. Wampanoag Indians—Missions. I. Title.

HARE, Lloyd Custer Mayhew, 1893- 974.4'94'0924 B
Thomas Mayhew, patriarch to the Indians (1593-1682); the life of the worshipful governor and chief magistrate of the Island of Martha's Vineyard; proprietary of Martha's Vineyard, Nantucket and the Elizabeth Islands, and lord of the Manor of Tisbury in North America, by Lloyd C. M. Hare. New York, D. Appleton and Company, 1932. St. Clair Shores, Mich., Scholarly Press, 1971. xii, 231 p. illus., facsim., geneal. table, maps, port. 22 cm. [F67.M526 1971] 76-145070 ISBN 0-403-01012-8
1. Mayhew, Thomas, 1593?-1682. 2. Martha's Vineyard, Mass.—History. 3. Nantucket, Mass.—History. 4. Indians of North America—Massachusetts. 5. Wampanoag Indians—Missions. I. Title.

Maymi, Carmen R.—Juvenile literature.

WHEELOCK, Warren. 973'.04'68 S
Carmen Rosa Maymi, to serve American women ; Roberto Clemente, death of a proud man ; Jose Feliciano, one voice, one guitar / written by Warren H. Wheelock and J. O. "Rocky" Maynes, Jr. ; consultants, Jorge Vadivieso, Amalia Perez, Ruben A. Soruco B. St. Paul : EMC Corp., [1976] p. cm. (Their Hispanic heroes of the U.S.A. ; 3) Brief biographies of three Spanish Americans: the director of the Women's Bureau in the Department of Labor, a popular singer, and a major league baseball star. [E184.S75W5 vol. 3] 920'.0092'6873 75-40230 ISBN 0-88436-244-2. ISBN 0-88436-245-0 pbk.
1. Maymi, Carmen R.—Juvenile literature. 2. Clemente, Roberto, 1934-1972—Juvenile literature. 3. Feliciano, Jose—Juvenile literature. I. Maynes, J. O., joint author. II. Title. III. Title: Roberto Clemente, death of a proud man. IV. Title: Jose Feliciano, one voice, one guitar.

WHEELOCK, Warren H. 973'.04'68
Carmen Rosa Maymi, para servir a las mujeres americanas. Roberto Clementes, la muerte de un hombre orgulloso. Jose Feliciano, una voz, una guitarra / Warren H. Wheelock ; adaptacion, J. O. "Rocky" Maynes ; consultantes, Jorge Valdivieso, Amalia Perez, Fabiola Franco. St. Paul, Minn. : EMC, 1976. p. cm. (His Ilustres hispanos de los EE. UU. ; 3) Translation of Carmen Rosa Maymi, to serve American women. Brief biographies of three Spanish Americans: the director of the Women's Bureau in the Department of Labor, a major league baseball star, and a popular singer. [E184.S75W517 vol. 3] 920'.0092'6873 920 76-2421 ISBN 0-88436-252-3. ISBN 0-88436-253-1 pbk.
1. Maymi, Carmen R.—Juvenile literature. 2. Clemente, Roberto, 1934-1972—Juvenile literature. 3. Feliciano, Jose—Juvenile literature. I. Maynes, J. O. II. Title. III. Title: Roberto Clemente, la muerte de un hombre orgulloso. IV. Title: Jose Feliciano, una voz, una guitarra.

Maynard, Joyce, 1953-

MAYNARD, Joyce, 1953- 917.3'03'920924 B
Looking back; a chronicle of growing up old in the sixties. [1st ed.] Garden City, N.Y., Doubleday, 1973. 160 p. 22 cm. [CT275.M46518A34] 72-76233 ISBN 0-385-02972-1 5.95
1. Maynard, Joyce, 1953- I. Title.

Mayo, Charles Horace, 1865-1939.

CLAPESATTLE, Helen B 926.1
The Doctors Mayo. New York, Pocket Books [1956, c1941] 484p. 17cm. (A Cardinal giant, 30) [R154] 56-58118
1. Mayo, William Worrell, 1819-1911. 2. Mayo, Charles Horace, 1865-1939. 3. Mayo, William James, 1861-1939. I. Title. BIP

CLAPESATTLE, Helen B v. 12
The Doctors Mayo. [2d ed.] Minneapolis, University of Minnesota Press [1960] xiii, 426 p. illus., map. 66-10813
1. Mayo, Charles Horace, 1865-1939. 2. Mayo, William James, 1961-1939. 3. Mayo, William Worrall, 1819-1911. 4. Mayo Clinic, Rochester, Minn. I. Title.

CLAPESATTLE, Helen B. 926.1
The Doctors Mayo. [2d ed., condensed] Minneapolis, University of Minnesota Press [1954, c1941] 426 p. illus. 23 cm. [R154.M33C3 1954] 54-11771
1. Mayo, William Worrell, 1819-1911. 2. Mayo, Charles Horace, 1865-1939. 3. Mayo, William James, 1861-1939. I. Title.

Mayo, Charles Horace, 1865-1939—Juvenile literature.

JOHNSON, Spencer. 610'.92'2
The value of sharing : the story of the Mayo brothers / by Spencer Johnson. 1st ed. La Jolla, Calif. : Value Communications, c1978. p. cm. (ValueTales series) The Mayo brothers, knowing the importance of sharing, enter a career in which they can share their knowledge, skills, and money with sick people and other doctors. [RD27.35.M38J63] 920 B 78-10578 ISBN 0-916392-28-7 lib.bdg. : 5.95
1. Mayo, Charles Horace, 1865-1939—Juvenile literature. 2. Mayo, William James, 1861-1939—Juvenile literature. 3. Surgeons—Minnesota—Rochester—Biography—Juvenile literature. I. Title.
Distributed by Oak Tree Publications, San Diego, CA 92121 BIP

Mayo, Charles W.

MAYO, Charles W. 610'.924 B
Mayo; the story of my family and my career [by] Charles W. Mayo. [1st ed.] Garden City, N.Y., Doubleday, 1968. viii, 351 p. illus., ports. 22 cm. [R154.M33A3] 68-22502 6.95

Mayo, William James, 1861-1939.

CLAPESATTLE, Helen B v. 12
The Doctors Mayo. [2d ed.] Minneapolis, University of Minnesota Press [1960] xiii, 426 p. illus., map. 66-10813
1. Mayo, Charles Horace, 1865-1939. 2. Mayo, William James, 1861-1939. 3. Mayo, William Worrall, 1819-1911. 4. Mayo Clinic, Rochester, Minn. I. Title.

Mayo, William James, 1861-1939—Juvenile literature.

GOODSELL, Jane 610.924
The Mayo brothers, illustrated by Louis S. Glazeman New York, Thomas Y. Crowell [1975] 42 p. ill. 23 cm. (Crowell biography) [R154.M33665] ISBN 0-690-00639-X 1.25 (pbk.)
1. Mayo, William James, 1861-1939—Juvenile literature. 2. Mayo, Charles Horace, 1865-1939—Juvenile literature. 3. Physicians. I. Title.
L.C. card number for original edition: 70-139104. BIP

GOODSELL, Jane. 610'.92'2 B
The Mayo brothers. Illustrated by Louis S. Glanzman. New York, Crowell [1972] 41 p. illus. (part col.) 24 cm. (A Crowell biography) Easy-to-read biography of the two brothers whose life-long interest in medicine resulted in the world-famous Mayo Clinic. [R154.M33G65] 920 70-139104 ISBN 0-690-52750-0 3.75
1. Mayo, William James, 1861-1939—Juvenile literature. 2. Mayo, Charles Horace, 1865-1939—Juvenile literature. I. Glanzman, Louis S., 1922- illus. II. Title.

Mayo, William Worrell, 1819-1911.

CLAPESATTLE, Helen B 926.1
The Doctors Mayo. New York, Pocket Books [1956, c1941] 484p. 17cm. (A Cardinal giant, 30) [R154] 56-58118
1. Mayo, William Worrell, 1819-1911. 2. Mayo, Charles Horace, 1865-1939. 3. Mayo, William James, 1861-1939. I. Title. BIP

CLAPESATTLE, Helen B. 926.1
The Doctors Mayo. [2d ed., condensed] Minneapolis, University of Minnesota Press [1954, c1941] 426 p. illus. 23 cm. [R154.M33C3 1954] 54-11771
1. Mayo, William Worrell, 1819-1911. 2. Mayo, Charles Horace, 1865-1939. 3. Mayo, William James, 1861-1939. I. Title.

Mayo, William Worrell, 1819-1911—Juvenile literature.

RICHARDSON, James P 922.273
Mother Alfred and the Doctors Mayo. Illus. by Charles Dougherty. New York, Benziger Bros. [1959] 177p. illus. 22cm. (Banner books [10]) [BX4705.A515R5] 59-15177
1. Mayo, William Worrell, 1819-1911—Juvenile literature. 2. Alfred, Mother, 1827 or 8-1899—Juvenile literature. 3. Saint Mary's Hospital Rochester, Minn.—Juvenile literature. I. Title.

Mays, Benjamin Elijah,

MAYS, Benjamin Elijah, 1895- 378.1'12'0924 B
Born to rebel; an autobiography, by Benjamin E. Mays. New York, Scribner [1971] xix, 380 p. illus., ports. 24 cm. [LC2851.M72M38] 77-123857 10.00
I. Title.

Mays, Willie, 1931-

EINSTEIN, Charles. 927.96357
Willie Mays: coast to coast Giant. New York, Putnam [1963] 191 p. illus. 21 cm. [GV865.M38E5] 63-9693
1. Mays, Willie, 1931- I. Title. BIP

EINSTEIN, Charles. 927.96357
Willie Mays: coast to coast Giant. New York, Putnam [1963] 191 p. illus. 21 cm. [GV865.M38E5] 63-9693
1. Mays, Willie, 1931-

EINSTEIN, Charles. 796.357'092'4 B
Willie's time : a memoir / edited by Joan Ervin 1st ed. New York : Lippincott, c1979. 352 p. ; 24 cm. [GV865.M38F53] 79-10097 ISBN 0-397-01329-9 : 9.95
1. Mays, Willie, 1931- 2. Baseball players—United States—Biography. I. Title.

HANO, Arnold, 1922- 796.3570924
Willie Mays. New York, Grosset & Dunlap [1966] 190 p. 20 cm. (Grosset sports library) [GV865.M38H29] 66-17205
1. Mays, Willie, 1931-

HANO, Arnold, 1922- 796.357'0924
Willie Mays. New York, Grosset & Dunlap [1970] 216 p. 18 cm. (Tempo books, 5337) [GV865.M38H29 1970] 79-112491 0.75
1. Mays, Willie, 1931-

HANO, Arnold, 1922- 927.96357
Willie Mays, the say-hey kid. New York, Bartholomew House [1961] 159p. 18cm. (Sport magazine library, no. 6) [GV865.M38H3] 61-65431
1. Mays, Willie, 1931- I. Title.

MAYS, Willie, 1931- 796.357
Born to play ball, by Willie Mays, as told to Charles Einstein. New York, Putnam [1955] 168 p. illus. 20 cm. [GV865.M38A3] 55-5779
I. Einstein, Charles. II. Title. BIP

MAYS, Willie, 1931- 796.3570924 B
Willie Mays: My life in and out of baseball, as told to Charles Einstein. [1st ed.] New York, Dutton, 1966. 320 p. illus., ports. 22 cm. [GV865.M38A32] 66-11554
I. Einstein, Charles. II. Title. III. Title: My life in and out of baseball.

MAYS, Willie, 1931- 796.357'092'4 B
Willie Mays: my life in and out of baseball, as told to Charles Einstein. Rev. ed. New York, E. P. Dutton, 1972. 320 p. illus. 22 cm. [GV865.M38A32 1972] 72-89530 ISBN 0-525-23465-9 6.95
I. Einstein, Charles. II. Title. III. Title: My life in and out of baseball.

SCHOOR, Gene. 927.96357
Willie Mays, modest champion. New York, Putnam [1960] 187 p. 21 cm. [GV865.M38S3] 60-5642
1. Mays, Willie, 1931-

SHAPIRO, Milton J. 927.96357
The Willie Mays story. New York, J. Messner [c.1960] 192p. illus. (front.) 22cm. 60-7055 2.95
1. Mays, Willie, 1931- I. Title.

SMITH, Ken, 1902- 927.96357
The Willie Mays story. New York, Greenberg, c1954. 94p. illus. 22cm. [GV865.M38S6] 54-12558
1. Mays, Willie, 1931- I. Title.

Mays, Willie, 1931- —Juvenile literature.

EPSTEIN, Samuel, 1909- 796.357'092'4 B
Willie Mays : baseball superstar / by Sam and Beryl Epstein ; illustrated by Victor Mays. Champaign, Ill. : Garrard Pub. Co., [1975] 96 p. : ill. (some col.) ; 24 cm. A biography of the record-setting baseball player who is one of three in the game's history to hit 600 home runs. [GV865.M38E67] 92 74-20954 ISBN 0-8116-6671-9 lib.bdg. : 3.28
1. Mays, Willie, 1931- —Juvenile literature. I. Epstein, Beryl Williams, 1910- joint author. II. Mays, Victor, 1927- ill. III. Title. BIP

MAY, Julian. 796.357'092'4 B
Willie Mays, most valuable player. Mankato, Minn., Crestwood House [1972] 47 p. illus. 24 cm. (Sports close-up books) A brief biography of the baseball star who spent most of his career with the Giants and was twice named Most Valuable Player. [GV865.M38M3 1972] 92 72-77305 ISBN 0-87191-204-X
1. Mays, Willie, 1931- —Juvenile literature. I. Title.

SULLIVAN, George, 1927- 796.357'092'4 B 92
Willie Mays. Illustrated by David Brown. New York, Putnam [1973] 64 p. illus. 23 cm. (A See and read beginning to read biography) An easy-to-read biography of the recordsetting baseball player who is one of three in the game's history to hit 600 home runs. [GV865.M38S94 1973] 796.357'092'4 B 92 72-97227 72-97227 ISBN 0-399-60824-9 3.39
1. Mays, Willie, 1931- —Juvenile literature. I. Brown, David, 1926- illus. II. Title. BIP

Mazarin, Hortense (Mancini) de La Porte, duchesse de, 1646-1699.

ROSVALL, Toivo David. 944'.033'0924 B
The Mazarine legacy; the life of Hortense Mancini, Duchess Mazarin. New York, Viking Press [1969] 244 p. illus., geneal. table, ports. 22 cm. "Bibliographical note": p. 233-236. [DC130.M39R6 1969] 69-18802 6.95
1. Mazarin, Hortense (Mancini) de La Porte, duchesse de, 1646-1699. I. Title.

Mazarin, Jules, Cardinal, 1602-1661.

HASSALL, Arthur, 1853-1930. 944'.033'0924
Mazarin. Freeport, N.Y., Books for Libraries Press [1970] xv, 187 p. geneal. tables. 23 cm. Reprint of the 1903 ed. [DC130.M4H3 1970b] 73-137379 ISBN 0-8369-5580-3
1. Mazarin, Jules, Cardinal, 1602-1661. 2. France—History—Louis XIV, 1643-1715.

HASSALL, Arthur, 1853-1930. 944'.033'0924
Mazarin. Port Washington, N.Y., Kennikat Press [1970] xv, 187 p. geneal. tables. 21 cm. Reprint of the 1903 ed. Bibliography: p. 183. [DC130.M4H3 1970] 74-112806
1. Mazarin, Jules, Cardinal, 1602-1661. 2. France—History—Louis XIV, 1643-1715. BIP

Mazarin, Jules, Cardinal, 1602-1661—Childhood and youth.

DETHAN, Georges, 1929- 944'.033'0924 B
The young Mazarin / Georges Dethan. London : Thames & Hudson, c1977. 199 p., [8] leaves of plates : ill. ; 23 cm. (Men in office) Translation of Mazarin et ses amis. Includes bibliographical references and index. [DC130.M4D413] 77-371027 ISBN 0-500-87004-7 : 16.95
1. Mazarin, Jules, Cardinal, 1602-1661—Childhood and youth. 2. Statesmen—France—Biography. I. Title.
Distributed by W.W. Norton. BIP

Mazepa, Ivan Stepanovich, hetman of the Cossacks, d. 1709.

MANNING, Clarence Augustus, 1893- 923.247
Hetman of Ukraine: Ivan Mazeppa. New York, Bookman Associates [1957] 234p. 23cm. [DK508.6.M3M3] 57-2869
1. Mazepa, Ivan Stepanovich, hetman of the Cossacks, d. 1709. I. Title.

Mazumdar, Shudha.

†MAZUMDAR, Shudha. 301.41'2'095414 B
A pattern of life : the memoirs of an Indian woman / Shudha Mazumdar ; translated and edited, Geraldine H. Forbes. Columbia, Mo. : South Asia Books, 1977. viii, 246 p. ; 23 cm. Includes index. [HQ1742.M3813] 77-82539 ISBN 0-8364-0009-7 : 12.50 ISBN 0-8364-0014-3 pbk. : 7.00
1. Mazumdar, Shudha. 2. Women—India—Bengal—Biography. I. Forbes, Geraldine Hancock, 1943- II. Title.

Mazzei, Filippo, 1730-1816.

MAZZEI, Filippo, 1730-1816. 917.3 B
Memoirs of the life and peregrinations of the Florentine, Philip Mazzei, 1730-1816. Translated by Howard R. Marraro. New York, Columbia University Press, 1942. Millwood, N.Y., Kraus, 1973. xvi, 447 p. illus. 24 cm. Bibliography: p. [419]-429. [E203.M472 1973] 73-15 19.00
1. Mazzei, Filippo, 1730-1816. 2. United States—Politics and government—Revolution. 3. United States—Description and travel—To 1783. 4. Virginia—History—Revolution. I. Title. BIP

MAZZEI, Filippo, 1730-1816. 973.3'092'4 B
Philip Mazzei, Jefferson's "Zealous Whig" / translated and edited by Margherita Marchione. New York : American Institute of Italian Studies, c1975. 350 p. : ill. ; 24 cm. Translation of v. 1 of Recherches historiques et politiques sur les Etats-Unis de l'Amerique Septentrionale. Bibliography: p. 67-69. [E188.M39213 1975] 75-29945 ISBN 0-916322-01-7 : 7.95. ISBN 0-916322-02-5 pbk. : 4.95
1. Mazzei, Filippo, 1730-1816. 2. United States—History—Colonial period, ca. 1600-1775. 3. United States—Politics and government—1783-1789. I. Marchione, Margherita. II. Title.

Mazzini, Giuseppe, 1805-1872.

BARR, Stringfellow, 1897- 945'.08'0924 B
Mazzini : portrait of an exile / by Stringfellow Barr. New York : Octagon Books, 1975, c1935. viii, 308 p., [1] leaf of plates : port., maps (on lining papers) ; 23 cm. Reprint of the ed. published by H. Holt, New York. Includes index. Bibliography: p. 267-277. [DG552.8.M3B3 1975] 75-29313 ISBN 0-374-90415-4 lib.bdg. : 13.00
1. Mazzini, Giuseppe, 1805-1872. BIP

GRIFFITH, Gwilym Oswald, 1882- 320.1'0924 B
Mazzini: prophet of modern Europe, by Gwilym O. Griffith. New York, H. Fertig, 1970. 381 p. 23 cm. Reprint of the 1932

ed. Bibliography: p. 373-374. [DG552.8.M3G7 1970] 78-80552
1. Mazzini, Giuseppe, 1805-1872. 2. Italy—History—1815-1870. I. Title.

HINKLEY, Edyth. 945'.08'0924 B
Mazzini; the story of a great Italian. Freeport, N.Y., Books for Libraries Press [1970] 287 p. map, port. 23 cm. "First published 1924." Includes bibliographical references. [DG552.8.M3H5 1970] 73-114883
1. Mazzini, Giuseppe, 1805-1872. BIP

HINKLEY, Edyth. 945'.08'0924 B
Mazzini; the story of a great Italian. Port Washington, N.Y., Kennikat Press [1970] 287 p. map, port. 22 cm. Originally published in 1924. Includes bibliographical references. [DG552.8.M3H5 1970b] 78-112807
1. Mazzini, Giuseppe, 1805-1872.

SALVEMINI, Gaetano, 1873- 923.245
Mazzini. Tr. from Italian by I. M. Rawson. New York, Collier [1962] 158p. 18cm. (AS261V) .95 pap.,
1. Mazzini, Giuseppe, 1805-1872. I. Title.

SALVEMINI, Gaetano, 1873- 923.245
Mazzini. Translated from the Italian by I. M. Rawson. Stanford, Stanford University Press [1957] 192p. 23cm. [DG552.8.M3S253] 57-7972
1. Mazzini, Giuseppe, 1805-1872. I. Title.

Mazzuchelli, Samuel Charles, 1806-1864.

ALDERSON, Jo Bartels. 282'.092'4 B
The man Mazzuchelli, pioneer priest [by] Jo Bartels Alderson and J. Michael Alderson. [1st ed. Madison, Wisconsin House, 1974] 1 v. (unpaged) illus. 24 cm. Includes bibliography. [BX4705.M475] 73-89029 ISBN 0-88361-026-4
1. Mazzuchelli, Samuel Charles, 1806-1864. I. Alderson, Jim Michael, joint author. II. Title.

EVANS, Mary Ellen, 1912- 922.273
The seed and the glory; the career of Samuel Charles Mazzuchelli, O. P., on the mid-American frontier. New York, McMullen Books, 1950. 250 p. 22 cm. [BX4705.M475E8] 51-194
1. Mazzuchelli, Samuel Charles, 1806-1864. I. Title.

Mboya, Tom.

RAKE, Alan. 967.62
Tom Mboya: young man of new Africa. [1st ed.] Garden city, N. Y., Doubleday, 1962. 264 p. illus. 22 cm. [DT434.E26M36] 62-11463
1. Mboya, Tom.

McAdoo, Bob, 1951- —Juvenile literature.

TUTTLE, Anthony. 796.32'3'0924 B
Bob McAdoo / by Anthony Tuttle ; illustrated by John Keely. Mankato, Minn. : Creative Education, [1976] p. cm. A brief biography of the basketball star of the Buffalo Braves, Bob McAdoo. [GV884.M2T88] 92 75-34491 ISBN 0-87191-497-2
1. McAdoo, Bob, 1951- —Juvenile literature. 2. Basketball Juvenile literature. I. Keely, John. II. Title. BIP

McAdoo, William Gibbs, 1863-1941.

BROESAMLE, John J. 973.91'3'0924 B
William Gibbs McAdoo; a passion for change, 1863-1917 [by] John J. Broesamle. Port Washington, N.Y., Kennikat Press, 1973. xii, 304 p. 24 cm. (Kennikat Press national university publications. Series in American studies) Bibliography: p. 262-288. [E748.M14B76] 73-83261 ISBN 0-8046-9043-X 15.00
1. McAdoo, William Gibbs, 1863-1941. BIP

McAlmon, Robert, 1896-1956.

MCALMON, Robert Menzies, 1896-1956 928.1
McAlmon and the Lost Generation; a self-portrait. Ed., commentary by robert E. Knoll. Lincoln. Univ. of Neb. Pr. [c.]1962. 396p. illus. 24cm. 62-7872 7.50
I. Knoll, Robert E., ed. II. Title.

ROBERT McAlmon, v. 12
expatriate publisher and writer. Lincoln, University of Nebraska Press, 1959. xiii, 96p. 23cm. 'Nebraska paperback.' 'First published in a series sponsored by the Senate Committee on University Studies (University of Nebraska studies; New series no. 18) 'Contact editions, including books printed at the Treee Mountains Press': p. 81-84. 'The published works of Robert McAlmon': p. 85-89.
1. McAlmon, Robert, 1896-1956. I. Knoll, Robert E BIP

SMOLLER, Sanford J. 818'.5'209 B
Adrift among geniuses; Robert McAlmon, writer and publisher of the twenties [by] Sanford J. Smoller. University Park [Pa.] Pennsylvania State University Press [1974, c1975] 389 p. ports. 24 cm. Bibliography: p. [373]-381. [PS3525.A1143Z88] 74-12257 ISBN 0-271-01173-4
1. McAlmon, Robert, 1896-1956—Biography. 2. Authors—Correspondence, reminiscences, etc. I. Title. BIP

McAnally, David Rice, 1810-1895.

HILLIARD, Frances McAnally Blackburn. 287'.631'0924 B
Stepping stones to glory : from circuit rider to editor and the years in between : life of David Rice McAnally, 1810-1895 / by Frances McAnally Blackburn Hilliard. Baltimore : Gateway Press, 1975. 139 p. : ill. ; 23 cm. [BX8495.M14H54] 75-18536 10.00
1. McAnally, David Rice, 1810-1895. I. Title.

McAstocker, David Plante, 1884-1958.

SCHOENBERG, Wilfred P 922.273
Father Dave, David Plante McAstocker, S. J. Milwaukee, Bruce Pub. Co. [1960] 123p. illus. 22cm. [BX4705.M128S3] 60-8431
1. McAstocker, David Plante, 1884-1958. I. Title.

McAuley, Jeremiah, 1839-1884.

BONNER, Arthur. 267'.1'097471
Jerry McAuley and his mission. Neptune, N.J., Loizeaux Bros. [1967] 123 p. illus., plans, ports. 27 cm. Bibliography: p. 120. [BV2657.M3B6] 67-31009
1. McAuley, Jeremiah, 1839-1884. 2. New York. McAuley Water Street Mission. I. Title.

McAuley, Mary Catherine, 1787-1841.

DEGNAN, Bertrand, Sister. 922.273
Mercy unto thousands; life of Mother Mary Catherine McAuley, foundress of the Sisters of Mercy. With a foreword by Edmund F. Gibbons, titular bishop of Verbe. Westminster, Md., Newman Press, 1957. 394p. illus. 24cm. [BX4705.M13D4] 57-11809
1. McAuley, Mary Catherine, 1778-1841. I. Title.

RAYMOND MARIE, Sister. 922.273
Courageous Catherine; Mother Mary Catherine the first Sister of Mercy. Illustrated by Sister Mary. Milwaukee, Bruce Pub. Co. [1958] 152p. illus. 22cm. (Catholic treasury books) [BX4705.M13R3] 58-122
1. McAuley, Mary Catherine, 1778-1841. 2. Sisters of Mercy. I. Title.

ROBERTO, Brother, 1927- 922.273
Kitty! Come quickly! A story of Mother Catherine McAuley. Illus. by Anthony Joyce. Notre Dame, Ind., Dujarie Press [1955] 94p. illus. 24cm. [BX4705.M13R6] 55-12870
1. McAuley, Mary Catherine, 1787-1841. I. Title.

McBeth, Sue L., d. 1893.

MORRILL, Allen Conrad. 266'.510922 B
Out of the blanket : the story of Sue and Kate McBeth, missionaries to the Nez Perces / by Allen Conrad Morrill, Eleanor Dunlap Morrill ; ill. & cover by Gregory Pole. Moscow : University Press of Idaho, c1978. 420 p. : ill. ; 21 cm. (A Gem book) Includes index. Bibliography: p. 412-416. [E99.N5M63] 78-54426 ISBN 0-89301-056-1 : 11.95
1. McBeth, Sue L., d. 1893. 2. McBeth, Kate C., 1832- 3. Nez Perce Indians—Missions. 4. Missionaries—Idaho—Biography. 5. Indians of North America—Idaho—Missions. I. Morrill, Eleanor Dunlap, joint author. II. Title.

McBey, James, 1883-1959.

MCBEY, James, 1883-1959. 769'.92'4 B
The early life of James McBey : an autobiography, 1883-1911 / edited by Nicolas Barker. Oxford [Eng.] ; New York : Oxford University Press, 1977. ix, 131 p., [8] leaves of plates : ill. ; 25 cm. [NE2047.6.M32A24] 77-6395 ISBN 0-19-211738-6 : 12.00
1. McBey, James, 1883-1959. 2. Etchers—Scotland—Biography. I. Barker, Nicolas. II. Title. BIP

McBride, Grace, 1885-1918.

WATSON, Lila. 922.651
Grace McBride, missionary nurse. Illustrated by Reed McBride. Nashville, Convention Press [1958] 131 p. illus. 19 cm. [BV3487.M2W3] 58-8933
1. McBride, Grace, 1885-1918. I. Title.

McBride, Michele, 1945-

MCBRIDE, Michele, 1945- 362.1'9'7110926 B
The fire that will not die / Michele McBride. Palm Springs, Calif. : ETC Publications, c1979. x, 240 p., [3] leaves of plates : ill. ; 24 cm. [RD96.4.M28] 78-31781 ISBN 0-88280-066-3 : 8.95
1. McBride, Michele, 1945- 2. Our Lady of the Angels (School)—Fire, 1958. 3. Burns and scalds—Biography. 4. Chicago—Fire, 1958. I. Title. BIP

McBride, William John, 1940-

MCBRIDE, William John, 1940- 796.33'3'0924 B
Willie John / the autobiography of Willie John McBride as told to Edmund Van Esbeck. Dublin : Gill & Macmillan, c1976. 160 p., [8] leaves of plates : ports. ; 23 cm. Includes index. [GV944.9.M28A38] 76-383301 ISBN 0-7171-0803-1 : £3.95
1. McBride, William John, 1940- 2. Rugby football players—Ireland—Biography. I. Van Esbeck, Edmund. II. Title.

McBurney, Laressa Cox, 1883- — Biography.

MCBURNEY, Laressa Cox, 1883- 811'.5'4 B
Dr. Charlie's wife : [autobiography] / by Laressa Cox McBurney. San Antonio : Naylor Co., [1975] p. cm. [PS3525.A1199Z52] 75-17546 ISBN 0-8111-0582-2 : 5.95
1. McBurney, Laressa Cox, 1883- — Biography. I. Title.

McCabe, Herb, 1936-

MCCABE, Herb, 1936- 253'.2 B
Love letters of Herb and Sandy McCabe. St. Louis, Concordia Pub. House [1973] 188 p. 18 cm. [CT275.M29A45 1973] 73-78879 ISBN 0-570-03169-9 0.95 (pbk)
1. McCabe, Herb, 1936- 2. McCabe, Sandy. I. McCabe, Sandy, joint author. II. Title. BIP

McCabe, Robin.

RUTTENCUTTER, Helen Drees. 786.1'092'4 B
Pianist's progress / by Helen Drees Ruttencutter. 1st ed. New York : Crowell, c1979. 158 p. ; 22 cm. "Much of this work appeared originally in The New Yorker." [ML417.M17R9] 78-22464 ISBN 0-690-01761-8 : 8.95
1. McCabe, Robin. 2. Pianists—United States—Biography. I. Title. BIP

McCall, Dorothy Lawson.

MCCALL, Dorothy Lawson. 917.95'03'40924 B
The Copper King's daughter; from Cape Cod to Crooked River. With an introd. by Tom Lawson McCall. [1st ed.] Portland, Or., Binfords & Mort [1972] vii, 190 p. illus. 23 cm. [CT275.M32A3] 74-188836 ISBN 0-8323-0203-1 4.95
I. Title.

McCall, Tom, 19132-

MCCALL, Tom, 1913- 979.5'04'0924 B
Tom McCall, Maverick : an autobiography / with Steve Neal. 1st ed. Portland, Or. : Binford & Mort, c1977. xiii, 296 p. : ill. ; 22 cm. Includes index. [F881.35.M33A37] 77-85394 ISBN 0-8323-0288-0 : 12.50. ISBN 0-8323-0289-9 pbk. : 7.50
1. McCall, Tom, 19132- 2. Oregon—Governors—Biography. 3. Oregon—Politics and government—1951- I. Neal, Steve, 1949- II. Title.

McCall, William Anderson, 1891- — Biography.

MCCALL, William Anderson, 1891- 370'.92'4 B
I thunk me a thaut / William A. McCall. New York : Teachers College Press, [1975] vii, 40 p. : ill. ; 23 cm. Autobiographical. [LA2317.M14A34] 74-32566 4.00
1. McCall, William Anderson, 1891- — Biography. I. Title. BIP

McCarthy, Eugene J., 1916-

MCCARTHY, Abigail Quigley. 973.923'092'4 B
Private faces/public places [by] Abigail McCarthy. [1st ed.] Garden City, N.Y., Doubleday, 1972. 448 p. illus. 25 cm [E840.8.M27A3] 70-171305 8.95
1. McCarthy, Eugene J., 1916- I. Title.

MCCARTHY, Eugene J., 1916- 973.923'0924
The McCarthy wit, edited and compiled by Bill Adler. Greenwich, Conn., Fawcett Publications [1969] 127 p. illus. 18 cm. (A Fawcett gold medal book) [E840.8.M3A5] 73-12527 0.75
I. Adler, Bill, ed. II. Title.

McCarthy. Glenn Herbert, 1907-

DAVIS, Wallace, 1902- 926.22338
Corduroy road, the story of Glenn H. McCarthy. Houston, Tex., A. Jones Press, 1951. 282 p. illus. 24 cm. [TN140.M23D3] 52-18397
1. McCarthy. Glenn Herbert, 1907- I. Title.

McCarthy, Joseph Raymond, 1908-1957.

ANDERSON, Jack, 1922- 923.273
McCarthy: the man, the Senator, the "ism", by Jack Anderson and Ronald W. May. Boston, Beacon Press [1952] 431 p. 22 cm. [Beacon studies in freedom and power] [E748.M143A5] 52-11115
1. McCarthy, Joseph Raymond, 1908-1957. 2. Communism—U.S.—1917- I. Title.

BUCKLEY, William Frank, 1925- 973.918
McCarthy and his enemies; the record and its meaning [by] Wm. F. Buckley & L. Brent Bozell. Prologue by William Schlamm. [New ed.] Chicago, H. Regnery Co., 1954 [i. e. 1961] 425 p. 24 cm. Includes bibliography. [E748.M143B8 1961] 61-66796
1. McCarthy, Joseph Raymond, 1909-1957. 2. Subversive activities—U.S. 3. Communism—U.S.—1917- I. Bosell, L. Brent, joint author. II. Title.

COHN, Roy M. 973.921'0924 B
McCarthy, by Roy Cohn. [New York] New American Library [1968] xiii, 292 p. illus., ports. 22 cm. [E748.M143C6] 68-23035
1. McCarthy, Joseph Raymond, 1908-1957. I. Title.

COOK, Fred J. 973.918'0924
The nightmare decade; the life and times of Senator Joe McCarthy [by] Fred J. Cook. New York, Random House [1971] xi, 626 p. ports. 24 cm. Includes bibliographical references. [E748.M143C64] 74-102320 ISBN 0-394-46270-X 10.00
1. McCarthy, Joseph Raymond, 1908-1957. 2. Subversive activities—U.S. 3. Communism—U.S.—1917- 1. Title.

CROSBY, Donald F., 1933- 973.918'092'4
God, church, and flag : Senator Joseph R. McCarthy and the Catholic Church, 1950-1957 / by Donald F. Crosby. Chapel Hill : University of North Carolina Press, c1978. xv, 307 p. ; 22 cm. Includes index. Bibliography: p. 279-291. [E748.M143C76] 77-14064 ISBN 0-8078-1312-5 : 16.95
1. McCarthy, Joseph Raymond, 1908-1957. 2. United States. Congress. Senate—Biography. 3. Catholics—United States—History. 4. United States—Politics and government—1953-1961. 5. United States—Politics and government—1953-1961. 6. Legislators—United States—Biography. I. Title. BIP

FORD, Sherman, 1929- 923.273
The McCarthy menance; an evaluation of the facts and an interpretation of the evidence. New York, William-Frederick Press, 1954. 94p. 22cm. [E748.M143F6] 54-12422
1. McCarthy, Joseph Raymond, 1909- I. Title.

GOLDSTON, Robert C. 973.921'092'4
The American nightmare; Senator Joseph R. McCarthy and the politics of hate [by] Robert Goldston. Indianapolis, Bobbs-Merrill [1973] 202 p. illus. 24 cm. Bibliography: p. 191-194. [E748.M143G58] 73-1748 5.95
1. McCarthy, Joseph Raymond, 1908-1957. I. Title.

MATUSOW, Allen J., comp. 973.921'0924
Joseph R. McCarthy, edited by Allen J. Matusow. Englewood Cliffs, N.J., Prentice-Hall [1970] vii, 181 p. 21 cm. (Great lives observed) (A Spectrum book.) Bibliography: p. 175-177. [E748.M143M3] 73-104846 5.95
1. McCarthy, Joseph Raymond, 1908-1957. BIP

OSHINSKY, David M., 1944- 322'.2'0924
Senator Joseph McCarthy and the American labor movement / David M. Oshinsky. [Columbia] : University of Missouri Press, 1976. 206 p. ; 24 cm. Includes index. Bibliography: p. [185]-198. [E748.M143O83] 75-23426 ISBN 0-8262-0188-1 : 10.50
1. McCarthy, Joseph Raymond, 1908-1957. 2. Trade-unions—United States—Political activity—History. I. Title. BIP

RORTY, James, 1890- 923.273
McCarthy and the Communists [by] James Rorty and Moshe Decter. Boston, Beacon Press [1954] viii, 163p. 20cm. [E748.M143R6] 54-11622
1. McCarthy, Joseph Raymond, 1909- 2. Communism—U. S.—1917- 3. Internal security— U. S. I. Decter, Moshe, joint author. II. Title.

RORTY, James, 1890- 973.918'0924 B
McCarthy and the Communists [by] James Rorty and Moshe Decter. Westport, Conn., Greenwood Press [1972, c1954] viii, 163 p. 22 cm. [E748.M143R6 1972] 78-138179 ISBN 0-8371-5636-X
1. McCarthy, Joseph Raymond, 1908-1957. 2. Communism—United States—1917- 3. Internal security—United States. I. Decter, Moshe, joint author. II. Title. BIP

ROVERE, Richard Halworth 923.273
Senator Joe McCarthy. New York, Meridian Books [1960, c.1959] 280p. 19cm. (M 98) 1.25 pap.,
1. McCarthy, Joseph Raymond, 1909-1957 I. Title BIP

ROVERE, Richard Halworth, 1915- v. 12
Senator Joe McCarthy. New York, Meridian Books [1960] 280 p. (Meridian books. M98) 63-56619
1. McCarthy, Joseph Raymond, 1909-1957. I. Title.

ROVERE, Richard Halworth, 1915- 923.273
Senator Joe McCarthy. [1st ed.] New York, Harcourt, Brace [1959] 280 p. 21 cm. [E748.M143R62] 59-9464
1. McCarthy, Joseph Raymond, 1908-1957.

WISCONSIN Citizens' Committee on McCarthy's Record 923.273
The McCarthy record. Madison, Wis., c1952. 134 p. illus. 19 cm. [E813.M3W5] 52-34613
1. McCarthy, Joseph R., 1909- I. Title.

McCarthy, Joseph Raymond, 1908-1957—Addresses, essays, lectures.

REEVES, Thomas C., 1936- comp. 322.4'2
McCarthyism / edited by Thomas C. Reeves. Huntington, N.Y. : R. E. Krieger Pub. Co., 1978, c1973. 139 p. ; 23 cm. (The American problem studies) Reprint of the ed. published by Dryden Press, Hinsdale, Ill., which was issued in series: American problem studies. Contents.Contents.—Joseph R. McCarthy: the man and his methods: Griffith R. The making of a demagogue. Glazer N. The methods of Senator McCarthy. Wechsler, J. A. To be called before the McCarthy Committee. Buckley, W. F., Jr. and Bozell, L. B. McCarthy and his evidence. Cohn, R. History will vindicate him.—McCarthyism and partisan politics: Theoharis, A. Truman and the Red scare. Latham, E. Republicans and the defeat of 1948. Rovere, R. McCarthyism and a bipartisan doctrine.—McCarthyism and mass movements: Viereck, P. Populism gone sour. Bell, D. The Status theory. Rogin, M. P. Pluralists and agrarian radicalism. Lipset, S. M. and Raab, E. An instrument rather than creater. Bibliography: p. 136-139. [E743.5.R43 1978]OMcCarthyism / edited by Thomas C. Reeve
1. McCarthy, Joseph Raymond, 1908-1957—Addresses, essays, lectures. 2. United States. Congress. Senate—Biography—Addresses, essays, lectures. 3. Internal security—United States—Addresses, essays, lectures. 4. Legislators—United States—Biography—Addresses, essays, lectures. 5. Communism—United States—1917- —Addresses, essays, lectures. 6. Subversive activities—United States—Addresses, essays, lectures. I. Title.
Contents omitted BIP

McCarthy, Kitty (Lynch) 1858-

MCCARTHY, Mary Eunice. 920.7
Meet Kitty. New York, Crowell [1957] 186p. illus. 21cm. [CT275.M335M3] 57-11092
1. McCarthy, Kitty (Lynch) 1858- I. Title.

McCarthy, Mary Therese, 1912- —Bibliography.

GOLDMAN, Sherli Evens. 016.818'5'209
Mary McCarthy; a bibliography. [1st ed.] New York, Harcourt, Brace & World [1968] ix, 80 p. 21 cm. [Z8531.8.G6] 68-12574
1. McCarthy, Mary Therese, 1912- —Bibliography. BIP

McCartney, Paul.

MCCARTNEY, Paul. 784'.092'4 B
Paul McCartney in his own words / written and edited by Paul Gambaccini ; designed by Pearce Marchbank. New York : Flash : [distributed by Quick Fox], 1976. 111 p. : ill. ; 26 cm. [ML410.M115A3] 76-8068 ISBN 0-8256-3910-7 pbk. : 3.95
1. McCartney, Paul. 2. Rock musicians—England—Biography. I. Gambaccini, Paul, 1949- II. Title.

McClary, Clebe.

MCCLARY, Clebe. 248'.2 B
Living proof / Clebe McClary, [with Diane Barker]. Atlanta, GA : Cross Roads Publishers, c1978. 150 p. : ill. ; 22 cm. [BR1725.M3117A34] 78-66754 3.95
1. McClary, Clebe. 2. Christian biography—United States. 3. Vietnamese Conflict, 1961-1975—Personal narratives, American. 4. Soldiers—United States—Biography. I. Barker, Diane, joint author. II. Title.

McClellan, George Brinton,

MCCLELLAN, George Brinton, 1865-1940. 923.273
The gentleman and the tiger; the autobiography of George B. McClellan, Jr. Edited from the original manuscript in the possession of the New-York Historical Society by Harold C. Syrett. [1st ed.] Philadelphia, Lippincott [c1956] 375p. illus. 22cm. [E748.M145A3] 56-5859
I. Title.

McClellan, George Brinton, 1826-1885.

HASSLER, Warren W. 923.573
General George B. McClellan, shield of the Union. [1st ed.] Baton Rouge, Louisiana State University Press [1957] 350 p. illus. 24 cm. Includes bibliography. [E467.1.M2H4] 57-7497
1. McClellan, George Brinton, 1826-1885.

HASSLER, Warren W 923.573
General George B. McClellan, shield of the Union. [1st ed.] Baton Rouge, Louisiana State University Press [1957] 350p. illus. 24cm. Includes bibliography. [E467.1.M2H4] 57-7497
1. McClellan, George Brinton, 1826-1885. I. Title.

HASSLER, Warren W. 973.7'41'0924
General George B. McClellan, shield of the Union, by Warren W. Hassler, Jr. Westport, Conn., Greenwood Press [1974, c1957] xvi, 350 p. illus. 24 cm. Reprint of the 1st ed. published by Louisiana State University Press, Baton Rouge. Bibliography: p. 331-342. [E467.1.M2H4 1974] 74-9619 ISBN 0-8371-7606-9
1. McClellan, George Brinton, 1826-1885. BIP

WILLIAMS, Thomas Harry, 1909- 923.573
McClellan, Sherman, and Grant. New Brunswick, N.J., Rutgers [c.1962] 113p. illus. 20cm. (Brown and Haley lectures, 1962) Bibl. 62-21246 3.50 bds.,
1. McClellan, George Brinton 1826-1885. 2. Sherman, William Tecumseh, 1820-1891. 3. Grant, Ulysses Simpson, Pres. U. S., 1822-1885. I. Title. BIP

WILLIAMS, Thomas Harry, 1909- 355.3'31'0922 B
McClellan, Sherman, and Grant / T. Harry Williams. Westport, Conn. : Greenwood Press, 1976 [c1962] p. cm. Reprint of the ed. published by Rutgers University Press, New Brunswick, N.J., in series: The Brown & Haley lectures, 1962. Bibliography: p. [E467.W5 1976] 76-29654 ISBN 0-8371-9280-3 lib.bdg. : 10.75
1. McClellan, George Brinton, 1826-1885. 2. Sherman, William Tecumseh, 1820-1891. 3. Grant, Ulysses Simpson, Pres. U.S., 1822-1885. 4. Generals—United States—Biography. I. Title. II. Series: The Brown & Haley lectures ; 1962.

McClenahan, William U., 1899-

MCCLENAHAN, William U., 1899- 610'.92'4 B
G. P. / by William U. McClenahan ; edited by John L. McClenahan. Philadelphia : Dorrance, c1974. 132 p. : ill. ; 22 cm. [R154.M193A33] 74-15159 ISBN 0-8059-2075-7 : 8.95
1. McClenahan, William U., 1899- 2. Physicians (General practice)—Correspondence, reminiscences, etc. I. Title.

McClendon, Sarah.

MCCLENDON, Sarah. 070.4'3'0924 B
My eight presidents / Sarah McClendon. 1st ed. New York : Wyden Books : trade distribution by Simon and Schuster, c1978. 239 p., [8] leaves of plates : ill. ; 22 cm. Includes index. [PN4874.M345A35] 78-3713 ISBN 0-88326-150-2 : 10.00
1. McClendon, Sarah. 2. Journalists—United States—Biography. 3. Presidents—United States. I. Title.

McCloskey, Eunice Mildred (Lon Coske)

MCCLOSKEY, Eunice Mildred (Lon Coske) 1906- 818.5203
Potpourri; an autobiography, by Eunice McCloskey. Philadelphia, Dorrance [1966] 157 p. illus., ports. 21 cm. [PS3525.A1548P6] 66-24869
I. Title.

McClure, Alexander Kelly, 1828-1909.

MCCLURE, Alexander Kelly, 1828-1909. 973
Colonel Alexander K. McClure's Recollections of half a century. New York : AMS Press, 1976. viii, 502 p., [7] leaves of plates : ill. ; 23 cm. Reprint of the 1902 ed. published by Salem Press Co., Salem, Mass. Includes index. [E415.7.M12 1976] 76-172762 ISBN 0-404-00086-X : 31.50
1. McClure, Alexander Kelly, 1828-1909. 2. United States—History—1849-1877—Addresses, essays, lectures. 3. United States—History—Civil War, 1861-1865—Addresses, essays, lectures. 4. United States—History—1865-1898—Addresses, essays, lectures. 5. United States—Biography. I. Title. II. Title: Recollections of half a century. BIP

McClure, Samuel Sidney, 1857-1949.

LYON, Peter, 1915- 920.5
Success story, the life and times of S. S. McClure. New York, Scribner 1963 viii, 433 p. illus., ports. 24 cm. "Author's note and bibliography": p. 413-422. [PN4874.M35L9] 63-16757
1. McClure, Samuel Sidney, 1857-1949. 2. McClure's magazine. I. Title.

McCollum, Elmer Verner,

MCCOLLUM, Elmer Verner, 1879- 925.4
From Kansas farm boy to scientist; the autobiography of Elmer Verner McCollum. Lawrence, Univ. of Ken. Pr. [c.]1964. 253p. ports. 24cm. 64-14559 5.00
I. Title.

McCollum, Ruby.

HUIE, William Bradford, 1910- v. 12
Ruby McCollum; woman in the Suwannee jail. Rev. ed. [New York] New American Library [1964] 190 p. illus., port. 18 cm. (A Signet book) 65-5658
1. McCollum, Ruby. I. Title.

McConnell, Francis John,

MCCONNELL, Francis John, Bp., 1871- 922.773
By the way, an autobiography. New York, Abingdon-Cokesbury Press [1952] 286 p. illus. 23 cm. [BX8495.M18A3] 52-402
I. Title.

McCormack, John, 1884-1945.

FOXALL, Raymond 927.8
John McCormack. Foreword by Sir Compton Mackenzie. Staten Island, N. Y., Alba [1964, c.1963] 185p. illus., ports. 23cm. 63-20090 3.95 bds.,
1. McCormack, John, 1884-1945. I. Title.

MCCORMACK, John, 1884-1945. 782.1'092'4 B
John McCormack; his own life story. Transcribed by Pierre V. R. Key. Edited and with an introd. by John Scarry. New York, Vienna House, 1973. xlii, 433 p. illus. 22 cm. Reprint with new introd. of the 1918 ed. published by Small, Maynard, Boston. [ML420.M13A3 1973] 72-93828 ISBN 0-8443-0092-6 15.00
1. McCormack, John, 1884-1945. 2. Musicians—Correspondence, reminiscences, etc. I. Key, Pierre Van Rensselaer, 1872-1945. II. Scarry, John, ed.

McCormack, John, 1884-1945—Juvenile literature.

HUME, Ruth (Fox) 1922- 927.8
The king of song: the story of John McCormack, by Ruth and Paul Hume. Illus. by Irene Murray. New York, Hawthorn [c.1964] 185p. illus. 22cm. (Credo bks., 23) [ML3930.M12H8] 64-19486 2.95
1. McCormack, John, 1884-1945—Juvenile literature. I. Hume, Paul, joint author. II. Title.

SHEA, Richard. j92
In the palm of his hand; a story of John McCormack. Illus. by Carolyn Lee Jagodits. Notre Dame, Ind., Dujarie Press [1962] 95 p. illus. 24 cm. [ML3930.M12S5] 62-6334
1. McCormack, John, 1884-1945 — Juvenile literature. I. Title.

McCormick, Cyrus Hall, 1809-1884.

CASSON, Herbert Newton, 1869- 681'.763'0924 B
Cyrus Hall McCormick: his life and work, by Herbert N. Casson. Freeport, N.Y., Books for Libraries Press [1971] xii, 264 p. illus., facsims., ports. 23 cm. Reprint of the 1909 ed. [HD9486.U4M33 1971] 74-152977 ISBN 0-8369-5729-6
1. McCormick, Cyrus Hall, 1809-1884. 2. Harvesting machinery.

HUTCHINSON, William Thomas, 1895- 681'.7 B
Cyrus Hall McCormick, by William T. Hutchinson. [1st ed.] New York, Da Capo Press, 1968 [c1930-35] 2 v. illus., facsims., map, ports. 24 cm. (The American scene) (A Da Capo Press reprint series.) Contents.Contents.—v. 1. Seed-time, 1809-1856.—v. 2. Harvest, 1856-1884. "Bibliographical guide": v. 1, p. 473-476; v. 2, p. 773-775. [HD9486.U4M35 1968] 68-8127 37.50
1. McCormick, Cyrus Hall, 1809-1884. 2. Harvesting machinery.

McCormick, Edna Haynes,

MCCORMICK, Edna Haynes, 1889- 920
William Lee McCormick; a study in tolerance, with genealogy. [1st ed.] Dallas, Book Craft [1956] 300p. illus. 24cm. 'Denton, Texas, centennial edition.' qMcCormick, William Lee, 1863-1945. [CT275.M4175M3 1956] 57-205
I. Title.

McCormick family.

HARLAN, Roma C., 1912- 929.2'0973
William McCormick 1732-1812; a soldier in the American Revolution: his ancestors and descendants 1570-1969. Compiled [by] Roma C. Harlan [and] Hazel S. Wright. [Washington] 1969. a-c, 25 l. 30 cm. [CS71.M13 1969] 78-3148
1. McCormick family. I. Wright, Hazel Sproul, 1899- joint author.

McCormick, Nettie (Fowler), 1835-1923.

BURGESS, Charles O. 923.673
Nettie Fowler McCormick: profile of an American philanthropist. Madison, State Hist. Soc. of Wis. [c.]1962. 88p. 23cm. (Logmark eds.) Bibl. 62-34857 3.00
1. McCormick, Nettie (Fowler), 1835-1923. I. Title.

RODERICK, Stella Virginia. 923.673
Nettie Fowler McCormick. Rindge, N. H., R. R. Smith, 1956. 332p. illus. 25cm. [HD9486.U4M39] 56-11748
1. McCormick, Nettie (Fowler) 1835-1923. I. Title.

McCormick, Robert Rutherford, 1880-1955.

GIES, Joseph. 070.4'092'4 B
The Colonel of Chicago / by Joseph Gies. 1st ed. New York : Dutton, c1979. 261 p., [7] leaves of plates : ill. ; 25 cm. Includes index. Bibliography: p. 246-250. [PN4874.M36G5] 79-967 ISBN 0-525-08267-0 : 12.95
1. McCormick, Robert Rutherford, 1880-1955. 2. The Chicago tribune. I. Title. **BIP**

WALDROP, Frank C. 070.5'092'4
McCormick of Chicago : an unconventional portrait of a controversial figure / by Frank C. Waldrop. Westport, Conn. : Greenwood Press, 1975, c1966. p. cm. Reprint of the ed. published by Prentice-Hall, Englewood Cliffs, N.J. Includes index. Bibliography: p. [PN4874.M36W3 1975] 74-1782 ISBN 0-8371-7401-5 lib.bdg. : 19.00
1. McCormick, Robert Rutherford, 1880-1955. I. Title.

McCormick, William Fergus.

VEYSEY, Alex, 1927- 796.33'3'0924 B
Fergie / Alex Veysey. Christchurch : Whitcoulls, 1976. 194 p., [16] leaves of plates : ill. ; 22 cm. [GV944.9.M3V49] 76-377459 ISBN 0-7233-0469-6
1. McCormick, William Fergus. 2. Rugby football players—New Zealand—Biography. I. Title.

McCormick, William Lee, 1863-1945.

MCCORMICK, Edna Haynes, 1889- 920
William Lee McCormick, a study in tolerance; with genealogy. Dallas, Book Craft [1952] 234p. illus. 24cm. [CT275.M4175M3] 53-16566
1. McCormick, William Lee, 1863-1945. I. Title.

McCowen, Alec.

MCCOWEN, Alec. 792'.028'0924 B
Young Gemini / by Alec McGowen. New York : Atheneum, 1979. p. cm. [PN2598.M17A33] 79-1991 ISBN 0-689-11004-9 : 6.95
1. McCowen, Alec. 2. Actors—Great Britain—Biography. I. Title. **BIP**

McCown, Joseph Albert, 1865-1934.

GASSMAN, McDill (McCown). 926.146
Daddy was an undertaker; illustrated by John V. Graven. New York, Vantage Press [1952] 248 p. illus. 23 cm. [RA622.7.M3G3] 52-8132
1. McCown, Joseph Albert, 1865-1934. I. Title.

McCoy, Frank Ross, 1874-1954.

BIDDLE, William S. 355.3'32'0924 B
Major General Frank Ross McCoy, 1874-1954: soldier-statesman-American by William S. Biddle. Lewistown, Pa., Mifflin County Historical Society, 1956. [15] p. port. 23 cm. [E745.M32B52] 74-173042
1. McCoy, Frank Ross, 1874-1954.

McCoy, Herbert Newby, 1870-1945.

ROBERTSON, George Ross, 1888- v. 12
Herbert Newby McCoy, 1870-1945, a biographical sketch, by G. Ross Robertson. Early American researches in the chemistry of radioactivity and rare earths. Los Angeles, 1964. 69 p. ports. 20 cm. "Scientific writings of Herbert McCoy": p. 20-30. 66-47710
1. McCoy, Herbert Newby, 1870-1945. 2. Radio — chemistry — Hist. I. Title.

McCoy, Kid, 1873-1940.

CANTWELL, Robert, 1908- 796.8'3'0924 B
The real McCoy; the life and times of Norman Selby. Princeton [N.J., Auerbach Publishers, 1971] 184 p. illus., ports. 25 cm. "A Vertex book." Bibliography: p. 179-180. [GV1132.M2C3] 70-147202 ISBN 0-87769-072-3
1. McCoy, Kid, 1873-1940. I. Title.

McCoy, Marie Bell.

MCCOY, Marie Bell. 920.9617712
Journey out of darkness. New York, McKay [1963] ix, 205 p. 21 cm. Autobiographical. [HV1792.M2A3] 63-19346
I. Title.

McCoy, Tim.

MCCOY, Tim. 978'.03'0924 B
Tim McCoy remembers the West : an autobiography / by Tim McCoy with Ronald McCoy. 1st ed. Garden City, N.Y. : Doubleday, 1977. p. cm. Includes index. [F595.M14A37] 76-56316 ISBN 0-385-12798-7 : 8.95
1. McCoy, Tim. 2. Pioneers—The west—Biography. 3. The west—History—1848-1950—Sources. I. McCoy, Ronald, joint author. II. Title.

McCracken, Harold,

MCCRACKEN, Harold, 1894- 917.98'03'40924
Roughnecks and gentlemen. [1st ed.] Garden City, N.Y., Doubleday, 1968. xi, 441 p. illus., ports. 24 cm. Autobiographical. [PS3525.A1748Z53] 68-22530 7.95
I. Title.

McCracken, Walter E.

MCCRACKEN, Walter E. 920
Hey, Crackie! New York, Vantage Press [c.1960] 118p. 22cm. 2.75 bds.,
I. Title.

McCrary, Sherman.

TRAINER, Orvel. 345'.73'02523
Deathroads : the story of the donut shop murders / by Orvel Trainer, with Robert N. Miller and Joseph A. Fanciulli. 1st ed. [Boulder, Colo.] : Pruett Pub. Co., [1979] p. cm. Includes index. [HV6533.C2T7] 79-15827 ISBN 0-87108-538-0 : 13.95
1. McCrary, Sherman. 2. Murder—California. 3. Crime and criminals—United States—Biography. I. Miller, Robert N., joint author. II. Fanciulli, Joseph A., joint author. III. Title. **BIP**

McCullers, Carson (Smith) 1917-1967.

GRAVER, Lawrence, 1931- 813'.5'2
Carson McCullers. Minneapolis, University of Minnesota Press [1969] 48 p. 21 cm. (University of Minnesota pamphlets on American writers, no. 84) Bibliography: p. 46-48. [PS3525.A1772Z65] 77-628287 0.95
1. McCullers, Carson (Smith) 1917-1967. I. Series: Minnesota. University. Pamphlets on American writers, no. 84 **BIP**

McCullers, Carson Smith, 1917-1967—Biography.

CARR, Virginia Spencer. 813'.5'2
The lonely hunter : a biography of Carson McCullers / by Virginia Spencer Carr. Garden City, N.Y. : Anchor Press, 1976, c1975 xix, 600 p., [24] leaves of plates : ill. ; 24 cm. Includes index. Bibliography: p. [580]-583. [PS3525.A1772Z58 1976] 76-10141 ISBN 0-385-12289-6 pbk. : 5.95
1. McCullers, Carson Smith, 1917-1967—Biography. I. Title.

CARR, Virginia Spencer. 813'.5'2 B
The lonely hunter : a biography of Carson McCullers / by Virginia Spencer Carr. 1st ed. Garden City, N.Y. : Doubleday, 1975. xix, 600 p., [24] leaves of plates : ill. ; 24 cm. Includes index. Bibliography: p. [580]-583. [PS3525.A1772Z58] 74-9478 ISBN 0-385-04028-8 : 12.50
1. McCullers, Carson Smith, 1917-1967—Biography. I. Title. **BIP**

McCulloch, Ben, 1811-1862.

THE life and service of Gen. Ben McCulloch; by Victor M. Rose. Philadelphia, Pictorial bureau of the press, 1888; Austin, Tex., Steck [1958] 2p. l., [25]-260p. illus., ports. 24cm. Facsimile reproduction of the 1st ed. v. 12
1. McCulloch, Ben, 1811-1862. 2. Texas rangers. 3. U. S.—Hist. War with Mexico, 1845-1848— Personal narratives. I. Rose, Victor M d. 1893.

McCulloch, Oscar C., 1843-1891.

WEEKS, Genevieve C. 285'.8'0924 B
Oscar Carleton McCulloch, 1843-1891 : preacher and practitioner of applied Christianity / Genevieve C. Weeks. Indianapolis : Indiana Historical Society, 1976. xvii, 248 p. : ill. ; 24 cm. Includes index. Bibliography: p. 223-235. [BX7260.M216W43] 77-150445
1. McCulloch, Oscar C., 1843-1891. 2. Congregational churches—Clergy—Biography. 3. Clergy—Indiana—Indianapolis—Biography. 4. Indianapolis—Biography.

McCutchan, Robert Guy, 1877-

MCCUTCHAN, Helen Cowles. 783.9'08 S
Born to music : the ministry of Robert Guy McCutchan / by Helen Cowles McCutchan. New York : Hymn Society of America, c1972. 24 p. : port. ; 23 cm. (The Papers of the Hymn Society of America ; 28) [ML3270.H9 no. 28] 780'.92'4 b 74-185596
1. McCutchan, Robert Guy, 1877- I. Title. II. Series: Hymn Society of America. Papers ; 28.

McDaniel, Audrey—Biography.

MCDANIEL, Audrey. 811'.5'4 B
Touched by the Master : reflections on my life and mission / by Audrey McDaniel ; floral designs by Hazel Hoffman. Norwalk, Conn. : C. R. Gibson Co., c1975. 88 p. : ill. ; 22 cm. (C. R. Gibson gift books) [PS3563.A27Z517] 74-83777 ISBN 0-8378-1770-6
1. McDaniel, Audrey—Biography. I. Title.

McDaniel, Eugene B.

MCDANIEL, Eugene B. 959.704'37
Before honor / by Eugene B. McDaniel, with James L. Johnson. 1st ed. Philadelphia : A. J. Holman Co., [1975] 192 p., [4] leaves of plates : ill. ; 22 cm. [DS559.4.M3] 75-20213 ISBN 0-87981-046-7 : 6.95
1. McDaniel, Eugene B. 2. Vietnamese Conflict, 1961-1975—Prisoners and prisons, North Vietnamese. 3. Vietnamese Conflict, 1961-1975—Personal narratives, American. I. Johnson, James Leonard, 1927- joint author. II. Title. BIP

McDermott, R. B.

MCDERMOTT, R. B. 920.5
Country printer; copy I didn't turn in. Philadelphia, Dorrance [1953] 153p. 20cm. [CT275.M428A3] 53-10198
I. Title.

McDonald, David John, 1902-

KELLY, George Edward, 1908- 923.373
Man of steel; the story of David J. McDonald [by] George Kelly and Edwin Beachler. New York, North American Book Co. [1954] 181p. illus. 22cm. [HD8073.M2K4] 54-7228
1. McDonald, David John, 1902- 2. United Steel Workers of America. I. Beachler, Edwin, joint author. II. Title.

McDonald, Iverach.

MCDONALD, Iverach. 327.4'047
A man of The Times : talks and travels in a disrupted world / by Iverach McDonald. London : Hamilton, 1976. xv, 220 p., [8] p. of plates : ill., ports . ; 23 cm. Includes index. [PN5123.M26A3 1976] 76-366819 ISBN 0-241-89404-2 : £5.50
1. McDonald, Iverach. 2. Journalists—Correspondence, reminiscences, etc. 3. Russia—Foreign relations. 4. World politics—20th century. I. Title.

McDonald, Simon, 1907-1968.

ANDERSON, Hugh. 784'.092'4 B
Time out of mind : Simon McDonald of Creswick / Hugh Anderson. Melbourne : National Press, 1974. 153 p., [4] leaves of plates : ill. ; 23 cm. [ML420.M136A8] 75-328986 ISBN 0-909470-16-2
1. McDonald, Simon, 1907-1968. 2. Musicians—Correspondence, reminiscences, etc. I. Title.

McDonald, Tommy.

MCDONALD, Tommy. 927.9633
They pay me to catch footballs, by Tommy McDonald as told to Ed Richter. Foreword by Sonny Jurgensen. [1st ed.] Philadelphia, Chilton Co., Book Division [1962] 123p. illus. 21cm. [GV939.M3A3] 62-16844
I. Richter, ed. II. Title.

McDonald, William Jesse, 1852-1918.

BAUGH, Virgil E. 363.2'09764
A pair of Texas rangers: Bill McDonald and John Hughes [by] Virgil E. Baugh. Washington, Potomac Corral, The Westerners, 1970. vi, 26 p. illus., ports. 23 cm. (The Great western series, no. 9) Includes bibliographies. [F391.B29] 70-147372
1. McDonald, William Jesse, 1852-1918. 2. Hughes, John Reynolds, 1855-1947. I. Title.

McDonald, Worden.

MCDONALD, Worden. 973.91'092'4 B
An old guy who feels good / by Worden McDonald. Berkeley, Calif. : Thorp Springs Press, [1978] p. cm. [CT275.M4334A32] 78-2956 ISBN 0-914476-68-8 pbk. : 4.50
1. McDonald, Worden. 2. United States—Biography. I. Title. BIP

McDougall, Alexander, 1732-1786.

MACDOUGALL, William L. 973.3'092'4 B
American revolutionary : a biography of General Alexander McDougall / William L. MacDougall ; foreword by Richard B. Morris. Westport, Conn. : Greenwood Press, 1977. xiii, 186 p. : ill. ; 22 cm. (Contributions in American history ; no. 57) Includes index. Bibliography: p. [179]-181. [E207.M12M3] 76-15324 ISBN 0-8371-9035-5 lib.bdg. : 13.95
1. McDougall, Alexander, 1732-1786. 2. United States. Army. Continental Army—Biography. 3. Generals—United States—Biography. 4. Statesmen—United States—Biography. I. Title. BIP

McDowall, Sue Ellen (Pride)

MCDOWALL, Sue Ellen (Pride) 1877- 920.7
Cotton and jasmine, a southern mosaic. [1st ed.] New York, Vantage Press [1956] 131p. illus. 21cm. Autobiographical. [CT275.M43415.A3] 56-5524
I. Title.

McDowell, Ephraim, 1771-1830.

RICH, Josephine. 926.1
Pioneer surgeon, Dr. Ephraim McDowell. New York, J. Messner [1959] 192 p. 22 cm. Includes bibliography. [R134.M28R48] 59-7018
1. McDowell, Ephraim, 1771-1830. I. Title.

McDuffie, John, 1883-1950.

MCDUFFIE, John, 1883-1950. 347'.73'2234 B
To inquiring friends if any; autobiography of John McDuffie, farmer, lawyer, legislator, judge. As told to and edited by Mary Margaret Flock. Mobile, Ala., Azalea City Printers [1970?] 300 p. 22 cm. [KF373.M216A3] 75-308752 5.75
1. McDuffie, John, 1883-1950. 2. Alabama—History. I. Flock, Mary Margaret. II. Title.

McEachern, Daniel Victor, 1879-

NANCE, Ellwood Cecil, 1900- 926.2
The Daniel V. McEachern story; saga of a Seattle Scot. College Place, Wash., College Press [1958] 246 p. illus. 24 cm. [CT275.M43414N3] 58-13976
1. McEachern, Daniel Victor, 1879-

McEnroe, John, 1959- —Juvenile literature.

BURCHARD, S. H. 796.34'2'0924 B
John McEnroe / S. H. Burchard. 1st ed. New York : Harcourt Brace Jovanovich, c1979. p. cm. (Sports star) A biography of the tennis star who at the age of 18 became the youngest semifinalist in the 100-year history of Wimbledon. [GV994.M26B87] 92 79-87509 ISBN 0-15-278017-3 : 5.95 ISBN 0-15-684787-6 pbk. : 2.95
1. McEnroe, John, 1959- —Juvenile literature. 2. Tennis players—United States—Biography—Juvenile literature. I. Title.

McFall, Charles H., 1887-

MCFALL, Charles H., 1887- 917.66'14'0350924
The first eighty-five years of my life; an autobiography, by Chas. H. McFall. [Frederick? Okla.] 1972. 53 p. port. 23 cm. [CT275.M434145A33] 74-163525
1. McFall, Charles H., 1887- I. Title.

McFarland, George Bradley, 1866-1942.

MCFARLAND, Bertha (Blount) 926.1
McFarland of Siam; the life of George Bradley McFarland, M. D., D. D. S., afterwards Phra Ach Vidyagama. Edited by George E. McCracken. [1st ed.] New York, Vantage Press [1958] 313p. illus. 21cm. Includes bibliography. [R644.S5M3] 58-14970
1. McFarland, George Bradley, 1866-1942. I. Title.

McFarlin, Robert Martin, 1866-1942.

TYSON, Carl N. 338.7'66'550922 B
The McMan : the lives of Robert M. McFarlin and James A. Chapman / by Carl N. Tyson, James H. Thomas, Odie B. Faulk. 1st ed. [Norman] : Published for the Oklahoma Heritage Association by the University of Oklahoma Press, c1977. xiii, 224 p. : ill. ; 22 cm. (Oklahoma trackmaker series) Includes index. Bibliography: p. 213-217. [HD9570.M22T97] 77-9113 ISBN 0-8061-1446-0 : 7.75
1. McFarlin, Robert Martin, 1866-1942. 2. Chapman, James Allen, 1881-1966. 3. McMann Oil Company—History. 4. McMan Oil and Gas Company—History. 5. Petroleum industry and trade—Oklahoma—History. 6. Businessmen—Oklahoma—Biography. I. Thomas, James Harold, 1943- joint author. II. Faulk, Odie B., joint author. III. Oklahoma Heritage Association. IV. Title. V. Series. BIP

McFee, William, 1881- —Addresses, essays, lectures.

MAULE, Harry Edward, 1886- 823'.912
William McFee, author—engineer : a note on his life and works containing a complete chronological bibliography / by Harry E. Maule. Brooklyn, N.Y. : Haskell House Pub., 1978, c1923 p. cm. Reprint of the 1st ed. published by Doubleday, Page, Garden City, N.Y. "McFee bibliography": p. [PR6025.A225Z77 1977] 77-10734 ISBN 0-8383-2204-2 lib.bdg. : 9.95
1. McFee, William, 1881- —Addresses, essays, lectures. 2. Authors, English—20th century—Biography—Addresses, essays, lectures. I. Title.

McGarrity, Joseph, 1874-1940.

TARPEY, Marie Veronica. 941.5082'1'0924
The role of Joseph McGarrity in the struggle for Irish independence / Maric Veronica Tarpey. New York : Arno Press, 1976, c1970. 363 p. ; 21 cm. (The Irish Americans) Reprint of the author's thesis, St. John's University, New York. Bibliography: p. 351-363. [DA959.T37 1976] 76-6368 ISBN 0-405-09360-8 : 22.00
1. McGarrity, Joseph, 1874-1940. 2. Irish question. I. Title. II. Series. BIP

McGarvey, John William,

MCGARVEY, John William, 1829-1911. 922.673
Autobiography. Lexington, Ky., College of the Bible, 1960. 93 p. 23cm. [BX7343.M24A3] 60-16285
I. Title.

McGavock, Randal William

MCGAVOCK, Randal William 920
Pen and sword; the life and journals of Randal W. McGavock. The biography [by] Herschel Gower, editor. The political and civil War journals, 1853-1862; Jack Allen, editor. Nashville 3; Historical Commission [State Library and Archives Bldg.], 1959,[c1960] 695 p. Bibliographical footnotes. illus. ports., map. 25cm. 60-9243
I. Gower, Herschel. II. Title.

McGehee, Florence.

MCGEHEE, Florence. 817.5
Sailors kiss everybody. New York, Macmillan, 1955. 224 p. 22 cm. Memoirs. [CT275.M43415A3] 55-14797
I. Title.

McGehee, Helen.

UMANA, A., 1910- 793.3'092'4
Helen McGehee, dancer / [conceived by] Alfonso Umana. New York : Editions Heraclita, 1974. [84] p. : ill. ; 22 cm. "List of dance compositions by Helen McGehee": P. [82] [GV1785.M24U42] 74-189546
1. McGehee, Helen. 2. Modern dance. I. Title.

McGiffin, Philo Norton, 1860-1897.

MCGIFFIN, Lee. 952.031
Yankee of the Yalu; Philo Norton McGiffin, American captain in the Chinese Navy, 1885-1895. [1st ed.] New York, Dutton [1968] 160 p. map. 21 cm. Bibliography: p. 158-160. [DS763.M3M3] 68-18350
1. McGiffin, Philo Norton, 1860-1897. I. Title.

McGill, Walter Marshall.

BATES, Lucille M. 285'.1'0924 B
Walter McGill; preacher and penman, by Lucille M. Bates. San Antonio, Tex., Naylor Co. [1971] xv, 110 p. illus., maps, ports. 22 cm. [BX9225.M217B38] 70-152303 ISBN 0-8111-0402-8 5.95
1. McGill, Walter Marshall.

McGillicuddy, Cornelius, 1862-1956—Juvenile literature.

VAN RIPER, Guernsey, 1909- 796.357'092'2
The mighty Macs; three famous baseball managers, by Guernsey Van Riper, Jr. Illustrated by Dom Lupo. Champaign, Ill., Garrard Pub. Co. [1972] 96 p. illus. (part col.) 24 cm. Brief biographies of three of baseball's best known managers. [GV865.A1V3] 920 76-164608 ISBN 0-8116-6663-8
1. McGillicuddy, Cornelius, 1862-1956—Juvenile literature. 2. McGraw, John Joseph, 1873-1934—Juvenile literature. 3. McCarthy, Joe, 1887- —Juvenile literature. I. Lupo, Dom, illus. II. Title. BIP

McGillivray, Alexander, 1740 ca.-1793.

ORRMONT, Arthur. 970.3 B
Diplomat in warpaint; Chief Alexander McGillivray of the Creeks. London, New York [etc.] Abelard-Schuman, 1968. 192 p. illus., map, ports. 22 cm. Bibliography: p. 187-188. A biography of a man of mixed Scottish and Indian blood who, as chief of the Creek Indians and friend of the British, defended his people's rights against Spanish and American encroachments during and after the American Revolution. [E99.C9O7 1968] 92 AC 68
1. McGillivray, Alexander, 1740 ca.-1793. 2. Creek Indians. I. Title.

McGinley, Gerard,

MCGINLEY, Gerard, 1906-1955. 922.273
A Trappist writes home: letters of Abbot Gerard McGinley, O. C. S. O., to his family. Introd. by Father Raymond. Milwaukee. Bruce Pub. Co. [1960] 175p. illus. 22cm. [BX4705.M193A4] 60-10195
I. Title.

McGinnis, George, 1950- —Juvenile literature.

ARMSTRONG, Robert, 1938- 796.32'3'0924 B
George McGinnis / by Robert Armstrong. Mankato, Minn. : Creative Education, c1977. 31 p. : col. ill. ; 25 cm. (Creative education Sports Superstars) A brief biography of the star player of the Philadelphia 76ers basketball team. [GV884.M23A83] 92 76-42262 ISBN 0-87191-538-3 lib.bdg. 4.95
1. McGinnis, George, 1950- —Juvenile

literature. 2. Basketball players—United States—Biography—Juvenile literature. I. Title.

HASKINS, James, 1941- 796'.32'3'0924 B
George McGinnis / by James Haskins. New York : Hastings House, [1978] p. cm. A biography of the Philadelphia 76er famous for his one-handed shots and fast-paced game. [GV884.M23H37] 92 78-17875 ISBN 0-8038-2688-5 : 6.95
1. McGinnis, George, 1950- —Juvenile literature. 2. Basketball players—United States—Biography—Juvenile literature. I. Title.

McGinnis, Vera.

MCGINNIS, Vera. 791.8 B
Rodeo road; my life as a pioneer cowgirl. New York, Hastings House [1974] 225 p. illus. 22 cm. [GV1834.M32] 74-12317 ISBN 0-8038-2670-2
1. McGinnis, Vera. 2. Rodeos. I. Title. **BIP**

McGlashan, Charles Fayette, 1847-1931.

MCGLASHAN, M. Nona. 979.4'37'0924 B
Give me a mountain meadow : the life of Charles Fayette McGlashan, 1847-1931, imaginative lawyer-editor of the High Sierra, who saved the Donner story from oblivion and launched winter sports in the West / M. Nona McGlashan. Fresno, [Calif.] : Valley Publishers, 1977. viii, 248 p. : ill. ; 24 cm. [F869.T8M32] 77-79315 ISBN 0-913548-41-3 : 12.00 ISBN 0-913548-42-1 pbk. : 4.95
1. McGlashan, Charles Fayette, 1847-1931. 2. McGlashan, M. Nona. 3. Truckee, Calif.—Biography. 4. Nevada Co., Calif.—Biography. 5. Pioneers—California—Truckee—Biography. I. Title.

McGlynn, Edward, 1837-1900.

BELL, Stephen, 1864- 282'.092'4 B
Rebel, priest, and prophet : a biography of Dr. Edward McGlynn / by Stephen Bell. Westport, Conn. : Hyperion Press, 1975, c1937. p. cm. (The Radical tradition in America) Reprint of the ed. published by Devin-Adair, New York. [BX4705.M2B4 1975] 75-301 ISBN 0-88355-206-X : 18.00
1. McGlynn, Edward, 1837-1900. I. Title. **BIP**

MALONE, Sylvester L., ed. 282'.092'4 B
Dr. Edward McGlynn / Sylvester L. Malone. New York : Arno Press, 1978. viii, 135 p., [23] leaves of plates : ill. ; 24 cm. (The American Catholic tradition) Reprint of the 1918 ed. published by Dr. McGlynn Monument Association, New York. [BX4705.M2M3 1978] 77-11298 ISBN 0-405-10841-9 : 12.00
1. McGlynn, Edward, 1837-1900. 2. Catholic Church—Clergy—Biography. 3. Clergy—New York (State)—Biography. 4. New York (State)—Biography. I. Title. II. Series.

McGovern, Ann

MCGOVERN, Ann 92
Christopher Columbus. Illus. by Joe Lasker. New York, Scholastic [c.1962] 63p. col. illus. 16x21cm. (TW382) .35 pap., *I. Title.*

*MCGOVERN, Ann 92
Runaway Slave, the story of Harriet Tubman. Pictures by R. M. Powers. New York, Scholastic [c.1965] unpaged. illus. 15x21cm. (TW638) .45 pap.,
I. Title.

McGovern, Eleanor, 1921-

MCGOVERN, Eleanor, 1921- 328.73'092'4 B
Uphill; a personal story [by] Eleanor McGovern, with Mary Finch Hoyt. Illustrated with photos. Boston, Houghton Mifflin, 1974. xi, 234 p. illus. 22 cm. [E840.8.M338A38] 74-11065 ISBN 0-395-19414-8 7.95
1. McGovern, Eleanor, 1921- 2. McGovern, George Stanley, 1922- I. Hoyt, Mary Finch, joint author. II. Title.

McGovern, George Stanley, 1922-

ANSON, Robert Sam, 1945- 328.73'092'4 B
McGovern: a biography. [1st ed.] New York, Holt, Rinehart and Winston [1972] xiii, 303 p. illus. 22 cm. [E840.8.M34A8 1972] 72-183538 ISBN 0-03-091345-4 7.95
1. McGovern, George Stanley, 1922-

MCGOVERN, George Stanley, 1922- 329.3'01
An American journey; the Presidential campaign speeches of George McGovern. [1st ed.] New York, Random House [1974] xvii, 246 p. illus. 22 cm. [E840.8.M34A52] 73-20595 8.95
1. McGovern, George Stanley, 1922- 2. United States—Politics and government—1969- —Addresses, essays, lectures. 3. Presidents—United States—Election—1972. I. Title.

MCGOVERN, George Stanley, 1922- 973.924'092'4 B
Grassroots : the autobiography of George McGovern. 1st ed. New York : Random House, c1977. p. cm. Includes index. [E840.M29] 77-5999 ISBN 0-394-41941-3 : 12.50
1. McGovern, George Stanley, 1922- 2. United States. Congress. Senate—Biography. 3. Legislators—United States—Biography. 4. United States—Politics and government—1945- I. Title. **BIP**

MCGOVERN, George Stanley, 1922- 328.73'092'4 B
McGovern: the man and his beliefs. Selected and edited by Shirley MacLaine. New York, Norton [1972] 125 p. illus. 21 cm. [E840.8.M34A25 1972] 72-6760 ISBN 0-393-05341-5
I. MacLaine, Shirley, 1934- ed. II. Title.

McGrady, Mike.

MCGRADY, Mike. 301.42'7
The kitchen sink papers : my life as a househusband / Mike McGrady. 1st ed. Garden City, N.Y. : Doubleday, 1975. 185 p. ; 22 cm. [HQ756.M23] 75-5263 ISBN 0-385-04879-3 : 6.95
1. McGrady, Mike. 2. Husbands. 3. Home economics—Biography. I. Title.

McGrail, Joie.

MCGRAIL, Joie. 362.1'9'699424
Fighting back : one woman's struggle against cancer / Joie Harrison McGrail. 1st ed. New York : Harper & Row, c1978. 196 p. ; 22 cm. [RC280.L8M23 1978] 76-26244 ISBN 0-06-012958-1 : 8.95
1. McGrail, Joie. 2. Lungs—Cancer—Biography. I. Title. **BIP**

McGravock, Willie Elizabeth Harding, 1833-1895.

MRS. D. H. M'Gavook; v. 12
life-sketch and thoughts, by Mrs. F. A. Butler. Nashville, Tenn., Barbee & Smith [n. d.] 272p. illus.
1. McGravock, Willie Elizabeth Harding, 1833-1895. I. Butler, Sarah Frances Stringfield.

McGraw, John Joseph, 1873-1934.

DURSO, Joseph. 796.357'0924 B
The days of Mr. McGraw. Englewood Cliffs, N.J., Prentice-Hall [1969] 243 p. illus., ports. 25 cm. [GV865.M3D8] 69-16633 7.95
1. McGraw, John Joseph, 1873-1934. 2. Baseball. I. Title.

MCGRAW, Blanche (Sindall) 927.96357
The real McGraw, by Mrs. John J. McGraw; edited by Arthur Mann. New York, D. McKay Co. [1953] 336p. illus. 21cm. [GV865.M3M2] 53-7549
1. McGraw, John Joseph, 1873-1934. I. Title.

MCGRAW, John Joseph, 1873-1934. 796.357'092'4 B
My thirty years in baseball. New York, Arno Press, 1974 [c1923] xiii, 265 p. illus. 21 cm. (Popular culture in America) Reprint of the ed. published by Boni & Liveright, New York. [GV865.M3A3 1974] 74-15746 ISBN 0-405-06381-4 17.00
1. McGraw, John Joseph, 1873-1934. 2. Baseball. I. Title. II. Series. **BIP**

McGraw, John Joseph, 1873-1934—Juvenile literature.

VAN RIPER, Guernsey, 1909- 796.357'092'2
The mighty Macs; three famous baseball managers, by Guernsey Van Riper, Jr. Illustrated by Dom Lupo. Champaign, Ill., Garrard Pub. Co. [1972] 96 p. illus. (part col.) 24 cm. Brief biographies of three of baseball's best known managers. [GV865.A1V3] 920 76-164608 ISBN 0-8116-6663-8
1. McGillicuddy, Cornelius, 1862-1956—Juvenile literature. 2. McGraw, John Joseph, 1873-1934—Juvenile literature. 3. McCarthy, Joe, 1887- —Juvenile literature. I. Lupo, Dom, illus. II. Title. **BIP**

McGraw, Tug, 1944-

MCGRAW, Tug, 1944- 796.357'092'4
Screwball [by] Tug McGraw [and] Joseph Durso. Boston, Houghton Mifflin, 1974. x, 178 p. illus. 22 cm. [GV865.M312A37] 74-2132 ISBN 0-395-18646-3 6.95
1. McGraw, Tug, 1944- 2. New York (City). Baseball club (National League, Mets) 3. Baseball. I. Durso, Joseph, joint author. II. Title. **BIP**

McGreevy, Grace.

MCGREEVY, Grace. 917.48
I'm thirsty too! South Brunswick [N.J.] A. S. Barnes [1968] 154 p. illus. 22 cm. Autobiography. [CT275.M43423A3] 68-11076 4.95
I. Title. **BIP**

McGregor, Charlie.

MCGREGOR, Charlie. 791.43'028'0924 B
Up from the walking dead : the Charles McGregor story / written by Sharon Sopher as told by Charles McGregor. 1st ed. Garden City, N.Y. : Doubleday, 1978. 490 p., [4] leaves of plates : ill. ; 22 cm. [HV9468.M34A37] 76-2795 ISBN 0-385-06674-0 : 8.95
1. McGregor, Charlie. 2. Prisoners—United States—Biography. 3. Moving-picture actors and actresses—United States—Biography. I. Sopher, Sharon, joint author. II. Title.

McGregor, Jim.

MCGREGOR, Jim. 796.32'3'0924 B
Called for travelling / Jim McGregor & Ron Rapoport. New York : Macmillan, 1978. p. cm. [GV884.M25A33] 78-9430 ISBN 0-02-583350-2 : 9.95
1. McGregor, Jim. 2. Basketball coaches—United States—Biography. I. Rapoport, Ron, joint author. II. Title.

McGriff family.

HILL, Joseph Edward, 1904- 929'.2'0973
Colonel Patrick McGriff of Chester County, South Carolina, and Montgomery County, Georgia; his children and grandchildren and some others named McGriff. [Leesburg? Fla., 1973] 66 l. 28 cm. On spine: McGriff & allied families. [CS71.M14785 1973] 73-159475
1. McGriff family. 2. McGriff, Patrick, ca. 1745-1810. I. Title. II. Title: McGriff & allied families.

McGrigor, James, Sir, bart., 1771-1858.

BLANCO, Richard L. 355.3'45'0924 B
Wellington's surgeon general, Sir James McGrigor / Richard L. Blanco. Durham, N.C. : Duke University Press, 1974. xiv, 235 p., [4] leaves of plates : ill. ; 25 cm. Includes bibliographies and index. [UH347.M26B5] 74-75477 ISBN 0-8223-0318-3 : 9.75
1. McGrigor, James, Sir, bart., 1771-1858. 2. Medicine, Military—Great Britain—History. I. Title.

McGuckin, Jack.

MCGUCKIN, Jack. 269'.2'0924 B
Split second from hell / Jack McGuckin. Scottsdale, Ariz. : Good Life Productions, c1979. 196 p., [4] leaves of plates : ill. ; 23 cm. [BV3785.M225A37] 79-52536 7.95
1. McGuckin, Jack. 2. Evangelists—United States—Biography. I. Title.

McGuffey, William Holmes, 1800-1873.

CRAWFORD, Benjamin Franklin, 1887- 370'.92'4 B
The life of William Holmes McGuffey. Delaware, Ohio, Carnegie Church Press [1974] 125 p. port. 18 cm. [LA2317.M2C69] 74-180268
1. McGuffey, William Holmes, 1800-1873. I. Title.

McGuffey, William Holmes, 1800-1873—Juvenile literature.

WILLIAMS, Barbara. 372.4'12'0924 B
William H. McGuffey: boy reading genius. Illustrated by Robert Doremus. Indianapolis, Bobbs-Merrill [1968] 200 p. col. illus. 20 cm. (Childhood of famous Americans) Bibliography: p. 198. A biography, concentrating on the boyhood, of the nineteenth-century educator whose series of six Eclectic Readers taught many generations of Americans to read. [LA2317.M2W5] 92 68-57788
1. McGuffey, William Holmes, 1800-1873—Juvenile literature. I. Doremus, Robert, illus. II. Title.

McGuire family.

CALHOUN, F. D. 979.4 B
49er Irish : one Irish family in the California mines / F. D. Calhoon. 1st ed. Hicksville, N.Y. : Exposition Press, c1977. xiii, 194 p. ; 22 cm. (An Exposition-Lochinvar book) [F865.C135] 77-72534 ISBN 0-682-48792-9 : 8.50
1. McGuire family. 2. California—Gold discoveries. 3. Irish Americans—California—History. I. Title.

McGuire, Maria.

MCGUIRE, Maria. 941.609'092'4
To take arms; my year with the IRA Provisionals. New York, Viking Press [1973] 185 p. illus. 21 cm. [DA990.U452M33 1973b] 73-4173 ISBN 0-670-71775-4 6.95
1. McGuire, Maria. 2. Irish Republican Army. 3. Guerrillas—Northern Ireland—Correspondence, reminiscences, etc. I. Title.

McIndoe, Sir Archibald Hector, 1900-1960.

MOSLEY, Leonard Oswald, 1911-- 926.1
Faces from the fire; the biography of Sir Archibald McIndoe. [1st American ed.] Englewood Cliffs, N. J., Prentice-Hall [c1962] 268 p. illus. 23 cm. [R489.M19M6] 63-11038
1. McIndoe, Sir Archibald Hector, 1900-1960. I. Title.

McIntire, Samuel, 1757-1811.

COUSINS, Frank, 1851- 720'.924 B
The wood-carver of Salem; Samuel

McIntire, his life and work, by Frank Cousins and Phil M. Riley. New York, AMS Press [1970] xx, 168 p. illus., facsims., plans. 23 cm. Reprint of the 1916 ed. [NA737.M25C6 1970] 74-119649
1. McIntire, Samuel, 1757-1811. I. Riley, Phil Madison, 1882- joint author. II. Title. BIP

KIMBALL, Sidney Fiske, 1888-1955. 720.97445 B
Mr. Samuel McIntire, carver, the architect of Salem. [Salem, Mass.] Essex Institute of Salem, 1940. Gloucester, Mass., P. Smith, 1966. xiii, 157 p. illus., fold. map, plans, ports. 28 cm. [NA737.M25K5 1966] 67-297
1. McIntire, Samuel, 1757-1811. I. Essex Institute, Salem, Mass. II. Title. III. Title: The architect of Salem. BIP

McIntosh, Lachlan, 1725-1806.

JACKSON, Harvey H. 975.8'03'0924 B
Lachlan McIntosh and the politics of Revolutionary Georgia / Harvey H. Jackson. Athens : University of Georgia Press, c1979. xi, 209 p., [1] leaf of plates : ill. ; 23 cm. Includes index. Bibliography: p. [91]-202. [E207.M13J32] 78-8995 ISBN 0-8203-0459-X : 16.00
1. McIntosh, Lachlan, 1725-1806. 2. Generals—United States—Biography. 3. Politicians—Georgia—Biography. 4. Georgia—Politics and government—1775-1865. 5. United States—History—Revolution, 1775-1783—Campaigns and battles. I. Title. BIP

McIntyre, Fred,

MCINTYRE, Fred, 1877- 920
The true life story of a pioneer. Syracuse, Ind., Nonpareil Press, c1955. 240p. 21cm. [CT275.M4344A3] 56-21050
I. Title.

McIntyre, Oscar Odd, 1884-1938.

DRISCOLL, Charles Benedict, 1885-1951. 070'.92'4 B
The life of O. O. McIntyre. New York, Beekman Publishers, 1974. 344 p. illus. 23 cm. (American newspapermen, 1790-1933) Reprint of the 1938 ed. published by Greystone Press, New York. [PN4874.M373D7 1974] 74-570 ISBN 0-8464-0022-7 16.00
1. McIntyre, Oscar Odd, 1884-1938. I. Title. BIP

McJunkin, George—Juvenile literature.

FOLSOM, Franklin, 1907- 917.89'23 B
The life and legend of George McJunkin: Black cowboy. [1st ed.] Nashville, T. Nelson [1973] 162 p. illus. 21 cm. Bibliography: p. 159. A biography of the Black cowboy whose skill with horses was renowned and whose curiosity led him to discover important archaeological relics. [F596.M145F6] 92 73-6446 ISBN 0-8407-6326-3
1. McJunkin, George—Juvenile literature. 2. Cowboys—Juvenile literature. I. Title.

McKay, Cecil Newton, 1899-1968.

MCKAY, Marjory, 1902- 338.7'63'130924 B
Cecil McKay : it wasn't all sunshine / [by] Marjory McKay. Melbourne : The Hawthorn Press, 1974. 245 p., [2] leaves of plates : ill. ; 25 cm. Includes index. [HD9486.A8M335] 75-316261 ISBN 0-7256-0127-2 : 12.50
1. McKay, Cecil Newton, 1899-1968.

McKay, Claude,

MCKAY, Claude, 1890-1948. 818'.5'209 B
A long way from home. New York, Arno Press, 1969 [c1937] 354 p. 21 cm. (The American Negro, his history and literature) [PS3525.A24785Z5 1969] 74-77507
I. Title. II. Series.

MCKAY, Claude, 1890-1948. 818'.5'209 B
A long way from home. Introd. by St. Clair Drake. New York, Harcourt, Brace & World [1970] xxi, 354 p. 21 cm. (A Harvest book, HB 172) An autobiography. [PS3525.A24785Z5 1970] 76-11560 2.85
I. Title. BIP

McKay, Claude, 1890-1948—Biography Youth.

MCKAY, Claude, 1890-1948 818'.5'209 B
My green hills of Jamaica / Claude McKay. Washington : Howard University Press, 1975. p. cm. Autobiography. [PS3525.A24785Z52 1975] 74-32394 ISBN 0-88258-052-3 : 7.95
1. McKay, Claude, 1890-1948—Biography—Youth. I. Title.

McKay, David Oman, 1873-1970.

MCKAY, Llewelyn R 922.8373
Home memories of President David O. McKay, compiled. and written by Llewelyn R. McKay. Salt Lake City, Desert Book Co., 1956. 280p. illus. 24cm. [BX8695.M27M3] 56-26187
1. McKay, David Oman, 1873- I. Title.

STEWART, John J. 289.3'0922 B
Remembering the McKays; a biographical sketch with pictures of David O. and Emma Ray McKay, by John J. Stewart. Salt Lake City, Deseret Book Co., 1970. 48 p. ports. 23 cm. [BX8695.M27S8] 70-136243
1. McKay, David Oman, 1873-1970. 2. McKay, Emma Ray, 1877- I. Title.

McKay, Donald, 1810-1880.

JUDSON, Clara (Ingram) 1879-1960 623.82
Yankee clippers; the story of Donald McKay. Line-and-wash drawings by Yukio Tashiro. Chicago, Follett [c.1943, 1965] 158p. illus. 23cm. First ed. pub. in 1943 under title: Donald McKay, designer of clipper ships. [VM140.M3J8] 65-18967 3.50
1. McKay, Donald, 1810-1880. I. Title.

McKay, Frances Peabody.

MCKAY, Frances Peabody. 975.8'794
More fun than heaven / by Frances Peabody McKay. 1st ed. St. Petersburg, Fla. : Valkyrie Press, c1978. 138 p. : ill. ; 22 cm. [F294.W3M3] 78-68465 ISBN 0-912760-86-9 pbk. : 3.95
1. McKay, Frances Peabody. 2. Waycross, Ga.—Biography. 3. St. Simon's Island, Ga.—Biography. BIP

McKay, Leo Hugh, 1895-

MCKAY, Leo Hugh, 1895- 347'.73'2234 B
The trials of a trial judge / Leo H. McKay. 1st ed. New York : Vantage Press, c1977. 95 p. ; 22 cm. [KF220.M3] 77-151093 ISBN 0-533-02583-4 : 5.95
1. McKay, Leo Hugh, 1895- 2. Trials—Pennsylvania—Mercer Co. 3. Judges—Pennsylvania—Mercer Co.—Biography. 4. Mercer Co., Pa.—History. I. Title.

McKay, Llewelyn R

MCKAY, Llewelyn R 922.8373
Home memories of President David O. McKay. compiled. and written by Llewelyn R. McKay. Salt Lake City, Desert Book Co., 1956. 280p. illus. 24cm. [BX8695.M27M3] 56-26187
I. McKay, David Oman, 1873- II. Title.

McKean, Thomas, 1734-1817.

COLEMAN, John M. 973.3'092'4 B
Thomas McKean, forgotten leader of the Revolution / by John M. Coleman. Rockaway, N.J. : American Faculty Press, [1975] xv, 332 p., [6] leaves of plates : ill. ; 25 cm. Includes index. Bibliography: p. 293-318. [E302.6.M13C64] 74-19952 ISBN 0-912834-07-2 : 16.95
1. McKean, Thomas, 1734-1817. I. Title.

ROWE, Gail Stuart, 1936- 973.3'092'4 B
Thomas McKean : the shaping of an American republicanism / G. S. Rowe. Boulder : Colorado Associated University Press, c1978. xiv, 503 p. : ports. ; 24 cm. Includes index. Bibliography: p. [475]-484. [E302.6.M13R68] 77-94085 ISBN 0-87081-100-2 : 15.00
1. McKean, Thomas, 1734-1817. 2. Politicians—United States—Biography. 3. Lawyers—United States—Biography. 4. Political science—United States—History. 5. United States—Politics and government—Revolution, 1775-1783. 6. United States—Politics and government—1783-1809. BIP

McKenna, Joseph, 1843-1926.

MCDEVITT, Matthew, Brother, 1904- 347'.73'2634 B
Joseph McKenna: Associate Justice of the United States. New York, Da Capo Press, 1974 [c1946] x, 250 p. geneal. table. 24 cm. (Da Capo Press reprint in American constitutional and legal history) Thesis—Catholic University, 1945. Reprint of the ed. published by Catholic University of America Press, Washington, D.C. Bibliography: p. 232-245. [KF8745.M25M3 1974] 73-21874 ISBN 0-306-70632-6 12.95
1. McKenna, Joseph, 1843-1926.

McKenna, Mary.

MCKENNA, Mary 301.42'7
A family / by Mary McKenna. St. Paul, Minn. : Carillon Books, c1978. vii, 185 ; 22 cm. [HQ759.M29] 78-111138 ISBN 0-89310-029-3 : 8.95. ISBN 0-89310-030-7 pbk. : 3.95
1. McKenna, Mary. 2. Mothers—United States—Biography. I. Title. BIP

McKenney, Thomas Loraine, 1785-1859.

VIOLA, Herman J. 353.008'48'4 B
Thomas L. McKenney : architect of America's early Indian policy, 1816-1830 / Herman J. Viola. 1st ed. Chicago : Sage Books, [1974] xii, 365 p., 10 leaves of plates : ill. ; 24 cm. Includes index. Bibliography: p. 345-355. [E93.M152V56] 74-18075 ISBN 0-8040-0668-7 : 15.00
1. McKenney, Thomas Loraine, 1785-1859. 2. Indians of North America—Government relations—1789-1869.

McKenzie, James Hewat.

HANKEY, Muriel 920.9133
James Hewat McKenzie, pioneer of psychical research. A personal memoir. New York, Helix Pr., 29 W. 57th St. [c.1963] 157p. front. port. 23cm. 4.50
1. McKenzie, James Hewat. I. Title.

McKibbin, Alma Estelle (Baker)

MCKIBBIN, Alma Estelle (Baker) 1871- 920.7
Step by step, an autobiography sketch. Washington, D.C., Review & Herald [1964] 96p. illus. 22cm. 63-19763 price unreported
I. Title.

McKim, Charles Follen, 1847-1909.

GRANGER, Alfred Hoyt, 1867-1939. 720'.92'4 B
Charles Follen McKim; a study of his life and work. New York, B. Blom, 1972. xii, 145 p. illus. 24 cm. Reprint of the 1913 ed. [NA737.M3G7 1972b] 79-152623 15.75
1. McKim, Charles Follen, 1847-1909. BIP

GRANGER, Alfred Hoyt, 1867-1939. 720'.92'4 B
Charles Follen McKim: a study of his life and work. Boston, Houghton Mifflin, 1913. [New York, AMS Press, 1972] xii, 145 p. illus. 24 cm. [NA737.M3G7 1972] 70-168178 ISBN 0-404-02890-X 7.00
1. McKim, Charles Follen, 1847-1909.

MOORE, Charles, 1855-1942. 720'.924 B
The life and times of Charles Follen McKim. New York, Da Capo Press, 1970 [c1929] xii, 356 p. illus., ports. 24 cm. (Da Capo Press series in architecture and decorative art, v. 32) (A Da Capo Press reprint edition.) [NA737.M3M6 1970] 70-99857
1. McKim, Charles Follen, 1847-1909. I. Title. BIP

McKinley, William, Pres. U.S., 1843-1901.

HEALD, Edward Thornton 923.173
The William McKinley story [Canton, Ohio] Stark County Hist. Soc., 1964. 125p. illus., facsims., ports. 23cm. 64-54780 2.50
1. McKinley, William, Pres. U.S., 1843-1901. I. Title.

HOYT, Edwin Palmer. 92
William McKinley, by Edwin P. Hoyt. Chicago, Reilly & Lee Co. [1967] 138 p. ports. 22 cm. ([His President series]) Bibliography: p. 133. A biography of the twenty-fifth President, emphasizing his term in office during which the U.S. emerged from isolation to win the Spanish-American war and begin its role as an international power. [E711.6.H85] AC 67
1. McKinley, William, Pres. U.S., 1843-1901. I. Title.

MORGAN, Howard Wayne 923.173
William McKinley and his America. [Syracuse, N.Y.] Syracuse Univ. [c.]1963. xi, 595p. illus., ports. 24cm. Bibl. 63-19723 9.00
1. McKinley, William, Pres, U.S., 1843-1901. I. Title.

OLCOTT, Charles Sumner, 1864-1935. 973.8'8'0924 B
William McKinley. Boston, Houghton, Mifflin. [New York, AMS Press, 1972] 2 v. illus. 18 cm. (American statesmen, v. 38-39) Reprint of the 1916 ed. First published under title: The life of William McKinley. [E711.6.O43 1972] 79-128946 ISBN 0-404-50893-6
1. McKinley, William, Pres. U.S., 1843-1901. 2. United States—Politics and government—1865-1900. I. Title. II. Series.

SPIELMAN, William Carl, 1884- 923.173
William McKinley, stalwart Republican; a biographical study. [1st ed.] New York, Exposition Press [1954] 215 p. illus. 21 cm. Bibliography: p. [207]-210. [E711.6.S73] 54-5557
1. McKinley, William, Pres. U.S., 1843-1901.

THOMPSON, Charles Willis, 1871-1946. 973.9'0922
Presidents I've known and two near Presidents. Freeport, N.Y., Books for Libraries Press [1970, c1956] 386 p. 23 cm. (Essay index reprint series) Contents.Contents.—Hanna-McKinley.—Bryan.—Roosevelt.—Taft.—Wilson.—Harding.—Coolidge. [E176.1.T45 1970] 71-93383
1. Hanna, Marcus Alonzo, 1837-1904. 2. McKinley, William, Pres. U.S., 1843-1901. 3. Bryan, William Jennings, 1860-1925. 4. Roosevelt, Theodore, Pres. U.S., 1858-1919. 5. Taft, William Howard, Pres. U.S., 1857-1930. 6. Wilson, Woodrow, Pres. U.S., 1856-1924. 7. Harding, Warren Gamaliel, Pres. U.S., 1865-1923. 8. Coolidge, Calvin, Pres. U.S., 1872-1933. I. Title. BIP

McKinley, William, Pres. U.S., 1843-1901—Juvenile literature.

HOYT, Edwin Palmer. 973.8'8'0924 B
William McKinley, by Edwin P. Hoyt. Chicago, Reilly & Lee [1967] 138 p. ports. 22 cm. ([His President series]) Bibliography: p. 133. [E711.6.H85] 67-14663
1. McKinley, William, Pres. U.S., 1843-1901—Juvenile literature.

Mckinney, Marion (White)

MCKINNEY, Marion (White) 928.1
1912-
Ned White, Arizona's 'Bard of Brewery Gulch.' Denver, Golden Bell [c.1965] viii, 152p. illus., ports. 23cm. [PS3545.H5183Z75] 64-8887 3.95
1. White, Edward P. II. Title.

McKinstry, Arthur R.

MCKINSTRY, Arthur R 283'.092'4 B
All I have seen : the McKinstry memoirs / by the fifth bishop of Delaware, 1939-1954 [A. R. McKinstry]. Wilmington, Del. : Serendipity Press, c1975. 266 p. : ill. ; 24 cm. [BX5995.M32A34] 75-24664 ISBN 0-914988-02-6 : 10.00
1. McKinstry, Arthur R. I. Title.

McKinstry, Byron Nathan, 1818-1894.

MCKINSTRY, 917.3'04'640924 B
Byron Nathan, 1818-1894.
The California gold rush overland diary of Byron N. McKinstry, 1850-1852 / with a biographical sketch and comment on a modern tracing of his overland travel by Bruce L. McKinstry. Glendale, Calif. : A. H. Clark Co., 1975. 401 p. : ill. ; 25 cm. (American trails series ; 10) Title on spine: Gold rush overland diary of Byron N. McKinstry, 1850-1852. Includes index. [F593.M25] 75-10033 ISBN 0-87062-114-9 : 15.00
1. McKinstry, Byron Nathan, 1818-1894. 2. Overland journeys to the Pacific. 3. California—Gold discoveries. I. McKinstry, Bruce L. II. Title. III. Title: Gold rush overland diary of Byron N. McKinstry, 1850-1852. IV. Series: American trail series ; 10. BIP

McKnight, William Lester, 1887-

COMFORT, Mildred Houghton, 926.5
1886-
William L. McKnight, industrialist; a biographical sketch of the chairman of the board, Minnesota Mining and Manufacturing Company. Minneapolis, Denison [c.1962] 202p. 22cm. (Her Men of achievement ser.) 62-14153 3.00
1. McKnight, William Lester, 1887- 2. Minnesota Mining and Manufacturing Company. I. Title.

McKuen, Rod—Biography.

MCKUEN, Rod. 811'.5'4 B
Finding my father : one man's search for identity / Rod McKuen. Los Angeles : Cheval Books, c1976. 253 p. : ill. ; 22 cm. [PS3525.A264Z515] 76-20809 ISBN 0-698-10774-8 : 7.95
1. McKuen, Rod—Biography. 2. Poets, American—20th century—Biography. I. Title. BIP

McLain, Denny.

MCLAIN, Denny. 796.357'092'4
Nobody's perfect / Denny McLain ; with Dave Diles. New York : Dial Press, 1975. xi, 208 p. ; 24 cm. [GV865.M313A33] 75-7541 ISBN 0-8037-5758-1 : 7.95
1. McLain, Denny. 2. Baseball. I. Diles, Dave. II. Title. BIP

McLain, Denny—Juvenile literature.

JACKSON, Robert B. 796.357'0924 B
Thirty-one and six; the story of Denny McLain, by Robert B. Jackson. New York, H. Z. Walck [1969] 69 p. illus., ports. 22 cm. A brief biography stressing the baseball career of the first major league pitcher since 1934 to win thirty games in one season. [GV865.M313J3] 92 69-17915 3.25
1. McLain, Denny—Juvenile literature. I. Title.

McLane, Louis,

MCLANE, Louis, 359.3'3'20924 B
1819-1905.
The private journal of Louis McLane, U.S.N., 1844-1848. Edited by Jay Monoghan. Illus. by Russell A. Ruiz. Los Angeles, Published for the Santa Barbara Historical Society by Dawson's Book Shop, 1971. 120 p. illus., facsims., map (on lining papers) 25 cm. [V63.M29A3] 74-148696 ISBN 0-87093-155-5
I. Monaghan, James, 1891- ed. II. Santa Barbara Historical Society. III. Title. BIP

McLane, Louis, 1786-1857.

MUNROE, John A., 973.5'092'4 B
1914-
Louis McLane: Federalist and Jacksonian [by] John A. Munroe. New Brunswick, N.J., Rutgers University Press [1973] xi, 763 p. illus. 25 cm. Bibliography: p. 699-720. [E302.6.M137M86] 73-17240 22.50
1. McLane, Louis, 1786-1857. 2. United States—Politics and government—1783-1865.

McLane, Robert Milligan, 1815-1898.

MCLANE, Robert 975.2'04'0924
Milligan, 1815-1898.
Reminiscences 1827-1897, Governor Robert M. McLane. Wilmington, Del., Scholarly Resources [1972] 165 p. port. 23 cm. Reprint of the 1903 ed. [E664.M157M2 1972] 72-79831 ISBN 0-8420-1375-X
1. McLane, Robert Milligan, 1815-1898. I. Title.

McLaren, Bruce Leslie, 1937-1970.

BEECHING, Jeanne. 796.7'5'0924B
The last season; the life of Bruce McLaren. Newfoundland, N.J., W. R. Haessner, 1972. 231 p. illus. 24 cm. Includes bibliographical references. [GV1032.M26B43] 74-188895 ISBN 0-87799-014-X 7.95
1. McLaren, Bruce Leslie, 1937-1970. I. Title.

YOUNG, Eoin S. 796.7'2'0924 B
McLaren! The man, the cars & the team [by] Eoin S. Young. Newport Beach, Calif., Bond, Parkhurst Publications [1971] 272 p. illus., ports. 24 cm. [GV1032.M26Y68] 72-155023 ISBN 0-87880-007-7 7.95
1. McLaren, Bruce Leslie, 1937-1970. BIP

McLaughlin, Henry Woods, 1869-1950.

CARR, James McLeod. 922.773
Glorious ride; the story of Henry Woods McLaughlin. 'Little jet' sketches by the author. Atlanta, Church and Community Press [1958] 156p. illus. 21cm. [BX9225.M2549C3] 58-8225
1. McLaughlin, Henry Woods, 1869-1950. 2. Rural churches. I. Title.

McLaughlin, James, 1842-1923.

PFALLER, 353.008'4'840924 B
Louis.
James McLaughlin, the man with an Indian heart / by Louis L. Pfaller. 1st ed. New York : Vantage Press, c1978. xvi, 440 p. : ill. ; 22 cm. Includes index. Bibliography: p. 429-436. [E93.M156P46] 79-102400 ISBN 0-533-03181-8 : 15.00
1. McLaughlin, James, 1842-1923. 2. Dakota Indians—Government relations. 3. Indians of North America—Government relations—1869-1934. 4. Indian agents—United States—Biography. I. Title.

McLean, Evalyn Walsh, 1886-1947.

MCLEAN, Evalyn 975.3'03'0924 B
Walsh, 1886-1947.
Father struck it rich / Evalyn Walsh McLean, with Boyden Sparkes. New York : Arno Press, 1975 [c1936] p. cm. (The Leisure class in America) Reprint of the ed. published by Little, Brown, Boston. [CT275.M44A3 1975] 75-1856 ISBN 0-405-06922-7 : 22.00
1. McLean, Evalyn Walsh, 1886-1947. I. Sparkes, Boyden, 1890-1954, joint author. II. Title. III. Series. BIP

McLean, Francis Herbert, 1869-1945.

ORMSBY, Ralph. 362.8'2'0924 B
A man of vision, Francis H. McLean, 1869-1945. New York, Family Service Association of America [1969] xi, 142 p. port. 24 cm. Includes bibliographical references. [HV28.M315O7] 75-99972
1. McLean, Francis Herbert, 1869-1945. I. Title.

McLean, John, 1785-1861.

WEISENBURGER, 347'.7326'34 B
Francis Phelps, 1900-
The life of John McLean; a politician on the United States Supreme Court, by Francis P. Weisenburger. New York, Da Capo Press, 1971 [c1937] ix, 244 p. port. 24 cm. (Da Capo Press reprints in American constitutional and legal history) (Ohio State University studies. Contributions in history and political science, no. 15) Bibliography: p. 230-236. [E340.M2W45 1971] 76-150296 ISBN 0-306-70106-5
1. McLean, John, 1785-1861. I. Title. II. Series: Ohio. State University, Columbus. Contributions in history and political science, no. 15

McLean, Marrs, 1883-1953.

CLARK, James 338.2'7'2820924 B
Anthony, 1907-
Marrs McLean, a biography, by James A. Clark. Houston, Tex., Priv. print. by Clark Book Co., 1969. xi, 194 p. illus., ports. (part col.) 24 cm. [HD9570.M25C55] 75-77621
1. McLean, Marrs, 1883-1953.

McLemore, Henry.

MCLEMORE, Henry. 920.5
One of us is wrong! Illustrated by the Strimbans. [1st ed.] New York, Holt [1953] 242 p. illus. 22 cm. Autobiography. [PN4874.M42A3] 53-5502
I. Title.

McLeod, Barry.

JORDAN, Pat. 796.32'3'0922 B
Chase the game / Pat Jordan. New York : Dodd, Mead, c1979. 216 p. ; 22 cm. [GV884.A1J67] 78-31848 ISBN 0-396-07632-7 : 10.00
1. Oleynick, Frank. 2. McLeod, Barry. 3. Luckett, Walter. 4. Basketball players—United States—Biography. I. Title. BIP

McLeod, Ceil.

MCLEOD, Ceil. 248'.2'0924 B
Another day, another miracle / Ceil McLeod. Wheaton, Ill. : Tyndale House Publishers, c1975. 115 p. ; 22 cm. Includes bibliographical references. [BR1725.M3154A32] 74-21964 2.95 (pbk.)
1. McLeod, Ceil. I. Title.

McLoughlin, John, 1784-1857.

FOGDALL, Alberta 979.5'03'0924 B
Brooks, 1912-
Royal family of the Columbia : Dr. John McLoughlin and his family / Alberta Brooks Fogdall. Fairfield, Wash. : Ye Galleon Press, 1978. 328 p. : ill. ; 29 cm. Includes index. Bibliography: p. 311-320. [F880.M17F63] 78-17170 ISBN 0-87770-168-7 : 14.95
1. McLoughlin, John, 1784-1857. 2. Hudson's Bay Company. 3. Pioneers—Northwest, Pacific—Biography. 4. Merchants—Northwest, Pacific—Biography. 5. Oregon—History—To 1859. 6. Northwest, Pacific—History. 7. Fur trade—Northwest, Pacific—History. I. Title.

JOHNSON, Robert Cummings, 979.5
1864-1938.
John McLoughlin: father of Oregon. [Portland, Or.] Binfords & Mort [1958, c1935] Boston, Allyn and Bacon, 1962. 302p. illus. 23cm. 714p. illus. 24cm. ohn McLoughlin: patriarch of the Northwest. First published in 1935 under title: management. Includes bibliography. [F880.M173 1958] 58-11483
1. McLoughlin, John, 1784-1857. 2. Oregon—Hist.—To 1859. 3. Hudson's Bay Company. 4. Fur trade—Oregon. I. Title. II. Series. BIP

McLoughlin, John, 1784-1857—Juvenile literature.

MORRISON, Dorothy 979.5'03'0924 B
N.
The eagle and the fort : the story of Dr. John McLoughlin / by Dorothy Nafus Morrison. New York : Atheneum, 1979. p. cm. Includes index. Bibliography: p. A biography of the man who was the chief factor and developer of Fort Vancouver for the Hudson's Bay Company. Under his direction the fort became the center of settlement and civilization for the Pacific Northwest. [F880.M17M67] 78-12911 ISBN 0-689-30691-1 : 7.95
1. McLoughlin, John, 1784-1857—Juvenile literature. 2. Hudson's Bay Company—Juvenile literature. 3. Oregon—History—To 1859—Juvenile literature. 4. Northwest, Pacific—History—Juvenile literature. 5. Pioneers—Oregon—Biography—Juvenile literature. I. Title.

McLuhan, Herbert Marshall.

MILLER, Jonathan, 001.5'0924
1934-
Marshall McLuhan. New York, Viking Press [1971] 133 p. 20 cm. (Modern masters) Bibliography: p. [125]-126. [P92.5.M3M5 1971b] 71-104150 ISBN 0-670-45876-7 4.95
1. McLuhan, Herbert Marshall.

McMahon, Ed.

MCMAHON, Ed. 791'.092'4 B
Here's Ed : or, How to be a second banana, from midway to midnight / by Ed McMahon, as told to Carroll Carroll. New York : Putnam, c1976. 319 p. : ill. ; 22 cm. [PN1992.4.M25A34 1976] 75-37084 7.95
1. McMahon, Ed. I. Carroll, Carroll. II. Title. III. Title: How to be a second banana, from midway to midnight. BIP

McMains, O. P.

TAYLOR, Morris F. 333.1'6 B
O. P. McMains and the Maxwell land grant conflict / Morris F. Taylor. Tucson : University of Arizona Press, c1979. xvi, 365 p. : ill. ; 23 cm. Includes index. Bibliography: p. 329-341. [F802.M38M327] 78-14227 ISBN 0-8165-0575-6 pbk. : 9.50
1. McMains, O. P. 2. Maxwell Land Grant—Biography. 3. Land settlement—New Mexico—History. 4. Land settlement—Colorado—History. 5. New Mexico—History. 6. Colorado—History—To 1876. I. Title. BIP

McMann Oil Company—History.

TYSON, Carl N. 338.7'66'550922 B
The McMan : the lives of Robert M. McFarlin and James A. Chapman / by Carl N. Tyson, James H. Thomas, Odie B. Faulk. 1st ed. [Norman] : Published for the Oklahoma Heritage Association by the University of Oklahoma Press, c1977. xiii, 224 p. : ill. ; 22 cm. (Oklahoma trackmaker series) Includes index. Bibliography: p. 213-217. [HD9570.M22T97] 77-9113 ISBN 0-8061-1446-0 : 7.75
1. McFarlin, Robert Martin, 1866-1942. 2. Chapman, James Allen, 1881-1966. 3. McMann Oil Company—History. 4. McMan Oil and Gas Company—History. 5. Petroleum industry and trade—Oklahoma—History. 6. Businessmen—Oklahoma—Biography. I. Thomas, James Harold, 1943- joint author. II. Faulk, Odie B., joint author. III. Oklahoma Heritage Association. IV. Title. V. Series. BIP

McManus, George Henry, 1867-1954.

NEWELL, Gordon R. 355.3'31'0924 B
Duty, honor, country : the biography of

George H. McManus, Brigadier General, United States Army / written and designed by Gordon Newell ; researched and published by H. W. McCurdy. [Seattle] : H. W. McCurdy, [1973 or 1974] 168 p. : ill. ; 24 cm. Two hundred copies printed. No. 61. [U53.M28N48] 74-31125
1. McManus, George Henry, 1867-1954. I. Title.

McMaster, Anew.

PINTER, Harold, 1930- 792'.092'4 B
Mac / Harold Pinter. Ann Arbor, Mich. : University Microfilms, 1979. p. cm. Reprint of the 1968 ed. published by Grove Press, New York. [PN2601.M35P5 1979] 79-23984 ISBN 0-8357-0485-8 : 7.00
1. McMaster, Anew. 2. Pinter, Harold, 1930- —Friends and associates. 3. Shakespeare, William, 1564-1616—Stage history—Ireland. 4. Actors—Ireland—Biography. I. Title.

McMaster, John Bach, 1852-1932.

GOLDMAN, Eric Frederick, 1915- 973'.072'024 B
John Bach McMaster, American historian, by Eric F. Goldman. New York, Octagon Books, 1971 [c1943] xi, 194 p. facsim., ports. 24 cm. Bibliography: p. 179-186. [E175.5.M2G6 1971] 73-154664 ISBN 0-374-93179-8
1. McMaster, John Bach, 1852-1932. BIP

McMein, Neyss, 1890 -1949.

BARAGWANATH, John, 1888- 818.52
A good time was had. [1st ed.] New York, Appleton-Century -Crofts [1962] 245p. 21cm. Autobiographical. [NC139.M23B3] 62-8496
1. McMein, Neyss, 1890 -1949. I. Title.

McMillan, John, 1752-1833.

GUTHRIE, Dwight Raymond, 1902- 922.573
John McMillan, the apostle of Presbyterianism in the West, 1752-1833. [Pittsburgh] University of Pittsburgh Press [1952] x, 296p. illus., ports., maps. 24cm. Bibliography: p. 277-287. [BX9225.M28G85] 53-579
1. McMillan, John, 1752-1833. I. Title.

GUTHRIE, Dwight Raymond, 1902- 922.573
John McMillan, the apostle of Presbyterianism in the West, 1752-1833. [Pittsburgh] University of Pittsburgh Press [1952] x, 296 p. illus., port., maps. 24 cm. Bibliography: p. 277-287. [BX9225.M28G85] 53-579
1. McMillan, John, 1752-1833.

McMillan, Margaret 1860-1931.

LOWNDES, George Alfred Norman 923.742
Margaret McMillan, 'the children's champion.' [dist. SportShelf, New Rochelle, N. Y., 1961, c.1960] 110p. illus. 4.25 bds.,
1. McMillan, Margaret 1860-1931. I. Title.

LOWNDES, George Alfred Norman. 923.742
Margaret McMillan, 'the children's champion.' [London] Museum Press [1961, c1960; stamped: distributed by Sportshelf, New Rochelle, N. Y.] 110p. illus. 23cm. [LA2377.M25L6] 61-1242
1. McMillian, Margaret, 1860-1931. I. Title.

McNabb, Vincent Joseph, 1868-1943.

SIDERMAN, Edward A 922.242
A saint in Hyde Park; memories of Father Vincent McNabb, o. p. Westminster, Md., Newman Press, 1950. 159 p. port. 20 cm. [BX4705.M2535S45 1950a] 50-11141
1. McNabb, Vincent Joseph, 1868-1943. I. Title.

McNally, Ward.

MCNALLY, Ward. 365'.9'24 B
Cry of a man running. [1st American ed.] South Brunswick [N.J.] A. S. Barnes [1969, c1968] 209 p. 22 cm. Autobiographical. [HV6248.M253A3 1969] 76-83390 4.95
I. Title.

McNamara, Robert S., 1916-

LIBERTY Lobby. 353.6'0924
Robert Strange McNamara: the true story of Dr. Strangebob; special report. [Washington, 1967] 126 p. 18 cm. Bibliographic footnotes. [UA23.L55] 67-31623
1. McNamara, Robert S., 1916- 2. U. S.—Defenses. I. Title.

LIBERTY Lobby. 353.6'0924
Robert Strange McNamara: the true story of Dr. Strangebob; special report. [Washington, 1967] 126 p. 18 cm. Bibliographic footnotes. [UA23.L55] 67-31623
1. McNamara, Robert S., 1916- 2. United States—Defenses.

McNary, James Graham 1877-

MCNARY, James Graham, 1877- 920
This is my life. Albuquerque, University of New Mexico Press, 1956. xvi, 271 p. illus., ports. 24 cm. [CT275.M4442A3] 56-7038
1. McNary, James Graham 1877- I. Title.

McNay, Marion Koogler.

BURKHALTER, Lois (Wood) 704'.36'0924 B
Marion Koogler McNay; a biography, 1883-1950. San Antonio, Marion Koogler McNay Art Institute [1968] 97 p. illus. (part col.), ports. 28 cm. [N8410.B8] 68-26507
1. McNay, Marion Koogler. I. Marion Koogler McNay Art Institute, San Antonio.

McNeil, Marian W.

MCNEIL, Marian W. 266'.5'10924 B
Lord, "give me this mountain" / by Marian W. McNeil. Collingswood, N.J. : Christian Beacon Press, 1976. 187 p., [7] leaves of plates : ill. ; 22 cm. [BV3625.K42M285] 76-42948
1. McNeil, Marian W. 2. Missionaries—Kenya—Biography. 3. Missionaries—United States—Biography. I. Title.

McNeir, Forest W

MCNEIR, Forest W 1875- 920
Forest McNeir of Texas. San Antonio, Naylor Co. [1956] 316p. illus. 22cm. [CT275.M4444A3] 56-42825
I. Title.

McNutt, Paul Vories, 1891-1955.

BLAKE, Israel George, 1902- 351.000924 B
Paul V. McNutt; portrait of a Hoosier statesman, by I. George Blake. Indianapolis, Central Pub. Co., 1966. xv, 399 p. illus., ports. 24 cm. Includes bibliographical references. [E748.M157B55] 66-30664
1. McNutt, Paul Vories, 1891-1955.

McPhee, Colin, 1901-1964—Journeys—Bali (Island)

MCPHEE, Colin, 1901-1964. 915.98'6
A house in Bali / Colin McPhee ; with photos. by the author. New York : AMS Press, 1980, c1946. p. cm. Reprint of the ed. published by the J. Day Co., New York. [ML410.M17A3 1980] 77-86965 ISBN 0-404-16766-7 : 26.50
1. McPhee, Colin, 1901-1964—Journeys—Bali (Island) 2. Bali (Island)—Description and travel. 3. Composers—United States—Biography. I. Title. BIP

McPherson, Aimee Semple, 1890-1944.

BAHR, Robert. 289.9 B
Least of all saints : the story of Aimee Semple McPherson / by Robert Bahr. Englewood Cliffs, N.J. : Prentice-Hall, c1979. 308 p., [8] leaves of plates : ill. ; 24 cm. Bibliography: p. 302-308. [BX7990.I68M273] 78-26530 ISBN 0-13-527978-X : 12.95
1. McPherson, Aimee Semple, 1890-1944. 2. Evangelists—United States—Biography. I. Title.

MCPHERSON, Aimee Semple, 1890-1944. 922
The story of my life. In memoriam, Echo Park Evangelistic Association, Los Angeles. Hollywood, Calif. [1951] 246 p. ports. 24 cm. "An International Correspondents' publication." [BV3785.M28A32] 51-9965
I. Title.

MCPHERSON, Aimee Semple, 289.9 B
The story of my life. Waco, Tex., Word Books [1973] 255 p. illus. 23 cm. [BX7990.I68M285] 72-96350 5.95
1. McPherson, Aimee Semple, 1890-1944. I. Title.

MCPHERSON, Aimee Semple, 1890-1944. 289.9 B
The story of my life. Waco, Tex., Word Books [1973] 255 p. illus. 23 cm. [BX7990.I68M285] 72-96350 5.95
1. McPherson, Aimee Semple, 1890-1944. I. Title.

STEELE, Robert V. P. 289.9 B
Storming heaven; the lives and turmoils of Minnie Kennedy and Aimee Semple McPherson [by] Lately Thomas. New York, Morrow, 1970. 364 p. illus. 25 cm. Includes bibliographical references. [BX7990.I68M33] 74-118057 10.00
1. McPherson, Aimee Semple, 1890-1944. 2. Kennedy, Minnie, 1871-1947. I. Title.

THOMAS, Lately, pseud. 922
The vanishing evangelist: the Aimee Semple McPherson kidnaping affair. New York, Viking Press, 1959. 334 p. illus. 23 cm. [BX7990.I68M3] 59-8351
1. McPherson, Aimee Semple, 1890-1944. I. Title.

McPherson, James, 1841-1895.

MCCARTHY, Patrick Hubert. 364.1'6 B
The wild Scotsman : a biography of James McPherson, the Queensland bushranger / P. H. McCarthy. Melbourne : Hawthorn, 1974. 123 p., [2] leaves of plates : ill. ; 23 cm. Includes bibliographical references and index. [DU272.M28M3] 75-320977 ISBN 0-7256-0128-0 : 9.50
1. McPherson, James, 1841-1895. 2. Bushrangers. I. Title.

McPherson, James Birdseye, 1828-1864.

WHALEY, Elizabeth J 923.573
Forgotten hero: General James B. McPherson; the biography of a Civil War general. [1st ed.] New York, Exposition Press [c1955] 203p. 21cm. Includes bibliography. [E467.M3W45] 54-11323
1. McPherson, James Birdseye, 1828-1864. I. Title.

McPherson, William, 1885-1964.

MEADOWS, Don. 917.94'9'0350924 B
A California paisano; the life of William McPherson. Claremont, Calif., Honnold Library Society, 1972. viii, 75, [1] p. illus. 22 cm. "Writings of William McPherson": p. [76] [F868.O6M39] 72-88325
1. McPherson, William, 1885-1964. I. Title.

McQuade White, E.

MCQUADE White, E. 355.3'45'0924 B
Reminiscences of an Australian Army nurse, by E. McQuade White. [Brisbane, Eager & Lamb, 1950?] 56 p. illus. 22 cm. [UH347.M3A33] 75-307937
1. McQuade White, E. 2. Military nursing. I. Title.

McQuaid, John Charles.

FEENEY, John, 1948- 282'.092'4 B
John Charles McQuaid : the man and the mask / by John Feeney. Dublin : Mercier Press, 1974. 88 p. ; 18 cm. [BX4705.M2555F43] 75-304534 ISBN 0-85342-377-6 : 0.75
1. McQuaid, John Charles.

McQueen, Steve, 1930-

MCCOY, Malachy 796.7'4 B
Steve McQueen. the unathorized biography. Chicago, H. Regnery Co. [1974] 233 p. illus. 22 cm. [PN2287.M19M25 1974] 73-19731 ISBN 0-8092-9056-1 7.95
1. McQueen, Steve, 1930-

McQueen, Steve, 1930-—Juvenile literature.

NOLAN, William F., 1928- 796.7'092'4 B
Steve McQueen: star on wheels, by William F. Nolan. New York, Putnam [1972] 159 p. port. 21 cm. A biography of a popular actor whose achievements in racing equal or surpass those in his first career. [GV1060.2.M25N64 1972] 92 73-182994 ISBN 0-399-20261-7 4.29
1. McQueen, Steve, 1930-—Juvenile literature. 2. Motorcycle racing—Juvenile literature. I. Title.

McQuilkin, Robert Crawford, 1886-1952.

MCQUILKIN, Marguerite. 922.573
Always in triumph, the life of Robert C. McQuilkin. Columbia, S. C., Bible College Bookstore [1956] 255p. 21cm. [BX9225.M315M3] 56-7444
1. McQuilkin, Robert Crawford, 1886-1952. I. Title.

McShean, Gordon.

MC SHEAN, Gordon 362.1'9'74120924 B
Bum ticker : a hearty traveler's tale / Gordon McShean. Scotts Valley, Calif. : Multinational Media, c1976. xii, 202 p. ; 21 cm. First published in 1970 under title: Operation New Zealand. [RD598.M16 1976] 76-13744 ISBN 0-917112-01-6 : 9.95 ISBN 0-917112-62-8 pbk. :
1. McShean, Gordon. 2. Heart—Valves—Transplantation—Personal narratives. I. Title.
Publisher's address: Multinational Media, 16 Jolley Way, Scotts Valley,Ca. 95066 BIP

McSorley, Rita (Cosgrove) 1887-1952.

MCSORLEY, Richard T., 1914- 922.273
The more, the merrier; the story of a mother of fifteen children. Washington, D.C., Georgetown Univ. Pr. [c.1963] 175p. illus. 23cm. 63-15818 1.95 pap.,
1. McSorley, Rita (Cosgrove) 1887-1952. I. Title.

McTyeire, Holland Nimmons, Bp., 1824-1889.

TIGERT, John James, 1882- 922.773
Bishop Holland Nimmons McTyeire, ecclelsiastical and educational architect. Nashville, Vanderbilt University Press, 1955. 279p. illus., ports. 24cm. Bibliography: p. 269-271. [BX8495.M26T5] 55-12869
1. McTyeire, Holland Nimmons, Bp., 1824-1889. I. Title.

McWhirter, Alan Ross.

MCWHIRTER, Norris Dewar. 070'.92'4 B
Ross : the story of a shared life / [by]

Norris McWhirter. London : Churchill Press Limited, 1976. ix, 240 p. : ill., ports. ; 23 cm. Includes index. [CT788.M19M3] 77-376118 ISBN 0-902782-23-1 : £4.50
1. McWhirter, Alan Ross. 2. England—Biography. I. Title.

McWilliams, Carey, 1905-

MCWILLIAMS, Carey, 1905- 070.4'092'4 B
The education of Carey McWilliams / by Carey McWilliams. New York : Simon and Schuster, c1979. 363 p. ; 24 cm. Includes index. Bibliography: p. 332-344. [PN4874.M475A33] 78-31675 ISBN 0-671-22876-5 : 10.95
1. McWilliams, Carey, 1905- 2. Journalists—United States—Biography. I. Title. BIP

Meacham, Joseph, 1742-1796.

EVANS, Frederick William, 1808-1893. 289.8
Shakers : compendium of the origin, history, principles, rules and regulations, government, and doctrines of the United Society of Believers in Christ's Second Appearing ... / by F. W. Evans. 4th ed. New York : AMS Press, 1975. 190 p. ; 19 cm. (Communal societies in America) Reprint of the 1867 ed. published in New Lebanon, N.Y. Bibliography: p. [188]-190. [BX9771.E85 1975] 72-2985 ISBN 0-404-10747-8
1. Shakers. 2. Shakers—Biography. 3. Lee, Ann, 1736-1784. 4. Lee, William, 1740-1784. 5. Whittaker, James, 1751-1787. 6. Hocknell, John, 1723?-1799. 7. Meacham, Joseph, 1742-1796. 8. Wright, Lucy, 1760-1821. I. Title: Compendium of the origin, history, principles, rules and regulations, government, and doctrines of the United Society of Believers in Christ's Second Appearing. BIP

Mead Corporation.

IN quiet ways; 338.7'67'620924 B
George H. Mead, the man and the company. Dayton, Ohio, Priv. print. [by] Mead Corporation, 1970. xii, 306 p. illus., ports. (part col.) 26 cm. [HD9829.M4I6] 72-22127
1. Mead Corporation. 2. Mead, George Houk, 1877-1963.

Mead, Eleanor Tyler.

MEAD, Eleanor Tyler. 248'.2'0924 B
Lay up your treasures in heaven / Eleanor Tyler Mead. Plainfield, N.J. : Logos International, c1977. 105 p. ; 21 cm. [BR1725.M357A34] 77-89182 ISBN 0-88270-257-2 pbk. : 2.95
1. Mead, Eleanor Tyler. 2. Christian biography—United States. 3. Consolation. 4. Bereavement. 5. Children—Death and future state. I. Title. BIP

Mead, George Jackson, 1891-1949.

MEAD, Cary Hoge, 1897- 629.13'00924 B
Wings over the world; the life of George Jackson Mead. Wauwatosa, Wis., Swannet Press [1971] x, 314 p. illus., ports. 23 cm. Includes bibliographical references. [TL540.M374M4] 74-141967
1. Mead, George Jackson, 1891-1949. I. Title.

Mead, Margaret,

MEAD, Margaret, 1901- 301.2'092'4 [B]
Blackberry winter; my earlier years New York, Pocket Books [1975, c1972] 337 p. illus. 18 cm. [GN21.M36A32] 72-7187 ISBN 0-671-78731-4 1.95 (pbk.)
I. Title.

Mead, Margaret, 1901-

MEAD, Margaret, 1901- 301.2'092'4 [B]
Blackberry winter; my earlier years New York, Pocket Books [1975, c1972] 337 p. illus. 18 cm. [GN21.M36A32] 72-7187 ISBN 0-671-78731-4 1.95 (pbk.)
I. Title.

MOSS, Allyn 925.72
Margaret Mead: shaping a new world. Chicago, Ency. Britannica [c.1963] 192p. illus., ports. 22cm. (Britannica bkshelf: Great lives) 63-13516 2.95 2.36 bds., lib. ed.,
1. Mead, Margaret, 1901- I. Title. II. Title: Shaping a new world.

MOSS, Allyn. 925.72
Margaret Mead; shaping a new world. Chicago, Encyclopaedia Britannica Press [c1963] 192 p. illus., ports. 22 cm. (Britannica bookshelf: Great lives) [GN21.M36M6] 63-13516
1. Mead, Margaret, 1901- I. Title. II. Title: Shaping a new world.

Mead, Margaret, 1901- —Juvenile literature.

JOHNSON, Spencer. 301.2'092'4 B
The value of understanding : the story of Margaret Mead / by Spencer Johnson ; illustrated by Pileggi. 1st ed. La Jolla, Calif. : Value Communications, c1979. 63 p. : col. ill. ; 28 cm. (ValueTales series) A biography, stressing the understanding and tolerance, of an anthropologist who did extensive studies of primitive cultures. [GN21.M36J63] 92 79-9800 ISBN 0-916392-37-6 : 5.95
1. Mead, Margaret, 1901- —Juvenile literature. 2. Anthropologists—United States—Biography—Juvenile literature. I. Pileggi, Steve. II. Title. BIP

RICE, Edward. 301.2'092'4 B
There's no one like Margaret! : A portrait of Margaret Mead / by Edward Rice. 1st ed. New York : Harper & Row, 1979. p. cm. Includes index. Bibliography: p. A biography of Margaret Mead as seen through her work. [GN21.M36R5 1979] 92 76-3827 ISBN 0-06-025001-1 : 10.00. ISBN 0-06-025002-X lib. bdg. : 9.89
1. Mead, Margaret, 1901- —Juvenile literature. 2. Anthropologists—United States—Juvenile literature. I. Title.

Mead, Richard, 1673-1754.

MEADE, Richard Hardaway, 1897- 610'.92'4 B
In the sunshine of life; a biography of Dr. Richard Mead, 1673-1754, by Richard H. Meade. Philadelphia, Dorrance [1974] 196 p. illus. 22 cm. Bibliography: p. 168-173. [R489.M4M4] 73-85546 ISBN 0-8059-1921-X 7.95
1. Mead, Richard, 1673-1754. I. Title.

Meade Co., S.D.—History.

MATO Paha: land of the pioneers; 917.83'44
northwest Meade County, South Dakota. [Marceline, Mo., Wallsworth, 1969] 650 p. illus., facsims., maps (on lining papers), ports. 29 cm. A history project sponsored by the Alkali Community Club. Pages 645-650, blank for clippings and recording dates. [F657.M4M3] 70-277419
1. Meade Co., S.D.—History. 2. Meade Co., S.D.—Biography. I. Alkali Community Club. II. Title: Mato Paha.

Meade, George Gordon, 1815-1872.

CLEAVES, Freeman, 1904- 923.573
Meade of Gettysburg. Norman, University of Oklahoma Press [1960] xi, 384 p. illus., ports., maps. 24 cm. Bibliography: p. 359-368. [E467.1.M38C45] 60-7735
1. Meade, George Gordon, 1815-1872. BIP

Meagher, Thomas Francis, 1823-1867.

ATHEARN, Robert G. 973.7'092'4 B
Thomas Francis Meagher : an Irish revolutionary in America / Robert G. Athearn. New York : Arno Press, 1977 182 p. : port. ; 24 cm. (The Irish-Americans) Reprint of the 1949 ed. published by University of Colorado Press, Boulder, which was issued as no. 1 of University of Colorado studies, Series in history. Includes index. Bibliography: p. 172-178. [E467.1.M4A83 1976] 76-6321 ISBN 0-405-09318-7 : 12.00
1. Meagher, Thomas Francis, 1823-1867. I. Title. II. Series. III. Series: Colorado. University. University of Colorado studies : Series in history ; no. 1. BIP

Meagher, Thomas Francis, 1823-1867— Juvenile literature.

LAMERS, William Mathias, 1900- 923.573
The thunder maker, General Thomas Meagher. Illustrated by Vera Yttri. Milwaukee, Bruce Pub. Co. [1959] 154p. illus. 22cm. (Catholic treasury books) [E467.1.M4L3] 59-10973
1. Meagher, Thomas Francis, 1823-1867—Juvenile literature. I. Title.

Meagher, Thomas Francis, 1823-1867—Juvenile literature.

ABODAHER, David J. 973.7'0924
Rebel on two continents: Thomas Meagher, by David J. Abodaher. New York, J. Messner [1970] 190 p. 22 cm. Bibliography: p. 186. A biography of the nineteenth-century Irish patriot who, after being exiled from his homeland, came to the United States where he served as a Union general and Governor of the Montana Territory. [E467.1.M4A2 1970] 92 70-123168 3.50
1. Meagher, Thomas Francis, 1823-1867—Juvenile literature. I. Title.

Means, Gaston Bullock, 1879-1938.

HOYT, Edwin Palmer. 923.4173
Spectacular rogue: Gaston B. Means. [1st ed.] Indianapolis, Bobbs-Merrill [1963] 352 p. illus. 22 cm. Includes bibliography. [CT275.M46552H6] 63-11643
1. Means, Gaston Bullock, 1879-1938. I. Title.

*Means, Marianne

*MEANS, Marianne 920.7
The woman in the White House; the lives, times, and influence of twelve notable first ladies [New York] New Amer. Lib. [1964, c.1963] 288p. 18cm. (Signet bk. T2512) .75 pap.,
I. Title.

Meany, George, 1894-

GOULDEN, Joseph C. 331.88'33'0924 B
Meany [by] Joseph C. Goulden. [1st ed.] New York, Atheneum, 1972. 504 p. 25 cm. Includes bibliographical references. [HD8073.M4G6] 72-82681 12.95
1. Meany, George, 1894-

Meany, George, 1894-—Juvenile literature.

FINKE, Blythe Foote. 331.88'33'0924 B
George Meany: modern leader of the American Federation of Labor. Charlotteville, N.Y., SamHar Press, 1972. 26 p. 23 cm. (Outstanding personalities, no. 38) Bibliography: p. 24-26. A biography of one of the most influential men in the labor movement with emphasis on his accomplishments in the last two decades. [HD8073.M4F55] 72-81899
1. Meany, George, 1894-—Juvenile literature. I. Title.

Mears, Henrietta Cornelia, 1890-

POWERS, Barbara Hudson. 922.573
The Henrietta Mears story. Introd. by Billy Graham. [Westwood, N. J.] Revell [1957] 191p. 22cm. [BV1518.M4P6] 57-8135
1. Mears, Henrietta Cornelia, 1890- I. Title.

Mears, Norman B., 1904-

COHN, Angelo. 686.2'092'4 B
Norman B. Mears, the man behind the shadow mask. Minneapolis, T. S. Denison [1972] 228 p. illus. 23 cm. (Men of achievement series of biographies) A biography of the Minnesota businessman who developed a small graphic arts company into a large business dealing in printing, photo-engraving, and electronics. [TR140.M38C63] 92 76-183713 ISBN 0-513-01231-1
1. Mears, Norman B., 1904- I. Title.

Mecherle, George Jacob, 1877-1951.

SCHRIFTGIESSER, Karl, 1903- 923.673
The farmer from Merna; a biography of George J. Mecherle and a history of the State Farm Insurance Companies of Bloomington, Illinois. New York, Random House, 1955. 243p. illus. 24cm. [HG8963.S67M47] 55-10628
1. Mecherle, George Jacob, 1877-1951. 2. State Farm Mutual Automobile Insurance Company. 3. State Farm Life Insurance Company. I. Title.

Mechnikov, Ilia Ilich, 1845-1916.

MARDUS, Elaine. 500.9'0924 B
Man with a microscope: Elie Metchnikoff. New York, J. Messner [1968] 223 p. 22 cm. Bibliography: p. 217-218. [QR31.M4M3] 68-25095 3.50
1. Mechnikov, Il'ia Il'ch, 1845-1916. I. Title.

MARDUS, Elaine. 500.9'0924 B
Man with a microscope: Elie Metchnikoff. New York, J. Messner [1968] 223 p. 22 cm. Bibliography: p. 217-218. [QR31.M4M3] 68-25095 3.50
1. Mechnikov, Il'ia Il'ch, 1845-1916. I. Title.

MECHNIKOVA, Olga. 591'.092'4 B
Life of Elie Metchnikoff, 1845-1916, by Olga Metchnikoff. With a pref. by Ray Lankester. Freeport, N.Y., Books for Libraries Press [1972] xxiii, 297 p. port. 22 cm. Translation of Vie d'Elie Metchnikoff. Reprint of the 1921 ed. Bibliography: p. 285-290. [QH31.M4M4 1972] 72-7248 ISBN 0-8369-6949-9
1. Mechnikov, Il'ia Il'ich, 1845-1916. I. Title. BIP

MECHNIKOVA, Olga. 591'.092'4 B
Life of Elie Metchnikoff, 1845-1916, by Olga Metchnikoff. With a pref. by Ray Lankester. Freeport, N.Y., Books for Libraries Press [1972] xxiii, 297 p. port. 22 cm. Translation of Vie d'Elie Metchnikoff. Reprint of the 1921 ed. Bibliography: p. 285-290. [QH31.M4M4 1972] 72-7248 ISBN 0-8369-6949-9
1. Mechnikov, Il'ia Il'ich, 1845-1916. I. Title. BIP

MEDINA Centennial Celebration, 1952 928.6
Jose Toribio Medina, humanist of the Americas; an appraisal. Contributors: Maury A. Bromsen [and others] Edited by Maury A. Bromsen [and others] Edited by Maury A. Bromsen. Washington, Pan American Union, 1960. iiv, 295p. illus., ports. 24cm. Papers presented at an international symposium on Medina's contributions to Americanist studies, held in Washington, Nov. 6-8, 1952, as part of the Medina Centennial Celebration. Includes bibliographical references. [Z1004.M49M4 1952] 60-60020
1. Medina, Jose Toriblo, 1852-1930. I. Bromsen, Maury A., ed. II. Pan American Union. III. Title.

SLOSSON, Edwin Emery, 1865-1929. 920.04
Major prophets of to-day, by Edwin E. Slosson. Freeport, N.Y., Books for

Libraries Press [1968] xii, 299 p. ports. 23 cm. (Essay index reprint series) Reprint of the 1914 ed. "The chapters of this volume have appeared in the Independent ... in a series under the general title of Twelve major prophets of to-day." Contents.Contents.—Maurice Maeterlinck.—Henri Bergson.—Henri Poincare.—Elie Metchnikoff.—Wilhelm Ostwald.—Ernst Haeckel. [CT119.S6 1968] 68-8493
1. Maeterlinck, Maurice, 1862-1949. 2. Bergson, Henri Louis, 1859-1941. 3. Poincare, Henri, 1854-1912. 4. Mechnikov, Il'ia Il'ich, 1845-1916. 5. Ostwald, Wilhelm, 1853-1932. 6. Haeckel, Ernst Heinrich Philipp August, 1834-1919. I. Title. BIP

Mecom, Jane (Franklin) 1712-1794.

VAN DOREN, Carl 973.3'2'0924 B
Clinton, 1885-1950.
Jane Mecom, the favorite sister of Benjamin Franklin: her life here first fully narrated from their entire surviving correspondence. Clifton [N.J.] A. M. Kelley, 1973 [c1950] vii, 255 p. illus. 22 cm. (Viking reprint editions) [E302.6.F8V37 1973] 78-122067 ISBN 0-678-03174-6
1. Mecom, Jane (Franklin) 1712-1794. 2. Franklin, Benjamin, 1706-1790.

VAN DOREN, Carl 973.3'2'0924 B
Clinton, 1885-1950.
Jane Mecom, the favorite sister of Benjamin Franklin: her life here first fully narrated from their entire surviving correspondence. Clifton [N.J.] A. M. Kelley, 1973 [c1950] vii, 255 p. illus. 22 cm. (Viking reprint editions) [E302.6.F8V37 1973] 78-122067 ISBN 0-678-03174-6 11.50
1. Mecom, Jane (Franklin) 1712-1794. 2. Franklin, Benjamin, 1706-1790.

Medalists—Dictionaries.

FORRER, Leonard. 737'.03
Biographical dictionary of medallists: coin, gem, and seal-engravers, mint-masters, &c., ancient and modern, with references to their works, B.C. 500-A.D. 1900, compiled by L. Forrer. New York, B. Franklin [1970] 8 v. illus. 24 cm. (Burt Franklin bibliography & reference series, 319) Reprint of the 1902 30 ed. Bibliography: v. 1, p. xxxix-xlvii. [CJ5535.F72] 71-118749
1. Medalists—Dictionaries. I. Title.

Medaris, John B., 1902-

HARRIS, Gordon L. 283'.092'4 B
A new command : the life of Bruce Medaris, Major General, USA, retired / Gordon Harris. Plainfield, N.J. : Logos International, c1976. v, 313 p., [7] leaves of plates : ill. ; 21 cm. [BX5995.M43H37] 76-10533 ISBN 0-88270-181-9 : 3.50
1. Medaris, John B., 1902- 2. Protestant Episcopal Church in the U.S.A.—Clergy—Biography. 3. Clergy—United States—Biography. 4. Generals—United States—Biography. I. Title.

Medem, Vladimir Davidovich, 1880-1923.

MEDEM, Vladimir 335.43'092'4 B
Davidovich, 1880-1923.
Vladimir Medem, the life and soul of a legendary Jewish socialist / [translated by] Samuel A. Portnoy. New York : Ktav Pub. House, c1979. xxxvi, 583 p., [9] leaves of plates : ;ill. ; 24 cm. Translation of Fun mayn leben. Includes index. [HX312.M413] 78-11146 ISBN 0-87068-332-2 : 20.00
1. Medem, Vladimir Davidovich, 1880-1923. 2. Socialists—Russia—Biography. 3. Jews in Russia—Biography. 4. Jews in Russia—Social conditions. I. Title.

Medema, Ken.

MEDEMA, Ken. 780'.92'4 B
Come and see / Ken Medema, with Joyce Norman. Waco, Tex. : Word Books, c1976. 142 p. : ports. ; 23 cm. [ML410.M455A3] 76-19533 ISBN 0-87680-438-5 : 5.95
1. Medema, Ken. 2. Composers—United States—Biography. I. Norman, Joyce, joint author. II. Title. BIP

Medical jurisprudence—Cases, clinical reports, statistics.

SMITH, Sir Sydney Alfred. 923.442
Mostly murder. With a foreword by Erle Stanley Gardner. New York, D. McKay Co. [1960, c1959] 318 p. illus. 22 cm. Autobiographical. [RA1025.S55A3] 60-16253
1. Medical jurisprudence — Cases, clinical reports, statistics. I. Title.

SMITH, Sydney Alfred Sir 923.442
Mostly murder. With a foreword by Erle Stanley Gardner. Ew York, D. McKay Co. [1960, c.1959] 318p. illus. 22cm. 60-16253 4.95
1. Medical jurisprudence—Cases, clinical reports, statistics. I. Title.

Medical microbiology—History.

REID, Robert, 1933- 616.01'09
Microbes and men / Robert Reid. [New York] : Saturday Review Press, 1975. 170 p. : ill. ; 24 cm. [QR46.R43] 74-24326 ISBN 0-8415-0348-6 : 8.95
1. Medical microbiology—History. 2. Microbiologists. I. Title. BIP

Medici, House of.

HALE, John Rigby, 320.9'45'51
1923-
Florence and the Medici : the pattern of control / J. R. Hale. [London] : Thames and Hudson, c1977. 208 p., [8] leaves of plates : ill. ; 24 cm. Includes index. Bibliography: p. 197-202 [DG737.42.H34] 78-306330 ISBN 0-500-25059-6 : 14.95
1. Medici, House of. 2. Florence—History—1421-1737. 3. Florence—Kings and rulers—Biography. I. Title.
Distributed by W. W. Norton, New York BIP

POTTINGER, George. 945'.51
The court of the Medici / George Pottinger. London : Croom Helm ; Totawa, N.J. : Rowman and Littlefield, c1978. 141 p. ; 23 cm. Includes index. Bibliography: p. 135-137. [DG735.6.P67 1978] 78-303056 ISBN 0-8476-6024-9 (Rowman and Littlefield) : 12.50
1. Medici, House of. 2. Florence—Civilization. 3. Florence—Court and courtiers. I. Title. BIP

Medici, Lorenzo de', il Magnifico, 1449-1492.

ADY, Cecilia Mary, 1881- 923.1455
Lorenzo dei Medici and Renaissance Italy. New York, Collier [1962] 157p. 18cm. (Men and hist. AS421V) Bibl. .95 pap.,
1. Medici, Lorenzo de', il Magnifico, 1449-1492. 2. Renaissance—Italy. I. Title.

ADY, Cecilia Mary, 1881- 923.1455
1958.
Lorenzo dei Medici and Renaissance Italy. New York, Macmillan [1952?] 176 p. illus. 18 cm. (Teach yourself history library) [DG737.9.A6] 55-4109
1. Medici, Lorenzo de', il Magnifico, 1449-1492. 2. Renaissance—Italy.

ARMSTRONG, 945'.51'050924 B
Edward, 1846-1928.
Lorenzo de' Medici and Florence in the fifteenth century. Freeport, N.Y., Books for Libraries Press [1973] p. Reprint of the 1896 ed. published by Putnam, New York, in series: Heroes of the nations. [DG737.9.A7 1973] 73-4531 ISBN 0-518-19013-7
1. Medici, Lorenzo de', il Magnifico, 1449-1492. 2. Florence—History—1421-1737. I. Title.

ROSS Williamson, 945'.51'050924 B
Hugh, 1901-
Lorenzo the Magnificent. New York, Putnam [1974] 288 p. illus. (part col.) 26 cm. Bibliography: p. 282. [DG737.9.R74] 73-93068 ISBN 0-399-11361-4 15.95
1. Medici, Lorenzo de', il Magnifico, 1449-1492. I. Title.

ROWDON, Maurice. 945.51'05'0924 B
Lorenzo the Magnificent / Maurice Rowdon. Chicago : H. Regnery Co., 1974. 237 p. : ill. ; 26 cm. Includes index. Bibliography: p. 225. [DG737.9.R76 1974b] 73-15043 ISBN 0-8092-1146-7 : 14.95
1. Medici, Lorenzo de', il Magnifico, 1449-1492. 2. Florence—History—1421-1737. I. Title.

WELLIVER, Warman, 1913- 923.1455
Lorenzo and Florence. Indianapolis, Clio Press [1961] 88 p. illus. 22 cm. [DG737.55.W4] 61-18214
1. Florence — Hist. 2. Medici, Lorence de', il Magnifico, 1449-1462. I. Title.

Medicine—Addresses, essays, lectures.

NEWMAN, George, Sir, 610'.922
1870-1948.
Interpreters of nature; essays. Freeport, N.Y., Books for Libraries Press [1968] 296 p. 22 cm. (Essay index reprint series) "First published 1927." Contents.Contents.—The great Paduans; a century of medicine at Padua.—Thomas Sydenham, reformer of English medicine.—Hermann Boerhaave; the disciples of Boerhaave in Edinburgh.—John Hunter, the private practitioner as pioneer in preventive medicine.—John Keats: apothecary and poet.—Louis Pasteur: The character of Louis Pasteur.—William Osler: a physician of two continents.—Modern interpreters; fifty years' progress in public health.—Future interpreters; everyman in preventive medicine. Bibliographical footnotes. [R117.N4 1968] 68-20325
1. Medicine—Addresses, essays, lectures. 2. Medicine—Biography. 3. Medicine—History. I. Title. BIP

Medicine, Ancient—Collected works.

EDELSTEIN, Ludwig, 610'.9'01
1902-1965.
Ancient medicine; selected papers of Ludwig Edelstein. Edited by Owsei Temkin and C. Lilian Temkin. Translations from the German by C. Lilian Temkin. Baltimore, Johns Hopkins Press [1967] xiv, 496 p. port. 24 cm. Bibliographical footnotes. [R135.E3] 67-12425
1. Medicine, Ancient—Collected works. I. Temkin, Owsei, 1902- ed. II. Temkin, Clarice Lilian (Shelley) 1906- ed. III. Title.

Medicine—Biography.

CHANDLER, Caroline Augusta, 926.1
1906-
Famous men of medicine. New York, Dodd, Mead, 1950. 140 p. illus., ports. 23 cm. [R134.C44] 50-617
1. Medicine—Biog. I. Title.

GIBSON, John, 1907- 610'.922
Great doctors and medical scientists. London, Melbourne [ect.] Macmillan; New York, St. Martin's P., 1967. vi, 122 p. 16 plates (incl. ports.), diagrs. 20 1/2 cm. (The Venturers biographies) 7/6 [R134] 67-69591
1. Medicine—Biog. I. Title.

GREENWOOD, Major, 1880- 614'.0922
Some British pioneers of social medicine. Freeport, N.Y., Books for Libraries Press [1970, c1948] 118 p. 23 cm. (University of London. Heath Clark lectures, 1946) (Biography index reprint series.) [R489.A1G7 1970] 71-126320
1. Medicine—Biography. 2. Hygiene, Public—Gt. Brit. I. Title. II. Series: London. University. Heath Clark lectures, 1946 BIP

MCGRADY, Mike 926.1
Jungle doctors. Philadelphia, Lippincott [c.1962] 191p. illus. 21cm. 62-18011 3.95
1. Medicine—Biog. 2. Tropics—Diseases and hygiene. 3. Missions, Medical. I. Title.

PERSPECTIVES in biology and 926.1
medicine.
A dozen doctors; autobiographic sketches. Edited by Dwight J. Ingle. Chicago, University of Chicago Press [1963] vii, 286 p. 24 cm. "Originally published in Perspectives in biology and medicine." Includes bibliographies. [R134.P48] 63-20908
*1. Medicine—Biog. 2. Biology—Biog. I. Ingle, Dwight Joyce, 1907- ed. II. Title.*BIP

PERSPECTIVES in biology and 926.1
medicine A dozen doctors; autobiographic sketches. Ed. by Dwight J. Ingle. Chicago, Univ. of Chic. Pr. [c.1958-1963] vii, 286p. 24cm. Bibl. 63-20908 5.50
1. Medicine—Biog. 2. Biology—Biog. I. Ingle, Dwight Joyce, 1907- ed.

POOLE, Lynn. 610.922
Doctors who saved lives, by Lynn and Gray Poole. New York, Dodd, Mead [1966] xii, 148 p. ports. 21 cm. (Makers of our modern world books) [R134.P65] 66-20318
1. Medicine—Biography. I. Poole, Gray, joint author. II. Title.

TALBOTT, John Harold, 610'.922 B
1902-
A biographical history of medicine: excerpts and essays on the men and their work [by] John H. Talbott. New York, Grune & Stratton [1970] 1211 p. illus., ports. 27 cm. Includes bibliographical references. [R134.T35] 78-109574
1. Medicine—Biography. I. Title. BIP

WALKER, M. E. M. 614'.0922
Pioneers of public health; the story of some benefactors of the human race, by M. E. M. Walker. With a foreword by Sir Humphrey Rolleston. Freeport, N.Y., Books for Libraries Press [1968] xv, 270 p. facsim., ports. 23 cm. (Essay index reprint series) Reprint of the 1930 ed. Includes bibliographies. [R134.W17 1968] 68-26483
1. Medicine—Biography. 2. Hygiene, Public—History. I. Title. BIP

WALSH, James Joseph, 610'.922 B
1865-1942.
Makers of modern medicine. Freeport, N.Y., Books for Libraries Press [1970] viii, 362 p. port. 23 cm. (Essay index reprint series) Reprint of the 1907 ed. Contents.Contents.—The making of medicine.—Morgagni, father of pathology.—Auenbrugger, inventor of percussion.—Jenner, discoverer of vaccination.—Galvani, founder of animal electricity.—Laennec, Father of physical diagnosis.—The Irish school of medicine - Graves, Stokes, Corrigan.—Muller, father of German medicine.—Schwann, founder of the Cell doctrine.—Claude Bernard, discoverer in physiology.—Pasteur, father of preventive medicine.—O'Dwyer, inventor of Intubation. [R134.W2 1970] 70-107741
1. Medicine—Biography. I. Title. BIP

WELLS, Walter Augustine, 926.1
1870-1964.
Doctors you know by name, by Walter A. Wells. Philadelphia, Dorrance [1964] xiv, 190 p. port. 21 cm. [R134.W4] 64-15897
1. Medicine — Biog. I. Title.

WILLIAMS, John Hargreaves 926.1
Harley, 1901-
The healing touch. Springfield, Ill., Thomas [1951] 370 p. illus. 21 cm. [R134.W6 1951] 51-6347
1. Medicine—Biog. 2. Medicine—Hist. I. Title.

Medicine—Biography—Juvenile literature.

CHANDLER, Caroline 610.922
Augusta, 1906-
Famous modern men of medicine, by Caroline A. Chandler. New York, Dodd, Mead [1965] 155 p. illus., ports. 22 cm. (Famous biographies for young people) [R153.C46] 65-19601
1. Medicine—Biography—Juvenile literature. I. Title.

CHANDLER, Caroline 610.922
Augusta, M.D., 1906-
Famous modern men of medicine. New York, Dodd [c.1965] 155p. illus., ports. 22cm. (Famous biogs. for young people) [R153.C46] 65-19601 3.25
1. Medicine—Biog.—Juvenile literature. I.

Title.

FARR, Muriel 920
Children in medicine. Illus. by Elinor Jaeger. Englewood Cliffs. N.J., Prentice [c.1964] 71p. illus., ports. 22cm. (P-H jr. res. bks.) 64-14981 3.25
1. Medicine—Biog. —Juvenile literature. I. Title.

FARR, Muriel. j920
Children in medicine. Illustrated by Elinor Jaeger. Englewood Cliffs, N.J., Prentice-Hall [1964] 71 p. illus., ports. 22 cm. (P-H junior research books) [R134.F3] 64-14981
1. Medicine — Biog. — Juvenile literature. I. Title.

RICH, Josephine. 610/.922
Women behind men of medicine. New York, Messner [1967] 190p. 22cm. [R134.R58] 67-216630 3.34
1. Medicine—Biog.—Juvenile literature, 2. Women in medicine—Juvenile literature. I. Title.
Contents Omitted.

Medicine—Cases, clinical reports, statistics.

FABRICANT, Noah Daniel 616.092
13 famous patients: Franklin D. Roosevelt [and others. 1st ed.] Philadelphia, Chilton Co. [c.1960] ix, 231p. Bibl.: p.215-221 illus. 21cm. 60-14578 3.50
1. Medicine—Cases, clinical reports, statistics. I. Title.

LOOMER, Alice. 616'.09
Famous flaws / Alice Loomer. New York : Macmillan, 1976. p. cm. Includes index. [R703.L66] 76-8411 ISBN 0-02-575101-8
1. Medicine—Cases, clinical reports, statistics. 2. Biography. 3. Physically handicapped—Biography. 4. Deformities—Cases, clinical reports, statistics. I. Title. **BIP**

OBER, William B. 809
Boswell's clap and other essays : medical analyses of literary men's afflictions / by William B. Ober. Carbondale : Southern Illinois University Press, c1979. xiv, 291 p. : ill., facsims. (on lining papers) ; 25 cm. Includes bibliographical references. [R703.O23] 78-16018 ISBN 0-8093-0889-4 : 17.50
1. Medicine—Cases, clinical reports, statistics. 2. Authors—Diseases and hygiene—Cases, clinical reports, statistics. 3. Authors—Biography—Addresses, essays, lectures. 4. Literature and medicine—Addresses, essays, lectures. I. Title. **BIP**

ROUECHE, Berton, 1911- 616.092
A man named Hoffman, and other narratives of medical detection. [1st ed.] Boston, Little, Brown [1965] 276 p. 21 cm. [RC66.R65] 65-16876
1. Medicine—Cases, clinical reports, statistics. I. Title.

TENEMENTS of clay : 616'.09
an anthology of medical biographical essays / chosen and edited by Arnold Sorsby. New York : Scribner, [1975] c1974. 258 p. : ill. ; 22 cm. Includes bibliographical references. [R703.T46 1975] 74-14010 ISBN 0-684-14035-7 : 7.95
1. Medicine—Cases, clinical reports, statistics. 2. Biography—Addresses, essays, lectures. I. Sorsby, Arnold, 1900-
Contents omitted

Medicine—China—Biography.

UNITED States. 610'.92'2 B
Library of Congress.
Chinese personalities in biomedicine / prepared under an interagency agreement with the Library of Congress. [Bethesda, Md.] : U.S. Dept. of Health, Education, and Welfare, Public Health Service, National Institutes of Health, 1975. v, 87 p. ; 27 cm. (A Publication of Geographic Health Studies, John E. Fogarty International Center for Advanced Study in the Health Sciences) (DHEW publication ; no. (NIH) 75-783) Includes index. [R604.A1U54 1975] 75-600973
1. Medicine—China—Biography. 2. Physicians—China—Biography. I. Title. II. Series: John E. Fogarty International Center for Advanced Study in the Health Sciences. Geographic Health Studies. A publication of the Geographic Health Studies, John E. Fogarty International Center for Advanced Study in the Health Sciences. III. Series: United States. Dept. of Health, Education, and Welfare. DHEW publication ; no. (NIH) 75-783.

Medicine—History.

HATHAWAY, Esse Virginia, 609.22
1871-1939.
Partners in progress [by] Esse V. Hathaway. Illustrated by Edmund F. Ward. Freeport, N.Y., Books for Libraries Press [1968] vii, 303 p. ports. 22 cm. (Essay index reprint series) Reprint of the 1935 ed. Bibliography: p. 293-295. [CB151.H35 1968] 68-29213
1. Medicine—History. 2. Medicine—Biography. 3. Inventions—History. 4. Inventors. 5. Machinery—History. 6. Charities—History. I. Title. **BIP**

SIGERIST, Henry Ernest, v. 12
1891-.
The great doctors; a biographical history of medicine. Tr. by Eden and Cedar Paul. [2. ed.] Garden City, Doubleday [1933; reprinted 1958] xv, [2], 422 p. 18 cm. (Anchor Book A 140) Bibliography: p. 389-401.
1. Medicine — Hist. 2. Physicians — Biog. I. Title. **BIP**

SIGERIST, Henry 610'.922 B
Ernest, 1891-1957.
The great doctors; a biographical history of medicine. Translated by Eden and Cedar Paul. Freeport, N.Y., Books for Libraries Press [1971] 436 p. illus., ports. 23 cm. (Essay index reprint series) Translation of Grosse Arzte. Reprint of the 1933 ed. Bibliography: p. 405-415. [R134.S4613 1971b] 74-156716 ISBN 0-8369-2297-2
1. Medicine—History. 2. Physicians—Biography. I. Title.

SIGERIST, Henry Ernest, 610'.922
1891-1957.
The great doctors; a biographical history of medicine. Translated by Eden and Cedar Paul. New York, Dover Publications [1971] 436 p. illus., ports. 22 cm. (Dover histories, biographies, and classics of medicine) Reprint of the 1933 ed., a translation of the 2d ed. of Grosse Arzte. Bibliography: p. 405-415. [R134.S4613 1971] 78-143674 ISBN 0-486-22696-4 4.50
1. Medicine—History. 2. Physicians—Biography. I. Title.

Medicine—Latin America.

MOLL, Aristides 610'.98
Alcibiades, 1882-
Aesculapius in Latin America, by Aristides A. Moll. [New York] Argosy-Antiquarian, 1969. xii, 639 p. illus., facsims., plans, ports. 23 cm. Reprint of the 1944 ed. Bibliography: p. 582-594. [R464.5.M6 1969] 76-101589
1. Medicine—Latin America. 2. Physicians—Biography. I. Title.

Medicine, Military—Biography.

EDELSON, Edward, 1932- 610'.922 B
Healers in uniform. [1st ed.] Garden City, N.Y., Doubleday, 1971. 184 p. 22 cm. Contents.Contents.—Benjamin Rush: a tradition is born.—William Beaumont: the magic window.—John Shaw Billings: the master builder.—George Miller Sternberg: frontier Pasteur.—Walter Reed: the conquest of yellow jack.—Bailey K. Ashford: beating the laziness bug.—Oswald H. Robertson: blood for the wounded.—A victory without a hero: typhus in Naples.—David N. W. Grant: wings for the wounded.—William Randolph Lovelace II: the high horizon.—Harry G. Armstrong: the farthest frontier.—John Paul Stapp: the human machine. [UH341.E32] 78-131072 3.95
1. Medicine, Military—Biography. I. Title.

Medicine—New Hampshire—Sullivan Co.—History.

STEARNS, Carl M. 610'.92'2 B
The early history of medicine in Sullivan County, N.H. / by Carl M. Stearns. 1st ed. [s.l. : s.n., 1974] (Springfield, Vt. : Hurd's Offset Print.) 197 p. : ill. ; 24 cm. [R280.S84S83] 74-195194 7.95
1. Medicine—New Hampshire—Sullivan Co.—History. 2. Physicians—New Hampshire—Sullivan Co.—Biography. 3. Sullivan Co., N.H.—Biography. I. Title.

Medicine—Pennsylvania—Montgomery Co.—History.

MEIER, Louis Alois, 610'.9748'12
1930-
Early Pennsylvania medicine : a representative early American medical history, Montgomery County, Pennsylvania, 1682 to 1799 / by Louis A. Meier. [Boyertown, Pa. : Gilbert Print. Co., 1976]. xx, 264 p. : ill. ; 24 cm. Includes index. Bibliography: p. 241-246. [R314.M66M45] 76-366974
1. Medicine—Pennsylvania—Montgomery Co.—History. 2. Physicians—Pennsylvania—Montgomery Co.—Biography. 3. Montgomery Co., Pa.—Biography. I. Title.

Medicine—Russia.

PONDOEV, Gavriil 926.1
Sergeevich.
Notes of a Soviet doctor. [2d ed., rev. and enl., translated from Russian by Basil Haigh] New York, Consultants Bureau, 1959. 238p. 24cm. [R532.P613 1959] 59-9232
1. Medicine—Russia. 2. Medicine—Practice. 3. Physicians—Russia. I. Title.

Medicine—15th-18th cent.

SYDENHAM, Thomas, 1624- 610.924
1689
Dr. Thomas Sydenham. 1624-1689; his life and original writings [by] Kenneth Dewhurst. Berkeley, Univ. of Calif. Pr., 1966. viii. 191p. illus., facsims., map. port. 23cm. Bibl. [R489.S85A2 1966] 66-19348 6.00 bds.,
1. Medicine—15th-18th cent. I. Dewhurst, Kenneth. II. Title.

Medina, Harold Raymond, 1888-

DANIEL, Hawthorne, 1890- 923.473
Judge Medina, a biography. New York, W. Funk [1952] 373 p. illus. 21 cm. 52-9783
1. Medina, Harold Raymond, 1888- I. Title.

Medina, Jose Toribio, 1852-1930.

PAN American Union 928.6
Jose Toribio Medina, humanist of the Americas; an appraisal. Ed. by Maury A. Bromsen. Washington, D. C. [Author, c.] 1960. liv, 295p. illus., ports. Papers presented at an international symposium on Medina's contributions to Americanist studies, held in Washington, Nov. 6-8, 1952, as part of the Medina centennial celebration. Bibl. 60-60020 6.00; 4.00 lim. ed. pap.,
1. Medina, Jose Toribio, 1852-1930. I. Bromsen, Maury A., ed. II. Title.

Meditation (Buddhism)

SUNNO Bhikku, 1945- 294.3'4'43
Living Buddhist masters / Sunno Bhikku. Santa Cruz, Calif. : Unity Press, 1975. p. cm. (Mindfulness series) Includes index. Bibliography: p. [BQ5612.S93] 75-20291 ISBN 0-913300-03-9 : 9.95. ISBN 0-913300-04-7 : 4.95
1. Meditation (Buddhism) 2. Buddhist monks—Burma—Biography. 3. Buddhist monks—Thailand—Biography. I. Title.

Meditations.

NADEN, Roy C. 221.9'22 B
Without a doubt / by Roy C. Naden. Mountain View, Calif. : Pacific Press Pub. Association, c1975. 78 p. : ill. ; 19 cm. [BS571.N3 1975] 75-32709
1. Bible. O.T.—Biography. 2. Meditations. I. Title. **BIP**

Medvedev, Zhores Aleksandrovich.

MEDVEDEV, Zhores 364.1'3 B
Aleksandrovich.
A question of madness / Zhores A. Medvedev, Roy A. Medvedev ; translated from the Russian by Ellen de Kadt. New York : Norton, 1979, c1971. p. cm. Translation of Kto sumasshedshii? [DK275.M35A3513 1979] 79-1106 ISBN 0-393-00921-1 : 3.95
1. Medvedev, Zhores Aleksandrovich. 2. Medvedev, Roi Aleksandrovich. 3. Political prisoners—Russia—Biography. 4. Psychiatric hospitals—Russia. I. Medvedev, Roi Aleksandrovich, joint author. II. Title. **BIP**

Medwin, Thomas, 1788-1869.

LOVELL, Ernest James, Jr., 928.2
1918-
Captain Medwin, friend of Byron and Shelly. Austin, Univ. of Texas Pr. [c.1962] 348p. 24cm. Bibl. 62-9788 5.75
1. Medwin, Thomas 1788-1869. I. Title.

LOVELL, Ernest James, 1918- 928.2
Captain Medwin, friend of Byron and Shelley. Austin, University of Texas Press [1962] 348 p. 24 cm. Includes bibliography. [PR4990.M37Z77] 62-9788
1. Medwin, Thomas, 1788-1869. I. Title.

Mee, Charles L.

MEE, Charles L. 070.4'092'4 b
A visit to Haldeman and other states of mind / Charles L. Mee, Jr. New York : M. Evans ; Philadelphia : distributed in the United States by Lippincott, c1977. 226 p. ; 24 cm. [CT275.M46554A38 1977] 76-30775 ISBN 0-87131-229-8 : 8.95
1. Mee, Charles L. 2. United States—Biography. 3. Watergate Affair, 1972- I. Title. **BIP**

Meed, Samuel Williams, 1895-

COLWELL, Robert T 926.591
The one world of Sam Meek as told to Robert T. Colwell by Sam Meek's friends and associates. New York, 1964. 75 p. ports. 27 cm. "Limited to five hundred copies." [HF5810.M4C6] 65-82
1. Meed, Samuel Williams, 1895- I. Title.

Meegeren, Han van, 1889-1947.

KILBRACKEN, John Raymond 927.5
Godley, baron, 1920-
The master forger; the story of Han van Meegeren. New York, W. Funk [1951?] 223p. illus. 20cm. [ND653.M58K53 1951a] 51-7661
1. Meegeren, Han van, 1889-1947. 2. Vermeer, Johannes, 1632-1675. 3. Hooch, Pieter de, 17th cent. 4. Forgery of works of art. 5. Paintings—Expertising. I. Title.

KILBRACKEN, John Raymond 759.9492
Godley, Baron, 1920-
Van Meegeren, master forger [by] Lord Kilbracken. New York, Scribner [1968, c1967] 197 p. illus., ports. 22 cm. [ND653.M58K56 1968] 68-17337
1. Meegeren, Han van, 1889-1947.

Meek, Joseph Lafayette, 1810-1875.

VESTAL, Stanley, 1887- 923.973
Joe Medk, the Merry Mountain man a biography. Lincoln Univ. of Nebr. Pr. [1963, c.1952] 336p. 21cm. (Bison bk. 154) Bibl. 1.60 pap.,

1. Meek, Joseph Lafayette, 1810-1875. I. Title.

VESTAL, Stanley, 1887- 923.973
Joe Meek; the merry mountain man, a biography. Caldwell, Idaho, Caxton Printers, 1952. 336 p. illus. 24 cm. Bibliography: p. [332]-336. [F880.M513] 52-5211
1. Meek, Joseph Lafayette, 1810-1875.

Meeks, Cathy.

MEEKS, Cathy. 248'.2'0924 B
I want somebody to know my name / by Cathy Meeks. Nashville : T. Nelson, c1978. 153 ; 21 cm. Includes index. [BR1725.M358A34] 78-670 ISBN 0-8407-5642-9 pbk. : 3.95
1. Meeks, Cathy. 2. Christian biography—United States. 3. Afro-Americans—Biography. I. Title. **BIP**

Meeman, Edward John, 1889-1966.

MEEMAN, Edward John, 1889-1966. 070.4'092'4 B
The editorial we : a posthumous autobiography / by Edward J. Meeman ; compiled and edited by Edwin Howard. Memphis : Memphis State University, c1976. p. cm. [PN4874.M485A33] 75-40139
1. Meeman, Edward John, 1889-1966. I. Howard, Edwin, 1924- II. Title.

Megan, Thomas M., 1899-1951.

WOJNIAK, Edward J 1909- 922.273
Atomic apostle, Thomas M. Megan, s.v.d. Techny, Ill., Divine Word Publications [1957] 279 p. illus. 21 cm. [BX4705.M4835W6] 58-17591
1. Megan, Thomas M., 1899-1951. I. Title.

Mehegan, Mary Xavier, Mother, 1825-1915.

MCENIRY, Blanche Marie, Sister, 1906- 922.273
Woman of decision; the life of Mother Mary Xavier Mehegan, foundress of the Sisters of Charity of Saint Elizabeth, Convent, New Jersey. New York, McMullen Books [1953] 232p. illus. 21cm. [BX4705.M484M3] 53-8121
1. Mehegan, Mary Xavier, Mother, 1825-1915. 2. Sisters of Charity of Saint Elizabeth, Convent Station, N. J. I. Title.

Meher Baba, 1894-1969.

ANZAR, Naosherwan. 294.5'6'3 B
The beloved : the life and work of Meher Baba / by Naosherwan Anzar. North Myrtle Beach, S.C. : Sheriar Press, [1974] xi, 146 p. : ill. ; 27 cm. [BL1175.M4A66] 75-301349 10.00
1. Meher Baba, 1894-1969. I. Title.

HOPKINSON, Henry Thomas, 1905- 294.5'6'3 B
Much silence : Meher Baba, his life and work / Tom and Dorothy Hopkinson. New York : Dodd, Mead, 1975, c1974. 191 p. : port. ; 22 cm. Includes bibliographical references. [BL1175.M4H66 1975] 74-26821 ISBN 0-396-07141-4 : 7.95
1. Meher Baba, 1894-1969. I. Hopkinson, Dorothy, joint author. II. Title. **BIP**

MEHER BABA, 1894- 922.94
The wisdom of Meher Baba. With interpretive verse by Ruth Whitte. [Charleston S. C., 1957] 68p. port. 21cm. [BL1270.M43] 58-16289
I. White, Ruth. II. Title.

Mehl, Duane.

MEHL, Duane. 362.2'93'0926
No more for the road : one man's journey from chemical dependency to freedom / Duane Mehl ; drawings by Siegfried Reinhardt. Minneapolis : Augsburg Pub. House, c1976. 159 p. : ill. ; 20 cm. [HV5805.M43A35] 75-22721 ISBN 0-8066-1515-X pbk. : 3.50
1. Mehl, Duane. 2. Drug abuse—Biography. 3. Alcoholics—Biography. I. Title. **BIP**

Mehmet II, the Great, Sultan of the Turks, 1430 (ca.)-1481.

BABINGER, Franz Carl Heinrich, 1891-1967. 956.1'01'0924 B
Mehmed the Conqueror and his time / Franz Babinger ; translated from the German by Ralph Manheim ; edited, with a pref., by William C. Hickman. Princeton, N.J. : Princeton University Press, 1977,c1978 p. cm. (Bollingen series ; 96) Translation of Mehmed der Eroberer und seine Zeit. Includes bibliographical references and index. [DR501.B313] 77-71972 ISBN 0-691-09900-6 : 30.00
1. Mehmet II, the Great, Sultan of the Turks, 1430 (ca.)-1481. 2. Turkey—History—Mehmet II, 1451-1481. I. Title. II. Series. **BIP**

KRITOBOULOS, 15thcent. 949.6
History of Mehmed the Conqueror, by Kritovoulos. Translated from the Greek by Charles T. Riggs. Westport, Conn., Greenwood Press [1970, c1954] ix, 222 p. 23 cm. Translation of Kritoboulou bios tou Moameth Deuterou (romanized form) [DR501.K713 1970] 79-90541
1. Mehmet II, the Great, Sultan of the Turks, 1430 (ca.)-1481. I. Title. **BIP**

Mehring, Walter, 1896- —Books and reading.

MEHRING, Walter, 1896- 928.3
The lost library, the autobiography of a culture; translated by Richard and Clara Winston. [1st ed.] Indianapolis, Bobbs-Merrill [1951] 290 p. 23 cm. [PT2625.E24L6] 51-11567
1. Mehring, Walter, 1896- —Books and reading. I. Title.

Mehta, Amolak Ram, 1895-

MEHTA, Ved Parkash. 915.4'5
Daddyji [by] Ved Mehta. New York, Farrar, Straus and Giroux [1972] 195 p. ports. 22 cm. [DS481.M367M43] 78-179793 ISBN 0-374-13438-3 6.95
1. Mehta, Amolak Ram, 1895 2. India—Social life and customs. I. Title. **BIP**

MEHTA, Ved Parkash. 362.1'092'4 B
Daddyji / Ved Mehta. Oxford ; New York : Oxford University Press, 1979, c1972. 195 p., [8] leaves of plates : ports. ; 21 cm. Reprint of the ed. published by Farrar, Straus, and Giroux, New York. [RA424.5.M43M43 1979] 79-15154 ISBN 0-19-502619-5 pbk. : 3.95
1. Mehta, Amolak Ram, 1895- 2. Health-officers—Punjab—Biography. 3. India—Social life and customs. 4. Fathers—India—Biography. I. Title.

Mehta, Pherozeshah Merwanji, Sir 1845-1915.

MADY, Hormasji Peroshaw, Sir 1881- 923.254
Sir Pherozeshah Mehta, political biography, by Homi Mody [1st ed., reprinted with minor amendments] New York, Asia Pub. [dist. Taplinger, 1964, c.1963] xviii, 400p. ports. 23cm. 64-55587 16.75
1. Mehta, Pherozeshah Merwanji, Sir 1845-1915. 2. India.—Pol. & govt.—1765-1947. I. Title.

Mehta, Shanti Devi.

MEHTA, Ved Parkash. 954'.5 B
Mamaji / Ved Mehta. New York : Oxford University Press, 1979. 334 p., [11] leaves of plates : ill. ; 22 cm. [CT1508.M347M43] 79-15065 ISBN 0-19-502640-3 : 12.95
1. Mehta, Shanti Devi. 2. Mehta, Ved Parkash. 3. India—Biography. 4. Mothers—India—Biography. I. Title. **BIP**

Mehta, Zubin.

BOOKSPAN, Martin. 785'.092'4 B
Zubin : the Zubin Mehta story / Martin Bookspan, Ross Yockey. 1st ed. New York : Harper & Row, c1978. 226 p., [8] leaves of plates : ill. ; 24 cm. Includes index. [ML422.M24B6] 77-11822 ISBN 0-06-010429-5 : 10.00
1. Mehta, Zubin. 2. Conductors (Music)—Biography. I. Yockey, Ross. II. Title. **BIP**

Mei, Kuang-hsien, 1887-1950.

MOYER, Elgin Sylvester, 1890- 922.651
Moy Gwong of South China; the story of Moy Gwong Han, who burned out for the Lord. Elgin, Ill., Brethren Pub. House [1951] 77 p. illus., ports. 20 cm. [BV3427.M4M6] 51-10485
1. Mei, Kuang-hsien, 1887-1950. I. Title.

Meierkhol'd, Vsevolod Emil'evich, 1874-1940.

BRAUN, Edward. 792'.0233'0924 B
The theatre of Meyerhold : revolution on the modern stage / Edward Braun. New York : Drama Book Specialists, c1979. 299 p. : ill. ; 24 cm. Copyright date stamped on verso of t.p. Bibliography: p. [287]-291. [PN2728.M4B7] 78-11864 ISBN 0-89676-003-0 : 13.95 ISBN 0-89676-004-9 pbk. : 10.00
1. Meierkhol'd, Vsevolod Emil'evich, 1874-1940. 2. Theatrical producers and directors—Russia—Biography. I. Title. **BIP**

Meiggs, Henry, 1811-1877—Juvenile literature.

MYERS, Elisabeth P. 625.1'00924 B
South America's Yankee genius, Henry Meiggs, by Elisabeth P. Myers. New York, Messner [1969] 190 p. 22 cm. Bibliography: p. 181-182. A biography of a self-taught Yankee railroad builder who opened a new era of progress in South America by constructing railways over impossible terrain. [HE2898.2.M4M9] 92 76-79696 3.50
1. Meiggs, Henry, 1811-1877—Juvenile literature. I. Title.

Meinertzhagen, Ricahrd, 1878-1967.

LORD, John, 1924- 355.3'32'0924
Duty, honor, Empire; the life and times of Colonel Richard Meinertzhagen. [1st ed.] New York, Random House [1970] 412 p. 25 cm. Bibliography: p. [397]-402. [DA69.3.M4L67 1970] 77-85600 10.00
1. Meinertzhagen, Ricahrd, 1878-1967. I. Title.

Meir, Golda (Mabovitz) 1898-

AGRES, Eliyahu. 956.94'0924
Golda Meir; portrait of a Prime Minister, by Eliyahu Agress. Translated by Israel I. Taslitt. Foreword by Israel Galili. New York, Sabra Books [1969] 157 p. illus., ports. 26 cm. Translation of Goldah (romanized form) [DS126.6.M42A6513] 73-18555 7.95
1. Meir, Golda (Mabovitz) 1898-

MANN, Peggy. 956.94'05'0924 B
Golda; the life of Israel's Prime Minister. New York, Coward, McCann & Geoghegan [1971] 287 p. ports. 23 cm. Bibliography: p. 282. [DS126.6.M42M3] 70-132591 5.95
1. Meir, Golda (Mabovitz) 1898- I. Title. **BIP**

MANN, Peggy. 956.94'05'0924
Golda; the life of Israel's Prime Minister. Updated ed. New York, Pocket Books [1973 c1971] 260 p. photos. 18 cm. Bibliography: p. 253-254. [DS126.6.M42M3] ISBN 0-671-48132-0 pap. 1.25
1. Meir, Golda (Mabovitz) 1898- I. Title.
L.C. card no. for original ed. 70-132591.

MEIR, Golda (Mabovitz) 1898- 956.94'05'0924 B
A land of our own: an oral autobiography, by Golda Meir. Edited by Marie Syrkin. New York, Putnam [1973] 251 p. 22 cm. [DS126.6.M42A36] 72-87630 ISBN 0-399-11069-0 6.95
1. Meir, Golda (Mabovitz), 1898- 2. Israel—Politics and government. I. Syrkin, Marie, 1900- comp. II. Title.

MEIR, Golda Mabovitz, 1898- 956.94050924
My life / Golda Meir. New York : Dell, 1976c1975. 459p. : ill. ; 18 cm. Includes index. [DS126.6M42A37] pbk. : 1.95
1. Meir, Golda Mabovitz,1898- I. Title.
L.C. card no. for 1975 Putnam edition: 75-25620

MEIR, Golda Mabovitz, 1898- 956.94'05'0924 B
My life / by Golda Meir. 1st American ed. New York : Putnam, 1975. 480 p., [8] leaves of plates : ill. ; 24 cm. Includes index [DS126.6.M42A37 1975] 75-25620 ISBN 0-399-11669-9 : 12.50
1. Meir, Golda Mabovitz, 1898- I. Title.

MORRIS, Terry, 1914- 956.94'05'0924 B
Shalom Golda. New York, Hawthorn Books [1971] xiv, 208 p. illus., ports. 22 cm. Bibliography: p. 195. [DS126.6.M42M67] 70-146296 5.95
1. Meir, Golda (Mabovitz) 1898- I. Title.

SYRKIN, Marie, 1900- 956.94'05'0924 B
Golda Meir: Israel's leader. [New rev. ed.] New York, Putnam [1969] 366 p. illus., ports. 22 cm. First ed. published in 1963 under title: Golda Meir: woman with a cause. [DS126.6.M42S9 1969] 76-94238 6.95
1. Meir, Golda (Mabovitz) 1898-

SYRKIN, Marie, 1900- 923.25694
Golda Meir: woman with a cause. New York, Putnam [1963] 320 p. illus., ports. 22 cm. [DS126.6.M42S9] 64-10403
1. Meir, Golda Mabovitz, 1898-

Meir, Golda Mabovitz, 1898- —Juvenile literature.

DAVIDSON, Mickie. 956.94'05'0924 B
The Golda Meir story / by Margaret Davidson. New York : Scribner, c1976. x, 211 p. : ill. ; 22 cm. Includes index. Bibliography: p. 203-205. A biography of Golda Meir, whose childhood memories of Russia helped her work to establish the independent state of Israel. [DS126.6.M42D38] 92 75-39297 ISBN 0-684-14610-X : 6.95
1. Meir, Golda Mabovitz, 1898- —Juvenile literature. I. Title. **BIP**

DOBRIN, Arnold. 956.94'05'0924 B
A life for Israel: the story of Golda Meir. New York, Dial Press [1974] 98 p. illus. 22 cm. A biography of the woman who dedicated her life to the creation and preservation of a Jewish state. [DS126.6.M42D6] 92 73-15442 ISBN 0-8037-6187-2 4.95
1. Meir, Golda Mabovitz, 1898- —Juvenile literature. I. Title.
Library binding 4.58; ISBN 0-8037-4817-5. **BIP**

NOBLE, Iris. 956.94'05'0924 B
Israel's Golda Meir; pioneer to Prime Minister. New York, J. Messner [1972] 189 p. 22 cm. Bibliography: p. 183-184. Relates the history of a new nation and the service of one of its first citizens who rose from an almond picker to national leader. [DS126.6.M42N62] 92 70-182945 ISBN 0-671-32516-7 4.50
1. Meir, Golda (Mabovitz) 1898- —Juvenile literature. I. Title.

NOBLE, Iris. 956.94'05'0924 B
Israel's Golda Meir; pioneer to Prime Minister. [Rev. ed.] New York, J. Messner [1974] 189 p. 22 cm. Bibliography: p. 183-184. Relates the history of a new nation and the service of one of its first citizens who rose from almond picker to national leader. [DS126.6.M42N62 1974] 92 74-178267 ISBN 0-671-32516-7 5.29

1. Meir, Golda Mabovitz, 1898- —Juvenile literature. I. Title.

Meissonnier, Juste Aurele.

MEISSONNIER, Juste Aurele. 709'.24
Ouvre de Juste Aurele Meissonnier. Introd. by Dorothea Nyberg. [New York] B. Blom, 1969. 43 p. illus., 74 plates (incl. plans; part fold.) 41 cm. "First published Paris ca. 1750." Includes bibliographical references. [N6853.M4N9 1969] 69-16909
I. Nyberg, Dorothea. II. Title.

Melady, Thomas Patrick.

MELADY, Thomas Patrick. 967.6'104'0924 B
Idi Amin Dada : Hitler in Africa / by Thomas and Margaret Melady. Kansas City, Kan. : Sheed Andrews and McMeel, c1977. p. cm. [DT433.282.A55M44] 77-11706 ISBN 0-8362-0783-1 : 7.95
1. Amin, Idi, 1925- 2. Melady, Thomas Patrick. 3. Melady, Margaret Badum. 4. Uganda—Presidents—Biography. 5. Uganda—Politics and government—1962- I. Melady, Margaret Badum, joint author. BIP

Melanchthon, Philipp, 1497-1560.

ALAND, Kurt. 280'.4 B
Four reformers : Luther, Melanchthon, Calvin, Zwingli / Kurt Aland ; translated by James L. Schaff. Minneapolis : Augsburg Pub. House, c1979. 174 p. ; 20 cm. Translation of Die Reformatoren. Bibliography: p. 159-174. [BR315.A4513] 79-50091 ISBN 0-8066-1709-8 pbk. : 4.95
1. Luther, Martin, 1483-1546. 2. Melanchthon, Philipp, 1497-1560. 3. Calvin, Jean, 1509-1564. 4. Zwingli, Ulrich, 1484-1531. 5. Reformation—Biography. 6. Reformation. I. Title.

MANSCHRECK, Clyde Leonard, 1917- 922.443
Melanchthon, the quiet reformer. New York, Abingdon Press [1958] 350 p. illus. 25 cm. Includes bibliography. [BR335.M3] 58-5147
1. Melanchthon, Philipp, 1497-1560.

MANSCHRECK, Clyde Leonard, 1917- 270.6'092'4 B
Melanchthon, the quiet reformer / Clyde Leonard Manschreck. Westport, Conn. : Greenwood Press, 1975, c1958. 350 p., [1] leaf of plates : ill. ; 23 cm. Reprint of the ed. published by Abingdon Press, New York. Includes index. Includes bibliographical references. [BR335.M3 1975] 73-21263 ISBN 0-8371-6131-2 : 17.50
1. Melanchthon, Philipp, 1497-1560. I. Title.

RICHARD, James William, 1843-1909. 270.6'092'4 B
Philip Melanchthon, the Protestant preceptor of Germany, 1497-1560. New York, B. Franklin Reprint [1974] xv, 399 p. illus. 23 cm. (Burt Franklin research & source work series, 139. Philosophy and religious history monographs) Reprint of the 1898 ed. published by Putnam, New York, which was issued as v. 2 of the series, Heroes of the Reformation. Includes bibliographical references. [BR335.R5 1974] 72-82414 ISBN 0-8337-4341-4 18.50
1. Melanchthon, Philipp, 1497-1560.

STUPPERICH, Robert, 1904- 284.10924
Melanchthon. Translated by Robert H. Fisher. Philadelphia, Westminster Press [1965] 175 p. 21 cm. Bibliography: p. 160-166. [BR335.S733] [B] 65-20620
1. Melanchthon, Philipp, 1497-1560.

STUPPERICH, Robert, 1904- 284.10924 (B)
Melanchthon, Translated by Robert H. Fischer. Philadelphia, Westminster Press [1965] 175 p. 21 cm. Bibliography: p. 160-166. [BR335.S733] 65-20620
1. Melanchthon, Phillipp, 1497-1560. I. Title.

STUPPERICH, Robert, 1904- 284.10924
Melanchtnon. [from German] by Robert H. Fischer. Philadelphia, Westminster [c1965] 175p. 21cm. Bibl. [BR335.S733] 65-20620 3.95
1. Melanchtnon, Philipp, 1497-1560. I. Title.

URBAN, Georg, ed. 270.6'092'4
Philipp Melanchthon, 1497-1560; Gedenkschrift zum 400. Todestag des Reformators 19. April 1560/1560. 2. erweiterte Aufl. Bretten, Melanchthonverein, 1960. 224 p. illus., ports., facsims. 24 cm. Includes bibliographies. [BR335.U6] 61-42769
I. Melanchthon, Philipp, 1497-1560. II. Title.

Melba, Nellie, Dame, 1861-1931.

MURPHY, Agnes G. 782.1'092'4 B
Melba : a biography / by Agnes G. Murphy ; with chapters by Madame Melba on the selection of music as a profession & on the science of singing. New York : Da Capo Press, 1977. xiv, 348 p., [36] leaves of plates : ill. ; 22 cm. (Da Capo Press music reprint series) Reprint of the 1909 ed. published by Doubleday, Page, New York. Includes index. [ML420.M35M9 1977] 77-8029 ISBN 0-306-77428-3 : 25.00
1. Melba, Nellie, Dame, 1861-1931. 2. Singers, Australian—Biography. BIP

WECHSBERG, Joseph, 1907- 927.8
Red plush and black velvet; the story of Melba and her times. [1st ed.] Boston. Little, Brown [1961] 372 p. 22 cm. [ML420.M35W4] 61-12821
1. Melba, Nellie, 1861-1931. I. Title.

Melbourne, William Lamb, 2d viscount, 1779-1848.

CECIL, David, Lord 1902- 923.242
Melbourne [Bobbs, dist. New York, Macfadden, 1962, c.1939, 1954] 450p. illus. 21cm (Charter bks.,101) "Pts.1-2 were pub. in 1939 under the title: The young Melboure." Bibl. 2.75 pap.,
1. Melbourne, William Lamb, 2d viscount, 1779-1848. 2. Lamb, Lady Caroline Ponsonby 1785-1828. 3. Victoria, Queen of Great Britain, 1819-1901. I. Title.

CECIL, David, Lord, 1902- 923.242
Melbourne. Indianapolis, Bobbs-Merrill [1954] 450 p. ports. 22 cm. "Parts I and II were published in 1939 under the title of The young Melbourne." [DA536.M5C5 1954] 54-9486
1. Melbourne, William Lamb, 2d viscount, 1779-1848. 2. Lamb, Caroline Ponsonby, Lady, 1785-1828. 3. Victoria, Queen of Great Britain, 1819-1901. BIP

CECIL, David, Lord, 1902- 942.07'3'0924 B
Melbourne. Westport, Conn., Greenwood Press [1971, c1954] 450 p. ports. 23 cm. Parts 1 and 2 were published in 1939 under the title of The young Melbourne. [DA536.M5C48 1971] 76-138583 ISBN 0-8371-5782-X
1. Melbourne, William Lamb, 2d Viscount, 1779-1848. 2. Lamb, Caroline (Ponsonby) Lady, 1785-1828. 3. Victoria, Queen of Great Britain, 1819-1901.

CECIL, David, Lord, 1902- 942.0730924 [B]
Melbourne Indianapolis, Bobbs-Merrill [1974, c1966] 450 p. illus. 24 cm. Pts. 1 & 2 were pub. in 1939 under the title of The Young Melbourne. [DA536.M5C48 1974] ISBN 0-672-52038-9 8.95
1. Melbourne, William Lamb, 2d Viscount, 1779-1848. 2. Lamb, Lady Caroline (Ponsonby) 1785-1828 3. Victoria, Queen of Great Britain, 1819-1901. I. Title.
L.C. card no. for original ed.: 54-9486

CECIL, David, Lord, 1902- 942.07'3'0924 B
Melbourne / by Lord David Cecil. New York : Harmony Books, [1979] c1954. p. cm. Pts. 1 and 2 published in 1939 under title, The young Melbourne. [DA536.M5C48 1979] 78-21315 ISBN 0-517-53782-6 pbk. : 6.95
1. Melbourne, William Lamb, 2d Viscount, 1779-1848. 2. Lamb, Lady Caroline (Ponsonby) 1785-1828. 3. Victoria, Queen of Great Britain. 1819-1901. 4. Great Britain—Politics and government—1830-1837. 5. Prime ministers—Great Britain—Biography. I. Title.

ZIEGLER, Philip. 941.07'5'0924 B
Melbourne : a biography of William Lamb, 2nd Viscount Melbourne / Philip Ziegler. 1st American ed. New York : Knopf, 1976. 400, x p., [8] leaves of plates : ill. ; 25 cm. Includes bibliographical references and index. [DA536.M5Z54 1976] 76-13683 ISBN 0-394-49159-9 : 15.00
1. Melbourne, William Lamb, 2d Viscount, 1779-1848. 2. Prime ministers—Great Britain—Biography. I. Title.

Melchior, Marcus.

MELCHIOR, Marcus. 296.6'1'0924
A rabbi remembers. [Tr. from Danish by Werner Melchior] New York, Lyle Stuart [1968] 256p. 21cm. Tr. of Levet og oplevet; erindringer. [BM755.M445A313] 67-15887 4.95
I. Title.

Melies, Georges, 1861-1938.

HAMMOND, Paul. 791.43'0232'0924 B
Marvellous Melies / Paul Hammond. New York : St. Martin's Press, 1975, c1974. 159 p. : ill. ; 22 cm. Includes bibliographical references, filmographies, and index. [PN1998.A3M42 1975] 74-82161 10.00
1. Melies, Georges, 1861-1938. I. Title.

Mellenthin, Friedrich Wilhelm von, 1904-

MELLENTHIN, Friedrich Wilhelm von, 1904- 940.54'09'43 B
German generals of World War II : as I saw them / by F. W. von Mellenthin. 1st ed. Norman : University of Oklahoma Press, c1977. xix, 300 p. : ill. ; 22 cm. Includes index. Bibliography: p. 291-294. [D757.M369] 76-62518 ISBN 0-8061-1406-1 : 8.95
1. Mellenthin, Friedrich Wilhelm von, 1904- 2. World War, 1939-1945—Germany. 3. Generals—Germany. 4. World War, 1939-1945—Personal narratives, German. I. Title.

Mellon, Paul.

HOFFMAN, William S. 338.7'62'233820924 B
Paul Mellon : portrait of an oil baron / William S. Hoffman. Chicago : Follett Pub. Co., [1974] 204 p. ; 22 cm. Bibliography: p. 191-204. [HD9569.G8H63] 74-80330 ISBN 0-695-80503-7 : 7.95
1. Mellon, Paul. 2. Gulf Oil Corporation.

Mellon, William Larimer, 1910-

MICHELMORE, Peter. 926.1
Dr. Mellon of Haiti. New York, Dodd, Mead [1964] vii, 176 p. illus., ports. 22 cm. [R154.M53M5] 64-22401
1. Mellon, William Larimer, 1910- I. Title.

Mellors, John, 1920-

MELLORS, John, 1920- 338.7'61'65910924 B
Memoirs of an advertising man / [by] John Mellors. London : London Magazine Editions, 1976. 220 p. ; 20 cm. [HF5810.M43A35] 76-382651 £3.75
1. Mellors, John, 1920- 2. Advertising—England—Biography. I. Title.

Melton, Ann Eliza.

KERSTING, Marjorie. 977.4'26 B
Bringing in the sheaves : a true story of pioneer days / Marjorie Kersting. 1st ed. St. Petersburg, Fla. : Valkyrie Press, c1978. 141 p. : ill. ; 22 cm. [F574.M367M444] 78-56807 ISBN 0-912760-75-3 : 6.95
1. Melton, Ann Eliza. 2. Mason, Mich.—Biography. I. Melton, Ann Eliza. II. Title.

Melton, Sparks White, 1870-1957.

LUMPKIN, William Latane 922.273
Doctor Sparks; a biography of Sparks White Melton, 1870-1957. Norfolk, Va., Phaup Print Co., 541 W. 35 St. [c.1963] 178p. port. 21cm. 63-23064 3.00
1. Melton, Sparks White, 1870-1957. I. Title.

Meltzer, Milton,

MELTZER, Milton, 1915- ed. 928.1
A Thoreau profile, by Milton Meltzer and Walter Harding. New York, Crowell [1962] viii, 310 p. illus., ports., map, facsims. 24 cm. "Derived for the most part from Thoreau's own autobiographical writings, supplemented ... by the writings of his friends and contemporaries." Includes bibliographical references. [PS3053.M4] 62-16548
I. Thoreau, Henry David, 1817-1862. II. Harding, Walter Roy. 1917- joint ed. III. Title. BIP

Melville, Herman, 1819-1891.

ANDERSON, Charles Roberts, 1902- 813.3
Melville in the South Seas. New York, Dover Publications [1966] 514 p. 22 cm. Bibliography: p. 489-497. [PS2386.A6 1966] 66-17122
1. Melville, Herman, 1819-1891. 2. Voyages and travels. 3. Pacific Ocean. I. Title.

ARVIN, Newton, 1900- 928.1
Herman Melville. [New York] Sloane [1950] xiii, 316 p. port. 22 cm. (The American men of letters series) "Bibliographical note": p. 301-304. [PS2386.A7 1950] 50-7584
1. Melville, Herman, 1819-1891. I. Title. II. Series.

BIXBY, William. 813'.3 B
Rebel genius: the life of Herman Melville. New York, McKay [1970] 133 p. 21 cm. [PS2386.B5] 78-120815 3.95
1. Melville, Herman, 1819-1891. I. Title.

FREEMAN, John, 1880-1929. 813'.3 B
Herman Melville. New York, Haskell House Publishers, 1974. x, 200 p. 23 cm. Reprint of the 1926 ed. published by Macmillan, London, in series: English men of letters. Bibliography: p. 197-198. [PS2386.F7 1974] 73-18099 ISBN 0-8383-1733-2 11.95
1. Melville, Herman, 1819-1891.

FREEMAN, John, 1880-1929. 813'.3 B
Herman Melville / by John Freeman. Folcroft, Pa. : Folcroft Library Editions, 1974. x, 200 p. ; 23 cm. Reprint of the 1926 ed. published by Macmillan, London, in series: English men of letters. Includes index. Bibliography: p. 197-198. [PS2386.F7 1974b] 74-22059 ISBN 0-8414-4228-2 lib. bdg.
1. Melville, Herman, 1819-1891.

FREEMAN, John, 1880-1929. 813'.3 B
Herman Melville / by John Freeman. Norwood, Pa. : Norwood Editions, 1976. x, 200 p. ; 24 cm. Reprint of the 1926 ed.

published by Macmillan, London, in series: English men of letters. Includes index. Bibliography: p. 197-198. [PS2386.F7 1976] 76-13211 ISBN 0-8482-0758-0 lib. bdg. : 17.50
1. Melville, Herman, 1819-1891.

FREEMAN, John, 1880-1929. 813'.3 B
Herman Melville / John Freeman. Folcroft, Pa. : Folcroft Library Editions, 1974. p. cm. Reprint of the 1926 ed. published by Macmillan, London, in series: English men of letters. Includes index. Bibliography: p. [PS2386.F7 1974b] 74-22059 ISBN 0-8414-4228-2 lib.bdg.: 17.50
1. Melville, Herman, 1819-1891.

GILMAN, William Henry, 1911- 813'.3 B
Melville's early life and Redburn, by William H. Gilman. New York, Russell & Russell [1972, c1951] ix, 378 p. illus. 25 cm. Includes bibliographical references. [PS2386.G46 1972] 77-173545
1. Melville, Herman, 1819-1891. 2. Melville, Herman, 1819-1891. Redburn. **BIP**

GILMAN, William Henry, 1911- 928.1
Melville's early life and Redburn. New York, New York University Press, 1951 ix, 378 p. illus., geneal. tables (on lining papers) 25 cm. Bibliographical references included in "Notes" (p. [289]-368) [PS2386.G46] 51-12126
1. Melville, Herman, 1819-1891. 2. Melville, Herman, 1819-1891. Redburn.

GOULD, Jean, 1909- 928.1
Young mariner Melville; illustrated by Donald McKay. New York, Dodd, Mead, 1956. 280 p. illus. 21 cm. [PS2386.M62G6] 56-10917
1. Melville, Herman, 1819-1891. I. Title.

HABERSTROH, Charles. 813'.3
Melville and male indentity / Charles J. Haberstroh. Cranbury, N.J. : Fairleigh Dickinson University Press, 1980. p. cm. Bibliography: p. [PS2386.H3] 78-75178 ISBN 0-8386-2321-2 : 12.00
1. Melville, Herman, 1819-1891. 2. Melville, Herman, 1819-1891—Biography—Character. 3. Masculinity (Psychology) 4. Novelists, American—19th century—Biography. I. Title.

HERMAN Melville v. 12
New York, Viking Press [1957, c1950] viii, 312p. 20cm. (Compass books, C20) Bibliography: p. 301-304.
1. Melville, Herman, 1819-1891. I. Arvin, Newton, 1900- **BIP**

HILLWAY, Tyrus. v. 12
Herman Melville. New Haven, College and University Press [1963] 176 p. 22 cm. (Twayne's United States author series, 37) Includes bibliography. 65-39184
1. Melville, Herman, 1819-1891. I. Title.

HILLWAY, Tyrus. 813'.3 B
Herman Melville / by Tyrus Hillway. Rev. ed. Boston : Twayne Publishers, 1979. 177 p. : port. ; 21 cm. (Twayne's United States authors series ; TUSAS 37) Includes index. Bibliography: p. 163-171. [PS2386.H5 1979] 78-11937 ISBN 0-8057-7256-1 : 9.95
1. Melville, Herman, 1819-1891. 2. Authors, American—19th century—Biography.

HOWARD, Leon. 928.1
Herman Melville, a biography. Berkeley, University of California Press [1951] xi, 354 p. illus. 24 cm. [PS2386.H6] 51-62667
1. Melville, Herman, 1819-1891.

HUMPHREYS,[Arthur Raleigh. v. 12
Herman Melville. New York, Barnes & Noble [1962] 120 p. 19 cm. (Writers and critics, 14) Includes bibliography. 67-96438
1. Melville, Herman, 1819-1891. I. Title. II. Series.

JAMES, Cyril Lionel Robert, 1901- v. 12
Mariners, renegades, and castaways; the story of Herman Melville and the world we live in. New York, 1953. 203p. 17cm. A55
1. Melville, Herman, 1819-1891. I. Title. **BIP**

LEYDA, Jay, 1910- ed. 813'.3 B
The Melville log; a documentary life of Herman Melville, 1819-1891. With a new supplementary chapter. New York, Gordian Press, 1969 [c1951] 2 v. (xxxiv, 966 p.) illus., facsims., ports. 24 cm. [PS2386.L4 1969] 73-81564
1. Melville, Herman, 1819-1891. I. Title.

MELVILLE, Herman 928.1
The letters of Herman Melville, edited by Merrill R. David pand William H. Gilman. New Haven Conn., Bale University Press [c.]1960. xxxi, 398p. Bibiographical references included in 'Textual notes' (p. 321-385) illus., facsims. 25cm. 60-7822 6.50
I. Title.

MELVILLE, Herman, 1819-1891. 928.1
The letters of Herman Melville, edited by Merrell R. Davis and William H. Gilman. New Haven, Yale University Press, 1960. xxxi, 398p. illus., facsims. 25cm. Bibliographical references included in 'Textual notes' (p. 321-385) [PS2386.A57] 60-7822
I. Title.

MUMFORD, Lewis, 1895- 928.1
Herman Melville, a study of his life and vision. Rev. ed. New York, Harcourt, Brace & World [1963, c1962] 256 p. 22 cm. [PS2386.M8 1963] 62-21847
1. Melville, Herman, 1819-1891.

STONE, Geoffrey. 813'.3 B
Melville / by Geoffrey Stone. New York : Octagon Books, 1976, c1949. 336 p. : port. ; 23 cm. Reprint of the ed. published by Sheed & Ward, New York, which was issued as no. 4 of Great writers of the world. Includes index. Bibliography: p. 320-326. [PS2386.S8 1976] 76-18221 ISBN 0-374-97632-5 : 14.50
1. Melville, Herman, 1819-1891. I. Title. II. Series: Great writers of the world ; [4]. **BIP**

WEAVER, Raymond Melbourne, 1888-1948. 928.1
Herman Melville, mariner and mystic. Introd. by Mark Van Doren. New York, Pageant Books, 1961. 399 p. illus. 24 cm. Includes bibliography. [PS2386.W4 1961] 59-13250
1. Melville, Herman, 1819-1891. **BIP**

Melville, Herman, 1819-1891—Addresses, essays, lectures.

SEALTS, Merton M., comp. 813'.3 B
The early lives of Melville : nineteenth-century biographical sketches and their authors / [selected by] Merton M. Sealts, Jr. Madison : University of Wisconsin Press, 1974. xiii, 280 p. : ill. ; 25 cm. Includes bibliographical references and index. [PS2386.S38] 74-5906 ISBN 0-299-06570-7 : 12.50
1. Melville, Herman, 1819-1891—Addresses, essays, lectures. 2. Melville, Herman, 1819-1891—Biography—Sources. 3. American prose literature—19th century. I. Title. **BIP**

Melville, Herman, 1819-1891—Biography.

MILLER, Edwin Haviland. 813'.3 B
Melville / Edwin Haviland Miller. New York : G. Braziller, c1975. 382 p., [4] leaves of plates : ill. ; 25 cm. (A Venture book) Includes index. Bibliography: p. 371-375. [PS2386.M49] 75-7958 ISBN 0-8076-0787-8 : 15.00
1. Melville, Herman, 1819-1891—Biography. I. Title. **BIP**

Melville, Herman, 1819-1891—Juvenile literature.

HOUGH, Henry Beetle, 1896- 928.1
Melville in the South Pacific. Illustrated by Frank Nicholas. Boston, Houghton Mifflin, 1960. 179p. illus. 22cm. (North Star books [22]) Includes bibliography. [PS2386.H57] 60-6386
1. Melville, Herman, 1819-1891—Juvenile literature. I. Title.

Melville, Jean Pierre.

NOGUEIRA, Rui. 791.43'023'0924
Melville on Melville. Edited by Rui Nogueira. New York, Viking Press [1972, c1971] 176 p. illus. 20 cm. (Cinema one, 16) "Filmography": p. 168-175. [PN1998.A3M445 1972] 79-173871 ISBN 0-670-46757-X 6.95
1. Melville, Jean Pierre. I. Melville, Jean Pierre. II. Title.

Mel'nikov, Konstantin Stepanovich, 1890-

STARR, S. Frederick. 720'.92'4 B
Melnikov : solo architect in a mass society / S. Frederick Starr. Princeton, N.J. : Princeton University Press, c1978. xvii, 276 p. : ill. ; 29 cm. Includes index. Bibliography: p. [263]-270. [NA1199.M37S7] 77-85566 ISBN 0-691-03931-3 : 25.00
1. Mel'nikov, Konstantin Stepanovich, 1890- 2. Architects—Russian Republic—Biography. I. Title. **BIP**

Memling, Hans, 1430?-1494.

DUMONT, Georges Henri. 759.9493'1
Hans Memling. [Translator: Haydn Barnes. Editor: Anthony Bosman] New York, Barnes & Noble [1967, c1966] 88 p. plate (part col.) 18 cm. (Barnes & Noble art series) "No. 628." [ND673.M5D813] 67-1532
1. Memling, Hans, 1430?-1494. I. Bosman, Anthony, ed.

MCFARLANE, Kenneth Bruce. 759.9493
Hans Memling, by K. B. McFarlane. Edited by Edgar Wind with the assistance of G. L. Harriss. Oxford [Eng.] Clarendon Press, 1971. xv, 74 p. 153 illus. 30 cm. Bibliography: p. [61] - 66. [ND673.M5M3] 72-200900 ISBN 0-19-817179-X 19.50 (U.S.)
1. Memling, Hans, 1430? 1494.

Memphis. Calvary Episcopal Church.

DAVIES-RODGERS, Ellen, 1903- 283'.768'19
The great book: Calvary Protestant Episcopal Church, 1832-1972, Memphis, Shelby County, Tennessee. Photography by Nadia. Memphis, Plantation Press [1973] 994 p. illus. 24 cm. Bibliography: p. 973. [BX5980.M4C343] 72-84829 20.00
1. Memphis. Calvary Episcopal Church. 2. Memphis—Biography. I. Title.
Publisher's Address: Brunswick, Memphis, Tenn. 38128.

Men—United States—Biography.

ROSE, Frank. 301.41'1
Real men / by Frank Rose & [photos. by] George Bennett. 1st ed. Garden City, N.Y. : Doubleday, [1980] p. cm. (A Dolphin book) [HQ1090.R67] 78-20096 ISBN 0-385-14421-0 : 8.95
1. Men—United States—Biography. 2. Masculinity. 3. Sex role. I. Bennett, George, 1945- II. Title. **BIP**

Menael, Gregor, 1822-1884—Juvenile literature.

WEBB, Robert N. 920
Gregor Mendel and heredity. New York, Watts [c.1963] 114p. illus. 22cm. (Immortals of Sci.) 63-16918 2.95
1. Menael, Gregor, 1822-1884—Juvenile literature. I. Title.

Mencius.

VERWILGHEN, Albert Felix. 181'.09'512 B
The character of Mencius / by Albert Felix Verwilghen. [Seattle : s.n.], 1964. xviii, 152 leaves ; 29 cm. Thesis (M.A.)—University of Washington. Bibliography: leaves [129]-152. [B128.M35V39] 75-309041
1. Mencius. I. Title.

Mencken, Henry Louis, 1880-1956.

ANGOFF, Charles, 1902- 928.1
H. L. Mencken, a portrait from memory. New York, T. Yoseloff [1956] 240p. 22cm. [PS3525.E43Z539] 56-9094
1. Mencken. Henry Louis. 1880-1956. I. Title.

ANGOFF, Charles, 1902- 928.1
H. L. Mencken, a portrait from memory. New York, T. Yoseloff [1956] 240 p. 22 cm. [PS3525.E43Z539] 56-9094
1. Mencken, Henry Louis, 1880-1956.

BODE, Carl, 1911- 818'.5'209 B
Mencken. Carbondale, Southern Illinois University Press [1969] ix, 452 p. illus., ports. 25 cm. Bibliographical references included in "Notes" (p. 390-436) [PS3525.E43Z5398] 69-16116 10.00
1. Mencken, Henry Louis, 1880-1956. **BIP**

BODE, Carl, 1911- 818'.5'209 B
Mencken. Carbondale, Southern Illinois University Press [1973, c1969] 452 p. illus. 20 cm. (Arcturus books, AB107) Includes bibliographical references. [PS3525.E43Z5398 1973] 72-11997 ISBN 0-8093-0627-1 3.95 (pbk.)
1. Mencken, Henry Louis, 1880-1956.

BOYD, Ernest Augustus, 1887-1946. 818'.5'209 B
H. L. Mencken / by Ernest Boyd. Norwood, Pa. : Norwood Editions, 1975, c1925. 89 p., [1] leaf of plates : port. ; 23 cm. Reprint of the ed. published by R. M. McBride, New York, in series: Modern American writers, 4. Bibliography: p. 87-89. [PS3525.E43Z54 1975] 75-42394 ISBN 0-88305-963-0 lib. bdg. : 8.00
1. Mencken, Henry Louis, 1880-1956. **BIP**

FECHER, Charles A. 818'.5'209 B
Mencken : a study of his thought / by Charles A. Fecher ; with a foreword by Alfred A. Knopf. 1st ed. New York : Knopf : distributed by Random House, 1978. xxi, 391 p., [4] leaves of plates : ill. ; 25 cm. Includes index. Bibliography: p. [367]-370. [PS3525.E43Z553 1978] 77-21154 ISBN 0-394-41354-7 : 15.00
1. Mencken, Henry Louis, 1880-1956. 2. Authors, American—20th century—Biography. **BIP**

GOLDBERG, Isaac, 1887-1938. 818'.5'209 B
The man Mencken; a biographical and critical survey. New York, AMS Press [1968] xiv, 388 p. illus. 24 cm. Reprint of the 1925 ed. "A Mencken miscellany": p. [299]-381. [PS3525.E43Z57 1968] 68-54271

1. Mencken, Henry Louis, 1880-1956. I. Title. BIP

H. L. Mencken. 818'5.'209
Fanfare by Burton Rascoe. [Folcroft, Pa.] Folcroft Library Editions, 1973. 32 p. ports. 24 cm. Reprint of the 1920 ed. published by Knopf, New York. [PS3525.E43Z576 1973] 73-9953 6.50
1. Mencken, Henry Louis, 1880-1956. I. Rascoe, Burton, 1892-1957. II. O'Sullivan, Vincent, 1872-1940. III. Henderson, F. C. BIP

JOHNS, Bud. 818'.5'209
The ombibulous Mr. Mencken; a drinking biography. [1st ed.] San Francisco, Synergistic Press [1968] 63 p. illus., ports. 23 cm. [PS3525.E43Z585] 68-8421 2.95
1. Mencken, Henry Louis, 1880-1956. I. Title.

KEMLER, Edgar 928.1
The irreverent Mr. Mencken. Boston, Atlantic-Little. [1963, c.1948, 1950] x, 317p. 20cm. Bibl. 2.25 pap.,
1. Mencken, Henry Louis, 1880- I. Title.

KEMLER, Edgar. 928.1
The irreverent Mr. Mencken [1st ed.] Boston, Little, Brown, 1950. x, 317 p. illus., ports. 21 cm. "An Atlantic Monthly Press book." Bibliographical references included in "Notes" (p. [295]-308) "Chronology of ... [H. L. Mencken's] books": p. [304]-306. [PS3525.E43Z59 1950] 50-7313
1. Mencken, Henry Louis, 1880-1956. I. Title.

MANCHESTER, William R 928.1
Disturber of the peace; the life of H. L. Mencken. With an introd. by Gerald W. Johnson. [1st ed.] New York, Harper [1951] xiv, 336 p. ports. 22 cm. "Bibliographical note": p. 317-322. [PS3525.E43Z67] 51-9028
1. Mencken, Henry Louis, 1880- I. Title.

MANCHESTER, William Raymond, 1922- 928.1
Disturber of the peace; the life of H. L. Mencken. Introd. by Gerald W. Johnson. New York, Collier [1962, c.1950, 1951] 382p. 18cm. (AS230) Bibl. .95 pap.,
1. Mencken, Henry Louis, 1880- I. Title.

MAYFIELD, Sara. 818'.5'209
The constant circle; H. L. Mencken and his friends. New York, Delacorte Press [1968] 307 p. 24 cm. [PS3525.E43Z68] 68-16641
1. Mencken, Henry Louis, 1880-1956. I. Title.

MENCKEN, Henry Louis, 1880-1956 928.1
Letters. Selected and annotated by Guy J. Forgue. Personal note by Hamilton Owens. New York, Knopf [c.]1961. xxxviii, 506, xxiip. front. port. 25cm. 61-12312 7.95
I. Title.

STENERSON, Douglas C. 818'.5'209 B
H. L. Mencken: iconoclast from Baltimore [by] Douglas C. Stenerson. Chicago, University of Chicago Press [1971] xv, 287 p. illus. 23 cm. Includes bibliographical references. [PS3525.E43Z83] 78-158683 ISBN 0-226-77249-7 7.95
1. Mencken, Henry Louis, 1880-1956.

Mencken, Henry Louis, 1880-1956—Manuscripts—Indexes.

ADLER, Betty, 1918- 016.070'924 B
Man of letters; a census of the correspondence of H. L. Mencken. Baltimore, Enoch Pratt Free Library, 1969. xi, 335 p. 23 cm. [Z6616.M53A33] 74-20128
1. Mencken, Henry Louis, 1880-1956—Manuscripts—Indexes. I. Title.

Mendel, Gregor, 1822-1884.

ILTIS, Hugo, 1882- 575.110924
Life of Mendel. Tr. [from German] by Eden and Cedar Paul. New York, Hafner, 1966. 336p. illus., ports. 23cm. [QH31.M45I52] 66-5640 5.75
1. Mendel, Gregor, 1822-1884. I. Title.

SOOTIN, Harry. 925.7
Gregor Mendel: father of the science of genetics. New York, Vanguard Press [1959] 223 p. illus 22 cm. [QH31.M45S6] 59-7933
1. Mendel, Gregor, 1822-1884. I. Title. BIP

Mendel, Gregor, 1822-1884—Juvenile literature.

[GARRISON, Webb B.] 92
The man who found out why: the story of Gregor Mendel, by Gary Webster [pseud.] illus. by Greg and Tim Hildebrandt. New York, Guild [1965, c.1963] 176p. 18cm. (Turret bks., 31503) .50 pap.,
1. Mendel, Gregor, 1822-1884—Juvenile literature. I. Title.

[GARRISON, Webb B.] 920
The man who found out why: the story of Gregor Mendel, by Gary Webster [pseud.] Illus. by Greg and Tim Hildebrandt. New York, Hawthorn [c.1963] 188p. illus. (pt. col.) 22cm. (Credo bks.) Bibl. 63-8787 2.95
1. Mendel, Gregor, 1822-1884—Juvenile literature. I. Title.

GARRISON, Webb B. 92
The man who found out why; the story of Gregor Mendel, by Gary Webster [pseud.] Illustrated by Greg and Tim Hildebrandt. New York, Hawthorn Books [1963] 188 p. illus. 22 cm. (Credo books) Includes bibliography. [QH31.M45G3] 63-8787
1. Mendel, Gregor, 1822-1884 — Juvenile literature. I. Title.

GREENE, Carla, 1906- 575.1'1'0924 B
Gregor Mendel. Illustrated by Richard Cuffari. New York, Dial Press [1970] 79 p. illus., ports. 24 cm. "Books about Gregor Mendel and genetics": p. 75-76. The life and work of the Austrian monk who discovered the laws of genetics in the nineteenth century. [QH31.M45G68] 92 69-18226 3.95
1. Mendel, Gregor, 1822-1884—Juvenile literature. I. Cuffari, Richard, 1925- illus. II. Title.

Mendeleev, Dmitrii Ivanovich, 1834-1907.

KELMAN, Peter. 540'.924 B
Mendeleyev: prophet of chemical elements, by Peter Kelman and A. Harris Stone. Illustrated by Henry Gorski. Englewood Cliffs, N.J., Prentice-Hall [1970] 68 p. illus. 22 cm. (History of science series) The biography of the Russian scientist whose discovery of the Periodic Law ordered the chemical elements and established the foundations of modern chemistry. [QD22.M43K4] 92 76-93770 3.95
1. Mendeleev, Dmitrii Ivanovich, 1834-1907. I. Stone, A. Harris, joint author. II. Gorski, Henry, illus. III. Title.

Mendelsohn, Erich, 1887-1958.

WHITTICK, Arnold, 1898- 927.2
Eric Mendelsohn. [2d ed.] New York, F. W. Dodge Corp. [1956] 219p. illus., ports.

Mendelssohn-Bartholdy, Felix, 1809-1847.

BLUNT, Wilfrid, 1901- 780'.92'4 B
On wings of song; a biography of Felix Mendelssohn. New York, Scribner [1974] 288 p. illus. 26 cm. Bibliography: p. [279]-281. [ML410.M5B62] 73-10840 ISBN 0-684-13633-3 17.50
1. Mendelssohn-Bartholdy, Felix, 1809-1847. I. Title.

DEVRIENT, Eduard, 1801-1877. 780'.92'4 B
My recollections of Felix Mendelssohn-Bartholdy, and his letters to me. Translated from the German by Natalia Macfarren. New York, Vienna House [1972] vii, 307 p. music, port. 23 cm. "Originally published by Richard Bentley, London, 1869." [ML410.M5D5 1972] 72-163799 ISBN 0-8443-0002-0
1. Mendelssohn-Bartholdy, Felix, 1809-1847. I. Macfarren, Clara Natalia (Andrae) lady, 1827-1916, tr. BIP

HILLER, Ferdinand, 1811-1885. 780'.92'4 B
Mendelssohn. Letters and recollections. Translated with the consent and revision of the author, by M. E. von Glehn. With an introd. by Joel Sachs. New York, Vienna House, [1973 c1972] xxxiv, 223 p. port. 22 cm. [ML410.M5H593 1972] 70-163790 ISBN 0-8443-0003-9 11.50
1. Mendelssohn-Bartholdy, Felix, 1809-1847. BIP

HURD, Michael. 780'.924 B
Mendelssohn. New York, T. Y. Crowell Co. [1971, c1970] 87 p. illus., facsims., music, ports. 26 cm. (The Great composers) Bibliography: p. 83. A biography of the nineteenth-century composer whose important works before the age of eighteen included the Overture to "A Midsummer's Night Dream." [ML410.M5H9 1971] 92 75-121384 ISBN 0-690-53105-2 4.50
1. Mendelssohn-Bartholdy, Felix, 1809-1847. I. Title.

JACOB, Heinrich Eduard, 1889- 927.8
Felix Mendelssohn and his times. Tr. from German by Richard and Clara Winston. Englewood Cliffs, N. J., Prentice [c.1963] 356p. illus. 26cm. Bibl. 63-18599 6.95
1. Mendelssohn-Bartholdy, Felix, 1809-1847. I. Title.

JACOB, Heinrich Eduard, 1889-1967. 780'.92'4 B
Felix Mendelssohn and his times. Translated from the German by Richard and Clara Winston. Westport, Conn., Greenwood Press [1973, c1963] vi, 356 p. illus. 24 cm. Translation of Felix Mendelssohn und seine Zeit. Reprint of the ed. published by Prentice-Hall, Englewood Cliffs, N.J. Includes bibliographical references. [ML410.M5J33 1973] 73-3024 ISBN 0-8371-6823-6
1. Mendelssohn-Bartholdy, Felix, 1809-1847. I. Title. BIP

JACOB, Heinrich Eduard, 1889-1967. 780'.92'4 B
Felix Mendelssohn and his times. Translated from the German by Richard and Clara Winston. Westport, Conn., Greenwood Press [1973, c1963] vi, 356 p. illus. 24 cm. Translation of Felix Mendelssohn und seine Zeit. Reprint of the ed. published by Prentice-Hall, Englewood Cliffs, N.J. Includes bibliographical references. [ML410.M5J33 1973] 73-3024 ISBN 0-8371-6823-6 15.00
1. Mendelssohn-Bartholdy, Felix, 1809-1847. I. Title.

KAUFMAN, Schima. 780'.924 B
Mendelssohn, "a second Elijah". Westport, Conn., Greenwood Press [1971, c1962] xiv, 353 p. illus. 23 cm. Reprint of the 1934 ed. Bibliography: p. 341-343. [ML410.M5K3 1971] 78-110829 ISBN 0-8371-3229-0
1. Mendelssohn-Bartholdy, Felix, 1809-1847. I. Title.

KUPFERBERG, Herbert. 780'.924 B
The Mendelssohns; three generations of genius. New York, C. Scribner's Sons [1972] ix, 272 p. illus. 24 cm. Bibliography: p. 253-259. [ML410.M5K88] 76-172947 ISBN 0-684-12681-8 8.95
1. Mendelssohn-Bartholdy, Felix, 1809-1847. 2. Mendelssohn family. I. Title.

LAMPADIUS, Wilhelm Adolf, 1812-1892. 780'.92'4 B
Life of Felix Mendelssohn Bartholdy / from the German of W. A. Lampadius ; edited and translated by William Leonhard Gage. Boston : Longwood Press, 1978. p. cm. Reprint of the 1865 ed. published by O. Ditson, Boston. [ML410.M5L22 1978] 77-92443 ISBN 0-89341-427-1 lib.bdg. : 25.00
1. Mendelssohn-Bartholdy, Felix, 1809-1847. 2. Composers—Biography. I. Gage, William Leonard, 1832-1889. II. Title. BIP

MENDELSSOHN-BARTHOLDY, Felix, 1809-1847 780'.92'4
Letters of Felix Mendelssohn Bartholdy from Italy and Switzerland / translated by Lady Wallace ; with a biographical notice by Julie de Marguerittes. Boston : Longwood Press, 1978. p. cm. Translation of Reisebriefe aus den Jahren 1830 bis 1832. Reprint of the 1869 ed. published by Leypoldt and Holt, New York. [ML410.M5A316 1978] 78-2022 ISBN 0-89341-429-8 lib.bdg. : 30.00
1. Mendelssohn-Bartholdy, Felix, 1809-1847. 2. Composers—Correspondence. 3. Europe—Description and travel—1800-1918. BIP

MENDELSSOHN. v. 12
London, Dent; New York, Farrar, Straus and Cudahy [1957] xi, 208p. illus., ports., facsims., music. 19cm. (The Master musicians. New ser.) 'Catalogue of works': p. 175-190. Bibliography: p. 196-198.
1. Mendelssohn-Bartholdy, Felix, 1809-1847. I. Radcliffe, Philip. BIP

MENDELSSOHN-BARTHOLDY, Felix, 1809-1847. 780'.92'4 B
Felix Mendelssohn: letters. Edited by G. Selden-Goth. New York, Vienna House [1973, c1945] 372 p. illus. 21 cm. [ML410.M5A28 1973] 73-86922 ISBN 0-8443-0108-6 4.45
1. Mendelssohn-Bartholdy, Felix, 1809-1847. 2. Musicians—Correspondence, reminiscences, etc. I. Selden-Goth, Gisella, 1884- ed.

MENDELSSOHN-BARTHOLDY, Felix, 1809-1847 780'.924
Letters from Italy and Switzerland. Translated from the German by Lady Wallace. With a biographical notice by Julie de Marguerittes. 3d ed. Freeport, N.Y., Books for Libraries Press [1970] xv, 360 p. illus., music. 23 cm. Translation of Reisebriefe aus den Jahren 1830 bis 1832. Reprint of the 1865 ed. [ML410.M5A316 1970] 70-114866
1. Europe—Description and travel—1800-1918. BIP

MENDELSSOHN-BARTHOLDY, Felix, 1809-1847. 780'.924
Letters of Felix Mendelssohn Bartholdy from 1833 to 1847. Edited by Paul Mendelssohn Bartholdy and Carl Mendelssohn Bartholdy. With catalogue of all his musical compositions compiled by Julius Rietz. Translated by Lady Wallace. Freeport, N.Y., Books for Libraries Press [1970] vi, 421 p. music. 23 cm. "First

published 1864." [ML410.M5A333 1970] 73-114867 201

MENDELSSOHN-BARTHOLDY, 780'.92'4
Felix, 1809-1847
Letters of Felix Mendelssohn Bartholdy from 1833 to 1847 / edited by Paul Mendelssohn Bartholdy and Carl Mendelssohn Bartholdy ; with a catalogue of all his musical compositions by Julius Rietz ; translated by Grace Wallace. Boston : Longwood Press, 1978. p. cm. Reprint of the 1868 ed. published by Leypoldt and Holt, New York. [ML410.M5A333 1978] 77-92441 ISBN 0-89341-426-3 lib.bdg. : 30.00
1. Mendelssohn-Bartholdy, Felix, 1809-1847. 2. Composers—Germany—Correspondence. **BIP**

RADCLIFFE, Philip 927.8
Mendselssohn. New York, Collier [1963] 224p. 18cm. (Great composers ser. BS160V) 1.50 pap.,
1. Mendelssohn-Bertholdy, Felix, 1809-1847. I. Title. II. Series.

SCHUMANN, Robert Alexander, 927.8
1810-1856.
Memoirs of Felix Mendelssohn-Bartholdy; from private notes and memoranda, letters, and dairies, [sic] of Robert Schumann. Translated for the Schumann Memorial Foundation, inc., by James A. Galston. [1st American ed. Rochester, N.Y.] 1950 [i.e. 1951] 83 p. ports. 16 cm. Translation of Erinnerungen an F. Mendelssohn. [ML410.M5S16] 51-5963
1. Mendelssohn-Bartholdy, Felix, 1800-1847. I. Title.

WERNER, Eric. 927.8
Mendelssohn; a new image of the composer and his age. Translated from the German by Dika Newlin. [New York] Free Press of Glencoe [1963] xv, 545 p. illus., ports., facsims., geneal. table, music. 24 cm. Bibliographical footnotes. [ML410.M5W37] 63-17629
1. Mendelssohn-Bartholdy, Felix, 1809-1847. I. Title. **BIP**

WERNER, Eric. 780'.92'4 B
Mendelssohn, a new image of the composer and his age / Eric Werner ; translated from the German by Dika Newlin. Westport, Conn. : Greenwood Press, 1978, c1963. xv, 545 p. : ill. ; 24 cm. Reprint of the ed. published by Free Press of Glencoe, New York. Includes bibliographical references and index. [ML410.M5W37 1978] 78-1750 ISBN 0-313-20302-4 lib bdg. : 29.75
1. Mendelssohn-Bartholdy, Felix, 1809-1847. 2. Composers—Germany—Biography.

Mendelssohn-Bartholdy, Felix, 1809-1847—Juvenile literature.

KUPFERBERG, Herbert. 780'.92'4 B
Felix Mendelssohn; his life, his family, his music. New York, C. Scribner's Sons [1972] xii, 176 p. illus. 24 cm. A biography of the German composer of "Midsummer Night's Dream" with emphasis on his happy family life and analyses of his music. [ML3930.M44K9] 92 72-1172 ISBN 0-684-12952-3 5.95
1. Mendelssohn-Bartholdy, Felix, 1809-1847—Juvenile literature. I. Title.

Mendelssohn family.

HENSEL, Sebastian, 1830- 780'.924
1898.
The Mendelssohn family 1729-1847; from letters and journals. With eight ports. from drawings by Wilhelm Hensel. 2d rev. ed. Translated by Carl Klingemann and an American collaborator. With a notice by George Grove. New York, Greenwood Press, 1968. 2 v. music, ports. 22 cm. First published in 1882 by Harper & Bros. The letters for the most part by Felix Mendelssohn and his sister, Fanny, frau Hensel. [ML385.H542 1968] 68-31000
1. Mendelssohn family. I. Mendelssohn-Bartholdy, Felix, 1809-1847. II. Hensel, Fanny Cacilia (Mendelssohn-Bartholdy) 1805-1847. III. Klingemann, Karl, d. 1862, tr.

HENSEL, Sebastian, 1830- 780'.922
1898.
The Mendelssohn family, 1729-1847, from letters and journals. With eight portraits from drawings by Wilhelm Hensel. 2d rev. ed. Translated by Carl Klingemann and an American collaborator, with a notice by George Grove. New York, Haskell House Publishers, 1969. 2 v. music, ports. 23 cm. First published in 1882 by Harper & Bros. The letters for the most part by Felix Mendelssohn and his sister Fanny, frau Hensel. [ML385.H542 1969] 68-25290
1. Mendelssohn family. I. Mendelssohn-Bartholdy, Felix, 1809-1847. II. Hensel, Fanny Cacilia (Mendelssohn-Bartholdy) 1805-1847. III. Klingemann, Karl, d. 1862, tr.

Mendelssohn, Moses, 1729-1786.

ALTMANN, Alexander, 1906- 193 B
Moses Mendelssohn; a biographical study. University, University of Alabama Press [1973] xvi, 900 p. illus. 25 cm. Includes bibliographical references. [B2693.A64] 72-12430 ISBN 0-8173-6860-4 15.00
1. Mendelssohn, Moses, 1729-1786. **BIP**

WALTER, Hermann, 1863- 193 B
Moses Mendelssohn, critic and philosopher. New York, Arno Press, 1973 [c1930] vii, 220 p. illus. 21 cm. (The Jewish people: history, religion, literature) Reprint of the ed. published by Bloch Pub. Co., New York. Bibliography: p. 213-217. [B2693.W3 1973] 73-2230 ISBN 0-405-05291-X 15.00
1. Mendelssohn, Moses, 1729-1786. I. Title. II. Series.

Mendes-France, Pierre, 1907-

WERTH, Alexander, 1901- 923.244
Lost statesman, the strange story of Pierre Mendes-France. New York, Abelard-Schuman [1958] 428 p. illus. 23 cm. [DC407.M4W4 1958] 58-6091
1. Mendes-France, Pierre, 1907- 2. France — Pol. & govt. — 1945- I. Title.

Mendoza, Antonio de, conde de Tendilla, 1491-1552.

AITON, Arthur Scott, 972'02'0924
1894-1955.
Antonio de Mendoza, first viceroy of New Spain. New York, Russell & Russell [1967] xii, 240 p. illus., map, port. 23 cm. Reprint of the 1927 ed. Bibliography: p. [196]-221. [F1231.A37 1967] 66-24664
1. Mendoza, Antonio de, conde de Tendilla, 1491-1552. 2. Mexico—History—Conquest, 1519-1540. 3. Mexico—History—Spanish colony, 1540-1810. **BIP**

Mendoza, Daniel, 1764-1836.

MENDOZA, Daniel, 1764- 927.9683
1836.
The memoirs of the life of Daniel Mendoza; edited, and with an introd. by Paul Magriel. London, New York, Batsford [1951] 115 p. illus. 24 cm. [GV1132.M4A3] 51-13258
1. Boxing — Hist. I. Title. **BIP**

MENDOZA, Daniel, 796.8'3'0924 B
1764-1836.
The memoirs of the life of Daniel Mendoza. New York : Arno Press, 1975. xii, 115 p., [9] leaves of plates : ill. ; 23 cm. (The Modern Jewish experience) Reprint of the 1951 ed. published by Batsford, London. Includes index. [GV1132.M4A3 1975] 74-29507 ISBN 0-405-06734-8 : 10.00
1. Mendoza, Daniel, 1764-1836. 2. Boxing—History. I. Title. II. Series.

RIBALOW, Harold Uriel, 1919- JUV
Fighter from Whitechapel the story of Daniel Mendoza. Illus. by Simon Jeruchim. [New York] Jewish Pubn. Soc. [dist. Farrar, c.1962] 148p. illus. 22cm. (Covenant bks., 15) 62-18412 2.95
I. Mendoza, Daniel, 1764-1836. I. Title.

RIBALOW, Harold 796.8'3'0922
Uriel, 1919-
Fighter from Whitechapel; the story of Daniel Mendoza. Illustrated by Simon Jeruchim. [New York] Farrar, Straus and Cudahy [1962] 148p. illus. 22cm. (Covenant books, 15) [GV1132.M4R5] 62-18412
1. Mendoza, Daniel, 1764-1836. I. Title.

Mendoza, George—Biography.

MENDOZA, George. 811'.5'4 B
Secret places of trout fishermen / George Mendoza. New York : Macmillan, c1977. xi, 112 p. : ill. ; 24 cm. [PS3563.E49Z524] 77-22442 ISBN 0-02-584300-1 : 9.95
1. Mendoza, George—Biography. 2. Authors, American—20th century—Biography. 3. Trout fishing. I. Title. **BIP**

Menelik II, Negus of Ethiopia, 1844-1913.

DARKWAH, R. H. 963'.04'0924 B
Kofi.
Menilek and the rise of the Ethiopian Kingdom of Shewa, 1813-89 / R. H. Kofi Darkwah. New York : Africana Pub. Co., 1975, c1974. p. cm. Bibliography: p. [DT390.S5D37 1975] 74-30137 ISBN 0-8419-0193-7
1. Menelik II, Negus of Ethiopia, 1844-1913. 2. Shoa—Politics and government. I. Title.

MARCUS, Harold G. 963'.04'0924 B
The life and times of Menelik II : Ethiopia 1844-1913 / by Harold G. Marcus. Oxford : Clarendon Press, 1975. viii, 298 p. : 2 maps ; 23 cm. (Oxford studies in African affairs) Includes index. Bibliography : p. [283]-291. [DT387.M37] 75-308576 ISBN 0-19-821674-2 : £5.25
1. Menelik II, Negus of Ethiopia, 1844-1913. 2. Ethiopia—History—1889- I. Title. II. Series. **BIP**

Menendez de Aviles, Pedro, 1519-1574.

BARRIENTOS, 975.9010924
Bartolome, ca.1518-1568
Pedro Menendez de Aviles, founder of Florida. Tr., introd. by Anthony Kerrigan. Introd. foreword by Archbishop Joseph P. Hurley & containing a facsim. repro of the sole printed ed. of the orig. Spanish work. Gainesville. Univ. of Fla. Pr. [c.1965] xxviii, 161, 149p. fold. maps (on lining papers) port. 26cm. Completed in 1567 and first pub. in 1902. [F314.M54B313] 65-29105 12.50, lim. ed.
1. Menendez de Aviles, Pedro, 1519-1574. 2. Florida—Hist.—Spanish colony, 1565-1763. I. Title.

Menendez de Aviles, Pedro, 1519-1574—Juvenile literature.

STONE, Elaine 975.9'01'0924 B
Murray, 1922-
Pedro Menendez de Aviles and the founding of St. Augustine. Illustrated by Unada. New York, P. J. Kennedy [1968, c1969] 187 p. illus. 22 cm. (American background books, 36) Bibliography: p. 180-182. A biography of the man who founded the oldest permanent settlement in the United States, St. Augustine, Florida, in 1565 and promoted Catholic missionary work among the natives. [F314.M54S7] 92 68-57046
1. Menendez de Aviles, Pedro, 1519-1574—Juvenile literature. 2. St. Augustine—History—Juvenile literature. I. Unada, illus. II. Title. III. Series. **BIP**

Mengs, Anton Raphael, 1728-1779.

PELZEL, Thomas. 759.3
Anton Raphael Mengs and neoclassicism / Thomas Pelzel. New York : Garland Pub., 1979. p. cm. (Outstanding dissertations in the fine arts) Originally presented as the author's thesis, Princeton, 1968. Bibliography: p. [ND588.M4P44 1979] 78-74375 ISBN 0-8240-3962-9 pbk. : 25.00
1. Mengs, Anton Raphael, 1728-1779. 2. Painters—Germany—Biography. 3. Neoclassicism (Art) I. Title. II. Series. **BIP**

Menicus.

VERWILGHEN, Albert Felix. 181'.11
Menicus: the man and his ideas. New York, St. John's University Press, 1967. xix, 122 p. 21 cm. (Asian philosophical studies, no. 3) Bibliography: p. 110-122. [B128.M35V4] 67-7616
1. Menicus. I. Title. II. Series.

Menjhin, Yehudi, 1916-

WYMER, Norman 927.8
Yehudi Menuhin. [New York] Roy Publishers. c.1961] 107p. illus. (Living biographies series) 61-1756 2.50 bds.,
1. Menjhin, Yehudi, 1916- I. Title.

Menken, Adah Isaacs, 1835-1868.

GERSON, Noel Bertram, 927.92
1914-
Queen of the Plaza; a biography of Adah Isaacs Menken, by Paul Lewis. New York, Funk & Wagnalls Co. [1964] 307 p. 22 cm. Bibliography: p. 295-296. [PN2287.M6G4] 64-20967
1. Menken, Adah Isaacs, 1835-1868. I. Title.

LESSER, Allen, 792'.028'0924 B
1907-
Enchanting rebel; the secret of Adah Isaacs Menken. Port Washington, N.Y., Kennikat Press [1973, c1947] 284 p. illus. 22 cm. "The poems and essays of Adah Isaacs Menken": p. 265-269. Bibliography: p. 271-273. [PN2287.M6L4 1973] 72-85325 ISBN 0-8046-1746-5 12.50
1. Menken, Adah Isaacs, 1835-1868. I. Title.

Menno Simons, 1496-1561.

LITTELL, Franklin 922.87492
Hamlin
A tribute to Menno Simons. Scottdale, Pa., Herald Pr. [c.1961] 72p. bibl. 61-15955 1.25 pap.,
1. Menno Simons, 1496-1561. I. Title.

Mennonites—Biography.

DYCK, Cornelius J. 289.7'092'2 B
Twelve becoming; biographies of Mennonite disciples from the sixteenth to the twentieth century [by] Cornelius J. Dyck. Illustrated by Richard Loehle. Newton, Kan., Faith and Life Press [1973] 126 p. illus. 28 cm. [BX8141.D9] 73-75174 ISBN 0-87303-865-7 4.50 (pbk.)
1. Mennonites—Biography. I. Title. **BIP**

FULL circle : 289.7'092'2 B
stories of Mennonite women / Mary Lou Cummings, editor. Newton, Kan. : Faith and Life Press, c1978. viii, 204 p. : ill. ; 23 cm. Includes bibliographical references. [BX8141.F84] 78-66879 ISBN 0-87303-014-1 pbk. : 5.25
1. Mennonites—Biography. 2. Women—Biography. I. Cummings, Mary Lou. **BIP**

Menotti, Gian Carlo, 1911-

GRUEN, John. 782.1'092'4 B
Menotti : a biography / John Gruen. New York : Macmillan, c1978. xiii, 242 p., [12] leaves of plates : ill. ; 24 cm. Includes index. [ML410.M52G8] 77-9304 ISBN 0-02-546320-9 : 14.95
1. Menotti, Gian Carlo, 1911- 2. Composers—Biography.

Mense, Hugo, 1879-

BURKS, Arthur J., 1898- 922.281
Bells above the Amazon. New York, McKay [1951] 241 p. illus. 21 cm. "A Story Press book." [BV2853.B6B8] 51-14366
1. Mense, Hugo, 1879- 2. Mundurucu Indians—Missions. I. Title.

Mental healing—Biography.

ST. Clair, David. 615'.852'0922
Psychic healers. [1st ed.] Garden City, N.Y., Doubleday, 1974. viii, 328 p. ports. 22 cm. [RZ407.S23] 74-2833 8.95
1. Mental healing—Biography. 2. Mental healing. I. Title. **BIP**

Mental illness-Personal narratives.

BARNES, Mary, 1923- 362.2'092'4
Mary Barnes: two accounts of a journey through madness, by Mary Barnes and Joseph Berke. New York, Ballantine, [1973, c1971] 374 p. illus. 18 cm.

[[RC463.B7 1972]] ISBN 0-345-03221-7 pap. 1.95
1. Mental illness—Personal narratives. I. Burke, Joseph, joint author. II. Title. III. Title: Two accounts of a journey through madness.
L.C. card no. for original ed. 76-187704
BIP

BARNES, Mary, 1923- 362.2'092'4 B
Mary Barnes: two accounts of a journey through madness, by Mary Barnes and Joseph Berke. [1st American ed.] New York, Harcourt Brace Jovanovich [1972, c1971] 351 p. illus. 22 cm. [RC463.B7 1972] 76-187704 ISBN 0-15-157730-7 7.50
1. Mental illness—Personal narratives. I. Berke, Joseph. II. Title: Two accounts of a journey through madness.

MOELLER, Helen. 616.89
Tornado; my experience with mental illness. Westwood, N.J., F. H. Revell Co. [1968, c1967] 109 p. 21 cm. [RC464.M57A3] 68-11366
1. Mental illness—Personal narratives. I. Title.

MY fight for sanity. v. 12
Greenwich Conn., Flawcett Publications [c1959] 256p. (Crest giants, d409) 'A Crest reprint.'
1. Mental illness-Personal narratives. I. Kruger, Judith.

Mentally handicapped children.

LALOR, Thomas F. 371.9'28
Tom Tom [by] Thomas F. Lalor. [1st ed.] New York, Harper & Row [1973] 106 p. 21 cm. [HQ773.7.L28 1973] 73-6323 ISBN 0-06-064914-3 4.95
1. Mentally handicapped children. I. Title.

Mentally handicapped children—Personal narratives.

JUNKER, Karin Stensland. 362.78
The child in the glass ball. Translated by Gustaf Lannestock. New York, Abingdon Press [1964] 256 p. 23 cm. Translation of De ensamma, natur och kultur. Autobiographical. [HQ773.7.J813] 64-10602
1. Mentally handicapped children—Personal narratives. I. Title.

MURRAY, John B. 362.3'092'4 B
And say what he is : the life of a special child / J. B. Murray and Emily Murray. Cambridge, Mass. : MIT Press, [1975] viii, 232 p. ; 21 cm. [RJ506.M4M87] 75-5810 ISBN 0-262-13115-3 : 9.95
1. Mentally handicapped children—Personal narratives. I. Murray, Emily, joint author. II. Title.
BIP

Mentally ill—Care and treatment.

BEERS, Clifford Whittingham, 1876-1943. 920.8
A mind that found itself; an autobiography. Garden City, N.Y., Doubleday, 1953. 394 p. illus. 21 cm. Supplement (p. [301]-394): 1. The mental hygiene movement, 1908-33, and its founder, by C. E. A. Winslow and others.—2. The mental hygiene movement, more recent developments, by L. E. Woodward—3. The mental hygiene movement, 1948 through 1952, by N. Ridenour.—4. The American Foundation for Mental Hygiene. [RC439.B4 1953] 132.1 53-3324
1. Mentally ill—Care and treatment. 2. Mental hygiene. I. Title. II. Title: The mental hygiene movement.

Menuhin family.

ROLFE, Lionel Menuhin, 1941- 780'.92'2 B
The Menuhins : a family odyssey / by Lionel Menuhin Rolfe ; ill. by Michael Cornier. San Francisco : Panjandrum/Aris, 1978. p. cm. Includes index. [ML418.M27R6] 78-13051 ISBN 0-915572-22-2 : 10.95
1. Menuhin family. 2. Menuhin, Yehudi, 1916- 3. Musicians—Biography. I. Title.
BIP

Menuhin, Yehudi, 1916-

DANIELS, Robin, 1941- 787'.1'0924 B
Conversations with Menuhin / by Robin Daniels. New York : St. Martin's Press, 1980. p. cm. [ML418.M27D3] 79-3137 ISBN 0-312-16943-4 : 14.95
1. Menuhin, Yehudi, 1916- I. Title. BIP

MAGIDOFF, Robert, 1905- 927.8
Yehudi Menuhin; the story of the man and the musician. [1st ed.] Garden City, N. Y., Doubleday, 1955. 319 p. illus. 22 cm. [ML418.M27M3] 55-11333
1. Menuhin, Yehudi, 1916-

MAGIDOFF, Robert, 1905- 787'.1'0924 B
Yehudi Menuhin; the story of the man and the musician. Westport, Conn., Greenwood Press [1973, c1955] 319 p. illus. 22 cm. Reprint of the ed. published by Doubleday, Garden City, N.Y. "Recordings by Yehudi Menuhin": p. [299]-308. [ML418.M27M3 1974] 73-10753 ISBN 0-8371-7020-6 14.00
1. Menuhin, Yehudi, 1916-

MENUHIN, Yehudi, 1916- 787'.1'0924 B
Unfinished journey / Yehudi Menuhin. New York : Knopf : distributed by Random House, 1977, c1976. xvii, 393 p., [24] leaves of plates : ill. ; 25 cm. Includes index. [ML418.M27A3] 76-48114 12.50
1. Menuhin, Yehudi, 1916- 2. Violinists, violoncellists, etc.—United States—Biography. I. Title.
BIP

Menus.

MURPHY, Patricia. 926.4
Glow of candlelight; the story of Patricia Murphy. Englewood Cliffs, N. J., Prentice-Hall [1961] 260p. illus. 22cm. [TX910.5.M8A3] 61-15517
1. Menus. 2. Cookery. I. Title.

Menzel family.

CURTIN, Elisabeth (Mead) 920.7
We Swiss children in the Castle of Prangins. Boston, Christopher [c.1963] 149p. illus. 21cm. 63-14332 3.75
1. Menzel family. 2. Prangins (Castle) I. Title.

CURTIN, Elisabeth (Mead) 920.7
We Swiss children in the Castle of Prangins. Boston, Christopher [c.1963] 149p. illus. 21cm. 63-14332 3.75
1. Menzel family. 2. Prangins (Castle) I. Title.

CURTIN, Elisabeth (Menzel) 920.7
We Swiss children in the Castle of Prangins. Boston, Christopher Pub. House [1963] 149 p. illus. 21 cm. Autobiographical. 63-14332
1. Menzel family. 2. Prangins (Castle) I. Title.

Menzies, Ivan, 1896-

MAGOR, Cliff. 782.8'1'0924 B
The song of a merryman : Ivan Menzies of the D'Oyly Carte Gilbert & Sullivan operas / by Cliff & Edna Magor. London : Grosvenor Books, 1976. 108 p., [8] p. of plates : ill., ports ; 19 cm. (A Grosvenor biography) [ML420.M383M3] 76-374941 ISBN 0-901269-18-2 : £1.00
1. Menzies, Ivan, 1896- 2. Singers—Biography. 3. Evangelists—Biography. I. Magor, Edna, joint author. II. Title.

Menzies, Sir Robert Gordon, 1894-

MENZIES, Robert Gordon, Sir, 1894- 994'.040924
Afternoon light; some memories of men and events. [1st American ed.] New York, Coward-McCann [1968] 384 p. group port. 22 cm. [DU114.M4A3 1968] 68-19223
1. World politics—20th century. I. Title.

PERKINS, Kevin. 994'.04'0924
Menzies; last of the Queen's men. [Adelaide] Rigby [1968] 264p. ports. 25cm. [DU114.M4P4] (B) 68-16578 9.50
1. Menzies, Sir Robert Gordon, 1894- I. Title.

Distributed by Tri-Ocean, San Francisco.

Mercader del Rio Hernandez, Jaime Ramon, 1914-

LEVINE, Isaac Don, 1892- 923.247
The mind of an assassin. New York, Farrar, Straus, and Cudahy [1959] 232 p. illus. 21 cm. [DK254.T6L48] 59-10190
1. Mercader del Rio Hernandez, Jaime Ramon, 1914- 2. Trotskii, Lev, 1879-1940—Assassination. I. Title.
BIP

LEVINE, Isaac Don, 1892- 923.247
The mind of an assassin. [New York] New American Lib. [1960, c.1959, 1960] 190p. illus. (Signet bk. D1854) Bibl. notes p. 184-185 .50 pap.,
1. Mercader del Rio Hernandez, Jaime Ramon, 1914- 2. Trotskii, Lev, 1879-1940—Assassination. I. Title.

Mercer, George, 1733-1784.

JAMES, Alfred Procter, 1886- 923.573
George Mercer of the Ohio Company; a study in frustration. [Pittsburg] University of Pittsburgh Press [1963] 96 p. 23 cm. Bibliographical references included in "Notes" (p. 85-90) [F229.M5J3] 63-21101
1. Mercer, George, 1733-1784. 2. Ohio Company (1747-1779) I. Title.

Mercer, Hugh, 1725 (ca.)-1777.

ENGLISH, Frederick. 973.3'092'4 B
General Hugh Mercer, forgotten hero of the American Revolution / by Frederick English. 1st ed. New York : Vantage Press, [1975] x, 108 p. : ill. ; 21 cm. Bibliography: p. 105-108. [E207.M5E53] 75-316987 ISBN 0-533-01263-5 : 5.00
1. Mercer, Hugh, 1725 (ca.)-1777. I. Title.

Merchant seamen — U.S.

WILLIAMS, James h 1864-1927. 923.873
Blow the man down! A Yankee seaman's adventures under sail; an autobiographical narrative based upon the writings of James H. Williams as arranged and edited by Warren F. Kuehl. [1st ed.] New York, Dutton, 1959. 255 p. illus. 22 cm. [HD8039.S42U74] 59-5821
1. Merchant seamen — U.S. I. Kuehl, Warren F., 1924- ed. II. Title.

Merchants, American.

FAMOUS merchants, 923.873
by Sigmund A. Lavine. New York, Dodd, Mead [1965] 154 p. illus., ports. 22 cm. (Famous biographies for young people) Contents. -- Charles Lewis Tiffany. -- Rowland Hussey Macy. -- John Wanamaker. -- Frank Winfield Woolworth. -- James Buchanan Brady. -- George Ludlum Hartford. -- James Cash Penney. -- Robert Elkington Wood. -- Elizabeth Arden. -- Margaret Fogharty Rudkin. -- Howard Deering Johnson. -- Eugene J. Ferkouf. [HF3023.A2L3] 65-15969
1. Merchants, American.

LAVINE, Sigmund A 923.873
Famous merchants, by Sigmund A. Lavine. New York, Dodd, Mead [1965] 154 p. illus., ports. 22 cm. (Famous biographies for young people) Contents. -- Charles Lewis Tiffany. -- Rowland Hussey Macy. -- John Wanamaker. -- Frank Winfield Woolworth. -- James Buchanan Brady. -- George Ludlum Hartford. -- James Cash Penney. -- Robert Elkington Wood. -- Elizabeth Arden. -- Margaret Fogharty Rudkin. -- Howard Deering Johnson. -- Eugene J. Ferkouf. [HF3023.A2L3] 65-15969
1. Merchants, American. I. Title.
BIP

Merchants—New York (City)

SCOVILLE, Joseph Alfred, 1815-1864. 381'.0922
The old merchants of New York City, by Walter Barrett. First[-fifth] series. New York, Greenwood Press, 1968. 5 v. 21 cm. Reprint of the 1863-69 ed. [HF3163.N7S32] 68-28645
1. Merchants—New York (City) 2. New York (City)—Biography. I. Title.
BIP

Merchants—United States.

HUNT, Freeman, 1804-1858, ed. 338'.0922
Lives of American merchants. [1st ed.] New York, A. M. Kelley, 1969. 2 v. ports. 22 cm. (Library of early American business & industry, 3) (Reprints of economic classics.) Reprint of the 1856 ed. [HF3023.A2H8 1969] 66-21679
1. Merchants—United States. I. Title.

Mercier, Ernest, 1878-1955.

KUISEL, Richard F. 320.5 B
Ernest Mercier; French technocrat, by Richard F. Kuisel. Berkeley, University of California Press, 1967. x, 184 p. port. 24 cm. Bibliography: p. [165]-180. [HF3554.5.M4K8] 67-22604
1. Mercier, Ernest, 1878-1955.

Mercouri, Melina,

MERCOURI, Melina, 1925- 791.43'028'0924 B
I was born Greek. [1st ed.] Garden City, N.Y., Doubleday, 1971. 253 p. ports. 22 cm. [PN2668.M4A3] 75-157610 6.95
I. Title.

MERCOURI, Melina, 1925- 791.43'028'0924 B
I was born Greek. [New York] [Dell] [1973, c.1971] 288 p. 18 cm. [PN2668.M4A3] pap., 1.50
I. Title.
L.C. card no. for original ed.: 75-157610.

Mercy, Randolph Barnes, 1812-1887.

HOLLON, W Eugene. 923.573
Beyond the cross timbers; the travels of Randolph B. Marcy, 1812-1887. [1st ed.] Norman, University of Oklahoma Press [c1955] 270p. illus. 22cm. Includes bibliography. [F593.M34H6] 55-6357
1. Mercy, Randolph Barnes, 1812-1887. I. Title.

Meredith, George, 1828-1909.

BUTCHER, Alice Mary (Brandreth) Lady. 823'.8
Memories of George Meredith. Port Washington, N.Y., Kennikat Press [1970] viii, 151 p. illus. 20 cm. Reprint of the 1919 ed. [PR5013.B8 1970] 72-103172
1. Meredith, George, 1828-1909. I. Title.
BIP

ELLIS, Stewart Marsh. 823'.8 B
George Meredith; his life and friends in relation to his work, by S. M. Ellis. [Folcroft, Pa.] Folcroft Library Editions, 1973. p. Reprint of the 1920 ed. published by G. Richards, London. [PR5013.E5 1973] 73-11362 ISBN 0-8414-1914-0 (lib. bdg.)
1. Meredith, George, 1828-1909.

GRETTON, Mary Sturge. 823'.8
The writings & life of George Meredith: a centenary study. New York, Haskell House, 1970. 250 p. 23 cm. Reprint of the 1926 ed. Includes bibliographical references. [PR5013.G7 1970] 70-117580
1. Meredith, George, 1828-1909. I. Title.

HAMMERTON, John Alexander, Sir, 1871-1949. 823'.8 B
George Meredith, his life and art in anecdote and criticism. A new and rev. ed. [Folcroft, Pa.] Folcroft Library Editions, 1973. xi, 391 p. illus. 22 cm. Reprint of the 1911 ed. published by J. Grant, Edinburgh. [PR5013.H3 1973] 73-16288 ISBN 0-8414-4799-3 (lib. bdg.)
1. Meredith, George, 1828-1909.

JOHNSON, Diane. 823'.8 B
The true history of the first Mrs. Meredith and other lesser lives. [1st ed.] New York, A. A. Knopf, 1972. xiv, 232 p. illus. 22 cm. Running title: Lesser lives. Bibliography: p. [231]-232. [CT788.M378J64] 72-2227 ISBN 0-394-48034-1 7.95
1. Meredith, Mary Ellen, 1821-1861. 2.

Meredith, George, 1828-1909. 3. Wallis, Henry, b. 1830. I. Title. II. Title: Lesser lives.

LINDSAY, Jack, 1900- 823'.8 B
George Meredith, his life and work. London, Bodley Head. Millwood, N.Y., Kraus Reprint Co., 1973. 420 p. port. 24 cm. Reprint of the 1956 ed. Includes bibliographical references. [PR5013.L5 1973] 73-9718 ISBN 0-527-57230-6 18.00
1. Meredith, George, 1828-1909. BIP

PHOTIADES, Constantin. 823'.8
George Meredith: his life, genius & teaching. From the French of Constantin Photiades rendered into English by Arthur Price. Port Washington, N.Y., Kennikat Press [1970] 253 p. 21 cm. Reprint of the 1913 ed. Includes bibliographical references. [PR5013.P52 1970] 79-113318
1. Meredith, George, 1828-1909. I. Title.

SASSOON, Siegfried 823'.8 B
Lorraine, 1886-1967.
Meredith. Port Washington, N.Y., Kennikat Press [1969, c1948] 269 p. port. 22 cm. [PR5013.S3 1969] 68-26214
1. Meredith, George, 1828-1909. BIP

STEVENSON, Lionel, 1902- 928.2
The ordeal of George Meredith, a biography. New York, Scribner, 1953. viii, 368p. port. 25cm. Bibliography: p. [355]-359. [PR5013.S7] 53-12025
1. Meredith, George, 1828-1909. I. Title.

Meredith, Mary Ellen, 1821-1861.

JOHNSON, Diane. 823'.8 B
The true history of the first Mrs. Meredith and other lesser lives. [1st ed.] New York, A. A. Knopf, 1972. xiv, 232 p. illus. 22 cm. Running title: Lesser lives. Bibliography: p. [231]-232. [CT788.M378J64] 72-2227 ISBN 0-394-48034-1 7.95
1. Meredith, Mary Ellen, 1821-1861. 2. Meredith, George, 1828-1909. 3. Wallis, Henry, b. 1830. I. Title. II. Title: Lesser lives.

Mergenthaler, Ottmar, 1854-1899.

MENGEL, Willi. 926.55
Ottmar Mergenthaler and the printing revolution. With an introd. by Lin Yutang. Brooklyn, Mergenthaler Linotype Co., 1954. 63p. illus. 26cm. [Z232.M56M4] 54-34221
1. Mergenthaler, Ottmar, 1854-1899. 2. Linotype. I. Title.

Mergenthaler, Ottmar, 1854-1899—Juvenile literature.

LEVINE, Israel E. 920
Miracle man of printing: Ottmar Mergenthaler. New York, Messner [c.1963] 190p. 22cm. Bibl. 63-16784 3.25; 3.19 lib. ed. net,
1. Mergenthaler, Ottmar, 1854-1899—Juvenile literature. I. Title.

Merideth, Robert.

MERIDETH, Robert. 979.4'05'0924 B
Transformations : a dictionary of contemporary changes / Robert Merideth. 1st ed. Bolinas, CA : Connections Press, c1979. x, 240 p. ; 23 cm. Includes index. [CT275.M472A37] 77-82555 ISBN 0-930474-00-7 pbk. : 6.00
1. Merideth, Robert. 2. California—Biography. I. Title. BIP

Merie-Smith, Van Santvoord, 1889-1943.

HUBER, Richard M. 923.373
Big all the way through; the life of Van Santvoord Merle-Smith. Princeton, N. J., 1952. 64 p. illus. 23 cm. [HC102.5.M4H8] 52-1794
1. Merie-Smith, Van Santvoord, 1889-1943. I. Title.

Merimee, Prosper, 1803-1870.

RAITT, Alan William. 848'.7'09 B
Prosper Merimee [by] A. W. Raitt. New York, Scribner [1970] 453 p. illus., ports. 25 cm. Bibliography: p. 429-442. [PQ2362.Z5R3 1970b] 77-122336 15.00
1. Merimee, Prosper, 1803-1870.

Meriwether, Elizabeth (Avery)

MERIWETHER, Elizabeth 928.1
(Avery) 1824-1917.
Recollections of 92 years. 1824-1916. Nashville. Tennessee Historical Commission [1958] 249p. illus. 25cm. [PS2389.M253R4] 58-63771
I. Title.

Merlo, Thecla, 1894-1964.

DAUGHTERS of St. Paul 271.979
Women of faith; a profile of Mother Thecla Merlo, confoundress of the Daughters of St. Paul. [Boston, Author, 1966, c.1965] 226p. illus. 21cm. [BX4334.Z8A5] 65-29133 3.00, 2.00 pap.,
1. Merlo, Thecla, 1894-1964. 2. Daughters of St. Paul. I. Title.

LUCARINI, Spartaco. 271'.9 B
A woman for our time: the servant of God, Mother Thecla Merlo, co-foundress of the Daughters of St. Paul. Translated by the Daughters of St. Paul. [Boston] St. Paul Editions [1974] 253 p. illus. 22 cm. [BX4334.Z8L8] 74-77253 3.95
1. Merlo, Thecla, 1894-1964. 2. Daughters of St. Paul. I. Title.

Merman, Ethel.

MERMAN, Ethel. 782.8'1'0924 B
Merman / by Ethel Merman with George Eells. New York : Simon and Schuster, c1978. 320 p., [8] leaves of plates : ill. ; 25 cm. Includes index. [ML420.M39A32] 78-92 ISBN 0-671-22712-2 : 9.95
1. Merman, Ethel. 2. Singers—United States—Biography. I. Eells, George, joint author. BIP

MERMAN, Ethel. 927.8
Who could ask for anything more, as told to Pete Martin. [1st ed.] Garden City, N. Y., Doubleday, 1955. 252 p. illus. 22 cm. [ML420.M39A3] 55-5495
1. Musicians—Correspondence, reminiscences, etc. I. Martin, Thornton, 1901- II. Title.

Merrett, John Donald, 1908-1954.

TULLETT, Tom. 923.4142
Portrait of a bad man. New York, Rinehart [1956] 196p. illus. 21cm. [HV6248.M49T8 1956a] 56-11655
1. Merrett, John Donald, 1908-1954. I. Title.

Merriam, Clinton Hart, 1855-1942.

STERLING, Keir 574'.092'4 B
Brooks.
Last of the naturalists: the career of C. Hart Merriam. New York, Arno Press, 1974. xv, 478 p. illus. 24 cm. (Natural sciences in America) A revision of the author's thesis, Columbia University. Bibliography: p. 441-478. [QH31.M452S7] 73-17847 ISBN 0-405-05770-9
1. Merriam, Clinton Hart, 1855-1942. 2. Naturalists—Biography. I. Title. II. Series.

Merrick, John, 1862 or 3-1890.

MONTAGU, Ashley, 155.9'16'0924
1905-
The elephant man; a study in human dignity [by] Ashley Montagu. New York, Ballantine [1973] xiii, 153 p., 18 cm. References: p. 151-153. [CT9983.M47M65 1973] pap. 1.25
1. Merrick, John, 1862 or 3-1890. I. Treves, Frederick, Sir, 1853-1923. The elephant man. II. Title.
L.C. card no. for orig. ed.: 79-16770 BIP

MONTAGU, Ashley, 155.9'16'0924
1905-
The elephant man; a study in human dignity. New York, Outerbridge & Dienstfrey; distributed by E. P. Dutton [1971] x, 140 p. illus., ports. 22 cm. "The elephant man, by Sir Frederick Treves": p. 13-38. Includes bibliographical references. [CT9983.M47M65 1971] 79-167770 ISBN 0-87690-037-6 5.95
1. Merrick, John, 1862 or 3-1890. I. Treves, Frederick, Sir, bart., 1853-1923. The elephant man. 1971. II. Title.

Merrill, Harriet Elizabeth, 1832-1861.

MERRILL, Harriet 910'.45 B
Elizabeth, 1832-1861.
Hattie. Edited by M. Virginia Wirtz. [Honolulu, Hawaii, Printed by Edward Enterprises, 1973] 146 p. port. 23 cm. Diary extracts and correspondence. [CT275.M482A33 1973] 73-166154
1. Merrill, Harriet Elizabeth, 1832-1861. I. Wirtz, M. Virginia, ed. II. Title.

Merrill, John,

MERRILL, John, 1875- 923.773
Son of Salem, the autobiography of John Merrill. New York, Vantage Press [c1953] 202p. illus. 23cm. [PN2237.M62A3] 53-10301
I. Title.

Merrill, Melissa.

MERRILL, Melissa. 289.3'3 B
Polygamist's wife / by Melissa Merrill. Salt Lake City : Olympus Pub. Co., c1975. 167 p. : ill. ; 24 cm. [BX8695.M37A36] 74-29659 ISBN 0-913420-52-2 : 7.95
1. Merrill, Melissa. 2. Polygamy. I. Title. BIP

Merritt, Charles E.

MERRITT, Charles 797.5'3'0924 B
E.
The big flight after 35 years of disappointments / by Charles E. Merritt. Phoenix : Ship Inc. Publications, c1974. ix, 175, a-j p. : ill. (1 fold. map) ; 24 cm. Fold. map on p. [2] of cover. [TL540.M394A32] 75-311869
1. Merritt, Charles E. 2. Air pilots—Correspondence, reminiscences, etc. I. Title.

Merry del Val, Raphael, Cardinal, 1865-1930.

QUINN, Mary Bernetta. 922.242
Give me souls; a life of Raphael Cardinal Merry del Val. Westminster, Md., Newman Press, 1958. 277 p. illus. 22 cm. Includes bibliography. [BX4705.M525Q5] 57-11804
1. Merry del Val, Raphael, Cardinal, 1865-1930. I. Title.

Mersfelder, Nick, 1858-1939.

SCOBEE, 917.64'934'0360924 B
Barry, 1885-
Nick Mersfelder: a remarkable man. Fort Davis, Tex., Fort Davis Historical Society [1969] 63 p. illus., ports. 23 cm. [F391.M56S3] 70-259753
1. Mersfelder, Nick, 1858-1939. I. Title.

Mershon, Ralph Davenport, 1868-1952.

COCKINS, Edith D 621.3'092'4
Ralph Devenport Merschon. Columbus, Ohio, 1956. 2 v. illus. 29cm. Vol. 2 contains articles and papers by Mershon. [TK140.M4C6] 56-35568
1. Mershon, Ralph Davenport, 1868-1952. 2. Electric engineering. I. Title.

Merson, Ralph Waldo,

MERSON, Ralph Waldo, 1803- 928.1
1882
Journals and miscellaneous notebooks; v.5. Ed. by William H. Gilman [others] Cambridge, Mass., Belknap Pr. of Harvard [c.]1965 xx, 542p. illus., facsims. 25cm. Contents.v.5. 1835-1838. Bibl. [PS1631.A3] 60-11554 12.50
I. Title.

Merton, Thomas, 1915-1968.

ADAMS, Daniel J. 271'.125'024 B
Thomas Merton's shared contemplation : a Protestant perspective / Daniel A. Adams. Kalamazoo, Mich. : Cistercian Publications, 1979. 361 p. ; 23 cm. (Cistercian studies series ; no. 62) Bibliography: p. 347-361. [BX4705.M542A64] 78-6549 ISBN 0-87907-862-6 : 17.95
1. Merton, Thomas, 1915-1968. 2. Trappists in the United States—Biography. I. Title. II. Series. BIP

MCINECRY, Dennis 255'.125'00924 B
Q.
Thomas Merton; the man and his work [by] Dennis Q. McInerny. Kalamazoo, Mich., Cistercian Publications, 1974. p. cm. (Cistercian studies series, no. 27) [BX4705.M542M3] 74-4319 ISBN 0-87907-827-8 7.95
1. Merton, Thomas, 1915-1968. I. Title. II. Series.

MCINERNY, Dennis 271'.125'024 B
Q.
Thomas Merton; the man and his work [by] Dennis Q. McInerny. [Spencer, Mass.] Cistercian Publications; [distributed by] Consortium Press, Washington, 1974. xii, 128 p. 23 cm. (Cistercian studies series, no. 27) [BX4705.M542M3] 74-4319 ISBN 0-87907-827-8
1. Merton, Thomas, 1915-1968. I. Title. II. Series.

MERTON, Thomas, 271'.125'024 B
1915-1968.
The seven storey mountain / Thomas Merton. New York : Harcourt-Brace Jovanovich, [1978] c1948. p. cm. (A Harvest/HBJ book) Autobiography. [BX4705.M542A3 1978] 78-7109 ISBN 0-15-680679-7 pbk. : 4.95
1. Merton, Thomas, 1915-1968. 2. Trappists in the United States—Biography. I. Title.

MERTON, Thomas, 271'.125'024
1915-1968.
The seven storey mountain / Thomas Merton. New York : Octagon Books, 1978, c1948. 429 p. ; 23 cm. Reprint of the ed. published by Harcourt, Brace, New York. Includes index. [BX4705.M542A3 1978b] 78-15504 lib.bdg. : 17.50
1. Merton, Thomas, 1915-1968. 2. Trappists in the United States—Biography. I. Title. BIP

MERTON, Thomas, 271'.125'024
1915-1968.
The sign of Jonas / Thomas Merton. 1st Harvest/HBJ ed. New York : Harcourt Brace Jovanovich, 1979, c1953. p. cm. (A Harvest/HBJ book) [BX4705.M542A32 1979] 79-10283 ISBN 0-15-682529-5 : 4.95
1. Merton, Thomas, 1915-1968. 2. Trappists in the United States—Biography. I. Title. BIP

RICE, Edward E., 818'.5'409 B
1918-
The man in the sycamore tree; the good times and hard life of Thomas Merton. An entertainment, with photos., by Edward Rice. [1st ed.] Garden City, N.Y., Doubleday, 1970. 139 p. illus., ports. 27 cm. [BX4705.M542R5] 76-121809 7.95
1. Merton, Thomas, 1915-1968. I. Title.

VOIGT, Robert J. 191
Thomas Merton: a different drummer [by] Robert J. Voigt. Liguori, Mo., Liguori Publications [1972] 127 p. 18 cm. Bibliography: p. 125-127. [BX4705.M542V65] 72-80829 1.50
1. Merton, Thomas, 1915-1968. 2. War and religion. 3. United States—Race question. 4. Perfection. I. Title.

WOODCOCK, George, 818'.5'409 B
1912-
Thomas Merton, monk and poet : a critical study / George Woodcock. 1st American ed. New York : Farrar, Straus, Giroux, 1978. 200 p., [1] leaf of plates : port. ; 24 cm. Includes index. Bibliography: p. 189-192. [PS3525.E7174Z95 1978b] 78-73396 ISBN 0-374-27635-8 : 7.95
1. Merton, Thomas, 1915-1968. 2. Poets, American—20th century—Biography. 3. Trappists in the United States—Biography. I. Title.

Merton, Thomas, 1915-1968—Juvenile literature.

SUSSMAN, Cornelia Silver. 271'.125'024 B
Thomas Merton : the daring young man on the flying belltower / Cornelia & Irving Sussman. New York : Macmillan, c1976. 177 p. : port. ; 22 cm. Includes index. Bibliography: p. 169-171. A biography of the Trappist monk and Zen mystic who gained fame as a writer, social critic, and radical peace activist. [BX4705.M542S9] 92 76-34236 ISBN 0-02-788630-1 : 6.95
1. Merton, Thomas, 1915-1968—Juvenile literature. I. Sussman, Irving, joint author. BIP

Merz, Henry, 1833-1905.

MERZ, Elsie, 1883-1950. 920
The long path. South Orange, N.J., 1951. 226 p. illus., ports. 24 cm. 125 copies printed. [CT275.M496A3] 51-26715
1. Merz, Henry, 1833-1905. 2. Merz, Augusta (Heller), 1837-1927. I. Title.

Mesmer, Franz Anton, 1734-1815.

BURANELLI, Vincent. 615'.8512'0924 B
The wizard from Vienna : Franz Anton Mesmer / by Vincent Buranelli. New York : Coward, McCann & Geoghegan, [1975] 256 p., [4] leaves of plates : ill. ; 22 cm. Includes index. Bibliography : p. 239-245. [BF1127.M4B87 1975] 75-24072 ISBN 0-698-10697-0 : 8.95
1. Mesmer, Franz Anton, 1734-1815. 2. Mesmerism. I. Title. BIP

BURANELLI, Vincent. 615'.8512'0924 B
The wizard from Vienna / by Vincent Buranelli. London : Owen, 1976. 256 p., [8] p. of plates : ill., facsim., map, ports. ; 23 cm. Includes index. Bibliography: p. 239-245. [BF1127.M4B87 1976] 77-359456 ISBN 0-7206-0464-8 : £5.25
1. Mesmer, Franz Anton, 1734-1815. 2. Mesmerism. 3. Mesmerists—Austria—Vienna—Biography. 4. Vienna—Biography. I. Title.

JENSEN, Ann (Oden) 1902- 610'.924
Franz Anton Mesmer, physician extraordinaire, by Ann Jensen and Mary Lou Watkins. New York, Garrett Publications [1967] 253 p. 22 cm. [R507.M39J4] 66-28499
1. Mesmer, Franz Anton, 1734-1815. I. Watkins, Mary Lou, joint author. II. Title. BIP

WYCKOFF, James. 615'.8512'0924 B
Franz Anton Mesmer : between God and Devil / by James Wyckoff. Englewood Cliffs, N.J. : Prentice-Hall, [1975] x, 148 p., [4] leaves of plates : ill. ; 22 cm. Includes bibliographical references and index. [BF1127.M4W9] 75-11759 ISBN 0-13-577379-2 : 8.95
1. Mesmer, Franz Anton, 1734-1815. 2. Mesmerism.

ZWEIG, Stefan, 1881-1942. 615.851
Mental healers: Franz Anton Mesmer, Mary Baker Eddy, Sigmund Freud. [Tr. from German by Eden and Cedar Paul] New York, Unger [1962, c.1932] 363p. 22cm. 62-14082 5.50
1. Mesmer, Franz Anton, 1734—1815. 2. Eddy, Mary (Baker) 1821-1910. 3. Freud, Sigmund, 1856-1939. 4. Mental healing. I. Title. BIP

Messing, Shep.

MESSING, Shep. 796.33'4'0924 [B]
The education of an American soccer player / Shep Messing, with David Hirshey. New York : Bantam Books, 1979, c1978. 257p., [8] leaves of plates : ill. ; 18 cm. [GV942.7.M47A33] ISBN 0-553-12619-9 pbk. : 2.25
1. Messing, Shep. 2. Soccer players — United States — Biography. I. Hirshey, David, joint author. II. Title.
L.C. card no. for 1978 Dodd, Mead ed.:78-8099. BIP

Mesta, Perle (Skirvin)

MESTA, Perle (Skirvin) 923.273
Perle--my story, by Perle Mesta, Robert Cahn. New York, Avon [1961, c.1960] 223p. illus. (G-1066) .50 pap.,
I. Title.

MESTA, Perle (Skirvin) 923.273
Perle --my story, by Perle Mesta with Robert Cahn. [1st ed.] New York, McGraw-Hill [1960] 251p. illus. 22cm. [CT275.M498A3] 60-10478
I. Title.

Mestrovic, Ivan,

MESTROVIC, Ivan, 1883-1962. 730'.0924 B
Ivan Mestrovic, [text] by Dusko Keckemet. New York, McGraw-Hill [1970] [71] p., 124 plates (56 col.) 31 cm. Translation of Ivan Mestrovic: Jedini put da se bude umjetnik jest raditi. Bibliography: p. [63-67] [NB593.M4K39913] 76-150462 17.95
I. Keckemet, Dusko. II. Babic, Milan, illus.

Meszaros, Andor, 1900-1972.

SEMMENS, Kelman. 730'.92'4
Andor Meszaros. Melbourne, Hawthorn Press, 1972. 32 p. illus. 25 cm. [NB522.5.M47S45] 73-163010 ISBN 0-7256-0091-8 8.50
1. Meszaros, Andor, 1900-1972. I. Meszaros, Andor, 1900-1972.

Metastasio, Pietro Antonio Domenico Buonaventura, 1698-1782.

BURNEY, Charles, 1726-1814. 851'.5 B
Memoirs of the life and writings of the Abate Metastasio, including translations of his principal letters. New York, Da Capo Press, 1971. 3 v. port. 23 cm. (Da Capo Press music reprint series) Reprint of the 1796 ed. [PQ4719.A2 1971] 76-162295 ISBN 0-306-71110-9
1. Metastasio, Pietro Antonio Domenico Buonaventura, 1698-1782.

Methodist Church—Biog.

CLARK, Elmer Talmage 1886- ed. 922.773
Who's who in Methodism; edited under the auspices of the Association of Methodist Historical Societies, USA, and the International Methodist Historical Society, an affiliate of the Ecumenical Conference. Elmer T. Clark, editor-in-chief; T.A. Stafford, cooperating editor. Chicago, A.N. Marquis Co., 1952. x, 860 p. 24 cm. [BX8213.W52] 52-8040
1. Methodist Church—Biog. I. Title.

MORROW, Thomas Manser. 287'1'0922
Early Methodist women [by] Thomas M. Morrow, London, Epworth Pr., 1967. 119p. 20cm. [BX8493.M6] 68-96621 3.00 bds.,
1. Methodist Church—Biog. 2. Woman—Biog. I. Title.
American distributor: Verry, Mystic, Conn.

SHULER, Robert Pierce, 1880- 922.773
Bob Shuler met these on the trail. Wheaton, Ill., Sword of the Lord Publishers [1955] 185p. 21cm. [BX8491.S46] 56-178740
1. Methodist Church—Biog. I. Title.

Methodist Church—Clergy—Correspondence, reminiscences, etc.

BAGBY, James Thomas, 1879- 922.773
From the tablets of my heart. [1st ed.] New York, Vantage Press [1957] 103p. 21cm. Autobiography. [BX8495.B23A3] 56-12208
1. Methodist Church—Clergy—Correspondence, reminiscences, etc. I. Title.

HILBISH, Benjamin F 922.773
Tales of a frontier preacher, by Benj. F Hilbish, edited by his daughter, Florence May Anna Hilbish. [1st ed.] New York, Pageant Press [1959] 156p. illus. 21cm. [BX8495.H54A3] 59-12475
1. Methodist Church—Clergy—Correspondence, reminiscences, etc. I. Hilbish, Florence May Anna, 1892- ed. II. Title.

MARTIN, Issac Patton, 1867- 922.778
A minister in the Tennessee Valley, sixty-seven years. Knoxville, Tenn., Methodist Historical Society of Holston Conference [1954] 234p. illus. 24cm. [BX8495.M32A3] 54-24793
1. Methodist Church—Clergy—Correspondence, remiaiacences, etc. I. Title.

Methodist Church—Bishops—Biography.

OXNAM, Garfield Bromley, Bp., 1891-1963. 287'.6'0924 B
I protest / by G. Bromley Oxnam. Westport, Conn. : Greenwood Press, 1979, c1954. 186 p. ; 23 cm. Reprint of the ed. published by Harper, New York. [BX8495.O93A34 1979] 78-21506 ISBN 0-313-21154-X : 16.00
1. Oxnam, Garfield Bromley, Bp., 1891-1963. 2. Methodist Church—Bishops—Biography. 3. United States. Congress. House. Committee on Un-American Activities. 4. Bishops—United States—Biography. I. Title.

Methodist Church—Clergy—Biography.

BRACE, Beverly Waltmire, 1924- 287'.632'0924 B
The Humboldt years, 1930-1939 / Beverly Waltmire Brace. Chicago : Adams Press, c1977. iv, 206 p. ; 22 cm. [BX8495.W2444B7] 77-154518 pbk. : 4.50
1. Waltmire, Baily, 1896-1962. 2. Methodist Church—Clergy—Biography. 3. Humboldt Park Community Methodist Episcopal Church, Chicago, Ill.—History. 4. Clergy—Illinois—Chicago—Biography. 5. Chicago—Biography. 6. Chicago—Church history. I. Title. BIP

Methodist Church in Montana.

WEST, Roberta B. 287'.09786
How they brought the good news of Methodism to north Montana / by Roberta B. West. [Chinook? Mont.] : West, [1974] 537 p. : ill. ; 29 cm. Includes index. Bibliography: p. 113-116. [BX8248.M9W47] 75-303211
1. Methodist Church in Montana. 2. Montana—Biography. I. Title.

Methodist Church in Norfolk Co., Va.—Clergy.

STEVENSON, Arthur Linwood, 1891- 287'.6755'51
Native Methodist preachers of Norfolk and Princess Anne Counties, Virginia / by Arthur L. Stevenson. Brevard, N.C. : Stevenson, 1975. 49 p. ; 22 cm. (His Native Methodist preacher series ; 6th) [BX8491.S69] 76-351183
1. Methodist Church in Norfolk Co., Va.—Clergy. 2. Methodist Church in Princess Anne Co., Va.—Clergy. 3. Norfolk Co., Va.—Biography. 4. Princess Anne Co., Va.—Biography. I. Title: Native Methodist preachers of Norfolk and Princess Anne Counties ...

Metro-Goldwyn-Mayer, inc.

PARISH, James Robert. 791.43'028'0922 B
The MGM stock company; the golden era [by] James Robert Parish and Ronald L. Bowers. Editor: T. Allan Taylor. Research associates: John Robert Cocchi [and] Florence Solomon. Photo associate: Gene Andrewski. New Rochelle, N.Y., Arlington House [1973] 862 p. illus. 24 cm. [PN1998.A2P394] 72-91640 ISBN 0-87000-128-0 14.95
1. Metro-Goldwyn-Mayer, inc. 2. Moving-picture actors and actresses—United States—Biography. I. Bowers, Ronald L., joint author. II. Title.

Metternich, Tatiana, furstin von Metternich—Winneburg.

METTERNICH, Tatiana, Furstin von Metternich-Winneburg. v. 12
Tatiana : five passports in a shifting Europe / by Tatiana Metternich. London : Heinemann, 1976. x, 285 p., 24 p. of plates : ill., ports. ; 25 cm. American ed. published under title: Purgatory of fools. [CT1495.M47A36 1976b] 77-372729 ISBN 0-434-46525-9 : £6.00
1. Metternich, Tatiana, furstin von Metternich—Winneburg. 2. Europe—Nobility—Biography. I. Title.

Metternich-Winneburg, Clemens Lothar Wenzel, Furst von, 1773-1859.

ARCHER, Jules. 940.2'7'0924 B
Colossus of Europe: Metternich. New York, J. Messner [1970] 191 p. 22 cm. Bibliography: p. 186. A biography of the Foreign Minister of Austria whose diplomatic foresight forged national alliances that ultimately vanquished Napoleon and helped sustain peace in Europe for forty years. [DB80.8.M57A7] 92 75-107397 3.50
1. Metternich-Winneburg, Clemens Lothar Wenzel, Furst von, 1773-1859—Juvenile literature. I. Title.

CECIL, Algernon, 1879-1953 923.2436
Metternich, 1773-1859; a study of his period and personality [3d ed.] London, Eyre and Spottiswoode [dist. Chester Springs, Pa., Dufour] 324p. ports. 22cm. Bibl. 5.00
1. Metternich-Winneburg, Clemens Lothar Wenzel, Furstvon, 1773-1859. 2. Europe—Politics—1789-1900. I. Title.

METTERNICH-WINNEBURG, Clemens Lothar Wenzel, Furst von, 1773-1859. 940.2'7'0924 B
Memoirs of Prince Metternich, 1773-1815. Edited by Prince Richard Metternich. The papers classified and arr. by M. A. de Klinkowstrom. Translated by Mrs. Alexander Napier. New York, H. Fertig, 1970. 5 v. facsims., port. 24 cm. Reprint of the 1880 ed. Translation of Aus Metternich's nach gelassenen papieren. Volume 5, 1830-1835 translated by Gerald W. Smith. [DB80.8.M52 1970] 68-9611
1. Europe—Politics and government—1789-1815. 2. Europe—Politics and government—1815-1848. 3. Austria—History—1789-1900. I. Metternich-Winneburg, Richard Clemens Lothar, Furst von, 1829-1895, ed. II. Klinkowstrom, Alfons, Freiherr von, 1818-1891, joint ed. III. Napier, Robina, trans. IV. Smith, Gerard W., trans. BIP

MILNE, Andrew. 940.2'7'0924 B
Metternich. Totowa, N.J., Rowman and Littlefield [1975, c1974] p. cm. (London history series) Bibliography: p. [DB80.8.M57M47 1975] 74-18347 ISBN 0-87471-591-1 11.00
1. Metternich-Winneburg, Clemens Lothar Wenzel, Furst von, 1773-1859.

PALMER, Alan Warwick. 940.2'7'1924 B
Metternich [by] Alan Palmer. [1st U.S. ed.] New York, Harper & Row [1972] vii, 405 p. illus. 24 cm. Bibliography: p. [376]-382. [DB80.8.M57P33 1972b] 70-190094 ISBN 0-06-013261-2 12.50
1. Metternich-Winneburg, Clemens Lothar Wenzel, Furst von, 1773-1859.

SCHWARZ, Henry Frederick, 1906- ed. 923.2436
Metternich, the "coachman of Europe": stateman or evil genius? Boston, Heath [1962] 107 p. 24 cm. (Problems in European civilization) Includes bibliography. [DB80.8.M57S35] 62-19748
1. Metternich-Winneburg, Clemens Lothar Wenzel, Furst von, 1773-1859.

Metzger, Max Josef, 1887-1944.

†SWIDLER, Leonard J. 282'.092'4 B
Bloodwitness for peace and unity : the life of Max Josef Metzger / by Leonard Swidler. Philadelphia : Ecumenical Press, c1977. vi, 122 p. ; 23 cm. Includes bibliographical references. [BX4705.M546S94] 77-76430 3.95

1. Metzger, Max Josef, 1887-1944. 2. Catholic Church—Clergy—Biography. 3. Clergy—Germany—Biography. I. Title. Publisher's address : 3725 Chestnut St., Philadelphia, PA

Meulen, Adam Franz van der, 1632-1690.

MORRIS, Inga, 1924- 759.4
Adam Franz van der Meulen (1632-1690) [Munster?] 1970 [cover 1973] viii, 147 p. 21 cm. Inaug.-Diss.—Munster. Bibliography: p. 81-87. [ND553.M52M67] 74-175820
1. Meulen, Adam Franz van der, 1632-1690.

Mexican American women—Middle West—Biography.

LINDBORG, Kristina. 301.41'2'0922
Five Mexican-American women in transition : a case study of migrants in the Midwest / Kristina Lindborg and Carlos J. Ovando. San Francisco, Calif. : R & E Research Associates, 1977. iv, 111 p. : 28 cm. Bibliography: p. 106-111. [HQ1412.L56] 76-56558 ISBN 0-88247-444-8 pbk. : 8.00
1. Mexican American women—Middle West—Biography. 2. Migrant agricultural laborers—Middle West. I. Ovando, Carlos Julio. II. Title. **BIP**

Mexican Americans—Bio-bibliography.

MARTINEZ, Julio A. 016.92'00092'6873
Chicano scholars and writers : a bio-bibliographical directory / edited & compiled by Julio A. Martinez. Metuchen, N.J. : Scarecrow Press, 1979. x, 579 p. ; 22 cm. Includes index. [E184.M5M385] 78-32076 ISBN 0-8108-1205-3 : 26.50
1. Mexican Americans—Bio-bibliography. I. Title. **BIP**

Mexican Americans—Biography.

NEWLON, Clarke. 920'.073
Famous Mexican Americans. Foreword by Uvaldo H. Palomares. New York, Dodd, Mead [1972] 187 p. illus. 22 cm. (Famous biographies for young people) Bibliography: p. 181. Brief biographies of twenty Mexican Americans who have made significant contributions in government, sports, entertainment, education, and other fields. [E184.M5N38] 920 79-178224 ISBN 0-396-06489-2 3.95
1. Mexican Americans Biography. I. Title. **BIP**

Mexican Americans—Social life and customs.

GALARZA, Ernesto, 1905- 301.451'687'2073
Barrio boy. Notre Dame [Ind.] University of Notre Dame Press [1971] vii, 275 p. 21 cm. "This study was produced through the United States-Mexico Border Studies Project at the University of Notre Dame." [E184.M5G3] 70-146805 ISBN 0-268-00440-4 7.95
1. Mexican Americans—Social life and customs. I. Title. **BIP**

Mexicans in Texas—Biography.

INSTITUTE of Texan Cultures. 917.64'06'6872
The Mexican Texans. [San Antonio, 1971] 32 p. illus. 22 x 28 cm. (The Texians and the Texans) Cover title. [F395.M4I57] 72-611950
1. Mexicans in Texas—Biography. I. Title. II. Series.

Mexico

CROWSON, Benjamin Franklin, 1918- 354.72'000922
Biographical sketches of the governors in Mexico. Washington, Crowson International Publications, 1951- no. ports. 22 cm. [F1205.C75] 66-91613
1. Mexico — Governors. I. Title.

Mexico—Biography.

ALISKY, Marvin. 354.72'000922
Who's who in Mexican government. Tempe, Center for Latin American Studies of Arizona State University, 1969. 64 p. 22 cm. Bibliography: p. 56-59. [F1235.5.A2A4] 77-625171
1. Mexico—Biography. 2. Statesmen—Mexico. I. Title.

LANSING, Marion Florence, 1883- 972'.0099 B
Liberators and heroes of Mexico and Central America, by Marion Lansing. Freeport, N.Y., Books for Libraries Press [1971, c1941] xviii, 299 p. illus., ports. 23 cm. (Essay index reprint series) Bibliography: p. 289-292. [F1205.L25 1971] 72-152186 ISBN 0-8369-2237-9
1. Mexico—Biography. 2. Central America—Biography. I. Title. **BIP**

MAGNER, James Aloysius, 1901- 920.072
Men of Mexico [by] James A. Magner. Freeport, N.Y., Books for Libraries Press [1968, c1942] x, 614 p. map, ports. 23 cm. (Essay index reprint series) Contents.Contents.—Moctezuma II.—Hernando Cortes.—Bartolome de Las Casas.—Juan de Zumarraga.—Don Vasco de Quiroga.—Antonio de Mendoza.—Count Revilla Gigedo II.—Miquel Hidalgo.—Jose Maria Morelos.—Agustin de Iturbide.—Antonio Lopez de Santa Anna.—Benito Juarez.—Maximilian.—Porfirio Diaz.—Venustiano Carranza.—Plutarco Elias Calles.—Lazaro Cardenas. Bibliographical footnotes. [F1205.M23 1968] 68-55849
1. Mexico—Biography. 2. Mexico—History. I. Title. **BIP**

NEWLON, Clarke. 972'.00992 B
The men who made Mexico. Illustrated with photos. New York, Dodd, Mead [1973] xii, 273 p. illus. 22 cm. Bibliography: p. 261-263. [F1205.N48] 72-12543 ISBN 0-396-06778-6 4.95
1. Mexico—Biography. I. Title. **BIP**

Mexico—History—Conquest, 1519-1540.

CORTES, Hernando, 1485-1547. 972'.02
Five letters, 1519-1526. Translated by J. Bayard Morris, with an introd. New York, Norton [196-] xlvii, 388 p. 20 cm. On cover: 5 letters of Cortes to the Emperor. [F1230.C8524] 76-7405 1.95
1. Mexico—History—Conquest, 1519-1540. I. Morris, John Bayard, ed. II. Title: 5 letters of Cortes to the Emperor. **BIP**

CORTES, Hernando, 1485-1547. 972'.02'0924 B
Letters from Mexico. Translated and edited by A. R. Pagden. With an introd. by J. H. Elliott. New York, Grossman Publishers, 1971. lxvii, 565 p. illus. 24 cm. (An Orion Press book) At head of title: Hernan Cortes. Translation of Cartas de relacion. Bibliography: p. 537-549. [F1230.C83213 1971] 73-114946 15.00
1. Mexico—History—Conquest, 1519-1540. I. Title.

Mexico—History—1810-

SANTA ANNA, Antonio Lopez de Pres. Mexico, 1794?-1876. 972 B
The eagle; the autobiography of Santa Anna. Edited by Ann Fears Crawford. Austin, Pemberton Press, 1967. xix, 299 p. illus., facsims., maps, plans, ports. 27 cm. Bibliography: p. [283]-287. [F1232.S23A32] 68-5896
1. Mexico—History—1810- I. Crawford, Ann Fears, ed. II. Title.

Mexico—Social life and customs.

TREVINO, Elizabeth (Borton) 1904- 917.2'03'82
My heart lies south; the story of my Mexican marriage, with epilogue, by Elizabeth Borton de Trevino. New York, Crowell [1972] 252 p. ports. 21 cm. [F1210.T675 1972] 72-185629 ISBN 0-690-56905-X 5.95
1. Mexico—Social life and customs. I. Title.

Meyer, Agnes Elizabeth Ernst,

MEYER, Agnes Elizabeth Ernst, 1887- 920.5
Out of these roots; the autobiography of an American woman. [1st ed.] Boston, Little, Brown [1953] 385 p. illus. 21 cm. "An Atlantic Monthly Press book." [CT275.M5124A3] 53-10236
I. Title.

Meyer, Annie (Nathan)

MEYER, Annie (Nathan) 1867-1951. 920.7
It's been fun; an autobiography. New York, Schuman [1951] 302 p. illus. 22 cm. [CT275.M5126A3] 51-13631
I. Title.

Meyer, Bernard F., 1891-1975.

DONOVAN, John F. 266'.2'0924 B
A priest named Horse / by John F. Donovan. Huntington, IN : Our Sunday Visitor, c1977. 256 p. : ill. ; 21 cm. [BV3427.M47D66] 76-53703 ISBN 0-87973-748-4 pbk. : 4.95
1. Meyer, Bernard F., 1891-1975. 2. Missionaries—China—Biography. 3. Missionaries—United States—Biography. I. Title. **BIP**

Meyer, Edith Patterson.

MEYER, Edith Patterson. 917.4 B
For goodness' sake! Growing up in a New England parsonage. Nashville, Abingdon Press [1973] 176 p. illus. 23 cm. Autobiography. [CT275.M51265A3] 73-6787 ISBN 0-687-13290-8 4.95
1. Meyer, Edith Patterson. I. Title.

Meyer, Eugene, 1875-1959.

PUSEY, Merlo John, 1902- 332'.092'4 B
Eugene Meyer [by] Merlo J. Pusey. [1st ed.] New York, Knopf, 1974. xiii, 397, xiii p. illus. 25 cm. Includes bibliographical references. [HG172.M5P87 1974] 74-7174 ISBN 0-394-47897-5
1. Meyer, Eugene, 1875-1959. **BIP**

Meyer family.

GREER, Georgeanna H. 738.3'7
The Meyer family: master potters of Texas [by] Georgeanna H. Greer [and] Harding Black. San Antonio, Published for the San Antonio Museum Association, by Trinity University Press [1971] 97 p. illus. (part col.) 24 cm. "Published in conjunction with an exhibit of Meyer pottery held at the Witte Memorial Museum, Brackenridge Park, San Antonio, Texas from October 10 to December 31, 1971." [NK4210.M15G7] 72-179912 ISBN 0-911536-43-4
1. Meyer family. I. Black, Harding, joint author. II. San Antonio Museum Association. III. Witte Memorial Museum, San Antonio. IV. Title.

Meyer, Lewis,

MEYER, Lewis, 1913- 917.3'03'910924 B
Mostly mama. [1st ed.] Garden City, N.Y., Doubleday, 1971. 216 p. 22 cm. [CT275.M5127A3] 72-144281 5.95
I. Title.

Meyers, Harvey, 1940-

MEYERS, Harvey, 1940- 294.5 B
Hariyana / by Harvey Meyers ; illustrated by Regina Meyers. San Francisco, Ca. : Omkara Press, c1979- v. : ill. ; 22 cm. Contents.Contents.—pt. 1. The yoga of dejection. [BL1175.M46A34] 79-84779 ISBN 0-934094-01-2 (v. 1) : 6.00
1. Meyers, Harvey, 1940- 2. Hindus—Biography. I. Title.
Publisher's address: 51 Scott St., San Francisco, CA 94117.

Meyers, Michael.

MEYERS, Michael. 610'.92'4 B
Goodbye, Columbus, hello medicine / Michael Meyers. New York : Morrow, 1976. p. cm. [R154.M58A33] 76-15403 ISBN 0-688-03090-4 : 8.95
1. Meyers, Michael. 2. Medical students—New Jersey—Correspondence, reminiscences, etc. 3. Actors—United States—Correspondence, reminiscences, etc. I. Title.

Meyers, Robert.

MEYERS, Robert. 362.3'092'6 B
Like normal people / Robert Meyers. New York : McGraw-Hill, c1978. ix, 203 p., [4] leaves of plates : ill. ; 24 cm. Bibliography: p. [202]-203. [RC570.5.U6M47] 78-9347 ISBN 0-07-041761-X : 9.95
1. Meyers, Robert. 2. Mental deficiency—United States—Biography. I. Title. **BIP**

Meyerson, Emile, 1859-1933.

LALUMIA, Joseph. 121
The ways of reason; a critical study of the ideas of Emile Meyerson. New York, Humanities Press, 1966. 154 p. 24 cm. Errata slip inserted. Bibliography: p. 146-151. [B2430.M44L3] 65-27892
1. Meyerson, Emile, 1859-1933. I. Title.

Meynell, Alice Christiana (Thompson) 1847-1922.

MEYNELL, Viola, 1886-1956. 821'.8 B
Alice Meynell; a memoir. New York, Scribner, 1929. St. Clair Shores, Mich., Scholarly Press, 1971. 354 p. illus., ports. 22 cm. [PR5021.M3M4 1971] 79-145182 ISBN 0-403-00804-2
1. Meynell, Alice Christiana (Thompson) 1847-1922.

Mezieres, Athanase de, d. 1779.

VIVIAN, Julia, 1901- 923.273
A cavalier in Texas. San Antonio, Naylor Co. [1953] 114p. illus. 22cm. [F373.V77] 53-9101
1. Mezieres, Athanase de, d. 1779. I. Title.

Mezvinsky, Edward.

MEZVINSKY, Edward. 328.73'092'4 B
A term to remember / Edward Mezvinsky, with Kevin McCormally & John Greenya. New York : Coward, McCann & Geoghegan, c1977. 256 p., [6] leaves of plates : ill. ; 22 cm. Autobiographical. Includes index. [E840.8.M49A37 1977] 77-3833 ISBN 0-698-10751-9 : 8.95
1. Mezvinsky, Edward. 2. Legislators—United States—Biography. 3. Watergate Affair, 1972- I. McCormally, Kevin. II. Greenya, John. III. Title. **BIP**

Mi Mi Khaing, Daw.

MI Mi Khaing, Daw. 959.1
Burmese family / Mi Mi Khaing ; illustrated by E. G. N. Kinch. 1st AMS ed. New York : AMS Press, 1979, c1962. 200 p. : ill. ; 23 cm. Reprint of the ed. published by Indiana University Press, Bloomington. [DS527.9.M5 1979] 76-6607 ISBN 0-404-15291-0 : 22.50
1. Mi Mi Khaing, Daw. 2. Burma—Social life and customs. 3. Women—Burma—Biography. I. Title. **BIP**

Miami University, Oxford, Ohio—Alumni.

HAVIGHURST, Walter, 1901- 920'.073
Men of old Miami, 1809-1873; a book of portraits. New York, Putnam [1974] 248 p. illus. 22 cm. Contents.Contents.—The road not traveled: Carter Bassett Harrison.—Robert Cumming Schenck: son of Miami.—The education of Charles Anderson.—William S. Groesbeck: the old Roman.—War governor: William Dennison.—The gift of Samuel Spahr Laws.—The years of Benjamin Harrison.—Homage to David Swing.—Byline "Agate":

the rise of Whitelaw Reid.—The church and the schoolhouse: Henry MacCracken.—The mind of John Shaw Billings.—The world of Calvin Brice.—Bibliography (p. 227-236) [E176.H37 1974] 73-93732 ISBN 0-399-11329-0 7.95
1. Miami University, Oxford, Ohio—Alumni. 2. United States—Biography. I. Title.

Miaskovskii, Nikolai IAkovlevich, 1881—

IKONNIKOV, Aleksei A. 780'.924 B
Myaskovsky; his life and work, by Alexei A. Ikonnikov. Translated from the Russian. New York, Greenwood Press [1969, c1946] 162 p. facsims. (music), port. 23 cm. [ML410.M64I4 1969] 70-90150
1. Miaskovskii, Nikolai IAkovlevich, 1881- BIP

Michalowicz, Konstanty, b. ca. 1435.

MICHAIOWICZ, Konstanty, b.ca.1435. 949.7'101'0924
Memoirs of a janissary / Konstantin Mihailovic ; translated by Benjamin Stolz ; historical commentary and notes by Svat Soucek. Ann Arbor : Published under the auspices of the Joint Committee on Eastern Europe, American Council of Learned Societies, by the Dept. of Slavic Languages and Literatures, University of Michigan, 1975. xxx, 255 p. : ill. ; 23 cm. (Michigan Slavic translations ; no. 3) Translation of Pamietniki janczara. English and Czech. Errata sheet inserted. Includes index. Bibliography: p. 239-250. [DR338.5.M47A3513] 75-16784
1. Michalowicz, Konstanty, b. ca. 1435. 2. Serbia—History—To 1456—Sources. 3. Turkey—History—Sources. 4. Turks in Serbia. I. Title. II. Series. BIP

Micheaux, Oscar,

MICHEAUX, Oscar, 1884- 917.8'03'30924
The conquest; the story of a Negro pioneer. College Park, Md., McGrath Pub. Co. [1969] 311 p. illus., port. 23 cm. Reprint of the 1913 ed. [E185.97.M62 1969] 78-76117
I. Title. BIP

MICHEAUX, Oscar, 1884- 917.8'03'30924 B
The conquest; the story of a Negro pioneer, by the pioneer. Lincoln, Neb., Woodruff Press, 1913. Miami, Fla., Mnemosyne Pub. Co. [1969] 311 p. illus., port. 23 cm. [E185.97.M62 1969b] 75-89391
I. The pioneer. II. Title.

Michel, Virgil George, 1890-1938.

MARX, Paul B 922.273
Virgil Michel and the liturgical movement. [Collegeville, Minn.] Liturgical Press [1957] ix, 466p. illus., ports. 24cm. (American Benedictine Academy [Latrobe, Pa.] Historical studies. Biographies, no.1) Issued also as thesis, Catholic University of America. Includes bibliographical references. 'Bibliography of Virgil Michel': p.421-434. [BX4705.M5512M3 1957] 57-59084
1. Michel, Virgil George, 1890-1938. 2. Liturgical movement. I. Title. II. Series.

Michelson, Albert Abraham, 1852-1931.

JAFFE, Bernard, 1896- 530'.092'4 B
Michelson and the speed of light / Bernard Jaffe. Westport, Conn. : Greenwood Press, 1979, c1960. 197 p. : ill. ; 23 cm. Reprint of the 1st ed. published by Anchor Books, Garden City, N.Y., which was issued as no. S13 of Science study series. "The more important of the 78 papers of Michelson; books by Michelson": p. 177-180. Includes index. Bibliography: p. 183-184. [QC16.M56J3 1979] 78-25969 ISBN 0-313-20777-1 lib. bdg. : 16.75
1. Michelson, Albert, 1852-1931. 2. Physicists—United States—Biography. 3. Optics—History. 4. Light—Speed—History. I. Title. II. Series: Science study series ; S13. BIP

LIVINGSTON, Dorothy Michelson. 530'.092'4 B
The master of light; a biography of Albert A. Michelson. New York, Scribner [1973] xi, 376 p. illus. 24 cm. Bibliography: p. 367. [QC16.M56L58] 72-1178 ISBN 0-684-13443-8 12.50
1. Michelson, Albert Abraham, 1852-1931. I. Title. BIP

MCALLISTER, D. T. 530'.092'4 B
Albert Abraham Michelson: the man who taught a world to measure [by D. T. McAllister. China Lake, Calif., Technical Information Dept., Naval Weapons Center, 1970] 30 p. illus. 28 cm. (Publications of the Michelson Museum, no. 3) Includes bibliographical references. [QC16.M56M3] 73-170834
1. Michelson, Albert Abraham, 1852-1961. I. Series: Michelson Museum. Publications, no. 3.

MCALLISTER, D. T. 530'.092'4 B
Albert Abraham Michelson: the man who taught a world to measure [by D. T. McAllister. China Lake, Calif., Technical Information Dept., Naval Weapons Center, 1970] 30 p. illus. 28 cm. (Publications of the Michelson Museum, no. 3) Includes bibliographical references. [QC16.M56M3] 73-170834
1. Michelson, Albert Abraham, 1852-1961. I. Series: Michelson Museum. Publications, no. 3.

Michigan

MILLBROOK, Minnie (Dubbs) 973.7'6
Michigan Medal of Honor winners in the Civil War; a study in valor. [Lansing] Michigan Civil War Centennial Observance Commission [1966] viii, 155 p. ports. 23 cm. Bibliography: p. 6-7. [E514.M664] 66-65600
1. Michigan — Hist. — Civil War — Biog. 2. Medal of Honor. 3. Heroes. I. Michigan. Civil War Centennial Observance Commission. II. Title.

Michigan—Governors—Wives—Biography.

WEDDON, Willah. 977.4'00992 B
First ladies of Michigan : a collection of information about first ladies of the State of Michigan, many of whom were never accorded recognition for their roles as Governor's wives in early historical accounts / by Willah Weddon. 1st ed. Grand Rapids : The Printers, 1977. 86 p. : ill. ; 21 cm. [F565.W4] 77-156002
1. Michigan—Governors—Wives—Biography. I. Title.

Michigan—Politics and government—1951-

HARE, James M. 320.9'774'04
With malice towards none; the musings of a retired politician [by] James M. Hare. With a foreword by Russel B. Nye. [East Lansing] Michigan State University Press, 1972. x, 196 p. port. 22 cm. Autobiographical. [JK5825 1972.H3] 74-185416 ISBN 0-87013-168-0 7.50
1. Michigan Politics and government—1951- I. Title.

Michigan. State University, East Lansing—Football.

STABLEY, Fred W. 796.33'263'0977427
The Spartans : a story of Michigan State football / by Fred W. Stabley. Huntsville, Ala. : Strode Publishers, c1975. 313 p. : ill. ; 24 cm. [GV958.M5S82] 75-12206 ISBN 0-87397-067-5 : 7.95
1. Michigan. State University, East Lansing—Football. 2. Football—Biography. I. Title. BIP

Michigan. University—Biographies.

BABST, Earl D., 1870-1967, ed. 973.8'092'2 B
Michigan and the Cleveland era; sketches of University of Michigan staff members and alumni who served the Cleveland administrations, 1885-89, 1893-97. Edited by Earl D. Babst and Lewis G. Vander Velde. Freeport, N.Y., Books for Libraries Press [1971, c1948] xi, 372 p. illus. 23 cm. (Biography index reprint series) [LD3272.B3 1971] 70-179724 ISBN 0-8369-8092-1
1. Michigan. University—Biographies. 2. Statesmen—United States—Biography. I. Vander Velde, Lewis George, 1890- joint ed. II. Title. BIP

Michotte, Edmond.

MICHOTTE, Edmond. 780'.922
Richard Wagner's visit to Rossini (Paris 1860); and, An evening at Rossini's in Beau-Sejour (Passy) 1858. Translated from the French and annotated, with an introd. and appendix, by Herbert Weinstock. Chicago, University of Chicago Press [1968] xi, 144 p. illus., facsims., music, ports. 23 cm. Translation of Souvenirs personnels. La visite de R. Wagner a Rossini (Paris 1860) and Souvenirs: Une soiree chez Rossini a Beau-Sejour (Passy) 1858. [ML410.W11M42] 68-16706
I. Wagner, Richard, 1813-1883. II. Rossini, Gioacchino Antonio, 1792-1868. III. Weinstock, Herbert, 1905- IV. Michotte, Edmond. Souvenirs: Une soiree chez Rossini a Beau-Sejour (Passy) 1858. V. Title. VI. Title: An evening at Rossini's in Beau-Sejour (Passy) 1858.

Mickiewicz, Adam, 1798-1855.

BUFFALO. University. 928.9185
Mickiewicz and the West; a symposium [by] Zbigniew Folejewski [and others] Edited by B. R. Bugelski. [Buffalo] 1956. 75p. 23cm. (The University of Buffalo studies, v.23, no.1) 'Essays ... first presented as lectures delivered on August 4th, 1955 at the annual convention of the American Council of Polish Cultural Clubs at the University of Buffalc. Bibliographical footnotes. [AS36.B95 vol.23, no.1] 56-58752
1. Mickiewez, Adam, 1798-1855. I. Folejewaski, Zbigniew, 1910 aFolejewski, Zbigndew, 1910- II. Bugelski, Bergen Richard, ed. III. Title. IV. Series: Buffalo. University. The University of Buffalo studies, v.23, no.1

BUFFALO. University. 928.9185
Mickiewicz and the West; a symposium [by] Zbigniew Folejewski [and others] Edited by B. R. Bugelski. [Buffalo] 1956. 75p. 23cm. (The University of Buffalo studies, v.23, no.1) 'Essays ... first presented as lectures delivered on August 4th, 1955 at the annual convention of the American Council of Polish Cultural Clubs at the University of Buffalc. Bibliographical footnotes. [AS36.B95 vol.23, no.1] 56-58752
1. Mickiewez, Adam, 1798-1855. I. Folejewaski, Zbigniew, 1910 aFolejewski, Zbigndew, 1910- II. Bugelski, Bergen Richard, ed. III. Title. IV. Series: Buffalo. University. The University of Buffalo studies, v.23, no.1

COLEMAN, Marion (Moore) 1900- 928.9185
Young Mickiewicz. Cambridge Springs, Pa., Alliance College [1956] 380p. illus. 23cm. [PG7158.M5Z869] 55-9778
1. Mickiewicz, Adam, 1796-1855. I. Title.

GARDNER, Monica Mary, d.1941. 891.8'5'16 B
Adam Mickiewicz, the national poet of Poland. New York, Arno Press, 1971. xv, 317 p. port. 23 cm. (The Eastern Europe collection) Reprint of the 1911 ed. Bibliography: p. 301-302. [PG7158.M51G3 1971] 74-135807 ISBN 0-405-02749-4
1. Mickiewicz, Adam, 1798-1855.

Mickle, Isaac.

MICKLE, Isaac. 974.9'8'030924 B
A gentleman of much promise : the diary of Isaac Mickle, 1837-1845 / edited, with an introd. by Philip English Mackey. [Philadelphia] : University of Pennsylvania Press, 1977. 2 v. (xxviii, 531 p.) : ill., maps (on lining papers) ; 24 cm. Title on spine: The diary of Isaac Mickle. Includes indexes. [F144.C2M52] 76-53190 ISBN 0-8122-7722-8 : 25.00
1. Mickle, Isaac. 2. Camden, N.J.—Biography. I. Mackey, Philip English. II. Title. III. Title: The diary of Isaac Mickle.

Middle States—Biog.—Dictionaries.

WHO'S who in the East and Eastern Canada. 11th ed. 1968-69. 920.07
Chicago, Marquis- Who's Who. v. 24-27cm. biennial. A biographical dictionary of noteworthy men and women of the Middle Atlantic and Northeastern States and Eastern Canada. Title and sutitle vary slightly [E176.W643] 43-18522 30.00
1. Middle States—Biog.—Dictionaries. 2. New England—Biog.—Dictionaries. 3. Canada—Biog.—Dictionaries.

Middle West—Hist.

GRANT, Clarence G. 923.9
Vanishing wagon tracks; the autobiography of an ex-saddle tramp and homesteader in the Middle West. New York, Exposition Press [c.1961] 100p. (Exposition-Lochinvar bk.) 2.50
1. Middle West—Hist. I. Title.

Middle West—Description and travel.

MALLORY, Mary Alice Shutes. 917.7'04'2
Diary: eight hundred miles [in] thirty-six days [by] covered wagon—1862 [from] Wyandott County, Ohio [to] Carroll County, Iowa [by] Mary Alice Shutes. [Bloomington, Ill., L. L. Shutes, 1967] 45 l. port. 28 cm. Cover title. [F353.M3] 67-5976
1. Middle West—Description and travel. 2. Pioneers—Middle West. I. Title.

Middlesex, Lionel Cranfield, 1st earl of, 1575-1645.

TAWNEY, Richard Henry, 1880-1962. 941.06'1'0924 B
Business and politics under James I : Lionel Cranfield as merchant and minister / by R.H.Tawney New York : Russell & Russell, 1976. 324 p. ; 23 cm. Reprint of the 1958 ed. published by Cambridge University Press, Cambridge. Includes indexes. Bibliography: p. 303-313. [HF3504.5.M5T38 1976] 73-94147 ISBN 0-8462-1790-2 : 20.00
1. Middlesex, Lionel Cranfield, 1st earl of, 1575-1645. 2. Merchants—Great Britain—Biography. 3. Statesmen—Great Britain—Biography. I. Title. BIP

Middleton, Charles Middleton, 2d Earl of, 1650?-1719.

JONES, George Hilton. 942.06/0924
Charles Middleton; the life and times of a Restoration politician. Chicago, Univ. of Chicago Pr. [1967] 332p. fold. map. 23cm. [DA437.M5J65] (B) 67-25532 10.00
1. Middleton, Charles Middleton, 2d Earl of, 1650?-1719. I. Title. BIP

JONES, George Hilton. 942.06'0924 (B)
Charles Middleton; the life and times of a Restoration politician. Chicago, University of Chicago Press [1967] 332 p. fold. map. 23 cm. Bibliography: p. [305]-317. [DA437.M5J65] 67-25532
1. Middleton, Charles Middleton, 2d Earl of, 1650?-1719. I. Title.

Middleton, David C., 1851-1913.

HUTTON, Harold. 364.1'5'0924 B
Doc Middleton; life and legends of the notorious Plains outlaw. [1st ed.] Chicago, Swallow Press [1974] 290 p. illus. 24 cm.

Bibliography: p. 272-277. [F666.M5H87] 67-14260 ISBN 0-8040-0532-X 10.00
1. Middleton, David C., 1851-1913. I. Title.

Middleton, Richard Barham, 1882-1911.

MIDDLETON, Richard Barham, 1882-1911. 821'.9'12
Richard Middleton's letters to Henry Savage. Edited, with an introd. and comments by the recipient. New York, Haskell House Publishers [1972] p. Reprint of the 1929 ed. [PR6025.I3Z548 1972] 72-3570 ISBN 0-8383-1554-2
I. Savage, Henry, ed. II. Title. BIP

SAVAGE, Henry. 821'.9'12
Richard Middleton, the man and his work. Port Washington, N.Y., Kennikat Press [1972] xi, 209 p. illus. 23 cm. Reprint of the 1922 ed. Bibliography: p. 197-200. [PR6025.I3Z7 1972] 70-160780 ISBN 0-8046-1612-4
1. Middleton, Richard Barham, 1882-1911.

Middleton, Samuel Henry, 1884-1964.

FORSBERG, Roberta J 371.975
Chief Mountain; the story of Canon Middleton [by] Roberta A. Forsberg. Whittier, Calif., 1964. viii, 119 p. illus. ports. 22 cm. [E97.6.S17F6] 65-1498
1. Middleton, Samuel Henry, 1884-1964. 2. St. Paul's Indian Residential School, Cardston, Alta. I. Title.

Middleton, Troy H., 1889-

PRICE, Frank James, 1917- 355.3'31'0924 B
Troy H. Middleton : a biography / Frank James Price. Baton Rouge : Louisiana State University Press, [1974] xiv, 416 p. : ill. ; 24 cm. Includes index. Bibliography: p. 403-409. [U53.M5P75] 73 90869 ISBN 0-8071-0067-6 : 10.00
1. Middleton, Troy H., 1889- BIP

Midhat, Pasa, 1822-1884.

MIDHAT, Ali Haydar. 956.1'01'0924
The life of Midhat Pasha. New York, Arno Press, 1973. xii, 292 p. port. 23 cm. (The Middle East collection) Translation of Mithat Pasanin hayat-i siyasiyesi, hidemati, sehadeti. Reprint of the 1903 ed. published by Murray, London. Includes bibliographical references. [DR568.8.M6M513 1973] 73-6290 ISBN 0-405-05348-7 16.00
1. Midhat, Pasa, 1822-1884. I. Title. II. Series. BIP

Midler, Bette.

MIDLER, Bette. 784'.092'4 B
A view from a broad / Bette Midler. New York : Simon and Schuster, 1980. p. cm. [ML420.M43A3] 79-23656 ISBN 0-671-24780-8 : 12.50
1. Midler, Bette. 2. Singers—United States—Biography. I. Title. BIP

Miedzyrzecki, Feigele Peltel.

MIEDZYRZECKI, Feigele Peltel.
On both sides of the wall : memoirs from the Warsaw ghetto / Vladka Meed [i.e. F. P. Miedzyrzecki] ; introd. by Elie Wiesel ; translated by Steven Meed ; [cover design by Morris Wyszogrod]. New York : Holocaust Library : [distributed by Schocken Books], c1979. 276 p., [1] leaves of plates : ill. ; 22 cm. Translation of Fun beyde zaytn geto-moyer. Includes indexes. [DS135.P62W32413 1979] 78-71300 ISBN 0-89604-012-7 : 9.95 ISBN 0-89604-013-5 (pbk.) : 4.95
1. Miedzyrzecki, Feigele Peltel. 2. Holocaust, Jewish (1939-1945)—Poland—Warsaw—Personal narratives. 3. Warsaw—History—Uprising of 1943. 4. Jews in Warsaw—Biography. I. Title.

Mielke, Arthur W.

MIELKE, Arthur W. 242'.4
Through the valley / Arthur W. Mielke. New York : Association Press, c1976. xi, 112 p. ; 19 cm. Bibliography: p. 111-112. [BV4905.2.M5] 76-10353 ISBN 0-8096-1917-2 pbk. : 4.95
1. Mielke, Arthur W. 2. Grief. 3. Consolation. I. Title. BIP

Mier Expedition, 1842.

WALKER, Samuel Hamilton, 1817-1847. 976.4'04'0924 B
Samuel H. Walker's account of the Mier expedition / edited with an introd. by Marilyn McAdams Sibley. [Austin] : Texas State Historical Association, c1978. 110 p. : ill. ; 27 cm. Includes bibliographical references and index. [F390.W194 1978] 78-63306 ISBN 0-87611-040-5 : 10.50 ISBN 0-87611-038-3 collector's ed. : 50.00
1. Mier Expedition, 1842. 2. Walker, Samuel Hamilton, 1817-1847. 3. Texas Rangers—Biography. 4. Soldiers—Texas—Biography. I. Sibley, Marilyn McAdams. II. Texas State Historical Association. III. Title. IV. Title: The Mier expedition. BIP

Mier Expedition, 1842—Personal narratives.

STAPP, William Preston. 976.4'04'0924
The prisoners of Perote : containing a journal kept by the author, who was captured by the Mexicans, at Mier, December 25, 1842, and released from Perote, May 16, 1844 / by William Preston Stapp. Austin : University of Texas Press, c1977. p. cm. (Barker Texas History Center series ; no. 1) Reprint of the 1845 ed. published by G. B. Zieber, Philadelphia; with new foreword. [F390.S79 1977] 77-22425 ISBN 0-292-76442-1 : 8.95
1. Mier Expedition, 1842—Personal narratives. 2. Stapp, William Preston. 3. Texas—Militia—Biography. 4. Soldiers—Texas—Biography. 5. Mexico—Description and travel. I. Title. II. Series: Eugene C. Barker Texas History Center. Barker Texas History Center series ; no. 1.

Mies van der Rohe, Ludwig, 1886-1969—Juvenile literature.

HOAG, Edwin. 720'.922 B
Masters of modern architecture : Frank Lloyd Wright, Le Corbusier, Mies van der Rohe, and Walter Gropius / by Edwin and Joy Hoag. Indianapolis : Bobbs-Merrill, c1977. xiii, 209 p., [8] leaves of plates : ill. ; 23 cm. Includes index. Bibliography: p. 193-197. Discusses the founding of modern architecture through the lives and works of four important architects. [NA680.H54] 920 77-76888 ISBN 0-672-52365-5 pbk. : 10.00
1. Wright, Frank Lloyd, 1867-1959—Juvenile literature. 2. Le Corbusier-Galerie Heidi Weber—Juvenile literature. 3. Mies van der Rohe, Ludwig, 1886-1969—Juvenile literature. 4. Gropius, Walter, 1883-1969—Juvenile literature. 5. Architecture, Modern—20th century—Juvenile literature. 6. Architects—Biography—Juvenile literature. I. Hoag, Joy, joint author. II. Title.

Mifflin, Thomas, 1744-1800.

ROSSMAN, Kenneth R 923.273
Thomas Mifflin and the politics of the American Revolution. [Chapel Hill] University of North Carolina Press [1952] 344 p. illus., ports. 22 cm. Based on the author's thesis. Iowa State University. "Bibliographical note": p. [326]-330. [E207.M6R6] 52-13499
1. Mifflin, Thomas, 1744-1800. 2. U.S. — Pol. & govt. — Revolution. I. Title.

Migrant agricultural laborers—California.

[ERICKSON, Bruce] 331.5'44'0922 B
The whole works: the autobiography of a young American couple [by Bruce and Gail Erickson, as recorded by] Starry Krueger. New York, Vintage Books [1974, c1973] xviii, 205 p. 19 cm. [HD1527.C2E7 1974] 74-4256 ISBN 0-394-71144-0 1.95 (pbk.)
1. Migrant agricultural laborers—California. I. Erickson, Gail. II. Krueger, Starry. III. Title.

Migueis, Jose Rodrigues, 1901- —Bibliography.

KERR, John Austin, 1934- 869'.3'41 B
Migueis, to the seventh decade / by John Austin Kerr, Jr. University, Miss. : Romance Monographs, inc., 1978. p. cm. (Romance monographs ; no. 29) Bibliography: p. [Z8574.37.K47] [PQ9261.M568] 77-02965 12.50
1. Migueis, Jose Rodrigues, 1901- —Bibliography. 2. Migueis, Jose Rodrigues, 1901- —Biography. 3. Authors, Portuguese—20th century—Biography. I. Title. BIP

Miguelito, Navaho Indian, 1865 (ca.)-1936.

REICHARD, Gladys Amanda, 1893-1955. 299'.7
Navajo medicine man : sandpaintings / by Gladys A. Reichard. New York : Dover Publications, 1977. x, 83 p., [25] leaves of plates : ill. (some col.) ; 31 cm. Reprint of the 1939 ed. published by J. J. Augustin, New York. [E99.N3R37 1977] 77-73298 ISBN 0-486-23329-4 : 6.95
1. Miguelito, Navaho Indian, 1865 (ca.)-1936. 2. Sandpaintings. 3. Navaho Indians—Relgion and mythology. 4. Navaho Indians—Biography. I. Title.

Mihailovic, Draza, 1893-1946.

COMMITTEE for a Fair Trial for Gen. Draza Mihailovich. Commission of Inquiry. 345'.497'02310264
Patriot or traitor : the case of General Mihailovich : proceedings and report of the Commission of Inquiry of the Committee for a Fair Trial for Draja Mihailovich / introductory essay by David Martin ; foreword by Frank J. Lausche. Stanford, Calif. : Hoover Institution Press, c1978. xviii, 499 p. : ill. ; 24 cm. (Hoover Institution publication ; 191) (Hoover archival documentaries) Includes bibliographical references and index. [DR359.M5C63 1978] 78-83123 19.00
1. Mihailovic, Draza, 1893-1946. 2. Yugoslavia. Armija—Officers—Biography. 3. Generals Yugoslavia Biography. I. Martin, David, 1914- II. Title. III. Series. IV. Series: Stanford University. Hoover Institution on War, Revolution, and Peace. Publications ; 191.

COMMITTEE for a Fair Trial for Gen. Draza Mihailovich. Commission of Inquiry. 345'.497'02310264
Patriot or traitor : the case of General Mihailovich : proceedings and report of the Commission of Inquiry of the Committee for a Fair Trial for Draja Mihailovich / introductory essay by David Martin ; foreword by Frank J. Lausche. Stanford, Calif. : Hoover Institution Press, c1978. xviii, 499 p. : ill. ; 24 cm. (Hoover Institution publication ; 191) (Hoover archival documentaries) Includes bibliographical references and index. [DR359.M5C63 1978] 78-83123 19.00
1. Mihailovic, Draza, 1893-1946. 2. Yugoslavia. Armija—Officers—Biography. 3. Generals—Yugoslavia—Biography. I. Martin, David, 1914- II. Title. III. Series. IV. Series: Stanford University. Hoover Institution on War, Revolution, and Peace. Publications ; 191.

SEITZ, Albert Blazier, 1898- 923.5497
Mihailovic, hoax or hero? Pen and ink sketches by Sally Seitz. [Memorial ed.] Columbus, Ohio, Leigh House [1953] 143p. illus. 24cm. [DR359.M5S4] 53-23025
1. Mihailovic, Drazs, 1893-1946. I. Title.

Mihal I, King of Rumania, 1921-

LEE, Arthur Stanley Gould. 923.1498
Crown against sickle, the story of King Michael of Rumania. London, New York, Hutchinson [1950] 199 p. illus., ports., map (on lining paper) 24 cm. [DR265.L44 1950] 50-4859
1. Mihal I, King of Rumania, 1921- 2. Communism—Rumania. I. Title.

Mikhail Aleksandrovich, Grand Duke of Russia, 1878-1918.

GRAY, Pauline. 947.08'092'2 B
The Grand Duke's woman : the story of the morganatic marriage of Michael Romanoff, the Tsar Nicholas II's brother and Nathalia Cheremetevskaya / [by] Pauline Gray. London : Macdonald and Jane's, 1976. ix, 201 p., [24] p. of plates : ill., ports. ; 23 cm. Includes index. Bibliography: p. 195-196. [DK254.M513G73] 76-375979 ISBN 0-356-08313-6 : £5.50
1. Mikhail Aleksandrovich, Grand Duke of Russia, 1878-1918. 2. Brassow, Nathalia Sergeievna, Countess, 1888-1952. 3. Russia—Princes and princesses—Biography. 4. Russia—Court and courtiers—Biography. I. Title.

Mikimoto, Kokichi, 1858-1954.

EUNSON, Robert, 1912- 926.39412
The Pearl King; the story of the fabulous Mikimoto. New York, Greenberg [1955] 243 p. illus. 22 cm. [SH377.J3E8] 55-10964
1. Mikimoto, Kokichi, 1858-1954. I. Title.

Mikita, Stan—Juvenile literature.

MIKITA, Stan. 796.9'62'0924 B
I play to win. New York, Morrow, 1969. 223 p. ports. 22 cm. Biography of a professional hockey player for the Chicago Black Hawks who has won many awards for scoring and sportsmanship. [GV848.5.M5A3] 92 73-95308 5.95
1. Hockey—Juvenile literature. I. Title.

YOUNG, Scott. 796.9'62'0924 B
Stan Mikita, tough kid who grew up. St. Paul, EMC Corp. [1974] 38 p. illus. 24 cm. (His Hockey heroes series) A biography emphasizing the career of a star player for the Chicago hockey team. [GV848.5.M5Y68 1974] 92 74-8366 ISBN 0-88436-100-4 4.95
1. Mikita, Stan—Juvenile literature. 2. Hockey—Juvenile literature. I. Title.
Pbk. 2.95; ISBN 0-88436-101-2.

Milam, Carl Hastings, 1884-1963.

MILAM, Carl Hastings, 1884-1963. 020'.92'4
Carl H. Milam and the United Nations Library / edited and with an introd. by Doris Cruger Dale. Metuchen, N.J. : Scarecrow Press, 1976. xvii, 132 p. ; 23 cm. Includes index. Bibliography: p. xvi-xvii. [Z720.M62A32 1976] 76-14866 ISBN 0-8108-0941-9 : 6.00
1. Milam, Carl Hastings, 1884-1963. 2. United Nations. Dag Hammarskjold Library. I. Dale, Doris Cruger. II. Title.

SULLIVAN, Peggy, 1929- 020'.92'4 B
Carl H. Milam and the American Library Association / by Peggy Sullivan. New York : H. W. Wilson, 1976. x, 390 p. : ill. ; 24 cm. Includes index. Bibliography: p. 365-377. [Z720.M62S84] 76-3686 ISBN 0-8242-0592-8 17.50
1. Milam, Carl Hastings, 1884-1963. 2. American Library Association. I. Title. BIP

Milani, Felix, 1905-

MILANI, Felix, 365'.6'0924 B
1905-1975.
The convict / Felix Milani, in collaboration with Micha Grin ; translated by Anita Barrows. New York : St. Martin's Press, c1977. xiv, 297 p. ; 25 cm. Translation of Il forzato. [HV8956.G8M5313 1977] 77-10288 ISBN 0-312-16948-5 : 10.00
1. Milani, Felix, 1905- 2. Convict labor—French Guiana. 3. Crime and criminals—France—Biography. I. Grin, Micha, joint author. II. Title.

Milarepa, 1040-1143.

GTSAN-SMYON He-ru-ka, 294.3'61 B
1452-1507.
The life of Milarepa / a new translation from the Tibetan by Lobsang P. Lhalungpa, in collaboration with Far West Translats. 1st ed. New York : Dutton, c1977. xxix, 221 p. ; 21 cm. Translation of Mi-la-ras-pa'i rnam thar. Includes bibliographical references. [BQ7950.M557G813 1977] 76-46374 pbk. : 5.95
1. Mi-la-ras-pa, 1040-1123. 2. Lamas—Tibet—Biography. I. Lhalungpa, Lobsang Phuntshok, 1926- II. Title. **BIP**

GTSAN-SMYON He-ru-ka, 294.3'61 B
1452-1507.
The life of Milarepa / a new translation from the Tibetan by Lobsang P. Lhalungpa, in collaboration with Far West Translats. 1st ed. New York : Dutton, c1977. xxix, 221 p. ; 21 cm. Translation of Mi-la-ras-pa'i rnam thar. Includes bibliographical references. [BQ7950.M557G813 1977] 76-46374 pbk. : 5.95
1. Mi-la-ras-pa, 1040-1123. 2. Lamas—Tibet—Biography. I. Lhalungpa, Lobsang Phuntshok, 1926- II. Title. **BIP**

RAS-CHUN. 294.3'61 B
Tibet's great yogi, Milarepa: a biography from the Tibetan, being the Jetsun-kahbum, or biographical history of Jetsun-Milarepa, according to the late Lama Kazi Dawa-Samdup's English rendering; edited with introduction and annotations by W. Y. Evans-Wentz. 2nd ed. London, New York, Oxford U.P., 1969. xxviii, 315 p., 6 plates. illus. 21 cm. (A Galaxy book, GB294) Translation of Mi-la-ras-pa'i rNam-thar. [BL1473.M54R313 1969] 71-514047 20/-
1. Mi-la-ras-pa, 1038-1122. 2. Lamaism. I. Zla-ba-Bsam-'grub, Kazi, 1868-1922, tr. II. Wentz, Walter Yeeling Evans, ed. III. Title.

Mildford, Matilda.

RUSSELL, James. 973'.04'97 S
Matilda : or, The Indian's captive / James Russell. New York : Garland Pub., 1977. p. cm. (The Garland library of narratives of North American Indian captivities ; v. 51) Reprint of the 1833 ed. printed by G. Stobbs, Three-Rivers, Canada. [E85.G2 vol. 51] [E87.M63] 971.02'092'4 B 75-7073 ISBN 0-8240-1675-0 lib.bdg. : 25.00
1. Mildford, Matilda. 2. Indians of North America—Canada—Captivities. 3. Canada—Biography. I. Title. II. Title: The Indian's captive. III. Series.

Mildmay, Sir Walter, 1520?-1989.

LEHMBERG, Stanford E 923.242
Sir Walter Mildmay and Tudor government [by] Stanford E. Lehmberg. Austin, University of Texas Press [1964] xii, 835 p. illus., ports. 24 cm. Bibliography: p. 315-322. [DA358.M5L4] 64-19415
1. Mildmay, Sir Walter, 1520?-1989. I. Title. **BIP**

Miles, Nelson Appleton, 1839-1925.

JOHNSON, Virginia Weisel. 923.573
The unregimented general; a biography of Nelson A. Miles. Illustrated with photos. and with maps prepared by Brigadier General W. M. Johnson. Boston, Houghton Mifflin, 1962. 401 p. illus., maps. 23 cm. Includes bibliography. [E181.M53J6] 62-8138
1. Miles, Nelson Appleton, 1839-1925. I. Title.

TOLMAN, Newton F. 355.3'32'0924 B
The search for General Miles, by Newton F. Tolman. New York, Putnam [1968] 252 p. 22 cm. [E83.866.M66T6] 68-15612 5.95
1. Miles, Nelson Appleton, 1839-1925. I. Title.

Mileto, Cecile.

MILETO, Cecile. 364.1'523'0924 B
Louie's widow : one woman's vengeance against the underworld / by Cecile Mileto, with Dave Fisher. 1st ed. Chicago : Playboy Press, c1975. 309 p. ; 22 cm. [CT275.M51427A34] 75-17266 ISBN 0-87223-443-6 : 8.95
1. Mileto, Cecile. I. Fisher, David, 1946- II. Title.

Miley, Michael, 1841-1918.

FISHWICK, Marshall William. 927.7
General Lee's photographer; the life and work of Michael Miley. [Chapel Hill] Published for the Virginia Historical Society by the University of North Carolina Press, 1954. 94 p. illus., col. plates, ports. 29 cm. "The Robert E. Lee series of negatives ... owned by the Virginia Historical Society": p. 77-87. Bibliographical footnotes. [TR140.M5F5] 54-13385
1. Miley, Michael, 1841-1918. 2. Lee, Robert Edward, 1807-1870. I. Virginia Historical Society, Richmond. II. Title.

Military biography.

BLUMENSON, Martin. 355.3'3'0922 B
Masters of the art of command / Martin Blumenson, James L. Stokenbury. Boston : Houghton Mifflin, 1975. xiv, 393 p. : maps ; 22 cm. Includes index. [U51.B58] 75-19020 ISBN 0-395-17212-8 : 12.95
1. Military biography. 2. Military history. 3. Leadership. I. Stokesbury, James L., joint author. II. Title.

*CONNOLLY, Gerard J., 923.2 B
1929-
Grand view farm; an autobiography, [by] Gerard J. Connolly. 1st. ed. Jericho, N.Y. Exposition [1974] 72 p. 22 cm. [CT220] ISBN 0-682-47943-8 4.00
1. Military biography. 2. Political science. I. Title.

*DENNIS, Peter. 923.2
Soldiers as statesmen. edited by Peter Dennis and Adrian Preston. New York : Harper & Row, Barnes & Noble Import Division, c1976. 184 p. ; 23 cm. Includes bibliographical references and index. [CT6900] [B] 76-7173 ISBN 0-06-491669-3 : 17.50
1. Military biography. 2. Political science. I. Preston, Adrian, joint compiler. II. Title. **BIP**

KEEGAN, John, 355.3'31'0922 B
1934-
Who's who in military history : from 1453 to the present day / John Keegan and Andrew Wheatcroft. London : Weidenfeld and Nicolson, c1976. 367 p. : ill. (some col.) ; 26 cm. [U51.K43] 76-373661 ISBN 0-297-77138-8 : £6.95
1. Military biography. I. Wheatcroft, Andrew, joint author. II. Title.

MARTELL, Paul. 355'.0092'2 B
World military leaders / Paul Martell and Grace P. Hayes, editors ; Trevor N. Dupuy, executive editor. New York : Bowker, [1974] 268 p. ; 29 cm. [U51.M35] 74-78392 ISBN 0-8352-0785-4 25.00
1. Military biography. I. Hayes, Grace P., joint author. II. Title. **BIP**

THE War lords : 355.3'31'0922 B
military commanders of the twentieth century / edited by Sir Michael Carver. London : Weidenfeld and Nicolson, c1976. xvi, 624 p., [8] leaves of plates : ill. ; 25 cm. Includes index. [U51.W32 1976b] 76-373174 ISBN 0-297-77084-5 : £10.00
1. Military biography. 2. Military history, Modern—20th century. I. Carver, Michael, Sir, 1915-

THE War lords : 355.3'31'0922 B
military commanders of the twentieth century / edited by Sir Michael Carver. 1st American ed. Boston : Little, Brown, c1976. xvi, 624 p., [8] leaves of plates : ill. ; 24 cm. Includes index. [U51.W32 1976] 76-14402 ISBN 0-316-13060-5 : 17.95
1. Military biography. 2. Military history, Modern—20th century. I. Carver, Michael, Sir, 1915-

WINDROW, Martin 355.3'31'0922 B
C.
A concise dictionary of military biography : two hundred of the most significant names in land warfare, 10th-20th century / [compiled by] Martin Windrow and Francis K. Mason. Reading : Osprey Publishing, 1975. xi, 337 p. ; 24 cm. [U51.W53] 75-330853 ISBN 0-85045-199-X : £5.95
1. Military biography. I. Mason, Francis K., joint author. II. Title.

Military history—Juvenile literature.

TOWNSON, William Duncan. 904'.7
Famous generals / [author, Duncan Townson ; ill., Gerry Embleton, W. Francis Phillips, Joyce Tuhill]. New York : Warwick Press, 1979, c1975. 48 p. ill. (some col.) ; 28 cm. (Modern knowledge library) Includes index. Brief biographies of some outstanding commanders throughout history with descriptions of the campaigns which have earned them a place in military history. [D25.T64 1979] 920 78-70608 ISBN 0-531-09120-1 lib. bdg. : 5.90
1. Military history—Juvenile literature. 2. Generals—Biography—Juvenile literature. I. Embleton, Gerry. II. Phillipps, W. Francis. III. Tuhill, Joyce. IV. Division of Watts V. Title. **BIP**

Mill, Harriet (Hardy) Taylor,

MILL, John Stuart, 1806- v. 12
1873.
John Stuart Mill and Harriet Taylor; their correspondence [i.e. friendship] and subsequent marriage, by F. A. Hayek. Chicago, University of Chicago Press [1951] 320 p. ports., facsim., geneal. tables. 22 cm. Errata slip (inserted) indicates correct title. Bibliographical reference included in "Notes" (p. 283-314) A51
1. Mill, Harriet (Hardy) Taylor, 1807-1858. I. Hayek, Friedrich August von, 1809- ed. II. Title.

Mill, James, 1773-1836.

BAIN, 330.15'3'0924 (B)
Alexander, 1818-1903.
James Mill, a biography. 1882. New York, A. M. Kelley, 1967. xxxii, 466 p. port. 21 cm. (Reprints of economic classics) [B1598.B2] 66-19689
1. Mill, James, 1773-1836. I. Title.

BATN, Alexander. 330.15'3'0924(B)
1818-1903
James Mill, a biography. 1882. New York, Kelley, 1967. xxxii, 466p. port. 21cm. (Reprints of econ. classics) [B1598.B2 1967] 66-196894 10.00
1. Mill, James, 1773-1836. I. Title.

CAVENAGH, Francis 370.1
Alexander, 1884-1946, comp.
James & John Stuart Mill on education / edited by F. A. Cavenagh. Westport, Conn. : Greenwood Press, 1979. xxvii, 208, [1] p. ; 23 cm. Reprint of the 1931 ed. published at the University Press, Cambridge, Eng., issued in series: Landmarks in the history of education. Bibliography: p. [209] [LB675.M5142C38 1979] 78-27822 ISBN 0-8371-4282-2 lib. bdg. : 15.00
1. Mill, James, 1773-1836. Article on education. 2. Mill, John Stuart, 1806-1873. Autobiography. 3. Mill, John Stuart, 1806-1873. Inauguaral address at St. Andrews. 4. Education—Philosophy. I. Title. II. Series: Landmarks in the history of education.

MAZLISH, Bruce, 1923- 192 B
James and John Stuart Mill : father and son in the nineteenth century / Bruce Mazlish. New York : Basic Books, [1975] xii, 484 p. ; 25 cm. Includes bibliographical references and indexes. [B1606.M39] 74-79278 ISBN 0-465-03630-9 : 16.95
1. Mill, James, 1773-1836. 2. Mill, John Stuart, 1806-1873.

MILL, John Stuart, 1806- 921.2
1873
John Mill's boyhood visit to France; being a Journal and Notebook written by John Stuart Mill in France, 1820-21. Edited, with an introd., by Anna Jean Mill. [Toronto] University of Toronto Press [1960] xxxi, 133p. Bibl.: p.[126]-128. facsims. 24cm. The text of a Journal of a visit to France (1820) in the form of letters to his father . . . is reproduced . . . [from] British Museum (Add. ms 31909). . . 80 folios made up of 12 sections . . . Except for . . . a few . . . items. the Notebook [now in the editor's possession] is the earlier draft . . . of corresponding parts of the Journal; and, like the Journal (from section 8 on), is in French.' 60-4877 5.00
1. Mill, James, 1773-1836. I. Title. **BIP**

Mill, John Stuart,

MILL, John Stuart, 1806- 921.2
1873
Autobiography. Garden City, N.Y., Doubleday [1961] 240p. (Dolphin, C 179) .95 pap.,
I. Title.

*MILL, John Stuart, 1806- 921.2
1873
Autobiography. Foreword by Asa Briggs [New York] New Amer. Lib. [1964] 224p. 18cm. (Signet classic, CT269) Bibl. .75 pap.,
I. Title.

MILL, John Stuart, 1806- 921.2
1873.
Autobiography. With an introd. by Currin V. Shields. New York, Liberal Arts Press [c1957] xviii, 201p. 21cm. (The Library of liberal arts, no. 91) Bibliography: p. xvii-xviii. [B1606.A2 1957] 57-14630
I. Title.

MILL, John Stuart, 1806- 921.2
1873
Autobiography. Published from the original manuscript in the Columbia University library; with a preface by John Jacob Coss. New York, Columbia University Press [1960, c.1924] 24op. (Columbia paperback 6) 1.50 pap.,
I. Title.

MILL, John Stuart, 1806- 921.2
1873.
The early draft of John Stuart Mill's autobiography. Edited by Jack Stillinger. Urbana, University of Illinois Press, 1961. 218p. 24cm. Bibliographical footnotes. [B1606.A2 1961] 61-62769
I. Stillinger, Jack, ed. II. Title.

Mill, John Stuart, 1806-1873.

BAIN, Alexander, 1818- 300'.924 B
1903.
John Stuart Mill; a criticism with personal recollections. New York, A. M. Kelley, 1969. xiii, 201 p. 22 cm. (Reprints of economic classics) Reprint of the 1882 ed. [B1607.B3 1969] 69-16521
1. Mill, John Stuart, 1806-1873.

BRITTON, Karl, 1909- 192 B
John Stuart Mill; [life and philosophy] 2d ed. New York, Dover Publications [1969] 224 p. 22 cm. Bibliography: p. 219-220. [B1607.B7 1969] 70-78798
1. Mill, John Stuart, 1806-1873.

BRITTON, Karl, 1909- 192.7
John Stuart Mill; [an introduction to the life and teaching of a great pioneer of modern social philosophy and logic] London, Baltimore, Penguin Books [1953] 224p. illus. 18cm. (Pelican books, A 274) Pelican philosophy series. [B1606.B7] 54-1927
1. Mill, John Stuart, 1806-1873. I. Title.

CAVENAGH, Francis 370.1
Alexander, 1884-1946, comp.
James & John Stuart Mill on education / edited by F. A. Cavenagh. Westport, Conn. : Greenwood Press, 1979. xxvii, 208, [1] p. ; 23 cm. Reprint of the 1931 ed. published at the University Press,

Cambridge, Eng., issued in series: Landmarks in the history of education. Bibliography: p. [209] [LB675.M5142C38 1979] 78-27822 ISBN 0-8371-4282-2 lib. bdg. : 15.00
1. Mill, James, 1773-1836. Article on education. 2. Mill, John Stuart, 1806-1873. Autobiography. 3. Mill, John Stuart, 1806-1873. Inaugural address at St. Andrews. 4. Education—Philosophy. I. Title. II. Series: Landmarks in the history of education.

ELLERY, John B. 921.2
John Stuart Mill, by John B. Ellery. New York, Twayne Publishers [1964] 134 p. 21 cm. (Twayne's English authors series, #5) Bibliography: p. 127-129. [B1607.E55] 64-19030
1. Mill, John Stuart, 1806-1873. BIP

KAMM, Josephine. 192 B
John Stuart Mill in love / Josephine Kamm. London : Gordon & Cremonesi, 1977. 253 p. : ill. ; 23 cm. Includes index. Bibliography: p. 242-246. [B1606.K35] 78-300962 ISBN 0-86033-020-6 : 14.95
1. Mill, John Stuart, 1806-1873. 2. Mill, Harriet Hardy Taylor, 1807-1858. 3. Philosophers—England—Biography. 4. Wives—England—Biography. I. Title.
Available from Mouton, 3 Westchester Plaza, Flmsford, NY 10523 BIP

MILL, John Stuart, 1806-1873 921.2
Autobiography. Garden City, N.Y., Doubleday [1961] 240p. (Dolphin, C 179) .95 pap.,
I. Title.

*MILL, John Stuart, 1806-1873 921.2
Autobiography. Foreword by Asa Briggs [New York] New Amer. Lib. [1964] 224p. 18cm. (Signet classic, CT269) Bibl. .75 pap.,
I. Title.

MILL, John Stuart, 1806-1873. 921.2
Autobiography. With an introd. by Currin V. Shields. New York, Liberal Arts Press [c1957] xviii, 201p. 21cm. (The Library of liberal arts, no. 91) Bibliography: p. xvii-xviii. [B1606.A2 1957] 57-14630
I. Title.

MILL, John Stuart, 1806-1873 921.2
Autobiography. Published from the original manuscript in the Columbia University library; with a preface by John Jacob Coss. New York, Columbia University Press [1960, c.1924] 24op. (Columbia paperback 6) 1.50 pap.,
I. Title.

MILL, John Stuart, 1806-1873. 921.2
The early draft of John Stuart Mill's autobiography. Edited by Jack Stillinger. Urbana, University of Illinois Press, 1961. 218p. 24cm. Bibliographical footnotes. [B1606.A2 1961] 61-62769
I. Stillinger, Jack, ed. II. Title.

PACKE, Michael St. John. 921.2
The life of John Stuart Mill. With a pref. by F. A. Hayek. New York, Macmillan, 1954. xvi, 567 p. illus., ports. 25 cm. Bibliography: p. 532-542. [B1606.P3 1954a] 54-4589
1. Mill, John Stuart, 1806-1873. BIP

Mill, John Stuart, 1806-1873—Addresses, essays, lectures.

JOHN Stuart Mill : 192 B
his life and works : twelve sketches / by Herbert Spencer, Henry Fawcett, Frederic Harrison, and other distinguished authors. Folcroft, Pa. : Folcroft Library Editions, 1976. Reprint of the 1873 ed. published by J. R. Osgood, Boston. [B1606.J63 1976] 76-8395 ISBN 0-8414-7845-7 lib. bdg. : 10.00
1. Mill, John Stuart, 1806-1873—Addresses, essays, lectures. I. Spencer, Herbert, 1820-1903.
Contents omitted

Mill, John Stuart, 1806-1873—Political science.

HALLIDAY, Richard John. 320.5'1'0924 B
John Stuart Mill / R. J. Halliday. New York : Barnes & Noble, 1976. 151 p. ; 23 cm. Includes index. Bibliography: p. 144-148. [JC223.M66H34 1976] 76-19969 ISBN 0-06-492665-6 : 12.50
1. Mill, John Stuart, 1806-1873 Political science. BIP

Milla y Vidaurre, Jose, 1827-1882.

PAYNE, Walter A 928.6
A Central American historian, Jose Milla (1822-1882) Gainesville, University of Florida Press, 1957. vi, 77p. 23cm. (Latin American monographs, no. 2) Bibliography: p. 73-77. [PQ7499.M5Z8] 57-14812
1. Milla y Vidaurre, Jose, 1827-1882. I. Title. II. Series.

Millais, John Everett, Sir, bart., 1829-1896.

BAYLISS, Wyke, Sir, 1835-1906. 759.2
Five great painters of the Victorian era: Leighton, Millais, Burne-Jones, Watts, Holman Hunt. New York, AMS Press [1971] vii, 159 p. illus., ports. 19 cm. Reprint of the 1902 ed. [ND467.B4 1971] 72-129384 ISBN 0-404-00696-5
1. Leighton, Frederic Leighton, Baron, 1830-1896. 2. Millais, John Everett, Sir, bart., 1829-1896. 3. Burne-Jones, Edward Coley, Sir, bart., 1833-1898. 4. Watts, George Frederick, 1817-1904. 5. Hunt, William Holman, 1827-1910.

MILLAIS, John Guille, 1865-1931. 759.2 B
The life and letters of Sir John Everett Millais, president of the Royal Academy. New York, F. A. Stokes, 1899. [New York, AMS Press, 1973] 2 v. illus. 24 cm. [ND497.M6M5 1973] 72-148280 ISBN 0-404-04326-7 95.00
1. Millais, John Everett, Sir, bart., 1829-1896. BIP

Milland, Ray.

MILLAND, Ray. 791.43'028'0924 B
Wide-eyed in Babylon; an autobiography. New York, Morrow, 1974. 264 p. illus. 24 cm. [PN2287.M633A38] 74-4016 ISBN 0-688-00257-9 7.95
1. Milland, Ray. I. Title.

MILLAND, Ray. 791.430280 B
Wide-eyed in Babylon, an autobiography. New York: Ballantine Books, [1975 c 1974] 304 p.: illus.; 18 cm. [PN2287.M633A38] 1.75 (pbk.)
1. Milland, Ray I. Title.
L.C. card no. for original edition: 74-4016. BIP

Millar, John,

MILLAR, John, 1735-1801 921.2
John Millar of Glasgow, 1735-1801; his life and thought and his contributions to sociological analysis by William C. Lehman [New York] Cambridge University Press, 1960[ ] xvi, 430p. port. (Publications of the Dept. of Social and Economic Researh, University of Glasgow, Social and economic studies) 60-51984 10.00
I. Lehmann, William Christian,, 1888- II. Title. III. Series: Glasgow. University. Dept. of Social and Economic Research. Publications. Series: Glasgow. University. Dept. of Social and Economic Research. Social and economic studies, 4

Millay, Edna St. Vincent, 1892-1950.

DASH, Joan. 920.72
A life of one's own; three gifted women and the men they married. [1st ed.] New York, Harper & Row [1973] xx, 388 p. ports. 22 cm. Bibliography: p. [365]-369. [CT3260.D37 1973] 76-138717 ISBN 0-06-010949-1 10.00
1. Sanger, Margaret, 1879-1966. 2. Millay, Edna St. Vincent, 1892-1950. 3. Mayer, Maria (Goeppert) 1906-1972. I. Title.

GOULD, Jean, 1909- 811'.5'2 B
The poet and her book; a biography of Edna St. Vincent Millay. New York, Dodd, Mead [1969] xii, 308 p. illus., ports. 24 cm. Bibliography: p. 292-299. [PS3525.I495Z64] 69-17603 6.50
1. Millay, Edna St. Vincent, 1892-1950. I. Title.

GRAY, James, 1899- 818'.5'209
Edna St. Vincent Millay. Minneapolis, University of Minnesota Press [1967] 48 p. 21 cm. (University of Minnesota. Pamphlets on American writers, no. 64) Bibliography: p. 47-48. [PS3525.I495Z65] 67-26664
1. Millay, Edna St. Vincent, 1892-1950. I. Series: Minnesota. University. Pamphlets on American writers, no. 64 BIP

GURKO, Miriam. 928.1
Restless spirit; the life of Edna St. Vincent Millay. New York, Crowell [1962] 271 p. 21 cm. Includes bibliography. [PS3525.I495Z67] 62-16544
1. Millay, Edna St. Vincent, 1892-1950. I. Title.

MILLAY, Edna St. Vincent, 1892-1950. 928.1
Letters; ed. by Allan Ross Macdougall. New York, Grosset [1961, c.1952] 384p. (Universal lib., 0103) 1.65 pap.,
I. Macdougall, Allan Ross, 1893- ed. II. Title.

MILLAY, Edna St. Vincent, 1892-1950. 928.1
Letters; edited by Allan Ross Macdougall. [1st ed.] New York, Harper [1952] xii, 384 p. port., facsims. 22 cm. [PS3525.I495Z53] 52-7291
I. Macdougall, Allan Ross, 1893- ed.

MILLAY, Edna St. Vincent, 1892 1950. 811'.5'2 B
Letters of Edna St. Vincent Millay. Edited by Allan Ross Macdougall. Westport, Conn., Greenwood Press [1972, c1952] xii, 384 p. front. 22 cm. [PS3525.I495Z53 1972] 72-6177 ISBN 0-8371-6482-6 15.25

SHAFTER, Toby. 928.1
Edna St. Vincent Millay; America's best-loved poet (February 22, 1892-October 19, 1950) New York, J. Messner [1957] 192 p. 22 cm. Includes bibliography. [PS3525.I495Z78] 57-6838
1. Millay, Edna St. Vincent, 1892-1950.

SHAFTER, Toby. 812.5
Edna St. Vincent Millay; America's best-loved poet (February 22, 1892-October 19, 1950) New York, J. Messner [1957] 192 p. 22 cm. Includes bibliography. [PS3525.I495Z78] [QT 928.1] 57-6838
1. Millay, Edna St. Vincent, 1892-1950. I. Title.

SHEEAN, Vincent, 1899- 928.1
The indigo bunting; a memoir of Edna St. Vincent Millay. [1st ed.] New York, Harper [1951] 131 p. illus. 22 cm. Full name: James Vincent Sheean. [PS3525.I 495Z8] 51-13495
1. Millay, Edna St. Vincent, 1802- I. Title. BIP

SHEEAN, Vincent, 1899- 811'.5'2 B
The indigo bunting; a memoir of Edna St. Vincent Millay. New York, Schocken Books [1973, c1951] 131 p. 21 cm. [PS3525.I495Z8 1973] 73-79054 ISBN 0-8052-3518-3 2.95 (pbk.)
1. Millay, Edna St. Vincent, 1892-1950. I. Title.

Millay, Edna St. Vincent, 1892-1950—Biography.

CHENEY, Anne, 1944- 811'.5'2 B
Millay in Greenwich Village / Anne Cheney. University : University of Alabama Press, [1975] p. cm. Includes index. Bibliography: p. [PS3525.I495Z63] 74-23424
1. Millay, Edna St. Vincent, 1892-1950—Biography. I. Title. BIP

Miller, Ann,

MILLER, Ann, 1923- 790.2'092'4
Miller's high life, by Ann Miller with Norma Lee Browning. [1st ed.] Garden City, N.Y., Doubleday, 1972. 283 p. illus. 22 cm. [PN2287.M635A3] 72-76193 ISBN 0-385-03440-7 7.95
I. Browning, Norma Lee, joint author. II. Title.

Miller, Arthur, 1915-

NELSON, Benjamin. 812'.5'2 B
Arthur Miller; portrait of a playwright. [1st American ed.] New York, McKay [1970] 336 p. 21 om. Bibliography: p. [323]-329. [PS3525.I5156Z83 1970] 70-94503 5.95
1. Miller, Arthur, 1915-

*Miller, Basil

*MILLER, Basil 285.00924 (B)
Charles G. Finney; official biography for the Finney Sesquicentennial Conference Chicago 1942. Minneapolis, Bethany Fellowship [1966, c.1941] 137p. 19cm. (BF 150) 1.50 pap.,
I. Title.

Miller, Ben Robertson.

MILLER, Ben Robertson. 340'.092'4 B
Memoirs of a southern lawyer. Baton Rouge, La., Priv. print. by B. R. Miller, 1973. xii, 333 p. illus. 24 cm. No. 316 of 350 copies. Includes bibliographical references. [KF373.M53A32] 73-87892
1. Miller, Ben Robertson. 2. Lawyers—Baton Rouge, La.—Correspondence, reminiscences, etc. 3. Baton Rouge, La.—History. I. Title.

Miller, Bertha E. (Mahony)

ROSS, Eulalie Steinmetz. 028.5 B
The spirited life: Bertha Mahony Miller and children's books. Selected bibliography, compiled by Virginia Haviland. Boston, Horn Book, 1973. 274 p. illus. 25 cm. Bibliography: p. 251-257. [Z1004.M64R65] 73-84132 ISBN 0-87675-057-9 12.00
1. Miller, Bertha E. (Mahony) 2. Children's literature—History and criticism. I. Haviland, Virginia, 1911- II. Title.

Miller, Bill, 1932-

MILLER, Bill, 1932- 791.44'092'4 B
You're on open line! : Inside the wacky world of late-night talk radio / by Bill Miller as told to John McCarty. Brattleboro, Vt. : S. Greene Press, c1978. p. cm. [PN1991.4.M5A37] 78-58682 ISBN 0-8289-0335-2 : 8.95
1. Miller, Bill, 1932- 2. Radio broadcasters—United States—Biography. 3. Talk shows—United States. I. McCarty, John, 1944- II. Title. BIP

Miller, Carolyn Paine.

MILLER, Carolyn Paine. 959.704'37
Captured! / Carolyn Paine Miller. 1st ed.

Chappaqua, N.Y. : Christian Herald Books, c1977. 288 p., [4] leaves of plates : ill. ; 23 cm. Autobiographical. [DS559.4.M54] 77-81401 ISBN 0-915684-17-9 : 6.95
1. Miller, Carolyn Paine. 2. Vietnamese Conflict, 1961-1975—Prisoners and prisons, Vietnamese. 3. Missionaries—Vietnam—Biography. 4. Vietnamese Conflict, 1961-1975—Personal narratives, American. I. Title. BIP

Miller, Edward S., 1888-

MILLER, Edward S., 1888- 338.2'7'440978968
The story of "King Solomon's Mine" at Gage, New Mexico / by Edward S. Miller. Ramona, Calif. : Miller, [1974] 13 leaves : ill. ; 28 cm. [TN24.N6M54] 74-187911
1. Miller, Edward S, 1888- 2. Mines and mineral resources—New Mexico—Gage—History. I. Title.

Miller, Glenn, 1909-1944—Discography.

FLOWER, John. 016.7899'12
Moonlight serenade; a bio-discography of the Glenn Miller civilian band. New Rochelle, N.Y., Arlington House [1972] 554 p. illus. 24 cm. [ML156.7.M5F6] 74-179717 ISBN 0-87000-161-2 10.00
1. Miller, Glenn, 1909-1944—Discography. I. Title.

Miller, Henry, 1827-1916.

TREADWELL, Edward Francis, 1875- 926.3
The Cattle King, a dramatized biography. [Rev. ed.] Boston, Christopher Pub. House [1950] xi, 375 p. ports., map (on lining paper) 22 cm. Biography of Henry Miller. [F596.M64] Agr
1. Miller, Henry, 1827-1916. I. Title.

Miller, Henry, 1891-

MILLER, Henry, 1891- 818'.5'209 B
My life and times. [Chicago] Playboy Press [1971] 204 p. illus. 32 cm. (A Gemini Smith book) [PS3525.I5454Z524] 79-151843 17.95
I. Title.

PERLES, Alfred 928.1
My friend, Henry Miller. New York, Belmont [c.1956, 1962] 189p. 18cm. (L92-546) Bibl. .50 pap.,
1. Miller, Henry, 1891- I. Title.

PERLES, Alfred. 928.1
My friend, Henry Miller; an intimate biography. With a pref. by Henry Miller. New York, J. Day Co. [1956] 255p. port. 21cm. Bibliography: p. 241-250. [PS3525.I5454Z8 1956] 56-7351
1. Miller, Henry, 1891- I. Title.

Miller, Henry, 1891- —Biography.

MARTIN, Jay. 818'.5'209 B
Always merry & bright : the life of Henry Miller / Jay Martin. Santa Barbara, Calif. : Capra Press, 1978. p. cm. Bibliography: p. [PS3525.I5454Z716] 78-6912 ISBN 0-88496-082-X : 15.00
1. Miller, Henry, 1891- —Biography. 2. Authors, American—20th century—Biography. I. Title. BIP

MILLER, Henry, 1891- 818'.5'209 B
On turning eighty ; Journey to an antique land ; foreword to The angel is my watermark / by Henry Miller ; drawings by Bob Nash. Santa Barbara, Calif. : Capra Press, 1972. 34 p. : ill. ; 18 cm. (Yes! Capra chapbook series ; no. 1) [PS3525.I5454Z525 1972] 75-318511 ISBN 0-912264-43-8 : 2.50
1. Miller, Henry, 1891- —Biography. I. Miller, Henry, 1891- Journey to an antique land. 1972. II. Miller, Henry, 1891- The angel is my watermark. 1972. III. Title.

Miller, Henry, 1891- —Correspondence.

MILLER, Henry, 1891- 818'.5'209 B
Henry Miller : years of trail & triumph, 1962-1964 : the correspondence of Henry Miller and Elmer Gertz / edited by Elmer Gertz and Felice Flanery Lewis. Carbondale : Southern Illinois University Press, c1978. xxiii, 345 p., [8] leavesof plate : ill ; 25 cm. Includes bibliographical references and index. [PS3525.I5454Z552] 78-3547 ISBN 0-8093-0860-6 : 17.50
1. Miller, Henry, 1891- —Correspondence. 2. Gertz, Elmer, 1906- 3. Miller, Henry, 1891- Tropic of Cancer. 4. Authors, American—20th century—Correspondence. 5. Lawyers—United States—Correspondence. 6. Censorship—United States. I. Gertz, Elmer, 1906- joint author. II. Lewis, Felice Flanery.

MILLER, Henry, 1891- 818'.5'209 B
Letters of Henry Miller and Wallace Fowlie, 1943-1972 / by Henry Miller and Wallace Fowlie; with an introd. by Wallace Fowlie New York : Grove Press : distributed by Random House, [1975] 184 p., [1] leaf of plates : ports. ; 22 cm. Includes index. [PS3525.I5454Z544] 74-24859 ISBN 0-394-49737-6 : 9.50
1. Miller, Henry, 1891- —Correspondence. 2. Fowlie, Wallace, 1908- 3. Authors—Correspondence, reminiscences, etc. I. Fowlie, Wallace, 1908- joint author. II. Title.

Miller, Henry, 1891- —Friends and associates.

MILLER, Henry, 1891- 818'.5'209 B
Henry Miller's book of friends :a tribute to friends of long ago. Santa Barbara [Calif.] : Capra Press, 1976. 138 p. : ill. ; 24 cm. [PS3525.I5454Z518] 75-38790 ISBN 0-88496-050-1 : 7.95. ISBN 0-88496-051-X pbk. : 4.95. ISBN 0-88496-052-8 lim. ed. : 20.00
1. Miller, Henry, 1891- —Friends and associates. 2. Miller, Henry, 1891- —Biography—Youth. I. Title. II. Title: Book of friends.

MILLER, Henry, 1891- 818'.5'209 B
Henry Miller's book of friends ; (with Brooklyn Street photos by Jim Lazarus). Santa Barbara [Calif.] : Capra Press, 1976. p. cm. [PS3525.I5454Z518] 75-38790 ISBN 0-88496-050-1 : 7.95. ISBN 0-88496-051-X pbk. : 4.95. ISBN 0-88496-052-8 lim. ed. : 20.00
1. Miller, Henry, 1891- —Friends and associates. 2. Miller, Henry, 1891- —Biography—Youth. I. Title. II. Title: Book of friends.

MILLER, Henry, 1891- 818'.5'209
My bike and other friends / by Henry Miller. Santa Barbara, Calif. : Capra Press, c1978. p. cm. Continues the author's Book of friends. [PS3525.I5454Z5236] 77-18967 ISBN 0-88496-075-7 : 7.95. ISBN 0-88496-076-5 pbk. : 3.95. ISBN 0-88496-081-1 signed lim. ed. : 25.00
1. Miller, Henry, 1891- —Friends and associates. 2. Authors, American—20th century—Biography. I. Title. BIP

Miller, Henry, 1891- —Friends and associates—Addresses, essays, lectures.

MILLER, Henry, 1891- 818'.5'209 B
Joey : a loving portrait of Alfred Perles together with some bizarre episodes relating to the opposite sex / Henry Miller. Santa Barbara, Calif. : Capra Press, 1979. p. cm. (Book of friends ; v. 3) (Series: Miller, Henry, 1891- Book of friends ; v. 3.) [PS3525.I5454Z52 1979] 79-9304 ISBN 0-88496-136-2 : 8.95 ISBN 0-88496-137-0 pbk. : 3.95 pbk. : 3.95
1. Miller, Henry, 1891- —Friends and associates—Addresses, essays, lectures. 2. Miller, Henry, 1891- —Relationship with women—Addresses, essays, lectures. 3. Perles, Alfred—Biography—Addresses, essays, lectures. 4. Authors, American—20th century—Biography—Addresses, essays, lectures. I. Title. II. Series. BIP

Miller, Henry, 1891- —Relationship with women—Addresses, essays, lectures.

MILLER, Henry, 1891- 818'.5'209 B
Joey : a loving portrait of Alfred Perles together with some bizarre episodes relating to the opposite sex / Henry Miller. Santa Barbara, Calif. : Capra Press, 1979. p. cm. (Book of friends ; v. 3) (Series: Miller, Henry, 1891- Book of friends ; v. 3.) [PS3525.I5454Z52 1979] 79-9304 ISBN 0-88496-136-2 : 8.95 ISBN 0-88496-137-0 pbk. : 3.95 pbk. : 3.95
1. Miller, Henry, 1891- —Friends and associates—Addresses, essays, lectures. 2. Miller, Henry, 1891- —Relationship with women—Addresses, essays, lectures. 3. Perles, Alfred—Biography—Addresses, essays, lectures. 4. Authors, American—20th century—Biography—Addresses, essays, lectures. I. Title. II. Series. BIP

Miller, J. Wesley, 1869-1934.

MILLER, J. Wesley, 1869-1934. 287'.632'0924 B
"All my days for Jesus"; the diary of the Rev. J. Wesley Miller of Bethel, Vermont. Edited by J. W. Miller, III. Springfield, Mass., 1959. [50] l. 28 cm. [BX8495.M525A3] 75-304150
1. Miller, J. Wesley, 1869-1934. 2. Registers of births, etc.—Bethel, Vt. 3. Bethel, Vt.—History. I. Title.

Miller, Jacob,

MILLER, Jacob, 1835-1911. 289.3'0924 B
Journal. Prepared for publication by Joseph Royal Miller and Elna Miller. [Salt Lake City] Mercury Pub. Co., 1967, c1968. 199 p. illus., port. 26 cm. [CT275.M52527A3] 68-5134
I. Miller, Joseph Royal, ed. II. Miller, Elna, joint ed.

Miller, Jim, 1866-1909.

SHIRLEY, Glenn. 364.15'5'0924 B
Shotgun for hire; the story of "Deacon" Jim Miller, killer of Pat Garrett. [1st ed.] Norman, University of Oklahoma Press [1970] ix, 131 p. illus., facsim., ports. 20 cm. Bibliography: p. 117-123. [F786.M66S5] 78-108794 4.95
1. Miller, Jim, 1866-1909. I. Title. BIP

Miller, joaquin, 1841?-1913.

MARBERRY, M. Marion, 1908- 928.1
Splendid poseur: Josquin Miller, American poet. New York, Crowell [1953] 310p. illus. 21cm. Includes bibliography. [PS2398.M3] 53-8435
1. Miller, Joaquin, 1841?-1913. I. Title.

MILLER, Juanita Joaquina, 1880- 928.1
My father, C. H. Joaquin Miller, poet, by Juanita J. Miller. Oakland, Calif., Tooley-Towne [1964] 218 p. illus., facsims., music, ports. 24 cm. [PS2398.M52] 64-54634
1. Miller, joaquin, 1841?-1913. I. Title.

Miller, Joe.

MILLER, Joe. 817'.5'4
Funny you should ask. New York, Carlton Press [1965] 94 p. 21 cm. Autobiographical. [CT275.M52528A3] 79-1292 2.50
I. Title.

Miller, Johnny, 1947- —Juvenile literature.

HASEGAWA, Sam. 796.352'092'4 B
Johnny Miller / by Sam Hasegawa ; illustrated by Fred Dingler. Mankato, Minn. : Creative Education, [1975] p. cm. A brief biography concentrating on the career of golf pro Johnny Miller. [GV964.M54H37] 92 75-20436 ISBN 0-87191-455-7 lib.bdg. : 4.95
1. Miller, Johnny, 1947- —Juvenile literature. 2. Golf—Juvenile literature. I. Dingler, Fred. II. Title. BIP

Miller, Orie O., 1892-

ERB, Paul, 1894- 289.7'0924 B
Orie O. Miller; the story of a man and an era. Scottdale, Pa., Herald Press [1969] 304 p. illus., ports. 23 cm. Includes bibliographies. [BX8143.M54E7] 75-76624 7.95
1. Miller, Orie O., 1892- BIP

Miller, Polly Rawlins.

*MILLER, Kathryn Smith 973.6
Polly Rawlins Miller: a biography. [Lancaster, Texas] [1973] ii, 57 p, illus., ports, 21 cm. [E415.9] 6.95
1. Miller, Polly Rawlins. I. Title.
Available from author, 701 W. Main St., Lancaster, Texas 75146

Miller, Queen Elizabeth (Taylor)

BLACKFORD, Audrey 920.7
The royal Queen Elizabeth Miller; the inspiring true story of a woman who built a kingdom for children whom the world had cast away. New York, Greenwich [1962, c.1961] 52p. 21cm. 60-53447 2.50
1. Miller, Queen Elizabeth (Taylor) I. Title.

Miller, Robin.

MILLER, Robin. 610.73'092'4 B
Flying nurse. New York, Taplinger [1972, c1971] 220 p. illus. 22 cm. Autobiographical. [RT37.M55A3 1972] 70-174244 ISBN 0-8008-2892-5 5.50
I. Title. BIP

Miller, Sammy, 1934-

CLEW, Jeffrey Robert. 796.7'5'0924 B
Sammy Miller : the will to win / [by] Jeff Clew. Yeovil : Foulis, 1976. 3-165 p., leaf of plate : ill., ports. ; 24 cm. (A Foulis motorcycling book) [GV1060.2.M47C53] 77-355303 ISBN 0-85429-219-5 : £3.95
1. Miller, Sammy, 1934- 2. Mortorcyclists—Great Britain—Biography. 3. Motorcycle racing—Great Britain.

Miller, Thelma Kay.

MILLER, Thelma Kay. 917.97'48'034
Grass is gold; a biographical history. North Quincy, Mass., Christopher Pub. House [1969] 171 p. illus. 21 cm. [CT275.M719A3] 76-101361 4.95
I. Title.

Miller, William, 1782-1849.

BLISS, Sylvester, d.1863. 286'.73 B
Memoirs of William Miller, generally known as a lecturer on the prophecies, and the second coming of Christ. Boston, J. V. Himes, 1853. [New York, AMS Press, 1971] vi, 426 p. port. 22 cm. Includes bibliographical references. [BX6193.M5B6 1971] 72-134374 ISBN 0-404-08422-2 17.50
1. Miller, William, 1782-1849.

Miller, William, 1795-1861.

MILLER, John. 980'.02'0924 B
Memoirs of General Miller, in the service of the Republic of Peru. 2d ed. London, Printed for Longman, Rees, Orme, Brown, and Green, 1829. [New York, AMS Press, 1973] 2 v. illus. 23 cm. [F3446.M65 1973] 70-172731 ISBN 0-404-04339-9 47.50
1. Miller, William, 1795-1861. 2. Peru—History—War of Independence, 1820-1829. 3. South America—History—Wars of Independence, 1806-1830. BIP

Millerand, Alexandre, pres. France, 1859-1943.

DERFLER, Leslie. 944.081'5'0924 B
Alexandre Millerand : the socialist years / Leslie Derfler. The Hague : Mouton, [1977] x, 326 p., [4] leaves of plates : ill. ; 24 cm. (Issues in contemporary politics ; 4) Includes index. Bibliography: p. [313]-317.

[HX263.M57D47] 77-467617 ISBN 9-02-797991-X : 48.00
1. Millerand, Alexandre, pres. France, 1859-1943. 2. Socialists—France—Biography. 3. France—Politics and government—1870-1940. I. Title. II. Series.
Distributed by Walter de Gruyter, NY **BIP**

Millet, Kate.

MILLETT, Kate. 301.41'2'0924
Sita / Kate Millett. New York : Farrar, Straus and Giroux, c1977. 321 p. ; 22 cm. [HQ75.4.M54A36 1977] 77-2267 ISBN 0-374-26546-1 : 10.00
1. Millett, Kate. 2. Lesbians—United States—Biography. 3. Feminists—United States—Biography. I. Title.

MILLETT, Kate. 301.41'2'0924
Sita / by Kate Millett. New York : Ballantine Books 1978,c1977. 313 p. ; 18 cm. [HQ75.4.M54A36 1977] ISBN 0-345-27362-1 pbk. : 2.25
1. Millet, Kate. 2. Lesbians-United States — Biography. 3. Feminists — united states — biography. I. Title.
L.C. card no. for 1977 Farrar, Straus and Giroux ed.:77-2267. **BIP**

Millet, Pierre, 1635-1709.

MILLET, Pierre, 973'.04'97 S
1635-1709.
Captivity of Father Milet / Pierre Milet. New York : Garland, 1978. 18 p. ; 23 cm. (The Garland library of narratives of North American Indian captivities ; v. 96) Reprint of the 1888 ed. published in New York. Issued with the reprint of the 1897 ed. of Millet, P. Captivity among the Oneidas of Father Milet. New York, 1978, the reprint of the 1888 ed. of Nystel, O. T. Lost and found. New York, 1978, the reprint of the 1890 ed. of Wehman, H. J. Wehman's book on the scalping knife. New York, 1978, and with the reprint of the 1882 ed. of Fuller, E. L. Left by the Indians. New York, 1978. [E85.G2 vol. 96] [E99.O45] 970'.004'97 B 77-27517 ISBN 0-8240-1720-X lib.bdg. : 29.50
1. Millet, Pierre, 1635-1709. 2. Jesuits—New York (State)—Biography. 3. Oneida Indians—Captivities. 4. Indians of North America—Captivities. 5. United States—History—King William's War, 1689-1697—Personal narratives. I. Title. II. Series.

Millette, Ernest Schlee.

MILLETTE, Ernest 791.3'4'0924 B
Schlee.
The circus that was; the autobiography of a star performer, by Ernest Schlee Millette, as told to Robert Wyndham. Philadelphia, Dorrance [1971] 180 p. illus. (part col.), ports. (part col.) 22 cm. [GV1811.M33A3] 71-148919 4.95
I. Hyndman, Robert Utley, 1906- II. Title.

Milligan, Terence Alan.

MILLIGAN, Terence 940.54'81'42
Alan.
Adolf Hitler; my part in his downfall [by] Spike Milligan. [1st U.S. ed.] New York, Harper's Magazine Press [1974, c1971] 146 p. illus. 21 cm. [D811.M5252 1974] 73-18653 ISBN 0-06-126380-X 5.95
1. Milligan, Terence Alan. 2. World War, 1939-1945—Personal narratives, English. 3. World War, 1939-1945—Humor, caricatures, etc. I. Title.

Millikan, Robert Andrews,

MILLIKAN, Robert Andrews, 925.3
1868-
Autobiography. [1st ed.] New York, Prentice-Hall [1950] xiv, 311 p. illus., ports. 24 cm. [QC16.M58A3] 50-7302

Millin, Philip, 1888-1952.

MILLIN, Sarah Gertrude 928.2
(Liebson) 1889-
The measure of my days. New York, Abelard-Schuman [1956, c1955] 394p. 23cm. Autobiographical. [PR6025] 56-6381
1. Millin, Philip, 1888-1952. I. Title.

Millionaires.

ARMOUR, Lawrence A. 658.4'09
The young millionaires [by] Lawrence A. Armour. Foreword by James J. Ling. Afterword by Nick J. Mileti. [1st ed. Chicago] Playboy Press, [1973] xxi, 264 p. 22 cm. [HC102.5.A2A74] 73-76283 7.95
1. Millionaires. 2. Capitalists and financiers—United States. I. Title.

RATNER, Sidney, 1908- ed. 923.373
New light on the history of great American fortunes; American millionaires of 1892 and 1902. [1st ed.] New York, A. M. Kelley, 1953. xxvii, 106p. 24cm. Includes reprints of 'a 93 page document published by the New York tribune in its supplement, the Tribune monthly, June, 1892, under the title 'American millionaries' ... [and] a twelve-and-a-half page ... list of 'American milionaires published in the New York World almanac and encyclopedia 1902.' Bibliographical footnotes. [HC102.5.A2R3] 53-13296
1. Millionaries. 2. Capitalists and financiers—U. S. 3. U. S.—Biog. 4. American millionaries. I. New York tribune. II. Title.

REES, Goronwy, 1909- 923.3
The multimillionaires; six studies in wealth. New York, Macmillan, 1961. 128p. 22cm. [CT105.R4] 61-8757
1. Millionaires. I. Title.

REES, Goronwy [Morgan 923.3
Goronwy Rees] 1909-
The multimillionaires; six studies in wealth. New York, Macmillan [c.]1961. 128p. 61-8757 3.50
1. Millionaires. I. Title.

WALL Street journal (The) 923.373
The new millionaires and how they made their fortunes, by the eds. of the Wall Street journal. [New York] Macfadden [1962, c.1960, 1961] 127p. (40103) .40 pap.,
1. Millionaires. I. Title.

Millionaires—Case studies.

GUNTHER, Max, 1927- 330.12'2'0922
The very, very rich and how they got that way. Ed. by Max Gunther [New York] Playboy Pr. [1973, c.1972] 316 p. 18 cm. (Playboy Pr. executive lib., 16191) Bibl. [HC102.5.A2G9] 74-187402 pap., 1.50
1. Millionaires—Case studies. 2. Capitalists and financiers—United States—Case studies. I. Title. **BIP**

WOOD, Robert, 1948- 301.44'1
comp.
Cool millions : life among the super rich / edited by Robert A. Wood ; illustrated by Walter Scott. Kansas City, Mo. : Hallmark Cards, [1974] 61 p. : ill. ; 20 cm. (Hallmark editions) [HG172.A2W6] 73-89442 ISBN 0-87529-383-2 : 3.50
1. Millionaires—Case studies. 2. Wealth—United States—Case studies. I. Title.

Millionaires—United States.

GREENE, Bert, 1923- 332'.092'2
Pity the poor rich / Bert Greene with Phillip Stephen Schulz. Chicago : Contemporary Books, c1978. ix, 236 p. ; 24 cm. Includes bibliographical references and index. [HG172.A2G73 1978] 78-57451 ISBN 0-8092-8198-8 : 9.95
1. Millionaires—United States. I. Schulz, Phillip Stephen, joint author. II. Title. **BIP**

Millionaires—United States—Biography.

LE BLANC, Jerry. 332'.092'2 B
Suddenly rich / Jerry LeBlanc & Rena Dictor LeBlanc. Englewood Cliffs, N.J. : Prentice-Hall, c1978. xix, 191 p. ; 22 cm. [HG172.A2L4] 78-3491 ISBN 013-875609-0 : 8.95
1. Millionaires—United States—Biography. 2. Wealth—United States. I. Le Blanc, Rena Dictor, 1939- joint author. II. Title.

Millionairesses—United States—Biography.

RICH-MCCOY, Lois 338'.092'2 B
Millionairess : self-made women of America / by Lois Rich-McCoy. 1st ed. New York : Harper & Row, c1978. xiii, 235 p. : ill. ; 22 cm. [HF5386.R49 1978] 78-2142 ISBN 0-06-012852-6 : 8.95
1. Millionairesses—United States—Biography. I. Title. **BIP**

Mills, Charles Wright.

PRESS, Howard. 301'.092'4 B
C. Wright Mills / by Howard Press. Boston : Twayne Publishers, c1978. 172 p. : port. ; 21 cm. (Twayne's world leaders series ; TWLS 57) Includes index. Bibliography: p. 166-169. [HM22.U6M456] 77-16057 ISBN 0-8057-7708-3 : 9.95
1. Mills, Charles Wright. 2. Sociologists—United States—Biography. **BIP**

Mills, Nettie Elizabeth (West)

MILLS, Nettie Elizabeth 920.7
(West) 1880-
The lady driller; the autobiography of N. Elizabeth Mills. [1st ed.] New York, Exposition Press [1955] 176p. 21cm. [CT275.M533A3] 55-8209
I. Title.

Mills, Robert, 1781-1855.

GALLAGHER, Helen Mar v. 12
Pierce.
Robert Mills, architect of the Washington monument, 1781-1855 [by] H.M. Pierce Gallagher. New York, AMS Press, 1966 [c1935] xxv, 233 p. illus., front., plates, maps, facsims. 24 cm. Bibliography: p. [217]-220. 68-42445
1. Mills, Robert, 1781-1855. I. Title. **BIP**

GALLAGHER, Helen Mar 720'.92'4 B
(Pierce) d.1942.
Robert Mills, architect of the Washington Monument, 1781-1855. New York, AMS Press, 1966 [c1935] xxv, 233 p. illus. 24 cm. Bibliography: p. [217]-220. [NA737.M5G3 1966] 72-183878
1. Mills, Robert, 1781-1855.

MARSH, Blanche. 720'.92'4
Robert Mills; architect in South Carolina. [Columbia, S.C.] R. L. Bryan Co., 1970. xi, 178 p. illus. 28 cm. Bibliography: p. 177-178. [NA737.M5M37] 72-125882
1. Mills, Robert, 1781-1855. 2. Architecture—South Carolina.

Milne, Alan Alexander, 1882-1956.

MILNE, Christopher, 828'.9'1209
1920-
The enchanted places / Christopher Milne. Harmondsworth ; New York [etc.] : Penguin, 1978. 183 p., [8] p. of plates : ill., map, ports. ; 18 cm. [PR6025.I65Z8 1976] 78-317933 ISBN 0-14-003449-8 pbk. : 1.95
1. Milne, Alan Alexander, 1882-1956. 2. Milne, Christopher. 3. Authors, English—20th century—Biography. 4. Children in England—Biography. I. Title. **BIP**

Milne, Christopher, 1920-

MILNE, 942.082'092'4 B
Christopher, 1920-
The path through the trees / Christopher Milne ; drawings by Tim Wood. 1st ed. New York : Dutton, c1979. xv, 268 p. : ill. ; 22 cm. [CT788.M547A36 1979] 78-26317 ISBN 0-525-17630-6 : 9.95
1. Milne, Christopher, 1920- 2. England—Biography. I. Title. **BIP**

Milne, George Francis Milne, Baron, 1866-1948.

NICOL, Graham, 355.3'31'0924 B
1933-
Uncle George : Field-Marshal Lord Milne of Salonika and Rubislaw / Graham Nicol. London : Reedminster, 1976. 341 p., [12] leaves of plates : ill. ; 23 cm. Includes index. Bibliography: p. 333-336. [DA69.3.M5N5] 77-354078 ISBN 0-85945-004-X : £6.75
1. Milne, George Francis Milne, Baron, 1866-1948. 2. Great Britain. Army—Biography. 3. Generals—Great Britain—Biography. 4. Great Britain—History, Military—20th century. I. Title.

Milner, Alfred Milner, 1st viscount, 1854-1925.

CRANKSHAW, Edward. 325.342'0968'7
The forsaken idea; a study of Viscount Milner. Westport, Conn., Greenwood Press [1974] ix, 178 p. 22 cm. Reprint of the 1952 ed. published by Longmans, Green, London. [DT776.M6C7 1974] 73-17918 ISBN 0-8371-7278-0 9.25
1. Milner, Alfred Milner, 1st Viscount, 1854-1925. 2. Africa, South—History. I. Title. **BIP**

MARLOWE, John. 941.083'092'4 B
Milner : apostle of Empire : a life of Alfred George, the Right Honourable Viscount Milner of St James's and Cape Town, KG, GCB, GCMG, 1854-1925 / [by] John Marlowe. London : Hamilton, 1976. xi, 394 p., [8] p. of plates : ports. ; 24 cm. Includes index. Bibliography: p. [377]-381. [DA566.9.M5M37 1976] 76-383431 ISBN 0-241-89433-6 : £9.50
1. Milner, Alfred Milner, 1st viscount, 1854-1925. 2. Statesmen—Great Britain—Biography.

Milner family.

MILNER, Edwin W., 929'.2'0973
1906-1969.
The autobiography of Edwin W. Milner, 1906-1969. Edited by Anita Cheek Milner. [La Mesa, Calif., 1973] 100 p. illus. 28 cm. Cover title. [CS71.M6576 1973] 73-83848
1. Milner family. 2. Milner, Edwin W., 1906 1969.

Milton, Billy.

MILTON, Billy. 791'.092'4 B
Milton's paradise mislaid / Billy Milton. London : Jupiter, 1976. vii, 218 p. : ill. ; 24 cm. Includes index. [PN2598.M56A35] 77-368057 ISBN 0-904041-67-0 : £3.75
1. Milton, Billy. 2. Entertainers—Great Britain—Biography. I. Title.

Milton, John,

MILTON, John, 1608-1674. 821'.4 B
Autobiography of John Milton; or, Milton's life in his own words. Edited by James J. G. Graham. London, Longmans, Green, 1872. [Folcroft, Pa.] Folcroft Library Editions, 1972. p. [PR3581 A2 1972] 72-7271 ISBN 0-8414-0287-6
I. Graham, James J. G., ed. **BIP**

Milton, John—Juvenile literature.

STROUSSE, Flora, 1897- 920
John Milton, clarion voice of freedom New York, Vanguard [c.1962] 283p. 21cm. 62-13343 3.50
1. Milton, John—Juvenile literature. I. Title.

Milton, John — Political and social views.

SENSABAUGH, George Frank, 928.2
1906-
That grand Whig, Milton. Stanford, Calif., Stanford University Press, 1952. ix, 213 p. 24 cm. (Stanford University publications. University series. Language and literature, v. 11) Bibliographical footnotes. [PR3592.P7S45] [AS36.L55] 52-5981
1. Milton, John — Political and social views. 2. Gt. Brit. — Pol. & govt. — 1603-1714. 3. Whig Party (Gt. Brit.) I. Title. II. Series: Stanford University. Stanford University publication. University series. Language and literature, v. 11 **BIP**

Milton, John, 1608-1674.

BAILEY, John Cann, 1864- 821'.4 B
1931.
Milton / John Bailey. Norwood, Pa. :

Norwood Editions, 1975. 256 p. ; 24 cm. Reprint of the 1945 ed. published by Oxford University Press, London, New York, as no. 103 of the Home university library of modern knowledge. Includes index. Bibliography: p. 250-253. [PR3581.B3 1975] 75-38789 ISBN 0-88305-916-9 lib. bdg. : 15.00
1. Milton, John, 1608-1674.

BRENNECKE, Ernest, 1896- 784'.1'00924 B
John Milton the elder and his music, by Ernest Brennecke, Jr. New York, Octagon Books, 1973 [c1938] xiii, 224 p. illus. 23 cm. Reprint of the ed. published by Columbia University Press, New York, in series: Columbia University studies in musicology, no. 2. Bibliography: p. 154-161. [ML410.M679B7 1973] 73-1770 ISBN 0-374-90980-6. 10.50
1. Milton, John, 1563 (ca.)-1647. 2. Milton, John, 1608-1674. I. Title. II. Series: Columbia University studies in musicology, no. 2. BIP

FLETCHER, Harris Francis, 1892- 928.2
The intellectual development of John Milton. Urbana, University of Illinois Press, 1956- v. illus. 27cm. Contents.v. 1. The institution to 1625: from the beginnings through grammar school. [PR3581.F5] 56-8058
1. Milton, John, 1608-1674. 2. Milton, John—Knowledge and learning. I. Title. BIP

FULLER, Edmund, 1914- 92
John Milton. New York, Seabury Press [1967] 242 p. 22 cm. A biography of the sixteenth-century English poet who refused to let blindness hinder his creative talent. [PR3581.F8 1967] AC 67
1. Milton, John, 1608-1674.

†HAYLEY, William, 1745-1820. 821'.4 B
The life of Milton, in three parts : to which are added conjectures on the origin of Paradise lost ; with an appendix / by William Hayley. Folcroft, Pa. : Folcroft Library Editions, 1976. xxiii, 328 p. ; 29 cm. Reprint of the 2d ed., enl., printed in 1796 for T. Cadell and W. Davies, London. "Appendix, containing extracts from the Adamo of Andreini, with an analysis of another Italian drama on the same subject": p. [281]-328. Includes bibliographical references. [PR3581.H3 1976] 76-26849 ISBN 0-8414-4739-X lib. bdg. : 40.00
1. Milton, John, 1608-1674. 2. Poets, English—Early modern, 1500-1700—Biography. I. Title.

HOOD, Edwin Paxton, 1820-1885. 821'.4 B
John Milton: the patriot and poet; illustrations of the model man. [Folcroft, Pa.] Folcroft Library Editions, 1970. 235 p. 22 cm. "Limited to 150 copies." Reprint of the 1852 ed. [PR3581.H6 1970] 72-190920
1. Milton, John, 1608-1674.

HUTCHINSON, Francis Ernest, 1871-1947. v. 12
Milton and the English mind. New York, Collier Books [1962] 156 p. 18 cm. (Men and history AS27OV) "This title first appeared as a volume in the Teach yourself history series under the general editorship of A. L. Rowse." 63-23806
1. Milton, John, 1608-1674. I. Title. BIP

IVIMEY, Joseph, 1773-1834. 821'.4
John Milton: his life and times, religious and political opinions: with an appendix, containing animadversions upon Dr. Johnson's Life of Milton, &c. &c. [Folcroft, Pa.] Folcroft Press, 1970. xvi, 397 p. port. 23 cm. Reprint of the 1833 ed. "An exact catalogue of all Milton's works": p. 345-347. [PR3581.I8 1970] 72-190658
1. Milton, John, 1608-1674. 2. Milton, John, 1608-1674—Religion and ethics. 3. Milton, John, 1608-1674—Political and social views. 4. Milton, John, 1608-1674—Contemporary England.

IVIMEY, Joseph, 1773-1834. 821'.4
John Milton, his life and times, religious and political opinions : with an appendix, containing animadversions upon Dr. Johnson's Life of Milton, &c. &c. / by Joseph Ivimey. Norwood, Pa. : Norwood Editions, 1974. xvi, 397 p., [1] leaf of plates : port. ; 23 cm. Reprint of the 1833 ed. published by E. Wilson, London. "An exact catalogue of all Milton's works": p. 345-347. [PR3581.I8 1974] 74-31400 ISBN 0-88305-851-0 lib. bdg. : 30.00
1. Milton, John, 1608-1674. 2. Milton, John, 1608-1674—Religion and ethics. 3. Milton, John, 1608-1674—Political and social views. 4. Milton, John, 1608-1674—Contemporary England.

IVIMEY, Joseph, 1773-1834. 821'.4
John Milton, his life and times, religious and political opinions : with an appendix, containing animadversions upon Dr. Johnson's Life of Milton, &c. &c. / by Joseph Ivimey. Norwood, Pa. : Norwood Editions, 1974 [i.e.,1975] xvi, 397 p., [1] leaf of plates : port. ; 23 cm. Reprint of the 1833 ed. published by E. Wilson, London. "An exact catalogue of all Milton's works": p. 345-347. [PR3581.I8 1974] 74-31400 ISBN 0-88305-851-0 lib. bdg. : 30.00
1. Milton, John, 1608-1674. 2. Milton, John, 1608-1674—Religion and ethics. 3. Milton, John, 1608-1674—Political and social views. 4. Milton, John, 1608-1674—Contemporary England.

LE COMTE, Edward Semple, 1916- 821'.4 B
Milton and sex / Edward Le Comte. New York : Columbia University Press, 1977. p. cm. Includes index. Bibliography: p. [PR3581.L37 1977] 77-1081 ISBN 0-231-04340-6 : 12.00
1. Milton, John, 1608-1674. 2. Poets, English—Early modern, 1500-1700—Biography. 3. Sex in literature. I. Title. BIP

LILJEGREN, Sten Bodvar, 1885- 942.06'2
Studies in Milton, by S. B. Liljegren. Folcroft, Pa., Folcroft Press [1969] xlii, 160 p. 26 cm. Reprint of the 1918 ed. Bibliography: p. [153]-158. [PR3588.L5 1969] 72-195245
1. Milton, John, 1608-1674. 2. Galilei, Galileo, 1564-1642. 3. Eikon basilike ([Eikon Vasilike (romanized form)]) 4. Eikon basilike ([Eikon Vasilike (romanized form)])—Bibliography. I. Title. BIP

MACAULAY, Rose, Dame. 821'.4 B
Milton [by] Rose Macaulay. New York, Haskell House Publishers, 1974. 141, [2] p. 21 cm. Reprint of the 1934 ed. published by Duckworth, London, which was issued as no. 26 of Great lives. Bibliography: p. [143] [PR3581.M17 1974] 74-7050 ISBN 0-8383-1911-4
1. Milton, John, 1608-1674. BIP

MILTON. v. 12
[2d ed., rev.] London, Duckworth; New York, Macmillan [1957] 141p. front. (Great lives)
1. Milton, John, 1608-1674. I. Macaulay, Dame Rose.

MILTON, John, 1608-1674. 821'.4 B
Autobiography of John Milton; or, Milton's life in his own words. Edited by James J. G. Graham. London, Longmans, Green, 1872. [Folcroft, Pa.] Folcroft Library Editions, 1972. p. [PR3581.A2 1972] 72-7271 ISBN 0-8414-0287-6
I. Graham, James J. G., ed. BIP

PARKER, William Riley, 1906-1968. 821'.4 B
Milton: a biography. Oxford, Clarendon P., 1968. 2 v. (xxi, 1489 p.) plates, facsim., 3 ports. (1 col.). 23 cm. Contents.Contents.—v. 1. The life.—v. 2. Commentary, notes, index, and finding list. Bibliography: p. 1205-1213. [PR3581.P27] 68-141367 £12/12/-
1. Milton, John, 1608-1674.

PATTISON, Mark, 1813-1884. 821'.4 B
Milton. New York, AMS Press [1968] vi, 220 p. 22 cm. (English men of letters) "Reprinted from the edition of 1887, London." [PR3581.P3 1968] 68-58393
1. Milton, John, 1608-1674. BIP

RACINE, Louis, 1692-1763. 821'.4
Life of Milton, together with observations on Paradise lost. Translated with an introd. by Katherine John. [Folcroft, Pa.] Folcroft Library Editions, 1973. 158 p. 23 cm. Reprint of the 1930 ed. published by L. and V. Woolf, London. [PR3581.R2513 1973] 73-16189 ISBN 0-8414-7258-0 (lib. bdg.)
1. Milton, John, 1608-1674. 2. Milton, John, 1608-1674. Paradise lost. I. Title.

SAILLENS, Emile. 821.4
John Milton: man, poet, polemist. New York, Barnes & Noble, 1964. xxii, 371 p. illus., maps (on lining papers) ports. 23 cm. Translation of John Milton, poete combattant. Bibliography: p. 355-366. [PR3581.S313] 64-7267
1. Milton, John, 1608-1674. I. Title.

TRENT, William Peterfield, 1862-1939. 821'.4
John Milton; a short study of his life and works. [Folcroft, Pa.] Folcroft Press, 1970. xii, 285 p. 24 cm. 150 copies printed. Reprint of the 1899 ed. [PR3581.T7 1970] 72-187004
1. Milton, John, 1608-1674. BIP

TRENT, William Peterfield, 1862-1939. 821'.4
John Milton; a short study of his life and works. New York, Macmillan, 1899. [New York, AMS Press, 1973] xii, 285 p. 19 cm. [PR3581.T7 1973] 71-177572 ISBN 0-404-06523-6 13.50
1. Milton, John, 1608-1674.

TRENT, William Peterfield, 1862-1939. 821'.4
John Milton : a short study of his life and works / by William P. Trent. Norwood, Pa. : Norwood Editions, 1975. xii, 285 p. ; 23 cm. Reprint of the 1899 ed. published by Macmillan, New York. Includes index. [PR3581.T7 1975] 75-35957 ISBN 0-88305-667-4 : 20.00
1. Milton, John, 1608-1674.

WAGENKNECHT, Edward Charles, 1900- 821'.4
The personality of Milton [by] Edward Wagenknecht. Norman, University of Oklahoma Press [1970] xiii, 170 p. 24 cm. Includes bibliographical references. [PR3581.W29] 71-108807 5.00
1. Milton, John, 1608-1674. I. Title. BIP

WARNER, Rex, 1905- 928.2
John Milton. New York, Chanticleer Press [1950] 95 p. illus., ports. 19 cm. (Personal portraits) [PR3581.W35] 50-7115
1. Milton, John, 1608-1674. I. Title. II. Series.

WARNER, Rex, 1905- 821'.4 B
John Milton. [Folcroft, Pa.] Folcroft Library Editions, 1973. p. Reprint of the 1949 ed. published by Parrish, London, issued in series: Personal portraits. [PR3581.W35 1973] 73-12371 12.50
1. Milton, John, 1608-1674. I. Series: Personal portraits. BIP

WARNER, Rex, 1905- 821'.4 B
John Milton. [Folcroft, Pa.] Folcroft Library Editions, 1974. 95 p. illus. 24 cm. Reprint of the 1949 ed. published by Parrish, London, issued in series: Personal portraits. [PR3581.W35 1974] 73-12371 ISBN 0-8414-9389-8 (lib. bdg.)
1. Milton, John, 1608-1674. I. Series: Personal portraits.

WARNER, Rex, 1905- 821'.4 B
John Milton / Rex Warner. New York : Haskell House, [1976] p. cm. Reprint of the 1949 ed. published by Parrish, London, in series: Personal portraits. [PR3581.W35 1976] 75-30812 ISBN 0-8383-2097-X pbk. : 9.95
1. Milton, John, 1608-1674. I. Series: Personal portraits.

WILLIAMSON, George Charles, 1858-1942. 821'.4 B
Milton. [Folcroft, Pa.] Folcroft Press [1969] 113 p. illus. 20 cm. Reprint of the 1905 ed., issued in series: Bell's miniature series of great writers. Bibliography: p. 106-108. [PR3581.W45 1969] 72-194902
1. Milton, John, 1608-1674. I. Series: Bell's miniature series of great writers. BIP

Milton, John, 1608-1674—Biography.

BERRY, William Grinton, 1873-1926. 821'.4 B
John Milton. [Folcroft, Pa.] Folcroft Library Editions, 1973. xi, 150 p. illus. 22 cm. Reprint of the 1909 ed. published by Jarrold, London, which was issued as no. 2 of the Men of fame series. [PR3581.B44 1973] 73-10007 17.50
1. Milton, John, 1608-1674—Biography.

BROWN, Eleanor Gertrude, 1888-1964. 821'.4 B
Milton's blindness / by Eleanor Gertrude Brown. Darby, Pa. : Arden Library, 1978 [c1934] 167 p. ; 26 cm. Reprint of the ed. published by Columbia University Press, New York. Includes index. Bibliography: p. [147]-159. [PR3582.B7 1978] 78-18890 ISBN 0-8495-0413-9 lib. bdg. : 25.00
1. Milton, John, 1608-1674—Biography. 2. Poets, English—Early modern, 1500-1700—Biography. 3. Blindness. I. Title. BIP

CARPENTER, William, 1797-1874. 821'.4
The life and times of John Milton / by William Carpenter. Folcroft, Pa. : Folcroft Library Editions, 1976. p. cm. Reprint of the 1836 ed. published by Wakelin, London. Includes bibliographical references. [PR3581.C34 1976] 76-28954 ISBN 0-8414-3485-9 lib. bdg. : 20.00
1. Milton, John, 1608-1674—Biography. 2. Authors, English—Early modern, 1500-1700—Biography. I. Title.

COOKE, John, M.A. 821'.4 B
John Milton, 1608-1674. [Folcroft, Pa.] Folcroft Library Editions, 1974. p. cm. "A lecture, delivered in the Parochial Hall, St. Bartholomew's, Dublin, on the occasion of Milton's Tercentenary, December 9, 1908." Reprint of the ed. published by Hodges, Figgis, Dublin. [PR3581.C6 1974] 74-5138 ISBN 0-8414-3549-9 (lib. bdg.)
1. Milton, John, 1608-1674—Biography.

DARBISHIRE, Helen, 1881-1961, ed. 828.409
The early lives of Milton. New York, Barnes andNoble [1965] ixi, 353p. illus., facsims., port. 23cm. [PR3579.D3] 66-193 8.00 bds.,
1. Milton, John, 1608-1674—Biog. I. Title.

DARBISHIRE, Helen, 1881-1961, ed. 821'.4 B
The early lives of Milton, edited with introd. and notes by Helen Darbishire. London, Constable, 1932. St. Clair Shores, Mich., Scholarly Press, 1972. p. The anonymous life, printed from Bodleian MS. Wood D. 4, is ascribed by the editor to John Phillips. Contents.Contents.—Aubrey, J. Mr. John Milton: minutes, 1681.—Phillips, J. The life of Mr. John Milton.—Wood, A. a. John Milton, master of arts: from Fasti oxonienses, 1691.—Phillips, E. The life of Mr. John Milton, 1694.—Toland, J. The life of John Milton, 1698. Richardson, J. The life of Milton, and a discourse on Paradise lost, 1734. [PR3579.D3 1972] 77-144966
1. Milton, John, 1608-1674—Biography. I. Title. BIP

EDMONDS, Cyrus R. 821'.4 B
John Milton : a biography, especially designed to exhibit the ecclesiastical principles of that illustrious man / by Cyrus R. Edmonds. Norwood, Pa. : Norwood Editions, 1976. viii, 251 p. : port. ; 23 cm. Reprint of the 1851 ed. published by A. Cockshaw, London. Includes bibliographical references. [PR3581.E3 1976] 76-2637 ISBN 0-88305-527-9 : 15.00
1. Milton, John, 1608-1674—Biography.

FRENCH, Joseph Milton, 1895- 821'.4 B
Milton in chancery : new chapters in the lives of the poet and his father / by J. Milton French. Millwood, N.Y. : Kraus Reprint Co., 1975, c1939. x, 428 p., [10] leaves of plates : ill. ; 24 cm. Reprint of the ed. published by Modern Language Association of America, New York, which was issued as its Monograph series, 10. Includes index. Bibliography: p. 209-212. [PR3583.F7 1975] 74-20581 ISBN 0-527-31550-8 : 29.00
1. Milton, John, 1608-1674—Biography. 2. Milton, John, 1608-1674—Knowledge—Law. 3. Milton, John, 1563 (ca.)-1647. I. Title. II. Series: Modern Language Association of America. Monograph series ; 10. BIP

GARNETT, Richard, 1835-1906. 821'.4
Life of John Milton. New York, AMS Press [1970] 205, xxxix p. 22 cm. Reprint of the 1890 ed. "Bibliography by John P.

Anderson": p. [i]-xxxix. [PR3581.G3 1970] 77-112638 ISBN 0-404-02686-9
1. Milton, John, 1608-1674—Biography.

GARNETT, Richard, 1835-1906. 821'.4 B
Life of John Milton. [Folcroft, Pa.] Folcroft Library Editions, 1973. p. Reprint of the 1890 ed. published by W. Scott, London, in series: Great writers. Bibliography, by John P. Anderson: p. [PR3581.G3 1973] 73-12143 9.75
1. Milton, John, 1608-1674—Biography. BIP

GARNETT, Richard, 1835-1906. 821'.4 B
Life of John Milton. [Folcroft, Pa.] Folcroft Library Editions, 1973. p. Reprint of the 1890 ed. published by W. Scott, London, in series: Great writers. Bibliography, by John P. Anderson: p. [PR3581.G3 1973] 73-12143 ISBN 0-8414-4402-1 (lib. bdg.)
1. Milton, John, 1608-1674—Biography. BIP

HAMILTON, John Arthur, 1845- 821'.4 B
The life of John Milton, Englishman, partly in his own words. [Folcroft, Pa.] Folcroft Library Editions, 1974. 72 p. illus. 23 cm. Reprint of the ed. published by the Congregational Union of England & Wales, London. [PR3581.H23 1974] 74-16133 ISBN 0-8414-4874-4 (lib. bdg.)
1. Milton, John, 1608-1674—Biography.

HAYLEY, William, 1745-1820. 821'.4 B
The life of Milton. [2d ed.] New York, Garland Pub., 1971. xxiii, 328 p. 26 cm. "Facsimile ... made from a copy in the Yale University Library [originally published in 1796]" Original t.p. reads: The life of Milton, in three parts. To which are added, conjectures on the origin of Paradise lost: with an appendix. By William Hayley, Esq. London: Printed for T. Cadell, Junior, and W. Davies, (successors to Mr. Cadell) in the Strand, MDCCXCVI. "Appendix, containing extracts from the Adamo of Andreini: with an analysis of another Italian drama on the same subject": p. [281]-328. [PR3581.H3 1796a] 79-112144
1. Milton, John, 1608-1674—Biography. 2. Milton, John, 1608-1674. Paradise lost. I. Andreini, Giovanni Battista, b. 1578. II. Title. BIP

LAWSON, McEwan. 821'.4 B
Master John Milton of the citie of London. [Folcroft, Pa.] Folcroft Library Editions, 1972. 46 p. port. 24 cm. Reprint of the 1923 ed. [PR3581.L29 1972] 72-10632 6.50
1. Milton, John, 1608-1674—Biography. I. Title. BIP

MARTYN, Carlos, 1841-1917. 821'.4 B
Life and times of John Milton / by W. Carlos Martyn. Folcroft, Pa. : Folcroft Library Editions, 1976. p. cm. Reprint of the 1866 ed. published by the American Tract Society, New York. Includes bibliographical references. [PR3581.M27 1976] 76-39970 ISBN 0-8414-6009-4 lib. bdg. : 30.00
1. Milton, John, 1608-1674—Biography. 2. Milton, John, 1608-1674—Contemporary England. 3. Poets, English—Early modern, 1500-1700—Biography. 4. Great Britain—History—Stuarts, 1603-1714. I. Title. BIP

RAYMOND, Dora (Neill) 1889-1961. 821'.4 B
Oliver's secretary; John Milton in an era of revolt. New York, Minton, Balch, 1932. [New York, AMS Press, 1973] xiv, 341 p. illus. 23 cm. Includes bibliographical references. [PR3581.R35 1973] 71-174302 ISBN 0-404-05229-0 14.50
1. Milton, John, 1608-1674—Biography. I. Title.

†TODD, Henry John, 1763-1845. 821'.4
Some account of the life and writings of John Milton : derived principally from documents in His Majesty's State-Paper Office, now first published / by H. J. Todd. Folcroft, Pa. : Folcroft Library Editions, 1977. vi, 370 lxvii, p., [1] leaf of plates : facsim. ; 26 cm. Reprint of the 1826 ed. printed for C. and J. Rivington, and others, London. Includes bibliographical references. [PR3581.T6 1977] 77-22935 ISBN 0-8414-8637-9 lib. bdg. : 50.00
1. Milton, John, 1608-1674—Biography. 2. Poets, English—Early modern, 1500-1700—Biography. I. Title.

Milton, John, 1608-1674—Juvenile literature.

FULLER, Edmund, 1914- 821.4 B
John Milton. New York, Seabury Press [1967] 242 p. 22 cm. [PR3581.F8 1967] 67-14496
1. Milton, John, 1608-1674—Juvenile literature.

Milton, John, 1608-1674—Knowledge—Law.

FRENCH, Joseph Milton, 1895- 821'.4 B
Milton in chancery : new chapters in the lives of the poet and his father / by J. Milton French. Millwood, N.Y. : Kraus Reprint Co., 1975, c1939. x, 428 p., [10] leaves of plates : ill. ; 24 cm. Reprint of the ed. published by Modern Language Association of America, New York, which was issued as its Monograph series, 10. Includes index. Bibliography: p. 209-212. [PR3583.F7 1975] 74-20581 ISBN 0-527-31550-8 : 29.00
1. Milton, John, 1608-1674—Biography. 2. Milton, John, 1608-1674—Knowledge—Law. 3. Milton, John, 1563 (ca.)-1647. I. Title. II. Series: Modern Language Association of America. Monograph series ; 10. BIP

Milton, John, 1608-1674—Political and social views.

IVIMEY, Joseph, 1773-1834. 821'.4
John Milton: his life and times, religious and political opinions: with an appendix, containing animadversions upon Dr. Johnson's Life of Milton, &c. &c. [Folcroft, Pa.] Folcroft Press, 1970. xvi, 397 p. port. 23 cm. Reprint of the 1833 ed. "An exact catalogue of all Milton's works": p. 345-347. [PR3581.I8 1970] 72-190658
1. Milton, John, 1608-1674. 2. Milton, John, 1608-1674—Religion and ethics. 3. Milton, John, 1608-1674—Political and social views. 4. Milton, John, 1608-1674—Contemporary England.

IVIMEY, Joseph, 1773-1834. 821'.4
John Milton, his life and times, religious and political opinions : with an appendix, containing animadversions upon Dr. Johnson's Life of Milton, &c. &c. / by Joseph Ivimey. Norwood, Pa. : Norwood Editions, 1974. xvi, 397 p., [1] leaf of plates : port. ; 23 cm. Reprint of the 1833 ed. published by E. Wilson, London. "An exact catalogue of all Milton's works": p. 345-347. [PR3581.I8 1974] 74-31400 ISBN 0-88305-851-0 lib. bdg. : 30.00
1. Milton, John, 1608-1674. 2. Milton, John, 1608-1674—Religion and ethics. 3. Milton, John, 1608-1674—Political and social views. 4. Milton, John, 1608-1674—Contemporary England.

IVIMEY, Joseph, 1773-1834. 821'.4
John Milton, his life and times, religious and political opinions : with an appendix, containing animadversions upon Dr. Johnson's Life of Milton, &c. &c. / by Joseph Ivimey. Norwood, Pa. : Norwood Editions, 1974 [i.e.,1975] xvi, 397 p., [1] leaf of plates : port. ; 23 cm. Reprint of the 1833 ed. published by E. Wilson, London. "An exact catalogue of all Milton's works": p. 345-347. [PR3581.I8 1974] 74-31400 ISBN 0-88305-851-0 lib. bdg. : 30.00
1. Milton, John, 1608-1674. 2. Milton, John, 1608-1674—Religion and ethics. 3. Milton, John, 1608-1674—Political and social views. 4. Milton, John, 1608-1674—Contemporary England.

Milton, John, 1608-1674—Religion and ethics.

IVIMEY, Joseph, 1773-1834. 821'.4
John Milton: his life and times, religious and political opinions: with an appendix, containing animadversions upon Dr. Johnson's Life of Milton, &c. &c. [Folcroft, Pa.] Folcroft Press, 1970. xvi, 397 p. port. 23 cm. Reprint of the 1833 ed. "An exact catalogue of all Milton's works": p. 345-347. [PR3581.I8 1970] 72-190658
1. Milton, John, 1608-1674. 2. Milton, John, 1608-1674—Religion and ethics. 3. Milton, John, 1608-1674—Political and social views. 4. Milton, John, 1608-1674—Contemporary England.

IVIMEY, Joseph, 1773-1834. 821'.4
John Milton, his life and times, religious and political opinions : with an appendix, containing animadversions upon Dr. Johnson's Life of Milton, &c. &c. / by Joseph Ivimey. Norwood, Pa. : Norwood Editions, 1974. xvi, 397 p., [1] leaf of plates : port. ; 23 cm. Reprint of the 1833 ed. published by E. Wilson, London. "An exact catalogue of all Milton's works": p. 345-347. [PR3581.I8 1974] 74-31400 ISBN 0-88305-851-0 lib. bdg. : 30.00
1. Milton, John, 1608-1674. 2. Milton, John, 1608-1674—Religion and ethics. 3. Milton, John, 1608-1674—Political and social views. 4. Milton, John, 1608-1674—Contemporary England.

IVIMEY, Joseph, 1773-1834. 821'.4
John Milton, his life and times, religious and political opinions : with an appendix, containing animadversions upon Dr. Johnson's Life of Milton, &c. &c. / by Joseph Ivimey. Norwood, Pa. : Norwood Editions, 1974 [i.e.,1975] xvi, 397 p., [1] leaf of plates : port. ; 23 cm. Reprint of the 1833 ed. published by E. Wilson, London. "An exact catalogue of all Milton's works": p. 345-347. [PR3581.I8 1974] 74-31400 ISBN 0-88305-851-0 lib. bdg. : 30.00
1. Milton, John, 1608-1674. 2. Milton, John, 1608-1674—Religion and ethics. 3. Milton, John, 1608-1674—Political and social views. 4. Milton, John, 1608-1674—Contemporary England.

Milwaukee Bucks (Basketball team)

DOUCETTE, Eddie. 796.32'364'0977595
The Milwaukee Bucks and the remarkable Abdul-Jabbar / by Eddie Doucette ; photography by Malcolm Emmons. Englewood Cliffs, N.J. : Prentice-Hall, [1974] 127 p. : ill. ; 28 cm. (Reward books) "A Stuart L. Daniels book." Presents a brief history of the Milwaukee Bucks basketball team with short biographies of the team members and special focus on Kareem Abdul Jabbar. [GV885.52.M54D68] 920 74-9352 ISBN 0-13-583237-3 pbk. : 3.95
1. Milwaukee Bucks (Basketball team) 2. Abdul-Jabbar, Kareem, 1947- 3. Basketball. 4. Basketball—Biography. I. Title.

Minakshisundaram Pillai, 1815-1876—Biography.

GURUSWAMY, Sridharam K., 1906- 894'.811'13 B
A poet's poet : life of Maha Vidwan Sri Meenakshisundaram Pillai, based on the biography in Tamil by Mahamahopadhyaya Dr. U. V. Swaminathaiyer / [Sridharam K. Guruswamy]. 1st ed. Madras : Mahamahopadhyaya Dr. U. V. Swaminatha Iyer Library, 1976. v, 129 p., [2] leaves of plates: ill. ; 22 cm. [PL4758.9.M45Z68] 76-905180 Rs6.00
1. Minakshisundaram Pillai, 1815-1876—Biography. 2. Poets, Tamil—19th century—Biography. I. Swaminathaiyar, Uttamadanapuram Venkata Subba Ayyar, 1855-1942. Tiruvavatuturai yatinattu makavittuvan Tiricirapuram Sri Minatciuntaram Pillaiyavarkal carittirac curukkam. II. Title.

Mindszenty, Jozsef, Cardinal, 1892—

VECSEY, Josef. 262'.135'0924 B
Mindszenty the man, by Joseph Vecsey, as told to Phyllis Schlafly. St. Louis, Cardinal Mindszenty Foundation [1972] 241 p. illus. 21 cm. Bibliography: p. 231-235. [BX4705.M5565V4] 72-93906 2.00
1. Mindszenty, Jozsef, Cardinal, 1892- I. Schlafly, Phyllis. II. Title. BIP

Miner, Myrtilla, 1815-1864.

O'CONNOR, Ellen M. 370'.9753
Myrtilla Miner; a memoir [by Ellen M. O'Connor] Boston, Houghton, Mifflin, 1885. Miami, Fla., Mnemosyne Pub. Co. [1969] 129 p. 23 cm. [LC2853.W45O25] 79-89384
1. Miner, Myrtilla, 1815-1864. BIP

O'CONNOR, Ellen M. 376'.9'24 B
Myrtilla Miner; a memoir [by] Ellen M. O'Connor. The School for Colored Girls; [an address by] Myrtilla Miner. New York, Arno Press, 1969. xx, 129, 12 p. port. 21 cm. (The American Negro, his history and literature) Reprint of two works originally issued separately in 1885 and 1854, respectively with new prefatory matter added. [LC2853.W45O25 1969b] 73-92235
1. Miner, Myrtilla, 1815-1864. 2. Miner Teachers College, Washington, D.C.—History. I. Miner, Myrtilla, 1815-1864. The School for Colored Girls. 1969. II. Title. III. Title: The School for Colored Girls. IV. Series.

Mines and mineral resources—The West

ALBERT, Herman W 917.8'03'30924
Odyssey of a desert prospector, by Herman W. Albert. [1st ed.] University of Oklahoma Press [1967] ix, 260 pl 20 cm. (The Western frontier library) [F595.A5] 67-15590
1. Mines and mineral resources—The West 2. Frontier and pioneer life—The West. I. Title. BIP

Miniature painters, British—Biography—Dictionaries.

FOSKETT, Daphne. 759.2
A dictionary of British miniature painters. New York, Praeger Publishers [1972] 2 v. 1069 illus. (100 col.) 29 cm. Vol. 2 consists of the monochrome illus. Bibliography: v. 1, p. 592-596. [ND1337.G7F463 1972] 72-112634 135.00
1. Miniature painters, British—Biography—Dictionaries. 2. Miniature painting, British. I. Title. II. Title: British miniature painters. BIP

FOSKETT, Daphne. 759.2
A dictionary of British miniature painters. London, Faber and Faber, 1972. 2 v. (3-596 p., 31 leaves; 3-108, [1], 400 p.) ports. (some col.) 29 cm. Bibliography: v. 1, p. 592-596. [ND1337.G7F463 1972b] 72-193605 ISBN 0-571-08295-5
1. Miniature painters, British—Biography—Dictionaries. 2. Miniature painting, British. I. Title. II. Title: British miniature painters Available from Praeger, 135.00.

Minnehaha County, S.D.—Genealogy.

PIONEER history : 978.3'371 B
Minnehaha County's Norwegian pioneers : history from the year 1866 to 1896 / gathered and published by Minnehaha County's Norwegian Pioneer Organization ; editors, Iver I. Oien ... [et al.] ; translated and reprinted 1976 by Emily Brende Sittig and Clara Brende Christenson. [Sious Falls, S.D.] : Sittig, 1976. viii, 595 p. : illus. ; 24 cm. Translation of Norske pionerers historie of Minnehaha County, Syd Dakota, fra 1866 til 1896. Cover title: Norwegian pioneers history of Minnehaha County, South Dakota. On spine: Minnehaha Norwegian pioneers history. "Originally published by Historical Organization's publication, Sioux Falls, South Dakota, 1928. Fremad weekly by Mr. Strass, publisher." Includes index. [F657.M6P56] 76-11048
1. Minnehaha County, S.D.—Genealogy. 2. Norwegian Americans—South Dakota—Minnehaha County—Genealogy. 3. Minnehaha County, S.D.—Biography. 4. Norwegian Americans—South Dakota—Minnehaha County—Biography. I. Oien, Iver I. II. Norwegian Pioneer Organization. III. Title: Norwegian pioneers history of Minnehaha County, South Dakota. IV. Title: Minnehaha Norwegian pioneers history.

Minnelli, Liza.

PARISH, James Robert. 791'.092'4 B
Liza! : An unauthorized biography / by James Robert Parish with Jack Ano. New York : Pocket Books, 1975. 176 p., [16] leaves of plates : ill. ; 18 cm. [PN2287.M644P3] 75-316177 ISBN 0-671-78946-5 : 1.50
1. Minnelli, Liza. I. Ano, Jack, joint author. II. Title.

Minnelli, Liza—Juvenile literature.

PAIGE, David. 790.2'092'4 B
Liza Minnelli / written by David Paige ; designed by Gene Kohler. [Mankato, Minn.] : Creative Education, [c1977] 31 p. : ill. ; 25 cm. (Stars of stage and screen) A biography of the young entertainer who, before the age of thirty, won an Academy Award and, at nineteen, was the youngest person ever to win the Tony Award. [PN2287.M644P28] 92 76-28385 ISBN 0-87191-558-8 lib.bdg. 4.95
1. Minnelli, Liza—Juvenile literature. 2. Entertainers—United States—Biography—Juvenile literature. I. Title. BIP

Minnelli, Vincente.

MINNELLI, Vincente. 791.43'0233'0924 B
I remember it well [by] Vincente Minnelli with Hector Arce. Foreword by Alan Jay Lerner. [1st ed.] Garden City, N.Y., Doubleday, 1974. xiv, 391 p. illus. 25 cm. Filmography: p. 381-382. [PN1998.A3M467 1974] 73-14052 ISBN 0-385-09522-8 10.95
1. Minnelli, Vincente. I. Arce, Hector. II. Title. BIP

Minnesota—Biography.

KENNEDY, Roger G. 917.76'03'0922
Men on the moving frontier, by Roger G. Kennedy. Palo Alto, Calif., American West Pub. Co. [1969] 199 p. illus., facsims., maps, ports. 25 cm. Contents.Contents.—Character and circumstance.—Giacomo Constantino Beltrami; Stephen Harriman Long.—Henry Hastings Sibley; Alexander Ramsey.—Harvey Ellis; Daniel H. Burnham.—Ignatius Donnelly; Frank Billings Kellogg.—F. Scott Fitzgerald; William Gray Purcell.—Bibliographic notes (p. 190-193) [F605.K4] 78-88203 5.95
1. Minnesota—Biography. 2. Middle West—Biography. I. Title.

Minor, Robert, 1884-1952.

NORTH, Joseph 923.373
Robert Minor, Artist and crusader; an informal biography. New York, International Publishers [1956] 284p. illus. 21cm. [HX84.M5N6] 56-420
1. Minor, Robert, 1884-1952. I. Title.

Minorities—United States.

THE Emerging minorities in America; 016.30145'0973 a resource guide for teachers. Contributions of significance which members of minority groups have made to the historical and cultural development of the United States of America. Santa Barbara, Calif., ABC-Clio [Press, 1972] xix, 256 p. 27 cm. Prepared for Santa Barbara County Board of Education. Includes bibliographies. [E184.A1E55 1972] 72-77550 ISBN 0-87436-092-7
1. Minorities—United States. 2. United States—Biography. I. Santa Barbara Co., Calif. Board of Education.

Minorities—United States—Biography—Juvenile literature.

TALES of the elders : 301.32'9'73 a memory book of men and women who came to America as immigrants, 1900-1930 / written and photographed by Carol Ann Bales. Chicago : Follett, c1977. 160 p. : ports. ; 23 cm. Bibliography: p. 159-160. The recollections of twelve people who immigrated to the United States during the period of the Great Migration between 1900 and 1930. [E184.A1T34] 920 76-19886 ISBN 0-695-80671-8 : 6.95. ISBN 0-695-40671-X lib.bdg. : 6.95
1. Minorities—United States—Biography—Juvenile literature. 2. United States—Emigration and immigration—Juvenile literature. 3. Assimilation (Sociology)—Juvenile literature. 4. United States—Biography—Juvenile literature.

Minot, George Richards, 1885-1950.

RACKEMANN, Francis Minot, 1887- 926.1
The inquisitive physician: the life and times of George Richards Minot, A. B., M. D., D. SC. Cambridge, Harvard University Press, 1956. 288 p. illus. 25 cm. [R154.M645R3] 56-6521
1. Minot, George Richards, 1885-1950. I. Title.

RACKEMANN, Francis Minot, 1887- 926.1
The inquisitive physician: the life and times of George Richards Minot, A. B., M. D., D. sC. Cambridge, Harvard University Press, 1956. 288p. illus. 25cm. [R154.M645R3] 56-6521
1. Minot, George Richards, 1885-1950. I. Title.

Minto, Gilbert John Elliot-Murray-Kynynmound, 4th earl of, 1845-1914.

WASTI, Syed Razi. 954.03'5'0924
Lord Minto and the Indian nationalist movement, 1905 to 1910 / by Syed Razi Wasti. 1st Pakistan ed. Lahore : People's Pub. House, 1976. viii, 254 p., [1] leaf of plate : port. ; 22 cm. A revision of the author's thesis, University of London, 1962. Reprint of the 1964 ed., published by Clarendon Press, Oxford. Includes index. Bibliography: p. [238]-247. [DS480.2.W37 1976] 76-938781 Rs52.00
1. Minto, Gilbert John Elliot-Murray-Kynynmound, 4th earl of, 1845-1914. 2. India—History—20th century. 3. Nationalism—India. 4. Statesmen—India—Biography. I. Title.

Mira de Amescua, Antonio, fl. 1600.

CASTANEDA, James A. 862'.3 B
Mira de Amescua / by James A. Castaneda. Boston : Twayne Publishers, c1977. 217 p. ; 21 cm. (Twayne's world authors series ; TWAS 449 : Spain) Includes index. Bibliography: p. 195-205. [PQ6413.M7Z59] 77-1956 ISBN 0-8057-6285-X lib.bdg. : 9.50
1. Mira de Amescua, Antonio, fl. 1600. 2. Dramatists, Spanish—17th century—Biography. BIP

Mirabeau, Honore Gabriel Riquetti, comte de, 1749-1791.

BARTHOU, Louis, 1862-1934. 944.04'1'0924 B
Mirabeau; from the French of Louis Barthou. Freeport, N.Y., Books for Libraries Press [1972] vii, 351 p. illus. 22 cm. Reprint of the 1913 ed. [DC146.M7B213 1972] 72-7091 ISBN 0-8369-6923-5
1. Mirabeau, Honore Gabriel Riquetti, comte de, 1749-1791. BIP

VALLENTIN, Antonina, 1893-1957. 944.04'1'0924 B
Mirabeau. Translated by E. W. Dickes. Clifton [N.J.] A. M. Kelley, 1973 [c1948] vi, 542 p. illus. 22 cm. (Viking reprint editions) A translation of the author's works: Mirabeau avant la Revolution and Mirabeau dans la Revolution. Reprint of the ed. published by Viking Press, New York. Bibliography: p. 529-532. [DC146.M7V2715 1973] 70-122070 ISBN 0-678-03173-8 16.50
1. Mirabeau, Honore Gabriel Riquetti, comte de, 1749-1791. I. Title.

WELCH, Oliver John Grindon. 944.04'1'0924 B
Mirabeau; a study of a democratic monarchist, by Oliver J. G. Welch. Port Washington, N.Y., Kennikat Press [1968, c1951] 355 p. facsims., ports. 21 cm. Bibliographical references included in "Notes" (p. 341-346) [DC146.M7W4 1968] 67-27662
1. Mirabeau, Honore Gabriel Riquetti, comte de, 1749-1791.

WILLERT, Paul Ferdinand, 1844-1912. 944.04'1'0924
Mirabeau. Port Washington, N.Y., Kennikat Press [1970] xi, 230 p. 21 cm. Reprint of the 1898 ed. [DC146.M7W7 1970] 74-112822
1. Mirabeau, Honore Gabriel Riquetti, comte de, 1749-1791. BIP

Miracles.

SANFORD, Agnes Mary (White) 221
The healing power of the Bible [by] Agnes Sanford. [1st ed.] Philadelphia, Lippincott [1970, c1969] 221 p. 21 cm. [BS571.S25] 75-88737 4.95
1. Bible. O.T.—Biography. 2. Miracles. I. Title. BIP

Mirambo, d. 1884.

UNOMAH, A. C. 967'.828'010924 B
Mirambo of Tanzania / [by] A. C. Unomah. London : Heinemann Educational, 1977. 47 p. : ill., maps, ports. ; 15 x 21 cm. (African historical biographies ; 12) [DT447.2.M57U55] 78-301574 ISBN 0-435-94374-X : pbk : 1.50
1. Mirambo, d. 1884. 2. Tanganyika—History. 3. Nyamwezi—Kings and rulers—Biography. 4. Tanganyika—Biography. I. Title. II. Series. Distributed by Heinemann Educational, Salem, NH BIP

Miranda, Francisco de, 1750-1816.

SHERIDAN, Philip John. 923.58
Francisco de Miranda: forerunner of Spanish-American independence. San Antonio, Naylor Co. [1960] 83 p. illus. 22 cm. Includes bibliography. [F2323.M715] 59-14817
1. Miranda, Francisco de, 1750-1816.

THORNING, Joseph Francis, 1896- 923.58
Miranda: world citizen. Introd. by Galo Plaza, foreword by Sumner Welles. Gainesville, University of Florida Press, 1952. xxii, 324 p. illus., ports. 24 cm. Full name: Joseph Francis Xavier Thorning. "Bibliographical essay": p. [313]-316. [F2323.M725] 52-10002
1. Miranda, Francisco de, 1750-1816. I. Title. BIP

Miriam Teresa, Sister, 1901-1927.

MAYNARD, Theodore, 1890- 922.273
The better part; the life of Teresa Demjanovich. New York, Macmillan, 1952. 276p. illus. 21cm. [BX4705.M57M35] 53-177
1. Miriam Teresa, Sister, 1901-1927. I. Title.

Miro, Joan, 1893—

DUPIN, Jacques. 759.6
Miro. [Translated from the French by Norbert Guterman] New York, H. N. Abrams [1961 or 2] 596 p. illus. (part mounted, part col.) ports. 31 cm. Bibliography: p. 577-591. [ND813.M5D83] 62-19132
1. Miro, Joan, 1893-

PENROSE, Roland, Sir. 759.6
Miro [by] Roland Penrose. New York, H. N. Abrams [1970?] 215 p. illus. (part col.) 22 cm. Bibliography: p. 205-206. [ND813.M5P4 1970b] 69-17033 ISBN 0-8109-0304-0
1. Miro, Joan, 1893-

Mironov, Filipp Kuz'mich, 1872-1921.

STARIKOV, Sergei. 947.084'1'0924 B
Philip Mironov and the Russian Civil War / Sergei Starikov & Roy Medvedev ; translated by Guy Daniels. 1st ed. New York : Knopf, 1978. p. cm. Includes bibliographical references and index. [DK254.M56S7213 1978] 77-20353 ISBN 0-394-40681-8 : 17.95
1. Mironov, Filipp Kuz'mich, 1872-1921. 2. Russia (1917- R.S.F.S.R.). Armiia—Biography. 3. Revolutionists—Russia—Biography. 4. Soldiers—Russia—Biography. I. Medvedev, Roi Aleksandrovich, joint author. II. Title. BIP

Misconduct in office—United States.

CAINE, James R. 345'.73'0232
Attorney in public office: his crimes, his accomplices, how he eludes prosecution; biography and commentary by James R. Caine. Rev. Akron, Ohio [1970] xii, 101 p. 22 cm. (His The criminal in public office, v. 1, pt. 1) Includes bibliographical references. [KF9409.Z9C3 1970] 73-157173
1. Misconduct in office—United States. 2. Government attorneys—United States. I. Title.

Misheiker, Betty.

MISHEIKER, Betty. 818.5
Wings on her petticoat. New York, Morrow, 1953 [c1952] 224p. 21cm. Autobiographical. First published in London in 1952 under title: Strange odyssey. [CT1968.M5A3 1953] 53-9230
I. Title.

Mishima, Yukio, pseud.

NATHAN, John, 1940- 895.6'3'5 B
Mishima: a biography. [1st ed.] Boston, Little, Brown [1974] xx, 300 p. illus. 22 cm. "The major plays and novels of Yukio Mishima": p. [283]-286. [PL833.I7Z6984] 74-12184 ISBN 0-316-59844-5 8.95
1. Mishima, Yukio, pseud.

SCOTT-STOKES, Henry, 1938- 895.6'3'5 B
The life and death of Yukio Mishima. New York, Farrar, Straus and Giroux [1974] 344 p. illus. 24 cm. Bibliography: p. 333-336. [PL833.I7Z874] 74-4192 ISBN 0-374-18620-0 10.00
1. Mishima, Yukio, pseud. I. Title. BIP

Missionaries.

BACH, Thomas John 922
Vision and valor: missionary biographies from St. Paul to Malla Moe. Illus. by Warner Sallman. Grand Rapids. Mich., Barker Bk., 1963[c.1955] 111p. 20cm. First pub. under title: Pioneer missionaries for Christ and his church. Bibl. 63-432 1.00 pap.,
1. Missionaries. I. Title.

CREEGAN, Charles Cole, 1850-1939. 266'.00922
Great missionaries of the church, by Charles C. Creegan and Josephine A. B. Goodnow. With an introd. by Francis E. Clark. Freeport, N.Y., Books for Libraries Press [1972] xvi, 404 p. port. 23 cm. (Essay index reprint series) Reprint of the 1895 ed. [BV3700.C67 1972] 73-37522 ISBN 0-8369-2541-6
1. Missionaries. I. Goodnow, Josephine A. B., joint author. II. Title. BIP

GREER, Genevieve, 1907- ed. 922.6
More than conquerors; intermediate missionary biographies. Nashville, Broadman Press [1956] 159p. illus. 20cm. (Missionary biographies) [BV3700.G69] 56-8669
1. Missionaries. 2. Baptists—Missions. I. Title.

GREER, Genevieve, 1907- ed. 922.6
Much to dare; junior missionary biographies. Nashville, Broadman Press [1956] 143p. illus. 20cm. [BV3700.G7] 56-8670
1. Missionaries. 2. Baptists— Missions. I. Title.

*KANE, J. Herbert. 266.0092
The making of a missionary, by J. Herbert Kane. Grand Rapids, Baker Book House [1975] 114 p. 23 cm. Bibliography: p. 113-1149 [BV2063] ISBN 0-8010-5358-7 2.95 (pbk.)
1. Missionaries. I. Title. BIP

KERRISON, Raymond. 922.273
Bishop Walsh of Maryknoll, a biography. New York, Putnam [1962] 314p. 22cm. [BX4705.W2573K40] SS61
1. Walsh, James Edward, Bp., 1891- II. Title.

MCBETH, Leon. 266
Men who made missions. Nashville, Broadman Press [1967, c1968] 128 p. 20 cm. Bibliography: p. 127-128. Describes briefly the life and dogma of nine Christians who extended the boundaries of their church through missionary work: Gregory, Patrick, Boniface, Ramon Lull, Francis Xavier, David Brainerd, William Carey, Livingstone, and Judson. [BV3700.M24] AC 68
1. Missionaries. I. Title.

MORRISON, James Horne, 1872- 266'.023'0922 B
The missionary heroes of Africa, by J. H. Morrison. New York, Negro Universities Press [1969] xii, 267 p. map. 23 cm. Reprint of the 1922 ed. [BV3503.M6 1969] 79-89010
1. Missionaries. 2. Missions—Africa. I. Title. BIP

SCHNITTKIND, Dana Arnold, 1918- 922
Crusaders for God [by] Dana Thomas [pseud.] New York, A. A. Wyn [1952] 340 p. 22 cm. [BV3700.S32] 52-11577
1. Missionaries. I. Title.

THOMAS, Dana Lee, 1918- 922
Crusaders for God. New York, A. A. Wyn [1952] 340p. 22cm. [BV3700.T45] 52-11577
1 Missionaries. I. Title.

YONGE, Charlotte Mary, 1823-1901. 266'.0092'2 B
Pioneers and founders; or, recent workers in the mission field. Plainview, N.Y., Books for Libraries Press [1974] p. cm. (Essay index reprint series) Reprint of the ed. published by Macmillan, London, in series: The Sunday library for household reading. [BV3700.Y7 1974] 74-4273 ISBN 0-518-10193-2 17.50
1. Missionaries. I. Title. II. Series: The Sunday library for household reading.

Missionaries—Correspondence, reminiscences, etc.

MELROSE, Paul C 922.551
On being a missionary. 1st ed. New York, Pageant Press [1957] 73p. 21cm. Autobiographical. [BV3427.M43A3] 57-8231
1. Missionaries Correspondence, reminiscences, etc 2. Missions—China. I. Title.

Missionaries, Women—Biography.

BRISTER, Elaine H. 266'.023'0922 B
The joy of discovery / Elaine H. Brister. Nashville : Broadman Press, c1976. 153 p., [2] leaves of plates : ports. ; 20 cm. Bibliography. p. [iv] [BV3703.B74] 76-21567 ISBN 0-8054-7217-7 bds. : 3.95
1. Missionaries, Women Biography. I. Title. BIP

Missions—Asia.

MUELLER, John Theodore, 1885- 266'.023'0922 B
Great missionaries to the Orient. Freeport, N.Y., Books for Libraries Press [1972, c1948] 133 p. 23 cm. (Biography index reprint series) Bibliography: p. 133. [BV3150.M8 1972] 78-38330 ISBN 0-8369-8125-1
1. Missions—Asia. 2. Missionaries. I. Title. BIP

Missions—California—History—Sources.

SERRA, Junipero, 1713-1784. 266.2'0924 B
Diario: the journal of Padre Serra, from Loreto, the capital of Baja California, to San Diego, capital of the new establishments of Alta California, in three months and three days, March 28 to July 1, 1769. A new grass roots translation by Ben F. Dixon. [2d ed.] San Diego, Calif., Don Diego's Libreria, 1967. xi, 116 p. illus., facsims., maps, ports. 22 cm. "The Song of Padre Serra" (unacc.) on inside front cover. Includes San Diego's water rights document. [F864.S393 1967] 71-276685 2.00
1. Missions—California—History—Sources. 2. Franciscans in California—History—Sources. I. Title.

Missions—China.

BARR, Pat, 1934- 266'.023'0951
To China with love; the lives and times of Protestant missionaries in China, 1860-1900. [1st ed. in the U.S.A.] Garden City, N.Y., Doubleday, 1973 [c1972] xiii, 210 p. illus. 22 cm. Bibliography: p. 200-203. [BV3415.2.B37 1973] 72-84888 ISBN 0-385-03864-X 7.95
1. Missions—China. 2. Missionaries, British. 3. Protestant churches—Missions. I. Title.

LANE, Ortha May, 1894- 266.7'6'0924 B
Under marching orders in North China. [1st ed.] Tyler, Tex., Story-Wright [1971] iii, 276 p. illus., ports. 24 cm. Autobiographical. [BV3427.L325A3] 72-155433
1. Missions—China. 2. Methodist Church—Missions. I. Title.

MUELLER, John Theodore, 1885- 266'.023'0922 B
Great missionaries to China. Freeport, N.Y., Books for Libraries Press [1972, c1947] 135 p. 23 cm. (Biography index reprint series) [BV3427.A1M8 1972] 73-38329 ISBN 0-8369-8124-3
1. Missions—China. 2. Missionaries. I. Title. BIP

WHITE, Mary Culler. 1875- 922.752
The days of June; the life story of June Nicholson. Kingstree, S.C., Kingstree Lithographic Co. [1952] 128 p. 18 cm. [BV3427.N6W5] 52-42362
1. Missions—China. I. Nicholson, June, 1870-1907. II. Title.

Missions—Congo.

MABIE, Catharine Louise Roe, 1872- 922.6675
Congo cameos. [1st ed.] Philadelphia, Judson Press [1952] 191 p. illus. 21 cm. Autobiography. [BV3625.C63M3] 52-10624
1. Missions—Congo, Belgiam I. Title.

Missions—Congo (Leopoldville)

CARLSON. LOIS 266.00924
Monganga Paul. the Congo ministry and martvrdom of Paul Carlson, M.D. New York, Harper [c. 1966] viii,197p. illus. 21cm. (Harper jungle missionary classics) [BV3625.C63C34] 66-11482 4.95
1. Missions—Cqngo (Leopoldville) I. Carlson, Paul Earle, 1928-1964. II. Title.

ROSEVEARE, Helen. 266'.023'0924
Give me this mountain; an autobiography. [1st ed.] Grand Rapids, Eerdmans [1966] 166 p. 18 cm. [BV3625.C63R643] 67-3299
1. Missions—Congo. I. Title.

Missions—Hawaii.

LYMAN, Sarah Joiner, 1805-1885. 266'.023'0924
Sarah Joiner Lyman of Hawaii—her own story. Compiled from the journal and letters of Sarah Joiner Lyman by Margaret Greer Martin. [Hilo, Hawaii, Lyman House Memorial Museum, 1970] 201 p. illus., ports. 23 cm. [BV3680.H4L83] 78-12188
1. Missions—Hawaii. I. Martin, Margaret Greer. II. Title.

Missions—Iran.

BEITZAKHAR, Michael Simonivitch. 922.655
Light through the shadows: the true life story of Michael Simonivitch Beitzakhar; translated and edited by Daniel V. Kubrock. Washington, Review & Herald Pub. Association [1953] 184p. illus. 20cm. [BV3217.B4A33] 54-21714
1. Missions—Iran. 2. Seventh-Day Adventists—Missions. I. Kubrock, Daniel Victor, ed. and tr. II. Title.

Missions—Mozambique.

KEYS, Clara Evans, 1884- 922.7679
We pioneered in Portuguese East Africa; a Methodist missionary's memoirs of planting Christian civilization in Mozambique. Foreword by Bishop Glenn R. Phillips. Tribute by Julian S. Rea. [1st ed.] New York, Exposition Press [1959] 89p. illus. 21cm. [BV3625.M65K4] 59-16220
1. Missions—Mozambique. I. Title.

Missions—Liberia.

PRICE, Frederick A. 922.7666
Liberian odyssey "by hammock and surfboat"; the autobiography of F. A. Price. [1st ed.] New York, Pageant Press [1954] 260 p. illus. 26 cm. [BV3625.L6P7] 54-9267
1. Missions—Liberia. I. Title.

Missions, Medical.

HEFLEY, James C. 266'.025'0922 B
The Cross and the scalpel [by] James C. Hefley. Waco, Tex., Word Books [1971] 158 p. illus., ports. 23 cm. [R722.H44] 76-134935 4.95
1. Missions, Medical. I. Title.

SEAGRAVE, Gordon S., M.D. 926.1
The life of a Burma surgeon. Introd. by Chester Bowles. New York, Ballantine Bks. [c.1943-1960] 224p. double map. 19cm. (F374K) .50 pap.,
1. Missions, Medical. 2. Medicine—Burma. 3. World war, 1939-1945—Burma. 4. World war, 1939-1945—Medical and sanitary affairs. I. Title.

Missions, Medical—Zululand.

MCCORD, James Bennett. 926.1
My patients were Zulus, by James B. McCord with John Scott Douglas. New York, Rinehart [1951] 308 p. port. 22 cm. [R722.M26 1951] 51-9899
1. Missions, Medical—Zululand. I. Douglas, John Scott. II. Title.

Missions, Medical—Korea.

RUSSELL, Riley. 266.6'73'0924 B
It came in handy; the story of Riley Russell, M.D., physician extraordinary to the people of Korea, as told to Stella Parker Peterson. Washington, Review and Herald Pub. Association [1969] 160 p. illus., map, ports. 22 cm. [R154.R96A3] 76-81310
1. Missions, Medical—Korea. I. Peterson, Stella Parker II. Title.

Missions—Rhodesia.

JENKINS, David Ernest. 266'.023'0922
They led the way: Christian pioneers of central Africa [by] David Jenkins & Dorothy Stebbing. Cape Town, London, Oxford U.P., 1966. [7], 80 p. illus. (incl. ports.). 19 cm. [BV3625.R5J4] 67-87883
1. Missions—Rhodesia. I. Stebbing, Dorothy, joint author. II. Title.

Missions—Theory—Addresses, essays, lectures.

ANDERSON, Rufus, 1796-1880. 266'.023'01
To advance the Gospel; selections from the writings of Rufus Anderson. Edited with an introd. by R. Pierce Beaver. Grand Rapids, Eerdmans [1967] 225 p. 24 cm. "The literary works of Rufus Anderson": p. 39-44. Bibliographical footnotes. [BV2063.A75] 66-22949
1. Missions—Theory—Addresses, essays, lectures. I. Beaver, Robert Pierce, 1906- ed. II. Title.

Missions—Vietnam.

HEFLEY, James C. 266'.023'09597
By life or by death; the dramatic story of the valiant missionary martyrs who have lived and died for Christ in war-torn Viet Nam [by] James C. Hefley. [1st ed.] Grand Rapids, Mich., Zondervan Pub. House [1969] 208 p. illus., maps, ports. 23 cm. Bibliographical footnotes. [BV3325.A6H4] 68-58932 4.95
1. Missions—Vietnam. 2. Christian and Missionary Alliance—Missions. 3. Missionaries. I. Title.

Missisippi

WILLIAMSON, Henry Cuthbert, 1851or2-1919. 973.80924
Memoirs of a statesman, being an account of the events in the career of a Mississippi journalist-legislator. Edited by C. Fred Thompson. Rochester, N.Y., Press of the Good Mountain [c1964] xii, 168 p. 24 cm. Limited edition of 50 copies. [F341.W5] 66-4887
1. Missisippi — Pol. & govt. — 1865- 2. The West — Descr. & trav. I. Thompson, C. Fred, ed. II. Title.

Mississippi—Biography.

SMITH, Frank Ellis, 1918- 920.0762
Mississippians all, by Frank E. Smith and Audrey Warren. New Orleans, Pelican Pub. House, 1968. 86 p. ports. 22 cm. Contents.Contents.—Jake W. Lindsey.—Milton Olive.—Eudora Welty.—Leontyne Price.—Blanche Kelso Bruce.—Lucius Q. C. Lamar.—Jake Gibbs.—George Scott. [F340.S6] 68-54601
1. Mississippi—Biography. I. Warren, Audrey. II. Title. BIP

Mississippi—Governors—Biography.

SUMNERS, Cecil Lamar, 1920- 976.2'009'92 B
The governors of Mississippi / by Cecil L. Sumners. Gretna, La. : Pelican Pub. Co., 1980. p. cm. Includes index. [F340.S9] 79-16813 ISBN 0-88289-237-1 : 12.95
1. Mississippi—Governors—Biography. 2. Mississippi—Politics and government. I. Title. BIP

Mississippi Valley.

PECK, John Mason, 1789-1855 286.10924
Forty years of pioneer life; memoir of John Mason Peck, D.D. Ed. from his journals and correspondence by Rufus Babcock. Introd. by Paul H. Harrison. Foreword by Herman R. Lantz. Carbondale, Southern Ill. Univ. Pr. [c.1965] lxxviii, 360p. port. 22cm. (Perspectives in sociol.) [F353.P35] 65-12394 10.00
1. Mississippi Valley. 2. Baptists—U. S. I. Babcock, Rufus, 1798-1875, ed. II. Title. III. Series.

PECK, John Mason, 1789-1855. 286.10924
Forty years of pioneer life; memoir of John Mason Peck, D. D. Edited from his journals and correspondence by Rufus Babcock. Introd. by Paul M. Harrison. Foreword by Herman R. Lantz. Carbondale, Southern Illinois University Press, [1965] ixxviii, 360 p. port. 22 cm. (Perspectives in sociology) [F353.P35] 65-12394
1. Mississippi Valley. 2. Baptists—U. S. I. Babcock, Rufus, 1798-1875 ed. II. Title. III. Series.

Missouri—Genealogy.

BRYAN, William Smith, 1846-1940. 977.8'03
A history of the pioneer families of Missouri, with numerous sketches, anecdotes, adventures, etc., relating to early days in Missouri : also the lives of Daniel Boone and the celebrated Indian chief Black Hawk, with numerous biographies and histories of primitive institutions by Wm. S. Bryan and Robert Rose. Baltimore : Genealogical Pub. Co., 1977. xvii, 569 p., [2] leaves of plates : ill.

; 23 cm. Reprint of the 1935 ed. published by Bryan, Brand, St. Louis. Includes indexes. [F465.B79 1977] 76-55479 ISBN 0-8063-0753-6 : 18.50
1. Missouri—Genealogy. 2. Missouri—Biography. 3. Frontier and pioneer life—Missouri. I. Rose, Robert, d. ca. 1878, joint author. II. Title: A history of the pioneer families of Missouri ...

Mistral, Frederic, 1830-1914.

EDWARDS, Tudor 928.49
The lion of Arles; a portrait of Mistral and his circle. New York, Fordham [c.1964] 215p. 22cm. Bibl. 63-16396 4.50
1. Mistral, Frederic, 1830-1914. I. Title.

LYLE, Rob. 928.49
Mistral. New Haven, Yale University Press, 1953. 68p. 22cm. (Studies in modern European literature and thought) [PC3402.M5Z742] A 53
1. Mistral, Frederic, 1830-1914. I. Title.

Mistrot family.

CARTIER, Gustave Mistrot, 1894-. 929'.2'0973
The Mistrot-Segura story in Louisiana and Texas, by Mistrot Cartier. [Houston, 1965] 82, xii l. illus. ports. 29 cm. Bibliography: leaf xii. [CS71.M66716] 65-51590
1. Mistrot family. 2. Segura family. I. Title.

Mitchel, John Purroy,

LEWINSON, Edwin R. 352.074710924
John Purroy Mitchel, the boy mayor of New York. New York, Astra Bks. [dist. Twayne, c.] 1965. 299p. 22cm. Bibl. [F128.5.M7L4] 65-15010 6.50
1. Mitchel, John Purroy, 2. New York (City)—Pol. & govt.—1898-1951. I. Title.

Mitchelhill, John Percy, 1879-1966.

COTES, Peter, 1912- 792'.023'0924 B
J. P., the man called Mitch : a memoir / by Peter Cotes ; foreword by Dame Anna Neagle. London : P. Elek, 1978 100 p., [1] leaf of plates : ill. ; 23 cm. [PN2598.M57C67 1977] 78-313886 ISBN 0-236-40119-X : 9.95
1. Mitchelhill, John Percy, 1879-1966. 2. Duchess Theatre. 3. Theatrical managers—England—Biogrpahy. I. Title.
Distributed by Technical Impex, Salem, NH

Mitchell, Albert Graeme, 1889-1941.

CRONIN, John Francis, 1903- 618.9'2'000924
Albert Graeme Mitchell, [by] John F. Cronin and Robert A. Lyon. Sponsored by the Mitchell Memorial Committee: George M. Guest [and others. Cincinnati 1964] v. 104 p. port. 24 cm. Bibliography: p. 97-104. [RJ43.M5C7] 926 64-5671
1. Mitchell, Albert Graeme, 1889-1941. I. Lyon, Robert Aaron, 1900- joint author. II. Title.

Mitchell, Arthur, 1934- —Juvenile literature.

TOBIAS, Tobi. 792.8'092'4 B
Arthur Mitchell. Illustrated by Carole Byard. New York, Crowell [1975] 32 p. col. illus. 24 cm. A biography of the black ballet dancer who gave up his career as a star with the New York City Ballet to found the Dance Theatre of Harlem. [GV1785.M53T62 1975] 92 74-13730 ISBN 0-690-00661-6 4.50
1. Mitchell, Arthur, 1934- —Juvenile literature. 2. Dance Theatre of Harlem—Juvenile literature. 3. Ballet—Juvenile literature. I. Byard, Carole M., illus. II. Title. BIP

Mitchell, Bill, 1850-1928.

SONNICHSEN, Charles Leland, 1901- 364.370924
Outlaw; Bill Mitchell alias Baldy Russell,his life and times. Denver, Sage Bks. [dist. Swallow. c.1965] 197p. illus., map (on lining papers) ports., 23cm. Bibl. [F801.M5S6] 65-25798 4.75 bds.,
1. Mitchell, Bill, 1850-1928. 2. Frontier and pioneer life—New Mexico. I. Title. BIP

Mitchell, Burroughs.

MITCHELL, Burroughs. 070.4'092'4 B
The education of an editor / Burroughs Mitchell. 1st ed. Garden City, N.Y. : Doubleday, 1980. p. cm. [PN149.9.M5A33] 79-7204 ISBN 0-385-15032-6 : 10.00
1. Mitchell, Burroughs. 2. Editors—United States—Biography. I. Title. BIP

Mitchell, Elizabeth Ann (Oldacre)

MITCHELL, Elizabeth Ann (Oldacre) 1876- 922.89
Anchored to the Rock. Anderson, Ind., Printed for the author by Gospel Trumpet Co. [1950] 142 p. 20 cm. [BX7094.C678M5] 50-31157
I. Title.

Mitchell, Elsie P., 1926-

MITCHELL, Elsie P., 1926- 294.3'927
Sun Buddhas, moon Buddhas: a Zen quest by Elsie P. Mitchell. With a foreword by Aelred Graham. [1st ed.] New York, Weatherhill [1973] 214 p. 22 cm. Includes bibliographical references. [BQ972.I87A37 1973] 73-4037 ISBN 0-8348-0083-7 7.50
1. Mitchell, Elsie P., 1926- 2. Religious life (Zen Buddhism) I. Title.

Mitchell family.

MITCHELL, Harry Elwood, 1877- 929'.2'0973
A Mitchell group: Adam, Jane, and Robert, and some of their descendants. [Long Beach? Calif.,] 1963. 177 p. illus., ports., maps, facsims. 23 cm. Bibliography: p. 177. [CS71.M6672 1963] 64-1265
1. Mitchell family. I. Title.

Mitchell, Frank, 1881-1967.

MITCHELL, Frank, 1881-1967. 784.7'51'0924 B
Navajo Blessingway singer : the autobiography of Frank Mitchell, 1881-1967 / edited by Charlotte J. Frisbie and David P. McAllester. Tucson : University of Arizona Press, c1978. x, 446 p. : ill. ; 24 cm. Includes index. Bibliography: p. 406-418. [E99.N3M64 1978] 77-75661 ISBN 0-8165-0611-6 : 14.50 ISBN 0-8165-0568-3 pbk. : 8.50
1. Mitchell, Frank, 1881-1967. 2. Navaho Indians—Biography. 3. Navaho Indians—Religion and mythology. 4. Indians of North America—Southwest, New—Religion and mythology. I. Title. BIP

Mitchell, Grant, 1874-

DUBOIS, Aaron 927.92
The House of Van Du; a vignette biography of the stage and screen actor, Grant Mitchell. New York, ,william-Frederick [c.]1962. 126p. illus. 23cm. 62-10878 4.50
1. Mitchell, Grant, 1874- I. Title.

Mitchell, Henry Laurens, 1831-1903.

CHURCH, George B. 975.9'06'0924 B
The life of Henry Laurens Mitchell, Florida's 16th Governor / by George B. Church, Jr. 1st ed. New York : Vantage Press, c1978. 144, [1] p. ; 21 cm. Bibliography: p. 141-[145] [F316.M57C49] 78-102423 ISBN 0-533-03070-6 : 7.50
1. Mitchell, Henry Laurens, 1831-1903. 2. Florida—Governors—Biography. I. Title.

Mitchell, James Leslie, 1901-1935.

YOUNG, Douglas F. 823'.9'12
Beyond the sunset; a study of James Leslie Mitchell (Lewis Grassic Gibbon). Aberdeen, Impulse Publications, 1973. viii, 162 p. 23 cm. Includes index. Bibliography: p. [160] [PR6025.I833Z9] 74-176489 ISBN 0-901311-40-5 £3.50
1. Mitchell, James Leslie, 1901-1935. I. Title.

Mitchell, John, d. 1768.

BERKELEY, Edmund. 570'.92'4 B
Dr. John Mitchell: the man who made the map of North America, by Edmund Berkeley and Dorothy Smith Berkeley. Chapel Hill, University of North Carolina Press [1974] xix, 283 p. illus. 24 cm. Bibliography: p. 269-276. [QK31.M48B47] 73-16162 ISBN 0-8078-1221-8 12.50
1. Mitchell, John, d. 1768. 2. Botany—United States—History. I. Berkeley, Dorothy Smith, joint author. II. Title.

Mitchell, John, 1870-1919.

GLUCK, Elsie. 331.88'12'2330924 B
John Mitchell, miner; labor's bargain with the gilded age. New York, Greenwood Press [1969, c1929] xvi, 270 p. 23 cm. Bibliography: p. [263]-265. [HD8073.M5G6 1969] 69-13909 ISBN 0-8371-2170-1
1. Mitchell, John, 1870-1919. 2. Coal-miners—United States. 3. Arbitration, Industrial—United States. BIP

Mitchell, Joni.

FLEISCHER, Leonore. 784'.092'4 B
Joni Mitchell / by Leonore Fleischer. New York : Flash Books, c1976. 79 p. : ill. ; 26 cm. [ML410.M6823F6] 75-29868 ISBN 0-8256-3907-7 pbk. : 3.95
1. Mitchell, Joni. BIP

Mitchell, Margaret, 1900-1949.

FARR, Finis. 813.52
Margaret Mitchell of Atlanta, the author of Gone with the wind. New York, Morrow, 1965. 244 p. illus., ports. 25 cm. [PS3525.I972Z67] 65-22974
1. Mitchell, Margaret, 1900-1949. I. Title.

FARR, Finis. 813.52
Margaret Mitchell of Atlanta. [New York] Avon [1974, c1965] 283 p. illus. 18 cm. [PS3525.I972Z67] 1.75 (pbk.)
1. Mitchell, Margaret, 1900-1949. I. Title.
L.C. card number for original ed.: 65-22974. BIP

Mitchell, Margaret, 1900-1949—Correspondence.

MITCHELL, Margaret, 1900-1949. 813'.5'2 B
Margaret Mitchell's Gone with the wind letters, 1936-1949 / edited by Richard Harwell. New York : Macmillan, 1976. p. cm. Includes index. [PS3525.I972Z53 1976] 76-13190 ISBN 0-02-548650-0 : 12.95
1. Mitchell, Margaret, 1900-1949—Correspondence. I. Harwell, Richard Barksdale. II. Title. III. Title: Gone with the wind letters, 1936-1949. BIP

Mitchell, Maria,

MITCHELL, Maria, 1818-1889. 520'.924 B
Maria Mitchell: life, letters, and journals. Compiled by Phebe Mitchell Kendall. Freeport, N.Y., Books for Libraries Press [1971] vi, 293 p. ports. 23 cm. Reprint of the 1896 ed. [QB36.M7K5 1971] 79-152989 ISBN 0-8369-5741-5
I. Kendall, Phebe Mitchell, comp.

Mitchell, Maria, 1818-1889—Juvenile literature.

BAKER, Rachel (Mininberg) 925.2
America's first woman astronomer, Maria Mitchell, by Rachel Baker and Joanna Baker Merlen. New York, J. Messner [c.1960] 192p. illus. 22cm. (Julian Messner shelf of biographies) 60-12450 2.95
1. Mitchell, Maria, 1818-1889—Juvenile literature. I. Merlen, Joanna (Baker) joint author. II. Title.

BAKER, Rachel (Mininberg) 1903- 925.2
America's first woman astronomer, Maria Mitchell, by Rachel Baker and Joanna Baker Merlen. New York, J. Messner [1960] 192p. illus. 22cm. [QB36.M7B35] 60-12450
1. Mitchell, Maria, 1818-1889—Juvenile literature. I. Merlen, Joanna (Baker) joint author. II. Title.

MORGAN, Helen L. 520'.92'4 B
Maria Mitchell, first lady of American astronomy / Helen L. Morgan. 1st ed. Philadelphia : Westminster Press, c1977. 141 p. ; 21 cm. Includes index. Bibliography: p. 135. A biography of a feminist who was the first woman science professor at Vassar College and the first American woman astronomer. [QB36.M7M67] 92 77-5871 ISBN 0-664-32614-5 : 7.95
1. Mitchell, Maria, 1818-1889—Juvenile literature. 2. Astronomers—United States—Biography—Juvenile literature. I. Title. BIP

WAYNE, Bennett. 920.72
Women who dared to be different. Edited, with commentary by Bennett Wayne. Champaign, Ill., Garrard Pub. Co. [1973] 168 p. illus. 22 cm. (A Torch book) Brief biographies of four women who pioneered in professions traditionally reserved for men. [CT3260.W39] 920 72-6802 ISBN 0-8116-4902-4 3.48
1. Oakley, Annie, 1860-1926—Juvenile literature. 2. Mitchell, Maria, 1818-1889—Juvenile literature. 3. Earhart, Amelia, 1898-1937—Juvenile literature. 4. Cochrane, Elizabeth, 1867-1922—Juvenile literature. 5. Women in the United States—Biography—Juvenile literature. 6. Women in the United States—Biography. I. Title. BIP

WILKIE, Katharine Elliott, 1904- 92 (J)
Maria Mitchell, stargazer, by Katharine E. Wilkie. Illustrated by Paul Kennedy. Champaign, Ill., Garrard Pub. Co. [1966] 80 p. illus. 23 cm. (A Discovery book) [QB36.M7W5] 67-10019
1. Mitchell, Maria, 1818-1889—Juvenile literature.

Mitchell, Martha, 1918-

*ASHMAN, Charles. 320.9'73
Martha: the mouth that reared, [by] Charles Ashman and Sheldon Engelmayer. New York, Berkley Publishing Corp., 1973. 212 p. 18 cm. (Berkley Medallion Books, TM757375) ISBN 0-425-02468-7 1.25 (pbk)
1. Mitchell, Martha (Mrs.), 1918- I. Engelmayer, Sheldon, joint author. II. Title.

MCLENDON, Winzola. 301.41'2'0924 B
Martha : the life of Martha Mitchell / by Winzola McLendon. 1st ed New York : Random House, c1979. xi, 440 p., [8] leaves of plates : ill. ; 25 cm. Includes index. [HQ1413.M57M3] 77-90289 ISBN 0-394-41124-2 : 12.50
1. Mitchell, Martha, 1918- 2. Mitchell, John Newton, 1913- 3. Wives—United States—Biography. 4. Lawyers—United States—Biography. I. Title.

MITCHELL, Martha, 1918- 973.924'0924
On with the wind: Martha Mitchell speaks. Additional dialogue by John Mitchell. Produced by Amram M. Ducovny. Drawings by Peter Green. New York, Ballantine Books [1971] 62 p. illus. 18 cm.

[E840.8.M55A3] 76-22006 ISBN 0-345-02100-2 1.00
1. Mitchell, John Newton, 1913- II. Title.

Mitchell, Silas Weir, 1829-1914.

EARNEST, Ernest Penney, [928.1]
1901-
S. Weir Mitchell, novelist and physician. Philadelphia, University of Pennsylvania Press, 1950. vii, 279 p. illus., ports. 23 cm. Bibliographical references included in "Notes" (p. 245-274) [R154.M66E3] 926.1 50-8063
1. Mitchell, Silas Weir, 1829-1914. I. Title.

WALTER, Richard D., 616.8'0924 B
1921-
S. Weir Mitchell, M.D., neurologist; a medical biography, by Richard D. Walter. Springfield, Ill., Thomas [1970] viii, 232 p. illus. 24 cm. Bibliography: p. 205-225. [R154.M66W3] 71-97540
1. Mitchell, Silas Weir, 1829-1914. I. Title.

Mitchell, Thomas Livingstone, Sir 1792-1855.

CUMPSTON, John Howard 923.294
Lidgett, 1880--
Thomas Mitchell, surveyor general & explorer. London, Oxford University Press, 1954[i. e. 1955] 270p. illus. 23cm. [DU114.M5C8] 55-40737
1. Mitchell, Thomas Livingstone, Sir 1792-1855. I. Title.

Mitchell, William, 1879-1936.

BURLINGAME, Roger, 1889- 923.573
General Billy Mitchell, champion of air defense. New York, McGraw-Hill [1952] 212 p. illus. 21 cm. (They made America) [UG633.M45B8] 52-12689
1. Mitchell, William, 1879-1936. I. Title.

BURLINGAME, 358.4'13'310924 B
Roger, 1889-1967.
General Billy Mitchell, champion of air defense / Roger Burlingame. Westport, Conn. : Greenwood Press, 1978, c1952. ix, 212 p., [4] leaves of plates : ill. ; 22 cm. Reprint of the ed. published by McGraw-Hill, New York, in series: They made America. Includes index. Bibliography: p. 193-199. [UG626.2.M57B87 1978] 77-26823 ISBN 0-313-20170-6 lib.bdg. : 17.75
1. Mitchell, William, 1879-1936. 2. Generals United States—Biography. 3. Aeronautics, Military—United States—History. I. Title.

DAVIS, Burke. 355.3'32'0924 B
The Billy Mitchell affair. New York, Random House [1967] 373 p. illus. 25 cm. Includes bibliographical references. [UG633.M45D3] 66-21474
1. Mitchell, William, 1879-1936. I. Title.

GENERAL Billy Mitchell, v. 12
champion of air defense. [New York] New American Library [1956, c1955] 159p. illus. 18cm. (Signet books, S1280) 'Sources': p. [148]-152.
1. Mitchell, William, 1879-1936. I. Burlingame, Roger, 1889- BIP

HURLEY, Alfred F. 923.573
Billy Mitchell: crusader for air power. New York, Watts [c.1964] x, 180p. illus., ports. 25cm. (Watts aerospace lib.) Bibl. 64-11917 5.95
1. Mitchell, William, 1879-1936. I. Title. BIP

HURLEY, Alfred 358.4'13'320924 B
F.
Billy Mitchell, crusader for air power / Alfred F. Hurley. New ed. Bloomington : Indiana University Press, 1975. ix, 190 p., [6] leaves of plates : ill. ; 25 cm. Includes index. Bibliography: p. 178-184. [UG633.M45H8 1975] 74-22831 ISBN 0-253-31203-5 : 10.00 ISBN 0-253-20181-0 pbk : 2.95
1. Mitchell, William, 1879-1936. I. Title.

LEVINE, Isaac Don, 1892- 923.573
Mitchell, pioneer of air power. [Rev. ed.] New York, Duell, Sloan and Pearce [1958] 420p. illus. 22cm. [UG633.M45L4 1958] 58-4461
1. Mitchell, William, 1879-1906. 2. Aeronautics, Military—U. S. I. Title.

LEVINE, Isaac Don, 1892- 923.573
Mitchell, pioneer of air power. [Rev. ed.] New York, Duell, Sloan and Pearce [1958] 420p. illus. 22cm. [UG633.M45L4 1958] 58-4461
1. Mitchell, William, 1879-1906. 2. Aeronautics, Military—U. S. I. Title.

LEVINE, Isaac 358.4'13'320924 B
Don, 1892-
Mitchell: pioneer of air power. [New York] Arno Press [1972, c1943] viii, 420 p. illus. 23 cm. (Literature and history of aviation) "Mitchell's own writings": p. 401-405. [UG633.M45L4 1972] 71-169426 ISBN 0-405-03777-5
1. Mitchell, William, 1879-1936. 2. Aeronautics, Military—United States. I. Title. II. Series. BIP

MITCHELL, Ruth. 923.573
My brother Bill, the life of General 'Billy' Mitchell; with an introd. by Gerald W. Johnson. [1st ed.] New York, Harcourt, Brace [c1953] 344p. 21cm. [UG633.M45M45] 52-9855
1. Mitchell, William, 1879-1936. I. Title.

Mitchell, William, 1879-1936 — Juvenile literature.

DAVIS, Burke. 355.3'32'0924 B
The Billy Mitchell story. [1st ed.] Philadelphia, Chilton Book Co. [1969] 149 p. illus., ports. 21 cm. A biography of "the apostle of air power" who forecast the attack on Pearl Harbor seventeen years in advance and whose constant prodding of the military to improve air power resulted in his being court martialed. [UG633.M45D32 1969] 92 76-94995 4.95
1. Mitchell, William, 1879-1936 Juvenile literature. I. Title.

DAVIS, Burke. 355.3'32'0924 B
The Billy Mitchell story. [1st ed.] Philadelphia, Chilton Book Co. [1969] 149 p. illus., ports. 21 cm. A biography of "the apostle of air power" who forecast the attack on Pearl Harbor seventeen years in advance and whose constant prodding of the military to improve air power resulted in his being court martialed. [UG633.M45D32 1969] 92 76-94995 4.95
1. Mitchell, William, 1879-1936—Juvenile literature. I. Title.

MOONEY, Booth, 355.3'32'0924 B
1912-
General Billy Mitchell. Illustrated with photos. Chicago, Follett Pub. Co. [1968] 157, [3] p. illus., ports. 23 cm. (Library of American heroes) Bibliography: p. [158] A biography of the general, Billy Mitchell, whose insistence that the United States change its defense policy and stress air power resulted in his court-martial and professional ruin. [UG633.M45M6] 67-21162 1.95
1. Mitchell, William, 1879-1936—Juvenile literature. I. Title.

MOONEY, Booth, 355.3'32'0924 B
1912-
General Billy Mitchell. Illustrated with photos. Chicago, Follett Pub. Co. [1968] 157, [3] p. illus., ports. 23 cm. (Library of American heroes) Bibliography: p. [158] A biography of the general, Billy Mitchell, whose insistence that the United States change its defense policy and stress air power resulted in his court-martial and professional ruin. [UG633.M45M6] 67-21162 1.95
1. Mitchell, William, 1879-1936—Juvenile literature. I. Title.

WHITEHOUSE, Arthur George j92
Joseph, 1895-
Billy Mitchell; America's eagle of air power, by Arch Whitehouse. New York, Putnam [1962] 192 p. 21 cm. (Lives to remember series) [UG633.M45W5] 62-8035
1. Mitchell, William, 1879-1936 — Juvenile literature. I. Title.

WOODWARD, Helen (Rosen) 923.573
1882-
General Billy Mitchell, pioneer of the air. Based on Mitchell, pioneer of air power, by Isaac Don Levine. [1st ed.] New York, Duell, Sloan and Pearce [c1959] 181 p. 21 cm. [UG633.M45W6] 59-12237
1. Mitchell, William, 1879-1936 — Juvenile literature. I. Title.

Mitchiner, Margaret

MITCHINER, Margaret 928.4
A muse in love, Julie de Lespinasse. London, Bodley Head [dist. Chester Springs, Pa., Dufour, 1964, c.1962] 222p. ports. 23cm. Bibl. 64-91892 5.00 bds.,
I. Lespinasse, Julie Jeanne Eleonore de, 1732-1776. II. Title.

Mitchum, Robert, 1917-

*BELTON, John. 791.43'028'0924
Robert Mitchum / by John Belton. New York : Pyramid Publications, 1976. 159p. : ill., ports. ; 20 cm. (A Pyramid illustrated history of the movies) Includes index. Bibliography: p. 141. [PN2287] 76-3340 pbk. : 1.75
1. Mitchum, Robert, 1917- I. Title.

TOMKIES, Mike. 791.43'028'0924
The Robert Mitchum story: "It sure beats working." New York, Ballantine [1973, c.1972] xvi, 235 p. illus. 18 cm. [PN2287.M648T6] ISBN 0 345 23484-7 1.25 (pbk.)
1. Mitchum, Robert. I. Title.
L.C. card no. for the hardbound edition: 72-80944.

TOMKIES, Mike. 791.43'028'0924
The Robert Mitchum story: "It sure beats working." New York, Ballantine [1973, c.1972] xvi, 235 p. illus. 18 cm. [PN2287.M648T6] ISBN 0-345-23484-7 1.25 (pbk.)
1. Mitchum, Robert. I. Title.
L.C. card no. for the hardbound edition: 72-80944.

TOMKIES, Mike. 791.43'028'0924
The Robert Mitchum story: "It sure beats working." Chicago, Regnery [1972] 271 p. illus. 23 cm. [PN2287.M648T6] 72-80944 6.95
1. Mitchum, Robert.

Mitford, Jessica,

MITFORD, Jessica, Hon. 920.7
1917-
Daughters and rebels [New York] Avon [1964, c.1960] 255p. 18cm. (V2091) .75 pap.,
I. Title.

MITFORD, Jessica, Hon., 920.7
1917-
Daughters and rebels; the autobiography of Jessica Mitford. Boston, Houghton Mifflin, 1960. 284 p. illus. 22 cm. [CT788.M56A3] 60-7569
I. Title.

Mitford, Jessica, Hon., 1917-

MITFORD, Jessica, Hon. 920.7
1917-
Daughters and rebels [New York] Avon [1964, c.1960] 255p. 18cm. (V2091) .75 pap.,
I. Title.

MITFORD, Jessica, Hon., 920.7
1917-
Daughters and rebels; the autobiography of Jessica Mitford. Boston, Houghton Mifflin, 1960. 284 p. illus. 22 cm. [CT788.M56A3] 60-7569
I. Title.

MITFORD, Jessica, 335.43'092'4 B
Hon., 1917-
A fine cold conflict / Jessica Mitford. 1st ed. New York : Knopf, 1977. xiv, 333 p., [4] leaves of plates : ill. ; 22 cm. Includes bibliographical references. [HX84.M55A34 1977] 77-2324 ISBN 0-394-49995-6 : 10.00
1. Mitford, Jessica, Hon., 1917- 2. Communists—United States—Biography. I. Title.

MITFORD, Jessica, 335.43'092'4 B
Hon., 1917-
A fine old conflict / Jessica Mitford. 1st Vintage Books ed. New York : Vintage Books, 1978, c1977. xiv, 333 p., [4] leaves of plates : ill. ; 21 cm. [HX84.M55A34 1978] 78-54656 pbk. : 4.95
1. Mitford, Jessica, Hon., 1917- 2. Communists—United States—Biography. I. Title. BIP

Mitford, Mary Russell,

MITFORD, Mary 828'.7'09 B
Russell, 1787-1855.
The letters of Mary Russell Mitford. Selected with an introd. by R. Brimley Johnson. Port Washington, N.Y., Kennikat Press [1972] ix, 236 p. 21 cm. [PR5023.A35 1972] 76-160763 ISBN 0-8046-1583-7
I. Johnson, Reginald Brimley, 1867-1932. II. Title. BIP

Mitford, Mary Russell, 1787-1855—Books and reading.

MITFORD, Mary 828'.7'09 B
Russell, 1787-1855.
Recollections of a literary life : or, Books, places, and people / by Mary Russell Mitford. New York : AMS Press, 1975. xii, 558 p. 19 cm. (Women of letters) Reprint of the 1852 ed. published by Harper, New York. [PR5023.A5 1975] 74-178342 ISBN 0-404-56789-4 : 34.50
1. Mitford, Mary Russell, 1787-1855—Books and reading. 2. Authors—Correspondence, reminiscences, etc. 3. English literature—History and criticism. 4. American literature—History and criticism. I. Title.

Mitford, Mary Russell, 1787-1855—Correspondence.

MITFORD, Mary 828'.7'09 B
Russell, 1787-1855.
The letters of Mary Russell Mitford. Selected with an introd. by R. Brimley Johnson. Port Washington, N.Y., Kennikat Press [1972] ix, 236 p. 21 cm. [PR5023.A35 1972] 76-160763 ISBN 0-8046-1583-7
I. Johnson, Reginald Brimley, 1867-1932. II. Title. BIP

MITFORD, Mary 828'.7'09 B
Russell, 1787-1855.
The letters of Mary Russell Mitford / selected with an introd. by R. Brimley Johnson. Folcroft, Pa. : Folcroft Library Editions, 1977. ix, 236 p. ; 23 cm. Reprint of the 1925 ed. published by Dial Press, New York. [PR5023.A4 1977] 77-16515 ISBN 0-8414-5403-5 lib. bdg. : 25.00
1. Mitford, Mary Russell, 1787-1855—Correspondence. 2. Authors, English—19th century—Correspondence. I. Johnson, Reginald Brimley, 1867-1932. II. Title. BIP

Mitford, Nancy, 1904-1973—Biography.

ACTON, Harold Mario 823'.9'14 B
Mitchell, 1904-
Nancy Mitford : a memoir / Harold Acton. 1st U.S. ed. New York : Harper & Row, c1975. xvi, 252 p., [6] leaves of plates : ill. ; 25 cm. (A Cass Canfield book) Includes index. "A list of Nancy Mitford's books": p. [241] [PR6025.I88Z56 1975b] 75-34580 ISBN 0-06-010018-4 : 10.00
1. Mitford, Nancy, 1904-1973—Biography. BIP

Mitford, Unity, 1914-1948.

PRYCE-JONES, David, 1936- 942.082'092'4 B
Unity Mitford : a quest / David Pryce-Jones. London : Weidenfeld & Nicolson, 1976. 276 p., [8] leaves of plates : ill. ; 25 cm. Includes index. Bibliography: p. [266]-267. [CT788.M564J66] 77-350383 ISBN 0-297-77156-6 : £6.50
1. Mitford, Unity, 1914-1948. 2. Hitler, Adolf, 1889-1945. 3. England—Biography.

PRYCE-JONES, David, 1936- 942.082'092'4 B
Unity Mitford : an inquiry into her life and the frivolity of evil / David Pryce-Jones. New York : Dial Press, 1977. 292 p., [8] leaves of plates : ill. ; 24 cm. Includes index. Bibliography: p. 283-284 [CT788.M564P79 1977] 77-23170 ISBN 0-8037-8865-7 : 9.95
1. Mitford, Unity, 1914-1948. 2. Hitler, Adolf, 1889-1945. 3. England—Biography. I. Title.

Mithridates VI, Eupator, King of Pontus, d. 63 B. C.

DUGGAN, Alfred Leo, 1903-1964. 923.13933
King of Pontus; the life of Mithradates Eupator. New York, Coward-McCann [1959] 208 p. 22 cm. First published in 1958 under title: He died old, Mithradates Eupator, King of Pontus. [DS156.P8D8 1959] 59-7175
1. Mithridates VI, Eupator, King of Pontus, d. 63 B. C. I. Title.

Mitrione, Dan.

LANGGUTH, A. J., 1933- 327'.12'0924 B
Hidden terrors / by A. J. Langguth. 1st ed. New York : Pantheon Books, c1978. 339 p. ; 22 cm. Includes index. Bibliography: p. [313]-327. [JK468.I6L35 1978] 77-88769 ISBN 0-394-40674-5 : 10.00
1. Mitrione, Dan. 2. Intelligence agents—United States—Biography. 3. Police—United States—Biography. 4. Kidnapping—Uruguay—Case studies. 5. Murder—Uruguay—Case studies. I. Title. BIP

Mitropoulos, Dimitri, 1896-1960.

MITROPOULOS, Dimitri, 1896-1960. 785'.092'4 B
Dimitri Mitropoulos, Katy Katsoyanis: a correspondence, 1930-1960. Foreword by George Seferis. Introductions by Louis Biancolli [and] Katy Katsoyanis. New York, Martin Dale, 1973. 187 p. illus. 23 cm. [ML422.M59A28] 73-75338
1. Mitropoulos, Dimitri, 1896-1960. 2. Katsogianne, Kaite. 3. Musicians—Correspondence, reminiscences, etc. I. Katsogianne, Kaite.

Mitscher, Marc Andrew, 1887-1947.

TAYLOR, Theodore, 1922- 923.573
The magnificent Mitscher. With a foreword by Arthur W. Radford. [1st ed.] New York, Norton [1954] 364 p. illus. 22 cm. [E745.M5T3] 54-12896
1. Mitscher, Marc Andrew, 1887-1947. I. Title.

Mitson, Eileen Nora.

MITSON, Eileen Nora. 248'.48'610924 B
Reaching for God / Eileen Mitson. 1st ed. Chappaqua, N.Y. : Christian Herald Books, c1978. 192 p. ; 21 cm. [BX6495.M524A34] 77-90115 6.95
1. Mitson, Eileen Nora. 2. Baptists—England—Biography. I. Title. BIP

Mitsuko, Iolana.

MITSUKO, Iolana. 818'.5'408
Honolulu madam. Los Angeles, Holloway House Pub. Co.; [distributed by All America Distributors Corp., 1969] 316 p. 18 cm. [PS3563.I84Z5] 68-58868 0.95
I. Title. BIP

Mittermaier, Rosi, 1950- —Juvenile literature.

SMITH, Jay H. 796.9'3'0924 B
Rosi Mittermaier / by Jay H. Smith. ; illustrated by John Keely. Mankato, Minn. : Creative Education, c1977. 31 p. : col. ;ill. : 25 cm. (Creative Education sports superstars) A biography of the German skier whose performances in the 1976 Olympics and World Cup competition have won her worldwide acclaim. [GV854.2.M57S63] 92 76-39923 ISBN 0-87191-544-8 lib.bdg. : 4.95
1. Mittermaier, Rosi, 1950- —Juvenile literature. 2. Skiers—Germany, West—Biography—Juvenile literature. I. Keely, John. II. Title. BIP

Miura, Ayako, 1922- —Biography.

MIURA, Ayako, 1922- 894.6'3'5 B
The wind is howling / Ayako Miura ; translated and abridged, Valerie Griffiths. Downers Grove, Ill. : InterVarsity Press, 1977 printing. 190 p. ; 21 cm. Translation of Michi ariki. Autobiographical. [PL856.I8Z5213 1977] 77-74845 ISBN 0-87784-782-7 pbk. : 3.95
1. Miura, Ayako, 1922- —Biography. 2. Authors, Japanese—20th century—Biography. I. Title. BIP

Miura, Yuichiro, 1932-

MIURA, Yuichiro, 1932- 796.9'3'0924 B
The men who skied down Everest / Yuichiro Miura, with Eric Perlman. 1st ed. San Francisco : Harper & Row, c1978. 170 p. : ill. ; 24 cm. [GV854.2.M58A35 1978] 78-3355 ISBN 0-06-250575-0 : 10.00
1. Miura, Yuichiro, 1932- 2. Skiers—Japan—Biography. 3. Everest, Mount—Description. I. Perlman, Eric, joint author. II. Title.

Mivart. St. George Jackson, 1827-1900.

GRUBER, Jacob W 213.5
A conscience in conflict: the life of St. George Jackson Mivart. New York, Published for Temple University Publications by Columbia University Press, 1960. 266p. illus. 24cm. [BL263.G68 1960] 60-10645
1. Mivart. St. George Jackson, 1827-1900. 2. Religion and science—1860-1899. 3. Evolution. I. Title. BIP

Mix, Tom, 1880- 1940.

MIX, Olive (Stokes) 927.92
The fabulous Tom Mix, by Olive Stokes Mix with Erio Heath. Englewood Cliffs, N. J., Prentice-Hall [1957] 177p. illus. 22cm. [PN2287.M65M5] 57-11473
1. Mix, Tom, 1880- 1940. I. Title.

MIX, Paul E. 791.43'028'0924 B
The life and legend of Tom Mix [by] Paul E. Mix. South Brunswick, A. S. Barnes [1972] 206 p. illus. 27 cm. Bibliography: p. [185]-186. [PN2287.M65M48] 71-146780 ISBN 0-498-07881-7 8.95
1. Mix, Tom, 1880-1940. I. Title.

Miyamoto, Musashi, 1584-1645.

DENING, Walter, 1846-1913. 952'.025
Japan in days of yore / Walter Denning [sic]. London : East-West Publication, 1978. 4 v. in 1 : col. ill. ; 21 cm. Reprint of the 1887-88 ed. published by The Hakubunsha, Tokyo. Contents.Contents.—[1] Human nature in a variety of aspects.—[2] Wounded pride and how it was healed.—[3-4] The life of Miyamoto Musashi. [DS822.2.D4 1978] 79-316994 ISBN 0-85692-001-0 : 16.95
1. Miyamoto, Musashi, 1584-1645. 2. Japan—Social life and customs—1600-1868. 3. Swordsmen—Japan—Biography. I. Title.
Distributed by Great Eastern Book, P.O. Box 271, Boulder,CO 80306 BIP

Miyoshi, Tami.

MIYOSHI, Tami. 301.41'5
The cherry dance. Los Angeles, Holloway House Pub. Co. [1969] 293 p. 18 cm. (Holloway House publication, HH-164) Autobiography. [HQ462.M56] 69-19949 0.95
I. Title.

Mizner, Addison, 1872-1933.

JOHNSTON, Alva. 920
The legendary Mizners; illustrated by Reginald Marsh. New York, Farrar, Straus and Young [1953] 304p. illus. 22cm. [CT275.M568J6] 53-7790
1. Mizner, Addison, 1872-1933. 2. Mizner, Wilson, 1876-1933. I. Title.

Mizner, Wilson, 1876-1933.

O'CONNOR, Richard, 1915-1975 364.1'63'0924 B
Rogue's progress : the fabulous adventures of Wilson Mizner / by John Burke [i.e. R. O'Connor]. New York : Putnam, [1975] xi, 304 p. ; 22 cm. Includes index. Bibliography: p. 295-296. [CT275.M569O26 1975] 74-16879 ISBN 0-399-11423-8 : 8.95
1. Mizner, Wilson, 1876-1933. I. Title.

Mlynarski, Bronislaw, 1899-1971.

MlYNARSKI, Bronislaw, 1899-1971. 940.54'05'094762 B
The 79th survivor / [by Bronis aw Mynarski; translated from the Polish by Casimir Zdziechowski: foreword by Arthur Rubinstein London : Bachman and Turner, 1976. 246 p. : map, port. ; 23 cm. Translation of Z niewoli sowieckiej. [D805.R9M5813] 77-350494 ISBN 0-85974-030-7 : £5.50
1. Mlynarski, Bronislaw, 1899-1971. 2. World War, 1939-1945—Prisoners and prisons, Russian. 3. World War, 1939-1945—Personal narratives, Polish. 4. Starobel'sk, Ukraine. 5. Prisoners of war—Ukraine—Starobel'sk—Biography. I. Title.

Mohammad, the prophet.

MUIR, William, Sir, 1819-1905. 297'.63 B
The life of Mohammad from original sources / by Sir William Muir. A new and rev. ed. / by T. H. Weir. New York : AMS Press, [1975] p. cm. Reprint of the 1923 ed. published by J. Grant, Edinburgh. [BP75.M8 1975] 78-180366 ISBN 0-404-56306-6 : 57.50
1. Mohammad, the prophet. I. Weir, Thomas Hunter, d. 1928, ed. II. Title. BIP

Mo, Ti, fl. 400 B.C.

MEI, Yi-pao. 181'.11 B
Motse, the neglected rival of Confucius. Westport, Conn., Hyperion Press [1973] xi, 222 p. 23 cm. Reprint of the 1934 ed. published by A. Probsthain, London, which was issued as no. 20 of Probsthain's oriental series. Bibliography: p. [203]-207. [B128.M8M4 1973] 73-892 ISBN 0-88355-084-9 12.75
1. Mo, Ti, fl. 400 B.C. I. Title.

Moats, Alice Leone.

MOATS, Alice Leone. 920.5
A violent innocence. New York, Duell, Sloan and Pearce [1951] vii, 312 p. 23 cm. [CT275.M57A3] 51-9604
I. Title.

Mocsanyi, Paul.

VAN LOEN, Alfred 730.9492
Alfred Van Loen, by Paul Mocsanyi. Great Neck, N.Y., Channel Press [c.1960] [63]p. illus. 32cm. 60-16162 5.95 half cloth,
1. Mocsanyi, Paul. I. Title.

Modernism—Catholic Church.

LOISY, Alfred Firmin, 1857-1940. 282'.0924 B
My duel with the Vatican; the autobiography of a Catholic modernist. Authorized translation by Richard Wilson Boynton. With a new introd. by E. Harold Smith. New York, Greenwood Press, 1968 [c1924] xiii, 357 p. 22 cm. Translation of Choses passees. Includes bibliographical references. [BX4705.L7A3 1968] 68-19290
1. Modernism—Catholic Church. I. Title. BIP

Modigliani, Amedeo, 1884-1920.

AMEDEO Modigliani 759.5
(1884-1920) Text by Jacques Lipchitz. New York, H. N. Abrams in association with Pocket Books [1954] [74] p. 64 illus. (part col.) port. 18cm. (The Pocket library of great art, A16) An Abrams art book. Bibliography: p. [74] [ND623.M67L57] 927.5 54-4310
1. Modigliani, Amedeo, 1884-1920. II. Lipchitz, Jacques, 1891-

FIFIELD, William, 1916- 759.5 B
Modigliani / by William Fifield. New York : Morrow, 1976. 317 p., [12] leaves of plates : ill. ; 24 cm. Includes index. [ND623.M67F53] 75-41362 ISBN 0-688-03039-4 : 9.95
1. Modigliani, Amedeo, 1884-1920.

MODIGLIANI, Amedeo, 1884-1920. 759.5
Medigliani. New York, Skira [1955?] [4] p., 6 col. plates (in portfolio) 32cm. [ND623.M67A5] 55-3120
I. Title.

MODIGLIANI, Amedeo, 1884-1920. 759.5
Medigliani. New York, Skira [1955?] [4] p., 6 col. plates (in portfolio) 32cm. [ND623.M67A5] 55-3120
I. Title.

MODIGLIANI, Amedeo, 1884-1920. 741.9'45
Modigliani : disegni / Osvaldo Patani. [Oggiono] : Edizioni della seggiola, 1976. 138, [1] p. : ill. ; 29 cm. (Documenti del disegno ; 1) English, French, and Italian. Bibliography: p. 138-[139] [NC257.M6P37] 77-474520
1. Modigliani, Amedeo, 1884-1920. I. Patani, Osvaldo. II. Title. III. Series.

MODIGLIANI, Jeanne. 927.5
Modigliani: man and myth. Translated from the Italian by Esther Rowland Clifford. New York, Orion Press; distributed by Crown Publishers [1958] 116 p. illus. 25 cm. Includes bibliography. [ND623.M67M63] 759.5 58-13185
1. Modigliani, Amedeo, 1884-1920.

ROY, Claude, 1915- 759.5
Modigliani. Translated by James Emmons and Stuart Gilbert. [New York?] Skira [1958] 133p. mounted col. illus. (part fold.) 19cm. (The Taste of our time, 23) Bibliography: p. 123-[124] [ND623.M67R63] 927.5 58-8336
1. Modigliani, Amedeo, 1884-1920. I. Title.

SALMON, Andre, 1881- 759.5
Modigliani, a memoir. [Tr. from French] by Dorothy and Randolph Weaver. New York, Putnam [1961, c.1957, 1961] 216p. illus. (part col.) 61-6898 5.00
1. Modigliani, Amedeo, 1884-1920. I. Title.

SICHEL, Pierre. 759.5
Modigliani; a biography of Amedeo Modigliani. [1st ed.] New York, Dutton, 1967. 597 p. illus., ports. 25 cm.

Bibliography: p. 582-588 [ND623.M67S5] 67-11841
1. Modigliani, Amedeo, 1884-1920.

Modisane, Bloke.

MODISANE, Bloke. 920
Blame me on history. [1st ed.] New York, Dutton, 1963. 311 p. 22 cm. Autobiography. [CT1929.M6A3] 63-20846
I. Title.

Modjeska, Helena,

MODJESKA, Helena, 792'.028'0924 B
1840-1909.
Memories and impressions of Helena Modjeska; an autobiography. New York, B. Blom [1969] v, 571 p. illus., ports. 24 cm. Reprint of the 1910 ed. [PN2618.M6A3 1969] 75-81212
I. Title.

Modjeska, Helena, 1840-1909.

COLEMAN, Arthur Prudden, 927.92
1897-
Wanderers twain; Modjeska and Sienkiewicz: a view from California, by Arthur Prudden Coleman, Marion Moore Coleman. Cheshire, Conn., Cherry Hill-Bks., 202 Highlane Ave., [c.]1964. ix, 111p. illus., ports. 23cm. 63-20948 5.00
1. Modjeska, Helena, 1840-1909. 2. Sienkiewicz, Henryk, 1846-1916. I. Coleman, Marion (Moore) 1900- joint author. II. Title.

COLEMAN, Marion 792'.028'0924 B
(Moore) 1900-
Fair Rosalind: the American career of Helena Modjeska. Cheshire, Conn., Cherry Hill Books, 1969. iv, 1019 p. illus., ports. 24 cm. Bibliographical references included in "Notes" (p. 969-990) [PN2618.M6C59] 69-10370 20.00
1. Modjeska, Helena, 1840-1909. I. Title.

GRONOWICZ, Antoni, 1913- 927.92
Modjeska, her life and loves. New York, T. Yoseloff [1956] 254 p. 22 cm. [PN2618.M6G7] 56-8956
1. Modjeska, Helena, 1840-1909.

MODJESKA, Helena, 792'.028'0924 B
1840-1909.
Memories and impressions of Helena Modjeska; an autobiography. New York, B. Blom [1969] v, 571 p. illus., ports. 24 cm. Reprint of the 1910 ed. [PN2618.M6A3 1969] 75-81212
I. Title.

Modotti, Tina, 1896-1942.

CONSTANTINE, Mildred. 770'.92'4 B
Tina Modotti : a fragile life : an illustrated biography / Mildred Constantine. New York : Paddington Press, [1975] 224 p. : ill. ; 29 cm. Includes index. Bibliography: p. 219. [TR140.M58C66] 73-20956 ISBN 0-8467-0027-1 : 14.95
1. Modotti, Tina, 1896-1942.

Moe, Petra Malena, 1863-1953.

NILSEN, Maria. 922
Malla Moe, by Maria Nilsen, as told to Paul H. Sheetz. Illus. by Warner Sallman. Chicago, Moody Press [1956] 253p. illus. 22cm. [BV3557.M67N5] 56-14618
1. Moe, Petra Malena, 1863-1953. I. Sheetz, Paul H. II. Title.

NILSEN, Maria 922
Malla Moe. by Maria Nilsen, as told to Paul H. Sheetz. Illus. by Warner Sallman. Chicago, Moody Press [1966, c.1956] 253p. illus. 22cm. [BV3557.M67N5] .89 pap.,
1. Moe, Petra Malena, 1863-1953. I. Sheetz, Paul H. II. Title.

Moen, John, 1869-1949.

MOEN, Esten, 1904- 920
Tales my father told me. [1st ed. Fosston, Minn., Thirteen Towns, 1954] 82p. illus. 27cm. [CT275.M572M6] 54-13107
1. Moen, John, 1869-1949. I. Title.

Moffat, Elaine Therese (Moore) 1930- -Juvenile literature.

[MOORE, Isabel] 92
Elaine Moore Moffat, blue ribbon horsewoman; the complete life story of a champion rider who learned to cope with life by learning to deal with horses. by Grace Walker. New York, Nelson [c.1965] 128p. illus., ports. 22cm. (Champion bks.; Rutledge bk.) [SF33.M6M6] 65-22519 2.75 bds.,
1. Moffat, Elaine Therese (Moore) 1930- —Juvenile literature. I. Title.

MOORE, Isabel. j92
Elaine Moore Moffat, blue ribbon horsewoman; the complete life story of a champion rider who learned to cope with life by learning to deal with horses, by Grace Walker. London, New York, T. Nelson [1965] 128 p. illus., ports. 22 cm. (Champion books) "A Rutledge book." [SF33.M6M6] 65-22519
1. Moffat, Elaine Therese (Moore) 1930- -Juvenile literature. I. Title.

Moffat, Gwen.

MOFFAT, Gwen. 927.9652
Space below my feet. Boston, Houghton, Mifflin, 1961. 302p. illus. 22cm. [G512.M6A3] 61-5371
I. Title. **BIP**

MOFFAT, Gwen. 796.5'22'0924 B
Space below my feet / Gwen Moffat. Harmondsworth, Eng. : Penguin Books, 1976, c1961. 304 p., [4] leaves of plates : ill. ; 19 cm. [GV199.92.M63A38 1976] 76-379334 ISBN 0-14-003991-0 pbk. : 2.95
1. Moffat, Gwen. 2. Mountaineers—Wales—Biography. I. Title.
Distributed by Penguin, Baltimore,Md.

Moffat, John Smith,

MOFFAT, John 266'.023'0924 B
Smith, 1835-1918.
John Smith Moffat, C.M.G. missionary; a memoir [compiled] by his son Robert U. Moffat. New York, Negro Universities Press [1969] xix, 388 p. illus., map, ports. 23 cm. Reprint of the 1921 ed. [DT776.M7A5 1969] 73-88443
I. Moffat, Robert Unwin, 1866-1947, comp.

Moffat, Robert, 1795-1883.

MOFFAT, Robert, 1795- 916.89'1
1883.
The Matabele journals of Robert Moffat, 1829-1860 / edited by J. P. R. Wallis. Salisbury : National Archives of Rhodesia, 1976. 2 v. : ill. ; 26 cm. Reprint of the 1945 ed. published by Chatto & Windus, London, which was issued as no. 1 of the Oppenheimer series. Includes index. Bibliography: v. 2, p. 281-282. [DT962.9.M37M63 1976] 77-359339 ISBN 0-86923-102-2
1. Moffat, Robert, 1795-1883. 2. Moffat, Mary Smith, 1795-1871. 3. Matabeleland—Description and travel. 4. Matabeleland—History—Sources. 5. Matabele. 6. Missionaries—Rhodesia, Southern—Matabeleland—Correspondence. 7. Missionaries—Scotland—Correspondence. I. Title. II. Series: Rhodesia, Southern. Central African Archives. Oppenheimer series ; no. 1. **BIP**

NORTHCOTT, William Cecil, 922.768
1902-
Robert Moffat: pioneer in Africa, 1817-1870. New York, Harper & Row [1962, c.1961] 357p. illus. 23cm. Bibl. 62-7296 7.50
1. Moffat, Robert, 1795-1883. 2. Missions—Africa, South. I. Title.

Moffat, Robert, 1795-1883—Juvenile literature.

ADVENTURES of a 266'.023'0924 B
missionary; or, Rivers of water in a dry place; being an account of the introduction of the Gospel of Jesus into South Africa and of Mr. Moffat's missionary travels and labors. New York, Carlton & Porter. [n.d.] Miami, Fla., Mnemosyne Pub. Co. [1969] 295 p. illus. 23 cm. Recounts the part played by the nineteenth century English missionary, Robert Moffat, in introducing the Gospel to South Africa. [BV3557.M7A65] 92 70-89387
1. Moffat, Robert, 1795-1883—Juvenile literature. 2. Missions—Africa, South—Juvenile literature. 3. Missionary stories.

Moffatt, David Halliday, 1839-1911.

BONER, Harold A. 923.373
The giant's ladder: David H. Moffat and his railroad. [Milwaukee, Kalmbach, c.1962] 224p. illus., map 29cm. Bibl. 62-12083 12.00
1. Moffatt, David Halliday, 1839-1911. 2. Denver, Northwestern and Pacific Railway. I. Title.

BONER, Harold A. 923.373
The giant's ladder: David H. Moffat and his railroad. [Milwaukee, Kalmbach Pub. Co., 1962] 224 p. illus. 29 cm. (A Kaimbach publication) [HE2791.D451] 62-12083
1. Moffatt, David Halliday, 1839-1911. 2. Denver, Northwestern and Pacific Railway. I. Title.

Moffett, William Adger, 1869-1933.

ARPEE, Edward, 1899- 923.573
From frigates to flat-tops; the story of the life and achievements of Rear Admiral William Adger Moffett, U. S. N., 'the father of naval aviation,' October 31, 1869-April 4, 1933. [Lake Forest, Ill., 1953] 276p. illus. 27cm. Includes bibliography. [E746.M6A7] 54-1129
1. Moffett, William Adger, 1869-1933. 2. Aeronautics, Military—U. S. I. Title.

Moffitt, Frederick James,

MOFFITT, Frederick James, 883 (J)
1896-
Diary of a warrior king: adventures from the Odyssey, by Frederick J. Moffitt. Consultant: M. A. Jagendorf [and] Carolyn W. Field. Illustrated by Bill Shields. Morristown, N.J., Silver Burdett Co. [1967] 90 p. col. illus., col. map. 25 cm. (Folk literature around the world) [PZ8.1.M698Di] 67-18717
I. Homerus. Odyssea. II. Title.

Mohamed Ibrahim, Munshi.

MOHAMED 915.95'1'0430924 B
Ibrahim, Munshi.
The voyages of Mohamed Ibrahim Munshi / translated, with an introd. and notes, by Amin Sweeney and Nigel Phillips. Kuala Lumpur ; New York : Oxford University Press, 1975. xxxiii, 145 p., [1] leaf of plates : ill. ; 23 cm. (Oxford in Asia historical memoirs) Translation of Kesah pelayaran Mohamed Ibrahim Munshi. Includes index. Bibliography: p. [135]-137. [DS592.4.M6313] 76-358691 ISBN 0-19-580267-5 : 20.50
1. Mohamed Ibrahim, Munshi. 2. Malaya—Description and travel. 3. Malaya—History—Sources. I. Title.

Mohammed Reza Pahlavi, Shah of Iran, 1919-

HOYT, Edwin 955'.05'0924 B
Palmer.
The Shah : the glittering story of Iran and its people / Edwin P. Hoyt. New York : P. S. Eriksson, c1976. xi, 244 p., [10] leaves of plates : ill. ; 24 cm. Includes index. Bibliography: p. 234-240. [DS318.H69 1976] 75-16501 ISBN 0-8397-7753-1 : 10.00.
1. Mohammed Reza Pahlavi, Shah of Iran, 1919- 2. Iran—History—1909- I. Title.

KARANJIA, Rustom 955'.05'0924 B
Khurshedji, 1912-
The mind of a monarch / R. K. Karanjia. London : G. Allen & Unwin, 1977. 265 p., [1] leaf of plates : 1 ill. ; 25 cm. [DS318.K32] 77-368137 ISBN 0-04-923069-7 : 16.00
1. Mohammed Reza Pahlavi, Shah of Iran, 1919- 2. Iran—Politics and government—1945- 3. Iran—Kings and rulers—Biography. I. Title.
Distributed by Allen & Unwin, 198 Ash St. Reading, Mass. 01867 **BIP**

SANGHVI, Ramesh. 955.05'0924 B
The Shah of Iran. New York, Stein and Day [1969, c1968] xxvi, 390 p. illus., maps (part col.) 23 cm. Half title: Aryamehr, the Shah of Iran; a political biography. Bibliography: p. 375-378. [DS318.S25 1969] 69-17944 10.00
1. Mohammed Reza Pahlavi, Shah of Iran, 1919- I. Title. II. Title: Aryamehr, the Shah of Iran.

Mohammed Reza Pahlavi, Shah of Iran, 1919- —Juvenile literature.

EDMONDS, I. G. 955'.05'0924 B
The Shah of Iran : the man and his land / I. G. Edmonds ; photos. by the author. New York : Holt, Rinehart and Winston, c1976. 192 p. : ill. ; 24 cm. Includes index. Bibliography: p. [186] A history of Iran and a biography of the man who has ruled that empire since 1941. [DS318.E35] 76-8457 ISBN 0-03-015561-4 : 6.95
1. Mohammed Reza Pahlavi, Shah of Iran, 1919- —Juvenile literature. 2. Iran—History—1909- —Juvenile literature. I. Title. **BIP**

Mohawk Valley, N.Y.—Biography.

WILLIAMS, Emily. 974.7'57
Stagecoach country : Utica to Sackets Harbor / text, Emily Williams ; photography, Helen Cardamone ; foreword, David M. Ellis. [Turin, N.Y.] : William, c1976. 115, [7] p. : ill. ; 32 cm. Bibliography: p. [118]-[119] [F127.M55W54] 77-152773 14.95
1. Mohawk Valley, N.Y.—Biography. 2. Mohawk Valley, N.Y.—History, Local. 3. Jefferson Co., N.Y. Biography. 4. Jefferson Co., N.Y.—History, Local. 5. Historic buildings—New York (State)—Mohawk Valley. 6. Historic buildings—New York (State)—Jefferson Co. I. Cardamone, Helen. II. Title.

Mohler, Johann Adam, 1796-1838.

SAVON, Herve 230.924
Johann Adam Mohler, the father of modern theology. Tr. by Charles McGrath. Glen Rock, N.J., Paulist [1966] 128p. 19cm. (Deus bks.) Bibl. [BX4705.M59S33] 66-28321 .95 pap.,
1. Mohler, Johann Adam, 1796-1838. I. Title.

Moises, Rosalio, 1896-1969.

MOISES, Rosalio, 1896- 970.3
1969.
The tall candle; the personal chronicle of Yaqui Indian, by Rosalio Moises, Jane Holden Kelley, and William Curry Holden. Introd. by Jane Holden Kelley. Lincoln, University of Nebraska Press [1971] lviii, 251 p. illus., geneal. table, map. 24 cm. Bibliography: p. lvii-lviii. [E99.Y3M6] 71-100809 ISBN 0-8032-0747-6 7.50
1. Yaqui Indians. I. Kelley, Jane Holden, 1928- II. Holden, William Curry, 1896- III. Title.

MOISES, Rosalio, 970'.004'97 B
1896-1969.
A Yaqui life : the personal chronicle of a Yaqui Indian / by Rosalio Moises, Jane Holden Kelley, and William Curry Holden ; introd. by Jane Holden Kelley. Lincoln : University of Nebraska Press, 1977, c1971. p. cm. Previous ed. (c1971) published under title: The tall candle. [E99.Y3M6 1977] 76-56789 ISBN 0-8032-5857-7 pbk. : 3.50
1. Moises, Rosalio, 1896-1969. 2. Yaqui Indians—Biography. I. Kelley, Jane Holden, 1928- joint author. II. Holden,

William Curry, 1896- joint author. III. Title. BIP

Moiseev, Ivan Vasil'evich, 1952-1972.

GRANT, Myrna. 286.1'092'4 B
Vanya. Carol Stream, Ill., Creation House [1974] 222 p. ports. 22 cm. Map on lining-paper. [BX6495.M53G72] 73-89729 ISBN 0-88419-071-4 4.95
1. Moiseev, Ivan Vasil'evich, 1952-1972. 2. Persecution—Russia. I. Title. BIP

Mojica, Jose, 1895-1974.

GONZALO de Jesus, fray, O.F.M. 271'.3'024 B
Fray Jose G. Mojica, O.F.M., mi guia y mi estrella / por fray Gonzalo de Jesus, O.F.M. Chicago: Franciscan Herald Press, [1975] p. cm. [BX4705.M5965G66] 75-9951 ISBN 0-8199-0570-4
1. Mojica, Jose, 1895-1974. I. Title: Mi guia y mi estrella.

I, a sinner . . . 927.8
autobiography.[Tr. from Spanish by Fanchon Royer] Chicago, Franciscan Herald [c.1963] v, 393p. illus., ports., facsims. 22cm. 63-12851 4.95
1. N I. Mojica, Jose Francisco de Guadalupe, 1895-

Mojica, Jose Francisco de Guadalupe,

I, a sinner . . . 927.8
autobiography.[Tr. from Spanish by Fanchon Royer] Chicago, Franciscan Herald [c.1963] v, 393p. illus., ports., facsims. 22cm. 63-12851 4.95
1. N I. Mojica, Jose Francisco de Guadalupe, 1895-

Mokgatle, Naboth,

MOKGATLE, Naboth, 1911- 916.8'06'96 B
The autobiography of an unknown South African. Berkeley, University of California Press [1971] vii, 349 p. map. 23 cm. (Perspectives on southern Africa, 1) [CT1968.M6A3] 79-138285 ISBN 0-520-01845-1 7.95
I. Title. BIP

Moldavia.

GIRS, Nikolai Karlovich, 1820-1895 923.247
The education of a Russian statesman, the memoirs Nicholas Karlovich Giers [Tr.,] ed. by Charles and Barbara Jelavich. Berkeley, Univ. of Calif. Pr. [c.] 1962. 241p. illus. 24cm. (Russian and East European studies) Bibl. 62-14297 6.00
1. Moldavia. 2. Education—Russia. I. Jelavich, Charles, ed. II. Jelavich, Barbara (Brightfield) ed. III. Title.

Molden, Fritz.

MOLDEN, Fritz. 940.53'436
Exploding star : a young Austrian against Hitler / Fritz Molden ; translated by Peter and Betty Ross. New York : Morrow, 1979. 280 p. ; 22 cm. Translation of Fepolinski und Waschlapski auf dem berstenden Stern. Includes index. [D802.A9M6413 1979] 78-69727 ISBN 0-688-03381-4 : 10.00
1. Molden, Fritz. 2. World War, 1939-1945—Underground movements—Austria—Biography. 3. World War, 1939-1945 Personal narratives, Austrian. 4. Guerrillas—Austria—Biography. I. Title. BIP

Moldovsky, Joel.

MOLDOVSKY, Joel. 345'.73'00924 B
The best defense / Joel Moldovsky and Rose DeWolf. New York : Macmillan, 1975. xiii, 249 p. ; 21 cm. [KF373.M54D4] 75-1154 ISBN 0-02-585590-5 : 7.95
1. Moldovsky, Joel. 2. Lawyers—Philadelphia—Correspondence, reminiscences, etc. 3. Philadelphia—Biography. I. DeWolf, Rose, joint author. II. Title. BIP

Molek, Ivan, 1882-1962.

MOLEK, Ivan, 1882-1962. 973'.049184 B
Slovene immigrant history, 1900-1950 : autobiographical sketches / by Ivan (John) Molek ; translated by Mary Molek ; including an annotated bibliography, researched, compiled, and with English translation and appendices A, B, C, D, E by Mary Molek. Dover, Del. : M. Molek, 1979. xxxvii, 537 p. : ill. ; 23 cm. Translated from ms. Supplements "Folklore and Growing up in old Slovenia" and unpublished mss.: p. 493-512. Includes bibliographies and index. [E184.S65M64213] 78-65725 ISBN 0-9603142-3-7 : 8.50
1. Molek, Ivan, 1882-1962. 2. Slovene Americans—Biography. I. Title.
Publisher's address: PO Box 453, Dover, DE 19901

Molesworth, Mary Louisa (Stewart) 1842-1921.

GREEN, Roger Lancelyn 823.8
Mrs. Molesworth. New York, Walck [1964, c.1961] 80p. port. 19cm. Bibl. 64-20839 2.50
1. Molesworth, Mary Louisa (Stewart) 1842-1921. I. Title.

Moley, Raymond, 1886-

MOLEY, Raymond, 1886- 320'.092'4 B
Realities and illusions, 1886-1931 : the autobiography of Raymond Moley / edited with foreword and prologue by Frank Freidel. New York : Garland Pub., 1979. p. cm. (The History of the United States, 1876-1976) Includes bibliographical references and index. [JC251.M56A37] 78-13887 ISBN 0-8240-9692-4 : 18.00
1. Moley, Raymond, 1886- 2. Political scientists—United States—Biography. I. Freidel, Frank Burt. II. Title. III. Series.

Moliere, Jean Baptiste Poquelin, 1622-1673.

FERNANDEZ, Ramon, 1894-1944. 928.4
Moliere: the man seen through the plays. Translated from the French by Wilson Follett. New York, Hill and Wang [1958] 212 p. 19 cm. Translation of La vie de Moliere. [PQ1852.F413] 58-14200
1. Moliere, Jean Baptiste Poquelin, 1622-1673. BIP

LEWIS, Dominic Bevan Wyndham, 1894- 928.4
Moliere: the comic mask. New York, Coward-McCann [c1959] 214p. 22cm. [PQ1852.L4 1959] 59-13103
1. Mollere, Jean Baptiste Poquelin, 1622-1673. I. Title.

PALMER, John Leslie, 1885-1944. 842'.4 B
Moliere. With a new index. New York, B. Blom, 1970. 518 p. illus., facsim., ports. 24 cm. Reprint of the 1930 ed. "Bibliographical note": p. 493-494. [PQ1852.P3 1970] 65-16246
1. Moliere, Jean Baptiste Poquelin, 1622-1673. BIP

TILLEY, Arthur Augustus, 1851-1942. 842'.4
Moliere. New York, Russell & Russell [1968] vii, 363 p. port. 20 cm. Reprint of the 1921 ed. Bibliographical footnotes. [PQ1852.T5 1968] 68-10950
1. Moliere, Jean Baptiste Poquelin, 1622-1673. BIP

TURNELL, Martin. 842'.4'09
The classical moment; studies of Corneille, Moliere, and Racine. Westport, Conn., Greenwood Press [1971] xv, 261 p. ports. 23 cm. "Originally published in 1948." Bibliography: p. 251-257. [PQ527.T8 1971] 79-138601 ISBN 0-8371-5803-6
1. Corneille, Pierre, 1606-1684. 2. Moliere, Jean Baptiste Poquelin, 1622-1673. 3. Racine, Jean Baptiste, 1639-1699. I. Title. BIP

Moliere, Jean Baptiste Poquelin, 1622-1673—Biography.

FERNANDEZ, Ramon, 1894-1944. 842'.4
Moliere : the man seen through the plays / by Ramon Fernandez ; translated from the French by Wilson Follett. New York : Octagon Books, 1980, c1958. p. cm. Trnslation of La vie de Moliere. Reprint of the ed. published by Hill and Wang, New York, in series: A dramabook. Includes index. [PQ1852.F413 1980] 79-28249 ISBN 0-374-92739-1 : 13.50
1. Moliere, Jean Baptiste Poquelin, 1622-1673—Biography. 2. Dramatists, French—17th century—Biography. I. Title.

TROLLOPE, Henry Merivale, b.1846. 842'.4 B
The life of Moliere. [Folcroft, Pa.] Folcroft Library Editions, 1974. p. cm. Reprint of the 1905 ed. published by A. Constable, London. [PQ1852.T7 1974] 74-9801 50.00 (lib. bdg.).
1. Moliere, Jean Baptiste Poquelin, 1622-1673—Biography. I. Title. BIP

Molinari, Guido, 1933-

THEBERGE, Pierre. 759.11 B
Guido Molinari : [exposition : catalogue] / par Pierre Theberge. Ottawa : Galerie nationale du Canada, 1976. vii, 160 p. : ill. (some col.) ; 26 cm. English and French. Bibliography: p. 153-159. [N6549.M6T48] 77-457773 ISBN 0-88884-307-0
1. Molinari, Guido, 1933- 2. Artists—Canada—Biography. I. Molinari, Guido, 1933- II. National Gallery of Canada.

Molk, Isador.

MOLK, Isador. 338.272820924 (B)
The making of an oilman. [1st ed.] New York, Citadel Press [1958] 252p. 21cm. Autobiographical. [HD9570.M6A3 926.22338] 56-13899
I. Title.

Moll family.

HEFFNER, Earl S. 338.4'7'683400974822
The Moll gunsmiths, by Earl S. Heffner, Jr. [Point Lookout, Mo., School of the Ozarks, Book Division, 1972] 44 p. illus. 22 cm. "Published especially for the Hellertown, Northampton County, Centennial Celebration." Bibliography: p. 42-44. [TS533.3.P4H43] 72-86701
1. Moll family. 2. Northampton Co., Pa.—Industries. 3. Hellertown, Pa.—Industries. 4. Gunsmiths—Pennsylvania. I. Title.

Molloy, Georgiana (Kennedy) 1805-1843.

HASLUCK, Alexandra. 994.1'02'0924
Portrait with background: a life of Georgianna Molloy. Melbourne, New York [etc.] Oxford U.P., 1966. xii, 284 p. 8 plates (incl. ports.) 20 cm. 20/- (B 67-11805) Bibliography: p. 275-277. [DU372.M58H3] [994'.1'020924 (B)] 67-101965
1. Molloy, Georgiana (Kennedy) 1805-1843. 2. Western Australia — Hist. I. Title.

Mollusks

KONDO, Yoshio. 925.9
Charles Montague Cooke, Jr., a bio-bibliography, by Yoshio Kondo and William J. Clench. Honolulu, The Museum, 1952. 56p. illus., ports., map. 26cm. (Bernice P. Bishop Museum. Special publication 4qCooke, Charles Montague, 1874-1948. [QL31.C67K6] 53-3899
1. Molluska)0s. I. Clench, William James, 1897- II. Title. III. Series: Bernice Pauahi Bishop Museum, Honolulu. Special publication 42

Moltke, Alfred William,

MOLTKE, Alfred William, 1895- 926.3
Memoirs of a logger, by Alfred W. Moltke. [1st ed.] Wenatchee, Wash. [1965] 415 p. illus., ports. 24 cm. [SD129.M57A3] 65-17538
I. Title.

Moltke, Helmuth Karl Bernhard, Graf von, 1800-1891.

MORRIS, William O'Connor, 1824-1904. 943.08'1'0924 B
Moltke; biographical and critical study. New York, Haskell House, 1971. xv, 419 p. maps, ports. 23 cm. Reprint of the 1893 ed. Bibliography: p. iv-ix. [DD219.M7M8 1971] 68-25254 ISBN 0-8383-0222-X
1. Moltke, Helmuth Karl Bernhard, Graf von, 1800-1891. 2. Franco-German War, 1870-1871. BIP

Molzahn, Kurt Emil Bruno.

MOLZAHN, Kurt Emil Bruno. 922.473
Prisoner of war. Philadelphia, Muhlenberg Press [1962] 251p. 20cm. Autobiographical. [BX8080.M 556A3] 62-8203
I. Title.

Momaday, N. Scott,1934-Biography-Youth.

MOMADAY, N. Scott, 1934- 813'.5'4
The names : a memoir / by N. Scott Momaday. New York : Harper and Row, 1977. 170p. : ill. ; 22 cm. (Harper Colophon Books) [PS3563.O47Z52] pbk. : 4.95
1. Momaday, N. Scott,1934-Biography-Youth. 2. Authors, American-20th century-Biography. I. Title.
L.C. card no. for 1976 Harper and Row ed.:75-138749. BIP

Momoko.

MOMOKO. 915.2'1'03330924 B
Never forever; the story of Momoko. Edited by Ruth Pratt. Philadelphia, Dorrance [1974] 216 p. 22 cm. [CT275.M5765A36] 73-87876 ISBN 0-8059-1946-5 6.95
1. Momoko. I. Title.

Monaghan, James, 1891-

MONAGHAN, James, 1891- 978'.03'0924 B
Schoolboy, cowboy, Mexican spy / Jay Monaghan ; with a foreword by Ray Allen Billington. Berkeley : University of California Press, c1977. xii, 218 p., [8] leaves of plates : ill. ; 24 cm. Autobiographical. Includes index. [E175.5.M64A37] 76-55565 ISBN 0-520-03408-2 : 10.95
1. Monaghan, James, 1891- 2. Historians—United States—Biography. 3. The West—Description and travel—1880-1950. 4. Frontier and pioneer life—The West. I. Title.

Monardes, Nicolas, 1512 (ca.)-1588.

GUERRA, Francisco 926.1
Nicolas Bautista Monardes: su vida y su obra, ca. 1493-1588. Mexico, D.F. Compania Fundidora de Fierro y Acero de Monterrey [dist. New York, Lothrop C. Harper, 1962] 225p. facsims. 23cm. [Yale Univ. Dept. of the Hist. of Medicine. Pubn. no. 41] Bibl. 62-52276 12.50
1. Monardes, Nicolas, 1512 (ca.)-1588. I. Title. II. Series: Yale University. Dept. of the History of Science and Medicine. Publication no. 41

Monasticism and religious orders — Brothers.

BURTON, Doris. 922.2
Heroic brothers: ten great religious. Fresno, Calif., Academy Guild Press [1962] 132 p. 23 cm. [BX2835.B8] 62-20459
1. Monasticism and religious orders —

Brothers. 2. Monasticism and religious orders — Biog. I. Title.

Monasticism and religious orders for women—Biog.

BURTON, Doris 922.2
The loveliest flower; ten foundresses of religious congregations. Fresno, Calif., Academy Guild Press [1960] vi, 186p. 20cm. 60-9246 2.95 bds.,
1. Monasticism and religious orders for women—Biog. I. Title.

Monasticism and religious orders—Great Britain—Registers.

KNOWLES, David, 1896- 271'.00942
The heads of religious houses, England and Wales, 940-1216; edited by David Knowles, C. N. L. Brooke [and] Vera C. M. London. Cambridge [Eng.] University Press, 1972. xlviii, 277 p. 24 cm. Bibliography: p. xix-xlvii. [BX2592.K55] 79-171676 ISBN 0-521-08367-2
1. Monasticism and religious orders—Great Britain—Registers. 2. Superiors, Religious Great Britain. I. Brooke, Christopher Nugent Lawrence, joint author. II. London, Vera C. M., joint author. III. Title. BIP

Monasticism and religious orders—History.

NIGG, Walter, 1903- 271
Warriors of God; the great religious orders and their founders. Edited and translated from the German by Mary Ilford. [1st American ed.] New York, Knopf, 1959. 353 p. illus. 25 cm. Translation of Vom Geheimnis der Monche. [BX2432.N513] 59-5429
1. Monasticism and religious orders—History. 2. Monasticism and religious orders—Biography. I. Title.

Monasticism and religious orders—Ireland.

RYAN, John, 1894- ed. 922.22
Irish monks in the golden age, by various writers. Dublin, Clonmore Reynolds [Chester Springs, Pa., Dufour, 1964] 114p. 19cm. Thomas Davis lects., broadcast over Radio Eireann, under the title: The Irish monks in a falling world. 64-7424 2.95
1. Monasticism and religious orders—Ireland. 2. Saints, Irish. I. Title.

Monboddo, James Burnett, Lord, 1714-1799.

CLOYD, E. L. 347'.41'03334 B
James Burnett, Lord Monboddo. Oxford, Clarendon Press, 1972. xii, 196 p. ports. 22 cm. Bibliography: p. [180]-187. [B1520.Z7C58] 72-190765 ISBN 0-19-812437-6 £4.50
1. Monboddo, James Burnett, Lord, 1714-1799. BIP

Monchanin, Jules.

MONCHANIN, Jules. 282'.092'4 B
In quest of the absolute : the life and work of Jules Monchanin / edited and translated by Joseph Weber. Kalamazoo, Mich. : Cistercian Publications, 1977. p. cm. (Cistercian studies series ; no. 51) Bibliography: p. [BX4705.M6312A34] 77-3596 ISBN 0-87907-851-0 : 10.95
1. Monchanin, Jules. 2. Catholics in India—Biography. 3. Theology—Addresses, essays, lectures. I. Weber, Joseph, 1931- II. Title. III. Series.

Monck, Charles Stanley Monck, 4th Viscount, 1819-1894.

BATT, Elisabeth, 971.04'092'4 B
1908-
Monck : governor general, 1861-1868 / Elisabeth Batt ; with a foreword by W. L. Morton. Toronto : McClelland and Stewart, c1976. 191 p. : ill. ; 24 cm. Includes bibliographical references and index. [F1032.M73B37] 76-365287 ISBN 0-7710-1157-1 : 10.00
1. Monck, Charles Stanley Monck, 4th Viscount, 1819-1894. 2. Canada—Politics and government—1841-1867.

Moncrif, Francois Augustin Paradis de, 1687-1770.

SHAW, Edward Pease, 1911- 928.4
Francois-Augustin Paradis de Moncrif, 1687-1770. New York, Bookman Associates [1958] 179 p. 23 cm. (Bookman monograph series) Includes bibliography. [PQ2007.M85Z85] 58-4922
1. Moncrif, Francois Augustin Paradis de, 1687-1770. I. Title.

Mondale, Walter F., 1928-

LEWIS, Finlay. 973.926'092'4 B
Mondale : portrait of an American politician / by Finlay Lewis. 1st ed. New York : Harper & Row, c1980. p. cm. Includes index. [E840.8.M66L48 1980] 79-1672 ISBN 0-06-012599-3 : 10.00
1. Mondale, Walter F., 1928- 2. United States. Congress. Senate—Biography. 3. Vice-Presidents—United States—Biography. 4. Legislators—United States—Biography. BIP

Mondriaan, Pieter Cornelis, 1872-1944.

PIET Mondrian, life and work v. 12
[par] Michel Seuphor [pseud.] New York, H. N. Abrams [1956] 433p. illus., plates (part mounted col.) ports. (part mounted col.) map. Bibliography: p.435-440.
1. Mondriaan, Pieter Cornelis, 1872-1944. I. Perckelaers, Ferdinand Louis, 1901-

WELSH, Robert P. 759.9492
Piet Mondrian's early career : the "naturalistic" periods / Robert P. Welsh. New York : Garland Pub., 1977. xvi, 232 p., [67] leaves of plates : ill. ; 21 cm. (Outstanding dissertations in the fine arts) Reprint of the ed. originally presented as the author's thesis, Princeton University, 1965. Bibliography: p. 228-232. [ND653.M76W4 1977] 76-23659 ISBN 0-8240-2738-8 lib.bdg. : 40.00
1. Mondriaan, Pieter Cornelis, 1872-1944. 2. Painters—Netherlands—Biography. I. Title. II. Series. BIP

Monet, Claude, 1840-1926.

MONET at Giverny / 759.4 B
text by Claire Joyes ; photographic and editorial research by Robert Gordon and Jean-Marie Toulgouat ; with a commentary on the paintings at Giverny, by Andrew Forge. New York : Two Continents Pub. Group, 1976, c1975. p. cm. Includes index. Bibliography: p. [ND553.M7M56 1976] 76-16720 ISBN 0-8467-0200-2 : 16.95
1. Monet, Claude, 1840-1926. 2. Monet, Claude, 1840-1926—Homes and haunts—France—Giverny. I. Joyes, Claire. II. Monet, Claude, 1840-1926. BIP

MONET, Claude, 1840-1926. 759.4
Claude Monet, 1840-1926. Text by Margaretta Salinger. New York, H. N. Abrams [1957] unpaged. illus. 17cm. (Pocket library of great art, A29) [ND553.M7S26] 927.5 58-4089
I. Salinger, Margaretta, 1907- II. Title.

MOUNT, Charles Merrill. 759.4
Monet, a biography. New York, Simon and Schuster [1967, c1966] 444 p. illus., ports. 25 cm. Bibliographical references included in "Notes" (p. 395-427) [ND553.M7M6] 66-24032
1. Monet, Claude, 1840-1926.

TAILLANDIER, Yvon 759.4
Monet. [Tr. from French by A. P. H. Hamilton] New York, Crown [1963] 94p. col. illus. (pt. mounted) 29cm. Bibl. 63-24889 3.50 bds.,
1. Monet, Claude, 1840-1926. I. Title.

WILDENSTEIN, Daniel, 1917- 750.92
Monet; impressions. [Translated by Diana Imber] New York, French & European Publications [1967] 66 p. col. illus. 21 cm. (Rhythm and colour, no. 10) [ND553.M7W5313] 759.4 68-1830
1. Monet, Claude, 1840-1926. I. Title. Impressions.

Monfreid, Henri de.

MONFREID, Henri 364.1'57'0924 B
de.
Hashish; the autobiography of a Red Sea smuggler. Translated by Helen Buchanan Bell. [New York] Stonehill [1973] vi, 287 p. 23 cm. Translation of La croisiere du hachich. [HJ7289.R42M6613 1973] 73-80672 ISBN 0-88373-006-5 7.95
1. Monfreid, Henri de. 2. Smuggling—Red Sea region. 3. Hashish.

Mongkut, King of Thailand, 1804-1868.

GRISWOLD, Alexander B. 923.1593
King Mongkut of Siam. New York, Asia Society [112 E. 64 St.] [c.1961] 60p. front.(part.) 61-1018 1.00 pap.,
1. Mongkut, King of Siam, d. 1868. I. Title.

MOFFAT, Abbot Low, 1901- 923.1593
Mongkut, the King of Siam. Ithaca, N. Y., Cornell [c.1961] 254p. illus. Bibl. 61-16666 3.75
1. Mongkut, King of Thailand, 1804-1868. I. Title.

MOFFAT, Abbot Low, 1901- 923.1593
Mongkut, the King of Siam. Ithaca, N.Y., Cornell Univ. Pr. [1968,c.1961] 254p. illus. 19cm. (CP 69) [DS581.M6] 61-16666 1.95 pap.,
1. Mongkut, King of Thailand, 1804-1868. I. Title. BIP

Mongolism—Personal narratives.

HUNT, Nigel, 616.85'8842'0924
1947-
The world of Nigel Hunt; the diary of a Mongoloid youth. Foreword by L. S. Penrose. New York, Garrett Publications [1967] 126 p. ports. 20 cm. [RC571.H9] 66-28498
1. Mongolism—Personal narratives. I. Title.

HUNT, Nigel, 616.85'8842'0924
1947-
The world of Nigel Hunt: the diary of a mongoloid youth; foreword by Professor L. S. Penrose. Beaconsfield (Bucks.), Darwen Finlayson, 1967. 126 p. 4. illus. (ports). 19 cm. (SBN 85208 008 5) [RC571.H9] 67-114570
1. Mongolism—Personal narratives. I. Title.

Monica, Saint, d. 387.

CRISTIANI, Leon, 270.2'092'4 B
1879-
Saint Monica (331-387 A.D.) : a biography / by Leon Cristiani; translated by M. Angeline Bouchard Boston : Daughters of St. Paul, c1975. p. cm. Translation of Sainte Monique, 331-387. [BX4700.M63C7413] 75-43832
1. Monica, Saint, d. 387. I. Title.

Monk, Maria d. ca. 1850.

MONK, Maria, 271'.97 B
d.ca.1850.
Awful disclosures of the Hotel Dieu Nunnery of Montreal / Maria Monk. New York : Arno Press, 1977. 376 p. ; 21 cm. (Anti-movements in America) Maria Monk's personal narrative as related to T. Dwight. Has also been ascribed to J. J. Slocum and to W. K. Hoyte. Cf. New York herald, Aug. 12, 1836, p. 2, column 1; The Colophon, pt. 17, 1934; Sabin and Gagnon, P. Essai de bibl. can. Reprint of the rev. ed. published in 1836 for M. Monk by Hoisington & Trow, New York. [BX4216.M6A3 1977] 76-46089 ISBN 0-405-09962-2 : 21.00
1. Monk, Maria d. ca. 1850. 2. Nuns—Quebec (Province)—Montreal—Biography. 3. Montreal, Que.—Biography. I. Dwight, Theodore, 1796-1866. II. Slocum John Jay, 1803-1863. III. Hoyte, William K. IV. Title. V. Series.

Monmouth, James Scott, Duke of, 1649-1685.

WATSON, J. N. P. 941.06'6'0924 B
Captain-General and rebel chief : the life of James, Duke of Monmouth / by J. N. P. Watson ; foreword by His Grace the Duke of Buccleuch and Queensberry. London ; Boston : G. Allen & Unwin, 1979. xxiii, 311 p., [9] leaves of plates : ill. ; 25 cm. Includes index. Bibliography: p. [294]-298. [DA448.9.W37] 78-41158 ISBN 0-04-920058-5 : 27.50
1. Monmouth, James Scott, Duke of, 1649-1685. 2. Great Britain. Army—Biography. 3. Great Britain—History—Restoration, 1660-1688. 4. Generals—Great Britain—Biography. I. Title. BIP

WYNDHAM, Violet. 941.06'6'0924 B
The Protestant Duke : a life of Monmouth / Violet Wyndham. London : Weidenfeld and Nicolson, c1976. 193 p., [4] leaves of plates : ill. ; 23 cm. Includes index. Bibliography: p. 185-186. [DA448.9.W94] 76-367070 ISBN 0-297-77099-3 : £4.95
1. Monmouth, James Scott, Duke of, 1649-1685. I. Title.

Monnet, Julien Charles, 1868-1951.

MCKOWN, Dave R., 340'.092'4 B
1895-
The dean; the life of Julien C. Monnet, by Dave R. McKown. [1st ed.] Norman, University of Oklahoma Press [1973] xiii, 294 p. illus. 23 cm. [KF373.M55M3] 73-7418 ISBN 0-8061-1132-1 7.95
1. Monnet, Julien Charles, 1868-1951. 2. Oklahoma. University. College of Law. I. Title.

Monnier, Henri Bonaventure, 1799-1877.

MELCHER, Edith, 1901- 927.41
The life and times by Henry Monnier, 1799-1877. Cambridge, Harvard University Press, 1950. xiv, 253 p. illus., ports. 22 cm. Bibliography: p.[223]-235. [NC1499.M6M4] 50-7071
1. Monnier, Henri Bonaventure, 1799-1877. I. Title.

Monro, David, Sir, 1813-1877.

WRIGHT-ST. Clair, 993.102'092'4 B
Rex Earl.
Thoroughly a man of the world; a biography of Sir David Monro, M.D. [by] Rex E. Wright-St Clair. [Christchurch] Whitcombe & Tombs [1971] 331 p. illus., facsims., maps, ports. 23 cm. Includes bibliographical references. [DU422.M55W75] 72-181730 ISBN 0-7233-0297-9
1. Monro, David, Sir, 1813-1877. I. Title.
Distributed by Verry 9.50

Monro, Harold, 1879-1932.

GRANT, Joy. 821'.9'12
Harold Monro and the Poetry Bookshop. Berkeley, University of California Press, 1967. x, 286 p. illus., ports. 23 cm. Bibliography: p. 276-279. [PR6025.O35Z67 1967a] 67-31919
1. Monro, Harold, 1879-1932. 2. Poetry Bookshop. I. Title. BIP

Monroe, Bill, 1911-

ROONEY, James, 1938- 784'.0922 B
Bossmen: Bill Monroe & Muddy Waters. New York, Dial Press, 1971. 159 p. illus., ports. 22 cm. [ML394.R66] 70-131181 5.95
1. Monroe, Bill, 1911- 2. Waters, Muddy, 1915- 3. Music, Popular (Songs, etc.)—U.S.—History and criticism. I. Title.

Monroe, Earl, 1944- —Juvenile literature.

JACKSON, Robert B. 796.32'3'0924 B
Earl the pearl; the story of Earl Monroe, by Robert B. Jackson. New York, H. Z. Walck [1969] 63 p. illus., ports. 21 cm. A biography of high scoring basketball guard, Earl Monroe, concentrating on his career with the Baltimore Bullets. [GV884.M6J3] 92 76-87243 3.75
1. Monroe, Earl, 1944- —Juvenile literature. I. Title.

JACKSON, Robert B. 796.32'3'0924 B
Earl the pearl; the story of Earl Monroe, by Robert B. Jackson. [Rev. ed.] New York, H. Z. Walck [1974] 72 p. illus. 21 cm. A biography of the high scoring basketball guard, Earl Monroe, concentrating on his careers with the Baltimore Bullets and the New York Knicks. [GV884.M6J3 1974] 92 74-5476 ISBN 0-8098-2100-1
1. Monroe, Earl, 1944- —Juvenile literature. 2. Basketball—Juvenile literature. I. Title.

JACKSON, Robert B. 796.32'3'0924 B
Earl the pearl; the story of Earl Monroe, by Robert B. Jackson. [Rev. ed.] New York, H. Z. Walck [1971] 64 p. illus. 21 cm. A biography of high scoring basketball guard, Earl Monroe, concentrating on his career with the Baltimore Bullets. [GV884.M6J3 1971] 92 75-174748 ISBN 0-8098-2064-1 1.25
1. Monroe, Earl, 1944- —Juvenile literature. 2. Basketball—Juvenile literature. I. Title.

Monroe, Elizabeth (Kortright) 1768-1830.

MINNIGERODE, Meade, 1887-1967. 973.4'0922
Some American ladies; seven informal biographies. Freeport, N.Y., Books for Libraries Press [1969] viii, 287 p. illus., ports. 23 cm. (Essay index reprint series) "First published 1926." Contents.Contents.—Martha Washington.—Abigail Adams.—Dolly Madison.—Elizabeth Monroe and Louisa Adams.—Rachel Jackson.—Peggy Eaton. [E176.M65 1969] 70-93361
1. Washington, Martha (Dandridge) Custis, 1731-1802. 2. Adams, Abigail (Smith) 1744-1818. 3. Madison, Dolley (Payne) Todd, 1768-1849. 4. Monroe, Elizabeth (Kortright) 1768-1830. 5. Adams, Louisa Catherine (Johnson) 1775-1852. 6. Jackson, Rachel (Donelson) 1767-1828. 7. Eaton, Margaret L. (O'Neale) Timberlake, 1799(?)-1879. I. Title.

Monroe, Harriet, 1860-1936—Biography—Editing career.

MONROE, Harriet, 1860-1936. 811'.5'2 B
A poet's life; seventy years in a changing world. New York, AMS Press [1969] viii, 488 p. facsims., ports. 23 cm. Reprint of the 1938 ed. [PS2423.A4 1969] 71-93777
1. Authors—Correspondence, reminiscences, etc. I. Title.

WILLIAMS, Ellen, 1930- 811'.5'05 B
Harriet Monroe and the poetry Renaissance : the first ten years of Poetry, 1912-22 / Ellen Williams. Urbana : University of Illinois Press, c1976. p. cm. Includes index. Bibliography: p. [PS301.P623W5] 76-45403 ISBN 0-252-00478-7 : 8.95
1. Monroe, Harriet, 1860-1936—Biography—Editing career. 2. Poetry (Chicago) 3. American poetry—20th century—History and criticism. 4. Journalists—United States—Biography. I. Title.

Monroe, James, Pres. U.S., 1758-1831.

CRESSON, William Penn, 1873-1932. 973.5'4'0924 B
James Monroe. [Hamden, Conn.] Archon Books, 1971 [c1946] xiv, 577 p. illus., ports. 23 cm. Bibliography: p. 549-559. [E372.C7 1971] 75-124098 ISBN 0-208-01089-0
1. Monroe, James, Pres. U.S., 1758-1831.

GILMAN, Daniel Coit, 1831-1908. 973.5'4'0924 B
James Monroe. New Rochelle, N.Y., Arlington House [1970] 312 p. ports. 21 cm. (Giants of America. The Founding Fathers) Originally published in 1883. Bibliography: p. 262-294. [E372.G523] 72-111227 ISBN 0-87000-089-6
1. Monroe, James, Pres. U.S., 1758-1831.

HOYT, Edwin Palmer. 973.5'4'0924 B
James Monroe, by Edwin P. Hoyt. Chicago, Reilly & Lee Co. [1968] 127 p. illus., map, ports. 21 cm. (President series) Bibliography: p. 121. A biography of the man whose Presidential years were known as "the era of good feeling," during which the Monroe Doctrine proclaimed opposition to further European control in the Western hemisphere. [E372.H6] 92 AC 68
1. Monroe, James, Pres. U.S., 1758-1831. I. Title.

MONROE, James, Pres. U.S., 1758-1831. 923.173
Autobiography. Edited, and with an introd., by Stuart Gerry Brown, with the assistance of Donald G. Baker. [Syracuse] Syracuse University Press [1959] xi, 236 p. illus., ports., facsims. 23 cm. [E372.A3] 59-13117

MORGAN, George, 1854-1936. 973.54'0924 B
The life of James Monroe. New York, AMS Press [1969] xvi, 484 p. illus., facsims., ports. 23 cm. Reprint of the 1921 ed. [E372.M84 1969] 76-106979
1. Monroe, James, Pres. U.S., 1758-1831. BIP

Monroe, James, Pres. U.S., 1758-1831—Juvenile literature.

GERSON, Noel Bertram, 1914- 973.5'4'0924 B
James Monroe; hero of American diplomacy, by Noel B. Gerson. Illustrated by Tommy Upshur. Englewood Cliffs, N.J., Prentice-Hall [1969] 141 p. illus. 22 cm. A Rutledge book. Bibliography: p. 141. A biography of the President who originated the Monroe Doctrine, still the basis of the foreign policy of the United States. [E372.G45] 92 69-10330 4.50
1. Monroe, James, Pres. U.S., 1758-1831—Juvenile literature. I. Title.

MARBLE, Harriet Clement. 973.5'4'0924 B
James Monroe; patriot and president. New York, Putnam [1970] 189 p. 22 cm. (Lives to remember) Bibliography: p. [183]-186. A biography of the man who, as fifth President of the United States, was responsible for one of the earliest foreign policy doctrines. [E372.M2 1970] 92 78-113516 3.86
1. Monroe, James, Pres. U.S., 1758-1831—Juvenile literature. I. Title.

Monroe, Marilyn, 1926-1962.

CARPOZI, George, Jr. 927.92
Marilyn Monroe. [New York] Belmont [dist. Belmont Prodns., c.1961] 222p. illus. (Belmont bks., L508) 61-4052 .50 pap.,
1. Monroe, Marilyn, 1926- I. Title.

CARPOZI, George. 791.43'028'0924 B
Marilyn Monroe: "her own story," by George Carpozi, Jr. UPD special ed. [New York, Universal-Award House, 1973] 112 p. illus. 28 cm. [PN2287.M69C34] 73-180272 1.50 (pbk.)
1. Monroe, Marilyn, 1926-1962.

FRANKLIN, Joe. 927.92
The Marilyn Monroe story, by Joe Franklin and Laurie Palmer. New York, R. Field Co.; Greenberg, trade distributors [1953] 63p. illus. 23cm. [PN2287.M69F7] 53-12986
1. Monroe, Marilyn, 1926- I. Palmer, Laurie, joint author. II. Title.

GUILES, Fred Lawrence. 791.43'028'0924 B
Norma Jean; the life of Marilyn Monroe. [1st ed.] New York, McGraw-Hill [1969] x, 341 p. 23 cm. [PN2287.M69G8] 69-18712
1. Monroe, Marilyn, 1926-1962. I. Title.

HOYT, Edw n Palmer 791.43028
Marilyn, the tragic Venus. New York, Duell [dist. Meredith, c.1965] xv, 279p. ports. 21cm. [PN2287.M69H6] 65-24854 5.95 bds.,
1. Monroe, Marilyn, 1926-1962. I. Title.

HOYT, Edwin Palmer. 791.43028
Marilyn, the tragic Venus, by Edwin P. Hoyt. [1st ed.] New York, Duell, Sloan and Pearce [1965] 279 p. ports. 21 cm. [PN2287.M69H6] 65-24854
1. Monroe, Marilyn,1926-1962. I. Title.

HOYT, Edwin Palmer. 791.43'028'0924 B
Marilyn, the tragic Venus, by Edwin P. Hoyt. New ed. Radnor, Pa., Chilton Book Co. [1973] xvi, 279 p. 21 cm. [PN2287.M69H6 1973] 73-9951 ISBN 0-8019-5915-2 6.95
1. Monroe, Marilyn, 1926-1962. I. Title.

KOBAL, John. 791.43'028'0924
Marilyn Monroe; a life on film; introduction by David Robinson; compiled and edited by John Kobal. London, New York, Hamlyn, 1974. 176 p. illus. (some col.), ports. (some col.) 31 cm. Includes index. Bibliography: p. 174. [PN2287.M69K6] 74-185832 ISBN 0-600-36172-1 £2.50
1. Monroe, Marilyn, 1926-1962.

LEMBOURN, Hans Jorgen, 1923- 791.43'028'0924 B
Diary of a lover of Marilyn Monroe / Hans Jorgen Lembourn ; translated by Hallberg Hallmundsson. New York : Arbor House, c1979. 214 p. ; 22 cm. Translation of 40 [i.e. Fyrre] dage med Marilyn. [PN2287.M69L413] 78-73861 ISBN 0-87795-216-7 : 8.95
1. Monroe, Marilyn, 1926-1962. 2. Moving-picture actors and actresses—United States—Biography. I. Title. BIP

MAILER, Norman. 791.43'028'0924 B
Marilyn, a biography. Pictures by the world's foremost photographers. [New York, Grosset & Dunlap, 1973] 270 p. illus. 28 cm. [PN2287.M69M28] 73-6899 ISBN 0-448-01029-1 19.95
1. Monroe, Marilyn, 1926-1962. I. Title.

MARTIN, Thornton, 1901- 927.92
Will acting spoil Marilyn Monroe? [By] Pete Martin [1st ed.] Garden City, N. Y., Doubleday, 1956. 128p. illus. 22cm. [PN2287.M69M3] 56-10769
1. Monroe, Marilyn, 1926- I. Title.

MARTIN, Thornton, 1901- 927.92
Will acting spoil Marylin Monore? [By] Pete Martin. [1st ed.] Garden City, N. Y., Doubleday, 1956. 128p. illus. 22cm. [PN2287.M69M3] 56-10769
1. Monroe, Marllyn, 1926- I. Title.

MELLEN, Joan. 791.43'028'0924
Marilyn Monroe. New York, Pyramid Publications [1973] 157 p. illus. 20 cm. (Pyramid illustrated history of the movies) Bibliography: p. 147-149. "The films of Marilyn Monroe": p. 150-153. [PN2287.M69M4] 73-78304 ISBN 0-515-03129-1 1.45 (pbk.)
1. Monroe, Marilyn, 1926-1962.

MELLEN, Joan. 791.43'028'0924
Marilyn Monroe / by Joan Mellen. New York : Galahad Books, [1974] c1973. 157 p. : ill. ; 22 cm. (The Pictorial treasury of film stars) Includes index. Bibliography: p. 147-149. [PN2287.M69M4 1974] 73-90218 ISBN 0-88365-165-3 : 4.95
1. Monroe, Marilyn, 1926-1962.

MONROE, Marilyn, 1926-1962. 791.43'028'0924 B
My story. New York, Stein and Day [1974] 143 p. 22 cm. [PN2287.M69A35] 74-77341 ISBN 0-8128-1707-9 5.95
1. Monroe, Marilyn, 1926-1962. I. Title.

MURRAY, Eunice. 791.43'028'0924 B
Marilyn, the last months / Eunice Murray, with Rose Shade. New York : Pyramid Books, 1975. 157 p., [4] leaves of plates : ports. ; 18 cm. [PN2287.M69M8] 74-25438 pbk. : 1.75
1. Monroe, Marilyn, 1926-1962. I. Shade, Rose, joint author. II. Title.

PEPITONE, Lena. 791.43'028'0924 B
Marilyn Monroe confidential : an intimate personal account / by Lena Pepitone and William Stadiem. New York : Simon and Schuster, c1979. 251 p., [8] leaves of plates : ill. ; 22 cm. [PN2287.M69P4] 78-26159 ISBN 0-671-24289-X : 9.95
1. Monroe, Marilyn, 1926-1962. 2. Moving-picture actors and actresses—United States—Biography. I. Stadiem, William, joint author. II. Title.

SLATZER, Robert F. 791.43'028'0924 B
The life and curious death of Marilyn Monroe / by Robert F. Slatzer. New York : Pinnacle House, 1974. xix, 348 p., [16] leaves of plates : ill. ; 24 cm. Includes index. Bibliography: p. 323-325. [PN2287.M69S55] 74-76796 8.95
1. Monroe, Marilyn, 1926-1962. I. Title. BIP

VIOLATIONS of the child 927.92
Marilyn Monroe. By her psychiatrist friend. [Prelude signed by H. P. S.] Cover, illus. by Veno. New York, Bridge-Bks., 1962. 159p. illus 22cm. 62-21278 3.95
1. Monroe, Marilyn, 1926-1962. I. S., H. P.

WAGENKNECHT, Edward Charles, 1900- comp. 791.43'028'0924
Marilyn Monroe; a composite view. Edited by Edward Wagenknecht. [1st ed.] Philadelphia, Chilton Book Co. [1969] xvii, 200 p. 24 cm. [PN2287.M69W3 1969] 75-90000
1. Monroe, Marilyn, 1926-1962.

WEATHERBY, William J. 791.43'028'0924 B
Conversations with Marilyn / W. J. Weatherby. New York : Mason/Charter, 1976. 229 p. ; 22 cm. [PN2287.M69W4] 75-45368 ISBN 0-88405-148-X : 7.95
1. Monroe, Marilyn, 1926-1962. I. Monroe, Marilyn, 1926-1962. II. Title.

ZOLOTOW, Maurice 927.92
Marilyn Monroe. New York, Harcourt, Brace [c.1960] xii, 340p. illus. 22cm. 60-10934 5.75 half cloth,
1. Monroe, Marilyn. I. Title.

ZOLOTOW, Maurice, 1913- v. 12
Marilyn Monroe. New York, Bantam Books [1961, c1960] 338 p. illus. 22 cm. 67-7281
1. Monroe, Marilyn, 1926- I. Title.

Monroe, Robert A.

MONROE, Robert A. 133.9'2
Journeys out of the body / Robert A. Monroe. Updated. Garden City, N.Y. : Anchor Press, 1977. 280 p. ; 21 cm. [BF1283.M582A3 1977] 77-154512 ISBN 0-385-00861-9 pbk. : 3.95
1. Monroe, Robert A. 2. Psychical research—Biography. 3. Astral projection. I. Title. BIP

Monroe, William G.

MONROE, William G. 920.9
It was fun while it lasted: the memories and musings of a real American 'old-timer.' New York, Greenwich Book Publishers [c.1959] 153p. 22cm. 59-12562 2.75

I. Title.

MONROE, William G 1905- 920
It was fun while it lasted; the memories and musings of a real American 'old-timer.' [1st ed.] New York, Greenwich Book Publishers [1959] 153p. 21cm. [CT275.M578A3] 59-12562
I. Title.

Monsarrat, Nicholas,

MONSARRAT, Nicholas, 823'.9'12 B
1910-
Breaking in, breaking out; an autobiography. New York, Morrow, 1971 [c1970] 542 p. illus. 24 cm. "An abridged version of the book published in Great Britain in two volumes under the title Life is a four-letter word." [PR6025.O36Z523 1971] 70-151917 12.50
I. Title.

Monsarrat, Nicholas, 1910-

MONSARRAT, Nicholas, 823'.9'12 B
1910-
Breaking in, breaking out; an autobiography. New York, Morrow, 1971 [c1970] 542 p. illus. 24 cm. "An abridged version of the book published in Great Britain in two volumes under the title Life is a four-letter word." [PR6025.O36Z523 1971] 70-151917 12.50
I. Title.

NICHOLAS Monsarrat [a biographical sketch] New York [1956] broadside. 28 x22cm. v. 12
1. Monsarrat, Nicholas, 1910- I. Morrow (William) and Company, New York.

Monsarrat, Nicholas, 1910- — Biography.

MONSARRAT, 940.54'59'41 B
Nicholas, 1910-
Monsarrat at sea / Nicholas Monsarrat. New York : Morrow, 1976, c1975. p. cm. Contents.Contents.—The longest love, the longest hate.—Three corvettes: H.M. corvette. East coast corvette. Corvette command.—I was there.—A ship to remember.—"H.M.S. Marlborough will enter harbour."—It was cruel.—The ship that died of shame. [PR6025.O36Z526 1976] 76-14864 ISBN 0-688-03103-X : 10.00
1. Monsarrat, Nicholas, 1910- — Biography. 2. World War, 1939-1945—Personal narratives, English. 3. Sea stories, English. I. Title. **BIP**

Monson, Todd.

MONSON, Gabriele. 248'.2 B
Say hi to Jesus for me / Gabriele Monson. Minneapolis : Augsburg Pub. House, c1979. 175 p. ; 20 cm. [BR1725.M524M66] 78-66951 ISBN 0-8066-1690-3 : 3.95
1. Monson, Todd. 2. Monson, Gabriele. 3. Christian biography—United States. 4. Cancer—Biography. I. Title.

Montagu, Edwin Samuel, 1879-1924.

WALEY, Sigismund David, 923.242
Sir 1887-1962
Edwin Montagu: a memoir and an account of his visits to India. New York, Asia Pub. [dist. Taplinger, c.1964] ix, 343p. ports. 23cm. [DS413.W29] 65-631 11.00
1. Montagu, Edwin Samuel, 1879-1924. 2. India—Descr. & trav.—1901-1946. I. Title.

WALEY, Sir Sigismund 923.242
David, 1887-1962.
Edwin Montagu: a memoir and an account of his visits to India. New York, Asia Pub. House [1964] ix, 343 p. ports. 23 cm. "Part II ... consists of extracts from Montagu's] 1912-13 diary." [DS413.W29 1964] 65-631
1. Montagu, Edwin Samuel, 1879-1924. 2. India—Descr. & trav.—1901-1946. I. Title.

Montagu, Elizabeth Robinson, 1720-1800.

BUSSE, John. 828'.6'09 B
Mrs. Montagu, Queen of the Blues / by John Busse. Folcroft, Pa. : Folcroft Library Editions, 1977. 83 p., [1] leaf of plates : port. ; 23 cm. Reprint of the 1928 ed. published by G. Howe, London, which was issued in series: Representative women. Bibliography: p. 83. [PR3603.M2Z55 1977] 77-16149 ISBN 0-8414-9905-5 lib. bdg. : 10.00
1. Montagu, Elizabeth Robinson, 1720-1800. 2. Authors, English—19th century—Biography. I. Title. II. Series: Representative women (London) **BIP**

DORAN, John, 914.2'03'720924 B
1807-1878.
A lady of the last century (Mrs. Elizabeth Montagu): illustrated in her unpublished letters; collected and arranged, with a biographical sketch, and a chapter on blue stockings. 2d ed. London, R. Bentley, 1873. [New York, AMS Press, 1973] xvi, 372 p. 23 cm. On spine: WOL. [DA483.M7D7 1973] 75-37690 ISBN 0-404-56744-4 19.50
1. Montagu, Elizabeth (Robinson) 1720-1800. I. Title.

MONTAGU, 914.2'03'720924 B
Elizabeth Robinson, 1720-1800.
The letters of Mrs. Elizabeth Montagu, with some of the letters of her correspondents. London, Printed for T. Cadell and W. Davies, 1809-1813. [New York, AMS Press, 1974] 4 v. port. 18 cm. (Women of letters) Contents.Contents.—pt. 1. Containing her letters from an early age to the age of twenty-three. 2 v.—pt. 2. Containing her letters from the age of twenty-three to forty, ending with the coronation of George the Third. 2 v. [DA483.M7A4 1974] 72-37704 ISBN 0-404 56800-9
1. Montagu, Elizabeth Robinson, 1720-1800. I. Title.

Montagu, Lady Mary (Pierrepont) Wortley, 1689-1762.

HALSBAND, Robert 928.2
The life of Lady Mary Wortley Montagu. New York, Oxford University Press, [c.] 1960. xii, 313p. (Bibl. footnotes) illus. 21cm. (A Galaxy book, GB44) 60-50029 2.25 pap.,
1. Montagu, Lady Mary (Pierrepont) Wortley, 1689-1762. I. Title.

HALSBAND, Robert, 1914- 928.2
The life of Lady Mary Wortley Montagu. Oxford, Clarendon Press, 1956 [i.e. 1957] 313p. illus. 23cm. [DA501.M7H3] 56-14373
1. Montagu, Lady Mary (Pierrepont) Wortley, 1689-1762. I. Title. **BIP**

HALSBAND, Robert, 1914- 928.2
The life of Lady Mary Wortley Montagu. New York, Oxford University Press, 1960. 313p. illus. 21cm. (A Galaxy book, GB44) [DA501.M7H3 1960] 60-50029
1. Montagu, Lady Mary (Pierrepont) Wortley, 1689-1762. I. Title.

MONTAGU, Mary (Pierrepont) 826'.5
Wortley, Lady, 1689-1762.
The selected letters of Lady Mary Wortley Montagu. Edited by Robert Halsband. New York, St. Martin's Press [1971, c1970] 310 p. port. 26 cm. Includes bibliographical references. [DA501.M7A4 1971] 74-141076 15.00
I. Title.

Montagu, Lilian Helen,

CONRAD, Eric, 1911- 923.642
Lily H. Montagu, prophet of a living Judaism. With a foreword by Leo Baeck. New York, National Federation of Temple Sisterhoods [1953] 111p. illus. 20cm. [DS135.E6M685] 54-21438
1. Montagu, Lilian Helen, I. Title.

Montagu, Mary (Pierrepont) Wortley,

MONTAGU, Mary (Pierrepont) 826'.5
Wortley, Lady, 1689-1762.
The selected letters of Lady Mary Wortley Montagu. Edited by Robert Halsband. New York, St. Martin's Press [1971, c1970] 310 p. port. 26 cm. Includes bibliographical references. [DA501.M7A4 1971] 74-141076 15.00
I. Title.

Montague, Andrew Jackson, 1862-1937.

LARSEN, William E., 320.0924
1936-
Montague of Virginia; the making of a Southern progressive. [Baton Rouge] La. State Univ. Pr. [1966, c.1965] xiii, 314p. map, ports. 24cm. (Southern biog. ser.) Bibl. [E748.M65L3] 65-20299 7.50
1. Montague, Andrew Jackson, 1862-1937 2. Virginia—Pol. & govt.—1865-1950. 3. U.S.—Pol. & govt.—20th cent. 4. Progressivism (U.S. politics) I. Title. II. Series.

Montaigne, Michel Eyquem de, 1533-1592.

DOWDEN, Edward, 1843- 844'.3 B
1913.
Michel de Montaigne. Port Washington, N.Y., Kennikat Press [1972] 383 p. port. 21 cm. Reprint of the 1905 ed. Bibliography: p. 361-370. [PQ1643.D6 1972] 77-153266 ISBN 0-8046-1562-4
1. Montaigne, Michel Eyquem de, 1533-1592. **BIP**

FRAME, Donald Murdoch, 844.3
1911-
Montaigne: a biography, by Donald M. Frame. [1st ed.] New York, Harcourt, Brace & World [1965] viii, 408 p. illus., facsims, geneal, table, map (on lining papers) ports. 25 cm. "Table of contents of Montaigne's essays": p. 324-326. Bibliographical references included in "Notes" (p. 329-393) [PQ1643.F69] 65 19055
1. Montaigne, Michel Eyquem de, 1533-1592. **BIP**

FRAME, Donald Murdoch, 844'.3 B
1911-
Montaigne in France, 1812-1852 / Donald Murdoch Frame. New York : Octagon Books, 1976, c1940. xii, 308 p. ; 24 cm. Reprint of the ed. published by Columbia University Press, New York. Includes index. Bibliography: p. [237]-294. [PQ1643.F7 1976] 75-43855 ISBN 0-374-92845-2 : 13.00
1. Montaigne, Michel Eyguem de, 1533-1592—Appreciation—France. 2. French literature—19th century—History and criticism. I. Title. **BIP**

Montaigne, Michel Eyquem de, 1533-1592—Biography.

LOWNDES, Mary E. 844'.3 B
Michel de Montaigne : a biographical study / by M. E. Lowndes. Folcroft, Pa. : Folcroft Library Editions, 1976. p. cm. Reprint of the 1898 ed. published by the University Press, Cambridge. [PQ1643.L6 1976] 76-18077 ISBN 0-8414-5738-7 lib. bdg. : 27.50
1. Montaigne, Michel Eyquem de, 1533-1592—Biography. **BIP**

Montalembert, Charles Forbes Rene de Tryon, comte de, 1810-1870.

FINLAY, James 320.5'1'0924 B
Charles, 1922-
The liberal who failed [by] James C. Finlay. With a foreword by John H. Hallowell. Washington, Corpus Books [1968] 286 p. 21 cm. Bibliographical references included in "Notes" (p. 214-278) [DC255.M7F47] 68-10451
1. Montalembert, Charles Forbes Rene de Tryon, comte de, 1810-1870. I. Title.

Montana—Biography.

MCCARTHY, Donald. 917.86'03'3
Afternoons in Montana, by Don McCarthy. Chapter drawings by Mary Ann McCarthy. [1st ed. Aberdeen, S.D., North Plains Press, 1971] 124 p. illus. 24 cm. "Language of the mosshorn": p. [85]-[122] [F730.M3] 77-179451 5.95
1. Montana—Biography. 2. Cowboys—Language (New words, slang, etc.) I. McCarthy, Donald, ed. Language of the mosshorn. 1971. II. Title. **BIP**

Montano, Walter Manuel.

PEARSON, Benjamin Harold, 922.585
1893-
The monk who lived again. Los Angeles, Cowman Publications [1952] 178 p. 20 cm. [BX1777.M6P4 1952] 52-44957
1. Montano, Walter Manuel. I. Title.

Montcalm-Gozon, Louis Joseph de, marquis de Saint-Veran, 1712-1759.

LEWIS, Meriwether Liston 923.5
Montcalm, the marvelous marquis. New York, Vantage [c.1961] 178p. front port. Bibl. 3.50 bds.,
1. Montcalm-Gozon, Louis Joseph de, marquis de Saint Veran, 1712-1759. I. Title.

LEWIS, Meriwether Liston. 923.544
Montcalm, the marvelous marquis. [1st ed.] New York, Vantage Press [1961] 178p. illus. 21cm. Includes bibliography. [E199.M7375] 62-1169
1. Montcalm-Gozon, Louis Joseph de, marquis de Saint-Veran, 1712-1759. I. Title.

Monteith, John, 1788-1868.

BONISTEEL, Roscoe 378.1'12'0924
Osmond, 1888-
John Monteith, first president of the University of Michigan [by] Roscoe O. Bonisteel. Ann Arbor, University of Michigan [1967] 23 p. illus., port. 23 cm. (Michigan Historical Collections. Bulletin no. 15) "A sesquicentennial publication." Bibliography: p. 22-23. [LD3275 1817.B59] 68-65895
1. Monteith, John, 1788-1868. 2. Michigan University—History. I. Series: Michigan. University. Michigan Historical Collections. Bulletin no. 15

Monteith, Robert, 1878- 1956.

LYNCH, Florence 923.5415
Monteith.
The mystery man of Banna Strand; the life and death of Captain Robert Monteith. [1st ed.] New York, Vantage Press [1959] 203p. illus., ports., facsims. 22cm. [DA965.M6L9] 59-14294
1. Monteith, Robert, 1878- 1956. 2. Casement, Roger, Sir 1864-1916. I. Title.

Montejo, Esteban,

MONTEJO, 917.291'03'50924
Esteban, 1860-
The autobiography of a runaway slave. Edited by Miguel Barnet. Translated from the Spanish by Jocasta Innes. [1st American ed.] New York, Pantheon Books [1968] 223 p. 21 cm. Translation of Biografia de un cimarron. [CT518.M6A33 1968] 68-25640 4.95
I. Barnet, Miguel, 1940- ed. II. Title.

MONTEJO, 917.291'03'50924 B
Esteban, 1860-
The autobiography of a runaway slave; edited by Miguel Barnet. Translated from the Spanish by Jocasta Innes. New York, Vintage Books [1973, c1968] 223 p. 19 cm. Translation of Biografia de un cimarron. [HT869.M6A313 1973] 72-1752 ISBN 0-394-71832-1 1.95 (pbk.)
I. Barnet, Miguel, 1940- II. Title.

Montesquieu, Charles Louis de Secondat, baron de La Brede et de, 1689-1755.

SOREL, Albert, 1842- 320.5'0924
1906.
Montesquieu. Translated by Melville B. Anderson and Edward Playfair Anderson. Port Washington, N.Y., Kennikat Press [1969] vi, 218 p. 17 cm. (The Great French writers) Reprint of the 1888 ed. [PQ2012.S62 1969] 68-26254
1. Montesquieu, Charles Louis de Secondat, baron de La Brede et de, 1689-1755. I. Title. II. Series. **BIP**

Montesquieu, Charles Louis de Secondat, baron de La Brede et de, 1689-1755.

SHACKLETON, Robert. 928.4
Montesquieu; a critical biography. [London] Oxford University Press, 1961. siv, 432 p. illus. port. 23 cm. "Bibliography of Montesquieu": 0. [400]-418. Bibliographical footnotes. [JC179.M8S35 1961] 61-4884
1. Montesquieu, Charles Louis de Secondat, baron de La Brede et de, 1689-1755. I. Title. **BIP**

Montesquiou-Fezensac, Robert, comte de, 1855-1921.

JULLIAN, Philippe. 841'.9'12 B
Prince of aesthetes: Count Robert de Montesquiou, 1855-1921. Translated from the French by John Haylock and Francis King. New York, Viking Press [1968, c1967] 288 p. illus., ports. 22 cm. Translation of Robert de Montesquiou, un prince 1900. [PQ2625.O39Z753 1968] 68-11419
1. Montesquiou-Fezensac, Robert, comte de, 1855-1921. I. Title.

Montessori, Maria, 1870-1952.

KRAMER, Rita. 372.1'3'0924 B
Maria Montessori : a biography / by Rita Kramer. New York : Putnam, c1976. 410 p., [8] leaves of plates : ill. ; 24 cm. Includes bibliographical references and index. [LB775.M8K7 1976] 75-37486 ISBN 0-399-11304-5 : 10.00
1. Montessori, Maria, 1870-1952.

SMARIDGE, Norah. 372.21092
The light within; the story of Maria Montessori. Illustrated by Janet and Alex D'Amato. New York, Hawthorn Books [1965] 172 p. illus. 22 cm. Bibliography: p. [165] [LB775.M8S56] 65-12732
1. Montessori, Maria, 1870-1952. I. Title.

STANDING, E. Mortimer 923.745
Maria Montessori, her life and work. [New York] New Amer. Lib. [c.1957, 1962] 382p. illus. 18cm. (Mentor-Omega bk., MQ425) Bibl. .95 pap.,
1. Montessori, Maria, 1870-1952. I. Title.

STANDING, E. Mortimer. 923.745
Maria Montessori, her life and work. [1st American ed.] Fresno, Calif., Academy Library Guild [1959, c1957] 354 p. illus. 22 cm. [LB775.M8S78 1959] 59-12591
1. Montessori, Maria, 1870-1952.

Monteux, Pierre, 1875-

MONTEUX, Doris Gerald 927.8
(Hodgkins)
Everyone is someone [by] Fifi Monteux. New York, Farrar, Straus Cudahy [1962] 138p. 21cm. The story of Pierre Monteux as supposedly seen and told by his dog Fifi to his wife Doris. [ML422.M72M7] 62-16687
1. Monteux, Pierre, 1875- 2. Musicians—Correspondence, reminiscences, etc. I. Title.

Monteverdi, Claudio, 1567-1643.

ARNOLD, Denis 927.8
Monteverdi. London, J. M. Dent; New York, Farrar, [c.1963] 212p. illus. 20cm. (Master musicians ser.) Bibl. 63-2544 3.50
1. Monteverdi, Claudio, 1567-1643. I. Title. **BIP**

PRUNIERES, Henry, 784.092'4 [B]
1886-1942.
Monteverdi; his life and work. Translated from the French by Marie D. Mackie. [Magnolia, Mass.] [Peter Smith] [1973 c.1972] vii, 293 p. music, port. 21 cm. (Dover bk. rebound) Reprint of the 1926 ed. Bibliography: p. 288-290. [ML410.M77P771 1972] 70-159686 ISBN 0-486-22770-7 5.50
1. Monteverdi, Claudio, 1567-1643. I. Title. **BIP**

PRUNIERES, Henry, 784'.092'4 B
1886-1942.
Monteverdi; his life and work. Translated from the French by Marie D. Mackie. Westport, Conn., Greenwood Press [1973] vii, 293 p. illus. 22 cm. Reprint of the 1926 ed. published by J. M. Dent, London, in series: Dent's international library of books on music. Bibliography: p. 288-290. [ML410.M77P771 1973] 70-100830 ISBN 0-8371-3996-1 11.75
1. Monteverdi, Claudio, 1567-1643.

REDLICH, Hans 784'.0924 B
Ferdinand, 1903-
Claudio Monteverdi, life and works. Translated by Kathleen Dale. Westport, Conn., Greenwood Press [1970] vi, 204 p. illus., music, ports. 23 cm. Reprint of the 1952 ed. Bibliography: p. [192]-194. [ML410.M77R432 1970] 70-104253 ISBN 0-8371-4003-X
1. Monteverdi, Claudio, 1567-1643.

REDLICH, Hans Ferdinand, 927.8
1903-
Claudio Monteverdi, life and works. Translated by Kathleen Dale. London, New York, Oxford University Press, 1952. vi, 204 p. illus., ports., music. 23 cm. "Several chapters and continuous paragraphs have been specially written for this [English] edition." Bibliography: p. [192]-194. [ML410.M77R432] 52-7825
1. Monteverdi, Claudio, 1567-1643. I. Title.

SCHRADE, Leo, 1903- 784'.092'4 B
*1903-1964.
Monteverdi : creator of modern music / Leo Schrade. New York : Da Capo Press, 1979, c1950. 384 p., [5] leaves of plates : ill. ; 24 cm. (Da Capo Press music reprint series) Reprint of the ed. published by W. W. Norton, New York. Includes index. Bibliography: p. 371-377. [ML410.M77S35 1979] 79-12292 ISBN 0-306-79565-5 : 25.00
1. Monteverdi, Claudio, 1567-1643. 2. Composers—Italy—Biography.

Montez, Lola, 1818-1861.

DARLING, Amanda. 793.3'2'0924 B
Lola Montez. New York, Stein and Day [1972] 240 p. 24 cm. [DD801.B383M59 1972] 74-185956 ISBN 0-8128-1436-3 7.95
1. Montez, Lola, 1818-1861.

GOLDBERG, Isaac, 793.3'2'0924 B
1887-1938.
Queen of hearts; the passionate pilgrimage of Lola Montez. New York, B. Blom [1969] 308 p. port. 21 cm. Reprint of the 1936 ed. Bibliography: p. 301-308. [DD801.B383M63 1969] 75-91505
1. Montez, Lola, 1818-1861. I. Title. **BIP**

GOLDBERG, Isaac, 793.3'2'0924 B
1887-1938.
Queen of hearts; the passionate pilgrimage of Lola Montez. New York, B. Blom [1969] 308 p. port. 21 cm. Reprint of the 1936 ed. Bibliography: p. 301-308. [DD801.B383M63 1969] 75-91505
1. Montez, Lola, 1818-1861. I. Title. **BIP**

HOLDREDGE, Helen 927.93
O'Donnell.
The woman in black; the life of Lola Montez. New York, Putman [1955] 309 p. illus. 22 cm. Includes bibliographies. [DD801.B383M635] 55-10419
1. Montez, Lola, 1818-1861. I. Title.

LOLA Montes: 793.3'2'0924 B
the tragic story of a liberated woman. Melbourne, Heritage Publications, 1973. 90 p. plates. 26 cm. Index. Bibliography: p. 86-88. [DD801.B383M654] 74-170007 ISBN 0-9599841-8-6 7.50
1. Montez, Lola, 1818-1861. **BIP**

ROSS, Ishbel, 793.3'2'0924 B
1897-
The uncrowned queen; life of Lola Montez. [1st ed.] New York, Harper & Row [1972] xiv, 349 p. illus. 22 cm. Bibliography: p. 327-336. [DD801.B383M684 1972] 70-181641 ISBN 0-06-013662-6 8.95
1. Montez, Lola, 1818-1861. I. Title.

Montezuma, Carlos, 1866-1923.

ARNOLD, Oren. 926.1
Savage son. [Albuquerque] [University of New Mexico Press] [1951] 273 p. illus. 21 cm. [R154.M718A7] 51-13912
1. Montezuma, Carlos, 1866-1923. I. Title.

Montezuma, Carlos, 1866-1923—Juvenile literature.

ARNOLD, Adele R. 610'.92'4 B
Red son rising [by] Adele R. Arnold. Minneapolis, Dillon Press [1974] 103 p. illus. 22 cm. A biography of Apache Indian Carlos Montezuma, who became a well-known physician. [E99.A6A75] 92 74-17283 ISBN 0-87518-077-9 5.95
1. Montezuma, Carlos, 1866-1923—Juvenile literature. I. Title. **BIP**

Montezuma I, Emperor of Mexico, ca. 1398-ca. 1468.

GILLMOR, Frances, 1903- 923.172
The King danced in the marketplace. Illustrated by Carolyn Huff Kinsey. Tucson, University of Arizona Press, 1964. xvi, 271 p. illus., map (on lining papers) geneal. table. 24 cm. Issued also as thesis, Universidad Nacional Autonoma de Mexico. Bibliography: p. 243-265. [F1219.G47 1964] 63-11970
1. Montezuma I, Emperor of Mexico, ca. 1398-ca. 1468. I. Title. **BIP**

Montezuma II, Emperor of Mexico, 1480 (ca.)-1520.

BURLAND, Cottie Arthur, 970.3 B
1905-
Montezuma: Lord of the Aztecs [by] C. A. Burland. Color photography by Werner Forman. New York, Putnam [1973] 269 p. illus. 26 cm. Bibliography: p. 265. [F1219.M8B87 1973b] 73-78633 ISBN 0-399-11176-X 15.00
1. Montezuma II, Emperor of Mexico, 1480 (ca.)-1520. 2. Mexico—History—Conquest, 1519-1540. I. Title.

COLLIS, Maurice, 1889- 923.572
Cortes and Montezuma. [1st American ed.] New York, Harcourt, Brace [1955, c1954] 256p. illus. 21cm. [F1230.C73 1955] 55-9377
1. Montezuma. Emperor of Exico, 1480 (ca.)-1520. I. Cortes, Hernando, 1485-1547. II. Title.

MONTERDE GARCIA 972'.02'0924
IEAZOALCETA, Francisco 1894-
Moctezuma, el de la silla de oro. Edited by Donald G. Castanien and Frederick S. Stimsn. New York, Oxford University Press, 1958. 107p. illus. 21cm. (Oxford Spanish readers) Includes bibliography. [F1230.M6M6 1958] 58-5376
1. Montezuma II. Emperor of Mexico, 1483 (ca.)-1520. 2. Mexico —Hist.—Conquest, 1519-1540. I. Title.

Montfort, Simon of, Earl of Leicester, 1208?-1265.

BEMONT, Charles, 942.03'4'0924 B
1848-1939.
Simon de Montfort, Earl of Leicester, 1208-1265. A new ed. translated by E. F. Jacob. Westport, Conn., Greenwood Press [1974] xxxix, 303 p. illus. 22 cm. Reprint of the 1930 ed. published by the Clarendon Press, Oxford. Bibliography: p. [xxxi]-xxxix. [DA228.M7B413 1974] 74-9223 ISBN 0-8371-7625-5 17.75
1. Montfort, Simon of, Earl of Leicester, 1208?-1265. **BIP**

JACOB, Ernest Fraser, 942.03'4
1894-
Studies in the period of baronial reform and rebellion, 1258-1267, by E. F. Jacob. New York, Octagon Books, 1974. xiv, 443 p. 23 cm. Reprint of the 1925 ed. published by the Clarendon Press, Oxford, which was issued as v. 8, no. 14 of Oxford studies in social and legal history. Includes bibliographical references. [DA227.5.J3 1974] 73-22287 ISBN 0-374-96167-0 22.50
1. Montfort, Simon of, Earl of Leicester, 1208?-1265. 2. Barons' War, 1263-1267. 3. Great Britain—Politics and government—1216-1272. I. Title. II. Series: Oxford studies in social and legal history, v. 8, no. 14.
Part of a nine volume set selling for 160.00.

LABARGE, Margaret Wade 923.242
Simon de Montfort, New York, Norton [1963, c.1962] 312p. illus. 23cm. Bibl. 63-6618 7.95
1. Montfort, Simon of, earl of Leicester, 1208?-1265. I. Title. **BIP**

LABARGE, Margaret 942.03'4'0924 B
Wade.
Simon de Montfort / by Margaret Wade Labarge. Westport, Conn. : Greenwood Press, 1975, c1962. xi, 312 p. : ill. ; 22 cm. Reprint of the 1963 ed. published by Norton, New York. Includes index. Bibliography: p. 297-303. [DA228.M7L3 1975] 75-22643 ISBN 0-8371-8359-6 : 16.00
1. Montfort, Simon of, Earl of Leicester, 1208?-1265.

Montgomery, Ala. First Presbyterian Church.

MAHONEY, William 285'.1761'47
James.
One hundred and fifty years : a sesquicentennial history of Montgomery's First Presbyterian Church / by William James Mahoney, Jr. ; introd. by Harry N. Miller, Jr. MOntgomery, Ala. : First Presbyterian Church of Montgomery, [1974] xiv, 146 p. : ill. ; 23 cm. Includes index. Bibliography: p. 137. [BX9211.M75F575] 75-304560
1. Montgomery, Ala. First Presbyterian Church. 2. Montgomery, Ala.—Biography. I. Title.

Montgomery, Bernard Law Montgomery, 1st viscount, 1887- —Juvenile literature.

CLARK, Ronald William 923.542
Montgomery of Alamein. New York, Roy Publishers [1961, c.1960] 109p. illus. 19cm. (The 'Living biographies' series) 60-14081 2.50 bds.,
1. Montgomery, Bernard Law Montgomery, 1st viscount, 1887- —Juvenile literature. I. Title.

CLARK, Ronald William. 923.542
Montgomery of Alamein. London, Phoenix House; New York, Roy Publishers [1960] 109p. illus. 19cm. (The 'Living biographies' series) [DA69.3.M56C6] 60-14081
1. Montgomery, Bernard Law Montgomery. 1st viscount, 1887- —Juvenile literature. I. Title.

Montgomery Co., Md.—History.

BOYD, Thomas Hulings 975.2'84
Stockton.
The history of Montgomery County, Maryland, from its earliest settlement in 1650 to 1879, by T. H. S. Boyd. With a new index. Baltimore, Regional Pub. Co., 1968. x, 187 p. 23 cm. Reprint of the 1879 ed. [F187.M7B7 1968] 68-31727
1. Montgomery Co., Md.—History. 2. Montgomery Co., Md.—Biography. 3. Montgomery Co., Md.—Directories. I. Title. **BIP**

Montgomery, Elizabeth Rider.

MONTGOMERY, 785.4'2'0924
Elizabeth Rider.
Duke Ellington; King of jazz, by Elizabeth Rider Montgomery. Illustrated by Paul Frame. [New York: Dell, 1975 c1972] 96 p.: illus.; 20 cm. (A Yearling book) (Americans all) Biography of an internationally acclaimed jazz musician who as a young man was torn between a career in art and music. [B] [ML3930.E44M6] 0.95 (pbk.)
I. Title.
L.C. card no. for original edition: 70-179401. **BIP**

Montgomery, Ernesto Alexander, 1925-

LINEDECKER, Clifford 133.8'092'4
L.
Psychic spy : the story of an astounding man / Clifford L. Linedecker. 1st ed.

Garden City, N.Y. : Doubleday, 1976. xiv, 178 p. ; 22 cm. Bibliography: p. [176]-178. [BF1283.M585L45] 76-3003 ISBN 0-385-11457-5 : 7.95
1. Montgomery, Ernesto Alexander, 1925- I. Title.

Montgomery, George Thomas, Abp. 1847-1907.

WEBER, Francis J 262.120924
George Thomas Montgomery, California churchman, by Francis J. Weber. Los Angeles. Westernlore, Pr. 1966. xii, 57p. illus., ports. 21cm. Bibl. [BX4705.M654W4] 66-23591 6.00
1. Montgomery, George Thomas, Abp. 1847-1907. I. Title.

Montgomery, Helen (Barrett) 1861-1934.

CATTAN, Louise 266'.023'0922 B
Armstrong.
Lamps are for lighting; the story of Helen Barrett Montgomery and Lucy Waterbury Peabody. Grand Rapids, Mich., Eerdmans [1972] 123 p. 22 cm. (Christian world mission books) Bibliography: p. 119-120. [BV2610.C37] 72-77184 ISBN 0-8028-1480-8 2.45
1. Montgomery, Helen (Barrett) 1861-1934. 2. Peabody, Lucy (McGill) Waterbury, 1861-1949. I. Title.

Montgomery, Janet Livingston, 1743-1828.

BABBITT, Katherine 973.3'092'4 B
M., 1915-
Janet Montgomery : Hudson River squire / by Katherine M. Babbitt. Monroe, N.Y. : Library Research Associates, [1975] 55 p. ; 23 cm. (Cameo series of notable women) Includes index. Bibliography: p. 43-52. [E207.M69B32] 75-9600 ISBN 0-912526-18-1 pbk. : 2.45
1. Montgomery, Janet Livingston, 1743-1828. 2. Montgomery, Richard, 1738-1775. BIP

Montgomery, Joe, 1876-

MONTGOMERY, Joe, 1876- 978.6'03 B
Colonel Joe, the last of the Rough Riders : recollections of a centenarian / as told to Claudia J. Brownlee. 1st ed. Hicksville, N.Y. : Exposition Press, c1978. 215 p. ; 21 cm. [E714.6.M66A33] 77-15346 ISBN 0-682-48988-3 : 8.00
1. Montgomery, Joe, 1876- 2. United States—History—War of 1898. 3. Montana—Social life and customs. 4. Soldiers—United States—Biography. I. Brownlee, Claudia J. II. Title. BIP

Montgomery, John Joseph, 1858-1911.

SPEARMAN, Arthur 629.13'00924 (B)
Dunning, 1899-
John Joseph Montgomery, 1858-1911 father of basic flying. A documentation by Arthur Dunning Spearman. Santa Clara, Calif., University of Santa Clara [1967] xx, 241 p. illus., facsims., map, ports. 27 cm. Bibliography: p. 222-236. [TL540.M62S65] 67-31889
1. Montgomery, John Joseph, 1858-1911. I. Title.

SPEARMAN, Arthur 629.13'00924 B
Dunning, 1899-
John Joseph Montgomery, 1858-1911, father of basic flying. A documentation by Arthur Dunning Spearman. Santa Clara, Calif., University of Santa Clara [1967] xx, 241 p. illus., facsims., map, ports. 27 cm. Bibliography: p. 222-236. [TL540.M62S65] 67-31889
1. Montgomery, John Joseph, 1858-1911.

Montgomery, Lucy Maud, 1874-1942—Biography.

GILLEN, Mollie. 813'.5'2
The wheel of things : a biography of L. M. Montgomery, author of Anne of Green Gables / Mollie Gillen. New York : Seabury Press, c1977. p. cm. (A Continuum book) Includes index. Bibliography: p. [PR9199.3.M6Z7 1977] 76-56154 ISBN 0-8164-9311-1 : 9.95
1. Montgomery, Lucy Maud, 1874-1942—Biography. 2. Authors, Canadian—20th century—Biography. I. Title.

GILLEN, Mollie. 813'.5'2 B
The wheel of things : a biography of L. M. Montgomery, author of Anne of Green Gables / Mollie Gillen. London : Harrap, 1976. [15], 200 p., [32] p. of plates : ill., facsims., ports. ; 24 cm. Includes index. Bibliography: p. 193-195. [PR9199.3.M6Z7 1976] 76-380508 ISBN 0-245-52971-3 : £4.95
1. Montgomery, Lucy Maud, 1874-1942—Biography. 2. Novelists, Canadian—20th century—Biography. I. Title.

Montgomery, Minn.—History.

MONTGOMERY 977.6'553 B
Bicentennial Committee.
Montgomery : from the "Big Woods" to the "Kolacky Capital," 1856-1976 : a project of Montgomery's Bicentennial Committee. [Montgomery? Minn. : The Committee, c1976- v. : ill. ; 29 cm. Bibliography: v. 1, 2d prelim. page. [F614.M68M66 1976] 77-353023
1. Montgomery, Minn.—History. 2. Czech Americans—Minnesota—Montgomery—History. 3. Montgomery, Minn.—Genealogy. 4. Registers of births, etc.—Minnesota—Montgomery. I. Title.

Montgomery of Alamein, Bernard Law Montgomery, 1st Viscount, 1887-

LEWIN, Ronald. 940.54 B
Montgomery as military commander. New York, Stein and Day [1972, c1971] 288 p. illus. 25 cm. Bibliography: p. [277]-279. [DA69.3.M56L4 1972] 77-163496 ISBN 0-8128-1426-6 10.00
1. Montgomery of Alamein, Bernard Law Montgomery, 1st Viscount, 1887- I. Title.

MONTGOMERY, 941.082'092'4 B
Brian.
A field-marshal in the family : a personal biography of Montgomery of Alamein / Brian Montgomery. New York : Taplinger Pub. Co., 1974, c1973. xii, 372 p., [9] leaves of plates : ill. ; 22 cm. Includes index. [DA69.3.M56M58 1974] 74-3873 ISBN 0-8008-2635-3 : 14.95
1. Montgomery of Alamein, Bernard Law Montgomery, 1st Viscount, 1887- I. Title. BIP

MONTGOMERY of Alamein, 923.542
Bernard Law Montgomery, 1st viscount, 1887
The memoirs of Field-Marshal the Viscount Montgomery of Alamein. [1st ed.] Cleveland, World Pub. Co. [1958] 508 p. illus., facsims., plans, ports. 25 cm. [DA69.3.M56A3] 58-9414
1. World War, 1939-1945 — Campaigns. I. Title.

THOMPSON, 940.54'21'0924 B
Reginald William.
Montgomery / R. W. Thompson. New York : Ballantine Books, 1974. 159 p. : ill. ; 21 cm. (War leader book ; no. 29) (Ballantine's illustrated history of the violent century) [DA69.3.M56T528] 75-306815 pbk. : 2.00
1. Montgomery of Alamein, Bernard Law Montgomery, 1st Viscount, 1887-

Montgomery, Richard, 1738-1775.

MAJOR General 973.33'1'0924
Richard Montgomery: a contribution toward a biography from the Clements Library. Ann Arbor [Published for the Clements Library Associates by] University of Michigan, 1970. 23 p. port. 24 cm. Includes letters by Richard and Janet Montgomery (p. 12-23) [E207.M7M3] 76-256028
1. Montgomery, Richard, 1738-1775. I. Montgomery, Janet (Livingston), 1743-1828. II. Michigan. University. William L. Clements Library. Clements Library Associates. III. Title.

Montgomery, Richard, 1738-1775—Juvenile literature.

TODD, Alden 973.33'1'0924
Richard Montgomery, rebel of 1775, by A. L. Todd. Maps, decorations by Leonard Vosburgh. New York, McKay [1967, c.1966] vii, 216p. 21cm. Bibl. [E207.M7T6] 67-17532 4.50
1. Montgomery, Richard, 1738-1775—Juvenile literature. 2. Canadian Invasion, 1775-1776—Juvenile literature. I. Title.

Montgomery, Robert Hiester, 1872-1953.

MONTGOMERY, Robert 657'.092'4 B
Hiester, 1872-1953.
Fifty years of accountancy / Robert H. Montgomery. New York : Arno Press, 1978 [c1939] xi, 678 p. ; 24 cm. (The Development of contemporary accounting thought) Autobiographical. Reprint of the ed. privately printed by Ronald Press Co., New York. [HF5616.U5M65 1978] 77-87280 ISBN 0-405-10908-3 : 40.00
1. Montgomery, Robert Hiester, 1872-1953. 2. Accounting—United States—History. 3. Accountants—Biography. I. Title. II. Series. BIP

Montherlant, Henry de, 1896-

BECKER, Lucille 848'.9'1209 B
Frackman.
Henry de Montherlant; a critical biography. With a pref. by Harry T. Moore. Carbondale, Southern Illinois University Press [1970] xi, 137 p. 22 cm. (Crosscurrents: modern critiques) Bibliography: p. 125-131. [PQ2625.O45Z558] 70-83666 4.95
1. Montherlant, Henry de, 1896- BIP

Montpensier, Anne Marie Louise d'Orleans, duchesse de, 1627-1693.

SACKVILLE-WEST, Victoria 920.7
Mary. Hon., 1892-1962.
Daughter of France; the life of Anne Marie Louise d'Orleans, duchesse de Montpensier, 1627-1693, la Grande Mademoiselle. [1st ed.] Garden City, N.Y., Doubleday, 1959. 336 p; illus. 22 cm. [DC130.M8S3 1959a] 59-9140
1. Montpensier, Anne Marie Louise d'Orleans, duchesse de, 1627-1693. I. Title.

STEEGMULLER, Francis, 1906- 920.7
The Grand Mademoiselle. New York, Farrar, Straus and Cudahy [1956] 308 p. illus. 22 cm. [DC130.M8S75] 55-11441
1. Montpensier, Anne Marie Louise d'OrlAns, duchesse de, 1627-1693. I. Title.

Montrose, James Graham, 1st marquis of, 1612-1650.

BUCHAN, John, 1875-1940. 923.541
Montrose. London, New York, T. Nelson [1965?] 419 p. maps, plans, ports. 23 cm. "First published in this edition, 1931." Bibliographical footnotes. [DA803.7] 65-7429 CD
1. Montrose, James Graham, 1st marquis of, 1612-1650. 2. Scotland — Hist. — Charles I, 1625-1649. I. Title.

MONTROSE. v. 12
With an introduction by Keith Feiling. London, Oxford University Press, 1957. xxii, 449p. maps. e(The 'world's classics. 555) Bibliographical footnotes.
1. Montrose, James Graham, 1st marquis of, 1612-1650. 2. Scotland—Hist.—Charles I, 1625— 1649. I. Buchan, John, 1875-1940.

WEDGWOOD, Cicely 941.060924
Veronica, 1910-
Montrose, by C. V. Wedgwood. Hamden, Conn., Archon 1966. 158p. maps, ports. 21cm. (Makers of hist.) [DA803.7.A3W4 1966] 66-21094 4.00
1. Montrose, James Graham, 1st marquis of, 1612-1650. I. Title.

Moody, Anne,

MOODY, Anne, 917.62'25'0360924 B
1940-
Coming of age in Mississippi. New York, Dial Press, 1968. 348 p. 22 cm. Autobiographical. [E185.97.M65A3] 68-55153 5.95
I. Title. BIP

Moody, Deborah, Lady, 1600-1659.

CRAWFORD, Deborah. 973.2'2'0922 B
Four women in a violent time: Anne Hutchinson (1591-1643) Mary Dyer (1591?-1660) Lady Deborah Moody (1600-1659) Penelope Stout (1622-1732). New York, Crown Publishers [1970] 191 p. 22 cm. Bibliography: p. 185-186. Traces the lives of four women who struggled for civil rights and justice in seventeenth-century America. [E187.5.C7 1970] 920 74-127519 4.50
1. Hutchinson, Anne (Marbury) 1591-1643. 2. Dyer, Mary, d. 1660. 3. Moody, Deborah, Lady, 1600-1659. 4. Stout, Penelope, 1622-1732. I. Title.

Moody, Dwight Lyman, 1837-1899.

BRADFORD, Gamaliel, 269'.2'0924 B
1863-1932.
D. L. Moody; a worker in souls. Freeport, N.Y., Books for Libraries Press [1972] 320 p. illus. 22 cm. Reprint of the 1927 ed. Bibliography: p. 305-308. [BV3785.M7B7 1972] 72-1275 ISBN 0-8369-6821-2
1. Moody, Dwight Lyman, 1837-1899.

CURTIS, Richard Kenneth, 922
1924-
They called him Mr. Moody. Grand Rapids, Mich., Eerdmans [1967, c.1962] 378p. 22cm. Bibl. 2.45 pap.,
1. Moody, Dwight Lyman, 1837-1899. I. Title.

CURTIS, Richard Kenneth, 922
1924-
They called him Mister Moody. [1st ed.] Garden City, N. Y., Doubleday, 1962. 378 p. 22 cm. Includes bibliography. [BV3785.M7C84] 62-7618
1. Moody, Dwight Lyman, 1837-1899. I. Title.

FINDLAY, James F., 269'.2'0924
1930-
Dwight L. Moody, American evangelist, 1837-1899 [by] James F. Findlay, Jr. With a foreword by Martin E. Marty. Chicago, University of Chicago Press [1969] ix, 440 p. 23 cm. "A note on sources": p. 422-426. Bibliographical footnotes. [BV3785.M7F47] 69-13200 10.00
1. Moody, Dwight Lyman, 1837-1899. I. Title. BIP

GERICKE, Paul. 269'.2'0924 B
Crucial experiences in the life of D. L. Moody / Paul Gericke. New Orleans : Insight Press, 1978. p. cm. Bibliography: p. [BV3785.M7G43] 78-7570 ISBN 0 914520-12-1 pbk. : 1.50
1. Moody, Dwight Lyman, 1837-1899. 2. Evangelists—United States—Biography. I. Title. BIP

GOODSPEED, Edgar 269'.2'0922 B
Johnson, 1833-1881.
A full history of the wonderful career of Moody and Sankey in Great Britain and America. New York, H. S. Goodspeed, 1876. [New York, AMS Press, 1973] 617 p. illus. 23 cm. [BV3785.M7G6 1973] 70-168154 ISBN 0-404-07227-5 25.00
1. Moody, Dwight Lyman, 1837-1899. 2. Sankey, Ira David, 1840-1908. 3. Evangelistic work. I. Title. BIP

MOODY, Paul Dwight, 1879- v. 12
The shorter life of D. L. Moody. Chicago, Moody Press [n.d.] 128 p. 18 cm. 68-38459
1. Moody, Dwight Lyman, 1837-1899. I. Fitt, Arthur Percy. II. Title.

POLLOCK, John Charles 922
Moody: a biograpical portrait of the pacesetter in modern mass evangelism. New York, Macmillan [1963] 336p. illus. 22cm. 63-11807 5.95
1. Moody, Dwight Lyman, 1837-1899. I. Title.

POLLOCK, John Charles. 269'.2'0924 B
Moody; a biographical portrait of the pacesetter in modern mass evangelism [by] J. C. Pollock. Grand Rapids, Zondervan Pub. House [1967, c1963] xii, 336 p. illus., ports. 21 cm. Bibliography: p. 319-325. [BV3785.M7P6 1967] 67-22692
1. Moody, Dwight Lyman, 1837-1899.

Moody, Dwight Lyman, 1837-1899—Juvenile literature.

ROBINSON, Virgil E. 269'.2'0924 B
Magnificent missionary; the story of Dwight L. Moody, by Virgil E. Robinson. Nashville, Southern Pub. Association [1969] 96 p. illus. 21 cm. A biography of the nineteenth-century evangelist who traveled extensively gathering converts to Christianity. [BV3785.M7R62] 69-19418 2.95
1. Moody, Dwight Lyman, 1837-1899—Juvenile literature. I. Title.

Moody, Howard—Addresses, essays, lectures.

A Voice in the Village 286'.131 B
: Howard Moody, twenty years on Washington Square / edited by Annette Kuhn. New York : Judson Memorial Church, [1977] p. cm. Bibliography: p. [BX6495.M548V64] 77-4288 5.50
1. Moody, Howard—Addresses, essays, lectures. 2. Judson Memorial Church—Addresses, essays, lectures. 3. Baptists—Clergy—Biography—Addresses, essays, lectures. 4. Clergy—New York (City)—Biography—Addresses, essays, lectures. 5. New York (City)—Biography—Addresses, essays, lectures. I. Kuhn, Annette, 1945-
Publisher's address: 55 Washington Square, New York, NY 10012

Moody, John, 1868-1958.

MOODY, John, 1868-1958. 332.6'092'4 B
The long road home : an autobiography / John Moody. New York : Arno Press, 1975, c1933. x, 263 p. ; 22 cm. (Wall Street and the security markets) Reprint of the ed. published by Macmillan, New York. Includes index. [HG172.M66A33 1975] 75-2650 ISBN 0-405-06975-8 : 17.00
1. Moody, John, 1868-1958. 2. Capitalists and financiers—United States—Correspondence, reminiscences, etc. I. Title. II. Series. BIP

Moody, Joseph P.

MOODY, Joseph P. 926.1
Arctic doctor, by Joseph P. Moody with W. de Groot van Embden. New York, Dodd, Mead [1955] 274 p. illus. 21 cm. [R464.M6A3] 55-6713
I. Embden, Willem de Groot van, joint author. II. Title.

Moody, Ralph,

MOODY, Ralph, 1898- 818.54
Shaking the nickel bush. Illustrated by Tran Mawicke. [1st ed.] New York, Norton [1962] 234p. illus. 22cm. Autobiographical. [CT275.M5853A327] 62-10101
I. Title.

Moody, Sewell Prescott, d. 1875.

MORTON, James W., 1922- 338.4'7'6740971133
The enterprising Mr. Moody, the bumptious Captain Stamp : the lives and colourful times of Vancouver's lumber pioneers / James Morton. North Vancouver : J. J. Douglas, 1978 vii, 183 p., [8] leaves of plates : ill., map, ports. ; 24 cm. Includes index. Bibliography: p. 177-180. [HD9764.C4V365] 78-315013 ISBN 0-88894-147-1 : 13.95
1. Moody, Sewell Prescott, d. 1875. 2. Stamp, Edward, 1814-1872. 3. Lumber trade—British Columbia—Vancouver—History. 4. Businessmen—British Columbia—Vancouver—Biography. 5. Vancouver, B.C.—Industries—History. I. Title.
Distributed by ISBS Dist. by ISBS, forest grove. or

Moon, Charlotte, 1840-1912—Juvenile literature.

SUMMERS, Jester. 266.6'1'0924 B
Lottie Moon of China. Illustrated by James Ponter. Nashville, Broadman Press [1970] 62 p. illus., port. 23 cm. A biography of the Virginia-born girl who spent forty years of her life as a Baptist missionary in China. [BV3427.M55S9] 92 70-117304 2.50
1. Moon, Charlotte, 1840-1912—Juvenile literature. I. Ponter, James, illus. II. Title.

*Mooney, Booth

*MOONEY, Booth 923.173
The Lyndon Johnson story. [New York] Avon [c.1956-1964] 191p. 18cm. (S148) .60 pap.,
I. Title.

Mooney, Jesse, 1866-1915.

MOONEY, Charles W. 610'.92'4 B
Doctor in Belle Starr country / by Charles W. Mooney. 1st ed. Oklahoma City : Century Press, 1975. xii, 291 p. : ill. ; 23 cm. [R154.M723M66] 74-30947 7.95
1. Mooney, Jesse, 1866-1915. 2. Starr, Belle Shirley, 1848-1889. 3. Indian Territory—Biography. I. Title. BIP

Mooney, Thomas J., 1882-1942.

GENTRY, Curt, 1931- 364.14'3
Frame-up; the incredible case of Tom Mooney and Warren Billings. [1st ed.] New York, Norton [1967] 496 p. illus., ports. 24 cm. Bibliography: p. 479-488. [KF224.M6G4] 65-18033
1. Mooney, Thomas J., 1882-1942. 2. Billings, Warren K., 1894- I. Title.

Moor, Elisabeth.

MOOR, Elisabeth. 610'.92'4 B
An impossible woman : the memories of Dottoressa Moor of Capri / edited and with an epilogue by Graham Greene. New York : Viking Press, 1976, c1975. 205 p. ; 23 cm. [R520.M66A34 1976] 75-42796 ISBN 0-670-39421-1 : 7.95
1. Moor, Elisabeth. 2. Women physicians—Italy—Capri—Correspondence, reminiscences, etc. I. Greene, Graham, 1904- II. Title.

Moore, Anne Carroll, 1871-1961.

SAYERS, Frances (Clarke) 1897- 020'.92'4
Anne Carroll Moore; a biography. [1st ed.] New York, Atheneum, 1972. xiv, 303 p. illus. 22 cm. Bibliography: p. [285]-289. [Z720.M68S29] 72-78291 8.95
1. Moore, Anne Carroll, 1871-1961. BIP

Moore, Archie,

MOORE, Archie, 1916- 796.8'3'0924 B
Any boy can: the Archie Moore story, by Archie Moore and Leonard B. Pearl. Englewood Cliffs, N.J., Prentice-Hall [1971] 263 p. illus. 22 cm. [GV1132.M75A29] 76-163398 ISBN 0-13-038562-X 6.95
I. Pearl, Leonard B., joint author. II. Title.

MOORE, Archie, 1916- 927.9683
The Archie Moore story. [1st ed.] New York, McGraw-Hill [1960] 240p. illus. 21cm. [GV1132.M75A3] 60-12825
I. Title.

Moore. Archie [Lee]

MOORE. ARCHIE [LEE] 927.9683
The Archie Moore story. New York, McGraw-Hill [c.1960] 240p. illus. 21cm. 60-12825 4.95 bds.
I. Title.

Moore, Arthur James, Bp., 1888-

MOORE, Arthur James, Bp., 1888- 287'.6'0924 B
Bishop to all peoples [by] Arthur J. Moore. Nashville, Abingdon Press [1973] 144 p. 23 cm. Autobiography. [BX8495.M567A3] 73-6701 ISBN 0-687-03571-6 5.95
1. Moore, Arthur James, Bp., 1888- I. Title. BIP

Moore, Austin Leigh,

MOORE, Austin Leigh, 1901- 818.54
My career as a knight errant [by] Austin L. Moore. Denver, Big Mountain Press [c1964] 51 p. 22 cm. Autobiographical. [CT275.M587A3] 65-1488
I. Title.

Moore, Bobby, 1941-

POWELL, Jeff. 796.33'4'0924 B
Bobby Moore : the authorised biography / [by] Jeff Powell. London : Everest, 1976. 192 p., [32] p. of plates : ill., ports. ; 24 cm. Includes index. [GV942.7.M6P68] 77-356219 ISBN 0-905018-20-6 : £4.25
1. Moore, Bobby, 1941- 2. Soccer players—Great Britain—Biography.

Moore, Charles Herbert, 1840-1960.

MATHER, Frank Jewett, 1868-1953. 759.13
Charles Herbert Moore, landscape painter. Princeton, Princeton University Press, 1957. xv, 85p. illus., ports. 22cm. [ND237.M65M3] [ND237.M65M3] 927.5 57-5450 57-5450
1. Moore, Charles Herbert, 1840-1960. I. Title.

Moore, Clement Clarke, 1779-1863.

PATTERSON, Samuel White, 1883- 928.1
The poet of Christmas Eve, a life of Clement Clarke Moore, 1779-1863. New York, Morehouse-Gorham Co. [1956] 180p. illus. 21cm. Includes bibliography. [PS2429.M5Z8] 56-10121
1. Moore, Clement Clarke, 1779-1863. I. Title.

Moore, Clifford H

MOORE, Clifford H 1889- 923.773
A new look: history in four dimensions; an archaeological approach to politics and education. [1st ed.] New York, Exposition Press [1955] 53p. illus. 21cm. Autobiographical. [CT275.M588A3] 55-9407
I. Title.

Moore, Colleen,

MOORE, Colleen, 1902- 791.43'0924
Silent star. [1st ed.] Garden City, N.Y., Doubleday, 1968. 262 p. illus., ports. 24 cm. Autobiographical. [PN2287.M695A3] 68-10562
I. Title.

Moore, Edward, 1712-1757.

CASKEY, John Homer, 1895- 822'.5 B
The life and works of Edward Moore. [Hamden, Conn.] Archon Books, 1973. iv, 197 p. 22 cm. Reprint of the 1927 ed., which was issued as v. 75 of Yale studies in English. Originally presented as the author's thesis, Yale, 1923. Bibliography: p. [168]-189. [PR3605.M3Z57 1973] 72-8823 ISBN 0-208-01125-0 6.50
1. Moore, Edward, 1712-1757. I. Series: Yale studies in English, v. 75. BIP

Moore, Ellen, 1915-

MOORE, Ellen, 1915- 973.9'092'4 B
Lead me to the exit / Ellen Moore. Washington : Ariadne Press, [1977] p. cm. Autobiography. [CT275.M5894A34] 77-9949 ISBN 0-918056-01-2 : 6.95
1. Moore, Ellen, 1915- 2. United States—Biography. I. Title. BIP

Moore, George,

MOORE, George, 1852-1933. 823'.8 B
Conversations with George Moore / Geraint Goodwin. Norwood, Pa. : Norwood Editions, 1975. p. cm. Reprint of the 1929 ed. published by E. Benn, London. [PR5042.C66 1975] 75-35648 ISBN 0-88305-893-6 : 20.00
I. Goodwin, Geraint. II. Title.

MOORE, George, 1852-1933. 823'.8 B
Conversations with George Moore. New York, Haskell House, 1974. 249 p. 20 cm. At head of title: Geraint Goodwin. Reprint of the 1940 ed. published by J. Cape, London, in series: The Saint Giles library. [PR5042.C66 1974] 73-21564 ISBN 0-8383-1811-8 18.95
I. Goodwin, Geraint. II. Title.

MOORE, George, 1852-1933. 823'.8 B
Letters from George Moore to Ed. Dujardin, 1886-1922. [Folcroft, Pa.] Folcroft Library Editions, 1970. 116 p. 24 cm. "Limited to 150 copies." English translation of letters originally written in French. Reprint of the 1929 ed. [PR5043.A45 1970] 72-187174
I. Dujardin, Edouard, 1861-1949. II. Title. BIP

Moore, George Fletcher.

MOORE, George Fletcher. 994.102
Diary of ten years eventful life of an early settler in Western Australia, and also A descriptive vocabulary of the language of the Aborigines / by George Fletcher Moore ; with an introduction by C. T. Stannage. Facsimile ed. Nedlands, W.A. : University of Western Australia Press, 1978. xi, 423, xi, 119 p. ; 23 cm. (Historical reprint series) Photoreprint of the 1884 ed. published by M. Walbrook, London. [DU372.M6A3 1978] 79-670397 ISBN 0-85564-137-1 : 35.00
1. Moore, George Fletcher. 2. Frontier and pioneer life—Australia—Western Australia. 3. Western Australia—Description and travel. 4. Nyungar dialects—Glossaries, vocabularies, etc. 5. Western Australia—Officials and employees—Biography. I. Title. II. Title: Descriptive vocabulary of the language of the Aborigines.
Distributed by International Scholarly Book Services Inc., Forest Grove, OR BIP

Moore, George, 1852-1933—Biography.

HONE, Joseph Maunsell, 1882-1959. 823'.8 B
The life of George Moore. With an account of his last years by his cook and housekeeper, Clara Warville. Westport, Conn., Greenwood Press [1973] 515 p. illus. 22 cm. "The achievement of George Moore, by Desmond Shawe-Taylor": p. [465]-492. Reprint of the 1936 ed. Bibliography: p. [498]-502. [PR5043.H6 1973] 73-141483 ISBN 0-8371-5868-0
1. Moore, George, 1852-1933—Biography. I. Warville, Clara. II. Shawe-Taylor, Desmond. BIP

MOORE, George, 1852-1933. 823'.8 B
A communication to my friends. [Folcroft, Pa.] Folcroft Library Editions, 1974. 86 p. 25 cm. Reprint of the 1933 ed. published by Nonesuch Press, London. Includes index. [PR5043.A42 1974] 74-11471 ISBN 0-8414-6162-7 (lib. bdg.)
1. Moore, George, 1852-1933—Biography. 2. London—Intellectual life. I. Title.

MOORE, George, 1852-1933. 823'.8 B
A communication to my friends. New York, Haskell House [1974] p. cm. Reprint of the 1933 ed. published by Nonesuch Press, London. [PR5043.A48 1974] 74-8663 ISBN 0-8383-1910-6 9.95 (lib. bdg.).
1. Moore, George, 1852-1933—Biography. 2. London—Intellectual life. I. Title. BIP

MOORE, George, 1852-1933. 823'.8 B
Conversations with George Moore / Geraint Goodwin. Norwood, Pa. :

Norwood Editions, 1975. p. cm. Reprint of the 1929 ed. published by E. Benn, London. [PR5042.C66 1975] 75-35648 ISBN 0-88305-893-6 : 20.00
I. Goodwin, Geraint. II. Title.

MOORE, George, 1852- 1933. 823'.8 B
Conversations with George Moore. New York, Haskell House, 1974. 249 p. 20 cm. At head of title: Geraint Goodwin. Reprint of the 1940 ed. published by J. Cape, London, in series: The Saint Giles library. [PR5042.C66 1974] 73-21564 ISBN 0-8383-1811-8 18.95
I. Goodwin, Geraint. II. Title.

MOORE, George, 1852-1933. 823'.8
Hail and farewell : ave, salve, vale / [by] George Moore. [2nd ed. reprinted with new introduction and notes] / edited by Richard Cave. Gerrards Cross : Smythe, 1976. 774 p., [16] p. of plates : ill., ports. ; 24 cm. Includes index. Bibliography: p. 755-756. [PR5042.H3 1976] 77-373885 ISBN 0-900675-64-0 : £20.00
1. Moore, George, 1852-1933—Biography. 2. Authors, Irish—20th century—Biography. 3. Ireland—Intellectual life. I. Cave, Richard. II. Title.

MOORE, George, 1852- 1933. 823'.8 B
Letters from George Moore to Ed. Dujardin, 1886-1922. [Folcroft, Pa.] Folcroft Library Editions, 1970. 116 p. 24 cm. "Limited to 150 copies." English translation of letters originally written in French. Reprint of the 1929 ed. [PR5043.A45 1970] 72-187174
I. Dujardin, Edouard, 1861-1949. II. Title. BIP

Moore, George, 1852-1933—Correspondence.

MOORE, George, 1852-1933. 823'.8
Letters of George Moore / with an introd. by John Eglinton [i.e. W. K. Magee] to whom they were written. Folcroft, Pa. : Folcroft Library Editions, 1977. p. cm. Reprint of the 1942 ed. published by Sydenham, Bournemouth, Eng. [PR5043.A46 1977] 77-1316 ISBN 0-8414-3980-X lib. bdg. : 17.50
1. Moore, George, 1852-1933—Correspondence. 2. Magee, William Kirkpatrick—Correspondence. 3. Novelists, Irish—20th century—Correspondence. I. Magee, William Kirkpatrick. BIP

MOORE, George, 1852- 1933. 823'.8 B
Letters to Lady Cunard, 1895-1933 / George Moore ; edited with an introd. and notes by Rupert Hart-Davis. Westport, Conn. : Greenwood Press, 1979. 208 p., [8] leaves of plates : ill. ; 23 cm. Reprint of the 1957 ed. published by R. Hart-Davis, London. Includes bibliographical references and index. [PR5043.A444 1979] 78-12712 ISBN 0-313-20645-7 lib. bdg. : 17.50
1. Moore, George, 1852-1933—Correspondence. 2. Cunard, Maud Alice Burke, Lady, 1872-1948. 3. Authors, Irish—20th century—Correspondence. I. Hart-Davis, Rupert, Sir. II. Title.

Moore, Glover, 1859-1930.

MOORE, Glover, 1911- 976.1'63'060924 B
A Calhoun County, Alabama, boy in the 1860's / Glover Moore, Jr. Jackson : University Press of Mississippi, c1978. p. cm. Includes bibliographical references. [F332.C25M66] 78-15256 ISBN 0-87805-081-7 : 5.00
1. Moore, Glover, 1859-1930. 2. Calhoun Co., Ala.—Biography. 3. Jefferson Co., Ala.—Biography. I. Title. BIP

Moore, Grace, 1901-1947.

MOORE, Grace, 1901- 1947. 782.1'092'4 B
You're only human once / Grace Moore. New York : Arno Press, 1977, c1944. 275 p., [3] leaves of plates : ill. ; 23 cm. (Opera biographies) Reprint of the ed. published by Doubleday, Doran, New York. [ML420.M57A3 1977] 76-29958 ISBN 0-405-09698-4 : 17.00
1. Moore, Grace, 1901-1947. 2. Singers—United States—Biography. I. Title. BIP

Moore, Henry Spencer, 1898-

HALL, Donald, 1928- 730.924
Henry Moore; the life and work of a great sculptor. [1st ed.] New York, Harper [1966] 181p. illus., ports. 24cm. [NB497.M6H3 1966] 66-15732 7.50
1. Moore, Henry Spencer, 1898- I. Title.

READ, Herbert Edward, Sir, 1893- 730.924 B
Henry Moore; a study of his life and work [by] Herbert Read. New York, Praeger [1966, c1965] 284 p. illus. (part col.), ports. 22 cm. (A Praeger world of art profile) Bibliography: p. 265-266. [NB497.M6R39 1966] 66-12041
1. Moore, Henry Spencer, 1898-

Moore, Jerome Aaron, 1903-

HAMMOND, John Hays, 1912- 378.1'12'0924 B
Jerome A. Moore : a man of TCU / by John H. Hammond. Fort Worth : Texas Christian University Press, [1974] 86 p. : port. ; 24 cm. Includes index. [LD5311.T3818M664] 74-75867
1. Moore, Jerome Aaron, 1903- 2. Texas Christian University, Fort Worth. BIP

Moore, John, Sir, 1761-1809.

PARKINSON, Roger. 355.3'32'0924 B
Moore of Corunna / [by] Roger Parkinson. London : Hart-Davis MacGibbon, 1976. viii, 245 p. : ill., facsim., plans, ports. ; 24 cm. Includes index. Bibliography: p. 240-241. [DA68.M66P37 1976] 76-371009 ISBN 0-246-10755-3 : £5.95
1. Moore, John, Sir, 1761-1809. 2. Great Britain Army—Biography. 3. Generals Great Britain—Biography. 4. Europe—History—1789-1815. I. Title.

Moore, John Thomas,

MOORE, John Thomas, 1876- 926.1
Dr. Tom; memoirs. [Nashville?] Printed by The Parthenon Press [1957] 204p. illus. 21cm. [R154.M732A3] 57-38996
I. Title.

MOORE, John Thomas, 1876- 926.1
Dr. Tom; memoirs. [Nashville?] Printed by The Parthenon Press [1957] 204p. illus. 21cm. [R154.M732A3] 57-38996
I. Title.

Moore, John Trotwood, 1858-1929.

GREEN, Claud Bethune, 1914- 928.1
John Trotwood Moore; Tennessee man of letters. Athens, University of Georgia Press [1957] x, 189p. port. 25cm. 'The writings of John Trotwood Moore;: p. 121-161. Bibliographical references included in 'Notes' (p.162-185) [PS2429.M8Z67] 57-10861
1. Moore, John Trotwood, 1858-1929. I. Title.

Moore, Langdon W.,

MOORE, Langdon W., 1830- 364.16'2'0924 B
Langdon W. Moore: his own story of his eventful life. Freeport, N.Y., Books for Libraries Press [1971] 659 p. illus., ports. 23 cm. Reprint of the 1892 ed. Title on spine: Moore's own story. [HV6248.M7A3 1971] 70-164617 ISBN 0-8369-5901-9
I. Title: Moore's own story.

Moore, Mary Tyler, 1937- —Juvenile literature.

*BRYARS, Chris 791.450280924
The real Mary Tyler Moore / Chris Bryars. New York : Pinnacle Books ,1977 c1976 164 p. : ill. ; 18 cm. [PN1992.4] ISBN 0-523-00988-7 pbk. : 1.50
1. Moore, Mary Tyler I. Title. BIP

PAIGE, David. 791.45'028'0924 B
Mary Tyler Moore / written by Danid Paige ; designed by Gene Kohler. [Mankato, Minn.] : Creative Education. [c1977] 30 p. : ill. ; 25 cm. (Stars of stage and screen) A biography of actress Mary Tyler Moore who has won several Emmys for her television series. [PN2287.M697P3] 92 76-44010 ISBN 0-87191-559-6 lib.bdg. : 4.95
1. Moore, Mary Tyler, 1937- —Juvenile literature. 2. Entertainers—United States—Biography—Juvenile literature. I. Title. BIP

Moore, Paul, 1942-

MOORE, Paul, 1942- 289.9 B
Shepherd of Times Square / by Paul Moore & Joe Musser. Nashville : T. Nelson, c1979. 249 p. ; 21 cm. [BX8699.N38M665] 79-16249 ISBN 0-8407-5166-4 : 8.95
1. Moore, Paul, 1942- 2. Church of the Nazarene—Clergy—Biography. 3. Clergy—United States—Biography. I. Musser, Joe, joint author. II. Title.

Moore, Ronnie, 1933-

MOORE, Ronnie, 1933- 796.7'5'0924 B
The Ronnie Moore story / as told to Rod Dew. Christchurch, N.Z. : Pegasus, 1976. 190 p., [8] leaves of plates : ill. ; 23 cm. [GV1060.2.M63A34] 77-362696 ISBN 0-908568-01-0
1. Moore, Ronnie, 1933- 2. Motorcyclists—New Zealand—Biography. I. Dew, Rod. II. Title.

Moore, Stewart—Biography.

MOORE, Stewart. 818'.5409 B
Over the hill to the Moorehouse / Stewart Moore. 1st ed. Detroit : Orion Press, c1975. 127 p., [8] leaves of plates : ill. ; 22 cm. [PS3563.O665Z52] 75-22706 ISBN 0-915824-01-9
1. Moore, Stewart—Biography. I. Title.

Moore, Thomas Overton, 1804-1876.

THOMAS Overton Moore, a v. 12
Confederate governor. Clinton, Commercial Printing Co., 1960. 78p. illus., port. 24cm.
1. Moore, Thomas Overton, 1804-1876. I. Moore, Claude Hunter.

Moore, Thomas Sturge, 1870-1944.

GWYNN, Frederick Landis, 1916- 928.2
Sturge Moore and the life of art. Lawrence, University of Kansas Press, 1951. 159p. ports. 22cm. 'A bibliography of Sturge Moore': p. [123]-135. [PR6025.O58Z7] 51-14941
1. Moore, Thomas Sturge, 1870-1944. I. Title. BIP

Moore, Thomas, 1779-1852.

GWYNN, Stephen Lucius, 1864-1950. 821'.7 B
Thomas Moore. [Folcroft, Pa.] Folcroft Library Editions, 1973. p. Reprint of the 1905 ed. published by Macmillan, New York, in series: English men of letters. [PR5056.G8 1973] 73-13838 15.00
1. Moore, Thomas, 1779-1852.

JONES, Howard Mumford, 1892- 821'.7 B
The harp that once—; a chronicle of the life of Thomas Moore. New York, Russell & Russell [1970, c1937] xvi, 365 p. illus., facsims., ports. 25 cm. Includes bibliographical references. [PR5056.J6 1970] 75-102508
1. Moore, Thomas, 1779-1852. I. Title. BIP

MOORE, Thomas, 1779-1852. 928.2
Journal, 1818-1841. Edited by Peter Quennell. [Rev. ed.] New York, Macmillan [1964] xv, 256 p. illus., ports. 21 cm. Selections from Memoirs, journal, and correspondence of Thomas Moore, first published 1853-56. [PR5056.A5 1964] 64-13351
I. Quennell, Peter, 1905- ed.

MOORE, Thomas, 1779-1852. 821'.7
Memoirs, journal, and correspondence of Thomas Moore. Edited by Lord John Russell. London, Longman, Brown, Green, and Longmans, Boston, Little, Brown, 1853-56. St. Clair Shores, Mich., Scholarly Press, 1971-72 [v. 1, 1972] 8 v. illus. 21 cm. Vol. 5 has imprint: Boston, Little, Brown, 1853. St. Clair Shores, Mich., Scholarly Press, 1971. [PR5056.A5 1972] 71-115258 ISBN 0-403-00527-2 (v. 1)

MOORE, Thomas, 1779- 1852. 828'.7'03
Tom Moore's diary; a selection edited, with an introd., by J. B. Priestley. Cambridge, University Press, 1925. St. Clair Shores, Mich., Scholarly Press, 1970. xv, 218 p. port. 21 cm. [PR5056.A55 1970] 76-131783
I. Title. BIP

SYMINGTON, Andrew James, b.1825. 821'.7 B
Thomas Moore, the poet; his life and works. [Folcroft, Pa.] Folcroft Press [1970] 255 p. port. 23 cm. Reprint of the 1880 ed. [PR5056.S8 1970] 72-190653
1. Moore, Thomas, 1779-1852.

Moore, Thomas, 1779-1852—Biography.

MACKEY, Herbert O. 821'.7 B
The life of Thomas Moore, Ireland's national poet, by Herbert O. Mackey. 2d ed. [Folcroft, Pa.] Folcroft Library Editions, 1973. 39 p. illus. 24 cm. Reprint of the 1951 ed. published by Apollo Press, Dublin. [PR5056.M27 1973] 73-11363 ISBN 0-8414-5968-1 (lib. bdg.)
1. Moore, Thomas, 1779-1852—Biography.

Moorehead, Agnes, 1906-1974.

SHERK, Warren Arthur. 791'.092'4 B
Agnes Moorehead : a very private person / by Warren Sherk. Philadelphia : Dorrance, c1976. x, 137 p. : ill. ; 23 cm. [PN2287.M698S5] 76-150177 ISBN 0-8059-2317-9 : 5.95
1. Moorehead, Agnes, 1906-1974. 2. Actors—United States—Biography. BIP

Moorehead, Alan,

MOOREHEAD, Alan, 1910- 907.2'024 B
A late education; episodes in a life. [1st U.S. ed.] New York, Harper & Row [1971, c1970] 175 p. group port. 22 cm. (A Cass Canfield book) [D15.M65A3 1971] 73-138751 ISBN 0-06-013027-X 5.95
I. Title.

Moorhouse, Geoffrey, 1931-

MOORHOUSE, Geoffrey, 1931- 916.6'04
The fearful void. Philadelphia, Lippincott [1974] 288 p. illus. 24 cm. [DT333.M58] 73-19977 ISBN 0-397-01019-2 10.00
1. Moorhouse, Geoffrey, 1931- 2. Sahara—Description and travel. I. Title. BIP

Moorman, Lewis Jefferson,

MOORMAN, Lewis Jefferson, 1875- 926.1
Pioneer doctor. [1st ed.] Norman, University of Oklahoma Press [1951] xvii, 252 p. illus., ports. 22 cm. Autobiographical. [R154.M734A3] 51-10218
I. Title.

Mooso, Josiah, b. 1803.

THE Life and travels *of Josiah Mooso* / Josiah Mooso. 973'.04'97 S New York : Garland Pub., 1977. 400 p. ; 19 cm. (The Garland library of narratives of North American Indian captivities ; v. 97) Reprint of the 1888 ed. published by Telegram Print, Winfield, Kan. [E85.G2 vol. 97] [F593] 978'.02 B 75-7124 ISBN 0-8240-1721-8 lib.bdg. : 25.00
1. Mooso, Josiah, b. 1803. 2. Pioneers—The West—Biography. 3. Frontier and pioneer life—The West. 4. Cowley Co., Kan.—History. 5. Indians of North America—Captivities. I. Series.

Mores, Antoine Amedee Marie Vincent, Manca de Vallombrosa, Marquis de, 1858-1896.

DRESDEN, Donald W. 978.4'9'020924 B
The Marquis de Mores: Emperor of the Bad Lands, by Donald Dresden. [1st ed.] Norman, University of Oklahoma Press [1970] xi, 282 p. illus., facsims., maps, ports. 22 cm. Bibliography: p. 268-272. [F641.M6D7] 69-16720 5.95
1. Mores, Antoine Amedee Marie Vincent Manca de Vallambrosa, Marquis de, 1858-1896. 2. North Dakota—History. I. Title.

TWETON, D. Jerome. 978.4'9'020924 B
The Marquis de Mores; Dakota capitalist, French nationalist [by] D. Jerome Tweton. Fargo, North Dakota Institute for Regional Studies, 1972. x, 249 p. illus. 24 cm. Bibliography: p. 240-244. [DC342.8.M7T9] 72-619655 8.95
1. Mores, Antoine Amedee Marie Vincent, Manca de Vallombrosa, Marquis de, 1858-1896. I. Title.

Moraes, Dom F.,

MORAES, Dom F., 1938- 828'.9'1409
My son's father; a poet's autobiography [by] Dom Moraes. [1st American ed. New York] Macmillan [1969, c1968] 241 p. 22 cm. [PR6063.O67Z5 1969] 69-11178
I. Title.

Moran, Thomas, 1837-1926.

CALIFORNIA. University, Riverside. v. 12
Thomas Moran, 1837-1926 Exhibition Selection and catalogue by William H. Gerdts with additional essays by Louise Nelson and Samuel Sachs II. The Picture Gallery, University of California, Riverside April 7th to June 7th, 1963. Thomas Moran eighteen thirty-seven-nineteen twenty-six Riverside, 1963. 48 p. illus. Errata slip inserted. Bibliography: 1. 22-23. 64-69360
1. Moran, Thomas, 1837-1926. I. Gerdts, William H. II. Title.

Morandi, Giorgio, 1890-1964.

GIUFFRE, Guido. 759.5
Morandi; [translated from the Italian]. London, New York, Hamlyn, 1971. 94 p. illus. (some col.). 32 cm. (Twentieth-century masters) Distributed in the U.S.A. by Crown Publishers, Inc. Bibliography: p. 92-94. [ND623.M687G513 1971] 72-177787 ISBN 0-600-35930-1 £2.25
1. Morandi, Giorgio, 1890-1964.

Morang, Alfred, 1901-1958.

MORANG, Alfred, 1901-1958. 760'.092'4 B
Alfred Morang, a neglected master / by Walt Wiggins. 1st ed. Roswell, N.M. : Pintores Press, c1979. 95 p. : ill. (some col.) ; 32 cm. Bibliography: p. 95. [ND237.M72A4 1979] 79-87716 ISBN 0-934116-01-6 : 25.00 ISBN 0-934116-00-8 casebound : 150.00
1. Morang, Alfred, 1901-1958. 2. Painters—United States—Biography. I. Wiggins, Walt. II. Title.

Moravec, Frantisek, 1895 or 6-1966.

MORAVEC, Frantisek, 1895or6-1966. 327'.12'0924 B
Master of spies : the memoirs of General Frantisek Moravec / Frantisek Moravec. 1st ed. in U.S.A. Garden City, N.Y. : Doubleday, 1975. xx, 240 p. ; 22 cm. [UB271.C952M675] 74-24488 ISBN 0-385-08585-0 : 7.95
1. Moravec, Frantisek, 1895 or 6-1966. 2. Espionage—Czechoslovak Republic—History. I. Title.

Moravia, Alberto, 1907—

COTTRELL, Jane E. 853'.9'12
Alberto Moravia [by] Jane E. Cottrell. New York, Ungar [1974] viii, 166 p. 21 cm. (Modern literature monographs) Bibliography: p. 151-156. [PQ4829.O62Z6] 73-84599 ISBN 0-8044-2131-5 6.00
1. Moravia, Alberto, 1907- BIP

Moravian Church—Missions.

ZEISBERGER, David, 1721-1808. 970.4'71
Diary of David Zeisberger; a Moravian missionary among the Indians of Ohio. Translated from the original German manuscript and edited by Eugene F. Bliss. Cincinnati, R. Clarke for the Historical and Philosophical Society of Ohio, 1885. St. Clair Shores, Mich., Scholarly Press, 1972. 2 v. 21 cm. Original ed. issued as new ser., v. 2-3, of Publications of the Cincinnati Historical Society. [E98.M6Z37 1972] 73-108557 ISBN 0-403-00253-2
1. Moravian Church—Missions. 2. Indians of North America—Missions. 3. Indians of North America—Ohio. 4. Delaware Indians. I. Series: Cincinnati Historical Society (Founded 1831). New series, v. 2-3.

More, Hannah, 1745-1833.

YONGE, Charlotte Mary, 1823-1901. 828'.6'09 B
Hannah More / by Charlotte M. Yonge. Folcroft, Pa. : Folcroft Library Editions, 1976, c1888. p. cm. Reprint of the ed. published by Roberts Bros., Boston, issued in series: Famous women. [PR3605.M6Y62 1976] 76-17900 ISBN 0-8414-9751-6 lib. bdg. : 25.00
1. More, Hannah, 1745-1833. I. Series: Famous women. BIP

More, Hannah, 1808-1868—Juvenile literature.

DAVIS, Susan. 286'.73 B
I was a stranger : the story of Jesus in the person of Hannah More / by Susan Davis. Mountain View, Calif. : Pacific Press Pub. Association, c1979. 96 p. : map ; 22 cm. (A Destiny book ; D-174) [BX6193.M67D38] 78-58077 ISBN 0-8163-0237-5 pbk. : 3.95
1. More, Hannah, 1808-1868—Juvenile literature. 2. Seventh-Day Adventists—United States—Biography—Juvenile literature. I. Title.

More, Paul Elmer,

MORE, Paul Elmer, 1864-1937. 818'.5'203 B
Pages from an Oxford diary. Port Washington, N.Y., Kennikat Press [1972, c1937] [85] p. 20 cm. [PS2431.P3 1972] 74-159095 ISBN 0-8046-1638-8
I. Title. BIP

More, Paul Elmer, 1864-1937.

DAKIN, Arthur Hazard 928.1
Paul Elmer More. Princeton, N. J., Princeton University Press [c.] 1960. xvii, 416p. (bibl. footnotes) illus. 23cm. 59-11076 7.50
1. More, Paul Elmer, 1864-1937. I. Title.

MORE, Paul Elmer, 1864-1937. 818'.5'203 B
Pages from an Oxford diary. Port Washington, N.Y., Kennikat Press [1972, c1937] [85] p. 20 cm. [PS2431.P3 1972] 74-159095 ISBN 0-8046-1638-8
I. Title. BIP

More, Sir Thomas, Saint, 1478-1535.

BA. RO. 923.242
The lyfe of Syr Thomas More, sometymes Lord Chancellor of Negland, by Ro: Ba: and edited from ms. Lambeth 179, with collations from seven manuscripts, by Elsie Vaughan Hitchcock and P. E. Hallett, with additional notes and appendices by A. W. Reed. London, Oxford University Press, 1950. xxv, 340 p. facsim. 22 cm. (Early English Text Society. [Publications] Original series, no. 222, 1930 (for 1945)) [PR1119.A2 no. 222] A51
1. More, Sir Thomas, Saint, 1478-1535. I. Ro. Ba. ni. Hitchcock, Elsie Vaughan, ed. II. Hallett, Phillip Edward, 1884-1948, ed. III. Lambeth Palace. Library. Mss. (no. 179) IV. Title. V. Series.

CHAMBERS, Raymond Wilson, 1874-1942. 942.05'2'0924 B
The saga and the myth of Sir Thomas More. [Folcroft, Pa.] Folcroft Library Editions, 1974. p. cm. Reprint of the 1927 ed. published by Oxford University Press, London, in series: The British Academy literary history lecture. Includes bibliographical references. [PR2322.C5 1974] 74-7444 5.50 (lib. bdg.)
1. More, Thomas, Sir, Saint, 1478-1535. I. Title. II. Series: British Academy, London (Founded 1901). Literary history lecture. BIP

CHAMBERS, Raymond Wilson, 1874-1942. 942.05'2'0924 B
The saga and the myth of Sir Thomas More / by R. W. Chambers. Norwood, Pa. : Norwood Editions, 1976. p. cm. Reprint of the 1927 ed. published by H. Milford, Oxford University Press, London, which was issued as the 1926 British Academy literary history lecture. Includes bibliographical references. [PR2322.C5 1976] 76-16828 ISBN 0-8482-0375-5 lib. bdg. : 6.50
1. More, Thomas, Sir, Saint, 1478-1535. I. Title. II. Series: British Academy, London (Founded 1901). Literary history lecture ; 1926.

CHAMBERS, Raymond Wilson, 1874-1942. 923.242
Thomas More. [Ann Arbor] University of Michigan Press [1958] 416 p. 21 cm. (Ann Arbor paperbacks, AA18) [DA334.M8C45 1958] 58-927
1. More, Thomas, Sir, Saint, 1478-1535.

FARROW, John, 1904- 923.242
The story of Thomas More. New York, Sheed and Ward, 1954. 242p. illus. 22cm. [DA334.M8F33] 54-11147
1. More, Sir Thomas, Saint, 1478-1535. I. Title.

GAVIN, Tadhg 922.22
High above the sun; lives of St. Thomas More and Bp. Edmund Campion. Pulaski,Wis., Franciscan Pubs. [c.]1961. 63p. illus. p.25 pap., 61-1019
1. More, Sir Thomas, Saint, 1478-1535. 2. Campion, Edmund, 1540-1581. I. Title.

HOLLIS, Christopher, 1902- 923.242
Sir Thomas More. [Rev. ed.] London, Burns & Oates [dist. Fresno, Calif., Acad. Lib. Guild, 1963, c.1961] 248p. 19cm. (Universe double bk.) Bibl. 1.95
1. More, Thomas Sir 1478-1535. I. Title.

THE life of Syr Thomas *More,* sometymes Lord Chancellor of England, by Ro: Ba: and edited from ms. Lambeth 179, with collations from seven manuscripts, by Elsie Vaughan Hitchcock and P. E. Hallett, with additional notes and appendices by A. W. Reed. London, Oxford University Press, 1957. xxv, 340p. facsim. 22cm. (Early English Text Society.[Publications] Original series, no. 222, 1950 (for 1945)) v. 12
1. More, Sir Thomas, Saint, 1478-1535. I. Ba., Ro. Ba. II. Hitchcock, Elsie Vaughan, ed. III. Hallett, Philip Edward, 1884-1948, ed. IV. Lambeth Palace. Library. Mss. (no. 179) V. Title: The lyf of Syr Thomas More. VI. Series.

MAYNARD, Theodore, 1890-1956. 942.05'2'0924 B
Humanist as hero; the life of Sir Thomas More. New York, Hafner Pub. Co., 1971. viii, 261 p. 23 cm. "Facsimile of the 1947 edition." [DA334.M8M3 1947a] 74-153580
1. More, Thomas, Sir, Saint, 1478-1535. I. Title. BIP

MORE, Thomas, Sir, Saint, 1478-1535. 942.05'2'0924 B
The correspondence of Sir Thomas More, edited by Elizabeth Frances Rogers. Freeport, N.Y., Books for Libraries Press [1970, c1947] xxii, 584 p. facsim., ports. 24 cm. (Library of English Renaissance literature) Bibliography: p. 567-574. [PR2322.A3 1970] 74-119961 202

NEWELL, Virginia. v. 12
His own good daughter, story of Sir Thomas More and his family. Illustrated by Vera Bock. New York, David McKay Co. [c1961, 1962] 150 p. illus. 64-51433
1. More, Sir Thomas, Saint, 1478-1535. 2. Roper, Margaret (More) 1505-1544. I. Title.

PAUL, Leslie Allen 923.242
Sir Thomas More. New York, Roy Publishers [1959] 22p. (2p. bibl.) illus. (pors.) 21cm. 59-12872 3.50
1. More, Thomas, Saint, Sir 1478-1535. I Title.

PAUL, Leslie Allen, 1905- 942.05'2'0924 B
Sir Thomas More [by] Leslie Paul. Freeport, N.Y., Books for Libraries Press [1970] 222 p. ports. 23 cm. (Library of English Renaissance literature) Reprint of the 1953 ed. Bibliography: p. 214-215. [BX4700.M717P3 1970] 75-128882
1. More, Thomas, Sir, Saint, 1478-1535.

REYNOLDS, Ernest Edwin, 1894- 942.05'2'0924 B
The field is won; the life and death of Saint Thomas More, by E. E. Reynolds. Milwaukee, Bruce Pub. Co. [1968] xv, 396 p. illus., maps, ports. (part col.) 23 cm. Bibliographical footnotes. [DA334.M8R38 1968b] 68-8827 6.50
1. More, Thomas, Sir, Saint, 1478-1535. I. Title.

REYNOLDS, Ernest Edwin, 1894- 942.05'2'0924 B
The life and death of St. Thomas More : the field is won / by E. E. Reynolds. London : Burns & Oates ; New York : Barnes & Noble Books, 1978, c1968. xiii, 396 p. : ill. ; 23 cm. Originally published under title: The field is won. Includes bibliographical references and index. [DA334.M8R38 1978] 78-322932 ISBN 0-06-495854-X : 13.50
1. More, Thomas, Sir, Saint, 1478-1535. 2. Statesmen—Great Britain—Biography. 3. Christian saints—England—Biography. 4. Great Britain—History—Henry VIII, 1509-1547. I. Title.

REYNOLDS, Ernest Edwin, 1894- 923.242
Saint Thomas More. New York, Kenedy [1954] 390p. illus., ports., map. geneal. table. 23cm. Bibliographical footnotes. Bibliography: p. 371-378. [DA334] 54-6531
1. More, Thomas, Saint, Sir 1478-1535. I. Title.

REYNOLDS, Ernest Edwin, 1894- 248.0924
Thomas More and Erasmus. New York, Fordham [1966, c.1965] x, 260p. illus., ports. 23cm. Bibl. [DA334.M8R43] 65-26739 5.00
1. More, Thomas, Saint, Sir 2. Erasmus, Desiderius, d. 1536. I. Title. BIP

ROPER, William, 1496-1578 922.242
Lives of Saint Thomas More [by] William Roper, Nicholas Harpsfield. Ed., introd. by E. E. Reynolds. London, Dent, New York, Dutton [c.1963] xv, 175p. 19cm. (Everyman's lib., no. 19) Bibl. 63-1812 1.95
1. More, Sir Thomas, Saint, 1478-1535. I. Harpsfied, Nicholas, 1519-1575. II. Title. III. Series.

ROPER, William, 1496-1578. 923.242
The lyfe of Sir Thomas Moore, knighte; edited by James Mason Cline. New York, Swallow Press, 1950. 120 p. 21 cm. (Books of the Renaissance) Bibliography: p. 120. [DA334.M8R72 1950] 50-7058
1. More, Sir Thomas, Saint, 1478-1535. 2. First published in 1626 under title: The Mirrour of vertue in worldly greatnes. I. Cline, James Mason, 1898- ed. II. Title.

RUPP, Ernest Gordon. 942.05'2'0924 B
Thomas More : the King's good servant / [by] Gordon Rupp ; [photography by Helmuth Nils Loose]. London ; New York : Collins, 1978. 63 p., [56] p. of plates : ill. (chiefly col.), 2 coats of arms (1 col.), facsims. (1 col.), ports. (chiefly col.) ; 24 cm. Photos. by H. N. Loose are identical with those in Thomas Morus by W. Nigg, published in Freiburg by Herder in 1978. Bibliography: p. 63. [DA334.M8R86 1978] 78-56261 ISBN 0-529-05494-9 : 14.95
1. More, Thomas, Sir, Saint, 1478-1535. 2. Statesmen—Great Britain—Biography. 3. Christian saints—England—Biography. 4. Great Britain—History—Henry VIII, 1509-1547. I. Loose, Helmuth Nils. II. Title. BIP

SAINT Thomas More. v. 12
Garden City, N.Y., Image Books [1958] x, 350p. geneal. table. 19cm. Bibliography: p. [333]-340.
1. More, Sir Thomas, Saint, 1478-1535. I. Reynolds, Ernest Edwin, 1894-

SARGENT, Daniel, 1890- 942.05'2'0924 B
Thomas More. Freeport, N.Y., Books for Libraries Press [1970] 299 p. 22 cm. (Library of English Renaissance literature) "First published 1933." [DA334.M8S3 1970] 71-119963
1. More, Thomas, Sir, Saint, 1478-1535.

SCHMID, Evan, Brother, 1920- 923.242
The merry saint; a story of Saint Thomas More. Illus. by Bernard Howard. Notre Dame, Inc., Dujarie Press [1951] 95 p. illus. 24 cm. [BX4700.M717S3] 52-19917
1. More, Sir Thomas, Saint, 1478-1585. I. Title.

SCHOECK, Richard J. 942.05'2'0924 B
The achievement of Thomas More, aspects of his life and works / Richard J. Schoeck. Victoria, B.C. : English Literary Studies, University of Victoria, 1976. 83 p. ; 23 cm. (ELS monograph series ; no. 7) Includes bibliographical references. [DA334.M8S35] 76-383800
1. More, Thomas, Sir, Saint, 1478-1535. I. Title. II. Series: English literary studies : ELS monograph series ; no. 7.

STAPLETON, Thomas, 1535-1598. 942.05'2'0924 B
The life and illustrious martyrdom of Sir Thomas More. In the translation of Philip E. Hallett. Edited and annotated by E. E. Reynolds. [Bronx, N.Y.] Fordham [1967, c1966] xviii, 206 p. geneal. table. 21 cm. Translation of Vita Thomae Mori. Includes bibliographical references. [DA334.M8S743 1966a] 66-23617
1. More, Thomas, Sir, Saint, 1478-1535. I. Hallett, Philip Edward, 1884-1948, tr. II. Title.

More, Thomas, Sir, Saint, 1478-1535—Addresses, essays, lectures.

ESSENTIAL 954.05'2'0924 B
articles for the study of Thomas More / edited with an introd. and bibliography by R. S. Sylvester and G. P. Marc'hadour. Hamden, Conn. : Archon Books, 1977. xxiii, 676 p. ; 23 cm. (The Essential articles series) Bibliography: p. xvii-xxiii. [DA334.M8E85] 76-42303 ISBN 0-208-01554-X : 20.00
1. More, Thomas, Sir, Saint, 1478-1535—Addresses, essays, lectures. 2. More, Thomas, Sir, Saint, 1478-1535. Utopia. 3. Christian saints—Great Britain—Biography—Addresses, essays, lectures. 4. Statesmen—Great Britain—Biography—Addresses, essays, lectures. 5. Utopias. 6. Consolation—Early works to 1800. I. Sylvester, Richard Standish. II. Marc'hadour, Germain.
Distributed by Shoe String Pr. BIP

More, Thomas, Sir, Saint, 1478-1535—Juvenile literature.

BRADY, Charles Andrew, 1912- 942.05'2'0924 B
St. Thomas More of London Town, by Charles A. Brady. Pictures by S. Ohrvel Carlson. Paterson, N.J., St. Anthony Guild Press [1969] 56 p. illus., coat of arms. 23 cm. A biography of the English statesman and author executed for treason by Henry VIII when he upheld the supremacy of the church over the crown. [DA334.M8B67] 92 75-82871
1. More, Thomas, Sir, Saint, 1478-1535—Juvenile literature. I. Carlson, S. Ohrvel, illus. II. Title.

NEWELL, Virginia 920
His own good daughter; story of Sir Thomas More and his family. Illus. by Vera Bock. New York, Longmans [c.]1961. 149p. 61-14323 3.25
1. More, Sir Thomas, Saint, 1478-1535 — Juvenile literature. 2. Roper, Margaret (More) 1505-1544—Juvenile literature. I. Title.

STANLEY-WRENCH, Margaret. 920
The conscience of a king; the story of Thomas More. Illus. by Kenneth Ody. New York, Hawthorn [1962, c.1961] 186p. 22cm. (Credo bks.) 62-19674 2.95
1. More,Thomas, Saint, Sir 1478-1535—Juvenile literature. I. Title.

HAUGHTON, Rosemary. 92
The young Thomas More. London, Parrish; New York, Roy [1966] 128 p. illus. 20 1/2 cm. 12/6 (B66-22819) [DA334.M8H34] 67-72988
1. More, Sir Thomas, Saint, 1478-1535 — Juvenile literature. I. Title.

Morea, Andre.

MOREA, Andre. 266'.023'0924 B
Surrounded by angels : the miraculous story of a Bible courier behind the Iron Curtain / Andre Morea. 1st U.S. ed. Minneapolis : Bethany Fellowship, 1976. 157 p. ; 18 cm. (Dimension books) [BV2369.5.E852M67 1976] 76-22930 ISBN 0-87123-503-X pbk. : 1.95
1. Morea, Andre. 2. Bible—Publication and distribution—Europe, Eastern. I. Title.

Moreau, Basile Antoine Marie, 1799-1873.

BARROSSE, Thomas. 271'.79 B
Moreau; portrait of a founder. Notre Dame, Ind., Fides Publishers [1969] viii 392 p. 23 cm. Includes bibliographical references. [BX4705.M72B37] 75-92021
1. Moreau, Basile Antoine Marie, 1799-1873. 2. Congregation of Holy Cross.

CATTA, Etienne. 922.244
Basil Anthony Mary Moreau, by Etienne Catta and Tony Catta. English translation by Edward L. Heston. Milwaukee, Bruce Pub. Co. [c1955] 2v. illus. 24cm. [BX4705.M72C33] 55-11616
1. Moreau, Basile Antolne Marie, 1799-1878. 2. Congregation of Holy Cross. I. Catta, Tony, joint author. II. Title.

CATTA, Etienne. 922.244
Mother Mary of the Seven Dolors and the early origins of the Marinites of Holy Cross (1818-1900) [by] Etienne Catta and Tony Catta. English translation by Edward L. Heston. Milwaukee, Catholic Life Publications [1959] 495p. illus. 24cm. Includes bibliography. [BX4705.M3815C3] 59-43143
1. Moreau, Basile Antoine Marie, 1799-1873. 2. Marie des Sept. Doubleurs, 1818-1900. 3. Sisters Marianites of Holy Cross. I. Catta, Tony, joint author. II. Title.

MARY Immaculate, Sister, 1908- 922.244
The cross against the sky; a book for children based on the life of Father Basil Anthony Moreau, the founder and first Superior General of the Congregation of the Holy Cross. With drawings by Sister M. Rose Ellen and Dorothy Van V. Young. South Bend [Ind.] Fides Publishers [1950] 133 p. col. illus. 23 cm. Secular name: Helen Creek. [BX4705.M72M3] 50-14978
1. Moreau, Basile Antoine Marie, I. Title.

Moreau, Gustave, 1826-1898.

MOREAU, Gustave, 1826-1898. 759.4
Gustave Moreau [by] Julius Kaplan. [Los Angeles] Los Angeles County Museum of Art [1974] 149 p. illus. (part col.) 28 cm. Catalog. "Exhibition dates: Los Angeles County Museum of Art, July 23-September 1, 1974. California Palace of the Legion of Honor, September 14-November 3, 1974." Bibliography: p. 145-148. [ND553.M8K36] 74-76953 ISBN 0-87587-059-7 7.00 (pbk.).
1. Moreau, Gustave, 1826-1898. I. Kaplan, Julius. II. Los Angeles Co., Calif. Museum of Art, Los Angeles. III. California Palace of the Legion of Honor, San Francisco.

SELZ, Jean. 759.4 B
Gustave Moreau / by Jean Selz ; [translated from the French by Alice Sachs]. New York : Crown Publishers, [1979] p. cm. [ND553.M8S4413] 78-12107 ISBN 0-517-53449-5 : 5.95
1. Moreau, Gustave, 1826-1898. 2. Painters—France—Biography. BIP

Morecambe, Eric, 1926-

MORECAMBE, Eric, 1926- 791'.092'2 B
Eric & Ernie: the autobiography of Morecambe & Wise; referee Dennis Holman. London, New York, W. H. Allen, 1973. [4], 214, [32] p. illus., facsim., ports. 23 cm. [PN2598.M66A3] 73-177788 ISBN 0-491-01211-X £2.25
1. Morecambe, Eric, 1926- 2. Wise, Ernie, 1925- I. Wise, Ernie, 1925- joint author. II. Holman, Dennis, 1915- ed. III. Title.

Morehead, Willie Carhart.

MOREHEAD, Willie Carhart. 926.1
The saving grace. New York, Vantage Press [1953] 57p. 23cm. [RT37.M56A3] 53-11504

I. Title.

Morehouse, Ward,

MOREHOUSE, Ward, 1898- 928.1
Just the other day; from Yellow Pines to Broadway. New York, McGraw-Hill [1953] 240p. 21cm. Autobiographical. [PS3525.O617J8] 53-5190
I. Title.

Morelos y Pavon, Jose Maria Teclo, 1765-1815.

TIMMONS, Wilbert H. 923.272
Morelos; priest, soldier, statesman of Mexico. El Paso, Texas Western Coll. Pr. [c.]1963. 184p. illus. map. (pt. col. on lining pap.) 24cm. Bibl. 63-13351 5.00; special coin inlaid ed., 8.00
1. Morelos y Pavon, Jose Maria Teclo, 1765-1815. I. Title.

Morewski, Awrom.

MOREWSKI, Awrom. 792
There and back; memories and thoughts of a Jewish actor, by Abraham Morevski. Translated from the Yiddish by Joseph Leftwich. St. Louis, Warren H. Green [1967] 256 p. illus., ports. 23 cm. Translation of Ahin un tsurik (romanized form) [PN2859] 791.43'028'0924 68-1539
I. Title.

Morey, Lloyd W.

MOREY, Lloyd W. 615'.533'0924 B
Magic city doctor / by Lloyd W. Morey, Sr. Boston : Branden press, c1977. 266 p. ; 22 cm. [RZ332.M67A35] 77-152638 ISBN 0-8283-1685-6 pbk. : 7.50
1. Morey, Lloyd W. 2. Osteopaths—Maine—Millinocket—Biography. 3. Millinocket, Me.—Biography. I. Title. BIP

Morgan, Charles, 1930-

MORGAN, Charles, 1930- 301.45'1'09761781
A time to speak / by Charles Morgan, Jr. 1st Holt ed. New York : Holt, Rinehart and Winston, 1979, c1964. x, 177 p. ; 22 cm. Original edition published by Harper & Row Publishers, Inc., New York. [F334.B69N45 1979] 78-14177 ISBN 0-03-013956-2 pbk. : 4.95 ISBN 0-03-050576-3. : 9.95
1. Morgan, Charles, 1930- 2. Birmingham, Ala.—Race relations. 3. Afro-American—Alabama—Birmingham—Civil rights. 4. Birmingham, Ala.—Biography. 5. Lawyers—Alabama—Birmingham—Biography. I. Title. BIP

Morgan, Daniel Edgar, 1877-1949.

CAMPBELL, Thomas F. 977.1'32'0924 B
Daniel E. Morgan, 1877-1949; the good citizen in politics, by Thomas F. Campbell. Cleveland, Press of Western Reserve University, 1966. ix, 196 p. 24 cm. Bibliography: p. 179-187. [F499.C6C25] 66-28143
1. Morgan, Daniel Edgar, 1877-1949. 2. Cleveland—Politics and government. BIP

Morgan, Daniel, 1736?-1802.

CALLAHAN, North. 923.573
Daniel Morgan, ranger of the Revolution. [1st ed.] New York, Holt, Rinehart and Winston [1961] 342 p. illus. 22 cm. Includes bibliography. [E207.M8C3] 61-5300
1. Morgan, Daniel, 1736?-1802.

HIGGINBOTHAM, Don. 923.573
Daniel Morgan, Revolutionary rifleman Chapel Hill, Published for the Institute of Early American History and Culture at Williamsburg, Va. by the University of North Carolina Press [1961] 239p. illus. 24cm. Includes bibliography. [E207.M8H5] 61-17062
1. Morgan, Daniel, 1736?-1802. I. Title.

HIGGINBOTHAM, Don 923.573
Daniel Morgan, Revolutionary rrifleman. Chapel Hill, Pub. for the Inst. of Early Amer. Hist. and Culture at Williamsburg, Va. by the Univ. of N. C. Pr. [c.1961] 239p. illus. Bibl. 61-17062 6.00
1. Morgan, Daniel, 1736?-1802. I. Title.

Morgan, Daniel, 1830-1865.

CARNEGIE, Margaret. 364.3'092'4 B
Morgan : the bold bushranger / [by] Margaret Carnegie. Melbourne : Hawthorn Press, 1974. 136 p., 8 p. of plates : map on lining papers ; 25 cm. Includes indexes. Bibliography: p. 123-131. [DU172.M67C37] 75-317594 ISBN 0-7256-0109-4 : 8.95
1. Morgan, Daniel, 1830-1865. 2. Bushrangers.

Morgan, Edwin Denison, 1811-1883.

RAWLEY, James A 923.273
Edwin D. Morgan, 1811-1883; merchant in politics. New York, Columbia University Press, 1955. 321p. port., map. 24cm. (Columbia studies in the social sciences. no. 582) Bibliography: p. [309]-317. [H31.C7 no. 582] 54-11918
1. Morgan, Edwin Denison, 1811-1883. I. Title. II. Series. BIP

RAWLEY, James A. 973.6'0924 B
Edwin D. Morgan, 1811-1883; merchant in politics, by James A. Rawley. [1st AMS ed.] New York, AMS Press [1968] 321 p. port. 23 cm. (Columbia studies in the social sciences, no. 582) Series statement also appears as: Columbia University studies in the social sciences, 582. Reprint of the 1955 ed. Bibliography: p. [309]-317. [E415.9.M84R3 1968] 68-59261
1. Morgan, Edwin Denison, 1811-1883. I. Title. II. Series.

Morgan, George Campbell, 1863-1945.

MORGAN, Jill. 285'.8'0924
A man of the word; life of G. Campbell Morgan. New York, F. H. Revell [1951] 404p. plates. 22cm. [BX7260.M] A53
1. Morgan, George Campbell, 1863-1945. I. Title.

Morgan, George, 1846-1903.

ALLRED, Berten Wendell, 1904- 929.2'0973
George Morgan, pioneer importer and breeder of American herefords, by B. W. Allred. With appendixes prepared by W. R. Pagel. Oldtown, Md., 1967. 22, 4, 6, 6 l. ports. 30 cm. [CS71.M848 1967b] 77-7609
1. Morgan, George, 1846-1903. 2. Morgan family. 3. Hereford cattle. I. Pagel, William Rush.

Morgan, Godfrey,

MORGAN, Godfrey, 1898- 919.4'3'00924 B
We are borne on as a river (my first seventy years); autobiography. Brisbane, W. R. Smith & Paterson, 1971. xii, 410 p. ports. 25 cm. [CT2808.M58A3] 71-886069
I. Title.

Morgan, Helen, 1900-1941.

MAXWELL, Gilbert, 1910- 784'.092'4 B
Helen Morgan : her life and legend / Gilbert Maxwell. New York : Hawthorn Books, c1974. 192 p., [9] leaves of plates : ill. ; 22 cm. [ML420.M617M4] 73-21319 ISBN 0-8015-4526-9 : 8.95
1. Morgan, Helen, 1900-1941. I. Title.

Morgan, Henry, Sir, 1635?-1688.

ALLEN, Hubert Raymond. 941.06'6'0924 B
Buccaneer : admiral Sir Henry Morgan / H. R. Allen. London : Barker, [1976] xi, 193 p. : ill. ; 23 cm. Includes index. Bibliography: p. [187] [F2161.M83] 76-358701 ISBN 0-213-16569-4 : £3.95
1. Morgan, Henry, Sir, 1635?-1688. I. Title.

POPE, Dudley. 972.9'03'0924 B
The buccaneer king : the biography of Sir Henry Morgan, 1635-1688 / Dudley Pope. New York : Dodd, Mead, 1978, c1977. xx, 379 p., [8] leaves of plates : ill. ; 24 cm. Includes index. Bibliography: p. 366-368. [F2161.M83P66 1978] 77-17962 ISBN 0-396-07566-5 : 11.95
1. Morgan, Henry, Sir, 1635?-1688. 2. Buccaneers—Caribbean area—Biography. I. Title.

Morgan, Henry, Sir, 1635?-1688—Juvenile literature.

SYME, Ronald, 1910- 92
Sir Henry Morgan, buccaneer. Illustrated by William Stobbs. New York, W. Morrow, 1965. 96 p. illus. 22 cm. Bibliography: p. 96. [F2161.M85] 64-21736
1. Morgan, Henry, Sir, 1635?-1688—Juvenile literature. I. Stobbs, William, illus.

Morgan, James, 1786-1866.

SWARTWOUT, Samuel, 1783-1856. 976.4'04'0922
Fragile empires : the Texas correspondence of Samuel Swartwout and James Morgan, 1836-1856 / edited by Feris A. Bass, Jr. and B. R. Brunson. Austin : Shoal Creek Publishers, 1978. p. cm. Includes bibliographical references and index. [F390.S94 1978] 78-13968 ISBN 0-88319-032-X : 27.50
1. Morgan, James, 1786-1866. 2. Swartwout, Samuel, 1783-1856. 3. Texas—History—To 1846—Sources. 4. Pioneers—Texas—Biography. 5. Merchants—Texas—Biography. 6. Customs administration—New York (City)—Officials and employees—Biography. I. Morgan, James, 1786-1866, joint author. II. Bass, Feris A., 1915- III. Brunson, Billy Ray. IV. Title.

Morgan, Joe, 1943-—Juvenile literature.

BURCHARD, Marshall. 796.357'092'4 B
Sports hero, Joe Morgan / by Marshall Burchard. New York : Putnam, c1978. 91 p. : ill. ; 22 cm. (Sports hero biographies) A biography of the All-Star second baseman of the Cincinnati Reds who excels in fielding, hitting, and stealing bases. [GV865.M64B87 1978] 92 77-15509 ISBN 0-399-61095-2 lib. bdg. : 5.49
1. Morgan, Joe, 1943- —Juvenile literature. 2. Cincinnati. Baseball Club (National League)—Juvenile literature. 3. Baseball players—United States—Biography—Juvenile literature. I. Title.

COHEN, Joel H. 796.357'092'4 B
Joe Morgan, great little big man / by Joel H. Cohen. New York : Putnam, c1978. 192 p. : ill. ; 21 cm. (Putnam sports shelf) Includes index. A career biography of Joe Morgan, Cincinnati Red who possesses all the ballplaying abilities. [GV865.M64C63 1978] 92 78-7493 ISBN 0-399-61125-8 lib.bdg. : 5.96
1. Morgan, Joe, 1943-—Juvenile literature. 2. Baseball players—United States—Biography—Juvenile literature. I. Title.

Morgan, John Hunt, 1825-1864.

BUTLER, Lorine Letcher. 923.573
John Morgan and his men. Philadelphia, Dorrance [1960] 357 p. illus. 24 cm. Includes bibliography. [E467.1.M86B8] 60-8555
1. Morgan, John Hunt, 1825-1864.

THOMAS, Edison H. 973.7'42'0924 B
John Hunt Morgan and his raiders / Edison H. Thomas. Lexington : University Press of Kentucky, c1975. xii, 119, [1] p., [4] leaves of plates : ill. ; 21 cm. (The Kentucky bicentennial bookshelf) Bibliography: p. 117-[120] [E475.18.T46] 75-3553 ISBN 0-8131-0214-6 : 3.95
1. Morgan, John Hunt, 1825-1864. 2. Morgan's Raid, 1863. I. Title. II. Series. BIP

Morgan, John Pierpont, 1837-1913.

ALLEN, Frederick Lewis, 1890- 923.373
The great Pierpoint Morgan. New York, Harper [1965, c.1948, 1949] 250p. 18cm. (Perennial lib. P56B) Bibl. [CT275.M6A6] 49-8274 .60 pap.,
1. Morgan, John Pierpont, 1837-1913. I. Title.

CANFIELD, Cass, 1897- 332.1'092'4 B
The incredible Pierpont Morgan; financier and art collector. New York, Harper & Row [1974] 176 p. illus. 26 cm. Bibliography: p. 172. [HG2463.M6C35] 73-15000 ISBN 0-06-010599-2 17.50
1. Morgan, John Pierpont, 1837-1913. I. Title. BIP

THE great Pierpont v. 12
Morgan. New York, Bantom Books, 1956. 244p. 18cm. (A Bantom biography)
1. Morgan, John, Pierpont, 1837-1913. I. Allen, Frederick Lewis, 1890-

HOVEY, Carl, 1875- 332.1'0924 B
The life story of J. Pierpont Morgan. Freeport, N.Y., Books for Libraries Press [1971] 352 p. illus. 23 cm. Reprint of the 1912 ed. [HG2463.M6H58 1971] 72-37345 ISBN 0-8369-6692-9
1. Morgan, John Pierpont, 1837-1913.

SATTERLEE, Herbert Livingston, 1863-1947. 332.1'092'4 B
J. Pierpont Morgan : an intimate portrait / Herbert L. Satterlee. New York : Arno Press, 1975, c1939. xvi, 595 p., [28] leaves of plates : ill. ; 24 cm. (Wall Street and the security markets) Reprint of the ed. published by Macmillan, New York. [HG172.M67S28 1975] 75-2667 ISBN 0-405-07230-9 : 40.00
1. Morgan, John Pierpont, 1837-1913. 2. Capitalists and financiers—United States—Biography. I. Title. II. Series. BIP

Morgan, John, 1735-1789.

BELL, Whitfield Jenks 926.1
John Morgan, continental doctor. Philadelphia, Univ. of Pa. Pr. [c.1965] 301p. illus., facsims., ports. 22cm. Bibl. [R154.M74B4] 65-12020 6.50
1. Morgan, John, 1735-1789. I. Title. BIP

BELL, Whitfield Jenks. 926.1
John Morgan, continental doctor, by Whitfield J. Bell, Jr. Philadelphia, University of Pennsylvania Press [1965] 301 p. illus. facsims., ports. 22 cm. Bibliographical references included in "Notes" (p. 267-291) [R154.M74B4] 65-12020
1. Morgan, John. 1735-1789. I. Title.

Morgan, Lewis Henry, 1818-1881.

STERN, Bernhard Joseph, 1894-1956. 390'.0924
Lewis Henry Morgan, social evolutionist. New York, Russell & Russell [1967] ix, 221 p. 22 cm. Reprint of the 1931 ed. Bibliography: p. 202-216. [GN21.M8S8 1967] 66-24763
1. Morgan, Lewis Henry, 1818-1881. BIP

Morgan, Martha, 1932-

FIBUSH, Esther, 1913- 616.8'914'0926 B
Forgive me no longer : the liberation of Martha / by Esther Fibush and Martha Morgan. New York : Family Service Association of America, c1977. 442 p. ; 23 cm. Bibliography: p. 435. [RC465.F49] 75-27965 ISBN 0-87304-148-8 : 17.95
1. Morgan, Martha, 1932- 2. Psychotherapy—Cases, clinical reports, statistics. 3. Psychotherapy patients—United States—Biography. 4. Women—Mental health. 5. Feminism. I. Morgan, Martha, 1932- joint author. II. Title. BIP

Morgan, Sir Henry, 1635?-1688.

THE great buccaneer; [923.41]
being the life, death, and extraordinary

adventures of Sir Henry Morgan, buccaneer and Lieutenant Governor of Jamaica. New York, W. Funk [1951] 305 p. 21 cm. Bibliography: p. 293-294. [F2161.M8448 1951] 923.242 51-3835
1. Morgan, Sir Henry, 1635?-1688. I. Lindsay, Philip, 1906-

THE great buccaneer, [923.41] being the life, death and extraordinary adventures of Sir Henry Morgan, Buccaneer and Lieutenant Governor of Jamaica. London, New York, P. Nevill [1950] 305 p. illus., ports. 22 cm. Bibliography: p. 293-294. [F216.M8448 1950] 923.242 50-58253
1. Morgan, Sir Henry, 1635?-1688. I. Lindsay, Philip, 1906-

Morgan, Sydney (Owenson) lady, 1783?-1859.

MORGAN, Sydney 914.4'03'60924 (Owenson) Lady, 1783?-1859.
Lady Morgan in France; edited by Elizabeth Suddaby and P. J. Yarrow. Newcastle upon Tyne, Oriel Press, 1971. [9], 339 p., plate. port. 23 cm. "The three books in which Lady Morgan records her impressions of France, and which are the source of the present volume are: France, 2 vols., London, Colburn, 1817. France in 1829-30, 2 vols., London, Saunders & Othey, 1830. Passages from my autobiography, London, Bentley, 1859." [DC33.5.M89] 74-133983 ISBN 0-85362-103-9 £3.00
1. France—Civilization—1789-1830. I. Suddaby, Elizabeth, ed. II. Yarrow, Philip John, ed. III. Title. BIP

SYMONDS, Emily Morse, 920.042 d.1936.
Little memoirs of the nineteenth century. Freeport, N.Y., Books for Libraries Press [1969] ix, 375 p. ports. 23 cm. (Essay index reprint series) Reprint of the 1902 ed. Contents.Contents.—Benjamin Robert Haydon.—Lady Morgan (Sydney Owenson)—Nathaniel Parker Willis.—Lady Hester Stanhope.—Prince Puckler-Muskau in England.—William and Mary Howitt. [DA531.1.S9 1969] 70-86787 ISBN 8-369-11970-
1. Puckler-Muskau, Hermann Ludwig Heinrich, furst von, 1785-1871. 2. Morgan, Sydney (Owenson) lady, 1783?-1859. 3. Haydon, Benjamin Robert, 1786-1846. 4. Willis, Nathaniel Parker, 1806-1867. 5. Stanhope, Hester Lucy, Lady, 1776-1839. 6. Howitt, William, 1792-1879. 7. Howitt, Mary (Botham) 1799-1888. I. Title. BIP

Morgan, Sydney Owenson, Lady, 1783?-1859—Biography.

MORGAN, Sydney 828'.7'09 B Owenson, Lady, 1783?-1859.
Lady Morgan's Memoirs : autobiography, diaries, and correspondence. New York : AMS Press, 1975. 2 v. : ports. ; 22 cm. (Women of letters) Reprint of the 1862 ed. published by W. H. Allen, London. Includes indexes. [PR5059.M3Z5 1975] 76-37705 87.50
1. Morgan, Sydney Owenson, Lady, 1783?-1859—Biography. 2. Morgan, Sydney Owenson, Lady, 1783-1859—Correspondence. I. Title: Memoirs.

STEVENSON, Lionel, 1902- 823 B
The wild Irish girl; the life of Sydney Owenson, Lady Morgan (1776-1859) New York, Russell & Russell [1969] 330 p. port. 23 cm. Reprint of the 1936 ed. Bibliography: p. 317-324. [PR5059.M3Z9 1969] 68-27864
1. Morgan, Sydney (Owenson) Lady, 1783?-1859—Biography. I. Title. BIP

Morgan, Ted, 1932-

MORGAN, Ted, 1932- 301.45'0973 B
On becoming American / Ted Morgan. Boston : Houghton Mifflin, 1978. 336 p. ; 24 cm. [E184.A1M676] 77-16662 ISBN 0-395-26283-6 : 10.95
1. Morgan, Ted, 1932- 2. Minorities—United States—Biography. 3. Minorities—United States—History. 4. United States—Biography. I. Title. BIP

Morgan, Thomas Hunt, 1866-1945.

ALLEN, Garland E. 575.1'092'4 B
Thomas Hunt Morgan : the man and his science / Garland E. Allan. Princeton, N.J. : Princeton University Press, c1978. p. cm. Includes index. Bibliography: p. [QH429.2.M67A44] 77-85526 ISBN 0-691-08200-6 : 22.50
1. Morgan, Thomas Hunt, 1866-1945. 2. Geneticists—United States—Biography.

SHINE, Ian. 575.1'092'4 B
Thomas Hunt Morgan, pioneer of genetics / Ian Shine and Sylvia Wrobel ; foreword by George W. Beadle. Lexington : University Press of Kentucky, c1976. xiv, 159 p., [4] leaves of plates : ill. ; 21 cm. (The Kentucky Bicentennial bookshelf) [QH31.M62S54 1976b] 76-40551 ISBN 0-8131-0095-X : 7.50
1. Morgan, Thomas Hunt, 1866-1945. 2. Geneticists—United States—Biography. I. Wrobel, Sylvia, joint author. II. Title. III. Series.

Morgenstern, Joseph,

MORGENSTERN, Joseph, 1889- 920
I have considered my days. New York, YKUF Publishers [c1964] 237 p. illus., port. 23 cm. Autobiographical. Translation of [CT275.M5944A33] 66-49117
I. Title.

Morike, Eduard Friedrich, 1804-1875.

MARE, Margaret Laura. 831'.7 B
Eduard Morike; the man and the poet [by] Margaret Mare. Westport, Conn., Greenwood Press [1973] ix, 275 p. illus. 22 cm. Reprint of the 1957 ed. Bibliography: p. 270. [PT2434.Z5M33 1973] 72-7860 ISBN 0-8371-6538-5 12.25
1. Morike, Eduard Friedrich, 1804-1875. BIP

Morike, Eduard Friedrich, 1804-1875. Mozart auf der Reise nach Prag.

FARRELL, Ralph, Barstow 927.8
Morike: Mozart auf der Reise nach Prag [In English] Gt. Neck,N.Y., Barron s [1962, c.1960] 62p. 18cm. (Studies in German lit., no. 3) Bibl. 62-20079 .85 pap.,
1. Morike, Eduard Friedrich, 1804-1875. Mozart auf der Reise nach Prag. I. Title.

Morillo y Morillo, Pablo, marques de la Puerta, 1778-1837.

STOAN, Stephen K. 987'.04'0924
Pablo Morillo and Venezuela, 1815-1820 [by] Stephen K. Stoan. Columbus, Ohio State University Press [1974] xi, 249 p. map. 22 cm. Bibliography: p. [237]-244. [F2274.M853S83] 74-11468 ISBN 0-8142-0219-5
1. Morillo y Morillo, Pablo, marques de la Puerta, 1778-1837. 2. Venezuela—History—War of Independence, 1810-1823. I. Title. BIP

Morison, George Abbot, 1879-1966.

GEORGE Abbott 658'.92'41520924 B
Morison, 1879-1966. Peterborough, N.H., Peterborough Historical Society, 1967. 30 p. illus., ports. 23 cm. [CT275.M629A3] 68-4488
1. Morison, George Abbot, 1879-1966. I. Peterborough Historical Society, Peterborough, N.H.

Morison, James, 1818-1882.

MORISON, James, 910'.45'091642 1818-1882.
By sea to San Francisco, 1849-50 : the journal of Dr. James Morison / edited by Lonnie J White and William R Gillaspie Memphis, TN : Memphis State University Press, c1976. p. cm. (Memphis State University Press primary source publications) Includes bibliographical references and index. [F865.M8 1976] 76-40153 ISBN 0-87870-036-6 pbk. : 5.95
1. Morison, James, 1818-1882. 2. Voyages to the Pacific coast. 3. California—Gold discoveries. 4. Physicians—California—Biography. I. Title. II. Series.

Morison, Priscilla Barton, 1906-1973.

MORISON, Samuel 784'.3'0924 B Eliot, 1887-
Vita nuova : a memoir of Priscilla Barton Morison / Samuel Eliot Morison. Northeast Harbor, Me. : Morison, 1975. xviii, 414 p., [31] leaves of plates : ill. (some col.) ; 24 cm. [ML420.M618M7] 75-13485
1. Morison, Priscilla Barton, 1906-1973. I. Title.

Morison, Stanley, 1889-1967.

BARKER, Nicolas. 686.2'092'4
Stanley Morison. Cambridge, Mass., Harvard University Press, 1972. 566 p. illus. 25 cm. Includes bibliographical references. [Z250.A2B15] 76-189157 ISBN 0-674-83425-9
1. Morison, Stanley, 1889-1967.

BARKER, Nicolas. 655.2'0924
Stanley Morison, 1889-1967: a radio portrait; compiled by Nicholas Barker & Douglas Cleverdon from recollections by T. F. Burns [and others]. Ipswich, Cowell, 1969. 5-39 p. plate. port. 22 cm. First broadcast in the B.B.C. third programme on Sunday, Feb. 2, 1969. [Z250.A2B16] 73-479161
1. Morison, Stanley, 1889-1967. I. Cleverdon, Douglas. II. Burns, Thomas F., 1873-

JONES, Herbert, 686.2'2'0924 B 1905-
Stanley Morison displayed : an examination of his early typographic work / by Herbert Jones ; foreword by William Emrys Williams. London : F. Muller, 1976. 127 p. : ill. ; 26 cm. Includes bibliographical references and index. [Z250.A2M688 1976] 76-374574 ISBN 0-584-10352-2 : £8.50
1. Morison, Stanley, 1889-1967. 2. Type designers—England—Biography. 3. Printers—England—Biography. 4. Printing—Specimens. I. Morison, Stanley, 1889-1967. II. Title.

MORAN, James. 686.2'2'0924
Stanley Morison; his typographic achievement. [1st ed.] New York, Hastings House [1971] 184 p. illus. 31 cm. (Visual communication books) Bibliography: p. 171-177. [Z250.A2M69 1971b] 77-163559 ISBN 0-8038-6706-9 17.50
1. Morison, Stanley, 1889-1967.

Moritz, Karl Philipp, 1757-1793.

BOULBY, Mark. 833'.6 B
Karl Philipp Moritz : at the fringe of genius / Mark Boulby. Toronto ; Buffalo : University of Toronto Press, c1978. p. cm. Includes index. Bibliography: p. [PT2435.M3Z555] 78-13651 ISBN 0-8020-5414-5 : 25.00
1. Moritz, Karl Philipp, 1757-1793. 2. Novelists, German—18th century—Biography. BIP

Morland, Samuel, Sir, bart., 1625-1695.

DICKINSON, Henry 609'.2'4 B Winram, 1870-1952.
Sir Samuel Morland: diplomat and inventor, 1625-1695, by H. W. Dickinson. Cambridge, Heffer for the Newcomen Society, 1970. xvi, 135 p., 13 plates. illus., facsims., ports. 24 cm. (Newcomen Society for the Study of the History of Engineering and Technology. Extra publications, no. 6) "Morland's literary works": p. 109-111. [Q143.M8D5] 72-177772 ISBN 0-85270-061-X £2.50
1. Morland, Samuel, Sir, bart., 1625-1695.

Morley, Christopher Darlington, 1890-1957.

OAKLEY, Helen 818'.5'209 B McKelvey.
Christopher Morley on Long Island; a biographical sketch, by Helen McK. Oakley. Roslyn, N.Y., Christopher Morley Knothole Association, 1967. 28 p. illus., ports. 22 cm. Bibliographical references included in "Foreword" (p. 1) [PS3525.O71Z78] 68-4633
1. Morley, Christopher Darlington, 1890-1957. I. Title.

Morley, Felix, 1894-

MORLEY, Felix, 070.4'092'4 B 1894-
For the road / Felix Morley. South Bend, Ind. : Regnery/Gateway, c1979. 472 p. ; 24 cm. Includes bibliographical references and index. [PN4874.M5855A34] 78-74437 ISBN 0-89526-687-3 : 15.00
1. Morley, Felix, 1894- 2. Journalists—United States—Biography. I. Title.

Morley, John Morley, Viscount, 1838-1923.

HAMER, David 942.081'0924 B Allan.
John Morley: liberal intellectual in politics [by] D. A. Hamer. Oxford, Clarendon P., 1968. xvi, 412 p. plate, port. 23 cm. Bibliography: p. [390]-402. [DA565.M78H3] 75-363580 ISBN 0-19-821398-0 65/-
1. Morley, John Morley, Viscount, 1838-1923.

WOLPERT, Stanley A., 954.03'0924 1927-
Morley and India, 1906-1910 [by] Stanley A. Wolpert. Berkeley. Univ. of Calif. Pr., 1967. x, 299p. 25cm. Bibl. [DS480.2.W6] 67-141187 6.95
1. Morley. John Morley, viscount. 1838-1923. 2. India—Pol. & govt.—1765-1947. I. Title.

Morley, Robert.

MORLEY, Robert. 828'.9'1207
Morley marvels / Robert Morley ; with a preface by William Davis. London : Robson Books, 1976. 192 p. ; 25 cm. [PN2598.M67A28] 77-350497 ISBN 0-903895-81-1 : £3.75
1. Morley, Robert. 2. Actors—Great Britain—Biography. I. Title. BIP

MORLEY, Robert. 828'.91207
Morley marvels : memoirs, notes, and essays of the famed actor, raconteur, collector, hotel guest, and man of leisure / Robert Morley ; [editor, Sheridan Morley]. 1st American ed. South Brunswick [N.J.] : A. S. Barnes, 1979, c1976. 192 p. : ill. ; 22 cm. [PN2598.M67A28 1979] 79-50770 ISBN 0-498-02397-4 : 8.95
1. Morley, Robert. 2. Actors—Great Britain—Biography. I. Morley, Sheridan, 1941- II. Title.

MORLEY, Robert. 790.2'092'4 B
A musing Morley / preface by Alan Coren. London : Coronet, 1976. 255 p., [4] p. of plates : ill., ports. ; 18 cm. [PN2598.M67A35 1976b] 77-360019 ISBN 0-340-19997-0 : £0.85
1. Morley, Robert. 2. Actors—Great Britain—Biography. I. Title.

MORLEY, Robert. 790'.20924 B
Robert Morley; a reluctant autobiography, by Robert Morley & Sewell Stokes. New York, Simon and Schuster [1967, c1966] 285 p. illus., ports. 25 cm. [PN2598.M67A3] 67-12917
I. Stokes, Sewell, 1902- BIP

Morley, Robert—Biography.

MORLEY, Robert. 790.2'092'4 B
The Robert Morley bedside reader. Chicago : H. Regnery, 1976, c1974. xiv, 208 p., [2] leaves of plates : ill. ; 24 cm. British ed. published under title: A musing Morley. [PN2598.M67A35 1976] 75-29027 ISBN 0-8092-8130-9
1. Morley, Robert—Biography. I. Title.

Morley, Sylvanus Griswold, 1883-1948.

SANTA Fe, N.M. Schools of American Research. 925.71
Morleyana; a collection of writings in memoriam Sylvanus Griswold Morley, 1883-1948. Santa Fe, N.M., School of American Research and the Museum of New Mexico [c1950] xii, 268 p. mounted port. 24 cm. "500 copies." "Writings of Sylvanus Griswold Morley, by Margaret W. Harrison": p. 73-84. [F1435.M752S3] 51-2663
1. Morley, Sylvanus Griswold, 1883-1948. 2. Mayas — Antiq. I. Santa Fe, N.M. Museum of New Mexico. II. Title.

Mormons and Mormonism.

CANNON, Elaine. 808.066'92
Putting life in your life story / Elaine Cannon. Salt Lake City : Desert Book Co., 1977. 94 p. ; 23 cm. Includes index. [BX8638.C36] 77-15451 ISBN 0-87747-679-9 pbk. : 2.95
1. Mormons and Mormonism. 2. Diaries—Authorship. 3. Biography (as a literary form) I. Title. **BIP**

FISH, Joseph, 1840-1926. 289.3'0924 B
The life and times of Joseph Fish, Mormon pioneer. Edited by John H. Krenkel. Danville, Ill., Interstate Printers & Publishers [1970] 543 p. 3 maps (2 on lining papers), port. 24 cm. Includes bibliographical references. [BX8695.F57A3 1970] 70-110886
1. Mormons and Mormonism. I. Title.

HUNTER, Rodello. 289.3
A daughter of Zion. Drawings by Allan P. Nielson. [1st ed.] New York, Knopf, 1972. xiv, 285 p. illus. 22 cm. [BX8695.H83A3] 74-171116 ISBN 0-394-47032-X 6.95
1. Mormons and Mormonism. I. Title. **BIP**

MERKLEY, Christopher, 1808- 289.3'3 B
Biography of Christopher Merkley. Written by himself. Freeport, N.Y., Books for Libraries Press [1972] 46 p. 23 cm. Reprint of the 1887 ed. [BX8695.M35A3 1972] 70-38363 ISBN 0-8369-6780-1
1. Mormons and Mormonism.

Mormons and Mormonism—Biography.

BURGESS-OLSON, Vicky, 1945- 289.3'3 B
Sister saints / by Vicky Burgess-Olson. Provo, Utah : Brigham Young University Press, c1978. xiv, 494 p. : ports. ; 23 cm. (Studies in Mormon history ; v. 5) Includes bibliographical references. [BX8693.B87] 78-5080 ISBN 0-8425-1235-7 : 5.95
1. Mormons and Mormonism—Biography. 2. Women—United States—Biography. I. Title. II. Series. **BIP**

GREEN, Doyle L. ed. 922.8373
Our leaders. Salt Lake City, Deseret Book Co. [1951] 112 p. illus. 19 cm. [BX8693.G7] 52-16007
1. Mormons and Mormonism—Blog. I. Title.

HETTRICK, Ric. 289.3'3 B
From among men : biographies of 26 Latter-Day apostles / Ric and Marcia Hettrick. Independence, Mo. : Herald Pub. House, c1976. 220 p. : ports. ; 21 cm. [BX8693.H44] 76-27242 ISBN 0-8309-0170-1
1. Mormons and Mormonism—Biography. I. Hettrick, Marcia, joint author. II. Title.

HINCKLEY, Bryant S 1867- 922.8373
The faith of our pioneer fathers. Salt Lake City, Deseret Book Co., 1956. 268p. illus: 24cm. [BX8693.H5] 56-2877
1. Mormons and Mormonism—Biog. I. Title.

NIBLEY, Preston. 922.8373
Stalwarts of Mormonism. Salt Lake City, Deseret Book Co., 1954. 215p. illus. 24cm. [BX8693.N53] 54-4997
1. Mormons and Mormonism—Biog. I. Title.

PEARSON, Carol Lynn. 289.3'3 B
The flight and the nest / Carol Lynn Pearson. Salt Lake City : Bookcraft, 1975. xiii, 121 p. : ill. ; 24 cm. Includes bibliographical references and index. [BX8693.P4] 75-31079 ISBN 0-88494-288-0 : 3.50
1. Mormons and Mormonism—Biography. 2. Women—Biography. 3. Women. I. Title.

REECE, Colleen L. 288.3'092'2 B
The unknown witnesses, by Colleen L. Reece. [Independence, Mo., Herald Pub. House, 1974] 159 p. 18 cm. [BX8693.R43] 73-87642 ISBN 0-8309-0107-8 5.00
1. Bible—Biography. 2. Mormons and Mormonism—Biography. I. Title. **BIP**

SESSIONS, Gene Allred. 289.3'3 B
Latter-day patriots : nine Mormon families and their Revolutionary War heritage / Gene Allred Sessions. Salt Lake City : Deseret Book Co., 1975. xiv, 219 p., [1] leaf of plates : ill. ; 24 cm. Includes bibliographical references and index. [BX8693.S47] 75-37276 ISBN 0-87747-600-4
1. Mormons and Mormonism—Biography. 2. United States—History—Revolution, 1775-1783. I. Title.

YOUNG, Brigham, 1801-1877. 289.3'0924
Manuscript history of Brigham Young, 1846-1847. [Edited by] Elden J. Watson. [Salt Lake City, Utah, J. Watson, 1971] 672 p. illus. 23 cm. [BX8695.Y7A3 1971] 77-27431
I. Watson, Elden Jay. II. Title.

Morny, Charles Auguste Louis Joseph, duc de, 1811-1865.

PFLAUM, Rosalynd. 944.07'0924 B
The emperor's talisman; the life of the Duc de Morny. [1st ed.] New York, Meredith Press [1968] xiii, 270 p. illus., ports. 23 cm. Bibliography: p. [259]-264. [DC280.5.M7P4] 68-9523 7.95
1. Morny, Charles Auguste Louis Joseph, duc de, 1811-1865. I. Title.

Moro Sheeba.

KING, Beatrice (Tannehill) 922
Moro Sheeba. Chicago, Moody Press [1957] 128p. 22cm. [BV3625.C63M6] 57-20942
1. Moro Sheeba. I. Title.

KING, Beztrice (Tannehill) 922
Moro Sheeba. Chicago, Moody Press [1957] 128p. 22cm. [BV3625.C63M6] 57-20942
1. Moro Sheeba. I. Title.

Moroz, Valentyn IAkovych, 1936—

MOROZ, Valentyn IAkovych, 1936- 323.44'092'4 B
Boomerang; the works of Valentyn Moroz. Introd. by Paul L. Gersper. Edited by Yaroslav Bihun. Baltimore, Smoloskyp [1974] xxiii, 272 p. 23 cm. Includes bibliographical references. [DK508.8.M58] 74-77633 ISBN 0-914834-00-2
1. Moroz, Valentyn IAkovych, 1936- 2. Ukraine—Politics and government—1917- 3. Dissenters—Ukraine. I. Title.

Morrall, Earl,

MORRALL, Earl, 1934- 796.332'0924 B
Comeback quarterback; the Earl Morrall story, by Earl Morrall and George Sullivan. New York, Grosset & Dunlap [1971] 216 p. 21 cm. (Grosset sports library) 1969 ed. published under title: In the pocket; my life as a quarterback. [GV939.M62A3 1971] 73-158750 2.50
I. Sullivan, George, 1927- joint author. II. Title.

MORRALL, Earl, 1934- 796.332'0924 B
In the pocket; my life as a quarterback, by Earl Morrall and George Sullivan. New York, Grosset & Dunlap [1969] x, 210 p. illus., ports. 22 cm. 1971 ed. published under title: Comeback quarterback; the Earl Morrall story. [GV939.M62A3] 74-86669 5.95
I. Sullivan, George, 1927- joint author. II. Title.

Morrell, Ottoline Violet Anne Cavendish-Bentinck, Lady, 1873-1938.

DARROCH, Sandra Jobson. 941.083'0924 B
Ottoline : the life of Lady Ottoline Morrell / Sandra Jobson Darroch. 1st American ed. New York : Coward, McCann & Geoghegan, 1975. 317 p., [16] leaves of plates : ill. ; 24 cm. Includes index. Bibliography: p. 307-309. [DA566.9.M63D37 1975] 74-16641 ISBN 0-698-10634-2 : 12.50
1. Morrell, Ottoline Violet Anne Cavendish-Bentinck, Lady, 1873-1938. 2. England—Intellectual life—20th century.

MORRELL, Ottoline Violet Anne Gavendish-Bentinck, Lady, 1873-1938. 941.083'092'4 B
Ottoline at Garsington : memoirs of Lady Ottoline Morrell, 1915-1918 / edited with an introd. by Robert Gathorne-Hardy. 1st American ed. New York : Knopf : distributed by Random House, 1975, c1974. 304 p. ; 24 cm. Continues Memoirs of Lady Ottoline Morrell. Includes index. [DA566.9.M63A36 1975] 75-8253 ISBN 0-394-49636-1 : 12.50
1. Morrell, Ottoline Violet Anne Cavendish-Bentinck, Lady, 1873-1938. 2. England—Intellectual life—20th century. I. Title. **BIP**

Morrell, William Parker, 1889-

MORRELL, William Parker, 1889- 993.103'092'4 B
Memoirs / W. P. Morrell. Dunedin : McIndoe ; New York : available from International Publications Service, 1979. 157 p., [4] leaves of plates : ill., 23 cm. Distributor statement from label. [DU419.3.M67A35] 79-670387 ISBN 0-908565-99-2 : 17.50
1. Morrell, William Parker, 1889- 2. Historians—New Zealand—Biography. I. Title.

Morrill, Justin Smith, 1810-1898.

PARKER, William Belmont, 1871-1934. 973.6'6'0924 B
The life and public services of Justin Smith Morrill. New York, Da Capo Press, 1971 [c1924] viii, 378 p. illus., port. 23 cm. (The American scene: comments and commentators) [E664.M8P2 1971] 79-87371 ISBN 0-306-71595-3
1. Morrill, Justin Smith, 1810-1898. I. Title. **BIP**

Morris, Ann Axtell, 1900-

MORRIS, Ann Axtell, 1900- 979
Digging in the Southwest / by Ann Axtell Morris ; illustrated with photos. Santa Barbara [Calif.] : P. Smith, 1978. p. cm. Reprint of the 1933 ed. published by Doubleday, Doran, Garden City, N.Y., with 8 new photos. added. [E78.S7M76 1978] 78-2705 ISBN 0-87905-045-4 pbk. : 5.95
1. Morris, Ann Axtell, 1900- 2. Indians of North America—Southwest, New—Antiquities. 3. Southwest, New—Antiquities. 4. Archaeologists—Southwest, New—Biography. I. Title. **BIP**

Morris, David D

MORRIS, David D 923.144
The greatest queen of France, her life and times, written and illustrated by David D. Morris. Albion, Mich. c1956. 103 l. illus. 30cm. [DC91.6.B5M6] 56-9535
I. Blanche de Castille, consort of Louis VIII, King of France, 1188-1252. II. Title.

Morris, Edita, 1902- —Biography—Youth.

MORRIS, Edita, 1902- 813'.5'2 B
Straitjacket : autobiography / Edita Morris. New York : Crown Publishers, c1978. 147 p. ; 24 cm. [PS3525.O7376Z47] 77-28755 ISBN 0-517-53257-3 : 7.95
1. Morris, Edita, 1902- —Biography—Youth. 2. Novelists, American—20th century—Biography. 3. Sweden—Biography. I. Title.

Morris, Gouverneur, 1752-1816.

MINTZ, Max M., 1919- 973.3'0924 B
Gouverneur Morris and the American Revolution, by Max M. Mintz. [1st ed.] Norman, University of Oklahoma Press [1970] xiii, 284 p. illus., ports. 23 cm. Bibliography: p. 241-262. [E302.6.M7M5] 70-108792 ISBN 8-06-109009-
1. Morris, Gouverneur, 1752-1816. I. Title. **BIP**

ROOSEVELT, Theodore, Pres. U.S., 1858-1919. 973.4'0924 B
Gouverneur Morris. New York, Haskell House Publishers, 1968. x, 370 p. 23 cm. Reprint of the 1888 ed. [E302.6.M7R75] 68-24996
1. Morris, Gouverneur, 1752-1816. **BIP**

ROOSEVELT, Theodore, Pres. U.S., 1858-1919. 973.4'0924 B
Gouverneur Morris. Boston, Houghton, Mifflin. [New York, AMS Press, 1972] vi, 341 p. illus. 19 cm. (American statesmen, v. 8) Reprint of the 1898 ed. [E302.6.M7R763] 76-128972 ISBN 0-404-50858-8
1. Morris, Gouverneur, 1752-1816. I. Title. II. Series.

ROOSEVELT, Theodore, Pres. U.S., 1858-1919. 973.4'0924 B
Gouverneur Morris. New Rochelle, N.Y., Arlington House [1970] 341 p. illus., ports. 21 cm. (Giants of America. The Founding Fathers) Originally published in 1898. [E302.6.M7R762] 79-111226 ISBN 0-87000-090-X
1. Morris, Gouverneur, 1752-1816.

SWIGGETT, Howard, 1891- 923.273
The extraordinary Mr. Morris. [1st ed.] Garden City, N.Y., Doubleday, 1952. xix, 483 p. illus., ports., facsims. 22 cm. Bibliography: p. [463]-472. [E302.6.M7S9] 52-5540
1. Morris, Gouverneur, 1752-1816. I. Title.

Morris, Henry, 1889-1961.

REE, Harry. 370'.92'4 B
Educator extraordinary; the life and achievements of Henry Morris, 1889-1961. [London] Longman [1973, i.e.1974] viii, 163 p. illus. 24 cm. Bibliography: p. 159-160. [LA2375.G72M677] 73-180577 ISBN 0-582-36312-8
1. Morris, Henry, 1889-1961. I. Title.
Distributed by Longman, New York, 7.95.

Morris, Jan, 1926-

MORRIS, Jan, 1926- 301.41'5 B
Conundrum [New York] New American Library [1975, c1974] 194 p. 18 cm. (A Signet book) Autobiographical [CT788.M637A33] 74-525 1.50 (pbk.)
1. Morris, Jan, 1926- 2. Change of sex—Personal narratives. I. Title.

MORRIS, Jan, 1926- 301.41'5 B
Conundrum. [1st ed.] New York, Harcourt Brace Jovanovich [1974] xi, 174 p. 21 cm. "A Helen and Kurt Wolff book." Autobiographical. [CT788.M637A33] 74-525 ISBN 0-15-122563-X 5.95
1. Morris, Jan, 1926- 2. Change of sex—Personal narratives. I. Title. **BIP**

Morris, Kathy.

MEE, Charles L. 616.9'93'810926 B
Seizure / Charles L. Mee, Jr. New York : M. Evans, c1978. 216 p. ; 22 cm. [RC280.B7M43] 77-26884 ISBN 0-87131-254-9 : 8.95
1. Morris, Kathy. 2. Brain—Tumors—Biography. I. Title.
Distributed by Lippincott,NY **BIP**

Morris, Robert, 1734-1806.

CHERNOW, Barbara Ann. 333'.0092'4 B
Robert Morris, land speculator, 1790-1801 / Barbara Ann Chernow. New York : Arno Press, 1978, c1974. p. cm. (Dissertations in American economic history) Reprint of the author's thesis, Columbia University, 1974. Bibliography: p. [E302.6.M8C47 1978] 77-14762 ISBN 0-405-11029-4 : 20.00

1. Morris, Robert, 1734-1806. 2. Capitalists and financiers—United States—Biography. I. Title. II. Series.

YOUNG, Eleanor May. 923.273
Forgotten patriot: Robert Morris. New York, Macmillan, 1950. xii, 280 p. ports. 22 cm. Bibliography: p. 268-271. [E302.6.M8Y6] 50-7836
1. Morris, Robert, 1734-1806. I. Title.

Morris, Thomas, b. 1732.

MORRIS, Thomas, 973'.04'97 S
b.1732?
Miscellanies in prose and verse / Thomas Morris. New York : Garland Pub., 1977. p. cm. (The Garland library of narratives of North American Indian captivities ; v. 20) Reprint of the 1791 ed. printed for J. Ridgway, London. Issued with the reprint of Bleecker, A. E. S. The history of Maria Kittle. Hartford, 1797. [E85.G2 vol. 20] [E83.76] 973.2'7 B 75-7041 ISBN 0-8240-1644-0 lib.bdg. : 29.50
1. Morris, Thomas, b. 1732. 2. Pontiac's Conspiracy, 1763-1765. 3. Indians of North America—Captivities. 4. United States—Biography. I. Title. II. Series.

Morris, Thomas Francis, 1852-1898.

MORRIS, Thomas 769'.924 B
Francis, 1890-
The life and work of Thomas F. Morris, 1852-1898, by Thomas F. Morris, II. Edited by Barbara R. Mueller. [Larchmont? N.Y., 1968] 159 p. illus., ports. 26 cm. [HE6185.U5M65] 70-1130
1. Morris, Thomas Francis, 1852-1898. 2. Postage-stamp design. 3. Paper money design. I. Title.

Morris, William, 1834-1896.

ARNOT, Robert Page, 335'.0092'4
1890-
William Morris, the man and the myth : including letters of William Morris to J. L. Mahon and Dr. John Glasse / by R. Page Arnot. Westport, Conn. : Greenwood Press, 1976, c1964. 131 p. ; 23 cm. Reprint of the ed. published by Monthly Review Press, New York. Includes bibliographical references and index. [HX243.A8 1976] 76-107 ISBN 0-8371-8652-8 lib.bdg. : 10.25
1. Morris, William, 1834-1896. 2. Mahon, John Lincoln. 3. Glasse, John. 4. Socialists—Great Britain. I. Morris, William, 1834-1896. II. Mahon, John Lincoln. III. Glasse, John. IV. Title.

BLOOMFIELD, Paul. 821'.8 B
William Morris. [Folcroft, Pa.] Folcroft Library Editions, 1973. ix, 314 p. illus. 26 cm. Reprint of the 1934 ed. published by A. Barker, London. Bibliography: p. 312. [PR5083.B6 1973] 73-15902 ISBN 0-8414-3322-4 (lib. bdg.)
1. Morris, William, 1834-1896.

BRADLEY, Ian C. 821'.8 B
William Morris and his world / Ian Bradley. New York : Scribner, c1978. 127 p. : ill. ; 24 cm. Includes index. Bibliography: p. 119. [NX547.6.M67B7 1978b] 78-53937 ISBN 0-684-15867-1 : 10.95
1. Morris, William, 1834-1896. 2. Artists—Great Britain—Biography. BIP

CARY, Elisabeth 709'.2'4 B
Luther, 1867-1936.
William Morris: poet, craftsman, socialist. [Folcroft, Pa.] Folcroft Library Editions, 1974 [c1902] ix, 296 p. illus. 23 cm. Reprint of the ed. published by Putnam, New York. Bibliography: p. 269-290. [PR5083.C3 1974] 74-18214 ISBN 0-8414-3545-6 (lib. bdg.)
1. Morris, William, 1834-1896. I. Title. BIP

COMPTON-RICKETT, 709'.24 B
Arthur, 1869-1937.
William Morris; a study in personality. With an introd. by R. B. Cunninghame Graham. Port Washington, N.Y., Kennikat Press [1972] xxii, 325 p. ports. 23 cm. Reprint of the 1913 ed. "Analytical biography and synopsis of events contemporary with Morris' career": p. [269]-317. [PR5083.C6 1972] 73-160749 ISBN 0-8046-1563-2
1. Morris, William, 1834-1896. I. Title.

ESHLEMAN, Lloyd 709'.24 B
Wendell, 1902-
A Victorian rebel; the life of William Morris. New York, Octagon Books, 1971 [c1940] xiv, 386 p. illus., port. 24 cm. Revision of the author's thesis, Princeton University, 1937, issued under title: William Morris: artist-philosopher and practical-socialist. Bibliography: p. 369-381. [PR5083.E75 1971] 74-168557 ISBN 0-374-92627-1
1. Morris, William, 1834-1896. 2. Socialism. I. Title. BIP

EVANS, Benjamin Ifor, 821'.8
Sir, 1899-
William Morris & his poetry, by B. Ifor Evans. London, G. G. Harrap. [New York, AMS Press, 1972] 155, [1] p. port. 19 cm. (Poetry and life series) Reprint of the 1925 ed. Bibliography: p. 155-[156] [PR5083.E8 1972] 74-120987 ISBN 0-404-52512-1
1. Morris, William, 1834-1896. I. Title. II. Series.

EVANS, Benjamin Ifor, 821'.8
Sir, 1899-
William Morris & his poetry / by B. Ifor Evans. Norwood, Pa. : Norwood Editions, 1976. p. cm. Reprint of the 1925 ed. published by G. G. Harrap, London, which was issued as no. 33 of Poetry & life series. Bibliography: p. [PR5083.E8 1976] 76-17047 ISBN 0-8482-0657-6 : 8.50
1. Morris, William, 1834-1896. I. Title. II. Series: Poetry and life series ; 33. BIP

EVANS, Benjamin Ifor, 821'.8
Sir, 1899-
William Morris & his poetry / by B. Ifor Evans. Folcroft, Pa. : Folcroft Library Editions, 1974. 155, [1] p., [1] leaf of plates : port. ; 24 cm. Reprint of the 1925 ed. published by G. G. Harrap, London, which was issued as no. 33 of Poetry & life series. Bibliography: p. 155-[156] [PR5083.E8 1974] 74-23889 ISBN 0-8414-3947-8 : 7.00
1. Morris, William, 1834-1896. I. Title. II. Series: Poetry & life series ; 33.

FAULKNER, Peter. 821.912
William Morris and W. B. Yeats. Dublin, Dolmen Press; [distributed outside Ireland by the Oxford University Press] 1962. 30 p. 21 cm. [PR5083.F3] 63-2833
1. Morris, William, 1834-1896. 2. Yeats, William Butler, 1865-1939. I. Title.

GODWIN, Edward F. 709'.24 B
Warrior bard; the life of William Morris [by] Edward and Stephani Godwin. Illustrated by the authors. Port Washington, N.Y., Kennikat Press [1970] 175 p. illus. 21 cm. Reprint of the 1947 ed. [PR5083.G6 1970] 70-103190
1. Morris, William, 1834-1896. I. Godwin, Stephani (Allfree) II. Title. BIP

GRENNAN, Margaret Rose, 709.24
1912-
William Morris, medievalist and revolutionary [by] Margaret R. Grennan. New York, Russell & Russell [1970, c1945] x, 173 p. 25 cm. Bibliography: p. [161]-167. [PR5087.S6G7 1970] 76-102500
1. Morris, William, 1834-1896. 2. Socialism. BIP

HENDERSON, Philip, 1906- 821'.8
William Morris: his life, work, and friends. Foreword by Allan Temko. New York, McGraw-Hill [1967] 388 p. 90 illus. (8 col. incl. facsims., ports.) 25 cm. Bibliographical references included in "Notes and sources" (p. 370-379) [PR5083.H4 1967b] 67-22695
1. Morris, William, 1834-1896.

JACKSON, Holbrook, 709'.24 B
1874-1948.
William Morris. Westport, Conn., Greenwood Press [1971] 160 p. 23 cm. Reprint of the 1926 ed. Bibliography: p. 159-160. [NK942.M8J3 1971] 79-110848 ISBN 0-8371-4515-5
1. Morris, William, 1834-1896.

LINDSAY, Jack, 1900- 821'.8 B
William Morris : his life and work / Jack Lindsay. New York : Taplinger Pub. Co., 1979, c1975. 432 p., [4] leaves of plates : ill. ; 24 cm. Includes index. Bibliography: p. 409-418. [PR5083.L5 1979] 79-13075 ISBN 0-8008-8339-X : 14.95
1. Morris, William, 1834-1896. 2. Authors, English—19th century—Biography. 3. Artists—England—Biography. 4. Socialists—England—Biography. I. Title. BIP

MACKAIL, John William, 709.24 B
1859-1945.
The life of William Morris. New York, Haskell House, 1970. 2 v. illus., port. 23 cm. Reprint of the 1899 ed. [PR5083.M25 1970] 79-118180
1. Morris, William, 1834-1896. I. Title.

MACKAIL, John William, 700'.924 B
1859-1945.
The life of William Morris. New York, B. Blom, 1968. 2 v. illus., ports. 24 cm. Reprint of the 1899 ed. [PR5083.M25 1968] 68-57988
1. Morris, William, 1834-1896. I. Title. BIP

MACKAIL, John William, 709'.24
1859-1945.
The life of William Morris. With an introd. by Sir Sydney Cockerell. London, Oxford University Press [1950] 2 v. in 1. 16 cm. (The World's classics, 521) [PR5083.M] A52
1. Morris, William, 1834-1896. I. Title.

MACKAIL, John William, 709'.2'4
1859-1945.
William Morris and his circle. New York, Haskell House Publishers, 1971. 22 p. 23 cm. "A lecture delivered in the examination schools, Oxford, at the summer meeting of the University Extension Delegacy, on August 6, 1907." Reprint of the 1907 ed. [PR5083.M3 1971] 79-117585 ISBN 0 8383 1018 4
1. Morris, William, 1834-1896. I. Title. BIP

MACKAIL, John William, 709'.2'4
1859-1945.
William Morris and his circle; a lecture delivered in the examination schools, Oxford, at the summer meeting of the University Extension Delegacy, on August 6, 1907. [Folcroft, Pa.] Folcroft Library Editions, 1973. 22 p. 26 cm. Reprint of the 1907 ed. published by Clarendon Press, Oxford. [PR5083.M3 1973] 73-12455 ISBN 0-8414-5999-1 (lib. bdg.)
1. Morris, William, 1834-1896. I. Title.

NOYES, Alfred, 1880- 709'.24 B
1958.
William Morris. New York, B. Blom, 1971. viii, 156 p. 22 cm. Reprint of the 1908 ed. [PR5083.N6 1971] 70-173176
1. Morris, William, 1834-1896.

NOYES, Alfred, 1880-1958. 821'.8
William Morris. Freeport, N.Y., Books for Libraries Press [1972] viii, 156 p. 23 cm. Reprint of the 1908 ed., issued in series: English men of letters. [PR5083.N6 1972] 72-39201 ISBN 0-8369-6803-4
1. Morris, William, 1834-1896.

THOMPSON, Edward Palmer, 821'.8 B
1924-
William Morris : romantic to revolutionary / E. P. Thompson. 1st American ed. New York : Pantheon Books, c1977. x, 829 p. ; 25 cm. Includes bibliographical references and index. [PR5083.T6 1977] 76-62712 ISBN 0-394-41136-6 : 17.95
1. Morris, William, 1834-1896. 2. Authors, English—19th century—Biography. 3. Socialism in Great Britain. BIP

THOMPSON, Edward Palmer, 928.2
1924-
William Morris, romantic to revolutionary. New York, Monthly Review Press, 1961 [i.e. 1962, c1955] 908 p. illus. 23 cm. [PR5083.T6 1962] 61-17951
1. Morris, William, 1834-1896. 2. Socialism in Great Britain. I. Title.

THOMPSON, Edward Palmer, 928.2
1924-
William Morris, romantic to revolutionary. New York, Monthly Review Press, 1961 [i. e. 1962, c1955] 908 p. illus. 23 cm. [PR5083.T6 1962] 61-17951
1. Morris, William, 1834-1896. 2. Socialism in Great Britain.

VALLANCE, Aymer, 1862- 709'.24
1943.
William Morris: his art, his writings, and his public life; a record. Kennebunkport, Me., Milford House, 1971. xiv, 462 p. illus., facsims., col. plate, port. 24 cm. Reprint of the 1897 ed. "Chronological list of the printed works of William Morris": p. [447]-452. [PR5083.V3 1971] 72-79486 ISBN 0-87821-015-6
1. Morris, William, 1834-1896.

VALLANCE, Aymer, 1862- 709'.24
1943.
William Morris, his art, his writings, and his public life : a record / by Aymer Vallance. Boston : Longwood Press, 1977. p. cm. Reprint of the 1898 ed. published by G. Bell, London. Includes index. "Chronological list of the printed works of William Morris": p. [PR5083.V3 1977] 77-6968 ISBN 0-89341-208-2 lib.bdg. : 50.00
1. Morris, William, 1834-1896. 2. Authors, English—19th century—Biography. 3. Artists—England—Biography.

WARWICK, Frances Evelyn 709'.2'4
(Maynard) Greville, Countess of, 1861-1938.
William Morris, his homes and haunts. With twelve drawings in crayon by A. Forestier and other illus. [Folcroft, Pa.] Folcroft Library Editions, 1974. xi, 68 p. illus. 24 cm. Reprint of the 1912 ed. published by T. C. & E. C. Jack, London, in series: The Pilgrim books. [PR5083.W3 1974] 73-13851 ISBN 0-8414-3462-X (lib. bdg.)
1. Morris, William, 1834-1896.

WATKINSON, Raymond. 709'.42
William Morris as designer. New York, Reinhold Pub. Co. [1967] 81 p. 92 illus. (incl. facsims., ports.; part col.) 26 cm. Bibliography: p. 80-[82]. [NK1498.M6W3 1967] 67-24704
1. Morris, William, 1834-1896. I. Title.

WEEKLEY, Montague. 709'.2'4 B
William Morris. London, Duckworth. [Folcroft, Pa.] Folcroft Library Editions, 1973. p. Reprint of the 1934 ed., which was issued as no. 33 of Great lives. Bibliography: p. [PR5083.W4 1973] 73-908 ISBN 0-8414-2800-X
1. Morris, William, 1834-1896. BIP

Morris, William, 1834-1896—Addresses, essays, lectures.

DUNLAP, Joseph 686.2'092'4 B
Riggs, 1913-
On the heritage of William Morris : some considerations, typographic & otherwise : an address delivered by the annual Typophiles Christmas luncheon, December 12, 1974. New York : The Typophiles, 1976. 26 p. ; 19 cm. (A Typophile monograph) [Z250.A2D86] 77-352486
1. Morris, William, 1834-1896—Addresses, essays, lectures. I. Title. II. Series: The Typophiles, New York. Typophile monographs.

Morris, William, 1834-1896—Correspondence.

MORRIS, William, 1834- 821'.8 B
1896.
The letters of William Morris to his family and friends / edited with introd. and notes by Philip Henderson. New York : AMS Press, 1978. lxvii, 406 p., [3] leaves of plates : ill. ; 23 cm. Reprint of the 1950 ed. published by Longmans, Green, London. Includes indexes. [PR5083.A4 1978.] 75-41199 ISBN 0-404-14711-9 : 24.50
1. Morris, William, 1834-1896—Correspondence. 2. Poets, English—19th century—Correspondence. 3. Socialists—England—Correspondence. I. Henderson, Philip, 1906- II. Title. BIP

Morris, William, 1834-1896—Journeys—Iceland.

PURKIS, John 914.91'2'0440924 B
Arthur, 1933-
The Icelandic jaunt : a study of the expeditions made by Morris to Iceland in 1871 and 1873 / John Purkis. Folcroft, Pa. : Folcroft Library Editions, 1977. p. cm. Reprint of the 1962 ed. published by the William Morris Society, Surrey, England. Includes bibliographical references. [PR5083.P8 1977b] 77-8166 ISBN 0-8414-6792-7 lib. bdg. : 10.00
1. Morris, William, 1834-1896—Journeys—Iceland. 2. Morris, William, 1834-1896.

Icelandic journeys. 3. Authors, English—19th century—Biography. 4. Iceland—Description and travel—History. I. Title. BIP

Morris, Willie.

MORRIS, Willie. 917.62'49 [B]
Good old boy. [New York] Avon [1974, c.1971] 128 p. 18 cm. Summary: The author's boyhood escapades in his hometown of Yazoo City, Mississippi. [CT275.M59444A296 1974] 75-157897 0.95 (pbk.)
I. Title. BIP

MORRIS, Willie. 973.92'0924
North toward home. Boston, Houghton Mifflin, 1967. 438 p. 22 cm. "A Houghton Mifflin literary fellowship book." Autobiographical. [CT275.M59444A3] 67-25803
I. Title. BIP

Morris, Wright, 1910-

HOWARD, Leon. 813'.5'2
Wright Morris. Minneapolis, University of Minnesota Press [1968] 48 p. 21 cm. (University of Minnesota pamphlets on American writers, no. 69) Bibliography: p. 44-48. [PS3525.O7475Z66] 68-64752
1. Morris, Wright, 1910- I. Series: Minnesota. University. Pamphlets on American writers, no. 69

Morriseau, Norval.

MORRISEAU, Norval. 759.11 B
The art of Norval Morriseau / Lister Sinclair and Jack Pollock. Toronto ; New York : Methuen, 1979. p. cm. Includes index. Bibliography: p. [ND249.M63A4 1979] 79-17652 ISBN 0-458-93820-3 : 50.00
1. Morriseau, Norval. 2. Painters—Canada—Biography. I. Sinclair, Lister. II. Pollock, Jack. III. Title.

Morrison, Anna (Daly)

MORRISON, Anna (Daly) 1884- 920.7
Diary. Illus. by Carl Hoobing. Boise, Idaho, Em-Kayan Press [1951] 446 p. illus., port. 23 cm. On spine: Those were the days. "A chronological revision and enlargement of a series of narratives published monthly in the Em-Kayan magazine under the serial heading: Those were the days." [CT275.M6453A3] 51-26031
I. Title: Those were the days. II. Title.

Morrison, DeLesseps Story, 1912-1964.

HAAS, Edward F. 320.9'763'3506
DeLesseps S. Morrison and the image of reform : New Orleans politics, 1946-1961 / Edward F. Haas. Baton Rouge : Louisiana State University Press, c1974. xii, 368 p., [8] leaves of plates : ill. ; 24 cm. Includes index. Bibliography: p. 341-354. [F379.N553M63] 73-90867 ISBN 0-8071-0073-0 : 12.95
1. Morrison, DeLesseps Story, 1912-1964. 2. New Orleans—Politics and government. I. Title. BIP

Morrison, Donald.

WALLACE, Clarke. 364.1'525'0924 B
Wanted—Donald Morrison : the true story of the Megantic outlaw / by Clarke Wallace. 1st ed. Toronto, Ont. : Doubleday Canada Ltd. ; Garden City, N.Y. : Doubleday, 1977. viii, 221 p., [4] leaves of plates : ill. ; 22 cm. [HV6248.M774W34] 76-42409 ISBN 0-385-12647-6 : 7.95
1. Morrison, Donald. 2. Crime and criminals—Quebec (Province)—Biography. I. Title.

Morrison, George Ernest, 1862-1920.

MORRISON, George Ernest, 1862-1920. 951'.03
The correspondence of G. E. Morrison / edited by Lo Hui-Min. Cambridge ; New York : Cambridge University Press, 1976-1978. 2 v. : ill. ; 24 cm. Includes indexes. Contents.Contents.—1. 1895-1912.—2. 1912-1920. [DS764.M67] 78-11354 82.50
1. Morrison, George Ernest, 1862-1920. 2. China—History—1900-—Sources. 3. Journalists—Correspondence. I. Lo, Hui-min.

PEARL, Cyril. 951'.03'0924 B
Morrison of Peking. [Harmondsworth, Eng.] Penguin Books [1970, c1967] 431 p. 20 cm. Bibliography: p. 415-416. [DS795.23.M6P4 1970] 72-193241 ISBN 0-14-003173-1 1.55
1. Morrison, George Ernest, 1862-1920. I. Title.

Morrison, George, 1919- —Juvenile literature.

KOSTICH, Dragos D. 759.13 B
George Morrison / by Dragos D. Kostich. Minneapolis : Dillon Press, c1976. 66 p. : ill. ; 24 cm. (The Story of an American Indian) A biography of the Chippewa Indian whose many artistic achievements were crowned when in 1970 he began teaching at the University of Minnesota not only art, but American Indian studies. [E99.C6M864] 92 75-45210 ISBN 0-87518-110-4 : 4.95
1. Morrison, George, 1919- —Juvenile literature. 2. Chippewa Indians—Juvenile literature. I. Title. BIP

Morrison, Henry Clay, 1857-1942.

WESCHE, Percival A 242'.4
Henry Clay Morrison; crusador saint. [Berne, Ind., Herald Press, c1963] 208 p. 21 cm. Imprint on mounted label. Bibliographical references included in "Footnotes" (p. 206-208) [BX8495.M68W4] 64-1036
1. Morrison, Henry Clay, 1857-1942. I. Title.

Morrison, Joseph Grant.

CORBETT, C T 922.89
Soldier of the cross; the life story of J. G. Morrison, 1871-1939. Kansas City, Mo., Beacon Hill Press [1956] 128p. 19cm. [BX8699.N32M63] 56-33591
1. Morrison, Joseph Grant. I. Title.

Morrow, Dwight Whitney, 1873-1931.

NICOLSON, Harold George, Sir, 1886-1968. 332.1'092'4 B
Dwight Morrow / Harold Nicholson. 1st ed. New York : Arno Press, 1975, c1935. xvi, 409 p., [10] leaves of plates : ill. ; 23 cm. (Wall Street and the security markets) Reprint of the ed. published by Harcourt, Brace, New York. [E748.M75N5 1975] 75-2657 ISBN 0-405-06982-0 : 26.00
1. Morrow, Dwight Whitney, 1873-1931. I. Title. II. Series. BIP

Morrow, Stanley J., 1843-1921.

HURT, Wesley Robert, 1917- 927.7
Frontier photographer; Stanley J. Morrow's Dakota years [by] Wesley R. Hurt and William E. Lass. [Vermillion] University of South Dakota [1956] 135 p. illus. 24 cm. Includes bibliography. [TR140.M6H87] 56-10996
1. Morrow, Stanley J., 1843-1921. 2. Northwestern States—History. 3. Dakota Indians. 4. Photography—History—U.S. I. Lass, William E., joint author. II. Title.

Morse, Henry, 1595-1645.

CARAMAN, Philip, 1911- 922.242
Henry Morse, priest of the plague. New York, Farrar, Straus and Cudahy [1957] 201p. illus. 22cm. Includes bibliography. [BX4705.M7254C3] 57-1742
1. Morse, Henry, 1595-1645. I. Title.

Morse, John Torry,

MORSE, John Torry, 1840-1937. 973.4'4'0924 B
John Adams. New Rochelle, N.Y., Arlington House [1970] 338 p. ports. 21 cm. (Giants of America. The Founding fathers) Originally published in 1884. [E322.M884] 70-111221 ISBN 0-87000-085-3
1. Adams, John, Pres. U.S., 1735-1826.

Morse, Philip McCord, 1903-

MORSE, Philip McCord, 1903- 530'.092'4 B
In at the beginnings : a physicist's life / Philip M. Morse. Cambridge, Mass. : MIT Press, c1977. vii, 375 p., [6] leaves of plates : ill. ; 21 cm. Includes index. [QC16.M66A34] 76-40010 ISBN 0-262-13124-2 : 14.95
1. Morse, Philip McCord, 1903- 2. Physicists—United States—Biography. I. Title. BIP

Morse, Samuel Finley Breese, 1791-1872.

LARKIN, Oliver W. 927.5
Samuel F. B. Morse and American democratic art. [1st ed.] Boston, Little, Brown, 1954. viii, 215 p. illus., ports. 21 cm. (The Library of American biography) "A note on the sources": p. [201]-203. [ND237.M75L3] 926.2 54-8284
1. Morse, Samuel Finley Breese, 1791-1872. 2. Art—United States.—History. I. Title. II. Series.

LATHAM, Jean Lee 927.5
Medals for Morse, artist and inventor; illus. by Albert Micale. New York, Scholastic Bk. Servs. [c.1954, 1962] 123p. (TX-412) 20cm. .35 pap.,
1. Morse, Samuel Finley Breese, 1791-1872. I. Title.

LATHAM, Jean Lee. 926.2
Medals for Morse, artist and inventor; illustrated by Douglas Gorsline. [1st ed.] New York, Aladdin Books, 1954. 192p. illus. 21cm. (American heritage series) [TK5243.M7L3] 927.5 54-6154
1. Morse, Samuel Finley Breese, 1791-1872. I. Title.

LATHAM, Jean Lee. 621.382'0924 B
Samuel F. B. Morse, artist-inventor. Illustrated by Jo Polseno. Champaign, Ill., Garrard Press [1961] 80 p. illus. 23 cm. (A Discovery book) A brief biography of the inventor of the telegraph and Morse code, who planned from early childhood to be a painter of great historical pictures but first won recognition as a portrait painter. [ND237.M75L34] 92 AC 68
1. Morse, Samuel Finley Breese, 1791-1872. I. Polseno, Jo, illus. II. Title.

MABEE, Carleton, 1914- 621.382'0924 B
The American Leonardo; a life of Samuel F. B. Morse. With an introd. by Allan Nevins. New York, Octagon Books, 1969 [c1943] xix, 420, xv p. illus., ports. 25 cm. "References": p. 381-420. [TK5243.M7M3 1969] 72-76512
1. Morse, Samuel Finley Breese, 1791-1872. I. Title. BIP

MORSE, Samuel Finley Breese, 1791-1872. 621.382'092'4 B
Samuel F. B. Morse; his letters and journals, edited by Edward Lind Morse. New York, Da Capo Press, 1973- [c1914- v. 22 cm. (Library of American art) [TK5243.M7A3 1973] 76-75279 ISBN 0-306-71304-7 37.50 (2 vols; Lib. ed.)
1. Morse, Samuel Finley Breese, 1791-1872. I. Morse, Edward Lind, 1857-1923, ed. BIP

PRIME, Samuel Irenaus, 1812-1885. 621.382'092'4 B
The life of Samuel F. B. Morse. New York, Arno Press, 1974 [c1874] xii, 776 p. illus. 24 cm. (Telecommunications) Reprint of the 1875 ed. published by D. Appleton, New York. [TK5243.M7P8 1974] 74-4691 ISBN 0-405-06054-8
1. Morse, Samuel Finley Breese, 1791-1872. I. Title. II. Series: Telecommunications (New York, 1974-)

Morse, Samuel Finley Breese, 1791-1872—Juvenile literature.

HAYS, Wilma Pitchford 927.5
Samuel Morse and the telegraph. Pictures by Richard Mayhew. New York F. Watts [c.1960] 66p. illus. 23cm. (A First biography) 60-5580 1.95
1. Morse, Samuel Finley Breese, 1791-1872—Juvenile literature. I. Title.

Morse, Wayne Lyman, 1900-

SMITH, Arthur Robert, 1925- 923.273
The tiger in the Senate; the biography of Wayne Morse. [1st ed.] Garden City, N. Y., Doubleday, 1962. 455 p. illus. 22 cm. [E748.M76S55] 61-12583
1. Morse, Wayne Lyman, 1900- I. Title.

Mort, Thomas Sutcliffe, 1816-1878.

BARNARD, Alan. 382'.092'4
Thomas Sutcliffe Mort. Melbourne, New York, Oxford University Press [1962] 30 p. illus., port. 19 cm. (Great Australians) Bibliography: p. 30. [HC602.5.M6B28] 65-32029
1. Mort, Thomas Sutcliffe, 1816-1878. I. Title.

Mortimer, Charles K.

MORTIMER, Charles K. 796.7'5'0924 B
Brooklands and beyond / [by] Charles Mortimer. [Norwich] : Goose, 1974. 240 p., [8] p. of plates, leaf of plate : ill., ports. ; 23 cm. Includes index. [GV1032.M56A33] 74-188461 ISBN 0-900404-23-X : 15.95
1. Mortimer, Charles K. 2. Weybridge, Eng. Brooklands. 3. Motorcycle racing. 4. Automobile racing. I. Title.
Distributed by British Book Center. BIP

Mortimer, Penelope, 1918- —Biography—Youth.

MORTIMER, Penelope, 1918- 823'.9'14 B
About time : an aspect of autobiography / by Penelope Mortimer. 1st ed. in the U.S.A. Garden City, N.Y. : Doubleday, 1979. 215 p. ; 22 cm. [PR6063.O815Z463 1979] 78-14707 ISBN 0-385-08457-9 : 8.95
1. Mortimer, Penelope, 1918- —Biography—Youth. 2. Authors, English—20th century—Biography. I. Title. BIP

Morton, Ferdinand Joseph, 1885-1941.

LOMAX, Alan, 1915- 927.8
Mister Jelly Roll; the fortunes of Jelly Roll Morton, New Orleans Creole and inventor of jazz. New York, Grove Press [1956, c1950] xv, 302p. map, music. 21cm. (Evergreen books, E-35) 'Chronological list of Morton's compositions': p. 276-280. Discography: p. 281-302. [ML410.M82L6 1956] 56-8441
1. Morton, Ferdinand Joseph, 1885-1941. 2. Morton, Ferdinand Joseph, 1885-1941—Discography. 3. Jazz music—Discography. I. Title.

LOMAX, Alan, 1915- 927.8
Mister Jelly Roll; the fortunes of Jelly Roll Morton, New Orleans Creole and "inventor of jazz." Drawings by David Stone Martin. [1st ed.] New York, Duell, Sloan and Pearce [1950] xvii, 318 p. illus., port., map, music. 22 cm. "Chronological list of Morton's compositions": p. 292-296. Discography: p. 297-318. [ML410.M82L6] 50-8436
1. Morton, Ferdinand Joseph, 1885-1941. 2. Morton, Ferdinand Joseph, 1885-1941—Discography. 3. Jazz music—Discography. I. Title.

LOMAX, Alan, 1915- 785.4'2'0924 B
Mister Jelly Roll; the fortunes of Jelly Roll Morton, New Orleans Creole and inventor of jazz. Drawings by David Stone Martin. 2d ed. Berkeley, University of California Press [1973] xvii, 318 p. illus. 21 cm. "Chronological list of Morton's compositions": p. 292-296. Discography: p. 297-318. [ML410.M82L6 1973] 74-189222 ISBN 0-520-02402-8 10.95; 3.45 (pbk.)
1. Morton, Ferdinand Joseph, 1885-1941. 2. Morton, Ferdinand Joseph, 1885-1941—Discography. 3. Jazz music—Discography. I. Title.

Morton, Ferinand Joseph, 1885-1941.

WILLIAMS, Martin T v. 12
Jelly Roll Morton. New York, A. S. Barnes and company [1963] 3 p. l., 85 p. ports. 21 cm. (Kings of jazz) "A Perpetua book" 67-22953
1. Morton, Ferinand Joseph, 1885-1941. I. Title. II. Series. **BIP**

Morton, Henry Albert.

MORTON, Henry Albert. 993.1
And now New Zealand / Harry Morton. Dunedin : John McIndoe, 1976. 191 p. : map ; 22 cm. An abridgement of And now New Zealand, first published in 1969. [DU412.M662] 77-353297 ISBN 0-908565-07-0
1. Morton, Henry Albert. 2. New Zealand—Description and travel—1951- 3. National characteristics, New Zealand. I. Title. **BIP**

Morton, John.

WILKINSON, Sylvia, 796.7'2'0924 1940-
The stainless steel carrot; an auto racing odyssey. Illustrated with photos. Boston, Houghton Mifflin, 1973. xvi, 335 p. illus. 22 cm. [GV1032.M57W54] 73-13756 7.95
1. Morton, John. 2. Automobile racing. I. Title.

Morton, Laura Elizabeth, 1871-1943.

DAUGHERTY, Wilna 976.4'822 B Morton.
She did what she could : history of a pioneer woman / by Wilna Morton Daugherty. [s.l. : s.n.], c1977 (Waco, Tex. : Texian Press) ix, 108 p. [3] leaves of plates : ill. ; 23 cm. [F394.D83M673] 77-89281
1. Morton, Laura Elizabeth, 1871-1943. 2. Dumas, Tex.—Biography. I. Title.

Morton, Levi Parsons, 1824-1920.

MCELROY, Robert 973.8'6'0924 B McNutt, 1872-1959.
Levi Parsons Morton : banker, diplomat, and statesman / Robert McNutt McElroy. New York : Arno Press, 1975 [c1930] xvii, 340 p., [4] leaves of plates : ill. ; 23 cm. (Wall Street and the security markets) Reprint of the ed. published by Putnam, New York. Includes index. [E664.M85M14 1975] 75-2646 ISBN 0-405-06971-5 : 22.00
1. Morton, Levi Parsons, 1824-1920. I. Title. II. Series. **BIP**

Morton, Oliver Perry, 1823-1877.

FOULKE, William 328.73'092'4 B Dudley, 1848-1935.
Life of Oliver P. Morton, including his important speeches. Indianapolis, Bowen-Merrill Co., 1899. [New York, AMS Press, 1974] 2 v. port. 23 cm. [E506.M87 1974] 77-168129 ISBN 0-404-04592-8 45.00
1. Morton, Oliver Perry, 1823-1877. I. Morton, Oliver Perry, 1823-1877. II. Title.

Morton, William Thomas Green, 1819-1868.

LUDOVICI, Laurence James. 926.1
The discovery of anaesthesia. New York, Crowell [1962, c1961] 230 p. 21 cm. London ed. (Parrish, 1961) has title: Cone of oblivion. Includes bibliography. [RD80.M9L8 1962] 62-18233
1. Morton, William Thomas Green, 1819-1868. 2. Jackson, Charles Thomas, 1805-1880. I. Title.

MACQUITTY, Betty. 617.96'0924 B
Victory over pain; Morton's discovery of anaesthesia. With a foreword by Christiaan Barnard. New York, Taplinger Pub. Co. [1971, c1969] 208 p. illus., port. 24 cm. First published in London under title: The battle for oblivion. Bibliography: p. 195-199. [RD80.M9M25 1971] 75-107007 ISBN 0-8008-8014-5 5.95
1. Morton, William Thomas Green, 1819-1868. I. Title.

WOODWARD, Grace Steele. 926.1
The man who conquered pain; a biography of William Thomas Green Morton. Pref. by William S. Derrick. Boston, Beacon Press [1962] 175 p. illus. 22 cm. [RD80.M9W6] 62-16635
1. Morton, William Thomas Green, 1819-1868. I. Title.

Moscheles, Ignaz, 1794-1870.

MENDELSSOHN-BARTHOLDY, 780'.924 Felix, 1809-1847.
Letters of Felix Mendelssohn to Ignaz and Charlotte Moscheles. Translated from the originals in his possession, and edited by Felix Moscheles. Freeport, N.Y., Books for Libraries Press [1970] xx, 306 p. illus., facsims., ports. 23 cm. "First published 1888." [ML410.M5A36 1970] 77-107822
1. Moscheles, Ignaz, 1794-1870. 2. Moscheles, Charlotte (Embden) d. 1889. I. Moscheles, Felix, 1833-1917, ed.

MENDELSSOHN-BARTHOLDY, 780'.924 B Felix, 1809-1847.
Letters of Felix Mendelssohn to Ignaz and Charlotte Moscheles. Translated from the originals in his possession, and edited by Felix Moscheles. [New York] B. Blom [1971] xx, 306 p. illus. 22 cm. Reprint of the 1888 ed. [ML410.M5A36 1971] 76-173116
1. Moscheles, Ignaz, 1794-1870. 2. Moscheles, Charlotte (Embden) d. 1889. I. Moscheles, Felix, 1833-1917, ed.

Moscow. Moskovskii Khudozhestvennyi akademicheskii teatr.

NEMIROVICH-DANCHENKO, 792'.0924 Vladimir Ivanovich, 1858-1943.
My life in the Russian theatre [by] Vladimir Nemirovitch-Dantchenko. Translated by John Cournos. With an introd. by Joshua Logan. A foreword by Oliver M. Sayler and a chronology by Elizabeth Reynolds Hapgood. New York, Theatre Arts Books [1968] xxv, 365 p. illus., ports. 25 cm. Translation of Iz proshlogo (romanized form) [PN2728.N4A3 1968b] 67-18053 9.50
1. Moscow. Moskovskii Khudozhestvennyi akademicheskii teatr. 2. Chekhov, Anton Pavlovich, 1860-1904. I. Title. **BIP**

Moseley, Henry Gwyn Jeffreys, 1887-1915.

HEILBRON, J. L. 530'.092'4 B
H. G. J. Moseley; the life and letters of an English physicist, 1887-1915 [by] J. L. Heilbron. Berkeley, University of California Press [1974] xiii, 312 p. illus. 24 cm. Bibliography: p. [283]-302. [QC16.M68H44] 72-93519 ISBN 0-520-02375-7 15.00
1. Moseley, Henry Gwyn Jeffreys, 1887-1915. I. Moseley, Henry Gwyn Jeffreys, 1887-1915. Correspondence. 1974. **BIP**

Moseley, Thomas, 1886-1959.

MOSELEY, Eva M v. 12
Moh Ta-Iu, "man of great plans"; the biography of Dr. Thomas Moseley, missionary-educator. Harrisburg, Pa., Christian Publications [1963] 224 p. illus. 68-101205
1. Moseley, Thomas, 1886-1959. I. Title.

Moser, Albert, 1870-1903.

DAVENPORT, Horace 610'.92'4 B Willard, 1912-
An eagle-feather: the short life of Albert Moser, M.D.; a footnote to the life of Walter B. Cannon [by] Horace W. Davenport. Boston, Francis A. Countway Library of Medicine, 1974. 41 p. illus. 23 cm. (Countway Library Associates. Historical publication no. 2) Includes bibliographical references. [R154.M8D38] 74-175991
1. Moser, Albert, 1870-1903. 2. Cannon, Walter Bradford, 1871-1945. 3. Deglutition. I. Title. II. Series.

Moser, Tilmann, 1938-

MOSER, Tilmann, 616.8'917'0924 B 1938-
Years of apprenticeship on the couch : fragments of my psychoanalysis / Tilmann Moser ; introd. by Heinz Kohut ; translated from the German by Anselm Hollo. New York : Urizen Books, 1977. 168 p. ; 23 cm. Translation of Lehrjahre auf der Couch. 76-58387 ISBN 0-916354-45-8 : 10.00
1. Moser, Tilmann, 1938- 2. Psychoanalysis—Biography. I. Title.

Moses.

AUERBACH, Elias, 222'.1'0924 1882-
Moses. Translated and edited by Robert A. Barclay and Israel O. Lehman, with annotations by Israel O. Lehman. Detroit, Wayne State University Press, 1975. 253 p. ; 24 cm. Includes bibliographical references. [BS580.M6A813] 72-6589 ISBN 0-8143-1491-0
1. Moses. 2. Bible. O.T. Pentateuch—Criticism, interpretation, etc. **BIP**

BEEGLE, Dewey M. 222'.1'0924 B
Moses, the servant of Yahweh [by] Dewey M. Beegle. Grand Rapids, Mich., Eerdmans [1972] 368 p. illus. (on lining paper) 23 cm. Includes bibliographical references. [BS580.M6B44] 73-162029 ISBN 0-8028-3406-X 7.95
1. Moses. I. Title. **BIP**

DAICHES, David, 222'.1'0924 B 1912-
Moses, the man and his vision / David Daiches. New York : Praeger, 1975. 264 p. : ill. ; 26 cm. Includes index. Bibliography: p. 257-258. [BS580.M6D3] 74-11918 ISBN 0-275-33740-5 : 19.95
1. Moses. I. Title.

GILPIN, Richard O. 222'.1'0924 B
Moses—born to be a slave, but God ... / Richard O. Gilpin. 1st ed. Hicksville, N.Y. : Exposition Press, c1977. 119 p. ; 22 cm. [BS580.M6G48] 77-366950 ISBN 0-682-48843-7 : 5.50
1. Bible. O.T.—Biography. 2. Moses. I. Title. **BIP**

GILPIN, Richard O. 222'.1'0924 B
Moses—born to be a slave, but God ... / Richard O. Gilpin. 1st ed. Hicksville, N.Y. : Exposition Press, c1977. 119 p. ; 22 cm. [BS580.M6G48] 77-366950 ISBN 0-682-48843-7 : 5.50
1. Bible. O.T.—Biography. 2. Moses. I. Title. **BIP**

GREGORIUS, Saint, Bp. 222'.1'0924 of Nyssa, fl.379-394.
The life of Moses / Gregory of Nyssa ; translation, introd. and notes by Abraham J. Malherbe and Everett Ferguson ; pref. by John Meyendorff. New York : Paulist Press, c1978. xvi, 208 p. ; 23 cm. (The Classics of Western spirituality) Translation of De vita Moysis. Includes indexes. Bibliography: p. 139-140 [BS580.M6G7313] 78-56352 ISBN 0-8091-2112-3 pbk. : 6.95
1. Moses. 2. Bible. O.T.—Biography. 3. Mysticism—Early church, ca.30-600. I. Title. II. Series.

KLAGSBRUN, Francine. 221.92'4
The story of Moses. New York, Watts [1968] xvii., 171p. map. 22cm. Immortals of phil. & religion) [BS580.M6K55] 68-27403 3.95; 2.96 lib. ed.,
1. Moses. I. Title. **BIP**

KLAGSBRUN, 222'.1'0924 B Francine.
The story of Moses. London, New York, Franklin Watts Ltd. [1971] xvii, 171 p. map. 23 cm. (Immortals of philosophy and religion) Bibliography: p. v-vii. [BS580.M6K55 1971] 72-180143 ISBN 0-85166-290-0 £1.25
1. Moses. I. Title.

MUNOWITZ, Ken. 222'.1'0924 B
Moses, Moses / pictures by Ken Munowitz ; text by Charles L. Mee, Jr.. 1st ed. New York : Harper & Row, c1977. [32] p. : ill. ; 26 cm. Retells the early events in the life of Moses. [BS580.M6M8 1977] 76-41516 ISBN 0-06-024178-0 : 4.95. lib.bdg. : 4.79
1. Bible. O.T.—Biography—Juvenile literature. 2. Moses—Juvenile literature. I. Mee, Charles L. II. Title.

PETERSEN, Mark E. 222'.1'0924 B
Moses : man of miracles / Mark E. Petersen. Salt Lake City : Deseret Book Co., 1977. 198 p. ; 24 cm. Includes index. [BS580.M6P445] 77-21553 ISBN 0-87747-651-9 : 4.95
1. Bible. O.T.—Biography. 2. Moses. 3. Mormons and Mormonism—Doctrinal and controversial works.

PETERSEN, Mark E. 222'.1'0924 B
Moses : man of miracles / Mark E. Petersen. Salt Lake City : Deseret Book Co., 1977. 198 p. ; 24 cm. Includes index. [BS580.M6P445] 77-21553 ISBN 0-87747-651-9 : 4.95
1. Bible. O.T.—Biography. 2. Moses. 3. Mormons and Mormonism—Doctrinal and controversial works.

PONDER, Catherine. 131'.32
The millionaire Moses : his prosperity secrets for you! / Catherine Ponder. Marina del Rey, Ca. : DeVorss, c1977. ix, 219 p. ; 21 cm. (The Millionaires of the Bible series) [BJ1611.2.P624] 77-71459 ISBN 0-87516-232-0 pbk. : 3.95
1. Moses. 2. Bible. O.T.—Biography. 3. Success. I. Title.

ROSHWALD, Mordecai, 222'.1'0924 1921-
Moses: leader, prophet, man; the story of Moses and his image through the ages [by] Mordecai and Miriam Roshwald. New York, T. Yoseloff [1969] 233 p. illus. 22 cm. Bibliography: p. 215-228. [BS580.M6R62] 69-15773 6.00
1. Moses. I. Roshwald, Miriam, joint author. II. Title.

SANFORD, John A. 221.9'22 B
The man who wrestled with God; a study of individuation (personal growth toward wholeness) based on four Bible stories [by] John A. Sanford. King of Prussia, Pa., Religious Pub. Co. [1974] 126 p. 22 cm. Errata slip inserted. Includes bibliographical references. [BS571.S26] 74-79994 5.95
1. Jacob, the patriarch. 2. Joseph, the patriarch. 3. Moses. 4. Adam (Biblical character) 5. Eve (Biblical character) I. Title.
Publisher's address: 198 Allendale Road, King of Prussia, Pa. 19406.

Moses, Anna Mary (Robertson) 1860-1961.

KALLIR, Otto, 1894- 759.13
Grandma Moses. New York, Abrams [1973] 357 p. illus. (part col.) 31 x 35 cm. Bibliography: p. 341-342. [ND237.M78K32] 73-6930 ISBN 0-8109-0166-8 32.50
1. Moses, Anna Mary (Robertson) 1860-1961. I. Moses, Anna Mary (Robertson) 1860-1961.

KALLIR, Otto, 1894- 759.13
Grandma Moses / Otto Kallir. New York : H. N. Abrams, [1975] p. cm. An abridgement of the 1973 ed. published by Abrams. [ND237.M78K322] 74-31269 ISBN 0-8109-2053-0
1. Moses, Anna Mary (Robertson) 1860-1961. I. Moses, Anna Mary Robertson, 1860-1961.

MOSES, Anna Mary 759.13 (Robertson) 1860-1961.
Art and life of Grandma Moses. Edited by Otto Kallir. New York, Gallery of Modern Art, 1969. 168 p. illus., ports. 24 cm. Includes catalogues of exhibitions. [ND237.M78K3] 76-13522
I. Kallir, Otto, 1894- ed. II. Title.

MOSES, Anna Mary (Robertson) 1860-1961. 927.5
Grandma Moses: my life's history. Edited by Otto Kallir. [1st ed. New York] Harper [1952] xi, 140 p. plates (part col.) ports., facsims. 25 cm. [ND237.M78A22] 51-11940
1. Artists—Correspondence, reminiscences, etc.

Moses, Anna Mary (Robertson) 1860-1961—Juvenile literature.

ARMSTRONG, William Howard, 1914- 759.13
Barefoot in the grass; the story of Grandma Moses, by William H. Armstrong. [1st ed.] Garden City, N.Y., Doubleday [1970] 96 p. illus. (part col.) 24 cm. The life of the artist who began her prolific career at the age of seventy. [ND237.M78A8] 92 74-122338 4.95
1. Moses, Anna Mary (Robertson) 1860-1961—Juvenile literature. I. Title. **BIP**

GRAVES, Charles Parlin, 1911- 759.13 B
Grandma Moses: favorite painter, by Charles P. Graves. Illustrated by Victor Hays. Champaign, Ill., Garrard Pub. Co. [1969] 96 p. illus. (part col.), ports. 24 cm. (Americans all) A biography of the New England grandmother who began painting seriously at age seventy and kept it up until she was over a hundred years old. [ND237.M78G7] 92 69-14830 2.49
1. Moses, Anna Mary (Robertson) 1860-1961—Juvenile literature. I. Mays, Victor, 1927- illus. II. Title.

LAING, Martha. 759.13
Grandma Moses: the grand old lady of American art. Charlotteville, N.Y., SamHar Press, 1972. 30 p. 23 cm. (Outstanding personalities, no. 13) Bibliography: p. 29-30. A biography of the famous American painter who did not begin painting seriously until age seventy-eight when arthritis forced her to give up embroidery. [ND237.M78L34] 92 71-190231
1. Moses, Anna Mary (Robertson) 1860-1961—Juvenile literature. I. Title.

Moses ben Maimon, 1135-1204.

BRATTON, Fred Gladstone, 1896- 296.1'72
Maimonides, medieval modernist. Boston, Beacon Press [1967] ix, 159 p. 21 cm. Bibliography: p. 152-154. [BM755.M6B7] 67-24893
1. Moses ben Maimon, 1135-1204. I. Title.

FELSHIN, Max, 1895- 921.9
Moses Maimonides, Rambam. New York, Book Guild, 1956. 205p. 21cm. [BM755.M6F4] 57-59236
1. Moses ben Maimon, 1135-1204. I. Title.

YELLIN, David, 1864-1941. 296.6'1'0924 B
Maimonides: his life and works, by David Yellin and Israel Abrahams. 3d rev. ed., with introd., bibliography and supplementary notes, by Jacob I. Dienstag. New York, Hermon Press [1972 i.e. 1973] xxxiv, 193 p. illus. 20 cm. Reprint of the 1903 ed. published by Jewish Publication Society of America, Philadelphia; with new material. Bibliography: p. xvii-xxix. [BM755.M6Y4 1972] 72-83937 ISBN 0-87203-031-8 7.95
1. Moses ben Maimon, 1135-1204. I. Abrahams, Israel, 1858-1925, joint author.

ZEITLIN, Solomon, 1892- 921.9
Maimonides, a biography. 2d ed. New York, Bloch Pub. Co., 1955. 234p. illus. 21cm. [B759.M34Z4 1955] 55-8133
1. Moses ben Maimon, 1135-1204. I. Title.

Moses ben Maimon, 1135-1204—Addresses, essays, lectures.

MOSES ben Maimon, 1135-1204. 296.6'1'0924 B
Letters of Maimonides / translated and edited with introductions and notes by Leon D. Stitskin. New York : Yeshiva University Press, 1977. 199 p. ; 24 cm. Includes bibliographical references. [BM545.A45S8 1977] 77-78152 ISBN 0-89362-006-8 : 10.00
1. Moses ben Maimon, 1135-1204—Addresses, essays, lectures. 2. Judaism—Addresses, essays, lectures. 3. Rabbis—Egypt—Biography—Addresses, essays, lectures. I. Stitskin, Leon D.

Moses ben Maimon, 1135-1204—Fiction.

LE PORRIER, Herbert. FIC
The doctor from Cordova : a biographical novel about the great philosopher Maimonides / Herbert Le Porrier ; translated from the French by Barbar Wright. 1st ed. Garden City, N.Y. : Doubleday, c1979. 280 p. ; 22 cm. Translation of Le medecin de Cordoue. [PZ4.L5864Do] [PQ2623.E563] 843'.9'14 77-16930 ISBN 0-385-11472-9 : 8.95
1. Moses ben Maimon, 1135-1204—Fiction. I. Title. **BIP**

Moses ben Maimon, 1135-1204—Juvenile literature.

MARCUS, Rebecca B. 296.6'1'0924 B
Moses Maimonides: rabbi, philosopher, and physician, by Rebecca B. Marcus. New York, F. Watts [1969] ix, 114 p. illus., facsims., ports. 22 cm. (Immortals of philosophy and religion) Bibliography: p. 108-109. A biography of the Spanish-born Jewish philosopher, rabbi, and physician of the Middle Ages who spent a good deal of his life in Egypt and whose works influenced the thinking of Jews, Christians, and Moslems. [BM755.M6M28] 92 69-12594 3.95
1. Moses ben Maimon, 1135-1204—Juvenile literature. I. Title.

Moses ben Nahman, ca. 1195-ca. 1270.

CHAVEL, Charles Ber, 1906- 296.8'1
Ramban, his life and teachings. New York, P. Feldheim [c1960] 128 p. 23 cm. Includes bibliography. [BM755.M62C4] 63-1543
1. Moses ben Nahman, ca. 1195-ca. 1270. I. Title. **BIP**

Moses, George Higgins, 1869-1944.

GALLAGHER, Edward J., 1890- 328.73'092'4 B
George H. Moses : a profile / [Edward J. Gallagher]. Laconia, N.H. : Citizen Pub. House, c1975. 114 p. : ill., ports. ; 22 cm. Includes index. [E748.M768G34] 75-22987 6.50
1. Moses, George Higgins, 1869-1944.

Moses—Juvenile literature.

KLAGSBRUN, Francine. 222'.1'0924 B
The story of Moses. New York, F. Watts [1968] vxii, 171 p. map. 22 cm. (Immortals of philosophy and religion) Presents the life and teachings of the prophet and lawgiver who, after a revelation from God, devoted his life to leading his people out of slavery to the promised land. [BS580.M6K55] 68-27403 3.95
1. Moses—Juvenile literature. I. Title.

MUNOWITZ, Ken. 222'.1'0924 B
Moses, Moses / pictures by Ken Munowitz ; text by Charles L. Mee, Jr.. 1st ed. New York : Harper & Row, c1977. [32] p. : ill. ; 26 cm. Retells the early events in the life of Moses. [BS580.M6M8 1977] 76-41516 ISBN 0-06-024178-0 : 4.95. lib.bdg. : 4.79
1. Bible. O.T.—Biography—Juvenile literature. 2. Moses—Juvenile literature. I. Mee, Charles L. II. Title.

WHEELER, Opal 920
Moses. Illus. by Linford Donovan. New York, Dutton [c.1962] 94p. 24cm. 62-7497 3.50
1. Moses—Juvenile literature. I. Title.

YOUNG, William Edgar, 1928- 222'.1'0924 B
Moses : God's helper / William E. Young ; illustrated by J. William Myers. Nashville : Broadman Press, c1976. 48 p. : col. ill. ; 24 cm. (Biblearn series) Discusses the life of Moses who led the Hebrews out of Eygpt and received the Ten Commandments from God. [BS580.M6Y68] 76-382766 ISBN 0-8054-4225-1 : 3.95
1. Moses—Juvenile literature. 2. Bible. O.T.—Biography—Juvenile literature. I. Myers, James William. II. Title. **BIP**

Moses, Robert, 1888-

CARO, Robert A. 974.7'04'0924 B
The power broker : Robert Moses and the fall of New York / Robert A. Caro. New York : Vintage Books, 1975, c1974. 1246, xxxiv p., [25] leaves of plates : ill. ; 24 cm. Includes index. Bibliography: p. [1173]-1177. [NA9085.M68C37 1975] 75-9557 ISBN 0-394-72024-5 pbk. : 7.95
1. Moses, Robert, 1888- I. Title. **BIP**

CARO, Robert A. 974.7'04'0924 B
The power broker: Robert Moses and the fall of New York, by Robert A. Caro. [1st ed.] New York, Knopf, 1974. ix, 1246, xxxiv p. illus. 25 cm. Bibliography: p. [1170]-1177. [NA9085.M68C37 1974] 73-20751 ISBN 0-394-48076-7 15.00
1. Moses, Robert, 1888- I. Title.

RODGERS, Cleveland, 1885- 927.1
Robert Moses, builder for democracy. Introd. by H. V. Kaltenborn. [1st ed.] New York, Holt [1952] 356 p. illus. 22 cm. [NA9085.M68R6] 52-10302
1. Moses, Robert, 1888- I. Title.

Mosher, Thomas Bird, 1852-1923.

HATCH, Benton Le Roy, 1913- p16.686209
A check list of the publications of Thomas Bird Mosher of Portland, Maine, MDCCCXCI [to] MDCCCCXXIII, compiled & edited by Benton L. Hatch and with a biographical essay by Ray Nash. [Northampton] Printed at the Gehenna Press for the University of Massachusetts Press, 1966. 211 p. 21 facsims. (part col.), port. 28 cm. "500 copies ... Fifty copies, not for sale, are numbered I to L ... number XL." Bibliography: p. [43] [Z232.M886H3] 65-26239
1. Mosher, Thomas Bird, 1852-1923. I. Nash, Ray, 1905- II. Title.

Moshesh, Basuto Chief, d. 1870.

THOMPSON, Leonard Monteath. 968'.601'0924 B
Survival in two worlds : Moshoeshoe of Lesotho, 1786-1870 / by Leonard Thompson. Oxford [Eng.] : Clarendon Press, 1975. xx, 389 p., [7] leaves of plates : ill. ; 23 cm. Includes index. Bibliography: p. [338]-362. [DT787.2.M67T45] 76-359632 ISBN 0-19-821693-9 : 30.50 pbk. : 6.95
1. Moshesh, Basuto Chief, d. 1870. 2. Lesotho—History—To 1966. I. Title.
Distributed by Oxford University Press N.Y. N.Y. **BIP**

Mosley, Diana, Lady, 1910-

MOSLEY, Diana, Lady, 1910- 941.082'092'4 B
A life of contrasts : the autobiography of Diana Mitford Mosley. New York : Times Books, c1977. vi, 296 p., [6] leaves of plates : ill. ; 22 cm. Includes index. [CT788.M66A35 1977] 77-27584 ISBN 0-8129-0758-2 : 10.95
1. Mosley, Diana, Lady, 1910- 2. Mosley, Oswald, Sir, bart., 1896- 3. England—Biography. I. Title.

*Mosley, Leonard

*MOSLEY, Leonard 963.050924
Haile Selassie: the conquering lio. New York, Hillary House [1966, c.1964] 306p. illus. 23cm. 6.00
I. Title.

Mosley, Oswald, Sir, bart., 1896-

MOSLEY, Oswald, Sir, bart., 1896- 942.084'0924 B
My life. New Rochelle, N.Y., Arlington House [1972, c1968] 521 p. illus. 24 cm. Includes bibliographical references. [DA574.M6A35 1972] 78-179718 ISBN 0-87000-160-4 12.95
I. Title.

SKIDELSKY, Robert Jacob Alexander, 1939- 329'.0092'4 B
Oswald Mosley / Robert Skidelsky. London ; New York : Macmillan, 1975. 578 p., [4] leaves of plates : ill. ; 23 cm. American ed. published under title: Sir Oswald Mosley. Includes index. Bibliography: p. [545]-555. [DA574.M6S55 1975b] 75-316960 ISBN 0-333-02986-0 : £6.95
1. Mosley, Oswald, Sir, bart., 1896-

SKIDELSKY, Robert Jacob Alexander, 1939- 329'.0092'4 B
Sir Oswald Mosley, by Robert Skidelsky. [1st ed.] New York, Holt, Rinehart and Winston [1975] p. cm. [DA574.M6S55] 74-6941 ISBN 0-03-086580-8
1. Mosley, Oswald, Sir, bart., 1896-

Mosley, Zack.

MOSLEY, Zack. 741.5'973 B
Brave coward Zack / by Zack Smilin' Jack Mosley. St. Petersburg, Fla. : Valkyrie Press, c1976. 99 p. : ill. ; 26 cm. Includes index. [TL540.M678A34] 76-43566 ISBN 0-912760-30-3 pbk. : 6.95
1. Mosley, Zack. 2. Mosley, Zack. Smilin' Jack. 3. Air pilots—United States—Biography. I. Title. **BIP**

Moss family.

MOSS, William Paul, 1886- 929'.2'0973
Biographical sketches of the Mosses: Paul Moss, Thaddeus A. Moss, Howell Moss, Howell C. Moss, Henry Moss, Amanda Holden Moss. [Odessa? Tex.] c1960. 1 v. (unpaged) ports. (part col.) col. coat of arms. 37cm. [CS71.M918 1960] 61-20890
1. Moss family. I. Title.

Moss, James E.,

MOSS, James E., 1875- 922.8373
Jimmy Moss, by Himself. Salt Lake City, Deseret [c.]1963. 243p. illus. 24cm. 63-5831 3.50
I. Title.

MOSS, James E 1875- 922.8373
Jimmy Moss. Sal[t] Lake City, Deseret Book Co., 1963. 243 p. illus. 24 cm. Autobiography. [BX8695.M6A3] 63-5831
I. Title.

Moss, Stirling, 1929-

MOSS, Stirling, 1929- 796.7'2'0924 B
All but my life; Stirling Moss face to face with Ken W. Purdy. [2d ed.] London, W. Kimber [1973, c1963] 239 p. illus. 22 cm. Stamped on t.p.: Distributed in the United States by Motorbooks International, Minneapolis, Minnesota. [GV1032.M6A3 1973] 74-162867 ISBN 0-7183-0173-0 8.95
1. Moss, Stirling, 1929- 2. Automobile racing. I. Purdy, Ken W. II. Title.

Mossman, Burton C., 1867-

HUNT, Frazier, 1885- 923.973
Cap Mossman, last of the great cowmen; with sixteen illus. by Ross Santee. New York, Hastings House [1951] 277 p. illus. 21 cm. [F786.M87H8] 51-14166
1. Mossman, Burton C., 1867- 2. Frontier and pioneer life—Southwest, New. 3. Cattle trade—Southwest, New. 4. Ranch life.

Mostel, Kate.

MOSTEL, Kate. 792'.028'0922 B
170 years of show business / Kate Mostel and Madeline Gilford, with Jack Gilford and Zero Mostel. 1st ed. New York : Random House, c1978. xi, 175 p., [16] leaves of plates : ill. ; 24 cm. [PN2285.M63] 77-90300 ISBN 0-394-41181-1 : 8.95
1. Mostel, Kate. 2. Gilford, Madeline. 3. Gilford, Jack. 4. Mostel, Zero, 1915-1977. 5. Actors—United States—Biography. I. Gilford, Madeline, joint author. II. Title.

Mothers.

DAVIS, Elisabeth Logan. 920.7
Mothers of America: the lasting influence of the Christian home. [Westwood, N. J.] F. H. evell Co. [1954] 191p. sWomen in the U. S.--Biog. [CT3260.D39] 54-7999
I. Title.

*HUGHES, Elmer R. 220.92
Famous mothers from the Bible and history: the stories of great men and the women behind them. New York, Exposition [c.1963] 156p. 21cm. 3.00
I. Title.

HUGHES, Elmer Ray 920.02
More famous mothers from the Bible and history, by Elmer R. Hughes. [1st ed] New York, Exposition [1966] 96p. 21cm. Companion vol. to the author's Famous mothers from the Bible and history. [CT3203.H82] 66-31668 3.50
1. Mothers. I. Title.

Motherwell, William, 1797-1835—Addresses, essays, lectures.

DOUGLAS, George 821'.7 B
Brisbane, Sir, bart., 1856-1935.
James Hogg. [Folcroft, Pa.] Folcroft Library Editions, 1974. 154 p. 23 cm. Contains also brief essays on Robert Tannahill, William Motherwell, and William Thom. Reprint of the 1899 ed. published by O. Anderson & Ferrier, Edinburgh, issued in series: Famous Scots series. Includes bibliographical references. [PR4792.D6 1974] 74-10889 ISBN 0-8414-3762-9 (lib. bdg.)
1. Hogg, James, 1770-1835—Biography. 2. Tannahill, Robert, 1774-1810—Addresses, essays, lectures. 3. Motherwell, William, 1797-1835—Addresses, essays, lectures. 4. Thom, William, 1798?-1848—Addresses, essays, lectures. BIP

Motion picture actors and actresses—U.S.—Biography.

REAGAN, Ronald. 927.92
Where's the rest of me? By Ronald Reagan with Richard G. Hubler. [1st ed.] New York, Duell, Sloan and Pearce [1965] 316 p. illus. 21 cm. [PN2287.R25A3] 65-11684
1. Motion picture actors and actresses—U.S.—Biography. I. Hubler, Richard Gibson, 1912- II. Title.

Motley, John Lothrop, 1814-1877.

HOLMES, Oliver 949.2'007'2024
Wendell, 1809-1894.
John Lothrop Motley. A memoir. Freeport, N.Y., Books for Libraries Press [1972] vii, 278 p. 23 cm. Reprint of the 1878 ed. [PS2436.H6 1972] 71-38358 ISBN 0-8369-6775-5
1. Motley, John Lothrop, 1814-1877. BIP

MOTLEY, John Lothrop, 949.2'008 S
1814-1877.
The correspondence of John Lothrop Motley. Edited by George William Curtis. Netherlands ed. New York, Harper, 1900. [New York, AMS Press, 1973] 3 v. ports. 19 cm. (Motley, John Lothrop, 1814-1877. Works, v. 15-17. 1973.) [DH186.5.M6 1973 vol. 15-17] [D15.M67] 949.2'008 73-8834 ISBN 0-404-04535-9 (v. 1)
1. Motley, John Lothrop, 1814-1877. I. Title. II. Series.

Motley, Willard, 1909-1965—Diaries.

MOTLEY, Willard, 1909- 813'.5'4 B
1965.
The diaries of Willard Motley / edited and with an introd. by Jerome Klinkowitz ; foreword by Clarence Majors. 1st ed. Ames : Iowa State University Press, 1979. xxiii, 196 p. : port. ; 24 cm. Includes index. Bibliography: p. xxi, xxiii. [PS3563.O888Z463 1979] 78-16782 ISBN 0-8138-0140-0 : 12.95
1. Motley, Willard, 1909-1965—Diaries. 2. Novelists, American—20th century—Biography. I. Klinkowitz, Jerome.

Moton, Robert Russa, 1867-1940.

HUGHES, William Hardin, 923.773
1881- ed.
Robert Russa Moton of Hampton and Tuskegee, edited by William Hardin Hughes [and] Frederick D. Patterson. Chapel Hill, University of North Carolina Press [1956] 238p. illus. 24cm. 'Volume of tributes to the life of Dr. Robert Russa Moton.' [E185.97.M92H8] 56-14299
1. Moton, Robert Russa, 1867-1940. 2. Tuskegee Institute. 3. Hampton Institute, Hampton, Va. I. Patterson, Frederick Douglas, 1901- joint ed. II. Title.

MOTON, Robert Russa, 378.1'1'0924
1867-1940.
Finding a way out; an autobiography. New York, Negro Universities Press [1969, c1920] ix, 295 p. 23 cm. [E185.97.M9 1969b] 75-89044
I. Title.

MOTON, Robert 378.1'1'0924 B
Russa, 1867-1940.
Finding a way out; an autobiography. College Park, Md., McGrath Pub. Co. [1969, c1920] ix, 295 p. 23 cm. [E185.97.M9 1969] 69-17091
I. Title. BIP

Motorcycle racing—History.

LANNING, Dave. 796.7'5
Speedway and short track racing / by Dave Lanning. London ; New York : Hamlyn, 1974. 128 p. : ill. (some col.), ports. (some col.). ; 30 cm. Includes index. Introduces the history of motorcycle racing, the important races around the world, and well-known riders with a discussion of their techniques and the types of motorbikes they ride. [GV1060.L34] 920 75-317916 ISBN 0-600-38701-1 : £2.50
1. Motorcycle racing—History. 2. Motorcycle racing—Biography. I. Title.

Motorcyclists—United States—Biography—Juvenile literature.

OLNEY, Ross 796.7'5'0922 B
Robert, 1929-
Modern motorcycle superstars / Ross R. Olney. New York : Dodd, Mead, [1980] p. cm. Career biographies of five motorcycle racing "stars": Jay Springsteen, Bob Hannah, Don Vesco, Gary Nixon, and Kenny Roberts. [GV1060.2.A1O44] 920 79-22021 ISBN 0-396-07786-2 : 5.95
1. Motorcyclists—United States—Biography—Juvenile literature. I. Title. BIP

Mott, Frank Luther, 1886-1964.

LONG, Howard Rusk, 378.1'11'0924
1906-
Frank Luther Mott; scholar, teacher, human being. Introd. by A. Craig Baird. [Carbondale, Ill., Hornstone Press, c1968] [23] l. 29 cm. No. 139 of 247 copies. Includes bibliographical references. [LA2317.M65L6] 68-58485
1. Mott, Frank Luther, 1886-1964.

MOTT, Frank Luther, 070'.92'4 B
1886-1964.
Time enough; essays in autobiography. Westport, Conn., Greenwood Press [1972, c1962] 248 p. 24 cm. [PN4874.M59A3 1972] 72-5654 ISBN 0-8371-6445-1
1. Journalists—Correspondence, reminiscences, etc. I. Title. BIP

Mott, John Raleigh 1865-1955.

MACKIE, Robert C. 267.0924
Layman extraordinary: John R. Mott, 1865-1955, by Robert C. Mackie, others, Foreword by W. A. Visser't Hooft [New York] Association [1965] 127p. 18cm. [BV1085.M75M26] 65-27832 1.25 pap.,
1. Mott, John Raleigh 1865-1955. I. Title.

Mott, Lucretia (Coffin), 1793-1880—Juvenile literature.

FABER, Doris, 322'.43'0924 B
1924-
Lucretia Mott, foe of slavery. Illustrated by Russell Hoover. Champaign, Ill., Garrard Pub. Co. [1971] 80 p. col. illus. 24 cm. (A Discovery book) A brief biography of the nineteenth-century Quaker woman important participant in the cause of abolition and who was an later in women's rights. [E449.M93F3] 92 70-151992
1. Mott, Lucretia (Coffin), 1793-1880 Juvenile literature. I. Hoover, Russell, illus. II. Title.

KURLAND, Gerald, 301.41'2'0924 B
1942-
Lucretia Mott, early leader of the women's liberation movement. Charlotteville, N.Y., SamHar Press, 1972. 32 p. 22 cm. (Outstanding personalities, no. 39) Includes bibliographical references. A biography of the nineteenth-century Quaker woman who was an important participant in the cause of abolition and women's rights. [HQ1413.M68K87] 92 72-81902
1. Mott, Lucretia (Coffin) 1793-1880—Juvenile literature. 2. Woman—Rights of women—Juvenile literature. 3. Woman—Suffrage—United States—Juvenile literature. I. Title.

Mott, Lucretia (Coffin) 1793-1880.

CROMWELL, Otelia. 326'.0924 B
Lucretia Mott. New York, Russell & Russell [1971, c1958] x, 241 p. port. 25 cm. Includes bibliographical references. [E449.M93C7 1971] 79-139913
1. Mott, Lucretia (Coffin) 1793-1880. BIP

HARE, Lloyd Custer 326'.0924 B
Mayhew, 1893-
The greatest American woman, Lucretia Mott, by Lloyd C. M. Hare. New York, Negro Universities Press [1970, c1937] 307 p. plates, port. 24 cm. [E449.M93H3 1970] 76-109327
1. Mott, Lucretia (Coffin) 1793-1880. I. Title. BIP

Mott, Thomas Bentley, 1865-

MOTT, Thomas 355.3'432'0924 B
Bentley, 1865-
Twenty years as military attache / Thomas Bentley Mott. New York : Arno Press, 1979. p. cm. (American military experience) Reprint of the 1937 ed. published by the Oxford University Press, New York. [E745.M6A37 1979] 78-22390 ISBN 0-405-11867-8 : 20.00
1. Mott, Thomas Bentley, 1865- 2. United States—Foreign relations—1865-1921. 3. European War, 1914-1918—United States. 4. Military attaches—United States—Biography. I. Title. II. Series. BIP

Motta, Dick.

MOTTA, Dick. 796.32'3'0924 B
Stuff it : the story of Dick Motta, toughest little coach in the NBA / Dick Motta, with Jerry Jenkins. 1st ed. Radnor, Pa. : Chilton Book Co., [1975] xii, 187 p. : ill. ; 22 cm. [GV884.M64A37 1975] 74-28178 ISBN 0-8019-5967-5 : 7.50
1. Motta, Dick. 2. Basketball. 3. Basketball coaching. I. Jenkins, Jerry B. II. Title.

Mount Cashell, Margaret Jane (King) Moore, countess of, 1772-1835.

MCALEER, Edward C 928.2
The sensitive plant; a life of Lady Mount Cashell. Chapel Hill, University of North Carolina Press [1958] 242p. illus. 23cm. Includes bibliography. [PR5101.M343Z75] 58-14919
1. Mount Cashell, Margaret Jane (King) Moore, countess of, 1772- 1835. I. Title.

Mount, Charles Merrill.

JOHN Singer Sargent, 759.13
a biography. [1st ed.] New York, W. W. Norton [1955] xv, 464p. illus. 25cm. Bibliographical references included in 'Notes' (p. 403-426) [ND237.S3M6] 927.5 55-13654
I. Mount, Charles Merrill. II. Sargent, John Singer, 1856-1925.

Mount Holyoke College.

WELLS, Anna 378.1'12'0974423
Mary.
Miss Marks and Miss Woolley / by Anna Mary Wells. Boston : Houghton Mifflin, 1978. xviii, 268 p., [8] leaves of plates : ill. ; 24 cm. Bibliography: p. [267]-268. [LD7092.7 1901 W44] 78-1391 ISBN 0-395-25724-7 : 10.95
1. Woolley, Mary Emma, 1863-1947. 2. Mount Holyoke College. 3. Marks, Jeannette Augustus, 1875-1964. 4. Wellesley College. 5. Lesbians—United States—Biography. I. Title.

Mount Holyoke College—History.

GREEN, Elizabeth 378.744'23
Alden, 1908-
Mary Lyon and Mount Holyoke ; opening the gates / Elizabeth Alden Green. Hanover, N.H. : University Press of New England, 1979. xviii, 406 p. : ill. ; 23 cm. Includes index. Bibliography: p. 347-350. [LD7092.65.L9G73] 78-68857 17.50
1. Mount Holyoke College—History. 2. Lyon, Mary, 1797-1849. 3. Education of women—United States—History. 4. College administrators—United States—Biography. I. Title. BIP

Mountaineers—Biography.

CROUCHER, Norman. 796.5'22'0924 B
High hopes / by Norman Croucher. London : Hodder and Stoughton, 1976. 160 p., [8] p. of plates. : ill., ports. ; 21 cm. [GV199.92.C76A34] 77-353871 ISBN 0-340-20556-3 : £3.50
1. Mountaineers—Biography. 2. Amputees—Biography. I. Title.

Mountaineers—Correspondence, reminiscences, etc.

STYLES, Showell, 796.5'22'0922
1908- comp.
Men and mountaineering; an anthology of writings by climbers. New York, D. White [1968] 207 p. 23 cm. (A David White collection) Contents.Contents.—The frozen battlements, by A. Wills.—Success and tragedy, by E. Whymper.—The climbing lasso, by C. King.—Alone on Monte Rosa, by J. Tyndall.—Alpine lodging, by J. Ormsby.—The ridge of the Rothhorn, by L. Stephen.—Grepon, by A. F. Mummery.—Mallory's last climb, by G. H. L. Mallory and E. F. Norton.—Waiting at Camp Four, by E. Knowlton.—Escape to the summit, by G. W. Young.—Notes on the Abominable Snowman, by H. W. Tilman.—Catastrophe on K2, by R. Bates.—The singing axes, by G. Moffat.—

The fourth day, by H. Harrer.—Stanley Peak, by N. Ellena.—First on the highest, by E. Hillary.—Zero Gully, by T. Patey.—The Matterhorn North Face, by T. Carruthers.—Night out on Everest, by W. W. Sayre.—On the stance, by D. Gregory.—Beyond the summit, by N. G. Dyhrenfurth.—Eigerwandering, by D. Haston.—The North America Wall, by R. Robbins. [G507.OMen and mountaineer
1. Mountaineers—Correspondence, reminiscences, etc. I. Title.

Mountbatten family.

HATCH, Alden, 1898- 923
The Mountbattens; the last royal success story. New York, Random [c.1965] viii, 472p. illus., geneal. table, ports. 25cm. Bibl. [CS439.M79] 65-11283 8.95
1. Mountbatten family. I. Title.

HOUGH, Richard Alexander, 1922- 929.7
The Mountbattens : the illustrious family who, through birth and marriage, from Queen Victoria and the last of the Tsars to Queen Elizabeth II, enriched Europe's royal houses / by Richard Hough. 1st ed. New York : Dutton, 1975. xvii, 424 p., [16] leaves of plates : ill. ; 24 cm. Includes bibliographical references and index. [CS439.M79 1975] 74-25027 ISBN 0-525-16038-8 : 14.95
1. Mountbatten family. 2. Battenberg family. I. Title.

Mountbatten, Louis Mountbatten, Earl, 1900-

SWINSON, Arthur. 942.082'0924 B
Mountbatten. [New York, Ballantine Books, 1971] 160 p. illus. 21 cm. (Ballantine's illustrated history of the violent century. War leader book no. 6) Cover title. Bibliography: p. 160. [DA89.1.M59S94] 72-175107 ISBN 0-345-02317-X 1.00
1. Mountbatten, Louis Mountbatten, Earl, 1900-

Mountbatten, Louis Mountbatten, Earl, 1900- —Juvenile literature.

WERSTEIN, Irving. 942.082'0924 B
The Supremo: Lord Louis Mountbatten and the testing of democracy. Philadelphia, Macrae Smith Co. [1971] 143 p. illus., ports. 24 cm. A biography of Queen Victoria's great-grandson who became a well-known British naval leader in World War II and subsequently an important statesman and educator. [DA89.1.M59W47 1971] 92 71-150678 ISBN 0-8255-9203-8 4.95
1. Mountbatten, Louis Mountbatten, Earl, 1900- —Juvenile literature. I. Title.

Mountevans, Edward Ratcliffe Garth Russell Evans, baron, 1880-1957.

MOUNTEVANS, Edward Ratcliffe Garth Russell Evans, baron, 1880-1957. v. 12
Happy adventurer, an autobiography. Illus. by S. Drigin. New York, W. Funk, 1951. 130 p. illus. (part col.) 20 cm. A 52
1. Antarctic regions. I. Title.

POUND, Reginald 923.542
Evans of the Broke; a biography of Admiral Lord Mountevans, K. C. B., D. S. O., LL. D. New York, Oxford [c.]1963. xii323p. illus., ports. 23cm. Bibl. 63-25233 6.75
1. Mountevans, Edward Ratcliffe Garth Russell Evans, baron, 1880-1957. 2. Almirante Uribe (Destroyer) I. Title.

Mouton, Alfred, 1829-1864.

ARCENEAUX, William. 973.7'3013'0924 B
Acadian general Alfred Mouton and the Civil War. Lafayette, La., University of Southwestern Louisiana, 1972. 159 p. illus. 22 cm. (The U.S.L. history series, no. 5) Bibliography: p. 140-149. [E467.1.M88A9] 72-187926
1. Mouton, Alfred, 1829-1864. 2. United States—History—Civil War, 1861-1865—Campaigns and battles. I. Title. II. Series: Louisiana. University of Southwestern Louisiana, Lafayette. The U.S.L. history series, no. 5.

Movimiento de Liberacion Nacional.

JACKSON, Geoffrey, Sir, 1915- 364.1'54'0924 B
Surviving the long night : an autobiographical account of a political kidnapping / Geoffrey Jackson. New York : Vanguard Press, [1974] 225 p., [4] leaves of plates : 10 ill. ; 22 cm. Published in 1973 under title: People's prison. [HV9628.J13 1974] 74-83673 ISBN 0-8149-0756-3 : 7.95
1. Movimiento de Liberacion Nacional. 2. Political prisoners—Uruguay—Personal narratives. I. Title. BIP

Moving-picture actors and actresses.

*AGAN, Patrick. 791.43'028'0922
Whatever happened to- New York, Ace Books [1974] 201 p., illus., 18 cm. [PN2287] 1.50 (pbk.)
1. Moving-picture actors and actresses. I. Title.

BRUNO, Michael, 1921- 791.43'09
Venus in Hollywood; the continental enchantress from Garbo to Loren. New York, L. Stuart [1970] 257 p. ports. 21 cm. Bibliography: p. 245-250. [PN1998.A2B74] 71-90838 6.95
1. Moving-picture actors and actresses. I. Title. BIP

CAMERON, Ian Alexander, 1937- 791.43'0922 B
Dames [by] Ian & Elisabeth Cameron. [New York] Praeger [1969] 144 p. illus. 18 cm. London ed. (Studio Vista) has title: Broads. [PN1998.A2C28] 75-91694 4.95
1. Moving-picture actors and actresses. I. Cameron, Elisabeth, joint author. II. Title.

*CHAMBERS, Marilyn. 791.43'028'0924 B
Marilyn Chambers: my story. [New York] Warner [1975] 206 p. illus. 18 cm. [PN2287] 1.95 (pbk.)
1. Moving-picture actors and actresses. I. Title. BIP

GRIFFITH, Richard, 1912- 791.43'028'0922
The movie stars. [1st ed.] Garden City, N.Y., Doubleday, 1970. xiii, 498 p. ports. 32 cm. [PN1998.A2G75] 72-126382 19.95
1. Moving-picture actors and actresses. I. Title.

HUGHES, Elinor. 792'.028'0922 B
Famous stars of filmdom (women). Freeport, N.Y., Books for Libraries Press [1970] x, 341 p. illus., ports. 23 cm. (Essay index reprint series) Reprint of the 1931 ed. [PN1998.A2H8 1970] 70-107717
1. Moving-picture actors and actresses. I. Title.

TWOMEY, Alfred E. 791.43'028'0922
The versatiles; a study of supporting character actors and actresses in the American motion picture, 1930-1955, by Alfred E. Twomey and Arthur F. McClure. South Brunswick [N.J.] A. S. Barnes [1969] 304 p. ports. 26 cm. [PN1998.A2T9] 68-27218 10.00
1. Moving-picture actors and actresses. I. McClure, Arthur F., joint author. II. Title.

Moving-picture actors and actresses, American.

WALKER, Alexander, film critic. 791.43'028'0922
Stardom; the Hollywood phenomenon. New York, Stein and Day [1970] 392 p. ports. 25 cm. Bibliography: p. 379-381. [PN1998.A2W3 1970b] 70-108320 10.00
1. Moving-picture actors and actresses, American. I. Title.

WRIGHT, Jacqueline 927.92
The life and loves of Lana Turner. New York 36, Wisdom House, 520 Fifth Ave. [c.1961] 160p. (Timely bks., W104) .50 pap.,
I. Title.

Moving-picture actors and actresses—Biography.

BECK, Calvin Thomas. 791.43'028'0922[B]
Scream queens : heroines of the horrors / Calvin Thomas Beck. New York : Macmillan, c1978. p. cm. Includes index. Bibliography: p. [PN1998.A2B383] 78-15336 ISBN 0-02-012140-7 pbk. : 7.95
1. Moving-picture actors and actresses—Biography. 2. Horror films—Biography. I. Title. BIP

FOX, Charles Donald, ed. 791.43'028'0922 B
Who's who on the screen / edited by Charles Donald Fox and Milton L. Silver. New York : Gordon Press, [1976] c1920. p. cm. Reprint of the ed. published by Ross Pub. Co., New York. [PN1998.A2F6 1976] 75-44363 ISBN 0-87968-277-9 lib.bdg. : 65.00
1. Moving-picture actors and actresses—Biography. I. Silver, Milton L., joint ed. II. Title. BIP

JONES, Ken D. 791.43'028'0922 B
Character people / Ken D. Jones, Arthur F. McClure, and Alfred E. Twomey. South Brunswick : A. S. Barnes, c1976. 209 p. : ill. ; 29 cm. [PN1998.A2J6 1976] 74-30972 ISBN 0-498-01697-8 : 17.50
1. Moving-picture actors and actresses—Biography. I. McClure, Arthur F., joint author. II. Twomey, Alfred E., joint author. III. Title.

JONES, Ken D. 791.43'028'0922 B
Character people / Ken D. Jones, Arthur F. McClure, and Alfred E. Twomey. South Brunswick : A. S. Barnes, c1975. p. cm. Includes index. [PN1998.A2J6] 74-30972 ISBN 0-498-01697-8 : 17.50
1. Moving-picture actors and actresses—Biography. I. McClure, Arthur F., joint author. II. Twomey, Alfred E., joint author. III. Title. BIP

MERCER, Jane, 1942- 791.43'028'0922
Great lovers of the movies / [by] Jane Mercer ; filmographies researched by Sandy Graham ; picture research by Sheila Whitaker. London ; New York : Hamlyn, 1975. 176 p. : ill. (some col.), ports. (some col.) ; 30 cm. Bibliography: p. 176. [PN1998.A2M39] 75-325158 ISBN 0-600-34454-1 : £2.95
1. Moving-picture actors and actresses—Biography. I. Title.

PARISH, James Robert. 791.43'028'0922 B
The debonairs / James Robert Parish and Don E. Stanke ; editor, T. Allan Taylor ; research associates, John Robert Cocchi, Michael R. Pitts, Florence Solomon ; introd. by Earl Anderson. New Rochelle, N.Y. : Arlington House, c1975. 511 p. : ill. ; 29 cm. Includes filmographies and index. [PN1998.A2P388] 75-29375 ISBN 0-87000-293-7 : 25.00
1. Moving-picture actors and actresses—Biography. I. Stanke, Don E., joint author. II. Title.

PARISH, James Robert. 791.43'028'0922
The swashbucklers / James Robert Parish & Don E Stanke ; editor, T. Allan Taylor ; research associates, Earl Anderson ... [et al.]. New Rochelle, N.Y. : Arlington House, c1976. 672 p. : ill. ; 24 cm. Includes bibliographies and index. [PN1998.A2P413] 76-4540 ISBN 0-87000-326-7 : 17.95
1. Moving-picture actors and actresses—Biography. I. Stanke, Don E., joint author. II. Title. BIP

THOMAS, Tony, 1927- 791.43'028'0922 B
Cads and cavaliers; the gentlemen adventurers of the movies. Illustrated by John Lebold. South Brunswick, A. S. Barnes [1973] 242 p. illus. 29 cm. Contents.Contents.—Douglas Fairbanks, pere et fils.—John Barrymore.—George Sanders.—Vincent Price.—David Niven.—Basil Rathbone.—Errol Flynn.—A gallery of adventurers. [PN1998.A2T5] 72-5177 ISBN 0-498-01192-5 15.00
1. Moving-picture actors and actresses—Biography. I. Title.

TRUITT, Evelyn Mack, 1931- 791.43'028'0922 B
Who was who on screen. New York, R. R. Bowker Co., 1974. vii, 363 p. 28 cm. Bibliography: p. 363. [PN1998.A2T73] 74-4325 ISBN 0-8352-0719-6 22.50
1. Moving-picture actors and actresses—Biography. I. Title.

TRUITT, Evelyn Mack, 1931- 791.43'028'0922 B
Who was who on screen / by Evelyn Mack Truitt. 2d ed. New York : Bowker, 1977. p. cm. Bibliography: p. [PN1998.A2T73 1977] 77-22651 ISBN 0-8352-0914-8 : 25.95
1. Moving-picture actors and actresses—Biography. I. Title. BIP

WLASCHIN, Ken. 791.43'028'0922 B
The illustrated encyclopedia of the world's great movie stars and their films : from 1900 to the present day / by Ken Wlaschin. New York : Harmony Books, 1979. p. cm. (A Salamander book) Includes index. [PN1998.A2W64] 78-26866 ISBN 0-517-53714-1. : 19.95 ISBN 0-517-53715-X pbk. : 8.95
1. Moving picture actors and actresses—Biography. 2. Moving-pictures—Dictionaries. 3. Moving-pictures—Catalogs. I. Title.

ZIEROLD, Norman J. 791.43'028'0922
Sex goddesses of the silent screen, by Norman Zierold. Chicago, H. Regnery Co. [1973] x, 207 p. illus. 24 cm. Contents.Contents.—The wickedest woman in the world: Theda Bara.—The too-beautiful girl: Barbara Lamarr.—The wildcat: Pola Negri.—The girl with the bee-stung lips: Mae Murray.—The it girl: Clara Bow.—Conclusion: the others. [PN1998.A2Z55] 72-11191 7.95
1. Moving-picture actors and actresses—Biography. I. Title.

Moving-picture actors and actresses—Biography—Bibliography.

SCHUSTER, Mel. 016.79143'028'0922
Motion picture performers; a bibliography of magazine and periodical articles, 1900-1969. Compiled by Mel Schuster. Metuchen, N.J., The Scarecrow Press, 1971. 702 p. 22 cm. [Z5784.M9S35] 70-154300 ISBN 0-8108-0407-7
1. Moving-picture actors and actresses—Biography—Bibliography. I. Title. BIP

Moving-picture actors and actresses—Portraits, caricatures, etc.

FINCH, John R. 791.43'092'2 B
Close-ups (from the Jorifin collection) / John R. Finch, Paul A. Elby. Cranbury, N.J. : A. S. Barnes, c1975. p. cm. Includes indexes. [PN1998.A2F535] 74-30974 ISBN 0-498-01723-0 (v. 1). ISBN 0-498-01778-8 (v. 2) : 17.50 per vol.
1. Moving-picture actors and actresses—Portraits, caricatures, etc. 2. Moving-picture actors and actresses—Biography. I. Elby, Paul A., joint author. II. Title.

*STEIGER, Brad 792.0924
Valentino [by] Brad Steiger, Chaw Mank. Illus. with photographs from Valentino's private scrapbooks [New York] Macfadden [c.1966] 192p. illus. 18cm. (75-171) .75 pap.,
I. Title.

TRENT, Paul, 1940- 799'.2
The image makers: sixty years of Hollywood glamour. Text by Paul Trent. Designed by Richard Lawton. New York, McGraw-Hill [1972] 327 p. ports. 32 cm. [PN1998.A2T66] 70-39064 ISBN 0-07-065138-8 20.00
1. Moving-picture actors and actresses—Portraits. I. Lawton, Richard, 1943- II. Title.

Moving-picture actors and actresses—Sweden—Biography.

BAINBRIDGE, John 927.92
Garbo. [New York] Dell [1961, c.1955] 319p. illus. (S26) .60 pap.,
I. Title.

COWIE, Peter. 791.43'028'0922 [B]
Stars and players / by Peter Cowie. London : Tantivy Press ; South Brunswick [N.J.] : A. S. Barnes, c1977. 128 p. : ill. ; 18 cm. (Film in Sweden) Includes index. [PN1998.A2C68] 76-24619 ISBN 0-498-02013-4 : 7.95
1. Moving-picture actors and actresses—Sweden—Biography. I. Title. II. Series.

Moving-picture actors and actresses—United States—Biography.

BEST, Marc, 1948- 791.43'028'0922 B
Their hearts were young and gay / Marc Best. South Brunswick : A. S. Barnes, [1975] 269 p. : ill. ; 26 cm. Continues Those endearing young charms. [PN1998.A2B43] 74-9287 ISBN 0-498-01512-2 : 10.00
1. Moving-picture actors and actresses—United States—Biography. 2. Children as actors. I. Title.

BEST, Marc, 1948- 791.43'028'0922
Those endearing young charms; child performers of the screen. South Brunswick, A. S. Barnes [1971] 278 p. illus. 27 cm. Continued by their hearts were young and gay. [PN1998.A2B45] 73-124218 ISBN 0-498-07729-2 10.00
1. Moving-picture actors and actresses—United States—Biography. 2. Children as actors. I. Title.

BODEEN, DeWitt. 791.43'028'0922 B
From Hollywood : the careers of 15 great American stars / DeWitt Bodeen. South Brunswick : A. S. Barnes, [1975] c1974. p. cm. [PN1998.A2B62 1975] 73-15158 ISBN 0-498-01346-4 : 15.00
1. Moving-picture actors and actresses—United States—Biography. I. Title.
Contents omitted.

BODEEN, DeWitt. 791.43'028'0922 B
More from Hollywood! : The careers of 15 great American stars / DeWitt Bodeen. South Brunswick [N.J.] : A. S. Barnes, c1977. 355 p. : ill. ; 26 cm. Includes index. Contents.Contents.—Elsie Ferguson.—Pauline Frederick.—Greta Garbo.—Dorothy Gish.—Frances Marion.—May McAvoy.—Antonio Moreno.—Nazimova.—Ramon Novarro.—Charles Ray.—Blanche Sweet.—Florence Bates.—Clint Eastwood.—Val Lewton.—Jeanette MacDonald. [PN1998.A2B623 1977] 77-3213 ISBN 0-498-01533-5 : 15.00
1. Moving-picture actors and actresses—United States—Biography. I. Title.
Contents omitted

†BRUNDIDGE, Harry T. 791.43'028'0922 B
Twinkle, twinkle, movie star! / Harry T. Brundidge. New York : Garland Pub., 1977, c1930. xii, 284 p., [1] leaf of plates : ports. ; 19 cm. (The Garland classics of film literature) Reprint of the ed. published by Dutton, New York. [PN1998.A2B7 1977] 76-52094 lib. bdg. 18.00
1. Moving-picture actors and actresses—United States—Biography. I. Title. II. Series. **BIP**

CARR, Larry. 791.43'028'0922 B
More fabulous faces : the evolution and metamorphosis of Dolores Del Rio, Myrna Loy, Carole Lombard, Bette Davis, and Katharine Hepburn / by Larry Carr. 1st ed. Garden City, N.Y. : Doubleday, 1979. xi, 264 p. : ill. ; 29 cm. [PN1998.A2C344] 77-16904 ISBN 0-385-12819-3 : 19.95
1. Moving-picture actors and actresses—United States—Biography. 2. Moving-picture actors and actresses—United States—Portraits. I. Title.

CORNEAU, Ernest N. 791.43'028'0922
The hall of fame of western film stars [by] Ernest N. Corneau. North Quincy, Mass., Christopher Pub. House [1969] 307 p. illus. 27 cm. [PN2285.C6] 70-91805 ISBN 0-8158-0124-6 9.75
1. Moving-picture actors and actresses—United States—Biography. 2. Western films. I. Title.

EELLS, George. 791.43'.028'0922 [B]
Ginger, Loretta, and Irene who? / by George Eells. New York : Pocket Books, 1978,c1976. 438 [32]p. : ill., photos ; 18 cm. (A Kangaroo Book) Includes index. Filmography: p.301-405. [PN1998.A2E35] ISBN 0-671-81805-8 pbk. : 1.95
1. Moving-picture actors and actresses — United States — Biography. I. Title.
L.C card no. for 1976 Putnam ed.: 76-20806. **BIP**

FRITCH, Charles E. 927.92
Kim Novak, goddess of love. Derby, Conn., Monarch [c.1962] 139p. 18cm. (K63) .35 pap.,
I. Title.

JACOBS, Jack, 1919- 791.43'028'0922 B
The golden age of the character actor / Jack Jacobs. New York : Drake Publishers, [1975] p. cm. [PN1998.A2J3] 75-10921 ISBN 0-8473-1014-0 : 12.95
1. Moving-picture actors and actresses—United States—Biography. I. Title.

LAHUE, Kalton C. 791.43'092'2
Gentlemen to the rescue; the heroes of the silent screen [by] Kalton C. Lahue. South Brunswick, A. S. Barnes [1972] 244 p. illus. 26 cm. [PN1998.A2L28] 74-146762 ISBN 0-498-07802-7 8.50
1. Moving-picture actors and actresses, American—Biography. I. Title.

LAHUE, Kalton C. 791.43'028'0922 B
Ladies in distress [by] Kalton C. Lahue. South Brunswick, A. S. Barnes [1971] 334 p. illus., ports. 26 cm. [PN1998.A2L3] 72-124207 ISBN 0-498-07634-2
1. Moving-picture actors and actresses—United States—Biography. I. Title.

LAHUE, Kalton C. 791.43'028'0922
Riders of the range; the sagebrush heroes of the sound screen, by Kalton C. Lahue. South Brunswick, A. S. Barnes [1973] 259 p. illus. 27 cm. [PN1998.A2L32] 77-168370 ISBN 0-498-07931-7 10.00
1. Moving-picture actors and actresses, American—Biography. 2. Western films. I. Title.

MCCLURE, Arthur F. 791.43'028'0922 B
Star quality; screen actors from the golden age of films [by] Arthur F. McClure and Ken D. Jones. South Brunswick, A. S. Barnes [1973] p. cm. [PN1998.A2M253] 73-2770 ISBN 0-498-01374-X 15.00
1. Moving-picture actors and actresses—United States—Biography. I. Jones, Ken D., joint author. II. Title.

MCCREADIE, Marsha, 1943- 791.43'028'0922
The American movie goddess. Edited by Marsha McCreadie. New York, Wiley [1973] xi, 92 p. illus. 23 cm. (Perception in communication) Includes bibliographical references. [PN1998.A2M26] 72-14279 ISBN 0-471-58320 0 3.50
1. Moving-picture actors and actresses, American—Biography. 2. United States—Popular culture. I. Title.

MALTIN, Leonard. 791.43'092'2 B
The great movie comedians : from Charlie Chaplin to Woody Allen / by Leonard Maltin. New York : Crown Publishers, c1978. xvii, 238 p. : ill. ; 26 cm. Includes filmographies and index. [PN1998.A2M274 1978] 77-20233 ISBN 0-517-53241-7 : 12.95
1. Moving-picture actors and actresses—United States—Biography. 2. Comedians—United States—Biography. 3. Comedy films—Catalogs. I. Title.

PARISH, James Robert. 791.43'028'0922 B
The all-Americans / James Robert Parish & Don E. Stanke, with Michael R. Pitts ; editor, T. Allan Taylor ; research associates, John Robert Cocchi, Florence Solomon. New Rochelle, N.Y. : Arlington House, c1977. 448 p. : ill. ; 29 cm. Includes filmographies and index. [PN1998.A2P387] 77-643 ISBN 0-87000-363-1 : 25.00
1. Moving-picture actors and actresses—United States—Biography. I. Stanke, Don E., joint author. II. Pitts, Michael R., joint author. III. Title. **BIP**

PARISH, James Robert. 791.43'028'0922
The glamour girls / James Robert Parish and Don E. Stanke. New Rochelle, N.Y. : Arlington House, [1975] 752 p. : ill. ; 25 cm. Includes index. [PN1998.A2P3915] 75-5650 ISBN 0-87000-244-9 : 17.95
1. Moving-picture actors and actresses—United States—Biography. I. Stanke, Don E., joint author. II. Title. **BIP**

PARISH, James Robert. 791.43'028'0922
Great movie heroes / James Robert Parish. New York : Harper & Row, 1975. 115 p. : ill. ; 21 cm. (A Barnes & Noble entertainment book) [PN1998.A2P3917] 75-549 ISBN 0-06-465039-1 pbk. : 1.95
1. Moving-picture actors and actresses—United States—Biography. I. Title. **BIP**

PARISH, James Robert. 791.43'028'0922 B
Great western stars / James Robert Parish. New York : Ace Books, 1976. 256 p. : ill. ; 18 cm. [PN1998.A2P39173] 76-150284 pbk. : 1.75
1. Moving-picture actors and actresses—United States—Biography. 2. Western films—History and criticism. I. Title.

PARISH, James Robert. 791.43'028'0922 B
The Hollywood beauties / James Robert Parish. New Rochelle, N.Y. : Arlington House, c1978. p. cm. Includes index. [PN1998.A2P39176] 78-18306 ISBN 0-87000-412-3 : 25.00
1. Moving-picture actors and actresses—United States—Biography. I. Title. **BIP**

PARISH, James Robert. 791.43'028'0922 B
Hollywood character actors / James Robert Parish, with Earl Anderson [et al.] ; research associates, Robert A. Evans, William T. Leonard, Florence Solomon. New Rochelle, N.Y. : Arlington House, c1978. 542 p. : ill. ; 29 cm. [PN1998.A2P39177] 78-17553 ISBN 0-87000-384-4 : 30.00
1. Moving-picture actors and actresses—United States—Biography. I. Title.

PARISH, James Robert. 791.43'028'0922
Hollywood players : the forties / by James Robert Parish and Lennard DeCarl, with William T. Leonard and Gregory W. Mank ; introd. by Jack Ano ; editor, T. Allan Taylor ; research associates, John Robert Cocchi and Florence Solomon. New Rochelle, N.Y. : Arlington House Publishers, c1976. 544 p. : ill. ; 29 cm. Includes index. [PN1998.A2P3918] 75-33146 ISBN 0-87000-322-4
1. Moving-picture actors and actresses—United States—Biography. I. DeCarl, Lennard, joint author. II. Title.

PARISH, James Robert. 791.43'028'0922 B
Hollywood players, the Thirties / James Robert Parish and William T. Leonard ; editor, T. Allan Taylor ; research associates, John Robert Cocchi, Don E. Stanke, Florence Solomon ; introd., DeWitt Bodeen. New Rochelle, N.Y. : Arlington House, c1976. 576 p. : ill. ; 24 cm. Includes index. [PN1998.A2P3919] 76-17647 ISBN 0-87000-365-8 : 25.00
1. Moving-picture actors and actresses—United States—Biography. I. Leonard, William T., joint author. II. Title.

PARISH, James Robert. 791.43'028'0922 B
The leading ladies / by James Robert Parish & Don E. Stanke ; editor, T. Allan Taylor ; research associates, John Robert Cocchi, Florence Solomon, Richard Wentzler ; introd. by Gerald Weales. New Rochelle, N.Y. : Arlington House, c1977. p. cm. Includes index. [PN1998.A2P393] 77-24565 ISBN 0-87000-388-7 : 25.00
1. Moving-picture actors and actresses—United States—Biography. I. Stanke, Don E., joint author. II. Title. **BIP**

PARISH, James Robert. 791.43'028'0922 B
The tough guys / James Robert Parish. New Rochelle, N.Y. : Arlington House Publishers, c1976. 635 p. : ill. ; 24 cm. Includes index. Contents.Contents.—James Cagney.—Kirk Douglas.—Burt Lancaster.—Robert Mitchum.—Paul Muni.—Edward G. Robinson.—Robert Ryan. [PN1998.A2P415] 76-16867 ISBN 0-87000-338-0 : 25.00
1. Moving-picture actors and actresses—United States—Biography. I. Title.
Contents omitted **BIP**

RAGAN, David. 791.43'028'0922 B
Who's who in Hollywood, 1900-1976 / David Ragan New Rochelle, N.Y. : Arlington House, c1976. p. cm. [PN1998.A2R3] 76-25542 ISBN 0-87000-349-6 : 20.00
1. Moving-picture actors and actresses—United States—Biography. I. Title. **BIP**

SLIDE, Anthony. 791.43'028'0922
The idols of silence / Anthony Slide. South Brunswick : A. S. Barnes, c1976. 208 p. : ill. ; 29 cm. Includes bibliographies. [PN1998.A2S56 1976] 73-125 ISBN 0-498-01611-0 : 15.00
1. Moving-picture actors and actresses—United States—Biography. 2. Moving-pictures, Silent—History. I. Title. **BIP**

*STEIGER, Brad 792.0924
Valentino [by] Brad Steiger, Chaw Mank. Illus. with photographs from Valentino's private scrapbooks [New York] Macfadden [c.1966] 192p. illus. 18cm. (75-171) .75 pap.,
I. Title.

TASHMAN, George. 791.43'028'0922 B
I love you, Clark Gable, etc. : male sex symbols of the silver screen / by George Tashman ; foreword by Natalie Wood. Richmond, Calif. : Brombacher Books, c1976. 159 p. : ill. ; 21 cm (Read and grow ; 8) [PN1998.A2T36] 76-1674 ISBN 0-89085-082-8 pbk. : 2.95
1. Moving-picture actors and actresses—United States—Biography. I. Title.

WELSCH, Janice R. 791.43'028'0922 B
Film archetypes : sisters, mistresses, mothers and daughters / Janice R. Welsch. New York : Arno Press, 1978, c1976. p. cm. (Dissertations on film series) Originally presented as the author's thesis, Northwestern University, 1975. Bibliography: p. [PN1998.A2W417 1978] 77-22913 22.00
1. Moving-picture actors and actresses—United States—Biography. 2. Women in moving-pictures. I. Title. II. Series. III. The Arno Press cinema program **BIP**

*WHITNEY, Steven. 791.43'028'0922
Charles Bronson: superstar. [New York] Dell [1975] 284 p. illus. 18 cm. [PN2287] 1.50 (pbk.)
I. Title.

ZOLOTOW, Maurice, 1913- 927.92
Marilyn Monroe. New York, Bantam Bks. [1961, c.1960] xxi, 338p. illus. (S2282) .75 pap.,
I. Title.

Moving-picture actors and actresses—United States—Biography—Addresses, essays, lectures.

CLOSE-UPS : 791.43'028'0922 B
intimate profiles of movie stars by co-stars, directors, screen writers, and friends / edited by Danny Peary. New York : Workman Pub., [1978] p. cm. Includes indexes. [PN2285.C55 1978] 78-7113 ISBN 0-89480-044-2 : 15.95. ISBN 0-89480-043-4 : 8.95
1. Moving-picture actors and actresses—United States—Biography—Addresses, essays, lectures. 2. Moving-pictures—United States—Catalogs. I. Peary, Danny, 1949-

REED, Rex. 791.43'028'0922 B
Travolta to Keaton / by Rex Reed. 1st ed. New York : Morrow, 1979. 222 p. : ports. ; 24 cm. [PN1998.A2R35 1979] 78-27028 ISBN 0-688-03434-9 : 9.95
1. Moving-picture actors and actresses—United States—Biography—Addresses, essays, lectures. 2. Moving-pictures—United States—Biography—Addresses, essays, lectures. I. Title. **BIP**

Moving-picture actors and actresses—United States—Biography—Juvenile literature.

EDELSON, Edward, 1932- 791.43'028'0922 B
Great kids of the movies / Edward Edelson. 1st ed. Garden City, N.Y. : Doubleday, c1979. p. cm. Includes index. [PN1998.A2E27] 78-14697 ISBN 0-385-14127-0 : 6.95. ISBN 0-385-14128-9 lib.bdg. : 7.90
1. Moving-picture actors and actresses—United States—Biography—Juvenile literature. 2. Children as actors—Juvenile literature. I. Title. BIP

EDELSON, Edward, 1932- 791.43'028'0922 B
Tough guys and gals of the movies / Edward Edelson. 1st ed. Garden City, N.Y. : Doubleday, c1978. 133 p. : ill. ; 21 cm. A look at the traditional "bad guys" and gals from the movies with special emphasis on the careers of Humphrey Bogart, James Cagney, and Edward G. Robinson. [PN1998.A2E29] 920 77-17002 ISBN 0-385-12788-X : 5.95. ISBN 0-385-12789-8 lib.bdg. : 5.95
1. Moving-picture actors and actresses—United States—Biography—Juvenile literature. I. Title. BIP

Moving-picture actors and actresses—United States—Correspondence, reminiscences, etc.

ASTOR, Mary, 1906- 791.43'028'0924 B
A life on film. With an introd. by Sumner Locke Elliott. New York, Delacorte Press [1971] x, 245 p. illus. 24 cm. [PN2287.A8A32] 77-164844 7.50
1. Moving-picture actors and actresses—United States—Correspondence, reminiscences, etc. I. Title.

Moving-picture producers and directors—Biography.

COWIE, Peter. 791.43'023'0922 B
Fifty major film-makers / edited by Peter Cowie. South Brunswick : A. S. Barnes, [1974] p. cm. Includes filmographies and index. [PN1998.A2C67] 73-107 ISBN 0-498-01255-7 : 20.00
1. Moving-picture producers and directors—Biography. I. Title. BIP

Moving-picture producers and directors—Biography—Addresses, essays, lectures.

GREAT film 791.43'0233'0922
directors : a critical anthology / edited by Leo Braudy and Morris Dickstein. New York : Oxford University Press, 1978. xi, 778 p. ; 23 cm. Includes bibliographical references. [PN1998.A2G74] 76-42668 ISBN 0-19-502312-9 pbk. : 7.00
1. Moving-picture producers and directors—Biography—Addresses, essays, lectures. I. Braudy, Leo. II. Dickstein, Morris. BIP

Moving-picture producers and directors—Biography—Bibliography.

SCHUSTER, Mel. 016.79143'0233'0922
Motion picture directors: a bibliography of magazine and periodical articles, 1900-1972. Metuchen, N.J., Scarecrow Press, 1973. 418 p. 22 cm. [Z5784.M9S34] 73-780 ISBN 0-8108-0590-1 12.00
1. Moving-picture producers and directors—Biography—Bibliography. I. Title. BIP

Moving-picture producers and directors—Interviews.

SARRIS, Andrew, comp. 791.43'0233'0922
Interviews with film directors. Indianapolis, Bobbs-Merrill [1968, c1967] x, 478 p. ports. 24 cm. Published in 1972 under title: Hollywood voices. Bibliographical footnotes. [PN1995.9.P7S2] 67-20455
1. Moving-picture producers and directors—Interviews. I. Title. BIP

Moving-picture producers and directors—Japan—Biography.

BOCK, Audie, 1945- 791.43'0232'0922
Japanese film directors / Audie Bock ; pref. by Donald Richie. 1st ed. New York : Published for the Japan Society by Kodansha International, 1978. 307 p., [24] leaves of plates : ill. ; 22 cm. Includes index. Filmography: p. 356-362. [PN1998.A2B618] 77-75968 ISBN 0-87011-304-6 : 12.95
1. Moving-picture producers and directors—Japan—Biography. I. Title. BIP

Moving-picture producers and directors—Russia—Biography.

BIRKOS, Alexander S. 791.43'0233'0922
Soviet cinema : directors and films / compiled by Alexander S. Birkos. Hamden, Conn. : Archon Books, 1976. x, 344 p. : ill. ; 23 cm. Bibliography: p. [341]-344. [PN1998.A2B56] 76-7082 ISBN 0-208-01581-7 : 17.50
1. Moving-picture producers and directors—Russia—Biography. 2. Moving-pictures—Russia—Catalogs. I. Title. BIP

Moving-picture producers and directors—United States.

ADAMSON, Joe. 791.43'0233'0924
Tex Avery, king of cartoons / by Joe Adamson. New York : Popular Library, c1975. 237 p. : ill. ; 28 cm. (The Big apple film series) (Big apple books) Filmography: p. [201]-[233] [NC1766.U52A922] 76-357684 pbk. : 3.95
I. Title.

*ADLER, Bill v. 12 B
Woody Allen clown prince of American humor, by Bill Adler & Jeffrey Feinman. New York, Pinnacle Books [1975] 178 p. illus. 18 cm. [PN2287] 791.43'028'0924 ISBN 0-523-00786-8 1.75 (pbk.)
I. Feinman, Jeffrey, joint author. II. Title. BIP

FRENCH, Philip. 791.43'0232'0922
The movie moguls; an informal history of the Hollywood tycoons. Chicago, H. Regnery Co. [1971, c1969] 170 p. ports. 22 cm. Bibliography: p. 159-163. [PN1998.A2F75 1971] 79-143851 5.95
1. Moving-picture producers and directors—United States. I. Title.

PHILLIPS, Gene D. 791.43'0233'0922
The movie makers: artists in an industry [by] Gene D. Phillips. Chicago, Nelson-Hall Co. [1973] xv, 249 p. illus. 21 x 27 cm. Bibliography: p. 241-244. [PN1998.A2P48] 73-75524 ISBN 0-911012-43-5 15.00
1. Moving-picture producers and directors—United States. 2. Moving-picture producers and directors—Great Britain. I. Title.

ZIEROLD, Norman J. 791.43'023'0922
The moguls [by] Norman Zierold. New York, Coward-McCann [1969] 354 p. illus., ports. 23 cm. Contents.Contents.—The Selznick saga.—"Uncle Carl" Laemmle.—"Samuel Goldwyn presents"—The gentlemen from Paramount.—White Fang.—The films' forgotten man: William Fox.—The brothers Warner.—The "goy" studio: Twentieth Century-Fox.—Mayer's ganz-mispochen. [PN1998.A2Z53] 69-14649 6.95
1. Moving-picture producers and directors—United States. I. Title.

Moving-picture producers and directors—United States—Biography.

CLOSE up : 791.43'023'0922
the contract director / general editor, Jon Tuska, associate editor, Vicki Piekarski, research editor, Karl Thiede. Metuchen, N.J. : Scarecrow Press, 1976. p. cm. Includes index. [PN1998.A2C55] 76-41345 ISBN 0-8108-0961-3 : 17.50
1. Moving-picture producers and directors—United States—Biography. I. Tuska, Jon. II. Piekarski, Vicki. III. Thiede, Karl. BIP

CLOSE-UP : 791.43'0233'0922
the Hollywood director / general editor, Jon Tuska, associate editor, Vicki Piekarski, research editor, David Wilson. Metuchen, N.J. : Scarecrow Press, 1978. ix, 444 p. : ill. ; 23 cm. Includes filmographies and index. [PN1998.A2C555] 77-14114 ISBN 0-8108-1085-9 : 17.50
1. Moving-picture producers and directors—United States—Biography. I. Tuska, Jon. II. Piekarski, Vicki. III. Wilson, David, 1942- BIP

JACOBS, Diane. 791.43'0233'0922 B
Hollywood Renaissance / Diane Jacobs. South Brunswick : A. S. Barnes, c1977. 192 p. : ill. ; 25 cm. Contents.Contents.—John Cassavetes.—Robert Altman.—Francis Ford Coppola.—Martin Scorsese.—Paul Mazursky. Bibliography: p. 175-177. [PN1998.A2J28] 76-18796 ISBN 0-498-01785-0 : 12.00
1. Moving-picture producers and directors—United States—Biography. 2. Moving-pictures—United States. I. Title. BIP

Moving-picture producers and directors—United States—Correspondence, reminiscences, etc.

HIGHAM, Charles, 1931- 791.43'0233'0922 B
The celluloid muse; Hollywood directors speak [by] Charles Higham and Joel Greenberg. Chicago, Regnery [1971, c1969] 268 p. plates, ports. 24 cm. "Filmographies": p. 255-260. [PN1998.A2H5 1971] 72-143852 7.95
1. Moving-picture producers and directors—United States—Correspondence, reminiscences, etc. I. Greenberg, Joel, joint author. II. Title.

Moving-picture producers and directors—United States—Juvenile literature.

FRIEDLAND, Ronald, 1937- 791.43'0233'0922
American film directors : the world as they see it / Ronald Lloyd [i.e. R. Friedland]. New York : F. Watts, 1976. 143 p. : ill. ; 24 cm. Includes index. Examines the work of six major American film directors and, more briefly, several newer directors. [PN1998.A2F76] 75-37949 ISBN 0-531-01110-0 lib.bdg. : 6.90
1. Moving-picture producers and directors—United States—Juvenile literature. I. Title. BIP

Moving pictures.

*MALTIN, Leonard. 791.43'.0233'0924
Movie comedy teams. With an introduction by Billy Gilbert. New York, New American Lib. [1974 c.1970] 352 p. photos 18 cm. (Signet Film Series) [PN1998] 1.50 (pbk.)
1. Moving pictures. I. Title. BIP

Moving-pictures—Biography.

BURDICK, Loraine. 791.43'028'0922
Child star dolls and toys. [New York, Macmillan, c1968] 170 p. illus., ports. 29 cm. (Quest books) Cover title. [PN1998.A2B8] 70-2382
1. Moving-pictures—Biography. 2. Children as actors. 3. Toys. I. Title.

CHANELES, Sol. 791.43'028'0922 B
The movie makers [edited] by Sol Chaneles and Albert Wolsky. Secaucus, N.J., Derbibooks [1974] 544 p. illus. 29 cm. "A Vineyard book." [PN1998.A2C46] 74-6443 ISBN 0-89009-002-5 19.95
1. Moving-pictures—Biography. I. Wolsky, Albert, joint author. II. Title.

*GRAHAM, Peter 927.9143
A dictionary of the cinema. London, Tantivy Pr.; New York, A. S. Barnes [c.1964] 158p. ports. 17cm. 1.95 pap.,
1. Moving-pictures—Biog. 2. Moving-pictures—Dictionaries. I. Title.

GRAHAM, Peter John, 1939- 927.9143
A dictionary of the cinema, by Peter Graham. London, Tantivy Press; New York, A. S. Barnes [1964] 158 p. ports. 16 cm. [PN1998.A2G7] 65-41
1. Moving-pictures — Biog. 2. Moving-pictures — Dictionaries. I. Title.

HOLLYWOOD s young 790.2'092'2
stars. v. 1- 1955- [New York] v. illus. 28cm. [PN1998.A2H65] 55-33178
1. Moving-pictures—Biog.

JESSEL, George Albert, 1898- 811.54
Halo over Hollywood. Van Nuys, Calif., Toastmaster Pub. Co. [1963] 176 p. illus. 21 cm. Biographical sketches in verse. [[PN1998.A2J4]] 63-13717
1. Moving-pictures — Biog. I. Title.

MEYERS, Warren B. 791.43'028'0922
"Who is that?" The late late viewers guide to the old old movie players, by Warren B. Meyers. Designed and illustrated by Jerry Lang & Gosta Viertel. [New York, Personality Posters, 1967] 63p. illus. (pt. col.), ports. 21x26cm. [PN1998.A2M4] 67-7843 1.50 pap.,
1. Moving-pictures—Biog. I. Title.

PARSONS, Louella (Oettinger) 1885- 927.92
Tell it to Louella. New York, Putnam [1961] 316p. 22cm. [PN1998.A2P42] 61-16721
1. Moving-pictures—Biog. 2. Journalists—Correspondence, reminiscences, etc. I. Title.

PARSONS, Louella (Oettinger) 1885- 927.92
Tell it to Louella. New York, Lancer [1963, c.1961] 256p. 18cm. (73-423) .60 pap.,
1. Moving-pictures—Biog. 2. Journalists—Correspondence, reminiscences, etc. I. Title.

ROSENBERG, Bernard, 1923- 791.43'09794'94
The real tinsel [by] Bernard Rosenberg and Harry Silverstein. [New York] Macmillan [1970] xi, 436 p. illus., ports. 25 cm. [PN1998.A2R65] 73-112854 9.95
1. Moving-pictures—Biography. 2. Moving-picture industry—California—Hollywood. I. Silverstein, Harry, joint author. II. Title. BIP

SAYRES, B. W. v. 12
Who's whose in Hollywood; a sorta saga of screenland. Hollywood [n. d.] 75 p. 67-72128
1. Moving-pictures—Biog. 2. Actors and actresses. I. Title.

STUART, Ray, 1899- 791.430922
Immortals of the screen. Book design by Czeslaw Z. Banasiewicz. [1st American ed.] Los Angeles, Sherbourne Press [1965] 224 p. illus., ports. 29 cm. [PN1998.A2S7] 66-661
1. Moving-pictures — Biog. I. Title.

STUART, Ray, 1899- 791.430922
Immortals of the screen. Book design by Czeslaw Z. Banasiewicz. [1st American ed.] Los Angeles, Sherbourne Press [1965] 224 p. illus., ports. 29 cm. [PN1998.A2S7 1965] 66-661
1. Moving-pictures—Biography. I. Title.

TAYLOR, John Russell. 791.4309
Cinema eye, cinema ear; some key film-makers of the sixties. [1st American ed.] New York, Hill and Wang [1964] 294 p. illus., ports. 21 cm. Bibliography: p. [278]-283. [PN1998.A2T38] 64-15384
1. Moving-pictures—Biography. 2. Moving-pictures. I. Title. BIP

THIS was Hollywood. 790.2'092'2
v.1-1955- [New York, Affiliated Magazines] v. illus. 28cm. annual. [PN1998.A2T47] 55-33179
1. Moving- pictures—Biog. 2. Moving-pictures—Yearbooks.

VOICES of film 791.43'028'0922 B
experience : 1894-to the present / edited by Jay Leyda ; research by Doug Tomlinson and John Hagan. New York : Macmillan, c1977. xxxviii, 544 p. ; 24 cm. Includes index. Bibliography: p. xi-xxxvii.

[PN1998.A2V66] 77-2569 ISBN 0-02-571600-X : 19.95
1. Moving-pictures—Biography. I. Leyda, Jay, 1910-

WHO'S who in Hollywood. 927.92
New York, Dell Pub. Co. v. illus., ports. 28 cm. Editors: F. Epstein, C. Kane. [PN1998.A2W47] 51-30858
1. Moving-pictures—Biog. 2. Actors, American. Florence, ed.

Moving-pictures—Biography—Dictionaries.

THOMSON, David, 1941- 791.43'092'2 B
A biographical dictionary of film / David Thomson. New York : Morrow, 1976, c1975. ix, 629 p. ; 24 cm. Published in 1975 under title: A biographical dictionary of the cinema. [PN1998.A2T55 1976] 75-20044 ISBN 0-688-02974-4 : 16.95
1. Moving-pictures—Biography—Dictionaries. I. Title. BIP

Moving-pictures—Catalogs.

PARISH, James Robert. 791.43'0233'0922
Film directors: a guide to their American films, by James Robert Parish and Michael R. Pitts. Research associate: William T. Leonard. Research assistants: Pierre Guinle, Norman Miller [and] Florence Solomon. Metuchen, N.J., Scarecrow Press, 1974. vii, 436 p. illus. 22 cm. [PN1998.P24] 74-17398 ISBN 0-8108-0752-1 15.00
1. Moving-pictures—Catalogs. 2. Moving-picture producers and directors—United States. I. Pitts, Michael R., joint author. II. Title. BIP

SPRECHER, Daniel. 791.43'8
Guide to films (16mm) about famous people. [1st ed.] Alexandria, Va., Serina Press [1969] x, 206 p. 23 cm. "Containing synopses of over 1450 motion picture films (16mm) concerning, in whole or in part, the lives, the times, the works, or the activities of over 1180 famous or well-known persons, contemporary and historical." [PN1998.S694] 76-110326
1. Moving-pictures—Catalogs. 2. Biography—Film catalogs. I. Title.

Moving-pictures—History.

VIDOR, King Wallis, 1895- 927.914
A tree is a tree. [1st ed.] New York, Harcourt, Brace [1953] 315p. illus. 21cm. Autobiography. [PN1998.A3V5] 53-9221
1. Moving-pictures Hist. I. Title.

WAGENKNECHT, Edward Charles, 1900- 791.4309
The movies in the age of innocence. [1st ed.] Norman, University of Oklahoma Press [1962] xii, 280 p. illus., ports. 24 cm. Bibliographical footnotes. [PN1993.5.A1W2] 62-16473
1. Moving-pictures—History. 2. Moving pictures—Biography. I. Title. BIP

ZUKOR, Adolph, 1873- 927.92
The public is never wrong; the autobiography of Adolph Zukor, with Dale Kramer. New York, Putnam [1953] 309p. illus. 22cm. [PN1998.A3Z8] 53-8164
1. Moving- pictures—Hist. I. Title.

Moving-pictures—Production and direction.

HOCHMAN, Stanley, comp. 791.43'0233'0922
American film directors. With filmographies and index of critics and films. New York, Ungar [1974] xiv, 590 p. 25 cm. (A Library of film criticism) [PN1995.9.P7H57] 73-92923 ISBN 0-8044-3120-5 18.50
1. Moving-pictures—Production and direction. 2. Moving-picture producers and directors—United States. I. Title.

VIDOR, King Wallis, 1895- 791.43'0233'0924
King Vidor on film making. New York, McKay [1972] xi, 239 p. illus. 22 cm. [PN1998.A3V48 1972] 72-86969 6.95
1. Moving-pictures—Production and direction. I. Title.

Moving-pictures—Production and direction—Addresses, essays, lectures.

HOLLYWOOD directors, 1914-1940 / [compiled by] Richard Koszarski. New York : Oxford University Press, 1976. xx, 364 p. : ill. ; 22 cm. Includes index. [PN1995.9.P7H64] 76-9262 ISBN 0-19-502085-5 : 13.95 792'.023'0922
1. Moving-pictures—Production and direction—Addresses, essays, lectures. 2. Moving-picture producers and directors—United States—Biography. I. Koszarski, Richard. BIP

HOLLYWOOD directors, 1941-1976 / [compiled by] Richard Koszarski. New York : Oxford University Press, 1977. xvii, 426 p. : ill. ; 22 cm. Includes index. [PN1995.9.P7H63] 76-51716 ISBN 0-19-502217-3 : 15.00 791.43'0233'0922
1. Moving-pictures—Production and direction—Addresses, essays, lectures. 2. Moving-picture producers and directors—United States—Biography. I. Koszarski, Richard.

Moving-pictures—United States—Biography.

PLATT, Frank Cheney, 1932- comp. 791.43'0922
Great stars of Hollywood's golden age, compiled by Frank C. Platt. [New York] New American Library [1966] 214 p. illus. 18 cm. (A Signet book, P2979) Contents.Contents.—Valentino, the life story of "The Shiek," by A. R. St. Johns.—Garbo, the mystery of Hollywood, by A. R. St. Johns.—The private life of Charlie Chaplin, by C. R. Robinson.—The loves of John Barrymore, by F. L. Collins.—Why Jean Harlow died, by E. Doherty.—Carole Lombard, by A. R. St. Johns. [PN1998.A2P55] 67-4407
1. Moving-pictures—United States—Biography. 2. Hollywood, Calif. I. Title.

STEEN, Mike. 791.43'092'2 B
Hollywood speaks; an oral history. New York, Putnam [1974] 379 p. 23 cm. Biographical interviews. [PN1998.A2S66] 73-78617 ISBN 0-399-11162-X 8.95
1. Moving pictures United States—Biography. 2. Moving-picture industry—United States. I. Title.
Contents omitted.

WAGNER, Walter, 1927- 791.43'092'2 B
You must remember this / Walter Wagner. New York : Putnam, [1975] 320 p. ; 23 cm. [PN1998.A2W24] 75-12699 ISBN 0-399-11274-X : 8.95
1. Moving-pictures—United States—Biography. I. Title.

Movius, Herbert John,

MOVIUS, Herbert John, 1888- 610.924
Doctor! doctor! Incredible stories of medical genius by a country doctor who became one of Hollywood's leading surgeons [by] Herbert J. Movius. [1st ed.] New York, Vantage Press [1966] 166 p. illus., port. 21 cm. Autobiographical. [R154.M8533A3] 66-3344
I. Title.

Mowat, Farley.

MOWAT, Farley. 940.54'81'71 B
And no birds sang / by Farley Mowat. 1st American ed. Boston : Little, Brown, c1979. p. cm. "An Atlantic Monthly Press book." [D811.M683 1979] 79-23231 ISBN 0-316-58695-1 : 10.95
1. Mowat, Farley. 2. World War, 1939-1945—Personal narratives, Canadian. 3. Soldiers—Canada—Biography. I. Title. BIP

Mowat, Oliver, Sir, 1820-1903.

BIGGAR, Charles Robert Webster, 1847-1909. 971.3'03'0924 B
Sir Oliver Mowat; a biographical sketch. Toronto, Warwick Bro's & Rutter, 1905. [New York, AMS Press, 1971] 2 v. ports. 22 cm. Includes bibliographical references. [F1033.M93B5 1971] 71-136404 ISBN 0-404-08021-9 (v. 1)
1. Mowat, Oliver, Sir, 1820-1903. 2. Canada—Politics and government—19th century. 3. Ontario—Politics and government. BIP

Moye, Jean Martin, 1730-1793.

CALLAHAN, Mary Generosa, 1901- 922.2
The life of Blessed John Martin Moye. Milwaukee, Bruce Press [1964] ix, 262 p. maps, port. 24 cm. (Catholic life publications) [BX4700.M68C3] 65-364
1. Moye, Jean Martin, 1730-1793. I. Title.

PLUS, Raoul, 1882- 922.2
Shepherd of untended sheep; John Martin Moye, priest of the Society of the Foreign Missions of Paris, founder of the Sisters of Divine Providence. Translated from the French by Sister James Aloysius [and] Sister Mary Generose. Westminster, Md., Newman Press, 1950. xv, 180 p. illus., ports. 21 cm. Translation of J. M. Moye. [BX4705.M74P52] 51-9450
1. Moye, Jean Martin, 1730-1793. 2. Sisters of Divine Providence. I. Title.

Moyer, Kenneth Allan, 1913-

MOYER, Kenneth Allan, 1913- 287'.92'0924 B
Preacher on the roof / by Kenneth A. Moyer ; illustrated by Joanne Jackson. [s.l. : s.n.], c1976. 74 p. : ill. ; 28 cm. Cover title. [BX9883.M65A35] 77-366089
1. Moyer, Kenneth Allan, 1913- 2. United Church of Canada—Clergy—Biography. 3. Clergy—Canada—Biography. I. Title.

Moylan, Stephen, 1734-1811.

GRIFFIN, Martin Ignatius Joseph, 1842-1911. 973.3'3'0924 B
Stephen Moylan, muster-master general secretary and aide-de-camp to Washington. New York, MSS Information Corp. [1972] p. Reprint of the 1909 ed. [E207.M9G8 1972] 72-8106 ISBN 0-8422-8062-6
1. Moylan, Stephen, 1734-1811.

Moyle, James Henry, 1858-1946.

HINCKLEY, Gordon Bitner, 1910- 923.273
James Henry Moyle, the story of a distinguished American and an honored churchman. Based in part on the research and manuscript writings of John Henry Evans. Salt Lake City, Deseret Book Co. ['1951] 399 p. illus. 24 cm. [F826.M8H5] 52-19491
1. Moyle, James Henry, 1858-1946. 2. Utah—Pol. & govt. I. Title.

MOYLE, James Henry, 1858-1946. 353'.00092'4 B
Mormon Democrat : the religious and political memoirs of James Henry Moyle / edited by Gene A. Sessions. [Salt Lake City] : Historical Dept. of the Church of Jesus Christ of Latter-day Saints, 1975. xix, 503 p. ; 29 cm. Includes bibliographical references and index. [F826.M795 1975] 75-312702
1. Moyle, James Henry, 1858-1946. I. Title.

Moynihan, Daniel Patrick.

SCHOEN, Douglas E., D.Phil. 973.92'092'4 B
Daniel Patrick Moynihan : a biography / by Douglas Schoen. 1st ed. New York : Harper & Row, c1979. xiii, 322 p. : ill. ; 24 cm. Includes bibliographical references and index. [E840.8.M68S35 1979] 78-20184 ISBN 0-06-013998-6 12.95
1. Moynihan, Daniel Patrick. 2. United States. Congress. Senate—Biography. 3. Statesmen—United States—Biography. 4. Sociologists—United States—Biography.

Moynihan, Donald T.

MOYNIHAN, Donald T. 617'.95'00924 B
Skin deep : the making of a plastic surgeon / by Donald T. Moynihan and Shirley Hartman. 1st ed. Boston : Little, Brown, c1979. viii, 339 p. ; 22 cm. [RD27.35.M68A33] 79-10552 ISBN 0-316-58700-1 : 9.95
1. Moynihan, Donald T. 2. Plastic surgeons—California—Biography. 3. Residents (Medicine)—California—Biography. I. Hartman, Shirley, joint author. II. Title. BIP

Mozart, Johann Chrysostom Wolfgang Amadeus, 1756-1791.

BARNE, Kitty, 1883- 927.8
Introducing Mozart. With drawings by J. J. Crockford. New York, Roy Publishers [1957] 89p. illus. 19cm. [ML3930] 57-10086
1. Mozart. Johann Chrysostom Wolfgang Amadeus, 1756-1791. 2. Music—Juvenile literature. I. Title.

BEYLE, Marie Henri, 780'.92'2 B
1783-1842.
Haydn, Mozart and Metastasio, by Stendhal. Translated, introduced & edited by Richard N. Coe. New York, Grossman Publishers, 1972. xxxii, 370 p. illus. 23 cm. London ed. (Calder & Boyars) has title: Lives of Haydn, Mozart and Metastasio. Translation of Vies de Haydn, de Mozart et de Metastase. Bibliography: p. 283-291. [ML390.B555V53 1972b] 77-188310 ISBN 0-670-36417-7 15.00
1. Haydn, Joseph, 1732-1809. 2. Mozart, Johann Chrysostom Wolfgang Amadeus, 1756-1791. 3. Metastasio, Pietro Antonio Domenico Buonaventura, 1698-1782. I. Coe, Richard N., ed. II. Title.

BIANCOLLI, Louis Leopold, 927.8
ed.
The Mozart handbook; a guide to the man and his music. [1st ed.] Cleveland, World Pub. Co. [1954] xxi, 629p. illus., ports., facsims. 24cm. 'Classified list of Mozart's works':p. [579]-593. Bibliography: p. 602-605. [ML410.M9B38] 54-8174
1. Mozart, Johann Chrysostom Wolfgang Amadeus, 1756-1791. I. Title.

BIANCOLLI, Louis 780'.92'4
Leopold, ed.
The Mozart handbook : a guide to the man and his music / compiled and edited by Louis Biancolli. Westport, Conn. : Greenwood Press, 1975, c1954. p. cm. Reprint of the ed. published by World Pub. Co., Cleveland. Includes index. Bibliography: p. [ML410.M9B38 1975] 75-32504 ISBN 0-8371-8496-7 lib.bdg. : 32.00
1. Mozart, Johann Chrysostom Wolfgang Amadeus, 1756-1791. I. Title.
BIP

BISHOP, Claire 780'.924 B
(Huchet)
Mozart; music magician. Illustrated by Paul Frame. Champaign, Ill., Garrard Pub. Co. [1968] 138 p. illus., music. 22 cm. (Creative arts biographies) A biography of the eighteenth-century musical prodigy who discovered the piano at age three, played for the Empress of Austria at age six, and grew up to be a great composer, unrecognized however in his own times. [ML3930.M9B6] 92 AC 68
1. Mozart, Johann Chrysostom Wolfgang Amadeus, 1756-1791. I. Frame, Paul, illus. II. Title.

BLOM, Eric, 1888- 927.8
Mozart. New York, Collier [1962] 348p. 18cm. (Great composers ser. AS401X) Bibl. .95 pap.,
1. Mozart, Johann Chrysostom Wolfgang Amadeus, 1756-1791. I. Title. II. Series.
BIP

BLOM, Eric, 1888-1959. v. 12
Mozart. [1st Collier Books ed.] New York, Collier Books [1962] 348 p. illus. (Great composers series) Includes bibliography. NUC64
1. Mozart, Johann Chrysostom Wolfgang Amadeus, 1756-1791. I. Title.

BURK, John Naglee, 1891- 927.8
Mozart and his music. New York, Random House [1959] x, 453p. 21cm. 'The Kochel chronology': p. [412]-444. [ML410.M9B97] 59-9481
1. Mozart, Johann Chrysostom Wolfgang Amadeus, 1756-1791. I. Title.

DAVENPORT. MARCIA (GLUCK) 927.8
1903-
Mozart. New York, Watts [1965, c.1932, 1956] 402p. facsim. 29cm. (Keith Jennison bk., large type ed.) Bibl. [ML410.M9D18] 8.95; 6.10 lib. ed.,
1. Mozart, Johann Chrysostom Wolfgang Amadeus, 1756-1791. I. Title.

DAVENPORT, Marcia (Gluck) 927.8
1903-
Mozart. [Bicentenary ed.] New York, Scribner, 1956. xix, 402 p. illus., ports., facsims. 23 cm. Bibliography: p. 389-393. [ML410.M9D18 1956] 56-13557
1. Mozart, Johann Chrysostom Wolfgang Amadeus, 1756-1791.

DAVENPORT, Marcia (Gluck), 927.8
1903-
Mozart / Marcia Davenport. New York : Avon Books, 1979, c.1960 402 p. ; ill. ; 18 cm. (A Discus Book) Includes bibliographic references and index. [ML410.M9D18] ISBN 0-380-45534-X pbk. : 3.50
1. Mozart, Johann Chrysostom Wolfgang Amadeus, 1756-1791. I. Title.
L.C. card no. for 1960 Scribner's ed.:56-13557

DEUTSCH, Otto Erich, 1883- 927.8
Mozart, a documentary biography. Tr. by Eric Blom, Peter Branscombe, Jeremy Noble. Stanford, Stanford Univ. Pr. [c.1965] ix. 680p. 24cm. Bibl. [ML410.M9D4782] 64-12077 17.50
1. Mozart, Johann Chrysostom Wolfgang Amadeus, 1756-1791. I. Title.

EINSTEIN, Alfred 927.8
Mozart, his character, his work. Tr. [from German] by Arthur Mendel, Nathan Broder. New York, Oxford 1962[1945] 492 p. illus. 21 cm (Hesperides bk. hsb) pap. 2.65
1. Mozart, Johann Chrysostom Wolfgang Amadeus, 1756-1791. 2. Medel Arthur, 1905-tr. Border Nathan, joint tr. I. Title.

EINSTEIN, Alfred, 1880- 927.8
Mozart, his character, his work [by] Alfred Einstein; tr. [from German] by Arthur Mendel, Nathan Broder. New York. Oxford [1966, c.1945] viii, 492p. front. (facsim.) illus. (music) ports. 21cm. (Galaxy bk., GB162) [ML410-M9E4] 45-1487 2.85 pap.,
1. Mozart, Johann Chrysostom Wolfgang Amadeus, 1756-1791. I. Mendel, Arthur, 1905- tr. II. Broder, Nathan, joint tr. III. Title.

EINSTEIN, Alfred, 1880-1952 927.8
Mozart, his character, his work. Tr. [from German] by Arthur Mendel. Nathan Broder. New York, Oxford. 1962 [c.1945* 492p. illus. 21cm. (Jesperides bk., HS8) 2.65 pap.,
1. Mozart, Johann Chrysostom Wolfgang Amadeus, 1756-1791. I. Mendel, Arthur, 1908- tr. II. Broder, Nathan, joint ed. III. Title.

GEHRING, Franz Eduard, 780'.924 B
1838-1884.
Mozart. Freeport, N.Y., Books For Libraries Press [1972] viii, 131 p. 23 cm. Reprint of the 1883 ed, issued in series: The Great musicians. [ML410.M9G3 1972] 78-37881 ISBN 0-8369-6718-6
1. Mozart, Johann Chrysostom Wolfgang Amadeus, 1756-1791.

HALDANE, Charlotte 927.8
(Franken)
Mozart. London, New York, Oxford University Press, 1960[ ] x, 149p. (Bibl. footnotes) illus. 23cm. 60-4617 4.25
1. Mozart, Johann Chrysostom Wolfgang Amadeus, 1756-1791. I. Title.

HALDANE, Charlotte 780'.92'4 B
Franken, 1894-1969.
Mozart / by Charlotte Haldane. Westport, Conn. : Greenwood Press, 1976, c1960. p. cm. Reprint of the ed. published by Oxford University Press, London, New York. Includes index. [ML410.M9H15 1976] 75-3733 lib.bdg. : 17.00
1. Mozart, Johann Chrysostom Wolfgang Amadeus, 1756-1791.

HOLMES, Edward, 1797- 780'.92'4 B
1859.
The life of Mozart / by Edward Holmes ; with a new introd. by Percy M. Young. New York : Da Capo Press, 1979. p. cm. (Da Capo Press music reprint series) Reprint of the 1854 ed. published in London. [ML410.M9H82 1979] 79-18093 25.00
1. Mozart, Johann Chrysostom Wolfgang Amadeus, 1756-1791. 2. Composers—Austria—Biography. I. Title.

HOLMES, Edward, 1797- 780'.92'4 B
1859.
The life of Mozart / by Edward Holmes. Westport, Conn. : Greenwood Press, 1980. p. cm. Reprint of the 1912 ed. published by J. M. Dent, London, and E. P. Dutton, New York, in series: Everyman's library. Includes index. [ML410.M9H82 1980] 79-25356 ISBN 0-313-22283-5 lib. bdg. : 24.25
1. Mozart, Johann Chrysostom Wolfgang Amadeus, 1756-1791. 2. Composers—Austria—Biography. I. Title.

HUSSEY, Dyneley, 1893- 780'.924 B
Wolfgang Amadeus Mozart Westport, Conn., Greenwood Press [1971] xiii, 368 p. port. 23 cm. Reprint of the 1928 ed. [ML410.M9H9 1971] 70-104288 ISBN 0-8371-3957-0
1. Mozart, Johann Chrysostom Wolfgang Amadeus, 1756-1791.
BIP

HUSSEY, Dyneley, 1893- 780'.924 B
Wolfgang Amadeus Mozart. Freeport, N.Y., Books for Libraries Press [1969] xiii, 368 p. port. 23 cm. (Select bibliographies reprint series) "Chronological table of Mozart's life and works": p. [333]-357. [ML410.M9H9 1969] 73-94272
1. Mozart, Johann Chrysostom Wolfgang Amadeus, 1756-1791.

HUTCHINGS, Arthur, 780'.92'4 B
1906-
Mozart : the man, the musician / [by] Arthur Hutchings. London : Thames and Hudson, 1976. viii, 113, 131 p., 48 p. of plates : ill. (some col.), facsims., map, music, ports. (some col.) ; 31 cm. Includes indexes. [ML410.M9H92 1976b] 77-352558 ISBN 0-500-01161-3 : £16.00
1. Mozart, Johann Chrysostom Wolfgang Amadeus, 1756-1791. 2. Composers—Austria—Biography.

JAHN, Otto, 1813-1869. 780'.924 B
Life of Mozart. Translated from the German by Pauline Townsend, with a pref. by George Grove. New York, Cooper Square Publishers, 1970. 3 v. facsims., music, ports. 22 cm. Translation of W. A. Mozart. Reprint of the 1891 ed. Includes bibliographical references. [ML410.M9J413 1970] 78-125917
1. Mozart, Johann Chrysostom Wolfgang Amadeus, 1756-1791.
BIP

KENYON, Max. 780'.92'4 B
Mozart in Salzburg : a study and guide / Max Kenyon. Westport, Conn. : Hyperion Press, 1979. p. cm. Reprint of the 1953 ed. published by Putnam, New York. Includes indexes. Bibliography: p. [ML410.M9K37 1979] 78-23817 22.50
1. Mozart, Johann Chrysostom Wolfgang Amadeus, 1756-1791. 2. Composers—Austria—Salzburg—Biography. I. Title.

KEYS, Ivor 780'.92'4 B
Christopher Banfield.
Mozart : his music in his life / Ivor Keys. New York : Holmes & Meier Publishers, c1979. p. cm. Includes index. Bibliography: p. [ML410.M9K4] 79-19028 ISBN 0-8419-0576-2 : 22.50
1. Mozart, Johann Chrysostom Wolfgang Amadeus, 1756-1791. 2. Composers—Austria—Biography.

KING, Alexander Hyatt. 780'.924 B
Mozart: a biography, with a survey of books, editions & recordings, by Alec Hyatt King. [Hamden, Conn.] Archon Books [1970] 114 p. 23 cm. (The Concertgoer's companions) [ML410.M9K54] 78-13319
1. Mozart, Johann Chrysostom Wolfgang Amadeus, 1756-1791.

KING, Alexander 785.7'00924
Hyatt.
Mozart chamber music [by] A. Hyatt King. Seattle, University of Washington Press [1969, c1968] 68 p. music. 20 cm. (BBC music guides, 4) [MT145.M7K55 1969] 79-80512 0.95
1. Mozart, Johann Chrysostom Wolfgang Amadeus, 1756-1791. Works, chamber music. I. Title.
BIP

KOLB, Annette, 1875- 927.8
Mozart. With an introd. by Jean Giraudoux. Chicago, H. Regnery Co., 1956. 299p. illus. 22cm. [ML410] 56-13893
1. Mozart, Johann Chrysostom Wolfgang Amadeus, 1756-1791. I. Title.

KOLB, Annette, 1875- 780'.92'4 B
1967.
Mozart / Annette Kolb ; with an introd. by Jean Giraudoux. Westport, Conn. : Greenwood Press, 1975. 300 p., [7] leaves of plates : ill ; 21 cm. Reprint of the 1956 ed. published by H. Regnery, Chicago. [ML410.M9K772 1975] 74-29634 ISBN 0-8371-7977-7 lib.bdg. : 16.00
1. Mozart, Johann Chrysostom Wolfgang Amadeus, 1756-1791.

KOMROFF, Manuel, 1890- 780'.924 B
Mozart. Decorations by Warren Chappell. [1st ed.] New York, Knopf, 1956. 171 p. illus. 22 cm. A biography of the musical prodigy who composed his first symphony when he was eight years old, and completed almost a thousand works in his short life. [ML3930.M9K6] 92 AC 68
1. Mozart, Johann Chrysostom Wolfgang Amadeus, 1756-1791. I. Title.

LEVEY, Michael. 780'.924 B
The life & death of Mozart. New York, Stein and Day [1971] 278 p. illus. 25 cm. Bibliography: p. 271-272. [ML410.M9L35] 70-163451 ISBN 0-8128-1407-X 8.95
1. Mozart, Johann Chrysostom Wolfgang Amadeus, 1756-1791. I. Title.
BIP

MOZART, Johann Chrysostom 927.8
Wolfgang Amadeus, 1756-1791
Letters. Ed., introd. by Eric Blom. Selected from The letters of Mozart and his family, tr., annotated by Emily Anderson. Baltimore, Penguin [1968] vii, 277p. 18cm. (Pelican bk., A238) [ML410.M9A1954 1961] 62-3230 1.25 pap.,
I. Blom, Eric, 1888- ed. II. Title.

MOZART, Johann Chrysostom 780.924
Wolfgang Amadeus, 1756-1791
The letters of Mozart and his family [2v.] Chronologically arr., tr. [from German] ed., introd., notes, & indexes, by Emily Anderson. 2d ed., prep. by A. Hyatt King. Moica Carolan. London, Macmillan; New York, St. Martin's [c.]1966. [ML410.M9A187 1966] 64-7562
I. Mozart, Leopold, 1719-1787. II. Anderson, Emily. ed. and tr. III. Mozart, Leopold, 1719-1787. IV. Anderson, Emily. ed. and tr. V. King, Alexander Hyatt, ed. VI. Carolan, Monica, ed. VII. Title.

MOZART, Johann Chrysostom 927.8
Wolfgang Amadeus, 1756-1791
Mozart, the man and the artist revealed in his own words. Comp. annotated by Friedrich Kerst. Tr. [from German] ed., with additional notes, by Henry Edward Krehbiel [Gloucester, Mass., P. Smith, 1965] vii, 99p. (Dover bk. rebound) [ML410.M9A182] 3.00
I. Kerst, Friedrich, comp. II. Krehbiel, Henry Edward, 1854-1923, ed. and tr. III. Title.

MOZART, Johann Chrysostom 927.8
Wolfgang Amadeus, 1756-1791
Mozart, the man and the artist revealed in his own words. Comp., annotated by Friedrich Kert. Tr. [from German] ed., additional notes, by Henry Edward Krehbiel. New York, Dover [1965] vii, 99p. 22cm. Unabridged, unaltered repubn. of the work first pub. by Geoffrey Bles, London, in 1926. [ML410.M9A182] 64-18855 1.00 pap.,
I. Kerst, Friedrich, comp. II. Krehbiel, Henry Edward, 1854-1923, ed. and tr. III. Title.

MOZART, Johann Chrysostom 927.8
Wolgang Amadeus, 1756-1791
Letters. Ed., introd. by Eric Blom. Selected from The letters of Mozart and his family [Magnolia, Mass., Peter Smith, 1968] vii, 277p. 18cm. (Pelican bk., A238 rebound) [ML410.M9 A1954 1961] 3.50
I. Blom, Eric, 1888- ed. II. Title.

NETTL, Paul, 1889- 780'.924
Mozart and masonry. New York, Da Capo Press, 1970 [c1957] 150 p. 8 plates (facsims., ports.) 24 cm. (Da Capo Press music reprint series) Includes bibliographical references. [ML410.M91N4 1970] 78-114564 ISBN 3-06-719223-
1. Mozart, Johann Chrysostom Wolfgang Amadeus, 1756-1791. 2. Freemasons—Songs and music—History and criticism. I. Title.

NIEMTSCHEK, Franz Xaver. 780'.92'4 B
Life of Mozart = Leben des K.K. Kapellmeisters Wolfgang Gottlieb Mozart : 1798 / by Frank Niemetschek ; translated by Helen Mautner ; with an introd. by A. Hyatt King. Westport, Conn. : Hyperion Press, 1979. p. cm. (Encore music editions) Reprint of the 1956 ed. published by L. Hyman, London. [ML410.M9N33 1979b] 78-66914 ISBN 0-88355-754-1 : 12.50
1. Mozart, Johann Chrysostom Wolfgang Amadeus, 1756-1791. 2. Composers—Austria—Biography. I. Title. II. Title: Leben des K. K. Kapellmeisters Wolfgang Gottlieb Mozart. III. Series.

PEYSER, Herbert Francis, 1886- 927.8
Wolfgang Amadeus Mozart. New York, Grosset & Dunlap [1951] 59 p. illus. 18 cm. [ML410.M9P292] 51-7953
1. Mozart, Johann Chrysostom Wolfgang Amadeus, 1756-1791. I. Title.

POHL, Karl Ferdinand, 1819-1887. 780'.92
Mozart und Haydn in London, by C. F. Pohl. New York, Da Capo Press, 1970. 2 pts. in 1 v. facsim. 23 cm. (Da Capo Press music reprint series) Reprint of the 1867 ed. Contents.Contents.—1. Abth. Mozart in London.—2. Abth. Haydn in London. Bibliography: p. [vii]-xiv (2d pt.) [ML390.P74 1970] 70-125059
1. Mozart, Johann Chrysostom Wolfgang Amadeus, 1756-1791. 2. Haydn, Joseph, 1732-1809. 3. Music—England—London. I. Title. **BIP**

RAYNOR, Henry. 780'.92'4 B
Mozart / Henry Raynor. London : Macmillan, 1978. 152 p. : ill. (some col.) ; 25 cm. Includes index. Bibliography: p. 149. [ML410.M9R42] 78-312253 ISBN 0-333-21615-6 : 45.00
1. Mozart, Johann Chrysostom Wolfgang Amadeus, 1756-1791. 2. Composers—Biography.

SACHS, David. 780'.92'4 B
Mozart : a biography / by David Sachs. New York : Quick Fox, c1979. 120 p. : ill. ; 26 cm. "Recommended records": p. 117-118. [ML410.M9S14] 79-65943 ISBN 0-8256-3159-9 pbk. : 5.95
1. Mozart, Johann Chrysostom Wolfgang Amadeus, 1756-1791. 2. Composers—Austria—Biography.

SADIE, Stanley. 780'.92'4 B
Mozart. New York, Grossman, 1970 [c1965] 192 p. illus. 21 cm. ([Library of composers, 1]) [ML410.M9S15 1970] 70-94089 ISBN 0-670-49197-7 7.95
1. Mozart, Johann Chrysostom Wolfgang Amadeus, 1756-1791. I. Title. II. Series.

SAIDE, Stanley 780.924 (B)
Mozart. London, Calder & Boyars, 1965 [i.e. 1967] 192p. front. illus. (incl. music, ports.) facsims. tables. 21cm. (Illus. Calderbk. CB71) Bibl. [ML410.M9S15] 66-72252 4.00
1. Mozart, Johann Chrysostom Wolfgang Amadeus, 1756-1791. I. Title.
American distributor: Hillary House, New York.

SCHENK, Erich, 1902- 927.8
Mozart and his times. Edited and translated from the German by Richard & Clara Winston. [1st American ed.] New York, Knopf, 1959. xiv, 452, xxiii p. illus., ports., facsims. 25cm. Translation of Wolfgang Amadeus Mozart; eine Biographie. [ML410.M9S272] 59-9068
1. Mozart, Johann Chrysostom Wolfgang Amadeus, 1756-1791. I. Title.

SEROFF, Victor Ilyitch, 1902- 927.8
Wolfgang Amadeus Mozart. New York, Macmillan [c.1965] 124p. illus., ports. (pt. col.) 23cm. Selected discography [ML410.M9S4752] 65-11566 3.50; 3.64 lib. ed.,
1. Mozart, Johann Chrysostom Wolfgang Amadeus, 1756-1791. I. Title. **BIP**

SITWELL, Sacheverell, Sir, Bart., 1897- 780'.924 B
Mozart. Freeport, N.Y., Books for Libraries Press [1970] 191 p. port. 23 cm. Reprint of the 1932 ed. Bibliography: p. 185-186. [ML410.M9S58 1970] 71-114896
1. Mozart, Johann Chrysostom Wolfgang Amadeus, 1756-1791.

SITWELL, Sacheverell, Sir, bart., 1897- 780'.924 B
Mozart. Westport, Conn., Greenwood Press [1971] 191 p. port. 23 cm. Reprint of the 1932 ed. Bibliography: p. 185-186. [ML410.M9S58 1971] 78-100840
1. Mozart, Johann Chrysostom Wolfgang Amadeus, 1756-1791. **BIP**

TENSCHERT, Roland, 1894- 784'.092'4
Wolfgang Amadeus Mozart. Translated from the German by Emily Anderson. New York, Macmillan [1953] 152p. illus. 21cm. [ML410.M9T] A 54
1. Mozart, Johann Chrysostom Wolfgang Amadeus, 1756-1791. I. Title.

TURNER, Walter James, 1889-1946. 927.8
Mozart: the man and his works. Garden City, N. Y., Doubleday, 1954 [c1938] 390p. illus. 19cm. (Doubleday anchor books, A24) [ML410] 54-14920
1. Mozart, Johann Chrysostom Wolfgang Amadeus, 1756-1791. I. Title. **BIP**

TURNER, Walter James, 1889-1946 780.924
Mozart: the man and his works. This ed. rev., ed. by Christopher Raeburn. New York, Barnes & Noble [1966] xii, 376p. facsims., music, ports. 22cm. Bibl. [MN410.M9T9] 66-3544 7.00; 3.95 bds., pap.,
1. Mozart, Johann Chrysostom Wolfgang Amadeus, 1756-1791 I. Title.

TURNER, Walter James, 1889-1946. 780'.92'4
Mozart, the man and his works / by W. J. Turner. Westport, Conn. : Hyperion Press, 1979. p. cm. (Encore music editions) Reprint of the 1938 ed. published by V. Gollancz, London. "Catalogue of works": p. Bibliography: p. [ML410.M9T9 1979b] 78-20497 ISBN 0-88355-873-4 : 28.50
1. Mozart, Johann Chrysostom Wolfgang Amadeus, 1756-1791. 2. Composers—Austria—Biography. I. Title. II. Series.

VALENTIN, Erich, 1906- 927.8
Mozart, a pictorial biography. [Translated by Margaret Shenfield] New York, Viking Press [1960, c1959] 143 p. illus., ports., facsims. 24 cm. (A Studio book) [ML410.M9V272] 60-825
1. Mozart, Johann Chrysostom Wolfgang Amadeus, 1756-1791. 2. Mozart, Johann Chrysostom Wolfgang Amadeus, 1756-1791—Iconography.

YOUNG, Percy Marshall, 1912- 780.924 (B)
Mozart, [by] Percy M. Young. New York, D. White [c1966] viii, 72 p. illus., music. 23 cm. (Masters of music) [ML410.M9Y7] 66-25606
1. Mozart, Johann Chrysostom Wolfgang Amadeus, 1756-1791. I. Title. **BIP**

Mozart, Johann Chrysostom Wolfgang Amadeus—Fiction.

KAUFMANN, Helen (Loeb) 927.8
The story of Mozart; illustrated by Eric M. Simon. New York, Grosset Dunlap [c1955] 179p. illus. 22cm. (Signature books [34]) [ML3930.M9K4] 55-6741
1. Mozart, Johann Chrysostom Wolfgang Amadeus—Fiction. 2. Music—Juvenile literature. 3. Musical fiction. I. Title.

Mozart, Johann Chrysostom Wolfgang Amadeus, 1756-1791—Juvenile literature.

BISHOP CLARE (HUCHET). 780.924
Mozart; music magician. Illus. by Paul Frame. Champaign, Ill., Garrard [1968] 138p. illus., music. 22cm. (Creative arts biogs.) [ML3930.M9B6] 67-16856 2.49
1. Mozart, Johann Chrysostom Wolfgang Amadeus, 1756-1791—Juvenile literature. I. Title.

JENKINS, Alan. 92
The Young Mozart. Illustrated by Anne Linton. New York, Roy Publishers [1961] 135p. illus. 21cm. [ML3930.M9J4] 61-11041
1. Mozart, Johann Chrysostom Wolfgang Amadeus—Juvenile literature. I. Title.

MIRSKY, Reba Paeff. 927.8
Mozart. Illustrated by W. T. Mars. Chicago, Follett Pub. Co. [1960] 144p. illus. 25cm. [ML3930.M9M57] 60-13358
1. Mozart, Johann Chrysostom Wolfgang Amadeus—Juvenile literature. I. Title.
1. Mozart, Johann Chrysostom Wolfgang Amadeus, 1756-1791—Juvenile literature. I. Title.

WOODFORD, Peggy 780.924
Mozart. Illus. by David Knight. [1st Amer. ed.] New York, Walck, 1966. 103p. illus. 21cm. (Composers and their times) Bibl. [ML3930.M9W6 1966] 66-7042 3.50

Mozier, Aloysius Eugene Francis Patrick,

MOZIER, Aloysius Eugene Francis Patrick, 1903- 923.573
A bell in the heart, the autobiography of Patty Gardenseed, America's ambassador of good will [as told to] Trixie-Ann Schubert. [1st ed.] Los Angeles, Western Publishers, 1963. 285 p. 22 cm. Patty Gardenseed, pseud. of Aloysius Eugene Francis Patrick Mozier. [CT275.M676A3] 63-11701
I. Schubert, Trixie Ann (Gehrung) II. Title.

Mqhayi, Samuel Edward Krune, 1875-1945—Biography.

MQHAYI, Samuel Edward Krune, 1875-1945. 896'.39
Mqhayi in translation / edited by Patricia E. Scott. Grahamstown : Department of African Languages, Rhodes University, 1976. 47 p. ; 21 cm. (Communication - Dept. of African Languages, Rhodes University ; no. 6) Contents.Contents.—A short autobiography of Samuel Krune Mqhayi, translated by W. G. Bennie.—The death of Hintsa and The dismissal of Sir Benjamin D'Urban, translated by J. K. Bokwe. Bibliography: p. 39-42 [PL8795.9.M7Z5213 1976] 77-566249 ISBN 0-949980-72-2 : R1.00
1. Mqhayi, Samuel Edward Krune, 1875-1945—Biography. 2. Authors, Xosa—Biography. I. Scott, Patricia Elena. II. Title. III. Series: Rhodes University, Grahamstown, South Africa. Dept. of African Languages. Communication — Dept. of African Languages, Rhodes University ; no. 6.

Mrabet, Mohammed, 1940- —Biography.

MRABET, Mohammed, 1940- 892'.7'36 B
Look & move on / Mohammed Mrabet ; taped and translated from the Moghrebi by Paul Bowles. Santa Barbara : Black Sparrow Press, 1976. 125 p. ; 23 cm. [PJ7850.R3Z52] 75-41349 ISBN 0-87685-255-X : 10.00. ISBN 0-87685-256-8 signed : 15.00. ISBN 0-87685-254-1 pbk. : 4.00
1. Mrabet, Mohammed, 1940- —Biography. I. Title. **BIP**

Mtusu, Daniel, d. 1917.

FRASER, Donald, 1870-1933. 286'.6'0924 B
The autobiography of an African; retold in biographical form & in the wild African setting of the life of Daniel Mtusu. Westport, Conn., Negro Universities Press [1970] 209 p. illus., port. 23 cm. Reprint of the 1925 ed. [BV3625.N82F7 1970] 78-138006 ISBN 0-8371-5653-X
1. Mtusu, Daniel, d. 1917. 2. Missions to Angoni. I. Title.

Mucha, Alphonse Marie, 1860-1939.

MUCHA, Jiri, 1915- 709.437(B)
Alphonse Mucha: his life and art, by his son; research by M. K. London, Heinemann, 1966. viii, 391p. 24 plates (incl. ports.) 23cm. Bibl. [N6838.M8M79] 67-70081 10.00
1. Mucha, Alphonse Marie, 1860-1939. I. Title.
American distributor: Humanities, New York.

Mudd, Samuel Alexander, 1833-1883.

HIGDON, Hal. 926.1
The Union vs. Dr. Mudd. Chicago, Follett Pub. Co., 1964. 235 p. illus., map, ports. 22 cm. Bibliography: p. 221-222. [E457.5.M93] 64-15332
1. Mudd, Samuel Alexander, 1833-1883. 2. Lincoln, Abraham, Pres. U.S., 1809-1865—Assassination. I. Title.

Muddiman, Henry, 1629?-1692.

MUDDIMAN, Joseph George, 1862?- 942.06'6
The king's journalist, 1659-1689; studies in the reign of Charles II. New York, A. M. Kelley, 1971. x, 294 p. illus., facsims., ports. 22 cm. (The English book trade) Reprint of the 1923 ed. Includes bibliographical references. [DA447.M8M8 1971] 74-125774 ISBN 0-678-00729-2
1. Muddiman, Henry, 1629?-1692. 2. Gt. Brit.—History—Charles II, 1660-1685. 3. Journalism—Gt. Brit. I. Title.

Mudgett, Herman W., alias H. H. Holmes, 1861-1896.

FRANKE, David. 364.1'523'0924 B
The torture doctor / David Franke. New York : Hawthorn Books, c1975. xix, 231 p. : ill. ; 25 cm. Includes index. [HV6248.M8F7 1975] 75-2561 ISBN 0-8015-7832-9 : 8.95
1. Mudgett, Herman W., alias H. H. Holmes, 1861-1896. I. Title.

FRANKE, David. 364.15230924
The torture doctor David Franke. New York : Avon Books ,1976 c1975. 256 p. : ill. ; 18 cm. Includes index. [HV6248.M8F7] ISBN 0-8015-7832-9 pbk. : 1.75
1. Mudgett, Herman W., alias H. H. Holmes, 1861-1896 I. Title.
L.C. card no. for 1975 Hawthorn Books edition: 75-2561. **BIP**

Mueller, Gustav Emil,

MUELLER, Gustav Emil, 1898- 191
Instead of a biography. New York, Philosophical Library [1970] viii, 237 p. port. 23 cm. [B945.M82A3] 79-97936 5.95
I. Title.

Muggeridge, Malcolm, 1903-

MUGGERIDGE, Malcolm, 1903- 070'.92'4 B
The infernal grove. New York, Morrow, 1974 [c1973] 280 p. 24 cm. (His Chronicles of wasted time, 2) [PR6025.U5Z5152 vol. 2] 74-1258 ISBN 0-688-00300-1 8.95
1. Muggeridge, Malcolm, 1903- I. Title. II. Series. **BIP**

Muhammad 'Abduh, 1849-1905.

AMIN, 'Uthman, 1905- 922.97
Muhammad 'Abduh [by] Osman Amin; translated from the Arabic by Charles Wendell. Washington, American Council of Learned Societies. 1953. vi. 103 p. 23 cm. (American Council of learned Societies. Near Eastern Translation Program. [Publication] no. 4) Bibliographical references included in "Notes" (p. 100-103) [BP80.M8A713] 54-781
1. Muhammad 'Abduh, 1849-1905. I. Title. II. Series: American Council of Learned Societies Devoted to Humanistic Studies. Near Eastern Translation Program. [Publication] no. 4

Muhammad 'Abduh, 1849-1905.

MUHAMMAD Zaki Badawi. 301.24'2'0962
The reformers of Egypt / M. A. Zaki Badawi. London : Croom Helm, c1978. 160 p. ; 23 cm. Includes bibliographical references and index. [BP64.E3M84 1978] 78-312985 ISBN 0-85664-651-2 : 19.00
1. al-Afghani, Jamal al-Din, 1838-1897. 2. Muhammad 'Abduh, 1849-1905. 3. Muhammad Rashid Rida. 4. Muslims in Egypt—Biography. 5. Islam—Egypt—History. I. Title.

Muhammad 'Ali, khedive of Egypt, 1769-1849.

TUGAY, Emine Foat, 1897- 929.2
Three centuries; family chronicles of Turkey and Egypt. Foreword by the Dowager Marchioness of Reading. New York, Oxford [c.]1963. x, 324p. illus., ports., geneal. tables. 23cm. Bibl. 63-6071 6.75
1. Muhammad 'Ali, khedive of Egypt, 1769-1849. 2. Turkey—Biog. 3. Egypt—Biog. I. Title.

Muhammad Ali, 1942-

*ATYEO, Don 796.830924
The holy Warrior Muhammad Ali; an illustrated biography by Don Atyeo and Felix Dennis. New York, Simon and Schuster, 1975 112 p. ill. 28 cm. (A Fireside Book) Bibliography: p. 112. [GV1132.M84] ISBN 0-671-22201-5 2.95 (pbk.)
1. Muhammad Ali, 1942- 2. Boxing—Biography. I. Dennis, Felix, joint author. II. Title.

*BURCHARD, Marshall. 796.8'3'0924 B
Muhammad Ali. New York, G. P. Putnam's Sons, [1975] 98 p. ill. 22 cm. (Sports hero) [GV1132.M84] 75-10445 ISBN 0-399-60888-5 4.99 (Lib. bdg.)
1. Muhammad Ali, 1942- 2. Boxing. I. Title.

COTTRELL, John. 796.8'3'0924
Muhammad Ali, who once was Cassius Clay. New York, Funk & Wagnalls [1968, c1967] 363 p. ports. 22 cm. First published in London under title: Man of destiny. [GV1132.C55C6 1968] 68-13265
1. Muhammad Ali, 1942- I. Title.

*KING, David. 796.830924
I am King; a photographic biography of Muhammad Ali. [Baltimore] Penguin Books [1975] 1 vol. (unpaged) ill. 30 cm. [GV1132.M84] 4.95 (pbk.)
1. Muhammad Ali, 1942- 2. Boxing—Biography. I. Title.

MUHAMMAD Ali, 1942- 796.8'3'0924 B
The greatest : my own story / Muhammad Ali, with Richard Durham. London : Hart-Davis, MacGibbon, 1976. xvi, 413 p. ; 25 cm. [GV1132.M84A33 1976] 76-358732 ISBN 0-246-10944-0 : £3.95
1. Muhammad Ali, 1942- 2. Boxing. I. Durham, Richard. II. Title. BIP

MUHAMMAD 'Ali, 1942- 796.8'3'0924 B
The greatest, my story [by] Muhammad Ali as told by Richard Durham. New York, Ballantine Books [1976 c1975] 528 p. 18 cm. [GV1132.M84A33] 1.95 (pbk.)
1. Muhammad Ali, 1942- 2. Boxing. I. Durham, Richard. II. Title.
L.C. card no. of 1975 Random House edition: 75-10293.

PACHECO, Ferdie. 796.8'3'0924 B
Fight doctor / Ferdie Pacheco. New York : Simon and Schuster, c1977. p. cm. [GV1132.M84P3] 77-7064 ISBN 0-671-22894-3 : 8.95
1. Muhammad Ali, 1942- 2. Pacheco, Ferdie. 3. Boxers (Sports)—United States—Biography. 4. Physicians—Florida—Miami—Biography. 5. Sports medicine. I. Title. BIP

SCHULBERG, Budd. 796.8'3'0924
Loser and still champion: Muhammad Ali. [1st ed.] Garden City, N.Y., Doubleday, 1972. 158 p. illus. 21 cm. [GV1132.M84S3] 76-176351 5.95
1. Muhammad Ali, 1942- I. Title.

SHEED, Wilfrid. 796.8'3'0924 B
Muhammad Ali : a portrait in words and photographs / by Wilfrid Sheed. [New York] : Crowell, c1975. 255 p. : ill. ; 29 cm. "An Alskog book." [GV1132.M84S47] 75-18714 ISBN 0-690-00958-5 : 19.95
1. Muhammad Ali, 1942- 2. Boxing.

SULLIVAN, George Edward, 1927- 796.83
The Cassius Clay story, by George Sullivan. New York, Fleet Pub. Corp. [1964] 116 p. ports. 21 cm. [GV1132.C55S9] 64-7713
1. Muhammad Ali, 1942- I. Title.

TORRES, Jose, 1936- 796.8'3'0924 B
Sting like a bee; the Muhammad Ali story. Pref. by Norman Mailer; epilogue by Budd Schulberg; sketches by Le Roy Neiman. London, New York, Abelard-Schuman [1971] 223 p. illus. 22 cm. [GV1132.M84T6] 70-157988 ISBN 0-200-71840-1 6.95 (U.S.)
1. Muhammad Ali, 1942- I. Title.

Muhammad Ali, 1942- —Juvenile literature.

EDWARDS, Audrey. 796.8'3'0924 B
Muhammad Ali: the people's champ/ by Audrey Edwards with Gary Wohl. 1st ed. Boston : Little, Brown, c1977. p. cm. A biography of an Olympic gold medal winner who went on to become heavyweight champion of the world. [GV1132.M84E39] 92 77-4719 ISBN 0-316-21172-9 : 6.95
1. Muhammad Ali, 1942- —Juvenile literature. 2. Boxers—Unites States—Biography—Juvenile literature. I. Wohl, Gary, joint author. II. Title. BIP

EDWARDS, Audrey. 796.8'3'0924 B
The picture life of Muhammad Ali / by Audrey Edwards and Gary Wohl. New York : Watts, 1976. [48] p. : ill. ; 23 cm. Easy-to-read biography of Muhammad Ali who fights for what he believes and usually wins. [GV1132.M84E4] 92 76-10999 ISBN 0-531-00327-2 lib.bdg. : 3.90
1. Muhammad Ali, 1942- —Juvenile literature. 2. Boxing—Juvenile literature. I. Wohl, Gary, joint author. II. Title. BIP

ELDRED, Patricia Mulrooney. 796.830924 B
Boxing's world champion, Muhammad Ali / by Patricia Mulrooney Eldred. Mankato, MN : Creative Education/Childrens Press, 1977. 30 p. ; 19 cm. (All-star series) A brief profile of a Heavyweight Champion of the World focusing on his recent fights. [GV1132.M84E44] 92 76-44212 ISBN 0-87191-586-3 lib.bdg. : 4.95
1. Muhammad Ali, 1942- —Juvenile literature. 2. Boxers (Sports)—United States—Biography—Juvenile literature. I. Title.

HANO, Arnold, 1922- 796.8'3'0924 B
Muhammad Ali, the champion / by Arnold Hano. New York : Putnam, c1977. p. cm. (Putnam sports shelf) Includes index. A biography of the heavyweight champion whose colorful antics in and out of the ring have made him a legend all over the world. [GV1132.M84H36 1977] 92 76-50101 ISBN 0-399-61091-X lib. bdg. : 5.29
1. Muhammad Ali, 1942- —Juvenile literature. 2. Boxers (Sports)—United States—Biography—Juvenile literature. I. Title.

OLSEN, James T. 796.8'3'0924 B
Muhammad Ali: "I am the greatest," by James T. Olsen. Illustrated by Harold Henriksen. Mankato, Minn., Creative Education; distributed by Childrens Press, Chicago [1974] 30 p. illus. (part col.) 25 cm. (Creative's superstars) "Prepared for the publisher by Educreative Systems, inc." A biography of a prizefighter whose dreams were realized when at twenty-two he became heavyweight champion of the world. [GV1132.M84O42] 92 73-10367 ISBN 0-87191-262-7 4.95
1. Muhammad Ali, 1942- —Juvenile literature. I. Henriksen, Harold, illus. II. Title.

RUDEEN, Kenneth. 796.8'3'0924 B
Muhammad Ali / by Kenneth Rudeen ; illustrated by George Ford. New York : Crowell, [1976] p. cm. Biography of Muhammad Ali whose boxing career has involved amateur championships, the Olympics, and professional world titles. [GV1132.M84R82] 92 76-12093 ISBN 0-690-01128-8 : 5.95
1. Muhammad Ali, 1942- —Juvenile literature. 2. Boxing—Juvenile literature. I. Ford, George Cephas. II. Title.

THOMAS, Linda, 1947- 796.8'3'0924 B
Muhammad Ali / by Linda Thomas ; illustrated by Harold Henriksen. Mankato, Mich. : Creative Education, [1975] c1976. p. cm. A brief biography of the world heavyweight boxing champion, Muhammad Ali. [GV1132.M84T46] 92 75-28194 ISBN 0-87191-262-7 lib.bdg. : 4.95
1. Muhammad Ali, 1942- —Juvenile literature. 2. Boxing—Juvenile literature. I. Henriksen, Harold. II. Title.

WILSON, Beth P. 796.8'3'0924 B
Muhammad Ali / by Beth P. Wilson ; illustrated by Floyd Sowell. New York : Putnam, [1974] 62 p. : ill. ; 23 cm. A brief biography of the prizefighter whose skill won him an Olympic gold medal and the heavyweight championship of the world. [GV1132.M84W54 1974] ISBN 0-399-60885- lib. bdg. : 3.86
1. Muhammad Ali, 1942- —Juvenile literature. 2. Boxing—Juvenile literature. I. Sowell, Floyd, ill. II. Title. BIP

Muhammad, the prophet.

ANDRA, Tor, Bp., 1885-1947. 922.97
Mohammed, the man and his faith. Translated by Theophil Menzel. New York, Harper [1960] 194 p. 21 cm. (Harper torchbooks, TB62. The Cloister library) [BP75.A57 1960] 60-5489
1. Muhammad, the prophet. BIP

ANDRa, Tor, Bp., 1885-1947. 297'.63 B
Mohammed; the man and his faith. Translated by Theophil Menzel. Freeport, N.Y., Books for Libraries Press [1971] 274 p. facsim. 23 cm. Reprint of the 1936 ed. Includes bibliographical references. [BP75.A57 1971] 79-160954 ISBN 0-8369-5821-7
1. Muhammad, the prophet.

ANDRAE, Tor. Bp., 1885-1947. 297
Mohammed, the man and his faith. Trenlsated by Theophil Menzel. New York, Barnes and Noble [1957] 196p. illus. 22cm. Bibliographical footnotes. [BP75.A] A 58
1. Muhammad, the prophet. I. Title.

DERMENGHEM, Emile, 1872- 297'.63 B
Muhammad and the Islamic tradition. Translated from the French by Jean M. Watt. Westport, Conn., Greenwood Press [1974, c1958] 191 p. illus. 22 cm. (Men of wisdom, MW6) Reprint of the ed. published by Harper, New York, which was issued as no. MW6 of Men of wisdom. Bibliography: p. 188-191. [BP75.D393 1974] 73-15204 ISBN 0-8371-7163-6
1. Muhammad, the prophet. 2. Islam. I. Title. II. Series. BIP

GLUBB, John Bagot, Sir, 1897- 297.63 B
The life and times of Muhammad, by John Bagot Glubb (Glubb Pasha). New York, Stein and Day [1970] 416 p. geneal. tables, maps. 25 cm. Bibliography: p. [403]-405. [BP75.G58] 74-87954 10.00
1. Muhammad, the prophet. I. Title. BIP

HOSAIN, Safdar. 297'.63'0924
Who was Mohammed. [Hyderabad, India, 1967] 122 p. 22 cm. Rs 3 [BP75.H67] S A
1. Muhammad, the prophet. I. Title.

IRVING, Washington, 1783-1859. 297'.63 B
Mahomet and his successors. New York, Putnam. [New York, AMS Press, 1973] 2 v. illus. 19 cm. (The works of Washington Irving, v. 15-16) At head of title: Hudson edition. Reprint of the 1889 ed. [DS38.3.176 1973] 73-8685 20.00 ea.
1. Muhammad, the prophet. 2. Islamic Empire—History. I. Title.

IRVING, Washington, 1783-1859. 297'.63 B
Mahomet and his successors. Edited by Henry A. Pochmann and E. N. Feltskog. Madison, University of Wisconsin Press, 1970. xiv, 651 p. facsims., map. 24 cm. (The Complete works of Washington Irving) Includes bibliographical references. [DS38.3.176 1970] 77-15207
1. Muhammad, the prophet. 2. Islamic Empire—History. I. Pochmann, Henry August, 1901- ed. II. Feltskog, E. N., ed. III. Title.

MARGOLIOUTH, David Samuel, 1858-1940. 297'.63 B
Mohammed and the rise of Islam. Freeport, N.Y., Books for Libraries Press [1972] xxvi, 481 p. illus. 23 cm. Reprint of the 1905 ed., issued in series: Heroes of the nations. Bibliography: p. xxiii-xxvi. [BP75.M3 1972] 73-38361 ISBN 0-8369-6778-X
1. Muhammad, the prophet. I. Title. II. Series: Heroes of the nations. BIP

MARGOLIOUTH, David Samuel, 1858-1940. 297'.63 B
Mohammed and the rise of Islam / by D. S. Margoliouth. New York : AMS Press, 1978. xxvi, 481 p., [27] leaves of plates (1 fold.) : ill. ; 19 cm. Reprint of the 1905 ed. published by Putnam, New York, in series: Heroes of the nations. Includes index. Bibliography: p. xxiii-xxvi. [BP75.M3 1978] 73-14455 ISBN 0-404-58273-7 : 30.00
1. Muhammad, the prophet. 2. Muslims in Saudi Arabia—Biography. I. Title. II. Series: Heroes of the nations.

RODINSON, Maxime. 297'.63 B
Mohammed. Translated by Anne Carter. [1st American ed.] New York, Pantheon Books [1971] xix, 360 p. illus. 22 cm. Bibliography: p. 315-324. [BP75.R5713 1971] 69-20189 ISBN 0-394-47110-5 8.95
1. Muhammad, the prophet.

RODINSON, Maxime. 297'.63 B
Mohammed. Translated by Anne Carter. New York, Vintage Books [1974, c1971] xix, 360 p. maps. 19 cm. Bibliography: p. 343-[346] [BP75.13.R613 1974] 73-14953 ISBN 0-394-71011-8 2.45 (pbk.)
1. Muhammad, the prophet.

SUGANA, Gabriele Mandel. 297'.63
The life and times of Mohammed; translator [from the Italian] Francis Koval. London, New York, Hamlyn, 1968. [1], 77 p. (chiefly illus. (chiefly col.) col. maps) 30 cm. (Portraits of greatness) German translation has title: Mohammed und seine zeit. Col. illus. on lining papers. [BP75.S9 1968] 70-433824 ISBN 0-600-03149-7 17/6
1. Muhammed, the prophet. I. Title.

WARREN, Ruth. 922.97
Muhammad, prophet of Islam. New York, F. Watts [1965] 133 p. 22 cm. (Immortals of philosophy and religion) [BP75.W296] 65-13070
1. Muhammad, the prophet.

WARREN, Ruth 922.97
Muhammad, prophet of Islam. New York, Watts [c.1965] 133p. 22cm. (Immortals of philo. and rel.) [BP75.W296] 65-13070 2.95
1. Muhammad, the prophet. I. Title.

WATT, William Montgomery. 922.97
Muhammad: prophet and statesman. [London] Oxford University Press, 1961. 250 p. illus. 19 cm. "Essentially an abridgement of the [author's] . . . Muhammad at Mecca and Muhammad at Medina." Includes bibliography. [BP75.W33] 61-2473
1. Muhammad, the prophet. I. Title.

WATT, William Montgomery 922.97
Muhammad: prophet and statesman [New York] Oxford [1964, c.1961] 250p. map. 19cm. (78) Abridgement of the author's Muhammad at Mecca and Muhammad at Medina. Bibl. 1.85 pap.,
1. Muhammad, the prophet. I. Title. BIP

WATT, William Montgomery, 922.97
Muhammad at Mecca. Oxford, Clarendon Press, 1953. xvi. 192p. 23cm. Sequel: Muhammad at Medina. Bibliography: p. [viii]-ix. [BP75.W3] 53-13179
1. Muhammad. the prophet. I. Title.

WATT, William Montgomery. 922.97
Muhammad at Medina. Oxford, Clarendon Press, 1956. xiv, 418 p. map. 23 cm. "Sequel to Muhammad at Mecca." Bibliographical footnotes. [BP75.W32] 56-4035
1. Muhammad, the prophet. I. Title.

WATT, William Montgomery. 922.97
Muhammad at Medina. Oxford. Clarendon Press, 1956. xiv. 418p. map. 23cm. 'Sequel to Muhammad at Mecca.' Bibliographical footnotes. [BP75.W32] 56-4035
1. Muhammad. the prophet. I. Title. **BIP**

WATT, William Montgomery 922.97
Muhammad: prophet and statesman. [New York] Oxford Univ. Press [c.]1961. 250p. illus. Bibl. 61-24730 4.00
1. Muhammad, the prophet. I. Title.

WATT, William 297'.63 B
Montgomery.
Muhammad: prophet and statesman [by] W. Montgomery Watt. London, New York, Oxford University Press [1974, c1961] 250 p. 21 cm. (A Galaxy book, 409) "Essentially an abridgement of the ... [author's] Muhammad at Mecca and Muhammad at Medina." Includes bibliographical references. [BP75.W33 1974] 74-163338 ISBN 0-19-881078-4 2.95 (pbk.)
1. Muhammad, the prophet.

Muhammad, the prophet—Biography.

RODINSON, Maxime. 297'.63 B
Mohammed / Maxime Rodinson ; translated from the French by Anne Carter ; with a new introd. on contemporary Islam by the author. New York : Pantheon Books, 1979. p. cm. Translation of Mahomet. Reprint of the 1971 ed. published by Pantheon Books, New York. Includes index. Bibliography: p. [BP75.13.R613 1979] 79-17158 ISBN 0-394-50908-0 : 15.00 ISBN 0-394-73822-5 pbk. : 4.95
1. Muhammad, the prophet—Biography. 2. Muslims—Saudi Arabia—Biography. I. Title.

Muhammad, the prophet—Juvenile literature.

KELEN, Betty. 297'.63 B
Muhammad : the messenger of God / by Betty Kelen. 1st ed. Nashville: T. Nelson, [1975] 278 p. ; 21 cm. Includes index. Bibliography: p. 261. [BP75.K43] 75-5792 ISBN 0-8407-6440-5 : 6.95
1. Muhammad, the prophet—Juvenile literature. **BIP**

PIKE, Edgar Royston, 297'.63 B
1896-
Mohammed; prophet of the religion of Islam [by] E. Royston Pike. New York, F. A. Praeger [1969, c1965] viii, 117 p. illus. 23 cm. (Praeger pathfinder biographies) 1962 and 1964 editions published under title: Mohammed, founder of the religion of Islam. Bibliography: p. 113-114. A biography of the founder of Islam who is revered by his followers as the first prophet of Allah. Includes chapters of the Koran, what a Muslim believes, and how he practices his faith. [BP75.P5 1969] 92 68-55017
1. Muhammad, the prophet—Juvenile literature. I. Title.

Muhlenberg, Henry Melchior,

MUHLENBERG, Henry 922.473
Melchior, 1711-1787.
The journals of Henry Melchior Muhlenberg. Translated by Theodore G. Tappert and John W. Doberstein. Philadelphia, Evangelical Lutheran Ministerium of Pennsylvania and Adjacent States, 1942-58. 3v. port. 27cm. [BX8080.M9A4] 42-18316
I. Title.

MUHLENBERG, Henry 922.473
Melchior, 1711-1787.
The notebook of a colonial clergyman, condensed from the Journal of Henry Melchior Muhlenberg. Translated and edited by Theodore G. Tappert and John W. Doberstein. Philadelphia. Muhlenberg Press, 1959. vi, 250p. 21cm. [BX8080.M9A43] 59-10536
I. Title.

Muhoz Rivera, Luis. 1859-1916.

LEBRON, Ramon, 1868- 923.27295
La vida del procer. [1. ed.] San Juan, P. R., 1954. 76p. 17cm. [F1975.M8L4] 56-34040
1. Muhoz Rivera, Luis. 1859-1916. I. Title.

Muir, Edwin, 1887-1959.

BUTTER, Peter H. 828'.9'1209 B
Edwin Muir: man and poet [by] P. H. Butter. New York, Barnes & Noble [1967, c1966] viii, 314 p. 23 cm. Bibliography: p. 301-308. [PR6025.U6Z58 1967] 67-1820
1. Muir, Edwin, 1887-1959.

BUTTER, Peter H. 828'.9'12 B
Edwin Muir, man and poet / P. H. Butter. Westport, Conn. : Greenwood Press, 1976, c1966. viii, 314 p. ; 23 cm. Reprint of the ed. published by Oliver & Boyd, Edinburgh, which was issued as no. 7 in Biography and criticism. Includes index. Bibliography: p. 301-308. [PR6025.U6Z58 1976] 76-11018 ISBN 0-8371-8169-0 lib.bdg. : 18.00
1. Muir, Edwin, 1887-1959. I. Title.

HIXSON, Allie Corbin. 828'.9'1209
Edwin Muir : a critical study / by Allie Corbin Hixson. 1st ed. New York : Vantage Press, c1977. 247 p. : ill. ; 22 cm. Bibliography: p. 241-247. [PR6025.U6Z66] 77-151304 ISBN 0-533-02270-3 : 8.95
1. Muir, Edwin, 1887-1959. 2. Authors, Scottish—20th century—Biography. **BIP**

MUIR, Edwin, 1887- 928.2
An autobiography. New York, W. Sloane Associates [1954] 287p. illus. 23cm. [PR6025] 54-14937
I. Title.

MUIR, Edwin, 1887-1959 928.2
An autobiography. New York, Seabury [1968, c.1954] 287p. map. 20cm. (SP52) [PR6025] 2.45 pap.,
I. Title.

Muir, John, 1838-1914.

BADE, William 333.7'2'0924 B
Frederic, 1871-1936.
The life and letters of John Muir. Boston, Houghton Mifflin, 1924. [New York, AMS Press, 1973] 2 v. illus. 19 cm. [QH31.M9B3 1973] 77-153302 45.00
1. Muir, John, 1838-1914. **BIP**

DOUGLAS, William Orville, 925.9
1898-
Muir of the mountains. Illustrated by Harve Stein. Boston, Houghton Mifflin, 1961. 183 p. illus. 22 cm. (North star books [25]) [QH31.M9D6] 61-5633
1. Muir, John, 1838-1914. I. Title.

MORRILL, Madge (Haines) 925.9
John Muir, protector of the wilds [by] Madge Haines and Leslie Morrill. Illustrated by Avery Johnson. New York, Abingdon Press [1957] 128p. illus. 21cm. (Makers of America) [QH31.M9M6] 57-13737
1. Muir, John, 1838-1914. I. Morrill, Leslie, joint author. II. Title.

MORRILL, Madge (Haines) 925.9
John Muir, protector of the wilds [by] Madge Haines and Leslie Morrill. Illustrated by Avery Johnson. New York, Abingdon Press [1957] 128p. illus. 21cm. (Makers of America) [QH31.M9M6] 57-13737
1. Muir, John, 1838-1914. I. Morrill. Leslie, joint author. II. Title.

MUIR, John, 1838- 917.94'04'4
1914.
John of the mountains : the unpublished journals of John Muir / edited by Linnie Marsh Wolfe. Madison : University of Wisconsin Press, [1979] c1938. xviii, 459 p. ; 22 cm. Includes index. [QH105.C2M8 1979] 79-83859 ISBN 0-299-07880-9 : 22.50 ISBN 0-299-07884-1 pbk. : 6.95
1. Muir, John, 1838-1914. 2. Natural history—California. 3. California—Description and travel. 4. Alaska—Description and travel. 5. Naturalists—United States—Biography. I. Wolfe, Linnie Marsh, 1881-1945. II. Title.

MUIR, John, 1838- 917.94'4'044
1914.
My first summer in the Sierra / by John Muir. Boston : Houghton Mifflin, 1979, c1916. x, 271 p., [23] leaves of plates : ill. ; 21 cm. Includes index. [QH31.M9A34 1979] 79-119676 ISBN 0-395-28521-6 : 5.95
1. Muir, John, 1838-1914. 2. Natural history—Sierra Nevada Mountains. 3. Sierra Nevada Mountains. 4. Naturalists—United States—Biography. I. Title. **BIP**

MUIR, John, 1838-1914 925.9
The story of my boyhood and youth. Foreword by Vernon Carstensen. Madison, Univ. of Wisc. Pr., 1965[c.1912-1965] xviii, 227p. illus. 19cm. [QH31.M9A35] 65-14539 6.00; 1.95 pap.,
I. Title.

MUIR, John, 1838-1914. 925.9
The wilderness world of John Muir. With an introd. and interpretive comments by Edwin Way Teale; illustrated by Henry B. Kane. Boston, Houghton Mifflin, 1954. xx, 332p. illus. 22cm. 'Selections from Muir's writings.' [QH31.M9A37] 54-9040
I. Teale, Edwin Way, 1899- ed. II. Title.

NORMAN, Charles, 1904- 925.9
John Muir, father of our national parks. New York, Messner [1957] 191p. 22cm. Includes bibliographies. [QH31.M9N6] 57-6591
1. Muir, John, 1838-1914. I. Title.

NORMAN, Charles, 1904- 925.9
John Muir, father of our national parks. New York, Messner [1957] 191 p. 22 cm. Includes bibliographies. [QH31.M9N6] 57-6591
1. Muir, John, 1838-1914.

SARGENT, 917.94'47'040924 B
Shirley.
John Muir in Yosemite. [1st ed.] Yosemite, Calif., Flying Spur Press [1971] 48 p. illus. 28 cm. On cover: Foreword by John Muir's granddaughter. Bibliography: p. 48. [F868.Y6S23] 77-32109
1. Muir, John, 1838-1914. 2. Yosemite Valley. I. Title.

SWIFT, Hildegarde (Hoyt) 925.9
From the eagle's wing; a biography of John Muir. Illustrated by Lynd Ward. New York, Morrow, 1962. 287 p. illus. 22 cm. [QH31.M9S9] 62-7055
1. Muir, John, 1838-1914. I. Title.

SWIFT, Hildegarde Hoyt. 925.9
From the eagle's wing; a biography of John Muir. Illustrated by Lynd Ward. New York, Morrow, 1962. 287 p. illus. 22 cm. [QH31.M9S9] 62-7055
1. Muir, John, 1838-1914. I. Title.

WOLFE, Linnie Marsh, 500.9'2'4 B
1881-1945.
Son of the wilderness : the life of John Muir / Linnie Marsh Wolfe. Madison : University of Wisconsin Press, 1978, c1945. xix, 364 p., [14] leaves of plates : ill. ; 22 cm. Reprint of the 1st ed. published by Knopf, New York. Includes index. Bibliography: p. 349-350. [QH31.M9W6 1978] 78-53294 ISBN 0-299-07730-6 : 20.00 ISBN 0-299-07734-9 pbk. : 6.95
1. Muir, John, 1838-1914. 2. Naturalists—United States—Biography. I. Title. **BIP**

Muir, John, 1838-1914—Juvenile literature.

CLARK, Margaret 333.7'2'0924 B
Goff.
John Muir, friend of nature. Illustrated by Cary. Champaign, Ill., Garrard Pub. Co. [1974] 80 p. col. illus. 23 cm. (A Discovery book) A biography of the nineteenth-century naturalist, explorer, and writer who was influential in establishing our national park system. [QH31.M9C53] 92 73-13571 ISBN 0-8116-6315-9 2.84
1. Muir, John, 1838-1914—Juvenile literature. I. Cary, Louis F., 1915- illus. II. Title.

DINES, Glen. 333.7'2'0924 B
John Muir / written and illustrated by Glen Dines. New York : Putnam, [1974] 64 p. : ill. (some col.) ; 23 cm. (A See and read biography) A simple biography of the man responsible for the preservation of the Yosemite Valley and other beautiful places in the United States. [QH31.M9D56] 92 73-87217 ISBN 0-399-60880-X lib. bdg. : 3.96
1. Muir, John, 1838-1914—Juvenile literature. I. Title.

GRAVES, Charles 574'.092'4 B
Parlin, 1911-1972.
John Muir, by Charles P. Graves. Illustrated by Robert Levering. New York, Crowell, [1973] 33 p. illus. 24 cm. (A Crowell biography) Biography of an explorer, naturalist, writer, founder of the Sierra Club, and early proponent of wilderness preservation who was influential in establishing our national park system. [QH31.M9G66] 92 75-158693 ISBN 0-690-46412-6 3.75
1. Muir, John, 1838-1914—Juvenile literature. I. Levering, Robert, 1919- illus. II. Title.

GROSSMAN, Adrienne Moss. 92
Trails of his own; the story of John Muir and his fight to save our national parks [by] Adrienne Grossman and Valerie Beardwood. Illustrated by Larry Toschik. New York, Longmans, Green [1961] 206p. illus. 21cm. [QH31.M9G7] 61-13101
1. Muir, John, 1838-1914—Juvenile literature. 2. National parks and reserves—U. S.—Juvenile literature. I. Beardwood, Valerie, joint author. II. Title.

SILVERBERG, Robert. 574'.092'4 B
John Muir, prophet among the glaciers. New York, Putnam [1972] 255 p. illus. 21 cm. (Lives to remember) Bibliography: p. 250-251. A biography of the nineteenth-century naturalist who devoted his life to studying American wildlife, climate, and geology. [QH31.M9S55] 92 74-183391 4.69
1. Muir, John, 1838-1914—Juvenile literature. I. Title.

STEWART, John, 333.7'2'0924 B
1920-
Winds in the woods : the story of John Muir / by John Stewart. Philadelphia : Westminster Press, [1975] 126 p. : ill. ; 23 cm. Includes index. Bibliography: p. 121. A biography of the naturalist, geologist, inventor, adventurer, writer, and artist who gave up thoughts of engineering and medical school in favor of a life of exploring wilderness areas. [QH31.M9S74] 92 74-20708 ISBN 0-664-32556-4
1. Muir, John, 1838-1914—Juvenile literature. I. Title. **BIP**

Muir, Thomas, 1765-1798.

EARNSHAW, John. 914.12'5
Thomas Muir, Scottish martyr; some account of his exile to New South Wales. his adventurous escape in 1796 across the Pacific to California, and thence, by way of New Spain, to France. Cremorne, N.S.W., Stone Copying Co., 1959. 84 p. illus. 26 cm. (Studies in Australian and Pacific history, no. 1) [CT828.M78E2] 65-66585
1. Muir, Thomas, 1765-1798. I. Title.

Muktananda Paramhamsa, Swami.

MUKTANANDA Paramhamsa, 294.5'6 B
Swami.
Guru: Chitshaktivilas; the play of consciousness. [1st ed.] New York, Harper & Row [1971] xxx, 175 p. illus. 22 cm. [BL1175.M77A313 1971] 77-148442 ISBN 0-06-066045-7 5.95
1. Muktananda Paramhamsa, Swami. 2. Spiritual life (Hinduism) I. Title.

Mulattoes.

JOHNSON, James Weldon, 928.1
1871-1938.
The autobiography of an ex-coloured man Introd. by Arna Bontemps. New York, Hill and Wang [c.1960] 211p. (American Century ser., AC32) 1.45 pap.,
1. Mulattoes. 2. Negroes. I. Title.

JOHNSON, James Weldon, v. 12
1871-1938.
The autobiography of an ex-coloured man.

With an introd. by Carl Van Vechten. New York, A. A. Knopf, 1961. xii, 211 p. 21 cm. First pub. in 1912. 65-90940
1. Mulattoes. 2. Negroes. I. Title. BIP

Mulhall, Lucille.

DAY, Beth (Feagles) 1924- 927.98
America's first cowgirl, Lucille Mulhall. Introd. by Charles Mulhall. New York, Messner [1955] 192p. illus. 22cm. [F596.M8D3] 55-9850
1. Mulhall, Lucille. I. Title.

Mulholland, Roger, 1740-1818.

BRETT, Charles Edward Bainbridge, 1928- 720'.92'4 B
Roger Mulholland : architect, of Belfast, 1740-1818 / by C. E. B. Brett. [Belfast] : Ulster Architectural Heritage Society, 1976. 20 p. : ill., map, plans, port. ; 26 cm. [NA997.M8B73] 77-363170 ISBN 0-900457-20-1 : £0.80
1. Mulholland, Roger, 1740-1818. 2. Architecture—Northern Ireland—Belfast.

Muli.

FREEMAN, James M. 301.44'94'0924 B
Untouchable : an Indian life history / James M. Freeman. Stanford, Calif. : Stanford University Press, 1979. viii, 421 p. : ill. ; 24 cm. Includes index. Bibliography: p. 408-411. [DS422.C3F73] 78-55319 ISBN 0-8047-1001-5: 18.95
1. Muli. 2. Untouchables—Biography. I. Title. BIP

Mullan, Fitzhugh.

MULLAN, Fitzhugh. 362.1'092'4 B
White coat, clenched fist / Fitzhugh Mullan. New York : Macmillan, [1976.] p. cm. [R154.M856A33] 76-18992 ISBN 0-02-587910-3 : 9.95
1. Mullan, Fitzhugh. 2. Physicians—United States—Correspondence, reminiscences, etc. 3. Medicine—United States. I. Title.

Mullen, Bernard F., 1825-1879.

MULLEN, Andrew. 973.7'472'0924 B
Col. Bernard F. Mullen, commander of the 35th Indiana Volunteers, 1st Irish Regiment, Civil War. [Celina, Ohio] 1968. 10, a-c p. 28 cm. Caption title. Includes bibliographies. [E506.5 35th.M84] 73-171695
1. Mullen, Bernard F., 1825-1879. 2. United States. Army. 35th Indiana Volunteers. 3. United States—History—Civil War, 1861-1865—Regimental histories—35th Indiana Volunteers.

Mullen, Herbert William.

LUNDE, Donald T. 364.1'523'0924 B
The die song : a journey into the mind of a mass murderer / Donald T. Lunde and Jefferson Morgan. 1st ed. New York : Norton, c1980. p. cm. [HV6248.M82L86 1980] 80-47 ISBN 0-393-01315-4 : 11.95
1. Mullen, Herbert William. 2. Crime and criminals—California—Biography. 3. Murder—California—Case studies. 4. Criminal psychology—Case studies. I. Morgan, Jefferson, joint author. II. Title. BIP

Mullen, John Joseph.

MULLEN, John Joseph. 974.8'14 B
In a year of our Lord : a memoir of American innocence / by John Mullen. New York : Arbor House, c1977. ix, 228 p. ; 22 cm. [F159.C5M8] 76-48772 ISBN 0-87795-160-8 : 8.95
1. Mullen, John Joseph. 2. Chester, Pa.—Biography. I. Title. BIP

Mullen, Thomas Richard, 1920-1948.

MULLEN, Thomas Richard, 1893- 920
Thomas R. Mullen, Jr.; a biography by his father. [New York? 1950] 107p. illus., ports. 23cm. [CT275.M716M8] 55-36376
1. Mullen, Thomas Richard, 1920-1948. I. Title.

Muller, Filip.

MULLER, Filip. 940.54'72'43
Eyewitness Auschwitz : three years in the gas chambers at Auschwitz / Filip Muller. New York : Stein and Day, 1979. p. cm. [D805.P7M83] 78-66257 ISBN 0-8128-2601-9 : 10.95
1. Muller, Filip. 2. Oswiecim (Concentration camp) 3. World War, 1939-1945—Personal narratives, Czech. 4. Prisoners of war—Czechoslovakia—Biography. 5. Prisoners of war—Poland—Biography. I. Title.

Muller, Friedrich Max, 1823-1900.

MULLER, Friedrich Max, 1823-1900 409'.2'4 B
The life and letters of the Right Honourable Friedrich Max Muller / edited by his wife. New York : AMS Press, 1976. 2 v. : ill. ; 23 cm. Reprint of the 1902 ed. published by Longmans, Green, New York. Includes index. Bibliography: v. 2, p. 487-488. [PJ64.M8A4 1976] 73-18820 ISBN 0-404-11445-8 : 57.50 2 vols.
1. Muller, Friedrich Max, 1823-1900. I. Title.

Muller, George, 1805-1898.

BAILEY, Faith Coxe. 923.642
Young rebel in Bristol; biography of George Mueller for teenagers. Chicago, Moody Press [1958] 159p. 19cm. (Moody pocket books, 32) [HV247.M8B3] 59-34876
1. Muller, George, 1805-1898. I. Title.

Muller, Jack, 1923-

NEIMARK, Paul G. 363.2'092'4 B
Cycle cop : the true story of Jack Muller, the Chicago giant killer who feared no evil / Paul Neimark. New York : Putnam, c1976. 124 p. ; 21 cm. Includes index. Biography of Jack Muller who has used his love of motorcycles to excel as a Chicago policeman. [HV7911.M854N44] 92 76-10792 ISBN 0-399-20534-9 : 5.95.
1. Muller, Jack, 1923- 2. Chicago—Police—Juvenile literature. I. Title. BIP

Mullings, Gwedolyn Lydia, 1928-

MULLINGS, Gwendolyn Lydia, 1928- 209'.2'4 B
My pilgrim journey : the making of an evangelist / by Gwendolyn Lydia Mullings. New York : William-Frederick Press, 1976. 91 p. ; 22 cm. [BX8809.M84A35] 76-47764 ISBN 0-87164-035-X : 3.50
1. Mullings, Gwedolyn Lydia, 1928- 2. Plymouth Brethren in New York (City)—Biography. 3. New York (City)—Biography. I. Title. BIP

Mullins, Eustace Clarence,

MULLINS, Eustace Clarence, 1923- 248
My life in Christ, by Eustace Mullins. Staunton, Va., Faith and Service Books, Aryan League of America [1968] 90 p. 22 cm. [CT275.M723A3] 68-25403
I. Title.

Mulloy, Gardnar,

MULLOY, Gardnar, 1913- 927.96342
The will to win; an inside view of the world of tennis. New York, A. S. Barnes [1960] 206p. illus. 22cm. Autobiographical. [GV994.M8A3 1960] 60-13083
I. Title.

Mumford, Geddes, 1925-1944.

MUMFORD, Lewis, 1895- 917.3'03'91
Green memories; the story of Geddes Mumford. Westport, Conn., Greenwood Press [1973, c1947] vi, 342 p. ports. 22 cm. Reprint of the ed. published by Harcourt, Brace, New York. [CT275.M73M8 1973] 73-6213 ISBN 0-8371-6892-9 14.25
1. Mumford, Geddes, 1925-1944. I. Title. BIP

Mumford, Lawrence Quincy, 1903-

L. Quincy Mumford, 020'.92'4 B
twenty years as Librarian of Congress, September 1, 1954-September 1, 1974 : a record of progress / presented by Librarian's conference. [Washington : Office of the Librarian, Library of Congress, 1974] 22 p. : graphs. ; 23 cm. [Z720.M83L14] 74-602517
1. Mumford, Lawrence Quincy, 1903-

Mumford, Lewis, 1895-

MUMFORD, Lewis, 1895- 818'.5'209 B
My works and days : a personal chronicle / Lewis Mumford. 1st ed. New York : Harcourt Brace Jovanovich, c1979. 545 p. ; 25 cm. Includes index. [CT275.M734A35] 78-53893 19.95
1. Mumford, Lewis, 1895- 2. Social reformers—United States—Biography. 3. City planners—United States—Biography. 4. Architects—United States—Biography. I. Title. BIP

Mun, Albert, comte de, 1841-1914.

MARTIN, Benjamin F., 1947- 320.9'44'081 B
Count Albert de Mun, paladin of the Third Republic / Benjamin F. Martin. Chapel Hill : University of North Carolina Press, c1978. xix, 367 p. ; 23 cm. Includes index. Bibliography: p. 337-338. [DC342.8.M8M34] 78-1739 ISBN 0-8078-1325-7 : 20.00
1. Mun, Albert, comte de, 1841-1914. 2. France—Politics and government—1870-1940. 3. Politicians—France—Biography. 4. Church and social problems—France. I. Title.

Munby, Arthur Joseph, 1828-1910.

HUDSON, Derek. 821'.8 B
Munby, man of two worlds; the life and diaries of Arthur J. Munby, 1828-1910. [Boston] Gambit [1972] ix, 461 p. illus. 24 cm. Bibliography: p. 452-454. [PR5101.M39Z6 1972b] 72-83706 ISBN 0-87645-066-4 12.50
1. Munby, Arthur Joseph, 1828-1910. I. Munby, Arthur Joseph, 1828-1910.

Munch, Edvard, 1863-1944.

DEKNATEL, Frederick B. [927.5]
Edvard Munch. With an introd. by Johan H. Langaard. Boston, Institute of Contemporary Art [1950] 120 p. illus. (part col.) ports. 26 cm. Published also as Oslo kommunes Kunstsamlinger catalog no. 6. Bibliography: p. 116-120. [ND773.M8D4 1950a] 759.81 50-58176
1. Munch, Edvard, 1863-1944. I. Title.

HODIN, Josef Paul. 759.81
Edvard Munch [by] J. P. Hodin. New York, Praeger [1972] 216 p. illus. (part col.) 22 cm. Bibliography: p. 211. [N7073.M8H59] 76-99313 10.00
1. Munch, Edvard, 1863-1944. BIP

MUNCH, Edvard, 1863-1944. 709'.2'4
Edvard Munch / Ian Dunlop. New York : St. Martin's Press, 1977. p. cm. [N7073.M8D86] 77-71078 ISBN 0-312-23822-3 pbk. : 5.95
1. Munch, Edvard, 1863-1944. I. Dunlop, Ian, 1940-

SELZ, Jean. 769'.92'4
E. Munch / by Jean Selz ; [translated from the French by Eileen B. Hennessy]. New York : Crown Publishers, [1974] 95 p. : ill. (some col.) ; 29 cm. Bibliography: p. 94. [N7073.M8S4413] 74-76242 ISBN 0-517-51571-7 : 3.95
1. Munch, Edvard, 1863-1944.

STANG, Ragna Thiis. 709'.2'4 B
Edvard Munch, man and artist / by Ragna Stang ; translation from the Norwegian by Geoffrey Culverwell. New York : Abbeville Press, c1979. p. cm. Translation of Edvard-Munch. Includes indexes. Bibliography: p. [N7073.M8S7313] 78-31813 ISBN 0-89659-025-9 : 39.95
1. Munch, Edvard, 1863-1944. 2. Artists—Norway—Biography. I. Title.

Mundahoi.

ROTH, Don A., 1927- 248'.246'0924 B
Mundahoi, Borneo witch doctor / by Don A. Roth. Nashville : Southern Pub. Association, c1975. 126 p. : ports. ; 21 cm. (A Crown book) [BV3342.M86R67] 75-11398 ISBN 0-8127-0098-8 pbk. : 2.95
1. Mundahoi. 2. Seventh-Day Adventists—Missions. 3. Missions—Sabah.

Mundus, Frank.

BOGGS, Robert F. 799.1'7'310924 B
Captain Frank Mundus, shark man : master hunter of the deep / by Robert F. Boggs. Dayton, Ohio : Lorenz Press, c1977. 202 p. ; 22 cm. [SH691.S4B63] 77-357140 ISBN 0-89328-007-0 : 7.95
1. Mundus, Frank. 2. Shark fishing—New York (State)—Montauk Point. 3. Charter boat captains—New York (State)—Biography. I. Title. II. Title: Shark man.

Muni, Paul, 1895-1967.

DRUXMAN, Michael B., 1941- 791.43'028'0924 B
Paul Muni; his life and his films [by] Michael B. Druxman. South Brunswick, A. S. Barnes [1974] 227 p. illus. 26 cm. [PN2287.M79D7] 73-10519 ISBN 0-498-01413-4 10.00
1. Muni, Paul, 1895-1967.

LAWRENCE, Jerome, 1915- 791'.092'4
Actor, the life and times of Paul Muni / by Jerome Lawrence. New York : Putnam, [1974] 380 p. : ill. ; 24 cm. Includes index. [PN2287.M79L3] 73-93734 ISBN 0-399-11341-X : 10.00
1. Muni, Paul, 1895-1967. I. Title.

Munk, Jens, 1579-1628.

HANSEN, Thorkild, 1927- 910'.924 B
The way to Hudson Bay; the life and times of Jens Munk. Translated by James McFarlane and John Lynch. [1st American ed.] New York, Harcourt, Brace & World [1970] 348 p. illus., facsims., maps, ports. 24 cm. "The English translation is a somewhat abridged version of the Danish original, Jens Munk." "A Helen and Kurt Wolff book." [G650 1619.H3132] 76-95854 7.95
1. Munk, Jens, 1579-1628. 2. America—Discovery and exploration—Danish. 3. Northwest Passage. I. Title.

Munk, Kaj Harold-Leininger, 1898-1944.

HARCOURT, Melville 248.0922
Portraits of destiny. Illus. by Giles Harcourt. New York, Sheed [1966] 239p. ports. 22cm. [BR1700.2.H3] 66-22014 5.50
1. Dolci, Danilo. 2. Luthuli, Albert John, 1898- 3. Munk, Kaj Harold-Leininger, 1898-1944. 4. Szabo, Violette (Bushnell) 1921-1945. I. Title.

Munoz Marin, Luis, 1898—

AITKEN, Thomas, 1910- 923.27295
Poet in the fortress; the story of Luis Munoz Marin, by Thomas Aitken, Jr. [New York] New American Library [1964] xiv, 241 p. illus., ports. 22 cm. (An NAL-World book) Bibliography: p. [229]-236. [F1975.M76A5] 64-20564
1. Munoz Marin, Luis, 1898- I. Title.

MATHEWS, Thomas G., 1925- 972.95'05'0924 B
Luis Munoz Marin; a concise biography by Thomas Mathews. New York, American R.D.M. Corp. [1967] 61 p. group ports. 21 cm. (A Study master publication, 909) Bibliography: p. 61. [F1976.M76M3] 66-28701
1. Munoz Marin, Luis, 1898-

Munoz Marin, Luis, 1898- —Juvenile literature.

MANN, Peggy. 972.95'05'0924 B
Munoz Marin : the man who remade Puerto Rico / by Peggy Mann. New York : Coward, McCann & Geoghegan, c1976. p. cm. Includes index. Bibliography: p. A biography of the man responsible for transforming Puerto Rico from an island of poverty, disease, and squalor into "the Showplace of the Caribbean." [F1976.M76M26 1976] 92 76-6117 ISBN 0-698-20362-3. ISBN 0-698-30614-7 lib. bdg. : 5.86
1. Munoz Marin, Luis, 1898- —Juvenile literature. 2. Puerto Rico—Politics and government—1952- —Juvenile literature. I. Title.

Munoz Rivera, Luis, 1859-1916.

NORRIS, Marianna. 972.95'04'0924 B
Father and son for freedom; the story of Puerto Rico's Luis Munoz Rivera and Luis Munoz Marin. New York, Dodd, Mead [1968] xvi, 166 p. illus., ports. 24 cm. Recounts the lives of Munoz Rivera, who sought Puerto Rican independence from Spain, and his son Munoz Marin, a poet, who worked to obtain justice from rich landowners and became governor of his country. [F1975.M8N6] 92 AC 68
1. Munoz Rivera, Luis, 1859-1916. 2. Munoz Marin, Luis, 1898- I. Title.

STERLING, Philip. 920
The quiet rebels; four Puerto Rican leaders Jose Celso Barbosa, Luis Munoz Rivera, Jose de Diego, Luis Munoz Marin by Philip Sterling and Maria Brau Illus. by Tracy Sugarman [1st ed.] Garden City, N.Y., Doubleday, 1968. 118 p. col. illus., col. map, col. ports. 21 cm. (Zenith books) Profiles of four Puerto Ricans who fought for independence and equal rights for their island people. [F1955.S7] AC 68
1. Barbosa, Jose Celso, 1857-1921. 2. Munoz Rivera, Luis, 1859-1916. 3. Diego, Jose de, 1866-1918. 4. Munoz Marin, Luis, 1898- I. Brau, Maria, joint author. II. Sugarman, Tracy, 1921- illus. III. Title.

Munoz Rivera, Luis, 1859-1916—Juvenile literature.

REYNOLDS, Mack. 972.95'04'0924 B
Puerto Rican patriot; the life of Luis Munoz Rivera. Illus. by Arthur Shilstone. [New York] Crowell-Collier Press [1969] 101 p. illus. 21 cm. Puerto Rican history, from the discovery of the island by Columbus through the twentieth century, serves as a background for this biography of a prominent politician who gained autonomy for the island from Spain. [F1973.M8R4] 92 73-81548
1. Munoz Rivera, Luis, 1859-1916—Juvenile literature. I. Shilstone, Arthur, illus. II. Title. BIP

STERLING, Philip. 920(J)
The quiet rebels; four Puerto Rican leaders: Jose Celso Barbosa, Luis Munoz Rivera, Jose de Diego, Luiz Munoz Marin, by Philip Sterling and Maria Brau. Illustrated by Tracy Sugerman. [1st ed.] Garden City, N.Y., Doubleday, 1968. 118 p. col. illus., col. map, col. ports. 21 cm. (Zenith books) [F1955.S7] 67-11153 2.95
1. Barbosa, Jose Celso, 1851-1921—Juvenile literature. 2. Munoz Rivera, Luis, 1859-1916—Juvenile literature. 3. Diego, Jose de, 1866-1918—Juvenile literature. 4. Munoz Marin, Luis, 1898- —Juvenile literature. I. Brau, Maria M., 1932- joint author. II. Title.

Munroe, Kirk, 1850-1930—Biography.

MUNROE, Kirk, 1850-1930. 813'.4 B
The Florida adventures of Kirk Munroe : narrative and biographical / by Irving Leonard. Chuluota, Fla. : Mickler House, 1975. 213 p., [1] leaf of plates : ill., map (on lining papers) ; 23 cm. Leonard's forename on t.p. corrected in manuscript from Irvin to Irving. Contains 22 articles by the author which were originally published in various periodicals. Includes index. Bibliography: p. 205-213. [PS2449.M54F4 1975] 75-21373 12.50
1. Munroe, Kirk, 1850-1930—Biography. 2. Munroe, Kirk, 1850-1930—Bibliography. 3. Florida—Description and travel—1865-1950. I. Leonard, Irving Albert, 1896- II. Title.

Munsey, Frank Andrew, 1854-1925.

BRITT, George, 1895- 070.5'0924 B
Forty years—forty millions; the career of Frank A. Munsey. Port Washington, N.Y., Kennikat Press [1972, c1935] vi, 309 p. port. 23 cm. [PN4874.M8B7 1972] 72-153203 ISBN 0-8046-1513-6
1. Munsey, Frank Andrew, 1854-1925. I. Title.

Munson, Charles J.

MUNSON, Charles J. 978
Westward to paradise / by Charles J. Munson ; edited and with an introd. by Kenneth B. Platt. Moscow : University Press of Idaho, c1978. 174 p. : ill. ; 21 cm. (A Gem book) (Local history paper ; no. 4) Includes index. [F754.M8M86] 78-54429 ISBN 0-89301-054-5 : 5.95
1. Munson, Charles J. 2. Moscow, Idaho—Biography. 3. Frontier and pioneer life—Idaho. 4. Frontier and pioneer life—Colorado. I. Platt, Kenneth B. II. Title. III. Series. BIP

Munson, Rachel Hall, d. 1870.

NARRATIVE of the 973'.04'97 S
capture of the Hall sisters. New York : Garland Pub., 1975. p. cm. (The Garland library of narratives of North American Indian captivities ; v. 49) Bound with the reprint of the 1834 ed. of Wakefield, J. A. History of the war between the United States and the Sac and Fox nations of Indians. New York, 1975. The reprint of the 2d ed., 1915, of Scanlan, C. M. Indian Creek massacre and captivity of Hall girls. New York, 1975. Bound with the reprint of the 1834 ed. of Wakefield, J. A. History of the war between the United States and the Sac and Fox nations of Indians. New York, 1975. The reprint of the 2d ed., 1915, of Scanlan, C. M. Indian Creek massacre and captivity of Hall girls. New York, 1975. [E85.G2 vol. 49] [E83.83] 973.5'6 75-25684 ISBN 0-8240-1673-4 lib.bdg. : 21.00
1. Munson, Rachel Hall, d. 1870. 2. Horn, Sylvia Hall, 1813-1899. 3. Indians of North America—Captivities. 4. Black Hawk War, 1832. I. Title. II. Series.

Munson, Thurman, 1947-

MUNSON, Thurman, 1947- 796.357'092'4 B
Thurman Munson / an autobiography with Martin Appel. New York : Coward, McCann & Geoghegan, c1978. 199 p., [10] leaves of plates : ill. ; 22 cm. [GV865.M78A35 1978] 78-8924 ISBN 0-698-10917-1 : 8.95
1. Munson, Thurman, 1947- 2. Baseball players—United States—Biography. I. Appel, Martin, joint author. BIP

Munson, Thurman, 1947- —Juvenile literature.

LIBBY, Bill. 796.357'092'4 B
Thurman Munson : pressure player / by Bill Libby. New York : Putnam, c1978. 191 p. : ill. ; 21 cm. (Putnam sport shelf) A biography of the New York Yankee catcher whose unlikely appearance belies his outstanding athletic ability and achievements. [GV865.M78L52 1978] 92 78-2843 ISBN 0-399-61124-X lib. bdg. : 5.96
1. Munson, Thurman, 1947- —Juvenile literature. 2. Baseball players—United States—Biography—Juvenile literature. I. Title. BIP

Munthe, Axel Martin Fredrik, 1857-1949.

MUNTHE, Axel Martin Fredrik, 1857-1949. 928.397
The story of San Michele. With a new introd. by George N. Shuster. Silver anniversary ed. New York, Dutton [1953, c1929] 534 p. 21 cm. Reminiscences. [PR6025.U69S7 1953] 53-10863
I. Title. II. Title: San Michele.

MUNTHE, Gustaf Lorentz, 1896- 928.397
The story of Axel Munthe, by Gustaf Munthe and Gudrun Uexkull; translated from the Swedish by Malcolm Munthe and from the German by Lord Sudley. [1st American ed.] New York, Dutton, 1953. 217 p. illus. 21 cm. An expansion of Gustaf Munthe's work, Axel Munthe, published in Swedish in 1949. [PT9875.M8Z852 1953a] 53-10862
1. Munthe, Axel Martin Fredrik, 1857-1949. I. Uexkull, Gudrun von Schwerin, Baronin von, 1878-

Muntz, Harry J

MUNTZ, Harry J 926.55
Tramp printer. [1st ed.] New York, Pageant Press [1953] 99p. 21cm. Autobiographical. [Z232.M925A3] 53-8099
I. Title.

Munzer, Martha E.

MUNZER, Martha E. 371.1'0092'4 B
Full circle / Martha Munzer. New York : Knopf : distributed by Random House, [1978] p. cm. [LA2317.M85A33 1978] 78-5852 ISBN 0-394-83903-X. lib.bdg. : 5.99 ISBN 0-394-93903-4 lib.bdg. : 5.95
1. Munzer, Martha E. 2. Teachers—United States—Biography. I. Title.

Munzer, Thomas, 1490 (ca.)-1525.

GRITSCH, Eric W. 284'.3 B
Reformer without a church; the life and thought of Thomas Muentzer, 1488?-1525, by Eric W. Gritsch. Philadelphia, Fortress Press [1967] xiv, 214 p. map, port. 24 cm. Bibliography: p. 199-208. [BX4946.M8G7] 67-20144
1. Munzer, Thomas, 1490 (ca.)-1525. I. Title.

Munzenberg, Willi.

GROSS, Babette. 329'.074'0924 B
Willi Munzenberg: a political biography. Translated by Marian Jackson. [East Lansing] Michigan State University Press, 1974. 337 p. 24 cm. Includes bibliographical references. [HX273.M76G76] 72-85878 ISBN 0-87013-173-7 12.50
1. Munzenberg, Willi.

Murch, James DeForest, 1892-

MURCH, James DeForest, 1892- 269'.2'0924 B
Adventuring for Christ in changing times; an autobiography of James DeForest Murch. [Louisville, Ky.] Restoration Press, 1973. 348 p. port. 25 cm. [BX7343.M8A33] 73-84633
1. Murch, James DeForest, 1892- I. Title.

Murder.

LIPSIG, Frances 364.152
Murder--family style. New York, Collier [c.1962] 188p. (Collier bks. orig., AS182) 62-11015 .95 pap.,
1. Murder. 2. Crime and criminals—Biog. I. Title.

WILSON, Colin Henry, 1931- 364.152
Encyclopedia of murder [by] Colin Wilson, Patricia Pitman. New York, Putnam [1962, c.1961] 576p. illus. Bibl. 61-12748 5.95
1. Murder. 2. Crime and criminals—Biog. I. Pitman, Patricia, joint author. II. Title.

Murder—Collections.

DE FORD, Miriam Allen, 1888- 364.15230926
Murderers sane & mad; case histories in the motivation and rationale of murder. New York, Abelard [c.1965] 239p. 22cm. [HV6515.D44] 65-15792 5.00
1. Murder—Collections. I. Title.
Contents omitted.

Murder — Minnesota.

TRENERRY, Walter N 364.152
Murder in Minnesota; a collection of true cases. St. Paul, Minnesota Historical Society, 1962. vii, 252 p. illus., ports. 23 cm. (Publications of the Minnesota Historical Society) Bibliographical references included in "Footnotes" (p. 229-243) [HV6533.M6T7] 62-63717
1. Murder — Minnesota. 2. Crime and criminals — Minnesota — Biog. 3. (Series: Minnesota Historical Society. Publications) I. Title. BIP

Murder—Biography.

GAUTE, J. H. H. 364.1'523'0922 B
The murderers' who's who : outstanding international cases from the literature of murder in the last 150 years / J. H. H. Gaute and Robin Odell ; with a foreword by Colin Wilson. 1st American ed. New York : Methuen, 1979. 269 : ill. ; 25 cm. Includes index. Bibliography: p. 253-269. [HV6245.G38 1979] 78-64828 ISBN 0-458-93900-5 : 17.95
1. Murder—Biography. I. Odell, Robin, joint author. II. Title.

Murder—Case studies.

FURNEAUX, Rupert. 364.15'23
The medical murderer. New York, Abelard-Schuman [1967, c1957] 152 p. illus., ports. 23 cm. [HV6245.F9 1967] 66-25009
1. Murder—Case studies. 2. Physicians—Biography. I. Title.

Murder—Gt. Brit.

SHEW, Edward Spencer, 1908- 364.152
A second companion to murder; a dictionary of death ... 1900 1950. With a note on the British judicial system. [1st American ed.] New York, Knopf, 1962. xii, 292 p. 22 cm. Bibliography: p. 279-287. [HV6945.S482 1962] 62-11116
1. Murder—Gt. Brit. 2. Crime and criminals—Gt. Brit.—Biography. I. Title. II. Title: Companion to murder.

Murder—Missouri—Case studies.

SADLER, Ella Jo. 364.1'523'0977864
Murder in the afternoon / Ella Jo Sadler. Grand Rapids : Zondervan Pub. House, c1975. 169 p. ; 23 cm. Autobiographical. [HV6533.M45S25] 74-25342 5.95
1. Murder—Missouri—Case studies. 2. Assault and battery—Missouri—Case studies. I. Title. BIP

Murdoch, Royal,

MURDOCH, Royal, 1898- 928.1
Poet's letters, 1942. New York, Fine Editions Press [1958] 157p. 21cm. [PS3525.U6535Z55] 58-2484
I. Title.

Murdoch, Rupert, 1931-

REGAN, Simon. 070.4'092'4 B
Rupert Murdoch : a business biography / [by] Simon Regan. London : Angus and Robertson, 1976. viii, 246 p., [8] p. of plates : ill., ports. ; 22 cm. Ill. on lining papers. Includes index. [PN4734.R4] 76-367536 ISBN 0-207-95509-3 : £3.80
1. Murdoch, Rupert, 1931-

Murdoch, Walter, Sir, 1874-1970.

LA NAUZE, John Andrew, 1911- 824 B
Walter Murdoch : a biographical memoir / John La Nauze. Carlton [Australia] : Melbourne University Press ; Forest Grove, Or. : [distributed by] International Scholarly Book Services, 1977. xiii, 189 p. : ill. ; 22 cm. Includes bibliographical references and index. [PR9619.3.M74Z74] 77-374845 ISBN 0-522-84119-8 : 18.00
1. Murdoch, Walter, Sir, 1874-1970. 2. Authors, Australian—20th century—Biography.
Distributed by ISBS

Murdoch, Walter, Sir, 1874-1970—Correspondence.

MURDOCH, Walter, Sir, 1874-1970. 828 B
Walter Murdoch and Alfred Deakin on Books and men : letters and comments, 1900-1918 / edited by J. A. La Nauze and Elizabeth Nurser. Clayton, Vic. : Melbourne University Press, 1974. ix, 108 p. ; 23 cm. [PR9619.3.M74Z543 1974] 75-330060 ISBN 0-522-84056-6 : 7.95
1. Murdoch, Walter, Sir, 1874-1970—Correspondence. 2. Deakin, Alfred, 1856-1819. 3. Australian literature—History and criticism—Addresses, essays, lectures. I. Deakin, Alfred, 1856-1819. II. La Nauze, John Andrew, 1911- ed. III. Nurser, R. M. Elizabeth, ed. IV. Title.

Murdock, Charles Albert, 1841-1928.

HARDING, George Laban, 1893- 686.2'092'4
Charles A. Murdock; printer & citizen of San Francisco: an appraisal, by George L. Harding. Berkeley, Tamalpais Press, 1973. x, 83 p. illus. 28 cm. Three hundred ten copies printed. [Z232.M927H36] 72-189653
1. Murdock, Charles Albert, 1841-1928.

Murdock, Stephen.

MURDOCK, Alma 920.9
Crowned. San Antonio, Tex., Naylor [c.1962] 51p. illus. 23cm. 62-13062 1.95; 1.00 pap.,
1. Murdock, Stephen. I. Title.

Murfree, Mary Noailles, 1850-1922.

PARKS, Edd Winfield, 1906-1968. 813'.4 B
Charles Egbert Craddock (Mary Noailles Murfree) Port Washington, N.Y., Kennikat Press [1972, c1941] x, 258 p. facsim., ports. 21 cm. Bibliography: p. [237]-249. [PS2456.P3 1972] 75-159098 ISBN 0-8046-1641-8
1. Murfree, Mary Noailles, 1850-1922.

Murnau, Friedrich Wilhelm, 1889-1931.

EISNER, Lotte H. 791.43'0233'0924
Murnau, by Lotte H. Eisner. [Rev. and enl.] Berkeley, University of California Press [1973, c1964] 287 p. illus. 22 cm. (A Shadows book) A rev. translation of the French work published in 1964 under title: F. W. Murnau. Bibliography: p. 280-283. [PN1998.A3M843 1973] 72-82222 ISBN 0-520-02285-8 10.95
1. Murnau, Friedrich Wilhelm, 1889-1931. Pbk. 4.50; ISBN 0-520-02425-7. **BIP**

Murphey, Cecil B.

MURPHEY, Cecil B. 266'.5'20924 B
But God has promised / Cecil B. Murphey. Carol Stream, Ill. : Creation House, c1976. 169 p. ; 22 cm. [BV3625.K42M87 1976] 76-16283 ISBN 0-88419-001-3 pbk. : 2.95
1. Murphey, Cecil B. 2. Missionaries—Kenya—Biography. 3. Missionaries—United States—Biography. I. Title. **BIP**

MURPHEY, Cecil B. 248'.4
Somebody knows I'm alive / by Cecil B. Murphey. Atlanta : John Knox Press, c1977. vi, 168 p. ; 21 cm. [BX9225.M8A37] 76-44967 ISBN 0-8042-2206-1 : 4.95
1. Murphey, Cecil B. 2. Presbyterian Church—Clergy—Biography. 3. Clergy—Georgia—Biography. I. Title. **BIP**

Murphy, Audie, 1924-1971.

SIMPSON, Harold B. 940.54'21'0924 B
Audie Murphy, American soldier / by Harold B. Simpson ; introd. by Olin E. Teague. Bi-centennial ed. Hillsboro, Tex. : Hill Jr. College Press, 1975. xv, 466 p., [1] leaf of plates : ill. ; 29 cm. Includes index. Bibliography: p. 450-457. [U53.M87S55] 75-27587 ISBN 0-912172-20-7 : 12.50
1. Murphy, Audie, 1924-1971. I. Title. **BIP**

Murphy, Bob.

MURPHY, Bob. 248'.246 B
Christianity rubs holes in my religion / by Bob Murphy. Houston : Hunter Ministries Pub. Co., c1976. 113 p. ; 20 cm. [BV4935.M84A33] 76-150938 1.95
1. Murphy, Bob. 2. Converts—United States—Biography. 3. Christian life—1960- I. Title. **BIP**

Murphy, Castle H

MURPHY, Castle H 1886- 922.83
Castle of Zion -- Hawaii; autobiography and episodes from life. Salt Lake City, Deseret Book Co., 1963. 180 p. 24 cm. [BV3680.H4M8] 63-4641
I. Title.

Murphy, Charles Francis, 1858-1924.

WEISS, Nancy Joan. 974.71'04'0924
Charles Francis Murphy, 1858-1924; respectability and responsibility in Tammany politics. Northampton, Mass., Smith Coll., 1968. x, 139p. illus., map, port. 24cm. (Edwin H. Land prize essays) Bibl. [F128.47.W45] (B) 67-21037 2.00
1. Murphy, Charles Francis, 1858-1924. 2. Tammany Hall. I. Title. II. Title: Respectability and responsibility in Tammany politics. III. Series.

Murphy, Daniel Richard, 1802-1875.

MUSTAIN, Claud J 266.60924
Wilderness prophet; a biography of Daniel Richard Murphy, pioneer preacher, missionary, colporteur, 1802-1875 [by] Claud J. Mustain. Springfield, Mo., Cain-Service Print. Co. [1966] ii, 54 p. illus. 22 cm. [BX6495.M85M8] 66-6533
1. Murphy, Daniel Richard, 1802-1875. I. Title.

Murphy, Edward Francis,

MURPHY, Edward Francis, 1892- 922.273
Yankee priest; an autobiographical journey, with certain detours, from Salem to New Orleans. [1st ed.] Garden City N.Y., Doubleday, 1952. 316 p. 22 cm. [BX4705.M975A3] 52-5117
I. Title.

Murphy, Francis Xavier,

MURPHY, Francis Xavier, 1914- 922.21
John XXIII, the story of the Pope. Orig. title: John XXIII comes to the Vatican New York, Avon [1961, c.1959] 159p. illus. (G-1093) .50 pap.,
I. Title.

Murphy, Frank, 1890-1949.

FINE, Sidney, 1920- 347'.73'2634 B
Frank Murphy / by Sidney Fine. Ann Arbor : University of Michigan Press, c1975- v. : ill. ; 24 cm. Includes index. Contents.Contents.—[1] The Detroit years. Bibliography: v. 1, p. 565-577. [KF8745.M8F49] 74-25945 ISBN 0-472-32949-9 : 20.00
1. Murphy, Frank, 1890-1949.

FINE, Sidney, 1920- 940.4'83'73 B
Frank Murphy in World War I Ann Arbor, Michigan Historical Collections, University of Michigan [1968] 44 p. ports. 23 cm. (Michigan Historical Collections. Bulletin, no. 17) Includes bibliographical references. [KF8745.M8F5] 78-631685
1. Murphy, Frank, 1890-1949. I. Title. II. Series: Michigan. University. Michigan Historical Collections. Bulletin no. 17.

HOWARD, J. Woodford. 347.99'73 B
Mr. Justice Murphy; a political biography, by J. Woodford Howard, Jr. Princeton, N.J., Princeton University Press, 1968. x, 578 p. illus., ports. 25 cm. "Documentary footnotes": p. [503]-558. [KF8745.M8H6] 68-11444 12.50
1. Murphy, Frank, 1890-1949. I. Title.

LUNT, Richard D 923.273
The high ministry of government: the political career of Frank Murphy, by Richard D. Lunt. Detroit, Wayne State University Press, 1965. 263 p. illus. ports. 24 cm. Bibliographical references included in "Notes" (p. 223-250) Bibliography: p. 251-258. [E748.M868L8] 65-10195
I. Title. **BIP**

MURPHY, Frank, 1916- 365'.64'0924
The Frank Murphy story; his years in Florida prisons, his rehabilitation, and his conquest of alcoholism, as told to Thomas Helm. New York, Dodd, Mead [1968] 312 p. 22 cm. [HV6248.M85A3] 68-8280 6.50
I. Helm, Thomas. II. Title.

Murphy, George,

MURPHY, George, 1902- 328.73'07'10924 B
"Say ... didn't you used to be George Murphy?" By George Murphy, with Victor Lasky. [New York] Bartholomew House [1970] 438 p. illus., ports. 21 cm. [E840.8.M8A3] 76-110744 6.95
I. Lasky, Victor. II. Title.

Murphy, Martin, 1807-1884.

SULLIVAN, Gabrielle. 917.94'03'40924 B
Martin Murphy, Jr., California pioneer, 1844-1884 / Gabrielle Sullivan. 1st ed. Stockton, Calif. : Pacific Center for Western Historical Studies, University of the Pacific, [1974] iii, iv, 76 p., [2] leaves of plates : ill. ; 23 cm. (Monograph - Pacific Center for Western Historical Studies ; no. 4) Includes index. Bibliography: p. 70-74. [F864.M98S94] 74-194420
1. Murphy, Martin, 1807-1884. 2. California—History—Miscellanea. I. Series: Pacific Center for Western Historical Studies. Monograph ; no. 4.

Murphy, Patrick V., 1920-

MURPHY, Patrick V., 1920- 363.2'092'4 B
Commissioner : a view from the top of American law enforcement / by Patrick V. Murphy and Thomas Plate. New York : Simon and Schuster, c1977. 280 p., [8] leaves of plates : ill. ; 25 cm. Includes index. [HV7911.M89A32] 77-21876 ISBN 0-671-22751-3 : 9.95
1. Murphy, Patrick V., 1920- 2. Police chiefs—New York (City)—Biography. I. Plate, Thomas Gordon, joint author. II. Title.

Murphy, Seamus.

MURPHY, Seamus. 736'.5'0924 B
Stone mad / Seamus Murphy ; with illustrations by William Harrington and initial letters by the author. [New and revised ed.]. London : Routledge and Kegan Paul, 1977 [i.e. 1976] x, 229 p. : ill., port. ; 22 cm. [NB497.M8A2 1977] 77-375105 ISBN 0-7100-8542-7 pbk. : 5.00
1. Murphy, Seamus. 2. Sculptors—Ireland—Biography. 3. Stone carving—Ireland. 4. Ireland—Social life and customs. I. Title.
Distributed by Routledge and Kegan Paul, Boston.

Murphy, Terry.

MURPHY, Terry. 596
Some of my best friends are animals / by Terry Murphy. New York : Paddington Press, 1979. p. cm. [QL31.M92A33] 79-10717 ISBN 0-448-22683-9 (U.S. & Can. only) : 10.00
1. Murphy, Terry. 2. Zoologists—Ireland—Biography. I. Title. **BIP**

Murphy, Willie, 1933-

†MURPHY, Willie, 1933- 269'.2'0924 B
Black and trying / by Willie Murphy. Harrison, Ark. : New Leaf Press, c1976. 165 p. : port. ; 23 cm. Written by W. Murphy with C. Dudley. [BV4935.M86A33] 76-22272 ISBN 0-89221-023-0 : 5.95
1. Murphy, Willie, 1933- 2. Converts—United States—Biography. 3. Evangelists—United States—Biography. I. Dudley, Cliff, joint author. II. Title. **BIP**

Murray, Arthur, 1895-

MURRAY, Kathryn (Kohnfelder) 1906- 927.933
My husband, Arthur Murray, by Kathryn Murray with Betty Hannah Hoffman. New York, Avon [1961, c.1959, 1960] 128p. illus. (T510) .35 pap.,
1. Murray, Arthur, 1895- I. Title.

Murray, Gilbert [George Gilbert Aime Murray],

MURRAY, Gilbert [George Gilbert Aime Murray], 1866-1957 928.2
Gilbert Murray: an unfinished autobiography, with contributions by his friends. Edited by Jean Smith and Arnold Toynbee. London, Allen and Unwin [dist. New York, Oxford University Press, 1960] 225p. illus. (front. port.) 23cm. 60-3252 4.00
I. Title.

Murray, James Augustus Henry, Sir, 1837-1915.

MURRAY, Katharine Maud Elisabeth. 423'.092'4 B
Caught in the web of words : James A. H. Murray ahd the Oxford English dictionary / K. M. Elisabeth Murray ; with a pref. by R. W. Birchfield. New Haven : Yale University Press, 1977. 386 p. : ill. ; 24 cm. Includes bibliographical references and index. [PE64.M8M78] 77-76309 ISBN 0-300-02131-3 : 15.00
1. Murray, James Augustus Henry, Sir, 1837-1915. 2. Murray, James Augustus Henry, Sir, 1837-1915. A new English dictionary. 3. Lexicographers—Great Britain—Biography. I. Title.

Murray, John, 1778-1843.

SMILES, Samuel, 1812-1904. 070.5'092'4 B
A publisher and his friends; memoir and correspondence of the late John Murray, with an account of the origin and progress of the house, 1768-1843. London, J. Murray; New York, Scribner, 1891. [New York, AMS Press, 1973] 2 v. ports. 23 cm. [Z325.M9S6 1973] 77-148304 ISBN 0-404-07492-8 20.00 ea.
1. Murray, John, 1778-1843. 2. Murray, John, publisher, London. I. Title.
Set of 2 volumes selling for 40.00.

Murray, John Courtney.

PELOTTE, Donald E. 261.7'092'4
John Courtney Murray : theologian in conflict / by Donald E. Pelotte. New York : Paulist Press, c1976. xi, 210 p. ; 24 cm. Includes index. Bibliography: p. 191-206. [BX4705.M977P44] 76-18046 ISBN 0-8091 0212 9 : 9.95
1. Murray, John Courtney. 2. Catholic Church—Biography. 3. Theologians—United States—Biography. BIP

Murray, John Hubert Plunkett, Sir, 1861-1940.

MURRAY, John Hubert Plunkett, Sir, 1861-1940. 995'.3
Selected letters of Hubert Murray, edited by Francis West. Melbourne, New York, Oxford University Press, 1970. xiii, 255 p. geneal. table. 23 cm. [DU746.M8A4 1970] 76-568716 ISBN 0-19-550313-9 6.50
I. West, Francis James, ed. BIP

WEST, Francis James. 995'.3 B
Hubert Murray; the Australian pro-consul [by] Francis West. Melbourne, New York [etc.] Oxford University Press, 1968. vii, 296 p. illus., map (on lining papers) ports. 23 cm. Bibliography: p. 277-282. [DU740.W4] 75 373297 7.50
1. Murray, John Hubert Plunkett, Sir, 1861-1940. BIP

Murray, Ken

MURRAY, Ken 927.92
Life on a pogo stick; autobiography of a comedian. Philadelphia, Winston [c.1960] xii, 180p. illus. 22cm. 60-7100 3.95
I. Title.

MURRAY, Ken, 1903- 927.92
Life on a pogo stick; autobiography of a comedian. [1st ed.] Philadelphia, Winston [1960] 180p. illus. 22cm. [PN2287.M82A3] 60-7100
I. Title.

Murray, Mae.

ARDMORE, Jane Kesner (Morris) 927.92
The self-enchanted: Mae Murray, image of an era. [1st ed.] New York, McGraw-Hill [1959] 262p. illus. 22cm. [PN2287.M83A75] 59-14436
1. Murray, Mae. I. Title.

Murray, Pauli,

MURRAY, Pauli, 1910- 920
Proud shoes; the story of an American family. [1st ed.] New York, Harper [1956] 276 p. 22 cm. [E185.97.M95] 55-10698
I. Title. BIP

Murray, Terence Aubrey, 1810-1873.

WILSON, Gwendoline. 994'.4'030924 B
Murray of Yarralumla. Melbourne, New York, [etc.] Oxford University Press, 1968. xvii, 334 p. illus., ports. 23 cm. Bibliography: p. 319-323. [DU172.M8W5] 72-356973 8.50
1. Murray, Terence Aubrey, 1810-1873. I. Title. BIP

Murray, William Henry, 1869-1956.

BRYANT, Keith L. 976.6'05'924 B
Alfalfa Bill Murray, by Keith L. Bryant, Jr. [1st ed.] Norman, University of Oklahoma Press [1968] xiii, 287 p. illus., maps, ports. 24 cm. Bibliography: p. 277-278. [F700.M697] 68-10299
1. Murray, William Henry, 1869-1956. I. Title.

Murray, William Vans, 1760-1803.

HILL, Peter P., 1926- 327'.44'073
William Vans Murray, Federalist diplomat; the shaping of peace with France, 1797-1801 [by] Peter P. Hill. [1st ed. Syracuse, N.Y.] Syracuse University Press [1971] ix, 241 p. ports. 24 cm. Includes bibliographical references. [E183.8.F8I15] 71-150347 ISBN 0-8156-0078-X 8.50
1. Murray, William Vans, 1760-1803. 2. U.S.—Foreign relations—France. 3. France—Foreign relations—U.S. BIP

Murrieta, Joaquin, 1828 or 9-1853.

NADEAU, Remi A. 364.1'5'0924 B
The real Joaquin Murieta : Robin Hood hero or Gold Rush gangster? / by Remi Nadeau. 1st ed. Corona del Mar, Calif. : Trans-Anglo Books, c1974. 160 p. : ill. ; 24 cm. Includes index. Bibliography: p. 149-156. [F865.M9665] 73-87362 ISBN 0-87046-027-7 : 5.95
1. Murrieta, Joaquin, 1828 or 9 1853. I. Title.

Murrow, Edward R.

KENDRICK, Alexander. 070'.924
Prime time; the life of Edward R. Murrow. [1st ed.] Boston, Little, Brown [1969] viii, 548 p. illus., ports. 24 cm. Bibliography: p. [519]-520. [PN4874.M89K4] 78-83740 8.95
1. Murrow, Edward R. I. Title.

LICHELLO, Robert, 1926- 384.54'0924
Edward R. Murrow, broadcaster of courage. Charlotteville, N.Y., SamHar Press, 1971. 31 p. 22 cm. (Outstanding personalities, no. 4) Bibliography: p. 31. [PN4874.M89L5] 75-185660
1. Murrow, Edward R. I. Title.

SMITH, Robert Franklin, 1929-1973. 070.4'3'0924
Edward R. Murrow, the war years / by R. Franklin Smith. [Kalamazoo : New Issues Press, c1978] vi, 156 p.; 23 cm. Bibliography: p. 149. [PN4874.M89S58 1978] 78-104357 5.95
1. Murrow, Edward R. 2. Journalists—United States—Biography. I. Title.

Murrow, Edward R.—Juvenile literature.

MYERS, Hortense. 070.9'24 B
Edward R. Murrow, young newscaster, by Hortense Myers and Ruth Burnett. Illustrated by James Cummins. Indianapolis, Bobbs-Merrill [1969] 200 p. col. illus. 20 cm. (Childhood of famous Americans) A biography of the news commentator whose broadcasts from London during World War II made his name familiar to all Americans. [PN4874.M89M9] 92 76-77817
1. Murrow, Edward R.—Juvenile literature. I. Burnett, Ruth, joint author. II. Cummins, James, illus.

Murry, Colin, 1926- —Biography.

MURRY, Colin, 1926- 823'.9'14 B
I at the keyhole : an autobiography / by Colin Murry. New York : Stein and Day, [1975] p. cm. [PR6063.U82Z52] 74-26998 ISBN 0-8128-1758-3 : 7.95
1. Murry, Colin, 1926- —Biography. I. Title.

Murry, John Middleton, 1889-1957.

CARSWELL, John. 820'.9'00912
Lives and letters : A. R. Orage, Beatrice Hastings, Katherine Mansfield, John Middleton Murry, S. S. Koteliansky : 1906-1957 / by John Carswell. New York : New Directions Pub. Corp., 1978. p. cm. Includes index. Bibliography: p. [PR106.C37] 77-15986 ISBN 0-8112-0681-5 : 15.00
1. Orage, Alfred Richard, 1873-1934. 2. Hastings, Beatrice. 3. Mansfield, Katherine, 1888-1923. 4. Murry, John Middleton, 1889-1957. 5. Koteliansky, Samuel Solomonovitch, 1880-1955. 6. Authors, English—20th century—Biography. I. Title. BIP

CARSWELL, John. 820'.9'00912
Lives and letters : A. R. Orage, Beatrice Hastings, Katherine Mansfield, John Middleton Murry, S. S. Koteliansky, 1906-1957 / by John Carswell. London ; Boston : Faber and Faber, 1978. 306 p., [4] leaves of plates : ill. ; 23 cm. Includes index. Bibliography: p. 294-297. [PR106.C37 1978] 78-313376 ISBN 0-571-10596-3 : 15.00
1. Orage, Alfred Richard, 1873-1934. 2. Hastings, Beatrice. 3. Mansfield, Katherine, 1888-1923. 4. Murry, John Middleton, 1889-1957. 5. Koteliansky, Samuel Solomonovitch, 1880-1955. 6. Authors, English—20th century—Biography. I. Title.
Distributed by New Directions Publishing Corp., 333 Ave of the Americas, New York, NY 10014

LEA, Frank Alfred 928.2
The life of John Middleton Murry. New York, Oxford University Press [1960] 378p. (2p bibl. and 17p. bibl. notes) illus. 23cm. 60-1543 6.50
1. Murry, John Middleton, 1889-1957. I. Title.

Muse, Dan Thomas, Bp., 1882-

ODEN, Margaret (Muse) 1916- 922.89
Steps to the sun. Franklin Springs, Ga., Publishing House of the Pentecostal Holiness Church [1955] 129p. illus. 21cm. [BX8795.P25O3] 55-36602
1. Muse, Dan Thomas, Bp., 1882- I. Title.

Musial, Stanley Frank, 1920-

MUSIAL, Stanley Frank, 1920- 927.96357
Stan Musial: "the man's" own story, as told to Bob Broeg. [1st ed.] Garden City, N. Y., Doubleday, 1965. vi, 328 p. ports. 22 cm. [GV865.M8A3] 64-11753
I. Broeg, Robert M.

ROBINSON, Ray, Dec.4,1920- 927.96357
Stan Musial: baseball's durable "man." New York, Putnam [1963] 192 p. illus. 21 cm. [GV865.M8R6] 63-9694
1. Musial, Stanley Frank, 1920-

SCHOOR, Gene. 927.96357
The Stan Musial story, by Gene Schoor with Henry Gilfond. New York, J. Messner [1955] 192 p. illus. 22 cm. [GV865.M8S3] 55-6929
1. Musial, Stanley Frank, 1920-

Music.

ALEXANDER, Lloyd. 927.8
My love affair with music. Decorations by Vasiliu. New York, Crowell [1960] 274 p. illus. 21 cm. [ML64.A46] 60-8249
1. Music. I. Title.

STRAVINSKII, Igor Fedorovich, 1882- 927.8
Conversations with Igor Stravinsky [by] Igor Stravinsky and Robert Craft. [1st ed.] Garden City, N.Y., Doubleday, 1959. 162 p. illus. 22 cm. [ML410.S932A33] 59-6375
1. Music. 2. Craft, Robert. I. Title.

STRAVINSKII, Igor' Fedorovich, 1882-1971 927.8
Conversations with Igor Stravinsky [by] Igor Stravinsky and Robert Craft. [1st ed.] Garden City, N. Y., Doubleday, 1959. 162 p. illus. 22 cm. [ML410.S932A33] 59-6375
1. Music. I. Craft, Robert. II. Title.

STRAVINSKII, Igor Fedorovich, 1882-1971. 927.8
Dialogues and a diary [by] Igor Stravinsky and Robert Craft. [1st ed.] Garden City, N. Y., Doubleday, 1963. 279 p. group ports. 22 cm. [ML410.S932A335] 63-20511
1. Music. I. Craft, Robert. II. Title.

STRAVINSKII, Igor' Fedorovich, 1882-1971. 927.8
Memories and commentaries [by] Igor Stravinsky and Robert Craft. [1st ed.] Garden City, N. Y., Doubleday, 1960 [c1958] 167 p. illus. 22 cm. [ML410.S932A35] 60-10684
1. Music. I. Craft, Robert. II. Title.

Music—Addresses, essays, lectures.

APTHORP, William Foster, 1848-1913. 780'.922
Musicians and music-lovers, and other essays. Freeport, N.Y., Books for Libraries Press [1972] viii, 346 p. music. 23 cm. (Essay index reprint series) Reprint of the 1894 ed. Contents.Contents.—Musicians and music-lovers.—Johann Sebastian Bach.—Additional accompaniments to Bach's and Handel's scores.—Giacomo Meyerbeer.—Jacques Offenbach.—Two modern classicists [Robert Franz and Otto Dresel]—John Sullivan Dwight.—Some thoughts on musical criticism.—Music and science. [ML60.A65 1972] 74-39633 ISBN 0-8369-2736-2
1. Music—Addresses, essays, lectures. 2. Musicians—Biography. I. Title.

APTHORP, William Foster, 1848-1913. 780'.92'2
Musicians and music-lovers, and other essays / by William Foster Apthorp. Boston : Longwood Press, 1978. p. cm. Reprint of the 1894 ed. published by Scribner, New York. Contents.Contents.—Musicians and music-lovers.—Johann Sebastian Bach.—Additional accompaniments to Bach's and Handel's scores.—Giacomo Meyerbeer.—Jacques Offenbach.—Two modern classicists [Robert Franz and Otto Dresel].—John Sullivan Dwight.—Some thoughts on musical criticism.—Music and science. [ML60.A65 1978] 78-58194 ISBN 0-89341-433-6 lib.bdg. : 35.00
1. Music—Addresses, essays, lectures. 2. Musicians—Biography. I. Title. BIP

SAINT-SAENS, Camille, 1835-1921. 780
Musical memories. Translated by Edwin Gile Rich. New York, Da Capo Press, 1969. 282 p. illus., ports. 24 cm. (Da Capo Press music reprint series) Translation of Ecole buissonniere. Reprint of the 1919 ed. [ML60.S14R4 1969] 70-93980
1. Music—Addresses, essays, lectures. 2. Musicians—Correspondence, reminiscences, etc. BIP

Music—Anecdotes, facetiae, satire, etc.

BORGE, Victor. 782'.0922 B
My favorite intermissions, by Victor Borge and Robert Sherman. Drawings by Thomas Winding. Garden City, N.Y., Doubleday [1971] 187 p. illus. 22 cm. [ML65.B675M9] 77-163733 4.95
1. Music—Anecdotes, facetiae, satire, etc. I. Sherman, Robert, 1931- joint author. II. Title. BIP

Music—Bibliography.

GILDER, Eric. 016.78
The dictionary of composers and their music : every listener's companion : arranged chronologically and alphabetically / Eric Gilder, June G. Port. New York : Paddington Press : distributed by Grosset & Dunlap, c1978. 406, [25] p. ; 24 cm. [ML113.G4] 77-15998 ISBN 0-448-22364-3 : 12.95
1. Music—Bibliography. 2. Music—Chronology. I. Port, June G., 1930- joint author. II. Title. BIP

GILDER, Eric. 016.78
The dictionary of composers and their music : every listener's companion : arranged chronologically and alphabetically / Eric Gilder, June G. Port. New York : Ballantine Books, 1979, c1978. 593p. ; 18 cm. [ML113.G4] ISBN 0-345-28041-5 pbk. : 2.75
1. Music — Bibliography. 2. Music — Chronology. I. Port, June G., 1930- joint author. II. Title.
L.C. card no. for 1978 Paddington Press ed.: 77-15998.

THOMPSON, Kenneth. 016.78'0904
A dictionary of twentieth-century composers (1911-1971) New York, St. Martin's Press [1973] 666 p. 25 cm. Catalogs of the works of Bartok, Berg, Bloch, Busoni, Debussy, Delius, Elgar, De Falla, Faure, Hindemith, Holst, Honegger, Ives, Janacek, Kodaly, Mahler, Martinu, Nielsen, Poulenc, Prokofiev, Puccini, Rachmaninov, Ravel, Roussel, Satie, Schoenberg, Sibelius, Richard Webren, with bibliographies and biographical sketches. [ML118.T5 1973b] 78-175526 30.00
1. Music—Bibliography. I. Title.

Music—Bio-bibliography.

BAKER, Theodor, 1851-1934. 927.8
Biographical dictionary of musicians. 5th ed., completely rev. by Nicolas Slonimsky. New York, G. Schirmer [1958] xv, 1855p. 24cm. [ML105.B16 1958] 58-4953
1. Music—Bio-bibl. I. Slonimsky, Nicolas, 1894- ed. II. Title.

BAKER, Theodore, 1851-1934. 780'.92'2 B
Baker's Biographical dictionary of musicians. 6th ed. / completely rev. by Nicolas Slonimsky. New York : Schirmer Books, c1978. p. cm. [ML105.B16 1978] 78-3205 ISBN 0-02-870240-9 : 75.00
1. Music—Bio-bibliography. I. Slonimsky, Nicolas, 1894- BIP

BAKER, Theodore, 1851-1934. 927.8
Biographical dictionary of musicians. 5th ed., completely rev. by Nicolas Slonimsky. New York, G. Schirmer [1958] xv, 1855 p. 24 cm. [ML105.B16 1958] 58-4953
1. Music—Bio-bibliography. I. Slonimsky, Nicolas, 1894- ed.

BAKER, Theodore, 1851-1934. 780'.92'2 B
Biographical dictionary of musicians. 5th ed. Completely rev. by Nicolas Slonimsky, with 1971 suppl. New York, G. Schirmer [1971] xvi, 1855, 262 p. 24 cm. [ML105.B16 1971] 78-183534 ISBN 0-911320-62-8
1. Music—Bio-bibliography. I. Slonimsky, Nicolas, 1894- ed.

BAKER, Theodore, 1851-1934. 780.922
Biographical dictionary of musicians. 5th ed., completely rev. by Nicolas Slonimsky. New York, G Schirmer [1958] New York, G. Schirmer, 1965. xv, 1855 p. 24 cm. vii, 143 p. 24 cm. Supplement, by Nicolas Slonimsky. [ML105.B16 1958] 58-4953
1. Music—Bio-bibl. I. Sionimsky, Nicolas, 1894- ed. II. Title.

CARLSON, Effie B. 780'.922
A bio-bibliographical dictionary of twelve-tone and serial composers, by Effie B. Carlson. Metuchen, N.J., Scarecrow Press, 1970. 233 p. 22 cm. Bibliography: p. 212-233. [ML105.C39] 79-8959
1. Music—Bio-bibliography. I. Title.

EWEN, David, 1907- ed., 780.922
Great composers, 1300-1900: a biographical and critical guide. New York, Wilson [c.]1966. 429p. ports. 27cm. [ML105.E944] 65-24585 10.00
1. Music—Bio-bibl. 2. Composers. I. Title.

EWEN, David, 1907- 780.922
Great composers, 1300-1900; a biographical and critical guide New York, H. W. Wilson Co., 1966. 429 p. ports. 27 cm. [ML105.E944] 65-24585
1. Music — Bio-bibl. 2. Composers. I. Title.

EWEN, David, 1907- 780'.92'2 B
Musicians since 1900 : performers in concert and opera / compiled and edited by David Ewen. New York : H. W. Wilson Co., 1978. p. cm. [ML105.E97] 78-12727 ISBN 0-8242-0565-0 : 35.00
1. Music—Bio-bibliography. 2. Opera—Bio-bibliography. I. Title.

FEATHER, Leonard G. 785.4'2'0922
The encyclopedia of jazz in the seventies / by Leonard Feather and Ira Gitler ; introduction by Quincy Jones. New York : Horizon Press, c1976. 393 p. : ill. ; 27 cm. "Bibliography: books 1966-1975", p. [391]-393. [ML105.F36] 76-21196 ISBN 0-8180-1215-3 : 20.00
1. Music—Bio-bibliography. 2. Jazz musicians—Biography. 3. Jazz music—Discography. I. Gitler, Ira, joint author. II. Title. BIP

FEATHER, Leonard G. 785.420922
The encyclopedia of jazz in the sixties, by Leonard Feather. Foreword by John Lewis. New York, Horizon Press [1966] 1 v. (unpaged) ports. 26 cm. Includes bibliography and discographies. [ML105.F35] 66-26705
1. Music—Bio-bibliography. 2. Jazz musicians. 3. Jazz music—Discography. I. Title. BIP

HISTORICAL Records Survey. District of Columbia. 016.78'092'2
Bio-bibliographical index of musicians in the United States of America since colonial times. St. Clair Shores, Mich., Scholarly Press, 1972. xxiii, 439 p. 28 cm. Prepared under the supervision of Leonard Ellinwood and Keyes Porter. Reprint of the 1956 ed. Bibliography: p. xvii-xxiii. [ML106.U3H6 1972b] 76-166235 ISBN 0-403-01362-3
1. Music—Bio-bibliography. 2. Music—United States—Bio-bibliography. I. Ellinwood, Leonard Webster, 1905- ed. II. Porter, Keyes, 1887- ed. III. Title.

HISTORICAL Records Survey. District of Columbia. 016.78'0922
Bio-bibliographical index of musicians in the United States of America since colonial times. Prepared under the supervision of Leonard Ellinwood and Keyes Porter. New York, Da Capo Press, 1971. xxiii, 439 p. 27 cm. (Da Capo Press music reprint series) Reprint of the 1956 ed. Bibliography: p. xvii-xxiii. [ML106.U3H6 1971] 76-159677 ISBN 0-306-70183-9
1. Music—Bio-bibliography. 2. Music—U.S.—Bio-bibliography. I. Ellinwood, Leonard Webster, 1905- ed. II. Porter, Keyes, 1887- ed. III. Title.

HISTORICAL Records Survey. District of Columbia. 780'.922 B
Bio-bibliographical index of musicians in the United States of America since colonial times. Washington, Music Section, Pan American Union, 1956. 2d ed. [New York, AMS Press, 1972] xxiii, 439 p. 27 cm. Prepared under the supervision of Leonard Ellinwood and Keyes Porter. Reprint of the 1956 ed. Bibliography: p. xvii-xxiii. [ML106.U3H6 1972] 76-39375 ISBN 0-404-08075-8 20.00
1. Music—Bio-bibliography. 2. Music—United States—Bio-bibliography. I. Ellinwood, Leonard Webster, 1905- ed. II. Porter, Keyes, 1887- ed. III. Title.

HISTORICAL Records Survey. District of Columbia. 016.78071
Bio-bibliographical index of musicians in the United States of America since colonial times. 2d ed. Washington, Music Section, Pan American Union, 1956. xxiii, 439p. 28cm. 'This Index was first planned in 1936 by Keyer Porter ... It was revived and expanded in January 1940 under the supervision of Dr. Leonard Ellinwood.' Bibliography: p. xvii-xxiii. 'A list of special studies, biographies, and autobiographies pertaining to the persons whose names appear in the Index': p. 421-439. [ML106.U3H6 1956] PA57
1. Music—Bio-bibl. 2. Music—U. S.—Bio-bibl. I. Title. BIP

HUGHES, Rupert, 1872-1956, ed. 780'.922
The biographical dictionary of musicians, originally compiled by Rupert Hughes. Completely rev. and newly edited by Deems Taylor and Russell Kerr. St. Clair Shores, Mich., Scholarly Press, 1971. 481 p. 22 cm. Reprint of the 1940 ed. [ML100.H892T2 1971] 73-166237
1. Music—Bio-bibliography. I. Taylor, Deems, 1885-1966, ed. II. Kerr, Russell, ed. BIP

THE music makers / 780'.92'2 B
editorial director, Victor Stevenson ; editor, Clive Unger-Hamilton. New York : H. N. Abrams, 1979. 255, [19] p. : ill. (some col.) ; 31 cm. Includes index. Bibliography: p. [264] [ML105.M9] 78-56318 ISBN 0-8109-1327-5 : 35.00
1. Music—Bio-bibliography. I. Stevenson, Victor. II. Unger-Hamilton, Clive.

PANASSIE, Hugues. 785.4'2
Guide to jazz, by Hugues Panassie and Madeleine Gautier. Translated by Desmond Flower; edited by A. A. Gurwitch. Introd. by Louis Armstrong. Westport, Conn., Greenwood Press [1973, c1956] vii, 312 p. illus. 23 cm. [ML102.J3P33 1973] 73-435 ISBN 0-8371-6766-3 15.00
1. Music—Bio-bibliography. 2. Jazz music—Dictionaries. 3. Jazz musicians. I. Gautier, Madeleine, 1905- joint author. II. Title. BIP

SIMMONS, David, ed. 927.8
Who's who in music and musicians' international directory. New York, Hafner Pub. Co. v. 26 cm. Began publication in 1935. Editor: 19 D. Simmons. [ML106.G7W44] 62-1554
1. Music — Bio-bibl. I. Title.

Music—California—San Francisco.

HAUSER, Miska, 1822-1887. 780'.9794'61 S
The letters of Miska Hauser, 1853. [Translated from the German by Eric Benson, Donald Peet Cobb, and Horatio F. Stoll, Jr.] New York, AMS Press [1972] 185 p. illus. 27 cm. (History of music in San Francisco series, v. 3) Originally published by the History of Music Project. Reprint of the 1939 ed. Bibliography: p. 178. [ML200.8.S2H4 vol. 3, 1972] 77-38303 ISBN 0-404-07243-7 12.50
1. Music—California—San Francisco. 2. Violinists, violoncellists, etc.—Correspondence, reminiscences, etc. 3. Musicians—San Francisco. I. History of Music Project. II. Title. III. Series.

HAUSER, Miska, 1822-1887. 780'.9794'61 S
The letters of Miska Hauser, 1853. [Translated from the German by Eric Benson, Donald Peet Cobb, and Horatio F. Stoll, Jr.] New York, AMS Press [1972] 185 p. illus. 27 cm. (History of music in San Francisco series, v. 3) Originally published by the History of Music Project. Reprint of the 1939 ed. Bibliography: p. 178. [ML200.8.S2H4 vol. 3, 1972] 77-38303 ISBN 0-404-07243-7 12.50
1. Music—California—San Francisco. 2. Violinists, violoncellists, etc.—Correspondence, reminiscences, etc. 3. Musicians—San Francisco. I. History of Music Project. II. Title. III. Series.

Music—Canada—Bio-bibliography.

CANADIAN Broadcasting Corporation. 016.78'092'2
Catalogue of Canadian composers; edited by Helmut Kallmann. Rev. and enl. ed. St. Clair Shores, Mich., Scholarly Press, 1972. 254 p. 21 cm. Reprint of the 1952 ed. Bibliography: p. 19-21. [ML106.C3C3 1972] 75-166240 ISBN 0-403-01375-5
1. Music—Canada—Bio-bibliography. 2. Musicians, Canadian. I. Kallmann, Helmut, ed. II. Title. BIP

Music—Dictionaries.

THOMPSON, Oscar, 1887-1945. 781.91
The international cyclopedia of music and musicians. Editor in chief: Oscar Thompson. Editor, 9th ed.: Robert Sabin. New York, Dodd, Mead, 1964. 2476 p. music, ports. 29 cm. [ML100.T47 1964] 64-23285
1. Music—Dictionaries. 2. Music—Biobibliography. I. Sabin, Robert, ed. II. Title. BIP

Music—History and criticism.

BROCKWAY, Wallace, 1905- 927.8
Men of music; their lives, times, and achievements [by] Wallace Brockway & Herbert Weinstock. Rev. and enl. ed. New York, Simon and Schuster, 1950. xvi, 649 p. ports. 24 cm. [ML390.B85 1950] 50-10706
1. Music—Hist. & crit. 2. Composers. I. Weinstock, Herbert, 1905- joint author. II. Title.

BROCKWAY, Wallace, 1905- 927.8
Men of music; their lives, times, and achievements [by] Wallace Brockway & Herbert Weinstock. Rev. and enl. ed. New York, Simon and Schuster [1958] 649 p. illus. 22 cm. [ML390.B85 1958] 58-14928
1. Music—History and criticism. 2. Composers. I. Weinstock, Herbert, 1905- joint author. II. Title.

Music—History and criticism—Outlines, syllabi, etc.

LOVELOCK, William. 780'.922 B
Brief biographies. Melbourne, Allans Music (Australia) Pty. [197-?] 44 p. 25 cm. (Imperial edition no. 1083) Cover title. [ML161.L69] 72-882823 0.75
1. Music—History and criticism—Outlines, syllabi, etc. 2. Composers—Biography. I. Title.

Music—History and criticism—19th century.

MASON, Daniel Gregory, 1873-1953. 780'.922
From Grieg to Brahms. New York, AMS Press [1971] ix, 259 p. ports. 19 cm. Reprint of the 1927 ed. Contents.Contents.—Introduction: The appreciation of music.—Edvard Grieg.—Antonin Dvorak.—Camille Saint-Saens.—Cesar Franck.—Peter Ilyitch Tschaikowsky.—Johannes Brahms.—Epilogue: The meaning of music.—Postscript: After twenty-five years. Bibliography: p. 256-259. [ML390.M4 1971] 79-149689 ISBN 0-404-04199-X 9.00
1. Music—History and criticism—19th century. 2. Composers—Biography. I. Title. BIP

Music—History and criticism—20th century.

EWEN, David, 1907- 780'.92'2 B
Composers of tomorrow's music : a non-technical introduction to the musical avant-garde movement / by David Ewen. Westport, Conn. : Greenwood Press, 1980, c1971. p. cm. Reprint of the ed. published by Dodd, Mead, New York. Includes index. [ML197.E85 1980] 79-18514 ISBN 0-313-22107-3 : 17.75
1. Music—History and criticism—20th century. 2. Composers. I. Title. BIP

ROSSI, Nick, writer on music. 780'.922
Music of our time; an anthology of works of selected contemporary composers of the 20th century, by Nick Rossi and Robert A. Choate. Boston, Crescendo Pub. Co. [1970, c1969] xi, 406 p. illus., music, ports. 24 cm. Bibliography: p. 390-396. [ML197.R77] 69-16933 12.50
1. Music—History and criticism—20th century. I. Choate, Robert A., joint author. II. Title.

Music, Jewish—History and criticism.

HOLDE, Artur. 781.7'2'924
Jews in music : from the age of enlightenment to the mid-twentieth century / Artur Holde. New ed. / prepared by Irene Heskes. New York : Bloch Pub. Co., c1974. xv, 366 p. ; 22 cm. [ML3776.H64 1974] 74-83942 ISBN 0-8197-0372-9 : 7.95
1. Music, Jewish—History and criticism. 2. Musicians, Jewish—Biography. I. Title. **BIP**

Music—Juvenile literature.

WHEELER, Opal. 927.8
Peter Tschaikowsky and the Nutcracker Ballet. [1st ed.] New York, E. P. Dutton [1959] 95 p. illus. 24 cm. [ML3930.C4W45] 59-5843
1. Music—Juvenile literature.

Music, Popular (Songs, etc.)—Bio-bibliography.

BROWN, Len. 784.4'9'22 B
The encyclopedia of country and western music, by Len Brown and Gary Friedrich. [New York, Tower Publications, 1971] 191 p. ports. 18 cm. (A Tower book) Bio-bibliographical. [ML102.P66B75] 70-24299 1.25
1. Music, Popular (Songs, etc.)—Bio-bibliography. I. Friedrich, Gary, joint author. II. Title.

BROWN, Len. 784'.0922 B
Encyclopedia of rock & roll, by Len Brown and Gary Friedrich. [New York, Tower Publications, 1970] 217 p. ports. 18 cm. (A Tower book) [ML102.P66B8] 75-21353 1.25
1. Music, Popular (Songs, etc.)—Bio-bibliography. I. Friedrich, Gary, joint author. II. Title.

EMERSON, Lucy. 784'.092'2 B
The Gold record / Lucy Emerson. New York : Fountain Pub. Co., c1976. p. cm. [ML102.P66E45] 76-23396 4.95
1. Music, Popular (Songs, etc.)—Bio-bibliography. 2. Rock musicians—Biography. I. Title. **BIP**

Music, Popular (Songs, etc.)—Dictionaries.

STAMBLER, Irwin. 784'.092'2 B
Encyclopedia of pop, rock and soul / by Irwin Stambler. New York : St. Martin's Press, [1975] c1974. 609 p. : ports. ; 25 cm. Bibliography: p. 605-609. [ML102.P66S8] 73-87393 19.95
1. Music, Popular (Songs, etc.)—Dictionaries. 2. Music, Popular (Songs, etc.)—Bio-bibliography. 3. Rock music—Dictionaries. 4. Rock music—Bio-bibliography. 5. Blues (Songs, etc.)—Dictionaries. 6. Blues (Songs, etc.)—Bio-bibliography. I. Title. **BIP**

STAMBLER, Irwin. 784'.092'2 B
Encyclopedia of pop, rock & soul / Irwin Stambler. New York : St. Martin's Press, c1977. 609 p. : ports. ; 24 cm. Bibliography: p. 605-609. [ML102.P66S8 1977] 77-362433 ISBN 0-312-25025-8 : 6.95
1. Music, Popular (Songs, etc.)—Dictionaries. 2. Music, Popular (Songs, etc.)—Bio-bibliography. 3. Rock music—Dictionaries. 4. Rock music—Bio-bibliography. 5. Blues (Songs, etc.)—Dictionaries. 6. Blues (Songs, etc.)—Bio-bibliography. I. Title.

Music, Popular (Songs, etc.)—U.S.—History and criticism.

COLBERT, Warren E. 784'.092'2
Who wrote that song? : or, Who in the hell is J. Fred Coots? : an informal survey of American popular songs and their composers / by Warren E. Colbert. New York : Revisionist Press, 1975. 195 p. : port. ; 24 cm. "Alphabetical listing of most popular songs": p. 113-195. [ML3561.P6C64] 74-27665 ISBN 0-87700-216-9 lib.bdg. : 29.00
1. Music, Popular (Songs, etc.)—United States—History and criticism. 2. Music, Popular (Songs, etc.)—United States—Bio-bibliography. I. Title.

COUNTRY music who's who (The); 784.092025 1966 [Denver, Colo. 80227, 3258 Sd. Wadsworth Blvd., Heather Pubns.] 1965. iv. (unpaged) illus. (pt. col.) ports. 29cm. Title varies. Ed.: 1966-- Thurston Moore. [ML1.C918] 60-1664 10.00
1. Music, Popular (songs, etc.)—U.S. Hist. and crit. I. Moore, Thurston, ed. II. Title: The Original country music who's who.

EWEN, David, 1907- 784'.0922
Great men of American popular song; the history of the American popular song told through the lives, careers, achievements, and personalities of its foremost composers and lyricists-from William Billings of the Revolutionary War to the "folk-rock" of Bob Dylan. Englewood Cliffs, N.J., Prentice-Hall [1970] x, 387 p. 25 cm. [ML3551.E83] 79-110079 12.95
1. Music, Popular (Songs, etc.)—U.S.—History and criticism. 2. Composers, American—Biography. I. Title.

WILK, Max. 784'.092'2 B
They're playing our song; from Jerome Kern to Stephen Sondheim - the stories behind the words and music of two generations. [1st ed.] New York, Atheneum, 1973. xv, 295 p. 25 cm. [ML3561.P6W5] 72-94250 ISBN 0-689-10554-1 10.00
1. Music, Popular (Songs, etc.)—United States—History and criticism. 2. Music, Popular (Songs, etc.)—United States—Bio-bibliography. I. Title.

Music—Russia—History and criticism.

MONTAGU-NATHAN, Montagu. 780'.92'2 B
A history of Russian music / by M. Montagu-Nathan. Boston : Longwood Press, 1977. p. cm. Reprint of the 1914 ed. published by Scribner, New York. [ML300.M78 1977] 77-8740 ISBN 0-89341-129-9 : 25.00
1. Music—Russia—History annd criticism. 2. Composers—Russia—Biography. I. Title. **BIP**

MONTAGU-NATHAN, Montagu. 780'.92'2 B
A history of Russian music, being an account of the rise and progress of the Russian school of composers, with a survey of their lives and a description of their works, by M. Montagu-Nathan. Boston, Milford House [1973] viii, 346 p. port. 22 cm. Running title: A short history of Russian music. Reprint of the 1914 ed. published by Scribner, New York. [ML300.M78 1973] 73-12306 ISBN 0-87821-061-X 22.50
1. Music—Russia—History and criticism. 2. Composers, Russian—Biography. I. Title.

Music—Russia—1917-

KREBS, Stanley Dale. 780'.922
Soviet composers and the development of Soviet music, by Stanley D. Krebs. New York, W. W. Norton [1970] 364 p. music. 23 cm. Bibliography: p. [344]-357. [ML300.5.K74] 69-14702 11.50
1. Music—Russia—1917- 2. Composers, Russian. I. Title.

Music—United States.

MARKS, Edward Bennet, 1865-1945. 782'.092'2 B
They all had glamour, from the Swedish Nightingale to the naked lady. Westport, Conn., Greenwood Press [1972, c1944] xvii, 448 p. illus. 23 cm. [ML3551.M3 1972] 79-154104 ISBN 0-8371-6075-8
1. Music—United States. 2. Theater—United States. 3. Singers—Biography. 4. Musicians—Correspondence, reminiscences, etc. I. Title.

Music—United States—Bio-bibliography.

AMERICAN Society of Composers, Authors and Publishers. 780.922
The ASCAP biographical dictionary of composers, authors and publishers. [3d ed.] Compiled and edited by the Lynn Farnol Group, Inc. New York, 1966. 845 p. 22 cm. [ML106.U3A5 1966] 66-20214
1. Music—United States—Bio-bibliography. I. Farnol (Lynn) Group, inc., ed. II. Title.

AMERICAN Society of Composers, Authors and Publishers. 927.8
The ASCAP biographical dictionary of composers, authors, and publishers, Edited by Daniel I. McNamara. 2d ed. New York, Crowell [1952] 636 p. 22 cm. (A Crowell reference book) [ML106.U3A5 1952] 52-7038
1. Music—U. S.—Bio-bibl. I. McNamara, Daniel Ignatius, 1885- ed. II. Title.

CLAGHORN, Charles Eugene, 1911- 780'.92'2 B
Biographical dictionary of American music. West Nyack, N.Y., Parker Pub. Co. [1973] 491 p. 24 cm. [ML106.U3C6] 73-5534 ISBN 0-13-076331-4 12.95
1. Music—United States—Bio-bibliography. I. Title. **BIP**

SOUTHEASTERN Composers' League. 780'.92'2
Catalogue. [Hattiesburg, Miss., Tritone Press] v. 28 cm. "Contains biographies and lists of compositions." [ML106.U3S7] 63-47639
1. Music—U.S.—Bio-bibl. 2. Composers—Southern States. I. Title.

Musical revue, comedy, etc.—Great Britain—Dictionaries.

BUSBY, Roy. 792.7'092'2 B
British music hall : an illustrated who's who from 1850 to the present day / Roy Busby. London ; Salem, N.H. : Elek, 1976. 191 p. : ill. ; 25 cm. [ML102.M88B9] 77-351040 ISBN 0-236-40053-3 : 24.95
1. Musical revue, comedy, etc.—Great Britain—Dictionaries. 2. Musicians—Biography. 3. Entertainers—Biography. I. Title.

Musicians.

BAKELESS, Katherine (Little) 1895- 927.8
In the big time; career stories of American entertainers, illustrated from photos. [1st ed.] Philadelphia, Lippincott [1953] 211p. illus. 21cm. [ML385.B18] 53-10217
1. Musicians. 2. Entertainers. I. Title.

BINGLEY, William, 1774-1823. 780'.922 B
Musical biography; memoirs of the lives and writings of the most eminent musical composers and writers who have flourished in the different countries of Europe during the last three centuries. New York, Da Capo Press, 1971. 2 v. 23 cm. (Da Capo Press music reprint series) Reprint of the 1834 ed. [ML385.B61 1971] 70-127286 ISBN 0-306-70032-8
1. Musicians. 2. Music—Bio-bibliography.

CHOTZINOFF, Samuel, 1889- 927.8
A little nightmusic; intimate conversations with Jascha Heifetz, Vladimir Horowitz, Gian Carlo Menotti, Leontyne Price, Richard Rodgers, Artur Rubinstein, Andres Segovia. Drawings by Olga Koussevitzky. [1st ed.] New York, Harper & Row [c1964] 151 p. illus. 22 cm. [ML385.C48] 63-21742
1. Musicians. I. Title.

EWEN, David, 1907- 927.8
Famous instrumentalists. New York, Dodd [c.1965] 159p. ports. 23cm. (Famous biographies for young people) [ML395.E9] 65-14118 3.25
1. Musicians. I. Title.

GELATT, Roland, 1920- 927.8
Music makers, some outstanding musical performers of our day. [1st ed.] New York, Knopf, 1953. 286p. illus. 22cm. [ML394.G4] 51-11983
1. Musicians. I. Title. **BIP**

GELATT, Roland, 1920- 780'.922
Music makers, some outstanding musical performers of our day. New York, Da Capo Press, 1972 [c1953] xvi, 286, xiv p. ports. 22 cm. (Da Capo Press music reprint series) [ML394.G4 1972] 72-2334 ISBN 0-306-70519-2
1. Musicians. I. Title.

GREAT musicians as children. v. 12 Garden City, N. Y., Doubleday [1960?] ix, 238p. 22cm.
1. Musicians. 2. Children as musicians. I. Schwimmer, Franciska. II. Title: Musicians as children.

NETTI, Paul, 1889- 927.8
Forgotten musicians. New York, Philosophical Library [1951] 352 p. 23 cm. [ML385.N5] 51-14690
1. Musicians. I. Title.

TERKEL, Louis. 927.8
Giants of jazz, by Studs Terkel. Sketches by Robert Galster. New York, Crowell [1957] 215 p. illus. 21 cm. [ML385.T45] 57-9251
1. Musicians. 2. Jazz music. I. Title. **BIP**

YOUNG, Patricia, writer on music. 920
Great performers. New York, H. Z. Walck, 1967. 71 p. illus., ports. 22 cm. (The Young reader's guides to music) Sketches the lives of five artists of the performing arts: Nicolo Paganini, Franz Liszt, Enrico Caruso, Anna Pavlova, and Arturo Toscanini. [ML3930.A2Y5 1967] AC 67
1. Musicians. I. Title.

Musicians—Correspondence, reminiscence etc.

ALDA, Frances. 782.1'0924
Men, women, and tenors. Freeport, N.Y., Books for Libraries Press [1970] 307 p. illus., ports. 23 cm. Reprint of the 1937 ed. [ML420.A56A3 1970] 72-107790
1. Musicians—Correspondence, reminiscences, etc. 2. Opera—New York (City) 3. Singers. I. Title. **BIP**

ALVAREZ, Marguerite d, 1886-1953. 927.8
All the bright dreams, an autobiography. [1st American ed.] New York, Harcourt, Briance [1956] 313p. illus. 21cm. First published in London in 1954 under title: Forsaken altara [ML420.A584A3 1956] 56-58562
1 Musicianc Correspondence, reminiscenes, etc. I. Title.

AMRAM, David. 780'.924
Vibrations; the adventures and musical times of David Amram. New York, Macmillan Co. [1968] 469 p. 22 cm. [ML410.A534A3] 68-23627
1. Musicians—Correspondence, reminiscences, etc. I. Title.

ANDERSON, Marian, 1902- 927.8
My Lord, what a morning; an autobiography. New York, Watts [1966, c.1956] 312p. 29cm. (Keith Jennison large type ed.) [ML420.A6A3] 6.95
1. Musicians—Correspondence, reminiscences, etc. I. Title.

ANDERSON, Marian, 1902- 927.8
My Lord, what a morning. an autobiography. New York, Viking Press, 1956. 312p. illus. 22cm. 'A condensed version ... appeared in serial form in the Woman's home companion.' [ML420.A6A3] 56-10402
1. Musicians—Correspondence, reminiscences, etc. I. Title.

ANDERSON, Marian, 1902- 927.8
My Lord, what a morning; an autobiography. New York, Viking Press, 1956. 312 p. illus. 22 cm. "A condensed version ... appeared in serial form in the Woman's home companion." [ML420.A6A3] 56-10402
1. Musicians—Correspondence, reminiscences, etc. I. Title.

ARMSTRONG, Louis, 1900- v. 12
Satchmo; my life in New Orleans. [New York] New American Library [c1954 1961] 191 p. illus. 18 cm. (Signet Book D 1970) NUC66
1. Musicians — Correspondence, reminiscences, etc. 2. Jazz music. I. Title.

ARMSTRONG, Louis, 1900- 927.8
1971.
Satchmo; my life in New Orleans. New York, Prentice-Hall [1954] 240 p. illus. 21 cm. [ML419.A75A3] 54-9628
1. Musicians—Correspondence, reminiscences, etc. 2. Jazz music. I. Title.

ARNOLD, Eddy. 784.4'9'24 B
It's a long way from Chester County. Old Tappan, N.J., Hewitt House [1969] 154 p. illus., ports. 22 cm. Autobiographical. [ML420.A77A3] 69-20149 4.95
1. Musicians—Correspondence, reminiscences, etc. I. Title.

ATWOOD, Rudy. 786.1'0924 B
The Rudy Atwood story. Old Tappan, N.J., Revell [1970] 126 p. 21 cm. [ML417.A89A3] 75-123066 3.50
1. Musicians—Correspondence, reminiscences, etc. I. Title.

AZNAVOUR, Charles. 784'.092'4 B
Aznavour by Aznavour; an autobiography. Translated by Ghilaine Boulanger. Chicago, Cowles Book Co. [1972] 283 p. ports. 24 cm. [ML410.A888A33] 75-183824 7.95
1. Musicians—Correspondence, reminiscences, etc.

BAEZ, Joan. 784.4'9'24
Daybreak. New York, Dial Press, 1968. 159 p. 21 cm. [ML420.B114A3] 68-29756
1. Musicians—Correspondence, reminiscences, etc. I. Title.

BAILEY, Pearl. 784'.0924
The raw Pearl. [1st ed.] New York, Harcourt, Brace & World [1968] 206 p. ports. 22 cm. [ML420.B123A3] 67-11963
1. Musicians—Correspondence, reminiscences, etc. I. Title. BIP

BAILEY, Pearl. 784'.0924
The raw Pearl. [1st ed.] New York, Harcourt, Brace & World [1968] 206 p. ports. 22 cm. [ML420.B123A3] 67-11963
1. Musicians—Correspondence, reminiscences, etc. I. Title. BIP

BAILEY, Pearl. 784'.0924
Talking to myself. [1st ed.] New York, Harcourt Brace Jovanovich [1971] xiv, 233 p. 22 cm. [ML420.B123A33] 78-153679 ISBN 0-15-187990-7
1. Musicians—Correspondence, reminiscences, etc. I. Title. BIP

BARTOK, Bela, 1881- 780'.924 B
1945.
Bela Bartok letters. Collected, selected, edited, and annotated by Janos Demeny. Prefaced by Sir Michael Tippett. Translated into English by Peter Balaban and Istvan Farkas. Translation rev. by Elisabeth West and Colin Mason. New York, St. Martin's Press [1971] 466 p. illus. 25 cm. Bibliography: p. 453-454. [ML410.B26A42 1971b] 70-124146 20.00
1. Musicians—Correspondence, reminiscences, etc. I. Demeny, Janos, ed.

BECHET, Sidney. 927.8
Treat it gentle. Among those who helped record and edit the tapes on which this book is based are: Joan Reid, Desmond Flower, and John Ciardi. New York, Hill and Wang [1960] 245 p. illus. 22 cm. Includes discography. [ML419.B23A3 1960a] 60-15935
1. Musicians—Correspondence, reminiscences, etc. I. Title.

BECHET, Sidney. 788'.66'0924 B
Treat it gentle / by Sidney Bechet. New York : Da Capo Press, 1975. p. cm. (The Roots of jazz) Reprint of the 1st ed., 1960, published by Cassell, London. "A catalogue of the recordings of Sidney Bechet, compiled by David Mylne": p. [ML419.B23A3 1975] 74-23412 ISBN 0-306-70657-1 : 12.50.
1. Musicians—Correspondence, reminiscences, etc. I. Title.

BERG, Alban, 1885- 780'.924 B
1935.
Alban Berg, letters to his wife. Edited, translated and annotated by Bernard Grun. New York, St. Martin's Press [1971] 456 p. illus., facsims., ports. 23 cm. Translation of Briefe an seine Frau. [ML410.B47A473 1971b] 79-145592 15.00
1. Musicians—Correspondence, reminiscences, etc. I. Berg, Helene (Nahowski)

BERLIOZ, Hector, 1803- 780.924
1869
Hector Berlioz: a selection from his letters; selected, edited, and translated by Humphrey Seale. New York, Vienna House, 1973 224 p. illus., 21 cm. Bibliography: p. [217]-218. [ML410.B5A517] 73-87555 ISBN 0-8443-0114-0 2.95 (pbk.)
1. Musicians—Correspondence, reminiscences, etc. I. Seale, Humphrey, ed. and tr. II. Title.

BERLIOZ, Hector, 780'.92'4 B
1803-1869.
New letters of Berlioz, 1830-1868. With introd., notes, and English translation by Jacques Barzun. [2d ed.] Westport, Conn., Greenwood Press [1974] xxxi, 322 p. illus. 22 cm. (Columbia bicentennial editions and studies) French and English; added t.p. in French. Bibliography: p. 310-312. [ML410.B5A33 1974] 75-100144 ISBN 0-8371-3251-7 14.50
1. Musicians—Correspondence, reminiscences, etc. I. Barzun, Jacques, 1907- ed. II. Title. BIP

BING, Rudolf, Sir, 782.1'092'4 B
1902-
5000 nights at the opera. [1st ed. Garden City, N.Y. Doubleday, 1972. 360 p. illus. 22 cm. [ML429.B52A3] 72-76124 ISBN 0-385-09259-8 10.00
1. Musicians—Correspondence, reminiscences, etc. I. Title.

BING, Rudolf, 782.1'092'4 [B]
Sir, 1902-
5000 nights at the opera. New York, Popular Library [1973, c.1972] 360 p. illus. 18 cm. At head of title: The memoirs of Sir Rudolf Bing. [ML429.B52A3] 1.25 (pbk.)
1. Musicians—Correspondence, reminiscences, etc. I. Title.
L.C. card no. for the hardbound edition: 72-76124.

BOULTON, Laura Theresa 781.7'0924
(Craytor)
The music hunter, the autobiography of a career, by Laura Boulton. [1st ed.] Garden City, N.Y., Doubleday, 1969. xiv, 513 p. illus., maps, ports. 22 cm. [ML423.B53A3] 67-11154 8.95
1. Musicians—Correspondence, reminiscences, etc. 2. Ethnomusicology. I. Title.

BRADFORD, Perry 927.8
Born with the blues; Perry Bradford's own story. The true story of the pioneering blues singers and musicians in the early days of jazz. New York, Oak [1966, c.1966, c.1965] 175p. illus. 26cm. [ML410.B779B6] 65-16635 2.95 pap.,
1. Musicians—Correspondence, reminiscences, etc. 2. Jazz music. 3. Negro musicians. I. Title.

BROONZY, William, 1893-1958 927.8
Big Bill blues, William Broonzy's story as told to Yannick Bruynoghe. With 9 pages of half-tone illus. and 4 drawings by Paul Oliver [Rev., updated] foreword by Charles Edward Smith. New York, Oak Pubns. [1964, c.1955] 176p. illus., ports. 22cm. (CT 2034 Discography [ML420.B78A3] 64-8787 2.95 pap.,
1. Musicians—Correspondence, reminiscences, etc. I. Bruynoghe, Yannick. II. Title.

BRYANT, Anita. 780'.924 B
Mine eyes have seen the glory. Old Tappan, N.J., Revell [1970] 159 p. illus., ports. 21 cm. Autobiographical. [ML420.B84A3] 78-96246 3.95
1. Musicians—Correspondence, reminiscences, etc. I. Title. BIP

BUSCH, Fritz, 1890- 785'.0924
1951.
Pages from a musician's life. Translated by Marjorie Strachey. Westport, Conn., Greenwood Press [1971] 223 p. illus., ports. 23 cm. Reprint of the 1953 ed. Translation of Aus dem Leben eines Musikers. [ML422.B95A32 1971] 71-106715 ISBN 0-8371-3445-5
1. Musicians—Correspondence, reminiscences, etc. I. Title.

BUSCH, Fritz, 1890- 785'.092'4 B
1951.
Pages from a musician's life. Translated by Marjorie Strachey. London, Hogarth Press, 1953. St. Clair Shores, Mich., Scholarly Press, 1972. 223 p. illus. 22 cm. Translation of Aus dem Leben eines Musikers. [ML422.B95A32 1972] 71-181120 ISBN 0-403-01519-7
1. Musicians—Correspondence, reminiscences, etc. I. Title. BIP

CARMICHAEL, Hoagy, 780'.924 B
1899-
The stardust road. New York, Greenwood Press [1969, c1946] 156 p. ports. 23 cm. First published in 1946. [ML410.C327A3 1969] 79-94603
1. Musicians—Correspondence, reminiscences, etc. I. Title. BIP

CASALS, Pablo, 787'.3'0924 B
1876-
Joys and sorrows; reflections, by Pablo Casals as told to Albert E. Kahn. New York, Simon and Schuster [1970] 314 p. illus., facsims., ports. 24 cm. [ML418.C4A35] 73-101879 7.95
1. Musicians—Correspondence, reminiscences, etc. I. Kahn, Albert Eugene, 1912- II. Title.

CASALS, Pablo, 1876- 787'.3'0924
1974.
Joys and sorrows [by] Pablo Casals as told to Albert E. Kahn. [New York] Simon and Schuster [1974, c1970] 314 p. illus. 23 cm. (A Touchstone book) [ML418.C4A35] [[B]] 0-671-21774-7 3.95 (pbk.)
1. Musicians-Correspondence, reminiscences, etc. I. Kahn, Albert Eugene, 1912- II. Title.
L.C. card number for original ed.: 73-101879

CASELLA, Alfredo, 1883- 927.8
1947.
Music in my time; the memoirs of Alfredo Casella. Translated and edited by Spencer Norton. [1st English ed.] Norman, University of Oklahoma Press [c1955] 254p. illus. 23cm. Translation of I segreti della giara. 'List of compositions': p. 239-243. [ML410.C34A25] 55-6360
1. Musicians—Correspondence, reminiscences, etc. I. Title.

CHEVALIER, Maurice, 784'.0924
1888-
I remember it well. Pref. by Marcel Pagnol. Translated from the French by Cornelia Higginson. [New York] Macmillan [1970] 221 p. illus., ports. 22 cm. Translation of Mome a cheveux blancs. [ML420.C473A383] 79-126515
1. Musicians—Correspondence, reminiscences, etc. I. Title.

CHEVALIER, Maurice, 784'.0924 B
1888-
I remember it well. Pref. by Marcel Pagnol. Translated from the French by Cornelia Higginson. Boston, G. K. Hall, 1972 [c1970] 315 p. 25 cm. "Large print" ed. Translation of Mome a cheveux blancs. [ML420.C473A383 1972] 73-38980 ISBN 0-8161-6022-8 (l. print)
1. Musicians—Correspondence, reminiscences, etc. I. Title.

CHEVALIER, Maurice, 1888- 927.8
1972.
With love, by Maurice Chevalier, as told to Eileen and Robert Mason Pollock. [1st ed.] Boston, Little, Brown [1960] 424 p. illus. 23 cm. Autobiographical. [ML420.C473A39] 60-11641
1. Musicians—Correspondence, reminiscences, etc. I. Pollock, Eileen. II. Title.

CHOTZINOFF, Samuel, 1889- 927.8
Day's at the morn. Pref. by Sir Osbert Sitwell. [1st ed.] New York, Harper & Row [1964] x, 309 p. 22 cm. Autobiographical. Continuation of the author's A lost paradise. [ML423.C564A32] 64-21653
1. Musicians—Correspondence, reminiscences, etc. I. Title.

CHOTZINOFF, Samuel, 1889- 927.8
Day's at the morn. Pref. by Sir Osbert Sitwell. [1st ed.] New York, Harper & Row [1964] x, 309 p. 22 cm. Autobiographical. Continuation of the author's A lost paradise. [ML423.C564A32] 64-21653
1. Musicians—Correspondence, reminiscences, etc. I. Title.

CHOTZINOFF, Samuel, 1889- 927.8
A lost paradise; early reminiscences. [1st ed.] New York, Knopf, 1955. 373 p. 22 cm. [ML423.C564A3] 54-7202
1. Musicians—Correspondence, reminiscences, etc. I. Title. BIP

CHRISTENSEN, Inga Hoegsbro, 927.8
1872-
Inga--Play! The memoirs of Inga Hoegsbro Christensen, pianist and leading exponent of Scandinavian and Finnish music in America; written in collaboration with Molly Winston Pearson, Alice Randall, and Peggy London. Foreword by James Francis Cooke. [1st ed.] New York, Exposition Press [1952] 202p. illus. 21cm. [ML417.C47A3] 52-8628
1. Musicians—Correspondence, reminiscences, etc. I. Title.

CORNISH, Nellie 923.773 B
Centennial, 1876-1956.
Miss Aunt Nellie; the autobiography of Nellie C. Cornish. Edited by Ellen Van Volkenburg Browne and Edward Nordhoff Beck; foreword by Nancy Wilson Ross. Seattle, University of Washington Press [1964] xvi, 283 p. illus., ports. 24 cm. [ML429.C643.M6] 64-25730
1. Musicians—Correspondence, Reminiscences, etc. 2. Cornish School, Seattle, Wash. I. Title.

CROFUT, Bill. 784'.0922
Troubadour; a different battlefield, by William Crofut. Foreword by Robert F. Kennedy. [1st ed.] New York, E. P. Dutton, 1968. 283 p. illus., map, ports. 22 cm. [ML420.C925A3] 67-11385
1. Musicians—Correspondence, reminiscences, etc. 2. Voyages and travels. I. Title.

CROSBY, Bing, 1901- 927.92
Call me lucky, by Bing Crosby as told to Pete Martin. New York, Simon and Schuster, 1953. 344p. illus. 23cm. [ML420.C93A3] 53-10768
1. Musicians—Correspondence, reminiscences, etc. I. Title.

DALE, Alan, Musician. 784.092
The spider and the marionettes, an autobiography. New York, L. Stuart, 1965. 317 p. 21 cm. 65-20565
1. Musicians — Correspondence, reminiscences, etc. I. Title.

DAMROSCH, Walter 780'.92'4 B
Johannes, 1862-1950.
My musical life. Westport, Conn., Greenwood Press [1972, c1923] viii, 376 p. illus. 22 cm. [ML422.D16A3 1972] 71-109725 ISBN 0-8371-4215-6 14.75
1. Musicians—Correspondence, reminiscences, etc. I. Title. BIP

DAVIS, Lorrie. 782.8'1'0924 B
Letting down my hair; two years with the love rock tribe—from dawning to downing of Aquarius, by Lorrie Davis with Rachel Gallagher. New York, A. Fields Books [1973] 279 p. illus. 22 cm. [ML420.D32A3] 72-94680 ISBN 0-525-63005-8 6.95
1. Musicians—Correspondence, reminiscences, etc. I. Gallagher, Rachel, joint author. II. Title.
Distributed by E. P. Dutton.

DAWSON, Peter, 1882- 927.8
Fifty years of song. London, New York, Hutchinson [1951] 239 p. illus. 22 cm. [ML420.D36A3] 52-1553
1. Musicians—Correspondence, reminiscences, etc. I. Title.

DE LARA, Adelina, 786.1'092'4 B
1872-
Finale. In collaboration with Clare H-Abrahall. [London] Burke. St. Clair Shores, Mich., Scholarly Press, 1972. 222 p. illus. 24 cm. Autobiography. Reprint of the 1955 ed. [ML417.D35A3 1972] 78-181138 ISBN 0-403-01539-1
1. Musicians—Correspondence, reminiscences, etc. I. Abrahall, Clare

Constance (Drury) Hoskyns. II. Title. **BIP**

DITTERS von Dittersdorf, Karl, 1739-1799. 780'.924
The autobiography of Karl von Dittersdorf. Translated from the German by A. D. Coleridge. New York, Da Capo Press, 1970. xx, 316 p. 23 cm. (Da Capo Press music reprint series) Translation of Lebensbeschreibung. Reprint of the 1896 ed. [ML410.D6A33 1970] 77-100655
1. Musicians—Correspondence, reminiscences, etc. **BIP**

DUKE, Vernon, 1903- 927.8
Passport to Paris. [1st ed.] Boston, Little, Brown [1955] 502p. illus. 22cm. Autobiographical. [ML410.D87A3] 54-8311
1. Musicians—Correspondence, reminiscences, etc. I. Title.

ELGAR, Edward William, Sir 1857-1934 784.092
Letters to Nimrod; Edward Elgar to August Jaeger, 1897-1908. Ed., annotated by Percy M. Young. London, D. Dobson [New York, Dover, c.1965] xix, 298p. illus., facsims. (incl. music), ports. 22cm. [ML410.E4A48] 65-8458 8.00 bds.,
1. Musicians—Correspondence, reminiscences, etc. I. Jaeger, August Johannes, 1860-1909. II. Young, Percy Marshall, 1912- ed. III. Title.

FARRAR, Geraldine, 1882-1967. 782.1'0924 B
The autobiography of Geraldine Farrar: Such sweet compulsion. New York, Da Capo Press, 1970 [c1938] xii, 303 p. illus., ports. 24 cm. (Da Capo Press music reprint series) [ML420.F27A2 1970b] 70-100656
1. Musicians—Correspondence, reminiscences, etc. I. Title: Such sweet compulsion.

FIELDS, Gracie, 1898- 927.8
Sing as we go; the autobiography of Gracie Fields. [1st ed. in the United States of America] New York, Doubleday, 1961 [c1960] 216 p. illus. 22 cm. [ML420.F46A3 1961] 61-9192
1. Musicians—Correspondence, reminiscences, etc. I. Title.

FINCK, Henry Theophilus, 1854-1926. 780.15
My adventures in the golden age of music. New York, Da Capo Press, 1971 [c1926] xvi, 462 p. illus. 23 cm. (Da Capo Press music reprint series) [ML423.F46 1971] 70-87496 ISBN 0-306-71448-5
1. Musicians—Correspondence, reminiscences, etc. 2. Music—New York (City) I. Title. **BIP**

FORD, Ernest Jennings, 1919- 927.8
This is my story, this is my song [by] Tennessee Ernie Ford. Line drawings by Larin Thompson. Englewood Cliffs, N. J., Prentice-Hall [1963] viii, 177 p. illus., ports. 21 cm. [ML420.F7A3] 63-20776
1. Musicians—Correspondence, reminiscences, etc. I. Title.

FOUNTAIN, Pete. 785.06'72'0924 B
A closer walk; the Pete Fountain story [by] Pete Fountain with Bill Neely. Chicago, Regnery [1972] viii, 202 p. illus. 22 cm. [ML419.F69A3] 78-183806 5.95
1. Musicians—Correspondence, reminiscences, etc. I. Neely, Bill. II. Title.

FROMM, Herbert 780'.924
The key of see; travel journals of a composer. Boston, Plowshare Pr. [1967] 191p. 22cm. [ML410.F963A3] 67-14404 4.00
1. Musicians—Correspondence, reminiscences, etc. I. Title. **BIP**

GAL, Hans, 1890- ed. 780.922
The musicians's world; great composers in their letters. New York, Arco Pub. Co. [1966, c1965] 464 p. illus., facsims. (incl. music), ports. 24 cm. (Arco music library) "References and sources to text": p. [455]-457. [ML90.G34 1966] 66-15140
1. Musicians—Correspondence, reminiscences, etc. I. Title.

GALLO, Fortune T. 782.1'0924
Lucky rooster; the autobiography of an impressario [by] Fortune T. Gallo. [1st ed.] New York. Exposition [c.1967] 304p. 21cm. [ML429 G153A3] (B) 67-26392 6.00.
1. Musicians—Correspondence. reminiscences, etc. 2. Impresarios. I. Title.

GARDEN, Mary, 1877- 927.8
Mary Garden's story, by Mary Garden and Louis Biancolli. New York, Simon and Schuster [1951] xii, 302 p. illus., ports. 21 cm. [ML420.G25A3] 51-10603
1. Musicians—Correspondence, reminiscences, etc. I. Biancolli, Louis Leopold.

GARDEN, Mary, 1877-1967. 927.8
Mary Garden's story, by Mary Garden and Louis Biancolli. New York. Simon and Schuster [1951] xii. 302 p. illus., ports. 21 cm. 51-10603
1. Musicians — Correspondence, reminiscences, etc. I. Biancolli, Louis Leopold. II. Title.

GERHARDT, Elena, 1883- 784'.092'4
1961.
Recital. With a pref. by Dame Myra Hess. London, Methuen. St. Clair Shores, Mich., Scholarly Press, 1972. x, 183 p. illus. 19 cm. Autobiography. Reprint of the 1953 ed. [ML420.G35A3 1972] 78-181162 ISBN 0-403-01564-2
1. Musicians—Correspondence, reminiscences, etc. I. Title. **BIP**

GLINKA, Mikhail Ivandvich, 1804-1857. 927.8
Memoirs. Tr. from Russian by Richard B. Mudge. Norman, Univ. of Okla. Pr. [c.1963] xi, 264p. illus., ports, music. 24cm. 63-8993 5.95
1. Musicians—Correspondence, reminiscences,etc. I. Title.

GLINKA, Mikhail Ivanovich, 1804-1857. 927.8
Memoirs, Translated from the Russian by Richard B. Mudge. [1st ed.] Norman, University of Oklahoma Press [1963] xi, 264 p. illus., ports., music. 24 cm. [ML410.G46A25] 63-8993 MN
1. Musicians — Correspondence, reminiscences, etc. I. Title.

GLUCK, Christoph Willibald, Ritter von, 1714-1787. 927.8
Collected correspondence and papers. Edited by Hedwig and E. H. Mueller von Asow. Translated by Stewart Thomson. New York, St. Martin's Press [1963, c1962] xi, 239 p. ports., facsims. 23 cm. "The sources": p. 217-223. Includes bibliographical references. [ML410.G5A413] 62-18209
1. Musicians—Correspondence, reminiscences, etc. I. Mueller von Asow, Hedwig, 1911- ed. II. Mueller von Asow, Erich Hermann, 1892- ed.

GOTTSCHALK, Louis Moreau. 1829-1869 927.8
Notes of a pianist [Tr. from French] Ed., prelude postlude, explanatory notes, by Jeanne Behrend. New York, Knopf [c.] 1964. 420p. illus. 22cm. 64-12302 6.95
1. Musicians—Correspondence, reminiscences, etc. 2. U.S.—Descr. & trav.—1848-1865. 3. South American—Descr. & trav. I. Behrend, Jeanne, 1911- ed. II. Title.

GOTTSCHALK, Louis Moreau, 1829-1869. 927.8
Notes of a pianist. Edited, with a prelude, a postlude, and explanatory notes, by Jeanne Behrend. 1st Borzoi Ed. New York, A. A. Knopf, 1964. 420 p. illus. 22 cm. (A Borzoi book) [ML410.G68G6 1964] 64-12302 mn
1. Musicians — Correspondence, reminiscences, etc. 2. u.s. — Descr. & trav. — 1848-1865. 3. South America — Descr. & Trav. I. Behrend, Jeanne, 1911- ed. II. Title. **BIP**

GOUNOD, Charles Francois, 1818-1893. 780'.924
Autobiographical reminiscences, with family letters and notes on music. Translated by W. Hely Hutchinson. New York, Da Capo Press, 1970. ix, 267 p. port. 23 cm. (Da Capo Press music reprint series) Translation of Memoires d'un artiste. Reprint of the 1896 London ed. [ML410.G7A33 1970] 68-16235
1. Musicians—Correspondence, reminiscences, etc. **BIP**

GRECHANINOV, Aleksandr Tikhonovich, 1864- v. 12
My life. Introd. and translation by Nicolas Slonimsky. New York, Coleman-Ross Co., 1952. xviii, 204p. ports. 21cm. Catalogue of works by Alexandre Gretchaninoff: p. 175-204. A53
1. Musicians—Correspondence, reminiscences, etc. I. Title.

HINES, Jerome, 1921- 782.1'0924
This is my story, this is my song. Westwood, N.J., F.H. Revell Co. [1968] 160 p. ports. 21 cm. [ML420.H452A3] 68-19054
1. Musicians—Correspondence, reminiscences, etc. I. Title. **BIP**

HOLIDAY, Billie, 1915- 927.8
Lady sings the blues [by] Billie Holiday with William Dufty. [1st ed.] Garden City, N. Y., Doubleday, 1956. 250p. illus. (on linning papers) 22cm. Autobiography. [ML420.H58A3] 56-5962
1. Musicians—Correspondence, reminiscences, etc. I. Title.

HOLIDAY, Billie, 1915- v. 12
Lady sings the blues by Billie holiday with William Dufty. New York, Lancer Books [1965] 191 p. 18 cm. (A Lancer book, 74-839) Autobiography. "Complete and unabridged." 67-18956
1. Musicians — Correspondence, reminiscences, etc. I. Title. **BIP**

HOLIDAY, Billie, 1915- 927.8
Lady sings the blues [by] Billie Holiday with William Dufty. [New lYork] Avon [1976 c1956] 192 p. 18 cm. [ML420.H58A3] ISBN 0-380-00491-7 1.50 (pbk.)
1. Musicians—Correspondence, reminiscences, etc. I. Title.
L.C. card no. of 1956 Doubleday edition: 56-5962.

HORNE, Lena. 927.8
In person, Lena Horne; as told to Helen Arstein and Carlton Moss. [New York] Greenberg [1950] 249 p. illus. 21 cm. [ML420.H65A3 1950] 50-10230
1. Musicians—Correspondence, reminiscences, etc. I. Arstein, Helen. II. Moss, Carlton. III. Title.

HORNE, Lena. 792.7 B
Lena, by Lena Horne and Richard Schickel. [1st ed.] Garden City, N.Y., Doubleday, 1965. 300 p. illus., ports. 22 cm. [ML420.H65A35] 65-18388
1. Musicians—Correspondence, reminiscences, etc. I. Schickel, Richard, joint author. II. Title.

HOWARD, Joseph Edgar, 1880- 927.8
Gay nineties troubadour; autobiography. [Miami Beach, Fla., Jo e Howard Music House, 1956] 127 p. illus. 18cm. [ML410.H883G4] 60-50040
1. Musicians—Correspondence, reminiscences, etc. I. Title.

IVES, Charles Edward, 1874-1954. 780'.92'4 B
Memos. Edited by John Kirkpatrick. [1st ed.] New York, W. W. Norton [1972] 355 p. illus. 25 cm. "Memos" (Ives' own title): p. [25]-142; "Appendices": p. [143]-324. [ML410.I94A3] 76-77407 ISBN 0-393-02153-X 12.50
1. Musicians—Correspondence, reminiscences, etc. I. Kirkpatrick, John, 1905- ed. II. Title.

KAMINSKY, Max, 1908- 927.8
My life in jazz, by Max Kaminsky with V. E. Hughes. [1st ed.] New York, Harper & Row [1963] 242 p. 22 cm. [ML419.K34A3] 63-10602
1. Musicians—Correspondence, reminiscences, etc. 2. Jazz music. I. Hughes, V. E., joint author. II. Title.

KITT, Eartha. 927.8
Thursday's child. [1st ed.] New York, Duell, Sloan and Pearce [1956] 250p. illus. 21cm. Autobiographical. [ML420.K5A3] 56-9590
1. Musicians—Correspondence, reminiscences, etc. I. Title.

KLEMPERER, Otto, 1885- 780.92
Minor recollections [Tr. from German by J. Maxwell Browniohn] London, D. Dobson [New York, Dover, 1965.c.1964] 124p. illus., facsims., ports. 21cm. [ML422.K67A335] 65-80183 2.50
1. Musicians—Correspondence, reminiscences, etc. I. Title.

LEHMANN, Lotte. 782.1'0924 B
Midway in my song; the autobiography of Lotte Lehmann. Freeport, N.Y., Books for Libraries Press [1970] xi, 250 p. illus., ports. 23 cm. "First published 1938." London ed. (K. Paul, Trench, Trubner) has title: Wings of song. Translation of Anfang und Aufstieg. [ML420.L33A33 1970] 73-107813
1. Musicians—Correspondence, reminiscences, etc. I. Title.

LEIDER, Frida, 1888- 784.0924
Playing my part. Translated by Charles Osborne. New York, Meredith Press [1966] 217 p. facsims., ports. 21 cm. Discography: p. 211-214. [ML420.L34A33 1966a] 66-9410
1. Musicians—Correspondence, reminiscences, etc. I. Title.

LEMARE, Edwin Henry, 1865-1934. 927.8
Organs I have met; the autobiography of Edwin H. Lemare, 1866-1934. Together with reminiscences by his wife and friends. Los Angeles, Schoolcraft Co. [c1956] 122p. illus., ports., facsim., music. 24cm. 'List of compositions by Edwin Lemare': p.118-122. [ML416.L44A3] 61-41641
1. Musicians— Correspondence, reminiscences, etc. I. Title.

LEVANT, Oscar, 1906- 780.924
The memoirs of an amnesiac. New York, Putnam [c.1965] 320p. 22cm. [ML417.L64A3] 65-10856 5.95 bds.,
1. Musicians—Correspondence, reminiscences, etc. I. Title.

LEVANT, Oscar, 1906- 786.1'0924
The unimportance of being Oscar. New York, Putnam [1968] 255 p. illus., ports. 22 cm. [ML417.L64A35] 68-20949
1. Musicians—Correspondence, reminiscences, etc. I. Title.

LILLENAS, Haldor. 784'.092'4
Down melody lane, an autobiography. Kansas City, Mo., Beacon Hill Press [1953] 80p. 19cm. [ML410.L66A3] 57-19912
1. Musicians—Correspondence, reminiscences, etc. I. Title.

LOPEZ, Vincent 927.8
Lopez speaking, an autobiography. New York, Citadel Press [c.1960] 351p. illus. 22cm. 60-9381 4.95
1. Musicians—Correspondence, reminiscences, etc. I. Title.

LOPEZ, Vincent, 1894- 927.8
Lopez speaking, an autobiography, [1st ed.] New York, Citadel Press [1960] 351p. illus. 22cm. [ML422.L77A3] 60-9381
1. Musicians—Correspondence, reminiscences, etc. I. Title.

MAL'KO, Nikolai Andreevich, 1883-1961 780.922
A certain art, by Nicolai Malko. [Comp., tr., ed. by Bertha Malko, Elizabeth Green, George Malko] Introd. by George Malko. New York, Morrow, [c.]1966. 235p. illus., facsims. (Incl. music) ports. 22cm. [ML422.M14A3] 66-16403 5.00
1. Musicians—Correspondence, reminiscences, etc. 2. Music—Russia—Hist. & crit. 3. Composers, Russian. I. Title.

MARETZEK, Max, 1821-1897. 782.1'0924
Revelations of an opera manager in 19th-century America. Crotchets and quavers & Sharps and flats. With a new introd. by Charles Haywood. New York, Dover Publications [1968] xxxv, 346, 94 p. facsims., ports. 22 cm. "This Dover edition is an unabridged and slightly corrected republication of Crotchets and quavers, originally published in 1855, and Sharps and flats, originally published in 1890." [ML429] [.M32A3] 68-19548
1. Musicians—Correspondence, Reminiscences, etc. I. Title. II. Title: Crotchets and quavers. III. Title: Sharps and flats.

MASON, Daniel Gregory, 1873-1953. 780'.924
Music in my time, and other reminiscences. Freeport, N.Y., Books for Libraries Press [1970] 409 p. illus., facsims., ports. 24 cm. "First published 1938." [ML410.M397A2 1970] 71-107818
1. Musicians—Correspondence, reminiscences, etc. I. Title.

MASON, Daniel Gregory, 1873-1953. 780'.924
Music in my time, and other reminiscences. Westport, Conn., Greenwood Press [1970] 409 p. illus., facsims, music, ports. 23 cm. Reprint of the 1938 ed. [ML410.M397A2 1970b] 71-109784
1. Musicians—Correspondence, reminiscenses, etc. I. Title.

MASON, William, 1829-1908. 786.1'0924 B
Memories of a musical life. New York, AMS Press [1970] xii, 306 p. illus., facsims., ports. 23 cm. Reprint of the 1901 ed. [ML417.M412 1970b] 70-133825 ISBN 0-404-07216-X
1. Musicians—Correspondence, reminiscences, etc. I. Title. **BIP**

MASON, William, 1829-1908. 786.1'0924 B
Memories of a musical life. New York, Da Capo Press, 1970. xii, 306 p. illus., facsims. (music), ports. 20 cm. (Da Capo Press music reprint series) Reprint of the 1901 ed. [ML417.M412 1970] 70-125056
1. Musicians—Correspondence, reminiscences, etc. I. Title.

MASSENET, Jules Emile Frederic, 1842-1912. 782.1'0924
My recollections. The authorized translation done at the master's express desire by his friend H. Villiers Barnett. Freeport, N.Y., Books for Libraries Press [1970] 304 p. illus., ports. 23 cm. "First published 1919." [ML410.M41A33 1970] 75-107819
1. Musicians—Correspondence, reminiscences, etc. **BIP**

MASSENET, Jules Emile Frederic, 1842-1912. 780'.92'2 B
My recollections, by Jules Massenet. The authorized translation done at the master's express desire by his friend H. Villiers Barnett. Westport, Conn., Greenwood Press [1970] 304 p. illus., ports. 23 cm. "Originally published in 1919." [ML410.M41A33 1970b] 79-109786 ISBN 0-8371-4276-8
1. Musicians—Correspondence, reminiscences, etc.

MASSENET, Jules Emile Frederic, 1842-1912. 782.1'0924 B
My recollections (1848-1912). [1st a M S New York, AMS Press, 1971] 304 p. illus., facsim., ports. 19 cm. Reprint of the 1919 ed. Translation of Mes souvenirs. [ML410.M41A33 1971] 70-137259 ISBN 0-404-04229-5
1. Musicians—Correspondence, reminiscences, etc. I. Title.

MELBA, Nellie, Dame, 1861-1931. 782.1'0924 B
Melodies and memories. New York, AMS Press [1971] 339 p. ports. 23 cm. Reprint of the 1926 ed. [ML420.M35M41 1971] 71-126694 ISBN 0-404-04287-2
1. Musicians—Correspondence, reminiscences, etc. I. Title.

MELBA, Nellie, Dame, 1861-1931. 782.1'0924
Melodies and memories. Freeport, N.Y., Books for Libraries Press [1970] 339 p. ports. 23 cm. "First published 1926." [ML420.M35M41 1970] 73-107821 ISBN 8-369-51921-
1. Musicians—Correspondence, reminiscences, etc. I. Title. **BIP**

MERMAN, Ethel. 927.8
Who could ask for anything more, as told to Pete Martin. [1st ed.] Garden City, N. Y., Doubleday, 1955. 252 p. illus. 22 cm. [ML420.M39A3] 55-5495
1. Musicians—Correspondence, reminiscences, etc. I. Martin, Thornton, 1901- II. Title.

MERRILL, Robert, 1919- 784.0924 (B)
Once more from the beginning [by] Robert Merrill, with Sandford Dody. New York, Macmillan [1965] 286 p. illus., ports. 21 cm. [ML420.M42A2] 65-25062
1. Musicians — Correspondence, reminiscences, etc. I. Dody, Sandford. II. Title.

MILHAUD, Darius, 1892- 927.8
Notes without music, an autobiography. [Translated from the French by Donald Evans. 1st American ed.] New York, Knopf, 1953. 355, xxii p. illus. 22cm. [ML410.M674A32 1953] 52-12205
1. Musicians—Correspondence, reminiscences, etc. I. Title.

MILHAUD, Darius, 1892- 780'.924
Notes without music; an autobiography. [Translated from the French by Donald Evans] New York, Da Capo Press, 1970 [c1953] x, 355, xxii p. illus., ports. 24 cm. (Da Capo Press music reprint series) [ML410.M674A32 1970] 72-87419
1. Musicians—Correspondence, reminiscences, etc. I. Title.

MINGUS, Charles, 1922- 785.4'2'0924 B
Beneath the underdog; his world as composed by Mingus. Edited by Nel King. [1st ed.] New York, Knopf, 1971. 365 p. 22 cm. Autobiography. A portion of the book first appeared in Changes, v. 1, no. 3. [ML410.M6795A3] 72-111243 ISBN 0-394-43622-9 6.95
1. Musicians—Correspondence, reminiscences, etc. I. Title.

MOORE, Gerald. 927.8
Am I too loud, a musical autobiography. New York, Macmillan [1962] 288p. illus. 22cm. [ML417.M85A3] 62-11924
1. Musicians—Correspondence, reminiscences, etc. I. Title.

MOORE, Gerald. 786.10924
Am I too loud? Memoirs of an accompanist. Harmondsworth (Mddx.), Penguin, 1966. 286 p. 8 plates (ports.) 18 cm. 6/- [ML417.M85A3] 66-66840
1. Musicians — Correspondence, reminiscences, etc. I. Title.

NABOKOV, Nicolas, 1903- 927.8
Old friends and new music. [1st ed.] Boston, Little, Brown, 1951. 294 p. 22 cm. "An Atlantic Monthly Press book." [ML410.N2A3] 51-176
1. Musicians—Correspondence, reminiscences, etc. I. Title. **BIP**

OTIS, Johnny, 1921- 780'.924
Listen to the lambs. [1st ed.] New York, W. W. Norton [1968] 256 p. 22 cm. Autobiography. [ML419.O85A3] 67-12446
1. Musicians—Correspondence, reminiscences, etc. I. Title.

OWENS, Harry. 780'.924 B
Sweet Leilani: the story behind the song; an autobiography. [1st ed.] Pacific Palisades, Calif., Hula House [1970] a-d, 313, xi p. illus., facsims., ports. (part col.) 24 cm. [ML410.O93A3] 73-17610 6.95
1. Musicians—Correspondence, reminiscences, etc. I. Title.

PETSCHNIKOFF, Lili, 1876- 787'.1'0924
The world at our feet. [1st ed.] New York, Vantage Press [1968] 221 p. illus., ports. 23 cm. Autobiographical. [ML418.P49A3] 72-639 4.50
1. Musicians—Correspondence, reminiscences, etc. I. Title.

PIAF, Edith, 1915-1963. 784.0924
The wheel of fortune; the autobiography of Edith Piaf. Translated by Peter Trewartha and Andree Masoin de Virton. Philadelphia, Chilton Books [1965] 192 p. ports. 23 cm. [ML420.P52A33] 66-22872
1. Musicians—Correspondence, reminiscences, etc. I. Title.

PIATIGORSKY, Gregor, 1903- 927.8
Cellist. Garden City, N. Y., Doubleday, 1965. viii, 273 p. 27 plates (ports.) 22 cm. [ML418.P63A3] 65-14340
1. Musicians—Correspondence, reminiscences, etc. I. Title.

PORTER, Cole, 1891-1961 782.810924
The Cole Porter story, as told to Richard G. Hubler. Introd. by Arthur Schwartz. Cleveland, World [c.1965] xii, 140p. ports. 21cm. Bibl. [ML410.P7844A3] 65-23352 3.75 bds.,
1. Musicians—Correspondence, reminiscences, etc. I. Hubler, Richard Gibson, 1912- II. Title.

PORTER, Cole, 1891-1964. 782.810924
The Cole Porter story, as told to Richard G. Hubler. With an introd. by Arthur Schwartz. Cleveland, World Pub. Co. [1965] xii, 140 p. ports. 21 cm. "Bibliography: Cole Porter songs": p. 125-140. [ML410.P7844A3] 65-23352
1. Musicians—Correspondence, reminiscences, etc. I. Hubler, Richard Gibson, 1912- II. Title.

ROBERTS, Joan. 927.8
Never alone. New York, McMullen Books [c1954] 204p. 21cm. Autobiographical. [ML420.R7A3] 54-12242
1. Musicians—Correspondence, reminiscences, etc. I. Title.

ROOT, George Frederick, 1820-1895. 780'.924 B
The story of a musical life; an autobiography. New York, Da Capo Press, 1970. ix, 256 p. music, port. 23 cm. (Da Capo Press music reprint series) Reprint of the 1891 ed. [ML410.R68A3 1970] 70-126072
1. Musicians—Correspondence, reminiscences, etc. I. Title.

ROOT, George Frederick, 1820-1895. 780'.92'4 B
The story of a musical life; an autobiography. Cincinnati; J. Church Co., 1891. [New York, AMS Press 1973] ix, 256 p. port. 19 cm. Music: p. 228-256. [ML410.R68A3 1973] 71-174964 ISBN 0-404-07205-4 9.50
1. Musicians—Correspondence, reminiscences, etc. I. Title. **BIP**

ROREM, Ned, 1923- 780.924
The Paris diary of Ned Rorem. With a port. of the diarist by Robert Phelps. [1st ed.] New York, G. Braziller [1966] xv, 240 p. ports. 22 cm. [ML410.R693A3] 66-20187
1. Musicians—Correspondence, reminiscences, etc. I. Title.

RUBINSTEIN, Artur, 1886- 786.1'092'4 B
My young years [by] Arthur Rubinstein. [1st ed.] New York, Knopf; [distributed by Random House] 1973. xi, 478, xiii p. illus. 25 cm. [ML417.R79A3] 70-171147 ISBN 0-394-46890-2 10.00
1. Musicians—Correspondence, reminiscences, etc. I. Title.

RUBINSTEIN, Artur, 1896- 786.1'092'4 B
My young years [by] Arthur Rubinstein. New York, Popular Library [1974, c1973] 511 p. illus. 18 cm. [ML417.R79A3] 1.75 (pbk.)
1. Musicians—Correspondence, reminiscences, etc. I. Title.
L.C. card number for original ed.: 70-171147 **BIP**

SARGEANT, Winthrop, 1903- 780'.924 B
In spite of myself; a personal memoir. [1st ed.] Garden City, N.Y., Doubleday, 1970. 264 p. 22 cm. [ML423.S3A3] 75-86330 6.95
1. Musicians—Correspondence, reminiscences, etc. I. Title.

SCHNABEL, Artur, 1882-1951 927.8
My life and music. Introd. by Edward Crankshaw. New York, St. Martin's [1963, c.1961] xv, 223p. front. port. 22cm. 62-16965 4.50 bds.,
1. Musicians—Correspondence, reminiscences, etc. I. Title.

SCHNABEL, Artur, 1882-1951. 786.1'092'4 B
My life and music; &, Reflections on music. With a foreword by Sir Robert Mayer and an introd. by Edward Crankshaw. New York, St. Martin's Press [1972, c1961] xv, 248 p. 22 cm. (St. Martin's music paperbacks) [ML417.S36A3 1972] 70-166527 3.50
1. Musicians—Correspondence, reminiscences, etc. I. Schnabel, Artur, 1882-1951. Reflections on music. 1972. II. Title.

SCHOENBERG, Arnold, 1874-1951 927.8
Letters. Selected. ed. by Erwin Stein. Tr. from German by Eithne Wilkins, Ernst Kaiser. New York, St Martin's [1965, c.1964] 309p. music, port, 24cm. [ML410.S283A42] 65-12618 8.75
1. Musicians—Correspondence, reminiscences, etc. I. Stein, Erwin, 1885- ed. II. Title.

SCHONBERG, Arnold, 1874-1951. 927.8
Letters. Selected and edited by Erwin Stein. Translated from the original German by Eithne Wilkins and Ernst Kaiser. New York, St. Martin's Press [1965, 1964] 309 p. music, port. 24 cm. First pub. in 1958 under title Arnold Schonberg: Ausgewahite Briefe. [ML410.S283A42] 65-12618
1. Musicians—Correspondence, reminiscences, etc. I. Stein, Erwin, 1885- ed. II. Title.

SCOTT, Toni Lee. 784'.0924 B
A kind of loving. Edited by Curt Gentry. New York, World Pub. Co. [1970] xv, 205 p. ports. 22 cm. [ML420.S43A3] 76-115803 5.95
1. Musicians—Correspondence, reminiscences, etc. I. Title.

SHALIAPIN, Fedor Ivanovich, 1873-1938 782.1/0924
Chaliapin, an autobiography as told to Maxim Gorky; with supplementary correspondence and notes, tr. from Russian, comp. & ed. by Nina Froud, James Hanley. New York, Stein & Day [c.1967] 320p. col. front., 89 plates (incl. facsims., ports.) 24cm. (romanized: Fedor Ivanovich Shaliapin) Tr. of selections from Bibl. [ML420.S53A2533 1967] (B) 67-25616 10.00
1. Musicians—Correspondence, reminiscences, etc. I. Gor'kii, Maksim, 1868-1936. II. Froud, Nina. ed. III. Hanley, James, 1901- ed. IV. Title.

SHALIAPIN, Fedor Ivanovich, 1873-1938. 782.1'0924 (B)
Chaliapin, an autobiography as told to Maxim Gorky; with supplementary correspondence and notes, translated from the Russian, compiled and edited by Nina Froud and James Hanley. New York, Stein and Day [c1967] 320 p. col. front., 89 plates (incl. facsims., ports.) 24 cm. Translation of selections from (romanized: Fedor Ivanovich Shaliapin) Bibliography: p. 307-308. [ML420.S53A2533] 67-25616
1. Musicians—Correspondence, reminiscences, etc. I. Gor'kii, Maksim, 1868-1936. II. Froud, Nina, ed. III. Hanley, James, 1901- ed. IV. Title. **BIP**

SHALIAPIN, Fedor Ivanovich, 1873-1938. 782.1'092'4 B
Man and mask; forty years in the life of a singer, by Feodor Chaliapin. Translated by Phyllis Megroz. London, V. Gollancz, 1932. St. Clair Shores, Mich., Scholarly Press, 1973. 413 p. illus. 22 cm. Translation of Maska i dusha. [ML420.S53A312 1973] 73-181256 ISBN 0-403-01679-7
1. Musicians—Correspondence, reminiscences, etc. I. Title. **BIP**

SHAW, Artie, 1911- 927.8
The trouble with Cinderella; an outline of identity. New York, Collier [1963, c.1952] 352p. 18cm. (AS540) .95 pap.,
1. Musicians—Correspondence, reminiscences, etc. I. Title.

SHAW, Artie, 1911- 927.8
The trouble with Cinderella; an outline of identity. New York, Farrar, Straus and Young [1952] 394 p. 22 cm. Autobiographical. [ML410.S498A3] 52-10229
1. Musicians—Correspondence, reminiscences, etc. I. Title.

SHORT, Bobby. 786.1'0924 B
Black and white baby. New York, Dodd, Mead [1971] 304 p. ports. 22 cm. [ML417.S6A3] 70-150167 ISBN 0-396-06348-9 7.95
1. Musicians—Correspondence, reminiscences, etc. I. Title.

SMART, George Thomas, Sir, 1776-1867. 785'.0924 B
Leaves from the journals of Sir George Smart, by H. Bertram Cox and C. L. E. Cox. New York, Da Capo Press, 1971. x, 355 p. illus., facsim., port. 24 cm. (Da Capo Press music reprint series) Reprint of the 1907 ed. Bibliography: p. 341. [ML410.S6A3 1971] 72-154696 ISBN 0-306-70164-2
1. Musicians—Correspondence, reminiscences, etc. I. Cox, Hugh Bertram, 1861-1930, ed. II. Cox, C. L. E., ed. **BIP**

SMITH, Kate [Kathryn Elizabeth Smith] 927.8
Upon my lips a song. New York, Funk & Wagnalls [c.1960] 213p. illus. 22cm. 60-12755 3.95 half cloth,
1. Musicians—Correspondence, reminiscences, etc. I. Title.

SMITH, Willie, 1897-1973. 786.1'092'4 B
Music on my mind : the memoirs of an American pianist / by Willie the Lion Smith, with George Hoefer. New York : Da Capo Press, 1975, c1964. xvi, 318 p. ; 22 cm. (The Roots of jazz) Reprint of the ed. published by Doubleday, Garden City, N.Y. Includes bibliographies, a discography, and index. [ML417.S675A3 1975] 74-23406 ISBN 0-306-70684-9 : 15.00.
1. Musicians—Correspondence, reminiscences, etc. 2. Jazz music. I. Hoefer, George. II. Title. **BIP**

SPALDING, Albert, 1888-1953. 787'.1'0924 B
Rise to follow; an autobiography. St. Clair Shores, Mich., Scholarly Press [1972, c1943] 328 p. port. 19 cm. [ML418.S7A2 1972] 74-181267 ISBN 0-403-01755-6
1. Musicians—Correspondence, reminiscences, etc. I. Title. **BIP**

SPOHR, Louis, 1784-1859. 780'.924 B
Autobiography. Translated from the German. New York, Da Capo Press, 1969. 2 v. in 1. music. 24 cm. (Da Capo Press music reprint series) Translation of Selbstbiographie. "This Da Capo Press edition is an unabridged republication of the first English edition published in 1865." [ML410.S7A32 1969] 69-12693 27.50
1. Musicians—Correspondence, reminiscences, etc.

STAUFFER, Teddy. 785'.092'4 B
Forever is a hell of a long time : an autobiography / by Teddy Stauffer. Chicago : H. Regnery, c1976. 309 p., [8] leaves of plates : ill. ; 24 cm. Translation of Es war und ist ein herrliches Leben. Includes index. [ML422.S65A33] 76-3635 ISBN 0-8092-8089-2 : 9.95
1. Musicians—Correspondence, reminiscences, etc. I. Title.

STRAVINSKII, Ignor' Fedrovich, 1882- 927.8
Expositions and developments [by] Igor Stravinsky, Robert Craft. Garden City, N. Y., Doubleday, 1962[c.1959-1962] 192p. illus. 61-12588 4.95
1. Musicians—Correspondence, reminiscences etc. I. Craft, Robert. II. Title.

SYMINGTON, Maude Fay, 1878-1964. 782.1'0924 B
Living in awe. Edited by Marshall Dill, Jr. San Francisco [Printed by Lawton and A. Kennedy] 1968. 173 p. illus. 27 cm. [ML420.S982A3] 70-9033
1. Musicians—Correspondence, reminiscences, etc. I. Title.

THOMAS, Theodore, 1835-1905. 785'.0924
A musical autobiography. Edited by George P. Upton. With a new introd. by Leon Stein. New York, Da Cape Press, 1964. A1-A69, 378 p. illus., facsims., ports. 24 cm. A reprint ed. based on the original 2 v. work of 1905. "Pages 35 through 356 of volume II, an enumeration of Thomas' 'Concert Programmes, 1855-1905,' were omitted in order to include the new introduction and appendices." [ML422.T46A33 1964] 64-18990
1. Musicians — Correspondence, reminiscences, etc. I. Upton, George Putnam, 1834-1919, ed. II. Stein, Leon, 1910- . III. Title.

THOMSON, Virgil, 1896- 780.924
Virgil Thomson. [1st ed.] New York, A. A. Knopf, 1966. x, 424, xiii p. illus., facsim., music, ports. 22 cm. [ML410.T452A3] 66-19403
1. Musicians—Correspondence, reminiscences, etc. I. Title. **BIP**

TIOMKIN, Dimitri. 927.8
Please don't hate me [by] Dimitri Tiomkin and Prosper Buranelli. [1st ed.] Garden City, N.Y., Doubleday, 1959. 261 p. illus. 22 cm. The story of Dimitri Tiomkin's musical career. [ML410.T465A26] 59-12650
1. Musicians—Correspondence, reminiscences, etc. I. Buranelli, Prosper, 1890- joint author. II. Title.

TRAPP, Maria Augusta 784.092
The story of the Trapp family singers, New York, Scholastic [1965, c.1949] 380p. illus. 17cm (T753) [ML400.T7] .50 pap.,
1. Musicians—Correspondence, reminiscences, etc. I. Title. II. Title: The Trapp family singers. **BIP**

TRAUBEL, Helen. 927.8
St. Louis woman. In collaboration with Richard G. Hubler. With an introd. by Vincent Sheean. [1st ed.] New York, Duell, Sloan and Pearce [1959] 296 p. illus. 21 cm. Autobiography. [ML420.T5A3] 59-5557
1. Musicians — Correspondence, reminiscences, etc. I. Title. **BIP**

VALLEE, Rudy, 1901- 927.8
My time is your time; the story of Rudy Vallee, by Rudy Vallee with Gil McKean. New York,.I. Obolensky [1962] 244 p. illus. 25 cm. [ML419.V2A3] 62-18783
1. Musicians — Correspondence, reminiscences, etc. I. Title.

VALLEE, Rudy, 1901- [Realname:HubertPriorVallee 927.8
My time is your time; the story of Rudy Vallee, by Rudy Vallee, Gil McKean. New York, Obolensky [c.1962] 244p. illus. 25cm. 62-18783 4.95
1. Musicians—Correspondence, reminiscences, etc. I. Title.

WALTER, Bruno, 1876- 927.8
Of music and music-making. Translated by Paul Hamburger. [1st American ed.] New York, W. W. Norton [1961] 222 p. illus. 22 cm. [ML422.W27A312] 61-5616
1. Musicians — Correspondence, reminiscences, etc. 2. Music — Addresses, essays, lectures. I. Title. **BIP**

WATERS, Ethel, 1900- v. 12
His eye is on the sparrow; an autobiography by Ethel Waters with Charles Samuels. New York, Bantam Books [1952; reprinted 1959] 278 p. 18 cm. (Bantam F 1976)
1. Musicians — Correspondence, reminiscences, etc. 2. Jazz music. I. Title.

WATERS, Ethel, 1900- 927.8
His eye is on the sparrow; an autobiography by Ethel Waters with Charles Samuels. [1st ed.] Garden City, N.Y., Doubleday, 1951. 278 p. illus. 22 cm. [ML420.W24A3] 51-9726
1. Musicians—Correspondence, reminiscences, etc. 2. Jazz music. I. Title. **BIP**

WATERS, Ethel, 1900- 927.8
His eye is on the sparrow; an autobiography by Ethel Waters with Charles Samuels. New York, Pyramid [1967, c.1951] 278p. 18cm. (T-1613) [ML420.W24A3] .75 pap.,
1. Musicians—Correspondence, reminiscence etc. 2. Jazz music I. Title.

WATERS, Thorold. 927.8
Much besides music; memoirs. Melbourne, Georgian House [1951] 231 p. 22 cm. [ML420.W26A3] 52-27419
1. Musicians — Correspondence reminiscences, etc. I. Title.

WEISS, Piero, comp. 780'.922
Letters of composers through six centuries. Compiled and edited by Piero Weiss. Foreword by Richard Ellmann. [1st ed.] Philadelphia, Chilton Book Co. [1967] xxix, 619 p. music. 24 cm. [ML90.W44] 67-28895
1. Musicians—Correspondence, reminiscences, etc. I. Title.

WELK, Lawrence, 1904- 785.4'1'0924 [B]
Wunnerful, wunnerful! The autobiography of Lawrence Welk, by Lawrence Welk with Bernice McGeehan. New York, Bantam [1973, c.1971] 404 p. illus. 18 cm. [ML422.W33A3] pap., 1.95
1. Musicians—Correspondence, reminiscences, etc. I. McGeehan, Bernice.

WELK, Lawrence, 1904- 785.4'1'0924 B
Wunnerful, wunnerful; the autobiography of Lawrence Welk, by Lawrence Welk with Bernice McGeehan. Englewood Cliffs, N.J., Prentice-Hall [1971] 294 p. illus. 24 cm. [ML422.W33A3] 70-155983 ISBN 0-13-971515-0 7.95
1. Musicians—Correspondence, reminiscences, etc. I. McGeehan, Bernice. II. Title.

WELLS, Dicky, 1910- 785.4'2'0924
The night people; reminiscences of a jazzman, by Dicky Wells, as told to Stanley Dance. Foreword by Count Basie. Boston, Crescendo, [1975 c1971] vi, 122 p. ports. 22 cm. Includes index. [ML419.W44A3] ISBN 0-87597-068-0 5.00 (pbk.)
1. Musicians—Correspondence, reminiscences, etc. 2. Jazz musicians. I. Title.
L.C. card no. for original ed.: 72-143284.

WHITING, Chester Earl. 785'.0924
The baton and the pendulum. [n.p., 1963] 176 p. illus., ports. 23 cm. [ML422.W39A3] 64-34
1. Musicians — Correspondence, reminiscences, etc. 2. Bands (Music) — U.S. I. Title.

WHYTHORNE, Thomas, b.ca.1528. 927.8
Autobiography. Edited by James M. Osborn. Oxford, Clarendon Press, 1961. 328 p. ports., facsims. (incl. music). 22 cm. [ML410.W647A3] 61-1880
1. Musicians — Correspondence, reminiscences, etc. 2. Music — England — Hist. & crit. I. Osborn, James Marshall, ed. II. Title.

WHYTHORNE, Thomas, b.ca.1528. 927.8
Autobiography. Modern spelling ed. edited by James M. Osborn. London, New York, Oxford University Press, 1962. 241 p. illus. 23 cm. [ML410.W647A3 1962] 62-51316
1. Musicians — Correspondence, reminiscences, etc. 2. Music — England — Hist. & crit. I. Osborn, James Marshall, ed. II. Title.

WHYTHORNE, Thomas, b ca. 1528. 927.8
Autobiography. Ed. by James M. Osborn. [dist. New York, Oxford Univ. Press, c.] 1961[ ] 328p. illus. Bibl. 61-1880 7.20
1. Musicians—Correspondence, reminiscences, etc. 2. Music—England—Hist. & crit. I. Osborn, James Marshall. ed. II. Title.

WILLSON, Meredith, 1902- 927.8
Eggs I have laid. [1st ed.] New York, Holt [1955] 185 p. 21 cm. [ML422.W63A32] 55-9878
1. Musicians—Correspondence, reminiscences, etc. I. Title.

WINKLER, Max, 1888- 926.555
A penny from Heaven. New York, Appleton-Century-Crofts [1951] 310 p. 21 cm. [ML427.W5A3] 51-10743
1. Musicians—Correspondence, reminiscences, etc. I. Title.

WOOD, Henry Joseph, Sir, 1869-1944. 785'.0924 B
My life of music. With an introd. by Sir Hugh Allen. Freeport, N.Y., Books for Libraries Press [1971] 384 p. music, port. 23 cm. Reprint of the 1946 ed. [ML422.W86A2 1971] 72-157359 ISBN 0-8369-5820-9
1. Musicians—Correspondence, reminiscences, etc. I. Title. **BIP**

Musicians, American.

BRIDGES, Glenn D. 780.924
Pioneers in brass, by Glenn Bridges. [Detroit, Sherwood Publications, 1965] 113 p. illus., facsims., ports. 28 cm. Cover title. Includes discographies. [ML399.B7] 65-4882
1. Musicians, American. 2. Music — Discography. I. Title.

KRAMER, Daniel. 780'.924
Bob Dylan. New York, Pocket Bks. [1968, c1967] 210p. ports. 18cm. (77029) [ML420.D98K7] .95 pap.,
1. Dylan, Bob, 1941- II. Title.

Musicians, American—Biography.

METCALF, Frank Johnson, 1865-1945. 783'.0922
American writers and compilers of sacred music, by Frank J. Metcalf. New York, Russell & Russell [1967, c1925] 373 p. facsims. (incl. music), ports. 21 cm. "Reissued." [ML106.U3M3 1967] 66-24731
1. Musicians, American—Biography. 2. Church music—United States. 3. Hymns, English—History and criticism. I. Title. **BIP**

MONTGOMERY, Elizabeth Rider. 785.4'2'0924
Duke Ellington; King of jazz, by Elizabeth Rider Montgomery. Illustrated by Paul Frame. [New York: Dell, 1975 c1972] 96 p.: illus.; 20 cm. (A Yearling book) (Americans all) Biography of an internationally acclaimed jazz musician who as a young man was torn between a career in art and music. [B] [ML3930.E44M6] 0.95 (pbk.)
1. Title.
L.C. card no. for original edition: 70-179401. **BIP**

Musicians, American—Biography—Juvenile literature.

SIGNIFICANT American musicians, composers, and singers. 780'.92'2 B Chicago : Childrens Press, [1976] p. cm. Includes index. Brief biographies of 183 musicians, composers, and singers arranged in chronological-alphabetical order. [ML3930.A2S484] 920 75-20691 ISBN 0-516-05306-X : 9.25
1. Musicians, American—Biography—Juvenile literature. I. Title: Musicians, composers, and singers.

Musicians, American Juvenile literature.

LEIPOLD, L. Edmond, 1902- 780'.92'2 B
Famous American musicians, by L. E. Leipold. Minneapolis, T. S. Denison [1972] 80 p. 25 cm. (His Famous American heroes and leaders series) Contents.Contents.—James Bland.—Louis Moreau Gottschalk.—John Philip Sousa.—Irving Berlin.—Louis Armstrong.—Marian Anderson.—Lena Horne.—Van Cliburn.—Leonard Bernstein.—Paul Revere and the Raiders. [ML3930.A2L43] 920 73-178993 ISBN 0-513-01166-8
1. Musicians, American—Juvenile literature. I. Title.

Musicians—Bio-bibliography.

EWEN, David, 1907- comp. 780'.92'2 B
Composers of yesterday : a biographical and critical guide to the most important composers of the past / compiled and edited by David Ewen. St. Clair Shores, Mich. : Scholarly Press, 1977. viii, 488 p. : ports ; 22 cm. Reprint of the 1937 ed. published by The H. W. Wilson Co., New York. Includes index. "A selected bibliography": p. [481]-486. [References cited at end of each biography.] [ML105.E94 1977] 73-181150 ISBN 0-403-01551-0 : 27.00
1. Musicians—Bio-bibliography. I. Title.

Musicians—Biography.

ENGEL, Louis. 780'.92'2 B
From Handel to Halle: biographical sketches. With autobiographies of Prof. Huxley and Prof. Herkomer. Freeport, N.Y., Books for Libraries Press [1972] viii, 251 p. ports. 23 cm. (Essay index reprint series) Reprint of the 1890 ed. Contents.Contents.—Handel.—Gluck.—Beethoven.—Sir Arthur Sullivan.—Joseph Barnby.—Madame Emma Albani-Gye.—Professor Huxley.—Hubert Herkomer.—Sir Charles and Lady Halle.—Three prodigies [Patti, Hofmann, Hegner] [ML385.E57 1972] 72-8544 ISBN 0-8369-7312-7
1. Musicians—Biography. I. Title.

GAISBERG, 789.9'1'0924 B
Frederick William.
The music goes round / Frederick William Gaisberg. New York : Arno Press, 1977, [c1942] 273 p., [15] leaves of plates : ill. ; 24 cm. (Opera biographies) Reprint of the ed. published by Macmillan, New York. Includes index. [ML1055.G15 1977] 76-29936 ISBN 0-405-09678-X : 20.00
1. Musicians—Biography. 2. Phonograph—History.

GAISBERG, 789.9'1'0924 B
Frederick William.
The music goes round / Frederick William Gaisberg. New York : Arno Press, 1977, [c1942] 273 p., [15] leaves of plates : ill. ; 24 cm. (Opera biographies) Reprint of the ed. published by Macmillan, New York. Includes index. [ML1055.G15 1977] 76-29936 ISBN 0-405-09678-X : 20.00
1. Musicians—Biography. 2. Phonograph—History. BIP

KLEINHANS, Theodore J 927.8
The music master; the story of Johann Sebastian Bach. Philadelphia, Muhlenberg Press [1962] 156p. 21cm. [ML410.B13K6] 62-8199
I. Bach, Johann Sebastian, 1685-1750. II. Title. BIP

NETTL, Paul, 1889- 780'.922 B
Forgotten musicians. New York, Greenwood Press [1969, c1951] 352 p. 23 cm. Bibliography: p. 339-340. [ML385.N5 1969] 76-94613 ISBN 0-8371-2463-8
1. Musicians—Biography. I. Title. BIP

PARKER, John R. 780'.92'2 B
A musical biography / by John Rowe Parker ; with new introd. by Frederick Freedman. Detroit : Information Coordinators, 1975. viii, 250 p. ; 26 cm. (Music for the Bicentennial) (Detroit reprints in music) Reprint of the 1825 ed. published by Stone & Fovell, Boston. Includes bibliographical references in introd. [ML385.P24 1975] 74-75895 ISBN 0-911772-73-1 : 10.50
1. Musicians—Biography. I. Title. BIP

ROWLANDS, Walter, 780'.92'2 B
1855-
Among the great masters of music : scenes in the lives of famous musicians : thirty-two reproductions of famous paintings with text / by Walter Rowlands. Boston : Longwood Press, 1978. 233 p., [31] leaves of plates : ill. ; 22 cm. Reprint of the 1900 ed. published by D. Estes, Boston. [ML385.R84 1978] 77-90805 ISBN 0-89341-422-0 lib.bdg. : 30.00
1. Musicians—Biography. 2. Musicians—Portraits. 3. Music in art. I. Title.

SIMON, George Thomas. 780'.92'2 B
The best of the music makers / George T. Simon. New York : Doubleday, c1979. p. cm. [ML385.S587] 78-22358 ISBN 0-385-14380-X : 19.95
1. Musicians—Biography. 2. Music, Popular (Songs, etc.)—History and criticism. I. Title. BIP

Musicians, Black—Biography.

ABDUL, Raoul. 780'.92'2 B
Blacks in classical music : a personal history / by Raoul Abdul. New York : Dodd, Mead, c1977. 253 p., [8] leaves of plates : ill. ; 22 cm. Includes index. [ML385.A27] 77-11645 ISBN 0-396-07394-8 : 8.95
1. Musicians, Black—Biography. I. Title. BIP

Musicians, British.

BROWN, James Duff, 780'.922 B
1862-1914.
British musical biography; a dictionary of musical artists, authors, and composers born in Britain and its colonies, by James D. Brown and Stephen S. Stratton. New York, Da Capo Press, 1971. ii, 462 p. 24 cm. (Da Capo Press music reprint series) Reprint of the 1897 ed. [ML106.G7B8 1971] 76-139197 ISBN 0-306-70076-X
1. Musicians, British. 2. Music—Gt. Brit.—Bio-bibliography. I. Stratton, Stephen Samuel, 1840-1906, joint author. BIP

*TREMLETT, George. 784'.092'4 B
The Rolling Stones. [New York] Warner Books [1975] 174 p. illus. 18 cm. [ML420] 1.25 (pbk.)
I. Title.

Musicians—Juvenile literature.

SCHWIMMER, Franciska. 927.8
Great musicians as children. Illustrated by M. Lois Murphy. New York, Doubleday, Doran, 1938. 238 p. 21 cm. [ML3930.A2S39] 40-3130
1. Musicians—Juvenile literature. 2. Music—Juvenile literature. I. Title. II. Title: Musicians as children.

Musicians—Portraits.

BRASK, Ole. 785.4'2'0922 B
Jazz people / photographs by Ole Brask ; text by Dan Morgenstern ; foreword by Dizzy Gillespie ; introd. by James Jones. New York : H. N. Abrams, 1976. p. cm. Includes index. Bibliography: [ML87.B65] 76-14462 ISBN 0-8109-1152-3 : 25.00
1. Musicians—Portraits. 2. Jazz musicians. I. Morgenstern, Dan. II. Title.

OUZER, Louis. 780'.92'2
Contemporary musicians in photographs / taken at the Eastman School of Music by Louis Quzer ; with text by Francis Crociata. New York : Dover Publications, c1979. 118 p. : chiefly ill. ; 29 cm. Includes index. [ML87.O84] 79-54808 ISBN 0-486-23859-8 pbk. : 6.00
1. Musicians—Portraits. I. Title. BIP

Musicians, Russian—Biography.

VODARSKY-SHIRAEFF, 780'.922
Alexandria, comp.
Russian composers and musicians; a biographical dictionary. New York, Greenwood Press [1969, c1940] 158 p. 23 cm. Bibliography: p. [155]-158. [ML106.R8V6 1969b] 78-97322
1. Musicians, Russian—Biography. I. Title. BIP

VODARSKY-SHIRAEFF, 780'.922
Alexandria.
Russian composers and musicians; a biographical dictionary. New York, Da Capo Press, 1969. 158 p. 24 cm. (Da Capo Press music reprint series) "An unabridged republication of the first edition published in 1940." Bibliography: p. [155]-158. [ML106.R8V6 1969] 71-76422
1. Musicians, Russian—Biography. I. Title.

Musicians—San Francisco.

HISTORY of Music 780'.9794'61 S
Project.
Celebrities in El Dorado, 1850-1906. New York, AMS Press [1972] 270 p. 27 cm. (History of music in San Francisco series, v. 4) Reprint of the 1940 ed. Bibliography: p. 263-266. [ML200.8.S2H4 v. 4, 1972] 73-38302 ISBN 0-404-07244-5 (v. 4)
1. Musicians—San Francisco. I. Title. II. Series.

Musicians, Scottish—Bio-bibliography.

BAPTIE, David, 1822- 780'.92'2 B
1906.
Musical Scotland, past and present. Being a dictionary of Scottish musicians from about 1400 till the present time, to which is added a bibliography of musical publications connected with Scotland from 1611. Hildesheim, New York, G. Olms, 1972. iv, 253 p. 22 cm. Reprint of the ed. published in Paisley by J. and R. Parlane in 1894. Bibliography: p. [243]-247. [ML106.S36B3] 72-185680 ISBN 3-487-04292-4
1. Musicians, Scottish—Bio-bibliography. I. Title.

Musicians, Women—Juvenile literature.

JONES, Hettie. 784'.092'2 B
Big star fallin' mama; five women in Black music. [1st ed.] New York, Viking Press [1974] 150 p. illus. 24 cm. Discography: p. [139]-140. Portraits of five black women and the kind of music they sang during a period of social change. Includes Ma Rainey, Bessie Smith, Mahalia Jackson, Billie Holiday, and Aretha Franklin. [ML82.J65] 920 73-5152 ISBN 0-670-16408-9 6.95
1. Musicians, Women—Juvenile literature. 2. Negro musicians—Juvenile literature. 3. Blues (Songs, etc.)—United States—Juvenile literature. I. Title. BIP

Muskie, Edmund S., 1914-

LIPPMAN, Theo. 973.924'0924
Muskie, by Theo Lippman, Jr. and Donald C. Hansen. [1st ed.] New York, Norton [1971] 237 p. illus., ports. 22 cm. [E840.8.M85L5 1971] 78-141941 6.95
1. Muskie, Edmund S., 1914- I. Hansen, Donald C., joint author.

MUSKIE, Edmund 973.924'092'4 B
S., 1914-
Journeys [by] Edmund S. Muskie. [1st ed.] Garden City, N.Y., Doubleday, 1972. 204 p. 22 cm. [E840.8.M85A34] 71-190432 5.95
I. Title.

NEVIN, David, 973.924'0924 B
1927-
Muskie of Maine. New York, Random House [1972] 238 p. 22 cm. [E840.8.M85N4] 72-159361 6.95
1. Muskie, Edmund S., 1914- I. Title.

Musonius Rufus, C.

CHARLESWORTH, Martin 920.037
Percival, 1895-1950.
Five men; character studies from the Roman Empire. Freeport, N.Y., Books for Libraries Press [1967] viii, 170 p. 22 cm. (Essay index reprint series) Martin classical lectures, v.6. Reprint of the 1936 ed. Includes bibliographical references. [PA25.M3 vol. 6 1967] 67-30202
1. Agrippa I, King of Judea, B. C. 10 (ca.)-A. D. 44. 2. Musonius Rufus, C. 3. Josephus, Flavius. 4. Agricola, Cn. Julius, 37-93. 5. Rome—Civilization. I. Title. II. Series: Martin classical lectures, v. 6 BIP

CHARLESWORTH, Martin 920.037
Percival, 1895-1950.
Five men; character studies from the Roman Empire. Freeport, N.Y., Books for Libraries Press [1967] viii, 170 p. 22 cm. (Essay index reprint series) (Martin classical lectures, v. 6.) Reprint of the 1936 ed. Includes bibliographical references. [PA25.M3 vol. 6 1967] 67-30202
1. Agrippa I, King of Judea, B.C. 10 (ca.)-A.D. 44. 2. Agricola, Cn. Julius, 37-93. 3. Musonius Rufus, C. 4. Josephus, Flavius. 5. Rome—Civilization. I. Title. II. Series.

Musorgskii, Modest Petrovich, 1839-1881.

RIESEMANN, Oskar von, 780'.924 B
1880-1934.
Moussorgsky. Translated from the German by Paul England. New York, AMS Press [1970] ix, 412, xvii p. 23 cm. Originally published as v. 2 of the author's Monographien zur russischen Musik, with title: Modest Petrowitsch Mussorgski. Bibliography: p. 409-412. [ML410.M97R53 1970] 74-121278
1. Musorgskii, Modest Petrovich, 1839-1881. BIP

RIESEMANN, Oskar von, 780'.92'4 B
1880-1934.
Moussorgsky. Translated from the German by Paul England. New York, Dover Publications [1971] ix, 429 p. 22 cm. Originally published as v. 2 of the author's Monographien zur russischen Musik, with title: Modest Petrowitsch Mussorgski. Bibliography: p. 409-412. [ML410.M97R53 1971] 78-138388 ISBN 0-486-22496-1 3.50
1. Musorgskii, Modest Petrovich, 1839-1881. BIP

Musset, Alfred de, 1810-1857.

HALDANE, Charlotte 928.4
(Franken) 1894-
Alfred; the passionate life of Alfred de Musset. New York, Roy [1961, c.1960] 222p. illus. Bibl. 60-15428 5.00
1. Musset, Alfred de, 1810-1857. I. Title. BIP

SEDGWICK, Henry Dwight, 841'.7 B
1861-1957.
Alfred deMusset, 1810-1857. Port Washington, N.Y., Kennikat Press [1973, c1931] 343 p. 22 cm. Bibliography: p. 329-330. [PQ2370.S35 1973] 70-113321 ISBN 0-8046-1738-4 13.75
1. Musset, Alfred de, 1810-1857. BIP

Mussolini, Benito, 1883-1945.

ARCHER, Jules. 923.245
Twentieth century Caesar, Benito Mussolini. New York, J. Messner [1964] 192 p. 22 cm. Bibliography: p. [186]-187. [DG575.M8A683] 64-20159
1. Mussolini, Benito, 1883-1945. I. Title.

ARCHER, Jules. 945.091'0924 B
Twentieth century Caesar, Benito Mussolini. New York, J. Messner [1964] 192 p. 22 cm. Bibliography: p. [186]-187. As organizer of the Fascist blackshirts, dictator of Italy, and visionary of a second Roman Empire, Mussolini exercised power and paved the way to Italy's downfall. [DG575.M8A683] 92 AC 68
1. Mussolini, Benito, 1883-1945. I. Title.

BAYNE-JARDINE, 945'.091'0924
Colin Charles.
Mussolini and Italy. Foreword by William J. Jacobs. New York, McGraw-Hill [1968, c1966] viii, 120 p. illus., maps, ports. 23 cm. Bibliography: p. [118] [DG575.M8B32 1968] 68-15464
1. Mussolini, Benito, 1883-1945. I. Title.

BORGHI, Armando. 945.091'092'4 B
Mussolini, red and black. With an epilogue, Hitler: Mussolini's disciple. Translated by Dorothy Daudley. New York, Haskell House Publishers, 1974. 207 p. 21 cm. Translation of Mussolini in camicia. Reprint of the 1938 ed. published by Freie Arbeiter Stimme, New York. [DG575.M8B63 1974] 73-20389 ISBN 0-8383-1765-0
1. Mussolini, Benito, 1883-1945. 2. Hitler, Adolf, 1889-1945. 3. Fascism—Italy.

BOX, Pelham Horton, 909.82 B
1898-1937.
Three master builders and another; studies in modern revolutionary and liberal statesmanship. With an introd. by Ernest Barker. Freeport, N.Y., Books for Libraries Press [1968] 395 p. ports. 22 cm. (Essay index reprint series) Reprint of the 1925 ed. Contents.Contents.—Nikolai Lenin.—Benito Mussolini.—Eleutherios Venizelos.—Woodrow Wilson. Includes bibliographies. [D412.6.B6 1968] 68-22904
1. Lenin, Vladimir Il'ich, 1870-1924. 2. Mussolini, Benito, 1883-1945. 3. Venizelos, Eleutherios, 1864-1936. 4. Wilson, Woodrow, Pres. U.S., 1856-1924. I. Title. BIP

BRADFORD, Gamaliel, 1863- 920.02
1932.
The quick and the dead. Port Washington, N.Y., Kennikat Press [1969, c1931] x, 282 p. ports. 22 cm. (Essay and general literature index reprint series)

Contents.Contents.—Theodore Roosevelt.—Woodrow Wilson.—Thomas Alva Edison.—Henry Ford.—Nikolai Lenin.—Benito Mussolini.—Calvin Coolidge. Bibliographical references included in "Notes" (p. [259]-[274]) [CT120.B65 1969] 70-85991
1. Roosevelt, Theodore, Pres. U.S., 1858-1919. 2. Wilson, Woodrow, Pres. U.S., 1856-1924. 3. Edison, Thomas Alva, 1847-1931. 4. Ford, Henry, 1863-1947. 5. Lenin, Vladimir Il'ich, 1870-1924. 6. Mussolini, Benito, 1883-1945. 7. Coolidge, Calvin, Pres. U.S., 1872-1933. I. Title.

COLLIER, Richard, 1924- 945.091'0924 B
Duce! A biography of Benito Mussolini. New York, Viking Press [1971] 447 p. illus. 24 cm. Bibliography: p. [395]-419. [DG575.M8C63 1971b] 70-157972 ISBN 0-670-28603-6 12.50
1. Mussolini, Benito, 1883-1945. I. Title.

DABROWSKI, Roman. 945.091
Mussolini: twilight and fall, by Roman Dombrowski. Translated and with a pref. by H. C. Stevens. New York, Roy Publishers [1956] 248 p. illus. 22 cm. Translation of Sto dni Mussoliniego. [DG575.M8D32] 55-9308
1. Mussolini, Benito, 1883-1945.

DEAKIN, Frederick William Dampier, 1913- 945.091
The brutal friendship: Mussolini, Hitler and the fall of Italian fascism, by F. W. Deakin. Revised ed. Harmondsworth, Penguin, 1966. 575 p. 18 1/2 cm. (Pelican books, A817) Previous ed. published as Part 1 of The brutal friendship. London, Weidenfeld & Nicolson, 1962. Bibliography: p. 533-537. [DG572.D382 1966b] 67-70231
1. Mussolini, Benito, 1883-1945. 2. Hitler, Adolf, 1889-1945. 3. World War, 1939-1945 Italy. 4. Germany—Foreign relations—Italy. 5. Italy—Foreign relations—Germany. I. Title.

FERMI, Laura. 923.245
Mussolini. [Chicago] University of Chicago Press [1961] 477 p. illus. 23 cm. Includes bibliography. [DG575.M8F42] 61-17075
1. Mussolini, Benito, 1883-1945. BIP

GOURLAY, Jack. 945.091'0924(B)
Benito Mussolini; a biography. Edited by Ellie Kurtz. New York, Distributed by Monarch Press [c1966] 172 p. 22 cm. (Monarch notes and study guides, 895-3) [DG575.M8] 66-27313
1. Mussolini, Benito, 1883-1945. I. Title.

HIBBERT, Christopher, 1924- 923.245
Il Duce; the life of Benito Mussolini. [1st ed.] Boston, Little, Brown [1962] 367 p. illus. 24 cm. "Published in England under the title of Benito Mussolini." Includes bibliography. [DG575.M8H47 1962a] 62-8069
1. Mussolini, Benito, 1883-1945.

HIBBERT, Christopher, 1924- 945.091'092'4 B
Mussolini. [New York, Ballantine Books, 1972] 160 p. illus. 21 cm. (Ballantine's illustrated history of the violent century. War leader book, no. 13) Bibliography: p. 160. [DG575.M8H48] 72-190011 ISBN 0-345-02648-9 1.00
1. Mussolini, Benito, 1883-1945.

KIRKPATRICK, Ivone, Sir. 945.091'092'4 B
Mussolini : a study in power / by Ivone Kirkpatrick. Westport, Conn. : Greenwood Press, 1976, c1964. 726 p., [16] leaves of plates : ill. ; 23 cm. Reprint of the 1st ed. published by Hawthorn Books, New York. Includes index. Bibliography: p. 697-707. [DG575.M8K5 1976] 75-26215 ISBN 0-8371-8400-2 lib.bdg. : 35.00
1. Mussolini, Benito, 1883-1945.

KIRKPATRICK, Ivone, Sir. 923.245
Mussolini, a study in power. [1st ed.] New York, Hawthorn Books [1964] 726 p. illus., ports., maps, geneal. table. 24 cm. Bibliography: p. 697-707. [DG575.M8K5] 64-13278
1. Mussolini, Benito, 1883-1945. I. Title. BIP

MEGARO, Gaudens, 1903- 945.091'0924
Mussolini in the making. New York, Ferting, 1967. 347p. illus., ports 21cm. Reprint of the 1938 ed. [DG575.M8M4 1967] 67-13634 8.00
1. Mussolini, Benito, 1883-1945. I. Title.

MONELLI, Paolo, 1891- 923.245
Mussolini; the intimate life of a demagogue. [Translated from the Italian by Brigid Maxwell] New York, Vanguard Press [1954] 304p. illus. 22cm. Translation of Mussolini, piccolo borghese. Includes bibliography. [DG575.M8M614 1954] 54-6996
1. Mussolini, Benito, 1883-1945. 2. Fascism—Italay. I. Title.

MUSSOLINI, Benito, 1883-1945. 945.091'092'4 B
The fall of Mussolini : his own story / by Benito Mussolini ; translated from the Italian by Frances Frenaye ; edited and with a pref. by Max Ascoli. Westport, Conn. : Greenwood Press, 1975, c1948. 212 p. ; 22 cm. Translation of Il tempo del bastone e della carota. Reprint of the ed. published by Farrar, Straus, New York. [DG575.M8A5423 1975b] 75-2699 ISBN 0-8371-8035-X lib.bdg. : 14.25
1. Mussolini, Benito, 1883-1945. 2. World War, 1939-1945—Italy. 3. Italy—History—1922-1945—Sources. I. Title.

MUSSOLINI, Benito, 1883-1945. 945,091'092'4 B
My autobiography. With a foreword by Richard Washburn Child. Westport, Conn., Greenwood Press [1970] xix, 318 p. illus., ports 23 cm. Reprint of the 1928 ed. [DG575.M8A2 1970] 78-109803 ISBN 8-371-42946-
1. Italy—Politics and government—1914-1945. I. Child, Richard Washburn, 1881-1935. BIP

MUSSOLINI, Rachele Guidi, 1892- 945.091'092'4 B
Mussolini: an intimate biography by his widow, Rachele Mussolini, as told to Albert Zarca. New York, Morrow, 1974. vi, 291 p. illus. 22 cm. Translation of Mussolini sans masque. [DG575.M8M835313 1974] 74-1129 ISBN 0-688-00266-8 8.95
1. Mussolini, Benito, 1883-1945. I. Zarca, Albert. II. Title.

MUSSOLINI, Vittorio, 1916- 945.091'092'2 B
Mussolini: the tragic women in his life. Translated from the Italian and with an introd. by Graham Snell. New York, Dial Press, 1973. ix, 148 p. illus. 22 cm. [DG575.M8A353] 73-3453 6.95
1. Mussolini, Benito, 1883-1945. I. Title.

PALEY, Alan L. 945.091'092'4 B
Benito Mussolini, Fascist dictator of Italy / by Alan L. Paley ; D. Steve Rahmas, editor ; compiled with the assistance of the research staff of SamHar Press. Charlotteville, N.Y. : SamHar Press, 1975. p. cm. (Outstanding personalities ; 81) Bibliography: p. [DG575.M8P24] 75-16324 lib.bdg. : 2.29 pbk. : 1.25
1. Mussolini, Benito, 1883-1945. I. Title. BIP

Muste, Abraham John, 1885-

HENTOFF, Nat. 923.673
Peace agitator; the story of A. J. Muste. New York, Macmillan [1963] 269 p. illus. 21 cm. Includes bibliography. [JX1962.M8H4] 63-15283
1. Muste, Abraham John, 1885- I. Title.

Muybridge, Eadweard, 1830-1904.

HAAS, Robert Bartlett. 770'.92'4 B
Muybridge : man in motion / by Robert Bartlett Haas. Berkeley : University of California Press, c1976. x, 207 p. : ill. ; 24 cm. Includes bibliographical references and index. [TR849.M87H3] 73-78542 ISBN 0-520-02464-8 : 18.50
1. Muybridge, Eadweard, 1830-1904. BIP

HENDRICKS, Gordon. 770'.92'4 B
Eadweard Muybridge : the father of the motion picture / Gordon Hendricks. New York : Grossman Publishers, 1975. xvi, 271 p. : ill. ; 28 cm. Includes index. Bibliography: p. 245-254. [TR849.M87H46] 73-16572 ISBN 0-670-28679-6 : 25.00
1. Muybridge, Eadweard, 1830-1904.

MACDONNELL, Kevin. 779'.092'4
Eadweard Muybridge, the man who invented the moving picture. [1st ed.] Boston, Little, Brown [1972] 158 p. illus. 28 cm. Bibliography. p. 155-158. [TR849.M87M3] 72-1800 ISBN 0-316-54190-7 12.50
1. Muybridge, Eadweard, 1830-1904.

Muzorewa, Abel Tendekayi, 1925-

MUZOREWA, Abel Tendekayi, 1925- 968.9'1'040924 B
Rise up & walk : the autobiography of Bishop Abel Tendekai Muzorewa / edited by Norman E. Thomas. Nashville : Abingdon, 1978. 289 p., [8] leaves of plates : ill. ; 23 cm. Includes index. [DT962.76.M88A37 1978] 78-19546 ISBN 0-687-36450-7 : 9.95
1. Muzorewa, Abel Tendekayi, 1925- 2. Methodist Church—Bishops—Biography. 3. Rhodesia, Southern—Politics and government—1965- 4. Rhodesia, Southern—Church history. 5. Statesmen—Rhodesia, Southern—Biography. 6. Bishops—Rhodesia, Southern—Biography. I. Title.

Myddleton, Sir Hugh, 1560?-1631.

GOUGH, John Wiedhofft 926.5
Sir Hugh Myddleton, entrepreneur and engineer [New York, Oxford, c.]1964. xii, 155p. illus., port. 23cm. Bibl. [TA140.M9G6] 65-620 4.80
1. Myddleton, Sir Hugh, 1560?-1631. I. Title.

Myer, Norman, Sir, 1897-1956.

WARRENDER, Pamela. 381'.45'000924 B
Prince of merchants; the story of Sir Norman Myer. Melbourne, Gold Star Publications, 1972. 266 p. illus., map, ports.; 18 cm. [HF3944.5.M93W37] 73-163016 ISBN 0-7260-0115-5 2.50
1. Myer, Norman, Sir, 1897-1956. I. Title.

Myers, Albert P

MYERS, Albert P 1878- 920
The lone dinner plate. New York, Vantage Press [1952] 187 p. illus. 22 cm. Autobiography. [CT275.M84A3] 52-6942
I. Title.

Myers, Carlton H., 1924-

MYERS, Carlton H., 1924- 353.008'233 B
I had to watch my country die / [Carlton H. Myers]. [Columbus, Ga.?] : Myers, c1976. ii, 275, 52 p. : ill. ; 24 cm. [TS197.M93] 76-54665
1. Myers, Carlton H., 1924- 2. Poultry inspectors—United States—Biography. I. Title.

Myers, George Sprague, 1905-

FESTSCHRIFT for George Sprague Myers in honor of his sixty-fifth birthday. 508'.1 S
San Francisco, The Academy, 1970. 437 p. illus., ports. 26 cm. (Proceedings of the California Academy of Sciences, 4th ser., v. 38) Includes bibliographies. [Q11.C253 vol. 38] 73-25199
1. Myers, George Sprague, 1905- 2. Fishes—Addresses, essays, lectures. 3. Amphibians—Addresses, essays, lectures. 4. Reptiles—Addresses, essays, lectures. I. Myers, George Sprague, 1905- II. Series: California Academy of Sciences, San Francisco. Proceedings, 4th ser., v. 38

Myers, Robert,

MYERS, Robert, 1892- 926.21
Shtimmer, the boy who couldn't talk; the story of a Jewish immigrant from Romania and his role in the American labor movement. [1st ed.] New York, Exposition Press [c1959] 249p. illus. 21cm. Autobiographical. [CT275M847A3] 60-437
I. Title.

Myers, Robert [Name originally; Myer Rubinstein]

MYERS, Robert [Name originally; Myer Rubinstein] 926.21
Shtimmer, the boy who couldn't talk; the story of a Jewish immigrant from Romania and his role in the American labor movement. New York, Exposition Press [c.1959] 249p. illus. 21cm. 60-437 3.50
I. Title.

Myrdal, Gunnar, 1898- —Biography.

BOHRN, Harald, 1904- 081
Gunnar Myrdal : a bibliography, 1919-1976 / by Harald Bohrn. Stockholm : [Kungliga biblioteket], 1976. 188 p. ; 24 cm. (Acta Bibliothecae Regiae Stockholmiensis ; 27) Includes index. [Z674.S8 no. 27] [Z7164.E2] [HB179.S8] 025.2 016.657 77-458577 ISBN 9-17-000060-3
1. Myrdal, Gunnar, 1898- —Biography. 2. Economics—Bibliography. I. Series: Stockholm. Kungliga biblioteket. Acta Bibliothecae Stockholmiensis ; 27.

Mystic Seaport, Mystic, Conn.

DICKERMAN, Marion. 917.46'5 B
The three founders: Dr. Charles Kirtland Stillman, Carl C. Cutler [and] Edward Eugene Bradley. With a foreword by Philip R. Mallory. [Mystic, Conn.] Marine Historical Association, 1965. 42 p. illus., ports. 23 cm. Cover title: The three founders of Mystic Seaport. [F104.M99D5] 71-17343
1. Mystic Seaport, Mystic, Conn. 2. Stillman, Charles Kirtland, 1879-1938. 3. Cutler, Carl C., 1878-1966. 4. Bradley, Edward Eugene, 1857-1938. I. Marine Historical Association. II. Title.

Mysticism.

SINGH, Sundar, 1889- 922
The cross is heaven; the life and writings of Sadhu Sundar Singh. Edited by A. J. Appasamy. New York, Association Press [1957] 93 p. 20 cm. (World Christian books) [BV5082.S52 1957] 57-6879
1. Mysticism. I. Title.

Mysticism—Addresses, essays, lectures.

SILENT fire : 248'.22'0922 B
an invitation to Western mysticism / by Walter Holden Capps and Wendy M. Wright [editors]. 1st ed. San Francisco : Harper & Row, c1978. p. cm. (A Harper forum book) Includes index. Bibliography: p. [BV5072.S54 1978] 78-3366 ISBN 0-06-061314-9 pbk. : 5.95
1. Mysticism—Addresses, essays, lectures. 2. Mystics—Biography—Addresses, essays, lectures. I. Capps, Walter H. II. Wright, Wendy M.

Mysticism—Catholic Church

GRAEF, Hilda C. 922.2
Mystics of our times. Garden City, N.Y., Hanover House, [c]1962. 240p. Bibl. 62-7636 4.50
1. Mysticism—Catholic Church I. Title. BIP

GRAEF, Hilda C 922.2
Mystics of our times. Glen Rock, N.J., Paulist Press [1963, c1962] 240 p. 18 cm. (Deus books) Bibliography: p. [239]-240. [BV5095.A1G68 1963] 63-20220
1. Mysticism — Catholic Church. 2. Catholic Church — Biog. I. Title.

Mysticism—Gt. Brit.

COLEMAN, Thomas William, 1884- 248.2'2'0922
English mystics of the fourteenth century, by T. W. Coleman. Westport, Conn., Greenwood Press [1971] 176 p. 23 cm. Reprint of the 1938 ed. Contents.Contents.—Christian

mysticism.—The times of the English mystics.—The Ancren riwle.—Richard Rolle.—The Cloud of unknowing.—Walter Hilton.—The Lady Julian.—Margery Kemp. Includes bibliographical references. [BV5077.G7C6 1971] 74-109723 ISBN 0-8371-4213-X
1. Mysticism—Gt. Brit. I. Title. **BIP**

Mysticism—Middle Ages.

ANGELA, of Foligno, 1248?-1309. 242'.1
The book of divine consolation of the Blessed Angela of Foligno. Translated from the Italian by Mary G. Steegmann. Introd. by Algar Thorold. New York, Cooper Square Publishers, 1966. xliv, 265 p. illus., facsims. 17 cm. (The Medieval library) Translation of Liber de vera fidelium experientia. [BV5080.A52 1966] 66-30731
1. Mysticism—Middle Ages. I. Steegmann, Mary G., tr. II. Thorold, Algar Labouchere, 1866-1936. III. Title.

Mysticism—Russia—History.

BOLSHAKOFF, Serge. 248'.22'0922 B
Russian mystics / by Sergius Bolshakoff ; introd. by Thomas Merton. Kalamazoo, Mich. : Cistercian Publications, 1977, c1976. xxx, 303 p. ; 23 cm. (Cistercian studies series ; no. 26) Italian translation has title: I mistici russi. Bibliography: p. 285-303. [BV5077.R8B6413] 76-15485 ISBN 0-87907-826-X : 13.95 ISBN 0-87907-926-6 pbk. : 5.50
1. Mysticism—Russia—History. 2. Mysticism—Orthodox Eastern Church, Russian—History. 3. Monasticism and religious orders—Russia—History. I. Title. II. Series. **BIP**

Mzilikazi, Matabele King, 1790-1868.

RASMUSSEN, R. Kent. 968.9'1'010924 B
Mzilikazi of the Ndebele / [by] R. Kent Rasmussen. London : Heinmann Educational, 1977. 48 p. : ill., maps, ports. ; 15 x 21 cm. (African historical biographies ; 13) Bibliography: p. 48. [DT962.9.M37M946] 78-305609 ISBN 0-435-94475-4 : pbk. : 1.95
1. Mzilikazi, Matabele King, 1790-1868. 2. Matabeleland—History. 3. Africa, Southern—History. 4. Matabele—Kings and rulers—Biography. 5. Matabeleland—Kings and rulers—Biography. I. Title. II. Series.
Distributed by Heinemann, Salem N.H. **BIP**

Nabokov, Nicolas, 1903-

NABOKOV, Nicolas, 1903- 780'.92'4 B
Bagazh : memoirs of a Russian cosmopolitan / Nicolas Nabokov. 1st ed. New York : Atheneum, 1975. ix, 307 p., [8] leaves of plates : ill. ; 25 cm. Includes index. [ML410.N2A28] 75-13677 ISBN 0-689-10656-4 : 12.95
1. Nabokov, Nicolas, 1903- I. Title.

NABOKOV, Nicolas, 1903- 780'.92'4 B
Old friends and new music. Westport, Conn., Greenwood Press, 1974. p. cm. Reprint of the 1951 ed. published by Little, Brown, Boston. [ML410.N2A3 1974] 74-7776 ISBN 0-8371-7594-1 13.75
1. Nabokov, Nicolas, 1903- 2. Musicians—Correspondence, reminiscences, etc. I. Title.

Nabokov, Vladimir Dmitrievich, 1869-1922.

NABOKOV, Vladimir Dmitrievich, 1869-1922. 320.9'47'0841
V. D. Nabokov and the Russian Provisional Government, 1917 / edited by Virgil D. Medlin and Steven L. Parsons ; introd. by Robert P. Browder. New Haven : Yale University Press, 1976. viii, 188 p. : port. ; 22 cm. Includes bibliographical references and index. [DK265.7.N26 1976] 75-18177 ISBN 0-300-01820-7 : 12.50
1. Nabokov, Vladimir Dmitrievich, 1869-1922. 2. Russia—History—Revolution, 1917-1921—Personal narratives. 3. Russia (1917. Provisional government) I. Title.

Nabokov, Vladimir Vladimirovich,

NABOKOV, Vladimir [Vladimirovich] 928.2
Speak, memory; a memoir, original title: Conclusive evidence. New York, Grosset & Dunlap [1960, c.1947-1951] 240p. 21cm. (The Universal library, UL-76) 60-2453 1.45 pap.,
I. Title.

NABOKOV, Vladimir Vladimirovich, 1899- 928.2
Conclusive evidence, a memoir. [1st ed.] New York, Harper [1951] 240 p. 22 cm. [PS3527.A15Z5] 51-9454
I. Title.

NABOKOV, Vladimir Vladimirovich, 1899- 891.7'8'4203 B
Speak, memory; an autobiography revisited, by Vladimir Nabokov. [Rev. ed.] New York, Putnam [1966] 316 p. illus., col. map (on lining papers) ports. 22 cm. First published in 1951 under title: Conclusive evidence. [PG3476.N3Z5 1966] 66-23330
I. Title.

Nabokov, Vladimir Vladimirovich, 1899-

DEMBO, L. S. 818'.5'209
Nabokov: the man and his work; studies ed. by L. S. Dembo. Madison, Univ. of Wis. Pr., 1967. x, 280p. 23cm. Bibl. [PS3527.A15Z62] 67-26625 6.50
1. Nabokov, Vladimir Vladimirovich, 1899- I. Title.

MOYNAHAN, Julian, 1925- 813'.5'4
Vladimir Nabokov. Minneapolis, University of Minnesota Press [1971] 47 p. 21 cm. (University of Minnesota pamphlets of American writers, no. 96) Bibliography: p. 46-47. [PG3476.N3Z75] 71-633325 ISBN 0-8166-0600-5 0.95
1. Nabokov, Vladimir Vladimirovich, 1899- I. Series: Minnesota. University. Pamphlets on American writers, no. 96 **BIP**

NABOKOV, Vladimir [Vladimirovich] 928.2
Speak, memory; a memoir, original title: Conclusive evidence. New York, Grosset & Dunlap [1960, c.1947-1951] 240p. 21cm. (The Universal library, UL-76) 60-2453 1.45 pap.,
I. Title.

NABOKOV, Vladimir Vladimirovich, 1899- 928.2
Conclusive evidence, a memoir. [1st ed.] New York, Harper [1951] 240 p. 22 cm. [PS3527.A15Z5] 51-9454
I. Title.

NABOKOV, Vladimir Vladimirovich, 1899- 891.7'8'4203 B
Speak, memory; an autobiography revisited, by Vladimir Nabokov. [Rev. ed.] New York, Putnam [1966] 316 p. illus., col. map (on lining papers) ports. 22 cm. First published in 1951 under title: Conclusive evidence. [PG3476.N3Z5 1966] 66-23330
I. Title.

Nabokov, Vladimir Vladimirovich, 1899- —Biography.

FIELD, Andrew, 1938- 813'.5'4 B
Nabokov, his life in part / Andrew Field. New York : Viking Press, [1977] p. cm. Includes index. [PG3476.N3Z65] 76-47042 ISBN 0-670-50367-3 : 12.50
1. Nabokov, Vladimir Vladimirovich, 1899- —Biography. 2. Authors, Russian—20th century—Biography. 3. Authors, American—20th century—Biography. I. Title.

Nabuco, Joaquim, 1849-1910.

NABUCO, Carolina. 923.231
The life of Joaquim Nabuco; translated and edited by Ronald Hilton in collaboration with Lee B. Valentine, Frances E. Coughlin [and] Joaquim M. Duarte, Jr. Stanford, Stanford University Press [1950] xxv, 373 p. port., map (on lining papers) 24 cm. "Bibliographical note": p. 364. [F2536.N173 1950] 50-8549
1. Nabuco, Joaquim, 1849-1910. I. Title. **BIP**

NABUCO, Carolina. 328.81'0924 B
The life of Joaquim Nabuco. Translated and edited by Ronald Hilton, in collaboration with Lee B. Valentine, Frances E. Coughlin [and] Joaquin M. Duarte, Jr. New York, Greenwood Press, 1968 [c1950] xxv, 373 p. map, port. 24 cm. Translation of A vida de Joaquim Nabuco. Bibliography: p. 364. [F2536.N173 1968] 69-10140
1. Nabuco, Joaquim, 1849-1910. I. Title.

Nader, Ralph.

ACTON, Jay. 340'.092'4 B
Ralph Nader: a man and a movement, by Jay Acton and Alan LeMond. New York, Warner Paperback Library [1972] 239 p. 18 cm. (A New earth book) Bibliography: p. 238-239. [KF373.N3A25] 73-160658 ISBN 0-446-66992-X 1.25
1. Nader, Ralph. I. Le Mond, Alan, joint author.

BUCKHORN, Robert F., 1927- 340'.0924 B
Nader: the people's lawyer, by Robert F. Buckhorn. Englewood Cliffs, N.J., Prentice-Hall [1972] viii, 310 p. 22 cm. Bibliography: p. 307-310. [KF373.N3B8] 76-38579 ISBN 0-13-609222-5 6.95
1. Nader, Ralph. I. Title.

GOREY, Hays. 343'.73'070924 B
Nader and the power of everyman / Hays Gorey. New York : Grosset & Dunlap, [1975] 320 p. ; 22 cm. Includes index. Bibliography: p. [313]-315. [KF373.N3G6] 74-14385 ISBN 0-448-02010-6 : 10.00
1. Nader, Ralph. I. Title.

MCCARRY, Charles. 340'.092'4 B
Citizen Nader. New York, Saturday Review Press [1972] xiv, 335 p. 22 cm. [HC110.C63M23] 70-182488 ISBN 0-8415-0163-7 7.95
1. Nader, Ralph. I. Title.

Nader, Ralph—Juvenile literature.

CURTIS, Richard. 340'.092'4 B
Ralph Nader's crusade. Philadelphia, Macrae Smith, [1972] 136 p. 21 cm. A biography of the man who investigates large corporations and government agencies on behalf of the consumer. [HC110.C63C85] 92 72-4379 ISBN 0-8255-2794-5 4.95
1. Nader, Ralph—Juvenile literature. I. Title.

OLSEN, James T. 340'.092'4 B
Ralph Nader: voice of the people, by James T. Olsen. Illustrated by Harold Henriksen. Mankato, Minn., Creative Education; [distributed by Childrens Press, Chicago, 1974] 29 p. col. illus. 25 cm. (Close-ups) A brief biography of Ralph Nader whose interest in consumer protection sparked the first major legislation which dictated safety standards for automobiles. [HC110.C63O37] 92 74-6421 ISBN 0-87191-355-0
1. Nader, Ralph—Juvenile literature. I. Henriksen, Harold, illus. II. Title.

Nader Shah, Shah of Iran, 1688-1747.

LOCKHART, Laurence. 955'.03'0924 B
Nadir Shah; a critical study based mainly upon contempoary sources, by L. Lockhart. With a foreword by E. Denison Ross. London, Luzac, 1938. [New York, AMS Press, 1973] xv, 344 p. illus. 24 cm. Bibliography: p. 314-328. [DS294.L6 1973] 78-180358 ISBN 0-404-56290-6 21.50
1. Nader Shah, Shah of Iran, 1688-1747. 2. Iran—History—16th-18th centuries. 3. India—History—1500-1765.

Nagal, Kafu, 1879-1959.

SEIDENSTICKER, Edward G 1921- 895.634
Kafu the Scribbler; the life and writings of Nagai Kafu, 1879-1959 [by] Edward Seidensticker. Stanford, Calif., Stanford University Press, 1965. vi, 360 p. illus., map (on lining papers) port. 24 cm. "Bibliographical note": p. [350]-352. [PL812.A4Z88] 65-21492
1. Nagal, Kafu, 1879-1959. I. Title. **BIP**

Nagel, Gottlieb, 1787-1827.

AMMON, Friedrich von. 940.2'7'0924 B
Soldier of freedom; the life of Dr. Christian Nagel, 1787-1827, director of the Royal Prussian Gymnasium in Cleve, knight of the Iron Cross, by Friedrich von Ammon and Theodor Herold. Translated and annotated by Gunther W. Nagel. San Francisco [Printed by L. and R. Kennedy] 1968. 154 p. illus., maps., port. 27 cm. Translation of Das Leben Dr. Christian Samuel Gottlieb Ludwig Nagel ... 1829. [DD416.N17A613] 68-59206
1. Nagel, Gottlieb, 1787-1827. I. Herold, Theodor, joint author. II. Nagel, Gunther W., tr. III. Title.

Nagle, Nano, 1718-1784.

MARY Thomas, Sister, P.B.V.M. 255'.977'0924 B
Not words but deeds; the story of Nano Nagle. Illustrated by Carolyn Lee Jagodits. Notre Dame, [Ind.] Dujarie Press [1968] 92 p. illus. 22 cm. A biography of the Irish woman who, despite the strictness of the English Penal Laws, opened schools for poor Catholic children, and founded the order of the Sisters of the Presentation. [PZ7.M3688No] 92 AC 68
1. Nagle, Nano, 1718-1784. I. Jagodits, Carolyn Lee, illus. II. Title.

Nagurski, Bronko, 1908- —Juvenile literature.

COLLINS, David R. 796.33'2'0922 B
Football running backs : three ground gainers / by David R. Collins. Champaign, Ill. : Garrard Pub. Co., c1976. 96 p. : ill. (some col.) ; 24 cm. Biographies of three running backs who helped popularize football: Red Orange, Bronko Nagurski, and Gale Sayers. [GV939.A1C64] 75-23346 ISBN 0-8116-6677-8 : 3.58
1. Grange, Harold Edward, 1903- —Juvenile literature. 2. Nagurski, Bronko, 1908- —Juvenile literature. 3. Sayers, Gale, 1943- —Juvenile literature. 4. Football—Biography—Juvenile literature. I. Title. **BIP**

Nahi'ena'ena, Princess of the Hawaiian Islands, 1815?-1836.

SINCLAIR, 996.9'02'0924 B
Marjorie Jane Putnam.
Nahi'ena'ena, sacred daughter of Hawai'i / Marjorie Sinclair. Honolulu : University Press of Hawaii, c1976. p. cm. Includes index. Bibliography: p. [DU627.17.N34S56] 76-27896 ISBN 0-8248-0367-1 : 9.95
1. Nahi'ena'ena, Princess of the Hawaiian Islands, 1815?-1836. 2. Hawaii—Princes and princesses—Biography. I. Title.

Nahman ben Simhah, of Bratzlav, 1770?-1810?

GREEN, Arthur, 296.6'1'0924 B
1941-
Tormented master : a life of Rabbi Nahman of Bratslav. University : University of Alabama Press, 1979. p. cm. (Judaic studies series ; 9) Bibliography: p. [BM755.N25G73] 78-16674 ISBN 0-8173-6907-4 : 19.50
1. Nahman ben Simhah, of Bratzlav, 1770?-1810? 2. Hasidim—Poland—Biography. 3. Hasidim—Poland—Biography. I. Title. II. Series: Judaic studies ; 9. **BIP**

Naima, Mustafa, 1652-1715.

THOMAS, Lewis 949.6'007'2024
Victor, 1914-1965.
A study of Naima. Edited by Norman Itzkowitz. New York, New York University Press, 1972. xii, 163 p. 24 cm. (Studies in Near Eastern civilization, no. 4) Edited from the author's thesis, Free University of Brussels, 1949. Bibliography: p. 161-163. [DR438.9.N35T48 1972] 71-189129 ISBN 0-8147-8150-0
1. Naima, Mustafa, 1652-1715. I. Title. II. Series: New York University. Studies in Near Eastern civilization, no. 4. **BIP**

Naimbana, d. 1793.

IJAGBEMI, E. Adeleye. 966'.4 B
Naimbana of Sierra Leone / [by] Adeleye Ijagbemi. London : Heinemann, 1976. 48 p. : ill., maps, plans ; 15 x 21 cm. (African historical biographies ; 8) Bibliography: p. [7] [DT516.72.N34I37] 77-363495 ISBN 0-435-94474-6 : £0.50
1. Naimbana, d. 1793. 2. Koya Chiefdom, Sierra Leone—History—Juvenile literature. 3. Sierra Leone—Colonization—Juvenile literature. 4. Slave-trade—Sierra Leone—Juvenile literature. 5. Koya Chiefdom, Sierra Leone—Kings and rulers—Biography—Juvenile literature. 6. Temne (African people)—Kings and rulers—Biography—Juvenile literature. I. Title. II. Series. **BIP**

Naipaul, Vidiadhar Surajprasad.

WALSH, William, 1916- 823 B
V. S. Naipaul. New York, Barnes & Noble Books [1973] 94 p. 20 cm. (Modern writers) Bibliography: p. 93-94. [PR9272.9.N32Z95 1973b] 73-175222 ISBN 0-06-497405-7 7.95
1. Naipaul, Vidiadhar Surajprasad.

Nairne, Carolina Oliphant Nairne, Baroness, 1766-1845—Biography.

NAIRNE, Carolina 784'.092'4 B
Oliphant Nairne, Baroness, 1766-1845.
The life and songs of the Baroness Nairne, with a memoir and poems of Caroline Oliphant the younger / edited by Charles Rogers. New York : AMS Press, 1976. 303 p. : ill. ; 19 cm. Reprint of the 1896 ed. published by J. Grant, Edinburgh. [PR5102.N3 1976] 70-144571 ISBN 0-404-08577-6 : 16.00
1. Nairne, Carolina Oliphant Nairne, Baroness, 1766-1845—Biography. I. Oliphant, Caroline, 1807-1831. II. Rogers, Charles, 1825-1890. III. Title. **BIP**

Nairne family.

WRONG, George McKinnon, 971.4'17
1860-1948.
A Canadian manor and its seigneurs; the story of a hundred years, 1761-1861. Freeport, N.Y., Books for Libraries Press [1972] p. Reprint of the 1908 ed. Bibliography: p. [F1054.5.L15W7 1972] 72-8431 ISBN 0-8369-6996-0
1. Nairne family. 2. Nairne, John, d. 1802. 3. La Malbaie, Que. I. Title.

Naismith, James, 1861-1939.

WEBB, Bernice 796.32'3'0924 B
Larson.
The basketball man, James Naismith. Lawrence, University Press of Kansas [1973] xi, 381 p. illus. 24 cm. Bibliography: p. 365-372. [GV884.N34W42] 72-87821 ISBN 0-7006-0098-1 11.50
1. Naismith, James, 1861-1939. I. Title.

Najder, Zdzislaw,

NAJDER, Zdzislaw, ed. 928.2
Conrad's Polish background; letters to and from Polish friends. Translated by Halina Carroll. London, New York, Oxford University Press, 1964. vii, 313 p. geneal. tables. 22 cm. Contents. -- Tadeusz Bobrowski's letters to Conrad. -- Two letters from Tadeusz Bobrowski to Stefan Buszczynski. -- Tadeusz Bobrowski's "Document." -- Conrad's letters. -- Conrad's Political memorandum (1914) -- The Bobrowski and Korzeniowski families. -- Bibliography (p. 307-308) [PR6005.O4Z532] 64-4657
I. Conrad, Joseph, 1857-1924. II. Bobrowski, Tadeusz, 1829-1894. III. Title.

Nakahama, Manjiro, 1827-1898.

KANEKO, Hisakazu. 923.952
Manjiro, the man who discovered America. Boston, Houghton Mifflin, 1956. 149 p. illus. 22 cm. [DS881.5.N3K3] 56-7239
1. Nakahama, Manjiro, 1827-1898. I. Title.

WARINNER, Emily V. 923.952
Voyager to destiny; the amazing adventures of Manjiro, the man who changed worlds twice. Indianapolis, Bobbs-Merrill [1956] 267 p. illus. 23 cm. [DS881.5.N3W3] 56-11321
1. Nakahama, Manjiro, 1827-1898. I. Title.

Nakanoin Masatada no musume, b. 1258—Biography.

NAKANOIN Masatada no 895.6'3'2 B
musume, b.1258.
Lady Nijo's own story; Towazu-gatari: the candid diary of a thirteenth-century Japanese imperial concubine. Translated by Wilfrid Whitehouse & Eizo Yanagisawa. Rutland, Vt., Tuttle [1974] 395 p. 20 cm. [PL792.N3Z5213 1974] 73-93503 ISBN 0-8048-1117-2 10.00
1. Nakanoin Masatada no musume, b. 1258—Biography. 2. Japan—Court and courtiers. I. Whitehouse, Wilfrid, tr. II. Yanagisawa, Eizo, 1902- tr. III. Title.

Nakhimov, Pavel Stepanovich, 1803-1855.

GOLEC, T R. 335.0947
The Russian John Paul Jones; a biographical sketch submitted to the head of the Department of English, History and Government. Annapolis, 1951. 42, [4] l. map (inserted) 29 cm. At head of title: U. S. Naval Academy. Bibliography: leaves [48]-[49] [DK209.6.N3G6] 51-31637
1. Nakhimov, Pavel Stepanovich, 1803-1855. I. Title.

Namath, Joe Willie, 1943-

ALLEN, Maury, 1932- 796.332'0924
Joe Namath's sportin' life. New York, Paperback Library [1969] 191 p. illus., ports. 18 cm. [GV939.N28A64] 75-6996 0.75
1. Namath, Joe Willie, 1943- I. Title.

BORTSTEIN, Larry. 796.332'0924 B
SuperJoe; the Joe Namath story. New York, Grosset & Dunlap [1969] 246 p. illus., ports. 21 cm. [GV939.N28B6] 72-86671 4.95
1 Namath, Joe Willie, 1943 I. Title.

*BURKE, Jim. 796.332092
Joe Willie. New York, Belmont Tower Books [1975] 207 p., illus. 18 cm. [GV939] 1.50 (pbk.)
1. Namath, Joe Willie, 1943- I. Title.

JACKSON, Robert B. 92 (J)
Joe Namath, superstar, by Robert B. Jackson. New York, H. Z. Walck [1968] 48 p. illus., ports. 21 cm. [GV939.N29J3] 68-23887 3.25
1. Namath, Joe Willie, 1943- I. Title.

LIPMAN, David. 92 (J)
Joe Namath; a football legend. New York, Putnam [1968] 193 p. 21 cm. [GV939.N28L5] 68-15063
1. Namath, Joe Willie, 1943-

SZOLNOKI, Rose 796.33'2'0924 B
Namath, 1912-
Namath, my son Joe / by Rose Namath Szolnoki, with Bill Kushner. Birmingham, Ala. : Oxmoor House, 1975. ix, 131 p., [16] leaves of plates : ill. ; 24 cm. Includes bibliographical references. [GV939.N28S96] 75-12417 7.95
1. Namath, Joe Willie, 1943- 2. Football. I. Kushner, Bill, joint author. II. Title.

Namath, Joe Willie, 1943- —Juvenile literature.

BURCHARD, 796.332'0924 B
Marshall.
Sports hero Joe Namath, by Marshall and Sue Burchard. New York, Putnam [1971] 96 p. illus., ports. 23 cm. An easy-to-read biography of the New York Jet's quarterback whose personal life style won him the nickname Broadway Joe. [GV939.N28B8] 92 79-145454 3.69
1. Namath, Joe Willie, 1943- —Juvenile literature. I. Burchard, S. H., joint author. II. Title.

ELDRED, Patricia 796.33'2'0924 B
Mulrooney.
Football's great quarterback, Joe Namath / by Patricia Mulrooney Eldred. Mankato, MN : Creative Education, [1976] p. cm. [GV939.N28E4] 76-27359 ISBN 0-87191-580-4 : 4.95
1. Namath, Joe Willie, 1943- —Juvenile literature. 2. Quarterback (Football)—Biography—Juvenile literature. I. Title.

ELDRED, Patricia 796.33'2'0924 B
Mulrooney.
Joe Namath / written by Patricia Mulrooney Eldred ; illustrated by John Keely. Mankato, Minn. : Creative Education, [1976] p. cm. A biography of Joe Namath, whose ability to pass has made him an outstanding professional quarterback. [GV939.N28E43] 92 76-16187 ISBN 0-87191-265-1 : 4.95
1. Namath, Joe Willie, 1943- —Juvenile literature. 2. Football—Juvenile literature. I. Keely, John. II. Title.

JACKSON, Robert 796.33'2'0924 B
B.
Joe Namath, superstar, by Robert B. Jackson. Rev. ed. New York, H. Z. Walck [1974] 69 p. illus. 21 cm. A biography of the football player who rose to fame as quarterback for the New York Jets. [GV939.N28J32 1974] 92 74-5475 ISBN 0-8098-2102-8 4.95
1. Namath, Joe Willie, 1943- —Juvenile literature. 2. Football—Juvenile literature.

OLSEN, James T. 796.33'2'0924 B
Joe Namath: the king of football, by James T. Olsen. Illustrated by Montie Salmela. Mankato, Minn., Creative Education; distributed by Childrens Press, Chicago [1974] 28 p. illus. (part col.) 25 cm. (Creative's superstars) "Prepared for the publisher by Educreative Systems, inc." A biography of the football player who rose to fame as quarterback of the New York Jets. [GV939.N28O47] 92 73-10388 ISBN 0-87191-265-1 4.95
1. Namath, Joe Willie, 1943- —Juvenile literature. I. Salmela, Montie, illus. II. Title.

Namboodiripad, E. M. S., 1909-

NAMBOODIRIPAD, E. 335.43'092'4 B
M. S., 1909-
How I became a Communist / E. M. S. Namboodiripad ; translated from Malayalam by P. K. Nair. Trivandrum : Chinta Publishers, 1976. viii, 211 p. ; 22 cm. Translation of Atmakatha. [HX392.N2513] 76-904093 Rs25.00
1. Namboodiripad, E. M. S., 1909- 2. Communists—India—Biography. I. Title.

Names, Personal—United States.

SMITH, Elsdon Coles, 929'.4'0973
1903-
New dictionary of American family names [by] Elsdon C. Smith. [1st ed.] New York, Harper & Row [1972, c1973] xxix, 570 p. 24 cm. Published in 1956 under title: Dictionary of American family names. [CS2481.S55 1973] 72-79693 ISBN 0-06-013933-1 12.95
1. Names, Personal—United States. I. Title.

Namier, Lewis Bernstein, Sir, 1888-1960.

NAMIER, Julia, Lady. 907'.2'024 B
Lewis Namier: a biography by Julia Namier. London, New York, Oxford University Press, 1971. xvii, 347 p., 12 plates; illus., 2 maps, ports. 23 cm.

Bibliography: p. 337-338. [D15.N3N35 1971] 76-852488 ISBN 0-19-211706-8 £4.25
1. Namier, Lewis Bernstein, Sir, 1888-1960.

Namkhan, Burma. Medical Center.

SEAGRAVE, Gordon Stifler, 1897- 926.1
The life of a Burma surgeon. Introd. by Chester Bowles. New York, Ballantine Books [1960] 224p. illus. 19cm. (Ballantine books, F374K) 'A compendium of material from Dr. Gordon S. Seagrave's ... Burma surgeon, and Burma surgeon returns, including excerpts from his combat diary. The epilogue, dealing with the years since World War II, was written ... by Dr. Seagrave in 1960.' [R154.S3545A3] 60-1867
1. Namkhan, Burma. Medical Center. I. Title.

Nampeyo, ca. 1856-1942.

COLLINS, John E. 738.3'092'4 B
Nampeyo, Hopi potter: her artistry and her legacy. Foreword by Barton Wright. Introd. by John E. Collins. Fullerton, Calif., Muckenthaler Cultural Center. [1974] 50 p. illus. (part col.) 27 cm. Exhibition held at the Muckenthaler Cultural Center Apr. 19-May 26, 1974. Bibliography: p. 49-50. [E99.H7C58] 74-78055
1. Nampeyo, ca. 1856-1942. 2. Hopi Indians—Pottery—Exhibitions. I. Nampeyo, ca. 1856-1942. II. Muckenthaler Cultural Center.

Nampeyo, Daisy Hooee, 1910- — Juvenile literature.

FOWLER, Carol. 730'.092'4 B
Daisy Hooee Nampeyo / by Carol Fowler. Minneapolis : Dillon Press, c1977. 74 p. : ill. ; 24 cm. (The Story of an American Indian) A biography of the Hopi Indian artist famous for her pottery, sculpture, and jewelry. [E99.H7F64] 92 76-54809 ISBN 0-87518-141-4 : 4.95
1. Nampeyo, Daisy Hooee, 1910- — Juvenile literature. 2. Hopi Indians—Biography—Juvenile literature. 3. Artists—Arizona—Biography—Juvenile literature. I. Title. BIP

Nance, Berta Hart, 1883-1958—Biography.

TURNER, Elsa McFarland, 1909- 811'.5'2 B
Berta Hart Nance; a brand of innocence, by Elsa McFarland Turner. [Albany? Tex., 1974] 243 p. illus. 25 cm. Includes correspondence and selected works of B. H. Nance. Bibliography: p. 242-243. [PS3527.A255Z9] 74-176081 ISBN 0-89015-059-1
1. Nance, Berta Hart, 1883-1958—Biography. I. Nance, Berta Hart, 1883-1958. Berta Hart Nance. 1974. II. Title.

Nansen, Fridtjof, 1861-1930.

HALL, Anna Gertrude, 1882- v. 12
Nansen, by Anna Gertrude Hall; illustrated by Boris Artzybasheff. New York, The Viking press [1959, c1940] 168 p. illus. 24 cm. Illustrated lining-papers. 65-86782
1. Nansen, Fridtjof, 1861-1930. I. I. Artzybasheff, Boris, 1899- illus. II. Title.

NANSEN, Fridtjof, 1861-1930. 915.66'2'043
Armenia and the Near East / by Fridtjof Nansen. New York : Da Capo Press, 1976. 324 p., [17] leaves of plates : ill. ; 23 cm. (The Middle East in the twentieth century) Translation of Gjennem Armenia. Reprint of the 1928 ed. published by Allen & Unwin, London. Includes bibliographical references. [DS165.N3413 1976] 76-25120 ISBN 0-306-70760-8 : 20.00
1. Nansen, Fridtjof, 1861-1930. 2. Armenia—Description and travel. 3. Armenia—History. 4. Reconstruction (1914-1939)—Armenia. I. Title. BIP

NOEL-BAKER, Francis Edward, 1920- 923.9481
Fridtjof Nansen, Arctic explorer. Illustrated by Robert Doremus. [1st American ed.] New York, Putnam [1958] 126p. illus. 21cm. (Lives to remember) [G635.N3N63] 58-13312
1. Nansen, Fridtjof, 1861-1930. I. Title.

VOGT, Per [Nils Peter Vogt] 1903- 923.9481
Fridtjof Nansen: explorer, scientist, humanitarian, by Per Vogt [others. Dist. New York, Vanous, 1962] 197p. illus. (pt. col.) map. 27cm. 62-6888 11.90
1. Nansen, Fridtjof, 1861-1930. I. Title.

Nansen, Fridtjof, 1861-1930—Juvenile literature.

BEST, Allena (Champlin) 1892- 919.8 B
A world explorer: Fridtjof Nansen, by Erick Berry. Illustrated by William Hutchinson. Champaign, Ill., Garrard Pub. Co. [1969] 96 p. col. illus., col. map (on lining papers) 24 cm. (World explorer books) A biography of a Norwegian explorer, author, scientist, and statesman who made many important expeditions to the North Pole. [G635.N3B4] 92 69-19017 2.59
1. Nansen, Fridtjof, 1861-1930—Juvenile literature. I. Hutchinson, William M., illus. II. Title.

Napear, Jane Emerson, 1962-

NAPEAR, Peggy. 362.3'092'4 B
Brain child; a mother's diary. [1st ed.] New York, Harper & Row [1973] p. Bibliography: p. [RJ506.M4N36 1973] 72-9141 ISBN 0-06-013156-X 5.95
1. Napear, Jane Emerson, 1962- 2. Brain-damaged children—Personal narratives. I. Title. BIP

Napoleon I, Emperor of the French, 1769-1821.

AUBRY, Octave, 1881-1946. 923.144
Napoleon. [Translated by Margaret Crosland and Sinclair Road] New York, Crown Publishers [1964] 384 p. illus., facisms., maps, ports. (part col.) [DC203.A8613] 64-23814
1. Napoleon I, Emperor of the French, 1769-1821. I. Title.

BAINVILLE, Jacques, 1879-1936. 944.05'0924 B
Napoleon. Translated from the French by Hamish Miles. With an introd. by H. A. L. Fisher. Port Washington, N.Y., Kennikat Press [1970] 475 p. illus., port. 23 cm. Reprint of the 1932 ed. "Survey of Napoleonic bibliography": p. 459-465. [DC203.B176 1970] 74-112794
1. Napoleon I, Emperor of the French, 1769-1821.

BALLARD, Colin Robert, 1868-1941. 944.05'092'4 B
Napoleon; an outline. Freeport, N.Y., Books for Libraries Press [1971] 325 p. illus. 23 cm. Reprint of the 1924 ed. Bibliography: p. 323-325. [DC203.B18 1971] 76-179503 ISBN 0-8369-6632-5
1. Napoleon I, Emperor of the French, 1769-1821. 2. France—History—1789-1815. BIP

BARNETT, Correlli. 944.05'092'4 B
Bonaparte / Correlli Barnett. New York : Hill and Wang, 1978. 224 p., [8] leaves of plates : ill. ; 26 cm. Includes index. Bibliography: p. 219. [DC203.B25 1978] 77-21833 ISBN 0-8090-3049-7 : 19.95
1. Napoleon I, Emperor of the French, 1769-1821. 2. France—Kings and rulers—Biography. I. Title. BIP

BEYLE, Marie Henri, 1783-1842. 944.05'092'4 B
A life of Napoleon / by Stendhal [i.e. M. H. Beyle]. New York : H. Fertig, 1977. 184 p. ; 22 cm. Translation of Vie de Napoleon. Reprint of the 1956 ed. published by Rodale Press, London. [DC203.B5713 1977] 76-13154 12.00
1. Napoleon I, Emperor of the French, 1769-1821. 2. France—Kings and rulers—Biography. I. Title. BIP

BUTTERFIELD, Herbert, 1900- v. 12
Napoleon. [1st Collier Books ed.[New York, N.Y., Collier Books [1962] 125 p. 18 cm. Bibliography: p. 121-125. 63-26320
1. Napoleon I, Emperior of the French, 1769-1821. I. Title.

CASTELOT, Andre. 944.05'0924 B
Napoleon. Translated from the French by Guy Daniels. [1st ed.] New York, Harper & Row [1971] vii, 627 p. illus. 25 cm. [DC203.C2713 1971] 70-83587 ISBN 0-06-010678-6 12.50
1. Napoleon I, Emperor of the French, 1769-1821. I. Title.

CHANDLER, David G 944.05'092'4 B
Napoleon [by] David Chandler. New York, Saturday Review Press [1974, c1973] 224 p. illus. 26 cm. (The great commanders, vol. II.) Bibliography: p. 217. [DC203.C45] 73-75721 ISBN 0-8415-0254-4 12.50
1. Napoleon I, Emperor of the French, 1769-1821. I. Title.

CRONIN, Vincent. 944.05'092'4 B
Napoleon Bonaparte; an intimate biography. New York, Morrow, 1972 [c1971] 480 p. illus. 25 cm. Includes bibliographical references. [DC203.C9 1972] 72-166356 12.50
1. Napoleon I, Emperor of the French, 1769-1821. I. Title.

CRONIN, Vincent. 944.05'092'4 [B]
Napoleon Bonaparte; an intimate biography. [New York] [Dell] [1973, c.1971] 544 p. 18 cm. Bibliographical references. [DC203.C9 1972] pap., 1.95
1. Napoleon I, Emperor of the French, 1769-1821. I. Title.

DURANT, William James, 1885- 909 S
The age of Napoleon : a history of European civilization from 1789 to 1815 / by Will and Ariel Durant. New York : Simon and Schuster, 1975. xxi, 872 p., [32] leaves of plates : ill. ; 25 cm. (His The story of civilization ; pt. 11) Includes index. Bibliography: p. 781-789. [CB53.D85 pt. 11] [CB411] 940.2'7 75-6888 14.95
1. Napoleon I, Emperor of the French, 1769-1821. 2. Europe—Civilization. 3. Europe—History—1789-1815. I. Durant, Ariel, joint author. II. Title.

GUERARD, Albert Leon, 1880-1959. 923.144
Napoleon I; a great life in brief. [1st ed.] New York, Knopf, 1956. 199 p. 19 cm. (Great lives in brief: a new series of biographies) [DC203.G867] 56-5803
1. Napoleon I, Emperor of the French, 1769-1821.

HEADLEY, Joel Tyler, 1813-1897. 944'.05'0924
Napoleon and his marshals. Freeport, N.Y., Books for Libraries Press [1973] p. (Essay index reprint series) Reprint of the 1847 ed. [DC198.A1H4 1973] 72-14140 ISBN 0-518-10011-1
1. Napoleon I, Emperor of the French, 1769-1821. 2. Marshals—France. I. Title.

HORTENSE, consort of Louis, King of Holland, 1783-1837. 949.2'05'0924 B
The memoirs of Queen Hortense. Published by arrangement with Prince Napoleon. Edited by Jean Hanoteau. Translated by Arthur K. Griggs. Freeport, N.Y., Books for Libraries Press [1973] p. Translation of Memoires de la reine Hortense. Reprint of the 1927 ed. published by Cosmopolitan Book Corp., New York. [DC216.4.A35 1973] 73-5999 ISBN 0-518-19050-1
1. Hortense, consort of Louis, King of Holland, 1783-1837. 2. Napoleon I, Emperor of the French, 1769-1821. 3. Bonaparte family. 4. France—History—1789-1815.

JONES, R. Ben. 944.05'092'4 B
Napoleon, man and myth / R. Ben Jones. New York : Holmes & Meier, 1978. p. cm. Includes bibliographies and index. [DC203.J68 1978] 78-15801 ISBN 0-8419-0440--5 : 12.50 ISBN 0-8419-0441-3 pbk. : 7.50
1. Napoleon I, Emperor of the French, 1769-1821. 2. France—Politics and government—1789-1815. 3. France—Kings and rulers—Biography. I. Title.

KIRCHEISEN, Friedrich Max, 1877-1933. 944.05'092'4 B
Napoleon. Translated by Henry St. Lawrence. Freeport, N.Y., Books for Libraries Press [1972] p. Translation of Napoleon I: ein Lebensbild. Reprint of the 1932 ed. [DC203.K582 1972] 72-8400 ISBN 0-8369-6981-2
1. Napoleon I, Emperor of the French, 1769-1821.

KOMROFF, Manuel, 1890- 944.05'0924 B
Napoleon. New York, J. Messner [1954] 189 p. 22 cm. A biography of the Frenchman whose empire dominated all of Europe in 1812, until his retreat from Moscow began his downfall. [DC203.K65 1954] 92 AC 68
1. Napoleon I, Emperor of the French, 1769-1821. I. Title.

LANFREY, Pierre, 1828-1877. 944.05'092'4 B
The history of Napoleon the First. London, New York, Macmillan, 1894. 2d ed. [New York, AMS Press, 1973] 4 v. 18 cm. Contents.—v. 1. 1769-1800.—v. 2. 1800-1804.—v. 3. 1805-1808.—v. 4. 1808-1811. Includes bibliographical references. [DC203.L27 1973] 77-171654 ISBN 0-404-07340-9 19.00 ea.
1. Napoleon I, Emperor of the French, 1769-1821. 2. France—History—1789-1815. I. Title.
Set of 2 vols. selling for $75.00. BIP

LARNED, Josephus Nelson, 1836-1913. 153.9'8'0922 B
A study of greatness in men. Freeport, N.Y., Books for Libraries Press [1972] 303 p. 23 cm. (Essay index reprint series) Reprint of the 1911 ed. Contents.Contents.—What goes into the making of a great man?—Napoleon: a prodigy, without greatness.—Cromwell: imperfect in greatness.—Washington: impressive in greatness.—Lincoln: simplest in greatness. [BF412.L4 1972] 73-156677 ISBN 0-8369-2557-2
1. Napoleon I, Emperor of the French, 1769-1821. 2. Cromwell, Oliver, 1599-1658. 3. Washington, George, Pres. U.S., 1732-1799. 4. Lincoln, Abraham, Pres. U.S., 1809-1865—Addresses, essays, lectures. 5. Genius. I. Title. BIP

MARKHAM, Felix Maurice Hippisley. 923.144
Napoleon. [New York] New American Library [1964, c1963] xiii, 292 p. illus., ports., maps, facsims., geneal. table. 22 cm. Bibliography: p. [259]-272. [DC203.M26] 64-13811
1. Napoleon I, Emperor of the French, 1769-1821.

MOSSIKER, Frances. 923.144
Napoleon and Josephine; the biography of a marriage. New York, Simon and Schuster, 1964. 447 p. illus., ports. 22 cm. Bibliography: p. 425-429. [DC216.1.M65] 64-12483
1. Napoleon I, Emperor of the French, 1769-1821. 2. Josephine, consort of Napoleon I, 1763-1814. I. Title.

NAPOLEON I, Emperor of the French, 1769-1821. 944.05'092'4 B
Correspondance de Napoleon Ier : publiee par l'ordre de l'empereur Napoleon III. New York : AMS Press, [1974] p. cm. Vols. 29-32 have also special title: Ouvres de Napoleon Ier a Sainte-Helene. Reprint of the 1858-70 ed. published by H. Plon, Paris. [DC213.N2 1974] 77-173013 ISBN 0-404-07400-6
1. Napoleon I, Emperor of the French, 1769-1821.

NAPOLEON I, Emperor of the French, 1769-1821. 923.144

Letters and documents. Selected and translated by John Eldred Howard. New York, Oxford University Press, 1961- v. illus., ports., maps, facsims., geneal. table. 23 cm. Contents.Contents.—v. 1. The rise to power. Includes bibliographical references. [DC213.H6] 61-4572
I. Howard, John Eldred, ed. and tr.

NAPOLEON I, Emperor of the French, 1769-1821. 923.144
Law, love, and religion of Napoleon Bonaparte in his own words. Edited by Hiram E. Casey. New York, Carlton Press, 1961. 93p. 21cm. (A Reflection book) [DC214.N2113] 62-312
I. Casey, Hiram E., ed. II. Title.

NAPOLEON I, Emperor of the French, 1769-1821. 923.144
Letters; selected, translated, and edited by J. M. Thompson. London, Dent; New York, Dutton [1954] 312p. 19cm. (Everyman's library, no. 995) Bibliography: p. 11-12. [AC1.E8 no.995] 54-2838
I. Thomps James Matthew, 1878- ed. and tr. II. Title.

NAPOLEON I, Emperor of the French, 1769-1821 923.144
Napoleon Bonaparte: citizen and soldier, his words on war and peace and his aphorisms. Comp., ed. by Hiram E. Casey. New York, Exposition [c.1963] 93p. illus. 22cm. 63-4046 3.00
I. Casey, Hiram E., ed. II. Title.

SAVANT, Jean, ed. v. 12
Napoleon in his time. Translated from the French by Katherine John. New York, Nelson [1958] 440p. ports. 22cm. Translation of Napoleon: Pacnle par los temolns de as vie. Bibliography: p.421-424. A58
1. Napoleon I. Emperor of the French, 1769-1821. I. Title.

SLOANE, William Milligan, 1850-1928. 944.0460924
The life of Napoleon Bonaparte. Rev. and enl., with ports. New York, AMS Press [1969] 4 v. illus. 23 cm. Reprint of the 1910 ed. Bibliography: v. 4, p. 307-353. [DC203.S65 1969] 76-107767
1. Napoleon I, Emperor of the French, 1769-1821. 2. Napoleon I, Emperor of the French, 1769-1821—Bibliography. 3. France—History—Consulate and Empire, 1799-1815—Bibliography. 4. France—History—Consulate and Empire, 1799-1815. I. Title. BIP

THOMPSON, James Matthew, 1878- 923.144
Napoleon Bonaparte. New York, Oxford University Press, 1952. ix, 463 p. ports., maps (on lining papers) facsims. 25 cm. English ed. (Oxford, B. Blackwell) has title: Napoleon Bonaparte, his rise and fall. Bibliographical references included in "Notes" (p. 443-451) [DC203.T53 1952a] 52-9576
1. Napoleon I, Emperor of the French, 1769-1821.

VOX, Maximilien 923.144
Napoleon. Tr. [from French] by Maurice Thornton. New York, Grove Press [1961] 192p. illus. (Evergreen profile book, 18) Bibl. 60-7388 1.35 pap.,
1. Napoleon I. Emperor of the French, I. Title.

Napoleon I, Emperor of the French, 1769-1821—Campaigns of 1813-1814.

LAWFORD, James Philip. 944.05'092'4
Napoleon : the last campaigns, 1813-15 / James Lawford. New York : Crown Publishers, 1977. 160 p. : ill. ; 32 cm. Pt. I co-written by P. Young. Includes index. [DC236.L35 1977] 77-6392 ISBN 0-517-52634-4 : 12.95
1. Napoleon I, Emperor of the French, 1769-1821—Campaigns of 1813-1814. 2. Napoleon I, Emperor of the French, 1769-1821—Elba and the Hundred Days, 1814-1815. I. Young, Peter, joint author. BIP

Napoleon I, Emperor of the French, 1769-1821—Captivity, 1815-1821.

BALMAIN, Aleksandr Antonovich, Graf, d.1848. 944.05'0924 B
Napoleon in captivity; the reports of Count Balmain, Russian commissioner on the island of St. Helena, 1816-1820. Translated and edited with introd. and notes by Julian Park. Freeport, N.Y., Books for Libraries Press [1971] xxv, 243 p. illus., facsims., ports. 23 cm. Reprint of the 1927 ed. [DC211.B3 1971] 72-160955 ISBN 0-8369-5822-5
1. Napoleon I, Emperor of the French, 1769-1821—Captivity, 1815-1821. I. Title. BIP

O'MEARA, Barry Edward, 1786-1836. 944.05'0924
Napoleon in exile; or, A voice from St. Helena. The opinions and reflections of Napoleon on the most important events in his life and government, in his own words, by Barry E. O'Meara. New York, AMS Press [1969] 2 v. illus., plan, port. 23 cm. Reprint of the 1853 ed. [DC211.O565 1969] 74-106520
1. Napoleon I, Emperor of the French, 1769-1821—Captivity, 1815-1821. I. Napoleon I, Emperor of the French, 1769-1821. II. Title.

Napoleon I, Emperor of the French, 1769-1821—Elba and the Hundred days, 1814-1815.

DUHAMEL, Jean. 944.05'0924 B
The fifty days; Napoleon in England. Translated by R. A. Hall. Coral Gables, Fla., University of Miami Press [1970] 141 p. illus., map, ports. 23 cm. Translation of Les cinquante jours de Waterloo a Plymouth. Bibliography: p. 137-138. [DC239.D813 1970] 71-102696
1. Napoleon I, Emperor of the French, 1769-1821—Elba and the Hundred days, 1814-1815. I. Title. BIP

Napoleon I, Emperor of the French, 1769-1821—Elba and the Hundred Days, 1814-1815.—Juvenile literature.

PRINGLE, Patrick. 944.05'0924
Napoleon's hundred days. Illustrated by Sheila Bewley. New York, F. Warne [1969, c1968] 95 p. illus. 21 cm. Recounts Napoleon's last bid for power after his escape from Elba until his defeat at Waterloo slightly more than one hundred days later. [DC239.P7 1969] 69-17699 2.95
1. Napoleon I, Emperor of the French, 1769-1821—Elba and the Hundred Days, 1814-1815.—Juvenile literature. I. Bewley, Sheila, illus. II. Title.

Napoleon I, Emperor of the French, 1769-1821—Invasion of Russia, 1812.

CAULAINCOURT, Armand Augustin Louis, marquis de, duc de Vicence, 1773-1827. 940.2'7'0924 B
With Napoleon in Russia : the memoirs of General de Caulaincourt, Duke of Vicenza : from the original memoirs / as edited by Jean Hanoteau ; abridged, edited, and with an introd. by George Libaire. Westport, Conn. : Greenwood Press, 1976, c1935. p. cm. Translation of Memoires du general de Caulaincourt. Reprint of the ed. published by W. Morrow, New York. Includes index. Bibliography: p. [DC198.C35A33 1976] 75-40914 ISBN 0-8371-8689-7 lib.bdg. : 25.00
1. Caulaincourt, Armand Augustin Louis, marquis de, duc de Vicence, 1773-1827. 2. Napoleon I, Emperor of the French, 1769-1821—Invasion of Russia, 1812. 3. France. Armee—Biography. 4. France—History—Consulate and Empire, 1799-1815. 5. Generals—France—Biography. I. Libaire, George. II. Title.

Napoleon I, Emperor of the French, 1769-1821—Juvenile literature.

CAMMIADE, Audrey 92
Napoleon. Illus. by Horace Vernet. Maps by R. R. Sellman. New York, Roy [1963] 112p. illus. 22cm. Bibl. 61-12338 3.75 bds.,
1. Napoleon I—Juveniel literature. I. Title.

CAMMIADE, Audrey 92
Napoleon. Illus. by Horace Vernet. Maps by R. R. Sellman. New York, Roy [1963] 112p. illus. 22cm. Bibl. 61-12338 3.75 bds.,
1. Napoleon I—Juveniel literature. I. Title.

COOPER, Leonard 92
The young Napoleon. Illus. by Anne Linton. New York, Roy [1963] 134p. illus. 21cm. 62-18436 3.00 bds.,
1. Napoleon I, Emperor of the French, 1769-1821—Juvenile literature. I. Title.

CORLEY, Thomas Anthony Buchanan, 1923- 92
The true story of Napoleon, Emperor of France. Chicago, Childrens [c.1958, 1964] 143p. col. illus., fold. col. map. 23cm. First pub. in London in 1959 under title: The true book about Napoleon. 64-19881
1. Napoleon I—Juvenile literature. I. Title.

CORLEY, Thomas Anthony Buchanan, 1923- 92
The true story of Napoleon, Emperor of France. Chicago, Childrens [c.1958, 1964] 143p. col. illus., fold. col. map. 23cm. First pub. in London in 1959 under title: The true book about Napoleon. 64-19881
1. Napoleon I—Juvenile literature. I. Title.

DUPUY, Trevor Nevitt, 1916- 940.2'7'0924
The military life of Napoleon, Emperor of the French. New York, F. Watts [1969] xv, 221 p. illus., maps, plans, ports. 23 cm. Reviews the military career of Napoleon, who learned his strategies from the defeats and victories of history's great military leaders. [DC203.D94] 73-87927 3.95
1. Napoleon I, Emperor of the French, 1769-1821—Juvenile literature. I. Title. BIP

Napoleon. I—Portraits, caricatures, etc.

MAUROIS, Andre, 1885- 923.144
Napoleon, a pictorial biography [Tr. from French by D. J. S. Thomson] New York, Viking [1961, c.1963] 160p. illus., ports., facsims. 24cm. (Studio bk.) 63-19194
1. Napoleon. I—Portraits, caricatures, etc. I. Title.

Napoleon I, Emperor of the French, 1769-1821—Relations with women.

DELDERFIELD, Ronald Frederick, 1912-1972. 944.05'092'4 B
Napoleon in love / R. F. Delderfield. New York : Simon and Schuster, [1979] c1959. 285 p., [8] leaves of plates : ill. ; 23 cm. Bibliography: p. 283-285. [DC204.D4 1979] 79-159 ISBN 0-671-24041-2 : 9.95
1. Napoleon I, Emperor of the French, 1769-1821—Relations with women. 2. France—Kings and rulers—Biography. I. Title.

DELDERFIELD, Ronald Frederick, 1912-1972. 923.144
Napoleon in love. [1st American ed.] Boston, Little, Brown [1960, c1959] 304 p. illus. 22 cm. Includes bibliography. [DC204.D4 1960] 60-9351
1. Napoleon I, Emperor of the French, 1769-1821—Relations with Women. I. Title. BIP

Napoleon III, Emperor of the French, 1808-1873

GOOCH, Brison Dowling, 1925- 923.144
Napoleon III, man of destiny; enlightened statesman or proto-fascist? New York, Holt, Rinehart and Winston [1963] 122 p. 24 cm. (European problem studies) Includes bibliography. [DC280.G66] 63-13324
1. Napoleon III, Emperor of the French, 1808-1873 I. Title. BIP

NAPOLEON III, Emperor of the French, 1808-1873. 944.07'092'4
Oeuvres de Napol III. New York : AMS Press, [1976] p. cm. Reprint of the 1869 ed. published by Plon, Paris. [DC275.2.N3 1976] 74-173015 ISBN 0-404-07380-8
1. France—History—1848-1870—Sources. 2. France—Politics and government—1848-1870—Sources. 3. Military history.

Napoleon, Joseph Charles Paul Bonaparte, Prince, 1822-1891.

FERRI-PISANI, Camille 917.3'04'7 B
Prince Napoleon in America, 1861; letters from his aide-de-camp. Translated with a pref. by Georges J. Joyaux. Foreword by Bruce Catton. Illustrated by Gil Walker. Port Washington, N.Y., Kennikat Press [1973, c1959] 317 p. illus. 22 cm. Letters written to Colonel de Franconiere. Translation of Lettres sur les Etats-Unis d'Amerique. Includes bibliographical references. [E167.F383 1973] 72-85279 ISBN 0-8046-1695-7 12.50
1. Napoleon, Joseph Charles Paul Bonaparte, Prince, 1822-1891. 2. United States—Description and travel—1848-1865. I. Franconiere, Paul Et. Ch. de Lamorte Charens. II. Title. BIP

Narain, Jai Prakash.

LAL, Lakshmi Narain, 1925- 954.03'5'0924 B
Jayaprakash : rebel extraordinary / Lakshmi Narain Lal. New Delhi : Indian Book Company, 1975. 179 p. ; 22 cm. [DS481.N3L35] 75-902427 ISBN 0-89253-006-5 9.95
1. Narain, Jai Prakash.
Distributed in the U.S. by Interculture

NARAIN, Jai Prakash. 365'.45'0924
Prison diary, 1975 / Jayaprakash Narayan ; edited with an introd. by A. B. Shah. [2d ed.]. Seattle : University of Washington Press, 1978, c1977. p. cm. Includes index. [HV9793.N37 1978] 78-5471 ISBN 0-295-95613-5 : 8.95
1. Narain, Jai Prakash. 2. Political prisoners—India—Biography. 3. India—Politics and government—1947- I. Shah, Amritlal B., 1920-

Naranjo, Michael—Juvenile literature.

NELSON, Mary Carroll. 730'.92'4 B
Michael Naranjo / by Mary Carroll Nelson. Minneapolis : Dillon Press, [1975] 66 p. : ill. ; 23 cm. A biography of the Pueblo Indian sculptor who was blinded in Vietnam in 1968. [E99.P9N276] 92 75-14366 ISBN 0-87518-111-2 : 4.95
1. Naranjo, Michael—Juvenile literature. 2. Naranjo, Michael. 3. Pueblo Indians—Juvenile literature. I. Title. **BIP**

Narayan, R. K., 1906- —Biography.

NARAYAN, R. K., 1906- 823 B
My days [by] R. K. Narayan. New York, Viking Press [1974] 186 p. 22 cm. [PR9499.3.N3Z52 1974] 73-20908 ISBN 0-670-49818-1 8.95
1. Narayan, R. K., 1906- —Biography. I. Title.

Narayan, R. K.1906-Criticism and interpretation.

HOLMSTROM, Lakshmi. 823
The novels of R. K. Narayan. [Calcutta,] Writers Workshop [1975c1973] 130.[5]p. 22 cm. (A Writers Workshop greybird book) Bibliography:p. [131]-135. [PR9499.3N3Z7] 73-904285 ISBN 0-88253-584-6
1. Narayan, R. K.1906-Criticism and interpretation. I. Title.
Distributed by Interculture Associates for 9.50. Pbk. 6.00 ISBN0-88253-538-8. **BIP**

Narcotic addicts—Rehabilitation.

CASRIEL, Daniel. 362.2'93
Daytop; three addicts and their cure, by Daniel Casriel and Grover Amen. New York, Hill and Wang [1971] xxv, 150 p. 21 cm. [HV5831.N7C35] 73-163566 ISBN 0-8090-3777-7 5.95
1. Narcotic addicts—Rehabilitation. 2. Narcotic addicts—Personal narratives. I. Amen, Grover, joint author. II. Title.

Narcotic habit.

ROSS, Barney. 927.9683
No man stands alone; the true story of Barney Ross, by Barney Ross and Martin Abramson. Foreword by Eddie Cantor. [1st ed.] Philadelphia, Lippincott [1957] 256p. illus. 22cm. 'A short version of Barney Ross's life story apeared in Coronet magazine under the title, 'God was in my corner.' [GV1132.R65A3] 57-13211
1. Narcotic habit. I. Abramson, Martin, 1915- joint author. II. Title.

Narcotics, control of.

LARKIN, R. T. 364.1570924
Pusher / R. T. Larkin New York : Belmont Tower ,1976 189 p. ; 18 cm. [HV5805] pbk. : 1.50
1. Narcotics, control of. I. Title.

Narcotics, Control of—Personal narratives.

BERDIN, Richard. 363.4'5'0924 B
Code name Richard. Translated and edited by Jeannette and Richard Seaver. [1st ed.] New York, Dutton, 1974. 309 p. 24 cm. "A Merlin House book." [HV5805.B47A3313 1974] 74-8268 ISBN 0-525-08240-9 8.95
1. Narcotics, Control of—Personal narratives. I. Title.

Narino, Antonio, 1765-1823.

BLOSSOM, Thomas, 1912- 986.1'03'0924 B
Narino, hero of Colombian independence. Tucson, University of Arizona Press [1967] xxix, 212 p. illus., map, port. 24 cm. Bibliography: p. 175-199. [F2274.N2436] 66-20661
1. Narino, Antonio, 1765-1823. I. Title.

Narodnaia volia (Political party)

FOOTMAN, David, 1895- 947.08'092'4 B
The Alexander conspiracy; a life of A. I. Zhelyabov. LaSalle, Ill., Open Court [1974, c1968] xvi, 354 p. illus. 21 cm. Previous editions published in London under title: Red prelude. "A library press book." Bibliography: p. [343]-348. [DK219.6.Z5F6 1974] 74-57 ISBN 0-912050-47-0 8.95
1. Zheliabov, Andrei Ivanovich, 1851-1881. 2. Narodnaia volia (Political party) 3. Alexander II, Emperor of Russia, 1818-1881. I. Title.

FOOTMAN, David, 1895- 322.4'2'0924 B
Red prelude : the life of the Russian terrorist Zhelyabov / by David Footman. Westport, Conn. : Hyperion Press, [1979] p. cm. Reprint of the 1945 ed. published by Yale University Press, New Haven. Includes index. Bibliography: p. [DK219.6.Z5F6 1979] 78-14119 22.00
1. Zheliabov, Andrei Ivanovich, 1851-1881. 2. Narodnaia volia (Political party) 3. Alexander II, Emperor of Russia, 1818-1881. 4. Revolutionist—Russia—Biography. 5. Terrorism—Russia. I. Title. **BIP**

Nasaw, Jonathan Lewis, 1947-

NASAW, Jonathan Lewis, 1947- 362.4'3'0924 B
Easy walking / Jonathan Lewis Nasaw. 1st ed. Philadelphia : Lippincott, [1975] 224 p. ; 22 cm. Autobiographical. [RD796.N37A33] 74-23446 ISBN 0-397-01078-8 : 7.50
1. Nasaw, Jonathan Lewis, 1947- 2. Paralysis—Personal narratives. 3. Paraplegics—Rehabilitation. I. Title.

Nascimento, Edson Arantes do, 1940-

BODO, Peter. 796.33'4'0924 B
Pele's new world / by Peter Bodo and David Hirshey, with Pele. 1st ed. New York : Norton, c1977. 223 p., [8] leaves of plates : ill. ; 22 cm. [GV942.7.N3B6 1977] 76-46961 ISBN 0-393-08758-1 : 8.95
1. Nascimento, Edson Arantes do, 1940- 2. Soccer players—Biography. I. Hirshey, David, joint author. II. Nascimento, Edson Arantes do, 1940- joint author. III. Title. **BIP**

KOWET, Don. 796.33'4'0924 B
Pele / Don Kowet. 1st ed. New York : Atheneum, 1976. 129 p. : ill. ; 22 cm. [GV942.7.N3K68] 75-38344 ISBN 0-689-10713-7 : 6.95
1. Nascimento, Edson Arantes do, 1940- 2. Soccer. I. Title. **BIP**

MARCUS, Joe, 1933- 796.33'4'0924 B
The world of Pele / by Joe Marcus. New York : Mason/Charter, 1976. x, 200 p., [7] leaves of plates : ill. ; 24 cm. [GV942.7.N3M36] 76-14214 ISBN 0-88405-366-0 : 8.95
1. Nascimento, Edson Arantes do, 1940- I. Title.

NASCIMENTO, Edson Arantes do, 1940- 796.33'4'0924 B
My life and the beautiful game : the autobiography of Pele / by Pele [i.e. E. Arantes do Nascimento] with Robert L. Fish. 1st ed. Garden City, N.Y. : Doubleday, 1977. x, 371 p., [24] leaves of plates : ill. ; 22 cm. [GV942.7.N3A35] 76-42382 ISBN 0-385-12185-7 : 10.00
1. Nascimento, Edson Arantes do, 1940- 2. Soccer players—Biography. I. Fish, Robert L., joint author. II. Title.

NASCIMENTO, Edson, Arantes do, 1940- 796.33'4'0924 [B]
My life and the beautiful game : the autobiography of Pele. / by Pele [i.e. E.Arantes do Nascimento] with Robert L. Fish 1st ed. new York : Warner Books, 1978,c1977. 398p., [24] leaves of plates : ill. ; 18 cm. [GV942.7N3A35] ISBN 0-446-81639-6 pbk. : 2.50
1. Nascimento, Edson Arantes do, 1940- 2. Soccer players — Biography. I. Fish, Robert L. joint author. II. Title.
L.C. card no. for 1977 Doubleday ed.: 76-42382

THEBAUD, Francois. 796.33'4'0924 B
Pele / Francois Thebaud ; translated from the French by Leo Weinstein. 1st ed. New York : Harper & Row, c1976. viii, 166 p., [8] leaves of plates : ill. ; 24 cm. [GV942.7.N3T4713 1976] 75-30348 ISBN 0-06-014254-5 : 8.95
1. Nascimento, Edson Arantes do, 1940- 2. Soccer. I. Title. **BIP**

Nascimento, Edson Arantes do, 1940- —Juvenile literature.

BURCHARD, S. H. 796.33'4'0924 B
Pele / S. H. Burchard ; illustrated with photos. and with drawings by Paul Frame. 1st ed. New York : Harcourt Brace Jovanovich, c1976. 64 p. : ill. ; 22 cm. (Sports star) A biography of the Brazilian who has earned the reputation as the greatest soccer player in the world. [GV942.7.N3B87] 92 75-33707 ISBN 0-15-278001-7 : 4.95 pbk. : 1.95
1. Nascimento, Edson Arantes do, 1940- —Juvenile literature. 2. Soccer—Juvenile literature. I. Frame, Paul, 1913- II. Title.

FAGO, John Norwood. 796'.0922 B
Vince Lombardi / [written by John Norwood Fago ; illustrated by Tony Caravana]. Pele / [written by John Norwood Fago ; illustrated by Nardo Cruz]. West Haven, Conn. : Pendulum Press, c1979. 63 p. : chiefly ill. ; 21 cm. (Pendulum illustrated biography series : Sports) Brief biographies in cartoon format highlight the lives of a well-known football coach and a famous soccer player. [GV697.A1F29] 920 79-83616 ISBN 0-88301-370-3 : 4.50 ISBN 0-88301-358-4 pbk. : 1.45
1. Nascimento, Edson Arantes do, 1940- —Juvenile literature. 2. Lombardi, Vince—Juvenile literature. 3. Football—Managers—Biography—Juvenile literature. 4. Soccer players—Brazil—Biography—Juvenile literature. I. Caravana, Tony. II. Cruz, Nardo. III. Fago, John Norwood. Pele. IV. Title. V. Series.

GAULT, Frank. 796.33'4'0924 B
Pele, the king of soccer / by Clare and Frank Gault. New York : Walker, 1975. 62 p. : ill. ; 21 cm. A biography of the Brazilian soccer star who was tempted out of retirement by an invitation to come to the United States to interest its people in the sport for which he is world-famous. [GV942.7.N3G38 1975] 92 75-27119 ISBN 0-8027-6240-9 : 5.95
1. Nascimento, Edson Arantes do, 1940- —Juvenile literature. 2. Soccer—Juvenile literature. I. Gault, Clare, joint author. II. Title. **BIP**

GUTMAN, Bill. 796.33'4'0924 B
Pele / by Bill Gutman. New York : Grosset & Dunlap, c1976. 93 p. : ill. ; 22 cm. (A Thistle book) A biography of the Brazilian who has become known as the greatest soccer player in the world. Includes notes on the origin and rules of the game. [GV942.7.N3G87] 92 76-17436 ISBN 0-448-26259-2
1. Nascimento, Edson Arantes do, 1940- —Juvenile literature. 2. Soccer players—Brazil—Biography—Juvenile literature. I. Title.

HASKINS, James, 1941- 796.33'4'0924 B
Pele : a biography / James S. Haskins. 1st ed. Garden City, N.Y. : Doubleday, 1976. 185 p. ; [8] leaves of plates : ill. ; 22 cm. Bibliography: p. 183-184. Biography of Pele, Brazilian soccer player who has become an international star. Also includes introductory material about the game of soccer. [GV942.7.N3H37] 92 75-39123 ISBN 0-385-11565-2 : 5.95
1. Nascimento, Edson Arantes do, 1940- —Juvenile literature. 2. Soccer—Juvenile literature. I. Title. **BIP**

SABIN, Louis. 796.33'4'0924 B
Pele, soccer superstar / by Louis Sabin. New York : Putnam, c1976. p. cm. (Putnam sports shelf) Includes index. A biography of Pele, the Brazilian soccer star who has achieved international notoriety because of his athletic achievements. [GV942.7.N3S2 1976] 92 76-26504 ISBN 0-399-61034-0 lib. bdg. : 5.29
1. Nascimento, Edson Arantes do, 1940- —Juvenile literature. 2. Soccer players—Brazil—Biography—Juvenile literature. I. Title.

TAYLOR, Paula. 796.33'4'0924 B
Pele / written by Paula Taylor ; illustrated by John Keely. Mankato, Minn. : Creative Education, [1976] p. cm. A biography of the world's soccer king who came to the United States to help make soccer a major sport here. [GV942.7.N3T38] 92 76-5818 ISBN 0-87191-513-8
1. Nascimento, Edson Arantes do, 1940- —Juvenile literature. 2. Soccer—Juvenile literature. I. Keely, John.

Nash, John Henry, 1871-1947.

HARLAN, Robert D. 686.2'0924 B
John Henry Nash: the biography of a career, by Robert D. Harlan. Berkeley, University of California Press, 1970. xi, 167 p. illus., ports. 25 cm. (University of California publications. Librarianship, 7) Bibliography: p. 151-159. [Z674.C3 vol. 7] 70-628359 ISBN 0-520-01712-9
1. Nash, John Henry, 1871-1947. I. Title. II. Series: California. University. University of California publications in librarianship, 7

Nash, John, 1752-1835.

DAVIS, Terence, 1924- 720'.924
John Nash, the Prince Regent's architect. [1st American ed.] South Brunswick [N.J.] A. S. Barnes [1967, c1966] 115 p. illus., plans. 26 cm. Bibliographical footnotes. [NA997.N3D33 1967] 67-20198
1. Nash, John, 1752-1835.

DAVIS, Terence, 1924- 720'.92'4
John Nash: the Prince Regent's architect. [New] ed. with corrections. Newton Abbot, David and Charles, 1973. 118, [43] p. illus., map, plans, ports. 26 cm. Includes index. Bibliography: p. 111-112. [NA997.N3D33 1973] 73-173291 ISBN 0-7153-5959-2
1. Nash, John, 1752-1835.
Distributed by David and Charles, Vermont, 12.00.

Nason, Joseph, 1814 or 15-1873.

KING, Alice. 926.2
Gallant heritage. [1st ed.] New York, Vantage Press [1965] 335 p. 21 cm. [CT275.N32K5] 65-1917
1. Nason, Joseph, 1814 or 15-1873. I. Title.

Nassau, N.Y.—History.

HUEY, Paul R. 974.7'245 B
The early history of Nassau Village, 1609-1830 : with brief biographical sketches of early settlers / by Paul R. Huey and Ralph D. Phillips. 2d ed. Nassau, N.Y. : Nassau Free Library, 1976. 42, vii p. : ill. ; 29 cm. Includes index. Bibliography: p. 41-42. [F129.N2H83 1976] 77-358361
1. Nassau, N.Y.—History. 2. Nassau, N.Y.—Genealogy. I. Phillips, Ralph D., joint author. II. Title.

Nasser, Gamal Abdel, Pres. United Arab Republic, 1918-1970.

DEKMEJIAN, R. Hrair, 1933- 962'.05
Egypt under Nasir; a study in political dynamics, by R. Hrair Dekmejian. [1st ed.] Albany, State University of New York Press, 1971. xvi, 368 p. illus., port. 25 cm. Bibliography: p. [344]-358. [DT107.83.D43] 70-152520 ISBN 0-87395-080-1 10.00
1. Nasser, Gamal Abdel, Pres. United Arab

HAYKAL, Muhammad Hasanayn. 962'.05'0924 B
The Cairo documents; the inside story of Nasser and his relationship with world leaders, rebels, and statesmen [by] Mohamed Hassanein Heikal. Introd. by Edward R. F. Sheehan. [1st ed. in the United States of America] Garden City, N.Y., Doubleday, 1973. xxxv, 360 p. ports.
Republic, 1918-1970. 2. Egypt—Politics and government—1952- I. Title. **BIP**

24 cm. [DT107.83.H367 1973] 76-182696 ISBN 0-385-06447-0 10.00
1. Nasser, Gamal Abdel, Pres. United Arab Republic, 1918-1970. 2. Egypt—Foreign relations. I. Title.

JOESTEN, Joachim, 1907- 962'.05'0924 B
Nasser; the rise to power. Westport, Conn., Greenwood Press [1974, c1960] 224 p. illus. 22 cm. Reprint of the ed. published by Odhams Press, London. [DT107.83.J59 1974] 74-3752 ISBN 0-8371-7471-6 11.75
1. Nasser, Gamal Abdel, Pres. United Arab Republic, 1918-

LACOUTURE, Jean. 960
The demigods: charismatic leadership in the third world. [Translated from the French by Patricia Wolf. 1st American ed.] New York, Knopf, 1970. 300, vi p. 22 cm. Translation of Quatre hommes et leurs peuples. Bibliography: p. [295]-300. [D839.5.L2513 1970] 72-111235 7.95
1. Nasser, Gamal Abdel, Pres. United Arab Republic, 1918-1970. 2. Bourguiba, Habib, Pres. Tunisia, 1903- 3. Norodom Sihanouk Varman, King of Cambodia, 1922- 4. Nkrumah, Kwame, Pres. Ghana, 1909- I. Title.

LACOUTURE, Jean. 962'.05'0924 B
Nasser, a biography. Translated from the French by Daniel Hofstadter. [1st American ed.] New York, Knopf; [distributed by Random House] 1973. xvi, 399, xi p. 23 cm. Bibliography: p. [397]-399. [DT107.83.L1713 1973] 71-154914 ISBN 0-394-46625-X 10.00
1. Nasser, Gamal Abdel, Pres. United Arab Republic, 1918-1970. I. Title.

NUTTING, Anthony. 962'.05'0924
Nasser. [1st ed.] New York, E. P. Dutton, 1972. xvii, 493 p. 22 cm. [DT107.83.N79 1972b] 74-189474 ISBN 0-525-16415-4 10.00
1. Nasser, Gamal Abdel, Pres. United Arab Republic, 1918-1970.

ST. John, Robert, 1902- 923.162
The boss; the story of Gamal Abdel Nasser. [1st ed.] New York, McGraw-Hill [1960] 325 p. 22 cm. [DT107.83.S3] 60-14047
1. Nasser, Gamal Abdel, Pres. United Arab Republic, 1918-1970. 2. Egypt—Politics and government—1952- I. Title.

STEPHENS, Robert Henry, 1920- 962'.05'0924 B
Nasser; a political biography [by] Robert Stephens. New York, Simon and Schuster [1972, c1971] 631 p. maps. 23 cm. Bibliography: p. [599]-607. [DT107.83.S74 1972] 79-183762 ISBN 0-671-21224-9 12.50
1. Nasser, Gamal Abdel, Pres. United Arab Republic, 1918-1970. 2. Egypt—History—1952-

Nast, Thomas,

NAST, Thomas, 1840-1902. 741.5973
Thomas Nast, political cartoonist, by J. Chal Vinson. Athens, University of Georgia Press [1967] x, 46 p., 154 illus. 29 cm. Bibliography: p. 42. [NC1429.N3V5] 66-27605
I. Vinson, John Chalmers.

Nast, Thomas, 1840-1902.

NAST, Thomas, 1840-1902. 741.5973
Thomas Nast, political cartoonist, by J. Chal Vinson. Athens, University of Georgia Press [1967] x, 46 p., 154 illus. 29 cm. Bibliography: p. 42. [NC1429.N3V5] 66-27605
I. Vinson, John Chalmers.

PAINE, Albert Bigelow, 1861-1937. 741.5'973
Th. Nast, his period and his pictures / by Albert Bigelow Paine. Princeton : Pyne Press, [1974] xxi, 583, xx p., [1] leaf of plates : ill. ; 24 cm. Reprint of the 1904 ed. published by Macmillan, New York. Includes indexes. [NC1429.N3P3 1974] 74-80488 ISBN 0-87861-079-0 : 12.50
1. Nast, Thomas, 1840-1902.

Nast, William, 1807-1899.

WITTKE, Carl Frederick, 1892- 922.743
William Nast, Patriarch of German Methodism, Detroit, Wayne State University Press, 1959 [c1960] 248 p. illus. 21 cm. Includes bibliography. [BX8495.N323W5] 60=5382
1. Nast, William, 1807-1899. I. Title.

Nastase, Ilie, 1946-

EVANS, Richard, 1939- 796.34'2'0924 B
Nasty, Ilie Nastase vs. tennis / Richard Evans. 1st American ed. New York : Stein and Day, 1979. xii, 242 p., [8] leaves of plates : ill. ; 24 cm. [GV994.N37E9 1979] 78-588815 ISBN 0-8128-2540-3 : 10.00
1. Nastase, Ilie, 1946- 2. Tennis players—Romania—Biography. I. Title.

Natal—History—Sources.

WOLSELEY, Garnet Joseph Wolseley, Viscount, 1833-1913. 968'.4'0924
The South African diaries of Sir Garnet Wolseley, 1875. Edited with an introd. by Adrian Preston. Cape Town, A. A. Balkema, 1971. x, 293 p. 26 cm. (South African biographical & historical studies, 11) Bibliography: p. 280-284. [Da68.32W7A32] 72-187560
1. Natal—History—Sources. I. Preston, Adrian W., ed. II. Title. III. Series.
Dist. by Verry 15.00.

Natchez, Miss.—Social life and customs.

JOHNSON, William, 1809-1851. 917.62'26'0350924
William Johnson's Natchez; the ante-bellum diary of a free Negro. Edited by William Ransom Hogan and Edwin Adams Davis. With a critical introd. by Frank A. Burdick. Port Washington, N.Y., Kennikat Press [1968, c1951] 2 v. (ix, 812 p.) illus., facsims. 24 cm. (Kennikat Press series in Negro culture and history) [E185.97.J697A3 1968] 68-25203
1. Natchez, Miss.—Social life and customs. I. Title.

Nathan, George Jean, 1882-1958—Biography—Addresses, essays, lectures.

MENCKEN, Henry Louis, 1880-1956. 818'.5'209
Pistols for two / by Owen Hatteras [i.e. H. L. Mencken and G. J. Nathan]. Folcroft, Pa. : Folcroft Library Editions, 1977. 42 p. ; 23 cm. Reprint of the 1917 ed. published by Knopf, New York. [PS3527.A72Z8 1977] 77-4002 ISBN 0-8414-4910-4 lib. bdg. : 10.00
1. Nathan, George Jean, 1882-1958—Biography—Addresses, essays, lectures. 2. Mencken, Henry Louis, 1880-1956—Biography—Addresses, essays, lectures. 3. Authors, American—20th century—Biography—Addresses, essays, lectures. I. Nathan, George Jean, 1882-1958, joint author. II. Title.

Nathan, Matthew, Sir, 1862-1939.

HAYDON, Anthony P. 325'.31'0924 B
Sir Matthew Nathan : British colonial governor and civil servant / [by] Anthony P. Haydon. St. Lucia, Q. : University of Queensland Press, 1977. viii, 280 p. : ill. ; 22 cm. Includes index. Bibliography: p. 247-271. [JV1009.N37H38] 77-375831 ISBN 0-7022-0965-1 : 26.65
1. Nathan, Matthew, Sir, 1862-1939. 2. Colonial administrators—Great Britain—Biography.
Distributed by Technical Impex. **BIP**

Nathan, Maud Nathan, 1862-

NATHAN, Maud Nathan, 1862- 324'.3'0924 B
Once upon a time and today [by] Maud Nathan. New York, Arno Press, 1974 [c1933] 327 p. illus. 23 cm. (Women in America: from colonial times to the 20th century) Reprint of the ed. published by Putnam, New York. [CT275.N34A3 1974] 74-3964 ISBN 0-405-06113-7
1. Nathan, Maud Nathan, 1862- I. Title. II. Series. **BIP**

Nathanson, Bernard N., 1926-

NATHANSON, Bernard N., 1926- 301
Aborting America / Bernard N. Nathanson, with Richard N. Ostling. 1st ed. Garden City, N.Y. : Doubleday, 1979. p. cm. Includes index. Bibliography: p. [HQ766.5.U5N28] 79-7069 ISBN 0-385-14461-X : 10.00
1. Nathanson, Bernard N., 1926- 2. Abortion—United States. 3. Abortion—Law and legislation—United States. 4. Physicians—United States—Biography. I. Ostling, Richard N., joint author. II. Title. **BIP**

Nation, Carry Amelia (Moore) 1846-1911.

TAYLOR, Robert Lewis. 364.170924 B
Vessel of wrath; the life and times of Carry Nation. [New York] New American Library [1966] 373, [2] p. illus. ports. 24 cm. Bibliographical references included in "Acknowledgments" (p. [375]) [HV5232.N3T3] 66-28648
1. Nation, Carry Amelia (Moore) 1846-1911. I. Title.

National Association for the Advancement of Colored People—History.

ROSS, Barbara Joyce. 301.45'19'6073062 B
J. E. Spingarn and the rise of the NAACP, 1911-1939 [by] B. Joyce Ross. [1st ed.] New York, Atheneum, 1972. xii, 305 p. 21 cm. (Atheneum [paperbacks] Studies in American Negro life, NL 32) Originally presented as the author's thesis, American University. Bibliography: p. [253]-296. [E185.5.N276R67 1972] 78-139326 3.95
1. National Association for the Advancement of Colored People—History. 2. Spingarn, Joel Elias, 1875-1939. I. Title. **BIP**

National Basketball Association.

PEPE, Phil. 796.32'3'0922
Greatest stars of the NBA. Englewood Cliffs, N.J., Prentice-Hall [1970] iii, 218 p. illus., ports. 24 cm. (The Official NBA library) "An Associated Features book." A close look at the careers of fifteen members of the National Basketball Association. [GV884.A1P4] 71 100632 6.95
1. National Basketball Association. 2. Basketball—Biography. 3. Basketball—Juvenile literature. I. Title.

National Basketball Association—Juvenile literature.

AASENG, Nathan. 796.32'364'0922 B
Basketball's high flyers / Nathan Aaseng. Minneapolis : Lerner Publications Co., c1979. p. cm. (The Sports heroes library) Presents biographies of 10 contemporary professional basketball players including Julius Erving, Bill Walton, Elvin Hayes, Bob McAdoo, and Moses Malone. [GV884.A1A23 1979] 920 79-17137 ISBN 0-8225-1058-8 (lib. bdg.) : 5.95
1. National Basketball Association—Juvenile literature. 2. Basketball players—United States—Biography—Juvenile literature. I. Title. II. Title: High flyers. **BIP**

ARMSTRONG, Robert, 1938- 796.32'3'0922 B
The coaches / by Robert Armstrong. Mankato, Minn. : Creative Education, c1977. 47 p. : col. ill. ; 28 cm. (Stars of the NBA) Focuses on the relationship between basketball coaches Red Holzman, Bill Fitch, K. C. Jones, Bill Sharman, and Al Attles and their respective NBA teams. [GV885.3.A84] 920 76-45181 ISBN 0-87191-566-9 lib.bdg. : 5.95
1. National Basketball Association—Juvenile literature. 2. Basketball coaching—Juvenile literature. 3. Basketball coaches—United States—Biography—Juvenile literature. I. Title. II. Series.

National Cash Register Company, Dayton, Ohio.

ALLYN, Stanley C 338.7'68'1140924
My half century with NCR [by] Stanley C. Allyn. [1st ed.] New York, McGraw-Hill [1968, c1967] vi, 209 p. ports. 21 cm. [HD9999.B94N37] 67-14890
1. National Cash Register Company, Dayton, Ohio. I. Title.

National characteristics, American.

BASSO, Hamilton, 1904-1964. 917.3'03'0922
Mainstream. Freeport, N.Y., Books for Libraries Press [1970, c1943] xii, 246 p. 23 cm. (Essay index reprint series) Contents.Contents.—Cotton Mather and John Smith.—Farewell and hail to Thomas Jefferson.—John Calhoun of Fort Hill.—Let us kneel to good Abe Lincoln.—Andrew Carnegie, or From rags to riches.—P. T. Barnum sits for a portrait.—Henry Adams and William Jennings Bryan.—Theodore Roosevelt feels fit as a bull moose.—Huey P. Long: Kingfish.—Franklin Delano Roosevelt. [E169.1.B24 1970] 73-106406
1. National characteristics, American. 2. U.S.—Biography. I. Title. **BIP**

National characteristics, English.

PRIESTLEY, John Boynton, 1894- 914.2'03
The English [by] J. B. Priestley. New York, Viking Press [1973] 256 p. illus. 28 cm. (A Studio book) [DA118.P68 1973] 73-1638 ISBN 0-670-29630-9 17.95
1. National characteristics, English. 2. Great Britain—Biography. I. Title.

National Dental Association (Founded 1932)—Biography.

WEBB, Harvey, 1929- 617.6'0092'2 B
The book of presidents : leaders of organized dentistry / by Harvey Webb, Jr., Lloyd Cecil Rhodes. [Charlottesville, Va.] : National Dental Association, 1977. [63] p. : ports. ; 29 cm. [RK1.N33W43] 77-10178
1. National Dental Association (Founded 1932)—Biography. 2. Afro-American dentists—Biography. 3. Dentists—United States—Biography. I. Rhodes, Lloyd Cecil, joint author. II. National Dental Association (Founded 1932) III. Title.

National Football League.

ANDERSON, Dave. 796.332240922
Great quarterbacks of the NFL. New York, Random House [1965] viii, 182 p. illus., ports. 22 cm. (The Punt, pass, and kick library, 2) Contents.Contents.—Johnny Unitas.—Sammy Baugh.—Sid Luckman.—Y. A. Tittle.—Otto Graham.—Norm Van Brocklin.—Frank Ryan.—Bart Starr.—Fran Tarkenton.—Charley Johnson. [GV939.A1A5] 65-22658
1. National Football League. 2. Football—Biography. I. Title. **BIP**

DEVANEY, John. 796.33'2'0922 B
Star pass receivers of the NFL. Illustrated with photos. New York, Random House [1972] 153 p. illus. 22 cm. (The Punt, pass, and kick library, # 17) Brief career biographies of nine pass receivers in pro football. Included are Otis Taylor, Fred Biletnikoff, Paul Warfield, Lance Alworth, Charlie Sanders, Bob Hayes, Raymond Berry, Don Maynard, and Danny Abramowicz. [GV939.A1D42] 920 72-1591 ISBN 0-394-82439-3 1.95
1. National Football League. 2. Football—Biography—Juvenile literature. I. Title. **BIP**

GUTMAN, Bill. 796.33'2'0922
Gamebreakers of the NFL. Illustrated with photos. New York, Random House [1973] 151 p. illus. 22 cm. (Punt, pass & kick library, 18) Profiles of seven notable football players of the NFL: Alan Page, George Blanda, Larry Little, Jim Plunkett, Jan Stenerud, Bruce Taylor, Willie Lanier.

[GV939.A1G87 1973] 920 73-4234 ISBN 0-394-82501-2 1.95
1. National Football League. 2. Football—Biography—Juvenile literature. I. Title.
Library binding 3.37; ISBN 0-394-92501-7. BIP

KAPLAN, Richard. 796.332'0922
Great linebackers of the NFL. New York, Random House [1970] vii, 144 p. illus., ports. 22 cm. (The Punt, pass, and kick library, 12) Highlights the football careers of ten National Football League linebackers of past and present: Butkus, Hein, Turner, Nitschke, Baughan, Walker, Robinson, Howley, Curtis, and Nobis. [GV939.A1K3] 920 70-90291
1. National Football League. 2. Football—Biography—Juvenile literature. I. Title. BIP

LIBBY, Bill. 796.332'0922
Star quarterbacks of the NFL. New York, Random House [1970] viii, 176 p. illus., ports. 22 cm. (The punt, pass, and kick library, 13) Brief biographies highlighting the football careers of ten quarterbacks: Gabriel, Cook, Griese, Jurgensen, Namath, Morton, Nelsen, Kapp, Lamonica, Dawson. [GV939.A1L48] 920 70-117548
1. National Football League. 2. Football—Biography—Juvenile literature. 3. Quarterback (Football) I. Title. BIP

SAHADI, Lou. 796.33'2'0922 B
Pro football's gamebreakers / Lou Sahadi ; foreword by Pete Rozell. Chicago : Contemporary Books, c1977. xiii, 284 p., [16] leaves of plates : ill. ; 29 cm. [GV939.A1S25 1977] 77-75847 ISBN 0-8092-7753-0 : 14.95
1. National Football League. 2. Football players—Biography. I. Title.

National Football League—Biography—Juvenile literature.

RUBIN, Bob. 796.33'2'0922 B
All-stars of the NFL / by Bob Rubin. New York : Random House, c1976. 153 p. : ill. ; 22 cm. (The Punt, pass and kick library) Includes index. Biographical sketches of eight outstanding players from the National Football League: Bradshaw, Bergey, Guy, Houston, Little, Curtis, Greene, and Simpson. [GV939.A1R82] 920 76-8133 ISBN 0-394-83258-2 : 2.50 lib.bdg. : 3.69
1. National Football League—Biography—Juvenile literature. 2. Football—Biography—Juvenile literature. I. Title. BIP

National Football League—Juvenile literature.

AASENG, Nathan. 796.33'2'0922 B
Football's fierce defenses / Nathan Aaseng. Minneapolis : Lerner Publications Co., c1979. p. cm. (The Sports heroes library) Biographies of defensive linemen of professional ball, including the "Fearsome Foursome" of the Los Angeles Rams, "Purple People Eaters" of the Minnesota Vikings, and "Orange Crush" of the Denver Broncos. [GV951.18.A27 1979] 920 79-16315 ISBN 0-8225-1057-X (lib. bdg.): 5.95
1. National Football League—Juvenile literature. 2. Football—Defense—Juvenile literature. 3. Football players—United States—Biography—Juvenile literature. I. Title. BIP

RUBIN, Bob. 796.33'2'0922 B
Little men of the NFL. Illustrated with photos. New York, Random House [1974] 153 p. illus. 22 cm. (The Punt, pass, and kick library) Brief biographies emphasizing the careers of seven professional football stars who are of smaller and lighter build than the average player. [GV955.5.N35R82 1974] 920 74-5145 ISBN 0-394-82807-0 1.95
1. National Football League—Juvenile literature. 2. Football—Juvenile literature. I. Title.
Library binding; 3.77, ISBN 0-394-92807-5. BIP

THORNE, Ian. 796.33'2'0922 B
Meet the defensive linemen / by Ian Thorne ; photos., Vernon J. Biever, John E. Biever. Mankato, Minn. : Creative Education, [1975] p. cm. Brief sketches of four defensive linemen of the National Football League : Alan Page, Bubba Smith, Bob Lilly, and Jim Marshall. [GV939.A1T44] 75-26720 ISBN 0-87191-467-0 lib.bdg. : 4.95
1. National Football League—Juvenile literature. 2. Football—Biography—Juvenile literature. 3. Line play (Football)—Juvenile literature. I. Biever, Vernon J. II. Biever, John. III. Title. BIP

THORNE, Ian. 796.33'2'0922 B
Meet the receivers / by Ian Thorne ; photos., Vernon J. Biever, John E. Biever. Mankato, Minn. : Creative Education, [1975] p. cm. Brief descriptions of the professional careers of four outstanding receivers: Charley Taylor, Fred Biletnikoff, John Gilliam, and Paul Warfield. [GB939.A1T45] 92 75-26565 ISBN 0-87191-468-9 lib.bdg. : 4.95
1. National Football League—Juvenile literature. 2. Football—Biography—Juvenile literature. 3. Passing (Football)—Juvenile literature. I. Biever, Vernon J. II. Biever, John. III. Title. BIP

National Hockey League—Biography—Juvenile literature.

THOMAS, Linda, 796.9'62'0922 B
1947-
Meet the goalies / written by Linda Thomas ; photos. from the National Hockey League. [Mankato, Minn.] : Creative Education, [1976] p. cm. Biographical sketches of four hockey goalies: Ken Dryden, Tony Esposito, Bernie Parent, and Gilles Gilbert. [GV848.5.A1T432] 920 76-21057 ISBN 0-87191-533-2 lib.bdg. : 4.95
1. National Hockey League—Biography—Juvenile literature. 2. Hockey—Biography—Juvenile literature. I. Title. BIP

National Maritime Union of America.

RUBIN, 331.88'11'38750924 B
Charles R.
The log of Rubin the sailor, by Charles Rubin. [1st ed.] New York, International Publishers [1973] 358 p. 22 cm. [HD8039.S42U665] 73-77809 ISBN 0-7178-0384-8 7.50
1. National Maritime Union of America. 2. Merchant seamen—Correspondence, reminiscences, etc. I. Title. BIP

National Museum of Natural History.

NATIONAL Museum of 500.9'07'2
Natural History.
The magnificent foragers / [writer, Thomas Harney ; consulting editor, Edward S. Ayensu, Alfred Meyer, editor]. Washington : National Museum of Natural History, Smithsonian Institution ; New York : distributed to the trade by W. W. Norton, 1978. 223 p. : ill. (some col.) ; 27 cm. Includes index. [QH51.N238 1978] 78-61066 ISBN 0-89599-001-6 : 16.95
1. National Museum of Natural History. 2. Natural history—Research. 3. Naturalists—United States—Biography. I. Harney, Thomas R. II. Title.

National socialism.

FEST, Joachim C., 943.086'0922
1926-
The face of the Third Reich; portraits of the Nazi leadership [by] Joachim C. Fest. Translated from the German by Michael Bullock. [1st American ed.] New York, Pantheon Books [1970] xiii, 402 p. 25 cm. Translation of Das Gesicht des Dritten Reiches. Bibliography: p. 386-391. [DD256.5.F413 1970b] 66-10412 10.00
1. National socialism. 2. Germany—Biography. I. Title. BIP

MESKIL, Paul, 1923- 923.543
Hitler's heirs. New York, Pyramid Books [1961] 191p. 19cm. [DD256.5.M48] 61-66170
1. National socialism. 2. Fascism. 3. Germany—Biog. I. Title.

Nationalism—India.

SHIVA RAO, B., 954.03'5'0922 [B]
1891-
India's freedom movement; some notable figures. [New Delhi] Orient Longman [1973, c.1972] viii, 336 p. 22 cm. [DS480.45.S4728] 72-906860
1. Nationalism—India. 2. India—Politics and government—1919-1947. 3. India—Biography. I. Title.
Available from International Publications Service, New York, for 13.50. BIP

Nationalsozialistische Deutsche Arbeiter-Partei—Biography.

DUTCH, Oswald, 943.086'0922
pseud.
Hitler's 12 apostles, by Otto Deutsch (Oswald Dutch, pseud.) Freeport, N.Y., Books for Libraries Press [1969] 249 p. ports. 24 cm. (Essay index reprint series) Reprint of the 1940 ed. Contents.Contents.—The frame.—Hermann Goering.—Dr. Josef Geobbels.—Alfred Rosenberg.—Rudolf Hess.—Heinrich Himmler.—Dr. Robert Ley.—Joachim von Ribbentrop.—Julius Streicher.—General Walther von Brauchitsch.—Dr. Walther Funk.—Dr. Wilhelm Frick.—Baldur von Schirach.—The martyrs.—The "would-be" apostles.—Twelve faces and a world philosophy.—Chronological summary of the National socialist movement. [DD244.D8 1969] 75-93333 ISBN 8-369-12861-
1. Nationalsozialistische Deutsche Arbeiter-Partei—Biography. 2. National socialism. 3. Germany—Politics and government—1933-1945. I. Title.

KELLEY, Douglas 920.043
McGlashan, M.D., 1912-
22 cells in Nuremberg; a psychiatrist examines the Nazi criminals, by Douglas M. Kelley. [New York, Hillman-Macfadden, 1961, c.1947] 176p. (Macfadden bk., 50-116) .50 pap.,
1. Nationalsozialistische deutsche arbeiter-partei—Biog. 2. Germany—Biog. I. Title.

Nationalsozialistische Duetsche Arbeiter-Partei. Bund der Jungmadel—Juvenile literature.

KOEHN, Ilse. 943.086'092'4 B
Mischling, second degree : my childhood in Nazi Germany / Ilse Koehn ; with a foreword by Harrison E. Salisbury. New York : Greenwillow Books, c1977. p. cm. The memoirs of a German girl who became a leader among the Hitler Youth while her Social Democratic family kept from her the secret of her partial Jewish heritage. [DD253.47.K63] 92 77-6189 ISBN 0-688-80110-2 : 7.95 ISBN 0-688-84110-4 lib.bdg. : 7.35
1. Nationalsozialistische Duetsche Arbeiter-Partei. Bund der Jungmadel—Juvenile literature. 2. Jews in Germany—History—1933-1945—Juvenile literature. 3. Koehn, Ilse—Juvenile literature. 4. Jews in Germany—Biography—Juvenile literature. I. Title.

KOEHN, Ilse. JUV
Mischling, second degree: my childhood in Nazi Germany / by Ilse Koehn; with a foreword by Harrison E. Salisbury. New York : Bantam Books, 1978. 213p. ; 18 cm. [DD253.47L63] 943.086'092'4[B] 92 ISBN 0-553-11968-0 pbk. : 1.95
1. Nationalsozialistiche Arbeiter-Parter Bunder jungmadel — Juvenile literature. 2. Jews in Germany — History — 3. Koehm Ilse — Juvenile literature 4. Jews in Germany — , Biography — Juvenile literature. I. Title.
L.C. card no. for 1977 Morrow ed.: 77-6189 BIP

Nationalsozialistische Deutsche Arbeiter-Partei. Waffenschutzstaffel. 33. Grenadier-Division [Charlemagne."

LA MAZIERE, 940.54'12'44
Christian de.
The captive dreamer. Translated by Francis Stuart. New York, Saturday Review Press, 1974. p. Autobiographical. Translation of Le reveur casque. [D757.85.L3513] 73-20004 7.95
1. Nationalsozialistische Deutsche Arbeiter-Partei. Waffenschutzstaffel. 33. Grenadier-Division [Charlemagne." 2. La Maziere, Christian de. 3. World War, 1939-1945—Campaigns—Eastern. 4. World War, 1939-1945—Personal narratives, French. I. Title.

Natural history—Florida.

CHAPMAN, Frank 500.9'09759
Michler, 1864-1945.
Frank M. Chapman in Florida: his journals & letters. Compiled and edited by Elizabeth S. Austin. Gainesville, University of Florida Press, 1967. vii, 228 p. illus., map (on lining paper) ports. 24 cm. "Chapman's published writings": p. 177-187. Bibliography: p. 222-225. [QH105.F6C47] 66-30436
1. Natural history—Florida. I. Austin, Elizabeth S., ed. II. Title.

Naturalists.

BLASSINGAME, Wyatt 925.7
Naturalist-explorers. Illus. by Fred Sweney. New York, Watts [c.1964] 145p. illus. 22cm. 64-17785 3.95
1. Naturalists. I. Title.

BLASSINGAME, Wyatt. 925.7
Naturalist-explorers. Illustrated by Fred Sweney. New York, F. Watts [1964] 145 p. illus. 22 cm. [QH26.B57] 64-17785
1. Naturalists. I. Title.

MIALL, Louis Compton, 574'.0922 B
1842-1921.
The early naturalists; their lives and work, 1530-1789. New York, Hafner Pub. Co., 1969. xi, 396 p. 22 cm. Facsimile of the ed. published in London by Macmillan in 1912. [QH26.M5 1912a] 72-104389
1. Naturalists. I. Title.

MILNE, Lorus Johnson, 925.74
1910-
Famous naturalists, by Lorus J. and Margery J. Milne. New York, Dodd, Mead, 1952. 178 p. illus. 23 cm. (Famous biographies for young people) [QH26.M53] 52-8118
1. Naturalists. I. Title.

MUIR, John 1838-1914. 925.009
The wilderness world of John Muir / with an introduction and interpretive comments by Edwin Way Teale ; illustrated by Henry B. Kane. Boston : Houghton Mifflin [1975c1954] xx, 332p. : ill. ; 21 cm. Includes index. [QH31M9A37] ISBN 0-395-24083-2 pbk. : 4.95
1. Naturalists. I. Title.
L. C. card no. for original edition: 54-9040.

Naturalists, American.

POOLE, Lynn. 925
Scientists who work outdoors, by Lynn and Gray Poole. New York, Dodd, Mead [1963] 178 p. illus. 21 cm. ("Makers of our modern world" books) [QH26.P6] 63-3024
1. Naturalists, American. 2. Scientists, American. I. Poole, Gray, joint author. II. Title. BIP

Naturalists—Biography.

ADAMS, Alexander B. 500.9'0922
Eternal quest: the story of the great naturalists, by Alexander B. Adams. New York, Putnam [1969] 509 p. illus., facsims., ports. 24 cm. Bibliography: p. 449-458. [QH26.A3] 68-25427 10.95
1. Naturalists—Biography. I. Title.

Naturalists—United States—Biography.

COATES, Ruth Allison. 500.9'22 B
Great American naturalists. Minneapolis, Lerner Publications Co. [1974] 103 p. illus. 22 cm. (A Pull ahead book) Brief biographies of fourteen men and women who dedicated their lives to studying some aspect of nature. [QH26.C6] 920 73-21989 ISBN 0-8225-0467-7 3.95
1. Naturalists—United States—Biography. I. Title. BIP

ELMAN, Robert. 500.9'2'2 B
First in the field : America's pioneering naturalists / by Robert Elman. ; foreword by Dean Amadon. New York : Van Nostrand Reinhold Co., 1978. p. cm. Includes index. Bibliography: p. [QH26.E44 1978] 78-16263 ISBN 0-442-80358-3 : 12.50
1. Naturalists—United States—Biography. I. Title. BIP

ELMAN, Robert. 500.9'2'2 B
First in the field : America's pioneering naturalists / by Robert Elman ; foreword by Dean Amadon. New York : Mason/Charter, 1977. xx, 231 p., [8] leaves of plates : ill. ; 24 cm. Includes index. Bibliography: p. 219-225. [QH26.E44] 77-3437 ISBN 0-88405-499-3 : 9.95
1. Naturalists—United States—Biography. I. Title.

KASTNER, Joseph. 500.92'2 3
A species of eternity / by Joseph Kastner. New York : Knopf, 1977. p. cm. Includes index. Bibliography: p. [QH26.K38] 77-74983 ISBN 0-394-49033-9 : 15.00
1. Naturalists—United States—Biography. I. Title. BIP

Naude, Beyers.

BRYAN, G. McLeod. 285'.732'0924 B
Naude, prophet to South Africa / G. McLeod Bryan. Atlanta : John Knox Press, c1978. vii, 151 p. : group port. ; 21 cm. [BX9595.S63N383] 77-15746 ISBN 0-8042-0942-1 pbk. : 5.95
1. Naude, Beyers. 2. Reformed Church—Clergy—Biography. 3. Clergy—South Africa—Biography. I. Title.

Naude, Gabriel, 1600-1653.

CLARKE, Jack Alden, 010'.924 B 1924-
Gabriel Naude, 1600-1653, by Jack A. Clarke. Hamden, Conn., Archon Books, 1970. 183 p. 22 cm. Bibliography: p. 168-179. [Z1004.N29C55] 74-100405
1. Naude, Gabriel, 1600-1653. I. Title. BIP

Nauer, Barbara.

NAUER, Barbara. 248'.2'0924 B
Rise up and remember / Barbara Nauer. 1st ed. Garden City, N.Y. : Doubleday, 1977. viii, 110 p. ; 21 cm. [BX4705.N284A37] 76-54011 ISBN 0-385-12955-6 pbk. : 2.95
1. Nauer, Barbara. 2. Catholics in the United States—Biography. 3. Pentecostalism—Catholic Church. I. Title. BIP

Navaho Indians—Biography.

STORIES of 970'.004'97
traditional Navajo life and culture / by twenty-two Navajo men and women ; editor, Broderick H. Johnson ; illustrators, Raymond Johnson and Hoke Denetsosie. 1st ed. Tsaile, Navajo Nation, Ariz. : Navajo Community College Press, 1977. p. cm. [E99.N3S84] 77-22484 ISBN 0-912586-23-0 : 9.95
1. Navaho Indians—Biography. 2. Navaho Indians—Social life and customs. I. Johnson, Broderick H. BIP

Navaho Indians—Biography—Juvenile literature.

HOFFMAN, Virginia, 970.3'0922 1938-
Navajo biographies, by Virginia Hoffman and Broderick H. Johnson. Illustrated by Hoke Denetsosie, Andy Tsinajinnie, and Clifford Beck, Jr. [1st ed. Rough Rock, Ariz.] Dine, 1970. 342 p. illus., maps, ports. 29 cm. On cover: Navaho Curriculum Center, Rough Rock Demonstration School, Rough Rock, Arizona. Contents.Contents.—A message to Navajo students.—Biographies by V. Hoffman: Narbona. Antonio Cebolla Sandoval. Zarcillos Largos. Manuelito. Barboncito. Ganado Mucho. Jesus Arviso. Henry Chee Dodge. Sam Ahkeah.—Biographies by B. H. Johnson: Albert George (Chic) Sandoval. Paul Jones. Chabah Davis Watson. Annie Dodge Wauneka. Dr. Taylor McKenzie. Raymond Nakai.—Bibliography (p. 340-342) [E99.N3H63] 920 70-113723
1. Navaho Indians—Biography—Juvenile literature. I. Johnson, Broderick H. II. Denetsosie, Hoke, illus. III. Tsinajinnie, Andy, illus. IV. Beck, Clifford, illus. V. Navaho Curriculum Center. VI. Title. BIP

Naval biography.

BOWEN, Frank Charles, 1894- 923.5
Men of the wooden walls. London, New York, Staples Press [1952] 152 p. illus. 26 cm. [V61.B6] 52-40660
1. Naval biography. I. Title.

FROTHINGHAM, Jessie 359.3'31'0922 Peabody.
Sea fighters from Drake to Farragut. Freeport, N.Y., Books for Libraries Press [1967] vii, 396 p. illus. 22 cm. (Essay index reprint series) Reprint of the 1902 ed. [D27.F8 1967] 67-26743
1. Naval biography. 2. Naval history, Modern. I. Title. BIP

HILL, Jim Dan, 1897- 923.573
Sea dogs of the sixties. Farragut and seven contemporaries [Gloucester, Mass., P. Smith, 1963,c.1935] 265p. illus., map. 21cm. (Perpetua bk. rebound) Bibl. 4.00
I. Title.

LEWIS, Charles Lee, 1886- 359'.09
Famous old-world sea fighters. Freeport, N.Y., Books for Libraries Press [1969] 362 p. illus., map (on lining papers), ports. 23 cm. (Essay index reprint series) London ed. (G. G. Harrap) has title: Famous sea-fighters. Reprint of the 1929 ed. Contents.Contents.—Phormio.—Marcus Vipsanius Agrippa.—Olaf Tryggvesson.—Barbarossa.—Francis Drake.—Robert Blake.—Michel de Ruyter.—Comte de Tourville.—Edward Hawke.—Comte de Grasse.—Bailli de Suffren.—Horatio Nelson.—Wilhelm von Tegetthoff.—Heihachiro Togo.—David Beatty.—Bibliography (p. 349-354) [D27.L4 1969] 70-99708
1. Naval biography. 2. Naval history. I. Title. BIP

WILSON, Harold 928.2
The private life of Mr. Pepys [New York] Dell [1961, c.1959] 287p. (F141) Bibl. .50 pap.,
I. Pepys, Samuel, 1633-1703. II. Title.

Navarro, Jose Antonio, 1795-1871.

DAWSON, Joseph 976.4'03'0924 B Martin, 1879-
Jose Antonio Navarro, co-creator of Texas. [Waco, Tex., Printed by Baylor University Press, c1969] xiv, 127 p. illus., map, ports. 24 cm. Includes bibliographical references. [F390.N38D3] 73-112732 6.50
1. Navarro, Jose Antonio, 1795-1871.

Navratilova, Martina, 1956- — Juvenile literature.

DOLAN, Edward F., 796.34'2'0924 B 1924-
Martina Navratilova / Edward F. Dolan, Jr., and Richard B. Lyttle. 1st ed. Garden City, N.Y. : Doubleday, c1977. vi, 81 p., [12] leaves of plates : ill. ; 22 cm. (A Doubleday Signal book) A biography of the tennis player who defected from Czechoslovakia to join the Cleveland Nets tennis team. [GV994.N38D64] 92 76-56282 ISBN 0-385-12525-9 : 6.95
1. Navratilova, Martina, 1956- —Juvenile literature. 2. Tennis players—Biography—Juvenile literature. I. Lyttle, Richard B., joint author. II. Title. BIP

JACOBS, Linda. 796.34'2'0924 B
Martina Navratilova, tennis fury / by Linda Jacobs. St. Paul : EMC Corp., 1976. 40 p. : ill. ; 23 cm. (Women who win 4) A biography of the Czech tennis star who asked for political asylum in the United States in 1975. [GV994.N38J3] 92 76-8421 ISBN 0-88436-237-X pbk. : 2.95
1. Navratilova, Martina, 1956- —Juvenile literature. 2. Tennis—Juvenile literature. I. Title.

Navrozov, Lev.

NAVROZOV, Lev. 300'.92'4 B
The education of Lev Navrozov : a life in the closed world once called Russia / by Lev Navrozov. 1st ed. New York : Harper's Magazine Press, [1975] 628 p. ; 24 cm. Includes index. Bibliography: p. [620] [H59.N38A33 1975] 73-6314 ISBN 0-06-126415-6 : 12.95
1. Navrozov, Lev. I. Title.

Naylor, Phyllis Reynolds.

NAYLOR, Phyllis 616.8'97'09 B Reynolds.
Crazy love : an autobiographical account of marriage and madness / Phyllis Naylor. New York : Morrow, 1977. 192 p. ; 22 cm. [RC464.N37A34] 76-56359 ISBN 0-688-03178-1 : 7.95
1. Naylor, Phyllis Reynolds. 2. Mental illness—Biography. 3. Mental illness—United States—Biography. I. Title. BIP

Naylor, Phyllis Reynolds—Biography—Juvenile literature.

NAYLOR, Phyllis 813'.5'4 B Reynolds.
How I came to be a writer / by Phyllis Reynolds Naylor. 1st ed. New York : Atheneum, 1978. 133 p. : ill. ; 21 cm. Details the career of one writer from stories composed in grade school through first published pieces to novels written to date. [PS3564.A9Z52] 92 77-23919 ISBN 0-689-30625-3 : 6.95
1. Naylor, Phyllis Reynolds—Biography—Juvenile literature. 2. Authors, American—20th century—Biography—Juvenile literature. 3. Authorship—Juvenile literature. I. Title. BIP

Ndadi, Vinnia, 1928-

NDADI, Vinnia, 1928- 968'.8 B
Breaking contract : the story of Vinnia Ndadi / [recorded and edited by Dennis Mercer]. Richmond, B.C. : LSM Information Center, c1974. 116 p. : ill. ; 21 cm. (Life histories from the revolution : Namibia, SWAPO ; 1) [DT715.N4A33] 76-350807
1. Ndadi, Vinnia, 1928- 2. Africa, Southwest—Politics and government. I. Mercer, Dennis. II. Title. III. Series.

Neal, John, 1793-1876.

LEASE, Benjamin. 813'.2 B
That wild fellow John Neal and the American literary revolution. Chicago, University of Chicago Press [1972] xii, 229 p. illus. 23 cm. Bibliography: p. 205-216. [PS2459.N28Z75] 72-81630 ISBN 0-226-46969-7
1. Neal, John, 1793-1876. I. Title. BIP

SEARS, Donald A. 813'.2 B
John Neal / by Donald A. Sears. Boston : Twayne Publishers, 1978. 154 p. : port. ; 21 cm. (Twayne's United States authors series ; TUSAS 307) Includes index. Bibliography: p. 145-150.. [PS2459.N28Z85] 78-5224 ISBN 0-8057-7230-8 lib. bdg. : 9.95
1. Neal, John, 1793-1876. 2. Authors, American—19th century—Biography. BIP

Nearing, Scott, 1883-

NEARING, Scott, 335'.00924 B 1883-
The making of a radical: a political autobiography. [1st ed.] New York, Harper & Row [1972] xi, 308 p. 21 cm. (Harper colophon books, CN 251) "Chronological bibliography of the author's works": p. [303]-308. [HX84.N4A3] 78-180725 ISBN 0-06-090251-5 2.45
I. Title.

WHITFIELD, Stephen 335'.0092'4 J., 1942-
Scott Nearing: apostle of American radicalism [by] Stephen J. Whitfield. New York, Columbia University Press, 1974. ix, 269 p. port. 24 cm. Bibliography: p. [247]-261. [HX84.N4W5] 74-10641 ISBN 0-231-03816-X
1. Nearing, Scott, 1883- I. Title.

Nebeker, Phebe Almira (Hulme) 1865-1948.

ADAMS, Luella (Nebeker) 920.7 1887
Phebe Almira Hulme Nebeker, 1865-1948. [Salt Lake City? 1955] 82p. illus. 23cm. [CT275.N415A6] 55-30036
1. Nebeker, Phebe Almira (Hulme) 1865-1948. I. Title.

Nebel, Long John.

BAIN, Donald, 791.44'092'4 B 1935-
Long John Nebel: radio talk king, master salesman, and magnificent charlatan. New York, Macmillan [1974] xix, 268 p. illus. 22 cm. [HF5438.B223] 74-1077 ISBN 0-02-505950-5 7.95
1. Nebel, Long John.

Nebraska—Biog.

JOHNSON, John Reuben, 920.0782 1897-
Representative Nebraskans; illustrated by Clarence E. Struble. Lincoln, Neb., Johnson Pub. Co. [1954] 198p. illus. 23cm. Includes bibliography. [F665.J6] 54-3445
1. Nebraska—Biog. I. Title.

Nebraska Marie Josephine, 1859-1894—Juvenile literature.

HILGER, Mary Ione 920
The first Sioux nun, Sister Marie-Josephine Nebraska, 1859-1894. Illus.: Mary Michael Kaliher. Milwaukee, Bruce [c.1963] 157p. illus. 22cm. 63-11880 3.50
1. Nebraska Marie Josephine, 1859-1894—Juvenile literature. I. Title.

Necchi, Lodovico, 1876-1930.

DE ROBECK, Nesta [Mary 926.1 Emily]
Vico Necchi. Chicago, Franciscan Herald Press [c.1960] 163p. illus. (front.) 21cm. 60-8643 2.95 bds.,
1. Necchi, Lodovico, 1876-1930. I. Title.

Nechaev, Sergei Gennadievich, 1847-1882.

[CHAROL, Michael] 1894- 923.247
The unmentionable Nechaev, a key to Bolshevism [by] Michael Prawdin [pseud.] New York, Roy [1963, c.1961] 198p. illus. 23cm. Bibl. 63-16461 4.00 bds.,

1. Nechaev, Sergei Gennadievich, 1847-1882. I. Title.

Necker, Jacques, 1732-1804.

HARRIS, Robert D. 354'.44'00720924
Necker, reform statesman of the Ancien Regime / Robert D. Harris. Berkeley : University of California Press, c1979. 259 p. : port. ; 25 cm. Includes index. Bibliography: p. [245]-252. [HJ1075.H37] 77-93464 ISBN 0-520-03647-6 : 14.00
1. Necker, Jacques, 1732-1804. 2. Finance, Public—France—To 1789. I. Title.

Neckers, James Winfred, 1902-

NECKERS, James Winfred, 1902- 540'.7'11773994 B
The building of a department : chemistry at Southern Illinois University, 1927-1967 / James W. Neckers. Carbondale : Southern Illinois University Press, c1979. 187 p. ; 23 cm. Includes index. [QD22.N36A34] 78-13384 ISBN 0-8093-0901-7 : 12.95
1. Neckers, James Winfred, 1902- 2. Illinois. Southern Illinois University, Carbondale. Dept. of Chemistry and Biochemistry. 3. Chemists—United States—Biography. I. Title. BIP

Neerskov, Hans Kristian.

NEERSKOV, Hans Kristian. 266'.0092'4 B
Mission possible / Hans Kristian, with Dave Hunt. Old Tappan, N.J. : Revell, [1975] 191 p. ; 21 cm. [BV3777.E93N43] 74-26808 ISBN 0-8007-0717-6 pbk. : 2.95
1. Neerskov, Hans Kristian. 2. Evangelistic work—Europe, Eastern. I. Hunt, Dave, joint author. II. Title.

Nef, Elinor (Castle)

NEF, Elinor (Castle) 1894or5-1953. 928.1
Letters & notes; edited by John U. Nef. [Los Angeles] W. Ritchie Press, 1953- v. illus. 24cm. [PS3527.E274Z52] 54-18284
I. Title.

Nef, John Ulric, 1899-

NEF, John Ulric, 1899- 917.3'03'920924
Search for meaning; the autobiography of a nonconformist, by John U. Nef. Washington, Public Affairs Press [1973] vi, 349 p. 24 cm. Bibliography of the author's works: p. 333-343. [CT275.N424A37] 73-82014 10.00
1. Nef, John Ulric, 1899- I. Title.

Nefertiti, Queen of Egypt, 14th cent., B.C.

HARTEL, Klaus Dieter. 932'.01'0924 B
Nefertiti : an archaeological biography / Philipp Vandenberg [i.e. K. D. Hartel] ; translated from the German by Ruth Hein. 1st English-language ed. Philadelphia : Lippincott, c1978. 161 p., [8] leaves of plates : ill. ; 22 cm. Translation of Nofretete. Bibliography: p. 160-161. [DT87.45.H3713] 77-28107 ISBN 0-397-01256-X : 10.00
1. Nefertiti, Queen of Egypt, 14th cent. B.C. 2. Egypt—History—To 332 B.C. 3. Egypt—Antiquities. 4. Egypt—Queens—Biography. I. Title.

PATTERSON, Emma Lillie. 189.4
Sun Queen; a novel about Nefertiti, by Emma L. Patterson. New York, D. McKay Co., 1967. 312 p. 21 cm. [PZ3.P27604Su] 67-28223
1. Nefertiti, Queen of Egypt, 14th cent., B.C.—Fiction. I. Title.

WELLS, Evelyn. 932
Nefertiti. [1st ed.] Garden City, N.Y., Doubleday, 1964. xii, 300 p. illus., ports. 24 cm. Bibliography: p. 288-290. [DT87.45.W4] 64-11391
1. Nefertiti, Queen of Egypt, 14th cent. B.C.

WELLS, Evelyn. 932
Nefertiti. [1st ed.] Garden City, N.Y., Doubleday, 1964. xii, 300 p. illus., ports. 24 cm. Bibliography: p. 288-290. [DT87.45.W4] 64-11391
1. Nefertiti, Queen of Egypt, 14th cent. B.C.

Neff, Hildegarde,

NEFF, Hildegarde, 1925- 792'.0924 B
The gift horse; report on a life [by] Hildegard Knef. Translated from the German by David Anthony Palastanga. [1st ed.] New York, McGraw-Hill [1971] 384 p. 23 cm. Translation of Der geschenkte Gaul. [PN2658.N35A313] 74-160709 ISBN 0-07-035085-X
I. Title.

Negre, Charles, 1820-1880.

NEGRE, Charles, 1820-1880. 779'.092'4
Charles Negre 1820-1880 / James Borcoman. Ottawa : National Gallery of Canada, 1976. 261 p. : chiefly ill. ; 30 cm. English and French in parallel columns. Includes indexes. Bibliography: p. 257-258. [TR652.N43 1976] 76-378760 ISBN 0-88884-268-6
1. Negre, Charles, 1820-1880. 2. Photography, Artistic. 3. Photographers—France—Biography. I. Borcoman, James.

Negri, Pola,

NEGRI, Pola, 1897- 791.43'028'0924 B
Memoirs of a star. [1st ed.] Garden City, N.Y., Doubleday, 1970. 453 p. illus., ports. 25 cm. [PN2287.N35A3] 70-97675 7.95
I. Title.

Negro artists—U.S.

FAX, Elton C. 709'.22
Seventeen black artists [by] Elton C. Fax. New York, Dodd, Mead [1971] xiv, 306 p. illus., ports. 22 cm. [N6538.N5F3] 72-165671 ISBN 0-396-06391-8 7.95
1. Negro artists—U.S. I. Title. BIP

Negro arts—United States—Biography.

*CEDERHOLM, Theresa Dickason. 700'.973
Afro-American artists; a bio-bibliographical directory, comp. and edited by Theresa Dickason Cederholm. [Boston, Mass.] Trustees of the Boston Public Library, 1973. 348 p. 24 cm. Bibliography: p. 325-348. [PS153] 73-84951 10.00 (pbk.)
1. Negro arts—United States—Biography. 2. Negroes in art—United States—Biography. I. Title.
Order from Information Office, Boston Public Library, Box 286, Boston, MA 02117. BIP

Negro athletes.

CHALK, Ocania. 796'.092'2 B
Black college sport / Ocania Chalk. New York : Dodd, Mead, c1976. 376 p. : ill. ; 24 cm. Includes index. [GV583.C45] 75-43833 ISBN 0-396-07023-X : 8.95
1. Negro athletes. 2. College sports—History. 3. Sports—United States—History. I. Title. BIP

YOUNG, Andrew Sturgeon Nash, 1919- 927.96
Negro firsts in sports, by A. S. "Doc" Young. With illus. by Herbert Temple. Chicago, Johnson Pub. Co. [1963] 301 p. illus. 22 cm. [GV697.A1Y6] 62-21535
1. Negro athletes. I. Title. BIP

Negro athletes—Biography.

CHALK, Ocania. 796'.092'2 B
Pioneers of Black sport : the early days of the Black professional athlete in baseball, basketball, boxing, and football / Ocania Chalk. New York : Dodd, Mead, [1975] xiii, 305 p. : ill. ; 24 cm. Includes bibliographical references and index. Brief biographies emphasizing the career achievements of well-known black athletes in baseball, basketball, boxing, and football. [GV697.A1C47] 920 73-15035 ISBN 0-396-06868-5 : 7.95
1. Negro athletes—Biography. I. Title.

Negro athletes—Juvenile literature.

HOLLANDER, Phyllis. 796'.092'2
They dared to lead: America's Black athletes. Edited by Phyllis and Zander Hollander. New York, Grosset & Dunlap [1972] 184 p. illus. 21 cm. "An Associated Features book." "A W. W. Norton book." [GV697.A1H58] 920 78-182013 ISBN 0-448-21429-6
1. Negro athletes—Juvenile literature. I. Hollander, Zander, joint author. II. Title.

Negro authors.

BRAWLEY, Benjamin Griffith, 1882-1939, ed. 810.9'9'174
Early Negro American writers; selections with biographical and and critical introductions. Freeport, N.Y., Books for Libraries Press [1968] ix, 305 p. 23 cm. (Essay index reprint series) Reprint of the 1935 ed. [PS508.N3B7 1968] 68-25601
1. Negro authors. 2. American literature—Negro authors. I. Title.

BRAWLEY, Benjamin Griffith, 1882-1939 920.0973
The Negro genius; a new appraisal of the achievement of the American Negro in literature and the fine arts. New York, Biblo &Tannen. 1966[c.1937] xiii, 366p. illus., ports. 21cm. xiii. 366p. illus., ports. 21cm. Bibl. [E185.82.B816 1966] 66-17517 7.50
1. Negro authors. 2. Negro artists. 3. Negro musicians. 4. American literature—Negro authors—Hist. & crit. 5. Negro art. I. Title.

Negro authors—Juvenile literature.

ROLLINS, Charlemae Hill 928.1
Famous American Negro poets. New York, Dodd, [c.1965] 95p. ports. 22cm. (Famous biogs. for young people) [PS153.N5R6] 65-11811 3.25
1. Negro authors—Juvenile literature. I. Title. BIP

Negro children—Juvenile literature.

ADLER, Bill, comp. 920.073
Black roots; an anthology, edited by Jay David and Catherine J. Greene. With an introd. by Charlemae Rollins. New York, Lothrop, Lee & Shepard Co. [1971] 224 p. 22 cm. Consists of excerpts from individual works.
1. Negro children—Juvenile literature. I. Greene, Catherine J., joint comp. II. Title.

Negro clergy—U.S.—Biography—Dictionaries.

WILLIAMS, Ethel L. 262.140922 B
Biographical directory of Negro ministers, by Ethel L. Williams. New York, Scarecrow Press, 1965. xi, 421 p. 22 cm. Bibliography: p. 407-412. [BR563.N4W5] 65-13562
1. Negro clergy—United States—Biography—Dictionaries. I. Title. BIP

WILLIAMS, Ethel L. 262'.14'0922 B
Biographical directory of Negro ministers, by Ethel L. Williams. 2d ed. Metuchen, N.J., Scarecrow Press, 1970. 605 p. 22 cm. Bibliography: p. 575-580. [BR563.N4W5 1970] 78-18496 ISBN 8-10-803283-
1. Negro clergy—U.S.—Biography—Dictionaries. I. Title.

WILLIAMS, Ethel L. 280'.092'2 B
Biographical directory of Negro ministers / by Ethel L. Williams. 3d ed. Boston : G. K. Hall, 1975. p. cm. Includes index. Bibliography: p. [BR563.N4W5 1975] 74-34109 ISBN 0-8161-1183-9 lib.bdg. : 28.00
1. Negro clergy—United States—Biography—Dictionaries. I. Title.

Negro clergy—United States—Biography.

BODDIE, Charles Emerson. 253'.2'0922 B
God's "bad boys." Valley Forge [Pa.] Judson Press [1972] 125 p. ports. 23 cm. [BR563.N4B64] 72-75360 ISBN 0-8170-0534-X 4.95
1. Negro clergy—United States—Biography. I. Title.

Negro inventors.

BAKER, Henry Edwin, 1859- 608.7'174'960922
The colored inventor [by] Henry E. Baker. New York, Arno Press, 1969. 12 p. ports. 26 cm. (The American Negro, his history and literature.) Reprint of the 1913 ed. [E185.8.B16 1969] 71-75851
1. Negro inventors. 2. Inventions—U.S. I. Title. II. Series.

Negro inventors—Juvenile literature.

HAYDEN, Robert C. 609'.2'2 B
Eight Black American inventors [by] Robert C. Hayden. [Reading, Mass.] Addison-Wesley [1972] 142 p. illus. 21 cm. "An Addisonian press book." Contents.Contents.—Garrett A. Morgan.—Lewis Temple.—Frederick McKinley Jones.—Jan E. Matzeliger.—Lewis H. Latimer.—Elijah McCoy.—Norbert Rillieux.—Granville T. Woods. [E185.8.H35] 920 78-164402 ISBN 0-201-02823-9 4.75
1. Negro inventors—Juvenile literature. I. Title.

Negro minstrels.

FLETCHER, Tom, 1873-1954. 927.8
100 years of the Negro in show business; the Tom Fletcher story. 1st ed. New York, Burdge [1954] 337p. illus. 23cm. [ML3561.N4F5] 55-1843
1. Negro minstrels. 2. Theater—U. S.—Hist. I. Title.

Negro musicians.

FAMOUS Negro music makers; illustrated with photos. New York, Dodd, Mead, 1957. 179p. illus. 22cm. (Famous biographies for young people) v. 12
1. Negro musicians. I. Hughes, Langston, 1902-

HUGHES, Langston, 1902-1967. 927.8
Famous Negro music makers; illustrated with photos. New York, Dodd, Mead, 1955. 179 p. illus. 22 cm. (Famous biographies for young people) [ML3556.H9] 55-9419
1. Negro musicians. I. Title.

RIVELLI, Pauline, comp. 780'.922 B
The Black giants. Edited by Pauline Rivelli and Robert Levin. New York, World Pub. Co. [1970] 126 p. ports. 22 cm. ([Jazz & pop book series]) [ML385.R59] 70-133474 5.95
1. Negro musicians. 2. Jazz musicians. 3. Jazz music. I. Levin, Robert, 1939- joint comp. II. Title.

Negro musicians—Biography.

BLACK music / 784'092'2 B
[editor and designer Gavin Petrie]. London ; New York : Hamlyn, 1974. 128 p. : ill., ports. (some col.) ; 28 cm. [ML385.B635] 75-309707 ISBN 0-600-31343-3 : £1.95
1. Negro musicians—Biography. 2. Negro music—Addresses, essays, lectures. 3.

Music, African—Addresses, essays, lectures. I. Petrie, Gavin.

DOBRIN, Arnold. 784'.092'2 B
Voices of joy, voices of freedom: Ethel Waters, Sammy Davis, Jr., Marian Anderson, Paul Robeson, Lena Horne. New York, Coward, McCann & Geoghegan [1972] 127 p. illus. 24 cm. Bibliography: p. [123] [ML394.D62] 71-189240 ISBN 0-698-20170-1 5.95
1. Negro musicians—Biography. I. Title.

Negro press—U.S.

PENN, Irvine Garland, 1867-1930. 070'.922
The Afro-American press and its editors. New York, Arno Press, 1969. 565 p. illus., ports. 21 cm. (The American Negro, his history and literature) Reprint of the 1891 ed. [PN4888.N4P4 1969] 69-18574
1. Negro press—U.S. 2. Negroes—Biography. I. Title. II. Series. **BIP**

Negro Race—Biography.

FELDMAN, Eugene P Romayn, ed. 920.067
Figures in Negro history, edited by Eugene P. Romayn Feldman. Chicago, Museum of Negro History and Art [1964] 98 p. ports. 22 cm. [DT18.F4] 65-1092
1. Negro race—Biog. I. Title.

ROGERS, Joel Augustus, 1880-1966. 920'.0092'96
World's great men of color, edited with an introd., commentary, and new bibliographical notes by John Henrik Clarke. New York, MacMillan [1972 c.1946-7] 2 v., ports., 22 cm. Includes bibliographies [DT18.R592] 73-186437 8.95 each vol.
1. Negro Race—Biography. I. Title.
Paperback ed. 3.95 each vol. **BIP**

Negro scientists.

HABER, Louis. 509'.22 B
Black pioneers of science and invention. [1st ed.] New York, Harcourt, Brace & World [1970] viii, 181 p. illus., facsims., ports. 24 cm. Bibliography: p. 168-176. [Q141.H2] 77-109090 4.50
1. Negro scientists. 2. Negro inventors. I. Title. **BIP**

HABER, Louis. 509'.22 B
The role of the American Negro in the fields of science. [New York?] 1966. 70 l. 28 cm. "Final report ... project number 6-8353, contract number OEC 1-6-068353-1684 [with the U.S. Office of Education, Curriculum Branch, Division of Elementary and Secondary Education, Bureau of Research]" Bibliography: leaves 67-70. [Q141.H212] 67-62053
1. Negro scientists. 2. Scientists—U.S. I. Title.

Negro sociologists—United States—Congresses.

BLACK sociologists : 301'.0973
historical and contemporary perspectives / edited by James E. Blackwell and Morris Janowitz. Chicago : University of Chicago Press, 1974. xxii, 415 p. ; 21 cm. (The heritage of sociology) Papers based on a National Conference on Black Sociologists, University of Chicago, May 5-6, 1972. Includes bibliographies and index. [HM22.U5B55] 73-84187 ISBN 0-226-05565-5
1. Negro sociologists—United States—Congresses. I. Blackwell, James Edward, 1925- II. Janowitz, Morris. III. National Conference on Black Sociologists, University of Chicago, 1972. **BIP**

Negro teachers— Correspondence, reminscences, etc.

CLARK, Septima (Poinsette) 1898- 923.773
Echo in my soul, by Septima Poinsette Clark with LeGette Blythe. Foreword by Harry Golden. [1st ed.] New York, Dutton, 1962. 243p. illus. 21cm. An autobiography. [E185.97.C59A3] 62-14718
1. Negro teachers— Correspondence, reminscences, etc. I. Blythe, Legette 1900- II. Title.

MORTON, Lena Beatrice. 923.773
My first sixty years: passion for wisdom. New York, Philosophical Library [1965] 175 p. port.22 cm. [LC2731.M6] 65-11951
1. Negro teachers — Correspondence, reminscences, etc. I. Title.

WILLS, Millicent A. 371.1'0092'4
Believe the works, and (memoirs of a traveler and teacher) by Millicent A. Wills. [Ann Arbor, Mich., 1973] ix, 84 p. illus. 24 cm. [LC2731.W54] 72-95824
1. Negro teachers—Correspondence, reminscences, etc. I. Title.

Negroes.

CHERRY, Gwendolyn 920
Portraits in color; the lives of colorful Negro women, by Gwendolyn Cherry, Ruby Thomas, Pauline Willis. New York, Pageant [c.1962] 224p. illus. 21cm. Bibl. 61-18864 4.00
1. Negroes—Biog.—Juvenile literature. 2. Women, Negro—Juvenile literature. I. Title.

CHILD, Lydia Maria (Francis) 1802-1880. 973'.0974'96
The freedmen's book. New York, Arno Press, 1968. vi, 277 p. 21 cm. (The American Negro, his history and literature) Reprint of the 1865 ed. [E185.86.C46 1968] 68-28989
1. Negroes. 2. Negroes—Biography. 3. Freedman. I. Title. II. Series. **BIP**

CHRISTIAN, Malcolm Henry, 1904- 920
My country and I; the interracial experiences of an American Negro. With essays on interracial understanding. New York, Exposition [c.1963] 96p. 22cm. 63-496 3.00
1. Negroes. I. Title.

CHRISTIAN, Malcolm Henry, 1904- 920
My country and I; the interracial experience of an American Negro. With essays on interracial understanding. [1st ed.] New York, Exposition Press [1963] 96 p. 22 cm. [E185.97.C5A3] 63-496
1. Negroes. I. Title.

DANIELS, Jonathan Myrick, 1939-1965. 973.92'0924
The Jon Daniels story, with his letters and papers. Edited, with an introd., by William J. Schneider. New York, Seabury Press [1967] 111 p. 21 cm. [E185.98.D3A4] 67-20940
1. Negroes—Civil rights. I. Schneider, William J., ed. II. Title.

DOBLER, Lavinia G. 920
Pioneers and patriots: the lives of six Negroes of the Revolutionary era [by] Lavinia Dobler, Edgar A. Toppin. Illus. by Colleen Browning. Garden City, N.Y., Doubleday [c.]1965. 118p. illus., facsims., ports. 22cm. (Zenith bks Z6) [E185.96.D6] 65-17241 1.45 pap.,
1. Negroes—Biog.—Juvenile literature. I. Toppin, Edgar Allan, 1928- joint author. II. Title.

GREGORY, Dick 927.92
Nigger, an autobiography, by Dick Gregory with Robert Lipsyte. New York, Pocket Bks. [1965, c.1964] 209p. illus. 18cm. (75091) .75 pap.,
1. Negroes—Civil rights. I. Title.

GREGORY, Dick. 927.92
Nigger; an autobiography by Dick Gregory with Robert Lipsyte. 1st ed. New York, Dutton, 1964. 224 p. illus., ports. 21 cm. [PN2287.G68A3] 64-11067
1. Negroes—Civil rights. I. Title. **BIP**

KING, John Taylor, 1921- 920.073
Famous Negro Americans; stories of twentythree, by John T. King, Marcet H. King. Austin, Tex., Steck Vaughan [1967] v, 120p. 21cm. [E185.96K5] 67-22745 1.65
1. Negroes—Biog.—Juvenile literature. I. King, Marcet H. joint author. II. Title.

LEIPOLD, L. Edmond, 1902- 920
Famous American Negroes, by L. Edmond Leipold. Minneapolis, Denison [1967] 75p. 25cm. (His Famous Amer. heroes and leaders ser.) [E185.96.L4] 67-26344 3.69
1. Negroes—Biog.—Juvenile literature. I. Title.
Contents Omitted.

MOORE, Geraldine (Hamilton) 976.1'98'050924
Behind the ebony mask. [Birmingham, Ala.] Southern University Press, 1961. 220p. illus. 23cm. [F334.B6M57] 62-4060
1. Negroes—Birmingham, Ala. I. Title.

ROBINSON, John Roosevelt, 1919-1972. 796.357'092'4
I never had it made, by Jackie Robinson as told to Alfred Duckett. New York, Putnam [1972] 287 p. 22 cm. [GV865.R6A29 1972] 75-175272 ISBN 0-399-11010-0 7.95
1. Negroes. I. Duckett, Alfred. II. Title. **BIP**

ROBINSON, John Roosevelt, 1919-1972. 796.357'092'4
I never had it made, by Jackie Robinson as told to Alfred Duckett. Greenwich, Conn., Fawcett [1974, c1972] 256 p. 18 cm. (Fawcett world library) [GV865.R6A29 1974] 75-175272 1.25 (pbk.)
1. Negroes. I. Duckett, Alfred. II. Title.

STRATTON, Madeline Robinson 920
Negroes who helped build America. Pref. by Joseph E. Penn. Boston, Ginn [c.1965] ix, 165, [1] p. illus., ports. 24cm. Bibl. [E185.96.S8] 65 2838 2.80
1. Negroes—Biog.—Juvenile literature. I. Title.

STRATTON, Madeline Robinson. 920
Negroes who helped build America. Pref. by Joseph E. Penn. Boston, Ginn [1965] ix, 165, [1] p. illus., ports. 24 cm. Bibliography: p. 164-[166] [E185.96.S8] 65-2838
1. Negroes — Biog. — Juvenile literature. I. Title.

STRINGFELLOW, William. v. 12
My people is the enemy; an autobiographical polemic. [1st ed.] Garden City, N.Y., Doubleday [1966, c1964] 151 p. 19 cm. (Anchor books [498]) 68-27054
1. Negroes—New York (City) 2. Poverty. I. Title.

WASHINGTON, Booker Taliaferro, 1859?-1915. 301.451'96'0924
My larger education; being chapters from my experience. Miami, Fla., Mnemosyne Pub. Inc., 1969. viii, 313 p. illus. 23 cm. Reprint of the 1911 ed. [E185.97.W28 1969] 70-79019
1. Negroes. I. Title.

WHITE, Walter Francis, 1893-1955. 323.4'0924 B
A man called White. New York, Arno Press, 1969. viii, 382 p. port. 23 cm. (The American Negro, his history and literature) Reprint of the 1948 ed. [E185.97.W6A3 1969] 69-18561
1. Negroes. I. Title. II. Series. **BIP**

WHITE, Walter Francis, 1893-1955. 323'.4'0924 B
A man called White; the autobiography of Walter White. Bloomington, Indiana University Press [1970, c1948] viii, 382 p. port. 20 cm. (A Midland book, MB135) [E185.97.W6A3 1970] 76-108216 3.25
1. Negroes. I. Title. **BIP**

Negroes—Addresses, essays, lectures.

CLEAVER, Eldridge, 1935- 301.451'96'073
Eldridge Cleaver: post-prison writings and speeches. Edited and with an appraisal by Robert Scheer. New York, Random House [1969] xxxiii, 211 p. 22 cm. [E185.615.C63] 77-76279 5.95
1. Negroes—Addresses, essays, lectures. I. Scheer, Robert, ed.

DU BOIS, William Edward Burghardt, 1868-1963. 370'.924 B
A W. E. B. Du Bois reader. Edited by Andrew G. Paschal. Introd. by Arna Bontemps. New York, Macmillan [1971] xxix, 376 p. 21 cm. Bibliography: p. [371]-376. [E185.97.D73A25 1971] 70-150672
1. Negroes—Addresses, essays, lectures. 2. Africa—Addresses, essays, lectures. I. Title.

Negroes—Albany.

JOHNSON, William Henry, 1833-1901. 917.47'43'097496 B
Autobiography of Dr. William Henry Johnson, respectfully dedicated to his adopted home, the capital city of the Empire State. New York, Haskell House, 1970. 295 p. illus., ports. 24 cm. Reprint of the 1900 ed. [E185.97.J7 1970] 72-129569
1. Negroes—Albany.

Negroes—Arkansas.

RICHARDS, Eugene. 309.2'63'09767
Few comforts or surprises: the Arkansas Delta. Cambridge, Mass., MIT Press [1973] 123 p. 24 x 29 cm. [E185.93.A8R5] 72-8704 ISBN 0-262-18062-6 9.95
1. Negroes—Arkansas. 2. Rural poor—Arkansas. I. Title. II. Title: Arkansas Delta. **BIP**

Negroes as businessmen.

SEDER, John. 338.0922
Getting it together; Black businessmen in America [by] John Seder and Berkeley G. Burrell. [1st ed.] New York, Harcourt Brace Jovanovich [1971] xvii, 233 p. illus., ports. 22 cm. [E185.8.S43] 70-142096 ISBN 0-15-135275-5 6.95
1. Negroes as businessmen. 2. Negroes—Biography. I. Burrell, Berkeley G., joint author. II. Title. **BIP**

Negroes—Atlanta.

CARTER, Edward R. 301.451'96073'0758231
The Black side. Freeport, N.Y., Books for Libraries Press, 1971. ix, 323 p. illus. 23 cm. (The Black heritage library collection) Reprint of the 1894 ed. [F294.A8C17 1971] 78-170692 ISBN 0-8369-8882-5
1. Negroes—Atlanta. I. Title. II. Series.

Negroes Bibliography.

ROBINSON, Wilhelmena S. 920'.009'17496
Historical Negro biographies, by Wilhelmena S. Robinson. [2d ed., rev.] New York, Publishers Co. [1969] xii, 291 p. illus. ports. 29 cm. (International library of Negro life and history) "Under the auspices of the Association for the Study of Negro Life and History." Bibliography: p. 271-281. [E185.96.R56 1969] 78-6620
1. Negroes—Bibliography. 2. Negro race—Biography. I. Title. II. Series.

Negroes—Biographies—Juvenile literature.

HUGHES, Langston, 1902- 920.932526
Famous Negro heroes of America. Illustrated by Gerald McCann. New York, Dodd, Mead, 1958. 202 p. illus. 22 cm. (Famous biographies for young people) [E185.96.H82] 58-9293
1. Negroes—Biographies—Juvenile literature. I. Title. **BIP**

Negroes—Biography.

*ABDUL, Raoul 927
Famous Black entertainers of today by Raoul Abdul. New York Dodd, Mead 1974 159 p. illus. 22 cm. [E185] 73-7096 ISBN 0-396-06849-9 4.50
1. Negroes—Biography. I. Title. **BIP**

ADAMS, Russell L. 920.06
Great Negroes, past and present. Illus. by Eugene Winslow. David P. Ross, Jr., ed. Chicago 80, Afro-Am Pub., Main Post Office [1964, c.1963] x, 182p. illus. (pt. col.) maps (pt. col.) ports. (pt. col.) 29cm. Bibl. 64-805 4.95
1. Negroes—Biog. 2. Negroes in Africa—Biog. I. Title.

ADLER, Bill, comp. 973'.0992
Black defiance; Black profiles in courage. Edited by Jay David. New York, Morrow, 1972. 240 p. 22 cm. Contents.Contents.—From Richard Allen, by M. M. Mathews.—From Anti-slavery leaders of North Carolina, by J. S. Bassett.—From the book of life; or, Narrative of Sojourner Truth, edited by O. Gilbert.—From The slave narrative of William Wells Brown.—From I bring you General Tubman, by E. Conrad.—From Bursting bonds, by W. Pickens.—We wear the mask, by P. L. Dunbar.—From Daniel Hale Williams: Negro surgeon, by H. Buckler.—From A northern Negro's autobiography, by F. B. Williams.—From A Negro and a mob.—From 13 against the odds, by E. R. Embree.—From Communist councilman from Harlem, by B. J. Davis.—You go South, by T. Poston.—From The hard kind of courage, by J. Baldwin.—From The challenge to Negro leadership, by J. Mayfield.—From Boycott in Philadelphia, by H. Lees.—Portrait of three heroes, by T. Dent.—On Eldridge Cleaver, by K. Cleaver.—From I remember papa, by H. Dolan.—FOBlack defiance; Black profiles in courage. Edited by Jay David. New York, Morrow, 1972. 240 p. 22 cm. Contents.Contents.—From Richard Allen, by M. M. Mathews.—From Anti-slavery leaders of North Carolina
1. Negroes—Biography. I. Title.

ADLER, Bill, comp. 301.5'92
Growing up black. New York, Morrow, 1968. 256 p. 22 cm. [E185.96.D283] 68-26436 6.50
1. Negroes—Biography. I. Title.

ADLER, Bill, comp. 920.073
Living Black in white America. Edited by Jay David and Elaine Crane. With a foreword by David L. Lewis. New York, Morrow, 1971. 317 p. 22 cm. Contents.Contents.—From On being Negro in America, by S. Redding.—From Along this way, by J. W. Johnson.—From Yes I can, by S. Davis, Jr.—From Notes of a native son, by J. Baldwin.—From The life of Olaudah Equiano; or, Gustavus Vassa, written by himself.—From Fifty years in chains; or, The life of an American slave, by C. Ball.—From Behind the scenes, by E. Keckley.—From The life and adventures of Nat Love, by N. Love.—From Blackthink, by J. Owens.—From A Colored woman in a white world, by M. C. Terrell.—From Lady sings the blues, by B. Holiday.—From The big sea, by L. Hughes.—From The third door, by E. Tarry.—From Nat Turner's Confession, by N. Turner.—From The life and times of Frederick Douglass, by F. Douglass.—From Stride toward freedom, by M. L. King, Jr.—From Coming of age in Mississippi, by A. Moody.—From The long shadow of LOLiving Black in white America. Edited by Jay David and Elaine Crane. With a foreword by David L. Lewis. New York, Morrow, 1971. 317 p. 22 cm. Contents.Contents.—From On being Negro in America, by S. Redding.—From Along this
1. Negroes—Biography. I. Crane, Elaine, joint comp. II. Title. BIP

ALEXANDER, Rae Pace, comp. 920'.073
Young and Black in America. Introductory notes by Julius Lester. New York, Random House [1973, c1970] 137 p. ports. 21 cm. (A Vintage sundial book, VS-4) Contents.Contents.—Teaching myself to read and write, by F. Douglass.—Apprentice, by R. Wright.—How my mother died, by D. Bates.—Turning point, by Malcolm X.—I was a teen-age warlord, by J. Brown.—Sitting and hiding out, by A. Moody.—The revolt of the Black athlete, by H. Edwards.—G.I. in Vietnam, by D. Parks.—Bibliography: p. [138] [E185.96.A5 1973] 920 72-3160 ISBN 0-394-70804-0 1.50
1. Negroes—Biography. I. Title. BIP

ALLEN, Harold C. 920.073
Great Black Americans [by] Harold C. Allen. West Haven, Conn., Pendulum Press [1971] 126 p. ports. 18 cm. (Now age books) [E185.96.A52] 73-24542 0.75
1. Negroes—Biography. I. Title. BIP

BARDOLPH, Richard, 1915- 325.2670973
The Negro vanguard. New York, Rinehart [1959] 388 p. 24 cm. Includes bibliography. [E185.96.B28] 59-6571
1. Negroes—Biography. 2. Negroes—History. I. Title. BIP

BARDOLPH, Richard, 1915- 325.2670973
The Negro vanguard. New York, Rinehart [1959] 388 p. 24 cm. Includes bibliography. [E185.96.B28] 59-6571
1. Negroes—Biography. 2. Negroes—History. I. Title. BIP

BARDOLPH, Richard, 1915- 917.3'06'96073 B
The Negro vanguard. Westport, Conn., Negro Universities Press [1971, c1959] 388 p. 24 cm. "Essay on authorities": p. 343-369. [E185.B267 1971] 77-135592 ISBN 0-8371-5183-X
1. Negroes—Biography. 2. Negroes—History.

BASKIN, Wade. 917.3'06'96003
Dictionary of Black culture, by Wade Baskin and Richard N. Runes. New York, Philosophical Library [1973] 493 p. 22 cm. [E185.96.B33] 72-78162 ISBN 0-8022-2090-8 15.00
1. Negroes—Biography. 2. Negroes—Dictionaries. I. Runes, Richard N., joint author. II. Title.

BENNETT, Lerone, 1928- 323.4'0922
Pioneers in protest, by Lerone Bennett, Jr. [1st ed.] Chicago, Johnson Pub. Co., 1968. 267 p. ports. 24 cm. [E185.96.B4] 68-55366 5.95
1. Negroes—Biography. 2. Abolitionists. I. Title. BIP

BONING, Richard A. 920.073
Profiles of Black Americans, by Richard A. Boning. Illustrated by Joseph Forte. [Rockville Centre, N.Y., Dexter and Westbrook, 1969- Cases (col. ports.) 27 cm. Title from case. [E185.96.B57] 73-90005
1. Negroes—Biography. I. Forte, Joseph, illus. II. Title.

BROUDY, Eric. 973'.0974'96 B
They had a dream; true stories about Blacks in America and their achievements [by] Eric Broudy, Warren Halliburton [and] Laurence Swinburne. New York, Pyramid Books [1969] 124 p. 18 cm. (A Pyramid hi-lo original, H-706) [E185.96.B7] 74-7398 0.60
1. Negroes—Biography. I. Halliburton, Warren, joint author. II. Swinburne, Laurence, joint author. III. Title.

BROWN, William Wells, 1815-1884. 970'.00974'96
The Black man. New York, Arno Press, 1969. 288 p. 23 cm. (The Anti-slavery crusade in America) Reprint of the 1863 ed. "Memoir of the author": p. 11-30. [E185.96.B863 1969c] 77-82179
1. Negroes—Biography. I. Title. II. Series.

BROWN, William Wells, 1815-1884. 970'.00974'96
The black man; his antecedents, his genius, and his achievements. 4th ed. Miami, Fla., Mnemosyne Pub. Inc., 1969. 312 p. 23 cm. Reprint of the 1865 ed. "Memoir of the author": p. 11-30. [E185.96.B863 1969] 76-79018
1. Negroes—Biography. I. Title. BIP

BROWN, William Wells, 1815-1884. 970'.00974'96
The Black man: his antecedents, his genius, and his achievements. Boston, J. Redpath, 1863. New York, Kraus Reprint Co., 1969. 312 p. front. 24 cm. "Memoir of the author": p. 11-30. [E185.96.B863 1969b] 71-12418
1. Negroes—Biography. I. Title. BIP

BRYANT, Lawrence Chesterfield. 328.757'0922
Negro lawmakers in the South Carolina Legislature, 1869-1902. Lawrence C. Bryant, editor. Orangeburg, School of Graduate Studies, South Carolina State College [1968] iii, 142 p. 28 cm. Bibliographical footnotes. [E185.93.S7B75] 68-65585
1. Negroes—Biog. 2. Legislators—South Carolina. 3. South Carolina—Pol. & govt.—1865-1950. I. South Carolina. State College, Orangeburg. School of Graduate Studies. II. Title. BIP

BULLOCK, Ralph W. 920
In spite of handicaps; brief biographical sketches with discussion outlines of outstanding Negroes now living who are achieving distinction in various lines of endeavor [by] Ralph W. Bullock. With a foreword by Channing H. Tobias. Freeport, N.Y., Books for Libraries Press [1968] x, 140 p. ports. 23 cm. (Essay index reprint series) Reprint of the 1927 ed. Bibliography: p. 131-140. [E185.96.B93 1968] 68-25602
1. Negroes—Biography. I. Title. BIP

CHRISTMAS, Walter, ed. 920.073
Negroes in public affairs and government. Contributors: Clifford A. Bradshaw [and others] Photographic editor: Roland Mitchell. Pref.: Alfred E. Cain. [1st ed.] Yonkers [N.Y.] Educational Heritage [1966- v. illus., ports. 29 cm. (Negro heritage library) Bibliography: v. 1, p. 342-345. [E185.96.C47] 67-31903
1. Negroes—Biography. 2. United States—Officials and employees—Biography. I. Title. II. Series.

DANNETT, Sylvia G L 1909- 920.7
Profiles of Negro womanhood, by Sylvia G. L. Dannett. Illus.: Horace Varela. Roll of honor ports.: Tom Feelings, [1st ed.] Yonkers, N.Y., Educational Heritage [1964- v. illus., facsims., ports. 29 cm. (Negro heritage library) Contents.V. 1. 1619-1900. Bibliography: v. 1. p. 339-345. [E185.96.D25] 64-25018
1. Negroes — Biog. 2. Women in the U.S. — Biog. I. Title.

DAVID, Jay. comp. 920.073
Growing up black. New York, Morrow, 1968. 256p. 22cm. [E185.96.D283] 68-26436 6.50
1. Negroes—Biog. I. Title. BIP

DROTNING, Phillip T. 920.073
Up from the ghetto, by Phillip T. Drotning and Wesley W. South. [1st ed.] New York, Cowles Book Co. [1970] xii, 207 p. ports. 22 cm. Stories of fourteen blacks who determined to escape from the ghetto and succeeded. [E185.96.D7 1970] 920 70-90066 5.95
1. Negroes—Biography. I. South, Wesley W., joint author. II. Title. BIP

EDMONDS, Helen G. 320.9'73'09 B
Black faces in high places; Negroes in government, by Helen G. Edmonds. New York, Harcourt Brace Jovanovich [1971] vi, 277 p. illus. 22 cm. [E185.96.E3] 77-30068 ISBN 0-15-371073-X
1. Negroes—Biography. I. Title.

EMBREE, Edwin Rogers, 1883-1950. 920.073
13 against the odds. Port Washington, N.Y., Kennikat Press [1968, c1944] 261 p. ports. 23 cm. (Kennikat Press series in Negro culture and history) Contents.Contents.—Mary McLeod Bethune, Amazon of God.—Richard Wright, native son.—Charles S. Johnson, a scholar and a gentleman.—Walter White, little David.—George Washington Carver, sweet potato wizard.—Langston Hughes, Shakespeare in Harlem.—Marian Anderson, deep river of song.—W. E. B., Du Bois, elder statesman.—Mordecai W. Johnson, lord high chancellor.—William Grant Still, music maker.—A Philip Randolph, Saint Philip of the Pullman porters.—Joe Louis, champion of the world.—Paul Robeson, voice of freedom. [E185.96.E4 1968] 68-25201
1. Negroes—Biography. I. Title.

FAX, Elton C. 301.451'96'073
Contemporary Black leaders [by] Elton C. Fax. New York, Dodd, Mead [1970] x, 243 p. ports. 22 cm. [E185.96.F38] 79-134322 4.95
1. Negroes—Biography. I. Title. BIP

FLYNN, James J. 920.009174'96
Negroes of achievement in modern America, by James J. Flynn. Introd. by Roy E. Wilkins. New York, Dodd, Mead [1970] 272 p. ports. 22 cm. Bibliography: p. [267]-268. [E185.96.F55] 70-111911 4.50
1. Negroes—Biography. I. Title.

GOODSON, James A. 301.45'1'96073 B
The current Black man: decade '70 [by James A. Goodson Jr.] 1st ed. Los Angeles, Record Pub. Co. [1971- v. ports. 28 cm. [E185.96.G66] 72-200271
1. Negroes—Biography. I. Title.

HASKINS, James, 1941- 301.45'19'6073022 B
Profiles in Black power. [1st ed.] Garden City, N.Y., Doubleday, 1972. 259 p. 22 cm. Contents.Contents.—Introduction.—Black power.—A chronology.—A short history of Black power.—Adam Clayton Powell, Jr.—The Reverend Albert B. Cleage.—Floyd McKissick.—Dr. Nathan Wright, Jr.—Malcolm X.—James Forman.—Eldridge Cleaver.—Huey P. Newton.—Stokely Carmichael.—Ron Ndabezitha Everett-Karenga.—H. Rap Brown.—Glossary.—Bibliography (p. [253]-259) [E185.96.H36] 74-157598 3.95
1. Negroes—Biography. 2. Black power—United States. I. Title.

JENNESS, Mary, d.1947. 920.073
Twelve Negro Americans. Freeport, N.Y., Books for Libraries Press [1969] x, 180 p. 23 cm. (Essay index reprint series) Reprint of the 1936 ed. Contents.Contents.—Better farms for better farmers; Thomas Monroe Campbell.—For the one-room cabin schools; Matilda Moseley Booker.—A city pastor; William Lloyd Imes.—A social worker for blind Americans; Lillian S. Proctor.—A Negro cooperative makes good; Lewis E. Anthony.—Making bricks without straw; Mary E. Branch.—A home-made school in the Deep South; Laurence Clifton Jones.—Young Negro leaders of Americans; Martin L. Harvey, Juanita E. Jackson, Esther Brown.—A leader of students; Howard Thurman.—Her unfinished task; Juliette Derricotte. Bibliographical footnotes. [E185.96.J46 1969] 74-86764
1. Negroes—Biography. I. Title. BIP

KAPLAN, Sidney, 1913- 973.3'092'2 B
The Black presence in the era of the American Revolution, 1770-1800. [Greenwich, Conn.] New York Graphic Society, 1973. xii, 241 p. illus., facsims., ports. 29 cm. Illustrations selected from the exhibition The Black presence in the era of the American Revolution, 1770-1800, held at the National Portrait Gallery, July 1973. [E185.96.K36 1973] 73-79335 ISBN 0-8212-0541-2 15.00
1. Negroes—Biography. 2. United States—History—Revolution, 1775-1783—Negroes. I. Title. BIP

KEEGAN, Frank L. 322'.4'0922 B
Blacktown, U.S.A., by Frank L. Keegan. [1st ed.] Boston, Little, Brown [1971] xiii, 430 p. illus., ports. 22 cm. Bibliography: p. 429-430. [E185.96.K43 1971] 70-149472 8.95
1. Negroes—Biography. 2. Negroes—Race identity. I. Title.

LARRIE, Reginald, 1928- 917.3'06'96073
Corners of Black history. [1st ed.] New York, Vantage Press [1971] 69 p. illus. 21 cm. Bibliography: p. 64-66. [E185.96.L28] 70-30598 3.75
1. Negroes—Biography. I. Title.

LOTZ, Philip Henry, 1889- ed. 301.451'96073'0922 B
Rising above color. Freeport, N.Y., Books for Libraries Press [1972, c1943] viii, 112 p. 23 cm. (Essay index reprint series) Original ed. issued as vol. 5 of Creative personalities series. Contents.Contents.—George Washington Carver, man with a magic wand, by F. G. Lankard.—Marian Anderson, singer, by H. B. Hunting.—W. E. B. DuBois, scholar and fighter, by H. B. Hunting.—Robert Russa Moton, co-operator and educator, by G. B. Hunting.—Samuel Coleridge-Taylor, musician, by F. W. Clelland.—Richard Allen, first Negro bishop, by M. E. Moxcey.—Frederick Douglass, orator, by M. E. Moxcey.—Daniel Hale Williams, surgeon, by M. E. Moxcey.—Booker T.

Washington, "Up from slavery", by F. G. Lankard.—Roland Hayes, world-renowned tenor, by F. G. Lankard.—Paul Laurence Dunbar, poet, by F. G. Lankard.—James Weldon Johnson, poet and diplomat by L. Desjardins.—Walter White, crusader for justice, by R. Wilkins. Includes bibliographies. [E185.96.L68 1972] 78-152190 ISBN 0-8369-2605-6
1. Negroes—Biography. I. Title. **BIP**

MAJOR, Geraldyn Hodges, 929'.373
1894-
Black society / Geraldyn Hodges Major, Doris E. Saunders. Chicago : Johnson Pub. Co., 1976. p. cm. [E185.96.M22] 75-39546 ISBN 0-87485-075-4 : 16.95
1. Negroes—Biography. 2. Negroes—Genealogy. 3. Upper classes—United States. I. Saunders, Doris E., joint author. II. Title. **BIP**

METCALF, George R., 323.4'0922
1914-
Black profiles, by George R. Metcalf. Expanded ed. New York, McGraw-Hill [1970] ix, 405 p. 22 cm. Includes bibliographical references. [E185.96.M48 1970] 75-121664
1. Negroes—Biography. I. Title.

METCALF, George R., 323.4'0922 B
1914-
Black profiles, by George R. Metcalf. New York, McGraw-Hill [1971, c1970] viii, 229 p. 21 cm. (McGraw-Hill paperbacks) Contents.Contents.—Martin Luther King, Jr.—William E. B. Du Bois.—Harriet Tubman.—Medgar Wiley Evers.—Whitney Moore Young, Jr.—Malcolm X.—Eldridge Cleaver.—A note on sources (p. 227-229) Includes bibliographical references [E185.96.M48 1971] 70-31607 ISBN 0-07-041663-X 2.95
1. Negroes—Biography. I. Title.

METCALF, George R., 323.4'0922
1914-
Black profiles, by George R. Metcalf. [1st ed.] New York, McGraw-Hill [1968] x, 341 p. 21 cm. Contents.Contents.—Martin Luther King, Jr.—William E. B. Du Bois.—Roy Wilkins.—Thurgood Marshall.—Jackie Robinson.—Harriet Tubman.—Medger Wiley Evers.—James H. Meredith.—Rosa Parks.—Edward W. Brooke.—Whitney Moore Young, Jr. Bibliographical references included in "A note on sources" (p. 337-340) [E185.96.M48] 68-30977
1. Negroes—Biography. I. Title.

METCALF, George 301.451'96'073
R., 1914-
Up from within; today's new Black leaders, by George R. Metcalf. [1st ed.] New York, McGraw-Hill [1971] xvi, 302 p. 22 cm. Contents.Contents.—John Conyers, Jr.—Kenneth Allen Gibson.—Clifton Reginald Wharton, Jr.—Shirley Chisholm.—Horace Julian Bond.—John Mackey.—Alvin F. Poussaint.—Andrew F. Brimmer. Includes bibliographical references. [E185.96.M483] 77-167558 ISBN 0-07-041661-3 7.95
1. Negroes—Biography. I. Title.

MILLER, Basil William, 326.92
1897-
Ten slaves who became famous. Grand Rapids, Zondervan Pub. House [1951] 71 p. illus. 29 cm. [E444.M66] 51-14997
1. Negroes — Biog. I. Title.

MOTT, Abigail 917.3'06'96073
(Field) 1766-1851, comp.
Narratives of colored Americans, by Lindley Murray. Compiled by Alexander [sic] Mott and M. S. Wood. Freeport, N.Y., Books for Libraries Press, 1971. iv, 276 p. 23 cm. (The Black heritage library collection) Reprint of the 1877 collection by A. Mott and M. S. Wood, published originally with funds from the estate of Lindley Murray. [E185.96.M92 1971] 70-170702 ISBN 0-8369-8892-2
1. Negroes—Biography. I. Murray, Lindley, 1745-1826. Narratives of colored Americans. II. Wood, M. S., joint comp. III. Title. IV. Series.

OVINGTON, Mary 301.451'96073'0922
White, 1865-1951.
Portraits in color. Freeport, N.Y., Books for Libraries Press [1971, c1927] x, 241 p. 23 cm. (Essay index reprint series) Contents.Contents.—James Weldon Johnson.—Marcus Garvey.—Max Yergan.—Mordecai W. Johnson.—Lucy Laney.—Robert Russa Moton.—W. E. Burghardt Du Bois.—Scipio Africanus Jones.—Walter White.—Robert S. Abbott.—Maggie Lena Walker.—Eugene Kinckle Jones.—Louis Tompkins Wright.—Ernest Everett Just.—George Washington Carver.—Janie Porter Barrett.—Langston Hughes.—Paul Robeson.—Meta Vaux Warrick Fuller.—Roland Hayes. [E185.96.O96 1971] 77-37121 ISBN 0-8369-2516-5
1. Negroes—Biography. I. Title. **BIP**

PARKS, Gordon, 301.451'96'073
1912-
Born Black. With photos. by the author. [1st ed.] Philadelphia, Lippincott [1971] 192 p. illus. 24 cm. [E185.96.P36] 78-146692 7.95
1. Negroes—Biography. I. Title. **BIP**

PETERSON, Frank Loris. 920
Climbing high mountains. Illustrated by Harry Baerg. Washington, Review and Herald Pub. Association [1962] 144 p. illus. 22 cm. [E185.96.P4] 62-14169
1. Negroes—Biog. I. Title.

RICHARDSON, Ben 325.260973
Albert.
Great American Negroes; rev. by William A. Fahey, illustrated by Robert Hallock. New York, Crowell [1956] 339 p. illus. 21 cm. Second rev. ed. published in 1976 under title: Great Black Americans. [E185.96.R5 1956] 56-9803
1. Negroes—Biography. I. Title.

RICHARDSON, Ben Albert. 920'.073
Great Black Americans = (formerly titled Great American Negroes) / by Ben Richardson and William A. Fahey. 2d rev. ed. New York : Crowell, [1976] p. cm. [E185.96.R5 1976] 75-12841 ISBN 0-690-00994-1
1. Negroes—Biography. I. Fahey, William A. II. Title.

ROBINSON, 920.009'174'96
Wilhelmena S.
Historical Negro biographies, by Wilhelmena S. Robinson. [2d ed.] New York, Publishers Co. [1968] xii, 291 p. illus. 28 cm. (International library of Negro life and history) Published under the auspices of the Association for the Study of Negro Life and History. Bibliography: p. 271-281. [E185.96.R56 1968] 68-2920
1. Negroes—Biography. I. Title. II. Series.

ROBINSON, 920.009'174'96
Wilhelmena S.
Historical Negro biographies, by Wilhelmena S. Robinson. [1st ed.] New York, Publishers Co. [1967] xii, 291 p. ports. 29 cm. (International library of Negro life and history) Published under the auspices of the Association for the Study of Negro Life and History. Bibliography: p. 271-281. [DT18.R57] 67-7209
1. Negroes—Biography. 2. Negro race—Biography. I. Title. II. Series.

ROLLINS, Charlemae Hill. 920.073
They showed the way; forty American Negro leaders. New York, Crowell [1964] 165 p. 21 cm. [E185.96.R6] 64-20692
1. Negroes—Biography. I. Title. **BIP**

SIMMONS, William J., 920'.073
1849-
Men of mark; eminent, progressive, and rising. Chicago, Johnson Pub. Co., 1970 [c1887] xix, 829 p. ports. 24 cm. (Ebony classics) [E185.96.S45 1970] 78-102983 12.50
1. Negroes—Biography. I. Title.

SIMMONS, William J., 920'.073
1849-
Men of mark; eminent, progressive and rising [by] William J. Simmons. New York, Arno Press, 1968. 1141 p. ports. 23 cm. (The American Negro, his history and literature) Reprint of the 1887 ed. [E185.96.S45 1968] 68-29017
1. Negroes—Biography. I. Title. II. Series.

SOCIOLOGICAL 301.15'5097
Resources for the Social Studies.
Leadership in American society; a case study of Black leadership. Boston, Allyn and Bacon [1969] vii, 68 p. illus., ports. 23 cm. (Episodes in social inquiry series) Includes bibliographical references. [E185.96.S67] 73-101059
1. Negroes—Biography. 2. Leadership. I. Title.

STERNE, Emma (Gelders) 323.40922
1894-
I have a dream. Illustrated by Tracy Sugarman. New York, Knopf [1965] x, 229, iv p. illus. 22 cm. Contents.Contents.—Lift every voice and sing. Marian Anderson.—For life, liberty, and the pursuit of jobs: Asa Phillip Randolph.—Freedom on the seas: Hugh Muizac.—Hammer of justice: Thurgood Marshall.—Tired feet and rested hearts: Rosa Lee Parks.—At the point of the bayonet: Daisy Bates.—When freedom is a cup of coffe: James Farmer.—The man with the bulletproof soul: Fred Shuttlesworth.—We shall overcome: John Lewis.—One day out of a long tomorrow. Bibliography: p. [i]-iv (3d group) [E185.96.S79] 65-12076
1. Negroes—Biography. 2. Negroes—Civil rights. I. Title. **BIP**

TURNER, Morrie. 301.45'19'6073 B
Famous Black Americans, by Morrie and Letha Turner. Valley Forge [Pa.] Judson Press [1973] 1 v. (unpaged) illus. 15 cm. Contents.Contents.—Crispus Attucks.—Benjamin Banneker.—Jean Baptiste Pointe de Sable.—Sojourner Truth.—Frederick A. Douglass.—Ira Aldridge.—Hiram Revels.—Matthew A. Henson.—William Edward Burghart Du Bois.—Bill Pickett.—George Washington Carver.—Mary McLeod Bethune.—Dr. Charles Drew.—W. C. Handy.—Langston Hughes. [E185.96.T87 1973] 920 72-11224 ISBN 0-8170-0591-9 0.95 (pbk.)
1. Negroes—Biography. I. Turner, Letha, joint author. II. Title. **BIP**

WHO'S who of the 920'.0092'96073
colored race : a general biographical dictionary of men and women of African descent / edited by Frank Lincoln Mather. Volume 1. Detroit : Gale Research Co., [1975] c1915. p. cm. No more published. Reprint of the ed. published in Chicago. [E185.96.W6 1975] 79-178669 ISBN 0-8103-4247-2 : 18.00
1. Negroes—Biography. I. Mather, Frank Lincoln.

WILEY, Joseph Harold. 920.073
From nowhere to somewhere [by] Jos. Harold Wiley, Kenneth Jeffries [and] Charles T. Brooker. [1st ed.] Philadelphia, Chilton Book Co. [1970] 132 p. 21 cm. (American society series) [E185.96.W57 1970] 71-123893
1. Negroes—Biography. 2. Negroes—Social conditions—To 1964. I. Jeffries, Kenneth. II. Brooker, Charles T. III. Title.

Negroes—Biography—Bibliography.

BELL, Barbara L. 016.92'0073
Black biographical sources: an annotated bibliography [by] Barbara L. Bell. New Haven, Yale University Library, 1970. 20 p. 28 cm. (Yale University Library. Bibliography series no. 1) [Z1361.N39B46] 70-130440 2.00
1. Negroes—Biography—Bibliography. I. Title. II. Series.

BRIGNANO, 016.9173'06'96073022 B
Russell Carl.
Black Americans in autobiography; an annotated bibliography of autobiographies and autobiographical books written since the Civil War [by] Russell C. Brignano. Durham, N.C., Duke University Press, 1974. ix, 118 p. 25 cm. [Z1361.N39B67] 73-92535 5.75
1. Negroes—Biography—Bibliography. 2. Slavery in the United States—Personal narratives—Bibliography. I. Title. **BIP**

Negroes—Biography—Juvenile literature.

ACHIEVEMENTS of Black 920.073 B
Americans. Wilkinsburg, Pa., Hayes School Pub. Co. [1969] 24 p. illus., ports. 28 cm. Cover title. "No. SS417." Bibliography: p. 24. Briefly summarizes the achievements and contributions of black Americans in many fields including exploration, medicine, politics, entertainment, science, and sports. [E185.96.A2] 920 76-22290 1.00
1. Negroes—Biography—Juvenile literature.

ADAMS, Russell L. 920
Great Negroes, past and present, by Russell L. Adams. Illustrated by Eugene Winslow. Edited by David P. Ross, Jr. 3d ed. Chicago, Afro-Am Pub. Co., 1969. ix, 212 p. illus. (part col.), maps (part col.), ports. (part col.) 29 cm. Bibliography: p. 207-208. Brief one- or two-page biographies of important Negroes from ancient to modern times and from many professions including science, education, art, music, and religion. [E185.96.A4 1969] 72-87924
1. Negroes—Biography—Juvenile literature. 2. Negroes in Africa—Biography—Juvenile literature. I. Winslow, Eugene, illus. II. Title. **BIP**

ALEXANDER, Rae Pace, 920.073
comp.
Young and Black in America. Introductory notes by Julius Lester. New York, Random House [1970] 139 p. ports. 22 cm. Contents.Contents.—Teaching myself to read and write, by F. Douglass.—Apprentice, by R. Wright.—How my mother died, by D. Bates.—Turning point, by Malcolm X.—I was a teen-age warlord, by J. Brown.—Sitting in and hiding out, by A. Moody.—The revolt of the Black athlete, by H. Edwards.—G.I. in Vietnam, by D. Parks.—Bibliography (p. 139) [E185.96.A5] 920 70-117005 ISBN 0-394-90482-6
1. Negroes—Biography—Juvenile literature. I. Title.

ANDERSON, 917.8'06'96073 B
LaVere.
Saddles and sabers: Black men in the Old West. Illustrated by Herman Vestal. Champaign, Ill., Garrard Pub. Co. [1975] 128 p. illus. 22 cm. (Toward freedom series) Brief biographies of black cowboys, lawmen, and cavalry soldiers who helped settle the West during the latter half of the nineteenth century. [E185.925.A65] 920 74-18122 ISBN 0-8116-4805-2 3.48 (lib. bdg.)
1. Negroes—Biography—Juvenile literature. 2. Negroes—The West—Juvenile literature. 3. The West—Biography—Juvenile literature. I. Vestal, Herman B., illus. II. Title. III. Series.

BRIMBERG, 917.3'06'96073 B
Stanlee.
Black stars. New York, Dodd, Mead [1974] 159 p. ports. 22 cm. Profiles of twelve black people—a poet, scientist, athlete, cowboy, militant, civil rights worker, and others—representative of the black struggle for freedom and self-identity. [E185.96.B83] 920 73-17868 ISBN 0-396-06914-2 3.95
1. Negroes—Biography—Juvenile literature. I. Title. **BIP**

BROWN, Vashti. 920 (J)
Proudly we hail [by] Vashti Brown [and] Jack Brown. With illus. by Don Miller. Boston, Houghton Mifflin [1968] x, 118 p. illus. 24 cm. [E185.96.B85] 68-4017
1. Negroes—Biography.—Juvenile literature. I. Brown, Jack, 1905- joint author. II. Title.

BRUNER, Richard. 320.9'73
Black politicians. New York, McKay [1971] 119 p. 21 cm. Contents.Contents.—Julian Bond: politics is the only game in town.—Richard Hatcher: the importance of being organized.—Kenneth A. Gibson: creating opportunities.—Shirley Chisholm: a fighter.—Carl B. Stokes: using the system.—John Conyers, Jr.: working against the odds. [E185.96.B9] 79-144020 4.00
1. Negroes—Biography—Juvenile literature. 2. Statesmen—United States—Juvenile literature. I. Title.

BURT, Olive (Woolley) 1894- 978
Negroes in the early West, by Olive W. Burt. Illustrated by Lorence F. Bjorklund. New York, Messner [1969] 96 p. illus. 22 cm. Bibliography: p. 91-92. Brief biographies of thirteen Negro men and two women who were among the first explorers, trappers, soldiers, businessmen, cowboys, and settlers in the "early West." [E185.96.B96] 920 74-81390 3.95

1. Negroes—Biography—Juvenile literature. I. Bjorklund, Lorence F., illus. II. Title. BIP

CHERRY, Gwendolyn 920
Portraits in color; the lives of colorful Negro women, by Gwendolyn Cherry, Ruby Thomas, Pauline Willis. New York, Pageant [c.1962] 224p. illus. 21cm. Bibl. 61-18864 4.00
1. Negroes—Biog.—Juvenile literature. 2. Women, Negro—Juvenile literature. I. Title.

DERRICOTTE, Elise Palmer. 973'.04'96073 B
Word pictures of great Negroes / by Elise Palmer Derricotte, Geneva Calcier Turner, Jessie Hailstalk Roy ; illustrated by Lois Mailou Jones. Washington : Associated Publishers, c1964. xiii, 313 p. : ill. ; 22 cm. Rev. and expanded version of the author's Word pictures of the great. Includes bibliographical references and index. Brief biographies of twenty-eight black men and women who gained prominence in a variety of fields. [E185.96.D4 1964] 920 75-309826
1. Negroes—Biography—Juvenile literature. I. Turner, Geneva Calcier, joint author. II. Roy, Jessie Hailstalk, 1896- joint author. III. Title.

DOBLER, Lavinia G. 920
Pioneers and patriots: the lives of six Negroes of the Revolutionary era [by] Lavinia Dobler, Edgar A. Toppin. Illus. by Colleen Browning. Garden City, N.Y., Doubleday [c.]1965. 118p. illus., facsims., ports. 22cm. (Zenith bks Z6) [E185.96.D6] 65-17241 1.45 pap.,
1. Negroes—Biog.—Juvenile literature. I. Toppin, Edgar Allan, 1928- joint author. II. Title.

DUCKETT, Alfred. 320.9'2'2 B
Changing of the guard; the new breed of Black politicians. New York, Coward, McCann & Geoghegan [1972] 126 p. illus. 22 cm. (Challenge books: eye witness reports) Contents.Contents.—Soul on Capitol Hill.—Don't let the anger show: Percy Sutton.—Youth power in action: Clarence Mitchell.—Young man to watch: Julian Bond.—Promises to keep: Charles Evers.—Congresswoman from Bedford-Stuyvesant: Shirley Chisholm.—They did beat City Hall: Charles Stokes, Kenneth Gibson, Richard Hatcher.—Soul sisters in politics: Fannie Lou Hamer, Anna Langford, Constance Baker Motley, Myrlie Evers.—A new generation: the Congressional Black Caucus. [E840.6.D8 1972] 920 70-132600 3.40
1. Negroes—Biography—Juvenile literature. 2. Negroes—Politics and suffrage—Juvenile literature. I. Title. BIP

EMANUEL, Myron. 973.3'0922 B
Faces of freedom: Crispus Attucks, Benjamin Banneker, Gabriel Prosser, James Forten. [New York] Scholastic Book Services [1971] 128 p. illus., facsims., ports. 21 cm. (Firebird books) Brief biographies of four Negroes who made significant contributions to American history. [E185.96.E38] 920 77-131368
1. Negroes—Biography—Juvenile literature. I. Title.

HUGHES, Langston, 1902- 920.932526
Famous Negro heroes of America. Illustrated by Gerald McCann. New York, Dodd, Mead, 1958. 202 p. illus. 22 cm. (Famous biographies for young people) [E185.96.H82] 58-9293
1. Negroes—Biographies—Juvenile literature. I. Title. BIP

HUGHES, Langston, 1902-1967. 325.260973
Famous American Negroes. New York, Dodd, Mead, 1954. 147 p. illus. 23 cm. (Famous biographies for young people) 325.260973 301.451* [E185.96.H8] 301.451* 54-5985
1. Negroes—Biography—Juvenile literature. I. Title.

JOHNSTON, Johanna. 92 (J)
A special bravery. Illustrated by Ann Grifalconi. New York, Dodd, Mead [1967] 94 p. illus. 24 cm. [E185.96.J6] 67-20777
1. Negroes—Biography—Juvenile literature. I. Grifalconi, Ann, illus. II. Title. BIP

KING, John Taylor, 1921- 920.073
Famous Negro Americans; stories of twentythree, by John T. King, Marcet H. King. Austin, Tex., Steck Vaughan [1967] v, 120p. 21cm. [E185.96K5] 67-22745 1.65
1. Negroes—Biog.—Juvenile literature. I. King, Marcet H. joint author. II. Title.

KING, John Taylor, 1921- 920.073
Famous Negro Americans, stories of twenty-three, by John T. King and Marcet H. King. Austin, Tex., Steck-Vaughn Co. [1967] v, 120 p. 21 cm. [E185.96.K5] 67-22745
1. Negroes—Biography—Juvenile literature. I. King, Marcet H., joint aduthor. II. Title.

LEIPOLD, L. Edmond, 1902- 920
Famous American Negroes, by L. Edmond Leipold. Minneapolis, Denison [1967] 75p. 25cm. (His Famous Amer. heroes and leaders ser.) [E185.96.L4] 67-26344 3.69
1. Negroes—Biog.—Juvenile literature. I. Title.
Contents Omitted.

PETERS, Margaret. 920.073
The Ebony book of Black achievement. Designed and illustrated by Cecil L. Ferguson. [1st ed.] Chicago, Johnson Pub. Co., 1970. 90, [2] p. ports. 25 cm. On spine: Black achievement. Bibliography: p. [91]-[92] Brief biographies of twenty-one lesser known black men and women who made significant contributions to history and the black heritage from the fourteenth to the twentieth centuries. [E185.96.P39] 920 79-128544 ISBN 0-87485-040-1 4.95
1. Negroes—Biography—Juvenile literature. I. Ferguson, Cecil L., illus. II. Title. III. Title: Black achievement. BIP

ROTH, R. S. 920 (J)
Negro heroes show the way, by R. S. Roth. Simplified reading. Miami Beach, Fla., Scher Pub. Co. [1967] 107 p. ports. 24 cm. [E185.96.R85] 68-3312
1. Negroes—Biography—Juvenile literature. I. Title.

SCHRAFF, Anne E. 920.073
Black courage [by] A. E. Schraff. Illus. by Len Ebert. Philadelphia, Macrae Smith Co. [1969] 158 p. illus. 22 cm. Brief sketches of twenty-one Negroes who participated in some important events of American history. [E185.96.S35] 920 76-87984 ISBN 0-8255-7800-0 3.95
1. Negroes—Biography—Juvenile literature. I. Ebert, Len, illus. II. Title. BIP

SIGNIFICANT 920'.0092'96073 B
American Blacks. Chicago : Childrens Press, [1976] p. cm. Includes index. Brief biographies of 144 prominent blacks arranged in chronological and alphabetical order. [E185.96.S43] 920 75-20676 ISBN 0-516-05304-3 : 6.95
1. Negroes—Biography—Juvenile literature. I. Title: Blacks.

STEETER, James. 301.45'19'6073 B
Home is over the mountains; the journey of five black children. Illustrated by Victor Mays. Champaign, Ill., Garrard Pub. Co. [1972] 64 p. col. illus. 24 cm. The author recounts the events of his journey with four brothers and sisters from Mississippi to Tennessee to rejoin their parents who had fled from an angry white man. [E185.97.S87A33] 92 70-181763 ISBN 0-8116-4256-9 2.95
1. Negroes—Biography—Juvenile literature. I. Mays, Victor, 1927- illus. II. Title. BIP

STRATTON, Madeline Robinson 920
Negroes who helped build America. Pref. by Joseph E. Penn. Boston, Ginn [c.1965] ix, 165, [1] p. illus., ports. 24cm. Bibl. [E185.96.S8] 65-2838 2.80
1. Negroes—Biog.—Juvenile literature. I. Title.

STRATTON, Madeline Robinson. 920
Negroes who helped build America. Pref. by Joseph E. Penn. Boston, Ginn [1965] ix, 165, [1] p. illus., ports. 24 cm. Bibliography: p. 164-[166] [E185.96.S8] 65-2838
1. Negroes — Biog. — Juvenile literature. I. Title.

STRATTON, Madeline Robinson. 920'.0092'96073
Strides forward: Afro-American biographies [by] Madeline R. Stratton. [Lexington, Mass.] Ginn [1973] vi, 120 p. illus. 24 cm. Brief biographies of nine black Americans: Shirley Chisholm, Arthur Ashe, Charles Hamilton, David Crosthwait, Jr., Malcolm X, Sadie Alexander, John Hope Franklin, Edward Brooke, and Gordon Parks. [E185.96.S815] 920 72-80719 ISBN 0-663-24750-0 2.28 (pbk.)
1. Negroes—Biography—Juvenile literature. I. Title.

STULL, Edith (Gilbert) 1919- 920.073
Unsung Black Americans, by Edith G. Stull. Pictures by Ernest Crichlow. New York, Grosset & Dunlap [1971] 69 p. col. illus. 24 cm. Brief biographies of lesser-known blacks from all walks of life and all periods of United States history who made important contributions to the development of their country. [E185.96.S82] 920 76-106317 ISBN 0-448-02810-7 2.95
1. Negroes—Biography—Juvenile literature. I. Crichlow, Ernest T., 1914- illus. II. Title.

WAYNE, Bennett, comp. 301.45'19'6073 B
Black crusaders for freedom. Edited, with commentary by Bennett Wayne. Champaign, Ill., Garrard Pub. Co. [1974] 168 p. illus. (part col.) 22 cm. (A Target book) Contents.Contents.—Peterson, H. S. Sojourner Truth.—Patterson, L. Frederick Douglass.—Epstein, S. and Epstein, B. Harriet Tubman.—Patterson, L. Booker T. Washington. [E185.96.W38] 920 74-3154 ISBN 0-8116-4910-5 4.75
1. Negroes—Biography—Juvenile literature. I. Title. BIP

YOUNG, Margaret B. 320.9'22
Black American leaders, by Margaret B. Young. New York, Watts [1969] 120 p. ports. 23 cm. Brief biographies of thirty-seven Negro men and women who have been leaders in international, national, and local politics and civil rights movements. [E185.96.Y6] 920 75-83651 3.95
1. Negroes—Biography—Juvenile literature. I. Title.

Negroes—Cincinnati.

DABNEY, Wendell Phillips, 1865-1952. 301.451'96'077178
Cincinnati's colored citizens; historical, sociological and biographical. New York, Negro Universities Press [1970] 440 p. illus., ports. 23 cm. Reprint of the 1926 ed. [F499.C5D12 1970] 73-100287 ISBN 8-371-29176-
1. Negroes—Cincinnati. I. Title.

Negroes—Civil rights—Juvenile literature.

MACK, John, 1935- 020'.924
Nobody promised me, by John Mack, with Don Arthur Torgersen and Emmett Smith. [Chicago, Childrens Press, 1970] 64 p. illus., ports. 19 cm. (Open door books) A black teacher and librarian tells of his struggles against discrimination to achieve his career goals. [E185.97.M16A3] 92 70-107500
1. Negroes—Civil rights—Juvenile literature. I. Torgersen, Don Arthur, 1934- II. Smith, Emmett. III. Title.

STEVENSON, Janet. 323.4'0922 B
Soldiers in the civil rights war; adventures in courage. Chicago, Reilly & Lee Books [1971] 155, [1] p. ports. 24 cm. Bibliography: p. [156] Biographical profiles of seven men devoted to gaining equal rights for black people. Includes Thaddeus Stevens, W. E. B. DuBois, Robert Smalls, Monroe Trotter, J. Waties Waring, Martin Luther King, and James Meredith. [E185.61.S824] 920 70-143870 5.95
1. Negroes—Civil rights—Juvenile literature. I. Title. II. Title: Adventures in courage.

Negroes—Cleveland.

DAVIS, Russell H. 977.1'32 B
Memorable Negroes in Cleveland's past, by Russell H. Davis. Cleveland, Western Reserve Historical Society, 1969. 58 p. illus., maps, ports. 23 cm. [F499.C6D3] 68-58107
1. Negroes—Cleveland. 2. Cleveland—Biography. I. Title.

Negroes—Collections.

ADLER, Bill, comp. 301.45'19'6073022 B
Black joy, edited by Jay David. [1st ed. Chicago] Cowles Book Co. [1971] 244 p. 23 cm. Contents.Contents.—From Narrative of the life of Frederic Douglass, an American slave, written by himself.—From The life and adventures of Deadwood Dick written by himself (Nat Love).—From Running a thousand miles for freedom, by W. Craft.—From Up from slavery, by B. T. Washington.—A Negro love song, by P. L. Dunbar.—From The autobiography of an ex-colored man, by J. W. Johnson.—From Jelly Roll Morton remembers, by F. Morton.—From The big Sea, by L. Hughes.—From The autobiography of W. E. B. DuBois.—The Black finger, by A. Grimke.—The gilded six-bits and High John de Conquer, by Z. N. Hurston.—The Negro speaks of rivers, by L. Hughes.—From The boy who painted Christ Black, by J. H. Clarke.—The dark side of Hopkinsville, by T. Poston.—Home thoughts, by C. McKay.—The pocketbook game, by A. Childress.—From It's good to be Black, by R. Goodwin.—Old man Cassius, by Muhammad Ali.—From From thOBlack joy, edited by Jay David. [1st ed. Chicago] Cowles Book Co. [1971] 244 p. 23 cm. Contents.Contents.—From Narrative of the life of Frederic Douglass, an American slave, written by himself.—From The life and adventures of Deadwood Dick written b
1. Negroes—Collections. I. Title.

Negroes—Education.

BROWNE, Rose Butler. 371.9'7 B
Love my children; an autobiography, by Rose Butler Browne and James W. English. [1st ed.] New York, Meredith Press [1969] 245 p. 21 cm. [LC2717.B7] 69-19048 5.95
1. Negroes—Education. I. English, James W., joint author. II. Title.

Negroes—Florida—Biography—Juvenile literature.

NEYLAND, Leedell W. 917.59'06'96073
Twelve Black Floridians, by Leedell W. Neyland. Tallahassee, Florida Agricultural and Mechanical University Foundation, 1970. vii, 98 p. ports. 23 cm. Contents.Contents.—Jonathan C. Gibbs: Florida's only Black cabinet member.—Matthew M. Lewey: Florida's first Black newspaper editor.—Mary McLeod Bethune: a life directed by faith.—John Robert Edward Lee, Sr.: a pioneer in Florida education.—Eartha M. White: Jacksonville's "angel of mercy".—Zora Neale Hurston: author and folklorist.—Abrams Lincoln Lewis: founder of the Afro-American Life Insurance Company.—George Henry Starke: physician with a mission.—Alonzo Smith "Jake" Gaither: a legend in athletics.—Robert Lee "Bob" Hayes: "world's fastest human".—Harry Tyson Moore: martyr for freedom.—Father John Edwin Culmer: builder of churches and men. [E185.93.F5N4] 920 72-630133
1. Negroes—Florida—Biography—Juvenile literature. 2. Negroes—Biography—Juvenile literature. I. Title.

Negroes—Georgia.

LEIGH, Frances (Butler) 1838-1910. 309.1'758'04
Ten years on a Georgia plantation since the war. New York, Negro Universities Press [1969] xi, 347 p. 23 cm. Reprint of the 1883 ed. [F291.L52 1969] 74-76857 ISBN 0-8371-1177-3
1. Negroes—Georgia. 2. Georgia—Social life and customs. I. Title. BIP

T CORNELIUS V. 920.0758
Distinguished Negro Georgians. Dallas, Royal Pub. Co. [1962] 203 p. 21 cm.

Includes bibliography. [E185.93.G4T7] 61-52066
1. Negroes — Georgia. 2. Georgia — Biog. I. Title.

TROUP, Conelius V. 920.0758
Distinguished Negro Georgians. Dallas, Royal [c.1962] 203p. 21cm. Bibl. 62-52066 3.95
1. Negroes—Georgia. 2. Georgia—Biog. I. Title.

Negroes—Hackensack, N.J.—Biography.

MORROW, 301.45'19'6073074921 B
Everett Frederic, 1909-
Way down South up North, by E. Frederic Morrow. Philadelphia, United Church Press [1973] 128 p. 22 cm. "A Pilgrim Press book." Includes bibliographical references. [F144.H13M67] 72-13451 ISBN 0-8298-0246-0 4.95
1. Negroes—Hackensack, N.J.—Biography. I. Title. BIP

Negroes—History.

BROWN, William 910.03'174'96
Wells, 1815-1884.
The rising son; or, The antecedents and advancement of the colored race. Miami, Fla., Mnemosyne Pub. Inc., 1969. 552 p. port. 23 cm. Reprint of the 1874 ed. [E185.B884 1969] 79-79008
1. Negroes—History. 2. Negro race. 3. Slavery in the United States. 4. Negroes—Biography. I. Title. BIP

HENRY, 301.451'96073'024 B
George, b.1819.
Life of George Henry. Together with a brief history of the colored people in America. Freeport, N.Y., Books for Libraries Press, 1971. 123 p. port. 23 cm. (Black heritage library collection) "First published 1894." [E185.97.H45 1971] 73-164389 ISBN 0-8369-8848-5
1. Negroes—History. I. Title. II. Series.

REDDING, Jay Saunders, 325.260973
1906-
The lonesome road; the story of the Negro's part in America. [1st ed.] New York, Doubleday, 1958. 355 p. 24 cm. (Mainstream of America series) Includes bibliography. [E185.61.R298] 301.451* 58-6647
1. Negroes—History. 2. Negroes Biography. 3. United States—Race question. I. Title.

WEYL, Nathaniel, 973'.04'96073
1910-
American statesmen on slavery and the Negro [by] Nathaniel Weyl and William Marina. New Rochelle, N.Y., Arlington House [1971] 440 p. 24 cm. Includes bibliographical references. [E185.61.W55] 79-143275 ISBN 0-87000-117-5 11.95
1. Negroes—History. 2. Statesmen—United States. I. Marina, William, 1937- joint author. II. Title.

Negroes—History—Exhibitions.

ANACOSTIA 973.8'0924 B
Neighborhood Museum.
The Frederick Douglass years; a cultural history exhibition. Organized by the Anacostia Neighborhood Museum, Smithsonian Institution. Circulated by the Smithsonian Institution Traveling Exhibition Service. Washington, Smithsonian Institution Press, 1970. v, 46 p. illus., ports. 28 cm. Larry Erskine Thomas, author and designer of the exhibition. [E185.53.W3A54] 70-610380
1. Negroes—History—Exhibitions. I. Douglass, Frederick, 1817?-1895. II. Thomas, Larry Erskine. III. Title.

Negroes—History—1877-1964.

BONTEMPS, Arna 325.2670973
Wendell, 1902-
100 years of Negro freedom. New York, Dodd, Mead, 1961. 276 p. illus. 22 cm. Includes bibliography. [E185.6.B74] 61-11716
1. Negroes—History—1877-1964. 2. Negroes—Biography. I. Title.

BONTEMPS, Arna Wendell, 301.32973
1902-
Anyplace but here [by] Arna Bontemps and Jack Conroy. New York, Hill and Wang [1966] viii, 372 p. 21 cm. "A revised and expanded version of They seek a city."—Dust jacket. Bibliography: p. 349-360. [E185.6.B75 1966] 66-15898
1. Negroes—History—1877-1964. 2. Negroes—Biography. 3. Migration, Internal—United States. I. Conroy, Jack, 1899- joint author. II. Title.

Negroes in Africa—Biography.

GOLLOCK, Georgina Anne, 320.096
1861-1940.
Lives of eminent Africans. New York, Negro Universities Press [1969] viii, 152 p. maps, ports. 23 cm. Reprint of the 1928 ed. [DT18.G6 1969] 70-91256 ISBN 8-371-20624-
1. Negroes in Africa—Biography. I. Title. BIP

GOLLOCK, Georgina Anne, 920.06
1861-1940.
Sons of Africa. New York, Negro Universities Press [1969] 247 p. 23 cm. Reprint of the 1928 ed. Includes bibliographical references. [DT18.G65 1969] 75-89001
1. Negroes in Africa—Biography. I. Title. BIP

Negroes—Juvenile literature.

HEARD, Joseph 301.451'96'073
Norman, 1922-
The Black frontiersmen; adventures of Negroes among American Indians, 1528-1918 [by] J. Norman Heard. New York, John Day Co. [1969] 128 p. illus. 21 cm. Bibliography: p. 121-124. Traces the adventures of ten Negroes who participated in the struggle between Indians and whites during the development of the American frontier. [E185.H4 1969] 79-89317 3.95
1. Negroes—Juvenile literature. 2. Indians of North America—Juvenile literature. 3. Frontier and pioneer life—U.S.—Juvenile literature. I. Title. BIP

Negroes—Kentucky—Biography.

JOHNSON, 301.45'19'60730769
William Decker.
Biographical sketches of prominent Negro men and women of Kentucky ... by W. D. Johnson. Freeport, N.Y., Books for Libraries Press, 1973. p. (The Black heritage library collection) Reprint of the 1897 ed. [E185.93.K3J63 1973] 72-12958 ISBN 0-8369-9225-3
1. Negroes—Kentucky—Biography. I. Title. II. Title: Prominent Negro men and women of Kentucky. III. Series.

Negroes—Little Rock, Ark.

BATES, Daisy (Gatson) 920.7
The long shadow of Little Rock, a memoir. New York, David McKay Co. [1962] 234 p. illus. 21 cm. [F419.L7B3] 62-20233
1. Negroes—Little Rock, Ark. 2. Little Rock, Ark.—Public schools. I. Title.

Negroes—Ohio.

MALVIN, John, 301.451960924 B
1795-1880.
North into freedom; the autobiography of John Malvin, free Negro, 1795-1880. Edited and with an introd. by Allan Peskin. Cleveland, Press of Western Reserve University, 1966. vii, 87 p. 23 cm. "A book from Cleveland State University." Bibliographical references included in "Notes to the introduction" (p. 22-24) [E185.97.M26A3 1966] 66-28142
1. Negroes—Ohio. 2. Negroes—Civil rights. I. Peskin, Allan, ed. II. Title.

Negroes—Pennsylvania—Biography.

BLOCKSON, 974.8'004'96073 B
Charles L.
Pennsylvania's Black history / by Charles L. Blockson ; edited by Louise D. Stone. Philadelphia : Portfolio Associates, 1975. i, 150 p. : ill. ; 22 cm. Includes index. Bibliography: p. 144-148. [E185.93.P41B56] 75-39135
1. Negroes—Pennsylvania—Biography. 2. Negroes—Pennsylvania—History. 3. Pennsylvania—History, Local. I. Title.

Negroes—Politics and suffrage.

HASKINS, James, 1941- 973
A piece of the power; four Black mayors. New York, Dial Press [1972] xiv, 174 p. illus. 24 cm. Traces the life and careers of four black mayors: Carl Stokes of Cleveland, Ohio; Richard Hatcher of Gary, Indiana; Charles Evers of Fayette, Mississippi; and Kenneth Gibson of Newark, New Jersey. [E185.615.H33] 920 71-181790 4.95
1. Negroes—Politics and suffrage. 2. Negroes—Biography. I. Title. BIP

Negroes—Religion.

FISK University, 248.2'46
Nashville. Social Science Institute.
God struck me dead; religious conversion experiences and autobiographies of ex-slaves. Clifton H. Johnson, editor. Foreword by Paul Radin. Philadelphia, Pilgrim Press [1969] xix, 171 p. 22 cm. [BV4930.F5 1969] 78-77839 3.45
1. Negroes—Religion. 2. Conversion. I. Johnson, Clifton H., ed. II. Title.

Negroes—Rhode Island.

BROWN, 301.451'096073'07452
William J., b.1814.
The life of William J. Brown, of Providence, R.I.; with personal recollections of incidents in Rhode Island. Freeport, N.Y., Books for Libraries Press, 1971. 230 p. 23 cm. (The Black heritage library collection) Reprint of the 1883 ed. [E185.97.B88 1971] 78-164382 ISBN 0-8369-8841-8
1. Negroes—Rhode Island. 2. Rhode Island—Social life and customs. I. Title. II. Series. BIP

Negroes—Social conditions—1964-

GREEN, Ely, 301.451'96'024 B
1893-1968.
Ely: too black, too white. Edited by Elizabeth N. & Arthur Ben Chitty. Amherst, University of Massachusetts Press, 1970. xiii, 637 p. 24 cm. Running title: Too black, too white. [E185.97.G795A3 1970] 75-76048 ISBN 0-87023-047-6 10.00
1. Negroes—Social conditions—1964- 2. Mulattoes—United States. I. Chitty, Elizabeth N., ed. II. Chitty, Arthur Benjamin, ed. III. Title. IV. Title. Too black, too white.

Negroes—Social life and customs.

GUFFY, Ossie, 301.451'96'073024 B
1931
Ossie: the autobiography of a Black woman, by Ossie Guffy as told to Caryl Ledner. [1st ed.] New York, Norton [1971] 224 p. 22 cm. [E185.97.G9A3 1971] 74-141940 ISBN 0-393-07458-7 6.50
1. Negroes—Social life and customs. 2. Negroes—Social conditions. I. Ledner, Caryl. II. Title.

Negroes soldiers—Personal narratives.

ADLER, Bill, comp. 973'.099
The Black soldier: from the American Revolution to Vietnam. Edited by Jay David and Elaine Crane. New York, Morrow, 1971. 248 p. 22 cm. Contents.—Marching song of the First Arkansas, by L. Miller.—From The narrative of James Roberts, soldier in the Revolutionary War, by J. Roberts.—From The trial record of Denmark Vesey.—From Proud shoes, by P. Murray.—Men of color, to arms, by F. Douglass.—From Army life in a Black regiment, by T. W. Higginson.—The abduction of the planter, by B. Quarles.—A soldier's plea for equal pay, by J. H. Gooding.—From The Buffalo soldiers: a narrative of the Negro cavalry in the West, by W. Leckie.—From The Colored regulars in the United States Army, by T. G. Steward.—From Harlem to the Rhine, by A. Little.—From Yes I can, by S. Davis, Jr.—From A choice of weapons, by G. Parks.—From Ebony brass, by J. Johnson.—From This is my country too, by J. A. Williams.—Armed defense, an interview with C. R. Sims.—From G.I. diary, by D. Parks.—When the BlacOThe Black soldier: from the American Revolution to Vietnam. Edited by Jay David and Elaine Crane. New York, Morrow, 1971. 248 p. 22 cm. Co
1. Negroes soldiers—Personal narratives. I. Crane, Elaine, joint comp. II. Title.

Negroes—South Carolina.

BRYANT, Lawrence 328.757'0922 B
Chesterfield.
Negro senators and representatives in the South Carolina Legislature, 1868-1902. Lawrence C. Bryant, editor. Orangeburg, S.C. [1968] ix, 199 p. 28 cm. Cover title. Bibliographical footnotes. [E185.93.S7B76] 68-6277
1. Negroes—South Carolina. 2. Legislators—South Carolina. 3. South Carolina—Politics and government—1865-1950. I. Title. BIP

Negroes—South Carolina—Biography.

BRYANT, Lawrence 328.757'092'2 B
Chesterfield.
South Carolina Negro legislators: a glorious success; State and local officeholders; biographies of Negro representatives, 1868-1902. Orangeburg, South Carolina State College [1974] 119 p. 29 cm. "Commemorating South Carolina tricentennial, 1970." Includes bibliographical references. [E185.93.S7B77] 74-164338
1. Negroes—South Carolina—Biography. 2. Legislators—South Carolina. 3. South Carolina—Politics and government—1865-1950. I. Title.

Nehemiah.

SEUME, Richard H. 221.9'24 B
Nehemiah : God's builder / by Richard H. Seume. Chicago : Moody Press, c1978. 121 p. ; 22 cm. Bibliography: p. 120-121. [BS580.N45S48] 77-29141 ISBN 0-8024-5868-8 : 2.95
1. Nehemiah. 2. Bible. O.T. Nehemiah—Criticism, interpretation, etc. 3. Bible. O.T.—Biography. BIP

Nehru, Jawaharlal, 1889-1964.

APSLER, Alfred 954.040924(B)
Fighter for independence, Jawaharlal Nehru. New York, Messner [1966] 191p. 22cm. Bibl. [DS481.N35 A8 1966] 66-17094 3.25
1. Nehru, Jawaharlal, 1889-1964. I. Title.

BUTLER, Richard Austen 954.03'5
baron, 1902-
Jawaharlal Nehru: the struggle for independence [by] the Right Honourable Lord Butler. Cambridge, Cambridge U.P., 1966. 28 p. 18 1/2 cm. (B66-23555) (Jawaharlal Nehru memorial lecture 1 1966) Bibliographical footnotes. [DS481.N35J32 no. 1 1966] 66-30619
1. Nehru, Jawaharlal, 1889-1964. I. Title. II. Series.

CROCKER, Walter 954.040924
Russell, 1902-
Nehru; a contemporary's estimate, by Walter Crocker. With a foreword by Arnold Toynbee. New York, Oxford University Press, 1966. 186 p. port. 23 cm. Bibliographical footnotes. [DS481.N35C7] 66-31908
1. Nehru, Jawaharlal, 1889-1964.

EDWARDES, Michael. 954.04'092'4 B
Nehru, a political biography. New York, Praeger Publishers [1972, c1971] 351 p. port. 23 cm. [DS481.N35E33 1972] 78-173442 8.95
1. Nehru, Jawaharlal, 1889-1964. I. Title.

GOPAL, Sarvepalli. 954.04'092'4
Jawaharlal Nehru : a biography / Sarvepalli Gopal. Cambridge, Mass. : Harvard University Press, 1976- v. : ill. ;

24 cm. Includes index. Contents.Contents.—v. 1. 1889-1947. Bibliography: v. 1, p. 376-382. [DS481.N35G66 1976] 17.50
1. Nehru, Jawaharlal, 1889-1964. 2. India—Politics and government—20th century.

LAMB, Beatrice 954.0350922
Pitney, 1904-
The Nehrus of India; three generations of leadership. New York, Macmillan [1967] vii, 276 p. illus., maps, ports. 22 cm. Bibliography: p. 262-264. [DS481.N4L3] 67-17209
1. Nehru, Motilal, 1861-1931. 2. Nehru, Jawaharlal, 1889-1964. 3. Gandhi, Indira Nehru, 1917- I. Title. BIP

LENGYEL, Emil, 954'.04'0924 B
1895-
Jawaharlal Nehru; the Brahman from Kashmir. New York, F. Watts [1968] 216 p. illus., ports. 22 cm. (Immortals of history) Bibliography: p. 211-212. [DS481.N35L43] 68-17704
1. Nehru, Jawaharlal, 1889-1964.

SETON, Marie. 954.04'0924 B
Panditji; a portrait of Jawaharlal Nehru. New York, Taplinger [1967] 515 p. illus., facsims., map (on end papers), ports. 23 cm. [DS481.N35S4 1967a] 67-11036
1. Nehru, Jawaharlal, 1889-1964. I. Title.

SHORTER, Bani. 954.04'0924 B
Nehru: a voice for mankind. New York, J. Day Co. [1970] vii, 312 p. illus., ports. 22 cm. [DS481.N35S484] 71-89307 7.95
1. Nehru, Jawaharlal, 1889-1964. I. Title.

TYSON, Geoffrey 954.040924
William, 1898-
Nehru; the years of power [by] Geoffrey Tyson. New York, F. A. Praeger [1966] 206 p. 23 cm. Bibliography: p. [199]-200. [DS481.N35T9 1966a] 66-17927
1. Nehru, Jawaharlal, 1889-1964.

Nehru, Jawaharlal, 1889-1964—Political and social views.

PRASHAD, Ganesh, 320.5'092'4
1913-
Nehru : a study in colonial liberalism / Ganesh Prashad. New Delhi : Sterling Publishers, c1976. vi, 218 p. ; 23 cm. Includes bibliographical references and index. [JC273.N43P7] 76-903941 15.00
1. Nehru, Jawaharlal, 1889-1964—Political and social views. 2. Political science—India—History. I. Title.
Distributed by Verry BIP

Nehru, Jawaharlal, 1889-1964—Portraits, caricatures. etc.

JAWAHARLAL NEHRU SOUVENIR 923.254
VOLUMES COMMITTEE
Jawaharlal Nehru, a memorial album. Foreword by S. Radhakrishnan. [Bombay, Popular Prakashan, on behalf of the Jawaharlal Nehru Souvenir Volumes Comm. [Dist. New York. Heinman. 1965] 1v. unpaged. (chiefly illus., ports.) 29cm. [DS481.N35J35] SA 65 10.00
1. Nehru, Jawaharlal, 1889-1964—Portraits, caricatures. etc. I. Title.

Nehru, Kamala, 1899-1936.

KALHAN, Promilla. 954.03'5'0924 B
Kamala Nehru; an intimate biography. Delhi, Vikas Pub. House [1973] vi, 145 p. illus. 23 cm. [DS481.N36K33] 73-905766
1. Nehru, Kamala, 1899-1936. I. Title.
Distributed by International Publication Service; 9.00. BIP

Nehru, Motilal, 1861-1931.

LAMB, Beatrice 954.0350922
Pitney, 1904-
The Nehrus of India; three generations of leadership. New York, Macmillan [1967] vii, 276 p. illus., maps, ports. 22 cm. Bibliography: p. 262-264. [DS481.N4L3] 67-17209
1. Nehru, Motilal, 1861-1931. 2. Nehru, Jawaharlal, 1889-1964. 3. Gandhi, Indira Nehru, 1917- I. Title. BIP

NANDA, Bal Ram. 929.20954
The Nehrus, Motilal and Jawaharlal. [1st American ed.] New York, J. Day Co. [1963, c1962] 357 p. illus. 23 cm. [DS481.N4N3 1963] 62-21017
1. Nehru, Motilal, 1861-1931. 2. Nehru, Jawaharlal, 1889-1964. I. Title. BIP

PANDIT Motilal 954.03'5'0924 B
Nehru, a great patriot / editorial board, D. C. Goswami, R. K. Nayak, executive editor, Shankar Dayal Singh ; foreword by D. K. Borooah ; introd. by Rajni Patel ; a homage by B. Bhagavati. New Delhi : National Forum of Lawyers and Legal Aid, [1976] xx, 215 p., [12] leaves of plates : ill. ; 25 cm. Contents.—Nehru, M. The family.—Nehru, J. My father.—Andrews, C. F. A maker of modern India.—Prasad, R. Reminiscence.—Radhakrishnan, S. A magnanimous man.—Panikkar, K. M. A great statesman and parliamentarian.—Asaf Ali. A fascinating figure.—Hailey, M. I should have rejoiced.—Sinha, S. Pt. Motilal Nehru.—Das, D. In the assembly.—Schuster, G. A true aristocrat.—Rau, M. C. 'The independent'.—Nanda, B. R. A great lawyer.—Lawrence, P. An anecdote.—Diwaker, S. C. Wit and wisdom of Panditji.—Gandhi, I. The story of Swaraj Bhawan.—Presidential address, Amritsar, 1919.—Presidential address, Calcutta, 1928.—Report of the Nehru Committee, 1928.—Thoughts.—Tributes.—Some selected letters. [DS481.N4P36] 76-903311 Rs25.0edit
1. Nehru, Motilal, 1861-1931. 2. Statesmen—India—Biography. I. Goswami, D. C. II. Nayak, R. K. III. Singh, Shankar Dayal, 1937-

Neihardt, John Gneisenau, 1881-1973.

ALY, Lucile Folse, 811'.5'2 B
1913-
John G. Neihardt : a critical biography / by Lucile F. Aly. Amsterdam : Rodopi, 1977. 307 p. ; 22 cm. (Melville studies in American culture ; v. 7) Includes bibliographical references. [PS3527.E35Z574] 77-371666 ISBN 90-620-3109-9 pbk. : 19.00
1. Neihardt, John Gneisenau, 1881-1973. 2. Poets, American—20th century—Biography.
Distributed by Humanities Press, Atlantic Highlands, N.J. BIP

Neihardt, John Gneisenau, 1881-1973—Biography.

NEIHARDT, John 811'.5'2
Gneisenau, 1881-1973.
Patterns and coincidences : a sequel to All is but a beginning / John G. Neihardt. Columbia : University of Missouri Press, 1978. viii, 122 p. ; 21 cm. [PS3527.E35Z523 1978] 77-24199 ISBN 0-8262-0233-0 : 9.50
1. Neihardt, John Gneisenau, 1881-1973—Biography. 2. Poets, American—20th century—Biography. I. Title. BIP

Neilson, Francis,

NEILSON, Francis, 1867- 928.1
My life in two worlds. Appleton, Wis., C. C. Nelson Pub. Co., 1952-53. 2v. illus. 24cm. [CT788.N35A3] 52-34905
I. Title.

NEILSON, Francis, 1867- 928.1
My life in two worlds. Appleton, Wis., C. C. Nelson Pub. Co., 1952- v. illus. 24 cm. [CT788.N35A3] 52-34905
I. Title. BIP

Neilson, John Shaw, 1872-1942.

ANDERSON, Hugh. 821 B
John Shaw Neilson [by] Hugh Anderson [and] L. J. Blake. [Adelaide] Rigby [1972] 216 p. illus. 22 cm. Bibliography: p. [219]-[225] [PR6027.E43Z532] 79-183423 ISBN 0-85179-357-6 8.50
1. Neilson, John Shaw, 1872-1942. I. Blake, Leslie James, joint author.
Distributed by Verry. BIP

Neilson, William Allan, 1869-1946.

THORP, Margaret (Farrand) 923.773
1891-
Neilson of Smith. New York, Oxford University Press, 1956. vii, 363p. illus., ports. 24cm. [LD7152.7 1918.T4] 56-5767
1. Neilson, William Allan, 1869-1946. I. Title.

THORP, Margaret (Farrand) 923.773
1891-
Neilson of Smith. New York, Oxford University Press, 1956. vii, 363 p. illus., ports. 24 cm. [LD7152.7 1918.T4] 56-5767
1. Neilson, William Allan, 1869-1946. I. Title.

Nekipelov Viktor, 1928-

NEKIPELOV, Viktor, 362.2'1'0947
1928-
Institute of fools : notes from Serbsky / Victor Nekipelov ; edited and translated from the Russian by Marco Carynnyk and Marta Horban. New York : Farrar, Straus, Giroux, c1980. p. cm. Includes index. Bibliography: p. [RC451.R9N44 1980] 79-21569 ISBN 0-374-17703-1 : 10.95
1. Nekipelov Viktor, 1928- 2. Moscow. TSentral'nyi nauchno-issledovatel'skii institut sudebnoi psikhiatrii. 3. Psychiatry—Russia. 4. Dissenters—Russia—Biography. I. Carynnyk, Marco. II. Horban, Marta. III. Moscow. TSentral'nyi nauchno-issledovatel'skii institut sudebnoi psikhiatrii. IV. Title. BIP

Nekrasov, Nikolai Alekseevich, 1821-1877—Biography—Character.

CHUKOVSKII, Kornei 891.7'1'3 B
Ivanovich, 1882-1969.
The poet and the hangman (Nekrasov and Muravyov) / Kornei Chukovsky ; translated by R. W. Rotsel. Ann Arbor, Mich. : Ardis, c1977. 95 p. ; 19 cm. (Ardis essay series ; no. 5) Translation of Poet i palach. Includes bibliographical references. [PG3337.N4Z62813 1977] 77-154958 ISBN 0-88233-217-1 : 7.95.
1. Nekrasov, Nikolai Alekseevich, 1821-1877—Biography—Character. 2. Murav'ev, Mikhail Nikolaevich, graf, 1796-1866. 3. Poets, Russian—19th century—Biography. I. Title.

Nelson, Cindy, 1955- —Juvenile literature.

JACOBS, Linda. 796.9'3'0924 B
Cindy Nelson, North Country skier / by Linda Jacobs. St. Paul : EMC Corp., 1976. 40 p. : ill. ; 23 cm. (Women who win ; 4) A biography of the girl from Minnesota who recuperated from serious injury in the 1972 Olympics in time to realize victory in the 1974 games. [GV854.2.N44J3] 92 76-7592 ISBN 0-88436-232-9 lib.bdg. : 4.95 pbk. : 2.95
1. Nelson, Cindy, 1955- —Juvenile literature. 2. Skis and skiing—Juvenile literature. I. Title.

Nelson, Erik Alfred, 1862-1939.

BRATCHER, Lewis Malen, 922.673
1888-
The apostle of the Amazon. Nashville, Broadman Press ['1951] 138 p. illus. 20 cm. [BV2853.B6B719] 52-6512
1. Nelson, Erik Alfred, 1862-1939. 2. Missions—Brazil. I. Title.

Nelson, Hallie F., 1905-

NELSON, Hallie F., 973.9'092'4 B
1905-
South of the cottonwood tree / by Hallie F. Nelson. [1st ed.]. [Broken Bow, Neb. : Purcells, c1977] 304 p. : ill., map (on lining papers) ; 23 cm. Autobiographical. [CT275.N4427A37] 76-42114 10.00
1. Nelson, Hallie F., 1905- 2. United States—Biography. I. Title. BIP

Nelson, Horatia, 1801-1881.

GERIN, Winifred. 914.2'03'730924
Horatia Nelson. Oxford, Clarendon P., 1970. xvii, 350 p. 17 plates. illus., geneal. tables, ports. 23 cm. [CT788.N414G4] 74-135874 ISBN 0-19-822331-5 65/-
1. Nelson, Horatia, 1801-1881. BIP

Nelson, Horatio Nelson,

NELSON, Horatio 940.2'7'0924
Nelson, Viscount, 1758-1805.
Nelson's last diary. A facsimile edited by Oliver Warner. [Kent, Ohio] Kent State University Press [1971] 80 p. illus. 25 cm. Contains a photocopy of the hand-written diary for the period Sept. 13/14-Oct. 21, 1805 with a printed transcription. [DA87.1.N4A45 1971] 70-165752 ISBN 0-87338-121-1 6.00
I. Warner, Oliver, 1903- ed. II. Title.

Nelson, Horatio Nelson, Viscount, 1758-1805.

BENNETT, Geoffrey 359.3'3'10924 B
Martin.
Nelson, the commander [by] Geoffrey Bennett. New York, Scribner [1972] xii, 322 p. illus. 23 cm. [DA87.1.N4B37 1972b] 71-38567 ISBN 0-684-12886-1 12.00
1. Nelson, Horatio Nelson, Viscount, 1758-1805. I. Title.

BRADFORD, Ernle 940.2'7'0924 B
Dusgate Selby.
Nelson : the essential hero / Ernle Bradford. 1st American ed. New York : Harcourt Bruce Jovanovich, c1977. 368 p., [4] leaves of plates : ill. ; 24 cm. Includes index. [DA87.1.N4B66 1977] 77-73114 ISBN 0-15-112240-7 : 12.95
1. Nelson, Horatio Nelson, Viscount, 1758-1805. 2. Great Britain. Navy—Biography. 3. Admirals—Great Britain—Biography.

GRENFELL, Russell. 940.2'7'0924 B
Horatio Nelson : a short biography / Russell Grenfell ; with a foreword by S. W. Roskill. Westport, Conn. : Greenwood Press, 1978. xv, 247 p., [4] leaves of plates : ill. ; 23 cm. First published in 1949 under title: Nelson, the sailor. Reprint of the 2d ed. published in 1968 by Faber and Faber, London. Includes index. [DA87.1.N4G7 1978] 78-6150 ISBN 0-313-20481-0 lib.bdg. : 19.50
1. Nelson, Horatio Nelson, Viscount, 1758-1805. 2. Great Britain—History, Naval—18th century. 3. Admirals—Great Britain—Biography. BIP

GRENFELL, Russell. 923.542
Nelson, the sailor. New York, Macmillan, 1950 [c1949] 235 p. illus., port. 21 cm. [DA87.1.N4G7 1950] 50-7050
1. Nelson, Horatio Nelson, Viscount, 1758-1805.

HATTERSLEY, Roy. 359.3'31'0924 B
Nelson. New York, Saturday Review Press [1974] 223 p. illus. (part col.) 26 cm. Bibliography: p. 215. [DA87.1.N4H33 1974] 73-87558 ISBN 0-8415-0288-9 12.50
1. Nelson, Horatio Nelson, Viscount, 1758-1805.

HEWITT, James. 940.2'7
Eye-witnesses to Nelson's battles; edited by James Hewitt. Reading, Osprey, 1972. x, 206, [16] p. illus., facsims., plans, ports. 22 cm. (His Eye-witnesses to history) Bibliography: p. 199-201. [DA87.1.N4H4] 72-169497 ISBN 0-85045-048-9 £2.50
1. Nelson, Horatio Nelson, Viscount, 1758-1805. 2. Great Britain—History, Naval—18th century. 3. Great Britain—History, Naval—19th century. I. Title.

HOWARTH, David Armine, 940.2'7
1912-
Trafalgar : the Nelson touch / David Howarth. New York : Galahad Books, [1975] c1969. 254 p. : ill. ; 24 cm. Includes index. [DA88.5 1805.H612 1975] 74-77013 ISBN 0-88365-272-2 : 8.95
1. Nelson, Horatio Nelson, Viscount, 1758-1805. 2. Trafalgar (Cape), Battle of, 1805. I. Title.

LENANTON, Carola 942.07'3'0924 B
Mary Anima (Oman) 1897-
Lord Nelson, by Carola Oman. Hamden, Conn., Archon Books [1968, c1954] 160 p. illus., maps, ports. 21 cm. (Makers of history) Bibliographical references included in "A note on sources" (p. 157-158) [DA87.1.N4L37 1968] 68-3770

1. Nelson, Horatio Nelson, Viscount, 1758-1805.

LENANTON, Carola 942.07'3'0924 B
Mary Anima (Oman) 1897-
Nelson, by Carola Oman (Carola Mary Anima Lenanton) Westport, Conn., Greenwood Press [1970, c1946] xiv, 748 p. illus., facsim., geneal. table, ports. 24 cm. Includes bibliographical references. [DA87.1.N4L4 1970] 77-100166 ISBN 0-8371-3976-7
1. Nelson, Horatio Nelson, Viscount, 1758-1805.

LLOYD, 359.3'3'10924 B
Christopher, 1906-
Nelson and sea power. London, English Universities Press, 1973. 156, [8] p. illus., maps, ports. 23 cm. (Men and their times) Bibliography: p. [148] [DA87.1.N4L53] 73-161901 ISBN 0-340-12413-X
1. Nelson, Horatio Nelson, Viscount, 1758-1805. I. Title.
Distributed by Verry; 5.00 BIP

MAHAN, Alfred 942.07'3'0924 B
Thayer, 1840-1914.
The life of Nelson; the embodiment of the sea power of Great Britain. New York, Greenwood Press, 1968. 2 v. maps, plans, ports. 24 cm. Reprint of the 1897 ed. Bibliographical footnotes. [DA87.1.N4M3 1968] 68-23312
1. Nelson, Horatio Nelson, Viscount, 1758-1805. I. Title. BIP

MAHAN, Alfred 942.07'3'0924
Thayer, 1840-1914.
The life of Nelson, the embodiment of the sea power of Great Britain. 2d ed., rev. Boston, Little, Brown, 1899. Grosse Pointe, Mich., Scholarly Press, 1968. xvi, 764 p. illus., maps, plans, ports. 23 cm. Bibliographical footnotes. [DA87.1.N4M3 1968b] 79-8486
1. Nelson, Horatio Nelson, Viscount, 1758-1805. I. Title.

MAHAN, Alfred 942.07'3'0924 B
Thayer, 1840-1914.
The life of Nelson, the embodiment of the sea power of Great Britain. 2d ed., rev. New York, Haskell House, 1969. xvi, 764 p. illus., maps, plans, ports. 23 cm. This ed. was first published in 1899. Bibliographical footnotes. [DA87.1.N4M3 1969] 68-26361
1. Nelson, Horatio Nelson, Viscount, 1758-1805. I. Title.

NELSON, Horatio 940.2'7'0924
Nelson, Viscount, 1758-1805.
Nelson's last diary. A facsimile edited by Oliver Warner. [Kent, Ohio] Kent State University Press [1971] 80 p. illus. 25 cm. Contains a photocopy of the hand-written diary for the period Sept. 13/14-Oct. 21, 1805 with a printed transcription. [DA87.1.N4A45 1971] 70-165752 ISBN 0-87338-121-1 6.00
I. Warner, Oliver, 1903- ed. II. Title.

POCOCK, Tom. 942.07'3'0924 B
Nelson and his world. New York, Viking Press [1968] 142 p. illus., facsims., ports. 24 cm. (A Studio book) Bibliography: p. 139. [DA87.1.N4P6 1968b] 68-16445 ISBN 0-670-50597-8 6.95
1. Nelson, Horatio Nelson, Viscount, 1758-1805.

POCOCK, Tom. 359.3'3'10924 B
Nelson and his world. New York, Viking Press [1968] 142 p. illus., facsims., ports. 24 cm. (A Studio book) Bibliography: p. 139. A biography of the English admiral whose exploits assured his country's supremacy on the seas. [DA87.1.N4P6 1968b] 92 AC 68
1. Nelson, Horatio Nelson, Viscount, 1758-1805. I. Title.

POPE, Dudley. 359.3'3'10924 B
The great gamble. New York, Simon and Schuster [1972] 579 p. illus. 25 cm. Bibliography: p. 531-565. [DL276.P63 1972b] 72-82202 ISBN 0-671-21404-7 12.50
1. Nelson, Horatio Nelson, Viscount, 1758-1805. 2. Copenhagen, Battle of, 1801. I. Title. BIP

RUSSELL, Jack, 942.07'3'0922
1928-
Nelson and the Hamiltons. New York, Simon and Schuster [1969] 448 p. illus., ports. 25 cm. Bibliography: p. 427-435. [DA87.1.N4R77 1969b] 70-79638 10.00
1. Nelson, Horatio Nelson, Viscount, 1758-1805. 2. Hamilton, Emma, Lady, 1761?-1815. 3. Hamilton, William, Sir, 1730-1803. I. Title. BIP

SABATINI, Rafael, 1875- 920.02
1950.
Heroic lives; Richard I: Saint Francis of Assisi: Joan of Arc: Sir Walter Ralegh: Lord Nelson: Florence Nightingale. Freeport, N.Y., Books for Libraries Press [1971, c1934] 416 p. 23 cm. (Essay index reprint series) [D106.S28 1971] 70-99648 ISBN 0-8369-2071-6
1. Richard I, King of England, 1157-1199. 2. Francesco d'Assisi, Saint, 1182-1226. 3. Jeanne d'Arc, Saint, 1412-1431. 4. Raleigh, Walter Sir, 1552?-1618. 5. Nelson, Horatio Nelson, Viscount, 1758-1805. 6. Nightingale, Florence, 1820-1910. I. Title.

SOUTHEY, Robert, 1774- 923.542
1843.
Life of Nelson. Garden City, N.Y., Doubleday [1961] 277p. (Dolphin bk. C112) .95 pap.,
1. Nelson, Horatio Nelson, viscount, 1758-1805. I. Title.

SOUTHEY, Robert, 1774-1843. v. 12
Life of Nelson. Introd.by Carola Oman. London, J.M. Dent; New York, E.P. Dutton [1962] x, 278 p. 19 cm. (Half-title: Everyman's library, ed. by Ernest Rhys. Biography, no. 52) First published in Everyman's Library 1906. Select bibliography: p. x. 63-54985
1. Nelson, Horatio Nelson, viscount, 1758-1805. I. Title.

SOUTHEY, Robert, 942.0730924
1774-1843
The life of Nelson. Ed. introd., notes and an appendix, by E. R. H. Harvey. London, Macdonald [Boston, Ginn, 1966] lxxiii, 339p. illus., facsims., maps, ports. 19cm. (Macdonald illus. classics) [DA87.1.N4S7] 66-5598 3.50
1. Nelson, Horatio Nelson, viscount, 1758-1805. I. Harvey, E. R. H., ed. II. Title.

WALDER, David. 940.2'7'0924 B
Nelson, a biography / by David Walder. New York : Dial Press/J. Wade, 1978. xxi, 538 p., [8] leaves of plates : ill. ; 24 cm. Includes index. Bibliography: p. [520]-525. [DA87.1.N4W24 1978] 78-2697 ISBN 0-8037-6431-6 : 14.95
1. Nelson, Horatio Nelson, Viscount, 1758-1805. 2. Great Britain—History, Naval—18th century. 3. Admirals—Great Britain—Biography.

WARNER, Oliver, 359.3'31'0924 B
1903-
Nelson / Oliver Warner ; introd. by Elizabeth Longford. Chicago : Follett Pub. Co., 1975. 231 p. : ill. ; 26 cm. Includes index. Bibliography: p. 222-223. [DA87.1.N4W277 1975b] 74-21370 ISBN 0-695-80541-X : 10.00
1. Nelson, Horatio Nelson, Viscount, 1758-1805. I. Title.

WARNER, Oliver, 1903- 923.542
Victory; the life of Lord Nelson. [1st ed.] Boston, Little, Brown [1958] 393 p. illus. 22 cm. [DA87.1.N4W3] 58-6026
1. Nelson, Horatio Nelson, viscount, 1758-1805. I. Title.

WHIPPLE, Addison 359'.00941
Beecher Colvin, 1918-
Fighting sail / by A. B. C. Whipple and the editors of Time-Life Books. Alexandria, Va. : Time-Life Books, c1978. 184 p. : ill. ; 29 cm. (The Seafarers ; v. 2) Includes index. Bibliography: p. 178-179. [DA87.1.N4W55] 78-52043 ISBN 0-8094-2654-4 : 9.95
1. Nelson, Horatio Nelson, Viscount, 1758-1805. 2. Great Britain. Navy—Sea life. 3. Great Britain—History, Naval—18th century. 4. Admirals—Great Britain—Biography. I. Time-Life Books. II. Title. III. Series. BIP

Nelson, Horatio Nelson, viscount, 1758-1805—Juvenile literature.

GIMPEL, Herbert J. 942.0730924
Lord Nelson. New York, Watts [c.1966] x,228p. illus. ports. 22cm. (Immortals of hist.) [DA87.1.N4G5] 66-14564 2.95; 2.21 lib. ed.,
1. Nelson, Horatio Nelson, viscount, 1758-1805—Juvenile literature. I. Title.

HOUGHTON, Richard 920
The true story of Lord Nelson, naval hero. Chicago, Childrens [c.1958, 1964] 141p. col. illus. 23cm. First pub. in London in 1958 under title: The true book about Nelson. 64-12908 3.50; 2.63 lib. ed.,
1. Nelson, Horatio Nelson, viscount, 1758-1805—Juvenile literature. I. Title.

SYME, Ronald 1910- 920
The young Nelson. Illus. by Susan Groom, Trevor Parkin. New York, Roy [1963] 125p. illus. 21cm. Bibl. 62-18437 3.00 bds.,
1. Nelson, Horatio Nelson, Viscount, 1758-1805—Juvenile literature. I. Title.

WHIPPLE, Addison Beecher 920
Colvin, 1918-
Hero of Trafalgar; the story of Lord Nelson. Illus. by William Hofmann. New York, Random [c.1963] 186p. col. illus. 22cm. (World landmark bks., W-55) Bibl. 63-7806 1.95; 2.28 lib.ed.,
1. Nelson, Horatio Nelson, viscount, 1758-1805—Juvenile literature. I. Title.

Nelson, James Boyce.

NELSON, James Boyce. 922.573
Papa remembers me. [1st ed.] New York, Vantage Press [1957] 117p. 21cm. [BX9225.N43A3] 57-9684
I. Title.

Nelson, Michael, 1921- —Biography.

NELSON, Michael, 823'.9'14 B
1921-
Captain Blossom in civvy street / Michael Nelson. London ; New York : Gordon & Cremonesi, c1978. 185 p. ; 24 cm. [PR6064.E53Z465] 77-30505 ISBN 0-86033-052-4 : 16.95
1. Nelson, Michael, 1921- —Biography. 2. Authors, English—20th century—Biography. I. Title. BIP

Nelson, Nels J.

NELSON, Rueben 917.73'38'0340924
H., 1912-
Little Nels and The Partner; over 75 years of living the great American adventure as seen through the highlights in the lives of a Swedish-American farmer and his wife in the Cambridge Ulah, Red Oak, and Bishop Hill communities of Henry County, Illinois, 1882-1964, by Rueben H. Nelson. [Tempe? Ariz., 1968] 28 p. illus., ports. 23 cm. [CT275.N443N4] 74-3573
1. Nelson, Nels J. 2. Nelson, Hilma. I. Title.

Nelson, Ozzie, 1906-

NELSON, Ozzie, 790.2'092'4 B
1906-
Ozzie. Englewood Cliffs, N.J., Prentice-Hall [1973] viii, 309 p. illus. 24 cm. Autobiography. [PN2287.N36A32] 73-11063 ISBN 0-13-647768-2 7.95
1. Nelson, Ozzie, 1906-

Nelson, Reuben Emmanuel, 1905-1960.

TORBET, Robert George, 922.673
1912-
Reuben E. Nelson: free churchman [by] Robert G. Torbet, Henry R. Bowler. Chicago, Judson Pr. [c.1961] 64p. illus. 61-12687 1.50
1. Nelson, Reuben Emmanuel, 1905-1960. I. Bowler, Henry R., joint author. II. Title.

Nelson, Teresa (Leopando) Lucero,

NELSON, Teresa (Leopando) 926.1
Lucero, 1917-
White cap and prayer. [1st ed.] New York, Vantage Press [1955] 226p. 21cm. An autobiography. [RT37.N4A3] 55-9074
I. Title.

Nelson, Thomas Amos Rogers, 1812-1878.

ALEXANDER, Thomas 923.273
Benjamin, 1918-
Thomas A. R. Nelson of east Tennessee. Nashville, Tennessee Historical Commission [1956] x, 186p. illus., ports., fold. map, facsims. 25cm. 'Critical essay on authorities': p.170-175. [F442.1.N4A4] 56-63418
1. Nelson, Thomas Amos Rogers, 1812-1878. I. Title. BIP

Nemerov, Howard.

MEINKE, Peter. 811'.5'4
Howard Nemerov. Minneapolis, University of Minnesota Press [1968] 48 p. 21 cm. (University of Minnesota pamphlets on American writers, no. 70) Bibliography: p. 46-48. [PS3527.E5Z77] 68-64753 0.95
1. Nemerov, Howard. I. Title. II. Series: Minnesota. University. Pamphlets on American writers, no. 70 BIP

Neo-Kantianism.

WILLEY, Thomas E., 1934- 142'.3
Back to Kant : the revival of Kantianism in German social and historical thought, 1860-1914 / Thomas E. Willey. Detroit : Wayne State University Press, 1978. 231 p. ; 24 cm. Includes index. Bibliography: p. 210-223. [B3192.W54] 77-29215 ISBN 0-8143-1590-9 : 17.95
1. Neo-Kantianism. 2. Philosophers—Germany—Biography. I. Title. BIP

Nerinckx, Charles,

MAGARET, Helene, 1906 922.273
Giant in the wilderness, a biography of Father Charles Nerinckx. Milwaukee, Bruce Pub. Co. [1952] 200 p. illus. 22 cm. [BX4705.N4M33] 52-1753
1. Nerinckx, Charles, I. Title.

Nero, Emperor of Rome, 37-68.

BISHOP, John H. 923.137
Nero, the man and the legend. New York, A. S. Barnes [1965, c.1964] 208p. illus., maps, ports. 24cm. Bibl. [DG285.B4] 65-14237 5.00
1. Nero, Emperor of Rome, 37-68. I. Title.

FRANZERO, Charles Marie, v. 12
1892-
The life and times of Nero. New York, Philosophical Library, 1956. 334p. illus. Includes bibliography.
1. Nero, Emperor of Rome, 37-68. 2. Rome—Soc. life & cust. I. Title.

GRANT, Michael, 937'.07'0924
1914-
Nero, Emperor in revolt. New York, American Heritage Press [1970] 272 p. illus. (part col.), geneal. tables, maps, ports. (part col.) 26 cm. Includes bibliographical references. [DG285.G73 1970] 79-116178 12.95
1. Nero, Emperor of Rome, 37-68.

WALTER, Gerard, 937'.07'0924 B
1896-1974.
Nero / Gerard Walter ; translated by Emma Craufurd. Westport, Conn. : Greenwood Press, [1976], c1957. 334 p. : ill., geneal. tables ; 23 cm. Translation of Neron. Reprint of the ed. published by Allen & Unwin, London. Includes index. Bibliography: p. 321-328. [DG285.W3413 1976] 76-45165 ISBN 0-8371-9302-8 lib. bdg. : 18.75
1. Nero, Emperor of Rome, 37-68. 2. Roman emperors—Biography. BIP

WARMINGTON, Brian 937'.07'0924 B
Herbert.
Nero: reality and legend [by] B. H. Warmington. New York, Norton [1970, c1969] 180 p. illus., maps. 21 cm. (Ancient culture and society) Includes bibliographical references. [DG285.W36 1970] 71-95885 6.00
1. Nero, Emperor of Rome, 37-68. I. Title.

Neroccio de' Landi, 1447-1500.

COOR, Gertrude Marianne, 927.595
1915-
Neroccio de' Landi, 1447-1500. Princeton, N. J., Princeton [c.]1961. xvii, 235p. illus. 31cm. Bibl. 61-7415 20.00
1. Neroccio de' Landi, 1447-1500. I. Title.

Neruda, Pablo, 1904-1973—Biography.

NERUDA, Pablo, 1904-1973. 861 B
Memoirs / Pablo Neruda ; translated from the Spanish by Hardie St. Martin. New York : Farrar, Straus and Giroux, [1976] p. cm. Includes index. [PQ8097.N4Z52313] 76-27329 10.00
1. Neruda, Pablo, 1904-1973—Biography.

NERUDA, Pablo, 1904-1973. 861 B
Memoirs / Pablo Neruda; translated from the Spanish by Hardie St. Martin. New York : Penguin Books, 1978, c1967. 370 p. ; 20 cm. Translation of Confieso que he vivido. Autobiography. Includes index. [PQ8097.N4Z52313 1978] 77-14170 ISBN 0-14-004661-5 pbk. : 2.95
1. Neruda, Pablo, 1904-1973—Biography. 2. Poets, Children—20th century—Biography.

Nervous system.

RAMON Y CAJAL, 611.01880924
Santiago, 1852-1934
Recollections of my life. Tr. [from Spanish] by E. Horne Craigie with Juan Cano. Cambridge, Mass., M. I. T. Pr. [1966] xi, 638p. illus., ports. 21cm. Bibl. [QM16.R3A23] 66-3339 10.00
1. Nervous system. I. Title.

RAMON Y CAJAL, 611.01880924
Santiago, 1852-1934.
Recollections of my life. Translated by E. Horne Craigie with the assistance of Juan Cano. Cambridge, Mass., M.I.T. Press [196-?] xi, 638 p. illus., ports. 21 cm. "Works by the author": p. 607-623. [QM16.R3A23] 66-3339
1. Nervous system. I. Title.

Nesbit, Evelyn.

MOONEY, Michael 364.1'523'0922
Macdonald, 1930-
Evelyn Nesbit and Stanford White : love and death in the gilded age / by Michael Macdonald Mooney. New York : Morrow, 1976. p. cm. Includes index. [HV6534.N5M66] 76-18111 ISBN 0-688-03079-3 : 10.95
1. Nesbit, Evelyn. 2. White, Stanford, 1853-1906. 3. Thaw, Harry Kendall, 1871-1947. I. Title. **BIP**

Nesbitt, Cathleen, 1888-

NESBITT, Cathleen, 791'.092'4 B
1888-
A little love & good company / Cathleen Nesbitt. Owings Mills, Md. : Stemmer House Publishers, [1976] p. cm. Includes index. [PN2598.N43A34 1976] 76-43369 ISBN 0-916144-10-0 : 8.95
1. Nesbitt, Cathleen, 1888- 2. Actors—England—Biography. I. Title. **BIP**

Nesbitt, Lowell, 1933-

NESBITT, Lowell, 1933- 759.13
Lowell Nesbitt, an autobiography : January 23-February 21, 1976, Andrew Crispo Gallery. New York : The Gallery, c1976. [110] p. : ill. (some col.) ; 23 x 27 cm. Errata slip inserted. Bibliography: p. [6] [ND237.N445A83] 75-42999
1. Nesbitt, Lowell, 1933- I. Andrew Crispo Gallery. II. Title.

Nestor, Agnes.

NESTOR, Agnes. 331.88'092'4 B
Woman's labor leader : an autobiography of Agnes Nestor. Washington : Zenger Pub. Co., 1975, c1954. p. cm. Reprint of the ed. published by Bellevue Books Pub. Co., Rockford, Ill. Includes index. [HD6095.N37A3 1975] 75-37823 ISBN 0-89201-020-7 : 15.00
1. Nestor, Agnes. 2. Women in trade-unions—United States—History. 3. Women—Employment—United States. I. Title.

Nestorius, Patriarch of Constantinople, fl. 428.

LOOFS, Friedrich, 230'.1'40924 B
1858-1928.
Nestorius and his place in the history of Christian doctrine / by Friedrich Loofs. New York : B. Franklin, [1975] p. cm. Reprint of the 1914 ed. published by the University Press, Cambridge, Eng. [BR65.N384L66 1975] 75-1225 ISBN 0-8337-4903-X
1. Nestorius, Patriarch of Constantinople, fl. 428. I. Title. **BIP**

Nettlau, Max, 1865-1944.

†MUNOZ, 335'.83'0924 B
Vladimiro, 1920-
Max Nettlau, historian of anarchism / by Vladimir Munoz ; translated from the Spanish by Lucy Ross. New York : Revisionist Press, 1977. p. cm. (Men and movements in the history and philosophy of anarchism) Translation of Una Cronologia de Max Nettlau. Bibliography: p. [HX828.M8613] 73-75690 ISBN 0-87700-179-0 lib.bdg. : 39.95
1. Nettlau, Max, 1865-1944. 2. Anarchism and anarchists—Historiography. 3. Historians—Biography. I. Title. II. Series.

Neugeboren, Jay.

NEUGEBOREN, Jay. 813'.5'4
Parentheses; an autobiographical journey. [1st ed.] New York, Dutton, 1970. 221 p. 22 cm. [PS3564.E844Z5 1970] 73-95489 5.95
I. Title.

Neuharth, Steven, 1952-1975.

UTT, Richard H. 286'.73 B
Once you start climbing-don't look down : the story of Steve Neuharth / by Richard H. Utt, with Ruben and Nancy Neuharth. Mountain View, Calif. : Pacific Press Pub. Association, c1978. 122 p. : ill. ; 18 cm. (A Redwood paperback ; 110) [BX6193.N48U77] 78-50438 pbk. : 2.50
1. Neuharth, Steven, 1952-1975. 2. Seventh-Day Adventists—United States—Biography. I. Neuharth, Ruben, joint author. II. Neuharth, Nancy, joint author. III. Title. IV. Title: Don't look down.

Neuman, Therese, 1898-

SCHIMBERG, Albert Paul, 922.243
1885-
The story of Therese Neumann. Bruce paperback pub. in collaboration with All Saints. New York. [1962,c.1947] 211p. 17cm. (AS-233) .50 pap.,
1. Neuman, Therese, 1898- 2. Stigmatization. I. Title.

Neumann, Emanuel, 1893-

NEUMANN, 956.94'001'0924 B
Emanuel, 1893-
In the arena : an autobiographical memoir / by Emanuel Neumann. New York : Herzl Press, 1976. xx, 374 p., [7] leaves of plates : ill. ; 23 cm. Includes bibliographical references and index. [DS151.N46A34] 75-38195 10.00
1. Neumann, Emanuel, 1893- 2. Zionists—Biography. 3. Zionism—History. I. Title.

Neumann, John Nepomucene, Bp., 1811-1860.

CURLEY, Michael Joseph, v. 12
1900--
Venerable John Neumann, C. SS. R., fourth bishop of Philadelphia. Washington, Catholic University of America Press [c1952] xv, 547p. illus., port. 24cm. Bibliography:p. 489-512. A52
1. Neumann, John Nepomucene, Bp., 1811-1860. I. Title.

FLAVIUS, Brother, 1927- 92
The house on Logan Square; a story of Blessed John Neumann. Illus. by Carolyn Lee Jagodits. Notre Dame, Ind., Dujarie Press [1964] 94 p. illus., port. 24 cm. [BX4700.N4F5] 65-934
1. Neumann, John Nepomucene, Bp., 1811-1860. I. Title.

FLAVIUS, Brother, 1927- 92
The house on Logan Square; a story of Blessed John Neumann. Illus. by Carolyn Lee Jagodits. Notre Dame, Ind., 46556, Dujarie Pr. [c.1964] 94p. illus. port. 24cm. [BX4700.N4F5] 65-934 2.25
1. Neumann, John Nepomucene, Bp., 1811-1860. I. Title.

GALVIN, James J 1911- 922.273
Blessed John Neumann, Bishop of Philadelphia. Forword by John J. Krol. Baltimore, Helicon [1964] ix, 261 p. 21 cm. [BX4700.N4G28] 64-14665
1. Neumann, John Nepomucene, Bp., 1811-1860. I. Title.

LANGAN, Tom. 282'.092'4 B
John Neumann : harvester of souls / Tom Langan. Huntington, IN : Our Sunday Visitor, c1976. 155 p. ; 21 cm. [BX4700.N4L35] 76-21416 ISBN 0-87973-758-1 pbk. : 2.95
1. Neumann, John Nepomucene, Bp., 1811-1860. 2. Catholic Church—Bishops—Biography. 3. Bishops—Pennsylvania—Philadelphia—Biography. 4. Philadelphia—Biography.

WILSON, Robert H. 282'.092'4 B
St. John Neumann, 1811-1860, fourth Bishop of Philadelphia / Robert H. Wilson. Philadelphia : Institutional Services, Archdiocese of Philadelphia, c1977. 39 p. : ill. (some col.) ; 24 cm. [BX4705.N45W54] 77-70313
1. Neumann, John Nepomucene, Bp., 1811-1860. 2. Catholic Church—Bishops—Biography. 3. Bishops—Pennsylvania—Philadelphia—Biography. 4. Philadelphia—Biography. I. Title.

Neumann, Therese, 1898-

GRAEF, Hilda C. 922.243
The case of Therese Neumann. Westminster, Md., New man Press, 1951. xix, 162 p. 23 cm. Bibliographical footnotes. [BX4705.N47G7] 51-108577
1. Neumann, Therese, 1898- 2. Stigmatization. I. Title.

SIWEK, Paul. 922.243
The riddle of Konnersreuth, a psychological and religious study; translated by Ignatius McCormick. Milwaukee, Bruce Pub. Co. [1953] xvi, 228p. 23cm. Translation and revision of Une stigmatisee de nos jours. Bibliographical footnotes. [BX4705.N47S52] 53-13490
1. Neumann, Therese, 1898- 2. Stigmatization. I. Title.

THE two stigmatists, v. 12
Padre Pio and Teresa Neumann; containing the autobiography of Teresa Neumann, a critical account of the phenomena in her life and a comparison with Padre Pio. A reply to the apostles of hysteria. 2d ed. St. Paul, Radio Replies Press Society, [1956?] xxxii, 212p. illus. 22cm.
1. Neumann, Therese, 1898- 2. Pio da Pietralcina, Father, 1887- 3. Stigmatization. I. Carty, Charles Mortimer. II. Neumann, Therese, 1898-

Neurologists —Biog.

HAYMAKER, Webb, 1902- ed. 926.1
The founders of neurology; one hundred and thirty-three biographical sketches prepared for the Fourth International Neurological Congress in Paris by eighty-four authors. Edited by Webb Haymaker, with the bibliographical and editorial assistance of Karl A. Baer. Springfield, Ill., C. C. Thomas [1953] xxvii, 479p. ports. 24cm. Includes bibliographies. [R134.H29 1953] 53-9273
1. Neurologists —Biog. I. Title.

HAYMAKER, Webb, 616.8'0922 B
1902- ed.
The founders of neurology; one hundred and forty-six biographical sketches by eighty-eight authors. Compiled and edited by Webb Haymaker [and] Francis Schiller. 2d ed. Springfield, Ill., Thomas [1970] xxi, 616 p. ports. 24 cm. Includes bibliographical references. [R134.H29 1970] 70-94212
1. Neurologists—Biography. I. Schiller, Francis, 1909- joint ed. II. Title. **BIP**

Nevada—Governors.

MYLES, Myrtle Tate, 979.3'00992 B
1886-
Nevada's Governors from territorial days to the present, 1861-1971. [Sparks, Nev., Western Print. & Pub. Co., c1972] xvi, 310 p. illus. 24 cm. [F840.M94] 70-184056 10.00
1. Nevada—Governors. I. Title.

Nevada—History.

ANGEL, Myron, ed. 979.3
History of Nevada. New York, Arno Press, 1973 [c1881] 680 p. illus. 32 cm. (The Far Western frontier) Reprint of the 1881 ed. published by Thomas & West, Oakland, Calif. Caption and running titles: History of the State of Nevada. [F841.A5 1973] 72-9424 ISBN 0-405-04956-0 50.00
1. Nevada—History. 2. Nevada—Biography. I. Title. II. Title: History of the State of Nevada. III. Series. **BIP**

Neve, Felipe de, 1740 (ca.)-1784.

BEILHARZ, Edwin 979.4'02'0924 B
A.
Felipe de Neve, first Governor of California, by Edwin A. Beilharz. San Francisco, California Historical Society, 1971. 194 p. 24 cm. (California Historical Society. Special publication no. 49) Bibliography: p. 183-186. [F864.N52B44] 72-178276
1. Neve, Felipe de, 1740 (ca.)-1784. 2. California—History—To 1846. I. Title. II. Series.

Neve, Rosemary, 1923-

NEVE, Rosemary, 283'.092'4 B
1923-
At the name of Jesus / by Rosemary Neve. Evesham : James, 1976. 110 p. ; 19 cm. [BX5199.N53A34] 77-363320 ISBN 0-85305-189-5 : £2.25
1. Neve, Rosemary, 1923- 2. Anglicans—Biography. I. Title.

Nevelson, Louise, 1900-

GLIMCHER, Arnold B. 730'.92'4
Louise Nevelson [by] Arnold B. Glimcher. New York, Praeger [1972] 172 p. illus. 29 cm. Includes bibliographical references. [NB237.N43G55] 70-145946 29.50
1. Nevelson, Louise, 1900- **BIP**

GLIMCHER, Arnold B. 730'.92'4 B
Louise Nevelson / Arnold B. Glimcher. 2d ed., rev. and enl. New York : Dutton, c1976. 197 p., [5] leaves of plates : ill. (some col.) ; 28 cm. [NB237.N43G55 1976] 76-150542 ISBN 0-525-47439-0 : 11.95
1. Nevelson, Louise, 1900- 2. Sculptors—United States—Biography.

NEVELSON, Louise, 730'.92'4 B
1900-
Dawns and dusks : taped conversations with Diana Mackown / Louise Nevelson. New York : Scribner, [1976] p. cm. [NB237.N43A23] 76-20634 ISBN 0-684-14781-5 : 9.95
1. Nevelson, Louise, 1900- 2. Sculptors—United States—Correspondence, reminiscences, etc. I. Mackown, Diana. II. Title. **BIP**

Nevers, Ernie, 1903- —Juvenile literature.

SCOTT, Jim, 1912- 796.332'0924 B
Ernie Nevers, football hero. Minneapolis, T. S. Denison [1969] 175 p. illus., ports. 22 cm. (Men of achievement series) A biography of fullback Ernie Nevers, tracing his successful career as player and coach in college and professional football. [GV939.N4S3] 92 72-91357
1. Nevers, Ernie, 1903- —Juvenile literature. I. Title.

Neville, Emily Cheney.

NEVILLE, Emily Cheney. 818'.5'403
Traveler from a small kingdom. Pictures by George Mocniak. New York, Harper & Row [1968] 197 p. illus. 22 cm. Autobiographical. [PS3564.E85Z5] 67-20584
I. Title. BIP

Nevin, John Williamson,

NEVIN, John Williamson, 922.473
1803-1886
My own life: the earlier years. Lancaster, Pa., Hist. Soc. of the Evangelical and Reformed Church, c/o Fackenthal Lib., Franklin & Marshall Coll., 1964. i, 160p. 23cm. (Paps. of the Eastern Chapter, Hist. Soc. of the Evangelical and Reformed Church, no. 1) (Evangelical and Reformed Church, Historical Society. Eastern Chapter. Papers, no.1) [BX9593.N4A3] 64-57065 1.75
I. Title. II. Series. BIP

Nevin, John Williamson, 1803-1886.

APPEL, Theodore, 285'.7'0924 B
1823-1907.
The life and work of John Williamson Nevin. New York, Arno Press, 1969. 776 p. facsim., port. 24 cm. (Religion in America) Reprint of the 1889 ed. [BX9593.N4A6 1969] 71-83409
1. Nevin, John Williamson, 1803-1886. I. Title. BIP

NEVIN, John Williamson, 922.473
1803-1886
My own life: the earlier years. Lancaster, Pa., Hist. Soc. of the Evangelical and Reformed Church, c/o Fackenthal Lib., Franklin & Marshall Coll., 1964. i, 160p. 23cm. (Paps. of the Eastern Chapter, Hist. Soc. of the Evangelical and Reformed Church, no. 1) (Evangelical and Reformed Church, Historical Society. Eastern Chapter. Papers, no.1) [BX9593.N4A3] 64-57065 1.75
I. Title. II. Series. BIP

New Denver, B.C. Relocation Center—Juvenile literature.

TAKASHIMA, 940.54'72'710971144
Shizuye.
A child in prison camp [by] Takashima. [1st ed. Plattsburg, N.Y.] Tundra Books, 1971. [74] p. illus. 20 x 25 cm. For three years during World War Two, a Japanese-Canadian girl and her family are imprisoned with thousands of others considered possible security threats. [D768.15.T34] 74-179429 ISBN 0-912766-00-X 7.95
1. New Denver, B.C. Relocation Center—Juvenile literature. 2. Takashima, Shizuye—Juvenile literature. 3. Japanese in British Colombia—Juvenile literature. 4. World War, 1939-1945—Evacuation of civilians—Juvenile literature. I. Title. BIP

New England—Biography.

BARKER, Shirley. 974.0922
Builders of New England. New York, Dodd, Mead [1965] 238 p. illus., ports. 21 cm. [F3.B37] 65-21420
1. New England—Biography. I. Title.

BOULEY, Charles Henry. 920.074
Biographical sketches of the pioneer settlers of New England, and their descendants in Worcester, Massachusetts. Barre, Mass., Barre Publishers [1964] xi, 643 p. geneal. tables. 24 cm. [F3.B6] 64-22850
1. New England — Biog. 2. Worcester, Mass. — Biog. I. Title.

POTTER, Gail M. 920.074
Stories behind the stones [by] Gail M. Potter. South Brunswick [N.J.] A. S. Barnes [1969] 244 p. illus., facsim., ports. 26 cm. Bibliography: p. 235-238. [F3.P6] 68-27250 8.50
1. New England—Biography. 2. Epitaphs—New England. I. Title.

WHITEHILL, Walter Muir, 920.074
1905-
Analecta biographica; a handful of New England portraits. Brattleboro, Vt., Stephen Greene Press [1969] xi, 243 p. ports. 23 cm. [CT240.W5] 78-76527 10.00
1. New England—Biography. I. Title.

New England—Church history.

MATHER, Cotton, 1663-1728. 277.4
Magnalia Christi Americana : or, The ecclesiastical history of New-England from its first planting in the year 1620 unto the year of our Lord 1698 / Cotton Mather. New York : Arno Press, 1972. 7 v. in 1 : ill. ; 27 cm. (Research library of colonial Americana) Reprint of the 1702 ed. printed for T. Parkhurst, London. [BR530.M34 1972] 74-141092 ISBN 0-405-03297-8
1. New England—Church history. 2. New England—History—Colonial period, ca. 1600-1775. 3. New England—Biography. I. Title. II. Series. BIP

New England—Description and travel—To 1775.

KNIGHT, Sarah 917.4'04'20924 B
Kemble, 1666-1727.
The journal of Madam Knight, including an introductory note by Malcolm Freiberg and wood engravings by Michael McCurdy. Boston, D. R. Godine, 1972 [c1971] 39 p. illus. 24 cm. Includes bibliographical references. [F7.K724 1972] 71-172647 ISBN 0-87923-044-4 10.00
1. New England—Description and travel—To 1775. I. Title. BIP

New England—Social life and customs.

HALE, Edward Ev erett, 922.8173
1822-1909.
A New England boyhood. With a new introd. by Nancy Hale. Boston, Little, Brown [1964] x. 208 p. illus. 20 cm. [PS1773.A2] 64-3439
1. New England—Soc. life & cust. 2. Boston—Soc. life & cust. I. Title.

HALE, Edward Everett, 818'.4'09 B
1822-1909.
A New England boyhood. Upper Saddle River, N.J., Literature House [1970] xxv, 267 p. illus. 22 cm. Reprint of the 1893 ed. [PS1773.A4 1970] 70-104469
1. New England—Social life and customs. 2. Boston—Social life and customs. I. Title BIP

HALE, Edward Everett, 818'.4'09
1822-1909.
A New England boyhood. A new ed. with foreword by Edwin D. Mead. New York, Grosset & Dunlap. St. Clair Shores, Mich., Scholarly Press, 1970 [c1927] xxxii, 208 p. illus., facsims., ports. 21 cm. [PS1773.A4 1970b] 72-131731 ISBN 0-403-00618-X
1. New England—Social life and customs. 2. Boston—Social life and customs. I. Title.

LARCOM, Lucy, 1824-1893 928.1
A new England girlhood. Introd. by Charles T. Davis [Gloucester, Mass., Peter Smith, c.1961] 274p. illus. (Amer. experience ser., AE9: Corinth bk. rebound) 3.75
1. New England—Soc. life & cust. I. Title.

LARCOM, Lucy, 1824-1893. 928.1
A New England girlhood. Introd. by Charles T. Davis. New York, Corinth Books [1961] 274p. illus. 19cm. (The American experience series, AE9) [PS2223.A3 1961] 61-8154
1. New England—Soc. life & cust. I. Title.

LARCOM, Lucy, 1824-1893. 928.1
A New England girlhood. Introd. by Charles T. Davis. Gloucester, Mass., Peter Smith, 1973 [c.1961] 274 p. illus. 21 cm. Reprint of the 1961 Corinth Books ed., The American experience series. [PS2223.A3 1961] ISBN 0-8446-2431-4 4.50
1. New England—Social life and customs. I. Title.
L.C. card no. for the Corinth ed.: 61-8154. BIP

New France—Discovery and exploration.

CHAMPLAIN, Samuel de, 971.01*13
1567-1635.
Voyages of Samuel de Champlain. Translated from the French by Charles Pomeroy Otis. With historical illus. and a memoir by Edmund F. Slafter. New York, B. Franklin [1966] 3 v. illus. 22 cm. (Burt Franklin research and source works series, #131. American classics in history and social science, #2) Reprint of the 1880 ed., which was issued as no. 11-13 of the Prince Society publications. Translation of the author's "Des savages, or, Voyages," 1604; "Les voyages ... or, Journal," 1613; and "Voyages et descouvertures faites en la Nouvelle France," 1619. [F1030.1.C438 1966] 72-184502
1. New France—Discovery and exploration. 2. America—Discovery and exploration—French. 3. Indians of North America—Canada. I. Title. II. Series: Prince Society, Boston. Publications, v. 11-13. BIP

New Jersey — Biog.

GRISCOM, Lloyd E 929'.3749
The down-Jerseymen: spirited adventurers; informal history. [Riverton? N.J., 1963] 118 p. illus., maps. 23 cm. [F133.G7] 64-4367
1. New Jersey — Biog. 2. New Jersey — Hist. I. Title.

New Mexico

FALL, Albert Bacon, 978.9040924
1861-1944.
The memoirs of Albert B. Fall. Edited with annotations by David H. Stratton. [El Paso, Texas Western Press] 1966. 63 p. illus., ports. 23 cm. (Southwestern studies, v. 4 no. 3. Monography no. 15) Cover title. "References": p. 53-62. [E748.F22A3] 66-65634
1. New Mexico — Pol. & govt. I. Stratton, David Hodges, 1927- ed. II. Title. III. Series. IV. Series: Southwestern studies, v. 4, no. 3

New Mexico—Biography.

CLARK, Ann (Nolan) 1898- 920.0789
These were the valiant; a collection of New Mexico profiles. [1st ed.] Albuquerque, N.M., C. Horn [1969] xiii, 150 p. 24 cm. Revision of a series of articles published originally in New Mexico magazine. [F795.C55] 71-102984 6.50
1. New Mexico—Biography. I. Title.

NEW Mexico. Historical 920.0789
Society.
Hall of fame essays. 1963- [Albuquerque] v. ports. 25 cm. annual. [F795.N48] 63-63709
1. New Mexico — Biog. I. Title.

WOODS, Dora 978.9'00992 B
Elizabeth Ahern, 1904-
101 men and women of New Mexico : 101 men and 101 women who contributed to New Mexico's history / by Betty Woods i.e. D. E. A. Woods Santa Fe, N.M. : Sunstone Press, c1976. 24 p. ; 23 cm. [F795.W66] 76-362749 ISBN 0-913270-58-X : 1.95
1. New Mexico—Biography. I. Title.

New Orleans—Biography.

FRENCH Quarter 917.63'03'60922
interviews. [New Orleans, Vagabond Press] 1969. 96 p. ports. 23 cm. Contents.Contents.—Danny Barker, curator of the Jazz Museum.—The Reverend Joseph E. Fogle.—Little Joe, bartender at the Seven Seas.—Rocque Brown, mayor of the French Quarter.—Nancy Davis, artist.—Tinker Bell, human being.—Bill Jones, manager of the Red Garter.—Roger Lovin, editor and publisher of The Word.—Frenchy, dancer and barmaid. [F379.N5F75] 70-80116 1.75 (pbk)
1. New Orleans—Biography.

New Orleans—History.

CLAPP, Theodore, 285'.8'0924 B
1792-1866.
Autobiographical sketches and recollections, during a thirty-five years' residence in New Orleans. Freeport, N.Y., Books for Libraries Press [1972] viii, 419 p. port. 23 cm. Reprint of the 1857 ed. [BX9225.C547A3 1972] 77-38346 ISBN 0-8369-6763-1
1. New Orleans—History. I. Title.

CLAPP, Theodore, 1792- 922.8173
1866.
Parson Clapp of the Strangers' Church of New Orleans, edited by John Duffy. Baton Rouge, Louisiana State University Press [1957] ix, 191p. illus., port., facsim. 24cm. (Louisiana State University studies. Social science series, no. 7) Selections from the author's Autobiographical sketches and recollections, during a thirty-five years' residence in New Orleans, with an account of his life by the editor. Bibliographical references included in 'Notes' (p. 175-188) [F379.N5C584] 57-9481
1. New Orleans—Hist. I. Duffy, John, 1915- ed. II. Title. III. Series.

New Orleans—Schools.

MEYER, Robert 371'.01'0976335
Eugene, 1911-
Names over New Orleans public schools / Robert Meyer, Jr. New Orleans : Namesake Press, [1975] v, 269 p. ; 23 cm. Includes bibliographical references and index. [LA297.N4M49] 75-314596
1. New Orleans—Schools. 2. United States—Biography. I. Title.

New South Wales. District Courts—Biography.

HOLT, Henry 347'.944'0234 B
Thomas Eulert.
A court rises : history of the judges of the District Court of New South Wales / [by] H. T. E. Holt. Sydney : Law Foundation of New South Wales, 1976. xxi, 258 p. : ill. ; 24 cm. Includes bibliographical references and index. [LAW] 76-379996 ISBN 0-909136-02-5
1. New South Wales. District Courts—Biography. 2. Judges—New South Wales—Biography. I. Title.

New Thought—United States—Directories.

BEEBE, Tom. 289.9 B
Who's who in New Thought : biographical dictionary of New Thought : personnel, centers, and authors' publications / by Tom Beebe. Lakemont, Ga. : CSA Press, c1977. 318 p. : maps ; 24 cm. Bibliography: p. 286-311. [BF648.A1B43] 77-152019 ISBN 0-87707-189-6 : 6.95
1. New Thought—United States—Directories. I. Title.

New York Association for the Blind.

HOLT, Winifred. 923.673
First lady of the Lighthouse, a biography of Winifred Holt Mather, edited by Edith Holt Bloodgood, in collaboration with Rufus Graves Mather. New York, The Lighthouse, New York Association for the Blind [1952] 207 p. illus. 20 cm. [HV1792.H65B5] 52-10597
1. New York Association for the Blind. I. Bloodgood, Edith (Holt). ed. II. Title.

New York. Baseball Club (American League)

ROBINSON, Ray, 796.357'0922
Dec.4,1920-
The greatest Yankees of them all. New

York, Putnam [1969] viii, 223 p. ports. 21 cm. (Putnam sports shelf) Contents.Contents.—Mickey Mantle.—Whitey Ford.—Red Ruffing.—Babe Ruth.—Roger Maris.—Allie Reynolds.—Herb Pennock.—Phil Rizzuto.—Lefty Gomez.—Yogi Berra.—Bill Dickey.—Red Rolfe.—Tony Lazzeri.—Joe Di Maggio.—Lou Gehrig. [GV865.A1R58] 68-24543 3.49
1. New York. Baseball Club (American League) 2. Baseball—Biography. I. Title.

New York (City). Baseball club (National League, Mets)

FISHMAN, Lew. 796.357'64'097471
New York's Mets : miracle at Shea / by Lew Fishman. Englewood Cliffs, N.J. : Prentice-Hall, [1974] 126 p. : ill. ; 28 cm. "A Stuart L. Daniels book." [GV875.N45F55] 74-7517 ISBN 0-13-620559-3 : 3.95
1. New York (City). Baseball club (National League, Mets) 2. Baseball. 3. Baseball—Biography. I. Title.

JACOBSON, Steve. 796.357'22
The pitching staff / Steve Jacobson. New York : Crowell, [1975] ix, 221 p., [4] leaves of plates : ports. ; 21 cm. [GV871.J32 1975] 75-6836 ISBN 0-690-00696-9 : 7.95
1. New York (City) Baseball club (National League, Mets) 2. Pitching (Baseball) 3. Pitchers (Baseball)—Biography. I. Title.

New York (City)—Biography.

TALESE, Gay 920.07471
The overreachers. Illus. by Stanislav Zagorski. New York, Harper [c.1961-1965] 190p. illus. 22cm. [F128.25.T13] 64-20542 3.95
1. New York (City)—Biog. I. Title.

TALESE, Gay. 920.07471
The overreachers. With illus. by Stanislav Zagorski. [1st ed.] New York, Harper & Row [c1965] 190 p. illus. 22 cm. [F128.25.T13] 64-20542
1. New York (City)—Biog. I. Title.

ULMANN, Albert, 1861-1948. 920.07471
New Yorkers from Stuyvesant to Roosevelt. With a new introd. by Ralph Adams Brown. Port Washington, N.Y., I. J. Friedman [1969, c1928] 267 p. illus., ports. 24 cm. (Empire State historical publications series, no. 62) [F128.25.U43 1969] 68-58929
1. New York (City)—Biography. I. Title. II. Series: Empire State historical publication no. 62

New York (City). Calvary Baptist Church.

DE PLATA, William R. 286'.1747'1
Tell it from Calvary; the record of a sustained Gospel witness from Calvary Baptist Church of New York City since 1847, by William R. De Plata. New York, Calvary Baptist Church [1973 c1972] xii, 189 p. illus. 24 cm. [BX6480.N5C33] 72-92842 4.95
1. New York (City). Calvary Baptist Church. 2. Baptists—Biography. 3. Baptists—Sermons. 4. Sermons, American. I. Title.
pap. 3.50.

New York (City)—Description—1951-

HAYES, Helen, 1900- 917.47'1'034
Twice over lightly; New York then and now [by] Helen Hayes and Anita Loos. [1st ed.] New York, Harcourt Brace Jovanovich [1972] 343 p. illus. 21 cm. [F128.52.H33] 72-75417 ISBN 0-15-192150-4
1. New York (City)—Description—1951- I. Loos, Anita, 1894- joint author. II. Title.

New York (City)—History—Anecdotes.

WHALEN, Grover Aloysius, 1886- 923.273
Mr. New York; the autobiography of Grover A. Whalen. New York, Putnam [1955] 312 p. illus. 22 cm. [F128.5.W54] 55-10103
1. New York (City)—History—Anecdotes. 2. Visits of state—New York (City) I. Title.

New York (City)—History—1775-1865.

HONE, Philip, 1780-1851. 917.471'03'3
The diary of Philip Hone, 1828-1851. Allan Nevins, editor. With a pref. by Churchill Rodgers. New York, Arno Press, 1970 [c1927] 2 v. in 1 (xxvii, 962 p.) ports. 23 cm. (The Rise of urban America) [F128.44.H77 1970] 77-112559
1. New York (City)—History—1775-1865. 2. New York (City)—Social life and customs. 3. U.S.—Politics and government—1815-1861. I. Title. II. Series. BIP

New York (City)—Mayors.

HAMBURGER, Philip Paul, 1914- 917.47'1'034
Mayor watching and other pleasures [by] Philip Hamburger. Freeport, N.Y., Books for Libraries Press [1973] p. (Essays index reprint series) Reprint of the 1958 ed. [F128.25.H3 1973] 72-10778 ISBN 0-8369-7221-X
*1. New York (City)—Mayors. 2. New York (City)—Biography. 3. New York (City)—Social life and customs. I. Title.*BIP

New York (City)—Police.

RADANO, Gene. 363.2'2
Walking the beat; a New York policeman tells what it's like on his side of the law. Cleveland, World Pub. Co. [1968] 192 p. 22 cm. [HV7914.R23] 68-13709
1. New York (City)—Police. 2. Police—Correspondence, reminiscences, etc. I. Title.

New York (City)—Police—Correspondence, reminiscences, etc.

*DROGE, Edward F. 363.2'092'4 [B]
The patrolman: a cop's story, by Edward F. Droge, Jr. [New York] New American Lib. [1973] 240 p. 18 cm. (Signet, Y5468) [HV7911] 1.25 (pbk.)
1. New York (City)—Police—Correspondence, reminiscences, etc. I. Title.

New York (City)—Social life and customs.

CHURCHILL, Allen, 1911- 309.1'7471
The upper crust; an informal history of New York's highest society. Englewood Cliffs, N.J., Prentice-Hall [1970] 290 p. illus., facsims., map, ports. 32 cm. Bibliography: p. 277-278. [F128.47.C47] 78-96270 ISBN 0-13-939157-6 12.95
1. New York (City)—Social life and customs. 2. New York (City)—Biography. I. Title.

DANA, Ethel Nathalie (Smith) 1878- 920.7
Young in New York; a memoir of a Victorian girlhood. Garden City, N. Y., Doubleday, 1963[c.1962, 1963] 205p. illus. 22cm. 63-16632 4.50
1. New York (City)—Soc. life & cust. I. Title.

SCHOENSTEIN, Ralph, 1933- 818.54
The block. New York, Random House [1960] 137p. illus. 22cm. The author's story of his boyhood in New York City. [CT275.S34475A3] 60-12138
1. New York (City)—Soc. life & cust. I. Title.

New York (City) Metropolitan Opera.

NOBLE, Helen Klaffky. 782
Life with the Met. New York, Putnam [1954] 250 p. illus. 22 cm. Autobiographical. [ML1711.8.N32M468] 54-5490
1. New York (City) Metropolitan Opera. I. Title.

New York Cosmos (Soccer team)

ROTH, Werner, 1948- 796.33'463'09747
Werner Roth's Cosmos book of soccer / Werner Roth with Frank Coffey. New York : Stein and Day, 1979. p. cm. Includes index. [GV943.6.N466R67] 78-66259 ISBN 0-8128-2609-4 : 14.95
1. New York Cosmos (Soccer team) 2. Roth, Werner, 1948- 3. Soccer players—United States—Biography. I. Coffey, Frank, joint author. II. Title. III. Title: Cosmos book of soccer.

New York Herald Tribune. European edition.

HAWKINS, Eric 920.5
Hawkins of the Paris Herald. With Robert N. Sturdevant. New York, S. & S. [c.]1963. 284p. 24cm. 63-10855 5.95
1. New York Herald Tribune. European edition. I. Title.

HAWKINS, Eric. 920.5
Hawkins of the Paris Herald. With Robert N. Sturdevant. New York, Simon and Schuster, 1963. 284 p. 24 cm. [PN4874.H275A3] 63-10855
1. New York herald tribune. European edition. I. Title.

New York Knickerbockers (Basketball team)

DEBUSSCHERE, Dave, 1940- 796.32'3'64097471
The open man; a championship diary. Edited by Paul D. Zimmerman and Dick Schaap. [1st ed.] New York, Random House [1970] 267 p. illus. ports. 22 cm. (A Maddick manuscripts book) [GV884.D4A3] 79-117648 6.95
1. New York Knickerbockers (Basketball team) I. Title.

New York Rangers (Hockey club)

FISCHLER, Stan. 796.9'62'097471
New York's Rangers : the icemen cometh / by Stan Fischler ; photography, Melchior Di Giacomo ; introd. by Mary Albert. Englewood Cliffs, N.J. : Prentice-Hall, [1974] 127 p. : ill. ; 28 cm. (Reward books) "A Stuart L. Daniels book." Text and photographs present a brief history of the New York Rangers hockey team with short biographies of the team members. [GV848.N43F56] 920 74-9237 ISBN 0-13-620567-4 pbk. : 3.95
1. New York Rangers (Hockey club) 2. Hockey—Biography. I. Title.

New York (State)—Biography.

FISKE, Stephen, 1840-1916. 920'.0747
Off-hand portraits of prominent New Yorkers / by Stephen Fiske. New York : Arno Press, 1975 [c1884] p. cm. (The Leisure class in America) Reprint of the ed. published by Lockwood, New York. [F118.F53 1975] 75-1847 ISBN 0-405-06914-6 : 21.00
1. New York (State)—Biography. 2. New York (City)—Biography. I. Title. II. Series. BIP

New York. State Prison, Attica.

COONS, William R. 365'.6'0924 B
Attica diary [by] William R. Coons. New York, Stein and Day [1972] 238 p. 22 cm. [HV9475.N716C66 1972] 72-187100 ISBN 0-8128-1469-X 6.95
1. New York. State Prison, Attica. 2. Prisoners—New York (State)—Personal narratives. I. Title.

MELVILLE, Samuel, 1935- 365'.6'0924 B
Letters from Attica. New York, Morrow, 1972. x, 181 p. 21 cm. Contents.Contents.—Foreword, by W. Kunstler.—Profile of Sam Melville, by J. Alpert.—Introduction, by J. Cohen.—Letters, by S. Melville.—The Attica Liberation Faction Manifesto of demands and Anti-depression platform. [HV9475.N716M4] 71-187806 ISBN 0-688-06031-5 1.95
1. New York. State prison, Attica. 2. Prisoners—Personal narratives. I. Title. BIP

New York University. Hall of American Artists.

PARIS, William Francklyn, 1871-1954. 709'.22
Personalities in American art. Freeport, N.Y., Books for Libraries Press [1970- v. ports. 23 cm. (Essay index reprint series) Vols. 2-10 have title: The Hall of American Artists. Reprint of the 1930- ed. [N6536.P32] 72-107731
1. New York University. Hall of American Artists. 2. Artists, American. I. Title. II. Title: The Hall of American Artists. BIP

New Zealand—Biog.

WHO'S who in New Zealand. G. C. Petersen, ed. 7th ed. [Dist. New York, Heinman, 1962] 307p. 23cm. Title varies: 7th ed., 1961. Who's who in New Zealand. Ed.: 1961, G. C. Petersen. 27-18903 15.00 920.0931
1. New Zealand—Biog. I. Petersen, G. C., ed.

New Zealand—Description and travel—To 1840.

BURNS, Barnet, b.ca.1807. 919.3'1'0310924 B
A brief narrative of a New Zealand chief, being the remarkable history of Barnet Burns, an English sailor, with a faithful account of the way in which he became a chief of one of the tribes of New Zealand; together with a few remarks on the manners and customs of the people, and other interesting matter, written by himself. Belfast, Printed by R. & D. Read, 1844. [Dunedin, Hocken Library, 1970] facsim: 26 p. illus. 22 cm. (Hocken Library. Facsimile no. 11) [DU410.B86] 75-871941 0.95
1. New Zealand—Description and travel—To 1840. 2. Maoris. I. Title. II. Series: Dunedin, N.Z. University of Otago. Library. Hocken Collection. Facsimile no. 11.

Newbold, Douglas, Sir, 1894-1945.

NEWBOLD, Douglas, Sir, 1894-1945. 962.4'03 B
The making of the modern Sudan; the life and letters of Sir Douglas Newbold ... by K. D. D. Henderson. With an introd. by Margery Perham. Westport, Conn., Greenwood Press [1974] xlii, 601 p. illus. 22 cm. Reprint of the 1953 ed. published by Faber and Faber, London, in series: Colonial and comparative studies. [DT108.6.N4 1974] 73-16800 ISBN 0-8371-7233-0
1. Newbold, Douglas, Sir, 1894-1945. 2. Sudan—History—1899-1956. I. Henderson, Kenneth David Druitt, 1903- ed. II. Title. III. Series: Colonial and comparative studies.

Newby, Elizabeth Loza.

†NEWBY, Elizabeth Loza. 301.44'43'0924 B
A migrant with hope / Elizabeth Loza Newby. Nashville : Broadman Press, c1977. 138 p. ; 20 cm. [BX7795.N43A34] 76-53980 ISBN 0-8054-7218-5 : 4.95
1. Newby, Elizabeth Loza. 2. Friends, Society of—United States—Biography. 3. Mexican Americans—Biography. I. Title. BIP

Newcastle, Margaret (Lucas) Cavendish, duchess 66, 1624?-1674.

GRANT, Douglas. 928.2
Margaret the First; a biography of Margaret Cavendish, duchess of Newcastle, 1623-1673. [Toronto] University of Toronto Press, 1957. 252p. illus. 23cm. [PR3605.N2G7 1957] 57-32605

1. Newcastle, Margaret (Lucas) Cavendish, duchess 66, 1624?-1674. I. Title.

Newcastle, Thomas Pelham-Holles, 1st Duke of, 1693-1768.

BROWNING, Reed. 941.07'2'0924 B
The Duke of Newcastle / Reed Browning. New Haven : Yale University Press, 1975. xiv, 388 p. : port. ; 24 cm. Includes index. Bibliography: p. 355-371. [DA501.N5B76] 74-77597 ISBN 0-300-01746-4 : 20.00
1. Newcastle, Thomas Pelham-Holles, 1st Duke of, 1693-1768. I. Title. **BIP**

KELCH, Ray A. 914.2'03'72 B
Newcastle; a duke without money; Thomas Pelham-Holles, 1693-1768 [by] Ray A. Kelch. Berkeley, University of California Press, 1974. x, 222 p. 23 cm. Bibliography: p. 211-216. [DA501.N5K44] 73-83064 ISBN 0-520-02537-7 12.00
1. Newcastle, Thomas Pelham-Holles, 1st Duke of, 1693-1768. I. Title.

Newcastle-upon-Tyne—Biography.

BELL, David, 1924- 920.0428'1
Characters of old Tyneside; evoked by David Bell and Edwin Patterson. Newcastle upon Tyne, Oriel P., 1969. [31] p. ports. 22 cm. [DA690.N6B38] 73-466532 ISBN 8-536-20695- 5/-
1. Newcastle-upon-Tyne—Biography. I. Patterson, Edwin, joint author. II. Title.

Newcastle, William Cavendish, Duke of, 1592-1676.

TREASE, Geoffrey, 1909- 941.06'2'0924 B
Portrait of a cavalier : William Cavendish, first Duke of Newcastle / Geoffrey Trease. New York : Taplinger Pub. Co., 1979. 223 p., [4] leaves of plates : ill. ; 23 cm. Includes index. Bibliography: p. 216-219. [DA407.N5T73 1979] 79-4929 ISBN 0-8008-6418-2 : 12.95
1. Newcastle, William Cavendish, Duke of, 1592-1676. 2. Great Britain. Army—Biography. 3. Great Britain—History—Charles I, 1625-1649. 4. Great Britain—History—Commonwealth and Protectorate, 1649-1660. 5. Great Britain—History—Charles II, 1660-1685. 6. Great Britain—Court and courtiers—Biography. 7. Generals—Great Britain—Biography. I. Title.

Newcomb. Kate (Pelham)

COMANDINI, Adele. 926.1
Doctor Kate, angel on snowshoes; the story of Kate Pelham Newcomb. New York, Rinehart [1956] 339p. illus. 22cm. [R154.N5C6] 56-5290
1. Newcomb. Kate (Pelham) I. Title.

Newell, Alton S., 1913- —Juvenile literature.

LEIPOLD, L. Edmond, 1902- 338.4'7'60460924 B
Alton S. Newell: recycling expert; up from poverty to become a worldwide recycling merchant, by L. E. Leipold. Minneapolis, T. S. Denison [1973] 201 p. illus. 23 cm. (Men of achievement series) A biography of a pioneer in the business of recycling scrap metal who began his career with a small auto-wrecking yard. [TS140.N48L46] 92 72-96412 ISBN 0-513-01306-7 4.98 (lib. bdg.)
1. Newell, Alton S., 1913- —Juvenile literature. I. Title.

Newell, Harriett Chase,

NEWELL, Harriett Chase, 1881- 917.42'6'034
In retrospect, an autobiography. [Littleton, N.H., Printed by Courier Print. Co.] 1967 [c1968] 165 p. illus., ports. 23 cm. [CT275.N476A3] 68-3504
I. Title.

NEWELL, Harriett Chase, 1881- 917.42'6'034
In retrospect, an autobiography. [Littleton, N. H., Printed by Courier Print, Co.] 1967 [1968] 165 p. illus., ports. 23 cm. [CT275.N476A3] 68-3504
I. Title.

Newhall, Beaumont, 1908- — Bibliography.

BEAUMONT Newhall. 016.709'24
[Rochester, N.Y., George Eastman House, 1971] [19] l. 28 cm. Chiefly a bibliography of the works of B. Newhall, compiled by R. Sobieszek and P. A. Slahucka. [Z8621.75.B4] 70-28255
1. Newhall, Beaumont, 1908- — Bibliography. I. Sobieszek, Robert A., 1943- II. Slahucka, Patricia A. III. George Eastman House, Rochester, N.Y.

Newhart, Robert, 1929- —Juvenile literature.

PAIGE, David. 791'.092'4 B
Bob Newhart / written by David Paige ; designed by Gene Kohler. [Mankato, Minn.] : Creative Education, [c1977] 30 p. : ill. ; 25 cm. (Stars of stage and screen) A biography of the popular comedian who stars in his own television show and sometimes appears in serious dramatic roles in movies. [PN2287.N43P3] 92 76-44013 ISBN 0-87191-561-8 lib.bdg. : 4.95
1. Newhart, Robert, 1929- —Juvenile literature. 2. Comedians—United States—Biography—Juvenile literature. I. Title. **BIP**

Newlands, Francis Griffith, 1848-1917.

ATWOOD, Albert William, 1879- 328.73'0924 B
Francis G. Newlands, a builder of the Nation, by Albert W. Atwood. [Washington? 1969] 64 p. port. 24 cm. [E664.N54A8] 78-105106
1. Newlands, Francis Griffith, 1848-1917. I. Title.

Newman, Barnett, 1905-1970.

ROSENBERG, Harold. 709'.2'4
Barnett Newman / by Harold Rosenberg. New York : Abrams, [1978] p. cm. (Contemporary artists series) Includes index. Bibliography: p. [N6537.N48R67] 77-25433 ISBN 0-8109-1360-7 : 45.00
1. Newman, Barnett, 1905-1970. 2. Artists—United States—Biography. I. Title. II. Series. **BIP**

Newman, Cecil E., 1903-—Juvenile literature.

LEIPOLD, L. Edmond, 1902- 655.4'24 B
Cecil E. Newman, newspaper publisher, by L. E. Leipold. Minneapolis, T. S. Denison [1969] 203 p. illus., ports. 22 cm. (Men of achievement series) Biography of a black journalist who currently publishes two newspapers. [PN4874.N39Z75] 92 72-104886
1. Newman, Cecil E., 1903-—Juvenile literature. I. Title.

Newman, Ernest, 1868-1959.

NEWMAN, Vera, 1895- 927.8
Ernest Newman; a memoir by his wife. New York, Knopf, 1964 [c.1963] 278p. illus., ports. 22cm. 64-14420 6.00
1. Newman, Ernest, 1868-1959. I. Title.

Newman, Howard Walker, 1840-1904.

NEWMAN, Earle S. 973.7'468'0924 B
Biography of Howard Walker Newman / by Earle S. Newman. [Alexandria, Va.] : Newman, c1975. iv p., 20 leaves ; 29 cm. Bibliography: leaf 20. [E579.9.N48N48] 75-40236
1. Newman, Howard Walker, 1840-1904. I. Title.

Newman, John Henry, Cardinal, 1801-1890.

BOUYER, Louis 922.242
Newman; his life and spirituality [Tr. from the French by J. Lewis May] New York, Meridian Books [1960, c.1958] xii, 391p. (Bibl. footnotes) 19cm. (M87) 1.55 pap.,
1. Newman, John Henry, Cardinal, 1801-1890. I. Title.

BOUYER, Louis, 1913- 922.242
Newman; his life and spirituality. [Translated by J. Lewis May] New York, Meridian Books [1960, c1958] xiii, 391 p. 19 cm. (Meridian books) "M87." [BX4705.N5B653] 60-6782
1. Newman, John Henry, Cardinal, 1801-1890. I. Title.

DARK, Sidney, 1874-1947. 262'.135'0924 B
Newman. [Folcroft, Pa.] Folcroft Library Editions, 1973. p. Reprint of the 1934 ed. published by Duckworth, London, which was issued as no. 36 of Great lives. Bibliography: p. [BX4705.N5D3 1973] 73-7641 10.00
1. Newman, John Henry, Cardinal, 1811-1890. **BIP**

DARK, Sidney, 1874-1947. 262'.135'0924 B
Newman. [Folcroft, Pa.] Folcroft Library Editions, 1973. p. Reprint of the 1934 ed. published by Duckworth, London, which was issued as no. 36 of Great lives. Bibliography: p. [BX4705.N5D3 1973] 73-7641 ISBN 0-8414-1870-5 (lib. bdg.)
1. Newman, John Henry, Cardinal, 1811-1890.

DONALD, Gertrude. 283'.43
Men who left the movement: John Henry Newman, Thomas W. Allies, Henry Edward Manning, Basil William Maturin. Freeport, N.Y., Books for Libraries Press [1967] viii, 422 p. 21 cm. (Essay index reprint series) Reprint of the 1933 ed. [BX5100.D6 1967] 67-23207
1. Newman, John Henry, Cardinal, 1801-1890. 2. Allies, Thomas William, 1813-1903. 3. Manning, Henry Edward, Cardinal, 1808-1892. 4. Maturin, Basil William, 1847-1915. 5. Oxford movement. I. Title.

ELWOOD, J. Murray. 201'.11
Kindly light : the spiritual vision of John Henry Newman / J. Murray Elwood ; [front cover line drawing after a portrait by George Richardson]. Notre Dame, Ind. : Ave Maria Press, c1979. 127 p. : ill. ; 23 cm. Includes bibliographical references. [BX4705.N5E48] 79-52444 ISBN 0-87793-185-2 (pbk.) : 2.95
1. Newman, John Henry, Cardinal, 1801-1890 2. Cardinals—England—Biography. I. Title. **BIP**

GARNETT, Emmeline, 1924- 262.1350924
Tormented angel; a life of John Henry Newman. New York, Ariel Bks. [1966] 136p. 22cm. Bibl. [BX4705.N5G3] 66-10431 3.25
1. Newman, John Henry, Cardinal, 1801-1890. I. Title.
Ages 14-up. Available from Farrar.

HUTTON, Richard Holt, 1826-1897. 262'.135'0924 B
Cardinal Newman / by Richard H. Hutton. 2d ed. New York : AMS Press, 1977. xi, 268 p. : port. ; 18 cm. Reprint of the 1891 ed. published by Methuen, London, in series: English leaders of religion. Includes bibliographical references. [BX4705.N5H8 1977] 75-30029 ISBN 0-404-14033-5 : 16.00
1. Newman, John Henry, Cardinal, 1801-1890. 2. Cardinals—England—Biography. I. Series: English leaders of religion.

MAY, James Lewis, 1873- 922.242
Cardinal Newman. Westminster, Md., Newman Press, 1951. 309 p. port. 22 cm. "A list of Newman's works": p. 305-306. [BX4705.N5M43 1951] 51-8610
1. Newman, John Henry, Cardinal, I. Title. **BIP**

MIDDLETON, Robert Dudley. 262'.135'0924 B
Newman & Bloxam; an Oxford friendship, by R. D. Middleton. Westport, Conn., Greenwood Press [1971] x, 261 p. illus. 23 cm. Reprint of the 1947 ed. Includes bibliographical references. [BX4705.N5M5 1971] 74-104246 ISBN 0-8371-3986-4
1. Newman, John Henry, Cardinal, 1801-1890. 2. Bloxam, John Rouse, 1807-1891. **BIP**

NEWMAN, John Henry, Cardinal, 1801-1890. 922.242
Apologia pro vita sua. Edited with an introd. and note by A. Dwight Culler. Boston, Houghton Mifflin [1956] 384p. 21cm. (Riverside editions, B10) [BX4705.N5A3 1956] 56-2548
1. Catholic Church—Doctrinal and controversial works—Catholl authors. I. Title.

NEWMAN, John Henry, 230.2'0924
Apologia pro vita sua: being a history of his religious opinions; ed. introd. notes, by Martin J. Svaglic. Oxford, Clarendon. Pr., 1967. ardinal, 1801-1890 1x, 604p. 23cm. Bibl. [BX4705.N5A3 1967] 68-75872 bds., price unreported
1. Catholic Church—Doctrinal and controversial works—Catholic authors. I. Svaglic, Martin J. ed. II. Title.
Available from Oxford Univ. Pr., New York. **BIP**

NEWMAN, John Henry, Cardinal, 1801-1890. 922.242
Apologia pro vita sua. With an introd. by Philip Hughes. Garden City, N. Y., Image Books [1956] 440p. 19cm. (A Doubleday image book, D37) 'Newman's list of his writings': p. 434-435. [BX4765.N5A3 1956a] 56-8735
1. Catholic Church—Doctrinal and controversial works—Catholic authors. I. Title.

NEWMAN, John Henry, Cardinal, 1801-1890. 230.2'0924
Apologia pro vita sua: being a history of his religious opinions; edited, with an introduction and notes, by Martin J. Svaglic. Oxford, Clarendon P., 1967. ix, 604 p. 22 1/2 cm. (B67-17788) Bibliographical references. [BX4705.N5A3] 68-75872
1. Catholic Church—Doctrinal and controversial works—Catholic authors. I. Svaglic, Martin J., ed. II. Title.

NEWMAN, John Henry, Cardinal, 1801-1890. 922.242
Apologia pro vta sua, Edited with an introd. and notes by A. Dwight Culler. Boston, Houghton Mifflin [1956] 384p. 21cm. (Riverside editions, B10) [BX4705.N5A3 1956] 56-2548
1. Catholic Church—Doctrinal and controversial works—Catholic authors. I. Title.

NEWMAN, John Henry, Cardinal, 1801-1890. 922.242
Autobiographical writings; edited with introductions by Henry Tristram. Enw York, Sheed and Ward [1957] 338p. 22cm. [BX4705.N5A15] 57-6045
1. Catholic Church—Clergy—Correspondence, reminiscences, etc. I. Title.

NEWMAN, John Henry, Cardinal, 1801-1890. 922.242
Letters; a selection, edited and introduced, by Derek Stanford and Muriel Spark. Westminster, Md., Newman Press, 1957. i51p, port. 22cm. Bibliographical footnotes. [BX4705.N5A43] 57-11825
1. Catholic Church—Clergy—Correspondence, reminiscences, etc. I. Title.

NEWMAN, John Henry, Cardinal 1801-1890 922.242
Letters and diaries; v.12, Ed. at the Birmingham Oratory with notes, introd. by Charles Stephen Dessain. New York, Nelson [1962] 441p. 25cm. Contents.v.12, Rome to Birmingham: Jan. 1847 to Dec. 1848. 61-65738 15.00
1. Catholic Church—Clergy—Correspondence, reminiscences, etc. I. Dessain, Charles Stephen, ed. II. Title.

NEWMAN, John Henry, Cardinal, 1801-1890. 922.242
Apologia pro vita sua [by] John Henry Cardinal Newman, being a history of his religious opinions. With an introd. by Basil Willey. London, Oxford University Press, 1964. xxxiv, 405 p. 16 cm. (The World's classics, 601) [BX4705.N5A3] 64-4741
1. Catholic Church — Doctrinal and controversial works — Catholic authors. I. Title. **BIP**

O'FAOLAIN, Sean, 1900- 922.242
Newman's way. London, New York,

Longmans, Green [1952] 286p. 22cm. [BX4705.N5O35 1952a] 54-2834
1. Newman, John Henry, Cardinal, 1801-1890. I. Title.

O'FAOLAIN, Sean, 1900- 922.242
Newman's way; the odyssey of John Henry Newman. New York, Devin-Adair Co., 1952. 335 p. illus. 23 cm. [BX4705.N5O35] 52-12280
1. Newman, John Henry, Cardinal, 1801-1890. I. Title.

PATTERSON, Webster T. 262'.15'0924
Newman: pioneer for the layman [by] Webster T. Patterson. Foreword by Robert W. Gleason. Washington, Corpus Books [1968] xxii, 193 p. 21 cm. Bibliography: p. 183-189. [BX4705.N5P3] 68-9475 7.50
1. Newman, John Henry, Cardinal, 1801-1890. 2. Laity. I. Title.

REYNOLDS, Ernest Edwin, 1894- 922.242
Three cardinals: Newman, Wiseman, Manning. New York, Kenedy [1958] 278p. illus. 22cm. Includes bibliography. [BX4665.G7R4] 58-10991
1. Newman, John Henry, Cardinal, 1801-1890. 2. Wiseman, Nicholas Patrick Stephen, Cardinal, 1802-1895. 3. Manning, Henry Edward, Cardinal, 1808-1892. 4. Cardinals—Gt. Brit. I. Title.

ROBBINS, William 262.1350924
The Newman brothers; an essay in comparative intellectual biography. Cambridge, Mass., Harvard [c.]1966. xii, 202p. ports. 23cm. Bibl. [BX4705.N5 R57] 66-4976 6.00
1. Newman, John Henry, Cardinal, 1801-1890. 2. Newman, Francis, 1805-1897. I. Title. BIP

ROBBINS, William. 262.1350924
The Newman brothers; an essay in comparative intellectual biography. London, Heinemann, 1966. xii, 202 p. front., 6 plates (ports.) 22 1/2 cm. 35/ -- [BX4705.N5R57] 66-71850
1. Newman, John Henry, Cardinal, 1801-1890. 2. Newman, Francis William, 1805-1897. I. Title.

SHERIDAN, Thomas L., 1926- 234'.7'0924
Newman on justification; a theological biography, by Thomas L. Sheridan. Staten Island, N.Y., Alba [1967] 265p. 22cm. Bibl. [BX4705.N5S4] 67-21427 6.50
1. Newman, John Henry, Cardinal, 1801-1890. 2. Justification—History of doctrines. I. Title.

TREVOR, Meriol. 922.242
Newman, the pillar of the cloud. Garden City, N.Y., Doubleday, 1962- v. illus. 22 cm. Includes bibliography. [BX4705.N5T662] 62-13341
1. Newman, John Henry, Cardinal, 1801-1890. Full name: Lucy Meriol Trevor. I. Title.

TREVOR, Meriol [Lucy Merial Trevor] 922.242
Newman, v.2. Garden City, N.Y., Doubleday, 1963[c.1962] 659p. illus. 22cm. Contents.v.2, Light in winter. Bibl. 62-13341 7.95
1. Newman, John Henry, Cardinal, 1801-1890. I. Title.

TREVOR, Meriol [Lucy Meriol Trevor] 922.242
Newman, the pillar of the cloud [v.1] Garden City, N.Y., Doubleday [c.]1962. 649p. illus. 22cm. Bibl. 62-13341 7.95
1. Newman, John Henry, Cardinal, 1801-1890. I. Title.

WALLER, Alfred Rayney, 1867-1922. 262'.135'0924 B
John Henry, Cardinal Newman / by A. R. Waller and G. H. S. Burrow [i.e. Barrow]. Norwood, Pa. : Norwood Editions, 1976. xviii, 150 p. ; 23 cm. Reprint of the 1901 ed. published by Kegan Paul, Trench, Trubner, London, in series: The Westminster biographies. Bibliography: p. [148]-150. [BX4705.N5W25 1976] 76-45369 ISBN 0-8482-2954-1 : 17.50
1. Newman, John Henry, Cardinal, 1801-1890. 2. Cardinals—England—Biography. I. Barrow, G. H. S., joint author. II. Series: The Westminster biographies. BIP

WEATHERBY, Harold L., 1934- 262'.135'0924 B
Cardinal Newman in his age; his place in English theology and literature [by] Harold L. Weatherby. Nashville, Vanderbilt University Press, 1973. xv, 296 p. 23 cm. Includes bibliographical references. [BX4705.N5W4] 72-1347 ISBN 0-8265-1182-1 11.50
1. Newman, John Henry, Cardinal, 1801-1890. I. Title. BIP

Newman, John Henry, Cardinal, 1801-1890—Juvenile literature.

SCHMID, Evan, 1920- 922.242
Cardinal from Oxford; a story of John Henry Cardinal Newman. Notre Dame, Ind., Dujarie Press [1959] 143p. illus. 22cm. [BX4705.N5S37] 59-3345
1. Newman, John Henry, Cardinal, 1801-1890—Juvenile literature. I. Title.

Newman, John Henry, Cardinal, 1801-1890—Political science.

KENNY, Terence. 320.5'092'4
The political thought of John Henry Newman. Westport, Conn., Greenwood Press [1974] x, 208 p. 22 cm. Reprint of the 1957 ed. published by Longmans, Green, London, New York. Bibliography: p. 194-201. [JC223.N5K4 1974] 73-16741 ISBN 0-8371-7226-8 10.00
1. Newman, John Henry, Cardinal, 1801-1890—Political science. I. Title.

Newman, Paul, 1925-

GODFREY, Lionel. 791.43'028'0924 B
Paul Newman, superstar : a critical biography / by Lionel Godfrey. New York : St. Martin's Press, 1979, c1978. 208 p., [8] leaves of plates ; 23 cm. Includes index. Bibliography: p. [189]-190. [PN2287.N44G6 1979] 76-66404 ISBN 0-312-59819-X : 8.95
1. Newman, Paul, 1925- 2. Moving-picture actors and actresses—United States—Biography. I. Title.

HAMBLETT, Charles. 791.43'028'0924 B
Paul Newman / by Charles Hamblett. Chicago : H. Regnery, 1975. xvii, 232 p., [8] leaves of plates : ill. ; 24 cm. Filmography: p. 210-230. [PN2287.N44H3 1975b] 75-13222 ISBN 0-8092-8236-4 : 8.95
1. Newman, Paul, 1925-

Newman, Robert, 1752-1804.

SHEETS, Robert Newman, 1934- 973.3'31'0924 B
Robert Newman : his life and letters in celebration of the bicentennial of his showing of two lanterns in Christ Church, Boston, April 18, 1775 / Robert Newman Sheets. Denver : Sheets, 1975. 60 p. : ill. ; 23 cm. Bibliography: p. 60. [F69.N58S53] 75-10151
1. Newman, Robert, 1752-1804. 2. Revere, Paul, 1735-1818. 3. Boston. Christ Church. 4. Boston—Siege, 1775-1776.

Newsboys—Personal narratives.

LARREA, Jean-Jacques. 381'.45'070172
The diary of a paper boy. Illustrated by Jacqueline Chwast. New York, Putnam [1972] [63] p. illus. 24 cm. The diary entries of a ten-year-old relate his adventures at school, at home, and on his paper route. [HD6247.N5U45] 73-189881 ISBN 0-399-20255-2 3.95
1. Newsboys—Personal narratives. I. Chwast, Jacqueline, illus. II. Title. BIP

Newton Co., Tex. — Biog.

WILSON, Thomas Asbury, 1866-1944. 929.2
Some early southeast Texas families, by Thomas A. Wilson. Edited by Madeleine Martin. Houston, Lone Star Press [1965] 174 p. illus., maps (on lining papers) ports. 25 cm. [F392.N4W5] 65-18183
1. Newton Co., Tex. — Biog. 2. Jasper Co., Tex. — Biog. I. Martin, Madeleine, ed. II. Title.

Newton, Isaac, Sir, 1642-1727.

ANDRADE, Edward Neville da Costa, 1887- 925.3
Isaac Newton. New York, Chanticleer Press [1950] 111 p. illus., ports. 19 cm. (Personal portraits) [QC16.N7A55] 50-7104
1. Newton, Isaac, Sir, 1642-1727. I. Series.

ANDRADE, Edward Neville da Costa, 1887-1971. 509'.2'4 B
Isaac Newton / E. N. da C. Andrade. Folcroft, Pa. : Folcroft Library Editions, 1979. p. cm. Reprint of the 1950 ed. published by M. Parrish, London, in series: Personal portraits. [QC16.N7A55 1979] 79-24430 ISBN 0-8414-3014-4 lib. bdg. : 12.50
1. Newton, Isaac, Sir, 1642-1727. 2. Scientists—Great Britain—Biography. I. Series: Personal portraits.

DE VILLAMIL, Richard, 1850- 509.2'4 B
Newton: the man. With a foreword by Albert Einstein and a new introd. by I. Bernard Cohen. New York, Johnson Reprint Corp., 1972. xii, vi, 111 p. port. 22 cm. (The Sources of science, no. 118) Reprint of the 1931 ed. "Catalogue of the library of Dr. James Musgrave": p. 62-103. "Supplementary list of Sir Isaac Newton's books": p. 104-111. [QC16.N7D47 1972] 71-166282
1. Newton, Isaac, Sir, 1642-1727. I. Title. BIP

ENGLISH, James Seymour. 530'.092'4 B
"... and all was light" : the life and work of Sir Isaac Newton / by J. S. English. [Lincoln] : Lincolnshire Library Service, 1977. 32 p. : ill., facsim., port. ; 21 cm. (Lincolnshire history series) Bibliography: p. 21-32. [QC16.N7E5] 77-372282
1. Newton, Isaac, Sir, 1642-1727. 2. Physicists—Great Britain—Biography. I. Title. II. Series.

MANUEL, Frank Edward. 509'.24 B
A portrait of Isaac Newton [by] Frank E. Manuel. Cambridge, Belknap Press of Harvard University Press, 1968. xvi, 478 p. illus., map, ports. 25 cm. Bibliographical references included in "Notes" (p. 395-467) [QC16.N7M3] 68-29180 11.95
1. Newton, Isaac, Sir, 1642-1727. I. Title. BIP

MANUEL, Frank Edward. 509'.2'4 B
A portrait of Isaac Newton / Frank E. Manuel. Washington : New Republic Books, 1979. xvi, 478 p. ; 24 cm. Reprint of the 1968 ed. published by Belknap Press of Harvard University Press, Cambridge, Mass. Includes bibliographical references and index. [QC16.N7M3 1979] 78-31108 ISBN 0-915220-52-0 : 17.50. ISBN 0-915220-53-9 pbk. : 7.95
1. Newton, Isaac, Sir, 1642-1727. 2. Physicists—Great Britain—Biography. I. Title.

NEWTON, Isaac, Sir 1642-1727 925.3
Correspondence, v. 3. Ed. by H. W. Turnbull. [New York] Cambridge Publisjed for the Royal Society. [c.]1961[ ] 445p. illus. 29cm. Contents.v. 3. 1688-1694. Bibl. 59-65134 25.00
1. Scientists—Correspondence, reminscences, etc. I. Turnbull, Herbert Western, 1885- ed. II. Title.

NEWTON, Isaac, Sir 1642-1727. 925.3
Correspondence, Edited by H. W. Turnbull. Cambridge [Eng.] Published for the Royal Society at the University Press, 1959- v. illus., port., facsims. 29cm. Includes bibliographical references. Contents.v. 1. 1661-1675. [QC16.N7A4] 59-65134
1. Scientists—Correspondence, reminscences, etc. I. Turnbull, Herbert Westren, 1885- ed. II. Title.

NEWTON, Issac, Sir 1642-1727 925.3
Correspondence. Ed. by H. W. Turnbull Cambridge [Eng.] Pub. for the Royal Soc. at the Univ. Pr., [1967] v. illus., port., facsims. 29cm. Contents.v.4 1694-1709, ed. by J. F. Scott. [QC16.N7A4] 59-65134 38.50
1. Scientists — Correspondence, reminscences, etc. I. turbull, Herbert Western, 1885- ed. II. Title.

SOOTIN, Harry. 925.3
Isaac Newton. New York, Messner [1955] 191 p. 22 cm. [QC16.N7S65] 55-9868
1. Newton, Isaac, Sir, 1642-1727.

Newton, Isaac, Sir, 1642-1727—Juvenile literature.

LAND, Barbara. 925.3
The quest of Isaac Newton, by Barbara and Myrick Land. Illustrated by Arthur Renshaw. [1st ed.] Garden City, N. Y., Garden City Books [1960] 56 p. illus. 32 cm. [QC16.N7L34] 60-12463
1. Newton, Isaac, Sir, 1642-1727—Juvenile literature. I. Land, Myrick, 1922- joint author. II. Title.

TINER, John Hudson, 1944- 509'.2'4 B
Isaac Newton : the true story of his life as inventor, scientist, & teacher / John Hudson Tiner ; illustrated by Jonathan & David Inc. Milford, Mich. : Mott Media, 1976 144 p. : ill. ; 23 cm. (The Sowers) Includes index. Bibliography: p. [143]-144. A biography of the seventeenth-century English scientist who developed the theory of gravity, discovered the secrets of light and color, and formulated the system of calculus. [QC16.N7T56] 92 75-32562 ISBN 0-915134-06-3 : 5.95
1. Newton, Isaac, Sir, 1642-1727—Juvenile literature. I. Jonathan & David Inc.

HOUSTON, W. Robert 925.3
Sir Isaac Newton, scientist-mathematician [by] W. Robert Houston [and] M. Vere DeVault. Illustrated by Betty Cobb. Austin, Tex., Steck Co. [c.1960] 48p. illus. (part col.) 23cm. 60-8934 1.75
1. Newton, Sir Isaac, 1642-1727—juvenile literature. I. DeVault, M. Vere, joint author. II. Title.

KNIGHT, David C. 925.3
Isaac Newton, mastermind of modern science. Pictures by John Griffin. New York, F. Watts [c.1961] 153p. illus. (Firt0)st biography) 61-5278 1.95; 'reinforced picture cloth binding, 2.95
1. Newton, Sir Isaac, 1642-1727—Juvenile literature. I. Title.

KNIGHT, David C 925.3
Isaac Newton, mastermind of modern science. Pictures by John Griffin. New York, F. Watts [1961] 153p. illus. 22cm. (A First biography) [QC16.N7K57] 61-5278
1. Newton, Sir Isaac, 1642-1727—Juvenile literature. I. Title.

Newton, Isaac, Sir, 1642-1727—Religion and ethics.

MANUEL, Frank Edward. 283'.092'4
The religion of Isaac Newton / Frank E. Manuel. Oxford : Clarendon Press, 1974. vi, 141 p. ; 23 cm. (Fremantle lectures ; 1973) Includes bibliographical references and index. [QC16.N7M32] 75-302605

ISBN 0-19-826640-5 : 11.25
1. Newton, Isaac, Sir, 1642-1727—Religion and ethics. I. Title. II. Series.

Newton-John, Olivia—Juvenile literature.

JACOBS, Linda. 784'.092'4 B
Olivia Newton-John, sunshine supergirl / by Linda Jacobs St. Paul : EMC Corp., 1975. p. cm. (Behind the bright lights) A biography of an English-born singer who won awards and became famous in the United States before she had even made her first visit. [ML3930.N495J2] 92 75-15757 ISBN 0-88436-184-5 lib.bdg. : 4.95 ISBN 0-88436-185-3 pbk. : 2.95
1. Newton-John, Olivia—Juvenile literature. I. Title.

MORSE, Ann. 784'.092'4 B
Olivia Newton-John / text, Ann Morse ; ill., John Keely. Mankato, Minn. : Creative Education, [1975] p. cm. [ML3930.N495M6] 75-25849 ISBN 0-87191-475-1
1. Newton-John, Olivia—Juvenile literature. I. Keely, John. II. Title.

MORSE, Ann. 784'.092'4 B
Olivia Newton-John / text Ann Morse ill John Keely Mankato, Minn. : Creative Education, [1975] p. cm. [ML3930.N495M6] 75-25849 ISBN 0-87191-475-1 lib.bdg. : 4.95
1. Newton-John, Olivia—Juvenile literature. I. Keely, John. II. Title.

RUFF, Peter. 784'.092'4 B
Olivia Newton-John / by Peter Ruff. New York : Quick Fox, c1979. 96 p. : ill. ; 26 cm. Discography: p. 93-96. A biography of the Australian female vocalist who won nearly 40 awards for her music in a little over three years. [ML3930.N495R8] 92 79-63527 0825639343 : 4.95
1. Newton-John, Olivia—Juvenile literature. 2. Singers—Australia—Biography. I. Title. **BIP**

Newton, John, 1725-1807.

DEAL, Williams 283'.092'4 B
John Newton, author of the song "Amazing grace," by William Deal. Westchester, Ill., Good News Publishers [1974] 80 p. 18 cm. (One evening book OE140) [BX5199.N55D35] 74-76011 0.95 (pbk.).
1. Newton, John, 1725-1807.

MARTIN, Bernard, 1897- 922.342
An ancient mariner: a biography of John Newton. [Rev. ed] Nashville, Abingdon [1961, c.1950, 1960] 240p. (Apex bk., G2) 1.25 pap.,
1. Newton, John, 1725-1807. I. Title.

Ney, Michel, duc d'Elchingen, prince de la Moskowa, 1769-1815.

FOSTER, John T. 940.2'7'0924 B
Napoleon's Marshal; the life of Michel Ney, by John Foster. Front. by Leonard Everett Fisher. Maps by Cynthia Basil. New York, Morrow [1968] 224 p. maps, port. 22 cm. Bibliography: p. [215]-216. A biography of the controversial French soldier who, switching loyalties, served Napoleon, then Louis XVIII, then Napoleon again. Although executed for treason, he was restored to honor by the French people thirty-eight years later. [DC198.N6F6] 92 AC 68
1. Ney, Michel, duc d'Elchingen, prince de la Moskowa, 1769-1815. I. Title. **BIP**

FOSTER, John T. 940.2'7'0924 B
Napoleon's Marshal; the life of Michel Ney, by John Foster. Front. by Leonard Everett Fisher. Maps by Cynthia Basil. New York, Morrow [1968] 224 p. maps, port. 22 cm. Bibliography: p. [215]-216. [DC198.N6F6] 68-9179 3.95
1. Ney, Michel, duc d'Elchingen, prince de la Moskowa, 1769-1815. I. Title.

KURTZ, Harold. 923.544
The trial of Marshal Ney; his last years and death. New York, Knopf, 1957. 335p. illus. 23cm. [DC198.N6K8] 57-13909
1. Ney, Michel, duc d'Elchingen, prince de la Moskowa, 1769-1815. I. Title.

Neyer, Dix.

NEYER, Dix. 616.8'9'09 B
Wander, wander / by Dix Neyer. Englewood Cliffs, N.J. : Prentice-Hall, c1977. 204 p. ; 22 cm. [RC464.N49A38 1977] 76-46580 ISBN 0-13-945774-7 : 7.95
1. Neyer, Dix. 2. Mental illness—Biography. I. Title.

Nez Perce Indians.

MOORE, Albert Thomas, 1861- 970.3 1965.
The life history of a Nez Perce Indian [by] Piluyekin [as told to] Anthony E. Thomas. [Ann Arbor, Mich., University Microfilms, 1970] iv, 68 p. illus., maps, ports. 28 cm. (Anthropological studies, 3) Bibliography: p. 68. [E99.N5M6 1970] 76-102046
1. Nez Perce Indians. I. Thomas, Anthony E., ed. II. Title. III. Series.

Nezahualcoyotl, King of Texcoco, fl.

FLUTE of the Smoking 970.3'0924
Mirror; a portrait of Nezahualcoyotl, poet-king of the Aztecs. [Tucson] Univ. of Ariz. Pr. [1968,c.1949] 183p. illus., col. map (on lining papers) 24cm. Bibl. [F1219.N48G55 1968] (B) 68-7596 6.50
1. Nezahualcoyotl, King of Texcoco, fl. 2. Mexico—Hist.—To 1519. I. Gillmor, Frances, 1903-

Nezahualcoyotl, King of Texcoco, fl. 1400-1470.

GILLMOR, Frances, 970.3'0924 B 1903-
Flute of the Smoking Mirror; a portrait of Nezahualcoyotl, poet-king of the Aztecs. [Tucson] University of Arizona Press [1968, c1949] 183 p. illus., col. map (on lining papers) 24 cm. Bibliography: p. 172-176. [F1219.N48G55 1968] 68-7596 6.50
1. Nezahualcoyotl, King of Texcoco, fl. 1400-1470. 2. Mexico—History—To 1519. I. Title.

Ngidulu.

BARTON, Roy Franklin, 959.9'1 1883-1947.
Philippine pagans : the autobiographies of three Ifugaos / by R. F. Barton. 1st AMS ed. New York : AMS Press, 1979. xxi, 271 p., [20] leaves of plates : ill. ; 22 cm. Reprint of the 1938 ed. published by G. Routledge, London. [DS666.I15B35 1979] 76-44686 ISBN 0-404-15903-6 : 24.50
1. Ngidulu. 2. Bugan nak Manghe. 3. Kumiha. 4. Ifugaos—Biography. 5. Ifugaos—Social life and customs. I. Title. **BIP**

Ng Poon Chew, 1866-1931—Juvenile literature.

HOEXTER, Corinne K. 979.4'004'951
From Canton to California : the epic of Chinese immigration / by Corinne K. Hoexter. New York : Four Winds Press, c1976. p. cm. Includes index. Bibliography: p. A history of the Chinese in the United States from their early days in California to the present, including the biography of Dr. Ng Poon Chew, who, as editor of the first Chinese language newspaper in the United States became a leader of all Chinese Americans. [F855.2.C5H63] 92 76-14504 ISBN 0-590-07344-3 : 8.95
1. Ng Poon Chew, 1866-1931—Juvenile literature. 2. Chinese Americans—California—History—Juvenile literature. 3. Chinese Americans—California—Biography—Juvenile literature. 4. Journalists—California—Biography—Juvenile literature. I. Title. **BIP**

Ngawang Lobsang Yishey Tenzing Gyatso, Dalai Lama, 1935-

THOMAS, Lowell Jackson, 922.943 1923-
The Dalai Lama. [1st ed.] New York, Duell, Sloan and Pearce [1961] 151 p. illus. 21 cm. [BL1489.N44T5] 61-7992
1. Ngawang Lobsang Yishey Tenzing Gyatso, Dalai Lama, 1935- I. Title.

Ngo-dinh-Diem, Pres. Vietnam, 1901-1963.

BOUSCAREN, Anthony 923.1597 Trawick.
The last of the mandarins; Diem of Vietnam. Pittsburgh, Duquesne University Press, 1965. 174 p. group port. 21 cm. Bibliography: p. 172-174. Bibliographical footnotes. [DS557.A6B6] 65-16136
1. Ngo-dinh-Diem, Pres. Vietnam, 1901-1963. I. Title.

Nguyen Thi Cinh, 1920—

NGUYEN Thi 959.704'3322'0924 B Cinh, 1920-
No other road to take : memoir of Mrs. Nguyen Thi Cinh / translated by Mai Elliott. Ithaca, N.Y. : Southeast Asia Program, Dept. of Asian Studies, Cornell University, 1976. viii, 77 p. : ill. ; 28 cm. (Data paper - Southeast Asia Program, Cornell University ; no. 102) Translation of Khong con duong nao khac. Includes bibliographical references. [DS556.93.N526A3613] 76-151065 ISBN 0-87727-102-X : 5.00
1. Nguyen Thi Cinh, 1920- 2. Revolutionists—Vietnam—Biography. 3. Ben Tre, Vietnam—Politics and government. I. Title. II. Series: Cornell University. Southeast Asia Program. Data paper ; no. 102.

Nguyen-cao-Ky.

NGUYEN-CAO-KY 959.704'3'0924 B
How we lost the Vietnam war / Nguyen Cao Ky. New York : Stein and Day, 1978, c1976. 239p. ; 24 cm. (A Scarborough book) Autobiographical. Includes index. [DS556.93N52A36] 78-59797 ISBN 0-8128-6016-0 pbk. : 3.95
1. Nguyen-cao-Ky. 2. Vietnam — Politics and government. I. Title.
LC card no. for 1976 Stein and Day hadcover ed.: 75-35895 **BIP**

Niarchos, Stavros.

LILLY, Doris. 387.5'0922 B
Those fabulous Greeks: Onassis, Niarchos, and Livanos. [1st ed.] New York, Cowles Book Co. [1970] ix, 373 p. illus., ports. 22 cm. Bibliography: p. 365-366. [HE569.A2L5] 72-90061 7.95
1. Onassis, Aristotle Socrates, 1906- 2. Niarchos, Stavros. 3. Livanos, Stavros George, 1890-1963. I. Title.

Niblack (Ship)

DONAHUE, Joseph A. 940.54'59'73
Tin cans and other ships : a war diary, 1941-1945 / by Joseph A. Donahue. North Quincy, Mass. : Christopher Pub. House, c1979. 255 p. : ill. ; 22 cm. [D774.N48D66] 78-74696 ISBN 0-8158-0378-8 : 7.50
1. Niblack (Ship) 2. Donahue, Joseph A. 3. Oklahoma City (Ship) 4. United States. Navy—Biography. 5. World War, 1939-1945—Personal narratives, American. 6. World War, 1939-1945—Naval operations, American. 7. Seamen—United States—Biography. I. Title.

Niccacci, Rufino.

NICCACCI, Rufino. 940.53'45'651
The Assisi underground : the priests who rescued Jews / Rufino Niccacci, with Alexander Ramati. New York : Stein and Day, 1978. p. cm. [D810.J4N475] 77-17837 ISBN 0-8128-2315-X : 8.95
1. Niccacci, Rufino. 2. Catholic Church—Clergy—Biography. 3. World War, 1939-1945—Jews—Rescue—Italy—Assisi. 4. Clergy—Italy—Assisi—Biography. 5. Assisi—Biography. I. Ramati, Alexander, 1921- joint author. II. Title.

Niccolo di Giovanni Fiorentino.

SCHULZ, Anne Markham, 730'.92'4 B 1938-
Niccolo di Giovanni Fiorentiono and Venetian sculpture of the early Renaissance / Anne Markham Schulz. New York : Published by New York State University Press for the College Art Association of America, 1978. xxiv, 136 p. : ill. ; 29 cm. (Monographs on archaeology and fine arts ; 33) Includes index. "Digest of documents concerning the life and works of Niccolo di Giovanni Fiorentino": p. 81-89. [NB623.N515S38] 77-6903 ISBN 0-8147-7786-4 : 22.50
1. Niccolo di Giovanni Fiorentino. 2. Sculptors—Italy—Biography. 3. Sculpture, Renaissance—Italy—Venice. I. College Art Association of America. II. Title. III. Series.

Nice family.

HASSAN, Hazel Nice, 929.2'0973 1925-
The biography of Mary Catherine, eleventh child of Philip and Rebecca (Meek) Nice. Rockford, Ill., 1969. xii, 115 p. illus., fold. facsims., fold. geneal. table., maps, ports. 21 cm. Includes bibliographical references. [CS71.N59 1969] 74-10899
1. Nice family.

Nichiren, 1222-1282.

ANESAKI, 294.3'92'0924 B Masaharu, 1873-1949.
Nichiren, the Buddhist prophet. Gloucester, Mass., P. Smith, 1966 [c1916] viii, 160 p. 21 cm. Bibliographical footnotes. [BL1442.N53A5 1966] 67-2824
1. Nichiren, 1222-1282. 2. Buddha and Buddhism—Japan. I. Title. **BIP**

RODD, Laurel Rasplica. 294.3'64 B
Nichiren, a biography / Laurel Rasplica Rodd. [Tempe] : Arizona State University, 1978. 86 p. ; 23 cm. (Occasional paper - Arizona State University ; no. 11) Contents.—Nichiren.—Letter from Sado.—Letter to the wife of Lord Shijo Kingo.—Letter from Mt. Minobu. Bibliography: p. 77-86. [BQ8349.N577R6] 78-624123 pbk. : 2.50
1. Nichiren, 1222-1282. 2. Priests, Nichiren—Japan—Biography. I. Title. II. Series: Arizona State University, Tempe. Center for Asian Studies. Occasional paper ; no. 11

Nichois. Loring.

JOHNSON, Grady. 927
The five pennies, the biography of jazz band leader, Red Nichols. Containing a novelization of Dena Pictures' Paramount release...The five pennies...Screenplay by Jack Rose and Melville Shavelson story by Robert Smith. [New York, Dell Pub. Co., 1959] 191p. 17cm. (A Dell first edition B128) [ML419.N65J6] 59-4278
1. Nichois. Loring. I. Title.

Nichol, Charles Ready, 1876-

UNDERWOOD, Maude Jones. 922.89
C. R. Nichol, a preacher of righteousness. Clifton, Tex., Nichol Pub. Co., 1952. 320p. illus. 23cm. [BX7094.C95U57] 53-23289
1. Nichol, Charles Ready, 1876- I. Title.

Nichol, Francis David, 1897-1966.

WOOD, Miriam. 286'.73
His initials were F. D. N.; a life story of elder F. D. Nichol, for twenty-one years editor of the Review and herald, by Miriam and Kenneth Wood. [Washington] Review and Herald Publishing Association, 1967. 256 p. illus., ports. 22 cm. [BX6193.N5W6] 67-21872
1. Nichol, Francis David, 1897-1966. I. Wood, Kenneth H., joint author. II. Title.

Nicholas I, Emperor of Russia, 1796-1855.

GRUNWALD, Constantin de. D923.147
Tsar Nicholas I. Translated from the French by Brigit Patmore. New York, Macmillan, 1955. ix, 294 p. port. 22 cm. Translation of La vie de Nicolas Ier. Bibliographical footnotes. [DK210.G72 1955] 55-13563
1. Nicholas I, Emperor of Russia, 1796-1855.

GRUNWALD, Constantin de. 923.147
Tsar Nicholas I. Translated from the French by Brigit Patmore. Tsar Nicholas the First New York, Macmillan, 1955. ix, 294p. port. 22cm. Translation of La vie de Nicolas I. Bibliographical footnotes. [DK210.G72 1955] 55-13563
1. Nicholas I, Emperor of Russia, 1796-1855. I. Title.

LINCOLN, W. Bruce. 447'.07'0924 B
Nicholas I / by W. Bruce Lincoln. Bloomington : Indiana University Press, c1978. 424 p. ; 24 cm. Includes index. Bibliography: p. [395]-414. [DK210.L56] 77-15764 ISBN 0-253-34059-4 : 12.50
1. Nicholas I, Emperor of Russia, 1796-1855. 2. Russia—Kings and rulers—Biography. 3. Russia—History—Nicholas I, 1825-1855. I. Title.

Nicholas II, Emperor of Russia, 1868-1918.

GILLIARD, Pierre, 1879- 947.08
Thirteen years at the Russian court. [Translated by F. Appleby Holt] New York, Arno Press, 1970. xiii, 304 p. illus., facsim., ports. 24 cm. (Russia observed) Translation of Treize annees a la cour de Russia. Originally published in 1921. [DK258.G513] 75-115539 ISBN 0-405-03029-0
1. Nicholas II, Emperor of Russia, 1868-1918. 2. Romanov, House of. 3. Russia—History—Revolution, 1917-1921—Personal narratives. I. Title.

MASSIE, Robert K., 947.08'0924 B
1929-
Nicholas and Alexandra [by] Robert K. Massie. [1st ed.] New York, Atheneum, 1967. xvii, 584 p. illus., geneal. tables. maps (on lining papers), ports. 25 cm. Bibliography: p. 563-568. [DK258.M3] 67-24627
1. Nicholas II, Emperor of Russia, 1868-1918. 2. Alexandra, consort of Nicholas II, Emperor of Russia, 1872-1918. 3. Russia—Politics and government—1894-1917. I. Title. BIP

NICHOLAS II, 947.08'092'4 B
Emperor of Russia, 1868-1918.
The letters of the Tsar to the Tsaritsa, 1914-1917 / translated by A. L. Hynes from the official ed. of the Romanov correspondence ; edited, with notes and an index, by C. E. Vulliamy ; with an introd. by C. T. Hagberg. Westport, Conn. : Hyperion Press, [1979] p. cm. Reprint of the 1929 ed. published by J. Lane, London. "Bibliography of works quoted": p. [DK258.N47 1979] 75-37207 ISBN 0-88355-447-X : 23.50
1. Nicholas II, Emperor of Russia, 1868-1918. 2. Alexandra, consort of Nicholas II, Emperor of Russia, 1872-1918. 3. Russia—Kings and rulers—Correspondence. I. Alexandra, consort of Nicholas II, Emperor of Russia, 1872-1918. II. Vulliamy, Colwyn Edward, 1886- III. Title. BIP

NICHOLAS II, Emperor 947.08'0924
of Russia, 1868-1918.
The Nicky-Sunny letters; correspondence of the Tsar and Tsaritsa, 1914-1917. [Hattiesburg, Miss.] Academic International, 1970. 2 v. in 1. geneal. table, port. 24 cm. (Russian series, v. 2) "Reprint of The letters of the Tsar to the Tsaritsa, 1914-1917 (London, 1929) and The letters of the Tsaritsa to the Tsar, 1914-1916 (London, 1923)" Each part has special t.p. and separate paging. [DK258.A4A6 1970] 78-111538
1. Nicholas II, Emperor of Russia, 1868-1918. The letters of the Tsar to the Tsaritsa, 1914-1917. 1970. II. Alexandra, Empress Consort of Nicholas II, Emperor of Russia, 1872-1918. Letters of the Tsari

OL'DENBURG, Sergei 947.08'092'4 B
Sergeevich.
Last tsar : Nicholas II, his reign & his Russia / S. S. Oldenburg ; translated by Leonid I. Mihalap and Patrick J. Rollins ; edited by Patrick J. Rollins ; with Searching for the last tsar by Patrick J. Rollins. Gulf Breeze, Fla. : Academic International Press, 1975- v. : ill. ; 23 cm. (The Russian series ; v. 25) Translation of TSarstvovanie Imperatora Nikolaia II. Contents.Contents.—v. 1. Rollins, P. J. Searching for the last tsar. The autocracy, 1894-1900. Includes bibliographical references. [DK262.O413] 76-351188 ISBN 0-87569-063-7 : 8.95
1. Nicholas II, Emperor of Russia, 1868-1918. 2. Russia—History—Nicholas II, 1894-1917. I. Title.

WASHBURN, Kitsos, 947.08'092'4 B
1958-
Nicholas II last Tsar of all Russias. Washington, 1971. [8] p. 25 cm. [DK258.W36] 73-153284
1. Nicholas II, Emperor of Russia, 1868-1918.

Nicholas II, Emperor of Russia, 1868-1918—Assassination.

BULYGIN, Paul. 947.08 B
The murder of the Romanovs : the authentic account / by Paul Bulygin. Including The road to the tragedy / by Alexander Kerensky ; with an introd. by Sir Bernard Pares. Westport, Conn. : Hyperion Press, 1975, c1935. 286 p., [16] leaves of plates : ill. ; 23 cm. "Translated from the Russian by Gleb Kerensky." Reprint of the ed. published by R. M. McBride, New York. Includes index. [DK258.B83 1975] 74-10075 ISBN 0-88355-183-7 : 22.00
1. Nicholas II, Emperor of Russia, 1868-1918—Assassination. 2. Nicholas II, Emperor of Russia, 1868-1918—Family. 3. Russia—History—Nicholas II, 1894-1917. I. Kerenskii, Aleksandr Fedorovich, 1881-1970. The road to the tragedy. 1975. II. Title.

Nicholas II, Emperor of Russia, 1868-1918—Portraits, caricatures, etc.

LYONS, Marvin. 947.08'092'4 B
Nicholas II : the last tsar / by Marvin Lyons ; edited by Andrew Wheatcroft. New York : St. Martin's Press, 1974. 224 p. : chiefly ill. ; 30 cm. [DK259.4.L93 1974b] 74-81713 16.95
1. Nicholas II, Emperor of Russia, 1868-1918—Portraits, caricatures, etc. 2. Nicholas II, Emperor of Russia, 1868-1918—Family—Portraits.

Nicholas, Saint, Bp. of Myra.

ANCELET-HUSTACHE, Jeanne 922.2392
Saint Nicholas. Tr. by Rosemary Sheed. New York, Macmillan, 1962[c.1959-1962] 96p. 18cm. (Your name--Your saint ser.) Bibl. 61-16725 2.50
1. Nicholas, Saint, Bp. of Myra. I. Title.

EBON, Martin. 282'.092'4 B
Saint Nicholas : life and legend / Martin Ebon. 1st ed. New York : Harper & Row, [1975] p. cm. Bibliography: p. [BX4700.N55E26 1975] 75-9329 ISBN 0-06-062113-3 : 8.95
1. Nicholas, Saint, Bp. of Myra. 2. Santa Claus.

JONES, Charles 282'.092'4 B
Williams, 1905-
Saint Nicholas of Myra, Bari, and Manhattan : biography of a legend / Charles W. Jones. Chicago : University of Chicago Press, c1978. p. cm. Includes indexes. Bibliography: p. [BX4700.N55J63] 77-15487 ISBN 0-226-40699-7 lib. bdg. : 28.00
1. Nicholas, Saint, Bp. of Myra. 2. Christian saints—Turkey—Lysia—Biography. 3. Lysia—Biography. I. Title. BIP

LORD, Daniel Aloysius, 922.1
1888-1955.
The man who was really Santa Claus. Illus. by Lee G. Hines. [St. Louis 1954] 71p. illus. 22cm. [BX4700.N55L6] 55-25501
1. Nicholas, Saint, Bp. of Myra. I. Title.

LUCKHARDT, Mildred 922.1
Madeleine (Corell)
The story of Saint Nicholas. Illustrated by Gordon Laite. New York, Abingdon Press [c.1960] 112p. illus. (part col.) 23cm. 60-6815 2.75
I. Title.

Nicholas, Saint, Bp. of Myra—Juvenile literature.

BRYSON, Bernarda. 922.1
The twenty miracles of Saint Nicolas. With illus. by the author. [1st ed.] Boston, Little, Brown [1960] 88 p. illus. 28 cm. [BX4700.N55B7] 59-7338
1. Nicholas, Saint, Bp. of Myra—Juvenile literature. I. Title.

LUCKHARDT, Mildred 922.1
Madeleine (Corell) 1898-
The story of Saint Nicholas. Illustrated by Gordon Laite. New York, Abingdon Press [1960] 112p. illus. 23cm. [BX4700.N55L8] 60-6815
1. Nicholas, Saint, Bp. of Myra—Juvenile literature. I. Title.

SMITH, Verena 92
The life of Saint Nicholas; pictures by Emile Probst. London, Burns &Oates; New York, Herder & Herder [1966, i.e., 1967] 26p. col. front., col. illus. 19x21cm. [BX4700.N55S6 1966] 67-82365 1.75 bds.,
1. Nicholas, Saint, Bp. of Myra— Juvenile literature. I. Probst, Emile, illus. II. Title.

Nicholls, Douglas Ralph, Sir, 1906-

CLARK, Mavis Thorpe. 286'.63 B
Pastor Doug: the story of Sir Douglas Nicholls, Aboriginal leader [by] Mavis Thorpe Clark. Rev. ed. Melbourne, Lansdowne Press, 1972. 259 p., 6 plates. 23 cm. [BV3667.N5C55 1972] 73-176912 ISBN 0-7018-0017-8 6.95
1. Nicholls, Douglas Ralph, Sir, 1906- 2. Missions—Australia. I. Title.

Nichols, Beverley,

NICHOLS, Beverley, 828'.9'209 [B]
1899-
Father figure. New York, Pocket Books [1973, c.1972] 219 p. illus., ports. 18 cm. Autobiographical. [PR6027.I22Z5] 72-82217 ISBN 0-671-78309-2 1.25 (pbk.)
I. Title.

Nichols, George,

NICHOLS, George, 382.'0924 B
1778-1865.
George Nichols, Salem shipmaster and merchant; an autobiography, edited with introd. and notes by his granddaughter, Martha Nichols. Freeport, N.Y., Books for Libraries Press [1970] xvi, 89 p. illus., ports. 23 cm. On spine: Salem shipmaster and merchant. "First published 1913." [CT275.N63A3 1970] 74-124245
I. Nichols, Martha, ed. II. Title: Salem shipmaster and merchant.

Nichols, James Calvin Kid, 1883-1962.

PATRICK, Lucille 796.8'12'0924 B
Nichols.
The Candy Kid: James Calvin "Kid" Nichols, 1883-1962. [1st ed. Cheyenne, Wyo., Manufactured by Flintlock Pub. Co., 1969] ix, 179 p. illus., ports. 29 cm. [CT275.N6517P3] 72-98532 10.00
1. Nichols, James Calvin Kid, 1883-1962. I. Title.

Nichols, James Wilson,

NICHOLS, James 917.64'03'0924 (B)
Wilson, 1820-1891.
Now you hear my horn; the journal of James Wilson Nichols, 1820-1887. Edited by Catherine W. McDowell. Illustrated by Eldridge Hardie. Austin, University of Texas Press [1968, c1967] xvi, 212 p. illus., facsims., maps, group port. 26 cm. [CT275.N652A3] 66-15698
I. Title.

Nichols, John Gough, 1806-1873, ed.

HALKETT, Anne (Murray) 942.06
lady, 1622-1699
The autobiography of Anne lady Halkett. Ed. by John Gough Nichols. [Westminster] Printed for the Camden Soc., 1875. New York, Johnson Reprint, 1965 [4], xxi, [3], 118p. 22cm. [Camden Soc. Pubns., new ser., no 13) [DA20.C17 new ser., no 13] A17 13.50
1. Nichols, John Gough, 1806-1873, ed. I. Title.

Nichols, Nina Belle Suits (Hurst)

NICHOLS, Nina Belle Suits 923.773
(Hurst) 1882-
Vinegar pie, being the story of a teacher who taught fortyfive years in the public elementary schools of the United States of North America, by Ninabelle [pseud.] San Antonio, Naylor Co. [1957] 259p. illus. 22cm. Prose and verse. [LA2317.N5A3] 57-3458
I. Title.

NICHOLS, Nina Belle Suits. 923.773
(Hurst) 1882-
Vinegar pie, being the story of a teacher who taught fortyfive years in the public elementary schools of the United States of North America, by Ninabelle [pseud.] San Antonio, Naylor Co. [1957] 259p. illus. 22cm. Prose and verse. [LA2317.N5A3] 57-3458
I. Title.

Nicholson, Charles, Sir, 1808-1903.

MACMILLAN, David 378.1'011'0924 B
S.
Charles Nicholson [by] David S. Macmillan. Melbourne, New York, Oxford University Press [1969] 30 p. illus. 19 cm. (Great Australians) Bibliography: p. 30. [LG704.N5M3] 79-494266 0.60
1. Nicholson, Charles, Sir, 1808-1903. 2. Sydney. University—History.

Nicholson, Frank J., 1915-

JONES, Olwen M. 974.6'9 B
Growing up on Lewis Street in the 1920's : oral history interview with Frank J. Nicholson / by Olwen M. Jones. [Greenwich, Conn. : Friends of the Greenwich Library, 1976], c1975. 48, [14] p., [2] leaves of plates : ill. ; 23 cm. Includes index. [F104.G8J66 1976] 76-360152
1. Nicholson, Frank J., 1915- 2. Greenwich, Conn.—Biography. I. Nicholson, Frank J., 1915- joint author. II. Title.

Nicholson, John, 1822-1857.

ABDULLAH, 909'.09'712420810922
Achmed, 1881-1945.
Dreamers of empire, by Achmed Abdullah [and] T. Compton Pakenham. Illustrated by B. K. Morris. Freeport, N.Y. Books for Libraries Press [1968] xiv, 368 p. ports. 23 cm. (Essay index reprint series) Reprint of the 1929 ed. Contents.Contents.—Cecil

John Rhodes.—Richard Francis Burton.—John Nicholson.—Henry Montgomery Lawrence.—William Walker.—Charles George Gordon. [DA531.1.A2 1968] 68-57300
1. Rhodes, Cecil John, 1853-1902. 2. Burton, Richard Francis, Sir, 1821-1890. 3. Nicholson, John, 1822-1857. 4. Lawrence, Henry Montgomery, Sir, 1806-1857. 5. Walker, William, 1824-1860. 6. Gordon, Charles George, 1833-1885. I. Pakenham, Thomas Compton, joint author. II. Title.
BIP

Nicholson, Lillie M., 1892-1975.

NICHOLSON, Lillie M., 1892-1975. 371.'0092'4 B
The vagabond schoolmarm / by Lillie M. Nicholson. [s.l. : s.n.], c1977 (North Newton, Kan. : Mennonite Press) 173 p., [4] leaves of plates : ill. ; 24 cm. [LA2317.N53A38] 76-48499
1. Nicholson, Lillie M., 1892-1975. 2. Teachers—Kansas—Biography. I. Title.

Nicholson, Ralph,

NICHOLSON, Ralph, 1899- 070'.924 B
A long way from Greens Fork: autobiography. [Tallahassee, Peninsular Pub. Co., 1968] 224 p. port. 24 cm. [PN4874.N53A3] 79-1915
I. Title.

Nicholson, Renton,

NICHOLSON, Renton, 1809-1861 914.21
Rougue's progress; the autobiography of 'Lord Chief Baron' Nicholson. Ed., introd., by John L. Bradley. Boston, Houghton [c.] 1965. xiii, 330p. illus. 21cm. First pub. in 1860 under title: The Lord Chief Baron Nicholson [CT788.N5A3] 65-10328 5.95
I. Bradley, John Lewis, ed. II. Title.

Nick the Greek, 1883-1966.

RICE, Cy. 795'.0924 B
Nick the Greek, King of the Gamblers. New York, Funk & Wagnalls [1969] xiii, 235 p. 22 cm. [GV1301.R48] 79-83723 7.95
1. Nick the Greek, 1883-1966.

Nicklaus, Jack.

NICKLAUS, Jack. 796.352'092'4 B
On and off the fairway : a pictorial autobiography / by Jack Nicklaus with Ken Bowden. New York : Simon and Schuster, c1978. p. cm. Includes index. [GV964.N5A34] 78-15160 ISBN 0-671-24306-3 : 10.95
1. Nicklaus, Jack. 2. Golfers—United States—Biography. I. Bowden, Ken. II. Title.
BIP

Nicklaus, Jack—Juvenile literature.

DEEGAN, Paul J., 1937- 796.352'092'4 B
Jack Nicklaus, the golden bear, by Paul Deegan. Illustrated by John Nelson. [Mankato, Minn., Creative Education; distributed by Childrens Press, Chicago, 1973, c1974] [32] p. illus. (part col.) 25 cm. (Creative's superstars) A biography of the professional golfer who is one of only four who have won the Masters, the two Opens, and the PGA during a career. [GV964.N5D43] 73-12190 ISBN 0-87191-259-7 4.95
1. Nicklaus, Jack—Juvenile literature. I. Nelson, John, 1928- illus. II. Title.

TAYLOR, Paula. 796.352'092'4
Golf's great winner, Jack Nicklaus / by Paula Taylor. [Mankato, Minn.] : Creative Educations, [c1977] 30 p. : ill. ; 19 cm. (The Allstars) Concentrates on the famous golfer's style and his competitiveness with Arnold Palmer. [GV964.N5T39] 92 76-45375 lib. bdg. 4.95
1. Nicklaus, Jack—Juvenile literature. 2. Golfers—United States—Biography—Juvenile literature. I. Title.

VAN RIPER, Guernsey, 1909- 796.352'092'2 B
Golfing greats: two top pros. Champaign, Ill., Garrard Pub. Co. [1975] 95 p. illus. 24 cm. Sketches the golfing careers of two of the game's pros, Jack Nicklaus and Lee Trevino. [GV964.N5V36] 920 74-16266 ISBN 0-8116-6669-7 3.28 (lib. bdg.)
1. Nicklaus, Jack—Juvenile literature. 2. Trevino, Lee—Juvenile literature. 3. Golf—Juvenile literature. I. Title.

Nicolaus Cusanus, Cardinal, 1401-1464.

BETT, Henry, 1876-1953. 230'.2'0924 B
Nicholas of Cusa / by Henry Bett. Merrick, N.Y. : Richwood Pub. Co., 1976. x, 210 p. ; 23 cm. Reprint of the 1932 ed. published by Methuen & Co., London, issued in series: Great medieval churchmen. Includes bibliographical references and index. [BX4705.N58B4 1976] 76-1131 ISBN 0-915172-05-4 lib.bdg. : 18.50
1. Nicolaus Cusanus, Cardinal, 1401-1464. I. Title. II. Series: Great medieval churchmen.
BIP

Nicolay, John George, 1832-1901.

NICOLAY, Helen, 1866-1954. 973.7'0924 B
Lincoln's secretary; a biography of John G. Nicolay. Westport, Conn., Greenwood Press [1971, c1949] x, 363 p. illus. 23 cm. [E467.1.N5N5 1971] 70-138169 ISBN 0-8371-5626-2
1. Nicolay, John George, 1832-1901. I. Title.
BIP

Nicolet, Jean, d. 1642.

BUTTERFIELD, Consul Willshire, 1824-1899. 977
History of the discovery of the Northwest by John Nicolet in 1634, with a sketch of his life. Port Washington, N.Y., Kennikat Press [1969] ix, 113 p. 21 cm. Reprint of the 1881 ed. Bibliographical footnotes. [F482.B88 1969] 68-26262
1. Nicolet, Jean, d. 1642. 2. Northwest, Old—Discovery and exploration. I. Title.

Nicoll, Maurice, 1884-1953.

POGSON, Beryl, 1895- 926.1
Maurice Nicoll. a portrait. New York, Nelson [c.1961] 288p. illus. 61-65131 6.50
1. Nicoll, Maurice, 1884-1953. I. Title.

POGSON, Beryl, 1895- 926.1
Maurice Nicoll, a portrait. [1st American ed.] New York, T. Nelson [1961] 288p. illus. 23cm. [R489.N52P6 1961a] 61-65131
1. Nicoll, Maurice, 1884-1953. I. Title.

Nicolson, William, Abp. of Cashel, 1655-1727.

JAMES, Francis Godwin. 922.342
North Country bishop; a biography of William Nicolson. New Haven, Yale University Press, 1956. xiv, 330p. port., map, geneal. table. 25cm. (Yale historical publications. Miscellany, 65) Bibliographical essay': p. 281-295. [BX5595.N5J3] 56-11797
1. Nicolson, William, Abp. of Cashel, 1655-1727. I. Title. II. Series.
BIP

Niebuhr, Helmut Richard, 1894-1962.

GODSEY, John D. 230'.0924 B
The promise of H. Richard Niebuhr, by John D. Godsey. [1st ed.] Philadelphia, Lippincott [1970] 122 p. 22 cm. (The Promise of theology) Bibliography: p. 119-122. [BX4827.N47G6] 75-103600 3.95
1. Niebuhr, Helmut Richard, 1894-1962. I. Title.

KLIEVER, Lonnie D. 230'.092'4 B
H. Richard Niebuhr / by Lonnie D. Kliever. Waco, Tex. : Word Books, c1977. 205 p. ; 23 cm. (Makers of the modern theological mind) Bibliography: p. 203-205. [BX4827.N47K56] 77-92452 ISBN 0-8499-0078-6 : 7.95
1. Niebuhr, Helmut Richard, 1894-1962.
BIP

Niebuhr, Reinhold, 1892-1971.

BINGHAM, June, 1919- 922.473
Courage to change; an introduction to the life and thought of Reinhold Niebuhr. New York, Scribner [1961] 414 p. 24 cm. Includes bibliography. [BX4827.N5B5] 61-13362
1. Niebuhr, Reinhold, 1892-1971. I. Title.
BIP

BINGHAM, June, 1919- 230'.0924 B
Courage to change; an introduction to the life and thought of Reinhold Niebuhr. New York, Scribner [1972] xii, 414 p. illus. 24 cm. "Books by Reinhold Niebuhr": p. 405-406. Includes bibliographical references. [BX4827.N5B5 1972] 72-37467 ISBN 0-684-12789-X 10.00
1. Niebuhr, Reinhold, 1892-1971. I. Title.

HARLAND, Gordon. 922.473
The thought of Reinhold Niebuhr. New York, Oxford University Press, 1960. xvii, 298 p. 22 cm. Bibliographical references included in "Notes" (p. [275]-294) [BX4827.N5H3] 60-7061
1. Niebuhr, Reinhold, 1892-1971. I. Title.

LANDON, Harold R., ed. 230'.092'4 B
Reinhold Niebuhr: a prophetic voice in our time. Essays in tribute by Paul Tillich, John C. Bennett [and] Hans J. Morgenthau. Harold R. Landon, editor. Plainview, N.Y., Books for Libraries Press [1974, c1962] 126 p. 22 cm. (Essay index reprint series) Papers and discussions from the colloquium in honor of Reinhold Niebuhr on October 20, 1961, at the Cathedral Church of St. John the Divine, New York City. Reprint of the ed. published by the Seabury Press, Greenwich, Conn. Includes bibliographical references. [BX4827.N5L3 1974] 74-841 ISBN 0-518-10150-9 9.50
1. Niebuhr, Reinhold, 1892-1971.
BIP

MERKLEY, Paul. 200.92
Reinhold Niebuhr : a political account / Paul Merkley. Montreal : McGill-Queen's University Press, 1975. xii, 289 p. ; 24 cm. Includes index. Bibliography: p. [273]-277. [BX4827.N5M47] 76-351874 ISBN 0-7735-0216-5 : 13.50
1. Niebuhr, Reinhold, 1892-1971.
Distributed by McGill-Queen's University Press, Irvington, N.Y.
BIP

NIEBUHR, Reinhold, 1892-1971. 230'.092'4 B
Leaves from the notebook of a tamed cynic / by Reinhold Niebuhr. New York : Da Capo Press, 1976, c1929. p. cm. (Prelude to depression) Reprint of the ed. published by Willett, Clark & Colby, Chicago. [BX4827.N5A34 1976] 76-27833 ISBN 0-306-70852-3 : 15.00
1. Niebuhr, Reinhold, 1892-1971. 2. Clergy—Michigan—Detroit—Biography. 3. Detroit—Biography. I. Title.

PATTERSON, Bob E. 230'.092'4 B
Reinhold Niebuhr / by Bob E. Patterson. Waco, Tex. : Word Books, c1977. 163 p. ; 23 cm. (Makers of the modern theological mind) Bibliography: p. 161-163. [BX4827.N5P37] 76-46783 ISBN 0-87680-508-X : 6.95
1. Niebuhr, Reinhold, 1892-1971.
BIP

STONE, Ronald H. 230'.0924
Reinhold Niebuhr, prophet to politicians [by] Ronald H. Stone. Nashville, Abingdon Press [1971, c1972] 272 p. 24 cm. Includes bibliographical references. [BX4827.N5S74 1972] 71-172813 ISBN 0-687-36272-5 8.00
1. Niebuhr, Reinhold, 1892-1971. 2. Christianity and politics. I. Title.

Niehans, Paul, 1882-1971.

HANNON, Leslie F. 615'.36 B
The second chance: the life and work of Dr. Paul Niehans [by] Leslie F. Hannon. London, New York, W. H. Allen, 1972. 242 p., leaf. port. 23 cm. Label mounted on t.p.: Transatlantic Arts, inc., New York, sole distributor for the U.S.A. Bibliography: p. 227-236. [R489.N54H36] 72-305148 ISBN 0-491-00469-9 £3.50
1. Niehans, Paul, 1882-1971. I. Title.

Niekro, Phil, 1939- —Juvenile literature.

BINETTE, Wilfred. 796.357'0924 B
Knuckler, the Phil Niekro story. [1st ed.] Atlanta, Ga., Hallux [1970] 132 p. illus., ports. 22 cm. A biography of the man who overcame many odds to become a top major league pitcher known for his knuckleball. [GV865.N5B5] 92 78-114836 3.95
1. Niekro, Phil, 1939- —Juvenile literature. 2. Pitching (Baseball) I. Title.

Nielsen, Carl, 1865-1931.

SIMPSON, Robert Wilfred Levick, 1921- 780.92
Carl Nielsen, symphonist, 1865-1931. Introd. by Count Reventlow. Biographical appendix by Torben Meyer. London, J. M. Dent [dist. Mystic, Conn., Verry, 1964] xiv, 236p. illus., ports., facsims., music. 22cm. Bibl. 53-1764 4.50
1. Nielsen, Carl, 1865-1931. 2. Nielsen, Carl, 1865-1931—Discography. I. Title.

Nielsen, Maren (Jacobsen)

JENKINS, Flora Berg. 920.7
Voices beyond the sea; the life story of Maren Jacobsen Nielsen, bu Flora Berg Jenkins; Irene W. Campbell, coauthor. [n.p., c1959] 283p. illus. 20cm. [CT275.N667J4] 60-22306
1. Nielsen, Maren (Jacobsen) I. Campbell, Irene W., joint author. II. Title.

Nielson, Jens, 1820-1906.

LYMAN, Albert R 1880- v. 12
Bishop Jens Nielson history and genealogy [written by Albert R. Lyman and others; compiled by Jay P. Nielson and others. n.p., 1866?] 1 v. (unpaged) illus., photos, facsims. 22 x 36 cm. 67-101258
1. Nielson, Jens, 1820-1906. I. Nielson, Jay P., comp. II. Title.

Niemoller, Martin, 1892-

DAVIDSON, Clarissa Start. 284'.1'0924 B
God's man : the story of Pastor Niemoeller / by Clarissa Start Davidson. Westport, Conn. : Greenwood Press, 1979, c1959. x, 242 p., [1] leaf of plates : port. ; 22 cm. Reprint of the ed. published by I. Washburn, New York. Bibliography: p. 241-242. [BX8080.N48D3 1979] 78-10131 ISBN 0-313-21065-9 lib. bdg. : 19.75
1. Niemoller, Martin, 1892- 2. Lutheran Church—Clergy—Biography. 3. Clergy—Germany, West—Biography. I. Title.
BIP

Niepce, Joseph Nicephore, 1765-1833.

FOUQUE, Victor, b.1802. 770'.92'4
The truth concerning the invention of photography: Nicephore Niepce, his life, letters, and works [Translated by Edward Epstean] New York, Arno Press, 1973. 163 p. 23 cm. (The Literature of Photography) Translation of Laverite surl'invention de la photographie. Reprint of the 1935 ed. Includes bibliographical references. [TR140.N5F72 1973] 72-9198 ISBN 0-405-04907-2 10.00.
1. Niepce, Joseph Nicephore, 1765-1833. 2. Photography—History. I. Title. II. Series.
BIP

Nietzsche, Friedrich Wilhelm,

NIETZSCHE, Friedrich Wilhelm, 1844-1900. 193
The Nietsche-Wagner correspondence. Edited by Elizabeth Foerster-Nietzsche. Translated by Caroline V. Kerr. Introd. by H. L. Mencken. New York, Liveright [1970? c1921] xvii, 312 p. 22 cm. [B3316.A47 1970] 72-131285 2.75
I. Wagner, Richard, 1813-1883. II. Forster-Nietzsche, Elisabeth, 1846-1935, ed. III. Kerr, Caroline V., tr. IV. Title.

Nietzsche, Friedrich Wilhelm, 1844-1900.

ABRAHAM, Gerald Ernest Heal, 1904- 193 B
Nietzsche, by Gerald Abraham. New York, Haskell House Publishers, 1974. 144 p. 20 cm. Reprint of the 1933 ed. published by Duckworth, London, which was issued as no. 23 of Great lives. Bibliography: p. 144. [B3316.A6 1974] 73-20387 ISBN 0-8383-1764-2 12.95 (lib. bdg.).
1. Nietzsche, Friedrich Wilhelm, 1844-1900.

BRANDES, Georg Morris Cohen, 1842-1927. 193 B
Friedrich Nietzsche. New York, Haskell House Publishers, 1972. 117 p. port. 23 cm. Reprint of the 1914 ed. [B3316.B6713 1972] 72-2133 ISBN 0-8383-1463-5 8.95
1. Nietzsche, Friedrich Wilhelm, 1844-1900.

BRINTON, Clarence Crane, 1898- 921.3
Nietzsche, by Crane Brinton. New York, Harper [1965] ix, 269p. ports. 21cm. (Harper torchbks. The acad. lib., TB1197L) Bibl. [B3316.B75] 65-4240 1.95 pap.,
1. Nietzsche, Friedrich Wilhelm, 1844-1900. I. Title.

DYCK, J. W. 438.6'42
Nietzsche [by] J. W. Dyck. Waltham, Mass., Blaisdell [1967] vii, 88p. port. 21cm. (Blaisdell bk. in the modern lang.) Text in German. [B3317.D9] 67-11446 1.25 pap.,
1. Nietzsche, Friedrich Wilhelm, 1844-1900. I. Title.

FRENZEL, Ivo. 193 B
Friedrich Nietzsche, an illustrated biography. Translated from the German by Joachim Neugroschel. New York, Pegasus [1967] 126 p. illus., facsims., ports. 22 cm. Translation of Friedrich Nietzsche in Selbstzeugnissen und Bilddokumenten. Bibliographical references included in "Notes" (p. 122-123) Bibliography: p. 124. [B3316.F813] 67-25499
1. Nietzsche, Friedrich Wilhelm, 1844-1900. I. Title.

KAUFMANN, Walter Arnold. 921.3
Nietzsche: Philosopher, psychologist, antichrist. New York, Meridian Books, 1956 [c1950] 412p. 19cm. (Meridian books, M25) [B3316] 56-6572
1. Nietzsche, Friedrich Wilhelm, 1844-1900. I. Title.

KAUFMANN, Walter Arnold. 921.3
Nietzsche: philosopher, psychologist, antichrist. New York, Meridian Books, 1956 [c1950] 412p. 19cm. (Meridian books, M25) [B3316] 56-6572
1. Nietzsche, Friedrich Wilhelm, 1844-1900. I. Title.

KENNEDY, John McFarland. 193
Nietzsche, by J. M. Kennedy. New York, Haskell House Publishers, 1974. 192 p. 20 cm. Reprint of the 1914 ed. published by T. W. Laurie, London, first issued in 1909 under title: The quintessence of Nietzsche. Includes bibliographical references. [B3317.K4 1974] 73-21622 ISBN 0-8383-1791-X 12.95
1. Nietzsche, Friedrich Wilhelm, 1844-1900. **BIP**

LEA, Frank Alfred, 1915- 193.9
The tragic philosopher; a study of Friedrich Nietzsche. New York, Philosophical Library [1957] 834p. illus. 23cm. [B3317.L37] 57-13831
1. Nietzsche, Friedrich Wilhelm, 1844-1900. I. Title.

LOVE, Frederick R. 928.3
Young Nietzsche and the Wagnerian experience. Chapel Hill, Univ. of N. C. Pr., 1963. xi, 103p. 23cm. (Univ. of N. C. Studies in the Germanic langs. & lits., no.39) Bibl. 63-63585 4.50; 3.00 pap.,
1. Nietzsche, Friedrich Wilhelm, 1844-1900. 2. Wagner, Richard, 1813-1883. I. Title. II. Series: North Carolina, University. Studies in the Germanic language and literature, no.39 **BIP**

MUGGE, Maximilian August, 1878- 193
Friedrich Nietzsche, by Maximilian A. Mugge. Port Washington, N.Y., Kennikat Press [1970] 94 p. port. 18 cm. Reprint of the 1912 ed. Bibliography: p. 91-92. [B3316.M87 1970] 78-103207
1. Nietzsche, Friedrich Wilhelm, 1844-1900. **BIP**

NIETZSCHE, v. 12
philosopher, psychologist, antichrist. Cleveland, World Pub. Co. [1961] 412p. 18cm. (Meridian books, M25) Bibliography: p.361-364.
1. Nietzsche, Friedrich Wilhelm, 1844-1900. I. Kaufmann, Walter Arnold.

NIETZSCHE, Friedrich Wilhelm, 1844-1900. 193
Briefwechsel : krit. Gesamtausg. / hrsg. von Giorgio Colli u. Mazzino Montinari. Berlin ; New York : de Gruyter, 1975- v. in ; 23 cm. Contents.Contents.—Abt. 1, Bd. 1. Friedrich Nietzsche Briefe, Juni 1850-Sept. 1864. Briefe an Friedrich Nietzsche, Okt. 1849-Sept. 1864.—Abt. 1, Bd. 2. Friedrich Nietzsche Briefe, Sept. 1864-Apr. 1869.—Abt. 1. Bd. 3. Briefe an Friedrich Nietzsche, Okt. 1864-Marz 1869. [B3316.A253 1975] 75-504997 ISBN 3-11-005912-6 (v. 1) : DM90.00 (v. 1)
1. Philosophers—Germany—Correspondence, reminiscences, etc. I. Colli, Giorgio. II. Montinari, Mazzino.

NIETZSCHE, Friedrich Wilhelm, 1844-1900. 193 S
Ecce homo (Nietzsche's autobiography) / Friedrich Nietzsche ; translated by Anthony M. Ludovici ; poetry rendered by Paul V. Cohn ... [et al.]. New York : Gordon Press, 1974. xiv, 207 p. : music ; 24 cm. (The complete works of Friedrich Nietzsche ; v. 17) [B3312.E5L6 1974 vol. 17] [B3316.A6] 193 75-321821 ISBN 0-87968-211-6
1. Nietzsche, Friedrich Wilhelm, 1844-1900. I. Title. **BIP**

NIETZSCHE, Friedrich Wilhelm, 1844-1900. 193
The Nietsche-Wagner correspondence. Edited by Elizabeth Foerster-Nietzsche. Translated by Caroline V. Kerr. Introd. by H. L. Mencken. New York, Liveright [1970? c1921] xvii, 312 p. 22 cm. [B3316.A47 1970] 72-131285 2.75
I. Wagner, Richard, 1813-1883. II. Forster-Nietzsche, Elisabeth, 1846-1935, ed. III. Kerr, Caroline V., tr. IV. Title.

NIETZSCHE, Friedrich Wilhelm, 1844-1900. 193 B
Nietzsche: a self-portrait from his letters. Edited and translated by Peter Fuss and Henry Shapiro. Cambridge, Mass., Harvard University Press, 1971. viii, 196 p. ports. 23 cm. Bibliography: p. 185-190. [B3316.A26] 73-134953 ISBN 0-674-62425-4 8.00
1. Philosophers, German—Correspondence, reminiscences, etc. I. Title.

O'BRIEN, Edward Joseph Harrington, 1890-1941. 193 B
Son of the morning; a portrait of Friedrich Nietzsche. New York, Haskell House Publishers [1972, c1932] p. Bibliography: p. [B3316.O2 1972] 72-2085 ISBN 0-8383-1469-4
1. Nietzsche, Friedrich Wilhelm, 1844-1900. I. Title.

PETERS, Heinz Frederick. 193 B
Zarathustra's sister : the case of Elisabeth and Friedrich Nietzsche / by H. F. Peters. New York : Crown, c1976. p. cm. "The writings of Elisabeth Forster-Nietzsche": p. Includes bibliographical references. [B3316.P47 1976] 76-18996 ISBN 0-517-52725-1 : 8.95
1. Nietzsche, Friedrich Wilhelm, 1844-1900. 2. Forster-Nietzsche, Elisabeth, 1846-1935. I. Title.

REYBURN, Hugh Adam. 193 B
Nietzsche; the story of a human philosopher, by H. A. Reyburn in collaboration with H. E. Hinderks and J. G. Taylor. Westport, Conn., Greenwood Press [1973] viii, 499 p. 22 cm. Reprint of the 1948 ed. Includes bibliographical references. [B3316.R43 1973] 72-11685 ISBN 0-8371-6674-8 18.25
1. Nietzsche, Friedrich Wilhelm, 1844-1900. **BIP**

Nietzsche, Friedrich Wilhelm, 1844-1900—Addresses, essays, lectures.

STUDIES in Nietzsche and the classical tradition / edited by James C. O'Flaherty, Timothy F. Sellner, and Robert M. Helm. Chapel Hill : University of North Carolina Press, 1976. p. cm. (University of North Carolina studies in the Germanic languages and literatures ; no. 85) Includes bibliographical references. [B3317.S78] 75-22444 ISBN 0-8078-8085-X 193
1. Nietzsche, Friedrich Wilhelm, 1844-1900—Addresses, essays, lectures. I. O'Flaherty, James C. II. Sellner, Timothy F., 1938- III. Helm, Robert Meredith. IV. Series: North Carolina. University. Studies in the Germanic languages and literatures ; no. 85. **BIP**

Nigeria—Biography.

ORIMOLOYE, S. A. 920'.0669
Biographia Nigeriana : a biographical dictionary of eminent Nigerians / S. A. Orimoloye. Boston : G. K. Hall, c1977. xiii, 368 p. ; 25 cm. (Bibliographies and guides in African studies) [CT2526.O74] 77-4132 ISBN 0-8161-8049-0 lib.bdg. : 40.00
1. Nigeria—Biography. I. Title. II. Series. **BIP**

Nightingale, Florence, 1820-1910.

COOPER, Lettice Ulpha, 1897- 926.1
The young Florence Nightingale. Illus. by Denise Brown. New York, Roy Publishers [c.1960] 143p. 60-14479 3.00 bds.,
1. Nightingale, Florence, 1820-1910. I. Title.

FFRENCH, Yvonne. 920.72'094
Six great Englishwomen : Queen Elizabeth I, Sarah Siddons, Charlotte Bronte, Florence Nightingale, Queen Victoria, Gertrude Bell / by Yvonne Ffrench. Folcroft, Pa. : Folcroft Library Editions, 1976. p. cm. Reprint of the 1953 ed. published by Hamilton, London. [DA28.7.F42 1976] 76-10646 ISBN 0-8414-4219-3 lib. bdg. : 17.50
1. Elizabeth, Queen of England, 1533-1603. 2. Siddons, Sarah Kemble, 1755-1831. 3. Bronte, Charlotte, 1816-1855. 4. Nightingale, Florence, 1820-1910. 5. Victoria, Queen of Great Britain, 1819-1901. 6. Bell, Gertrude Lowthian, 1868-1926. I. Title.

LADY with a lamp; 920.7
the story of Florence Nightingale. New York, Roy Publishers [1957?] 96p. illus. 20cm. (Stories of faith and fame) [UH347] [UH347] 926.1 57-7193 57-7193
1. Nightingale, Florence, 1820-1910. I. Davey, Cyril James.

NIGHTINGALE, Florence, 1820-1910. 610'.8
Florence Nightingale : her wit and wisdom / compiled and edited by Evelyn R. Barritt ; with ill. by Jeff Hill. Mount Vernon, N.Y. : Peter Pauper Press, [1975] 61 p. : ill. ; 20 cm. [RT37.N53A33 1975] 75-306791 1.95
1. Nightingale, Florence, 1820-1910. I. Hill, Jeff.

NIGHTINGALE, Florence, 1820-1910. 610'.8
Florence Nightingale : her wit and wisdom / compiled and edited by Evelyn R. Barritt ; with ill. by Jeff Hill. Mount Vernon, N.Y. : Peter Pauper Press, [1975] 61 p. : ill. ; 20 cm. [RT37.N53A33 1975] 75-306791 1.95
1. Nightingale, Florence, 1820-1910. I. Hill, Jeff.

NIGHTINGALE, Florence, 1820-1910. 610.73'092'4 B
Letters of Florence Nightingale in the History of Nursing Archive, Special Collections, Boston University Libraries / edited by Lois A. Monteiro ; with an introd. by Irene S. Palmer. Boston : Boston University, Mugar Memorial Library, Nursing Archive, 1974. xxiv, 69 p. : ill. ; 23 cm. Includes index. [UH347.N6A4 1974] 74-187754
1. Nightingale, Florence, 1820-1910. I. Mugar Memorial Library. Nursing Archive. II. Title.

STRACHEY, Giles Lyton, 1880-1932 920.042
Eminent Victorians: Cardinal Manning, Florence Nightingale, Dr. Arnold, General Gordon. New York [Putnam, 1963] vii, 338p. (Capricorn bk., 83) Bibl. 1.65 pap.,
1. Manning, Henry Edward, cardinal, 1808-1892. 2. Nightingale, Florence, 1820-1910. 3. Arnold, Thomas, 1795-1842. 4. Gordon, Charles George, 1833-1885. I. Title.

STRACHEY, Giles Lytton, 1880-1932. 920.042
Eminent Victorians: Cardinal Manning, Florence Nightingale, Dr. Arnold, General Gordon. New York, Capricorn Books [1963] vii, 338 p. 18 cm. Includes bibliographies. [CT782.S8] 64-4150
1. Nightingale, Florence, 1820-1910. 2. Arnold, Thomas, 1795-1842. 3. Gordon, Charles George, 1833-1885. 4. Manning, Henry Edward, Cardinal, 1808-1892. I. Title.

WOODHAM smith, Cecil Blanche (Fitzgerald), 1896- 920.7
Florence Nightingale. New York, Avon [1963, c.1961] 384p. 18cm. (V2063) Bibl. .75 pap.,
1. Nightingale, Florence, 1820-1910. I. Title.

WOODHAM Smith, Cecil Blanche (Fitzgerald) 1896- [920.7] 926.1
Florence Nightingale, 1820-1910. New York, McGraw-Hill [1951] 382 p. illus., ports. 24 cm. Bibliography: p. 367-372. [UH347.N6W6 1951] 51-9544
1. Nightingale, Florence, 1820-1910. I. Title.

WOODHAM Smith, Cecil Blanche (Fitzgerald) 1896- 920.7
Lonely crusader; the life of Florence Nightingale, 1820-1910. An abridged edition of the definitive biography, Florence Nightingale, by the same author. New York, Bantam [1963, c.1951] 196p. 18cm. (Pathfinder Ed., FP2) Bibl. .50 pap.,
1. Nightingale, Florence, 1820-1910. I. Title.

WOODHAM SMITH, Cecil Blanche (FitzGerald) 1896- [920.7] 929.1
Florence Nightingale, 1820-1910. New York, Grosset & Dunlap [1958, c1951] 382 p. illus. 22 cm. (Biographies of distinction) [UH347.N6W6] 58-14625
1. Nightingale, Florence, 1820-1910. I. Title.

WOODHAM SMITH, Cecil Blanche (Fitzgerald) 1896- [920.7] 926.1
Lonely crusader; the life of Florence Nightingale, 1820-1910. An abridged edition of the definitive biography, Florence Nightingale, by the same author. New York, Whittlesey House [1951] 255 p. illus., ports. 21 cm. Bibliography: p. 243-248. [UH347.N6W6 1951a] 51-12704
1. Nightingale, Florence, 1820-1910. I. Title.

Nightingale, Florence, 1820-1910 — Juvenile literature.

GRAFF, Polly Anne (Colver) 1908- 92
Florence Nightingale, war nurse. Illustrated by Gerald McCann. Champaign,Ill., Garrard Press [1961] 80 p. illus. 23 cm. (A Discovery book) [UH347.N6G7] 61-5485
1. Nightingale, Florence, 1820-1910 — Juvenile literature. I. Title.

HUME, Ruth (Fox) 926.1
Florence Nightingale. Illustrated by Robert Frankenberg. New York, Random House [c.1960] 184p. Bibl. col. illus., endpaper map 22cm. (World landmark books, W-46) 60-10021 1.95
1. Nightingale, Florence, 1820-1910—Juvenile literature. I. Title.

WEBB, Robert N. 920
The how and wonder book of Florence Nightingale Illus. by Leonard Vosburgh. [Deluxe ed.] New York, Grosset [c.1962] 48p. illus. (pt. col.) 29 cm. (How and why wonder bks.) 62-12795 bds., 1.00
1. Nightingale, Florence, 1820-1910—Juvenile literature. I. Title.

Nightingale, Florence, 1820-1910—Juvenile literature.

HARMELINK, Barbara. 610.73'0924 B
Florence Nightingale, founder of modern nursing. New York, F. Watts [1969] viii, 116 p. illus., ports. 22 cm. (Immortals of history) Includes bibliographies. A biography of Florence Nightingale, whom the author labels a reluctant saint and describes as a woman who despite great compassion and dedication was embittered by the many hardships and opposition she endured. [RT37.N5H3] 92 69-13709
1. Nightingale, Florence, 1820-1910—Juvenile literature. I. Title.

HYNDMAN, Jane 610.73'0924 B
Andrews (Lee) 1912-
Florence Nightingale; nurse to the world [by] Lee Wyndham. Illustrated by Richard Cuffari. New York, World Pub. Co. [1969] 175 p. illus. 21 cm. Bibliography: p. 174-175. A biography of the aristocratic woman who defied social convention in order to establish nursing as a respectable career for women and bring about great reforms in hospital conditions and nursing care. [RT37.N5H9 1969] 92 78-82782 3.95
1. Nightingale, Florence, 1820-1910—Juvenile literature. I. Cuffari, Richard, 1925- illus. II. Title.

KOCH, Charlotte, 610.73'092'4 B
1923-
Florence Nightingale / by Charlotte Koch ; illustrated by Michele Chessare. New York : Dandelion Press, 1979. [32] p. : col. ill. ; 18 x 23 cm. A brief biography of the well-to-do woman who defied social convention in order to establish nursing as a respectable career for women and bring about great reforms in hospital conditions and nursing care. [RT37.N5K62] 92 78-64424 ISBN 0-89799-105-2 : 3.50 ISBN 0-89799-038-2 pbk. : 1.50
1. Nightingale, Florence, 1820-1910—Juvenile literature. 2. Nurses—England—Biography—Juvenile literature. I. Chessare, Michele. II. Title.

Nijinsky, Waslaw,

NIJINSKY, Waslaw, 792.8'0924
1890-1950.
The diary of Vaslav Nijinsky. Edited by Romola Nijinsky. Berkeley, University of California Press, 1968 [c1936] xvi, 187 p. illus., ports. 21 cm. [GV1785.N6A3 1968] 68-12426
I. Nijinsky, Romola (de Pulszky) ed. II. Title. **BIP**

Nijinsky, Waslaw, 1890-1950.

BEAUMONT, Cyril 792.8'2'0924
William, 1891-
Vaslav Nijinsky, by Cyril W. Beaumont New York, Haskell House Publishers, 1974. 28 p. illus. 24 cm. Reprint of the 1932 ed. published by C. W. Beaumont, London, which was issued as no. 2 of Essays in dancing & dancers. [GV1785.N6B4 1974] 74-1080 ISBN 0-8383-1752-9
1. Nijinsky, Waslaw, 1890-1950. **BIP**

BOURMAN, Anatole. 792.8'0924 B
The tragedy of Nijinsky. In collaboration with D. Lyman. Westport, Conn., Greenwood Press [1970] xx, 291 p. ports. 21 cm. Reprint of the 1936 ed. [GV1785.N6B6 1970] 70-98822
1. Nijinsky, Waslaw, 1890-1950. I. Lyman, Dorothy, 1902- joint author. II. Title.

KRASOVSKAIA, Vere 792.8'092'4 B
Mikhailovna.
Nijinsky / Vera Krasovskaya ; translated from the Russian by John E. Bowlt. New York : Schirmer books, 1979. p. cm. Translation of Nizhinskii. "A Dance Horizons Book." Includes index. [GV1785.N6K7213] 79-7368 ISBN 0-02-871870-4 : 15.00
1. Nijinsky, Waslaw, 1890-1950. 2. Dancers—Russia—Biography. 3. Choreographers—Russia—Biography. **BIP**

NIJINSKY, v. 12
by Romola Nijinsky, his wife. [Harmondsworth] Penguin Books, 1960. 348p. 8 plates (incl. ports.) 19cm.
1. Nijinsky, Waslaw, 1890-1950. I. Nijinsky, Romola (de Pulszky)

NIJINSKY, Pavlova, 792.8'092'4 B
Duncan : three lives in dance / edited by Paul Magriel. New York : Da Capo Press, 1977. 260 p. in various pagings : ill. ; 24 cm. (A Da Capo paperback) Reprint of 3 works: Nijinsky (1946), Pavlova (1947), and Isadora Duncan (1947), which were edited by P. D. Magriel and published by Holt, New York. Includes bibliographies. [GV1785.A1N54 1977b] 76-30403 ISBN 0-306-70845-0 : 22.50
1. Nijinsky, Waslaw, 1890-1950. 2. Pavlova, Anna, 1881-1931. 3. Duncan, Isadora, 1878-1927. 4. Dancers—Biography. I. Magriel, Paul David, 1906- II. Magriel, Paul David, 1906- ed. Nijinsky, 1977. III. Magriel, Paul David, 1906- ed. Pavlova. 1977. IV. Magriel, Paul David, 1906- ed. Isadora Duncan. 1977.

NIJINSKY, Pavlova, 792.8'092'4 B
Duncan : three lives in dance / edited by Paul Magriel. New York : Da Capo Press, 1977. 260 p. in various pagings : ill. ; 24 cm. (A Da Capo paperback) Reprint of 3 works: Nijinsky (1946), Pavlova (1947), and Isadora Duncan (1947), which were edited by P. D. Magriel and published by Holt, New York. Includes bibliographies. [GV1785.A1N54 1977b] 76-30403 ISBN 0-306-70845-0 : 22.50
1. Nijinsky, Waslaw, 1890-1950. 2. Pavlova, Anna, 1881-1931. 3. Duncan, Isadora, 1878-1927. 4. Dancers—Biography. I. Magriel, Paul David, 1906- II. Magriel, Paul David, 1906- ed. Nijinsky, 1977. III. Magriel, Paul David, 1906- ed. Pavlova. 1977. IV. Magriel, Paul David, 1906- ed. Isadora Duncan. 1977. **BIP**

NIJINSKY, Romola de 927.93
Pulszk.
The last years of Nijinsky. New York, Simon and Schuster, 1952. 260 p. illus. 22 cm. [GV1785 N6N58] 52-10206
1. Nijinsky, Waslaw, 1890-1950. 2. World War, 1939-1945—Personal narratives. **BIP**

NIJINSKY, Romola (de 792.8'2'0924
Pulszky)
Nijinsky, by Romola Nijinsky. Foreword by Paul Claudel. New York, AMS Press [1968] xvii, 447 p. illus. 24 cm. Reprint of the 1934 ed. [GV1785.N6N6 1968] 68-54285
1. Nijinsky, Waslaw, 1890-1950. **BIP**

NIJINSKY, Waslaw, 792.8'0924
1890-1950.
The diary of Vaslav Nijinsky. Edited by Romola Nijinsky. Berkeley, University of California Press, 1968 [c1936] xvi, 187 p. illus., ports. 21 cm. [GV1785.N6A3 1968] 68-12426
I. Nijinsky, Romola (de Pulszky) ed. II. Title **BIP**

REISS, FRANCOISE. 927.928
Nijinsky, a biography. Translated by Helen and Stephen Haskell. New York, Pitman Pub. Corp. [c1960] 208p. illus. 24cm. 'English translation ... from 'Nijinsky, on La grace, tome 1: La vie de Nijinsky." [GV1785.N6R43] 61-2326
1. Nijinsky, Waslaw, 1890-1950. I. Title.

Nikephoros of Chios, Saint.

CAVARNOS, 281.9'092'4 B
Constantine.
St. Nikephoros of Chios, outstanding writer of liturgical poetry and lives of saints, educator, spiritual striver, and trainer of martyrs : an account of his life, character, and message, together with a comprehensive list of his publications, selections from them, and brief biographies of eleven neomartyrs and other Orthodox saints who are treated in his works / by Constantine Cavarnos. Belmont, Mass. : Institute for Byzantine and Modern Greek Studies, c1976. 124 p. : port. ; 21 cm. (His Modern Orthodox saints ; 4) Includes index. Bibliography: p. 111-114. [BX395.N46C38] 76-3152 ISBN 0-914744-32-1 : 6.50. ISBN 0-914744-33-X pbk. : 3.95
1. Nikephoros of Chios, Saint. 2. Christian saints—Biography. I. Title: St. Nikephoros of Chios, outstanding writer of liturgical poetry ...

Nikitenko, Aleksandr Vasil'evich, 1804?-1877—Biography.

NIKITENKO, Aleksandr 891.7'09 B
Vasil'evich, 1804?-1877.
The diary of a Russian censor / Aleksandr Nikitenko ; abridged, edited & translated by Helen Saltz Jacobson. Amherst : University of Massachusetts Press, [1975] xxii, 397 p. : port. ; 24 cm. Translation of Dnevnik. Includes index. [PG2947.N5A3613 1975] 74-78977 ISBN 0-87023-152-9 : 20.00
1. Nikitenko, Aleksandr Vasil'evich, 1804?-1877—Biography. 2. Censorship—Russia. 3. Russia—Intellectual life. I. Jacobson, Helen Saltz. II. Title.

Nikodemos Hagioreites, 1748 or 9-1809.

CAVARNOS, 281.9'092'4 B
Constantine.
St. Nicodemos the Hagiorite, great theologian and teacher of the Orthodox Church ... : an account of his life, character, and message ... / by Constantine Cavarnos. Belmont, Mass. : Institute for Byzantine and Modern Greek Studies, [1974] 167 p. : port. ; 21 cm. (His Modern Orthodox saints ; 3) Includes index. Bibliography: p. 157-158. [BX619.N5C38] 74-79388 ISBN 0-914744-17-8 : 6.00 ISBN 0-914744-18-6 pbk. : 3.95
1. Nikodemos Hagioreites, 1748 or 9-1809. I. Title: St. Nicodemos the Hagiorite, great theologian and teacher ...

Nikolaeva, Valentina Vladimirovna Tereshkova, 1937—Juvenile literature.

SHARPE, Mitchell 629.45'0092'4 B
R.
"It is I, Sea gull," Valentina Tereshkova, first woman in space, by Mitchell R. Sharpe. New York, Crowell [1975] 214 p. illus. 24 cm. Bibliography: p. 205-208. A biography of the first woman astronaut and history of the Russian manned space program. [TL789.85.N48S5 1975] 92 74-14698 ISBN 0-690-00646-2 5.95
1. Nikolaeva, Valentina Vladimirovna Tereshkova, 1937—Juvenile literature. 2. Astronautics—Russia—History—Juvenile literature. I. Title.

Nikolai, Metropolitan of Krutitsy and Kolomna, 1892-1961.

FLETCHER, William C. 281.9'0924 B
Nikolai; portrait of a dilemma, by William C. Fletcher. New York, Macmillan [1968] ix, 230 p. 22 cm. Includes bibliographical references. [BX597.N49F55 1968] 68-13209
1. Nikolai, Metropolitan of Krutitsy and Kolomna, 1892-1961.

Nikolaus von der Fliie, Saint, 1417-1487.

LAMB, George Robert. 922.2494
Brother Nicholas, a life of St. Nicholas of Flue. New York, Sheed and Ward [1955] 191p. 20cm. [BX4700.N66L3] 55-9450
1. Nikolaus von der Fliie, Saint, 1417-1487. I. Title.

Niles, John, 1775-1812.

PARKER, Sarah W 922.573
The Reverend John Niles, 1775-1812. Prepared for the one hundred and fiftieth anniversary of the Church of Christ in Bath, Presbyterian Congregation, January 3-5, 1958. Bath, N. Y., 1958. 80p. illus. 23cm. Includes bibliography. [BX9225.N47P3] 58-20659
1. Niles, John, 1775-1812. I. Title.

Nimeth, Albert J.,

NIMETH, Albert J., tr. 922.245
To live the Gospel; tr. from French by Albert J. Nimeth. Chicago, Franciscan Herald [c. 1963] 51p. 18cm. .65 pap.,
I. Title.

Nimitz, Chester William, 1885-1966.

POTTER, Elmer 940.54'26'0924 B
Belmont, 1908-
Nimitz / E. B. Potter. Annapolis, Md. : Naval Institute Press, c1976. xiii, 507 p., [10] leaves of plates : ill. ; 27 cm. Includes index. Bibliography: p. 474-481. [V63.N55P67] 76-1056 ISBN 0-87021-492-6 : 16.95
1. Nimitz, Chester William, 1885-1966. 2. United States. Navy—Biography. 3. Admirals—United States—Biography. **BIP**

Nin, Anais, 1903- —Biography.

NIN, Anais, 1903- 818'.5'203
The diary of Anais Nin. Edited, and with an introd., by Gunther Stuhlmann. New York, Swallow Press [1969- ,c1966- v. 21 cm. "A Harvest book." Contents.—[1] 1931-1934.—[2] 1934-1939. [PS3527.I865Z5 1969] 77-2085
1. Nin, Anais, 1903- —Biography. I. Stuhlmann, Gunther, ed. II. Title. **BIP**

NIN, Anais, 1903- 818'.5'203 B
The diary of Anais Nin. Edited, and with an introd., by Gunther Stuhlmann. [1st ed.] New York, Swallow Press [1966- v. illus. 22 cm. Vol. 3 has imprint: New York, Harcourt, Brace & World; v. 4- New York, Harcourt, Brace, Jovanovich. Contents.Contents.—v. 1. 1931-1934.—v. 2. 1934-1939.—[3] 1939-1944.—[4] 1944-1947.—[5] 1947-1955. [PS3527.I865Z5] 66-12917 ISBN 0-15-125593-8 (v. 5)
1. Nin, Anais, 1903- —Biography. I. Stuhlmann, Gunther, ed. II. Title.

Nin, Anais, 1903- —Interviews.

SCHNEIDER, Duane. 813'.5'2 B
An interview with Anais Nin [by] Duane Schneider. [1st ed.] Athens, Ohio [D. Schneider Press] 1970. 35 p. 23 cm. 176 copies printed. No. 52. [PS3527.I865Z9] 75-16651
1. Nin, Anais, 1903- —Interviews. I. Nin, Anais, 1903- II. Title.

Nin, Anais, 1903-1977—Diaries.

NIN, Anais, 1903- 818'.5'203 B
1977.
The diary of Anais Nin / edited and with a pref. by Gunther Stuhlmann. New York : Harcourt Brace Jovanovich, [1977] c1976- p. cm. (A Harvest/HBJ book) Includes index. Contents.Contents.— [6] 1955-1966. [PS3527.I865Z5 1977] 77-3599 ISBN 0-15-626032-8 pbk. : 3.95
1. Nin, Anais, 1903-1977—Diaries. 2. Authors, American—20th century—Biography. I. Stuhlmann, Gunther. II. Title.

NIN, Anais, 1903- 818'.5'203 B
1977.
Linotte : the early diary of Anais Nin, 1914-1920 / translated from the French by Jean L. Sherman ; with a pref. by Joaquin Nin-Culmell. New York : Harcourt Brace Jovanovich, 1978 p. cm. (A Harvest/HBJ book) [PS3527.I865Z522 1980] 79-18962 14.95
1. Nin, Anais, 1903-1977—Diaries. 2. Authors, American—20th century—Biography. I. Title.

NIN, Anais, 1903- 818'.5'203
1977.
Linotte : the early diary of Anais Nin, 1914-1920 / with a pref. by Joaquin Nin-Culmel ; translated from the french by Jean L. Sherman. 1st ed. New York : Harcourt, Brace, Jovanovich, c1978. x, 518 p. : ill. ; 24 cm. Includes index. [PS3527.I865Z522 1978] 77-20314 ISBN 0-15-152488-2 : 14.95
1. Nin, Anais, 1903-1977—Diaries. 2. Authors, American—20th century—Biography. I. Title.

Nitschke, Ray, 1936-

NITSCHKE, Ray, 796.33'2'0924 B
1936-
Mean on Sunday; The autobiography of Ray Nitschke, as told to Robert W. Wells. [1st ed.] Garden City, N.Y., Doubleday, 1973. 302 p. illus. 22 cm.

[GV939.N57A35] 72-97256 ISBN 0-385-06898-0 7.95
1. Nitschke, Ray, 1936- 2. Football. I. Wells, Robert W. II. Title.

Niven, David,

NIVEN, David, 1910- 791.43'028'0924 B
The moon's a balloon. New York, Putnam [1971 c1972] 380 p. illus. 23 cm. [PN2598.N5A3 1972] 78-175270 7.95
I. Title. BIP

Niven, David, 1910-

NIVEN, David, 1910- 791.43'028'0924 B
Bring on the empty horses / David Niven. New York : Putnam, [1975] 369 p., [8] leaves of plates : ill. ; 22 cm. [PN2598.N5A29 1975] 75-17646 ISBN 0-399-11542-0
1. Niven, David, 1910- 2. Moving-picture actors and actresses—United States—Correspondence, reminiscences, etc. 3. Moving-picture industry—United States—Hollywood, Calif. I. Title.

NIVEN, David, 1910- 791.43'028'0924 B
Bring on the empty horses / David Niven. Boston : G. K. Hall, 1976, c1975. 2 v. ; 24 cm. "Large print." [PN2598.N5A29 1976] 76-8885 ISBN 0-8161-6369-3 : 18.95
1. Niven, David, 1910- 2. Moving-picture actors and actresses—United States—Correspondence, reminiscences, etc. 3. Moving-picture industry—California—Hollywood. 4. Sight-saving books. I. Title.

NIVEN, David, 1910- 791.43'028'0924 B
Bring on the empty horses / David Niven. New York : Putnam, [1975] p. cm. Includes index. [PN2598.N5A29] 75-17524 ISBN 0-399-11542-0 : 9.95
1. Niven, David, 1910- 2. Moving-picture actors and actresses—United States—Correspondence, reminiscences, etc. 3. Moving-picture industry—United States—Hollywood, Calif. I. Title. BIP

NIVEN, David, 1910- 791.43'028'0924 B
The moon's a balloon. New York, Putnam [1971 c1972] 380 p. illus. 23 cm. [PN2598.N5A3 1972] 78-175270 7.95
I. Title. BIP

Niven, Thornton MacNess, 1806-1895.

DOWNS, Arthur Channing, 1930- 720'.924
The architecture and life of the Hon. Thornton MacNess Niven (1806-1895), with accounts of architecture and building practices in Newburgh, Goshen, Monticello, and Riverhead, N.Y., and of newly discovered architecture by Andrew J. Downing, A. J. Davis, Russell Warren, and Calvin Pollard [by] Arthur Channing Downs, Jr. [1st ed. Goshen, N.Y., Orange County Community of Museums & Galleries, 1971] 60 p. illus. 28 cm. Cover title. Includes bibliographical references. [NA737.N5D6] 71-174676
1. Niven, Thornton MacNess, 1806-1895.

Nixon family.

HOYT, Edwin Palmer. 929'.2'0973
The Nixons: an American family [by] Edwin P. Hoyt. [1st ed.] New York, Random House [1972] xii, 307 p. ports. 22 cm. [CS71.N74 1972] 74-37052 ISBN 0-394-47324-8 7.95
1. Nixon family. 2. Milhous family. I. Title.

Nixon, Gary, 1941-

SCALZO, Joe. 796.7'0924 B
Racer: the story of Gary Nixon. [Long Beach, Calif., Parkhurst Pub. Co., 1970] 192 p. illus., ports. 23 cm. (Cycle world library) [GV1060.2.N5S3] 74-21393 5.95
1. Nixon, Gary, 1941- 2. Motorcycle racing—Biography. I. Title.

Nixon, Patricia, 1912-

DAVID, Lester. 973.924'092'4 B
The lonely lady of San Clemente : the story of Pat Nixon / Lester David. 1st ed. New York : Crowell, c1978. 235 p., [8] leaves of plates : ill. ; 24 cm. Includes index. Bibliography: p. 225-226. [E857.N58D38 1978] 78-3299 ISBN 0-690-01688-3 : 9.95
1. Nixon, Patricia, 1912- 2. Presidents—United States—Wives—Biography. I. Title. BIP

DAVID, Lester. 973.924'0092'4 B
The lonely lady of San Clemente : the story of Pat Nixon / Lester David. New York : Berkely Pub. Corp., 1979, c1978. 277p. : ill. ; 18 cm. (A Berkley Book) Includes index. [E857.N58D38 1978] ISBN 0-425-04253-7 pbk. : 2.50
1. Nixon, Patricia, 1912- 2. Presidents — United States — Wives — Biography. I. Title.
L.C. card no. for 1978 Crowell's ed.: 78-3299

Nixon, Patrick Ireland, 1883-

NIXON, Patrick Ireland, 1883- 610'.92'4 B
Pat Nixon of Texas : autobiography of a doctor / by Pat Ireland Nixon ; edited with an introd. by Herbert H. Lang. College Station : Texas A&M University Press, 1979. p. cm. Includes bibliographical references and index. [R154.N66A34] 78-65575 ISBN 0-89096-072-0 : 13.50
1. Nixon, Patrick Ireland, 1883- 2. Physicians—Texas—San Antonio—Biography. 3. Medical historians—Texas—San Antonio—Biography. 4. Public health—Texas—San Antonio—History—20th century. I. Lang, Herbert H., 1921- II. Title. BIP

Nixon, Richard Milhous, 1913-

ALLEN, Gary. 973.924'0924 B
Richard Nixon: the man behind the mask. Boston, Western Islands [1971] 433 p. 21 cm. Includes bibliographical references. [E855.A78] 73-31048 8.00
1. Nixon, Richard Milhous, 1913- 2. United States—Politics and government—1969-1974. I. Title.

ALSOP, Stewart [Johonnot Oliver] 923.273
Nixon & Rockefeller: a double portrait. Garden City, N.Y., Doubleday, [c.]1960. 240p. 22cm. 60-6855 3.95
1. Nixon, Richard Milhous, 1913- 2. Rockefeller, Nelson Aldrich, 1908- 3. U.S.—Pol. & govt.—1953- I. Title.

ANDREWS, Phillip, 1911- 923.273
This man Nixon; the life story of California Senator Richard M. Nixon, Republican candidate for Vice President of the United States, his rise to fame, his prosecution of the Hiss case, his nomination; including the text of the famous radio and TV vindication speech. Philadelphia, Winston [1952] 62 p. illus. 23 cm. [E816.A6] 52-13954
1. Nixon, Richard Milhous, 1913- I. Title.

ARNOLD, William A. 973.924'092'4 B
Back when it all began : the early Nixon years : being some reminiscences of President Nixon's early political career by his first administrative assistant and press secretary / William A. Arnold. 1st ed. New York : Vantage Press, c1975. 45 p., [2] leaves of plates : ill. ; 21 cm. [E856.A89] 75-323198 ISBN 0-533-01713-0 : 4.50
1. Nixon, Richard Milhous, 1913- 2. Arnold, William A. I. Title.

COSTELLO, William, 1904- 923.273
The facts about Nixon; an unauthorized biography. New York, Viking Press, 1960. 306 p. 22 cm. [E748.N5C6] 60-5834
1. Nixon, Richard Milhous, 1913- I. Title.

DE TOLEDANO, Ralph 923.273
Nixon. Rev. and expanded ed. New York, Duell, Sloan and Pearce [c.1956, 1960] 250p. (bibl. footnotes) 21cm. 60-2443 3.95
1. Nixon, Richard Milhous, 1913- I. Title.

DE TOLEDANO, Ralph, 1916- 973.924'0924 B
One man alone: Richard Nixon. New York, Funk & Wagnalls [1969] 386 p. 22 cm. [E856.D4] 71-97942 6.95
1. Nixon, Richard Milhous, 1913- I. Title.

HUGHES, Arthur J. 973.924'0929'4
Richard M. Nixon, by Arthur J. Hughes. New York, Dodd, Mead [1972] viii, 181 p. illus. 21 cm. Bibliography: p. 171-172. [E856.H83] 72-3152 ISBN 0-396-06642-9 4.95
1. Nixon, Richard Milhous, 1913-

JOHNSON, George 923.273
Richard Nixon; an intimate and revealing portrait of one of America's key political figures. Derby, Conn., Monarch [c.1961] 158p. (K57) 61-18603 .35 pap.,
1. Nixon, Richard Milhous, 1913- I. Title.

JOHNSON, George, 1917- 923.273
Richard Nixon; an intimate and revealing portrait of one of America's key political figures. Derby, Conn., Monarch Books [1961] 158p. 19cm. (Monarch books, K57) [E748.N5J6] 61-18603
1. Nixon, Richard Milhous, 1913- I. Title.

KEOGH, James. 923.273
This is Nixon. New York, Putnam [1956] 191 p. illus. 22 cm. [E748.N5K4] 56-8617
1. Nixon, Richard Milhous, 1913- I. Title.

KISSINGER, Henry Alfred. 327.73
White House years / Henry Kissinger. 1st ed. Boston : Little, Brown, c1979. xxiv, 1521 p., [24] leaves of plates : ill. ; 25 cm. Includes bibliographical references and index. [E855.K57] 79-90006 ISBN 0-316-49661-8 : 22.50
1. Nixon, Richard Milhous, 1913- 2. Kissinger, Henry Alfred. 3. United States—Foreign relations—1969-1974. 4. Statesmen—United States—Biography. I. Title. BIP

KORNITZER, Bela. 923.273
The real Nixon, an intimate biography. New York, Rand McNally [1960] 352 p. illus. 21 cm. [E748.N5K6] 60-10346
1. Nixon, Richard Milhous, 1913- I. Title.

MANKIEWICZ, Frank, 1924- 973.924'0924
Perfectly clear; Nixon from Whittier to Watergate. [New York] Quadrangle [1973] xiii, 239 p. 25 cm. [E856.M26 1973] 73-82532 ISBN 0-8129-0405-2 8.95
1. Nixon, Richard Milhous, 1913- 2. Watergate Affair, 1972- I. Title.

MAZLISH, Bruce, 1923- 973.924'092'4 B
In search of Nixon; a psychohistorical inquiry. New York, Basic Books [1972] x, 187 p. illus. 22 cm. Bibliography: p. 181-182. [E856.M27] 71-189669 ISBN 0-465-03219-2 6.95
1. Nixon, Richard Milhous, 1913- I. Title. BIP

MAZLISH, Bruce, 1923- 973.924'092'4 [B]
In search of Nixon; a psychohistorical inquiry. Baltimore, Penguin Books [1973] xxviii, 187 p. illus., ports. 18 cm. (Pelican books) Bibliography: p. 181-182. [E856.M27] ISBN 0-14-021771-1 1.50 (pbk.)
1. Nixon, Richard Milhous, 1913- I. Title.
L.C. card no. for the hardbound edition: 71-189669.

MAZO, Earl 923.273
Richard Nixon; a political and personal portrait. This edition has been specially revised by the author to include new material covering Mr. Nixon's recent activities. New York, Avon [c.1959, 1960] 270p. 18cm. (T-416) .35 pap.,
1. Nixon, Richard Milhous. 1913- I. Title.

MAZO, Earl, 1919- 973.92'0924 B
Nixon; a political portrait [by] Earl Mazo and Stephen Hess. [1st ed.] New York, Harper & Row [1968] viii, 326 p. 22 cm. [E748.N5M3 1968] 68-31363
1. Nixon, Richard Milhous, 1913- I. Hess, Stephen, joint author.

MAZO, Earl, 1919- 923.273
Richard Nixon; a political and personal portrait. [1st ed.] New York, Harper [1959] 309 p. 22 cm. [E748.N5M3] 59-6313
1. Nixon, Richard Milhous, 1913-

MILLEN, William Arthur, 1896- 973.924'0924
Nixonia; fact, fable, fantasy, by William A. Millen. [1st ed.] New York, Exposition Press [1970] 153 p. illus., ports. 22 cm. [E855.M54] 75-126372 ISBN 0-682-47119-4 6.00
1. Nixon, Richard Milhous, 1913- 2. United States—Politics and government—1969-1974. I. Title.

OSBORNE, John, 1907- 320.9'73'0924
The fifth year of the Nixon watch. Caricatures by David Levine. New York, Liveright [1974] viii, 241 p. illus. 22 cm. Consists of articles that appeared in The New republic, Jan. 1973-Jan. 1974. [E855.O85] 73-93125 ISBN 0-87140-582-2 7.95
1. Nixon, Richard Milhous, 1913- 2. United States—Politics and government—1969- 3. Watergate Affair, 1972- I. Title.

PRICE, Raymond, 1930- 973.924'092'4
With Nixon / Raymond Price. New York : Viking Press, [1977] p. cm. Includes index. [E856.P74] 77-13248 ISBN 0-670-77672-6 : 10.00
1. Nixon, Richard Milhous, 1913- 2. Price, Raymond, 1930- 3. United States—Politics and government—1969-1974. 4. Presidents—United States—Biography. 5. Presidents—United States—Staff—Biography. I. Title. BIP

SPALDING, Henry D. 973.924'092'4 B
The Nixon nobody knows, by Henry D. Spalding. Middle Village, N.Y., J. David [1972] 456 p. illus. 22 cm. [E856.S62] 70-188240 ISBN 0-8246-0139-4 8.95
1. Nixon, Richard Milhous, 1913- I. Title. BIP

WHITNEY, David C. 327.73'051
The week that changed the world; President Richard M. Nixon's historic visit to Communist China, February 21-28, 1972, by David C. Whitney. [Chicago, J. G. Ferguson Pub. Co., 1972] [32] p. illus. 28 cm. [E856.W47] 72-85827
1. Nixon, Richard Milhous, 1913- 2. Visits of state—China. I. Title.

WILLS, Garry, 1934- 973.924'0924
Nixon Agonistes; the crisis of the self-made man. Boston, Houghton Mifflin, 1970. xiv, 617 p. 22 cm. [E856.W53] 72-80426 10.00
1. Nixon, Richard Milhous, 1913- 2. U.S.—Politics and government—1945- I. Title. BIP

WOODSTONE, Art 973.9240924
Nixon's head / Arthur Woodstone New York : Popular Library, 1976. viii, 286 p. ; 17 cm. [E856.] [66] ISBN 0-445-08576-2 pbk. : 1.95
1. Nixon, Richard Milhous, 1913-—Personality. I. Title.
L.C. card no. for 1972 St. Martins Press ed.: 73-162872.

THE Young Nixon : 973.924'092'4 B
an oral inquiry / edited by Renee K. Schulte. 1st ed. Fullerton : California State University, Fullerton, Oral History Program, Richard M. Nixon Project, c1978. xxvi, 279 p. : ill. ; 24 cm. Includes index. [E856.Y66] 78-66711 ISBN 0-930046-02-1 : 13.95 ISBN 0-930046-01-3 pbk. : 7.95
1. Nixon, Richard Milhous, 1913- 2. Presidents—United States—Biography. I. Schulte, Renee K. BIP

Nixon, Richard Milhous, 1913- — Cartoons, satire, etc.— Exhibitions.

WATERGATE, the unmaking of a President : 760'.074'016947 S
Lexington, January 12-February 9, 1975 / organized and edited for the University of Kentucky Art Gallery by Richard B. Freeman. [Lexington : University of Kentucky Art Gallery, 1975] 96 p. : chiefly ill. ; 28 cm. (Graphics ; 17, 1975) Catalog of the

exhibition held at the University of Kentucky Art Gallery. [NE45.K4K45 no. 17, 1975] [E860] 364.1'32 75-312669
1. Nixon, Richard Milhous, 1913- — Cartoons, satire, etc.—Exhibitions. 2. Watergate Affair, 1972- —Caricatures and cartoons—Exhibitions. 3. American wit and humor, Pictorial—Exhibitions. I. Freeman, Richard B., 1908- II. Series: Kentucky. University. Art Gallery. Graphics ; 17, 1975.

Nixon, Richard Milhous, 1913- — Chronology.

NIXON, Richard Milhous, 1913- 973.924'092'4
Richard M. Nixon, 1913 : chronology, documents, bibliographical aids / edited by Howard F. Bremer. Dobbs Ferry, N.Y. : Oceana Publications, 1975. v, 250 p. ; 24 cm. Includes index. Bibliography: p. 237-245. A chronology of the life of former president Richard M. Nixon, a compilation of twenty-four of his speeches, and a bibliography of books, articles, and documents by and about him. [E838.5.N57] 92 75-23324 ISBN 0-379-12083-6 : 12.50
1. Nixon, Richard Milhous, 1913- — Chronology. 2. United States—Politics and government—1969-1974—Sources. I. United States. President, 1969-1974 (Nixon) II. Bremer, Howard F.

Nixon, Richard Milhous, 1913- — Impeachment.

WHITE, Theodore Harold, 1915 364.1'32'0973
Breach of faith : the fall of Richard Nixon / Theodore H. White. 1st ed. New York : Atheneum Publishers, 1975. 373 p. ; 25 cm. Includes bibliographical references and index. [E860.W48] 74-20350 ISBN 0-689-10658-0 : 10.95
1. Nixon, Richard Milhous, 1913- — Impeachment. 2. Watergate Affair, 1972- I. Title. **BIP**

Nixon, Richard Milhous, 1913- — Juvenile literature.

CAMPBELL, Ann Raymond. 973.924'0924 B
The picture life of Richard Milhous Nixon, by Ann Campbell. New York, F. Watts [1969] 57 p. illus. 22 cm. Describes briefly in text and photograph the life of Richard M. Nixon, thirty-seventh President of the United States. [E856.C3] 92 76-87933
1. Nixon, Richard Milhous, 1913- — Juvenile literature. I. Title.

LEIPOLD, L. Edmond, 1902- 973.9240924 B
Richard M. Nixon, President, by L. E. Leipold. Minneapolis, Denison [1969] 199 p. ports. 23 cm. (Men of achievement series) A biography of the Quaker boy who wanted to be "a lawyer his father would be proud of," but went much further to become the thirty-seventh President of the United States. [E856.L4] 92 68-59425
1. Nixon, Richard Milhous, 1913- — Juvenile literature. I. Title.

OLDS, Helen (Diehl) 1895- 973.924'0924 B
Richard Nixon, by Helen D. Olds. Illustrated by Frank Aloise. New York, Putnam [1970] 61 p. illus. 23 cm. (A See and read beginning to read biography) An easy-to-read biography of the thirty-seventh President of the United States. [E856.O4 1970] 92 74-110320 2.68
1. Nixon, Richard Milhous, 1913- — Juvenile literature. I. Aloise, Frank E., illus. II. Title. **BIP**

Nixon, Richard Milhous, 1913- — Personality.

ABRAHAMSEN, David, 1903- 973.924'092'4 B
Nixon vs. Nixon : an emotional tragedy / David Abrahamsen. 1st ed. New York : Farrar, Straus and Giroux, 1977. xvi, 267 p. : ill. ; 22 cm. Includes bibliographical references and index. [E856.A65 1977] 76-49827 ISBN 0-374-22275-4 : 8.95
1. Nixon, Richard Milhous, 1913- — Personality. 2. Presidents—United States—Biography. I. Title. **BIP**

CHESEN, Eli S. 973.924'092'4 B
President Nixon's psychiatric profile; a psychodynamic-genetic interpretation, by Eli S. Chesen. New York, P. H. Wyden [1973] 245 p. 21 cm. Bibliography: p. 245. [E856.C47] 73-90919 ISBN 0-88326-069-7 6.95
1. Nixon, Richard Milhous, 1913- — Personality. I. Title.

WOODSTONE, Art. 973.924'092'4 B
Nixon's head, by Arthur Woodstone. New York, St. Martin's Press [1972] vii, 248 p. 20 cm. Includes bibliographical references. [E856.W66 1972b] 72-96437 6.95
1. Nixon, Richard Milhous, 1913- — Personality. I. Title.

Nizer, Louis, 1902-

NIZER, Louis, 1902- 340'.92'4 [B]
Reflections without mirrors : an autobiography of the mind / Louis Nizer. 1st ed. New York : Berkley Pub. Corp., 1979, c1978. 532p. ; 18 cm. (A Berkley book) Includes index. [KF373.N56A37] ISBN 0-425-04143-3 pbk. : 2.75
1. Nizer, Louis, 1902- 2. Lawyers — New York (City) — Biography. I. Title.
L.C. card no. for 1978 Doubleday ed.: 77-79559.

NIZER, Louis, 1902- 340'.092'4 B
Reflections without mirrors an autobiography of the mind / Louis Nizer. 1st ed. Garden City, N.Y. : Doubleday, 1978. vi, 469 p. ; 25 cm. Includes index. [KF373.N56A37] 77-79559 ISBN 0-385-12670-0 : 10.96
1. Nizer, Louis, 1902- 2. Lawyers—New York (City)—Biography. I. Title.

Njau, Elimo, 1932-

CRANE, Louise, 1917- 709'.2'4 B
The antelope rises : Elimo Njau, East African artist / Louise Crane. Thompson, Conn. : InterCulture Associates, c1978. 60 p., [1] leaf of plates : ill. ; 21 cm. (The Africa sketches series) [N7397.6.T343N533] 77-94635 ISBN 0-89253-103-7 pbk. : 1.95
1. Njau, Elimo, 1932- 2. Artists—Tanzania—Biography. I. Title. II. Series.

Nkrumah, Kwame, Pres. Ghana, 1909-

ALEXANDER, Henry Templer, Maj.-Gen. 1911- 966.7050924
African tightrope; my two years as Nkrumah's Chief of Staff. New York, Praeger [1966, c.1965] xii, 152p. illus., ports. 23cm. [DT512.A72] 66-11566 4.95
1. Nkrumah, Kwame, Pres. Ghana, 1909- 2. Ghana—History. Military. 3. Congo (Leopoldville)—1960- I. Title. **BIP**

THE autobiography of Kwame Nkrumah. v. 12 Edinburgh, T. Nelson, 1957 310p. illus.
1. Ghana—Hist. I. Nkrumah, Kwame, 1909-

BRETTON, Henry L. 1916- 966.7050924
The rise and fall of Kwame Nkrumah; a study of personal rule in Africa [by] Henry L. Bretton. New York, Praeger [1967, c1966] xii, 232 p. 22 cm. Bibliography: p. 219-222. [DT510.6.N5B7] 66-26548
1. Nkrumah, Kwame, Pres. Ghana, 1909- I. Title.

NKRUMAH, Kwame, Pres. Ghana, 1909- 966.7'05'0924 B
Ghana; the autobiography of Kwame Nkrumah. New York, International Publishers [1971, c1957] xiii, 310 p. maps, port. 21 cm. [DT510.6.N5A33 1971] 70-148514 ISBN 0-7178-0293-0 7.50
1. Ghana—Politics and government—To 1957. **BIP**

OMARI, T. Peter. 966.7'05'0924
Kwame Nkrumah; the anatomy of an African dictatorship, by T. Peter Omari. With a foreword by Nii Amaa Ollennu. New York, Africana Pub. Corp. [1970] xix, 229 p. 23 cm. Appendices (p. 179-220):—A. Speech in Parliament by J. A. Braimah during debate on Preventive detention bill, 1958.—B. Nkrumaism—African socialism: Ghana's conception of socialism, by K. Baako—C. Eulogy on Dr. J. B. Danquah, by N. Azikiwe.—D. Last wills of Kwame Nkrumah. Bibliography: p. 221-223. [DT510.6.N5O43] 74-103939 8.50
1. Nkrumah, Kwame, Pres. Ghana, 1909- 2. Ghana—Politics and government—1957- **BIP**

TIMOTHY, Bankole 923.1667
Kwame Nkrumah: his rise to power. Foreword by Kojo Botsio. [2d ed. Evanston, Ill.] Northwestern Univ. Pr. 1963[c.1955, 1963] xiii, 191p. illus., ports. 23cm. 63-19756 3.50 bds.,
1. Nkrumah, Kwame, Pres. Ghana, 1909- I. Title.

Nkrumah, Kwame, Pres. Ghana, 1909-1972—Addresses, essays, lectures.

MCKENZIE-RENNIE, Rhoda. 966.7'05'0924 B
Nkrumah : greatest of modern philosophers / Rhoda McKenzie-Rennie. 1st ed. New York : Vantage Press, c1977. 125 p. : ill. ; 22 cm. [DT512.3.N57M3] 77-151891 ISBN 0-533-02338-6 : 5.95
1. Nkrumah, Kwame, Pres. Ghana, 1909-1972—Addresses, essays, lectures. I. Title.

Nkrumah, Kwame, Pres. Ghana, 1909-1972—Bibliography.

KWAME Nkrumah : 016.96 S
a select bibliography. Accra : Research Library on African Affairs, 1976. iv, 69 p. ; 25 cm. (Special subject bibliography - Research Library on African Affairs ; no. 7) Cover title. Includes index. [Z3785.G4 no. 7] [Z8629.7] [DT512.3.N57] 016.9667'05'0924 77-366781
1. Nkrumah, Kwame, Pres. Ghana, 1909-1972—Bibliography. I. George Padmore Research Library on African Affairs, Accra. II. Series: George Padmore Research Library on African Affairs, Accra. Special subject bibliography ; no. 7.

Noah.

LESSING, Erich. 221.95 (J)
The story of Noah. [Told in photographs by Erich Lessing. Text from the King James Bible. Pictures and text edited by Barbara Brakeley Miller. New York, Time-Life Books, 1968?] 1 v. (unpaged) illus. (part col.) 26 cm. [BS580.N6L4] 68-23127
1. Noah. 2. Bible. O.T. Genesis—Pictures, illustrations, etc. I. Miller, Barbara Brakeley, ed. II. Title.

Noah—Juvenile literature.

HUTTON, Warwick. 222'.11'09505
Noah and the great flood / Warwick Hutton. New York : Atheneum, 1977. p. cm. "A Margaret K. McElderry book." An interpretation of the familiar Bible story using a simple text based on the King James version. [BS658.H87] 77-3217 ISBN 0-689-50098-X : 7.95
1. Noah—Juvenile literature. 2. Bible. O.T.—Biography—Juvenile literature. 3. Deluge—Juvenile literature. I. Title. **BIP**

Nobel, Alfred Bernhard, 1833-1896.

BERGENGREN, Erik 926.6
Alfred Noble, the man and his work. With a suppl. on the Nobel institutions and the Nobel prizes by Nils K. Stahle. Tr. [from Swedish] by Alan Blair. New York, Nelson [1962, c.1960] 222p. illus. 23cm. Bibl. 62-51742 6.50
1. Nobel, Alfred Bernhard, 1833-1896. I. Title.

GRAY, Tony. 327'.172'0922
Champions of peace : the story of Alfred Nobel, the peace prize and the laureates / Tony Gray. New York : Paddington Press, c1976. p. cm. Includes index. Bibliography: p. [JX1962.A2G7] 76-3812 ISBN 0-8467-0143-X : 10.95
1. Nobel, Alfred Bernhard, 1833-1896. 2. Peace—Biography. 3. Nobel prizes—History. I. Title. **BIP**

HALASZ, Nicholas, 1895- 926.6
Nobel; a biography of Alfred Nobel. New York, Orion Press [c1959] 281p. 22cm. [TP268.5.N7H3] 59-13326
1. Nobel, Alfred Bernhard, 1833-1896. I. Title.

MEYER, Edith Patterson. 926.6
Dynamite and peace; the story of Alfred Nobel. [1st ed.] Boston, Little, Brown [1958] 298 p. illus. 21 cm. [TP268.5.N7M4] 58-8487
1. Nobel, Alfred Bernhard, 1833-1896. I. Title.

NOBELSTIFTELSEN, Stockholm. 926.6
Nobel, the man and his prizes, by H. Schuck [and others] Norman, University of Oklahoma Press [1951, c1950] 620 p. port. 25 cm Swedish ed. has title: Nobelprisen 50 Ar. Forkskare, diktare, fredskampar. [TP268.3.N7N763 1951] 51-12693
1. Nobel, Alfred Bernhard, 1833-1896. 2. Nobel prizes. I. Schuck, Henrik, 1855-1947. II. Title.

Nobel family.

*TOLF, Robert W. 929.'2
The Russian Rockefellers : the saga of the Nobel family and the Russian oil industry Robert W. Tolf. Stanford, Calif : Hoover Institution Pr. / Stanford University, c1976. xv, 269p. : ill. ; 24 cm. (Hoover institution publication ; 158) Includes index. Bibliography: pp. [235]-258. [TP690.2R9] 76-284 ISBN 0-8179-6581-5 : 14.95
1. Nobel family. 2. Oil industries-Russia-History. I. Title. **BIP**

Nobel prizes.

OPFELL, Olga S. 001.4'4
The lady laureates : women who have won the Nobel Prize / by Olga S. Opfell. Metuchen, N.J. : Scarecrow Press, 1978. p. cm. Bibliography: p. [AS911.N9O63] 78-15995 ISBN 0-8108-1161-8 : 11.50
1. Nobel prizes. 2. Women authors—Biography. 3. Women scientists—Biography. 4. Women—Biography. I. Title. **BIP**

Nobili, Roberto de', 1577-1656.

CRONIN, Vincent. 922.254
A pearl to India; the life of Roberto de Nobili. New York, Dutton, 1959. 297 p. illus. 21 cm. Includes bibliography. [BV3269.N6C7 1959] 59-5815
1. Nobili, Roberto de', 1577-1656. I. Title.

Nobility—England.

POPE-HENNESSY, James. 928.2
Monckton Milnes. New York, Farrar, Straus & Cudahy [1955- v. illus., ports. 22cm. Contents.v. 1. The years of promise, 1809-1851.--v. 2. The flight of youth, 1851-1885 Bibliographical footnotes. [PR4808.P57] 55-13770
I. Houghton, Richard Monckton-Millnes, baron, 1809-1885. II. Title.

TURNER, Ernest Sackville, 1909- 390'.23'0922
Amazing grace : the great days of dukes / [by] E. S. Turner. London : Joseph, 1975. 316 p., [8] p. of plates : ill., ports. ; 23 cm. Includes bibliographical references and index. [DA28.1.T75 1975] 76-366894 ISBN 0-7181-1362-4 : 17.50
1. Nobility—England. 2. England—Biography. I. Title.
Distributed by International Publications Service.

*WILLIAMS, Norman Lloyd 942.0550924
Sir Walter Raleigh. Baltimore. Penguin [1965, c.1962] 275p. 18cm. (2147) 1.25 pap.,
I. Title.

Noble, Cora (Moore)

NOBLE, Cora (Moore) 920.7
Memories. Boston, Christopher [c.1964] 238p. illus., ports. 21cm. 64-18970 4.00
I. Title.

Noble, Margaret Elizabeth, 1867-1911.

ATMAPRANA, Pravrajika 921.9
Sister Nivedita of Ramakrishna-Vivekananda. [dist. Hollywood, Calif., Vendanta, 1962, c.1961] 297p. illus. 23cm. 62-3355 3.50 bds.,
1. Noble, Margaret Elizabeth, 1867-1911. I. Title.

REYMOND, Lizelle. 921.9
The dedicated, a biography of Nivedita. New York, J. Day Co. [1953] 374p. illus. 21cm. (An Asia book) Translation of Nivedita, fille de i'Inde. [B133.N64R43] 52-12681
1. Noble, Margaret Elizabeth, 1867-1911. I. Title.

Noble, William Alexander, 1895-

HANSEN, Lillian E. 266'.025'0924 B
The double yoke; the Story of William Alexander Noble, M.D., Fellow of the American College of Surgeons, Fellow of the International College of Surgeons, Doctor of Humanities, medical missionary extraordinary to India, his adopted land, by Lillian E. Hansen. Drawings by Ernest L. Reedstrom. New York, Citadel Press [1968] 268 p. illus., col. maps (on lining papers) 21 cm. [BX9743.N6H3 1968] 68-28451 5.95
1. Noble, William Alexander, 1895- 2. Missions, Medical—India. I. Title.

Nock, Albert Jay, 1872 or 3-1945.

NOCK, Albert Jay, 1872or3-1945. 928.1
Selected letters. Collected and edited by Francis J. Nock, with Memories of Albert Jay Nock, by Ruth Robinson. Caldwell, Idaho, Caxton Printers, 1962. 201p. 22cm. [PS3527.O2Z53] 62-8189
1. Authors—Correspondence, reminiscences, etc. I. Title.

WRESZIN, Michael. 814'.5'2
The superfluous anarchist: Albert Jay Nock. Providence, Brown University Press [1972, c1971] xi, 196 p. port. 23 cm. Bibliography: p. 179-188. [PS3527.O2Z9 1972] 75-154339 ISBN 0-87057-130-3 8.50
1. Nock, Albert Jay, 1872 or 3-1945. I. Title.

Nodier, Charles, 1780-1844.

OLIVER, Alfred Richard, 1912- 928.4
Charles Nodier, pilot of romanticism [by] A. Richard Oliver. [Syracuse, N.Y.] Syracuse University Press, 1964. xi, 276 p. illus., ports. 22 cm. Bibliographical references included in "Notes to chapters" (p. 255-262) [PQ2376.N6Z66] 64-8670
1. 1. Nodier, Chalres, 1780-1844. I. Title.

Nodier, Charles, 1780-1844—Bibliography.

BELL, Sarah Fore. 016.848'7'09
Charles Nodier: his life and works; a critical bibliography, 1923-1967. Chapel Hill, University of North Carolina Press [1971] 187 p. 24 cm. (University of North Carolina studies in the Romance languages and literatures, no. 95.) [PC13.N67 no. 95] [Z8630.5] 76-28870 5.00
1. Nodier, Charles, 1780-1844—Bibliography. I. Series: North Carolina. University. Studies in the Romance languages and literatures, no. 95. BIP

Noel, Conrad, 1869-1942.

GROVES, Reginald, 1908- 283'.0924
Conrad Noel and the Thaxted Movement; an adventure in Christian socialism, by Reg Groves. New York, A. M. Kelley [1968] 334 p. port. 23 cm. Bibliographical references included in "Sources and acknowledgements" (p. 327-328) [BX5199.N65G7 1968] 68-3219
1. Noel, Conrad, 1869-1942. I. Title.

Noethen, Joseph C., 1892-

NOETHEN, Joseph C., 1892- 974.7'1'040924 B
Ah! Youth : growing up between wars, 1892-1918 / by Joseph C. Noethen. New York : New Voices Pub. Co., c1978. 181 p. : port. ; 22 cm. [F128.5.N76] 77-86154 ISBN 0-911024-24-7 pbk. : 6.50
1. Noethen, Joseph C., 1892- 2. New York (City)—Biography. I. Title: Ah! Youth.

Noguchi, Isamu, 1904-

HUNTER, Sam, 1923- 730'.92'4
Isamu Noguchi / by Sam Hunter. New York : Abbeville Press, c1978. p. cm. Includes index. [NB237.N6H86] 78-5288 65.00
1. Noguchi, Isamu, 1904- 2. Sculptors—United States—Biography. BIP

Noguchi, Isamu, 1904- —Juvenile literature.

TOBIAS, Tobi. 730'.92'4 B
Isamu Noguchi; the life of a sculptor. New York, Crowell [1974] 42 p. illus. 23 cm. (A Biography for young people) A brief biography of the renowned Japanese-American sculptor. [NB237.N6T56 1974] 92 72-7560 ISBN 0-690-45014-1 5.95
1. Noguchi, Isamu, 1904- —Juvenile literature. I. Title. BIP

Nolan, Philip, d. 1801.

WEEMS, John Edward. 976
Men without countries; three adventurers of the early Southwest. Illustrated by Rick Duiker. Boston, Houghton Mifflin, 1969. 272 p. illus., map (on lining papers) 22 cm. Bibliography: p. [267]-272. [F396.W38] 69-19567 5.95
1. Wilkinson, James, 1757-1825. 2. Nolan, Philip, d. 1801. 3. Bean, Ellis Peter, 1783-1846. 4. Southwest, Old—History. I. Title.

Nolen, William A.,

NOLEN, William A., 1928- 617'.0924 B
The making of a surgeon [by] William A. Nolen. [1st ed.] New York, Random House [1970] xvi, 269 p. 22 cm. [R154.N68A3] 72-102325 6.95
I. Title. BIP

Nollekens, Joseph, 1737-1823.

COLSON, Percy, 1873-1952. 920.71
Their ruling passions. Foreword by James Laver. Freeport, N.Y., Books for Libraries Press [1970] 221 p. illus., ports. 24 cm. (Biography index reprint series) Reprint of the 1949 ed. Contents.Contents.—Baron Stockmar, a study in wire-pulling.—Lord George Gordon, a study in fanaticism.—Dr. Samuel Parr, a study in egoism.—Joseph Nollekens, a study in avarice.—The young Disraeli, a study in ambition. Includes bibliographies. [DA531.2.C78 1970] 70-136645
1. Stockmar, Christian Friedrich, Freiherr von, 1787-1863. 2. Gordon, George, Lord, 1751-1793. 3. Parr, Samuel, 1747-1825. 4. Nollekens, Joseph, 1737-1823. 5. Beaconsfield, Benjamin Disraeli, 1st Earl of, 1804-1881. I. Title. BIP

Nonesuch Press, London.

MEYNELL, Francis, Sir, 1891- 070.5'092'4 B
My lives. [1st American ed.] New York, Random House [1971] 331 p. illus. 23 cm. [Z232.N82M46 1971b] 70-159358 ISBN 0-394-46418-4 10.00
1. Nonesuch Press, London. I. Title.

Nonviolence—Juvenile literature.

HASKINS, James, 1941- 301
Resistance; profiles in nonviolence. [1st ed.] Garden City, N.Y., Doubleday, 1970. 164 p. 22 cm. Discusses the concept of non-violence as practised by eight famous people, including Martin Luther King, Cesar Chavez, and Jesus of Nazareth. [HM278.H34] 920 71-116212 3.95
1. Nonviolence—Juvenile literature. I. Title.

Nordau, Max Simon, 1849-1923.

MAX Nordau, v. 12
Philosopher of human solidarity. With foreword by Salo W. Baron. New York, Conference on Jewish Social Studies, 1956. xiv, 309p. (Jewish social studies. Publication no. 6)
1. Nordau, Max Simon, 1849-1923. I. Ben-Horin, Meir, 1918- II. Series.

Nordica, Lillian, 1859-1914.

GLACKENS, Ira, 1907- 927.8
Yankee diva; Lillian Nordica and the golden days of opera. With Lillian Nordica's Hints to singers. New York, Coleridge Pr. [dist. Taplinger, c.1963] xiv, 366p. illus., ports. 24cm. Bibl. 63-22042 10.00
1. Nordica, Lillian, 1859-1914. I. Title. II. Title: Hinds to singers.

Nordtvedt, Matilda.

NORDTVEDT, Matilda. 248'.86
Living beyond depression / by Matilda Nordtvedt. Minneapolis, Minn. : Bethany Fellowship, c1978. 128 p. ; 18 cm. (Dimension books) Includes bibliographical references. [BR1725.N54A35] 78-58082 ISBN 0-87123-339-8 pbk. : 1.95
1. Nordtvedt, Matilda. 2. Christian biography—United States. 3. Christian life—1960- 4. Depression, Mental—Biography. I. Title. BIP

Norfolk, Thomas Howard, 2d duke of, 1443-1524.

TUCKER, Melvin J. 942.05
The life of Thomas Howard, earl of Surrey and second duke of Norfolk, 1443-1524. The Hague, Mouton [New York, Humanities, 1965, c.1964] 170p. geneal. tables, map, ports. 25cm. (Studies in European hist., 4) Bibl. [DA330.8.N6T8] 65-4159 7.50
1. Norfolk, Thomas Howard, 2d duke of, 1443-1524. I. Title.

Norfolk, Thomas Howard, 4th duke of, 1538-1572.

WILLIAMS, Neville, 1924- 923.242
Thomas Howard, fourth duke of Norfolk. New York, Dutton [1965, c.1964] xiii, 289p. facsims., ports. 23cm. Bibl. [DA317.8.N6W5] 64-66165 7.50
1. Norfolk, Thomas Howard, 4th duke of, 1538-1572. I. Title.

Norman, Chares,

NORMAN, charles. 1904- 928.1
To a different drum; the story of Henry David Thoreau. Pictures by Margaret Bloy Graham. New York, Harper & Row [1962, c.1954] 113p. 22cm. 54-8977 2.44 lib. ed.,
I. Thoreau, Henry David, 1817-1862. II. Title.

Norman, Elof.

†NORMAN, Elof. 979.7'71 B
The coffee chased us up : Monte Cristo memories / Elof Norman. Seattle : Mountaineers, c1977. 115 p. : ill. ; 24 cm. [F899.M66N67 1977] 77-72254 ISBN 0-916890-48-1 pbk. : 3.95
1. Norman, Elof. 2. Monte Cristo, Wash.—Biography. I. Title.

Norman, Frank.

NORMAN, Frank. 828'.9'1409 B
The lives of Frank Norman: told in extracts from his autobiographical books Banana boy, Stand on me, Bang to rights, The guntz; with an introduction by C. H. Rolph. Harmondsworth, Penguin, 1972. 316 p. 18 cm. [PR6064.O74Z515] 73-154072 ISBN 0-14-003326-2 £0.45
1. Norman, Frank. I. Title.

Norman, Henry, Sir bart 1858-1939

NORMAN, Henry, Sir, bart., 1858-1939. 914.7.04.8
All the Russias; Travels and studies in contemporary European Russia, Finland, Siberia, the Caucasus and Central Asia. Boston, Milford House [1974] Reprint of the 1914 ed. published by Scribner, New York [DK26.N84974] 73-16178 ISBN 0-87821-237-X
1. Norman, Henry, Sir bart 1858-1939 2. Russia—Description and Travel. 3. Russia—Economic Conditions. 4. Finland—Description and Travel. I. Title.

Norman, Joyce.

NORMAN, Joyce. 248'.24 B
Personal assignment; a newspaperwoman's search for the good news. Old Tappan, N.J., F. H. Revell [1973] 127 p. 22 cm. [BV4935.N59A3] 73-16193 ISBN 0-8007-0639-0 3.95
1. Norman, Joyce. 2. Conversion. I. Title.

Norman, Montagu Collet Norman, Baron, 1871-1950.

BOYLE, Andrew, 1919- 332.1'1'0924 B
Montagu Norman; a biography. New York, Weybright and Talley [1968, c1967] ix, 348 p. 22 cm. Bibliography: p. 333-336. [HG1552.N65B65 1968] 68-17748
1. Norman, Montagu Collet Norman, Baron, 1871-1950.

CLAY, Henry, Sir, 1883-1954. 332.1'1'0924 B
Lord Norman / Henry Clay. New York : Arno Press, 1978 p. cm. (International finance) Reprint of the 1957 ed. published by Macmillan, London. Includes index. [HG2994.C53 1979] 78-3906 ISBN 0-405-11211-4 lib. bdg. : 32.00
1. Norman, Montagu Collet Norman, Baron, 1871-1950. 2. Bank of England—History. 3. Bankers—Great Britain—Biography. 4. Banks and banking—Great Britain—History. 5. Currency question—Great Britain—History. I. Title. II. Series: International finance (New York, 1979-)

Norman, Montagu, 1871-1950.

CLAY, Henry, Sir 1883-1954. 923.342
Lord Norman. London, Macmillan; New York, St. Martin's Press, 1957. 495p. illus. 23cm. [HG2994.C53] 57-4257
1. Norman, Montagu, 1871-1950. 2. Banks and banking—Gt. Brit. 3. Currency question—Gt. Brit. I. Title. BIP

Normandy—Social life and customs.

HENREY, Robert, Mrs., 1906- 914.422
Madeleine, young wife; the autobiography of a French girl. [1st ed.] New York, Dutton, 1954. 380 p. 23 cm. [D811.5.H4475] 54-9306
1. Normandy—Social life and customs. 2. World War, 1939-1945—Personal narratives, French. I. Title.

Norodom Sihanouk Varman, King of Cambodia, 1922-

LACOUTURE, Jean. 960
The demigods: charismatic leadership in the third world. [Translated from the French by Patricia Wolf. 1st American ed.] New York, Knopf, 1970. 300, vi p. 22 cm. Translation of Quatre hommes et leurs peuples. Bibliography: p. [295]-300. [D839.5.L2513 1970] 72-111235 7.95
1. Nasser, Gamal Abdel, Pres. United Arab Republic, 1918-1970. 2. Bourguiba, Habib, Pres. Tunisia, 1903- 3. Norodom Sihanouk Varman, King of Cambodia, 1922- 4. Nkrumah, Kwame, Pres. Ghana, 1909- I. Title.

Norris, Clarence.

NORRIS, Clarence. 976.1'06'0924 B
The last of the Scottsboro boys : an autobiography / by Clarence Norris and Sybil D. Washington. New York : Putnam,

c1979. 281 p., [4] leaves of plates : ill. ; 22 cm. [E185.93.A3N676 1978] 78-23428 ISBN 0-399-12018-1 : 10.95
1. Norris, Clarence. 2. Scottsboro Case. 3. Afro-Americans—Alabama—Biography. 4. Alabama—Biography. I. Washington, Sybil D., joint author. II. Title. **BIP**

Norris, Frank,

NORRIS, Frank, 1870-1902. 928.1
Letters; edited by Franklin Walker. San Francisco, Book Club of California, 1956. xiii, 98p. port. 29cm. 'Three hundred and fifty copies printed.' [PS2473.A45 1956] 56-3156
I. Title.

Norris, Frank Kingsley,

NORRIS, Frank Kingsley, Sir, 1893- 355.3'45'0924 B
No memory for pain; an autobiography [by] F. Kingsley Norris. Melbourne, Heinemann [1970] 392 p. illus., map, ports. 23 cm. [UH347.N65A3] 70-585295 ISBN 0-85561-007-7 7.50
I. Title.

Norris, Frank, 1870-1902.

DILLINGHAM, William B. 813'.4
Frank Norris, instinct and art [by] William B. Dillingham. Lincoln, University of Nebraska Press [1969] ix, 179 p. 22 cm. Includes bibliographical references. [PS2473.D5] 69-15257 5.95
1. Norris, Frank, 1870-1902. I. Title.

NORRIS, Charles Gilman, 1881-1945. 813'.4
Frank Norris [by Charles G. Norris. Folcroft, Pa.] Folcroft Library Editions, 1973. p. Reprint of the 1914 ed. published by Doubleday Page, New York. [PS2473.N6 1973] 73-9950 7.50
1. Norris, Frank, 1870-1902. **BIP**

NORRIS, Charles Gilman, 1881-1945. 813'.4
Frank Norris 1870-1902; an intimate sketch of the man who was universally acclaimed the greatest American writer of his generation. [Folcroft, Pa.] Folcroft Library Editions, 1973. 28 p. illus. 24 cm. Reprint of the 1914 ed. published by Doubleday Page, New York. Bibliography: p. 19-28. [PS2473.N6 1973] 73-9950 ISBN 0-8414-2366-0 (lib. bdg.)
1. Norris, Frank, 1870-1902.

NORRIS, Frank, 1870-1902. 928.1
Letters; edited by Franklin Walker. San Francisco, Book Club of California, 1956. xiii, 98p. port. 29cm. 'Three hundred and fifty copies printed.' [PS2473.A45 1956] 56-3156
I. Title.

WALKER, Franklin Dickerson, 1900- 928.1
Frank Norris, a biography. New York, Russell & Russell, 1963. 317 p. illus. 23 cm. [PS2473.W3 1963] 63-15186
1. Norris, Frank, 1870-1902. **BIP**

Norris, Frank, 1870-1902—Biography.

NORRIS, Charles Gilman, 1881-1945. 813'.4 B
Frank Norris, 1870-1902 : an intimate sketch of the man who was universally acclaimed the greatest American writer of his generation / by Charles G. Norris. Norwood, Pa. : Norwood Editions, 1976. 28 p., [1] leaf of plates : ill. ; 24 cm. Reprint of the 1914 ed. published by Doubleday Page, New York. Bibliography: p. 19-28. [PS2473.N6 1976] 76-9794 ISBN 0-8482-1909-0 : 6.50
1. Norris, Frank, 1870-1902—Biography.

Norris, George William, 1861-1944.

LIEF, Alfred, 1901- 328.73'092'4 B
Democracy's Norris : the biography of a lonely crusade / by Alfred Lief. New York : Octagon Books, 1977, c1939. p. cm. Reprint of the ed. published by Stackpole Sons, New York. Includes index. Bibliography: p. [E748.N65L5 1977] 77-21901 ISBN 0-374-94998-0 lib.bdg. : 25.00
1. Norris, George William, 1861-1944. 2. United States—Politics and government—1901-1943. 3. Legislators—United States—Biography. I. Title. **BIP**

LOWITT, Richard, 1922- 923.273
George W. Norris; the making of a progressive, 1861-1912. [Syracuse, N.Y.] Syracuse [c.]1963. xiv, 341p. illus., ports. 24cm. Bibl. 63-19724 7.95
1. Norris, George William, 1861-1944. I. Title. **BIP**

LOWITT, Richard, 1922- 923.273
George W. Norris; the making of a progressive, 1861-1912. [Syracuse, N.Y.,] Syracuse University Press, 1963. xiv, 341 p. illus., ports. 24 cm. Bibliographical references included in "Notes to chapters" (p. 279-335) [E748.N65L6] 63-19724
1. Norris, George William, 1861-1944. I. Title.

LOWITT, Richard, 1922- 328.73'092'4 B
George W. Norris : the triumph of a progressive, 1933-1944 / Ricard Lowitt. Urbana : University of Illinois Press, c1978. xiii, 493 p., [9] leaves of plates : ill. ; 24 cm. Includes index. Bibliography: p. [378]-382. [E748.N65L622] 78-2033 ISBN 0-252-00223-7 : 20.00
1. Norris, George William, 1861-1944. 2. United States. Congress. Senate—Biography. 3. Legislators—United States—Biography. 4. United States—Politics and government—1933-1945. 5. Progressivism (United States politics) I. Title.

LOWITT, Richard, 1922- 328.73'092'4 B
George W. Norris : the making of a progressive, 1861-1912 / Richard Lowitt. Westport, Conn. : Greenwood Press, [1980] c1963. p. cm. Reprint of the ed. published by Syracuse University Press, Syracuse, N.Y. Includes bibliographical references and index. [E748.N65L6 1980] 79-18826 ISBN 0-313-22103-0 : 29.00
1. Norris, George William, 1861-1944. 2. United States. Congress—Biography. 3. Progressivism (United States politics) 4. United States—Politics and government—1901-1953. 5. Legislators—United States—Biography.

ZUCKER, Norman L. 328.73
George W. Norris; gentle knight of American democracy. Urbana, Univ. of Ill. Pr. [c.] 1966. x, 186p. port. 24cm. Bibl. [E748.N65Z8] 66-10060 5.00
1. Norris, George William, 1861-1944. I. Title. **BIP**

Norris, John Franklyn, 1877-1952.

TATUM, E Ray. 286.100924(B)
Conquest or failure? Biography of J. Frank Norris by E. Ray Tatum. Dallas, Baptist Historical Foundation.[1966] 295 p. illus., ports. 21 cm. Bibliographical footnotes. [BX6495.N59T3] 66-8241
1. Norris, John Franklyn, 1877-1952. I. Title.

Norris, Lynne, 1931-

NORRIS, Lynne, 1931- 301.42'7
Can a woman over forty? / Lynne Norris. Manhattan Beach, Calif. : Olive Press Publications, 1979. p. cm. [HQ759.N63] 79-12587 ISBN 0-933380-41-0: 8.95. ISBN 0-933380-42-9 lib. bdg. : 10.95. ISBN 0-933380-47-X pbk. : 5.95
1. Norris, Lynne, 1931- 2. Mothers—Biography. 3. Childbirth in middle age—United States. I. Title. **BIP**

North American Soccer League—Juvenile literature.

GUTMAN, Bill. 796.33'4'0922 B
Modern soccer superstars / Bill Gutman. New York : Dodd, Mead, 1979. p. cm. Includes index. Spotlights six outstanding professional soccer players: Pele, Jim McAlister, Kyle Rote, Werner Roth, Al Trost, and Shep Messing. [GV942.7.A1G87] 920 79-52048 ISBN 0-396-07731-5 : 5.95
1. North American Soccer League—Juvenile literature. 2. Soccer players—Biography—Juvenile literature. I. Title. **BIP**

North Carolina—Biography.

BASSETT, John Spencer, 1867-1928. 326
Anti-slavery leaders of North Carolina. Spartanburg, S.C., Reprint Co. [1971] 74 p. 23 cm. (Johns Hopkins University. Studies in historical and political science, ser. 16, no. 6) Pages also numbered 268-334. Reprint of the 1898 ed. [E445.N8B28 1971] 76-149341 ISBN 0-87152-061-3
1. North Carolina—Biography. 2. Slavery in the United States—North Carolina. I. Title. II. Series. **BIP**

BASSETT, John Spencer, 1867-1928. 327.73'042 S
Anti-slavery leaders of North Carolina. Baltimore, Johns Hopkins Press, 1898. [New York, Johnson Reprint Corp., 1973] 74 p. 22 cm. Pages also numbered 268-334. Original ed. issued as no. 6 of Anglo-American relations and Southern history, which forms the 16th series of Johns Hopkins University studies in historical and political science. [E183.8.G7A67 no. 6] [E445.N8] 326'.092'2 B 72-14355 ISBN 0-384-03526-4 pap. 4.00
1. North Carolina—Biography. 2. Slavery in the United States—North Carolina. I. Title. II. Series: Johns Hopkins University. Studies in historical and political science, 16th ser., 6. III. Series: Anglo-American relations and Southern history, no 6.

DICTIONARY of North Carolina biography / edited by William S. Powell. Chapel Hill : University of North Carolina Press, c1979- p. cm. Includes bibliographies. [CT252.D5] 79-10106 ISBN 0-8078-1329-X : 45.00 920'.0756
1. North Carolina—Biography. I. Powell, William Stevens, 1919-

EDMUNDS, Pocahontas Wight. 920.0756
Tar Heels track the century: Andrew Johnson, Z. B. Vance, M. W. Ransom, C. B. Aycock, O. Henry, J. B. Duke, W. H. Page, F. M. Simmons, Josephus Daniels, Thomas Wolfe. Raleigh, N. C., Edwards & Broughton Co., 1966. 355 p. ports. 23 cm. Bibliographical references included in "Footnotes" (p. 307-318) Bibliography: p. 319-335. [F253.E3] 66-28600
1. North Carolina—Biography. I Title.

EDMUNDS, Pocahontas Wight. 920.0756
Tar Heels track the century: Andrew Johnson, Z. B. Vance, M. W. Ransom, C. B. Aycock, O. Henry, J. B. Duke, W. H. Page, F. M. Simmons, Josephus Daniels, Thomas Wolfe. Raleigh, N.C., Edwards & Broughton Co., 1966. 355 p. ports. 23 cm. Bibliographical references included in "Footnotes" (p. 307-318) [F253.E3] 66-28600
1. North Carolina—Biography. I. Title.

POWELL, William Stevens, 1919- ed. 920.0756
North Carolina lives; the Tar Heel who's who. A reference edition recording the biographies of contemporary leaders in North Carolina with special emphasis on their achievements in making it one of America's greatest States. Written and prepared under the supervision of William S. Powell. Hopkinsville, Ky., Historical Record Association, 1962. 1358 p. ports. 27 cm. [F253.N88] 62-62984
1. North Carolina — Biog. I. Title.

North Carolina—Governors.

NORTH Carolina. State Dept. of Archives and History. 975.6 B
North Carolina Governors, 1585-1968; brief sketches, by Beth G. Crabtree. Rev. Raleigh, 1968. 142 p. ports. 23 cm. Includes bibliographical references. [F253.N8612 1968] 79-626446
1. North Carolina—Governors. I. Crabtree, Elizabeth G. II. Title. **BIP**

North Carolina—Governors—Biography.

NORTH Carolina. 975.6'00992 B
Division of Archives and History.
North Carolina Governors, 1585-1974 : brief sketches / by Beth G. Crabtree. Rev. Raleigh : Division of Archives and History, Dept. of Cultural Resources, 1974. viii, 189 p. : ports. ; 23 cm. Previous editions issued by the body under its earlier name: State Dept. of Archives and History. Bibliography: p. 146-148. [F253.N84 1974] 75-305645 3.00
1. North Carolina—Governors—Biography. I. Crabtree, Elizabeth G. II. North Carolina. State Dept. of Archives and History. North Carolina Governors. III. Title.

North Dakota—Biog.

ROLFSRUD, Erling Nicolai, 1912- 920.0784
Extraordinary North Dakotans. Alexandria, Minn., Lantern Books [1954] 228p. illus. 22cm. [F635.R58] 54-44007
1. North Dakota—Biog. I. Title.

ROLFSRUD, Erling Nicolai, 1912- 920.0784
Lanterns over the prairies. Brainerd, Minn., Lakeland Color Press [1949-50] 2 v. illus., ports. 21 cm. Vol. 2: 1st ed. Includes bibliographies. [F635.R6] 50-1052
1. North Dakota — Biog. 2. Frontier and pioneer life — North Dakota. I. Title.

WHITE, Hugh L., ed. 920.0784
Who's who for North Dakota. 1955- Bismarck, H. L. White. v. illus., ports. 27 cm. Triennial. Vols. for 1955- published with the cooperation of the State Historical Society of North Dakota. Editor: 1955- H. L. White. [F635.W5] 60-51394
1. North Dakota — Biog. 2. North Dakota. State Historical Society. I. Title.

North Dakota. Constitutional Convention, 1971-1972.

WRIGHT, Boyd L. 342'.784'029 B
Convention profile and individual biographics / by Boyd L. Wright and Lloyd A. Bakken. Grand Forks : Bureau of Governmental Affairs, University of North Dakota, 1971. i, 102 p. ; 28 cm. (Resource publication [for the] North Dakota Constitutional Convention delegates ; C) Cover title. [JK6425 1971.W74] 74-624051
1. North Dakota. Constitutional Convention, 1971-1972. 2. North Dakota—Biography. I. Bakken, Lloyd A., joint author. II. Title. III. Series.

WRIGHT, Boyd L. 342'.784'029 B
North Dakota Constitutional Convention: biographies of delegates and staff. Edited by Boyd L. Wright. Grand Forks, Bureau of Governmental Affairs, University of North Dakota, 1971. v, 116 p. 28 cm. Cover title. [JK6425 1971.W75] 72-611361
1. North Dakota. Constitutional Convention, 1971-1972. 2. North Dakota—Biography. I. Title.

North Dakota. Legislative Assembly—Biography.

NORTH Dakota. 328.784'092'2
University. Bureau of Governmental Affairs.
Biographical sketches, 1975 legislature. [Grand Forks] : Bureau of Governmental Affairs, University of North Dakota, [1975?] 172 p. : map ; 28 cm. Cover title. [JK6431 1975.N67 1975] 75-623574
1. North Dakota. Legislative Assembly—Biography. I. Title.

North, Dudley Burton Napier, Sir, 1881-1961.

PLIMMER, Charlotte. 359.1'14'0924 B
A matter of expediency : the jettison of Admiral Sir Dudley North / [by] Charlotte and Denis Plimmer. London ; New York [etc.] : Quartet Books, 1978. [12], 179 p., [8] p. of plates : ill., map, ports. ; 23 cm. Distributed in the U.S.A. by Horizon Press, New York. Includes index. Bibliography: p. 173-[174]

[DA89.1.N6P56] 78-321013 ISBN 0-7043-2169-6 : 12.50
1. North, Dudley Burton Napier, Sir, 1881-1961. 2. Great Britain. Navy—Biography. 3. World War, 1939-1945—Naval operations, British. 4. World War, 1939-1945—Mediterranean Sea. 5. World War, 1939-1945—Naval operations, French. 6. Admirals—Great Britain—Biography. I. Plimmer, Denis, joint author. II. Title.
Dist. by Horizon Press, NY.

North, Frederick North, Baron, 1732-1792.

THOMAS, Peter 941.07'3'0924 B
David Garner.
Lord North / Peter D. G. Thomas. New York : St. Martin's Press, 1976. viii, 176 p. ; 23 cm. (British political biography) Includes index. Bibliography: p. [163]-167. [DA506.N7T48 1976] 75-29819 12.95
1. North, Frederick North, Baron, 1732-1792. I. Title. BIP

VALENTINE, Alan 942.07'3'0924 (B)
Chester 1901-
Lord North [by] Alan Valentine. [1st ed.] Norman, Univ. of Okla. Pr. [1967] 2 v. ports. 23cm. Bibl. [DA506.N7V3] 67-15575 19.95 set bxd.
1. North, Frederick North, Baron, 1732-1792. I. Title.

Northcliffe, Alfred Charles William Harmsworth, 1st viscount, 1865-1922.

FYFE, Henry Hamilton, 655.4'24 B
1869-1951.
Northcliffe; an intimate biography. New York, AMS Press [1969] ix, 357 p. illus., facsims., ports. 23 cm. Reprint of the 1930 ed. [DA566.9.N7F87 1969] 74-100527
1. Northcliffe, Alfred Charles William Harmsworth, 1st Viscount, 1865-1922.

PIERCE, Robert N. 070'.08 S
Lord Northcliffe, trans-atlantic influences / Robert N. Pierce. [Lexington, Ky.] : Association for Education in Journalism, 1975. 41 p. ; 23 cm. (Journalism monographs ; no. 40) Cover title. Includes bibliographical references. [PN4722.J6 no. 40] [PN5123] 070.5'092'4 B 76-360688 2.00
1. Northcliffe, Alfred Charles William Harmsworth, 1st Viscount, 1865-1922. I. Title. II. Series: Journalism monographs (Austin) ; no. 40.

POUND, Reginald 920.5
Northcliffe [by] Reginald Pound and Geoffrey Harmsworth. New York, Praeger [1959, i.e., 1960] xvi, 933p. Bibl.: p.887-897 illus. (col. port) 24cm. 60-13897 10.00 buck.,
1. Northcliffe, Alfred Charles William Harmsworth, 1st viscount, 1865-1922. I. Harmsworth, Geoffrey, joint author. II. Title.

Northeastern States—Description and travel.

BAILEY, Anthony. 917.4
Through the great city. New York, Macmillan [1967] 276 p. map. 21 cm. Autobiographical. "Most of the material...appeared originally in the New Yorker in slightly different form." Bibliography: p. 267-269. [F106.B16] 67-13585
1. Northeastern States—Description and travel. 2. Urbanization—Northeastern States. I. Title. BIP

Northern Ireland—Politics and government.

DEVLIN, Bernadette, 328.42'0924 B
1947-
The price of my soul. [1st ed.] New York, Knopf, 1969. viii, 224 p. 22 cm. [DA990.U46D45] 78-98650 5.95
1. Northern Ireland—Politics and government. I. Title.

Northfield, Mass.

MABIE, Janet. 818.5
Heaven on earth. [1st ed.] New York, Harper [1951] 242 p. illus., map (on lining papers) 20 cm. Autobiographical. [CT275.M13A3] 51-9460
1. Northfield, Mass. I. Title.

Northmen in Great Britain—History.

SMYTH, Alfred P. 941'.01'60922
Scandinavian kings in the British Isles, 850-880 / by Alfred P. Smyth Oxford [Eng.] ; New York : Oxford University Press, 1977. p. cm. (Oxford historical monographs) Includes index. Bibliography: p. [DA152.S63] 77-6391 ISBN 0-19-821865-6 : 22.00
1. Northmen in Great Britain—History. 2. Great Britain—History—Edmund, 855-870. 3. Great Britain—History—Alfred, 871-901. I. Title. BIP

Northrop, Will H

NORTHROP, Will H 920
The true story of Northrop pioneering in North Dakota. [Fargo? 1960] 92p. illus. 22cm. Autobiographical. [CT275.N745A3] 60-36372
I. Title.

Northumberland, John Dudley, 1st Duke of, 1502-1553.

BEER, Barrett L. 942.05'2'0924 B
Northumberland; the political career of John Dudley, Earl of Warwick and Duke of Northumberland [by] Barrett L. Beer. [Kent, Ohio] Kent State University Press [1974, c1973] xi, 235 p. illus. 24 cm. Bibliography: p. 218-227. [DA345.1.N6B43 1974] 73-77386 ISBN 0-87338-140-8 10.00
1. Northumberland, John Dudley, 1st Duke of, 1502-1553. 2. Great Britain—Politics and government—1509-1547. 3. Great Britain—Politics and government—1547-1553. BIP

Northwest, Canadian—Description and travel—To 1821.

MACKENZIE, Alexander, 917.1'04
Sir, 1763-1820.
Voyages from Montreal on the river St. Laurence, through the continent of North America to the Frozen and Pacific Oceans in the years 1789 and 1793, with a preliminary account of the rise, progress, and present state of the fur trade of that country. [New ed.] Rutland, Vt., Tuttle [1971] xx, cxxxii, 412 p. fold. maps. 27 cm. Title on spine: Voyages from Montreal through the continent of North America. Includes vocabularies of the Knisteneax, Algonquin, Chepewyan, Nagailer and Atnah Indian languages. [F1060.7.M1785] 78-170101 ISBN 0-8048-1006-0 19.25
1. Northwest, Canadian—Description and travel—To 1821. 2. Indians of North America—Northwest, Canadian. 3. Fur trade—Northwest, Canadian. 4. Indians of North America—Canada—Languages—Glossaries, vocabularies, etc. I. Title. BIP

Northwest coast of North America.

COLNETT, James, 910.09'1'665
1755?-1806.
Colnett's journal aboard the Argonaut. A facsim. ed. New York, Greenwood Press, 1968. xxxi, 328 p. illus., maps. 24 cm. (Champlain Society publication 26) Reprint of the 1940 ed. published under title: The journal of Captain James Colnett aboard the Argonaut. [F851.5.C8 1940a] 68-28614
1. Northwest coast of North America. 2. Nootka Sound. 3. Pacific coast—Description and travel. 4. Pacific Ocean. I. Title. II. Title: Journal aboard the Argonaut. III. Series: Champlain Society, Toronto. Publications, 26

Northwest, Pacific—Biography.

EMINENT men of the 920.0795
Northwest, 1955- Palo Alto, Calif., C. W. Taylor. v. ports. 27 cm. [F852.E48] 55-36551
1. Northwest, Pacific—Biog. I. Taylor, Charles William, 1896-

JOHNSON, Jalmar, 1905- 923.973
Builders of the Northwest. With an introd. by Stewart H. Holbrook. New York, Dodd, Mead [1963] 242 p. illus. 21 cm. Includes bibliography. [F851.J677] 63-11086
1. Northwest, Pacific—Biography. 2. Northwest, Pacific—History. I. Title.

Northwood, N.H.—Biography.

BAILEY, Joann Weeks. 917.42'6
A guide to the history and old dwelling places of Northwood, New Hampshire. [Concord, N.H., Printed by Capital Offset Co., 1973] xi, 275 p. illus. 24 cm. Bibliography: p. 272-273. [F44.N88B34] 73-166247
1. Northwood, N.H.—Biography. 2. Northwood, N.H.—Historic houses, etc. I. Title.

Norton, Bertha Stemm,

NORTON, Bertha Stemm, 917.71'03'4
1872-1967.
Bertie and May [by] Bertha Stemm Norton and Andre Norton. Illustrated by Fermin Rocker. New York, World Pub. Co. [1969] 174 p. illus. 22 cm. A year in the life of two little girls living in rural Ohio in the 1880's. [CT275.N748A3 1969] 72-82778 4.25
I. Norton, Alice Mary, joint author. II. Rocker, Fermin, illus. III. Title.

Norton, Caroline Sheridan, 1808-1877—Correspondence.

NORTON, Caroline 821'.8 B
Sheridan, 1808-1877.
The letters of Caroline Norton to Lord Melbourne. Edited by James O. Hoge and Clarke Olney. [Columbus] Ohio State University Press [1974] xvii, 182 p. illus. 22 cm. Bibliography: p. 173-174. [PR5112.N5A845 1974] 74-12344 ISBN 0-8142-0208-X 10.75
1. Norton, Caroline Sheridan, 1808-1877—Correspondence. 2. Melbourne, William Lamb, 2d Viscount, 1779-1848. I. Melbourne, William Lamb, 2d Viscount, 1779-1848. II. Hoge, James O., ed. III. Olney, Clark, 1901- ed. IV. Title. BIP

Norton, Charles Eliot, 1827-1908.

NORTON, Charles 818'.4'09 B
Eliot, 1827-1908.
Letters of Charles Eliot Norton, with biographical comment by his daughter Sara Norton and M. A. DeWolfe Howe. Boston, Houghton Mifflin, 1913. [New York, AMS Press, 1973] 2 v. illus. 19 cm. Bibliography: v. 2, p. 461-465. [PS2478.A4 1973] 76-148817 ISBN 0-404-04800-5 21.50 (per vol.)
1. Norton, Charles Eliot, 1827-1908. I. Norton, Sara, 1864- ed. II. Howe, Mark Antony De Wolfe, 1864-1960, ed. III. Title.
Two volume set 42.50.

VANDERBILT, Kermit. 928.1
Charles Eliot Norton; apostle of culture in a democracy. Cambridge, Mass., Belknap Press, 1959. xiii, 286 p. illus., ports., facsim. 22 cm. Bibliography: p. [243]-257. [PS2478.V3] 59-10321
1. Norton, Charles Eliot, 1827-1908. I. Title. II. Title: Apostle of culture in a democracy. BIP

Norton, Joshua Abraham, 1819-1880.

KRAMER, William 979.4'61'040924 B
M.
Emperor Norton of San Francisco : a look at the life and death and strange burials of the most famous eccentric of gold rush California / by William M. Kramer. Santa Monica, Calif. : N. B. Stern, 1974. 66 p., [1] leaf of plates : ill. ; 21 cm. Three hundred copies printed. Includes bibliographical references. [CT275.N75K7] 74-84446
1. Norton, Joshua Abraham, 1819-1880. 2. Jews in San Francisco. I. Title.

Norway—Hist.—German occupation, 1940-1945.

SONSTEBY, Gunnar 940.534810924
Fridtjof Thurmann, 1918-
Report from no. 24. Prepared from a tr. from Norwegian by Maurice Michael. New York, L. Stuart [c.1965] 192p. 21cm. Autobiographical. [DL532.S613] 63-14969 4.95 bds.,
1. Norway—Hist.—German occupation, 1940-1945. 2. World War, 1939-1945—Underground movements—Norway. I. Title.

*[Norway, Nevil Shute]

*[NORWAY, Nevil Shute] 926.2
1899-1960
Slide rule; the autobiography of an engineer, by Nevil Shute [pseud.] New York, Ballantine [1964, c.1954] 224p. 18cm. (U5006) .60 pap.,
I. Title.

Norway, Nevil Shute, 1899-1960.

*[NORWAY, Nevil Shute] 926.2
1899-1960
Slide rule; the autobiography of an engineer, by Nevil Shute [pseud.] New York, Ballantine [1964, c.1954] 224p. 18cm. (U5006) .60 pap.,
I. Title.

SMITH, Julian, 1937- 823'.9'12 B
Nevil Shute (Nevil Shute Norway) / by Julian Smith. Boston : Twayne Publishers, c1976. p. cm. (Twayne's English authors series ; TEAS 190) Includes index. Bibliography: p. [PR6027.O54Z9] 76-8018 lib.bdg. : 7.50
1. Norway, Nevil Shute, 1899-1960. I. Title. BIP

Notre Dame, Ind. University—Football.

RAPPOPORT, 796.33'263'0977289
Ken.
Wake up the echoes : Notre Dame football / by Ken Rappoport. Huntsville, Ala. : Strode Publishers, c1975. 464 p. : ill. ; 24 cm. [GV958.N6R36] 75-26072 ISBN 0-87397-053-5 : 8.95
1. Notre Dame, Ind. University—Football. 2. Football—Biography. I. Title.

Nottingham, Eng.—Biography.

MELTORS, Robert, 1835- 920.0425'2
Men of Nottingham and Nottinghamshire. [1st ed.] republished. Wakefield, S. R. Publishers, 1969. [4], iii-viii, 368 p. 20 cm. ([County history reprints]) First published in 1924. [DA670.N9M4 1969] 70-472186 63/-
1. Nottingham, Eng.—Biography. 2. Nottinghamshire, Eng.—Biography. I. Title.

Nouwen, Henri J. M.

NOUWEN, Henri J. 248'.48'20924 B
M.
The Genesee diary : report from a Trappist monastery / Henri J. M. Nouwen. 1st ed. Garden City, N.Y. : Doubleday, 1976. xiv, 195 p. ; 22 cm. Includes bibliographical references. [BX4705.N87A33] 75-38169 ISBN 0-385-11368-4 : 6.95
1. Nouwen, Henri J. M. 2. Spiritual life—Catholic authors. I. Title.

Nova Scotia—Biography.

ARCHIBALD, Frank E. 920'.0716
Mostly maritimers / by Frank E. Archibald. Windsor, N.S. : Lancelot Press, 1972. 127 p. ; 22 cm. [CT290.A7] 75-309723
1. Nova Scotia—Biography. I. Title.

Nova Scotia—History—1763-1867—Sources.

PERKINS, Simeon, 971.6'02'0924 B
1735-1812.
The diary of Simeon Perkins. New York, Greenwood Press, 1969- v. illus., facsim., map, port. 24 cm. (Champlain

Society publication 29, 36) Reprint of the ed. first published 1948- Contents.Contents.—[1] 1766-1780, edited with introd. and notes by H. A. Innis.—[2] 1780-1789, edited with an introd. by D. C. Harvey, with notes by C. B. Fergusson. [F1038.P48A32] 69-14503
1. Nova Scotia—History—1763-1867—Sources. 2. United States—History—Revolution, 1775-1783—Sources. I. Series: Champlain Society, Toronto. Publications, 29 [etc.] BIP

Novak, Frank, 1884-

ALLEE, George Franklin, 1897- 922
Beyond prison walls; the story of Frank Novak, once a desperate criminal and convict, now national prison chaplain no. 1 by the grace of God. Kansas City, Mo., Beacon Hill Press [1960] 96p. 20cm. [BV4465.A4] 60-12063
1. Novak, Frank, 1884- 2. Prisons—Missions and charities. I. Title.

Novak, Kim.

FRITCH, Charles E v. 12
Kim Novak; goddess of love. The fascinating life story of the world's most desirable woman. Derby, Conn., Monarch Books [1962] 139 p. 19 cm. (Monarch books, K63) 67-14976
1. Novak, Kim. I. Title.

Novelists.

THOMAS, Henry, 1886- 928
Living biographies of famous novelists, by Henry Thomas and Dana Lee Thomas. Garden City, N.Y., Garden City Books [1959] 305 p. illus. 22 cm. [PN3463.T5 1959] 59-2708
1. Novelists. I. Thomas, Dana Lee, 1918- joint author. II. Title.

Novelists, American.

COURNOS, John, 1881- 928.1
Famous modern American novelists, by John Cournos and Sybil Norton. New York, Dodd, Mead, 1952. 181 p. illus. 23 cm. (Famous biographies for young people) [PS128.C65] 52-7209
1. Novelists, American. I. Title.

Novelists, English—19th century—Biography.

BIGLAND, Eileen. 928.2
Ouida, the passionate Victorian. London, New York, Jarrolds, 1950. 272 p. illus., ports., facsims. 22 cm. Bibliography: p. 265-266. [PR4528.B5 1950] 51-4032
1. D 2. De la Ramee, Louise, 1839-1908. DelaRamee Louise 1839 1908 I. Title.

WATT, James Crabb. 823'.03
Great novelists: Scott, Thackeray, Dickens, Lytton. [Folcroft, Pa.] Folcroft Library Editions, 1975. 260 p. illus. 24 cm. (Series: Lardner, Dionysius, 1793-1859, ed. The cabinet cyclopadia.) Reprint of the 1880 ed. published by F. Warne, London, in series: Cabinet of biography. Includes bibliographical references. [PR863.W3 1975] 74-8661 ISBN 0-8414-9523-8
1. Novelists, English—19th century—Biography. I. Title. II. Series.

Noverre, Jean Georges, 1727-1810.

LYNHAM, Deryck. 927.93
The chevalier Noverre, father of modern ballet; a biography. London, Sylvan Press; New York, British Book Centre [1950] 204 p. illus., ports. 22 cm. "The known productions of Jean Georges Noverre": p. 165-178. Bibliography: p. 192-194. [GV1785.N7L9] 50-9771
1. Noverre, Jean Georges, 1727-1810. I. Title.

Noyes, Alfred,

NOYES, Alfred, 1880- 928.2
Two worlds for memory. [1st ed.] Philadelphia, Lippincott [1953] 348p. illus., ports. 22cm. Autobiography. [PR6027.O8Z5] 53-5420
I. Title.

Noyes, John Humphrey, 1811-1886.

NOYES, George Wallingford, ed. 289.9 B
Religious experience of John Humphrey Noyes, founder of the Oneida Community. Freeport, N.Y., Books for Libraries Press [1971] xiii, 416 p. illus., ports. 23 cm. Reprint of the 1923 ed. [BX8795.P4N8 1971] 72-152998 ISBN 0-8369-5750-4
1. Noyes, John Humphrey, 1811-1886.

PARKER, Robert Allerton. 335'.9'74764 B
A Yankee saint; John Humphrey Noyes and the Oneida Community. Philadelphia, Porcupine Press, 1972. 322 p. illus. 22 cm. (The American utopian adventure) Reprint of the 1935 ed. Bibliography: p. 313-316. [HX656.O5P3 1972] 75-187456 ISBN 0-87991-009-7
1. Noyes, John Humphrey, 1811-1886. 2. Oneida Community. I. Title. BIP

ROBERTSON, Constance (Noyes) comp. 335'.9747'64
Oneida Community; an autobiography, 1851-1876. Edited, with an introd. and prefaces, by Constance Noyes Robertson. [1st ed. Syracuse] Syracuse University Press [1970] xvi, 364 p. illus., ports. 24 cm. Bibliography: p. 362-364. [HX656.O5R62] 75-115417 11.50
1. Noyes, John Humphrey, 1811-1886. 2. Oneida Community.

THOMAS, Robert David, 1939- 335'.9'74764 B
The man who would be perfect : John Humphrey Noyes and the Utopian impulse / Robert David Thomas. [Philadelphia] : University of Pennsylvania Press, 1977. xii, 199 p. : port. ; 24 cm. Includes index. Bibliography: p. 177-194. [HX656.O5N697] 76-53198 ISBN 0-8122-7724-4 : 12.95
1. Noyes, John Humphrey, 1811-1886. 2. Oneida Community. 3. Social reformers—United States—Biography. I. Title. BIP

Nu, U.

BUTWELL, Richard A 923.2591
U Nu of Burma. Stanford, Calif., Stanford University Press, 1963. x, 301 p. illus., ports. 23 cm. Bibliography: p. 279-291. [DS485.B892B8] 63-14126
1. Nu, U. I. Title. BIP

NU, U. 959.1'05'0924 B
U Nu, Saturday's son / by U Nu ; translated by U Law Yone ; edited by U Kyaw Win. New Haven : Yale University Press, 1975. xv, 358 p., [2] leaves of plates : ill. ; 25 cm. Includes index. [DS530.53.N9A3513] 74-79835 ISBN 0-300-01776-6 : 15.00
1. Nu, U. 2. Burma—Politics and government. I. Title.

Nuffield, William Richard Morris, 1st Viscount, 1877-1963.

OVERY, R. J. 338.7'62'920924 B
William Morris, Viscount Nuffield / R. J. Overy. London : Europa Publications, c1976. xlvi, 151 p., [3] leaves of plates : ill. ; 23 cm. (The Europa library of business biography) Includes index. Bibliography: p. 142-148. [HD9710.G72N845] 76-382883 ISBN 0-900362-84-7 : £4.50
1. Nuffield, William Richard Morris, 1st Viscount, 1877-1963. 2. Morris Motors, ltd., Cowley, Eng.—History. 3. Businessmen—Great Britain—Biography.

Nugent, Elliott,

NUGENT, Elliott, 1900- 792.0924
Events leading up to the comedy; an autobiography. NewYork, Trident [c.]1965. 304p. group port. 22cm. [PN2287.N78A3] 65-28310 4.95 bds.,
I. Title.

Nugent, James.

DUNNING, Harold Marion, 1891- 978.8'68
The life of Rocky Mountain Jim (James Nugent). Boulder, Colo., Johnson Pub. Co., [1967] 48 p. illus., ports. 23 cm. Based on A lady's life in the Rocky Mountains, by I. L. Bishop. [F782.L2D8] 67-8953
1. Nugent, James. 2. Estes Park, Colo.—History. I. Bishop, Isabella Lucy (Bird) 1831-1904. A lady's life in the Rocky Mountains. II. Title.

Nugent, William Lewis, 1832-1897.

NUGENT, William Lewis, 1832-1897. 973.7'82
My dear Nellie : the Civil War letters of William L. Nugent to Eleanor Smith Nugent / edited by William M. Cash and Lucy Somerville Howorth. Jackson : University Press of Mississippi, 1977. p. cm. Includes index. [E605.N83 1977] 77-24597 ISBN 0-87805-036-1 : 10.95
1. Nugent, William Lewis, 1832-1897. 2. Confederate States of America. Army—Biography. 3. United States—History—Civil War, 1861-1865—Personal narratives—Confederate side. 4. Soldiers—Confederate States of America—Biography. I. Nugent, Eleanor Smith. II. Title. BIP

Nunez Cabeza de Vaca, Alvar, 16th cent.

BISHOP, Morris, 1893- 973.1'6'0924 B
The odyssey of Cabeza de Vaca. Westport, Conn., Greenwood Press [1971, c1933] vii, 306 p. illus. 23 cm. Bibliography: p. 293-298. [E125.N9B56 1971] 70-139123 ISBN 0-8371-5739-0
1. Nunez Cabeza de Vaca, Alvar, 16th cent. 2. America—Discovery and exploration—Spanish. I. Title. BIP

FERNANDEZ, Jose B., 1948- 918.1'1'042
Alvar Nunez Cabeza de Vaca, the forgotten chronicler / Jose B. Fernandez. Miami, Fla. : Ediciones Universal, c1975. 144 p. ; 22 cm. (Hispanic studies collection) English or Spanish. Includes index. Bibliography: p. 135-141. [E125.N9F47] 75-16777
1. Nunez Cabeza de Vaca, Alvar, 16th cent. La relacion. 2. Nunez Cabeza de Vaca, Alvar, 16th cent. 3. Narvaez, Pan Filo de, d. 1528. 4. America—Discovery and exploration—Spanish. 5. Indians of North America. I. Title. II. Series.

FERNANDEZ, Jose B., 1948- 918.1'1'042
Alvar Nunez Cabeza de Vaca, the forgotten chronicler / Jose B. Fernandez. Miami, Fla. : Ediciones Universal, c1975. 144 p. ; 22 cm. (Hispanic studies collection) English or Spanish. Includes index. Bibliography: p. 135-141. [E125.N9F47] 75-16777
1. Nunez Cabeza de Vaca, Alvar, 16th cent. La relacion. 2. Nunez Cabeza de Vaca, Alvar, 16th cent. 3. Narvaez, Pan Filo de, d. 1528. 4. America—Discovery and exploration—Spanish. 5. Indians of North America. I. Title. II. Series.

Nunez Cabeza de Vaca, Alvar, 16th cent.—Juvenile literature.

KERMAN, Gertrude Lerner. 970.01'6'0924 B
Cabeza de Vaca, defender of the Indians / by Gertrude Kerman ; illustrated by Ray Abel. Irvington-on-Hudson, N.Y. : Harvey House, [1974] 142, [2] p. : ill. ; 23 cm. Bibliography: p. [143] A brief biography of the sixteenth-century explorer who traveled from Florida to Mexico and sought freedom and peace for the Indians. [E125.N9K47] 92 73-79455 ISBN 0-8178-5111-9. ISBN 0-8178-5112-7 lib. bdg.
1. Nunez Cabeza de Vaca, Alvar, 16th cent.—Juvenile literature. I. Abel, Raymond, ill. II. Title.

[RODMAN, Maia (Wojciechowska)] 973.16
Odyssey of courage; the story of Alvar Nunez Cabeza de Vaca [by] Maia Wojciechowska. Decorations by Alvin, Smith. New York, Atheneum [c.]1965. x, 182p. illus., maps. 22cm. Bibl. [E125.N9R6] 65-10477 3.75
1. Nunez Cabeza de Vaca, Alvar, 16th cent.—Juvenile literature. I. Title.

SYME, Ronald 920
First man to cross America; the story of Cabeza de Vaca. Illus. by William Stobbs. New York, Morrow [c.]1961. 190p. illus., map 61-8104 2.95
1. Nunez Cabeza de Vaca, Alvar, 16th cent.—Juvenile literature. I. Title.

Nunez de Reinoso, Alonso, fl. 1552.

ROSE, Constance Hubbard. 863'.3
Alonso Nunez de Reinoso: the lament of a sixteenth-century exile. Rutherford [N.J.] Fairleigh Dickinson University Press [1971] 309 p. 22 cm. Appendix "Algunas rimas" (p. 179-306) contains facsim. of the 1552 text of the 2d vol. of Nunez de Reinoso's Historia de los amores de Clareo y Florisea y de los trabajos de Isea con otras obras en verso parte al estilo espanol y parte al italiano agora nuevamente sacada a luz, entitled: Libro segundo de las Obras en coplas castellanas y versos al estilo italiano. Bibliography: p. 165-175. [PQ6419.N84Z85] 77-99324 ISBN 0-8386-7612-X 15.00
1. Nunez de Reinoso, Alonso, fl. 1552. I. Nunez de Reinoso, Alonso, fl. 1552. Libro segundo de las Obras en coplas castellanas y versos al estilo italiano. 1971.

Nunez, Tommy, 1938- —Juvenile literature.

WHEELOCK, Warren H. 973'.04'68 S
Raul H. Castro, la adversidad es mi angel. Tommy Nunez, arbitro del NBA. !Presentando a Vikki Carr! / Warren H. Wheelock ; adaptacion, J. O. "Rocky" Maynes ; consultantes, Jorge Valdivieso, Amalia Perez, Ruben A. Soruco B. St. Paul, Minn. : EMC, 1976. p. cm. (His Ilustres hispanos de EE. UU. ; 1) Translation of Raul H. Castro, adversity is my angel. Brief biographies of three Spanish Americans: the Arizona governor, a professional basketball referee, and a popular female singer. [E184.S75W517 vol. 1] 920'.0092'6873 920 76-2420 ISBN 0-88436-248-5. ISBN 0-88436-249-3 pbk.
1. Castro, Raul Hector, 1916- —Juvenile literature. 2. Nunez, Tommy, 1938- —Juvenile literature. 3. Carr, Vikki—Juvenile literature. I. Maynes, J. O. II. Title. III. Title: Tommy Nunez, arbitro del NBA. IV. Title: !Presentando a Vikki Carr!

Nunn-Bush Shoe Company.

NUNN, Henry Lightfoot, 1878- 926.85
The whole man goes to work; the life story of a businessman [1st ed.] New York, Harper [1953] 214p. 22cm. Autobiography. [HD9787.U6N82] 53-8548
1. Nunn-Bush Shoe Company. I. Title.

Nunn, Robert Tipton, 1871-1957.

NUNN, Roy, 1897- 926.3
Texan by choice. San Antonio, Naylor Co. [1961] 247p. illus. 22cm. [CT275.N786N8] 61-142737
1. Nunn, Robert Tipton, 1871-1957. I. Title.

Nuns.

CODE, Joseph Bernard, 1899- 248.8'943'0922
Great American foundresses, by Joseph B. Code. Freeport, N.Y., Books for Libraries Press [1968] xviii, 512 p. ports. 22 cm. (Essay index reprint series) "First published 1929."
1. Nuns. 2. Women—United States—Biography. I. Title. BIP

WALSH, James Joseph, 1865-1942, comp. 271'.9 B
These splendid Sisters, compiled by James Joseph Walsh with introd. Freeport, N.Y., Books for Libraries Press [1970] 252 p. 23 cm. (Essay index reprint series) Reprint of the 1927 ed.
1. Nuns. I. Title. BIP

Nuns—Correspondence, reminiscences, etc.

QUIN, Eleanor. 271'.976'0924 B
Last on the menu, by Sister Eleanor Quin (Sister M. Vincent dePaul, C.S.J.) Englewood Cliffs, N.J., Prentice-Hall [1969] 182 p. 22 cm. Autobiographical. [BX4210.Q5] 78-80997 ISBN 0-13-524033-6 4.95
1. Nuns—Correspondence, reminiscences, etc. I. Title.

Nureyev, Rudolph Hametovitch,

NUREYEV, Rudolph Hametovitch, 1938- 927.933
Nureyev: an autobiography. With pictures by Richard Avedon and others. Introduced by Alexander Bland. [1st ed.] New york, Dutton, 1963[c1962] 160 p. illus. 24 cm. [GV1785.N8A3] 63-8605

Nureyev, Rudolph Hametovitch, 1938-

NUREYEV. 792.8'092'4 B
London : Dance Books [for] Victor Hochhauser Ltd, 1976. [64] p. : ill., ports. ; 29 cm. [GV1785.N8N87] 77-367258 ISBN 0-903102-23-4 : £3.00. ISBN 0-903102-24-2 pbk.

1. Nureyev, Rudolf Hametovitch, 1938-

NUREYEV, Rudolph 927.933
Hametovitch, 1938-
Nureyev: an autobiography. With pictures by Richard Avedon and others. Introduced by Alexander Bland. [1st ed.] New york, Dutton, 1963[c1962] 160 p. illus. 24 cm. [GV1785.N8A3] 63-8605

PERCIVAL, John. 792.8'092'4 B
Nureyev : aspects of the dancer : a biography / by John Percival. New York : Putnam, [1975] 256 p., [16] leaves of plates : ill. ; 22 cm. Includes indexes. [GV1785.N8P47] 75-21519 ISBN 0-399-11544-7 : 8.95
1. Nureyev, Rudolph Hametovitch, 1938- 2. Ballet.

PERES, Louis. 792.8'092'4
Rudolf Nureyev / photos. by Louis Peres ; text by Arthur Todd ; additional photos. by Arthur Todd. New York : Dance Horizons, [1975] 21 p. : ill. ; 23 cm. (Dance Horizons spotlight series) Caption title. [GV1785.N8P48] 75-9155 ISBN 0-87127-059-5
1. Nureyev, Rudolph Hametovitch, 1938- 2. Ballet. I. Todd, Arthur.

Nurses and nursing—Biog.

WRIGHT, Helen, 1914- ed. 926.1
Great adventures in nursing, edited by Helen Wright and Samuel Rapport. [1st ed.] New York Harper [1960] 288 p. 22 cm. [RT34.W7] 60-5785
1. Nurses and nursing — Biog. I. Rapport, Samuel Berder, 1903- joint ed. II. Title.

WRIGHT, Helen, [Mary Helen 926.1
Wright] ed.
Great adventures in nursing, edited by Helen Wright and Samuel Rapport. New York, Harper [c.1960] x, 288p. 22cm. 60-5785 3.50
1. Nurses and nursing—Biog. I. Rapport, Samuel Berder, joint ed. II. Title.

Nurses and nursing—Biography—Juvenile literature.

MCKOWN, Robin. 610.730922
Heroic nurses. New York, Putnam [1966] 320 p. illus., ports. 23 cm. Bibliography: p. 311-313. [RT34.M3] 66-9762
1. Nurses and nursing—Biography—Juvenile literature. I. Title.

Nurses—United States—Biography—Juvenile literature.

COLLINS, David R. 610.73'0922 B
Great American nurses, by David R. Collins. Illustrated by Haris Petie. New York, J. Messner [1971] 96 p. illus. 22 cm. Contents.Contents.—Sister Anthony: angel of the battlefield.—Linda Richards; America's first trained nurse.—Mary Breckinridge: nurse on horseback.—Sally Zumaris McKinney: combat nurse.—Dee O'Hara: Aerospace nurse. [RT34.C65] 920 70-141836 ISBN 0-671-32395-4 4.50
1. Nurses—United States—Biography—Juvenile literature. I. Petie, Haris, illus. II. Title.

Nursing—United States—History.

SAFIER, Gwendolyn. 610.73'092'2 B
Contemporary American leaders in nursing : an oral history / Gwendolyn Safier. New York : McGraw-Hill, c1977. vii, 392 p. : ports. ; 24 cm. "A Blakiston publication." Includes bibliographical references. [RT4.S23] 76-46352 ISBN 0-07-054412-3 : 11.50
1. Nursing—United States—History. 2. Nurses—United States—Interviews. I. Title.

Nussbaum, Jean, 1888-1967.

LOEWEN, Gertrude. 286'.7'0924 B
Crusader for freedom; the story of Jean Nussbaum. Nashville, Southern Pub. Association [1969] 227 p. ports. 22 cm. [BX6193.N8L6] 77-86336
1. Nussbaum, Jean, 1888-1967. I. Title.

Nuttall, Thomas, 1786-1859.

GRAUSTEIN, Jeannette 574'.0924(B)
E.
Thomas Nuttall, naturalist; expolrations in America, 1808-1841 [by] Jeannette E. Graustein. Cambridge, Harvard, 1967. xiii, 481p. illus., port. 25cm. Bibl. [QH31.N8G7] 67-13253 11.95
1. Nuttall, Thomas, 1786-1859. I. Title.

Nutting, Mary Adelaide, 1858-1948.

MARSHALL, Helen E. 610.73'092'4 B
Mary Adelaide Nutting, pioneer of modern nursing [by] Helen E. Marshall. Baltimore, Johns Hopkins University Press [1972] ix, 396 p. port. 24 cm. Bibliography: p. 371-384. [RT37.N87M37] 72-174557 ISBN 0-8018-1365-4 12.00
1. Nutting, Mary Adelaide, 1858-1948. I. Title.

Nuvolari, Tazio, 1892-1953.

LURANI Cernuschi, 927.9672
Giovanni,
Nuvolari, by Count Giovanni Lurani with the collaboration of Luigi Marinatto. Translated by John Eason Gibson. With an appendix of racing successes. New York, Morrow [1960, c1959] 223 p. illus. 22 cm. [GV1032.N8L813 1960] 60-12291
1. Nuvolari, Tazio, 1892-1953.

LURANI CERNUSCHI, 927.9672
Giovanni.
Nuvolari, by Count Giovanni Lurani with the collaboration of Luigi Marinatto. Translated by John Eason Gibson. With an appendix of racing successes. [Abridged and rev. New York, Sports Car Press; [distributed by Crown Publishers, 1963, c1959] 120 p. illus. 21 cm. (Modern sports car series) [GV1032.NSL813 1963] 63-13381
1. Nuvolari, Tazio, 1892-1953. I. Title.

Nyad, Diana.

NYAD, Diana. 797.2'1'0924
Other shores / Diana Nyad. 1st ed. New York : Random House, c1978. 174 p. ; 22 cm. [GV838.N9A34] 78-56910 ISBN 0-394-50175-6 : 8.95
1. Nyad, Diana. 2. Swimmers—United States—Biography. I. Title. BIP

Nye, Edgar Wilson,

NYE, Edgar Wilson, 1850- 817'.4 B
1896.
Bill Nye, his own life story. Continuity by Frank Wilson Nye. Freeport, N.Y., Books for Libraries Press [1970] xx, 412 p. illus., ports. 23 cm. Reprint of the 1926 ed. [PS2482.A3 1970] 78-124246
I. Nye, Frank Wilson, 1887- BIP

Nyein Tha, Daw.

PROCTER, Marjorie. 286'.1'0924 B
The world my country : the story of Daw Nyein Tha of Burma / by Marjorie Procter. London : Grosvenor Books, 1976. 142 p., [8] p. of plates : ill., ports. ; 19 cm. (A Grosvenor biography) [BX6495.N88P76] 77-364619 ISBN 0-901269-22-0 : £1.25
1. Nyein Tha, Daw. 2. Baptists—Burma—Biography. I. Title.

Nyerere, Julius Kambarage, Pres. Tanzania, 1922-

SMITH, William 967'.804'0924 B
Edgett.
We must run while they walk; a portrait of Africa's Julius Nyerere. [1st ed.] New York, Random House [1972, c1971] 296 p. 22 cm. [DT446.N9S57] 78-159376 ISBN 0-394-46752-3 7.95
1. Nyerere, Julius Kambarage, Pres. Tanzania, 1922- I. Title.

Nyerere, Julius Kambarage, Pres. Tanzania, 1922- —Juvenile literature.

DUBOIS, Shirley 967.8'04'0924 B
Graham, 1906-
Julius K. Nyerere : teacher of Africa / by Shirley Graham. New York : Julian Messner, [1975] 191 p. ; 22 cm. Includes index. Bibliography: p. 188. A biography of the African nationalist who led Tanganyika to independence, united that country with Zanzibar, and became the first president of Tanzania. [DT448.25.N9D8] 92 74-30239 ISBN 0-671-32717-8 lib.bdg. : 5.29
1. Nyerere, Julius Kambarage, Pres. Tanzania, 1922- —Juvenile literature. I. Title. BIP

Nygaard, Norman Eugene,

NYGAARD, Norman Eugene, 1897- FIC
They sought a country. [1st ed.] New York, Longmans, Green, 1950. 211 p. 21 cm. A novel. [PZ3.N98815Th] fic 50-5476
I. Title.

Nyiregyhazi, Erwin, 1903—

REVESZ, Geza, 1878- 780.07'12
1955.
The psychology of a musical prodigy. Freeport, New York, Books for Libraries Press [1970] ix, 180 p. illus., music, port. 23 cm. Translation of Erwin Nyiregyhazi. Reprint of the 1925 ed. [ML81.R413 1970] 70-114890 ISBN 0-8369-5294-4
1. Nyiregyhazi, Erwin, 1903- 2. Children as musicians. 3. Music—Psychology. I. Title. BIP

O'Brien, Edna.

ECKLEY, Grace. 823'.9'14
Edna O'Brien. Lewisburg [Pa.] Bucknell University Press [1974] 88 p. 20 cm. (The Irish writers series) Bibliography: p. 85-88. [PR6065.B7Z65] 79-168806 ISBN 0-8387-7838-0
1. O'Brien, Edna. BIP

O'Brien, Edna—Biography.

O'BRIEN, Edna. 823'.9'14 B
Mother Ireland / Edna O'Brien ; with photos. by Fergus Bourke. 1st American ed. New York : Harcourt Brace Jovanovich, c1976. 144 p. : ill. ; 24 cm. [PR6065.B7Z515 1976b] 76-381695 ISBN 0-15-162587-5 : 12.95
1. O'Brien, Edna—Biography. 2. O'Brien, Edna—Homes and haunts—Ireland. 3. Ireland—Description and travel—1951- 4. Ireland—Social life and customs. 5. Authors, Irish—20th century—Biography. I. Title. BIP

O'Brien, Edward, 1910-

SUCCOP, Margaret Phillips, v. 12
1914-
Painter into artist; the progress of Edward O'Brien, as recorded by Margaret Phillips and Merle Armitage. [Yucca Valley, Calif.] Manzanita Press, 1964. 53 l. 18 plates [part col.] 23 cm. 66-85698
1. O'Brien, Edward, 1910- I. Armitage, Merle, 1893- II. Title.

O'Brien, Joe, 1917-

HILL, Marie, 1931- 798'.4'00924 B
Gentleman Joe : the story of harness driver Joe O'Brien / Marie Hill. New York : Arco Pub. Co., [1975] 192 p. : ill. ; 22 cm. Includes index. [SF336.O18H54] 74-14204 ISBN 0-668-03624-9 : 7.95
1. O'Brien, Joe, 1917- 2. Harness racing. I. Title. BIP

O'Brien, Johnny, 1851-1931—Juvenile literature.

HERRON, Edward Albert, 92 (J)
1912-
Dynamite Johnny O'Brien, Alaska's sea captain. New York, J. Messner [1962] 189 p. 22 cm. [VK140.O2H4] 62-10198
1. O'Brien, Johnny, 1851-1931—Juvenile literature. I. Title.

O'Brien, Lawrence F.

O'BRIEN, Lawrence F. 329'.0092'4
No final victories; a life in politics - from John F. Kennedy to Watergate [by] Lawrence F. O'Brien. New York, Ballantine [1975 c1974] 407 p. 18 cm. [E840.8.O24A36] ISBN 0-345-24762-01 1.95 (pbk.)
1. O'Brien, Lawrence F. 2. United States—Politics and government—1945- I. Title.
L.C. card no. of 1974 Doubleday edition: 73-22535.

O'BRIEN, Lawrence 329'.0092'4 B
F.
No final victories; a life in politics - from John F. Kennedy to Watergate [by] Lawrence F. O'Brien. [1st ed.] Garden City, N.Y., Doubleday, 1974. 394 p. illus. 25 cm. Autobiographical. [E840.8.O24A36] 73-22535 ISBN 0-385-02484-3 12.50
1. O'Brien, Lawrence F. 2. United States—Politics and government—1945- I. Title.

O'Bryant, Tilmon B.

FRIEDMAN, Ina R. 363.2'092'4 B
Black cop, by Ina R. Friedman. Philadelphia, Westminster Press [1974] 159 p. illus. 21 cm. A biography of Tilmon B. O'Bryant, who, despite obstacles, rose to the position of Assistant Chief of Police in Washington, D.C. [HV7911.O27F74] 92 73-20142 ISBN 0-664-32546-7 5.95
1. O'Bryant, Tilmon B. 2. Negro policemen—Biography—Juvenile literature. I. Title.

O'Casey, Eileen.

O'CASEY, Eileen. 792'.028'0924 B
Eileen / Eileen O'Casey ; edited with an introd. by J. C. Trewin. London : Macmillan, 1976. 224 p., [4] leaves of plates : ill. ; 23 cm. Includes index. [PR6029.C3Z52] 77-350754 ISBN 0-333-13472-9 : £4.50
1. O'Casey, Eileen. 2. O'Casey, Sean, 1880-1964—Biography—Marriage. 3. Dramatists, Irish—20th century—Biography. 4. Actors—Ireland—Biography. I. Title. BIP

O'Casey, Sean,

O'CASEY, Sean 928.2
Drums under the windows, by Sean O'Casey . . . New York, The Macmillan company, 1960 [c.1946, 1960] 431p. 22cm. A continuation of the author's I knock at the door; swift glances back at things that made me, published 1939, and Pictures in the hallway, published 1942. (Macmillan Paperback, 30) 1.65 pap.,
I. Title.

O'CASEY, Sean, 1880- 928.2
Mirror in my house: the autobiographies of Sean O'Casey. New York, Macmillan, 1956. 2 v. illus., ports. 22 cm. Each part has special t.p. and separate paging. Also issued separately. Contents.-- v. 1. I knock at the door. Pictures in the hallway Drums under the windows. -- v. 2. Inishfallen, fare thee well. Rose and crown. Sunset and evening star. [PR6029.C33Z555] A57
I. Title.

O'CASEY, Sean, 1880- 928.2
Rose and crown. New York, Macmillan, 1952. 323 p. illus. 22 cm. Autobiographical [PR6029.C33R6] 52-4597
I. Title.

O'CASEY, Sean, 1880- 928.2
Sunset and evening star. New York, Macmillan, 1954. 339 p. illus. 22 cm. Autobiographical. [PR6029.C33Z58 1954] 54-4920
I. Title.

O'CASEY, Sean, 1880-1964. 928.2
Rose and crown. New York, Macmillan, 1952. 323 p. illus. 22 cm. Autobiographical. [PR6029.C33R6 1952a] 52-4597
I. Title.

O'CASEY, Sean, 1884- 928.2
Inishfallen, fare thee well. New York, Macmillan Co., 1960 [c.1949] 396p. 21cm. The 4th vol. in an autobiographical cycle. 1.65 pap.,

I. Title.

O'CASEY, Sean, 1884- 928.2
Rose and crown. New York, Macmillan, 1961 [c.1952] 323p. (Macmillan paperback 42) 1.45 pap.,
I. Title.

O'Casey, Sean, 1880-1964.

AYLING, Ronald, 1932- 822'.9'12
comp.
Sean O'Casey. Nashville, Aurora Publishers [1970] 274 p. 22 cm. (Modern judgements) Bibliography: p. [261]-269. [PR6029.C33Z588 1970] 79-127563 ISBN 0-87695-097-7 2.50
1. O'Casey, Sean, 1880-1964. **BIP**

FALLON, Gabriel. 822.912
Sean O'Casey, the man I knew. [1st American ed.] Boston, Little, Brown [1965] 213 p. illus., ports. 22 cm. [PR6029.C33Z63 1965] 65-21349
1. O'Casey, Sean, 1880-1964.

KOSLOW, Jules, 1916- 822
Sean O'Casey; the man and his plays. [Rev. and expanded ed.] New York, Citadel Press [1966] 117 p. 21 cm. First published in 1950 under title: The green and the red: Sean O'Casey, the man and his plays. [PR6029.C33Z67 1966] 66-24062
1. O'Casey, Sean, 1880-1964. I. Title. **BIP**

KOSLOW, Jules, 1916- 822
Sean O'Casey; the man and his plays. [Rev., expanded ed.] New York, Citadel [c.1950, 1966] 117p. 21cm. First pub. in 1950 under title: The green and the red: Sean O'Casey, the man and his plays. (C-227) [PR6029.C33Z67] 66-24062 1.75 pap.,
1. O'Casey, Sean, 1880-1964. I. Title.

*KRAUSE, David. 822.'9'12
Sean O'Casey and his world / David Krause. New York : Charles Scribners' Sons, 1976. 128p. : ill., ports. ; 24 cm. Includes index. Bibliography: p. 117-118. [PR6029.C33] 76-7182 ISBN 0-684-14727-0 : 8.95
1. O'Casey, Sean, 1880-1964. I. Title. **BIP**

KRAUSE, David, 1917- 822'.9'12
Sean O'Casey: the man and his work. An enl. [i.e. 2d] ed. New York, Macmillan [1975] xii, 390 p. 21 cm. Includes bibliographical references. [PR6029.C33Z68 1975] 74-11129 ISBN 0-02-566640-1 8.95
1. O'Casey, Sean, 1880-1964.

O'CASEY, Sean 928.2
Drums under the windows, by Sean O'Casey . . . New York, The Macmillan company, 1960 [c.1946, 1960] 431p. 22cm. A continuation of the author's I knock at the door; swift glances back at things that made me, published 1939, and Pictures in the hallway, published 1942. (Macmillan Paperback, 30) 1.65 pap.,
I. Title.

O'CASEY, Sean, 1880- 928.2
Mirror in my house: the autobiographies of Sean O'Casey. New York, Macmillan, 1956. 2 v. illus., ports. 22 cm. Each part has special t.p. and separate paging. Also issued separately. Contents.-- v. 1. I knock at the door. Pictures in the hallway Drums under the windows. -- v. 2. Inishfallen, fare thee well. Rose and crown. Sunset and evening star. [PR6029.C33Z555] A57
I. Title.

O'CASEY, Sean, 1880- 928.2
Rose and crown. New York, Macmillan, 1952. 323 p. illus. 22 cm. Autobiographical [PR6029.C33R6] 52-4597
I. Title.

O'CASEY, Sean, 1880- 928.2
Sunset and evening star. New York, Macmillan, 1954. 339 p. illus. 22 cm. Autobiographical. [PR6029.C33Z58 1954] 54-4920
I. Title.

O'CASEY, Sean, 1880-1964. 928.2
Rose and crown. New York, Macmillan, 1952. 323 p. illus. 22 cm. Autobiographical. [PR6029.C33R6 1952a] 52-4597
I. Title.

O'CASEY, Sean, 1884- 928.2
Inishfallen, fare thee well. New York, Macmillan Co., 1960 [c.1949] 396p. 21cm. The 4th vol. in an autobiographical cycle. 1.65 pap.,
I. Title.

O'CASEY, Sean, 1884- 928.2
Rose and crown. New York, Macmillan, 1961 [c.1952] 323p. (Macmillan paperback 42) 1.45 pap.,
I. Title.

O'Casey, Sean, 1880-1964—Biography.

KRAUSE, David, 1917- 822'.9'12 B
Sean O'Casey and his world / David Krause. London : Thames & Hudson, c1976. 128 p. : ill. ; 24 cm. Includes index. Bibliography: p. 117-118. [PR6029.C33Z678] 77-355569 ISBN 0-500-13055-8 : £3.50
1. O'Casey, Sean, 1880-1964—Biography. 2. Dramatists, Irish—20th century—Biography. I. Title.

O'Casey, Sean, 1880-1964—Biography—Youth.

MARGULIES, Martin B. 822'.9'12 B
The early life of Sean O'Casey [by] Martin B. Margulies. [Dublin] Dolmen Press; [distributed in the U.S.A. by Dufour Editions, Chester Springs, Pa., 1970] 87 p. 23 cm. [PR6029.C33Z757] 72-200011 ISBN 0-19-647543-0
1. O'Casey, Sean, 1880-1964—Biography—Youth. I. Title.

O'Casey, Sean, 1880-1964—Correspondence.

O'CASEY, Sean, 1880- 822'.9'12 B
1964.
The letters of Sean O'Casey. Edited by David Krause. New York, Macmillan [1975- v. illus. 25 cm. Contents.Contents.—v. 1. 1910-41. Includes bibliographical references. [PR6029.C33Z53 1975] 74-11442 ISBN 0-02-566660-6 (v. 1)
1. O'Casey, Sean, 1880-1964—Correspondence. I. Krause, David, 1917- ed. II. Title. **BIP**

O'Connell, Daniel Peter, 1885-

ROBINSON, Frank S. 320.9'747'4304
Albany's O'Connell machine; an American political relic, by Frank S. Robinson. Albany, Washington Park Spirit [1973] vi, 249 p. ports. 24 cm. [JS512.R6] 73-176487 4.50
1. O'Connell, Daniel Peter, 1885- 2. Albany—Politics and government. I. Title.

O'Connell, Daniel, 1775-1847.

GWYNN, Denis Rolleston, 923.1415
1893-
Daniel O'Connell. Rev. centenary ed. Cork Univ. Pr. [dist. Mystic, Conn., Verry, 1964] 262p. 23cm. Bibl. 3.50
1. O'Connell, Daniel, 1775-1847. 2. Ireland— Pol. & govt.—19th cent. I. Title.

O'FAOLAIN, 941.5081'092'4 B
Sean, 1900-
King of the beggars : a life of Daniel O'Connell, the Irish liberator, in a study of the rise of the modern Irish democracy (1775-1847) / by Sean O'Faolain. Westport, Conn. : Greenwood Press, 1975, c1938. 338 p., [8] leaves of plates : ill. ; 22 cm. Reprint of the ed. published by Viking Press, New York. Includes index. [DA950.22.O4 1975] 75-7242 ISBN 0-8371-8104-6 lib.bdg. : 15.00
1. O'Connell, Daniel, 1775-1847. 2. Ireland—Politics and government—19th century. I. Title.

O'Connell, Eugene, 1815-1891.

DWYER, John T. 282'.092'4 B
Condemned to the mines : the life of Eugene O'Connell, 1815-1891, pioneer bishop of Northern California and Nevada / by John T. Dwyer. 1st ed. New York : Vantage Press, c1976. xxiii, 302 p. : ill., ports. ; 21 cm. Includes bibliographical references and index. [BX4705.O293D88] 76-150322 ISBN 0-533-02130-8 : 8.95
1. O'Connell, Eugene, 1815-1891. 2. Catholic Church—Bishops—Biography. 3. Bishops—California—Biography. I. Title.

O'Connell, William Henry, Cardinal, 1859-1944.

WAYMAN, Dorothy (Godfrey) 922.273
1893-
Cardinal O'Connell of Boston; a biography of William Henry O'Connell, 1859-1944. New York, Farrar, Straus and Young [ci955] 307p*2cm. [BX4705.O3W3] 55-5834
1. O'Connell, William Henry, Cardinal, 1859-1944. I. Title.

O'Connor, C. Y., 1843-1902.

TAUMAN, Merab. 624'.092'4 B
The chief, C. Y. O'Connor / Merab Tauman. Nedlands [Australia] : University of Western Australia Press ; Forest Grove, Or. : [sold by] International Scholarly Book Services, 1978. xiv, 290 p., [7] leaves of plates : ill. ; 25 cm. Includes bibliographical references and index. [TA140.O36T38 1978] 79-308921 ISBN 0-85564-123-1 : 26.00
1. O'Connor, C. Y., 1843-1902. 2. Civil engineers—Australia—Western Australia—Biography. I. Title.

O'Connor, Flannery.

FEELEY, Kathleen. 813'.5'4
Flannery O'Connor: voice of the peacock. New Brunswick, N.J., Rutgers University Press [1972] xii, 198 p. 22 cm. Bibliography: p. [187]-192. [PS3565.C57Z667] 76-163958 ISBN 0-8135-0705-7 9.00
1. O'Connor, Flannery. I. Title.

HENDIN, Josephine. 813'.5'4
The world of Flannery O'Connor. Bloomington, Indiana University Press [1970] xi, 177 p. 22 cm. Bibliography: p. 159-164. [PS3565.C57Z69] 76-108208 ISBN 0-253-19340-0 5.75
1. O'Connor, Flannery. I. Title. **BIP**

O'Connor, Flannery—Correspondence.

O'CONNOR, Flannery. 813'.5'.4 B
The habit of being : letters / Flannery O'Connor ; edited and with an introd. by Sally Fitzgerald. New York : Farrar, Straus, Giroux, c1979. xviii, 617 p. ; 24 cm. Includes index. [PS3565.C57Z48 1979] 78-11559 15.00
1. O'Connor, Flannery—Correspondence. 2. Novelists, American 20th century—Correspondence. I. Fitzgerald, Sally. II. Title. **BIP**

O'CONNOR, Flannery. 813'.5'4 B
The habit of being : letters / Flannery O'Connor ; edited and with an introd. by Sally Fitzgerald. New York : Vintage Books, [1980] p. cm. Reprint of the 1978 ed. published by Farrar, Strauss & Giroux, New York. Includes index. [PS3565.C57Z48 1980] 79-23319 ISBN 0-394-74259-1 pbk. : 6.95
1. O'Connor, Flannery—Correspondence. 2. Novelists, American—20th century—Correspondence. I. Fitzgerald, Sally. II. Title.

O'Connor, Frank, 1909-

HURLEY, Edward 329'.00924 B
Francis, 1895-
The last poor man. [1st ed.] New York, Emblem Enterprises [1968] viii, 208 p. 22 cm. [E840.8.O25H8] 68-29090 6.00
1. O'Connor, Frank, 1909- 2. Elections—New York (State)—Campaign funds. 3. New York (State)—Politics and government—1951- I. Title.

O'Connor, Jack,

O'CONNOR, Jack, 1902- 917.91'73
Horse and buggy West; a boyhood on the last frontier. Illus. by Irving Boker. [1st ed.] New York, Knopf, 1969 [c1968] ix, 302 p. illus. 22 cm. [PS3565.C58Z5] 68-23938 5.95
I. Title.

O'Connor, Jimmy.

O'CONNOR, Jimmy. 364.1'092'4 B
The eleventh commandment / Jimmy O'Connor. St. Peter Port, Channel Islands : Seagull, 1976. 191 p. ; 23 cm. [HV6248.O43A34] 76-371802 ISBN 0-905353-00-5 : £4.95
1. O'Connor, Jimmy. 2. Crime and criminals—England—Biography. I. Title.

O'Connor, Joseph,

O'CONNOR, Joseph, 1877- 923.5415
Hostage to fortune. Dublin, M. F. Moynihan [1951] 291 p. 22 cm. Autobiography. [DA965.O25A3] 52-41071
I. Title.

O'Connor, Rachel Swayze, 1774-1846.

CRAVEN, Avery Odelle, 976.3 B
1886-
Rachel of old Louisiana / Avery O. Craven ; with ill. by the author. Baton Rouge : Louisiana State University Press, [1975] xiii, 122 p. : ill. ; 21 cm. [F374.C72] 74-15921 ISBN 0-8071-0095-1 : 6.95
1. O'Connor, Rachel Swayze, 1774-1846. 2. Plantation life—Louisiana. 3. Louisiana—Social life and customs. 4. Slavery in the United States—Louisiana. I. Title. **BIP**

O'Connor, William Douglas, 1832-1889.

LOVING, Jerome, 1941- 814'.4 B
Walt Whitman's champion : William Douglas O'Connor / by Jerome Loving. 1st ed. College Station : Texas A&M University Press, c1978. xx, 252 p., [4] leaves of plates : ill. ; 24 cm. Includes index. Bibliography: p. [243]-245. [PS2486.O5Z75] 77-89511 ISBN 0-89096-039-9 : 11.50
1. O'Connor, William Douglas, 1832-1889. 2. Whitman, Walt, 1819-1892—Friends and associates. 3. Authors, American—19th century—Biography. I. O'Connor, William Douglas, 1832-1889. II. Title. **BIP**

O Crohan, Tomas, 1856-1937.

O CROHAN, Tomas, 1856- 941.96
1937.
The islandman / Tomas O Crohan ; translated from the Irish by Robin Flower. Oxford [Eng.] ; New York : Oxford University Press, 1978. xiv, 245 p., [7] leaves of plates : ill. ; 20 cm. (Oxford paperbacks) Translation of An t-oileanach. [DA990.B65O3 1978] 77-30567 pbk. : 4.50
1. O Crohan, Tomas, 1856-1937. 2. Blasket Islands, Ire.—Social life and customs. 3. Blasket Islands, Ire.—Biography. I. Title. **BIP**

O'Donovan, Michael,

O'DONOVAN, Michael, 1903- 821 B
1966.
My father's son [by] Frank O'Connor. [1st American ed.] New York, Knopf, 1969 [c1968] 235 p. ports. 22 cm. [PR6029.D58Z523 1969] 70-79323 6.95
I. Title.

O'DONOVAN, Michael, 1903- 928.2
1966.
An only child [by] Frank O'Connor [pseud. 1st ed.] New York, Knopf, 1961. 275 p. illus. 22 cm. Autobiography. [PR6029.D58Z52] 60-15873
I. Title.

O'Donovan, Michael, 1903-1966.

O'DONOVAN, Michael, 1903- 821 B
1966.
My father's son [by] Frank O'Connor. [1st American ed.] New York, Knopf, 1969 [c1968] 235 p. ports. 22 cm. [PR6029.D58Z523 1969] 70-79323 6.95

I. Title.

O'DONOVAN, Michael, 1903-1966. 928.2
An only child [by] Frank O'Connor [pseud. 1st ed.] New York, Knopf, 1961. 275 p. illus. 22 cm. Autobiography. [PR6029.D58Z52] 60-15873
I. Title.

WOHLGELERNTER, Maurice. 828'.9'12 B
Frank O'Connor : an introduction / Maurice Wohlgelernter. New York : Columbia University Press, 1977. xx, 222 p. : port. ; 24 cm. Includes index. Bibliography: p. [207]-213. [PR6029.D58Z98] 76-45085 ISBN 0-231-04194-2 : 10.95
1. O'Donovan, Michael, 1903-1966. 2. Authors, Irish—20th century—Biography. I. Title.

O'Dowd, Bernard, 1866-1953.

ANDERSON, Hugh. 821 B
The poet militant: Bernard O'Dowd. [Rev. and enl. ed.] Melbourne, Hill of Content [1969] 158 p. 23 cm. Originally published, New York, Twayne Publishers, 1968, under the title, Bernard O'Dowd. Bibliography: p. 151-155. [PR6029.D6Z57 1969] 71-460777 5.60
1. O'Dowd, Bernard, 1866-1953. I. Title.

O'Dwyer, Paul, 1907-

O'DWYER, Paul, 1907- 340'.092'4 B
Counsel for the defense : the autobiography of Paul O'Dwyer. New York : Simon and Schuster, c1979. p. cm. Includes index. [KF373.O38A3] 79-13936 ISBN 0-671-22573-1 : 10.95
1. O'Dwyer, Paul, 1907- 2. Lawyers—New York (City)—Biography. 3. City Councilmen—New York (City)—Biography. I. Title.

O'Dwyer, William, 1890-1964.

WALSH, George, 1931- 974.7'1'040924 B
Public enemies : the mayor, the mob, and the crime that was / George Walsh. 1st ed. New York : Norton, c1980. p. cm. Includes index. Bibliography: p. [F128.5.W23 1980] 79-17943 ISBN 0-393-01306-5 : 12.95
1. O'Dwyer, William, 1890-1964. 2. Costello, Frank. 3. Corruption (in politics)—New York (City) 4. New York (City)—Politics and government—1898-1951. 5. New York (City)—Mayors—Biography. 6. Crime and criminals—New York (City)—Biography. I. Title. **BIP**

O'Hair family.

O'HAIR, K. R., 1887- 929.2'0973
Michael O'Hair, 1749-1813; soldier of the revolution, by K. R. O'Hair. [Paris, Ill., 1971] 284 p. front. 24 cm. Includes bibliographical references. [CS71.O37 1971] 78-30769 7.95
1. O'Hair family. 2. O'Hair, Michael, 1749-1813. I. Title.

O'Hara, Dolores, 1935-

MCDONNELL, Virginia B. 926.1
Dee O'Hara, astronauts' nurse; the complete life story of the first aerospace nurse. New York, Nelson [c.1965] 126p. illus., ports. 22cm. (Rutledge bk.) [RC1097.M3] 65-16505 2.75; 2.78 lib. ed.,
1. O'Hara, Dolores, 1935- I. Title.

O'Hara, Edwin Vincent, Bp., 1881-

SHAW, James Gerard. 922.273
Edwin Vincent O'Hara: American prelate. Foreword by Matthew F. Brady. New York, Farrar, Straus and Dudahy [1957] 274 p. illus. 22 cm. [BX4705.O43S5] 57-6500
1. O'Hara, Edwin Vincent, Bp., 1881- I. Title.

O'Hara, John, 1905-1970.

BRUCCOLI, Matthew Joseph, 1931- 813'.5'2 B
The O'Hara concern : a biography of John O'Hara / by Matthew J. Bruccoli. 1st ed. New York : Random House, 1975. xxix, 417 p. : ill., maps (on lining papers) ; 25 cm. Includes index. "John O'Hara's works": p. 358-386. [PS3529.H29Z59] 75-9736 ISBN 0-394-48446-0 : 15.00
1. O'Hara, John, 1905-1970. I. Title. **BIP**

FARR, Finis. 813'.5'2 B
O'Hara: a biography. [1st ed.] Boston, Little, Brown [1973] 300 p. illus. 25 cm. [PS3529.H29Z67] 72-10474 ISBN 0-316-27473-9 8.50
1. O'Hara, John, 1905-1970.

O'Higgins, Bernardo, Supreme Director of Chile, 1778-1842.

CLISSOLD, Stephen. 983'.04'0924 B
Bernardo O'Higgins and the independence of Chile. New York, Praeger [1969] 254 p. maps, ports. 23 cm. Includes bibliographical references. [F3094.O35517 1969] 69-11332 6.50
1. O'Higgins, Bernardo, Supreme Director of Chile, 1778-1842. 2. O'Higgins, Ambrosio, marques de Osorno, 1720-1801. 3. Chile—History—War of Independence, 1810-1824. I. Title.

KINSBRUNER, Jay. 983'.04
Bernardo O'Higgins. New York, Twayne [1968] 183p. map. 21cm. (Twayne's rulers & statesmen of the world ser., 8) Bibl. [F3094.O357] (B) 67-28863 4.95
1. O'Higgins, Bernardo, Supreme Director of Chile, 1778-1842. I. Title.

KINSBRUNER, Jay. 983'.04'0924 B
Bernardo O'Higgins. New York, Twayne Publishers [1968] 183 p. map. 21 cm. (Twayne's rulers and statesmen of the world series, 8) Includes bibliographical references. [F3094.O357] 67-28863
1. O'Higgins, Bernardo, Supreme Director of Chile, 1778-1842.

O'Higgins, Kevin Christopher, 1892-1927.

WHITE, Terence De Vere 923.2415
Kevin O'Higgins [Tralee, Ireland] Anvil Bks. [New Rochelle, N.Y., SportShelf, 1966, c. 1948] 249p. port. 18cm. Bibl. [DA965.O5W5] 1.75 pap,
1. O'Higgins, Kevin Christopher, 1892-1927. I. Title.

O'Kane, Richard H., 1911-

O'KANE, Richard H., 1911- 940.54'51
Clear the bridge! : The war patrols of the U.S.S. Tang / by Richard H. O'Kane. Chicago : Rand McNally, c1977. 480 p. : ill. ; 24 cm. Includes index. [D783.5.T35O38] 77-7158 ISBN 0-528-81058-8 : 10.00
1. Tang (Ship) 2. O'Kane, Richard H., 1911- 3. United States. Navy—Biography. 4. World War, 1939-1945—Naval operations—Submarine. 5. World War, 1939-1945—Pacific Ocean. 6. World War, 1939-1945—Naval operations, American. 7. World War, 1939-1945—Personal narratives, American. 8. Seamen—United States—Biography. I. Title. **BIP**

O'Keeffe, John,

O'KEEFFE, John, 1747-1833. 792'.028'0924 B
Recollections of the life of John O'Keeffe. New York, B. Blom, 1969. 2 v. in 1. port. 21 cm. Reprint of the 1826 ed. [PR3605.O3A8 1969] 70-89711
I. Title. **BIP**

O'Kelly, Seumas, 1881-1918.

SAUL, George Brandon, 1901- 828'.9'1209
Seumas O'Kelly. Lewisburg, Bucknell University Press [1971] 101 p. 21 cm. (The Irish writers series) Bibliography: p. 81-101. [PR6029.K4Z9] 74-126030 ISBN 0-8387-7765-1 4.50
1. O'Kelly, Seumas, 1881-1918. 2. O'Kelly, Seumas, 1881-1918—Bibliography. **BIP**

O'Leary, John, 1830-1907.

BOURKE, Marcus. 941.5'8'0924 B
John O'Leary; a study in Irish separatism. Athens, University of Georgia Press [1968, c1967] 251 p. illus., ports. 22 cm. Bibliographical references included in "Sources and notes" (p. 236-244) [DA950.23.O4B6 1968] 70-4108 6.00
1. O'Leary, John, 1830-1907. I. Title.

O'Meara, Walter—Biography.

O'MEARA, Walter. 813'.5'2 B
We made it through the winter: a memoir of northern Minnesota boyhood. St. Paul, Minnesota Historical Society, 1974. xi, 128 p. illus. 23 cm. (Publications of the Minnesota Historical Society) Includes bibliographical references. [PS3529.M4Z527] 74-18369 ISBN 0-87351-092-5
1. O'Meara, Walter—Biography. I. Title. II. Series: Minnesota Historical Society. Publications.

O'Neal, John—Juvenile literature.

COHEN, Tom. 323.4'0922 B
Three who dared. [1st ed.] Garden City, N.Y., Doubleday [1969] 144 p. illus. 22 cm. (A Doubleday signal book) Contents.Contents.—The Henry M. Aronson story.—The John O'Neal story.—The Eric Weinberger story. Describes the activities of three young men who risked their lives to participate in the Freedom Marches and Civil Rights Movement of the early 1960's. [E185.61.C637] 920 69-10998 3.50
1. Aronson, Henry M.—Juvenile literature. 2. O'Neal, John—Juvenile literature. 3. Weinberger, Eric, 1932- —Juvenile literature. 4. Negroes—Civil rights—Juvenile literature. 5. Civil rights—Southern States—Juvenile literature. I. Title. **BIP**

O'Neil, Kitty—Juvenile literature.

THACHER, Alida M. 796.7'2'0924 B
Fastest woman on earth / Alida Thacher ; ill., Ken Bachaus. Milwaukee : Raintree Publishers, c1980. p. cm. Traces the death-defying career of Kitty O'Neil, a drag racer, stunt woman, and the holder of land speed records. [GV1032.T48A33] 92 79-21047 ISBN 0-8172-1566-2 (lib. bdg.) : 7.99
1. O'Neil, Kitty—Juvenile literature. 2. Automobile racing drivers—United States—Biography—Juvenile literature. 3. Stunt men and women—United States—Biography—Juvenile literature. I. Bachaus, Ken. II. Title. **BIP**

O'Neill, Eugene Gladstone, 1888-1953.

BOULTON, Agnes. 928.1
Part of a long story. [1st ed.] Garden City, N. Y., Doubleday, 1958. 331 p. 22 cm. Autobiographical. [PS3529.N5Z57] 58-9374
1. O'Neill, Eugene Gladstone, 1888-1953. I. Title.

BOWEN, Croswell 928.1
The curse of the misbegotten; a tale of the house of O'Neill, by Croswell Bowen, with the assistance of Shane O'Neill. New York, Ballantine [1962,c.1959] 382p. 18cm. (S653) .75 pap.,
1. O'Neill, Eugene Gladstone, 1888-1953. 2. O'Neill family. I. Title.

BOWEN, Croswell. 928.1
The curse of the misbegotten; a tale of the house of O'Neill, by Croswell Bowen, with the assistance of Shane O'Neill. [1st ed.] New York, McGraw-Hill [1959] 384 p. 22 cm. [PS3529.N5Z573] 58-59657
1. O'Neill, Eugene Gladstone, 1888-1953. 2. O'Neill family. I. Title.

COOLIDGE, Olivia E. 812.52
Eugene O'Neill, by Olivia Coolidge. New York, Scribner [1966] 223 p. port. 22 cm. [PS3529.N5Z627] 66-24498
1. O'Neill, Eugene Gladstone, 1888-1953.

FRENZ, Horst, 1912- 812'.5'2
Eugene O'Neill. [Translated from the German by Helen Sebba. Revisions and additions for the American edition by the author] New York, Ungar [1971] v, 121 p. 20 cm. (Modern literature monographs) Bibliography: p. 111-113. [PS3529.N5Z64413] 79-143188 ISBN 0-8044-2211-7 5.00
1. O'Neill, Eugene Gladstone, 1888-1953.
1.75 pap. ISBN 0-8044-6159-7

GELB, Arthur, 1924- 928.1
O'Neill [by] Arthur & Barbara Gelb. [1st ed.] New York, Harper [1962] 970 p. illus. 24 cm. [PS3529.N5Z653] 61-13602
1. O'Neill, Eugene Gladstone, 1888-1953. I. Gelb, Barbara, joint author. **BIP**

GELB, Arthur, 1924- 928.1
O'Neill [by] Arthur & Barbara Gelb. Abridged by the authors [New York, Dell, c.1960-1965] 575p. 18cm. (Laurel ed., 6629) [PS3529.N5Z653] .95 pap.,
1. O'Neill, Eugene Gladstone, 1888-1953. I. Gelb, Barbara, joint author. II. Title.

GELB, Arthur, 1924- 812'.5'2 B
O'Neill [by] Arthur & Barbara Gelb. New York, Harper & Row [1974, c1973] xx, 990 p. illus. 24 cm. [PS3529.N5Z653 1974] 73-6760 ISBN 0-06-011487-8 17.50
1. O'Neill, Eugene Gladstone, 1888-1953. I. Gelb, Barbara, joint author.

SHEAFFER, Louis. 812'.5'2
O'Neill, son and playwright. [1st ed.] Boston, Little, Brown [1968] xx, 543p. illus. facsim., ports. 24cm. Bibl. [PS3529.N5Z798] 68-17278 10.00
1. O'Neill, Eugene Gladstone, 1888-1953. I. Title.

O'Neill, Felix J., 1860-1937.

YOUNG, Thomas E 811.52
Felix J. O'Neill, poet priest of New England. [n. p. 1960] 105 p. illus. 21 cm. [PS3529.N52Z95] 61-22588
1. O'Neill, Felix J., 1860-1937. I. Title.

O'Neill, John Edward, 1892-1961.

O'NEILL, Bill. 338.7'63'0924 B
A mountain never too high : the story of J. E. O'Neill / by Bill O'Neill. Fresno, Calif. : Valley Publishers, c1977. ix, 106 p. : ill. ; 29 cm. Includes index. [HD9005.O63] 77-82899 ISBN 0-913548-46-4 : 15.00
1. O'Neill, John Edward, 1892-1961. 2. Businessmen—California—San Joaquin Valley—Biography. 3. Agricultural industries—California—San Joaquin Valley—Biography. 4. Farmers—California—San Joaquin Valley—Biography. I. Title. **BIP**

O'Neill, Rose Cecil, 1874-1944.

MCCANSE, Ralph Alan. 740'.924 B
Titans and kewpies; the life and art of Rose O'Neill. [1st ed.] New York, Vantage Press [1968] 220 p. illus., ports. 21 cm. [NC139.O5M3] 68-1950
1. O'Neill, Rose Cecil, 1874-1944. I. Title.

RUGGLES, Rowena Fay (Godding) 741.6
The one Rose, mother of the immortal Kewpies; a biography of Rose O'Neill and the story of her work, by Rowena Godding Ruggles. [Oakland? Calif., 1964] xi, 80 p. plates, ports. 25 cm. [NC139.05R8] 64-6933
1. O'Neill, Rose Cecil, 1874-1944. I. Title.

O'Neill, William Owen, 1860-1898.

EATON, Jeanette. 923.573
Buckey O'Neill of Arizona; illus. by Edward Shenton. New York, W. Morrow, 1949. 219p. illus. 21cm. [F811.O5E3] 49-11000
1. O'Neill, William Owen, 1860-1898. I. Title.

O'Reilly, John Boyle, 1844-1890.

SCHOFIELD, William Greenough, 1909- 928.1
Seek for a hero; the story of John Boyle O'Reilly. New York, Kenedy [c1956] 309p. 21cm. [PS2493.S3] 56-5747
1. O'Reilly, John Boyle, 1844-1890. I. Title.

O'Reilly, John Boyle, 1844-1890—Biography—Journalistic career.

MCMANAMIN, Francis G. 070.4'092'4 B
The American years of John Boyle O'Reilly, 1870-1890 / Francis G McManamin New York : Arno Press, 1976, c1959. p. cm. (The Irish-Americans) Reprint of the author's thesis, Catholic University of America. Includes bibliographical references. [PS2493.M3 1976] 76-6356 ISBN 0-405-09349-7 : 20.00
1. O'Reilly, John Boyle, 1844-1890—Biography—Journalistic career. I. Title. II. Series.

O'Rourke, John H., 1856-1929.

NEVILS, Coleman, 1878- 922.273
A moulder of men, John H. O'Rourke, s. j.; a memoir. New York, Apostleship of Prayer, 1953. 284p. illus. 20cm. [BX4705.O67N4] 53-7495
1. O'Rourke, John H., 1856-1929. I. Title.

O'Sullivan, Timothy H.

HORAN, James David, 1914- 770.924 B
Timothy O'Sullivan, America's forgotten photographer; the life and work of the brilliant photographer whose camera recorded the American scene from the battlefields of the Civil War to the frontiers of the West, by James D. Horan. [1st ed.] Garden City, N.Y., Doubleday, 1966. xiv, 334 p. illus. 29 cm. Bibliography: p. 324-326. [TR140.O8H6] 66-20922
1. O'Sullivan, Timothy H. 2. Photography—History—United States. 3. The West—Description and travel—Views. 4. United States—History—Civil War, 1861-1865—Pictorial works.

Oakes, Harry, Sir, bart., 1874-1943.

BOCCA, Geoffrey. 364.152
The life and death of Sir Harry Oakes. [1st ed.] Garden City, N. Y., Doubleday, 1959. 238 p. 22 cm. [CT348.O17B6] 59-9779
1. Oakes, Harry, Sir, bart., 1874-1943.

Oakie, Jack, 1903-

OAKIE, Jack, 1903- 791.43'028'0924 B
Jack Oakie's double takes / Jack Oakie. San Francisco : Strawberry Hill Press, [1979] p. cm. Includes index. [PN2287.O17A34] 79-12432 ISBN 0-89407-019-3 pbk. : 9.95
1. Oakie, Jack, 1903- 2. Comedians—United States—Biography. 3. Moving-picture actors and actresses—United States—Biography. I. Title.

Oakland Athletics (Baseball team)

CLARK, Tom, 1941- 796.357'64'0979466
Champagne and baloney : the rise and fall of Finley's A's / by Tom Clark ; with drawings by the author. 1st ed. New York : Harper & Row, c1976. p. cm. Includes index. [GV875.O24C42 1976] 75-26878 ISBN 0-06-010832-0 : 7.95
1. Oakland Athletics (Baseball team) 2. Finley, Charles Oscar, 1918- 3. Baseball. I. Title.

Oakland, Manitoba—Biography.

ROME, J. B., 1897- 917.127'4
Oakland echoes, published by J. B. Rome. Compiled by Connie Davidson. [Brandon, Man.] 1970. 309 p. illus., ports. 23 cm. Available from the author, Apt. 18, 312 Fourth St., Brandon, Manitoba, R7A 3G9. [F1064.5.O23R65] 73-161744 5.50 (pbk.)
1. Oakland, Manitoba—Biography. 2. Oakland, Manitoba—History. I. Davidson, Connie. II. Title.

Oakley, Annie, 1860-1926.

GARST, Doris Shannon, 1899- 927.993
Annie Oakley, born August 13, 1860, died November 3, 1926. New York, J. Messner [1958] 190 p. 22 cm. Includes bibliography. [GV1157.O3G3] 58-6015
1. Oakley, Annie, 1860-1926.

Oakley, Annie, 1860-1926—Juvenile literature.

ALDERMAN, Clifford Lindsey. 799.3'092'4 B
Annie Oakley and the world of her time / Clifford Lindsey Alderman. New York : Macmillan, c1979. ix, 91 p., [3] leaves of plates : ill. ; 22 cm. Includes index. Bibliography: p. 85-86. Examines the life and times of sharpshooter Annie Oakley with emphasis on her role as entertainer in Buffalo Bill's West Show and other shows of the time. [GV1157.O3A64] 92 78-31838 ISBN 0-02-700270-5 : 8.95
1. Oakley, Annie, 1860-1926—Juvenile literature. 2. Shooters (of arms)—United States—Biography—Juvenile literature. I. Title. BIP

KRASKE, Robert. 791'.092'2 B
Daredevils do amazing things / by Robert Kraske ; illustrated by Ivan Powell. New York : Random House, c9178. 69 p. : ill. ; 22 cm. (Step-up books ; 26) Describes the daring feats of adventures Blondin, Harry Houdini, Annie Oakley, Harry Rieseberg, and Evel Knievel. [GV1811.A1K7] 920 77-90194 ISBN 0-394-83623-5 : 2.95. ISBN 0-394-93623-X lib. bdg. : 3.99
1. Houdini, Harry, 1874 1926—Juvenile literature. 2. Oakley, Annie, 1860-1926—Juvenile literature. 3. Rieseberg, Harry Earl—Juvenile literature. 4. Knievel, Evel, 1938- —Juvenile literature. 5. Blondin, Jean Francois Gravelet, known as, 1824-1897—Juvenile literature. 6. Entertainers—United States—Biography—Juvenile literature. I. Powell, Ivan. II. Title. BIP

WAYNE, Bennett. 920.72
Women who dared to be different. Edited, with commentary by Bennett Wayne. Champaign, Ill., Garrard Pub. Co. [1973] 168 p. illus. 22 cm. (A Torch book) Brief biographies of four women who pioneered in professions traditionally reserved for men. [CT3260.W39] 920 72-6802 ISBN 0-8116-4902-4 3.48
1. Oakley, Annie, 1860-1926—Juvenile literature. 2. Mitchell, Maria, 1818-1889—Juvenile literature. 3. Earhart, Amelia, 1898-1937—Juvenile literature. 4. Cochrane, Elizabeth, 1867-1922—Juvenile literature. 5. Women in the United States—Biography—Juvenile literature. 6. Women in the United States—Biography. I. Title. BIP

Oastler, Richard, 1789-1861.

DRIVER, Cecil Herbert. 942.081'0924 B
Tory radical; the life of Richard Oastler [by] Cecil Driver. New York, Octagon Books, 1970 [c1946] ix, 597 p. illus., ports. 24 cm. Bibliography: p. 563-583. [DA541.O3D7 1970] 75-120249
1. Oastler, Richard, 1789-1861. I. Title.

Oatman family.

STRATTON, Royal B., d.1875. 970.3
Captivity of the Oatman girls. Upper Saddle River, N.J., Literature House [1970] 290 p. illus., ports. 23 cm. Reprint of the 1859 ed. [E87.O12 1970] 76-104572
1. Oatman family. 2. Indians of North America—Captivities. I. Title. BIP

STRATTON, Royal B., d.1875. 973'.04'97 S
Captivity of the Oatman girls / Royal B. Stratton. 2d ed., changed. New York : Garland Pub., 1977, c1857. xiii, 231 p. : ill. ; 19 cm. (The Garland library of narratives of North American Indian captivities ; v. 71) Reprint of the ed. published by Whitton, Towne & Co.'s Excelsior Steam Power Presses, San Francisco. Issued with a reprint of the author's Captivity of the Oatman girls. New York, 1977. [E85.G2 vol. 71] [E87] 970'.004'97 75-7096 ISBN 0-8240-1695-5 : part of a 7 vol. set : 29.50 (set)
1. Oatman family. 2. Indians of North America—Captivities. 3. Apache Indians—Captivities. 4. Mohave Indians—Captivities. I. Title. II. Series.

STRATTON, Royal B., d.1875. 973'.04'97 S
Life among the Indians : Captivity of the Oatman girls / Royal B. Stratton. New York : Garland Pub., 1977. p. cm. (The Garland library of narratives of North American Indian captivities ; v. 71) Reprint of the 1857 ed. published by Whitton, Towne, San Francisco. [E85.G2 vol. 71] [E87] 970'.004'97 76-56808 ISBN 0-8240-1695-5 lib.bdg. : 25.00
1. Oatman family. 2. Indians of North America—Captivities. 3. Apache Indians—Captivities. 4. Mohave Indians—Captivities. I. Title. II. Series.

Oberth, Hermann, 1894-

WALTERS, Helen B 926.294
Hermann Oberth: father of space travel. Introd. by Hermann Oberth. New York, Macmillan [1962] 109 p. illus. 22 cm. Includes bibliography. [TL781.85.O3W3] 62-21204
1. Oberth, Hermann, 1894- I. Title.

Obituaries.

LEVY, Felice D. 920'.02
Obituaries on file / compiled by Felice Levy New York : Facts on File, c1979. p. cm. Includes index. [CT120.L43] 79-12907 ISBN 0-87196-372-8 : 75.00
1. Obituaries. I. Facts on File, inc., New York. II. Title.

OBITUARIES from the Times, 1971-1975, including an index to all obituaries and tributes appearing in the Times during the years 1971-1975 / 920'.02
compiler, Frank C. Roberts. Reading, Eng. : Newspaper Archive Developments Lit. : Westport, Conn. : distributed in North America by Meckler Books, 1978 647 p. : 31 cm. Includes index. [CT120.O17] 77-22500 ISBN 0-913672-18-1 lib.bdg. : 85.00
1. The Times, London—Indexes. 2. Obituaries. 3. Biography—20th century. 4. Obituaries—Indexes. I. Roberts, Frank C. II. The Times, London.

Obolensky, Serge,

OBOLENSKY, Serge, 1890- 923.247
One man in his time; the memoirs of Serge Obolensky. New york, McDowell, Obolensky [1958] 433 p. illus. 24 cm. [CT275.O22A3] 58-12582
I. Title.

Obookiah, Henry, 1792?-1818.

DWIGHT, Edwin Welles, 1789-1841. 266'.022'0924
Memoirs of Henry Obookiah, a native of Owhyhee and a member of the Foreign Mission School, who died at Cornwall, Connecticut, February 17, 1818, aged 26 years. Honolulu [Woman's Board of Missions for the Pacific Islands] 1968. xiv, 112 p. illus., facsims., map, ports. 21 cm. "150th anniversary edition." [BV3680.H4O33 1968] 68-7300 1.50
1. Obookiah, Henry, 1792?-1818. I. Woman's Board of Missions for the Pacific Islands. II. Title.

Observer Transatlantic Singlehanded Sailing Race.

FRANCIS, Clare. 797.1'4
Woman alone : sailing solo across the Atlantic / by Clare Francis. New York : D. McKay Co., c1977. p. cm. [GV832.F695] 77-8708 ISBN 0-679-50758-2 : 8.95
1. Observer Transatlantic Singlehanded Sailing Race. 2. Francis, Clare. I. Title.

Observer Transatlantic Singlehanded Sailing Race—History.

ASARIA, Gerald. 797.1'4
Challenge, lone sailors of the Atlantic / by Gerald Asaria. New York : Mayflower Books, [1979] p. cm. Translation of Les Heros solitaires de l'Atlantique. Bibliography: p. [GV832.A8213] 79-10041 ISBN 0-8317-1242-2 : 19.95
1. Observer Transatlantic Singlehanded Sailing Race—History. 2. Seamen—Biography. I. Title.

Obstetrics—Algeria.

YOUNG, Ian, 1941- 362.1'9'8209653
The private life of Islam. New York, Liveright [1974] vi, 306 p. 22 cm. [RG67.A4Y68 1974] 74-13842 ISBN 0-87140-597-0 8.95
1. Obstetrics—Algeria. 2. Physicians—Correspondence, reminiscences, etc. I. Title.

Ocampo, Melchor, 1814-1861.

ALMANZO, Robert M. 972'.06'0924 B
To break rather than bend; a biographical sketch of Melchor Ocampo, by Robert M. Almanzo. Los Angeles, c1966. 83 p. 23 cm. Bibliography:p. 82-83. [F1233.O3A55] 67-7399
1. Ocampo, Melchor, 1814-1861. I. Title.

Ocampo, Victoria, 1891- —Biography.

MEYER, Doris. 868 B
Victoria Ocampo / by Doris Meyer. New York : G. Braziller, [1978] p. cm. Includes fifteen essays by V. Ocampo translated from the Spanish by D. Meyer. Includes index. [PQ7797.O295Z78] 78-56302 ISBN 0-8076-0900-5 : 12.50
1. Ocampo, Victoria, 1891- —Biography. 2. Authors, Argentine—20th century—Biography. I. Ocampo, Victoria, 1891-

Occult sciences.

WILSON, Colin, 1931- 133
They had strange powers / by Colin Wilson. Garden City, N.Y. : Doubleday, 1975. 142 p. : ill. ; 27 cm. (A New library of the supernatural) British ed. published under title : Mysterious powers. [BF1411.W54 1975] 75-16748 7.95
1. Occult sciences. 2. Occult sciences—Biography. I. Title. II. Series.

Occult sciences—Biography.

COHEN, Daniel. 133'.0922
Masters of the occult. New York, Dodd, Mead [1971] x, 234 p. illus. 22 cm. Bibliography: p. 221-225. [BF1408.C63] 74-165669 ISBN 0-396-06407-8 5.95
1. Occult sciences—Biography. I. Title. BIP

INDEX to occult sciences. 133'.092'2 B
Garden City, N.Y. : Doubleday, 1977. 128 p. : ill. ; 27 cm. (A New library of the supernatural) Includes index to the 1st 19 volumes of the series. "Also published as guide to index." [BF1408.I5] 76-40569 ISBN 0-385-11326-9 : 8.95
1. A New library of the supernatural—Indexes. 2. Occult sciences—Biography. 3. Psychical research—Biography. BIP

LILLIE, Arthur, b.1831. 133'.092'2
Modern mystics and modern magic; containing a full biography of the Rev. William Stainton Moses, together with sketches of Swedenborg, Boehme, Madame Guyon, the Illuminati, the kabbalists, the theosophists, the French spiritists, the Society of Psychical Research, etc. Freeport, N.Y., Books for Libraries Press [1972] vii, 172 p. illus. 22 cm. (Essay index reprint series) Reprint of the 1894 ed. [BF1408.L53 1972] 72-5680 ISBN 0-8369-2996-9
1. Occult sciences—Biography. I. Title.

Occult sciences—California.

ST. Clair, David. 133'.09794
The psychic world of California. [1st ed.] Garden City, N.Y., Doubleday, 1972. x, 323 p. 22 cm. Bibliography: p. [317]-319. [BF1434.U6S23] 75-178834 7.95
1. Occult sciences—California. 2. Occult sciences—Biography. 3. Psychical research—California. 4. Psychical research—Biography. I. Title.

Ocean travel.

DIARIES from the days of sail / edited by R. C. Bell ; introd. by Alan Villiers ; technical editor, C. P. Seyd. 910'.45
[London] : Barrie & Jenkins, c1974. 160 p. : ill. ; 26 cm. Contents.Contents.—Villiers, A. Introduction.—Clarke, C. H. American journey.—Whitehead, A. China and back.—Lacey, E. Clipper and Adelaide. [G540.A1D46 1974] 74-4411 ISBN 0-03-012941-9 : 10.00
1. Ocean travel. 2. Sailing ships. I. Bell, Robert Charles, 1917-
Distributed by Holt Rinehart & Winston.

Oceania—Biography.

MORE Pacific Islands portraits / Deryck Scarr, editor. Canberra : Australian National University Press ; Norwalk, Conn. : [distributed by] Books Australia, 1978 i.e. 1979. xi, 297 p. : maps ; 22 cm. Continues Pacific Islands portraits. Includes bibliographical references and index. [CT2775.M67 1979] 77-95353 ISBN 0-7081-1801-1 : 24.95 920'.099
1. Oceania—Biography. I. Scarr, Deryck.
Available from Books Australia, 21 Brookhedge Rd., Trumbulle, CT 06611

Oceanographers.

COX, Donald William. 551.4'6'00922
Explorers of the deep; pioneers of oceanography, by Donald W. Cox. Portrait illus. by Jack Woodson. Maplewood, N. J., Hammond [1968] 93 p. col. illus., maps (part col.), col. ports. 27 cm. (Profile series) [GC30.A1C6] 68-27451 3.50
1. Oceanographers. 2. Oceanographic research—History I. Title.

Ochbaum, Elfrieda,

OCHBAUM, Elfrieda, 1877-1962. 920
Burning arrows. Boston, B. Humphries [c1963] 320 p. illus., ports. 23 cm. Autobiographical. [CT275.H6283A3] 63-19546
I. Title.

Ochs, Adolph Simon, 1858-1935.

JOHNSON, Gerald White, 1890- 070.4'0924 B
An honorable Titan, a biographical study of Adolph S. Ochs, by Gerald W. Johnson. Westport, Conn., Greenwood Press [1970, c1946] ix, 313 p. 23 cm. Includes bibliographical references. [PN4874.O4J6 1970] 74-109293 ISBN 0-8371-3836-1
1. Ochs, Adolph Simon, 1858-1935. I. Title.

Ochs, Adolph Simon, 1858-1935—Juvenile literature.

FABER, Doris, 1924- 920.5
Printer's devil to publisher: Adolph S. Ochs of the New York Times. New York, Messner [c.1963] 191p. 22cm. Bibl. 63-8651 3.25; 3.19 lib. ed.,
1. Ochs, Adolph Simon, 1858-1935—Juvenile literature. I. Title.

Ochs, Phil.

ELIOT, Marc. 784.4'92'4 B
Death of a rebel / Marc Eliot. 1st ed. Garden City, N.Y. : Anchor Press, 1979. 316 p., [24] leaves of plates : ill. ; 21 cm. Includes index. Discography: p. [285]-293. [ML420.O29E4] 77-25586 ISBN 0-385-13610-2 pbk. : 4.95
1. Ochs, Phil. 2. Singers—United States—Biography. I. Title.

Ockenga, Harold John, 1905-

LINDSELL, Harold, 1913- 922.573
Park Street prophet, a life of Harold John Ockenga. Wheaton, Ill., Van Kampen Press [1951] 175 p. illus., ports. 20 cm. [BX7260.O3L5] 51-10787
1. Ockenga, Harold John, 1905- 2. National Association of Evangelicals for United Action. I. Title.

Oddie, Tasker Lowndes, 1870-1950.

CHAN, Loren Briggs, 1943- 979.3'03'0924 B
Sagebrush statesman: Tasker L. Oddie of Nevada. Reno, University of Nevada Press, 1973. 189 p. illus. 23 cm. (Nevada studies in history and political science, no. 12) Bibliography: p. [173]-182. [F841.C45] 73-77715 ISBN 0-87417-038-9 4.00 (pbk.)
1. Oddie, Tasker Lowndes, 1870-1950. 2. Nevada—Politics and government. I. Title. II. Series.

Odets, Clifford, 1906-1963.

WEALES, Gerald Clifford, 1925- 812'.5'4 B
Clifford Odets, playwright. New York, Pegasus [1971] 205 p. 21 cm. (Pegasus American authors) Includes bibliographical references. [PS3529.D46Z9] 75-124824 6.95
1. Odets, Clifford, 1906-1963. I. Title.

Odets, Clifford, 1906-1963—Criticism and interpretation.

CANTOR, Harold, 1926- 812'.5'4
Clifford Odets, playwright-poet / by Harold Cantor. Metuchen, N.J. : Scarecrow Press, 1978. viii, 235 p. ; 22 cm. Includes index. Bibliography: p. 214-229. [PS3529.D46Z6] 77-27284 ISBN 0-8108-1107-3 : 10.00
1. Odets, Clifford, 1906-1963—Criticism and interpretation. I. Title.

Odo, Abbot of Cluny, Saint 879 (ca.)-942.

JOANNES, monk of Cluny,fl. 945. 922.244
St. Odo of Cluny; being the Life of St. Odo of Cluny by John of Salerno, and the Life of St. Gerald of Aurillac by St. Odo. Translated and edited by Gerard Sitwell. London, New York, Sheed and Ward [1958] xxix, 186p. 22cm. (The Makes of Christendom) 'Odo's writings': p. xxv-xxvi. Bibliography: p. [xxvii]-xxix. eraldus Aurillaechsis, Saint, 855 (ca.)-909. [BX4700.O35J63 1958] 59-793
1. Odo, Abbot of Cluny, Saint 879 (ca.)-942. I. Odo, Abbot of Cluny, Saint 879 (ca.)-942. Life of St. Gerald of Aurillac. II. Sitwell, Gerard, ed. and tr. III. Title. IV. Series.

Oenslager, Donald, 1902-1975.

OENSLAGER, Donald, 1902-1975. 792'.025'0924 B
The theatre of Donald Oenslager / Donald M. Oenslager. 1st ed. Middletown, Conn. : Wesleyan University Press, c1978. xv, 176 p., [8] leaves of plates : ill. ; 23 x 29 cm. "Productions designed by Donald Oenslager": p. 147-167. Includes index. [PN2096.O4A37 1978] 77-16026 ISBN 0-8195-5025-6 : 30.00
1. Oenslager, Donald, 1902-1975. 2. Set designers—United States—Biography. 3. Theater—New York (City)—History. 4. Theater—United States—Stage-setting and seenery. I. Title.

Offenbach, Jacques, 1819-1880.

MOSS, Arthur, 1889- 782.8'1'0924 B
Cancan and barcarolle : the life and times of Jacques Offenbach / Arthur Moss & Evalyn Marvel. Westport, Conn. : Greenwood Press, 1975, c1954. p. cm. Reprint of the ed. published by Exposition Press, New York, in series: A Banner book. Bibliography: p. [ML410.O41M7 1975] 75-2629 ISBN 0-8371-8045-7 : 14.50
1. Offenbach, Jacques, 1819-1880. I. Marvel, Evalyn, joint author. II. Title. **BIP**

Offenberg, Bernice

OFFENBERG, Bernice 923.673
The Angel of Hell's Kitchen. [New York] B. Geis Assocs.; dist. Random [c.1962] 277p. 62-9158 4.50 bds.,
I. Title.

Ofstie, Hollis Lynn, 1920- 1946.

JURGENSEN, Barbara. 616.836
Leaping upon the mountains. Minneapolis, Augsburg Pub. House [1960] 100p. 21cm. The story of a victim of spastic paralysis. [RC388.J8] 60-8896
1. Ofstie, Hollis Lynn, 1920- 1946. I. Title.

Ogata, Kenzam, 1663-1743.

LEACH, Bernard Howell, 1887- 709.52
Kenzan and his tradition: the lives and times of Koetsu, Sotatsu, Korin and Kenzan. New York, Transatlantic Arts [1967] 3-173p. col. front., illus., 108 plates (incl. ports., facsims.) table, diagr. 26cm. [corrected entry] [ND1059.035 L4] 27.50
1. Honami, Koetsu, 1558-1637. 2. Ogata, Korin, 1658-1716. 3. Ogata, Kenzam, 1663-1743. 4. Tawaraya, Sotatsu, d. 1643. I. Title.

Ogata, Korin, 1658-1716.

LEACH, Bernard Howell, 1887- 709.52
Kenzan and his tradition: the lives and times of Koetsu, Sotatsu, Korin and Kenzan. New York, Transatlantic Arts [1967] 3-173p. col. front., illus., 108 plates (incl. ports., facsims.) table, diagr. 26cm. [corrected entry] [ND1059.035 L4] 27.50
1. Honami, Koetsu, 1558-1637. 2. Ogata, Korin, 1658-1716. 3. Ogata, Kenzam, 1663-1743. 4. Tawaraya, Sotatsu, d. 1643. I. Title.

Ogden, Charles Kay, 1889-1957.

C. K. Ogden : a collective memoir / by J. R. L. Anderson ... [et al.] ; edited by P. Sargant Florence and J. R. L. Anderson. London : Elek, P., 1977. 252 p., [2] leaves of plates : ill. ; 23 cm. "List of books edited by Ogden": p. [245]-252. Includes bibliographical references. [CT788.O32C13 1977] 78-304679 ISBN 0-301-76061-6 : 14.95 ISBN 0-301-76062-4 pbk. : 6.95 150'.92'4
1. Ogden, Charles Kay, 1889-1957. 2. England—Biography. I. Ogden, Charles Kay, 1889-1957. II. Anderson, John Richard Lane, 1911- III. Florence, Philip Sargant, 1890-
Distributed by P.Elek, Salem, N.H **BIP**

Ogden, Peter Skene, 1790-1854.

CLINE, Gloria Griffen. 971.2'092'4 B
Peter Skene Ogden and the Hudson's Bay Company. [1st ed.] Norman, University of Oklahoma Press [1974] xv, 279 p. illus. 23 cm. (The American exploration and travel series) Bibliography: p. 219-239. [F880.O34C53] 72-9266 ISBN 0-8061-1073-2
1. Ogden, Peter Skene, 1790-1854. 2. Hudson's Bay Company. I. Title. II. Series. **BIP**

PHILLIPS, Fred M. 979'.02
Desert people and mountain men : exploration of the Great Basin, 1824-1865 / Fred M. Phillips. Bishop, Calif. : Chalfant Press, c1977. 62 p. : ill. ; 23 cm. Bibliography: p. 62. [F592.P47] 77-2335 ISBN 0-912494-25-5 pbk. : 3.95
1. Fremont, John Charles, 1813-1890. 2. Ogden, Peter Skene, 1790-1854. 3. Smith, Jedediah Strong, 1799-1831. 4. Walker, Joseph Reddeford, 1798-1876. 5. Great Basin—Discovery and exploration. 6. Explorers—Great Basin—Biography. 7. Indians of North America—Great Basin. I. Title. **BIP**

Ogilvie family.

FARWELL, George, 1911- 919.44'03'20924
Squatter's castle, the story of a pastoral dynasty; life and times of Edward David Stewart Ogilvie, 1814-96. Melbourne, Lansdowne, 1973. 340 p. ill., geneal. tables on end papers, maps, 8 col. plates. 25 cm. Aus Bibliography: p. [338]-340. [CS2009.O33 1973] 74-155194 ISBN 0-7018-0255-3 9.95
1. Ogilvie family. 2. Ogilvie, Edward David Stewart, 1814-1896. I. Title.

Ogilvie, John, 1580?—1615.

MARTYR in Scotland v. 12
the life and time of John Ogilvie. [1st America n ed.] New York, Macmillan [1956] xi, 268p. plates. Bibliography: p. [xi]
1. Ogilvie, John, 1580?—1615. I. Collins, Thomas, 1913-

Ogilvie, William, 1736-1819.

DAVIDSON, John Morrison. 330.1'0922
Concerning four precursors of Henry George and the single tax, as also the land gospel according to Winstanley "the Digger", by J. Morrison Davidson. Port Washington, N.Y., Kennikat Press [1971] 151 p. 21 cm. Half title: Four precursors of Henry George. Reprint of 1899 ed. [HD1313.D2 1971] 77-115317
1. Ogilvie, William, 1736-1819. 2. Spence, Thomas, 1750-1814. 3. Paine, Thomas, 1737-1809. 4. Dove, Patrick Edward, 1815-1873. 5. Winstanley, Gerrard, b. 1609. I. Title. II. Title: Four precursors of Henry George.

Ogilvy, David, 1911-

OGILVY, David, 1911- 659.1'092'4 B
Blood, brains & beer : the autobiography of / David Ogilvy. 1st ed. New York : Atheneum Publishers, 1978. vii, 181 p. ; 22 cm. Includes index. [HF5810.034A32 1978] 77-76541 ISBN 0-689-10809-5 : 7.95
1. Ogilvy, David, 1911- 2. Advertising—Biography. I. Title. **BIP**

OGILVY, David, 1911- 659.112
Confessions of an advertising man. [1st ed.] New York, Atheneum, 1963. 172 p. 24 cm. [HF5810.O34A3] 63-17855
1. Advertising—United States. I. Title. **BIP**

Oglethorpe, Anne Henrietta, b. 1683?

HILL, Patricia Kneas. 942.07'092'2
The Oglethorpe ladies and the Jacobite conspiracies / by Patricia Kneas Hill. Atlanta : Cherokee Pub. Co., 1977. ix, 177 p. : ill. ; 24 cm. Includes index. Bibliography: p. 164-172. [DA483.O36H54] 76-26441 ISBN 0-87797-039-4 : 7.95
1. Oglethorpe, Anne Henrietta, b. 1683? 2. Oglethorpe, Eleanor, d. 1775. 3. Jacobites—Biography. I. Title. **BIP**

Oglethorpe, James Edward, 1696-1785.

ETTINGER, Amos Aschbach, 1901- 975.8'01'0924 B
James Edward Oglethorpe, imperial idealist. [Hamden, Conn.] Archon Books, 1968. xi, 348 p. illus., facsims., fold. map, ports. 22 cm. Reprint of the 1936 ed. Bibliographical footnotes. [F289.033 1968] 68-20378
1. Oglethorpe, James Edward, 1696-1785. 2. Georgia—History—Colonial period, ca. 1600-1775. **BIP**

RADFORD, Ruby Lorraine, 1891- 975.8'02'0924 B
James Edward Oglethorpe; a colony leader, by Ruby Radford and Charles P. Graves. Illustrated by Nathan Goldstein. Champaign, Ill., Garrard Pub. Co. [1968]

64 p. col. illus., port. 24 cm. (Colony leaders) A biography of the man who devoted his life to helping the poor and oppressed in England and whose principal achievement was the founding of the colony of Georgia. [F289.O365] 92 AC 68
1. Oglethorpe, James Edward, 1696-1785. I. Graves, Charles Parlin, 1911- joint author. II. Goldstein, Nathan, illus. III. Title.

SPALDING, Phinizy. 975.8'02'0924 B
Oglethorpe in America / Phinizy Spalding. Chicago : University of Chicago Press, 1977. xi, 207 p., [2] leaves of plates : ill. ; 22 cm. Includes index. Bibliography: p. 191-199. [F289.O367] 76-8092 ISBN 0-226-76846-5 lib.bdg. 12.50
1. Oglethorpe, James Edward, 1696-1785. 2. Statesmen—Georgia—Biography. 3. Georgia—History—Colonial period, ca. 1600-1775. I. Title. **BIP**

Oglethorpe, James Edward, 1696-1785—Juvenile literature.

BLACKBURN, Joyce. 975.8'02'0924 B
James Edward Oglethorpe. [1st ed.] Philadelphia, Lippincott [1970] 144 p. map. 21 cm. A biography of the English founder of the colony of Georgia who was active in politics and penal reform and a supporter of the American Revolution. [F289.O28] 92 75-117245 3.95
1. Oglethorpe, James Edward, 1696-1785—Juvenile literature. I. Title. **BIP**

RADFORD, Ruby Lorraine, 1891- 92 (J)
James Edward Oglethorpe; a colony leader, by Ruby Radford and Charles P. Graves. Illustrated by Nathan Goldstein. Champaign, Ill., Garrard Pub. Co. [1968] 64 p. col. illus., port. 24 cm. (Colony leaders) [F289.O365] 68-11354
1. Oglethorpe, James Edward, 1696-1785—Juvenile literature. I. Graves, Charles Parlin, 1911- joint author.

VAETH, Joseph Gordon, 1921- 975.8'01'0924 B
The man who founded Georgia [by] J. Gordon Vaeth. New York, Crowell-Collier Press [1968] 134 p. illus., facsims., maps, ports. 21 cm. Bibliography: p. [130] A biography of the English gentleman who founded the colony of Georgia in 1733 for settlement by the unemployed and "worthy poor." [F289.O369] 92 68-19026
1. Oglethorpe, James Edward, 1696-1785—Juvenile literature. I. Title.

Ohio — Governors.

PHILLIPS, Hazel Spencer, 1896- 923.2771
Governors of Ohio [by] Hazel Spencer Phillips and Lawrence Jordan Gray. [Lebanon? Ohio] c1952. 61 p. illus. 22 cm. [F490.P47] 52-40966
1. Ohio — Governors. I. Title.

Ohio—Hist.—Civil War.

WHEELER, Kenneth W. 973.7'471'0922
For the Union; Ohio leaders in the Civil War. Ed. by Kenneth W. Wheeler. [Columbus] Ohio State Univ. Pr. [1968] viii, 497p. 22cm. Bibl. refs. [E525.W5] 67-25693 10.00
1. Ohio—Hist.—Civil War. 2. Ohio—Biog. I. Title.
Contents Omitted.

Ohio—Politics and government—1865-1950.

JOHNSON, Tom Loftin, 1854-1911. 977.1'32'040924 B
My story. Edited by Elizabeth J. Hauser. New York, AMS Press [1970] xli, 326 p. illus., ports. 23 cm. Reprint of the 1911 ed. [F496.J69 1970b] 77-127899 ISBN 0-404-03593-0
1. Ohio—Politics and government—1865-1950. 2. Cleveland—Politics and government. I. Title.

JOHNSON, Tom Loftin, 1854-1911. 977.1'32'040924 B
My story. Edited by Elizabeth J. Hauser. Introd. by Melvin G. Holli. Seattle, University of Washington Press [1970, c1911] lvi, 326 p. illus., ports. 23 cm. (Americana library, 18) Includes bibliographical references. [F496.J69 1970] 71-125181
1. Ohio—Politics and government—1865-1950. 2. Cleveland—Politics and government. I. Title.

Ohio. State University, Columbus—Football.

VARE, Robert. 796.33'263'0977157
Buckeye : a study of Coach Woody Hayes and the Ohio State football machine / by Robert Vare. 1st ed. New York : Harper's Magazine Press, [1974] 243 p., [8] leaves of plates : ill. ; 22 cm. [GV958.O35V37 1974] 74-3904 ISBN 0-06-129150-1 : 7.95
1. Ohio. State University, Columbus—Football. 2. Hayes, Wayne Woodrow. 3. Football. I. Title.

Ohrt, Wallace L.

OHRT, Wallace L. 979.5'21
The Rogue I remember / Wallace L. Ohrt ; ill. by George Daly. Seattle : The Mountaineers, 1979. p. cm. [F882.R6O476] 79-17166 ISBN 0-916890-94-5 pbk. : 6.95
1. Ohrt, Wallace L. 2. Rogue River Valley, Or.—Social life and customs. 3. Rogue River Valley, Or.—Biography. I. Title. **BIP**

Okakura, Kakuzo, 1862-1913.

HORIOKA, Yasuko 927.5
The life of Kakuzo, author of The book of tea [Tokio] Hokuseido Pr. [dist. Rutland, Vt., Japan Pubns., c.1963] x, 97p. illus., ports., facsims. 19cm. Bibl. 64-1207 3.75
1. Okakura, Kakuzo, 1862-1913. I. Title.

Oklahoma City (Ship)

DONAHUE, Joseph A. 940.54'59'73
Tin cans and other ships : a war diary, 1941-1945 / by Joseph A. Donahue. North Quincy, Mass. : Christopher Pub. House, c1979. 255 p. : ill. ; 22 cm. [D774.N48D66] 78-74696 ISBN 0-8158-0378-8 : 7.50
1. Niblack (Ship) 2. Donahue, Joseph A. 3. Oklahoma City (Ship) 4. United States. Navy—Biography. 5. World War, 1939-1945—Personal narratives, American. 6. World War, 1939-1945—Naval operations, American. 7. Seamen—United States—Biography. I. Title.

Oklahoma—Governors—Biography.

TERRITORIAL 976.6'04'0922 B
governors of Oklahoma / edited by LeRoy H. Fischer. 1st ed. Oklahoma City : Oklahoma Historical Society, 1975. vii, 150 p. : ill. ; 23 cm. (The Oklahoma series ; v. 1) Includes bibliographical references and index. [F693.T47] 75-15045
1. Oklahoma—Governors—Biography. 2. Oklahoma—Politics and government—To 1907. I. Fischer, LeRoy Henry, 1917- II. Title. III. Series.

Oklahoma—History.

COLCORD, Charles Francis, 1859-1934. 917.8 B
The autobiography of Charles Francis Colcord, 1859-1934. [Tulsa, Okla., C. C. Helmerich?, 1970] 245 p. illus., facsims., col. map, ports. 27 cm. [F700.C6A3] 73-140435
1. Oklahoma—History. 2. Frontier and pioneer life—The West. I. Title.

Okubo, Toshimichi, 1830-1878.

IWATA, Masakazu 923.252
Okubo Toshimichi, the Bismarck of Japan. Berkeley, Univ. of Calif. Pr. [c.]1964. viii, 376p. 25cm. (Pubns. of the Ctr. for Japanese and Korean Studies) Bibl. [DS881.5.O419] 64-25533 7.00
1. Okubo, Toshimichi, 1830-1878. I. Title. II. Title: The Bismarck of Japan. (Series California. University. Center for Japanese and Korean Studies. Publications)

Okuma, Shigenobu, 1838-1922.

LEBRA, Joyce C. 952.03'1'0924 B
Okuma Shigenobu: statesman of Meiji Japan [by] Joyce C. Lebra. Canberra, Australian National University Press, 1973. 195 p. 22 cm. Includes index. Bibliography: p. [174]-181. [DS884.O4L4] 73-81467 ISBN 0-7081-0400-2
1. Okuma, Shigenobu, 1838-1922. 2. Japan—Politics and government—1868-1912. I. Title.
Distributed by International Scholarly Book Service, 12.25.

Ol'ga Aleksandrovna, grand duchess of Russia, 1882-1960.

VORRES, Ian 923.247
The last grand duchess, Her Imperial Highness Grand Duchess Olga Alexandrovna, 1 June 1882-24 November 1960. New York, Scribners [c.1964, 1965] xix, 264p. illus., geneal. tb0)ables, ports. 24cm. [DK254.O4V6] 65-15784 5.95
1. Ol'ga Aleksandrovna, grand duchess of Russia, 1882-1960. I. Title.

Olafsson, Eggert, 1726-1768.

HERMANNSSON, Halldor, 1878-1958. v. 12
Eggert Olafsson, a biographical sketch. Ithaca, N.Y., Cornell University Library, 1925. [New York, Kraus Reprint Corp., 1966] 56 p. illus. (incl. facsims.) plates. 23 cm. (Islandica; an annual relating to Iceland and the Fiske Icelandic collection in Cornell University Library, v. 16) 67-37339
1. Olafsson, Eggert, 1726-1768. I. Title. **BIP**

Olcott, Henry Steel, 1832-1907.

MURPHET, Howard. 212'.52'0924 B
Hammer on the mountain: life of Henry Steel Olcott (1832-1907) Wheaton, Ill., Theosophical Pub. House [1972] xii, 339 p. illus. 23 cm. "H. S. Olcott's works": p. [326]-327. [BP585.O4M8] 72-76427 ISBN 0-8356-0210-9 7.95
1. Olcott, Henry Steel, 1832-1907. I. Title.

Old age.

SCOTT-MAXWELL, Florida Pier, 1884- 301.43'5'0924
The measure of my days / Florida Scott-Maxwell. New York : Penguin Books, 1979, c1968. 150 p. ; 20 cm. Reprint of the 1st ed. published by Knopf, New York. [HQ1061.S36 1979] 78-27682 ISBN 0-14-005164-3 pbk. : 2.50
1. Old age. 2. Aged women—United States—Biography. I. Title. **BIP**

Old Concord Presbyterian Church, Appomattox Co., Va.

CHILTON, Harriett A. 929'.3755'625
Register of Old Concord Presbyterian Church, Appomattox County, Virginia - 1826-1878; baptism 1826-1876, membership 1826-1878, obituary 1829-1854. Transcribed and edited by Harriett A. Chilton and Mitzi Chilton Wilkerson. [Falls Church? Va.] 1973. 51 p. illus. 23 cm. [BX9211.A6O42] 74-160732
1. Old Concord Presbyterian Church, Appomattox Co., Va. 2. Appomattox Co., Va.—Biography. 3. Registers of births, etc.—Appomattox Co., Va. I. Wilkerson, Mitzi Chilton, joint author. II. Title.

Old family.

ORMSBEE, Mary Chalfant, 1912- comp. 929'.2'0973
Letters to Sarah Ann Olds Johnson, written to her by her relatives and friends between 1857 and 1887. [Boulder, Colo., c1972] 222 p. illus. 24 cm. [CS71.J7 1972d] 74-151343
1. Johnson family. 2. Old family. 3. Johnson, Sarah Ann Olds, 1834-1901. I. Johnson, Sarah Ann Olds, 1834-1901. II. Title.

Old Persian inscriptions—Juvenile literature.

SILVERBERG. ROBERT 915.5030924
To the rock of Darius: the story of Henry Rawlinson. [1st ed.] New York. Holt [1966] 218p. illus., map. 21cm. Bibl. [PJ3164.R3S5] 66-8309 3.95 3.59 bds. lib. ed. qRawlinson, Henry Creswicke, bart., Sir 1810-1895--Juvenile literature.
1. Old Persian inscriptions—Juvenile literature. I. Title.

Oldcastle, Sir John, styled Lord Cobham, d. 1417.

FIEHLER, Rudolph. 270.50924 (B)
The strange history of Sir John Oldcastle. [1st ed.] New York, American Press [c1965] 243 p. 21 cm. "Notes on the sources": p. 239-243. [BX4906.O6F5] 65-25021
1. Oldcastle, Sir John, styled Lord Cobham, d. 1417. I. Title.

Oldenbarnevelt, Johan van, 1547-1619.

MOTLEY, John Lothrop, 1814-1877. 949.2'008 S
The life and death of John of Barneveldt, advocate of Holland; with a view of the primary causes and movements of the Thirty Years' War. Netherlands ed. New York, Harper, 1900. [New York, AMS Press, 1973] 3 v. illus. 19 cm. (Motley, John Lothrop, 1814-1877. Works, v. 12-14. 1973.) [DH186.5.M6 1973 vol. 12-14] [DH188.O4] 949.2'03'0924 B 73-8882 ISBN 0-404-04532-4 (v. 1)
1. Oldenbarnevelt, Johan van, 1547-1619. 2. Thirty Years' War, 1618-1648. I. Title. II. Series.

TEX, Jan den. 949.2'03'0924 B
Oldenbarnevelt. [Translated from the Dutch by R. B. Powell] Cambridge [Eng.] University Press, 1973. 2 v. illus. 24 cm. Contents.Contents.—v. 1. 1547-1606.—v. 2. 1606-1619. Bibliography: p. 710-717. [DH188.O4T4813] 73-177937 ISBN 0-521-08429-6 (set) £21.00 ($55.00 U.S.) (set)
1. Oldenbarnevelt, Johan van, 1547-1619.

Oldenburg, Henry.

*OLDENBURG, Henry. 509'.2'4
The correspondence of Henry Oldenburg / edited and translated by A. Rupert Hall & Marie Boas Hall. London : Mansell, 1977. xxiv, 543p. ; 24 cm. Includes index. Contents.Contents: Vol. XI: May 1674-September 1675: Letters 2490-2754. [Q143] ISBN 0-7201-0630-3 : 42.50
1. Oldenburg, Henry. 2. Scientists — Correspondence, reminiscences, etc. I. Hall, A. Rupert. II. Hall, Marie Boas. III. Title.
Distributed by Merrimack Book Service.

Oldfield, Barney, 1878-1946.

NOLAN, William F 1928- 927.9672
Barney Oldfield; the life and times of America's legendary speed king. New York, Putnam [1961] 251p. illus. 22cm. [GV1032.O4N6] 61-12739
1. Oldfield, Barney, 1878-1946. I. Title.

Oldham, Dale.

OLDHAM, Dale. 269'.2'0924 B
Giants along my path; my fifty years in the ministry. Anderson, Ind., Warner Press [1973] 288 p. illus. 21 cm. [BX7027.Z8O4] 73-16413 ISBN 0-87162-165-7 10.00
1. Oldham, Dale. I. Title.
Pbk. 3.95; ISBN 0-87162-162-2.

Oldham, Joseph Houldsworth, 1874-1969.

LEYS, Norman Maclean. 320.9'676'203
By Kenya possessed : the correspondence of Norman Leys and J. H. Oldham, 1918-1926 / edited and with an introd. by John W. Cell. Chicago : University of Chicago Press, 1976. ix, 382 p. : ports. ; 23 cm. (Studies in imperialism) Includes

bibliographical references and index. [DT433.575.L48 1976] 75-27894 ISBN 0-226-09971-7 lib.bdg. : 20.00
1. Oldham, Joseph Houldsworth, 1874-1969. 2. Leys, Norman Maclean. 3. Kenya—Politics and government. I. Oldham, Joseph Houldsworth, 1874-1969. II. Cell, John Whitson. III. Title.

Olds, Ransom Eli, 1864-1950.

MAY, George 338.7'62'920924 B
Smith, 1924-
R. E. Olds, auto industry pioneer / by George S. May. Grand Rapids : Eerdmans, c1977. viii, 458 p. : ill. ; 24 cm. Includes index. Bibliography: p. 407-413. [HD9710.U52Q435] 77-7988 ISBN 0-8028-7028-7 : 9.95
1. Olds, Ransom Eli, 1864-1950. 2. Automobile industry and trade—United States—History. 3. Businessmen—United States—Biography. I. Title.

NIEMEYER, Glenn A. 926.292
The automotive career of Ransom E. Olds. East Lansing, Bur. of Bus. and Economic Res., Graduate Sch. of Bus. Adm., Mich. State Univ. [c.]1963. xiii, 233p. illus., ports., diagrs., tables. 24cm. (MSU bus. studies) Bibl. 63-63708 6.50
1. Olds, Ransom Eli, 1864-1950. 2. Automobile industry and trade—U.S. I. Title. II. Series: Michigan. State University, East Lansing. Bureau of Business and Econimic Research. Business studies BIP

Olds, Sarah E., 1875-1963.

OLDS, Sarah E., 979.3'55'030924 B
1875-1963.
Twenty miles from a match : homesteading in western Nevada / Sarah E. Olds ; foreword by Leslie Zurfluh. Reno : University of Nevada Press, 1978. xiii, 182 p., [4] leaves of plates : ill. ; 21 cm. (A Bristlecone paperback) [F847.W3O47] 78-13766 ISBN 0-87417-052-4: 5.50
1. Olds, Sarah E., 1875-1963. 2. Washoe Co., Nev.—Biography. 3. Pioneers—Nevada—Washoe Co.—Biography. 4. Frontier and pioneer life—Nevada—Washoe Co. I. Title. BIP

*Olender, Terrys T.

*OLENDER, Terrys T. 340.0924
My life in crime. [Rev. ed.] Foreword by J. W. Ehrlich. Los Angeles, Holloway House [c.1961, 1966] 224p. 18cm. (HH125) .75 pap.
I. Title.

Olesha, IUrii Karlovich, 1899-1960—Biography—Addresses, essays, lectures.

OLESHA, IUrii 891.7'8'4209 B
Karlovich, 1899-1960.
No day without a line / Yuri Olesha ; translated & edited by Judson Rosengrant. Ann Arbor : Ardis, c1979. 314 p. ; 24 cm. Translation of Ni dniabez strochki. Includes bibliographical references. [PG3476.O37Z5213 1979] 79-118377 ISBN 0-88233-211-2 pbk. : 7.00
1. Olesha, IUrii Karlovich, 1899-1960—Biography—Addresses, essays, lectures. 2. Authors, Russian—20th century—Biography—Addresses, essays, lectures. I. Title. BIP

Oleynick, Frank.

JORDAN, Pat. 796.32'3'0922 B
Chase the game / Pat Jordan. New York : Dodd, Mead, c1979. 216 p. ; 22 cm. [GV884.A1J67] 78-31848 ISBN 0-396-07632-7 : 10.00
1. Oleynick, Frank. 2. McLeod, Barry. 3. Luckett, Walter. 4. Basketball players—United States—Biography. I. Title. BIP

Olf, Lillian (Browne)

OLF, Lillian 262'.13'0922 B
(Browne) 1880-
Their name is Pius; portraits of five great modern popes [by] Lillian Browne-Olf. Freeport, N.Y., Books for Libraries Press [1970] xv, 382 p. ports. 23 cm. (Essay index reprint series) Reprint of the 1941 ed. Bibliography: p. 371-374. [BX1365.O4 1970] 74-107729
I. Title.

Oliphant, Laurence, 1829-1888—Biography.

OLIPHANT, Margaret 828'.8'09 B
Oliphant Wilson, 1828-1897.
Memoir of the life of Laurence Oliphant and of Alice Oliphant, his wife / Margaret Oliphant W. Oliphant. New York : Arno Press, 1976. p. cm. (The Occult) Reprint of the 1892 ed. published by W. Blackwood, Edinburgh. [PR5112.O8O7 1976] 75-36915 ISBN 0-405-07970-2 : 24.00
1. Oliphant, Laurence, 1829-1888—Biography. I. Title. II. Series: The Occult (New York, 1976-) BIP

Oliphant, Samuel Duncan, 1842-1904.

SMITH, Fred, 1908- 929.2
Samuel Duncan Oliphant, the indomitable campaigner, his Scottish, colonial and American family history with emphasis on his heroic Civil War record. [1st ed.] New York, Exposition Press [1967] 203 p. illus., facsims., map (on lining paper), ports. 21 cm. Includes music. Bibliography: p. [201]-203. [CS71.O468 1967] 67-24269
1. Oliphant, Samuel Duncan, 1842-1904. 2. Oliphant family.

Oliva, Tony, 1941-

OLIVA, Tony, 1941- 796.357'092'4
Tony O! The trials and triumphs of Tony Oliva, by Tony Oliva, with Bob Fowler. New York, Hawthorn Books [1973] x, 199 p. illus. 22 cm. "An Associated Features book." [GV865.O44A37 1973] 72-7782 6.95
1. Oliva, Tony, 1941- 2. Baseball. I. Fowler, Bob. II. Title.

Oliveira Lima, Manuel de, 1867-1928.

OLIVEIRA Lima 016.981'05'0924
Library.
Manoel de Oliveira Lima; catalogue of the exhibit held in the Mullen Library of the Catholic University of America, by R. J. Luke Williams and Elmer Broxson, in cooperation with the Special Services Department of the Catholic University of America Libraries. [Washington, 1968] 15 p. port. 21 cm. Cover title. [F2537.O488] 72-187726
1. Oliveira Lima, Manuel de, 1867-1928. I. Williams, Robert Joseph Luke, 1942- II. Broxson, Elmer.

Oliver, Alfred Richard.

OLIVER, Alfred Richard. 928.4
1912-
Charles Nodier, pilot of romanticism. [Syracuse, N.Y.] Syracuse Univ. Pr. [c.] 1964. xi, 276 p. illus., ports. 22cm. Bibl. [PQ2376.N6Z66] 64-8670 5.95
I. Nodier, Charles, 1780-1844. II. Title.

Oliver, Joseph, 1885-1968.

WILLIAMS, Martin T 927.8
King Oliver, by Martin Williams. New York, Barnes [1961] 80 p. group ports. 21 cm. (A Perpetua book) Kings of jazz, P-4036. [ML419] 60-16826
1. Oliver, Joseph, 1885-1968. I. Title. BIP

Oliver, Robert, 1757?-1834.

BRUCHEY, Stuart Weems. 382
Robert Oliver, merchant of Baltimore, 1783-1819. Baltimore, Johns Hopkins Press, 1956. 411p. port. 23cm. (The Johns Hopkins University studies in historical and political science, ser. 74, no. 1) Bibliography: p. 399-405. [HF3163.B2O42] 56-11638
1. Oliver, Robert, 1757?-1834. 2. Baltimore—Comm. I. Title. II. Series. BIP

BRUCHEY, Stuart 382'.092'4 B
Weems.
Robert Oliver, merchant of Baltimore, 1783-1819 / Stuart Weems Bruchey. New York : Arno Press, 1979, c1956. 411 p. : port. ; 24 cm. (Small business enterprise in America) Reprint of the ed. published by Johns Hopkins Press, Baltimore, which was issued as ser. 74, no. 1, of the Johns Hopkins University studies in historical and political science. Includes index. Bibliography: p. 399-405. [HF3163.B2O42 1979] 78-18954 ISBN 0-405-11458-3 : 28.00
1. Oliver, Robert, 1757?-1834. 2. Baltimore—Commerce—History. 3. Merchants—Baltimore—Biography. I. Title. II. Series. III. Series: Johns Hopkins University. Studies in historical and political science; ser. 74, no. 1. BIP

Oliver, Susan Lawrence,

OLIVER, Susan Lawrence, 920.7
1881-
Reminiscences of a Bostonian. [Boston? 1952] 88p. 24cm. [CT275.O47A3] 52-68595
I. Title.

Olivi, Pierre Jean, 1248 or 9-1298.

BURR, David, 1934- 271'.3'024 B
The persecution of Peter Olivi / David Burr. Philadelphia : American Philosophical Society, 1976. 98 p. ; 30 cm. (Transactions of the American Philosophical Society ; new ser., v. 66, pt. 5 ISSN 0065-9746s) Includes index.IBibliography: p. 93-96.I[BX4705.O48543B87].76-24254 ISBN 0-87169-665-7 pbk. : 6.00
1. Olivi, Pierre Jean, 1248 or 9-1298. 2. Franciscans in France—Biography. I. Title. II. Series: American Philosophical Society, Philadelphia. Transactions ; new ser., v. 66, pt. 5. BIP

Olivier, Laurence Kerr, Baron Olivier, 1907-

COTTRELL, John. 791'.092'4 B
Laurence Olivier / by John Cottrell. Englewood Cliffs, N.J. : Prentice-Hall, [1975] 433 p., [16] leaves of plates : ill. ; 24 cm. Includes index. Bibliography: p. 412-416. [PN2598.O55C6] 75-4768 ISBN 0-13-526152-X : 10.00
1. Olivier, Laurence Kerr, Baron Olivier, 1907-

DANIELS, Robert L. 791'.092'4 B
Laurence Olivier, theater and cinema / Robert L. Daniels. South Brunswick [N.J.] : A. S. Barnes ; London : T. Yoseloff, 1979, c1980. p. cm. Includes index. Filmography: p. [PN2598.O55D28] 78-75346 ISBN 0-498-02287-0 : 19.95
1. Olivier, Laurence Kerr, Baron Olivier, 1907- 2. Actors—Great Britain—Biography. I. Title.

FAIRWEATHER, Virginia. 791'.0924
Olivier: An informal portrait. [1st American ed.] New York, Coward-McCann [1969] 183 p. illus., port. 22 cm. London ed. (Calder & Boyars) has title: Cry God for Larry. [PN2598.O55F3 1969b] 77-96775 4.95
1. Olivier, Laurence Kerr, Baron Olivier, 1907- I. Title.

GOURLAY, Logan. 791'.092'4
Olivier, edited by Logan Gourlay. New York, Stein and Day [1974, c1973] 208 p. illus. 24 cm. Theatre and film chronology: p. 196-208. [PN2598.O55G6 1974] 73-88745 ISBN 0-8128-1648-X 8.95
1. Olivier, Laurence Kerr, Baron Olivier, 1907- 2. Actors—England—Correspondence, reminiscences, etc.

HIRSCH, Foster. 791.43'028'0924 B
Laurence Olivier / Foster Hirsch. Boston : Twayne Publishers, 1979. 190 p. : ill. ; 21 cm. (Twayne's theatrical arts series) Includes index. Bibliography: p. 171-173. [PN2598.O55H5] 78-21675 ISBN 0-8057-9260-0 : 10.95
1. Olivier, Laurence Kerr, Baron Olivier, 1907- 2. Shakespeare, William, 1564-1616—Film adaptations. 3. Actors—Great Britain—Biography. BIP

LASKY, Jesse Lenard, 791'.092'2 B
1910-
Love scene : the story of Laurence Olivier and Vivien Leigh / Jesse Lasky, Jr., with Pat Silver. 1st U.S. ed. New York : Crowell, c1978. 256 p. : ill. ; 25 cm. Includes index. Bibliography: p. 252-253. [PN2598.O55L3 1978] 78-4765 10.95
1. Olivier, Laurence Kerr, Baron Olivier, 1907- 2. Leigh, Vivien, 1913-1967. 3. Actors—Great Britain—Biography. I. Silver, Pat, joint author. II. Title. BIP

Olivieri, Umberto, 1884-1973.

ABELOE, William N. 282'.092'4 B
To the top of the mountain : the life of Father Umberto Olivieri, "Padre of the Otomis" / William N. Abeloe ; with a foreword by Miguel Dario Cardinal Miranda. 1st ed. Hicksville, N.Y. : Exposition Press, c1976. 160 p., [11] leaves of plates : ill. ; 22 cm. [BX4705.O48545A63] 76-7187 ISBN 0-682-48558-6 : 8.00
1. Olivieri, Umberto, 1884-1973. 2. Catholic Church—Clergy—Biography. 3. Clergy—United States—Biography. I. Title. BIP

Ollveira Salazar, Antonio de, 1889-

GARNIER, Christine, 923.2469
1915-
Salazar, an intimate portrait. Translated from the French. New York, Farrar, Straus & Young [1954] 217p. illus. 21cm. Cover title: Salazar in Portugal. Translation of Vacances avec Salazar. [DP676.O5G313] 54-11069
1. Ollveira Salazar, Antonio de, 1889- I. Title. II. Title: Salazar in Portugal.

Olmstead, Alan H.

OLMSTEAD, Alan H. 301.43'5
Threshold : the first days of retirement : recording some of the disappointments, pleasures, and reflections of a new traveler into that state of joblessness sometimes known as the Golden Age / Alan H. Olmstead. 1st ed. New York : Harper & Row, [1975] 214 p. ; 21 cm. [HQ1062.O45 1975] 75-6351 ISBN 0-06-013271-X : 8.95
1. Olmstead, Alan H. 2. Retirement—Biography. I. Title.

OLMSTEAD, Alan H. 301.43'5
Threshold : the first days of retirement : recording some of the disappointments, pleasures, and reflections of a new traveler into that state of joblessness sometimes known as the Golden Age / Alan H. Olmstead. Boston : G. K. Hall, 1978, c1975. 399 p. ; 24 cm. "Published in large print." [HQ1062.045 1978] 77-15470 ISBN 0-8161-6531-9 lib.bdg. : 11.95
1. Olmstead, Alan H. 2. Retirement—Biography. I. Title.

Olmsted, Frederick Law,

OLMSTED, Frederick Law, 712'.08
1822-1903.
Frederick Law Olmsted, landscape architect, 1822-1903. Edited by Frederick Law Olmsted, Jr., and Theodora Kimball. New York, B. Blom, 1970. 131, xviii, 575 p. illus., facsim., 2 fold. maps (1 col.) 24 cm. Reprint of the 1922-28 ed. Includes bibliographies. [SB470.O5A53] 68-57756
I. Olmsted, Frederick Law, 1870-1957, ed. II. Hubbard, Theodora (Kimball), Mrs., 1887-1935, ed. BIP

Olmsted, Frederick Law, 1822-1903.

FABOS, Julius Gy. 712'.0924 B
Frederick Law Olmsted, Sr.; founder of landscape architecture in America [by] Julius Gy. Fabos, Gordon T. Milde, & V. Michael Weinmayr. [Amherst] University of Massachusetts Press, 1968. 114 p. illus. (part fold.), maps, plans, ports. 26 cm. [SB470.O5F32] 68-19670 12.00
1. Olmsted, Frederick Law, 1822-1903. 2. Parks—United States. I. Milde, Gordon T., joint author. II. Weinmayr, V. Michael, joint author.

OLMSTED, Frederick Law, 712'.08 S
1822-1903.
The formative years, 1822 to 1852 / Charles Capen McLaughlin, editor, Charles E. Beveridge, associate editor. Baltimore :

Johns Hopkins University Press, c1977. xx, 423 p. : ill. ; 25 cm. (The Papers of Frederick Law Olmstead ; v. 1) Includes bibliographical references and indexes. [SB470.O5A2 1977 vol. 1] 712'.08 76-47378 ISBN 0-8018-1798-6 : 20.00
1. Olmsted, Frederick Law, 1822-1903. 2. Landscape architects—United States—Correspondence. 3. Landscape architects—United States—Biography. I. Title.

OLMSTED, Frederick Law, 1822-1903. 712'.08
Frederick Law Olmsted, landscape architect, 1822-1903. Edited by Frederick Law Olmsted, Jr., and Theodora Kimball. New York, B. Blom, 1970. 131, xviii, 575 p. illus., facsim., 2 fold. maps (1 col.) 24 cm. Reprint of the 1922-28 ed. Includes bibliographies. [SB470.O5A53] 68-57756
I. Olmsted, Frederick Law, 1870-1957, ed. II. Hubbard, Theodora (Kimball), Mrs., 1887-1935, ed. BIP

STEVENSON, Elizabeth, 1919- 712'.092'4 B
Park maker : a life of Frederick Law Olmstead / by Elizabeth Stevenson. New York : Macmillan, c1977. xxv, 484 p., [8] leaves of plates : ill. ; 25 cm. Includes index. Bibliography: p. 453-469. [SB470.O5S73] 76-52942 ISBN 0-02-614440-9 : 17.95
1. Olmsted, Frederick Law, 1822-1903. 2. Landscape architects—United States—Biography. I. Title.

Olmsted, Frederick Law, 1822-1903—Collected works.

OLMSTED, Frederick Law, 1822-1903. 712'.08
The papers of Frederick Law Olmstead / Charles Capen McLaughlin, editor, Charles E. Beveridge, associate editor. Baltimore : Johns Hopkins University Press, c1977- v. : ill. ; 25 cm. Contents.Contents.—v. 1. The formative years, 1822 to 1852. Includes bibliographical references and index. [SB470.O5A2 1977] 77-741 ISBN 0-8018-1798-6 (v.1) : 20.00
1. Olmsted, Frederick Law, 1822-1903—Collected works. 2. Landscape architects—United States—Correspondence—collected works. 3. Landscape architects—United States—Biography—Collected works.

Olmsted, Frederick Law, 1822-1903—Juvenile literature.

JOHNSTON, Johanna. 712'.092'4 B
Frederick Law Olmsted : partner with Nature / Johanna Johnston. New York : Dodd, Mead, [1975] 125 p. ; 24 cm. Includes index. Bibliography: p. 121-122. A biography of the self-taught landscape architect who designed many large park systems, including the first large city park in America, Central Park in New York. [SB470.O5J63] 92 74-25519 ISBN 0-396-07079-5 : 4.95
1. Olmsted, Frederick Law, 1822-1903—Juvenile literature. 2. Parks—United States—Juvenile literature. 3. Landscape architecture—United States—Juvenile literature. I. Title. BIP

NOBLE, Iris. 712'.092'4 B
Frederick Law Olmsted, park designer. New York, J. Messner [1974] 190 p. 21 cm. Bibliography: p. 185-186. A biography of the nineteenth-century park and city planner and conservationist who designed New York's Central Park, among countless others, and was instrumental in the creation of the National Park Service. [SB470.O5N62] 92 74-7585 ISBN 0-671-32675-9 5.95
1. Olmsted, Frederick Law, 1822-1903—Juvenile literature. 2. Parks—United States—History—Juvenile literature. 3. Landscape architecture—United States—History—Juvenile literature. I. Title.
Library binding; 5.29, ISBN 0-671-3267-7.

Olney, Richard, 1835-1917.

JAMES, Henry, 1879-1947. 973.8'7'0924
Richard Olney and his public service. With documents, including unpublished diplomatic correspondence. New York, Da Capo Press, 1971 [c1923] xi, 335 p. illus., map, ports. 24 cm. (The American scene: comments and commentators) "List of published articles about Olney and by Olney": p. [319]-323. [E664.O45J2 1971] 70-87445 ISBN 0-306-71516-3
1. Olney, Richard, 1835-1917. 2. U.S.—Foreign relations—1901-1909. 3. Venezuela—Boundaries—Guyana. 4. Guyana—Boundaries—Venezuela. I. Title.

Olomu, Nana, 1852?-1916.

IKIME, Obaro. 966.9'3'030924 B
Merchant prince of the Niger delta; the rise & fall of Nana Olomu, last governor of the Benin River. New York, Africana Pub. Corp. [1969, c1968] xiii, 218 p. illus., maps. 23 cm. Bibliography: p. 208-210. [DT515.6.O4138 1969] 72-80852 8.95
1. Olomu, Nana, 1852?-1916. 2. Benin, Nigeria (Province)—History. I. Title.

Olsen, Viggo B.

OLSEN, Viggo B. 954.9'205
Daktar diplomat in Bangladesh, by Viggo B. Olsen with Jeanette Lockerbie. Chicago, Moody Press [1973] 352 p. illus. 24 cm. Includes bibliographical references. [DS395.5.O45] 72-95021 ISBN 0-8024-1745-0 5.95
1. Olsen, Viggo B. 2. Bangladesh—History—Revolution, 1971—Medical and sanitary affairs. 3. Bangladesh—History—Revolution, 1971—Personal narratives. I. Lockerbie, Jeanette W., joint author. II. Title.

Olson, Bruce.

OLSON, Bruce. 266'.023'0987
Bruchko by Bruce Olson. Carol Stream, Ill. : Creation House, 1978. 208p. ; 18 cm. First ed. published in 1973 under title: For this cross I'll Kill you [F2319.2M6044 1978] 78-107540 ISBN 0-88419-133-8 pbk. : 1.95
1. Olson, Bruce. 2. Motilon Indians — Missions. 3. Yuko Indians — Missions. 4. Indians of South America — Venezuela — Missions. 5. Missionaries — Venezuela — Biography. 6. Missionaries — United States — Biography. I. Title. BIP

Olson, Charles, 1910-1970—Biography—Last years and death.

BOER, Charles, 1939- 818'.5'409
Charles Olson in Connecticut / Charles Boer. 1st ed. Chicago : Swallow Press, c1975. 156 p., [2] leaves of plates : ports. ; 23 cm. [PS3529.L655Z57] 74-19869 ISBN 0-8040-0649-0 : 7.95
1. Olson, Charles, 1910-1970—Biography—Last years and death. I. Title. BIP

Olson, David C. B., 1904-

OLSON, David C. B., 1904- 977.4'9'040924
Life on the upper Michigan frontier / by David C. B. Olson. Boston : Branden Press, [1974] 307 p. : ill. (on lining papers) ; 23 cm. Autobiographical. [F572.N8O47] 74-76304 ISBN 0-8283-1544-2 : 8.95
1. Olson, David C. B., 1904- 2. Frontier and pioneer life—Michigan, Northern Peninsula. 3. Michigan, Northern Peninsula—History. I. Title. BIP

Olson, Lois Ellen, 1941-

OLSON, Lois Ellen, 1941- 287'.6'0924 B
Meeting Him in the wilderness : a true story of adventure and faith / Lois Ellen Olson. 1st ed. Garden City, N.Y. : Doubleday, 1980. p. cm. "A Doubleday-Galilee original." [BX8495.O47A35] 79-7504 ISBN 0-385-15132-2 : 9.95
1. Olson, Lois Ellen, 1941- 2. Olson, Tom. 3. Methodist Church—United States—Biography. I. Title. BIP

Olson, Tom.

OLSON, Lois Ellen, 1941- 287'.6'0924 B
Meeting Him in the wilderness : a true story of adventure and faith / Lois Ellen Olson. 1st ed. Garden City, N.Y. : Doubleday, 1980. p. cm. "A Doubleday-Galilee original." [BX8495.O47A35] 79-7504 ISBN 0-385-15132-2 : 9.95
1. Olson, Lois Ellen, 1941- 2. Olson, Tom. 3. Methodist Church—United States—Biography. I. Title. BIP

Olsson, Olof, 1841-1900.

LINDQUIST, Emory Kempton, 1908- 978.1'55
Vision for a valley; Olof Olsson and the early history of Lindsborg, by Emory Lindquist. Rock Island, Ill., Augustana Historical Society, 1970. xiii, 138 p. illus., facsim., ports. 25 cm. (Augustana Historical Society. Publication no. 22) Includes bibliographical references. [F536.A96 no. 22] 77-142012 4.95
1. Olsson, Olof, 1841-1900. 2. Lindsborg, Kan.—History. I. Title. II. Series: Augustana Historical Society, Rock Island, Ill. Publications, no. 22

Olympic games—Biography.

LAKLAN, Carli. 796.4'8
Olympic champions: why they win. New York, Funk & Wagnalls [1968] 168 p. illus., ports. 25 cm. [GV721.5.L3] 68-21128 4.95
1. Olympic games—Biography. I. Title.

Olympic games—History—Juvenile literature.

WALSH, John Evangelist, 1924- 796.4'8'09
The Summer Olympics / by John Walsh. 4th ed., rev. ed. / rev. by Frank Litsky. New York : Watts, 1979. 88 p. : ill. ; 23 cm. (A First book) A revision of part of the author's The first book of the Olympic games. Includes bibliographical references and index. Presents a history of the summer Olympic Games, including brief sketches of 16 outstanding competitors, a tally of medals won by each country, and track and field records from 1896 through 1976. [GV721.5.W262 1979] 78-23777 ISBN 0-531-02935-2 : 5.90
1. Olympic games—History—Juvenile literature. 2. Athletes—Biography—Juvenile literature. I. Litsky, Frank. II. Walsh, John Evangelist, 1927- The first book of the Olympic games. III. Title.

Olympic games (Winter)—History—Juvenile literature.

LITSKY, Frank. 796.9'8
The winter Olympics / by Frank Litsky. New York : F. Watts, 1979. 87 p. : ill. ; 22 cm. (A First book) Includes index. Bibliography: p. 84. Explores the origins of the Winter Olympics, recaps the games from 1924-1976, and presents profiles of some of the athletes participating in these games. [GV841.5.L55] 79-10600 ISBN 0-531-02946-8 : 5.90
1. Olympic games (Winter)—History—Juvenile literature. 2. Athletes—Biography—Juvenile literature. I. Title. BIP

Omar Khayyam—Contemporary Iran.

ROTHFIELD, Otto, 1876-1932. 891'.55'11
Umar Khayyam and his age, by Otto Rothfeld. [Folcroft, Pa.] Folcroft Library Editions, 1974 [c1922] iii, 89 p. 24 cm. Reprint of the ed. published by Simpkin, Marshall, Hamilton, Kent, London. [PK6524.R6 1974] 74-11126 ISBN 0-8414-7309-9 (lib. bdg.)
1. Omar Khayyam—Contemporary Iran. I. Title.

Omar Khayyam—Religion and ethics.

SAKLATWALLA, Jamshedji Edulji. 891'.55'11 B
Omar Khayyam as a mystic, by J. E. Saklatwalla. [Folcroft, Pa.] Folcroft Library Editions, 1974. p. cm. Reprint of the 1928 ed. published by the British India Press, Bombay, which was issued as no. 10 of Dorab J. Saklatwalla memorial series. [PK6525.S28 1974] 74-9971 6.50
1. Omar Khayyam—Religion and ethics. I. Title. II. Series: Dorab Saklatwalla memorial series, no. 10. BIP

Omarr, Sydney.

BROWNING, Norma Lee. 133.5'092'4 B
Omarr : astrology and the man / Norma Lee Browning. 1st ed. Garden City, N.Y. : Doubleday, 1977. 311 p. ; 22 cm. [BF1708.1.B76] 73-11628 ISBN 0-385-04443-7 : 8.95
1. Omarr, Sydney. 2. Astrology. BIP

Omohundro, John Burwell, 1846-1880.

LOGAN, Herschel C., 1901- 923.973
Buckskin and satin; the life of Texas Jack (J. B. Omohundro) buckskin clad scout, Indian fighter, plainsman, cowboy, hunter, guide, and actor, and his wife, Mlle. Morlacchi, premiere danseuse in satin slippers. With a foreword by Paul I. Wellman. [1st ed.] Harrisburg, Pa., Stackpole Co. [1954] 218 p. illus. 23 cm. Includes bibliography. [F594.O5L6] 54-11498
1. Omohundro, John Burwell, 1846-1880. 2. Morlacchi, Giuseppina, 1846-1886. I. Title.

Onassis, Aristotle Socrates, 1906-1975.

ARISTOTLE Onassis 387.5'092'4 B
/ by Nicholas Fraser ... [et al.]. 1st ed. Philadelphia : Lippincott, c1977. x, 372 p., [16] leaves of plates : ill. ; 24 cm. Includes index. Bibliography: p. 361-363. [HE569.O5A74] 77-24417 ISBN 0-397-01218-7 : 12.50
1. Onassis, Aristotle Socrates, 1906-1975. 2. Merchant marine—Biography. I. Fraser, Nicholas, 1948 BIP

BRADY, Frank, 1934- 387.5'092'4 B
Onassis, an extravagant life / Frank Brady. Englewood Cliffs, N.J. : Prentice-Hall, c1977. 218 p., [8] leaves of plates : ill. ; 24 cm. Includes index. [HE569.O5B7] 77-24418 ISBN 0-13-634378-3 : 12.50
1. Onassis, Aristotle Socrates, 1906-1975. 2. Merchant marine—Biography. I. Title.

CAFARAILIS, Christian. 387.5'092'4
The fabulous Onassis: his life and loves, by Christian Cafarakis, with Jacques Harucy. Tr. from French by John Minhan. [New York,] [Pocket Books] [1973, c1972] 158 p. 18 cm. [HE569.O5C313] 73-188186 ISBN 0-671-78272-X 1.25 (pbk)
1. Onassis, Aristotle Socrates, 1906-

FRISCHAUER, Willi, 1906- 387.5'0924 B
Onassis. [1st ed.] New York, Meredith Press [1968] v, 277 p. illus. 24 cm. Bibliography: p. 269. [HE569.O5F7 1968b] 68-19027 6.95
1. Onassis, Aristotle Socrates, 1906-

JOESTEN, Jaochim, 1907- 923.382
Onassis, a biography. New York, Abelard [1964, c.1963] 192p. 22cm. 63-12464 3.95
1. Onassis, Aristotle Socrates, 1906- I. Title.

LILLY, Doris. 387.5'0922 B
Those fabulous Greeks: Onassis, Niarchos, and Livanos. [1st ed.] New York, Cowles Book Co. [1970] ix, 373 p. illus., ports. 22 cm. Bibliography: p. 365-366. [HE569.A2L5] 72-90061 7.95
1. Onassis, Aristotle Socrates, 1906- 2. Niarchos, Stavros. 3. Livanos, Stavros George, 1890-1963. I. Title.

Onassis, Jacqueline Kennedy, 1929-

BIRMINGHAM, Stephen. 973.922'092'4 B
Jacqueline Bouvier Kennedy Onassis / by Stephen Birmingham. New York : Grossett & Dunlap, 1978. [10], 242 p., [18] leaves of plates : ports. ; 24 cm. Includes index. Bibliography: 8th prelim. page. [CT275.O552B57] 77-87799 ISBN 0-448-14306-2 : 12.95

1. Onassis, Jacqueline Kennedy, 1929- 2. United States—Biography. BIP

*DAVID, Lester. 973.922'092'4
Jackie and Ari [by] Lester David [and] Jhan Robbins. New York, Pocket Books [1976] 190 p. illus. 18 cm. [CT275] ISBN 0-671-80383-2 1.95 (pbk.)
1. Onassis, Jacqueline Kennedy, 1929- 2. Onassis, Aristotle, 1905-1975. I. Robbins, Jhan, joint author II. Title.

DAVID, Lester. 387.5'092'4 B
Jackie and Ari / Lester David and Jhan Robbins. New York : Pocket Books, 1976. 190 p., [8] leaves of plates : ill. ; 18 cm. [CT275.O552D38] 76-354015 ISBN 0-671-80383-2 : 1.95
1. Onassis, Jacqueline Kennedy, 1929- 2. Onassis, Aristotle Socrates, 1906-1975. I. Robbins, Jhan, joint author. II. Title.

FARNUM, Henry 973.922'092'2 B Merritt.
Jackie, with love (We, the people of Camelot). New York, Farnum Films [1973] 94 p. 23 cm. [CT275.O552F37] 73-181291
1. Onassis, Jacqueline Kennedy, 1929- 2. Kennedy, John Fitzgerald, Pres. U.S., 1917-1963. I. Title. BIP

FRISHAUER, Willi, 973.922'092'4 B 1906-
Jackie / [by] Willi Frischauer. London : Joseph, 1976. 255 p., [8] p. of plates : ill., ports. ; 23 cm. Bibliography: p. 253-[255] [CT275.O552F74 1976] 77-354598 ISBN 0-7181-1545-7 : £4.95
1. Onassis, Jacqueline Kennedy, 1929- 2. Presidents—United States—Wives—Biography. 3. United States—Biography. I. Title.

GALLAGHER, Mary 973.922'0924 Barelli.
My life with Jacqueline Kennedy. Edited by Frances Spatz Leighton. New York, D. McKay Co. [1969] x, 396 p. illus., ports. 22 cm. [E843.K4G3] 77-97224 7.95
1. Onassis, Jacqueline Kennedy, 1929- I. Title.

GUTHRIE, Lee. 973.922'092'4 B
Jackie : the price of the pedestal / by Lee Guthrie. New York : Drake Publishers, 1978. p. cm. Includes index. [CT275.O552G84] 78-3212 ISBN 0-8473-1801-X : 10.95
1. Onassis, Jacqueline Kennedy, 1929- 2. United States—Biography. BIP

KELLEY, Kitty. 973.922'092'4 B
Jackie Oh! / By Kitty Kelley ; with photos. by Ron Galella. 1st ed. Secaucus, N.J. : L. Stuart, c1978. 352 p., [16] leaves of plates : ill. ; 24 cm. Includes index. Bibliography: p. 343-345. [E843.K4K44 1978] 78-14373 ISBN 0-8184-0265-2 : 12.00
1. Onassis, Jacqueline Kennedy, 1929- 2. Kennedy, John Fitzgerald, Pres. U.S., 1917-1963. 3. Presidents—United States—Wives—Biography. 4. Presidents—United States—Biography. I. Title. BIP

KRAMER, Freda. 973.922'092'4 B
Jackie / Freda Kramer. New York : Award Books, 1975. 202 p. : ill. ; 18 cm. Bibliography: p. 202. [CT275.O552K7] 75-315892 pbk. : 1.50
1. Onassis, Jacqueline Kennedy, 1929- I. Title.

MALKUS, Alida Sims, 1895- 92
The story of Jacqueline Kennedy. Illustrated by Michael Lowenbein. Cover portrait by Earl Mayan. New York, Grosset & Dunlap [1967] viii, 179 p. illus., ports. 22 cm. (Signature books) Biography of the wife of the youngest American President, whose poise and good looks ushered in a new era of youth and style to the White House. [E843.K4M3] AC 67
1. Onassis, Jacqueline Kennedy, 1929- I. Lowenbein, Michael, illus. II. Title.

MOORE, Marcia. 133.5'48
An astroanalysis of Jacqueline Onassis [by] Marcia Moore [and] Mark Douglas. [1st ed.] York, Me., Arcane Publications [1970] xvi, 336 p. illus. 24 cm. [BF1728.O5M6 1970] 78-129250 6.95
1. Onassis, Jacqueline Kennedy, 1929- 2. Astrology. I. Douglas, Mark, joint author. II. Title.

ONASSIS, 914'.04'550924 Jacqueline Kennedy, 1929-
One special summer / written and illustrated by Jacqueline and Lee Bouvier. New York : Delacorte Press, [1974] [63] p. : ill. ; 34 cm. "An Eleanor Friede book." [CT275.O552A36] 74-193210 ISBN 0-440-06037-0 : 7.95.
1. Onassis, Jacqueline Kennedy, 1929- 2. Radziwill, Lee Bouvier, 1933- 3. Europe—Description and travel—1945- I. Radziwill, Lee Bouvier, 1933- joint author. II. Title.

THAYER, Mary Van 973.922'0924 B Rensselaer.
Jacqueline Kennedy, the White House years. [1st ed.] Boston, Little, Brown [1971] xx, 362 p. illus., facsims., ports. 24 cm. [E843.K4T53 1971] 78-121429 7.95
1. Onassis, Jacqueline Kennedy, 1929- I. Title.

Onassis, Jacqueline Kennedy, 1929-

BIRMINGHAM, 973.922'092'4 [B] Stephen.
Jacqueline Baurier Kennedy Onassis / by Stephen Birmingham. New York : Pocket Book, 1978, c1977. x.,262p., [16] leaves of plates : ports. ; 18 cm. Includes index. [CT275.O552B57] ISBN 0-671-82862-2 pbk. : 2.50
1. Onassis, Jacqueline Kennedy, 1929- 2. United States — Biography. I. Title.
L.C. card no. for 1978 Grosset & Dunlap ed.:77-87799.

Onassis, Jacqueline Kennedy, 1929- —Juvenile literature.

MARTIN, Patricia 973.922'0924 B Miles.
Jacqueline Kennedy Onassis. Illustrated by Paul Frame. New York, Putnam [1969] 62 p. illus. (part col.) 23 cm. (A See and read beginning to read biography) A simple biography of the woman who was married to the thirty-fifth President of the United States. [CT275.O552M3 1969] 92 69-11474 2.68
1. Onassis, Jacqueline Kennedy, 1929- — Juvenile literature. I. Frame, Paul, 1913- illus. II. Title.

Onassis, Jacqueline Kennedy, 1929- —Portraits, caricatures, etc.

GALELLA, Ron. 973.922'092'4 B
Jacqueline. [New York] Sheed and Ward [1974] 200 p. illus. ports. 29 cm. [CT275.O552G34] 74-1535 ISBN 0-8362-0573-1 12.95
1. Onassis, Jacqueline Kennedy, 1929- — Portraits, caricatures, etc. I. Title.

Oneida, ltd.

NOYES, Pierrepont Burt, 926.7 1870-
A goodly heritage. New York, Rinehart [1958] 275 p. illus. 22 cm. Autobiography. [HD9536.U54O65] 58-7314
1. Oneida, ltd. I. Title.

*Ongaro, A. Cremonini

*ONGARO, A. Cremonini 922.22
Saint Pancratius. Illus. by G. de Luca. Boston, Daughters of St. Paul, c.1964. 28p. col. illus. 21cm. (St. Paul eds.) .50;.35 pap., *I. Title.*

Onon, Urgungge.

ONON, Urgungge. 915.1'7'034'0924
My childhood in Mongolia [by] Urgunge Onon. London, Oxford University Press, 1972. 112 p. illus. 23 cm. [CT1828.O56A35] 73-161145 ISBN 0-19-917022-3 £1.25
1. Onon, Urgungge. 2. Mongolia—Social life and customs. I. Title. BIP

ONON, Urgungge. 915.1'7'034'0924
My childhood in Mongolia [by] Urgunge Onon. London, Oxford University Press, 1972 i.e.1973] 112 p. illus. 23 cm. [CT1828.O56A35] 73-161145 ISBN 0-19-917022-3 4.00
1. Onon, Urgungge. 2. Mongolia—Social life and customs. I. Title.
Distributed by Oxford University Press N.Y.

Ontario—Biography.

SMITH, William, 971.3'03'0922 1859-1932.
Political leaders of upper Canada. Freeport, N.Y., Books for Libraries Press [1968] xxxii, 292 p. map, ports. 22 cm. (Essay index reprint series) Reprint of the 1931 ed. Contents.Contents.—John Graves Simcoe.—Robert Gourlay.—John Beverley Robinson.—William Lyon Mackenzie.—Sir Francis Bond Head.—Bishop Strachan.—Egerton Ryerson.—Sir George Arthur.—Durham's administration.—Reception of the Durham report in Canada. [F1058.S64 1968] 68-26475
1. Ontario—Biography. 2. Ontario—Politics and government. I. Title. BIP

WISMER, Cathy. 917.13'03 B
Faces of the old north. Toronto, New York, McGraw-Hill Ryerson [1974] 133 p. illus. 25 cm. [F1056.8.W6] 74-175956 ISBN 0-07-077774-8 8.95
1. Ontario—Biography. 2. Ontario—Social life and customs. I. Title.

Ontario—Social life and customs.

HAIGHT, 917.13'03'20924 B Canniff, 1825-1901.
Country life in Canada, with a new introduction by Arthur R. M. Lower and a full index appended. Belleville, Ont., Mika Silk Screening, 1971. ii, 303, 7 p. illus. 23 cm. (Canadiana reprint series, no. 2) Facsimile reprint of 1885 ed. published by Hunter, Rose & Co., Toronto. Includes bibliographical references. [F1057.H16 1971] 72-184198
1. Ontario—Social life and customs. 2. Frontier and pioneer life—Ontario. I. Title. II. Series.

Open plan schools.

HERSHEY, Myrliss, 1928- 372.1'3
Teacher was a white witch. Philadelphia, Westminster Press [1973] 108 p. 20 cm. Bibliography: p. 105-108. [LB1029.O6H47] 72-12981 ISBN 0-664-20963-7 5.00
1. Open plan schools. 2. School integration—United States. 3. Teaching. I. Title.

Open spaces—United States.

HECKSCHER, August, 309.2'62'0973 1913-
Open spaces : the life of American cities / by August Heckscher, with Phyllis Robinson ; maps by Dyck Fledderus. 1st ed. New York : Harper & Row, c1977. x, 386 p. : ill. ; 24 cm. "A Twentieth Century Fund essay." Includes bibliographical references and index. [HT167.H38 1977] 76-12064 ISBN 0-06-011801-6 : 20.00 ISBN 0-06-011804-0 pbk. : 8.95 6.95
1. Open spaces—United States. 2. City planning—United States. 3. Urban renewal—United States. I. Robinson, Phyllis, joint author. II. Title. BIP

Open Theater.

CHAIKIN, Joseph, 792'.028'0922 1935-
The presence of the actor. [1st ed.] New York, Atheneum, 1972. xii, 161 p. illus. 21 cm. Autobiographical. [PN2287.C46A3] 70-175287 6.95
1. Open Theater. 2. Actors—Correspondence, reminiscences, etc. I. Title. BIP

Opera—Biography—Dictionaries.

WHO'S who in opera 782.1'092'2 B : an international biographical directory of singers, conductors, directors, designers, and administrators, also including porfiles of 101 opera companies / Maria F. Rich, editor. 1st ed. New York : New York Times Co., 1976. xxi, 684 p. ; 25 cm. [ML102.O6W5] 75-7963 ISBN 0-405-06652-X : 65.00
1. Opera—Biography—Dictionaries. 2. Opera—Directories. I. Rich, Maria F.

Opera—History and criticism.

ROLLAND, Romain, 1866- 780'.922 1944.
Some musicians of former days. Translated by Mary Blaiklock. Freeport, N.Y., Books for Libraries Press [1968] vii, 374 p. 22 cm. (Essay index reprint series) Translation of Musiciens d'autrefois. Reprint of 1915 ed. Contents.Contents.—The beginnings of opera.—The first opera played in Paris: Luigi Rossi's Orfeo.—Notes on Lully.—Gluck.—Gretry.—Mozart.—Musical supplement: "The despair of Orpheus," from Orfeo. Bibliographical footnotes. [ML390.R662 1968] 68-8490
1. Opera—History and criticism. 2. Composers—Biography. I. Blaiklock, Mary, tr. II. Title. BIP

Opera—London.

MAPLESON, James Henry, 782.0924 1830-1901.
The Mapleson memoirs; the career of an operatic impresario, 1858-1888. Edited and annotated by Harold Rosenthal. New York, Appleton-Century [1966] 346 p. illus., ports. 26 cm. [ML429] 66-20000
1. Opera—London. 2. Opera—United States. I. Rosenthal, Harold D., ed. II. Title.

Ophthalmology—Addresses, essays, lectures.

LEBENSOHN, James Elzar, 617'.7'08 1893- comp.
An anthology of ophthalmic classics. Edited, with comments, biographical notes, and portrait illustrations [by] James E. Lebensohn. Foreword by C. Wilbur Rucker. Baltimore, Williams & Wilkins, 1969. xx, 407 p. ports. 27 cm. Includes bibliographies. [RE61.L4] 76-94010
1. Ophthalmology—Addresses, essays, lectures. 2. Ophthalmologists—Biography. I. Title.

Opie, Amelia Alderson, 1769-1853—Biography.

OPIE, Amelia Alderson, 823'.7 B 1769-1853.
Memorials of the life of Amelia Opie / selected and arranged from her letters, diaries, and other manuscripts by Cecilia Lucy Brightwell. 2d ed. New York : AMS Press, 1975. xii, 410 p. : port. ; 23 cm. (Women of letters) Reprint of the 1854 (2d) ed. published by Fletcher and Alexander, Norwich, Eng. [PR5115.O3Z5 1975] 79-37711 ISBN 0-404-56774-6 : 30.00
1. Opie, Amelia Alderson, 1769-1853—Biography. 2. Opie, Amelia Alderson, 1769-1853—Correspondence. I. Title. BIP

Oppen, Mary, 1908- —Biography.

OPPEN, Mary, 1908- 811'.5'2
Meaning a life : an autobiography / Mary Oppen. Santa Barbara, Calif. : Black Sparrow Press, 1978. 212 p. : ill. ; 23 cm. [PS3529.P54Z8] 78-6223 ISBN 0-87685-375-0 : 14.00. ISBN 0-87685-376-9 signed : 17.50. ISBN 0-87685-374-2 pbk. : 4.50
1. Oppen, Mary, 1908- —Biography. 2. Oppen, George—Biography. 3. Wives—United States—Biography. 4. Poets, American—20th century—Biography. I. Title.

Oppenheimer, J. Robert,

CHEVALIER, Haakon Maurice, v. 12 1902-
Oppenheimer; the story of a friendship, by Haakon Chevalier. New York, Pocket Books [1966] xvi, 204 p. 22 cm. Bibliography: p. 193-194. 67-80030
1. Oppenheimer, J. Robert, I. Title.

Oppenheimer, J. Robert, 1904-

ALSOP, Joseph, 1910- 925.3
We accuse! The story of the miscarriage of American justice in the case of J. Robert Oppenheimer, by Joseph and Stewart Alsop. New York, Simon and Schuster,

1954. 88p. 28cm. [HD9698.U52A66] 54-12966
1. Oppenheimer, J. Robert, 1904- I. Alsop, Stewart Johonot Oliver, 1913- joint author. II. Title.

ALSOP, Joseph Wright, 1910- 925.3
We accuse; The story of the miscarriage of American justice in the case of J. Robert Oppenheimer, by Joseph and Stewart Alsop. New York, Simon and Schuster, 1954. 88 p. 28 cm. [HD9698.U52A66] 54-12966
1. Oppenheimer, J. Robert, 1904- I. Alsop, Steward Johonot Oliver, 1913- joint author. II. Title.

CHEVALIER, Haakon 323.20973
Maurice, 1902-
Oppenheimer; the story of a friendship. New York, Braziller [c.1965] xvi, 219p. 22cm. Bibl. [QC16.O62C5] 65-23175 5.00
1. Oppenheimer, J. Robert, 1904- I. Title.

CHEVALIER, Haakon 323.20973
Maurice, 1902-
Oppenheimer; the story of a friendship, by Haakon Chevalier. New York, G. Braziller [1965] xvi, 219 p. 22 cm. Bibliography: p. [209]-210 [QC16.O62C5] 65-23175
1. Oppenheimer, J. Robert, 1904- I. Title.

CURTIS, Charles Pelham, 925.3
1891--
The Oppenheimer case; the trial of a security system. New York, Simon and Schuster, 1955. 281p. 22cm. [QC16.O62C8] 55-8808
1. Oppenheimer, J. Robert, 1904 I. Title.

KUGELMASS, J. Alvin. 925.3
J. Robert Oppenheimer and the atomic story. Decorations by William Metzig. New York, J. Messner [1953] 179 p. illus. 22 cm. Includes bibliography. [QC16.O62K8] 53-10508
1. Oppenheimer, J. Robert, 1904-1967. I. Title.

MICHELMORE, Peter. 530'.0924 B
The swift years; the Robert Oppenheimer story. New York, Dodd, Mead [1969] viii, 273 p. ports. 24 cm. Bibliography: p. 259-261. [QC16.O62M5] 71-88070 6.95
1. Oppenheimer, J. Robert, 1904-1967. I. Title.

OPPENHEIMER 530'.0924 B
[by] I. I. Rabi [and others] New York, Scribner [1969] x, 90 p. illus., ports. 24 cm. "The speeches on which this book is based originated as lectures given at the Oppenheimer memorial session of the American Physical Society meeting held in Washington, D.C., in April 1967 and appeared subsequently in the October 1967 issue of Physics today, under the title A memorial to Oppenheimer." Contents.Contents.—Introduction, by I. I. Rabi.—The early years, by R. Serber.—The Los Alamos years, by V. F. Weisskopf.—The Princeton period, by A. Pais.—Public service and human contributions, by G. T. Seaborg.—Reference notes (p. 63-66).—Selected bibliography of Oppenheimer's writings (p. 81-86) [QC16.O62O6] 68-57086 5.95
1. Oppenheimer, J. Robert, 1904-1967. I. Oppenheimer, J. Robert, 1904-1967. II. Rabi, Isidor Isaac, 1898-

ROYAL, Denise. 530'.0924 B
The story of J. Robert Oppenheimer. New York, St. Martin's Press [1969] x, 196 p. illus., ports. 22 cm. Bibliography: p. [185]-189. [QC16.O62R62] 68-29074 5.95
1. Oppenheimer, J. Robert, 1904-1967. I. Title.

STERN, Philip M. 353.001'83 B
The Oppenheimer case; security on trial, by Philip M. Stern with the collaboration of Harold P. Green. With a special commentary by Lloyd K. Garrison. [1st ed.] New York, Harper & Row [1969] xii, 591 p. 25 cm. Bibliographical references included in "Notes and sources" (p. 551-580) [QC16.O62S69] 76-81869 10.00
1. Oppenheimer, J. Robert, 1904-1967. I. Green, Harold P. II. Title.

STROUT, Cushing, 530'.092' [B]
ed.
Conscience, science and security: the case of Dr. J. Robert Oppenheimer. Chicago, Rand McNally [1963] 58 p. 22 cm. (The Berkeley series in American history) "Further reading": p. 58. [QC16.O62S7] 63-8260
1. Oppenheimer, J. Robert, 1904-1967. I. Title. II. Series.

Oprescu, George, 1881-

GRIGORESCU, Nicolae, 759.9498
1838-1907
Grigorescu, 1838-1907 [by] G. Oprescu. [dist. New York, Vanous, 1962] 180p. illus. (pt. mounted col.) col. plates. 30cm. 62-2910 13.90
1. Oprescu, George, 1881- I. Title.

Orage, Alfred Richard, 1873-1934.

CARSWELL, John. 820'.9'00912
Lives and letters : A. R. Orage, Beatrice Hastings, Katherine Mansfield, John Middleton Murry, S. S. Koteliansky : 1906-1957 / by John Carswell. New York : New Directions Pub. Corp., 1978. p. cm. Includes index. Bibliography: p. [PR106.C37] 77-15986 ISBN 0-8112-0681-5 : 15.00
1. Orage, Alfred Richard, 1873-1934. 2. Hastings, Beatrice. 3. Mansfield, Katherine, 1888-1923. 4. Murry, John Middleton, 1889-1957. 5. Koteliansky, Samuel Solomonovitch, 1880-1955. 6. Authors, English—20th century—Biography. I. Title.
BIP

CARSWELL, John. 820'.9'00912
Lives and letters : A. R. Orage, Beatrice Hastings, Katherine Mansfield, John Middleton Murry, S. S. Koteliansky, 1906-1957 / by John Carswell. London ; Boston : Faber and Faber, 1978. 306 p., [4] leaves of plates : ill. ; 23 cm. Includes index. Bibliography: p. 294-297. [PR106.C37 1978] 78-313376 ISBN 0-571-10596-3 : 15.00
1. Orage, Alfred Richard, 1873-1934. 2. Hastings, Beatrice. 3. Mansfield, Katherine, 1888-1923. 4. Murry, John Middleton, 1889-1957. 5. Koteliansky, Samuel Solomonovitch, 1880-1955. 6. Authors, English—20th century—Biography. I. Title. Distributed by New Directions Publishing Corp., 333 Ave of the Americas, New York, NY 10014

MAIRET, Philippe, 1886- 072
A. R. orage; Orage; a memoir. New Hyde Park, N.Y., University Bks. [c.1966] xxxii,140p. ports. 25cm. [PN5123.O7M3] 66-15076 6.00
1. Orage, Alfred Richard, 1873-1934. I. Title.

Oraison, Marc.

ORAISON, Marc. 282'.0924 B
Strange voyage; the autobiography of a non-conformist. Translated by J. F. Bernard. [1st ed.] Garden City, N.Y., Doubleday, 1970 [c1969] 236 p. 22 cm. Translation of Tete dure. [BX4705.O498A33] 77-116243 5.95
I. Title.

Orake, Francis, Sir 1540 -1596—Juvenile literature.

[WOOD, William Hollingsworth] 920
1914-
The true story of Sir Francis Drake, privateer, by Will Holwood [pseud.] Chicago, Childrens [c.1964] 139p. col. illus. 23cm. First pub. in London in 1958 under title: The true book about Sir Francis Drake. 64-12905 3.50 2.63 lib. ed. net,
1. Orake, Francis, Sir 1540 -1596—Juvenile literature. I. Title.

Orators, American.

JONES, Edgar De Witt, 808'.00922
1876-1956.
Lords of speech; portraits of fifteen American orators. Freeport, N.Y., Books for Libraries Press [1969, c1937] xi, 256 p. 23 cm. (Essay index reprint series) Contents.Contents.—Patrick Henry.—Henry Clay.—Daniel Webster.—Edward Everett.—Wendell Phillips.—Seargent S. Prentiss.—Abraham Lincoln.—Henry W. Grady.—Henry Ward Beecher.—Robert G. Ingersoll.—The Breckinridges.—Phillips Brooks.—Albert J. Beveridge.—William Jennings Bryan.—Woodrow Wilson.—Bibliography (p. [249]-256) [PS400.J6 1969] 68-58799
1. Orators, American. I. Title.

Orchard, Hugh Anderson.

ORCHARD, Hugh Anderson. 630.1
Old Orchard Farm, the story of an Iowa boyhood. Edited by Paul F. Sharp; illustrated by John Huseby. Ames, Iowa State College Press [1952] 235 p. illus. 20 cm. [CT275.O57A3] 52-44490
I. Title.

Orcutt, Charles Russell, 1864-1929.

DUSHANE, Helen. 500.9'72'2
The Baja California travels of Charles Russell Orcutt. Los Angeles, Dawson's Book Shop, 1971. 75 p. illus., facsims., fold. map (in pocket), port. 22 cm. (Baja California travels series, 23) On spine: Charles Russell Orcutt. 500 copies. Includes bibliographical references. [QH31.O68D8] 70-113983 ISBN 0-87093-223-3
1. Orcutt, Charles Russell, 1864-1929. 2. Baja California—Description and travel. I. Title. II. Title: Charles Russell Orcutt. III. Series.

Oregon—Biography.

COGSWELL, Philip. 920'.0795
Capitol names : individuals woven into Oregon's history / by Philip Cogswell, Jr. Portland : Oregon Historical Society, c1977. 133 p. : ill. ; 21 cm. Bibliography: p. 133. [CT256.C63] 76-56657 ISBN 0-87595-054-X pbk. : 1.00
1. Oregon—Biography. I. Title. **BIP**

Orff, Carl, 1895-

LIESS, Andreas, 1903- 782.0924
Carl Orff. Translated by Adelheid and Herbert Parkin. New York, St. Martin's Press [1966] 184 p. illus., facsim., music, ports. 21 cm. Bibliography: p. [171]-174. [ML410.O65L57] 64-16423
1. Orff, Carl, 1895- I. Title.

Organisation Gehlen.

GEHLEN, Reinhard, 327'.12'0924 B
1902-
The service; the memoirs of General Reinhard Gehlen. Translated by David Irving. Introd. by George Bailey. New York, World Pub. [1972] xxvii, 386 p. illus. 24 cm. Translation of Der Dienst. [DD247.G37A313 1972] 73-183092 ISBN 0-529-04455-2 10.00
1. Organisation Gehlen. 2. World War, 1939-1945—Secret Service. I. Title.

Organized crime—United States.

*BARBOZA, Joe. 364'.1'060924
Barboza, by Joe Barboza, with Hank Messick. [New York, Dell 1975] 204 p. 18 cm. [HV6783] 1.25 (pbk.)
1. Organized crime—United States. I. Messick, Hank. joint author. II. Title.

Oriental Missionary Society—Biography.

ERNY, Edward. 266'.023'0922 B
No guarantee but God; the story of the founders of the Oriental Missionary Society, by Edward and Esther Erny. Greenwood, Ind., Oriental Missionary Society [1969] vii, 116 p. ports. 19 cm. Contents.—Charles Cowman.—Juji Nakada.—Ernest Kilbourne.—Lettie B. Cowman. [BV2360.O7E7] 78-16999
1. Oriental Missionary Society—Biography. I. Erny, Esther, joint author. II. Title.

Origo, Iris (Cutting)

ORIGO, Iris (Cutting) 818'.5'209
marchesa, 1902-
Images and shadows; part of a life [by] Iris Origo. [1st American ed.] New York, Harcourt Brace Jovanovich [1971, c1970] xi, 278 p. illus., ports. 23 cm. "A Helen and Kurt Wolff book." [PN75.O7A3 1971] 79-134574 ISBN 0-15-144101-4 8.50
I. Title. **BIP**

Orione, Luigi,1872-1940.

HYDE, Douglas Arnold, 922.245
1911-
God's bandit, the story of Don Orione, 'Father of the Poor.' Westminster, Md., Newman Press, 1957. 207p. illus. 21cm. [HV28.O7H9] 57-59081
1. Orione, Luigi,1872-1940. I. Title.

Orione, Luigi, 1872-1940.

HYDE, Douglas Arnold, 922.245
1911-
God's bandit, the story of Don Crione, Father of the Poor. Westminster, Md., Newman Press, 1957. 207p. illus. 21cm. [HV28.O7H9] 57-59081
1. Orione, Luigi, 1872-1940. I. Title.

Orlando, Tony—Juvenile literature.

MORSE, Ann. 784'.092'4 B
Tony Orlando / by Ann Morse ; designed by Mark Landkamer. Mankato, Minn. : Creative Education, c1978. 31 p. : ill. ; 25 cm. A biography of the singer of Greek and Puerto Rican descent who rose to television stardom. [ML3930.O74M7] 92 77-22682 ISBN 0-87191-616-9 : 4.95
1. Orlando, Tony—Juvenile literature. 2. Singers—United States—Biography—Juvenile literature. I. Title.
BIP

Orleans, Phillippe II, duc d', 1674-1723.

LEWIS, Warren Hamilton. 923.244
The scandalous regent; a life of Philippe, duc d'Orleans, 1674-1723 and of his family. [1st American ed.] New York, Harcourt, Brace & World [1961] 228 p. 23 cm. Includes bibliography. [DC132.L53] 61-6681
1. Orleans, Phillippe II, duc d', 1674-1723. I. Title.

SHENNAN, J. H. 944'.034'0924 B
Philippe, Duke of Orleans . Regent of France, 1715-1723 / J. H. Shennan. London : Thames and Hudson, c1979. 191 p., [8] leaves of plates : ill. ; 23 cm. (Men in office) Includes index. Bibliography: p. [152]-159. [DC132.S53] 78-62806 ISBN 0-500-87009-8 : 16.95
1. Orleans, Philippe II, duc d', 1674-1723. 2. France—History—Regency, 1715-1723. 3. France—Kings and rulers—Biography. Distributed by W. W. Norton, New York, NY **BIP**

Ornstein, Leo, 1895-

MARTENS, Frederick 786.1'092'4 B
Herman, 1874-1932.
Leo Ornstein : the man, his ideas, his work / Frederick H. Martens. New York : Arno Press, 1975, c1918. p. cm. (The Modern Jewish experience) Reprint of the ed. published by Breitkopf & Hartel, New York. [ML410.O67M2 1975] 74-29505 ISBN 0-405-06732-1 : 9.00
1. Ornstein, Leo, 1895- I. Title. II. Series.
BIP

Orozco, Jose Clemente, 1883-1949.

HELM, MacKinley, 1896- 759.972 B
Man of fire: J. C. Orozco; an interpretative memoir. Westport, Conn., Greenwood Press [1971, c1953] ix, 245 p. illus. 27 cm. Bibliography: p. 111-117. [ND259.O7H43 1971] 79-106689 ISBN 0-8371-3361-0

1. Orozco, Jose Clemente, 1883-1949. I. Title.

Orozco, Jose Clemente, 1883-1949.

HELM, MacKinley, 1896- 927.5
Man of fire: J. C. Orozco; an interpretative memoir. [1st ed.] New York, Harcourt, Brace [1953] ix, 245 p. illus., 67 plates (4 col.) port. 26 cm. Bibliography: p. 111-117. [ND259.O7H43] 759.972 52-13764
1. Orozco, Jose Clemente, 1883-1949. I. Title.

OROZCO, Jose Clemente, 1883-1949. 927.5
An autobiography. Translated by Robert C. Stephenson. Introd. by John Palmer Leeper. Austin, University of Texas Press [1962] 171 p. illus. 21 cm. (The Texas Pan-American series) [ND259.O7A213] 62-9790
1. Artists—Correspondence, reminiscences, etc.

REED, Alma M 759.972
Orozco. New York, Oxford University Press, 1956. 308p. illus. 25cm. [ND259.O7R4] 927.5 56-5428
1. Orozco, Jose Clemente, 1883-1949. I. Title.

Orphans and orphan asylums—Gt. Brit.

THOMAS, Leslie, 1931- 362.73
This time next week, the autobiography of a happy orphan. With illus. by Graham Byfield. [1st American ed.] Boston, Little, Brown [1965, c1964] 250 p. illus. 21 cm. [HV1148.T46 1965] 65-11586
1. Orphans and orphan asylums—Gt. Brit. I. Title.

Orr, Bobby, 1948-

FISCHLER, Stan. 796.9'62'0924 B
Bobby Orr and the big, bad Bruins. New York, Dodd, Mead [1969] x, 273 p. ports. 22 cm. [GV848.5.O7F5] 78-93942 5.95
1. Orr, Bobby, 1948- 2. Boston Bruins. I. Title.

ORR, Bobby, 1948- 796.9'62'0924 B
Bobby Orr: my game, with Mark Mulvoy. Special photography by Heinz Kluetmeier. [1st ed.] Boston, Little, Brown [1974] 237 p. illus. 27 cm. "A Sports illustrated book." [GV848.5.O7A32] 74-14685 ISBN 0-316-66490-1
1. Orr, Bobby, 1948- 2. Hockey. I. Mulvoy, Mark.

Orr, Bobby, 1948- —Juvenile literature.

BURCHARD, Marshall. 796.9'62'0924B92
Sports hero: Bobby Orr, by Marshall and Sue Burchard. New York, Putnam [1973] 94 p. illus. 23 cm. An easy-to-read biography of the Boston Bruins hockey star who began his professional career at age fourteen. [GV848.5.07B86 1973] 796.9'62'0924 B 92 72-85625 72-85625 ISBN 0-399-60795-1. 3.86 (Lib. bdg.)
1. Orr, Bobby, 1948- —Juvenile literature. I. Burchard, Sue, joint author. II. Title.

DEVANEY, John. 796.9'62'0924 B
The Bobby Orr story. New York, Random House [1973] 153 p. illus. 22 cm. (Pro hockey library, 6) A biography of the Boston Bruins' star defensive player considered by many to be one of the best all-round hockey players of all time. [GV848.5.O7D48 1973] 73-6661 ISBN 0-394-82612-4 1.95
1. Orr, Bobby, 1948- —Juvenile literature. I. Title. BIP

EDWARDS, Audrey. 796.9'62'0924 B
The picture life of Bobby Orr / by Audrey Edwards and Gary Wohl. New York : Watts, 1976. [48] p. : ill. ; 23 cm. Brief text and photographs present the life of Bobby Orr, star of the Boston Bruins hockey team. [GV848.5.O7E38] 92 76-16200 ISBN 0-531-01208-5 lib.bdg. : 3.90
1. Orr, Bobby, 1948- —Juvenile literature. 2. Hockey—Juvenile literature. I. Wohl, Gary, joint author. II. Title. BIP

HIRSHBERG, Albert, 1909-1973. 796.9'62'0924 B
Bobby Orr : fire on ice / by Al Hirshberg. New York : Putnam, c1975. 156 p. ; 22 cm. (Putnam sports shelf) This biography has been completed by Frank Orr. Includes index. Traces the development of the Canadian superstar's professional career which began at age fourteen. [GV848.5.O7H57 1975] 92 75-10436 ISBN 0-399-20464-4 : 5.29.
1. Orr, Bobby, 1948- —Juvenile literature. 2. Hockey—Juvenile literature. I. Orr, Frank. II. Title. BIP

JACKSON, Robert B. 796.9'62'0924 B
"Here comes Bobby Orr," by Robert B. Jackson. New York, H. Z. Walck [1971] 64 p. illus. 22 cm. Recounts the professional career of hockey player Bobby Orr, who was signed by the Boston Bruins at age fourteen. [GV848.5.O7J3] 77-163323 ISBN 0-8098-2080-3 4.25
1. Orr, Bobby, 1948- —Juvenile literature. I. Title.

LISS, Howard. 796.9'62'0924 B
Bobby Orr, lightning on ice / by Howard Liss ; illustrated by Victor Mays. Champaign, Ill. : Garrard Pub. Co., [1975] 96 p. : ill. (some col.) ; 24 cm. A biography of Bobby Orr from the time he learned to skate at age three until he became superstar of the Boston Bruins. [GV848.5.O7L57] 75-2423 ISBN 0-8116-6672-7 lib.bdg. : 3.28
1. Orr, Bobby, 1948- —Juvenile literature. 2. Hockey—Juvenile literature. I. Mays, Victor, 1927- ill. II. Title.

MAY, Julian. 796.9'62'0924 B
Bobby Orr, star on ice. Mankato, Minn., Crestwood House [1973] 46 p. illus. 24 cm. (Sports close-up books) A biography of the award-winning hockey player, groomed from his youth to play for the Boston Bruins. [GV848.5.O7M38 1973] 92 73-80422 ISBN 0-913940-02-X
1. Orr, Bobby, 1948- —Juvenile literature. I. Title.

SMITH, Jay H. 796.9'62'0924 B
Bobby Orr, by Jay H. Smith. Illustrated by Harold Henriksen. Mankato, Minn., Creative Education; [distributed by Childrens Press, Chicago, 1974] 31 p. col. illus. 25 cm. (Superstars) A biography of the Canadian boy who from the age of fourteen was primed to lead the Boston Bruins out of their losing streak into NHL victory. [GV848.5.O7S58] 92 74-8848 ISBN 0-87191-368-2
1. Orr, Bobby, 1948- —Juvenile literature. 2. Hockey—Juvenile literature. I. Henriksen, Harold, illus. II. Title. BIP

SMITH, Jay H. 796.9'62'0924 B
Hockey's legend, Bobby Orr / by Jay H. Smith. [Mankato, Minn.] : Creative Education, [c1977] 30 p. : ill. ; 19 cm. (The Allstars) Describes Bobby Orr's legendary ten-year career with the Boston Bruins. [GV848.5.O7S6] 92 76-45862 ISBN 0-87191-590-1 lib.bdg. 4.95
1. Orr, Bobby, 1948- —Juvenile literature. 2. Hockey players—Biography—Juvenile literature. I. Title.

Orrery, Roger Boyle, 1st earl of, 1621-1679.

LYNCH, Kathleen Martha 941.560924
Roger Boyle, first Earl of Orrery. Knoxville, Univ. of Tenn. Pr. [c.1965] ix, 308p. plates, ports. 23cm. Bibl. [DA940.5.O8L9] 65-17348 7.50
1. Orrery, Roger Boyle, 1st earl of, 1621-1679. 2. Ireland—Pol. & govt.—17th cent. I. Title. BIP

Orsini, Felice, 1819-1858.

PACKE, Michael St. John. 923.245
Orsini; the story of a conspirator. [1st American ed.] Boston, Little, Brown [1958, c1957] 313 p. illus. 22 cm. First published in London in 1957 under title: The bombs of Orsini. Includes bibliography. [DG552.8.O6P3 1958] 58-7857
1. Orsini, Felice, 1819-1858. 2. Europe—Politics—1815-1871.

Orsini, Joseph E.

ORSINI, Joseph E. 282'.092'4 B
Hear my confession / Joseph Orsini. New and updated ed. Plainfield, N.J. : Logos International, c1977. 144 p. ; 21 cm. [BX4705.O715A3 1977] 77-73151 ISBN 0-88270-231-9 pbk. : 2.95
1. Orsini, Joseph E. 2. Catholic Church—Clergy—Biography. 3. Clergy—New Jersey—Biography. 4. Pentecostalism—Catholic Church. I. Title.

Ortega y Gasset, Jose, 1883-1955.

MARIAS Aguilera, Julian. 196
Jose Ortega y Gasset, circumstance and vocation, by Julian Marias. Translated by Frances M. Lopez-Morillas. [1st ed.] Norman, University of Oklahoma Press [1970] xiii, 479 p. 25 cm. Includes bibliographical references. [B4568.O74M27] 71-88141 12.50
1. Ortega y Gasset, Jose, 1883-1955. I. Title.

NIEDERMAYER, Franz. 196'.1 B
Jose Ortega y Gasset. Translated by Peter Tirner. New York, Ungar [1973] ix, 138 p. 20 cm. (Modern literature monographs) Bibliography: p. 125-127. [B4568.O74N513] 71-163150 ISBN 0-8044-2659-7 5.00
1. Ortega y Gasset, Jose, 1883-1955. BIP

Ortiz de Ayala, Tadeo.

TIMMONS, Wilbert H. 976.4'03'0924 B
Tadeo Ortiz, Mexican colonizer and reformer / by Wilbert H. Timmons ; ill. by Jose Cisneros. [El Paso] : Texas Western Press, [1974] 82 p. : ill. ; 23 cm. (Southwestern studies ; monograph no. 43) Includes bibliographical references. [F1232.O854T55] 74-196046 ISBN 0-87404-101-5 : 3.00
1. Ortiz de Ayala, Tadeo. I. Title. II. Series: Southwestern studies (El Paso, Tex.) ; monograph no. 43. BIP

Ortiz, Juan, d. 1543?—Juvenile literature.

STEELE, William O., 1917- 973.1'6'0924 B
The wilderness tattoo; a narrative of Juan Ortiz, by William O. Steele. [1st ed.] New York, Harcourt Brace Jovanovich [1972] 184 p. illus. 21 cm. Bibliography: p. 183-184. After living eleven years among Indians in Florida, a Spaniard guides De Soto's troops in their fruitless search for gold. [E125.O66S8] 77-167838 ISBN 0-15-297325-7 4.95
1. Ortiz, Juan, d. 1543?—Juvenile literature. 2. Soto, Hernando de, 1500 (ca.)-1542—Juvenile literature. 3. Timucua Indians—Juvenile literature. I. Title. BIP

Ortman, Elmore Jan

ORTMAN, Elmore Jan 923.773
To rear the tender thought; the autobiography of a modern educator. New York, Exposition Press [c.1960] 124p. 22cm. (An Exposition-Banner bk.) 3.00
I. Title.

Orton, Arthur, calling himself Sir Roger Charles Doughty-Tichborne, bart., 1834-1808.

MACGREGOR, Geddes. 343
The Tichborne imposter. [1st ed.] Philadelphia, Lippincott [1957] 288p. illus. 21cm. 57-11952
1. Orton, Arthur, calling himself Sir Roger Charles Doughty-Tichborne, bart., 1834-1808. 2. Doughty-Tichborne, Roger Charles, 1829-1854. I. Title.

Orton, Joe.

LAHR, John, 1941- 822'.9'14 B
Prick up your ears : the biography of Joe Orton / John Lahr. 1st ed. New York : Knopf : distributed by Random House, 1978. p. cm. Includes index. Bibliography: p. [PR6065.R7Z77] 78-7130 ISBN 0-394-50153-5 : 15.00
1. Orton, Joe. 2. Dramatists, English—20th century—Biography. I. Title. BIP

Orwell, George, 1903-1950.

ATKINS, John Alfred, 1916- v. 12
George Orwell; a literary and biographical study. New York, Ungar [1965, c1954] 348 p. 23 cm. 68-34283
1. Orwell, George, 1903-1950. I. Title.

ATKINS, John Alfred, 1916- 820.81
George Orwell; a literary and biographical study. New York, Ungar [1955, c1954] 348p. 23cm. [PR6029] 55-8749
1. Orwell, George, 1903-1950. I. Title.

ATKINS, John Alfred, 1916- 828.912
George Orwell; a literary and biographical study [Reissue] New York, Ungar [1965, c.1954] 348p. 23cm. [PR6029] 55-8749 6.50
1. Orwell, George, 1903-1950. I. Title.

BRANDER, Laurence, 1903- v. 12
George Orwell. London, New York, Longmans, Green [1954] 212p. port. 20cm. Bibliography: p. 207-208. A55
1. Orwell, George, 1903-1950. I. Title.

HOLLIS, Christopher, 1902- 823.91
A study of George Orwell; the man and his works. Chicago, H. Regnery Co., 1956. 212p. 23cm. [PR6029.R8Z68] 56-14195
1. Orwell, George, 1903-1950. I. Title.

STANSKY, Peter. 828'.9'1209 B
The unknown Orwell [by] Peter Stansky and William Abrahams. [1st ed.] New York, Knopf, 1972. xx, 316, xiii p. illus. 22 cm. Includes bibliographical references. [PR6029.R8Z79] 72-2245 ISBN 0-394-47393-0 8.95
1. Orwell, George, 1903-1950. I. Abrahams, William Miller, 1919- joint author. II. Title. BIP

VOORHEES, Richard Joseph, 1916- 928.2
The paradox of George Orwell. [Lafayette, Ind., Purdue University, c.1961] 127p. (Purdue University studies: humanities series) Bibl. 61-62508 1.95 pap.,
1. Orwell, George, 1903-1950. I. Title. II. Series. BIP

WILLIAMS, Raymond. 828'.9'1209
George Orwell. New York, Viking Press [1971] 102 p. 20 cm. (Modern masters) Bibliography: p. [99]-100. [PR6029.R8Z86] 71-132184 ISBN 0-670-33702-1 4.95
1. Orwell, George, 1903-1950.

THE World of George Orwell. 828'.9'1209 B
Edited by Miriam Gross. New York, Simon and Schuster [1972, c1971] 182 p. illus. 26 cm. [PR6029.R8Z92 1972] 73-164705 ISBN 0-671-21124-2 12.95
1. Orwell, George, 1903-1950. I. Gross, Miriam, ed. BIP

Osborn, George Coleman,

OSBORN, George Coleman, 1904- 923.273
John Sharp Williams, planter-statesman of the Deep South. Gloucester, Mass., P. Smith [1965, c.1943] ix, 501p. illus., ports. 21cm. Bibl. [E664.W675O7] 65-1351 6.75
1. Williams, John Sharp, 1854-1932. II. Title. BIP

Osborn, Michael,

OSBORN, Michael, 1937- 387.7'0924 B
"Mr. Mac"; William P. MacCracken, Jr. on aviation, law, optometry, by Michael Osborn and Joseph Riggs. [1st ed.

Memphis,] Southern College of Optometry, 1970. viii, 228 p. illus., ports. 24 cm. Includes bibliographical references. [TL540.M225O8] 74-140202
1. MacCracken, William Patterson, 1888-1969. II. Riggs, Joseph Howard, 1928- joint author. III. Title.

Osborne, John, 1929-

CARTER, Alan, 1936- 822'.9'14
John Osborne. [2d ed.] New York, Barnes and Noble, a divn. of Harper [1973, c.1969] 213 p. 23 cm. (Biography and criticism, 14) Bibliography: p. 204-209. [PR6029.S39Z6] ISBN 0-06-491001-6 11.50
1. Osborne, John, 1929- I. Title.
L.C. card no. for 1st (British) edition: 79-463056.

HAYMAN, Ronald, 1932- 822'.9'14
John Osborne. New York, Ungar [1972] vii, 168 p. illus. 21 cm. (World dramatists) Bibliography: p. 161-162. [PR6029.S39Z65 1972] 79-153123 ISBN 0-8044-2386-5 6.50
1. Osborne, John, 1929- **BIP**

Osborne, Thomas Mott, 1859-1926.

CHAMBERLAIN, Rudolph 365'.9'24 B
Wilson, 1891-
There is no truce; a life of Thomas Mott Osborne, by Rudolph W. Chamberlain. Freeport, N.Y., Books for Libraries Press [1970] vi, 420 p. illus., ports. 23 cm. Reprint of the 1935 ed. [HV8978.O7C5 1970] 74-124229
1. Osborne, Thomas Mott, 1859-1926. I. Title.

Osceola Nikkanochee, Seminole Indian.

WELCH, Andrew. 970'.004'97
A narrative of the early days and remembrances of Oceola Nikkanochee, prince of Econchatti / written by his guardian. Facsim. reproductions of the 1841 ed. and of the pamphlets of 1837 and 1847 / with an introd. and indexes by Frank Laumer. Gainesville : University Presses of Florida, 1977i.e.1976 352 p. in various pagings ; 20 cm. (Bicentennial Floridiana facsimile series) "A University of Florida book." Photoreprint of the 1841 ed. published by Hatchard, London; of the 1837 ed. of A Narrative of the life and sufferings of Mrs. Jane Johns, printed by Burke & Giles, Charleston; and of the 1847 ed. of A narrative of the life of Benjamin Benson, published by the author, London. Includes bibliographical references and indexes. [E99.S28W44 1977] 76-54519 ISBN 0-8130-0411-X : 8.50
1. Osceola Nikkanochee, Seminole Indian. 2. Osceola, Seminole chief, 1804-1838. 3. Johns, Jane (Hall), Mrs., b. 1813. 4. Benson, Benjamin, b. 1818. 5. Seminole Indians—Biography. 6. United States—Biography. I. Welch, Andrew. A narrative of the life of Benjamin Benson. 1976. II. A Narrative of the life and sufferings of Mrs. Jane Johns. 1976. III. Title. IV. Title: A narrative of the early days and remembrances of Oceola Nikkanochee ... V. Series.

Osceola, Seminole chief, 1804-1838.

HARTLEY, William B. 970.3 B
Osceola, the unconquered Indian, by William and Ellen Hartley. New York, Hawthorn Books [1973] 293 p. illus. 23 cm. Includes bibliographical references. [E99.S28H37 1973] 73-341 8.95
1. Osceola, Seminole chief, 1804-1838. I. Hartley, Ellen, joint author.

WELCH, Andrew. 970'.004'97
A narrative of the early days and remembrances of Oceola Nikkanochee, prince of Econchatti / written by his guardian. Facsim. reproductions of the 1841 ed. and of the pamphlets of 1837 and 1847 / with an introd. and indexes by Frank Laumer. Gainesville : University Presses of Florida, 1977i.e.1976 352 p. in various pagings ; 20 cm. (Bicentennial Floridiana facsimile series) "A University of Florida book." Photoreprint of the 1841 ed. published by Hatchard, London; of the 1837 ed. of A Narrative of the life and sufferings of Mrs. Jane Johns, printed by Burke & Giles, Charleston; and of the 1847 ed. of A narrative of the life of Benjamin Benson, published by the author, London. Includes bibliographical references and indexes. [E99.S28W44 1977] 76-54519 ISBN 0-8130-0411-X : 8.50
1. Osceola Nikkanochee, Seminole Indian. 2. Osceola, Seminole chief, 1804-1838. 3. Johns, Jane (Hall), Mrs., b. 1813. 4. Benson, Benjamin, b. 1818. 5. Seminole Indians—Biography. 6. United States—Biography. I. Welch, Andrew. A narrative of the life of Benjamin Benson. 1976. II. A Narrative of the life and sufferings of Mrs. Jane Johns. 1976. III. Title. IV. Title: A narrative of the early days and remembrances of Oceola Nikkanochee ... V. Series.

Osceola, Seminole chief, 1804-1838—Juvenile literature.

GRANT, Matthew G. 970.3 B
Osceola and the Seminole War [by] Matthew G. Grant. Illustrated by Harold Henriksen and John Keely. [Mankato, Minn., Creative Education; distributed by Childrens Press, Chicago, 1973, c1974] 29 p. illus. (part col.) 25 cm. (His Gallery of great Americans series. Indians of America) A brief biography of the Seminole leader who fought against President Jackson's decree to move his people west. [E99.S28O82] 92 73-12407 ISBN 0-87191-266-X
1. Osceola, Seminole chief, 1804-1838—Juvenile literature. I. Henriksen, Harold, illus. II. Keely, John, illus. III. Title.

GRIDLEY, Marion Eleanor, 970.3 B
1906-
Osceola, by Marion E. Gridley. Illustrated by Lloyd E. Oxendine. New York, Putnam [1972] 60 p. illus. 23 cm. (A See and read beginning to read biography) A brief biography of the early nineteenth-century Seminole chief who fought a long battle to keep his people from being deported from their Florida homes. [E99.S28G74 1972] 92 79-161919 2.97
1. Osceola, Seminole chief, 1804-1838—Juvenile literature. I. Oxendine, Lloyd E., illus. II. Title.

JOHNSON, Robert Proctor, 970.3 B
1924-
Osceola, by R. P. Johnson. Minneapolis, Dillon Press [1973] 90 p. illus. 24 cm. (The Story of an American Indian) A biography of the Seminole Chief who was the guiding spirit and military genius behind the Second Seminole War, his people's attempt to resist forcible removal from their land. [E99.S28J64] 92 72-91158 ISBN 0-87518-055-8 3.95
1. Osceola, Seminole Chief, 1804-1838—Juvenile literature. 2. Seminole War, 2d, 1835-1842—Juvenile literature. I. Title. **BIP**

MCGOVERN, Ann. 973'.099 B
The defenders; Osceola, Tecumseh, Cochise. [New York] Scholastic Book Services [1970] 128 p. illus. (part col.), col. maps, ports. 21 cm. (Firebird books) Brief biographies of three Indian chiefs who struggled to save their people from the white man's oppression. [E99.S28O83] 920 75-116623
1. Osceola, Seminole chief, 1804-1838—Juvenile literature. 2. Tecumseh, Shawnee chief, 1768-1813—Juvenile literature. 3. Cochise, Apache chief, d. 1874—Juvenile literature. I. Title.

SYME, Ronald, 1910- 973'.04'97 B
Osceola, Seminole leader / by Ronald Syme ; illustrated by Ben F. Stahl. New York : Morrow, 1976. 96 p. : ill. ; 22 cm. Includes index. Bibliography: p. 94. A biography of the Seminole leader who spent his life fighting the white men's attempts to deport his people from Florida. [E99.S28S95] 92 75-22373 ISBN 0-688-22054-1 : 5.50 ISBN 0-688-32054-6 lib.bdg. : 4.81
1. Osceola, Seminole chief, 1804-1838—Juvenile literature. 2. Seminole Indians—Biography. 3. Indians of North America—Biography. I. Stahl, Ben F. II. Title. **BIP**

Osei Tutu, King of Ashanti, 1636-1712—Juvenile literature.

DAAKU, Kwame 966.7'01'0924 B
Yeboa.
Osei Tutu of Asante / [by] K. Yeboa Daaku. London : Heinemann Educational, 1976. 48 p. : ill., maps, ports. ; 15 x 21 cm. (African historical biographies ; 6) Bibliography: p. 6. [DT507.O83D33] 77-360248 ISBN 0-435-94470-3 pbk. : 1.25
1. Osei Tutu, King of Ashanti, 1636-1712—Juvenile literature. 2. Ashanti—History—Juvenile literature. 3. Ashanti—Kings and rulers—Biography—Juvenile literature. I. Title. II. Series.
Distributed by Heinemann Educ., Salem, New Hampshire **BIP**

Osgood, James Ripley, 1836-1892.

WEBER, Carl Jefferson 926.55
The rise and fall of James Ripley Osgood, a biography. Waterville, Me., Colby College Press, [c.]1959. 283p. illus., port., map, geneal. table. 24cm. (Colby College monograph no. 22) 60-9632 8.00 buck.,
1. Osgood, James Ripley, 1836-1892. I. Title. II. Series: Colby College, Waterville, Me. Colby College monograph no. 22

WEBER, Carl Jefferson, 926.55
1894-
The rise and fall of James Ripley Osgood, a biography. Waterville, Me., Colby College Press, 1959. 283 p. illus., port., map, geneal. table. 24 cm. (Colby College monography no. 22) [Z473.O8W4] 60-9632
1. Osgood, James Ripley, 1836-1892. I. Title. II. Series: Colby College, Waterville, Me. Colby College monography no. 22

Osler, William, bart, Sir 1849-1919.

NOBLE, Iris. 926.1
The doctor who dared, William Osler. New York, Messner [1959] 192p. 22cm. Includes bibliography. [R464.O8N6] 59-7139
1. Osler, William, bart, Sir 1849-1919. I. Title.

Osler, William, Sir, bart., 1849-1919.

HOLLEY, Howard L. 610'.924 B
A continual remembrance; letters from Sir William Osler to his friend Ned Milburn, 1865-1919, by Howard L. Holley. With a foreword by John W. Scott. Springfield, Ill., Thomas [1968] xxiii, 132 p. illus., ports. 24 cm. Includes bibliographical references. [R464.O8H6] 68-11692
1. Osler, William, Sir, bart., 1849-1919. I. Osler, William, Sir, bart., 1849-1919. II. Milburn, Ned, 1849-1926. III. Title.

Osmond Brothers.

DELANEY, Monica. 784'.092'2 B
The Osmonds / text, Monica Delaney & Shannon Laney ; illustrated by John Keely. Mankato, Minn. : Creative Education, [1975] p. cm. Bibliography: p. A biography of the family of Mormon background who have become world famous as a rock group. [ML3930.O85D4] 920 75-23185 ISBN 0-87191-461-1 : 4.95
1. Osmond Brothers. I. Laney, Shannon, joint author. II. Keely, John. III. Title.

DUNN, Paul H. 784.0922
The Osmonds: the official story of the Osmond family /by Paul H. Dunn. Garden City: Doubleday, 1976. ix, 246 p.: ill.; 23 cm. [ML421.O83D8] 75-45765 ISBN 0-385-12217-9: 6.95
1. Osmond Brothers. I. Title. **BIP**

DUNN, Paul H. 784'.092'2 B
The Osmonds : the official story of the Osmond family / by Paul H. Dunn. Salt Lake City : Bookcraft, inc., 1975. 246 p. : ill. ; 24 cm. [ML421.O83D8] 75-4325 ISBN 0-88494-278-3
1. Osmond Brothers. I. Title.

DUNN, Paul H. 784'.092'2 [B]
The Osmonds / by Paul H. Dunn. New York : Avon Books, 1977. 255p. : ill.,photos ; 18 cm. [ML421.O83D8] ISBN 0-380-01717-2 pbk. : 1.75
1. Osmond Brothers. I. Title. .
L.C. card no. for 1975 Bookcraft ed.: 75-4325.

DUNN, Paul H. 784'.092'2 [B]
The Osmonds / by Paul H. Dunn. New York : Avon Books, 1977. 255p. : ill.,photos ; 18 cm. [ML421.O83D8] ISBN 0-380-01717-2 pbk. : 1.75
1. Osmond Brothers. I. Title.
L.C. card no. for 1975 Bookcraft ed.: 75-4325.

DUNN, Paul H. 784'.092'2 B
The Osmonds : the official story of the Osmond family / by Paul H. Dunn. Salt Lake City : Bookcraft, inc., 1975. 246 p. : ill. ; 24 cm. [ML421.O83D8] 75-4325 ISBN 0-88494-278-3 : 5.95
1. Osmond Brothers. I. Title.

TREMLETT, George. 784'.092'2 B
The Osmond story / George Tremlett. New York : Warner Paperback Library, 1975, c1974. 158 p. : ports. ; 18 cm. [ML421.O83T7] 75-310211 ISBN 0-446-76788-3 pbk. : 1.25
1. Osmond Brothers. I. Title.

Osmond Brothers—Juvenile literature.

DELANEY, Monica. 784'.092'2 B
The Osmonds / text, Monica Delaney, Shannon Laney ; ill. John Kelly ; design concept, Mark Landkramer. Mankato, Minn. : Creative Education, c1976. 31 p. : col. ill. ; 25 cm. (Rock 'n pop stars) Bibliography: p. A biography of the family of Mormon background who have become world famous as a rock group. [ML3930.O85D4] 920 75-26783 ISBN 0 87191-461-1 : 4.95
1. Osmond Brothers—Juvenile literature. I. Laney, Shannon, joint author. II. Keely, John. III. Title.

DELANEY, Monica. 784'.092'2 B
The Osmonds / text, Monica Delaney, Shannon Laney ; ill. John Kelly ; design concept, Mark Landkramer. Mankato, Minn. : Creative Education, c1976. 31 p. : col. ill. ; 25 cm. (Rock 'n pop stars) Bibliography: p. A biography of the family of Mormon background who have become world famous as a rock group. [ML3930.O85D4] 920 75-26783 ISBN 0-87191-461-1 : 4.95
1. Osmond Brothers—Juvenile literature. I. Laney, Shannon, joint author. II. Keely, John. III. Title.

DELANEY, Monica. 784'.092'2 B
The Osmonds / text, Monica Delaney, Shannon Laney ; ill. John Kelly ; design concept, Mark Landkramer. Mankato, Minn. : Creative Education, c1976. 31 p. : col. ill. ; 25 cm. (Rock 'n pop stars) Bibliography: p. A biography of the family of Mormon background who have become world famous as a rock group. [ML3930.O85D4] 920 75-26783 ISBN 0-87191-461-1 : 4.95
1. Osmond Brothers—Juvenile literature. I. Laney, Shannon, joint author. II. Keely, John. III. Title.

Osmond, Donny.

MCMILLAN, Constance 784'.092'2 B
Van Brunt.
Donny and Marie Osmond : breaking all the rules / by Constance Van Brunt McMillan. St. Paul : EMC Corp., 1977. p. cm. (So young, so far) A biography of a brother and sister who quickly rose to the top of pop and country music and now host their own television variety program. [ML420.O83M2] 920 77-24069 ISBN 0-88436-408-9 lib.bdg. : 4.95 ISBN 0-88436-409-7 pbk. : 2.95
1. Osmond, Donny. 2. Osmond, Marie, 1959- 3. Singers—United States—Biography—Juvenile literature. I. Title. **BIP**

Osmond, Donny—Juvenile literature.

ELDRED, Patricia 784'.092'2 B
Mulrooney.
Donny and Marie / by Patricia Mulrooney Eldred ; designed by Mark Landkamer. Mankato, Minn. : Creative Education, c1978. 31 p. : ill. ; 25 cm. (Rock 'n pop stars) A brief biography of the well-known brother and sister singing team.

[ML3930.O83E4] 920 77-24654 ISBN 087191-618-5 : 4.95
1. Osmond, Donny—Juvenile literature. 2. Osmond, Marie, 1959- —Juvenile literature. 3. Singers—United States—Biography—Juvenile literature. I. Title. **BIP**

Ospital, John, 1915-

†OSPITAL, John, 1915- 940.54'81'73
We wore jump boots and baggy pants / by John Ospital. [Aptos, Calif.] : Willow House, c1977. ix, 118 p., [1] leaf of plates : ill. ; 26 cm. [D811.O85] 78-104903 ISBN 0-912450-15-0 pbk. : 7.95
1. Ospital, John, 1915- 2. United States. Army—Airborne troops—Biography. 3. World War, 1939-1945—Personal narratives, American. 4. Soldiers—United States—Biography. I. Title. **BIP**

Oss, John.

RUFFO, Vinnie. 266'.023'0922
Behind barbed wire. Mountain View, Calif., Pacific Press Pub. Association [1967] v, 121 p. 22 cm. [BV3427.O68R8] 67-27708
1. Oss, John. 2. Oss, Olga Bertine (Osnes) 1897- I. Title.

Ossoli, Sarah Margaret (Fuller) marchesa d', 1810-1850.

ANTHONY, Katharine Susan, 1877-1965. 818'.3'09 B
Margaret Fuller; a psychological biography. New York, Harcourt, Brace, 1921. St. Clair Shores, Mich., Scholarly Press, 1970. v, 223 p. 21 cm. Bibliography: p. 217-220. [PS2506.A8 1970] 78-131608
1. Ossoli, Sarah Margaret (Fuller) marchesa d', 1810-1850. **BIP**

ANTHONY, Katharine Susan, 1877-1965. 818'.3'09 B
Margaret Fuller; a psychological biography. Folcroft, Pa., Folcroft Press [1969, c1920] v, 223 p. port. 24 cm. Bibliography: p. 217-220. [PS2506.A8 1969] 72-195019
1. Ossoli, Sarah Margaret (Fuller) marchesa d', 1810-1850. I. Title.

BELL, Margaret, 1894- 818'.3'09 B
Margaret Fuller; a biography. With an introd. by Mrs. Franklin D. Roosevelt. Freeport, N.Y., Books for Libraries Press [1971] 320 p. 23 cm. Reprint of the 1930 ed. [PS2506.B4 1971] 72-164587 ISBN 0-8369-5871-3
1. Ossoli, Sarah Margaret (Fuller) marchesa d', 1810-1850.

BRAUN, Frederick Augustus. 818'.3'09 B
Margaret Fuller and Goethe; the development of a remarkable personality, her religion and philosophy, and her relation to Emerson, J. F. Clarke, and transcendentalism. [Folcroft, Pa.] Folcroft Library Editions, 1971 [c1910] vii, 271 p. 23 cm. "Limited to 150 copies." Bibliography: p. 259-261. [PS2506.B7 1971] 72-195018
1. Ossoli, Sarah Margaret (Fuller) marchesa d', 1810-1850. 2. Goethe, Johann Wolfgang von, 1749-1832. I. Title.

BROWN, Arthur W. 928.1
Margaret Fuller. Coll. & Univ. Pr.; dist. New York Grosset [c.1964] 159p. 21cm. (Twayne's United States authors ser., 48) Bibl. 1.95 pap.,
1. Ossoli, Sarah Margaret (Fuller) marchesa d', 1810-1850. I. Title. **BIP**

BROWN, Arthur W. 928.1
Margaret Fuller. New York, Twayne Publishers [1964] 159 p. 21 cm. (Twayne's United States authors series, 48) "Notes and references": p. 135-147. Bibliography: p. 148-153. [PS2506.B77] 63-20612
1. Ossoli, Sarah Margaret (Fuller) marchesa d', 1810-1850.

CHEVIGNY, Bell Gale. 818'.3'09 B
The woman and the myth : Margaret Fuller's life and writings / by Bell Gale Chevigny. Old Westbury, N.Y. : Feminist Press, 1976. p. cm. Includes a selection of writings by M. Fuller. Includes bibliographical references. [PS2506.C48] 76-19030 ISBN 0-912670-43-6 pbk. : 6.50
1. Ossoli, Sarah Margaret Fuller, marchesa d', 1810-1850. 2. Women—Social and moral questions. I. Ossoli, Sarah Margaret Fuller, marchesa d', 1810-1850. The woman and the myth. 1976. II. Title. **BIP**

CHIPPERFIELD, Faith. 928.1
In quest of love; the life and death of Margaret Fuller. New York, Coward-McCann [1957] 320 p. illus. 22 cm. [PS2506.C5] 57-7062
1. Ossoli, Sarah Margaret (Fuller) marchesa d', 1810-1850. I. Title.

DEISS, Joseph Jay. 818'.3'09 B
The Roman years of Margaret Fuller; a biography, by Joseph Jay Deiss. New York, Crowell [1969] 338 p. illus., map, ports. 21 cm. Bibliography: p. 314-320. [PS2506.D39] 70-81941 6.95
1. Ossoli, Sarah Margaret (Fuller) marchesa d', 1810-1850. I. Title.

HOWE, Julia (Ward) 1819-1910. 818'.3'09 B
Margaret Fuller (Marchesa Ossoli) New York, Haskell House Publishers, 1968. x, 298 p. 23 cm. Reprint of the 1883 ed. [PS2506.H6 1968] 68-24938
1. Ossoli, Sarah Margaret (Fuller) marchesa d', 1810-1850. **BIP**

HOWE, Julia (Ward) 1819-1910. 818'.3'09 B
Margaret Fuller (Marchesa Ossoli). Westport, Conn., Greenwood Press [1970] x, 298 p. 23 cm. (Famous women) Reprint of the 1883 ed. [PS2506.H6 1970] 69-13936 ISBN 0-8371-4089-7
1. Ossoli, Sarah Margaret (Fuller) marchesa d', 1810-1850. I. Title. II. Series.

OSSOLI, Sarah Margaret (Fuller) marchesa d', 1810-1850. 928.1
Margaret Fuller; American romantic; a selection from her writings and correspondence. Edited by Perry Miller. Garden City, N.Y., Doubleday, 1963. 319 p. 19 cm. (Anchor books) A Doubleday Anchor original. "A356." [PS2502.M5] 63-13082
I. Title.

OSSOLI, Sarah Margaret (Fuller) marchesa d'. 1810-1850 928.1
Margaret Fuller: American romantic; a selection from her writings and correspondence. Ed. by Perry Miller. Garden City, N.Y., Doubleday [c.]1963. 319p. 19cm. (Anchor bks., A356) Bibl. 63-13082 1.45 pap.,
I. Title.

OSSOLI, Sarah Margaret (Fuller) marchesa d'. 1810-1850 928.1
Margaret Fuller: American romantic; a selection from her writings and correspondence. Ed. by Perry Miller. Garden City, N.Y., Doubleday [c.]1963. 319p. 19cm. (Anchor bks., A356) Bibl. 63-13082 1.45 pap.,
I. Title.

STERN, Madeleine Bettina, 1912- 818'.3'09 B
The life of Margaret Fuller, by Madeleine B. Stern. New York, Haskell House, 1968 [c1942] xvi, 549 p. illus., facsims., ports. 24 cm. Bibliography: p. 493-523. [PS2506.S7 1968] 68-29738
1. Ossoli, Sarah Margaret (Fuller) marchesa d', 1810-1850. **BIP**

WADE, Mason, 1913- 818'.3'09 B
Margaret Fuller, whetstone of genius. Clifton [N.J.] A. M. Kelley, 1973 [c1940] xvi, 304 p. illus. 23 cm. (Viking reprint editions) Bibliography: p. 294-297. [PS2506.W3 1973] 72-122077 ISBN 0-678-03178-9 13.50
1. Ossoli, Sarah Margaret (Fuller) Marchessa d', 1810-1850.

Ossoli, Sarah Margaret Fuller, marchesa d', 1810-1850 - Biography.

BLANCHARD, Paula. 818'.3'09
Margaret Fuller : from Transcendentalism to revolution / Paula Blanchard. New York : Dell Pub. Co., 1979, c1978. xii, 370p., [4] leaves of plates : ill. ; 21 cm. (Delta/Seymour Lawrence) (Radcliffe biography series) Includes index. "A Merloyd Lawrence book." Bibliography: p. 353-360. [PS2506.B57] ISBN 0-440-56242-2 pbk. : 6.95
1. Ossoli, Sarah Margaret Fuller, marchesa d', 1810-1850 — Biography. 2. Authors, American — 19th century — Biography. I. Title.
L.C. card no. for 1978 Delacorte/S. Lawrence ed.: 78-739.

SLATER, Abby. 818'.3'09 B
In search of Margaret Fuller : a biography / by Abby Slater. New York : Delacorte Press, c1978. viii, 215 p. ; 22 cm. Includes index. Bibliography: p. [205]-208. A biography of a critic, journalist, and social reformer. [PS2506.S57] 92 77-86335 ISBN 0-440-03944-4 : 6.95
1. Ossoli, Sarah Margaret Fuller, marchesa d', 1810-1850—Biography. 2. Authors, American—19th century—Biography. I. Title. **BIP**

Ossoli, Sarah Margaret Fuller, marchesa d', 1810-1850—Biography—Juvenile literature.

WILSON, Ellen Janet Cameron. 818'.3'09 B
Margaret Fuller, bluestocking, romantic, revolutionary / Ellen Wilson. New York : Farrar, Straus and Giroux, c1977. 185 p. : ill. ; 21 cm. Includes index. Bibliography: p. 178-181. A biography of an American writer active in early women's rights activities and prominent in the transcendentalist movement of the early 1800's. [PS2506.W5] 92 77-381 ISBN 0-374-34807-3 : 7.95
1. Ossoli, Sarah Margaret Fuller, marchesa d', 1810-1850—Biography—Juvenile literature. 2. Authors, American—19th century—Biography—Juvenile literature. I. Title.

Ossoli, Sarah Margaret (Fuller) Marchessa d', 1810-1850.

WADE, Mason, 1913- 818'.3'09 B
Margaret Fuller, whetstone of genius. Clifton [N.J.] A. M. Kelley, 1973 [c1940] xvi, 304 p. illus. 23 cm. (Viking reprint editions) Bibliography: p. 294-297. [PS2506.W3 1973] 72-122077 ISBN 0-678-03178-9 13.50
1. Ossoli, Sarah Margaret (Fuller) Marchessa d', 1810-1850.

Ossorio, Alfonso, 1916-

FRIEDMAN, Bernard Harper, 1926- 709'.2'4
Alfonso Ossorio [by] B. H. Friedman. New York, H. N. Abrams [1972] 269 p. illus. (part col.) 28 x 30 cm. "Plates": p. [95]-[264] Bibliography: p. 267-269. [N6537.O77F74] 73-160154 ISBN 0-8109-0352-0
1. Ossorio, Alfonso, 1916- I. Ossorio, Alfonso, 1916- **BIP**

Ostrow, Sarah.

PICON, Molly 817.54
So laugh a little, by Molly Picon as told to Eth Clifford Rosenberg. New York, Paperback Lib. [1966, c.1962] 160p. 18cm. (53-353) .60 pap.,
1. Ostrow, Sarah. 2. Actors—Correspondence, reminiscences, etc. I. Rosenberg, Ethel Clifford II. Title.

PICON, Molly. 817.54
So laugh a little, by Molly Picon as told to Eth Clifford Rosenberg. New York, Messner [1962] 175 p. 21 cm. Autobiographical. [PN2287.P53A3] 62-19189
1. Ostrow, Sarah. 2. Actors—Correspondence, reminiscences, etc. I. Rosenberg, Ethel Clifford, 1915- II. Title.

Ostwald, Wilhelm, 1853-1932.

SLOSSON, Edwin Emery, 1865-1929. 920.04
Major prophets of to-day, by Edwin E. Slosson. Freeport, N.Y., Books for Libraries Press [1968] xii, 299 p. ports. 23 cm. (Essay index reprint series) Reprint of the 1914 ed. "The chapters of this volume have appeared in the Independent ... in a series under the general title of Twelve major prophets of to-day." Contents.Contents.—Maurice Maeterlinck.—Henri Bergson.—Henri Poincare.—Elie Metchnikoff.—Wilhelm Ostwald.—Ernst Haeckel. [CT119.S6 1968] 68-8493
1. Maeterlinck, Maurice, 1862-1949. 2. Bergson, Henri Louis, 1859-1941. 3. Poincare, Henri, 1854-1912. 4. Mechnikov, Il'ia Il'ich, 1845-1916. 5. Ostwald, Wilhelm, 1853-1932. 6. Haeckel, Ernst Heinrich Philipp August, 1834-1919. I. Title. **BIP**

Oswald, Lee Harvey.

LEE: 364.15/2/0924
a portrait of Lee Harvey Oswald. by his brother, Robert L. Oswald, with Myrick and Barbara Land. New York, Coward [1967] 246p. ports. 22cm. [E842.9.O8] (B) 67-29487 5.95
1. Oswald, Lee Harvey. I. Oswald, Robert L. II. Land, Myrick, 1922- joint author. III. Land, Barbara. joint author.

MCMILLAN, Priscilla Johnson. 973.922'092'4 B
Marina and Lee / by Priscilla Johnson McMillan. 1st ed. New York : Harper & Row, c1977. p. cm. Includes index. [CT275.O737M32 1977] 76-26238 ISBN 0-06-012953-0 : 15.00
1. Oswald, Marina, 1941- 2. Oswald, Lee Harvey. 3. Kennedy, John Fitzgerald, Pres. U.S., 1917-1963—Assassination. 4. United States—Biography. I. Title. **BIP**

OSWALD, Robert L. 364.15'24'0924 B
Lee; a portrait of Lee Harvey Oswald, by his brother, Robert L. Oswald, with Myrick and Barbara Land. New York, Coward-McCann [1967] 246 p. ports. 22 cm. [E842.9.O8] 67-29487
1. Oswald, Lee Harvey. I. Land, Myrick, 1922- joint author. II. Land, Barbara, joint author. III. Title.

SITES, Paul, 1926- 364.15'24'0924 B
Lee Harvey Oswald and the American dream. [1st ed.] New York, Pageant Press [1967] 261 p. 21 cm. Includes bibliographical references. [E842.9.S5] 67-66259
1. Oswald, Lee Harvey. I. Title.

Oswald, Marina, 1941-

MCMILLAN, Priscilla Johnson. 973.922'092'4 B
Marina and Lee / by Priscilla Johnson McMillan. 1st ed. New York : Harper & Row, c1977. p. cm. Includes index. [CT275.O737M32 1977] 76-26238 ISBN 0-06-012953-0 : 15.00
1. Oswald, Marina, 1941- 2. Oswald, Lee Harvey. 3. Kennedy, John Fitzgerald, Pres. U.S., 1917-1963—Assassination. 4. United States—Biography. I. Title. **BIP**

Oswald, Saint, King of Northumbria, 6057-642.

AELFRIC, Abbot of Eynsham. v. 12
Lives of three English saints; edited by G. I. Needham. New York, Appleton-Century-Crofts [1966] viii, 119 p. 19 cm. (Emthuen's Old English Library. Series B: Prose selections) Bibliography: p. 82-85. [NUC67-74378]

1. Oswald, Saint, King of Northumbria, 6057-642. 2. Edmund, Saint, King of East Anglia, 841-870. 3. Swithun, Saint, Bp. of Winchester, d. 862. I. Needbam, Geoffrey Ivor, ed. II. Title.
Contents Omitted.

Otani, Sadao, 1892-1969.

DR. Sadao Otani; 616.07'08
his contribution to American pathology. [New York? 1972] 1 v. (various pagings) illus. 27 cm. Contents.Contents.—Popper, H. Foreword.—Ehrlich, J. C. Sadao Otani, 1892-1969.—Mori, K. Dr. Otani's teaching of human pathology.—Otani, S. Large sessile mucosal polyps of the colon.—Otani, S. Malignant melanoma.—Otani, S. Excerpt from "Pathology of the breast".—Otani, S. Trabeculated adenoma of the thyroid gland and its malignant transformation.—Otani, S. Papillary adenomatous tumors of aberrant thyroid in cervical lymph nodes.—Kornblith, B. A. and Otani, S. Meconium ileus with congenital stenosis of main pancreatic duct.—Klemperer, P. and Otani, S. Malignant nephrosclerosis (Fahr).—Otani, S. and Ehrlich, J. C. Solitary granuloma of bone simulating primary neoplasm. Includes bibliographies. [RB6.D63] 73-170537
1. Otani, Sadao, 1892-1969. 2. Pathology—Addresses, essays, lectures. I. Churg, Jacob, ed. II. Strauss, Lillian Laser, ed.

Otero, Caroline, 1868-1965.

LEWIS, Arthur H., 1906- 301.41'5
La Belle Otero New York, Pocket Bks. [1968, c.1967] ix, 243p. 18cm. (77018) [HQ117.L43] .95 pap.,
1. Otero, Caroline, 1868-1965. I. Title.

Otero, Miguel Antonio, 1859-1944.

OTERO, Miguel 978.9'04'0924 B
Antonio, 1859-1944.
Otero: an autobiographical trilogy. New York, Arno Press, 1974. 293, xi, 306, viii, 404 p. 23 cm. (The Mexican American) Reprint of My life on the frontier, 1864-1882, first published 1935, by Press of the Pioneers, New York; of My life on the frontier, 1882-1897, first published 1939, by University of New Mexico Press, Albuquerque; and of My nine years as Governor of the Territory of New Mexico, 1897-1906, first published 1940, by University of New Mexico Press, Albuquerque. [F801.O893] 73-14420 ISBN 0-405-05685-0 52.00 (3 volumes)
1. Otero, Miguel Antonio, 1859-1944. 2. New Mexico—History—1848- I. Title. II. Series.

Otey, William Wesley, 1867-1961.

WILLIS, Cecil. 922.673
W. W. Otey, contender for the faith; a history of controversies in the Church of Christ from 1860-1960. Akron, Ohio [c1964] xi, 425 p. illus. ports. 22 cm. "A compendium of the writings of W. W. Otey": p. 393-416. Bibliography: p. 417-422. [BX7343.O8W5] 66-4455
1. Otey, William Wesley, 1867-1961. I. Title.

Otis, Charles Augustus,

OTIS, Charles Augustus, 923.373
1868-
Here I am; a rambling account of the exciting times of yesteryear. Cleveland, Buehler Printcraft Corp., 1951. 216p. illus. 23cm. [CT275.O744A3] 53-23409
I. Title.

Otis, James, 1725-1783.

GALVIN, John R., 973.2'7'0922
1929-
Three men of Boston / John R. Galvin. New York : Crowell, c1976. 326 p. ; 23 cm. Includes index. Bibliography: p. 303-305. [E302.5.G34] 75-20331 ISBN 0-690-01018-4 : 10.00
1. Hutchinson, Thomas, 1711-1780. 2. Otis, James, 1725-1783. 3. Adams, Samuel, 1722-1803. 4. United States—History—Revolution, 1775-1783—Causes. I. Title. BIP

TUDOR, William, 973.3'0924 B
1779-1830.
The life of James Otis, of Massachusetts. New York, Da Capo Press, 1970. xx, 508 p. illus., facsim., port. 24 cm. (The Era of the American Revolution) (A Da Capo Press reprint series.) Reprint of the 1823 ed. [E302.6.O8T9 1970] 70-118203
1. Otis, James, 1725-1783. BIP

Ott, Mel. 1909-1958

SHAPIRO, Milton J. 927.96357
The Mel Ott story. New York, Messner [1959] 192 p. illus. 22 cm. [GV865.O8S5] 59-12767
1. Ott, Mel. 1909-1958 I. Title.

Otterbein, Philip William, Bp., 1726-1813.

CORE, Arthur C. 289.9 B
Philip William Otterbein; pastor ecumenist ... By Arthur C. Core. Dayton, Ohio, Board of Publication, Evangelical United Brethren Church [1968] 127 p. illus., facsims., port. 22 cm. Includes bibliographical references. [BX9877.O8C6] 68-22446
1. Otterbein, Philip William, Bp., 1726-1813. I. Title.

MILHOUSE, Paul William, 289.9 B
1910-
Philip William Otterbein; pioneer pastor to Germans in America, by Paul W. Milhouse. Nashville, Upper Room [1968] 71 p. illus. 16 cm. Includes bibliographical references. [BX9877.O8M5] 68-19994
1. Otterbein, Philip William, Bp., 1726-1813.

Otto, Madeline (Bird) 1898-1960.

OTTO, Arnold Clarence, 920.7
1887-
Madeline Bird Otto; a memorial, with historical data of the Bird, Bourne, Sparkes, and Otto families, edited and published by Arnold C. Otto. Milwaukee, 1964. 342 p. illus., ports. 27 cm. "Private edition, limited to five hundred printings." [CT275.O78O8] 63-16438
1. Otto, Madeline (Bird) 1898-1960. I. Title.

Ouercia, Jacopo della, 1372?-1438.

HANSON, Anne Coffin 730.945
Jacopo della Quercia's Fonte Gaia [New York] Oxford [c.]1965. xiv, 123p. plates. 29cm. (Oxford-Warburg studies) Bibl. [NB623.O4I13] 65-2071 12.00
1. Ouercia, Jacopo della, 1372?-1438. 2. Siena. Fonte Gaia. I. Title. BIP

Our Lady of Mount Carmel Church, Baden, Mo.

BARRY, R. K. 282'.778'66
The history of Our Lady of Mount Carmel Parish, Baden, Missouri. Compiled by R. K. Barry. [Baden? Mo., 1972?] 48 p. illus. 28 cm. Cover title: Our Lady of Mt. Carmel centennial celebration, 1872-1972. [BX4603.B28O862] 74-152668
1. Our Lady of Mount Carmel Church, Baden, Mo. 2. Baden, Mo.—Biography. I. Title. II. Title: Our Lady of Mt. Carmel centennial celebration, 1872-1972.

Oursler, Fulton,

OURSLER, Fulton, 1893-1952. 928.1
Behold this dreamer! An autobiography. Edited and with commentary by Fulton Oursler, Jr. [1st ed.] Boston, Little, Brown [1964] x, 501 p. port. 22 cm. [PS3529.U65Z5] 64-23292
I. Title.

Oury, William Sanders, 1817-1887.

SMITH, Cornelius Cole, 917.91
1913-
William Sanders Oury: history-maker of the southwest [by] Cornelius C. Smith , Jr. Tucson, University of Arizona Press [1967] xv, 298 p. illus., maps, ports. 24 cm. Bibliography: p. 265-272. [F786.O9S5] 66-24301
1. Oury, William Sanders, 1817-1887. 2. Southwest, New—History.

Outlaws.

FAMOUS gunfighters of the v. 12
western frontier: Luke Short, Bill Tilghman, Ben Thompson, Doc Holliday [and] Wyatt Earp. Houston, Frontier Press of Texas, 1957. 112p. illus., plates, ports. 'Published in Human life magazine, 1907.'
1. Outlaws. 2. Crime and criminals—The West. I. Masterson, William Barclay, 1853-1921. II. Title: Gunfighters of the western frontier.

Outlaws—Biography.

MENDHAM, Roy, 364.1'55'0922 B
1890-
The dictionary of Australian bushrangers / compiled by Roy Mendham. Melbourne : Hawthorn Press, 1975. 179 p. : ill. ; 23 cm. Includes index. [HV6453.A7M45] 76-350665 ISBN 0-7256-0120-5 : 8.95
1. Outlaws—Biography. 2. Brigands and robbers—Australia—Biography. I. Title.

Outlaws—California—Biography.

JACKSON, Joseph 979.4'04'0922 B
Henry, 1894-1955.
Bad company : the story of California's legendary and actual stage-robbers, bandits, highwaymen, and outlaws from the fifties to the eighties / Joseph Henry Jackson. Lincoln : University of Nebraska Press, [1977] c1949. xx, 346 p., [8] leaves of plates : ill. ; 21 cm. Reprint of the 1st ed. published by Harcourt, Brace, New York. Four of the chapters were published in 1939 under the title: Tintypes in gold. "A Bison book". Includes index. "Notes on sources": p. 327-330. [F866.J24 1977] 77-7300 ISBN 0-8032-0930-4 : 15.00 ISBN 0-8032-5866-6 pbk. : 4.50
1. Outlaws—California—Biography. 2. California—Biography. 3. California—History—1850-1950. I. Title. BIP

Outlaws—The West—Biography.

HORAN, James 978'.02'0922 B
David, 1914-
The authentic wild West / by James D. Horan. New York : Crown Publishers, c1976- v. : ill. ; 29 cm. Contents.Contents.—v. [1] The gunfighters. Bibliography: v. [1], p. 302-308. [F594.H79 1976] 76-10758 ISBN 0-517-52680-8 : 12.95 ISBN 0-517-52818-5 leather : 100.00
1. Outlaws—The West—Biography. 2. The West—Biography. I. Title.

Ouvrard, Gabriel Julien, 1770-1846.

WOLFF, Otto, 1881- 923.344
Ouvrard, speculator of genius, 1770-1846. Tr. by Stewart Thomson. Introd., notes by T.A.B. Corley. New York, McKay [1963, c.1962] 239p. illus. 23cm. Bibl. 63-13474 5.95
1. Ouvrard, Gabriel Julien, 1770-1846. 2. Finance, Public—France—Hist. I. Title.

Overland journeys to the Pacific.

BIDLACK, Russell Eugene, 920.02
1920-
Letters home; the story of Ann Arbor's forty-niners. With an introd. by F. Clever Bald. Ann Arbor, Mich., Ann Arbor Publishers, 1960. 56 p. illus. 23 cm. Includes extracts from letters written by Ann Arbor residents en route to California and after their arrival. Includes bibliography. [F593.B6] 61-4483
1. Overland journeys to the Pacific. 2. California—Gold discoveries. 3. Ann Arbor, Michigan—Biography. I. Title.

DICKENSON, Luella. 978'.03
Reminiscences of a trip across the Plains in 1846 and early days in California / Luella Dickenson. Fairfield, Wash. : Ye Galleon Press, 1977. 48 p. : ill. ; 29 cm. Seven hundred eighty five copies printed. No. 32. Originally published in 1904 by Whitaker & Ray Co., San Francisco. [F592.D43 1977] 77-8983 ISBN 0-87770-180-6 : 10.00
1. Overland journeys to the Pacific. 2. Pioneers—California—Biography. 3. California—Biography. 4. Indians of North America—The West. I. Title. BIP

HEWITT, James. 917.8'04'208
Eye-witnesses to wagon trains west; Reading, Osprey Publishing, 1973. xi, 178, [16] p. illus., facsim., maps, ports. 23 cm. (His Eye-witnesses to history) Includes index. Bibliography: p. [168]-171. [F593.H48 1973] 73-173234 ISBN 0-85045-104-3 £2.50
1. Overland journeys to the Pacific. 2. Pioneers—United States. I. Title. BIP

PERKINS, Elisha Douglass, 978'.02
1823-1852.
Gold rush diary, being the journal of Elisha Douglass Perkins on the Overland Trail in the spring and summer of 1849. Edited by Thomas D. Clark. Lexington, University of Kentucky Press, 1967. xxv, 206 p. illus., maps, ports. 29 cm. Bibliography: p. 197-201 [F593.P46A3] 66-26690
1. Overland journeys to the Pacific. 2. California—Gold discoveries. 3. Frontier and pioneer life—California. I. Clark, Thomas Dionysius, 1903- ed. II. Title.

WOJCIK, Donna M. 979.5'03'0922
The brazen overlanders of 1845 / researched, compiled, and written by Donna M. Wojcik ; illustrations by Ralph Niader. Portland, Or. : Wojcik, c1976. xv, 566 p., [11] leaves of plates : ill. ; 23 cm. "Book no. 298." Includes index. Bibliography: p. 529-556. [F593.W64] 76-45289
1. Overland journeys to the Pacific. 2. Pioneers—Oregon—Biography. 3. Oregon—Genealogy. 4. Registers of births, etc.—Oregon. I. Title.

Ovidius Naso, Publius.

SORLEY, Herbert Tower, 1892- 928
Exile, a study in three books. Ilfracombe, Eng., A.H. Stockwell [Port Washington, N.Y., Clark McCutcheon, 176 Main, 1965] x, 203p. 29cm. Bibl. [CT105.S724] 65-7394 2.75
1. Ovidius Naso, Publius. 2. Charles Edward, the Young Pretender, 1720-1788. 3. Hugo, Victor Marie, comte, 1802-1885. 4. Exiles. I. Title.
Contents omitted.

Oviedo, Spain (Province)—History.

LOPEZ y Garcia Jove, 914.68
Luciano.
Historia de los reyes de la monarquia asturiana / por Luciano Lopez y Garcia Jove. 2. ed. Oviedo : [s.n.], 1974. 152 p. : ill. ; 16 cm. On cover: Los reyes de la monarquia asturiana. [DP302.O8L66 1974] 76-457792 ISBN 8-440-07750-5 : 40ptas
1. Oviedo, Spain (Province)—History. 2. Oviedo, Spain (Province)—Kings and rulers. I. Title. II. Title: Los reyes de la monarquia asturiana.

Owen, Goronwy, 1722-1769?

JONES, John Gwilym. 891.6'6'12
Goronwy Owen's Virginian adventure; his life, poetry, and literary opinions, with a translation of his Virginian letters. Lecture and translation by John Gwilym Jones. Williamsburg, Va., Botetourt Bibliographical Society, 1969. 35 p. 22 cm. (Botetourt publications, no. 2) Cover title. "Five-hundred copies." [Z732.V8B6 no. 2] 75-15078
1. Owen, Goronwy, 1722-1769? I. Botetourt Bibliographical Society. II. Title. III. Series.

Owen, John,

OWEN, John, 1616-1683. 274.2
The correspondence of John Owen (1616-1683): with an account of his life and work; edited by Peter Toon, foreword by Geoffrey F. Nuttall Cambridge, James Clarke, 1970. xv, 190 p. 23 cm. Bibliography: p. 187-188. [BX5207.O88A4

1970] 73-582713 ISBN 0-227-67736-6 £1.50
I. Toon, Peter, 1939- ed.

Owen, John, 1616-1683.

OWEN, John, 1616-1683. 274.2
The correspondence of John Owen (1616-1683): with an account of his life and work; edited by Peter Toon, foreword by Geoffrey F. Nuttall Cambridge, James Clarke, 1970. xv, 190 p. 23 cm. Bibliography: p. 187-188. [BX5207.O88A4 1970] 73-582713 ISBN 0-227-67736-6 £1.50
I. Toon, Peter, 1939- ed.

TOON, Peter, 1939- 285'.9'0924 B
God's statesman: the life and work of John Owen, pastor, educator, theologian. Grand Rapids, Mich., Zondervan Pub. House [1973, c1971] viii, 200 p. 23 cm. Bibliography: p. [188]-195. [BX5207.O88T66 1973] 72-95518 ISBN 0-85364-133-1 5.95
1. Owen, John, 1616-1683. I. Title.

Owen, Richard, Sir, 1804-1892.

OWEN, Richard Startin. 591'.092'4 B
The life of Richard Owen / by Richard Owen ; with the scientific portions rev. by C. Davies Sherborn ; also an essay on Owen's position in anatomical science by T. H. Huxley. New York : AMS Press, 1975. 2 v. : ill. ; 19 cm. Reprint of the 1894-95 ed. published by D. Appleton, 1894. Includes index. "Bibliography of Richard Owen, 1830-1889": v. 2, p. [333]-382. [QL31.O9O8 1975] 72-1697 ISBN 0-404-07995-4 : 57.50
1. Owen, Richard, Sir, 1804-1892. I. Title. **BIP**

Owen, Robert,

OWEN, Robert, 1771-1858. 335'.12'0924 B
The life of Robert Owen; written by himself, with selections from his writings & correspondence. v. 1-1A. New York, A. M. Kelley Publishers, 1967. 2 v. port. 22 cm. (Reprints of economic classics) Vol. 1A has title: A supplementary appendix to the first volume of the Life of Robert Owen. Containing a series of reports, addresses, memorials, and other documents, referred to in that volume. 1803-1820. Reprint of 1st ed., published in 1857-58. No more published. [HX696.O9A3 1967] 66-21690
I. Title. **BIP**

OWEN, Robert, 1771-1858. 335'.12 B
Robert Owen in the United States [edited by] Oakley C. Johnson. Foreword by A. L. Morton. New York, Published for A.I.M.S. by Humanities Press, 1970. xii, 86 p. port. 24 cm. (AIMS historical series, no. 6) Bibliography: p. 77-83. [HX696.O9J58] 73-10845 3.50
I. Johnson, Oakley C., 1890- ed. II. Title. III. Series: American Institute for Marxist Studies. AIMS historical series, no. 6

Owen, Robert Dale, 1801-1877.

LEOPOLD, Richard William. 973.6'0924 B
Robert Dale Owen, a biography. New York, Octagon Books, 1969 [c1940] xii, 470 p. port. 23 cm. "A list of the writings of Robert Dale Owen": p. [419]-428. Bibliography: p. [429]-440. [HX696.O9L56 1969] 71-96184
1. Owen, Robert Dale, 1801-1877.

Owen, Robert, 1771-1858.

COLE, George Douglas Howard, 1889-1959 335.120924
The life of Robert Owem. New introd. by Margaret Cole. [3d ed. Hamden. Conn.] Archon [dist. Shoe String, 1966.] xxii, 349p. illus., port. 22cm. Bibl. [HX696.O9C6] 66-864 10.00
1. Owen, Robert, 1771-1858. 2. Socialism in Great Britain. 3. Cooperation—Gt. Brit. I. Title.

COLE, Margaret Isabel (Postgate) 1893- 923.342
Robert Owen of New Lanark. New York, Oxford University Press, 1953. 231p. illus. 22cm. [HX696.O9C63 1953a] 53-12782
1. Owen, Robert, 1771-1858. I. Title. **BIP**

COLE, Margaret Isabel (Postgate) 1893- 335'.12'0924 B
Robert Owen of New Lanark, by Margaret Cole. [New York] A. M. Kelley [1969] vi, 231 p. port. 23 cm. "A note on books": p. 225-226. Bibliographical footnotes. [HX696.O9C63 1969] 75-77254
1. Owen, Robert, 1771-1858. I. Title.

JONES, Lloyd, 1811-1886. 335'.12'0924 B
The life, times, and labours of Robert Owen. London, S. Sonnenschein, 1890. [New York, AMS Press, 1971] 2 v. in 1. ports. 22 cm. Reprint of the 1890 ed. [HX696.O9J7 1971] 77-134406 ISBN 0-404-08449-4
1. Owen, Robert, 1771-1858. I. Title. **BIP**

MORTON, Arthur Leslie, 1903- 923.342
The life and ideas of Robert Owen. New York, Monthly Review, 1963[c.1962] 187p. 23cm. Bibl. 63-8631 3.50
1. Owen, Robert, 1771-1858. I. Title. **BIP**

MORTON, Arthur Leslie, 1903- 335'.12'0924
The life and ideas of Robert Owen, by A. L. Morton. [New and rev. ed.] New York, International Publishers [1969] 239 p. 20 cm. (New world paperbacks, NW-S-5) [HX696.O9M6 1969] 71-4923 1.35
1. Owen, Robert, 1771-1858. I. Title.

OWEN, Robert, 1771-1858. 335'.12'0924 B
The life of Robert Owen; written by himself, with selections from his writings & correspondence. v. 1-1A. New York, A. M. Kelley Publishers, 1967. 2 v. port. 22 cm. (Reprints of economic classics) Vol. 1A has title: A supplementary appendix to the first volume of the Life of Robert Owen. Containing a series of reports, addresses, memorials, and other documents, referred to in that volume. 1803-1820. Reprint of 1st ed., published in 1857-58. No more published. [HX696.O9A3 1967] 66-21690
I. Title. **BIP**

OWEN, Robert, 1771-1858. 335'.12 B
Robert Owen in the United States [edited by] Oakley C. Johnson. Foreword by A. L. Morton. New York, Published for A.I.M.S. by Humanities Press, 1970. xii, 86 p. port. 24 cm. (AIMS historical series, no. 6) Bibliography: p. 77-83. [HX696.O9J58] 73-10845 3.50
I. Johnson, Oakley C., 1890- ed. II. Title. III. Series: American Institute for Marxist Studies. AIMS historical series, no. 6

PODMORE, Frank, 1856-1910. 335'.12'0924 B
Robert Owen; a biography. New York, A. M. Kelley, 1968. 2 v. in 1 (xv, 688 p.) illus. 21 cm. (Reprints of economic classics) Reprint of a work first published in 2 vols. in 1906. Bibliography: p. 655-667. [HX696.O9P8 1968] 68-9762
1. Owen, Robert, 1771-1858.

PODMORE, Frank, 1856-1910. 335'.12'0924 B
Robert Owen; a biography. New York, Haskell House Publishers, 1971. 2 v. (xiii, 688 p.) illus., facsims., ports. 23 cm. "First published 1907." Bibliography: p. 655-667. [HX696.O9P8 1971] 78-156295 ISBN 0-8383-1265-9
1. Owen, Robert, 1771-1858.

ROBERT Owen: 335'.12'0924 B
aspects of his life and work. A symposium edited by John Butt. New York, Humanities Press, 1971. 265 p. illus., ports. 23 cm. "These essays on Robert Owen have evolved from discussions ... in the Department of Economic History at Strathclyde University." Includes bibliographical references. [HX696.O9R6 1971] 77-147784 ISBN 0-391-00154-X 11.50
1. Owen, Robert, 1771-1858. I. Butt, John, ed. II. Glasgow. University of Strathclyde. Dept. of Economic History. **BIP**

Owen, Robert, 1771-1858— Addresses, essays, lectures.

POLLARD, Sidney. 335'.12'0924 B
Robert Owen, prophet of the poor; essays in honour of the two hundredth anniversary of his birth. Edited by Sidney Pollard and John Salt. With an introd. by Sidney Pollard. [1st American ed.] Lewisburg, Bucknell University Press [1971] xi, 318 p. 23 cm. Contents.Contents.—A new view of Mr. Owen, by J. F. C. Harrison.—Robert Owen and revolutionary politics, by C. Tsuzuki.—Robert Owen and the community experiments, by R. G. Garnett.—Owen's reputation as an educationist, by H. Silver.—Robert Owen and radical culture, by E. Yeo.—J. E. Smith and the Owenite movement, 1833-4, by J. Saville.—Robert Owen, cotton spinner: New Lanark, 1800-25, by A. J. Robertson.—Owen in 1817: the Millennialist movement, by W. H. Oliver.—Owen's mind and methods, by M. Cole.—Owen and America, by W. H. G. Armytage.—Images and echoes of Owenism in nineteenth-century France, by H. Desroche.—The impact of Owen's ideas on German social and cooperative thought during the nineteenth century, by E. HasselmanORobert Owen, prophet of the poor; essays in honour of the two hundredth anniversary of his bir
1. Owen, Robert, 1771-1858—Addresses, essays, lectures. I. Owen, Robert, 1771-1858. II. Salt, John, joint author. III. Title.

Owen, Wilfred, 1893-1918.

OWEN, William Harold, 1897- 928.2
Journey from obscurity; Wilfred Owen, 1893-1918. Memoirs of the Owen family [v.2] New York, Oxford [c.]1964. 292p. illus. 23cm. Contents.[v.]2. Youth. 63-5999 5.60
1. Owen, Wilfred, 1893-1918. 2. Owen family. I. Title.

OWEN, William Harold, 1897- 928.2
Journey from obscurity: Wilfred Owen, 1893-1918. Memoirs of the Owen family [v.]3. New York, Oxford. 263p. illus. 23cm. Contents.[v.]3. War. [PR6029.W4Z8] 63-5999 5.60
1. Owen, Wilfred, 1893-1918. 2. Owen family. I. Title.

OWEN, William Harold, 1897- 821.912
Journey from obscurity; Wilfred Owen, 1893-1918. Memoirs of the Owen family. London, New York, Oxford University Press, 1963-65. 3 v. illus., ports. 23 cm. Contents.Childhood. -- Youth. -- War. [PR6029.W4Z8] 63-5999
1. Owen, Wilfred, 1893-1918. 2. Owen family. I. Title.

Owen, Wilfred, 1893-1918— Biography.

ORRMONT, Arthur. 821'.9'12 B
Requiem for war; the life of Wilfred Owen. New York, Four Winds Press [1972] 192 p. port. 25 cm. [PR6029.W4Z77] 74-182118 6.72
1. Owen, Wilfred, 1893-1918—Biography. I. Title.

STALLWORTHY, Jon. 821'.9'12
Wilfred Owen / Jon Stallworthy. London : Oxford University Press [etc.], 1974. xiv, 333 p. : ill., facsims, geneal. tables, maps (on lining papers), plans, ports. ; 25 cm. Includes index. Bibliography: p. [324] [PR6029.W4Z855] 75-301078 ISBN 0-19-211719-X : 17.50
1. Owen, Wilfred, 1893-1918—Biography. I. Title.
Distributed by Oxford University Press, New York. **BIP**

Owen, William Harold,

OWEN, William Harold, 1897- 759.2 B
Aftermath [by] Harold Owen. London, New York, Oxford U.P., 1970. xi, 199 p., 9 plates. illus. 23 cm. [CT788.O87A3 1970] 73-537524 ISBN 0-19-211195-7 55/-
I. Title. **BIP**

Owens, Claire Myers.

OWENS, Claire Myers. 920.7
Awakening to the good--psychological or religious? An autobiographical inquiry. Boston, Christopher Pub. House [1958] 273p. illus: 21cm. Includes bibliography. [CT275.O87A3] 58-6719
I. Title.

OWENS, Claire Myers. 294.3'927'0924 B
Zen and the lady : memoirs—personal and transpersonal in a world in transition / by Claire Myers Owens. New York : Baraka Books, c1979. v, 306 p. ; 23 cm. Includes index. Bibliography: p. 299-302. [BQ976.W457A35] 79-50288 ISBN 0-88238-996-3 : 5.95
1. Owens, Claire Myers. 2. Zen Buddhists—United States—Biography. 3. Spiritual life (Zen Buddhism) I. Title.

Owens, Jesse, 1913-

OWENS, Jesse, 1913- 301.451'96'0924
Blackthink; my life as black man and white man [by] Jesse Owens, with Paul G. Neimark. New York, Morrow, 1970. 215 p. 22 cm. [E185.61.O93] 73-106343 5.95
1. U.S.—Race question. 2. Negroes—Civil rights. I. Neimark, Paul G. II. Title.

OWENS, Jesse, 1913- 796.4'2'0924 B
Jesse, a spiritual autobiography / by Jesse Owens, with Paul Neimark. Plainfield, N.J. : Logos International, c1978. 206 p. ; 22 cm. [GV697.O9A29] 78-59857 ISBN 0-88270-314-5 : 5.95
1. Owens, Jesse, 1913- 2. Track and field athletes—United States—Biography. I. Neimark, Paul G., joint author. II. Title.

OWENS, Jesse, 1913- 796.4'26'0924 B
The Jesse Owens story, by Jesse Owens with Paul G. Neimark. New York, Putnam [1970] 109 p. 22 cm. The Negro athlete who won four gold medals in the 1936 Berlin Olympics tells his life story. [GV697.O9A3 1970] 92 72-90865 3.29
1. Track-athletics—Biography. 2. Track-athletics—Juvenile literature. I. Neimark, Paul G. **BIP**

Owens, Jesse, 1913- —Juvenile literature.

KAUFMAN, Mervyn D. 796.4'2'0924 B
Jesse Owens, by Mervyn Kaufman. Illustrated by Larry Johnson. New York, Crowell [1973] 33 p. illus. 24 cm. (Crowell biographies.) An easy-to-read biography of the black athlete who won four gold medals in the 1936 Olympics. [GV697.O9K38] 92 72-83787 ISBN 0-690-45934-3 3.75
1. Owens, Jesse, 1913- —Juvenile literature. I. Johnson, Larry, 1949- illus.
Library binding 4.50; ISBN 0-690-45935-1.

Owens, John, 1790-1846.

CLAPP, Brian William. 658'.00924
John Owens, Manchester merchant, by B. W. Clapp. New York, A. M. Kelley, 1967 [c1965] viii, 193 p. illus., facsims., port. 23 cm. Bibliographical footnotes. [HD9861.5.C55] 67-31834
1. Owens, John, 1790-1846. I. Title.

Owens, Tinker.

BRUNS, Bill. 796.33'2'0924
"Sooner" : a season as lived and played by Tinker Owens / text by Bill Bruns ; photos. by Rich Clarkson. Topeka, Kan. : Josten's Publications, 1974. 144 p. : ill. (some col.) ; 32 cm. [GV939.O83B78] 74-12784 12.50
1. Owens, Tinker. 2. Oklahoma. University—Football. 3. Football. I. Clarkson, Rich, ill. II. Title.

Owens, William A., 1905-

OWENS, William A., 1905- 917.64'263'0360924 B
A season of weathering, by William A. Owens. New York, Scribner [1973] xii, 258 p. 25 cm. Autobiographical. Continuation of the author's This stubborn soil. [F392.L36O89] 72-1196 ISBN 0-684-13022-X 7.95
1. Owens, William A., 1905- 2. Lamar Co., Tex.—Social life and customs. I. Title.

PILKINGTON, William T. 813'.5'2
William A. Owens, by William T. Pilkington. Austin, Tex., Steck-Vaughn Co. [1968] ii, 43 p. 21 cm. (Southwest writers series no. 17) Bibliography: p. 41-43. [PS3565.W58Z82] 68-8626 1.00
1. Owens, William A., 1905- I. Title. II. Series.

Owings, Nathaniel Alexander, 1903-

OWINGS, Nathaniel Alexander, 1903- 720'.92'4
The spaces in between; an architect's journey. Boston, Houghton Mifflin, 1973. xiv, 303 p. illus. 24 cm. Autobiographical. [NA737.O94A28] 72-9012 ISBN 0-395-15468-5 8.95
1. Owings, Nathaniel Alexander, 1903- I. Title.

Owsley, Alvin Mansfield, 1888-1967.

ADAMS, Marion S. 369'.1861'0924 B
Alvin M. Owsley of Texas, apostle of Americanism, by Marion S. Adams. Introd. by Mark W. Clark. [Waco, Tex., Texian Press, 1971] xiii, 272 p. illus. 24 cm. Bibliography: p. 271-272. [E748.O986A65] 70-175532 10.00
1. Owsley, Alvin Mansfield, 1888-1967.

Oxford and Asquith, Herbert Henry Asquith, 1st Earl of, 1852-1928.

KOSS, Stephen E. 941.083'092'4 B
Asquith / Stephen Koss. New York : St. Martin's Press, 1976. x, 310 p. ; 23 cm. (British political biography) Includes index. Bibliography: p. [285]-292. [DA566.9.O7K67 1976b] 76-20200 12.95
1. Oxford and Asquith, Herbert Henry Asquith, 1st Earl of, 1852-1928. 2. Prime ministers—Great Britain—Biography. 3. Great Britain—Politics and government—1901-1936. 4. Great Britain—Politics and government—1837-1901. I. Title. BIP

Oxford and Asquith, Margot Asquith,

OXFORD and Asquith, Margot Asquith, countess of [Emma Alice Margaret (Tennat) Asquith, Countess of Oxford and Asquith] 1865-1945. 920.7
Autobiography. Ed., introd. by Mark Bonham Carter. Boston, Houghton, 1963[c.1962] 342p. illus. 23cm. 63-7202 6.00
I. Title.

Oxford, Robert Harley, 1st Earl of, 1661-1724.

HAMILTON, Elizabeth, Lady, 1928- 942.06'9'0924 B
The backstairs dragon; a life of Robert Harley, Earl of Oxford. New York, Taplinger Pub. Co. [1970, c1969] 308 p. illus., ports. 25 cm. Bibliography: p. 283-286. [DA497.O8H3 1970] 75-97190 10.00
1. Oxford, Robert Harley, 1st Earl of, 1661-1724. I. Title. BIP

Oxford. University.

LANGSTAFF, John Brett, 1889- 378.4257
Oxford, 1914, by J. Brett Langstaff. [1st ed. New York, Vantage Press [1965] 317 p. illus., facsims. 22 cm. Autobiographical. [LF523.L3] 65-19607
1. Oxford. University. I. Title.

Oxford, University—Hist.

WOOD, Anthony a, 1632-1695 928.2
The life and times of Anthony a Wood, abridged from Andrew Clark's ed.; introd. by Llewelyn Powys. New York, Oxford [c.1962] 372p. 16cm. (World's classics, 580) 61-65392 2.75
1. Oxford, University—Hist. I. Clark, Andrew, 1856-1922, ed. II. Powys, Llewelyn, 1884-1939, ed. III. Title.

Oxford. University—Bio-bibliography.

WOOD, Anthony a, 1632-1695. 378.425'7 B
Athenae oxonienses, an exact history of all the writers and bishops who have had their education in the University of Oxford; to which are added the Fasti; or, Annals of the said university. A new edition, with additions and a continuation by Philip Bliss. New York, Johnson Reprint Corp., 1967. 4 v. illus. 29 cm. (The Sources of science, no. 55) The Fasti oxonienses is divided: Pt. 1 (1500-1640) in v. 2, and pt. 2 (1641-1691) in v. 4. Reprint of the 1813-20 ed. Bibliographical footnotes. [LF525.W84 1967] 68-1239
1. Oxford. University—Bio-bibliography. I. Bliss, Philip, 1787-1857, ed. II. Title. BIP

Oxford. University. Christ Church—Biog.

FEILING, Keith [Grahame] Sir 1884- 378.4257
In Christ Church Hall. New York, St. Martin's Press [c.] 1960 [1961] 208p. illus. 60-52195 5.75
1. Oxford. University. Christ Church—Biog. I. Title.

Oxford. University—Registers.

EMDEN, Alfred Brotherston, 1888- 378.425'72
A biographical register of the University of Oxford, A.D. 1501 to 1540, by A. B. Emden. Oxford, Clarendon Press, 1974. xxiv, 742 p. 24 cm. Bibliography: p. x-xiii. [LF525.E52] 74-171882 ISBN 0-19-951008-3
1. Oxford. University—Registers. 2. Oxford. University—Biography. I. Title. Distributed by Oxford University Press, New York; 58.00.

Oxnam, Garfield Bromley, Bp., 1891-1963.

OXNAM, Garfield Bromley, Bp., 1891-1963. 287'.6'0924 B
I protest / by G. Bromley Oxnam. Westport, Conn. : Greenwood Press, 1979, c1954. 186 p. ; 23 cm. Reprint of the ed. published by Harper, New York. [BX8495.O93A34 1979] 78-21506 ISBN 0-313-21154-X : 16.00
1. Oxnam, Garfield Bromley, Bp., 1891-1963. 2. Methodist Church—Bishops—Biography. 3. United States. Congress. House. Committee on Un-American Activities. 4. Bishops—United States—Biography. I. Title.

Ozanam, Antoine Frederic, 1813-1853.

THE brave never die; a story of Frederick Ozanam. v. 12 Illustrations by Carolyn Lee Jagodits. Notre Dame, Ind., Dujarie Press [c1958] 94p. illus. 24cm.
1. Ozanam, Antoine Frederic, 1813-1853. I. Roberto, Brother, 1927-

DERUM, James Patrick. 928.4
Apostle in a top hat; the life of Frederic Ozanam. 1st ed. Garden City, N.Y., Hanover House, 1960. 240 p. 22 cm. [BX4705.O8D4] 60-13515
1. Ozanam, Antoine Frederic, 1813-1853. I. Title.

Paez, Jose Antonio, Pres. Venezuela, 1790-1873.

GRAHAM, Robert Bontine Cunninghame, 1852-1936. 987'.061'0924 B
Jose Antonio Paez. Port Washington, N.Y., Kennikat Press [1970] xiii, 328 p. illus., facsim., map, ports. 22 cm. Reprint of the 1929 ed. Bibliography: p. 315-316. [F2322.8.P18 1970b] 72-112799
1. Paez, Jose Antonio, Pres. Venezuela, 1790-1873. 2. Venezuela—History—1810- BIP

GRAHAM, Robert Bontine Cunninghame, 1852-1936. 987'.061'0924 B
Jose Antonio Paez. Freeport, N.Y., Books for Libraries Press [1971] xiii, 328 p. illus., fold. map, ports. 23 cm. Reprint of the 1929 ed. Bibliography: p. 315-316. [F2322.8.P18 1971] 73-146857 ISBN 0-8369-5624-9
1. Paez, Jose Antonio, Pres. Venezuela, 1790-1873. 2. Venezuela—History—1810-

GRAHAM, Robert Bontine Cunninghame, 1852-1936. 987'.061'0924
Jose Antonio Paez. New York, Cooper Square Publishers, 1970. xiii, 328 p. illus., facsims., fold. map, ports. 23 cm. Reprint of the 1929 ed. Bibliography: p. 315-316. [F2322.8.P18 1970] 72-118638 ISBN 8-15-403291- 10.00
1. Paez, Jose Antonio, Pres. Venezuela, 1790-1873. 2. Venezuela—History—1810- BIP

Peguy, Charles Pierre, 1873-1914.

VILLIERS, Marjorie Howard, 1903- 848'.9'1209 B
Charles Peguy : a study in integrity / by Marjorie Villiers. Westport, Conn. : Greenwood Press, 1975, c1965. 412 p., [8] leaves of plates : ill. ; 22 cm. Reprint of the ed. published by Harper & Row, New York. Includes index. Bibliography: p. 401-404. [PQ2631.E25Z87 1975] 73-15321 ISBN 0-8371-7190-3 lib.bdg. : 20.00
1. Peguy, Charles Pierre, 1873-1914. BIP

Perez Galdos, Benito, 1843-1920.

PATTISON, Walter Thomas, 1903- 863'.5
Benito Perez Galdos / by Walter T. Pattison. New York : Twayne Publishers, [1975] 181 p. : port. ; 22 cm. (Twayne's world author's series ; TWAS 341 : Spain) Includes index. Bibliography: p. 173-177. [PQ6555.Z5P28] 74-20650 ISBN 0-8057-2689-6 : 5.95
1. Perez Galdos, Benito, 1843-1920. BIP

Perez, Tony, 1942- —Juvenile literature.

WHEELOCK, Warren H. 973'.04'68 S
Tony Perez, el superestrella callado. Lee Trevino, el supermexicano. Jim Plunkett, no se retiro / Warren H. Wheelock ; adaptacion, J. O. "Rocky" Maynes ; consultantes, Jorge Valdivieso ... [et al.]. St. Paul, Minn. : EMC, 1976. p. cm. (His Ilustres hispanos de los EE. UU. ; 4) Translation of Tony Perez, the silent superstar. Brief biographies of three Spanish Americans: a professional golfer, a major league baseball star, and a professional football quarterback. [E184.S75W517 vol. 4] [GV697.A1] 920'.0092'6873 920 76-2419 ISBN 0-88436-254-X. ISBN 0-88436-255-8 pbk.
1. Perez, Tony, 1942- —Juvenile literature. 2. Trevino, Lee—Juvenile literature. 3. Plunkett, Jim—Juvenile literature. I. Mayes, J. O. II. Title. III. Title: Lee Trevino, el supermexicano. IV. Title: Jim Plunkett, no se retiro.

Petain, Henri Philippe Benoni Omer, 1856-1951.

GRIFFITHS, Richard M. 944.081'092'4 B
Petain; a biography of Marshal Philippe Petain of Vichy [by] Richard Griffiths. [1st ed. in the U.S.] Garden City, N.Y., Doubleday, 1972 [c1970] xix, 379 p. illus. 25 cm. First published in London under title: Marshal Petain. Bibliography: p. 367-372. [DC342.8.P4G7 1972] 73-157595 10.00
1. Petain, Henri Philippe Benoni Omer, 1856-1951.

RYAN, Stephen, 1922- 944.081'0924 B
Petain the soldier. South Brunswick [N.J.] A. S. Barnes [1969] 315 p. illus. 25 cm. Bibliographical footnotes. [DC342.8.P4R9] 68-25388 8.00
1. Petain, Henri Philippe Benoni Omer, 1856-1951. I. Title.

SPEARS, Edward Louis, Sir, bart., 1886- 944.0810922
Two men who saved France: Petain and De Gaulle, by Sir Edward Spears. New York, Stein and Day [1966] 222 p. map. 22 cm. [DC342.8.P4S63] 66-24811
1. Petain, Henri Philippe Benoni Omer, 1856-1951. 2. Gaulle, Charles de, Pres. France, 1890- I. Title.

P'i, Jih-hsiu, ca. 834-ca. 883.

NIENHAUSER, William H. 895.1'1'3 B
P'i Jih-hsiu / by William H. Nienhauser, Jr. Boston : Twayne Publishers, 1979. 161 p. ; 21 cm. (Twayne's world authors series ; TWAS 530 : China) "Finding list of translations of P'i Jih-hsiu's works in this volume :" p. 151-152. Includes index. Bibliography: p. 137-150. [PL2677.P5Z79] 78-23230 ISBN 0-8057-6372-4 : 13.95
1. P'i, Jih-hsiu, ca. 834-ca. 883. 2. Poets, Chinese—Biography. BIP

Puckler-Muskau, Hermann Ludwig Heinrich, furst von, 1785-1871.

SYMONDS, Emily Morse, d.1936. 920.042
Little memoirs of the nineteenth century. Freeport, N.Y., Books for Libraries Press [1969] ix, 375 p. ports. 23 cm. (Essay index reprint series) Reprint of the 1902 ed. Contents.Contents.—Benjamin Robert Haydon.—Lady Morgan (Sydney Owenson)—Nathaniel Parker Willis.—Lady Hester Stanhope. Prince Puckler-Muskau in England.—William and Mary Howitt. [DA531.1.S9 1969] 70-86787 ISBN 8-369-11970-
1. Puckler-Muskau, Hermann Ludwig Heinrich, furst von, 1785-1871. 2. Morgan, Sydney (Owenson) lady, 1783?-1859. 3. Haydon, Benjamin Robert, 1786-1846. 4. Willis, Nathaniel Parker, 1806-1867. 5. Stanhope, Hester Lucy, Lady, 1776-1839. 6. Howitt, William, 1792-1879. 7. Howitt, Mary (Botham) 1799-1888. I. Title. BIP

Paar, Jack.

PAAR, Jack. 927.92
I kid you not, by Jack Paar, withJohn Reddy. Boston, Little, Brown [c.1960] xx, 226p. illus. 22cm. 60-9350 3.95
I. Title.

PAAR, Jack 927.92
My saber is bent. Introd. by Alexander King. New York, Pocket Bks. [1962, c.1961] 233p. illus. 17cm. (Cardinal ed., GC148) .50 pap.,
I. Title.

PAAR, Jack. 927.92
My saber is bent [by] Jack Paar, with John Reddy. New York, Simon and Schuster, 1961. 236 p. illus. 22 cm. [PN1992.4.P3A33] 62-9229
I. Title.

Pabst, Lettie (Little)

PABST, Lettie (Little) 1891- 920.7
Kansas heritage. [1st ed.] New York, Vantage Press [1956] 153p. 21cm. Autobiographical. [CT275.P12A3] 56-5523
I. Title.

Pacheco, Romualdo, 1831-1899—Juvenile literature.

RAMIREZ, Anthony. 979.4'04'0924 B
Romualdo Pacheco, Governor of California / by Anthony Ramirez, Jr. San Francisco : San Francisco Press, c1974. 30 p. : col. ill. ; 23 cm. Bibliography: p. 30. A brief biography of the man who became the twelfth governor of California in 1875, the first native Californian to hold that office. [F866.P112R35] 92 74-15571
1. Pacheco, Romualdo, 1831-1899—Juvenile literature. I. Title.

Pacheo, Francisco Perez, 1790-1860.

†SHUMATE, Albert. 979.4'9'030924 B
Francisco Pacheco of Pacheco Pass / by Albert Shumate. Stockton, Calif. : University of the Pacific, c1977. i, 47 p., [3] leaves of plates : ill. ; 23 cm. (Monograph - Holt-Atherton Pacific Center for Western Studies ; no. 7) Includes bibliographical references and index. [F867.P38S56] 78-104769 ISBN 0-931156-07-6 : 4.50
1. Pacheo, Francisco Perez, 1790-1860. 2. California, Southern—Biography. 3. Ranchers—California, Southern—Biography. I. Title. II. Series: Holt-Atherton Pacific Center for Western Studies. Monograph — Holt-Atherton Pacific Center for Western Studies ; no. 7. BIP

Pachman, Ludek.

PACHMAN, Ludek. 794.1'092'4 B
Checkmate in Prague : the memoirs of a grandmaster / Ludek Pachman ; translated by Rosemary Brown. 1st American ed. New York : Macmillan, 1975. 216 p. ; 21 cm. Translation of Jetzt kann ich sprechen. [GV1439.P32A3513 1975] 75-23432 ISBN 0-02-594300-6 : 8.95
1. Pachman, Ludek. 2. Chess. 3. Czechoslovak Republic—Politics and government—1945- I. Title. BIP

Pachomius, Saint.

THE life of 270.1'092'4 B
Pachomius : vita prima Graeca / translated by Apostolos N. Athanassakis ; introd. by Birger A. Pearson. Missoula, Mont. : Published by Scholars Press for the Society of Biblical Literature, c1975. xi, 201 p. : 24 cm. (Texts and translations - Society of Biblical Literature ; 7) (Early Christian literature series ; 2) English and Greek. "Contains the text of G1 [i.e. the Vita prima Graeca] as edited by F. Halkin." Bibliography: p. xi. [BR1720.P23V5613] 75-37766 ISBN 0-89130-065-1 : 2.80
1. Pachomius, Saint. I. Athanassakis, Apostolos N. II. Title. III. Series. IV. Series: Society of Biblical Literature. Texts and translations ; 7.

Pacific area—History.

DAY, Arthur Grove, 1904- 990
Adventurers of the Pacific, by A. Grove Day. Foreword by James A. Michener. [1st ed.] New York, Meredith Press [1969] xv, 303 p. illus., map, ports. 22 cm. Bibliography: p. 289-292. [DU28.3.D3] 69-14770 6.95
1. Pacific area—History. 2. Adventure and adventurers. I. Title.

Pacific coast — Biog.

WHO'S who on the Pacific coast; 920.079 a biographical dictionary of noteworthy men and women of the Pacific coast and the Western States. [1949]- Chicago, A. N. Marquis Co. v. 24 cm. Published also under title Who's who in the West. Supersedes in part Who's who in the South and Southwest, published by Larkin, Roosevelt & Larkin. [F851.W6] 49-49629
1. Pacific coast — Biog.

Pacific salmon fisheries—British Columbia.

LANDALE, Zoe, 1952- 636'.27'550924 B
Harvest of salmon : adventures in fishing the B.C. coast / by Zoe Landale. Seattle : Hancock House Publishers, c1977. p. cm. [SH349.L27] 77-2367 ISBN 0-919654-75-4 : 8.95
1. Pacific salmon fisheries—British Columbia. 2. Fishermen—Biography. I. Title. BIP

Pacific States — Bio.

WHO'S who on the Pacific coast 920.079 1949-51 Chicago, A. N. Marquis Co. 2 v. 24 cm. "A biographical dictionary of noteworthy men and women of the Pacific Coastal and Western States." Published also under title: Who's who in the West (later Who's who in the West and Western Canada) [E176.W648] 49-49629
1. Pacific States — Bio.

Pacifists—Biography—Juvenile literature.

MEYER, Edith Patterson. 327'.172'0922 B
In search of peace : the winners of the Nobel peace prize, 1901-1975 / by Edith Patterson Meyer ; illustrated by Billie Jean Osborne. Nashville : Abingdon, c1978. 208 p. : ill. ; 23 cm. Includes index. Presents information about the individuals and organizations who have been recipients of the Nobel Peace Prize. [JX1962.A2M42] 920 77-24599 ISBN 0-687-01360-7 : 13.95
1. Pacifists—Biography—Juvenile literature. 2. Nobel prizes—Juvenile literature. 3. Peace—Juvenile literature. I. Osborne, Billie Jean. II. Title. BIP

Pack family.

PACK, Wehrli D., 1889- 929.2'0973
A bit of Pack history or biography. Compiled and written by Wehrli D. Pack. Provo, Utah, J. G. Stevenson, 1969. vii, 283 p. illus., facsims., ports. 25 cm. [CS71.P118 1969] 74-7773
1. Pack family. I. Title.

Packard, Reynolds, 1903- —Biography—Journalistic career.

PACKARD, Reynolds, 1903- 070'.92'4 B
Rome was my beat / by Reynolds Packard. Secaucus, N.J. : L. Stuart, [1975] p. cm. [PS3531.A2156Z52] 74-31665 ISBN 0-8184-0216-4 : 8.95
1. Packard, Reynolds, 1903- —Biography—Journalistic career. 2. Rome (City)—Social life and customs. I. Title. BIP

Packer, Alferd, 1842-1907.

MAZZULLA, Fred M. 978.8'39
Al Packer; a Colorado cannibal [by] Fred and Jo Mazzulla. [Denver? 1968] 47 p. (chiefly illus.) 22 cm. [F781.P2M3] 68-29102
1. Packer, Alferd, 1842-1907. I. Mazzulla, Jo, joint author. BIP

Paddock, Paul.

PADDOCK, Paul. 327'.0951'8
China diary : crisis diplomacy in Dairen / Paul Paddock. 1st ed. Ames : Iowa State University Press, 1977. xix, 274 p. : map ; 22 cm. [E183.8.C5P25] 77-3229 ISBN 0-8138-0240-7 : 7.50
1. Paddock, Paul. 2. United States—Foreign relations—China. 3. China—Foreign relations—United States. 4. Dairen—History. 5. China—History—Civil War, 1945-1949. 6. Diplomats—United States—Biography. I. Title. BIP

Paddock, Robert Lewis, Bp., 1869-1939.

MINOR, Maria Sheerin. 922.373
Portrait of a rebel; the story of Robert Lewis Paddock, 1869-1939, by Maria Minor. New York, Seabury Press [1965] vii, 150 p. 22 cm. [BX5995.P26M5] 64-19628
1. Paddock, Robert Lewis, Bp., 1869-1939. I. Title.

Paderewaski, Ignacy Jan, 1860-1941.

KELLOGG, Charlotte (Hoffman) 927.8
Paderewski. New York, Viking Press, 1956. 224p. 22cm. [DK440.5.P4K4] 56-14300
1. Paderewaski, Ignacy Jan, 1860-1941. I. Title. BIP

LANDAU, Rom, 1899- 786.1'092'4 B
Ignace Paderewski, musician and statesman / by Rom Landau. New York : AMS Press, 1976. xiii, 314 p., [13] leaves of plates : ill. ; 23 cm. Reprint of the 1934 ed. published by Crowell, New York. Bibliography: p. 289-305. [ML410.P114L3 1976] 74-24137 ISBN 0-404-12999-4 : 20.00
1. Paderewski, Ignacy Jan, 1860-1941. 2. Composers—Poland—Biography.

PHILLIPS, Charles Joseph MacConaghy, 1880-1933. 786.1'092'4 B
Paderewski, the story of a modern immortal / by Charles Phillips ; with an introd. by Edward Mandell House. New York : Da Capo Press, 1978, [c1933] xiv, 563 p., [3] leaves of plates : ill. ; 24 cm. (Da Capo Press music reprint series) Reprint of the 1934 ed. published by Macmillan, New York. "A list of Paderewski's compositions": p. 547-550. [ML410.P114P5 1978] 77-17399 ISBN 0-306-77534-4 : 29.50
1. Paderewski, Ignacy Jan, 1860-1941. 2. Musicians—Poland—Biography.

Paderewski, Ignacy Jan, 1860-1941 — Juvenile literature.

LENGYEL, Emil, 1895- 786.1'0924
Ignace Paderewski, musician and statesman. New York, F. Watts [1970] 120 p. illus., ports. 22 cm. (Immortals of music) Bibliography: p. [115] A biography of the Polish piano virtuoso who became the first prime minister of a united Poland after World War I. [ML3930.P17L4] 92 70-115413
1. Paderewski, Ignacy Jan, 1860-1941—Juvenile literature. I. Title.

ROBERTO, Brother, 1927- 92
Music for millions; a story of Ignace Paderewski. Illus. by Carolyn Lee Jagodits. Notre Dame, Ind., Dujarie Press [1962] 94 p. illus. 24 cm. [ML3930.P11R6] 63-1247
1. Paderewski, Ignacy Jan, 1860-1941 — Juvenile literature. I. Title.

Padma Sambhava, ca. 717-ca. 762.

YE-SES-MTSHO-RGYAL, 8thcent. 294.3'6'30924 B
The life and liberation of Padmasambhava / as recorded by Yeshe Tsogyal [i.e. Ye-ses-mtsho-rgyal], rediscovered by Urgyan Linpa ; translated into French as de dict de Padma by Gustav-Charles Toussaint ; translated into English by Kenn Dougals and Gwendolyn Bays ; corrected with the original Tibetan manuscript and with an introduction by Tarthany Tulka. Berkeley, Calif. : Dharma Pub., 1978. 2 v. (xxxiv, 769 p. : ill. ; 26 cm. (Tibetan translation series) [BQ7950.P327Y4713] 78-17445 ISBN 0-913546-19-4 (v. 1) : 50.00. ISBN 0-913546-20-8 (vol. 2) : 50.00
1. Padma Sambhava, ca. 717-ca. 762. 2. Lamas—Tibet—Biography. I. O-rgyan-glin-pa, gter-ston, b. 1323. II. Tarthang Tulku. III. Title. IV. Series. BIP

Padmore, George, 1903-1959.

HOOKER, James R. 909'.09'74960820924 B
Black revolutionary; George Padmore's path from communism to pan-Africanism [by] James R. Hooker. New York, Praeger [1967] 168 p. port. 23 cm. (Praeger library of African affairs) Bibliography: p. 154-159. [CT3150.P3H6] 67-22702
1. Padmore, George, 1903-1959. I. Title.

Padow, Mollie Potter,

PADOW, Mollie Potter, 1888- 917.3'03
A saga of eighty years of living. Philadelphia, Dorrance [1971] 228 p. 22 cm. Autobiography. [CT275.P16A3] 72-134287 ISBN 0-8059-1509-5 4.50
I. Title.

Paganini, Nicolo, 1782-1840.

ACKER, Helen. 920.045
Five sons of Italy. New York, Nelson [1950] 191 p. 21 cm. Bibliography: p. 190-191. [DG463.A28] 50-8995
1. Leonardo da Vinci, 1452-1519. 2. Buonarroti, Michel Angelo, 1475-1564. 3. Galilei, Galileo, 1564-1642. 4. Paganini, Nicolo, 1782-1840. 5. Verdi, Giuseppe, 1813-1901. I. Title.

COURCY, Geraldine, I. C. de. 787'.1'0924 B
Paganini, the Genoese / by G. I. C. de Courcy. New York : Da Capo Press, 1977, c1957. 2 v. : ill. ; 24 cm. (Da Capo Press music reprint series) Reprint of the ed. published by the University of Oklahoma Press, Norman. Includes index. Bibliography: p. 393-411. [ML418.P2C73 1977] 76-58927 ISBN 0-306-70872-8 : 45.00 (2 vols.)
1. Paganini, Nicolo, 1782-1840. 2. Violinists, violoncellists, etc.—Italy—Biography. I. Title.

COURCY, Geraldine I. C. de 927.8
Paganini, the Genoese. [1st ed.] Norman, University of Oklahoma Press [1957] 2 v. ports., facsims. 25 cm. Bibliography: v. 2, p. 396-411. [ML410.P125C7] 57-5953
1. Paganini, Nicolo, 1782-1840.

FETIS, Francois Joseph, 1784-1871. 787'.1'0924 B
Biographical notice of Nicolo Paganini : with an analysis of his compositions and a sketch of the history of the violin / by F. J. Fetis. 2d ed., with port. and wood engravings. New York : AMS Press, 1976. 90 p., [1] leaf of plates : ill. ; 23 cm. Reprint of the 1876 ed. published by Schott, London. [ML418.P2F32 1976] 74-24081 ISBN 0-404-12909-9 : 15.00
1. Paganini, Nicolo, 1782-1840. 2. Violin—History.

PROD'HOMME, Jacques Gabriel, 1871-1956. 787'.1'0924 B
Nicolo Paganini : a biography / by J. G. Prod'homme ; translated from the original French ed. by Alice Mattullath. New York : AMS Press, [1976] c1911. 67 p., [12] leaves of plates : ill. ; 23 cm. Reprint of the ed. published by C. Fischer, New York, in series: Celebrated musicians. Bibliography: p. 66-67. [ML418.P2P913 1976] 74-24195 ISBN 0-404-13096-8 : 10.00
1. Paganini, Nicolo, 1782-1840. 2. Violinists, violoncellists, etc.—Italy—Biography.

PULVER, Jeffrey, 1884- 780'.924 B
Paganini, the romantic virtuoso. With a new bibliography compiled by Frederick Freedman. New York, Da Capo Press, 1970. 353 p. ports. 24 cm. (Da Capo Press music reprint series) "First published in 1936." Bibliography: p. 331-353. [ML418.P2P98 1970] 69-11669
1. Paganini, Nicolo, 1782-1840.

SAUSSINE, Renee de, 1897- 927.8
Paganini. Foreword by Jacques Thibaud. Translated by Marjorie Laurie. New York, McGraw-Hill Book Co. [1954] 271 p. illus. 21 cm. Translation of: Paganini le magicien. [ML418.P2S262 1954] 54-9708
1. Paganini, Nicolo, 1782-1840.

SAUSSINE, Renee de, 1897- 787'.1'0924 B
Paganini. Foreword by Jacques Thibaud. Translated by Marjorie Laurie. Westport, Conn., Greenwood Press [1970, c1954] xiv, 271 p. illus., facsim., ports. 23 cm. Translation of Paganini le magicien. Bibliography: p. 262-264. [ML418.P2S262 1970] 77-100174 ISBN 0-8371-4013-7
1. Paganini, Nicolo, 1782-1840.

STRATTON, Stephen Samuel, 1840-1906. 787'.1'0924 B
Nicolo Paganini: his life and work. Westport, Conn., Greenwood Press [1971] 205 p. 27 plates (incl. facsims., ports.) 23 cm. Reprint of the 1907 ed. Bibliography: p. [201]-205. [ML418.P2S6 1971] 75-109856 ISBN 0-8371-4347-0
1. Paganini, Nicolo, 1782-1840.

Page, Alan, 1945- —Juvenile literature.

BATSON, Larry, 1930- 796.33'2'0924 B
Alan Page / by Larry Batson. Mankato, Minn. : Creative Education, [1976] p. cm. A biography of the defensive lineman with the paradoxical nature who became a leader in a fight for players' rights. [GV939.P33B38 1976] 92 76-42274 ISBN 0-87191-569-3 lib.bdg. : 4.95
1. Page, Alan, 1945- —Juvenile literature. 2. Football players—Biography—Juvenile literature. I. Title. **BIP**

Page, Charles Grafton, 1812-1868.

†POST, Robert C. 621.3'092'4 B
Physics, patents, and politics : a biography of Charles Grafton Page / Robert C. Post. 1st ed. New York : Science History Publications, 1976. 227 p., [6] leaves of plates : ill. ; 24 cm. Includes index. Bibliography: p. 206-213. [TK140.P3P67] 75-44017 ISBN 0-88202-046-3 : 15.95
1. Page, Charles Grafton, 1812-1868. 2. United States. Patent office—History. 3. Electric engineers—United States—Biography. I. Title. **BIP**

Page, Rosewell,

PAGE, Rosewell, 1858-1939. 818'.5'203 B
When I was a little boy. With illus. by Ellen Bruce Baylor. Foreword and afterword by Harriet R. Holman. Coconut Grove, Fla., Field Research Projects, 1970. iii, 80 p. illus. 28 cm. Facsim. of the author's unfinished MS. in the Virginia State Library, Richmond, written in 1890. [PS3531.A237Z5 1970] 73-287587
I. Baylor, Ellen Bruce, illus. II. Holman, Harriet R. III. Title.

Page, Ruth.

MARTIN, John Joseph, 1893- 792.8'092'4 B
Ruth Page : an intimate biography / John Martin ; foreword by Margot Fonteyn. New York : M. Dekker, c1977. viii, 342 p., [11] leaves of plates : ill. ; 24 cm. ([The Dance program ; v. 4]) Includes index. [GV1785.P26M37] 76-18427 17.50
1. Page, Ruth. 2. Dancers—Biography. 3. Choreographers—United States—Biography. I. Title. II. Series. **BIP**

PAGE, Ruth. 792.8'092'4 B
Page by page / by Ruth Page ; edited and with an introd. by Andrew Mark Wentink. Brooklyn, N.Y. : Dance Horizons, c1978. xvi, 224 p. : ill. ; 25 cm. [GV1785.P26A36] 78-65648 ISBN 0-87127-102-8 : 14.95
1. Page, Ruth. 2. Dancers—United States—Biography. 3. Choreographers—United States—Biography. I. Wentink, Andrew Mark. II. Title. **BIP**

Page, Thomas Nelson, 1853-1922.

PAGE, Rosewell, 1858-1939. 813'.4 B
Thomas Nelson Page: a memoir of a Virginia gentleman, by his brother. Port Washington, N.Y., Kennikat Press, [1969, c1923] vi, 210 p. illus., port. 18 cm. [PS2516.P3 1969] 68-8238
1. Page, Thomas Nelson, 1853-1922.

Page, Thomas Nelson, 1853-1922—Correspondence.

PAGE, Thomas Nelson, 1853-1922. 818'.4'03
Mediterranean winter-1906; journal and letters. Edited by Harriet R. Holman. Coconut Grove, Fla., Field Research Projects, 1971. ii, 157 p. 28 cm. [PS2516.A45 1971] 75-303923
1. Page, Thomas Nelson, 1853-1922—Correspondence. 2. Page, Thomas Nelson, 1853-1922—Biography. 3. Europe—Description and travel—1800-1918. I. Holman, Harriet R., ed. II. Title.

Page, Walter Hines, 1855-1918.

COOPER, John Milton. 973.8'092'4 B
Walter Hines Page : the Southerner as American, 1855-1918 / by John Milton Cooper, Jr. Chapel Hill : University of North Carolina Press, c1977. xxx, 457 p., [7] leaves of plates : ill. ; 24 cm. (The Fred W. Morrison series in Southern studies) Includes index. Bibliography: p. 427-435. [E664.P15C66] 77-4390 ISBN 0-8078-1298-6 : 15.95
1. Page, Walter Hines, 1855-1918. 2. Ambassadors—United States—Biography. 3. Journalists—United States—Biography. 4. United States—Politics and government—1865-1933. 5. United States—Foreign relations—1913-1921. I. Title. II. Series. **BIP**

HENDRICK, Burton Jesse, 1870-1949. 070.4'0924 B
The life and letters of Walter H. Page. Garden City, N.Y., Doubleday, Page, 1925. St. Clair Shores, Mich., Scholarly Press, 1970. 3 v. illus., ports. 22 cm. Vol. 3 contains the letters to Woodrow Wilson. [E664.P15H4 1970] 79-145079 ISBN 0-403-00769-0
1. Page, Walter Hines, 1855-1918. 2. U.S.—Foreign relations—Gt. Brit. 3. Gt. Brit.—Foreign relations—U.S. I. Page, Walter Hines, 1855-1918. Letters. II. Wilson, Woodrow, Pres. U.S., 1856-1924. III. Title. **BIP**

HENDRICK, Burton Jesse, 1870-1949. 070.4'0924 B
The training of an American; the earlier life and letters of Walter H. Page, 1855-1913. Dunwoody, Ga., N. S. Berg, 1970 [c1928] xii, 444 p. illus., ports 24 cm. Includes bibliographical references. [E664.P15H3 1970] 78-11286 11.90
1. Page, Walter Hines, 1855-1918. I. Title.

Page, William 1811-1885.

TAYLOR, Joshua Charles, 1917- [759.13
William Page, the American Titian. [Chicago] University of Chicago Press [1957] xxii, 292 p. illus., ports. 28 cm. "Catalogue of works":p. 246-280. Bibliography: p. 281-286. [ND237.P17T3] 927.5 57-6991
1. Page, William 1811-1885. I. Title.

Paget, Florence Cecilia, Lady, 1842-1907.

BLYTH, Henry. 942.081'0922
The Pocket Venus; a Victorian scandal. New York, Walker [1967, c1966] xv, 301 p. illus., ports. 22 cm. Bibliography: p. 285-289. [DA565.H33B5 1967] 67-14564
1. Hastings, Henry Weysford Charles Plantagenet, 4th marquis of, 1842-1868. 2. Paget, Florence Cecilia, Lady, 1842-1907. 3. Chaplin, Henry Chaplin, 1st viscount, 1841-1923. 4. Horse-racing—Great Britain. I. Title.

Paget, Violet, 1856-1935.

GUNN, Peter 928.2
Vernon Lee: Violet Paget, 1856-1935. New York, Oxford [c.]1964. xi, 244p. facsim., ports. 23cm. Bibl. 64-6685 5.60
1. Paget, Violet, 1856-1935. I. Title. **BIP**

GUNN, Peter. 928.2
Vernon Lee: Violet Paget, 1856-1935. London, New York, Oxford University Press, 1964. xi, 244 p. facsim., ports. 23 cm. Bibliography: p. [233]-235. [PR5115.P2Z67] 64-6685
1. Paget, Violet, 1856-1935. I. Title.

Paget, Violet, 1856-1935—Biography.

GUNN, Peter. 824'.8 B
Vernon Lee : Violet Paget, 1856-1935 / Peter Gunn. New York : Arno Press, 1975, c1964. p. cm. (Homosexuality) Reprint of the ed. published by Oxford University Press, London. Bibliography: p. [PR5115.P2Z67 1975] 75-12323 ISBN 0-405-07357-7 : 12.00
1. Paget, Violet, 1856-1935—Biography. I. Title. II. Series.

Paget, William, Baron Paget of Beaudesert, 1505, or 6-1563.

GAMMON, Samuel Rhea, 1889- 942.05'092'4 B
Statesman and schemer; William, First Lord Paget, Tudor Minister. Hamden, Conn., Archon Books [1973] 296 p. ports. 23 cm. Bibliography: p. 285-289. [DA317.8.P33G35 1973b] 74-160925 ISBN 0-208-01405-5 13.50
1. Paget, William, Baron Paget of Beaudesert, 1505, or 6-1563. 2. Great Britain—Politics and government—1485-1603. I. Title. **BIP**

GAMMON, Samuel Rhea, 1924- 942.05'092'4 B
Statesman and schemer; William, First Lord Paget, Tudor Minister. Hamden, Conn., Archon Books [1973] 296 p. ports. 23 cm. Bibliography: p. 285-289. [DA317.8.P33G35 1973b] 74-160925 ISBN 0-208-01405-5 13.50
1. Paget, William, Baron Paget of Beaudesert, 1505, or 6-1563. 2. Great Britain—Politics and government—1485-1603. I. Title.

Pahk, Induk.

PAHK, Induk. 920.7
September monkey. [1st ed.] New York, Harper [1954] 283 p. 22 cm. [CT1848.P3A3] 54-8981
I. Title.

Paige, Leroy,

PAIGE, Leroy, 1906- 796.357
Maybe I'll pitch forever; a great baseball player tells the hilarious story behind the legend, by LeRoy (Satchel) Paige, as told to David Lipman. [1st ed.] Garden City, N.Y., Doubleday, 1962. 285 p. illus. 22 cm. [GV865.P3A28] 62-7670
I. Lipman, David. II. Title.

Paige, Leroy, 1906——Juvenile literature.

PAIGE, Leroy, 1906- 796.357
Maybe I'll pitch forever; a great baseball player tells the hilarious story behind the legend, by LeRoy (Satchel) Paige, as told to David Lipman. [1st ed.] Garden City, N.Y., Doubleday, 1962. 285 p. illus. 22 cm. [GV865.P3A28] 62-7670
I. Lipman, David. II. Title.

RUBIN, Robert, 1941- 796.357'092'4 B
Satchel Paige: all-time baseball great. New York, Putnam [1974] 157 p. 22 cm. (Putnam sports shelf) A biography of the black pitcher who might have been the greatest pitcher of major league history had his color not barred him from the majors until the last eight years of his career. [GV865.P3R82 1974] 73-87215 ISBN 0-399-20386-9 4.89 (lib. bdg.).
1. Paige, Leroy, 1906——Juvenile literature. 2. Pitching (Baseball)—Juvenile literature. I. Title.

Paige, Mabeth (Hurd)

ALDRICH, Darragh, pseud. 923.273
Lady in law, a biography of Mabeth Hurd Paige; sketching seventy five picturesque and dramatic years as seen through her eyes. Chicago, R. F. Seymour [1950] 347 p. illus., ports. 24 cm. [F606.P22A5] 51-9480
1. Paige, Mabeth (Hurd) I. Title.

Paine, Thomas, 1737-1809.

ALDRIDGE, Alfred Owen, 1915- 923.273
Man of reason, the life of Thomas Paine. [1st ed.] Philadelphia, Lippincott [1959] 348p. illus. 22cm. [JC178.V2A8] 59-7777
1. Paine, Thomas, 1737-1800. I. Title.

BUCHANAN, John G. 320.5'1'0924 B
Thomas Paine, American Revolutionary writer / by John G. Buchanan. Charlotteville, N.Y. : SamHar Press, 1976. p. cm. (Outstanding personalities ; 85) Bibliography: p. [JC178.V2B78] 76-40998 lib.bdg. : 2.45 pbk. : 1.25
1. Paine, Thomas, 1737-1809. 2. Political scientists—United States—Biography. I. Title. **BIP**

CONWAY, Moncure Daniel, 1832-1907. 320.5'1'0924 B
The life of Thomas Paine. New York, B. Blom, 1969 [i.e. 1970] xvi, 352 p. port. 27 cm. Reprint of the 1909 ed., with a new introd. Appendices (p. 328-348):—A. The Cobbett papers.—B. The Hall manuscripts.—C. Portraits of Paine.—D. Brief list of Paine's works (p. 348) [JC178.V2C7 1970] 68-56506
1. Paine, Thomas, 1737-1809. I. Title. **BIP**

CONWAY, Moncure Daniel, 1832-1907. 320.5'1'0924 B
The life of Thomas Paine, with a history of his literary, political, and religious career in America, France, and England. To which is added a sketch of Paine by William Cobbett. [Folcroft, Pa.] Folcroft Library Editions, 1974. p. cm. Reprint of the 1909 ed. published by Watts, London. Appendices (p.): A. The Cobbett papers.—B. The Hall manuscripts.—C. Portraits of Paine.—D. Brief list of Paine's works (p.) [JC178.V2C7 1974] 74-9716 20.00
1. Paine, Thomas, 1737-1809. I. Title.

CONWAY, Moncure Daniel, 1832-1907. 320.5'1'0924 B
The life of Thomas Paine, with a history of his literary, political, and religious career in America, France, and England. To which is added a sketch of Paine by William Cobbett. [Folcroft, Pa.] Folcroft Library Editions, 1974. p. cm. Reprint of the 1909 ed. published by Watts, London. Appendices (p.): A. The Cobbett papers.—B. The Hall manuscripts.—C. Portraits of Paine.—D. Brief list of Paine's works (p.) [JC178.V2C7 1974] 74-9716 ISBN 0-8414-3511-1 (lib. bdg.)
1. Paine, Thomas, 1737-1809. I. Title.

DAVIDSON, John Morrison. 330.1'0922
Concerning four precursors of Henry George and the single tax, as also the land gospel according to Winstanley "the Digger", by J. Morrison Davidson. Port Washington, N.Y., Kennikat Press [1971] 151 p. 21 cm. Half title: Four precursors of Henry George. Reprint of 1899 ed. [HD1313.D2 1971] 77-115317
1. Ogilvie, William, 1736-1819. 2. Spence, Thomas, 1750-1814. 3. Paine, Thomas, 1737-1809. 4. Dove, Patrick Edward, 1815-1873. 5. Winstanley, Gerrard, b. 1609 I. Title. II. Title: Four precursors of Henry George.

DEL VECCHIO, Thomas. 923.273
Tom Paine: American, a new perspective that restores Paine to his rightful position as a patriotic American with-out peer. New York, Whittier Books [c1956] 168p. 25cm. Includes bibliography. [JC178.V2D4] 57-3157
1. Paine, Thomas, 1737-1809 I. Title.

GERSON, Noel Bertram, 1914- 320.5'1'0924 B
Rebel! A biography of Tom Paine [by] Samuel Edwards. New York, Praeger [1974] 304 p. 24 cm. Bibliography: p. 293-296. [JC178.V2G47] 73-9062 8.95
1. Paine, Thomas, 1737-1809. I. Title.

GURKO, Leo, 1914- 923.273
Tom Paine, freedom's apostle. Illustrated by Fritz Kredel. New York, Crowell [1957] 213 p. illus. 21 cm. [JC178.V2G85] 57-6567
1. Paine, Thomas, 1737-1809.

HAWKE, David Freeman. 320.510924
Paine. New York, Harper & Row [1975 c1974] x, 500 p. illus. 21 cm. Bibliography: p. 463-474. [JC178.V2H34] ISBN 0-06-090470-4 3.75 (pbk.)
1. Paine, Thomas, 1737-1809. I. Title.
L.C. card no for original edition: 73-14264. **BIP**

MCKOWN, Robin. 923.273
Thomas Paine. New York, Putnam [1962] 192 p. 21 cm. (Lives to remember) Includes bibliography. [JC178.V2M2] 62-10977
1. Paine, Thomas, 1737-1809.

SEDGWICK, Ellery, 1872-1960. 320'.092'4 B
Thomas Paine / by Ellergy Sedgwick. Folcroft, Pa. : Folcroft Library Editions, 1978 [c1899] p. cm. Reprint of the ed. published by Small, Maynard, Boston, in series: The Beacon biographies of eminent Americans. Bibliography: p. [JC178.V2S4 1978] 78-10619 ISBN 0-8414-7910-0 lib. bdg. : 20.00
1. Paine, Thomas, 1737-1809. 2. Political scientists—United States—Biography. 3. Revolutionists—United States—Biography. I. Series: The Beacon biographies of eminent Americans. BIP

THOMPSON, Ira M. 923.273
The religious beliefs of Thomas Paine. New York, Vantage [c.1965] 134p. 21cm. Bibl. [JC178.V2T64] 65-4304 3.50 bds.,
1. Paine, Thomas, 1737-1809. I. Title.

WILLIAMSON, Audrey, 1913- 320.5'1'0924 B
Thomas Paine; his life, work, and times. New York, St. Martin's Press [1973] 296 p. illus. 25 cm. Bibliography: p. 285-287. [JC178.V2W54 1973] 72-93447 12.50
1. Paine, Thomas, 1737-1809.

WILSON, Jerome D. 320.5'1'0924 B
Thomas Paine / by Jerome D. Wilson and William F. Ricketson. Boston : Twayne Publishers, c1978. 170 p. : port. ; 21 cm. (Twayne's United States authors series ; TUSAS 301) Includes index. Bibliography: p. 162-167. [JC178.V2W56] 77-15478 ISBN 0-8057-7206-5 : 8.95
1. Paine, Thomas, 1737-1809. 2. Political scientists—United States—Biography. 3. Revolutionists—United States—Biography. I. Ricketson, William F., joint author. BIP

WOODWARD, William E., 1874-1950. 320.5'1'0924 B
Tom Paine: America's godfather, 1737-1809. Westport, Conn., Greenwood Press [1972, 1c.1973, c1945] 359 p. illus. 22 cm. Bibliography: p. 342-343. [JC178.V2W64 1972] 72-7512 ISBN 0-8371-6520-2 14.50
1. Paine, Thomas, 1737-1809.

Paine, Thomas, 1737-1809—Juvenile literature.

BRETT, Grace Neff. 92
The picture story and biography of Tom Paine. Illustrated by Robert C. Frankenberg. Chicago, Follett Pub. Co. [1965] 142 p. col. illus., col. port. 22 cm. (The Library of American heroes) [JC178.V2B69] 65-14468
1. Paine, Thomas, 1737-1809 — Juvenile literature. I. Frankenberg, Robert C., illus. II. Title.

COOLIDGE, Olivia E. 320'.0924 B
Tom Paine, revolutionary, by Olivia Coolidge. New York, Scribner [1969] ix, 213 p. port. 22 cm. Bibliography: p. [207]-208. The life of the political philosopher whose pamphlets Common Sense and The American Crisis greatly influenced colonial opinion during the Revolution. [JC178.V2C83] 92 69-17064 3.95
1. Paine, Thomas, 1737-1809—Juvenile literature. BIP

MYERS, Elisabeth P. 320.5'1'0924 B
Thomas Paine, common sense boy / by Elisabeth P. Myers ; illustrated by Robert Doremus. Indianapolis : Bobbs-Merrill, c1976. 192 p. : ill. ; 20 cm. (Childhood of famous Americans) [JC178.V2M94] 75-12448 ISBN 0-672-52189-X : 4.95 ISBN 0-672-71323-3 lib.bdg. : 3.73
1. Paine, Thomas, 1737-1809—Juvenile literature. 2. Political scientists—United States—Biography—Juvenile literature. I. Doremus, Robert. II. Title.

O'CONNOR, Richard, 1915- 320.0924 B
The common sense of Tom Paine. Illustrated by Richard Cuffari. New York, McGraw-Hill [1969] 125 p. illus. 21 cm. The life of the man whose pamphlet "Common Sense" became one of the basic tracts of the American Revolution. [JC178.V2O3] 92 69-19202 4.50
1. Paine, Thomas, 1737-1809—Juvenile literature. I. Cuffari, Richard, 1925- illus. II. Title.

Painters.

CHUBB, Edwin Watts, 1865-1959. 759.94
Sketches of great painters. Freeport, N.Y., Books for Libraries Press [1968] 263 p. illus. 22 cm. (Essay index reprint series) Reprint of the 1915 ed., from a copy in the collections of the New York Public Library, Astor, Lenox and Tilden Foundations. Contents.Contents.—Raphael.—Millet.—Leonardo da Vinci.—Rembrandt.—Whistler.—Turner.—Titian.—Rubens.—Corot.—Michelangelo.—Reynolds.—Murillo.—Velasquez.—Rosa Bonheur.—Van Dyck. [ND36.C5 1968] 68-55843
1. Painters. 2. Paintings. I. Title. BIP

DELOGU, Giuseppe, 1898- 759.5
Caravaggio [Tr. by John Shepley] New York, Abrams [1964] 163,[1]p. illus. (pt. col.) plates (pt. col.) 38cm. Bibl. 64-10759 17.50
I. Caravaggio, Michelangelo Merisi da, 1569?-1609. II. Title.

MCKINNEY, Roland Joseph, 1898- 927.5
Famous old masters of painting. New York, Dodd, Mead, 1951. 135 p. illus. 23 cm. [Famous biographies for young peoples] [ND150.M3] 51-11037
1. Painters. I. Title.

MYERS, Bernard Samuel, 1908- 927.5
50 great artists. [1st ed.] New York, Bantam Books, 1953] xviii, 232, [6] p. illus. (part col.) 18cm. (A Bantam fifty, F 1171) Bibliography: p. [234]-[236] [ND36.M9] 54-16488
1. Painters. I. Title.

SCHERMAN, Bernardine (Kielty) 759
Masters of painting: their works, their lives, their times [by] Bernardine Kielty. [1st ed.] Garden City, N.Y., Doubleday [1964] 183 p. illus. (part col.) ports. 33 cm. [ND36.S34] 63-15118
1. Painters. 2. Paintings. I. Title.

THOMAS, Henry, 1886- 927.5
Living biographies of great painters, by Henry Thomas and Dana Lee Thomas. Garden City, N.Y., Garden City Books [1959] 312 p. 22 cm. [ND36.T45 1959] 59-2814
1. Painters. I. Thomas, Dana Lee, 1918- joint author. II. Title.

TURNGREN, Annette. 927.5
Great artists; 26 master painters. New York, Abelard Press [1953] 286p. 22cm. [ND36.T79] 53-6814
1. Painters. I. Title.

Painters—Dictionaries.

BRYAN, Michael, 1757-1821 927.5
Dictionary of painters and engravers [5v.] New ed., rev., enl., under the supervision of George C. Williamson. Port Washington, N.Y., Kennikat Pr. [1964] 5v. (various p.) plates, ports. 26cm. First ed. pub. in 1816 under title: A biographical and critical dictionary of painters and engravers. 64-15534 124.50, set, lim. ed.
1. Painters—Dictionaries. 2. Engravers—Dictionaries. I. Williamson, George Charles, 1858-1942, ed. II. Title.

Painters, American.

JOHN Singer Sargent, 759.13
a biography. [1st ed.] New York, W. W. Norton [1955] xv, 464p. illus. 25cm. Bibliographical references included in 'Notes' (p. 403-426) [ND237.S3M6] 927.5 55-13654
I. Mount, Charles Merrill. II. Sargent, John Singer, 1856-1925.

MCKINNEY, Roland Joseph, 1898- 927.5
Famous American painters. Illustrated with reproductions of the artists' paintings. New York, Dodd, Mead, 1955. 125p. illus. 22cm. (Famous biographies for young people) [ND236.M26] 55-9420
1. Painters, American. I. Title.

RHYS, Hedley Howell 759.13
Maurice Prendergast, 1859-1924. Boston [dist.] Cambridge, Mass., Harvard Univ. Press, 1960. 156p. illus. (part col.) 60-16756 7.50
I. Prendergast Maurice Brazil, 1859-1924. II. Title.

Painters, American—Juvenile literature.

BRAIDER, Donald, 1923- 759.13 B
Five early American painters: Benjamin West, John Singleton Copley, Charles Willson Peale, Gilbert Stuart, John Trumbull. [1st ed.] New York, Meredith Press [1969] 188 p. ports. 24 cm. Brief biographies of five early American painters including Benjamin West, John Singleton Copley, Charles Willson Peale, Gilbert Stuart, and John Trumbull. [ND236.B67] 920 71-91007 5.95
1. Painters, American—Juvenile literature. I. Title.

LEIPOLD, L. Edmond, 1902- 759.13 B
Famous American artists, by L. Edmond Leipold. Minneapolis, Denison [1969] 83 p. 25 cm. (His Famous American heroes and leaders series) Brief portraits of ten outstanding American artists: James McNeill Whistler, Benjamin West, Gilbert Stuart, Arthur Davies, Grant Wood, Mary Cassatt, Charles Willson Peale, George Caleb Bingham, Winslow Homer, and John Singer Sargent. [ND236.L45] 920 75-91284
1. Painters, American—Juvenile literature. I. Title.

LEIPOLD, L. Edmond, 1902- 759.13
Great American artists, by L. Edmond Leipold. Minneapolis, T. S. Denison [1973] 62 p. illus. 25 cm. (Lives of great Americans) Brief biographies of five American painters: Benjamin West, Winslow Homer, James McNeil Whistler, Grant Wood, and Oscar Howe. [ND236.L46] 920 76-190688 ISBN 0-513-01240-0 3.99
1. Painters, American—Juvenile literature. I. Title. II. Series: Lives of great Americans (Minneapolis)

Painters—Biography.

CANADAY, John Edwin, 1907- 759 B
The lives of the painters [by] John Canaday. [1st ed.] New York, Norton [1969] 4 v. plates (part col.) 24 cm. Contents.Contents.—v. 1. Late Gothic to High Renaissance.—v. 2. Baroque.—v. 3. Neoclassic to post-impressionist.—v. 4. Plates and index. [ND35.C35] 67-17666
1. Painters—Biography. I. Title. BIP

†NORMAN, Geraldine. 759.05
Nineteenth-century painters and painting : a dictionary / Geraldine Norman. Berkeley : University of California Press, 1977. 240 p. : ill. (some col.) ; 28 cm. Bibliography: p. 223-229. [ND190.N57 1977b] 76-24594 ISBN 0-520-03328-0 : 35.00
1. Painters—Biography. 2. Painting, Modern—19th century. I. Title. BIP

Painters. British.

PROCTER, Ida. 759.2
Masters of British painting: an introduction to their lives and works. New York, Roy Publishers [1956?] 192p. illus. 21cm. [ND496.P73] 927.5 54-10463
1. Painters. British. I. Title.

Painters, England—Correspondence, reminiscences, etc.

WARD, Leslie, Sir, 1851-1922. 759.2 B
Forty years of "Spy". Detroit, Singing Tree Press, 1969. xvi, 351 p. illus., facsims., ports. 22 cm. [ND497.W255A3 1969] 70-81512
1. Painters, England—Correspondence, reminiscences, etc. I. Title. BIP

Painters—France—Biography.

BUSIGNANI, Alberto. 759.9492
Mondrian [the life and the work of the artist, illustrated with 80 full-color plates. Translated from the Italian by Caroline Beamish. 1st American ed.] New York, Grosset & Dunlap [1968] 39 p. illus., col. plates. 18 cm. (The New Grosset art library, 13) Bibliography: p. 29-32. [ND653.M76B83 1968b] 68-26687

VAN DYKE, John Charles, 1856-1932, ed. 759.4 B
Modern French masters : a series of biographical and critical reviews by American artists / edited by John C. Van Dyke ; with thirty-seven wood-engravings and twenty-eignt half-tone ill. New York : Garland Pub., 1976, c1896. p. cm. (The Art experience in late nineteenth-century America) Reprint of the ed. published by Century Co., New York. [ND547.V3 1976] 75-28885 ISBN 0-8240-2243-2 lib.bdg. : 35.00
1. Painters—France—Biography. 2. Painting, French. 3. Painting, Modern—19th century—France. I. Title. II. Series.
Conntents omitted

Painters, French.

WECHSLER, Herman Joel, 1904- 927.5
Lives of famous French painters, from Ingres to Picasso [new ed.] New York, Washington Sq. [1962, c.1952] 208p. illus. (W733) Bibl. .60 pap.,
1. Painters, French. I. Title.

WECHSLER, Herman Joel, 1904- 927.5
Lives of famous French painters, from Ingres to Picasso. New York, Pocket Books [1952] 208 p. illus. 16 cm. (A Cardinal ed., C-28) [ND552.W4] 52-28626
1. Painters. French. I. Title.

Painters, French—Juvenile literature.

MCKINNEY, Rola-d Joseph, 1898- 759.4
Famous French painters. Illustrated with reproductions of the artists' paintings. New York, Dodd, Mead, 1960. 157p. illus. 22cm. (Famous biographies for young people) [ND552.M25] 60-9152
1. Painters, French—Juvenile literature. I. Title.

MCKINNEY, Roland Joseph 759.4
Famous French painters. Illustrated with reproductions of the artists' paintings. New York, Dodd, Mead, [c.]1960. 157p. illus. 22cm. (Famous biographies for young people) 60-9152 3.00
1. Painters, French—Juvenile literature. I. Title.

Painters, German.

THE German 759.3
expressionists; a generation in revolt. New York, Praeger [1957] 401p. illus. (part mounted, part col.) ports. 29cm. Bibliography: p. 369-389. [ND568.M9] 927.5 57-11147
1. Painters, German. 2. Paintings, German. 3. Expressionism (Art) I. Myers, Bernard Samuel, 1908-

THE German 759.3
expressionists; a generation in revolt. New York, Praeger [1957] 401p. illus. (part mounted, part col.) ports. 29cm. Bibliography:p. 369-389. [ND568.M9] [ND568.M9] 927.5 57-11147 57-11147
1. Painters, German. 2. Paintings, German. 3. Expressionism (Art) I. Myers, Bernard Samuel, 1908-

Painters—Great Britain—Biography.

ROTHENSTEIN, John Knewstub Maurice, Sir, 1901- 759.2 B
Modern English painters / by John Rothenstein. Rev. ed. New York : St. Martin's Press, 1976- v. : ill. ; 23 cm. Contents.Contents.—v. 1. Sickert to Smith.—v. 2. Lewis to Moore. Includes bibliographical references and indexes. [ND496.R652 1976] 77-362026 11.95 per vol.
1. Painters—Great Britain—Biography. I. Title. BIP

Painters—Great Britain—Biography—Dictionaries.

FISHER, Stanley W. 759.2
A dictionary of watercolour painters, 1750-1900, by Stanley W. Fisher. London, New York, Foulsham, 1972. 245, [16] p. illus. 26 cm. Bibliography: p. 241-245. [ND1928.F54] 72-169716 ISBN 0-572-00794-9 £4.90
1. Painters—Great Britain—Biography—Dictionaries. 2. Water-color painting—Great Britain. I. Title.

Painters—Italy—Juvenile literature.

WILLIAMS, Francis S. 795.5
Painting in Mantua, Padua, Siena and Urbino, by Francis Williams. [1st ed.] Oxford, New York, Pergamon Press [1970] ix, 60 p. 23 illus. (part col.), 5 col. plates. 18 x 25 cm. (The Commonwealth and international library. Painting, sculpture and fine arts division) Profiles of the lives and works of twenty-seven early Renaissance painters from north-central Italy. [ND622.W53 1970] 920 78-99997
1. Painters—Italy—Juvenile literature. 2. Painting—Mantua. 3. Painting—Padua. 4. Painting—Siena. 5. Painting—Urbino. I. Title.

Painters—Netherlands—Correspondence, reminiscences, etc.

GOGH, Vincent van, 1853-1890. 759.9492
Van Gogh's "diary"; the artist's life in his own words and art. Edited by Jan Hulsker. New York, Morrow, 1971 [c1970] 168 p. illus. (part col.) 27 cm. Translation of "Dagboek" van Van Gogh. [ND653.G7A2813] 70-158078 12.50
1. Painters—Netherlands—Correspondence, reminiscences, etc. I. Hulsker, Jan, ed. II. Title.

Painters—United States—Correspondence, reminiscences, etc.

COPLEY, John Singleton, 1738-1815. 759.13 B
Letters & papers of John Singleton Copley and Henry Pelham, 1739-1776. New York, Kennedy Graphics, 1970 [c1914] xxii, 384 p. illus., facsims., ports. 24 cm. (Library of American art) Includes bibliographical references. [ND237.C7A3 1970] 78-100615 ISBN 0-306-71406-X
1. Painters—United States—Correspondence, reminiscences, etc. I. Pelham, Henry, 1749-1806. II. Title. BIP

COPLEY, John Singleton, 1738-1815. 759.13 B
Letters & papers of John Singleton Copley and Henry Pelham, 1739-1776. [Boston] Massachusetts Historical Society, 1914. [New York, AMS Press, 1972] xxii, 384 p. illus. 23 cm. Original ed. issued as v. 71 of Massachusetts Historical Society collections. [ND237.C7A3 1972] 72-456 ISBN 0-404-01719-3 15.00
1. Painters—United States—Correspondence, reminiscences, etc. I. Pelham, Henry, 1749-1806. II. Title. III. Series: Massachusetts Historical Society, Boston. Collections, v. 71.

Painters—United States—Juvenile literature.

HEIDERSTADT, Dorothy. 759.13
Painters of America. New York, D. McKay Co. [1970] x, 180 p. 15 illus. 21 cm. Contents.Contents.—Benjamin West.—John Trumbull.—George Catlin.—Thomas Cole.—Karl Bodmer.—Alfred Jacob Miller.—George Caleb Bingham.—Emanuel Leutze.—George Inness.—Alfred Bierstadt.—Winslow Homer.—Frederic Remington.—Charles Schreyvogel.—Charles Marion Russell.—Grant Wood.—Bibliography (p. 171-173) [ND236.H43] 920 75-125655 4.95
1. Painters—United States—Juvenile literature. I. Title.

Painters, Victorian—Biography—Dictionaries.

WOOD, Christopher. 759.2
Dictionary of Victorian painters; with guide to auction prices, ... and index to artists' monograms. [Woodbridge] Antique Collectors' Club, 1971. v-xvi, 435 p. illus. 28 cm. Bibliography: p. xiv-xv. [ND35.W6] 72-188506 ISBN 0-902028-10-3 £8.00
1. Painters, Victorian—Biography—Dictionaries. I. Title. BIP

Painting

WILENSKI, Reginald Howard 759.4
Modern French painters. v. 1, 1863-1903 v.2, 1904-1938. New York, Vintage Books [c.]1960 llus. 19cm. v. 1, 398, xx p. (Bibl. p. [351] -398; v. 2, 271, xvii p. (bibl. p. [247] -263) (K-97A, K-97B 1.65 pap., ea.
1. Painting—France—Hist. 2. Painters, French. 3. Art—Hist.—20th cent. I. Title.

WILENSKI, Reginald Howard, 1887- 759.4
Modern French painters. New York, Vintage Books, 1960. 2 v. illus. 10 cm. [ND547.W5 1960] 60-2590
1. Painting — France — Hist. 2. Painters, French. I. Title.

Painting, Abstract—Ecuador—Exhibitions.

BARNITZ, Jacqueline. 759.9866'074'01471
Abstract currents in Ecuadorian art : Araceli, Maldonado, Molinari, Rendon, Tabara, Villacis / Jacqueline Barnitz, guest curator. [New York] : Center for Inter-American Relations, c1977. 47 p. : ill. (some col.) ; 18 x 25 cm. [ND385.5.A26B37] 77-156050 6.00
1. Painting, Abstract—Ecuador—Exhibitions. 2. Paintings, Ecuadorian—Ecuador—Exhibitions. 3. Painting, Modern—20th century—Ecuador—Exhibitions. 4. Painters—Ecuador—Biography. I. Center for Inter-American Relations. II. Title.
Publisher's address: 680 Park Avenue, New York, NY 10021

Painting, American.

DAVIDSON, Abraham A. 759.13
The eccentrics and other American visionary painters / Abraham A. Davidson. 1st ed. New York : Dutton, c1978. xxii, 202 p., [6] leaves of plates : ill. (some col.) ; 21 cm. Includes index. Bibliography: p. 189-196. [ND210.5.R6D34 1978] 78-55775 ISBN 0-525-47500-1 : 9.95 ($12.50 Can)
1. Painting, American. 2. Romanticism in art—United States. 3. Surrealism—United States. 4. Fantasy in art. 5. Painting, Modern—19th century—United States. I. Title. BIP

YOUNG, Mahonri Sharp, 1911- 759.13 B
American realists, Homer to Hopper / by Mahonri Sharp Young. New York : Watson-Guptill Publications, 1977. 208 p. : chiefly ill. (some col.) ; 30 cm. Includes index. Bibliography: p. 204-205. [ND210.5.R4Y68] 77-5416 ISBN 0-8230-0215-2 : 35.00
1. Painting, American. 2. Realism in art—United States. 3. Painting, Modern—19th century—United States. 4. Painting, Modern—20th century—United States. 5. Painters—United States—Biography. I. Title.

Painting, American—Exhibitions.

ALBRIGHT-KNOX Art Gallery. 759.13'074'014797
American painting of the 1970s : with an essay / by Linda L. Cathcart. Buffalo : Albright-Knox Art Gallery, c1978. vi, 112 p. : col. ill. ; 28 cm. Bibliography: p. 110-111. [ND212.A4475 1978] 78-21790 ISBN 0-914782-22-3 pbk. : 18.50
1. Painting, American—Exhibitions. 2. Painting, Modern—20th century—United States—Exhibitions. 3. Painters—United States—Biography. I. Cathcart, Linda L. II. Title.

Painting—France.

GORDON, Jan, 1882-1944. 759.4
Modern French painters. Freeport, N.Y., Books for Libraries Press [1970] xii, 188 p. illus. 24 cm. (Essay index reprint series) Reprint of the 1923 ed. [ND548.G6 1970] 73-99697 ISBN 0-8369-1573-9
1. Painting—France. 2. Painting, Modern—20th century—France. 3. Painters—France. I. Title.

Painting, Gothic—Italy.

JAMESON, Anna Brownell (Murphy) 1794-1860. 759.5
Memoirs of the early Italian painters. Freeport, N.Y., Books for Libraries Press [1973] p. (Essay index reprint series) Reprint of the 1889 ed. published by Houghton, Mifflin, Boston. [ND614.J35 1973] 73-4569 ISBN 0-518-10085-5
1. Painting, Gothic—Italy. 2. Painting, Renaissance—Italy. 3. Painters, Italian. I. Title.

Painting, Mexican.

HELM, MacKinley, 1896- 759.972
Modern Mexican painters. Freeport, N.Y., Books for Libraries Press [1968, c1941] xxi, 205 p. illus. 26 cm. (Essay index reprint series) [ND255.H4 1968] 68-22917
1. Painting, Mexican. 2. Painters, Mexican. I. Title. BIP

HELM, MacKinley, 1896- 759.972
Modern Mexican painters. New York, Dover Publications [1974, c1941] xxi, 205 p. 82 plates. 24 cm. Reprint of the ed. published by Harper, New York. [ND255.H4 1974] 73-91489 ISBN 0-486-22889-4 5.00 (pbk.)
1. Painting, Mexican. 2. Painting, Modern—20th century—Mexico. 3. Painters—Mexico. I. Title.

Painting, Modern—19th century—Europe.

VENTURI, Lionello, 1885-1961. 759.4
Modern painters. New York, Cooper Square Publishers, 1973. 2 v. illus. 25 cm. Vol. 2 has title: Impressionists and symbolists. Translation of Pittori moderni. Reprint of the 1947-50 ed. published by Scribner, New York. Contents.Contents.—[v. 1] Goya, Constable, David, Ingres, Delacroix, Corot, Daumier, Courbet.—v. 2. Manet, Degas, Monet, Pissarro, Sisley, Renoir, Cezanne, Seurat, Gauguin, Van Gogh, Toulouse-Lautrec. Includes bibliographies. [ND457.V415 1973] 72-97507 12.50
1. Painting, Modern—19th century Europe. 2. Painters—Europe. I. Title. II. Title: Impressionists and symbolists. BIP

Painting, Modern—20th century—Australia.

GLEESON, James. 759.99'4
Modern painters 1931-1970. [Melbourne] Lansdowne [1971] 128 p. col. illus. 26 cm. (Australian painting studio series) (Australian art library) Bibliography: p. 128. [ND1100.G62] 71-883627 ISBN 0-7018-0174-3 4.50
1. Painting, Modern—20th century—Australia. 2. Painting, Australian. 3. Painters, Australian. I. Title.

Painting, Scottish—History.

IRWIN, David G. 759.9411
Scottish painters at home and abroad, 1700-1900 / David Irwin and Francina Irwin London : Faber, 1975. 508 p., [58] leaves of plates : ill. (some col.) ; 26 cm. Includes index. Bibliography: p. 453-477. [ND477.I78] 75-326635 ISBN 0-571-08822-8 : 49.95
1. Painting, Scottish—History. 2. Painting, Modern—17th-18th centuries—Scotland. 3. Painting, Modern—19th century—Scotland. 4. Painters—Scotland—Biography. I. Irwin, Francina, joint author. II. Title.
Distributed by Faber and Faber, Salem, New Hampshire

Paintings, Dutch

ART Association of Indianapolis, Indians. John Herron Art Institute. 759.9492
The young Rembrandt and his times, a loan dxhibition of Dutch painting of the first four decades of the seventeenth century. John Herron Art Museum, Indianapolis, Indiana, February 14-March 23, 1958. The Fine Arts Gallery, San Diego, California, April 11-May 18, 1958. [Indianapolis, 1958] [112]p. illus. (part col.) map. 25cm. [ND646.A82] [ND646.A82] 927.5 58-2164 58-2164
1. Paintings, Dutch—Exhibitions. 2. Rembrandt Hermanszoon van Rijn, 1606-1669. I. San Diego, Calif. Fine Arts Gallery. II. Title.

JACOBS, Alan. 759.9492 B
17th century Dutch and Flemish painters : a collectors' guide / compiled by Alan Jacobs. London ; New York : McGraw-Hill, 1977,c1976 297 p. : ill. (some col.) ; 22 x 28 cm. "A revision of A classified synopsis of the principal painters of the Dutch and Flemish schools, their scholars, imitators, and analogists, by George Stanley, published in London by Henry G. Bohn, 1855." Includes bibliographical references and index. [ND646.J32] 76-26521 ISBN 0-07-084477-1: 7.95
1. Paintings, Dutch—Catalogs. 2. Paintings, Modern—17th-18th centuries—Netherlands—Catalogs. 3. Paintings, Flemish—Catalogs. 4. Paintings, Modern—17th-18th centuries—Flanders—Catalogs. 5. Painters—Netherlands—Biography. 6. Painters—Flanders—Biography. I. Stanley, George. A classified synopsis of the principal painters of the Dutch and Flemish schools .... II. Title.

Paintings, Sienese.

SIENESE painting. 759.5
Greenwich, Conn., New York Graphic Society [c1956] 77p. illus., plates (part col.) 36cm. [The Great masters of the past, 7] [ND621.S6C32] [ND621.S6C32] 927.5 57-13102 57-13102
1. Paintings, Sienese. 2. Painters, Italian — Siens. I. Carli, Enzo, 1910- II. Series.

Paisiello, Giovanni, 1740-1816.

HUNT, Jno Leland 782.1'092'4 B
Giovanni Paisiello, his life as an opera composer / Jno Leland Hunt. [s.l.] : National Opera Association, 1975. vii, 88 p. ; 23 cm. (NOA monograph series ; v. 2) Bibliography: p. 87-88. [ML410.P14H8] 75-26158
1. Paisiello, Giovanni, 1740-1816. I. Series: National Opera Association. NOA monograph series ; v. 2.

Paisley, Oldham, 1893-

O'SHEA, Margaret N. 070.4'092'4 B
Oldham Paisley: a community editor and his newspapers, the Marion daily Republican and Marion weekly leader, 1915-1970, by Margaret N. O'Shea. Marion, Ill., Available from the Marion daily Republican [1974] 186 p. ports. 29 cm. Originally presented as the author's thesis (M.A.) Southern Illinois University. Includes bibliographical references. [PN4874.P235O8 1974] 74-167313 3.75
1. Paisley, Oldham, 1893- I. Title.

Pak, In-dok.

PAK, In-dok. 920.7
September monkey [by] Induk Pahk. [1st ed.] New York, Harper [1954] 283 p. 22 cm. [CT1848.P3A3] 54-8981
I. Title.

Pakenham, Simona.

PAKENHAM, Simona. 828.912
Pigtails and Pernod. London, Macmillan; New York, St. Martin's Press, 1961. 286p. illus. 23cm. Autobiographical. [CT788.P24A3 1961] 61-18330
I. Title.

Pakistan—Politics and government.

AYUB Khan, Mohammad, Pres. Pakistan, 1907- 954.9'04'0924 B
Friends not masters, a political autobiography. New York, Oxford University Press, 1967. xiv, 275 p. illus., maps, ports. 24 cm. [DS385.A9A3] 67-25583
1. Pakistan—Politics and government. I. Title.

AYUB KHAN, Mohammad, Pres. Pakistan, 1907- 954.9'04'0924(B)
Friends not masters: a political autobiography. London, New York [etc.] Oxford U.P., 1967. 275 p. front., 26 plates (incl. ports. maps) 25 cm. (B67-17732) [DS385.A9A3] 67-104032
1. Pakistan—Pol. & govt. I. Title.

Palavicino, Sir Horatio, 1540 (ca.)-1600.

STONE, Lawrence. 923.242
An Elizabethan: Sir Horatio Palavicino. Oxford, Clarendon Press, 1956. 345 p. illus. 22 cm. [HC252.5.P3S8] 56-2572
1. Palavicino, Sir Horatio, 1540 (ca.)-1600. 2. Finance, Public — Gt. Brit. — To 1688. I. Title. BIP

Pale Moon, Princess.

PALE Moon, Princess. 248'.2'0924 B
Pale Moon : the story of an Indian princess / by Princess Pale Moon. Wheaton, Ill. : Tyndale House Publishers, 1975. 110 p., [8] leaves of plates : ill. ; 22 cm. [E99.C5P25] 75-7227 ISBN 0-8423-4878-6 : 4.95
1. Pale Moon, Princess.

Paleontologists—Correspondence, reminiscences, etc.

TEILHARD de Chardin, Pierre. 925.72
Letters from a traveller. New York, Harper [1962] 380 p. illus. 22 cm. Translation of Lettres de voyage, 1923-1939, and Nouvelles lettres de voyage, 1939-1955. [QE707.T4A414 1962a] 62-11136
1. Paleontologists—Correspondence, reminiscences, etc. I. Title.

TEILHARD de Chardin, Pierre. 925.72
Letters from a traveller. New York, Harper [1968, c.1962] 380p. illus. 21cm. (Torchbk., 385) Tr. of Lettres de voyage, 1923-1939, and Nouvelles lettres de voyage, 1939-1955. [QE707.T4A414 1962a] 62-11136 2.45 pap.,
1. Paleontologists—Correspondence, reminiscences, etc. I. Title.

Palermo, Louie.

PALERMO, Louie. 783.7'092'2 B
'Atsa Louie, I'ma Phil / Louie and Phil Palermo, with Bernard Palmer. Wheaton, Ill. : Victor Books, c1975. 135 p. : ill. ; 21 cm. [ML420.P15A3] 75-18082 ISBN 0-88207-650-7 : 2.95
1. Palermo, Louie. 2. Palermo, Phil. 3. Gospel musicians—Correspondence, reminiscences, etc. I. Palermo, Phil, joint author. II. Palmer, Bernard Alvin, 1914- joint author. III. Title.

Palestine—Politics and government.

SAMUEL, Edwin, Viscount Samuel, 1898- 915.694'03'40924
A lifetime in Jerusalem; the memoirs of the second Viscount Samuel. London, New York, Abelard-Schuman [1970] ix, 335 p. ports. 22 cm. Includes bibliographical references. [DS125.3.S34A3 1970b] 71-124097 ISBN 0-200-71719-7 10.95 (U.S.)
1. Palestine—Politics and government. I. Title.

Palestrina, Giovanni Pierluigi da, 1525?-1594.

CAMETTI, Alberto, 1871-1935. 783'.026'20924 B
Palestrina / Alberto Cametti. 1st AMS ed. New York : AMS Press, 1979. 383 p. : ill. ; 19 cm. Reprint of the 1925 ed. published by Bottega di Poesia, Milan, in series: I Fascicoli musicali. Bibliography: p. [375]-378. [ML410.P15C18 1979] 74-24055 ISBN 0-404-12878-5 : 32.00
1. Palestrina, Giovanni Pierluigi da, 1525?-1594. 2. Composers—Italy—Biography. I. Series: Fascicoli musicali. BIP

COATES, Henry, 1880-1963. 783'.026'20924 B
Palestrina / by Henry Coates. Westport, Conn. : Hyperion Press, 1979. p. cm. (Encore music editions) (Reprint of the 1938 ed. published by Dent, London; Dutton, New York, in series: The Master musicians. New series.) "Catalogue of works": p. Bibliography: p. Includes index. [ML410.P15C7 1979] 78-66885 ISBN 0-88355-732-0 : 22.50
1. Palestrina, Giovanni Pierluigi da, 1525?-1594. 2. Composers—Italy—Biography. I. Series: The Master musicians. New series. BIP

KING, Ethel M. 780.92
Palestrina, the Prince of music. Brooklyn, N.Y., Gaus [1966, c.1965] 122p. port. 22cm. Bibl. [ML410.P15K5] 65-29275 3.00
1. Palestrina, Giovanni Pierluigi da, 1525?-1594. I. Title.

PYNE, Zoe Kendrick. 783'.0924 B
Giovanni Pierluigi da Palestrina, his life and times. Freeport, N.Y., Books for Libraries Press [1970] xxv, 232 p. illus., port. 23 cm. "First published 1922." [ML410.P15P9 1970] 79-107828
1. Palestrina, Giovanni Pierluigi da, 1525?-1594. BIP

PYNE, Zoe Kendrick. 783'.0924 B
Giovanni Pierluigi da Palestrina, his life and times. Westport, Conn., Greenwood Press [1970] xxv, 232 p. illus., music, port. 23 cm. Reprint of the 1922 ed. Includes bibliographical references. [ML410.P15P9 1970b] 74-100831 ISBN 0-8371-4002-1
1. Palestrina, Giovanni Pierluigi da, 1525?-1594.

Paley, William Samuel, 1901-

PALEY, William Samuel, 1901- 384.54'092'4 B
As it happened : a memoir / William S. Paley. 1st ed. Garden City, N.Y. : Doubleday, 1979. 418 p., [24] leaves of plates : ill. ; 24 cm. Includes index. [HE8689.8.P34] 78-73191 ISBN 0-385-14639-6 : 14.95
1. Paley, William Samuel, 1901- 2. Columbia Broadcasting System, inc. 3. Broadcasting—United States. 4. Businessmen—United States—Biography. I. Title.

Palfrey. John Gorham, 1796-1881.

AYER, Hannah (Palfrey), 1881- ed. 923.273
A legacy of New England; letters of the Palfrey family. [Milton? Mass.] Priv. print., 1950. 2 v. (xviii. 401 p.) illus., ports., facsims. 26 cm. "Printed in an edition of 150 copies." [E340.P2A9] 50-26911
1. Palfrey. John Gorham, 1796-1881. 2. Palfrey family. I. Title.

Palgrave, Francis Turner,

PALGRAVE, Francis Turner, 1824-1897. 821'.8 B
Francis Turner Palgrave; his journals and memories of his life, by Gwenllian F. Palgrave. New York, AMS Press [1971] ix, 276 p. illus., port. 23 cm. Reprint of the 1899 ed. Includes bibliographical references. [PR5115.P5A8 1971] 73-148283 ISBN 0-404-04867-6
I. Palgrave, Gwenllian Florence, 1867- ed. BIP

Palladio, Andrea, 1508-1580.

PUPPI, Lionello. 720'.92'4
Andrea Palladio / Lionello Puppi ; [translated by Pearl Sanders]. Boston : New York Graphic Society, 1975, c1973. 465 p. : ill. ; 29 cm. [NA1123.P2P8213 1975b] 74-21496 ISBN 0-316-03970-5 : 47.50
1. Palladio, Andrea, 1508-1580. BIP

Pallandt, Nina, Barones van, 1932-

PALLANDT, Nina, Barones van, 1932- 784'.092'4 B
Nina. New York, Walker [1973] 221 p. illus. 24 cm. Autobiographical. [ML420.P155A3] 72-83757 ISBN 0-8027-0399-2 6.95
1. Pallandt, Nina, Barones van, 1932- I. Title.

Palliko, Alan Joseph, 1937—

BUGLIOSI, Vincent. 345'.73'02523
Till death us do part : a true murder mystery / Vincent Bugliosi with Ken Hurwitz. 1st ed. New York : Norton, c1978. 384 p. ; 24 cm. [KF224.P34B83] 78-3840 ISBN 0-393-08821-9 : 10.95
1. Palliko, Alan Joseph, 1937- 2. Stockton, Sandra D., 1940- 3. Trials (Murder)—California—Los Angeles. 4. Crime and criminals—California—Biography. I. Hurwitz, Ken, joint author. BIP

Pallotti, Vincenzo, Saint, 1795-1850.

BONIFAZI, Flavian. 922.22
Soul of a saint; St. Vincent Pallotti, pioneer of Catholic action. Staten Island, N. Y., Alba House [1963] 192 p. 21 cm. Bibliography: p. [185]-186. [BX4700.P23B6] 63-19455
1. Pallotti, Vincenzo, Saint, 1795-1850. I. Title.

BURTON, Katherine (Kurz) 1890- 922.245
In haven we shall rest; the life of Vincenzo Pallotti, founder of the Congregation of the Catholic Apostolate. Foreword by Francis Cardinal Spellman. New York, Benziger Bros. [1955] 214p. illus. 21cm. [BX4705.P36B8] 55-12726
1. Palloti, Vincenzo, 1795-1850. I. Title.

GREENE, Ellis 282'.0924(B)
Champion of the apostolate; the life of St. Vincent Pallotti. Illustrated by Dorothy Koch. North Easton, Mass., Holy Cross Pr., 1967. 111p. illus. 22cm. [BX4700.P23G7] 67-25215 2.50
1. Pallotti, Vincenzo, Saint, 1795-1850 I. Title.

[WEBER, Eugen] 922.245
Vincent Pallotti an apostle and mystic [by] Eugene Weber. Tr. by Horst Vollmer. Staten Island, N. Y., Alba [c.1964] 460p. 23cm. 63-14572 5.95
1. Pallotti, Vincenzo, Saint, 1795-1850. I. Title.

WEBER, Eugene, 1890- 922.245
Vincent Pallotti; an apostle and mystic. Translated by Horst Vollner. Staten Island, N.Y., Alba House [1964] 460 p. 23 cm. [BX4700.P23W43] 63-14572
1. Pallotti, Vincenzo, Saint, 1795-1850. I. Title.

Palmer, Alexander Mitchell, 1872-1936.

COBEN, Stanley. 923.273
A. Mitchell Palmer: politician. New York, Columbia University Press, 1963. 351 p. illus. 24 cm. Includes Bibliography. [E748.P24C6] 63-9874
1. Palmer, Alexander Mitchell, 1872-1936. I. Title. BIP

COBEN, Stanley. 973.91'3'0924 B
A. Mitchell Palmer: politician. New York, Da Capo Press, 1972 [c1963] xii, 351 p. 23 cm. (Civil liberties in American history) Bibliography: p. [329]-338. [E748.P24C6 1972] 79-180787 ISBN 0-306-70208-8
1. Palmer, Alexander Mitchell, 1872-1936. I. Title. II. Series.

Palmer, Alice Elvira (Freeman) 1855-1902—Juvenile literature.

FLEMING, Alice (Mulcahey) 1928- 378.1'12'0924 B
Alice Freeman Palmer: pioneer college president, by Alice Fleming. Illustrated by Donn Albright. Englewood Cliffs, N.J., Prentice-Hall [1970] 143 p. illus. 22 cm. (Hall of Fame books) "A Rutledge book." Bibliography: p. 143. A biography of a woman who became president of Wellesley College and who was also one of the first women in America to receive a college degree. [LD7212.7 1882.F55] 92 75-92099 ISBN 0-13-022293-3 4.50
1. Palmer, Alice Elvira (Freeman) 1855-1902—Juvenile literature. I. Albright, Donn, illus. II. Title. III. Series.

Palmer, Arnold, 1929-

ARNOLD, Palmer, 796.352'74'0924
by the editors of Golf digest magazine. New York, Grosset & Dunlap [1967] 159 p. ports. 20 cm. (Grosset sports library) [GV964.P3A7] 67-14762
1. Palmer, Arnold, 1929- 2. Golf digest.

BISHER, Furman. 796.352'64'0924
The birth of a legend: Arnold Palmer's golden year, 1960. Murray Olderman, general editor. Englewood Cliffs, N.J., Prentice-Hall [1972] 174 p. illus. 22 cm. (The Golden year series) [GV964.P3B5] 72-38133 ISBN 0-13-077313-1
1. Palmer, Arnold, 1929- I. Title.

GOLF digest. 796.352'74'0924
Arnold Palmer, by the editors of Golf digest magazine. New York, Grosset & Dunlap [1967] 159 p. ports. 20 cm. (Grosset sports library) [GV964.P3G6] 67-14762
1. Palmer, Arnold, 1929- I. Title.

MCCORMACK, Mark H. 796.352'64'0924
Arnie, the evolution of a legend, by Mark H. McCormack. New York, S.&S. [1967] 318p. illus. 25cm. [GV964.P3M3] 67-22939 6.50 bds.,
1. Palmer, Arnold, 1929- I. Title.

Palmer, Arnold, 1929—Juvenile literature.

OLSEN, James T. 796.352'092'4 B
Arnold Palmer: king on the course, by James T. Olsen. Illustrated by Harold Henriksen. Mankato, Minn., Creative Education, distributed by Childrens Press, Chicago, [1974] 31 p. illus. (part col.) 25 cm. (Creative's superstars) Biography of the world-famous golfer who once worked as a paint salesman and now has eight companies worth millions of dollars. [GV964.P3O47] 92 73-13861 ISBN 0-87191-284-8 4.95
1. Palmer, Arnold, 1929—Juvenile literature. I. Henriksen, Harold, illus. II. Title.

Palmer, Daniel David, 1842-1913.

MAYWARD, Joseph Edward. 926.1
Healing hands; the story of the Palmer family, discoverers and developers of chiropractic. Freeport, N. Y., Jonorm Pub. Co. [c1959] 365p. illus. 24cm. [RZ232.P3M3] 59-14319
1. Palmer, Daniel David, 1842-1913. 2. Palmer, Bartlett Joshua, 1881- I. Title.

Palmer, Edward, 1831-1911.

BEATY, Janice J. 925.8
Plants in his pack; a life of Edward Palmer, adventurous botanist and collector. Illus. by Joan Berg [New York] Pantheon [c.1964] 182, [2]p. illus., maps. 22cm. Bibl. 64-18324 3.75; 3.29 lib. ed.,
1. Palmer, Edward, 1831-1911. I. Title.

BEATY, Janice J. 581'.0924 B
Plants in his pack; a life of Edward Palmer, adventurous botanist and collector, by Janice J. Beaty. Illus. by Joan Berg. [New York] Pantheon Books [1964] 182, [2] p. illus., maps. 22 cm. Bibliography: p. [184] A biography of botanist Edward Palmer who collected more than 100,000 plant specimens for museums, discovered 2,000 plants new to science, and had 200 plants named in his honor. [QK31.P3B4] 92 AC 68
1. Palmer, Edward, 1831-1911. I. Berg, Joan, illus. II. Title.

MCVAUGH, Rogers, 1909- 925.8
Edward Palmer, plant explorer of the American West. [1sted.] Norman,

University of Oklahoma Press [1956] xvii, 430p. illus., ports., maps, facsims. 24cm. 'References and sources : p.403-420 [QK31.P3M3] 56-11234
1. Palmer, Edward, 1831-1911. 2. Botany—The West. 3. Botany—Mexico. I. Title.

MCVAUGH, Rogers, 1909- 925.8
Edward Palmer, plant explorer of the American West. [1st ed.] Norman, University of Oklahoma Press [1956] xvii, 430p. illus., ports., maps, facsims. 24cm. 'References and sources': p. 403-420. [QK31.P3M3] 56-11234
1. Palmer, Edward, 1831-1911. 2. Botany—The West. 3. Botany—Mexico. I. Title.

MCVAUGH, Rogers, 581'.092'4 B
1909-
Edward Palmer, plant explorer of the American West / Rogers McVaugh. Sakonnet : Theophrastus, 1977. p. cm. Reprint of the 1st ed. published in 1956 by University of Oklahoma Press, Norman. Bibliography: p. [QK31.P3M3 1977] 77-10073 ISBN 0-913728-26-8 : 15.00
1. Palmer, Edward, 1831-1911. 2. Plant collectors—United States—Biography. 3. Botany—The West—History. 4. Botany—Mexico—History. I. Title. **BIP**

Palmer family.

PALMER, William 929'.2'0973
Preston, 1897-
George Ware Palmer, Jr. & Agnes Preston Palmer : a memoir / by their son, William Preston Palmer. New York : Palmer, 1972. 2 v. : ill. ; 29 cm. [CS71.P175 1972b] 75-308537
1. Palmer family. 2. Palmer, George Ware, 1861-1929. I. Title.

Palmer, George Herbert,

PALMER, George Herbert, 191 B
1842-1933.
The autobiography of a philosopher. New York, Greenwood Press, 1968 [c1930] vi, 137 p. port. 21 cm. [B945.P24A3 1968] 68-19291
I. Title. **BIP**

Palmer, Jim, 1945- —Juvenile literature.

COHEN, Joel H. 796.357'092'4 B
Jim Palmer : great comeback competitor / by Joel H. Cohen. New York : Putnam, c1978. 192 p. : ill. ; 21 cm. (Putnam sport shelf) Includes index. A biography of the pitcher who has the distinction of being the only American Leaguer to win the Cy Young Award three times. [GV865.P34C63 1978] 92 77-24311 ISBN 0-399-61114-2 lib. bdg. : 5.69
1. Palmer, Jim, 1945- —Juvenile literature. 2. Baltimore. Baseball club (American League)—Juvenile literature. 3. Pitchers (Baseball)—United States—Biography Juvenile literature. I. Title. **BIP**

Palmer, Kenyon T.,

PALMER, Kenyon T., 333.3'3'0924 B
1899-
For land's sake; the autobiography of a dynamic Arizonan [by] K. T. Palmer. [Flagstaff, Ariz.] Northland Press [1971] viii, 354 p. illus. 24 cm. [CT275.P343A3] 77-174995 ISBN 0-87358-073-7 10.50
I. Title.

Palmer, Lilli, 1914-.

PALMER, Lilli, 791'.0924'4 B
1914-
Change lobsters, and dance : an autobiography. New York : warner Books, 1976c1975. 366p. : ill. ; 18 cm. Translation of Dickie Lilli, gutes Kind [PN2658.P3A3313] pbk. : 1.95
1. Palmer, Lilli, 1914-. I. Title.
L.C. card no. of 1975 Macmillan edition: 75-15924

Palmer, Lilli, 1914-

PALMER, Lilli, 1914- 791'.092'4 B
Change lobsters, and dance : an autobiography / by Lilli Palmer. 1st American ed. New York : Macmillan, 1975. viii, 320 p., [12] leaves of plates : ill. ; 24 cm. Translation of Dicke Lilli, gutes Kind. [PN2658.P3A3313 1975] 75-15924 ISBN 0-02-594610-2
1. Palmer, Lilli, 1914- I. Title.

Palmer, Samuel, 1805-1881.

CECIL, David, Lord, 1902- 759.2 B
Visionary and dreamer; two poetic painters: Samuel Palmer and Edward Burne-Jones. [Princeton, N.J.] Princeton University Press [1970, c1969] xxii, 177 p. illus. (part col.) 27 cm. (Bollingen series, 35. The A. W. Mellon lectures in the fine arts, 15) Bibliography: p. 163-[166] [ND496.C4 1970] 68-57088
1. Palmer, Samuel, 1805-1881. 2. Burne-Jones, Edward Coley, Sir, bart., 1833-1898. I. Title. II. Series: Bollingen series, 35. III. Series: The A. W. Mellon lectures in the fine arts, 15 **BIP**

MALINS, Edward 760'.0924 B
Greenway.
Samuel Palmer's Italian honeymoon [by] Edward Malins. London, New York [etc.] Oxford U.P., 1968. xiv, 130 p. 20 plates, illus., facsims., map, ports. 23 cm. Bibliography: p. [123]-125. [ND497.P3M3] 79-356980 35/-
1. Palmer, Samuel, 1805-1881. 2. Linnell, John, 1792-1882. I. Title.

PALMER, Samuel, 1805- 759.2 B
1881.
The letters of Samuel Palmer / edited by Raymond Lister. Oxford : Clarendon Press, 1974, [i.e.1975] 2 v. ; 23 cm. Contents Contents.—v. 1. 1814-1859.—v. 2. 1860-1881. Includes bibliographical references and index. [ND497.P3A24] 75-311327 ISBN 0-19-817309-1 : 80.00
1. Palmer, Samuel, 1805-1881. 2. Painters—Great Britain—Correspondence, reminiscences, etc.
Distributed by Oxford University Press New York. **BIP**

PEACOCK, Carlos. 760'.0924 B
Samuel Palmer; Shoreham and after Greenwich, Conn., New York Graphic Society [1968] 144 p. illus. (part col.) 30 cm. [ND497.P3P4 1968b] 69-12901
1. Palmer, Samuel, 1805-1881.

SELLARS, James. 760'.092'4 B
Samuel Palmer / James Sellars. New York : St. Martin's Press, 1974. 159 p. : ill. (some col.) ; 32 cm. Includes index. Bibliography: p. [155] [ND497.P3S44 1974] 74-81700 ISBN 0-85670-148-3 : 45.00
1. Palmer, Samuel, 1805-1881.

Palmer, Thomas Waverly,

PALMER, Thomas Waverly, 923.473
1891-
Gringo lawyer. Gainesville, University of Florida Press, 1956. 176p. 24cm. Autobiographical. 56-9486
I. Title. **BIP**

Palmer, William Jackson, 1836-1909.

ANDERSON, George 385'.0924
LaVerne, 1905-
General William Jackson Palmer: man of vision [by] George L. Anderson. Colorado Springs, Colorado College, 1960. 24 p. 23 cm. (The Colorado College studies, no. 4) "Revision of a lecture delivered at Colorado College, April 22, 1959, as a memorial to General William Jackson Palmer, on the fiftieth anniversary of his death." Bibliographical footnotes. [AS36.C563 no. 4] 77-10767
1. Palmer, William Jackson, 1836-1909. I. Series: Colorado College, Colorado Springs. Research Committee. The Colorado College studies, no. 4

Palmerston, Henry John Temple, 3d viscount, 1784-1865.

BELL, Herbert Clifford 942.080924
Francis, 1881-
Lord Palmerston; 2v. Hamden, Conn., Archon. [dist. Shoe String] 1966. 2v. (various p.) illus., ports. 22cm. First pub. in 1936 by Longmans, Green, London. Bibl. [DA536.P2B4] 66-14604 18.00 set,
1. Palmerston, Henry John Temple, 3d viscount, 1784-1865. 2. Gt. Brit.—Pol. & govt.—19th cent. 3. Gt. Brit.—For. rel.—19th cent. 4. Europe—Politics—1815-1871. I. Title.

RIDLEY, Jasper 942.081'0924 B
Godwin.
Lord Palmerston [by] Jasper Ridley. New York, Dutton [1971, c1970] xiii, 688 p. illus., ports. 26 cm. Bibliography: p. 661-671. [DA536.P2R53 1971] 71-148470 ISBN 0-525-14873-6 12.50
1. Palmerston, Henry John Temple, 3d Viscount, 1784-1865.

SOUTHGATE, Donald 942.080924
The most English minister . . . The policies and politics of Palmerston London, Macmillan; New York St Martin's [c.] 1966. xxx,647p. maps, ports. 23cm. Bibl. [DA536.P2S6] 65-22794 15.00
1. Palmerston, Henry John Temple, 3d viscount, 1784-1865. I. Title.

Pambrum, Andrew Dominique, 1822-1895.

PAMBRUN, Andrew 979.5'03
Dominique, 1822-1895.
Sixty years on the frontier in the Pacific Northwest / Andrew Dominique Pambrun. Fairfield, Wash. : Ye Galleon Press, 1979. p. cm. Includes index. Bibliography: p. [F880.P1757] 79-14273 ISBN 0-87770-183-0 : 14.95
1. Pambrun, Andrew Dominique, 1822-1895. 2. Northwest, Pacific—Description and travel. 3. Indians of North America—Northwest, Pacific. 4. Northwest, Pacific—Biography. 5. Walla Walla, Wash.—Biography. 6. Pioneers—Northwest, Pacific—Biography. I. Title. **BIP**

Pan, Chao, 1st century.

SWANN, Nancy Lee, 895.1'8'209
1881-
Pan Chao, foremost woman scholar of China, first century A.D.; background, ancestry, life, and writings of the most celebrated Chinese woman of letters. New York, Russell & Russell [1968, c1932] xvii, 179 p. illus., maps. 23 cm. Half title in Chinese. Includes bibliographies. [PL2663.P3Z8 1968] 68-10946
1. Pan, Chao, 1st century.

Pandit, Vijaya Lakshmi Nehru, 1900-

ANDREWS, Robert 954.04'0924(B)
Douglas, 1903-
A lamp for India: the story of Madame Pandit [by] Robert Hardy Andrews. Englewood Cliffs, N. J., Prentice [1967] 406p. ports. 24cm. Bibl. [DS481.P3A8] 67-16380 7.95 bds.,
1. Pandit, Vijaya Lakshmi Nehru, 1900- I. Title.

GUTHRIE, Anne. 920.7
Madame Ambassador; the life of Vijaya Lakshmi Pandit. [1st ed.] New York, Harcourt, Brace and World [1962] 192 p. illus. 21 cm. [DS481.P3G8] 62-9478
1. Pandit, Vijaya Lakshmi Nehru, 1900- I. Title.

PANDIT, Vijaya 954.04'092'4 B
Lakshmi Nehru, 1900-
The scope of happiness : a personal memoir / by Vijaya Lakshmi Pandit. New York : Crown Publishers, c1979. xvii, 333 p., [16] leaves of plates : ill. ; 24 cm. Includes index. [DS481.P3A29 1979] 78-20901 ISBN 0-517-53688-9 : 12.95
1. Pandit, Vijaya Lakshmi Nehru, 1900- 2. India—History—20th century. 3. Statesmen—India—Biography. I. Title. **BIP**

Panella, Vincent.

PANELLA, Vincent. 974.7'1'00451
The other side : growing up Italian in America / by Vincent Panella ; photos. by Susan Sechel. 1st ed. Garden City, N.Y. : Doubleday, 1979. 189 p. : ill. ; 27 cm. [F128.9.I8P36] 78-22346 ISBN 0-385-14733-3 : 12.95
1. Panella, Vincent. 2. Panella family. 3. Italian Americans—New York (City)—Biography. 4. New York (City)—Biography. I. Sechel, Susan. II. Title. **BIP**

Panikkar, Kavalam Madhava.

PANIKKAR, Kavalam 327'.2'0924 B
Madhava, 1896-1963.
An autobiography / K. M. Panikkar ; translated from the Malayalam by K. Krishnamurthy. Madras : Oxford University Press, 1977. vi, 372 p., [4] leaves of plates : ill. ; 23 cm. Includes index. [DS481.P32A3313] 77-905441 12.50
1. Panikkar, Kavalam Madhava. 2. Diplomats—India—Biography. 3. Historians—India—Biography. I. Title.
Distributed by Oxford University Press, New York

Panizzi, Anthony, Sir 1797-1879.

FAGAN, Louis 020'.924 B
Alexander, 1845-1903.
The life of Sir Anthony Panizzi, K.C.B., late principal librarian of the British Museum, senator of Italy. With an etching and other illus. by the author. 2d ed. New York, B. Franklin [1970] 2 v. illus., port. 22 cm. (Burt Franklin research & source work series, 586. Essays in literature & criticism, 97) Includes letters in English, French, or Italian. Reprint of the 1880 ed. Includes bibliographical references. [Z720.P2F2 1970] 70-130597 ISBN 0-8337-1095-8
1. Panizzi, Anthony, Sir, 1797-1879.

MILLER, Edward 020'.924
Prince of librarians; the life and times of Antonio Panizzi of the British Museum. Athens, Ohio Univ. Pr. [1967] 356p. illus., ports. 23cm. Bibl. [Z720.P2M5 1967b] 67-26123 7.50
1. Panizzi, Anthony, Sir 1797-1879. I. Title. **BIP**

Pankey family.

PANKEY, William 286'.1'73
Russell.
Edge of paradise; fifty years in the pulpit. Parsons, W. Va., McClain Print. Co., 1972. x, 245 p. coat of arms. 23 cm. [BX6495.P26A3] 79-174564 ISBN 0-87012-111-1
1. Pankey family. I. Title. **BIP**

Pankey, Joe, 1892-

PANKEY, Joe, 1892- 636.2'0092'4 B
Land and cattle : conversations with Joe Pankey, a New Mexico rancher / by Jack Parsons and Michael Earney ; foreword by Brant Calkins ; photos. by Jack Parsons. 1st ed. Albuquerque : University of New Mexico Press, c1978. xii, 96 p. : ill. ; 22 cm. [SF194.2.P36A33] 78-56950 ISBN 0-8263-0491-5 : 15.00
1. Pankey, Joe, 1892- 2. Ranchers—New Mexico—Biography. 3. Cattle—New Mexico—History. I. Parsons, Jack, 1939- joint author. II. Earney, Michael, 1937- joint author. III. Title. **BIP**

Pankhurst, Emmeline (Goulden) 1858-1928.

KAMM, Josephine. 324'.3'0924 B
The story of Emmeline Pankhurst. [1st U.S. ed.] New York, Meredith Press [1968, c1961] ix, 181 p. illus., ports. 21 cm. Bibliography: p. 181. [JN979.P28K35 1968] 68-26328 4.95
1. Pankhurst, Emmeline (Goulden) 1858-1928. I. Title.

Pankhurst, Emmeline (Goulden) 1858-1928—Juvenile literature.

NOBLE, Iris. 324'.3'0922 B
Emmeline and her daughters: the Pankhurst suffragettes. New York, J. Messner [1971] 190 p. 22 cm. Bibliography: p. 185-186. A biography of the aristocratic English woman and her three daughters who led British women in their struggle to win the vote. [HQ1595.A3N6] 920 70-160303 ISBN 0-671-32437-3 3.95
1. Pankhurst, Emmeline (Goulden) 1858-1928—Juvenile literature. 2. Pankhurst, Estelle Sylvia, 1882-1960—Juvenile literature. 3. Pankhurst, Christabel, Dame, 1880-1958—Juvenile literature. 4. Feminism—Great Britain—Juvenile literature. I. Title. BIP

Pankhurst, Estelle Sylvia, 1882-1960—Juvenile literature.

NOBLE, Iris. 324'.3'0922 B
Emmeline and her daughters: the Pankhurst suffragettes. New York, J. Messner [1971] 190 p. 22 cm. Bibliography: p. 185-186. A biography of the aristocratic English woman and her three daughters who led British women in their struggle to win the vote. [HQ1595.A3N6] 920 70-160303 ISBN 0-671-32437-3 3.95
1. Pankhurst, Emmeline (Goulden) 1858-1928—Juvenile literature. 2. Pankhurst, Estelle Sylvia, 1882-1960—Juvenile literature. 3. Pankhurst, Christabel, Dame, 1880-1958—Juvenile literature. 4. Feminism—Great Britain—Juvenile literature. I. Title. BIP

Pannenberg, Wolfhart, 1928-

GALLOWAY, Allan Douglas, 1920- 230.0924
Wolfhart Pannenberg [by] Allan D. Galloway London, George Allen and Unwin [1975 c1973] 143 p. 22 cm. (Contemporary religious thinkers) Includes index. Bibliography: p. 139-140. [BX4827.P3G34] ISBN 0-04-230011-8
1. Pannenberg, Wolfhart, 1928- I. Title.
Distributed by Humanities Press for 9.75. L.C. card no. for original edition: 73-179423.

OLIVE, Don H. 230'.092'4 B
Wolfhart Pannenberg [by] Don H. Olive. Waco, Tex., Word Books [1973] 120 p. 23 cm. (Makers of the modern theological mind) Bibliography: p. 117-120. [BX4827.P3O44] 78-188068 4.95
1. Pannenberg, Wolfhart, 1928- I. Title. BIP

Panos, Chris.

PANOS, Chris. 269'.2'0924 B
God's spy / by Chris Panos. 1st ed. Plainfield, N.J.: Logos International, 1976. xiii, 270 p. ; 22 cm. [BV3785.P33A33] 76-55451 ISBN 0-88270-213-0 : 6.95. pbk. : 3.50
1. Panos, Chris. 2. Evangelists—United States—Biography. I. Title. BIP

Panov, Valery, 1938-

PANOV, Valery, 1938- 792.8'092'4 B
To dance / Valery Panov, with George Feifer. 1st ed. New York : Knopf : distributed by Random House, 1978. xv, 397 p., [20] leaves of plates : ill. ; 25 cm. Autobiography. Includes index. [GV1785.P275A37 1978] 77-20362 ISBN 0-394-49882-8 : 12.95
1. Panov, Valery, 1938- 2. Dancers—Biography. I. Feifer, George, joint author. II. Title. BIP

Panzram, Carl, 1891-1930.

GADDIS, Thomas E. 364.15'23'0924 B
Killer; a journal of murder [by] Thomas E. Gaddis & James O. Long. [New York] Macmillan [1970] 388 p. illus., facsim., ports. 21 cm. Includes excerpts from Carl Panzram's autobiography. [HV6248.P26G32] 74-129749
1. Panzram, Carl, 1891-1930. I. Long, James O., joint author. II. Title.

*GADDIS, Thomas E. 364.15'23'0924[B]
Killer: a journal of murder [by] Thomas E. Long & James O. Long. Greenwih, Conn., Fawcett Pubns. [1973, c.1970] 352 p. illus., facsim., ports. 18 cm. (Premier Book, P628) "Based on the papers of Henry Lesser." Includes excerpts from Carl Panzram's autobiography. [HV6248.P26G32] 1.25 (pbk.)
1. Panzram, Carl, 1891-1930. I. Long, James O., joint author. II. Title.
L.C. card no. for the hardbound edition: 74-129749.

Paoli, Pasquale, 1725-1807.

BOSWELL, James, 1740-1795. 828.6
Boswell on the Grand Tour: Italy, Corsica, and France, 1765-1766. Edited by Frank Brady and Frederick A. Pottle. [1st ed.] New York, McGraw-Hill [1955-) xxv, 356 p. illus., ports., 3 maps on fold. 1. 25 cm. (The Yale editions of the private papers of James Boswell) Contents.Contents.—Introduction, by F. Brady.—Boswell in Italy, 1765.—The journal of a tour to Corsica and memoirs of Pascal Paoli.—The voyage home, 1765-1766.—Appendix A. Correspondence with Girolama Piccolomini (Moma), 1766-1769.—Appendix B. Letters of Rousseau to Therese Le Vasseur.—Appendix C. Discarded portion of letter from Boswell to Rousseau.—Appendix D. Paragraphs from "The London chronicle" concerning Corsica and Boswell. [PR3325.A92] 55-7270
1. Paoli, Pasquale, 1725-1807. 2. Italy—Description and travel. 3. Corsica—Description and travel. 4. France—Description and travel. I. Brady, Frank, ed. II. Pottle, Frederick Albert, 1897- ed. III. Title. IV. Series.

BOSWELL, James, 1740-1795. 828'.6'03
Boswell on the grand tour: Italy, Corsica, and France, 1765-1766. Edited by Frank Brady and Frederick A. Pottle Melbourne [Australia] W. Heinemann [1955] xxviii, 383 p. illus., facsims., maps (on lining papers), ports. 24 cm. (The Yale editions of the private papers of James Boswell) Contents.Contents.—Introduction, by F. Brady.—Boswell in Italy, 1765.—The journal of a tour to Corsica and memoirs of Pascal Paoli.—The voyage home, 1765-1766.—Appendix A. Correspondence with Girolama Piccolomini (Moma), 1766-1769.—Appendix B. Letters of Rousseau to Therese Le Vasseur.—Appendix C. Discarded portion of letter from Boswell to Rousseau.—Appendix D. Paragraphs from the London chronicle concerning Corsica and Boswell. [PR3325] 68-4422
1. Paoli, Pasquale, 1725-1807. 2. Italy—Description and travel. 3. Corsica—Description and travel. 4. France—Description and travel. I. Brady, Frank, ed. II. Pottle, Frederick Albert, 1897- ed. III. Title. IV. Series.

BOSWELL, James, 1740-1795. 914.4'945'04340924
The journal of a tour to Corsica, and memoirs of Pascal Paoli / by James Boswell ; edited, with an introd., by Morchard Bishop. Folcroft, Pa. : Folcroft Library Editions, 1975. 127 p. : port. ; 23 cm. Reprint of the 1951 ed. published by Williams & Norgate, London. Bibliography: p. 5-6. [DC611.C811B75 1975] 75-17527 ISBN 0-8414-3155-8 lib. bdg. : 17.50
1. Paoli, Pasquale, 1725-1807. 2. Corsica. I. Title. BIP

THRASHER, Peter Adam, 1923- 945.9'5'0340924 B
Pasquale Paoli, an enlightened hero, 1725-1807. [Hamden, Conn.] Archon Books, 1970. 352 p. illus., maps, ports. 23 cm. Bibliography: p. 339-342. [DC611.C806P37 1970] 70-107866 9.00
1. Paoli, Pasquale, 1725-1807. I. Title.

Paolo della Croce, Saint, 1694-1775.

ALMERAS, Charles 922.245
St. Paul of the Cross, founder of the Passionists. Translated [from the French] by M. Angeline Bouchard. Garden City, N. Y., Hanover House [c.] 1960. 286p. Bibl. notes: p.262-277. 22cm. 60-15165 3.95
1. Paolo della Croce, Saint, 1694-1775. I. Title.

Paolo della Croce, Saint, 1694-1775—Juvenile literature.

ROBERTO, Brother, 1927- 922.245
A light on the mountain; a story of St. Paul of the Cross. Notre Dame, Ind., Dujarie Press [1960] 143p. illus. 22cm. [BX4700.P25R6] 60-52059
1. Paolo della Croce, Saint, 1694-1775—Juvenile literature. I. Title.

Paolozzi, Eduardo, 1924—

KIRKPATRICK, Diane. 709.24
Eduardo Paolozzi. Greenwich, Conn., New York Graphic Society [1969?] 144 p. illus. (part col.) 26 cm. Bibliography: p. 139-141. [N6797.P25K5] 71-125993 14.50
1. Paolozzi, Eduardo, 1924-

PAOLOZZI, Eduardo, 1924- 709'.2'4
Eduardo Paolozzi : sculpture, drawings, collages, and graphics : an Arts Council exhibition, Newcastle, Laing Art Gallery, 17 April-16 May 1976 ... . [London : Arts Council, 1976] 128 p. : chiefly ill. ; 20 cm. Includes bibliographical references. [N6797.P25A897] 77-357404 ISBN 0-7287-0090-5 : £1.65
1. Paolozzi, Eduardo, 1924- I. Arts Council of Great Britain. II. Laing Art Gallery, Newcastle-upon-Tyne.

Papacy—Hist.

FARROW, John, 1904- 922.21
Pageant of the popes; illustrated by Jean Charlot. Holy Year [i. e. 2d] ed. New York, Sheed & Ward, 1950. v, 394 p. ports. 22 cm. Bibliography: p. 381. [BX955.F33 1950] 50-6234
1. Papacy—Hist. I. Title.

Papacy—History—To 1309.

DUCHESNE, Louis Marie Olivier, 1843-1922. 945'.6
The beginnings of the temporal sovereignty of the popes, A.D. 754-1073. Authorised translation from the French by Arnold Harris Mathew. New York, B. Franklin [1972] xi, 312 p. 23 cm. (Burt Franklin research and source work series. Philosophy and religious history monographs, 121) Reprint of the 1908 ed., which was issued as v. 11 of International Catholic library. Translation of Les premiers temps de l'Etat pontifical. Includes bibliographical references. [BX1070.D83 1972] 73-185937 ISBN 0-8337-4079-2
1. Papacy—History—To 1309. 2. Popes—Temporal power. 3. Papal states—History. I. Title. II. Series: The International Catholic library, v. 11.

Papegoja, Armegott (Printz) 1626-1695.

MEIXNER, Esther (Chilstrom) 1904- 917.510320924 (B)
The Governor's daughter; the story of Armegott Printz, a fascinating personality of the early Colonial era, and a champion for women's rights. [Chester, Pa., 1965] vi, 45 p. illus., ports. 22 cm. [F167.P3M4] 65-29581
1. Papegoja, Armegott (Printz) 1626-1695. 2. New Sweden — Hist. I. Title.

Paper making and trade.

HUNTER, Dard, 1883-1966. 676.2*
My life with paper; an autobiography. [1st ed.] New York, Knopf, 1958. 236 p. illus. 22 cm. [TS1098.H8A32] 58-9672
1. Paper making and trade. I. Title.

Papini, Giovanni,

PAPINI, Giovanni, 1881-1956. 920.045
Labourers in the vineyard. Port Washington, N.Y., Kennikat Press [1970] xi, 250 p. 21 cm. (Essay and general literature index reprint series) Reprint of the 1930 ed. Translation of Gli operai della vigna. Essays. Contents.Contents.—Petrarch.—Michelangelo Buonarroti.—Giovanni Fattori.—Oscar Ghiglia.—Romano Romanelli.—The evangelists—Saint Francis of Assisi.—Jacopone da Todi.—Saint Ignatius of Loyola.—Joseph de Maistre.—Alessandro Manzoni.—Pius XI.—Domenico Giuliotti.—Casar and Virgil. Bibliographical footnotes. [PQ4835.A27G513 1970] 79-111313 ISBN 8-04-609330-
I. Title. BIP

Papp, Joseph.

LITTLE, Stuart W. 792'.0232'0924
Enter Joseph Papp : in search of a new American theater / Stuart W. Little. New York : Coward, McCann & Geoghegan, [1974] 320 p. ; 24 cm. Includes index. [PN2287.P23L5 1974] 73-93761 8.95
1. Papp, Joseph. I. Title.

Pappenheim, Bertha,

PAPPENHEIM, Bertha, 1859-1936. 301.41'2'0924
Bertha Pappenheim: Freud's Anna O. by Dora Edinger. [Highland Park, Ill., Congregation Solel, 1968] 102 p. illus., ports. 22 cm. Translated from the German. Includes bibliographical references. [DS135.G5P33] 78-5607
I. Edinger, Dora, ed. II. Title.

Papua New Guinea—Biography—Addresses, essays, lectures.

PAPUA New Guinea portraits : the expatriate experience / James Griffin, editor. Canberra ; Norwalk, Conn. : Australian National University Press : [available from] Books Australia, 1978. xxxi, 269 p., [4] leaves of plates : ill. ; 22 cm. Includes bibliographical references. [CT2950.P36 1978] 78-52790 ISBN 0-7081-1295-1 pbk. : 24.95 920'.095
1. Papua New Guinea—Biography—Addresses, essays, lectures. I. Griffin, James. BIP

Papua-New Guinea (Ter.)

WILLIAMS, Maslyn. 919.5'03
In one lifetime. [Melbourne] Cheshire [1970] 73 p. illus. (part col.), maps (on lining paper), ports. 32 cm. Label mounted on t.p.: Distributed by Lawrence Verry Inc., Mystic, Conn. [DU740.W535 1970] 70-96410 4.95 ($7.00 U.S.)
1. Papua-New Guinea (Ter.) 2. Papua-New Guinea (Ter.)—Biography. I. Title.

Paracelsus, 1493-1541.

PACHTER, Henry Maximilian, 1907- 921.9
Paracelsus; magic into science, being the true history of the troubled life, adventures, doctrines, miraculous cures, and prophecies of the most renowned, widely traveled, very learned and pious gentleman, scholar, and most highly experienced and illustrious physicus, the Honorable Philippus Theophrastus Aureolus Bombastus ab Hohenheim, Eremita, called Paracelsus. New York, Schuman [1951] x, 360 p. illus., ports., facsims. 22 cm. Bibliography: p. [341]-343. [B785.P24P3] 51-10192
1. Paracelsus, 1493-1541.

PAGEL. WALTER, 1898- 921.9
Paracelsus; an introduction to philosophical

medicine in the era of the Renaissance. Basel, New York, S. Karger, 1958. xii, 368p. illus. ports., facsims. 25cm. Bibliographical footnotes. [R128.6.P33P3] 59-2446
1. Paracelsus, 1493-1541. I. Title.

ROSEN, Sidney. 921.9
Doctor Paracelsus. Illustrated by Rafaello Busoni. [1st ed.] Boston, Little, Brown [1959] 214 p. illus. 22 cm. Includes bibliography. [R147.P2R6] 59-7359
1. Paracelsus, 1493-1541.

Paracelsus, 1493-1541—Juvenile literature.

SUSAC, Andrew. 610'.924 B
Paracelsus, monarch of medicine. [1st ed.] Garden City, N.Y., Doubleday [1969] 192 p. port. 22 cm. A biography of the sixteenth-century European physician who helped usher in the modern age of medicine by realizing the importance of the physician-patient relationship. [R147.P2S86] 92 71-76552 3.95
1. Paracelsus, 1493-1541—Juvenile literature. I. Title.

Paradis, Charles Alfred Marie, 1848-1926.

HODGINS, Bruce Willard, 1931- 971.4'03'0924 B
Paradis of Temagami : the story of Charles Paradis, 1848-1926 : northern priest, colonizer, and rebel / by Bruce W. Hodgins. Cobalt, Ont. : Highway Book Shop, 1976. 46 p. : ill. ; 22 cm. Includes bibliographical references. [F1053.P28H62] 77-372970 ISBN 0-88954-104-3
1. Paradis, Charles Alfred Marie, 1848-1926. 2. Catholic Church—Clergy—Biography. 3. Quebec (Province)—History. 4. Ontario—History. 5. Pioneers—Canada—Biography. 6. Clergy—Canada—Biography. I. Title.

Paralysis—Personal narratives.

WILLIS, Jack. 362.4'3'0924 B
But there are always miracles [by] Jack and Mary Willis. New York, Viking Press [1974] 181 p. 22 cm. Autobiographical. [RD796.W5A33 1974] 73-20946 ISBN 0-670-19757-2 6.95
1. Paralysis—Personal narratives. I. Willis, Mary, 1946- joint author. II. Title.

Paralysis. Spastic—Personal narratives.

NEAL, Elizabeth. 920.9616842
One of those children. [1st American ed.] New York, Taplinger Pub. Co. [1962, c1961] 198p. 23cm. [RC418.N4 1962] 62-8357
1. Paralysis. Spastic—Personal narratives. I. Title.

Paramount Pictures Corporation.

PARISH, James Robert. 791.43'028'0922
The Paramount pretties. Editor: T. Allan Taylor. Research associates: John Robert Cocchi [and] Florence Solomon. Photo associate: Gene Andrewski. New Rochelle, N.Y., Arlington House [1972] 587 p. illus. 25 cm. [PN1998.A2P395] 72-78482 ISBN 0-87000-180-9 12.95
1. Paramount Pictures Corporation. 2. Moving-picture actors and actresses, American—Biography. I. Title.

Paraplegia.

MCADAM, Terry. 616.83
Very much alive; the story of a paraplegic. Boston, Houghton Mifflin, 1955. 146 p. 22 cm. Autobiographical. [RC382.M2] 54-11452
1. Paraplegia. I. Title.

Pardee, Alice DeWolf.

PARDEE, Alice DeWolf. 920.7
Grandma wears blue jeans. Illustrated by Nancy Pardee Swenson. New York, Crowell [1959] 103 p. illus. 21 cm. Autobiographical. [CT275.P356A3] 59-6736
I. Title.

Pare, Ambroise, 1510?-1590.

AMRBOISE Pare, 128
surgeon of the Renaissance, by Wallace B. Hamby. St. Louis, W. H. Green [1967] xxi, 251p. illus., maps. 24cm. Bibl. [R507.P3H3] 617 9.50
1. Pare, Ambroise, 1510?-1590. I. Hamby, Wallace Bernard, 1903

PARE, Ambroise, 1510?-1590. 926.1
The apologie and treatise of Ambroise Pare, containing the voyages made into divers places, with many of his writings upon surgery. Edited and with an introd. by Geoffrey Keynes. Chicago, University of Chicago Press [1952] xxii, [1]. 227 p. illus., ports. 22 cm. (The Classics of science) Bibliography: p. [xxiii] [R507.P3A3 1952] 52-10208
1. Surgeons — Correspondence, reminiscences, etc. 2. Surgery — Early works to 1800. I. Title. II. Series.

PARE, Ambroise, 1510-1590 617.0924
The apologie and treatise of Ambroise Pare, containing the voyages made into divers places with many of his writings upon surgery. Ed., introd. by Geoffrey Keynes [Magnolia, Mass., Peter Smith. 1968] xxii, [1] 227p. illus., ports. 22cm. (Dover bk., T1902 rebound) Repubn. of the ed. pub. by the Univ. of Chicago Pr. in 1952. Bibl. [R507.P3A3 1968] 7.50
1. Surgeons—Correspondence, reminiscences, etc. 2. Surgery—Early works to 1800. I. Title.

PARE, Ambroise, 1510?-1590. 617'.0924
The apologie and treatise of Ambroise Pare, containing the voyages made into divers places with many of his writings upon surgery. Edited and with an introd. by Geoffrey Keynes. New York, Dover Publications [1968] xxii, [1] 227 p. illus., ports. 22 cm. A republication of the ed. published by the University of Chicago Press in 1952. Bibliography: p. [xxiii] [R507.P3A3 1968] 68-14763
1. Surgeons—Correspondence, reminiscences, etc. 2. Surgery—Early works to 1800. I. Title.

PARE, Ambroise, 1510?-1590. 617'.0924 B
Life and times of Ambroise Pare, 1510-1590, with a new translation of his Apology and an account of his journeys in divers places, by Francis R. Packard. New York, B. Blom, 1971. xii, 297 p. illus., 2 fold. maps. 21 cm. Translation of A. Pare's Apologie, et traite contenant les voyages faits en divers lieux, together with F. R. Packard's essay on Life and times of Ambroise Pare. [R507.P3A3 1971] 79-160607
1. Surgery History. 2. France—History—16th century. I. Packard, Francis Randolph, 1870-1950, ed. II. Title.

Pare, Ambroise, 1510?-1590—Juvenile literature.

CARBONNIER, Jeane. 92
A barber-surgeon; a life of Ambroise Pare, founder of modern surgery. Illustrated by Joseph Cellini. [New York] Pantheon Books [1965] 186 p. illus. 22 cm. Bibliography: p. 185-186. [R507.P3C3] 65-20653
1. Pare, Ambroise, 1510?-1590—Juvenile literature. I. Title.

Paree, Ambroise, 1510?-1590—Juvenile literature.

CARBONNIER, Jeanne, M.D. 92
A barber-surgeon; a life of Ambroise Pare, founder of modern surgery. Illus. by Joseph Cellini. [New York] Pantheon [c.1965] 186p. illus. 22cm. Bibl. [R507.P3C3] 65-20653 3.75; 3.49 lib. ed.,
1. Paree, Ambroise, 1510?-1590—Juvenile literature. I. Title.

Parent, Bernie, 1945-

PARENT, Bernie, 1945- 796.9'62'0924 B
Bernie! / by Bernie Parent, with Bill Fleischman and Sonny Schwartz. Englewood Cliffs, N.J. : Prentice-Hall, 1976c1975 272 p. : ill. ; 22 cm. [GV848.5.P28A33] 75-38542 ISBN 0-13-074526-X : 8.95
1. Parent, Bernie, 1945- 2. Hockey. I. Fleischman, Bill, 1939- II. Schwartz, Sonny. III. Title.

Pareto, Vilfredo, 1848-1923.

MEISEL, James Hans, 1900- ed. 301.0922
Pareto & Mosca, Edited by James H. Meisel. Englewood Cliffs, N.J., Prentice-Hall, [1965] 184 p. 21 cm. (Makers of modern social science) A Spectrum book. Bibliography: p. 181-182. Bibliographical footnotes. [HM59.M4] 65-20601
1. Pareto, Vilfredo, 1848-1923. 2. Mosca, Gaetano, 1858-1941. I. Title. II. Series.

Paris—Intellectual life.

GREEN, Julien, 1900- 928.4
Diary, 1928-1957. Selected by Kurt Wolff. Translated by Anne Green. [1st American ed.] New York, Harcourt, Brace & World [1964] 313 p. 22 cm. [PQ2613.R3Z533 1964] 64-22667
1. Paris—Intellectual life. 2. U.S.—Descr. & trav.—1920-1940. 3. Europe—Descr. & trav.—1919- I. Title.

Paris, Matthew, 1200-1259.

VAUGHAN, Richard, 1927- 942.034
Matthew Paris. Cambridge [Eng.] University Press, 1958. xii, 287 p. illus., facsims., diagrs. 23 cm. (Cambridge studies in medieval life and thought, new ser., v. 6) Bibliography: p. 267-275. [DA3.P3V3] 58-14636
1. Paris, Matthew, 1200-1259. I. Series. BIP

Paris. Peace Conference, 1919.

LANSING, Robert, 1864-1928. 940.3'141'0922
The Big Four and others of the Peace Conference. Freeport, N.Y., Books for Libraries Press [1972] 212 p. ports. 23 cm. (Essay index reprint series) Reprint of the 1921 ed. [D647.A2L3 1972] 73-177961 ISBN 0-8369-2556-4
1. Paris. Peace Conference, 1919. 2. Statesmen. 3. European War, 1914-1918—Biography. I. Title. BIP

LEVIN, Norman Gordon, comp. 940.3'141
Woodrow Wilson and the Paris Peace Conference. 2d ed. edited, and with an introd., by N. Gordon Levin, Jr. Lexington, Mass., Heath [1972] xv, 232 p. illus. 21 cm. (Problems in American civilization) Published in 1957 under title: Wilson at Versailles, edited by T. P. Greene. Bibliography: p. 229-232. [D644.L45 1972] 72-2914 ISBN 0-669-83915-9 2.50
1. Paris. Peace Conference, 1919. 2. Wilson, Woodrow, Pres. U.S., 1856-1924. 3. Versailles, Treaty of, June 28, 1919 (Germany) I. Greene, Theodore P., 1920- ed. Wilson at Versailles. II. Title. III. Series. BIP

Paris—Social life and customs.

HENREY, Robert, Mrs. 1906- 914.436
The little Madeleine; the autobiography of a young girl in Montmartre. [1st American ed.] New York, Dutton, 1953. 350 p. 23 cm. [DC736.H37 1953] 52-12157
1. Paris—Social life and customs. I. Title.

Park, Brad.

PARK, Brad. 796.9'62
Play the man [by] Brad Park with Stan Fischler. New York, Dodd, Mead [1971] viii, 211 p. illus. 22 cm. [GV848.5.P3A3] 73-181824 ISBN 0-396-06433-7 6.95
I. Fischler, Stan, joint author. II. Title.

Park, Brad—Juvenile literature.

BURCHARD, S. H. 796.9'62'0924 B
Sports star, Brad Park / S. H. Burchard ; illustrated with photos. and with drawings by Paul Frame. 1st ed. New York : Harcourt Brace Jovanovich, [1975] 64 p. : ill. ; 21 cm. A simple biography of Brad Park, defenseman for the New York Rangers hockey team. [GV848.5.P3B87] 92 75-11778 ISBN 0-15-277998-1 : 4.95
1. Park, Brad—Juvenile literature. 2. Hockey—Juvenile literature. I. Title.

PARK, Brad. 796.9'62
Play the man [by] Brad Park with Stan Fischler. New York, Dodd, Mead [1971] viii, 211 p. illus. 22 cm. [GV848.5.P3A3] 73-181824 ISBN 0-396-06433-7 6.95
I. Fischler, Stan, joint author. II. Title.

Park, Etta Wolcott,

PARK, Etta Wolcott, 1863-1938. 929.2'0973
A story for my children. [Edited by Nettie W. Park. 1st ed.] New York, Vantage Press [1968] 253 p. illus., coat of arms, geneal. tables, map (on lining papers), ports. 21 cm. Autobiographical. Bibliography: p. [7]-[8] [CT275.P358A3] 68-1458
I. Title.

Park, Mungo, 1771-1806.

BRENT, Peter Ludwig. 916.6'04'0924 B
Black Nile : Mungo Park and the search for the Niger / by Peter Brent. London : Gordon Cremonesi, 1977. 200 p., [8] leaves of plates : ill. ; 27 cm. Includes index. Bibliography: p. [193]-194. [DT356.P37B73] 77-30052 ISBN 0-86033-017-6 : 16.95
1. Park, Mungo, 1771-1806. 2. Africa, West—Discovery and exploration. 3. Niger River. 4. Explorers—Africa, West—Biography. I. Title.

LUPTON, Kenneth. 916.6'2'040924 B
Mungo Park, the African traveler / Kenneth Lupton. Oxford ; New York : Oxford University Press, 1979. xxii, 272 p., [6] leaves of plates : ill. ; 23 cm. Includes index. Bibliography: p. [241]-244. [DT356.P37L86] 78-40200 ISBN 0-19-211749-1 : 19.95
1. Park, Mungo, 1771-1806. 2. Africa, West—Discovery and exploration. 3. Niger River. 4. Explorers—Africa, West—Biography. 5. Explorers—Scotland—Biography. I. Title.

THOMSON, Joseph, 1858-1895. 916.62'04'0924 B
Mungo Park and the Niger. [New York] Argosy-Antiquarian, 1970. 338 p. illus., 11 maps. 23 cm. Reprint of the 1890 ed. [DT356.P37T4 1970] 70 122475 ISBN 0-87266-040-0
1. Park, Mungo, 1771-1806. 2. Niger River. I. Title. BIP

Park, Robert Ezra, 1864-1944.

RAUSHENBUSH, Winifred. 301'.092'4 B
Robert E. Park : biography of a sociologist / Winifred Raushenbush ; with a foreword and an epilogue by Everett C. Hughes. Durham, N.C. : Duke University Press, 1979. xii, 206 p. ; 25 cm. Includes index. "The publications of Robert E. Park": p. [195]-198. [HM22.U6P347] 77-88063 ISBN 0-8223-0402-3 : 12.75
1. Park, Robert Ezra, 1864-1944. 2. Sociologists—United States—Biography. I. Title. BIP

Parker, Adele.

*HULL, Robert Chareton. 978'.02'0924 B
The Search for Adele Parker. [Roslyn Heights, N.Y., Libra, 1974] xvi, 188 p. illus. 22 cm. [F594] 74-82751 6.95
1. Parker, Adele. I. Title. BIP

Parker, Bob.

PARKER, Audrey, 1923- 362.7'8'20926 B
We still love you, Bob! / Audrey Parker. Chappaqua, N.Y. : Christian Herald Books, [1979] p. cm. [RJ499.P37] 79-50947 ISBN 0-915684-34-9 : 7.95
1. Parker, Bob. 2. Child psychopathology—United States—Biography. I. Title. BIP

Parker, Calvin, d. 1939.

CHRISTENSEN, Alta (Hilliard) 922.69611
In strange peril, on dark trails. Washington, Review and Herald [1958] 251p. illus. 22cm. [BV3680.N6C5] 59-1964
1. Parker, Calvin, d. 1939. I. Title.

Parker, Charles Christopher, 1920-1955.

HARRISON, Max. 927.8
Charlie Parker. New York, Barnes [1961, c1960] 84p. illus. 21cm. (Kings of jazz) A Perpetua book, P-4034. [ML419.P4H4 1961] 60-16823
1. Parker, Charles Christopher, 1920-1955. I. Title.

REISNER, Robert George. 927.8
Bird: the legend of Charlie Parker. New York, Citadel Press [1962] 256 p. ports. 26 cm. Discography: p, 241-256. [ML419.P4R4] 61-16977
1. Parker, Charles Christopher, 1920-1955. I. Title. BIP

REISNER, Robert George. 788'.66'0924 B
Bird : the legend of Charlie Parker / by Robert George Reisner. New York : Da Capo Press, 1975, c1962. 256 p. : ill. ; 26 cm. (The Roots of jazz) Reprint of the ed. published by Citadel Press, New York. Discography: p. 241-255. [ML419.P4R4 1975] 74-30084 ISBN 0-306-70677-6 lib.bdg. : 12.95
1. Parker, Charles Christopher, 1920-1955. I. Title.

RUSSELL, Ross. 788'.66'0924 B
Bird lives; the high life and hard times of Charlie (Yardbird) Parker. New York, Charterhouse [1973] x, 404 p. illus. 24 cm. Bibliography: p. 381-383; discography: p. 384-388. [ML419.P4R9] 72-84214 8.95
1. Parker, Charles Christopher, 1920-1955. I. Title. BIP

Parker, Cynthia Ann, 1827?-1864.

DE SHIELDS, James T. 973'.04'97 S
Cynthia Ann Parker : the story of her capture / James T. DeShields. New York : Garland Pub., 1976, c1886. p. cm. (The Garland library of narratives of North American Indian captivities ; v. 95) Reprint of the 1886 ed. printed for the author, St. Louis. Issued with the reprint of the 1885 ed. of Gowanlock, Theresa. Two months in the camp of Big Bear. New York, 1976. [E85.G2 vol. 95] [E99.C85] 970'.004'97 B 75-7121 ISBN 0-8240-1719-6 lib.bdg. : 21.00
1. Parker, Cynthia Ann, 1827?-1864. 2. Parker, Quanah, 1854-1911. 3. Ross, Lawrence Sullivan, 1838-1898. 4. Comanche Indians—Captivities. 5. Indians of North America—Captivities. I. Title. II. Series.

Parker, Dorothy (Rothschild) 1893-1967.

KEATS, John, 1920- 070'.924 B
You might as well live; the life and times of Dorothy Parker. New York, Simon and Schuster [1970] 319 p. ports. 24 cm. Bibliography: p. 307-309. [PS3531.A5855Z7] 70-130195 ISBN 6-7120-6605- 7.50
1. Parker, Dorothy (Rothschild) 1893-1967. I. Title.

Parker, Dorothy Rothschild, 1893-1967.

KINNEY, Arthur F., 1933- 818'.5'209
Dorothy Parker / by Arthur F. Kinney. Boston : Twayne Publishers, 1978. p. cm. (Twayne's United States author series ; TUSAS 315) Includes index. Bibliography: p. [PS3531.A5855Z73] 78-16724 ISBN 0-8057-7241-3 lib. bdg. : 8.95
1. Parker, Dorothy Rothschild, 1893-1967. 2. Authors, American—20th century—Biography. BIP

Parker, Ely Samuel, 1828-1895.

ARMSTRONG, William Howard, 1932- 970'.004'97 B
Warrior in two camps : Ely S. Parker, Union general and Seneca chief / William H. Armstrong. 1st ed. Syracuse, N.Y. : Syracuse University Press, 1978. xi, 244 p. : ill. ; 24 cm. (An Iroquois book) Includes index. Bibliography: p. 216-229. [E99.S3P3253] 78-5719 ISBN 0-8156-0143-3 : 11.95
1. Parker, Ely Samuel, 1828-1895. 2. United States. Army—Biography. 3. Seneca Indians—Biography. 4. Generals—United States—Biography. I. Title. II. Series. BIP

Parker, Ely Samuel, 1828-1895—Juvenile literature.

FELTON, Harold W., 1902- 970.3 B
Ely S. Parker, spokesman for the Senecas [by] Harold W. Felton. Illustrated by Lorence F. Bjorkland. New York, Dodd, Mead [1973] 111 p. illus. 24 cm. A biography of the Iroquois Indian who rose to prominent leadership positions in both the Indian and white man's world by meeting the white men on their own ground instead of the battlefield. [E99.S3F44] 92 72-7748 ISBN 0-396-06736-0 4.25
1. Parker, Ely Samuel, 1828-1895—Juvenile literature. I. Bjorkland, Lorence F., illus. II. Title.

***Parker, Emma.**

*PARKER, Emma. 364.1'0924
The true story of Bonnie & Clyde as told by Bonnie's Mother and Clyde's Sister, [by Emma Parker, Nell Barrow Cowan] Introd. by Nelson Algren; comp., arr., ed. by Jan I. Fortune. New York, New Amer. Lib. [c. 1968] xxii, 175p. 18cm. (Signet bk., P3437) Formerly pub. under title: Fugitives. .60 pap.,
I. Title.

Parker, Francis Wayland, 1837-1902.

CAMPBELL, Jack K. 370'.924 B
Colonel Francis W. Parker, the children's crusader [by] Jack K. Campbell. New York, Teachers College Press, [1967] vi, 283 p. 22 cm. Bibliography: p. 245-270. [LB875.P259C3] 67-20114
1. Parker, Francis Wayland, 1837-1902. I. Title.

Parker, George LeRoy, 1867-

KELLY, Charles, 1889- 923.4173 b
The outlaw trail; a history of Butch Cassidy and his Wild Bunch. [Rev. and enl. ed.] New York, Devin-Adair Co., 1959. 374 p. illus. 21 cm. [F595.K324 1959] 58-9756
1. Parker, George LeRoy, 1867- 2. Outlaws. 3. Crime and criminals—The West. I. Title.

Parker, Horatio William, 1863-1919.

CHADWICK, George Whitefield, 1854-1931. 780'.92'4 B
Horatio Parker, 1863-1920. New Haven, Yale University Press, 1921. [New York, AMS Press, 1972] 26 p. 19 cm. [ML410.P163C4 1972] 72-1392 ISBN 0-404-08304-8 5.00
1. Parker, Horatio William, 1863-1919. BIP

SEMLER, Isabel (Parker) 780'.92'4 B
Horatio Parker; a memoir for his grandchildren. Compiled from letters and papers by Isabel Parker Semler, in collaboration with Pierson Underwood. New York, Da Capo Press, 1973 [c1942] 330 p. illus. 22 cm. (Da Capo Press music reprint series) [ML410.P163S3 1973] 72-8291 ISBN 0-306-70538-9 12.95
1. Parker, Horatio William, 1863-1919. I. Underwood, Pierson, joint author.

SEMLER, Isabel Parker. 780'.92'4 B
Horatio Parker : a memoir for his grandchildren, compiled from letters and papers / by Isabel Parker Semler, in collaboration with Pierson Underwood. New York : AMS Press, [1975] p. cm. Reprint of the 1942 ed. published by Putnam, New York. "Works of Horatio W. Parker, compiled by W. Oliver Strunk": p. [ML410.P163S3 1975] 72-1674 ISBN 0-404-08333-1 : 15.00
1. Parker, Horatio William, 1863-1919. I. Underwood, Pierson. II. Title. BIP

Parker, Isaac Charles, 1838-1896.

CROY, Homer, 1883- 923.473
He hanged them high; an authentic account of the fanatical judge who hanged eighty-eight men. [1st ed.] New York, Duell, Sloan and Pearce [1952] 278 p. illus. 21 cm. 52-6782
1. Parker, Isaac Charls, 1838-1896. I. Title.

HARRINGTON, Fred Harvey, 1912- 923.473
Hanging judge. Illus. from photos. Caldwell, Idaho, Caxton Printers, 1951. 204 p. illus. 24 cm. 51-11701
1. Parker, Isaac Charles, 1838-1896. I. Title.

Parker, Joan H.

PARKER, Joan H. 362.1'9'699449
Three weeks in spring / by Joan H. Parker & Robert B. Parker. Boston : Houghton Mifflin, 1978. 183 p. ; 22 cm. [RC280.B8P29] 77-12396 ISBN 0-395-26282-8 : 7.95
1. Parker, Joan H. 2. Breast—Cancer—Biography. I. Parker, Robert B., 1932- joint author. II. Title. BIP

Parker, Matthew, Abp. of Canterbury, 1504-1575.

BROOK, Victor John Knight, 1887- 922.342
A life of Archbishop Parker. [New York] Oxford [c.]1962[ ] 358p. Bibl. 62-2860 5.60
1. Parker, Matthew, Abp. of Canterbury, 1504-1575. I. Title.

BROOK, Victor John Knight, 1887- 922.342
A life of Archbishop Parker. Oxford [Eng.] Clarendon Press, 1962. 358p. 23cm. Includes bibliography. [BX5199.P3B7] 62-2860
1. Parker, Matthew, Abp. of Canterbury, 1504-1575. I. Title.

Parker, Maurice Wesley, 1873-

BREWER, Wilmon, 1895- v. 12
A life of Maurice Parker. Francestown, N. H., Marshall Jones [c1954] 55p. illus., ports. 21cm. A55
1. Parker, Maurice Wesley, 1873- I. Title. BIP

Parker, Morris B., 1871-1957.

PARKER, Morris B., 1871-1957. 338.2'092'4 B
Morris B. Parker's Mules, mines, and me in Mexico, 1895-1932 / edited with an introd. and notes by James M. Day. Tucson : University of Arizona Press, 1979. p. cm. Includes index. Bibliography: p. [TN28.P37 1979] 79-15206 ISBN 0-8165-0626-4 : 12.50
1. Parker, Morris B., 1871-1957. 2. Mines and mineral resources—Mexico—History. 3. Mining engineers—Mexico—Biography. I. Day, James M. II. Title. III. Title: Mules, mines, and me in Mexiico, 1895-1932.

Parker, Peter, 1804-1888.

STEVENS, George Barker, 1854-1906. 266'.0092'4 B
The life, letters, and journals of the Rev. and Hon. Peter Parker, M.D., missionary, physican, diplomatist ... by George B. Stevens, with the co-operation of W. Fisher Markwick. Wilmington, Del., Scholarly Resources [1972] 362 p. port. 23 cm. [R154.P253S8 1972] 72-79840 ISBN 0-8420-1357-1
1. Parker, Peter, 1804-1888. I. Markwick, William Fisher, 1848-1911, joint author.

Parker, Quanah, 1854-1911.

DE SHIELDS, James T. 973'.04'97 S
Cynthia Ann Parker : the story of her capture / James T. DeShields. New York : Garland Pub., 1976, c1886. p. cm. (The Garland library of narratives of North American Indian captivities ; v. 95) Reprint of the 1886 ed. printed for the author, St. Louis. Issued with the reprint of the 1885 ed. of Gowanlock, Theresa. Two months in the camp of Big Bear. New York, 1976. [E85.G2 vol. 95] [E99.C85] 970'.004'97 B 75-7121 ISBN 0-8240-1719-6 lib.bdg. : 21.00
1. Parker, Cynthia Ann, 1827?-1864. 2. Parker, Quanah, 1854-1911. 3. Ross, Lawrence Sullivan, 1838-1898. 4. Comanche Indians—Captivities. 5. Indians of North America—Captivities. I. Title. II. Series.

Parker, Quanah, 1854-1911—Juvenile literature.

ANDERSON, LaVere. 970.3 B
Quanah Parker, Indian warrior for peace. Illustrated by Russell Hoover. Champaign, Ill., Garrard Pub. Co. [1970] 96 p. illus. (part col.), ports. 24 cm. (Americans all) A biography of the Comanche Chief who led his people against confinement on reservations, but once confinement occured he helped the tribe accept and benefit from reservation life. [E90.P19A65] 92 71-103957 2.49
1. Parker, Quanah, 1854-1911—Juvenile literature. I. Hoover, Russell, illus. II. Title.

MAY, Julian. 970.3 B
Quanah, leader of the Comanche. Illustrated by Phero Thomas. Mankato, Minn., Creative Educational Society, 1973. [39] p. illus. 24 cm. (Personal close-up books) A biography of the last chief of the Commanches who tried to bridge the gap between the red man's world and the white. [E90.P19M39] 92 72-14173 ISBN 0-87191-227-9
1. Parker, Quanah, 1854-1911—Juvenile literature. I. Thomas, Phero, illus. II. Title.

Parker, Scudder M

PARKER, Scudder M 920
In all love and honor; the autobiography of a marriage. New York, Abingdon Press [1959] 159p. 21cm. [CT275.P3765A3] 59-5213
I. Title.

Parker, Theodore, 1810-1860.

ALBRECHT, Robert C. 288'.0924 B
Theodore Parker by Robert C. Albrecht. New York, Twayne Publishers [1971] 160 p. 21 cm. (Twayne's United States authors series, 179) Bibliography: p. 150-155. [BX9869.P3A43] 76-120521
1. Parker, Theodore, 1810-1860.

CHADWICK, John White, 1840-1904. 288'.0924 B
Theodore Parker, preacher and reformer. Boston, Houghton, Mifflin, 1900. St. Clair Shores, Mich., Scholarly Press, 1971. xx, 422 p., ports. 22 cm. Bibliography: p. [xi]-xx. [BX9869.P3C5 1971] 72-144939 ISBN 0-403-00925-1
1. Parker, Theodore, 1810-1860.

COMMAGER, Henry Steele 922.8173
Theodore Parker. With a new introd. by the author. Boston, Beacon Press

[c.1947,1960]. 339p. Includes bibliography. 21cm. (Beacon series in liberal religion, LR4) 59-10731 1.75 pap.,
1. Parker, Theodore, 1810-1860. I. Title.

COMMAGER, Henry Steele, v. 12
1902-
Theodore Parker; with a new introd., by the author. [2d ed.] Boston, Beacon Press [1962] xi, 339 p. Includes bibliography. 68-93464
1. Parker, Theodore, 1810-1860. I. Title.

PARKER, Theodore, 288'.092'4 B
1810-1860.
Theodore Parker: American transcendentalist; a critical essay and a collection of his writings, by Robert E. Collins. Metuchen, N.J., Scarecrow Press, 1973. v, 271 p. illus. 22 cm. Contents.Contents.—Essay: A forgotten American.—Selections from Theodore Parker: Transcendentalism. A discourse of the transient and permanent in Christianity. The position and duties of the American scholar. The political destination of America and the signs of the times. The writings of Ralph Waldo Emerson. A sermon of war.—Selected bibliography (p. 261-264) [BX9869.P3A25 1973] 73-9593 ISBN 0-8108-0641-X 7.50
1. Parker, Theodore, 1810-1860. 2. Emerson, Ralph Waldo, 1803-1882. 3. Transcendentalism—Collected works. I. Collins, Robert E., ed.

WEISS, John, 1818- 288'.0924 B
1879.
Life and correspondence of Theodore Parker. New York, Bergman Publishers [1969] 2 v. illus., ports. 24 cm. Reprint of the 1864 ed. [BX9869.P3W4 1969b] 68-28772
1. Parker, Theodore, 1810-1860. I. Parker, Theodore, 1810-1860. Correspondence. II. Title.

WEISS, John, 1818- 288'.0924 B
1879.
Life and correspondence of Theodore Parker. New York, Da Capo Press, 1970. 2 v. illus., ports. 24 cm. Reprint of the 1864 ed. [BX9869.P3W4 1970] 76-106987
1. Parker, Theodore, 1810-1860. I. Parker, Theodore, 1810-1860. Correspondence. 1970. II. Title. BIP

WEISS, John, 1818- 288'.0924 B
1879.
Life and correspondence of Theodore Parker. New York, Arno Press, 1969. 2 v. in 1 illus., facsim., ports. 24 cm. (Religion in American) Reprint of the 1864 ed. [BX9869.P3W4 1969d] 70-83446
1. Parker, Theodore, 1810-1860. I. Parker, Theodore, 1810-1860. Correspondence. 1969. II. Title.

WEISS, John, 1818- 288'.0924 B
1879.
Life and correspondence of Theodore Parker, minister of the Twenty-eighth Congregational Society, Boston. New York, D. Appleton, 1864, Freeport, N.Y., Books for Libraries Press [1969] 2 v. illus., facsim., ports. 23 cm. (Select bibliographies reprint series) [BX9869.P3W4 1969] 69-16854
1. Parker, Theodore, 1810-1860. I. Title.

WEISS, John, 1818-1879. 288'.0924
Life and correspondence of Theodore Parker, minister of the Twenty-eighth Congregational Society, Boston. New York, Negro Universities Press [1969] 2 v. 23 cm. Reprint of the 1864 ed. [BX9869.P3W4 1969c] 74-97443
1. Parker, Theodore, 1810-1860. I. Parker, Theodore, 1810-1860. Correspondence. 1969. II. Title.

Parker, Willie J.

†PARKER, Willie J. 363.2 B
Halt! : I'm a Federal game warden : the amazing career of "the toughest game warden of them all" / Willie J. Parker, with Conway Robinson ; foreword by Nathaniel P. Reed. New York : D. McKay Co., c1977. x, 210 p., [4] leaves of plates : ill. ; 22 cm. [SK354.P37A35] 77-10493 ISBN 0-679-50779-5 : 9.95
1. Parker, Willie J. 2. Game wardens—Tennessee—Biography. I. Robinson, Conway, joint author. II. Title.

Parkinson, Samuel Rose, 1831-1919.

TAYLOR, Lester 979.6'42'030924 B
Parkinson.
Samuel Rose Parkinson : portrait of a pioneer / by Lester Parkinson Taylor. [s.l.] : Claymont Co., 1977. v, 199 p. : ill. ; 23 cm. Includes bibliographical references and index. [F754.F73P377] 77-5290
1. Parkinson, Samuel Rose, 1831-1919. 2. Franklin, Idaho—Biography. 3. Mormons and Mormonism in Franklin, Idaho—Biography. 4. Pioneers—Idaho—Franklin—Biography.

Parkman, Ebenezer, 1703-1782.

PARKMAN, 917.44'3'0320924
Ebenezer, 1703-1782.
The diary of Ebenezer Parkman, 1703-1782 / edited by Francis G. Walett ; with a foreword by Clifford K. Shipton. Worcester, Mass. : American Antiquarian Society, 1974- v. : map ; 30 cm. Includes bibliographical references and index. [F74.W65P19] 68-30686 ISBN 0-912296-04-6 : 19.50(vol.1)
1. Parkman, Ebenezer, 1703-1782. 2. Westboro, Mass.—Social life and customs. I. Walett, Francis G., ed.

Parkman, Francis, 1823-1893.

DOUGHTY, Howard, 970'.007'2024 B
1904-
Francis Parkman / by Howard Doughty. Westport, Conn. : Greenwood Press, 1978, c1962. 414 p. ; 23 cm. Reprint of the ed. published by Macmillan, New York. Includes index. Bibliography: p. 402-403. [E175.5.P212 1978] 78-5521 ISBN 0-313-20387-3 : 24.50
1. Parkman, Francis, 1823-1893. 2. Historians—United States—Biography. BIP

FARNHAM, Charles 970'.0072'024 B
Haight, 1841-1929.
A life of Francis Parkman. [Champlain ed.] New York, Greenwood Press [1969, c1901] xv, 394 p. illus., ports. 23 cm. "Bibliography of Francis Parkman's writings": p. [359]-364 [E175.5.P215 1969] 69-13894
1. Parkman, Francis, 1823-1893. I. Title.

FARNHAM, Charles 970'.0072'024 B
Haight, 1841-1929.
A life of Francis Parkman. Frontenac ed. Boston, Little, Brown, 1901. St. Clair Shores, Mich., Scholarly Press, 1970. xv, 394 p. illus., ports. 22 cm. "Bibliography of Francis Parkman's writings": p. [359]-364. [E175.5.P215 1970] 71-108480
1. Parkman, Francis, 1823-1893. I. Title.

FARNHAM, Charles 970'.0072'024 B
Haight, 1841-1929.
A life of Francis Parkman. New York, Haskell House, 1968. xv, 394 p. port. 23 cm. Reprint of the 1900 ed. "Haskell House catalogue item # 938." "Bibliography of Francis Parkman's writings": p. [359]-364. [E175.5.P215 1968] 68-24975
1. Parkman, Francis, 1823-1893. I. Title. BIP

FARNHAM, Charles 970'.007'2024 B
Haight, 1841-1929.
A life of Francis Parkman. [1st AMS ed.] New York, AMS Press [1969] xv, 394 p. illus. 22 cm. ([Parkman, Francis, 1823-1893. Works] La Salle ed., v. 20) "Reprinted from the edition of 1902, Boston." Includes bibliographical references. [E175.5.P215 1969b] 72-186529
1. Parkman, Francis, 1823-1893. I. Title.

PARKMAN, Francis, 1823- 816'.4
1893.
The correspondence of Francis Parkman and Henry Stevens, 1845-1885. Edited by John Buechler. Philadelphia, American Philosophical Society, 1967. 36 p. 30 cm. (Transactions of the American Philosophical Society, new ser., v. 57, pt. 6) Bibliographical footnotes. [Q11.P6 n.s., vol. 57, pt. 6] 67-27070
I. Stevens, Henry, 1819-1886, joint author. II. Buechler, John, ed. III. Series: American Philosophical Society, Philadelphia. Transactions, new ser., v. 57, pt. 6.

PARKMAN, Francis, 1823-1893 928.1
Letters of Francis Parkman. Edited and with an introd. by Wilbur R. Jacobs. Norman, University of Oklahoma Press [c.1960] 2v. (Bibl. footnotes) illus., ports., map. facsims. 25cm. 'Published in co-operation with the Massachusetts Historical Society.' 60-8754 12.50, bxd.
I. Title.

WADE, Mason, 970'.007'2024 B
1913-
Francis Parkman; heroic historian. [Hamden, Conn.] Archon Books, 1972 [c1942] xiii, 466 p. illus. 23 cm. Includes bibliographical references. [E175.5.P28 1972] 72-6564 ISBN 0-208-01213-3 12.00
1. Parkman, Francis, 1823-1893. BIP

Parks, Charles C., 1922-

BRANDYWINE River 730'.92'2
Museum.
Three sculptors of American realism: Charles Parks, Eric Parks, Christopher Parks. Essay: Michael Richman. Photography: A. Cypen Lubitsh. Chadds Ford, Pa. [1973] 63 p. illus. (part col.) 26 cm. Catalog of an exhibition. [NB237.P27B72] 73-84334
1. Parks, Charles C., 1922- 2. Parks, Eric. 3. Parks, Christopher. 4. Realism in art. I. Parks, Charles C., 1922- II. Parks, Eric. III. Parks, Christopher. IV. Richman, Michael. V. Title.

Parks, Eric.

BRANDYWINE River 730'.92'2
Museum.
Three sculptors of American realism: Charles Parks, Eric Parks, Christopher Parks. Essay: Michael Richman. Photography: A. Cypen Lubitsh. Chadds Ford, Pa. [1973] 63 p. illus. (part col.) 26 cm. Catalog of an exhibition. [NB237.P27B72] 73-84334
1. Parks, Charles C., 1922- 2. Parks, Eric. 3. Parks, Christopher. 4. Realism in art. I. Parks, Charles C., 1922- II. Parks, Eric. III. Parks, Christopher. IV. Richman, Michael. V. Title.

Parks, Gordon, 1912-

PARKS, Gordon. 770.924 [B]
A choice of weapons. New York, Harper & Row [1973 c.1966] 222 p. 18 cm. (Perennial Library) [PS3566.A73C5] ISBN 0-06-080305-3 1.25 (pbk.)
I. Title.
L.C. card no. for original ed.: 64-25119.

PARKS, Gordon, 1912- 770.924 B
A choice of weapons. [1st ed.] New York, Harper & Row [1966] x, 274 p. 22 cm. [PS3566.A73C5] 64-25119
I. Title. BIP

PARKS, Gordon, 1912- 770.'92'4 B
To smile in autumn : a memoir / Gordon Parks. 1st ed. New York : Norton, c1979. p. cm. [TR140.P35A34 1979] 79-19225 ISBN 0-393-01272-7 : 12.95
1. Parks, Gordon, 1912- 2. Afro-American photographers—United States—Biography. I. Title.

Parks, Gordon, 1912- —Juvenile literature.

HARNAN, Terry. 770'.92'4 B
Gordon Parks: Black photographer and film maker. Illustrated by Russell Hoover. Champaign, Ill., Garrard Pub. Co. [1972] 96 p. illus. (part col.) 24 cm. (Americans all) A brief biography of the man who overcame many obstacles to become a renowned photographer and film maker. [TR140.P35H37] 92 76-182846 ISBN 0-8116-4572-X
1. Parks, Gordon, 1912- —Juvenile literature. I. Hoover, Russell, illus. II. Title.

TURK, Midge. 770'.924
Gordon Parks. Illus. by Herbert Danska. New York, T. Y. Crowell [1973, c.1971] 33 p. illus. (pt. col.) 23 cm. (Crowell crocodile) (Crowell biographies) An easy-to-read biography of the black man who became a well-known photographer and author. [TR140.P35T8 1971] [92] 75-113857 ISBN 0-690-33794-9 0.95 (pbk.)
1. Parks, Gordon, 1912- —Juvenile literature. I. Danska, Herbert, illus. II. Title.

Parks, Hazzard Forest.

LEE, Amy. 361.7'4'0924 B
Call him a man; the story of Hazzard Parks. New York, Friendship Press [1970] 95 p. 18 cm. (Bold believers series) [HV28.P34L4] 72-130777 ISBN 0-377-84191-9 1.50
1. Parks, Hazzard Forest. I. Title. BIP

Parks, Rosa, 1913- —Juvenile literature.

GREENFIELD, 323.4'.092'4 B
Eloise.
Rosa Parks. Illustrated by Eric Marlow. New York, Crowell [1973] 32 p. illus. (part. col.)24 cm. (Crowell biographies) A brief biography of the black woman sometimes known as the Mother of the Civl Rights Movement for her part in precipitating the Montgomery bus boycott. [E185.97.P3G74] 92 72-83782 ISBN 0-690-71210-3 3.75
1. Parks, Rosa, 1913- Juvenile literature. I. Marlow, Eric, illus. II. Title. BIP

MERIWETHER, Louise. 323.4'092'4 B
Don't ride the bus on Monday: the Rosa Parks story. Illustrated by David Scott Brown. Englewood Cliffs, N.J., Prentice-Hall [1973] [32] p. illus. 24 cm. A brief biography of the Alabama black woman whose refusal to give up her seat on the bus marked the beginning of the civil rights movement. [E185.97.P3M4] 92 72-6331 ISBN 0-13-218750-7 4.75
1. Parks, Rosa, 1913- —Juvenile literature. 2. Segregation in transportation—Montgomery, Ala.—Juvenile literature. 3. Montgomery, Ala.—Race question—Juvenile literature. I. Brown, David, 1926- illus. II. Title. BIP

Parmenter, Frederick Albert, 1874-1920.

SACCO, Nicola, 343'.5'230922
1891-1927, defendant.
The Sacco-Vanzetti case; transcript of the record of the trial of Nicola Sacco and Bartolomeo Vanzetti in the courts of Massachusetts and subsequent proceedings 1920-7. Prefatory essay by William O.

Douglas. 2d ed. Mamaroneck, N.Y., P. P. Appel, 1969. 5 v. (L, 5621 p.) illus., fold. plans, ports. 27 cm. Sacco and Vanzetti were tried at Dedham, in the Superior Court of Massachusetts for Norfolk County, May 31-July 14, 1921, for the murder of F. A. Parmenter and A. Berardelli at South Braintree, Apr. 15, 1920. An explanatory title page, not included in the paging, introduces the various sections of the text. [KF224.S2D6 1969] 68-56904
1. Parmenter, Frederick Albert, 1874-1920. 2. Berardelli, Alessandro, d. 1920. 3. Cox, Alfred Elmer, 1887?- 4. Sacco-Vanzetti case. I. Vanzetti, Bartolomeo, 1888-1927, defendant. II. Massachusetts. Superior Court (Norfolk Co.) III. Massachusetts. Supreme Judicial Court. IV. Massachusetts. Superior Court (Plymouth Co.) BIP

SACCO, Nicola, 343'.5'230926
1981-1927, defendant.
The Sacco-Vanzetti case, by Osmond K. Fraenkel. New York, Russell & Russell [1969, c1931] 550, xv p. illus., maps, ports. 25 cm. [KF224.S2F7 1969] 71-83851
1. Parmenter, Frederick Albert, 1874-1920. 2. Berardelli, Alessandro, d. 1920. 3. Sacco-Vanzetti case. I. Vanzetti, Bartolomeo, 1888-1927, defendant. II. Fraenkel, Osmond Kessler, 1888- ed. III. Massachusetts. Superior Court (Norfolk Co.) IV. Title.

Parnell, Charles Stewart, 1846-1891.

GILLGANNON, Mary 941'.08'0924
McAuley.
Charles Stewart Parnell, political paradox. [1st ed.] New York, Vantage Press [1967] 117 p. 21 cm. Includes bibliographical references. [DA958.P2G5] 67-5332
1. Parnell, Charles Stewart, 1846-1891.

LYONS, Francis 941.5081'092'4 B
Stewart Leland, 1923-
Charles Stewart Parnell / F. S. L. Lyons. New York : Oxford University Press, 1977. 704 p. ; 24 cm. Includes bibliographical references and index. [DA958.P2L89] 77-367920 ISBN 0-19-519949-9 : 20.00
1. Parnell, Charles Stewart, 1846-1891. 2. Home rule—Ireland. 3. Ireland—Politics and government—1837-1901. 4. Politicians—Ireland—Biography. BIP

O'BRIEN, Richard 941.5'8'0924 B
Barry, 1847-1918.
The life of Charles Stewart Parnell, 1846-1891 New York, Haskell House, 1968. 2 v. illus., port. 23 cm. Reprint of the 1898 ed. [DA958.P2O2 1968] 68-25256
1. Parnell, Charles Stewart, 1846-1891. I. Title. BIP

Parnell, Katharine Wood.

MARLOW, Joyce. 941.58'092'4 B
The uncrowned queen of Ireland : the life of Kitty O'Shea / Joyce Marlow. 1st U.S. ed. New York : Saturday Review Press, [1975] xii, 334 p., [8] leaves of plates : ill. ; 24 cm. Includes index. Bibliography: p. 319-321. [DA958.P2M27 1975] 74-28356 ISBN 0-8415-0374-5 : 13.95
1. Parnell, Katharine Wood. 2. Parnell, Charles Stewart, 1846-1891. I. Title.

Parr, Jack.

JOHNSON, George, 1917- 927.92
The real Jack Paar. Greenwich, Conn., Fawcett Publications [1962] 142 p. 18 cm. (Gold medal books, s1263) [PN1992.4.P3J6 1962] 63-567
1. Parr, Jack. I. Title.

Parr, Samuel, 1747-1825.

COLSON, Percy, 1873-1952. 920.71
Their ruling passions. Foreword by James Laver. Freeport, N.Y., Books for Libraries Press [1970] 221 p. illus., ports. 24 cm. (Biography index reprint series) Reprint of the 1949 ed. Contents.Contents.—Baron Stockmar, a study in wire-pulling.—Lord George Gordon, a study in fanaticism.—Dr. Samuel Parr, a study in egoism.—Joseph Nollekens, a study in avarice.—The young Disraeli, a study in ambition. Includes bibliographies. [DA531.2.C78 1970] 70-136645
1. Stockmar, Christian Friedrich, Freiherr von, 1787-1863. 2. Gordon, George, Lord, 1751-1793. 3. Parr, Samuel, 1747-1825. 4. Nollekens, Joseph, 1737-1823. 5. Beaconsfield, Benjamin Disraeli, 1st Earl of, 1804-1881. I. Title. BIP

Parrish, Jasper, 1767-1836.

PARRISH, Jasper, 973'.04'97 S
1767-1836.
The story of Captain Jasper Parrish. New York : Garland Pub., 1976. p. 527-546 ; 23 cm. (The Garland library of narratives of North American Indian captivities ; v. 105) Originally published in 1903 in Buffalo Historical Society Publications, v. 6, p. 527-546. "Personal recollections of Captains Jones and Parrish ... by Hon. Orlando Allen": p. 539-546. Issued with the reprint of the 1904 ed. of Tarble, H. M. The story of my capture and escape. New York, 1976. The reprint of the 1906 ed. of Parkman, E. The story of the Rice boys. New York, 1976. [E85.G2 vol. 105] [E99.M93] 970'.004'97 B 75-40953 ISBN 0-8240-1729-3 lib.bdg. : 25.00
1. Parrish, Jasper, 1767-1836. 2. Munsee Indians—Captivities. 3. Indians of North America—Captivities. 4. Iroquois Indians. I. Allen, Orlando, 1803-1874. Personal recollections of Captains Jones and Parrish. 1976. II. Title. III. Series.

PARRISH, Jasper, 973'.04'97 S
1767-1936.
The story of Captain Jasper Parrish. New York : Garland Pub., 1976. p. cm. (The Garland library of narratives of North American Indian captivities ; v. 105) Originally published in 1903 in Buffalo Historical Society Publications, v. 6, p. 527-546. "Personal recollections of Captains Jones and Parrish ... by Hon. Orlando Allen": p. Issued with the reprint of the 1904 ed. of Tarble, H. M. The story of my capture and escape. New York, 1976. The reprint of the 1906 ed. of Parkman, E. The story of the Rice boys. New York, 1976. [E85.G2 vol. 105] [E99.M93] 970'.004'97 B 75-40160 ISBN 0-8240-1729-3 lib.bdg. : 21.00
1. Parrish, Jasper, 1767-1836. 2. Munsee Indians—Captivities. 3. Indians of North America—Captivities. 4. Iroquois Indians. I. Allen, Orlando, 1803-1874. Personal recollections of Captains Jones and Parrish. 1976. II. Title. III. Series.

Parrish, Robert.

PARISH, Robert. 791.430230924 B
Growing up in Hollywood / Robert Parrish. New York : Harcourt Brace Jovanovich, [1977] c1976. p. cm. (A Harvest/HBJ book) Includes index. [PN1998.A3P27 1977] 77-4120 ISBN 0-15-637315-7 pbk. : 3.95
1. Parrish, Robert. 2. Moving-picture producers and directors—United States—Biography. I. Title.

PARRISH, Robert. 791.43'023 B
Growing up in Hollywood / Robert Parrish. 1st ed. New York : Harcourt Brace Jovanovich, c1976. 229 p., [12] leaves of plates : ill. ; 22 cm. Includes index. [PN1998.A3P27 1976] 75-29174 ISBN 0-15-137473-2 : 10.00
1. Parrish, Robert. I. Title. BIP

Parrott, Cecil, Sir, 1909-

PARROTT, Cecil, 327'.2'0924 B
Sir, 1909-
The serpent and the nightingale / Cecil Parrott. London : Faber, 1977, i.e.1978 224 p., [6] leaves of plates : ill. ; 23 cm. Sequel to The tightrope. Includes index. [DB2218.7.P37] 78-305291 ISBN 0-571-10869-5 : 11.95
1. Parrott, Cecil, Sir, 1909- 2. Czechoslovakia—Politics and government—1945- 3. Russia—Politics and government—1953- 4. Czechoslovakia—Foreign relations—Great Britain. 5. Great Britain—Foreign relations—Czechoslovakia. 6. Russia—Foreign relations—Great Britain. 7. Great Britain—Foreign relations—Russia. 8. Diplomats—Great Britain—Biography. I. Title.
Distributed by Faber & Faber, Salem, N.H. BIP

Parrott, John, 1811-1884.

JOSTES, Barbara 327'.2'0924 B
Donohoe.
John Parrott, consul, 1811-1884; selected papers of a western pioneer. San Francisco, Calif., 1972. iv, 236 p. illus. 32 cm. Includes bibliographical references. [HC102.5.P36J67] 72-191127
1. Parrott, John, 1811-1884. I. Parrott, John, 1811-1884. John Parrott, consul, 1811-1884. II. Title: Selected papers of a western pioneer.

Parry-William, Thomas Herbert, Sir, 1887-1975.

JONES, Robert Gerallt. 891.6'6'12
T. H. Parry-Williams / [by] R. Gerallt Jones. [Cardiff] : University of Wales Press [for] the Welsh Arts Council, 1978. [3], 108 p., plate : port. ; 25 cm. (Writers of Wales) Bibliography: p. 99-103. [PB2298.P33Z73] 78-316521 ISBN 0-7083-0670-5 pbk. : 5.00
1. Parry-William, Thomas Herbert, Sir, 1887-1975. 2. Poets, Welsh—20th century—Biography.
Distributed by Lawrence Verry, Mystic, CT BIP

Parsons, Frank, 1854-1908.

DAVIS, Howard 371.42'5'0924 B
Vaughn, 1915-
Frank Parsons; prophet, innovator, counselor [by] Howard V. Davis. Carbondale, Southern Illinois University Press [1969] xi, 163 p. 23 cm. Includes bibliographical references. [HF5381.P24D3] 69-11514 5.85
1. Parsons, Frank, 1854-1908.

Parsons, Geneve Shaffer.

PARSONS, Geneve 917.94'61'035 B
Shaffer.
Geneve. Forword by Lenore D. Underwood. [1st ed.] New York, Vantage Press [1969] 103 p. port. 21 cm. Autobiographical. [CT275.P3872A3] 75-4837 2.95
I. Title.

Parsons, Johnnie, 1918- —Juvenile literature.

OLNEY, Ross 796.7'2'0922 B
Robert, 1929-
Great auto racing champions, by Ross Olney. Illustrated by Victor Mays. Champaign, Ill. Garrard Pub. Co. [1973] 95 p. illus. (part col.) 24 cm. Biographies of three winners of the Indy 500: Ralph De Palma, Johnnie Parsons, and A. J. Foyt. [GV1032.A1O42] 920 73-5696 ISBN 0-8116-6666-2 2.98
1. De Palma, Ralph—Juvenile literature. 2. Parsons, Johnnie, 1918- —Juvenile literature. 3. Foyt, A. J., 1935- —Juvenile literature. I. Mays, Victor, 1927- illus. II. Title. BIP

Parsons, Levi, 1792-1822.

†MORTON, Daniel 226'.5'80924 B
Oliver, 1788-1852.
Memoir of Rev. Levi Parsons / compiled by Daniel Oliver Morton. New York : Arno Press, 1977. 431 p. ; 22 cm. (America and the Holy Land) Reprint of the 1824 ed. published by Smith & Shute, Poultney, Vt. [BV3202.P3M6 1977] 77-70730 ISBN 0-405-10271-2 : 25.00
1. Parsons, Levi, 1792-1822. 2. Missionaries—Palestine—Biography. 3. Missionaries—United States—Biography. I. Parsons, Levi, 1792-1822. II. Title. III. Series.

Parsons, Robert,

PARISH, John Edward, 1913- v. 12
Robert Parsons and the English counter-reformation [by] John E. Parish. Houston, William Marsh Rice University, 1966. 80 p. 23 cm. (Rice University studies, v. 52. no. 1. Monograph in English history) Bibliographical references included in "Notes" (p. 76-80) 67-59630
1. Parsons, Robert, 2. Counter-Reformation—England. I. Title.

Parsons, Schuyler Livingston,

PARSONS, Schuyler Livingston, 920
1892-
Untold friendships. Boston, Houghton Mifflin, 1955. 252 p. illus. 22 cm. Autobiographical. [CT275.P3875A3] 55-9001
I. Title.

Parsons, Theophilus,

PARSONS, Theophilus, 347.99'24 B
1797-1882.
Memoir of Theophilus Parsons, by Theophilus Parsons, Jr. New York, Da Capo Press, 1970. viii, 476 p. port. 23 cm. (Da Capo Press reprints in American constitutional and legal history) Reprint of the 1859 ed. [KF368.P36P3 1970] 71-118032
1. Parsons, Theophilus, 1750-1813. II. Title. BIP

Parsons, Thomas W., 1826-1915.

PARSONS, Thomas W., 973.7'81 B
1826-1915.
Incidents & experiences in the life of Thomas W. Parsons, from 1826 to 1900 / edited by Frank Furlong Mathias. Lexington : University Press of Kentucky, [1975] xix, 209 p. ; 27 cm. Includes index. Bibliography: p. 197-[203] [E601.P27] 74-7878 ISBN 0-8131-1319-9 : 13.50
1. Parsons, Thomas W., 1826-1915. 2. Kentucky Cavalry. 14th Regt., 1862-1864. 3. United States—History—Civil War, 1861-1865—Personal narratives. 4. United States—History—Civil War, 1861-1865—Regimental histories—Kentucky Cavalry—14th. 5. Frontier and pioneer life—Kentucky. 6. Kentucky—History. I. Title: Incidents & experiences in the life of Thomas W. Parsons ... BIP

Partai Kebangsaan Malayu Malaya—History.

RUHI Hayat, 1920- 329.9'595'1
Carving the path to the summit / by Ahmad Boestamam [i.e. Ruhi Hayat] ; translated with an introd. by William R. Roff. Athens : Ohio University Press, c1978. p. cm. (Southeast Asia translation series ; v. 2) Translation of Merintis jalan kepunchak. Includes bibliographical references and index. [JQ719.A8K43713] 79-11174 ISBN 0-8214-0397-4 : 12.00 ISBN 0-8214-0409-1 pbk : 5.50
1. Partai Kebangsaan Malayu Malaya—History. 2. Ruhi, Hayat, 1920- 3. Politicians—Malaysia—Biography. I. Title. II. Series: Southeast Asia Translation series ; 2. BIP

Partiia sotsialistov-revoliutsionerov.

SAVINKOV, Boris 947'.08'0924 B
Viktorovich, 1879-1925.
Memoirs of a terrorist. [Translated by Joseph Shaplen with a foreword and epilogue.] Millwood, N.Y., Kraus Reprint Co., 1972. 364 p. 26 cm. Translation of Vospominaniia terrorista. [DK254.S28A3413 1972] 72-5616 16.00
1. Partiia sotsialistov-revoliutsionerov. 2. Russia—Politics and government—1894-1917. I. Title. BIP

Partido Comunista de Espana.

GALLAGHER, Charles F. 338.1'094
La Pasionaria / by Charles F. Gallagher. Hanover, N.H. : American Universities Field Staff, c1976- v. : ill. ; 28 cm. (West Europe series ; v. 11, no. 6 : Spain) (Fieldstaff reports : Europe) Cover title. Contents.Contents.—pt. 1. Only yesterday. Bibliography: pt. 1, p. 12. [D1050.A4 vol. 11, no. 6, etc.] [HX344] 77-362393 1.00
1. Partido Comunista de Espana. 2. Ibarruri, Dolores, 1895- 3. Communism—Spain. 4. Communists—Spain—Biography. I. Title. II. Series: American Universities Field Staff. Fieldstaff reports. III. Series: West Europe series ; v. 11, no. 6 .

GALLAGHER, Charles F. 338.1'094
La Pasionaria / by Charles F. Gallagher. Hanover, N.H. : American Universities Field Staff, c1976- v. : ill. ; 28 cm. (West Europe series ; v. 11, no. 6 : Spain) (Fieldstaff reports : Europe) Cover title. Contents.Contents.—pt. 1. Only yesterday. Bibliography: pt. 1, p. 12. [D1050.A4 vol. 11, no. 6, etc.] [HX344] 77-362393 1.00
1. Partido Comunista de Espana. 2. Ibarruri, Dolores, 1895- 3. Communism—Spain. 4. Communists—Spain—Biography. I. Title. II. Series: American Universities Field Staff. Fieldstaff reports. III. Series: West Europe series ; v. 11, no. 6 .

Parton, Dolly.

BERMAN, Connie. 784'.092'4 B
The official Dolly Parton scrapbook/ by Connie Berman ; foreword by Dolly Parton. Abridged. New York : Grosset & Dunlap, [c1978] 79 p. : ill. ; 28 cm. (A Target book) Cover title: The Dolly Parton scrapbook Discography: p. 78-79. [ML420.P28B4] 79-121559 ISBN 0-448-15569-9 : 4.95
1. Parton, Dolly. 2. Country musicians—United States—Biography. I. Title. II. Title: Dolly Parton scrapbook.

JAMES, Otis. 784'.092'4 B
Dolly Parton / Otis James. New York : Quick Fox, c1978. 95 p. : ill. ; 26 cm. Discography: p. [92]-[96] A biography of the singer and composer of country music who has twice won the Country Music Association award and twice been Female Vocalist of the Year. [ML420.P28J3] 92 78-56222 ISBN 0-8256-3922-0 pbk. : 3.95
1. Parton, Dolly. 2. Country musicians—United States—Biography. BIP

Parton, Dolly—Juvenile literature.

KRISHEF, Robert K. 784.5'2'00924 B
Dolly Parton / Robert K. Krishef. Minneapolis : Lerner Publications Co., c1980. p. cm. (Country music library) Includes index. Discography: p. Traces the life of Dolly Parton from her childhood of poverty in the Great Smoky Mountains to her stardom as a performer and song writer. [ML3930.P25K7] 92 79-28247 ISBN 0-8225-1411-7 : 5.95
1. Parton, Dolly—Juvenile literature. 2. Country music—United States—Biography—Juvenile literature. I. Title. BIP

Parton, James, 1822-1891.

FLOWER, Milton Embick. 920'.00924 B
James Parton, the father of modern biography [by] Milton E. Flower. New York, Greenwood Press, 1968 [c1951] ix, 253 p. illus., ports. 24 cm. Bibliography: p. [203]-211 [E175.5.P3F6 1968] 68-29742
1. Parton, James, 1822-1891. BIP

Partridge, Bellamy,

PARTRIDGE, Bellamy, 1877 928.1
Salad days; illustrated by Richard Powers. New York, Crowell [1951] xi, 272 p. illus. 21 cm. Autobiographical. [PS3531.A710Z56] 51-2933
I. Title.

Partridge, Casper Appollos, 1846-

†PLIMPTON, Florus Beardsley, 1830-1886. 973'.04'97 S
The lost child / Florus Beardsley Plimpton. New York : Garland Pub., 1977. 79 p. ; 23 cm. (The Garland library of narratives of North American Indian captivities ; v. 64) Reprint of the ed. printed by Harris, Fairbanks, Cleveland. Issued with Diffenderffer, H. The young merchant and the Indian captive. New York, 1977. [E85.G2 vol. 64] [E99.M44] 970'.004'97 B 77-1961 ISBN 0-8240-1688-2 : 25.00
1. Partridge, Casper Appollos, 1846- 2. Menominee Indians—Captivities. 3. Indians of North America—Captivities. 4. Wisconsin—Biography. I. Title. II. Series.

Pascal, Blaise, 1623-1662.

BISHOP, Morris, 1893- 194
Blaise Pascal. [New York, Dell Pub. Co., 1966] 256 p. 19 cm. (The Laurel great lives and thought) Bibliography: p. [6] [BX4735.P26B5] 66-996
1. Pascal, Blaise, 1623-1662. I. Title.

BISHOP, Morris, 1893- 194 B
Pascal; the life of genius. New York, Greenwood Press, 1968 [c1964] x, 398 p. illus., ports. 24 cm. Bibliographical references included in "Notes" (p. 355-389) [B1903.B43 1968] 68-9538
1. Pascal, Blaise, 1623-1662. BIP

CAILLET, Emile, 1894- 921.4
Pascal: the emergence of genius. 2d ed., with appendix on recent research. Introd. by C. S. Duthie. New York, Harper [c.1945, 1961] 383p. (Harper torchbooks. The Cloister library, TB82) Bibl. 61-3102 1.85 pap.,
1. Pascal, Blaise, 1623-1662. I. Title.

CAILLIET, Emile, 1894- 921.4
Pasoal: the emergence of geneus. 2d ed., wtih an appedix on recent research. Introd. by C. S. Duthie. New York, Harper [1961] 383p. 21cm. (Harper torchbooks, The Closter library, TB82) Includes bibliography. [BX4735.P26C32 1961] 61-3102
1. Pascal, Blaise, 1623-1662. I. Title.

CALLIET, Emile, 1894- 921.4
Pascal: the emergence of genius. 2d ed., with appendix on recent research. Introd. by C. S. Duthie: [Gloucester, Mass., Peter Smith, c.1945, 1961] 383p. (Harper torchbks. Cloister lib., TB82, rebound) 3.85
1. Pascal, Blaise, 1623-1662. I. Title.

HAZELTON, Roger, 1909- 194 B
Blaise Pascal: the genius of his thought. Philadelphia, Westminster Press [1974] 218 p. 21 cm. Bibliography: p. [211]-212. [B1903.H33] 73-21951 ISBN 0-664-20999-8 7.50
1. Pascal, Blaise, 1623-1662. I. Title.

LAW, Reed G. 194
From reason to romanticism [by] Reed G. Law and Bobbie W. Law. New York, Haskell House, 1973 [c1965] 134 p. 23 cm. Includes bibliographical references. [B1903.L37 1973] 72-4541 ISBN 0-8383-1595-X 8.95
1. Pascal, Blaise, 1623-1662. I. Law, Bobbie W., joint author. II. Title.

MESNARD, Jean. 921.4
Pascal, his life and works. Pref. by Ronald Knox. [New York] Philosophical Library [1952] 210p. illus. 23cm. [B1903.M413] 53-5804
1. Pascal, Blaise, 1623-1662. I. Title.

MORTIMER, Ernest. 194 B
Blaise Pascal : the life and work of a realist / Ernest Mortimer. Westport, Conn. : Greenwood Press, 1976, c1959. 249 p., [4] leaves of plates : ill. ; 23 cm. Reprint of the ed. published by Harper, New York. Includes index. Bibliography: p. 231-235. [B1903.M63 1976] 76-847 ISBN 0-8371-8747-8 lib.bdg. : 14.75
1. Pascal, Blaise, 1623-1662. BIP

SOLTAU, Roger Henry, 1887-1953. 194
Pascal: the man and the message. Westport, Conn., Greenwood Press [1970] xiv, 216 p. port. 23 cm. Reprint of the 1927 ed. Bibliography: p. 210-213. [B1903.S6 1970] 73-109850 ISBN 0-8371-4341-1
1. Pascal, Blaise, 1623-1662. I. Title.

STEINMANN, Jean. 194
Pascal. Translated by Martin Turnell. [1st American ed.] New York, Harcourt, Brace & World [1966] xii, 304 p. illus., ports. 21 cm. [B1903.S713 1966] 65-21036
1. Pascal, Blaise, 1623-1662. I. Title.

Paschal, Agnes, 1776-1869.

PASCHAL, George Washington, 1812-1878. 917.58'175'0330924 B
Ninety-four years: Agnes Paschal. Spartanburg, S.C., Reprint Co., 1974 [c1871] 361 p. facsim. 22 cm. Reprint of the ed. printed by M'Gill & Witherow, Washington. [CT275.P388P3 1974] 74-2356 ISBN 0-87152-184-9 15.00
1. Paschal, Agnes, 1776-1869. I. Title. BIP

Pascin, Jules, 1885-1930.

DIEHL, Gaston. 760'.0924
Pascin. [Translated from the French by Rosalie Siegel] New York, Crown Publishers [1968] 94, [1] p. illus. (part col.), ports. (part col.) 29 cm. Bibliography: p. 94-[95] [ND893.P3D53] 68-9080 3.50
1. Pascin, Jules, 1885-1930. BIP

Pasek, Jan Chryzostom.

PASEK, Jan Chryzostom. 943.8'02'0924 B
The memoirs of Jan Chryzostom z Goslawic Pasek / translated, with an introd. and commentaries, by Maria A. J. Swiecicka. New York : Kosciuszko Foundation, 1978, c1971. 529 p. : ill. ; 20 cm. (The Library of Polish studies ; v. 8) Translation of Pamietniki. Bibliography: p. [56]-65. [DK4312.P3A3513 1978] 78-322489 ISBN 0-917004-15-9 : 8.95
1. Pasek, Jan Chryzostom. 2. Poland—History—17th century. 3. Poland—Gentry—Biography. I. Swiecicka, Maria A. J. II. Title. III. Series.

PASEK, Jan Chryzostom. 943.8'02'0924 B
Memoirs of the Polish Baroque : the writings of Jan Chryzostom Pasek, a squire of the Commonwealth of Poland and Lithuania / edited, translated, with an introduction and notes by Catherine S. Leach ; foreword by Wiktor Weintraub. Berkeley : University of California Press, c1976. lxiv, 327 p., [10] leaves of plates : ill. ; 25 cm. Translation of Pamietniki. Includes index. [DK4312.P3A3513] 74-77731 ISBN 0-520-02752-3 : 20.00
1. Pasek, Jan Chryzostom. 2. Poland—History—17th century. 3 Poland—Gentry—Biography. I. Title. BIP

Pasquier, Etienne Denis, duc, 1767-1862.

KIESWETTER, James K. 944.05'092'4 B
Etienne-Denis Pasquier, the last chancellor of France / James K. Kieswetter. Philadelphia : American Philosophical Society, 1977. 190 p. : port. ; 29 cm. (Transactions of the American Philosophical Society ; v. 67, pt. 1 ISSN 0065-9746s) Includes index.IBibliography: p. 175-179..[DC255.P3K53] 76-50179 ISBN 0-87169-671-1 pbk. : 15.00
1. Pasquier, Etienne Denis, duc, 1767-1862. 2. Statesmen—France—Biography. I. Series: American Philosophical Society. Philadelphia. Transactions ; v. 67, pt. 1.

PASQUIER, Etienne Denis, duc, 1767-1862. 944.05'0924 B
The memoirs of Chancellor Pasquier, 1767-1815. Translated by Douglas Garman. Introd. and notes by Robert Lacour-Gayet. [1st American ed.] Rutherford [N.J.] Fairleigh Dickinson University Press [1968, c1967] xv, 292 p. illus., ports. 23 cm. Translation of Souvenirs du Chancelier Pasquier. Bibliographical footnotes. [DC255.P3A353 1968] 68-9353 10.00
1. France—History—1789-1815. I. Lacour-Gayet, Robert, ed. II. Title. BIP

Pasternak, Boris Leonidovich, 1890-

RUGE, Gerd. 928.917
Pasternak, a pictorial biography. [Translated by Beryl and Joseph Avrach] New York, McGraw -Hill [1959] 143p. illus. 24cm. [PG3476.P27Z82] 59-2037
1. Pasternak, Boris Leonidovich, 1890- I. Title.

Pasternak, Boris Leonidovich 1890-1960 - relationship with women - ol'ga Ivinskaia

IVINSKAIA, Ol'ga Vsevolodovna, 1912- 891.7'1'42 B
A captive of time / Olga Ivinskaya ; translated by Max Hayward. 1st ed. Garden City, N.Y. : Doubleday, 1978. xl, 462 p., [14] leaves of plates : ill. ; 24 cm. Includes bibliographical references and index. [PG3476.P27Z714] 77-83420 ISBN 0-385-12731-6 : 12.50
1. Pasternak, Boris Leonidovich, 1890-1960—Relationship with women—Ol'ga Ivinskaia. 2. Ivinskaia, Ol'ga Vsevolodovna, 1912- 3. Authors, Russian—20th century—Biography. I. Title. BIP

IVINSKAIA, Ol'ga Vsevolodorna, 1912- 891.7'1 B
A captive of time : my years with pasternak / Olga Ivinskaya ; translted by Max Hayward. 1st ed. New York : Warner Books, 1979, c1978. 639 p., [16] leaves of plates : ill. ; 24 cm. Includes bibliographic references and index. [PG3476.P27Z7] ISBN 0-446-85968-0 pbk. : 2.95
1. Pasternak, Boris Leonidovich 1890-1960 — relationship with women — ol'ga Ivinskaia 2. Ivinskaia Ol'ga Vserolodovna, 1912- 3. Authors, Russian — 20th century — Biography. I. Title.
L.C. card no. for 1978 Doubleday ed.: 77-83420.

Pasternak, Boris Leonidovich, 1890-1960—Biography.

GLADKOV, Aleksander Konstantinovich. 891.7'1'42 B
Meetings with Pasternak : a memoir / by Alexander Gladkov ; translated from the Russian and edited with notes and introd. by Max Hayward. 1st American ed. New York : Harcourt Brace Jovanovich, c1977. 223 p. ; 23 cm. Translation of Vstrechi s Pasternakom. "Helen and Kurt Wolff book." [PG3476.P27Z68413 1977b] 77-153840 ISBN 0-15-158590-3 : 8.95
1. Pasternak, Boris Leonidovich, 1890-1960—Biography. 2. Authors, Russian—20th century—Biography. I. Hayward, Max. II. Title. BIP

PASTERNAK, Boris Leonidovich, 1890- 928.917
I remember; sketch for an autobiography. Translated with a pref. and notes by David Magarshack. With an essay on translating Shakespeare, translated by Manya Harari [1st ed. New York] Pantheon [1959] 191p. illus. 21cm. [PG3476.P27Z523] 59-8586
I. Title.

PASTERNAK, Boris Leonidovich, 1890- 927.917
I remember; sketch for an autobiography. Translated with a pref. and notes by David Magarshack. With an essay on translating Shakespeare, translated by Manya Harari. New York, Meridian Books [1960, c.1959] 191p. illus. 19cm. (Meridian Books M100) 1.35 pap.,
I. Title.

PASTERNAK, Boris Leonidovich, 1890-1960 928.917
I remember; sketch for an autobiography. Tr., pref., notes by David Magarshack. With an essay on translating Shakespeare, tr. by Manya Harari [Magnolia, Mass., P. Smith, 1967, c.1959] 191p. illus. 21cm. (Meridian bk. rebound) [PG3476.P27Z523] 3.50
I. Title.

SCHEWE, Heinz. 891.7'1'42
Pasternak privat / Heinz Schewe. Hamburg : Christians Verlag, [1974] 104 p., [2] leaves of plates : ill. ; 20 cm. Includes indexes. [PG3476.P27Z835] 75-566811 ISBN 3-7672-0283-2
1. Pasternak, Boris Leonidovich, 1890-1960—Biography. I. Title.

Pasternak, Joseph,

PASTERNAK, Joseph, 1901- 927.914
Easy the hard way, by Joe Pasternak as told to David Chandler. New York, Putnam [c1956] 301p. illus. 21cm. Autobiography. [PN1998.A3P3] 56-6624
I. Chandler, David. II. Title.

Pasteur, Louis, 1822-1895.

CUNY, Hilaire. v. 12
Louis Pasteur; the man and his theories. Translated by Patrick Evans. Greenwich, Conn., Fawcett [1967] 192 p. illus. 18 cm. (A Profile in science) Bibliography: p. 188. 68-44063

1. Pasteur, Louis, 1822-1895. I. Title.

CUNY, Hilaire 509.24
Louis Pasteur; the man and his theories. Tr. by Patrick Evans. [1st Amer. ed.] New York, Eriksson [dist. Hill & Wang, 1966, c.1963] 192p. illus., ports. 24cm. (Profile in sci.) Bibl. [Q143.P2C813] 65-24213 5.00
1. Pasteur, Louis, 1822-1895. I. Title.

DUBOS, Rene Jules, 1901- 925
Louis Pasteur, free lance of science. [1st ed.] Boston, Little, Brown, 1950. xii, 418 p. ports. 23 cm. Bibliography: p. [405]-408. [Q143.P2D78] 50-5543
1. Pasteur, Louis, 1822-1895.

DUBOS, Rene Jules, 1901- 591.2'322'0924 B
Louis Pasteur, free lance of science / Rene Dubos. New York : Scribner, c1976. xxxix, 420 p. : ill. ; 24 cm. Includes index. Bibliography: p. [409]-412. [Q143.P2D78 1976] 75-21919 ISBN 0-684-14500-6 : 12.50 pbk. : 4.95
1. Pasteur, Louis, 1822-1895.

DUBOS, Rene Jules, 1901- 925
Pasteur and modern science. [1st ed.] Garden City, N.Y., Anchor Books, 1960. 159 p. 18 cm. (Science study series, S15) [Q143.P2D79] 60-13520
1. Pasteur, Louis, 1822-1895.

DUCLAUX, Emile, 1840-1904. 591.2'322'0924 B
Pasteur; the history of a mind. [Translated by Erwin F. Smith and Florence Hedges] With a foreword by Rene Dubos. Metuchen, N.J., Scarecrow Reprint Corp., 1973 [c1920] viii, xxxii, 363 p. illus. 22 cm. (The History of medicine series, no. 39) "Published under the auspices of the Library of the New York Academy of Medicine." [Q143.P2D8 1973] 73-5913 ISBN 0-8108-0630-4
1. Pasteur, Louis, 1822-1895. I. Title. II. Series.

GRANT, Madeleine Parker, 1895- 925
Louis Pasteur, fighting hero of science. Illustrated with photos. and with line drawings by Clifford Geary. New York, Whittlesey House [1959] 220 p. illus. 21 cm. [Q143.P2G7] 59-8539
1. Pasteur, Louis, 1822-1895.

HOLMES, Samuel Jackson, 1868- 925
Louis Pasteur. New York, Dover [c.1924, 1961] 149p. illus. 61-19613 1.00 pap.,
1. Pasteur, Louis, 1822-1895. I. Title.

MANN, John Harvey. 925
Louis Pasteur, founder of bacteriology, by John Mann. New York, Scribner [1964] 160 p. port. 21 cm. Bibliography: p. 154. [Q143.P2M27] 64-22753
1. Pasteur, Louis, 1822-1895.

MECHNIKOV, il'ia Il'ich, 1845-1916. 610'.922 B
The founders of modern medicine: Pasteur, Koch, Lister, by Elie Metchnikoff. Including Etiology of wound infections, by Robert Koch, The antiseptic system, by Sir Joseph Lister, and Prevention of rabies, by Louis Pasteur. Freeport, N.Y., Books for Libraries Press [1971] 387 p. 23 cm. (Essay index reprint series) Reprint of 1939 ed. Translation of Trois fondateurs de la medecine moderne. [R134.M42 1971] 78-142669 ISBN 0-8369-2111-9
1. Pasteur, Louis, 1822-1895. 2. Lister, Joseph Lister, Baron, 1827-1912. 3. Koch, Robert, 1843-1910. I. Pasteur, Louis, 1822-1895. II. Lister, Joseph Lister, Baron, 1827-1912. III. Koch, Robert, 1843-1910. IV. Title.

NICOLLE, Jacques 925
Louis Pasteur. the story of his major discoveries. Greenwich, Conn., Fawcett [1966. c.1961] ix. 192p. 18cm. (Sci. & discovery ser.; premier bk. R290) [Q143.P2N513] .60 pap.,
1. Pasteur, Louis, 1822-1895. I. Title.

NICOLLE, Jacques. v. 12
Louis Pasteur, the story of his major discoveries. Greenwich, Conn., Fawcett [1966, c1961] 192 p. 19 cm. (A Fawcett premier book) 68-55192
1. Pasteur, Louis, 1822-1895. I. Title.

REGGIO, Edwin, 1933- 925
Microbe detective; a story of Louis Pasteur. Illus. by Carolyn Lee Jagodits. Notre Dame, Ind., Dujarie Press [1957] 95p. illus. 24cm. [Q143.P2R4] 57-41144
1. Pasteur, Louis, 1822-1895. I. Title.

ROWLANND, John, 1907- 925
The microscope man; the story of Louis Pasteur. New York, Roy Publishers [1964] 142 p. 21 cm. [Q143.P2R6] 64-20089
1. Pasteur, Louis, 1822-1895. I. Title.

VALLERY-RADOT, Pasteur, 1886- 925
Louis Pasteur; a great life in brief. [Translated from the French by Alfred Joseph] [1st ed.] New York, Knopf, 1958. 199 p. 19 cm. (Great lives in brief; a new series of biographies) [Q143.P2V243] 58-5828
1. Pasteur, Louis, 1822-1895.

VALLERY-RADOT, Rene 925
The life of Pasteur. Translated from the French by R. L. Devonshire. New York, Dover Publications [1960] xxi, 484p. 21cm. (T632) 60-3182 2.00 pap.,
1. Pasteur, Louis, 1822-1895. I. Title.

WOOD, Laura Newbold. 509.24 (B)
Louis Pasteur. by Laura N. Wood. New York, J. Messner.[1962, c1948] 217 p. 22 cm. [Q143.P2] [PR5852.B84] 66-5419 65-5651
1. Pasteur, Louis, 1822-1895. I. Title. **BIP**

Pasteur, Louis, 1822-1895—Juvenile literature.

BURTON, Mary June. 92
Louis Pasteur, founder of microbiology. New York, F. Watts [1963] vii, 197 p. illus. 22 cm. (Immortals of science) [Q143.2B75] 62-21748
1. Pasteur, Louis, 1822-1895 — Juvenile literature. I. Title.

BURTON, Mary June 92
Louis Pasteur, founder of microbiology. New York, Watts [c.1963] vii, 197p. illus. 22cm. (Immortals of sci.) 62-21748 2.95
1. Pasteur, Louis, 1822-1895—Juvenile literature. I. Title.

JOHNSON, Spencer. 591.2'3'220924 B
The value of believing in yourself : the story of Louis Pasteur / by Spencer Johnson ; illustrated by Pileggi. 2d ed. La Jolla, Calif. : Value Communications, c1976. 62 p. : col. ill. ; 29 cm. (ValueTales) Edition for 1975 published under title: The ValueTale of Louis Pasteur. Retells the story of Louis Pasteur, whose unwavering belief in the concept of germs led to a cure for rabies. [QR31.P37J63 1976] 92 76-55225 ISBN 0-916392-06-6 : 4.95
1. Pasteur, Louis, 1822-1895—Juvenile literature. 2. Self-reliance—Juvenile literature. 3. Bacteriologists—France—Biography—Juvenile literature. I. Title. **BIP**

LAUBER, Patricia. 925
The quest of Louis Pasteur. Illustrated by Lee J. Ames. [1st ed.] Garden City, N. Y., Garden City Books, 1960. 56p. illus. 32cm. [Q143.P2L27] 60-12061
1. Pasteur, Louis, 1822-1895—Juvenile literature. I. Title.

MANN, John Harvey 92
Louis Pasteur, the germ killer. Illus. by Herschel Levit. New York, Macmillan [c.1966] 40p. col. illus. 23cm. (Sci. story lib.) [Q143.P2M28] 65-15577 2.95; 3.24 lib. ed.,
1. Pasteur, Louis, 1822-1895—Juvenile literature. I. Levit, Herschel, illus. II. Title.

RICHARDSON, Joanna 92
The young Louis Pasteur. Illus. by Anne Linton. New York, Roy [1965, c.1964] 128p. illus. 21cm. [Q143.P2R5] 65-18883 3.25 bds.,
1. Pasteur, Louis, 1822-1895—Juvenile literature. I. Title.

Patchen, Kenneth, 1911-1972—Addresses, essays, lectures.

†KENNETH Patchen : 811'.5'4 B
a collection of essays / edited and with an introd. by Richard G. Morgan ; foreword by Miriam Patchen. New York : AMS Press, 1977. xxiii, 262 p., [2] leaves of plates : ill. (some col.) ; 23 cm. Bibliography: p. 255-262. [PS3531.A764Z73] 77-78319 ISBN 0-404-16005-0 : 19.50
1. Patchen, Kenneth, 1911-1972—Addresses, essays, lectures. 2. Authors, American—20th century—Biography—Addresses, essays, lectures. I. Morgan, Richard G. **BIP**

Patchin, Freegift, d. 1831.

PRIEST, Josiah, 1788-1851. 973'.04'97 S
The captivity and sufferings of Gen. Freegift Patchin / Josiah Priest. New York : Garland Pub., 1977. 50 p. ; 23 cm. (The Garland library of narratives of North American Indian captivities ; v. 52) Reprint of the 1833 ed. printed by Packard, Hoffman and White, Albany, N.Y. Issued with the 1835 ed. of United States. Congress. House. Committee on Claims. U.S. Congress report on claims of Samuel Cozad. New York, 1977. Reprint of the 1835 ed. of Baldwin, T. Narrative of the massacre of my wife and children. New York, 1977. Reprint of the 1836 ed. of Baldwin, T. Narrative of the massacre of my wife and children. New York, 1977. Reprint of the 1836 ed. of Narrative of the Seminole War and the miraculous escape of Mary Godfrey. New York, 1977. Reprint of an undated broadside, Captivity and sufferings of Mrs. Mason. New York, 1977. Reprint of the 1836 ed. of Priest, J. Stories of the Revolution. New York, 1977. Reprint of articles published in Columbian almanac for 1838, CaptivitiOThe captivity and sufferings of Gen. Freegift Patchin / Josiah Priest. New York : Garland Pub., 1977. 50 p. ; 23 cm. (The Ga
1. Patchin, Freegift, d. 1831. 2. Brant, Joseph, Mohawk chief, 1742-1807. 3. Iroquois Indians—Captivities. 4. United States—History—Revolution, 1775-1783—Personal narratives. 5. New York (State)—Biography. 6. Indians of North America—Captivities. I. Title. II. Series.

Pate, A. M.—Library.

MARY Couts Burnett Library. 016.973'00992 B
The Dr. and Mrs. A. M. Pate, Jr. collection on the American Presidency / Mary Couts Burnett Library, Texas Christian University. Fort Worth : Texas Christian University Press, 1977c1976. x, 152 p. : ill. ; 24 cm. Includes indexes. [Z1249.P7M37 1976] [E176.1] 76-10498 pbk. : 2.50
1. Pate, A. M.—Library. 2. Pate, Joyce—Library. 3. Presidents—United States—Biography—Bibliography—Catalogs. 4. United States—Politics and government—Bibliography—Catalogs. I. Title.

Patel, Vallabhbhai Jhaverbhai, Sardar, 1875-1950.

HOMAGE to Sardar 954.03'5'0924 B
Patel : birth centenary commemoration publication. Bangalore : Vallabhbhai Patel Institute, 1976. 40 p. : ill. ; 26 cm. Cover title. [DS481.P35H65] 76-905649 Rs3.50
1. Patel, Vallabhbhai Jhaverbhai, Sardar, 1875-1950. 2. Statesmen—India—Biography. I. Patel, Vallabhbhai Jhaverbhai, Sardar, 1875-1950. II. Vallabhbhai Patel Institute.

MURTHI, R. K., 1934- 954.03'5'0924 B
Sardar Patel : the man and his contemporaries / R. K. Murthi. 1st ed. New Delhi : Sterling Publishers, 1976. 220 p., [4] leaves of plates : ill. ; 23 cm. Includes index. Bibliography: p. [214] [DS481.P35M87] 76-902603 Rs35.00
1. Patel, Vallabhbhai Jhaverbhai, Sardar, 1875-1950. 2. Statesmen—India—Biography. I. Title.

Patel, Vithalbhai Jhaverbhai, 1873-1933—Addresses, essays, lectures.

VITHALBHAI Patel, 954.03'5'0924 B
patriot and president / message, Indira Gandhi ; foreword, D. K. Borooah ; pref., Rajni Patel ; homages, Jagjiwan Ram and B. Bhagavati ; editorial board, R. K. Nayak, executive editor ... [et al.]. New Delhi : National Forum of Lawyers and Legal Aid, c1976. xxxii, 464 p., [6] leaves of plates : ports. ; 25 cm. "Select letters": p. [375]-404. Includes bibliographical references and index. [DS481.P36V57] 77-901690 Rs70.00 ($12.00 U.S.)
1. Patel, Vithalbhai Jhaverbhai, 1873-1933—Addresses, essays, lectures. 2. Statesmen—India—Biography—Addresses, essays, lectures. I. Patel, Vithalbhai Jhaverbhai, 1873-1933. II. Nayak, R. K.

Pater, Walter Horatio,

PATER, Walter Horatio, 1839-1894. 824'.8
Letters of Walter Pater; edited by Lawrence Evans. Oxford, Clarendon P., 1970. iii-xlvii, 182 p. 9 plates. facsims., port. 23 cm. Includes bibliographical references. [PR5136.A43 1970] 73-504920 50/-
I. Evans, Lawrence, 1935- ed. II. Title. **BIP**

Pater, Walter Horatio, 1839-1894.

GREENSLET, Ferris, 1875-1959. 824'.8
Walter Pater. New York, Haskell House Publishers, 1974. viii, 163 p. port. 20 cm. Reprint of the 1903 ed. published by McClure, Phillips, New York, which was issued in the Contemporary men of letters series. [PR5136.G7 1974] 73-21634 ISBN 0-8383-1798-7 11.95
1. Pater, Walter Horatio, 1839-1894. I. Series: Contemporary men of letters series. **BIP**

MONSMAN, Gerald Cornelius. 824'.8 B
Walter Pater / by Gerald Monsman. Boston : Twayne Publishers, c1977. 213 p. : port. ; 21 cm. (Twayne's English authors series ; TEAS 207) Includes index. Bibliography: p. 197-201. [PR5136.M6] 76-58511 ISBN 0-8057-6676-6 lib.bdg. : 7.95
1. Pater, Walter Horatio, 1839-1894. 2. Authors, English—19th century—Biography.

PATER, Walter Horatio, 1839-1894. 824'.8
Letters of Walter Pater; edited by Lawrence Evans. Oxford, Clarendon P., 1970. iii-xlvii, 182 p. 9 plates. facsims., port. 23 cm. Includes bibliographical references. [PR5136.A43 1970] 73-504920 50/-
I. Evans, Lawrence, 1935- ed. II. Title. **BIP**

WRIGHT, Thomas, 1859-1936. 824'.8 B
The life of Walter Pater. New York, Haskell House, 1969. 2 v. illus., facsims., ports. 23 cm. Reprint of the 1907 ed. Bibliographical footnotes. [PR5136.W7 1969] 68-24928
1. Pater, Walter Horatio, 1839-1894. **BIP**

Pater, Walter Horatio, 1839-1894—Biography.

LEVEY, Michael. 824'.8 B
The case of Walter Pater / Michael Levey. [London] : Thames and Hudson, c1978. 232 p., [4] leaves of plates : ill. ; 25 cm. Includes index. "A list of Pater's writings published in his lifetime": p. 223-224. [PR5136.L4] 78-322216 ISBN 0-500-01193-1 : 14.95
1. Pater, Walter Horatio, 1839-1894—Biography. 2. Authors, English—19th century—Biography. I. Title.
Distributed by W.W. Norton, NYC **BIP**

Paterson, Andrew Barton, 1864-1941.

SEMMLER, Clement. 828.914
The Banjo of the bush; the work, life and times of A. B. Paterson. [Melbourne] Lansdowne [1967] xi, 263p. facsim., ports. 25cm. [PR6031.A75Z853] 66-66972 11.50 bds.,
1. Paterson, Andrew Barton, 1864-1941. I. Title.
Distributed by SportShelf, New Rochelle, N.Y.

Paterson, William, 1745-1806.

O'CONNOR, John E. 973.4'092'4 B
William Paterson, lawyer and statesman, 1745-1806 / by John E. O'Connor. New Brunswick, N.J. : Rutgers University Press, c1979. p. cm. Includes index. [E302.6.P3O27] 79-15966 ISBN 0-8135-0880-0 : 23.50
1. Paterson, William, 1745-1806. 2. United States. Congress. Senate—Biography. 3. New Jersey—Politics and government—Revolution, 1775-1783. 4. United States—Politics and government—1783-1809. 5. Legislators—United States—Biography. 6. New Jersey—Governors—Biography. 7. Judges—United States—Biography. I. Title.

Pathologists, Amer.

CASEY, Albert Eugene, 1903-. 610'.92'2
Biographical encyclopedia of pathologists: Southern United States of America. Persons trained in pathology before 1937 and resident in the South before the golden anniversay meeting of the Southern Medical Association, Washington, D.C., November 12-15, 1956; and including observations on the training for research, teaching, and practice in pathology. Birmingham, Ala., Published for Memorial Institute of Pathology by the Amite and Knocknagree Historical Fund, 1963. xvii, 920 p. ports., diagrs. 20 cm. Pages 377-[806] reduced in size and photo-reproduced on [105] pages. Bibliography: p. 917-920. [R153.C3] 63-25809
1. Pathologists, Amer. I. Title.

Patmore, Coventry Kersey Dighton, 1823-1896.

GOSSE, Edmund William, Sir, 1849-1928. 821'.8 B
Coventry Patmore. New York, Greenwood Press [1969] viii, 213 p. illus. 23 cm. (Literary lives) Reprint of the 1905 ed. [PR5144.G6 1969] 69-13915
1. Patmore, Coventry Kersey Dighton, 1823-1896. I. Title. II. Series. BIP

GOSSE, Edmund William, Sir, 1849-1928. 821'.8 B
Coventry Patmore. London, Hodder and Stoughton, 1905. St. Clair Shores, Mich., Scholarly Press, 1970. viii, 252 p. illus., ports. 22 cm. (Literary lives) [PR5144.G6 1970] 71-131720
1. Patmore, Coventry Kersey Dighton, 1823-1896. I. Title. II. Series.

OLIVER, Edward James, 1911- 821.89
Coventry Patmore. New York, Sheed & Ward, 1956. 211p. 21cm. [PR5143.O4] 56-6824
1. Patmore, Coventry Kersey Dighton, 1823-1896. I. Title. BIP

Paton family.

NOEL-PATON, M. H. 929'.2'0941
Tales of a grand-daughter. Elgin, M. H. Noel-Paton, 1970. 110 p., 23 plates (1 fold.). illus., geneal. table, ports. 28 cm. [CS479.P36 1970] 72-175544 ISBN 0-9501756-0-9 £4.50
1. Paton family. I. Title.

Paton, John Gibson, 1824-1907

BELL, Ralph R 922
John G. Paton, apostle to the New Hebrides. Butler, Ind., Higley Press [c1957] 240p. illus. 20cm. [BV3680.N6P35] 58-26406
1. Paton, John Gibson, 1824-1907 I. Title.

Paton, John Gibson, 1824-1907—Juvenile literature.

ROBINSON, Virgil E. 266'.6'73 B
Curse of the cannibals / Virgil E. Robinson ; [ill., John Gourley]. Washington : Review and Herald Pub. Association, c1976. 125 p. : ill. ; 21 cm. (Penguin series) "Originally published in Guide magazine under the title King of the cannibals." A biography of the Scottish missionary with emphasis on his work in the New Hebrides. [BV3680.N6P67 1976] 92 76-23025
1. Paton, John Gibson, 1824-1907—Juvenile literature. 2. Missionaries—Scotland—Biography—Juvenile literature. 3. Missionaries—New Hebrides—Biography—Juvenile literature. 4. Missions—New Hebrides—Juvenile literature. I. Title.

Patrick, Saint, 373?-463?

BEEBE, Catherine, 1898- 270.20924 B
Saint Patrick, apostle of Ireland. Drawings by S. Ohrvel Carlson. Paterson, N.J., Saint Anthony Guild Press [1968] 40 p. col. illus. 23 cm. Relates what is known of St. Patrick, whose feast day is celebrated March 17th, describing his servitude in Ireland, his journey to England and freedom, and his return to Ireland to teach Christianity. [BX4700.P3B4] 92 AC 68
1. Patrick, Saint, 373?-463? I. Carlson, S. Ohrvel, illus. II. Title.

BURY, John Bagnell, 1861-1927. 270.20924 B
The life of St. Patrick and his place in history. Freeport, N.Y., Books for Libraries Press [1971] xv, 404 p. maps. 23 cm. Reprint of the 1905 ed. Includes bibliographical references. [BX4700.P3B8 1971] 79-175691 ISBN 0-8369-6606-6
1. Patrick, Saint, 373?-463? I. Title.

CUSHING, Richard James, Cardinal, 1895- 922.2415
Saint Patrick and the Irish. [Boston] St. Paul Editions [1963] 114 p. illus. 22 cm. [BX4700.P3C8] 63-14892
1. Patrick, Saint, 373?-463? I. Title.

CUSHING, Richard James, Cardinal, 1895- 922.2415
Saint Patrick and the Irish. [Boston] St. Paul Eds. [dist Daughters of St. Paul, c.1963] 114p. illus. 22cm. 63-14892 2.50;1.50 pap.,
1. Patrick, Saint, 373?-463? I. Title.

ERNEST, Brother, 1897- 922.2415
Saint of the fighting Irish; a story of St. Patrick. Illus. by Brother Bernard Howard. Notre Dame, Ind., Dujarie Press [1953] 95p. illus. 24cm. [BX4700.P3E7] 53-2906
1. Patrick, Saint, 373?—163? I. Title.

HANSON, Richard Patrick Crosland. 270.2'0924
Saint Patrick, his origins and career, by R. P. C. Hanson. New York, Oxford University Press, 1968. 248 p. 22 cm. Bibliography: p. [230]-235. [BX4700.P3H27] 68-20360
1. Patrick, Saint, 373?-463? I. Title.

HARNEY, Martin Patrick, 1896- 270.2'092'4 B
The legacy of Saint Patrick as found in his own writings [by] Martin P. Harney. [Boston] St. Paul Editions [1972] 144 p. illus. 22 cm Includes bibliographical references. [BX4700.P3H29] 76-183441 3.00
1. Patrick, Saint, 373?-463? I. Title.

PATRICK, Saint, 373?-463? 270.2'092'4 B
Patrick in his own words. [Translated and with commentary by] Joseph Duffy. [Dublin] Veritas Publications [1972] 97 p. 19 cm. English translation and Latin original of the author's Confessio. Includes bibliographical references. [BX4700.P3P3713] 74-152587 £0.50
1. Patrick, Saint, 373?-463? I. Duffy, Joseph A. II. Title.

REYNOLDS, Quentin James, 1902-1965. 270.2'0924 B
The life of Saint Patrick, by Quentin Reynolds. Illustrated by Douglas Gorsline. New York, Random House [1955] 182 p. illus. 22 cm. (World landmark books [W-17]) A biography of the British boy, captured by raiding Irish warriors at age sixteen, who performed miracles, ended the power of the Druid priests over the Irish people, and converted the Irish kings and their people to Christianity. [BX4700.P3R4] 92 AC 68
1. Patrick, Saint, 373?-463? I. Gorsline, Douglas W., 1913- illus. II. Title.

RYAN, John, 1894- ed. 922.22
Saint Patrick. [Dublin] Published for Radio Eireann by the Stationery Off., 1958. 94p. 19cm. (Thomas Davis lectures, [4]) Added t. p., in Gaelic. [BX4700.P3R9] 58-46462
1. Patrick, Saint, 373?-463? I. Title. II. Series.

Patrick, Saint, 373?-463?—Juvenile literature.

BEEBE, Catherine, 1898- 92 (J)
Saint Patrick, apostle of Ireland. Drawings by S. Ohrvel Carlson. Paterson, N.J., Saint Anthony Guild Press [1968] 40 p. col. illus. 23 cm. [BX4700.P3B4] 68-25401
1. Patrick, Saint, 373?-463?—Juvenile literature. I. Title.

HAYS, Wilma Pitchford. 270.2'0924 B
Patrick of Ireland. Illustrated by Peter Burchard. New York, Coward-McCann [1970] 64 p. illus. (part col.) 23 cm. A biography of the fifth-century monk who brought Christianity to Ireland. [BX4700.P3H36] 92 71-87885 3.29
1. Patrick, Saint, 373?-463?—Juvenile literature. I. Burchard, Peter, illus. II. Title.

Patrick, William J., 1910-

PATRICK, William J., 1910- 978 B
The formative years : an autobiography / by William J. Patrick. Flushing, N.Y. : New Voices Pub. Co., c1977. 144 p. ; 21 cm. [CT275.P4A33] 77-79107 ISBN 0-911024-23-9 pbk. : 4.50
1. Patrick, William J., 1910- 2. United States—Biography. I. Title.

Patten, George Zeboim, 1929-

PATTEN, George Zeboim, 1929- 362.2'92'0924 B
You, too, can stop drinking / G. Z. (Bome) Patten ; with a foreword by Robert B. Hagood. 1st ed. Hicksville, N.Y. : Exposition Press, c1977. 256 p. ; 22 cm. [HV5293.P36A38] 76-57471 ISBN 0-682-48733-3 : 8.50
1. Patten, George Zeboim, 1929- 2. Alcoholics—Biography 3. Alcoholism. I. Title. BIP

Patten, Gilbert,

PATTEN, Gilbert, 1866-1945. 928.1
Frank Merriwell's "father"; an autobiography by Gilbert Patten ("Burt L. Standish") Edited by Harriet Hinsdale, assisted by Tony London. [1st ed.] Norman, University of Oklahoma Press [1964] xxv, 331 p. illus. 23 cm. [PS3531.A82Z5] 64-13591
I. Hinsdale, Harriet, 1900- ed. II. Title.

Patterson, Chippy, 1875-1933.

LEWIS, Arthur H., 1906- 923.473
The worlds of Chippy Patterson. [1st ed.] New York, Harcourt, Brace [1960] 311 p. 22cm. [KF373.P38L48 1960] 60-10928
1. Patterson, Chippy, 1875-1933. 2. Crime and criminals—Philadelphia. I. Title.

LEWIS, Arthur H. 1906- 923.473
The worlds of Chippy Patterson, [by] Arthur H. Lewis. New York, Pocket Books [1973, c1960] 354 p. 18 cm. ISBN 0-671-78336-X. 1.25 (pbk.)
1. Patterson, Chippy, 1875-1933. 2. Crime and criminals—Philadelphia. I. Title.
L.C. card no. for original ed. 60-10928.

Patterson, Eleanor Medill, 1881-1948.

HEALY, Paul F. 071.530924
Cissy; the biography of Eleanor M. "Cissy" Patterson, by Paul F. Healy. Garden City, N. Y., Doubleday, [c.]1966. 421p. plates, ports. 22cm. [PN4874.P3528H4] 66-13481 5.95
1. Patterson, Eleanor Medill, 1881-1948. I. Title.

MARTIN, Ralph G., 1920- 070'.92'4 B
Cissy / Ralph G. Martin. New York : Simon and Schuster, c1979. 512 p., [16] leaves of plates : ill. ; 25 cm. Includes index. Bibliography: p. 477-492. [CT275.P42M37] 79-10752 ISBN 0-671-22557-X : 12.50
1. Patterson, Eleanor Medill, 1881-1948. 2. United States—Biography. I. Title.

Patterson, Floyd.

NEWCOMBE, Jack 927.9683
Floyd Patterson, heavyweight king. New York, Bartholomew House [dist. MacFadden Bks., P c.1961] 159p. (Sport magazine lib., no. 7) 61-46759 .50 pap.,
1. Patterson, Floyd. I. Title. II. Series.

PATTERSON, Floyd 927.9683
Victory over myself. With Milton Gross. [New York] Scholastic [1963,c.1962] 315p. 16cm. (T421) .50 pap.,
I. Title.

PATTERSON, Floyd 927.9683
Victory over myself. With Milton Gross. [New York] Scholastic [1963,c.1962] 315p. 16cm. (T421) .50 pap.,
I. Title.

PATTERSON, Floyd. 927.9683
Victory over myself. With Milton Gross. [New York] B. Geis Associates; distributed by Random House [1962] 244 p. illus. 22 cm [GV1132.P3A3] 62-15657
I. Title.

Patterson, John Alvin,

PATTERSON, John Alvin, 1876- 917.64'03'60924 B
Life stories of J. A. Patterson; in Lampasas and Runnels Counties, by Clara Patterson Patton. Editorial consultant: Juanita Daniel Zachry. Ballinger, Tex. [1969] 89 p. illus., ports. 24 cm. [CT275.P444A3] 70-16359
I. Patton, Clara Patterson, 1911- II. Title.

Patterson, Paul, 1909-

PATTERSON, Paul, 1909- 976.4'06'0924 B
Crazy women in the rafters : memories of a Texas boyhood / by Paul Patterson. 1st ed. Norman : University of Oklahoma Press, c1976. xii, 242 p. ; 21 cm. [CT275.P453A33] 74-34035 ISBN 0-8061-1280-8 : 8.95
1. Patterson, Paul, 1909- I. Title. BIP

Patterson, William Allen, 1899-

TAYLOR, Frank J., 1894- 387.7'0924
'Pat' Patterson, by Frank J. Taylor. Illus. by Gordon Brusstar. Menlo Park, Calif., Lane [1967] 160p. illus. 28cm. [HD9711.U6T3] 67-15742 10.00
1. Patterson, William Allen, 1899- I. Title.

Patterson, William L.,

PATTERSON, William L., 1891- 323.4'0924 B
The man who cried genocide; an autobiography, by William L. Patterson. [1st ed.] New York, International Publishers [1971] 223 p. illus., ports. 21 cm. [E185.97.P32A3] 78-148516 ISBN 0-7178-0305-8 6.95
I. Title.

Patti, Adelina, 1843-1919.

KLEIN, Hermann, 1856-1934. 782.1'092'4 B
The reign of Patti / by Herman Klein. New York : Da Capo Press, 1978 [c1920] ix, 470 p., [32] leaves of plates : ill. ; 23 cm. (Da Capo Press music reprint series) Reprint of the ed. published by Century Co., New York. Includes index. [ML420.P32K5 1978] 77-17874 ISBN 0-306-77530-1 : 25.00
1. Patti, Adelina, 1843-1919. 2. Singers—Biography. I. Title.

KLEIN, Hermann, 1856-1934. 782.1'092'4 B
The reign of Patti / Herman Klein ; with a discography by W. R. Moran. New York : Arno Press, 1977 [c1920] ix, 470, v p., [31] leaves of plates : ill. ; 23 cm. (Opera biographies) Reprint of the ed. published by the Century Co., New York. Includes index. [ML420.P32K5 1977] 76-29944 ISBN 0-405-09686-0 : 32.00
1. Patti, Adelina, 1843-1919. 2. Singers—Biography. I. Title. BIP

Pattie, James Ohio, b. 1804?

COBLENTZ, Stanton Arthur, 1896- 923.973
The swallowing wilderness; the life of a frontiersman: James Ohio Pattie. New York, T. Yoseloff [1961] 188 p. 22 cm. [F800.P34] 61-6932
1. Pattie, James Ohio, b. 1804? 2. Frontier and pioneer life—Southwest, New. I. Title.

Pattillo, James William, 1806-1887.

GARLAND, Joseph E. 639.22 B
That great Pattilo, by Joseph E. Garland. [1st ed.] Boston, Little, Brown [1966] x, 342 p. illus., maps (on lining-papers) 21 cm. Bibliography: p. 339-342. [SH205.P3G3] B 66-16559
1. Pattillo, James William, 1806-1887. I. Title.

GARLAND. JOSEPH E. 639.22
That great Pattillo. Boston, Little [c.1966] x, 342p. illus., maps (on lining-papers) 21cm. Bibl. [SH205.P3G3] 66-16559 6.50 bds.,
1. Pattillo, James William, 1806-1887. I. Title.

Pattison, George.

FOULDS, Elfrida Vipont (Brown), 1902- 922.8642
Blow the man down, by Charles Vipont [pseud.] With which is published The fighting sailor turn'd peaceable Christian of Thomas Lurting, first printed in 1710. Illustrated by Norman Hepple. Philadelphia, Lippincott [1952] 248 p. illus. 19 cm. [BX7795.P28F6] 52-11570
1. Pattison, George. I. Lurting, Thomas. II. Title. III. Title: The fighting sailor turn'd peaceable Christian.

Patton, George Smith, 1885-1945-

AYER, Frederick. 923.573
Before the colors fade; portrait of a soldier: George S. Patton, Jr., by Fred Ayer, Jr. With a foreword by Omar N. Bradley. Boston, Houghton Mifflin, 1964, xvii, 266 p. ports. (part col.) 22 cm. [E745.P3A9] 64-18329
1. Patton, George Smith, 1885-1945. I. Title. BIP

ESSAME, Hubert, 1896- 940.54'21'0924 B
Patton; a study in command, by H. Essame. New York, Scribner [1974] x, 280 p. illus. 24 cm. Bibliography: p. [263]-265. [E745.P3E85] 73-15498 ISBN 0-684-13671-6 8.95
1. Patton, George Smith, 1885-1945. BIP

FARAGO, Ladislas 923.573
Patton: ordeal and triumph. New York, Obolensky [1964, c.1963] 885p. maps. 24cm. Bibl. 63-20479 9.95
1. Patton, George Smith, 1885-1945. I. Title. BIP

HATCH, Alden, 1898- 923.573
George Patton, general in spurs. New York, Messner [1950] x, 184 p. ports., map. 22 cm. [E745.P3H3] 50-9641
1. Patton, George Smith, 1885-1945.

PEARL, Jack 923.573
Blood-and-Guts Patton; the swashbuckling life story of America's most daring and controversial general. derby, Conn., Monarch Books [c.1961] 142p. (A Monarch Americana book, MA305) Bibl. 61-10782 .35 pap.,
1. Patton, George Smith, 1885-1945. I. Title.

SEMMES, Harry Hodges, 1892- 923.573
Portrait of Patton. New York, Appleton-Century-Crofts [1955] 308 p. illus. 22 cm. [E745.P3S3] 55-9434
1. Patton, George Smith, 1885-1945. I. Title.

WHITING, Charles, 1926- 940.542'1'0924
Patton. [New York, Ballantine Books, 1970] 160 p. illus., maps, ports. 21 cm. (Ballantine's illustrated history of World War II. War leader book, no. 1) Cover title. Bibliography: p. 160. [E745.P3W48] 73-19954 1.00
1. Patton, George Smith, 1885-1945. BIP

WILLIAMSON, Porter B., 1916- 940.54'21'0924 B
I remember General Patton's principles / by Porter B. Williamson. Tucson, Ariz. : Management and Systems Consultants, c1979. 167 p., [8] leaves of plates : ill. ; 20 cm. [E745.P3W54] 77-70779 ISBN 0-918356-03-2 : 5.95
1. Patton, George Smith, 1885-1945- 2. United States. Army—Biography. 3. Williamson, Porter B., 1916- 4. Generals—United States—Biography. I. Title.

Patton, George Smith, 1885-1945—Addresses, essays, lectures.

BLUMENSON, Martin. 355.3'31'0924
The many faces of George S. Patton, Jr. [Colorado Springs] U.S. Air Force Academy, 1972. 27 p. port. 20 cm. (The Harmon memorial lectures in military history, no. 14) Includes bibliographical references. [E745.P3B54] 72-603776
1. Patton, George Smith, 1885-1945—Addresses, essays, lectures. I. Title. II. Series.

Patton, George Smith, 1885-1945—Juvenile literature.

FINKE, Blythe Foote. 355.3'31'0924 B
General Patton, fearless military leader. Charlotteville, N.Y., SamHar Press, 1972. 27 p. 22 cm. (Outstanding personalities, no. 34) Bibliography: p. 25-27. A biography of the controversial commander of the Third Army in World War II. [E745.P3F56] 92 76-190251 ISBN 0-87157-534-5 1.98
1. Patton, George Smith, 1885-1945—Juvenile literature. I. Title.
Pap. $0.98 ISBN 0-87157-034-3

MELLOR, William Bancroft. 355.3'31'0924 B
General Patton: the last cavalier. New York, Putnam [1971] 191 p. illus., port. 22 cm. (Lives to remember) A biography of the controversial commander of the Third Army in World War II. [E745.P3M39 1971] 92 75-108745 3.86
1. Patton, George Smith, 1885-1945—Juvenile literature. I. Title.

Paul, Charles Kegan,

PAUL, Charles Kegan, 1828-1902. 070.5'0924 B
Memories. [Hamden, Conn.] Archon Books, 1971. x, 390 p. 20 cm. "Bibliographical note": p. 378-381. [Z325.P32 1971] 76-21644 ISBN 0-208-01157-9 7.50

Paul I, Emperor of Russia, 1754-1801.

WALISZEWSKI, Kazimierz, 1849-1935. 947'.07'0924 B
Paul the First of Russia, the son of Catherine the Great. [Hamden, Conn.] Archon Books, 1969. v, 495 p. port. 23 cm. Reprint of the 1913 ed. Translation of Le fils de la Grande Catherine. [DK186.W32 1969] 69-19221
1. Paul I, Emperor of Russia, 1754-1801. 2. Russia—History—Paul I, 1796-1801. I. Title.

Paul I, Emperor of Russia, 1754-1891—Addresses, essays, lectures.

PAUL I, a 947'.07'0924 B
reassessment of his life and reign / edited by Hugh Ragsdale. Pittsburgh : University Center for International Studies, University of Pittsburgh, [1978] p. cm. (UCIS series in Russian and East European studies ; 2) Bibliography: p. [DK186.P38] 78-14893 pbk. : 6.95
1. Paul I, Emperor of Russia, 1754-1891—Addresses, essays, lectures. 2. Russia—History—Paul I, 1796-1801—Addresses, essays, lectures. 3. Russia—Kings and rulers—Biography—Addresses, essays, lectures. I. Ragsdale, Hugh. II. Series: Pittsburgh. University. University Center for International Studies. UCIS series in Russian and East European studies ; 2.

Paul James Francis, Father, 1863-1940.

ANGELL, Charles. 248'.242'0924 B
Prophet of reunion : the life of Paul of Graymoor / Charles Angell, Charles LaFontaine ; with an introd. by James Stuart Wetmore. New York : Seabury Press, [1975] xi, 224 p. : ill. ; 22 cm. "A Crossroad book." [BX4705.P3842A8] 74-32239 ISBN 0-8164-0281-7 : 6.95
1. Paul James Francis, Father, 1863-1940. I. LaFontaine, Charles, joint author. II. Title.

CRANNY, Titus, 1921- 922.273
Father Paul, apostle of unity; a biographical study of the unity vocation of Father Paul James Francis, S. A., founder of the Society of the Atonement and originator of the Chair of Unity Octave. Peekskill, N. Y., Graymoor Press [1955] 94p. 21cm. [BX4705.P3842C7] 55-3361
1. Paul James Francis, Father, 1863-1940. 2. Friars of the Atonement. I. Title.

GANNON, David, Father, 1904- 922.273
Father Paul of Graymoor. New York, Macmillan, 1951. x, 372 p. illus., ports. 22 cm. [BX4705.P3842G3] 51-5046
1. Paul James Francis, Father, 1863-1940. 2. Friars of the Atonement. 3. Franciscan Sisters of the Atonement. I. Title.

Paul, Saint, apostie—Juvenile literature.

MARY Eleanor, Mother, 1903- 209'.22
The last apostle. Illustrated by George Pollard. Milwaukee, Bruce Pub. Co. [1956] 150p. illus. 22cm. (Catholic treasury books) [BS2505.M318] 56-11154
1. Paul, Saint, apostie—Juvenile literature. I. Title.

Paul, Saint, apostle.

ASHBROOK, James B., 1925- 230
Christianity for pious skeptics / James B. Ashbrook, Paul W. Walaskay. Nashville : Abingdon, c1977. 160 p. : ill. ; 21 cm. Includes bibliographical references. [BS2506.A83] 77-911 ISBN 0-687-07646-3 pbk. : 4.95
1. Paul, Saint, Apostle. 2. Bible. N.T.—Biography. 3. Christian saints—Turkey—Tarsus—Biography. 4. Tarsus, Turkey—Biography. 5. Faith and reason. 6. Christian life—1960- I. Walaskay, Paul W., 1939- II. Title. BIP

BALL, Charles Ferguson. [922.1]
The life and journeys of Paul Illus. by Francis Mason Holt Chicago, Moody Press ['1951] 315 p. illus. 21 cm. [BS2505.B232] 225.92 52-6727
1. Paul, Saint, apostle. I. Title. BIP

BARCLAY, William, lecturer in the University of Glasgow. 225.9'24 B
Ambassador for Christ; the life and teaching of Paul. Valley Forge, [Pa.] Judson Press [1974, c1973] 183 p. 22 cm. "Originally published in 1951 by the Church of Scotland Youth Committee." [BS2506.B34 1974] 73-9762 ISBN 0-8170-0631-1 1.95 (pbk)
1. Paul, Saint, apostle. I. Title.

BORNKAMM, Gunther. 225.9'24 B
Paul, Paulus. Translated by D. M. G. Stalker. [1st U.S. ed.] New York, Harper & Row [1971] xxviii, 259 p. 22 cm. [BS2506.B6213] 75-22728 7.50
1. Paul, Saint, apostle. 2. Bible. N.T. Epistles of Paul—Theology.

BRADFORD, Ernle Dusgate Selby. 225.9'24 B
Paul the traveller / Ernle Bradford. 1st American ed. New York : Macmillan, 1976, c1974. vii, 246 p., [6] leaves of plates : ill. ; 22 cm. Includes index. [BS2506.B7 1976] 75-28451 ISBN 0-02-514390-5 : 9.95
1. Paul, Saint, Apostle. I. Title. BIP

BRUCE, Frederick Fyvie, 1910- 225.9'2'4 B
Paul, apostle of the heart set free / F. F. Bruce. 1st American ed. Grand Rapids : Eerdmans, 1977. 491 p., [8] leaves of plates : ill. ; 24 cm. Includes index. Bibliography: p. 476-479. [BS2506.B755 1977] 77-26127 ISBN 0-8028-3501-5 : 9.95
1. Paul, Saint, Apostle. 2. Bible. N.T.—Biography. 3. Bible. N.T. Epistles of Paul—Theology. 4. Christian saints—Turkey—Tarsus—Biography. 5. Tarsus, Turkey—Biography. I. Title.

DEISSMANN, Gustav Adolf, 1866-1937. 225.92
Paul; a study in social and religious history. Translated by William E. Wilson. [1st Harper torchbook ed.] New York, Harper [1957] 323 p. illus. 21 cm. (Harper torchbooks, TB15) [BS2505.D42 1957] 922.1 57-7533
1. Paul, Saint, apostle.

DRANE, John William. 225.9'24 B
Paul : [an illustrated documentary on the life and writings of a key figure in the beginnings of Christianity] / John W. Drane. Berkhamsted : Lion Publishing, 1976. 127 p. : ill., facsims., maps ; 24 cm. Includes index. Bibliography: p. 123-125. [BS2506.D7] 77-373988 ISBN 0-85648-043-6 : £1.75
1. Paul, Saint, Apostle. 2. Bible. N.T Epistles of Paul—Criticism, interpretation, etc. 3. Christian saints—Turkey—Tarsus—Biography. 4. Tarsus, Turkey—Biography.

THE first Christian; 922.1
a study of St. Paul and Christian origins. New York, Farrar,Straus and Cudahy [1957] 275p. illus. 22cm. [BS2505.D36] [BS2505.D36] 225.92 57-14507 57-14507
1. Paul, Saint, apostle. 2. Christinaity-Origin. I. Davies, Arthur Powell.

FRANCISCUS, Brother, 1922- [922.1]
The tentmaker from Tarsus, a story of St. Paul. Illus. by Rosemary Donatino. Natre Dame, Ind., Dujarie Press [1950] 95 p. illus. 24 cm. [BS2505.F7] 225.92 50-2575
1. Paul, Saint, apostle. I. Title.

GIBBS, Paul T. 225.9'24 B
Paul the Conqueror [by] Paul T. Gibbs. Washington, Review and Herald Pub. Association [1972] 124 p. 22 cm. (Discovery paperbacks) [BS2506.G5] 75-178160
1. Paul, Saint, apostle. I. Title.

GRANT, Michael, 1914- 225.9'24 B
Saint Paul / Michael Grant. London : Weidenfeld and Nicolson, c1976. 250 p. : maps ; 24 cm. Includes index. Bibliography: p. 242-244. [BS2506.G68] 76-364100 ISBN 0-297-77082-9 : £5.95
1. Paul, Saint, Apostle. BIP

GRANT, Michael, 1914- 225.9'24 B
Saint Paul / Michael Grant. New York : Scribner, c1976. 250 p. : maps ; 25 cm. Includes index. Bibliography: p. 242-244. [BS2506.G68 1976b] 76-6024 ISBN 0-684-14682-7 : 14.95
1. Paul, Saint, Apostle. 2. Bible. N.T.—Biography. I. Title.

GRASSI, Joseph A. 225.9'2'4 B
The secret of Paul the Apostle / Joseph A. Grassi. Maryknoll, N.Y. : Orbis Books, c1978. 170 p. ; 21 cm. [BS2506.G693] 77-29045 ISBN 0-88344-454-2 pbk. : 7.95
1. Paul, Saint, Apostle. 2. Christian saints—Turkey—Tarsus—Biography. 3. Tarsus, Turkey—Biography. 4. Missions—History—Early church, ca. 30-600. I. Title.

BIP

GROLLENBERG, Lucas 225.9'2'4 B
Hendricus, 1916-
Paul / Lucas Grollenberg. Philadelphia : Westminster Press, c1978. 179 p. ; 20 cm. Translation of Die moeilijk Paulus. [BS2506.G7713] 78-14372 ISBN 0-664-24234-0 pbk. : 4.50
1. Paul, Saint, Apostle. 2. Bible. N.T.—Biography. 3. Bible. N.T. Epistles of Paul—Theology. 4. Christian saints—Turkey—Tarsus—Biography. 5. Tarsus, Turkey—Biography.

GUNTHER, John J. 225.9'2'4 B
Paul: messenger and exile; a study in the chronology of his life and letters [by] John J. Gunther. Valley Forge, Judson Press [1972] 190 p. map. 23 cm. Includes bibliographical references. [BS2506.G85] 70-181022 ISBN 0-8170-0504-8 6.95
1. Paul, Saint, apostle. I. Title.

HAUGHTON, Rosemary. 225.924 B
Paul and the world's most famous letters. [Nashville, Abingdon Press, 1970] 110 p. illus., maps. 27 cm. 1969 ed., London, published under title: Why the Epistles were written. Bibliography: p. 107. [BS2506.H3 1970] 72-105063 3.75
1. Paul, Saint, apostle. 2. Bible. N.T. Epistles of Paul—Criticism, interpretation, etc. I. Title.

HENDERLITE, Rachel. 922.1
Paul, Christian and world traveler. Student's book. With illus. by Dawn Kyoko Aoto. Richmond, Published for the Cooperative Publication Association by John Knox Press [1957] 66p. illus. 23cm. [BS2507.H4] 225.92 57-23346
1. Paul, Saint, apostle. I. Title

KALLAS, James G 225.924 (B)
The story of Paul, by James G. Kallas. Minneapolis, Augsburg Pub. House [1966] 151 p. 22 cm. Includes bibliographies. [BS2506.K3] 66-19206
1. Paul, Saint, apostle. I. Title. BIP

KNOX, John, 1900- 225.92
Chapters in a life of Paul. Nashville, Abingdon [1964, c.1950] 168p. 23cm. (Apex bks., P2) 1.25 pap.,
1. Paul, Saint, apostle. I. Title.

KNOX, John, 1900- [922.1]
Chapters in a life of Paul. New York, Abingdon-Cokesbury Press [1950] 168 p. 24 cm. [BS2505.K56] 225.92 50-5882
1. Paul, Saint, apostle. I. Title.

KRAELING, Emil 225.924 (B)
Gottlieb Heinrich, 1892-
I have kept the faith; the life of the apostle Paul, by Emil G. Kraeling. Chicago, Rand McNally [1965] 320 p. maps (on lining papers) 22 cm. "Notes and references": p. 276-307. [BS2506.K7] 65-15357
1. Paul, Saint, apostle. I. Title. BIP

THE life and epistles of 922.1
St. Paul. By W. J. Conybeare and J. S. Howson. New ed. Grand Rapids, W.B. Eerdmans Pub. Co., 1953. xxi, 850p. illus., maps. 22cm. Bibliographical footnotes. [BS2505.C65 1953] [BS2505.C65 1953] 225.92 53-1496 53-1496
1. Paul, Saint, apostle. I. Conybeare, William John, 1815-1857. II. Howson: John Saul, 1816-1885. III. Bible. N.T. Epistles of Paul. English. 1953.

THE life of Paul. 922.1
Philadelphia, Published for the Cooperative Publication Association by the Christian Education Press [1956, c1955] 81p. illus. 19cm. (The Cooperative series leadership training textbooks) [BS2507.M6] 225.92 56-7714
1. Paul, Saint, apostle. I. Moss, Robert V

LOHFINK, Gerhard, 225.9'24 B
1934-
The conversion of St. Paul : narrative and history in Acts / by Gerhard Lohfink; translated and edited by Bruce J. Malina Chicago : Franciscan Herald Press, [1975] p. cm. (Herald scriptural library) Translation of Paulus vor Damaskus, 3d. ed. (1967) Bibliography: p. [BS2506.L5713] 75-12796 ISBN 0-8199-0572-0 : 5.95
1. Paul, Saint, apostle. 2. Bible. N.T. Acts—Criticism, interpretation, etc. I. Title.

LONGENECKER, Richard 225.92'4 B
N.
The ministry and message of Paul [by] Richard Longenecker. Grand Rapids, Mich., Zondervan Pub. House [1971] 130 p. 21 cm. (Contemporary evangelical perspectives) Bibliography: p. 113-122. [BS2506.L598] 77-159661
1. Paul, Saint, apostle. I. Title. BIP

LUCE, Harry Kenneth, 1897- 922.1
St. Paul. Illustrated by G. S. Ronalds. [1st American ed.] New York, Putnam [1958] 118p. illus. 21cm. (Lives to remember) [BS2505.L7] 225.92 58-7445
1. Paul, Saint, apostle. I. Title.

THE man from Tarsus. 922.1
With an introd. by A. Victor Murray. Newtown, Montgomeryshire Print. Co., 1956. 375p. 22cm. [BS2505.E8] [BS2505.E8] 225.92 57-39876 57-39876
1. Paul, Saint, apostle. I. Eurich, H F A

MEYER, Frederick 922.1
Brotherton, 1847-1929.
Paul, a servant of Jesus Christ. Grand Rapids, Zondervan Pub. House [1953] 155p. 20cm. [BS2505.M43 1953] [BS2505.M43 1953] 225.92 53-13075 53-13075
1. Paul, Saint, apostle. I. Title.

MILLER, Donald G. 225.92
Conqueror in chains, a story of the apostle Paul; illustrated by Albert De Mee Jousset. Philadelphia, Westminster Press [1951] 271 p. illus. 22 cm. [BS2505.M52] 922.1 51-12690
1. Paul, Saint, apostle. I. Title.

MOE, Olaf Edvard, 1876- 225.92
The apostle Paul. Translated by L. A. Vigness. Minneapolis, Augsburg Pub. House [1950-54] 2 v. maps. 22 cm. Contents.Contents.—1. His life and his work.—2. His message and doctrine. Includes bibliographies. [BS2505.M5494] 922.1 50-7291
1. Paul, Saint, apostle.

NOCK, Arthur Darby, 1902- 922.1
St. Paul. New York, Harper [1963] 255p. 18cm. (Harper torchbk.; Cloister Lib., TB104) Bibl. 1.45 pap.,
1. Paul, Saint, apostle. I. Title.

NOCK, Arthur Darby, 1902- 225.92
St. Paul. New York, Harper & Row [1963] 255 p. 21 cm. (Harper torchbooks. The Cloister library) "TB 104." Bibliography: p. 249-251. [[BS2506]]
1. Paul, Saint, apostle.

PAUL, 922.1
the tent maker. Foreword byAbram Woodard. Boston, Christopher Pub. House [1957] 109p. illus. 21cm. [BS2505.D37] [BS2505.D37] 225.92 57-28030 57-28030
1. Paul, Saint, apostle. I. Day, Bertram, 1871-

PAUL. 922.1
Edited and completed by Werner Georg Kummel. Translated by Frank Clarke. Philadelphia, Westminster Press [1953] 172p. illus. 19cm. [BS2505.D495] [BS2505.D495] 225.92 53-1574 53-1574
1. Paul, Saint, apostle. I. Dibelius, Martin, 1883-1947. II. Kummel, Werner Georg, 1905- ed.

PAUL as a leader; 922.1
a study of the apostle's role and influence in the field of religious education. Foreword by W. L. Howse. [1st ed.] New York, Exposition Press [1955] 144p. 21cm. (Exposition--university book) [BS2505.C58] [BS2505.C58] 225.92 55-9397 55-9397
1. Paul, Saint, apostle. 2. Religious education. I. Collins, Carl A 1915-

PAUL'S life and letters. 922.1
[1st ed.] Salt Lake City, Bookcraft, 1955. 314p. illus. 24cm. [BS2505.S65] [BS2505.S65] 225.92 56-18630 56-18630
1. Paul, Saint, apostle. 2. Bible. N. T. Epsitles of Paul— Introductions. I. Sperry, Sidney Branton, 1895-

PHILLIPS, Harold L 922.1
A man of Tarsus; life and work of Paul. Anderson, Ind., Warner Press [1955] 104p. 20cm. [BS2505.P46] [BS2505.P46] 225.92 55-35795 55-35795
1. Paul, Saint, apostle. I. Title.

PITTENGER, William 225.92'4
Norman, 1905-
The life of Saint Paul [by] W. Norman Pittenger. New York, F. Watts [1968] ix, 141 p. map. 22 cm. (Immortals of philosophy and religion) Bibliography: p. 137-138. [BS2506.P5] 68-22145 3.95
1. Paul, Saint, apostle.

PITTENGER, William Norman, 225.92
1905-
The life of Saint Paul [by] W. Norman Pittenger. New York, F. Watts [1968] ix, 141 p. map. 22 cm. (Immortals of philosophy and religion) Bibliography: p. 137-138. A biography of the man known as "the first Christian missionary and theologian," including discussions of the world he lived in, other religions of the time, our sources of information about him, his teachings, and his influence on religious history. [BS2506.P5] AC 68
1. Paul, Saint, apostle. I. Title.

RICCIOTTI, Giuseppe, 1890- 922.1
Paul the apostle; translated by Alba I. Zizzamia. Milwaukee, Bruce Pub. Co. [1953] 540p. illus. 25cm. [BS2505.R5132] [BS2505.R5132] 225.92 53-13257 53-13257
1. Paul, Saint, apostle. I. Title.

ROBERTSON, Archibald 225.9'24
Thomas, 1863-1934.
Epochs in the life of Paul : a study of development in Paul's career / A. T. Robertson. Nashville : Broadman Press, 1974. xi, 337 p. ; 20 cm. (A. T. Robertson library) Reprint of the 1909 ed. published by Scribner, New York. Includes indexes. Bibliography: p. 321-327. [BS2505.R57 1974] 74-192551 ISBN 0-8054-1348-0 : pbk. 3.45
1. Paul, Saint, apostle. I. Title.

RUBENSTEIN, Richard L. 225.9'24 B
My brother Paul [by] Richard L. Rubenstein. [1st ed.] New York, Harper & Row [1972] x, 209 p. 22 cm. Includes bibliographical references. [BS2506.R8 1972] 72-124704 ISBN 0-06-067014-2 5.95
1. Paul, Saint, apostle. I. Title. BIP

SAINT Paul, 922.1
apostle of nations; translated by Jex Martin. Chicago, Fides Publishers Association [1953] 163p. 21cm. Translation of Saint Paul, conquerant du Christ. [BS2505.D3413] [BS2505.D3413] 225.92 53-11075 53-11075
1. Paul, Saint, apostle. I. Daniel- Rops, Henry, 1901-

SAINT Paul, the apostle of 922.1
the Gentiles. Translated from the Spanish by Paul Barrett. Westminster, Md., Newman Press, 1956. 430p. 23cm. [BS2505.P432] [BS2505.P432] 225.92 56-11428 56-11428
1. Paul, Saint, apostle. I. Perez de Urbel, Justo, 1895-

ST. Paul's journeys in the 922.1
Greek Orient [Translated by S. H. Hooke from the French] New York, Philosophical Library [1955*C75p. illus. 19cm. 75p. illus. 19cm. (Studies in biblical archaeology. no. 4) [BS2505.M423] [BS2505.M423] 225.92 56-2402 56-2402
1. Paul, Saint, apostle. I. Metzger. Benri.

SANNESS, Palmer. 225.924
The incomparable Paul. Boston, Branden Press [1969] 39 p. 22 cm. [BS2506.S17] 78-83704 1.00
1. Paul, Saint, apostle. I. Title. BIP

SHEPARD, John Watson, 1879- 227
The life and letters of St. Paul; an exegetical study. 1st ed. Grand Rapids, Eerdmans, 1950. 605 p. 24 cm. Bibliography: p. [601]-605. Bibliographical footnotes. [BS2650.s55] 50-11380
1. Paul, Saint, apostle. 2. Bible. N. T. Epistles of Paul—Commentaries. I. Title.

SMITH, Roy Lemon, 1887- 225.9'24
From Saul to Paul; the making of an apostle. Nashville, Tidings [1962] 104 p. 19 cm. [BS2506.S5] 62-20562
1. Paul, Saint, apostle. I. Title.

STALKER, James 225.92
Life of St. Paul; handbook for Bible classes. Grand Rapids, Mich., Zondervan [1960] 160p. Bibliographical references included in 'Hints to teachers and questions for pupils (p. 145-160)20cm. 1.25 bds.,
1. Paul, Saint, apostle. I. Title.

STALKER, James, [922.1] 225.92
1848-1927.
The life of St. Paul. New York, Revell [1950] 100 p. 20 cm. Bibliographical references included in "Hints to teachers and questions for pupils" (p. 145-160) [BS2505.S7 1950] 50-4996
1. Paul, Saint, apostle. I. Title. BIP

TAYLOR, William Mackergo, 225.92
1829-1895.
Paul, the missionary. Grand Rapids, Baker Book House, 1962. 570 p. 21 cm. (Bible biographies) [BX2505.T37 1962] 62-21707
1. Paul, Saint, apostle. I. Title.

TRESMONTANT, [922.1] 225.92
Claude.
Saint Paul and the mystery of Christ. Translated by Donald Attwater. New York, Harper Torchbooks [c1957] 190 p. illus., maps (on cover, 1 fold.) facsims. 18 cm. (Men of wisdom, 1) "Bibliographical note": p. 188-189. [BS2505.T673] 58-5220
1. Paul, Saint, apostle. I. Title.

VAN ETTEN, Isabel [922.1] 225.92
Upton.
Who was Saul of Tarsus. Los Angeles, Cole-Holmquist Press, 1957. 92 p. 24 cm. [BS2505.V3] 57-28029
1. Paul, Saint, apostle. I. Title.

WHITE, Reginald E. O 225.92
Apostle extraordinary, a modern portrait of St. Paul. Grand Rapids, Mich., Eerdmans [c.1962] 209p. 22cm. 62-18955 3.50 bds.,
1. Paul, Saint, apostle. I. Title.

WHITE, Reginald E O 225.92
Apostle extraordinary, a modern portrait of St. Paul. Grand Rapids, W. B. Eerdmans Pub. Co. [1962] 200 p. 22 cm. [BS2506.W5] 62-18955
1. Paul, Saint, apostle. I. Title.

WILLIAMS, Albert Nathaniel, 922.1
1914-
Paul, the world's first missionary; a biography of the Apostle Paul. New York, Association Press [1954] 157p. illus. 20cm. (Heroes of God series) [BS2505.W49] 225.92 54-8251
1. Paul, Saint, apostle. I. Title.

Paul, Saint, Apostle—Chronology.

JEWETT, Robert. 225.9'2'4 B
A chronology of Paul's life / by Robert Jewett. Philadelphia : Fortress Press, c1979. viii, 160 p., [1] fold. leaf of plates : graph ; 24 cm. "Submitted as part of a dissertation at the Eberhard-Karls-University in Tubingen," 1964. Includes bibliographical references and indexes. [BS2506.J49] 78-54553 ISBN 0-8006-0522-5 : 10.95
1. Paul, Saint, Apostle—Chronology. I. Title. BIP

Paul, Saint, apostle—Journeys.

PEROWNE, Stewart, 225.9'24 B
1901-
The journeys of St. Paul. London, New York, Hamlyn, 1973. 144 p. illus. (some col.), col. maps (on lining papers), ports. 29 cm. Bibliography: p. 142. [BS2506.P45 1973] 73-162279 £2.25
1. Paul, Saint, apostle—Journeys. I. Title.

Paul, Saint, Apostle—Juvenile literature.

BRUCE, Janet 225.92
The life of Saint Paul. Pictures by Emile Probst. London, Burns & Oates; New York, Herder & Herder [c.1965] [27]p. col. illus. 19cm. (Men of God 4) [BS2506.5.B7] 65-21948 1.50 bds.
1. Paul, Saint, apostle—Juvenile literature. I. Probst, Emile, illus. II. Title. III. Series.

PRIESTER, Gertrude 225.92'4 B
Ann.
Who are you, Lord? [By] Gertrude Priester. Illustrated by Shannon Stirnweis. Richmond, CLC Press [1969] 126 p. col. illus. 21 cm. (The Covenant life

curriculum) A biography of the Apostle Paul based largely on the Book of Acts telling how he traveled throughout the Biblical world preaching about Jesus Christ. [BS2506.5.P73] 92 70-13550
1. Paul, Saint, apostle—Juvenile literature. I. Stirnweis, Shannon, illus. II. Title. **BIP**

TUCKER, Iva Jewel. 225.9'24 B
Paul, the missionary / Iva Jewel Tucker ; illustrated by Ron Hester. Nashville : Broadman Press, c1976. 46 p. : col. ill. ; 24 cm. (Biblearn series) Discusses the conversion and ministry of Paul the missionary. [BS2506.5.T82] 76-382994 ISBN 0-8054-4228-6 : 3.95
1. Paul, Saint, Apostle—Juvenile literature. 2. Evangelists (Bible)—Biography—Juvenile literature. 3. Bible. N.T.—Biography—Juvenile literature. I. Hester, Ronald. II. Title.

Paul Wilhelm, Duke of Wurtemberg, 1797-1860.

PAUL Wilhelm, Duke of Wurttemberg, 1797-1860. 917.7'04'2
Travels in North America, 1822-1824. Translated by W. Robert Nitske. Edited by Savoie Lottinville. [1st ed.] Norman, University of Oklahoma Press [1973] xxxiv, 456 p. illus. 24 cm. (The American exploration and travel series, v. 63) Translation of Erste Reise nach dem nordlichen Amerika in den Jahren 1822 bis 1824. Bibliography: p. 415-426. [F353.P3213] 72-3596 20.00
1. Paul Wilhelm, Duke of Wurtemberg, 1797-1860. 2. Mississippi Valley—Description and travel. 3. United States—Description and travel—1783-1848. I. Title. II. Series.

Paulding, James Kirke,

PAULDING, James Kirke, 1778-1860. 928.1
Letters. Ed. by Ralph M. Aderman. Madison, Univ. of Wis. Pr. [c.]1962. xxiv, 631p. illus., ports., facsims., genaeal. table. 25cm. 62-17397 10.00
I. Title.

Pauley, Jane, 1950- —Juvenile literature.

JACOBS, Linda. 791.45'092'4 B
Jane Pauley, a heartland style / by Linda Jacobs. St. Paul : EMC Corp., 1978. 39 p. : ill. ; 23 cm. (Headliners I) A biography of the co-host of the Today Show, a popular early morning television news program. [PN1992.4.P35J3] 92 77-27805 ISBN 0-88436-474-7 lib. bdg. : 4.95. ISBN 0-88436-425-9 pbk. : 2.95
1. Pauley, Jane, 1950- —Juvenile literature. 2. Television personalities—United States—Biography—Juvenile literature. I. Title. II. Series.

Paulius VI, Pope, 1897-

DE VITO, Albert Conrad, Bp., 1904- 262.130924
Pope Paul VI; glimpses of his life before he became Pope. Allahabad, St Paul Publications [1964] 147 p. ports. 18 cm. "No. 136" [BX1378.3.D4] 65-2870
1. Paulius VI, Pope, 1897- I. Title.

Paulson, David, 1868-1916.

CLOUGH, Caroline Louise. 926.1
His name was David; the remarkable life of Dr. David Paulson, man of faith and founder of Hinsdale Sanitarium. Washington, Review and Herald Pub. Association [1955] 160p. illus. 23cm. [R154.P325C6] 55-12651
1. Paulson, David, 1868-1916. 2. Hinadale Sanitarium and Benevolent Association. I. Title.

Paulucci, Jeno F., 1918-

LEIPOLD, L. Edmond, 1902- 338.7'66'400924 B
Jeno F. Paulucci; merchant philanthropist, by L. E. Leipold. Minneapolis, T. S. Denison [1968] 227 p. illus., ports. 22 cm. (Men of achievement series) A biography of the multi-millionaire, founder of Chun King and other companies, who has received numerous awards for his philanthropic activities. [HD9010.P38L4] 92 68-56035
1. Paulucci, Jeno F., 1918- I. Title.

Paulus, Friedrich.

GORLITZ, Walter, 1913- 923.543
Paulus and Stalingrad; a life of Field-Marshal Friedrich Paulus, with notes, correspondence, and documents from his papers. Pref. by Ernst Alexander Paulus. Tr. [from German] by R. H. Stevens. New York, Citadel [1964, c.1963] xvi, 301p. illus., ports., maps. 22cm. Bibl. 63-21199 5.95 bds.,
1. Paulus, Friedrich. 2. Stalingrad, Battle of, 1942-1943. I. Title.

GORLITZ, Walter, 1913- 355.3'31'0924 B
Paulus and Stalingrad; a life of Field-Marshal Friedrich Paulus, with notes, correspondence and documents from his papers. With a pref. by Ernst Alexander Paulus. Translated by R. H. Stevens. Westport, Conn., Greenwood Press [1974, c1963] xvi, 301 p. illus. 23 cm. Translation of Paulus: "Ich stehe hier auf Befehl!" Reprint of the ed. published in 1964 by Citadel Press, New York. Includes bibliographical references. [DD247.P38G613 1974] 74-5782 ISBN 0-8371-7497-X
1. Paulus, Friedrich. 2. Stalingrad, Battle of, 1942-1943. I. Title.

Paulus, Thebaeus, Saint.

HIERONYMUS, Saint. 270.1'0924 B
The first desert hero: St. Jerome's Vita Pauli. With introd., notes, and vocabulary by Ignatius S. Kozik. Mount Vernon, N.Y., King Lithographers [1968] x, 67 p. illus. 22 cm. Text in Latin. "The Migne edition is the one mainly followed ... The following sections of the Vita have been omitted: Prologue (PL 23. 17-18), the story of the two martyrs (ibid. 19-20), and Anthony's journey through the desert (ibid. 22-24)." Bibliography: p. 12-14. Bibliographical footnotes. [BR1720.P28H5] 68-56001
1. Paulus, Thebaeus, Saint. I. Kozik, Ignatius S., ed. II. Title. III. Title: Vita Pauli.

Paulus, VI, Pope, 1897-

BARRETT, William Edmund, 1900- 922.21
Shepherd of mankind a biography of Pope Paul VI. Garden City, N. Y., Doubleday [c.]1964. 288p. illus., ports. 24cm. 64-16869 4.95
1. Paulus VI, Pope, 1897- I. Title.

BARRETT, William Edmund, 1900- 262.130924
Shepherd of mankind; a biography of Pope Paul VI. [1st ed.] Garden City, N.Y., Doubleday, 1964. 288 p. illus., ports. 24 cm. [BX1378.3.B6] 64-16869
1. Paulus VI, Pope, 1897- I. Title.

GONZALEZ, James L. 922.21
Paul VI, by J.A. Gonzalez, T. Perez. English version by Edward L. Heston. [Boston] St. Paul Eds. [dist. Daughters of St. Paul, c.1964] 338p. illus., ports. 22cm. [BX1378.3.G613] 64-7923 5.00; 4.00 pap.,
1. Paulus, VI, Pope, 1897- I. Perez, Thomas, joint author. II. Title.

GONZALEZ, Jose Luis. 922.21
Paul VI, by j.L. Gonzalez [and] T. Perez. English version by Edward L. Heston. [Boston] St. Paul Editions [1964] 338 p. illus., ports. 22 cm. [BX1378.3.G613] 64-7923
1. Paulus, VI, Pope, 1897- I. Perez, Thomas, joint author. II. Title.

HATCH, Alden, 1898- 262.13
Pope Paul VI. New York, Random House [1966] 279 p. ports. 22 cm. Bibliography: p. 267. [BX1378.3.H3] 66-12006
1. Paulus VI, Pope, 1897- I. Title.

HEBBLETHWAITE, Peter. 262'.13'09047
The year of the three popes / Peter Hebblethwaite. London : Collins, 1978. ix, 220 p. ; 22 cm. Includes index. Bibliography: p. 213-214. [BX1389.H36] 79-307264 ISBN 0-00-215047-6 : 8.95
1. Paulus VI, Pope, 1897- 2. John Paul I, Pope, 1912-1978. 3. John Paul II, Pope, 1920- 4. Papacy—History—20th century. 5. Popes—Biography. I. Title.
Distributed by Collins Publishers, Inc., Cleveland, OH 44111 **BIP**

MACGREGOR-HASTIE, Roy 922.21
Pope Paul VI. New York, Criterion [c. 1965] 162p. illus., ports. 22cm. (Criterion bk. for young people) [BX1378.3.M2] 64-22139 3.50
1. Paulus VI, Pope, 1897- I. Title.

PALLENBERG, Corrado, 1912- 922.21
The making of a Pope. [New York, Macfadden-Bartell Corp., 1964] 176 p. 18 cm. "A Macfadden original." "60-188." Bibliography: p. 175-176. [BX1378.3.P3] 64-55963
1. Paulus VI, Pope, 1897- I. Title.

PALLENBERG, Corrado, 1912- 262'.13'0924 B
Pope Paul VI. [Rev. ed.] New York, Putnam [1968] 224 p. 22 cm. (Lives to remember) First published in 1964 under title: The making of a Pope. Bibliography: p. 221-222. A biography of Pope Paul VI, covering his boyhood, education, the positions he held leading to his election as Pope, and the reform movements of his reign. [BX1378.3.P3 1968] 92 AC 68
1. Paulus VI, Pope, 1897- I. Title.

Paustovskii, Konstantin Georgievich,

PAUSTOVSKII, Konstantin Georgievich, 1893- 891.7842
The story of a life. Translated from the Russian by Joseph Barnes. New York, Pantheon Books [1964- v. port. 25 cm. Autobiography. [PG3476.P29Z513] 63-7344
I. Title.

PAUSTOVSKII, Konstantin Georgievich, 1893-1968. 891.7'3'42
The story of a life: Years of hope [by] Konstantin Paustovsky. Translated from the Russian by Manya Harari and Andrew Thomson. New York, Pantheon Books [1969, c1968] 223 p. 22 cm. Translation of Povest' o zhizni (romanized form) [PG3476.P29Z513 1969] 69-15479
I. Title. II. Title: Years of hope.

Pavlov, Ivan Petrovich, 1849-1936.

BABKIN, Boris Petrovich 926.12
Pavlov, a biography. [Chicago] University of Chicago Press [1960, c.1949] xiii, 364p. 'References': p. [347]-353. illus., ports. 22cm. (Chicago reprint series) 6.00
1. Pavlov, Ivan Petrovich, 1849-1936. I. Title.

BABKIN, Boris Petrovich, 1877-1950. v. 12
Pavlov, a biography. [Chicago] University of Chicago Press [1960, c1949] xiii, 364p. illus., ports. 22cm. (Chicago reprint series) 'References': p. [345]-353.
1. Pavlov, Ivan Petrovich, 1849-1936. I. Title. **BIP**

CUNY, Hilaire 152.32240924
Ivan Pavlov; the man and his theories. Tr. by Patrick Evans[1st Amer. ed.] New York, Eriksson [dist. Hill & Wang, 1965] 174p. illus., ports. 24cm. (Profile in sci) Bibl. [QP26.P35C83] 65-15778 5.00
1. Pavlov, Ivan Petrovich, 2. Conditioned response. I. Title.

CUNY, Hilaire 152.32240924
Ivan Pavlov; the man and his theories. Tr. [from French] by Patrick Evans. [1st Amer. ed.] New York, Fawcett [1966, c.1962] 174p. illus., ports. 24cm. (Fawcett premier bk., R308) Bibl. [QP26.P35C83] .60 pap.,
1. Pavlov, Ivan Petrovich, 1849-1936. 2. Conditioned response. I. Title.
Previously available from Paul Eriksson in 1965.

GRAY, Jeffrey Alan. 152.3'224'0924 B
Ivan Pavlov / Jeffrey A. Gray. New York : Viking Press, [1980] p. cm. (Modern masters) Includes index. Bibliography: p. [BF109.P38G72] 79-21591 ISBN 0-670-40457-8 : 10.00
1. Pavlov, Ivan Petrovich, 1849-1936. 2. Psychologists—Russia—Biography. 3. Classical conditioning. **BIP**

Pavlova, Anna, 1881-1931.

DANDRE, Victor. 792.8'2'0924 B
Anna Pavlova in art & life [by] V. Dandre. New York, B. Blom, 1972. 408 p. illus. 26 cm. Reprint of the 1932 ed. published under title: Anna Pavlova. [GV1785.P3D3 1972] 70-180025
1. Pavlova, Anna, 1881-1931. I. Title. **BIP**

KERENSKY, Oleg, 1930- 792.8'2'0924 B
Anna Pavlova. New York, Dutton, 1973. xvi, 160 p. illus. 22 cm. Bibliography: p. [154]-155. [GV1785.P3K47 1973] 73-79554 ISBN 0-525-17658-6 6.95
1. Pavlova, Anna, 1881-1931. 2. Ballet.

NIJINSKY, Pavlova, 792.8'092'4 B
Duncan : three lives in dance / edited by Paul Magriel. New York : Da Capo Press, 1977. 260 p. in various pagings : ill. ; 24 cm. (A Da Capo paperback) Reprint of 3 works: Nijinsky (1946), Pavlova (1947), and Isadora Duncan (1947), which were edited by P. D. Magriel and published by Holt, New York. Includes bibliographies. [GV1785.A1N54 1977b] 76-30403 ISBN 0-306-70845-0 : 22.50
1. Nijinsky, Waslaw, 1890-1950. 2. Pavlova, Anna, 1881-1931. 3. Duncan, Isadora, 1878-1927. 4. Dancers—Biography. I. Magriel, Paul David, 1906- II. Magriel, Paul David, 1906- ed. Nijinsky, 1977. III. Magriel, Paul David, 1906- ed. Pavlova. 1977. IV. Magriel, Paul David, 1906- ed. Isadora Duncan. 1977.

NIJINSKY, Pavlova, 792.8'092'4 B
Duncan : three lives in dance / edited by Paul Magriel. New York : Da Capo Press, 1977. 260 p. in various pagings : ill. ; 24 cm. (A Da Capo paperback) Reprint of 3 works: Nijinsky (1946), Pavlova (1947), and Isadora Duncan (1947), which were edited by P. D. Magriel and published by Holt, New York. Includes bibliographies. [GV1785.A1N54 1977b] 76-30403 ISBN 0-306-70845-0 : 22.50
1. Nijinsky, Waslaw, 1890-1950. 2. Pavlova, Anna, 1881-1931. 3. Duncan, Isadora, 1878-1927. 4. Dancers—Biography. I. Magriel, Paul David, 1906- II. Magriel, Paul David, 1906- ed. Nijinsky, 1977. III. Magriel, Paul David, 1906- ed. Pavlova. 1977. IV. Magriel, Paul David, 1906- ed. Isadora Duncan. 1977. **BIP**

OLIVEROFF, Andre. 792.8'092'4 B
Flight of the swan : a memory of Anna Pavlova / by Andre Oliveroff. New York : Da Capo Press, 1979 [c1932] xii, 258 p., [16] leaves of plates : ill. ; 23 cm. (Da Capo series in dance) "As told to John Gill." Reprint of the ed. published by Dutton, New York. [GV1785.P3O6 1979] 79-17906 19.50
1. Pavlova, Anna, 1881-1931. 2. Dancers—Russia—Biography. I. Gill, John, fl. 1932-1944. II. Title. **BIP**

PAVLOVA, a biography. v. 12
In collaboration with members of the Pavlova Commemoration Committee. New York, Macmillan, 1956. 144p. illus. 23cm.
1. Pavlova, Anna, 1881-1931. I. Franks, Arthur Henry, 1907- ed.

Pavlova, Anna, 1881-1931— Addresses, essays, lectures.

FRANKS, Arthur Henry, 1907- ed. 792.8'092'4 B
Pavlova, a biography / edited by A. H. Franks, in collaboration with members of the Pavlova Commemoration Committee. New York : Da Capo Press, 1979, c1956. 144 p., [16] leaves of plates : ill. ; 22 cm. (Da Capo series in dance) Reprint of the ed. published by Burke, London. Includes index. [GV1785.P3F7 1979] 79-1053 ISBN 0-306-79538-8 : 19.50
1. Pavlova, Anna, 1881-1931—Addresses, essays, lectures. 2. Dancers—Russia—Biography—Addresses, essays, lectures. I. Pavlova Commemoration Committee. II. Title.

Pavlova, Anna, 1881-1931—Juvenile literature.

ALMEDINGEN, Martha Edith, 927.933
1898-
The young Pavlova [by] E. M. Almedingen. Illustrated by Denise Brown. New York, Roy Publishers [1961, c1960] 138 p. illus. 21 cm. [GV1785.P3A82 1961] 60-14478
1. Pavlova, Anna, 1881-1931—Juvenile literature.

Paxton, Elisha Franklin, 1828-1863.

PAXTON, Elisha Franklin, 973.7'82
1828-1863.
The Civil War letters of General Frank "Bull" Paxton, CSA, a lieutenant of Lee & Jackson / edited by John Gallatin Paxton ; introduced by Harold B. Simpson. Hillsboro, Tex. : Hill Jr. College Press, 1978. viii, 102 p. : ill. ; 24 cm. Includes index. Bibliography: p. 100. [E581.5.S76P396] 78-68427 ISBN 0-912172-23-1 : 8.50
1. Paxton, Elisha Franklin, 1828-1863. 2. Confederate States of America. Army. Stonewall Brigade—Biography. 3. United States—History—Civil War, 1861-1865—Personal narratives—Confederate side. 4. United State—History—Civil War, 1861-1865—Regimental histories—Stonewall Brigade. 5. Generals—United States—Biography. I. Paxton, John Gallatin. II. Title.

Paxton, Harry T.

STENGEL, Casey [Charles 927.96357
Dillon Stengel]
Casey at the bat: the story of my life in baseball, as told to Harry T. Paxton. New York, Random [c.1961,1962] 254p. illus. 62-8465 3.95 bds.,
1. Paxton, Harry T. 2. Baseball—Hist. I. Title.

Paylin, Jolie, 1913-

PAYLIN, Jolie, 977.5'33'040924 B
1913-
Cutover country : Jolie's story / Jolie Paylin. 1st ed. Ames : Iowa State University Press, 1976. p. cm. [F587.M35P386] 76-10245 ISBN 0-8138-0015-3 : 6.95
1. Paylin, Jolie, 1913- 2. Marinette Co., Wis.—Biography. I. Title. **BIP**

Payne, Ben Iden, 1881-1976.

PAYNE, Ben Iden, 1881- 792'.092'4
1976.
A life in a wooden O : memoirs of the theatre / Ben Iden Payne. New Haven : Yale University Press, 1977. xvii, 204 p. : ill. ; 26 cm. Includes index. Bibliography: p. 197-199. [PN2287.P29A35 1977] 76-48988 ISBN 0-300-02064-3 : 12.50
1. Payne, Ben Iden, 1881-1976. 2. Shakespeare, William, 1564-1616—Dramatic production. 3. Theatrical producers and directors—United States—Biography. I. Title. **BIP**

Payne, Cril.

PAYNE, Cril. 364.12'092'4 B
Deep cover : an FBI agent infiltrates the radical underground / by Cril Payne. New York : Newsweek Books, c1979. p. cm. [HV7911.P38A33] 79-51632 ISBN 0-88225-274-7 : 12.95
1. Payne, Cril. 2. U.S. Federal Bureau of Investigation—Officials and employees—Biography. 3. Weather Underground Organization. 4. Radicalism—United States. I. Title.

Payne, John, fl. 1829-1859.

HARDING, Eric, 994.5'03'0924 B
1893-
Bogong Jack, the gentleman bushranger. [Melbourne] Yandoo [1967] 88 p. illus., maps. 19 cm. [CT2808.P3H3] 68-89634 1.95 Aust.
1. Payne, John, fl. 1829-1859. I. Title.

Payne, John Howard, 1791-1852.

HANSON, Willis 792'.028'0924 B
Tracy.
The early life of John Howard Payne, with contemporary letters heretofore unpublished, by Willis T. Hanson, Jr. New York, B. Blom, 1971. 226 p. illus. 22 cm. Reprint of the 1913 ed. Bibliography: p. 163-164. [PS2533.H25 1971] 76-91516
1. Payne, John Howard, 1791-1852. I. Title.

OVERMYER, Grace. 812'.3
America's first Hamlet / by Grace Overmyer. Westport, Conn. : Greenwood Press, 1975, c1957. p. cm. Reprint of the ed. published by New York University Press, New York. Includes index. Bibliography: p. [PS2533.O84 1975] 75-31964 ISBN 0-8371-8446-0 lib.bdg. : 21.75
1. Payne, John Howard, 1791-1852. I. Title. **BIP**

***Payton, Barbara**

*PAYTON, Barbara 927.91
I am not ashamed. Los Angeles. Holloway House [c.1963] 190p. illus. 18cm. (HI108) .75 pap.,
I. Title.

Payton, Everett Lee.

PAYTON, Everett J. 248'.86 B
I won't be crippled when I see Jesus / Everett J. Payton. Minneapolis, Minn. : Augsburg Pub. House, c1979. 158 p. ; 20 cm. [BR1725.P33P39] 79-50084 ISBN 0-8066-1716-0 pbk. : 3.95
1. Payton, Everett Lee. 2. Payton, Everett J. 3. Christian biography—United States. 4. Blind—Biography. 5. Hydrocephalus—Biography. 6. Cerebral palsy—United States—Biography. I. Title. **BIP**

Payton, Walter, 1954-

PAYTON, Walter, 796.33'2'0924 B
1954-
Sweetness / Walter Payton with Jerry B. Jenkins. Chicago : Contemporary Books, c1978. p. cm. [GV939.P39A35 1978] 78-7553 ISBN 0-8092-7544-9
1. Payton, Walter, 1954- 2. Chicago. Football club (National League) 3. Football players—United States—Biography. I. Jenkins, Jerry B., joint author. II. Title. **BIP**

Payton, Walter, 1954- —Juvenile literature.

CONRAD, Dick. 796.33'2'0924 B
Walter Payton, the running machine / by Dick Conrad. Chicago : Childrens Press, c1979. 42 p. : ill. ; 21 cm. (Sports stars) Highlights the career of running back Walter Payton who started playing professional ball in 1975 with the Chicago Bears. [GV939.P39C66] 92 78-11379 ISBN 0-516-04306-4 lib.bdg. : 6.00
1. Payton, Walter, 1954- —Juvenile literature. 2. Football players—United States—Biography. I. Title. II. Series.

SOUCHERAY, Joe. 796.33'2'0924 B
Walter Payton / by Joe Soucheray. Mankato, MN : Creative Education, [1979] p. cm. (Creative Education sports superstars) [GV939.P39S65] 79-9937 ISBN 0-87191-722-X : 5.95 ISBN 0-89812-160-4 pbk. : 2.75
1. Payton, Walter, 1954- —Juvenile literature. 2. Football players—United States—Biography—Juvenile literature. Publisher's Address : 123 South Broad St., Mankato, MN 56001 **BIP**

Penalosa, Diego Dionisio de, 1624-1687.

SCHOLES, France 978.9'02'0924 B
Vinton, 1897-
Troublous times in New Mexico, 1659-1670 / by France V. Scholes New York : AMS Press, [1977] p. cm. Reprint of the 1942 ed. published by the University of New Mexico Press, Albuquerque, which was issued as v. 11 of Publications in history of the Historical Society of New Mexico. Includes index. Bibliography: p. [F799.S36 1977] 75-41242 ISBN 0-404-14701-1 : 12.50
1. Penalosa, Diego Dionisio de, 1624-1687. 2. New Mexico—History—To 1848. 3. New Mexico—Governors—Biography. I. Title. II. Series: New Mexico. Historical Society. Publications in history ; v. 11. **BIP**

Peabody, Elizabeth Palmer, 1804-1894.

BAYLOR, Ruth M. 372.218
Elizabeth Palmer Peabody: kindergarten pioneer, by Ruth M. Baylor. Philadelphia, University of Pennsylvania Press [1965] 228 p. illus., facsims., ports. 22 cm. "List of books from Miss Peabody's library and bookshop": p. 175-176. Bibliography: p. 191-224. [LB695.P4B3] 64-24505
1. Peabody, Elizabeth Palmer, 1804-1894. I. Title.

BROOKS, Gladys. 920.7
Three wise virgins. [1st ed.] New York, Dutton, 1957. 244 p. illus. 21 cm. [HV28.D6B7] 57-12754
1. Dix, Dorothea Lynde, 1802-1887. 2. Peabody, Elizabeth Palmer, 1804-1894. 3. Sedgwick, Catharine Maria, 1789-1867. I. Title.

Peabody, Endicott, 1857-1944.

ASHBURN, Frank 373.1'2'0120924 B
Davis, 1903-
Peabody of Groton, a portrait [by] Frank D. Ashburn. [2d ed.] Cambridge [Mass.] Riverside Press, 1967. xiv, 446 p. illus., geneal. table, ports. 24 cm. [LD7501.G85G6172 1967] 68-942
1. Peabody, Endicott, 1857-1944. I. Title.

Peabody, George Foster, 1852-1938.

WARE, Louise, 1895- 923.373
George Foster Peabody, banker, philanthropist, publicist. Athens, University of Georgia Press [1951] x, 279 p. port. 23 cm. Bibliography: p. 257-272. [HG2463.P4W3] 51-11005
1. Peabody, George Foster, 1852-1938. I. Title.

Peabody, George, 1795-1869.

HIDY, Muriel E. 361.7'40924 B
George Peabody, merchant and financier : 1829-1854 / Muriel Emmie Hidy ; with a new pref. New York : Arno Press, 1978 i.e. 1979. xi, 398 p. ; 24 cm. (International finance) Originally presented as the author's thesis, Radcliffe, 1939. Bibliography: p 391 398. [HF3023.P38H52 1979] 78-3926 ISBN 0-405-11224-6 : 27.00
1. Peabody, George, 1795-1869. 2. Merchants—United States—Biography. 3. Capitalists and financiers—United States—Biography. I. Title. II. Series: International finance (New York, 1979-) **BIP**

PARKER, Franklin, 361.7'4'0924 B
1921-
George Peabody; a biography. Foreword by Merle Curti. Nashville, Vanderbilt University Press, 1971. x, 233 p. port. 25 cm. Bibliography: p. 211-219. [HV28.P4P29 1971] 79-157741 ISBN 0-8265-1170-8 8.95
1. Peabody, George, 1795-1869.

Peabody, Joseph, 1757-1844.

ENDICOTT, William 929'.2'0973
Crowninshield, 1860-1936.
Captain Joseph Peabody; East India merchant of Salem (1757-1844) A record of his ships and of his family, compiled by William Crowninshield Endicott. Edited and completed, with a sketch of Joseph Peabody's life, by Walter Muir Whitehill. Salem [Mass.] Peabody Museum, 1962. xv, 358 p. illus., ports. 26 cm. Bibliographical footnotes. [CS71.P35 1962] 63-5009
1. Peabody, Joseph, 1757-1844. 2. Peabody family. I. Salem, Mass. — Comm. II. Whitehill, Walter Muir, 1905- ed. III. Title.

Peace.

SUTTNER, Bertha Felicie 327'.172
Sophie (Kinsky) Freifrau von, 1843-1914.
Memoirs of Bertha von Suttner; the records of an eventful life. With a new introd. for the Garland ed. by Irwin Abrams. New York, Garland Pub., 1972 [c1910] 2 v. port. 22 cm. (The Garland library of war and peace) [JX1962.S8A313 1972] 75-147458 ISBN 0-8240-0317-9
1. Peace. I. Title. II. Series.

Peace—Biography.

LIEBERMAN, Mark, 327'.172'0922 B
1942-
The pacifists; soldiers without guns. New York, Praeger [1972] 127 p. illus. 22 cm. Bibliography: p. 123. [JX1962.A2L53] 74-189912 5.95
1. Peace—Biography. I. Title.

Peace—Biography—Juvenile literature.

FOX, Mary Virginia. 920'.02
Pacifists; adventures in courage. Chicago, Reilly & Lee Books [1971] 160 p. ports. 24 cm. Contents.Contents.—George Fox.—William Penn.—Albert Schweitzer.—Norman Thomas.—Mahatma Gandhi.—Jane Addams.—Jeannette Rankin.—Albert Luthuli.—Abraham Johannes Muste.—Dag Hammarskjold.—Bibliography (p. [159]-160) [JX1962.A2F65] 77-143872
1. Peace—Biography—Juvenile literature. I. Title.

WINTTERLE, John. 920.02
Portraits of Nobel laureates in peace [by] John Wintterle and Richard S. Cramer. London, New York, Abelard Schuman [1971] x, 246 p. ports. 22 cm. Bibliography: p. 240-241. Brief biographies of the men and women whose achivements on behalf of world peace earned them the Nobel peace prize. [JX1962.A2W55] 920 79-105263 ISBN 0-200-71678-6 £1.75 ($5.95 U.S.)
1. Peace—Biography Juvenile literature. 2. Nobel prizes—Juvenile literature. I. Cramer, Richard S., joint author. II. Title.

Peace, Charles Frederick, 1832-1879.

WARD, George David 923.4142
Allen, 1923-
The shortest route to paradise; the story of the master criminal Charles peace. [New York] Horizon Press [1964, c1963] 176 p. illus., ports. 23 cm. First published in London in 1963 under title: King of the lags. [HV6248.P37W3 1964] 64-15189
1. Peace, Charles Frederick, 1832-1879. I. Title.

Peace, Judy Boppell.

PEACE, Judy Boppell. 968.06
The boy child is dying : a South African experience / Judy Boppell Peace. Downers Grove, Ill. : InterVarsity Press, c1978. 91 p. ; 18 cm. True stories. [DT763.P39] 78-4445 ISBN 0-87784-635-9 : 2.25
1. Peace, Judy Boppell. 2. South Africa—Race relations—Anecdotes, facetiae, satire, etc. 3. Americans in South Africa—Biography. I. Title.

Peace officers—The West.

BREIHAN, Carl W 1915- v. 12
Great lawmen of the West [by] Carl W. Breihan. New york, Bonanza Books [c1963] 190 p. 22 cm. 68-81501
1. Peace officers—The West. 2. The West—Biog. 3. Crime and criminals—The West. I. Title.

PENFIELD, Thomas, 1903- 923.573
Western sheriffs and marshals. Illustrated by Robert Glaubke. New York, Grosset & Dunlap [1955] 145 p. illus. 29 cm. (Illustrated true books) Includes bibliography. [F591.P4] 55-29829
1. Peace officers—The West. 2. Crime and criminals—The West. 3. The West—Biography. I. Title.

Peace officers — The West — Juvenile literature.

JOHNSON, Dorothy M. 920
Famous lawmen of the Old West. New York, Dodd, Mead [1963] 151 p. illus. 22 cm. (Famous biographies for young people) Includes bibliography. [F591.J6] 63-15624
1. Peace officers — The West — Juvenile literature. 2. The West — Biog. — Juvenile literature. 3. Crime and criminals — The West — Juvenile literature. I. Title.

Peacock, Thomas Love, 1785-1866.

CAMPBELL, Olwen Ward. 928.2
Thomas Love Peacock. New York, Roy [1953] 104 p. 19 cm. (The English novelists) [[PR5163]] 53-10348
1. Peacock, Thomas Love, 1785-1866.

CAMPBELL, Olwen (Ward) 823'.7 B
Thomas Love Peacock, by Olwen W. Campbell. Freeport, N.Y., Books for Libraries Press [1971, c1953] 104 p. 23 cm. Bibliography: p. 102. [PR5163.C3 1971] 73-157327 ISBN 0-8369-5787-3
1. Peacock, Thomas Love, 1785-1866.

PRIESTLEY, John Boynton, 823'.7 B 1894-
Thomas Love Peacock, by J. B. Priestley. New York, Macmillan, 1927. St. Clair Shores, Mich., Scholarly Press, 1970. viii, 215 p. 22 cm. (English men of letters) [PR5163.P7 1970] 74-131808 ISBN 0-403-00695-3
1. Peacock, Thomas Love, 1785-1866.

PRIESTLEY, John Boynton, 1894- 828.709 (B)
Thomas Love Peacock, by J.B. Priestley. [New ed.] introduced by J.I.M. Stewart. London, Melbourne [etc.] Macmillan: New York, St. Martin's P., 1966. xxviii,215 p. 19 1/2 cm. 25/- [PR5163.P7 1966] 67-10203
1. Peacock, Thomas Love 1785-1866. I. Title.

VAN DOREN, Carl Clinton, 1885-1950. 828.7
The life of Thomas Love Peacock, by Carl Van Doren. New York, Russell & Russell, 1966. xi, 298 p. illus., ports. 23 cm. Reprint of work first published in 1911. Bibliography: p. 283-289. Bibliographical footnotes. [PR5163.V3 1966] 65-18838
1. Peacock, Thomas Love, 1785-1866. I. Title. BIP

Peake, Mervyn Laurence, 1911-1968— Biography.

WATNEY, John Basil, 1915- 741'.092'4 B
Mervyn Peake / John Watney. New York : St. Martin's Press, 1976. 255 p. : ill. ; 25 cm. Includes index. Bibliography: p. 246-249. [PR6031.E183Z95 1976] 76-17422 10.95
1. Peake, Mervyn Laurence, 1911-1968—Biography. 2. Authors, English—20th century—Biography. 3. Painters—England—Biography. BIP

Peale, Charles Willson, 1741-1827.

BRIGGS, Berta N. 927.5
Charles Willson Peale, artist & patriot. New York, McGraw-Hill [1952] 262 p. illus. 21 cm. (They made America) [ND237.P27B7] 52-9763
1. Peale, Charles Willson, 1741-1827.

SELLERS, Charles Coleman, 1903- 759.13 B
Charles Willson Peale. New York, Scribner [1969] xiv, 510 p. illus., facsims. (music), ports. 29 cm. Based on the author's Charles Willson Peale, published in 1947 as v. 23, pts. 1-2 of the Memoirs of the American Philosophical Society. Includes bibliographical references. [ND237.P27S44] 68-17345 20.00
1. Peale, Charles Willson, 1741-1827.

Peale, Charles Willson, 1741-1827— Juvenile—literature.

PEARE, Catherine Owens 920
Painter of patriots, Charles Willson Peale. New York, Holt [c.1964] 144p. illus. 21cm. 64-18255 3.25; 3.07 bds., lib. ed.,
1. Peale, Charles Willson, 1741-1827—Juvenile—literature. I. Title.

PLATE, Robert 973.3'0924(B)
Charles Willson Peale; son of liberty, father of art and science. New York, McKay, 1967. 276p. illus., ports. 21cm. Bibl. [E207.P4P55] 67-16505 5.50
1. Peale, Charles Willson, 1741-1827—Juvenile literature. I. Title.

PLATE, Robert. 973.3'0924 (B)
Charles Wilson Peale: son of liberty, father of art and science. New York, McKay Co., 1967. 276 p. illus., ports. 21 cm. Bibliography: p. 265-269. [E207.P4P55] 67-16505
1. Peale, Charles Wilson,1741-1827—Juvenile literature. I. Title.

Peale, Norman Vincent, 1898-

GORDON, Arthur. 287'.1'0924 B
One man's way; the story and message of Norman Vincent Peale, a biography. Rev. and enl. ed. of Minister to millions. Englewood Cliffs, N.J., Prentice-Hall [1972] 324 p. illus. 21 cm. Published in 1958 under title: Norman Vincent Peale; minister to millions. [BX9543.P4G6 1972] 72-3311 ISBN 0-13-636084-X 5.95
1. Peale, Norman Vincent, 1898- I. Title.

WESTPHAL, Clarence 922.573
Norman Vincent Peale, Christian crusader, a biography. Minneapolis, Denison [c.1964] 141p. 22cm. (Men of achievement ser.) [BX9543.P4W4] 64-7703 3.00
1. Peale, Norman Vincent, 1898- I. Title.

WESTPHAL, Clarence. 922.573
Norman Vincent Peale, Christian crusador, a biography. Minneapolis, Denison [1964] 141 p. 22 cm. (Men of achievement series) [BX9543.P4W4] 64-7703
1. Peale, Norman Vincent, 1898- I. Title.

Pearce, Bryan.

JONES, Ruth. 759.2 B
The path of the son : a biography of Bryan Pearce / by Ruth Jones. Sheviock : Sheviock Gallery Publications, 1976. 104 p., [20] p. of plates : ill. (some col.), ports. ; 22 cm. [N6797.P34J65] 76-380640 ISBN 0-9504904-0-7 : £3.95
1. Pearce, Bryan. 2. Artists, Mentally handicapped—England—Cornwall—Biography. I. Title.

Pearl, Joise (Reed)

SCHULMERICH, Alma 920.7
Josie Pearl. Salt Lake City, Deseret [c.] 1963. 273p. 24cm. 63-3537 2.95
1. Pearl, Joise (Reed) I. Title. BIP

Pearl, Ralph,

*PEARL, Ralph, 1914- 070.92'4 [B]
Las Vegas is my beat. With a foreword by Jack Benny. New York, Bantam Books [1974, c1973] 277 p. 18 cm. [PN4874] 1.50 (pbk.)
I. Title. BIP

Pearls.

ROSENTHAL, Leonard. 623.844
The pearl hunter, an autobiography; illustrated by Rachel Rosenthal, translated from the French by Herma Briffault. New York, H. Schuman [1952] 214 p. illus. 22 cm. "Revised edition of Memoares d'un chercheur de peries, published in Paris in 1919." [HD9747.A2R62] 52-9197
1. Pearls. 2. Jewelry trade. I. Title.

Pearse, Joseph, 1837-1911.

MOSS, Charles Frederick Arrowsmith. 266'.023'0924 B
A pioneer in Madagascar, Joseph Pearse of the L.M.S., by C. F. A. Moss. New York, Negro Universities Press [1969] xvi, 261 p. illus., map, ports. 23 cm. Reprint of the 1913 ed. [BV3625.M22P4 1969] 70-98738
1. Pearse, Joseph, 1837-1911. 2. Missions—Madagascar. I. Title.

Pearse, Padraic, 1879-1916.

EDWARDS, Ruth Dudley. 941.5082'1'0924 B
Patrick Pearse : the triumph of failure / by Ruth Dudley Edwards. New York : Taplinger Pub. Co., 1978, c1977. xv, 384 p. ; 22 cm. Includes index. Bibliography: p. [362]-372. [DA965.P4E28 1978] 78-58294 ISBN 0-8008-6267-8 : 14.95
1. Pearse, Padraic, 1879-1916. 2. Revolutionists—Ireland—Biography. 3. Ireland—History—Sinn Fein Rebellion, 1916. BIP

EDWARDS, Ruth Dudley. 941.5082'1'0924 B
Patrick Pearse : the triumph of failure / by Ruth Dudley Edwards. London : Gollancz, 1977. xv, 384 p., [4] leaves of plates : ill. ; 23 cm. Includes index. Bibliography: p. [362]-374. [DA965.P4E28] 77-367608 ISBN 0-575-02153-5 : 16.00
1. Pearse, Padraic, 1879-1916. 2. Revolutionists—Ireland—Biography. 3. Ireland—History—Sinn Fein Rebellion, 1916.
Distributed by Humanities Press

Pearson, Drew, 1897-

BEALLE, Morris Allison, 1891- 070.924
All America louse, a candid biography of Drew A. Pearson, by Morris A. Bealle. Washington, Columbia Pub. Co. [1965?] 89 p. illus. 22 cm. [PN4874.P38B4] 65-9451
1. Pearson, Drew, 1897- I. Title.

KLUCKHOHN, Frank L. 070.924
The Drew Pearson story, by Frank Kluckhohn and Jay Franklin. Chicago, C. Hallberg [1967] 181 p. 21 cm. [PN4874.P38K55] 66-30600
1. Pearson, Drew, 1897- I. Carter, John Franklin, 1897- joint author. II. Title.

KLURFELD, Herman. 070'.924
Behind the lines: the world of Drew Pearson. Englewood Cliffs, N.J., Prentice-Hall [1968] 281 p. illus., ports. 24 cm. [PN4874.P38K57] 68-28377 6.95
1. Pearson, Drew, 1897- I. Title.

PEARSON, Drew, 1897-1969. 070.4'092'4
Diaries, 1949-1959. Edited by Tyler Abell. [1st ed.] New York, Holt, Rinehart and Winston [1974] xiv, 592 p. 24 cm. [PN4874.P38A3 1974] 72-78142 ISBN 0-03-001426-3 15.00
1. Pearson, Drew, 1897-1969. 2. United States—Politics and government—1945-1953. 3. United States—Politics and government—1953-1961. I. Abell, Tyler, ed.

PILAT, Oliver Ramsay, 1903- 070'.92'4 B
Drew Pearson: an unauthorized biography, by Oliver Pilat. New York, Harper's Magazine Press [1973] 332 p. illus. 25 cm. [PN4874.P38P5] 72-79719 ISBN 0-06-126499-7 10.00
1. Pearson, Drew, 1897-1969.

Pearson, Haydn Sanborn.

PEARSON, Haydn Sanborn. 818.5
That darned minister's son. [1st ed.] Garden City, N. Y., Doubleday, 1950. xix, 262 p. 21 cm. Autobiographical. [BV4013.P4] 50-6636
I. Title.

Pearson, Irving Frederick,

PEARSON, Irving Frederick, 1897- 370'.924 B
Three score ten and more; an autobiography, by Irving F. Pearson. Chicago, Adams Press [1971] viii, 244 p. illus., ports. 23 cm. [LB885.P416] 76-168761
I. Title.

Pearson, Lester B.

BEAL, John Robinson, 1906- 923.271
Pearson of Canada. [1st ed.] New York, Duell, Sloan and Pearce [1964] xi, 210 p. ports. 22 cm. [F1034.P37B4] 64-13790
1. Pearson, Lester B. I. Title.

PEARSON, Lester B. 971.06'43'0924 B
Mike; the memoirs of the Right Honourable Lester B. Pearson. New York, Quadrangle Books [1972- v. illus. 24 cm. Half title and on spine: Memoirs. Contents.Contents.—v. 1. 1897-1948. [F1034.3.P4A35] 72-90360 12.50 (v. 1)
1. Canada—Politics and government—20th century. 2. Canada—Foreign relations. I. Title. BIP

STURSBERG, Peter. 971.064'3'0924 B
Lester Pearson and the dream of unity / Peter Stursberg. 1st ed. Toronto : Doubleday Canada ; Garden City, N.Y. : Doubleday, 1978. xv, 456 p., [8] leaves of plates : ports. ; 24 cm. Includes index. [F1034.3.P4S86] 77-16951 ISBN 0-385-13478-9 : 17.95
1. Pearson, Lester B. 2. Canada—Politics and government—1945- 3. Federal government—Canada. 4. Quebec (Province)—History—Autonomy and independence movements. 5. Prime ministers—Canada—Biography. I. Title. BIP

THORDARSON, Bruce. 971.064'3'0924 B
Lester Pearson : diploma and politician / Bruce Thordarson. Toronto : Oxford University Press, 1974. ix, 245 p. : ill. ; 20 cm. (Canadian lives) Includes index. Bibliography: p. [238]-241. [F1034.3.P4T48] 75-319338 ISBN 0-19-540225-1
1. Pearson, Lester B.

Peary, Robert Edwin, 1856-1920.

ANGELL, Pauline Knickerbocker, 1886- 923.973
To the top of the world; the story of Peary and Henson. Chicago, Rand McNally [1964] 288 p. illus., ports., maps. 22 cm. [G635.P4A65] 63-7431
1. Peary, Robert Edwin, 1856-1920. 2. Henson, Matthew Alexander, 1866-1955. 3. North Pole. I. Title.

CLARK, Electa. 923.973
Robert Peary, boy of the North;illustrated by Bernard Barton. [1st ed.] Indianapolis, Bobbs-Merrill [1953] 192p. illus. 21cm. (The Childhood of famous Americans series) [G635.P4C5] 53-8878
1. Peary, Robert Edwin, 1856-1920. I. Title.

HENSON, Matthew Alexander, 1866-1955. 919.8 B
A Black explorer at the North Pole; an autobiographical report by the Negro who conquered the top of the world with Admiral Robert E. Peary. Foreword by Robert E. Peary. Introd. by Booker T. Washington. New York, Walker [1969] xiv, 190 p. illus., map, ports. 21 cm. Originally published in 1912 under title: A Negro explorer at the North Pole. [G670 1909.H4A33] 69-14362 4.50
1. Peary, Robert Edwin, 1856-1920. 2. Arctic regions. 3. North Pole. I. Title.

STAFFORD, Marie (Peary) 1893- 923.973
Discoverer of the North Pole; the story of Robert E. Peary. Illustrated by Walter Buehr. New York, Morrow, 1950. 220 p. illus. 22 cm. [G635.P4S7] 59-8186
1. Peary, Robert Edwin, 1856-1920. I. Title.

WEEMS, John Edward. 919.8'04'0924 B
Peary, the explorer and the man, based on his personal papers. Boston, Houghton Mifflin, 1967. ix, 362 p. map (on lining paper) plates (incl. facsim., ports.) 23 cm. Includes bibliographical references. [G635.P4W4] 67-10925
1. Peary, Robert Edwin, 1856-1920. I. Title.

Peary, Robert Edwin, 1856-1920 — Juvenile literature.

BERRY, Erick, 1892- 93 (J)
Robert E. Peary, North Pole conqueror, by Erick Berry [pseud.] Illustrated by Frederick T. Chapman. Champaign, Ill., Garrard Pub. Co. [1963] 80 p. illus. 23 cm. (A Discovery book) [G635.P4B4] 63-7113
1. Peary, Robert Edwin, 1856-1920— Juvenile literature.

BEST, Allena (Champlin) 1892- 92
Robert E. Peary, North Pole conqueror, by Erick Berry [pseud.] Illustrated by Frederick T. Chapman. Champaign, Ill., Garrard Pub. Co. [1963] 80 p. illus. 23 cm. (A Discovery book) Full name: Evangel Allena (Champlin) Best. [G635.P4B4] 63-7113
1. Peary, Robert Edwin, 1856-1920 — Juvenile literature. I. Title.

EDUCATIONAL 919.8'04'0922 B
Research Council of America. Social Science Staff.
Explorers and discoverers, Peary and Henson / prepared by the Social Science Staff of the Educational Research Council of America. Learner-verified ed. 2. Boston : Allyn and Bacon, [1974] 52 p. : col. ill. ; 20 x 21 cm. (Concepts and inquiry, the ERC social science program) An easy-to-read account of the arctic expedition of Robert Peary and Matthew Henson that led them to the North Pole. [G635.P4E32 1974] 920 73-78348 pbk. : 1.76
1. Peary, Robert Edwin, 1856-1920— Juvenile literature. 2. Henson, Matthew Alexander, 1866-1955—Juvenile literature. 3. Arctic regions—Juvenile literature. I. Title. II. Series: Concepts and inquiry, the Educational Research Council social science program.

EDUCATIONAL 919.8'04'0924
Research Council of America. Social Science Staff.
Explorers and discoverers: Robert E. Peary. Boston, Allyn and Bacon [1970] 52 p. col. illus., col. maps. 21 cm. (Concepts and inquiry: the ERC social science program) An easy-to-read account of the Arctic expedition of Robert Peary, the first man to reach the North Pole. [G635.P4E3] 92 74-97104
1. Peary, Robert Edwin, 1856-1920— Juvenile literature. 2. North Pole—Juvenile literature. I. Title. II. Series: Concepts and inquiry: the Educational Research Council social science program

LISKER, Tom, 1928- 919.8'040924 B
First to the top of the world : Admiral Peary at the North Pole / by Tom Lisker ; illustrated by Gloria Priam. New York : C.P.I. ; Morristown, N.J. : distributors, Silver Burdett Co., c1978. 48 p. : col. ill. ; 24 cm. A biography of the man whose dream of being the first man to set foot on the North Pole became reality. [G635.P4L5] 92 78-14924 ISBN 0-89547-047-0 : 5.58
1. Peary, Robert Edwin, 1856-1920 — Juvenile literature. 2. North Pole—Juvenile literature. 3. Explorers—United States— Biography—Juvenile literature. I. Priam, Gloria. II. Title.
Distributed by Silver Burdell, Morristown, NJ 07960 **BIP**

Pease, Lucadia Christiana Niles.

LUCADIA Pease & the Governor : letters, 1850-1857 / edited by Katherine Hart & Elizabeth Kemp. [Austin, Tex.] : Encino Press for the Friends of the Austin Public Library, c1974. xii, 350 p., [1] leaf of plates : ill. ; 24 cm. (A Waterloo book ; no. 5) [F391.P35L8] 75-306450 12.50 976.4'05'0924 B
1. Pease, Lucadia Christiana Niles. 2. Pease, Elisha Marshall. I. Pease, Lucadia Christiana Niles. II. Pease, Elisha Marshall, 1812-1883. III. Hart, Katherine. IV. Kemp, Elizabeth. V. Title. VI. Series.

Pease, Mae (Townsend)

PEASE, Mae (Townsend) 1881- 920
Reminiscences from lamplight to satellite. Philadelphia, Dorrance [1960] 136p. illus. 20cm. [CT275.P512A3] 60-53217
I. Title.

Pechey-Phipson, Edith, 1845-1908.

LUTZKER, Edythe. 610'.92'4 B
Edith Pechey-Phipson, M.D.; the story of England's foremost pioneering woman doctor. [1st ed.] New York, Exposition Press [1973] xviii, 259 p. illus. 21 cm. (An Exposition-banner book) Bibliography: p. 249-252. [R489.P43L88] 72-90066 ISBN 0-682-47597-1 7.50
1. Pechey-Phipson, Edith, 1845-1908. 2. Women as physicians. **BIP**

Peck, Clara Temple (Boardman)

PECK, Clara Temple 920.7
(Boardman) 1885-1950.
Letters and verses of Clara Boardman Peck, edited by her husband. New York, Dodd, Mead, 1951. 432 p. ports. 23 cm. [PS3531.F2613 1951] 51-3894
I. Title.

Peck, Gregory, 1916-

THOMAS, Tony, 791.43'028'0924 B
1927-
Gregory Peck / by Tony Thomas. New York : Pyramid Publications, 1977. 160 p. : ill. ; 20 cm. (A Pyramid illustrated history of the movies) Includes index. Filmography: p. 145-153. [PN2287.P35T5] 76-57802 ISBN 0-515 04239-0 pbk. : 1.75
1. Peck, Gregory, 1916- 2. Moving-picture actors and actresses—United States— Biography. **BIP**

Peck, William Jay, 1853-1920.

MOORE, Helen (Peck) 1899- 922.573
William Jay Peck, a shepherd's heart. Narberth, Pa., Livingston Pub. Co., 1957. 84p. illus. 24cm. [BX7260.P46M6] 57-14828
1. Peck, William Jay, 1853-1920. I. Title.

Peckham, John. Abp. of Canterbury. d. 1292.

DOUIE, Decima Langworthy, 922.342
1901-
Archbishop Pecham. Oxford, Clarendon Press, 1952. 362p. 23cm. [BR754.P4D67] 53-546
1. Peckham, John. Abp. of Canterbury. d. 1292. I. Title.

Pecznick, Ira.

HOFFMAN, Paul, 364.1'06'0749
1934-
To drop a dime / by Paul Hoffman and Ira Pecznick. New York : Putnam, c1976. 320 p., [4] leaves of plates : ill. ; 22 cm. [HV6248.P374H63 1976] 76-9825 8.95
1. Pecznick, Ira. 2. Informers—New Jersey. 3. Organized crime—New Jersey. I. Pecznick, Ira, joint author. II. Title. **BIP**

Pediatricians—Correspondence, reminiscences, etc.

GOLDBLOOM, Alton, 1890- 926.1
Small patients; the autobiography of a children's doctor. [1st ed.] Philadelphia, Lippincott [1959] 316 p. 22 cm. [RJ43.G6A3] 59-6431
1. Pediatricians—Correspondence, reminiscences, etc. I. Title.

Pedro de Alcantara, Saint, 1499-1562.

ROBERTO, Brother, 1927- 922.246
Peter laughed at pain; a story of St. Peter of Alcantara. Illus. by William Pero. Notre Dame, Ind., Dujarie Press1[1956] 96p. illus. 24cm. [BX4700.P362R6] 56-42844
1. Pedro de Alcantara, Saint, 1499-1562. I. Title.

Pedro II, Emperor of Brazil, 1825-1891.

WILLIAMS, Mary 981.040924 B
Wilhelmine, 1878-1944.
Dom Pedro, the Magnanimous, second Emperor of Brazil. New York, Octagon Books, 1966 [c1937] xi, 414 p. illus., fold. map, ports. 24 cm. Bibliography: p. [386]-403. [F2536.P388 1966] 66-18031
1. Pedro II, Emperor of Brazil, 1825-1891. 2. Brazil—History—1822-1889. I. Title.

Peekskill, N. Y.— Biog.

SMITH, Chester Allen, 920.0747
1884-
Who's who in Peekskill. [1st ed.] Peekskill, N. Y., Friendly Town Association, 1954[c1955] 289p. illus. 24cm. [F129.P37S5] 54-11946
1. Peekskill, N. Y.— Biog. I. Title.

Peel, John Hugh Brignall, 1913-

PEEL, John Hugh 914.1'04'857
Brignall, 1913-
Along the green roads of Britain / [by] J. H. B. Peel. London : Cassell, 1976. [10], 214 p., [16] p. of plates : ill., maps ; 23 cm. Includes index. [DA632.P43] 77-353738 ISBN 0-304-29564-7 : £4.50
1. Peel, John Hugh Brignall, 1913- 2. Great Britain—Description and travel— 1971- I. Title.

Peel, Robert, Sir, bart., 1788-1850.

GASH, Norman 923.242
Mr. Secretary Peel; the life of Sir Robert Peel to 1830. Cambridge, Mass., Harvard Univ. Press [c.]1961. xiv, 693p. ports. Bibl. 61-9686 12.50
1. Peel, Robert, bart., Sir 1788-1850. I. Title.

GASH, Norman. 941.081'092'4 B
Peel / Norman Gash. London ; New York : Longman, 1976. 319 p., [8] leaves of plates : ill. ; 23 cm. "A condensed version of Mr. Secretary Peel (1961) and Sir Robert Peel (1972)." Includes index. Bibliography: p. 313-314. [DA536.P3G315] 75-25695 ISBN 0-582-48083-3 17.50
1. Peel, Robert, Sir, bart., 1788-1850.

GASH, Norman. 942.081'092'4
Sir Robert Peel; the life of Sir Robert Peel after 1830. Totowa, N.J., Rowman and Littlefield [1972] xx, 743 p. illus. 23 cm. Bibliography: p. 723-727. [DA536.P3G32 1972b] 72-171399 ISBN 0-87471-132-0 22.50
1. Peel, Robert, Sir, bart., 1788-1850. **BIP**

RAMSAY, Anna 942.07'5'0924 B
Augusta Whittall, 1894-
Sir Robert Peel. Freeport, N.Y., Books for Libraries Press [1969] viii, 385 p. port. 23 cm. (Select bibliographies reprint series) Reprint of the 1928 ed. Bibliography: p. 378-380. [DA536.P3R3 1969] 72-95076
1. Peel, Robert, Sir, bart., 1788-1850.

RAMSAY, Anna 942.07'5'0924 B
Augusta Whittall, 1894-
Sir Robert Peel. New York, Barnes & Noble [1971] xi, 383 p. port. 23 cm. "First published 1928." Original ed. issued in series: Makers of the nineteenth century. [DA536.P3R3 1971] 75-31611 ISBN 0-389-04182-3
1. Peel, Robert, Sir, bart., 1788-1850. **BIP**

THURSFIELD, James 942.07'5'0924 B
Richard, Sir, 1840-1923.
Peel. Freeport, N.Y., Books for Libraries Press [1972] vi, 246 p. 23 cm. Reprint of the 1891 ed., issued in series: Twelve English statesmen. [DA536.P3T5 1972] 77-39213 ISBN 0-8369-6815-8
1. Peel, Robert, Sir, bart., 1788-1850. I. Series: Twelve English statesmen. **BIP**

Peele, George,

PEELE, George, 1558?-1597? 928.2
The life and works of George Peele. Charles Tyler Prouty, general editor. [New Haven, Yale University Press, 1952-] v. illus. 24 cm. Contents.-- v.1. The life and minor works of George Peele, by D. H. Horne. [PR2731.P76] 52-4943
I. Title.

Peele, George, 1558?-1597?

HORNE, David Hamilton, v. 12
1912-
The life and minor workks of Goerge Peele. New Haven, Yale University Press [1963, c1952] 305 p. illus. 24 cm. (The Life and works of George Peele, v.1) Includes bibliography. 64-72030
1. Peele, George, 1558?-1597? I. Peele, George, 1558?-1597? II. Title.

HORNE, David Hamilton, 928.2
1912-
The life and minor works of George Peele. New Haven, Yale University Press, 1952. xvii, 305 p. illus. 24 cm. (The Life and works of George Peele, v. 1) Bibliography: p. 283-294. [PR2731.P76 vol. 1] 52-9265
1. Peele, George, 1558?-1597? I. Title. **BIP**

PEELE, George, 1558?-1597? 928.2
The life and works of George Peele. Charles Tyler Prouty, general editor. [New Haven, Yale University Press, 1952-] v. illus. 24 cm. Contents.-- v.1. The life and minor works of George Peele, by D. H. Horne. [PR2731.P76] 52-4943
I. Title.

Peele, George, 1558?-1597?— Biography.

HORNE, David Hamilton, 822'.3 B
1912-
The life and minor works of George Peele / by David H. Horne. Westport, Conn. : Greenwood Press, 1978, c1952. xvii, 305 p., [1] leaf of plates : ill. ; 24 cm. Reprint of the ed. published by Yale University Press, which was issued as v. 1 of The Life and works of George Peele. Includes index. Bibliography: p. 283-294. [PR2736.H6 1978] 78-6649 ISBN 0-8371-9071-1 lib.bdg. : 22.00
1. Peele, George, 1558?-1597?—Biography. 2. Dramatists, English—Early modern, 1500-1700—Biography. I. Peele, George, 1558?-1597? Selected works. 1978. II. Title.

Peerce, Jan, 1904-

PEERCE, Jan, 1904- 782.1'092'4 B
The bluebird of happiness : the memoirs of Jan Peerce / by Alan Levy. 1st ed. New York : Harper & Row, c1976. p. cm. Includes index. [ML420.P38A3] 75-25055 ISBN 0-06-013311-2 : 10.95
1. Peerce, Jan, 1904- 2. Singers—United States— Biography. I. Levy, Alan, joint author. II. Title. **BIP**

Peerman, Frank.

PEERMAN, Frank. 248'.86 B
See you in the morning / Frank Peerman. Nashville : Broadman Press, c1976. 94 p. ; 20 cm. [BJ1487 P4] 76 5296 ISBN 0-8054-5237-0 : 3.50
1. Peerman, Frank. 2. Grief. 3. Baptists— Biography. I. Title. **BIP**

Pefley, Peter Jackson, 1830-1906.

PHIPPS, Maude (Pefley) 923.273
Peter Jackson Pefley, my father, written by his loving daughter, Maude Pefley Phipps in collaboration with Edwin Pefley Phipps and Paul Pefley Phipps, his grandsons. [n. p., 1952, c1953] 51p. illus. 22cm. [CT275.P523P4] 53-17558
1. Pefley, Peter Jackson, 1830-1906. I. Title.

Pegler, Westbrook, 1894-

PILAT, Oliver Ramsay, 1903- 920.5
Pegler, angry man of the press. Boston, Beacon [c.1963] 288p. illus. 22cm. Bibl. 63-11391 5.00 bds.,
1. Pegler, Westbrook, 1894- I. Title. **BIP**

PILAT, Oliver Ramsay, 070.4'092'4
1903-
Pegler, angry man of the press, by Oliver Pilat. Westport, Conn., Greenwood Press [1973, c1963] vii, 288 p. port. 22 cm. Reprint of the ed. published by Beacon

Press, Boston. Bibliography: p. 281-282. [PN4874.P43P5 1973] 73-3236 ISBN 0-8371-6838-4 12.50
1. Pegler, Westbrook, 1894- I. Title.

Peguy, Charles Pierre, 1873-1914.

DRU, Alexander. 928.4
Peguy. New York, Harper [1957, c1956] 121p. 22cm. [PQ2631] 56-12064
1. Peguy, Charles Pierre, 1873-1914. I. Title.

SERVAIS, Yvonne. 928.4
Charles Peguy; the pursuit of salvation. Westminster, Md., Newman Press, 1953. 401p. 22cm. Bibliography: p. 391-397. [PQ2631] 53-12310
1. Peguy, Charles Pierre, 1873-1914. I. Title.

Peirce, Charles Santiago Sanders, 1839-1914.

GOUDGE, Thomas Anderson, 1910- v. 12
The thought of C. S. Peirce. [Toronto] University of Toronto Press, 1950. xii, 360 p. diagr., facsim. 23 cm. A51
1. Peirce, Charles Santiago Sanders, 1839-1914. I. Title. BIP

KNIGHT, Thomas Stanley, 1921- 191
Charles Peirce [by] Thomas S. Knight. New York, Washington Square Press [1965] vi, 200 p. illus. 18 cm. (The Great American thinkers series) "W885." Bibliography: p. 192-194. [B945.P4K6] 65-2960
1. Peirce, Charles Santiago Sanders, 1889-1914. I. Title.

Pelham, Benjamin B., 1862-1948.

MALLAS, Aris A 923.573
Forty years in politics; the story of Ben Pelham, by Aris A. Mallas, Jr., Rea McCain [and] Margaret K. Hedden. Detroit, Wayne State University Press, 1957. 92p. illus. 24cm. [F572.W4P4] 57-10562
1. Pelham, Benjamin B., 1862-1948. 2. Finance, Public—Wayne Co., Mich. 3. Wayne Co., Mich.—Pol. & govt. I. Title.

Pelham, Henry, 1695?-1754.

OWEN, John Beresford. 942.07'2
The rise of the Pelhams, by John B. Owen. New York, Barnes & Noble [1971] x, 357 p. 23 cm. Reprint of the 1957 ed. Includes bibliographical references. [DA500.O85 1971] 76-24488 ISBN 0-389-04145-9 12.50
1. Pelham, Henry, 1695?-1754. 2. Gt. Brit.—Politics and government—1727-1760. I. Title.

Pelham, John, 1838-1863.

HASSLER, William Woods. 923.573
Colonel John Pelham; Lee's boy artillerist. Illus. by Sidney E. King. Richmond, Garrett & Massie [1960] 185 p. illus. 21 cm. Includes bibliography. [E467.1.P36H3] 60-10349
1. Pelham, John, 1838-1863. BIP

MERCER, Philip. 923.573
The life of the gallant Pelham. Macon, Ga., J. W. Burke Co. [c1929]; Kennesaw, Ga., Continental Book Co., 1958. 180p. illus., ports., map. 23cm. [E467.1.P36M5 1958] 59-3928
1. Pelham, John, 1838-1863. I. Title. II. Title: The gallant Pelham.

MILHAM, Charles G 923.573
Gallant Pelham, American extraordinary. Introd. by U. S. Grant, 3rd. Washington, Public Affairs Press [1959] 250p. illus. 24cm. Includes bibliography. [E467.1.P36M56] 58-13402
1. Pelham, John, 1838-1863. I. Title.

Pell, Herbert Claiborne, 1884-1961.

BAKER, Leonard. 973.9'0924 B
Brahmin in revolt; a biography of Herbert C. Pell. [1st ed.] New York, Doubleday, 1972. 350 p. illus. 22 cm. Bibliography: p. [333]-337. [E748.P44B3] 75-160866 7.95
1. Pell, Herbert Claiborne, 1884-1961. I. Title.

Peller, Sigismund, 1890-

PELLER, Sigismund, 1890- 610'.92'4 B
Not in my time : the story of a doctor / Sigismund Peller. New York : Philosophical Library, c1979. xiv, 374 p. : ports. ; 22 cm. Includes indexes. [R154.P374A35] 79-83607 ISBN 0-8022-2239-0 : 15.00
1. Peller, Sigismund, 1890- 2. Physicians—New York (City)—Biography. 3. Medical scientists—United States—Biography. 4. Health-officers—Palestine—Biography. 5. Health-officers—Austria—Biography. 6. Cancer—Research. I. Title. BIP

Pellet, Elizabeth (Eyre)

PELLET, Elizabeth (Eyre) 923.273
"That Pellet woman!" By Betty Pellet, with Alexander Klein. New York, Stein and Day [1965] 379 p. illus., facsims., ports. 22 cm. [CT275.P552A3] 65-14396
I. Klein, Alexander, 1918- II. Title.

Pelletier, Marie de Sainte Euphrasie, Saint, 1796-1868.

BERNOVILLE, Gaetan [Marie Joseph] 922.244
Saint Mary Euphasia Pelletier, foundress of the Good Shepherd Sisters. [Translation from the French] Westminster, Md., Newman Press [1959] 196p. illus. 22cm. 60-47 3.50
1. Pelletier, Marie de Sainte Euphrasie, Saint, 1796-1868. 2. Sisters of Our Lady of Charity of the Good Shepherd. I. Title.

BOARDMAN, Anne (Cawley) 922.244
Good Shepherd's fold; a biography of St. Mary Euphrasia Pelletier, R. G. S., foundress of the Congregation of Our Lady of Charity of the Good Shepherd of Angers. [1st ed.] New York, Harper [c1955] 292p. illus. 22cm. [BX4700.P38B6] 54-12327
1. Pelletler, Arie de Sainte Euphrasie, Saint, 1796-1868. 2. Sisters of Our Lady of Charity of the Good Shepherd. I. Title.

MARY of our lady of the Angels, Sister. 922.244
The little white shepherdess, the story of the life of St. Mary Euphrasia: illustrated by Clifford Hickox, Milwaukee, Tower Press [1950] xviii, 220 p. illus. (part col.) 24 cm. [BX4700.P38M3] 50-11975
1. Pelletier, Marie de Sainte Euphrasie, Saint, I. Title.

Pelletier, Wilfred.

PELLETIER, Wilfred. 970.3 B
No foreign land: the biography of a Northern American Indian [by] Wilfred Pelletier and Ted Poole. [1st ed.] New York, Pantheon Books [1974, c1973] 212 p. 22 cm. [E99.O9P44 1974] 73-7029 ISBN 0-394-48033-3 6.95
1. Pelletier, Wilfred. 2. Indians of North America—Canada. I. Poole, Ted. II. Title.

Pellicer, Carlos, 1897-

†MULLEN, Edward J., 1942- 861 B
Carlos Pellicer / by Edward J. Mullen. Boston : Twayne Publishers, c1977. 173 p. : port. ; 21 cm. (Twayne's world authors series ; TWAS 451 : Mexico) Includes index. Bibliography: p. 165-167. [PQ7297.P3Z78] 77-1959 ISBN 0-8057-6288-4 : 9.50
1. Pellicer, Carlos, 1897- 2. Poets, Mexican—20th century—Biography. BIP

Pellico, Silvio, 1789-1854—Biography—Imprisonment.

PELLICO, Silvio, 1789-1854. 858'.7'09 B
My prisons = Le mie prigioni / Silvio Pellico ; translation, introd., and notes by I. G. Capaldi ; foreword by Archibald Colquhoun. Westport, Conn. : Greenwood Press, [1978] c1963. p. cm. Reprint of the ed. published by Oxford University Press, New York, issued in series: The Oxford library of Italian classics. Bibliography: p. [PQ4728.A2C3 1978] 78-12351 ISBN 0-313-21053-5 lib.bdg. : 18.00
1. Pellico, Silvio, 1789-1854—Biography—Imprisonment. 2. Italy—History—1815-1870—Sources. 3. Authors, Italian—19th century—Biography. 4. Political prisoners—Italy—Biography. I. Title. BIP

Pemberton, Brock, 1885-1950.

HILL, Charles R., 1928- 792'.0232'0924
Brock Pemberton, Broadway producer / by Charles R. Hill. Emporia : Emporia Kansas State College, 1975. 55 p. ; 23 cm. (The Emporia State research studies ; v. 23, no. 4) Based on the author's thesis—University of Kansas. Bibliography: p. 51-55. [PN2287.P38H5] 75-623339
1. Pemberton, Brock, 1885-1950. I. Title. II. Series.

Pembroke, Anne (Clifford) Herbert, countess of, 1590-1676.

NOTESTEIN, Wallace, 1878- 920.042
Four worthies: John Chamberlain, Anne Clifford, John Taylor, Oliver Heywood. New Haven, Yale University Press, 1957. 248p. illus. 21cm. [DA377.N6] 57-1426
1. Chamberlain, John, 1554?-1628. 2. Pembroke, Anne (Clifford) Herbert, countess of, 1590-1676. 3. Taylor, John, 1580-1653. 4. Heywood, Oliver, 1629-1702. I. Title.

WILLIAMSON, George Charles, 1858-1942. 942.06'0924 B
Lady Anne Clifford, Countess of Dorset, Pembroke & Montgomery, 1590-1676: her life, letters and work [by] George C. Williamson. 2nd ed. Wakefield (Yorks.), S. R. Publishers, 1967. xxiv, 547 p. 71 plates; illus., facsims. tables. 23 cm. Facsimile reprint of 1st ed., Kendal, Wilson, 1922. Bibliography: p. 521-526. [DA378.P4W5 1922b] 68-140869 6/6/-
1. Pembroke, Anne (Clifford) Herbert, Countess of, 1590-1676. 2. Great Britain—Court and courtiers. 3. Great Britain—Social life and customs—17th century. I. Title.

Pembroke, William Marshal, earl of, 1144?-1219.

CROSLAND, Jessie (Raven) 923.242
William the Marshal: the last great feudal baron. London, P. Owen [dist. Hollywood-by-the-Sea, Fla., Transatlantic, c.1962] 159p. front. 22cm. 63-226 5.25
1. Pembroke, William Marshal, earl of, 1144?-1219. I. Title.

PAINTER, Sidney, 1902- 923.242
William Marshal, Knight-errant, baron, and regent of England, by Sidney Painter. Baltimore, Hopkins [1967, c.1933] xi, 305p. 24cm. (JH-38) This biography was orig. written as a dissertation for the degree of doctor of phil. in Yale Univ. [1930]--Pref. [DA209.P4P3] 33-8958 2.95 pap.,
1. Pembroke, William Marshal, earl of 1144?-1219. 2. Gt. Brit.—Hist. —Angevin period, 1154-1216. I. Title.

Pembrokeshire, Wales—History, Local.

LEWIS, Ewart Thomas. 942.9'65
Local heritage from Efailwen to Whitland : comprising the history of the parishes of Climaenllwyd, Hellanfallteg, Llanboidy, Llandysilio, Llanddewi Velfrey, Whitland / by E. T. Lewis, with contributions by J. Towyn Jones and Haydn Lewis ; foreword by George Bancroft. [Clunderwen] : The author, 1976- v. : ill., ports. ; 21 cm. Includes index. [DA740.P3L46] 77-367797 ISBN 0-902126-05-9 (v. 2) : £1.20 (v. 2)
1. Pembrokeshire, Wales—History, Local. 2. Pembrokeshire, Wales—Biography. I. Jones, J. Towyn, joint author. II. Lewis, Haydn, joint author. III. Title.

Pend Oreille Co., Wash.—Biography.

†TAYLOR, Lee. 920'.0797'21
Pend Oreille profiles / Lee Taylor. Fairfield, Wash. : Ye Galleon Press, 1977. 334 p. : ill. ; 30 cm. [F897.P4T39] 77-151412 ISBN 0-87770-185-7 : 14.95
1. Pend Oreille Co., Wash.—Biography. I. Title. BIP

Pendar, Kenneth Whittemore.

PENDAR, Kenneth Whittemore. 940.53'22'73
Adventure in diplomacy : our French dilemma / by Kenneth Pendar. New York : Da Capo Press, 1976, c1945. p. cm. (The Politics and strategy of World War II) Reprint of the ed. published by Dodd, Mead, New York. [D766.82.P4 1976] 76-5479 ISBN 0-306-70774-8
1. Pendar, Kenneth Whittemore. 2. World War, 1939-1945—Africa, North. 3. World War, 1939-1945—Diplomatic history. 4. World War, 1939-1945—Personal narratives, American. I. Title.

Pender, William Dorsey, 1834-1863.

DIKET, A. L. 973.7'3
wha hae wi' [Pender] ... bled / by A. L. Diket. 1st ed. New York : Vantage Press, c1979. 165 p. ; 21 cm. Bibliography: p. 162-165. [E467.1.P367D54] 79-107767 ISBN 0-533-03517-1 : 7.50
1. Pender, William Dorsey, 1834-1863. 2. Pender, Mary Frances Shepperd. 3. United States—History—Civil War, 1861-1865—Campaigns and battles. 4. Generals—United States—Biography. I. Title. BIP

Pendleton, Alexander Swift, 1840-1864.

BEAN, William Gleason, 1891- 923.573
Stonewall's man: Sandie Pendleton. Chapel Hill, University of North Carolina Press [1959] 252p. illus. 24cm. Includes bibliography. [E467.1.P368B4] 59-9699
1. Pendleton, Alexander Swift, 1840-1864. I. Title.

Pendleton, Brian, 1599-1681.

PENDLETON, Everett Hall, 1878- 923.273
Brian Pendleton and his Massachusetts, 1634-1681. [South Orange? N.J., 1951] xi, 259 p. illus., facsims. 24 cm. Bibliographical footnotes. [F67.P4P4] 51-26593
1. Pendleton, Brian, 1599-1681. 2. Massachusetts — Hist. — Colonial period. I. Title.

Pendleton Edmund, 1721-1803.

MAYS, David John, 1896- 923.273
Edmund Pendleton, 1721-1803; a biography. Cambridge, Harvard University Press, 1952. 2 v. illus., ports., maps. 25 cm. Bibliography: v. 2, p. [407]-429. [F230.P425] 52-5036
1. Pendleton Edmund, 1721-1803. 2. Virginia—Politics and government—Colonial period. 3. Virginia—Politics and government—1775-1865.

Penet, Peter, d. 1789.

POWELL, Thomas F. 974.7'57'03
Penet's Square : an episode in the early history of northern New York / Thomas F. Powell. Lakemont, N.Y. : North Country Books, c1976. ix, 203 p. : ill. ; 24

cm. Bibliography: p. 201-203. [F127.J4P68] 76-373595 7.50
1. Penet, Peter, d. 1789. 2. Jefferson Co., N.Y.—History. 3. Oneida Indians. 4. Jefferson Co., N.Y.—Biography. I. Title.

Penfield, Wilder, 1891-

PENFIELD, Wilder, 1891- 616.8'092'4 B
No man alone : a surgeon's story / by Wilder Penfield ; with a foreword by Lord Adrian. 1st ed. Boston : Little, Brown, c1977. xv, 398 p. : ill. ; 22 cm. Includes bibliographical references and index. [RC339.52.P46A34] 77-22350 ISBN 0-316-69839-3 : 12.50
1. Penfield, Wilder, 1891- 2. McGill University, Montreal. Montreal Neurological Institute—History. 3. Neurosurgeons—Quebec (Province)—Biography. I. Title.

Peninsular War, 1807-1814—Personal narratives.

HARRIS, John, rifleman. 940.2'7'0924
Recollections of rifleman Harris, as told to Henry Curling. Edited and introduced by Christopher Hibbert. [Hamden, Conn.] Archon Books, 1970. ix, 128 p. 23 cm. [DC232.H37 1970] 77-15885 5.50
1. Peninsular War, 1807-1814—Personal narratives. I. Curling, Henry, 1803-1864, ed. II. Hibbert, Christopher, 1924- ed. III. Title.

Penn family.

PENN, William, 1644-1718. 974.8'02
Correspondence between William Penn and James Logan, and others, 1700-1750. From the original letters in possession of the Logan family. With notes by Deborah Logan. Edited with additional notes by Edward Armstrong. Philadelphia, Printed by J. B. Lippincott for the Historical Society of Pennsylvania. Sold by J. Pennington, 1870-72 [New York, AMS Press, 1972] 2 v. 23 cm. (Publications of the Historical Society of Pennsylvania) [F152.P2872] 72-173943 ISBN 0-404-04985-0
1. Penn family. 2. Pennsylvania—History—Colonial period, ca. 1600-1775—Sources. I. Logan, James, 1647-1751. II. Series: Pennsylvania. Historical Society. Memoirs.

Penn, Jack.

PENN, Jack. 617'.95'00924 B
The right to look human : an autobiography / Jack Penn. Johannesburg ; New York : McGraw-Hill Book Co., [1974] 254 p. : ill. ; 24 cm. [R654.P46A33] 75 308732 ISBN 0-07-091283-1 : 10.50
1. Penn, Jack. 2. Surgeons—Correspondence, reminiscences, etc. 3. Surgery, Plastic. I. Title.

Penn, William, 1644-1718.

BLUM, Herman, 1884- ed. 923.273
William Penn, 1644-1718; new light thrown on the Queker founder of Pennsylvania, through heretofore unpublished documents in the Blumhaven Library...An exhibition of holograph letters and autograph documents, selcted from source materials in the Blumhaven Collection. [Philadelphia, Blumhaven Library and Gallery, 1950] 48 p. illus., ports., facsims. 25 cm. Bibliography: p. 48. [F152.2.B55] 50-13149
1. Penn, William, 1644-1718. I. Blumhaven Library and Gallery. Philadelphia. II. Title.

BRAILSFORD, Mabel Richmond. 974.8'02'0924 B
The making of William Penn. With woodcut frontispiece by Clare Leighton and other illus. Freeport, N.Y., Books for Libraries Press [1970] xxiv, 367 p. illus., ports. 23 cm. Reprint of the 1930 ed. Bibliography: p. 361-363. [F152.2.B8 1970] 77-124227
1. Penn, William, 1644-1718. 2. Penn family. I. Title. BIP

DOBREE, Bonamy, 1891- 974.8'02'0924 B
William Penn, Quaker and pioneer / by Bonamy Dobree. Folcroft, Pa. : Folcroft Library Editions, 1978. p. cm. Reprint of the 1932 ed. published by Houghton Mifflin, Boston. Includes bibliographical references and index. [F152.2.D72 1978] 78-15258 lib. bdg. : 35.00
1. Penn, William, 1644-1718. 2. Friends, Society of—Pennsylvania—Biography. 3. Statesmen—United States—Biography. 4. Pioneers—Pennsylvania—Biography. 5. Pennsylvania—History—Colonial period, ca. 1600-1775. I. Title. BIP

DUNN, Mary Maples. 320.1
William Penn, politics and conscience. Princeton, N.J., Princeton University Press, 1967. x, 206 p. 23 cm. "Bibliographical note": p. 195-198. [JC153.P4D8] 66-21831
1. Penn, William, 1644-1718. I. Title.

FANTEL, Hans. 974.8'02'0924 B
William Penn; apostle of dissent. New York, Morrow, 1974. xiv, 298 p. port. 22 cm. Bibliography: p. 286-290. [F152.2.F36] 74-10626 ISBN 0-688-00310-9
1. Penn, William, 1644-1718.

HAUGHEY, Betty Ellen. 974.8'02'0924 B
William Penn, American pioneer. Illustrated by Steele Savage. New York, Putnam [1968] 63 p. col. illus. 24 cm. (An American pioneer biography) A brief biography of the Quaker whose constant battle for religious freedom for all people resulted in the establishment of a successful colony in the New World. [F152.2.H36 1968] 92 AC 68
1. Penn, William, 1644-1718. I. Savage, Stelle, illus. II Title.

HAVILAND, Virginia, 1911- 923.273
William Penn, founder and Friend; illustrated by Peter Burchard. New York, Abingdon-Cokesbury Press [1952] 127 p. illus. 22 cm. (Makers of America) [F152.2.H37] 52-8357
1. Penn, William, 1644-1718.

HULL, William Isaac, 1868-1939. 974.8'02'0924 B
William Penn, a topical biography. Freeport, N.Y., Books for Libraries Press [1971] xvi, 362 p. illus 23 cm. Reprint of the 1937 ed. Bibliography: p. 349-352. [F152.2.H936 1971] 78-179525 ISBN 0-8369-6654-6
1. Penn, William, 1644-1718.

JANNEY, Samuel Macpherson, 1801-1880. 974.8'02'0924
The life of William Penn; with selections from his correspondence and autobiography. Freeport, N.Y., Books for Libraries Press [1970] xi, 560 p. ports. 23 cm. "First published 1851." Includes bibliographical references. [F152.2.J34 1970] 74-130555
1. Penn, William, 1644-1718. I. Title. BIP

PEARE, Catherine Owens 923.273
William Penn: a biography. Ann Arbor, Univ. of Mich. Pr. [1966, c.1956] 448p. port. 21cm. (Ann Arbor Paperbacks, AA120) Bibl. [F152.2.P34] 2.95 pap.,
1. Penn, William, 1644-1718. I. Title.

PENN, William, 1644-1718. 974.8'02'0924
A collection of the works of William Penn, to which is prefixed a journal of his life with many original letters and papers not before published. New York, AMS Press [1974] 2 v. 32 cm. Reprint of 1726 ed. printed and sold by the assigns of J. Sowle, London, with an index of the works compiled in 1730 by Henry Portsmouth. [F152.2.P393 1974] 79-173942 ISBN 0-404-04982-6
1. Penn, William, 1644-1718. I. Title.

PENN, William, 1644-1718. 320.5'092'4
William Penn, 17th century founding father : selections from his political writings / Edward B. Bronner. Wallingford, Pa. : Pendle Hill Publications, 1975. 36 p. : facsim. ; 19 cm. (Pendle Hill pamphlet ; 204 ISSN 0031-4250s) Bibliography: p. 36. [JC153.P38 1975] 75-32728 ISBN 0-87574-204-1 : 0.95
1. Political science—Collected works. I. Bronner, Edwin B., 1920- II. Title.

VINING, Elizabeth (Gray) 1902- 248.2'2
William Penn: mystic, as reflected in his writings. [Wallingford, Pa., Pendle Hill Publications, 1969] 31 p. 19 cm. (Pendle Hill pamphlet 167) [F152.2.V79] 74-95891 0.55
1. Penn, William, 1644-1718. I. Title.

WALLACE, Willard Mosher, 1911- 923.273
Friend William. Illustrated by Gustav Schrotter. Edinburgh, New York, T. Nelson [1958] 157 p. illus. 21 cm. Includes bibliography. [F152.2.W22] 58-6115
1. Penn, William, 1644-1718. I. Title.

WILDES, Harry Emerson, 1890- 974.8'02'0924 B
William Penn. New York, Macmillan [1974] ix, 469 p. 24 cm. Includes bibliographical references. [F152.2.W46] 73-1857 ISBN 0-02-628570-3 12.95
1. Penn, William, 1644-1718. BIP

Penn, William, 1644-1718.

PEARE, Catherine Owens. 923.273
William Penn. Illustrated by Henry C. Pitz. [1st ed.] New York, Holt [1958] 192 p. illus. 21 cm. [F152.2.P33] 58-6513
1. Penn, William, 1644-1718.

PEARE, Catherine Owens. 923.273
William Penn; a biography. [1st ed.] Philadelphia, Lippincott, 1957 [c1956] 448 p. port. 22 cm. Bibliography: p. 427-444. [F152.2.P34] 56-10810
1. Penn, William, 1644-1718.

WALLOWER, Lucille, 1910- 974.8'02'0924 B
William Penn. Illustrated with drawings by Louis Cary and contemporary pictorial material. Chicago, Follett Pub. Co. [1968] 157, [3] p. illus., ports. 23 cm. (Library of American heros) Bibliography: p [158] The life of the English gentleman who became a Quaker and established the colony of Pennsylvania as a peaceful settlement with religious freedom for all and friendly relations with the Indians. [F152.2.W25] 92 AC 68
I. Cary, Louis F., illus. II. Title.

Penn, William, 1644-1718—Juvenile literature.

DOLSON, Hildegarde 92
William Penn Quaker hero, Illus. by Leonard Everett Fisher. New York, Random [c.1961] 186p. col. illus. (Landmark bks. [98]) Bibl. 61-13481 1.95
1. Penn, William, 1644-1718—Juvenile literature. I. Title.

SYME. RONALD, 1910- j92
William Penn. founder of Pennsylvania. Illustrated by William Stobbs. New York, W. Morrow, 1966. 95. [1] p. illus. 22 cm. Bibliography: p. [96] [F152.2.S97] 66-12614
1. Penn, William, 1644-1718 — Juvenile literature. I. Title.

WILKIE, Katharine Elliott, 1904- 920
William Penn, friend of all. Illus. by J. L. Pellicer. Champaign, Ill., Garrard [c.1964] 80p. col. illus. 23cm. (Discovery bk.) 64-10068 2.50
1. Penn, William, 1644-1718—Juvenile literature. I. Title.

Penn, William, 1644-1718—Juvenile literature.

BRANDENBERG, Aliki 974.8'02'0924 [B]
The story of William Penn. Written and illustrated by Aliki. Englewood Cliffs, N.J., Prentice-Hall [1975, c1964] 1 v. (unpaged, chiefly illus.) 23 cm. (A Treehouse paperback) [F152.2B83] [92] 64-14025 ISBN 0-13-846931-8 0.95 (pbk.)
1. Penn, William, 1644-1718—Juvenile literature. I. Title.

FOSTER, Genevieve (Stump) 1893- 974.8'02'0924 B
The world of William Penn, by Genevieve Foster. Illustrated by the author. New York, Scribner [1973] 192 p. illus. 24 cm. Traces the life of the Quaker founder of Pennsylvania with emphasis on the important people and events of his time. [D247.F63] 92 72-7531 ISBN 0-684-13188-9 5.95
1. Penn, William, 1644-1718—Juvenile literature. 2. History, Modern—17th century—Juvenile literature. I. Title. BIP

HAUGHEY, Betty Ellen. 92 (J)
William Penn, American pioneer. Illustrated by Steele Savage. New York, Putnam [1968] 63 p. col. illus. 24 cm. (An American pioneer biography) [F152.2.H36 1968] 68-15052
1. Penn, William, 1644-1718—Juvenile literature.

WALLOWER, Lucille, 1910- 92 (J)
William Penn; illustrated with drawings by Louis Cary and contemporary pictorial material. Chicago, Follett Pub. Co. [1968] 157, [3] p. illus., ports. 23 cm. (Library of American heros) Bibliography: p. [158] [F152.2.W25] 70-231 1.95
1. Penn, William, 1644-1718—Juvenile literature. I. Title.

WILKIE, Katharine Elliott, 1904- j92
William Penn, friend to all. Illustrated by J. L. Pellicer. Champaign, Ill., Garrard Pub. Co. [1964] 80 p. col. illus. 23 cm. (A Discovery book) [F152.2.W5] 64-10068
1. Penn, William 1644-1718 — Juvenile literature. I. Title.

Penney (J. C.) Company.

PENNEY, James Cash, 1875-1971. 923.873
Fifty years with the Golden Rule. [1st ed.] New York, Harper [1950] 245 p. port. 22 cm. Autobiography. [HF5465.U6P43] 50-10795
1. Penney (J. C.) Company. I. Title.

Penney, James Cash, 1875-

PLUMB, Beatrice, 1886- 923.873
J. C. Penney, merchant prince; a biography of a man who built a business empire based on the Golden rule. Minneapolis, Denison [c.1963] 156p. 23cm. (Men of achievement ser.) 63-13385 3.00
1. Penney, James Cash, 1875- I. Title.

Penney, James Cash, 1875-1971—Juvenile literature.

HUDSON, Wilma J. 381'.45 B
J. C. Penney; golden rule boy, by Wilma J. Hudson. Illustrated by Robert Doremus. Indianapolis, Bobbs-Merrill [1972] 200 p. col. illus. 20 cm. (Childhood of famous Americans) Bibliography: p. 198 A biography stressing the childhood of the boy whose knack for earning an honest dollar led to the establishment of a nationwide chain of dry goods stores. [HF5465.U6P452] 92 79-187335
1. Penney, James Cash, 1875-1971—Juvenile literature. I. Doremus, Robert, illus. II. Title. BIP

Pennsylvania—Biog.—Dictionaries.

PENNSYLVANIA who's who. 920.0748 *1957/58-* Pittsburgh. v. 28cm. [F148.P49] 58-1397
1. Pennsylvania—Biog.—Dictionaries.

Pennsylvania—Governors—Biog.

GREENE, Le Roy. 923.273
Shelter for His Excellency; the story of Pennsylvania's Executive Mansion and the one hundred governors of the Commonwealth. Harrisburg, Stackpole Books, 1951. 379 p. illus., ports. 24 cm. Bibliography: p. 375-379. [F148.G7] 51-100618
1. Pennsylvania—Governors—Blog. 2. Harrisburg, Pa. Executive Mansion. I. Title.

Pennsylvania—Biography.

SHARPLESS, Isaac, 1848-1920. 974.8'02'0922 B
Political leaders of provincial Pennsylvania. Freeport, N.Y., Books for Libraries Press

[1971] vii, 248 p. 23 cm. Reprint of the 1919 ed. Contents.Contents.—William Penn.—Thomas Lloyd.—David Lloyd.—James Logan.—John Kinsey.—Isaac Norris.—James Pemberton.—John Dickinson. [F152.S538 1971] 75-169774 ISBN 0-8369-5994-9
1. Pennsylvania—Biography. 2. Pennsylvania—Politics and government—Colonial period, ca. 1600-1775. I. Title. BIP

Pennsylvania. University.

SMITH, Horace 378.1'11'0924 B
Wemyss, 1825-1891.
Life and correspondence of the Rev. William Smith, D.D. New York, Arno Press, 1972 [c1878] 2 v. in 1. ports. 24 cm. (Religion in America, series II) [LD4525 1755.S62] 79-38786 ISBN 0-405-04084-9
1. Smith, William, 1727-1803. 2. Pennsylvania. University. 3. Washington College, Chestertown, Md. I. Title. BIP

Pennsylvania. Western State Penitentiary, Pittsburgh.

BERKMAN, 335'.83'0924 B
Alexander, 1870-1936.
Prison memoirs of an anarchist. Introductory by Hutchins Hapgood. With a new introd. by Paul Goodman. New York, Schocken Books [1970] 512 p. illus., facsims., ports. 21 cm. (Studies in the libertarian and utopian tradition) Reprint of the 1912 ed. [HX843.B5 1970] 77-130206
1. Pennsylvania. Western State Penitentiary, Pittsburgh. 2. Anarchism and anarchists—U.S. I. Title. BIP

Penny, James Cash, 1876-

ALBUS, Harry James, 1920- 923.873
Mr. Penney; the life of J. C. Penney in story form. Illus. by Macy Schwartz. Grand Rapids, Mich., Eerdams [c.1961] 89p. 61-10857 2.00 bds.,
1. Penny, James Cash, 1876- 2. Penney (J. C.) Company. I. Title.

Penrose, Boies, 1860-1921.

BOWDEN, Robert 973.91'0924 B
Douglas, 1889-
Boies Penrose, symbol of an era. Freeport, N.Y., Books for Libraries Press [1971] ix, 274 p. illus. 23 cm. Reprint of the 1937 ed. [E664.P41B67 1971] 75-175690 ISBN 0-8369-6605-8
1. Penrose, Boies, 1860-1921.

DAVENPORT, Walter. 328.73'0924 B
Power and glory; the life of Boies Penrose. New York, Putnam, 1931. St. Clair Shores, Mich., Scholarly Press, 1970. ix, 240 p. ports. 21 cm. [E664.P41D3 1970] 78-131683
1. Penrose, Boies, 1860-1921. I. Title. BIP

DAVENPORT, Walter. 328.73'0924
Power and glory, the life of Boies Penrose. New York, AMS Press [1969] ix, 240 p. ports. 23 cm. Reprint of the 1931 ed. [E664.P41D3 1969] 77-100525
1. Penrose, Boies, 1860-1921. I. Title. BIP

Penrose, Harald.

PENROSE, Harald. 629.13'092'4 B
No echo in the sky. [New York] Arno Press [1972, c1958] 134 p. illus. 23 cm. (Literature and history of aviation) Autobiographical. [TL540.P43A3 1972] 78-169433 ISBN 0-405-03776-7
I. Title. II. Series. BIP

Penrose, Richard Alexander Fullerton,

PENROSE, Richard Alexander 925.5
Fullerton, 1863-1931.
Life and letters of R. A. F. Penrose, Jr., by Helen R. Fairbanks and Charles P. Berkey. New York, [Geological Society of America] 1952. 765p. illus. 26cm. [CT99.P417A4] 53-23636
I. Fairbanks, Helen R., ed. II. Title.

Penslee, Edmund Randolph, 1814-1878.

MARR, James Pratt, 1898- 926.1
Pioneer surgeons of the Woman's Hospital; the lives of Sims, Emmet, Peaslee, and Thomas. Philadelphia, F. A. Davis Co., 1957. 148p. illus. 24cm. Includes bibliography. [RA982.N5W64] 57-8716
1. Sims, James Marlon, 1813-1883. 2. Emmet, Thomas Addis, 1828-1919. 3. Penslee, Edmund Randolph, 1814-1878. 4. Thomas, Theodore Gallard, 1832-1903. 5. New York. Woman's Hospital in the State of New York. I. Title.

Pentecostalism—Mennonites—Addresses, essays, lectures.

MY personal Pentecost 230'.9'7
/ edited by Roy S. and Martha Koch ; foreword by Kevin Ranaghan. Scottdale, Pa. : Herald Press, c1977. 275 p. : port. ; 20 cm. Includes bibliographical references. [BX8128.C47M9] 77-79229 ISBN 0-8361-1816-2 pbk. : 3.95
1. Pentecostalism—Mennonites—Addresses, essays, lectures. 2. Mennonites—United States—Biography—Addresses, essays, lectures. I. Koch, Roy S., 1913- II. Koch, Martha. BIP

Peoples Temple—Biography.

NUGENT, John Peer. 289.9 B
White night / John Peer Nugent. 1st ed. New York : Rawson, Wade Publishers, c1979. p. cm. Includes index. Bibliography: p. [BP605.P46N83 1979] 79-64720 ISBN 0-89256-116-5 : 10.95
1. Jones, Jim, 1931-1978. 2. Peoples Temple—Biography. 3. Peoples Temple. I. Title.

Pepitone, Joe.

PEPITONE, Joe. 796.357'092'4 B
Joe, you coulda made us proud / Joe Pepitone with Barry Stainback. New York : Dell, 1976c1975. 286p. : ill. ; 18 cm. [GV865.P45A35] pbk. : 1.75
1. Pepitone, Joe. 2. Baseball. I. Stainback, Berry. II. Title.
L.C. card no. of 1975 Play boy Press edition: 74-33557.

PEPITONE, Joe. 796.357'092'4 B
Joe, you coulda made us proud / by Joe Pepitone ; with Berry Stainback. 1st ed. Chicago : Playboy Press, [1975]. x, 246 p., [4] leaves of plates : ill. ; 22 cm. [GV865.P45A35] 74-33557 ISBN 0-87223-428-2 : 8.95
1. Pepitone, Joe. 2. Baseball. I. Stainback, Berry. II. Title.

Peploe. Samuel John, 1871-1935.

HONEYMAN, Tom John, 1891- 927.5
Three Scottish colourists: S. J. Peploe, F. C. B. Cadell, Leslie Hunter. London, New York, Nelson [1950] xi, 132 p. plates (part col.) ports. 24 cm. "As I remember them, by Ion R. Harrison": p. [117]-126. [ND496.H6 1950] 52-30535
1. Peploe. Samuel John, 1871-1935. 2. Cadell, Francis Campbell Bolleau, 1883-1937. 3. Hunter, Leslie, 1879-1931. I. Title.

Pepper, Art, 1925-

PEPPER, Art, 1925- 785.4'2'0924 B
Straight life : the story of Art Pepper / by Art and Laurie Pepper. New York : Schirmer Books, 1979. p. cm. Includes index. Discography: p. [ML419.P48A3] 79-7363 ISBN 0-02-871820-8 : 12.95
1. Pepper, Art, 1925- 2. Jazz musicians—United States—Biography. I. Pepper, Laurie, joint author. II. Title. BIP

Pepys, Samuel, 1633-1703.

BRADFORD, 941.06'6'0924 B
Gamaliel, 1863-1932.
Samuel Pepys / by Gamaliel Bradford. New York : Haskell House, [1976.] x, 261 p. ; 21 cm. First published in 1924 by Houghton, Mifflin, New York, under title: The soul of Samuel Pepys. Reprint of the 1924 ed. published by J. Cape, London. Includes bibliographical references and index. [DA447.P4B7 1975] 75-42291 ISBN 0-8383-2061-9 lib.bdg. : 15.95
1. Pepys, Samuel, 1633-1703. I. Title. BIP

BRADFORD, Gamaliel, 828'.4'08 B
1863-1932.
The soul of Samuel Pepys. Port Washington, N.Y., Kennikat Press [1969, c1924] x, 261 p. ports. 22 cm. Bibliographical references included in "Notes" (p. 241-[255]) [DA447.P4B7 1969] 78-85993
1. Pepys, Samuel, 1633-1703. I. Title. BIP

EMDEN, Cecil Stuart. 928.2
Pepys himself. London, New York, Oxford University Press, 1963. 146 p. 23 cm. [PR3618.P2E4] 63-1253
1. Pepys, Samuel, 1633-1703. I. Title.

HUNT, Percival, 941.06'6'0924
1878-
Samuel Pepys in the diary / Percival Hunt. Westport, Conn. : Greenwood Press, 1978, c1958. 178 p. ; 23 cm. Reprint of the ed. published by University of Pittsburgh Press, Pittsburgh. [DA447.P4H8 1978] 78-2747 lib.bdg. : 15.25
1. Pepys, Samuel, 1633-1703. Diary. 2. Pepys, Samuel, 1633-1703—Biography. 3. Statesmen—Great Britain—Biography. 4. Authors, English—Early modern, 1500-1700—Biography. I. Title.

KIRK, Clara 914.2'03'660922 B
Marburg, 1898-
Mr. Pepys and Mr. Evelyn / by Clara Marburg. [Folcroft, Pa.] : Folcroft Library Editions, 1974. p. cm. Reprint of the 1935 ed. published by University of Pennsylvania Press, Philadelphia. [DA447.P4K48 1974] 74-21000 ISBN 0-8414-5976-2 lib.bdg.: 12.50
1. Pepys, Samuel, 1633-1703. 2. Evelyn, John, 1620-1706. I. Title. BIP

KIRK, Clara 914.2'03'660922 B
Marburg, 1898-
Mr. Pepys and Mr. Evelyn / by Clara Marburg. Folcroft, Pa. : Folcroft Library Editions, 1974. xi, 156 p., [2] leaves of plates : facsim. ; 26 cm. Reprint of the 1935 ed. published by University of Pennsylvania Press, Philadelphia. Includes bibliographical references. [DA447.P4K48 1974] 74-21000 ISBN 0-8414-5976-2 lib. bdg.
1. Pepys, Samuel, 1633-1703. 2. Evelyn, John, 1620-1706. I. Title.

LUBBOCK, Percy, 914.2'03'660924 B
1879-
Samuel Pepys. [Folcroft, Pa.] Folcroft Library Editions, 1974. p. cm. Reprint of the 1909 ed. published by Scribner, New York, in series: Literary lives. [DA447.P4L8 1974] 74-9975 ISBN 0-8414-5731-X (lib. bdg.)
1. Pepys, Samuel, 1633-1703. I. Title. II. Series: Literary lives.

MEYNELL, Esther 942.06'6'0924 B
Hallam Moorhouse.
Samuel Pepys : administrator, observer, gossip / by E. Hallam Moorhouse. New York : Haskell House, [1975] p. cm. Reprint of the 1909 ed. published by Chapman and Hall, London. [DA447.P4M4 1975] 74-30375 ISBN 0-8383-1908-4 : 24.95
1. Pepys, Samuel, 1633-1703.

PONSONBY, Arthur 914.2'03'60924 B
Ponsonby, Baron, 1871-1946.
Samual Pepys. Port Washington, N.Y., Kennikat Press [1972] xiii, 160 p. 22 cm. Reprint of the 1928 ed. Bibliography: p. 153-154. [DA447.P4P6 1972] 72-153238 ISBN 0-8046-1548-9
1. Pepys, Samuel, 1633-1703.

PONSONBY, Arthur 828'.4'03 B
Ponsonby, Baron, 1871-1946.
Samuel Pepys. Freeport, N.Y., Books for Libraries Press [1971] xiii, 160 p. 23 cm. Reprint of the 1928 ed. Bibliography: p. 153-154. [DA447.P4P6 1971] 71-160987 ISBN 0-8369-5855-1
1. Pepys, Samuel, 1633-1703. BIP

TANNER, Joseph Robson, 828.4'03 B
1860-1931.
Mr. Pepys; an introduction to the Diary together with a sketch of his later life. Westport, Conn., Greenwood Press [1971] xv, 308 p. port. 23 cm. Reprint of the 1925 ed. Bibliography: p. 299-300. [DA447.P4T4 1971] 71-110870 ISBN 0-8371-4549-X
1. Pepys, Samuel, 1633-1703. I. Title.

TANNER, Joseph 914.2'03'660924 B
Robson, 1860-1931.
Mr. Pepys; an introduction to the Diary together with a sketch of his lter life. [Folcroft, Pa.] Folcroft Library Editions, 1973. p. Reprint of the 1925 ed. published by G. Bell, London. Bibliography: p. [DA447.P4T4 1973] 73-13907 ISBN 0-8414-8526-7 (lib. bdg.)
1. Pepys, Samuel, 1633-1703.

TANNER, Joseph 914.2'03'660924 B
Robson, 1860-1931.
Mr. Pepys; an introduction to the dairy together with a sketch of his later life. [Folcroft, Pa.] Folcroft Library Editions, 1973, [i.e. 1974] p. Reprint of the 1925 ed. published by G. Bell, London. Bibliography: p. [DA447.P4T4 1973] 73-13907 15.00 (lib. bdg.).
1. Pepys, Samuel, 1633-1703.

TREASE, 914.2'03'660924 B
Geoffrey, 1909-
Samuel Pepys and his world. New York, Putnam [1972] 128 p. illus. 24 cm. Bibliography: p. 119. Presents the life of Samuel Pepys as well as the social and historical events of the times. [DA447.P4T7 1972b] 92 73-189471 6.95
1. Pepys, Samuel, 1633-1703. I. Title. BIP

WHEATLEY, Henry 941.06'6'0924 B
Benjamin, 1838-1917.
Samuel Pepys and the world he lived in / by Henry B. Wheatley. 3d ed. New York : Haskell House Publishers, 1976 viii, 311 p. ; 21 cm. Reprint of the 1889 ed. published by S. Sonnenschein, London. Includes bibliographical references and index. [DA447.P4W5 1976] 75-34323 ISBN 0-8383-1895-9 lib.bdg. : 15.95
1. Pepys, Samuel, 1633-1703. 2. England—Social life and customs—17th century. I. Title. BIP

WILSON, John Harold, 1900- 928.2
The private life of Mr. Pepys. New York, Farrar, Straus, and Cudahy [1959] 249 p. illus. 22 cm. [DA447.P4W65] 59-14008
1. Pepys, Samuel, 1633-1703. I. Title.

Pepys, Samuel, 1633-1703—Juvenile literature.

GUNSTON, David 92
The young Samuel Pepys. Illus. by Joan Howell. New York, Roy [1966, c.1965] 125p. illus. 21cm. [PR3618.P2G8] 66-13353 3.25 bds.,
1. Pepys, Samuel, 1633-1703—Juvenile literature. I. Title.

Pepys, Samuel, 1633-1703—Biography.

OLLARD, Richard 914.2'03'660924 B
Lawrence.
Pepys: a biography, by Richard Ollard. New York, Holt, Rinehart and Winston [1975, c1974] 368 p. illus. 24 cm. Includes bibliographical references. [PR3618.P2O5 1975] 74-5541 ISBN 0-03-013146-4 10.00
1. Pepys, Samuel, 1633-1703—Biography.

PEPYS, Samuel, 941.06'6'0924 B
1633-1703.
The illustrated Pepys : extracts from the diary / selected & edited by Robert Latham ; [picture researcher, Barbara Fraser]. Berkeley : University of California Press, c1978. 240 p., [7] leaves of plates : ill. ; 26 cm. Includes index. [DA447.P4A4 1978] 77-78416 ISBN 0-520-03633-6 : 15.95
1. Pepys, Samuel, 1633-1703—Biography. 2. Great Britain—Social life and customs—17th century. 3. Statesmen—Great Britain—Biography. 4. Authors, English—Early modern, 1500-1700—Biography. I. Latham, Robert, 1912- II. Title. BIP

TREASE, Geoffrey, 941.06'6'0924
1909-
Samuel Pepys and his world / by Geoffrey Trease. New York : Scribner, [1978] c1972. 128 p. : ill. ; 24 cm. Includes index.

Bibliography: p. 119. [DA447.P4T7 1978] 77-83234 ISBN 0-684-15512-5 : 9.95
1. Pepys, Samuel, 1633-1703—Biography. 2. Statesmen—Great Britain—Biography. 3. Great Britain—History—Charles II, 1660-1685. 4. Great Britain—History—James II, 1685-1688. 5. Authors, English—Early modern, 1500-1700—Biography. I. Title.

Pepys, Samuel, 1633-1703—Correspondence.

HEATH, Helen Truesdell, ed. 941.06'6'0924
The letters of Samuel Pepys and his family circle / edited by Helen Truesdell Heath. Westport, Conn. : Greenwood Press, 1979, c1955. xl, 253 p., [2] leaves of plates (1 fold.) : ill. ; 24 cm. Reprint of the ed. published by Clarendon Press, Oxford. Includes bibliographical references and index. [DA447.P4H4 1979] 78-10795 ISBN 0-313-20656-2 lib. bdg. : 23.75
1. Pepys, Samuel, 1633-1703—Correspondence. 2. Statesmen—Great Britain—Correspondence. 3. Authors, English—Early modern, 1500-1700—Correspondence. I. Title.

Pepys, Samuel, 1633-1708. Diary.

HUNT, Percival, 1878- 928.2
Samuel Pepys in the diary. [Pittsburgh] University of Pittsburgh Press, 1958. 178p. 23cm. [DA447.P4H8] 58-13078
1. Pepys, Samuel, 1633-1708. Diary. I. Title. BIP

Peron, Eva Duarte, 1919-1952.

BARNES, John, 1935- 982'.06'0924 B
Evita, First Lady : a biography of Eva Peron / John Barnes. 1st ed. New York : Grove Press : distributed by Random House, 1978. 195 p., [8] leaves of plates : ill. ; 22 cm. Includes index. [F2849.P37B3] 78-3185 ISBN 0-8021-0163-1. ISBN 0-394-50289-2 (Random House) : 8.95
1. Peron, Eva Duarte, 1919-1952. 2. Argentine Republic—Presidents—Wives—Biography. 3. Women in politics—Argentine Republic—Biography. I. Title. BIP

EVITA : 982'.06'0924 B
Eva Duarte Peron tells her own story / by Evita. London : Proteus ; New York : Distributed by Two Continents, 1978, c1953. 235, [12] p., [4] leaves of plates : ill. ; 23 cm. Translation of La razon de mi vida. [F2849.P313 1978] 78-395643 ISBN 0-906071-07-0 : 10.00
1. Peron, Eva Duarte, 1919-1952. 2. Peron, Juan Domingo, Pres. Argentine Republic, 1895-1974. 3. Argentine Republic—Presidents Wives—Biography. 4. Argentine Republic—Social conditions.

MAIN, Mary (Foster) 920.7
The woman with the whip: Eva Peron, by Maria Flores[pseud. 1st ed.] Garden City, N. Y., Doubleday, 1952. 286 p. 22 cm. [F2849.P37M3] 52-10995
1. Peron, Eva (Duarte) 1919-1952. I. Title.

Peron, Juan Domingo, Pres. Argentine Republic, 1895-1974.

ALEXANDER, Robert Jackson, 1918- 982'.06'0924 B
Juan Domingo Peron : a history / Robert J. Alexander. Boulder, Colo. : Westview Press, 1979. xiii, 177 p. ; 24 cm. Includes index. Bibliography: p. 167-170. [F2849.P48A59] 78-21705 ISBN 0-89158-364-5 lib. bdg. : 15.00
1. Peron, Juan Domingo, Pres. Argentine Republic, 1895-1974. 2. Argentine Republic—Presidents—Biography. 3. Argentine Republic—History—1943- 4. Peronism.

BARAGER, Joseph R., comp. 982
Why Peron came to power; the background to Peronism in Argentina. Edited, with an introd., by Joseph R. Barager. New York, Knopf [1968] xi, 274 p. 19 cm. (Borzoi books on Latin America) Bibliography: p. [267]-274. Bibliographical footnotes. [F2849.B34] 67-20621
1. Peron, Juan Domingo, Pres. Argentine Republic, 1895- 2. Argentine Republic—Politics and government—1943-1955. 3. Argentine Republic—Politics and government—1810- I. Title.

PERON, Eva (Duarte) 1919-1952. 920.7
My mission in life; translated from the original by Ethel Cherry. New York, Vantage Press [c1953] 216p. illus. 23cm. Translation of La razon de mi vida. [F2849.P313] 53-11625
1. Peron, Juan Domingo, Pres. Argentine Republic, 1895- 2. Argentine Republic—Soc. condit. I. Title.

Perceval, Spencer, 1762-1812.

GRAY, Denis 923.242
Spencer Perceval; the evangelical Prime Minister, 1762-1812. [Manchester] Manchester Univ. Pr. [dist. New York, Barnes & Noble, c.1963] xii, 506p. illus., ports, 23cm. Bibl. 64-9 11.00
1. Perceval, Spencer, 1762-1812. I. Title.

Percival, Eleanor (Haas)

PERCIVAL, Eleanor (Haas) 917.71981
Duck Creek Acres. Columbus, Ohio, 1952. 153 p. illus. 24 cm. Autobiographical. [CT275.P566A3] 52-27199
I. Title.

Percy, Charles H.

CLEVELAND, Martha. 973.923'0924
Charles Percy: strong new voice from Illinois, a biography. [1st ed.] Jacksonville, Ill., Harris-Wolfe [1968] 228p. ports. 22cm. [E840.8.P4C55] (B) 67-31276 5.95
1. Percy, Charles H. I. Title.
Publisher's address: 255 N. Main, Jacksonville, Ill. 62650

MURRAY, David, 1925- 973.923'0924 B
Charles Percy of Illinois. [1st ed.] New York, Harper & Row [1968] x, 178 p. illus., ports. 22 cm. [E840.8.P4M8] 68-15967
1. Percy, Charles H. I. Title.

Percy, Walker, 1916-

COLES, Robert. 813'.5'4 B
Walker Percy, an American search / by Robert Coles. 1st ed. Boston : Little, Brown, c1978. xx, 250 p. ; 24 cm. "An Atlantic-Monthly Press book." Includes index. [PS3566.E6912Z6] 78-13629 ISBN 0-316-15160-2 : 15.00
1. Percy, Walker, 1916- 2. Christianity and existentialism in literature. 3. Authors, American—20th century—Biography. I. Title.

Percy, William Alexander, 1885-1942.

PERCY, William Alexander, 1885-1942. 813'.5'2
Lanterns on the levee; recollections of a planter's son. With an introd. by Walker Percy. Baton Rouge, Louisiana State University Press [1973 or 4, c1941] xviii, 347 p. 21 cm. (Library of Southern civilization) [PS3531.E65L3 1973] 73-90687 ISBN 0-8071-0072-2 3.95
1. Percy, William Alexander, 1885-1942. I. Title.

Perera, Edward Walter.

THE lion of 954.9'302'0924 B
Kotte : his life & times / by Douglas D. Ranasinghe. 1st ed. [Rajagiriya?] : Ranasinghe, 1976- v. : ill. ; 27 cm. "Centenary volume, 1875-1975." Includes index. Contents.Contents.—pt. 1. Birth of a patriot. [DS489.73.P47L56] 76-904393
1. Perera, Edward Walter. 2. Statesmen—Sri Lanka—Biography. 3. Sri Lanka—History—1505-1948—Sources. I. Ranasinghe, Douglas D.

Peretz, Isaac Loeb,

PERETZ, Isaac Loeb, 1851-1915. FIC
Peretz. Translated and edited by Sol Liptzin. Freeport, N.Y., Books for Libraries Press [1972, c1947] 379 p. port. 22 cm. (Biography index reprint series) Original ed. issued in series: Yivo bilingual series. English and Yiddish. [PJ5129.P4A6 1972] 839'.09'8309 B 72-5689 ISBN 0-8369-8137-5
I. Series: Yivo Institute for Jewish Research. Yivo bilingual series. BIP

PERETZ, Isaac Loeb, 1851-1915. FIC
Peretz. Translated and edited by Sol Liptzin. Freeport, N.Y., Books for Libraries Press [1972, c1947] 379 p. port. 22 cm. (Biography index reprint series) Original ed. issued in series: Yivo bilingual series. English and Yiddish. [PJ5129.P4A6 1972] 839'.09'8309 B 72-5689 ISBN 0-8369-8137-5
I. Series: Yivo Institute for Jewish Research. Yivo bilingual series. BIP

SAMUEL, Maurice. 928.9249
Prince of the ghetto. New York, Schocken Books [1973, c.1948] 294 p. 18 cm. [PJ5129.P4Z96] 73-81382 ISBN 0-8052-0401-6 2.95 (pbk.)
1. Peretz, Isaac Loeb, 1851-1915. I. Title. BIP

Peretz, Isaac Loeb, 1851-1915—Juvenile literature.

ROTHCHILD, Sylvia, 1923- 928.9249
Keys to a magic door: Isaac Leib Peretz. Illustrated by Bernard Krigstein. [New York] Farrar, Straus & Cudahy [and] Jewish Publication Society [1959] 175p. illus. 22cm. (Covenant books [7] [PJ5129.R67K4] 59-10192
1. Peretz, Isaac Loeb, 1851-1915—Juvenile literature. I. Title.

Perez, Leander Henry, 1871-1969.

CONAWAY, James. 345'.73'0750924 B
Judge: the life and times of Leander Perez. [1st ed.] New York, Knopf; [distributed by Random House] 1973. 204 p. 22 cm. [KF373.P47C65] 73-7267 ISBN 0-394-47429-5 6.95
1. Perez, Leander Henry, 1871-1969. I. Title.

Perez, Leander Henry, 1891-1969.

JEANSONNE, Glen, 1946- 345'.763'01 B
Leander Perez, boss of the Delta / Glen Jeansonne. Baton Rouge : Louisiana State University Press, c1977. p. cm. Includes index. Bibliography: p. [F375.P45J42] 77-4486 ISBN 0-8071-0191-5 : 25.00
1. Perez, Leander Henry, 1891-1969. 2. Politicians—Louisiana—Biography. 3. Judges—Louisiana—Biography. 4. Louisiana—Politics and government—1865-1950. 5. Louisiana—Politics and government—1951- 6. Plaquemines Parish, La.—Politics and government. 7. Louisiana—Race relations. I. Title.

Perez, Tony, 1942- —Juvenile literature.

WHEELOCK, Warren. 973'.04'68 S
Tony Perez, the silent superstar ; Lee Trevino, Supermex ; Jim Plunkett, he didn't drop out / written by Warren H. Wheelock and J. O. "Rocky" Maynes, Jr. ; consultants, Jorge Vadivieso, Amalia Perez, Ruben A. Soruco B. St. Paul : EMC Corp., [1976] p. cm. (Their Hispanic heroes of the U.S.A. ; 4) Brief biographies of three Spanish Americans: a professional golfer, a major league baseball star, and a professional football quarterback. [E184.S75W5 vol. 4] [GV697.A1] 920'.0092'6373 75-40231 ISBN 0-88436-246-9. ISBN 0-88436-247-7 pbk.
1. Perez, Tony, 1942- —Juvenile literature. 2. Trevino, Lee—Juvenile literature. 3. Plunkett, Jim—Juvenile literature. I. Maynes, J. O., joint author. II. Title. III. Title: Lee Trevino, Supermex. IV. Title: Jim Plunkett, he didn't drop out.

Performing arts—Biography.

GRUEN, John. 790.2'0922
Close-up. New York, Viking Press [1968] xvi, 206 p. ports. 25 cm. [PN1583.A2G7] 67-26916
1. Performing arts—Biography. 2. Artists. I. Title.

TREASE, Geoffrey, 1909- 790.20922
Seven stages. New York, Vanguard [1965, c1964] 194, [1] p. ports. 22cm. Bibl. [PN1583.A2T7] 65-26138 3.95
1. Performing arts—Biog. I. Title. BIP

Performing arts—London—Biography.

HIGHFILL, Philip H. 790.2'092'2 B
A biographical dictionary of actors, actresses, musicians, dancers, managers & other stage personnel in London, 1660-1800, by Philip H. Highfill, Jr., Kalman A. Burnim, and Edward A. Langhans. Carbondale, Southern Illinois University Press [1973- v. illus. 26 cm. Contents.Contents.—v. 1. Abaco to Belfille.—v. 2. Belfort to Byzand. Includes bibliographical references. [PN2597.H5] 71-157068 ISBN 0-8093-0518-6 19.85 (v. 1)
1. Performing arts—London—Biography. I. Burnim, Kalman A., joint author. II. Langhans, Edward A., joint author. III. Title. BIP

Performing arts—United States.

HARRIMAN, Margaret (Case) 791'.092'2
Take them up tenderly; a collection of Profiles. Freeport, N.Y., Books for Libraries Press [1972, c1944] xiii, 266 p. 22 cm. (Essay index reprint series) All except one of the Profiles originally appeared in the New Yorker. Contents.Contents.—Mr. Miller and Mr. Hyde: Gilbert Miller.—The old Max: Max Gordon.—The candor kid: Clare Boothe.—Hi-yo, Platinum! Moss Hart.—Miss Lily of New Orleans: Lillian Hellman.—Veni, vidi, Vicky: Helen Hayes.—The wise lived yesterday: Cole Porter.—Big-time urchin: Larry Adler.—Words and music: Rodgers and Hart.—The squarest little shooter on Vesey Street: Oscar Hammerstein II.—The boys: John-Frederics.—Hollywood agent: Leland Hayward.—Miss Fixit: Fanny Holtzmann.—Sweetheart: Mary Pickford.—Dance team: The De Marcos. [PN1582.U6H3 1972] 72-5763 ISBN 0-8369-2991-8
1. Performing arts—United States. 2. United States Biography. I. Title. BIP

Perham, Margery Freda, Dame, 1895-

PERHAM, Margery Freda, Dame, 1895- 916.8'04'50924 B
African apprenticeship; an autobiographical journey in southern Africa, 1929 [by] Margery Perham. New York, Africana Pub. Co. [1974] 268 p. illus. 23 cm. [DT732.P47] 74-78312 ISBN 0-8419-0169-4 12.50
1. Perham, Margery Freda, Dame, 1895- 2. Africa, Southern—Description and travel. I. Title. BIP

Perkins, Carl.

PERKINS, Carl. 784'.092'4 B
Disciple in blue suede shoes / Carl Perkins ; with Ron Rendleman. Grand Rapids : Zondervan Pub. House, c1978. 145 p., [4] leaves of plates. : ill. ; 22 cm. [ML420.P453A3] 78-57518 ISBN 0-310-36730-1 : 6.95
1. Perkins, Carl. 2. Country musicians—United States—Biography. 3. Christian biography—United States. I. Rendleman, Ron, joint author. II. Title. BIP

Perkins, Clifford Alan, 1908-1977.

PERKINS, Clifford Alan, 1908-1977. 363.2'32'0924 B
Border patrol : with the U.S. Immigration Service on the Mexican boundary, 1910-54

/ by Clifford Alan Perkins ; assisted by Nancy Dickey ; edited with an introd. by C. L. Sonnichsen. [El Paso] : Texas Western Press, University of Texas at El Paso, 1978. ix, 126 p. : ill. ; 24 cm. Includes index. [JV6493.P47 1978] 77-91576 ISBN 0-87404-058-2 : 10.00
1. Perkins, Clifford Alan, 1908-1977. 2. United States. Immigration Border Patrol—Officials and employees—Biography. I. Sonnichsen, Charles Leland, 1901- II. Title.

Perkins, Dexter,

PERKINS, Dexter, 1889- 973'.072'024 B
Yield of the years; an autobiography. [1st ed.] Boston, Little, Brown [1969] 245 p. port. 21 cm. [D15.P4A3] 69-16976 6.95
I. Title.

Perkins, Frances, 1882-1965.

MARTIN, George Whitney. 973.917'092'4 B
Madam Secretary, Frances Perkins / by George Martin. Boston : Houghton Mifflin, 1976. xv, 589 p., [8] leaves of plates : ill. ; 24 cm. Includes index. Bibliography: p. [557]-570. [HD8073.P38M37] 75-38637 ISBN 0-395-24293-2 : 16.95
1. Perkins, Frances, 1882-1965. 2. Women in politics—United States—Biography. 3. Labor policy—United States—History. I. Title.

Perkins, Frances, 1882-1965—Juvenile literature.

FRANCES Perkins, 353.83'0924
First Lady of the Cabinet. Illus. with photographs. London, New York, Abelard [1966,i.e.1967] 160p. ports. 22cm. Bibl. [HD8073.P38L3] (B) 68-92844 4.00
1. Perkins, Frances, 1882-1965—Juvenile literature. I. Lawson, Don.

LAWSON, Don. 353.83'0924 (B)
Frances Perkins, First Lady of the Cabinet. Illustrated with photographs. London, New York [etc.] Abelard-Schuman [1966] 160 p. ports. 22 cm. (B***) Bibliography: p. 154-155. [HD8073.P38L3] 68-92844 unpriced
1. Perkins, Frances, 1882-1965—Juvenile literature. I. Title.

MYERS, Elisabeth P. 973.917'092'4
Madam Secretary: Frances Perkins, by Elisabeth P. Myers. New York, J. Messner [1972] 190 p. 22 cm. Bibliography: p. 185-187. A biography of Franklin D. Roosevelt's Secretary of Labor, the first woman to be appointed to the United States Cabinet. [HD8073.P38M9] 92 74-176380 ISBN 0-671-32500-0 4.50
1. Perkins, Frances, 1882-1965—Juvenile literature. I. Title.

Perkins, George Walbridge, 1862-1920.

GARRATY, John Arthur 923.373
Right-hand man; the life of George W. Perkins. New York, Harper [c.1960] xii, 433p. (Bibl. notes: p.393-421) illus. 22cm. 60-10404 7.50
1. Perkins, George Walbridge, 1862-1920. I. Title. **BIP**

GARRATY, John Arthur, 1920- 338'.092'4 B
Right-hand man : the life of George W. Perkins / John A. Garraty. Westport, Conn. : Greenwood Press, 1978, c1960. xii, 433 p., [4] leaves of plates : ill. ; 23 cm. Reprint of the ed. published by Harper, New York. Includes bibliographical references and index. [HC102.5.P4G3 1978] 77-18807 ISBN 0-313-20186-2 lib.bdg. : 26.00
1. Perkins, George Walbridge, 1862-1920. 2. Businessmen—United States—Biography. I. Title.

Perkins, Lucy Fitch, 1865-1937.

PERKINS, Eleanor Ellis, 1893- 928.1
Eve among the Puritans; a biography of Lucy Fitch Perkins. Boston, Houghton Mifflin, 1956. 238 p. illus. 22 cm. [PS3531.E6744Z7] 56-5646
1. Perkins, Lucy Fitch, 1865-1937. I. Title.

perkins, Maxwell Evarts, 1884-19 47

BERG, Andrew Scott. 070.4'092'4 B
Max Perkins editor of Genius, / A. Scott Berg New York : Pocket Books, 1979, c1978. 640 p.: 18 cm. Includes index and bibliographic references [PN149.9P4B4] ISBN 0-671-82719-7 pbk. : 2.50
1. perkins, Maxwell Evarts, 1884-19 47 2. Editors — United States — Biography I. Title.
LC card no. for 1978 E.P. Dutton edition 77-25944

BERG, Andrew Scott. 070.4'092'4 B
Max Perkins, editor of genius / A. Scott Berg. 1st ed. New York : Dutton, c1978. viii, 498 p., [8] leaves of plates : ill. ; 24 cm. "Thomas Congdon books." Includes bibliographical references and index. [PN149.9.P4B4] 77-25944 ISBN 0-525-15427-2 : 15.00
1. Perkins, Maxwell Evarts, 1884-1947. 2. Editors—United States—Biography. I. Title.

PERKINS, Maxwell Evarts, 1884-1947. 070.5'2'0924
Editor to author, the letters of Maxwell E. Perkins / selected and edited, with commentary and an introd., by John Hall Wheelock ; and a new introd. by Marcia Davenport. New York : Scribner, [1979] c1950. xx, 315 p. : port ; 22 cm. Includes bibliographical references and index. [PN149.9.P4A34 1979] 78-66326 ISBN 0-684-16173-7 : 12.50
1. Perkins, Maxwell Evarts, 1884-1947. 2. Editors—Correspondence. I. Wheelock, John Hall, 1886- II. Title.

Perkins, Michael.

PERKINS, Michael. 760'.0924
Renie Perkins; the life and work of a young artist who died by her own hand at the age of twenty-five. Text by Michael Perkins. [1st ed.] New York, Croton Press; distributed by Small Publisher's Co., 1969. 57 p. illus., ports. 21 cm. [N6537.P4P4] 70-91411 1.50
1. Perkins, Renie, 1942-1968.

Perkins, Ralph,

PERKINS, Ralph, 1886- 920
Volume II. Perkinsiana. Cleveland, Gates Press, 1953. ix, 118p. illus. ports., col. coat of arms. 24cm. Companion volume to J. B.'s final [CT275.P573A3] 53-40556
I. Title.

Perkins, Simon, 1771-1844.

CONLIN, Mary Lou. 977.1'3'0924
Simon Perkins of the Western Reserve. [Cleveland] Western Reserve Hist. Soc., 1968. xii, 215p. illus., port. 23cm. (Western Reserve Hist. Soc. pubn. no. 120) Bibl. [F486.W58 no. 120] (B) 67-27800 5.95
1. Perkins, Simon, 1771-1844. I. Title. II. Series: Western Reserve Historical Society, Clevland. Publication no. 120

CONLIN, Mary Lou. 977.1'3'0924 (B)
Simon Perkins of the Western Reserve. [Cleveland] Western Reserve Historical Society, 1968. xii, 215 p. illus., port. 23 cm. (Western Reserve Historical Society publication no. 120) Bibliography: p. 193-205. [F486.W58] 67-27800
1. Perkins, Simon, 1771-1844. I. Title. II. Series: Western Reserve Historical Society, Cleveland. Publication no. 120

Perkins, Thomas Handasyd, 1764-1854.

CARY, Thomas Greaves, 1791-1859. 380.1'0924 B
Memoir of Thomas Handasyd Perkins, containing extracts from his diaries and letters, with an appendix. By Thomas G. Cary. New York, B. Franklin [1971] 304 p. port. 23 cm. (Burt Franklin research and source works series, 591. American classics in history and social sciences, 199) Reprint of the 1856 ed. [F69.P46 1971] 77-164040 ISBN 0-8337-0491-5
1. Perkins, Thomas Handasyd, 1764-1854. 2. Voyages and travels. 3. Massachusetts—Politics and government—1775-1865.

SEABURG, Carl. 380,1'0924 B
Merchant prince of Boston, Colonel T. H. Perkins, 1764-1854 [by] Carl Seaburg and Stanley Paterson. [Cambridge Mass., Harvard University Press] 1971. xi, 478 p. illus. 24 cm. (Harvard studies in business history, 26) Includes bibliographical references. [HF3023.P46S42] 71-165419 ISBN 0-674-56910-5 16.00
1. Perkins, Thomas Handasyd, 1764-1854. I. Paterson, Stanley, joint author. II. Title. III. Series.

Perley, Helen Mewer—Juvenile literature.

JOHNSON, Eleanor Noyes. 636'.00924 B
Mrs. Perley's people. Illustrated by Robert L. Jefferson. Philadelphia, Westminster Press [1970] 158 p. illus., port. 24 cm. Briefly relates the episodes in Helen Perley's life that fostered her interest in animals and describes at length the unusual animal farm she maintains. [SF406.J64] 92 72-117176 4.95
1. Perley, Helen Mewer—Juvenile literature. 2. Animal dealers—Juvenile literature. I. Jefferson, Robert Louis, 1929- illus. II. Title.

Perlman, John.

PERLMAN, John. 811'.5'4
Self portrait / John Perlman. New Rochelle, N.Y. : Elizabeth Press, c1976. 95 p. ; 24 cm. Two hundred and fifty copies printed. [PS3566.E6916S4] 76-379359
I. Title. **BIP**

Perls, Frederick S.

GAINES, Jack, 1918- 616.8'9'00924 B
Fritz Perls, here and now / Jack Gaines. Millbrae, Ca. : Celestial Arts, 1979, c1978. p. cm. Includes index. Bibliography: p. [RC339.52.P47G34] 78-9348 ISBN 0-89087-186-8 : 14.95. ISBN 0-89087-214-7 pbk. : 8.95
1. Perls, Frederick S. 2. Psychiatrists—United States—Biography. 3. Gestalt therapy. I. Title.

Pernet, Etienne Claude, 1824- 1899.

BURTON, Katherine (Kurz) 1890- 922.244
The stars beyond the storms: Father Etienne Pernet, founder of the Congregation of the Little Sisters of the Assumption. With a pref. by Francis Cardinal Spellman. New York, Benziger Bros. [1954] 204p. illus. 21cm. [BX4705.P429B8] 54-4346
1. Pernet, Etienne Claude, 1824- 1899. 2. Little Sisters of the Assumption. I. Title.

Peroff, Frank.

WHITTEMORE, L. H. 364.1'63'0924 B
Peroff : the man who knew too much / by L. H. Whittemore. New York : Morrow, 1975. 315 p. ; 24 cm. [HV6248.P415W48] 75-8767 ISBN 0-688-02934-5 : 8.95
1. Peroff, Frank. 2. Swindlers and swindling—Biography. I. Title: The man who knew too much. **BIP**

Perreault, Gil, 1950- —Juvenile literature.

YOUNG, Scott. 796.9'62'0924 B
Gil Perreault makes it happen. St. Paul, EMC Corp. [1974] 38 p. illus. 24 cm. (His Hockey heroes series) A biography of a Canadian hockey player who is a superstar of the Buffalo Sabres. [GV848.5.P47Y68 1974] 74-8374 ISBN 0-88436-106-3 4.95
1. Perreault, Gil, 1950- —Juvenile literature. 2. Hockey—Juvenile literature. I. Title.
Pbk. 2.95; ISBN 0-88436-107-1.

Perrella, Robert.

PERRELLA, Robert. 282'.092'4 B
They call me the showbiz priest, by Robert Perrella ("Father Bob"). New York, Trident Press [1973] 287 p. ports. 22 cm. [BX4705.P4325A33] 73-82874 ISBN 0-671-27112-1 7.95
1. Perrella, Robert. I. Title. **BIP**

Perrers, Alice, 1348 (ca.)-1400.

KAY, Frederick George, 1911- 942.0370924
Lady of the sun; the life and times of Alice Perrers [by] F. George Kay. New York, Barnes & Noble [1966] 205 p. illus. ports. 23 cm. Bibliography: p. 200. [DA233.K3 1966a] 66-9426
1. Perrers, Alice, 1348 (ca.)-1400. 2. Edward III, King of England, 1312-1377. I. Title.

Perreyve, Henri, 1831-1865.

HAMERTON, Philip Gilbert, 1834-1894. 920'.044
Modern Frenchmen; five biographies. Freeport, N.Y., Books for Libraries Press [1972] xiv, 422 p. 22 cm. (Essay index reprint series) Reprint of the 1878 ed. Contents.Contents.—Victor Jacquemont.—Henri Perreyve.—Francois Rude.—Jean Jacques Ampere.—Henri Regnault. [CT1012.H3 1972] 72-4579 ISBN 0-8369-2947-0 14.50
1. Jacquemont, Victor, 1801-1832. 2. Perreyve, Henri, 1831-1865. 3. Rude, Francois, 1784-1855. 4. Ampere, Jean Jacques Antoine, 1800-1864. 5. Regnault, Henri, 1843-1871. I. Title. **BIP**

Perrin, Elula.

PERRIN, Elula. 301.41'57'0924
Women prefer women / by Elula Perrin ; translated from the French by Harold J. Salemson. 1st ed. New York : Morrow, 1979, c1978. 239 p. ; 22 cm. Translation of Les femmes preferent les femmes. [HQ75.4.P47A3413] 78-13330 ISBN 0-688-03407-1 : 8.95
1. Perrin, Elula. 2. Lesbians—France—Biography. I. Title. **BIP**

Perrin, Henri

PERRIN, Henri 922.244
Priest and worker; the autobiography of Henri Perrin. Tr. [from French] introd. by Bernard Wall. Chicago, Regnery [1966, c.1958, 1964] v, 247p. 22cm. (Logos, 51L-711) [BX4705.P4334A43] 64-14356 1.95 pap.,
I. Title.

PERRIN, Henri. 922.244
Priest and worker; the autobiography of Henri Perrin. Translated and with an introd. by Bernard Wall. [1st ed.] New York, Holt, Rinehart and Winston [1964] v, 247 p. 22 cm. Translation of Itineraire d'Henri Perrin, pretre ouvrier, 1914-1954. [BX4705.P4334A43] 64-14356
I. Title.

Perry, Charies, 1807-1891.

ROBIN, Arthur de Quettevillef. 283'.0924
Charles Perry, Bishop of Melbourne; the challenges of a colonal episcopate, 1847-76 [by] A. de Q. Robin. [Nedlands, Perth] Univ. of Western Australia Pr. [1967] x, 229p. illus., facsim, maps (on lining-papers)

ports. 25cm. Bibl. [BX5720.P4R6] (B) 67-27319 8.50 bds.,
1. Perry, Charles, 1807-1891. I. Title.
Distributed by Verry, Mystic, Conn.

Perry-Cowen, Frances.

PERRY- COWEN, Frances. 784'.092'4 B
Chautauqua to opera : an autobiography of a voice teacher and daughter of a Chautauqua pioneer / Frances Perry-Cowen. 1st ed. Hicksville, N.Y. : Exposition Press, c1978. 127 p. : ill. ; 24 cm. [ML420.R455A3] 78-109572 ISBN 0-682-49112-8 : 8.00
1. Perry-Cowen, Frances. 2. Singers—United States—Biography. I. Title. BIP

Perry, Frederick, 1857-

PERRY, Frederick, 1857- 910'.45
Fair winds & foul : a narrative of daily life aboard an American clipper ship / by Frederick Perry. Stanfordville, N.Y. : E. M. Coleman, 1979. p. cm. (Seafaring men, their ships and time series) Reprint of the 1925 ed. published by C. E. Lauriat Co., Boston. [G540.P4 1979] 79-22111 ISBN 0-930576-25-X : 17.50
1. Perry, Frederick, 1857- 2. Clipper-ships. 3. Seafaring life. 4. Sailors—United States—Biography. I. Title. II. Series. BIP

Perry, Gaylord, 1938-

PERRY, Gaylord, 1938- 796.357'092'4 B
Me and the spitter; an autobiographical confession [by] Gaylord Perry with Bob Sudyk. [1st ed.] New York, Saturday Review Press [1974] 222 p. 22 cm. [GV865.P47A35 1974] 74-245 ISBN 0-8415-0299-4 6.95
1. Perry, Gaylord, 1938- 2. Pitching (Baseball) I. Sudyk, Bob, joint author. II. Title.

PERRY, Gaylord, 1938- 796.357'092'4 B
Me and the spitter; an autobiographical confession [by] Gaylord Perry with Bob Sudyk. [New York] New American Library [1974] 222 p. 18 cm. (A Signet book) [GV865.P47A35 1974] 1.25 (pbk.)
1. Perry, Gaylord, 1938- 2. Pitching (Baseball) I. Sudyk, Bob, joint author. II. Title.
L.C. card number for original ed.: 74-245.

Perry, George Sessions, 1910-1956.

HAIRSTON, Maxine. 818'.5'2 B
George Sessions Perry : his life and works / Maxine Cousins Hairston. Austin, Tex. : Jenkins Pub. Co., 1973. ix, 188 p. : ill. ; 23 cm. Bibliography: p. [179]-188. [PS3531.E687Z7] 73-84416 ISBN 0-8363-0119-6 : 8.95
1. Perry, George Sessions, 1910-1956. BIP

Perry, Jim, 1894 or 5-

PERRY, Jim, 1894or5- 975.5
Le's whittle awhile : my Blue Ridge neighbors and friends / Jim Perry, with Betsy White. Greenville, N.C. : Era Press, c1976. 134 p. : ill. ; 22 cm. [F262.B6P47] 76-41656
1. Perry, Jim, 1894 or 5- 2. Blue Ridge Mountains—Social life and customs. 3. Blue Ridge Mountains—Biography. I. White, Betsy, joint author. II. Title.

Perry, Lewis, 1877-1970.

SALTONSTALL, William Gurdon, 1905- 373.1'2'0120924 B
Lewis Perry of Exeter : a memoir / William G. Saltonstall. 1st ed. New York : Atheneum, 1980. p. cm. [LD7501.E936P477 1980] 79-23837 ISBN 0-689-11056-1 : 6.95
1. Perry, Lewis, 1877-1970. 2. Phillips Exeter Academy—History. 3. High school principals—New Hampshire—Biography. I. Title.

Perry, Matthew Calbraith, 1794-1858.

KUHN, Ferdinand. 923.573
Commodore Perry and the opening of Japan; illustrated by J. Graham Kaye. New York, Random House [1955] 183 p. illus. 22 cm. (Landmark books, 56) Includes bibliography. [E182.P464] 55-5821
1. Perry, Matthew Calbraith, 1794-1858. 2. United States Naval Expedition to Japan, 1852-1854.

MORISON, Samuel Eliot, 1887- 973.5'0924 (B)
"Old Bruin": Commodore Matthew C. Perry, 1794-1858; the American naval officer who helped found Liberia ... [1st ed.] Boston, Little Brown [1967] xxii, 482 p. illus., maps, ports. 24 cm. "An Atlantic Monthly Press book." Bibliography:p. [451]-465. [E182.P466] 67-16707
1. Perry, Matthew Calbraith, I. Title.

MORISON, Samuel Eliot, 1887- 973.5'0924 (B)
'Old Bruin': Commodore Matthew C. Perry, 1794-1858; the American naval officer who helped found Liberia . . . [1st ed.] Boston, Little, Brown [1967] xxii, 482p. illus., maps, ports. 24cm. Atlantic Monthly Pr. bk. Bibl [E182.P466] 67-16707 12.50
1. Perry, Mathew Calbraith, 1794-1858. I. Title.

Perry, Matthew Calbraith, 1794-1858—Juvenile literature.

ORRMONT, Arthur. 923.573
The indestructible Commodore Matthew Perry. New York, J. Messner [1962] 192 p. 22 cm. Includes bibliography. [E182.P467] 62-10195
1. Perry, Matthew Calbraith, 1794-1858—Juvenile literature. I. Title.

Perry, Newel Lewis, 1873-1960.

BUCKINGHAM, Thomas Hugh, 1883-1965. 371.9'11'0924 B
Blind educator : the story of Newel Lewis Perry / by T. Hugh Buckingham. Berkeley, Calif. : L. Buckingham, 1974. 200 p. : ill., ports. ; 24 cm. "100 copies." [HV1792.P47B8] 76-351634
1. Perry, Newel Lewis, 1873-1960. 2. Teachers of the blind—Biography. I. Title.

Perry, Oliver Hazard, 1785-1819.

HOYT, Edwin Palmer 973.4'0924 (B)
The tragic Commodore: the story of Oliver Hazard Perry, by Edwin P. Hovt. London, New York [etc.] Abelard [c.1966, i.e. 1967] 159p. illus., ports., maps, plan. 22cm. Bibl. [E353.1.P4H6] 67-99141 4.00
1. Perry, Oliver Hazard, 1785-1819. I. Title.

RHODES, James A 923.573
The court-martial of Commodore Perry, by James A. Rhodes and Dean Jauchius. [1st ed.] Indianapolis, Bobbs-Merrill [1961] 192p. illus. 22cm. Includes bibliography. [E353.1.P4R5] 61-7897
1. Perry, Oliver Hazard, 1785-1819. I. Jauchius, Dean, joint author. II. Title.

Perry, Pettis.

BOYER, Richard Owen, 1903-1973. 329'.82'00924
Pettis Perry : the story of a working class leader / by Richard O. Boyer. [New York : Self Defense Committee of the 17 Smith Act Victims, 1952] [24] p. : ports. ; 21 cm. First published in the Dec. 1951 issue of Masses & mainstream. [HX84.P47B69] 75-317088
1. Perry, Pettis.

Perry, Ralph Barton,

PERRY, Ralph Barton, 1876- 921.1
The thought and character of William James, as revealed in unpublished correspondence and notes, together with his published writings; 2 v. Boston, Atlantic-Little [1962, c.1935] 2 v. (xxx, 824; xxii, 786p.) illus. 25cm. Contents.v.1. Inheritance and vocations.--v.2. Philosophy and psychology. Bibl. 15.00 set,
I. Title.

Perry, Thomas Sergeant,

PERRY, Thomas Sergeant, 1845-1928. 809 B
Selections from the letters of Thomas Sergeant Perry. Edited, with an introd., by Edwin Arlington Robinson. New York, Macmillan, 1929. St. Clair Shores, Mich., Scholarly Press, 1971. 255 p. port. 22 cm. [PS2554.P16A8 1971] 78-131797 ISBN 0-403-00687-2
I. Robinson, Edwin Arlington, 1869-1935, ed. BIP

Perry, Thomas Sergeant, 1845-1928.

HARLOW, Virginia, 1890- 928.1
Thomas Sergeant Perry: a biography and letters to Perry from William, Henry and Garth Wilkinson James. Durham, N.C., Duke University Press, 1950. xi, 394 p. ports. 24 cm. Bibliography: p. [354]-385. [PS2554.P16H3] 51-383
1. Perry, Thomas Sergeant, 1845-1928.

PERRY, Thomas Sergeant, 1845-1928. 809 B
Selections from the letters of Thomas Sergeant Perry. Edited, with an introd., by Edwin Arlington Robinson. New York, Macmillan, 1929. St. Clair Shores, Mich., Scholarly Press, 1971. 255 p. port. 22 cm. [PS2554.P16A8 1971] 78-131797 ISBN 0-403-00687-2
I. Robinson, Edwin Arlington, 1869-1935, ed. BIP

Pershing, John Joseph, 1860-1948.

ARMY Times, Washington, D. C. 923.573
The Yanks are coming; the story of General John J. Pershing, by the editors of the Army Times. New York, Putnam [c.1960] 182p. Bibl.: p.181-182 illus. 27cm. 60-13667 5.95
1. Pershing, John Joseph, 1860-1948. I. Title.

GOLDHURST, Richard. 355.3'32'0924 B
Pipe clay and drill : John J. Pershing, the classic American soldier / Richard Goldhurst. New York : Reader's Digest Press : distributed by Crowell, 1976, c1977. p. cm. Includes index. Bibliography: p. [F181.P4695 1977] 76-44269 ISBN 0-88349-097-8 : 12.95
1. Pershing, John Joseph, 1860-1948. 2. United States. Army—Biography. 3. Generals—United States—Biography. I. Title.

O'CONNOR, Richard, 1915- 923.573
Black Jack Pershing [1st ed.] Garden City, N. Y., Doubleday, 1961. 431 p. illus. 22 cm. Includes bibliography. [E181.P487] 61-8899
1. Pershing, John Joseph, 1860-1948.

PALMER, Frederick, 1873-1958. 355.3'32'0924 B
John J. Pershing, General of the Armies; a biography. Westport, Conn., Greenwood Press [1970, c1948] xiii, 380 p. ports 23 cm. [E181.P512 1970] 77-100253 ISBN 0-8371-2986-9
1. Pershing, John Joseph, 1860-1948.

SMYTHE, Donald. 355.3'32'0924 B
Guerrilla warrior; the early life of John J. Pershing. New York, Scribner [1973] ix, 370 p. illus. 24 cm. Bibliography: p. 331-362. [E181.P518] 72-12584 ISBN 0-684-12933-7 10.95
1. Pershing, John Joseph, 1860-1948. I. Title.

VANDIVER, Frank Everson, 1925- 355.3'31'0924 B
Black Jack : the life and times of John J. Pershing / by Frank E. Vandiver. 1st ed. College Station : Texas A&M University Press, c1977. 2 v. (xxii, 1178 p., [17] leaves of plates) : ill. ; 24 cm. Includes index. Bibliography: p. [1099]-1122. [E181.P575] 76-51729 ISBN 0-89096-024-0 : 35.00
1. Pershing, John Joseph, 1860-1948. 2. United States. Army—Biography. 3. Generals—United States—Biography. I. Title. BIP

Pershing, John Joseph, 1860-1948—Juvenile literature.

FOSTER, John T. 355.3'32'0924 B
John J. Pershing, World War I hero, by John Foster. Illustrated by Herman B. Vestal. Champaign, Ill., Garrard Pub. Co. [1970] 112 p. illus. (part col.) 24 cm. A biography of "Black Jack" Pershing whose military service earned him the highest rank ever given to an American soldier. [E181.P469] 92 76-90815 2.69
1. Pershing, John Joseph, 1860-1948—Juvenile literature. I. Vestal, Herman B., illus. II. Title.

SCRIMSHER, Lila Gravatt 923.573
General Pershing, strong man. Decorations by Robert L. Allen. San Carlos, Calif., Golden Gate [c.1965] 166p. illus. 22cm. Bibl. [E181.P517] 65-10361 3.75; 3.49 lib. ed.,
1. Pershing, John Joseph, 1860-1948—Juvenile literature. I. Title.

SCRIMSHER, Lila Gravatt. 923.573
General Pershing, strong man. Decorations by Robert L. Allen. San Carlos, Calif., Golden Gate Junior Books [1965] 166 p. illus. 22 cm. Bibliography: p. [165]-166. [E181.P517] 65-10361
1. Pershing, John Joseph, 1860-1948—Juvenile literature. I. Title.

WHITEHOUSE, Arthur George Joseph, 1895- j92
John J. Pershing. New York, Putnam [1964] 191 p. 21 cm. Bibliography: p. 189. [E181.P58] 64-10425
1. Pershing, John Joseph, 1860-1948 —Juvenile literature. I. Title.

WHITEHOUSE ARTHUR GEORGE JOSEPH, 1895- 920
John J. Pershing. New York, Putnam [c.1964] 191p. 21cm. (Lives to remember ser.) Bibl. 64-10425 3.25
1. Pershing, John Joseph, 1860-1948—Juvenile literature. I. Title.

Persinger, Jacob.

PERSINGER, Joseph. 973'.04'97 S
The life of Jacob Persinger / Joseph Persinger. New York : Garland Pub., 1977. 24 p. ; 23 cm. (The Garland library of narratives of North American Indian captivities ; v. 76) Issued with the reprint of the 1860 ed. of Bone, J. H. A. The Indian captive. New York, 1977. Reprint of the 1861 ed. printed for the author by Moody & M'Michael, Sturgeon? Mo. [E85.G2 vol. 76] [E99.S35] 970'.004'97 B 76-54521 ISBN 0-8240-1700-5 : 25.00
1. Persinger, Jacob. 2. Shawnee Indians—Captivities. 3. Indians of North America—Captivities. 4. United States—Biography. I. Title. II. Series.

Perth, James Eric Drummond, 16th Earl of, 1876-

BARROS, James. 341.22'092'4 B
Office without power : Secretary General Sir Eric Drummond, 1919-1933 / by James Barros. Oxford : Clarendon Press ; New York : Oxford University Press, 1979. xii, 4213 p. ; 23 cm. Includes bibliographical references and index. [D413.P45B37] 78-40312 ISBN 0-19-822551-2 : 41.00
1. Perth, James Eric Drummond, 16th Earl of, 1876- 2. League of Nations. 3. League of Nations—Biography. 4. Europe—Politics and government—1918-1945. 5. Diplomats—Great Britain—Biography. I. Title.
Distributed by Oxford University Press, New York, NY BIP

Perth, N.Y.—History.

ZIERAK, Sylvia Jennings. 974.7'47 B
Perth : memories and reflections / by Sylvia Jennings Zierak. 1st ed. [s.l. : s.n.],

c1976 (Amsterdam, N.Y. : Franklin Press) [6], 186 p., [2] fold. leaves of plates : ill. ; 28 cm. Bibliography: 5th prelim. page. [F129.P398Z5] 77-151488
1. Perth, N.Y.—History. 2. Perth, N.Y.—Genealogy.

Peru—History—Conquest, 1522-1548.

ENRIQUEZ de Guzman, Alonso, b.1499. 985'.02'0924 B
The life and acts of Don Alonzo Enriquez de Guzman, a knight of Seville of the Order of Santiago, A.D. 1518 to 1543. Translated from an original and inedited MS. in the National Library at Madrid with notes and an introd. by Clements R. Markham. New York, B. Franklin [1970] xxv, 168 p. 23 cm. (Works issued by the Hakluyt Society, 1st ser., no. 29) Reprint of the 1862 ed. Translation of Libro de la vida y costumbres de don Alonso Enriquez de Guzman. [G161.H22 no. 29] 77-126272
1. Peru—History—Conquest, 1522-1548. I. Markham, Clements Robert, Sir, 1830-1916, ed. II. Series: Hakluyt Society. Works, no. 29

Peru—History—Conquest, 1522-1548—Biography.

LOCKHART, James Marvin. 985'.02'0922 B
The men of Cajamarca; a social and biographical study of the first conquerors of Peru, by James Lockhart. Austin, Published for the Institute of Latin American Studies by the University of Texas Press [1972] xvi, 496 p. map. 23 cm. (Latin American monographs, no. 27) Bibliography: p. [471]-480. [F3442.L77] 72-185236 ISBN 0-292-75001-3 10.00
1. Peru—History—Conquest, 1522-1548—Biography. I. Title. II. Series: Latin American monographs (Austin, Tex.) no. 27. BIP

Peskov, Vasikii Mikhailovich.

PESKOV, Vasilii Mikhailovich. 947
This is my native land : a Soviet journalist's travels / Vasili Peskov ; [translated from the Russian by Fainna Glagoleva]. Moscow : Progress, [1976] 196 p. : ill. (some col.) ; 27 cm. Translation of Otechestvo. [DK29.P4713] 77-361354
1. Peskov, Vasikii Mikhailovich. 2. Russia—Description and travel—1970- I. Title.

Pesqueira, Ignacio, 1818-1886.

ACUNA, Rodolfo. 972'.1'060924
Sonoran strongman: Ignacio Pesqueira and his times [by] Rodolfo F. Acuna. Tucson, University of Arizona Press [1974] x, 179 p. illus. 23 cm. Bibliography: p. 155-172. [F1346.P32A28] 73-76304 ISBN 0-8165-0370-2 4.50 (pbk.)
1. Pesqueira, Ignacio, 1818-1886. 2. Sonora, Mexico—History. I. Title.

Pestalozzi, Johann Heinrich, 1746-1827.

DOWNS, Robert Bingham, 1903- 370'.92'4 B
Heinrich Pestalozzi, father of modern pedagogy, by Robert B. Downs. Boston, Twayne Publishers [1975] 147 p. port. 22 cm. (Twayne's world leaders series) Bibliography: p. 143-144. [LB627.D68] 74-14554 ISBN 0-8057-3560-7 7.50
1. Pestalozzi, Johann Heinrich, 1746-1827.

GUTEK, Gerald Lee. 370.1'092'4
Joseph Neef : The Americanization of Pestalozzianism / Gerald Lee Gutek. University, Ala. : University of Alabama Press, c1977. p. cm. Includes index. Bibliography: p. [LB628.G76] 77-1456 ISBN 0-8173-9110-X : 7.95
1. Pestalozzi, Johann Heinrich, 1746-1827. 2. Neef, Joseph, 1770-1854. 3. Education—Philosophy. 4. Education—United States—Curricula. BIP

SILBER, Kate. 370'.92'4 B
Pestalozzi; the man and his work, by Kate Silber. [3d ed.] New York, Schocken Books [1973] xiv, 337 p. illus. 23 cm. Bibliography: p. 329-332. [LB627.S513 1973b] 73-78301 ISBN 0-8052-3521-3 11.50
1. Pestalozzi, Johann Heinrich, 1746-1827. BIP

SILBER, Kate 923.7494
Pestalozzi, the man and his work. New York, Humanities Press [1961, c.1960] 335p. illus. 60-50500 6.50
1. Pestalozzi, Johann Heinrich, 1746-1827. I. Title.

Petain, Henri Philippe Benoni Omer, 1856-1951.

TOURNOUX, Jean Raymond. 944.0810924
Sons of France: Petain and De Gaulle. Translated by Oliver Coburn. New York, Viking Press [1966] 245 p. illus., facsims., ports. 22 cm. Bibliography: p. 235-239. [DC342.8.P4T63 1966] 66-15876
1. Petain, Henri Philippe Benoni Omer, 1856-1951. 2. Gaulle, Charles de, Pres. France, 1890-1970. I. Title.

Peter I, the Great, Emperor of Russia, 1672-1725.

ANDERSON, Matthew Smith. 947'.05'0924 B
Peter the great / M. S. Anderson. London : Thames and Hudson, c1978. 207 p., [8] leaves of plates : ill. ; 23 cm. (Men in office) Includes index. Bibliography : p. 189-193. [DK131.A49 1978] 78-53047 ISBN 0-500-87008-X : 14.95
1. Peter I, the Great, Emperor of Russia, 1672-1725. 2. Russia—History—Peter I, 1689-1725. 3. Russia—Kings and rulers—Biography. I. Title.
Distributed by W.W. Norton, New York

BRUCE, Peter Henry, 1692-1757. 947'.05'0924
Memoirs of Peter Henry Bruce, esq., a military officer in the services of Prussia, Russia & Great Britain. Containing an account of his travels in Germany, Russia, Tartary, Turkey, the West Indies, &c. As also several very interesting private anecdotes of the Czar, Peter I. of Russia. New York, Da Capo Press, 1970. xv, 527 p. 23 cm. (Russia through European eyes, no. 9) Title on spine: Memoirs of Bruce. Reprint of the 1783 ed. [D285.8.B7A3 1970] 68-27009
1. Peter I, the Great, Emperor of Russia, 1672-1725. 2. Voyages and travels. I. Title. II. Series.

GRAHAM, Stephen, 1884- 947'.05'0924 B
Peter the Great; a life of Peter I of Russia, called the Great. Westport, Conn., Greenwood Press [1971] 376 p. illus., ports. 23 cm. Reprint of the 1929 ed. [DK131.G7 1971] 75-138241 ISBN 0-8371-5598-3
1. Peter I, the Great, Emperor of Russia, 1672-1725. 2. Russia—History—Peter I, 1689-1725.

GREY, Ian, 1918- 923.147
Peter the Great, Emperor of all Russia. [1st ed.] Philadelphia, Lippincott [1960] 505 p. 22 cm. [DK131.G75] 60-5109
1. Peter I, the Great, Emperor of Russia, 1672-1725.

JOSEPH, Joan. 947'.05'0924 B
Peter the Great. New York, J. Messner [1968] 190 p. map. 22 cm. Bibliography: p. 185. A biography of Russia's great Tsar who was responsible for westernizing his country against great opposition and making it a major sea power. [DK131.J66] 92 AC 68
1. Peter I, the Great, Emperor of Russia, 1672-1725. I. Title.

KLIUCHEVSKII, Vasilii Osipovich, 1842?-1911 923.147
Peter the Great, by Vasili Klyuchevsky. Tr. [from Russian] by Liliana Archibald. New York, Random [1961, c.1958] 282p. map (Vintage Russian lib., V-728) Bibl. 1.25 pap.,
1. Peter I, the Great, Emperor of Russia, 1672-1725. I. Archibald, Liliana, tr. II. Title.

OLIVA, Lawrence Jay, 1933- comp. 947'.05'0924 B
Peter the Great. Edited by L. Jay Oliva. Englewood Cliffs, N.J., Prentice-Hall [1970] viii, 181 p. 21 cm. (Great lives observed) (A Spectrum book.) "Bibliographical note": p. 178. [DK131.O39] 76-126813
1. Peter I, the Great, Emperor of Russia, 1672-1725.

PETER the Great. v. 12
Translated from the French by Viola Gervin. New York, Macmillan, 1956. 224p.
1. Peter I, the Great, Emperor of Russia, 1672-1725. I. Grunwald, Constantin de.

PUTNAM, Peter. 947'.05'0924 B
Peter, the revolutionary tsar, by Peter Brock Putnam. Maps and illus. by Laszlo Kubinyi. [1st ed.] New York, Harper & Row [1973] xiv, 269 p. illus. 25 cm. Bibliography: p. [255]-259. A biography of one of the most powerful Russian tsars who determined to "westernize" his country during his reign. [DK131.P88 1973] 92 78-105488 ISBN 0-06-024779-7 7.95
1. Peter I, the Great, Emperor of Russia, 1672-1725. I. Kubinyi, Laszlo, 1937- illus. II. Title. BIP

RAEFF, Marc, ed. 947'.05'0924
Peter the Great changes Russia. Edited and with an introd. by Marc Raeff. 2d ed. Lexington, Mass., Heath [1972] xxiv, 199 p. illus. 21 cm. (Problems in European civilization) First published in 1963 under title: Peter the Great, reformer or revolutionary? Bibliography: p. 195-199. [DK131.R3 1972] 72-1850 ISBN 0-669-82701-0 2.50 (pbk.)
1. Peter I, the Great, Emperor of Russia, 1672-1725. 2. Russia—History—Peter I, 1689-1725. I. Title. II. Series. BIP

RAEFF, Marc, ed. 923.147
Peter the Great, reformer or revolutionary? Boston, Heath [1963] xviii, 109 p. 24 cm. (Problems in European civilization) Second ed. published in 1972 under title: Peter the Great changes Russia. Bibliographical references included in footnotes. "Suggestions for additional reading and a bibliographical note": p. 107-109. [DK131.B14] 63-20379
1. Peter I, the Great, Emperor of Russia, 1672-1725. I. Title. II. Series.

SCHUYLER, Eugene, 1840-1890. 947'.05'0924 B
Peter the Great, Emperor of Russia; a study of historical biography. New York, Russell & Russell [1967] 2 v. illus., geneal. table, maps (1 fold.,) ports. 22 cm. Reprint of the 1884 ed. Bibliographical footnotes. [DK131.S39 1967] 66-24757
1. Peter I, the Great, Emperor of Russia, 1672-1725. I. Title.

STAEHLIN von Storcksburg, Jakob, 1709-1785. 947'.05'0924
Original anecdotes of Peter the Great. New York, Arno Press, 1970. viii, 448 p. 23 cm. (Russia observed) Reprint of the 1788 ed. [DK132.S813 1970] 74-115587 ISBN 0-405-03064-9
1. Peter I, the Great, Emperor of Russia, 1672-1725. I. Title.

WALISZEWSKI, Kazimierz, 1849-1935. 947'.05'0924 B
Peter the Great. Translated from the French by Lady Mary Loyd. [2d ed.] New York, Greenwood Press [1968] x, 562 p. port. 23 cm. Reprint of the 1897 ed. Bibliographical footnotes. [DK131.W173 1968] 69-14133
1. Peter I, the Great, Emperor of Russia, 1672-1725. 2. Russia—History—Peter I, 1689-1725. BIP

WALISZEWSKI, Kazimierz, 1849-1935. 947'.05'0924
Peter the Great. Translated from the French by Mary Loyd. New York, Haskell House, 1969. 2 v. port. 23 cm. Translation of Pierre le grand. Reprint of the 1897 ed. Bibliographical footnotes. [DK131.W173 1969] 68-25279 ISBN 08383-0265-3
1. Peter I, the Great, Emperor of Russia, 1672-1725. 2. Russia—History—Peter I. 1689-1725.

WALISZEWSKI, Kazimierz, 1849-1935. 947'.05'0924 B
Peter the Great. Translated form the French by Lady Mary Lloyd. [2d ed.] St. Clair Shores, Mich., Scholarly Press, 1972. x, 562 p. 22 cm. Translation of Pierre le grand. "Originally published in 1897." Includes bibliographical references. [DK131.W173 1972] 71-145349 ISBN 0-403-01258-9 14.50
1. Peter I, the Great, Emperor of Russia, 1672-1725. 2. Russia—History—Peter I, 1689-1725.

Peter I, the Great, Emperor of Russia, 1672-1725 — Fiction.

TOLSTOI, Aleksei Nikolaevich, graf, 1882-1945. FIC
Peter the First. [Translated by Tatiana Shebunina] New York, Macmillan, 1959. 768 p. 22 cm. Fictionized biograp,y. [PZ3.T58Pe2] 923.147 59-11459
1. Peter I, the Great, Emperor of Russia, 1672-1725 — Fiction. I. Title.

Peter I, the Great, Emperor of Russia, 1672-1725—Juvenile literature.

LIVERSIDGE, Douglas, 1913- 947'.05'0924 B
Peter the Great, the reformer-tsar. New York, F. Watts [1968] vi, 152 p. map. 22 cm. (Immortals of history) [DK131.L5] 68-18579
1. Peter I, the Great, Emperor of Russia, 1672-1725—Juvenile literature. I. Title.

Peter II, King of Yugoslavia, 1923-

ALEKSANDRA, consort of Peter II, King of Yugoslavia, 1921- 923.1497
For love of a king. [1st ed.] Garden City, N. Y., Doubleday, 1956. 318p. illus. 22cm. [DR369.A6] 56-7529
1. Peter II, King of Yugoslavia, 1923- I. Title.

PETER II King of Yugoslavia, 1923- 923.1497
A King's heritage. New York, Putnam [1954] 304 p. illus. 22 cm. [DR369.P4] 54-10501
1. Yugoslavia—History. I. Title.

Peter, Saint, apostle.

CLIFFORD, T. A., 1893- 225.9'24 B
Peter and the keys, by T. A. Clifford. Philadelphia, Dorrance [1972] 58 p. 22 cm. Includes bibliographical references. [BS2515.C54] 72-171930 ISBN 0-8059-1615-6 3.50
1. Peter, Saint, apostle. 2. Papacy. I. Title.

ELTON, Godfrey Elton, baron, 1892- 226.0905
Simon Peter [by] Lord Elton. [1st ed. in the U.S.A.] Garden City, N.Y., Doubleday, 1966 [c1965] xvii, 236 p. 22 cm. Bibliographical footnotes. [BS2515.E45 1966] 66-10918
1. Peter, Saint, apostle. I. Title.

ELTON, Godfrey Elton, baron, 1892- 226.0905
Simon Peter [1st ed. in the U.S.A.] Garden City, N.Y., Doubleday, 1966 [c.1965] xvii, 236p. 22cm. Bibl. [BS2515.E45] 66-10918 4.50
1. Peter, Saint, apostle. I. Title.

LOWE, John, 1899- 922.1
Saint Peter. New York, Oxford University Press, 1956. 65p. 20cm. [BS2515.L7] 225.92 56-8573
1. Peter, Saint, apostle. I. Title.

MARY Simeon, Mother, 225.92
Simon called Peter. Decorations by John F. Kelly. Westminster, Md., Newman Press, 1959[i.e., 1960] 111p. illus. 19cm. 60-1823 2.25 bds.,
1. Peter, Saint, apostle. I. Title.

MEYER, Frederick Brotherton, 1847-1929. v. 12
Peter, fisherman, disciple, apostle. [New ed.] Fort Washington, Pa., Christian Literature Crusade [1961] 190 p. This edition first published 1950. 66-51410
1. Peter, Saint, apostle. I. Title.

PALAU, Luis. 248'.4
Walk on water, Pete! / By Luis Palau. Glendale, Calif. : G/L Regal Books, [1974] 87 p. ; 18 cm. [BV4501.2.P27] 74-79563 ISBN 0-8307-0286-5 pbk. 1.25
1. Peter, Saint, apostle. 2. Christian life—1960- I. Title. BIP

PETER, disciple, apostle, 922.1
martyr; a historical and theological study. Translated from the German by Floyd V. Filson. Philadelphia, Westminster Press [1953] 252p. illus. 24cm. Bibliographical footnotes. [BS2515.C813] [BS2515.C813] 225.92 53-13084 53-13084
1. Peter, Saint, apostle. I. Cullmann, Oscar.

PITTENGER, William 225.9'24 B
Norman, 1905-
The life of Saint Peter, by W. Norman Pittenger. New York, Watts [1971] x, 116 p. 22 cm. (Immortals of philosophy and religion) Includes bibliographical references. The life of the disciple who founded the Christian Church. [BS2515.P58] 92 70-134659 ISBN 0-531-00963-7
1. Peter, Saint, apostle. I. Title.

SAINT Peter. v. 12
Oxford, Clarendon Press, 1956. 65p. 20cm.
1. Peter, Saint, apostle. I. Lowe, John, 1899-

SIMON Peter, 922.1
sinner and saint. Grand Rapids, Zondervan Pub. House [1954] 185p. 20cm. [BS2515.D4] [BS2515.D4] 225.92 54-11935 54-11935
1. Peter. Saint, apostle. I. De Haan, Martin Ralph, 1891-

Peter, Saint, apostle — Juvenile literature.

WOOD, Katharine Marie, 225.92
1910-
The holy apostles: Peter and Paul. Story and pictures by Katharine Wood. New York, P. J. Kenedy [1960] unpaged illus. 29 cm. [BS2515.W64] 60-13883
1. Peter, Saint, apostle — Juvenile literature. 2. Paul, Saint, apostle — Juvenile literature. I. Title.

Peter, Saint, apostle—Juvenile literature.

BLACKWELL, Muriel 225.9'24 B
Fontenot.
Peter, the prince of apostles / Muriel F. Blackwell ; illustrated by Paul Karch. Nashville : Broadman Press, c1976. 48 p. : col. ill. ; 24 cm. (Biblearn series) Discusses the conversion and ministry of Peter, the apostle chosen to lead Jesus' followers after the crucifixion. [BS2515.B52] 76-382762 ISBN 0-8054-4227-8 : 3.95
1. Peter, Saint, apostle—Juvenile literature. 2. Bible. N.T.—Biography—Juvenile literature. 3. Apostles—Biography—Juvenile literature. I. Karch, Paul. II. Title.

SCHRAFF, Francis. 225.9'22 B
The adventures of Peter and Paul : Acts of the Apostles for the young / Francis and Anne Schraff ; with 17 playlets by Suzanne Hockel ; [ill., Linda Harris]. Liguori, Mo. : Liguori Publications, c1978. 79 p. : col. ill. ; 28 cm. Brief stories and plays recount the deeds of Christ's apostles. [BS2515.S3] 78-64755 ISBN 0-89243-094-X : 2.95
1. Peter, Saint, apostle—Juvenile literature. 2. Paul, Saint, Apostle—Juvenile literature. 3. Apostles—Biography—Juvenile literature. 4. Christian saints—Turkey—Tarsus—Juvenile literature. 5. Tarsus, Turkey—Biography—Juvenile literature. I. Schraff, Anne E., joint author. II. Hockel, Suzanne. III. Harris, Linda. IV. Title. BIP

Peter, Sarah (Worthington) King, 1800-1877—Juvenile literature.

POWER-WATERS, Alma (Shelley) 92
1896-
Sarah Peter: the dream and the harvest. Illus. by John Lawn. New York, Farrar [c.1965] xii, 177p. illus. 22cm. (Vision bk. 68) [CT275.P58P6] 65-20919 2.25
1. Peter, Sarah (Worthington) King, 1800-1877—Juvenile literature. I. Title.

Peter I, the great, Emperor of Russia, 1672-1725.

KLIUCHEVSKII, Vasilii 923.147
Osipovich, 1841-1911.
Peter the Great. Translated by Liliana Archibald. [New York] St. Martin's Press, 1958. 282p. illus. 23cm. Translation of v. 4 of the author's Курс русской (transliterated: Kurs russkoi istorii) [DK131.K553] 59-1544
1. Peter I, the great, Emperor of Russia, 1672-1725. I. Title.

PETER the Great. v. 12
Translated by Liliana Archibald. London, Macmillan New York, St. Martin's Press [c1958] 282p. illus. Translation of v. 4 of the author's Kurs russkoi istorii.
1. Peter I, I. Kliuchevskii, Vasilii Osipovich, 1841-1911. II. The Great, Emperor of Russia, 1672-1725.

Peterkin, Myrna.

KUHLMAN, Kathryn. 616.7'2
Standing tall / Kathryn Kuhlman. Minneapolis : Bethany Fellowship, [1975] 87 p. : ill. ; 18 cm. (Dimension books) [RC933.K8] 74-28755 ISBN 0-87123-534-X pbk. : 0.95
1. Peterkin, Myrna. 2. Arthritis—Personal narratives. 3. Faith-cure. I. Title. BIP

Peters, Christina, 1942-

PETERS, Christina, 616.8'523 B
1942-
Tell me who I am before I die / Christina Peters, with Ted Schwarz. 1st ed. New York : Rawson Associates Publishers, c1978. 211 p. ; 22 cm. [RC569.5.M8P47 1978] 78-54689 ISBN 0-89256-063-0 : 9.95
1. Peters, Christina, 1942- 2. Multiple personality—United States—Biography. I. Schwarz, Theodore, joint author. II. Title. BIP

Peters, Frederick C., 1900-

BURGHARD, August, 630'.92'4 B
1901-
The story of Frederick C. Peters. Fort Lauderdale, Fla., Tropical Press, 1972. v, vii, 258 p. illus. 26 cm. Bibliography: p. 243-248. [S417.P44B87] 72-94217
1. Peters, Frederick C., 1900- 2. Potatoes—Florida. 3. Agriculture—Florida. 4. Plantation, Fla. (Broword Co.)

Peters, Hugh 1598-1660.

STEARNS, Raymond Phineas, 922.542
1904-
The strenous Puritan: Hugh Peters, 1598-1660. Urbana, University of Illinois, 1954. x, 463p. illus., ports. 27cm. Bibliographical footnotes. [DA407.P4S8] 53-9765
1. Peters, Hugh 1598-1660. 2. Gt. Brit.—Hist.—Puritan Revolution, 1642-1660. I. Title.

Peters, Jean, 1927-

STRAIT, 791.43'028'0924 B
Raymond.
Mrs. Howard Hughes. Los Angeles, Holloway House Pub. Co. [distributed by All American Pub. Co., 1970] 244 p. illus., ports. 18 cm. [PN2287.P4S8] 70-20746 ISBN 0-87067-408-0 1.50
1. Peters, Jean, 1927- I. Title.

Peters, Lloyd, 1902-

PETERS, Lloyd, 791.43'028'0924 B
1902-
Lionhead Lodge / Lloyd Peters. Fairfield, Wash. : Ye Galleon Press, 1976. 179 p. : ill. ; 25 cm. [PN2287.P42A35] 77-357244
1. Peters, Lloyd, 1902- 2. Moving-picture actors and actresses—United States—Biography. I. Title. BIP

Peters, Matthew William, 1742-1814.

TRIPP, Miles, 1923- FIC
A woman in bed / Miles Tripp. London : Macmillan, 1976. 160 p. ; 21 cm. Includes as an appendix a life of the painter Matthew William Peters, 1742-1814. Includes bibliographical references. [PZ4.T837Wp] [PR6070.R48] 823'.9'14 76-383145 ISBN 0-333-17807-6 : £2.95
1. Peters, Matthew William, 1742-1814. 2. Painters—England—Biography. I. Title.

Petersen, Johann.

PETERSEN, Johann. 920
I am a fugitive from injustice, from a cesspool of intolerance, greed, and corruption. [n.p.] 1952. 136p. illus. 21cm. Autobiographical. [CT275.P584A3] 56-21051
I. Title.

Peterson, Elmer George.

PETERSON, E. G., 630'.7'1179212 B
Mrs., 1890-
Remembering E. G. Peterson, his life and our story, by Mrs. E. G. Peterson. [Logan, Utah] Old Main Society [1974] 137 p. illus. 24 cm. [S537.U92P47] 74-13517 ISBN 0-87421-070-4
1. Peterson, Elmer George. 2. Utah. State University of Agriculture and Applied Science, Logan—History. I. Title. BIP

Peterson, Jim.

FLOWERS, M. 926.1
Doctor Jim. New York, Vantage Press [1952] 149 p. 23 cm. [R154.P475F55] 52-6934
1. Peterson, Jim. I. Title.

***Peterson, Norman E.**

*PETERSON, Norman E. 920
Beauty in a world of darkness: as lived by Norman E. Peterson. New York, Vantage [1966] 82p. 21cm. 2.50 bds.,
I. Title.

Peterson, Roger Tory, 1908-

DEVLIN, John C. 598.2'092'4 B
The world of Roger Tory Peterson : an authorized biography / by John C. Devlin and Grace Naismith ; foreword by Elliot Richardson. New York : Quadrangle/New York Times Book Co., c1977. p. cm. Includes index. [QL31.P45D48 1977] 77-5180 ISBN 0-8129-0694-2 : 14.95
1. Peterson, Roger Tory, 1908- 2. Ornithologists—United States—Biography. I. Naismith, Grace, joint author. II. Title. BIP

Pethick-Lawrence, Emmeline, 1867-

PETHICK-LAWRENCE, 324'.3'0924
Emmeline, 1867-
My part in a changing world / by Emmeline Pethick-Lawrence. Westport, Conn. : Hyperion Press, 1976. p. cm. (Pioneers of the woman's movement) Reprint of the 1938 ed. published by V. Gollancz, London. [HQ1595.P45A3 1976] 75-21811 ISBN 0-88355-260-4 : 22.50
1. Pethick-Lawrence, Emmeline, 1867- I. Title. BIP

Pethick-Lawrence, Frederick William, 1871-

BRITTAIN, Vera Mary 923.242
Pethick-Lawrence; a portrait. London, Allen & Unwin [Mystic, Conn., Verry, 1965, c.1963] 232p. illus., ports. 23cm. Bibl. [DA566.9.P4B7] 63-24260 5.00 bds.,
1. Pethick-Lawrence, Frederick William, 1871- I. Title.

Petigru, James Louis,

PETIGRU, James 340'.092'4 B
Louis, 1789-1863.
Life, letters, and speeches of James Louis Petigru, the Union man of South Carolina, by James Petigru Carson. With an introd. by Gaillard Hunt. Freeport, N.Y., Books for Libraries Press [1972] p. Reprint of the 1920 ed. [F273.P4814 1972] 72-8433 ISBN 0-8369-6969-3
I. Carson, James Petigru.

Petigru, James Louis, 1789-1863.

EDWARDS, Sally. 340'.0924 B
The man who said no. New York, Coward-McCann [1970] 191 p. 23 cm. Bibliography: p. 184-185. A biography of the South Carolina lawyer who remained faithful to the Union throughout the Civil War. [KF368.P44E3] 92 75-106925 4.95
1. Petigru, James Louis, 1789-1863. I. Title. BIP

PETIGRU, James 340'.092'4 B
Louis, 1789-1863.
Life, letters, and speeches of James Louis Petigru, the Union man of South Carolina, by James Petigru Carson. With an introd. by Gaillard Hunt. Freeport, N.Y., Books for Libraries Press [1972] p. Reprint of the 1920 ed. [F273.P4814 1972] 72-8433 ISBN 0-8369-6969-3
I. Carson, James Petigru.

Petit, Adolphe, 1822-1914.

ENRODY, Ladislas J 922.2493
Hope unlimited; little stories from the life of the saintly Father Petit. S. J. English translation by Sister Teresa Clare. [Boston] St Paul Editions [c1962] 113 p. illus. 22 cm. [BX4705.P435E5] 62-21100
1. Petit, Adolphe, 1822-1914. I. Title.

Petkoff, Teodoro, 1931-

GALL, Norman. 918 S
Teodoro Petkoff: the crisis of the professional revolutionary. [Hanover, N.H.] American Universities Field Staff [197 -73] v. illus. 29 cm. (Fieldstaff reports: East Coast South America series, ; v. 17, no. 9) Cover title. Contents.Contents.— —pt. 2. A new party. Bibliography: ; v. 2, p. 21-24. [F2214.A65 vol. 17, no. 9, etc.] [HX233.5] 322.4'2'0924 B 74-165260 1.00 ea. (nonsubscribers)
1. Petkoff, Teodoro, 1931- 2. Communism—Venezuela. I. Series: American Universities Field Staff. Fieldstaff reports. II. Series: East Coast South American series, v.

Petliura, Symon Vasyl'ovych, 1879-1926.

DESROCHES, Alain. 947'.71'084 B
The Ukrainian problem and Symon Petlura (the fire and the ashes). Chicago, Ukrainian Research and Information Institute, 1970. 108 p. port. 24 cm. [DK508.6.P4D413] 72-170484 3.00
1. Petliura, Symon Vasyl'ovych, 1879-1926. 2. Nationalism Ukraine. I. Title.

Petrarca, Francesco,

PETRARCA, Francesco, 1304- 928.5
1374.
Petrarch at Vaucluse; letters in verse and prose, translated by Ernest Hatch Wilkins. [Chicago] University of Chicago Press [1958] 215 p. 20 cm. [PQ4507.W5] 58-5688
I. Wilkins, Ernest Hatch, 1880- ed. and tr.

Petrarca, Francesco — Homes and haunts — Milan.

WILKINS, Ernest Hatch, 928.5
1880-
Petrarch's eight years in Milan. Cambridge, Mass., Mediaeval Academy of America, 1958. xx, 266 p. port. 24 cm. (Mediaeval Academy of America. Publication no. 69) Bibliographical references included in "Introductory notes" (p. ix-sv) [PQ4519.M5W5] 58-13250
1. Petrarca, Francesco — Homes and haunts — Milan. I. Title. II. Series. BIP

Petrarca, Francesco, 1304-1374.

BISHOP, Morris, 1893- 851'.1 B
Petrarch and his world. Drawings by Alison Mason Kingsbury. Port Washington, N.Y., Kennikat Press [1973, c1963] 399 p. illus. 22 cm. Bibliography: p. [376]-377.

[PQ4505.B5 1973] 72-85320 ISBN 0-8046-1730-9
1. Petrarca, Francesco, 1304-1374. I. Title. BIP

HOLLWAY-CALTHROP, Henry 851'.1 B Calthrop.
Petrarch: his life and times. New York, Cooper Square Publishers, 1972. x, 319 p. illus. 23 cm. [PQ4505.H7 1972] 75-187413 ISBN 0-8154-0406-9
1. Petrarca, Francesco, 1304-1374. 2. Italy—History—1268-1492.

JERROLD, Maud F. 851'.1
Francesco Petrarca, poet and humanist, by Maud F. Jerrold. Port Washington, N.Y., Kennikat Press [1970] xi, 350 p. illus. 23 cm. "First published in 1909." Bibliography: p. 335-344. [PQ4505.J4 1970] 78-103195
1. Petrarca, Francesco, 1304-1374. 2. Petrarca, Francesco, 1304-1374—Knowledge and learning.

PETRARCA, Francesco, 1304-1374. 928.5
Petrarch at Vaucluse; letters in verse and prose, translated by Ernest Hatch Wilkins. [Chicago] University of Chicago Press [1958] 215 p. 20 cm. [PQ4507.W5] 58-5688
I. Wilkins, Ernest Hatch, 1880- ed. and tr.

WILKINS, Ernest Hatch, 1880- 928.5
Petrach's later years. Cambridge, Mass., Mediaeval Academy of America, 1959. xiv, 322 p. facsim. 24 cm. (Mediaeval Academy of America. Publication no. 70) A continuation of the author's Petrarch's eight years in Milan. Bibliographical references included in "Introductory notes" (p. ix-xiv) [PQ4513,W5] 59-14351
1. Petrarca, Francesco, 1304-1374. I. Title. II. Series.

WILKINS, Ernest Hatch, 1880- 928.5
Studies in the life and works of Petrarch. Cambridge, Mass., Mediaeval Academy of America, 1955. xiv, 324p. 24cm. (Mediaeval Academy of America. Publication no. 63) Includes bibliographies. [PQ4505.Z5W5] 55-8492
1. Petrarca, Francesco, 1304-1374. I. Title. II. Series. BIP

WILKINS, Ernest Hatch, 1880-1966. 928.5
Life of Petrarch. [Chicago] University of Chicago Press [1961] 275 p. 23 cm. [PQ4505.W5 1961] 61-15939
1. Petrarca, Francesco, 1304-1374.

Petrarca, Francesco, 1304-1374—Congresses.

FRANCESCO Petrarca, 851'.1
citizen of the world / edited by Also S. Bernardo. Albany : State University of New York Press, 1979. p. cm. (Studi sul Petrarca ; v. 7) Major lectures delivered at the Congress dealing with Petrarca's life and works held Apr. 6-13, 1974 in Washington. [PQ4504.F7] 79-13968 ISBN 0-87395-392-4 : 35.00
1. Petrarca, Francesco, 1304-1374—Congresses. I. Bernardo, Also S. II. Title. III. Series.

Petre, Diana—Biography.

PETRE, Diana. 823'.9'14 B
The secret orchard of Roger Ackerley / Diana Petre. New York : G. Braziller, 1975. vii, 182 p., [4] leaves of plates : ill. ; 22 cm. [PR6066.E754Z525 1975] 75-13516 ISBN 0-8076-0799-1 : 6.95
1. Petre, Diana—Biography. 2. Ackerley, Alfred Roger. 3. Scott-Hewitt, Muriel Haidee Perry, 1890-1960. I. Title. BIP

Petre, William, Sir 1505?-1572.

EMMISON, Frederick George, 1907- 923.242
Tudor secretary: Sir William Petre at court and home. Cambridge, Mass., Harvard [c.] 1961[ ] 264p. illus. Bibl. 61-4859 8.50
1. Petre, William, Sir 1505?-1572. I. Title.

Petroleum Industry and trade.

GETTY, Jean Paul, 1892-1976. 923.373
My life and fortunes. [1st ed.] New York, Duell, Sloan and Pearce [1963] 300 p. illus. 24 cm. [HD9570.G4A3] 63-10344
1. Petroleum Industry and trade. I. Title.

Petroleum industry and trade—U.S.—History.

O'CONNOR, Richard, 1915- 338.2'7'2820922
The oil barons; men of greed and grandeur. [1st ed.] Boston, Little, Brown [1971] x, 502 p. map (on lining papers) 25 cm. Includes bibliographical references. [HD9565.O34] 75-135432 8.95
1. Petroleum industry and trade—U.S.—History. 2. Petroleum industry and trade—History. I. Title.

Petrosino, Joseph, 1860-1909.

PETACCO, Arrigo. 364.1'523'0924 B
Joe Petrosino. Translated by Charles Lam Markmann. [1st American ed.] New York, Macmillan [1974] viii, 195 p. illus. 21 cm. [HV7911.P45P4813] 73-17179 ISBN 0-02-595160-2 5.95
1. Petrosino, Joseph, 1860-1909. BIP

Petrovskaya, Kyra

PETROVSKAYA, Kyra 927.92
Kyra. [New York] New Americana Lib. [1961, c.1959] 320p. (Signet bk., T1888) .75 pap.,
I. Title.

PETROVSKAYA, Kyra. 927.92
Kyra. Englewood Cliffs, N. J., Prentice-Hall [1959] 344 p. illus. 22 cm. Autobiography. [PN2728.P38A3] 59-8767
I. Title.

Petrus Lombardus, bp. of Paris, ca.1100-1164. Sententiarum libri quatuor.

IN Petri Lombardi v. 12
Sententias theologicas commentariorum libri IIII. Venetiis ex Typographia Guerraea, 1571. Ridgewood, N.J., Gregg Press, 1964. 2 v. 66-42120
1. Petrus Lombardus, bp. of Paris, ca.1100-1164. Sententiarum libri quatuor.

SERIPTUM super super primum v. 12
Senterntiarum. Edited by Eligius M. Buytacrt. St. Binaventure. N. Y. Franciscan Institute, 1952-56. 2v. (xxviii, 1053 p.) (Franciscan Institute publications. Text series, no. 3) Includes bibliography.
1. Petrus Lombardus, Bp. of Paris, d.1164. Sententiarum libri. I. Aureoli, Petrus, Abp. of Aix, 1260-1322. II. Buytaert, Eloi Marie, 1913- ed. III. Series.

Petrus Thomasius, Saint, 1305-1366.

BOEHLKE, Frederick J 1926- 271.9710924 (B)
Pierre de Thomas, scholar, diplomat, and crusader [by] Frederick J. Boehlke, Jr. Philadelphia, University of Pennsylvania Press [1966] 360 p. 22 cm. Based on thesis, University of Pennsylvania. Bibliography: p. 328-352. [BX4700.P466B6 1966] 65-23579
1. Petrus Thomasius, Saint, 1305-1306. I. Title.

BOEHLKE, Frederick J., Jr., 1926- 271.9710924
Pierre de Thomas, scholar, diplomat, and crusader. Philadelphia, Univ. of Pa. Pr. [c.1966] 360p. 22cm. Bibl. [BX4700.P466B6] 65-23579 7.50
1. Petrus Thomasius, Saint, 1305-1366. I. Title.

Petteys, Anna C.

LUBCHENCO, Portia (McKnight) 926.1
Doctor Portia, her first fifty years in medicine, as told to Anna C. Petteys. Denver, Golden Bell [c.]1964. 315p. illus., ports. 23cm. 64-8450 5.00
1. Petteys, Anna C. I. Title.

Pettigrew, Charles, 1744-1807.

LEMMON, Sarah McCulloh. 283'.0924 B
Parson Pettigrew of the "Old Church", 1744-1807. Chapel Hill, University of North Carolina Press, 1970. 168 p. 23 cm. (The James Sprunt studies in history and political science, v. 52) Bibliography: p. [149]-155. [F251.J28 vol. 52] 76-132259 ISBN 0-8078-5052-7
1. Pettigrew, Charles, 1744-1807. I. Title. II. Series. BIP

Pettis, Jerry L., 1916-1975.

WOOD, Miriam. 328.73'092'4 B
Congressman Jerry L. Pettis, his story / by Miriam Wood. Mountain View, Calif. : Pacific Press Pub. Association, c1977. 128 p. : ill. ; 22 cm. (A Destiny book) [E840.8.P43W66] 77-80683 pbk. : 3.50
1. Pettis, Jerry L., 1916-1975. 2. United States. Congress. House—Biography. 3. Legislators—United States—Biography. I. Title.

Pettit, Hermon, 1894-

PETTIT, Hermon, 1894- 269'.2'0924 B
Jubilee! : Autobiography of Hermon Pettit / Hermon Pettit and Helen Wessel ; [cover photo, Jim Morgenstern]. Fresno, Calif. : Bookmates International, c1979. 177 p. : ill. ; 21 cm. [BV3785.P48A34] 78-73580 ISBN 0-933082-00-2 pbk. : 3.95
1. Pettit, Hermon, 1894- 2. Evangelists—United States—Biography. I. Wessel, Helen Strain, 1924- joint author. II. Title. BIP

Pettit, Robert E. Lee,

PETTIT, Robert E. Lee, 1932- 796.323640924
Bob Pettit: the drive within me, by Bob Pettit with Bob Wolff. Englewood Cliffs, N. J., Prentice-Hall [1966] 170 p. illus., ports. 24 cm. [GN885.P44] 66-14357
1. Wolff, Bob. II. Title. III. Title: The drive within me.

Pettus, John Jones, 1813-1867.

DUBAY, Robert W. 976.2'05'0924 B
John Jones Pettus, Mississippi fire-eater : his life and times, 1813-1867 / Robert W. Dubay. Jackson : University Press of Mississippi, c1975. xii, 234 p. ; 24 cm. Includes index. Bibliography: p. 209-228. [F341.P47D82] 74-33923 ISBN 0-87805-066-3 : 12.50
1. Pettus, John Jones, 1813-1867. I. Title. BIP

Pettus, Winston, 1912-1945.

HUME, Edward Hicks, 1876- 926.1
Dauntless adventurer; the story of Dr. Winston Pettus. New Haven, 1952. 195 p. illus. 25 cm. [R154.P48H8] 52-10894
1. Pettus, Winston, 1912-1945. I. Title.

Petty, Lee—Juvenile literature.

LIBBY, Bill. 796.7'2'0922 B
Superdrivers : three auto racing champions / by Bill Libby. Champaign, Ill. : Garrard Pub. Co., c1977. 96 p. : ill. ; 24 cm. Biographical sketches of three American racing car drivers: Rodger Ward, Lee Petty, and Don Garlits. [GV1032.A1L53] 920 76-47475 ISBN 0-8116-6681-6 lib.bdg. : 3.84
1. Ward, Rodger—Juvenile literature. 2. Petty, Lee—Juvenile literature. 3. Garlits, Don—Juvenile literature. 4. Automobile racing drivers—United States—Biography—Juvenile literature. I. Title. BIP

Petty, Richard.

LIBBY, Bill. 796.7'2'0924 B
"King Richard" : the Richard Petty story / by Bill Libby, with Richard Petty. 1st ed. Garden City, N.Y. : Doubleday, 1977. 322 p., [16] leaves of plates : ill. ; 22 cm. [GV1032.P47L52] 76-40884 ISBN 0-385-11404-4 : 9.95
1. Petty, Richard. 2. Automobile racing drivers—United States—Biography. I. Petty, Richard, joint author. II. Title.

PETTY, Richard. 796.7'2 B
Grand National; the autobiography of Richard Petty as told to Bill Neely. Chicago, Regnery [1971] 212 p. illus. 22 cm. [GV1032.P47A3] 78-163255 5.95
I. Neely, Bill. II. Title.

PETTY, Richard. 796.7'2 B
Grand National [by] Richard Perry as told to Bill Neely. [New York] Berkley Pub. Co. [1974, c1971] 175 p. 18 cm. (A Berkley medallion book) [GV1032.P47A3] ISBN 0-425-02455-5. 0.95 (pbk.)
I. Neely, Bill. II. Title.
L.C. card number for original ed.: 78-163255.

PETTY, Richard. 796.7'2'0924 B
King of the road / by Richard Petty ; photography and drawings by Ellen Griesedieck. New York : Macmillan, c1977. 200 p. : ill. ; 26 cm. "A Ruthledge book." [GV1032.P47A34] 76-44947 9.95
1. Petty, Richard. 2. Automobile racing drivers—United States—Biography. I. Title. BIP

Petty, Richard.

PETTY, Richard. 796.7'2 B
Grand National; the autobiography of Richard Petty as told to Bill Neely. Chicago, Regnery [1971] 212 p. illus. 22 cm. [GV1032.P47A3] 78-163255 5.95
I. Neely, Bill. II. Title.

PETTY, Richard. 796.7'2 B
Grand National [by] Richard Perry as told to Bill Neely. [New York] Berkley Pub. Co. [1974, c1971] 175 p. 18 cm. (A Berkley medallion book) [GV1032.P47A3] ISBN 0-425-02455-5. 0.95 (pbk.)
I. Neely, Bill. II. Title.
L.C. card number for original ed.: 78-163255.

Petty, Richard—Juvenile literature.

BURCHARD, Marshall. 796.7'2'0924 B
Sports hero, Richard Petty / by Marshall and Sue Burchard. New York : Putnam, [1974] 95 p. : ill. ; 23 cm. (The Sports hero biographies) An easy-to-read biography of the stock-car driver whose many record-breaking accomplishments have earned him the title King Richard. [GV1032.P47B87 1974] 92 74-77296 ISBN 0-399-20408-3. ISBN 0-399-60899-0 lib. bdg. : 4.69
1. Petty, Richard—Juvenile literature. 2. Automobile racing—Juvenile literature I. Burchard, S. H., joint author. II. Title.

Petty, Sir William, 1623-1687.

STRAUSS, Emil, 1889- 923.342
Sir William Petty; portrait of a genius. Glencoe, Ill., Free Press, 1954. 260p. illus. 22cm. [HB103] 55-26
1. Petty, Sir William, 1623-1687. I. Title.

STRAUSS, Erich, 1911- 923.342
Sir William Petty; portrait of a genius. Glencoe, Ill., Free Press, 1954. 260 p. illus. 22 cm. [HB103] 55-26
1. Petty, Sir William, 1623-1687. I. Title.

Peucer, Kaspar, 1525-1602.

KOLB, Robert. 027'.1'4347
Caspar Peucer's library : portrait of a Wittenberg professor of the mid-sixteenth century / Robert Kolb. St. Louis : Center for Reformation Research, 1976. vi, 76 p. ; 22 cm. (Sixteenth century bibliography ; 5) Includes bibliographical references. [Z725.P58K5] 76-364373 pbk. : 2.00
1. Peucer, Kaspar, 1525-1602. 2. Libraries, Private—Germany—Wittenberg—History. 3. Wittenberg—Libraries—History. I.

Peucer, Kaspar, 1525-1602. II. Title. III. Series.

Peyton, Patrick J.

PEYTON, Patrick J. 282.0924
All for her; the autobiography of Father Patrick Peyton, C.S.C. Garden City, N.Y., Doubleday [1967] 286 p. illus., ports. 22 cm. [BX4705.P4458A3] 67-22441
I. Title.

Peyton, Thomas Roy,

PEYTON, Thomas Roy, 1897- 926.1
Quest for dignity, an autobiography of a Negro doctor. Los Angeles, W. F. Lewis [1950] vii, 156 p. 24 cm. [R154.P49A3] 50-13642
I. Title. II. Title: Negro doctor.

PEYTON, Thomas Roy, M.D. 926.1
1897-
Quest for dignity; an autobiography of a Negro doctor. [Rev. reprinting] Los Angeles 18, Publishers Western, 1822 South Western Ave. 1963 [c.1950] 160p. illus. 18cm. 63-14047 1.85 pap.,
I. Title. II. Title: Negro doctor.

Pfaender, Maria Klara, 1827-1882.

PROBST, Brunilde. 922.243
The burning seal; biography of Mother Mary Clara Pfaender, foundress of the Franciscan Sisters of Salzkotten. Chicago, Franciscan Herald Press [1960] 129p. illus. 22cm. [BX4353.Z8P45] 60-11992
1. Pfaender, Maria Klara, 1827-1882. 2. Franciscan Sisters, Daughters of the Sacred Hearts of Jesus and Mary. I. Title.

Pfeifle, Robert, 1880-1958.

†ORPE, Frank. 974.8'22 B
Dare to be brave / Frank Orpe, Jean Pfeifle McQuade. Center Square, Pa. : Alpha Publications, c1977. 167 p. : ill., facsims. ; 24 cm. [F159.B5P446] 77-155695 ISBN 0-914416-02-2 : 10.00
1. Pfeifle, Robert, 1880-1958. 2. Bethlehem, Pa.—Mayors—Biography. 3. Bethlehem, Pa.—Politics and government. I. McQuade, Jean Pfeifle, 1929- joint author. II. Title. BIP

Phelan, James Duval, 1861-1930.

KAUCHER, Dorothy, 1892- 923.273
James Duval Phelan; a portrait, 1861-1930, by Dorothy Kaucher. Saratoga, Calif., Gallery Committee of the Montalvo Association [1965] 53, [46] p. illus., facsims., ports. 24 cm. [E748.P53K3] 65-4423
1. Phelan, James Duval, 1861-1930. I. Title.

Phelps, Edward John, 1822-1900.

PARSONS, Francis, 378.746'8 B
1871-1937.
Six men of Yale. Foreword by Charles Seymour. Freeport, N.Y., Books for Libraries Press [1971, c1939] xii, 145 p. ports. 23 cm. (Essay index reprint series) Contents.Contents.—Elisha Williams, 1694-1755.—Ezra Stiles, 1727-1795.—The young Silliman in Nelson's England, 1805-1806.—Edward J. Phelps, 1822-1900.—The second President Dwight, 1828-1916.—Henry Augustin Beer, 1847-1926. [LD6319.P3 1971] 72-156702 ISBN 0-8369-2329-4
1. Williams, Elisha, 1694-1775. 2. Stiles, Ezra, 1727-1795. 3. Silliman, Benjamin, 1779-1864. 4. Phelps, Edward John, 1822-1900. 5. Dwight, Timothy, 1828-1916. 6. Beers, Henry Augustin, 1847-1926. I. Title. BIP

Phelps, Humphrey.

PHELPS, 942.4'1'0840924 B
Humphrey.
Just across the fields / Humphrey Phelps ; illustrated by Brian Walker. New York : St. Martin's Press, 1976. 219 p. : ill. ; 23 cm. [S522.G7P46 1976] 76-20429 8.95
1. Phelps, Humphrey. 2. Farm life—England—Gloucestershire. 3. Gloucestershire, Eng.—Biography. I. Title.

Phelps, Richard.

PHELPS, Richard. 796.32'3'0924 B
A coach's world [by] Richard "Digger" Phelps and Larry Keith. New York, Crowell [1974] 254 p. illus. 21 cm. [GV884.P45A33] 74-17182 ISBN 0-690-00560-1
1. Phelps, Richard. 2. Notre Dame, Ind. University—Basketball. 3. Basketball. 4. Basketball coaching. I. Keith, Larry, joint author. II. Title.

Phelps, Samuel, 1804-1878.

ALLEN, Shirley S. 792'.028'0924 B
Samuel Phelps and Sadler's Wells Theatre, by Shirley S. Allen. [1st ed.] Middletown, Conn., Wesleyan University Press [1971] xvi, 354 p. illus., ports. 24 cm. Bibliography: p. 334-340. [PN2598.P4A4] 72-120259 ISBN 0-8195-4029-3 15.00
1. Phelps, Samuel, 1804-1878. 2. Sadler's Wells Theatre, London. I. Title. BIP

Philadelphia— Biog.

PROGRESSIVE Italo- 070.5'092'4
Americans, including who's who in Philadelphia v.1- 1925- Philadelphia, Stafford's National News Service. v. illus., ports. 30cm. [F158.25.P7] 56-53708
1. Philadelphia— Biog. 2. Italians in Philadelphia.

Philadelphia Athletics (Baseball team)—History.

BASEBALL 796.357'64'0974811
Padre.
The Mackmen : "Reflections on a baseball team" / by the Baseball Padre. 2d ed. [Upper Darby, Pa. : order from The Mackmen, 1712 S. State Road], c1979. viii, 139 p., [6] leaves of plates : ill. ; 23 cm. Bibliography: p. 138-139. [GV875.P45B37 1979] 79-67458 7.00
1. Philadelphia Athletics (Baseball team)—History. 2. McGillicuddy, Cornelius, 1862-1956. 3. Baseball players—United States—Biography. 4. Baseball managers—United States—Biography. I. Title.

Philadelphia Flyers (Hockey club)

CHEVALIER, Jack. 796.9'62'0974811
The Broad Street bullies : the incredible story of the Philadelphia Flyers / Jack Chevalier. New York : Collier Books, 1974. 192 p. : ill. ; 28 cm. "A Rutledge book." Text and photographs present a brief history of the Philadelphia Flyers hockey team with short biographies of the team members. [GV848.P48C47] 920 74-15131 pbk. : 5.95
1. Philadelphia Flyers (Hockey club) 2. Hockey. 3. Hockey—Biography. I. Title. BIP

FISCHLER, Stan. 796.9'62'0924 B
Bobby Clarke and the ferocious Flyers. New York, Dodd, Mead [1974] x, 213 p. illus. 22 cm. [GV848.P48F57] 73-15031 ISBN 0-396-06885-5 5.95
1. Philadelphia Flyers (Hockey club) 2. Clarke, Bobby, 1949- I. Title.

FISCHLER, Stan. 796.9'62'0974811
The Philadelphia Flyers : supermen of the ice / by Stan Fischler. Englewood Cliffs, N.J. : Prentice-Hall, [1974] 127 p. : ill. ; 28 cm. "A Stuart L. Daniels book." Text and photographs present a brief history of the Philadelphia Flyers hockey team with short biographies of the team members. [GV848.P48F58] 920 74-9239 pbk. : 3.95
1. Philadelphia Flyers (Hockey club) 2. Hockey—Biography.

Philadelphia Orchestra.

SIEGEL, 779'.9'785062748110924
Adrian.
Concerto for camera; a photographic portrait of the Philadelphia Orchestra. [Philadelphia, Philadelphia Orchestra Association, 1972] 207 p. illus. 26 cm. [ML200.8.P52O747] 72-8993
1. Philadelphia Orchestra. 2. Musicians—Portraits. I. Title.

Philanthropists.

BOLTON, Sarah 361.7'4'0922 B
(Knowles) 1841-1916.
Famous givers and their gifts. Freeport, N.Y., Books for Libraries Press [1971] x, 382 p. illus. 23 cm. (Essay index reprint series) Reprint of the 1896 ed. [HV27.B7 1971] 76-37129 ISBN 0-8369-2484-3
1. Philanthropists. I. Title. BIP

STEVENS, William Oliver, 923.6
1878-
Famous humanitarians. New York, Dodd, Mead, 1953. 131p. illus. 23cm. (Famous biographies for young people) [HV27.S8] 53-9025
1. Philanthropists. I. Title.

*Philby, Eleanor.

*PHILBY, Eleanor. 327'.12'0924
Kim Philby, the spy I married. New York, Ballantine [1968,c.1967,1968] 173p. 18cm. (U6141) First pub. in Britain as Kim Philby: the spy I loved. .75 pap.,
I. Title.

Philby, Harry St. John Bridger, 1885-1960.

PHILBY, Harry St. John 915.3'04'5
Bridger, 1885-1960.
Arabian highlands / by H. St. J. B. Philby. New York : Da Capo Press, 1976, c1952. xvi, 771 p., [15] leaves of plates : ill. ; 24 cm. (The Middle East in the Twentieth century) Reprint of the ed. published for the Middle East Institute, Washington, D.C., by Cornell University Press, Ithaca. Includes index. [DS207.P48 1976] 76-10643 ISBN 0-306 70765-9 : 39.50
1. Philby, Harry St. John Bridger, 1885-1960. 2. Arabia—Description and travel. I. Title. BIP

Philby, Kim, 1912-

PAGE, Bruce. 327'.12'0924 B
Philby: the spy who betrayed a generation [by] Bruce Page, David Leitch [and] Phillip Knightley; introduction by John le Carre. Revised ed. Harmondsworth, Penguin, 1969. 3-336 p. 16 plates, illus., ports. 19 cm. First published in 1968 under title: The Philby conspiracy. [UB271.R92P436 1969b] 77-548176 ISBN 0-14-002945-1 7/6
1. Philby, Kim, 1912- I. Leitch, David, joint author. II. Knightley, Phillip, joint author.

SEALE, Patrick. 327'.12'0924 B
Philby: the long road to Moscow [by] Patrick Seale and Maureen McConville. New York, Simon and Schuster [1973] xiv, 282 p. illus. 24 cm. Includes bibliographical references. [UB271.R92P46 1973b] 73-8705 ISBN 0-671-21509-4 8.95
1. Philby, Kim, 1912- 2. Espionage, Russian—Great Britain. I. McConville, Maureen, joint author.

SPIRO, Edward. 327'.12'0924 B
The third man [by] E. H. Cookridge. New York, Putnam [1968] 281 p. illus., ports. 22 cm. Bibliographical references included in "Notes" (p. 273-281) [UB271.R92P47 1968b] 68-20710
1. Philby, Kim, 1912- I. Title.

Philharmonic Society of San Mateo County, Calif.

ARMSBY, Leonora (Wood) 780'.922
Musicians talk. Freeport, N.Y., Books for Libraries Press [1969] xiii, 242 p. illus., ports. 23 cm. (Essay index reprint series) "First published 1935." The author's reminiscences as manager of the Philharmonic Society of San Mateo County, California. [ML65.A73M8 1969] 76-99679
1. Philharmonic Society of San Mateo County, Calif. 2. Musicians—Correspondence, reminiscences, etc. 3. Music—California. 4. Music—Anecdotes, facetiae, satire, etc. I. Title. BIP

Philidor, Francois Andre Danican, known as, 1726-1795.

ALLEN, George, 1808- 794.1'0924 B
1876.
The life of Philidor; musician and chess-player. Supplementary essay by Tassilo von Heydebrand und der Lasa. New York, Da Capo Press, 1971. xii, 156 p. 23 cm. (DaCapo Press Music reprint series) Includes bibliographical references. [ML410.P52 1971] 70-139198 ISBN 0-306-70075-1
1. Philidor, Francois Andre Danican, known as, 1726-1795. I. Heydebrand und der Lasa, Tassilo von, 1818-1899. BIP

Philip, duke of Edinburgh, 1921-

ALEKSANDRA, Consort of 923.242
Peter II, King of Yugoslavia, 1921-
Prince Philip; a family portrait. Indianapolis, Bobbs-Merrill [1960] 256 p. illus. 24 cm. [DA591.A2A65 1960a] 60-12628
1. Philip, duke of Edinburgh, 1921- I. Title.

BOOTHROYD, John 942.085'0924 B
Basil, 1910-
Prince Philip; an informal biography [by] Basil Boothroyd. [1st American ed.] New York, McCall Pub. Co. [1971] xviii, 311 p. illus. 25 cm. First published in Harlow, Eng., under title: Philip, an informal biography. Bibliography: p. 297-298. [DA591.A2B66 1971b] 73-154246 ISBN 0-8415-0116-5 8.95
1. Philip, Duke of Edinburgh, 1921- I. Title.

CATHCART, Helen 923.242
H. R. H. Prince Philip, sportsman. [Dist. New Rchelle, N.Y., SportShelf, c.1961] 208p. illus. 61-38566 5.75 bds.,
1. Philip, duke of Edinburgh, 1921- I. Title.

DEAN, John, 1921- 923.242
Prince Philip. [1st American ed.] New York, Holt [1955, c1954] 219 p. illus. 22 cm. First published in London in 1954 under title: H. R. H. Prince Philip, duke of Edinburgh. [DA591.A2D4 1955] 55-7916
1. Philip, duke of Edinburgh, 1921-

PEACOCKE, Marguerite D 923.242
H. R. H. the Duke of Edinburgh. New York, Roy Publishers [1961* 126p. illus. 20cm. (The Living biographies series) [DA591.A2P4] 61-12289
1. Philip, duke of Edinburgh, 1921- I. Title.

PEACOCKE, Marguerite D. 923.242
H. R. H. the Duke of Edinburgh. New York, Roy [c.1961] 126p. illus. (Living biographies ser.) 61-12289 2.50 bds.,
1. Philip, duke of Edinburgh, 1921- I. Title.

Philip II, King of Macedonia, 382-336 B.C.

CAWKWELL, George. 938'.1'070924 B
Philip of Macedon / George Cawkwell. London ; Boston : Faber & Faber, 1978. 215 p. : maps ; 23 cm. Includes index. Bibliography: p. [207]-209. [DF233.C38] 78-316519 ISBN 0-571-10958-6 : 19.95
1. Philip II, King of Macedonia, 382-336 B.C. 2. Macedonia—Kings and rulers—Biography. 3. Greece—Kings and rulers—Biography. I. Title.
Available from Faber and Faber, Salem, NH 03079 BIP

ELLIS, John R. 938'.1'070924
Philip II and Macedonian imperialism / [by]J. R. Ellis. London : Thames and Hudson, 1976. 312 p. : geneal. table, maps ; 23 cm. (Aspects of Greek and Roman life) Includes index. Bibliography: p. [240]-244. [DF233.E4] 76-380632 ISBN 0-500-40028-8 : £9.50
1. Philip II, King of Macedonia, 382-336 B.C. 2. Greece—History—To 146 B.C. 3. Macedonia—History. 4. Greece—Kings and rulers—Biography. I. Title. II. Series.

HOGARTH, David 938'.07'0922
George, 1862-1927.
Philip and Alexander of Macedon; two essays in biography. Freeport, N.Y., Books

for Libraries Press [1971] xi, 312 p. fold. map, ports. 23 cm. Reprint of the 1897 ed. [DF233.H72 1971] 75-154154 ISBN 0-8369-5770-9
1. Philip II, King of Macedonia, 382-336, B.C. 2. Alexander the Great, 356-323 B.C. I. Title.

WUST, Fritz R. 938'.07'0924 B
Philipp II. von Makedonien und Griechenland in den Jahren von 346 bis 338 von Fritz. R. Wust. New York, Arno Press, 1973. ix, 188 p. 24 cm. (Greek history) Reprint of the 1938 ed., published by Beck, Munich, in series: Munchener historische Abhandlungen. 1. Reihe: Allgemeine und politische Geschichte, Heft 14. A portion of this work was originally presented as the author's thesis, Munich. Includes bibliographical references. [DF233.W8 1973] 72-7910 ISBN 0-405-04806-8
1. Philip II, King of Macedonia, 382 B.C.-336. 2. Macedonia—History—To 168 B.C. 3. Greece—History. I. Title. II. Series: Munchener historische Abhandlungen. 1. Reihe: Allgemeine und politische Geschichte, Heft 14.

Philip, King (Metacomet) Sachem of the Wampanoags, d. 1676.

AVERILL, Esther Holden. 970.2
King Philip, the Indian chief; illustrated by Vera Belsky. [1st ed.] New York, Harper [1950] 147 p. illus. 22 cm. [E83.67.A9] 50-12861
1. Philip, King (Metacomet) Sachem of the Wampanoags, d. 1676.

Philip, King (Metacomet) Sachem of the Wampanoags, d. 1676—Juvenile literature.

EDWARDS, Cecile Pepin 92
King Philip: loyal Indian. Illus. by Forrest Orr. Boston, Houghton [c.1962] 189p. col. illus. 22cm. (Piper bks.) 62-9301 1.95; 2.20; 1.76; 1.16 lib. ed., text ed., pap.,
1. Philip, King (Metacomet) Sachem of the Wampanoags, d. 1676—Juvenile literature. I. Title.

Philip, Scotty, 1858-1911.

LEE, Wayne C. 639'.97'973580924 B
Scotty Philip, the man who saved the buffalo, by Wayne C. Lee. Caldwell, Idaho, Caxton Printers, 1974. p. cm. Bibliography: p. [F655.P55L43] 73-83113 ISBN 0-87004-241-6 7.95
1. Philip, Scotty, 1858-1911. I. Title.

Philip, Scotty, 1858-1911—Juvenile literature.

VEGLAHN, Nancy. 639'.97'973580924 B
The Buffalo King; the story of Scotty Philip. Illustrated by Donald Carrick. New York, Scribner [1971] 180 p. illus., ports. 22 cm. Bibliography: p. [179]-180. Biography of the Scottish immigrant who settled in Dakota Territory in the late 1800's and whose campaign to preserve the vanishing bison was so ardent he became known as "the buffalo king." [F655.P55V4] 92 79-161470 ISBN 0-684-12492-0 5.50
1. Philip, Scotty, 1858-1911—Juvenile literature. 2. Dakota Indians—Juvenile literature. I. Carrick, Donald, illus. II. Title.

Philip the evangelist, deacon—Juvenile literature.

NAISH, Jack. 226'.6'0924 B
Philip : traveling preacher / Jack Naish ; illustrated by Ron Hester. Nashville : Broadman Press, c1978. 48 p. : col. ill. ; 24 cm. (Biblearn series) Tells how a Jewish man converted to Christianity and spread the mission of the early church. [BS2520.P5N34] 78-105146 ISBN 0-8054-4241-3 : 3.95
1. Philip the evangelist, deacon—Juvenile literature. 2. Bible. N.T.—Biography—Juvenile literature. I. Hester, Ronald. II. Title. BIP

Philipp, Emanuel Lorenz, 1861-1925.

MAXWELL, Robert S 923.273
Emanuel L. Philipp, Wisconsin stalwart. Madison, State Historical Society of Wisconsin, 1959. 272p. illus. 24cm. Includes bibliography. [E586.P5M3] 59-62973
1. Philipp, Emanuel Lorenz, 1861-1925. I. Title.

Philipp I, der Grossmutige, Landgrave of Hesse, 1504-1567.

HILLERBRAND, Hans Joachim. 943'.41'0310924 B
Landgrave Philipp of Hesse, 1504-1567; religion and politics in the Reformation [by] Hans J. Hillerbrand. St. Louis, Foundation for Reformation Research, 1967. 40 p. port. 23 cm. (Reformation essays & studies, 1) Bibliographical footnotes. [DD801.H59H46] 68-4879
1. Philipp I, der Grossmutige, Landgrave of Hesse, 1504-1567. 2. Reformation—Germany. I. Title. II. Series.

Philippe II Auguste, King of France, 1165-1223.

HUTTON, William Holden, 1860-1930. 944'.023'0924 B
Philip Augustus. Port Washington, N.Y., Kennikat Press [1970] 228 p. 21 cm. Reprint of the 1896 ed. [DC90.H98 1970] 75-112809
1. Philippe II Auguste, King of France, 1165-1223. BIP

Philippe le Bon, Duke of Burgundy, 1396-1467.

VAUGHAN, Richard, 1927- 944'.4 B
Philip the Good; the apogee of Burgundy. New York, Barnes & Noble [1970] xvii, 456 p. maps, ports. 23 cm. Bibliography: p. 401-433. [DC611.B78V353 1970] 79-12645 16.00
1. Philippe le Bon, Duke of Burgundy, 1396-1467. 2. Burgundy—History.

Philippine Islands—History—1898-1946.

PIER, Arthur Stanwood, 1874-1966. 959.9'03'0922
American apostles to the Philippines. With an introd. by W. Cameron Forbes. Freeport, N.Y., Books for Libraries Press [1971, c1950] xxi, 156 p. illus., ports. 23 cm. (Biography index reprint series) Contents.Contents.—George Dewey.—Frederick Funston.—William Howard Taft.—Luke Edward Wright.—Leonard Wood.—Dean Conant Worcester.—Frank Watson Carpenter.—Warwick Greene.—John Sylvanus Leech.—John Joseph Pershing.—Richard Pearson Strong.—Charles Henry Brent. [DS685.P578 1971] 74-160926 ISBN 0-8369-8089-1
1. Philippine Islands—History—1898-1946. 2. U.S.—Biography. I. Title. BIP

Philips, Frits, 1905-

PHILIPS, Frits, 1905- 338.7'62'1381094 B
45 years with Philips : an industrialist's life / by Frederik Phillips. Poole : Blandford Press, 1978. viii, 280 p., [48] p. of plates : ill., map, ports. ; 24 cm. Translation of 45 [i.e. Vijfenveertig] jaar met Philips. Maps on lining papers. Includes index. [HD9695.N24P54413] 78-318952 ISBN 0-7137-0931-6 : 14.95
1. Philips, Frits, 1905- 2. Philips' Gloeilampenfabrieken, N.V., Eindhoven—History. 3. Businessmen—Netherlands—Biography. I. Title.
Distributed by Sterling Pub Co., 2 Park Ave., New York NY 10016

Philipson, Robin.

LINDSAY, John Maurice, 1918- 759.9411 B
Robin Philipson / by Maurice Lindsay. Edinburgh : Edinburgh University Press, c1976. 79 p. : ill. (some col.) ; 16 x 22 cm. (Modern Scottish painters ; no. 6) Bibliography: p. 75. [ND497.P48L56] 77-360047 ISBN 0-85224-302-2 : 5.00
1. Philipson, Robin. 2. Painters—Scotland—Biography. I. Philipson, Robin.
Distributed by Edinburgh Univ. Press, c/o Biblio Distribution Ctr., 81 Adams Dr., Totowa, NJ 07512

Philleo, Prudence (Crandall) 1803-1890.

YATES, Elizabeth, 1905- JUV
Prudence Crandall, woman of courage; illustrated by Nora S. Unwin. [1st ed.] New York, Aladdin Books, 1955. 246p. illus. 22cm. [PZ7.Y213Pr] JUV 55-10125
1. Philleo, Prudence (Crandall) 1803-1890. I. Title.

YATES, Elizabeth, 1905- v. 12
Prudence Crandall, woman of courage; illustrated by Nora S. Unwin. [1st ed.] New York, Dutton [1965] 246 p. illus. 22 cm. 68-58525
1. Philleo, Prudence (Crandall) 1803-1890. I. Title.

Phillip, Alma, 1891-1975—Portraits, etc.

PHILLIP, Alma, 1891-1975. 779'.9'978272503
Next-year country : one woman's view / photos. by Alma Phillip, 1891-1975 ; edited by Linda M. Hasselstrom. 1st ed. Hermosa, SD : Lame Johnny Press, c1978. 66 p., [1] leaf of plates : chiefly ill. ; 19 x 26 cm. [F672.K5P46 1978] 77-91463 ISBN 0-917624-09-2 : 9.95 ISBN 0-917624-07-6 (pbk.) : 7.95
1. Phillip, Alma, 1891-1975—Portraits, etc. 2. Phillips family—Portraits, etc. 3. Keya Paha Co., Neb.—Biography—Portraits. 4. Farm life—Nebraska—Keya Paha Co.—Pictorial works. I. Hasselstrom, Linda M. II. Title. BIP

Phillip, Arthur, 1738-1814—Juvenile literature.

LEVIS, Eve. 994'.4'020924 B
Arthur Phillip. Illustrated by A. van Ewijk. [Melbourne] Longmans [1967] 30 p. illus. (part col.), maps (1 col.) 21 cm. (Great people in Australian history) [DU172.P58L4 1967] 75-374444 unpriced
1. Phillip, Arthur, 1738-1814—Juvenile literature.

Phillipps, Thomas, Sir, bart, 1792-1872.

MUNBY, Alan Noel Latimer. 920.1
The family affairs of Sir Thomas Phillipps. Cambridge [Eng.] University Press, 1952. xiii, 119p. illus., ports. 22cm. (Phillipps studies, no. 2) [Z997.P553M83] 52-14633
1. Phillipps, Thomas, bart., Sir 1792-1872. I. Title. II. Series.

MUNBY, Alan Noel Latimer. 020'.75'0924 B
Portrait of an obsession; the life of Sir Thomas Phillipps, the world's greatest book collector; adapted by Nicolas Barker from the five volumes of Phillipps studies by A. N. L. Munby. New York, Putnam [1967] xvii, 278 p. illus., facsims., ports. (1 col.) 23 cm. [Z989.P49M8 1967b] 67-28090
1. Phillipps, Thomas, Sir, bart, 1792-1872. I. Title.

Phillips Academy, Andover, Mass.

FUESS, Claude Moore, 1885- 923.773
Independent schoolmaster. [1st ed.] Boston, Little, Brown [1952] 371 p. illus. 23 cm. "An Atlantic Monthly Press book." [LD7501.A5P317 1933] 52-9092
1. Phillips Academy, Andover, Mass. 2. Private schools. I. Title.

Phillips, Benjamin Dwight, 1885-1968.

MURCH, James DeForest, 1892- 286'.6'0924 B
B. D. Phillips; life and letters. Memorial ed. [Louisville, Ky., Printed by Standard Print. Co., 1969] x, 256 p. illus., ports. 24 cm. [BX6793.P47M8] 70-110433
1. Phillips, Benjamin Dwight, 1885-1968.

Phillips, Clare Doreen (Bowles)

PHILLIPS, Clare Doreen (Bowles) 920.9133
The autobiography of a fortuneteller. [1st ed.] New York, Vantage Press [1958] 215p. 21cm. [BF1408.2.P5A3] 58-866
I. Title.

Phillips, David Graham, 1867-1911.

FILLER, Louis, 1911- 813'.5'2 B
Voice of the democracy : David Graham Phillips, journalist, novelist, progressive / by Louis Filler. University Park : Pennsylvania State University Press, [1978] p. cm. Includes index. Bibliography: p. [PS3531.H5Z67] 77-13893 ISBN 0-271-00528-9 : 12.95
1. Phillips, David Graham, 1867-1911. 2. Novelists, American—20th century—Biography. 3. Journalists—United States—Biography. I. Title.

Phillips, Dorothea Sarah Florence Alexandra (Ortlepp) lady.

GUTSCHE, Thelma. 968'.05'0924
No ordinary woman; the life and times of Florence Phillips. Cape Town, H. Timmins, 1966. 432 p. illus., facsims., map (on lining paper) ports. 25 cm. "Select bibliography and references": p. 409-413. [CT1929.P5G8] 67-2091
1. Phillips, Dorothea Sarah Florence Alexandra (Ortlepp) lady. I. Title.

Phillips, Duncan, 1886-1966.

HORMATS, Bess. 709'.24
Retrospective for a critic: Duncan Phillips. "The critical writing of Duncan Phillips" and catalogue. Pref. [by] George Levitine. Introd. [by] William H. Gerdts. Foreword [by] J. William Fulbright. [College Park, University of Maryland, 1969] viii, 61 p. illus., port. 26 cm. An exhibition of paintings, sculpture, and watercolors from the Phillips Collection relating to the critical writing of Duncan Phillips, Feb. 12 through Mar. 16, 1969, University of Maryland Art Dept. and Art Gallery, J. Millard Tawes Fine Arts Center, College Park, Md. Includes bibliographical references. "The published writing of Duncan Phillips": p. 27-31. Bibliography: p. 32. [N5020.C7364] 79-625394
1. Phillips, Duncan, 1886-1966. 2. Art—Exhibitions. I. Phillips Collection, Washington, D.C. II. Maryland. University. Dept. of Art. III. Maryland. University. Art Gallery. IV. Title.

PHILLIPS, Marjorie, 1895- 750'.74'0153
Duncan Phillips and his collection. With a foreword by Laughlin Phillips. [1st ed.] Boston, Little, Brown [1970] xvi, 347 p. illus. (part col.), ports. (part col.) 26 cm. "An Atlantic Monthly Press book." [N5220.P55P5] 78-128359 20.00
1. Phillips, Duncan, 1886-1966. 2. Phillips Collection, Washington, D.C. I. Title.

Phillips, Everett Franklin, 1878-1951.

PHILLIPS, Mary (Geisler) 1878-1951. v. 12
The bee man; life and letters of Everett Franklin Phillips. Ithaca, N.Y., Available from Office of Apiculture, Dept. of Entomology, Cornell University, 1967. 112 p. 29 cm. 68-18860
1. Phillips, Everett Franklin, 1878-1951. 2. Bee culture. I. Phillips, Everett Franklin, 1878-1951. II. Title.

Phillips family.

PHILLIPS, C. Arthur. 929'.2'0973
Deacon Nicholas Phillips of Dedham and Weymouth, Mass., 1636-1672 / C. Arthur Phillips. Evansville, Ind. : Unigraphic, 1976. 62 p., [3] leaves of plates : ill. ; 22 cm. Includes indexes. [CS71.P555 1976] 76-6650

1. Phillips family. 2. Massachussetts—Genealogy. I. Title.

REZNECK, Samuel. 929'.2'0973
The saga of an American Jewish family since the Revolution : a history of the family of Jonas Phillips / by Samuel Rezneck ; with foreword by Malcolm H. Stern. Washington, D.C. : University Press of America, 1980. p. cm. Includes index. Bibliography: p. [E184.J5P557] 79-6725 ISBN 0-8191-0939-8 : 16.75 ISBN 0-8191-0940-1 (pbk.) : 9.25
1. Phillips family. 2. Jews in the United State—Biography. 3. United States—Biography. I. Title. BIP

Phillips John Aristotle

PHILLIPS, John Aristitle. 623.4'.5119
Mushroom : the story of the A-bomb kid / by John Aristotle Phillips and David Michaelis. New York : Pocket Books, 1979, c1978. 265 p. ; 18 cm. [QC774.PaaA33] [B] 0-671 ISBN pbk. : 2.50.
1. Phillips John Aristotle 2. Atomic bomb 3. Physicists — United States. I. Micaelis, David joint author. II. Title.
L.C. card no.: for 1978 Morrow edition 78-8411 BIP

Phillips, Kathryn (Sisson)

PHILLIPS, Kathryn (Sisson) 1879- 923.773
My room in the world; a memoir by Kathryn Sisson Phillips as told to Keith Jennison. New York, Abingdon Press [1964] 157 p. 21 cm. [CT275.P5929P45] 64-10604
I. Jennison, Keith Warren. II. Title.

Phillips, Lena Madesin, 1881-1955.

SERGIO, Lisa, 1905- 301.41'2'0924 B
A measure filled; the life of Lena Madesin Phillips drawn from her autobiography. New York, R. B. Luce [1972] 246 p. illus. 23 cm. [HQ1413.P5S4] 71-190073 5.95
1. Phillips, Lena Madesin, 1881-1955. I. Title.

Phillips, Wendell, 1811-1884.

AUSTIN, George Lowell, 1849-1893. 973.71'14'0924 B
The life and times of Wendell Phillips. Chicago, Afro-Am Press, 1969. 431 p. illus., port. 23 cm. Reprint of the 1884 ed. Imperfect: p. 15-16 wanting. Bibliographical footnotes. [E449.P543 1969] 74-99334
1. Phillips, Wendell, 1811-1884. BIP

BARTLETT, Irving H. 923.673
Wendell Phillips, Brahmin radical. Boston, Beacon Press [1961] 438 p. 21 cm. Includes bibliography. [E449.P5594] 61-10570
1. Phillips, Wendell, 1811-1884. BIP

BARTLETT, Irving H. 973.7'114'0924 B
Wendell Phillips, Brahmin radical, by Irving H. Bartlett. Westport, Conn., Greenwood Press [1973, c1961] viii, 438 p. 22 cm. Reprint of the ed. published by Beacon Press, Boston. Includes bibliographical references. [E449.P56B37 1973] 73-11849 ISBN 0-8371-7071-0 16.25
1. Phillips, Wendell, 1811-1884.

KORNGOLD, Ralph, 1886- 923.673
Two friends of man; the story of William Lloyd Garrison and Wendell Phillips, and their relationship with Abraham Lincoln. [1st ed.] Boston, Little, Brown, 1950. xii, 425 p. ports. 23 cm. Selected bibliography": p. [401]-410. [E449.G2556] 49-49461
1. Garrison, William Lloyd, 1805-1879. 2. Phillips, Wendell, 1811-1884. 3. Lincoln, Abraham, Pres. U.S., 1809-1865. 4. Slavery in the U.S.—Anti-slavery movements. I. Title.

MARTYN, Carlos, 1841-1917. 973.71140924 B
Wendell Phillips: the agitator. With an appendix containing three of the orator's masterpicces, never before published in book form, viz.: The lost arts; Daniel O'Connell; The scholar in a republic. Rev. ed. New York, Negro Universities Press [1969] 600 p. port. 23 cm. Reprint of the 1890 ed. Includes bibliographical references. [E449.P5546 1969] 71-92753
1. Phillips, Wendell, 1811-1884. BIP

MARTYN, Carlos, 1841-1917. 973.71'14'0924 B
Wendell Phillips: the agitator. With an appendix containing three of the orator's masterpieces, never before published in book form, viz.: The lost arts, Daniel O'Connell, The scholar in a republic. Rev. ed. Chicago, Afro-Am Press, 1969. xi, 600 p. 22 cm. Reprint of the 1890 ed. Bibliographical footnotes. [E449.P5546 1969b] 74-99393
1. Phillips, Wendell, 1811-1884.

SEARS, Lorenzo, 1838-1916. 973.71'14'0924 B
Wendell Phillips, orator and agitator. New York, B. Blom [1967] xv, 379 p. port. 20 cm. Reprint of the 1909 ed. [E449.P5597 1967] 67-13340
1. Phillips, Wendell, 1811-1884. I. Title.

SHERWIN, Oscar, 1902- 923.673
Prophet of liberty; the life and times of Wendell Phillips. New York, Bookman Associattes [1958] 814 p. illus. 24 cm. Includes bibliography. [E449.P5599] 58-2156
1. Phillips, Wendell, I. Title. BIP

SHERWIN, Oscar, 1902- 973.7'114'0924 B
Prophet of liberty : the life and times of Wendell Phillips / by Oscar Sherwin. Westport, Conn. : Greenwood Press, 1975, c1958. 814 p. : ports. ; 22 cm. Reprint of the ed. published by Bookman Associates, New York. Includes index. Bibliography: p. 765-801. [E449.P56S42 1975] 74-6754 ISBN 0-8371-7553-4 lib.bdg. : 33.25
1. Phillips, Wendell, 1811-1884. I. Title.

Philologists.

ANCIENT Greek and Roman rhetoricians; 808'.00922 a biographical dictionary. Compiled for the Speech Association of America by Robert W. Smith [and others] and edited by Donald C. Bryant. Columbia, Mo., Artcraft Press, 1968. [10], 104 p. 23 cm. Bibliography; 6th-8th prelim. pages. [PA83.A5] 70-1929
1. Philologists. 2. Rhetoric, Ancient. I. Smith, Robert Wayne, 1926- II. Bryant, Donald Cross, 1905- ed. III. Speech Association of America.

Philomena, Saint.

MOHR, Marie Helene, Sister. 922.245
Saint Philomena, powerful with God. Milwaukee, Bruce Pub. Co. [1956] 186p. illus. 23cm. [BX4700.P75M6 1956] 57-644
1. Philomena, Saint. I. Title.

MOHR, Marie Helene, Sister. 922.245
Saint Philomena, powerful with God. Milwaukee, Bruce [1953] 136p. illus. 23cm. [BX4700.P75M6] 53-2859
1. Philomena, Saint. I. Title.

Philosophers.

AYKROYD, Wallace Ruddell, 1899- 540'.922 B
Three philosophers (Lavoisier, Priestley and Cavendish), by W. R. Aykroyd. Westport, Conn., Greenwood Press [1970] xi, 227 p. illus., ports. 23 cm. "Originally published in 1935." Includes bibliographical references. [QD21.A95 1970] 77-98808 ISBN 0-8371-2890-0
I. Lavoisier, Antoine Laurent, 1743-1794. II. Priestley, Joseph, 1733-1804. III. Cavendish, Henry, 1731-1810. IV. Title.

DONDO, Mathurin Marius, 1884- 921.4
The French Faust, Henri de Saint-Simon. New York, Philosophical Library [c1955] 253p. illus. 22cm. Includes bibliography. [HX265.S4D66] 56-13574
I. Saint-Simon, Claude Henri, comte de, 1760-1825. II. Title.

THOMAS, Henry, 1886- 921
Living adventures in philosophy [by] Henry Thomas and Dana Lee Thomas. [1st ed.] Garden City, N. Y., Hanover House [1954] 320p. 22cm. [B72.T33] 54-5760
1. Philosophers. 2. Philosophy—Hist. I. Thomas, Dana Lee, 1918- joint author. II. Title.

THOMAS, Henry, 1886- 921
Living biographies of great philosophers, by Henry Thomas and Dana Lee Thomas. Garden City, N.Y., Garden City Books [1959] 335 p. 22 cm. [B72.T34 1959] 59-16322
1. Philosophers. I. Thomas, Dana Lee, 1918- joint author. II. Title.

THOMAS, Henry, 1886- 921
Living biographies of great philosophers, by Henry Thomas and Dana Lee Thomas. Garden City, N. Y., Perma Giants [1950, c1941] viii. 335p. 21cm. [B72.T34 1950] 50-54735
1. Philosophers. I. Thomas, Dana Lee, 1918- joint author. II. Title.

THOMAS, Henry, 1886- 921
Living biographies of great philosophers, by Henry Thomas and Dana Lee Thomas. Illustrations by Gordon Ross. New York, Garden City Pub. Co., Inc. 1959. viii, 335 p. front., ports. 24 cm. [B72.T34 1941] 41-3760
1. Philosophers. I. Thomas, Dana Lee, 1918- joint author. II. Title.

THOMAS, Henry, 1886- 109'.22 B
Living biographies of great philosophers, by Henry Thomas and Dana Lee Thomas (Henry Thomas Schnittkind and Dana Arnold Schnittkind) Illus. by Gordon Ross. Freeport, N.Y., Books for Libraries Press [1972, c1941] viii, 335 p. illus. 23 cm. (Essay index reprint series) [B72.T34 1972] 75-167414 ISBN 0-8369-2625-0
1. Philosophers. I. Thomas, Dana Lee, 1918- joint author. II. Title.

TOMLIN, Eric Walter Frederick, 1913- 921
The great philosophers. New York, A. A. Wyn [1952- v. illus. 22 cm. Contents.Contents. -- [1] The Western World. [B72.T42] 52-6922
1. Philosophers. 2. Philosophy — Hist. I. Title.

Philosophers, American—Biography—Dictionaries.

NAUMAN, St. Elmo. 191
Dictionary of American philosophy. Totowa, N.J., Littlefield, Adams, 1974 [c1973] viii, 273 p. 21 cm. (A Littlefield, Adams quality paperback, no. 275) [B851.N3 1974] 74-3062 ISBN 0-8226-0275-X 2.95 (pbk.)
1. Philosophers, American—Biography—Dictionaries. I. Title. BIP

Philosophers, American—Correspondence, reminiscences, etc.

SANTAYANA, George, 1863-1952. 921.1
Letters. Edited, with an introd. and commentary, by Daniel Cory. New York, Scribner, 1955. xxxi, 451 p. 24 cm. [B945.S24A4] 55-9677
1. Philosophers, American—Correspondence, reminiscences, etc.

Philosophers-Biography.

THE greatest thinkers : 920'.02 the thirty minds that shaped our civilization / edited by Edward de Bono ; dia grs. by Edward de Bono with George Daulby. New York : Putnam, c1976. 214p. ; ill. ; 25 cm. Includes index. Bibliography. [CT105.G73] 76-6034 ISBN 0-399-11762-8 : 15.95
1. Philosophers-Biography. I. De Bono, Edward, 1933-

Philosophers, British—Correspondence, reminiscences, etc.

LOCKE, John, 1632-1704. 192
The correspondence of John Locke and Edward Clarke. Edited, with a biographical study by Benjamin Rand. Freeport, N.Y., Books for Libraries Press [1973] p. Reprint of the 1927 ed. [B1296.A4 1973] 72-10623 ISBN 0-8369-7116-7
1. Philosophers, British—Correspondence, reminiscences, etc. I. Clarke, Edward, 1649?-1710. II. Rand, Benjamin, 1856-1934, ed. III. Title.

WIDGERY, Alban Gregory, 1887- 921.2
A philosopher's pilgrimage. New York, Crowell [c.1961] 204p. 61-10888 4.95
1. Philosophers, British—Correspondence, reminiscenses, etc. I. Title.

Philosophers—Dictionaries.

THOMAS, Henry, 1886- 921
Biographical encyclopaedia of philosophy. [1st ed.] Garden City, N. Y., Doubleday, 1965. xii, 273 p. 24 cm. [B41.T5] 64-22313
1. Philosophers—Dictionaries. I. Title.

THOMAS, Henry, 1886- 921
Biographical encyclopedia of philosophy. Garden City, N.Y., Doubleday [c.]1965. xii, 273p. 24cm. [B41.T5] 64-22313 5.50
1. Philosophers—Dictionaries. I. Title.

Philosophers, German—Correspondence, reminiscences, etc.

NIETZSCHE, Friedrich Wilhelm, 1844-1900. 193
Briefwechsel : krit. Gesamtausg. / hrsg. von Giorgio Colli u. Mazzino Montinari, Berlin ; New York : de Gruyter, 1975- v. in ; 23 cm. Contents.Contents.—Abt. 1, Bd. 1. Friedrich Nietzsche Briefe, Juni 1850-Sept. 1864. Briefe an Friedrich Nietzsche, Okt. 1849-Sept. 1864.—Abt. 1, Bd. 2. Friedrich Nietzsche Briefe, Sept. 1864-Apr. 1869.—Abt. 1. Bd. 3 Briefe an Friedrich Nietzsche, Okt. 1864-Marz 1869. [B3316.A253 1975] 75-504997 ISBN 3-11-005912-6 (v. 1) : DM90.00 (v. 1)
1. Philosophers—Germany—Correspondence, reminiscences, etc. I. Colli, Giorgio. II. Montinari, Mazzino.

NIETZSCHE, Friedrich Wilhelm, 1844-1900. 193 B
Nietzsche: a self-portrait from his letters. Edited and translated by Peter Fuss and Henry Shapiro. Cambridge, Mass., Harvard University Press, 1971. viii, 196 p. ports. 23 cm. Bibliography: p. 185-190. [B3316.A26] 73-134953 ISBN 0-674-62425-4 8.00
1. Philosophers, German—Correspondence, reminiscences, etc. I. Title.

Philosophers—Juvenile literature.

OZMON, Howard. 109'.22
Twelve great philosophers. Illustrated by Rodney Furan. Mankato, Minn., Oddo Publishing [1968] 48 p. illus. (part col.) 25 cm. (The Wonderful world of children's books) Contents.Contents.—Socrates.—Plato.—Aristotle.—Aquinas.—Descartes.—Spinoza.—Locke.—Voltaire.—Kant.—Hegel.—Dewey.—Russell. [B72.O9] 920 68-16403
1. Philosophers—Juvenile literature. I. Furan, Rodney, illus. II. Title.

Philosophers, Modern.

NEILL, Thomas Patrick, 1915- 921
Makers of the modern mind. 2d enl. ed. Milwaukee, Bruce Pub. Co. [1958] 420p. illus. 23cm. [B791.N4 1958] 58-1695
1. Philosophers, Modern. I. Title.

Philosophers, Modern—Biography—Collected works.

KAUFMANN, Walter Arnold. 193 S B
Discovering the mind / by Walter Kaufmann. New York : McGraw-Hill, c1980- p. cm. Includes index. Contents.Contents.—V. 1. Goethe, Kant, and Hegel. Bibliography: p. [B803.K38] 79-18015 ISBN 0-07-033311-4 (v.1) : 15.00
1. Philosophers, Modern—Biography—Collected works. 2. Philosophy, Modern—19th century—Collected works. 3. Philosophy, Modern—20th century—Collected works. 4. Philosophers—

Germany—Biography—Collected works. I. Title.

Philosophy and religion.

GILSON, Etienne Henry, 1884- 921.4
The philosopher and theology. Tr. from French by Cecile Gilson. New York, Random [c.1962] 236p. 24cm. 62-8440 3.75
1. Philosophy and religion. I. Title.

Philosophy, Confucian.

CREEL, Herrlee Glessner, 1905- 921.9
Confucius and the Chinese way. New York, Harper [1960] 363 p. illus. 21 cm. (Harper torchbooks, TB63. The Cloister library) First published in 1949 under title: Confucius, the man and the myth. Includes bibliography. [B128.C8C65 1960] 60-5492
1. Philosophy, Confucian. BIP

Philosophy—Introductions.

JOHNSON, Allison Heartz, 1910- 190
Philosophers in action / A. H. Johnson. Columbus, Ohio : Merrill, c1977. ix, 221 p. : ports. ; 25 cm. Includes bibliographical references and index. [BD21.J63] 77-70243 ISBN 0-675-08490-3 : 8.95
1. Philosophy—Introductions. 2. Philosophers—Biography. I. Title. BIP

Philosophy, Modern—20th century—Bio-bibliography.

WHO'S who in philosophy. 190 B
Dagobert D. Runes, editor. Lester E. Denonn, Ralph B. Winn, associate editors. New York, Greenwood Press [1969- v. 24 cm. Reprint of the 1942- ed. [B804.W52] 79-88971 ISBN 0-8371-2095-0
1. Philosophy, Modern—20th century—Bio-bibliography. 2. Philosophers—United States—Directories. 3. Philosophers, English—Directories. I. Runes, Dagobert David, 1902- ed. BIP

Philosophy, Renaissance—Bio-bibliography.

RIEDL, John Orth, 1905- 199'.4 B
A catalogue of Renaissance philosophers (1350-1650) [by] John O. Riedl. Hildesheim, New York, G. Olms, 1973. xi, 179 p. illus. 20 cm. Reprint of the 1940 ed., Milwaukee, Marquette University Press. Bibliography: p. 167-172. [Z7125.R54 1973] 73-180964 ISBN 3-487-04848-5
1. Philosophy, Renaissance—Bio-bibliography. I. Title. BIP

Phinehas ben Abraham, of Korets, 1726 or 8-1791.

WIESEL, Elie, 1928- 296.8'33
Four Hasidic masters and their struggle against melancholy / by Elie Wiesel ; foreword, Theodore M. Hesburgh. Notre Dame [Ind.] : University of Notre Dame Press, c1978. xix, 131 p., [1] leaf of plates : ill. ; 21 cm. (Ward-Phillips lectures in English language and literature ; v. 9) [BM198.W5125] 78-1419 ISBN 0-268-00944-9 : 7.95
1. Phinehas ben Abraham, of Korets, 1726 or 8-1791. 2. Baruch, of Tul'chin, 1757 (ca.)-1811. 3. Horowitz, Jacob Isaac, d. 1815. 4. Horowitz, Naphtali Zebi, 1760-1827. 5. Hasidim—Biography. I. Title. II. Series. BIP

Phips, William, Sir, 1651-1695.

ALDERMAN, Clifford Lindsey. 923.273
Stormy knight: the life of Sir William Phips. [1st ed.] Philadelphia, Chilton Books [1964] 171 p. 21 cm. Bibliography: p. 167-171. [F67.P566] 64-14290
1. Phips, William, Sir, 1651-1695. I. Title.

MATHER, Cotton, 1663-1728. 974.4'02'0924 B
The life of Sir William Phips. Edited with a pref. by Mark Van Doren. New York, Covici-Friede, 1929. [New York, AMS Press, 1971] xi, 208 p. port. 19 cm. Originally published in 1697 under title: Pietas in patriam: the life of His Excellency Sir William Phips, knt. [F67.P57 1971] 75-137260 ISBN 0-404-04249-X
1. Phips, William, Sir, 1651-1695. I. Van Doren, Mark, 1894- ed. II. Title. BIP

PERKINS, Virginia Chase, 1902- 923.273
The Knight of the Golden Fleece. Illustrated by Howard Simon. [1st ed.] Boston, Little, Brown [1959] 219 p. illus. 21 cm. [F67.P58] 59-5290
1. Phips, William, Sir, 1651-1695. I. Title.

Phlegar, Orrin King, 1876-

OWENS, Thelma (Phlegar) 1905- 926.1
Daddy was a doctor, by Lorena Owens (pseud.) Illustrated by Paul Galdone. [1st ed.] New York, Dutton, 1951. 221 p. illus. 21 cm. [R154.P497O9] 51-14107
1. Phlegar, Orrin King, 1876- I. Title.

Photographers.

FORSEE, Aylesa. 920
Famous photographers: excellence in professional photography as seen through the lives and works of five masters: Edward Steichen, Ansel Adams, Cecil Beaton, Yousuf Karsh and David D. Duncan Philadelphia, Macrae Smith [1968] 223 p. illus., ports. 24 cm. Bibliography: p. [213]-215. Biographies of five well-known photographers concentrating on their professional development as they sought to capture the illusive quality of greatness in man and nature. [TR139.F6] AC 68
1. Photographers. I. Title.

RAYFIELD, Stanley. 927.7
Life photographers, their careers and favorite pictures. [Garden City, N. Y.] Doubleday [1957] 89p. illus. 37cm. [TR139.R3] 57-10628
1. Photographers. 2. Life (Chicago) I. Title.

RAYFIELD, Stanley. 927.7
Life photographers, their careers and favorite pictures. [Garden City, N. Y.] Doubleday [1957] 89p. illus. 37cm. [TR139.R3] 57-10628
1. Photographers. 2. Life (Chicago) I. Title.

Photographers —Correspondence, reminiscences, etc.

BEATON, Cecil Walter Hardy, 1904- 927.7
Photobiography. [1st ed.] Garden City, N. Y., Doubleday, 1951. 255 p. illus., ports. 26 cm. [TR140.B4A3] 51-11655
1. Photographers—Correspondence, reminiscences, etc. I. Title.

DUNCAN, Charles. 927.7
A photographic pilgrim's progress; being the adventures of an itinerant photographer among cameras, cabbages, and kings. With a pref. by Percy W. Harris. London, New York, Focal Press [1954] 160p. 19cm. [TR140.D8A3] 55-20528
1. Photographers —Correspondence, reminiscences, etc. I. Title.

KIRKLAND, Wallace. 920.5
Recollections of a Life photographer. Photos. by the author. Boston, Houghton Mifflin, 1954. 272p. illus. 22cm. [TR140.K5A3] 54-9121
1. Photographers —Correspondence, reminiscences, etc. 2. Life (Chicago) I. Title.

PENDRIGH, Ernest. 927.7
The magic box; exploits of a street-photographer. London, New York, J. Long [1954] 156p. illus. 22cm. [TR140.P4A3] 54-44344
1. Photographers—Correspondence, reminiscences, etc. I. Title.

Photographers—Biography.

DIALOGUE with photography / [interviews conducted by] Paul Hill & Thomas Cooper. New York : Farrar, Straus, Giroux, c1979. 427 p. : ports. ; 22 cm. "Originally appeared in Camera magazine, Lucerne, Switzerland." Includes bibliographies and index. [TR139.D52 1979] 78-25851 ISBN 0-374-13893-1 : 12.95 770'.92'2 B
1. Photographers—Biography. I. Hill, Paul, 1941- II. Cooper, Thomas Joshua, 1947- III. Camera (Lucerne) BIP

Photographers, British.

BOORD, W. Arthur. 770'.92'2
Sun Artists, edited by W. Arthur Boord. New York, Arno Press, 1973. 60 p. illus. 32 cm. (Literature of Photography) Originally published in 1891. [TR139.B6 1973] 72-9184 ISBN 0-405-04895-5. 30.00.
1. Photographers, British. 2. Photography, Artistic. I. Title. II. Series.

Photographers—Interviews.

DANZIGER, James, 1953- 770'.92'2 B
Interviews with master photographers : Minor White, Imogen Cunningham, Cornell Capa, Elliott Erwitt, Yousuf Karsh, Arnold Newman, Lord Snowdon, Brett Weston / James Danziger, Barnaby Conrad III. New York : Paddington Press : distributed by Grosset & Dunlap, c1977. 175 p., [12] leaves of plates : ill. ; 24 cm. [TR139.D36] 76-53315 ISBN 0-448-22183-7 : 10.00
1. Photographers—Interviews. I. Conrad, Barnaby, 1953- joint author. II. Title.

Photographers—Juvenile literature.

FORSEE, Aylesa. 770.922
Famous photographers; excellence in professional photography as seen through the lives and work of five masters: Edward Steichen, Ansel Adams, Cecil Beaton, Yousuf Karsh [and] David D. Duncan. Philadelphia, Macrae Smith [1968] 223 p. illus., ports. 24 cm. Bibliography: p. [213]-215. [TR139.F6] 68-18810
1. Photographers—Juvenile literature. I. Title.

Photography — Biog.

SIPLEY, Louis Walton. 770.922
Photography's great inventors, selected by an international committee for the International Photography Hall of Fame. Philadelphia, American Museum of Photography [1965] xix, 170 p. illus., ports. 24 cm. "A selected chronology of photography" p. 137-150. Includes bibliographies. [TR139.S5] 65-28010
1. Photography — Biog. I. American Museum of Photography, Philadelphia. II. Title.

Photography, Advertising.

KEPPLER, Victor. 770'.924 B
Man + camera; a photographic autobiography [by] Victor Keppler. Designed by Hal Rogers. New York, Amphoto [1970] 215 p. illus. (part col.) 33 cm. [TR690.4.K46] 75-97872
1. Photography, Advertising. I. Title.

Photography, Artistic.

CARTIER-BRESSON, Henri, 1908- 779'.0924
The world of Henri Cartier Bresson. New York, Viking Press [1968] [16] p., 210 illus. 28 x 31 cm. (A Studio book) [TR650.C38] 68-23211 14.00
1. Photography, Artistic. I. Title.

COBURN, Alvin Langdon, 1882- 779.0924
Alvin Langdon Coburn, photographer; an autobiography. Edited by Helmut & Alison Gernsheim. New York, F. A. Praeger [1966] 143 p. illus., ports. 29 cm. Bibliography: p. 141-143. [TR140.C56A27 1966a] 66-21778
1. Photography, Artistic. I. Gernsheim, Helmut, 1913- ed. II. Gernsheim, Alison, ed. III. Title. BIP

ERWITT, Elliott. 779'.092'4
Photographs and anti-photographs. Biographical essay by Sam Holmes. Introd. by John Szarkowski. Greenwich, Conn., New York Graphic Society [1972] 128 p. (chiefly illus.) 25 x 30 cm. [TR654.E78] 72-183972 ISBN 0-8212-0440-8 15.00
1. Photography, Artistic. I. Title.

LARTIGUE, Jacques Henri, 1894- 779
Diary of a century. [Edited by Richard Avedon. Translation by Carla van Splunteren] New York, Viking Press [1970] 1 v. (unpaged) illus., ports. 34 cm. (A Studio book) [TR653.L37] 74-101776 27.50
1. Photography, Artistic. I. Title. BIP

STOUMEN, Louis Clyde. 791.43'092'4
Can't argue with sunrise : a paper movie / Lou Stoumen. Millbrae, Calif. : Celestial Arts, 1975. 185 p. : ill. ; 22 cm. "A Hand Press book." [TR654.S76] 75-262 ISBN 0-89087-052-7 : 14.95. pbk. : 9.45
1. Photography, Artistic. 2. Photography, Documentary. I. Title.

STRAND, Paul, 1890-1976. 779'.092'4
Paul Strand : sixty years of photographs : excerpts from correspondence, interviews, and other documents / profile by Calvin Tomkins. Millerton, N.Y. : Aperture, c1976. 183 p. : ill. ; 30 cm. Bibliography: p. 178-181. [TR654.S77 1976] 76-42103 ISBN 0-912334-81-9 : 25.00. ISBN 0-900406-82-8 pbk.
1. Photography, Artistic.

Photography—Biography.

BEATON, Cecil Walter Hardy, Sir, 1904- 770'.92'2 B
The magic image : the genius of photography from 1839 to the present day / Cecil Beaton and Gail Buckland. 1st American ed. Boston : Little, Brown, c1975. 304 p. : ill. (some col.) ; 29 cm. [TR139.B4 1975] 74-7107 19.95
1. Photography—Biography. 2. Photography—History. I. Buckland, Gail, joint author. II. Title. BIP

Photography, Journalistic.

QUICK, Watson, the camera : seventy-five years of news photography / edited by Delmar Watson ; text by Helen R. Weiner. Hollywood, CA : D Watson, 1975. 120 p. : chiefly ill. ; 29 cm. Includes index. [TR820.Q52] 75-15119 12.95 779'.092'2
1. Photography, Journalistic. I. Watson, Delmar. II. Weiner, Helen R.

SPINA, Tony. 778.5'38'07
Press photographer. Text and photos. by Tony Spina. South Brunswick, [N.J.] A. S. Barnes [1968] 185 p. (chiefly illus., ports) 29 cm. [TR820.S68] 67-10743
1. Photography, Journalistic. I. Title.

Photography of sailing ships.

BEESTON, Diane. 779'.37'0924
Of wind, fog and sail; sailing on San Francisco Bay. San Francisco, Chronicle Books [1972] 160 p. (chiefly illus.) 25 x 35 cm. [TR670.5.B44] 72-85167 12.95
1. Photography of sailing ships. I. Title.

Photography—Portraits.

*CAMERON, Julia Margaret. 779'2'0924
Victorian photographs of famous men & fair women. With introductions by Virginia Woolf & Roger Fry. Expanded and revised edition edited by Tristam Powell. New York, A & W Visual Library [1975 c1973] 32 p. 44 plates, 30 cm. [TR681] 75-12275 ISBN 0-88365-332-X 6.95 (pbk.)
1. Photography—Portraits. I. Title. BIP

GALELLA, Ron. 779'.2'0924
Offguard : a paparazzo look at the beautiful people / by Ron Galella ; with an introd. by Bruce Jay Freidman. New York

: McGraw-Hill, c1976. 192 p. : ill. ; 28 cm. Includes index. [TR681.F3G34] 75-46628 ISBN 0-07-022729-2 : 12.95. ISBN 0-07-022733-0 pbk. : 6.95
1. Photography—Portraits. 2. Photography, Journalistic. I. Title.

MATHERS, Michael H. 779'.2'0924
Portraits : friends and strangers / Michael Mathers ; foreword by Thomas Farber. Seattle : Madrona Publishers, c1979. ca. 150 p. : ill. ; 26 cm. [TR680.M365] 79-336 ISBN 0-914842-36-6 : 14.95. ISBN 0-914842-35-8 pbk. : 9.95
1. Photography—Portraits. 2. Mathers, Michael H. I. Title.

WEISSBERGER, L. Arnold. 779'.2'0924
Famous faces; a photograph album of personal reminiscences, by L. Arnold Weissberger. New York, H. N. Abrams [1973] 443 p. ports. 28 x 30 cm. [TR681.F3W44] 72-706 ISBN 0-8109-0115-3 35.00
1. Photography—Portraits. 2. Performing arts—Biography—Portraits. I. Title.

Photography—The West—History—Juvenile literature.

HOOBLER, Dorothy. 770'.92'2 B
Photographing the frontier / by Dorothy and Thomas Hoobler. New York : Putnam, c1979. p. cm. Includes index. Bibliography: p. Discusses early photographic images of the West and the photographers responsible for these photographic records. [TR23.6.H66 1979] 79-11130 ISBN 0-399-20694-9 : 9.95
1. Photography—The West—History—Juvenile literature. 2. Photographers—The West—Biography—Juvenile literature. I. Hoobler, Thomas, joint author. II. Title. BIP

Phreas, Joannes, 1430 (ca.)-1465.

MITCHELL, Rosamond Joscelyne, 1902- 923.742
John Free, from Bristol to Rome in the fifteenth century. London, New York, Longmans, Green [1955] 157p. illus. 23cm. [LA98.M5] 55-4398
1. Phreas, Joannes, 1430 (ca.)-1465. 2. Education, Medieval. I. Title.

Physical education and training—Biography.

GERBER, Ellen W. 613.7
Innovators and institutions in physical education [by] Ellen W. Gerber. Philadelphia, Lea & Febiger, 1971. xvii, 452 p. illus., ports. 24 cm. (Health education, physical education, and recreation series) Bibliography: p. 417-433. [GV331.G47] 79-115024 ISBN 0-8121-0301-7
1. Physical education and training—Biography. 2. Physical education and training—History. I. Title. BIP

Physical education and training—Dictionaries.

THE Oxford companion to sports & games / edited by John Arlott. 796'.03
London ; New York : Oxford University Press, 1975. vii, 1143 p. : ill. ; 25 cm. [GV207.O93] 75-319716 ISBN 0-19-211538-3 : 29.95
1. Physical education and training—Dictionaries. 2. Sports—Dictionaries. 3. Games—Dictionaries. 4. Athletes—Biography. I. Arlott, John.

Physically handicapped—Biography.

HENRICH, Edith (Dodd) 1907- ed. 920.93624
Experiments in survival. Commentary by Leonard Kriegel. New York, Association for the Aid of Crippled Children [1961] 199 p. 21 cm. [CT9983.A1H4] 61-16249
1. Physically handicapped—Biography. I. Title.

Physically handicapped—Personal narratives.

DEACON, Joseph John. 362.2'1'0924 B
Joey / Joseph Jones Deacon. New York : Scribner, c1974. 92 p., [2] leaves of plates : ill. ; 20 cm. Published in 1974 under title: Tongue tied. Autobiographical. [RD796.D4A35 1974b] 75-15452 ISBN 0-684-14474-3 : 5.95
1. Physically handicapped—Personal narratives. 2. Cerebral palsy—Personal narratives. I. Title.

*TILLMAN, Carolyn. 362.430924
Life on wheels by Carolyn Tillman. Los Angeles, Crescent [1975] 98 p. 21 cm. [RD796] 75-16527 ISBN 0-89144-001-1 3.25 (pbk.)
1. Physically handicapped—Personal narratives. I. Title. BIP

*VAN LINT, June 362.40924.
My new life [La Jolla, Ca.] June Van Lint, 1975 vi, 199. 22 cm. [CT9983] 75-183430 6.95.
1. Physically handicapped-Personal narratives. I. Title.
Pbk., 3.95. Author's address: 1032 Skylark Drive, 92037

Physicians.

BLAUVELT, Eva Burdick, 1877- 920.7
Gram's story. [1st ed.: New York, Pageant Press [1955] 69p. illus. 21cm. [CT275.B57936A3] 55-12137
I. Title.

CARDANO, Girolamo, 1501-1576. 925
The book of my life (De vita propria liber) Translated from the Latin by Jean Stoner. New York, Dover Publications [1962] xviii, 331 p. port. 22 cm. Bibliography: p. 329-331. [Q143.C3A3] 63-2615
1. "Unabridged and corrected republication of the work first published ... in 1930." I. Title.

*DOOLEY, Agnes (Wise) 926.1
Promises to keep; the life of Doctor Thomas A. Dooley. [New York] New Amer. Lib. [1964, c.1961, 1962] 190p. illus. 18cm. (Signet bk., P2405) .60 pap.,
I. Title.

GLASCOCK, Harold, 1880- 926.1
Plow and scalpel; a biography of Clemson MacFarland, M. D., by Robert Winfield [Pseud.] New York, Vantage Press [c1953] 218p. 22cm. [RZ332.G5A3] 53-12235
I. Title.

SOURKES, Theodore L. 610'.922
Nobel Prize winners in medicine and physiology, 1901-1965, by Theodore L. Sourkes. [New and rev. ed.] London, New York, Abelard-Schuman [1967, c1966] ix, 464 p. ports. 23 cm. (The Life of science library, no. 45) Revision of Lloyd G. Stevenson's Nobel Prize winners in medicine and physiology, 1901-1950. Includes bibliographical references. [R149.S6 1967] 65-24774
1. Physicians. 2. Physiologists. 3. Nobel prizes. I. Stevenson, Lloyd G. Nobel Prize winners in medicine and physiology, 1901-1950. II. Title.

STEVENSON, Lloyd G 378.32
Nobel prize winners in medicine and physiology, 1901-1950. New York, H. Schuman [1953] 291p. illus. 22cm. (The Life of science library, no. 29) [R134.S77] [R134.S77] 926.1 53-10370 53-10370
1. Physicians. 2. Physiologists. 3. Noblel prizes. I. Title.

NEW York Academy of Medicine. Library. 016.9261
Catalog of biographies. Boston, G. K. Hall, 1960. 165p. 37cm. [R134.N4] 60-50505
1. Physicians—Biog.—Catalogs. I. Title.

U.S. Joint Publications Research Service. v. 12
Biographic information on Soviet scientists. New York, 1960. a -- c, 104 p. (JPRS: 3666) Translated from the Bol'shaia meditsinskaia entsiklopediia and various Soviet periodicals.
1. Physicians — U.S.S.R. — Biog. 2. Science — U.S.S.R. — Biog. I. Title.

U.S. Joint Publications Research Service. v. 12
Biographical sketches of Soviet scientific personalities. New York, 1960. 387 p. (JPRS: 2893) Translated from the Bol'shaia sovetskaia entsiklopediia.
1. Physicians — U.S.S.R. — Biog. 2. Science — U.S.S.R. — Biog. I. Title.

Physicians, American.

BLASSINGAME, Wyatt Rainey 926.1
Frontier doctors, by Wyatt Blassingame, Richard Glendinning. New York, Watts [c.1963] 150p. 22cm. 62-21753 2.95
1. Physicians, American. I. Glendinning, Richard, joint author. II. Title.

Physicians—Biography.

CROWTHER, James Gerald, 1899- 926.1
Six great doctors: Harvey. Pasteur. Lister, Pavlov, Ross. Fleming. London, Hamilton [Chester Springs, Pa., Dufour. 1966] 207p. illus. 19cm. Bibl. A59 3.25 bds.,
1. Physicians—Biog. I. Title.

DENTI di Pirajno, Alberto, 1886- 926.1
A cure for serpents; a doctor in Africa. Translated by Kathleen Naylor. New York, W. Sloane Associates [1955] 277 p. illus. 22 cm. Autobiographical. [R520.D4A313 1955a] 55-9060
I. Title.

MARDUS, Elaine. 926.1
Doctors to the great, by Elaine Mardus and Miriam Lang. New York, Dial Press, 1962. 246p. 22cm. [R134.M3] 62-15397
1. Physicians—Biography. I. Lang, Miriam, joint author. II. Title.

MARTIN, Wayne. 610
Medical heroes and heretics / by Wayne Martin. Old Greenwich, Conn. : Devin-Adair Co., c1977. x, 242 p. ; 22 cm. Bibliography: p. 239-241. [R134.M33] 75-40912 ISBN 0-8159-6214-2 : 10.00
1. Physicians—Biography. 2. Medical research personnel—Biography. 3. Medicine—History. 4. Medical innovations—History. I. Title. BIP

SIGERIST, Henry Ernest, 1891-. v. 12
The great doctorss; a biographical history of medicine. Tr. by Eden and Cedar Paul. [3d ed.] Garden City, N.Y., Doubleday, 1958. xv, 422 p. (Doubleday Anchor books, no. A 140) Translation of Grosse Arzte; eine Geschichte der Heilkunde in Lebensbildern.
1. Physicians — Biog. I. Title.

TRUAX, Rhoda. 926.1
True adventures of doctors; illustrated by Paul Galdone [1st ed.] Boston, Little, Brown [1954] 216 p. illus. 20 cm. (The True adventure library) [R134.T7] 54-5118
1. Physicians—Biography. I. Title.

WHO'S who in industrial medicine. Chicago, Industrial Medicine Pub. Co. v. 24 cm. biennial. A51 v. 12
1. Physicians—Biog. 2. Surgeons—Biog. 3. Dentists—Biog.

Physicians—Biography—Juvenile literature.

SILVERBERG, Robert. 920
The great doctors. New York, Putnam [1964] 193 p. 21 cm. Bibliography: p. 187-191. [R134.S48] 64-13041
1. Physicians—Biography—Juvenile literature. I. Title.

Physicians, British.

WOLSTENHOLME, Gordon E. W., ed. 926.1
The Royal College of Physicians of London: portraits. The portraits described by David Piper. London, J. & A. Churchill [dist. Boston, Little] 1964. 468p. illus., col. front ports. 26cm. 64-1523 16.00
1. Physicians, British. 2. Physicians—Portraits. I. Piper, David. II. Royal College of Physicians of London. III. Title.

Physicians—Correspondence, reminiscences, etc.

BERCZELLER, Richard. 610'.924 B
Time was. New York, Viking Press [1971] 216 p. 22 cm. Autobiographical. [R502.B44A3 1971] 75-132859 ISBN 0-670-71563-8 6.95
1. Physicians—Correspondence, reminiscences, etc. I. Title.

FOTHERGILL, John, 1712-1780. 610'.924 B
Chain of friendship; selected letters of Dr. John Fothergill of London, 1735-1780. With introd. and notes by Betsy C. Corner & Christopher C. Booth. Cambridge, Belknap Press of Harvard University Press, 1971. xxiv, 538 p. illus., facsims., geneal. table, map, ports. 24 cm. Bibliography: p. 511-519. [R489.F6A4 1971] 75-127877 ISBN 0-674-10660-1 20.00
1. Physicians—Correspondence, reminiscences, etc. I. Title. BIP

HEISER, Victor George, 1873- 926.1
An American doctor's odyssey; adventures in forty-five countries. New York, Grosset & Dunlap [1957, c1936] 544p. illus. 21cm. (Grosset's universal library, UL-30) [R154] 57-4404
1. Physicians—Correspondence, reminiscences, etc. 2. Hygiene, Public—East (Far East) 3. Tropics—Diseases and hygiene. 4. Rockefeller Foundation. International Health Board. 5. Hygiene, Public—Phillippine Islands. I. Title.

KING, George Suthie, 1878- 926.1
Doctor on a bicycle. New York, Rinehart [1958] 275 p. 22 cm. Autobiography. [R154.K32A3] 58-11521
1. Physicians—Correspondence, reminiscences, etc. I. Title.

MARSHALL, Otis, 1884- 926.1
Memoirs of a G. P. [1st ed.] New York, Vantage Press [1958] 155p. 21cm. [R154.M2956A3] 58-10665
1. Physicians— Correspondence, reminiscences, etc. I. Title.

NOLEN, William A., 1928- 610'.973
A surgeon's world, by William A. Nolen. [1st ed.] New York, Random House [1972] xii, 366 p. 22 cm. [R154.N68A32] 72-7235 7.95
1. Physicians—Correspondence, reminiscences, etc. I. Title. BIP

NORRIS, Jack Clayton, 1899- 926.1
Gleanings from a doctor's eye. [Atlanta, 1953] 120p. illus. 20cm. [R154.N693A5] 54-275
1. Physicians—Correspondence, reminiscences, etc. I. Title.

POINDEXTER, Hildrus Augustus, 1901- 610'.92'4 B
My world of reality (an autobiography) [by] Hildrus A. Poindexter. Detroit, Balamp Pub. [1973] vii, 342 p. port. 24 cm. [R695.P64] 72-85752 9.95
1. Physicians—Correspondence, reminescences, etc. 2. Negro physicians. I. Title.

PRITZKE, Herbert. 926.1
Bedouin doctor. Translated from the German by Richard Graves. [1st American ed.] New York, Dutton, 1957. 255 p. illus. 21 cm. Translation of Nach Hause kommst du nie. [R512.P7A313 1957a] 57-8996
1. Physicians—Correspondence, reminiscences, etc. I. Title.

PURVINE, Mary (Bowerman) 926.1
Mary B. Purvine, pioneer doctor. Santa Barbara, Calif., 1958. 60p. illus., ports. 27cm. '100 copies printed by Johnck & Seeger, San Francisco.' Stories collected by Helen Purvine Burnett. [R154.P868A3] 58-46344
1. Physicians—Correspondence, reminiscences, etc. I. Burnett, Helen (Purvine) comp. II. Title.

RICHARDSON, Edward Henderson, 1877- 926.1
A doctor remembers. 1st ed. New York, Vantage Press [1959] 252p. illus. 21cm. [R154.R42A3] 59-8427

1. Physicians—Correspondence, reminiscences, etc. I. Title.

RUBIN, Theodore Isaac. 616'.025'0924 B
Emergency room diary. New York, Grosset & Dunlap [1972] viii, 193 p. 22 cm. [R154.R389A3] 72-79619 ISBN 0-448-01555-2 6.95
1. Physicians—Correspondence, reminiscences, etc. 2. Medical emergencies. I. Title.

RUSH, Benjamin, 1745-1813. 926.1
Letters. Edited by L. H. Butterfield. [Princeton] Published for the American Philosophical Society by Princeton University Press, 1951. 2 v. (lxxxvii, 1295 p.) illus., ports., fold. map. 25 cm. (Memoirs of the American Philosophical Society, v. 30, pts. 1-2) Contents.CONTENTS. -- v. 1. 1761-1792 -- v. 2. 1793-1813. Bibliography: p. 1219-1229. [R154.R9A4] 51-11569
1. Physicians — Correspondence, reminiscences, etc. I. Butterfield, Lyman Henry, ed. II. Title. III. Series: American Philosophical Society, Philadelphia. Memoirs, v. 30, pts. 1-2

SEEL, David John, 1925- 248.8'6
Does my father know I'm hurt? Illustrated by Peggy Bradford Long. Wheaton, Ill., Tyndale House Publishers [1971] 96 p. illus. 18 cm. [R630.S4A3] 70-155975 ISBN 0-8423-0670-6(pbk)
1. Physicians—Correspondence, reminiscences, etc. 2. Cancer—Korea. 3. Missions, Medical—Korea. I. Title.

SMITH, Elihu Hubbard, 1771-1798. 081 S
The diary of Elihu Hubbard Smith (1771-1798). Edited by James E. Cronin. Philadelphia, American Philosophical Society, 1973. xiii, 481 p. port. 32 cm. (Memoirs of the American Philosophical Society, v. 95) Includes bibliographical references. [Q11.P612 vol. 95] [R154] 610'.92'4 B 72-83462 ISBN 0-87169-095-0 15.00
1. Physicians—Correspondence, reminiscences, etc. I. Cronin, James E., ed. II. Title. III. Series: American Philosophical Society, Philadelphia. Memoirs, v. 95.

TREUE, Wilhelm, 1909- 926.1
Doctor at court. Translated from the German by Frances Fawcett. New York, Roy Publishers [c1958] 209 p. 23 cm. [R133.T683] 59-14347
1. Physicians — Correspondence, Reminiscences, etc. 2. Kings and rulers. I. Title.

TROUPA, Albert B 1881-1959. 926.1
Grass-roots doctor; memories of a mischievous boyhood and forty fruitful years as an M.D. [1st ed.] New York, Exposition Press [1959] 156 p. 21 cm. [R154.T676A3] 59-16447
1. Physicians — Correspondence, reminiscences, etc. I. Title.

WELCH, William J. 610'.92'4 B
What happened in between; a doctor's story [by] William J. Welch. New York, G. Braziller [1972] xi, 208 p. 22 cm. [R154.W323A3 1972] 72-80733 ISBN 0-8076-0660-X 6.95
1. Physicians—Correspondence, reminiscences, etc. I. Title. **BIP**

X, Doctor. 610
Intern. [1st ed.] New York, Harper & Row [1965] 404 p. 22 cm. Diary recorded by the author during his hospital internship. [R840.X2] 64-25118
1. Physicians—Correspondence, reminiscences, etc. 2. Interns (Medicine) I. Title. **BIP**

Physicians—Great Britain—Biography.

BETTANY, George Thomas, 1850-1891. 610'.922 B
Eminent doctors: their lives and their work. Freeport, N.Y., Books for Libraries Press [1972] 2 v. 23 cm. (Essay index reprint series) Reprint of the 1885 ed. [R489.A1B5 1972] 76-39663 ISBN 0-8369-2747-8
1. Physicians—Great Britain. 2. Medicine—Great Britain—History. I. Title.

HALE-WHITE, William, Sir, 1857-1949. 610'.922 B
Great doctors of the nineteenth century. Freeport, N.Y., Books for Libraries Press [1970] vii, 325 p. 23 cm. (Essay index reprint series) Reprint of the 1935 ed. [R489.A1H3 1970] 74-108639
1. Physicians—Gt. Brit. 2. Surgeons—Gt. Brit. 3. Medicine—Gt. Brit. I. Title. **BIP**

POWER, D'Arcy, Sir, 1855-1941, ed. 610'.922 B
British masters of medicine. Freeport, N.Y., Books for Libraries Press [1969] xv, 242 p. illus., ports. 23 cm. (Essay index reprint series) Reprint of the 1936 ed. Contents.—William Harvey.—Thomas Sydenham.—John Floyer.—William Cheselden.—Percivall Pott.—John Hunter.—John Coakley Lettsom.—Edward Jenner.—Robert Willan.—Richard Bright.—Thomas Addison.—William Stokes.—William Fergusson.—Robert Bentley Todd.—James Young Simpson.—James Paget.—Joseph Lister.—William Turner.—Hugh Owen Thomas.—Robert Jones.—Patrick Manson.—William Osler.—James Mackenzie.—Ernest H. Starling. [R489.A1P6 1969] 79-99721 ISBN 0-8369-1375-2
1. Physicians—Great Britain—Biography. I. Title. **BIP**

Physicians—Kent, Ont.—Biography.

LAURISTON, Victor, 1881- 610'.922
A centennial chronicle of Kent doctors. [Chatham, Ont., Shepherd Print. Co., c1967] 284 p. 24 cm. Sponsored by the Kent County Medical Society. [R464.A1L3] 68-137016
1. Physicians—Kent, Ont.—Biography. I. Kent County Medical Society. II. Title.

Physicians—Kentucky—Biography.

EBERSON, Frederick, 1892- 610'.92'2 B
Portraits: Kentucky pioneers in community health and medicine. Lexington, University of Kentucky Medical Center, 1968. ix, 121 p. illus., maps, ports. 23 cm. Bibliography: p. 111-117. [R231.E23] 75-312948
1. Physicians—Kentucky—Biography. 2. Medicine—Kentucky—History. 3. Hygiene, Public—Kentucky—History. 4. Kentucky—Biography. I. Title.

Physicians—Russia—Directories.

JOHN E. Fogarty International Center for Advanced Study in the Health Sciences. Geographic Health Studies. 610'.92'2 B
Soviet personalities in biomedicine : a publication of the Geographic Health Studies program of the John E. Fogarty International Center for Advanced Study in the Health Sciences ; prepared under an interagency agreement with the Library of Congress. [Bethesda, Md.] : U.S. Dept. of Health, Education and Welfare, Public Health Service, National Institutes of Health, 1974. xx, 968 p. ; 27 cm. (DHEW publicaton ; no. (NIH) 74-699) Includes indexes. [R713.57.J64 1974] 74-602670
1. Physicians—Russia—Directories. 2. Medical research personnel—Russia—Directories. 3. Public health personnel—Russia—Directories. I. United States. Library of Congress. II. Title. III. Series: United States. Dept. of Health, Education, and Welfare. DHEW publication ; no. (NIH) 74-699.

Physicians—U.S.

JIRKA, Frank Joseph, 1886-1963. 610'.922 B
American doctors of destiny; a collection of historical narratives of the lives of great American physicians and surgeons whose service to the Nation and to the world has transcended the scope of their profession. With an introd. by Harold W. Camp and twenty portraits by Raymond Warren. Freeport, N.Y., Books for Libraries Press [1970] xix, 361 p. ports. 23 cm. (Essay index reprint series) Reprint of the 1940 ed. Bibliography: p. 352-353. [R153.J5 1970] 76-121482
1. Physicians—U.S. 2. Surgeons—U.S. 3. Medicine—U.S. I. Title.

KELLY, Howard Atwood, 1858-1943. 610'.922 B
Dictionary of American medical biography; lives of eminent physicians of the United States and Canada, from the earliest times, by Howard A. Kelly and Walter L. Burrage. Boston, Milford House [1971] xxx, 1364 p. 26 cm. Reprint of the 1928 ed. First published in 1912 under title: A cyclopedia of American medical biography. Bibliography: p. ix-xxx. [R153.K3 1971] 74-78618 ISBN 0-87821-017-2
1. Physicians—U.S. 2. Physicians—Canada. I. Burrage, Walter Lincoln, 1860-1935, joint author. II. Title.

THACHER, James, 1754-1844. 610'.922
American medical biography; or, Memoirs of eminent physicians who have flourished in America, to which is prefixed a succinct history of medical science in the United States from the first settlement of the country. New York, Milford House, 1967. 2 v. in 1. ports. 24 cm. (A Milford House reprint) Reprint of the 1828 ed. Bibliographical footnotes. [R153.T3 1967] 67-30787
1. Physicians—United States. 2. Medicine—United States. I. Title. II. Title: Memoirs of eminent physicians who have flourished in America.

WILLIAMS, Stephen West, 1790-1855. 610'.922
American medical biography; or, Memoirs of eminent physicians; embracing principally those who have died since the publication of Dr. Thacher's initial work in 1828 on the same subject. New York, Milford House, 1967. xv, 664 p. ports. 24 cm. (A Milford House reprint) Reprint of the 1845 ed. [R153.W5 1967] 67-30786
1. Physicians—United States. 2. Medicine—United States. I. Thacher, James, 1754-1844. American medical biography. II. Title. III. Title: Memoirs of eminent physicians.

Physicians—United States—Biography.

AMERICAN Medical Political Action Committee. FIC
Threads of greatness : a Bicentennial tribute to physician-statesmen. [Chicago : American Medical Political Action Committee], 1976. 32 p. : ill. ; 28 cm. (Political stethoscope ; v. 15, no. 1) [R153.A53 1976] 610'.92'2 B 76-376610
1. Physicians—United States—Biography. 2. Statesmen—United States—Biography. I. Title. II. Series.

HENDIN, David. 610'.92'4 B
The life givers / by David Hendin. New York : Morrow, 1976. 260 p. ; 22 cm. Includes index. [R153.H46] 75-42119 ISBN 0-688-03035-1 : 8.95
1. Physicians—United States—Biography. I. Title. **BIP**

KELLY, Howard Atwood, 1858-1943. 610'.92'2
Dictionary of American medical biography : lives of eminent physicians of the United States and Canada, from the earliest times / by Howard A. Kelly and Walter L. Burrage. Boston : Longwood Press, 1978. p. cm. Reprint of the 1928 ed. published by Appleton, New York. Includes index. Bibliography: p. [R153.K3 1978] 78-13906 ISBN 0-89341-513-8 lib.bdg. : 75.00
1. Physicians—United States—Biography. 2. Physicians—Canada—Biography. I. Burrage, Walter Lincoln, 1860-1935, joint author. II. Title.

Physicians' wives—Manitoba—Biography.

PETERKIN, Audrey. 610'.92'2 B
Mrs. Doctor : reminiscences of Manitoba doctors' wives / Audrey Peterkin and Margaret Shaw. Winnipeg : Prairie, c1976. 168 p. : ill. ; 23 cm. [R464.A.1P47] 77-366008 ISBN 0-919576-07-9
1. Physicians' wives—Manitoba—Biography. 2. Manitoba—Biography. I. Shaw, Margaret Mason, joint author. II. Title.

Physicists.

HART, Ivor Blashka, 1889- 530'.0922 B
The great physicists, by Ivor B. Hart. Freeport, N.Y., Books for Libraries Press [1970] vi, 137 p. illus. 22 cm. (Essay index reprint series) Reprint of the 1927 ed. originally published by Methuen. [QC15.H3 1970] 71-117804
1. Physicists. 2. Physics—History. I. Title. **BIP**

HEATHCOTE, Niels Hugh de Vaudrey. 378.32
Nobel prize winners in physics, 1901-1950. With a foreword by Herbert Dingle. New York, H. Schuman [1953] 473p. illus. 22cm. (The Life of science library, no. 30) [QC15.H4] 925.3 53-10369
1. Physicists. 2. Nobel prizes. I. Title.

HEATHCOTE, Niels Hugh de Vaudrey. 530'.0922
Nobel prize winners in physics, 1901-1950, by Niels H. de V. Heathcote. With an introd. by Herbert Dingle. Freeport, N.Y., Books for Libraries Press [1971, c1953] xvi, 473 p. illus. 23 cm. (Essay index reprint series) "Originally published as part of the Life of science library." [QC15.H4 1971] 76-167354 ISBN 0-8369-2455-X
1. Physicists. 2. Nobel prizes. I. Title. **BIP**

ROWLAND, John, 1907- 539.70922
The atom. London, M. Parrish [1965] 120 p. illus., ports. 21 cm. (The Conquerors) Biographical sketches. Bibliography: p. 120. [QC15.R68] 66-1274
1. Physicists. 2. Atoms. I. Title.

ROWLAND, John, 1907- 539.7'0922
The atom. Worthington [Ohio] A. Lynn [1967, c1965] 120 p. illus., ports. 21 cm. (The Conquerors series) Biographical sketches. Bibliography: p. 120. [QC15] 67-7859
1. Physicists. 2. Atoms.

Physicists—Biography—Juvenile literature.

MANN, Alafded Leonard, 1930 925.3
Famous physicists, by A. L. Mann & A. C. Vivian. Illus. by Norma Ost. London, Museum Press [dist. Sportshelf, New Rochelle, N.Y., 1962] 127p. illus. 23cm. 61-17878 3.75
1. Physicists—Biog.—Juvenile literature. 2. Physics—Juvenile literature. I. Vivian, Charles 1917- joint author. II. Title.

MANN, Alfred Leonard, 1930- 920
Famous physicists [by] A. L. Mann, A. C. Vivian. Illus. by Norma Ost. New York, John Day [c.1961, 1963] 159p. illus. 21cm. 62-19715 3.25
1. Physicists—Biog.—Juvenile literature. 2. Physics—Juvenile literature. I. Vivian, Charles, 1917- joint author. II. Title.

MOORE, William, 1914- 530'.0922 B
The atomic pioneers; from Irish castle to Manhattan Project. New York, Putnam [1970] 159 p. illus., ports. 22 cm. Highlights in the lives of twelve scientists, dating from the seventeenth century to the present, whose experiments contributed to the coming of the Atomic Age. [QC15.M6] 920 78-113508 3.64
1. Physicists—Biography—Juvenile literature. 2. Chemists—Biography—Juvenile literature. I. Title.

RIEDMAN, Sarah Regal, 1902- 925.3
Men and women behind the atom. London, New York, Abelard-Schuman [1958] 228p. illus. 21cm. [QC15.R5] 58-12802
1. Physicists—Biog.—Juvenile literature. I. Title. **BIP**

Physicists—Correspondence, reminiscences, etc.

BITTER, Francis, 1902-1967. 538
Magnets: the education of a physicist. [1st ed.] Garden City, N.Y., Doubleday, 1959. 155 p. illus. 18 cm. (Science study series, S2) (Doubleday anchor books.) [QC16.B52A3] 59-9611
1. Physicists—Correspondence, reminiscences, etc. 2. Magnetism. I. Title.

FARADAY, Michael, 1791-1867. 530'.0924 B
The selected correspondence of Michael Faraday. Edited on behalf of the Royal Institution of Great Britain by L. Pearce Williams, with the assistance of Rosemary FitzGerald & Oliver Stallybrass. Cambridge [Eng.] University Press, 1971- v. port. 27 cm. English or French. Contents.Contents.—v. 1. 1812-1848. Includes bibliographical references. [QC16.F2A4 1971] 77-138377 ISBN 0-521-07908-X (v. 1)
1. Physicists—Correspondence, reminiscences, etc. I. Williams, Leslie Pearce, 1927- ed. II. FitzGerald, Rosemary, ed. III. Stallybrass, Oliver, ed. IV. Royal Institution of Great Britain, London. V. Title.

Physicists—India—Biography.

MISHRA, Debakanta, 1939- 530'.092'2 B
Five eminent scientists : their lives and work / D. K. Mishra. Delhi : Kalyani Publishers, c1976. xii, 214 p., [9] leaves of plates : ill. ; 23 cm. Includes bibliographical references. [QC15.M54] 76-900923 Rs18.00
1. Physicists—India—Biography. I. Title.

Physiocrats.

JEFFERSON, Thomas, Pres. U.S., 1743-1826. 973.4'6'0924
Correspondence between Thomas Jefferson and Pierre Samuel du Pont de Nemours, 1798-1817. Edited by Dumas Malone. Translations by Linwood Lehman. Supplement by Gilbert Chinard New York, Da Capo Press, 1970. xxv, 210, cxxiii p. facsim. 24 cm. The main work is a reprint of the 1930 ed., with Chinard's supplement, "Jefferson and the physiocrats," reprinted from The correspondence of Jefferson and du Pont de Nemours, published in 1931. [E302.J45 1970] 78-75282
1. Physiocrats. I. Du Pont de Nemours, Pierre Samuel, 1739-1817. II. Malone, Dumas, 1892- ed. III. Title. BIP

Physiology.

ZOTTERMAN, Yngve. 612'.00924 B
Touch, tickle, and pain. [1st ed.] Oxford, New York, Pergamon Press [1969-71] 2 v. illus., ports. 23 cm. An autobiography. [QP26.Z6A3] 70-91702 ISBN 0-08-015532-4
1. Physiology. I. Title. BIP

Piaf, Edith, 1915-1963.

BERTEAUT, Simone, 1918- 784'.092'4 B
Piaf; a biography. [1st ed.] New York, Harper & Row [1972] viii, 488 p. ports. 25 cm. Translated by June Guicharnaud. [ML420.P52B53 1972] 75-138706 ISBN 0-06-010313-2 10.00
1. Piaf, Edith, 1915-1963.

BERTEAUT, Simone, 1918- 784'092'4 [B]
Piaf; a biography [by] Simone Berteaut. Trans. by June Guicharnaud. [New York, Dell, 1973 c.1972] 475 p. 18 cm. [ML420.P52B53 1973] 1.75 (pbk)
1. Piaf, Edith, 1915-1963. I. Title.
L.C. card no. for original ed.: 75-138706

PIAF, Edith, 1915-1963. 784.0924
The wheel of fortune; the autobiography of Edith Piaf. Translated by Peter Trewartha and Andree Masoin de Virton. Philadelphia, Chilton Books [1965] 192 p. ports. 23 cm. [ML420.P52A33] 66-22872
1. Musicians—Correspondence, reminiscences, etc. I. Title.

Piaget, Jean, 1896-

BRINGUIER, Jean Claude. 155.4'13'0924
Conversations with Jean Piaget / Jean-Claude Bringuier ; translated by Basia M. Gulati. Chicago : University of Chicago Press, 1980. p. cm. Translation of Conversations libres avec Jean Piaget. [BF723.C5B6513] 79-15669 ISBN 0-226-07503-6 : 13.50
1. Piaget, Jean, 1896- 2. Cognition in children. 3. Intellect. 4. Knowledge, Theory of. I. Piaget, Jean, 1896- II. Title. BIP

Pianists.

CHASINS, Abram, 1903- 927.8
Speaking of pianists ... [1st ed.] New York, Knopf, 1957. 291 p. 22 cm. [ML397.C5] 57-12173
1. Pianists. I. Title.

FAMOUS pianists, for young people, [by] Gladys Burch. New York, Dodd, Mead, 1956. vii, 156p. incl. front., illus. (incl. ports.) 23 x 20cm. (Famous bibliographies for young people) First published under the title Famous pianists for boys and girls. v. 12
1. Piamists. 2. Music—Juvenile literature. I. Burch, Gladys, 1899-

GERIG, Reginald, 1919- 786.1'092'2 B
Famous pianists & their technique / Reginald R. Gerig. 2d ed. Washington : R. B. Luce, 1976. p. cm. Bibliography: p. [ML700.G44 1976] 75-37789 ISBN 0-88331-066-X
1. Pianists. 2. Piano music—Interpretation (Phrasing, dynamics, etc.) I. Title. BIP

GERIG, Reginald, 1919- 786.1'092'2 B
Famous pianists & their technique [by] Reginald R. Gerig. Washington, R. B. Luce [1974] xvi, 560 p. illus. 24 cm. Bibliography: p. 519-542. [ML700.G44] 73-18804 ISBN 0-88331-066-X 17.95
1. Pianists. 2. Piano music—Interpretation (Phrasing, dynamics, etc.) I. Title.

LENZ, Wilhelm von, 1808-1883. 786.1'092'2 B
The great piano virtuosos of our time from personal acquaintance: Liszt, Chopin, Tausig, Henselt. Translated from the German by Madeleine R. Baker. New York, Da Capo Press [1973, c1899] 169 p. 21 cm. (Da Capo Press music reprint series) [ML397.L57 1973] 72-8049 ISBN 0-306-70528-1 8.50
1. Pianists. I. Baker, Madeleine R., tr. II. Title.

Pianists—Biography.

BROOK, Donald. 786.1'0922 B
Masters of the keyboard. Westport, Conn., Greenwood Press [1971] 184 p. illus., ports. 23 cm. Reprint of the 1946 ed. [ML397.B57 1971b] 75-114479 ISBN 0-8371-4768-9
1. Pianists—Biography. I. Title. BIP

BROOK, Donald. 786.1'0922 B
Masters of the keyboard. Freeport, N.Y., Books for Libraries Press [1971, c1946] 184 p. illus., ports. 23 cm. (Biography index reprint series) Bibliography: p. 184. [ML397.B57 1971] 76-148206 ISBN 0-8369-8053-0
1. Pianists—Biography. I. Title.

BROWER, Harriette Moore, 1869-1928. 786.1'0922
Modern masters of the keyboard, by Harriet Brower. Edited by John C. Burton. Freeport, N.Y., Books for Libraries Press [1969] viii, 303 p. ports. 23 cm. (Essay index reprint series) "First published 1926." [ML397.B6 1969] 70-86736 ISBN 0-8369-1124-5
1. Pianists—Biography. 2. Piano—Instruction and study. I. Title.

CHAPIN, Victor. 786.1'0922
Giants of the keyboard. [1st ed.] Philadelphia, Lippincott [1967] 189 p. illus., ports. 22 cm. Discography: p. [181]-182. [ML397.C49] 67-2200
1. Pianists—Biography. 2. Piano music—Discography. I. Title.

SCHONBERG, Harold C. 927.8
The great pianists. New York, Simon and Schuster, 1963. 448 p. ports., music. 24 cm. [ML397.S3] 63-15367
1. Pianists—Biography. I. Title. BIP

Piankhi, King of Ethiopia, fla. 720 B.C. Juvenile literature.

JOHNSON, E. Harper 920
Piankhy the Great. Written, illus. by E. Harper Johnson. New York, Nelson [c.1962] 96p. col. illus. 22cm. 62-15987 2.95
1. Piankhi, King of Ethiopia, fla. 720 B.C. Juvenile literature. I. Title.

Piasecki, Victor.

PIASECKI, Victor. 940.54'72'470924
You'll need a guardian angel / [as told to] Alec Thackeray. New York : Norton, c1979. p. cm. [D805.R9P46 1979] 79-17903 ISBN 0-393-01274-3 : 10.95 10.95
1. Piasecki, Victor. 2. World War, 1939-1945—Prisoners and prisons, Russian. 3. World War, 1939-1945—Personal narratives, Polish. 4. Prisoners of war—Poland—Biography. 5. Prisoners of war—Russia—Biography. 6. Escapes—Russia. I. Thackeray, Alec. II. Title.

Piatigorsky, Gregor, 1903-

PIATIGORSKY, Gregor, 1903- 787'.3'0924 B
Cellist / Gregor Piatigorsky. New York : Da Capo Press, 1976, c1965. p. cm. (Da Capo Press music reprint series) Reprint of the ed. published by Doubleday, Garden City, N.Y. [ML418.P63A3 1976] 76-3697 ISBN 0-306-70822-1 : 17.50
1. Piatigorsky, Gregor, 1903- 2. Violinists, violoncellists, etc.—Correspondence, reminiscences, etc. I. Title.

Picabia, Francis, 1879-1953.

CAMFIELD, William A. 759.4 B
Francis Picabia : his art, life, and times / by William Camfield. Princeton, N.J. : Princeton University Press, c1978. p. cm. Includes index. Bibliography: p. [ND553.P47C36] 77-85533 ISBN 0-691-03932-1 : 35.00
1. Picabia, Francis, 1879-1953. 2. Painters—France—Biography. BIP

Picasso, Pablo, 1881-1973.

BERGER, John 759.6
The success and failure of Picasso [Magnolia, Mass., P. Smith, 1967, c.1965] 210p. illus. (inc. ports.) 20cm. (Penguin bk., 2383 rebound) [ND553.P5B45] 4.25
1. Picasso, Pablo, 1881- I. Title. BIP

BERGER, John 759.6
The success and failure of Picasso. [Harmondsworth, Eng., Baltimore] Penguin [1966, c.1965] 210p. 120 illus. (incl. ports.) 20cm. (2383) [ND553.P5B45] 66-757 2.25 pap.,
1. Picasso, Pablo, 1881- I. Title.

BUCHHEIM, Lothar Gunther. 759.6
Picasso, a pictorial biography. [translated by Michael Heron] New York, Viking Press [1959] 143 p. illus. (part col.) ports. 24 cm. (A Studio book) [ND553.P5B663] 59-165152
1. Picasso, Pablo, 1881-1973.

DUNCAN, David Douglas. 759.4
Goodbye Picasso / David Douglas Duncan. 1st ed. New York : Grosset & Dunlap, [1974] 299 p. : ill. (some col.) ; 33 cm. [ND553.P5D77] 74-4059 ISBN 0-448-11619-7 : 35.00
1. Picasso, Pablo, 1881-1973. I. Title.

ELGAR, Frank 759.6
Picasso. A study of his work by Frank Elgar. A biographical study by Robert Maillard. Translated from the French by Francis Scarfe. New York, Praeger [1960, c.1956] 268p. bBibl.: p.[259-260] illus. (part col.) plates 21cm. 2.95
1. Picasso, Pablo. I. Maillard, Robert. II. Title.

ELGAR, Frank. 709'.2'4
Picasso. Study of his work by Frank Elgar. Biographical study by Robert Maillard. [Translated from the French by Francis Scarfe] Rev. and enl. ed. New York, Tudor Pub. Co. [1972] 247, [7] p. illus. (part col.) 28 cm. Bibliography: p. [249]-[254] [ND553.P5E43 1972] 72-85393 ISBN 0-8148-0512-4 15.00
1. Picasso, Pablo, 1881- I. Maillard, Robert.

GILOT, Francoise, 1921- 927.5
Life with Picasso [by] Francoise Gilot, Carlton Lake. New York, McGraw [c.1964] 373p. illus., plates (incl. ports.) 23cm. 64-23276 6.95
1. Picasso, Pablo, 1881. I. Lake, Carlton. II. Title.

GILOT, Francoise, 1921- 927.5
Life with Picasso [by] Francoise Gulot and Charleto Lake New York New Amer. Lib. [1965, c.1964] 349p. 18cm. (Signet bk., Q2772) [ND553.P5G55] .95 pap.,
1. Picasso, Pablo, 1881- I. Lake, Carlton. II. Title.

GREENFELD, Howard. 759.4
Pablo Picasso; an introduction. Chicago, Follett [1971] 192 p. illus. (part col.) 25 cm. [ND553.P5G7] 70-118928 ISBN 0-695-80139-2 5.95
1. Picasso, Pablo, 1881-

LEYMARIE, Jean. 709'.2'4
Picasso : the artist of the century / text by Jean Leymarie ; with appreciations by poets and friends of the artist ; designed and edited by Albert Skira ; [translated from the French by James Emmons]. Geneva : Skira ; New York : Rizzoli, c1976. x, 309 p. : ill (some col.) ; 35 cm. Translation of Picasso, metamorphoses et unite. Includes index. Bibliography: p. 287-289. [ND553.P5L4413 1976] 76-62894 ISBN 0-8478-0090-3 (Rizzoli) : 50.00
1. Picasso, Pablo, 1881-1973. I. Picasso, Pablo, 1881-1973. BIP

MICHELI, Mario de. 759.6
Picasso. [Translated from the Italian by Pearl Sanders. 1st American ed.] New York, Grosset & Dunlap [1967] 39, [80] p. illus. (part col.) 18 cm. (The New Grosset art library, 4) On cover: Picasso; the life and work of the artist. Bibliography: p. 28-31. [ND553.P5M52 1967b] 67-24231
1. Picasso, Pablo, 1881-

O'BRIAN, Patrick. 759.4 B
Pablo Ruiz Picasso : a biography / Patrick O'Brian. London : Collins, 1976. 511 p., [8] p. of plates : ill., geneal. tables, ports. ; 24 cm. American ed. published under title: Picasso. Includes index. [ND553.P5O27 1976b] 77-362548 ISBN 0-00-211685-5 : £6.95
1. Picasso, Pablo, 1881-1973. 2. Painters—France—Biography.

O'BRIAN, Patrick. 759.4 B
Picasso : Pablo Ruiz Picasso : a biography / by Patrick O'Brian. New York : Putnam, c1976. 511 p. ; 24 cm. Includes index. [ND553.P5O27 1976] 75-41334 12.95 12.95
1. Picasso, Pablo, 1881-1973. 2. Painters—France—Biography. I. Title.

PARMELIN, Helene. 927.5
Picasso plain; an intimate portrait. Translated from the French by Humphrey Hare. New York, St. Martin's Press [1963] 250 p. illus. 22 cm. Translation of Picasso sur la place. [ND553.P5P333] 63-15854
1. Picasso, Pablo, 1881-1973.

PENROSE, Roland, Sir. 759.4
Picasso : his life and work / Roland Penrose. [Revised ed.]. Harmondsworth : Penguin, 1971. xv, 518 p., [16] leaves of plates : ill. ; 20 cm. (Pelican biographies) Includes index. Bibliography: p. [492]-498. [ND553.P5P42 1971] 75-309868 ISBN 0-14-021408-9
1. Picasso, Pablo, 1881-1973. I. Title. BIP

PENROSE, Roland, Sir. 759.6
Picasso: his life and work. New York, Harper [1959, c1958] 392 p. illus. 22 cm. Includes bibliography. [ND553.P5P42 1959] 58-8863
1. Picasso, Pablo, 1881-1973.

PENROSE, Roland, Sir. 759.6
Picasso: his life and work. [1st U.S. ed.]

New York, Harper & Row [1973] xv, 518 p. illus. 22 cm. (Icon editions, IN-16) [ND553.P5P42 1973] 72-180702 15.00
1. Picasso, Pablo, 1881-1973. I. Title.
Pbk. 5.95; ISBN 0-06-430016-1

PENROSE, Roland. 759.6
Portrait of Picasso. New York, Museum of Modern Art; distributed by Simon and Schuster [1957] 96p. illus., ports., map. 25cm. [ND553.P5P43] 927.5 57-7372
1. Picasso, Pablo, 1881- I. Title.

PICASSO; 759.6
a loan exhibition of his paintings, drawings, sculpture, ceramics, prints, and illustrated books, January 8-February 23, 1958. [Pref. by Henry Clifford. Philadelphia, 1958] 129p. illus., col. plates ports. 26cm. [N6853.P5P5] 927.5 58-2453
1. Picasso, Pablo, 1881- I. Philadelphia Museum of Art. II. Clifford, Henry, 1904-

PICASSO, Pablo, 1881- 759.6
Pablo Picasso: blue and rose periods. Text by William S. Lieberman. New York, H. N. Abrams in association with Pocket Books [1954] [74] p. 46 illus. (part col.) port. 18cm. (The Pocket library of great art, A20) An Abrams art book. Bibliography: p. [74] [ND553.P5L535] [ND553.P5L535] 927.5 54-14620 54-14620
I. Lieberman, William Slattery, 1924- II. Title.

PICASSO, Pablo, 1881- 759.6
Pablo Picasso: blue and rose periods. Text by William S. Lieberman. New York, H. N. Abrams in association with Pocket Books [1954] [74] p. 46 illus. (part col.) port. 18cm. (The Pocket library of great art, A20) An Abrams art book. Bibliography: p. [74] [ND553.P5L535] [ND553.P5L535] 927.5 54-14620 54-14620
I. Lieberman, William Slattery, 1924- II. Title.

PICASSO, Pablo 759.6
Picasso: the early years [by] Jiri Padrta. With a pref. by Jean Cocteau. [Translated by Iris Urwin] New York, Tudor Pub. Co. [1960] 16p. illus. 29 col. plates 28cm. 60-50595 7.95
I. Padrta, Jiri. II. Title.

PICASSO, Pablo 759.6
Picasso: the early years [by] Jiri Padrta. With a pref. by Jean Cocteau. [Translated by Iris Urwin] New York, Tudor Pub. Co. [1960] 16p. illus. 29 col. plates 28cm. 60-50595 7.95
I. Padrta, Jiri. II. Title.

STRUCHEN, Jeanette. 759.6 B
Pablo Picasso: master of modern art. New York, Watts [1969] 114 p. illus. 25 cm. (Immortals of art) Bibliography: p. 107-108. [ND553.P5S83] 69-11689 5.95
1. Picasso, Pablo, 1881-

VALLENTIN, Antonina, 1893-1957. 927.5
Picasso. Editorial consultant: Katherine Woods. Garden City, N.Y., Doubleday [1963] 275 p. illus. 23 cm. [ND553.P5V33] 61-12595
1. Picasso, Pablo, 1881- I. Title.

VALLENTIN, Antonina, 1893-1957 927.5
Picasso. Edit. consultant: Katherine Woods [Tr. from French] London, Cassell; New York, Doubleday [c.1957, 1963] 275p. illus. 23cm. 63-1873 7.50
1. Picasso, Pablo, 1881- I. Title.

Picasso, Pablo, 1881-1973—Friends and associates.

LAPORTE, Genevieve. 759.4 B
Sunshine at midnight : memories of Picasso and Cocteau / Genevieve Laporte ; translated and with annotations by Douglas Cooper. 1st American ed. New York : Macmillan, 1975. xii, 123 p., [4] leaves of plates : ill. ; 21 cm. Translation of Si tard le soir. Includes index. [ND553.P5L3213] 75-15633 ISBN 0-02-568300-4 : 6.95
1. Picasso, Pablo, 1881-1973—Friends and associates. 2. Laporte, Genevieve. I. Title.

Picasso, Pablo, 1881-1973—Juvenile literature.

BAKER, Donna. 759.4 B
Picasso / by Donna Baker. Chicago : Childrens Press, [1977] p. cm. (Artists in our world) A brief biography of one of the major artists of the twentieth century. [ND553.P5B24] 92 77-4848 ISBN 0-516-03683-1 lib.bdg. : 6.60
1. Picasso, Pablo, 1881-1973—Juvenile literature. 2. Painters—France—Biography—Juvenile literature. I. Title. II. Series.

RABOFF, Ernest Lloyd. 709'.24 (J)
Pablo Picasso, by Ernest Raboff. Garden City, N.Y., Doubleday, 1968. 1 v. (unpaged) illus. (part col.), port. 29 cm. (Art for children) (A Gemini-Smith book.) [ND553.P5R24] 68-26551 3.95
1. Picasso, Pablo, 1881- —Juvenile literature. BIP

SMITH, Miranda. 759.4 B
Pablo Picasso, master of modern art. Illustrated by Harold Henriksen. Mankato, Minn., Creative Education [distributed by Childrens Press, Chicago, 1974] 30 p. col. illus. 25 cm. (Creative Education close-ups) A brief biography of one of the major artists of the twentieth century considered the "father and master of modern art." [ND553.P5S57] 92 74-19319 ISBN 0-87191-411-5
1. Picasso, Pablo, 1881-1973—Juvenile literature. I. Henriksen, Harold, illus. II. Title.

Picasso, Pablo, 1881-1973—Portraits, etc.

QUINN, Edward. 759.4 B
Picasso : photographs from 1951-1972 / Edward Quinn ; [translator, Donna Pedini Simpson]. Woodbury, N.Y. : Barron's Educational Series, 1979, c1980. p. cm. Translated from the German. [ND553.P5Q5213] 80-11462 ISBN 0-8120-2109-6 pbk. : 2.95
1. Picasso, Pablo, 1881-1973—Portraits, etc. 2. Painters—France—Biography.

Piccard, Auguste, 1884-1962—Juvenile literature.

FIELD, Adelaide. 550'.924 B
Auguste Piccard; captain of space, admiral of the abyss. Boston, Houghton Mifflin, 1969. 150 p. illus., ports. 23 cm. Bibliography: p. 150. A biography of the French scientist who was the first to go up into the stratosphere in a balloon and who invented the bathyscaphe making it possible to explore the deepest oceans. [Q143.P45F5] 92 73-86299 3.50
1. Piccard, Auguste, 1884-1962—Juvenile literature. I. Title.

Piccard, Augute, 1884—juvenile literature.

MALKUS, Alida Sims, 1895- 920
Auguste and Jacques Piccard; exploring the sky and sea. Illus. by Robert Boehmer Chicago, Britanica Bks., div. of Ency. Britannica [1963, c.1961] 190p. col. illus. 22cm. (Britannica bkshelf.: Great lives for young Amers.) 2.36 lib. ed.,
1. Piccard, Augute, 1884—juvenile literature. 2. Piccard, Jacques—Juvenile literature. I. Title.

Piccard, Jean Felix, 1884-1963.

DE GRUMMOND, Lena Young. 629.133'22'0924 B
Jean Felix Piccard, boy balloonist, by Lena Young de Grummond and Lynn de Grummond Delaune. Illustrated by Robert Doremus. New York, Bobbs-Merrill [1968] 200 p. col. illus. 20 cm. (Childhood of famous Americans) Bibliography: p. 198. A biography that concentrates on the younger years of Jean Piccard who with his twin brother, Auguste, pioneered in balloon exploration of the stratosphere. [TL620.P5D4] 92 AC 68
1. Piccard, Jean Felix, 1884-1963. 2. Balloon ascensions. I. Delaune, Lynn (de Grummond) 1924- joint author. II. Doremus, Robert, illus. III. Title.

Picciano, John, 1947-

FRANKS, Lucinda. 959.704'38
Waiting out a war; the exile of Private John Picciano. New York, Coward, McCann & Geoghegan [1974] 222 p. 22 cm. [DS557.A68F7] 72-76680 ISBN 0-698-10463-3 6.95
1. Picciano, John, 1947- 2. Vietnamese Conflict, 1961- —Desertions—United States. I. Title.

Piccolo, Brian, 1943-1970.

MORRIS, Jeannie. 796.332'0924 B
Brian Piccolo; a short season. Chicago, Rand McNally [1971] 159 p. illus. 22 cm. [GV939.P5M6] 70-170647 5.95
1. Piccolo, Brian, 1943-1970. BIP

Pickens, Andrew, 1739-1817.

WARING, Alice Noble 923.573
The fighting elder: Andrew Pickens. 1738-1817. Columbia, Univ. of S. C. Pr. [c.] 1962. 252p. illus. 24cm. Bibl. 62-13875 6.00
1. Pickens, Andrew, 1739-1817. I. Title.

Pickering, Timothy, 1745-1829.

PRENTISS, Hervey Putnam, 1903- 973.4'0924 B
Timothy Pickering as the leader of New England Federalism, 1800-1815. New York, Da Capo Press, 1972. 118 p. illus. 22 cm. (The American scene: comments and commentators) Reprint of the 1934 ed., which consisted of chapters originally presented in the author's thesis, Northwestern University, 1932. [E302.6.P5P7 1972] 71-124882 ISBN 0-306-71052-8
1. Pickering, Timothy, 1745-1829. 2. Federal Party. New England. I. Title. BIP

Pickering, William, 1796-1854.

KEYNES, Geoffrey Langdon, Sir, 1887- 655.4'24
William Pickering, publisher: a memoir and a check-list of his publications. Rev. ed. New York, B. Franklin [1969] 125 p. illus., facsims. (part col.) 27 cm. (Burt Franklin bibliography and reference series, 283) Bibliography: p. 121. [Z325.P59K4 1969b] 77-99576
1. Pickering, William, 1796-1854. BIP

Pickersgill, J. W., 1905-

PICKERSGILL, J. W., 1905- 971.06'3'0924
My years with Louis St. Laurent : a political memoir / J. W. Pickersgill. Toronto ; Buffalo : University of Toronto Press, c1975. p. cm. Includes index. [F1034.3.P52A34] 75-24675 ISBN 0-8020-2215-4 : 17.50
1. Pickersgill, J. W., 1905- 2. St. Laurent, Louis Stephen, 1882- I. Title. BIP

PICKERSGILL, J. W., 1905- 971.06'3'0924
My years with Louis St. Laurent : a political memoir / J. W. Pickersgill. Toronto ; Buffalo : University of Toronto Press, c1975. viii, 334 p., [4] leaves of plates : ill. ; 24 cm. Includes index. [F1034.3.P52A34] 75-24675 ISBN 0-8020-2215-4 : 17.50
1. Pickersgill, J. W., 1905- 2. St. Laurent, Louis Stephen, 1882- I. Title.

Pickett, Bill, 1860 (ca.)-1932.

HANES, Bailey C. 791.8 B
Bill Pickett, bulldogger : the biography of a Black cowboy / by Bailey C. Hanes ; with a foreword by Bill Burchardt. 1st ed. Norman : University of Oklahoma Press, c1977. xx, 207 p. : ill. ; 21 cm. Includes index. Bibliography: p. 187-195. [GV1833.6.P5H38] 76-54937 ISBN 0-8061-1391-X : 7.95
1. Pickett, Bill, 1860 (ca.)-1932. 2. Cowboys—Biography. 3. Rodeos—United States. I. Title. BIP

Pickett, Bill, 1860 (ca.)-1932—Juvenile literature.

HANCOCK, Sibyl. 791.8 B
Bill Pickett : first Black rodeo star / by Sibyl Hancock ; illustrated by Lorinda Bryan Cauley. 1st ed. New York : Harcourt Brace Jovanovich, c1977. 61 p. : ill. ; 22 cm. (A Let me read book) A biography of the black Texan who introduced bulldogging to rodeos. [GV1833.6.P5H36] 92 76-41741 ISBN 0-15-207392-2 : 4.95 ISBN 0-15-207393-0 pbk. : 1.95
1. Pickett, Bill, 1860 (ca.)-1932—Juvenile literature. 2. Cowboys—Texas—Biography—Juvenile literature. I. Cauley, Lorinda Bryan. BIP

Pickett, Clarence Evan, 1884-1965.

KAHOE, Walter, ed. 289.60924(B)
Clarence Pickett, a memoir, [Moylan? Penn.] 1966. v, 52p. mounted ports. 23cm. Bibl. [BX7795.P55K3] 66-21720 2.00 bds.,
1. Pickett, Clarence Evan, 1884-1965. I. Title.
Available from the editor at the Rose Valley Pr., Moylan, Pa., 19065.

Pickford, Mary, 1893-

NIVER, Kemp R. 791.43'028'0924
Mary Pickford, comedienne, by Kemp R. Niver. Edited by Bebe Bergsten. [Los Angeles, Locare Research Group, c1969] 156 p. facsims., ports. 29 cm. Contains photos selected from films made 1909-1912 by the Biograph Company, with the Biograph handbills for each production. [PN2287.P5N5] 72-103050
1. Pickford, Mary, 1893- I. Bergsten, Bebe, ed. II. Biograph Company. III. Title.

PICKFORD, Mary, 1893- 927.92
Sunshine and shadow. Foreword by Cecil B. de Mille. [1st ed.] Garden City, N. Y., Doubleday, 1955. 382 p. illus. 22 cm. Autobiography. [PN2287.P5A3] 55-5580
1. Actors—Correspondence, reminiscences, etc. I. Title.

WINDELER, Robert. 791.43'028'0924 B
Sweetheart; the story of Mary Pickford. New York, Praeger [1974, c1973] x, 226 p. illus. 22 cm. Filmography: p. 204-218. [PN2287.P5W5 1974] 73-13349 7.95
1. Pickford, Mary, 1893- I. Title. BIP

WINDELER, Robert. 791.43'028'0924 B
Sweetheart; the story of Mary Pickford. Boston, G. K. Hall, 1974 [c1973] xxvii, 411 p. 25 cm. Large print ed. Bibliography: p. 409-411. [PN2287.P5W5 1974b] 74-13136 ISBN 0-8161-6234-4
1. Pickford, Mary, 1893- 2. Sight-saving books. I. Title.

Pickles, Wilfred, 1904-

PICKLES, Wilfred, 1904- 791.44'028'0924 B
Wilfred Pickles invites you to have another go. Newton Abbot ; North Pomfret, Vt. : David and Charles, 1978. 135 p. : ill. ; 23 cm. [PN2598.P44A38] 77-85039 ISBN 0-7153-7393-5 : 11.95
1. Pickles, Wilfred, 1904- 2. Actors—England—Biography. I. Title. II. Title: Invites you to have another go. BIP

Pickyavit, Joseph J., 1892-

BECKWITH, Frank A., 1892- 970'.004'97 B
Indian Joe, in person and in background : historical perspective into Piute life / by Frank A. Beckwith. 1st public ed. Delta, Utah : DuWil Pub. Co., c1975. xiii, 205 p., [1] leaf of plates : ill., map ; 27 cm. Includes index. [E99.U8P522] 76-357669
1. Pickyavit, Joseph J., 1892- 2. Ute Indians. I. Title.

Picon, Molly.

PICON, Molly. 792'.028'0924 B *Molly!* : An autobiography / by Molly Picon with Jean Bergantini Grillo. New York : Simon and Schuster, c1979. p. cm. Includes index. [PN2287.P53A28] 79-21067 ISBN 0-671-24016-1 : 6.95
1. Picon, Molly. 2. Kalich, Jacob, 1891-1975. 3. Actors—United States—Biography. 4. Theater—Jews. I. Grillo, Jean Bergantini, joint author. II. Title.

Pierce, Abel Head, 1834-1900.

EMMETT, Chris, 1886- 923.973 *Shanghai Pierce:* a fair likeness; with drawings by Nick Eggenhofer. [1st ed.] Norman, University of Oklahoma Press [1953] xiii, 326p. illus., ports., maps. 24cm. Bibliography: p. 313-319. [F391.P59E5] 53-5481
1. Pierce, Abel Head, 1834-1900. 2. Cattle trade—Texas. I. Title.

Pierce, Franklin, Pres. U.S., 1804-1869.

HAWTHORNE, Nathaniel, 1804-1864. 973.6'0924 B *The life of Franklin Pierce.* New York, Garrett Press, 1970. ix, 144 p. port. 19 cm. Reprint of the 1852 ed. with a new foreword by Richard C. Robey. [E432.H38 1970] 71-106758
1. Pierce, Franklin, Pres. U.S., 1804-1869. 2. Campaign literature, 1852—Democratic. I. Title. BIP

NICHOLS, Roy Franklin, 1896- 923.173 *Franklin Pierce,* Young Hickory of the Granite Hills. [2d ed., completely rev.] Philadelphia, University of Pennsylvania Press [1958] xvii, 625p. ports., maps. facsims. 24cm. Bibliography: p.577-593. [E432.N63 1958] 58-7750
1. Pierce, Franklin, Pres. U. S., 1804-1869. I. Title.

Pierce, Franklin, Pres. U.S., 1804-1869—Juvenile literature.

HOYT, Edwin Palmer. 973.6'6'0924 *Franklin Pierce;* the fourteenth President of the United States [by] Edwin P. Hoyt. Illustrated with photographs. London, New York, Abelard-Schuman [1972] 157 p. illus. 22 cm. Bibliography: p. [151] A biography of the New England politician who became the fourteenth President. [E432.H6] 92 74-156582 ISBN 0-200-71828-2 5.95 (U.S.)
1. Pierce, Franklin, Pres. U.S., 1804-1869—Juvenile literature. I. Title. BIP

Pierce, Josiah, b. 1861.

PIERCE, Josiah, b.1861. 620'.0092'4 B *Letters to Laura* : letters from Josiah Pierce, Jr., to Laura Dunham, 1884-1889 / with an introd. by Sarah Darney Letterts. Boston : Godine Press, 1974. ca. 100 p. : facsims ; 22 cm. "Privately printed." Five hundred copies printed. [TA140.P53A44] 75-318139
1. Pierce, Josiah, b. 1861. 2. Dunham, Laura, b. 1862. I. Dunham, Laura, b. 1862. II. Title. BIP

Pierce, W. H.

PIERCE, W. H. 917.98'04'3 *Thirteen years of travel and exploration in Alaska, 1877-1889* / W. H. Pierce ; edited and updated by R. N. De Armond. Anchorage : Alaska Northwest Pub. Co., c1977. xiv, 105 p. : ill. ; 21 cm. (Northern history library) Original ed., edited by Prof. and Mrs. J. H. Carruth, published in 1890 by the Journal Pub. Co., Lawrence, Kansas. [F908.P59 1977] 77-2893 ISBN 0-88240-076-2 pbk. : 3.95
1. Pierce, W. H. 2. Alaska—Description and travel—1867-1896. 3. Alaska—Gold discoveries. 4. Gold mines and mining—Alaska. I. Title. BIP

Pierce, William, 1590?-1641.

VOLLERTSEN, Dorothy F. 975.5'02'0924 B *Captain William Peirce, "ancient planter" and early settler of Mulberry Island in Virginia,* by Dorothy F. Vollertsen and Arthur H. Vollertsen. [Fort Eustis, Va., Historical and Archaeological Association, 1970] 13, [4] l. 29 cm. Caption title. Bibliography: p. [15]-[17] [F229.P6V64] 73-170247
1. Pierce, William, 1590?-1641. 2. Virginia—History—Colonial period, ca. 1600-1775. I. Vollertsen, Arthur H., 1919- joint author. II. Title.

Pierre de Dreux, Duke of Brittany, 13th century.

PAINTER, Sidney, 1902-1960. 944'.1'0230924 B *The scourge of the clergy;* Peter of Dreux, Duke of Brittany. New York, Octagon Books, 1969 [c1937] vii, 155 p. geneal. tables (part fold.), fold. map. 24 cm. (The Johns Hopkins historical publications) Includes bibliographical references. [DC611.B882P3 1969] 76-96188
1. Pierre de Dreux, Duke of Brittany, 13th century. 2. France—History—Philip II Augustus, 1180-1223. 3. France—History—Louis IX, 1226-1270. 4. Brittany—History. I. Title. II. Series. BIP

Pierres, Philippe Denis, 1741-1808.

WATTS, George Byron, 1890- 655.1'44 *Philippe-Denis Pierres: first printer ordinary of Louis XVI* [by] George B. Watts. [Charlotte, N.C., Printed by Heritage Printers, 1966] 56 p. 23 cm. Cover title. Bibliography: p. 52-56. [Z232.P59W3] 66-23874
1. Pierres, Philippe Denis, 1741-1808.

Pilsudski, Jozef, 1867-1935.

DZIEWANOWSKI, M. K. 943.8'04'0924 B *Joseph Pilsudski: a European federalist, 1918-1922,* by M. K. Dziewanowski. Stanford, Calif., Hoover Institution Press [1969] xvi, 379 p. maps (on lining papers) 24 cm. (Hoover Institution publications, 79) Bibliography: p. 355-372. [DK440.5.P5D97] 68-54094 8.70
1. Pilsudski, Jozef, 1867-1935. 2. Europe, Eastern—History. I. Title. II. Series. Stanford University. Hoover Institution on War, Revolution, and Peace. Publications, 79

Pike, Albert, 1809-1891.

DUNCAN, Robert Lipscomb, 1927- 928.1 *Reluctant general;* the life and times of Albert Pike. [1st ed.] New York, Dutton [1961] 289 p. 22 cm. Includes bibliography. [HS511.P6D8] 61-5035
1. Pike, Albert, 1809-1891. I. Title.

Pike, Diane Kennedy.

PIKE, Diane Kennedy. 242'.4 *Life is victorious!* : How to grow through grief : a personal experience / Diane Kennedy Pike. New York : Simon and Schuster, c1976. 209 p., [4] leaves of plates : ill. ; 23 cm. [BR1725.P54A34] 76-17328 ISBN 0-671-22335-6 : 7.95
1. Pike, Diane Kennedy. 2. Pike, James Albert, Bp., 1913-1969. 3. Grief. I. Title.

Pike, James Albert, Bp., 1913-1969.

PIKE, Diane Kennedy. 283'.0924 B *Search: the personal story of a wilderness journey.* [1st ed.] Garden City, N.Y., Doubleday, 1970, [c1969] xii, 198 p. col. map (on lining papers) 22 cm. [BX5995.P54P5] 74-108620 4.95
1. Pike, James Albert, Bp., 1913-1969. I. Title.

STRINGFELLOW, William. 283'.092'4 B *The death and life of Bishop Pike* / William Stringfellow and Anthony Towne. 1st ed. Garden City, N.Y. : Doubleday, 1976. xxxii, 446 p., [8] leaves of plates : ill. ; 22 cm. "Books by James A. Pike": [445]-446. [BX5995.P54S83] 75-32721 ISBN 0-385-07455-7 : 10.00
1. Pike, James Albert, Bp., 1913-1969. I. Towne, Anthony, joint author. II. Title.

UNGER, Merrill Frederick, 1909- 133.9 *The haunting of Bishop Pike;* a Christian view of The other side [by] Merrill F. Unger. Wheaton, Ill., Tyndale House Publishers [1971] 115 p. 22 cm. Includes bibliographical references. [BF1042.U5 1971] 76-144329 ISBN 0-8423-1340-0 2.95
1. Pike, James Albert, Bp., 1913-1969. 2. Pike, James Albert, Bp., 1913-1969. The other side. 3. Spiritualism—Controversial literature. I. Title.

Pike, James Shepherd, 1811-1882.

DURDEN, Robert Franklin. 973.6'092'4 *James Shepherd Pike* : Republicanism and the American Negro, 1850-1882 / Robert Franklin Durden. Westport, Conn. : Greenwood Press, 1978, c1957. v, 249 p. ; 22 cm. Reprint of the ed. published by Duke University Press, Durham, N.C. Includes index. Bibliography: p. [232]-242. [E415.9.P53D8 1978] 77-26867 ISBN 0-313-20168-4 lib.bdg. : 17.50
1. Pike, James Shepherd, 1811-1882. 2. Politicians—United States—Biography. 3. Intellectuals—United States—Biography. 4. Slavery in the United States—Anti-slavery movements. 5. Reconstruction—South Carolina. BIP

Pike. Zebulon Montgomery, 1779-1813.

BAKER, Nina (Brown) 1888- 923.573 *Pike of Pike's Peak;* illustrated by Richard Powers. [1st ed.] New York, Harcourt, Brace [1953] 140p. illus. 21cm. [F592.P654] 53-7859
1. Pike. Zebulon Montgomery, 1779-1813. I. Title.

CARTER, Carrol Joe. 917.88'33'042 *Pike in Colorado* / by Carrol Joe Carter ; ill. by Mark McMahon. Fort Collins, Colo. : Old Army Press, c1978 83 p. : ill. ; 19 x 26 cm. Bibliography: p. 82-83. [F592.P653C37] 78-60399 ISBN 0-88342-058-9 : 10.95 ISBN 0-88342-241-7 pbk. : 3.95
1. Pike, Zebulon Montgomery, 1779-1813. 2. San Luis Valley—Description and travel. 3. Frontier and pioneer life—San Luis Valley. 4. Explorers—United States—Biography. 5. Hiking—San Luis Valley. I. Title. BIP

PIKE of Pike's Peak; v. 12 illustrated by Richard Powers. New York, Harcourt, Brace [1960, c1953] 140p. illus. 21cm.
1. Pike, Zebulon Montgomery, 1779-1813. I. Baker, Nina (Brown) 1888-

PIKE, Zebulon Montgomery, 1779-1813. 917.8'04'2 *Zebulon Pike's Arkansaw journal:* in search of the southern Louisiana Purchase boundary line (interpreted by his newly recovered maps). Edited, with bibliographical resume, 1800-1810, by Stephen Harding Hart and Archer Butler Hulbert. Westport, Conn., Greenwood Press [1972, c1932] xcvi, 200 p. illus. 22 cm. Original ed. issued as vol. 1 of Overland to the Pacific series. The journal is part of the author's An account of expeditions to the sources of the Mississippi. [F592.P638 1972] 72-138172 ISBN 0-8371-5629-7
1. The West—Description and travel—To 1848. 2. United States—Exploring expeditions. I. Hart, Stephen Harding, ed. II. Hulbert, Archer Butler, 1873-1933, ed. III. Title. IV. Title: Arkansaw journal. V. Series: Overland to the Pacific; the Charles B. Voorhis series, v. 1

STEVENSON, Augusta. 973.4'8'0924 B *Zeb Pike, boy traveler.* Illustrated by James Ponter. Indianapolis, Bobbs-Merrill [1963] 200 p. illus. 20 cm. (Childhood of famous Americans) The boyhood of the Army officer and explorer who discovered the great Rocky Mountain peak in Colorado which bears his name. [PZ7.S8467Ze5] 92 AC 68
1. Pike, Zebulon Montgomery, 1779-1813. I. Ponter, James, illus. II. Title.

TERRELL, John Upton, 1900 973.4'8'0924 B *Zebulon Pike; the life and times of an adventurer.* New York, Weybright and Talley [1968] 250 p. 22 cm. Bibliography: p. 241-248. [F592.P658] 68-12871
1. Pike, Zebulon Montgomery, 1779-1813.

Pike, Zebulon Montgomery, 1779-1813—Juvenile literature.

ARONSON, Howard Stanley 92 *Zeb Pike:* Illus. by Fred Darge. San Antonio, Tex., Naylor [1963] 47p. col. illus., map (on lining papers) 27cm. (Amer. heroes: Explorers of the Western territories) 62-20636 3.95
1. Pike, Zebulon Montgomery, 1779-1813—Juvenile literature. I. Title.

KEATING, Bern. 92 *Zebulon Pike;* young America's frontier scout. Illustrated by Frank Aloise. New York, Putnam [1965] 159 p. illus. 21 cm. [F592.P6574] 65-25399
1. Pike, Zebulon Montgomery, 1779-1813 — Juvenile literature. I. Title.

WIBBERLEY, Leonard Patrick O'Connor, 1915- j92 *Zebulon Pike, soldier and explorer.* New York, Funk & Wagnalls [1961] 179 p. 22 cm. [F592.P66] 61-6817
1. Pike, Zebulon Montgomery, 1779-1818 — Juvenile literature. I. Title.

Pilate, Pontius, 1st cent.

CAILLOIS, Roger, 1913- 923.233 *Pontius Pilate.* Tr. [from French] by Charles Lam Markmann. New York, Macmillan [c.1963] 111p. 21cm. 63-13184 3.00
1. Pilate, Pontius, 1st cent. I. Title.

Pilcher, Joshua, 1790-1843.

SUNDER, John Edward. 970.5'0924 *Joshua Pilcher, fur trader and Indian agent* [by] John E. Sunder. [1st ed.] Norman, Univ. of Okla. Pr. [1968] xi, 203p. illus., maps, ports. 22cm. Bibl. [F598.P5S8] (B) 65-15680 5.95
1. Pilcher, Joshua, 1790-1843. 2. Fur trade—Missouri Valley. 3. Indians of North America—Government relations—1789-1869. I. Title.

SUNDER, John Edward. 970.5'0924 B *Joshua Pilcher, fur trader and Indian agent* [by] John E. Sunder. [1st ed.] Norman, University of Oklahoma Press [1968] xi, 203 p. illus., maps, ports. 22 cm. Bibliography: p. 175-190. [F598.P5S8] 68-15680
1. Pilcher, Joshua, 1790-1843. 2. Fur trade—Missouri Valley. 3. Indians of North America—Government relations—1789-1869.

Pilgrim Fathers.

STODDARD, Francis Russell, 1877- 973.2'2 *The truth about the Pilgrims,* by Francis R. Stoddard. Baltimore, Genealogical Pub. Co., 1973 [c1952] 206 p. illus. 20 cm. Reprint of the 1952 ed. published by the Society of Mayflower Descendents in the State of New York, New York. Bibliography: p. 188-195. [F68.S92 1973] 73-7218 ISBN 0-8063-0561-4 7.50
1. Pilgrim Fathers. I. Title. BIP

WILLISON, George Findlay, 1897- 974.402 *Saints and strangers.* New ed., specially rev., abridged by the author. N 380p.

18cm. Bibl. [F68.W75] [York,] BALLANTINE 65-3581 [1965 .75 pap., *1. Pilgrim Fathers. 2. Massachusetts—Hist.—Colonial period (New Plymouth) I. Title.*

Pilgrim Fathers — Juvenile literature.

SMITH, Edric Brooks. 923.273
The coming of the Pilgrims, told from Governor Bradford's firsthand account, by E. Brooks Smith and Robert Meredith. Illustrated by Leonard Everett Fisher. [1st ed.] Boston, Little, Brown [1964] 60 p. illus. (part col.) 20 x 26 cm. "Prepared in cooperation with and approved by Plimoth Plantation." [F68.S62] 64-10182
1. Pilgrim Fathers — Juvenile literature. I. Meredith, Robert K., joint author. II. Bradford, William, 1588-1657. III. Title.

Pilkington, Latitia van Lewen, 1712-1750.

PILKINGTON, Latitia van Lewen, 1712-1750. 828'.5'09 s
Memoirs with anecdotes of Dean Swift, 1748-1754 / by Ltitia Pilkington New York : Garland Pub., 1975. p. cm. (The Life & times of seven major British writers) (Swiftiana ; 17-19) Reprint of the 1748-1754 ed. printed by R. Griffiths, Dublin and London, under title: The memoirs of Mrs. Latitia Pilkington. [PR3726.S95 vols. 17-19] [CT788.P66] 821'.5 75-1027 ISBN 0-8240-1278-X lib.bdg. : 21.00
1. Pilkington, Latitia van Lewen, 1712-1750. 2. Swift, Jonathan, 1667-1745. I. Title. II. Series.

Pillet, Nettie Ethel,

PILLET, Nettie Ethel, 1877- 920.7
The kingdom of my soul. New York, Comet Press Books [1955] 109p. 23cm. Autobiography. [CT275.P6433A3] 55-9805
I. Title.

Pilon, Juliana Geran, 1947-

PILON, Juliana Geran, 1947- 949.8'004'924 B
Notes from the other side of night / Juliana Geran Pilon ; with an introd. by Mircea Eliade. South Bend, Ind. : Regnery/Gateway, cl979. xiii, 146 p. : ill. ; 21 cm. [DS135.R73P546] 78-74440 ISBN 0-89526-685-7 : 8.95
1. Pilon, Juliana Geran, 1947- 2. Jews in Romania—Biography. 3. Romania—Description and travel—1945-1977. I. Title. BIP

Pilsudski, Jozef, 1867-1935.

PILSUDSKA, Aleksandra (Szczerbinska) 943.8'04'0924 B
Pilsudski [by] Alexandra Pilsudska. New York, Arno Press, 1971. 352 p. map, port. 24 cm. (The Eastern Europe collection) Reprint of the 1941 ed. "Written in collaboration with Mrs. Jennifer Ellis." [DK440.5.P5P5 1971] 76-135829 ISBN 0-405-02771-0
1. Pilsudski, Jozef, 1867-1935. 2. Poland—History. I. Ellis, Jennifer.

Pinchot, Gifford, 1865-1946.

FAUSOLD, Martin L. 926.349
Gifford Pinchot, Bull Moose progressive. [Syracuse, N. Y.] Syracuse Univ. Pr. [c.] 1961. viii, 270p. illus. (Men and movements ser.) Bibl. 61-9763 4.50
1. Pinchot, Gifford, 1865-1946. I. Title.

FAUSOLD, Martin L. 329'.0092'4 B
Gifford Pinchot, Bull Moose progressive [by] Martin L. Fausold. Westport, Conn., Greenwood Press [1973, c1961] viii, 270 p. illus. 22 cm. (Men and movements series) Reprint of the ed. published by Syracuse University Press, Syracuse, N.Y. Bibliography: p. 251-262. [E664.P62F3 1973] 73-7672 ISBN 0-8371-6943-7
1. Pinchot, Gifford, 1865-1946. I. Series: Men and movements (Syracuse) BIP

FAUSOLD, Martin L. 329'.0092'4 B
Gifford Pinchot, Bull Moose progressive [by] Martin L. Fausold. Westport, Conn., Greenwood Press [1973, c1961] viii, 270 p. illus. 22 cm. (Men and movements series) Reprint of the ed. published by Syracuse University Press, Syracuse, N.Y. Bibliography: p. 251-262. [E664.P62F3 1973] 73-7672 ISBN 0-8371-6943-7 12.25
1. Pinchot, Gifford, 1865-1946. I. Series: Men and movements (Syracuse)

MCGEARY, Martin Nelson 926.349
Gifford Pinchot, forestr-politician. Princeton, N. J., Princeton University Press, [c.]1960. xi, 481p. Bibl.: p.467-471 illus. 25cm. 60-12232 8.50
1. Pinchot, Gifford, 1865-1946. I. Title.

PINCHOT, Gifford, 1865-1946. 333.7'5'0924 B
Breaking new ground. Introd. by James Penick, Jr. Seattle, University of Washington Press [1972, c1947] xxvi, 522 p. illus. 23 cm. (Americana library, AL-22) Autobiography. [E664.P62A3 1972] 75-172901 ISBN 0-295-95181-8
1. Pinchot, Gifford, 1865-1946. 2. Conservation of natural resources—United States. I. Title.

PINKETT, Harold T. 634.9'0924 B
Gifford Pinchot, private and public forester [by] Harold T. Pinkett. Urbana, University of Illinois Press [1970] 167 p. illus., ports. 24 cm. Bibliography: p. 151-161. [SD129.P5P5] 74-76830 6.95
1. Pinchot, Gifford, 1865-1946. 2. Forest conservation—U.S.—History. I. Title.

PLACE, Marian Templeton. 926.349
Gifford Pinchot, the man who saved the forests, by Dale White [pseud.] New York, Messner [1957] 192 p. 22 cm. Includes bibliographies. [SD129.P5P55] 57-9747
1. Pinchot, Gifford, 1865-1946.

Pinckney, Charles Cotesworth, 1746-1825.

ZAHNISER, Marvin R. 973.4'0924 B
Charles Cotesworth Pinckney, founding father, by Marvin R. Zahniser. Chapel Hill, Published for the Institute of Early American History and culture, Williamsburg, Va., by the University of North Carolina Press [1967] ix, 295 p. port. 24 cm. Bibliographical footnotes. [E302.6.P55Z3] 67-28010
1. Pinckney, Charles Cotesworth, 1746-1825. I. Institute of Early American History and Culture, Williamsburg, Va. II. Title.

Pinckney, Eliza (Lucas) 1723-1793.

PINCKNEY, Eliza (Lucas) 1723-1793. 975.7'02'0924 B
The letterbook of Eliza Lucas Pinckney, 1739-1762. Edited by Elise Pinckney, with the editorial assistance of Marvin R. Zahniser, and an introd. by Walter Muir Whitehill. Chapel Hill, University of North Carolina Press [1972] xxix, 195 p. illus. 24 cm. [F272.P6416] 76-174783 ISBN 0-8078-1182-3 9.95
I. Pinckney, Elise, ed. II. Title. BIP

RAVENEL, Harriott Horry (Rutledge) 1832-1912. 975.7'02'0924 B
Eliza Pinckney, by Harriott Horry Ravenel. [Spartanburg, S.C., Reprint Co., 1967] xi, 331 p. facsim. (on lining papers) 22 cm. (South Carolina heritage series, no. 10.) (Women of colonial and revolutionary times) Title page includes original imprint: New York, Scribner, 1896. Bound with Pinckney, E. L. Journal and letters of Eliza Lucas. [Spartanburg, S.C., 1967] [F266.S53 no. 10] 67-25800
1. Pinckney, Eliza (Lucas) 1723-1793. 2. Pinckney, Charles, d. 1758. 3. South Carolina—History—Colonial period. I. Title. II. Series. III. Series: South Carolina heritage series no. 10 BIP

Pinckney, Eliza Lucas, 1723-1793—Juvenile literature.

LEE, Susan. 975.7'02'0924 B
Eliza Pinckney / by Susan & John Lee ; illustrated by Andy Aldridge. Chicago : Childrens Press, c1977. 47 p. : col. ill. ; 24 cm. (Heroes of the Revolution) A biography of the industrious young woman who helped introduce the cultivation of the indigo plant in South Carolina. [F272.P642L43] 92 76-46445 ISBN 0-516-04658-6 lib.bdg. : 6.60
1. Pinckney, Eliza Lucas, 1723-1793—Juvenile literature. 2. South Carolina—Biography—Juvenile literature. 3. Plantation life—South Carolina—Juvenile literature. I. Lee, John, joint author. II. Aldridge, Andy. III. Title. BIP

Pinckney family.

ROGERS, George C. 975.7'915'02
Charleston in the age of the Pinckneys, by George C. Rogers, Jr. [1st ed.] Norman, University of Oklahoma Press [1969] xv, 187 p. 20 cm. (The Centers of civilization series) "Bibliographical note": p. 170-173. [F279.C457R6] 68-31371
1. Pinckney family. 2. Charleston, S.C.—History. I. Title. II. Series. BIP

Pinel, Philippe, 1745-1826.

MACKLER, Bernard. 616.89'00924 B
Philippe Pinel, unchainer of the insane. New York, F. Watts [1968] viii, 118 p. 22 cm. (Immortals of science) The life of the eighteenth-century French physician whose revolutionary theories on the treatment of the mentally ill became the foundation of modern psychiatry. [R507.P5M3] 92 68-11330
1. Pinel, Philippe, 1745-1826. I. Title. BIP

SEMELAIGNE, Rene. 616.8'9'00924 B
Philippe Pinel et son oeuvre au point de vue de la medecine mentale / Rene Semelaigne. New York : Arno Press, 1976. 173 p. ; 23 cm. (Classics in psychiatry) Reprint of the 1888 ed. published by Imprimeries reunies, Paris. Includes index. [RC339.52.P56S45 1976] 75-16733 ISBN 0-405-07454-9
1. Pinel, Philippe, 1745-1826. 2. Psychiatry—Early works to 1900. 3. Psychiatry—History. I. Title. II. Series. BIP

Pinero, Arthur Wing, Sir, 1855-1934.

DUNKEL, Wilbur Dwight. 822'.8
Sir Arthur Pinero; a critical biography with letters. Port Washington, N.Y., Kennikat Press [1967] 142 p. facsims., port. 22 cm. Reprint of the 1941 ed. "Bibliographical note": p. 137-138. [PR5183.D8 1967] 67-27594
1. Pinero, Arthur Wing, Sir, 1855-1934.

Pinero, Arthur Wing, Sir, 1855-1934—Correspondence.

PINERO, Arthur Wing, Sir, 1855-1934. 822'.8 B
The collected letters of Sir Arthur Pinero. Edited by J. P. Wearing. Minneapolis, University of Minnesota Press [1974] ix, 302 p. 24 cm. Title on spine: Pinero letters. [PR5183.A44 1974] 74-76742 ISBN 0-8166-0717-6 15.00
1. Pinero, Arthur Wing, Sir, 1855-1934—Correspondence. 2. Authors, English—Correspondence, reminiscences, etc. 3. Theater—Great Britain. I. Title: Pinero letters. BIP

Pinkerton, Allan, 1819-1884.

LAVINE, Sigmund A 923.673
Allan Pinkerton; America's first private eye. New York, Dodd, Mead [1963] 241 p. illus. 21 cm. [HV7911.P5L3] 63-16269
1. Pinkerton, Allan, 1819-1884. I. Title. II. Title: America's first private eye.

LAVINE, Sigmund A. 923.673
Allan Pinkerton; America's first private eye. New York, Dodd [c.1963] 241p. illus. 21cm. 63-16269 3.50
1. Pinkerton, Allan, 1819-1884. I. Title. II. Title: America's first private eye.

ORRMONT, Arthur 923.673
Master detective: Allan Pinkerton. New York, Messner [c.1965] 191p. 22cm. Bibl. [HV7911.P5O7] 65-10168 3.25; 3.19 lib. ed.,
1. Pinkerton, Allan, 1819-1884. I. Title.

ORRMONT, Arthur. 923.673
Master detective: Allan Pinkerton. New York, J. Messner [1965] 191 p. 22 cm. Bibliography: p. 185. [HV7911.P5O7] 65-10168
1. Pinkerton, Allan, 1819-1884. I. Title.

PINKERTON, Allan, 1819-1884. 364.1'62'09761
The expressman and the detective / Allan Pinkerton. New York : Arno Press, 1976 [c1874] 278 p., [12] leaves of plates : ill. ; 21 cm. (Literature of mystery and detection) Reprint of the 1875 ed. published by W. B. Keen, Cooke, Chicago. [HV7914.P58 1976] 75-32775 ISBN 0-405-07894-3 : 16.00
1. Pinkerton, Allan, 1819-1884. 2. Detectives—United States—Correspondence, reminiscences, etc. 3. Robbery—United States—Case studies. I. Title. II. Series. BIP

Pinkerton, Allan, 1819-1884—Juvenile literature.

ANDERSON, LaVere. 364.12'0924 B
Allan Pinkerton; first private eye. Illustrated by Frank Vaughn. Champaign, Ill., Garrard Pub. Co. [1972] 94 p. illus. (part. col.) 24 cm. (Americans all) A biography of the Scottish immigrant barrel-maker whose side line detective work developed into the oldest and most famous detective agency in the United States. [HV7911.P5A54] 92 77-182270 ISBN 0-8116-4575-4 2.79
1. Pinkerton, Allan, 1819-1884—Juvenile literature. I. Vaughn, Frank E., illus. II. Title.

Pinkerton, Kathrene Sutherland Gedney, 1887-1967.

PINKERTON, Kathrene Sutherland Gedney, 1887-1967. 971.3'11'030924 B
A home in the wilds / Kathrene Pinkerton. New York : Taplinger Pub. Co., 1976, c1939. 327 p., [6] leaves of plates : ill. ; 22 cm. Previous editions published under title: Wilderness wife. Reprint of the ed. published by Carrick and Evans, New York. [F1057.P66 1976] 76-11117 ISBN 0-8008-3922-6 : 9.95
1. Pinkerton, Kathrene Sutherland Gedney, 1887-1967. 2. Frontier and pioneer life—Ontario. 3. Ontario—Biography. I. Title. BIP

Pinkham, Lydia Estes, 1819-1883.

WASHBURN, Robert Collyer. 338.7'61'61510924 B
The life and times of Lydia E. Pinkham / Robert Collyer Washburn. New York : Arno Press, 1976, c1931. p. cm. (Getting and spending) Reprint of the ed. published by Putnam, New York. [HD9666.95.P5W37 1976] 75-39280 ISBN 0-405-08055-7 : 16.00
1. Pinkham, Lydia Estes, 1819-1883. 2. Medicines, Patent, proprietary, etc. I. Title. II. Series. BIP

Pinkney, William, 1764-1822.

PINKNEY, William, Bp., 1810-1883. 973.4 B
The life of William Pinkney, by William Pinkney. New York, Da Capo Press, 1969. 407 p. port. 24 cm. (A Da Capo Press reprint edition) Reprint of the 1853 ed. [E302.6.P6P6 1969] 75-75276
1. Pinkney, William, 1764-1822. BIP

Pinter, Harold, 1930- —Friends and associates.

PINTER, Harold, 792'.092'4 B
1930-
Mac / Harold Pinter. Ann Arbor, Mich. : University Microfilms, 1979. p. cm. Reprint of the 1968 ed. published by Grove Press, New York. [PN2601.M35P5 1979] 79-23984 ISBN 0-8357-0485-8 : 7.00
1. McMaster, Anew. 2. Pinter, Harold, 1930- —Friends and associates. 3. Shakespeare, William, 1564-1616—Stage history—Ireland. 4. Actors—Ireland—Biography. I. Title.

Pinzer, Maimie, 1885-

PINZER, Maimie, 301.41'54'0924
1885-
The Maimie papers / historical editor, Ruth Rosen, textual editor, Sue Davidson ; with an introd. by Ruth Rosen. [Old Westbury, N.Y.] : Feminist Press, [1977] p. cm. Letters written 1910-1922 chiefly to Fanny Quincy Howe. [HQ146.P4P56] 77-21693
1. Pinzer, Maimie, 1885- 2. Prostitutes—Pennsylvania—Philadelphia—Correspondence, reminiscences, etc. 3. United States—Moral conditions—Sources. I. Rosen, Ruth. II. Davidson, Sue. III. Howe, Fanny Quincy, 1870-1933. IV. Title.

Pinto, Vivian de Sola,

PINTO, Vivian de 828'.9'1209 B
Sola, 1895-
The city that shone; an autobiography, 1895-1922. [1st American ed.] New York, John Day Co. [1969] 308 p. illus., ports. 22 cm. [PR6031.I53Z5 1969b] 72-81151 6.50
I. Title.

Pinza, Ezio.

PINZA, Ezio. 927.8
Ezio Pinza, an autobiography, with Robert Magidoff. New York, Rinehart [1958] 307 p. illus. 21 cm. [ML420.P53A3] 58-9356
I. Magidoff, Robert, 1905- BIP

PINZA, Ezio. 782.1'092'4 B
Ezio Pinza : an autobiography / with Robert Magidoff. New York : Arno Press, 1977, [c1958] xi, 307 p., [11] leaves of plates : ill. ; 23 cm. (Opera biographies) Reprint of the ed. published by Rinehart, New York. Includes index. [ML420.P53A3 1977] 76-29962 ISBN 0-405-09702-6 : 21.00
1. Pinza, Ezio. 2. Singers—Biography. I. Magidoff, Robert, 1905-1970. II. Title.

Pio da Pietrelcina, Father.

CARROLL, Malachy Gerard, 922.245
1918-
Padre Pio. Chicago, H. Regnery Co., 1955. 80p. 18cm. (Angelus books) [BX4705.P49C34] 55-4768
1. Pio da Pietrelcina, Father. I. Title.

DE LISO, Oscar 922.245
Padre Pio. New York, All Saints Pr. [1962,c.1960] 183p. (AS-218) .50 pap.,
1. Pio da Pietralcina, Father. I. Title.

GAUDIOSE, Dorothy 271'.36'024 B
M., 1920-
Prophet of the people; a biography of Padre Pio, by Dorothy M. Gaudiose. Illustrated by George Lallas. New York, Alba House [1974] xviii, 237 p. illus. 22 cm. [BX4705.P49G38] 74-7123 ISBN 0-8189-0290-6
1. Pio da Pietrelcina, Father. I. Title. BIP

GIGLIOZZI, Giovanni. 271.360924 B
Padre Pio; a pictorial biography. Translation by Oscar DeLiso. [New York] Phaedra, 1965. 84 p. illus., map, ports. 23 cm. Translation of I monilli dello sposo. [BX4705.P49G53] 65-23441
1. Pio da Pietrelcina, Father. I. Title.

SCHUG, John A. 271'.36'024 B
Padre Pio / John A. Schug. Huntington, Ind. : Our Sunday Visitor, 1976. 256 p. : port. ; 21 cm. [BX4705.P49S38] 76-17953 ISBN 0-87973-856-1 pbk. : 4.95
1. Pio da Pietrelcina, father. 2. Capuchins—Biography. I. Title. BIP

THREE studies in 282'.092'2 B
simplicity, by Malachy Carroll and Pol de Leon Albaret. [Pol de Leon Albaret's Sainte Benedict l'Africain translated from the French by Malachy Carroll] Chicago, Franciscan Herald Press [1974] vii, 201 p. 21 cm. [BX4655.2.T45] 74-8284 ISBN 0-8199-0533-X 5.95
1. Pio da Pietrelcina, Father. 2. Martin de Porres, Saint, 1579-1639. 3. Benedetto da San Filadelfo, Saint, 1526-1589. I. Carroll, Malachy Gerard, 1918- Padre Pio. 1974. II. Carroll, Malachy Gerard, 1918- St. Martin de Porres. 1974. III. Albaret, Pol de Leon, Father, 1906- Benedict l'Africain. English. 1974.
Contents omitted.

Piomer, William Charles Franklyn,

PIOMER, William Charles 928.2
Franklyn, 1903-
Double lives, an autobiography. New York, Noonday Press [1956] 254p. 20cm. [PR6031] 56-12293
I. Title. BIP

Pioneers—California.

BANCROFT, Hubert Howe, 920.0794
1832-1918
Register of pioneer inhabitants of California, 1542 to 1848, and index to information concerning them in Bancroft's History of California, vs. i-v. Los Angeles, Dawson's, 1964. 5v. (various p.) 24cm. Cover title: Pioneer register. Reprint from vs. 2, 3, 4, and 5 of the History of California pub. in San Francisco in 1885 and 1886. 64-3538 3.75
1. Pioneers—California. 2. California—Biog. I. Title. II. Title: Pioneer register.

Pioneers — Georgia.

HUXFORD, Folks, 1893- 920.0758
Pioneers of Wiregrass Georgia; a biographical account of some of the early settlers of that portion of Wiregrass Georgia embraced in the original counties of Irwin, Appling, Wayne, Camden, and Glynn. [Homerville? Ga., 1951-60] 4 v. ports., maps, facsims. 24 cm. [F285.H8] 51-8247
1. Pioneers — Georgia. 2. Georgia — Biog. Georgia — Geneal. I. Title.

Pioneers—Texas—Biography—Addresses, essays, lectures.

BEARDEN, Donna. 920'.0764
A Texas sampler : a stitch in time / by Donna Bearden and Jamie Frucht. [Austin, Tex.] : Governor's Committee on Aging, c1976. 224 p. : ill. ; 27 cm. [F385.B42] 77-620738
1. Pioneers—Texas—Biography—Addresses, essays, lectures. 2. Texas—Biography—Addresses, essays, lectures. I. Frucht, Jamie, joint author. II. Title.

GREEN, Mary Rowena 923.973
(Maverick) 1874- ed.
Samuel Maverick, Texan: 1803-1870 a collection of letters, journals, and memoirs. San Antonic [Priv. print.] 1952 [i.e. 1953] 430p. illus. 24cm. Most of the letters are from Samuel Maverick to his wife, Mary A. Maverick; the memoirs are those of Mary A. Maverick. [F390.M498G7] 53-2583
I. Maverick, Samuel Augustus, 1803-1870. II. Maverick, Mary Ann (Adams) 1818-1918. III. Title.

Pioneers—The West.

BECHDOLT, Frederick 978 B
Ritchie, 1874-1950.
Giants of the Old West. Freeport, N.Y., Books for Libraries Press [1969, c1930] 245 p. illus., maps, ports. 23 cm. (Essay index reprint series) Contents.Contents.—John Colter.—Ashley and his young men.—Stephen Fuller Austin.—The Alamo had none.—William Becknell.—James Pattie.—Brigham Young.—John Augustus Sutter.—Alexander Majors.—Charles Goodnight. [F591.B39 1969] 73-80382
1. Pioneers—The West. 2. The West—Biography. I. Title. BIP

CUTLER, Samuel. 923.973
Famous pioneers; [true stories of Davy Crockett and others who won the West] Illustrated by William Moyers. New York, S. Gabriel Sons [1955] 63p. illus. 26cm. (A Trumpet book, BT30) [F591.C88] 55-4282
1. Pioneers—The West. 2. The West—Biog. I. Title.

Pioneers—The West—Juvenile literature.

FOLSOM, Franklin 923.973
Brewster, 1907-
Men who won the West. Illus. by Dick Priest. New York, Scholastic Bk. Servs. [c.1955, 1962] 96p. (TW 365) col. illus. 21cm. .50 pap.,
1. Pioneers—The West—Juvenile literature. 2. The West—Biog.—Juvenile literature. I. Title.

RALEIGH-KING, Robin Victor j920
Lethridge, 1920-
Pioneers, by Robin King [pseud.] Illustrated by Charles Beck. Racine, Wis., Whitman Pub. Co. [c1959] 92 p. (A Whitman badger book) [F591] 63-6969
1. Pioneers—The West—Juvenile literature. 2. The West—Hist.—Juvenile literature. I. Title.

Pioneers—U. S. —Biog.

MCSPADDEN, Joseph Walker, 923.973
1874-
Pioneer heroes. Ports. by Robert Hallock. [2d print.] New York, Crowell [1954] 215p. illus. 21cm. [E176.M175 1954] 54-9146
1. Pioneers—U. S. sU. S.—Biog. I. Title.

Pioneers—United States—Juvenile literature.

HEIDERSTADT, Dorothy. 920
Frontier leaders and pioneers Illustrated by Clifford N. Geary. [1st ed.] New York, D. McKay Co. [1962] 181p illus. 22cm. Includes bibliography. [E176.8.H4] 62-16722
1. Pioneers—U. S.—Juvenile literature. 2. Frontier and pioneer life—U. S. —Juvenile literature. 3. U. S.—Biog.—Juvenile literature. I. Title.

JOHNSTON, Charles 973'.099 B
Haven Ladd, 1877-1943.
Famous frontiersmen and heroes of the border, their adventurous lives and stirring experiences in pioneer days. Freeport, N.Y., Books for Libraries Press [1971, c1913] x, 359 p. illus., ports. 23 cm. (Essay index reprint series) Contents.Contents.—The frontiersman.—Daniel Morgan.—James Harrod.—Robert McLellan.—Colonel Benjamin Logan.—George Rogers Clark.—John Slover.—Lewis Wetzel.—Samuel Colter.—Meshack Browning.—"Bill" Bent.—Thomas Eddie.—Jim Bridger.—"Old Bill" Williams.—"Big Foot" Wallace.—Captain Jack Hays.—Bill Hamilton.—Uncle Job Witherspoon.—Henry Shane.—Poor Jerry Lane.—The song of the moose.—Retrospect. [E176.J64 1971] 920 72-152178 ISBN 0-8369-2231-X
1. Pioneers—U.S.—Juvenile literature. 2. Frontier and pioneer life—U.S.—Juvenile literature. I. Title.

MOYER, John 917.8'03'0922 B
William.
Famous frontiersmen, by John W. Moyer. Illustrated by James L. Vlasaty. Northbrook, Ill., Hubbard Press [1972] 116 p. illus. (part col.) 32 cm. Short biographies of Boone, Lewis, Clark, Crockett, Houston, Bowie, Bridges, Carson, Hickok, Custer, and Cody. [E178.3.M9] 920 71-188862 ISBN 0-8331-0009-2
1. Pioneers—United States—Juvenile literature. 2. Frontier and pioneer life—United States—Juvenile literature. I. Vlasaty, James L., illus. II. Title. BIP

Piozzi, Hester Lynch Salusbury Thrale, 1741-1821.

CLIFFORD, James Lowry, 928.2
1901-
Hester Lynch Piozzi (Mrs. Thrale) 2d ed. Oxford, Clarendon Press, 1952. 493 p. illus. 23 cm. [PR3619.P3C5 1952] 53-3106
1. Piozzi, Hester Lynch Salusbury Thrale, 1741-1821.

HYDE, Mary Morley 828'.6'09 B
(Crapo)
The impossible friendship; Boswell and Mrs. Thrale [by] Mary Hyde. Cambridge, Mass., Harvard University Press, 1972. xvi, 188 p. illus. 27 cm. Includes bibliographical references. [PR3325.H9] 72-88127 ISBN 0-674-44541-4 7.50
1. Boswell, James, 1740-1795. 2. Piozzi, Hester Lynch (Salusbury) Thrale, 1741-1821. 3. Johnson, Samuel, 1709-1784. I. Title. BIP

PIOZZI, Hester Lynch 914.4
(Salusbury) Thrale, 1741-1821.
The French journals of Mrs. Thrale and Doctor Johnson. Edited from the original manuscripts in the John Rylands library and in the British Museum, with introd. and notes, by Moses Tyson and Henry Guppy. New York, Haskell House, 1973. vii, 274 p. ports. 23 cm. Reprint of the 1932 ed. published by Manchester University Press, Manchester, Eng. Includes bibliographical reference. [DC25.P5 1973] 72-1263 ISBN 0-8383-1430-9 11.95
1. France—Description and travel. I. Johnson, Samuel, 1709-1784. II. Title.

Piozzi, Hester Lynch Salusbury Thrale, 1741-1821—Biography.

PIOZZI, Hester Lynch 828'.6'09 B
Salusbury Thrale, 1741-1821.
Autobiography, letters, and literary remains of Mrs. Piozzi (Thrale) / edited with notes and an introductory account of her life and writings by A. Hayward. New York : AMS Press, [1975] p. cm. (Women of letters) Reprint of the 1861 ed. published by Ticknor and Fields, Boston. Includes index. [PR3619.P5A8 1975] 70-178349 ISBN 0-404-56776-2 : 34.50
1. Piozzi, Hester Lynch Salusbury Thrale, 1741-1821—Biography. I. Title. BIP

PIOZZI, Hester Lynch 828'.6'09 B
Salusbury Thrale, 1741-1821.
The Thrales of Streatham Park / [edited] by Mary Hyde. Cambridge : Harvard University Press, [1977] p. cm. Annotated journal of Hester Thrale. Includes index. [PR3619.P5A827 1977] 77-24922 ISBN 0-674-88746-8 : 15.00
1. Piozzi, Hester Lynch Salusbury Thrale, 1741-1821—Biography. 2. Thrall family. 3. Salisbury family. 4. England—Social life and customs—18th century. I. Hyde, Mary Morely Crapo. II. Title.

Piper, William Thomas, 1881-1970.

FRANCIS, 338.7'62'91300924 [B]
Devon Earl, 1901-
Mr. Piper and his Cubs [by] Devon Francis. [First ed.] Ames, Iowa State University Press, 1973. 256 p. photos 24 cm. Bibliography: p. 243-244 [TL724.5.P5F7] 72-1890 ISBN 0-8138-1250-X 7.95
1. Piper, William Thomas, 1881-1970. 2. Piper Aircraft Corporation, Lock Haven, Pa. 3. Lock Haven, Pa.—Industries—History. I. Title. BIP

Pippin, Horace, 1888-1946.

PIPPIN, Horace, 1888-1946. 759.13
Horace Pippin : the Phillips Collection, Washington, D.C., Feb. 25-March 27,

1977, Terry Dintenfass Gallery, New York, N.Y., April 5-April 30, 1977, Brandywine River Museum, Chadds Ford, Pa., June 4-Sept. 5, 1977 / with an essay by Romare Bearden. Washington : [Phillips Collection], c1976. [64] p. : chiefly col. ill. ; 23 x 28 cm. Catalog of an exhibition. [ND237.P65P48] 76-52613
1. Pippin, Horace, 1888-1946. I. Phillips Collection, Washington, D.C. II. Terry Dintenfass, inc. III. Brandywine River Museum.

Pippin, Horace, 1888-1946—Juvenile literature.

RODMAN, Selden, 1909- 759.13
Horace Pippin; the artist as a Black American [by] Selden Rodman & Carole Cleaver. [1st ed.] Garden City, N.Y., Doubleday [1972] 91 p. illus. (part col.) 24 cm. A biography of the black artist who did not complete his first painting until the age of forty-nine. Includes reproductions of his works. [ND237.P65R63] 92 76-175397 4.95
1. Pippin, Horace, 1888-1946—Juvenile literature. I. Cleaver, Carole, joint author. II. Title.

Pirandello, Luigi, 1867-1936.

STARKIE, Walter Fitzwilliam, 1894- 858
Luigi Pirandello, 1867-1936 [3d ed., rev., enl.] Berkeley, Univ. of Calif. Pr. [c.]1965. xii, 304p. port. 20cm. Bibl. [PQ4835.I7Z8] 65-11819 5.00
1. Pirandello, Luigi, 1867-1936. I. Title.

Pirandello, Luigi, 1867-1936—Biography.

GIUDICE, Gaspare. 858'.9'1209 B
Pirandello : a biography / Gaspare Giudice ; translated by Alastair Hamilton. London ; New York : Oxford University Press, 1975. 238 p. : ill. ; 22 cm. Abridged translation of the 1963 work. "Works of Pirandello," compiled by F. Firth: p. [223]-226. Bibliography: p. [221]-222. [PQ4835.I7Z598 1975] 75-306382 ISBN 0-19-212582-6 : 12.50
1. Pirandello, Luigi, 1867-1936—Biography.

Pirates.

BROWN, Douglas 920.7
Anne Bonny, pirate queen. Derby, Conn., Monarch [c.1962] 138p. (MA320) .35 pap., *I. Title.*

EXQUEMELIN, Alexander Olivier 923.41729
The buccaneers of America; a true account of the most remarkable assaults committed of late years upon the coasts of the West Indies by the buccaneers of Jamaica and Tortuga, both English and French. Wherein are contained more especially the unparalleled exploits of Sir Henry Morgan, our English Jamaican hero, who sacked Porto Bello, burn Panama, etc. Rendered into English with facsims. of all the original engravings, etc. [dist. New York] Barnes & Noble 1962 xxxv, 272p. illus., map. 24cm. Reprinted from the first English ed. of 1684. 5.00
1. Pirates. 2. Buccaneers. 3. Spanish Main. 4. West Indies—Hist. I. Title.

GOSSE, Philip, 1879-1959. 364.13'5'0922
The pirates' who's who; giving particulars of the lives & deaths of the pirates & buccaneers. New York, B. Franklin [1968] 328 p. illus., ports. 23 cm. (Burt Franklin research & source works series 119) (Essays in history, economics & social science, 51.) Reprint of the 1924 ed. [G535] 68-56594
1. Pirates. I. Title.

Pirates—Biography—Juvenile literature.

SCHODER, Judith. 364.1'35 B
Brotherhood of pirates / by Judith Schoder ; illustrated by Paul Frame. New York : J. Messner, 1979. p. cm. Includes index. A brief description of the origins of the buccaneer brotherhood accompanies biographical sketches of seven infamous pirates, including two women who terrorised the Caribbean area during the 17th and 18th centuries. [G535.S28] 920 79-16061 ISBN 0-671-32965-0 lib. bdg. : 7.29
1. Pirates—Biography—Juvenile literature. I. Frame, Paul, 1913- II. Title. BIP

Pirc, Franc, 1785-1880.

FURLAN, William P. 922.273
In charity unfeigned; the life of Father Francis Xavier Pierz. [St. Cloud? Minn.] Diocese of St. Cloud, 1952. 270 p. illus. 23 cm. [BX4705.P496F8] 52-12087
1. Pirc, Franc, 1785-1880. I. Title.

Pirquet von Cesenatico, Clemens Peter, Freiherr, 1874-1929.

WAGNER, Richard, 1887- 610'.924 B
Clemens von Pirquet; his life and work. Baltimore, Johns Hopkins Press [1968] xx, 214 p. illus. 24 cm. Bibliographical footnotes. [R154.P63W3] 68-12899
1. Pirquet von Cesenatico, Clemens Peter, Freiherr, 1874-1929.

Pisan, Christine de, ca. 1363-ca. 1431.

MCLEOD, Enid. 841'.2 B
The Order of the Rose : the life and ideas of Christine de Pizan / by Enid McLeod. London : Chatto & Windus, 1976. 185 p., [5] leaves of plates : ill. ; 22 cm. Includes index. Bibliography: p. 178-182. [PQ1575.Z5M3 1976] 76-365251 ISBN 0-7011-1927-6 : £6.50
1. Pisan, Christine de, ca. 1363-ca. 1431. I. Title. BIP

Piscator, Erwin, 1893-1966.

WILLETT, John. 792'.0233'0924 B
The theatre of Erwin Piscator : half a century of politics in the theatre / John Willett. New York : Holmes & Meier, [1979] p. cm. Includes index. Bibliography: p. [PN2658.P5W55 1979] 79-11941 ISBN 0-8419-0501-0. : 22.50
1. Piscator, Erwin, 1893-1966. 2. Theatrical producers and directors—Germany—Biography. 3. Theater—Political aspects. I. Title. BIP

Pissarro, Camille, 1830-1903.

ADLER, Kathleen. 759.4 B
Camille Pissarro : a biography / Kathleen Adler. New York : St. Martin's Press, 1978, c1977. 208 p., [8] leaves of plates : ill. ; 25 cm. Includes bibliographical references and index. [ND553.P55A85 1977] 77-10307 ISBN 0-312-11459-1 : 12.95
1. Pissarro, Camille, 1830-1903. 2. Painters—France—Biography.

PISSARRO, Camille, 1830-1903. 759.4
Camille Pissarro (1830-1903) Text by John Rewald. New York, H. N. Abrams in association with Pocket Books [1954] [74] p. 42 illus. (part col.) port. 18cm. (The Pocket library of great art, A18) An Abrams art book. Bibliography: p. [74] [ND553.P55R42] [ND553.P55R42] 927.5 54-14621 54-14621
I. Rewald, John, 1912- II. Title.

PISSARRO, Camille, 1830-1903. 759.4 B
Camille Pissarro: letters to his son Lucien, edited with the assistance of Lucien Pissarro by John Rewald. 3d ed., rev. and enl. Mamaroneck, N.Y., P. P. Appel, 1972. 399 p. illus. 26 cm. Includes the letters of Lucien to Camille Pissarro published for the first time in English translation. [ND553.P55P4813 1972] 77-162499 ISBN 0-911858-22-9 22.50
1. Pissarro, Camille, 1830-1903. 2. Painters—France—Correspondence, reminiscences, etc. I. Rewald, John, 1912- ed. II. Pissarro, Lucien, 1863-1944. III. Title.

Pitchers (Baseball)—Biography—Juvenile literature.

BROSNAN, Jim. 927.96357
Great baseball pitchers. New York, Random House [1965] 183 p. illus., ports. 22 cm. (Little league library, 3) [GV865.A1B7] 65-10493
1. Pitchers (Baseball)—Biography—Juvenile literature. I. Title. BIP

LIBBY, Bill. 796.357'0922 B
Star pitchers of the major leagues. New York, Random House [1971] ix, 142 p. illus., ports. 22 cm. (Major league library, 15) Brief biographical sketches of nine major league pitchers: Tom Seaver, Juan Marichal, Dennis McLain, Jim Maloney, Don Drysdale, Jim Bunning, Hoyt Wilhelm, Sam McDowell, and Bob Gibson. [GV865.A1L5] 920 79-146652 ISBN 0-394-82112-2 1.95
1. Pitchers (Baseball)—Biography—Juvenile literature. I. Title.

SHAPIRO, Milton J. 796.3572'2'0922
Heroes of the bullpen; baseball's greatest relief pitchers, by Milton J. Shapiro. New York, J. Messner [1967] 186 p. ports. 22 cm. Contents.Contents.—General.—Hugh Casey, Joe Page.—Jim Konstanty.—Joe Black.—Hoyt Wilhelm.—Luis Arroyo, Ryne Duren.—Jim Brosnan.—Dick Radatz.—Ron Perranoski.—Heroes of the future.—Records. [GV865.A1S46] 67-3320
1. Pitchers (Baseball)—Biography—Juvenile literature. I. Title.

Pitchers (Baseball)—United States—Biography.

THORN, John, 1947- 796.357'22'0922 B
The relief pitcher : baseball's new hero / John Thorn. 1st ed. New York : Dutton, c1979. xiv, 241 p. : ill. ; 22 cm. Includes index. [GV865.A1T47 1979] 78-26834 ISBN 0-525-19048-1 : 10.95
1. Pitchers (Baseball)—United States—Biography. I. Title. BIP

Pitchers (Baseball)—United States—Biography—Juvenile literature.

SMITH, Jay H. 796.357'092'2 B
Meet the pitchers / by Jay H. Smith. Mankato, Minn. : Creative Education, [1976] c1977. 30 p. : ill. ; 19 cm. (Creative Education early sports books) Biographical sketches of five notable baseball pitchers: Nolan Ryan, Jim "Catfish" Hunter, Tom Seaver, Gaylord Perry, and Mike Marshall. [GV865.A1S5593] 920 76-28442 ISBN 0-87191-576-6 lib.bdg. 4.95
1. Pitchers (Baseball)—United States—Biography—Juvenile literature. I. Title. BIP

Pitkin family.

DANIELS, Bruce Colin. 974.6'02'0924
Connecticut's first family : William Pitkin and his connections / by Bruce Colin Daniels. Chester, Conn. : Pequot Press, 1975. 64 p. : ill. ; 23 cm. (Connecticut bicentennial series ; 11) "A publication of the American Revolution Bicentennial Commission of Connecticut." Includes bibliographical references. [F97.P62D36] 75-27800 ISBN 0-87106-060-4 pbk. : 2.50
1. Pitkin family. 2. Pitkin, William, 1694-1769. 3. Connecticut—Politics and government—Colonial period, ca. 1600-1775. I. Title. II. Series.

Pitseolak, Peter, 1902-

PITSEOLAK, Peter, 1902- 970'.004'97
People from our side : an Eskimo life story in words and photographs : an Inuit record of Seekooseelak, the land of the people of Cape Dorset, Baffin Island / Peter Pitseolak and Dorothy Eber ; [translator, Ann Meekitjuk Hanson ; interpreters for interviews, Ann Hanson ... et al.]. Bloomington : Indiana University Press, [1977] c1945. p. cm. Based on a manuscript written in Eskimo syllabics. [E99.E7P535 1977] 76-26420 ISBN 0-253-34334-8 : 17.95 pbk. : 12.95
1. Pitseolak, Peter, 1902- 2. Eskimos—Canada—Baffin Island. 3. Eskimos—Canada—Baffin Island—Biography. I. Eber, Dorothy, joint author. II. Title.

Pitt, Thomas, 2d Baron Camelford, 1775-1804.

TOLSTOY, Nikolai. 359.3'3'20924 B
The half-mad lord : Thomas Pitt, 2nd Baron Camelford (1775-1804) / Nikolai Tolstoy. 1st American ed. New York : Holt, Rinehart and Winston, 1979, c1978. xiv, 239 p., [8] leaves of plates : ill. ; 24 cm. Includes bibliographical references and index. [CT788.P664T64 1979] 78-14185 ISBN 0-03-047261-X. : 10.95
1. Pitt, Thomas, 2d Baron Camelford, 1775-1804. 2. England—Nobility—Biography. I. Title.

Pitt, William, 1st earl of Chatham, 1708-1778.

AYLING, Stanley Edward. 941'.07'3'0924 B
The elder Pitt, Earl of Chatham / [by] Stanley Ayling. London : Collins, 1976. 478 p., [16] p. of plates : ill., geneal. table (on lining papers), maps, ports. ; 24 cm. Includes index. Bibliography: p. 431-438. [DA483.P6A95] 76-365274 ISBN 0-00-216202-4 : £6.50
1. Pitt, William, 1st Earl of Chatham, 1708-1778. I. Title.

AYLING, Stanley Edward. 941.07'3'0924 B
The Elder Pitt, Earl of Chatham / Stanley Ayling. 1st American ed. New York : D. McKay, 1976. 478 p., [8] leaves of plates : ill. ; 24 cm. Includes index. Bibliography: p. 431-438. [DA483.P6A95 1976b] 76-40507 ISBN 0-679-50717-5 : 14.95
1. Pitt, William, 1st Earl of Chatham, 1708-1778. 2. Statesmen—Great Britain—Biography. 3. Great Britain—Politics and government—18th century. I. Title.

BROWN, Peter Douglas. 941.07'3'0924 B
William Pitt Earl of Chatham, the great commoner / Peter Douglas Brown. London : Allen & Unwin, 1978. 448 p. : port. ; 23 cm. Includes index. Bibliography: p. [430]-434. [DA483.P6B76] 78-305593 ISBN 0-04-942145-X : 29.75
1. Pitt, William, 1st Earl of Chatham, 1708-1778. 2. Great Britain—Politics and government—1714-1760. 3. Great Britain—Politics and government—1760-1789. 4. Statesmen—Great Britain—Biography. I. Title.
Distributed by Allen & Unwin, Inc. 198 Ash St., Reading, MA 01867

PLUMB, John Harold, 1911- 923.242
Chatham. Hamden, Conn., Archon [dist. Shoe String] 1965[c.1953, 1965] 158p. illus., maps, ports. 21cm. (Makers of hist.) [DA483.P6P5] 65-4286 4.00
1. Pitt, William, 1st earl of Chatham, 1708-1778. I. Title.

WILLIAMS, Basil, 1867-1950. 942.07'3'0924 B
The life of William Pitt, earl of Chatham. New York, Octagon Books, 1966. 2 v. illus., port. 23 cm. Bibliography: v. 2, p. 353-368. [DA483.P6W5 1966a] 66-30301
1. Pitt, William, 1st earl of Chatham, 1708-1778. 2. Great Britain—Politics and government—18th century. I. Title. BIP

Pitt, William, 1759-1806.

DERRY, John Wesley 923.242
William Pitt. New York, Arco [1963, c.1962] 160p. illus. 23cm. 63-17096 3.95
1. Pitt, William, 1759-1806. I. Title.

JARRETT, Derek. 942.07'3'0924 B
Pitt the younger / Derek Jarrett ; introd. by A. J. P. Taylor. New York : Scribner, [1974] 224 p. : ill. ; 26 cm. (British prime ministers) Includes index. Bibliography: p. 217-219. [DA522.P6J3 1974] 74-2679 ISBN 0-684-13868-9 : 10.00
1. Pitt, William, 1759-1806. I. Title.

REILLY, Robin. 941.07'3'0924 B
William Pitt the Younger / by Robin Reilly. 1st American ed. New York : Putnam, 1979, c1978. ix, 502 p., [4] leaves of plates : ill. ; 24 cm. Includes index. Bibliography: p. 476-485. [DA522.P6R44 1979] 78-13050 10.95
1. Pitt, William, 1759-1806. 2. Great Britain—Politics and government—1760-1820. 3. Prime ministers—Great Britain—Biography. I. Title. **BIP**

ROSEBERY, Archibald 942.07'3'0924
Philip Primrose, 5th Earl of, 1847-1929.
Pitt, by Lord Rosebery. New York, Haskell House, 1968. viii, 298 p. 23 cm. Reprint of the 1891 ed. [DA522.P6R8 1968] 68-25264
1. Pitt, William, 1759-1806. **BIP**

ROSEBERY, 942.07'3'0924 B
Archibald Philip Primrose, 5th Earl of, 1847-1929.
Pitt. New York, Greenwood Press [1969] viii, 297 p. 23 cm. (Twelve English statesmen) Reprint of the 1891 ed. [DA522.P6R8 1969] 69-14062
1. Pitt, William, 1759-1806.

STANHOPE, Philip 942.07'3'0924 B
Henry Stanhope, 5th Earl, 1805-1875.
Life of the Right Honourable William Pitt. 3d ed. New York, AMS Press [1970] 4 v. facsim., ports. 23 cm. Reprint of the 1867 ed. [DA522.P6S72] 71-108929
1. Pitt, William, 1759-1806. I. Title. **BIP**

Pittman, Key, 1872-1940.

ISRAEL, Fred L 923.273
Nevada's Key Pittman Lincoln, University of Nebraska Press [1963] 210 p. illus. 24 cm. Includes bibliography. [E748.P618] 63-8118
1. Pittman, Key, 1872-1940. I. Title.

Pittman, Portia Marshall Washington, 1883-

*HILL, Roy L. 378.1'11'0924
Booker T's child: the life and times of Portia Marshall Washington Pittman. [By] Roy L. Hill 1st. ed. Newark, N.J. McDaniel Press [1974] [94] p. ports. 23 cm. Bibliography: p. [93-94]. [E185] 7.95
1. Pittman, Portia Marshall Washington, 1883- I. Title.

Pittman, Vail M., 1883-1964.

MOODY, Eric N. 979.3'03'0924 B
Southern gentleman of Nevada politics: Vail M. Pittman, by Eric N. Moody. Reno, University of Nevada Press, 1974. 136 p. port. 23 cm. (Nevada studies in history and political science, no. 13) Bibliography: p. [125]-130. [F841.M57] 73-84927 ISBN 0-87417-039-7 3.50 (pbk.).
1. Pittman, Vail M., 1883-1964. 2. Nevada—Politics and government. I. Title. II. Series.

Pitts, Edith P.

PITTS, Edith P. 972.91'06
Cuba : from the Republic to Castro / by Edith P. Pitts. 1st ed. New York : Vantage Press, c1976. 131 p. ; 21 cm. Includes bibliographical references. [F1787.P57] 77-361294 ISBN 0-533-02411-0 : 5.95
1. Pitts, Edith P. 2. Cuba—History—1895- 3. Cuba—Social life and customs. 4. Florida—Biography. I. Title.

Pittsburgh—Biog.

VERMORCKEN, Elizabeth 920.0748
(Moorhead)
Pittsburgh portraits. Pittsburgh, Boxwood Press [1955] 101p. 22cm. [F159.P6V4] 55-32236
1. Pittsburgh—Biog. I. Title.

Pittsburgh Steelers (Football club)

DIDINGER, Ray. 796.33'264'0974886
Pittsburgh Steelers / by Ray Didinger. New York : Macmillan, 1974. 192 p. : ill. ; 27 cm. (Great teams' great years) "A National Football League book." [GV956.P57D52] 73-21303 8.95
1. Pittsburgh Steelers (Football club) 2. Footfall. 3. Football—Biography.

Pittsburgh Steelers (Football club)—History.

SAHADI, Lou. 796.33'264'0974886
Steelers, team of the decade / Lou Sahadi ; foreword by Art Rooney. New York : Times Books, c1979. p. cm. [GV956.P57S23 1979] 79-13214 ISBN 0-8129-0843-0 : 14.95
1. Pittsburgh Steelers (Football club)—History. 2. Football players—United States—Biography. I. Title.

Pius II, Pope, 1405-1464.

MITCHELL, Rosamond 922.21
Joscelyne, 1902-
The laurels and the tiara; Pope Pius II, 1458-1464. [1st ed. in the U.S.A.] Garden City, N.Y., Doubleday [1963, c1962] 286 p. 22 cm. [BX1308.M5 1963] 63-14329
1. Pius II, Pope, 1405-1464. I. Title.

PIUS II Pope, 1405-1464 922.21
Memoirs of a Renaissance Pope; the commentaries of Pius II, an abridgement. Translated by Florence A. Gragg. Edited with introd. by Leona C. Gabel. Illus. selected by Ruth Olitzky Rubinstein. New York, Putnam [1959] 381 p. illus., ports., map (on lining papers) 22 cm. [BX1308.A38] 59-5680
I. Title.

PIUS II, Pope, 1405-1464 922.21
Memoirs of a Renaissance Pope; the commentaries of Pius II, an abridgement. Tr. by Florence A. Gragg. Ed. with introd. by Leona C. Gabel. Illus. selected by Ruth Olitzky Rubinstein. New York [Capricorn Bks., dist.] Putnam [1961 c.1959] 381p. illus., map. (CAP gaint 210) 1.85 pap.,
I. Title.

PIUS II Pope, 1405-1464 922.21
Memoirs of a Renaissance Pope; the commentaries of Pius II, an abridgement. Translated by Florence A. Gragg. Edited with introd. by Leona C. Gabel. Illus. selected by Ruth Olitzky Rubinstein. New York, Putnam [1959] 381 p. illus., ports., map (on lining papers) 22 cm. [BX1308.A38] 59-5680
I. Title.

PIUS II, Pope, 1405-1464 922.21
Memoirs of a Renaissance Pope; the commentaries of Pius II, an abridgement. Tr. by Florence A. Gragg. Ed. with introd. by Leona C. Gabel. Illus. selected by Ruth Olitzky Rubinstein. New York [Capricorn Bks., dist.] Putnam [1961 c.1959] 381p. illus., map. (CAP gaint 210) 1.85 pap.,
I. Title.

Pius IX, Pope, 1792-1878.

THORNTON, Francis 922.21
Beauchesne, 1898-
Cross upon cross; the life of Pope Pius IX. New York, Benziger Bros. [1955] 263p. 21cm. Includes bibliography. [BX1373.T47] 55-3892
1. Plus IX, Pope, 1792-1878. I. Title.

Pius V, Saint, Pope, 1504-1572.

ANDERSON, Robin, 262'.13'0924 B
1913-
St. Pius V, a brief account of his life, times, virtues & miracles by Robin Anderson ; foreword by Alfredo Ottaviani. Rockford, Ill. : Tan Books and Publishers, 1978. 111 p. : ill. ; 18 cm. [BX1323.A52] 78-55637 ISBN 0-89555-068-7 : 2.00
1. Pius V, Saint, Pope, 1504-1572. 2. Popes—Biography. 3. Christian saints—Italy—Biography. I. Title. **BIP**

MCCARTHY, Gerontius, 1920- 922.21
Who is like to God; a story of Pope St. Pius v. Illus. by Frances Sheeran. Notre Dame, Ind., Dujarie Press [1955] 95p. illus. 24cm. [BX1323.M25] 55-3408
1. Plus v, Saint, Pope, 1504-1572. I. Title.

Pius VII, Pope, 1742-1823.

HALES, Edward 262'.13'0924 B
Elton Young, 1908-
The Emperor and the Pope : the story of Napoleon and Pius VII / E. E. Y. Hales. New York : Octagon Books, 1978, c1961. p. cm. Reprint of the ed. published by Doubleday, Garden City, N.Y. [BX1369.H34 1978] 78-14767 ISBN 0-374-93375-8 lib.bdg. : 12.00
1. Pius VII, Pope, 1742-1823. 2. Napoleon I, Emperor of the French, 1769-1821. 3. Popes—Biography. 4. France—Kings and rulers—Biography. I. Title.

WISEMAN, Nicholas 262'.13'0922
Patrick Stephen, Cardinal, 1802-1865.
Recollections of the last four popes and of Rome in their times. New and rev. ed. Freeport, N.Y., Books for Libraries Press [1973] p. (Essay index reprint series) "First published 1858." [BX1386.W5 1973] 72-14111 ISBN 0-518-10032-4
1. Pius VII, Pope, 1742-1823. 2. Leo XII, Pope, 1760-1829. 3. Pius VIII, Pope, 1761-1830. 4. Gregorius XVI, Pope, 1765 1846. I. Title. II. Title: The last four popes.

Pius VII, Pope, 1761-1830 —Juv. lit.

BREAK down the doors;! v. 12
a story of Pope Pius VII. Illustrations by Carolyn Lee Jagodits. Notre Dame, Ind., Dujarie Press [1961] 94p. illus. 24cm.
1. Pius VII, Pope, 1761-1830 —Juv. lit. I. Roberto, Brother, 1927-

Pius VIII, Pope, 1761-1830.

WISEMAN, Nicholas 262'.13'0922
Patrick Stephen, Cardinal, 1802-1865.
Recollections of the last four popes and of Rome in their times. New and rev. ed. Freeport, N.Y., Books for Libraries Press [1973] p. (Essay index reprint series) "First published 1858." [BX1386.W5 1973] 72-14111 ISBN 0-518-10032-4
1. Pius VII, Pope, 1742-1823. 2. Leo XII, Pope, 1760-1829. 3. Pius VIII, Pope, 1761-1830. 4. Gregorius XVI, Pope, 1765-1846. I. Title. II. Title: The last four popes.

Pius X, Saint, Pope, 1835-1914.

BURTON, Katherine (Kurz), 922.21
1890-
The great mantle; the life of Giuseppe Melchiore Sarto, Pope Pius x. [1st ed.] New York, Longmans, Green, 1950. xiv, 238 p. port. 22 cm. Bibliography: p. 225-226. [BX1375.B8 1950] 50-6259
1. Plus x, Pope, 1835-1914. I. Title.

DAL-GAL, Girolamo. 922.21
Pius, X, the life-story of the Beautus: the new Italian life of Pius X, translated and adapted by Thomas F. Murray. Westminster, Md., Newman Press, 1954. 246 p. illus. 22 cm. [BX1375.D323] 54-5661
1. Pius x, Pope, 1835-1914. I. Title.

DIETHELM, Walther. 922.21
Saint Pius X, the farm boy who became Pope. Illustrated by G.W. Thompson. New York, Vision Books [1956] 189p. illus. 22cm. (Vision books, 8) [BX1375.D52] 56-5990
1. Plus x. Saint. Pope, 1835-1914. I. Title.

ERNEST, Brother, 1897- 922.21
A story of Saint Pius X Pictures by John Roytek. Notre Dame, Ind., Dujarie Press [1957] unpaged. illus. 21cm. [BX1375.E7] 57-4989
1. Plus x, Saint, Pope, 1835-1914. I. Title.

FITCH, Lawrence, 1930- 922.21
The song of the shoemaker's son; a story of Blessed Pius X. Illus. by Harold Ruplinger. Notre Dame, Ind., Dujarie Press [1951] 92 p. illus. 24 cm. [BX1375.F5] 52-18159
1. Pius x, Pope, 1835-1914. I. Title.

GIORDANI, Igino, 1894- 922.21
Pius X, a country priest; translated by Thomas J. Tobin. Milwaukee, Bruce Pub. Co. [1954] 205p. illus. 21cm. [BX1375.G52] 54-7602
1. Plus x, Pope, 1835-1914. I. Title.

GIORDANI, Igino, 1894- 922.21
Pius X, a country priest; translated by Thomas J. Tobin. Milwaukee, Bruce Pub. Co. [1954] 219p. illus. 22cm. [BX1375.G52 1954a] 55-614
1. Pius x, Saint, Pope, 1835-1914. I. Title.

GRASHOFF, Raphael. 922.21
'A good shepherd he was; the life of Blessed Pius x. St. Meinrad, Ind, [1952] 79p. illus. 20cm. 'A Grail publication.; [BX1375.G7] 53-28243
1. Pius x, Pope, 1835-1914. I. Title.

HUNERMANN, Wilhelm. 922.21
Flame of white, a life of Saint Pius x. Translated from the German by M. Ida Adler. Chicago, Franciscan Herald Press [1959] 269p. 22cm. Translation of Brennendes Feuer. [BX1375.H813] 59-9332
1. Pius x, Saint, Pope, 1855-1914. I. Title.

MARTINI, Teri. 922.21
The Fisherman's ring; the life of Giuseppe Sarto, the children's Pope. Pref, by Edwin V. O Hara. Illustrated by June Roberts. Paterson, N. J., St. Anthony Guild Press, 1954. 117p. illus. 24cm. [BX1375.N37] 54-27102
1. Pius x, 1835-1914. I. Title.

MARYGROVE College, 922.21
Detroit.
St. Pius X. Detroit, 1954. 78p. illus. 31cm. A reprint of the commencement number of the Campus reporter.' [BX1375.M38] 55-22512
1. Pius x, Saint, Pope, 1835-1914. I. Title.

MATT, Leonard Von. 922.245
Pope Pius X [by] Leonard von Matt, Nello Vian. Tr. from German. New York, Universe [c.1963] 48p. 75illus., (incl. ports.) 18cm. [Orbis bks., 1) Summary of St. Pius X, a pictorial biography, orig. pub. in German under title: Pius X. 63-18342 1.75 pap.,
1. Pius X, Saint, Pope, 1835-1914. I. Vian, Nello. II. Title.

MATT, Leonard von. 922.21
St. Pius X, a pictorial biography, by Leonard von Matt and Nello Vian. Translated from the German by Sebastian Bullough. Chicago, H. Regnery Co. [1955] 90p. illus. 25cm. [BX1375.M3915] 55-13810
1. Plus x, Saint, Pope, 1835-1914. I. Vian, Nello. II. Title.

MERRY DEL VAL, Raphael, 922.21
Cardinal, 1865-1930.
Memories of Pope Pius X. Forewords by Cardinal Hinsley and Cardinal Hayes. Westminster, Md., Newman Press, 1951. 81 p. 19 cm. [BX1375.M43] 52-6152
1. Pius x, Pope, 1835-1914. I. Title.

O'BRIEN, Felicity. 262'.13'0924 B
St Pius X / by Felicity O'Brien. London : Catholic Truth Society, 1976. 20 p. ; 19 cm. Includes bibliographical references. [BX1375.O18] 77-359057 ISBN 0-85183-183-4 : £0.15
1. Pius X, Saint, Pope, 1835-1914. 2. Popes—Biography. I. Title.

SMIT, Jan Olav, Bp., 262.130924
D.D., 1883-
St. Pius X, Pope. Tr. by James H. Van der Veldt. Foreword by Richard Cardinal Cushing, Archbishop of Boston. Saint Pius the tenth Pope [Boston] St. Paul Eds. [dist. Daughters of St. Paul, c.1965] 185p. illus., facsim., ports. 22cm. [BX1375.S64] 64-7924 4.00; 3.00 pap.,
1. Pius X, Saint, Pope, 1835-1914. I. Title.

SMIT, Jan Olay, 262.130924 (B)
Bp., 1883-
St. Pius x, Pope. Translated by James H. Van der Veldt. With a foreword by Richard Cardinal Cushing, Archbishop of Boston. [Boston] St. Paul Editions [1965]

185 p. illus., facsim, ports. 22 cm. [BX1375.S64] 64-7924
1. Pius x, Saint, Pope, 1835-1914. I. Title.

THORNTON, Francis Beauchesne, 1898- 922.21
The burning flame; the life of Pope Pius x. New York, Benziger Bros. [1952] 216p. 21cm. [BX1375.T45] 53-85
1. Pius x, Pope, 1835-1914. I. Title.

Pius X, Saint, Pope, 1835-1914—Juvenile literature.

DIETHELM, Walther. 92
St. Pius x, the farm boy who became Pope. Illustrated by Charles Dolesch. Condensed for very young readers from the original Vision book. New York, Guild Press [1963] 76 p. illus. (port. col.) 24 cm. (A Junior Vision book) Condensed from translation of Ein Bauernbub wird Papst. [BX1375.D533] 63-24996
1. Pius x, Saint, Pope, 1835-1914 — Juvenile literature. I. Title.

FITCH, Lawrence, 1930- 92
The song of the shoemaker's son; a story of Saint Pius X. Illus. by Harold Ruplinger. Notre Dame, Ind., Dujarie, 1966[c.1951] 94p. illus. 24cm. [BX1375.F5] 66-3448 2.25
1. Pius X, Saint, Pope, 1835-1914—Juvenile literature. I. Title.

Pius XI, Pope, 1857-1939.

ARADI, Zsolt. 922.21
Pius XI, the Pope and the man. [1st ed.] Garden City, N. Y., Hanover House, 1958. 262 p. illus. 22 cm. Includes bibliography. [BX1377.A7] 58-6628
1. Pius XI, Pope, 1857-1939.

Pius XII, Pope, 1876-1958.

BARGELLINI, Piero, 1897- 922.21
Pius XII, the angelic shepherd. English translation. New York, Good Shepherd Pub. Corp. [1950] 181 p. illus., ports. 23 cm. [BX1378.B314] 50-11205
1. Pius XII, Pope, 1876- I. Title.

BURTON, Katherine (Kurz) 1890- 922.21
Witness of the light; the life of Pope Pius XII. [1st ed.] New York, Longmuns, Green, 1958. 248p. 22cm. Includes bibliography. [BX1378.B8] 58-7680
1. Pius XII, Pope, 1876- I. Title.

CONNIFF, James C G 922.21
Pope Pius XII; the holy life of Eugenio Pacelli. Greenwich, Conn., Fawcett Publications, c1955. 32p. illus. 29cm. [BX1378.C6] 55-1739
1. Pius xii, Pope, 1876- I. Title.

FITCH, Lawrence, 1930-- 922.21
The world and the white prince; a story of Pope Pius XII.Illus. by Harold Ruplinger. Notre Dame, Ind., Dujarie Press [1954] 98p. illus. 24cm. [BX1378.F5] 54-3699
1. Pius XII, Pope, 1876— I. Title.

FRIEDLANDER, Saul, 1932- 262.130924
Pius XII and the Third Reich; a documentation. Tr. from the French and German by Charles Fullman. [1st Amer. ed.] New York, Knopf, 1966. xxiv, 238p. 22cm. Bibl. [BX1378.F713] 66-10029 4.95
1. Pius XII, Pope, 1876-1958. 2. Catholic Church—Relations (diplomatic) with Germany. 3. Germany —For. rel.—Catholic Church. I. Title.

HATCH, Alden, 1898- v. 12
Crown of glory; the life of Pope Pius XII, by Alden Hatch and Seamus Walshe. Illustrated with drawings by Louis Priscilla. Garden City, Echo Books [1965] 273 p. illus. 19 cm. 67-30090
1. 1. Pius XII, Pope, 1876-1958. I. Walshe, Seamus, 1918- joint author. II. Title.

HATCH, Alden, 1898- 922.21
Crown of glory; the life of Pope Pius xii, by Alden Hatch, Seamus Walshe. Drawings by Louis Priscilla. Garden City, N. Y., Doubleday [c.1957-1965] 273p. illus. 18cm. (Echo bk. E1) [BX1378.H35] .85 pap.,
1. Pius xii, Pope, 1876-1958. I. Walshe, Seamus, 1918- joint author. II. Title.

HATCH, Alden, 1898- 922.21
Crown of glory the life of Pope Pius XII by Alden Hatch and Seamus Walshe. Illustrated with drawings by Louis Priscilla [Memorial ed., rev. and enl.] New York, Hawthorn Books [1957] 251p. illus. 24cm. [BX1378.H35] 57-6362
1. Pius XII, Pope, 1876- I. Walshe, Seamus, 1918- joint author. II. Title.

HATCH, Alden, 1898- 922.21
Crown of glory the life of Pope Pius XII by Alden Hatch and Seamus Walshe. Illustrated with drawings by Louis Priscilla. [Memorial ed., rev. and enl.] New York, Hawthorn Books [1958] 271p. illus. 24cm. [BX1378.H35 1958] 58-59703
1. Pius XII, Pope, 1876-1958. I. Walshe, Seamus, 1918- joint author. II. Title.

KONSTANTIN, Prince of Bavaria, 1920- 922.21
The Pope; a portriat from life. Translated by Diana Pyke. New York, Roy Publishers [1955?] 307p. illus. 23cm. [BX1378] 56-5048
1. Pius XII, Pope, 1876- I. Title.

LAVELLE, Elise. 922.21
The man who was chosen; the story of Pope Pius XII. New York, Whittlesey House [1957] 156p. illus. 21cm. [BX1378.L3] 57-6401
1. Pius XII, Pope, 1876- I. Title.

LENN, Lottie Helen, 1908- 922.21
Pope Pius XII, Rock of Peace, by Lottie H. Lenn and Mary A. Reardon; illustrated by Mary A. Reardon. Foreword by Richard J. Cushing. [1st ed.] New York, Dutton, 1950. 152 p. illus. 21 cm. Bibliography: p. 147-148. [BX1378.L39] 50-5908
1. Pius XII, Pope, 1876-1958. I. Reardon, Mary A., joint author.

O'MIKLE, Stephen, ed. 922.21
Pope Pius XII, his voice and life. New York, Wilson Pub. Co. [1958] 64p. (chiefly illus.) 25cm. and phonodisc (2 s. 6 in. 78 rpm) in pocket. [BX1378.O5] 59-291
1. Pius XII, Pope, 1876-1958. I. Title.

PADELLARO, Nazareno 1892- 922.21
Portrait of Pius XII. Translated by Michael Derrick. Foreword by Daniel-Rops. [1st American ed.] New York, Dutton, 1957 [c1956] 274 p. illus. 22 cm. Translation of Pio XII. [BX1378.P312 1957] 56-6317
1. Pius XII, Pope, 1876-

PFISTER, Pierre, 1895- 922.21
Pius XII; the life and work of a great Pope New York, Studio Publications [1955] 159p. illus. 26cm. [BX1378.P49] 55-7828
1. Pius xii, Pope, 1876- I. Title.

ROOSEVELT, Franklin Delano, Pres. U.S., 1882-1945. 940.53'2
Wartime correspondence between President Roosevelt and Pope Pius XII : with an introd. & explanatory notes / by Myson C. Taylor. New York : Da Capo Press, 1975, c1947. xiii, 127 p. : ports. ; 23 cm. (Franklin D. Roosevelt and the era of the New Deal) Reprint of the ed. published by Macmillan, New York. [D753.R69 1975] 74-31356 ISBN 0-306-70709-8 : 15.00
1. Roosevelt, Franklin Delano, Pres. U.S., 1882-1945. 2. Pius XII, Pope, 1876-1958. 3. Catholic Church—Relations (diplomatic) with the United States. 4. World War, 1939-1945—United States. 5. United States—Foreign relations—Catholic Church. I. Pius XII, Pope, 1876-1958. II. Taylor, Myron Charles, 1874-1959. III. Title. IV. Series.

SMIT, Jan Olva, Bp., 1883- 922.21
Angelic shepherd; the life of Pope Pius XII. Adapted into English by James H. Vanderveldt. New York, Dodd, Mead, 1950. x, 326 p. illus., ports. 22 cm. "References": p. 295-310. "Pius XII ... A checklist of published biographies and biographical notes, compiled by Elizabeth J. Barham": p. 311-318. [BX1378.S533] 50-6532
1. Pius XII, Pope, 1876- I. Title.

SMYTH, J Hilton LeBaron. 922.21
His Holiness Pope Pius XII; a memorial picture history of the Pope of Peace, with texts and notes [Stamped: New Rochelle, N.Y., Distributed by Sportshelf, 1958] 128 p. illus. 23 cm. [BX1378.S55] 58-4975
1. Pius XII, Pope, 1876-1958. I. Title.

TARDINI, Domenico, Cardinal. 922.21
Memories of Pius XII. Translated by Rosmarie Goldie. Goldie. Westminster, Md., Newman [c.]1961. 175p. ports. (col.) 60-53377 2.75
I. Title.

Pius, XII, Pope, 1876-1958—Juvenile literature.

DE WOHL, Louis, 1903- 922.21
Pope Pius XII, the world's shepherd. Illus by Harry Barton. New York, Farrar, Straus & Cudahy [c.1961] 190p. (Vision books, 50) 61-5897 1.95
1. Pius, XII, Pope, 1876-1958—Juvenile literature. I. Title.

HATCH, Alden, 1898- 92
Apostle of peace; the story of Pope Pius XII. Illustrated by Jo Polseno. New York, Hawthorn Books [1965] 191 p. illus. 22 cm. Bibliography: p. [175] [BX1378.H34] 65-12735
1. Pius XII, Pope, 1876-1958 — Juvenile literature. I. Title.

Pizarro, Francisco, marques, 1470?-1541—Juvenile literature.

SYME, Ronald, 1910- 923.185
Francisco Pizarro, finder of Peru. Illustrated by William Stobbs. New York, Morrow, 1963. 96 p. illus. 22 cm. [F3442.P729] 62-15758
1. Pizarro, Francisco, marques, 1470?-1541—Juvenile literature. I. Title: Finder of Peru.

Place, Francis,

PLACE, Francis, 1771-1854. 309.1'421'073 B
The autobiography of Francis Place (1771-1854), edited with an introd. and notes by Mary Thale. Cambridge [Eng.] University Press, 1972. xl, 308 p. port. 24 cm. Includes bibliographical references. [DA536.P7A3] 78-174265 ISBN 0-521-08399-0
I. Title. BIP

Placidus, Saint, ca. 515-ca. 550.

GALLOIS, Genevieve. 922.2
The life of little Saint Placid. Foreword by Marcelle Auclair. [Translated by the monks of Mount Saviour Monanstery. New York] Pantheon [1956] unpaged. illus. 20cm. [BX4700.P78G32] 56-6121
1. Placidus, Saint, ca. 515-ca. 550. I. Title.

Planche, James Robinson, 1796-1880—Biography—Theatrical career.

PLANCHE, Jams Robinson, 1796-1880. 822'.8 B
Recollections and reflections : a professional autobiography / by James Robinson Planche. Rev. ed. New York : Da Capo Press, 1978. p. cm. (Da Capo Press music reprint series) Reprint of the 1901 ed. published by S. Low, Marston, London. [PR5187.P2A827 1978] 78-17733 lib.bdg. : 35.00
1. Planche, James Robinson, 1796-1880—Biography—Theatrical career. 2. Authors, English—19th century—Biography. 3. Performing arts—England—History—19th century. I. Title.

Plant City, Fla.—History.

BRUTON, Quintilla Geer, 1907- 975.9'65
Plant City, its origin and history / by Quintilla Geer Bruton and David E. Bailey, Jr. 1st ed. St. Petersburg, Fla. : Valkyrie Press, c1977. 477 p. : ill. ; 27 cm. Bibliography: p. [6] [F319.P59B78] 76-42919 ISBN 0-912760-34-6 : 20.00
1. Plant City, Fla.—History. 2. Plant City, Fla.—Genealogy. 3. Plant City, Fla.—Biography. I. Bailey, David E., 1917- joint author. II. Title.

Plant collectors—Biography.

HEALEY, B. J. 581'.092'2 B
The plant hunters / B. J. Healey. New York : Scribner, [1975] vii, 214 p. : ill. ; 24 cm. Includes bibliographical references and index. [QK26.H37] 74-32295 ISBN 0-684-14214-7 8.95
1. Plant collectors—Biography. 2. Plant introduction—History. I. Title.

Plant collectors—England—Biography.

ALLAN, Mea. 635.9'075
Plants that changed our gardens / Mea Allan. Newton Abbot; North Pomfret, VT: David and Charles, 1974 [i.e., 1975] 208 p. : ill., ports. ; 23 cm. Includes indexes. [QK26.A44] 74-83306 ISBN 0-7153-6721-8 : 14.00
1. Plant collectors—England—Biography. 2. Plant collectors—Biography. 3. Plant introduction—England. 4. Plants, Ornamental. I. Title. BIP

Plant, Robert

*GROSS, Michael 784'.092'4 B
Robert Plant New York, Popular Library [1975] 160 p. 18 cm. [ML420] 1.50 (pbk.)
1. Plant, Robert I. Title.

Plantagenet, House of.

BROOKS, Janice Young. 942'.00992
Kings and queens : the Plantagenets of England / by Janice Young Brooks. 1st ed. Nashville : T. Nelson, [1975] p. cm. Includes index. [DA177.B76] 75-17843 ISBN 0-8407-6438-3 : 6.50
1. Great Britain—Kings and rulers—Biography. 2. Great Britain—History—Medieval period, 1066-1485. I. Title. BIP

HARVEY, John Hooper. 942.03'092'2
The Plantagenets / John Harvey. 3rd ed. London : Severn House : [Distributed by Hutchinson], 1976. xiv, 7-248 p. : facsims., geneal. table, map, music, ports. ; 21 cm. Includes index. Bibliography: p. 231-233. [DA177.H3 1976] 77-350820 ISBN 0-7278-0105-8 : £5.00
1. Plantagenet, House of. 2. Great Britain—Kings and rulers—Biography. 3. Great Britain—History—Medieval period, 1066-1485. I. Title. BIP

Plantation life—Louisiana.

NORTHUP, Solomon, b.1808. 301.45'22'0924 B
Twelve years a slave. With a new introd. by Philip S. Foner. New York, Dover Publications [1970] x, 336 p. illus. 21 cm. (Black rediscovery) Reprint of the 1854 ed. At head of title: Twentieth thousand. [E444.N87 1970] 72-105666
1. Plantation life—Louisiana. 2. Slavery in the United States—Louisiana. I. Title. II. Series. BIP

Plantation life—Louisiana—Juvenile literature.

KNIGHT, Michael. 301.44'93'0924 B
In chains to Louisiana; Solomon Northup's story, adapted by Michael Knight. [1st ed.] New York, Dutton [1971] 123 p. 22 cm. (Black autobiographies) "A Richard W. Baron book." Adapted from S. Northup's Twelve years a slave. A free black man

from New York, kidnapped and sold into slavery in 1841 at the age of thirty-three, tells of his twelve years as a slave in Louisiana. [E444.K57 1971] 92 73-108967 4.50
1. Plantation life—Louisiana—Juvenile literature. 2. Slavery in the United States—Louisiana—Juvenile literature. I. Northup, Solomon, b. 1808. Twelve years a slave. II. Title. III. Series. **BIP**

Plantation life—Southern States.

EPPES, Susan 917.5'03'4
(Bradford) 1845or6-1942.
Through some eventful years. Gainesville, University of Florida Press, 1968. xxviii, 378, 5 p. illus., coat of arms., geneal. table, ports. 24 cm. (Floridiana facsimile & reprint series) Reprint of the 1926 ed., with new introd. and index by J. D. Cushman, Jr. Bibliographical references included in "Notes" (p. xxvi-xxviii) [F213.E54 1968] 68-21660
1. Plantation life—Southern States. I. Title. II. Series. **BIP**

Plante, Jacques, 1929-

O'BRIEN, Andy, 796.9'62'0924 [B]
1910-
The Jacques Plante story, by Andy O'Brien with Jacques Plante. Toronto, New York, McGraw-Hill Ryersons [1973, c1972] 162 p. illus. 22 cm. [GV848.5.P55O2] 71-38295 ISBN 0-07-092991-2
1. Plante, Jacques, 1929- I. Plante, Jacques, 1929- II. Title.
Available from McGraw-Hill, New York, for 5.95

Plante, Jacques, 1929- —Juvenile literature.

ETTER, Les. 796.9'62'0922
Hockey's masked men : three great goalies / by Les Etter ; illustrated by Larry Noble. Champaign, Ill. : Garrard Pub. Co., c1976. 96 p. : ill. ; 24 cm. Biographies of three men who brought a new style of goaltending to hockey: Terry Sawchuk, Glenn Hall, and Jacques Plante. [GV848.5.A1E87] 920 75-28413 ISBN 0-8116-6676-X : 3.58
1. Hall, Glenn, 1931- —Juvenile literature. 2. Plante, Jacques, 1929- —Juvenile literature. 3. Sawchuk, Terry, 1929- —Juvenile literature. 4. Hockey—Biography—Juvenile literature. I. Noble, Larry. II. Title. **BIP**

Plantin, Christophe, 1514-1589.

CLAIR, Colin 926.255
Christopher Plantin. London, Cassell [New York, Hiliary House, 1966, c.1960] xv, 302p. illus., ports, facsims. 26cm. Bibl. [Z232.P71C55] 60-4116 7.50
1. Plantin, Christophe, 1514-1589. I. Title.

Plants, Ornamental—Collection and preservation—History.

COATS, Alice M. 581'.0922 B
The plant hunters; being a history of the horticultural pioneers, their quests, and their discoveries from the Renaissance to the twentieth century [by] Alice M. Coats. New York, McGraw-Hill [1970, c1969] 400 p. illus., maps, ports. 26 cm. First published in 1969 under title: The quest for plants. Bibliography: p. 379-384. [SB404.5.C63 1970] 77-101380
1. Plants, Ornamental—Collection and preservation—History. 2. Plant introduction—History. 3. Horticulturists. 4. Botanists. I. Title.

Plath, Sylvia, 1932-1963.

AIRD, Eileen M. 811'.5'4
Sylvia Plath [by] Eileen M. Aird. New York, Barnes & Noble Books [1973] 114 p. 20 cm. Bibliography: p. 113-114. [PS3566.L27Z56] 73-174111 ISBN 0-06-490038-X 5.25
1. Plath, Sylvia.

AIRD, Eileen M. 811'.5'4
Sylvia Plath; her life and work [by] Eileen M. Aird. New York, Harper and Row [1975, c1973] 114 p. 18 cm. (Perennial library) Original title: Sylvia Plath Bibliography: p. 113-114 [PS3566.L27Z56] ISBN 0-06-080341-X 1.25 (pbk.)
1. Plath, Sylvia I. Title.
L.C. card number for original ed.: 73-174111 **BIP**

SALOP, Lynne. 811'.5'4 B
Suisong / by Lynne Salop. 1st ed. New York : Vantage Press, c1978. 81 p. ; 21 cm. Bibliography: p. 79-81. [PS3566.L27Z89] 77-84844 ISBN 0-533-03104-4 : 4.95
1. Plath, Sylvia, 1932-1963. 2. Suicide. 3. Creation (Literary, artistic, etc.) 4. Poets, American—20th century—Biography. I. Title.

SYLVIA Plath : 811'.5'4
the woman and the work / edited, with an introd. by Edward Butscher. New York : Dodd, Mead, [1977] p. cm. Includes bibliographical references. [PS3566.L27Z92] 77-24700 ISBN 0-396-07497-9 : 8.95
1. Plath, Sylvia. 2. Authors, American—20th century—Biography. I. Butscher, Edward. **BIP**

Plath, Sylvia—Correspondence.

PLATH, Sylvia. 811'.5'4 B
Letters home : correspondence, 1950-1963 / by Sylvia Plath ; selected and edited with commentary by Aurelia Schober Plath. 1st ed. New York : Harper & Row, [1975] p. cm. Includes index. [PS3566.L27Z53 1975] 74-1849 ISBN 0-06-013372-4 : 12.50
1. Plath, Sylvia—Correspondence. 2. Plath, Aurelia Schober. I. Plath, Aurelia Schober. II. Title. **BIP**

Plato.

FRIEDLANDER, Paul, 1882- 184
1968.
Plato / Paul Friedlander ; translated from the German by Hans Meyerhoff. 2d ed., with revisions. Princeton, N.J. : Princeton University Press, 1973- c1969- v. : ill. ; 22 cm. (Bollingen series ; 59) Translation of Platon. Contents.Contents.—1. An introduction. "Bibliography of the writings of Paul Friedlander": v. 1, p. [433]-439. [B395.F7523 1973] 75-313712 ISBN 0-691-09812-3. ISBN 0-691-01795-6 pbk. : 3.95
1. Plato. I. Title. II. Series.

HUIT, Charles, 1845-1914. 184 B
La vie et l'ouvre de Platon / Charles Huit. Hildesheim ; New York : G. Olms, 1973. 2 v. : ill. ; 20 cm. Reprint of the 1893 ed. published by Thorin, Paris. Includes bibliographical references. [PA4291.H8 1973] 75-503790 ISBN 3-487-04528-1 (v. 1). ISBN 3-487-04529-X (v. 2)
1. Plato. I Title.

RITTER, Constantin, 1859- 184 B
1936.
Platon : sein Leben, seine Schriften, seine Lehre / Constantin Ritter. New York : Arno Press, 1976. 2 v. ; 23 cm. (History of ideas in ancient Greece) Reprint of the 1910-23 ed. published by C. H. Beck, Munchen. Includes bibliographical references and index. [B393.R5 1976] 75-13291 ISBN 0-405-07333-X
1. Plato. I. Title. II. Series. **BIP**

TAYLOR, Alfred Edward, 184.1
1869-1945.
Plato: the man and his work. New York, Meridian Books, 1956. xi, 562 p. 21 cm. (Meridian books, MG7) Includes bibliographies. [B395.T25 1956] 56-10023
1. Plato.

Plato—Juvenile literature.

PITTENGER, William Norman, 184 B
1905-
Plato, his life and teachings, by W. Norman Pittenger. New York, F. Watts [1971] ix, 118 p. map. 22 cm. (Immortals of philosophy and religion) Bibliography: p. 113-114. The life of the philosopher of fourth- and fifth-century Greece whose ideas have had a continuing influence on civilization. [B393.P58] 92 76-150375 ISBN 0-531-00964-5
1. Plato—Juvenile literature. I. Title.

Platt, Fanny Arabella (Hayes)

PLATT, Fanny Arabella (Hayes) 920
1820-1856.
Letters: Fanny Arabella Hayes Platt. Diary and correspondence: Fanny Platt Fullerton. 1847-1896. [Columbus? Ohio] c1956. A-C, 91p. 29cm. Cover title. [CT275.P6643A4] 56-28413
I. Fullerton, Fanny Hayes (Platt) 1847-1896. II. Title.

Platt, John A.

PLATT, John A. 979.6'86'0924
Whispers from old Genesee and echoes of the Salmon River / by John A. Platt. Memorial ed. Fairfield, Wash. : Galleon Press, 1975. p. cm. Reprint of the 1962 printing with a new introd., biographical sketches, and new illus. [F746.P53 1975] 75-2266 ISBN 0-87770-143-1 : 9.00
1. Platt, John A. 2. Frontier and pioneer life—Idaho. 3. Genesee, Idaho—History. 4. Salmon Valley, Idaho—History. I. Title. **BIP**

Platt, Orville Hitchcock, 1827-1905.

COOLIDGE, Louis 973.7'092'4 B
Arthur, 1861-1925.
An old-fashioned Senator: Orville H. Platt of Connecticut; the story of a life unselfishly devoted to the public service. Port Washington, N.Y., Kennikat Press [1971] 2 v. (xiv, 655 p.) port. 22 cm. (Kennikat Press scholarly reprints. Kennikat series on American history and culture in the nineteenth century) Reprint of the 1910 ed. [E664.P7C7 1971] 74-137907 ISBN 0-8046-1475-X
1. Platt, Orville Hitchcock, 1827-1905. I. Title.

Platt, Thomas Collier, 1833-1910.

PLATT, Thomas 973.8'092'4 B
Collier, 1833-1910.
The autobiography of Thomas Collier Platt. Compiled and edited by Louis J. Lang. New York, Arno Press, 1974 [c1910] xxiii, 556 p. ports. 23 cm. (Politics and people: the ordeal of self-government in America) Reprint of the ed. published by B. W. Dodge, New York. [E664.P72A32 1974] 73-19172 ISBN 0-405-05894-2 30.00
1. Platt, Thomas Collier, 1833-1910. I. Lang, Louis Jay, 1859- ed. II. Title. III. Series. **BIP**

Playboy.

MARSHE, Surrey, 778.9'24'0924 B
1947-
The girl in the centerfold; the uninhibited memoirs of Miss January, by Surrey Marshe with Robert A. Liston. New York, Delacorte Press [1969] 181 p. 22 cm. [TX910.5.M334A3] 72-78793 4.95
1. Playboy. I. Liston, Robert A. II. Title.

Player, Gary.

PLAYER, Gary. 796.352'092'4 B
Gary Player, world golfer / [written] with Floyd Thatcher. Waco, Tex. : Word Books, [1974] 193 p. : ill. ; 23 cm. [GV964.P55A29] 74-83674 6.95
1. Player, Gary. 2. Golf. I. Thatcher, Floyd W., joint author.

Pleasant, Mary Ellen.

HOLDREDGE, Helen 920.7
(O'Donnell)
Mammy Pleasant. 53New ed.] San Carlos, Calif., Nourse Pub. Co. [1961, c.1953] 311p. illus. [Her The San Francisco scandals, v. 1] Bibl. 61-4045 5.00
1. Pleasant, Mary Ellen. I. Title.

HOLDREDGE, Helen O'Donnell. 920.7
Mammy Pleasant. New York, Putnam [1953] 311 p. 22 cm. [E185.97.P6H6] 53-8160
1. Pleasant, Mary Ellen. I. Title.

Plekhanov, Georgii Valentinovich, 1856-1918.

BARON, Samuel Haskell, 923.247
1921-
Plekhanov; the father of Russian Marxism. Stanford, Calif., Stanford University Press, 1963. 400 p. illus. 24 cm. Includes bibliography. [HX312.P63B3] 63-10732
1. Plekhanov, Georgii Valentinovich, 1856-1918. I. Title.

Plimpton, George.

PLIMPTON, George. 796.33'2'0922
Mad ducks and bears. [1st ed.] New York, Random House [1973] vii, 421 p. 22 cm. Based on the contributions of the author, J. Gordy, and A. Karras. [GV939.A1P55] 73-85563 ISBN 0-394-48847-4 6.95
1. Plimpton, George. 2. Gordy, John. 3. Karras, Alex. 4. Football—Biography. I. Gordy, John. II. Karras, Alex. III. Title.

PLIMPTON, George 796.332640924
Paper Lion. New York, Pocket Bks. [1967, c.1966] 303p. ports. 18cm. (95053) Autobiographical. [GV939.P6A3] .95 pap.,
1. Football. I. Title. **BIP**

PLIMPTON, George. 796.332640924
Paper Lion. [1st ed.] New York, Harper & Row [1966] 362 p. ports. 22 cm. Autobiographical. [GV939.P6A3] 64-20541
1. Football. I. Title.

PLIMPTON, George. 796.332'0924
Paper lion. Large type ed. New York, Harper & Row [1969, c1966] 362 p. 29 cm. [GV939] 72-4051 9.95
1. Football. 2. Sight-saving books. I. Title.

Plinius Caecilius Secundus, C.—Correspondence.

PLINIUS Caecilius 876'.01
Secundus, C.,
Pliny : a selection of his letters / translated by Clarence Greig. Cambridge ; New York : Cambridge University Press, 1979. ix, 83 p. : ill. ; 22 cm. (Translations from Greek and Roman authors) Includes index. [PA6639.E5G7 1978] 77-91088 ISBN 0-521-21978-7 pbk. : 3.25
1. Plinius Caecilius Secundus, C.—Correspondence. I. Greig, Clarence, 1935- II. Title. III. Series.

Plisetskaia, Maiia Mikhailovna, 1926—

MAYA Plisetskaya 792.8'092'4 B
/ Andrei Voznesensky ... [et al. ; compiled by Galina Kapterova ; translated from the Russian by Kathleen Cook]. Moscow : Progress Publishers, 1976. 152 p. : ill. ; 27 cm. Translation of Maiia Plisetskaia. [GV1785.P55M3913] 77-358743
1. Plisetskaia, Maiia Mikhailovna, 1926 2. Dancers—Russia—Biography. I. Voznesenskii, Andrei Andreevich.

Pliushch, Leonid Ivanovich, 1939—

PLIUSHCH, Leonyd 364.1'3 B
Ivanovych, 1939-
History's carnival : a dissident's autobiography / Leonid Plyushch ; with a contribution by Tatyana Plyushch ; edited and translated by Marco Carynnyk. 1st ed. New York : Harcourt Brace Jovanovich, c1979. xvii, 429 p. ; 25 cm. Translated from the author's manuscript: V karnavale istorii. "A Helen and Kurt Wolff Book." Includes bibliographical references and index. [DK274.P5413] 77-92544 ISBN 0-15-141614-1. : 14.95
1. Pliushch, Leonid Ivanovich, 1939- 2. Russia—Politics and government—1953- 3. Political prisoners—Russia—Biography. 4. Psychiatric hospitals—Russia. I. Pliushch, Tania. II. Title. **BIP**

Plockhoy, Pieter Corneliszoon, fl.1659.

HARDER, Leland, 1926- 922.87492
Plockhoy from Zurik-Zee; the study of a Dutch reformer in Puritan England and colonial America [by] Leland Harder and Marvin Harder. Newton, Kan., Board of Education and Publication [General Conference Mennonite Church] 1952. x, 255p. illus., map. facsims. 20cm. The writings of Plockhoy;: p 108-205. (Mennonite historical series, no.2) Includes bibliographical references. [BX8129.G4M4 vol.2] A54
1. Plockhoy, Pieter Corneliszoon, fl.1659. I. Harder, Marvin Andrew, 1921- joint author. II. Title. III. Series.

Plomer, William Charles Franklyn, 1903-1973—Biography.

PLOMER, William Charles Franklyn, 1903- 928.2
Double lives, an autobiography. New York, Noonday Press [1956] 254p. 20cm. [PR6031] 56-12293
I. Title.

PLOMER, William Charles Franklyn, 1903-1973. 828'.9'1209 B
The autobiography of William Plomer / with a postscript by Simon Nowell-Smith. New York : Taplinger Pub. Co., 1976, c1975. 455 p., [6] leaves of plates : ill. ; 23 cm. Includes bibliographical references and index. [PR6031.L7Z524 1976] 75-10548 ISBN 0-8008-0543-7 : 20.00
1. Plomer, William Charles Franklyn, 1903-1973—Biography. I. Title. BIP

Plotinus.

PLOTINUS. 186'.4
The essence of Plotinus : extracts from the six Enneads and Porphyry's Life of Plotinus, based on the translation by Stephen Mackenna : with an appendix giving some of the most important Platonic and Aristotelian sources on which Plotinus drew, and an annotated bibliography / compiled by Grace H. Turnbull ; foreword by W. R. Inge. Westport, Conn. : Greenwood Press, 1976. p. cm. Reprint of the 1934 ed. published by Oxford University Press, New York. Includes index. Bibliography: p. [B693.E53M3 1976] 76-40320 ISBN 0-8371-9054-1 lib.bdg. : 18.75
1. Plotinus. 2. Philosophy. 3. Philosophers—Greece—Biography. I. Mackenna, Stephen, 1872-1934. II. Turnbull, Grace Hill, 1880- III. Porphyrius. Plotini vita. English. Selections. 1976. IV. Title.

Plotkin, Abe L.

PLOTKIN, Abe L. 926.3
Struggle for justice: the autobiography of Abe L. Plotkin; an immigrant's life as a farmer in Saskatchewan and apartment house builder in Los Angeles. Foreword by Oakland W. Valley. New York, Exposition Press 187p. illus. 21cm. 60-509 4.00
I. Title.

PLOTKIN, Abe L 1889- 926.3
Struggle for justice: the autobiography of Abe L. Plotkin; an immigrant's life as a farmer in Saskatchewan and apartment house builder in Los Angeles. Foreword by Oakland W. Valleau. [1st ed.] New York, Exposition Press [1960] 187p. illus. 21cm. [CT310.P55A3] 60-509
I. Title.

Plumer, William, 1759-1850.

PLUMER, William, 1789-1854. 328.73'0924 B
Life of William Plumer, by William Plumer, Jr. Edited by A. P. Peabody. New York, Da Capo Press, 1969. xvi, 543 p. ports. 24 cm. (A Da Capo Press reprint edition) Reprint of the 1857 ed. [E302.6.P73P7 1969] 77-87384
1. Plumer, William, 1759-1850. 2. U.S.—Politics and government—1801-1809. 3. New Hampshire—Politics and government—1775-1865. I. Peabody, Andrew Preston, 1811-1893, ed. BIP

TURNER, Lynn W. 923.273
William Plumer of New Hampshire, 1759-1850. Chapel Hill, Pub. for the Inst. of Early Amer. Hist. and Culture, Williamsburg, Va., by Univ. of N. C. Pr. [c.1962] 366p. illus. 24cm. Bibl. 62-4988 7.50
1. Plumer, William, 1759-1850. I. Title.

TURNER, Lynn W 923.273
William Plumer of New Hampshire, 1759-1850. Chapel Hill, Published for the Institute of Early American History and Culture. Williamsburg.,Va., by University of North Carolina Press [1962] 366 p. illus. 24 cm. Based on thesis, Harvard University. Includes bibliography. [E302.6.P73T8] 62-4988
1. Plumber, Williams, 1759-1850. I. Title. BIP

Plummer, Clarissa.

PLUMMER, Clarissa. 973'.04'97 S
Narrative of the captivity of Clarissa Plummer, 1838. New York : Garland Pub., 1977 [c1838] 23 p. : ill. ; 23 cm. (The Garland library of narratives of North American Indian captivities ; 54) Reprint of the ed. published by Perry and Cooke, New York, under title: Narrative of the captivity and extreme sufferings of Mrs. Clarissa Plummer. Issued with the reprint of the 1838 ed. of Harris, C. History of the captivity of Caroline Harris. New York, 1977; the reprint of the 1839 ed. of Horn, S. A. Narrative of the captivity of Mrs. Horn with Mrs. Harris. New York, 1977; the reprint of the 1851 ed. of Horn, S.A. Narrative of the captivity of Mrs. Horn with Mrs. Harris. New York, 1977; the reprint of the 1839 ed. of Clark, R. Narrative of Ransom Clark. New York, 1977; and with the reprint of the 1839 ed. of Hubbard, R. Historical sketches of Roswell Franklin and family. New York, 1977. [E85.G2 vol. 54] [E99.C85] 970'.004'97 76-51850 ISBN 0-8240-1678-5 lib.bdg. : 25.00
1. Plummer, Clarissa. 2. Harris, Caroline. 3. Comanche Indians—Captivities. 4. Indians of North America—Captivities. 5. United States—Biography. I. Title. II. Series.

Plummer, Henry Stanley, 1874-1936.

WILLIUS, Fredrick Arthur, 1888- 926.1
Henry Stanley Plummer, a diversified genius. Springfield, Ill., Thomas [c1960] viii, 71 p. illus., ports., map. 21 cm. [R154.P69W5 1960] 60-14762
1. Plummer, Henry Stanley, 1874-1936. I. Title.

Plunket, Jean Reasoner.

PLUNKET, Jean Reasoner. 741'.092'4
Faces that won't sit still : celebrated subjects by a prominent portrait artist and how they were captured / by Jean Reasoner Plunket, with Barbara Brandt Ward. Washington : Acropolis Books, c1978. 201 p. : ill. ; 29 cm. [NC139.P57A2 1978] 78-14259 ISBN 0-87491-261-X : 18.00. pbk. : 9.95. ISBN 0-87491-260-1 lim. deluxe ed. : 35.00
1. Plunket, Jean Reasoner. 2. Portrait painters—United States—Biography. 3. Children—Portraits. 4. Portrait drawing—Technique. I. Ward, Barbara Brandt, joint author. II. Title. BIP

Plunket, Oliver. Abp., 1629-1681.

CURTAYNE, Alice. 922.2415
The trial of Oliver Plunkett. London, New York, Sheed and Ward [1953] 239p. illus. 23cm. [BX4705.P6515C8 1953] 53-12997
1. Plunket, Oliver. Abp., 1629-1681. I. Title.

ROBERTO, Brother, 1927- 922.2415
Now comes the hangman; a story of Blessed Oliver Plunkett. Illus. by Brother Eagan. Notre Dame, Ind., Dujarie Press [1956] 95p. illus. 24cm. [BX4705.P6515R6] 56-25349
1. Plunket, Oliver, Abp., 1629-1681. I. Title.

Plunkett, Jim—Juvenile literature.

BATSON, Larry, 1930- 796.33'2'0924 B
Jim Plunkett / written by Larry Batson. Mankato, Minn. : Creative Education, [1976] p. cm. [GV939.P63B37] 76-27640 ISBN 0-87191-570-7 : 5.95
1. Plunkett, Jim—Juvenile literature. 2. Quarterback (Football)—Biography—Juvenile literature. I. Title.

Plunkett, Jim, 1947-

*GUTMAN, Bill. 796.33'2'0924
Jim Plunkett. New York, Grosset & Dunlap [1973] 87 p. photos. 21 cm. (A Thistle Book) [GV939] 72-92926 ISBN 0-448-21470-9 1.50 (pbk.)
1. Plunkett, Jim, 1947- I. Title.

Plunkett, John Hubert, 1802-1869.

MOLONY, John Neylon. 354'.944'0650924 B
An architect of freedom: John Hubert Plunkett in New South Wales, 1832-1869 [by] John N. Molony. Canberra, Australian National University Press, 1973. 313 p. front. (port.) 23 cm. Includes index. Bibliography: p. 281-302. [LAW] 72-97976 ISBN 0-7081-0462-2
1. Plunkett, John Hubert, 1802-1869. I. Title.
Distributed by Intl. Scholarly Book Service, 18.50

*Plutarch

*PLUTARCH 920.03
Lives of nine illustrious Greeks and Romans. The Dryden-Clough tr. Selected ed., introd. by Wendell Clausen. New York, Washington Sq. [c.1964] 416p. illus. 18cm. (W 509) .60 pap.,
I. Title.

PLUTARCH. 920.03
The rise and fall of Athens; nine Greek lives by Plutarch. Translated [from the Greek] by Ian Scott-Kilvert. [Baltimore] Penguin Books [1960] 318p. maps. 19cm. (Penguin Classics L102) 1.25 pap.,
I. Title.

Plutarchus.

JONES, Christopher Prestige. 938'.0072'024 B
Plutarch and Rome, [by] C. P. Jones. Oxford, Clarendon Press, 1971. xiii, 158 p. 23 cm. Bibliography: p. [139]-147. [PA4382.J6] 72-873625 ISBN 0-19-814363-X £2.75
1. Plutarchus. 2. Rome—History. I. Title. BIP

PLUTARCHUS. 920.03
Everybody's Plutarch. Arr. and edited for the modern reader from the "Parallel lives" and with an introd. by Raymond T. Bond. New York, Dodd, Mead [1962, c1931] ix, 780 p. illus., ports. 22 cm. (Great illustrated classics: Titan editions) "The translation used is that called Dryden's, corrected from the Greek and revised by Arthur Hugh Clough." [DE7.P5 1962] 62-9722
1. Greece—Biography. 2. Rome—Biography. I. Dryden, John, 1631-1700, tr. II. Clough, Arthur Hugh, 1819-1861, ed. III. Bond, Raymond Tostevin, 1893- ed. IV. Title.

WARDMAN, Alan. 329'.0092'2 B
Plutarch's Lives. Berkeley, University of California Press, 1974. xiii, 274 p. 23 cm. Bibliography: p. [259]-261. [PA4385.W3] 73-89369 ISBN 0-520-02663-2 11.95
1. Plutarchus. Vitae parallelae. I. Title. BIP

Plutarchus—Biography.

BARROW, Reginald Haynes, 1893- 938'.007'2024 B
Plutarch and his times / by R. H. Barrow. 1st AMS ed. New York : AMS Press, 1979. xv, 202 p. : map ; 23 cm. Reprint of the 1967 ed. published by Indiana University Press, Bloomington. Includes index. Bibliography: p. 199-200. [PA4382.B3 1979] 76-6599 ISBN 0-404-15276-7 : 19.00
1. Plutarchus—Biography. 2. Plutarchus—Contemporary Rome. 3. Rome—Civilization. I. Title. BIP

Po Sein, U, 1880-1952.

SEIN, Kenneth, 1918- 792.0924
The great Po Sein; a chronicle of the Burmese theater, by Kenneth (Maung Khe) Sein, J. A. Withey. Drawings by Ba Lose Lay. Bloomington, Indiana Univ. Pr. [1966, c.1965] xiv, 170p. illus., ports. 25cm. Bibl. [PN2960.B8S4] 65-19705 4.95
1. Po Sein, U, 1880-1952. 2. Theater—Burma. I. Withey, Joseph A., joint author. II. Title.

Poaching—Gt. Brit.

HAWKER, James, 1836-1921. 927.992
A Victorian poacher; James Hawker's journal. Edited and introduced by Garth Christian. London, New York, Oxford University Press, 1961. 113p. illus. 19cm. [SK17.H29A3] 61-66314
1. Poaching—Gt. Brit. I. Title.

Pobedonostsev, Konstantine Petrovich, 1827-1907.

BYRNES, Robert Francis. 947.08'0924 B
Pobedonostsev, his life and thought [by] Robert F. Byrnes. Bloomington, Indiana University Press [1968] xiii, 495 p. ports. 25 cm. (Indiana University international studies) Bibliography: p. 369-409. [DK236.P6B8] 68-14598
1. Pobedonostsev, Konstantine Petrovich, 1827-1907. I. Series: Indiana. University. International studies.

Pocahontas, d. 1617.

BARBOUR, Philip L. 975.5'01'0924 B
Pocahontas and her world; a chronicle of America's first settlement in which is related the story of the Indians and the Englishmen, particularly Captain John Smith, Captain Samuel Argall, and Master John Rolfe [by] Philip L. Barbour. Boston, Houghton Mifflin, 1970 [c1969] xx, 320 p. illus., maps, ports. 22 cm. Bibliography: p. [283]-299. [F234.J3B38] 70-100621 6.95
1. Pocahontas, d. 1617. 2. Jamestown, Va.—History. I. Title.

GERSON, Noel Bertram, 1914- 975.5'01'0924 B
First lady of America; a romanticized biography of Pocahontas, by Leon Phillips. Foreword by Clifford Dowdey. [1st ed.] Richmond, Va., Westover Pub. Co. [1973] 203, [2] p. 25 cm. (A Media General publication) Bibliography: p. [204]-[205] [E99.P85G47] 72-96994 ISBN 0-87858-033-6 8.95
1. Pocahontas, d. 1617. 2. Powhatan Indians. I. Title.

MOSSIKER, Frances. 975.5'01'0924 B
Pocahontas : the life and the legend / by Frances Mossiker. 1st ed. New York : Knopf : distributed by Random House, 1976. p. cm. Includes index. Bibliography: p. [E99.P85P575 1976] 76-13720 ISBN 0-394-46082-0 : 12.95
1. Pocahontas, d.1617.

WOODWARD, Grace Steele. 975.5'01'0924 B

Pocahontas. [1st ed.] Norman, University of Oklahoma Press [1969] xv, 227 p. illus., ports. (both part col.) 23 cm. (The Civilization of the American Indian series [93]) [E90.P6W6] 68-15687
1. Pocahontas, d. 1617. I. Title. II. Series. BIP

Pocahontas, d. 1617—Juvenile literature.

FABER, Doris, 1924- 92
The life of Pocahontas. Illus. by Elinor Jaeger. Englewood Cliffs, N.J., Prentice [c.1963] 72p. illus. 22cm. 63-13290 2.84 lib. ed.,
1. Pocahontas, d. 1617—Juvenile literature. I. Title.

MARTIN, Patricia Miles. 92
Pocahontas. Illustrated by Portia Takakjian. New York, Putnam [1964] 63 p. col. illus. 23 cm. (A See and read beginning to read biography) [E90.P6M3] 64-13037

RICHARDS, Dorothy 975.5'01'0924 B
Fay, 1915-
Child-Princess Pocahontas / by Dorothy Fay Richards ; illustrated by John Nelson. Elgin, Ill. : Child's World ; Chicago : distributed by Childrens Press, c1978. p. cm. A brief account of the life of the Indian princess who befriended Captain John Smith and the English settlers of Jamestown. [E99.P85P577] 78-7719 ISBN 0-89565-035-5 : 7.35
1. Pocahontas, d. 1617—Juvenile literature. 2. Smith, John, 1580-1631—Juvenile literature. 3. Powhatan Indians—Biography—Juvenile literature. I. Nelson, John, 1928- II. Title.

WILKIE, Katharine 975.5'01'0924 B
Elliott, 1904-
Pocahontas, Indian princess, by Katharine E. Wilkie. Illustrated by William Hutchinson. Champaign, Ill., Garrard Pub. Co. [1969] 80 p. illus., map (both col.) 23 cm. Brief biography of the Indian princess who saved the life of the leader of the Jamestown settlers and who later married an Englishman with whom she visited London. [E90.P6W5] 92 69-10375
1. Pocahontas, d. 1617—Juvenile literature. I. Hutchinson, William M., illus. II. Title.

Poe, Edgar Allan, 1809-1849.

ALLEN, Hervey, 1889- v. 12
Israfel, the life and times of Edgar Allan Poe. New York, Holt, Rinehart and Winston [1960, c1934] 748p. illus., ports., facsims. 22cm. Third printing, December, 1960.
1. Poe, Edgar Allan, 1809-1849. I. Title.

BAUDELAIRE, Charles 818'.3'09
Pierre, 1821-1867.
Edgar Allan Poe: sa vie et ses ouvrages. Edited by W. T. Bandy. [Toronto, Buffalo] University of Toronto Press [1973] xlvi, 128 p. 24 cm. (University of Toronto romance series, no. 22) Text in French; introd. and textual notes in English. Bibliography: p. [117]-128. [PS2631.B33 1973] 73-81753 ISBN 0-8020-5280-0 10.00
1. Poe, Edgar Allen, 1809-1849. I. Bandy, William Thomas, 1903- ed. II. Series: Toronto. University. University of Toronto romance series, no. 22.

BITTNER, William Robert 928.1
Poe, a biography. Boston, Atlantic-Little [c.1962] 306p. illus. 22cm. Bibl. 62-16955 6.50
1. Poe, Edgar Allan, 1809-1849. I. Title. BIP

BRADDY, Haldeen, 1908- 818'.3'07
Three dimensional Poe. El Paso, Texas Western Press, 1973. xi, 86 p. 24 cm. Bibliography: p. [51]-81. [PS2631.B72] 73-75915 ISBN 0-87404-045-0 10.00
1. Poe, Edgar Allan, 1809-1849. 2. Poe, Edgar Allan, 1809-1849—Bibliography. I. Title. BIP

CAMPBELL, Killis, 1872- 928.1
1937.
The mind of Poe, and other studies. New York, Russell & Russell, 1962. 237 p. 21 cm. [PS2631.C3 1962] 62-10679
1. Poe, Edgar Allan, 1809-1849. I. Title.

BIP

CHASE, Lewis Nathaniel, 811'.3
1873-1937.
Poe and his poetry. London, Harrap, 1913. [New York, AMS Press, 1971] 129, [2] p. port. 19 cm. (Poetry and life series) Bibliography: p. [131] [PS2631.C5 1971] 72-120973 ISBN 0-404-52506-7 8.00
1. Poe, Edgar Allan, 1809-1849. I. Title. II. Series.

CHASE, Lewis Nathaniel, 811'.3
1873-1937.
Poe and his poetry / by Lewis Chase. New York : Haskell House, [1976] p. cm. Reprint of the 1924 ed. published by Harrap, London, which was issued as v. 17 of Poetry and life series. [PS2631.C5 1976] 75-38649 ISBN 0-8383-2112-7 : 9.95
1. Poe, Edgar Allen, 1809-1849. I. Title. II. Series: Poetry and life series ; v. 17. BIP

†CHASE, Lewis Nathaniel, 811'.3
1873-1937.
Poe and his poetry / by Lewis Chase. Folcroft, Pa. : Folcroft Library Editions, 1976. 129, [2] p. : port. ; 23 cm. Reprint of the 1913 ed. published by G. G. Harrap, London, which was issued as no. 17 of Poetry and life series. Bibliography: p. [13] [PS2631.C5 1976b] 76-49656 ISBN 0-8414-3453-0 lib. bdg. : 8.00
1. Poe, Edgar Allan, 1809-1849. 2. Authors, American—19th century—Biography. I. Title. II. Series: Poetry and life series ; 17.

CHIVERS, Thomas Holley, 928.1
1809-1858.
Life of Poe; edited with an introd. by Richard Beale Davis, from the mss. in the Henry E. Huntington Library, San Marino, Calif. [1st ed.] New York, Dutton, 1952. 127 p. port. 22 cm. Bibliographical references included in "Explanatory notes" (p. [101]-121) [PS2631.C53] 52-5295
1. Poe, Edgar Allan. 1809-1849. I. Davis, Richard Beale. ed. II. Title.

DILLON, John Milton, 818'.3'09
1868-1911.
Edgar Allan Poe: his genius and character. [Folcroft, Pa.] Folcroft Library Editions, 1973 [c1911] xviii, 109 p. port. 23 cm. Reprint of the ed. published by Knichkerbocker Press, New York. [PS2631.D53 1973] 73-480 ISBN 0-8414-1334-7 (lib. bdg.)
1. Poe, Edgar Allan, 1809-1849.

EVELETH, George 818'.3'09 B
Washington.
The letters from George W. Eveleth to Edgar Allan Poe. Edited by Thomas Ollive Mabbott. [Folcroft, Pa.] Folcroft Library Editions, 1972. 27 p. illus. 33 cm. Reprint of the 1922 ed., published by the New York Public Library. Includes bibliographical references. [PS2631.E9 1973] 73 1872 ISBN 0-8414-5915-0 (lib. bdg.)
1. Poe, Edgar Allan, 1809-1849. I. Poe, Edgar Allan, 1809-1849. II. Mabbott, Thomas Ollive, 1898-1968, ed. BIP

HARRISON, James Albert, 818'.3'09
1848-1911.
Life of Edgar Allan Poe. New York, Haskell House, 1970. viii, 455 p. illus., facsims., ports. 23 cm. Reprint of the 1903 ed. "Bibliography of the writings of Edgar A. Poe": p. [431]-455. [PS2631.H4 1970] 70-115184
1. Poe, Edgar Allan, 1809-1849. I. Title. BIP

LEIGH, Oliver. 818'.3'09
Edgar Allan Poe; the man, the master, the martyr, by Oliver Leigh ("Geoffrey Quarles") [Folcroft, Pa.] Folcroft Library Editions, 1972 [c1906] 78 p. illus. 23 cm. Original ed. issued as no. 1 of the Dilettante series. 150 copies printed. [PS2635.L4 1972] 72-186977
1. Poe, Edgar Allan, 1809-1849. BIP

LINDSAY, Philip, 1906- 928.1
The haunted man; a portrait of Edgar Allan Poe. New York, Philosophical Library [1954] 276p. illus. 22cm. [PQ2631] 54-11394
1. Poe, Edgar Allan, 1809-1849. I. Title.

OLIVERO, Federico, 818'.3'09
1878-
Edgar Allan Poe. New York, AMS Press [1972] 234 p. 24 cm. Reprint of the 1932 ed. Bibliography: p. [213]-221. [PS2631.O6 1972] 79-144666 ISBN 0-404-04818-8 6.50
1. Poe, Edgar Allan, 1809-1849.

POE, Edgar Allan, 810'.9'003 B
1809-1849.
A chapter on autography / by Edgar Allan Poe ; edited by Don C. Seitz. New York : Haskell House, 1974 [i.e. 1975] 92 p. : ill. ; 20 cm. Reprint of the 1926 ed. published by L. Macveagh, New York. [PS128.P6 1975] 74-30363 ISBN 0-8383-2067-8 : 9.95
1. Authors, American—Autographs—Facsimiles. 2. Authors, American. I. Title.

POE, Edgar Allan 1809-1849. v. 12
Edgar Allan Poe; his life, letters, and opinions. Ingram, John Henry, 1842-1916. New York, Ams Press,[1965] vii, 488 p. 19 cm. 65-89000
1. Poe, Edgar Allan, 1809-1849 I. Title.

POE, Edgar Allan, 818'.3'09 B
1809-1849.
Edgar Allan Poe letters till now unpublished, in the Valentine Museum, Richmond, Virginia. Introductory essay and commentary by Mary Newton Stanard. With fac-similes of all letters. New York, Haskell House [1973] 327 p. illus. 24 cm. Reprint of the 1925 ed. published by Lippincott, Philadelphia. [PS2631.A34 1973] 72-11698 ISBN 0-8383-1692-1 24.95
I. Valentine Museum, Richmond, Va.

POE, Edgar Allan, 1809- 810.81
1849.
The enigma of Poe. Edited by Warren U. Ober, Paul S. Burtness, and William R. Seat, Jr. Boston, Heath [c1960] 149p. 24cm. 'The materials here presented fall into three general sections: 1. Imaginative and critical works by Poe. 2. Selected letters of Poe and his circle. 3. Biographical and critical evaluations of Poe.' [PS2602.O2] 61-2039
1. Poe, Edgar Allan, 1809-1849. I. Ober, Warren U., ed. II. Title.

POE, Edgar Allan, 1809- 818'.3'09
1849.
Poe—man, poet, and creative thinker, by Sherwin Cody. Port Washington, N.Y., Kennikat Press [1973, c1924] xiii, 485 p. 20 cm. [PS2603.C6 1973] 72-85316 ISBN 0-8046-1731-7 17.50
I. Cody, Sherwin, 1868-1959, ed. II. Title.

POE, Elisabeth 818'.3'09 B
Ellicott, 1888-1947.
Edgar Allan Poe, a high priest of the beautiful; a biographical essay supplemented by select Poe poems, including "The raven," "The bells," "Annabel Lee," etc., by Elisabeth Ellicott Poe and Vylla Poe Wilson. [Folcroft, Pa.] Folcroft Library Editions, 1973 [c1930] 112 p. 24 cm. [PS2631.P6 1973] 72-14322 12.50
1. Poe, Edgar Allan, 1809-1849. I. Wilson, Vylla (Poe) joint author.

POPE-HENNESSY, Una 818'.3'09 B
(Birch) Dame, 1876-1949.
Edgar Allan Poe, 1809-1849; a critical biography. New York, Haskell House, 1971. xii, 342 p. port. 23 cm. Reprint of the 1934 ed. Bibliography: p. 334-[335] [PS2631.P67 1971] 77-92977 ISBN 0-8383-0998-4
1. Poe, Edgar Allan, 1809-1849.

PORGES, Irwin. 928.1
Edgar Allan Poe. [1st ed.] Philadelphia, Chilton Books [1963] 191 p. 20 cm. Bibliography: p. 185. [PS2631.P68] 68-21333
1. Poe, Edgar Allan, 1800-1849. I. Title.

PORGES, Irwin 928.1
Edgar Allan Poe. Philadelphia, Chilton [c.1963] 191p. 20cm. Bibl. 63-21333 3.95
1. Poe, Edgar Allean, 1809-1849. I. Title.

QUINN, Arthur Hobson, 818'.3'09 B
1875-
Edgar Allan Poe, a critical biography. New York, Cooper Square, 1969 [c1941] xvi, 804 p. illus., facsims., ports. 24 cm. Bibliography: p. 763-770. [PS2631.Q5 1969] 76-97465 ISBN 0-8154-0313-5
1. Poe, Edgar Allan, 1809-1849.

QUINN, Arthur Hobson, 1875- v. 12
Edgar Allan Poe, a critical biography, by Arthur Hobson Quinn. New York, Appleton-Century Crofts [1963, c1941] xvi, 804 p. front., illus., plates, ports, facsims. 24 cm. Bibliography: p. 763-770. 68-10024
1. Poe, Edgar Allan, 1800-1849. I. Title. BIP

ROBERTSON, John 818'.3'09
Wooster, 1856-
Edgar A. Poe; a study, by John W. Robertson. New York, Haskell House Publishers, 1970. 424 p. illus., facsims., ports. 23 cm. Reprint of the 1921 ed. [PS2631.R6 1970] 71-117583
1. Poe, Edgar Allan, 1809-1849. 2. Poe, Edgar Allan, 1809-1849—Bibliography.

STOVALL, Floyd, 1896- 811'.3
Edgar Poe the poet; essays new and old on the man and his work. Charlottesville, University Press of Virginia [1969] vii, 273 p. port. 25 cm. [PS2631.S8] 75 82532
1. Poe, Edgar Allan, 1809-1849. I. Title.

SYMONS, Julian, 1912- 818'.3'09 B
The tell-tale heart : the life and works of Edgar Allan Poe / Julian Symons. 1st ed. New York : Harper & Row, c1978. x, 259 p. ; 25 cm. "A Joan Kahn book." Includes index. Bibliography: p. 242-245. [PS2631.S95] 77-15881 ISBN 0-06-014208-1 : 12.95
1. Poe, Edgar Allan, 1809-1849. 2. Authors, American—19th century—Biography. I. Title. BIP

WAGENKNECHT, Edward 928.1
Charles, 1900-
Edgar Allan Poe; the man behind the legend. New York, Oxford University Press, 1963. 276 p. port. 21 cm. Bibliographical references included in "Notes" (p. 223-260) "Note on Bibliography": p. 261-266. [PS2631.W3] 63-17740
1. Poe, Edgar Allan, 1809-1849.

WINWAR, Frances, pseud. 928.1
The haunted palace; a life of Edgar Allan Poe. [1st ed.] New York, Harper [1959] 408 p. illus. 22 cm. Includes bibliography. [PS2631.W57] 58-12457
1. Poe, Edgar Allan, 1809-1849. I. Title.

WOODBERRY, George Edward, 818.309
1855-1930
The life of Edgar Allan Poe, personal and literary; with his chief correspondence with men of letters. v. 1&2. New York, Biblo & Tannen. 1965. 2v. (383;481p.) illus., facsims., ports. 22cm. First pub., 1909. [PS2631.W7] 65-23484 15.00 set.
1. Poe, Edgar Allan, 1809-1849. I. Title.

Poe, Edgar Allan, 1809-1849—Bibliography.

PHILLIPS, Leona 016.818'3'09
Rasmussen.
Edgar Allan Poe : an annotated bibliography / by Leona Rasmussen Phillips. New York : Gordon Press, 1978. p. cm. (Gordon Press bibliographies for librarians series) [Z8699.P48] [PS2631] 78-6783 ISBN 0-8490-1392-5 lib. bdg. : 39.95
1. Poe, Edgar Allan, 1809-1849—Bibliography.

Poe, Edgar Allan, 1809-1849—Biography.

FACTS about Poe. 818'.3'09
[Folcroft, Pa.] Folcroft Library Editions, 1972 [c1926] 58 p. ports. 24 cm. Original ed. issued in series: University of Virginia record. Extension series, v. 10, no. 8. Contents.Contents.—Wilson, J. S. Facts about Poe; a brief sketch of the life of Edgar Allan Poe.—A selected bibliography of Poe (p. [23]-25)—Schulte, A. P. The portraits & daguerreotypes of Edgar Allan Poe. [PS2631F26 1972] 72-10098 ISBN 0-8414-0629-4 (lib. bdg.)
1. Poe, Edgar Allan, 1809-1849—Biography. 2. Poe, Edgar Allan, 1809-1849—Portraits, etc. I. Wilson, James Southall, 1880-1963. Facts about Poe; a brief sketch of the life of Edgar Allan Poe.

1972. II. Schulte, Amanda Pogue. The portraits & daguerreotypes of Edgar Allan Poe. 1972. III. Title. IV. Series: Virginia. University. School of General Studies. University of Virginia record. Extension series, v. 10, no. 8.

LINDSAY, Philip, 1906- 818'.3'09 B
The haunted man : a portrait of Edgar Allan Poe / by Philip Lindsay. Folcroft, Pa. : Folcroft Library Editions, 1978. p. cm. Reprint of the 1953 ed. published by Hutchinson, London. [PS2631.L49 1978] 78-23799 ISBN 0-8414-5841-3 lib. bdg. : 27.50
1. Poe, Edgar Allan, 1809-1849—Biography. 2. Authors, American—19th century—Biography. I. Title.

MACY, John Albert, 1877-1932. 818'.3'09 B
Edgar Allan Poe / by John Macy. New York : Haskell House Publishers, [1976] c1907. p. cm. Reprint of the ed. published by Small, Maynard, Boston, in series: The Beacon biographies of eminent Americans. Bibliography: p. [PS2631.M3 1976] 75-30869 ISBN 0-8383-2090-2 pbk. : 9.95
1. Poe, Edgar Allan, 1809-1849—Biography. I. Series: The Beacon biographies of eminent Americans (Boston)

MACY, John Albert, 1877-1932. 818'.3'09 B
Edgar Allan Poe / by John Macy. Folcroft, Pa. : Folcroft Library Editions, 1974, [c1907] p. cm. Reprint of the ed. published by Small, Maynard, Boston, in series: The Beacon biographies of eminent Americans. Bibliography: p. [PS2631.M3 1974] 74-22182 ISBN 0-8414-5955-X lib. bdg. : 10.00
1. Poe, Edgar Allan, 1809-1849—Biography. I. Series: The Beacon biographies of eminent Americans (Boston)

MANKOWITZ, Wolf. 818'.3'09 B
The extraordinary Mr. Poe : a biography of Edgar Allan Poe / by Wolf Mankowitz. New York : Summit Books, c1978. 248 p. : ill. : 26 cm. Includes index. Bibliography: p. [243] [PS2631.M35] 78-918 ISBN 0-671-40042-8 : 15.00
1. Poe, Edgar Allan, 1809-1849—Biography. 2. Authors, American—19th century—Biography. I. Title.

PALEY, Alan L. 818'.3'09 B
Edgar Allan Poe, American poet and mystery writer / by Alan L. Paley, compiled with the assistance of the research staff of SamHar Press. Charlotteville, N.Y. : SamHar Press, 1975. p. cm. (Outstanding personalities ; #84) Bibliography: p. [PS2631.P25] 75-16318 lib.bdg. : 2.29 pbk. : 0.98
1. Poe, Edgar Allan, 1809-1849—Biography. I. Title. BIP

POE, Elisabeth Ellicott, 1888-1947. 818'.3'09 B
Edgar Allan Poe, a high priest of the beautiful : a biographical essay supplemented by select Poe poems, including "The raven," "The bells," "Annabel Lee," etc. / by Elisabeth Ellicott Poe and Vylla Poe Wilson. Norwood, Pa. : Norwood Editions, 1976 [c1930] 112 p. ; 24 cm. Reprint of the ed. published by Stylus Pub. Co., Washington. [PS2631.P6 1976] 76-9796 ISBN 0-8482-2064-1 : 10.00
1. Poe, Edgar Allan, 1809-1849—Biography. I. Wilson, Vylla Poe, joint author. II. Poe, Edgar Allan, 1809-1849. Poems. 1976. III. Title.

REID, Mayne, 1818-1883. 818'.3'09 B
Edgar Allan Poe. [Folcroft, Pa.] Folcroft Library Editions, 1973. p. Reprint of the 1933 ed. published by E. B. Hill, Ysleta, Tex. Originally published in 1890 in Mayne Reid: a memoir of his life, by E. Reid. [PS2631.R4 1973] 73-13600 ISBN 0-8414-7223-8 (lib. bdg.)
1. Poe, Edgar Allan, 1809-1849—Biography.

SINCLAIR, David. 818'.3'09 B
Edgar Allan Poe / David Sinclair. Totowa, N.J. : Rowman and Littlefield, 1977. 272 p., [4] leaves of plates : ill. ; 24 cm. Includes index. Bibliography: p. [265]-268. [PS2631.S53 1977] 77-21661 ISBN 0-8476-6008-7 ; 13.50
1. Poe, Edgar Allan, 1809-1849—Biography. 2. Authors, American—19th century—Biography.

WEISS, Susan Archer Talley, 1835- 818'.3'09 B
The home life of Poe. [Folcroft, Pa.] Folcroft Library Editions, 1974 [c1907] 229 p. port. 23 cm. Reprint of the ed. published by Broadway Pub. Co., New York. [PS2631.W4 1974] 74-3361 30.00 (lib. bdg.).
1. Poe, Edgar Allan, 1809-1849—Biography. I. Title. BIP

Poe, Edgar Allan, 1809-1849—Biography—Last years.

NICHOLS, Mary Sargeant Gove, 1810-1884. 818'.3'09 B
Reminiscences of Edgar Allan Poe. [Folcroft, Pa.] Folcroft Library Editions, 1973. 14 p. 24 cm. Reprint of the 1931 ed. [PS2631.N5 1973] 73-1138 ISBN 0-8414-2350-4 4.00
1. Poe, Edgar Allan, 1809-1849—Biography—Last years. I. Title.

NICHOLS, Mary Sargeant Gove, 1810-1884. 818'.3'09 B
Reminiscences of Edgar Allan Poe. New York, Haskell House Publishers, 1974. 14 p. 20 cm. Reprint of the 1931 ed. published by Union Square Book Shop, New York. [PS2632.N5 1974] 74-4041 ISBN 0-8383-2068-6
1. Poe, Edgar Allan, 1809-1849—Biography—Last years. BIP

Poe, Edgar Allan, 1809-1849—Biography—Sources.

MILLER, John Carl. 818'.3'09 B
Building Poe biography / John Carl Miller. Baton Rouge : Louisiana State University Press, c1977. xix, 269 p. : ill. ; 24 cm. (Southern literary studies) Includes index. Bibliography: p. 254-260. [PS2630.5.M5] 76-47653 ISBN 0-8071-0195-8 : 20.00(v.1)
1. Poe, Edgar Allan, 1809-1849—Biography—Sources. 2. Ingram, John Henry, 1842-1916. 3. Authors, American—19th century—Biography. 4. Biographers—England—Correspondence. I. Title. BIP

WHITMAN, Sarah Helen Power, 1803-1878. 818'.3'09 B
Poe's Helen remembers / edited by John Carl Miller. Charlottesville : University Press of Virginia, 1979. p. cm. "Correspondence that passed between John Ingram and Sarah Helen Whitman from late 1873 through mid-1878." Includes index. [PS2630.5.W5 1979] 79-742 ISBN 0-8139-0771-3 : 24.95
1. Poe, Edgar Allan, 1809-1849—Biography—Sources. 2. Whitman, Sarah Helen Power, 1803-1878—Correspondence. 3. Ingram, John Henry, 1842-1916. 4. Authors, American—19th century—Biography. I. Ingram, John Henry, 1842-1916, joint author. II. Miller, John Carl. III. Title.

Poe, Edgar Allan, 1809-1849—Biography—Youth.

RUSSELL, John Thomas, 1935- 818'.3'09 B
Edgar Allan Poe: the Army years, by J. Thomas Russell. Foreword by Egon A. Weiss. West Point, N.Y., U.S. Military Academy, 1972. ix, 54 p. illus. 23 cm. (USMA Library bulletin, no. 10) Includes bibliographical references. [PS2632.R8] 73-601110
1. Poe, Edgar Allan, 1809-1849—Biography—Youth. 2. United States Military Academy, West Point. I. Series: United States. Military Academy, West Point. Library. USMA Library bulletin, no. 10.

Poe, Edgar Allan, 1809-1849—Correspondence.

POE, Edgar Allan, 1809-1849. 818'.3'09 B
Edgar Allan Poe letters till now unpublished, in the Valentine Museum, Richmond, Virginia. Introductory essay and commentary by Mary Newton Stanard. [Folcroft, Pa.] Folcroft Library Editions, 1974. p. cm. Reprint of the 1925 ed. published by Lippincott, Philadelphia. [PS2631.A34 1974] 74-14530 24.75 (lib. bdg.).
1. Poe, Edgar Allan, 1809-1849—Correspondence. 2. Allan, John, 1780-1834. I. Stanard, Mary Mann Page Newton, 1865-1929. II. Valentine Museum, Richmond, Va. III. Title.

POE, Edgar Allan, 1809-1849. 818'.3'09 B
The last letters of Edgar Allan Poe to Sarah Helen Whitman : in commemoration of the hundredth anniversary of Poe's birth, January 19, 1909 / edited by James A. Harrison. Folcroft, Pa. : Folcroft Library Editions, 1974 [c1909] viii, 50 p. : ports. ; 26 cm. "Published under the auspices of the University of Virginia." Reprint of the ed. published by Putnam, New York. [PS2631.A39 1974] 74-26841 ISBN 0-8414-4899-X lib. bdg. : 15.00
1. Poe, Edgar Allan, 1809-1849—Correspondence. 2. Whitman, Sarah Helen Power, 1803-1878. I. Whitman, Sarah Helen Power, 1803-1878. II. Harrison, James Albert, 1848-1911, ed. III. Title.

Poe, Edgar Allan, 1809-1849—Homes and haunts—Philadelphia.

ADELMAN, Seymour. 818'.3'09 B
Poe: Philadelphian; a keepsake. [Philadelphia] Friends of the Free Library of Philadelphia, [1972] 12 p. 23 cm. Cover title. [PS2634.A4] 72-189750
1. Poe, Edgar Allan, 1809-1849—Homes and haunts—Philadelphia. I. Philadelphia. Free Library. Friends. II. Title.

Poe, Edgar Allan, 1809-1849—Juvenile literature.

COOPER, Lettice Ulpha, 1897- 92
The young Edgar Allan Poe. Illus. by William Randell. New York, Roy [1965, c.1964] 135p. illus. 21cm [PS2631.C67] 64-23913 3.25 bds.,
1. Poe, Edgar Allan, 1809-1849—Juvenile literature. I. Title.

COOPER, Lettice Ulpha, 1897- 928'.1
The young Edgar Allan Poe [by] Lettice Cooper. Illustrated by William Randell. New York, Roy Publishers [1964] 135 p. illus. 21 cm. [PS2631.c67] 64-23913
1. Poe, Edgar Allan, 1809-1849—Juvenile literature. I. Title.

JACOBS, William Jay. 818'.3'09 B
Edgar Allan Poe : genius in torment / by William Jay Jacobs. New York : McGraw-Hill, [1975] 135 p. : port. ; 21 cm. Includes index. Bibliography: p. 130-131. A biography of the troubled nineteenth-century author with a discussion of his prose and poetry which greatly influenced prominent artists and writers throughout the world. [PS2631.J34] 92 74-32010 ISBN 0-07-032158-2 lib. bdg. : 5.72
1. Poe, Edgar Allan, 1809-1849—Juvenile literature. I. Title.

STERN, Philip Van Doren, 1900- 818'.3'09 B
Edgar Allan Poe, visitor from the night of time. New York, Crowell [1973] 172 p. 22 cm. Bibliography: p. [161]-164. Biography of an American writer who, in spite of his fame for such poems and stories as "The Raven," "Annabel Lee," "The Gold Bug," and "The Pit and the Pendulum," lived and died in poverty. [PS2631.S67] 92 72-83786 ISBN 0-690-25554-3 4.50
1. Poe, Edgar Allan, 1809-1849—Juvenile literature. I. Title.

Poe, Edgar Allan, 1809-1849—Miscellanea.

THE *Edgar Allan Poe scrapbook* : articles, essays, letters, anecdotes, illustrations, photographs, and memorabilia about the legendary American genius / edited by Peter Haining ; foreword by Robert Bloch. New York : Schocken Books, 1978, c1977. 144 p. : ill. ; 30 cm. [PS2631.E33 1978] 77-87863 ISBN 0-8052-3679-1 : 15.00 ISBN 0-8052-0583-7 pbk. : 7.95 818'.3'09 B
1. Poe, Edgar Allan, 1809-1849—Miscellanea. 2. Authors, American—19th century—Biography—Addresses, essays, lectures. I. Haining, Peter.

Poetry.

COBLENTZ, Stanton Arthur 928.1
My life in poetry. New York, Bookman Associates [c.1959] 182p. 23cm. 59-14624 3.50
1. Poetry. I. Title.

COBLENTZ, Stanton Arthur, 1896- 928.1
My life in poetry. New York, Bookman Associates [1959] 182p. 23cm. [PS3505.O144Z52] 59-14624
1. Poetry. I. Title.

SWIFT, Joan, 1926- 811'.5'4
This element : poems / by Joan Swift. New York : AMS Press, 1975, c1965. 41 p. ; 20 cm. Reprint of the ed. published by A. Swallow, Denver, in series: New poetry series. [PS3569.W5T5 1975] 71-179830 ISBN 0-404-56030-X : 12.50
I. Title.

Poets.

DA PONTE, Lorenzo, 1749-1838 709.'.24
Memoirs of Lorenzo Da Ponte. Tr. from Italian by Elisabeth Abbott. Ed., annotated by Arthur Livingston. New pref. by Thomas G. Bergin [Magnolia, Mass., P. Smith. 1968] x, 512p. illus., facsims., ports. 22cm. (Dover bk. on music, T1706 rebound) Unabridged, unaltered repubn. of the work first pub. in 1929 (B) 5.00
I. Title.

SCHNITTKIND, Henry Thomas, 1888- 928.2
Living biographies of great poets, by Henry Thomas [pseud.] and Dana Lee Thomas [pseud.] Garden City, N.Y., Perma Giants [1950, c1941] viii, 307 p. 22 cm. [PR503.S33 1950] 52-575
1. Poets. 2. Poets, English. 3. Poets, American I. Schnittkind, Dana Arnold, 1918- joint author. II. Title.

Poets, American.

BECKER, Kate Harbes. 928.1
Paul Hamilton Hayne: life and letters. Belmont, N. C., Outline Co., 1951. xi, 145 p. 23 cm. Bibliography: p. 139-141. [PS1908.B4] 51-12034
1. Hayne, Paul Hamilton, 1830-1886. II. Title.

BENET, Laura. 928.1
Famous American poets. New York, Dodd, Mead, 1950. 183 p. ports. 23 cm. (Famous biographies for young people) [PS303.B4] 50-6514
1. Poets, American. I. Title.

Poets, American—Biography—Juvenile literature.

LEIPOLD, L. Edmond, 1902- 811'.009 B
Great American poets, by L. Edmond Leipold. Minneapolis, Denison [1973] 59 p. col. illus. 25 cm. (His Lives of great Americans) Brief biographies of five American poets: Eugene Field, James Whitcomb Riley, Henry W. Longfellow, Edna St. Vincent Millay, and Robert Frost. [PS129.L43] 920 74-190690 3.99 (Lib. bdg.)
1. Poets, American—Biography—Juvenile literature. I. Title.

Poets, American—Juvenile literature.

LEIPOLD, L. Edmond, 1902- 811'.009
Famous American poets, by L. Edmond Leipold. Minneapolis, Denison [1969] 88 p. 25 cm. (His Famous American heroes and leaders series) Brief biographies of ten American poets: James Whitcomb Riley, Phillis Wheatley, Henry Wadsworth Longfellow, Langston Hughes, Edna St. Vincent Millay, Robert Frost, Walt Whitman, Eugene Field, Allen Tate, and Vachel Lindsay. [PS305.L4] 920 74-91281

1. Poets, American—Juvenile literature. I. Title. II. Series.

Poets, American—19th century—Juvenile literature.

HOFF, Rhoda. 811'.3
Four American poets: why they wrote; Dickinson, Longfellow, Poe, Whitman. New York, H. Z. Walck [1969] 143 p. 24 cm. Bibliography: p. 139-140. Brief biographical sketches and discussions of the poetry of four major American poets of the nineteenth century. Includes selections from their works. [PS321.H6] 920 69-17906 ISBN 0-8098-3078-7 4.50
1. Poets, American—19th century—Juvenile literature. 2. American poetry. I. Title.

Poets, American—20th century.

ALLEN, Everett S. 811'.009
Famous American humorous poets, by Everett S. Allen. New York, Dodd, Mead [1968] 127 p. ports. 22 cm. (Famous biographies for young people) Contents.Contents.—Franklin Pierce Adams.—Richard Willard Armour.—Margaret Fishback.—Arthur Guiterman.—Oliver Herford.—Samuel Goodman Hoffenstein.—Donald Robert Perry Marquis.—Phyllis McGinley.—Christopher Darlington Morley.—Ogden Nash.—Dorothy Parker.—James Whitcomb Riley.—Bert Leston Taylor. [PS129.A5] 68-16178
1. Poets, American—20th century. 2. Humorists, American. I. Title.

ALLEN, Everett S. 920
Famous American humorous poets, by Everett S. Allen. New York, Dodd, Mead [1968] 127 p. ports. 22 cm. (Famous biographies for young people) Biographical sketches of thirteen contemporary American writers of humorous verse: Franklin Pierce Adams, Richard Willard Armour, Margaret Fishback, Arthur Guiterman, Oliver Herford, Samuel Goodman Hoffenstein, Donald Robert Perry Marguis, Phyllis McGinley, Christopher Darlington Morley, Ogden Nash, Dorothy Parker, James Whitcomb Riley, and Bert Leston Taylor. [PS129.A5] AC 68
1. Poets, American 20th century. 2. Humorists, American. I. Title.

RICHARDS, Norman. 811'.5'2 B
Robert Frost. Chicago, Childrens Press [1968] 94 p. illus., ports. 29 cm. (People of destiny: a humanities series) Bibliography: p. 90. A biography of the man who became known as America's "national poet," stressing the rural emphasis of his poetry and his determination to succeed in spite of poverty and personal tragedy. Includes some of his poems. [PS3511.R94Z915] 92 AC 68
I Title.

Poets—Biography.

HARRISON, James Albert, 1848-1911. 809.1 B
A group of poets and their haunts. Freeport, N.Y., Books for Libraries Press [1973] p. (Essay index reprint series) Reprint of the 1875 ed. [PN452.H3 1973] 73-1177 ISBN 0-518-10044-8
1. Poets—Biography. I. Title.

VIZETELLY, Ernest Alfred, 1853-1922. 809.1 B
Loves of the poets. London, H. Hardingham, 1915. [Folcroft, Pa., Folcroft Library Editions, 1972] p. "Owing to the unfortunate illnes of Mr. E. A. Vizetelly, the last two chapters of this book were written by Mr. Walter M. Gallichan." Contents.Contents.—Introduction: troubadours and trouveres.—Some early Italian poets.—Some English poets of Tudor and Stuart days.—Some British poets: from Congreve to Goldsmoth.—Other English poets: from Churchill to Lytton.—Poets of recent days.—Loves of some French poets.—The love-life of Goethe. [PN481.V5 1972] 72-12901 ISBN 0-8414-1003-8 (lib. bdg.)
1. Poets—Biography. 2. Woman—Biography. I. Gallichan, Wlater M., 1861- II. Title. BIP

Poets, English.

BREGY, Katherine Marie Cornelia, 1888-1967. 821'.009
The poets' chantry. Port Washington, N.Y., Kennikat Press [1970] 181 p. ports. 21 cm. Reprint of the 1912 ed. The essays originally appeared in The Catholic world. Contents.Contents.—Robert Southwell.—William Habington.—Richard Crashaw.—Aubrey de Vere.—Gerard Hopkins.—Coventry Patmore.—Lionel Johnson.—Francis Thompson.—Alice Meynell.—Bibliography (p. 173-176) [PR106.B7 1970] 70-105766
1. Poets, English. I. Title. BIP

COURNOS, Helen Sybil Norton (Kestner), 1893- 928.2
Famous British poets, by Sybil Norton [pseud,] and John Cournos. New York, Dodd, Mead, 1952. 202 p. illus. 23 cm. (Famous biographies for young people). [PR504.C68] 52-9256
1. Poets, English. I. Title.

EMDEN, Cecil Stuart. 821'.009 B
Poets in their letters, by Cecil S. Emden. With drawings by Lynton Lamb. London, Oxford University Press, 1959. St. Clair Shores, Mich., Scholarly Press, 1971. xii, 232 p. illus. 22 cm. Includes bibliographical references. [PR106.E4 1971] 74-158501 ISBN 0-403-01300-3
1. Poets, English. 2. English letters—History and criticism. I. Title. BIP

HUDSON, Gertrude Reese, ed. 928.2
Browning to his American friends; letters between the Brownings, the Storys and James Russell Lowell, 1841-1890 edited with introd. and notes by Gertrude Reese Hudson. New York, Barnes and Noble [1965] xvi, 382 p. ports. 23 cm. Bibliography: p. 368-370. [PR4231.A3H8] 65-2653
I. Browning, Robert, 1812-1889. II. Title.

JOHNSON, Samuel, 1709-1784. 928.2
Lives of the English poets Introd. by Warren L. Fleisachauer. Chicago, Gateway Editions; distributed by H. Regnery Co. [1955] 400, [1]p. 18cm. Bibliography: p. [401] [PR553.J7 1955] 55-4216
1. Poets, English. 2. English poetry—Early modern (to 1700)—Hist. & crit. 3. English poetry—18th cent.—Hist. & crit. I. Title. BIP

JOHNSON, Samuel, 1709-1784. 928.2
Lives of the English poets. Introd., notes and bibliography by Warren L. Fleischauer. Chicago, H. Regnery Co. [1964] viii, 406 p. 17 cm. (A Gateway edition) "6014." Bibliography: p. [407]-408. [PR553.J8] 63-21415
1. Poets, English. 2. English poetry — Early modern (to 1700) — Hist. & crit. 3. English poetry — 18 cent. — Hist & crit. I. Title.

JOHNSON, Samuel, 1709-1784 821'.00922
Lives of the English poets. Ed. by George Birkbeck Hill. With brief memoir of Birkbeck Hill by Harold Spencer Scott. New York, Octagon 1967. 3 v. 24cm. This ed. first pub. in 1905. Titles of many of the works quoted in the notes: v. 3, p. [559]-568. Contents.v. 1. Cowley-Dryden. -- v. 2. Smith-Savage. -- v. 3. Swift-Lyttelton [PR553.J7 1967] 67-20301 45.00 set,
1. Poets, English. 2. English poetry — Early modern (to 1700) — Hist. & crit. 3. English poetry — 18th cent. — Hist. & crit. I. Hill, George Birkbeck Norman, 1835-1903, ed. II. Title.

JOHNSON, Samuel, 1709-1784. 821.'4'09
The six chief lives, from Johnson's Lives of the poets, with Macaulay's Life of Johnson. Edited, with a pref. by Matthew Arnold. New York, Russell & Russell [1968] xxv, 466 p. 20 cm. Reprint of the 1881 ed. [PR553.R8 1968] 68-25025
1. Poets, English. I. Macaulay, Thomas Babington Macaulay, Baron, 1800-1859. II. Arnold, Matthew, 1822-1888, ed. III. Title.

JONES, Frederick Lafayette, 1901- 928.2
The Shelley legend in White, Newman Ivey, 1892-1948. An examination of The Shelley legend. Philadelphia, Univ. of Pennsylvania Press, 1951. [PR5431.S76W5] 51-12162
I. Title.

LIVES of the English poets, v. 12 with an introduction by Arthur Waugh. London, New York, Oxford University Press [1955-56] 2v. (World's classics. 83-84) Reset in 1952 and reprinted in 1955-1956.
1. Poets, English. 2. English poetry—Early modern (to 1700)—Hist. & crit. 3. English poetry—18th cent.—Hist. & crit. I. Johnson, Samuel, 1709-1784.

ROSSETTI, William Michael, 1829-1919. 821'.009
Lives of famous poets. [Folcroft, Pa.] Folcroft Library Editions, 1971. xii, 406 p. port. 23 cm. 150 copies printed. Reprint of the 1878 ed., issued in series: Moxon's popular poets. [PR106.R6 1971b] 72-187861
1. Poets, English. I. Title. BIP

THOMAS, Henry, 1886- 928.2
Living biographies of great poets, by Henry Thomas and Dana Lee Thomas. Garden City, N.Y., Garden City Books [1959] 307 p. 22 cm. [PR503.T47 1959] 59-2802
1. Poets, English. 2. Poets, American. I. Thomas, Dana Lee, 1918- joint author. II. Title.

THOMAS, Henry, 1886- 928.2
Living biographies of great poets, by Henry Thomas and Dana Lee Thomas. Garden City, N. Y., Perma Giants [1950, c1941] viii. 307p. 22cm. [PR503.T47 1950] 52-575
1. Poets, English. 2. Poets, American. I. Thomas, Dana Lee, 1918- joint author. II. Title.

WINSTANLEY, William, 1628?-1698. 928.1
The lives of the most famous English poets (1687) Facsimile reproduction. Introd. by William Riley Parker. Gainesville, Fla., Scholars' Facsimiles. 1963. viii p. facsim.: 221p. illus. 23cm. 63-7095 7 50
1. Poets, English. I. Title.

Poets, English—Juvenile literature.

BENET, Laura 928.1
Famous poets for young people. New York, Dodd [c.1964] 160p. ports. 22cm. (Famous biogs. for young people) 64-13081 3.25
1. Poets, English—Juvenile literature. 2. Poets, American—Juvenile literature. 3. Children's poetry—Hist. & crit. I. Title.

Poets, English—Biography.

MASSON, David, 1822-1907. 821'.009 B
In the footsteps of the poets, by David Masson and others. [Folcroft, Pa.] Folcroft Library Editions, 1970. 381 p. illus. 24 cm. Reprint of the 1893 ed. "Limited to 150 copies." Contents.Contents.—Masson, D. Milton.—Brown, J. Herbert.—Benham, Rev. C. Cowper.—Haliburton, H. Thomson.—Ewart, H. C. Wordsworth.—Dennis, J. Scott.—Lord Bishop of Ripon. Mrs. Browning.—Hutton, R. H. Robert Browning.—Canton, W. Tennyson. [PR109.I6 1970] 72-192501
1. Poets, English—Biography. 2. Literary landmarks—Great Britain. I. Title.

THOMAS, Henry, 1886- 821'.009 B
Living biographies of great poets, by Henry Thomas and Dana Lee Thomas. Illus. by Gordon Ross. Freeport, N.Y., Books for Libraries Press [1972, c1959] viii, 307 p. illus. 23 cm. (Essay index reprint series) [PR105.T5 1972] 79-167415 ISBN 0-8369-2626-9
1. Poets, English—Biography. 2. Poets, American—Biography. I. Thomas, Dana Lee, 1918- joint author. II. Title.

Poets, English—20th century—Biography.

STALLWORTHY, Jon. 821'.9'1209 B
Poets of the First World War / Jon Stallworthy. [London] : Oxford University Press [for] the Imperial War Museum, 1974. 32 p. : ill., facsims., ports ; 25 cm. Bibliography: p. [32] [PR106.S8] 75-312259 ISBN 0-19-211847-1 : £0.45
1. Poets, English—20th century—Biography. 2. European War, 1914-1918—Literature and the war. I. Title.

Poets, French.

BRERETON, Geoffrey. 841'.009
An introduction to the French poets: Villon to the present day. 2nd ed. London, Methuen, 1973. xii, 320 p. 23 cm. Distributed in the USA by Harper & Row Publishers, Barnes & Noble Import Division. Bibliography: p. [303]-314. [PQ401.B7 1973] 73-162190 ISBN 0-416-76620-X 12.75
1. Poets, French. 2. French poetry—History and criticism. I. Title.
Pbk. 6.50; ISBN 0-416-67550-6.

QUENNELL, Peter, 1905- 841'.8'09
Baudelaire and the symbolists. 2d rev. ed. Freeport, N.Y., Books for Libraries Press [1971] xii, 164 p. illus. 23 cm. (Essay index reprint series) Reprint of the 1954 ed. Includes bibliographical references. [PQ438.Q4 1971] 72-142689 ISBN 0-8369-2423-1
1. Poets, French. 2. French poetry—19th century—History and criticism. 3. Symbolism in literature. I. Title. BIP

Poets, French—Biography.

MACKWORTH, Cecily. 841'.8'09 B
English interludes; Mallarme, Verlaine, Paul Valery, Valery Larbaud in England, 1860-1912 London, Boston, Routledge & K. Paul [1974] 220 p. ports. 22 cm. Includes bibliographical references. [PQ146.M25] 75-300160 ISBN 0-7100-7878-1 15.50
1. Poets, French—Biography. 2. French in London. 3. England—Intellectual life—19th century. I. Title.

Poets, Irish—Bio-bibliography.

O'DONOGHUE, David James, 1866-1917. 016.821
The poets of Ireland; a biographical and bibliographical dictionary of Irish writers of English verse. Dublin, H. Figgis, 1912. Detroit, Gale Research Co., 1968. iv, 504 p. 22 cm. [Z2037.O26 1968] 68-30622
1. Poets, Irish—Bio-bibliography. 2. English poetry—Irish authors—Bibliography. I. Title. BIP

Poets, Women—Biography.

ROBERTSON, Eric Sutherland. 821'.009 B
English poetesses: a series of critical biographies, will illustrative extracts. Freeport, N.Y., Books for Libraries Press [1973] p. (Essay index reprint series) Reprint of the 1883 ed. published by Cassell, London and New York. [PR111.R6 1973] 73-5628 ISBN 0-518-10129-0
1. Poets, Women—Biography. 2. Poets, English—Biography. I. Title.

Pohl, Frederik.

POHL, Frederik. 813'.5'4 B
The way the future was : a memoir / Frederik Pohl. 1st ed. New York : Ballantine Books, 1978. vii, 312 p., [8] leaves of plates : ill. ; 22 cm. "A Del Rey book." [PS3566.O36Z47] 78-19050 ISBN 0-345-27714-7 : 8.95
1. Pohl, Frederik. 2. Authors, American—20th century—Biography. 3. Science fiction, American—History and criticism. I. Title. BIP

Poincare, Henri, 1854-1912.

SLOSSON, Edwin Emery, 1865-1929. 920.04
Major prophets of to-day, by Edwin E. Slosson. Freeport, N.Y., Books for Libraries Press [1968] xii, 299 p. ports. 23 cm. (Essay index reprint series) Reprint of the 1914 ed. "The chapters of this volume have appeared in the Independent ... in a series under the general title of Twelve major prophets of to-day." Contents.Contents.—Maurice Maeterlinck.—Henri Bergson.—Henri Poincare.—Elie Metchnikoff.—Wilhelm

Ostwald.—Ernst Haeckel. [CT119.S6 1968] 68-8493
1. Maeterlinck, Maurice, 1862-1949. 2. Bergson, Henri Louis, 1859-1941. 3. Poincare, Henri, 1854-1912. 4. Mechnikov, Il'ia Il'ich, 1845-1916. 5. Ostwald, Wilhelm, 1853-1932. 6. Haeckel, Ernst Heinrich Philipp August, 1834-1919. I. Title. BIP

Poincare, Raymond, Pres. France, 1860-1934.

POINCARE, Raymond, Pres. France, 1860-1934. 944.081'092'4
The memoirs of Raymond Poincare / translated and adapted by Sir George Arthur ; with a pref. by the Duke of Northumberland. New York : AMS Press, 1975. 4 v. : port. ; 18 cm. Translation of Au service de la France. Reprint of the 1926-1931 ed. published by Doubleday, Garden City, N.Y. Includes index. [DC385.A63 1975] 70-160452 ISBN 0-404-09090-7
1. Poincare, Raymond, Pres. France, 1860-1934. 2. France—Foreign relations—1870-1940. 3. Europe—Politics and government—1871-1918. I. Arthur, George Compton Archibald, Sir, bart., 1860-1946. II. Title. BIP

WRIGHT, Gordon, 1912- 944.081/0924
Raymond Poincare and the French presidency. New York, Octagon, 1967[c.1932] ix, 271p. 24cm. (Hoover Lib. on War, Revolution, & Peace. Pubn. no. 19) Bibl. [DC385.W7 1967] 67-18792 7.50
1. Poincare, Raymond, Pres. France, 1860-1934. 2. France—Pol. & govt.—1914-1940. 3. France—Presidents. I. Title. II. Series: Stanford University. Hoover Instituion on War, Revoluution, and Peace. Publication no. 19
Originally published by Stanford Univ. Pr. BIP

Pointe de Sable, Jean Baptiste, 1745?-1818—Juvenile literature.

CORTESI, Lawrence. 977.3'11'020924 B
Jean duSable: father of Chicago. [1st ed.] Philadelphia, Chilton Book Co. [1972] 177 p. 21 cm. Bibliography: p. 169-171. A biography of the black Haitian who was the first non-Indian to settle and establish a trading community on the site of present-day Chicago. [F548.4.P742] 92 72-3791 ISBN 0-8019-5678-1
1. Pointe de Sable, Jean Baptiste, 1745?-1818—Juvenile literature. 2. Chicago—History—To 1875—Juvenile literature. I. Title.

Poiret, Paul.

WHITE, Palmer. 746.9'2 B
Poiret. [1st American ed.] New York, C. N. Potter [1973] 192 p. illus. (part col.) 30 cm. Bibliography: p. 183-185. [TT505.P6W47] 73-78881 ISBN 0-517-50537-1 20.00
1. Poiret, Paul. I. Title.

Poitier, Sidney.

HOFFMAN, William, 1937- 791.43'028'0924 B
Sidney. New York, L. Stuart [1971] 175 p. illus., ports. 24 cm. [PN2287.P57H6] 76-118620 5.95
1. Poitier, Sidney. I. Title.

Poitier, Sidney—Juvenile literature.

PAIGE, David. 92
Sidney Poitier / written by David Paige. Mankato, Minn. : Creative Education, [1976] p. cm. A brief biography of the black actor who rose from abject poverty to become a superstar in films and on the stage. [PN2287.P57P3] 76-27844 ISBN 0-87191-556-1 : 4.95
1. Poitier, Sidney—Juvenile literature. 2. Actors—United States—Biography—Juvenile literature. I. Title. BIP

Poitiers, Diane de, Duchess of Valentinois, 1499-1566.

STRAGE, Mark. 944'.028'0922 B
Women of power : the life and times of Catherine de Medici / Mark Strage. 1st ed. New York : Harcourt Brace Jovanovich, c1976. xiv, 368 p., [16] leaves of plates : ill. ; 22 cm. "A Helen and Kurt Wolff book." Includes index. Bibliography: p. 349-356. [DC119.8.S75] 75-35771 ISBN 0-15-198370-4 : 12.95
1. Catherine de Medicis, Consort of Henry II, King of France, 1519-1589. 2. Poitiers, Diane de, Duchess of Valentinois, 1499-1566. 3. Marguerite de Valois, Consort of Henry IV, King of France, 1553-1615. I. Title. BIP

Poland—Politics and government—1945-

BETHELL, Nicholas. 943.8'05'0924[B]
Gomulka; his Poland and his communism. [Baltimore] Penguin [1972] 307 p. illus., plates, facsims., maps. 18 cm. (Pelican Books: Leaders of the twentieth century, A1470) Bibliography: p. [296]-299 [DK443.B4] ISBN 0-14-021470-4 pap., 2.65
1. Poland—Politics and government—1945- I. Gomulka, Wladyslaw, 1906- II. Title.
L.C. card no. for London edition: 75-436368.

Pole, Charles, 1910-

POLE, Charles, 1910- 610'.92'4 B
Medicine, murder and merriment : a doctor's life / [by] Charles Pole. 2nd ed. Pinner : Pentagon, 1976. xix, 407 p. : ill., map, ports. ; 23 cm. Includes index. Bibliography: p. 392-394. [R489.P57A33 1976] 77-352389 ISBN 0-904288-11-0 : £4.95
1. Pole, Charles, 1910- 2. Physicians (General practice)—Great Britain—Biography. 3. World War, 1939-1945—Personal narratives, Polish. I. Title.

Pole, Hilary.

WILSON, Dorothy Clarke. 362.4'3'0924 B
Hilary; the brave world of Hilary Pole. New York, McGraw-Hill [1973, c1972] 259 p. illus. 22 cm. [RD796.P65W55 1973] 72-11230 ISBN 0-07-070753-7 5.95
1. Pole, Hilary. 2. Physically handicapped—Personal narratives.

Pole, Reginald, Cardinal, 1500-1558. Harvard Univ. Library

HALLE, Marie. v. 12
Life of Reginald Pole, by Martin Haile [pseud.] New York, Longmans, Green, 1910. xiii, 554 p. illus., ports. 23 cm. A10
1. Pole, Reginald, Cardinal, 1500-1558. Harvard Univ. Library I. Title.

Polgar, Franz J.,

POLGAR, Franz J., 1900- 920.9134
The story of a hypnotist [by] Franz J. Polgar with Kurt Singer. New York, Hermitage House [1951] 222 p. illus. 22 cm. [BF1127.P6A3] 51-13883
I. Title.

Polhem, Christopher, 1661-1751.

JOHNSON, William A. ed. v. 12
Christopher Polhem, the father of Swedish technology. Translated from Christopher Polhem (Minnesskrift utgifven af Svenska Teknologforeningen, 1911) Hartford, Conn., Published by the Trustees of Trinity College, under a grant from Karl William Hallden, 1963. xxi, 259 p. illus., ports. 27 cm. 64-12681
1. Polhem, Christopher, 1-61-1751. I. Title.

SVENSKA TEKNOLOGFORENINGEN, Stockholm 926.71
Christopher Polhem, the father of Swedish technology. Tr.from [Swedish] by William A. Johnson. Hartford, Conn., Trustees of Trinity Coll. [c.]1963. 259p. illus. (col. front.) 28cm. Bibl. 63-13636 8.00
1. Polhem, Christopher, 1661-1751. I. Title.

Police—Correspondence, reminiscences, etc.

WHITED, Charles. 363.232 B
Chiodo undercover cop. New York Playboy Press [1974, c1973] 315 p. 18 cm. Originally published under title: The decoy man; the extraordinary adventures of an undercover cop. [HV8148.N52W45] 1.50 (pbk.)
1. Police—Correspondence, reminiscences, etc. 2. Undercover investigation. I. Title.
L.C. card number for original ed.: 73-84921.

Police—History—Addresses, essays, lectures.

PIONEERS in 363.2'092'2 B
policing / [edited by] Philip John Stead. Montclair, N.J. : Patterson Smith, c1977. 307 p. : ill. ; 24 cm. (Patterson Smith series in criminology, law enforcement & social problems ; publication no. 213) Includes bibliographies and index. [HV7903.P56] 78-19648 ISBN 0-87585-213-0 : 15.00 ISBN 0-87585-803-1 pbk. : 6.75
1. Police—History—Addresses, essays, lectures. 2. Police—Biography. I. Stead, Philip John. BIP

Policewomen—Correspondence, reminiscences, etc.

SCHNABEL, Martha, 1926- 363.2'092'4 B
Officer Mama. San Antonio, Naylor Co. [1973] xiii, 100 p. illus. 22 cm. Autobiographical. [HV7911.S35A3] 73-4059 ISBN 0-8111-0491-5 7.95
1. Policewomen—Correspondence, reminiscences, etc. I. Title.

Polidori, John William, 1795-1821—Diaries.

POLIDORI, John William, 1795-1821. 828'.7'03
The diary of Dr. John William Polidori, 1816, relating to Byron, Shelley, etc. / edited and elucidated by William Michael Rossetti. Folcroft, Pa. : Folcroft Library Editions, 1975. p. cm. Reprint of the 1911 ed. published by E. Mathews, London. [PR5187.P5A8 1975] 75-29345 ISBN 0-8414-7320-X lib. bdg. : 30.00
1. Polidori, John William, 1795-1821—Diaries. 2. Byron, George Gordon Noel Byron, Baron, 1788-1824—Friends and associates. 3. Shelley, Percy Bysshe, 1792-1822—Friends and associates. 4. Authors, English—19th century—Correspondence, reminiscences, etc. I. Rossetti, William Michael, 1829-1919. II. Title.

Poling, Daniel Alfred,

POLING, Daniel Alfred, 1884- 922.573
Mine eyes have seen. [1st ed.] New York, McGraw-Hill [1959] 297 p. illus. 22 cm. Autobiography. [BX9543.P62A3] 59-14960
I. Title.

Poliomyelitis—Personal narratives.

SEIBERT, Florence Barbara. 616.2'46'0072024 B
Pebbles on the hill of a scientist [by] Florence B. Seibert. [1st ed.] St. Petersburg, Fla. [1968] x, 162 p. illus., ports. 24 cm. Autobiographical. "Bibliography of publications": p. 148-154. [QP26.S44A3] 79-437
1. Poliomyelitis—Personal narrative. I. Title.

WARREN, Mary Phraner. 362.4'3'0924 B
Bottom high to the crowd, by Mary Phraner Warren and Don Kirkendall. New York, Walker [1973] 222 p. 24 cm. [RC180.2.W33 1973] 72-95742 ISBN 0-8027-0409-3 6.95
1. Poliomyelitis—Personal narratives. I. Kirkendall, Don, joint author. II. Title.

Polis, Harry.

POLIS, Harry. 922.96
The struggle of an orphan for life and education. Chicago, Published by the author in cooperation with the Jewish way journal, 1956. 444p. illus. 23cm. Autobiographical. [DS135.R95P6] 57-20107
I. Title.

Polish Americans—Biography.

HAIMAN, Miecislaus, 1888-1949. 973'.04'9185 B
Polish past in America, 1608-1865 / by Miecislaus (Miecysaw) Haiman. Chicago : Polish Museum of America, 1974. c-u, xiv, 178 p. : ill. ; 23 cm. Reprint of the 1939 ed. published by the Polish Roman Catholic Union Archives and Museum, Chicago, with a new pref. and introd. "Polish war song ... music composed by Ch. Zeuner": p. 73-74. Includes bibliographies and index. [E184.P7H136 1974] 75-327195
1. Polish Americans—Biography. I. Title.

WANDYCZ, Damian S. 917.3'09'1749185
Register of Polish American scholars, scientists, writers & artists. Edited by Damian S. Wandycz. New York, Polish Institute of Arts and Sciences in America, 1969. 80 p. 23 cm. [E184.P7W34] 71-15219 2.00
1. Polish Americans—Biography. I. Title. BIP

WHO'S who in Polish 920.073
America. Francis Bolek, editor. New York, Arno Press, 1970 [c1943] 579 p. 24 cm. (The American immigration collection. Series II) [E184.P7W49 1970] 75-129390 ISBN 0-405-00545-8
1. Polish Americans—Biography. I. Bolek, Francis, 1886- ed.

Polish Americans—Juvenile literature.

PILARSKI, Laura. 920.0438
They came from Poland; the stories of famous Polish-Americans. New York, Dodd, Mead [1969] 178 p. illus., maps, ports. 22 cm. Bibliography: p. 163-[167] Brief biographies of famous Poles or descendants of Polish immigrants emphasizing their unique contributions to their adopted homeland. [E184.P7P55] 69-17599 3.75
1. Polish Americans—Juvenile literature. I. Title.

Political prisoners—China—Personal narratives.

DUNLAP, Albert Menzo, 1884- 951.05
Behind the Bamboo Curtain; the experiences of an American doctor in China, by A. M. Dunlap. Illus. by Eva Wyman Dunlap. Foreword by Daniel T. MacDougal. Introd. by John Leighton Stuart. Westport, Conn., Greenwood Press [1973, c1956] viii, 208 p. illus. 23 cm. [DS777.55.D8 1973] 72-14086 ISBN 0-8371-6752-3
1. Political prisoners—China—Personal narratives. I. Title.

Political prisoners—Greece, Modern—Personal narratives.

FLEMING, Amalia, Lady. 949.5'07 B
A piece of truth. [1st American ed.] Boston, Houghton Mifflin, 1973. 257 p. illus. 22 cm. Includes bibliographical references. [DF852.F5 1973] 72-6810 ISBN 0-395-15474-X 6.95
1. Political prisoners—Greece, Modern—Personal narratives. I. Title.

Political prisoners—Russia—Personal narratives.

SOLOMON, Michael. 365'.45'0924 B
Magadan. Foreword by Irving Layton. Montreal, New York, Chateau Books

[1971] 243 p. map. 24 cm. [HV8959.R9S65 1971b] 70-149290 ISBN 0-88870-003-2 7.95
1. Political prisoners—Russia—Personal narratives. 2. Political prisoners—Romania—Personal narratives. 3. Antisemitism—Russia. I. Title.

SOLOMON, Michael. 365'.45'0924 B
Magadan. Foreword by Irving Layton. Princeton, [Auerbach Publishers, 1971] x, 243 p. map (on lining papers) 24 cm. "A Vertex book." [HV8959.R9S65] 73-151236 ISBN 0-87769-085-5 7.95
1. Political prisoners—Russia—Personal narratives. 2. Political prisoners—Romania—Personal narratives. 3. Antisemitism—Russia. I. Title.

Political prisoners—United States—Personal narratives.

SOBELL, Morton. 365'.6'0924
On doing time. New York, Bantam Books [1976 c1974] 436 p. illus. 18 cm. [HV9468.S7] 2.25 (pbk.)
1. Political prisoners—United States—Personal narratives. 2. Espionage—United States. I. Title.
L.C. card no. of 1974 Scribner edition: 74-11203.

Political science—Collected works.

PENN, William, 1644-1718. 320.5'092'4
William Penn, 17th century founding father : selections from his political writings / Edward B. Bronner. Wallingford, Pa. : Pendle Hill Publications, 1975. 36 p. : facsim. ; 19 cm. (Pendle Hill pamphlet ; 204 ISSN 0031-4250s) Bibliography: p. 36. [JC153.P38 1975] 75-32728 ISBN 0-87574-204-1 : 0.95
1. Political science—Collected works. I. Bronner, Edwin B., 1920- II. Title.

Politicians—Australia Queensland—Biography.

QUEENSLAND political 320.9'943 B
portraits 1859-1952 / edited by D. J. Murphy and R. B. Joyce. St. Lucia, Q. : University of Queensland Press, 1978. viii, 518 p. : ports. ; 23 cm. Includes bibliographical references and index. [DU272.A2Q43] 78-317434 ISBN 0-7022-1127-3 : 24.25
1. Politicians—Australia—Queensland—Biography. 2. Queensland—Biography. 3. Queensland—Politics and government. I. Murphy, D. J. II. Joyce, R. B.
Available from Technical Impex Corp., Lawrence, MA

Politicians—United States—Biography—Juvenile literature.

LEVY, Elizabeth. 329'.0092'2
Politicians for the people / by Elizabeth Levy and Mara Miller. New York : Knopf : distributed by Random House, c1979. p. cm. Presents career biographies of men and women noted for their non-traditional approach to politics. [E840.6.L48 1979] 920 79-2197 6.95 ISBN 0-394-84068-2. lib. bdg. : 6.95
1. Politicians—United States—Biography—Juvenile literature. 2. United States—Politics and government—1945- —Juvenile literature. I. Miller, Mara. II. Title.

Polk, Frank, 1908-

POLK, Frank, 1908- 978'.03'0924 B
F-F-F-Frank Polk : an uncommonly Frank autobiography / illustrated by Joe Beeler ; with a foreword by Slim Pickins. 1st ed. Flagstaff, [Ariz.] : Northland Press, c1978. x, 123 p. : ill. ; 25 cm. [F596.P64A33] 78-51848 ISBN 0-87358-174-1 : 10.50
1. Polk, Frank, 1908- 2. Cowboys—The West—Biography. 3. The West—Biography. **BIP**

Polk, James Knox, Pres. U.S., 1795-1849.

MCCORMAC, Eugene Irving, 1872-1943 923.173
James K. Polk; a political biography. New York, Russell & Russell, 1965. x, 746p. port. 23cm. Reissue of 1922 ed. Bibl. [E417.M12] 64-66402 12.50
1. Polk, James Knox, Pres. U. S., 1795-1849. I. Title. **BIP**

MCCOY, Charles Allan, 1920- 973.6'1'0924 B
Polk and the Presidency, by Charles A. McCoy. New York, Haskell House Publishers, 1973, [c1960] xiii, 238 p. illus. 23 cm. Bibliography: p. 227-234. [E417.M15 1973] 72-10451 ISBN 0-8383-1686-7 10.95 (Lib. bdg.)
1. Polk, James Knox, Pres. U.S., 1795-1849. 2. Executive power—United States. I. Title. **BIP**

POLK, James Knox, Pres. U.S., 1795-1849. 923.173
Polk; the diary of a president, 1845-1849, covering the Mexican War, the acquisition of Oregon, and the conquest of California and the Southwest, edited by Allan Nevins. London, New York, Longmans, Green, 1952. xxxiv, 412. [1] p. 24 cm. "Bibliographical note": p. [413] [E416.P77 1952] 52-8933
1. "A selection from "The diary of James K. Polk during his Presidency, 1845-1849,' edited and annotated by Milo Milton Quaife." 2. U.S. — Pol. & govt. — 1845-1849. 3. U.S. — Hist. — War with Mexico, 1845-1848 — Sources. I. Nevins, Allan, 1890- ed. II. Title.

SELLERS, Charles Grier. 973.610924 B
James K. Polk, Jacksonian, 1795-1843. Princeton, N.J., Princeton University Press, 1957- v. illus. 25 cm. Vol. 2 has title: James K. Polk, continentalist, 1843-1846. Includes bibliography. [E417.S4] 57-5457
1. Polk, James Knox, Pres. U.S., 1795-1849.

Polk, James Knox, Pres. U.S., 1795-1849—Juvenile literature.

HOYT, Edwin Palmer. 973.610924 B
James Knox Polk, by Edwin P. Hoyt. Chicago, Reilly & Lee, 1965. 155 p. illus., ports. 21 cm. Bibliography: p. 155. [E417.H75] 65-21486
1. Polk, James Knox, Pres. U.S., 1795-1849—Juvenile literature.

LOMASK, Milton. j92
This slender reed; a life of James K. Polk. New York, Farrar, Straus and Giroux [1966] 176 p. 22 cm. (An Ariel book) Bibliography: p. 171-172. [E417.L6] 66-5504
1. Polk, James Knox, Pres. U.S., 1795-1849 — Juvenile literature. I. Title.

Polk, Leonidas, Bp., 1806-1864.

PARKS, Joseph Howard. 922.375
General Leonidas Polk, C.S.A., the fighting bishop. [Baton Rouge] Louisiana State University Press [1962] 408 p. illus., maps, ports. 24 cm. (Southern biography series) "Critical essay on authorities.": p. [387]-395. [E467.1.P7P3] 62-15028
1. Polk, Leonidas, Bp., 1806-1864. I. Title. II. Series.

Polk, Sarah Childress, 1803-1891.

CLAXTON, Jimmie Lou Sparkman. 973.6'1'0924 B
88 years with Sarah Polk. [1st ed. New York, Vantage Press [1972] 222 p. illus. 21 cm. Bibliography: p. 208. [E417.1.C55] 72-195234 ISBN 0-533-00222-2 6.95
1. Polk, Sarah (Childress) 1803-1891. I. Title.

NELSON, Anson. 973.6'1'0924 B
Memorials of Sarah Childress Polk, wife of the eleventh President of the United States, by Anson and Fanny Nelson. Spartanburg, S.C., Reprint Co. [1974, c1892] xiv, 284 p. illus. 22 cm. Reprint of the ed. published by A. D. F. Randolph, New York. [E417.1.N44 1974] 73-22435 ISBN 0-87152-163-6 15.00
1. Polk, Sarah Childress, 1803-1891. I. Nelson, Fanny, joint author. II. Title.

Pollitt, Basil Hubbard,

POLLITT, Basil Hubbard, 1896- 920
The life and loves of Baron Von Audax, some time private, corporal, 'tenny-anty,' and first lieutenant in the United States Marine Corps, as told to Basil H. Pollitt. New York, Vantage [c.1962] 200p. 21cm. 3.50 bds.,
I. Title.

Pollitt, Harry, 1890-1960.

MAHON, John, 1901-1975. 320.5'32'0924 B
Harry Pollitt : a biography / by John Mahon. London : Lawrence and Wishart, 1976. 567 p., [8] leaves of plates : ill., ports. ; 23 cm. Includes bibliographical references and indexes. [HX243.P59M3 1976] 76-366223 ISBN 0-85315-327-2 : £6.00
1. Pollitt, Harry, 1890-1960.

Pollock, Donald.

POLLOCK, Donald. 365'.64 B
Call me a good thief / by Donald Pollock. London : H. Baker, 1976. [2], 236 p., [4] p. of plates : facsims., ports. ; 23 cm. [HV6248.P58A33] 77-360833 ISBN 0-7030-0088-8 : £3.50. ISBN 0-7030-0095-0 pbk.
1. Pollock, Donald. 2. Crime and criminals—Canada—Biography. I. Title.

Pollock, Jackson, 1912-1956.

BUSIGNANI, Alberto. 759.13
Pollock [translated from the Italian] London, New York, Hamlyn, 1971. 96 p. (chiefly illus. (chiefly col.), ports.) 32 cm. (Twentieth-century masters) Distributed in the United States by Crown Publishers. Bibliography: p. 96. [ND237.P73B813] 72-182352 ISBN 0-600-36914-5 £2.25
1. Pollock, Jackson, 1912-1956.

POLLOCK, Jackson, 1912-1956. 759.13
Pollock; [the life and work of the artist, illustrated with 80 full-color plates, by] Italo Tomassoni. [Translated from Italian by Caroline Beamish. 1st American ed.] New York, Grosset & Dunlap [1969, c1968] 39 p. illus., plates (part col.) 18 cm. (The New Grosset art library, 24) Bibliography: p. 27-29. [ND237.P73T63 1969] 69-11563 ISBN 0-448-00473-9 1.50
I. Tomassoni, Italo.

Pollock, Oliver, 1737-1823.

JAMES, James Alton, 1864-1962. 973.31'0924 B
Oliver Pollock; the life and times of an unknown patriot. Freeport, N.Y., Books for Libraries Press [1970] xiii, 376 p. facsim., map. 23 cm. Reprint of the 1937 ed. Bibliography: p. 360-368. [E302.6.P84J3 1970] 70-130554
1. Pollock, Oliver, 1737-1823.

Polo, Marco, 1254-1323.

GANNON, Jack. 796.35'3'0924 B
Before the colours fade : polo, pig, India, Pakistan, and some memories : a collection from the writings of Brigadier Jack Gannon. London: J. A. Allen, 1976. 117 p. : port. ; 22 cm. Limited ed. of 500 copies. [GV1011.G36] 76-378345 ISBN 0-85131-227-6 : £5.00
1. Polo. I. Title.

DOLAN, Ellen M. 92
Marco Polo. Pictures by Raymond Renard. Adapted by Ellen M. Dolan from the original text. St. Louis, Webster Division, McGraw-Hill [1967] [28 p.] col. illus., port. 19 x 21 cm. (Men of genius books) (Around the world library) A short biography of the man who as a youth journeyed eastward to the court of the Kublai Khan where he spent twenty-four years before he returned to Venice with tales and treasures of an unknown land. [G370.P9D6] AC 67
1. Polo, Marco, 1254-1323? I. Renard, Raymond, illus. II. Title.

EDUCATIONAL Research Council of America. Social Science Staff. 372.8'9
Explorers and discoverers: Marco Polo, and people Marco Polo met. Boston, Allyn and Bacon [1970] 48 p. col. illus. 21 cm. (Concepts and inquiry: the ERC social science program) Relates briefly the high points of Marco Polo's twenty-one year journey through the Orient. In a separate section describes the Mongols and their way of life. [G370.P9E3] 92 70-97100
1. Polo, Marco, 1254-1323?—Juvenile literature. I. Title. II. Title: Marco Polo, and people Marco Polo met. III. Series: Concepts and inquiry: the Educational Research Council social science program

EDUCATIONAL Research Council of America. Social Science Staff. 910'.92'4 B
Explorers and discoverers, Marco Polo, and people Marco Polo met / prepared by the Social Science Staff of the Educational Research Council of America. Learner-verified ed. 2. Boston : Allyn and Bacon, [1974] 52 p. : col. ill. ; 21 cm. (Concepts and inquiry, the ERC social science program) Relates briefly the high points of Marco Polo's twenty-one year journey through the Orient and describes the Mongols and their way of life. [G370.P9E3 1974] 73-78347 pbk. : 1.76
1. Polo, Marco, 1254-1323?—Juvenile literature. 2. Mongols—Juvenile literature. I. Title. II. Title: Marco Polo, and people Marco Polo met. III. Series: Concepts and inquiry, the Educational Research Council social science program.

HART, Henry Hersch, 1886- 910.4
Marco Polo, Venetian adventurer [by] Henry H. Hart. [1st ed. Norman, Univ. of Okla. Pr., 1967] xxvii, 306p. illus., facsims., ports, maps. 23cm. Bibl. [G370.P9H28] (B) 67-16685 5.95
1. Polo, Marco, 1254-1323? I. Title.

HART, Henry Hersch, 1886- 910.4 B
Marco Polo, Venetian adventurer [by] Henry H. Hart. [1st ed. Norman, University of Oklahoma Press, 1967] xxviii, 306 p. illus., facsims., ports, maps. 23 cm. Bibliography: p. 270-299. [G370.P9H28] 67-15585
1. Polo, Marco, 1254-1323?

HUMBLE, Richard. 910'.92'4 B
Marco Polo / Richard Humble ; introd. by Elizabeth Longford. 1st Amercian ed. New York : Putnam, 1975, C1974. 232 p. : ill. ; 26 cm. Includes index. Bibliography: p. 224. [G370.P9H85 1975b] 75-326241 ISBN 0-399-11473-4 : 12.95
1. Polo, Marco. 2. Asia—Description and travel.

KOMROFF, Manuel, 1890- 923.95
Marco Polo; illustrated by Edgard Cirlin. New York, Messner [1952] 171 p. illus. 22 cm. [G370.P9K6] 52-12731
1. Polo, Marco, 1254-1323? **BIP**

KOMROFF, Manuel, 1890- 910.4 B
Marco Polo; illustrated by Edgard Cirlin. New York, Messner [1952] 171 p. illus. 22 cm. A biography of the Venetian traveler whose trips throughout Asia and China gave the European world its first knowledge of the Far East. [G370.P9K6] 92 AC 68
1. Polo, Marco, 1254-1323? I. Cirlin, Edgard, 1913- illus. II. Title.

POLO, Marco, 1254-1323? 910.4
The travels of Marco Polo, the Venetian. The translation of Marsden rev., with a selection of his notes. Edited by Thomas Wright. London, H. G. Bohn, 1854. New York, AMS Press [1968] xxviii, 508 p. 21 cm. Original ed. issued in series: Bohn's

antiquarian library. [G370.P72 1968b] 68-57871
1. Voyages and travels. 2. Asia—Description and travel. 3. Mongols—History. I. Wright, Thomas, 1810-1877, ed. II. Marsden, William, 1754-1836, tr.

PRESTON, Edna Mitchell. 910.4 B
Marco Polo; a story of the Middle Ages. Illustrated by Edward Leight. New York, Crowell-Collier Press [1968] 115 p. illus., map. 24 cm. Bibliography: p. 111. A biography of the Venetian who travelled at the age of seventeen to the court of Kublai Khan and did not return to Venice until twenty-four years later. His account of his travels afforded the European world its first knowledge of the East. [G370.P9P7] 92 AC 68
1. Polo, Marco, 1254-1323? I. Leight, Edward, illus. II. Title. BIP

PRESTON, Edna Mitchell. 92 (J)
Marco Polo; a story of the Middle Ages. Illustrated by Edward Leight. New York, Crowell-Collier Press [1968] 115 p. illus., map. 24 cm. Bibliography: p. 111. [G370.P9P7] 68-11269
1. Polo, Marco, 1254-1323?—Juvenile literature.

ROSS, Edward Denison, Sir, 1871-1940. 910'.92'4 B
Marco Polo and his book / by Sir E. Denison Ross. Folcroft, Pa. : Folcroft Library Editions, 1975. 27 p. ; 26 cm. Reprint of the 1934 ed. published by H. Milford, London, in series: Annual Italian lecture of the British Academy. Includes bibliographical references. [G370.P9R67 1975] 75-20116 ISBN 0-8414-7384-6 : 7.50
1. Polo, Marco, 1254-1323? 2. Voyages and travels. I. Title. II. Series: British Academy, London (Founded 1901). Italian lecture.

VENETIAN adventurer, v. 12
being an account of the life and times and of the book of Messer Marco Polo. New York, Bantam Books [1956] x, 256p. 18cm. (A Bantam biography FB403)
1. Polo, Marco, 1254-1323? I. Hart, Henry Hersch, 1886-

WEBB, Robert N. 910.4'0924(B)
Marco Polo: the great traveler. New York, Watts [1967] 105p. map. 22cm. (Immortals of hist.) [G370.P9W4] 67-16531 2.95
1. Polo, Marco, 1254-1323? I. Title.

Polo, Marco, 1254-1323?—Juvenile literature.

BUEHR, Walter. 923.95
The world of Marco Polo. Written and illustrated by Walter Buehr. New York, Putnam [1961] 91p. illus. 23cm. [G370.P9B8] 61-8236
1. Polo, Marco, 1254-1323?—Juvenile literature. I. Title.

KOMROFF, Manuel, 1890- j92
Marco Polo. Illustrated by Robin Jacques. Garden City, N.Y., Junior Deluxe Editions [1966] 186 p. illus. (1 col.) map. 22 cm. [G370.P9K6] 66-6188
1. Polo, Marco, 1254-1323? — Juvenile literature. I. Title.

Polska Zjednoczona Partia Robotnicza—History.

DE WEYDENTHAL, Jan B. 329.9'438
The communists of Poland : an historical outline / Jan B. de Weydenthal. Stanford, Calif. : Hoover Institution Press, Stanford University, c1978. xviii, 217 p. ; 23 cm. (Hoover Institution publication ; 202) (Histories of ruling Communist parties) Includes index. Bibliography: p. [203]-210. [JN6769.A52D49] 78-59465 pbk. : 7.95
1. Polska Zjednoczona Partia Robotnicza—History. 2. Poland—Politics and government—1945- I. Title. II. Series. III. Series: Stanford University. Hoover Institution on War, Revolution, and Peace. Publications ; 202. BIP

Poltoratskii, Ellen Sarah (Southee) 1819-1908.

ALMEDINGEN, Martha Edith, 1898- 914.7'03'80924 B
Ellen (Ellen Sarah Southee de Poltoratzky, 1819-1908) [by] E. M. Almedingen. [1st ed.] New York, Farrar, Straus & Giroux [1970] x, 274 p. 21 cm. (An Ariel book) Biographical. A biography of the author's grandmother, a nineteenth-century English girl who married one of the richest men in Russia. [CT1218.P587A64] 92 76-125150 4.50
1. Poltoratskii, Ellen Sarah (Southee) 1819-1908. I. Title.

Polybius.

WALBANK, Frank William. 907'.2'024 B
Polybius, by F. W. Walbank. Berkeley, University of California Press [1972 i.e. 1973] ix, 201 p. 24 cm. (Sather classical lectures, v. 42) Bibliography: p. [184]-188. [DG206.P65W34] 72-189219 ISBN 0-520-02190-8 8.50
1. Polybius. I. Title. II. Series. BIP

Pombal, Sebastiao Jose de Carvalho e Mello, marquez de, 1699-1782.

CHEKE, Marcus, Sir. 946.9'03'0924 B
Dictator of Portugal; a life of the Marquis of Pombal, 1699-1782. Freeport, N.Y., Books for Libraries Press [1969] viii, 315 p. port. 23 cm. (Select bibliographies reprint series) Reprint of the 1938 ed. Bibliography: p. 305-306. [DP641.C5 1969] 74-94267
1. Pombal, Sebastiao Jose de Carvalho e Mello, marquez de, 1699-1782. I. Title. BIP

Pomeroy, Marcus Mills, 1833-1896.

TUCKER, Mary Eliza (Perine) 1838- 070.4'0924 B
Life of Mark M. Pomeroy. [New York] Arno [1970] 230 p. port. 23 cm. (The American journalists) Reprint of the 1868 ed. [E664.P77T8 1970] 77-125721 ISBN 0-405-01704-9
1. Pomeroy, Marcus Mills, 1833-1896. BIP

Pompadour, Jeanne Antoinette Poisson, marquise de, 1721-1764.

LEVRON, Jacques, 1906- 920.7
Pompadour. Tr. [from French] by Claire Eliane Engle. New York, St Martin's [c.1961, 1963] 279p. illus., ports. 23cm. 63-8552 6.95 bds.,
1. Pompadour, Jeanne Antoinette (Poisson) marquise de, 1721-1764. I. Title.

LEVRON, Jacques, 1906- 920.7
Pompadour. Translated by Claire Eliane Engel. New York, St. Martin's Press [1963] 279 p. illus., ports. 23 cm. Translation of Secrete Madame de Pompadour. [DC135.P8L443] 63-8552
1. Pompadour, Jeanne Antoinette (Poisson) marquise de, 1721-1764. I. Title.

MITFORD, Nancy, 1904- 920.7
Madame de Pompadour. New York, Random House [1954, c1953] 324p. illus. 22cm. [DC135] 54-5957
1. Pompadour, Jeanne Antoinette (Poisson) marquise de, 1721-1764. I. Title. BIP

MITFORD, Nancy, 1904- 944'.034'0924
Madame de Pompadour. New York, Harper & Row [1968] 304 p. illus. (part col.), maps, ports. (part col.) 27 cm. Bibliography: p. 296. [DC135.P8M6 1968] 68-23423 15.00
1. Pompadour, Jeanne Antoinette (Poisson) marquise de, 1721-1764.

SMYTHE, David Mynders. 920.7
Madame de Pompadour: mistress of France. New York, W. Funk [1953] 370 p. illus. 22 cm. [DC135.P8S5] 52-14009
1. Pompadour, Jeanne Antoinette Poisson, marquise de, 1721-1764.

Pompeius Magnus, Cn.

LEACH, John, 1938- 937'.05'0924 B
Pompey the Great / John Leach. London : Croom Helm ; Totowa, N.J. : Rowman and Littlefield, 1978. 265 p. : maps ; 23 cm. Includes indexes. Bibliography: p. 249-254. [DG258.L4 1978] 77-18826 ISBN 0-8476-6035-4 : 15.00
1. Pompeius Magnus, Cn. 2. Rome—History—265-30 B.C. 3. Consuls, Roman—Biography. 4. Generals—Rome—Biography. I. Title. BIP

†RAWSON, Beryl. 937'.05'0924 B
The politics of friendship : Pompey and Cicero / [by] Beryl Rawson. Sydney : Sydney University Press, 1977. vi, 217 p. ; 22 cm. (Sources in ancient history) Stamped on t.p.: Exclusive distributor: ISBS, Inc., Forest Grove, Or. Includes index. Bibliography: p. 211-212. [DG258.R38] 78-320651 ISBN 0-424-06800-1 : 9.00 (U.S.)
1. Pompeius Magnus, Cn. 2. Cicero, Marcus Tullius. 3. Rome—History—265-30 B.C. 4. Statesmen—Rome—Biography. I. Title. II. Series. BIP

Ponce de Leon, Juan, 1460?-1521.

BLASSINGAME, Wyatt. 917.29'04'20924 B
A world explorer: Ponce de Leon. Illustrated by Russ Hoover Champaign, Ill., Garrard Pub. Co. [1965] 96 p. col. illus., col. map. 24 cm. (World explorer books) A biography of the Spanish explorer which concentrates on his travels in the Caribbean, his discovery of Florida, and his lifelong quest for a fountain of youth. [E125.P7B5] 92 AC 68
1. Ponce de Leon, Juan, 1460?-1521. I. Hoover, Russ, illus. II. Title.

WISNIEWSKI, Jerome Joseph, 1885- v. 12
Jean Ponce de Leon. Saint Leo, Florida, Abbey Press, 1962. 61, [2] p. ports., map. 20 cm. "Partial list of sources consulted": p. [63] 65-74083
1. Ponce de Leon, Juan, 1460?-1521. I. Title.

Pond, Cornelia Jones, b. 1834.

POND, Cornelia Jones, b.1834. 917.58 B
Life on a Liberty County plantation; the journal of Cornelia Jones Pond. Edited by Josephine Bacon Martin. Illus. by Anne Lee Haynes. Darien, Ga., Priv. print. [by the Darien News, 1974] xiii, 146 p. illus. 21 cm. [F292.L6P66] 74-177244
1. Pond, Cornelia Jones, b. 1834. 2. Plantation life—Liberty Co., Ga. 3. Liberty Co., Ga.—History—Civil War, 1861-1865. I. Title.

Pond, Jean, 1929-

POND, Jean, 1929- 616.9'93'81 B
Surviving / Jean Pond. 1st ed. New York : Hill and Wang, 1978. 135 p. ; 21 cm. [RC280.B7P64] 77-19357 ISBN 0-8090-9028-7 : 7.95
1. Pond, Jean, 1929- 2. Cerebellum—Tumors—Biography. 3. Gliomas—Biography. I. Title. BIP

Pond, Peter, 1740-1807?

KELSEY, Vera. 978
Young men so daring; fur traders who carried the frontier west. [1st ed.] Indianapolis, Bobbs-Merrill [1956] 288 p. illus. 22 cm. [F592.K38] 56-7606
1. Pond, Peter, 1740-1807? 2. Lisa, Manuel, 1772-1820. 3. Astor, John Jacob, 1763-1848. 4. Bridger, James, 1804-1881. I. Title.

WAGNER, Henry Raup, 1862- v. 12
Peter Pond, fur trader & explorer. [New Haven] Yale University Library, 1955. 103p. 3 fold. maps. 19cm. (Yale University. Library. Western historical series, no. 2) Maps, which arein separate folder, and text volume issued together in case. One of an ed. of 50 copies on special paper. A 57
1. Pond, Peter, 1740-1807? 2. Fur trade—Northwest, Canadian. I. Title. II. Series.

Pontecorvo, Bruno, 1913-

MOOREHEAD, Alan, 1910- 364.13
The traitors. With a new pref. [Rev. ed.] New York, Harper & Row [1963] 236 p. illus. 22 cm. Includes bibliography. [HD9698.A28M6 1963] 63-10606
1. Fuchs, Klaus Emil Julius, 1911- 2. Pontecorvo, Bruno, 1913- 3. May, Allan Nunn, 1911- 4. Atomic energy. I. Title.

Pontiac, Ottawa chief, d. 1769.

HOLLMANN, Clide Anne. 970.3 B
Pontiac, king of the Great Lakes, by Clide Hollmann. New York, Hastings House Publishers [1968] 151 p. illus., map (on lining papers) 24 cm. Bibliography: p. 146. A biography of the Ottawa chief who aided the French in the French and Indian War, united the Great Lakes Indian tribes in the first organized resistance to the white man, and led the Indians' siege of Fort Detroit. [E83.76.H76] 92 AC 68
1. Pontiac, Ottawa chief, d. 1769. I. Title. BIP

PECKHAM, Howard Henry, 1910- 973.2'7'0924 B
Pontiac and the Indian uprising [by] Howard H. Peckham. New York, Russell & Russell [1970] xviii, 346 p. illus., facsims., maps, ports. 22 cm. "Reproduced from the second edition of 1961." Bibliography: p. 326-332. [E83.76.P4 1970] 70-102528
1. Pontiac, Ottawa chief, d. 1769. 2. Pontiac's Conspiracy, 1763-1765. I. Title. BIP

Pontiac, Ottawa chief, d. 1769—Juvenile literature.

GRANT, Matthew G. 970.3 B
Pontiac, Indian general and statesman [by] Matthew G. Grant. Illustrated by Harold Henriksen. [Mankato, Minn., Creative Education; distributed by Childrens Press, Chicago, 1973, c1974] 28 p. illus. (part col.) 25 cm. (His Gallery of great Americans series. Indians of America) A biography of the Ottawa war chief whose almost successful plan to join many tribes together to defeat the British was known as Pontiac's Conspiracy. [E83.76.P2G72] 92 73-12193 ISBN 0-87191-268-6 3.95
1. Pontiac, Ottawa chief, d. 1769—Juvenile literature. I. Henriksen, Harold, illus. II. Title.

GRIDLEY, Marion Eleanor, 1906- 973.2'7'0924 B
Pontiac, by Marion E. Gridley. Illustrated by Unada. New York, Putnam [1970] 57 p. illus. (part col.) 23 cm. (A See and read beginning to read biography) An easy-to-read biography of the Ottawa chief who fought a losing battle against the white man. [E83.76.G73] 92 79-92345 2.68
1. Pontiac, Ottawa chief, d. 1769—Juvenile literature. I. Unada, illus. II. Title. BIP

HAYS, Wilma Pitchford 970.2
Pontiac, lion in the forest. Illus. by Lorence Bjorklund. Boston, Houghton [c.1965] 189p. col. illus., col. maps (1 fold.) 22cm. (Piper bks.) [E83.76.H3] 65-10518 1.96; 2.20; 1.32 lib. ed., pap.,
1. Pontiac, Ottawa chief, d. 1769—Juvenile literature. I. Title.

HAYS, Wilma Pitchford. 970.2
Pontiac, lion in the forest. Illustrated by Lorence Bjorklund. Boston, Houghton Mifflin [1965] 189 p. col. illus., col. maps (1 fold.) 22 cm. (Piper books) [E83.76.H3] 65-105186
1. Pontiac, Ottawa chief, d. 1769—Juvenile literature. I. Title.

VOIGHT, Virginia Frances. 973.2'7'0924 B
Pontiac, mighty Ottawa Chief / by Virginia F. Voight ; illustrated by William Hutchinson. Champaign, Ill. : Garrard Pub. Co., [1977] p. cm. A biography of the Ottawa patriot and war chief who united the Great Lakes tribes against the intruding British, laying siege to Detroit in 1763 in a culmination of what has come to be known as Pontiac's Conspiracy. [E99.O9P668] 76-25244 ISBN 0-8116-6613-1 lib.bdg. : 3.58
1. Pontiac, Ottawa Chief, d. 1769—Juvenile literature. I. Hutchinson, William M. II. Title.

Ponting, Herbert George.

ARNOLD, Harry John 770'.92'4 B Philip, 1932- *Photographer of the world;* the biography of Herbert Ponting [by] H. J. P. Arnold. [1st American ed.] Rutherford [N.J.] Fairleigh Dickinson University Press [1972, c1969] 175 p. illus. 26 cm. Includes bibliographical references. [TR140.P6A7 1972] 75-156270 ISBN 0-8386-7959-5 8.50
1. Ponting, Herbert George. I. Title. **BIP**

Pontoppidan, Henrik, 1857-1943.

MITCHELL, Philip 839.8'1'36 B Marshall, 1916- *Henrik Pontoppidan* / by P. M. Mitchell. Boston : Twayne Publishers, 1979. 158 p. : port. ; 21 cm. (Twayne's world authors series ; TWAS 524 : Denmark) Includes index. Bibliography: p. 149-155. [PT8175.P6Z728] 78-21609 ISBN 0-8057-6366-X : 13.95
1. Pontoppidan, Henrik, 1857-1943. 2. Authors, Danish—19th century—Biography. 3. Authors, Danish—20th century—Biography. **BIP**

Ponzi, Charles.

DUNN, Donald H. 364.1'63'0924 B *Ponzi!* : The Boston swindler / by Donald H. Dunn. New York : McGraw-Hill, [1975] xii, 254 p., [8] leaves of plates : ill. ; 24 cm. [HV6698.Z9P53] 74-32253 ISBN 0-07-018270-1 : 7.95
1. Ponzi, Charles. I. Title.

Ponzi, Tom.

VON BLOCK, B. W. 364.12'092'4 B *Super-detective;* the many lives of Tom Ponzi, Europe's master investigator [by] B. W. von Block. With a foreword by Tom Ponzi. [1st ed. Chicago] Playboy Press; [distributed by Simon & Schuster, New York, 1973, c1972] 243 p. illus. 22 cm. [HV7911.P65V65] 72-75966 7.95
1. Ponzi, Tom. I. Title.

Poole, Ernest,

POOLE, Ernest, 1880- 813'.5'2 B 1950. *The bridge;* my own story. New York, Macmillan, 1940. New York, Johnson Reprint Corp., 1971. 422 p. illus., ports. 23 cm. (Series in American studies) [PS3531.O53Z5 1971] 78-156934
I. Title. **BIP**

Poole, Sam.

POOLE, Victoria. 617'.412 B *Thursday's child* / Victoria Poole. 1st ed. Boston : Little, Brown, c1979. p. cm. [RD598.P55 1979] 79-25767 ISBN 0-316-71334-1 : 10.95
1. Poole, Sam. 2. Heart—Transplantation—Biography. I. Title. **BIP**

Poole, William Frederick, 1821-1894.

WILLIAMSON, William 920.2 Landram, 1920- *William Frederick Poole and the modern library movement.* New York, Columbia University Press, 1963. x, 203 p. ports. 24 cm. (Columbia University studies in library service, no. 13) Based on thesis, University of Chicago. Bibliography: p. [193]-196. [Z720.P6W5] 63-14110
1. Poole, William Frederick, 1821-1894. I. Series.

Pooley family.

STIGALL, Phyllis 929'.2'0973 Graham. *Samuel John Pooley, widow's son* / by Phyllis Graham Stigall. Scarborough, N.Y. : Stigall, 1976. xvi, 102 p. : ill. ; 27 cm. Includes bibliographical references and index. [CS71.P822 1976] 76-150831
1. Pooley family. 2. Pooley, Samuel John, 1868-1965. 3. Iowa—Genealogy. 4. United States—Genealogy. 5. Iowa—Biography. I. Title.

Poon, Lim—Juvenile literature.

BONING, Richard A. 910'.45 B *Alone* / Richard A. Boning ; illustrated by Harry Schaare. Baldwin, N.Y. : Dexter & Westbrook, [1975] 47 p. : col. ill. ; 24 cm. (The Incredible series) Relates the adventures and struggle for survival of a Chinese steward who drifted 1200 miles on a raft to the coast of Brazil after being shipwrecked in the middle of the Atlantic Ocean. [G530.P746B65] 74-33583 ISBN 0-87966-108-9 lib.bdg. : 4.95
1. Poon, Lim—Juvenile literature. 2. Survival (after airplane accidents, shipwrecks, etc.)—Juvenile literature. I. Schaare, Harry J. II. Title. **BIP**

Pope, Alexander, 1688-1744.

AYRE, William. 821'.5 S *Memoirs of the life and writings of Alexander Pope, 1745.* New York, Garland Pub., 1974. p. cm. (The Life & times of seven major British writers. Popeiana, 20-21) Attributed to Edmund Curll. Cf. R. Straus, The unspeakable Curll. Reprint of the ed. printed by His Majesty's authority for the author; sold by the Booksellers of London and Winchester. [PR3633.P58 vol. 20-21] 821'.5 74-14944 ISBN 0-8240-1257-7 22.00
1. Pope, Alexander, 1688-1744. I. Curll, Edmund, 1675-1747. II. Title. III. Series: Popeiana, 20-21.

DEQUINCEY, Thomas, 1785- 809 B 1859. *Biographies of Shakspeare, Pope, Goethe, and Schiller, and on the policial parties of modern England.* New York, AMS Press [1972] vii, 376 p. port. 19 cm. Reprint of the ed. issued in 1862 by A. and C. Black, Edinburgh, as: De Quincey's works, v. 15. [PN452.D4 1972] 75-164822 ISBN 0-404-02079-8 17.50
1. Shakespeare, William, 1564-1616—Biography. 2. Pope, Alexander, 1688-1744. 3. Goethe, Johann Wolfgang von, 1749-1832—Biography. 4. Schiller, Johann Christoph Friedrich von, 1759-1805—Biography. 5. Political parties—Great Britain.

DILWORTH, W. H. 821'.5 S *The life of Alexander Pope, Esq.* New York, Garland Pub., 1974. p. cm. (The Life and times of seven major British writers. Popeiana 23) Reprint of the 1759 ed. printed for G. Wright, London. [PR3633.P58 vol. 23] 821'.5 B 74-16269 ISBN 0-8240-1259-3 22.00
1. Pope, Alexander, 1688-1744. I. Title. II. Series.

DOBREE, Bonamy, 1891- 928.2 *Alexander Pope.* New York, Oxford, 1963. 100p. 20cm. (Oxford paperback, no. 70) 1.50 pap.,
1. Pope, Alexander, 1688-1744. I. Title. **BIP**

DOBREE, Bonamy, 1891- 928.2 *Alexander Pope.* [New York] Philosophical Library [1952] 125 p. 22 cm. [PR3633.D6 1952] 52-7252
1. Pope, Alexander, 1688-1744.

DOBREE, Bonamy, 1891- 821'.5 B *Alexander Pope.* New York, Greenwood Press [1969] 125 p. 23 cm. Reprint of the 1951 ed. [PR3633.D6 1969] 72-94604
1. Pope, Alexander, 1688-1744.

EDMUNDS, Edward William. 821'.5 B *Pope and his poetry,* by E. W. Edmunds. [Folcroft, Pa.] Folcroft Library Editions, 1974. p. Reprint of the 1913 ed. published by G. G. Harrap, London, which was issued as no. 19 of Poetry and life series. Includes bibliographical references. [PR3633.E4 1974b] 74-7051 7.00 (lib. bdg.).
1. Pope, Alexander, 1688-1744. I. Title. II. Series: Poetry and life series, no. 19. **BIP**

FRASER, George Sutherland, 821'.5 1915- *Alexander Pope* / by George S. Fraser. London ; Boston : Routledge and Paul, 1978. x, 134 p. ; 22 cm. Includes index. Bibliography: p. 124-128. [PR3633.F7] 78-40731 ISBN 0-7100-8990-2 : 11.75
1. Pope, Alexander, 1688-1744. 2. Poets, English—18th century—Biography.

GRIFFIN, Dustin H. 821'.5 *Alexander Pope the poet in the poems* / Dustin H. Griffin. Princeton, N.J. : Princeton University Press, c1978. p. cm. Includes index. [PR3633.G7] 78-51167 ISBN 0-691-06371-0 : 17.50
1. Pope, Alexander, 1688-1744. 2. Poets, English—18th century—Biography. I. Title.

POPE, Alexander, 1688-1744. 923.2 *Correspondence.* Edited by George Sherburn. Oxford, Clarendon Press, 1956- v. illus., ports. facsim. 23cm. Contents.v. 1704-1718--v.2. 1719-1728.--v. 4. 1738-1744.--v. 5. Index. Includes bibliographies. [PR3633.A4] 57-528
I. Title.

POPE. ALEXANDER, 1688-1744. 928.2 *Correspondence.* Edited by George. Sherburn. Oxford, Clarendon Press, 1956-- v. illus., ports., facsim. 23cm. Contents.v. 1. 1704-1718.--v. 2. 1719-1728.--v. 4. 1736-1744.--v. 5. Index. Includes bibliographies. [PR3633.A4] 57-528
I. Title.

QUENNELL, Peter, 1905- 821'.5 B *Alexander Pope;the education of genius, 1688-1728.* New York, Stein and Day [1968] 278 p. illus., ports. 24 cm. Bibliography: p. 258-260. [PR3633.Q4] 68-31610 7.95
1. Pope, Alexander, 1688-1744.

ROOT, Robert Kilburn, 1877- 928.2 *The poetical career of Alexander Pope.* Gloucester, Mass., Peter Smith, 1962[c.1938] 248p. 28cm. Bibl. 4.25
1. Pope, Alexander, 1688 1744. I. Title. **BIP**

RUFFHEAD, Owen, 1723- 821'.5 S 1769. *The life of Alexander Pope.* New York, Garland Pub., 1974. p. cm. (The Life & times of seven major British writers. Popeiana, 22) Reprint of the 1769 ed. printed for S. Powell Dublin. [PR3633.P58 vol. 22] 821'.5 B 74-17008 ISBN 0-8240-1258-5 22.00
1. Pope, Alexander, 1688-1744. I. Title. II. Series: Popeiana, 22. **BIP**

SHERBURN, George Wiley, 821'.5 B 1884- *The early career of Alexander Pope,* by George Sherburn. Oxford, Clarendon P., 1968. vi, 326 p. illus. 23 cm. "First published 1934." Bibliographical footnotes. [PR3633.S45 1968] 76-401360 ISBN 1-9811675-6- unpriced
1. Pope, Alexander, 1688-1744. I. Title. **BIP**

SITWELL, Dame Edith, 1887- 928.2 *Alexander Pope.* New York, Norton [1963] 256p. 20cm. (Norton lib., N182) 63-5366 1.75 pap.,
1. Pope, Alexander, 1688-1744. I. Title.

SITWELL, Edith, Dame, 821'.5 B 1887-1964. *Alexander Pope.* Freeport, N.Y., Books for Libraries Press [1972] 368 p. illus. 21 cm. Reprint of the 1930 ed. [PR3633.S5 1972] 72-7190 ISBN 0-8369-6953-7
1. Pope, Alexander, 1688-1744.

STEPHEN, Leslie, Sir, 821'.5 B 1832-1904. *Alexander Pope.* New York, AMS Press [1968] vii, 210 p. 22 cm. (English men of letters) [PR3633.S7 1968] 68-58397
1. Pope, Alexander, 1688-1744. I. Title. **BIP**

THORNTON, Francis 928.2 Beauchesne, 1898- *Alexander Pope:* Catholic poet. New York, Pellegrini & Cudahy [1952] viii, 312 p. 22 cm. Bibliography: p. 302-308. [PR3633.T5] 51-12760
1. Pope, Alexander, 1688-1744. I. Title.

THREE biographical 821'.5 B *pamphlets, 1744-1745* New York, Garland Pub., 1974. p. cm. (The Life & times of seven major British writers. Popeiana, 24) Reprint of the 1745 ed. of Remarks on 'Squire Ayre's Memoirs of the life and writings of Mr. Pope, in a letter to Mr. Edmund Curl, bookseller, printed for M. Cooper, London; of the 1744 ed. of The life of Alexander Pope, esq., with remarks on his works: to which is added his last will, printed for W. Bickerton, London; and of the 1744 ed. of The life of Alexander Pope, esq., with a true copy of his last will and testament, printed for C. Corbett, London. [PR3633.P58 vol. 24] 74-16034 ISBN 0-8240-1260-7 22.00
1. Pope, Alexander, 1688-1744. I. Remarks on 'Squire Ayre's Memoirs of the life and writings of Mr. Pope, in a letter to Mr. Edmund Curl, bookseller. 1974. II. The Life of Alexander Pope, esq., with remarks on his works: to which is added, his last will. 1974. III. The Life of Alexander Pope, esq., with a true copy of his last will and testament. 1974. IV. Series: Popeiana, 24.

Pope, Alexander, 1688-1744, in fiction, drama, poetry, etc.

SMEDLEY, Jonathan, 828'.5'09 S 1671-1729. *Gulliveriana, 1728* New York, Garland Pub., 1974 p. cm. (The Life & times of seven major British writers. Swiftiana, 8) Reprint of the ed. printed for J. Roberts, London. [PR3726.S95 vol. 8] [PR3687.S75] 828'.5'09 74-17378 ISBN 0-8240-1269-0 22.00
1. Swift, Jonathan, 1667-1745, in fiction, drama, poetry, etc. 2. Pope, Alexander, 1688-1744, in fiction, drama, poetry, etc. 3. Swift, Jonathan, 1667-1745. Miscellanies in prose and verse. I. Title. II. Series: Swiftiana, 8. **BIP**

Pope-Hennessy, James.

POPE-HENNESSY, James. 928.2 *Monckton Milnes.* New York, Farrar, Straus & Cudahy [1955- v. illus., ports. 22cm. Contents.v. 1. The years of promise, 1809-1851.--v. 2. The flight of youth, 1851-1885. Bibliographical footnotes. [PR4808.P57] 55-13770
I. Houghton, Richard Monckton Millnes, baron, 1809-1885. II. Title.

Pope, Vyvyan Vavasour, 1891-1941.

LEWIN, Ronald. 358'.18'0924 B *Man of armour* : a study of Lieut-General Vyvyan Pope and the development of armoured warfare / by Ronald Lewin. London : Lee Cooper, 1976. 152 p., [2] leaves of plates : ill. ; 22 cm. Includes bibliographical references and index. [U55.P65L48 1976] 76-372349 ISBN 0-85052-050-9 : £4.95
1. Pope, Vyvyan Vavasour, 1891-1941. 2. Great Britain. Army—Biography. 3. Generals—Great Britain—Biography. 4. Mechanization, Military—History. I. Title.

Popes.

CHAMBERLIN, Eric 262'.13'0922 Russell. *The bad Popes* [by] E. R. Chamberlin. New York, Dial Press, 1969. 310 p. illus. (part col.) 25 cm. "A Brahmin book." Bibliography: p. 291-296. [BX955.2.C45] 78-83475 12.50
1. Popes. I. Title.

MANN, Horace Kinder, 1859- 922.21 1928 *The lives of the popes in the early Middle Ages,* by the Rev. Horace K. Mann ... London, K. Paul, Trech, Trubner & Co., 1902-1932. Nendeln, Liechtenstein, Kraus-Thomson Org., 1968. 18v. in 19. fronts., illus., plates, maps (pt. fold.) plan, facsims. fold. geneal. tab. 23cm. Vols. vi- have title: The lives of the popes in the middle ages. V. 16, pt. 2 prepd. by Johannes

Hollnsteiner. Bibl. ... [BX1070.M3] 4-16966 198.00
1. Popes. I. Hollnsteiner, Johannes, 1865- II. Title.
Order from Kraus-Thomson Org., 9491 Nendeln, Liechtenstein.

MATT, Leonard von 922.21
The Popes; papal history in picture and word, by Leonard. von Matt, Hans Kuhner. [Tr. from German by Salvator Attnaasio.] New York, Universe Bks. [c.1963] 239p. illus., ports., coats of arms. 20cm. 63-18341 10.50
1. Popes. 2. Papacy—Hist.—Pictures, illustrations, etc. I. Kuhner, Hans, joint author. II. Title.

MURPHY, Francis Xavier, 1914- 922.21
John XXIII, the story of the Pope. Orig. title: John XXIII comes to the Vatican New York, Avon [1961, c.1959] 159p. illus. (G-1093) .50 pap.,
I. Title.

Popov, Dusko.

POPOV, Dusko. 940.54'86'420924 B
Spy/counterspy; the autobiography of Dusko Popov. Foreword by Ewen Montagu. New York, Grosset & Dunlap [1974] ix, 339 p. illus. 22 cm. [D810.S8P6 1974] 73-14131 ISBN 0-448-11606-5 7.95
1. Popov, Dusko. 2. World War, 1939-1945—Secret service—Great Britain. 3. World War, 1939-1945—Secret service—Germany. I. Title.

Porsche, Ferdinand, 1875-1951.

FRANKENBERG, Richard Alexander, Freiherr von, 1922- 629.2'0924 B
Porsche; the man and his cars, by Richard von Frankenberg. English version by Charles Meisl. Rev. ed. Cambridge, Mass., R. Bentley, 1969. ix, 236 p. illus. 23 cm. Translation of Die ungewohnliche Geschichte des Hauses Porsche. [TL140.P6F713 1969b] 70-77459 10.95
1. Porsche, Ferdinand, 1875-1951. 2. Porsche automobile. I. Title.

FRANKENBERG, Richard Alexander, Freiherr von, 1922- 926.292
Porsche: the man and his car. English version [from German] by Charles Meisl. Cambridge, Mass., Robert Bentley [c.] 1961. 223p. illus. 61-16133 7.50
1. Porsche, Ferdinand, 1875-1951. 2. Porsche automobile. I. Title.

Porson, Richard, 1759-1808.

CLARKE, Martin Lowther. 880'.9 B
Richard Porson, a biographical essay, by M. L. Clarke. [Folcroft, Pa.] Folcroft Library Editions, 1973. viii, 132 p. port. 24 cm. Reprint of the 1937 ed. published by the University Press, Cambridge, Eng. Bibliography: p. 123-127. [PA85.P6C5 1973] 73-11484 17.50
1. Porson, Richard, 1759-1808. **BIP**

Porson, Richard, 1759-1808—Anecdotes.

ROGERS, Samuel, 1763-1855. 821'.7 B
Recollections of the table-talk of Samuel Rogers : to which is added Porsoniana / edited by Alexander Dyce. Folcroft, Pa. : Folcroft Library Editions, 1975. p. cm. Reprint of the 1887 ed. published by H. A. Rogers, New Southgate, Eng. [PR5234.A3 1975] 75-30733 ISBN 0-8414-3724-6 lib. bdg. : 65.00
1. Porson, Richard, 1759-1808—Anecdotes. I. Title.

Porta, Giovanni Battista della, 1535?-1615.

CLUBB, Louise George 852.4
Giambattista della Porta, dramatist. Princeton, N.J., Princeton [c.]1965. xvi, 359p. port. 21cm. Bibl. [PQ4630.P6Z6] 64-25757 8.50
1. Porta, Giovanni Battista della, 1535?-1615. I. Title. **BIP**

CLUBB, Louise George. 852.4
Giambattista della Porta, dramatist. Princeton, N.J., Princeton University Press, 1965. xvi, 359 p. port. 21 cm. Bibliography: p. 315-342. [PQ4630.P6Z6] 64-25757
1. Porta, Giovanni Battista della, 1535?-1615. I. Title.

Porter, Alexander, 1785-1844.

STEPHENSON, Wendell Holmes, 1899-1970. 328.73'092'4 B
Alexander Porter, Whig planter of old Louisiana. New York, Da Capo Press, 1969 [c1934] 154 p. port. 24 cm. (The American scene: comments and commentators) (Reprint of the ed. published by Louisiana State University Press, Baton Rouge, which was issued as no. 16 of Louisiana State University studies.) Bibliography: p. [145]-148. [F374.P73S73 1969] 69-19761
1. Porter, Alexander, 1785-1844. 2. Louisiana—Politics and government—1803-1865. **BIP**

Porter, Anthony Toomer,

PORTER, Anthony Toomer, 1828-1902. 283'.0924 B
Led on! Step by step, scenes from clerical, military, educational, and plantation life in the South, 1828-1898; an autobiography. New York, Putnam, 1898. Miami, Fla., Mnemosyne Pub. Co. [1969] xv, 462 p. illus., ports. 23 cm. [BX5995.P6A3 1969] 75-89383
I. Title.

Porter Co., Ind.—Biography.

AMERICAN Revolution Bicentennial Committee of Porter County. Bicentennial History Book Committee. 977.2'98
A biographical history, Porter County, Indiana, 1976 / Bicentennial History Book Committee. Valparaiso, Ind. : American Revolution Bicentennial Committee of Porter County, [1976?] 183 p. : ill. ; 32 cm. At head of title: American Bicentennial, 1776-1976. [F532.P8A45 1976] 77-153812
1. Porter Co., Ind.—Biography. 2. Porter Co., Ind.—History. I. Title.

Porter, Cole, 1891-1964.

EELLS, George. 782.8'1'0924 B
The life that late he led; a biography of Cole Porter. New York, G. P. Putnam's Sons [1967] 383 p. illus., ports. 22 cm. "Cole Porter's works": p. 327-367. [ML410.P7844E3] 66-20276
1. Porter, Cole, 1891-1964. I. Title.

EWEN, David, 1907- 782.810924 B
The Cole Porter story. [1st ed.] New York, Holt, Rinehart and Winston [1965] 192 p. port. 22 cm. Bibliography: p. 185-186; discography: p. 182-185. [ML410.P7844E9] 65-21542
1. Porter, Cole, 1891-1964. I. Title.

KIMBALL, Robert, comp. 782.8'1'0924 B
Cole. Edited by Robert Kimball. A biography essay by Brendan Gill. Designed by Bea Feitler. [1st ed.] New York, Holt, Rinehart & Winston [1971] xix, 283 p. illus. 32 cm. The essay (p. [ix]-xix) is followed by a chronological collection of illustrations, correspondence, anecdotes, etc., and Cole Porter's lyrics. [ML410.P7844K55] 76-155521 ISBN 0-03-086710-X 25.00
1. Porter, Cole, 1891-1964. I. Gill, Brendan, 1914- II. Porter, Cole, 1891-1964. Songs. Texts. Selections. English. 1971. III. Title.

PORTER, Cole, 1891-1961 782.810924
The Cole Porter story, as told to Richard G. Hubler. Introd. by Arthur Schwartz. Cleveland, World [c.1965] xii, 140p. ports. 21cm. Bibl. [ML410.P7844A3] 65-23352 3.75 bds.,
1. Musicians—Correspondence, reminiscences, etc. I. Hubler, Richard Gibson, 1912- II. Title.

PORTER, Cole, 1891-1964. 782.810924
The Cole Porter story, as told to Richard G. Hubler. With an introd. by Arthur Schwartz. Cleveland, World Pub. Co. [1965] xii, 140 p. ports. 21 cm. "Bibliography: Cole Porter songs": p. 125-140. [ML410.P7844A3] 65-23352
1. Musicians—Correspondence, reminiscences, etc. I. Hubler, Richard Gibson, 1912- II. Title.

SCHWARTZ, Charles. 782.8'1'0924 B
Cole Porter : a biography / by Charles Schwartz. New York : Dial Press, 1977. xvi, 365 p., [8] leaves of plates : ill. ; 24 cm. Includes index. "Works by Cole Porter": p. [241]-293. [ML410.P7844S4] 77-6907 ISBN 0-8037-1464-5 : 9.95
1. Porter, Cole, 1891-1964. 2. Composers—United States—Biography.

SCHWARTZ, Charles. 782.8'1'0924 B
Cole Porter : a biography / by Charles Schwartz. New York : Da Capo Press, 1979, c1977. p. cm. (A Da Capo paperback) Reprint of the ed. published by Dial Press, New York. "Works by Cole Porter": p. [ML410.P7844S4 1979] 78-20840 ISBN 0-306-80097-7 pbk. : 6.95
1. Porter, Cole, 1891-1964. 2. Composers—United States—Biography. **BIP**

Porter, Cole, 1891-1964—Juvenile literature.

SALSINI, Paul. 782.8'1'0924 B
Cole Porter; twentieth century composer of popular songs. Charlotteville, N.Y., SamHar Press, 1972. 31 p. 23 cm. (Outstanding personalities, no. 41) Bibliography: p. 30-31. The biography of the American songwriter who composed some 1000 popular songs during his lifetime. [ML3930.P67S2] 92 72-89206
1. Porter, Cole, 1891-1964—Juvenile literature. I. Title. **BIP**

Porter, David Dixon, 1813-1891.

GERSON, Noel Bertram, 1914- 973.75'0924 B
Yankee admiral; a biography of David Dixon Porter, by Paul Lewis. [New York] D. McKay Co. [1968] 210 p. 21 cm. [E467.1.P78G4] 68-55047 4.95
1. Porter, David Dixon, 1813-1891. I. Title.

Porter, David, 1780-1843.

LONG, David Foster, 1917- 973.5'0924 B
Nothing too daring; a biography of Commodore David Porter, 1780-1843 [by] David F. Long. Annapolis, Md., U.S. Naval Institute [1970] xiv, 396 p. illus., maps, ports. 25 cm. Bibliography: p. 361-380. [E353.1.P7L6] 78-94781 ISBN 0-87021-494-2 12.50
1. Porter, David, 1780-1843. I. Title. **BIP**

Porter, Gene Stratton, 1863-1924.

KING, Rollin Patterson. 818'.5'209 B
Gene Stratton-Porter, a lovely light / by Rollin Patterson King. 1st ed. Chicago : Adams Press, c1979. 172 p. : ill. ; 23 cm. "Books by Gene Stratton-Porter": p. 169. [PS3531.O7345Z57] 79-50501 12.95
1. Porter, Gene Stratton, 1863-1924. 2. Authors, American—20th century—Biography. I. Title.
Publisher's Address : P.O. Box 102 Hastings, Ne 68901

MEEHAN, Jeannette (Porter) 818'.5'209 B
Life & letters of Gene Stratton-Porter. Port Washington, N.Y., Kennikat Press [1972] 287 p. ports. 22 cm. First published in 1928 under title: The Lady of the Limberlost. [PS3531.O7345Z6 1972] 77-160774 ISBN 0-8046-1606-X
1. Porter, Gene (Stratton) 1863-1924.

Porter, Hal

PORTER, Hal 928.2
The watcher on the cast-iron balcony, an Australian autobiography. London, Faber & Faber [dist. Hollywood-by-the-Sea, Fla., Transatlantic, 1964, c.1963] 255p. 21cm. [PR6066.O7W3] 64-57899 5.00
I. Title.

Porter, Lewis B., 1895-

PORTER, Lewis B., 1895- 920'.0764'512
Early civilization on the Washboard / by Lewis B. Porter, Sr. Goldthwaite, Tex. : Porter, 1975. 230 p., [2] leaves of plates : ill. ; 23 cm. Includes index. [F392.M56P67] 75-320666
1. Porter, Lewis B., 1895- 2. Mills Co., Tex.—Biography. 3. Mills Co., Tex.—History. I. Title.

Porter, Rufus, 1792-1884.

LIPMAN, Jean (Herzberg) 1909- 759.13 B
Rufus Porter, Yankee pioneer [by] Jean Lipman. Foreword by Gerard Piel. Pref. by John I. H. Baur. [1st ed.] New York, C. N. Potter; distributed by Crown [1968] ix, 202 p. illus. (part col.), coat of arms, facsims., ports. 29 cm. Bibliography: p. 189-192. [ND237.P8135L48] 68-26881 12.50
1. Porter, Rufus, 1792-1884.

Porter, Russell Williams, 1871-1959.

PORTER, Russell Williams, 1871-1949. 919.8 B
The Arctic diary of Russell Williams Porter / edited by Herman Friis. Charlottesville : University Press of Virginia, 1976. xii, 171, [1] p. : ill. ; 27 cm. Bibliography: p. 171-[172] [G606.P67] 75-45375 ISBN 0-8139-0649-0 : 20.00
1. Porter, Russell Williams, 1871-1949. 2. Arctic regions. I. Title. **BIP**

WILLARD, Berton C. 919.8 B
Russell W. Porter, arctic explorer, artist, telescope maker / by Berton C. Willard ; with a pref. by David O. Woodbury. Freeport, Me. : Bond Wheelwright Co., c1976. xiii, 274 p. : ill. ; 24 cm. Bibliography: p. 269-274. [QB36.P63W54 1976] 76-8090 ISBN 0-87027-168-7 : 12.50. pbk. : 7.95
1. Porter, Russell Williams, 1871-1959. 2. Astronomers—Biography. 3. Polar regions—Biography. 4. Artists—United States—Biography. 5. Telescope. **BIP**

Porter, William Sydney, 1862-1910.

ARNETT, Ethel Stephens. 928.1
O. Henry from Polecat Creek. [2d ed.] Greensboro, N.C., Piedmont Press, 1963 [c1962] 250 p. illus. 24 cm. Includes bibliography. [PS2649.P5Z63] 63-16928
1. Porter, William Sydney, 1862-1910. I. Title.

LONG, Eugene Hudson, 1908- 928.1
O, Henry, the man and his work [Gloucester, Mass., Peter Smith, 1962, c.1949] 158p. front. port. (Perpetua bk. rebound) Bibl. 3.50
1. Porter, William Sydney, 1862-1910. I. Title.

LONG, Eugene Hudson, 1908- 813'.5'2
O. Henry, the man and his work, by E. Hudson Long. New York, Russell & Russell [1969, c1949] xi, 158 p. port. 22 cm. Bibliography: p. 149-152. [PS2649.P5Z714 1969] 68-27073
1. Porter, William Sydney, 1862-1910.

NOLAN, Jeannette (Covert) 1896- v. 12
O Henry; the story of William Sydney Porter. Illus. by Hamilton Greene. New York, J. Messner Inc. [1964, c1943] 253 p. illus. "Thirteenth printing." Includes bibliographies. 68-6792
1. Porter, William Sydney, 1862-1910. I. Title.

O. Henry papers; 813'.5'2 B
containing some sketches of his life together with an alphabetical index to his

complete works. New rev. ed. [Folcroft, Pa.] Folcroft Library Editions, 1973. 68 p. illus. 24 cm. Reprint of the ed. published by Doubleday, Doran, Garden City, N.Y. Contents.—Introductory note.—MacAdam, G. O. Henry's only autobiographia.—Page, A. W. Little pictures of O. Henry.—Wootten, K. H. and Barker, T. D. Bibliography.—O. Henry index. [PS2649.P5Z759 1973] 73-3464 ISBN 0-8414-1722-9
1. Porter, William Sydney, 1862-1910. 2. Porter, William Sydney, 1862-1910—Bibliography.

O'CONNOR, Richard, 1915- 817'.5'2
O. Henry: the legendary life of William S. Porter. [1st ed.] Garden City, N.Y., Doubleday, 1970. x, 252 p. illus., ports. 22 cm. Bibliography: p. [245]-246. [PS2649.P5Z758] 70-108035 6.95
1. Porter, William Sydney, 1862-1910. I. Title.

Porter, William Trotter, 1809-1858.

BRINLEY, Francis, 1800-1889. 070.4'0924 B
The life of William T. Porter. [New York] Arno [1970, c1860] vii, 273 p. port. 23 cm. (The American journalists) [PN4874.P59B7 1970] 79-125680 ISBN 0-405-01655-7
1. Porter, William Trotter, 1809-1858. I. Title. **BIP**

YATES, Norris Wilson. 920.5
William T. Porter and the Spirit of the times; a study of the Big Bear school of humor. Baton Rouge, Louisiana State University Press [1957] xi, 222 p. illus. 24 cm. Bibliographical footnotes. Bibliography: p. [205]-210. [PN4874.P59Y3] 56-9520
1. Porter, William Trotter, 1809-1858. 2. Spirit of the times.

†YATES, Norris Wilson. 070.4'092'4 B
William T. Porter and the Spirit of the times / Norris W. Yates. New York : Arno Press, 1977, c1957. xi, 222 p. ; 24 cm. (International folklore) Reprint of the ed. published by Louisiana State University Press, Baton Rouge. Includes index. Bibliography: p. [205]-210. [PN4874.P59Y3 1977] 77-70630 ISBN 0-405-10134-1 : 14.00
1. Porter, William Trotter, 1809-1858. 2. Spirit of the times. 3. Journalists—United States—Biography. 4. American wit and humor—History and criticism. I. Title. II. Series.

Porterfield, Bill.

PORTERFIELD, Bill. 976.4'06'0922
A loose herd of Texans / by Bill Porterfield. 1st ed. College Station : Texas A&M University Press, c1978. xiv, 198 p. ; 24 cm. [F391.P84] 77-99277 ISBN 0-89096-044-5 : 10.00
1. Porterfield, Bill. 2. Texas—Social life and customs. 3. Texas—Biography. I. Title. **BIP**

Porters—Correspondence, reminiscences, etc.

TURNER, Robert Emanuel, 1875- 923.873
Memories of a retired Pullman porter. [1st ed.] New York, Exposition Press [1954] 191p. illus. 21cm. [HD8039.R37T8] 54-10978
1. Porters—Correspondence, reminiscences, etc. I. Title.

Porter, William Sydney,

LANGFORD, Gerald, 1911- 928.1
Alias O. Henry; a biography of William Sidney Porter. New York. Macmillan, 1957. xix, 294p. ports. 22cm. 'Notes and references': p. 259-286. [PS2649.P5Z7126] 57-8270
1. Porter, William Sydney, I. Title.

Porteus, Stanley David,

PORTEUS, Stanley David, 1883- 150'.924 B
A psychologist of sorts; the autobiography and publications of the inventor of the Porteus maze tests [by] Stanley D. Porteus. Palo Alto, Calif., Pacific Books [1969] x, 325 p. illus., maps, ports. 24 cm. "Annotated list of publications": p. [251]-325. [BF109.P6A3] 68-31287 7.50
I. Title. **BIP**

Portland, William Bentinck, 1st Earl of, 1649-1709.

GREW, Marion Ethel (Tuckwell) 942.06'8'0922
William Bentinck and William III (Prince of Orange); the life of Bentinck Earl of Portland from the Welbeck correspondence, Marion E. Grew Port Washington, N.Y., Kennikat Press [1971] ix, 433 p. geneal. tables, ports. 22 cm. Reprint of the 1924 ed. Includes bibliographical references. [DA462.P7G7 1971] 77-118473
1. Portland, William Bentinck, 1st Earl of, 1649-1709. 2. William III, King of Great Britain, 1650-1702. 3. Gt. Brit.—History—William and Mary, 1689-1702. I. Title.

Portman, John Calvin.

PORTMAN, John Calvin. 728.5
The architect as developer / by John Portman and Jonathan Barnett. New York : McGraw-Hill, c1976. p. cm. [NA737.P63B37] 76-19062 ISBN 0-07-050536-5 : 22.95
1. Portman, John Calvin. 2. Atlanta. Hyatt Regency Atlanta. 3. San Francisco. Hyatt Regency San Francisco. I. Barnett, Jonathan, joint author. II. Title. **BIP**

Portrait-painters, American.

SHERMAN, Frederic Fairchild, 1874-1940. 757
Early American portraiture. New York, B. Blom, 1972. 65 p. ports. 26 cm. Reprint of the 1930 ed. [ND1311.S5 1972] 72-84107
1. Portrait-painters, American. 2. Portraits, American. I. Title. **BIP**

Portraits.

PLAUT, Frederick. 927
The unguarded moment, a photographic interpretation. Englewood Cliffs, N. J., Prentice-Hall [1964] v. (unpaged) ports. 32 cm. Bibliographical references included in "Acknowledgements": p. [5] [CT206.P6] 64-22799
1. Portraits. 2. Biography. I. Title.

Portraits, American—Catalogs.

NATIONAL Portrait Gallery, Washington, D.C. 704.94'2'0973
This new man: a discourse in portraits. Edited by J. Benjamin Townsend and introd. by Charles Nagel. With an essay by Oscar Handlin. Washington, Published for the National Portrait Gallery by the Smithsonian Institution Press; [distributed by Random House, New York] 1968. 217 p. ports. (part col.) 27 cm. (Smithsonian publication 4752) [N7593.N23] 68-8535 6.95
1. Portraits, American—Catalogs. 2. United States—Biography—Portraits. I. Townsend, James Benjamin, 1918- II. Handlin, Oscar, 1915- III. Title.

Portsmouth, Gerard Vernon Wallop, 9th earl of,

PORTSMOUTH, Gerard Vernon Wallop, 9th earl of, 1898- 320.924
A knot of roots; an autobiography, by Gerard Wallop, Earl of Portsmouth [New York] New Amer. Lib. [c.1965] xi, 336p. illus., port. 22cm. (NAL bk.) [DA566.9.P63A3] 65-26639 6.95
I. Title.

Portsmouth, Louise Renee de Penancoet de Keroualle, duchess of, 1649-1734.

DELPECH, Jeanine. 920.7
The life & times of the Duchess of Portsmouth. [Translated from the French by Ann Lindsay] New York, Roy Publishers [1953] 212p. illus. 23cm. Translation of Louise de Keroualle. [DA447] 53-10349
1. Portsmouth, Louise Renee de Penancoet de Kerouaile, duchess of, 1649-1734. I. Title.

Portugal—Descr. &trav.

BECKFORD, William, 1760-1844. 928.2
The journal of William Beckford In Portugal and Spain, 1787-1788. Edited with an introd. and notes by Boyd Alexander. New York, J. Day Co., 1955 [c1954] 340p. illus., ports., fold. maps, facsims., geneal. tables. 22cm. [PR4092] 55-14393
1. Portugal—Descr. &trav. 2. Spain—Descr. &trav. I. Title.

Posselt, Teresia Renata de Spiritu Sancto,

POSSELT, Teresia Renata de Spiritu Sancto, Sister, 1891- 922.243
Edith Stein; translated by Cecily Hastings and Donald Nicholl. New York, Sheed and Ward, 1952. 238 p. illus. 21 cm. Secular name: Teresia Posselt. [BX4705.S814P63 1952 a] 52-4323
I. Stein, Edith, 1891-1942. II. Title.

POSSELT, Teresia Renata de Spiritu Sancto, Sister, 1891- 922.243
Edith Stein; translated by Cecily Hastings and Donald Nicholl. London, New York, Sheed and Ward [1952] 238 p. illus. 21 cm. Secular name: Teresia Posselt. [BX4705.S814P63 1952] 52-2160
I. Stein, Edith, 1891-1942. II. Title.

Post, Charles William, 1854-1914.

MAJOR, Nettie Leitch 926.6
C. W. Post: the hour and the man a biography with genealogical supplement. Washington 8, D.C. Pr. of Judd & Detweiler [dist. Author, 2231 Bancroft Pl., N.W., c.]1963. xx, 318p. illus. (pt. col.) ports. (pt. col.) col. coat of arms, facsim. 27cm. 63-22290 12.00
1. Post, Charles William, 1854-1914. I. Title.

Post, Emily Price, 1873-1960.

POST, Edwin. 928.1
Truly Emily Post. New York, Funk & Wagnalls Co. [1961] 249 p. illus. 22 cm. [BJ1853.P68P6] 61-7298
1. Post, Emily Price, 1873-1960. I. Title.

Post, Marjorie Merriweather.

WRIGHT, William 1930- 361.7'4'0924 B
Heiress : the rich life of marjorie Merriweather Post / William Wright. New York : Pocket Books, 1979, c1978. 315p. : ill. ; 18 cm. [HV28.P6W74] pbk. : 2.50
1. Post, Marjorie Merriweather. 2. Philanthropists — United States — Biography. I. Title.
L.C. card no. for 1978 New Republic edition: 77-26168 **BIP**

WRIGHT, William, 1930- 361.7'4'0924 B
Heiress : the rich life of Marjorie Merriweather Post / William Wright. Washington : New Republic Books ; New York : trade distribution by Simon and Schuster, 1978. xvii, 265 p., [16] leaves of plates : ill. ; 24 cm. Includes index. [HV28.P6W74] 77-26168 ISBN 0-915220-36-9 : 12.50
1. Post, Marjorie Merriweather. 2. Philanthropists—United States—Biography. I. Title.

Post, Melville Davisson, 1871-1930.

NORTON, Charles A. 813'.5'2 B
Melville Davisson Post: man of many mysteries [by] Charles A. Norton. Bowling Green, Ohio, Bowling Green University Popular Press [1974, c1973] 261 p. illus. 23 cm. Bibliography of Post's works: p. 246-255. [PS3531.O76427Z8 1974] 73-83359 ISBN 0-87972-056-5 8.95
1. Post, Melville Davisson, 1871-1930.
Pbk. 3.95; ISBN 0-87972-060-3.

Postage-stamps—Forgeries.

TYLER, Varro E. 769'.562'0922 B
Philatelic forgers, their lives and works / by Varro E. Tyler. London : Lowe, 1976. iv, 60 p. : facsims., ports. ; 25 cm. Includes bibliographical references and index. [HE6184.F6T94] 77-362339 £4.00
1. Postage-stamps—Forgeries. I. Title.

Postal service—U.S.

DAY, James Edward, 1914- 383.4973092
My appointed round; 929 days as Postmaster General. New York, Holt [c.1965] 152p. 22cm. [HE6371.D3] 65-14437 3.95
1. Postal service—U.S. I. Title. **BIP**

GEDDES, Virgil, 1897- 383.4973
Country postmaster. New York, Austin-Phelps, 1952. 230 p. 21 cm. Autobiographical. [HE6385.G4A3] 52-12228
1. Postal service—U.S. I. Title.

Postel, Guillaume, 1510-1581.

BUTLER, Geoffrey Gilbert, Sir, 1887- 341.1'1'094
Studies in statecraft: being chapters, biographical, and bibliographical, mainly on the sixteenth century. Port Washington, N.Y., Kennikat Press [1970] vi, 138 p. 22 cm. Reprint of the 1920 ed. Contents.Contents.—Bishop Roderick and Renaissance pacificism.—The French "civilians." Roman law, and the new monarchy.—William Postel; world peace through world power.—Sully and his grand design.—"The grand design" of Emerich Cruce.—Appendices: A. Passages quoted in Chapter I. B. A bibliography of Rodericus Sancius, Bishop of Calahorra (p. [108]-113). C. English version of passages quoted in Chapter II. D. A bibliography of William Postel (p. [117]-131) [D234.B8 1970] 79-110899 ISBN 0-8046-0882-2
1. Sanchez de Arevalo, Rodrigo, Bp., 1404-1470. 2. Postel, Guillaume, 1510-1581. 3. Sully, Maximilien de Bethune, duc de, 1559-1641. 4. Cruce, Emeric, 1590?-1648. 5. Europe—Politics and government—1517-1648. 6. Peace. I. Title.

Poston, Charles Debrille, 1825-1902.

GRESSINGER, A. W. 923.273
Charles D. Poston, sunland seer. Drawings by Harold A. Wolfinbarger, Jr. Globe, Ariz., D. S. King, Six Shooter Canyon [c.1961] 212p. maps. Bibl. 61-18211 5.00; 3.75 pap.,
1. Poston, Charles Debrille, 1825-1902. 2. Arizona—Hist. I. Title.

Potter, Andrew, 1886-1951.

SCANTLAN, Sam W 922.673
Andrew Potter, Baptist builder. [Oklahoma City c1955] 204p. illus. 21cm. [BX6495.P55S35] 58-25951
1. Potter, Andrew, 1886-1951. I. Title.

Potter, Andrey Abraham, 1882-

ECKLES, Robert 620'.007'1177295 B
B.
The dean : a biography of A. A. Potter / by Robert B. Eckles. West Lafayette, Ind. : Purdue University, 1974. xi, 172 p., [4] leaves of plates : ill. ; 24 cm. Includes index. Bibliography: p. 159-166. [TA140.P65E34] 74-82793 6.50
1. Potter, Andrey Abraham, 1882- I. Title.

Potter, Beatrix, 1866-1943.

CROUCH, Marcus. 928.2
Beatrix Potter. [1st American ed.] New York, H. Z. Walck [1961, c1960] 75 p. illus. 29 cm. [PR6031.O72Z58 1961] 61-8578
1. Potter, Beatrix, 1866-1943.

LANE, Margaret, 1907- 823'.8 B
The magic years of Beatrix Potter / by Margaret Lane. London ; New York : F. Warne, 1978. 216 p. : ill. (some col.), facsims., ports. ; 26 cm. Includes index. Bibliography: p. [211]-212. [PR6031.O72Z59] 78-52636 ISBN 0-7232-2108-1 : 17.95
1. Potter, Beatrix, 1866-1943. 2. Authors, English—20th century—Biography. 3. Artists—England—Biography. I. Potter, Beatrix, 1866-1943. II. Title. **BIP**

LANE, Margaret, 1907- 928.2
The tale of Beatrix Potter, a biography by Margaret Lane. Baltimore, Penguin [1963, c.1962] 192p. illus. (pt. col.) 18cm. (1849) Bibl. .95 pap.,
1. Potter, Beatrix, 1866-1943. I. Title.

LANE, Margaret, 1907- 741'.0924 B
The tale of Beatrix Potter: a biography. Revised ed. London, New York, F. Warne, 1968. 173 p. 47 plates, illus. (some col.), ports. 22 cm. "The Beatrice Potter books": p. 167-168. [PR6031.O72Z6 1968] 68-22444 ISBN 0-7232-0138-2 30/-
1. Potter, Beatrix, 1866-1934—Biography. I. Title. **BIP**

Potter, Beatrix, 1866-1943—Biography—Juvenile literature.

ALDIS, Dorothy (Keeley) 823'.8 B
1896-1966.
Nothing is impossible; the story of Beatrix Potter. Drawings by Richard Cuffari. [1st ed.] New York, Atheneum, 1969. xi, 156 p. illus. 22 cm. "A list of Beatrix Potter's books": p. 155-156. A biography of the woman who created Peter Rabbit as well as other stories read by children all over the world. [PR6031.O72Z56 1969] 92 69-13528 4.50
1. Potter, Beatrix, 1866-1943—Biography—Juvenile literature. I. Cuffari, Richard, 1925- illus. II. Title. **BIP**

MAYER, Ann Margaret, 823'.8 B
1938-
The two worlds of Beatrix Potter. Illustrated by Harold Henriksen. Mankato, Minn., Creative Education; [distributed by Childrens Press, Chicago, 1974] 36 p. illus. (part col.) 25 cm. (Creative Education close-ups) A brief biography of the creator of "Peter Rabbit" and many other books whose characters became world famous. [PR6031.O72Z7] 92 74-2082 ISBN 0-87191-324-0
1. Potter, Beatrix, 1866-1943—Biography—Juvenile literature. I. Henriksen, Harold, illus. II. Title.

Potter, Charles Francis,

POTTER, Charles Francis, 922.8173
1885-1962.
The preacher and I, an autobiography. New York, Crown Publishers [1951] 429 p. 22 cm. [BX9869.P74A3] 51-12006
I. Title.

Potter, Jared, 1742-1810.

THOMAS, Herbert, 1885- 926.1
The Doctos Jared of Connecticut: Jared Eliot, Jared Potter, Jared Kirtland. Hamden, Conn., Shoe String Press, 1958. 76 p. illus. 22 cm. (Dept. of the History of Medicine, Yale University School of Medicine. Publication no. 35) [R153.T35] 58-59573
1. Ellot, Jared, 1685-1763. 2. Potter, Jared, 1742-1810. 3. Kirtland, Jared Potter, 1793-1877. I. Title.

Potter, Mary, 1847-1913.

WORDLEY, Dick. 271'.97 B
No one dies alone / [by] Dick Wordley, with assisted creative research by Sister Jeanne Hyland and Frank S. Greenop. [Sydney] : Australian Creative Workshop for The Little Company of Mary, 1976. 244 p., [16] p. of col. plates : ill. ; 25 cm. [BX4390.Z8W67] 77-373919 ISBN 0-909246-33-5 : 14.95
1. Potter, Mary, 1847-1913. 2. Little Company of Mary—History. 3. Nuns—Australia—Biography. I. Hyland, Jeanne, joint author. II. Greenop, Frank Sydney, joint author. III. Title.

Potter, Philip.

GENTZ, William H., 262'.001 B
1918-
The world of Philip Potter [by] William H. Gentz. New York, Friendship Press [1974] 96 p. illus. 20 cm. Includes excerpts from P. Potter's speeches. Includes bibliographical references. [BX6.8.P67G46] 74-9918 ISBN 0-377-00006-X 2.95 (pbk.)
1. Potter, Philip. I. Potter, Philip. The world of Philip Potter. 1974. II. Title. **BIP**

Potter, Robert, 1799?-1842.

FISCHER, Ernest 976.4'04'0924 B
G.
Robert Potter : founder of the Texas navy / by Ernest G. Fischer ; foreword by Stephen L. Walter. Gretna [La.] : Pelican Pub. Co., 1975. p. cm. Includes index. Bibliography: p. [F390.P88F57] 75-33771 ISBN 0-88289-081-6 : 12.50
1. Potter, Robert, 1799?-1842. 2. Texas (Republic). Navy. 3. Texas—History—Republic, 1836-1846.

Potterbaum, Charlene.

POTTERBAUM, 248'.2'0924 B
Charlene.
His eye is on the sparrow so ... this is really for the birds / Charlene Potterbaum. Plainfield, N.J. : Logos International, c1979. ix, 190 p. ; 21 cm. On spine: This is really for the birds. [BR1725.P63A34] 79-83788 ISBN 0-88270-354-4 pbk. : 3.50
1. Potterbaum, Charlene. 2. Christian biography—United States. 3. Christian life—1960- I. Title. II. Title: This is really for the birds.

POTTERBAUM, Charlene. 248'.4
Thanks, Lord, I needed that! / By Charlene Potterbaum. Plainfield, N.J. : Logos International, c1977. ix, 155 p. : ill. ; 20 cm. [BR725.P63A35] 77-86470 ISBN 0-88270-248-3 pbk. : 2.95
1. Potterbaum, Charlene. 2. Christian biography—United States. 3. Christian life—1960- I. Title. **BIP**

Potters—Great Britain—Interviews.

POTTERS on pottery / 738'.092'2
[edited by] Elisabeth Cameron and Philippa Lewis. London : Evans, 1976. 168 p. : ill. (some col.) ; 26 cm. [NK4085.P59 1976b] 77-359493 ISBN 0-237-44855-6 : £6.50
1. Potters—Great Britain—Interviews. 2. Pottery, British. I. Cameron, Elisabeth. II. Lewis, Philippa.

Pottery—Marks.

BARBER, Edwin Atlee, 738'.027'8
1851-1916.
Marks of American potters. Southampton, N.Y., Cracker Barrel Press [1971?] 174 p. illus., facsims., ports. 21 cm. Reprint of the 1904 ed. [NK4215.B3 1971] 70-21077 3.00
1. Pottery—Marks. 2. Potters—United States. I. Title. **BIP**

Pottery, Mexican.

WHITAKER, Irwin. 738'.0972
A potter's Mexico / Irwin & Emily Whitaker. 1st ed. Albuquerque : University of New Mexico Press, c1978. xvi, 136 p., [8] leaves of plates : ill. (some col.) ; 27 cm. Includes index. Bibliography: p. 130-133. [NK4031.W47] 77-29047 ISBN 0-8263-0472-9 : 17.50
1. Pottery, Mexican. 2. Pottery—20th century—Mexico. 3. Potters—Mexico—Biography. I. Whitaker, Emily. II. Title. **BIP**

Potts, Abbie Findlay, 1884-1964—Correspondence.

POTTS, Abbie 371.1'0092'4 B
Findlay, 1884-1964.
Letters written to Winifred Comstock Bowman, 1923-1963 / [by] Abbie Findlay Potts. London ; New York : Regency Press, 1975. 232 p. ; 23 cm. Abbie Findlay Potts, publications: p. [232] [PS3531.O784Z544 1975] 75-327458 ISBN 0-7212-0396-5 : 10.00
1. Potts, Abbie Findlay, 1884-1964—Correspondence. 2. Bowman, Winifred Comstock. I. Bowman, Winifred Comstock. II. Title.

Pouget, Guillaume, 1847-1933.

GUITTON, Jean. 922.244
Abbee Pouget discourses. Translated from the French by Fergus Murphy with a biographical note by the Earl of Wicklow. Baltimore, Helicon Press [1959] 163p. 22cm. Translation of Portrait de m. Pouget. [BX4705.P658G83] 59-6711
1. Pouget, Guillaume, 1847-1933. I. Title.

Poulenc, Francis, 1899-1963.

POULENC, Francis, 780'.92'4 B
1899-1963.
My friends and myself : conversations [with] Francis Poulenc / assembled by Stephane Audel ; translated [from the French] by James Harding. London : Dobson, 1978. 152 p., leaf of plate, [8] p. of plates : 1 ill., ports. ; 23 cm. Translation of Moi et mes amis. Includes index. [ML410.P787A33] 79-348638 ISBN 0-234-77251-4 : 9.95
1. Poulenc, Francis, 1899-1963. 2. Composers—France—Biography. I. Audel, Stephane. II. Title.
Distributed by Southwest Books Service, Dallas, TX 75247

Poulsen, James, 1831-1920.

JAMES Poulsen; v. 12
a faithful Dane. Salt Lake City, Granite Pub. Co., 1960. viii, 98p. illus., ports.
1. Poulsen, James, 1831-1920. I. Poulsen, Ezra James, 1889-

Pound, Ezra Loomis,

POUND, Ezra Loomis, 1885- 928.1
Letters, 1907-1941, ed. by D. D. Paige. New York, Harcourt [1962, c.1950] xxv, 358p. 21cm. (Harvest bk., HB54) 2.25 pap.,
I. Title.

Pound, Ezra Loomis, 1885-1972.

HUTCHINS, Patricia. 928.1
Ezra Pound's Kensington; an exploration 1885-1913. Chicago, Regnery [1965] 180 p. illus., ports. 23 cm. Bibliographical references included in "Notes" (p. 161-170) [PS3531.O82Z65] 65-2305
1. Pound, Ezra Loomis, 1885- 2. Kensington, Eng. I. Title.

MEACHAM, Harry M. 811'.5'2
The caged panther; Ezra Pound at Saint Elizabeths, by Harry M. Meacham. New York, Twayne Publishers [1967] 222 p. facsims., ports. 22 cm. Bibliographical references included in "Notes" (p. 205-212) [PS3531.O82Z753] 811'.5'2 67-30723
1. Pound, Ezra Loomis, 1885- I. Title.

MULLINS, Eustace Clarence, 928.1
1923-
This difficult individual, Ezra Pound. New York, Fleet Pub. Corp. [1961] 388p. illus. 21cm. [PS3531.O82Z755] 61-7628
1. Pound, Ezra Loomis, 1885- I. Title. **BIP**

NORMAN, Charles, 1904- 811'.5'2 B
The case of Ezra Pound. New York, Funk and Wagnalls [1968] x, 209 p. illus., ports. 24 cm. [PS3531.O82Z77 1968] 68-16761
1. Pound, Ezra Loomis, 1885- I. Title. **BIP**

NORMAN, Charles, 1904- 928.1
Ezra Pound. New York, Macmillan, 1960. 493p. illus. 22cm. Includes bibliography. [PS3531.O82Z785] 60-13141
1. Pound, Ezra Loomis, 1885- I. Title.

NORMAN, Charles, 1904- 811'.5'2 B
Ezra Pound. Rev. ed. [New York] Minerva Press [1969] xvi, 493 p. illus., ports. 21 cm. Bibliographical references included in "Notes" (p. 469-477) [PS3531.O82Z773 1969b] 72-9512 2.95
1. Pound, Ezra Loomis, 1885-

OLSON, Charles, 1910- 811'.5'2 B
1970.
Charles Olson & Ezra Pound : an encounter at St. Elizabeths / by Charles Olson ; edited by Catherine Seelye. New York : Grossman Publishers, 1975. xxvi, 143 p. ; 25 cm. Includes bibliographical references and index. [PS3531.O82Z7853 1975] 75-14299 ISBN 0-670-52400-X : 8.95
1. Pound, Ezra Loomis, 1885-1972. I. Title.

POUND, Ezra Loomis, 1885- 928.1
Letters, 1907-1941, ed. by D. D. Paige. New York, Harcourt [1962, c.1950] xxv, 358p. 21cm. (Harvest bk., HB54) 2.25 pap.,
I. Title.

RECK, Michael. 811'.5'2
Ezra Pound; a close-up. [1st ed.] New York, McGraw-Hill [1967] xi, 205 p. 22 cm. [PS3531.O82Z792] 67-22962
1. Pound, Ezra Loomis, 1885-

RECK, Michael. 811'.5'2 B
Ezra Pound; a close-up. New York, McGraw-Hill [1973] ix, 210 p. 21 cm. (McGraw-Hill paperbacks) [PS3531.O82Z792 1973] 73-7893 ISBN 0-07-051351-1 2.95
1. Pound, Ezra Loomis, 1885-1972.

SIMPSON, Louis Aston 811'.5'209
Marantz, 1923-
Three on the tower : the lives and works of Ezra Pound, T. S. Eliot, and William Carlos Williams / by Louis Simpson. New York : Morrow, 1975. ix, 373 p. ; 24 cm. Includes index. Bibliography: p. 356-362. [PS3531.O82Z836] 74-26952 ISBN 0-688-02899-3 : 12.50
1. Pound, Ezra Loomis, 1885-1972. 2. Eliot, Thomas Stearns, 1888-1965. 3. Williams, William Carlos, 1883-1963. I. Title. **BIP**

STOCK, Noel. 811'.5'2 B
The life of Ezra Pound. [1st American ed.] New York, Pantheon Books [1970] xvii, 472 p. illus., facsims., ports. 25 cm. [PS3531.O82Z839] 73-110127 10.00
1. Pound, Ezra Loomis, 1885- I. Title. **BIP**

STOCK, Noel. 811'.5'2 B
The life of Ezra Pound [New York, Avon, 1974, c1970] 610 p. illus. facsims. ports. 18 cm. (Discus books.) [PS3531.082Z839] ISBN 0-380-00191-8 2.65 (pbk.)
1. Pound, Ezra Loomis, 1885-1972. I. Title.
L.C. card no. for original ed.: 73-110127.

YALE literary magazine. v. 12
Ezra Pound: a new montage. [New Haven, Conn., 1958] 50 p. illus., ports. 26 cm. Cover title. Consists of vol. 126, no. 5 (Dec. 1958) of the magazine. Includes Pound's Canto C.
1. Pound, Ezra Loomis, 1885- I. Pound, Ezra Loomis, 1885- II. Title.

Pound, Ezra Loomis, 1885-1972—Biography.

DOOLITTLE, Hilda, 811'.5'2 B
1886-1961.
End to torment : a memoir of Ezra Pound / by H. D. ; edited by Norman Holmes Pearson and Michael King ; with the poems from "Hilda's book" by Ezra Pound.

New York : New Directions Pub. Corp., 1979. xii, 84 p. : ill. ; 21 cm. Includes bibliographical references. [PS3531.O82Z595 1979] 78-27149 ISBN 0-8112-0719-6 : 8.50 ISBN 0-8112-0720-X pbk. : 3.95
1. Pound, Ezra Loomis, 1885-1972—Biography. 2. Doolittle, Hilda, 1886-1961—Friends and associates. 3. Poets, American—20th century—Biography. I. H. D. II. D., H. III. Pearson, Norman Holmes, 1909-1976. IV. King, Michael John. V. Pound, Ezra Loomis, 1885-1972. Hilda's book. 1979. VI. Title. **BIP**

HEYMANN, Clemens David, 1945- 811'.5'2 B
Ezra Pound, the last rower : a political profile / by C. David Heymann. New York : Viking Press, 1976. xii, 372 p. : ill. ; 24 cm. "A Richard Seaver book." Includes bibliographical references and index. [PS3531.O82Z645] 74-4803 ISBN 0-670-30391-7 : 10.00
1. Pound, Ezra Loomis, 1885-1972—Biography. 2. Pound, Ezra Loomis, 1885-1972—Political and social views.

RACHEWILTZ, Mary de. 811'.5'2 B
Ezra Pound, father and teacher : discretions / Mary de Rachewiltz. New York : Published for J. Laughlin by New Directions Pub. Corp., 1975. 312 p., [8] leaves of plates : ill. ; 21 cm. (New Directions paperbook ; 405) (A New Directions book) First ed. published in 1971 under title: Discretions. Includes bibliographical references. [PS3531.O82Z79 1975] 76-352215 ISBN 0-8112-0589-4 pbk. : 4.75
1. Pound, Ezra Loomis, 1885-1972—Biography. 2. Rachewiltz, Mary de—Biography—Youth. I. Title. II. Title: Discretions. **BIP**

Pound, Ezra Loomis, 1885-1972—Correspondence.

POUND, Ezra Loomis, 1885 811'.5'2 B
The letters of Ezra Pound, 1907-1941, edited by D. D. Paige. New York, Haskell House Publishers, 1974. 464 p. 21 cm. Reprint of the 1951 ed. published by Faber and Faber, London. [PS3531.O82Z53 1974] 74-11145 ISBN 0-8383-1991-2
1. Pound, Ezra Loomis, 1885-1972—Correspondence. **BIP**

POUND, Ezra Loomis, 1885- 811'.5'2 B
The selected letters of Ezra Pound, 1907-1941. Edited by D. D. Paige. [New York, New Directions Pub. Corp., 1971] xxv, 358 p. 21 cm. (A New Directions paperbook, NDP317) First published in 1950 under title: The letters of Ezra Pound, 1907-1941. [PS3531.O82Z53 1971] 71-145933 2.95
1. Pound, Ezra Loomis, 1885-1972—Correspondence. I. Title. **BIP**

POUND, Ezra Loomis, 1885-1972. 811'.5'2
Letters to Ibbotson, 1935-1952 / Ezra Pound ; edited by Vittoria I. Mondolfo and Margaret Hurley ; introd. by Walter Pilkington. Orono : National Poetry Foundation, University of Maine, c1979. 145 p. : facsims. ; 24 cm. (Ezra Pound scholarship series) "Limited edition: 400." Includes bibliographical references and index. [PS3531.O82Z5328] 78-55724 ISBN 0-915032-10-4 : 12.95
1. Pound, Ezra Loomis, 1885-1972—Correspondence. 2. Ibbotson, Joseph Darling, 1869- 3. Poets, American—20th century—Correspondence. I. Ibbotson, Joseph Darling, 1869- II. Mondolfo, Vittoria I. III. Hurley, Margaret. IV. Title. V. Series. **BIP**

Pound, Ezra Loomis, 1885-1972—Homes and haunts—Pennsylvania.

STOCK, Noel. 811'.5'4 B
Ezra Pound's Pennsylvania : compiled for the most part from Mr. Carl Gatter's researches into original sources and documents / by Noel Stock. Toledo, Ohio : Friends of the University of Toledo Libraries, 1976. 111 p. : ill. ; 23 cm. "A shorter version ... appeared in 1973 in Poetry Australia no. 46." Includes bibliographical references. [PS3531.O82Z838] 75-39838 pbk. : 10.00
1. Pound, Ezra Loomis, 1885-1972—Homes and haunts—Pennsylvania. I. Gatter, Carl. II. Title.

Pound, Roscoe, 1870-1964.

WIGDOR, David. 340'.092'4 B
Roscoe Pound; philosopher of law. Westport, Conn., Greenwood Press [1974] xi, 356 p. port. 21 cm. (Contributions in American history, no. 33) Includes bibliographical references. [KF373.P6W5] 72-852 ISBN 0-8371-6419-2 12.95
1. Pound, Roscoe, 1870-1964.

Pourier, Bat, 1841-1933.

GILBERT, Hila. 978'.02'0924 B
Big Bat Pourier; [guide & interpreter, Fort Laramie, 1870-1880] By Hila Gilbert, with George Harris and Bernice Pourier Harris. Sheridan, Wyo., Mills Co., [1968] 82 p. illus., ports. 23 cm. Includes bibliographical references. [F597.P6G5] 68-7879 2.95
1. Pourier, Bat, 1841-1933. 2. Northwestern States—History. I. Harris, George. II. Harris, Bernice Pourier. III. Title.

Poussin, Nicolas, 1594?-1665.

MACGREEVY, Thomas 759.4
Nicolas Poussin. [dist. Chester Springs, Pa., Dufour Eds., c.1960] 47p. illus. 26cm. 61-3099 4.50, pap., limited ed.
1. Poussin, Nicolas, 1594?-1665. I. Title.

Povich, Shirley.

POVICH, Shirley. 070'.924 B
All these mornings. Englewood Cliffs, N.J., Prentice-Hall [1969] x, 240 p. ports. 22 cm. Autobiography. [PN4784.S6P6] 69-17499 5.95
I. Title.

Powell, Adam Clayton, 1908-1972

COLEMAN, Emmett. 973.92'0924 (B)
The rise, fall, and...? of Adam Clayton Powell. Rise fall and of Adam Clayton Powell. [New York, Bee-Line Books, 1967] 169 p. illus., ports. 18 cm. [E748.P86C6] 67-6445
1. Powell, Adam Clayton, 1908- I. Title.

HICKEY, Neil. 923.273
Adam Clayton Powell and the politics of race, by Neil Hickey and Ed Edwin. New York, Fleet Pub. Corp. [1965] 308 p. illus., ports. 21 cm. Bibliography: p. 200-300. [E748.P86H5] 65-16313
1. Powell, Adam Clayton, 1908- I. Edwin, Ed. joint author. II. Title.

LEWIS, Claude 923.273
Adam Clayton Powell. Greenwich, Conn., Fawcett [c.1963] 127p. 18cm. (Gold medal bks., K1361) 64-703 40 pap.,
1. Powell, Adam Clayton, 1908- I. Title.

POWELL, Adam Clayton, 1908- 973.92'0924 B
Adam by Adam; the autobiography of Adam Clayton Powell, Jr. New York, Dial Press, 1971. x, 260 p. ports. 22 cm. [E748.P86A3] 71-163587 6.95
I. Title.

Powell, Adam Clayton, 1908-1972—Juvenile literature.

HASKINS, James, 1941- 973.92'092'4 B
Adam Clayton Powell: portrait of a marching Black. New York, Dial Press [1974] 174 p. illus. 22 cm. A biography of the well-known Black political figure whose flamboyant conduct led to the denial of his seat in Congress. [E748.P86H37] 73-6026 ISBN 0-8037-1809-8 4.95
1. Powell, Adam Clayton, 1908-1972—Juvenile literature. I. Title.

POWELL, Adam Clayton, 1908- 973.92'0924 B
Adam by Adam; the autobiography of Adam Clayton Powell, Jr. New York, Dial Press, 1971. x, 260 p. ports. 22 cm. [E748.P86A3] 71-163587 6.95
I. Title.

Powell, Anthony, 1905-—Biography.

POWELL, Anthony, 1905- 823'.9'12 B
Infants of the spring : the memoirs of Anthony Powell. New York : Holt, Rinehart and Winston, 1977, c1976. 214 p. [8] p. : ill. ; 24 cm. (His To keep the ball rolling) Includes index. [PR6031.O74Z516 1977] 77-71357 ISBN 0-03-020991-9 : 10.00
1. Powell, Anthony, 1905-—Biography. 2. Novelists, English—20th century—Biography. I. Title. II. Series.

Powell, Anthony, 1905-Biography London life.

POWELL, Anthony, 1905- 823'.9'12 B
Messengers of day : the memoirs of Anthony Powell. 1st ed. New York : Holt, Rinehart, and Winston, c1978. p. cm. (His To keep the ball rolling ; 2) Includes index. [PR6031.O74Z52] 78-4703 ISBN 0-03-020996-X : 10.95
1. Powell, Anthony, 1950- —Biography—London life. 2. Novelists, English—20th century—Biography. 3. London—Intellectual life. I. Title. II. Series.

Powell, Dilys.

POWELL, Dilys. 828.9
Coco, a biography. New York, Oxford University Press, 1953 [c1952] 121 p. illus. 20 cm. [QL795.D6P65 1953] 636.78 53-6621
I. Title.

Powell, John Benjamin, 1888-1947.

POWELL, John Benjamin, 1888-1947. 320.9'51'04
My twenty-five years in China / by John B. Powell. New York : Da Capo Press, 1976, c1945. 436 p. ; 23 cm. (China in the 20th century) Reprint of the ed. published by Macmillan, New York. Includes index. [DS775.P67 1976] 76-27721 ISBN 0-306-70761-6 : 25.00
1. Powell, John Benjamin, 1888-1947. 2. China—Politics and government—1912-1949. 3. Journalists—China—Biography. I. Title. **BIP**

Powell, John Enoch, 1912-

SCHOEN, Douglas E., D. Phil. 941.085'092'4 B
Enoch Powell and the Powellites / Douglas E. Schoen. New York : St. Martin's Press, 1977. xviii, 317 p. : graphs ; 23 cm Includes index. Bibliography: p. 280-287. [DA591.P64S36 1977] 77-70333 ISBN 0-312-25672-8 : 18.95
1. Powell, John Enoch, 1912- 2. Great Britain—Politics and government—1964- 3. Statesmen—Great Britain—Biography. I. Title. **BIP**

Powell, John Wesley, 1834-1902.

CARLSON, Vada F. 917.91'3'0440924 B
John Wesley Powell : conquest of the canyon / by Vada F. Carlson ; drawings by Richard Cuffari. Irvington-on-Hudson, N.Y. : Harvey House, [1974] 158, [2] p. : ill. ; 23 cm. Bibliography: p. [159] A biography of the geologist who led the first expedition down the canyons of the Green and Colorado rivers in 1869. [Q143.P8C37] 73-79453 ISBN 0-8178-5131-3. ISBN 0-8178-5132-1 lib. bdg.
1. Powell, John Wesley, 1834-1902. I. Cuffari, Richard, 1925- ill.

DARRAH, William Culp, 1909- 925
Powell of the Colorado. Princeton, Princeton University Press, 1951. ix, 426 p. illus., ports. 25 cm. Bibliography: p. [401]-412. [Q143.P8D25] 51-11671
1. Powell, John Wesley, 1834-1902. I. Title.

STEGNER, Wallace Earle, 1909- 925
Beyond the hundredth meridian: John Wesley Powell and the second opening of the West. With an introd. by Bernard De Voto. Boston, Houghton, Mifflin, 1954. xxiii, 438 p. illus., maps. 22 cm. Bibliographical references included in "notes" (p. [369]-419) [Q143.P8S8] 53-9245
1. Powell, John Wesley, 1834-1902. 2. The West. I. Title.

TERRELL, John Upton, 1900- 550'.924 B
The man who rediscovered America; a biography of John Wesley Powell. New York, Weybright and Talley [1969] 281 p. maps. 22 cm. Bibliography: p. 271-273. [Q143.P8T4 1969] 76-85151 6.95
1. Powell, John Wesley, 1834-1902. I. Title.

U.S. Geological Survey. 550'.924 B
John Wesley Powell: soldier, explorer, scientist. [Washington, 1969] 23 p. illus., ports. 23 cm. Bibliography: p. 23. [Q143.P8U5] 71-603443
1. Powell, John Wesley, 1834-1902. I. Title.

WATSON, Elmo Scott, 1892-1951, ed. 925
The professor goes West: Illinois Wesleyan University reports of Major John Wesley Powell's explorations, 1867-1874. Bloomington, Illinois Wesleyan University Press, 1954. vii, 138p. 24cm. [F786.W35] 55-34567
1. Powell, John Wesley, 1834-1902. 2. U. S.—Exploring expeditions. 3. Southwest, New—Descr. & trav. I. Title.

WIBBERLEY, Leonard Patrick O'Connor, 1915- 925
Wes Powell, conqueror of the Grand Canyon. New York, Ariel Books [1958] 216 p. 22 cm. Includes bibliography. [Q143.P8W5] 58-10764
1. Powell, John Wesley, 1834-1902.

Powell, John Wesley, 1834-1902—Juvenile literature.

PLACE, Marian (Templeton) 509'.2'2
John Wesley Powell: canyon's conqueror, Illustrated by Harve Stein Boston, Houghton Mifflin [c1963] 191 p. col. illus. 22 cm. (Piper books) [Q143.P8P54] 63-15656
1. Powell, John Wesley, 1834-1902—Juvenile literature. I. Title.

Powell, Lawrence Clark,

POWELL, Lawrence Clark, 1906- 027.7'0924 B
Fortune & friendship, an autobiography. New York, R. R. Bowker Co., 1968. xiii, 227 p. ports. 23 cm. [Z720.P65] 67-29798
I. Title.

Powell, Lawrence Clarke, 1906-—Addresses, essays, lectures.

POWELL, Lawrence Clark, 1906- 027.7'0924 B
Fortune & friendship, an autobiography. New York, R. R. Bowker Co., 1968. xiii, 227 p. ports. 23 cm. [Z720.P65] 67-29798
I. Title.

POWELL, Lawrence Clark, 1906- 920'.073
From the heartland : profiles of people and places of the Southwest and beyond / by Lawrence Clark Powell ; ill. by Bettina Steinke. 1st ed. Flagstaff [Ariz.] : Northland Press, c1976. xi, 167 p. : ill. ; 24 cm. [CT260.5.P68] 75-43347 ISBN 0-87358-155-5 : 9.50
1. Powell, Lawrence Clarke, 1906-—Addresses, essays, lectures. 2. Southwest, New—Biography—Addresses, essays, lectures. 3. Southwest, New—Description and travel—Addresses, essays, lectures. I. Title.

Powell, Margaret.

POWELL, Margaret. 641'.0924 B
Below stairs. New York, Dodd, Mead [1970, c1968] 176 p. 22 cm. [TX649.P68A3 1970] 77-108042 4.95
I. Title. BIP

Powell, Sandy, 1900-

POWELL, Sandy, 1900- 792.7 B
"Can you hear me mother" : Sandy Powell's lifetime of music-hall / Sandy Powell's story told to Harry Stanley. London : Jupiter Books, 1976. 3-192 p. : ill., facsims., ports. ; 24 cm. [PN2598.P68A33] 76-371411 ISBN 0-904041-38-7 : £3.50
1. Powell, Sandy, 1900- 2. Entertainers—Great Britain—Biography. I. Stanley, Harry. II. Title.

Powell, Tyrone, 1914-1958.

ARCE, Hector. 791.43'028'0924 B
The secret life of Tyrone Power / by Hector Arce. 1st ed. New York : Morrow, 1979. 317 p. : ill. ; 25 cm. Bibliography: p. 315-317. [PN2287.P62A83] 79-51789 ISBN 0-688-03484-5 : 9.95
1. Power, Tyrone, 1914- 2. Moving-picture actors and actresses—United States—Biography. I. Title. BIP

BELAFONTE, Dennis. 792'.028'0924 B
The films of Tyrone Power / by Dennis Belafonte with Alvin H. Marill ; foreword by Henry King. 1st ed. Secaucus, N.J. : Citadel Press, c1979. 224 p. : ill. ; 29 cm. [PN2287.P62B4] 79-102089 ISBN 0-8065-0477-3 : 14.95
1. Power, Tyrone, 1914- 2. Moving-picture actors and actresses—United States—Biography. I. Marill, Alvin H., joint author. II. Title. BIP

CHRISTIAN, Linda. 927.92
Linda, my own story. New York, Crown Publishers [1962] 280p. illus. 23cm. [PN2287.C54A3] 62-20060
1. Power, Tyrone, 1914- I. Title.

CHRISTIAN, Linda [Blanca Rosa (Welter) Purdom] 927.92
Linda, my own story. New York, Crown [c.1962] 280p. illus. 23cm. 62-20060 4.95
1. Power, Tyrone, 1914- I. Title.

GUILES, Fred Lawrence. 791.43'028'0924 B
Tyrone Power : the last idol / by Fred Lawrence Guiles. 1st ed. Garden City, N.Y. : Doubleday, 1979. xvii, 389 p., [32] leaves of plates : ill. ; 22 cm. Includes index. Bibliography: p. [369]-371. [PN2287.P62G8] 79-6978 ISBN 0-385-14383-4 : 10.00
1. Power, Tyrone, 1914- 2. Moving-picture actors and actresses—United States—Biography. BIP

WINTER, William, 1836-1917. 792'.028'0924 B
Tyrone Power. New York, B. Blom, 1972. 192 p. illus. 21 cm. Reprint of the 1913 ed., issued in series: Lives of the players. [PN2287.P6W5 1972] 76-91591 12.50
1. Power, Tyrone, 1869-

Powell, Vavasor, 1617-1670.

NUTTALL, Geoffrey Fillingham, 1911- v. 12
The Welsh saints, 1640-1660: Walter Cradock, Vavasor Powell, Morgan Llwyd. iCardiff, University of Wales Press, 1957. x, 93p. 22cm. 'Delivered as a course of lectures (under the title 'The Welsh saints, 1640-1660') at the University College of North Wales during March 1957.' Bibliographical references included in 'Notes' (p.79-90) A59
1. Cradock, Walter, 1606;-1659. 2. Powell, Vavasor, 1617-1670. 3. Lloyd(Morgan, 1619-1639. I. Title.

Powell, Violet Georgiana, Lady, 1912-—Biography.

POWELL, Violet Georgiana, Lady, 1912- 941.083'092'4 B
Within the family circle : an autobiography / [by] Violet Powell. London : Heinemann, 1976. xii, 243 p. : geneal. tables ; 23 cm. Includes index. [PR6066.O958Z518] 76-363630 ISBN 0-434-59955-7 : £4.50
1. Powell, Violet Georgiana, Lady, 1912-—Biography. I. Title.

Powell, W. H. R.

POWELL, W. H. R. 253'.0924 B
Illustrations from a supervised life, by W. H. R. Powell. [Philadelphia, Printed by Continental Press, 1968] 263 p. illus. 22 cm. Autobiographical. [BX6455.P65A3] 68-7980 4.50
I. Title.

Powell, William Stevens,

POWELL, William Stevens, 1919- 975.5'01'0924 B
John Pory, 1572-1636 : the life and letters of a man of many parts / by William S. Powell. Chapel Hill : University of North Carolina Press, c1977. xviii, 187 p., [8] leaves of plates : ill. ; 22 cm. Includes bibliographical references and index. [DA378.P6P68] 75-45074 ISBN 0-8078-1270-6 16.95

Powell, William, 1892-

MORELLA, Joe. 791.43'028'0922 B
Cable & Lombard & Powell & Harlow / [by] Joe Morella & Edward Z. Epstein. 1st British ed. London : W. H. Allen, 1976. 204 p., [8] p. of plates : ill., ports. ; 23 cm. [PN1998.A2M56 1976] 76-383446 ISBN 0-491-01975-0 : £3.50
1. Gable, Clark, 1901-1960. 2. Lombard, Carole, 1908-1942. 3. Powell, William, 1892- 4. Harlow, Jean, 1911-1937. 5. Moving-picture actors and actresses—United States—Biography. I. Epstein, Edward Z., joint author. II. Title.

Power, Emily, Mother, 1844-1909.

SYNON, Mary. 922.273
Mother Emily of Sinsinawa, American pioneer. Milwaukee, Bruce Pub. Co. [c1955] 279p. illus. 23cm. [BX4705.P6595S9] 55-1260
1. Power, Emily, Mother, 1844-1909. 2. Sisters of the Order of St. Dominic. Sinsinawa, Wis. I. Title.

Powers, Francis Gary, 1929-

POWERS, Barbara (Moore) 1934- 920
Spy wife [by] Barbara Powers with W. W. Diehl. New York, Pyramid [c.1965] 188p. 18cm. (X1240) Bibl. [DK266.3.P6] 65-8821 .60 pap.,
1. Powers, Francis Gary, 1929- 2. U-2 Incident, 1960. 3. U.S. Central Intelligence Agency. I. Diehl., W. W. II. Title.

Powers, Hiram, 1805-1873.

CRANE, Sylvia E. 730'.973
White silence; Greenough, Powers, and Crawford, American sculptors in nineteenth-century Italy [by] Sylvia E. Crane. Coral Gables [Fla.] University of Miami Press [1972] xviii, 499 p. illus. 27 cm. Bibliography: p. [459]-489. [NB236.C72] 79-156141 ISBN 0-87024-199-0 9.95
1. Greenough, Horatio, 1805-1852. 2. Powers, Hiram, 1805-1873. 3. Crawford, Thomas, 1813-1857. I. Title.

Powers, Jack, d. 1860.

ROSS, Dudley T. 364.1'55 B
Devil on horseback : a biography of the "notorious" Jack Powers / by Dudley T. Ross. Fresno, [Calif.] : Valley Publishers, 1975. xv, 185 p. : ill. ; 23 cm. Includes index. Bibliography: p. 175-177. [F865.P69R67] 74-84615 ISBN 0-913548-28-6 : 7.95
1. Powers, Jack, d. 1860. I. Title.

Powers, John G.

WOOD, Elizabeth (Lambert) 923.4173
The tragedy of the Powers Mine, an Arizona story. Portland, Or., Binfords & Mort. [c1957] 63 p. illus. 22 cm. [HV6248.P64W6] 58-1883
1. Powers, John G. I. Title.

Powhatan, Indian chief, d. 1618—Juvenile literature.

NEE, Kay Bonner. 970.3 B
Powhatan. Minneapolis, Dillon Press [1971] 41 p. illus. 24 cm. A biography of the Algonquian chief who assured the survival of the Jamestown colonists and is remembered as the builder of the Powhatan Confederacy of Indian tribes. [E99.P85P65] 92 73-140991 ISBN 0-87518-036-1
1. Powhatan, Indian chief, d. 1618—Juvenile literature. 2. Virginia—History—Colonial period, ca. 1600-1775—Juvenile literature. I. Title. BIP

Pownall, Henry, Sir, 1887-1961.

POWNALL, Henry, Sir, 1887-1961. 355.3'31'0924 B
Chief of staff; the diaries of Lieutenant-General Sir Henry Pownall. Edited by Brian Bond. [Hamden, Conn.] Archon Books, 1973- v. illus. 23 cm. Contents.—v. 1. 1933-1940.—v. 2. 1940-1944. [U55.P69A33] 73-160579 ISBN 0-208-01326-1 16.50 (v. 1)
1. Pownall, Henry, Sir, 1887-1961. I. Title.

Pownall, Thomas, 1722-1805.

SCHUTZ, John A 1919- 923.542
Thomas Pownall, British defender of American liberty; a study of Anglo-American relations in the eighteenth century. Glendale, Calif., A. H. Clark Co., 1951. 340 p. illus., ports., map., facsim. 25 cm. (Old Northwest historical series, 5) Bibliography: p. [291]-309. [F67.P893] 51-5674
1. Pownall, Thomas, 1722-1805. I. Title. II. Series.

Powys, John Cowper

POWYS, John Cowper 928.2
Autobiography. [New York] New Directions, 1960[ ] 652p. ports. 23cm. 60-9295 4.75 bds.,
I. Title.

POWYS, John Cowper, 1872-1963. 828'.9'1209 B
Confessions of two brothers [by] John Cowper Powys [and] Llewellyn Powys. Rochester, N.Y., Manas Press, 1916. St. Clair Shores, Mich., Scholarly Press, 1971. 265 p. 21 cm. [PR6031.O867C6 1971] 70-131804 ISBN 0-403-00691-0
I. Powys, Llewellyn, 1884-1939. II. Title. BIP

Premorel, Raoul de.

PREMOREL, Raoul de. 967.5'1'020924 B
Kassai : the story of Raoul de Premorel, African trader / [as told to] Reginald Ray Stuart. Stockton, Calif. : Pacific Center for Western Historical Studies, University of the Pacific, c1975. i, ii, 129 p., [8] leaves of plates : ill., coat of arms ; 23 cm. (Monograph - Pacific Center for Western Historical Studies ; special no. 1) Includes index. [DT655.2.P73A34] 75-330792
1. Premorel, Raoul de. 2. Zaire—Description and travel—1881-1950. 3. Zaire—Commerce. I. Stuart, Reginald Ray, 1882- II. Title. III. Series: Pacific Center for Western Historical Studies. Monograph ; special no. 1.

Prevost, Antoine Francois, called Prevost d'Exiles, 1697-1763.

HARRISSE, Henry, 1829-1910. 843'.5 B
L'abbe Prevost: histoire de sa vie et de ses oeuvres dapres des documents nouveaux. New York, B. Franklin [1972] 465 p. 22 cm. (Burt Franklin research & source works series. Selected essays & texts in literature & criticism, 182) Reprint of the 1896 ed. Includes bibliographical references. [PQ2021.Z5H3 1972] 72-87292 ISBN 0-8337-4159-4 20.00
1. Prevost, Antoine Francois, called Prevost d'Exiles, 1697-1763.

Proll, Annemarie, 1953- —Juvenile literature.

JACOBS, Linda. 796.9'3'0924 B
Annemarie Proell : queen of the mountain / by Linda Jacobs. St. Paul : EMC Corp., 1975. 40 p. : ill. ; 24 cm. (Women who win 3) A biography of the Austrian skiier whose record-breaking achievements include winning four World Cup titles in 1971-1974. [GV854.2.P7J32] 92 75-4501 ISBN 0-88436-170-5 lib.bdg. : 3.95 ISBN 0-88436-171-3 pbk. : 1.95
1. Proll, Annemarie, 1953- —Juvenile literature. 2. Skiers—Austria—Biography. I. Title.

Prados, Emilio, 1899-

EMILIO Prados; v. 12
vida y obra - bibliografia-antologia. New York, Hispanic Institute in the United States [1960] 136p. illus., ports., facsims. 26cm. Bibliography: p. [111]-113.
1. Prados, Emilio, 1899- I. Blanco Aguinaga, Carlos.

Praed, Rosa Caroline (Murray-Prior) 1851-1935—Juvenile literature.

POWNALL, Evelyn. 823 B
A pioneer daughter [by] Eve Pownall. Illustrated by Jane Walker. Melbourne, New York [etc.] Oxford University Press, 1968. 32 p. illus. 20 cm. (Early Australians) A brief and easy-to-read biography that concentrates on the childhood of the girl who became "Queenland's first woman author." [PR5189.P6Z85] 92 76-469611 unpriced
1. Praed, Rosa Caroline (Murray-Prior) 1851-1935—Juvenile literature. I. Walker, Jane, illus. II. Title.

Prang, Louis, 1824-1909.

FREEMAN, Graydon La Verne, 1904- 769'.92'4
Louis Prang; color lithographer; giant of a man [by] Larry Freeman. Watkins Glen, N.Y., Century House [1971] 190 p. illus. (part col.) 29 cm. (Library of Victorian culture) [NE2312.P7F7] 70-145867
1. Prang, Louis, 1824-1909.

Prasad, Rajendra, Pres. India, 1884-

PANJABI, Kewal Lalchand, 1898- 923.154
Rajendra Prasad, first President of India. New York, St. Martin's [1962, c.1960] 215p. illus. 61-4860 3.50
1. Prasad, Rajendra Pres. India, 1884- I. Title.

RAJENDRA Prasad, v. 12
first president of India. London, Macmillan New York, St. Martin's Press, 1960. 215p. plates, ports. 22cm.
1. Prasad, Rajendra, Pres. India, 1884- 2. India—Pol. & govt.—1947- I. Punjabi, Kewal L

Prassinos, Mario, 1916-

FERRIER, Jean Louis 759.4
Prassinos. [Paris, G. Fall, dist. New York, Efron] c.1962. 74p. col. illus. 19cm. (Le Musee de poche) 62-52236 1.50 pap.,
1. Prassinos, Mario, 1916- I. Title.

Prat, Arturo, 1848-1879.

ARTURO Prat : 983'.06
vida y obra de un hombre ejemplar / proyecto y fotografia, Walter Grohmann Borchers ; textos, Carlos Toledo de la Maza ; poesias, Ruben Dario ... [et al.] ; asesoria tecnica, Jorge Quezada Navarro, Joaquin Schmidt. 1. ed. Valparaiso : Ediciones Prat, 1975- v. : ill., ports. ; 24

cm. (Coleccion Fanal) [F3095.P885A77] 75-522485
1. Prat, Arturo, 1848-1879. 2. Chile—History, Naval. I. Grohmann Borchers, Walter. II. Toledo de la Maza, Carlos.

Praxedes Mother.

PATRICIA, Jean, Sister 922.273
Only one heart; the story of a pioneer nun in America. Garden City, N.Y., Doubleday [c.]1963. 312p. 22cm. Bibl. 63-10262 4.50
1. Praxedes Mother. I. Title.

Preaching—Addresses, essays, lectures.

GOD demands doctrinal 251
preaching / edited by Thomas B. Warren, Garland Elkins. Jonesboro, Ark. : National Christian Press, c1978. 332 p. ; 22 cm. (Spiritual sword lectureship ; 3) Includes bibliographical references. [BV4222.G6] 78-113413 9.95 pbk. : 7.95
1. Bible—Biography—Addresses, essays, lectures. 2. Bible—Criticism, interpretation, etc.—Addresses, essays, lectures. 3. Preaching—Addresses, essays, lectures. I. Warren, Thomas B. II. Elkins, Garland. III. Title. IV. Series. **BIP**

Preaching—Biblical teaching.

LAYMON, Charles M. 220.6'6
They dared to speak for God [by] Charles M. Laymon. Nashville, Abingdon Press [1974] 176 p. 22 cm. Includes bibliographical references. [BS511.2.L4] 73-17196 ISBN 0-687-41649-3 5.95
1. Bible—Criticism, interpretation, etc. 2. Bible—Biography. 3. Preaching—Biblical teaching. I. Title.

Preaching—History.

DEMARAY, Donald E. 251'.009'22 B
Pulpit giants: what made them great, by Donald E. Demaray. Chicago, Moody Press [1973] 174 p. ports. 22 cm. [BV4207.D38] 72-95026 ISBN 0-8024-6950-7 3.95
1. Preaching—History. 2. Christian biography. I. Title.
Contents Omitted.

Preaching—History—U.S.

JONES, Edgar De Witt, 251'.0922 B
1876-1956.
American preachers of to-day; intimate appraisals of thirty-two leaders. Freeport, N.Y., Books for Libraries Press [1971, 1933] 317 p. 23 cm. (Essay index reprint series) [BV4208.U6J65] 76-156667 ISBN 0-8369-2279-4
1. Preaching—History—U.S. I. Title. **BIP**

Preble, Edward, 1761-1807.

MCKEE, Christopher 359.3'31'0924
Edward Preble; a naval biography, 1761-1807. Annapolis, Naval Institute Press, 1972. x, 394 p. illus. 24 cm. Includes bibliographical references. [E335.P78M32] 76-151092 ISBN 0-87021-525-6 16.00
1. Preble, Edward, 1761-1807. I. Title.

Preddy, George Earl, 1919-1944.

NOAH, Joseph W. 940.54'49'730924
Wings God gave my soul: The story of George E. Preddy, Jr., American fighter pilot, WW II, by Joseph W. Noah; foreword by John C. Meyer. Annandale, Va. C. Baptie Studios, [1975 c1974] xiii, 209 p. ill. 22 cm. Includes index. [TL540.P7N6] 74-81677 ISBN 0-911720-81-2 9.95
1. Preddy, George Earl, 1919-1944. I. Title.
Distributed by Aviation Book. Pbk. 6.95; ISBN 0-911720-82-0.

Preece, William Henry, Sir, 1834-1913.

BAKER, Edward 621.3'092'4 B
Cecil.
Sir William Preece, F.R.S. : Victorian engineer extraordinary / [by] E. C. Baker. London : Hutchinson, 1976. xiv, 377 p., leaf of plate, [8] p. of plates : ill., facsims., map, ports. ; 24 cm. Includes indexes. "Principal lectures and publications": p. [356]-362. [TK140.P73B34] 76-373464 ISBN 0-09-126610-6 : £6.50
1. Preece, William Henry, Sir, 1834-1913. 2. Electric engineers—Great Britain—Biography. **BIP**

Prefontaine, Steve.

JORDAN, Tom. 796.4'26 B
Pre! / By Tom Jordan. Los Altos, Calif. : Tafnews, 1977. 128 p. : ill. ; 23 cm. [GV697.P73J67] 77-90084 ISBN 0-911520-79-1 pbk. : 6.00
1. Prefontaine, Steve. 2. Track and field athletes—United States—Biography. I. Title. **BIP**

Pregnancy—Personal narratives.

DEMORIANE, 618.2'4'0924 B
Hermine.
Life star. [1st American ed.] New York, Coward-McCann [1970, c1969] 103 p. illus. 20 cm. [RG525.D36 1970] 74-111431 3.95
1. Pregnancy—Personal narratives. I. Title.

Preminger, Marion Mill

PREMINGER, Marion Mill 927.92
All I want is everything [New York] Macfadden [1964, c.1957] 224p. 18cm. (75-127) .75 pap.,
I. Title.

PREMINGER, Marion Mill. 927.92
All I want is everything. New York, Funk & Wagnalls [1957] 328p. illus. 22cm. Autobiography. [PN2287.P7A3] 57-10581
I. Title.

Preminger, Otto.

FRISCHAUER, 791.43'0233'0924 B
Willi, 1906-
Behind the scenes of Otto Preminger; an unauthorized biography. New York, Morrow, 1974 [c1973] 278 p. illus. 21 cm. "The plays and films of Otto Preminger": p. [249]-268. [PN1998.A3P674 1974] 73-22614 ISBN 0-688-00262-5 7.95
1. Preminger, Otto. I. Title.

PREMINGER, 791.43'023'0924 B
Otto.
Preminger : an autobiography / by Otto Preminger. 1st ed. Garden City, N.Y. : Doubleday, 1977. 208 p., [16] leaves of plates : ill. ; 22 cm. Includes index. Filmography: p. [194]-199. [PN1998.A3P672 1977] 74-18825 ISBN 0-385-03480-6 : 8.95
1. Preminger, Otto. 2. Moving-picture producers and directors—United States—Biography.

***Premont, Brother Jeremy**

*PREMONT, Brother Jeremy 920
The cardinal said no: St. John Fisher, Valatie, N.Y., Holy Cross Pr. [c.1964] 140p. 22cm. 2.50
I. Title.

Prempeh, King of Ashanti.

BADEN-POWELL, Robert 966.7'03
Stephenson Smyth Baden-Powell, Baron, 1857-1941.
The downfall of Prempeh; a diary of life with the native levy in Ashanti, 1895-96. With a chapter on the political and commercial position of Ashanti, by Sir George Baden-Powell. Freeport, N.Y., Books for Libraries Press, 1972. 198 p. illus. 22 cm. (The Black heritage library collection) Reprint of the 1896 ed. [DT507.B2 1972] 72-6481 ISBN 0-8369-9157-5
1. Prempeh, King of Ashanti. 2. Ashanti—History. I. Title. II. Series.

Prentiss, Seargent Smith, 1808-1850.

SHIELDS, Joseph 328.73'092'4 B
Dunbar, 1820-1886.
The life and times of Seargent Smith Prentiss. Freeport, N.Y., Books for Libraries Press [1971] 442 p. illus. 23 cm. Reprint of the 1883 ed. [E340.P9S55 1971] 76-179538 ISBN 0-8369-6667-8
1. Prentiss, Seargent Smith, 1808-1850. 2. Prentice family (Henry Prentice, d. 1654) I. Title. **BIP**

Preobrazhenskaia, Ol'ga Osipovna, 1870-1962.

HALL, Fernau. 792.8'092'4 B
Olga Preobrazhenskaya : a portrait / Elvira Rone ; translated, adapted, and introduced by Fernau Hall. New York : M. Dekker, c1978. 159 p., [8] leaves of plates : ill. ; 24 cm. (The Dance program ; v. 9) Includes bibliographical references and index. [GV1785.P7H34] 77-27883 ISBN 0-8247-6663-6 : 14.75
1. Preobrazhenskaia, Ol'ga Osipovna, 1870-1962. 2. Dancers—Biography. I. Rone, Elvira. II. Title. III. Series.

Prepys, Samuel, 1633-1706.

HEATH, Helen Truesdell, ed. 928.2
The letters of Samuel Pepys and his family circle. Oxford, Clarendon Press, 1955. xi, 253p. port., facsim., geneal. tables. 28cm. 'Previous editions of the letters': p. 246. [DA447.P4H4] 55-1764
1. Prepys, Samuel, 1633-1706. I. Title. **BIP**

Presbyterian

ROBINSON, George 922.573
Livingstone, 1864-
Autobiography of George L. Robinson, a short story of a long life. Grand Rapids, Baker Book House, 1957. 142p. illus. 23cm. [BX9225.R713A3] 57-12192
1. Presbyterian I. Title.

Presbyterian Church—Clergy—Correspondence, reminiscences, etc.

BENJAMIN, Mooshie Sargis, 922.573
1889-
The Persian Yankee. [1st ed.] New York, Vantage Press [1957, c1956] 114p. illus. 21cm. Autobiographical. [BX9225.B534A3] 56-10558
1. Presbyterian Church—Clergy—Correspondence, reminiscences, etc. I. Title.

BROWN, Arthur Judson, 922.573
1856-
Memoirs of a centenarian; edited by William N. Wysham. New York, World Horizons, 1957. 174p. illus. 24cm. [BX9225.B758A3] 58-15906
1. Presbyterian Church— Clergy—Correspondence, reminiscences, etc. I. Title.

LEWIS, John, 1878- 922.573
The strange story of a minister's life. Boston, Christopher Pub. House [1956] 171p. illus. 21cm. [BX9225.L47A3] 57-177
1. Presbyterian Church—Clergy—Correspondence, reminiscences, etc. I. Title.

MCLEES, Richard Gustavus, 922.573
1864-
Opening doors my life's story. Weaverville, N. C., Southern Presbyterian journal, 1954. 87p. illus. 23cm. [BX9225.M2555A3] 54-24792
1. Presbyterian Church—Clergy—Correspondence, reminiscences, etc. I. Title.

Presbyterian Church—Biography.

PRESBYTERIAN 285'.133'02573
Church in the U.S.
Ministerial directory of the Presbyterian Church, U.S., 1861-1967. Compiled by E. D. Witherspoon, Jr. Published by order of the General Assembly. Doraville, Ga., Foote & Davies, 1967. vii, 648 p. 24 cm. Supplements Ministerial directory of 1941 and of 1951. Bibliography: p. 648. [BX9220.P7 1967] 68-3645
1. Presbyterian Church—Biography. 2. Presbyterian Church in the U.S.—Biography. I. Witherspoon, Eugene Daniel, 1932- II. Title.

Presbyterian Church in Canada.

BAILEY, Thomas Melville, 285'.271
1912-
The covenant in Canada / by T. M. Bailey. Hamilton, Ont. : Macnab, 1975. 160 p. : ill. ; 19 x 24 cm. Cover title. [BX9001.B34] 76-357174 ISBN 0-919874-02-9
1. Presbyterian Church in Canada. 2. Presbyterian Church in Canada—Biography. I. Title.

Presbyterian Church in Los Angeles.

YOUNG, Nellie 917.94'94'0340924
May.
William Stewart Young, 1859-1937: builder of California institutions; an intimate biography Glendale, Calif., A. H. Clark, 1967. 196 p. illus., ports. 25 cm. [F869.L8Y68] 67-18217
1. Young, William Stewart, 1859-1937. 2. Presbyterian Church in Los Angeles. 3. Los Angeles. Hollenbeck Home for the Aged. 4. Los Angeles. Occidental College. I. Title: Builder of California institutions.

Presbyterian Church—Missions.

CHAMBERS, John R. 917'.987
Arctic bush mission; the experiences of a missionary bush pilot in the Far North, by John R. Chambers. [1st ed.] Seattle, Superior Pub. Co. [1970] 174 p. illus., ports. 28 cm. [E99.E7C48] 79-125901 12.95
1. Presbyterian Church—Missions. 2. Eskimos—Alaska. 3. Eskimos—Missions. 4. Air pilots—Alaska. I. Title.

Prescott, Orville.

PRESCOTT, Orville. 920.5
The five-dollar gold piece; the development of a point of view. Illustrated by Vasiliu. New York, Random House [c1956] 242p. illus. 22cm. Autobiography [PN4874.P7A3] 56-5202
I. Title.

Prescott, William Hickling,

PRESCOTT, William 907.2024
Hickling, 1796-1859.
The correspondence of William Hickling Prescott, 1833 1847, transcribed and edited by Roger Wolcott New York, Da Capo Press, 1970 [c1925] xxi, 691 p. port. 24 cm. [PS2657.A3 1970] 76-112312
I. Wolcott, Roger, 1877- ed. II. Title. **BIP**

Prescott, William Hickling, 1796-1859.

CLINE, Howard Francis, ed. 928.1
William Hickling Prescott, a memorial. Edited by Howard F. Cline, C. Harvey Gardiner, and Charles Gibson. Durham, N. C., Duke University Press, 1959. 179p. port. 24cm. 'Clothbound edition of the Hispanic American historical review, volume xxxix, number 1, February 1959.'--Dust Jacket. Includes bibliographical references. [F1409.8.P7C5] 59-16153
1. Prescott, William Hickling, 1796-1859. I. Hispanic American Historical review. II. Title.

GARDINER, Clinton 907.2'024 B
Harvey.
William Hickling Prescott; a biography, by C. Harvey Gardiner. Introd. by Allan Nevins. Austin, University of Texas Press [1969] xxi, 366 p. port. 24 cm. Includes bibliographical references. [PS2657.G33] 72-96223 7.50
1. Prescott, William Hickling, 1796-1859. **BIP**

PECK, Harry Thurston, 818'.3'08
1856-1914.
William Hickling Prescott. Port Washington, N.Y., Kennikat Press [1968,

c1905] x, 186 p. 19 cm. [PS2657.P4 1968] 68-16284
1. Prescott, William Hickling, 1796-1859. **BIP**

PECK, Harry Thurston, 1856-1914. 907'.2'024
William Hickling Prescott. New York, Greenwood Press [1969, c1905] x, 186 p. 23 cm. (English men of letters) [PS2657.P4 1969] 69-14033
1. Prescott, William Hickling, 1796-1859.

PRESCOTT, William Hickling, 1796-1859. 907.2024
The correspondence of William Hickling Prescott, 1833-1847, transcribed and edited by Roger Wolcott New York, Da Capo Press, 1970 [c1925] xxi, 691 p. port. 24 cm. [PS2657.A3 1970] 76-112312
I. Wolcott, Roger, 1877- ed. II. Title. **BIP**

TICKNOR, George, 1791-1871. 907'.2'024
Life of William Hickling Prescott. With an introd. by Wilfred Harold Munro. Montezuma ed. New York, AMS Press [1968] xix, 626 p. illus. 22 cm. (The Works of William H. Prescott, v. 22) Reprint of the 1904 ed. "Translations of Mr. Prescott's histories": p. 600-603. [PS2657.T5 1968] 72-186523
1. Prescott, William Hickling, 1796-1859. 2. Prescott family. I. Title. **BIP**

Preshaw, George Ogilvy, 1839-1890.

PRESHAW, George Ogilvy, 1839-1890. 919.4'03'31
Banking under difficulties. New York, Arno Press, 1974. xii, 179 p. 23 cm. (Gold: historical and economic aspects) Reprint of the 1888 ed. published by Edwards, Dunlop, Melbourne. [DU102.P83 1974] 74-357 ISBN 0-405-05918-3 11.00
1. Preshaw, George Ogilvy, 1839-1890. 2. Gold mines and mining—Australia—Personal narratives. 3. Gold mines and mining—New Zealand—Personal narratives. I. Title. II. Series.

Presidents

BARZMAN, Sol. 973 B
The First Ladies. [1st ed.] New York, Cowles Book Co. [1970] xiii, 370 p. ports. 22 cm. Bibliography: p. 359-363. [E176.2.B3 1970] 73-102817 8.95
1. Presidents—U.S.—Wives. I. Title.

BASSETT, Margaret Byrd, 1902- 923.173
Profiles & portraits of American Presidents. With an introd. by Henry F. Graff. Photos. by the Bachrachs. Freeport, Me., B. Wheelwright Co. [1964] x. 126 p. ports. 29 cm. Bibliography: p. 123-126. [E176.1.B23] 64-18581
1. Presidents—U.S. 2. Presidents—U.S.—Portraits. I. Title. **BIP**

BROOKS, Gertrude Zeth. 973'.0922
First ladies of the White House. Edited by Jan Pitts. Chicago, C. Hallberg [1969] xi, 114 p. illus., ports. 29 cm. [E176.2.B76] 76-86857 5.95
1. Presidents—U.S.—Wives. I. Title.

CHAFFIN, Lillie D. 973
America's First Ladies [by] Lillie Chaffin [and] Miriam Butwin. Minneapolis, Lerner Publications Co. [1969] 2 v. illus., ports. 21 cm. (A Pull ahead book) Contents.Contents.—v. 1. 1789-1865.—v. 2. 1865 to present day. Brief biographies of thirty-eight First Ladies and White House hostesses from Martha Washington to Patricia Nixon. [E176.2.C45] 920 68-31499 ISBN 0-8225-0455-3 (v. 1)
1. Presidents—United States—Wives—Juvenile literature. I. Butwin, Miriam, joint author. II. Title.

DIETZ, August, 1869- 923.173
Presidents of the United States of America; portraits and biographies. [3d ed.] Richmond, Dietz Press [1953] 72p. illus. 20cm. [E176.1.D53 1953] 53-2764
1. Presidents—U. S. 2. Presidents—U. S.—Portraits. I. Title.

DURANT, John, 1902- 923.173
Pictorial history of American Presidents, by John and Alice Durant. New York, Barnes [1955] vii, 320p. illus., ports., facsims. 29cm. [E176.1.D9] 55-10214
1. Presidents —U. S.—Iconography. 2. Presidents—U. S.—Biog. I. Durant, Alice K. (Rand) II. Title.

DURANT, John, 1902- 923.173
Pictorial history of American Presidents, by John and Alice Durant. 2d rev. ed. New York, A. S. Barnes [c.1955-1962] 340p. illus. 29cm. 61-13916 7.95
1. Presidents—U. S.—Iconography. 2. Presidents—U. S.—Biog. I. Durant, Alice K. (Rand) joint author. II. Title.

DURANT, John, 1902- 923.173
Pictorial history of American Presidents, by John and Alice Durant. 3d rev. ed. New York, A.S. Barnes [1964] 348 p. illus., ports 29 cm. [E176.1.D9] 64-21452
1. Presidents — U.S. — Iconography. 2. Presidents — U.S. — Biog. I. Durant, Alice K. (Rand) joint author. II. Title. **BIP**

DURANT, John, 1902- 923.173
Pictorial history of American Presidents, by John and Alice Durant. 4th rev. ed. New York, A. S. Barnes [1965] 356 p. illus., ports., facsims. 29 cm. [E176.1.D9 1965] 65-15287
1. Presidents—U.S.—Iconography. 2. Presidents—U.S.—Biography. I. Durant, Alice K. Rand, joint author. II. Title.

DURANT, John, 1902- 973
Pictorial history of American Presidents, by John and Alice Durant. 5th rev. ed. South Brunswick [N.J.] A. S. Barnes [1969] 370 p. illus. 29 cm. [E176.1.D9 1969] 69-19632 12.50
1. Presidents—U.S.—Iconography. 2. Presidents—U.S.—Biography. I. Durant, Alice K. (Rand) joint author. II. Title.

DURANT, John, 1902- 923.173
The sports of our Presidents. New York, Hastings House Publishers [1964] 149 p. illus., ports. 24 cm. Bibliography: p. 141-143. [E176.1.D92] 64-13482
1. Presidents — U.S. — Sports. I. Title.

LINDOP, Edmund 923.173
White House sportsmen [by] Edmund Lindop, Joseph Jares. Boston, Houghton [c.]1964. 172p. ports. 23cm. Bibl. 64-20537 3.75
1. Presidents—U.S.—Sports. I. Jares, Joseph Frank, 1937- joint author. II. Title.

LINDOP, Edmund. 923.173
White House sportsmen [by] Edmund Lindop and Joseph Jares. Boston, Houghton Mifflin, 1964. 172 p. ports. 23 cm. Bibliography: p. [170]-172. [E176.1.L527] 64-20537
1. Presidents — U.S. — Sports. I. Jares, Joseph Frank, 1967- joint author. II. Title.

GERLINGER, Irene (Hazard) 973 B
Mistresses of the White House; narrator's tale of a pageant of First Ladies. Freeport, N.Y., Books for Libraries Press [1970, c1950] xx, 125 p. ports. 23 cm. (Biography index reprint series) Bibliography: p. 109-116 [E176.2.G4 1970] 71-117323
1. Presidents—U.S.—Wives. I. Title.

GOLTERMAN, Guy. 923.173
The book of the Presidents; a gallery of famous portraits of the Presidents of the United States. St. Louis, c1953. 1v. illus. 22cm. First published in 1949 under title: The White House collection of official portraits of the Presidents. [E176.1.G64 1953] 53-2834
1. Presidents I. Title.

GORDON, Lydia L. 973'.0992 B
From Lady Washington to Mrs. Cleveland, by Lydia L. Gordon. Freeport, N.Y., Books for Libraries Press [1972] 448 p. 22 cm. (Essay index reprint series) "First published 1888." [E176.2.G6 1972] 72-5675 ISBN 0-8369-2990-X
1. Presidents—United States—Wives. 2. Presidents—United States—Biography. I. Title. **BIP**

HADLEY, Arthur Twining, 1924- 973.0922
Power's human face; a unique American history. Introd. by Howard R. Lamar. New York, Morrow [c.]1965. 259p. 22cm. Bibl. [E176.1.H13] 65-22968 5.00 bds.,
1. Presidents—U. S. 2. Executive power. I. Title.

HADLEY, Arthur Twining, 1924- 973'.0922
Power's human face; a unique American history. Introd. by Howard R. Lamar. New York [Apollo, 1968,c.1965] 259p. 20cm. (A175) Bibl. [E176.1.H13] 1.95 pap.
1. Presidents—U.S. 2. Executive power. I. Title.

KANE, Joseph Nathan, 1899- 973'.0992
Facts about the Presidents; a compilation of biographical and historical data. 3d ed. New York, H. W. Wilson Co., 1974. viii, 407 p. ports. 27 cm. [E176.1.K3 1974] 74-5297 ISBN 0-8242-0538-3
1. Presidents—United States. I. Title.

KELLY, Frank K., 1914- 920
The martyred Presidents and their successors, by Frank K. Kelly. New York, Putnam [1967] 223 p. 22 cm. Bibliography: p. 216-220. Brief biographies of the assassinated presidents and the problems their successors faced in making the administrative transition. [E176.1.K4] AC 67
1. Presidents—Biography. 2. Presidents—Assassination. I. Title.

LOGAN, Logna B. 920.7
Ladies in the White House. New York, Vantage [c.1962] 194p. 21cm. 62-4766 3.50
1. Presidents—U.S.—Wives. I. Title.

LOGAN, Logna B 920.7
Ladies of the White House. [1st ed.] New York, Vantage Press [1962] 194p. 21cm. [E176.2.L6] 62-4766
1. Presidents—U. S.—Wives. I. Title.

MCCONNELL, Jane (Tomkins) 1898- 920.7
Our First Ladies, from Martha Washington to Mamie Eisenhower [by] Jane and Burt McConnell. Ports. by Isabel Dawson. New York, Crowell [1957] 342p. illus. 21cm. First published in 1953 under title: First Ladies. Includes bibliography. [E176.2.M3 1957] 57-8349
1. Presidents—U. S.—Wives. I. MConnell, Burt Morton, 1888- joint author. II. Title.

MCCONNELL, Jane (Tompkins) 1898- 920.7
First Ladies, from Martha Washington to Mamie Eisenhower [by] Jane and Burt McConnell. Ports. by Isabel Dawson. New York, Crowell [1953] 342p. illus. 21cm. Includes bibliography. [E176.2.T6] 53-8418
1. Presidents—U.S.—Wives. I. McConnell, Burt Morton, 1888- joint author. II. Title.

MCCONNELL, Jane (Tompkins) 1898- 920.7
Our First Ladies, from Martha Washington to Mamie Eisenhower [by] Jane and Burt McConnell. Ports. by Isabel Dawson. New York, Crowell [1957] 342p. illus. 21cm. First published in 1953 under title: First Ladies. Includes bibliography. [E176.2.M3 1957] 57-8349
1. Presidents—U.S.—Wives. I. McConnell, Burt Morton, 1888- joint author. II. Title.

MCCONNELL, Jane (Tompkins) 1898- 920.7
Our First Ladies, from Martha Washington to Lady Bird Johnson [by] Jane and Burt McConnell. Ports. by Isabel Dawson. New York, Crowell [1964] 373p. ports. 21cm. Bibl. 64-20800 4.95
1. Presidents—U.S.—Wives—Juvenile literature. I. McConnell, Burt Morton, 1888- joint author. II. Title.

MCCONNELL, Jane (Tompkins) 1898- 920
Our First Ladies, from Martha Washington to Jacqueline Lee Bouvier Kennedy [by] Jane and Burt McConnell. Ports. by Isabel Dawson. New York, Crowell [1961] 358p. illus. 21cm. First published in 1953 under title: First Ladies. Includes bibliography. [E176.2.M3 1961] 61-15585
1. Presidents— U. S.—Wives—Juvenile literature. I. McConnell, Burt Morton, 1888- joint author. II. Title.

MCCONNELL, Jane (Tompkins) 1898- 973 B
Our First Ladies, from Martha Washington to Pat Ryan Nixon [by] Jane and Burt McConnell. Ports. by Isabel Dawson. [Rev. ed.] New York, Crowell [1969] 379 p. ports. 21 cm. First published in 1953 under title: First Ladies. Bibliography: p. 369-373. Profiles of the lives of the thirty-seven women who served as White House hostesses. [E176.2.M3 1969] 920 78-89992 5.95
1. Presidents—U.S.—Wives—Juvenile literature. I. McConnell, Burt Morton, 1888-1960, joint author. II. Dawson, Isabel, illus. III. Title.

*MEANS, Marianne 920.7
The woman in the White House; the lives, times, and influence of twelve notable first ladies [New York] New Amer. Lib. [1964, c.1963] 288p. 18cm. (Signet bk. T2512) .75 pap.,
I. Title.

MEANS, Marianne. 920.7
The woman in the White House; the lives, times and influence of twelve notable first ladies. New York, Random House [1963] 299 p. 25 cm. [E176.2.M4] 63-14143
1. Presidents—U.S.—Wives. I. Title.

MORAN, Thomas Francis, 1866-1928. 973'.0992
American presidents; their individualities and their contributions to American progress, by Thomas Francis Moran. [New ed., rev. and enl. by Louis Martin Sears] Plainview, N.Y., Books for Libraries Press [1974, c1933] xii, 318 p. ports. 22 cm. (Essay index reprint series) Reprint of the ed. published by Crowell, New York. [E176.1.M82 1974] 74-847 ISBN 0-518-10157-6 16.25
1. Presidents—United States. I. Sears, Louis Martin, 1885- ed. II. Title.

PRINDIVILLE, Kathleen. 920.7
First ladies. Decorations by Undine Dunn. [Rev. ed.] New York, Macmillan, 1954. 309p. illus. 22cm. Includes bibliography. [E176.2.P88 1954] 54-4829
1. Presidents—U. S.—Wives. I. Title.

SADLER, Christine 920.7
America's First Ladies. [New York, Macfadeen, c.1963] 256p. ports. 18cm. (60-138) 63-24138 .60 pap.,
1. Presidents—U. S.—Wives. I. Title.

WHITTON, Mary Ormsbee. 973 B
First First Ladies, 1789-1865; a study of the wives of the early Presidents Freeport, N.Y., Books for Libraries Press [1969, c1948] x, 341 p. ports. 23 cm. (Biography index reprint series) Bibliography: p. 335-341. [E176.2.W5 1969] 76-101834
1. Presidents—U.S.—Wives. I. Title.

WILLIAMS, William Appleman. 973.9'092'2
Some presidents: Wilson to Nixon. [New York, New York Review]; distributed by Vintage Books [1972] 122 p. illus. 19 cm. (A New York review book. NYR 108) Includes bibliographical references. [E176.1.W723] 72-78148 1.95
1. Presidents—United States. I. Title.

Presidents—U.S.—Addresses, essays, lectures.

VIRGINIA born 973'.0922
Presidents; addresses delivered on the occasions of unveiling the busts of Virginia born Presidents at Old Hall of the House of Delegates, Richmond, Virginia. Compiled under the auspices of and with an introd. by Jno. Garland Pollard. Freeport, N.Y., Books for Libraries Press [1971] ix, 232 p. ports. 23 cm. (Essay index reprint series) Reprint of the 1932

ed. [E176.1.V72 1971] 79-156728 ISBN 0-8369-2300-6
1. Presidents—U.S.—Addresses, essays, lectures. 2. Virginia—Biography—Addresses, essays, lectures. 3. Virginia—Capital and capitol—Addresses, essays, lectures. I. Pollard, John Garland, 1871-1937.

Presidents—Biography—Juvenile literature.

BEARD, Charles Austin, 1874-1948. 973'.0992 B
Charles A. Beard's The presidents in American history / brought forward since 1948 by William Beard. 10th rev. ed. New York : J. Messner, c1977. viii, 212 p. : ports. ; 22 cm. Briefly summarizes the achievements of each presidential administration from Washington to Carter. Includes a biographical digest giving basic facts about each President, a list of Vice-Presidents and cabinet members, and the results of each presidential election. [E176.1.B35 1977] 920 77-908 ISBN 0-671-32838-7 lib.bdg. : 7.29
1. Presidents—United States—Biography—Juvenile literature. I. Beard, William, 1907- II. Title: The presidents in American history.

BEARD, Charles Austin, 1874-1948. 973'.0992 B
Charles A. Beard's The Presidents in American history / brought forward since 1948 by William Beard. 9th rev. ed. New York : J. Messner, 1974. viii, 205 p. : ports. ; 22 cm. Briefly summarizes the achievements of each presidential administration from Washington to Ford. Includes a biographical digest giving basic facts about each President, a list of Vice-Presidents and cabinet members, and the results of each presidential election. [E176.1.B35 1974] 920 73-5387 ISBN 0-671-32131-5. ISBN 0-671-32132-3 lib. bdg.
1. Presidents—United States—Biography—Juvenile literature. I. Beard, William, 1907- II. Title: The Presidents in American history.

BEARD, Charles Austin, 1874-1948. 973'.0992 B
The Presidents in American history. Brought forward since 1948 by William Beard. New York, J. Messner [1973] viii, 199 p. illus. 22 cm. Briefly summarizes the achievements of each presidential administration from Washington to Nixon. Includes a biographical digest giving basic facts about each President, a list of Vice-Presidents and cabinet members, and the results of each presidential election. [E176.1.B35 1973] 74-154447 ISBN 0-671-32131-5 5.95
1. Presidents—United States—Biography—Juvenile literature. I. Beard, William, 1907- II. Title. **BIP**

BERIE, Marcia. j 920
Famous Presidents of the United States. New York, Dodd, Mead [1963] 159 p. illus. 22 cm. (Famous biographies for young people) [E176.1.B78] 62-13002
1. Presidents — U.S. — Biog. — Juvenile literature. I. Title.

BLASSINGAME, Wyatt. 920 (J)
The look-it-up book of Presidents. Illustrated by Ted Lewin. New York, Random House [1968] 131 p. col. illus., col. ports. 29 cm. [E176.8.B55] 68-23656 3.95
1. Presidents—United States—Juvenile literature. I. Title. **BIP**

BORIE, Marcia 920
Famous Presidents of the United States. New York, Dodd [c.1963] 159p. illus. 22cm. (Famous biogs. for young people) 62-13002 3.00
1. Presidents—U. S.—Biog.—Juvenile literature. I. Title.

CARY, Sturges Flagler. 920 (J)
Arrow book of Presidents, by Sturges F. Cary. Illustrated by Leo Summers. New York, Four Winds Press [1966] 103 p. illus., ports. 24 cm. [E176.1.C26] 66-9349
1. Presidents—United States—Biography—Juvenile literature. I. Title.

CAVANAH, Frances. 001.2
Meet the Presidents. In collaboration with Elizabeth L. Crandall. Illustrated by Clifford Schule. Philadelphia, Macrae Smith [1964] 351 p. ports. 24 cm. [E176.1.C28] 64-4319
1. Presidents — U.S. — Biog. — Juvenile literature. I. Title.

CAVANAH, Frances. 920
Meet the Presidents, by Frances Cavanah in collaboration with Elizabeth L. Crandall. Illustrated by Clifford Schule. Philadelphia, Macrae Smith [1962] 352p. illus. 24cm. [E176.1.C28] 62-10288
1. Presidents—U. S.—Biog.—Juvenile literature. I. Title.

CAVANAH, Frances. 973.0922
Meet the Presidents, by Frances Cavanah, in collaboration with Elizabeth L. Crandall. Illustrated by Clifford Schule. Rev. ed. Philadelphia, Macrae Smith Co. [1965] 380 p. ports. 24 cm. Bibliography: p. 377-380. [E176.1.C28 1965] 65-25483
1. Presidents — U.S. — Biog. — Juvenile literature. I. Title.

COOKE, Donald Ewin, 1916- 923.173
Atlas of the Presidents, by Donald E. Cooke. Illustrated maps by Dwight Dobbins. Pictures of the Presidents based on photos. of portraits supplied by the Library of Congress. Maplewood, N.J., C. S. Hammond [1964] 93 p. col. maps, col. ports. 27 cm. (Profile series) [E176.1.C79] 64-25038
1. Presidents—United States—Biography—Juvenile literature. I. Title.

COOKE, Donald Ewin, 1916- j 920
Atlas of the Presidents, by Donald E. Cooke. Illustrated maps by Dwight Dobbins. Pictures of the Presidents based on photos of ports. supplied by the Library of Congress. [Rev. ed.] Maplewood, N. J., Hammond [c1967] 86 p. col. illus., col. maps, col. ports. 27 cm. (Profile series) [E176.1.C79] 68-2369
1. Presidents—U.S.—Biog.—Juvenile literature. I. Title. **BIP**

COOKE, Donald Ewin, 1916- 973'.099 B
Atlas of the Presidents, by Donald E. Cooke. Illustrated maps by Dwight Dobbins. [Rev. ed.] Maplewood, N.J., Hammond [1971] 93 p. illus. 26 cm. "Pictures of the Presidents based on photographs or portraits supplied by the Library of Congress." Brief biographies of the thirty-seven United States Presidents. Includes a section of constitutional laws pertaining to Presidential office. [E176.1.C79 1971] 920 70-30783
1. Presidents— U.S.—Biography—Juvenile literature. I. Dobbins, Dwight, illus. II. Title.

COOKE, Donald Ewin, 1916- 973 B
Presidents in uniform, by Donald E. Cooke. Illustrated by Floyd James Torbert. New York, Hastings House [1969] 184 p. illus. 24 cm. Bibliography: p. 178-179. Brief biographies of the eighteen Presidents who served in the armed forces of the United States with emphasis on their military careers. [E176.1.C7918] 920 69-14455
1. Presidents—U.S.—Biography—Juvenile literature. I. Torbert, Floyd James, illus. II Title. **BIP**

COY, Harold. 973'.0992 B
The first book of Presidents / by Harold Coy. 7th ed. New York : Watts, c1977. p. cm. (A First book) Includes index. Describes the general duties and responsibilities of the President and summarizes the careers of those who have held the office. [E176.1.C798 1977] 77-1600 ISBN 0-531-02906-9 lib.bdg. : 4.47
1. Presidents—United States—Biography—Juvenile literature. I. Title.

DAVIDSON, William John, 1918- 923.173
President Kennedy selects six brave Presidents. New York, Harper & Row [c.1961, 1962] 96p. illus. 22cm. 62-8874 2.95
1. Presidents—U.S.—Biog.—Juvenile literature. I. Title. II. Title: Six brave Presidents.

DAVIDSON, William John, 1918- 923.173
President Kennedy selects six brave Presidents. New York, Popular Lib. [1963, c.1961, 1962] 128p. 18cm. (K52) .40 pap.,
1. Presidents-U.S.—Biog. —Juvenile literature. I. Title. II. Title: Six brave Presidents.

*FORD, Thomas K. 923.173
The Golden stamp book of presidents of the United States. Pictures by Mel T. Crawford. Rev. ed. New York, Golden, c.1954, 1966. 48p. illus. col. stamps. 28cm. (Golden stamp bks., 2511) 50 pap.,
1. Presidents—U.S.—Biog.—Juvenile literature. I. Title.

GREEN, Margaret. 92
Defender of the Constitution: Andrew Johnson. New York, J. Messner [1962] 192p. 22cm. Includes bibliography. [E667.G7] 62-10193
1. Johnson. Andrew, Pres., 1808-1875—Juvenile literature. II. Title.

HOFF, Rhoda. 973'.099 B
They grew up to be President. [1st ed.] Garden City, N.Y., Doubleday, 1971. 167 p. illus., ports. 24 cm. Traces the childhood of thirty-six boys from diverse backgrounds who grew up to have one thing in common—each became President of the United States. [E176.1.H7] 920 72-123695 4.95
1. Presidents—U.S.—Biography—Juvenile literature. I. Title.

KENNETT, Teresa. 973'.0992
Presidents are also people / text, Teresa Kennett ; ill., John Tullis. Richmond, Calif. : Brombacher Books, c1976. 157 p. : ill. ; 21 cm. (Read and grow ; 7) Previous ed. (c1975) published under title: 37 personal portraits of the Presidents of the United States of America. [E176.1.K43 1976] 920 76-3199 pbk. : 2.95
1. Presidents—United States—Biography—Juvenile literature. 2. Presidents—United States—Portraits—Juvenile literature. I. Tullis, John, 1949- II. Title.

LENGYEL, Cornel Adam. 973 B
Presidents of the United States New York, Golden Press [1969] 106 p. illus., ports. (part col.) 29 cm. (A De Luxe golden book) "Adapted from Presidents of the U.S.A.: profiles and pictures." Brief biographical sketches describing the family life, social background, political careers, and administrations of each of the thirty-seven United States Presidents. [E176.1L35 1969] 920 79-8009
1. Presidents—U.S.—Biography—Juvenile literature. I. Title.

LENGYEL, Cornel Adam. 973'.0992 B
Presidents of the United States / Cornel Adam Lengyel. Rev. new ed. New York : Golden Press, c1977. 108 p. : ill. ; 29 cm. "Adapted from Presidents of the U.S.A." Includes index. Brief biographical sketches describing the family life, social background, political careers, and administrations of each of the Presidents from George Washington to Jimmy Carter. [E176.1.L35 1977] 920 77-150206 ISBN 0-307-17863-3 : 5.95 ISBN 0-307-67863-6 lib. bdg. : 7.95
1. Presidents—United States—Biography—Juvenile literature. I. Title.

MCCONNELL, Jane (Tompkins) 1898- 353.030922
Presidents of the United States; the story of their lives, closely interwoven with the vast political and economic changes of the Nation [by] Jane and Burt McConnell. Ports. by Constance Joan Naar. New York, Crowell [1965] 374p. ports. 21cm. Bibl. [E176.1.M15] 65-23775 5.00
1. Presidents—U. S.—Biog.—Juvenile literature. I. McConnell, Burt Morton, 1888- joint author. II. Title.

MCCONNELL, Jane (Tompkins) 1898- 923
Presidents of the United States; the story of their lives closely interwoven with the vast political and economic changes of the Nation [by] Jane and Burt McConnell. Ports. by Constance Joan Naar. New York, Crowell [c1961] 358p. illus. 21cm. Includes bibliography. [E176.1.M15 1961] 62-3209
1. Presidents—U. S.—Biog.—Juvenile literature. I. McConnell, Rurt Morton, 1888- joint author. II. Title.

MCCONNELL, Jane Tompkins, 1898- 353.030922
Presidents of the United States; the story of their lives closely interwoven with the vast political and economic changes of the Nation [by] Jane and Burt McConnell. Ports by Constance Joan Naar. New York, Crowell [1965] 374 p. ports. 21 cm. Bibliography: p. 362-366. [E176.1.M15 1965] 65-23775
1. Presidents—U.S.—Biography—Juvenile literature. I. McConnell, Burt Morton, 1888-1960. joint author. II. Title.

MCCONNELL, Jane (Tompkins) 1898- 973
Presidents of the United States; the story of their lives, closely interwoven with the vast political and economic changes of the Nation [by] Jane and Burt McConnell. Ports. by Constance Joan Naar. New York, Crowell [1970] xx, 383 p. illus., ports. 22 cm. Bibliography: p. 368-373. Brief biographies of thirty-seven men who served as President of the United States. [E176.1.M15 1970] 920 79-94784
1. Presidents—U.S.—Biography—Juvenile literature. I. McConnell, Burt Morton, 1888- joint author. II. Title.

MIERS, Earl Schenck, 1910- 973
America and its Presidents. [Rev. Tempo Books ed.] New York, Grosset & Dunlap [1970] 192 p. ports. 18 cm. (Tempo books, 5346) Brief biographies of the thirty-seven men who have served as President of the United States. [E176.1.M6 1970] 920 70-75327 0.75
1. Presidents—U.S.—Biography—Juvenile literature. 2. U.S.—History—Juvenile literature. I. Title.

*PEARSON, James R. 923.73
Presidents. New York, Golden [1965, c.1954-1964] 48p. col. illus. 14cm. (Jr. Golden guide: Quiz me, 5512) .25 pap.,
1. Presidents—U.S.—Juvenile literature. I. Title.

PETERSHAM, Maud (Fuller) 1890- 920
Story of the Presidents of the United States of America, by Maud and Miska Petersham. Rev. ed. New York, Macmillan [1966] 80p. col. illus. 26cm. (Their This is Amer. bks.) [E176.1.P49 1966] 66-16713 3.95
1. Presidents—U.S.—Biog.—Juvenile literature. I. Petersham, Miska, 1888- joint author. II. Title.

REINFELD, Don. 923.173
Picture book of the Presidents. [Rev. ed.] New York, Sterling Pub. Co. [1964] 64 p. illus. ports. 26 cm. (Visual history series) [E176.1.R35] 65-4066
1. Presidents — U.S. — Biog. — Juvenile literature. 2. Presidents — U.S. — Portraits — Juvenile literature. I. Title.

ROWE, Jeanne A. 973
An album of the Presidents, by Jeanne A. Rowe. New York, Watts [1969] 87 p. illus., ports. 29 cm. Summarizes the most outstanding events in the administration of each President of the United States. [E176.1.R8] 79-75723
1. Presidents—U.S.—Biography—Juvenile literature. I. Title.

SIGNIFICANT American 973'.0492 B
Presidents of the United States. Chicago : Childrens Press, [1976] p. cm. Includes index. Brief biographies of the first thirty-seven Presidents of the United States arranged in chronological and alphabetical order. [E176.1.S55] 920 75-20692 ISBN 0-516-05311-6 : 6.95
1. Presidents—United States—Biography—Juvenile literature. I. Title: Presidents of the United States.

Presidents—Childhood and youth—Juvenile literature.

PERRY, Enos Johnson, 1891- 973'.0922 B
The boyhood days of our Presidents, by Enos J. Perry. [Chicago, Adams Press, 1971] 315 p. 23 cm. Bibliography: p. 309-315. Selected childhood incidents provide insight into the characters of the men who later became United States Presidents. [E176.1.P45] 920 71-172821 7.75
1. Presidents—U.S.—Childhood and youth—Juvenile literature. I. Title.

Presidents Election—Juvenile literature.

GOLDMAN, David J. 973
Presidential losers [by] David J. Goldman. Minneapolis, Lerner Publications Co. [1970] 102 p. illus., ports. 22 cm. (A Pull ahead book) Brief biographies of eight Presidential candidates who lost the election: Burr, Clay, McClellan, Tilden, Bryan, Landon, Dewey, and Stevenson. [E183.G6 1970] 920 75-103678
1. Presidents—U.S.—Election—Juvenile literature. 2. U.S.—Biography—Juvenile literature. I. Title. BIP

Presidents Portraits.

GOLTERMAN, Guy. 923.173
The book of the Presidents: a gallery of famous portraits of the Presidents of the United States. Rev. ed. St. Louis, c1956. unpaged. illus. 22cm. First published in 1949 under title: The White House collection of official portraits of the Presidents. [E176.1.G64 1956] 57-1365
1. Presidents-U. S.-Portraits. I. Title.

KENNETT, Teresa. 973'.0992
37 personal portraits of the Presidents of the United States of America / text, Teresa Kennett; ill., John Tullis. Richmond, Calif. : Brombacher Books, c1975. 79 p. : 37 ports. ; 28 cm. [E176.1.K43] 75-30322 ISBN 0-89085-076-3 : 2.95
1. Presidents—United States—Portraits. 2. Presidents—United States—Biography. I. Tullis, John, 1949- II. Title.

Presidents Religion.

ISELY, Bliss, 1881- 923.173
The Presidents: men of faith. Boston, W. A. Wilde Co., 1953. 284 p. illus. 24 cm. [E176.1.I8] 53-6168
1. Presidents—U.S.—Religion. I. Title.

Presidents-United States-Biography.

ARMBRUSTER, Maxim Ethan, 1902- 923.173
The President of the United States: a new appraisal, from Washington to Kennedy. [Rev. and enl. ed.] New York, Horizon Press [1963] 350 p. illus. 22 cm. Includes bibliography. [E176.1.A75] 63-13202
1. Presidents — U.S. — Biog. I. Title.

ARMBRUSTER, Maxim Ethan, 1902- 923.173
The Presidents of the United States; a new appraisal, from Washington to Kennedy. [Rev., enl. ed.] New York, Horizon [c.1960, 1963] 350p. illus. 22cm. Bibl. 63-13202 5.95
1. Presidents—U. S.—Biog. I. Title.

ARMBRUSTER, Maxim Ethan, 1902- 973'.0992 B
The Presidents of the United States and their administrations from Washington to Ford / Maxim E. Armbruster. 6th rev. ed. New York : Horizon Press, [1975] 384 p. : ports. ; 23 cm. Includes index. Bibliography: p. [369]-376. [E176.1.A75 1975] 75-319642 ISBN 0-8180-0812-1 : 10.00
1. Presidents—United States—Biography. I. Title.

ARMBRUSTER, Maxim Ethan, 1902- 973'.0992 B
The Presidents of the United States, and their administrations from Washington to Nixon. 5th ed., rev. New York, Horizon Press [1973] 378 p. ports. 23 cm. Bibliography: p. [363]-370. [E176.1.A75 1973] 73-82069 ISBN 0-8180-0812-1 7.95
1. Presidents—United States—Biography. I. Title.

BASSETT, Margaret Byrd, 1902- 973'.0992 B
Profiles and portraits of American presidents / Margaret Bassett ; with an introd. by Henry F. Graff. New and updated ed. New York : McKay, c1976. x, 306 p. : ill. ; 26 cm. Bibliography: p. 297-306. [E176.1.B23 1976] 76-16022 ISBN 0-679-50618-7 : 10.95
1. Presidents—United States—Biography. 2. Presidents—United States—Portraits. I. Title.

BEARD, Charles Austin, 1874-1948. 923.173
Charles A. Beard's The Presidents in American history; brought forward since 1948 by William Beard. [Rev. ed.] New York, J. Messner [1965] viii. 190 p. ports. 22 cm. [E176.1.B35] 65-19366
1. Presidents — U.S. — Biog. I. Beard, William, 1907- II. Title.

BEARD, Charles Austin, 1874-1948 923.173
Charles A. Beard's The Presidents in American history; brought forward since 1948 by William Beard. [Rev. ed.] New York, Messner [c.1946-1965] viii, 190p. ports. 22cm. [E176.1.B35] 65-19366 3.25; 3.19 lib. ed.,
1. Presidents—U. S.—Biog. I. Beard, William, 1907- II. Title.

BEARD, Charles Austin, 1874-1948. 923.173
The Presidents in American history; brought forward since 1948 by William Beard. New York, J. Messner [1953] 177p. illus. 22cm. [E176.1.B35 1953] 53-9060
1. Presidents—U. S.—Biog. I. Title.

BEARD, Charles Austin, 1874-1948. 923.173
The Presidents in American history; brought forward since 1948 by William Beard, Rev. ed. New York, Messner [1957] 177p. illus. 22cm. [E176.1.B35 1957] 57-3485
1. Presidents—U. S.—Biog. I. Title.

BOOTH, Edward Townsend, 1890- 973'.0992 B
Country life in America as lived by ten presidents of the United States: John Adams, George Washington, Thomas Jefferson, Andrew Jackson, Martin Van Buren, William Henry Harrison, James Buchanan, Abraham Lincoln, Theodore Roosevelt, Calvin Coolidge. Westport, Conn., Greenwood Press [1973, c1947] xviii, 264, xii p. 22 cm. Reprint of the ed. published by Knopf, New York. Bibliography: p. [249]-264. [E176.1.B75 1973] 73-10578 ISBN 0-8371-7018-4 12.25
1. Presidents—United States—Biography. 2. Country life—United States. I. Title. BIP

DAYTON, Eldorous L 923.173
Give 'em Hell Harry; an informal biography of the terrible tempered Mr. T. New York, Devin-Adair Co., 1956. 250p. [E814.D34] 56-9833
I. Title.

FORSEE, Corinne, 1892- 923.173
Human interest stories about the Presidents. [Portland, Me.] J. W. Walch, c1954. unpaged. illus. 28cm. [E176.1.F76] 55-194
1. Presidents—U. S.—Biog. I. Title.

FREIDEL, Frank Burt. 973'.0992 B
Our country's Presidents, by Frank Freidel. Introd. by Richard M. Nixon. Foreword by Melville Bell Grosvenor. Prepared by National Geographic Special Publications Division. [5th ed.] Washington, National Geographic Society [1973] 258 p. illus. 26 cm. Bibliography: p. 257. [E176.1.F79 1973] 74-159895 ISBN 0-87044-024-1
1. Presidents—United States—Biography. I. National Geographic Society, Washington, D.C. Special Publications Division. II. Title.

FREIDEL, Frank Burt. 973'.0992
Our country's Presidents, by Frank Freidel. Introd. by Richard M. Nixon. Foreword by Melville Bell Grosvenor. Prepared by National Geographic Special Publications Division. [4th ed.] Washington, National Geographic Society [1972] 258 p. illus. 26 cm. Bibliography: p. 257. [E176.1.F79 1972] 73-150450 ISBN 0-87044-024-1 4.25
1. Presidents—United States—Biography. I. National Geographic Society, Washington, D.C. Special Publications Division. II. Title.

FREIDEL, Frank Burt. 973'.0992 B
Our country's Presidents / by Frank Freidel ; introd. by Gerald R. Ford ; foreword by Melville Bell Grosvenor ; prepared by National Geographic Special Publications Division. 6th ed. Washington : National Geographic Society, [1975] 266 p. : ill. (some col.) ; 27 cm. Includes index. Bibliography: p. 265. Brief biographies of the thirty-eight Presidents. [E176.1.F79 1975] 920 75-330343 ISBN 0-87044-024-1
1. Presidents—United States—Biography. I. National Geographic Society, Washington, D.C. Special Publications Division. II. Title.

FREIDEL, Frank Burt. 973'.0992 B
Our country's Presidents / by Frank Freidel ; introd. by Jimmy Carter ; foreword by Melville Bell Grosvenor ; prepared by National Geographic Special Publications Division. 8th ed. Washington : National Geographic Society, c1979. 278 p. : ill. (some col.) ; 27 cm. Includes bibliographical references and index. Presents brief biographies of the Presidents from George Washington to Jimmy Carter. [E176.1.F79 1979] 920 79-63364 ISBN 0-87044-024-1 pbk. : 5.75
1. Presidents—United States—Biography. I. National Geographic Society, Washington, D.C. Special Publications Division. II. Title.

FREIDEL, Frank Burt. 923.173
The Presidents of the United States of America, by Frank Freidel. Washington, White House Historical Association [1964] 79 p. illus. (part col.) col. ports, 26 cm. [E176.1.F8] 64-66269
1. Presidents — U.S. — Biog. I. White House Historical Association. II. Title.

FREIDEL, Frank Burt. 973'.0992 B
The Presidents of the United States of America, by Frank Freidel. [5th ed.] Washington, White House Historical Association [1973] 82 p. col. ports. 26 cm. [E176.1.F8 1973] 74-164320 1.25 (pbk.)
1. Presidents—United States—Biography. I. White House Historical Association. II. Title.

FREIDEL, Frank Burt. 973'.0992 B
The Presidents of the United States of America / by Frank Freidel. 6th ed. Washington : White House Historical Association, [1975] 83 p. : ill. (some col.) ; 26 cm. Includes index. Single-page biographies with pictures of the thirty-eight Presidents. [E176.1.F8 1975] 920 75-328478 2.00
1. Presidents—United States—Biography. I. White House Historical Association. II. Title.

GOLSON, K. K. 923.173
Presidents are people. New York, Carlton [c.1964] 270p. facsims., ports. 21cm. (Reflection bk.) 64-56026 4.50
1. Presidents—U.S.—Biog. 2. Graphology. I. Title.

GRAHAM, Alberta (Powell) 923.173
Thirty- three roads to the White House. [Rev.] Illustrated by George Avison. New York, Nelson [1953, c1944] 257p. illus. 25cm. [E176.1.G8 1953] 53-7069
1. Presidents—U. S.—Biog. I. Title.

HASKIN Service, Washington D.C. 923.173
Our Presidents and their wives. [Rev. ed. Washington, 1953, c1933] 54 p. ports, 23 cm. (The Haskin educational booklets, 3) Previous editions by Frederic J. Haskin have title: Presidents and their wives. [E176.1.H343] 53-3798
1. Presidents — U.S. — Biog. 2. Presidents — U.S. — Wives. I. Haskin, Frederic Jennings, 1872-1944. Presidents and their wives. II. Title. III. Series.

HASKIN Service, Washington, D. C. 923.173
The Presidents and their wives, from Washington to Kennedy. [Washington, 1961] 66p. illus. 23cm. Published in 1953 under title: Our Presidents and their wives. [E176.1.H343 1961] 61-9629
1. Presidents—U. S. —Biog. 2. Presidents—U. S.—Wives. I. Title.

JEFFRIES, Ona Griffin 923.173
In and out of the White House, from Washington to the Eisenhowers; an intimate glimpse into the social and domestic aspects of the Presidential life. New York, W. Funk [c.1960] xi, 404p. illus. 24cm. 60-6700 8.50
1. Presidents—U. S.—Biog. 2. Washington, D. C.—Soc. life & cust. 3. Washington, D. C. White House. 4. Etiquette—Washington, D. C. I. Title.

JEFFRIES, Ona Griffin. 923.173
In and out of the White House from Washington to the Eisenhowers an intimate glimpse into the social and domestic aspects of the Presidential life. New York, W. Funk [1960] 404p. illus. 24cm. [E176.1.J4] 60-6700
1. Presidents—U. S.—Biog. 2. Washington, D. C.—Soc. life & cust. 3. Washington, D. C. White House. 4. Etiquette—Washington, D. C. I. Title.

LA CARRUBA, Michael A. 923.173
Presidents and wives: portraits, facts. Washington 13, D.C., Historic Publications, P.O. Box 1511 47p. illus. 24cm. 59-15702 1.00 pap.,
1. Presidents—U.S.—Biog. 2. Presidents—U.S.—Wives. 3. Presidents—U.S.—Ports. I. Title.

LENGYEL, Cornel Adam 923.173
Presidents of the United States. New York, Golden [1964] 104p. illus. (pt. col.) ports. (pt. col.) 29cm. (Deluxe golden bk.) Adapted from Presidents of the U. S. A.: profiles and pictures. 64-12826 2.95
1. Presidents—U. S.—Biog. I. Title. BIP

LENGYEL, Cornel Adam. 001.2
Presidents of the U. S. A.; profiles and pictures. [New York, Bantam Books, 1961] 215p. illus., ports. 18cm. (A Bantam gallery edition, GDQ4) Bibliography: o. 215. [E176.1.L35] 62-1170
1. Presidents—U. S.—Biog. I. Title.

LUKE, James 923.173
Our glorious heritage; the presidents from Washington to Eisenhower. New York, Vantage Press [c.1961] 94p. illus. 2.50 bds.,
1. Presidents—U.S.—Biog. I. Title.

MCCONNELL, Jane (Tompkins) 1898- 923.173
Presidents of the United States; the story of their lives, closely interwoven with the vast political and economical changes of the nation [by] Jane and Burt McConnell. Ports. by Constance Joan Naar. New York, Crowell [1957] 342p. illus. 21cm. Includes bibliography. [E176.1.M15 1957] 57-7955
1. Presidents—U.S.—Biog. I. McConnell, Burt Morton, 1888- joint author. II. Title.

MCCONNELL, Jane (Tompkins) 1898- 923.173
Presidents of the United States; the story of their lives, closely interwoven with the vast political and economic changes of the nation [by] Jane and Burt McConnell. Ports. by Constance Joan Naar. New York, Crowell [1951] 324p. illus. 21cm. Includes bibliography. [E176.1.M15 1951] 51-12919
1. Presidents— U. S.—Biog. I. McConnell, Burt Morton, 1888- joint author. II. Title.

MIERS, Earl Schenck, 1910- 923.173
America and its Presidents. Ports. in color by Stanley Dersh. Line drawings by Paul Granger. New York, Grosset & Dunlap, 1959. 210p. illus. 28cm. [E176.1.M6] 59-16403
1. Presidents—U. S.—Biog. 2. U. S.—History, Juvenile. I. Title.

*MOONEY, Booth 923.173
The Lyndon Johnson story. [New York] Avon [c.1956-1964] 191p. 18cm. (S148) .60 pap.,
I. Title.

PARKS, Lillian (Rogers) 923.173
My thirty years backstairs at the White House [by] Lillian Rogers Parks in collaboration with Frances Spatz Leighton. New York [Avon, c.1961] 287p. (V2042) .75 pap.,
1. Presidents—U.S.—Biog. 2. Presidents—U.S.—Wives. 3. Washington, D.C. White House. I. Title.

PARKS, Lillian (Rogers) 923.173
My thirty years backstairs at the White House [by] Lillian Rogers Parks in collaboration with Frances Spatz Leighton. New York, Fleet Pub. Corp. [1961] 346p. 21cm. [E176.1.P37] 61-7626
1. Presidents—U. S.—Diog. 2. Presidents—U. S.—Wives. 3. Washington, D. C. White House. I. Title.

REINFELD, Don. 923.173
Picture book of the Presidents. New York,

Sterling Pub. Co. [1961] 64p. illus. 26cm. (Visual history series) [E176.1.R35] 61-15900
1. Presidents—U. S.—Biog. 2. Presidents—U. S. —Portraits. I. Title.

SOKOLSKY, Eric 923.173
Our seven greatest presidents. Foreword by James A. Farley. New York, Exposition [c.1964] 120p. 21cm. Bibl. 64-4868 3.00
1. Presidents—U. S.—Biog. I. Title.

WHITNEY, David C. 973'.0992 B
The American Presidents / by David C. Whitney ; illustrated by Richard Paul Kluga. [New expanded 4th ed.]. Garden City, N.Y. : Doubleday, c1978. xi, 532 p. : ports ; 22 cm. Includes index. [E176.1.W6 1978] 78-111091 10.95
1. Presidents—United States—Biography. I. Title.

WHITNEY, David C. 973'.0992
The graphic story of the American Presidents, by David C. Whitney. Edited by Thomas C. Jones. Chicago, J. G. Ferguson Pub. Co.; distributed to the book trade by Doubleday [1973] vii, 543 p. illus. 29 cm. Expanded and rearranged pictorial edition of the author's The American Presidents. [E176.1.W6 1973] 74-155403 ISBN 0-385-02418-5 19.95
1. Presidents—United States—Biography. I. Title.

WILSON, Phoebe. 923.173
Young reader's book of Presidents; illustrated by Stuyvesant Van Veen. New York, Wonder Books, c1956. 64p. illus. 21cm. (Young readers wonder books, 2533) [E176.1.W78] 56-4162
1. Presidents—U. S.—Biog. I. Title.

WILSON, Vincent. 001.2
The book of the Presidents. Maps by Peter Guilday. Silver Spring, Md., American History Research Associates [1962] 75 p. illus. 23 cm. [E176.1.W785] 62-17548
1. Presidents — U.S. — Biog. I. Title.

WILSON, Vincent, Jr. 923.173
The book of the Presidents [rev. ed.] Maps by Peter Guilday. Silver Spring, Md., American Hist. Res. Assos. [c.1962. 1963] 75p. illus. (pt. col.) 23cm. 62-17548 1.50 pap.,
1. Presidents—U. S.—Biog. I. Title.

WILSON, Vincent. 973'.0992 B
The book of the Presidents / Vincent Wilson, Jr. ; maps by Peter Guilday. 6th ed. Brookville, Md. : American History Research Associates, [1975] 81 p. : ports. ; 23 cm. On cover : Bicentennial edition. [E176.1.W785 1975] 75-317141 2.50
1. Presidents—United States—Biography. I. Title.

WILSON, Vincent. 973'.0992 B
The book of the Presidents. Maps by Peter Guilday. [5th ed.] Brookline, Md. American History Research Associates [1973] 79 p. illus. 24 cm. [E176.1.W785 1973] 73-160492 2.00
1. Presidents—United States—Biography. I. Title.
Publisher's Address: Box 140 Brookline, Md 20729. BIP

WOLFE, Harold, 1907- 923.173
Herbert Hoover: public servant and leader of the loyal opposition, a study of his life and career. [1st ed.] New York, Exposition Press [1956] 507p. 21cm. (A Banner book) Includes bibliography. [E802.W74] 56-8724
I. Hoover, Herbert Clark, Pres U. S., 1874- II. Title.

Presidents-United states-Biography.

ARMBRUSTER, Maxim Ethan, 1902- 923.173
The Presidents of the United States: a new appraisal. New York, Horizon Press, 1960. 342 p. illus. 22 cm. Includes bibliography. [E176.1.A75] 60-8159
1. Presidents—U.S.—Biography.

ARMBRUSTER, Maxim Ethan, 1902- 973 B
The Presidents of the United States, and their administrations from Washington to Nixon. 4th ed., rev. New York, Horizon Press [1969] 372 p. ports. 23 cm. Bibliography: p. [357]-364 [E176.1.A75 1969] 76-92714 6.50
1. Presidents—U.S.—Biography. I. Title. BIP

ASHLEY, Maurice Percy. 973'.099
Mr. President; an introduction to American history, by Maurice Ashley. Freeport, N.Y., Books for Libraries Press [1972] 448 p. ports. 23 cm. (Biography index reprint series) Reprint of the 1948 ed. Contents.Contents.—George Washington.—Thomas Jefferson.—Andrew Jackson.—Abraham Lincoln.—Theodore Roosevelt.—Woodrow Wilson.—Epilogue: the United States and Great Britain. Includes bibliographies. [E176.1.A8 1972] 79-38317 ISBN 0-8369-8115-4
1. Presidents—United States—Biography. I. Title. BIP

BARCLAY, Barbara. 973'.0922 B
Lamps to light the way; our presidents. Presidential portraits by Celeste Swayne-Courtney. [Glendale, Calif.] Bowmar [1970] xi, 444 p. illus. (part col.), facsims., maps, ports. (part col.) 32 cm. [E176.1.B22] 71-134284
1. Presidents—U.S.—Biography. I. Title.

BASSETT, Margaret Byrd, 1902- 973 B
Profiles & portraits of American Presidents & their wives, by Margaret Bassett. With an introd. on the Presidency by Henry F. Graff. Freeport, Me., B. Wheelwright Co.; distributed by Grosset & Dunlap, New York [1969] x, 449 p. ports. 27 cm. "Material on the Presidents, from George Washington through Lyndon B. Johnson, previously was published in Profiles & portraits of American Presidents." Bibliography: p. 440-449. [E176.1.B24] 68-11104 10.00
1. Presidents—U.S.—Biography. 2. Presidents—U.S.—Wives. I. Title.

BORDEN, Morton, ed. 973'.099 B
America's eleven greatest Presidents. Edited by Morton Borden. 2d ed. Chicago, Rand McNally [1971] xii, 295 p. 21 cm. (Rand McNally history series) First published in 1961 under title: America's ten greatest Presidents. Bibliography: p. 289-295. [E176.1.B77 1971] 70-167638
1. Presidents—U.S.—Biography. I. Title. BIP

BORDEN, Morton, ed. 923.173
America's ten greatest Presidents. Chicago, Rand McNally [1961] 269 p. 22 cm. (Rand McNally history series) Includes bibliography. [E176.1.B77] 61-6579
1. Presidents—United States—Biography. I. Title.

BRUCE, David Kirkpatrick Este. 923.173
Sixteen American Presidents. [1st ed.] Indianapolis, Bobbs-Merrill [1962] 336 p. illus. 24 cm. Revision of Revolution to Reconstruction, published in 1939. [E176.1.B887 1962] 62-14694
1. Presidents—U.S.—Biography. I. Title.

COY, Harold. 923.173
The first book of Presidents. Pictures by Manning De V. Lee. New York, F. Watts, c1952. 68 p. illus 23 cm. ([First book series] 28) [E176.1.C798] 52-11165
1. Presidents—U.S.—Biography. I. Title.

COYLE, David Cushman, 1887-1969. 923.273
Ordeal of the Presidency. With illus. collected by M. B. Schnapper. Washington, Public Affairs Press [1960] 408 p. illus. 24 cm. [E176.1.C8] 60-8580
1. Presidents—U.S.—Biography. I. Title. BIP

DURANT, John, 1902- 973'.0992 B
Pictorical history of American Presidents / by John and Alice Durant. New York : Castle Books, c1975. 375 p. : ill. ; 29 cm. Includes bibliographical references and index. [E176.1.D9 1975] 75-322484 12.50
1. Presidents—United States—Biography. 2. Presidents—United States—Iconography. I. Durant, Alice K. Rand, joint author. II. Title.

DURANT, John, 1902- 973'.0992 B
The Presidents of the United States : a history of the Presidents of the United States : with an encyclopedic supplement on the office and powers of the Presidency : chronologies, and records of Presidential elections / by John and Alice Durant. [Commemorative ed.]. Miami : A. A. Gache, c1976. 2 v (390 p.) : ill. ; 29 cm. Includes index. [E176.1.D9135] 76-381523
1. Presidents—United States—Biography. I. Durant, Alice K. Rand, joint author. II. Title.

FIRST Federal Savings and Loan Association of Worcester. 973'.099 B
A book of the Presidents; with portraits from the White House collection. [1st ed. Worcester, Mass., 1971] 72 p. illus. (part col.) 23 cm. Cover title: The Presidents of the United States. [E176.1.F52] 70-165258
1. Presidents—U.S.—Biography. I. Title. II. Title: The Presidents of the United States.

FREIDEL, Frank Burt. 353.030922
Our country's Presidents. Introd. by Lyndon B. Johnson. Foreword by Melville Bell Grosvenor. Prepared by National Geographic, Special Publications Division. Washington, National Geographic Society [1966] 248 p. illus. (part col.) ports. (part col.) 26 cm. [E176.1.F79] 66-18847
1. Presidents—United States—Biography. I. National Geographical Society, Washington, D.C. Special Publications Division. II. Title.

FREIDEL, Frank Burt. 973'.099 B
Our country's Presidents. Introd. by Richard M. Nixon. Foreword by Melville Bell Grosvenor. Prepared by National Geographic Special Publications Division. [2d ed.] Washington, National Geographic Society [1969] 258 p. illus., facsims., ports. 26 cm. [E176.1.F79 1969] 78-20468
1. Presidents—U.S.—Biography. I. National Geographic Society, Washington, D.C. Special Publications Division. II. Title. BIP

FREIDEL, Frank Burt. 973
The Presidents of the United States of America, by Frank Freidel. [2d ed.] Washington, White House Historical Association [1969] 82 p. col. ports. 26 cm. [E176.1.F8 1969] 79-2265
1. Presidents—U.S.—Biography. I. White House Historical Association. II. Title.

GOEBEL, Dorothy (Burne) 1898- 973'.099 B
Generals in the White House, by Dorothy Burne Goebel and Julius Goebel, Jr. Freeport, N.Y., Books for Libraries Press [1971, c1945] 276 p. maps. 23 cm. (Essay index reprint series) Contents.Contents.—American paradox.—The pedigree of prejudice.—What makes a general?—General Washington.—General Jackson.—General William Henry Harrison.—General Taylor.—General Pierce.—General Grant.—Generals Hayes, Garfield, and Benjamin Harrison.—Conclusion. [E176.1.G63 1971] 78-134082 ISBN 0-8369-2501-7
1. Presidents—United States—Biography. 2. Generals—United States. 3. United States—History, Military—To 1900. I. Goebel, Julius, 1892- joint author. II. Title. BIP

HATHAWAY, Esse Virginia, 1871-1939. 973 B
The book of American Presidents. Illustrated by Samuel Bernard Schaeffer. 2d ed. Freeport, N.Y., Books for Libraries Press [1970] xii, 399 p. ports. 23 cm. (Essay index reprint series) Reprint of the 1933 ed. [E176.1.H38 1970] 70-93345
1. Presidents—U.S.—Biography. I. Title. BIP

KANE, Joseph Nathan, 1899- 973'.0992
Facts about the Presidents : a compilation of biographical and historical data. New York : Ace Books, 1976. 698 p., [8] leaves of plates : ill. ; 18 cm. [E176.1.K3 1976] 76-366155 pbk. : 1.95
1. Presidents—United States—Biography. 2. Presidents—United States. I. Title.

MILLER, Hope Ridings. 973'.0992 B
Scandals in the highest office; facts and fictions in the private lives of our Presidents. [1st ed.] New York, Random House [1973] 280 p. 22 cm. Bibliography: p. [265]-273. [E176.1.M647] 73-5022 ISBN 0-394-46873-2 6.95
1. Presidents—United States—Biography. 2. Corruption (in politics)—United States. I. Title.

MORGAN, James, 1861-1955. 973 B
Our Presidents. Chapters on Kennedy and Johnson by Herbert S. Parmet. 3d ed. [New York] Macmillan [1969] xx, 548 p. illus., ports. 21 cm. [E176.1.M84 1969] 76-90874 8.95
1. Presidents—U.S.—Biography. I. Title.

MORGAN, James, 1861-1955. 923.173
Our Presidents; brief biographies of our chief magistrates from Washington to Eisenhower, 1789-1958. 2d enl. ed. New York, Macmillan, 1958. 470 p. illus. 21 cm. [E176.1.M84 1958] 58-13113
1. Presidents—U.S.—Biography. I. Title.

PERLING, Joseph Jerry. 973'.099
Presidents' sons; the prestige of name in a democracy, by Joseph J. Perling. Freeport, N.Y., Books for Libraries Press [1971, c1947] viii, 451 p. illus., facsims. 23 cm. (Biography index reprint series) Includes bibliographical references. [E176.1.P4 1971] 70-148226 ISBN 0-8369-8073-5
1. Presidents—U.S.—Biography. 2. Presidents—U.S.—Children. I. Title. BIP

PETERSHAM, Maud Fuller, 1890-1971. 923.173
Story of the Presidents of the United States of America, by Maud and Miska Petersham. New York, Macmillan [1953] 80 p. illus. 27 cm. [E176.1.P49] 53-7758
1. Presidents—U.S.—Biography. I. Petersham, Miska, 1888-1960, joint author. BIP

THE Presidents, 1789-1909 / compiled by T. G. Hamlin. [s.l.] : Tomlin Publications, c1976. [62] p. : ports. ; 23 cm [E176.1.P96] 77-357301 2.98 973'.0992 B
1. Presidents—United States—Biography. 2. Presidents—United States—Portraits. 3. United States—Politics and government—19th century. I. Hamlin, T. G.

ROSS, George Edward, 1904- 923.173
Know your Presidents and their wives. Illus. by Seymour Fleishman. Chicago, Rand McNally, c1960. 72 p. illus. 28 cm. [E176.1.R79] 60-8268
1. Presidents—United States—Biography. 2. Presidents—United States—Wives. I. Title.

SCHARA, August W. 973'.0992
All the Presidents, plus Time and biorhythms—the art and the science : an insight into moments of history through biorhythms / August W. Schara. 1st ed. Hicksville, N.Y. : Exposition Press, c1978. xiii, 178 p. : ill. ; 29 cm. Cover title: All the Presidents plus. Includes index. Bibliography: p. 175. [E176.1.S33] 78-100975 ISBN 0-682-48872-0 : 9.50
1. Presidents United States—Biography. 2. Biological rhythms. I. Title.

SIX Presidents from the Empire State. Edited by Harry J. Sievers. Tarrytown, N.Y., Sleepy Hollow Restorations [1974] x, 208 p. ports. 24 cm. Bibliography: p. 189-192. [E176.1.S59] 74-951 ISBN 0-912882-07-7 8.95 973'.0992 B
1. Presidents—United States—Biography. 2. United States—Politics and government—19th century—Addresses, essays, lectures. 3. United States—Politics and government—1901-1953—Addresses, essays, lectures. I. Sievers, Harry Joseph, 1920- ed. II. Sleepy Hollow Restorations, Tarrytown, N.Y. BIP

SMITH, A. Merriman, 1913-1970. 973.099 B
Merriman Smith's book of Presidents; a White House memoir. Edited by Timothy G. Smith, with a foreword by Robert J. Donovan. [1st ed.] New York, Norton [1972] 250 p. 21 cm. [E176.1.S62] 73-39298 ISBN 0-393-07469-2 7.95
1. Presidents—United States—Biography. I. Title. II. Title: A White House memoir.

TAYLOR, Tim, 1920- 973'.099 B
The book of presidents. [1st ed.] New York, Arno Press, 1972. viii, 703 p. ports. 25 cm. "The Constitution": p. 637-645. [E176.1.T226] 74-164708 ISBN 0-405-00226-2 12.95
1. Presidents—United States—Biography. I. United States. Constitution. 1972. II. Title.

TOMPKINS, Jane. 923.173
Presidents of the United States; the story of their lives, closely interwoven with the

vast political and economic changes of the nation [by] Jane and Burt McConnell. Ports. by Constance Joan Naar. New York, Crowell [1951] 324 p. illus. 21 cm. Includes bibliography. [E176.1.T65] 51-12919
1. Presidents—U.S.—Biography. I. McConnell, Burt Morton, 1888-1960, joint author. II. Title.

WHITE, William Allen, 1868-1944. 973'.099
Masks in a pageant. Westport, Conn., Greenwood Press [1971] xv, 507 p. illus., ports. 23 cm. Reprint of the 1928 ed. Contents.Contents.—The old kings: Croker. Platt.—The early Stuarts: Harrison. Grover Cleveland. McKinley.—Two Warwicks: Mark Hanna. Bryan.—The great rebellion: Theodore Roosevelt. Taft. Woodrow Wilson.—The restoration: Harding. Coolidge.—The young princes of democracy: Alfred Emanuel Smith. William Hale Thompson. [E176.1.W58 1971] 73-110884 ISBN 0-8371-4568-6
1. Presidents—United States—Biography. 2. Statesmen—United States. 3. United States—Politics and government. I. Title. BIP

WHITE, William Allen, 1868-1944. 973'.099 B
Masks in a pageant. New York, Macmillan, 1930. St. Clair Shores, Mich., Scholarly Press, 1970 [c1928] xv, 507 p. illus., map, ports. 22 cm. Contents.Contents.—The old kings: Croker. Platt.—The early Stuarts: Harrison. Grover Cleveland.—Two Warwicks: Mark Hanna. Bryan.—The great rebellion: Theodore Roosevelt. Taft. Woodrow Wilson.—The restoration: Harding. Coolidge.—The young princes of democracy: Alfred Emanuel Smith. William Hale Thompson. [E176.1.W58 1970] 79-145367 ISBN 0-403-01272-4
1. Presidents—United States—Biography. 2. Statesmen—United States. 3. United States—Politics and government—1865-1933. I. Title.

WHITNEY, David C. 973
The American Presidents, by David C. Whitney. Illustrated by Richard Paul Dluga. Garden City, N.Y., Doubleday [1967] x, 372 p. ports. 22 cm. [E176.1.W6] 67-20646
1. Presidents—United States—Biography. I. Title.

WHITNEY, David C. 973 B
The American Presidents, by David C. Whitney. Illustrated by Richard Paul Kluga. Garden City, N.Y., Doubleday [1969] x, 397 p. ports. 22 cm. [E176.1.W6 1969] 73-94327 5.95
1. Presidents—U.S.—Biography. I. Title.

WHITNEY, David C. 973
The graphic story of the American Presidents, by David C. Whitney. Edited by Thomas C. Jones. Chicago, J. G. Ferguson Pub. Co.; distributed by Doubleday [Garden City, N.Y., 1968] 523 p. illus. (part col.), ports. 29 cm. Expanded and rearranged pictorial edition of the author's The American Presidents. [E176.1.W6 1968] 68-55254 14.95
1. Presidents—United States—Biography. I. Title.

WHITNEY, David C. 973'.0922
The graphic story of the American Presidents, by David C. Whitney. Edited by Thomas C. Jones. Chicago, J. G. Ferguson Pub. Co.; distributed to the book trade by Doubleday [1969] 540 p. illus. (part col.), facsims., ports. 29 cm. Expanded and rearranged pictorial edition of the author's The American Presidents. [E176.1.W6 1969] 70-78472 14.95
1. Presidents—United States—Biography. I. Title.

WHITNEY, David C. 973'.0992 B
The graphic story of the American Presidents, by David C. Whitney. Edited by Thomas C. Jones. Chicago, J. G. Ferguson Pub. Co.; distributed to the book trade by Doubleday [Garden City? N.Y., 1972] 540 p. illus. 29 cm. Expanded and rearranged pictorial ed. of the author's The American Presidents. [E176.1.W6 1972] 72-179639 14.95
1. Presidents—United States—Biography. I. Title.

WHITNEY, David C. 973'.0992 B
The graphic story of the American Presidents, by David C. Whitney. Edited by Thomas C. Jones. Chicago, J. G. Ferguson Pub. Co.; distributed to the book trade by Doubleday [1971] 540 p. illus. (part col.), facsims., ports. 29 cm. Expanded and rearranged pictorial edition of the author's The American Presidents. [E176.1.W6 1971] 78-22359 14.95
1. Presidents—United States—Biography. I. Title.

WISE, John Sergeant, 1846-1913. 973
Recollections of thirteen presidents. Freeport, N.Y., Books for Libraries Press [1968] 284 p. ports. 22 cm. (Essay index reprint series) Reprint of the 1906 ed. Contents.Contents.—John Tyler.—Franklin Pierce.—James Buchanan.—Jefferson Davis.—Andrew Johnson.—Ulysses S. Grant.—Rutherford B. Hayes.—James A. Garfield.—Chester A. Arthur.—Grover Cleveland.—Benjamin Harrison.—William McKinley.—Theodore Roosevelt. [E176.1.W81 1968] 68-55865
1. Presidents—United States—Biography. 2. United States—Politics and government. I. Title. BIP

Presidents—United States—Election—Bibliography.

MILES, William, 1942- 016.329'01'0973
The image makers : a bibliography of American presidential campaign biographies / by William Miles. Metuchen, N.J. : Scarecrow Press, 1979. p. cm. Includes indexes. [Z7164.R4M63] [JK524] 79-19472 ISBN 0-8108-1252-5 : 12.50
1. Presidents—United States—Election—Bibliography. 2. Presidents—United States—Biography—Bibliography. 3. Campaign biography—Bibliography. I. Title. BIP

Presidents—United States—Homes.

UNITED States. National Park Service. 973'.0992 B
The Presidents : from the inauguration of George Washington to the inauguration of Jimmy Carter : historic places commemorating the Chief Executives of the United States. Rev. ed. Washington : U.S. Dept. of the Interior, National Park Service : for sale by the Supt. of Docs., U.S. Govt. Print., Off., 1977. p. cm. (The National survey of historic sites and buildings ; v. 20) Bibliography: p. [E159.U55 1977] 77-608061
1. Presidents—United States—Homes. 2. Presidents—United States—Biography. 3. Historic sites—United States. I. Title. II. Series.

Presidents—United States—Miscellanea.

FRANK, Sidney. 973'.0992
The Presidents : tidbits & trivia / edited by Sidney Frank. Maplewood, N.J. : Hammond Inc., [1975] p. cm. [E176.1.F789] 75-13655 ISBN 0-8437-3232-6 pbk. : 2.95
1. Presidents—United States—Miscellanea. I. Title. BIP

*KANE, Joseph Nathan 923.1
Facts about the Presidents from Washington to Johnson, rev & enl. New York, Pocket Bks. [1964, c.1959, 1964] 504p. 19cm. (75001) .75 pap.,
I. Title.

Presidents—United States—Mistresses—Biography.

HUNT, Irma. 973'.0992 B
Dearest madame : the Presidents' mistresses / by Irma Hunt. New York : McGraw-Hill, c1978. xi, 288 p. ; 24 cm.. Includes bibliographical references and index. [E176.4.H86] 78-8713 ISBN 0-07-031306-7 : 8.95
1. Presidents—United States—Mistresses—Biography. I. Title.

Presidents—United States—Mothers—Biography.

FABER, Doris, 1924- 973'.0992 B
The Presidents' mothers / Doris Faber. New York : St. Martin's Press, c1978. xv, 316 p. : ill. ; 22 cm. Includes index. Bibliography: p. 275-304. [E176.3.F32] 77-9175 ISBN 0-312-64132-X : 10.00
1. Presidents—United States—Mothers—Biography. I. Title. BIP

Presidents—United States—Religion—Juvenile literature.

SCHRAFF, Anne E. 973'.0992 B
The faith of the Presidents / compiled and written by Anne E. Schraff ; illustrated by Don Kueker. St. Louis : Concordia Pub. House, c1978. 80 p. : ports. ; 24 cm. (Greatness with faith) Sketches of ten Presidents focusing on inspirational moments in their lives. [E176.8.S35] 77-28723 ISBN 0-570-07877-6 : 4.95. ISBN 0-570-07882-2 pbk. : 2.95
1. Presidents—United States—Religion—Juvenile literature. 2. Presidents—United States—Biography—Juvenile literature. I. Kueker, Don. II. Title. III. Series. BIP

Presidents—United States—Staff.

ANDERSON, Patrick, 1936- 353'.03
The Presidents' men; White House assistants of Franklin D. Roosevelt, Harry S. Truman, Dwight D. Eisenhower, John F. Kennedy, and Lyndon B. Johnson. [1st ed.] Garden City, N.Y., Doubleday, 1968. viii, 420 p. 25 cm. Bibliographical references included in "Sources" (p. [401]-405) [E747.A75] 68-24832 6.95
1. Presidents—United States—Staff. 2. United States—Biography. I. Title.

Presidents—United States—Staff—Biography.

MEDVED, Michael. 353'.03'130922
The shadow Presidents : the secret history of the Chief Executives and their top aides / Michael Medved. New York : Times Books, c1979. xi, 401 p., [8] leaves of plates : ill. ; 24 cm. Includes index. Bibliography: p. 367-384. [E176.47.M42 1979] 78-20682 ISBN 0-8129-0816-3 : 12.50
1. Presidents—United States—Staff—Biography. 2. United States—Politics and government—19th century. 3. United States—Politics and government—20th century. I. Title.

Presidents—United States—Wives—Biography.

KLAPTHOR, Margaret Brown. 973'.0992 B
The First Ladies / by Margaret Brown Klapthor. 1st ed. Washington : White House Historical Association, c1975. 84 p. : ill., ports. ; 26 cm. "Published ... with the cooperation of the National Geographic Society." [E176.2.K48] 74-15419
1. Presidents—United States—Wives—Biography. I. White House Historical Association. II. Title.

LANGFORD, Laura Carter Holloway, b.1848. 973'.0992 B
The ladies of the White House : or, In the home of the Presidents, being a complete history of the social and domestic lives of the Presidents from Washington to the present time / by Laura C. Holloway. New York : AMS Press, [1975] p. cm. Reprint of the 1882 ed. published by A. Gorton, Philadelphia. [E176.2.L36 1975] 70-171655 ISBN 0-404-04608-8 : 38.50
1. Presidents—United States—Wives—Biography. 2. Presidents—United States—Biography. I. Title.

Presidents—United States—Wives—Biography—Juvenile literature.

BLUMBERG, Rhoda. 973'.0992 B
First ladies / by Rhoda Blumberg. New York : F. Watts, 1977. 63 p. : ports. ; 23 cm. (A First book) Includes index. Bibliography: p. 61. Brief biographies of the women who have been First Ladies of the United States. [E176.2.B58] 920 77-2617 ISBN 0-531-01286-7 lib.bdg. : 4.47
1. Presidents—United States—Wives—Biography—Juvenile literature. I. Title.

Presley, Bob, 1946-1975.

MICHELSON, Herb. 796.32'3'0924 B
Almost a famous person / Herb Michelson. 1st ed. New York : Harcourt Brace Jovanovich, c1980. p. cm. [GV884.P73M5] 79-2766 ISBN 0-15-105069-4 : 9.95
1. Presley, Bob, 1946-1975. 2. Basketball players—United States—Biography. I. Title. BIP

Presley, Elvis Aron. 1935-1977.

COCKE, Marian J., 1926- 784.5'4'00924 B
I called him Babe : Elvis Presley's nurse remembers / by Marian J. Cocke. Memphis : Memphis State University Press, c1979. 160 p. : ill. ; 24 cm. (20th-century reminiscence series) [ML420.P96C6] 79-124443 ISBN 0-87870-053-6 : 10.00
1. Presley, Elvis Aron. 2. Cocke, Marian J., 1926- 3. Singers—United States—Biography. 4. Nurses—Tennessee—Biography. I. Title. II. Series. BIP

DUNLEAVY, Steve. 784'.092'4 B
Elvis : what happened? / Steve Dunleavy. 1st ed. New York : Ballantine Books, 1977. p. cm. [ML420.P96D8] 77-6127 ISBN 0-345-27215-3 pbk. : 1.95
1. Presley, Elvis Aron. 2. Singers—United States—Biography. 3. Moving-picture actors and actresses—United States—Biography. I. Title. BIP

GREGORY, James, ed. 927.92
The Elvis Presley story. Introd. by Dick Clark. New York, Hillman Bks. 158p. illus., ports. (HB 130) .35 pap.,
I. Presley, Elvis Aron, 1935- II. Title.

*HANNA, David. 784.'092'4
Elvis : Lovely star at the top / David Hanna. New York : Nordon Pubns., c1977. 224p. : photos : 18 cm. (A Leisure Book) [ML420. 6] ISBN 0-8439-0532-8 pbk. : 1.95
1. Presley, Elvis,1935-1977. I. Title.

HARBINSON, William Allen, 1941- 784'.092'4 B
The illustrated Elvis / by W. A. Harbinson ; designed by Stephen Ridgeway. New York : Grosset & Dunlap, 1976, c1975. 160 p. : ill. ; 28 cm. First ed. published in 1975 under title: Elvis Presley. A pictorial biography of the popular singer who became "the quintessence of American popular music." [ML420.P96H4 1976] 92 77-74740 ISBN 0-448-12572-2 : 12.95 ISBN 0-448-12461-0 pbk. : 4.95
1. Presley, Elvis Aron. 2. Singers, American—Biography. 3. Moving-picture actors and actresses—United States—Biography. I. Title.

HARMS, Valerie. 784'.092'4 B
Trying' to get to you / by Valerie Harms. New York : Atheneum, 1979. p. cm. A biography of Elvis Presley, whose musical style, forged from gospel songs, black blues, and country ballads, altered the course of contemporary music. [ML3930.P73H4] 92 79-14641 ISBN 0-689-30726-8 : 8.95
1. Presley, Elvis Aron. 2. Rock musicians—United States—Biography—Juvenile literature. I. Title.

HOPKINS, Jerry. 784'.0924 B
Elvis; a biography. New York, Simon and Schuster [1971] 448 p. illus. 22 cm. "Discography": p. [429]-444. [ML420.P96H7] 77-156154 ISBN 0-671-20973-6 7.95
1. Presley, Elvis Aron. I. Title.

JONES, Peter, 1930- 784'.092'4 B
Elvis / [by] Peter Jones. London : Octopus Books, 1976. 88 p. : ill. (some col.), ports. (some col.) ; 31 cm. Col. ill. on lining papers. [ML420.P96J6] 77-354001 ISBN 0-7064-0550-1 : £1.99
1. Presley, Elvis Aron. 2. Entertainers—United States—Biography.

LICHTER, Paul, 1944- 784'.092'4 B
The boy who dared to rock: the definitive Elvis / by Paul Lichter. 1st ed. Garden City, N.Y. : Dolphin Books, 1978. 304 p., [8] leaves of plates : ill. ; 28 cm. Discography: p. 201-298. [ML420.P96L52] 76-52006 ISBN 0-385-12636-0 : 7.95
1. Presley, Elvis Aron. 2. Presley, Elvis Aron—Bibliography. 3. Singers—United States—Biography. I. Title. **BIP**

PANTA, Ilona. 784'.092'4 B
Elvis Presley, king of kings / Ilona Panta. 1st ed. Hicksville, N.Y. : Exposition Press, c1979. 247 p. ; 22 cm. [ML420.P96P23] 79-113136 ISBN 0-682-49266-3 : 10.00
1. Presley, Elvis Aron. 2. Singers—United States—Biography. 3. Moving picture actors and actresses—United States—Biography.

PARISH, James Robert. 784
The Elvis Presley Scrapbook / James Robert Parish. New York : Ballantine Books, c1977. 218 p. : ill. ; 30 cm. Discography: p. 177-196. [ML420.P96P25 1977] .092'4[B 78-107932 ISBN 0-345-27594-2 : 7.95
1. Presley, Elvis Aron. 2. Singers—United States—Biography. I. Title.

PARKER, Edmund K. 784'.092'4 B
Inside Elvis / Ed Parker ; sketches by George Bartell Limited 1st ed. Orange, CA : Rampart House, c1978. x, 197p. [9] leaves of plates : ill. ; 23 cm. [ML420.P96P28] 78-56562 ISBN 0-89773-000-3 pbk. : 2.25
1. Presley, Elvis Aron. 2. Singers — United States — Biography. 3. M0ving-picture actors and actresses — United States — Biography. I. Title. **BIP**

PRESLEY, Vester. 784'.092'4 B
A Presley speaks / by Vester Presley, as told to Deda Bonura. Memphis : Wimmer Brothers Books, c1978. vi, 150 p. : ill. ; 24 cm. [ML420.P96P7] 78-111857 ISBN 0-918544-10-6 : 10.00
1. Presley, Elvis Aron. 2. Singers—United States—Biography. I. Bonura, Deda. II. Title. **BIP**

REGGERO, John 784'.092'4 B
Elvis in concert / text and photos. by John Reggero ; with an introd. by David Stanley. New York : Distributed by Dell Pub., c1979. [128] p. : chiefly ill. ; 28 cm. "A Delta special/Lorelei." [ML420.P96R4] 79-53039 ISBN 0-440-02219-3 pbk. : 7.95
1. Presley, Elvis Aron. 2. Singers—United States—Biography. I. Title.

TAYLOR, Paula. 784'.092'4 B
Elvis Presley. Illus.: Dick Brude. Mankato, Minn., Creative Education; [distributed by Childrens Press, Chicago, 1974, c1975] 31 p. illus. (part col.) 25 cm. (Rock 'n pop stars) A biography of "the biggest selling record artist of all time" stressing his rise to fame as a singer. [ML3930.P73T4] 92 74-14546 ISBN 0 87191-394-1 4.95 (lib. bdg.)
1. Presley, Elvis Aron—Juvenile literature. I. Brude, Dick, illus. II. Title. **BIP**

YANCEY, Becky. 784'.092'4 B
My life with Elvis / Becky Yancey with Cliff Linedecker. New York : St. Martin's Press, c1977. xviii, 360 p. : ill. ; 22 cm. [ML420.P96Y3] 77-10377 8.95
1. Presley, Elvis Aron. 2. Rock musicians—United States—Biography. I. Linedecker, Cliff, joint author. II. Title. **BIP**

ZMIJEWSKY, Steve. 784'.092'4 B
Elvis : the films and career of Elvis Presley / by Steven Zmijewsky and Boris Zmijewsky. 1st ed. Secaucus, N.J. : Citadel Press, c1976. 223, [1] p. : ill. ; 29 cm. Discography: p. 216-[224] [ML420.P96Z6] 76-151058 ISBN 0-8065-0511-7 : 14.00
1. Presley, Elvis Aron. 2. Singers—United States—Biography. I. Zmijewsky, Boris, joint author. **BIP**

Presley, Elvis Avon.

ELVIS, we love you tender / Dee Presley ... [et al.], as told to Martin Torgoff. New York : Delacorte Press, 1980. p. cm. "A Delilah/Mike Franklin book." Includes index. [ML420.P96E47] 79-20830 ISBN 0-440-02323-8 : 14.95 784'.092'4 B
1. Presley, Elvis Aron. 2. Singers—United States—Biography. I. Presley, Dee. II. Torgoff, Martin. **BIP**

*HARBINSON, W. A. 784.'092'4 B
The illustrated Elvis / W. A. Harbinson ; designed by Stephen Ridgeway. New York : Grosset & Dunlap, 1976 c1975. 160 p. : ill. ; 27 cm. [ML420.P96] 76-556 0-448 ISBN 0-448-12572-2 : 10.00 ISBN pbk. : 4.95
1. Presley, Elvis Avon. I. Title. **BIP**

Press—Europe—Biog.

WHO'S who in the Common Market's press and advertising; a biographical dictionary containing about 4,000 biographies of prominent people in press and advertising in Belgium, France, Germany(West), Italy, Luxembourg and the Netherlands. Ed. by Helmut von der Heiden, Stephen S. Taylor [New York, 10010. Albert Daub, 257 Park Ave. South] 1965 New York, 10010. Albert Daub, 257 Park Ave. South 1965 557p. 21cm. 65-29193 16.80 070.922
1. Press—Europe—Biog. 2. Advertising—Biog. 3. European Economic Community. I. Heiden, Helmut von der, ed.

Preston, William, 1729-1783.

JOHNSON, Patricia Givens. 975.5'8'02
William Preston and the Allegheny patriots / by Patricia Givens Johnson. [s.l. : s.n.], c1976 (Pulaski, Va. : B. D. Smith) xiii, 318 p. : ill. ; 24 cm. Includes bibliographical references and index. [E230.5.A43J63] 76-9446 8.95
1. Preston, William, 1729-1783. 2. Allegheny Mountains—History—Revolution, 1775-1783. 3. Virginia—History—Revolution, 1775-1783. 4. United States—History—French and Indian War, 1755-1763. 5. Virginia—Biography. I. Title.

Pretty-shield, Crow Indian.

LINDERMAN, Frank Bird, 1868-1938. 970.3 B
Pretty-shield, medicine woman of the Crows. Illustrated by Herbert Morton Stoops. New York, John Day Co. [1972, c1932] 256 p. illus. 22 cm. [E99.C92L59 1972] 72-3273 7.95
1. Pretty-shield, Crow Indian. 2. Indians of North America—Women. 3. Crow Indians. I. Title. **BIP**

*LINDERMAN, Frank Bird, 1868-1938. 970.3 [B]
Pretty-shield, medicine woman of the Crows [by] Frank B. Linderman. Illus by Herbert Morton Stoops. Lincoln, University of Nebraska Press [1974, c1972] [1974, c1932] 256 p. illus. 20 cm. (Bison book, BB580) [E99.C92L59] ISBN 0-8032-5791-0 2.45 (pbk.)
1. Pretty-shield, Crow Indian. 2. Indians of North America—Women. 3. Crow Indians. I. Title.
L.C. card no. for the hardbound edition: 72-3273.

Preus, Herman Amberg, 1825-1894.

PREUS, Caroline Dorothea Margrethe (Keyser) 1829-1880. 920.7
Linka's diary, on land and sea, 1845-1864. Translated and edited by Johan Carl Keyser Preus and his wife Diderikke Margrethe, nee Brandt. Illus. by Mary Stalland, nee Kvaase. Minneapolis, Augsburg Pub. House [1952] 288 p. illus. 22 cm. [BX8080.P68A33] 52-338025
1. Preus, Herman Amberg, 1825-1894. I. Title.

Preus, Jacob Aall Ottesen, 1920-

ADAMS, James Edward, 1941- 284'.1'0924 B
Preus of Missouri and the great Lutheran civil war / James E. Adams. 1st ed. New York : Harper & Row, c1977. x, 242 p. ; 21 cm. Includes index. [BX8080.P73A65 1977] 76-62931 ISBN 0-06-060071-3 : 10.00
1. Preus, Jacob Aall Ottesen, 1920- 2. Lutheran Church—Clergy—Biography. 3. Lutheran Church—Missouri Synod—Doctrinal and controversial works. 4. Clergy—United States—Biography. I. Title.

Previn, Dory—Biography.

PREVIN, Dory. 818'.5'409 B
Bog-trotter : an autobiography with lyrics / by Dory Previn ; drawings by Joby Baker. 1st ed. Garden City, N.Y. : Doubleday, 1980. p. cm. [PS3566.R42Z515] 78-20094 ISBN 0-385-14708-2 : 12.00
1. Previn, Dory—Biography. 2. Authors, American—20th century—Biography. I. Title.

PREVIN, Dory. 818'.5'409 B
Midnight baby : an autobiography / Dory Previn. New York : Macmillan, c1976. x, 246 p. ; 22 cm. [PS3566.R42Z52] 76-20544 ISBN 0-02-599000-4 : 8.95
1. Previn, Dory—Biography. I. Title. **BIP**

Prevost, Antoine Francois, called Prevost d'Exiles, 1697-1763.

PREVOST, Antoine Francois, called Prevost d'Exiles, 1697-1763. 016.843'5
Manon Lescaut [by] Abbe Prevost [translated by D. C. Moylan] Carmen [by] Prosper Merimee [translated by Edmund H. Garrett. Introd. by Philip Henderson. Memoir of Merimee by Imogen Guiney] London, J. M. Dent; New York, E. P. Dutton [1951] viii, 216p. 18cm. (Everyman's library, no. 834. Fiction) Life and bibliography of Prevost: p. [1] Life and bibliography of Mermee: p. [152] [PQ2021.M3E5 1951] 56-22719
1. Merimee, Prosper, 1803-1870. Carmen. II. Title. III. Title: Carmen. IV. Series.

Prewett, Virginia.

PREWETT, Virginia. 918.17
Beyond the Great Forest. [1st ed.] New York, Dutton, 1953. 302 p. 22 cm. Autobiographical. [CT275.P8424A3] 52-12962
I. Title.

Price, Doughbelly,

PRICE, Doughbelly 920.8
Short stirrups; the saga of Doughbelly Price. Los Angeles, Westernlore Press [c.] 1960. 205p. Introd. by Richard G. Hubler illus. 21cm. 60-12695 5.75
I. Title.

PRICE, Doughbelly, 1897- 920.8
Short strrups; the saga of Doughbelly Price. Los Angeles, Westernlore Press, 1960. 205p. illus: 21cm. [GV1811.P7A3] 60-12695
I. Title.

Price, Eugenia.

PRICE, Eugenia. 248'.2 B
The burden is light! The autobiography of a transformed pagan who took God at His word. Boston, G. K. Hall, 1973 [c1955] 326 p. 25 cm. Large print ed. [BV4935.P75A32 1973] 73-9986 ISBN 0-8161-6137-2 9.95 (lib. bdg.)
1. Price, Eugenia. 2. Converts. I. Title.

Price, Eugenia—Biography.

PRICE, Eugenia. 813'.5'4
St. Simons memoir : the personal story of finding the island and writing the St. Simons trilogy of novels / Eugenia Price. 1st ed. Philadelphia : Lippincott, c1978. 224 p., [8] leaves of plates : ill. ; 24 cm. [PS3566.R47Z47] 78-1340 ISBN 0-397-01216-0 : 10.00
1. Price, Eugenia—Biography. 2. St. Simon's Island, Ga.—Biography. I. Title. **BIP**

Price, George McCready, 1870-

CLARK, Harold Willard, 1891- 213'.0924
Crusader for creation; the life and writings of Geroge McCrendy Price, by Harold W. Clark. Incorporating biographical materials prepared by R. Lyle James. Mountain View, Calif., Pacific Press Pub. Association [c1966] 102 p. 22 cm. (A Destiny book, D-110) "Books by George McCready Price": p. 101-102. [BX6193.P7C5] 66-28531
1. Price, George McCready, 1870- I. Title. II. Title: The life and writings of George McCready Price.

Price, Harry, 1881-1948.

HALL, Trevor H. 133'.092'4 B
Search for Harry Price / Trevor H. Hall. London : Duckworth, 1979. x, 237 p., [5] leaves of plates : ill. ; 22 cm. Includes bibliographical references and index. [BF1027.P67H34] 79-304531 ISBN 0-7156-1143-7 : 14.95
1. Price, Harry, 1881-1948. 2. Psychical research—England—Biography. 3. Phychical research—Controversial literature. I. Title.
Distributed by Biblio Distribution Centre, Totowa, NJ 07511 **BIP**

TABORI, Paul, 1908- 133.0924
Harry Price; the biography of a ghosthunter, With a pref, by Eileen J. Garrett. New York, Living Books [1966] xi, 316 p. illus., port. 23 cm. First published in 1950. Bibliography: p. 305-311. [BF1027.P67T3] 66-21596
1. Price, Harry, 1881-1948. I. Title.

Price, John Giles, 1808-1857.

BARRY, John Vincent, Sir 1903- 923.542
The life and death of John Price; a study of the exercise of naked power [Parkville] Melbourne Univ. Pr., New York, Cambridge [1965] xiii, 204p. illus., plan, ports. 23cm Bibl. [HV9872.D3] 63-2478 9.50
1. Price, John Giles, 1808-1857. 2. Prisons—Australia—Hist. I. Title.

BARRY, John Vincent Sir 1903- 923.542
The life and death of John Price; a study of the exercise of naked power. [Parkville] Melbourne University Press; New York, Cambridge University press [1964] xiii, 204 p. illus., plan, ports. 23 cm. Bibliographical references included in "Notes" (p. 185-196) Bibliography: p. 197-200. [HV9872.B3] 65-2478
1. Price, John Giles, 1808-1857 2. Prisons — Australia — Hist. I. Title.

Price, John Milburn, 1884-

MAGUIRE, Clyde (Merrill) 922.673
J. M. Price; portrait of a pioneer. Nashville, Broadman Press [c.1960] 138p. illus. 22cm. 60-14145 2.95 bds.,
1. Price, John Milburn. I. Title.

MAGUIRE, Clyde (Merrill) 922.673
J. M. Price; portrait of a pioneer. Nashville, Broadman Press. [1960] 138p. illus. 22cm. [BV1470.3.P7M3] 60-14145
1. Price, John Milburn, 1884- I. Title.

Price, Joseph Charles, 1854-1893.

WALLS, William Jacob, Bp., 1885- 370'.92'4 B
Joseph Charles Price, educator and race leader. Freeport, N.Y., Books for Libraries Press, 1973. p. (The Black heritage library collection) Reprint of the 1943 ed. Bibliography: p. [E185.97.P9W3 1973] 72-10404 ISBN 0-8369-9214-8
1. Price, Joseph Charles, 1854-1893. I. Title. II. Series.

YATES, Walter L ed. v. 12
He spoke, now they speak; a collection of speeches and writings of and on the life and works of J. C. Price. [Salisbury, N. C., Hood Theological Seminary] 1952. 165p. illus. 22cm. [BX8459.P7Y3] 54-43328
1. Price, Joseph Charles, 1854-1893. I. Title.

Price, Nina Mae, 1882-1974.

WHEELER, Shirley P. 616.8'55'00924 B
Dr. Nina and the panther / Shirley P. Wheeler. New York : Dodd, Mead, c1976. 278 p. ; 22 cm. [R154.P8627W48] 76-25814 ISBN 0-396-07348-4 : 8.95
1. Price, Nina Mae, 1882-1974. 2. Women physicians—Pennsylvania—Biography. 3. Monroe Co., Pa.—Biography. I. Title. **BIP**

Price, Samuel Woodson, 1828-1918.

COLEMAN, John Winston, 1898- 709'.2'2
Three Kentucky artists—Hart, Price, Troye / J. Winston Coleman, Jr. Lexington : University Press of Kentucky, [1974] 76 p., [4] leaves of plates : ill. ; 21 cm. (The Kentucky bicentennial bookshelf) "Partial list of portraits by Samuel Price": p. 44-[48] [N6530.K4C64] 74-7873 ISBN 0-8131-0202-2 pbk. : 3.95
1. Hart, Joel Tanner, 1810-1877. 2. Price, Samuel Woodson, 1828-1918. 3. Troye, Edward, 1808-1874. 4. Art—Kentucky. I. Title. II. Series.

Price, Sterling, 1809-1867.

CASTEL, Albert E. 973.7'0924
General Sterling Price and the Civil War in the West [by] Albert Castel. Baton Rouge, Louisiana State University Press [1968] xiii, 300 p. illus., facsims., maps, ports. 24 cm. Bibliography: p. 287-294. [E467.1.P87C3] 68-21804 8.95
1. Price, Sterling, 1809-1867. 2. The West—History—Civil War, 1861-1865. 3. United States—History—Civil War, 1861-1865—Campaigns and battles. I. Title. **BIP**

SHALHOPE, Robert E., 1941- 973.7'0924 B
Sterling Price; portrait of a Southerner [by] Robert E. Shalhope. Columbia, Mo., University of Missouri Press [1971] xii, 311 p. maps. 25 cm. Bibliography: p. [293]-303. [E467.1.P87S5] 79-130670 ISBN 0-8262-0103-2 12.00
1. Price, Sterling, 1809-1867.

Price, Thomas Frederick, 1860-1919.

MURRETT, John C 922.273
The story of Father Price: Thomas Frederick Price, cofounder of Maryknoll. New York, McMullen Books [1953] 116p. 20cm. 'An abridgment of the author's ... Tar Heel apostle.' [BX4705.P7M83] 53-12277
1. Price, Thomas Frederick, 1860-1919. I. Title.

Price, Vincent, 1911-

PARISH, James Robert. 791'.092'4 B
Vincent Price unmasked, by James Robert Parish with Steven Whitney. New York, Drake Publishers [1974] 266 p. illus. 24 cm. [PN2287.P72P3] 74-6151 ISBN 0-87749-667-6
1. Price, Vincent, 1911- I. Whitney, Steven, joint author. II. Title.

PRICE, Vincent, 1911- 707.5
I like what I know; a visual autobiography. Illustrated with photos. [1st ed.] Garden City, N. Y., Doubleday, 1959. 313 p. illus. 24 cm. [N8384.P7A3] 59-12830
1. Art—Collectors and collecting. I. Title.

Price, Vincent, 1911——Juvenile literature.

PRICE, Vincent, 1911- 791'.092'4 B
Vincent Price, his movies, his plays, his life / by Vincent Price ; conceived and produced by Whitehall, Hadlyme & Smith, inc. 1st ed. Garden City, N.Y. : Doubleday, c1978. 117 p. : ill. ; 22 cm. (An I want to know about book) Includes index. An actor well-known for his roles in spine-chillers describes his life, his career in the theater and movies, and his interest in the arts. [PN2287.P72A35] 92 77-16940 ISBN 0-385-11594-6 : 5.95.
1. Price, Vincent, 1911-—Juvenile literature. 2. Actors—United States—Biography—Juvenile literature. I. Whitehall, Hadlyme & Smith. II. Title.

Price, William Murray, 1904-1963.

PRICE, Edna Calkins. 917.8'03'30924 B
Burro Bill and me. Illustrated by Joyce Stolpe. Idyllwild, Calif., Strawberry Valley Press [1973] 275 p. illus. 21 cm. [F868.D2P7] 72-97363 ISBN 0-913612-00-6 pap. 4.95
1. Price, William Murray, 1904-1963. 2. Price, Edna Calkins. 3. Death Valley—Social life and customs. 4. Arizona—Social life and customs. 5. Nevada—Social life and customs. I. Title.
Publisher's Address: P.O. Box 157 Idyllwild, Calif. 92349. **BIP**

Pride, Charley—Juvenile literature.

BARCLAY, Pamela. 784'.092'4 B
Charley Pride. Illus.: Dick Brude. Mankato, Minn., Creative Education; [distributed by Childrens Press, Chicago, 1974, c1975] 31 p. illus. (part col.) 25 cm. (Rock 'n pop stars) A biography of the black man who broke the color line in country music. [ML3930.P75B3] [92] 74-14659 ISBN 0-87191-397-6
1. Pride, Charley—Juvenile literature. I. Brude, Dick, illus. II. Title. **BIP**

Priest, Ivy (Baker)

PRIEST, Ivy (Baker) 1905- 923.573
Green grows Ivy. [1st ed.] New York, McGraw-Hill [1958] 270p. illus. 21cm. Autobiographical. [E748.P89A3] 58-13015
I. Title.

Priestley, John Boynton, 1894-

BRAINE, John. 828'.9'1209 B
J. B. Priestley / John Braine. New York : Barnes & Noble Books, 1979, c1978. 163 p., [8] leaves of plates : ill. ; 24 cm. Includes index. [PR6031.R6Z559 1979] 78-26245 ISBN 0-06-490642-6 : 14.50
1. Priestley, John Boynton, 1894- 2. Authors, English—20th century—Biography. **BIP**

COOPER, Susan. 828'.9'1209 B
J. B. Priestley: portrait of an author. [1st U.S. ed.] New York, Harper & Row [1971, c1970] 240 p. port. 22 cm. "Works of J. B. Priestley": p. 239-240. [PR6031.R6Z563 1971] 72-138716 ISBN 0-06-010853-3 7.95
1. Priestley, John Boynton, 1894-

PRIESTLEY, John Boynton, 1894- 828.912
Margin released a writer's reminiscences and reflections. New York, Harper [1963, c.1962] 236p. illus. 22cm. 62-20114 4.95
1. Authors—Correspondence, reminiscences, etc. I. Title.

Priestley, John Boynton, 1894- — Biography.

PRIESTLEY, John Boynton, 1894- 824'.9'12
The happy dream : an essay / by J. B. Priestley. Andoversford : Whittington Press, 1976. [7], 35, [1] p. ; 21 cm. Limited ed. of 400 signed, numb. copies. [PR6031.R6H35] 77-358175 ISBN 0-904845-08-7 : £12.00
1. Priestley, John Boynton, 1894- — Biography. 2. Authors, English—20th century—Biography. 3. Dreams—Addresses, essays, lectures. I. Title.

PRIESTLEY, John Boynton, 1894- 828'.9'1209 B
Instead of the trees : a final chapter of autobiography / J. B. Priestley. New York : Stein and Day, 1977. 151 p. ; 22 cm. The 3d volume of the author's autobiography, the 1st of which is Midnight on the desert and the 2d, Rain upon Godshill. [PR6031.R6Z514] 77-2257 ISBN 0-8128-2265-X : 8.95
1. Priestley, John Boynton, 1894- — Biography. 2. Authors, English—20th century—Biography. I. Title. **BIP**

Priestley, Joseph, 1733-1804.

CROWTHER, James Gerald, 1899- 925
Scientists of the industrial revolution: Joseph Black, James Watt, Joseph Priestley [and] Henry Cavendish. Chester Springs. Pa., Dufour, 1963[c.1962] xii, 365p. ports. 23cm. Bibl. 63-21150 6.95
1. Black, Joseph, 1728-1799. 2. Watt, James, 1736-1819. 3. Priestley, Joseph, 1733-1804. 4. Cavendish, Henry, 1731-1810. I. Title.

GIBBS, Frederick William. 540'.0924 B
Joseph Priestley; revolutions of the eighteenth century [by] F. W. Gibbs. [1st ed.] Garden City, N.Y., Doubleday, 1967 [c1965] xii, 258 p. illus., facsim., map, ports. 22 cm. Bibliography: p. [250]-252. [QD22.P8G53] 67-14120
1. Priestley, Joseph, 1733-1804.

HOLT, Anne, 1899- 540'.924 B
A life of Joseph Priestley. With an introd. by Francis W. Hirst. Westport, Conn., Greenwood Press [1970] xviii, 221 p. port. 23 cm. Reprint of the 1931 ed. Bibliography: p. [xv]-xviii. [BX9869.P8H6 1970] 75-109750 ISBN 0-8371-4240-7
1. Priestley, Joseph, 1733-1804. I. Title. **BIP**

MARCUS, Rebecca B 925.4
Joseph Priestley, pioneer chemist. Pictures by Peter Costanza. New York, F. Watts [1961] 145p. illus. 22cm. (A First biography) [QD22.P8M3] 61-7500
1. Priestley, Joseph, 1733-1804. I. Title.

MARCUS, Rebecca B. 925.4
Joseph Priestly, pioneer chemist. Pictures by Peter Costanza. New York, Watts [c.1961] 145p. (First biography) 61-7500 1.95
1. Priestley, Joseph, 1733-1804. I. Title.

ORANGE, A. D. 540'.92'4 B
Joseph Priestley : an illustrated life of Joseph Priestley, 1733-1804, [by] A. D. Orange. Aylesbury : Shire Publications, 1974. 48 p. : ill., ports. ; 21 cm. (Lifelines ; 31) Includes index. Bibliography: p. 47. [QD22.P8O7] 75-308582 ISBN 0-85263-252-5 pbk. : 3.00
1. Priestley, Joseph, 1733-1804.
Distributed by International Publications Service.

PRIESTELEY, Joseph, 1733-1804 925.4
The memoirs of Dr. Joseph Priestley, eighteenth century religious liberal. Ed. by John T. Boyer. Washington, D.C., Barcroft Pr., Box 2009 [c.1964] 173p. 20cm. Abridged from 2-vol. 1806 ed. i0)entitled Memoirs of Dr. Joseph Priestley to the year 1795. A continuation of the Memoirs of Dr. Joseph Priestley, written by his son Joseph Priestley: p.105-168. Bibl. 64-20413 4.00; 2.00 pap.,
I. Priestley, Joseph, 1768-1833. II. Title.

PRIESTLEY, Joseph, 1733-1804 540'.924
Ascientific autobiography of Joseph Priestley, 1733-1804 selected scientific correspondence. Ed., commentary by Robert E. Schofield. Cambridge, M.I.T. Pr. [c.1966] xiv, 415p. port. 25cm. Bibl. [QD22.P8A4] 67-14099 13.50
I. Schofield, Robert E., ed. II. Title.

PRIESTLEY, Joseph, 1733-1804. 540'.924 B
Autobiography of Joseph Priestley. Memoirs written by himself. An account of further discoveries in air. Introd. by Jack Lindsay. [1st Amer. ed.] Teaneck [N.J.] Fairleigh Dickinson University Press [1971] 159 p. 23 cm. "An account of further discoveries in air, read 25 May 1775 [1st published in Royal Society of London] Philosophical transactions, 65 (1775), 384-394." Bibliography: p. [153]-154. [QD22.P8A33 1971] 71-137365 10.00
I. Lindsay, Jack, 1900- ed. II. Priestley, Joseph, 1733-1804. An account of further discoveries in air. 1971. III. Title: An account of further discoveries in air.

PRIESTLEY, Joseph, 1733- 925.4
The memoirs of Dr. Joseph Priestley, Eighteenth century religious liberal. Ed. by John T. Boyer. Washington, D.C., Barcroft Pr [1964] 173p. 20cm. Abridged from the 2-vol. 1806 ed. entitled Memoirs of Dr. Joseph Priestley to the year 1795. Bibl. 64-20413 4.00
I. Priestley, Joseph, 1768-1833. II. Title.

PRIESTLEY, Joseph, 1733-1804. 540'.92'4 B
Memoirs of Dr. Joseph Priestley to the year 1795, written by himself ; with a continuation to the time of his decease by his son, Joseph Priestley, and observations on his writings by Thomas Cooper and William Christie. Millwood, N.Y. : Kraus Reprint Co., 1978. v, 824, x p. ; 21 cm. Reprint of the 1806 ed. printed by J. Binns, Northumberland, Pa. "Catalogue of Dr. Priestley's smaller pamphlets and uncollected papers on philosophical subjects": p. 290-293; "A catalogue of books written by Doctor Priestley": p. i-x. [QD22.P8A33 1978] 78-3422 ISBN 0-527-72730-X : 50.00
1. Priestley, Joseph, 1733-1804. 2. Chemists—England—Biography. I. Priestley, Joseph, 1768-1833. **BIP**

PRIESTLEY, Joseph, 1733-1804. 540'.924
A scientific autobiography of Joseph Priestley, 1733-1804: selected scientific corresondence. Edited with commentary by Robert E. Schofield. Cambridge, M. I. T. Press [c1966] xiv, 415 p. port. 25 cm. Bibliography: p. 394-400. [QD22.P8A4] 67-14099
I. Schofield, Robert E., ed. II. Title.

THORPE, Thomas Edward, Sir, 1845-1925. 540'.92'4 B
Joseph Priestley / by T. E. Thorpe. New

York : AMS Press, 1976. viii, 228 p., [1] leaf of plates : ill. ; 18 cm. Reprint of the 1906 ed. published by J. M. Dent, London, in series: English men of science. "EMS #3." Includes index. [QD22.P8T5 1976] 70-177458 ISBN 0-404-07893-1 : 12.50
1. Priestley, Joseph, 1733-1804. 2. Chemists—England—Biograph. I. Series: English men of science.

Priestley, Joseph, 1733-1804—Juvenile literature.

CRANE, William Dwight. 920
The discoverer of oxygen: Joseph Priestley. New York, Messner [c.1962] 191p. 22 cm. Bibl. 62-15417 2.99
1. Priestley, Joseph, 1733-1804—Juvenile literature. I. Title.

Priestley, Joseph, 1733-1804—Congresses.

JOSEPH Priestley 540'.92'4
Symposium, Wilkes-Barre, Pa., 1974.
Joseph Priestley, scientist, theologian, and metaphysician : a symposium celebrating the two hundredth anniversary of the discovery of oxygen by Joseph Priestly in 1774 / Erwin N. Hiebert, Aaron J. Ihde, Robert E. Schofield ; edited by Lester Kieft and Bennett R. Willeford, Jr. Lewisburg [N.J.] : Bucknell University Press, 1980, c1979. p. cm. Symposium held during the ninth Middle Atlantic regional meeting of the American Chemical Society in Wilkes-Barre, Pa., Apr. 23-26, 1974. Includes bibliographical references. [QD22.P8J67] 77-92577 ISBN 0-8387-2202-4 : 10.00
1. Priestley, Joseph, 1733-1804—Congresses. 2. Chemistry—History—Congresses. 3. Chemists—Biography. I. Hiebert, Erwin N., 1919- II. Ihde, Aaron John, 1909- III. Schofield, Robert E. IV. Kieft, Lester, 1912- V. Willeford, Bennett R. VI. American Chemical Society. VII. Title.

Priests—Meditations.

SKWIRCZYNSKI, Wladyslaw. v. 12
My life in Christ, meditations for the reverend priests. New York, Arlington Print, Co., 1957. xviii, 217 p. 24 cm. Print. 68-103260
1. Priests—Meditations. I. Title.

Prigogine, Ilya.

FOR Ilya Prigogine / 541'.08 S
edited by Stuart A. Rice. New York : Wiley, c1978. 472 p. : ill. ; 24 cm. (Advances in chemical physics ; v. 38) "An Interscience publication." Includes bibliographical references and index. [QD453.A27 vol. 38] [QD455] 541 79-101799 ISBN 0-471-03883-0 ; 36.50
1. Prigogine, Ilya. 2. Chemistry, Physical and theoretical—Addresses, essays, lectures. 3. Chemists—United States—Biography. I. Prigogine, Ilya. II. Rice, Stuart Alan, 1932- III. Title. IV. Series.

Prime ministers

GILBERT, Martin. 941.08'092'4
Winston S. Churchill Boston, Mass. : Houghton Mifflin Volumes I and II were written by Randolph S. Churchill.
I. Title.
Vol. 5, 1977, entitled the Prophet of Truth, 1922-1939, is available for 30.00 L.C. card no. : 66-12065. ISBN 0-395-25104-4 **BIP**

HISTORY today. 923.242
British prime ministers; a portrait gallery introduced by Duff Cooper. New York, Roy Publishers [1953?] 177p. illus. 22cm. [DA28.4.H63] 53-10346
1. Prime ministers—Gt. Brit. I. Title.

MERSEY, Clive 354.42'000922
Bingham, 2d Viscount, 1872-1956
The chief ministers of England, 920-1720. Freeport, N.Y., Books for Libs. Pr. [1967] x, 422p. illus., facsims., ports. 24cm. (Essay index reprint ser.) Reprint of the 1923 ed. Bibl. [DA28.4.M42 1967] 67-30222 13.75
1. Prime ministers—Gt. Brit. I. Title. **BIP**

SMITH, George 942.081'092'2 B
Barnett, 1841-1909.
The prime ministers of Queen Victoria. Rev. ed. Freeport, N.Y., Books for Libraries Press [1973] p. (Essay index reprint series) Reprint of the 1888 ed. published by G. Routledge, London. [DA562.S64 1973] 73-4478 ISBN 0-518-10103-7
1. Prime ministers—Great Britain. 2. Great Britain—Politics and government—1837-1901. I. Title.

Prime ministers—Australia—Biography.

WHITINGTON, Don. 994'.00992 B
Twelfth man? Milton, Q., Jacaranda, 1972. 184 p. plates. 22 cm. [DU82.W48] 73-158609 ISBN 0-7016-0585-5 4.85
1. Prime ministers—Australia—Biography. I. Title.

Prime ministers—Canada—Biography

CROSBIE, John S., 1920- 971 B
Canada and its leaders. Toronto, New York [etc.] Baxter, 1968. 176 p. ports. 21 cm. Bibliography: p. 171-176. [F1033.C84] 68-143517
1. Prime ministers—Canada—Biography I. Title.

Prime ministers—Great Britain—Biography.

BRITISH prime 941.082'092'2
ministers in the twentieth century / edited by John P. Mackintosh. New York : St. Martin's Press, 1977- v. : 23 cm. Contents.Contents.—v. 1. Balfour to Chamberlain. Includes bibliographical references and index. [DA566.9.A1B74 1977b] 77-76542 ISBN 0-312-10517-7 : 14.95
1. Prime ministers—Great Britain—Biography. 2. Executive power—Great Britain. I. Mackintosh, John Pitcairn, 1929- **BIP**

HELLICAR, Eileen. 941'.00992
Prime ministers of Britain / Eileen Hellicar ; with drawings by Shirley Curzon. Newton Abbot ; North Pomfret, Vt. : David & Charles, c1978. 159 p. ports. ; 23 cm. Includes index. [DA28.4.H44] 77-85014 ISBN 0-7153-7486-9 : 12.95
1. Prime ministers—Great Britain—Biography. I. Title. **BIP**

MERSEY, Clive 942.07'0922 B
Bigham, 2d Viscount, 1872-1956.
The prime ministers of Britain, 1721-1921; with a supplementary chapter to 1924. 4th ed. Freeport, N.Y., Books for Libraries Press [1969] xiii, 384 p. ports. 23 cm. (Essay index reprint series) Reprint of the 1924 ed. Bibliography: p. 369-374. [DA28.4.M4 1969] 74-86772 ISBN 0-8369-1422-8
1. Prime ministers—Great Britain—Biography. I. Title.

ROTH, Cecil, 1899- 923.242
Benjamin Disraeli, earl of Beaconsfield. New York, Philosophical Library [1952] 178 p. illus. 22 cm. [DA564.B3R68] 52-11658
1. Beaconsfield, Benjamin Disraeli, 1st earl of, 1804-1881. II. Title.

VAN THAL, Herbert 942'.00992 B
Maurice, 1904-
The Prime Ministers / edited by Herbert Van Thal. New York : Stein and Day, [1975] p. cm. Vol. 2 introduced by Robert Blake. Contents.Contents.—Sir Robert Walpole to Sir Robert Peel.—From Lord John Russell to Edward Heath. Includes bibliographies. [DA28.4.V36] 74-26983 ISBN 0-8128-1738-9
1. Prime ministers—Great Britain—Biography. I. Title. **BIP**

WILSON, Harold, 941.08'092'2 B
1916-
A Prime Minister on Prime Ministers / Harold Wilson. New York : Summit Books, c1977. 334 p. : ill. ; 26 cm. Includes index. [DA531.2.W54] 77-14304 ISBN 0-671-40029-0 : 15.00
1. Prime ministers—Great Britain—Biography. 2. Great Britain—Politics and government—19th century. 3. Great Britain—Politics and government—20th century. 4. Great Britain—Biography. I. Title. **BIP**

Primitivism in art—Australia.

LEHMANN, Geoffrey, 759.994 B
1940-
Australian primitive painters / [by] Geoffrey Lehmann. St. Lucia, Q. : University of Queensland Press, 1977. 99 p. : ill. (some col.) ; 29 cm. Distributed in the United Kingdom by Prentice-Hall International, Hemel Hempstead, Eng. [ND1100.5.P7L43] 78-320865 ISBN 0-7022-1039-0 : 24.25
1. Primitivism in art—Australia. 2. Painting, Australian. 3. Painting, Modern—20th century—Australia. 4. Painters—Australia—Biography. I. Title.
Distributed by Technical Impex, 5 South Union St., Lawrence, MA 01843 **BIP**

Primrose, William, 1904

PRIMROSE, William, 787'.1'0924 B
1904-
Walk on the north side : memoirs of a violist / William Primrose. Provo, Utah : Brigham Young University Press, c1978. p. cm. Includes index. Discography: p. [ML418.P84A3] 78-4952 ISBN 0-8425-1263-2 : 12.95
1. Primrose, William, 1904 2. Violinists, violoncellists, etc.—Biography. I. Title. **BIP**

Prin, Alice, 1901-

KOHNER, Frederick. 301.41'2 B
Kiki of Montparnasse. New York, Stein and Day [1967] 222 p. 22 cm. [HQ196.P3K6] 67-25153
1. Prin, Alice, 1901- I. Title.

Prina, L. Edgar.

ILMA, Viola. 920.7
The political virgin, by Viola Ilma as fathomed by L. Edgar Prina. [1st ed.] New York, Duell, Sloan and Pearce [1958] 180p. 21cm. Autobiographical. [CT275.I45A3] 57-11063
1. Prina, L. Edgar. I. Title.

Prince, William Meade,

PRINCE, William Meade, 927.4
1893-
The southern part of heaven, with illustrations by the author. New York, Rinehart [1950] 314 p. illus. 22 cm. Autobiography. [NC139.P7A3] 50-5707
I. Title. **BIP**

PRINCE, William Meade, 917.56'565
1893-1951.
The southern part of heaven. With illus. by the author. Chapel Hill, University of North Carolina Press, [1969, c1950] 314 p. illus. 21 cm. Autobiography. [NC139.P7A3 1969] 71-6542 5.95
I. Title.

Princes.

HERBERT, Crystal, 1918- ed. 923.2
Royal children today. Englewood Cliffs [N. J.] Prentice-Hall [1955, c1954] 126p. illus. 26cm. 'Adapted from Enfants royaux d'aujourd'hui, edited by Jean de la Varende.' [D412.8.H4 1955] 55-11071
1. Princes. 2. Princesses. I. Title.

Princeton Theological Seminary — Biog.

KERR, Hugh Thomson, 1909- 922.5
ed.
Sons of the prophets; leaders in Protestantism from Princeton Seminary. Princeton, N. J., Princeton University Press, 1963. xix, 227 p. ports. 23 cm. "Essays in celebration of the sesquicentennial, Princeton Theological Seminary, Princeton, New Jersey, 1812-1962." Bibliographical footnotes. [BV4070.P759A2 1963] 63-12665
1. Princeton Theological Seminary — Biog. I. Title. **BIP**

Prinet, Jean.

PRINET, Jean. 779'.0924
Nadar, par Jean Prinet et Antoinette Dilasser. Paris, A. Colin, 1966. 287 p. illus., facsims., port. 18 cm. ([Collection] Klosque, 15) 8.50 F. (F***) Bibliography: p. 265-[268] [TR140.T6P7] 67-78251
I. Tournachon, Felix, 1820-1910. II. Dilasser, Antoinette, joint author. III. Title.

Pringle, William James, 1905-

SIBLEY, Ford. 338'.09
William James Pringle, the gentle logician of Foote, Cone & Belding. [Los Angeles, W. Ritchie Press, 1966] [10] p. illus., port. 17 cm. Cover title: The gentle logician. 100 copies printed. "This article ... appeared in the March 1949 issue of Western advertising." [HF5810.P7S5] 67-209
1. Pringle, William James, 1905- I. Title: The gentle logician.

Printing—Hist.—Texas.

HUNTER, John Marvin, 1880- 926.55
Peregrinations of a pioneer printer; an autobiography. Grand Prairie, Tex., Printed by Frontier Times Pub. House, c1954. 244p. illus. 23cm. [Z232.H85A3] 54-39743
1. Printing—Hist.—Texas. I. Title.

Printing—Italy—Bio-bibl.

COSENZA, Mario 016.6551'45
Emilio, 1880-
Biographical and bibliographical dictionary of the Italian printers, and of foreign printers in Italy from the introduction of the art of printing into Italy to 1800, Boston. Hall, 1968[c.1967] vii, 679p. 36cm. [Z155.C6] 67-17808 65.00
1. Printing—Italy—Bio-bibl. I. Title. **BIP**

Printing as a trade—U. S.

HICKS, John Edward. 926.55
Adventures of a tramp printer, 1880-1890. [1st ed.] Kansas City, Mo., Midamericana Press [1950] 285 p. 24 cm. Bibliography: p. 283-285. [Z243.U5H5] 50-9816
1. Printing as a trade U. S. I. Title.

Printmakers—Japan—Biography.

BLAKEMORE, Frances. 769'.92'2 B
Who's who in modern Japanese prints / by Frances Blakemore. 1st ed. New York : Weatherhill, 1975. 263 p. : ill. ; 22 cm. [NE771.B55] 74-28174 ISBN 0-8348-0101-9 : 12.50
1. Printmakers—Japan—Biography. I. Title. **BIP**

Printmakers—United States Biography.

ZIGROSSER, Carl, 769'.92'2 B
1891-
The artist in America : contemporary printmakers / by Carl Zigrosser. New York : Hacker Art Books, 1978, c1942. xxi, 207, v p., [46] leaves of plates : ill. ; 25 cm. Reprint of the 1st ed. published by Knopf, New York. Includes index. [NE508.Z45 1978] 77-73724 ISBN 0-87817-215-7 lib bdg : 30.00
1. Printmakers—United States—Biography. 2. Prints—20th century—United States. I. Title.

Prints, Australian.

KEMPF, Franz, 1926- 769'.92'2 B
Contemporary Australian printmakers / Franz Kempf. Melbourne : Landsdowne, 1976. 100, 32 p. : ill. ; 31 cm. Includes Directory of Australian printmakers, 1976. Bibliography: p. 100. [NE789.4.K45] 77-365474 ISBN 0-7018-0469-6
1. Prints, Australian. 2. Prints—20th century—Australia. 3. Printmakers—Australia—Biography. 4. Printmakers—Australia—Directories. I. Directory of Australian printmakers. 1976. II. Title.

Prinze, Freddie.

PRUETZEL, Maria. 791'.092'4 B
The Freddie Prinze story / as told by his mother, Maria Pruetzel and John A. Barbour. Kalamazoo, Mich. : Master's Press, c1978. xii, 275 p. : ill. ; 18 cm. [PN2287.P734P7] 78-54223 ISBN 0-89251-051-X pbk. : 2.25
1. Prinze, Freddie. 2. Entertainers—United States—Biography. I. Barbour, John Andrews, 1928- joint author. II. Title.

Prior, Matthew, 1664-1721.

EVES, Charles Kenneth, 1888- 821'.5 B
Matthew Prior, poet and diplomatist. New York, Octagon Books, 1973 [c1939] 436 p. ports. 24 cm. Originally presented as the author's thesis, Columbia. Original ed. issued as no. 144 of Columbia University studies in English and comparative literature. Bibliography: p. [411]-421. [PR3643.E9 1973] 73-1151 ISBN 0-374-92646-8 15.00 (Lib. bdg.)
1. Prior, Matthew, 1664-1721. I. Series: Columbia University studies in English and comparative literature, no. 144.

LEGG, Leopold George Wickham, 1877- 327.20924 B
Matthew Prior: a study of his public career and correspondence, by L. G. Wickham Legg. New York, Octagon Books, 1972. x, 348 p. port. 23 cm. Reprint of the 1921 ed. [DA497.P7L4 1972] 72-5135 ISBN 0-374-94890-9
1. Prior, Matthew, 1664-1721. 2. Great Britain—History—1689-1714. 3. Great Britain—Foreign relations—France. 4. France—Foreign relations—Great Britain. BIP

Prior, Matthew, 1664-1721—Biography.

BICKLEY, Francis Lawrance, 1885- 821'.5 B
The life of Matthew Prior, by Francis Bickley. [Folcroft, Pa.] Folcroft Library Editions, 1974. vii, 295 p. port. 24 cm. Reprint of the 1914 ed. published by I. Pitman, London. Includes bibliographical references. [PR3643.B5 1974] 74-2441 30.00
1. Prior, Matthew, 1664-1721—Biography. I. Title.

BICKLEY, Francis Lawrence, 1885- 821'.5 B
The life of Matthew Prior / by Francis Bickley. Norwood, Pa. : Norwood Editions, 1976. p. cm. Reprint of the 1914 ed. published by I. Pitman, London and New York. Includes bibliographical references and index. [PR3643.B5 1976] 76-17049 ISBN 0-8482-0175-2 lib bdg. : 30.00
1. Prior, Matthew, 1664-1721—Biography. BIP

BICKLEY, Francis Lawrence, 1885- 821'.5 B
The life of Matthew Prior / by Francis Bickley. Darby, Pa. : Arden Library, 1978. vii, 295 p. : port. ; 23 cm. Reprint of the 1914 ed. published by I. Pitman, London and New York. Includes bibliographical references and index. [PR3643.B5 1978] 78-18914 ISBN 0-8495-0340-X lib. bdg. : 35.00
1. Prior, Matthew, 1664-1721—Biography. 2. Poets, English—18th century—Biography. I. Title.

Prison Fellowship.

COLSON, Charles W. 248'.2'0924 B
Life sentence / by Charles W. Colson. Lincoln, Va. : Chosen Books Pub. Co., [1979] p. cm. [BX6495.C5687.A34] 79-18715 ISBN 0-912376-41-4 : 9.95
1. Colson, Charles W. 2. Prison Fellowship. 3. Fellowship House. 4. Baptists—United States—Biography. I. Title. BIP

Prisoners—French Guiana—Personal Narratives.

CHARRIERE, Henri. 365.64'0924 [B]
Papillon. With an introduction by Jean Pierre Castelnau. Translated by June P. Wilson and Walter B. Michaels. New York, Pocket Books [1973 c.1970] 458 p. maps 18 cm. [HV8956.G8C513] 75-123129 ISBN 0-671-78528-1. 1.95 (pbk)
1. Prisoners—French Guiana—Personal Narratives. I. Title.

CHARRIERE, Henri, 1906- 365'.64'0924 B
Papillon. With an introd. by Jean-Pierre Castelnau. Translated by June P. Wilson and Walter B. Michaels. New York, Morrow, 1970. xi, 434 p. map. 25 cm. [HV8956.G8C513 1970b] 75-123129 8.95
1. Prisoners—French Guiana—Personal narratives. I. Title. BIP

Prisoners—Personal narratives.

KAMPA, Leo. 364.3'092'4 B
The enigma of crime. Philadelphia, Dorrance [1972] x, 120 p. 22 cm. Autobiographical. [HV9468.K35A3] 77-170133 ISBN 0-8059-1607-5 3.95
1. Prisoners—Personal narratives. I. Title.

SHOBLAD, Richard H. 364.1'63'0924 B
Doing my own time [by] Richard H. Shoblad. [1st ed.] Garden City, N.Y., Doubleday, 1972. x, 270 p. 22 cm. Autobiography. [HV9468.S55A3] 70-175398 6.95
1. Prisoners—Personal narratives. I. Title.

WILLIAMSON, Henry, pseud. 364.15
Hustler! [By] Henry Williamson. Edited by R. Lincoln Keiser. With a commentary by Paul Bohannan. [1st ed.] Garden City, N. Y., Doubleday, 1965. xi, 222 p. 22 cm. Autobiographical. [HV6248.W49A3] 65-10686
1. Prisoners—Personal narratives. I. Keiser, R. Lincoln, 1937- ed. II. Title.

Prisoners—United States—Biography—Bibliography.

SAVAK, Daniel, 1947- 016.365'6'0924 B
Memoirs of American prisons : an annotated bibliography / by Daniel Suvak. Metuchen, N.J. : Scarecrow Press, 1979. viii, 227 p. ; 23 cm. Includes indexes. [Z5703.5.U5S9] [HV9468] 78-11107 ISBN 0-8108-1180-4 : 10.00
1. Prisoners—United States—Biography—Bibliography. 2. Prisons—United States—Bibliography. I. Title.

Prisoners—United States—Personal narratives.

JOHNSON, Lester Douglas, 1903- 365'.9'78138
The devil's front porch. Lawrence, University Press of Kansas [1970] xix, 226 p. 23 cm. [HV9468.J62] 78-107328 6.95
1. Prisoners—U.S.—Personal narratives. I. Title.

MCCUNE, Billy George, 1929- 364.1'53 B
The autobiography of Billy McCune. With an introd. by Danny Lyon. [San Francisco] Straight Arrow Books; [distributed by Quick Fox, New York, 1973] 154 p. ports. 22 cm. [HV9468.M32A3] 72-88838 ISBN 0-87932-049-4 5.95
1. Prisoners—United States—Personal narratives. I. Title.

Pritchett, Victor Sawdon,

PRITCHETT, Victor Sawdon, 1900- 828'.9'1203
A cab at the door; a memoir, by V. S. Pritchett. New York, Random House [1968] 244 p. 22 cm. [PR6031.R7Z5 1968b] 68-14504
I. Title.

Pritham, Frederick John, 1880-

WILSON, Dorothy Clarke. 610'.924 B
The big-little world of Doc Pritham. [1st ed.] New York, McGraw-Hill [1971] xii, 320 p. illus., maps (on lining papers) 24 cm. Bibliography: p. vi-vii. [R154.P864W5] 75-154241 ISBN 0-07-070751-0 6.95
1. Pritham, Frederick John, 1880- I. Title.

Pro Juarez, Miguel Agustin, 1891-1927—Juvenile literature.

ROYER, Fanchon, 1902- 920
Padre Pro, Mexican hero. Illus. by James J. Fox. New York, Kenedy [c.1963] 189p. illus. 22cm. (Amer. background bks. [23]) 63-11352 2.50
1. Pro Juarez, Miguel Agustin, 1891-1927—Juvenile literature. I. Title.

Pro Juarez, Miguel Augustin, 1891-1927.

DAUGHTERS of St. Paul 92
God s secret agent; the life of Michael Augustine Pro, S. J., written, illus. by the Daughters of St. Paul. [Boston] St. Paul Eds. [1967] 101p. illus. 22cm. (Their Encounter bks.) [BX4705.P75D34] 67-4290 1.50
1. Pro Juarez, Miguel Agustin, 1891-1927. I. Title.
Distributed by the Daughters of St. Paul.

DAUGHTERS of St. Paul. 92
God's secret agent; the life of Michael Augustine Pro, S.J., written and illustrated by the Daughters of St. Paul. [Boston] St. Paul Editions [1967] 101 p. illus. 22 cm. (Their Encounter books) A biography of a Jesuit priest and martyr for the Catholic faith in the early twentieth-century struggle between Church and State in Mexico. [BX4705.P72D34] AC 67
1. Pro Juarez, Miguel Agustin, 1891-1927. I. Title.

FATHER Michael Pro, v. 12
priest of the workingman. Based on a translation from the Spanish of Adro Xavier's 'Entre obreros'. Paterson, N. J., St. Anthony Guild Press, 1956. viii, 67p. ports. 19cm.
1. Pro Juarez, Miguel Augustin, 1891-1927. I. Donnelly, William Patrick. II. Xavier, Adro. Entre obreros.

MULLER, Gerald Francis, 1927- 271'.5'0924 B
With life and laughter; the life of Father Miguel Agustin Pro, by Gerald F. Muller. Notre Dame [Ind.] Dujarie Press [1969] 128 p. illus., ports. 22 cm. First ed. published in 1954 under title: The martyr laughed. [BX4705.P72M8 1969] 70-76774
1. Pro Juarez, Miguel Agustin, 1891-1927. I. Title.

ROBERTO, Brother, 1927- 922.272
Dawn brings glory; a story of Father Pro, S. J. Notre Dame, Ind., Dujarie Press [1956] 139p. illus. 22cm. High school ed. of the author's The martyr laughed. [BX4705.P72R57 1956] 56-59252
1. Pro Juarez, Miguel Augustin, 1891-1927. I. Title.

ROBERTO, Brother, 1927- 922.272
The martyr laughed; a story of Father Miguel Pro, S. J. Illus. by Anthony Joyce. Notre Dame, Ind., Dujarie Press [1954] 92p. illus. 24cm. [BX4705.P72R57] 54-41985
1. Pro Juar2s, Miguel Agustin, 1891-1927. I. Title.

ROYER, Fanchon, 1902- 922.272
Padre Pro. New York, P. J. Kenedy [1954] 248p. illus. 21cm. [BX4705.P72R6] 54-5016
1. Pro Juares, Miguel Agustin, 1891-1927. I. Title.

Probation—New York (City)

PORTER, Edward Sefton. 364.63097471
Conscience of the court. Englewood Cliffs, N. J. Prentice-Hall [1962] 203 p. 22 cm. Autobiographical. [HV9306.N6P6] 62-14739
1. Probation—New York (City) I. Title.

Problem children.

MORRISON, Ishbel. 155.45'3
The knot of love. Brattleboro, Vt., R. L. Dothard Associates, 1969. x, 109 p. illus. 21 cm. Autobiographical. [HQ773.M65] 70-93679
1. Problem children. I. Title. BIP

Probyn, Walter, 1931-

PROBYN, Walter, 1931- 364.2'5'0924 B
Angel face : the making of a criminal / by Walter Probyn ; with an introduction and commentary by Stan Cohen. London ; Boston : Allen & Unwin, 1977. 3-254 p. ; 23 cm. [HV6248.P77A33] 78-301173 ISBN 0-04-923070-0 : 11.50
1. Probyn, Walter, 1931- 2. Crime and criminals—England—Biography. 3. Corrections—England. I. Title. BIP

Prochnow, Herbert Victor, 1897-

ALTMAN, Frances. 332.1'0924 B
Herbert V. Prochnow, banker. Minneapolis, T. S. Denison [1969] 195 p. ports. 23 cm. (Men of achievement series) Bibliographical footnotes. [HG2463.P7A65] 78-79474
1. Prochnow, Herbert Victor, 1897-

Procopius of Sazava, Saint, d. 1053.

KADLEC, Jaroslav, doctor of theology. 922.22
Saint Procopius, guardian of the Cyrilo-Methodian legacy. Translated by Vitus Buresh. [Cleveland, Micro Photo Division, Bell & Howell Co., 1964. 331 p. illus. 23 cm. Photocopy of typescript reproduced by duopage process. Bibliograpical references included in "Footnotes" (p. 203-310) [BX4700.P8K313] 64-4477
1. Procopius of Sazava, Saint, d. 1053. I. Title.

Procter, Ben H

PROCTER, Ben H 923.273
Not without honor; the life of John H. Reagan. Austin, University of Texas Press [1962] xii, 361 p. illus., ports. 24 cm. Bibliography: p. [303]-328. [E664.R29P7] 62-9791
I. Reagan, John Henninger. 1818-1905. II. Title.

Procter, Bryan Waller, 1787-1874—Friends and associates.

FIELDS, James Thomas, 1816-1881. 821'.7 B
Old acquaintance. Barry Cornwall and some of his friends. [Folcroft, Pa.] Folcroft Library Editions, 1974 [c1876] 121 p. ports. 24 cm. Reprint of the ed. published by J. R. Osgood and Co., Boston, in series: Vest-pocket series of standard and popular authors. [PR5192.Z5F5 1974] 74-9554 10.00 (lib. bdg.).
1. Procter, Bryan Waller, 1787-1874—Friends and associates. 2. Authors, English—Correspondence, reminiscences, etc. I. Title. BIP

Proctor, Alexander Phimister,

PROCTOR, Alexander Phimister, 1862-1950. 730'.924
Alexander Phimister Proctor, sculptor in buckskin; an autobiography. Edited and with an introd. by Hester Elizabeth Proctor. Introd. by Vivian A. Paladin. [1st ed.] Norman, University of Oklahoma Press [1971] xvii, 266 p. illus., ports. 19 x 23 cm. [NB237.P74A2] 77-108803 ISBN 0-8061-0912-2

Proctor, Henry Hugh,

PROCTOR, Henry Hugh, 1868-1933. 285'.8'0924 B
Between Black and white, autobiographical sketches. Freeport, N.Y., Books for Libraries Press, 1971. xi, 189 p. illus. 23 cm. (The Black heritage library collection)

Reprint of the 1925 ed. [E185.97.P95 1971] 79-173611 ISBN 0-8369-8903-1
I. Title. II. Series.

Progressive Party of Wisconsin.

LAFOLLETTE, Philip Fox, 1897-1965. 977.5'04'0924 B
Adventure in politics: the memoirs of Philip LaFollette. Edited by Donald Young. [1st ed.] New York, Holt, Rinehart, and Winston [1970] xvii, 299 p. illus., ports. 22 cm. Bibliography: p. 285-288. [F586.L3A3] 78-84681 7.95
1. Progressive Party of Wisconsin. 2. LaFollette, Robert Marion, 1855-1925. 3. Wisconsin—Politics and government—1848-1950. I. Young, Donald, ed. II. Title.

Prokof'ev, Sergei Sergeevich, 1891-1953.

HANSON, Lawrence. 927.8
Prokofiev, a biography in three movements [by] Lawrence & Elisabeth Hanson. New York, Random House, 1964. xiii, 368 p. illus., ports. 22 cm. "Catalogue of works": p. 347-354. Bibliography: p. 355-358. [ML410.P865H3] 64-17936
1. Prokof'ev, Sergei Sergeevich, 1891-1953. I. Hanson, Elisabeth M., joint author.

KAUFMANN, Helen (Loeb) 780'.924 B
The story of Sergei Prokofiev, by Helen L. Kaufmann. [1st ed.] Philadelphia, J. B. Lippincott Co. [1971] 160 p. illus. 21 cm. A biography of the twentieth-century Russian composer of "Peter and the Wolf" and many popular symphonies, operas, and ballets. [ML3930.P77K35] 92 70-141458
1. Prokof'ev, Sergei Sergeevich, 1891-1953—Juvenile literature. I. Title.

NEST'EV, Izrail' Vladimirovich, 1911- 927.8
Prokofiev. Translated from the Russian by Florence Jonas; with a foreword by Nicolas Slonimsky. Stanford, Calif., Stanford University Press, 1960. 528p. illus., ports., facsim., music. 24cm. An extension and elaboration of the author's Sergei Prokofiev, his musical life. 1946 'Catalogue of Prokofiev's works': p. 505-513. [ML410.P865N463] 60-11631
1. Prokofev Sergei Sergeevich, 1891-1953. I. Jonas, Florence, tr. II. Title.

PROKOF'EV, Sergei Sergeevich, 1891-1953. 780'.92'4 B
Prokofiev by Prokofiev : a composer's memoir / Sergei Prokofiev ; edited by David H. Appel ; translated by Guy Daniels. Garden City, N.Y. : Doubleday, 1979. xii, 370 p., [24] leaves of plates : ill. ; 24 cm. Translation of Avtobiografiia. Includes bibliographical references and index. [ML410.P865A3153] 77-25605 ISBN 0-385-09960-6 : 14.00
1. Prokof'ev, Sergei Sergeevich, 1891-1953. 2. Composers—Russia—Biography. I. Title.

SAMUEL, Claude. 780'.92'4 B
Prokofiev. Translated by Miriam John. New York, Grossman Publishers, 1971. 192 p. illus. 22 cm ([Library of composers, 4]) [ML410.B365S35 1971b] 73-143540 ISBN 0-670-57955-6 7.95
1. Prokof'ev, Sergei Sergeevich, 1891-1953. I. Title. II. Series. BIP

SEROFF, Victor Ilyitch, 1902- 780'.924 B
Sergei Prokofiev, a Soviet tragedy: the case of Sergei Prokofiev, his life & work, his critics, and his executioners, by Victor Seroff. New York, Funk & Wagnalls [1968] 339 p. facsims., ports. 24 cm. Bibliography: p. 331-332. [ML410.P865S56] 67-29535
1. Prokof'ev, Sergei Sergeevich, 1891-1953. I. Title.

SEROFF, Victor Ilyitch, 1902- 780'.92'4 B
Sergei Prokofiev : a Soviet tragedy : the case of Sergei Prokofiev, his life & work, his critics, and his executioners / by Victor Seroff. New York : Taplinger Pub. Co., 1979, c1969. 339 p., [5] leaves of plates : ill. ; 24 cm. "A Crescendo book." Bibliography: p. 331-332. [ML410.P865S56 1979] 78-73657 ISBN 0-8008-7067-0 : 14.95 ISBN 0-8008-7068-9 pbk : 7.95
1. Prokof'ev, Sergei Sergeevich, 1891-1953. 2. Composers—Russia—Biography. I. Title.

Pronyuk, Yevhen, 1936-

THREE philosophers-political prisoners in the Soviet Union / translated and edited by Taras Zakydalsky. 364.1'3'0922 Baltimore : Smoloskyp Publishers, 1976. 18 p. : ill. ; 18 cm. (Smoloskyp samvydav series ; no. 4) (Documents of Ukrainian samvydav) [DK508.8.T45] 77-375724
1. Lisovy, Vasyl Semenovich, 1937- 2. Pronyuk, Yevhen, 1936- 3. Bondar, Mykola Vasylevich, 1939- 4. Political prisoners—Russia—Ukraine. 5. Ukraine—History—1917- I. Zakydalsky, Taras. II. Title. III. Series.

Prophecies.

NOTREDAME, Michel de, 1503-1566. v. 12
Nostradamus: life and literature. Including all the Prophecies in French and English, with complete notes and indexes. A critical biography of Nostradamus, his will, and personal letters. Bibliography of Nostradamus and his commentators. A review of theories about him, his method and other supplementary material. By Edgar Leoni. New York, Exposition Press [1961. Label: New York, Nosbooks, 1965] 823 p. illus. 24 cm. "Second edition 1965." 65-97819
1. Prophecies. 2. Astrology. I. Leoni, Edgar. II. Title.

Prophecies (Occult sciences)

DIXON, Jeane. 133.3'0924
Jeane Dixon: my life and prophecies; her own story as told to Rene Noorbergen. New York, W. Morrow, 1969. 219 p. 22 cm. [BF1283.D48A3] 70-94472 5.95
1. Prophecies (Occult sciences) I. Noorbergen, Rene. II. Title.

DIXON, Jeane. 133.3'0924 B
Jeane Dixon: my life and prophecies; her own story as told to Rene Noorbergen. Boston, G. K. Hall, 1971 [c1969] 373 p. 25 cm. Large print ed. [BF1283.D48A3 1971] 70-38008 ISBN 0-8161-6004-X 7.95
1. Prophecies (Occult sciences) I. Noorbergen, Rene. II. Title.

Prophets.

RAD, Gerhard von, 1901-1971. 224
The message of the prophets. [1st U.S. ed.] New York, Harper & Row [1972, c1965] 289 p. 22 cm. Translation of Die Botschaft der Propheten, a revised version of material from the author's Theologie des Alten Testaments. Includes bibliographical references. [BS1505.2.R313 1972] 72-183633 3.95
1. Bible. O.T. Prophets—Theology. 2. Prophets. I. Title. BIP

SKELTON, Eugene. 224
Meet the prophets! Nashville, Tenn., Broadman Press [1972] 160 p. illus. 22 cm. [BS1198.S5] 72-79176 ISBN 0-8054-1510-6
1. Prophets. I. Title BIP

VAN DOLSON, Bobbie Jane. 224'.09'22
Prophets are people, believe it or not / Bobbie Jane Van Dolson. Washington : Review and Herald Pub. Association, [1974] 92 p. : ill. ; 21 cm. [BS1560.V36] 74-78394 ISBN pbk. : 2.50
1. Prophets. I. Title.

WIFALL, Walter. 224'.06
Israel's prophets : envoys of the King / by Walter Wifall. Chicago : Franciscan Herald Press, [1975] p. cm. (Herald Biblical booklets) Bibliography: p. [BS1198.W5] 74-31167 ISBN 0-8199-0521-6 pbk. : 0.95
1. Prophets. I. Title. BIP

Prophets—Biography—Juvenile literature.

MCMINN, Tom. 224'.092'2 B
Prophets, preachers for God / Tom McMinn ; illustrated by H. Don Fields. Nashville : Broadman Press, c1979. 48 p. : ill. ; 24 cm. (Biblearn series) Presents accounts of the lives of five Old Testament prophets: Elisha, Amos, Jeremiah, Jonah, and Micah. Discussion questions accompany each selection. [BS1198.M19] 79-111901 ISBN 0-8054-4250-2 : 3.95
1. Bible. O.T.—Biography—Juvenile literature. 2. Prophets—Biography—Juvenile literature. I. Fields, H. Don. II. Title.

Proselytes and proselyting, Jewish—Converts from Christianity—Juvenile literature.

YOWA. 296.7'1
The becoming of Ruth; an autobiography. Written and illustrated by Yowa. New York, Crown Publishers [1972] 64 p. col. illus. 21 cm. A young girl's search for spiritual fulfillment leads her to convert from Christianity to Judaism. [BM729.P7Y69] 79-185069 4.95
1. Proselytes and proselyting, Jewish—Converts from Christianity—Juvenile literature. I. Title.

Proskauer, Joseph Meyer, 1877-1971.

HACKER, Louis Morton, 1899- 340'.092'4 B
Proskauer, his life and times / by Louis M. Hacker and Mark D. Hirsch. University, Ala. : University of Alabama Press, [1977] p. cm. Includes index. Bibliography: p. [E184.J5P943] 77-1697 ISBN 0-8173-9361-7 : 10.50
1. Proskauer, Joseph Meyer, 1877-1971. 2. Jews in the United States—Biography. 3. Lawyers—New York (State)—Biography. 4. United States—Biography. I. Hirsch, Mark David, 1910- joint author. II. Title. BIP

Prostitutes—Correspondence, reminiscences, etc.

JULIE. 301.41'54'0924
My nights and days / by Julie. New York : Putnam, [1974] 256 p. ; 22 cm. [HQ146.N7J84] 73-93729 ISBN 0-399-11360-6 : 6.95
1. Prostitutes—Correspondence, reminiscences, etc. I. Title.

KIMBALL, Nell, 1854-1934 338.7'61'301415 B
Nell Kimball; her life as an American madam, by herself. Edited and with an introd. by Stephen Longstreet. [New York] Macmillan [1970] ix, 286 p. 24 cm. [HQ146.N4K5] 74-101725
1. Prostitutes—Correspondence, reminiscences, etc. I. Longstreet, Stephen, 1907- ed. II. Title.

SUSAN. 301.41'5
Diary. Santa Fe, N.M. [1970] 150 p. 25 cm. Cover title: Peace & the puta & the day of the beautyful jail. [HQ151.A5S82] 73 84846 3.00
1. Prostitutes—Correspondence, reminiscences, etc. I. Title: Peace & the puta & the day of the beautyful jail.

Prostitution—Hollywood, Calif.

ELLIOT, Jack, 1919- v. 12
Confessions of a Hollywood call girl, by John O'Day [pseud.] Introd. by Leonard A. Lowag. Los Angeles, Sherbourne Press [c1964] 159 p. 68-52158
1. Prostitution—Hollywood, Calif. I. Title.

Prostitution—Paris.

ELLIOT, Jack, 1919- v. 12
Confessions of a Paris prostitute,, by John O'Day. Introd. by Leonard A. Lowag. Los Angeles, Sherbourne Press [1964] 160 p. 68-100430
1. Prostitution—Paris. I. Title.

Prostitution—Chicago.

WASHBURN, Charles. 301.41'54'0977311
Come into my parlor; a biography of the aristocratic Everleigh sisters of Chicago. New York, Arno Press, 1974 [c1934] 255 p. 23 cm. (Women in America: from colonial times to the 20th century) Reprint of the ed. published by Knickerbocker Pub. Co., New York. [HQ146.C4W3 1974] 74-3978 ISBN 0-405-06126-9
1. Prostitution—Chicago. 2. Chicago—Moral conditions. I. Title. II. Series. BIP

Prostitution—United States—Case studies.

HEYL, Barbara Sherman, 1942- 301.41'54'0722
The madam as entrepreneur : career management in house prostitution / Barbara Sherman Heyl. New Brunswick, N.J. : Transaction Books, [1978] p. cm. Includes index. Bibliography: p. [HG144.H48] 76-50329 ISBN 0-87855-211-1 : 14.95
1. Prostitution—United States—Case studies. 2. Prostitutes—United States—Biography. 3. Pimps—United States. 4. Sex and law—United States. 5. Prostitution—United States—Vocational guidance. I. Title. BIP

Protestant churches—Biography.

HARPER, Howard V. 280'.4'0922
Profiles of Protestant saints, by Howard V. Harper. Foreword by Richard Cardinal Cushing. New York, Fleet Press Corp. [1968] 231 p. 21 cm. [BX4825.H3] 67-24071
1. Protestant churches—Biography. I. Title. BIP

SMART, William James, 1895- v. 12
Six mighty men. New York, Macmillan [1957] 151 p. 19 cm.
1. Protestant churches — Biog. I. Title.

Protestant Episcopal Church in the U. S. A.—Clergy—Correspondence, reminiscences, etc.

ARGO, Fordyce Hubbard, 1872- 922.273
Chapters of memory; impressions, evaluations. [Delray Beach? Fla., 1954] 124p. illus. 23cm. [BX5995.A65A4] 56-21063
1. Protestant Episcopal Church in the U. S. A.—Clergy—Correspondence, reminiscences, etc. 2. Rockledge, Pa. Memorial Church of the Holy Nativity. I. Title.

SEAGLE, Nathan A 1868- 922.373
The memoirs of a metropolitan minister; sixty years of service in the Diocese of New York. Foreword by the Rt. Rev. Horace W. B. Donegan. [1st ed.] New York, Exposition Press [1955] 99p. illus. 21cm. [BX5995.S314A3] 55-11831
1. Protestant Episcopal Church in the U. S. A.—Clergy—Correspondence, reminiscences, etc. I. Title.

Protestants in the U. S.

SOPER, David Wesley, 1910- ed. 920
Highways to faith; autobiographies of Protestant Christians. Philadelphia, Westminster Press [1954] 168p. 22cm. [BR569.S63] 54-5289
1. Protestants in the U. S. 2. Christian biography. I. Title.

Proudhon, Pierre Joseph, 1809-1865.

HAYAMS, Edward S. 335'.2 B
Pierre-Joseph Proudhon, his revolutionary life, mind, and works / Edward Hyams. New York : Taplinger Pub. Co., 1979. 304 p. ; 22 cm. Includes bibliographical references and index. [HX263.P75H92 1979] 78-72023 ISBN 0-8008-6552-9 : 17.50
1. Proudhon, Pierre Joseph, 1809-1865. 2. Socialists—Frame—Biography. 3. Anarchism and anarchists—France—Biography.

LUBAC, Henri de, 1896- 301'.092'4 B
The un-Marxian socialist : a study of Proudhon / by Henri de Lubac ; translated by R. E. Scantlebury. New York : Octagon Books, 1978. xvi, 304 p. : port. ; 23 cm. Translation of Proudhon et le christianisme. Reprint of the 1948 ed. published by Sheed & Ward, London. Includes bibliographical references and

index. [HB105.P8L8 1978] 77-18871 lib.bdg. : 14.50
1. Proudhon, Pierre Joseph, 1809-1865. 2. Economists—France—Biography. 3. Socialists—France—Biography. I. Title.

PIERRE-JOSEPH Proudhon, v. 12
a biography. New York, Macmillan [1956] 291p. illus. 23cm.
1. Proudhon, Pierre Joseph, 1809-1865. I. Woodcock, George, 1912-

WOODCOCK, George, 1912- v. 12
Pierre-Joseph Proudhon, a biography. New York, Macmillan [1956] 291 p. illus. 23 cm.
1. Proudhon, Pierre Joseph, 1809-1865. I. Title.

WOODCOCK, George, 301'.092'4 B
1912-
Pierre Joseph Proudhon: his life and work [by] George Woodcock. New York, Schocken Books [1972] 295 p. port. 21 cm. (Studies in the libertarian and utopian tradition) (Schocken paperbacks) Originally published in 1956 under title: Pierre-Joseph Proudhon, a biography. Bibliography: p. 281-288. [HB105.P8W6 1972] 72-80045 ISBN 0-8052-0372-9 3.95
1. Proudhon, Pierre Joseph, 1809-1865.

Proust, Marcel, 1871-1922.

ALBARET, Celeste. 843'.9'12
Monsieur Proust / Celeste Albaret ; edited by Georges Belmont ; translated from the French by Barbara Bray. New York : McGraw-Hill, c1976. xi, 387 p., [8] leaves of plates : ill. ; 24 cm. Autobiographical. Includes index. [PQ2631.R63Z461613] 75-25859 ISBN 0-07-000945-7 : 12.50
1. Proust, Marcel, 1871-1922. 2. Albaret, Celeste. I. Belmont, Georges. II. Title.

BARKER, Richard Hindry, 928.4
1902-
Marcel Proust, a biography. New York, Grosset [1962, c.1958] 373p. 21cm. (Universal Lib. UL138) Bibl. 2.25 pap.,
1. Proust, Marcel, 1871-1922. I. Title.

BARKER, Richard Hindry, 928.4
1902-
Marcel Proust, a biography. New York, Criterion Books [1958] 373 p. illus. 22 cm. [PQ2631.R63Z465] 58-10617
1. Proust, Marcel, 1871-1922.

BREE, Germaine. 843.912
The world of Marcel Proust. Boston, Houghton Mifflin [1966] viii, 295 p. 21 cm. (Riverside studies in literature, L8) Includes bibliographies. [PQ2631.R63Z54526] 66-5642
1. Proust, Marcel, 1871-1922. I. Title. **BIP**

CATTAUI, Georges. 843'.9'12 B
Marcel Proust. Translated by Ruth Hall. With a foreword: The life and after-life of Marcel Proust, by P. de Boisdeffre. [1st American ed. New York] Minerva Press [1968, c1967] xvi, 125 p. 21 cm. Bibliography: p. 113-119. [PQ2631.R63Z54563 1968] 68-22179 1.95
1. Proust, Marcel, 1871-1922. I. Boisdeffre, Pierre de.

LEON, Derrick, 1908- 843'.9'12 B
1944.
Introduction to Proust, his life, his circle, and his work / Derrick Leon. Folcroft, Pa. : Folcroft Library Editions, 1976. p. cm. Reprint of the 1940 ed. published by K. Paul, Trench, Trubner & Co., London. Includes index. Bibliography: p. [PQ2631.R63Z67 1976] 76-18188 ISBN 0-8414-5734-4 lib. bdg. : 27.50
1. Proust, Marcel, 1871-1922. **BIP**

MAUROIS, Andre, 1885- 928.4
Proust; a biography, Translated from the French by Gerard Hopkins. New York, Meridian Books [1960, c1950] 346p. 19cm. (Meridian books, M54) Translation of A la recherche de Marcel Proust. Includes bibliography. [PQ2631.R63Z7822 1960] 58-8527
1. Proust, Marcel, 1871-1922. I. Title.

MAUROIS, Andre 1885- 928.4
The quest for Proust: tr. from French by Gerard Hopkins. London, Cape [dist. Mustic, Conn., Verry, 1964] 348p. illus., ports. 23cm. American ed. (New York, Harper) has title: Proust; portrait of a genius. Bibl. A51 price unreported
1. Proust, Marcel, 1871-1922. I. Title.

MILLER, Milton L 928.4
Nostalgia, a psychoanalytic study of Marcel Proust. Boston, Houghton Mifflin, 1956. xii, 306p. 22cm. Bibliography: p. [295]-299. [PQ2631.R63Z783] 56-11147
1. Proust, Marcel, 1871-1922. I. Title. **BIP**

PAINTER, George Duncan, 928.4
1914-
Proust, by George D. Painter. [Maps drawn by Samuel H. Bryant] Boston, Little, Brown [1968,c.1965] v. maps. 20cm. Orig. an Atlantic Monthly Pr. bk. Contents.[2] The later years. Bibl. [PQ2631.R63Z7896] 59-7629 2.95 pap.,
1. Proust, Marcel, 1871-1922. I. Title.

PROUST, Marcel, 1871-1922. 928.4
Marcel Proust: letters to his mother. Translated and edited with an introd. by George D. Painter, and with an essay by Pamela Hansford Johnson. [1st American ed.] New York, Citadel Press [1958, c1956] 237 p. ports., diagr. 21 cm. Bibliographical references included in "Notes" (p. 207-225) [PQ2631.R63Z4456 1958] 57-14237
I. Proust, Jeanne Weill, **BIP**

PROUST, Marcel, 1871- 843'.9'12 B
1922.
Marcel Proust; letters to his mother. Translated and edited with an introd. by George D. Painter, and with an essay by Pamela Hansford Johnson. Westport, Conn., Greenwood Press [1973] 237 p. illus. 21 cm. Reprint of the 1956 ed. Includes bibliographical references. [PQ2631.R63Z445413 1973] 72-13865 ISBN 0-8371-6760-4 10.95
1. Proust, Marcel, 1871-1922. 2. Proust, Jeanne (Weill) d. 1905. I. Proust, Jeanne (Weill) d. 1905. II. Painter, George Duncan, 1914- ed.

Proust, Marcel, 1871-1922—Friends and associates.

LE SAGE, Laurent, 1913- 928.4
Marcel Proust and his literary friends. Urbana, University of Illinois Press, 1958. vii, 113p. 26cm. (Illinois studies in language and literature, v. 45) Bibliographical footnotes. [PQ2631.R63Z6715] 57-6952
1. Proust, Marcel, 1871-1922—Friends and associates. 2. Authors, French. I. Title. II. Series: Illinois. University Illinois studies in language and literature, v. 45

Proust, Marcel, 1871-1922—Biography.

CATTAUI, Georges. 843'.9'12
Marcel Proust, translated [from the French] by Ruth Hall. With a foreword "The life and after-life of Marcel Proust" by P. de Boisdeffre. [1st American ed.] New York, Funk & Wagnalls [1968, c1967] xvi, 125 p. 21 cm. Bibliography: p. 113-119. [PQ2631.R63Z54563 1968b] 73-7328 3.95
1. Proust, Marcel, 1871-1922—Biography.

MAUROIS, Andre, 843'.9'12 B
1885-1967.
The world of Marcel Proust / Andre Maurois ; translated from the French by Moura Budberg, with the assistance of Barbara Creed ; special photos. and research by Andre Ostier. 1st U.S. ed. New York : Harper & Row, 1974. 288 p. : ill. (some col.) ; 30 cm. Original French version published in 1960 under title: Le monde de Marcel Proust. [PQ2631.R63Z782513 1974b] 74-5793 ISBN 0-06-012864-X : 22.50
1. Proust, Marcel, 1871-1922—Biography. I. Title.

PAINTER, George 843'.9'12 B
Duncan, 1914-
Marcel Proust : a biography / by George D. Painter. New York : Vintage Books, 1978, c1959. 2 v. : ill. ; 20 cm. Reprint of the ed. published by Chatto & Windus, London. [LPQ2631.R63Z78958 1978b] 77-90260 ISBN 0-394-72561-1 (v. 1). ISBN 0-394-72562-X (v. 2) pbk. : 4.95(set)
1. Proust, Marcel, 1871-1922—Biography. 2. Novelists, French—20th century—Biography.

PAINTER, George 843'.9'12 B
Duncan, 1914-
Marcel Proust : a biography / by George D. Painter. 1st ed. New York : Random House, [1978] c1959-1965. 2 v. : ill. ; 22 cm. Reprint of the ed. published by Chatto & Windus, London. Includes indexes. Bibliography: p. [365]-374. [PQ2631.R63Z78958 1978] 77-90263 ISBN 0-394-50040-7 (v. 1) : 12.95 ISBN 0-394-50041-5 (v. 2) : 12.95
1. Proust, Marcel, 1871-1922—Biography. 2. Novelists, French—20th century—Biography. **BIP**

STRAUS, Bernard. 843'.912 B
Maladies of Marcel Proust / Bernard Straus. New York : Holmes & Meier, 1980. p. cm. Includes index. Bibliography: p. [PQ2631.R63Z918] 80-11204 ISBN 0-8419-0546-0 : 19.50
1. Proust, Marcel, 1871-1922—Biography. 2. Diseases in literature. 3. Novelists, French—20th century—Biography. I. Title. **BIP**

Pruden, Edward Hughes.

PRUDEN, Edward 286'.1'0924 B
Hughes.
A window on Washington / Edward Hughes Pruden. 1st ed. New York : Vantage Press, c1976. 136 p. ; 21 cm. Includes bibliographical references. [BX6495.P78A38] 77-353145 ISBN 0-533-02086-7 : 5.95
1. Pruden, Edward Hughes. 2. Baptists—Clergy—Biography. 3. Clergy—Washington, D.C.—Biography. 4. Washington, D.C.—Biography. 5. Statesmen—United States—Biography. I. Title.

Prudhomme, Edward C.

PRUDHOMME, Edward C. 739.7'4
E. C. Prudhomme, master gun engraver; a retrospective exhibition: 1946-1973. April 1 to May 13, 1973, the R. W. Norton Art Gallery. [Shreveport, La., R. W. Norton Art Gallery, 1973] 32 p. illus. 29 cm. Catalogue. [TS532.2.U6S563] 73-78704 ISBN 0-913060-01-1
1. Prudhomme, Edward C. 2. Firearms—Exhibitions. I. Norton (R. W.) Art Gallery. II. Title.

Pruette, Lorine,

PRUETTE, Lorine, 1896- 191 B
G. Stanley Hall; a biography of a mind. With an introd. by Carl Van Doren. Freeport, N.Y., Books for Libraries Press [1970] xi, 266 p. 23 cm. Originally published in 1926. [B945.H24P7 1970] 73-126247
I. Hall, Granville Stanley, 1844-1924.

Pruitt, Ida.

PRUITT, Ida. 951.04'092'4 B
A China childhood / by Ida Pruitt ; with a foreword by John K. Fairbank. San Francisco : Chinese Materials Center, 1978. xiii, 205 p., [4] leaves of plates : ill., maps (on lining papers) ; 22 cm. (Asian library series ; no. 10) [DS721.P77] 79-100810 ISBN 0-89644-523-2 pbk. : 2.45
1. Pruitt, Ida. 2. China—Social life and customs. 3. Missionaries—China—Biography. 4. Missionaries—United States—Biography. I. Title. II. Series. **BIP**

Prussia. Armee—History.

SEATON, Albert, 1921- 355'.00943
Frederick the Great's army / text by Albert Seaton ; colour plates by Michael Youens. Reading : Osprey Publishing, 1973. 40, [8] p. : ill. (some col.), map ; 25 cm. (Men-at-arms series) [UA718.P9S4] 75-309684 ISBN 0-85045-151-5 : £1.25
1. Prussia. Armee—History. 2. Friedrich der Grosse, King of Prussia, King of Prussia, 1712-1786. I. Title.

YOUNG, Peter. 940.2'7
Blucher's army; text by Peter Young; colour plates by Michael Roffe. Reading, Osprey Publishing, 1973. 40, [8] p. illus. (some col.), ports. 25 cm. (Men-at-arms series) Includes bibliographical references. [UA718.P9Y68] 73-172909 ISBN 0-85045-117-5 £1.25
1. Prussia. Armee—History. 2. Blucher, Gebhard Leberecht von, 1742-1819. 3. Prussia—History—1806-1815. I. Title. **BIP**

Prussia, East—Bio-bibliography.

WEISFERT, Julius Nicol. v. 12
Biographisch-litterarisches Lexikon fur die Haupt- und Residenzstadt Konigsberg und Ostpreussen / Julius Nicolaus Weisfert. Hildesheim ; New York : G. Olms, 1975. 259 p. ; 19 cm. Reprint of the 1897 ed. published by G. Schadlofsky, Konigsberg. [DK4600.P776A27 1975] 75-521328 ISBN 3-487-05657-7
1. Prussia, East—Bio-bibliography. 2. Kaliningrad, Russia—Bio-bibliography. I. Title: Biographisch-litterarisches Lexikon fur die Haupt- und Residenzstadt Konigsberg ...

Pryor, Roger Atkinson, 1828-1919.

HOLZMAN, Robert S. 347'.73'3634 B
Adapt or perish : the life of General Roger A. Pryor, C.S.A. / by Robert S. Holzman. Hamden, Conn. : Archon Books, 1976. 209 p., [3] leaves of plates : ports. ; 23 cm. Includes index. Bibliography: p. 193-202. [KF368.P78H64] 76-6988 ISBN 0-208-01585-X : 13.50
1. Pryor, Roger Atkinson, 1828-1919. I. Title. **BIP**

PRYOR, Sara Agnes 973.78'2'0924
(Rice) 1830-1912.
Reminiscences of peace and war. Rev. and enl. ed. Freeport, N.Y., Books for Libraries Press [1970] xviii, 418 p. illus., plan, port. 23 cm. Reprint of the 1908 ed. Includes bibliographical references. [E415.7.P98 1970] 77-126248 ISBN 0-8369-5475-0
1. Pryor, Roger Atkinson, 1828-1919. 2. United States—Politics and government—1849-1861. 3. Washington, D.C.—Public life. 4. United States—History—Civil War, 1861-1865—Personal narratives—Confederate side. I. Title. **BIP**

Prywes, Raquela, 1924-

GRUBER, Ruth, 1911- 610.73'092'4
Raquela : a woman of Israel / Ruth Gruber. New York : New American Library, 1979, c1978. 416 p. ; 18 cm. (A Signet Book) [RT37.P79G78] pbk. : 2.50
1. Prywes, Raquela, 1924- 2. Nurses — Israel -biography 3. Israel — Social life and customs. I. Title.
L.C. card no. for 1978 Coward, McCann & Geoghegan ed.: 78-107 **BIP**

GRUBER, Ruth, 610.73'092'4 B
1911-
Raquela, a woman of Israel / Ruth Gruber. New York : Coward, McCann & Geoghegan, c1978. 379 p., [4] leaves of plates : ill. ; 24 cm. [RT37.P79G78] 78-107 ISBN 0-698-10895-7 : 10.95
1. Prywes, Raquela, 1924- 2. Nurses—Israel—Biography. 3. Israel—Social life and customs. I. Title.

Przheval'skii, Nikolai Mikhailovich, 1839-1888.

RAYFIELD, Donald, 915.8'04 B
1942-
The dream of Lhasa : the life of Nikolay Przhevalsky (1839-88) explorer of Central Asia / Donald Rayfield. London : P. Elek, 1976. xii, 221 p., [4] leaves of plates : ill. ;

23 cm. Includes indexes. Bibliography: p. [211]-214. [DS785.P93R38] 76-366567 ISBN 0-236-40015-0 : £6.95
1. Przheval'skii, Nikolai Mikhailovich, 1839-1888. 2. Asia, Central—Description and travel. I. Title. BIP

RAYFIELD, Donald, 915.8'04 B
1942-
The dream of Lhasa : the life of Nikolay Przhevalsky (1839-88) explorer of Central Asia / Donald Rayfield. [Athens] : Ohio University Press, 1976[i.e.1977] xii, 221 p., [4] leaves of plates : ill. ; 23 cm. Includes index. Bibliography: p. [211]-214. [DS785.P93R38 1976b] 76-20326 ISBN 0-8214-0369-9 lib.bdg. : 13.50
1. Przheval'skii, Nikolai Mikhailovich, 1839-1888. 2. Asia, Central—Description and travel. 3. Explorers—Asia, Central—Biography. I. Title.

Psteur, Louis, 1822-1895.

ROWLAND, John, 1907- 925
Tge microscope man the story of Louis Pasteur. New York, Roy [c.1964] 142p. 21cm. 64-20089 3.50
1. Psteur, Louis, 1822-1895. I. Title.

Psychiatric hospital care—Biography.

BLUE jolts : 362.2'1'0922 B
true stories from the cuckoo's nest / compiled by Charles Steir. Washington, D.C. : New Republic Books ; New York : trade distribution by Simon and Schuster, 1978. vii, 245 p. ; 24 cm. Includes index. Bibliography: p. 231-239. [RC464.A1B58] 77-21412 ISBN 0-915220-30-X : 8.95
1. Psychiatric hospital care—Biography. 2. Mental illness—Biography. I. Steir, Charles, 1947-

Psychiatrists—Correspondence, reminiscences, etc.

BOUDREAU, Eugene N 616.89'00924
A fifty-year view of psychiatry and the golden years of medicine, by Eugene N. Boudreau. [1st ed.] New York, Vantage Press [1967] 211 p. illus., ports. 21 cm. [R154.B755A3] 68-1667
I. Title.

BURROW, Trigant, 1875-1950. 926.1
A search for man's sanity; the selected letters of Trigant Burrow, with biographical notes. Prepared by the Editorial Committee of the Lifwynn Foundation: William E. Galt, chairman. Foreword by Herbert Read. New York, Oxford University Press, 1958. xxiv, 615p. 22cm. Bibliography: p. 595-601. [R154.B868A4] 58-7994
1. Psychiatrists—Correspondence, reminiscences, etc. I. Title.

VISCOTT, David 616.8'9'00924 [B]
S., 1938-
The making of a psychiatrist [by] David S. Viscott. Greenwich, Conn., Fawcett [1973 c.1972] 416 p. 18 cm. Autobiographical. [R154.V57A33] 72-82180 1.75 (pbk)
1. Psychiatrists—Correspondence, reminiscences, etc. 2. Psychiatry—Study and teaching. I. Title. BIP

Psychical research.

GANDEE, Lee R. 133
Strange experience; the autobiography of a hexenmeister [by] Lee R. Gandee. Englewood Cliffs, N.J., Prentice-Hall [1971] 355 p. illus. 24 cm. [BF1027.G25A3] 76-157053 ISBN 0-13-850966-2 6.95
1. Psychical research. 2. Occult sciences. 3. Reincarnation. I. Title.

MCDOUGALL, William, 1871- 133
1938.
William McDougall: explorer of the mind; studies in psychical research, compiled and edited by Raymond Van Over and Laura Oteri in collaboration with Angus McDougall. With a biographical introd. by J. Wainwright Evans and foreword by Eileen J. Garrett. [New York, Garrett Publications, c1967] 319 p. port. 24 cm. Includes bibliographical references. [BF1031.M34] 67-23366
1. Psychical research. I. Title: Explorer of the mind.

Psychical research—Biography.

BIOGRAPHICAL dictionary of 921
parapsychology. 1964-66. New York, Garrett [dist. Taplinger, c.]1964. v. 25cm. Eds.: 1964-66-- Helene Pleasants. (Helix Pr. bk.) 64-4288 9.00
1. Psychical research—Biolg. I. Pleasants, Helene, ed.

MAY, Antoinette. 133.8'092'2 B
Haunted ladies / by Antoinette May. San Francisco : Chronicle Books, [1975] p. cm. Bibliography: p. [BF1026.M39] 75-26670 7.95
1. Psychical research—Biography. I. Title.

PLEASANTS, Helene, ed. 921
Biographical dictionary of parapsychology. 1964-66- New York, Garrett Publications Heix Press. v. 25 cm. Editors: 1964-66- Helene Pleasants. [BF1026.B5] 64-4288
1. Psychical research—Biog. I. Title. BIP

TABORI, Paul, 1908- 133'.092'2
Pioneers of the unseen. New York, Taplinger Pub. Co. [1972] 243 p. ports. 22 cm. (The Frontiers of the unknown series) [BF1026.T3 1972b] 74-185948 ISBN 0-8008-6310-0 6.50
1. Psychical research—Biography. I. Title. BIP

VAN DER HURK, Pieter, 920.91338
1911-
Psychic; the story of Peter Hurkos by Peter Hurkos [pseud.] Indianapolis, Bobbs-Merrill, [1961] 224 p. 22 cm. [BF1027.V3A3] 61-15545
I. Title.

Psychical research—Biography—Juvenile literature.

KETTELKAMP, Larry. 133.8'092'2 B
Investigating psychics : five life histories / by Larry Kettelkamp. New York : Morrow, 1977. 128 p. : ill. ; 22 cm. Includes index. Biographical sketches of five psychics involved in studies of psychic consciousness. [BF1281.K47] 920 77-23957 ISBN 0-688-22123-8 : 5.95 ISBN 0-688-32123-2 lib. bdg. : 5.21
1. Psychical research—Biography—Juvenile literature. I. Title. BIP

Psychical research—Chicago.

STEIGER, Brad. 133'.09773'11
Psychic City Chicago : doorway to another dimension / Brad Steiger. 1st ed. Garden City, N.Y. : Doubleday, 1976. vi, 186 p., [4] leaves of plates : ill. ; 22 cm. [BF1028.5.U6S74] 74-33663 ISBN 0-385-01362-0 : 6.95
1. Psychical research—Chicago. 2. Occult sciences—Chicago. 3. Psychical research—Biography. 4. Occult sciences—Biography. I. Title.

Psychoanalysis.

AN autobiographical [921.36]
study; authorized translation by James Strachey. New York, Norton [1952] 141 p. 20 cm. "Appeared originally in 1925 in volume IV of Die Medizin der Gegenwart in Selbstdarstellungen (Leipzig: Felix Melner)" [BF173.F85A3 1952] 926.1 52-12426
1. Psychoanalysis. I. Freud, Sigmund, 1856-1939.

FREUD, Sigmund, 1856-1939 926.1
An autobiographical study; authorized tr. by James Strachev. New York, Norton [c.1952, 1963] 141p. 20cm. (N146) 1.25 pap.,
1. Psychoanalysis. I. Title.

Psychoanalysis—Dictionaries.

EIDELBERG, Ludwig, 150.19'52
1898-
Encyclopedia of psychoanalysis. Ludwig Eidelberg, editor-in-chief. New York, Free Press [1968] xxxvii, 571 p. 26 cm. Bibliography: p. 483-519. [BF173.E5] 67-28974
1. Psychoanalysis—Dictionaries. I. Title. BIP

Psychoanalysis—Personal narratives.

MITCHELL, 616.8'917'0924 B
Suzanne.
My own woman; the diary of an analysis. New York, Horizon Press [1973] 269 p. 22 cm. [RC506.M55] 73-77643 ISBN 0-8180-0221-2 7.95
1. Psychoanalysis—Personal narratives. I. Title. BIP

Psychologists, American—Correspondence, reminiscences, etc.

BATHURST, James E 921.1
And now I know. College Park, Ga., 1957. 197p. 21cm. [BF109.B3A3] 57-25434
1. Psychologists, American—Correspondence, reminiscences, etc. I. Title.

Psychologists—Biography.

COHEN, David, 1946- 150'.92'2
Psychologists on psychology / David Cohen. New York : Taplinger, 1977. 360 p. ; 24 cm. Contents.Contents.—David McClelland.—Donald Broadbent.—Noam Chomsky.—H. J. Eysenck.—Leon Festinger.—Liam Hudson.—Michael Jouvet.—R. D. Laing.—Leopold Lowenthal.—Neal Miller.—Burrhus Skinner.—Henri Tajfel.—Niko Tinbergen. Bibliography: p. 357-360. [BF109.A1C63 1977] 76-11687 ISBN 0-8008-6557-X : 12.95. ISBN 0-8008-6558-8 pbk. : 4.95
1. Psychologists—Biography. 2. Psychology—Methodology. I. Title. BIP

PERRY, Ralph Barton, 1876- 921.1
The thought and character of William James, as revealed in unpublished correspondence and notes, together with his published writings; 2 v. Boston, Atlantic-Little [1962, c.1935] 2 v. (xxx, 824; xxii, 786p.) illus. 25cm. Contents.v.1. Inheritance and vocations.--v.2. Philosophy and psychology. Bibl. 15.00 set,
I. Title.

Psychologists—United States—Correspondence, reminiscences, etc.

SPOERL, Howard Davis, 289.4'092'4
1903-
There was a man; the letters, papers and poems of Howard Davis Spoerl. Edited by Paul B. Zacharias. North Quincy, Mass., Christopher Pub. House [1972] 193 p. port. 21 cm. [BF109.S69A25 1972] 72-78904 4.95
1. Psychologists—United States—Correspondence, reminiscences, etc. I. Zacharias, Paul B., ed. II. Title.

Psychology—Abstracts.

GUTSCH, Kenneth Urial. 158'.08
Insights into human development : commentaries / Kenneth Urial Gutsch and Larry L. Thornton. Jackson : University Press of Mississippi, 1978. xxi, 176 p. ; 23 cm. "Authorized and sponsored by Delta State University, Cleveland, Mississippi. Includes bibliographies. [BF121.G87] 77-17020 ISBN 0-87805-043-4 : 8.95 ISBN 0-87805-044-2 pbk. : 3.95
1. Psychology—Abstracts. 2. Mental health—Abstracts. 3. Psychologists—Biography. 4. Mental health personnel—Biography. I. Thornton, Larry L., joint author. II. Delta State University. III. Title. BIP

Ptolemaeus, Claudius.

NEWTON, Robert R. 520'.92'4
The crime of Claudius Ptolemy / Robert R. Newton. Baltimore : Johns Hopkins University Press, c1977. p. cm. Includes index. Bibliography: p. [QB36.P83N47] 77-4211 ISBN 0-8018-1990-3 : 22.50
1. Ptolemaeus, Claudius. I. Title. BIP

Ptolemaeus I Soter, King of Egypt, d. 283 B.C.

KINCAID, Charles Augustus, 930'.4
1870-1954.
Successors of Alexander the Great. Chicago, Argonaut, 1969. 182 p. maps. 24 cm. (The Argonaut library of antiquities) Reprint of the 1930 ed. Bibliographical footnotes. [DF235.K5 1969] 73-7841
1. Ptolemaeus I Soter, King of Egypt, d. 283 B.C. 2. Pyrrhus, King of Epirus, 318-272 B.C. 3. Hiero II, King of Syracuse, d. 215? B.C. 4. Antiochus III, the Great, King of Syria, 238 (ca)-187 B.C. I. Title.

Public health personnel—Europe—Biography.

EBERSON, Frederick, 362.1'092'2 B
1892-
Apostles and prophets : medicine for society's ills / Frederick Eberson. 1st ed. Hicksville, N.Y. : Exposition Press, c1977. xi, 106 p. : ill. ; 21 cm. (An Exposition-university book) Includes index. Bibliography: p. 99-103. [RA424.4.E23] 76-42181 ISBN 0-682-48694-9 : 6.00
1. Public health personnel—Europe—Biography. 2. Physicians—Europe—Biography. 3. Social medicine—History. I. Title. BIP

Public relations—Biog.

BARBOUR, Robert L., ed. 926.591
Who's who in public relations, international. 1st- ed.; 1959-1960 Meriden, N. H., PR Pub. Co. v. 24 cm. Editor 1959- R. L. Barbour. [HM263.W45] 62-4348
1. Public relations — Biog. I. Title.

WHO'S who in public 926.591
relations, international. [2d ed.] Meriden, N.H., PR Pub. Co [c.1962] 547p. 24cm. d.: 1962--Robert L. Barbour. 62-4348 40.00 bds.,
1. Public relations—Biog. I. Barbour, Robert L., ed.

Publishers and publishing—Gt. Brit.

DICKSON, Lovat, 1902- 920.4
The house of words. [1st American ed.] New York, Atheneum Publishers, 1963. 304 p. illus. 22 cm. Autobiographical. 63-11351
1. Publishers and publishing — Gt. Brit. 2. Macmillan, firm, publishers, London. I. Title.

DICKSON, Lovat [Horatio 920.4
Henry Lovat Dickson] 1902-
The house of words. New York, Atheneum [c.]1963. 304p. illus. 22cm. 63-11351 5.00
1. Publishers and publishing—Gt. Brit. 2. Macmillan. firm,publishers, London. I. Title.

WARBURG, Fredric, 1898- 926.55
An occupation for gentlemen. [1st American ed.] Boston, Houghton Mifflin, 1960 [c1959] 287 p. illus. 22 cm. Autobiographical. [Z325.W29A3 1960] 60-5220
1. Publishers and publishing—Gt. Brit. I. Title.

Publishers and publishing—U.S.

LATHAM, Harold Strong, 655.40924
1887-
My life in publishing. Introd. by Sterling North. New York, Dutton, [c.]1965. 256p. 22cm. [Z473.L29A28] 65-19612 5.00
1. Publishers and publishing—U.S. 2. Authors and publishers. 3. Authors, American. 4. Authors, English. I. Title.

Publishers and publishing—Biography.

DICKSON, Lovat, 655.4'0924 B
1902-
The ante-room. Harmondsworth, Penguin, 1969. 250 p. 19 cm. [PR6007.I39Z52 1969] 79-440004 6/-
I. Title.

INTERNATIONAL 070.5'092'2 B
Publishers Association.
Who's who in publishing : [a list as of May

1, 1976 of participants in the 20th congress of the International Publishers Assocation in Kyoto and Tokyo, May 25-June 1, 1976]. [Tokyo : The Association, 1976] 206 p. ; 18 cm. Supplement: 18 p. inserted. [Z282.I62 1976] 77-358247
1. Publishers and publishing—Biography. 2. Publishers and publishing—Directories. I. Title.

Publishers and publishing—United States—Correspondence, reminiscences, etc.

DOUBLEDAY, Frank Nelson, 1862-1934. 070.5'092'4
The memoirs of a publisher. [1st ed.] Garden City, N.Y., Doubleday, 1972. ix, 304 p. port. 22 cm. [Z473.D74 1972] 72-76155
1. Publishers and publishing—United States—Correspondence, reminiscences, etc. I. Title.

Publishers and publishing—United States—Directories.

KURIAN, George Thomas. 070.5'025'73
The directory of American book publishing, from founding fathers to today's conglomerates / by George Thomas Kurian. New York : Simon and Schuster, c1975. 386 p., [1] leaf of plates : ill. ; 28 cm. Includes index. Bibliography: p. 321-332. [Z475.K87] 74-16534 ISBN 0-671-18745-7 lib.bdg. : 25.00
1. Publishers and publishing—United States—Directories. 2. Publishers and publishing—United States—Biography. I. Title: The directory of American book publishing ...

Puccini, Giacomo, 1858-1924.

CARNER, Mosco. 782.1'092'4 [B]
Puccini; a critical biography. [1st American ed.] New York, Knopf, 1959. xvi, 500 p. illus., ports., music. 24 cm. Bibliography: p. 488-489. [ML410.P89C3 1959] 59-8926
1. Puccini, Giacomo, 1858-1924. BIP

CARNER, Mosco. 782.1'092'4 B
Puccini : a critical biography / by Mosco Carner. 2d ed. New York : Holmes & Meier Publishers, 1977, c1974. xvi, 520 p., [11] leaves of plates : ill. ; 26 cm. Includes indexes. Bibliography: p. 507-508. [ML410.P89C3 1977] 76-30456 ISBN 0-8419-0302-6 : 25.00
1. Puccini, Giacomo, 1858-1924. 2. Composers—Italy—Biography.

DEL FIORENTINO, Dante 927.8
Immortal Bohemian; an intimate memoir of Giacomo Puccini. New York, Crown [1963, c.1954] 232p. 22cm. 63-5611 4.95
1. Puccini, Gia como, 1858-1924. I. Title.

DEL FIORENTINO, Dante, Father. 927.8
Immortal Bohemian; an intimate memoir of Giacomo Puccini. New York, Prentice-Hall [1952] 232 p. illus. 22 cm. [ML410.P89D4] 52-9190
1. Puccini, Giacomo, 1858-1924. I. Title.

DEL FLORENTINO, Dante. 927.8
Immortal Bohemian; an intimate memoir of Giacomo Puccini. New York, Prentice-Hall [1952] 232 p. illus. 22 cm. [ML410.P89D4] 52-9190
1. Puccini, Giacomo, 1858-1924. I. Title.

JACKSON, Stanley, 1910- 782.1'092'4 B
Monsieur Butterfly; the story of Puccini. London, New York, W. H. Allen, 1974. x, 267 p. illus. 23 cm. Bibliography: p. 263-264. [ML410.P89J2] 74-159124 ISBN 0-491-01162-8 £3.50
1. Puccini, Giacomo, 1858-1924. I. Title.

JACKSON, Stanley, 1910- 782.1'092'4 B
Monsieur Butterfly; the story of Giacomo Puccini. New York, Stein and Day [1974] x, 267 p. illus. 25 cm. Bibliography: p. 263-264. [ML410.P89J2 1974b] 73-90692 ISBN 0-8128-1651-X 10.00
1. Puccini, Giacomo, 1858-1924. I. Title.

MAREK, George Richard, 1902- 927.8
Puccini, a biography. New York, Simon and Schuster, 1951. xviii, 412 p. illus., ports., facsims. 24 cm. "The stories of Puccini's operas": p. 323-358. Bibliography: p. 395.397. [ML410.P89M25] 51-10114
1. Puccini, Giacomo, 1858-1924. 2. Operas—Stories, plots, etc. I. Title.

PUCCINI, Giacomo, 1858-1924. 782.1'092'4 B
Letters of Giacomo Puccini; mainly connected with the composition and production of his operas. Edited by Giuseppe Adami. Translated from the Italian and edited for the English ed. by Ena Makin. New York, Vienna House, 1973. 335 p. illus. 22 cm. Reprint of the 1931 ed. published by J. B. Lippencott Co., Philadelphia. [ML410.P89A23 1973] 74-183316 ISBN 0-8443-0036-5 3.95 (pbk.)
1. Puccini, Giacomo, 1858-1924. 2. Musicians—Correspondence, reminiscences, etc. I. Adami, Giuseppe, 1878-1946, ed.

PUCCINI, Giacomo, 1858-1924. 782.1'092'4
Letters of Giacomo Puccini : mainly connected with the composition and production of his operas / edited by Giuseppe Adami ; translated [from the Italian] by Ena Makin. New ed. / revised and introduced by Mosco Carner. London : Harrap, 1974. 341 p., leaf of plate, [6] p. of plates : ill., facsims., music, ports. ; 23 cm. Includes index. [ML410.P89A23 1974] 75-314529 ISBN 0-8405-0293-1
1. Puccini, Giacomo, 1858-1924. 2. Composers—Italy—Correspondence. I. Adami, Giuseppe, 1878-1946, ed.
Distributed by International Scholarly Book Services for 6.25 (pbk.)

SELIGMAN, Vincent Julian, 1896- 782.1'0924 B
Puccini among friends, by Vincent Seligman. New York, B. Blom, 1971. xi, 373 p. illus. 22 cm. Reprint of the 1938 ed. Bibliography: p. 363-364. [ML410.P89S3 1971] 75-174370
1. Puccini, Giacomo, 1858-1924. I. Title.

SPECHT, Richard, 1870-1932. 782.1'0924 B
Giacomo Puccini; the man, his life, his work. Translated by Catherine Alison Phillips. Westport, Conn., Greenwood Press [1970] xvi, 256 p. illus., facsims., ports. 23 cm. Reprint of the 1933 ed. Includes bibliographical references. [ML410.P89S61 1970] 72-100844 ISBN 8-371-40307-
1. Puccini, Giacomo, 1858-1924.

VALENTE, Richard. 782.1'0924
The verismo of Giacomo Puccini, from Scapigliatura to expressionism. Ann Arbor, Mich., Braun-Blumfield, 1971. vi, 274 p. illus. 23 cm. Bibliography: p. 252-274. [ML410.P89V3] 76-31728
1. Puccini, Giacomo, 1858-1924. Operas. I. Title.

WEAVER, William, 1923- 782.1'092'4 B
Puccini : the man and his music / William Weaver ; picture editor, Gerald Fitzgerald. 1st ed. New York : E. P. Dutton, 1977. 147 p. : ill. ; 24 cm. (The Metropolitan Opera Guild composer series) [ML410.P89W3] 77-6324 ISBN 0-525-18610-7 : 8.95
1. Puccini, Giacomo, 1858-1924. 2. Composers—Italy—Biography. I. Series: Metropolitan Opera Guild. The Metropolitan Opera Guild composer series. BIP

Pueblo Indians—Juvenile literature.

COUFFER, Jack. 979.1'32'050922 B
Canyon summer / Jack & Mike Couffer. New York : Putnam, c1977. 95 p. : ill. ; 24 cm. A father and son relate their summer experiences exploring the Arizona canyon country and living one day in the ancient way of the Anasazi Indians. [E99.P9C77 1977] 77-4323 ISBN 0-399-20585-3 : 6.95
1. Pueblo Indians—Juvenile literature. 2. Indians of North America—Arizona—Juvenile literature. 3. Arizona—Description and travel—1951- —Juvenile literature. I. Couffer, Mike, joint author. II. Title. BIP

Pueblo (Ship)

BUCHER, Lloyd M., 1927- 359.3'4'320924
Bucher: my story, by Lloyd M. Bucher, with Mark Rascovich. [1st ed.] Garden City, N.Y., Doubleday, 1970. 447 p. illus., charts (on lining papers), plans, ports. 22 cm. [VB230.B8] 77-119919 7.95
1. Pueblo (Ship) I. Rascovich, Mark.

Puerto Ricans in the United States.

GROWING up Puerto Rican. 917.3'06'687295
Edited by Paulette Cooper. With a foreword by Jose Torres. New York, Arbor House [1972] 216 p. 22 cm. [E184.P85G7 1972] 79-184881 ISBN 0-87795-033-4 6.95
1. Puerto Ricans in the United States. I. Cooper, Paulette, ed. BIP

Puerto Rico — Soc. life & cust.

LEE, Albert Edward, 1873- 923.27295
An island grows; memoirs of Albert E. Lee, Puerto Rico, 1873-1942. San Juan, P.R., A. E. Lee and Son [1963] 169 p. illus. 23 cm. [F1975.L4] 63-49145
1. Puerto Rico — Soc. life & cust. 2. Puerto Rico — Hist. I. Title.

Puerto Rico—Biography.

GEIGEL Polanco, Vicente, 1904- 920'.07295
Valores de Puerto Rico / Vicente Geigel Polanco. New York : Arno Press, 1975. p. cm. (The Puerto Rican experience) Reprint of the 1943 ed. published by Editorial Eugenio Maria de Hostos, San Juan, P.R. [F1955.G4 1975] 74-14242 ISBN 0-405-06229-X
1. Puerto Rico—Biography. 2. Puerto Rico—History—Addresses, essays, lectures. 3. Authors, Puerto Rican—Biography. I. Title. II. Series.

YURCHENCO, Henrietta. 917.295'03'53
!Hablamos! Puerto Ricans speak. Photos. by Julia Singer. New York, Praeger Publishers [1971] 136 p. illus. 25 cm. [F1960.Y87 1971] 73-121721 6.50
1. Puerto Rico—Biography. 2. Puerto Rico—Social life and customs. I. Title.

Puerto Rico—Biography—Juvenile literature.

NEWLON, Clarke. 920'.07295
Famous Puerto Ricans / by Clarke Newlon. New York : Dodd, Mead, [1975] 167 p., [4] leaves of plates : ill. ; 22 cm. (Famous biographies for young people) Includes index. [CT526.N48] 75-11436 ISBN 0-396-07149-X
1. Puerto Rico—Biography—Juvenile literature. I. Title. BIP

Puffer, Celia L.

PUFFER, Celia L. 929'.2'0973
From the grass to the rose / by Celia L. Puffer. [s.l.] : Puffer, c1976. 128, 27 p. : ill. ; 29 cm. [F59.T4P84] 76-21432
1. Puffer, Celia L. 2. Thetford, Vt.—Biography. 3. Vermont—Genealogy. I. Title.

Pugach, Burt.

STAINBACK, Berry. 973.9'092'4 B
A very different love story : Burt and Linda Pugach's intimate account of their triumph over tragedy. New York : Morrow, 1976. p. cm. [CT275.P8727S8] 76-10628 ISBN 0-688-03089-0 : 7.95
1. Pugach, Burt. 2. Pugach, Linda. I. Title. BIP

Puget, Peter John.

WING, Robert C., 1921- 979.7'7
Peter Puget : lieutenant on the Vancouver Expedition, fighting British naval officer, the man for whom Puget Sound was named / by Robert C. Wing, with Gordon Newell. Seattle : Gray Beard Pub., c1979. p. cm. Includes index. Bibliography: p. [F897.P9W634] 79-83741 ISBN 0-933686-00-5 : 24.95
1. Puget, Peter John. 2. Puget Sound area—History. 3. Puget Sound area—Description and travel. 4. Explorers—Great Britain—Biography. 5. Explorers—Washington (State)—Puget Sound area—Biography. I. Newell, Gordon R., joint author. II. Title.

Pugh, Emerson M.

PUGH, Emerson M. 530'.092'4 B
Wyoming scientist, horses to spaceships : memoirs / by Emerson M. Pugh. 1st ed. Hicksville, N.Y. : Exposition Press, c1979. ix, 283 p., [8] leaves of plates : ill. ; 24 cm. Bibliography: p. 279-283. [QC16.P73A33] 79-51268 ISBN 0-682-49392-9 : 15.00
1. Pugh, Emerson M. 2. Physicists—United States—Biography. I. Title.

Pugh, Herbert Lamont,

PUGH, Herbert Lamont, 1895- 926.1
Navy surgeon. [1st ed.] Philadelphia, Lippincott [1959] 459 p. 22 cm. Autobiography. [VG227.P8A3] 59-9326
I. Title.

Pugin, Augustus Welby Northmore, 1812-1852.

FERREY, Benjamin, 1810-1880. 720'.92'4 B
Recollections of A. N. Welby Pugin, and his father, Augustus Pugin; with notices of their works. With an appendix by E. Sheridan Purcell. New York, B. Blom, 1972. xv, 473 p. illus. 21 cm. "An appendix, in which the writings and character of Augustus Welby Northmore Pugin are considered in their Catholic aspect, by Edmund Sheridan Purcell": p. 307-465. Reprint of the 1861 ed. [NA997.P9F4 1972] 77-173143
1. Pugin, Augustus Welby Northmore, 1812-1852. 2. Pugin, Augustus Charles, 1762-1832. I. Purcell, Edmund Sheridan, 1824?-1899. II. Title.

STANTON, Phoebe B. 720.9'24
Pugin [by] Phoebe Stanton. Pref. by Nikolaus Pevsner. New York, Viking Press [1972, c1971] 216 p. illus. 22 cm. (A Studio book) Bibliography: p. 210-212. [NA997.P9S7 1972] 78-172898 ISBN 0-670-58216-6 7.95
1. Pugin, Augustus Welby Northmore, 1812-1852.

Pujol, Joseph, 1857-1945.

NOHAIN, Jean. 792'.0924
Le Petomane, 1857-1945, by Jean Nohain, F. Caradec. [Tr. by Warren Tute. 1st Amer. ed.] Los Angeles, Sherbourne [1968] 95p. illus., facsim., ports. 17cm. [PN2638.P8N613 1968] 68-2860 2.50 bds.,
1. Pujol, Joseph, 1857-1945. I. Caradec, Francois. joint author. II. Title.

Pulaski, Kazimiers, 1748-1779 — Juvenile literature.

ABODAHER, David J. 943.8'02'0924
Freedom fighter: Casimir Pulaski, by David J. Abodaher. New York, J. Messner [1969] 190 p. 22 cm. Bibliography: p. 183. A biography of the exiled Polish leader who joined the forces of George Washington to fight the British. [E207.P8A57] 92 69-13048 ISBN 0-671-32104-8 3.50
1. Pulaski, Kazimierz, 1747-1779—Juvenile literature. I. Title.

FLAVIUS, Brother 1927- 92
Father of the American Cavalry; a story of Brigadier General Casimir Pulaski. Illus. by Carolyn Lee Jagodits. Notre Dame, Ind., Dujarie Press [c1962] 96 p. illus. 24 cm. [E207.P8F5] 63-1457
1. Pulaski, Kazimiers, 1748-1779 — Juvenile literature. I. Title.

Pulaski, Kazimierz, 1748-1779.

ADAMS, Dorothy. 923.5438
Cavalry hero: Casimir Pulaski. Illustrated by Irena Lorentowicz. New York. Kenedy [1957] 190p. illus. 22cm. (American background books. 1) [E207.P8A6] 57-6512
1. Pulaski, Kazimlecz, 1748-1779. I. Title. II. Series.

ADAMS, Dorothy. 923.5438
Cavalry hero: Casimir Pulaski Illustrated by Irena Lorentowicz. New York, Kenedy [1957] 190p. illus. 22cm. (American background books, 1) [E207.P8A6] 57-6542
1. Pulaski, Kazimierz, 1748-1779. I. Title. II. Series.

Pulitzer, Joseph, 1847-1911.

HEATON, John Langdon, 070'.924
1860-1935.
The story of a page. [New York] Arno [1970, c1913] x, 364 p. port. 23 cm. (The American journalists) [PN4899.N42W65 1970] 75-125698 ISBN 0-405-01677-8
1. Pulitzer, Joseph, 1847-1911. 2. The World (New York, 1860-1931) 3. U.S.—History—1865- I. Title.

JUERGENS, George. 070.924
Joseph Pulitzer and the New York World. Princeton, N.J., Princeton University Press, 1966. xv, 392 p. illus., facsims., ports. 24 cm. Bibliography: p. 369-380. [PN4874.P8J8] 66-11974
1. Pulitzer, Joseph, 1847-1911. 2. The World (New York, 1860-1931) BIP

NOBLE, Iris. 920.5
Joseph Pulitzer; front page pioneer. New York, Messner [1957] 191 p. 22 cm. Includes bibliographies. [PN4874.P8N6] 57-6837
1. Pulitzer, Joseph, 1847-1911.

SEITZ, Don Carlos, 070'.924 B
1862-1935.
Joseph Pulitzer, his life & letters. New York, AMS Press [1970] xvi, 478 p. illus., facsim., map, ports. 23 cm. Reprint of the 1924 ed. [PN4874.P8S4 1970] 74-126692 ISBN 4-04-056997-
1. Pulitzer, Joseph, 1847-1911. I. Title. BIP

SMITH, Pattie 070'.92'4 B
Sherwood.
Joseph Pulitzer, giant of journalism. Charlotteville, N.Y., SamHar Press, 1973. 31 p. 22 cm. (Outstanding personalities, no. 58) Bibliography: p. 31. A biography of the newspaper editor who crusaded against corruption, established the Pulitzer Prize, and founded the School of Journalism at Columbia University. [PN4874.P836] 92 73-77602 0.98 (pbk.)
1. Pulitzer, Joseph, 1847-1911. I. Title. BIP

SWANBERG, W. A., 071'.3'0924 B
1907-
Pulitzer, by W. A. Swanberg. New York, Scribner [1967] xiv, 462 p. illus. 24 cm. Bibliography: p. 439-445. [PN4874.P8S9] 67-23695
1. Pulitzer, Joseph, 1847-1911.

Pulitzer, Joseph, 1885-1955.

GRANBERG, Wilbur J., 070.924
1906-
The world of Joseph Pulitzer. New York, Abelard [c.1965] 190p. illus., ports. 21cm. Bibl. [PN4874.P8G7] 65-12933 3.75
1. Pulitzer, Joseph, 1885-1955. I. Title.

Pulkingham, Betty.

PULKINGHAM, Betty. 283'.092'4 B
Little things in the hands of a big God / Betty Pulkingham. Waco, Tex. : Word Books, 1978,c1977. 142 p. : ill. ; 21 cm. [BR1725.P84A34] 79-63930 ISBN 0-8499-2855-9 : 4.95
1. Pulkingham, Betty. 2. Christian biography—United States. 3. Christian life—1960- I. Title. BIP

Pullen family.

*PULLEN, Lester Lafayette, 929.2
1892-
The biography of the Pumpkin Pullen family, by Les Pullen. Illus. by V. M. Banfield. Philadelphia, Dorrance [1968] 51p. illus. 21cm. 3.00
1. Pullen family. I. Title.

Puller, Lewis Burwell, 1898-

DAVIS, Burke 923.573
Marine! The life of Lt. Gen. Lewis B. (Chesty) Puller, USMC (ret.) New York, Bantam [1964, c.1962] 369 illus. 18cm. (S2745) .75 pap.,
1. Puller, Lewis Burwell, 1898- I. Title.

DAVIS, Burke. 923.573
Marine! The life of Lt. Gen. Lewis B. (Chesty) Puller, USMC (ret.) [1st ed.] Boston, Little, Brown [1962] 403 p. illus. 22 cm. [E746.P8D3] 61-14547
1. Puller, Lewis Burwell, 1898- I. Title.

Pupin, Michael Idvorsky, 1858-1965.

GREENE, Jay Elihu, 1914- 920.02
ed.
Four biographies. [School ed.] New York, Globe Book Co. [1956] 499p. illus. 21cm. [CT106.G65] 56-2582
1. Franklin, Benjamin, 1706-1790. 2. Blackwell, Elizabeth, 1821-1910. 3. Pupin, Michael Idvorsky, 1858-1965. 4. Rogers, Will, 1879-1935. I. Title.
Contents omitted.

Pupin, Michael Idvorsky, 1858-1935—Juvenile literature.

MARKEY, Dorothy 920
Explorer of sound: Michael Pupin. New York, Messner [c.1964] 191p. 22cm. Bibl. 64-12840 3.25; 3.19 lib. ed.,
1. Pupin, Michael Idvorsky, 1858-1935—Juvenile literature. I. Title.

PUPIN, Michael Idvorsky, 925.3
1858-1935.
From immigrant to inventor. With a foreword by Freeman J. Dyson. New York, Sceibner [1960, c.1922-1960] x, 396p. 20cm. (The Scribner library, SL26) 60-50388 1.45 pap.,
I. Title.

Puppets and puppet-plays.

STILL, William Frank. 745.59'22
Charming children with puppets, for 35 years, by Wm. Frank Still. Jacksonville, Fla., Paramount Press [1967] ix, 77 p. illus., facsim., ports. 26 cm. Autobiographical. [PN1972.S72] 68-558
1. Puppets and puppet-plays. I. Title.

Purcell, Henry, 1658 or 9-1695.

DUPRE, Henri, 780'.92'4 B
d.1929.
Purcell / Henri Dupre ; translated from the French by Catherine Alison Phillips and Agnes Bedford. New York : AMS Press, 1978. xv, 208, xv p., [6] leaves of plates : ill. ; 19 cm. Reprint of the 1928 ed. published by Knopf, New York. Includes index. Bibliography: p. 206-208. [ML410.P93D982 1978] 74-24071 ISBN 0-404-12899-8 : 18.50
1. Purcell, Henry, 1658 or 9-1695. 2. Composers—England—Biography.

WESTRUP, Sir Jack Allan, v. 12
1904-
Purcell. [Rev. ed.] London, Dent; New York, Farrar, Straus and Cudahy [1960] xi, 323 p. illus., music. 19 cm. (The Master musicians. New series) 63-72528
1. Purcell, Henry, 1658 or 9-1695. I. Title. II. Series.

WESTRUP, Jack Allan, 1904- 927.8
Purcell. New York, Collier [1962] 348p. 18cm. (Great Composers ser., BS114 x) Bibl. 1.50 pap.,
1. Purcell, Henry, 1658 or 9-1695. I. Title. II. Series. BIP

ZIMMERMAN, Franklin 780.924 (B)
B.
Henry Purcell, 1659-1695: his life and times [by] Franklin B. Zimmerman. London, Melbourne, Macmillan; New York, St. Martin's, 1967. xvii, 429p. front. (port.), illus. (incl. facsims.), 15 plates. diagrs 23cm. Illus. on endpapers. Bibl. [ML410.P93Z5] 67-14079 15.00
1. Purcell, Henry, 1658 org-1695. I. Title.

Purcell, Hugh Devereux

PURCELL, Hugh Devereux 923.873
Captain Forrester; the story of a Salem merchant prince. New York, Carlton [c.] 1962. 65p. 21cm. (Reflection bk.) 2.00
I. Title.

***Purcell, Mary**

*PURCELL, Mary 922.22
The first Jesuit, St. Ignatius Loyola. Garden City, N.Y., Doubleday [1965] 433p. 18cm. (Image bk., D189) Bill. .35 pap.,
I. Title.

Purnell, Benjamin Franklin.

STERLING, Anthony 922.89
King of the harem heaven; the amazing true story of a daring charlatan who ran a virgin love cult in America. Derby, Conn., Monarch Books [c.1960] 159p. 19cm. (Monarch Americana bk. MA300) .35 pap.,
1. Purnell, Benjamin Franklin. I. Title.

Pushkin, Aleksandr Sergeevich, 1799-1837.

MIRSKII, Dmitrii 891.783
Petrovich, 1890-
Pushkin, by D. S. Mirsky. Introd. by George Siegel. New York, Dutton, 1963. xii, 288 p. port. 19 cm. "D129." Bibliography: p. 227-242. "Chronological list of works": p. 276-277. [PG3350.M5 1963] 63-24657
1. Pushkin, Aleksandr Sergeevich, 1799-1837. I. Title.

MIRSKII, Dmitrii 891.7'1'3 B
Petrovich, 1890-
Pushkin / by D. S. Mirsky. New York : Haskell House, 1974. v, 266 p. : port. ; 22 cm. Reprint of the 1926 ed. published by G. Routledge, London. Includes index. Bibliography: p. 227-242. [PG3350.M5 1974] 74-34587 ISBN 0-8383-1998-X
1. Pushkin, Aleksandr Sergeevich, 1799-1837. I. Title.

PUSHKIN; 891.7'1'3
the man and the artist [by] Martha Warren Beckwith [and others] Freeport, N.Y., Books for Libraries Press, 1971. 245 p. 23 cm. (The Black heritage library collection) Reprint of the 1937 ed. Bibliography: p. 237-245. [PG3350.A4P83 1971] 75-168509 ISBN 0-8369-8862-0
1. Pushkin, Aleksandr Sergeevich, 1799-1837. I. Beckwith, Martha Warren, 1871-1959. II. Title. III. Series.

PUSHKIN; 891.7'1'3
a collection of articles and essays on the great Russian poet A. S. Pushkin. Freeport, N.Y., Books for Libraries Press, 1971. 187 p. illus. 27 cm. (The Black heritage library collection) Reprint of the 1939 ed. Contents.—The greatness of Pushkin, by I. Luppol.—The life and death of the poet: Alexander Sergeyevich Pushkin (a biographical essay), by V. Kirpotin. The lonely Pushkin, by A. Blagoi.—Pushkin's work: The father of modern Russian literature, by I. Lezhnev. Eugene Onegin, by A. Gurstein. Pushkin's lyrical poetry, by L. Timofeyev. Pushkin's epic poems, by M. Khrapchenko. Pushkin's prose, by V. Shklovski. Pushkin as a playwright, by G. Vinokur. Pushkin and folklore, by M. Azadovski. Gorky on Pushkin, by S. Balukhaty.—A genius of world significance: Western Europe and Pushkin, by V. Neustadt. Pushkin and Western literature, by V. Zhirmunski.—Theatre and music: Pushkin and the stage, by M. Zagorski. Pushkin in Russian music, by V. Ferman.—Pushkin in art. [PG3350.A4P8 1971] collection of articles and ess
1. Pushkin, Aleksandr Sergieevich, 1799-1837. I. Title. II. Series.

SIMMONS, Ernest Joseph, 928.917
1903-
Pushkin. New York, Random [c.1937, 1964] 456p. 19cm. (Vintage Russian lib., V-744) 64-55395 1.95 pap.,
1. Pushkin, Aleksandr Sergieevich, 1799-1837. I. Title.

SIMMONS, Ernest Joseph, 928.917
1903-
Pushkin [Gloucester, Mass., P. Smith, 1965, c.1937, 1964] 456p. 20cm. (Vintage bk., V744) [PG3350.S52] 4.00
1. Pushkin, Alexsandr Sergeevich, 1790-1837. I. Title. BIP

SIMMONS, Ernest Joseph, 928.917
1903-
Pushkin [by] Ernest J. Simmons. New York, Vintage Books [1964] 456 p. 19 cm. (Vintage Russian library, V-744) [PG3350.S52 1964] 64-55395
1. Pushkin, Alexandr Sergievich, 1799-1837. I. Title.

TROYAT, Henri, 1911- 928.917
Pushkin, a biography. Translation, by Randolp T. Weaver. [New York] Pantheon [1950] 508 p. illus., ports. 22 cm. [PG3350.T714] 50-5549
1. Pushkin, Aleksandr Sergeevich, 1799-1837. I. Title.

Pushkin, Aleksandr Sergeevich, 1799-1837—Biography.

MAGARSHACK, David. 891.7'1'3 B
Pushkin; a biography. New York, Grove Press [1968, c1967] 320 p. illus. 24 cm. Bibliography: p. 309-311. [PG3350.M28 1968] 68-9565 7.50
1. Pushkin, Aleksandr Sergeevich, 1799-1837—Biography.

TROYAT, Henri, 1911- 891.7'1'3 B
Pushkin. Translated from the French by Nancy Amphoux. Garden City, N.Y., Doubleday, 1970. xiii, 655 p. illus., ports. 25 cm. Translation of Pouchkine. Bibliography: p. [627]-631. [PG3350.T714 1970] 70-116181 10.00
1. Pushkin, Aleksandr Sergeevich, 1799-1837—Biography.

Pusinelli, Anton, 1815-1878.

WAGNER, Richard, 782.1'092'4 B
1813-1883.
The letters of Richard Wagner to Anton Pusinelli. Translated and edited with critical notes by Elbert Lenrow. New York, Vienna House, 1972 [c1932] xxvii, 293, x p. 24 cm. Reprint of the ed. published by A. A. Knopf, New York. [ML410.W1A4 1972] 72-93825 ISBN 0-8443-0104-3 12.50
1. Pusinelli, Anton, 1815-1878. 2. Wagner, Richard, 1813-1883. BIP

Pusser, Buford, 1937-

MORRIS, W. R., 1934- 363.2'0924 B
The twelfth of August; the story of Buford Pusser, by W. R. Morris. Nashville, Aurora Publishers [1971] xvi, 240 p. illus. 21 cm. [HV7911.P85M66 1971] 72-145849 ISBN 0-87695-121-3 4.95
1. Pusser, Buford, 1937- I. Title.

MORRIS, W. R., 363.2'0924 [B]
1934-
The twelfth of August; the story of Buford Pusser, by W. R. Morris. New York, Bantam Books [1974, c1971] 176 p. illus. 18 cm. [HV7911.P85M66 1974] 1.50 (pbk.)
1. Pusser, Buford, 1937- I. Title.
L.C. card number for hardbound ed.: 72-145849.

Putnam, Herbert, 1861-1955.

U.S. Library of Congress. 920.2
Herbert Putnam, 1861-1955; a memorial tribute. Washington, 1956. vii, 94 p. ports. 23 cm. Contents.Foreword, by L. Q. Mumford. -- Address: Herbert Putnam and his responsible eye, a memorial tribute, by D. C. Mearns. -- Bibliography: writings and addresses of Herbert Putnam and books and articles about him, by H. D. Hones. -- Herbert Putnam, a chronology, by D. C. Mearns. [Z720.P9U52] 56-60027
1. Putnam, Herbert, 1861-1955. 2. Mearns, David Chambers, 1890- I. Jones, Helen Gertrude (Dudenbostel) 1908- II. Title.

U. S. Library of Congress. 920.2
Herbert Putnam, 1861-1955 a memorial tribute Washington, 1956. vii, 94p. ports. 23cm. [Z720.P9U52] 56-60027
1. Putnam, Herbert, 1861-1955. I. Mearns, David Chambers, 1899- II. Jones, Helen Gertrude (Dudenbostel) 1908- III. Title.
Contents omitted.

Putnam, Israel, 1718-1790.

CUTTER, William, 1801-1867. 973.33'0924 B
The life of Israel Putnam, Major-General in the Army of the American Revolution, compiled from the best authorities. 4th ed. Port Washington, N.Y., Kennikat Press [1970] 383 p. illus., maps, port. 21 cm. (Kennikat American bicentennial series) Reprint of the 1850 ed. [E207.P9C9 1970] 78-120874
1. Putnam, Israel, 1718-1790.

HUMPHREYS, David, 1752-1818. 973.304'97 S
An essay on the life of the Honorable Major-General Israel Putnam / David Humphreys. New York : Garland Pub., 1977. p. cm. (The Garland library of narratives of North American Indian captivities ; v. 19) Reprint of the 1788 ed. printed by Hudson and Goodwin, Hartford. Issued with the reprint of the 1792 ed. of Howe, J. S. A genuine and correct account of the captivity, sufferings & deliverance of Mrs. Jemima Howe. New York, 1977. The reprint of the 1815 ed. of The Affecting history of Mrs. Howe. New York, 1977. [E85.G2 vol. 19] [E207.P9] 973.3'3'0924 B 77-6779 ISBN 0-8240-1643-2 lib.bdg. : 25.00
1. Putnam, Israel, 1718-1790. 2. United States. Army. Continental Army—Biography. 3. Indians of North America—Captivities. 4. Generals—United States—Biography. I. Title. II. Series. BIP

PUTNAM, Hamilton Staples, 1910- 973.2'6
Country on fire : Israel Putnam and the colonial struggle for survival, 1755-1765 / Hamilton S. Putnam. 1st ed. Concord, N.H. : H. S. Putnam, [1974] xxi, 210 p. : ill. ; 24 cm. Includes bibliographical references and index. [E199.P97] 74-24311
1. Putnam, Israel, 1718-1790. 2. United States—History—French and Indian War, 1755-1763. I. Title.

STEVENSON, Augusta. 973.33'0924 B
Israel Putnam, fearless boy. Illustrated by Jerry Robinson. Indianapolis, Bobbs-Merill [1959] 192 p. illus. 20 cm. (Childhood of famous Americans) A biography of an American patriot who fought in both the French and Indian and Revolutionary Wars, describing his boyhood and youth on the Massachusetts frontier. [PZ7.S8467Is] 92 AC 68
1. Putnam, Israel, 1718-1790. I. Robinson, Jerry, illus. II. Title.

TARBOX, Increase Niles, 1815-1888. 973.33'0924 B
Life of Israel Putnam ("Old Put"), major-general in the Continental Army. Port Washington, N.Y., Kennikat Press [1970] 389 p. illus., map, port. 22 cm. (Kennikat American bicentennial series) Reprint of the 1876 ed. [E207.P9T2 1970] 72-120894
1. Putnam, Israel, 1718-1790. 2. Bunker Hill, Battle of, 1775. I. Title.

Putnam, Israel, 1718-1790—Juvenile literature.

DWIGHT, Allan, pseud. 973.330924
Soldier and patriot: the life of General Israel Putnam. New York, Washburn [dist. McKay, c.1965] vi, 184p. 21cm. [E207.P9D9] 65-22019 3.75
1. Putnam, Israel, 1718-1790—Juvenile literature. I. Title. II. Title: The life of general Israel Putnam.

Putnam, Peter.

PUTNAM, Peter. 920.96177
Cast off the darkness. [1st ed.] New York, Harcourt, Brace [1957] 253p. 22cm. Autobiographical. [HV1792.P8A29] 362 57-10061
I. Title.

Puzo, Mario,

PUZO, Mario, 1920- 813'.5'4
The godfather papers & other confessions. New York, Putnam [1972] 252 p. 23 cm. [PS3566.U9Z5] 72-187892 6.95
I. Title. BIP

Pyle, Ernest Taylor, 1900-1945.

MILLER, Lee Graham, 1902- 920.5
The story of Ernie Pyle. New York, Viking Press, 1950. viii, 439 p. ports. 22 cm. [PN4874.P86M53 1950] 50-8918
1. Pyle, Ernest Taylor, 1900-1945. BIP

MILLER, Lee Graham, 1902-1961. 070.9'24 B
The story of Ernie Pyle. Westport, Conn., Greenwood Press [1970, c1950] viii, 439 p. ports. 23 cm. [PN4874.P86M53 1970] 78-100169 ISBN 0-8371-3743-8
1. Pyle, Ernest Taylor, 1900-1945. I. Title.

PYLE, Ernest Taylor, 1900-1945. 940.54'81'73
Brave men [by] Ernie Pyle. Westport, Conn., Greenwood Press [1974, c1944] 474 p. 22 cm. Reprint of the ed. published by H. Holt, New York. [D811.5.P88 1974] 74-70 ISBN 0-8371-7368-X 18.75
1. Pyle, Ernest Taylor, 1900-1945. 2. World War, 1939-1945—Personal narratives, American. 3. World War, 1939-1945—Campaigns—Italy. 4. World War, 1939-1945—Campaigns—France. I. Title. BIP

Pyle family.

PYLE, Carl Homer, 1898-1969. 929.2'0973
Colonel John Pyle and his people. Compiled by C. Homer Pyle. Edited by Bessie E. Pyle. Bethany, Mo., BB Engraving and Print. Co., 1970. 40 p. port. 28 cm. Bibliography: p. 39. [CS71.P995 1970] 78-18461
1. Pyle family. 2. Pyle, John, 1723-1804. I. Title.

Pyle, Howard, 1853-1911.

PITZ, Henry Clarence, 1895- 760'.092'4
Howard Pyle—writer, illustrator, founder of the Brandywine school / by Henry C. Pitz. 1st ed. New York : C. N. Potter : distributed by Crown Publishers, [1975] viii, 248 p., [16] leaves of plates : ill. (some col.) ; 32 cm. Includes index. Bibliography: p. 231-244. [ND237.P94P57 1975] 74-77563 ISBN 0-517-51665-9(Crown) : 25.00.
1. Pyle, Howard, 1853-1911. I. Title.

PYLE, Howard, 1853-1911. 759.13
Howard Pyle / introd. by Rowland Elzea. 1st U.S. ed. New York : Scribner, 1975. [5] p., 43 leaves of plates : chiefly col. ill. ; 30 cm. "An original Peacock Press/Bantam Book." [ND237.P94A44 1975] 75-5196 ISBN 0-684-14415-8 : 10.00
1. Pyle, Howard, 1853-1911.

Pym, John, 1584-1643.

SMITH, Goldwin, 1823-1910. 942.06 B
Three English statesmen: a course of lectures on the political history of England. Freeport, N.Y., Books for Libraries Press [1972] 328 p. 22 cm. (Essay index reprint series) Reprint of the 1867 ed. [DA307.S5 1972] 72-4587 ISBN 0-8369-2979-9 12.50

1. Pym, John, 1584-1643. 2. Cromwell, Oliver, 1599-1658. 3. Pitt, William, 1759-1806. I. Title. BIP

WADE, Charles Edward, 1864- 942.06'1'0924
John Pym, by C. E. Wade. Westport, Conn., Greenwood Press [1971] vii, 356 p. geneal. table, ports. 23 cm. Reprint of the 1912 ed. Includes bibliographical references. [DA396.P9W3 1971] 79-110880 ISBN 0-8371-4561-9
1. Pym, John, 1584-1643. 2. Gt. Brit.—History—Early Stuarts, 1603-1649. BIP

Pyrrhus, King of Epirus, 318-272 B.C.

KINCAID, Charles Augustus, 1870-1954. 930'.4
Successors of Alexander the Great. Chicago, Argonaut, 1969. 182 p. maps. 24 cm. (The Argonaut library of antiquities) Reprint of the 1930 ed. Bibliographical footnotes. [DF235.K5 1969] 73-7841
1. Ptolemaeus I Soter, King of Egypt, d. 283 B.C. 2. Pyrrhus, King of Epirus, 318-272 B.C. 3. Hiero II, King of Syracuse, d. 215? B.C. 4. Antiochus III, the Great, King of Syria, 238 (ca)-187 B.C. I. Title.

Pythagoras and Pythagorean school.

STANLEY, Thomas, 1625-1678. 182'.2
Pythagoras, his life and teachings. Foreword by Manly P. Hall. Introductory essay by Henry L. Drake. Los Angeles, Philosophical Research Society [1970?] x, 491-576 p. illus., ports. 34 cm. "Being a photographic facsimile of the ninth section of the 1687 edition of [the author's] the History of philosophy." [B243.S67 1687a] 74-26811
1. Pythagoras and Pythagorean school. I. Title.

Quain, Eric P

QUAIN, Eric P 1870- 926.1
Just memories. Eugene, Or., Printed by Valley Print. Co., c1951. 57 p. 20 cm. "A continuation of a series of personal experiences . . . published . . . in 1948 and entitled 'Unforgettable events.'" [R154.Q47A3] 51-37574
I. Title.

Quant, Mary

QUANT, Mary 687.120922
Quant by Quant. New York, Ballantine [1967, c.1966] 222p. illus. 18cm. (Mod bk., u6094) [TT505.Q3A3] .75 pap.,
I. Title.

Quantas Empire Airways, ltd.

FYSH, Wilmont Hudson Sir 387.70924
Qantas rising; the autobiography of the flying Fysh [by] Hudson Fysh. [Sydney] Angus & Robertson [San Francisco, Tri-Ocean, c.1965] xii, 296p. illus., fold, map. ports. 25cm. [HE9889.Q33] 65-25523 7.35
1. Quantas Empire Airways, ltd. I. Title.

Quantz, Johann Joachim, 1697-1773.

REILLY, Edward R. 788'.51'0924
Quantz and his Versuch; three studies [by] Edward R. Reilly. New York, American Musicological Society; distributor: Galaxy Music Corp. [1971] xi, 178 p. music. 23 cm. (American Musicological Society. Studies and documents, no. 5) "Studies dealing with Quantz's work as a composer, the dissemination of the Versuch in Germany and other European countries, and the musical and historical background of several topics dealt with in the treatise." Bibliography: p. 164-173. [ML410.Q12R4] 70-25592 5.50
1. Quantz, Johann Joachim, 1697-1773. Versuch einer Anweisung die Flote traversiere zu spielen. I. Title. II. Series.

Quarterback (Football)

SHAPIRO, Milton J. 796.332'0922 B
The pro quarterbacks, by Milton J. Shapiro. New York, J. Messner [1971] 189 p. ports. 22 cm. Contents.Contents.—Len Dawson.—Roman Gabriel.—Sonny Jurgensen.—Joe Namath.—Bart Starr.—Johnny Unitas.—The young quarterbacks.—Records. [GV939.A1S42] 73-147862 ISBN 0-671-32304-0 4.50
1. Quarterback (Football) 2. Football—Biography. I. Title. BIP

Quarterback (Football)-Biography.

KLOBUCHAR, Jim. 796.33'20924
Tarkenton / by Jim Klobucher and Fran Tarkenton. New York : Harper and Row, 1977. xiii, 336p. : ill. ; 18 cm. (Perennial Library) [GV939.T3K56] ISBN 0-06-080425-4 pbk. : 1.95
1. Quarterback (Football)-Biography. I. Tarkenton, Francis A., joint author. II. Title.
L.C. card no. for 1976 Harper and Row ed.: 76-30426. BIP

Queen, Ellery, pseud.

WHITE, William Anthony Parker, 1911- 928.1
Ellery Queen, a double profile, by Anthony Boucher [pseud. Boston, Little, Brown, 1951] 12 p. 23 cm. Cover title. Bibliography: p. 12. [PS3533.U4Z78] 51-3809
1. Queen, Ellery, pseud. I. Title.

Queens.

DAHMUS, Joseph Henry, 1909- 940.1'0922 B
Seven medieval queens [by] Joseph Dahmus. [1st ed.] Garden City, N.Y., Doubleday, 1972. 333 p. 22 cm. Contents.Contents.—Theodora, Byzantine Empress.—Brunhild, Merovingian Queen.—Theophano, Queen of Germany.—Zoe, Byzantine Empress.—Eleanor of Aquitaine, Queen of England.—Margaret, Queen of Denmark, Norway, and Sweden.—Margaret of Anjou, Queen of England.—Selected bibliography (p. 329-333) [D107.3.D24] 70-171285 7.95
1. Queens. I. Title.

FARJEON, Eleanor, 1881-1965, ed. 920
A cavalcade of queens, collected, ed. jointly by Eleanor Farjeon, William Mayne. Illus. by Victor Ambrus. New York, Walck [c.] 1965 xii, 243p. illus. 26cm. [D107.3.F18] 65-23251 5.95
1. Queens. I. Mayne, William, 1928- joint ed. II. Ambrus, Victor, illus. III. Title.

FARMER, Lydia (Hoyt) 1842-1903 923.1
A book of famous queens. Rev. by Willard A. Heaps. New York, Crowell [c.1964] vi, 246p. 21cm. First pub. in 1887 under title: The girls' book of famous queens. 63-18413 3.50
1. Queens—Juvenile literature. I. Heaps, Willard Allison, 1909- II. Title.

Queens—Biography.

BOYD, Mildred. 929.7
Rulers in petticoats. New York, Criterion Books [1967, c1966] 224 p. ports. 22 cm. Bibliography: p. 217-219. [D107.3.B6] 67-25848
1. Queens.—Biography. 2. Roman empresses. I. Title.

DARK, Sidney, 1874- 909'.00922 B
1947.
Twelve royal ladies. With ports. by Mabel Pugh. Freeport, N.Y., Books for Libraries Press [1970] 339 p. ports. 23 cm. (Essay index reprint series) Reprint of the 1929 ed. Contents.Contents.—Catherine de Medici.—Mary of England.—Mary Queen of Scots.—Henrietta Maria.—Queen Christina of Sweden.—Sophia, Electress of Hanover.—Louise de la Valliere.—Maria Theresa.—Catherine the Great.—Marie Antoinette.—Josephine de Beauharnais.—Caroline of Brunswick. [D107.3.D33 1970] 73-99689 ISBN 0-8369-1459-7
1. Queens—Biography. I. Title. BIP

Queens—Biography—Juvenile literature.

DAVIS, Mary Lee, 940'.0992 B
1935-
Women who changed history: five famous queens of Europe [by] Mary L. Davis. Minneapolis, Lerner Publications Co. [1974] 103 p. illus. 23 cm. Includes index. Contents.Contents.—Eleanor of Aquitaine.—Isabella of Spain.—Elizabeth I.—Marie Antoinette.—Catherine the Great. [D107.3.D38] 74-11899 ISBN 0-8225-0638-6 5.95 (lib. bdg.)
1. Queens—Biography—Juvenile literature. I. Title.
Contents omitted

TREASE, Geoffrey, 1909- 909
Seven sovereign queens. New York, Vanguard Press [1971? c1968] vii, 178, [1] p. illus., maps, ports. 23 cm. Contents.Contents.—Cleopatra, 'lass unparalleled'.—Boudicca, queen of the Iceni.—Galla Placidia, the empress in the West.—Isabella of Spain.—Christina of Sweden.—Maria Theresa, the empress-queen.—Catherine the Great. Bibliography: p. [179] [D107.3.T7 1971] 920 71-89662 ISBN 0-8149-0660-5 4.95
1. Queens—Biography—Juvenile literature. I. Title. BIP

Queensberry, William Douglas, 4th Duke of, 1725-1810.

BLYTH, Henry. 914.2'03'70924 B
Old Q, the rake of Piccadilly; a biography of the fourth Duke of Queensberry. Chicago, H. Regnery Co. [1970, c1967] xi, 238 p. illus., geneal. table, ports. 22 cm. Bibliography: p. 226-229. [DA506.Q3B54 1970] 73-126141 5.95
1. Queensberry, William Douglas, 4th Duke of, 1725-1810. I. Title.

Quennell, Peter, 1905- —Biography.

QUENNELL, Peter, 821'.9'12 B
1905-
The marble foot : an autobiography, 1905-1938 / Peter Quennell. New York : Viking Press, 1977, c1976. 254 p. : port. ; 22 cm. Includes index. [PR6033.U4Z52 1977] 76-49844 ISBN 0-670-45473-7 : 10.00
1. Quennell, Peter, 1905- —Biography. 2. Quennell, Charles Henry Bourne, 1872-1935. 3. Authors, English—20th century—Biography. I. Title.

Quetelet, Lambert Adolphe Jacques, 1796-1874.

HANKINS, Frank 001.4'22'0924 B
Hamilton, 1877-
Adolphe Quetelet as statistician, by Frank H. Hankins. New York, AMS Press [1968] 135 p. 23 cm. (Columbia University studies in the social sciences, 84) Originally presented as the author's thesis, Columbia University, 1908. Vita. Includes bibliographical references. [HA23.Q4H22 1968] 74-76680
1. Quetelet, Lambert Adolphe Jacques, 1796-1874. 2. Statistics—History. I. Title. II. Series: Columbia studies in the social sciences, no. 84 BIP

Quezon, Manuel Luis, Pres. Philippines, 1878-1944.

GOETTEL, Elinor. 991.4'035'0924 B
Eagle of the Philippines: President Manuel Quezon. New York, J. Messner [1970] 224 p. map. 22 cm. Bibliography: p. 215-217. [DS686.3.G6] 71-100561 3.95
1. Quezon, Manuel Luis, Pres. Philippines, 1878-1944. I. Title.

Quick, Thomas, 1734-1796.

LESLIE, Vernon. 974.9'02'0924 B
The Tom Quick legends / by Vernon Leslie. 1st ed. Middletown, N.Y. : T. E. Henderson, 1977. xi, 170 p. : ill. ; 26 cm. Includes index. Bibliography: p. 160-164. [F157.D4Q525] 76-55579 15.00
1. Quick, Thomas, 1734-1796. 2. Outlaws—Delaware Valley—Biography. 3. Indians of North America—Delaware Valley. I. Title.

Quicke, Kenneth.

QUICKE, Kenneth. 791.8
Immortal Henry : the story of a Lipizzaner stallion / Kenneth Quicke. London : P. Elek, 1977. 142 p., [4] leaves of plates : ill. ; 23 cm. [PN1995.9.A5Q5 1977] 77-370466 ISBN 0-236-40096-7 : 9.95
1. Quicke, Kenneth. 2. Henry (Horse) 3. Horsemen—England—Biography. I. Title.
Distributed by Technical Impex BIP

Quill, Michael J.

WHITTEMORE, L. 331.881'1'3880924
H.
The man who ran the subways; the story of Mike Quill [by] L. H. Whittemore. [1st ed.] New York, Holt, Rinehart and Winston [1968] xii, 308 p. illus., ports. 22 cm. Bibliography: p. 301-303. [HD6509.Q5W5] 68-12216
1. Quill, Michael J. I. Title.

Quimby, Paul Elmore.

†QUIMBY, Paul Elmore. 266'.6'73 B
Yankee on the Yangtze : one missionary's saga in revolutionary China / Paul Quimby with Norma Youngberg. Nashville, Tenn. : Southern Pub. Association, c1976. 176 p. ; 21 cm. [BV3427.Q55A36] 76-49387 ISBN 0-8127-0131-3 pbk. : 4.95
1. Quimby, Paul Elmore. 2. Missionaries—China—Biography. 3. Missionaries—United States—Biography. I. Youngberg, Norma R., joint author. II. Title.

Quimby, Phineas Parkhurst, 1802-1866.

HAWKINS, Ann Ballew, 922.8573
1892-
Phineas Parkhurst Quimby, revealer of spiritual healing to this age; his life and what he taught. [1st ed.] Jackson, Tenn. [1951] 56 p. 18 cm. "Based on the Quimby manuscripts and original letters in the Library of Congress." [RZ401.Q63] 51-5939
1. Quimby, Phineas Parkhurst, 1802-1866. I. Title.

Quin, James, 1693-1766.

THE Life of Mr. 792'.028'0924 B
James Quin, comedian, with the history of the stage from his commencing actor to his retreat to Bath. Anonymous. New York, Garland Pub., 1973. 116 p. port. 20 cm. Reprint of the 1766 ed. printed for S. Bladon, London. [PN2598.Q6L6 1973] 73-1287 ISBN 0-8240-0635-6
1. Quin, James, 1693-1766. 2. Theater—England—History.

Quincy, Josiah, 1744-1775.

QUINCY, Josiah, 973.3'0924 B
1772-1864.
Memoir of the life of Josiah Quincy. New York, Da Capo Press, 1971 [c1825] viii, 498 p. facsims. 23 cm. (The Era of the American revolution) "Observations on the act of Parliament commonly called the Boston port-bill; with thoughts on civil society and standing armies. By Josiah Quincy, Jun'r ... Boston ... 1774": p. [355]-469. Includes bibliographical references. [E263.M4Q72 1971] 78-146274 ISBN 0-306-70098-0
1. Quincy, Josiah, 1744-1775. 2. Massachusetts—Politics and government—Revolution, 1775-1783. I. Quincy, Josiah, 1744-1775. Observations on the act of Parliament commonly called the Boston port-bill. 1971. BIP

Quincy, Josiah, 1772-1864.

MCCAUGHEY, Robert 973.5'092'4 B
A.
Josiah Quincy, 1772-1864; the last Federalist [by] Robert A. McCaughey. Cambridge, Mass., Harvard University Press, 1974. xii, 264 p. port. 25 cm. (Harvard historical studies, v. 90) Includes bibliographical references. [E302.6.Q7M32] 73-89506 ISBN 0-674-48375-8 12.00
1. Quincy, Josiah, 1772-1864. I. Title. II. Series. BIP

Quinn, Clinton Simon, bp.

CHIDSEY, Alan Lake. 283.09
The bishop; a portrait of the Right Reverend Clinton S. Quin. Houston, Tex., Gulf Pub. Co. [1966] 239 p. 22 cm. [BX5995.15C5] 65-29026
1. 1. Quinn, Clinton Simon, Bp. I. Title.

Quinn, Edel Mary, 1907-1944.

BROWN, Evelyn M. 92
Edel Quinn, beneath the Southern Cross, by Evelyn M. Brown. Illustrated by Harold Lang. New York, Vision Books [1967] xv, 175 p. illus. 22 cm. A biography of an Irish girl who dedicated her life to missionary service in East Africa. [BV3557.Q8B7] AC 67
1. Quinn, Edel Mary, 1907-1944. 2. Missions—Africa, South.

MCAULIFFE, Marius 266'.2'0924 B
Envoy to Africa : the interior life of Edel Quinn / Marius McAuliffe. Chicago : Franciscan Herald Press, [1975] p. cm. [BV3557.Q8M32] 74-31153 ISBN 0-8199-0560-7 pbk. : 1.95
1. Quinn, Edel Mary, 1907-1944. I. Title. BIP

SUENENS, Leon Joseph, v. 12
Cardinal, 1904-
A heroine of the Apostolate (1907-1944), Edel Quinn, envoy of the Legion of Mary to Africa. Pref. by H. E. Archbishop Riberi. Dublin. C. J. Fallon; Distributed in U.S.A. by Publishers Printing Co. Louisville, Ky. [1956] xviii, 272 p. illus., ports., maps. 22 cm.
1. Quinn, Edel Mary, 1907-1944. 2. Legion of Mary. 3. Missions—Africa. I. Title.

Quinn, John, 1870-1924.

REID, Benjamin 704'.34'0924 B
Lawrence.
The man from New York; John Quinn and his friends [by] B. L. Reid. New York, Oxford University Press, 1968. xviii, 708 p. illus., ports. 24 cm. Bibliography: p. 687-691. [CT275.Q55R4] 68-29724 12.50
1. Quinn, John, 1870-1924. I. Title.

Quinn, Michael A., 1895-

QUINN, Michael 940.54'72'520924
A., 1895-
Love letters to Mike : forty months as a Japanese prisoner of war, April 9, 1942 to September 17, 1945 : the diary of Colonel Michael A. Quinn. 1st ed. New York : Vantage Press, c1977. 331 p. ; 21 cm. [D805.J3Q56] 78-100041 ISBN 0-533-02800-0 10.00
1. Quinn, Michael A., 1895- 2. World War, 1939-1945—Prisoners and prisons, Japanese. 3. World War, 1939-1945—Personal narratives, American. 4. Prisoners of war—Philippine Islands—Biography. 5. Prisoners of war—Taiwan—Biography. I. Title.

Quiroga, Juan Facundo, 1790-1835.

SARMIENTO, Domingo 982'.03 B
Faustino, Pres. Argentine Republic, 1811-1888.
Life in the Argentine Republic in the days of the tyrants : or, Civilization and barbarism / D. F. Sarmiento ; with a biographical sketch of the author by Mrs. Horace Mann. New York : Gordon Press, 1976. 288 p. ; 24 cm. Translation of Facundo. [F2846.S2472 1976] 76-19754 ISBN 0-87968-403-8
1. Quiroga, Juan Facundo, 1790-1835. 2. Argentine Republic—History—1817-1860. 3. Argentine Republic—Description and travel. 4. Generals—Argentine Republic—Biography. I. Title. II. Title: Civilization and barbarism.

Quisling, Vidkun, 1887-1945.

HAYES, Paul M. 948.1'04'0924 B
Quisling: the career and political ideas of Vidkun Quisling, 1887-1945 [by] Paul M. Hayes. Bloomington, Indiana University Press [1972, c1971] 368 p. port. 25 cm. Bibliography: p. 356-362. [DL529.Q5H38 1972] 78-184523 ISBN 0-253-34760-2 12.95
1. Quisling, Vidkun, 1887-1945.

HEWINS, Ralph. 940.53370924
Quisling, prophet without honor [1st Amer. ed.] New York, John Dar [1966, c1965] 384p. illus. ports. 22 cm. [DL529.Q5H46] 66-10515
1. Quisling, Vidkun, 1887-1945. I. Title.

Quispe Mamani, Modesto—Juvenile literature.

MANGURIAN, David. 980'.004'98
Children of the Incas / by David Mangurian. New York : Four Winds Press, c1979. 73 p. : ill. ; 26 cm. A 13-year-old Quechua Indian boy living in a village near Lake Titicaca describes his family, home, and day-to-day activities. [F2230.2.K4M37] 79-12186 ISBN 0-590-07500-4 : 8.95
1. Quispe Mamani, Modesto—Juvenile literature. 2. Quechua Indians—Juvenile literature. 3. Quechua Indians—Biography—Juvenile literature. I. Title. BIP

Quogue, N.Y.—Biography—Addresses, essays, lectures.

QUOGUE as we remember 974.7'25 B
it / prepared by the Quogue Historical Society on the occasion of the United States Bicentennial ; editors, Diana Stokes Callaway, Margaret B. Perry, Patricia D. Shuttleworth. [Quogue, N.Y. : The Society, c1976] 47 p. : ill. ; 28 cm. [F129.Q63Q63] 77-358357
1. Quogue, N.Y.—Biography—Addresses, essays, lectures. 2. Quogue, N.Y.—Social life and customs—Addresses, essays, lectures. I. Callaway, Diana Stokes. II. Perry, Margaret B. III. Shuttleworth, Patricia D. IV. Quogue Historical Society.

Rabbis—U. S.—Biog.

GOLDMAN, Alex J. 922.96
Giants of faith; great American rabbis, by Rabbi Alex J. Goldman. New York, Citadel [1965, c.1964] 349p. ports. 24cm. [BM750.G57] 64-8163 6.95
1. Rabbis—U. S.—Biog. I. Title.

Rabelais, Francois, 1490 (ca.)-1553?

CHAPPELL, Arthur Fred. 843'.3
The enigma of Rabelais; an essay in interpretation, by A. F. Chappell. [Folcroft, Pa.] Folcroft Library Editions, 1973. xvi, 196 p. 23 cm. Reprint of the 1924 ed. published by University Press, Cambridge, Eng. Includes bibliographical references. [PQ1694.C5 1973] 73-11356 ISBN 0-8414-3412-3 (lib. bdg.)
1. Rabelais, Francois, ca. 1490-1553? I. Title. BIP

CHAPPELL, Arthur Fred. 843'.3
The enigma of Rabelais; an essay in interpretation, by A. F. Chappell. [Folcroft, Pa.] Folcroft Library Editions, 1973. xvi, 196 p. 23 cm. Reprint of the 1924 ed. published by University Press, Cambridge, Eng. Includes bibliographical references. [PQ1694.C5 1973] 73-11356 ISBN 0-8414-3412-3 (lib. bdg.)
1. Rabelais, Francois, ca. 1490-1553? I. Title. BIP

DOCTOR Rabelais. v. 12
London and New York, Sheed and Ward [1957] 274p. illus. Bibliography: p.267.
1. Rabelais, Francois, 1490 (ca.)—1553? I. Lewis, Wyndham, 1886-1957.

ELDRIDGE, Paul, 1888- 843'.3 B
Francois Rabelais, the great story teller. South Brunswick, A. S. Barnes [1971] 215 p. 22 cm. [PQ1693.E4] 73-124198 ISBN 0-498-07799-3 5.95
1. Rabelais, Francois, 1490 (ca.)-1553?

FRAME, Donald Murdoch, 843'.3 B 1911-
Francois Rabelais : a study / Donald M. Frame. 1st ed. New York : Harcourt Brace Jovanovich, c1977. xviii, 238 p. : port. ; 25 cm. Includes index. Bibliography: p. 219-225. [PQ1693.F68] 76-62519 ISBN 0-15-133465-X : 12.95
1. Rabelais, Francois, 1490(ca.)-1553? 2. Authors, French—16th century—Biography.

LEWIS, Dominic Bevan 847.32 Wyndham, 1894-
Doctor Rabelais. London, New York, Sheed and Ward [1957] 274p. illus. 23cm. Includes bibliography. [PQ1693.L4] 57-3472
1. Rabelais, Francois, 1490 (ca.)-1553? I. Title.

LEWIS, Dominic Bevan 847.32 Wyndham, 1894-1969.
Doctor Rabelais. London, New York, Sheed and Ward [1957] 274 p. illus. 23 cm. Includes bibliography. [PQ1693.L4] 57-3472
1. Rabelais, Francois, 1490 (ca.)-1553?

LEWIS, Dominic Bevan 843'.3 B Wyndham, 1894-1969.
Doctor Rabelais, by D. B. Wyndham Lewis. New York, Greenwood Press, 1968. xii, 274 p. illus., facsims., map, port. 23 cm. Reprint of the 1957 ed. Bibliography: p. 267. [PQ1693.L4 1968] 69-10117
1. Rabelais, Francois, 1490 (ca.)-1553? I. Title.

POWYS, John Cowper, 1872- 928.4
Rabelais, his life; the story told by him, selections therefrom here newly translated, and an interpretation of his genius and his religion. New York, Philosophical Library [1951] 424 p. 23 cm. [PQ1693.P67 1951] 51-3374
1. Rabelais, Francois, 1490 (cs.)-1553? I. Title.

PUTNAM, Samuel, 1892-1950. 843'.3
Francois Rabelais, man of the Renaissance; a spiritual biography. Freeport, N.Y., Books for Libraries Press [1973] p. Reprint of the 1929 ed. [PQ1693.P8 1973] 73-2692 ISBN 0-8369-7167-1
1. Rabelais, Francois, 1490 (ca.)-1553?

TILLEY, Arthur Augustus, 843'.3 B 1851-1942.
Francois Rabelais. Port Washington, N.Y., Kennikat Press [1970] 388 p. port. 21 cm. Reprint of the 1907 ed. Bibliography: p. 359-365. [PQ1694.T5] 79-113326
1. Rabelais, Francois, 1490 (ca.)-1553? BIP

Rabin, Yitzhak, 1922-

RABIN, Yitzhak, 956.94'05'0924 B 1922-
The Rabin memoirs / by Yitzhak Rabin. 1st English language ed. Boston : Little, Brown, c1979. vi, 344 p., [8] leaves of plates : ill. ; 24 cm. Includes index. [DS126.6.R32A37] 79-9273 ISBN 0-316-73002-5 : 12.95
1. Rabin, Yitzhak, 1922- 2. Prime ministers—Israel—Biography. 3. Israel—History, Military. 4. Israel—Foreign relations—United States. 5. United States—Foreign relations—Israel. I. Title. BIP

Rabinowitz, Shalom,

RABINOWITZ, Shalom, 928.9249 1859-1916.
The great fair; scenes from my childhood [by] Sholom Aleichem [pseud.] Translated by Tamara Kahana. With a drawing of the author by Marc Chagall. New York, Noonday Press, 1955. 306 p. illus. 21 cm. [PJ5129.R2F83] 55-8229
I. Title.

Rabinowitz, Shalom, 1859-1916.

FALSTEIN, Louis. 892.49'7'3 B
The man who loved laughter; the story of Sholom Aleichem. Illustrated by Adrianne Onderdonk Dudden. [1st ed.] Philadelphia, Jewish Publication Society of America, 1968. 154 p. illus. 22 cm. (Covenant books, 21) [PJ5129.R2Z59] 68-19608 2.95
1. Rabinowitz, Shalom, 1859-1916. I. Title. BIP

RABINOWITZ, Shalom, 928.9249 1859-1916.
The great fair; scenes from my childhood [by] Sholom Aleichem [pseud.] Translated by Tamara Kahana. With a drawing of the author by Marc Chagall. New York, Noonday Press, 1955. 306 p. illus. 21 cm. [PJ5129.R2F83] 55-8229
I. Title.

WAIFE-GOLDBERG, 892.49'8'308 Marie.
My father, Sholom Aleichem. New York, Simon and Schuster [1968] 333 p. illus., ports. 24 cm. "Works of Sholom Aleichem in English translation": p. 318-319. [PJ5129.R2Z88] 68-11011
1. Rabinowitz, Shalom, 1859-1916. I. Title. BIP

Rachmaninoff, Sergei, 1873-1943.

BERTENSSON, Sergei, 1885- 927.8
Sergei Rachmaninoff, a lifetime in music, by Sergei Bertensson and Jay Leyda, with the assistance of Sophia Satin. New York, New York University Press, 1956. viii, 464p. illus., ports, facsims., music. 24cm. 'Works': p. 402-419. 'Work on records': p. 420-438. [ML410.R12B47] 55-10065
1. Rachmaninoff, Sergei, 1873-1943. 2. Rachmaninoff, Sergei, 1893-1943—Discography. I. Leyds, Jay, 1910- joint author. II. Satin, Sophia. III. Title.

BERTENSSON, Sergei, 1885- 927.8 1962.
Sergei Rachmaninoff, a lifetime in music, by Sergei Bertensson and Jay Leyda, with the assistance of Sophia Satin. New York, New York University Press, 1956. viii, 464 p. illus., ports., facsims., music. 24 cm. "Works": p. 402-419. "Work on records": p. 420-438. [ML410.R12B47] 55-10065
1. Rachmaninoff, Sergei, 1873-1943. 2. Rachmaninoff, Sergei, 1893-1943—Discography. I. Leyda, Jay, 1910- joint author. II. Satina, Sophie, 1879- BIP

LYLE, Watson. 780'.92'4 B
Rachmaninoff : a biography / by Watson Lyle. New York : AMS Press, 1976. xii, 247 p., [1] leaf of plates : port. ; 18 cm. "With portraits, list of works in order of opus number, and a critical survey of Rachmaninoff's gramophone recordings by Wilson G. Lyle." Reprint of the 1939 ed. published by W. Reeves, London. Includes index. [ML410.R12L9 1976] 74-24140 ISBN 0-404-13003-8 : 15.00
1. Rachmaninoff, Sergei, 1873-1943. 2. Composers—Russia—Biography.

NORRIS, Geoffrey. 780'.92'4
Rakhmaninov / by Geoffrey Norris. London : Dent, 1976. xi, 211 p., [8] p. of plates : ill., music, ports. ; 20 cm. (The Master musicians series) "Catalogue of works": p. 179-194. Includes index. Bibliography: p. 200-203. [ML410.R12N67] 76-366415 ISBN 0-460-03145-7 : 7.50
1. Rachmaninoff, Sergei, 1873-1943. I. Title. II. Series.
Distributed by Rowman & Littlefield. BIP

PIGGOTT, Patrick, 780'.92'4 B 1915-
Rachmaninov / Patrick Piggott. London : Faber and Faber, 1978. 110 p. : ill. ; 23 cm. (The Great composers) Includes index. Bibliography: p. 104. [ML410.R12P5] 78-314213 ISBN 0-571-10265-4 : 7.95
1. Rachmaninoff, Sergei, 1873-1943. 2. Composers—Russia—Biography.
Distributed by Faber & Faber, Salem, NH

SEROFF, Victor, Ilyitch, 927.8 1902-
Rachmaninoff. New York, Simon and Schuster, 1950. xiv, 269 p. ports. 22 cm. "List of Rachmaninoff's compositions": p. 241-251. Bibliogrphy: p. 252-263. [ML410.R12S4] 50-6037
1. Rachmaninoff, Sergei, 1873-1943. BIP

SEROFF, Victor 780'.924 B Ilyitch, 1902-
Rachmaninoff, by Victor I. Seroff. Freeport, N.Y., Books for Libraries Press [1970, c1950] xiv, 269 p. ports. 23 cm. (Biography index reprint series) Bibliography: p. 252-263. [ML410.R12S4 1970] 70-126328
1. Rachmaninoff, Sergei, 1873-1943.

Racine, Jean Baptiste, 1639-1699.

ABRAHAM, Claude Kurt, 842'.4 B 1931-
Jean Racine / by Claude Abraham. Boston : Twayne Publishers, c1977. 179 p. : port. ; 21 cm. (Twayne's world authors series ; TWAS 458 : France) Includes index. Bibliography: p. 173-176. [PQ1904.A66] 77-2377 ISBN 0-8057-6295-7 lib.bdg. : 8.95
1. Racine, Jean Baptiste, 1639-1699. 2. Dramatists, French—17th century—Biography. BIP

GOLDMANN, Lucien. 842'.4
Racine; translated [from the French] by Alastair Hamilton; with an introduction by Raymond Williams. Cambridge, Rivers Press Ltd, 1972. xxii, 105 p. 22 cm. Translation of Jean Racine. [PQ1904.G5813] 73-158514 £2.25
1. Racine, Jean Baptiste, 1639-1699. I. Title.

Racine, Jean Baptiste, 1639-1699—Biography.

DUCLAUX, Agnes Mary 842'.4 B Frances (Robinson) 1857-1944.
The life of Racine. Port Washington, N.Y., Kennikat Press [1972] 256 p. 22 cm. Reprint of the 1925 ed. Bibliography: p. 249. [PQ1904.D7 1972] 73-153904 ISBN 0-8046-1595-0
1. Racine, Jean Baptiste, 1639-1699—Biography. I. Title. BIP

Rackham, Arthur, 1867-1939.

HUDSON, Derek. 741.64
Arthur Rackham: his life and work. New York, Scribner [1960] 181 p. illus. (part mounted, part col.) ports. 29 cm. Bibliography: p. 159-160. "The printed work of Arthur Rackham, a check-list compiled by Bertram Rota": p. 164-181. [NC242.R3H8] 60-12994
1. Rackham, Arthur, 1867-1939.

Radar.

WATSON-WATT, Robert 926.2138 Alexander Sir, 1892-
The pulse of radar: the autobiography of Sir Robert Watson-Watt. New York, Dial Press, 1959. 438 p. illus. 21 cm. [UG610.W28] 58-11430
1. Radar. 2. Radio, Military. 3. World War, 1939-1945 — Technology. I. Title.

Radbill, Samuel X.,

RADBILL, Samuel X., ed. 926.1
The autobiographical ana of Robley Dunglison, M.D. Edited with notes and introd. by Samuel X. Radbill. Philadelphia, American Philosophical Society, 1963. 212 p. illus., ports., facsims. 30 cm. (Transactions of the Aemrican Philosophical Society, new ser., v. 53, pt. 8) Bibliography: p. 196-199. [Q11.P6 n.s., vol. 53, pt. 8] 63-22636
I. Title. II. Series. III. Series: American Philosophical Society, Philadelphia. Transactions, new ser., v. 53, pt. 8

Radcliffe, Ann (Ward) 1764-1823.

GRANT, Aline. 928.2
Ann Radcliffe, a biography. Denver, A. Swallow [1951] 153 p. 23 cm. Bibliography: p. 149-153. [PR5203.G7] 51-14495
1. Radcliffe, Ann (Ward) 1764-1823. I. Title.

Radcliffe, Anne Bonny, b. 1700.

CARLOVA, John 923.4173
Mistress of the seas. New York, Citadel [c.1964] 253p. port. 22cm. 64-15966 4.50 bds.,
1. Radcliffe, Anne Bonny, b. 1700. I. Title.

CARLOVA, John. 923.4173
Mistress of the seas. [1st ed.] New York, Citadel Press [1964] 253 p. port. 22 cm. [G537.43C3] 64-15966
1. Radcliffe, Anne Bonny, b. 1700. I. Title.

Radcliffe family.

MILNE, Maurice. 942.8'2'0810924 B
The strange story of the "Countess of Derwentwater": a Victorian tragi-comedy. Newcastle upon Tyne, Graham, 1970. 22 p. illus., facsims., geneal. table. 22 cm. (Northern historical booklets, no. 7) Bibliography: p. 22. [CS439.R2M53] 76-852260 5/-
1. Radcliffe family. I. Title. II. Title: Derwentwater, Countess of. III. Series: Northern history booklets, no. 7.

Raddall, Thomas Head, 1903—Biography.

RADDALL, Thomas Head, 813'.5'4 B 1903-
In my time : a memoir / Thomas H. Raddall. Toronto : McClelland and Stewart, c1976. viii, 365 p., [8] leaves of plates : ill. ; 24 cm. [PR9199.3.R23Z517] 77-353477 ISBN 0-7710-7250-3 : 14.95
1. Raddall, Thomas Head, 1903—Biography. 2. Authors, Canadian—20th century—Biography. I. Title.
Distributed by Lippincott,N.Y.

Radek, Karl, 1885-1939.

LERNER, Warren. 335.43'0924 B
Karl Radek, the last internationalist. Stanford, Calif., Stanford University Press, 1970. x, 240 p. illus., ports. 23 cm. Based on the author's thesis, Columbia University. "Radek's publications": p. [213]-219. Bibliography: p. [221]-223. [HX312.R3L4 1970] 70-97915 7.95
1. Radek, Karl, 1885-1939. I. Title.

Radford, Albert, 1862-1904.

RADFORD, Fred W. 738'.092'4 B
A. Radford; pottery, his life & works, by Fred W. Radford. [Columbia? S.C., 1973] 50 p. illus. 23 cm. [NK4210.R28R32] 73-161384
1. Radford, Albert, 1862-1904.

Radhakrishnan, Sarvepalli, Pres. India, 1888-

RADHAKRISHNAN: 370.1/0924
the portrait of an educationist. [1st ed.] Delhi, Sterling Publishers [1967] 147p. 23cm. Bibl. [LB775.R29S55] [PL480:I-E-8554] SA67 5.00 [corrected entry]
1. Radhakrishnan, Sarvepalli, Pres. India, 1888- I. Singh, Rajendra Pal, 1932-
Distributed by Verry, Mystic, Conn.

SAMARTHA, S J 1920- 181.4
Introduction to Radhakrishnan; the man and his thought. New York, Association Press [1964] 127 p. 21 cm. [B133.R16S3] 64-11596
1. Radhakrishnan, Sarvepalli, Pres. India, 1888- I. Title.

Radiguet, Raymond, 1903-1923—Biography.

CROSLAND, Margaret, 843'.9'12 B 1920-
Raymond Radiguet : a biographical study

with selections from his work / [by] Margaret Crosland. London : Owen, 1976. 153 p., [4] p. of plates : ports. ; 23 cm. Includes index. Bibliography: p. 148-150. [PQ2635.A25Z585] 77-351573 ISBN 0-7206-0413-3 : £4.95
1. Radiguet, Raymond, 1903-1923—Biography. 2. Authors, French—20th century—Biography.

Radini Tedeschi, Giacomo Maria, 1857-1914.

JOANNES XXIII, Pope, 282'.0924 B
1881-1963.
My bishop; a portrait of Mgr. Giacomo Maria Radini Tedeschi. With a foreword by H. E. Cardinale, and an introd. by Loris Capovilla. Translated by Dorothy White. New York, McGraw-Hill [1969] 143 p. illus., ports. 25 cm. Translation of Mons. Giacomo Maria Radini Tedeschi. [BX4705.R286J63] 69-13212 6.95
1. Radini Tedeschi, Giacomo Maria, 1857-1914. I. Title.

Radio—Biography.

DAYLIE, Daddy-O. 791.44'0924
You're on the air, by Daddy-O Daylie, with Emmett Smith. [Chicago, Childrens Press, c1969] 62 p. illus., ports. 19 cm. (An Open door book) Autobiographical. A black disc jockey tells about his background, how he got his break in radio, and his climb to success. [ML3930.D35A3] 92 70-101626
I. Smith, Emmett, joint author. II. Title.

DUNLAP, Orrin 621.3841'0922 B
Elmer, 1896-
Radio's 100 men of science; biographical narratives of pathfinders in electronics and television [by] Orrin E. Dunlap, Jr. Freeport, N.Y., Books for Libraries Press [1970, c1944] xx, 294 p. ports. 24 cm. (Essay index reprint series) [TK6545.A1D8 1970] 70-128235 ISBN 0-8369-1916-5
1. Radio—Biography. 2. Scientists—Biography. I. Title.

Radio broadcasting—Biog.

WHO'S who in TV & radio. 927.92
v. 1 [New York, Dell Pub. Co.] 1957 v. ports. 27 cm. annual. [PN1991.1.W467] 52-24598
1. Radio broadcasting—Biog. 2. Television broadcasting—Biog.

Radishchev, Aleksandr Nikolaevich, 1749-1802—Biography.

LANG, David Marshall. 197'.2 B
The first Russian radical, Alexander Radishchev, 1749-1802 / David Marshall Lang. Westport, Conn. : Greenwood Press, 1977, c1959. 298 p., [8] leaves of plates : ill. ; 23 cm. Reprint of the ed. published by Allen & Unwin, London. Includes index. Bibliography: p. [280]-288. [PG3317.R3Z72 1977] 77-5516 ISBN 0-8371-9637-X lib.bdg. : 19.25
1. Radishchev, Aleksandr Nikolaevich, 1749-1802—Biography. 2. Authors, Russian—18th century—Biography. I. Title.

Radisson, Pierre Esprit, 1620?-1710.

LAUT, Agnes Christina, 971.2'01
1871-1936.
Pathfinders of the West; being the thrilling story of the adventures of the men who discovered the great Northwest, Radisson, La Verendrye, Lewis, and Clark. Illus. by Remington, Goodwin, Marchand and others. Freeport, N.Y., Books for Libraries Press [1969] xxv, 380 p. illus., maps, ports. 23 cm. (Essay index reprint series) "First published 1904." [F1060.7.L38 1969] 74-90651
1. Radisson, Pierre Esprit, 1620?-1710. 2. La Verendrye, Pierre Gaultier de Varennes, sieur de, 1685-1749. 3. Hearne, Samuel, 1745-1792. 4. Mackenzie, Alexander, Sir, 1763-1820. 5. Lewis and Clark Expedition. 6. Northwest, Canadian—Discovery and exploration. I. Title.

NUTE, Grace Lee, 971.01'6'0922
1895-
Caesars of the wilderness : Medard Chouart, Sieur des Groseilliers and Pierre Esprit Radisson, 1618-1710 / by Grace Lee Nute. Reprint ed. St. Paul : Minnesota Historical Society Press, 1978, c1943. xx, 386 p., [7] leaves of plates : ill. ; 24 cm. (Publications of the Minnesota Historical Society) Reprint of the ed. published by Appleton-Century, New York. Includes index. Bibliography: p. 359-370. [F1060.7.C483N87 1978] 78-811 ISBN 0-87351-127-1 : 12.50 ISBN 0-87351-128-X pbk. : 5.95
1. Chouart, Medard, sieur des Groseilliers, 17th century. 2. Radisson, Pierre Esprit, 1620?-1710. 3. Hudson's Bay Company. 4. New France—Discovery and exploration. 5. Explorers—France—Biography. 6. Fur trade—New France. I. Title. II. Series: Minnesota Historical Society. Publications.
BIP

SYME, Ronald. 923.971
Bay of the North, the story of Pierre Radisson; illus. by Ralph Ray. New York, Morrow, 1950. 192 p. illus. 21 cm. [Morrow junior books] [F1060.7.R15S9] 50-5501
1. Radisson, Pierre Esprit, 1620?-1710. I. Title.

Radisson, Pierre Esprit, 1620?-1710—Juvenile literature.

RITCHIE, Cicero T. 1914- 923.971
Runner of the woods; the story of young Radisson. Illus. by WilliamWheeler. New York, St Martin's [1964, c.]1963. 160p. illus. (pt. col.) map (on lining papers) (Great stories of Canada, 28) 64-10300 2.95 bds.,
1. Radisson, Pierre Esprit, 1620?-1710—Juvenile literature. I. Title.

Radnor, William Pleydell-Bouverie, 3d Earl of, 1779-1869.

HUCH, Ronald K. 328.41'092'4 B
The radical Lord Radnor : the public life of Viscount Folkestone, Third Earl of Radnor, 1779-1869 / by Ronald K. Huch. Minneapolis : University of Minnesota Press, c1977. ix, 204 p. ; 23 cm. (Minnesota monographs in the humanities ; v. 10) Includes index. Bibliography: p. 189-195. [DA536.R17H8 1977] 76-55172 18.50
1. Radnor, William Pleydell-Bouverie, 3d Earl of, 1779-1869. 2. Legislators—Great Britain—Biography. 3. Great Britain—Politics and government—1800-1837. I. Title. II. Series.
BIP

Radowitz, Joseph Maria Ernst Christian Wilhelm von, 1797-1853.

MORRIS, Warren 943'.07'0924 B
Bayard, 1948-
The political career of Joseph Maria von Radowitz / by Warren Bayard Morris, Jr. [Stillwater, Okla.] : Morris, 1974. v, 234 leaves ; 28 cm. Thesis—Oklahoma State University. Vita. Bibliography: leaves 230-234. [DD205.R3M67] 74-193269
1. Radowitz, Joseph Maria Ernst Christian Wilhelm von, 1797-1853. I. Title.

Radziwill family.

NOWAKOWSKI, Tadeusz. 929'.2'09438
The Radziwills; the social history of a great European family. Translated from the German by E. B. Garside. [New York] Delacorte Press/S. Lawrence [1974] 325 p. illus. 24 cm. Translation of Die Radziwills. [CS879.R313 1974] 74-692 ISBN 0-440-07340-5 12.50
1. Radziwill family. I. Title.

Raffaele Sanzio, 1483-1520.

ERNEST, Brother, 1897- 927.5
Our Lady's portrait painter, a story of Raphael. Illus. reproductions from the works of Raphael. Notre Dame, Ind., Dujarie Press [1952] 94 p. illus. 24 cm. [ND623.R2E7] 52-3888
1. Raffaele Sanzio, 1483-1520. 2. Art—Juvenile literature. I. Title.

GILLETTE, Henry S. 92
Raphael; painter of the Renaissance, by Henry S. Gillette. New York, Watts [1967] 160 p. illus. 25 cm. (Immortals of art) Bibliography: p. 148-150. A biography of the sixteenth century Italian painter known for such works as the Sistine Madonna, La Belle Jardiniere, The School of Athens, and Triumph of Galatea. [ND623.R5G5] AC 67
1. Raffaele, Sanzio, 1483-1520. I. Title.

Raffalovich, Katharine Lightner,

RAFFALOVICH, 917.55'03'40924
Katharine Lightner, 1891-
Flying horses: an international autobiography. Lynchburg, Va., J. P. Bell Co., 1967. 227p. illus., ports. 24cm. [CT275.R2A3] 67-22184 7.50
I. Title.
Publisher's address: 816 Main St., Lynchburg, Va. 24505.

Raffalovich, Marc Andre, 1864-1934.

SEWELL, Brocard, ed. 821.8
Two friends: John Gray & Andre Raffalovich; essays biographical & critical with three letters from Andre Raffalovich to J.-K. Huysmans. [Aylesford, Kent] St. Albert's Pr. [dist. Chester Springs, Pa., Dufour] 1963. xiv, 193p. ports. 22cm. Gray, John Henry, 1866-1934. Bibl. 63-5998 12.50
1. Raffalovich, Marc Andre, 1864-1934. I. Title.

Rafferty, Max Lewis, 1917-

CUMMINS, Paul F. 371.2'011'0924
Max Rafferty; a study in simplicity, by Paul F. Cummins. Newhall, Calif., Hogarth Press [1968] 32 p. 21 cm. Bibliography: p. 32. [LB875.R3C8] 68-3171
1. Rafferty, Max Lewis, 1917-

O'NEILL, William 371.2'011'0924
F.
Readin, ritin, and Rafferty; a study of educational fundamentalism, by William O'Neill. Berkeley, Glendessary Press [1969] vii, 147 p. 22 cm. Bibliography: p. 142-147. [LA209.2.O5] 71-98146 2.45
1. Rafferty, Max Lewis, 1917- 2. Education—U.S.—1945-1964. 3. Education—U.S.—1965- I. Title.

Raffles, Thomas Stamford, Sir, 1781-1826.

COLLIS, Maurice, 942.07'3'0924 B
1889-
Raffles. [1st American ed.] New York, John Day Co. [1968] 227 p. illus., maps, ports. 22 cm. Bibliography: p. 221-222. [DS646.26.R3C58 1968] 68-11295
1. Raffles, Thomas Stamford, Sir, 1781-1826. I. Title.

RAFFLES, Thomas 941.07'3'0924 B
Stamford, Sir, 1781-1826.
Statement of the services of Sir Stamford Raffles / with an introd. by John Bastin. Kuala Lumpur ; New York : Oxford University Press, 1978. xi, 72 p. ; 29 cm. (Oxford in Asia historical reprints) [DS598.S7R267] 79-118509 ISBN 0-19-580318-3 : 17.50
1. Raffles, Thomas Stamford, Sir, 1781-1826 2. East India Company (English)—History. 3. Indonesia—Politics and government—1798-1942. 4. Singapore—Politics and government. 5. Colonial administrators—Indonesia—Biography. 6. Colonial administrators—Singapore—Biography. 7. Colonial administrators—Great Britain—Biography.
BIP

Rafinesque, Constantine Samuel, 1783-1840.

RAFINESQUE : 500.9'2'4 B
autobiography and lives / with an introd. by Keir B. Sterling. New York : Arno Press, 1978. p. cm. (Biologists and their world) Reprint of the 1836 ed. of A life of travels and researches in North America and south of Europe by C. S. Rafinesque, printed for the author by F. Turner, Philadelphia; of the 1895 ed. of The life and writings of Rafinesque by R. E. Call, published by J. P. Morton, Louisville, Ky.; and of the 1911 ed. of Rafinesque: a sketch of his life with bibliography by T. J. Fitzpatrick, published by the Historical Dept. of Iowa, Des Moines. [QH31.R13R33 1978] 77-83130 ISBN 0-405-10723-4 : 39.00
1. Rafinesque, Constantine Samuel, 1783-1840. 2. Naturalists—France—Biography. 3. Naturalists—United States—Biography. I. Rafinesque, Constantine Samuel, 1783-1840. A life of travels and researches in North America and south of Europe. 1978. II. Call, Richard Ellsworth, 1856- The life and writings of Rafinesque. 1978. III. Fitzpatrick, T. J., 1868- Rafinesque—a sketch of his life with bibliography. 1978. IV. Title. V. Series.
BIP

Raft, George.

PARISH, James 791.43'028'0924 B
Robert.
The George Raft file: the unauthorized biography, by James Robert Parish, with Steven Whitney. New York, Drake Publishers [1973] 279 p. illus. 24 cm. [PN2287.R22P3] 73-5565 ISBN 0-87749-520-3 7.95
1. Raft, George. I. Whitney, Steven. II. Title.

YABLONSKY, 791.43'028'0924 B
Lewis.
George Raft. New York, McGraw-Hill [1974] 289 p. illus. 24 cm. Bibliography: p. 265-266. [PN2287.R22Y3] 73-21842 ISBN 0-07-072235-8 8.95
1. Raft, George.

Raftery, Anthony,

RAFTERY, Anthony, 891.6'2'13
1784-1835.
Abhrain ata leagtha ar an Reachtuire. Songs ascribed to Raftery, being the fifth chapter of the Songs of Connacht. [Collected, edited, and translated by] Douglas Hyde (An chraoibhin aoibhinn) Introd. by Dominic Daly. New York, Barnes & Noble Books [1973] xii, 371, xvi p. port. 23 cm. English and Irish. Facsim. reprint of the 1st ed. published in 1903, Dublin. [PB1399.R3A63 1903a] 73-175231 10.00
I Hyde, Douglas, Pres. Irish Free State, 1860-1949, ed. II. Title. III. Title: Songs ascribed to Raftery.

Rahner, Karl, 1904-

ROBERTS, Louis. 201
The achievement of Karl Rahner. [New York] Herder and Herder [1967] viii, 312 p. 22 cm. Includes bibliographical references. [BX4705.R287R6] 67-25883
1. Rahner, Karl, 1904- I. Title.

VORGRIMLER, Herbert. 230.20924
Karl Rahner; his life, thought and works. Translated by Edward Quinn. Glen Rock, N.J., Paulist Press [1966, c1965] 96 p. 19 cm. (Deus books) Translation of Karl Rahner; Denkers over God en Wereld. "Notes and bibliography": p. 89-95. "Books by Karl Rahner available in English": p. 96. [BX4705.R287V63 1966a] 66-4765
1. Rahner, Karl, 1904- I. Title. II. Series.

Railroad engineers—Biography.

MARSHALL, John, 625.1'0092'2
1922(May1)-
A biographical dictionary of railway engineers / John Marshall. Newton Abbot [Eng.] ; North Pomfret, Vt. : David & Charles, c1978. 247 p. ; 23 cm. Includes index. [TF139.M35] 77-85011 ISBN 0-7153-7489-3 : 25.00
1. Railroad engineers—Biography. I. Title.
BIP

Railroads—U. S.—Biog.

*MURPHY, Nicholas V. 385.2
The fun and work of railroading. Philadelphia, Dorrance [1968] 94p. 21cm. (B) 3.00
1. Railroads—U. S.—Biog. I. Title.

Railroads—Juvenile literature.

MURPHY, Nicholas V. 625.1'00924
The fun and work of railroading, by Nicholas V. Murphy. Philadelphia, Dorrance [1968] 94 p. illus. 22 cm. Autobiographical. The author relates the exhilaration and thrills he experienced while working as fireman and engineer on steam locomotives during the days when railroading was "king." [TF148.M86] 68-31575 3.00
1. Railroads—Juvenile literature. I. Title.

Railroads—United States.

FRIMBO, Ernest M. 385'.092'4 B
All aboard with E. M. Frimbo; world's greatest railroad buff. [Compiled by] Rogers E. M. Whitaker & Anthony Hiss. New York, Grossman Publishers, 1974. 14 p. 21 cm. Excerpts from the author's autobiography. [HE2751.F68] 74-173597
1. Railroads—United States. 2. Railroads—United States—Commuter traffic. I. Whitaker, Rogers E. M. II. Hiss, Anthony. III. Title. BIP

Raine, Edgar C.

RAINE, Edgar C. 920
Here and there and everywhere; a factual story of unusual events encountered during forty-seven years of lecturing at universities, colleges, and clubs. New York, Greenwich Book Publishers [c.1959] 49p. 21cm. 59-15010 1.95
I. Title.

Raine, Kathleen Jessie, 1908- — Biography.

RAINE, Kathleen Jessie, 1908- 821'.9'12 B
The land unknown / Kathleen Raine. New York : G. Braziller, 1975. 207 p. ; 22 cm. [PR6035.A37Z524 1975] 75-10995 ISBN 0-8076-0800-9 : 6.95
1. Raine, Kathleen Jessie, 1908- — Biography. I. Title. BIP

RAINE, Kathleen Jessie, 1908- 821'.9'12 B
The lion's mouth / by Kathleen Raine. New York : G. Braziller, [1978] p. cm. Autobiography. [PR6035.A37Z525 1978] 77-6122 ISBN 0-8076-0877-7 : 7.95
1. Raine, Kathleen Jessie, 1908- — Biography. 2. Authors, English—20th century—Biography. I. Title. BIP

Raines, Robert Arnold.

RAINES, Robert Arnold. 287'632'0924 B
Going home / Robert A. Raines. 1st ed. San Francisco : Harper & Row, c1979. x, 145 p. ; 21 cm. [BR1725.R25A33 1979] 78-15834 ISBN 0-06-066768-0 : 6.95
1. Raines, Robert Arnold. 2. Christian biography—United States. I. Title. BIP

Rainey, Henry Thomas, 1860-1934.

WALLER, Robert A., 1931- 328.73'092'4 B
Rainey of Illinois : a political biography, 1903-34 / Robert A. Waller. Urbana : University of Illinois Press, c1977. p. cm. (Illinois studies in social sciences ; 60) Includes index. Bibliography: p. [E748.R22W34] 77-23859 ISBN 0-252-00647-X : 12.50
1. Rainey, Henry Thomas, 1860-1934. 2. Legislators—United States—Biography. 3. Illinois—Politics and government—1865-1950. 4. United States—Politics and government—1865-1933. I. Title. II. Series. BIP

Rainey, Joseph H., 1832-1887.

PACKWOOD, Cyril Outerbridge, 1930- 328.73'092'4 B
Detour—Bermuda, destination—U.S. House of Representatives : the life of Joseph Hayne Rainey / by Cyril Outerbridge Packwood. Hamilton, Bermuda : Baxter's, c1977. 39, [1] p. : ports. ; 23 cm. Bibliography: p. 39-[40] [E664.R15P3] 77-370339
1. Rainey, Joseph H., 1832-1887. 2. United States. Congress. House—Biography. 3. Reconstruction. 4. Legislators—United States—Biography. I. Title.

Rainsford, William Stephen,

RAINSFORD, William Stephen, 1850-1933. 283'.0924 B
The story of a varied life; an autobiography. Freeport, N.Y., Books for Libraries Press [1970] 481 p. illus., ports. 23 cm. Reprint of the 1922 ed. [BX5995.R3A35 1970] 70-126249
I. Title.

Rais, Gilles de Laval, seigneur de, 1404-1440.

WILSON, Thomas, 1832-1902. 944'.026'0924 B
Blue-beard; a contribution to history and folk-lore, being the history of Gilles de Retz of Brittany, France, who was executed at Nantes in 1440 A.D., and who was the original of Blue-beard in the tales of Mother Goose. New York, B. Blom, 1971. xv, 212 p. illus. 21 cm. Reprint of the 1899 ed. [DC102.8.R2N6 1971] 74-174394
1. Rais, Gilles de Laval, seigneur de, 1404-1440. I. Title.

Rajagopalachari, Chakravarti, 1878-1972.

CHATTERJEE, Bimanesh, 1907- 954'.82'0350924 B
Thousand days with Rajaji. New Delhi, Affiliated East-West Press [1973] 136 p. 24 cm. [DS481.R27C48] 73-906982
1. Rajagopalachari, Chakravarti, 1878-1972. I. Title.
Distributed by International Publication Service; 7.50. BIP

Raleigh, Sir Walter, 1552?-1618.

ADAMSON, Jack H. 942.05'5'0924 B
The shepherd of the ocean; an account of Sir Walter Raleigh and his times, by J. H. Adamson and H. F. Folland. Boston, Gambit, 1969. 464 p. illus., maps, ports. 24 cm. Bibliography: p. 454-456. [DA86.22.R2A3] 69-17747 8.95
1. Raleigh, Walter, Sir, 1552?-1618. I. Folland, H. F., 1906- joint author. II. Title.

BAKER, Nina (Brown), 1888- 923.242
Sir Walter Raleigh. [1st ed.] New York, Harcourt, Brace [1950] 191 p. port. 22 cm. Bibliography: p. 185-186. [DA86.22.R2B3] 923.942 50-9893
1. Raleigh. Sir Walter. 1552?-1618. I. Title.

BUCKMASTER, Henrietta, pseud. 923.942
Walter Raleigh: man of two worlds. Illustrated by H. B. Vestal. New York, Random House [1964] 181 p. col. illus. 22 cm. (World landmark books, w-58) Bibliography: p. [175]-176. [DA86.22.R2B83] 64-11176
1. Raleigh, Sir Walter, 1552?-1618 — Juvenile literature. I. Title. BIP

DE LEEUW, Adele Louise, 1899- 942.05'5'0924 B
A world explorer: Sir Walter Raleigh, by Adele deLeeuw. Illustrated by Adolph Le Moult. Champaign, Ill., Garrard Pub. Co. [1964] 96 p. col. illus. 24 cm. ([World explorer books]) A short biography of the Englishman who explored areas of America, made attempts to establish an English colony on Roanoke Island, and led expeditions to search for gold in South America. [DA86.88.R2D36] 92 AC 68
1. Raleigh, Walter, Sir, 1552?-1618. I. Le Moult, Adolph, illus. II. Title.

EDWARDS, Philip. 828'.3'09 B
Sir Walter Ralegh / by Philip Edwards. Folcroft, Pa. : Folcroft Library Editions, 1976. p. cm. Reprint of the 1953 ed. published by Longmans, Green, London, in series: Men and books. Includes index. Bibliography: p. [PR2335.E3 1976] 76-39784 ISBN 0-8414-3969-9 lib. bdg. : 20.00
1. Raleigh, Walter, Sir, 1552?-1618. 2. Authors, English—Early modern, 1500-1700—Biography. I. Title. II. Series: Men and books.

FECHER, Constance, 1911- 942.05'5'0924 B
The last Elizabethan; a portrait of Sir Walter Ralegh. New York, Farrar, Straus & Giroux [1972] xiii, 241 p. illus. 21 cm. Bibliography: p. [233]-235. [DA86.22.R2F4] 74-178882 ISBN 0-374-34361-6 5.50
1. Raleigh, Walter, Sir, 1552?-1618. I. Title.

GOSSE, Edmund William, Sir, 1849-1928. 942.05'5'0924 B
Raleigh. [Folcroft, Pa.] Folcroft Library Editions, 1974. p. cm. Reprint of the 1888 ed. published by Longmans, Green, London, in series: English worthies. [DA86.22.R2G6 1974] 74-14939 15.00
1. Raleigh, Walter, Sir, 1552?-1618. I. Series: English worthies.

GREENBLATT, Stephen Jay. 942.05'5'0924
Sir Walter Raleigh; the Renaissance man and his roles [by] Stephen J. Greenblatt. New Haven, Yale University Press, 1973. xii, 209 p. port. 23 cm. (Yale studies in English, 183) Includes bibliographical references. [PR2335.G7] 73-77150 7.95
1. Raleigh, Walter, Sir, 1552?-1618. I. Title. II. Series.

IRWIN, Margaret Emma Faith. 923.942
That great Lucifer; a portrait of Sir Walter Raleigh, [1st American ed.] New York, Harcourt, Brace [1960] 320 p. illus. 22 cm. [DA86.22.R17 1960a] 60-10925
1. Raleigh, Walter, Sir, 1552?-1618. I. Title.

LACEY, Robert. 942.05'5'0924 B
Sir Walter Ralegh. [1st American ed.] New York, Atheneum, 1974 [c1973] 415 p. illus. 25 cm. Includes bibliographical references. [DA86.22.R2L3 1974] 73-80750 ISBN 0-689-10570-3 10.95
1. Raleigh, Walter, Sir, 1552?-1618. BIP

MAGNUS, Philip Montefiore, Sir bart., 1906- 942.05'5'0924 (B)
Sir Walter Raleigh, by Philip Magnus. Hamden, Conn., Archon Books [1968] 158 p. maps, ports. 21 cm. (Makers of history) [DA86.22.R2M17] 68-3593
1. Raleigh, Sir Walter, 1552?-1618. I. Title.

MAGNUS, Philip Montefiore bart., Sir 1906- 942.05'5'0924
Sir Walter Raleigh, by Philip Magnus. Hamden, Conn., Archon [1968] 158p. maps, ports. 21cm. (Makers of hist.) [DA86.22.R2M17 1968] (B) 68-3583 4.00
1. Raleigh, Sir Walter, 1552?—1618. I. Title.

MAGNUS, Philip Montefiore, Sir Bart., 1906- 923.242
Sir Walter Raleigh. New York, Macmillan [1956] 158p. illus. 19cm. (Brief lives, no. 14) [DA86.22.R2M17 1956] 923.942 56-4868
1. Raleigh, Walter, Sir bart., 1552-1618. I. Title.

MAGNUS, Philip Montefiore, Sir, bart., 1906- 942.05'5'0924 B
Sir Walter Raleigh, by Philip Magnus. Hamden, Conn., Archon Books [1968] 158 p. maps, ports. 21 cm. (Makers of history) [DA86.22.R2M17 1968] 68-3593
1. Raleigh, Walter, Sir, 1552?-1618.

MAGNUS, Philip Montefiore, bart., Sir 1906- 923.242
Sir Walter Raleigh. New York, Macmillan [1956] 158p. illus. 19cm. (Brief lives, no.14) [DA86.22.R2M17 1956] [DA86.22.R2M17 1956] 923.942 56-4868 56-4868
1. Raleigh, Walter, bart., Sir 1552?-1618. I. Title.

QUINN, David Beers 923.942
Raeigh and the British Empire. [New, rev. ed.] New York, Collier [1962] 220p. 18cm. (Men & hist., AS386V) Bibl. .95 pap.,
1. Raleigh, Walter, Sir 1552?-1618. 2. America—Disc. & explor.—English. 3. Gt. Brit.—Colonies—Hist. I. Title.

RALEIGH, Walter, Sir, 1552?-1618. 942.05'5'0924
The works of Sir Walter Ralegh, kt., now first collected. To which are prefixed the lives of the author by Oldys and Birch. New York, B. Franklin [1965] 8 v. 24 cm. (Burt Franklin research and source works series, 73) Reprint of the 1829 ed. Contents.Contents.—v. 1. The life of Sir Walter Ralegh, by W. Oldys. The life of Sir Walter Ralegh, by T. Birch.—v. 2.-7. The history of the world.—v. 8. Miscellaneous works. [PR2334.A1 1965] 78-6383
1. Oldys, William, 1696-1761. The life of Sir Walter Ralegh. II. Birch, Thomas, 1705-1766. The life of Sir Walter Ralegh.

ROWSE, Alfred Leslie, 1903- v. 12
Ralegh and the Throckmortons. London, Macmillan; New York, St. Martin's Press, 1962. xi, 347 p. ports., facsims. 23 cm. American ed. (New York, Harper) has title: Sir Walter Ralegh; his family and private life. 63-56649
1. Raleigh, Sir Walter, 1552?-1618. I. Title.

ROWSE, Alfred Leslie, 1903- 923.942
Sir Walter Raleigh, his family and private life. [1st ed.] New York, Harper [1962] 348 p. illus. 25 cm. London ed. (Macmillan) has title: Ralegh and the Throckmortons. [DA86.22.R2R65 1962] 62-9895
1. Raleigh, Walter, Sir, 1552?-1618.

ROWSE, Alfred Leslie, 1903- 942.05'5'0924 B
Sir Walter Ralegh, his family and private life / by A. L. Rowse. Westport, Conn. : Greenwood Press, 1975, c1962. xi, 348 p., [4] leaves of plates : ill. ; 23 cm. Reprint of the ed. published by Harper, New York, which was published in London under title: Ralegh and the Throckmortons. Includes bibliographical references and index. [DA86.22.R2R65 1975] 73-21492 ISBN 0-8371-6388-9 lib.bdg. : 18.75
1. Raleigh, Walter, Sir, 1552?-1618. I. Title.

SABATINI, Rafael, 1875-1950. 920.02
Heroic lives; Richard I: Saint Francis of Assisi: Joan of Arc: Sir Walter Ralegh: Lord Nelson: Florence Nightingale. Freeport, N.Y., Books for Libraries Press [1971, c1934] 416 p. 23 cm. (Essay index reprint series) [D106.S28 1971] 70-99648 ISBN 0-8369-2071-6
1. Richard I, King of England, 1157-1199. 2. Francesco d'Assisi, Saint, 1182-1226. 3. Jeanne d'Arc, Saint, 1412-1431. 4. Raleigh, Walter Sir, 1552?-1618. 5. Nelson, Horatio Nelson, Viscount, 1758-1805. 6. Nightingale, Florence, 1820-1910. I. Title.

SAMS, Conway Whittle, 1864-1935. 975.5'01
The conquest of Virginia; the first attempt [being an account of Sir Walter Raleigh's colony on Roanoke Island, based on original records, and incidents in the life of Raleigh, 1584-1602] Spartanburg, S.C., Reprint Co. [1973, c1924] xxviii, 547 p. illus. 22 cm. Reprint of the ed. published by Keyser-Doherty Printing Corp, Norfolk, Va. Includes bibliographical references. [F229.S242 1973] 73-668 ISBN 0-87152-123-7 30.00
1. Raleigh, Walter, Sir, 1552?-1618. 2. Virginia—History—Colonial period. 3. Raleigh's Roanoke colonies, 1584-1590. I. Title.

THE shepherd of the ocean; Sir Walter Raleigh. A biography for young people. illustrated by Bruno Frost. New York, D. McKay Co. [1952] 179p. illus. 22cm. [DA86.22.R2N6] [DA86.22.R2N6] 923.942 52-12741 52-12741 923.242
1. Raleigh, Sir Walter, 1552?-1618. I. Norman, Charles, 1904-

STEBBING, William, 1832-1926. 942.05'5'0924 B
Sir Walter Ralegh; a biography. New York, Lemma Pub. Corp., 1972. xxvi, 413 p. port. 23 cm. Reprint of the 1899 ed.

Bibliography: p. [xiii]-xxvi. [DA86.22.R2S8 1972] 73-180772 ISBN 0-87696-033-6 22.50
1. Raleigh, Walter, Sir, 1552?-1618.

STRATHMANN, Ernest Albert, 1906- 211.7'092'4
Sir Walter Ralegh; a study in Elizabethan skepticism, by Ernest A. Strathmann. New York, Octagon Books, 1973 [c1951] ix, 292 p. 23 cm. Reprint of the ed. published by Columbia University Press, New York. Includes bibliographical references. [DA86.22.R2S86 1973] 73-8897 ISBN 0-374-97640-6 11.50
1. Raleigh, Walter, Sir, 1552?-1618. 2. Skepticism.

SYME, Ronald, 1910- j92
Walter Raleigh. Illustrated by William Stobbs. New York, Morrow, 1962. 96 p. illus. 22 cm. [DA86.22.R2S9] 62-7093
1. Raleigh, Sir Walter, 1552?-1618 — Juvenile literature. I. Title. **BIP**

THOREAU, Henry David, 1817-1862. 942.05'5'0924 B
Sir Walter Raleigh / by Henry David Thoreau ; introd. by Franklin Benjamin Sanborn ; edited by Henry Aiken Metcalf. New York : Gordon Press, 1976, c1905. p. cm. Reprint of the ed. published by the Bibliophile Society, Boston. [DA86.22.R2T6 1976] 76-1847 lib.bdg. : 34.95
1. Raleigh, Walter, Sir, 1552?-1618. I. Metcalf, Henry Aiken, 1845-1911.

TREASE, Geoffrey, 1909- 923.942
Sir Walter Raleigh, captain & adventurer. New York, Vanguard Press [1950] 248 p. 21 cm. [DA86.22.R2T78] 50-10458
1. Raleigh, Walter, Sir, 1552?-1618. **BIP**

WALLACE, Willard Mosher, 1911- 923.942
Sir Walter Raleigh. Princeton, N.J., Princeton University Press, 1959. 334 p. illus. 25 cm. Includes bibliography. [DA86.22.R2W33] 59-9677
1. Raleigh, Sir Walter, 1552?-1618. I. Title.

WILLIAMS, Norman Lloyd 923.942
Sir Walter Raleigh. [Chester Springs, Pa.] Dufour, 1963[c 1962] viii, 295p. illus., ports., map (on lining paper) 23cm. Bibl. 63-20550 6.00
1. Raleigh, Walter, Sir 1552?-1618. I. Title.

WINTON, John, pseud. 942.05'5'0924 B
Sir Walter Ralegh / John Winton. 1st American ed. New York : Coward, McCann & Geoghegan, 1975. 352 p., [8] leaves of plates : ill. ; 26 cm. Includes index. Bibliography: p. 344-348. [DA86.22.R2W68 1975] 74-22658 ISBN 0-698-10648-2 : 15.00
1. Raleigh, Walter, Sir, 1552?-1618.

Raleigh, Walter, Sir 1552?-1618—Juvenile literature.

BUCKMASTER, Henrietta, pseud. 923.942
Walter Raleigh: man of two worlds. Illus. by H. B. Vestal. New York, Random [c.1964] 181p. col. illus. 22cm. (World landmark bks., W-58) Bibl. 64-11176 1.95; 2.28 lib. ed.,
1. Raleigh, Walter, Sir 1552?-1618—Juvenile literature. I. Title.

SYME, Ronald 920
Walter Raleigh. Illus. by William Stobbs. New York, Morrow [c.]1962. 96p. 62-7093 2.75 bds.,
1. Raleigh, Walter, Sir 1552?-1618—Juvenile literature. I. Title.

Raley, John Wesley, 1902-1968.

RALEY, Helen Thames. 378.1'1'0924 B
An uncommon man; the life of John Wesley Raley. Waco, Tex., Word Books [1970] 264 p. illus., ports. 23 cm. [LD4291.O717 1934.R3] 78-135351 5.95
1. Raley, John Wesley, 1902-1968. I. Title.

Ralston family.

SMITH, Norma Dell. 929'.2'0973
Lewis Ralston / by Norma Dell Smith. [Atlanta] : Smith, [1974] 20, [5] leaves : ill. ; 29 cm. [CS71.R172 1974] 75-313355
1. Ralston family. 2. Ralston, Lewis, b. 1804.

Ralston, William Chapman, 1826-1875.

LAVENDER, David Sievert, 1910- 332.1'092'4 B
Nothing seemed impossible : William C. Ralston and early San Francisco / by David Lavender ; foreword by J. E. Wallace Sterling. 1st ed. Palo Alto, Calif. : American West Pub. Co., [1975] p. cm. (Western biography series) Includes index. Bibliography: p. [HG2463.R34L38] 75-6321 ISBN 0-910118-64-7 : 12.95
1. Ralston, William Chapman, 1826-1875. 2. Bankers—San Francisco. I. Title.

Rama, Swami, 1925-

BOYD, Doug. 181'.4
Swami / Douglas Boyd. 1st ed. New York : Random House, c1976. xx, 330 p. ; 22 cm. [BL2003.B6] 75-40566 ISBN 0-394-49603 5 : 10.00
1. Rama, Swami, 1925- 2. Boyd, Doug. 3. Sadhus—India. 4. India—Religion. I. Title. **BIP**

Ramakrishna, 1836-1886.

FRENCH, Harold W. 294.5'55
The swan's wide waters : Ramakrishna and Western culture / Harold W. French. Port Washington, N.Y. : Kennikat Press, 1974. viii, 220 p. ; 24 cm. (National university publications) Includes bibliographical references and index. [BL1270.R3F73] 74-77657 ISBN 0-8046-9055-3 : 11.95
1. Ramakrishna, 1836-1886. 2. Vivekananda, Swami, 1863-1902. I. Title. **BIP**

ISHERWOOD, Christopher, 1904- 921.9
Ramakrishna and his disciples. New York, Simon and Schuster [1965] 348 p. illus., map, ports. 24 cm. Bibliography: p. 335-337. [BL1270.R318] 65-17100
1. Ramakrishna, 1836-1886. I. Title. **BIP**

LEMAITRE, Solange. 294.5'55'0924 B
Ramakrishna and the vitality of Hinduism. Translated by Charles Lam Markmann. New York, Funk & Wagnalls [1969] xviii, 244 p. illus. 21 cm. Bibliography: p. 232-234. [BL1270.R3L43] 68-54059 4.95
1. Ramakrishna, 1836-1886. 2. Hinduism. I. Title.

MULLER, Friedrich Max, 1823-1900. 294.5'55'0924 B
Ramakrishna, his life and sayings / by F. Max Muller. New York : AMS Press, [1975] p. cm. Reprint of the 1899 ed. published by Scribner, New York. [B5134.R38M83 1975] 73-18812 ISBN 0-404-11452-0 : 14.50
1. Ramakrishna, 1836-1886. I. Ramakrishna, 1836-1886. Ramakrishna, his life and sayings. 1975. II. Title.

SATPRAKASHANANDA, Swami. 294.5'55'0924 B
The significance of Sri Ramakrishna's life and message in the present age : with the author's reminiscences of Holy Mother and some direct disciples / by Swami Satprakashananda. St. Louis : Vedanta Society of St. Louis, 1976. 208 p. ; 20 cm. On spine: Sri Ramakrishna's life and message in the present age. Includes bibliographical references and index. [BL1175.R26S26] 75-46386 ISBN 0-916356-54-X : 6.00
1. Ramakrishna, 1836-1886. 2. Hinduism—Biography. I. Title. II. Title: Sri Ramakrishna's life and message in the present age.

Ramakrishna, 1836-1886—Addresses, essays, lectures.

SRI Ramakrishna, in the eyes of Brahma and Christian admirers 294.5'55'0924 / edited by Nanda Mookerjee. 1st ed. Calcutta : Firma KLM, 1976. xiv, 141, [9] p., [2] leaves of plates : ill. ; 22 cm. Includes bibliographical references and index. [BL1175.R26S693] 76-904430 Rs22.00 ($4.00 U.S.)
1. Ramakrishna, 1836-1886—Addresses, essays, lectures. I. Mookerjee, Nanda. **BIP**

Ramamohana Raya, raja, 1774?-1833.

SINGH, Iqbal. v. 12
Rammohun Roy; a biographical inquiry into the making of modern India. New York, Asia Pub. House [1958- v. front. 23 cm.
1. Ramamohana Raya, raja, 1774?-1833. I. Title.

Ramana, Maharshi.

MAHADEVAN, Telliyavaram Mahadevan Ponnambalam, 1911 294.5'6'1 B
Ramana Maharshi : the sage of Arunacala / T. M. P. Mahadevan. London : Allen & Unwin, 1977. 186 p. ; 21 cm. Includes bibliographical references and index. [BL1175.R342M33] 77-354800 ISBN 0-04-149040-1 : 9.95 ISBN 0-04-149041-X pbk. : 4.50
1. Ramana, Maharshi. 2. Hindus—Biography. **BIP**

OSBORNE, Arthur, 1906- 294.5'6'10924 B
Ramana Maharshi and the path of self-knowledge. Foreword by S. Radhakrishnan. New York, S. Weiser [1970] 207 p. port. 21 cm. Reprint of the 1954 ed. [BL1146.R352O8 1970b] 76-18194 3.00 (pbk)
1. Ramana, Maharsi. **BIP**

Ramanujan Aiyangar, Srinivasa, 1887-1920.

RANGANATHAN, Shiyali Ramamrita, rao sahib, 1892- 510'.0924
Ramanujan, the man and the mathematician [by] S.R. Ranganathan. [1st ed.] Bombay, New York, Asia Pub. House [1967] 138 p. illus., facsims., ports. 23 cm. (Great thinkers of India series, 1) [QA29.R3R3] SA68
1. Ramanujan Aiyangar, Srinivasa, 1887-1920. I. Title.

RANGANATHAN, Shiyali Ramamrita, Rao Sahib, 1892- 510'.0924
Ramanujan, the man and the mathematician [by] S. R. Ranganathan. [1st ed.] Bombay, New York, Asia Pub. House [1967] 138 p. illus., facsims., ports. 23 cm. (Great thinkers of India series, 1) [QA29.R3R3] SA 68 Rs18
1. Ramanujan Aiyangar, Srinivasa, 1887-1920.

Ramarau, Rama V. M. G.,

RAMARAU, Rama V. M. G., 1910- 923.254
Of men, matter, and me. New York, Asia Pub. [dist. Taplinger, 1962, c.1961] 88p. 62-3050 3.75
I. Title. **BIP**

Rambo, Victor.

WILSON, Dorothy Clarke. 617.7'0092'4 B
Apostle of sight : the story of Victor Rambo, surgeon to India's blind / by Dorothy Clarke Wilson. Chappaqua, NY : Christian Herald Books, c1980. p. cm. [RE36.R35W54] 79-55678 ISBN 0-915684-54-3 : 7.95
1. Rambo, Victor. 2. Ophthalmologists—United States—Biography. 3. Ophthalmologists—India—Biography. 4. Christian life—1960- I. Title.

Rameau, Jean Philippe, 1683-1764.

GIRDLESTONE, Cuthbert Morton, 1895- 927.8
Jean-Philippe Rameau, his life and work. [Reissue] London, Cassell [dist. New York, Dover, 1965, c. 1957] viii, 627p. illus., ports., music. 22cm. [ML410.R2G5] 58-1564 12.50
1. Rameau, Jean Philippe, 1683-1764. I. Title.

GIRDLESTONE, Cuthbert Morton, 1895- 780'.924 B
Jean-Philippe Rameau: his life and work, by Cuthbert Girdlestone. [Rev. and enl. ed.] New York, Dover Publications [1969] x, 631 p. illus., music, ports. 22 cm. Bibliography: p. [578]-592. [ML410.R2G5 1969] 74-78058 5.00
1. Rameau, Jean Philippe, 1683-1764.

Rameses II, King of Egypt.

SCHMIDT, John D. 932'.01'0924
Ramesses II; a chronological structure for his reign [by] John D. Schnidt. Baltimore, Johns Hopkins University Press [1973] vii, 216 p. 26 cm. (The Johns Hopkins University Near Eastern studies) Originally presented as the author's thesis, Johns Hopkins, 1970. Bibliography: p. 195-207. [DT88.S34 1973] 72-6558 ISBN 0-8018-1455-3 10.00
1. Rameses II, King of Egypt. 2. Egypt—History—To 332 B.C.—Chronology. I. Title. II. Series: Johns Hopkins University. Near Eastern studies.

Ramirez, Armando Socarras—Juvenile literature.

SCHACHTEL, Roger. 972.91'064
Fantastic flight to freedom/ Roger Schachtel ; ill. Charles Shaw. Milwaukee : Raintree Publishers, c1980. p. cm. Relates the experiences of two teenage boys who decide to escape from Castro'sCuba by stowing away in the landing gear of an airplane. [F1788.S385] 79-23116 ISBN 0-8172-1551-4 (lib. bdg.) : 7.99
1. Ramirez, Armando Socarras—Juvenile literature. 2. Cuba—History—1959- —Juvenile literature. 3. Refugees, Political—Cuba—Biography—Juvenile literature. 4. Refugees, Political—United States—Biography—Juvenile literature. I. Shaw, Charles, 1941- II. Title. **BIP**

Rammohun Roy, Raja, 1772?-1833.

CARPENTER, Mary, 1807-1877. 294.5'562'0924 B
The last days in England of the Rajah Rammohun Roy / by Mary Carpenter. Riddhi ed. / edited by Swapan Majumdar. Calcutta : Riddhi, 1976. xii, 159 p., [1] leaf of plates : ill. ; 22 cm. Running title: Rammohun Roy. First published in 1866 by Trubner, London. Includes bibliographical references. [BL1265.R3C3 1976] 76-903877 Rs25.00
1. Rammohun Roy, Raja, 1772?-1833. 2. Brahma-samaj—Biography. 3. Hindus—Biography. I. Majumdar, Swapan, 1946- II. Title.

Ramose—Juvenile literature.

GLUBOK, Shirley. 932'.01'0924 B
The mummy of Ramose : the life and death of an ancient Egyptian nobleman / Shirley Glubok and Alfred Tamarin. 1st ed. New York : Harper & Row, c1978. 82 p. : ill. ; 23 cm. Includes index. Bibliography: p. 75-76. Describes the life of an Egyptian nobleman of the Eighteenth Dynasty and the mummification and funeral rites that followed his death. [DT62.M7G53 1978] 76-21392 ISBN 0-06-022039-2 : 6.95 ISBN 0-06-022042-2 lib.bdg. : 6.79
1. Ramose—Juvenile literature. 2. Mummies—Juvenile literature. 3. Funeral rites and ceremonies—Egypt—Juvenile

literature. 4. Egypt—Nobility—Biography—Juvenile literature. I. Tamarin, Alfred H., joint author. II. Title.

Ramsay, Allan, 1685?-1758.

MARTIN, Burns. 821'.5
Allan Ramsay, a study of his life and works. Westport, Conn., Greenwood Press [1973] vi, 203 p. front. 19 cm. Reprint of the 1931 ed. Bibliography: p. [187]-195. [PR3657.M3 1973] 72-605 ISBN 0-8371-5830-3
1. Ramsay, Allan, 1685-1758. **BIP**

SMEATON, William Henry Oliphant, 1856-1914. 821'.5
Allan Ramsay / by Oliphant Smeaton. New York : AMS Press, 1977. 160 p. ; 18 cm. Reprint of the 1896 ed. published by O. Anderson & Ferrier, Edinburgh, in series: Famous Scots series. [PR3657.S6 1977] 77-144486 ISBN 0-404-08599-7 : 12.00
1. Ramsay, Allan, 1685?-1758. 2. Poets, Scottish—18th century—Biography. I. Title. **BIP**

Ramsay. Andrew Michael, 1686-1743.

HENDERSON, George David, 1888- 920
Chevalier Ramsay. London, New York, Nelson [1952] 246 p. 22 cm. [CT788.R23H4] 52-3281
1. Ramsay. Andrew Michael, 1686-1743. I. Title.

Ramsay, Jack, 1925-

RAMSAY, Jack, 1925- 796.32'3'0924 [B]
The coach's art / by Jack Ramsay, with John Strawn. Forest Grove, Or. : Timber Press, c1978. x, 174 p. : ill. ; 22 cm. Stamped on t.p.: Exclusive distributor, ISBS, inc., P.O. Box 555, Forest Grove, OR. [GV884.R33A33] 78-5458 ISBN 0-917304-36-5 pbk. : 9.95
1. Ramsay, Jack, 1925- 2. Basketball coaches—United States—Biography. I. Strawn, John, joint author. II. Title. **BIP**

Ramsey, Arthur Michael, Abp. of Canterbury, 1904-

SIMPSON, James Beasley 922.342
The hundredth Archbishop of Canterbury. New York, Harper [c.1962] 262p. illus. 22cm. 62-14581 6.00
1. Ramsey, Arthur Michael, Abp. of Canterbury, 1904- I. Title.

Ramsey, Ian T.

EDWARDS, David Lawrence. 283'.092'4 B
Ian Ramsey, Bishop of Durham; a memoir [by] David L. Edwards. London, New York, Oxford University Press, 1973. 101 p. illus., port. 23 cm. [BX5199.R22E38] 73-179441 ISBN 0-19-213111-7 £2.00
1. Ramsey, Ian T. I. Title.

Ranade, Mahadev Govind, Rao Bahadur, 1842-1901.

PARVATE, Trimbak Vishnu, 1901- 923.254
Mahadev Govind Ranade, a biography [by] T. V. Parvate. New York, Asia Pub. [dist. Taplinger, 1964, c.1963] x, 326p. port. 23cm. Bibl. 64-5882 10.75
1. Ranade, Mahadev Govind,rao bahadur, 1842-1901. I. Title.

TUCKER, Richard P. 954.03'5'0924 B
Ranade and the roots of Indian nationalism / Richard P. Tucker. Chicago : University of Chicago Press, 1976, c1972. xiii, 259 p. : map ; 23 cm. (Midway reprint) Includes index. Bibliography: p. 241-254. [DS479.1.R32T8 1976] 72-80683 ISBN 0-226-81532-3 pbk. : 11.00
1. Ranade, Mahadev Govind, Rao Bahadur, 1842-1901. 2. Statesmen—India—Biography. 3. Nationalism—India. 4. Maharashtra, India (State)—Politics and government. I. Title. **BIP**

Ranch life.

ELLISON, Glenn R., 1891- 630.11'24 B
Cowboys under the Mogollon Rim [by] Glenn R. "Slim" Ellison. With sketches by the author. [Tucson] University of Arizona Press [1968] 274 p. illus. 24 cm. Autobiographical. [CT275.E3847A3] 68-9337 6.50
1. Ranch life. I. Title. **BIP**

JORDAN, Grace Edgington. 917.96
Home below Hell's Canyon. New York, Crowell [1954] 243 p. illus. 21 cm. Autobiographical. [F596.J6] 54-6332
1. Ranch life. 2. Frontier and pioneer life—Idaho. I. Title. **BIP**

RANDOLPH, Edmund, 1903- 917.86
Hell among the yearlings. Drawings by James Ryan. [1st ed.] New York, W. W. Norton [1955] 308 p. illus. 22 cm. Autobiographical. "Published in Great Britain under the title Don't fence them in." [F596.R3] 55-14919
1. Ranch life. I. Title.

Ranch life—Arizona.

JEFFERS, Jo (Johnson) 1931- 630.1
Ranch wife, by Jo Jeffers. With illus. by Ross Santee. [1st ed.] Garden City, N.Y., Doubleday, 1964. 273 p. illus. 22 cm. Autobiographical. [CT275.J45A3] 64-19298
1. Ranch life—Arizona. I. Title.

Ranch life—Queensland.

BRITT, Margaret. 364.14
Pardon my boots. Melbourne, Lansdowne Press [1963] 153 p. illus. 22 cm. Autobiographical [DU272.B7A3 1963] 68-46111
1. Ranch life—Queensland. I. Title.

Ranch life—San Pedro Valley, Ariz.

BOURNE, Eulalia. 917.91'75'0350924
Woman in levi's. Illustrated by Vic Donahue. [Tucson] University of Arizona Press [1967] xiv, 208 p. illus. 20 cm. Autobiographical. [F817.S25B6] 66-27382
1. Ranch life—San Pedro Valley, Ariz. 2. Rural schools—Arizona. I. Title. **BIP**

Randall, Dick.

CHENEY, Roberta Carkeek. 647'.94786'0924 B
Music, saddles & flapjacks : dudes at the OTO ranch / Roberta Cheney and Clyde Erskine. Missoula, Mont. : Mountain Press Pub. Co., [1978] p. cm. [TX910.5.R35C43] 78-13774 ISBN 0-87842-074-6 : 12.95
1. Randall, Dick. 2. OTO Ranch. 3. Dude ranchers—Montana—Biography. I. Erskine, Clyde, joint author. II. Title. **BIP**

Randall, James Garfield, 1881-1953.

RANDALL, Ruth (Painter) 973.7'072 B
I, Ruth: autobiography of a marriage; the self-told story of the woman who married the great Lincoln scholar, James G. Randall, and through her interest in his work became a Lincoln author herself. [1st ed.] Boston, Little, Brown [1968] xiv, 266 p. illus., ports. 21 cm. [E175.5.R34A3] 68-15389 5.95
1. Randall, James Garfield, 1881-1953. I. Title.

Randall, Margaret (Randall) 1936-

RANDALL, Margaret (Randall) 1936- 811'.5'4 B
Part of the solution; portrait of a revolutionary [by] Margaret Randall. [New York, New Directions, 1973] 192 p. 21 cm. (A New Directions book) [PS3535.A56277Z52] 72-93974 ISBN 0-8112-0470-7 9.95
1. Randall, Margaret (Randall) 1936- I. Title.
Pbk. 2.95; ISBN 0-8112-0471-5. **BIP**

Randle, Frank, 1901-1957.

NUTTALL, Jeff. 791'.092'4 B
King Twist : a portrait of Frank Randle / Jeff Nuttall. London ; Boston : Routledge and Paul, 1978. ix, 139 p., [10] leaves of plates : ill. ; 23 cm. [PN2598.R33N87] 78-40548 ISBN 0-7100-8977-5 : 14.25
1. Randle, Frank, 1901-1957. 2. Comedians—England—Biography. I. Title. **BIP**

Randolph, Asa Philip, 1889-

ANDERSON, Jervis. 323.4'092'4 B
A. Philip Randolph; a biographical portrait. New York, Harcourt Brace Jovanovich [1974, c1973] xiv, 398 p. illus. 21 cm. (A Harvest book, HB 280) Bibliography: p. 353-384. [E185.97.R27A82 1974] 73-12847 ISBN 0-15-671710-7 4.45 (pbk.)
1. Randolph, Asa Philip, 1889- **BIP**

*DAVIS, Daniel S. 331.88 [B]
Mr. Black Labor; the story of A. Philip Randolph, father of the Civil Rights movement. Introduction by Bayard Ruskin. New York, Dutton [1972] xii, 174 p., photos, 24 cm. Selected Bibliography: p. 165-167 [E176] 72-182599 ISBN 0-525-35325-9 6.50
1. Randolph, Asa Philip, 1889- I. Title.

DAVIS, Daniel S. 301.45'19'6073 B
Mr. Black labor; the story of A. Philip Randolph, father of the civil rights movement, by Daniel S. Davis. Introd. by Bayard Rustin. [1st ed.] New York, E. P. Dutton [1972] xii, 174 p. illus. 25 cm. Bibliography: p. 165-167. [E185.97.R27D38 1972] 72-82599 ISBN 0-525-35325-9 6.50
1. Randolph, Asa Philip, 1889- 2. Negroes—Civil rights. I. Title.

Randolph, Asa Philip, 1889- —Juvenile literature.

GREENLEAF, Barbara Kaye. 331.88'0924 B
Forward march to freedom; a biography of A. Philip Randolph. Illustrated by Charles Waterhouse. New York, Grosset & Dunlap [1971] 64 p. col. illus. 18 x 24 cm. "A New York times book." A biography of the black man whose efforts to help his people centered on gaining equal employment opportunities, equality in labor unions, and integration of the United States Army. [E185.97.R27G7] 92 79-145734 ISBN 0-448-02466-7 2.95
1. Randolph, Asa Philip, 1889- —Juvenile literature. I. Waterhouse, Charles H., illus. II. Title.

WILSON, Beth P. 920'.073
Giants for justice : Bethune, Randolph, and King / Beth P. Wilson. 1st ed. New York : Harcourt Brace Jovanovich, c1978. viii, 103 p., [26] leaves of plates : ill. ; 22 cm. Includes bibliographies and index. Biographical sketches of three outstanding black leaders who did much to pave the way toward dignity and freedom for their people in education, labor, and civil rights. [E185.96.W65] 920 77-88971 ISBN 0-15-230781-8 : 6.95
1. Bethune, Mary Jane McLeod, 1875-1955—Juvenile literature. 2. Randolph, Asa Philip, 1889- —Juvenile literature. 3. King, Martin Luther—Juvenile literature. 4. Afro-Americans—Biography—Juvenile literature. I. Title. **BIP**

Randolph, Edmund, 1753-1813.

REARDON, John J. 973.4'1'0924
Edmund Randolph; a biography [by] John J. Reardon. New York, Macmillan [1975, c1974] xvi, 517 p. illus. 24 cm. Bibliography: p. 483-502. [KF363.R35R42] 74-18458 ISBN 0-02-601200-6 11.95
1. Randolph, Edmund, 1753-1813.

Randolph, John, 1773-1833.

ADAMS, Henry, 1838-1918. v. 12
John Randolph. Introduction by Milton Cantor. Greenwich, Conn., Fawcett Publications [1961] 208p. (Premier Americana. d139)
1. Randolph, John, 1772-1833. I. Title.

ADAMS, Henry, 1838-1918. 973.4'0924 B
John Randolph. Boston, Houghton, Mifflin, 1899. [New York, AMS Press, 1972] 326 p. illus. 19 cm. (American statesmen, v. 16) [E302.6.R2A2 1972] 70-128968 ISBN 0-404-50865-0
1. Randolph, John, 1773-1833. I. Title. II. Series.

ADAMS, Henry, 1838-1918. 973.4'0924 B
John Randolph. Introd. by Milton Cantor. Gloucester, Mass., P. Smith, 1969 [c1961] xv, 208 p. 21 cm. (American lives) (Premier Americana.) Reprint of the 1961 ed. [E302.6.R2A2 1969] 73-8159
1. Randolph, John, 1773-1833. **BIP**

ADAMS, Henry Brooks, 1838-1918 923.273
John Randolph. Introd. by Milton Cantor. Greenwich, Conn., Fawcett [c.1961] 199p. (Premier Americana, d139) .50 pap.,
1. Randolph, John, 1773-1833. I. Title.

ADAMS, Henry Brooks, 1838-1918 923.273
John Randolph. Introd. by Milton Cantor. [Gloucester, Mass., Peter Smith, 1962, c.1961] 208p. 18cm. (Fawcett's Amer. lives ser. rebound) 2.00
1. Randolph, John, 1773-1833. I. Title.

BRUCE, William Cabell, 1860-1946. 973.4'0924 B
John Randolph of Roanoke, 1773-1833; a biography based largely on new material. New York, Octagon Books, 1970 [c1922] 2 v. illus., coats of arms, ports. 23 cm. Includes bibliographical references. [E302.6.R2B9 1970] 68-23979
1. Randolph, John, 1773-1833. I. Title.

DAWIDOFF, Robert. 973.4'092'4 B
The education of John Randolph / Robert Dawidoff. 1st ed. New York : Norton, c1979. p. cm. Includes index. Bibliography: p. [E302.6.R2D28 1979] 79-16178 ISBN 0-393-01242-5 : 16.95
1. Randolph, John, 1773-1833. 2. United States. Congress. House—Biography. 3. United States—Politics and government—1783-1865. 4. Legislators—United States—Biography. I. Title. **BIP**

GARLAND, Hugh A., 1805-1854. 973.4'0924 B
The life of John Randolph of Roanoke. 11th ed. New York, Haskell House, 1969. 2 v. illus., port. 23 cm. [E302.6.R2G25 1969] 68-24977
1. Randolph, John, 1773-1833. I. Title. **BIP**

GARLAND, Hugh A., 1805-1854. 973.4'0924 B
The life of John Randolph of Roanoke. 12th ed. New York, Greenwood Press [1969] 2 v. in 1. ports. 23 cm. Reprint of the 1859 ed. [E302.6.R2G25 1969b] 68-57603
1. Randolph, John, 1773-1833. I. Title.

GARLAND, Hugh A., 1805-1854. 973.4'0924 B
The life of John Randolph of Roanoke. 12th ed. New York, D. Appleton, 1859. St. Clair Shores, Mich., Scholarly Press, 1970. 2 v. in 1. ports. 22 cm. [E302.6.R2G25 1970] 70-108485
1. Randolph, John, 1773-1833. I. Title.

KIRK, Russell. 923.273
John Randolph of Roanoke; a study in American politics, with selected speeches and letters. Chicago, Regnery, 1964. 485 p. port. 25 cm. First published in 1951 under title: Randolph of Roanoke. Bibliography: p. 471-478. [E302.6.R2K5 1964] 64-14603
1. Randolph, John, 1773-1833. 2. United States—Politics and government—1783-1865. I. Title.

KIRK, Russell. 973.4'092'4
John Randolph of Roanoke : a study in American politics, with selected speeches and letters / Russell Kirk. [3d ed.]. Indianapolis : Liberty Press, c1978. 588 p. ; 24 cm. Includes indexes. Bibliography: p. [571]-579. [E302.6.R2K5 1978] 78-8659 ISBN 0-913966-39-8 : 9.00. ISBN 0-913966-40-1 pbk. : 3.50
1. Randolph, John, 1773-1833. 2. Legislators—United States—Biography. 3. United States—Politics and government—1783-1865. I. Title.

KIRK, Russell. 923.273
Randolph of Roanoke; a study in conservative thought. [Chicago] University of Chicago Press [1951] vii, 186 p. port. 21 cm. Bibliography: p. 177-183. [E302.6.R2K5] 51-12157
1. Randolph, John, 1773-1833. 2. U. S.—Pol. & govt.—1783-1865. I. Title.

Randolph, Martha (Jefferson) 1772-1836.

HALL, Gordon Langlev 973.460922
Mr. Jefferson's ladies. Boston, Beacon Pr. [c.1966] xvi. 239p. illus., ports. 21cm. Bibl. [E332.25.H3] 65-20787 4.95
1. Jefferson. Martha (Wayles) Skelton. 1748-1782. 2. Randolph. Martha (Jefferson) 1772-1836. 3. Eppes. Mary (Jefferson) 1778-1804. I. Title.

Randolph, Martha (Jefferson) 1772-1836—Juvenile literature.

KELLY, Regina 914.4'03'350924 B
(Zimmerman) 1898-
Miss Jefferson in Paris, by Regina Z. Kelly. Illustrated by Nena Allen. New York, Coward, McCann & Geoghegan [1971] 159 p. illus. 22 cm. Recounts twelve-year-old Patsy Jefferson's experiences during her visit to Paris in 1784 prior to the French revolution. [E332.25.R18K4 1971] 92 70-166586 5.09
1. Randolph, Martha (Jefferson) 1772-1836 Juvenile literature. I. Allen, Nena, illus. II. Title.

Randolph, Thomas Mann, 1768 1828.

GAINES, William Harris, 320.0924
Jr. 1918-
Thomas Mann Randolph, Jefferson's son-in-law. [Baton Rouge] La. State Univ. Pr. [c.1966] vii, 203p. illus., ports. 24cm. (Southern biog. ser.) Bibl. [E332.25.G3] 66-17579 7.50
1. Randolph, Thomas Mann, 1768-1828. 2. Jefferson, Thomas, Pres. U.S., 1743-1826. (Series) I. Title.

Ranga, N. G.

RANGA, N. G. 954.03'5'0924
Fight for freedom, autobiography of N. G. Ranga. Delhi, S. Chand, 1968. xv, 560p. illus., port. 23cm. [CT1508.R34A3] (B) SA68 7.50
I. Title.
Distributed by Verry, Mystic, Conn.

Range Riders Inc.

FANNING the 917.86'33'030922 B
embers. [Billings, Mont., Gazette Print. & Lithography, 1971] xii, 580 p. illus. 29 cm. [F737.C9F3] 71-30901
1. Range Riders Inc. 2. Range Riders Reps. 3. Custer County, Mont.—Biography.

Rank, Otto, 1884-1939.

TAFT, Jessie, [921.36] 926.L
1882-1960.
Otto Rank; a biographical study based on notebooks, letters, collected writings, therapeutic achievements, and personal associations. New York, Julian Press, 1958. xix, 299 p. port. 25 cm. "Published works of Otto Rank": p. 297-299. Bibliographical footnotes. [BF173.R36T2] 58-9814
1. Rank, Otto, 1884-1939. I. Title.

TAFT, Jessie, 1882- 921.36 926.1
1960.
Otto Rank; a biographical study based on notebooks, letters, collected writings, therapeutic achievements, and personal associations. New York, Julian Press, 1958. xix, 299 p. port. 25 cm. "Published works of Otto Rank": p. 297-299. Bibliographical footnotes. Full name: Julia Jessie Taft. [BF173.R36T2] 58-9814
1. Rank, Otto, 1884-1939. I. Title.

Ranke, Leopold von, 1795-1886.

GAY, Peter, 1923- 907'.2'022
Style in history. New York, Basic Books [1974] xiii, 242 p. illus. 22 cm. Bibliography: p. 219-238. [D14.G39] 73-91076 ISBN 0-465-08304-8 8.95
1. Gibbon, Edward, 1737-1794. 2. Ranke, Leopold von, 1795-1886. 3. Macaulay, Thomas Babington Macaulay, Baron, 1800-1859. 4. Burckhardt, Jakob Christoph, 1818-1897. 5. Historiography. I. Title. BIP

KRIEGER, Leonard. 907'.2'024
Ranke : the meaning of history / Leonard Krieger. Chicago : University of Chicago Press, 1977. xii, 402 p. ; 24 cm. Includes index. Bibliography: p. [388]-392. [D15.R3K74] 76-25633 ISBN 0-226-45349-9 lib.bdg. : 23.00
1. Ranke, Leopold von, 1795-1886. 2. History—Philosophy. 3. Historicism. 4. Historians—Germany—Biography. BIP

VON LAUE, Theodore H 928.3
Leopold Ranke, the formative years. Princeton,Princeton University Press, 1950. ix, 230 p. port. 23 cm. (Princeton studies in history, v. 4) "Bibliographical essay": p. 219.227. [D15.R3V6] 50-3230
1. Ranke. Leopold von, 1795-1886. I. Title. II. Series: Princeton University. Princeton studies in history, v. 4

VON LAUE, Theodore Hermann. 928.3
Leopold Ranke, the formative years. Princeton, Princeton University Press, 1950. ix, 230p. port. 23cm. (Princeton studies in history, v. 4) 'Bibliographical essay': p. 219-227. [D15.R3V6] 50-3230
1. Ranke, Leopold von, 1795-1886 I. Title. II. Series: Princeton University. Princeton studies in history, v. 4

Rankin, Jeannette.

BLOCK, Judy 328.73'092'4 B
Rachel, 1948-
The first woman in Congress : Jeannette Rankin / by Judy Rachel Block ; illustrated by Terry Kovalcik. New York : C.P.I., c1978. 48 p. : ill. (some col.) ; 24 cm. Traces the career of the first woman to hold a congressional office. [JK1030.R3B56] 92 78-14490 ISBN 0-89547-053-5 : 5.58
1. Rankin, Jeannette. 2. Legislators—United States—Biography—Juvenile literature. I. Kovalcik, Terry. II. Title.
Distributed by Silver Burdell, Morristown, NJ 07960

JOSEPHSON, Hannah 324'.3'0924 B
Geffen.
Jeannette Rankin, first lady in Congress : a biography / Hannah Josephson. Indianapolis : Bobbs-Merrill, [1974] xii, 227 p. : ill. ; 24 cm. Includes index. Bibliography: p. 213-216. [JK1030.R3J67] 74-3887 ISBN 0-672-51921-6 : 8.95
1. Rankin, Jeannette. I. Title.

Rankin, Milledge Theron, 1804-1953.

WEATHERSPOON, Jesse 922.651
Burton, 1886-
M. Theron Rankin, Apostle of Advance. Nashville, Broadman Press [1958] 137 p. illus. 21 cm. [BV3427.R2W4] 58-11550
1. Rankin, Milledge Theron, 1804-1953. I. Title.

Rankin, William Henry,

RANKIN, William Henry, 923.573
1920-
The man who rode the thunder. New York, Pyramid Bks. [1961, c.1960] 189p. (R660) .50 pap.,
I. Title. BIP

RANKIN, William Henry, 923.573
1920-
The man who rode the thunder. Englewood Cliffs, N.J., Prentice-Hall [1960] 208 p. illus. 21 cm. Autobiographical. [TL540.R28A3] 60-16622
I. Title.

Ransom, John Crowe, 1888-1974—Biography.

YOUNG, Thomas Daniel, 811'.5'2 B
1919-
Gentleman in a dustcoat : a biography of John Crowe Ransom / Thomas Daniel Young. Baton Rouge : Louisiana State University Press, c1976. xx, 528 p., [5] leaves of plates : ill. ; 23 cm. (Southern literary studies) Includes bibliographical references and index. [PS3535.A635Z9185] 75-27667 ISBN 0-8071-0190-7 : 32.50. ISBN 0-8071-0255-5 pbk. : 8.95
1. Ransom, John Crowe, 1888-1974—Biography. 2. Authors, American—20th century—Biography. I. Title. II. Series. BIP

Ransome, Arthur, 1884-1967.

SHELLEY, Hugh. 823.912
Arthur Ransome. [1st American ed.] New York, H. Z. Walck [1964, c1960] 71 p. port. 19 cm. Bibliography: p. 69-71. [PR6035.A63Z8 1964] 64-20836
1. Ransome, Arthur, 1884-1967.

Ransome, Arthur, 1884-1967—Biography.

RANSOME, Arthur, 823'.9'12 B
1884-1967.
The autobiography of Arthur Ransome / edited, with prologue and epilogue, by Rupert Hart-Davis. London : J. Cape, 1976. 368 p., [9] leaves of plates : ill. ; 23 cm. Includes index. [PR6035.A63Z513 1976] 76-380617 ISBN 0-224-01245-2 : £5.95
1. Ransome, Arthur, 1884-1967—Biography. 2. Authors, English—20th century—Biography. I. Title.

Raphael, 1483-1520.

BORTOLON, Liana. 759.5 B
The life and times of Raphael; text by Liana Bortolon, translator [from the Italian] Barbara Paterson. London, New York[etc.] Hamlyn, 1968. [1], 77 p. illus. (chiefly col.), ports. (some col.) 30 cm. (Portraits of greatness) [ND623.R2B64] 73-415496 ISBN 0-600-03134-9 17/6
1. Raphael, 1483-1520. I. Title.

CROWE, Joseph Archer, Sir, 759.5
1825-1896.
Raphael: his life and works. With particular reference to recently discovered records, and an exhaustive study of extant drawings and pictures, by J. A. Crowe and G. B. Cavalcaselle. Freeport, N.Y., Books for Libraries Press [1972] 2 v. 22 cm. Reprint of the 1882-85 ed. [ND623.R2C8 1972] 72-2584 ISBN 0-8369-6852-2
1. Raphael, 1483-1520. I. Cavalcaselle. Giovanni Battista, 1820-1897, joint author.

GILLETTE, Henry S. 759.5
Raphael; painter of the Renaissance by Henry S. Gillette New York, Watts [1967] 160 p. illus. 25 cm. (Immortals of art) Bibliography: p. 148-150. [ND623.R5G5] 67-14177
1. Raphael, 1483-1520. I. Title.

MUNTZ, Eugene, 1845- 759.5 B
1902.
Raphael, his life, works, and times / by Eugene Muntz. Rev. from the 2d French ed. / by Walter Armstrong. Boston : Longwood Press, 1977. p. cm. Reprint of the 1888 ed. published by Chapman and Hall, London. [ND623.R2M9 1977] 77-9327 ISBN 0-89341-202-3 lib.bdg. : 60.00
1. Raphael, 1483-1520. I. Armstrong, Walter, Sir, 1850-1918. II. Title.

PASSAVANT, Johann David, 759.5 B
1787-1861.
Raphael of Urbino and his father Giovanni Santi / Johann David Passavant. New York : Garland Pub., 1978. p. cm. (Conoisseurship, criticism, and art history in the nineteenth century) Reprint of the 1872 ed. published by Macmillan, London and New York. "Catalogue of Raphael's paintings": p. [ND623.R2P28 1978] 77-25762 ISBN 0-8240-3275-6 : 30.00
1. Raphael, 1483-1520. 2. Sanzio, Giovanni, 1435?-1494. 3. Painters—Italy—Biography. I. Title. II. Series. BIP

QUATREMERE de Quincy, 759.5 B
Antoine Chrysostome, 1755-1849.
History of the life and works of Raffaello / Quatremere de Quincy. New York : Garland Pub., 1979. p. cm. (Connoisseurship, criticism, and art history in the nineteenth century ; 19) Translation of Histoire de la vie et des ouvrages de Raphael. "Excerpted from a volume in the Lives of the Italian painters series, containing Michel Angelo by R. Duppa as well as de Quincy's Raffaelo, published by David Bogue, London, 1896." Includes index. [ND623.R2Q3713] 77-25764 ISBN 0-8240-3277-2 : 40.00
1. Raphael, 1483-1520. 2. Painters—Italy—Biography. I. Title. II. Series.

RIPLEY, Elizabeth, 1906- 759.5
Raphael; a biography. Philadelphia, Lippincott [1961] 68 p. illus. 26 cm. [ND623.R2R64] 61-6065
1. Raphael (Raffaelle Sansio da Urbino) 1483-1520.]

Rapier, James T., 1839-1883.

FELDMAN, Eugene 328.73'0924 B
Pieter Romayn.
Black power in old Alabama; the life and stirring times of James T. Rapier, Afro-American Congressman from Alabama, 1839-1883. Illus. by Margaret T. Burroughs [and] Jennie Washington. [Chicago] Museum of African American History [1968] 69, [7] p. illus., map, port. 22 cm. Bibliographical references included in "Footnotes" (p. [70]-[72]) Bibliography (annotated): p. [73]-[74] [E185.97.R3F4] 68-6846
1. Rapier, James T., 1839-1883. I. Title.

SCHWENINGER, 328.73'092'4 B
Loren.
James T. Rapier and Reconstruction / Loren Schweninger. Chicago : University of Chicago Press, c1978. xx, 248 p. ; 23 cm. (Negro American biographies and autobiographies) Includes index. Bibliography: p. 211-234. [E185.97.R3S38] 77-81734 ISBN 0-226-74240-7 lib.bdg. : 22.00
1. Rapier, James T., 1839-1883. 2. Reconstruction—Alabama. 3. Politicians—Alabama—Biography. I. Title. II. Series. BIP

Rapier, James T., 1839-1883—Juvenile literature.

BUCKMASTER, 328.73'09'22 B
Henrietta, pseud.
The fighting Congressmen: Thaddeus Stephens, Hiram Revels, James Rapier, Blanche K. Bruce. [New York] Scholastic Book Services [1971] 111 p. illus., facsims., ports. 21 cm. (Firebird books) Brief biographies of one white and three black congressmen active in the struggle to assure the rights of black people during the Reconstruction. [E663.B9] 920 75-131370
1. Stevens, Thaddeus, 1792-1868—Juvenile literature. 2. Revels, Hiram Rhoades, 1827?-1901—Juvenile literature. 3. Rapier, James T., 1839-1883—Juvenile literature. 4. Bruce, Blanche Kelso, 1841-1898—Juvenile literature. I. Title.

Rappleye, Willard C.

ATKINS, Harry. 610'.92'4 B
The Dean : Willard C. Rappleye and the evolution of American medical education / by Harry Atkins. New York : Josiah Macy, Jr. Foundation, c1975. 126 p. : port. ; 24 cm. Includes bibliographical references and index. [R154.R24A84] 75-43445
1. Rappleye, Willard C. 2. Columbia University. College of Physicians and Surgeons. 3. Medical education—United States—History. I. Title.

Raskin, Jonah, 1942- —Biography.

RASKIN, Jonah, 322.4'2'0924 B
1942-
Out of the whale : growing up in the

American left : an autobiography / by Jonah Raskin. New York : Links : distributed by Quick Fox, [1974] xiv, 216 p., [5] leaves of plates : ill. ; 22 cm. [PS3568.A713Z52] 74-78870 ISBN 0-8256-3039-8 pbk. : 4.95
1. Raskin, Jonah, 1942- —Biography. 2. Radicalism—United States—Personal narratives. I. Title.

Raskolniks.

AVVAKUM, Protopope, 1621?-1682 922.147
The life of the Archpriest Avvakum, by himself. Tr. from seventeenth century Russian by Jane Harrison, Hope Mirrlees. Pref. by Prince D. S. Mirsky. Hamden, Conn., Archon [dist. Shoe String, 1963] 155p. 18cm. 63-18279 5.00
1. Raskolniks. I. Title.

Rasmussen, Anne-Marie.

RASMUSSEN, Anne-Marie. 332'.092'4 B
There was once a time / Anne-Marie Rasmussen. 1st ed. New York : Harcourt Brace Jovanovich, [1975] xiii, 236 p., [16] leaves of plates : ill. ; 22 cm. Includes index. [CT275.R266A33] 74-20803 ISBN 0-15-189481-7 : 8.95
1. Rasmussen, Anne-Marie. 2. Rockefeller family. I. Title.

Raspail, Francois Vincent, 1794-1878.

WEINER, Dora B. 509'.24 B
Raspail; scientist and reformer, by Dora B. Weiner. With a chapter by Simone Raspail. New York, Columbia University Press, 1968. xiv, 336 p. illus., facsims., geneal. table, ports. 24 cm. Bibliography: p. 293-321. [Q143.R34W4] 68-19761
1. Raspail, Francois Vincent, 1794-1878.

Raspe, Rudolf Erich, 1737-1794.

CARSWELL, John 928.3
The prospector, being the life and times of Rudolf Erich Raspe, 1737-1794. London, Cresset Pr. [Chester Springs, Pa., Dufour, 1966] vi, 277p. illus., ports. 23cm. Bibl. [PT2452.R4C3] 51-1556 5.00 bds.,
1. Raspe, Rudolf Erich, 1737-1794. I. Title.

CARSWELL, John. 928.3
The romantic rogue; being the singular life and adventures of Rudolph Eric Raspe, creator of Baron Munchausen. New York, Dutton [1950] vi, 277 p. illus. 23 cm. London ed. (Cresset Press) has title: The prospector. [PT2452.R4C] A51
1. Raspe, Rudolf Erich, 1737-1794. I. Title.

Rasputin, Grigorii Efimovich, 1871-1916.

FULOP-MILLER, Rene, 1891- 922.147
Rasputin, the holy devil. New York, F. Ungar Pub. Co. [1962, c1955] 386 p. 21 cm. Translation of Der heilige Teufel. [DK254.R3F85 1962] 62-12959
1. Rasputin, Grigorii Efimovich, 1871-1916. 2. Russia—History—Nicholas II, 1894-1917. 3. Russia—Court and courtiers. BIP

JUDAS, Elizabeth, 1897- 281.90924
Rasputin, neither devil nor saint. [2d ed.] Miami, Fla. 33127, Allied Pubs. 220 N.W. 47 St. [c.1942-1965] 216p. illus. ports. 21cm. [DK254.R3J8] 65-8566 3.95
1. Rasputin, Grigorii Efimovich, 1871-1916. I. Title.

MINNEY, Rubeigh James, 1895- 947.08'092'4 B
Rasputin [by] R. J. Minney. [1st American ed.] New York, McKay [1973] 234 p. illus. 22 cm. Bibliography: p. 224-226. [DK254.R3M56 1973] 72-96479 6.95
1. Rasputin, Grigorii Efimovich, 1871-1916.

RASPUTINA, Mariia Grigor'evna. 947.08'092'4 B
Rasputin, the man behind the myth, a personal memoir / by Maria Rasputin and Patte Barham. Englewood Cliffs, N.J. : Prentice-Hall, c1977. 266 p., [4] leaves of plates : ill. ; 24 cm. Includes index. [DK254.R3R35 1977] 76-54231 ISBN 0-13-753129-X : 10.00
1. Rasputin, Grigorii Efimovich, 1871-1916. 2. Russia—Court and courtiers—Biography. I. Barham, Patte, joint author. II. Title.

RODZIANKO, Mikhail Vladimirovich, 1859-1924. 947.08'092'4 B
The reign of Rasputin: an empire's collapse. Memoirs of M. V. Rodzianko. Translated by Catherine Zvegintzoff. Introd. by Bernard Pares. With a new introd. by David R. Jones. [Gulf Breeze, Fla.] Academic International Press, 1973. xxvii, 278 p. port. 23 cm. (The Russian series, v. 55) Translation of Krushenie imperii. [DK262.R6313 1973] 72-97047 ISBN 0-87569-051-3 12.00
1. Rasputin, Grigorii Efimovich, 1871-1916. 2. Rodzianko, Mikhail Vladimirovich, 1859-1924. 3. Russia—History—Nicholas II, 1894-1917. I. Title.

VOGEL-JoRGENSEN, T., 1891- 947.08'0924 B
Rasputin: prophet, libertine, plotter, by T. Vogel-Jorgensen. Translated from the Danish by William Frederick Harvey. New Hyde Park, N.Y., University Books [1971, c1970] xvi, 143 p. 21 cm. Reprint of the 1917 ed., with a new foreword by Leslie Shepard. [DK254.R3V513 1971] 74-118609 5.00
1. Rasputin, Grigorii Efimovich, 1871-1916. I. Title.

WILSON, Colin, 1931- 922.147
Rasputin and the fall of the Romanovs. New York, Farrar, Straus [1964] 240 p. ports. 22 cm. Bibliography: p. 218-220. [DK254.R3W5] 64-23120
1. Rasputin, Grigorii Efimovich, 1871-1916. I. Title.

Rath, Charles.

RATH, Ida Ellen. 923.973
The Rath trail; non-fiction biography of Charles Rath, Indian trader, merchant, buffalo hunter, hide buyer, railroad grader, and organizer of early day towns and trading posts, a friend of Kit Carson and the Bents, a maker of trails. Wichita, Kan., McCormick-Armstrong [1961] 204p. illus. 24cm. [F594.R27] 61-16115
1. Rath, Charles. 2. Frontier and pioneer life—The West. I. Title.

Rathbone, Basil, 1892-1967.

DRUXMAN, Michael B., 1941- 791.43'028'0924 B
Basil Rathbone : his life and his films / Michael B. Druxman. South Brunswick, N.J. : A. S. Barnes, [1974] p. cm. [PN2598.R35D7] 74-3611 ISBN 0-498-01471-1 : 10.00
1. Rathbone, Basil, 1892-1967. BIP

RATHBONE, Basil, 1892- 927.92
In and out of character. [1st ed.] Garden City, N. Y., Doubleday, 1962. 278 p. illus. 22 cm. Autobiography. [PN2598.R35A3] 62-15316
1. Actors—Correspondence, reminiscences, etc. I. Title.

Rathbun, Benjamin.

NICHOLS, Thomas Low, 1815-1901. 071'.47'97
Journal in jail. [New York] Arno [1970] 247 p. 23 cm. (The American journalists) Reprint of the 1840 ed. [F129.B8N6 1970] 71-125709 ISBN 0-405-01690-5
1. Rathbun, Benjamin. 2. The Buffalonian. I. Title. BIP

Rathenau, Walther, 1867-1922.

FELIX, David, 1921- 940.3'1422
Walther Rathenau and the Weimar Republic; the politics of reparations. Baltimore, Johns Hopkins Press [1971] xii, 210 p. port. 24 cm. Bibliography: p. 191-205. [D649.G3F4] 76-132338 ISBN 0-8018-1175-9 9.00
1. Rathenau, Walther, 1867-1922. 2. European War, 1914-1918—Reparations. I. Title.

JOLL, James. 923.24
Three intellectuals in politics. [New York] Pantheon Books [1961, c1960] xiv, 203 p. 23 cm. Published in 1960 under title: Intellectuals in politics. Bibliographical references included in "Notes" (p. 185-197) [D412.6.J64] 61-10030
1. Blum, Leon, 1872-1950. 2. Rathenau, Walther, 1867-1922. 3. Marinetti, Fllippo Tommaso, 1876-1944. I. Title.

KESSLER, Harry Klemens Ulrich, Graf von, 1868-1937. 943.085'092'4 B
Walther Rathenau : his life and work / by Count Harry Kessler ; [translated by W. D. Robson-Scott and Lawrence Hyde under the author's supervision, with notes and additions for English readers] New York : AMS Press, 1975. 400 p., [4] leaves of plates : ill. ; 23 cm. Reprint of the 1930 ed., published by Harcourt, Brace and Co., New York. Includes indexes. [DD231.R3K43 1975] 70-181937 ISBN 0-404-03665-1 : 9.00
1. Rathenau, Walther, 1867-1922. 2. Germany—History—20th century. BIP

KESSLER, Harry Klemens Ulrich, Graf von, 1868-1937. 943.085'0924 B
Walther Rathenau; his life and work. [Translated by W. D. Robson-Scott and Lawrence Hyde, and rev. by the author, with notes and additions for English readers] New York, H. Fertig, 1969 [c1928] 400 p. facsim., ports. 23 cm. [DD231.R3K43 1969] 68-9663
1. Rathenau, Walther, 1867-1922. 2. Germany—History—20th century. BIP

Ratiu, Alexander.

RATIU, Alexander. 272'.9
Stolen church, martyrdom in Communist Romania / Alexander Ratiu & William Virtue. Huntington, Ind. : Our Sunday Visitor, c1979. 192 p. ; 21 cm. [BX4711.495.R37A37] 79-87926 ISBN 0-87973-730-1 pbk. : 4.95
1. Ratiu, Alexander. 2. Catholic Church—Clergy—Biography. 3. Catholic Church in Romania—Clergy. 4. Clergy—Romania—Biography. 5. Prisoners—Romania—Biography. 6. Persecution—Romania. I. Virtue, William, joint author. II. Title.

Rato Khyongla Nawang Losang.

RATO Khyongla Nawang Losang. 294.3'61'0924 B
My life and lives : the story of a Tibetan incarnation / Rato Khyongla Nawang Losang ; edited with an introd. by Joseph Campbell. 1st ed. New York : Dutton, c1977. p. cm. [BQ982.A767A35] 77-8399 ISBN 0-525-47480-3 pbk. : 3.50
1. Rato Khyongla Nawang Losang. 2. Lamas—Tibet—Biography. I. Campbell, Joseph, 1904- II. Title. BIP

Ratzel, Friedrich, 1844-1904.

WANKLYN, Harriet Grace 923.943
Friedrich Ratzel; a biographical memoir and bibliography. [New York] Cambridge [c.]1961[ ] ix, 96p. Bibl. 61-65229 2.25
1. Ratzel, Friedrich, 1844-1904. I. Title.

WANKLYN, Harriet Grace. 923.943
Friedrich Ratzel; a biographical memoir and bibliography. Cambridge [Eng.] University Press, 1961. ix, 96 p. 20 cm. [G69.R28W3] 61-65229
1. Ratzel, Friedrich, 1844-1904. I. Title.

Rauch, Friedrich August, 1806-1841.

ZIEGLER, Howard J B 1908- 921.1
Frederick Augustus Rauch, American Hegelian; with a foreword by Lee M. Erdman. Lancaster, Pa., Published by order of the college, 1953. xvii, 103p. facsims. 21cm. (Franklin and Marshall College studies, no. 8) Issued also as thesis, Columbia University, in microfilm form. Bibliography: p. 92-99. [B931.R34Z5 1953] 53-1472
1. Rauch, Friedrich August, 1806-1841. I. Title. II. Series.

Rauschenberg, Robert, 1925-

FORGE, Andrew. 709.24
Rauschenberg. New York, Abrams [1969] 230, [1] p. (incl. cover) illus. (part col.) 28 x 30 cm. Title page is p. [221] "Autobiography [of Rauschenberg]": p. 225-229. Bibliography: p. 230-[231] [N6537.R27F6] 69-12480
1. Rauschenberg, Robert, 1925-

Rauschenbusch, Walter, 1861-1918.

JAEHN, Klaus Juergen. 230'.6'10924 B
Rauschenbusch, the formative years / [Klaus Juergen Jaehn]. Valley Forge, PA : Judson Press, c1976. 58 p. ; 22 cm. A revision of the author's thesis (Master of Divinity) which was first published in two parts in Foundations, Oct.-Dec., 1973, v. 16, no. 4 and Jan.-Mar., 1974, v. 17, no. 1. Bibliography: p. 49-52. [BX6495.R3J3 1976] 75-38191 ISBN 0-8170-0707-5 pbk. : 1.50
1. Rauschenbusch, Walter, 1861-1918. I. Title.

Rauwolf, Leonhard, d. 1596.

DANNENFELDT, Karl H. 581'.0924 B
Leonhard Rauwolf; sixteenth-century physician, botanist, and traveler, by Karl H. Dannenfeldt. Cambridge, Harvard University Press, 1968. viii, 321 p. illus., maps. 24 cm. (Harvard monographs in the history of science) Bibliography: p. [283]-290. [DS47.D175] 68-15634
1. Rauwolf, Leonhard, d. 1596. 2. Levant—Description and travel. 3. Botany—Levant. BIP

Ravalli, Anthony, 1812-1884.

ALLEN, Harold, 1912- 720'.92'4
Father Ravalli's missions. Chicago, Good Lion [1972] 31, [104] p. illus. 30 cm. Bibliography: p. 31. [NA737.R3A7] 72-182080 ISBN 0-912844-03-5
1. Ravalli, Anthony, 1812-1884. 2. Missions—Northwest, Old. I. Title.

Ravel, Maurice, 1875-1937.

DEMUTH, Norman, 1898- 927.8
Ravel. New York, Collier [1962] 253p. 18cm. (Gt. composers ser., BS148v) Bibl. 1.50 pap.,
1. Ravel, Maurice, 1875-1937. I. Title. II. Series.

DEMUTH, Norman, 1898- 927.8
Ravel. New York, Collier [1962] 253p. 18cm. (Gt. composers ser., BS148v) Bibl. 1.50 pap.,
1. Ravel, Maurice, 1875-1937. I. Title. II. Series.

DEMUTH, Norman, 1898-1968. 780'.92'4 B
Ravel / by Norman Demuth. Westport, Conn. : Hyperion Press, 1979. p. cm. (Core collection reprints) Reprint of the 1947 ed. published by Dent, London, in series: The Master musicians. Includes index. "Catalogue of [Ravel's] works": p. [ML410.R23D4 1979] 78-59016 ISBN 0-88355-690-1 : lib.bdg. : 18.50
1. Ravel, Maurice, 1875-1937. 2. Composers—France—Biography. I. Series: The Master musicians.

JANEKELEVITCH, Vladimir 927.8
Ravel. Translated [from the French] by Margaret Crosland. New York, Grove Press [c.1959] 192p. Bibliography: p. 192. Discography: p. 190-191. illus., ports., music. 18cm. (Evergreen profile book 3) 59-6059 1.35 pap.,
1. Ravel, Maurice, 1875-1937. I. Title.

JANEKELEVITCH, Vladimir 927.8
Ravel. Translated [from the French] by Margaret Crosland. New York, Grove Press [c.1959] 192p. Bibliography: p. 192. Discography: p. 190-191. illus., ports., music. 18cm. (Evergreen profile book 3) 59-6059 1.35 pap.,
1. Ravel, Maurice, 1875-1937. I. Title.

JANKELEVITCH, Vladimir. 927.8
Ravel Translated by Margaret Crosland. New York, Grove Press [c1959] 192p.

illus., ports., music. 18cm. (Evergreen profile book 3) Bibliography: p. 192. Discography: p. 190-191. [ML410.R23J22] 59-6059
1. Ravel, Maurice, 1875- 1937. I. Title.

JANKELEVITCH, Vladimir. 780'.92'4 B
Ravel / Vladimir Jankelevitch ; translated by Margaret Crosland. Westport, Conn. : Greenwood Press, 1976, c1959. p. cm. Reprint of the ed. published by Grove Press, New York, which was issued as no. 3 of Evergreen profile books. Bibliography: p. [ML410.R23J22 1976] 75-28925
1. Ravel, Maurice, 1875-1937.

JANKELEVITCH, Vladimir. 780'.92'4 B
Ravel / Vladimir Jankelevitch ; translated by Margaret Crosland. Westport, Conn. : Greenwood Press, 1976, c1959. 192 p. : ill. ; 20 cm. Reprint of the ed. published by Grove Press, New York, which was issued as no. 3 of Evergreen profile books. Bibliography: p. 192. [ML410.R23J22 1976] 75-28925 17.50
1. Ravel, Maurice, 1875-1937.

JANKELEVITCH, Vladimir. 780'.92'4 B
Ravel / Vladimir Jankelevitch ; translated by Margaret Crosland. Westport, Conn. : Greenwood Press, 1976, c1959. 192 p. : ill. ; 20 cm. Reprint of the ed. published by Grove Press, New York, which was issued as no. 3 of Evergreen profile books. Bibliography: p. 192. [ML410.R23J22 1976] 75-28925 17.50
1. Ravel, Maurice, 1875-1937.

MYERS, Rollo H. 927.8
Ravel life works. New York, T. Yoseloff [1961, c.1960] 239p. illus. Bibl. 61-6931 5.00
1. Ravel, Maurice, 1875-1937. I. Title.

MYERS, Rollo H. 780'.92'4 B
Ravel: life & works, by Rollo H. Myers. Westport, Conn., Greenwood Press [1973, c1960] 239 p. illus. 22 cm. Reprint of the ed. published by Thomas Yoseloff, New York. Bibliography: p. 228-230. [ML410.R23M9 1973] 73-2340 ISBN 0-8371-6841-4 11.25
1. Ravel, Maurice, 1875-1937.

MYERS, Rollo H. 780'.92'4 B
Ravel: life & works, by Rollo H. Myers. Westport, Conn., Greenwood Press [1973, c1960] 239 p. illus. 22 cm. Reprint of the ed. published by Thomas Yoseloff, New York. Bibliography: p. 228-230. [ML410.R23M9 1973] 73-2340 ISBN 0-8371-6841-4 11.25
1. Ravel, Maurice, 1875-1937.

NICHOLS, Roger. 780'.92'4 [B]
Ravel / by Roger Nichols. London : J. M. Dent, 1977. xi, 199 p., [4] leaves of plates : ill. ; 20 cm. (The Master musicians series) Includes index. Bibliography: p. 186-189. [ML410.R23N5] 77-363348 ISBN 0-460-03146-5 : 9.95
1. Ravel, Maurice, 1875-1937. 2. Composers—France—Biography. I. Title. II. Series.
Distributed by Biblio Distribution Center,Totowa,N.J. BIP

ORENSTEIN, Arbie. 780'.92'4 B
Ravel : man and musician / by Arbie Orenstein. New York : Columbia University Press, 1975. xvi, 290 p., [16] leaves of plates : ill. ; 24 cm. "Catalogue of works": p. 219-[245] [ML410.R23O73] 74-34022 ISBN 0-231-03902-6 : 10.95
1. Ravel, Maurice, 1875-1937.

ORENSTEIN, Arbie. 780'.92'4 B
Ravel : man and musician / by Arbie Orenstein. New York : Columbia University Press, 1975. xvi, 290 p., [16] leaves of plates : ill. ; 24 cm. "Catalogue of works": p. 219-[245] [ML410.R23O73] 74-34022 ISBN 0-231-03902-6 : 10.95
1. Ravel, Maurice, 1875-1937.

SEROFF, Victor Ilyitch, 1902- 785'.0924 B
Maurice Ravel, by Victor I. Seroff. Freeport, N.Y., Books for Libraries Press [1970, c1953] viii, 310 p. illus., ports. 23 cm. (Biography index reprint series) Bibliography: p. 297-305. [ML410.R23S4 1970] 77-126327
1. Ravel, Maurice, 1875-1937. BIP

STUCKENSCHMIDT, Hans Heinz, 1901- 780.924
Maurice Ravel; variations on his life and work, by H. H. Stuckenschmidt. Tr. from German by Samuel R. Rosenbaum [1st ed.] Philadelphia, Chilton [1968] xiv, 271p. port. 21cm. [ML410.R23S753] 68-22690 6.50
1. Ravel, Maurice, 1875-1937. I. Title.

STUCKENSCHMIDT, Hans Heinz, 1901- 784'.092'4
Maurice Ravel; variations on his life and work, by H. H. Stuckenschmidt. Translated from the German by Samuel R. Rosenbaum. [1st ed.] Philadelphia, Chilton Book Co. [1968] xiv, 271 p. port. 21 cm. [ML410.R23S753] 68-22690
1. Ravel, Maurice, 1875-1937.

Raven, Charles Earle, 1885-1964.

DILLISTONE, Frederick William, 1903- 230'.3'0924 B
Charles Raven : naturalist, historian, theologian / by F. W. Dillistone. 1st ed. Grand Rapids, Mich. : Eerdmans, [1975] 448 p., [4] leaves of plates : ill. ; 24 cm. Includes index. "Bibliography of Charles Raven": p. 439-440. [BX5199.R26D54 1975] 74-20580 ISBN 0-8028-3455-8 : 12.95
1. Raven, Charles Earle, 1885-1964.

Ravenstein, Johann Theodore von, b. 1889.

RYDER, Rowland. 355.3'32'0924 B
Ravenstein : portrait of a German general / Rowland Ryder. New York : Hippocrene Books, c1978. x, 214 p., [4] leaves of plates : ill. ; 23 cm. Includes index. Bibliography: p. [206]-207. [U55.R35R92 1978b] 78-60443 ISBN 0-88254-470-5 : 14.95
1. Ravenstein, Johann Theodore von, b. 1889. 2. Germany. Heer—Biography. 3. Generals—Germany—Biography. BIP

Rawlinson, Alfred, Sir, bart., 1867-1934.

SMITHERS, A. J., 1919- 940.4'81'41
Toby : a real life ripping yarn / A. J. Smithers. London ; New York : Gordon & Cremonesi, c1978. 191 p. ; 26 cm. [DA574.R38S54] 78-40403 ISBN 0-86033-069-9 : 16.95
1. Rawlinson, Alfred, Sir, bart., 1867-1934. 2. Great Britain—Nobility—Biography. 3. European War, 1914-1918—Biography. I. Title. BIP

Ray, Ann, 1937-

RAY, Ann, 1937- 131.3
Journey into light / Ann Ray. Boulder Creek, Calif. : University of the Trees Press, c1977. vi, 298 p. : ill. ; 24 cm. [BF1408.2.R39A35] 76-53174 ISBN 0-916438-06-6 pbk. : 7.95
1. Ray, Ann, 1937- 2. Occult sciences—Biography. 3. Spiritual life. I. Title. BIP

Ray, Charles Henry.

MONAGHAN, James, 1891- 973.7'092'4
The man who elected Lincoln, by Jay Monaghan. Westport, Conn., Greenwood Press [1973, c1956] x, 334 p. port. 22 cm. Reprint of the ed. published by Bobbs-Merrill, Indianapolis. Bibliography: p. 301-318. [E415.9.R3M6 1973] 73-7310 ISBN 0-8371-6920-8 13.75
1. Ray, Charles Henry. 2. Lincoln, Abraham, Pres. U.S., 1809-1865. 3. United States—Politics and government—1849-1861. I. Title. BIP

Ray, Emma J.,

RAY, Emma J., 1859- 287'.873'0922 B
Twice sold, twice ransomed; autobiography of Mr. and Mrs. L. P. Ray. Introd. by C. E. McReynolds. Freeport, N.Y., Books for Libraries Press, 1971. 320 p. illus. 23 cm. (The Black heritage library collection) Reprint of the 1926 ed. [BX8473.R3A3 1971] 76-173613 ISBN 0-8369-8905-8
1. Ray, Lloyd P., 1860- II. Title. III. Series.

Ray, James Earl, 1928-

HUIE, William Bradford, 1910- 364.1'524'0924 B
Did the F.B.I. kill Martin Luther King? / By William Bradford Huie. Nashville : T. Nelson, c1977. p. cm. Contains the author's He slew the dreamer, with a new prologue and epilogue. [HV6248.R39H82 1977] 77-11881 ISBN 0-8407-4062-X pbk. : 3.95
1. Ray, James Earl, 1928- 2. King, Martin Luther. 3. United States. Federal Bureau of Investigation. 4. Crime and criminals—Biography. I. Title. BIP

MCMILLAN, George. 364.15'24'0924 B
The making of an assassin : the life of James Earl Ray / by George McMillan. 1st ed. Boston : Little, Brown, c1976. 318 p. ; 22 cm. Includes index. [HV6248.R39M33] 76-18685 ISBN 0-316-56241-6 : 8.95
1. Ray, James Earl, 1928- I. Title. BIP

Ray, Jefferson Davis, 1860-1951.

RAY, Georgia Miller, 1887- 922.673
The Jeff Ray I knew; a pioneer preacher in Texas. With introd. by W. R. White. San Antonio, Naylor Co. [1952] 192 p. illus. 22 cm. [BX6495.R35R3] 52-9348
1. Ray, Jefferson Davis, 1860-1951. I. Title.

Ray, John, 1627-1705.

RAVEN, Charles Earle, 1885- 925.7
John Ray, naturalist, his life and works. [2d ed.] Cambridge [Eng.] University Press, 1950. xix, 506p. port. 24cm. Sources : p. [xiii]-xv. Bibliographical footnotes. [QH31.R2R] A53
1. Ray, John, 1627-1705. I. Title.

RAY, John, 1627-1705. 574'.092'4 B
The correspondence of John Ray / edited by Edwin Lankester. New York : Arno Press, 1975. xvi, 502 p., [1] leaf of plates : ill. ; 23 cm. (History, philosophy, and sociology of science) Reprint of the 1848 ed. printed for the Ray Society, London, issued in series: Ray Society publications. Includes index. [QH31.R2A4 1975] 74-26287 ISBN 0-405-06613-9 : 29.00
1. Ray, John, 1627-1705. 2. Naturalists—Correspondence, reminiscences, etc. I. Title. II. Series. III. Series: Ray Society, London. Publications. BIP

Ray, Man,

RAY, Man, 1890- 927.5
Self portrait. [1st ed.] Boston, Little, Brown [1963] 402 p. illus. 24 cm. [ND237.R178A2] 63-8319
I. Title.

Ray, Satyajit, 1922-

SETON, Marie. 791.43'0233'0924
Portrait of a director: Satyajit Ray. Bloomington, Indiana University Press [1971] 350 p. illus., facsims., geneal. table, maps (on lining papers), ports. 23 cm. [PN1998.A3R37] 75-108946 ISBN 0-253-16815-5 8.95
1. Ray, Satyajit, 1922- I. Title.

Rayburn, Otto Ernest.

RAYBURN, Otto Ernest. 920
Forty years in the Ozarks; an autobiography. Foreword by Vance Randolph. Eureka Springs, Ark, Ozark Guide Press [1957] 101p. 21cm. [CT275.R286A3] 57-37895
I. Title.

Rayburn, Sam Taliaferro, 1882-1961.

DOROUGH, C. Dwight, 1912- 923.273
Mr. Sam. New York, Random [c.1962] 597p. illus. 25cm. Bibl. 62-14442 8.50
1. Rayburn, Sam Taliaferro, 1882-1961. I. Title.

STEINBERG, Alfred, 1917- 328.73'092'4 B
Sam Rayburn : a biography / Alfred Steinberg. New York : Hawthorn Books, [1975] xiii, 391 p., [4] leaves of plates : ill. ; 25 cm. Includes index. Bibliography: p. 369-374. [E748.R24S73 1975] 74-3604 ISBN 0-8015-5210-9 : 15.00
1. Rayburn, Sam Taliaferro, 1882-1961.

Rayburn, Sam Taliaferro, 1882-1961 — Juvenile literature.

ALLEN, Edward, 1929- 923.273
Sam Rayburn; leading the lawmakers. Chicago, Enclyclopaedia Britannica Press [1963] 191 p. 22 cm. (Britannica bookshelf: great lives) [E748.R24.A7] 63-13518
1. Rayburn, Sam Taliaferro, 1882-1961 — Juvenile literature. I. Title.

Rayleigh, John William Strutt, Baron, 1842-1919.

LINDSAY, Robert Bruce, 1900- 530'.0924 B
Men of physics: Lord Rayleigh—the man and his work. [1st ed.] Oxford, New York, Pergamon Press [1970] viii, 251 p. 20 cm. (The Commonwealth and international library. Selected readings in physics) Bibliography: p. 38-71. [QC16.R3L5 1970] 79-94934
1. Rayleigh, John William Strutt, baron, 1842-1919. I. Title.

RAYLEIGH, Robert John Strutt, Baron, 1875- 530'.0924
Life of John William Strutt, Third Baron Rayleigh, O.M., F.R.S., by Robert John Strutt, Fourth Baron Rayleigh. An augm. ed. with annotations by the author and foreword by John N. Howard. Madison, Univ. of Wis. Pr., 1968. xxvii, 439p. geneal. table, ports. 23cm. First ed. pub. in 1924 under title: John William Strutt, Third Baron Rayleigh. [QC16.R3R3 1968] (B) 68-16063 10.00
1. Rayleigh, John William Strutt, Baron, 1842-1919. I. Title.

RAYLEIGH, Robert John Strutt, Baron, 1875- 530'.0924 (B)
Life of John William Strutt, Third Baron Rayleigh, O. M., F. R. S., by Robert John Strutt, Fourth Baron Rayleigh. An augm. ed. with annotations by the author and foreword by John N. Howard. Madison, University of Wisconsin Press, 1968. xxvii, 439 p. geneal. table, ports. 23 cm. First ed. published in 1924 under title: John William Strutt, Third Baron Rayleigh. [QC16.R3R3] 68-16063
1. Rayleigh, John William Strutt, Baron, 1842-1919. I. Title.

Raymond, Antonin, 1888-

RAYMOND, Antonin, 1888- 720'.92'4 B
Antonin Raymond; an autobiography. Rutland, Vt., C. E. Tuttle [1973] 328 p. illus. (part col.) 32 cm. [NA737.R33A22] 72-91552 ISBN 0-8048-1044-3 27.50
1. Raymond, Antonin, 1888- BIP

Raymond, Father, 1903-

RAYMOND, Father, 1903- 271'.125'024 B
Forty years behind the wall / M. Raymond. Huntington, Ind. : Our Sunday Visitor, c1979. 336 p. ; 21 cm. [BX4705.R3744A29] 79-83875 ISBN 0-87973-644-5 : 5.95
1. Raymond, Father, 1903- 2. Trappists in the United States—Biography. I. Title.

Raymond, Henry Jarvis, 1820-1869.

BROWN, Ernest Francis, 1903- 070.4'0924 B
Raymond of the Times [by] Francis Brown. Westport, Conn., Greenwood Press

[1970, c1951] viii, 345 p. illus., ports. 23 cm. "Some notes on bibliography": p. [335]-340. [PN4874.R3B7 1970] 79-100216
1. Raymond, Henry Jarvis, 1820-1869. I. Title. **BIP**

Raymond III, of Tripolis, 1140 (ca.)-1187.

BALDWIN, Marshall Whithed, 1903- 956.94'4'030924
Raymond III of Tripolis and the fall of Jerusalem (1140-1187) / by Marshall Whitehead Baldwin. New York : AMS Press, 1978. viii, 177 p., [1] fold. leaf of plates : ill. ; 23 cm. Originally presented as the author's thesis, Princeton University, 1933. Reprint of the 1936 ed. published by Princeton University Press, Princeton, N.J. Includes index. Bibliography: p. [161]-172. [D194.R39B34 1978] 76-29830 ISBN 0-404-15411-5 : 22.50
1. Raymond III, of Tripolis, 1140 (ca.)-1187. 2. Jerusalem—History—Latin Kingdom, 1099-1244. 3. Crusades—Biography. I. Title. **BIP**

Raymond IV de Saint-Gilles, count of Toulouse, d. 1105.

HILL, John Hugh. 923.244
Raymond IV, count of Toulouse [by] John Hugh Hill and Laurita Lyttleton Hill. [Syracuse, N. Y.] Syracuse University Press, 1962. 177p. illus. 22cm. Includes bibliography. [D161.2.H5] 62-14120
1. Raymond IV de Saint-Gilles, count of Toulouse, d. 1105. 2. Crusades—First, 1096-1099. I. Hill, Laurita Lyttleton, joint author. II. Title.

Raymond, Robert S.

RAYMOND, Robert S. 940.54'49'410924 B
A Yank in Bomber Command / by Robert S. Raymond ; edited by Michael Moynihan ; pref. by Noble Frankland. Newton Abbot : David & Charles ; New York : Hippocrene Books, 1977. 159 p., [2] leaves of plates : ill. ; 23 cm. [D786.R37 1977] 76-46270 ISBN 0-88254-428-4 : 12.95
1. Raymond, Robert S. 2. Great Britain. Royal Air Force. Bomber Command—Biography. 3. World War, 1939-1945—Aerial operations, British. 4. World War, 1939-1945—Personal narratives, American. 5. Air pilots, Military—Great Britain—Biography. I. Title. **BIP**

Raymundus de Pennaforte, Saint, 1175?-1275.

ERNEST, Brother, 1897- 922.246
When all ships failed; a story of St. Raymond of Pennafort. Illus. by Brother Bernard Howard. Notre Dame, Ind., Dujarie Press [1953] 93p. illus. 24cm. [BX4700.R35E7] 53-3998
1. Raymundus de Pennaforte, Saint, 1175?-1275. I. Title.

Rayner, Betty.

CLARK, Mavis Thorpe. 792'.0226'0994
Joan & Betty Rayner, strolling players. Melbourne, Lansdowne, 1972. 164 p. illus. 23 cm. [PN3018.R3C5] 72-197047 ISBN 0-7018-0005-4 6.95
1. Rayner, Joan. 2. Rayner, Betty. 3. Australian Children's Theatre.

Rayner, Joan.

CLARK, Mavis Thorpe. 792'.0226'0994
Joan & Betty Rayner, strolling players. Melbourne, Lansdowne, 1972. 164 p. illus. 23 cm. [PN3018.R3C5] 72-197047 ISBN 0-7018-0005-4 6.95
1. Rayner, Joan. 2. Rayner, Betty. 3. Australian Children's Theatre.

Read, Grantly Dick, 1890-

THOMAS, A Noyes. 926.1
Doctor courageous: the story of Dr. Grantly Dick Read. New York, Harper [1957] 218 p. illus. 22 cm. [RG76.R4T47] 57-8196
1. Read, Grantly Dick, 1890- I. Title.

Read, Helen Calvert Maxwell,

READ, Helen Calvert Maxwell, 1750-1833. 917.55'03'20924 B
Memoirs of Helen Calvert Maxwell Read. Edited by Charles B. Cross, Jr. [Chesapeake, Va.] Norfolk County Historical Society of Chesapeake, Virginia, 1970. 83 p. illus., facsims., maps, ports. 25 cm. [CT275.R317A3] 74-15040
I. Cross, Charles Brinson, 1914- ed. II. Norfolk County Historical Society of Chesapeake, Virginia.

Read, Herbert Edward,

READ, Herbert Edward, Sir 1893- 928.2
The contrary experience; autobiographies. [1st American ed.] New York, Horizon Press [1963] 356 p. 23 cm. Includes the author's The innocent eye and part 2 of his Annals of innocence and experience, with new and previously unpublished material. [PR6035.E24Z55] 63-13207
I. Title.

Read, Herbert Edward, Sir, 1893-1968—Biography.

READ, Herbert Edward, Sir 1893- 928.2
The contrary experience; autobiographies. [1st American ed.] New York, Horizon Press [1963] 356 p. 23 cm. Includes the author's The innocent eye and part 2 of his Annals of innocence and experience, with new and previously unpublished material. [PR6035.E24Z55] 63-13207
I. Title.

READ, Herbert Edward, Sir, 1893-1968. 828'.9'1209 B
The contrary experience; autobiographies. Personal foreword by Graham Greene. New York, Horizon Press [1974, c1963] 352 p. 23 cm. "Re-issued with the revisions the author wished to incorporate."—Dust jacket. [PR6035.E24Z55 1974] 73-85856 ISBN 0-8180-0223-9 10.00
1. Read, Herbert Edward, Sir, 1893-1968—Biography. I. Title.

Read, Opie Percival, 1852-1939.

MORRIS, Robert Lee, 1903- 928.1
Opie Read, American humorist, 1852-1939. New York, Helios Bks. [c.1965] 247p. port. 21cm. [PS2679.R6Z75] 64-8665 4.95 bds.,
1. Read, Opie Percival, 1852-1939. I. Title.

MORRIS, Robert Lee, 1903- 928.1
Opie Read, American humorist, 1852-1939 [by] Robert L. Morris. [1st ed.] New York, Helios Books [1965] 247 p. port. 21 cm. [PS2679.R6Z75] 64-8665
1. Read, Opie Percival, 1852-1939. I. Title.

Reade, Charles, 1814-1884.

ELWIN, Malcolm, 1902- 828'.8'08 B
Charles Reade. New York, Russell & Russell [1969] 388 p. ports. 23 cm. Reprint of the 1931 ed. Bibliography: p. 365-372. [PR5216.E6 1969] 68-27056
1. Reade, Charles, 1814-1884. **BIP**

Reade, Charles, 1814-1884—Biography.

READE, Charles L. 828'.8'09 B
Charles Reade, dramatist, novelist, journalist : a memoir compiled chiefly from his literary remains / by Charles L. Reade and Compton Reade. Folcroft, Pa. : Folcroft Library Editions, 1977- v. ; 23 cm. Reprint of the 1887 ed. published by Chapman and Hall, London. [PR5216.R4 1977] 77-18092 ISBN 0-8414-7438-9 lib. bdg. : 85.00
1. Reade, Charles, 1814-1884—Biography. 2. Authors, English—19th century—Biography. I. Reade, Compton, 1834-1909, joint author. II. Title.

Reade, Lovel L.

STRACEY, P D 799.27'6'10924
Reade: elephant hunter [by] P. D. Stracey. London, Hale, 1967. 173 p. 12 plates (incl. ports.). 22 1/2 cm. [SK305.E3S7] 67-112898
1. Reade, Lovel L. 2. Elephant hunting. I. Title.

Readers and speakers—History.

SHAPP, Martha 920
Let's find out about Christopher Columbus, by Martha and Charles Shapp. Pictures by Gloria Gaulke. New York, Watts, c.1964. 44p. col. illus. 22cm. (Let's find out bks.) 64-20619 2.50
1. Readers and speakers—History. I. Shapp, Charles, joint author. II. Title.

Readers—Autobiography.

MYERS, Franklin G. 808'.0427
It's your life : autobiographical writing / Franklin G. Myers. Englewood Cliffs, N.J. : Prentice-Hall, c1978. 272 p. : ill. ; 25 cm. (Passport series) Includes index. A textbook containing instructions for writing an autobiography and basic language arts skills. Includes excerpts from several types of autobiography covering a range of ages and a variety of cultures. [PE1127.A9M9] 77-8653 ISBN 0-13-507665-X : 7.96
1. Readers—Autobiography. 2. Readers (Secondary) 3. English language—Composition and exercises. I. Title. II. Series.

Readers—Biography.

ADVENTURES with athletes and artists, by Henry Bamman [and others] Westchester, Ill., Benefic Press [1968] 319 p. illus. (part col.), ports. 24 cm. (Invitation to adventure series) [PE1127.A8A3] 68-20148 juv
1. Readers—Biography. 2. Athletes—United States—Biography—Juvenile literature. 3. Artists, American—Juvenile literature. I. Bamman, Henry A.

ADVENTURES with athletes and artists, by Henry Bamman [others] Westchester, Ill., Benefic [1968] 319p. illus. (pt. col.), ports. 24cm. (Invitation to adventure ser.) [PE1127.A8A3] 68-20148 3.40 92
1. Readers—Biography. 2. Athletes, American—Juvenile literature. 3. Artists, American—Juvenile literature. I. Bamman, Henry A.
Publisher's address: 10300 West Roosevelt Rd., Westchester, Ill. 60153

BISHOP, Curtis Kent, 1912- 920.073
America: ideals and men, by Curtis Bishop, Grace Bishop, and Clyde Inez Martin. Illus. by Leonard Vosburgh. Austin, Tex., W. S. Benson [1965] 414 p. illus. (part col.) 24 cm. (Adventure trails to reading) Teachers' edition. Bibliography: p. 411-414 [PE1127.H5B53] 63-4697
1. Readers—Biography. 2. U.S.—Biog.—Juvenile literature. I. Bishop, Grace, joint author. II. Martin, Clyde Inez, joint author. III. Title. IV. Series. **BIP**

BROWN, Vashti. 428.6
Above the crowd [by] Vashti Brown, Jack Brown [and] Margaret Lalor. With illus. by Don Miller. Boston, Houghton Mifflin [1970, c1971] vii, 152 p. col. illus., col. maps. 24 cm. Brief biographies of twenty men and women who used their lives to help others. Includes Indira Gandhi, Danny Kaye, Pope John XXIII, and Martin Luther King, Jr. [PE1127.H4B7 1971] 74-125120
1. Readers—Biography. 2. Biography—Juvenile literature. I. Brown, Jack, 1905- joint author. II. Lalor, Margaret, joint author. III. Miller, Don, 1923- illus. IV. Title.

BROWN, Vashti. 428.6
Above the crowd [by] Vashti Brown, Jack Brown [and] Margaret Lalor. With illus. by Don Miller. Boston, Houghton Mifflin [1970, c1971] vii, 152 p. col. illus., col. maps. 24 cm. Brief biographies of twenty men and women who used their lives to help others. Includes Indira Gandhi, Danny Kaye, Pope John XXIII, and Martin Luther King, Jr. [PE1127.H4B7 1971] 74-125120
1. Readers—Biography. 2. Biography—Juvenile literature. I. Brown, Jack, 1905- joint author. II. Lalor, Margaret, joint author. III. Miller, Don, 1923- illus. IV. Title.

KENAN, Lucette Rollet. 428.2
Modern American profiles / Lucette Rollet Kenan. New York : Harcourt Brace Jovanovich, [1975] viii, 213 p. : ill. ; 24 cm. [PE1127.H5K4] 74-25381 ISBN 0-15-559866-X pbk. : 3.95
1. Readers—Biography. I. Title. **BIP**

WOESSNER, Nina C., comp. 920.073
The big ones [compiled by] Nina Woessner [and] William D. Sheldon. Boston, Allyn & Bacon [1969] 328 p. illus. 21 cm. (Breakthrough) [PE1121.W698] 78-78564
1. Readers—Biography. I. Sheldon, William D., joint comp. II. Title.

Reading, Rufus Daniel Isaacs, 1st Marquis of, 1860-1935.

GOODHART, Arthur Lehman, Sir, 1891- 340'.57'0922 B
Five Jewish lawyers of the common law [by] Arthur L. Goodhart. With a new pref. to this ed. and a suppl. on Mr. Justice Felix Frankfurter. Freeport, N.Y., Books for Libraries Press [1971, c1949] vii, 81 p. 23 cm. (Biography index reprint series) Includes bibliograhical references. [KF299.J4G65 1971] 79-148212 ISBN 0-8369-8059-X
1. Benjamin, Judah Philip, 1811-1884. 2. Jessel, George, Sir, 1824-1883. 3. Brandeis, Louis Dembitz, 1856-1941. 4. Reading, Rufus Daniel Isaacs, 1st Marquis of, 1860-1935. 5. Cardozo, Benjamin Nathan, 1870-1938. I. Title. **BIP**

HYDE, Harford Montgomery, 1907- 942'.083'0924 B
Lord Reading; the life of Rufus Isaacs, First Marquess of Reading [by] H. Montgomery Hyde. [1st American ed.] New York, Farrar, Straus and Giroux [1968, c1967] 454 p. illus., ports. 23 cm. Bibliography: p. 428-433. [DA566.9.R3H9 1968] 68-11961
1. Reading, Rufus Daniel Isaacs, 1st Marquis of, 1860-1935.

Reagan, Green Pryor, 1835-1893.

REAGAN, Leroy Amons, 1883- 926.1
G. P. Reagan, country doctor, by Rocky Reagan. San Antonio, Naylor [c.1963] 39p. illus. 22cm. 63-11897 2.95
1. Reagan, Green Pryor, 1835-1893. I. Title.

Reagan, John Henninger, 1818-1905.

PROCTER, Ben H. 923.273
Not without honor; the life of John H. Reagan. Austin, Univ. of Texas Pr. [c.1962] xii, 361p. illus., ports. 24cm. Bibl. 62-9791 6.00
1. Reagan, John Henninger, 1818-1905. I. Title. **BIP**

Reagan, Nancy, 1923-

REAGAN, Nancy, 1923- 979.4'05'0924 B
Nancy / by Nancy Reagan, with Bill Libby. New York : Morrow, 1980. p. cm. [CT275.R323A36] 79-26509 ISBN 0-688-03533-7 : 9.95
1. Reagan, Nancy, 1923- 2. Reagan, Ronald. 3. Actors—United States—Biography. 4. California—Governors—Wives—Biography. I. Libby, Bill, joint author. II. Title. **BIP**

Reagan, Ronald.

BOYARSKY, Bill. 979.4'05'0924 B
The rise of Ronald Reagan. New York, Random House [1968] viii, 269 p. illus., ports. 22 cm. [F866.2.R39B6] 68-18261
1. Reagan, Ronald. I. Title.

BROWN, Edmund Gerald, 1905- 979.4'05'0924
Reagan and reality; the two Californias

[by] Edmund G. (Pat) Brown. New York, Praeger Publishers [1970] xii, 235 p. 22 cm. [F866.2.R39B7 1970] 71-108752 6.95
1. Reagan, Ronald. 2. California—Politics and government—1951- I. Title.

DAVIS, Kathy Randall. 979.4'05'0924
But what's he really like? Menlo Park, Calif., Pacific Coast Publishers [1970] 113 p. illus., ports. 27 cm. [F866.2.R39D3] 78-125093 3.95
1. Reagan, Ronald. I. Title. BIP

EDWARDS, Lee. 979.4'05'0924 B
Reagan; a political biography. San Diego, Calif., Viewpoint Books [1967] 252 p. 18 cm. [F866.2.R39E3] 68-3228
1. Reagan, Ronald. I. Title.

HOBBS, Charles D. 320.9'73'0925
Ronald Reagan : Ronald Reagan's call to action / by Charles D. Hobbs. Nashville : T. Nelson, c1976. 190 p., [4] leaves of plates : ill. ; 21 cm. [F866.2.R39H62] 75-45220 ISBN 0-8407-5605-4 : 7.95
1. Reagan, Ronald. 2. United States—Politics and government—1945- I. Title.

LEIPOLD, L. Edmond, 1902- 979.4'05'0924 B
Ronald Reagan, Governor and statesman, by L. Edmond Leipold. Minneapolis, T. S. Denison [1968] 240 p. illus., ports. 22 cm. (Men of achievement series) [F866.2.R39L4] 68-21247
1. Reagan, Ronald. I. Title.

REAGAN, Ronald. 927.92
Where's the rest of me? By Ronald Reagan with Richard G. Hubler. [1st ed.] New York, Duell, Sloan and Pearce [1965] 316 p. illus. 21 cm. [PN2287.R25A3] 65-11684
1. Motion picture actors and actresses—U.S.—Biography. I. Hubler, Richard Gibson, 1912- II. Title.

SMITH, George Henry, 1922- 979.4'05'0924 B
Who is Ronald Reagan? [By] George H. Smith. New York, Pyramid Books [1968] 173 p. ports. 18 cm. [F866.2.R39S6] 68-7410 0.75
1. Reagan, Ronald. I. Title.

Real estate business—U. S.

RACHLIS, Eugene. 923.373
The land lords [by] Eugene Rachlis & John E. Marquesee. New York, Random House [1963] 302 p. illus. 25 cm. Includes bibliography. [HD205.1963.R2] 63-8337
1. Real estate business—U. S. 2. Land—U. S.—Hist. I. Marquesee, John E., joint author. II. Title.

Real estate business — U.S. — Big.

NATIONAL Association of Real Estate Boards. 016.3015'4
Who's who in the Executive Officers Council of the National Association of Real Estate Boards. [Chicago?] v. 18 cm. [HD251.W45] 63-29559
1. Real estate business — U.S. — Big. I. Title.

Real estate business—Juvenile literature.

TRAVIS, Dempsey, 1920- 658.89'3333'3
Don't stop me now, by Dempsey Travis. With Lestre Brownlee and Leonard Grossman. [Chicago, Childrens Press, 1970] 64 p. ports. 19 cm. (Open door books) A Negro describes his youth in Chicago, his career as a musician, his stint in the Army, and his interest and subsequent career in real estate. [E185.97.T73A3] 92 78-123809
1. Real estate business—Juvenile literature. I. Brownlee, Lestre. II. Grossman, Leonard. III. Title.

Realino, Bernardino, Saint, 1530-1616.

†SWEENEY, Francis W., 1916- 282'.092'4 B
Every man my brother / Francis Sweeney. [Boston] : St. Paul Editions, c1976. 172 p. ; 22 cm. Includes index. Bibliography: p. 165-167. [BX4700.R36S83] 77-370075 4.00
1. Realino, Bernardino, Saint, 1530-1616. 2. Christian saints—Italy—Biography. I. Title. BIP

†SWEENEY, Francis W., 1916- 282'.092'4 B
Every man my brother / Francis Sweeney. [Boston] : St. Paul Editions, c1976. 172 p. ; 22 cm. Includes index. Bibliography: p. 165-167. [BX4700.R36S83] 77-370075 4.00
1. Realino, Bernardino, Saint, 1530-1616. 2. Christian saints—Italy—Biography. I. Title. BIP

Reaugh, Frank, 1860-1945.

HALEY, James Evetts 1901- 759.13
F. Reaugh: man and artist. El Paso, Tex., C. Hertzog, 1960. unpaged. illus. 24cm. [ND237.R25H3] 61-1411
1. Reaugh, Frank, 1860-1945. I. Title.

Reaves, James Robert, 1847-1940.

REAVES, Caroline Margaret, 1881- ed. v. 12
Grateful memories of James Robert Reaves, 1847-1940 and Sarah McMillan Reaves, 1851-1941. Edited by Caroline Margaret Reaves assisted by members of her family. Hartsville, S.C., 1962. iii, 132 p. 29 cm. 67-50248
1. Reaves, James Robert, 1847-1940. 2. Reaves, Sarah (McMillan) 1851-1941. 3. Reaves family. I. Title.

Reavis, James Addison, 1843-1914.

COCKRIDGE, E.H. v. 12
The baron of Arizona ... New York, J. Day [c1967] ix, 304 p. plates. 22 cm. "Documentation and selected bibliography": p. 291-293. 68-45574
1. Reavis, James Addison, 1843-1914. I. Title.

SPIRO, Edward. 364.16'3'0924 B
The Baron of Arizona [by] E. H. Cockridge. New York, John Day Co. [1967] ix, 304 p. map, ports. 22 cm. "Documentation and selected bibliography": p. 291-293. [F811.R4S65] 66-22931
1. Reavis, James Addison, 1843-1914. I. Title.

Recamler, Jeanne Francoise Julie Adedlaide Bernard, 1977-1849.

RECAMIER, Jeanne Francoise Julie Adelaide Bernard, 1777-1849. 944.06'092'4
Memoirs & correspondence of Madame Recamier / translated from the French and edited by Isaphene M. Luyster. New illustrated ed. New York : AMS Press, 1975. xxii, 408 p., [11] leaves of plates : ill. ; 19 cm. (Women of letters) Translation of Souvenirs et correspondance tires des papiers de Madame Recamier. Reprint of the 1867 ed. published by Knight and Millet, Boston. [DC255.R3A25 1975] 73-37715 ISBN 0-404-56808-4 : 21.50.
1. Recamier, Jeanne Francoise Julie Adelaide Bernard, 1777-1849. I. Title. BIP

Reconstruction.

LYNCH, John Roy, 1847-1939. 973.8'0924 B
Reminiscences of an active life; the autobiography of John Roy Lynch. Edited and with an introd. by John Hope Franklin. Chicago, University of Chicago Press [1970] xlii, 521 p. port. 23 cm. (Negro American biographies and autobiographies) Includes bibliographical references. [F341.L97A3] 70-110669 ISBN 0-226-49818-2
1. Reconstruction. 2. U.S.—Politics and government—1865-1900. 3. Mississippi—Politics and government—1865-1950. I. Title. II. Series. BIP

Recreation—U.S.—Blog.

BUTLER, George Daniel, 1893- 790.922
Pioneers in public recreation, by George D. Butler. Minneapolis, Burger Pub. Co. [1965] xi, 219 p. ports. 23 cm. Bibliography: p. 215-219. [GV161.B8] 65-26259
1. Recreation—U.S.—Blog. I. Title.

Red Cloud, Sioux Chief, 1822-1909.

GARST, Doris Shannon, 1899- 970.3 B
The picture story and biography of Red Cloud [by] Shannon Garst. Illustrated by Art Seiden. Chicago, Follett [1965] 141 p. col. illus. 22 cm. (The Library of American heroes) A biography of the Sioux chief Red Cloud, who joined Crazy Horse in leading their people in a prolonged assault against the white man and the confines of the Indian Reservation. [E99.O3G3] 92 AC 68
1. Red Cloud, Sioux Chief, 1822-1909. I. Seiden, Art, illus II. Title.

OLSON, James C 970.50924
Red Cloud and the Sioux problem [by] James C. Olson. Lincoln, University of Nebraska Press [1965] xiii, 375 p. illus., map. (on lining papers) ports. 24 cm. Bibliography: p. 350-359. [E99.O3O4] 65-10048
1. Red Cloud, Sioux chief, 1822-1909. 2. Oglala Indians — Hist. 3. Indians of North America-Government relations. I. Title. BIP

Red Cloud, Sioux Chief, 1822-1909 — Juvenile literature.

GARST, Doris Shannon 1899- 92
The picture story and biography of Red Cloud [by] Shannon Garst. Illustrated by Art Seiden. Chicago, Follett Pub. Co. [1965] 141 p. col. illus. 22 cm. (The Library of American heroes) [E99.O3G3] 65-14467
1. Red Cloud, Sioux Chief, 1822-1909 — Juvenile literature. I. Seiden, Arthur H., illus. II. Title.

MCGAA, Ed. 970.3 B
Red Cloud. Minneapolis, Dillon Press [1971] 54 p. illus. 24 cm. A biography of the Oglala Indian who rose to leadership in the Sioux nation because of his skill with weapons and words. [E99.O3R375] 92 73-146124 ISBN 0-87518-041-8
1. Red Cloud, Sioux Chief, 1822-1909—Juvenile literature. BIP

MCGAA, Ed. 970'.004'97
Red Cloud / by Ed McGaa. Minneapolis : Dillon Press, c1977. 54 p. : ill. ; 24 cm. (The Story of an American Indian) A biography of the Oglala Indian who rose to leadership in the Sioux nation because of his skill with weapons and words. [E99.O3R375 1977] 92 77-12662 ISBN 0-87518-151-1 lib. bdg. : 5.95
1. Red Cloud, Sioux chief, 1822-1909—Juvenile literature. 2. Oglala Indians—Biography—Juvenile literature. I. Title.

VOIGHT, Virginia Frances. 970.3 B
Red Cloud, Sioux war chief / by Virginia F. Voight ; illustrated by Victor Mays. Champaign, Ill. : Garrard Pub. Co., [1975] 80 p. : col. ill. ; 23 cm. A biography of the Sioux Indian who became chief through bravery in battle rather than through heredity and who tried unsuccessfully to save his people's land. [E99.O3R378] 92 74-20884 ISBN 0-8116-6611-5 lib.bdg. : 3.12
1. Red Cloud, Sioux chief, 1822-1909—Juvenile literature. I. Mays, Victor, 1927- ill. II. Title.

Red Cross—Biography.

DEMING, Richard. 361.5'0922 B
Heroes of the International Red Cross. [1st ed.] New York, Meredith Press [1969] xvi, 205 p. illus., ports. 21 cm. [HV569.A1D45] 69-14773 4.95
1. Red Cross—Biography. I. Title.

Red Jacket, Seneca chief, 1751?-1830.

HUBBARD, John Niles, 1815-1897. 973
An account of Sa-go-ye-wat-ha; or, Red Jacket and his people, 1750-1830. New York, B. Franklin [1971] xiv, 356 p. illus. 19 cm. (Burt Franklin research & source works series, 880. American classics in history and social science, 219) Reprint of the 1886 ed., which was issued as no. 13 of Munsell's historical series. [E99.S3R3 1971] 79-179394 ISBN 0-8337-1757-X
1. Red Jacket, Seneca chief, 1751?-1830. 2. Iroquois Indians—Government relations. I. Title.

PARKER, Arthur Caswell, 1881- *970.1 970.2
Red Jacket, last of the Seneca. Drawings by Jack Moment. New York, McGraw-Hill [1952] xi, 228 p. illus., map (on lining papers) 21 cm. (They made America) [E99.S3R37] 52-9764
1. Red Jacket, Seneca chief, 1751?-1830. I. Title.

STONE, William Leete, 1792-1844. 970.3'0924
The life and times of Red-Jacket, or Sa-go-ye-wat-ha; being the sequel to the history of Six Nations. New York, Wiley and Putnam, 1841. St. Clair Shores, Mich., Scholarly Press, 1970. x, 484 p. illus., port. 24 cm. On spine: Life and letters of Red-Jacket. Includes bibliographical references. [E99.S3R4 1970] 71-108543
1. Red Jacket, Seneca chief, 1751?-1830. 2. Farmer's Brother, Seneca chief. 3. Cornplanter, Seneca chief, 1732?-1836. I. Title.

Redd, Lemuel Hardison, 1856-1923.

REDD, Amasa Jay, 1895- 289.3'0924
Lemuel Hardison Redd, Jr., 1856-1923, pioneer, leader, builder. compiled and edited by Amasa Jay Redd. Biography written by Albert R. Lyman. Biographical contributions by family members. Photos. arr. by Amasa Mason Redd. Salt Lake City, 1967. 229 p. illus. 29 cm. Includes bibliographical references. [BX8695.R4R4] 68-4357
1. Redd, Lemuel Hardison, 1856-1923. I. Lyman, Albert R., 1880- II. Title.

REDD, Amasa Jay, 1895- 289.3'0924
Lemuel Hardison Redd, Jr., 1856 1923, pioneer, leader, builder, compiled and edited by Amasa Jay Redd. Biography written by Albert R. Lyman. Biographical contributions by family members. Photos arr. by Amasa Mason Redd Salt Lake City, 1967. 229 p. illus. 29 cm. Includes bibliographical references. [BX8695.R4R4] 68-4357
1. Redd, Lemuel Hardison, 1856-1923. I. Lyman, Albert R., 1880- II. Title.

Redding, Otis, d. 1967.

SCHIESEL, Jane. 784'.092'4 B
The Otis Redding story. [1st ed.] Garden City, N.Y., Doubleday, 1973. 143 p. front. 22 cm. "Otis Redding's albums": p. 139-143. [ML420.R295S3] 70-144294 ISBN 0-385-02335-9 3.95
1. Redding, Otis, d. 1967. I. Title. BIP

Redding, Robert H.

REDDING, Robert H. 917.98'03'4
North to the wilderness; the story of an Alaskan boy, by Robert H. Redding. [1st ed.] Garden City, N.Y., Doubleday [1970] 187 p. col. map (on lining papers) 22 cm. The author relates his boyhood experiences on the Alaskan frontier where he moved with his widowed mother, a schoolteacher, in 1928. [CT275.R3457A3] 92 76-97682 3.95
I. Title.

Reddix, Jacob L.

REDDIX, Jacob L. 378.1'12'0924 B
A voice crying in the wilderness : the memoirs of Jacob L. Reddix / by Jacob L. Reddix. Jackson : University Press of Mississippi, [1974] xi, 238 p., [2] leaves of plates : ill. ; 24 cm. Includes index.

[LA2317.R36A38] 73-86314 ISBN 0-87805-024-8 : 10.95
1. Reddix, Jacob L. 2. Negroes—Education. I. Title. BIP

Redelstein, Elisabeth.

OGLE, Mary S., 1905- 951.04'2'0924 B
China nurse : the life story of Elisabeth Redelstein / by Mary S. Ogle. Mountain View, Calif. : Pacific Press Pub. Association, c1974. 118 p., [5] leaves of plates : ports. ; 22 cm. (A Destiny book ; D-148) [R722.32.R4O36] 74-79164
1. Redelstein, Elisabeth. 2. Missions, Medical—China. 3. China—Description and travel—1901-1948. I. Title.

Redfield, Malissa—Homes and haunts—Vermont.

REDFIELD, Malissa. 813'.5'4 B
Scenes from country life / Malissa Redfield. Englewood Cliffs, N.J. : Prentice-Hall, c1979. 158 p. : ill. ; 22 cm. [PS3568.E345Z475] 78-31856 ISBN 0-13-791632-9 : 8.95
1. Redfield, Malissa—Homes and haunts—Vermont. 2. Novelists, American—20th century—Biography. 3. Country life—Vermont. I. Title. BIP

Redford, Robert—Juvenile literature.

PAIGE, David. 791.43'028'0924 B
Robert Redford / written by David Paige ; designed by Gene Kohler. [Mankato, Minn.] : Creative Education, [c1977] 30 p. : ill. ; 25 cm. (Stars of stage and screen) A biography of the popular actor who starred in the films, "Butch Cassidy and the Sundance Kid," "The Sting," and "All the President's Men." [PN2287.R283P3] 92 76-40604 ISBN 0-87191-554-5 lib.bdg. 4.95
1. Redford, Robert—Juvenile literature. 2. Moving-picture actors and actresses—United States—Biography—Juvenile literature. I. Title. BIP

Redgrave, Michael.

BAIN, Kenneth Bruce Findlater, 1921- 927.92
Michael Redgrave, actor, by Richard Findlater [pseud.] With an introd. by Harold Clurman. New York, Theatre Arts Books [c1956] 170p. illus. 23cm. [PN2598] 56-9609
1. Redgrave, Michael. I. Title.

Redlands, Calif.—Biography.

HINCKLEY, Edith Barrett (Parker) 1880- 917.94'95 B
Redlands and certain old-timers, by Edith Parker Hinckley. Claremont, Calif., Creative Press [1970] 72 p. ports. 22 cm. Contents.Contents.—Maria Armenta Bermudez.—Lewis Jacobs.—Scipio Craig.—Maud Garland.—Jose Rivera.—One of God's gentlemen.—Edith Rounds Smith.—Charles M. Brown.—Lulu Nash.—Arthur Gregory, Sr.—James William Kyle.—Jennie Davis.—Helen Cheney Kimberly. [F869.R3H518] 74-107859
1. Redlands, Calif.—Biography. I. Title. BIP

Redmond, John Edward, 1856-1918.

GWYNN, Denis Rolleston, 1893- 328.42'0924 B
The life of John Redmond, by Denis Gwynn. Freeport, N.Y., Books for Libraries Press [1971] 610 p. illus. 23 cm. Reprint of the 1932 ed. [DA952.R3G7 1971] 77-169761 ISBN 0-8369-5981-7
1. Redmond, John Edward, 1856-1918. 2. Ireland—Politics and government—1901-1910. 3. Ireland—Politics and government—1910-1921. I. Title. BIP

Redon, Odilon, 1840-1916.

MELLERIO, Andre, 1862- 760'.0924
Odilon Redon. New York, Da Capo Press, 1968. 166 p. 206 illus., port. 29 cm. (Da Capo Press series in graphic art, v. 4) "Unabridged republication of the first edition published in Paris in 1913... Also includes the supplementary catalogue that appeared in Mellerio's Odilon Redon: peintre, dessinateur et graveur, published in Paris in 1923." "Bibliographie et expositions": p. [129]-161. [NE650.R4M4] 67-27461
1. Redon, Odilon, 1840-1916. I. Title. BIP

REDON, Odilon, 1840-1916. 760'.092'4
Odilon Redon / edited by Carolyn Keay ; introd. by Thomas Walters. New York : Rizzoli, 1977. 80 p. : ill. (some col.) ; 31 cm. [N6853.R38K42] 76-62547 ISBN 0-8478-0070-9 : 13.95. ISBN 0-8478-0088-1 pbk.
1. Redon, Odilon, 1840-1916. I. Keay, Carolyn.

Reeb, James Joseph, 1927-1965.

HOWLETT, Duncan 288.330924
No greater love: the James Reeb Story. New York, Harper [c.1966] xii, 242p. illus., ports. 22cm. [BX9869.R4H6] 66-11489 4.95
1. Reeb, James Joseph, 1927-1965. I. Title.

Reed, Alfred Hamish,

REED, Alfred Hamish, 1875- 655.5'73'0924
An autobiography [by] A. H. Reed. Wellington, Auckland, Reed [1967] 316p. illus., ports. 25cm. [DU422.R42A3] (B) 68-80899 6.00 bds.,
I. Title.
American distributor: Tri-Ocean, San Francisco.

Reed, Ellis Emmons.

REED, Ellis Emmons. 928.1
Of all people. Philadelphia, Dorrance [196o] 174p. 20cm. Autobiographical. [PS3535.E266Z52] 60-15492
I. Title.

Reed, John, 1887-1920.

BAYES, Ronald H., 1932- 070.924 B
John Reed and the limits of idealism, by Ronald H. Bayes. Fort Smith, Ark., South and West, inc. [1967] 20 p. 24 cm. Bibliography: p. 17-18. [HX84.R4B3] 68-1464
1. Reed, John, 1887-1920. I. Title.

GELB, Barbara. 070'.92'4 B
So short a time; a biography of John Reed and Louise Bryant. [1st ed.] New York, Norton [1973] 304 p. 22 cm. [HX84.R4G4] 73-6630 ISBN 0-393-07478-1 7.50
1. Reed, John, 1887-1920. 2. Bryant, Louise, 1890-1936. I. Title.

O'CONNOR, Richard, 1915- 818'.5'209
The lost revolutionary; a biography of John Reed [by] Richard O'Connor [and] Dale L. Walker. [1st ed.] New York, Harcourt, Brace & World [1967] 328 p. 22 cm. Bibliography: p. [307]-309. [HX84.R4O23] 67-20314
1. Reed, John, 1887-1920. I. Walker, Dale L., joint author. II. Title.

ROSENSTONE, Robert A. 070'.092'4 B
Romantic revolutionary : a biography of John Reed / Robert A. Rosenstone. 1st ed. New York : Knopf : distributed by Random House, 1975. xiv, 430, xiii p., [4] leaves of plates : ill. ; 25 cm. Includes index. Bibliography: p. [411]-430. [HX84.R4R67 1975] 74-21311 ISBN 0-394-46103-7 : 15.00
1. Reed, John, 1887-1920. I. Title. BIP

Reed, John, 1887-1920—Juvenile literature.

HOVEY, Tamara. 070'.92'4 B
John Reed, witness to revolution / by Tamara Hovey. 1st ed. New York : Crown, [1975] xi, 227 p. : ill. ; 24 cm. Includes index. A biography of the "father of modern journalism" whose coverage of the turbulent events of his times earned him a world-wide reputation. [HX84.R4H68] 92 75-4933 ISBN 0-517-51694-2 : 6.95
1. Reed, John, 1887-1920—Juvenile literature. I. Title.

Reed, Joseph, 1741-1785.

ROCHE, John Francis, 1925- 923.573
Joseph Reed, a moderate in the American Revolution. New York, Columbia University Press, 1957 [c1954] x, 298p. port. 24cm. (Columbia studies in the social sciences, no. 595) An outgrowth of the author's thesis, Columbia University. Bibliography: p. [271]-285. [H31.C7 no.595] 57-7187
1. Reed, Joseph, 1741-1785. I. Title. II. Series.

ROCHE, John Francis, 1925- 923.576
Joseph Reed, a moderate in the American Revolution. New York, Columbia University Press, 1957 [c1954] x, 208p. port. 24cm. (Columbia studies in the social sciences, no. 595) An outgrowth of the author's thesis, Columbia University. Bibliography: p. [271]- 285. [H31.C7 no.595] 57-7187
1. Reed, Joseph, 1741-1785. I. Title. II. Series. BIP

ROCHE, John Francis, 1925- 973.33'0924 B
Joseph Reed: a moderate in the American Revolution, by John F. Roche. [1st AMS ed.] New York, AMS Press [1968] x, 298 p. port. 23 cm. (Columbia studies in the social sciences, no. 595) Series statement also appears as: Columbia University studies in the social sciences, 595. Reprint of the 1957 ed. Bibliography: p. [271]-285. [E302.6.R3R6 1968] 68-59259
1. Reed, Joseph, 1741-1785. I. Title. II. Series.

Reed, Nathaniel, 1862-1950.

REED, Nathaniel, 1862-1950. 364.1'62'0924 B
The life of Texas Jack: eight years a criminal—41 years trusting in God. With introd. and notes, by Glenn Shirley. Quanah, Tex., Nortex Press, 1973. xxii, 66 p. illus. 24 cm. (Mesquite collector series, no. 1) Autobiographical. Bibliography: p. 66. [F595.R37A34] 74-171062 4.95
1. Reed, Nathaniel, 1862-1950. 2. Crime and criminals—The West. 3. The West—History—1848-1950. I. Shirley, Glenn. II. Title.

Reed, Richard Brumback, 1891-1918.

REED, Ellen. v. 12
The story of one American's patriotism: Lieutenant Richard B. Reed. [Hartford, Conn., Privately printed, 1964] 197 p. illus. 29 cm. "This book is a personal family record." Foreword signed by Ellen Reed and Orville S. Reed. Limited ed. 67-60920
1. Reed, Richard Brumback, 1891-1918. I. Reed, Orville S., joint author. II. Title.

Reed, Thomas Brackett, 1839-1902.

MCCALL, Samuel Walker, 1851-1923. 973.8'0924 B
Thomas B. Reed. Boston, Houghton, Mifflin. [New York, AMS Press, 1972] x, 303 p. illus. 18 cm. (American statesmen, v. 35) Reprint of the 1914 ed. [E664.R3M14 1972] 74-128950 ISBN 0-404-50885-5
1. Reed, Thomas Brackett, 1839-1902. I. Title. II. Series. BIP

Reed, Walter, 1851-1902.

DOLAN, Edward F. 1924- 926.1
Vanquishing yellow fever: Walter Reed. Illus. by Dan Siculan. Chicago, Ency. Britannica [1963, c.1962] 192p. col. illus. 22cm. (Britannica bkshelf: Great lives for young Amers.) 62-10422 2.36 lib. ed.,
1. Reed, Walter, 1851-1902. I. Title.

DOLAN, Edward F 1924- 926.1
Vanquishing yellow fever: Walter Reed, by Edward F. Dolan, Jr. Illustrated by Dan Siculan. Chicago, Encyclopaedia Britannica Press [1964? c1962] 192 p. illus. 22 cm. (Britannica bookshelf: Great lives series) 64-57226
1. Reed, Walter, 1851-1902. I. Title.

HIGGINS, Helen Boyd. 926.1
Walter Reed, boy who wanted to know. Illustrated by Raymond Burns. [1st ed.] Indianapolis, Bobbs-Merrill Co. [1958] 192p. illus. 20cm. (Childhood of famous Americans series, 96) [R154.R3H48] 57-8695
1. Reed, Walter, 1851-1902. I. Title.

Reed, Walter, 1851-1902—Juvenile literature.

GROH, Lynn. 610'.924 B
Walter Reed, pioneer in medicine. Illustrated by Frank Vaughn. Champaign, Ill., Garrard Pub. Co. [1971] 94 p. illus. (part col.), ports. 24 cm. (Americans all) A biography of the Army doctor who is best known for his discovery of the way in which yellow fever is spread. [R154.R3G7] 92 74-126416 ISBN 0-8116-4563-0 2.49
1. Reed, Walter, 1851-1902—Juvenile literature. I. Vaughn, Frank, 1915- illus. II. Title.

Reeder, Lucille Lois.

REEDER, Lucille Lois. 248.40924
What faith can do. San Antonio, Naylor Co. [1966] 83 p. 22 cm. Autobiolgraphical. [BX6495.R43A3] 66-23434
I. Title.

REEDER, Lucille Lois 248.40924
What faith can do. San Antonio, Tex., Naylor [c.1966] 83p. 22cm. Autobiographical. [BX6495.R43A3] 66-23430 3.95
I. Title.

Reeder, Russell Potter.

REEDER, Russell Potter 355.1'0924
Army brat; life story of a West Pointer, by Red Reeder. [1st ed.] New York, Meredith [1967] x, 240p. port. 23cm. Condensed [U53.R4A32] 67-13910 4.95
I. Title.

REEDER, Russell Potter. 355.10924
Born at reveille, by Red Reeder. [1st ed.] New York, Duell, Sloan and Pearce [1966] xii, 270 p. port. 24 cm. Autobiography. [U53.R4A3] 66-10912
I. Title.

Reedy, Michael J., 1905-

REEDY, Michael J., 1905- 353.006'092'4 B
Play roles on Uncle's payrolls : doing one's thing / by Michael J. Reedy. Alexandria, Va. : Mount Vernon Pub. Co., c1976. iv, 111 p. : ill. ; 23 cm. Autobiographical. Includes index. [JK691.R43] 76-27579 4.00
1. Reedy, Michael J., 1905- 2. Civil service—United States. 3. United States—Officials and employees—Biography. I. Title.

Reedy, William Marion, 1862-1920.

KING, Ethel M. 920.5
Reflections of Reedy; a biography of William Marion Reedy of Reedy's Mirror. Brooklyn 1, N.Y., G. J. Rickard [1962, c.1961] 144p. illus. Bibl. 62-12333 2.75
1. Reedy, William Marion, 1862-1920. 2. The Mirror, St. Louis. I. Title.

PUTZEL, Max. 070.5'092'4
The man in the Mirror; William Marion Reedy and his magazine. Westport, Conn., Greenwood Press [1972, c1963] xiv, 351 p. port. 22 cm. Bibliography: p. 297-310. [PN4874.R36P8 1972] 72-6189 ISBN 0-8371-6453-2 14.50
1. Reedy, William Marion, 1862-1920. 2. The Mirror, St. Louis. I. Title.

PUTZEL, Max. 920.5
The man in the Mirror; William Marion Reedy and his magazine. Cambridge, Harvard University Press, 1963. xiv, 351 p. port. 22 cm. Bibliography: p. 297-310. Bibliographical references included in

"Notes" (p. 311-342) [PN4874.R36P8] 63-17208
1. Reedy, William Marion, 1862-1920. 2. The Mirror, St. Louis. I. Title. BIP

Rees, Emory J., 1870-1947.

EMERSON, Elizabeth Holaday. 266'.96'0924 B
Emory J. Rees language pioneer; a biographical sketch, by Elizabeth H. Emerson. [Gowanda, N.Y., Niagara Frontier Pub. Co., 1958] 25 p. 23 cm. Includes bibliographical references. [BV3625.K42R433] 74-156675
1. Rees, Emory J., 1870-1947. 2. Logooli language. I. Title.

Rees, Seth Cook, 1854-1933.

REES, Paul Stromberg. 922.89
Seth Cook Rees, the warrior-saint, by Paul S. Rees. Indianapolis, Ind., The Pilgrim book room, 1934. ix, p., 2 l., 194 p. front., pl., ports. 19 1/2 cm. [BX7990.H62R47] 44-22353
1. Rees, Seth Cook, 1854-1933. I. Title.

Rees, William Gilbert, 1827-1898.

GRIFFITHS, George John. 919.315'7 B
King Wakatip; how William Gilbert Rees, cousin and cricketing godfather of the incomparable W. G. Grace, emigrated to the colonies and founded the most beautiful township in New Zealand [by] G. J. Griffiths. Dunedin, McIndoe [1971] 156 p. illus., facsims., geneal. table, maps, ports. 22 cm. Bibliography: p. 149. [DU422.R43G7] 72-190294 4.50
1. Rees, William Gilbert, 1827-1898. I. Title.

Reese, Harold Henry, 1919-

SCHOOR, Gene. 927.96357
The Pee Wee Reese story. New York, J. Messner [1956] 190 p. illus. 22 cm. [GV865.R4S35] 56-6795
1. Reese, Harold Henry, 1919-

Reeves, George S.,

REEVES, George S., 1905- 920
A man from South Dakota. [1st ed.] New York, Dutton, 1950. 256 p. map. 21 cm. Autobiography. [CT275.R365A3] 50-7233
I. Title.

Reeves, Malachiah, 1843-1929.

EADS, Lelia Ione (Reeves) comp. v 12
M. Reeves and his family; containing the autobiographical sketch written by Malachiah Reeves, together with historical and genealogical addenda which fill out the story of this pioneer farmer-missionary-preacher. Edited by Mary Joe Reeves Young. Midland, Tex., 1966. 52 p. illus. 22 cm. 67-82924
1. Reeves, Malachiah, 1843-1929. 2. Reeves family. I. Young, Mary Joe (Reeves) ed. II. Title.

Reeves, Melvin.

REEVES, Melvin. 920
Marianna, Catherine and I. [1st ed.] New York, Pageant Press [1957] 150p. 21cm. [CT275.R367A3] 57-8310
I. Title.

Reeves, William Pember, 1857-1932.

SINCLAIR, Keith 354.931000924
William Pember Reeves, New Zealand Fabian. Oxford, Clarendon Pr. [New York, Oxford, c.]1965. x, 356p. ports. 23cm. Bibl. [DU422.R45S5] 65-9091 6.75
1. Reeves, William Pember, 1857-1932. I. Title.

SINCLAIR, Keith. 354.931000924 (B)
William Pember Reeves, New Zealand Fabian. Oxford, Clarendon Press, 1965. x, 356 p. ports. 23 cm. Bibliographical footnotes. [DU422.R45S5] 65-9091
1. Reeves, William Pember, 1857-1932. I. Title.

Reformation—Biography.

BAINTON, Roland Herbert, 1894- 277.6'0922 B
Women of the Reformation, from Spain to Scandinavia / Roland H. Bainton. Minneapolis : Augsburg Pub. House, c1977. 240 p. : ill. ; 22 cm. Includes bibliographies and index. [BR317.B28] 76-27089 ISBN 0-8066-1568-0 : 9.95
1. Reformation—Biography. 2. Women—Biography. I. Title.

BAINTON, Roland Herbert, 1894- 270.6'092'2 B
Women of the Reformation in France and England [by] Roland H. Bainton. Minneapolis, Augsburg Pub. House [1973] 287 p. illus. 23 cm. Bibliography: p. 277. [BR317.B29] 73-78269 ISBN 0-8066-1333-5 8.95
1. Reformation—Biography. 2. Woman—Biography. I. Title.

BAINTON, Roland Herbert, 1894- 270.6'092'2 B
Women of the Reformation in France and England / Roland H. Bainton. Boston : Beacon Press, 1975, c1973. 287 p. : ill. ; 20 cm. Reprint of the ed. published by Augsburg Pub. House, Minneapolis. Includes index. Bibliography: p. 277. [BR317.B29 1975] 75-19393 ISBN 0-8070-5649-9 pbk. : 4.45
1. Reformation—Biography. 2. Women—Biography. I. Title.

BAINTON, Roland Herbert, 1894- 270.6'0922 B
Women of the Reformation in Germany and Italy, by Roland H. Bainton. Minneapolis, Augsburg Pub. House [1971] 279 p. illus., facsims., geneal. table, maps, ports. 23 cm. Includes bibliographies. [BR317.B3 1971] 70-135235 7.95
1. Reformation—Biography. 2. Woman—Biography. I. Title.

BAINTON, Roland Herbert, 1894- 270.6'092'2 B
Women of the Reformation in Germany and Italy, by Roland H. Bainton. Boston, Beacon Press [1974, c1971] 279 p. illus. 21 cm. (Beacon paperback, 485) Reprint of the ed. published by Augsburg Pub. House, Minneapolis. Includes bibliographies. [BR317.B3 1974] 74-6085 ISBN 0-8070-5651-0 3.95
1. Reformation—Biography. 2. Woman—Biography. I. Title.

BELLOC, Hilaire, 1870-1953. 940.2'3'0922 B
Characters of the Reformation. Portraits by Jean Charlot. Freeport, N.Y., Books for Libraries Press [1970] 342 p. ports. 23 cm. (Essay index reprint series) Reprint of the 1936 ed. [BR315.B35 1970] 72-121449
1. Reformation—Biography. I. Title. BIP

GERRISH, Brian Albert, 1931- 270.6'0922
Reformers in profile. Ed. by B. A. Gerrish. Philadelphia, Fortress [1967] vii, 264p. 23cm. Bibl. [BR315.G4] 67-27134 5.95
1. Reformation—Biog. I. Title.
Contents Omitted.

STEINMETZ, David Curtis. 270.6'0922 B
Reformers in the wings [by] David C. Steinmetz. Philadelphia, Fortress Press [1971] viii, 240 p. 23 cm. Includes bibliographies. [BR315.S83] 75-135266 ISBN 0-8006-0051-7 8.50
1. Reformation—Biography. I. Title.

Reformed Church in the United States—Pennsylvania.

BOEHM, John Philip, 1683-1749. 285'.7'0924 B
Life and letters of the Rev. John Philip Boehm, founder of the Reformed Church in Pennsylvania, 1683-1749. Edited by the Rev. William J. Hinke. New York, Arno Press, 1972 [c1916] xxiv, 501 p. illus., map (1 fold.) 24 cm. (Religion in America, series II) [BX9593.B6A3 1972] 71-38784 ISBN 0-405-04069-5
1. Reformed Church in the United States—Pennsylvania. I. Hinke, William John, 1871-1947, ed.

Reformers—Biography.

CARTER, John Franklin, 1897-1967. 320'.0922
American messiahs, by the Unofficial observer. New introd. by Donald H. Stewart. Port Washington, N.Y., Kennikat Press [1969, c1935] 238 p. 22 cm. (Essay and general literature index reprint series) By John Franklin Carter and others. Cf. Who's who in America, 1942-43. [E806.C3843 1969] 68-26232
1. Reformers—Biography. 2. United States—Politics and government—1933-1945. 3. United States—Social conditions—1933-1945. I. Unofficial observer. II. Observer, Unofficial. III. Title.

Refugees, East Indian.

ANAND, Balwant Singh. 361.5'3'0924
Cruel interlude. Bombay, New York, Asia Pub. House [1961] 228 p. 22 cm. Autobiographical. [[HV640.5]] SA62
1. Refugees, East Indian. I. Title.

Refugees, Political.

PIRE, Dominique [Secular name: Georges Charles Clement Ghislain Pire] 923.6493
The story of Father Dominique Pire, winner of the Nobel peace prize, as told to Hugues Vehenne. Tr. from French by John L. Skeffington. New York, Dutton, 1961 [c.1960] 220p. illus., map 60-9747 4.50
1. Refugees, Political. 2. World War, 1939-1945—Displaced persons. I. Vehenne, Hugues. II. Title.

Refugees—Russia—Biography.

HANFMANN, Eugenia, 1905- 947.084'2'0922 B
Six Russian men : lives in turmoil / by Eugenia Hanfmann and Helen Beier. North Quincy, Mass. : Christopher Pub. House, c1976. 218 p. ; 24 cm. Bibliography: p. 217-218. [DK269.H35] 75-32060 ISBN 0-8158-0333-8 : 5.95
1. Refugees—Russia—Biography. 2. Russia—History—1925-1953. 3. Personality and culture. 4. National characteristics, Russian. I. Beier, Helen, joint author. II. Title.

Regional planning—Cambridgeshire and Isle of Ely, Eng.

CAMBRIDGESHIRE and Isle of Ely, Eng. County Planning Dept. 309.2'5'094259
Cambridge study area: a progress report. Cambridge, Cambridgeshire and Isle of Ely (County Planning Department) [1970] [1], 8 p. 30 cm. [HT395.G72C37] 72-175512 ISBN 0-902436 01 5
1. Regional planning—Cambridgeshire and Isle of Ely, Eng. I. Title.

Register, Susanne Haines, 1947-

REGISTER, Susanne Haines, 1947- 248'.246 B
Take it all off / Susanne Haines Register. San Diego : Beta Books ; [New York] : distributed by Two Continents Pub. Group, c1977. p. cm. Autobiography. [BV4935.R36A37] 77-17285 ISBN 0-89293-074-8 pbk. : 2.95
1. Register, Susanne Haines, 1947- 2. Converts—United States—Biography. 3. Entertainers—United States—Biography. I. Title. BIP

Registers of births, etc.—Wayne County, Ky.

BORK, June Baldwin. 929'.3769'64
Wayne County, Kentucky. [Huntington Beach, Calif.] 1972- v. illus. 28 cm. Contents.Contents.—v. 1. Marriages and vital records, 1801-1860: marriages "A-J".—v. 2. Marriages and vital records, 1801-1860: marriages "K-Z".—v. 3. Vital records: 1850 census.—v. 4. Pioneers: biographical sketches and civil court records. [F457.W4B67] 72-193505 15.00 per vol.
1. Registers of births, etc.—Wayne County, Ky. 2. Wayne County, Ky.—Genealogy. I. Title.

Regnery, Henry, 1912-

REGNERY, Henry, 1912- 070.5'092'4 B
Memoirs of a dissident publisher / Henry Regnery. 1st ed. New York : Harcourt Brace Jovanovich, c1979. xii, 260 p. ; 24 cm. Includes index. [Z473.R43A35] 78-22269 ISBN 0-15-173752-5 : 12.95
1. Regnery, Henry, 1912- 2. Publishers and publishing—United States—Biography. 3. Conservatism—United States. I. Title. BIP

Rehabilitation of criminals—Australia—Personal narratives.

MCNALLY, Ward. 365'.92'4 B
Man from zero [by] Ward McNally. Melbourne, Thomas Nelson (Australia), 1973. 214 p. 22 cm. [HV6248.M253A33] 74-194479 ISBN 0-17-001989-6 5.95
1. Rehabilitation of criminals—Australia—Personal narratives. I. Title.

Rehwinkel, Bessie Lee (Efner)

REHWINKEL, Bessie Lee (Efner) 926.1
Dr. Bessie; the life story and romance of a pioneer lady doctor on our Western and the Canadian frontier, as told by herself and here presented in a running narrative by her husband. St. Louis, Concordia [1964, c.1963] ix, 171p. illus., ports. 21cm. 62-21429 3.00 bds.,
I. Rehwinkel, Alfred Martin, 1887- II. Title.

Reich, Charles A.

REICH, Charles A. 340'.092'4 B
The sorcerer of Bolinas Reef / Charles Reich. 1st ed. New York : Random House, c1976. 266 p. ; 22 cm. [KF373.R4A32] 76-14193 ISBN 0-394-49192-0 : 10.00
1. Reich, Charles A. 2. Conduct of life. 3. Lawyers—United States—Biography. I. Title. BIP

Reich, Wilhelm, 1897-1957.

CATTIER, Michel. 615'.85 B
The life and work of Wilhelm Reich. Translated from the French by Ghislaine Boulanger. New York, Horizon Press [1971] 224 p. 22 cm. Translation of La vie et l'oeuvre du docteur Wilhelm Reich. Bibliography: p. 216-218. [BF109.R38C3813] 76-171016 ISBN 0-8180-0220-4 6.95
1. Reich, Wilhelm, 1897-1957. I. Title. BIP

CHESSER, Eustace, 1902- 150'.19
Salvation through sex; the life and work of Wilhelm Reich. New York, W. Morrow, 1973 [c1972] 114 p. 22 cm. Published in 1972 under title: Reich and sexual freedom. Bibliography: p. 113-114. [BF692.C53 1973] 73-9355 ISBN 0-688-00182-3 4.95
1. Reich, Wilhelm, 1897-1957. 2. Sex (Psychology) 3. Psychoanalysis. I. Title.

RADITSA, Leo. 150'.19'50924
Some sense about Wilhelm Reich / Leo Raditsa. New York : Philosophical Library, 1977 126 p. ; 22 cm. Includes bibliographical references. [RC339.52.R44R3] 77-9222 ISBN 0-8022-2212-9 : 6.00
1. Reich, Wilhelm, 1897-1957. 2. Psychoanalysts—United States—Biography. 3. Orgonomy. I. Title. BIP

REICH, Ilse Ollendorff. 615'.856
Wilhelm Reich; a personal biography. With an introd. by Paul Goodman. New York, St. Martin's Press, 1969. xxi, 167 p. illus., ports. 22 cm. Bibliography: p. 161-162. [RZ460.R4] 69-17316 5.95
1. Reich, Wilhelm, 1897-1957.

Reichel, Willy.

REICHEL, Willy. 133.9'092'4 B
An occultist's travels / by Willy Reichel. Philadelphia : Running Press, [1975] 244 p. ; 22 cm. Originally published in 1908. [BF1241.R3 1975] 74-31539 ISBN 0-914294-10-5 pbk. : 3.95
1. Reichel, Willy. 2. Spiritualism. I. Title. BIP

Reid, Forrest, 1875-1947—Biography.

REID, Forrest, 1875-1947. 823'.9'12 B
Private road / by Forrest Reid. New York : AMS Press, 1978. 243 p. ; 18 cm. Continues Apostate, the first part of the author's autobiography. Reprint of the 1940 ed. published by Faber and Faber, London. [PR6035.E43Z52 1978] 75-41225 ISBN 0-404-14587-6 : 14.00
1. Reid, Forrest, 1875-1947—Biography. 2. Authors, English—20th century—Biography. I. Title. BIP

Reid, James Seaton, 1793-1851.

ALLEN, Robert, 1904- 285'.2'0924
James Seaton Reid, a centenary biography. With a foreword by John Foster. Belfast, W. Mullan, 1951. 207p. illus. 22cm. [BX9225.R38A65] 55-17401
1. Reid, James Seaton, 1793-1851. I. Title.

Reid, Jim.

REID, Jim. 286'.132'0924 B
Praising God on the Las Vegas Strip / Jim Reid ; foreword by Creath Davis. Grand Rapids : Zondervan Pub. House, [1975] 183 p. ; 21 cm. [BV3775.L3R44] 74-25335 5.95
1. Reid, Jim. 2. Evangelistic work—Las Vegas, Nev. I. Title.

Reid, Jimmy, 1932-

REID, Jimmy, 1932- 335.43'4
Reflections of a Clyde-built man / [by] Jimmy Reid ; compiled by Ruth Wishart. London : Souvenir Press, 1977. viii, 166 p. ; 23 cm. (A Condor book) Label mounted on t.p.: Exclusive distributor, ISBS, Inc., Forest Grove, Or. [HD8393.R4A36] 78-315354 ISBN 0-285-64825-X pbk. : 4.95
1. Reid, Jimmy, 1932- 2. Upper Clyde Shipbuilders. 3. Trade-unions—Great Britain—Officials and employees—Biography. 4. Great Britain—Politics and government—1964- I. Title. BIP

Reid, Loren Dudley, 1905-

REID, Loren Dudley, 1905- 977.8'17 B
Hurry home Wednesday : growing up in a Missouri small town / Loren Reid. Columbia : University of Missouri Press, 1978. p. cm. [F474.G4R44] 77-25401 ISBN 0-8262-0247-0 : 12.95
1. Reid, Loren Dudley, 1905- 2. Gilman City, Mo.—Biography. 3. Gilman City, Mo.—History. I. Title.

Reid, Thomas, 1870-1958.

DONER, Mary Frances. 926.56
The salvager; the life of Captain Tom Reid on the Great Lakes. [1st ed.] Minneapolis, Ross and Haines, 1958. 312 p. illus. 23 cm. [VK1491.D65] 58-42628
1. Reid, Thomas, 1870-1958. 2. Salvage—Great Lakes. 3. Ship-wrecks—Great Lakes. I. Title.

Reid, Whitelaw, 1837-1912.

DUNCAN, Bingham. 070'.92'4 B
Whitelaw Reid : journalist, politician, diplomat / Bingham Duncan. Athens : University of Georgia Press, c1975. 305 p. : port. ; 25 cm. Includes index. Bibliography: p. 289-298. [E664.R35D86] 73-90844 ISBN 0-8203-0353-4 : 11.00
1. Reid, Whitelaw, 1837-1912.

DUNCAN, Bingham. 070'.92'4 B
Whitelaw Reid : journalist, politician, diplomat / Bingham Duncan. Athens : University of Georgia Press, c1975. 305 p. : port. ; 25 cm. Includes index. Bibliography: p. 289-298. [E664.R35D86] 73-90844 ISBN 0-8203-0353-4 : 11.00
1. Reid, Whitelaw, 1837-1912. BIP

Reigeluth, Ray John.

REIGELUTH, Ray John. 926.24
The heritage of an ancestor. New Haven, 1958. 162p. illus. 21cm. Autobiography. [CT275.R375A3] 59-21428
I. Title.

Reik, Theodor, 1888-1970.

REIK, Theodor, 1888-1969. 150'.19'50924 B
Fragment of a great confession; a psychoanalytic autobiography. Westport, Conn., Greenwood Press [1973, c1949] ix, 497 p. 23 cm. "Goethe's romance with Friederike": p. [31]-211. Reprint of the 1965 ed. published by Citadel Press, New York. [BF109.R4A3 1973] 73-2643 ISBN 0-8371-6812-0
1. Reik, Theodor, 1888-1969. 2. Goethe, Johann Wolfgang von, 1749-1832—Relationship with women—Friederike von Sesenheim. I. Reik, Theodor, 1888-1970. Warum verliess Goethe Friederike? English. 1973. II. Title.

REIK, Theodor, 1888-1969. 150'.19'50924
The search within; the inner experiences of a psychoanalyst. New York, Funk & Wagnalls [1968, c1956] xi, 657 p. facsim. 21 cm. Bibliographical footnotes. [BF173.R423 1968] 70-4368 8.95
1. Reik, Theodor, 1888-1969. 2. Psychoanalysis. I. Title.

REIK, Theodor, 1888-1970. 150'.19'50924 B
Fragment of a great confession; a psychoanalytic autobiography. Westport, Conn., Greenwood Press [1973, c1949] ix, 497 p. 23 cm. "Goethe's romance with Friederike": p. [31]-211. Reprint of the 1965 ed. published by Citadel Press, New York. [BF109.R4A3 1973] 73-2643 ISBN 0-8371-6812-0 17.50
1. Reik, Theodor, 1888-1970. 2. Goethe, Johann Wolfgang von, 1749-1832—Relationship with women—Friederike von Sesenheim. I. Reik, Theodor, 1888-1970. Warum verliess Goethe Friederike? English. 1973. II. Title.

Reilly, Sidney George, 1874-1925.

LOCKHART, Robin N. Bruce. 355'.3'432'0924
Ace of spies, by Robin Bruce Lockhart. New York, Stein and Day [1968, c1967] 192 p. illus., ports. 22 cm. [DA574.R4L6 1968] 68-16038
1. Reilly, Sidney George, 1874-1925. I. Title. BIP

Reines, Isaac Jacob, 1839-1915.

WANEFSKY, Joseph. 296.6'1'0924
Rabbi Isaac Jacob Reines; his life and thought. New York, Philosophical Library [1970] 171 p. 23 cm. Bibliography: p. 171. [BM755.R348W35] 79-118314 ISBN 0-8022-2349-4 5.95
1. Reines, Isaac Jacob, 1839-1915.

Reinhardt, Aurelia (Henry) 1877-1948.

HEDLEY, George Percy, 1899- 923.773
Aurelia Henry Reinhardt; portrait of a whole woman. [Oakland, Calif.] Mills College [c.]1961. 299p. illus. 27cm. Bibl. 61-18232 12.95
1. Reinhardt, Aurelia (Henry) 1877-1948. 2. Mills College, Calif.—Hist. I. Title.

Reinhardt, Max, 1873-1943.

REINHARDT, Gottfried. 792'.0233'0924 B
The genius : the memoir of Max Reinhardt / by his son Gottfried Reinhardt. New York : Knopf, 1979. p. cm. Translation of Der Liebhaber. Includes index. [PN2658.R4R413] 78-20600 ISBN 0-394-49085-1. : 15.95
1. Reinhardt, Max, 1873-1943. 2. Theatrical producers and directors—Germany—Biography. I. Title. BIP

Reinharz, Shulamit.

REINHARZ, Shulamit. 300'.7'2
On becoming a social scientist / Shulamit Reinharz. 1st ed. San Francisco : Jossey-Bass Publishers, 1979. xviii, 422 p. ; 24 cm. (Jossey-Bass social and behavioral science series) Includes index. Bibliography: p. 383-410. [H62.R417] 79-83577 ISBN 0-87589-416-X : 15.95
1. Reinharz, Shulamit. 2. Social sciences—Methodology. 3. Social science research—Case studies. 4. Sociological research. 5. Social scientists—Biography. 6. Socialization. I. Title.

Reinhold, Hans Ansgar,

REINHOLD, Hans Ansgar, 1897- 282'.0924 B
H.A.R.; the autobiography of Father Reinhold. [New York] Herder and Herder [1968] x, 150 p. 21 cm. [BX4705.R433A3] 67-29678
I. Title.

Reinsch, Paul Samuel, 1869-1923.

PUGACH, Noel H. 327.2'092'4
Paul S. Reinsch, open door diplomat in action / Noel H. Pugach. Millwood, N.Y. : KTO Press, 1979. xii, 310 p. : ill. ; 24 cm. (KTO studies in American history) Includes index. Bibliography: p. [294]-298. [E748.R33P83] 79-1503 ISBN 0-527-73050-5. : 19.95
1. Reinsch, Paul Samuel, 1869-1923. 2. United States—Relations (general) with China. 3. China—Relations (general) with the United States. 4. Eastern question (Far East) 5. Diplomats—United States—Biography. I. Title. II. Series.

Reis, Claire Raphael.

REIS, Claire Raphael. 780'.92'2
Composers, conductors, and critics / by Claire R. Reis ; with new introd. by the author ; new pref. by Aaron Copland ; foreword by Darius Milhaud. Detroit : Detroit Reprints in Music, 1974. xvi, xiii, 264 p., [2] leaves of plates : ill. ; 22 cm. (Music for the Bicentennial) Reprint of the 1955 ed. published by Oxford University Press, New York. Includes index. [ML423.R365A3 1974] 74-75896 ISBN 0-911772-62-6 : 8.50
1. Reis, Claire Raphael. 2. League of Composers, inc. 3. Musicians—Correspondence, reminiscences, etc. 4. Music—United States. I. Title.
A Division of Information Coordinators BIP

Reis, Philipp, 1834-1874.

THOMPSON, Silvanus Phillips, 1851-1916. 621.385'092'4 B
Philipp Reis, inventor of the telephone. New York, Arno Press, 1974. ix, 182 p. illus. 23 cm. (Telecommunications) Reprint of the 1883 ed. published by E. & F. N. Spon, London, New York. Includes bibliographical references. [TK6143.R4T5 1974] 74-4696
1. Reis, Philipp, 1834-1874. 2. Telephone—History. I. Title. II. Series: Telecommunications (New York, 1974-)

Reisman, Marty, 1930-

REISMAN, Marty, 1930- 796.34'6'0924 B
The money player; the confessions of America's greatest table tennis champion and hustler. New York, Morrow, 1974. 241 p. illus. 22 cm. [GV1005.22.R44A35] 74-6197 ISBN 0-688-00273-0 6.95
1. Reisman, Marty, 1930- 2. Table tennis. I. Title. BIP

Reissig family

SCHENCK, Lucy (Reissig) 920.7
Seven, eight shut the gate! The heartwarming story of an American family. [1st ed.] New York, Greenwich Book Publishers [1958] 86p. 22cm. Autobiographical. [CT275.S3434A3] 58-43949
1. Reissig family I. Title.

Rejlander, Oscar Gustav, 1813-1875.

JONES, Edgar Yoxall. 770'.92'4 B
Father of art photography, O. G. Rejlander, 1813-1875. Greenwich, Conn., New York Graphic Society [1973] 112 p. illus. 25 cm. Includes bibliographical references. [TR140.R43J66 1973b] 73-89945 ISBN 0-8212-0598-6
1. Rejlander, Oscar Gustav, 1813-1875. 2. Photography, Artistic. I. Rejlander, Oscar Gustav, 1813-1875. II. Title.

Religion and sports—Juvenile literature.

SAFE at home / 796.357'092'2 B
compiled by Rick Arndt. St. Louis : Concordia Pub. House, c1979. p. cm. [GV706.S22] 79-11145 ISBN 0-570-03619-4 : 3.95
1. Religion and sports—Juvenile literature. 2. Baseball players—United States—Biography—Juvenile literature. I. Arndt, Rick, 1956- BIP

Religion—Biography—Addresses, essays, lectures.

THE Biographical process : 200'.92
studies in the history and psychology of religion / edited by Frank E. Reynolds and Donald Capps. The Hague : Mouton, 1977 xi, 436 p. ; 23 cm. (Religion and reason ; 11) Based on seminars held at the Divinity School, University of Chicago, 1972 and 1973. Includes indexes. Bibliography: p. 413-426. [BL72.B56] 77-352279 ISBN 9-02-797522-1 : 31.25
1. Religion—Biography—Addresses, essays, lectures. 2. Biography (as a literary form)—Addresses, essays, lectures. I. Reynolds, Frank, 1930- II. Capps, Donald. III. Chicago. University. Divinity School.
Distributed by Humanities Press BIP

Religions—Biography.

BANCROFT, Anne, 1923- 200'.92'2 B
Twentieth century mystics and sages / Anne Bancroft. Chicago : Regnery, 1976. p. cm. Includes bibliographical references and index. [BL72.B36] 76-153 ISBN 0-8092-8148-1. ISBN 0-8092-8237-2 pbk.
1. Religions—Biography. I. Title.

BOWDEN, Henry Warner. 209'.2'2 B
Dictionary of American religious biography / Henry Warner Bowden ; Edwin S. Gaustad, advisory editor. Westport, Conn. : Greenwood Press, 1976. p. cm. Includes bibliographies and index. [BL72.B68] 76-5258 ISBN 0-8371-8906-3 lib.bdg. : 29.95
1. Religions—Biography. 2. United States—Biography. I. Title. BIP

BURROWS, Millar, 1889- 200'.92'2 B
Founders of great religions, being personal sketches of famous leaders. Freeport, N.Y., Books for Libraries Press [1973] p. (Essay index reprint series) Reprint of the 1931 ed. [BL72.B8 1973] 72-13272 ISBN 0-8369-8148-0
1. Religions—Biography. I. Title.

CHANLER, Julie (Olin) 1882-1961. 291.6'3'0922 B
His messengers went forth. Illustrated by Olin Dows. Freeport, N.Y., Books for Libraries Press [1971, c1948] 64 p. illus. 23 cm. (Biography index reprint series) [BL72.C45 1971] 77-148209 ISBN 0-8369-8056-5
1. Religions—Biography. I. Title. BIP

EASTMAN, Max, 1883-1969. 200'.922
Seven kinds of goodness. New York, Horizon Press [1967] 156 p. 22 cm. [BL72.E15] 67-17781
1. Religions—Biography. I. Title.

FREMANTLE, Anne (Jackson), 1909- 220'.922
Pilgrimage to people, by Anne Fremantle.

New York., McKay [1968] viii, 231p. 21cm. [BL72.F73] 68-10539 5.50
1. Religions—Biog. I. Title.

FREMANTLE, Anne 200'.922
(Jackson) 1909-
Pilgrimage to people, by Anne Fremantle. New York, McKay [1968] viii, 231 p. 21 cm. [BL72.F73] 68-10539
1. Religions—Biography. I. Title.

GAER, Joseph, 1897- 922
Young heroes of the living religions. Drawings by Anne Marie Jauss. [1st ed.] Boston, Little, Brown [1953] 201p. illus. 22cm. [BL72.G28] 53-7323
1. Religions—Biog. I. Title.

MIEROW, Charles Christopher, 922
1883-
The hallowed flame. Evanston, Ill., Principia Press of Illinois [c1956] 255p. 24cm. Includes bibliography. [BL72.M5] 58-14652
1. Religions—Biog. I. Title. BIP

*POWERS, Robert 922.777 B
Merrill.
Prairie preacher; a tale of our yesterdays along the middle border; memoirs. 1st. ed. [Jericho] N.Y. Exposition [1974] 165 p. 22 cm. [CT5500] ISBN 0-682-47854-7 7.00
1. Religions—Biography. I. Title.

STROUP, Herbert 200'.92'2 B
Hewitt, 1916-
Founders of living religions, by Herbert Stroup. Philadelphia, Westminster Press [1974] 256 p. 21 cm. Bibliography: p. [241] -244. [BL72.S8] 74-10934 ISBN 0-664-24994-9 4.25
1. Religions—Biography. 2. Religions. I. Title.

THOMAS, Henry, 1886- 922
Living biographies of religious leaders, by Henry Thomas and Dana Lee Thomas. Garden City, N.Y., Garden City Books [1959] 298 p. illus. 22 cm. [BL72.T36 1959] 59-3053
1. Religions — Biog. I. Thomas, Dana Lee, 1918- joint author. II. Title.

THOMAS, Henry, 1886 922
Living biographies of religious leaders, by Henry Thomas and Dana Lee Thomas. Garden City, N. Y., Perma Giants [1950, c1942] viii, 297p. 22cm. [BL72.T36 1950] 51-30711
1. Religions—Biog. I. Thomas, Dana Lee, 1918- joint author. II. Title.

VAN BUSKIRK, William 291.6'3 B
Riley.
The saviors of mankind. Freeport, N.Y. Books for Libraries Press [1969] xiv, 537 p. 23 cm. (Essay index reprint series) Reprint of the 1929 ed. Contents.Contents.—Lao-Tze.—Confucius.—Guatama.—Zoroaster.—Aakhnaton.—Moses.—Isaiah of Babylon.—Socrates.—Jesus of Nazareth.—Saul of Tarsus.—Mahomet. [BL72.V3 1969] 71-86790
1. Religions—Biography. 2. Prophets. I. Title. BIP

Religions—Biography—Juvenile literature.

BLOOM, Naomi, 1938- 209'2'2 B
Religion / by Naomi Bloom. Minneapolis : Dillon Press, c1978. 126, [1] p. : ill. ; 23 cm. (Contributions of women) Bibliography: p. [127] Six biographies of women who have made outstanding contributions to religion. Included are Anne Hutchinson, Ann Lee, Mary Baker Eddy, Amanda Smith, Henrietta Szold, and Dorothy Day. [BL72.B59] 920 77-20034 ISBN 0-87518-123-6 : 6.95
1. Religions—Biography—Juvenile literature. 2. Women—United States—Biography—Juvenile literature. 3. Reformers—United States—Biography—Juvenile literature. 4. Women in religion—Juvenile literature. I. Title.

HEIDERSTADT, Dorothy. 920
Ten torchbearers. Illustrated by Robert W. Arnold. New York, T. Nelson [1961] 192p. illus. 21cm. Includes bibliography [BR569.H4] 61-13831
1. —Religions biography —Juvenile literature. I. Title.

Religious — Biog.

SCHNITTKIND, Henry Thomas, 922
1888-
Living biographies of religious leaders, by Henry Thomas [pseud.] and Dana Lee Thomas [pseud.] Garden City, N.Y., Perma Giants [1950, c1942] viii, 297 p. 22 cm. [BL72.S37 1950] 51-30711
1. Religious — Biog. I. Schnittkind, Dana Arnold, 1918- joint author. II. Title.

Religious liberty.

BAINTON, Roland 261.7'2'0922
Herbert, 1894-
The travail of religious liberty; nine biographical studies, by Roland H. Bainton. [Hamden, Conn.] Archon Books, 1971 [c1951] 272 p. illus. 23 cm. Bibliography: p. [261]-266. [BV741.B26 1971] 76-122412 ISBN 0-208-01085-8 8.50
1. Religious liberty. 2. Christian biography. I. Title. BIP

Remarriage—Miscellanea.

ADLER, Bill. 301.42'7
The second time is better / by Bill Adler & Gary Wagner. 1st ed. Chicago : Playboy Press, 1979. 221 p. ; 18 cm. [HQ728.A34] 78-70091 ISBN 0-87216-515-9 pbk. : 1.95
1. Remarriage Miscellanea. 2. Actors—United States—Biography. 3. Actors—United States—Interviews. I. Wagner, Gary, joint author. II. Title. BIP

Rembrandt, Harmenszoon van Rijn, 1606-1669.

ABELES, Elivn, 1909- 759.9492
The magic painter; the story of Remhrandt, told by Kelwin Bowles [pseud.] Illustrated by Mitchell Foster. New York, Stravon Publishers [1951] 31 p. illus. 22 x 28 cm. (A Child's book of great artists) Stravon great artist series, 3. [ND653.R4A65] 927.5 51-8432
1. Rembrandt Hermanszoon van Rijn, 1606-1669. 2. Art—Juvenile literature. I. Title.

BAILEY, Anthony. 759.9492 B
Rembrandt's house / Anthony Bailey. Boston : Houghton Mifflin, 1978. 246 p. : ill. ; 24 cm. Includes index. Bibliography: p. 237-240. [N6953.R4B25] 77-26987 ISBN 0-395-25706-9 : 15.00
1. Rembrandt Harmenszoon van Rijn, 1606-1669. 2. Artists—Netherlands—Biography. 3. Rembrandthuis. 4. Amsterdam—Social life and customs. I. Title. BIP

CLARK, Kenneth 759.9492 B
McKenzie, Baron Clark, 1903-
An introduction to Rembrandt / Kenneth Clark. 1st U.S. ed. New York : Harper & Row, c1978. 153 p. : ill. ; 25 cm. (Icon editions) "Based on a series of television programmes ... made for the Ashwood Trust." Includes index. [N6953.R4C55 1978] 77-3745 ISBN 0-06-430860-X : 12.95
1. Rembrandt Harmenszoon van Rijn, 1606-1669. 2. Artists—Netherlands—Biography. I. Title. BIP

HAAK, B. 759.9492 B
Rembrandt; his life, his work, his time [by] Bob Haak. [Translated from the Dutch by Elizabeth Willems-Treeman] New York, H. N. Abrams [1969] 348 p. illus., facsims., maps, ports. 36 cm. Translation of Rembrandt, zijn leven, zijn werk, zijn tijd. Part of the illustrative matter is colored. Bibliography: p. 337-340. [ND653.R4H153 1969b] 69-12481
1. Rembrandt Harmenszoon van Rijn, 1606-1669. I. Title.

KUENZEL, Helga. 760'.0924
Rembrandt. Tr. from German by Anne Ross. New York, Crown [1967] 44p. illus., col. plates. 19cm. (Basic art lib.) [ND653.R4K813] 67-3094 1.00 bds.,
1. Rembrandt Hermanszoon van Rijn, 1606-1669. I. Title.

LEPORE, Mario, 1912- 759.9492
The life and times of Rembrandt; text by Mario Lepore, translator [from the Italian] Julia Shaw. London, New York [etc.] Hamlyn, 1968. 75 p. col. illus., facsim., ports. (some col.) 30 cm. (Portraits of greatness) Illus. on lining papers. [ND653.R4L413] 78-397565 ISBN 6-00-031543- 17/6
1. Rembrandt, Harmenszoon van Rijn, 1606-1669. I. Title.

REMBRANDT; 759.9492
biographical and critical study. Translated from the German by James Emmons. [New York] Skira [1957] 153p. mounted col. illus. 19cm. (The Taste of our time, v. 22) Bibliography: p.137-141. [ND653.R4B423] [ND653.R4B423] 927.5 57-11642 57-11642
1. Rembrandt Hermanszoon van Rijn, 1606-1669. I. Benesch, Otto, 1896-

REMBRANDT Harmenszoon 759.9492
van Rijn, 1606-1669.
Rembrandt [the life and work of the artist, illustrated with 80 full-color plates, by] Lionello Puppi. [Translated from the Italian by Pearl Sanders. 1st American ed. New York, Grosset & Dunlap [1970, c1969] 39 p. illus., col. plates. 18 cm. (The New Grosset art library, 27) [ND653.R4P813 1970] 69-13388
I. Puppi, Lionello.

REMBRANDT HERMANSZOON 759.9492
VAN RIJN, 1606-1669.
Rembrandt. Text by Ludwig Munz. [1st ed.] New York, H. N. Abrams [1954] 158p. (chiefly illus., col. plates)34cm (The Library of great painters) [An Abrams art book] [ND653.R4M785] [ND653.R4M785] 927.5 54-14560 54-14560
I. Munz, Ludwig. II. Title.

REMBRANDT HERMANSZOON 759.9492
VAN RIJN, 1606-1669.
Rembrandt (1606-1669) Text by Wilhelm Koehler, with illus. selected by the editorial staff. New York, H. N. Abrams in association with Pocket Books [1953] [74] p. 38illus. (part col.) 18cm. (The Pocket library of great art. A8) An Abrams art book. Bibliography: p.[74] [ND653.R4K6542] [ND653.R4K6542] 927.5 53-4519 53-4519
I. Koehler, Wilhelm Reinhold Walter, 1884- II. Title.

RIPLEY, Elizabeth, 1906- 927.5
Rembrandt, a biography. With drawings, etchings and paintings by Rembrandt. New York, Oxford University Press, 1955. 68 p. illus. 26 cm. (Oxford books for boys and girls) [ND653.R4R55] 55-8693
1. Rembrandt Harmenszoon van Rijn, 1606-1669.

ROSENBERG, Jakob, 1893- 760'.0924
Rembrandt: life & work. [3d ed.] London, New York, Phaidon [1968] xi, 386 p. illus., ports. 25 cm. (Paidon paperback, PH54) Includes bibliographical references. [ND653.R4R82 1968] 68-18911 ISBN 0-7148-1338-9 4.95
1. Rembrandt, Harmenszoon van Rijn, 1606-1669.

VAN LOON, Hendrik 759.9492
Willem, 1882-1944.
The life and times of Rembrandt, R. v. R., is an account of the last years and the death of one Rembrandt Harmenszoon Van Rijn, a painter and etcher of some renown who lived and worked in the town of Amsterdam, and died of general neglect and diverse other unfortunate circumstances on the fourth of October of the year of Grace, 1669, by Joannis Van Loon, doctor medicinae and chirurgeon in extraordinary, who during a most busy life yet found time to write down these personal recollections of the greatest of his fellow-citizens, which are now presented by his great-greatgrandson, nine times removed. Authorized abridgment. New York, Bantam Books [1957] 366p. illus. 18cm. (A Bantam biography, FB413) [ND653.R4V43 1957] [nD653.R4V43 1957] 927.5 927 57-11879 57-11879
1. Rembrandt Hermanszoon van Rijn, 1606-1669. I. Title.

WALLACE, Robert, 1919- 760'.0924
The world of Rembrandt, 1606-1669, by Robert Wallace and the editors of Time-Life Books New York, Time-Life Books [1968] 188 p. illus. (part col.) 31 cm. (Time-Life library of art) Issued in a case. Bibliography: p. 183. [ND653.R4W27 1968] 68-22321
1. Rembrandt Harmenszoon van Rijn, 1606-1669. I. Time-Life Books. II. Title. BIP

WHITE, Christopher. 927.5
Rembrandt and his world. New York, Viking Press [1964] 144 p. illus., facsims., map, col. plates, ports. 24 cm. (A Studio book) [ND653.R4W44] 64-18148
1. Rembrandt Harmenszoon van Rijn, 1606-1669. I. Title.

Remington, Frederic, 1861-1909.

MCKOWN, Robin. 927
Painter of the Wild West: Frederic Remington. New York, Messner [1959] 192 p. 22 cm. Includes bibliography. [ND237.R36M33] 59-7014
1. Remington, Frederic, 1861-1909. I. Title.

VORPAHL, Ben Merchant. 709'.2'4 B
Frederic Remington and the West : with the eye of the mind / by Ben Merchant Vorpahl. Austin : University of Texas Press, c1978. p. cm. Includes bibliographical references and index. [N6537.R4V67] 77-25953 ISBN 0-292-78703-0 : 15.95

1. Remington, Frederic, 1861-1909. 2. Artists—United States—Biography. 3. The West in art. I. Title. BIP

WEAR, Bruce. 730.924
The bronze world of Frederic Remington. [Tulsa, Okla., Gaylord, 1966] 149 p. illus. 29 cm. [NK7998.R4W4] 66-6580
1. Remington, Frederic, 1861-1909. I. Title.

Remington, Frederic, 1861-1909—Juvenile literature.

ANDERSON, LaVere. 759.13 B
Frederic Remington, artist on horseback. Champaign, Ill., Garrard Pub. Co. [1971] 152 p. illus. (part col.), ports. 22 cm. ([A People in the arts and sciences book]) The life of the painter whose canvases became pictorial diaries of American frontier life reflecting the artist's fascination with this now vanished era. [ND237.R36A83] 92 73-127181 ISBN 0-8116-4509-6 2.98
1. Remington, Frederic, 1861-1909—Juvenile literature. I. Title.

MOORE, Clyde B., 1886- 709'.24 B
Frederic Remington, young artist, by Clyde B. Moore. Illustrated by Robert Doremus. Indianapolis, Bobbs-Merrill [1971] 200 p. col. illus. 20 cm. (Childhood of famous Americans) Bibliography: p. 198. A biography stressing the childhood of the man who combined interests in horses, drawing, and the West to become a famous artist of western scenes. [ND237.R36M6] 92 72-146330
1. Remington, Frederic, 1861-1909—Juvenile literature. I. Doremus, Robert, illus. II. Title.

PETER, Adeline. 759.13
Frederic Remington, by Adeline Peter and Ernest Raboff. Garden City, N.Y., Doubleday [1973] [31] p. illus. (part col.) 29 cm. (Art for children) (A Gemini-Smith book) Introduces a selection of Frederic Remington's paintings and sculptures emphasizing social context and technical approach. Includes a brief biography of the artist. [ND237.R36P47] 73-75361 ISBN 0-385-05033-X 4.95
1. Remington, Frederic, 1861-1909—Juvenile literature. 2. The West in art—Juvenile literature. I. Raboff, Ernest Lloyd, joint author. II. Title.

Renaissance—Biog.

CHECKSFIELD, Muriel May 920.04
Portraits of Renaissance life and thought. New York, Barnes & Noble [1965, c.1964] x, 244p. illus., maps, ports. 23cm. Bibl. [CT116.C5] 65-3092 5.00 bds.,
1. Renaissance—Biog. I. Title.

Renaissance—Dictionaries.

SCHWEITZER, Frederick M., comp. 914'.03'2103
Dictionary of the Renaissance, edited by Frederick M. Schweitzer and Harry E. Wedeck. New York, Philosophical Library [1967] xxii, 646 p. 23 cm. [CB361.S45] 64-20429
1. Renaissance—Dictionaries. I. Wedeck, Harry Ezekiel, joint comp. II. Title.

Renaissance—Italy.

PETRARCA, Francesco, 1304-1374. 851'.1 B
Petrarch, the first modern scholar and man of letters. A selection from his correspondence with Boccaccio and other friends, designed to illustrate the beginnings of the Renaissance. Translated from the original Latin, together with historical introductions and notes by James Harvey Robinson with the collaboration of Henry Winchester Rolfe. New York, Haskell House, 1970. x, 436 p. 23 cm. Reprint of the 1898 ed. Includes bibliographical references. [PQ4507.R6 1970] 75-127999 ISBN 0-8383-1148-2
1. Renaissance—Italy. I. Robinson, James Harvey, 1863-1930, ed. II. Rolfe, Henry Winchester, 1858- ed.

Renaissance—Italy—Dictionaries.

THE New Century 914.5'03'503
Italian Renaissance encyclopedia. Edited by Catherine B. Avery. Editorial consultants: Marvin B. Becker [and] Ludovico Borgo. New York, Appleton-Century-Crofts [1972] xiii, 978 p. illus., map (on lining papers) 26 cm. [DG537.8.A1N48] 76-181735
1. Renaissance—Italy—Dictionaries. 2. Italy—Biography—Dictionaries. I. Avery, Catherine B., ed. II. Title: Italian Renaissance encyclopedia. BIP

Renault, Louis, 1877-1944.

RHODES, Anthony Richard Ewart. 629.22'22'0924 B
Louis Renault; a biography [by] Anthony Rhodes. With a foreword by Lord Montagu of Beaulieu. [1st American ed.] New York, Harcourt, Brace & World [1970, c1969] 233 p. illus., ports. 22 cm. Bibliography: p. 221-224. [TL140.R4R5 1970] 69-14841
1. Renault, Louis, 1877-1944. I. Title.

Rendall, Montague John, 1862-1950.

FIRTH, John D'Ewes, 1900- 923.742
Rendall of Winchester; the life and witness of a teacher. London, New York, Oxford University Press, 1954. 273p. illus. 23 cm. [LF795.W7F53] 54-13073
1. Rendall, Montague John, 1862-1950. I. Title.

Rene, Roy, 1892-1954.

PARSONS, Fredric Hundy. 791'.092'4 B
A man called Mo [by] Fred Parsons. With a foreword by Graham Kennedy. Melbourne, Heinemann, 1973. xi, 174 p. ill. 25 cm. [PN3018.R4P3] 74-182050 ISBN 0-85561-031-X 7.95
1. Rene, Roy, 1892-1954. I. Title.

Renfroe, Stephen S., 1843-1886.

ROGERS, William Warren. 364.1'55'0924 B
Stephen S. Renfroe, Alabama's outlaw sheriff, by William Warren Rogers and Ruth Pruitt. Tallahassee, Sentry Press, 1972. xi, 148 p. illus. 24 cm. Bibliography: p. 137-141. [HV7911.R43R64] 74-189833
1. Renfroe, Stephen S., 1843-1886. I. Pruitt, Ruth, joint author.

Rennert, Maggie—Homes and haunts—Israel—Beersheba.

RENNERT, Maggie. 956.94'05
Shelanu : an Israel journal / Maggie Rennert. Englewood Cliffs, N.J. : Prentice-Hall, c1979. viii, 446 p. ; 24 cm. [DS107.4.R43] 78-9561 ISBN 0-13-808808-X : 12.95
1. Rennert, Maggie—Homes and haunts—Israel—Beersheba. 2. Israel—Description and travel. 3. Authors, American—20th century—Biography. I. Title.

Rennie, John,

BOUCHER, Cecil Thomas Goodman. v. 12
John Rennie, 1761-1821. The life and work of a great engineer. New York, Augustus M. Kelley, 1967. x, 149 p. illus., port. 22 cm. (Reprints of economic classics) Imprint from label mounted on t.p. 68-104696
1. Rennie, John, I. Title.

Renoir, Auguste, 1841-1919.

CALLEN, Anthea. 759.4 B
Renoir / Anthea Gallen. 1st U.S. ed. New York : Two Continents/Oresko, 1978. p. cm. (Oresko art book series) Includes index. Bibliography: p. [ND553.R45C32 1977] 77-10354 ISBN 0-8467-0377-7 : 15.95
1. Renoir, Auguste, 1841-1919. 2. Painters—France—Biography. I. Title. II. Series.

HANSON, Lawrence. 759.4 B
Renoir: the man, the painter, and his world. New York, Dodd, Mead [1968] xi, 332 p. illus. 24 cm. Bibliography: p. 297-301. [ND553.R45H27] 68-21898 8.50
1. Renoir, Auguste, 1841-1919. I. Title.

RENOIR, Auguste, 1841-1919. 759.4
Pierre Auguste Renior (1841-1912) Text by Milton S. Fox. New York, H. N. Abrams in Pocket Books [1953] [74]p. 39 illus. (part col.) 18cm. (The association with Pocket library of great art. A11) An Abrams art book. Bibliography: p.[74] [ND553.R45F69] [ND553.R45F69] 927.5 53-4520 53-4520
I. Fox, Milton S., 1904- II. Title.

RENOIR, Auguste [Pierre Auguste Renoir] 1841-1919 759.4
Renoir, by Madeleine Ledivelic. New York, Crown [1963] 36p. illus. (pt. col.)18cm. (Little bks. on great artists) Biographical sketch in French, English, and German. 63-25372 .69
I. Ledivelec, Madeleine. II. Title.

RENOIR, Jean, 1894- 927.5
Renoir, my father. Translated by Randolph and Dorothy Weaver. [1st American ed.] Boston, Little, Brown [1962] 465 p. illus. 25 cm. [ND553.R45R43 1962] 62-17956
1. Renoir, Auguste, 1841-1919. I. Title. BIP

TRAZ, Georges de, 1881- 759.4 B
Renoir [by] Francois Fosca. [Translated from the French by Mary I. Martin] New York, H. N. Abrams [1969] 288 p. illus. (part col.), ports. (part col.) 22 cm. Translation of Renoir, l'homme et son ouvre. [ND553.R45T683 1969] 73-90892
1. Renoir, Auguste, 1841-1919.

TRAZ, Georges de, 1881- 759.4
Renoir, his life and work [by] Francois Fosca [pseud. Translated from the French by Mary I. Martin. 1st American ed.] Englewood Cliffs, N.J., Prentice-Hall [1962, c1961] 271 p. illus. 22 cm. [ND553.R45T683] 62-52349
1. Renoir, Auguste, 1841-1919. Full name: Georges Albert Edouard de Traz. I. Title.

TRAZ, Georges de, 1881- 759.4 B
Renoir : his life and work / Francois Fosca [i.e. G. de Traz] ; [translated from the French by Mary I. Martin]. New York : Praeger, 1975. 288 p. : ill. (some col.) ; 21 cm. (Praeger world of art paperbacks) (A Praeger world of art profile) Translation of Renoir, l'homme et son ouvre. Includes index. [ND553.R45T683 1975] 74-8442 ISBN 0-275-71670-8 : 5.95
1. Renoir, Auguste, 1841-1919.

Renoir, Jean, 1894-

DURGNAT, Raymond. 791.43'0233'0924
Jean Renoir / Raymond Durgnat. Berkeley : University of California Press, c1974. xiii, 429 p. : ill. ; 24 cm. Includes index. Bibliography: p. 407-414. [PN1998.A3R42] 72-82221 ISBN 0-520-02283-1 : 16.50
1. Renoir, Jean, 1894- BIP

RENOIR, Jean, 1894- 791.43'023'0924 B
My life and my films / by Jean Renoir ; translated by Norman Denny. 1st American ed. New York : Atheneum, 1974. 287 p., [16] leaves of plates : ill. ; 24 cm. Translation of Ma vie et mes films. Includes index. [PN1998.A3R45713] 74-77856 ISBN 0-689-10629-7 : 10.00
1. Renoir, Jean, 1894- 2. Moving-picture producers and directors—Correspondence, reminiscences, etc. I. Title. BIP

Renty, Gaston Jean Baptiste, baron de, 1611-1648.

SAINT JURE, Jean Baptiste de, 1588-1657. 922.244
An extract of the life of Monsieur de Renty, a late nobleman of France. Published by John Wesley. 1st American ed. Philadelphia, Printed by H. Tuckniss and sold by J. Dickins, 1795. 70 p. 19 cm. "Extracted from 'The holy life of Monr. de Renty...Written in French by John Baptist S. Jure...translated into English by E. S. Gent. London...1958.' "--Richard Green. The works of John and Charles Wesley. 2d ed. 1906. [BX4705.R44S322] 65-58543
1. Renty, Gaston Jean Baptiste, baron de, 1611-1648. I. Wesley, John, 1703-1791, ed. II. Title.

Reorganized Church of Jesus Christ of Latter-Day Saints—Biography.

CHEVILLE, Roy Arthur, 1897- 289.3'0922 B
They made a difference, by Roy Cheville. [Independence, Mo., Herald Pub. House, 1970] 350 p. ports. 21 cm. "A roster of thirty persons whose participation made significant impact upon the Latter Day Saint Movement: The Early Church, 1820-1844; the Reorganized Church, 1853-1970." [BX8678.A2] 78-101568 6.95
1. Reorganized Church of Jesus Christ of Latter-Day Saints—Biography. I. Title.

LIVING saints witness at work / compiled by T. Ed Barlow. 289.3'3 B
Independence, Mo. : Herald Pub. House, c1976. 126 p. : ill. ; 21 cm. [BX8678.A28] 76-27227 ISBN 0-8309-0153-1
1. Reorganized Church of Jesus Christ of Latter-Day Saints—Biography. 2. Christian life—Mormon authors. I. Barlow, T. Ed, 1931- BIP

PHILLIPS, Emma M 922.83
33 women of the restoration Independence, Mo., Herald House [1960] 197p. 21cm. Includes bibliography. [BX8678.A43] 60-14176
1. Reorganized Church of Jesus Christ of Latter-Day Saints—Biog. 2. Woman—Biog. I. Title.

RUOFF, Norman D. comp. 289.3/0922
Witness to the world; a collection of testimonies and inspirational writings from the pages of the Resforation witness, ed., comp. by Norman D. Ruoff. [Independence, Mo., Herald Pub., 1967] 216p. 20cm. [BX8678.A46] 67-30460 3.50
1. Reorganized Church of Jesus Christ of Latter-Day Saints—Biog. 2. Restoration witness. I. Title.

WHO'S who in service—a 289.3'3 B
look at areas of service participation by members of the Reorganizaed Church of Jesus Christ of Latter Day Saints. Independence, Mo. : Herald Pub. House, c1977. 164 p. ; 26 cm. [BX8678.A48] 76-29064 ISBN 0-8309-0173-6 : 12.00
1. Reorganized Church of Jesus Christ of Latter Day Saints—Biography. I. Herald Publishing House.

Repplier, Agnes, 1855-1950.

STOKES, George Stewart. 814'.4
Agnes Repplier, lady of letters. Westport, Conn., Greenwood Press [1970, c1949] xiii, 274 p. ports. 23 cm. Reprint of 1949 ed. Originally presented as the author's thesis, University of Pennsylvania, under title: Agnes Repplier: a critical biography. Bibliography: p. 267-268. [PS2697.S8 1970] 73-108400 ISBN 0-8371-3823-X
1. Repplier, Agnes, 1855-1950. BIP

WITMER, Emma (Repplier) 928.1
Agnes Repplier, a memoir, by her niece Emma Repplier (Mrs. Lightner Witmer) Philadelphia, Dorrance [1957] 171 p. illus. 20 cm. [PS2697.W5] 57-11237
1. Repplier, Agnes, 1855-1950. I. Title.

Republic Pictures Corporation.

SWANN, Thomas Burnett. 338.7'61'791430973
The heroine or the horse : leading ladies in Republic's films / Thomas Burnett Swann. South Brunswick [N.J.] : A. S. Barnes, c1977. 134 p. : ill. ; 29 cm. Includes index. Bibliography: p. 130-131. [PN1999.R4S95] 76-18483 ISBN 0-498-01962-4 : 17.50
1. Republic Pictures Corporation. 2. Moving-picture actors and actresses—United States—Biography. I. Title. BIP

Republican Party. National Convention. 25th, Chicago, 1952.

HOWARD, Katherine Graham, 1898- 329'.0092'4 B
With my shoes off / Katherine G. Howard. 1st ed. New York : Vantage Press, c1977. 347 p. : ill. ; 21 cm. [E748.H785A38] 77-74556 ISBN 0-533-02950-3 : 10.00
1. Howard, Katherine Graham, 1898- 2. United States. Federal Civil Defense Administration—Officials and employees—Biography. 3. Republican Party. National Convention. 25th, Chicago, 1952. 4. Eisenhower, Dwight David, Pres. U.S., 1890-1969. 5. Presidents—United States—Election—1952. 6. United States—Civil defense. I. Title. BIP

Rerat, Eugene A.

SEVAREID, Paul A. 923.473
The people's lawyer; the life of Eugene A. Rerat. Minneapolis, Ross & Haines [c.1963] 260p. illus., ports. 23cm. 63-25962 4.95
1. Rerat, Eugene A. I. Title.

Reresby, John, Sir, 2d bart., 1634-1689.

CHAPMAN, Hester W., 1899-1976. 941.06'092'4 B
Four fine gentlemen / Hester Chapman. Lincoln : University of Nebraska Press, 1978. 301 p., [4] leaves of plates : ports. ; 23 cm. Includes index. Bibliography: p. [289]-291. [DA377.3.C47 1977b] 77-20589 ISBN 0-8032-1401-4 : 12.50
1. Shaftesbury, Anthony Ashley Cooper, 1st Earl of, 1621-1683. 2. Temple, William, Sir, bart., 1628-1699. 3. Reresby, John, Sir, 2d bart., 1634-1689. 4. Shrewsbury, Charles Talbot, Duke of, 1660-1718. 5. Great Britain—History—17th century—Biography. 6. Statesmen—Great Britain—Biography. I. Title. BIP

Resnick, Rose.

RESNICK, Rose. 362.4'1'0924 B
Sun and shadow / Rose Resnick. 1st ed. New York : Atheneum, 1975. vii, 274 p. ; 22 cm. [HV1624.R47A37] 74-32614 ISBN 0-689-10666-1 : 10.00
1. Resnick, Rose. 2. Blind—Biography. I. Title.

Restif de La Bretonne, Nicolas Edme, 1734-1806.

PORTER, Charles Allan. 843'.5
Restif's novels; or, An autobiography in search of an author, by Charles A. Porter. New Haven, Yale University Press, 1967. viii, 441 p. facsims., port. 24 cm. (Yale Romanic studies, 2d ser.,16) "Restif bibliography since 1949": p. [421]-426. Bibliographical footnotes. [PQ2025.Z5P6] 66-21531
1. Restif de La Bretonne, Nicolas Edme, 1734-1806. I. Title. II. Title: An autobiography in search of an author. III. Series.

Retail trade.

REILLY, Philip J 658.8700922
Old masters of retailing, by Philip J. Reilly. New York, Fairchild Publications [1966] xiii, 210 p. 24 cm. [HF5429.R375] 65-27051
1. Retail trade. 2. Department stores. I. Title.

Rettew, Granville Raymond, 1903-1973.

RETTEW, Granville Raymond, 1903-1973. 615'.329'23 B
"A quiet man from West Chester"; memoirs. Introd. by Robert D. Coghill. Edited by Mary E. G. Robinson. West Chester, Pa., Chester County Historical Society [1974] 55 p. illus. 24 cm. Includes bibliographical references. [RS73.R47A33] 74-80873 3.68
1. Rettew, Granville Raymond, 1903-1973. 2. Penicillin—History. I. Title.

Retz, Jean Francois Paul de Gondi, cardinal de, 1613-1679.

SALMON, John Hearsey McMillan, 1925- 444'.033'0924 B
Cardinal de Retz: the anatomy of a conspirator [by] J. H. M. Salmon. [1st American ed. New York] Macmillan Co. [1970, c1969] 447 p. geneal. table (on lining papers) 23 cm. Bibliography: p. [419]-424. [DC130.R45S3 1970] 73-77973 8.95
1. Retz, Jean Francois Paul de Gondi, cardinal de, 1613-1679. I. Title.

Reu, Johann Michael, 1869-1943.

IN remembrance of Reu : 384'.1'0924 B an evaluation of the life and work of J. Michael Reu, 1868-1943, on the 100th anniversary of his birth by some of his friends and former students / edited by Robert C. Wiederaenders. Dubuque : Wartburg Seminary Association, 1969. 31 leaves : port. ; 28 cm. Cover title. Consists of presentations made at a luncheon sponsored by the Wartburg Seminary (Alumni) Association held Nov. 12, 1961. "Writings about J. Michael Rue": leaf 31. [BX8080.R38I5] 75-316286
1. Reu, Johann Michael, 1869-1943. 2. Reu, Johann Michael, 1869-1943—Bibliography. I. Reu, Johann Michael, 1869-1943. II. Wiederaenders, Robert C. III. Wartburg Seminary Association.

Reuter, Fritz, 1810-1874.

REUTER, Fritz, 1810-1874. 839'.4'8209 B
Seven years of my life. Translated from the low German with introd. and notes by Carl F. Bayerschmidt. New York, Twayne Publishers [1974, i.e.1975] p. cm. Translation of Ut mine Festungstid. "Twayne's international studies and translations program." Published in cooperation with the Germanic Society of America. [PT4848.R4U513] 74-10854 ISBN 0-8057-5740-6 7.95
1. Reuter, Fritz, 1810-1874. I. Title. BIP

Reuther, Ruth E

REUTHER, Ruth E 920.7
The wife of four hobbies 1st. ed New York, Pageant Press [1956] 81p. illus. 21cm. Autobiographical. [CT275.R44A3] 56-11350
I. Title.

Reuther, Victor G., 1912-

REUTHER, Victor G., 1912- 331.88'12'920924 B
The brothers Reuther and the story of the UAW : a memoir / by Victor G. Reuther. Boston : Houghton Mifflin, 1976. xiv, 523 p., [8] leaves of plates : ill. ; 24 cm. Includes index. [HD6509.R39A33] 76-840 ISBN 0-395-24304-1 : 16.95
1. Reuther, Victor G., 1912- 2. Reuther, Walter Philip, 1907-1970. 3. International Union, United Automobile, Aircraft and Agricultural Implement Workers of America. 4. Trade-unions—Automobile industry workers—United States—History. I. Title. BIP

Reuther, Walter Philip, 1907-1970.

CORMIER, Frank. 331.881'292'0924 B
Reuther [by] Frank Cormier and William J. Eaton. Englewood Cliffs, N.J., Prentice-Hall [1970] 475 p. port. 24 cm. Includes bibliographical references. [HD8073.R4C67] 71-131869 10.00
1. Reuther, Walter Philip, 1907-1970. I. Eaton, William J., joint author. II. Title.

REUTHER, Victor G., 1912- 331.88'12'920924 B
The brothers Reuther and the story of the UAW : a memoir / by Victor G. Reuther. Boston : Houghton Mifflin, 1976. xiv, 523 p., [8] leaves of plates : ill. ; 24 cm. Includes index. [HD6509.R39A33] 76-840 ISBN 0-395-24304-1 : 16.95
1. Reuther, Victor G., 1912- 2. Reuther, Walter Philip, 1907-1970. 3. International Union, United Automobile, Aircraft and Agricultural Implement Workers of America. 4. Trade-unions—Automobile industry workers—United States—History. I. Title. BIP

TYLER, Robert L. 331.88'12'920924 B
Walter Reuther, by Robert L. Tyler. [Grand Rapids, Mich.] W. B. Eerdmans [1973] 80 p. port. 22 cm. (Great men of Michigan) Bibliography: p. 79-80. [HD8073.R4T9] 72-77187 ISBN 0-8028-7027-9 pap. 1.95
1. Reuther, Walter Philip, 1907-1970.

Revel, Bernard, 1885-1940.

ROTHKOFF, Aaron. 296.8'32'0924 B
Bernard Revel: builder of American Jewish orthodoxy. [1st ed.] Philadelphia, Jewish Publication Society of America, 1972. xiv, 378 p. illus. 22 cm. Bibliography: p. 343-359. [BM755.R44R67] 71-188582 6.00
1. Revel, Bernard, 1885-1940.

Revels, Hiram Rhoades, 1827?-1901.

LAWSON, Elizabeth, 1904- 923.273
The gentleman from Mississippi: our first Negro Congressman, Hiram R. Revels. With an introd. by William L. Patterson. [New York, 1960] 63p. illus. 20cm. Includes bibliography. [E664.R4L3] 60-2439
1. Revels, Hiram Rhoades, 1827?-1901. I. Title.

Revels, Hiram Rhoades, 1827?-1901—Juvenile literature.

BUCKMASTER, Henrietta, pseud. 328.73'09'22 B
The fighting Congressmen. Thaddeus Stephens, Hiram Revels, James Rapier, Blanche K. Bruce. [New York] Scholastic Book Services [1971] 111 p. illus., facsims., ports. 21 cm. (Firebird books) Brief biographies of one white and three black congressmen active in the struggle to assure the rights of black people during the Reconstruction. [E663.B9] 920 75-131370
1. Stevens, Thaddeus, 1792-1868—Juvenile literature. 2. Revels, Hiram Rhoades, 1827?-1901—Juvenile literature. 3. Rapier, James T., 1839-1883—Juvenile literature. 4. Bruce, Blanche Kelso, 1841-1898—Juvenile literature. I. Title.

Revere, Paul, 1702-1754.

DOUGLAS, Donald. 284.573
The Huguenot; the story of the Huguenot emigrations, particularly to New England, in which is included the early life of Apollos Rivoire, the father of Paul Revere. With an introd. by C. C. Little. [1st ed.] New York, Dutton, 1954. 384 p. 22 cm. Includes bibliography. [BX9459.R4D6] 54-5035
1. Revere, Paul, 1702-1754. 2. Huguenots. I. Title.

Revere, Paul, 1735-1818.

FORBES, Allan, 1874-1955. 917.44'61'0641
The Boston French; a collection of facts and incidents with appropriate illustrations relating to some well-known citizens of France who found homes in Boston and New England, with which are included accounts of several visits made by one of the authors to La Rochelle and to the homes of the ancestors of Paul Revere. By Allan Forbes and Paul F. Cadman. Cottonport [La.] Polyanthos, 1971. 98 p. illus. 24 cm. Reprint of the 1938 ed. published under title: Boston and some noted emigres. Includes bibliographical references. [F73.9.F7F7 1971] 73-175218
1. Revere, Paul, 1735-1818. 2. French in Boston. 3. Boston—Biography. 4. Huguenots in the United States. 5. La Rochelle—History. I. Cadman, Paul Fletcher, 1889-1946, joint author. II. Title.

FORBES, Esther 923.273
Paul Revere & the world he lived in. Boston, Houghton [1963, c.1942] xiii, 510p. illus. 2icm. (Sentry, SE21) Bibl. 2.35 pap.,
1. Revere, Paul, 1735-1818. I. Title. BIP

GOSS, Elbridge Henry, 1830-1908. 973.33'11'0924 B
The life of Colonel Paul Revere, with portraits, many illustrations, fac-similes, etc. Freeport, N.Y., Books for Libraries Press [1971] 2 v. (xxiv, 689 p.) illus., facsims., ports. 23 cm. Reprint of the 1891 ed. [F69.R42 1971] 78-157339 ISBN 0-8369-5799-7
1. Revere, Paul, 1735-1818. 2. Penobscot Expedition, 1779.

GOSS, Elbridge Henry, 1830-1908. 973.3'311'0924 B
The life of Colonel Paul Revere. Boston, Gregg Press, 1972 [c1891] 2 v. (x, xxiv, 689 p.) illus. 24 cm. (The American Revolutionary series. American and French accounts of the American Revolution) Reprint of the ed. published by J. G. Cupples, Boston. Includes bibliographical references [F69.R42 1972] 72-8757 ISBN 0-8398-0670-1 25.00 (Lib. ed.)
1. Revere, Paul, 1735-1818. I. Title. II. Series: American and French accounts of the American Revolution. BIP

REVERE, Paul, 1735-1818. 973.3'311'0924
Paul Revere's three accounts of his famous ride / with an introd. by Edmund S. Morgan. 3d ed. [Boston : Massachusetts Historical Society], c1976. [36] p. : facsims. ; 28 cm. (A Massachusetts Historical Society picture book) Includes bibliographical references. [E216.R43 1976] 76-372845 2.00
1. Revere, Paul, 1735-1818. 2. Statesmen—Massachusetts—Biography. 3. Massachusetts—Biography. 4. United States History—Revolution, 1775-1783—Personnal narratives. I. Title. II. Series.

SHEETS, Robert Newman, 1934- 973.3'31'0924 B
Robert Newman : his life and letters in celebration of the bicentennial of his showing of two lanterns in Christ Church, Boston, April 18, 1775 / Robert Newman Sheets. Denver : Sheets, 1975. 60 p. : ill. ; 23 cm. Bibliography: p. 60. [F69.N58S53] 75-10151
1. Newman, Robert, 1752-1804. 2. Revere, Paul, 1735-1818. 3. Boston. Christ Church. 4. Boston—Siege, 1775-1776.

STEVENSON, Augusta. 973.33'11'0924 B
Paul Revere, boy of old Boston. Illustrated by Frank Nicholas. Indianapolis, Bobbs-Merrill [1962] 200 p. illus. 20 cm. (Childhood of famous Americans) The boyhood of the colonial Boston lad who became a renowned silversmith and great patriot of the Revolution, with his ride which warned that the British were coming. [PZ7.S8467Pau5] 92 AC 68
1. Revere, Paul, 1735-1818. I. Nicholas, Frank, illus. II. Title.

Revere, Paul, 1735-1818—Juvenile literature.

GREEN, Margaret 920
Paul Revere, the man behind the legend. New York, Messner [c.1964] 191p. 22cm. Bibl. 64-12775 3.25; 3.19 lib. ed.,
1. Revere, Paul, 1735-1818—Juvenile literature. I. Title.

KELLY, Regina (Zimmerman) 1898- 920
Paul Revere: colonial craftsman. Illus. by Harvey Kidder. Boston, Houghton [c.1963] 188p. illus. (pt. col.) col. maps (pt. fold.) 22cm. (Piper bks.) 63-15655 1.95
1. Revere, Paul, 1735-1818—Juvenile literature. I. Title.

WOLFE, Louis 920
Let's go with Paul Revere. Illus. by Charles Dougherty. New York, Putnam [c.1964] 47p. col. illus. 21cm. (Let's go hist. ser.) Bibl. 64-18031 1.86 lib. ed.,
1. Revere, Paul, 1735-1818—Juvenile literature. I. Title.

Revere, Paul, 1735-1818—Juvenile literature.

FRITZ, Jean. 973.3'311'0924 B
And then what happened, Paul Revere? Pictures by Margot Tomes. New York, Coward, McCann & Geoghegan [1973] 45 p. illus. (part col.) 24 cm. Describes some of the well-known as well as the lesser-known details of Paul Revere's life and exciting ride. [F69.R4178 1973] 92 73-77423 ISBN 0-698-20274-0 5.95
1. Revere, Paul, 1735-1818—Juvenile literature. I. Tomes, Margot, illus. II. Title. **BIP**

GRANT, Matthew G. 973.3'311'0924 B
Paul Revere; patriot and craftsman [by] Matthew G. Grant. Illustrated by John Keely and Dick Brude. [Mankato, Minn., Creative Education; distributed by Childrens Press, Chicago, 1974] 31 p. illus. (part col.) 25 cm. (His Gallery of great Americans series. War heroes of America) A brief biography of Paul Revere stressing his patriotic acts and his skill as a silversmith. [F69.R4215] 92 73-18076 ISBN 0-87191-303-8 3.95 (lib. bdg.)
1. Revere, Paul, 1735-1818—Juvenile literature. I. Keely, John, illus. II. Brude, Dick, illus. III. Title.

Revolutionists—Biography.

MEYERS, Jeffrey. 909.82'092'2 B
A fever at the core : the idealist in politics / Jeffrey Meyers. New York : Barnes & Noble Books, 1976. 172 p. ; 23 cm. Bibliography: p. [171]-172. [HM283.M52] 75-43049 ISBN 0-06-494791-2 : 15.00
1. Revolutionists—Biography. 2. Revolutionists—Psychology. 3. Idealism. I. Title. **BIP**

ROBERTSON, William Spence, 1872- 987'.04'0924 B
The life of Miranda. New York, Cooper Square Publishers, 1969. 2 v. illus., maps, ports. 24 cm. (Library of Latin American history and culture) Reprint of the 1929 ed. Bibliography: v. 2, p. [257]-276. [F2323.M6R62 1969] 77-79203
I. Miranda, Francisco de, 1750-1816. II. Title. **BIP**

Revolutionists—Russia—Correspondence, reminiscences, etc.

SERGE, Victor, 1890-1947. 923.347
Memoirs of a revolutionary, 1901-1941. Tr. [from French] ed. by Peter Sedgwick. New York, Oxford [c.]1963. 401p. illus. 23cm. Bibl. 63-5744 10.00
1. Revolutionists, Russian—Correspondence, reminiscences, etc. 2. Russia—Hist.—20th cent. I. Title.

SERGE, Victor, 1890-1947 923.347
Memoirs of a revolutionary, 1901-1941. Tr., ed. by Peter Sedgwick. London, New York, Oxford Univ. Pr., [1967,c.1963] 401p. illus. 21cm. (123) [DK254.S39A313] 63-5744 2.95 pap.,
1. Revolutionists, Russian—Correspondence, reminiscences, etc. 2. Russia—Hist.—20th cent. I. Title.

SERGE, Victor, 1890-1947. 947.084'0924 B
Memoirs of a revolutionary, 1901-1941; translated [from the French] and edited by Peter Sedgwick. [1st ed.] with corrections. London, New York [etc.] Oxford U.P. [1967]. iii, xxv, 401 p. 21 cm. (Oxford paperbacks, no. 123) Translation of Memoires d'un revolutionnaire. Bibliography: p. [387]-389. [DK254.S39A313 1967] 68-100796 12/6
1. Revolutionists—Russia—Correspondence, reminiscences, etc. 2. Russia—History—20th century. I. Title. **BIP**

TUTAEV, David, comp. 947.084'2'0922 B
The Alliluyev memoirs; recollections of Svetlana Stalina's maternal aunt Anna Alliluyeva and her grandfather Sergei Alliluyev. Translated and edited by David Tutaev. New York, Putnam [1968] 222 p. illus., ports. 22 cm. Translation of Vospominaniia (romanized form) by Anna Allilueva, and Proidennyi put' (romanized form) by Sergei Alliluev, compiled into one narrative with editorial matter interspersed. Bibliographical references included in "Notes" (p. 214-222). [DK254.A55T8 1968] 68-21917
1. Revolutionists—Russia—Correspondence, reminiscences, etc. I. Allilueva, Anna Sergeevna, 1896-1964. Vospominaniia. II. Alliluev, Sergei IAkovlevich, 1866-1945. Proidennyi put'. III. Title.

Revolutions.

BUTLER, Ed. 301.6333'0924
Revolution is my profession. [New York, Twin Circle, c1968] 248 p. illus. 19 cm. [HM281.B82] 71-20162 3.95
1. Revolutions. 2. Revolutionists. I. Title.

Revolutions—Addresses, essays, lectures.

ESSAYS on modern-European revolutionary history / by Stanley H. Palmer ... [et al.] ; introduction by Charles Tilly ; edited by Bede K. Lackner and Kenneth Roy Philip. Austin : University of Texas Press, c1977. xxiii, 132 p. ; 23 cm. (The Walter Prescott Webb memorial lectures ; 11) ISSN 0083-713X) Includes bibliographical references. [D359.7.E84] 76-43976 ISBN 0-292-72021-1 : 7.95 940.2'8
1. Revolutions—Addresses, essays, lectures. 2. Revolutionists—Biography—Addresses, essays, lectures. 3. Europe—History—19th century—Addresses, essays, lectures. 4. Europe—History—20th century—Addresses, essays, lectures. I. Palmer, Stanley H. II. Lackner, Bede K. III. Philp, Kenneth R., 1941- IV. Series.

Revson, Charles, 1906-1975.

TOBIAS, Andrew P. 338.7'66'850924 B
Fire and ice : the Charles Revson/Revlon story / by Andrew P. Tobias. New York : Morrow, 1976. p. cm. [HD9999.C93U62] 76-6124 ISBN 0-688-03023-8
1. Revson, Charles, 1906-1975. 2. Revlon, inc. I. Title. **BIP**

Revson, Peter.

REVSON, Peter. 796.7'2'0924 B
Speed with style; the autobiography of Peter Revson, by Peter Revson and Leon Mandel. [1st ed.] Garden City, N.Y., Doubleday, 1974. xviii, 221 p. illus. 22 cm. [GV1032.R47A37] 74-9201 ISBN 0-385-06166-8 8.95
1. Revson, Peter. 2. Automobile racing. I. Mandel, Leon. II. Title.

Reyes, Alfonso, 1889-1959.

APONTE, Barbara Bockus. 868 B
Alfonso Reyes and Spain; his dialogue with Unamuno, Valle-Inclan, Ortega y Gasset, Jimenez, and Gomez de la Serna. Austin, University of Texas Press [1972] 206 p. port. 24 cm. Bibliography: p. [197]-202. [PQ7297.R386Z58] 78-37254 ISBN 0-292-70300-7 7.50
1. Reyes, Alfonso, 1889-1959. **BIP**

HISPANIC Institute in the United States. v. 12
Alfonso Reyes; vida y obra, bibliografia, antologia. New York, Hispanic Institute in the United States, 1956. 112 p. illus. 26 cm. (Autores modernos, [25]) Bibliography: p. 60-81. 67-105653
1. Reyes, Alfonso, 1889- 2. Reyes, Alfonso, 1889- — Bibliography. I. Title.

Reyes, Antonio de los, Bp., 1729-1786.

STAGG, Albert. 266'.2'0924 B
The first Bishop of Sonora : Antonio de los Reyes / Albert Stagg. Tucson : University of Arizona Press, c1976. ix, 109 p. : ill. ; 24 cm. Includes index. Bibliography: p. 103-106. [F1219.3.M59R497] 76-379189 ISBN 0-8165-0549-7 : 8.50. ISBN 0-8165-0486-5 pbk. :
1. Reyes, Antonio de los, Bp., 1729-1786. 2. Indians of Mexico—Missions. 3. Franciscans in Mexico. 4. Missionaries—Mexico—Biography. 5. Missionaries—Spain—Biography. I. Title.

Reynard, Grant T., 1887-1968.

KNAUTZ, Harlan E. 759.13 B
Grant Reynard, N.A. : an American painter / by Harlan E. Knautz. Berea, Ohio : Baldwin-Wallace College, 1974. 172 p. : ill. (some col.) ; 29 cm. Includes index. Bibliography: p. 167-170. [ND237.R4K55] 74-15652
1. Reynard, Grant T., 1887-1968. I. Reynard, Grant T., 1887-1968.

Reynolds, Bede, 1892-

REYNOLDS, Bede, 1892- 271'.1'024 B
A rebel from riches : the autobiography of an unpremeditated monk / Bede Reynolds (ne Kenyon L. Reynolds). Canfield, Ohio : Alba Books, [1975] 150 p., [11] leaves of plates : ill. ; 18 cm. [BX4705.R446A34] 74-27608 pbk. : 1.65
1. Reynolds, Bede, 1892- I. Title.

Reynolds, Burt.

HURWOOD, Bernhardt J. 791.43'028'0924 B
Burt Reynolds / Bernhardt J. Hurwood ; [front cover photo. by Ron Galella]. New York : Quick Fox, c1979. 112 p. : ill. ; 26 cm. Filmography: p. 103-107. [PN2287.R447H87] 79-90893 ISBN 0-8256-3144-0 pbk. : 5.95
1. Reynolds, Burt. 2. Moving-picture actors and actresses—United States—Biography. **BIP**

WHITLEY, Dianna. 791.43'028'0924 B
Burt Reynolds, portrait of a superstar / by Dianna Whitley. New York : Grosset & Dunlap, c1979. 112 p. : ill. ; 28 cm. [PN2287.R447W5] 78-73640 ISBN 0-448-15479-X : 5.95
1. Reynolds, Burt. 2. Moving-picture actors and actresses—United States—Biography. I. Title.

Reynolds family.

LETTERS to William Frend from the Reynolds family of Little Paxton and John Hammond of Fenstanton 1793-1814 / edited by Frida Knight. Cambridge : Cambridge Antiquarian Records Society, 1974. 98 p., plate : 1 ill., geneal. table ; 25 cm. ([Publications] - Cambridge Antiquarian Records Society ; 1972, v. 1) Includes bibliographical references and index. [CS439.R47 1974] 75-312804 ISBN 0-904323-00-5 : £4.50 942.6'54'073
1. Reynolds family. 2. Frend, William. I. Frend, William, 1757-1841. II. Reynolds, Richard, 1730-1814. III. Reynolds, Mary C. IV. Hammond, John, b. 1755. V. Knight, Frida. VI. Series: Cambridge Antiquarian Records Society. Publications — Cambridge Antiquarian Records Society ; 1972, v. 1.

Reynolds, Frederic,

REYNOLDS, Frederic, 1764-1841. 822'.7 B
The life and times of Frederick Reynolds. New York, B. Blom, 1969. 2 v. in 1. port. 21 cm. Reprint of the 1827 ed. [PR5221.R3Z5 1969] 74-88489
I. Title. **BIP**

Reynolds, John Fulton, 1820-1863.

NICHOLS, Edward Jay, 1900- 923.573
Toward Gettysburg; a biography of General John F. Reynolds. [University Park] Pennsylvania State University Press, 1958. x, 276 p. illus., maps, ports. 25 cm. Bibliography: p. 259-264. [E467.1.R4N5] 58-6824
1. Reynolds, John Fulton, 1820-1863. 2. United States—History—Civil War, 1861-1865—Campaigns and battles. I. Title.

Reynolds, John Hamilton, 1794-1852.

REYNOLDS, John Hamilton, 1794-1852. 828'.7'09 B
The letters of John Hamilton Reynolds. Edited with an introd. by Leonidas M. Jones. Lincoln, University of Nebraska Press [1973] xxxviii, 82 p. 23 cm. Includes bibliographical references. [PR5221.R5Z53 1973] 72-90342 ISBN 0-8032-0827-8 8.50
1. Reynolds, John Hamilton, 1794-1852. I. Jones, Leonidas M., ed. **BIP**

Reynolds, Joshua, Sir, 1723-1792.

MORGAN, Eileen. 759.2
Sir Joshua Reynolds, 1723-1792; first president of the Royal Academy. [Plymouth, Plymouth Corporation and the Sir Joshua Reynolds Celebrations Committee, 1973] 44 p. illus. 21 cm. [ND497.R4M85] 74-162425 £0.40
1. Reynolds, Joshua, Sir, 1723-1792.

REYNOLDS, Joshua, Sir, 1723-1792. 759.2 B
Letters of Sir Joshua Reynolds / collected and edited by Frederick Whiley Hilles. New York : AMS Press, [1976] p. cm. Originally presented as the editor's thesis, Yale University, 1926. Reprint of the 1929 ed. published by the University Press, Cambridge, Eng. Includes index. Bibliography: p. [ND497.R4A35 1976] 75-4122 13.50
1. Reynolds, Joshua, Sir, 1723-1792. 2. Painters—Great Britain—Correspondence, reminiscences, etc. I. Title.

REYNOLDS, Joshua, Sir, 1723-1792. 759.2
Reynolds [by] Ellis Waterhouse. [New York] Phaidon; [distributed by Praeger, 1973] 192 p. 127 plates (part col.) 29 cm. Includes bibliographical references. [ND497.R4W3 1973] 78-158100 ISBN 0-7148-1519-5 25.00
1. Reynolds, Joshua, Sir, 1723-1792. I. Waterhouse, Ellis Kirkham, 1905-

STEEGMAN, John, 1899-1966. 759.2 B
Sir Joshua Reynolds / by John Steegmann [i.e. Steegman]. Folcroft, Pa. : Folcroft Library Editions, 1977. 136 p. ; 23 cm. Reprint of the 1933 ed. published by Macmillan, New York, in series: Great lives, 5. Bibliography: p. 136. [ND497.R4S75 1977] 77-17594 ISBN 0-8414-7867-8 lib. bdg. : 12.50
1. Reynolds, Joshua, Sir, 1723-1792. 2. Painters—England—Biography. **BIP**

Reynolds, Samuel, 1825-1901.

GILLISON, Joan Mary. 994.5
Colonial doctor and his town / [by] Joan Gillison. Melbourne : Cypress Books, 1974. 292 p., [8] p. of plates : ill., map on lining papers ; 22 cm. Includes index. Bibliography: p. 283-284. [R674.R48G55] 75-316646 ISBN 0-909807-15-9 : 8.50
1. Reynolds, Samuel, 1825-1901. 2. Mansfield, Australia—History. I. Title.

Reza Shah, Shah of Iran, 1878-1944.

WILBER, Donald Newton. 955'.05'0924 B
Riza Shah Pahlavi : the resurrection and reconstruction of Iran / Donald N. Wilber. 1st ed. Hicksville, N.Y. : Exposition Press, [1975] xii, 301 p., [8] leaves of plates : ill. ; 24 cm. (An Exposition-university book) Includes index. Bibliography: p. 269-291. [DS317.W54] 74-34518 ISBN 0-682-48206-4 : 15.00

1. Reza Shah, Shah of Iran, 1878-1944. 2. Iran—History—1909- BIP

Rezanov, Nikolai Petrovich, 1764-1807.

CHEVIGNY, Hector, 1904- 923.247
Lost empire; the life and adventures of Nikolai Petrovich Rezanov. Portland, Or., Binfords & Mort, 1958. 356p. illus. 23cm. Includes bibliography. [DK190.6.R4C5 1958] 58-11484
1. Rezanov, Nikolai Petrovich, 1764-1807. I. Title.

Rhea, Claude H.

RHEA, Claude H. 783.7'092'4 B
With my song I will prasie Him / Claude H. Rhea. Nashville : Broadman Press, c1977. 156 p. : ill. ; 21 cm. [ML420.R43A3] 76-17946 ISBN 0-8054-5571-X : 4.95
1. Rhea, Claude H. 2. Gospel musicians—United States—Biography. I. Title.

Rhee, Syngman, 1875-

ALLEN, Richard C. 923.1519
Korea's Syngman Rhee, an unauthorized portrait. Rutland, Vt., C. E. Tuttle Co. [1960] 259p. Bibl.: p.[253]-254 illus., ports. 23cm. 60-15606 3.75 half cloth,
1. Rhee, Syngman. I. Title.

OLIVER, Robert Tarbell, 1909- 923.1519
Syngman Rhee, the man behind the myth. New York, Dodd, Mead, 1954. 380p. illus. 22cm. [DS916.5.R5O4] 54-7714
1. Rhee, Syngman, 1875- 2. Korea—Pol. & govt. I. Title.

OLIVER, Robert Tarbell, 1909- 951.9'04'0924
Syngman Rhee, the man behind the myth, by Robert T. Oliver. Westport, Conn., Greenwood Press [1973, c1954] x, 380 p. illus. 22 cm. Bibliography: p. 331-336. [DS916.5.R5O4 1973] 72-13864 ISBN 0-8371-6759-0 16.00
1. Rhee, Syngman, 1875-1965. 2. Korea—Politics and government—1948-1960. I. Title.

Rhett, Robert Barnewell, 1800-1876.

WHITE, Laura Amanda 973.7130924
Robert Barnwell Rhett, father of secession. Gloucester, Mass., P. Smith [1966, c.1931] ix, 264p. illus., geneal. table. fold. map, ports. 21cm. At head of title: The American Historical Association. Bibl. [F273.R52] 66-824 5.00
1. Rhett, Robert Barnewell, 1800-1876. 2. South Carolina—Pol. & govt.—1775-1865. 3. Secession. I. American Historical Association. II. Title. BIP

Rhinelander, Philip Mercer, Bp., 1869-1939.

WASHBURN, Henry Bradford, 1869- 922.373
Philip Mercer Rhinelander, seventh Bishop of Pennsylvania, first warden of the College of Preachers. New York, Morehouse-Gorham Co., 1950. ix, 210 p. illus., port. 21 cm. [BX5995.R48W3] 50-10776
1. Rhinelander, Philip Mercer, Bp., 1869-1939. I. Title.

Rhoads, Bert.

ROTH, Don A., 1927- 286'.7'0924 B
The individualist; a biography of Bert Rhoads, by Don A. Roth. Nashville, Southern Pub. Association [1968] 126 p. port. 22 cm. A biography of the man who overcame poverty and ill health to serve most of his ninety-six years as an educator and writer for the Seventh-Day Adventist Church. [BX6193.R45R6] 92 AC 68
1. Rhoads, Bert. I. Title.

ROTH, Don A., 1927- 286.7'0924 B
The individualist; a biography of Bert Rhoads, by Don A. Roth. Nashville, Southern Pub. Association [1968] 126 p. port. 22 cm. [BX6193.R45R6] 68-20844
1. Rhoads, Bert. I. Title.

Rhode Island—Biography.

REVOLUTIONARY 974.5'03'0922 B
portraits : people, places, and events from Rhode Island's historic past / written by members of the Rhode Island Short Story Club. Providence : Rhode Island Bicentennial Foundation, 1976. i, 80 p. ; 28 cm. [F78.R46] 76-152142
1. Rhode Island—Biography. 2. United States—History—Revolution, 1775-1783—Biography. I. Rhode Island Short Story Club.

Rhodes, Cecil John, 1853-1902.

ABDULLAH, Achmed, 1881-1945. 909'.09'712420810922
Dreamers of empire, by Achmed Abdullah [and] T. Compton Pakenham. Illustrated by B. K. Morris. Freeport, N.Y. Books for Libraries Press [1968] xiv, 368 p. ports. 23 cm. (Essay index reprint series) Reprint of the 1929 ed. Contents.Contents.—Cecil John Rhodes.—Richard Francis Burton.—John Nicholson.—Henry Montgomery Lawrence.—William Walker.—Charles George Gordon. [DA531.1.A2 1968] 68-57300
1. Rhodes, Cecil John, 1853-1902. 2. Burton, Richard Francis, Sir, 1821-1890. 3. Nicholson, John, 1822-1857. 4. Lawrence, Henry Montgomery, Sir, 1806-1857. 5. Walker, William, 1824-1860. 6. Gordon, Charles George, 1833-1885. I. Pakenham, Thomas Compton, joint author. II. Title. BIP

BAKER, Herbert, Sir, 1862-1946. 968'.04'0924 B
Cecil Rhodes, by his architect, Herbert Baker. 2d ed. Freeport, N.Y., Books for Libraries Press [1969] xvi, 182 p. illus., facsims., plan, ports. 23 cm. (Select bibliographies reprint series) Reprint of the 1938 ed. [DT776.R4B3 1969] 77-102223
1. Rhodes, Cecil John, 1853-1902.

FLINT, John E. 968.04'092'4 B
Cecil Rhodes, by John Flint. [1st ed.] Boston, Little, Brown [1974] xx, 268 p. illus. 21 cm. (The Library of world biography) Bibliography: p. [253]-257. [DT776.R4F55] 74-13734 6.95
1. Rhodes, Cecil John, 1853-1902. BIP

GROSS, Felix, 1888- 923.242
Rhodes of Africa. New York, F. A. Praeger [1957] 433 p. illus. 22 cm. [DT776.R4G75 1957] 57-7632
1. Rhodes, Cecil John, 1853-1902. I. Title.

LOCKHART, John Gilbert, 1891- 923.242
Cecil Rhodes; the colossus of southern Africa, by J. G. Lockhart and C. M. Woodhouse. New York, Macmillan [1963] 525 p. illus. 25 cm. [DT776.R4L62] 63-11803
1. Rhodes, Cecil John, 1853-1902. 2. Africa, South—Politics and government—1836-1909. I. Woodhouse, Christopher Montague, 1917- joint author.

MCDONALD, James Gordon, Sir, 1867-1943. 968.04'092'4 B
Rhodes: a heritage. New York, Negro Universities Press [1969] 166 p. illus. 23 cm. Reprint of the 1943 ed. Bibliography: p. 159. [DT776.R4M26 1969] 79-98724 ISBN 0-8371-2763-7
1. Rhodes, Cecil John, 1853-1902.

MAUROIS, Andre, 1885-1967. 968'.04'0924 B
Cecil Rhodes. Translated from the French by Rohan Wadham. Hamden, Conn., Archon Books [1968, c1953] 140, [3] p. illus., map, ports. 21 cm. (Makers of history) Bibliographical references included in "A note on sources" (p. [142]) [DT776.R4M38 1968b] 68-3628
1. Rhodes, Cecil John, 1853-1902.

MICHELL, Lewis, Sir, 1842-1928. 968'.04'0924 B
The life and times of the Right Honourable Cecil John Rhodes, 1853-1902. New York, Negro Universities Press [1969] 2 v. illus., facsims., ports. 23 cm. Reprint of the 1910 ed. [DT776.R4M6 1969] 73-90135
1. Rhodes, Cecil John, 1853-1902. I. Title. BIP

MICHELL, Lewis, Sir, 1842-1928. 968.04'092'4 B
The life and times of the Right Honourable Cecil John Rhodes, 1853-1902 / Lewis Michell. New York : Arno Press, 1977 [c1910] p. cm. (European business) Reprint of the ed. published by M. Kennerley, New York. [DT776.R4M6 1977] 76-29768 ISBN 0-405-09782-4(2 vols.) : 43.00
1. Rhodes, Cecil John, 1853-1902. 2. Statesmen—Africa, Southern—Biography. I. Title. II. Series.

ROBERTS, Brian. 968.04'0924 B
Cecil Rhodes and the princess. Philadelphia, Lippincott [1969] 405 p. map. 23 cm. Bibliography: p. 378-380. [DT776.R4R6] 70-77869 6.95
1. Rhodes, Cecil John, 1853-1902. 2. Radziwill, Catherine, Princess, 1858-1941. I. Title.

WILLIAMS, Basil, 1867-1950. 968'.04'0924 B
Cecil Rhodes. New York, Greenwood Press [1968] xi, 353 p. fold. map. 24 cm. Reprint of the 1921 ed. Bibliography: p. 331-337. [DT776.R4W5 1968] 69-14152
1. Rhodes, Cecil John, 1853-1902. BIP

Rhodes, Cecil John, 1853-1902 — Juvenile literature.

BATES, Neil. 968.04'092'4 B
Cecil Rhodes / [by] Neil Bates. Hove : Wayland, 1976. 96 p. : ill., 2 facsims., maps, ports. ; 22 cm. (Wayland history makers) Includes index. Bibliography: p. 93-94. [DT776.R4B35] 77-356815 ISBN 0-85340-296-5 : £2.95
1. Rhodes, Cecil John, 1853-1902—Juvenile literature. 2. Statesmen—Africa, Southern—Biography—Juvenile literature. 3. Capitalists and financiers—Africa, Southern—Biography—Juvenile literature.

GIBBS, Peter. j 92
The true story of Cecil Rhodes in Africa. Chicago, Childrens Press [1964] 139 p. col. illus. 23 cm. First published in London in 1956 under title: The true book about Cecil Rhodes. [DT776.R4G5] 64-12910
1. Rhodes, Cecil John, 1853-1902 — Juvenile literature. I. Title.

Rhodes, Eugene Manlove, 1869-1934.

GASTON, Edwin W. 818'.5'209
Engene Manlove Rhodes; cowboy chronicler, by Edwin W. Gaston, Jr. Austin, Tex., Steck-Vaughn Co. [1967] ii, 44 p. 21 cm. (Southwest writers series no. 11) Bibliography: p. 41-44. [PS3535.H68Z6] 67-24563
1. Rhodes, Eugene Manlove, 1869-1934. I. Title. II. Series.

RHODES, Eugene Manlove, 1869-1934. 928.1
A Bar Cross man; the life & personal writings of Eugene Manlove Rhodes [by] W. H. Hutchinson. [1st ed.] Norman, University of Oklahoma Press [1956] xix, 432 p. illus., ports., maps, facsims. 24 cm. "Check list of Eugene Manlove Rhodes' writing": p. 392-407. [PS3535.H68Z54] 56-6001
I. Hutchinson, William Henry, 1910- II. Title.

Rhodes, Harrie Vernette,

RHODES, Harrie Vernette, 1871- 920.9133
In the one spirit; the autobiography of Harrie Vernette Rhodes as told to Marguerritte Harmon Bro. [1st ed.] New York, Harper [1951] 192 p. 20 cm. [BR1716.R5A3] 51-14400
I. Bro. Marguerritte (Harmon) 1894- II. Title.

Rhodes, James Ford, 1848-1927.

CRUDEN, Robert 928.1
James Ford Rhodes: the man, the historian, and his work. With a complete bibliography of the writings of James Ford Rhodes. [Cleveland] Pr. of Western Reserve Univ. [c.]1961. 290p. Bibl. 61-16743 6.00
1. Rhodes, James Ford, 1848-1927. I. Title.

Rhodesia—Biog.

**WHO'S who of Rhodesia,* 920.068
Mauritis, Central and East Africa supplement to the Who's who of Southern Africa. Johannesburg, Combined Pubs [New York, Intl. Pubns. Serv. 1966] illus., ports. 25cm. In this sect. page nos. appear as 1017-1 to 1237-221 in order to preserve the continuity in this and the Who's who of Southern Africa. 15.00
1. Rhodesia Biog. 2. Africa, Central—Biog. 3. Africa, East —Biog.

Rhododendron—Breeding.

HYBRIDS and 635.9'33'62
hybridizers, rhododendrons and azaleas for Eastern North America / edited by Philip A. Livingston and Franklin H. West ; introd. by David Goheen Leach. Newtown Square, Pa. : Harrowood Books, c1978. xvi, 256 p., [12] leaves of plates : ill. ; 29 cm. Includes indexes. Bibliography: p. 236. [SB413.R47H9] 77-16822 ISBN 0-915180-04-9 : 25.00
1. Rhododendron—Breeding. 2. Azalea—Breeding. 3. Plant breeders—United States—Biography. 4. Rhododendron—Varieties. 5. Azalea—Varieties. 6. Hybridization, Vegetable. I. Livingston, Philip A., 1901- II. West, Franklin H., 1921-
Publisher's address : 3943 N. Providence Rd., Newtown Square, PA 19073

Rhys, Hedley Howell

RHYS, Hedley Howell 759.13
Maurice Prendergast, 1859-1924. Boston [dist.] Cambridge, Mass., Harvard Univ. Press, 1960. 156p. illus. (part col.) 60-16756 7.50
I. Prendergast Maurice Brazil, 1859-1924. II. Title.

Ribot, Theodule, 1839-1916.

DAVIS, Donald Irvin. v. 12
Theodule Armand Ribot and the development of the fundamental concepts of an organic psychology. [n.p.] 1964. 1 v. Honors thesis -- Harvard. 67-7615
1. Ribot, Theodule, 1839-1916. I. Title.

Ricardo, David, 1772-1823.

GOOTZEIT, Michael J., 1939- 330.15'3'0924
David Ricardo / Michael J. Gootzeit. New York : Columbia University Press, 1975. ix, 90 p. : ill. ; 24 cm. (Columbia essays on the great economists) Bibliography: p. [89]-90. [HB103.R5G66] 75-5687 ISBN 0-231-03524-1 : 7.50 ISBN 0-231-03916-6 pbk. : 1.95
1. Ricardo, David, 1772-1823. BIP

WEATHERALL, David. 330.15'3'0924 B
David Ricardo : a biography / by David Weatherall. The Hague : Martinus Nijhoff, 1977. x, 201 p., [3] leaves of plates : ill. ; 24 cm. Includes index. Bibliography: p. [195]-196. [HB103.R5W4] 76-380023 ISBN 9-02-471865-1 : 14.75
1. Ricardo, David, 1772-1823. 2. Economists, British—Biography.
Distributed by Humanities Press

Ricasoli, Bettino, barone, 1809-1880.

HANCOCK, William Keith, Sir, 1898- 945'.5'080924
Ricasoli and the Risorgimento in Tuscany, by W. K. Hancock. New York, H. Fertig, 1969. x, 320 p. illus., port. 24 cm. Reprint of the 1926 ed. Bibliography: p. 296-308. [DG738.6.R5H3 1969] 68-9603
1. Ricasoli, Bettino, barone, 1809-1880. 2. Tuscany—History. 3. Italy—History—1815-1870. I. Title. BIP

WHITTAM, John. 945'.08'0924
Ricasoli as Prime Minister: the struggle for the recognition of the Kingdom of Italy 1861. Reading, University of Reading (Department of Italian Studies), 1971. [2], 30 p. 21 cm. (Centre for the Advanced Study of Italian Society. Occasional papers, no. 4) Includes bibliographical references. [DG738.6.R5W48] 75-882604 ISBN 0-903005-00-X £0.40
1. Ricasoli, Bettino, barone, 1809-1880. I. Title. II. Series: Reading, Eng. University. Centre for the Advanced Study of Italian Society. Occasional papers, no. 4

Ricci, Matteo, 1552-1610.

CRONIN, Vincent. 922.251
The wise man from the West. [1st American ed.] New York, Dutton, 1955. 300 p. illus. 22 cm. [BV3427.R46C7 1955a] 55-8331
1. Ricci, Matteo, 1552-1610. I. Title.

CRONIN, Vincent. 922.251
The wise man from the West. Garden City, N. Y., Image Books [1957, (1955] 276 p. 18 cm. (A Doubleday image book, D44) Includes bibliography. [BV3427] 57-273
1. Ricci, Matteo, 1552-1610. I. Title.

Ricci, Sebastiano, 1659-1734.

DANIELS, Jeffery. 759.5
Sebastiano Ricoi / [by] Jeffery Daniels. Hove : Wayland, 1976. xix, 172 p., leaf of plate, [136] p. of plates : ill. (some col.), facsim., plan, ports. ; 32 cm. Includes index. Bibliography: p. 158-164. [ND623.R644D35] 76-479298 ISBN 0-85340-057-1 : £45.00
1. Ricci, Sebastiano, 1659-1734.

Rice, Dan, 1823-1900.

GILLETTE, Don Carle. 791.33'0924
He made Lincoln laugh; the story of Dan Rice. [1st ed.] New York, Exposition Press [1967] 170 p. ports. 21 cm. (An Exposition-Lochinvar book) [GV1811.R4G54] 67-26393
1. Rice, Dan, 1823-1900. I. Title.

Rice family.

PARKMAN, Ebenezer, 1703-1782. 973'.04'97 S
The story of the Rice boys / Ebenezer Parkman. New York : Garland Pub., 1976. 6 p. : ill. ; 23 cm. (The Garland library of narratives of North American Indian captivities ; v. 105) Reprint of the 1906 ed. published by the Westborough Historical Society, Westboro, Mass. Issued with the reprint of the 1903 ed. of Parrish, J. The story of Captain Jasper Parrish. New York, 1976. [E85.G2 vol. 105] [E87.R49] 974.4'3'020922 75-7133 ISBN 0-8240-1729-3 lib.bdg. : 25.00
1. Rice family. 2. Indians of North America—Captivities. I. Title. II. Series.

Rice, Helen Steiner—Biography.

RICE, Helen Steiner. 811'.5'4 B
In the vineyard of the Lord : my life story / Helen Steiner Rice, as told to Fred Bauer. Old Tappan, N.J. : F. H. Revell Co., c1979. p. cm. [PS3568.I28Z467] 79-16686 ISBN 0-8007-1036-3 : 8.95
1. Rice, Helen Steiner—Biography. 2. Poets, American—20th century—Biography. 3. Christian biography—United States. I. Bauer, Fred, fl. 1968- II. Title.

Rice, Jim.

*GUTMAN, Bill. 796.357'092'2 [B]
Grand slammers : Rice, Luzinski, Foster, Hisle / by Bill Gutman. New York : Tempo Books, 1979. 182p. ; 18 cm. [GV865] ISBN 0-448-17344-1 pbk. : 1.50
1. Rice, Jim. 2. Luzinski, Greg. 3. Hisle, Larry. 4. Foster, George. 5. Baseball players — United States — Biography. I. Title.

Rice, Joan Moore—Juvneile literature.

JACOBS, Linda. 796.4'1'0924 B
Joan Moore Rice : the Olympic dream / by Linda Jacobs. St. Paul : EMC Corp., [1975] p. cm. (Women who win ; 3) A brief biography of the champion gymnast who gave up her amateur status to open a gymnastics training school. [GV333.R52J32] 92 75-5519 ISBN 0-88436-164-0 lib.bdg. : 4.95 ISBN 0-88436-165-9 pbk. : 2.95
1. Rice, Joan Moore—Juveneile literature. I. Title. BIP

Rice, John Holt, 1777-1831.

PRICE, Philip B. 922.573
The life of the Reverend John Holt Rice, D.D. Richmond, Lib. of Union Theological Seminary in Virginia, 1963. ix, 144 1. facsim. 28cm. Reprinted from the Central Presbyterian, 1886-1887. 63-23592 price on request
1. Rice, John Holt, 1777-1831. I. Title.

Rice, John R., 1895-

SUMNER, Robert Leslie, 1922- v. 12
Man sent from God; a biography of Dr. John R. Rice. Grand Rapids, Eerdmans [1959] c.262 p. illus. 23 cm.
1. Rice, John R., 1895- I. Title.

Rice, Justus Bulkley,

RICE, Justus Bulkley, 1896- 610'.924 B
My number two wife, by Justus B. Rice. [1st ed.] New York, Meredith Press [1968] viii, 213 p. 21 cm. [R154.R387A3] 68-26332 4.95
I. Title.

Rice, Luther, 1783-1836— Juvenile literature.

CARVER, Saxon Rowe. 920
Ropes to Burma; the story of Luther Rice. Illus. by Edward Shenton. Nashville, Broadman [c.1961] 183p. 61-7552 2.50
1. Rice, Luther, 1783-1836—Juvenile literature. I. Title.

CARVER, Saxon Rowe. 92
Ropes to Burma; the story of Luther Rice. Illustrated by Edward Shenton. Nashville, Broadman Press [1961] 183p. illus. 21cm. [BX6495.R55C3] 61-7552
1. Rice, Luther, 1783-1836— Juvenile literature. I. Title.

Rice, Merton Stacher, 1872-1943.

CHABUT, Elaine (Rice) 1910- 922.773
Preacher Mike; the life of Dr. Merton S. Rice. [1st ed.] New York, Citadel Press [1958] 226p. illus. 22cm. [BX495.R466C5] 58-7309
1. Rice, Merton Stacher, 1872-1943. I. Title.

*Rice, Robert H.,

*RICE, Robert H., 1886- 920.7
The book I'd like to write [by] Robert H. "Bob" Rice. New York, Vantage [1968] 196p. illus. 21cm. 3.95 bds.,
I. Title.

Rice, William Marsh, 1816-1900.

MORRIS, Sylvia Stallings. 378.764'1411 B
William Marsh Rice and his Institute; a biographical study. Edited by Sylvia Stallings Morris from the papers and research notes of Andrew Forest Muir. Houston, Tex., William Marsh Rice University, 1972. ix, 171 p. illus. 24 cm. "Originally published as vol. 58, no. 2 of Rice University studies." [LD6053.M67 1972] 72-87103
1. Rice, William Marsh, 1816-1900. I. Muir, Andrew Forest. II. Title. BIP

MORRIS, Sylvia Stallings. 080 S
William Marsh Rice and his institute; a biographical study. Edited by Sylvia Stallings Morris from the papers and research notes of Andrew Forest Muir. [Houston, Tex., William Marsh Rice University] 1972. ix, 171 p. illus. 23 cm. (Rice University studies, v. 58, no. 2) Bibliography: p. 125-148. [AS36.W65 vol. 58, no. 2] [LD6053] 378.764'1411 B 73-174009
1. Rice, William Marsh, 1816-1900. 2. William Marsh Rice University, Houston, Tex. I. Muir, Andrew Forest. II. Title. III. Series.

Rich, Barnabe, 1540?-1617.

CRANFILL, Thomas Mabry. 928.2
Barnaby Rich, a short biography, by Thomas M. Cranfill and Dorothy Hart Bruce. Austin, University of Texas Press, 1953. 135p. illus. 18cm. Based in part on D. H. Bruce's thesis (Stanford University) entitled Barnabe Riche and his acquaintances. [PR2336.R8Z6] 53-6002
1. Rich, Barnabe, 1540?-1617. I. Bruce, Dorothy Hart, joint author. II. Title.

Rich, Bernard, 1917-

BALLIETT, Whitney. 789'.1'0924
Super drummer: a profile of Buddy Rich. With photos. by Fred Seligo. Indianapolis, Bobbs-Merrill Co. [1968] 128 p. illus. 15 x 22 cm. [ML419.R52B3] 68-15809 3.95
1. Rich, Bernard, 1917- I. Title.

Rich, Charles Coulson, 1809-1883.

ARRINGTON, Leonard J. 289.3'092'4 B
Charles C. Rich, Mormon general and Western frontiersman [by] Leonard J. Arrington. Provo, Utah, Brigham Young University Press [1974] xvii, 386 p. illus. 24 cm. (Studies in Mormon history, v. 1) Includes bibliographical references. [BX8695.R46A77] 74-13624 ISBN 0-8425-1051-6 7.50
1. Rich, Charles Coulson, 1809-1883. I. Title. II. Series.

Rich, Charlie—Juvenile literature.

ERON, Judy. 784'.092'4 B
Charlie Rich / text, Judy Eron & Geoffrey Morgan ; ill., John Keely. Mankato, Minn. : Creative Education, [1975] p. cm. Bibliography: p. [ML3930.R5E7] 75-23079 ISBN 0-87191-463-8 : 4.95
1. Rich, Charlie—Juvenile literature. I. Morgan, Goeffrey, joint author. II. Keely, John. III. Title.

ERON, Judy. 784'.092'4 B
Charlie Rich / text, Judy Eron & Geoffrey Morgan ; ill., John Keely. Mankato, Minn. : Creative Education, [1975] p. cm. Bibliography: p. [ML3930.R5E7] 75-23079 ISBN 0-87191-463-8 lib.bdg. : 4.95
1. Rich, Charlie—Juvenile literature. I. Morgan, Goeffrey, joint author. II. Keely, John. III. Title. BIP

Richard, Cliff.

WINTER, David Brian. 784'.0924 B
New singer, new song: the Cliff Richard story, by David Winter. Waco, Tex., Word Books [1968] 160 p. ports. 23 cm. Relates the rise, success, and personal life of a popular British singer who got his start in 1958 during the rock and roll era. [ML420.R5W5 1968] 92 AC 68
1. Richard, Cliff. I. Title.

WINTER, David Brian. 784'.0924 B
New singer, new song: the Cliff Richard story, by David Winter. Waco, Tex., Word Books [1968] 160 p. ports. 23 cm. [ML420.R5W5 1968] 68-4867
1. Richard, Cliff. I. Title.

Richard, Duke of York, 1473-1483.

JENKINS, Elizabeth, 1907- 942.04'6'0924 B
The princes in the tower / by Elizabeth Jenkins. New York : Coward, McCann & Georghegan, c1978. p. cm. [DA260.J46] 78-14459 ISBN 0-698-10842-6 : 10.95 12.50
1. Richard III, King of England, 1452-1485. 2. Richard, Duke of York, 1473-1483. 3. Edward V, King of England, 1470-1483. 4. Great Britain—History—Richard III, 1483-1485. 5. Great Britain—Kings and rulers—Biography. I. Title. BIP

Richard. Gabriel, 1767-1832.

MAST, Dolorita 277.740924
Always the priest; the life of Gabriel Richard, S.S. Helicon [dist New York, Taplinger, c.1965] 368p. 21cm. Bibl. [F574.D4R517] 64-20229 6.95
1. Richard. Gabriel, 1767-1832. I. Title.

WOODFORD, Frank Bury, 1903- 922.273
Gabriel Richard; frontier ambassador, by Frank B. Woodford and Albert Hyma. With a foreword by Roscoe O. Bonisteel and an introd. by Edward J. Hickey. Detroit, Wayne State University Press, 1958. 158 p. illus. 27 cm. Includes bibliography. [F574.D4R53] 58-12331
1. Richard, Gabriel, 1767-1832. I. Hyma, Albert, 1893- joint author. II. Title.

Richard, Gabriel, 1767-1832 — Juvenile literature.

ABODAHER, David J j92
Under three flags; the story of Gabriel Richard, by David J. Abodaher. Illustrated by Richard Lewis. New York, Hawthorn Books [1965] 187 p. illus., maps. 22 cm. (Hawthorn junior biographies) Bibliography: p. [181] [F574.D4R525] 65-12734
1. Richard, Gabriel, 1767-1832 — Juvenile literature. I. Title.

Richard, Hetty Lawrence (Hemenway) 1890-1961.

GRAHAM, Elinor (Mish) 920.7
The story of Hetty Hemenway Richard, a journey worth the taking, by Elinor M. Graham. [New York? 1964] 304 p. illus., ports. 22 cm. [PS3535.I2445Z67] 63-23472
1. Richard, Hetty Lawrence (Hemenway) 1890-1961. I. Title.

Richard I, King of England, 1157-1199.

BRUNDAGE, James A. 942.03'2'0924 B
Richard Lion Heart [by] James A. Brundage. New York, Scribner [1974] viii, 278 p. maps. 24 cm. Bibliography: p. [264]-269. [DA207.B75] 73-1361 ISBN 0-684-13802-6 10.00
1. Richard I, King of England, 1157-1199. 2. Great Britain—History—Richard I, 1189-1199. I. Title. BIP

GILLINGHAM, John Bennett. 942.03'2'0924
Richard the Lionheart / John Gillingham. New York : Times Books, [1979] c1978. 318 p., [4] leaves of plates : ill. ; 22 cm. Includes index. Bibliography: p. [289]-290.

[DA207.G48 1979] 78-63599 ISBN 0-8129-0802-3 : 12.50
1. Richard I, King of England, 1157-1199. 2. Great Britain—Kings and rulers—Biography. I. Title.

HENDERSON, Philip, 1906- 923.142
Richard Coeur de Lion; a biography. [1st American ed.] New York, W. W. Norton [1959] 256 p. illus. 22 cm. [DA207.H4 1959] 59-11242
1. Richard I, King of England, 1157-1199. **BIP**

HENDERSON, Philip, 1906- 942.03'2'0924 B
Richard, Coeur de Lion : a biography / by Philip Henderson. Westport, Conn. : Greenwood Press, 1976, c1958. 256 p. : ill. ; 23 cm. Reprint of the 1959 ed. published by Norton, New York. Includes index. Bibliography: p. [249]-251. [DA207.H4 1976] 76-4 ISBN 0-8371-8724-9 lib.bdg. : 15.00
1. Richard I, King of England, 1157-1199.

NORGATE, Kate. 942.03'2'0924 B
Richard the Lion Heart. New York, Russell & Russell [1969] viii, 349 p. 23 cm. Reprint of the 1924 ed. Bibliographical references included in "Notes" (p. 330-339) [DA207.N6 1969] 69-17841
1. Richard I, King of England, 1157-1199. **BIP**

SABATINI, Rafael, 1875-1950. 920.02
Heroic lives; Richard I: Saint Francis of Assisi: Joan of Arc: Sir Walter Ralegh: Lord Nelson: Florence Nightingale. Freeport, N.Y., Books for Libraries Press [1971, c1934] 416 p. 23 cm. (Essay index reprint series) [D106.S28 1971] 70-99648 ISBN 0-8369-2071-6
1. Richard I, King of England, 1157-1199. 2. Francesco d'Assisi, Saint, 1182-1226. 3. Jeanne d'Arc, Saint, 1412-1431. 4. Raleigh, Walter Sir, 1552?-1618. 5. Nelson, Horatio Nelson, Viscount, 1758-1805. 6. Nightingale, Florence, 1820-1910. I. Title.

Richard I, King of England, 1157-1199—Juvenile literature.

PITTENGER, William Norman, 1905- 942.03'2'0924 B
Richard the Lion-Hearted: the crusader king [by] W. Norman Pittenger. London, New York, Franklin Watts Ltd., 1970. ix, 149 p. map. 23 cm. (Immortals of history) Bibliography: p. 145. [DA207.P54 1970b] 72-31002 ISBN 0-85166-302-8 £1.25
1. Richard I, King of England, 1157-1199—Juvenile literature. I. Title.

SUSKIND, Richard. 942.03'2'0924 B
The crusader king, Richard the Lionhearted. Illustrated by William Sauts Bock. [1st ed.] Boston, Little, Brown [1973] 120 p. illus. 22 cm. Bibliography: p. [115] A biography of the second king of the Plantagenet dynasty who lived in England only six months during his ten year reign. [DA207.S87] 92 72-6728 ISBN 0-316-82250-7 5.95
1. Richard I, King of England, 1157-1199—Juvenile literature. I. Bock, William Sauts, 1939- illus. II. Title.

SUSKIND, Richard. 942.03'2'0924 B
The crusader king: Richard the Lionhearted. Illustrated by William Sauts Bock. Boston, G. K. Hall, 1973. 157 p. illus. 25 cm. Large print ed. Bibliography: p. A biography of the second king of the Plantagenet dynasty who lived in England only six months during his ten year reign. [DA207.S87 1973b] 92 73-12281 ISBN 0-8161-6144-5 5.95
1. Richard I, King of England, 1157-1199—Juvenile literature. 2. Sight-saving books. I. Bock, William Sauts, 1939- illus. II. Title.

Richard II, King of England, 1367-1400.

HUTCHISON, Harold F 923.142
The hollow crown; a life of Richard II. [1st American ed.] New York, John Day Co. [1961] 276p. illus. 23cm. [DA235.H8 1961] 61-12719
1. Richard II, King of England, 1367-1400. I. Title.

Richard III, King of England, 1452-1485.

BUCK, George, Sir, d.1623. 942.04'6'0924 B
The history of the life and reigne of Richard the Third. With a new introd. by A. R. Myers. Totowa, N.J., Rowman and Littlefield [1973] ix, 150 p. illus. 27 cm. Reprint of the 1647 ed. published by W. Wilson, London. Includes bibliographical references. [DA260.B8 1973] 73-155139 ISBN 0-87471-143-6 10.00
1. Richard III, King of England, 1452-1485. 2. Great Britain—History—Richard III, 1483-1485. I. Title.

GAIRDNER, James, 1828-1912. 942.04'6'0924 B
History of the life and reign of Richard the Third, to which is added The story of Perkin Warbeck, from original documents. A new and rev. ed. New York, Greenwood Press [1969] xii, 388 p. ports. 23 cm. Reprint of the 1898 ed. Bibliographical footnotes. [DA260.G15 1969] 69-13900
1. Richard III, King of England, 1452-1485. 2. Warbeck, Perkin, 1474-1499. 3. Gt. Brit.—History—Richard III, 1483-1485. I. Title.

JENKINS, Elizabeth, 1907- 942.04'6'0924 B
The princes in the tower / by Elizabeth Jenkins. New York : Coward, McCann & Georghegan, c1978. p. cm. [DA260.J46] 78-14459 ISBN 0-698-10842-6 : 10.95 12.50
1. Richard III, King of England, 1452-1485. 2. Richard, Duke of York, 1473-1483. 3. Edward V, King of England, 1470-1483. 4. Great Britain—History—Richard III, 1483-1485. 5. Great Britain—Kings and rulers—Biography. I. Title. **BIP**

KENDALL, Paul Murray. 923.142
Richard the Third. [1st American ed.] New York, W. W. Norton [1956] 602p. illus. 22cm. [DA260.K4 1956] 56-10090
1. Richard III, King of England, 1452-1485. I. Title.

KENDALL, Paul Murray, ed. 923.142
Richard III: the great debate, ed. with introds by Paul Murray Kendall. New York, Norton [c.1965] 244p. 20cm. (Norton lib., N310) [DA260K4] 1.75 pap.,
1. Richard III, King of England, 1452-1485 I. Title.

KENDALL, Paul Murray. v. 12
Richard the Third. Garden City, N. Y. Doubleday & Co. [1965, c1956] 514 p. illus. (Anchor Books) Bibliographical references included in "Notes" (p. 437-499) Richard the Third was originally published by W. W. Norton in 1956, with whose arrangements this edition is published. Dibliography: p. 500 502. 66-85348
1. Richard III, King of England, 1425-1485. I. Title. **BIP**

KENDALL, Paul Murray. v. 12
Richard the Third. Garden City, N. Y. Doubleday & Co. [1965, c1956] 514 p. illus. (Anchor Books) Bibliographical references included in "Notes" (p. 437-499) Richard the Third was originally published by W. W. Norton in 1956, with whose arrangements this edition is published. Bibliography: p. 500-502. 66-85348
1. Richard III, King of England, 1425-1485. I. Title. **BIP**

KENDALL, Paul Murray, 1911-1973. 923.142
Richard the Third. New York: Norton, [1975 c1955] 602 p.; 20 cm. Bibliography: p. 580-583. [DA260.K4 1975] 56-10090 ISBN 0-393-00785-5 5.95 (pbk.)
1. Richard III, King of England, 1452-1485. I. Title. **BIP**

MACKINTOSH, Elizabeth, 1896- FIC
The daughter of time, by Josephine Tey [pseud.] New York, Macmillan, 1952 [c1951] 204 p. 21 cm. [PZ3.M2174Dau2] fic 52-7599
1. Richard III, King of England, I. Title.

MARKHAM, Clements Robert, Sir 1830-1916 942.04'6'0924
Richard III: his life and character, reviewed in the light of recent research. New York, Russell & Russell [1968] xix, 327p. 2 geneal. tables, fold. map, port. 23cm. Reprint of the 1906 ed. Bibl. footnotes. [DA260.M3 1968] (B) 67-16007 9.75
1. Richard III, King of England, 1452-1485. I. Title.

MORE, Thomas, Sir Saint, 1478-1535. 942.04'6'0924 B
The history of King Richard III and selections from the English and Latin poems / St. Thomas More ; edited by Richard S. Sylvester. New Haven, [Conn.] : Yale University Press, 1976. xxviii, 168 p. ; 21 cm. (The Yale edition of the works of St. Thomas More : Selected works) Includes index. Bibliography: p. xxiii-xxviii. [DA260.M6 1976] 76-372139 ISBN 0-300-01840-1 : 12.50 ISBN 0-300-01925-4 pbk. : 3.95
1. Richard III, King of England, 1452-1485. 2. Great Britain—History—Richard III, 1483-1485. I. Sylvester, Richard Standish. II. Title: The history of King Richard III and selections ...

MURPH, Roxane C. 942.04'6'0924 B
Richard III : the making of a legend / by Roxane C. Murph. Metuchen, N.J. : Scarecrow Press, 1977. v, 148 p. ; 23 cm. Includes index. Bibliography: p. 133-141. [DA260.M8] 77-4021 ISBN 0-8108-1034-4 : 6.00
1. Richard III, King of England, 1452-1485. 2. Richard III, King of England, 1452-1485, in fiction, drama, poetry, etc. 3. Great Britain—Kings and rulers—Biography. **BIP**

Richards, Barry.

RICHARDS, Barry. 796.358'092'4 B
The Barry Richards story / by Barry Richards. London ; Boston : Faber, 1978. 180 p., [8] leaves of plates : ill. ; 22 cm. [GV915.R48A32] 78-316283 ISBN 0-571-11187-4 : 10.95
1. Richards, Barry. 2. Cricket players—South Africa—Biography. I. Title. **BIP**

Richards, Dorothy.

RICHARDS, Dorothy. 599'.3232
Beaversprite : my years building an animal sanctuary / by Dorothy Richards, with Hope Sawyer Buyukmihci. San Francisco : Chronicle Books, c1977. 191 p. : ill. ; 24 cm. [QL795.B5R5] 77-24150 7.95
1. Richards, Dorothy. 2. Beavers—Legends and stories. 3. Beavers as pets. 4. Wildlife conservation—New York (State) 5. Naturalists—New York (State)—Biography. I. Buyukmihci, Hope Sawyer, joint author. II. Title. **BIP**

Richards, Edward, 1936-

RICHARDS, Edward, 1936- 616.5'44 B
Would you call it a miracle? / [By Edward and Elizabeth Richards]. St. Petersburg, Fla. : Valkyrie Press, c1977. 95 p. ; 19 cm. Includes bibliographical references. [RL451.R5] 77-77043 ISBN 0-912760-53-2 pbk. : 2.50
1. Richards, Edward, 1936- 2. Scleroderma (Disease)—Biography. 3. Scleroderma (Disease)—Nutritional aspects. I. Richards, Elizabeth Alice, 1940- joint author. II. Title.

Richards, Ellen Henrietta (Swallow) 1842-1911.

CLARKE, Robert, 1931- 574.5'092'4 B
Ellen Swallow: the woman who founded ecology. Chicago, Follett Pub. Co. [1973] xii, 276 p. illus. 23 cm. Bibliography: p. 256-262. [QH31.R5C55] 73-82198 ISBN 0-695-80388-3 7.95
1. Richards, Ellen Henrietta (Swallow) 1842-1911. 2. Ecologists—Biography. **BIP**

DOUTY, Esther (Morris) 926.4
America's first woman chemist, Ellen Richards. New York, Messner [c.1961] 191p. Bibl. 61-14455 2.95
1. Richards, Ellen Henrietta (Swallow) 1842-1911. I. Title.

HUNT, Caroline Louisa, 1865-1927. 926.4
The life of Ellen H. Richards, 1842-1911. Anniversary ed. Washington, American Home Economics Association, 1958. 202p. illus. 23cm. [TX140.R6H8 1958] 58-2706
1. Richards, Ellen Henrietta (Swallow) 1842-1911. I. Title.

Richards family.

PIERCE, Arthur Dudley 929.2
Family empire in Jersey iron; the Richards enterprises in the pine barrens. New Brunswick, N.J., Rutgers [1965, c.1964] xvii, 286p. illus., facsims., maps, ports. 22cm. [CS71.R5122] 64-24737 6.00
1. Richards family. 2. Iron industry and trade—New Jersey. I. Title.

Richards, Kenneth G.,

RICHARDS, Kenneth G., 1926- 720'.924 B
Frank Lloyd Wright [by] Kenneth G. Richards. Chicago, Childrens Press [1968] 95 p. illus., ports. 29 cm. (People of destiny: a humanities series) Bibliography: p. 92. A biography of the man whose new concept of design revolutionized the development of American architecture in the twentieth century. [NA737.W7R5] 92 AC 68
I. Title.

Richards, Laura Elizabeth (Howe)

RICHARDS, Laura Elizabeth (Howe) 1850-1943. 811'.3 B
Julia Ward Howe, 1819-1910, by Laura E. Richards and Maud Howe Elliott, assisted by Florence Howe Hall. Dunwoody, Ga., N. S. Berg, 1970 [c1915] 2 v. in 1. illus., facsim., ports. 24 cm. [PS2018.R5 1970] 78-11235
I. Howe, Julia (Ward) 1819-1910. II. Elliott, Maud (Howe) 1854-1948, joint author. III. Hall, Florence Marion (Howe) 1845-1922, joint author. **BIP**

Richards, Linda Ann Judson, 1841-1930—Juvenile literature.

COLLINS, David R. 610.73'092'4 B
Linda Richards: first American trained nurse, by David R. Collins. Illustrated by Cary. Champaign, Ill., Garrard Pub. Co. [1973] 80 p. col. illus. 23 cm. (A Discovery book) A brief biography of the woman whose concern for the sick led her to become the first professional nurse in the United States in 1873. [RT37.R6C64] 92 73-5889 2.84
1. Richards, Linda Ann Judson, 1841-1930 Juvenile literature. I. Cary, Louis F., 1915- illus. II. Title.

Richards, Norman.

RICHARDS, Norman. 362.4'0924 B
Helen Keller. Chicago, Childrens Press [1968] 94 p. illus. 29 cm. (People of destiny: a humanities series) A biography of Helen Keller that stresses her education and her efforts to aid and encourage the handicapped. [HV1624.K4R5] 92 AC 68
I. Title.

RICHARDS, Norman. 811'.5'2 B
Robert Frost. Chicago, Childrens Press [1968] 94 p. illus., ports. 29 cm. (People of destiny: a humanities series) Bibliography: p. 90. A biography of the man who became known as America's "national poet," stressing the rural emphasis of his poetry and his determination to succeed in spite of poverty and personal tragedy. Includes some of his poems. [PS3511.R94Z915] 92 AC 68
I. Title.

Richards, Theodore, 1867-1948.

ALLEN, Gwenfread Elaine, 1904- 285'.8'0922 B
Bridge builders; the story of Theodore and Mary Atherton Richards, by Gwenfread E. Allen. [Honolulu] Hawaii Conference Foundation, 1970. 260 p. illus. 24 cm. [BV3680.H4R4762] 75-131598
1. Richards, Theodore, 1867-1948. 2. Richards, Mary (Atherton) I. Title.

*Richards, Vyvyan

*RICHARDS, Vyvyan 923.242
Portrait of T. E. Lawrence. New York, Scholastic [1964,c.1939] 147p. 17cm. (T543) Orig. Eng. pubn. appeared under title: T.E. Lawrence in Duckworth's Gt. lives ser. Bibl. .35 pap.,
I. Lawrence, Thomas Edward, 1888-1935. II. Title.

Richards, Walter Scott, 1871-

TRAVIS, Lorena L 920
Walter Scott Richards, pioneer of the Southwest. Muskogee, Okla., American Print. [1956] 123 p. illus. 22 cm. [CT275.R548T7] 56-38460
1. Richards, Walter Scott, 1871- I. Title.

Richards, Willard, 1804-1854.

NOALL, Claire Augusta (Wilcox) 1892- 922.8373
Intimate disciple; a portrait of Willard Richards, apostle to Joseph Smith, cousin of Brigham Young, by Claire Noall. [Salt Lake City] University of Utah Press, 1957. xi, 630 p. illus., maps., ports. 24 cm. Bibliography: p. 621-630. [BX8695.R53N6] 64-57118
1. Richards, Willard, 1804-1854. I. Title.

Richardson, Dorothy Miller, 1873-1957.

FROMM, Gloria G., 1931- 823'.9'12 B
Dorothy Richardson : a biography / Gloria G. Fromm. Urbana : University of Illinois Press, c1977. p. cm. Includes index. Bibliography: p. [PR6035.I34Z68] 77-8455 ISBN 0-252-00631-3 : 16.00
1. Richardson, Dorothy Miller, 1873-1957. 2. Novelists, English—20th century—Biography. I. Title.

FROMM, Gloria G., 1931- 823'.9'12 B
Dorothy Richardson : a biography / Gloria G. Fromm. Urbana : University of Illinois Press, c1977. p. cm. Includes index. Bibliography: p. [PR6035.134Z68] 77-8455 ISBN 0-252-00631-3 : 16.00
1. Richardson, Dorothy Miller, 1873-1957. 2. Novelists, English—20th century—Biography. I. Title. BIP

ROSENBERG, John. 823'.9'12 B
Dorothy Richardson. [1st American ed.] New York, Knopf; [distributed by Random House] 1973. xi, 198, viii p. 22 cm. Bibliography: p. 179-184. [PR6035.I34Z9 1973] 73-7259 ISBN 0-394-48066-X 6.95
1. Richardson, Dorothy Miller, 1873-1957.

Richardson, Evelyn May Fox, 1902-

RICHARDSON, Evelyn May Fox, 1902- 940.54'81'71625 B
B...was for butter and enemy craft / Evelyn M. Richardson. Halifax, N.S. : Petheric Press, 1976. 122 p. ; 23 cm. [D811.5.R463] 77-374263 ISBN 0-919380-22-0 : 3.95
1. Richardson, Evelyn May Fox, 1902- 2. World War, 1939-1945—Personal narratives, Canadian. 3. Nova Scotia—Biography. I. Title.

Richardson family (Thomas Richardson, d. 1651)

RICHARDSON, Charles Albert, 1875- comp. 920
Richardson letters; letters written to Albert Richardson from 1832 to 1881, with biographical sketches and a partial genealogy of the Richardson family. Jefferson, Me., 1954 [i. e. 1955] xii, 318p. front., coat of arms. 23cm. 'Published privately for the Richardson family. The edition numbers fifty copies, none of which is for sale.' [CT275.R549R5] 55-30092
1. Richardson family (Thomas Richardson, d. 1651) 2. Jefferson, Me.—Soc. life & cust. I. Richardson, Albert, 1814-1898. II. Title.

Richardson, Henry Handel, pseud.

ELLIOTT, William D., 1938- 823 B
Henry Handel Richardson (Ethel Florence Lindesay Richardson) / by William D. Elliott. Boston : Twayne Publishers, c1975. 174 p. : port. ; 21 cm. (Twayne's world authors series : TWAS 366 : Australia) Includes index. Bibliography: p. 159-172. [PR9619.3.R5Z65] 75-12692 ISBN 0-8057-6217-5 lib.bdg. : 7.50
1. Richardson, Henry Handel, pseud.

Richardson, Henry Hobson, 1838-1886.

HITCHCOCK, Henry Russell, 1903- 720.924
Richardson as a Victorian architect. [Baltimore, Pub. by Smith College at the Barton-Gillet Co., 1966] 53p. illus., plans. 23cm. (Katharine Asher Engel lects. 1965) Bibl. [NA737.R5H54] 66-6442 2.00 pap.,
1. Richardson, Henry Hobson, 1838-1886. I. Title. II. Series.

Richardson, John, Sir, 1787-1865.

JOHNSON, Robert Eugene. 917.19'9'0410924 B
Sir John Richardson : Arctic explorer, natural historian, naval surgeon / by Robert E. Johnson with the assistance of ... [others]. London : Taylor and Francis, 1976. xii, 209 p., leaf of plate, [16] p. of plates : ill., facsims., maps, ports. ; 26 cm. "Distributed in the United States of America and its territories by Crane, Russak & Co. ... New York." Includes index. Bibliography: p. 145-165. [G635.R5J63] 77-357178 ISBN 0-85066-074-2 : £15.00
1. Richardson, John, Sir, 1787-1865. 2. Explorers—England—Biography. 3. Explorers—Arctic regions—Biography. BIP

Richardson, Ralph, 1902-

RALPH Richardson. v. 12
New York, Macmillan [1958] 98p. illus. 23cm. (Theatre world monograph, no. 11)
1. Richardson, Ralph, 1902- I. Hobson, Harold. II. Series.

Richardson, Robert Clinton

RICHARDSON, Robert Clinton 927.96357
The Bobby Richardson story. Westwood, N.J., Revell [c.1965] 159p. ports. 21cm. [GV865.R43A3] 65-20412 3.95
I. Title.

Richardson, Samuel, 1689-1761.

BRISSENDEN, R F v. 12
Samuel Richardson, by R. F. Brissenden. Henry Fielding, by John Butt. Laurence Sterne, by D. W. Jefferson. Tobias Smollett, by Laurence Brander. Lincoln, University of Nebraska Press [c1965] 146 p. ports. 21 cm. (British writers and their work, no. 6) A Bison book, BB455. Includes bibliographies. 68-107263
1. Richardson, Samuel, 2. Fielding, Henry, 3. Sterne, Laurence, 4. Smollett, Tobias George, I. Butt, John Everett, 1906-1965. Henry Fielding. II. Jefferson, Douglas William, 1912- Laurence Sterne. III. Brander, Laurence, 1903- Tobias Smollett. IV. Title. V. Series.

DOBSON, Austin, 1840-1921. 823'.6 B
Samuel Richardson. New York, Macmillan, 1902. Detroit, Gale Research Co., 1968. v, 214 p. 23 cm. (The Gale library of lives and letters: British writers series) [PR3666.D6 1968] 67-23877
1. Richardson, Samuel, 1689-1761.

DOBSON, Austin, 1840-1921. 823'.6 B
Samuel Richardson. London, Macmillan, 1902. St. Clair Shores, Mich., Scholarly Press [1968] 213 p. 22 cm. (English men of letters) Bibliographical footnotes. [PR3666.D6 1968b] 70-7894
1. Richardson, Samuel, 1689-1761. BIP

EAVES, Thomas Cary Duncan, 1918- 823'.6 B
Samuel Richardson: a biography, by T. C. Duncan Eaves and Ben D. Kimpel. Oxford, Clarendon Press, 1971. xvii, 728 p., 12 plates. facsims., ports. 24 cm. Includes bibliographical references. [PR3666.E2] 78-27067 ISBN 0-19-812431-7 £6.50
1. Richardson, Samuel, 1689-1761. I. Kimpel, Ben D., joint author. BIP

SALE, William Merritt, 1899- 686.2'092'4 B
Samuel Richardson : master printer / William M. Sale, Jr. Westport, Conn. : Greenwood Press, [1977?] c1950. vi, 389 p. : ill. ; 23 cm. Reprint of the ed. published by Cornell University Press, Ithaca, N.Y., which was issued as v. 37 of Cornel studies in English. Includes bibliographical references and index. [Z232.R595S3 1977] 77-22446 ISBN 0-8371-9732-5 lib.bdg. : 21.75
1. Richardson, Samuel, 1689-1761. 2. Printers—England—Biography. 3. Printing—England—History. I. Series: Cornell University. Cornell studies in English ; v. 37. BIP

THOMSON, Clara Linklater. 823'.6
Samuel Richardson; a biographical and critical study. Folcroft, Pa., Folcroft Press [1969] viii, 308 p. illus. 23 cm. Reprint of the 1900 ed. Bibliography: p. 292-301. [PR3666.T5 1969] 72-192842
1. Richardson, Samuel, 1689-1761. BIP

THOMSON, Clara Linklater. 823'.6 B
Samuel Richardson; a biographical and critical study. Port Washington, N.Y., Kennikat Press [1970] viii, 308 p. illus., ports. 21 cm. Reprint of the 1900 ed. Bibliography: p. [292]-301. [PR3666.T5 1970] 74-103214
1. Richardson, Samuel, 1689-1761.

Richardson, Victor York,

RICHARDSON, Victor York, 1894- 796.358/0924
The Vic Richardson story; the autobiography of a versatile sportsman [by] V. Y. Richardson in conjunction with R. S. Whitington. [Adelaide] Rigby; San Francisco, Tri-Ocean [1967] 209p. illus., ports. 23cm. [GV914.R5A3] 66-10443 6.45 bds.,
I. Whitington, Richard S. II. Title.

Richelieu, Armand Emmanuel Sophie Septimanie de Plessis, duc de, 1766-1822.

COX, Cynthia 923.244
Talleyrand's successor; Armand-Emmanuel du Plessis, Duc de Richelieu, 1766-1822. New York, Vanguard Press [1961, c.1959] 224p. illus. ports., Bibl. 25cm. 60-9722 5.95
1. Richelieu, Armand Emmanuel Sophie Septimanie de Plessis, duc de, 1766-1822. I. Title.

Richelieu, Armand Jean du Plessis, Cardinal, duc de, 1585-1642.

AUCHINCLOSS, Louis. 944'.032'0924 B
Richelieu. New York, Viking Press [1972] 263 p. illus. (part col.) 26 cm. (A Studio book) [DC123.9.R5A84 1972] 72-81676 ISBN 0-670-59755-4 16.95
1. Richelieu, Armand Jean du Plessis, Cardinal, duc de, 1585-1642.

BELLOC, Hilaire, 1870-1953. 944'.032'0924 B
Richelieu; a study. Westport, Conn., Greenwood Press [1972, c1929] 392 p. 22 cm. [DC123.9.R5B4 1972] 77-114466 ISBN 0-8371-4762-X
1. Richelieu, Armand Jean du Plessis, Cardinal, duc de, 1585-1642. 2. France—History—Louis XIII, 1610-1643. BIP

BURCKHARDT, Carl Jacob, 1891- 923.244
Richelieu; his rise to power. Translated and abridged, by Edwin and Willa Muir. Rev. ed. edited and with an introd. by Charles H. Carter. New York, Vintage Books [1964] xvi, 355 p. 19 cm. "V-250." [DC123.9.R5B82 1964] 64-11998
1. Richelieu, Armand Jean de Plessis, cardinal, duc de, 1585-1642. I. Muir, Edwin, 1887-1959, tr. II. Muir, Willa, 1890- tr. III. Title.

CHURCH, William Farr, 1912- 944'.032'0924
Richelieu and reason of state, by William F. Church. Princeton, N.J., Princeton University Press [1973, c1972] 554 p. 25 cm. Bibliography: p. 515-547. [DC123.9.R5C5] 76-181518 ISBN 0-691-05199-2 20.00
1. Richelieu, Armand Jean du Plessis, Cardinal, duc de, 1585-1642. 2. France—Politics and government—1610-1643. I. Title. BIP

ERLANGER, Philippe, 1903- 944'.032'0924 B
Richelieu. Translated by Patricia Wolf. New York, Stein and Day [1968- v. illus., ports. 25 cm. Contents.Contents.—The thrust for power. Bibliography: v. 1, p. 243-245. [DC123.9.R5E713] 68-31678 6.95
1. Richelieu, Armand Jean du Plessis, Cardinal, duc de, 1585-1642.

FEDERN, Karl, 1868-1942. 944'.032'0924
Richelieu. Translated by Bernard Miall. New York, Haskell House, 1970. 253 p. illus., facsim., ports. 23 cm. Reprint of the 1928 ed. [DC123.9.R5F413 1970] 72-132440
1. Richelieu, Armand Jean du Plessis, Cardinal, duc de, 1585-1642.

LODGE, Richard, Sir, 1855-1936. 944'.032'0924 B
Richelieu. Port Washington, N.Y., Kennikat Press [1970] x, 235 p. 21 cm. Reprint of the 1896 ed. Bibliography: p. [232]-233. [DC123.9.R5L8 1970] 77-112812
1. Richelieu, Armand Jean du Plessis, Cardinal, duc de, 1585-1642.

O'CONNELL, Daniel Patrick. 944'.032'0924 B
Richelieu [by] D. P. O'Connell. Cleveland, World Pub. Co. [1968] 509 p. illus., map, ports. 22 cm. Bibliography: p. 449-484. [DC123.9.R5O25 1968b] 68-27612 10.00
1. Richelieu, Armand Jean du Plessis, Cardinal, duc de, 1585-1642.

PERKINS, James Breck, 1847-1910. 944'.032'0924
Richelieu and the growth of French power. Freeport, N.Y., Books for Libraries Press [1971] xiii, 359 p. illus., map, ports. 23 cm. Reprint of the 1900 ed. [DC123.9.R5P4 1971] 70-157353 ISBN 0-8369-5814-4
1. Richelieu, Armand Jean du Plessis, Cardinal, duc de, 1585-1642. 2. France—History—Louis XIII, 1610-1643. I. Title. BIP

TREASURE, Geoffrey Russell Richards. 944'.032'0924 B
Cardinal Richelieu and the development of absolutism [by] G. R. R. Treasure. New York, St. Martin's Press [1972] 316 p. map. 23 cm. Bibliography: p. 288-297. [DC123.9.R5T7] 76-183397 10.95
1. Richelieu, Armand Jean du Plessis, Cardinal, duc de, 1585-1642. I. Title. BIP

WILKINSON, Burke, 1913- 944.0320924
Cardinal in armor. Illus. by Arthur Shilstone. New York, Macmillan [c.1966] 178p. illus., 2 col. maps. 21cm. Bibl. [DC123.9.R5W53] 66-16108 3.95
1. Richelieu, Armand Jean du Plessis, Cardinal, ducde, 1585-1642. I. Title.

WILKINSON, Burke, 1913- 944.0320924 (B)
Cardinal in armor. Illustrated by Arthur Shilstone. New York, Macmillan [1966] 178 p. illus., 2 col. maps. 21 cm. Bibliography: p. 173-174. [DC123.9.R5W53] 66-16108
1. Richelieu, Armand Jean du Plessis, Cardinal, duc de, 1585-1642. I. Title.

Richelieu, Louis Francois Armand du Plessis, duc de, 1696-1788.

COLE, Hubert. 923.244
First gentleman of the bedchamber; the life

of Louis-Francois-Armand, marechal duc de Richelieu. New York, Viking Press [1965] 310 p. illus., ports. 22 cm. Bibliography: p. 293-300. [DC135.R5C6] 65-14511
1. Richelieu, Louis Francois Armand du Plessis, duc de, 1696-1788. I. Title.

Richler, Mordecai, 1931- — Biography—Youth.

RICHLER, Mordecai, 1931- 813'.5'4 B
The street / Mordecai Richler. New York : Penguin Books, 1977, c1969. 128 p. ; 18 cm. [PR9199.3.R5Z52 1977] 76-49661 ISBN 0-14-004418-3 pbk. : 1.75
1. Richler, Mordecai, 1931- —Biography—Youth. 2. Jews in Montreal. 3. Novelists, Canadian—20th century—Biography. I. Title.

RICHLER, Mordecai, 1931- 813'.5'4 B
The street / Mordecai Richler. Washington : The New Republic Book Co., 1975, c1969. 128 p. ; 22 cm. [PR9199.3.R5Z52 1975] 75-15771 ISBN 0-915220-04-0 : 6.95. ISBN 0-915220-08-3 pbk. : 2.50
1. Richler, Mordecai, 1931- —Biography—Youth. 2. Jews in Montreal. I. Title. BIP

Richley, John William,

RICHLEY, John William, 1874- 926.292
Obstacles no barrier; an autobiography, with an introd. by Allen C. Shue. [York? Pa.] c1951. 599 p. illus. 23 cm. [TL140.R5A3] 51-32340
I. Title.

Richli, William C., 1913-

WOOLSEY, Raymond H. 610'.92'4 B
Flying doctor of the Philippines [by] Raymond H. Woolsey. Washington, Review and Herald Pub. Association [1972] 192 p. illus. 22 cm. [R621.R5W66] 72-172788 4.95
1. Richli, William C., 1913- I. Title.

Richmond and Lennox, Charles Lenn0x, 3d duke of, 1735-1806.

OLSON, Alison Gilbert 923.242
The radical duke: career and correspondence of Charles Lennox, third Duke of Richmond. [New York] Oxford [c.]1961[ ] 262p. (Oxford historical ser., 2d ser.) Bibl. 61-3904 5.60
1. Richmond and Lennox, Charles Lenn0x, 3d duke of, 1735-1806. I. Richmond and Lennox, Chales Lennox, 3d duke of, 1735-1806. II. Title.

Richter, Conrad, 1890

BARNES, Robert J. 813'.5'2
Conrad Richter, by Robert J. Barnes. Austin, Tex., Steck-Vaughn Co. [1968] ii, 44 p. 20 cm. (Southwest writers series, no. 14) Bibliography: p. 43-44. [PS3535.I429Z57] 68-22977 1.00
1. Richter, Conrad, 1890-

Richter. Ed.

MCDONALD, Tommy [Thomas Franklin McDonald] 927.9633
They pay me to catch footballs, by Tommy McDonald as told to Ed Richter. Foreword by Sonny Jurgensen. Philadelphia, Chilton [c.1962] 123p. illus. 21cm. 62-16844 2.95; 1.95 pap.,
1. Richter. Ed. I. Title.

Richter, Hans,

RICHTER, Hans, 1888- 700'.924
Hans Richter. Edited by Cleve Gray. New York, Holt, Rinehart and Winston [1971] 191 p. illus. (part col.) 29 cm. [NX93.R5G7] 75-155510 ISBN 0-03-083475-9 27.50
I. Gray, Cleve, ed. II. Title.

Richthofen family.

GREEN, Martin Burgess, 1927- 914 B
The von Richthofen sisters; the triumphant and the tragic modes of love: Else and Frieda von Richthofen, Otto Gross, Max Weber, and D. H. Lawrence, in the years 1870-1970 [by] Martin Green. New York, Basic Books [1974] xviii, 396 p. illus. 25 cm. Bibliography: p. [385]-388. [CS629.R514 1974] 73-81037 ISBN 0-465-09050-8 12.50
1. Richthofen family. 2. Jaffe-Richthofen, Else, 1874- 3. Lawrence, Frieda von Richthofen, 1879-1956. 4. Lawrence, David Herbert, 1885-1930. I. Title.

Richthofen, Manfred Albrecht, Freiherr von, 1892-1918.

BRIGGS, Raymond. 92
Richthofen, the Red Baron. [Illus. by] Raymond Briggs; text by Nicholas Fisk. 1st Amer. ed. New York, Coward [1968] 1v. (unpaged) illus. (pt. col.) 21cm. [Briggs' bks.] [UG635.G7B72 1968] 68-18042 3.29 lib. ed.,
1. Richthofen, Manfred Albrecht, Freiherr von, 1892-1918. I. Fisk, Nicholas. II. Title.

BURROWS, William E., 1937- 940.4'49'43 B
Richthofen; a true history of the Red Baron [by] William E. Burrows. [1st ed.] New York, Harcourt, Brace & World [1969] xvi, 268 p. illus., map (on lining paper), ports. 22 cm. Bibliography: p. 259-260. [D604.R529] 75-85010 6.50
1. Richthofen, Manfred Albrecht, Freiherr von, 1892-1918.

TITLER, Dale Milton, 1926- 940.4'49'43
The day the Red Baron died [by] Dale Titler. New York, Ballantine Books [1970] 331 p. illus., maps, ports. 18 cm. [TL540.R5T5] 75-17797 1.25
1. Richthofen, Manfred Albrecht, Freiherr von, 1892-1918. 2. European War, 1914-1918—Aerial operations, German I. Title. BIP

Richthofen, Manfred Albrecht, Freiherr von, 1892-1918—Juvenile literature.

FISK, Nicholas. 940.4'49'43
Richthofen, the Red Baron. [Illus. by] Raymond Briggs; text by Nicholas Fish. 1st American ed. New York, Coward McCann [1968] [40] p. illus. (part col.) 21 cm. ([Briggs' books]) Illustrations and brief text portray the major victories of Germany's World War I ace who won eighty air battles before being shot down in 1918. [D604.R5297 1968] 92 68-18042
1. Richthofen, Manfred Albrecht, Freiherr von, 1892-1918—Juvenile literature. I. Briggs, Raymond, illus. II. Title.

WRIGHT, Nicolas. 940.4'49'430924 B
The Red Baron / Nicolas Wright. New York : McGraw-Hill, 1977, c1976. 116 p. : ill. ; 22 cm. Includes index. A biography of the World War I ace known as the Red Baron who shot down 80 Allied planes before he himself was killed, a month before his twenty-sixth birthday. [UG626.2.R5W74 1977] 77-78759 ISBN 0-07-072040-1 lib. bdg. : 6.84
1. Richthofen, Manfred Albrecht, Freiherr von, 1892-1918—Juvenile literature. 2. Air pilots—Germany—Biography—Juvenile literature. 3. European War, 1914-1918—Aerial operations, German—Juvenile literature. I. Title. BIP

Rickard, Clinton, 1882-1971.

RICKARD, Clinton, 1882-1971. 970.3 B
Fighting Tuscarora; the autobiography of Chief Clinton Rickard. Edited by Barbara Graymont. [1st ed. Syracuse, N.Y.] Syracuse University Press, 1973. xxviii, 182 p. maps. 23 cm. (A York State book) Includes bibliographical references. [E99.T9R53 1973] 73-8208 ISBN 0-8156-0092-5 10.50
1. Rickard, Clinton, 1882-1971. 2. Tuscarora Indians. I. Graymont, Barbara. II. Title. BIP

Rickard, George Lewis, 1875-1929.

SAMUELS, Charles. 927.9683
The magnificent rube; the life and gaudy times of Tex Rickard. New York, McGraw-Hill [1957] 301 p. illus. 21 cm. [GV165.R5S3] 57-8627
1. Rickard, George Lewis, 1875-1929. I. Title.

Rickenbacker, Edward Vernon, 1890-1973.

FARR, Finis. 629.13'092'4 B
Richenbacker's luck : an American life / Finis Farr. Boston : Houghton Mifflin, 1979. x, 366 p., [4] leaves of plates : ill. ; 22 cm. Includes index. Bibliography: p. [347]-352. [TL540.R54F37] 79-377 ISBN 0-395-27102-9 : 15.95
1. Rickenbacker, Edward Vernon, 1890-1973. 2. Aeronautics—United States—Biography. I. Title.

RICKENBACKER, Edward Vernon, 1890- 973.9'0924
From father to son; the letters of Captain Eddie Rickenbacker to his son William, from boyhood to manhood. Edited, with notes and introd. by William F. Rickenbacker. New York, Walker [1970] x, 204 p. illus., ports. 24 cm. [TL540.R54A45 1970] 78-126110 6.95
I. Rickenbacker, William F., 1928- ed. II. Title.

RICKENBACKER, Edward Vernon, 1890-1973. 973.9'0924 B
Rickenbacker [by] Edward V. Rickenbacker. Englewood Cliffs, N.J., Prentice-Hall [1967] 458 p. illus. 24 cm. [E748.R4A3] 67-22580

Rickenbacker, Edward Vernon, 1890-1973—Juvenile literature

CLEVEN, Cathrine Seward, 1906- 629.13'092'4 B
Eddie Rickenbacker, young racer and flyer / by Catherine Cleven ; illustrated by Fred M. Irvin. Indianapolis : Bobbs-Merrill, c1974. 200 p. : ill. ; 20 cm. (Childhood of famous Americans) Bibliography: p. 198. A biography of an automobile racer and pilot who contributed a great deal towards the growth of military and commercial aviation in the United States. [TL540.R53C56] 92 74-15576
1. Rickenbacker, Edward Vernon, 1890-1973—Juvenile literature. I. Irvin, Fred M. II. Title.

Ricketts, Edward Flanders, 1896-1948.

†ASTRO, Richard. 574.97'6'0924 B
Edward F. Ricketts / by Richard Astro. Boise, Idaho : Boise State University, c1976. 48 p. ; 21 cm. (Boise State University Western writers series ; no. 21) Bibliography: p. 45-47. [QH31.R53A87] 76-46147 ISBN 0-88430-020-X pbk. : 1.50
1. Ricketts, Edward Flanders, 1896-1948. 2. Steinbeck, John, 1902-1968—Friends and associates. 3. Marine biologists—The West—Biography. I. Series: Boise State University. Boise State University Western writers series ; no. 21. BIP

Rickey, Branch, 1881-

MANN, Arthur William, 1901- 927.96357
Branch Rickey: American in action. Boston, Houghton Mifflin, 1957. 312p. illus. 22cm. [GV865.R45M3] 57-10787
1. Rickey, Branch, 1881- I. Title.

MANN, Arthur William, 1901- 927.96357
Branch Rickey: American in action. Boston, Houghton Mifflin, 1957. 312 p. illus. 22 cm. [GV865.R45M3] 57-10787
1. Rickey, Branch, 1881-

Rickey, Branch, 1881-1965.

LIPMAN, David 796.3570924
Mr. Baseball; the story of Branch Rickey. New York, Putnam [c.1966] 191p. 21cm. (Lives to remember) [GV865.R45L5] 66-14330 3.50; 3.29 lib. ed.,
1. Rickey, Branch, 1881-1965. I. Title.

Rickover, Hyman George.

DAVID, Heather M. 359.3'3'10924
Admiral Rickover and the nuclear navy, by Heather M. David. New York, Putnam [1970] 223 p. 22 cm. (Lives to remember series) Bibliography: p. 219. A biography of the American naval officer who pioneered in developing the Nautilus, the nuclear-powered submarine. [V63.R54D37 1970] 92 78-92807 3.64
1. Rickover, Hyman George. 2. Atomic ships. I. Title. BIP

Riddell, John Leonard, 1807-1867.

RIESS, Karlem. 550'.8 S
John Leonard Riddell : scientist-inventor, melter and refiner of the New Orleans Mint, 1839-1848, postmaster of New Orleans, 1859-1862 / by Karlem Riess. 1st ed. New Orleans : Louisiana Heritage Press, 1977. ii, 110 p. : ill. ; 25 cm. (Tulane studies in geology and paleontology ; v. 13, no. 1-2) Bibliography: p. 104-110. [QE1.T826 vol. 13, no. 1-2] [Q143.R52] 509'.2'4 B 77-84015
1. Riddell, John Leonard, 1807-1867. 2. Scientists—United States—Biography. 3. Inventors—United States—Biography. I. Title. II. Series. III. Special papers on the history of science ; 1

Rider, Fremont,

RIDER, Fremont, 1885- 920.2
And master of none; an autobiography in the third person. Middletown, Conn., Godfrey Memorial Library, 1955. xiv, 253p. illus., ports. 23cm. 'Of the first printing ... four hundred and fifty copies have been numbered and signed by the author, of which this is no. 146.' This copy not signed. [CT275.R562A3] 55-12741
I. Title.

Rider-Kelsey, Corinne, 1877-1947.

REED, Lynnel. 927.8
Be not afraid biography of Madame Rider-Kelsey. [1st ed.] New York, Vantage Press [1955] 168p. illus. 21cm. [ML420.R55R4] 55-7177
1. Rider-Kelsey, Corinne, 1877-1947. I. Title.

Ridgeway, Rick.

RIDGEWAY, Rick. 796.5'22'0954
The boldest dream : the story of twelve who climbed Mount Everest / Rick Ridgeway ; [map by Nicholas Fasciano]. 1st ed. New York : Harcourt Brace Jovanovich, c1979. xii, 244 p., [4] leaves of plates : ill. ; 22 cm. [GV199.44.E85R5] 78-11091 10.95
1. Ridgeway, Rick. 2. Mountaineering—Everest, Mount. 3. Mountaineers—United States—Biography. 4. Everest, Mount—Description. I. Title. BIP

Ridgway, John M.

RIDGWAY, John M. 797.1'4
Around the world with Ridgway / by John

and Marie-Christine Ridgway. 1st American ed. New York : Holt, Rinehart, and Winston, c1979. 317 p., [9] leaves of plates : ill. ; 25 cm. Includes index. [GV832.R5 1979] 78-11848 ISBN 0-03-043751-2 : 15.95
1. Whitbread Round the World Race. 2. Ridgway, John M. 3. Ridgway, Marie-Christine. 4. Seamen—Great Britain—Biography. I. Ridway, Marie-Christine, joint author. II. Title.

Ridgway, Matthew Bunker,

RIDGWAY, Matthew Bunker, 1895- 923.573
Soldier: the memoirs of Matthew B. Ridgway, as told to Harold H. Martin. [1st ed.] New York, Harper [1956] 371p. illus. 22cm. [E745.R5A35] 56-6032
I. Martin, Harold H. II. Title.

RIDGWAY, Matthew Bunker, 1895- 355.3'31'0924 B
Soldier: the memoirs of Matthew B. Ridgway, as told to Harold H. Martin. Westport, Conn., Greenwood Press [1974, c1956] 371 p. illus. 22 cm. Reprint of the 1st ed. published by Harper, New York. [E745.R52 1974] 74-11883 ISBN 0-8371-7700-6 16.75 (lib. bdg.)
1. Ridgway, Matthew Bunker, 1895- I. Martin, Harold H. II. Title.

Ridley, Nicholas, Bp. of London, 1500?-1555.

RIDLEY, Jasper Godwin. 922.342
Nicholas Ridley, a biography. London, New York, Longmans, Green [1957] 453p. illus. 21cm. Includes bibliography. [BX5199.R5R53] 57-13904
1. Ridley, Nicholas, Bp. of London, 1500?-1555. I. Title. BIP

Ridout, Thomas, d. 1829.

EDGAR, Matilda Ridout, Lady, 1844-1910. 973'.04'97 S
Ten years of upper Canada in peace and war (the Thomas Ridout captivity) / Matilda Edgar. New York : Garland Pub., 1977 [c1890] 389 p., [2] fold. leaves of plates : ill. ; 23 cm. (The Garland library of narratives of North American Indian captivities ; v. 98) Reprint of the ed. published by W. Briggs, Toronto. Includes index. [E85.G2 vol. 98] [E361] 971.3'02 75-7125 ISBN 0-8240-1722-6 lib.bdg. : 25.00
1. Ridout, Thomas, d. 1829. 2. United States—History—War of 1812—Personal narratives. 3. Ontario—History—Sources. 4. Indians of North America—Captivities. 5. England—Social life and customs—19th century. I. Title. II. Series.

Riedesel, Friederike Charlotte Luise (von Massow) Freifrau von. 1746-1808.

THARP, Louise (Hall) 1898- 920.7
The baroness and the general. 1st ed. Boston, Little, Brown [1962] 458 p. illus. 22 cm. Includes bibliography. [E268.R58T5] 62-17955
1. Riedesel, Friederike Charlotte Luise (von Massow) Freifrau von. 1746-1808. 2. Riedesel, Friedrich Adolf, Freiherr von, 1738-1800. 3. U.S. — Hist. — Revolution — German mercenaries. I. Title.

Riedesel, Friedrich Adolf, Freiherr von, 1738-1800.

EELKING, Max von, 1813-1873. 973.33'30924
Memoirs, letters, and journals of Major General Riedesel. Translated by William L. Stone. [New York] New York times [1969] 2 v. illus., port. 23 cm. (Eyewitness accounts of the American Revolution) Reprint of the 1868 ed. A translation of v. 2 and part of v. 3 of the author's Leben und Wirken des Herzoglich Braunschweig'schen General-Lieutenants Friedrich Adolph Riedesel, Leipzig, 1856. [E268.E2634 1969] 79-77109
1. Riedesel, Friedrich Adolf, Freiherr von, 1738-1800. 2. United States—History—Revolution, 1775-1783—Personal narratives. 3. United States—History—Revolution, 1775-1783—German mercenaries. 4. Burgoyne's campaign, 1777. I. Title. II. Series.

Riefenstahl, Leni.

INFIELD, Glenn B. 791.43'028'0924 B
Leni Riefenstahl and the fallen film goddess / by Glenn Infield. New York : Crowell, [1976] p. cm. Includes index. Bibliography: p. [PN1998.A3R528] 76-7084 ISBN 0-690-01167-9
1. Riefenstahl, Leni. I. Title.

Riegert, Wilbur A.

RIEGERT, Wilbur A. 978.3'004'97 B
Quest for the pipe of the Sioux : as viewed from Wounded Knee / by Wilbur A. Riegert. [Rapid City? S.D. : J. M. Fritze?, 1975] xiv, 164 p. : ill. ; 23 cm. Bibliography: p. 163-164. [E99.C6R57] 75-758
1. Riegert, Wilbur A. 2. Dakota Indians. 3. Chippewa Indians. I. Title.

Riel, Louis David, 1844-1885.

FLANAGAN, Thomas. 971.05'1'0924
Louis 'David' Riel : prophet of the new world / Thomas Flanagan. Toronto ; Buffalo : University of Toronto Press, c1979. ix, 216 p. ; 24 cm. Includes bibliographical references and index. [F1060.9.R53F57] 78-18497 ISBN 0-8020-5430-7 : 15.00
1. Riel, Louis David, 1844-1885. 2. Revolutionists—Northwest Territories—Biography. BIP

HOWARD, Joseph Kinsey, 1906-1951. 971.05'1
Strange empire; a narrative of the Northwest. Westport, Conn., Greenwood Press [1974, c1952] xii, 601 p. maps. 22 cm. Reprint of the ed. published by Morrow, New York. Bibliography: p. 567-588. [F1060.9.H7 1974] 73-19575 ISBN 0-8371-7290-X 23.00
1. Riel, Louis David, 1844-1885. 2. Red River Rebellion, 1869-1870. 3. Riel Rebellion, 1885. I. Title.

RIEL, Louis David, 1844-1885. 971.05'1'0924 B
The diaries of Louis Riel / edited by Thomas Flanagan. Edmonton : Hurtig, c1976. 187 p. ; 22 cm. Includes bibliographical references. [F1060.9.R5293 1976] 77-367581 ISBN 0-88830-116-2 : 9.95. ISBN 0-88830-117-0 pbk.
1. Riel, Louis David, 1844-1885. 2. Riel Rebellion, 1885. 3. Politicians—Northwest, Canadian—Biography. I. Flanagan, Thomas. II. Title.

STANLEY, George Francis Gilman. 971.05'1'0924 B
Louis Riel [by] George F. G. Stanley. Toronto, New York, McGraw-Hill Ryerson [1972] 431 p. 22 cm. Includes bibliographical references. [F1060.9.R563 1972] 72-196072 ISBN 0-07-092961-0
1. Riel, Louis David, 1844-1885.

Ries, Elias Elkan, 1862-1928.

RIES, Estelle H. 926
Elias E. Ries, inventor. New York, Philosophical Library [c1951] 369 p. illus. 23 cm. [TK140.R5R5] 52-6470
1. Ries, Elias Elkan, 1862-1928. I. Title.

Rieseberg, Harry Earl—Juvenile literature.

KRASKE, Robert. 791'.092'2 B
Daredevils do amazing things / by Robert Kraske ; illustrated by Ivan Powell. New York : Random House, c9178. 69 p. : ill. ; 22 cm. (Step-up books ; 26) Describes the daring feats of adventures Blondin, Harry Houdini, Annie Oakley, Harry Rieseberg, and Evel Knievel. [GV1811.A1K7] 920 77-90194 ISBN 0-394-83623-5 : 2.95. ISBN 0-394-93623-X lib. bdg. : 3.99
1. Houdini, Harry, 1874-1926—Juvenile literature. 2. Oakley, Annie, 1860-1926—Juvenile literature. 3. Rieseberg, Harry Earl—Juvenile literature. 4. Knievel, Evel, 1938- —Juvenile literature. 5. Blondin, Jean Francois Gravelet, known as, 1824-1897—Juvenile literature. 6. Entertainers—United States—Biography—Juvenile literature. I. Powell, Ivan. II. Title. BIP

Riesemann, Oskar von, 1880-1934.

RACHMANINOFF, Sergei, 1873-1943. 780'.924 B
Rachmaninoff's recollections, told to Oskar von Riesemann. [Translated from the German manuscript by Dolly Rutherford] Freeport, N.Y., Books for Libraries Press [1970] 272 p. illus., facsims. (music), ports. 23 cm. Reprinted from the 1934 ed. [ML410.R12A22 1970] 74-111100
1. Riesemann, Oskar von, 1880-1934. 2. Musicians—Correspondence, reminiscences, etc. BIP

Rigby, Cathy, 1952- —Juvenile literature.

JACOBS, Linda. 796.4'1'0924 B
Cathy Rigby : on the beam / by Linda Jacobs. St. Paul : EMC Corp., [1975] p. cm. (Her Women who win 2) Brief biography of the California girl who became the first American gymnast to win a medal in an international competition and placed in two Olympic competitions. [GV460.2.R53J32] 92 74-31424 ISBN 0-88436-168-3 lib.bdg. : 4.95 ISBN 0-88436-169-1 pbk. : 2.95
1. Rigby, Cathy, 1952- —Juvenile literature. 2. Gymnastics—Juvenile literature. I. Title. BIP

Riggs, Lynn, 1899-1954.

ERHARD, Thomas A., 1923- 812'.5'2 B
Lynn Riggs, Southwest playwright, by Thomas Erhard. Austin, Tex., Steck-Vaughn [1970] ii, 44 p. 21 cm. (Southwest writers series, no. 29) Bibliography: p. 40-44. [PS3535.I645Z65] 75-110697
1. Riggs, Lynn, 1899-1954. I. Title. II. Series.

Riggs, Robert Larimore, 1918-

RIGGS, Robert Larimore, 1918- 796.34'2'0924 B
Court hustler, by Bobby Riggs with George McGann. [1st ed.] Philadelphia, Lippincott [1973] 203 p. illus. 22 cm. [GV994.R54A29] 73-13818 ISBN 0-397-00893-7 6.95
1. Riggs, Robert Larimore, 1918- 2. Tennis. I. McGann, George. II. Title.

Riggs, Stephen Return, 1812-1883.

RIGGS, Stephen Return, 1812-1883. 970.3 B
Mary and I; forty years with the Sioux. With an introd. by S. C. Bartlett. Minneapolis, Ross & Haines, 1969 [c1887] xxxxv, 23-437 p. illus. 23 cm. [E99.D1R52 1969] 77-98193 12.50
1. Riggs, Stephen Return, 1812-1883. 2. Dakota Indians—Missions. I. Title. BIP

Riis, Jacob August, 1849-1914.

RIIS, Jacob August, 1849-1914. 923.6
The making of an American. Ed., introd. notes, by Roy Lubove. New York, Harper [c.1966] xxvi. 443p. illus. 21cm. (Amer. perspectives. Torchbk., Univ. lib., TB 3070) Orig. pub. in 1901 [CT275.R6A3] 2.75 pap.,
I. Title.

RIIS, Jacob August, 1849-1914. 818.408
The making of an American. Edited with an introd. and notes by Roy Lubove. New York, Harper & Row [1966] xxvi, 443 p. illus., port. 21 cm. (Harper torchbooks, TB 3070 P) Originally published in 1901. [CT275.R6A3 1966] 66-4327
I. Lubove, Roy, ed. II. Title.

RIIS, Jacob August, 1849-1914. 070.9'24 B
The making of an American. A new ed. with an epilogue by J. Riis Owre. [New York] Macmillan [1970] xiv, 347 p. illus. 19 cm. "The papers which form this autiobiography were originally published in the Outlook, the chapter telling of my going 'home to mother' in the Churchman, and parts of one or two others in the Century magazine." [CT275.R6A3 1970] 79-99110
I. Title. BIP

WARE, Louise, 1895- 070'.92'4 B
Jacob A. Riis: police reporter, reformer, useful citizen. Introd. by Allan Nevins. Freeport, N.Y., Books for Libraries Press [1973] p. Reprint of the 1938 ed., which was also presented as the author's thesis, Columbia. Bibliography: p. [CT275.R6W3 1973] 73-2616 ISBN 0-8369-7173-6
1. Riis, Jacob August, 1849-1914.

WARE, Louise, 1895- 070'.92'4 B
Jacob A. Riis, police reporter, reformer, useful citizen / by Louise Ware ; introd. by Allan Nevins. Millwood, N.Y. : Kraus Reprint Co., 1975, c1938. xxii, 335 p., [7] leaves of plates : ill. ; 23 cm. Reprint of the ed. published by D. Appleton-Century Co., New York. Originally presented as the author's thesis, Columbia, 1939. Includes index. Bibliography: p. 295-313. [CT275.R6W3 1975] 74-20795 ISBN 0-527-94503-X
1. Riis, Jacob August, 1849-1914. I. Title.

WARE, Louise, 1895- 070'.92'4 B
Jacob A. Riis, police reporter, reformer, useful citizen / by Louise Ware ; introd. by Allan Nevins. Millwood, N.Y. : Kraus Reprint Co., 1975, c1938. xxii, 335 p., [7] leaves of plates : ill. ; 23 cm. Reprint of the ed. published by D. Appleton-Century Co., New York. Originally presented as the author's thesis, Columbia, 1939. Includes index. Bibliography: p. 295-313. [CT275.R6W3 1975] 74-20795 ISBN 0-527-94503-X : 19.00
1. Riis, Jacob August, 1849-1914. I. Title.

Riklis, Meshulam, 1923-

SCHISGALL, Oscar, 1901- 658.1'6'0924 B
The magic of mergers; the saga of Meshulam Riklis. [1st ed.] Boston, Little, Brown [1968] xii, 236 p. port. 21 cm. [HF3023.R5S3] 68-11521
1. Riklis, Meshulam, 1923- I. Title.

Riley, James Whitcomb, 1849-1916.

CROWDER, Richard. 928.1
Those innocent years; the legacy and inheritance of a hero of the Victorian era, James Whitcomb Riley. [1st ed.]

Indianapolis, Bobbs-Merrill [1957] 288 p. illus. 23 cm. [PS2706.C7] 57-9342
1. Riley, James Whitcomb, 1849-1916. I. Title.

NOLAN, Jeannette (Covert) 928.1
1896-
Poet of the people; an evaluation of James Whitcomb Riley, by Jeannette Covert Nolan, Horace Gregory, and James T. Farrell. Bloomington, Indiana University Press, 1951. 106 p. 19 cm. Contents.CONTENTS. -- Riley as a children's poet, by J. C. Nolan. -- James Whitcomb Riley, a victorian American, by H. Gregory. -- The frontier and James Whitcomb Riley, by J. T. Farrell. [PS2706.N6] 51-3048
1. Riley, James Whitcomb, 1849-1916. I. Gregory, Horace, 1898- II. Farrell, James Thomas, 1904- III. Title.

RILEY, James Whitcomb, 811'.4 B
1849-1916.
Letters of James Whitcomb Riley. Edited by William Lyon Phelps. Indianapolis, Bobbs-Merrill, 1930. [New York, AMS Press, 1973] 349 p. illus. 23 cm. Includes bibliographical references. [PS2706.A53 1973] 78-153348 ISBN 0-404-05336-X 15.00
1. Riley, James Whitcomb, 1849-1916. **BIP**

Riley, Vincent, 1891-1951?

GLEN, Fred. 923.4142
Vincent Riley; the story of a "meth-elated spirit." Newcastle, Staffs., L. Orridge [1951] 133 p. illus. 20 cm. [HV5447.R5G55] 52-34444
1. Riley, Vincent, 1891-1951? 2. Wood-alcohol. I. Title.

Rilke, Rainer Maria, 1875-1926.

BUTLER, Eliza Marian, 831'.9'12 B
1885-1959.
Rainer Maria Rilke. New York, Octagon Books, 1973. xii, 437 p. port. 23 cm. Reprint of the 1946 ed. published by Cambridge University Press, Cambridge, England. Bibliography: p. [426]-428. [PT2635.I65Z65 1973] 73-8838 ISBN 0-374-91129-0 15.00 (lib. bdg.)
1. Rilke, Rainer Maria, 1875-1926. **BIP**

GRAFF, Willem Laurens, 928.3
1890-
Rainer Maria Rilke; creative anguish of a modern poet. Princeton, Princeton University Press, 1956. x, 353 p. 25 cm. Bibliography: p. 343-345. [PT2635.I65Z7345] 56-8381
1. Rilke, Rainer Maria, 1875-1926. **BIP**

HEERIKHUIZEN, F W van, 928.3
1910-
Rainer Maria Rilke, his life and work. Translated by Fernand G. Renier and Anne Cliff. New York, Philosophical Library [1952] 396 p. illus. 23 cm. [PT2635.I 65Z7413] 52-9006
1. Rilke, Rainer Maria, 1875-1926. I. Title.

HOLTHUSEN, Hans Egon, 831'.9'12 B
1913-
Portrait of Rilke; an illustrated biography. Translated by W. H. Hargreaves. [New York] Herder and Herder [1971] 175 p. illus. 21 cm. Translation of Rainer Maria Rilke in Selbstzeugnissen und Bilddokumenten. Bibliography: p. 174-175. [PT2635.I65Z742713] 74-167864 6.95
1. Rilke, Rainer Maria, 1875-1926. I. Title.

KNIGHT, Eric Mowbray, 831'.9'12 B
1897-1943.
The dedicated life and Rainer Maria Rilke. New York, Haskell House Publishers [1974] p. Reprint of the 1949 ed. published by Ridgeway House, Shorne, Eng., which was issued as no. 19 of the Burning glass papers. [PT2635.I65Z754 1974] 74-7280 ISBN 0-8383-1920-3 7.95
1. Rilke, Rainer Maria, 1875-1926. I. Title. **BIP**

PETERS, Heinz 831'.9'12 B
Frederick.
Rainer Maria Rilke : masks and the man / by H. F. Peters. New York : Gordian Press, 1977, c1960. xii, 226 p. ; 24 cm. Text in English, poems in English, French, or German. Reprint of the ed. published by University of Washington Press, Seattle. Includes index. Bibliography: p. 219. [PT2635.I65Z825 1977] 77-24731 ISBN 0-87752-198-0 : 9.50
1. Rilke, Rainer Maria, 1875-1926. 2. Authors, German—20th century—Biography. **BIP**

PURTSCHER, Nora (von 928.3
Wydenbruck) 1894-
Rilke, man and poet; a biographical study. New York, Appleton-Century-Crofts [1950] 373 p. plates, ports. 23 cm. Bibliography: p. 365-366. [PT2635.I65Z837 1950] 50-8340
1. Rilke, Rainer Maria, 1875-1926. I. Title.

PURTSCHER, Nora (von 831'.9'12 B
Wydenbruck) 1894-1959.
Rilke, man and poet; a biographical study, by Nora Wydenbruck. Westport, Conn., Greenwood Press [1972] 373 p. illus. 22 cm. Reprint of the 1950 ed. Bibliography: p. 365-366. [PT2635.I65Z837 1972] 71-169852 ISBN 0-8371-6247-5
1. Rilke, Rainer Maria, 1875-1926. I. Title.

RILKE, Rainer Maria, 1875- 928.3
1926.
The letters of Rainer Maria Rilke and Princess Marie von Thurn und Taxis. Translated and introduced by Nora Wydenbruck. [Norfolk, Conn.] New Directions [1958] x, 294p. 23cm. The present ed. is a translation of the letters edited by Ernst Zinn and published in 1951 under title: Briefwechsel [zwischen] Rainer Maria Rilke und Marie von Thurn und Taxis. 'Dr. Theodor Haemmerill to Marie Taxis': p. 267-269. [PT2635.I65Z5543] 58-11827
I. Thurn und Taxis, Marie (zu Hohenlohe) Fllrstin von, 1855-1934. II. Title.

RILKE, Rainer Maria, 1875 928.3
1926.
Rainer Maria Rilke: his last friendship; unpublished letter to Mrs. Elouibey, with a study by Edmond Jaloux and an introd. by Marcel Raval. [Translated from the French by William H. Kennedy] New York, Philosophical Library [1952] 114 p. ports. 21 cm. [PT2635.I65Z17] 52-8399
I. Eloui, Nimet, d. 1943. II. Jaloux, Edmond, 1878-1949. III. Title.

RILKE, Rainer Maria, 1875- 928.3
1926
Selected letters. Edited by Harry T. Moore. Garden City, N. Y., Doubleday, 1960. [c.1945-1960] 404p. 19cm. (Anchor books, A223) 60-13548 1.45 pap.,
I. Title.

SALIS, Jean Rodolphe de. 928.3
1901-
Rainer Maria Rilke: the years in Switzerland; a contribution to the biography of Rilke's later life. Re. [from German] by N. K. Cruickshank. Berkeley. Univ. of Calif. Pr. [1966, c.1964] 321p. 21cm. (Cal 118) Bibl. [PT2635.165Z8553] 1.75 pap.,
1. Rilke, Rainer Maria, 1875-1926. I. Title.

SALIS, Jean Rudolphe de, 928.3
1901-
Rainer Maria Rilke: the years in Switzerland; a contribution to the biography of Rilke's later life, by J. R. von Salis. Translated by N. K. Cruickshank. Berkeley, University of California Press, 1964. 321 p. illus., port. 23 cm. Translation of Rainer Maria Rilkes Schweizer Jahre. Bibliography: p. 316-318. [PT2635.I65Z8553 1964] 64-25912
1. Rilke, Rainer Maria, 1875-1926. I. Title.

Rillieux, Norbert, 1806-1894—Juvenile literature.

HARBISON, David. 920'.073
Reaching for freedom: Paul Cuffe, Norbert Rillieux, Ira Aldridge, James McCune Smith. [New York] Scholastic Book Services [1972] 128 p. illus. 22 cm. (Firebird biographies) (Firebird books) Short biographies of four men who overcame racial obstacles to become famous as a sea captain, an inventor, an actor, and a doctor. [E185.96.H33] 920 70-187886
1. Cuffe, Paul, 1759-1817—Juvenile literature. 2. Rillieux, Norbert, 1806-1894—Juvenile literature. 3. Aldridge, Ira Frederick, d. 1867—Juvenile literature. 4. Smith, James McCune—Juvenile literature. I. Title.

Rimbaud, Jean Nicholas Arthur, 1854-1891

STARKIE, Enid Mary 841.8
Arthur Rimbaud. [New York] New Directions [1962,c.1961] 491p. illus. Bibl. 61-18468 10.00
1. Rimbaud, Jean Nicholas Arthur, 1854-1891 I. Title. **BIP**

Rimbaud, Jean Nicolas Arthur, 1854-1891—Biography.

CARRE, Jean Marie, 841'.8 B
1887-1958.
A season in hell : the life of Arthur Rimbaud / by Jean-Marie Carre ; translated by Hannah and Matthew Josephson. 1st AMS ed. New York : AMS Press, 1979. 312 p. ; 19 cm. Translation of La vie aventureuse de Jean Arthur Rimbaund. Reprint of the 1931 ed. published by Macaulay, New York. [PQ2387.R5Z5613 1979] 77-10254 ISBN 0-404-16309-2 : 27.00
1. Rimbaud, Jean Nicolas Arthur, 1854-1891—Biography. 2. Poets, French—19th century—Biography. I. Title. **BIP**

HARE, Humphrey. 841'.8 B
Sketch for a portrait of Rimbaud. New York, Haskell House Publishers, 1974. 127 p. 21 cm. Reprint of the 1937 ed. published by Brendin Pub. Co., London. Bibliography: p. 126-127. [PQ2387.R5Z6962 1974] 74-7105 ISBN 0-8383-1922-X
1. Rimbaud, Jean Nicolas Arthur, 1854-1891—Biography. I. Title. **BIP**

Rimfire, 1868-1945.

STURM, Harry Price, 975.4'65'0924
1886-
Rimfire, his life story and selections from his own writings. A study of the typical mountaineer, Eli (Rimfire) hamrick, by Harry P. Sturm and Hesiter G. Rhawn. [Parsons, W.Va., McClain Print. Co., 1967] 67 p. illus., ports. 16 cm. [CT275.R605S7] 67-25902
1. Rimfire, 1868-1945. I. Rhawn, Heister G., joint author. II. Title.

STURM, Harry Price, 975.4'65'0924
1886-
Rimfire, his life story and selections from his own writings. A study of the typical mountaineer, Eli (Rimfire) Hamrick, by Harry P. Sturm and Heister G. Rhawn. [Parsons, W. Va., McClain Print. Co., 1967] 67 p. illus., ports. 16 cm. [CT275.R605S7] 67-25902
1. Rimfire, 1868-1945. I. Rhawn, Heister G., joint author.

Rimmer, William, 1816-1879.

BARTLETT, Truman Howe, 709'.24 B
1835-1923.
The art life of William Rimmer, sculptor, painter, and physician. New York, Kennedy Graphics, 1970. ix, xii, 147 p. illus., ports. 29 cm. (Library of American art) A reprint of the 1890 ed. with a new pref. by Leonard Baskin. [NB237.R6B3 1970] 68-27718
1. Rimmer, William, 1816-1879. I. Title.

KIRSTEIN, Lincoln, 1907- v. 12
William Rimmer, his life & art. [Amherst, Mass., Massachusetts Review, 1961?] unpaged. 16 illus. 23 cm. This "essay by Lincoln Kirstein is reprinted from the catalogue of the Rimmer exhibition of 1946-7, arranged by the Whitney Museum of American Art and the Museum of Fine Arts." 66-39780
1. Rimmer, William, 1816-1879. I. Title.

Rimskii-Korsakov, Nikolai Andreevich, 1844-1908.

ABRAHAM, Gerald 780'.92'4 B
Ernest Heal, 1904-
Rimsky-Korsakov : a short biography / by Gerald Abraham. New York : AMS Press, c1976] p. cm. Reprint of the 1945 ed. published by Duckworth, London. Bibliography: p. [ML410.R52A62 1976] 75-41002 ISBN 0-404-14500-0 : 10.00
1. Rimskii-Korsakov, Nikolai Andreevich, 1844-1908. 2. Composers—Russia—Biography.

RIMSKII-KORSAKOV, 780'.92'4 B
Nikolai Andreevich 1844-1908.
My musical life [by] Nikolay Andreyevich Rimsky-Korsakov. Translated from the 5th rev. Russian ed. by Judah A. Joffee. Edited with an introd. by Carl Van Vechten. New York, Vienna House, 1972 [ie. 1973] xliv, 480, xxi p. illus. 24 cm. Translation of Letopis' moei muzykal'noi zhizni. [ML410.R52A33 1972] 74-183332 ISBN 0-8443-0024-1 16.50
1. Rimskii-Korsakov, Nikolai Andreevich, 1844-1908. 2. Musicians—Correspondence, reminiscences, etc. I. Van Vechten, Carl, 1880-1964, ed. **BIP**

Rincon de Gautier, Felisa—Juvenile literature.

GRUBER, Ruth, 1911- 972.95 B
Felisa Rincon de Gautier: the mayor of San Juan. New York, Crowell [1972] 238 p. illus. 22 cm. (Women of America) Bibliography: p. 227-228. Biography of the Puerto Rican woman who served five terms as mayor of San Juan and believed in ruling with the "politics of love." [F1981.S2G78] 92 72-83789 ISBN 0-690-29475-1 4.50
1. Rincon de Gautier, Felisa—Juvenile literature. I. Title.

NORRIS, Marianna. 972.95
Dona Felisa, a biography of the Mayor of San Juan. Illustrated with photos. New York, Dodd, Mead [1969] 95 p. illus., ports. 23 cm. The biography of the first woman mayor of San Juan, Puerto Rico, who remained in office for twenty years and was responsible for many social reforms. [F1981.S2R56] 92 69-15557 3.50
1. Rincon de Gautier, Felisa—Juvenile literature. I. Title.

Rinehart, Mary Roberts, 1876-1958.

COHN, Jan, 1933- 813'.5'2 B
Improbable fiction : the life of Mary Roberts Rinehart / Jan Cohn. Pittsburgh : University of Pittsburgh Press, [1980] p. cm. Includes index. "Mary Roberts Rinehart, a chronological bibliography": p. [PS3535.I73Z6] 79-3997 ISBN 0-8229-3401-9 : 16.95
1. Rinehart, Mary Roberts, 1876-1958. 2. Authors, American—20th century—Biography. I. Title. **BIP**

Ringling Brothers.

NORTH, Henry Ringling, 1909- 927.913
The circus kings; our Ringling family story [by] Henry Ringling North, Alden Hatch [New York] Dell [1964, c.1960] 317p. 17cm. (1282) .60 pap.,
1. Ringling Brothers. I. Hatch, Alden, 1898- II. Title.

NORTH, Henry Ringling, 1909- 927.913
The circus kings; our Ringling family story [by] Henry Ringling North and Alden Hatch. [1st ed.] Garden City, N. Y., Doubleday, 1960. 383 p. illus. 22 cm. [GV1821.R5N6] 60-8877
1. Ringling Brothers. I. Hatch, Alden, 1898- II. Title.

NORTH, Henry Ringling, 1909- 927.913
The circus kings; our Ringling family story [by] Henry Ringling North and Alden Hatch. [1st ed.] Garden City. N. Y., Doubleday, 1960. 383p. illus. 22cm. [GV1821.R5N6] 60-8877
1. Ringling Brothers I. Hatch, Alden, 1898- II. Title.

Ringling Brothers—Juvenile literature.

CONE, Molly. 791.3'0922 B
The Ringling Brothers. Illustrated by James and Ruth McCrea. New York, Crowell [1971] 40 p. illus. (part col.), ports. 24 cm. (Crowell biographies) A brief biography of the seven Ringling Brothers emphasizing the beginning and development of their famous circus. [GV1821.R5C6] 920 70-132295 ISBN 0-690-70287-6 3.75
1. Ringling Brothers—Juvenile literature. I. McCrea, James, illus. II. McCrea, Ruth, illus. BIP

GLENDINNING, Richard. 791.3'092'2
The Ringling Brothers: circus family, by Richard and Sally Glendinning. Illustrated by William Hutchinson. [Champaign, Ill., Garrard Pub. Co., 1972] 80 p. col. illus. 23 cm. (A Discovery book) A brief biography of the Ringling Brothers concentrating on the five who developed the circus called the "Greatest Show on Earth." [GV1821.R5G55] 920 72-1401 ISBN 0-8116-6310-8 2.95
1. Ringling Brothers—Juvenile literature. I. Glendinning, Sally, joint author. II. Hutchinson, William M., illus. III. Title.

Ringling, John, 1866-1936.

THOMAS, Richard, 1902- 927.913
John Ringling, circus magnate and art patron; a biography. [1st ed.] New York, Pageant Press [1960] 268 p. 21 cm. [GV1811.R52T5] 60-2357
1. Ringling, John, 1866-1936. I. Title.

THOMAS, Richard [Garner] 927.913
John Ringling, circus magnate and art patron;a biography. New York, Pageant Press [c.1960] 268p. 21cm. 60-2357 3.50
1. Ringl2ng, John 1866-1936. I. Title.

Rinish, Erika F

RINISH, Erika F 1936- 920.7
From Germany to the U. S. A.; the autobiography of a German war bride. [1st ed.] New York, Greenwich Book Publishers [1960] 79p. 21cm. [CT1098.R47A3] 60-11447
I. Title.

Rink, Paul,

RINK, Paul, 1912- 973.35'0924 B
John Paul Jones: conquer or die. Illustrated by Tran Mawicke. New York, Putnam [1968] 95 p. illus. 24 cm. (An American pioneer biography) A biography of the young man who, though small of stature and quick of temper, became a courageous sea captain, America's first naval hero, and father of the United States Navy. [E207.J7R5 1968] 92 AC 68
I. Mawicke, Tran, illus. II. Title.

RINK, Paul, 1912- 980 B
Quest for freedom; Bolivar and the South American Revolution. Maps and drawings by Barry Martin. New York, J. Massner [1968] 188 p. illus., map. 22 cm. ([Milestones in history]) Bibliography: p. [183] The life of the South American revolutionary instrumental in liberating his continent from the domination of Spain. Also includes the historical and political background of South America. [F2235.3.R565] AC 68
I. Martin, Barry, illus. II. Title.

Rinker, Rosalind.

RINKER, Rosalind. 283'.092'4 B
Ask me, Lord, I want to say yes / Rosalind Rinker. Plainfield, N.J. : Logos International, c1979. 105 p. ; 18 cm. Bibliography: p. 105. [BX5995.R5A32] 79-53030 ISBN 0-88270-381-1 pbk. : 1.95
1. Rinker, Rosalind. 2. Episcopalians in the United States—Biography. 3. Baptism in the Holy Spirit. I. Title. BIP

RINKER, Rosalind. 248'.092'4 B
Within the circle. Grand Rapids, Zondervan Pub. House [1973] 120 p. illus. 21 cm. Bibliography: p. [119]-120. [BV3427.R526A33] 72-83867 1.95
1. Rinker, Rosalind. 2. Christian life—1960- I. Title.

Riordan, Patrick William, Abp., 1841-1914.

GAFFEY, James P. 282'.092'4 B
Citizen of no mean city: Archbishop Patrick Riordan of San Francisco (1841-1914) [by] James P. Gaffey. [Washington, Catholic University of America Press, 1974] p. cm. Includes bibliographical references. [BX4705.R555G33] 74-5435 ISBN 0-8132-0537-9
1. Riordan, Patrick William, Abp., 1841-1914. I. Title.

Riou, Roger, 1909-

RIOU, Roger, 1909- 266'.2'0924 B
The island of my life : from petty crime to priestly mission / Roger Riou ; translated from the French by Martin Sokolinsky. New York : Delacorte Press, [1975] 300 p., [7] leaves of plates : ill. ; 22 cm. [R722.R56A3313] 75-4980 ISBN 0-440-04559-2 : 7.95
1. Riou, Roger, 1909- 2. Missionaries, Medical—Correspondence, reminiscences, etc. 3. Missions, Medical—Haiti. I. Title.

Ripley, George, 1802-1880.

CROWE, Charles Robert, 1928- 818'.3'08
George Ripley, transcendentalist and utopian socialist, by Charles Crowe. Athens, University of Georgia Press [1967] x, 316 p. 25 cm. Bibliography: p. 292-304. [PS2713.C7] 67-26605
1. Ripley, George, 1802-1880.

FROTHINGHAM, Octavius Brooks, 1822-1895. 818'.3'08
George Ripley. New York, AMS Press [1970] vi, 321 p. port. 22 cm. Reprint of the 1883 ed. [PS2713.F6 1970] 75-101910
1. Ripley, George, 1802-1880. BIP

GOLEMBA, Henry L. 809 B
George Ripley / by Henry L. Golemba. Boston : Twayne Publishers, c1977. 172 p. ; 21 cm. (Twayne's United States authors series ; TUSAS 281) Includes index. Bibliography: p. 164-169. [PS2713.G6] 76-41768 ISBN 0-8057-7181-6 lib.bdg. 8.95
1. Ripley, George, 1802-1880. 2. Critics—United States—Biography. 3. Social reformers—United States—Biography. BIP

Ripley, Robert Le Roy, 1893-1949.

CONSIDINE, Robert Bernard, 1906- 927.4
Ripley, the modern Marco Polo. [1st ed.] Garden City, N. Y., Doubleday, 1961. 214 p. illus. 22 cm. [PN4874.R53C6] 60-13508
1. Ripley, Robert Le Roy, 1893-1949. I. Title.

Ripon, Frederick John Robinson, 1st Earl of, 1782-1859.

JONES, Wilbur Devereux. 942.07'4'0924
"Prosperity" Robinson: the life of Viscount Goderich, 1782-1859. London, Melbourne [etc.] Macmillan; New York, St. Martin's P., 1967. x, 324 p. 8 plates (ports.). 22 1/3 cm. 50/- Bibliographical references included in "Notes" (p. 281-313) [DA536.R48J6 1967] 67-18711
1. Ripon, Frederick John Robinson, 1st Earl of, 1782-1859. I. Title.

Rippy, James Fred,

RIPPY, James Fred, 1892- 378.120924 (B)
Bygones I cannot help recalling; the memoirs of a mobile scholar, by J. Fred Rippy. Austin, Tex., Steck [1966] ix, 195p. ports. 24cm. [CT275.R612A3] 66-12938 5.95
I. Title.

Rita da Cascia, Saint, 1381?-1457.

MOSIER, Bernardine, Brother, 1908- 922.245
Saint of the impossible; a story of St. Rita. Illus. by Brother Bernard Howard. Notre Dame, Ind., Dujarie Press [1953] 93p. illus. 24cm. [BX4700.R5M6] 53-34339
1. Rita da Cascia, Saint, 1381?-1457. I. Title.

SPENS, Willy de, 1911- 922.245
Saint Rita. Translated by Julie Kerman. [1st ed.] Garden City, N.Y., Hanover House [1962] 144 p. 22 cm. Includes bibliography. [BX4700.R5S73] 62-8295
1. Rita de Cascia, Saint, 1381?-1457. I. Title.

Ritchie, Anna Cora (Ogden) Mowatt, 1819-1870.

BARNES, Eric Wollencott. 927.92
The lady of fashion; the life and the theatre ofAnna Cora Mowatt. New York, Scribner [c1954] 402p. illus. 22cm. London ed. (Secker & Warburg) has title: Anna Cora. Includes bibliography. [PN2287.R54B3 1954] 54-10366
1. Ritchie, Anna Cora (Ogden) Mowatt, 1819-1870. I. Title.

Ritchie. Anna Cora (Ogden) Mowatt, 1819-1870—Juvenile literature.

BUTLER, Mildred Allen 792.0924
Actress in spite of herself; the life of Anna Cora Mowatt. New York, Funk & Wagnalls [c.1966] 188p. illus. 22cm. [PN2287.R54B8] 66-12577 3.95 bds.,
1. Ritchie. Anna Cora (Ogden) Mowatt, 1819-1870—Juvenile literature. I. Title.

Ritchie, Eveline.

RITCHIE, Eveline. 301.43'5
Taking out my bucketful / Eveline Ritchie with Violet T. Pearson. Denver : Accent Books, c1978. 160 p. : ill. ; 21 cm. [LA2317.R56A37] 78-67935 ISBN 0-89636-009-1 : 2.95
1. Ritchie, Eveline. 2. Teachers—Michigan—Biography. 3. Retirement. I. Pearson, Violet T. II. Title. BIP

Ritchie, George G., 1923-

RITCHIE, George G., 1923- 248'.2'0924 B
Return from tomorrow / George G. Ritchie, with Elizabeth Sherrill. Waco, Tex. : Chosen Books : distributed by Word Books, c1978. 124 p. ; 21 cm. [BR1725.R58A37] 77-27543 ISBN 0-912376-23-6 : 5.95
1. Ritchie, George G., 1923- 2. Christian biography—United States. 3. Psychiatrists—United States—Biography. 4. Death, Apparent—Case studies. I. Sherrill, Elizabeth, joint author. II. Title. BIP

Ritchley, Leonard Alvin,

GROVE, Margie (Ritchley) 1911- 920
Papa passes. [1st ed.] New York, Greenwich Book Publishers [1956] 85p. 21cm. [CT275.R613G7] 56-12254
1. Ritchley, Leonard Alvin, I. Title.

Ritschl, Albrecht Benjamin, 1822-1889.

RITSCHL, Albrecht Benjamin, 1822-1889. 230'.4
Three essays. Translated and with an introd. by Philip Hefner. Philadelphia, Fortress Press [1972] 301 p. 24 cm. Contents.Contents.—Theology and metaphysics.—"Prolegomena" to The history of pietism.—Instruction in the Christian religion. Includes bibliographical references. [B85.R58] 72-75654 ISBN 0-8006-0224-2 10.50
1. Ritschl, Albrecht Benjamin, 1822-1889. 2. Pietism. 3. Christianity—Philosophy. 4. Theological, Doctrinal. I. Title. BIP

Ritson, Joseph, 1752-1806.

BURD, Henry Alfred, 1889- v. 12
Joseph Ritson, a critical biography. [Urbana] University of Illinois, 1916. New York, Johnson Reprint [1967] 224 p. (University of Illinois studies in language and literature. vol. II, no. 3) 68-91638
1. Ritson, Joseph, 1752-1806. I. Title.

Ritt, Joseph Fels, 1893-1951. (Series: National Academy of Sciences. Washington, D.C. Biographical memoirs, v. 29, 10th memoir)

SMITH, Paul Althaus, 1900- v. 12
Joseph Fels Ritt, 1893-1951. (In National Academy of Sciences, Washington, D.C. Biographical memoirs. New York. 24 cm. v. 29 (1956) [10th memoir] p. [253]-264. port.) Bibliography of Joseph Fels Ritt: p. 259-264.
1. Ritt, Joseph Fels, 1893-1951. (Series: National Academy of Sciences. Washington, D.C. Biographical memoirs, v. 29, 10th memoir) I. Title.

Rittenhouse, David, 1732-1796.

HINDLE, Brooke 925.2
David Rittenhouse. Princeton, N.J., Princeton [c.]1964. ix, 394p. illus., maps, port. 23cm. Bibl. 63-23407 8.50
1. Rittenhouse, David, 1732-1796. I. Title. BIP

Ritter, Gerhard,

RITTER, Gerhard, 1888- 943'.053'0924
Frederick the Great; a historical profile. Tr. introd., by Peter Paret. Berkeley, Univ. of Calif. Pr. 1968. xiv, 207p. port. 23cm. [DD404.R513] (B) 68-15815 7.50
I. Frederick. II. der Grosse, King of Prussia, 1712-1786. III. Title.
Translation of the third edition of "Friedrich der Grosse: Ein Historisches Profil" published by Quelle & Meyer, Heidelberg, 1954.

Rivard, Paul Leon.

TRENT, Bill 926.1
Northwoods doctor. Philadelphia, Lippincott, [c.]1962. 320p. 22cm. 62-13990 5.95 bds.,
1. Rivard, Paul Leon. I. Title.

Rivera, Diego,

RIVERA, Diego, 1886-1957. 759.972
My art, my life; an autobiography [by] Diego Rivera, with Gladys March. [1st ed.] New York, Citadel Press [1960] 318p. illus., ports. 22cm. [ND259.R5A3] 60-15451
I. March, Gladys. II. Title.

RIVERA, Diego, 1886-1957. 759.972
My art, my life; an autobiography [by]

Diego Rivera, with Gladys March. [1st ed.] New York, Citadel Press [1960] 318p. illus., ports. 22cm. [ND259.R5A3] 60-15451
I. March, Gladys. II. Title.

RIVERA, Diego [Diego Maria 759.972
My art, my life; an autobiography [by] Diego Rivera, with Gladys March. New York, Citadel Press [c.1960] oncepcion Juan Nepomuceno Estanislao de la Rivera y Barrientos Acosta y Rodriguez] 1886-1957. 318p. illus., ports. 22cm. 60-15451 6.00
1. March, Gladys. I. Title.

WOLFE, Bertram David, 1896- 759.972
The fabulous life of Diego Rivera. New York, Stein and Day [1963] xxi, 457 p. illus., ports. 24 cm Bibliography: p. 433-442. [ND259.R5W.56] 63-20061
1. Rivera, Diego, 1886-1957. I. Title. **BIP**

Rivera, Geraldo—Juvenile literature.

ITZKOWITZ, Leonore K., 1933- 070'.92'4 B
Eyewitness to the 70's—The story of Geraldo Rivera [by] Leonore K. It kowitz. New York, Random House [1974] p. cm. A biography of the New York TV news reporter who through his job tries to improve the life of people with problems. [PN4874.R537I8] 92 74-1255 ISBN 0-394-12311-5
1. Rivera, Geraldo—Juvenile literature. 2. Rivera, Geraldo. I. Title.

Rivera, Jose Eustasio, 1888-1928.

NEALE-SILVA, Eduardo 928.6
Horizonte humano; vida de Jose Eustasio Rivera. Madison, University of Wisconsin Press, 1960[ ] 506p. illus. 22cm. 60-5842 7.50; 2.25 pap.,
1. Rivera, Jose Eustasio, 1888-1928. I. Title. **BIP**

Rivers, Larry, 1923-

HUNTER, Sam, 1923- 709'.2'4
Rivers [by] Sam Hunter. New York, H. N. Abrams [1972] 102 p. illus. (part col.) 21 x 23 cm. (Modern artists) Bibliography: p. [98]-102. [N6537.R57H82] 71-175945 ISBN 0-8109-4424-3 6.75
1. Rivers, Larry, 1923- I. Rivers, Larry, 1923- **BIP**

Rivers, Thomas Milton,

RIVERS, Thomas Milton, 1888-1962 576.'64'0924
Tom Rivers: reflections on a life in medicine and science; an oral history memoir, prepared by Saul Benison. Cambridge, Mass., M. I. T. Pr. [1967] xxi, 682p. ports. 24cm. Bibl. [QR31.R5A3] 67-16500 17.50
I. Benison, Saul, 1919- II. Title. III. Title. Reflections on a life in medicine and science.

RIVERS, Thomas Milton, 1888-1962. 576'.64'0924
Tom Rivers: reflections on a life in medicine and science; an oral history memoir, prepared by Saul Benison. Cambridge, Mass., M.I.T. Press [1967] xxi, 682 p. ports. 24 cm. Includes bibliographies. [QR31.R5A3] 67-16500
I. Benison, Saul, 1919- II. Title. III. Title: Reflections on a life in medicine and science.

Rivers, William Halse Rivers, 1864-1922.

SLOBODIN, Richard, 1915- 301.2 B
W. H. R. Rivers / Richard Slobodin. New York : Columbia University Press, 1978. xv, 295 p. : ill. ; 23 cm. (Leaders of modern anthropology series) Includes index. Bibliography: p. 271-288. [GN21.R53S57] 78-6393 20.00
1. Rivers, William Halse Rivers, 1864-1922. 2. Anthropologists—England—Biography. 3. Ethnology—Addresses, essays, lectures. 4. Psychology—Addresses, essays, lectures. I. Title. II. Series. **BIP**

Rizal y Alonso, Jose, 1861-1896.

COATES, Austin. 991.4'02'0924 B
Rizal, Philippine nationalist and martyr. Hong Kong, New York, Oxford University Press, 1968. xxxii, 378 p. illus., facsims., maps, ports. 23 cm. Bibliography: p. 363-369. [DS675.8.R5C57] 78-304
1. Rizal y Alonso, Jose, 1861-1896. I. Title.

Rizzi, Marcia Salo.

*RIZZI, Marcia Salo. 759.972[B]
Some pictures from my life; a diary by Marcia Salo Rizzi. [Washington N.J.] [Times Change Press] [1972] 1 v. (unpaged), illus., 18 cm. 72-87034 ISBN 0-87810-022-9 1.35 pap.
I. Title. **BIP**

Rizzo, Frank.

DAUGHEN, Joseph R. 352'.0083'0924 B
The cop who would be king : Mayor Frank Rizzo / Joseph R. Daughen and Peter Binzen. 1st ed. Boston : Little, Brown, c1977. viii, 344 p. : ill. ; 25 cm. Includes bibliographical references and index. [F158.52.R58D38] 77-24242 ISBN 0-316-09521-4 : 10.00
1. Rizzo, Frank. 2. Philadelphia—Mayors—Biography. I. Binzen, Peter, joint author. II. Title.

Rizzo, Frank L.

HAMILTON, Fred J. 352'.0083'0924 B
Rizzo [by] Fred Hamilton. New York, Viking Press [1973] 209 p. illus. 22 cm. [F158.52.R58H35] 72-91027 ISBN 0-670-60072-5 6.95
1. Rizzo, Frank L.

Rizzuto, Philip Francis, 1918-

SHAPIRO, Milton J. 927.96357
The Phil Rizzuto story. New York, Messner [1959] 192 p. illus. 22 cm. [GV865.R5S5] 59-7019
1. Rizzuto, Philip Francis, 1918- I. Title.

TRIMBLE, Joe. 927.96357
Phil Rizzuto, a biography of the Scooter. New York, A. S. Barnes [1951] viii, 184 p. illus., ports. 21 cm. (Most valuable player series) [GV865.R5T7] 51-10778
1. Rizzuto, Philip Francis, 1918-

RKO Radio Pictures, inc.

PARISH, James Robert. 791.43'028'0922 B
The RKO gals. Editor: T. Allan Taylor. Research associates: John Robert Cocchi [and] Florence Solomon. New Rochelle, N.Y., Arlington House [1974] 896 p. illus. 25 cm. Includes bibliographical references. [PN1998.A2P398] 74-8346 ISBN 0-87000-246-5 14.95
1. RKO Radio Pictures, inc. 2. Moving-picture actors and actresses—United States—Biography. I. Title. **BIP**

Roanoke Valley—History.

GINTHER, Herman. 975.5'6
Captain Staunton's River. Richmond, Dietz Press [1968] 106 p. illus., map, ports. 27 cm. "From ... [the author's] series of feature articles published in the Union star, Brookneal, Virginia." [F232.R63G5] 76-1838 5.00
1. Roanoke Valley—History. 2. Roanoke Valley—Biography. I. Title.

Robb, George Douglas,

ROBB, George Douglas, Sir, 1899- 610'.924 B
Medical odyssey [by] Sir Douglas Robb. [Springfield, Ill.] C. C. Thomas [1968] 201, [6] p. illus., ports. 22 cm. Bibliography: p. [203]-[206] [R674] 73-2530 5.50
I. Title.

Robb, James Henry.

CARVER, Saxon Rowe. v. 12
James Robb, pioneer. Illustrated by William Moyers. Atlanta, Home Mission Board, Southern Baptist Convention [1963] 75 p. illus. 20 cm. (Southern Baptist Convention. Home Mission Board. Home Mission studies. 1964 graded series) [Supplement] Teacher's guide [by] Margaret Sharp. [Atlanta, Home Mission Board, Southern Baptist Convention, 1963] 27 p. illus. 28 cm. 65-7967
1. Robb, James Henry. 2. Southern Baptist Convention — Missions. 3. Missions, Home — Juvenile literature. I. Title. II. Series.

Robb, Lynda Bird, 1944-

SIMMONS, Dawn Langley. 973.923'0922
Lady Bird and her daughters, by Gordon Langley Hall. Philadelphia, M. Smith Co. [1967] 254 p. ports. 22 cm. "Selected bibliography": p. [253]-254. [E848.S5] 66-26497
1. Johnson, Claudia Alta (Taylor) 1912- 2. Robb, Lynda Bird, 1944- 3. Nugent, Luci Baines (Johnson) 1947- I. Title.

Robben, John.

ROBBEN, John. 170'.202
Coming to my senses. New York, Crowell [1973] 197, [1] p. 22 cm. Bibliography: p. 197-[198] [CT275.R712A33] 73-8845 ISBN 0-690-00098-7 5.95
1. Robben, John. I. Title. **BIP**

Robbia, Andrea della, 1435?-1525?

CRUTTWELL, Maud. 730'.92'2
Luca & Andrea della Robbia and their successors. With over 150 illus. London, Dent; New York, Dutton, 1902. [New York, AMS Press, 1972] xix, 363 p. illus. 24 cm. Includes bibliographies. [NB623.R7C8 1972] 79-155625 ISBN 0-404-01869-6 12.50
1. Robbia, Luca della, 1400?-1482. 2. Robbia, Andrea della, 1435?-1525? 3. Robbia, Giovanni della, 1469-1529? I. Title.

MARQUAND, Allan, 1853-1924. 730'.92'4
Andrea della Robbia and his atelier. New York, Hacker Art Books, 1972 [i.e. 1973] 2 v. in 1. illus. 27 cm. Reprint of the 1922 ed. published by Princeton University Press as v. 11 of Princeton monographs in art and archaeology. Bibliography: v. 2, p. [267]-272. [NB623.R713M3 1972] 70-153007 ISBN 0-87817-102-9
1. Robbia, Andrea della, 1435?-1525? I. Title. II. Series: Princeton monographs in art and archaeology, 11.
Set of 8 vols. bound in four selling for 250.00.

Robbia, Luca della, 1400?-1482.

CRUTTWELL, Maud. 730'.92'2
Luca & Andrea della Robbia and their successors. With over 150 illus. London, Dent; New York, Dutton, 1902. [New York, AMS Press, 1972] xix, 363 p. illus. 24 cm. Includes bibliographies. [NB623.R7C8 1972] 79-155625 ISBN 0-404-01869-6 12.50
1. Robbia, Luca della, 1400?-1482. 2. Robbia, Andrea della, 1435?-1525? 3. Robbia, Giovanni della, 1469-1529? I. Title.

DOWNER, Marion. 730'.924 B
Long ago in Florence; the story of the della Robbia sculpture. Drawings by Mamoru Funai. New York, Lothrop, Lee & Shepard Co. [1968] 31 p. illus. 26 cm. A brief biography of an Italian sculptor well-known for his statues of children and for inventing the method of sculpting glazed enamel over terra-cotta. [NB623.R7D6] 92 AC 68
1. Robbia, Luca della, 1400?-1482. I. Funai, Mamoru, illus. II. Title. **BIP**

MARQUAND, Allan, 1853-1924. 730'.92'4
Luca della Robbia. New York, Hacker Art Books, 1972. xxxix, 286 p. illus. 27 cm. Reprint of the 1914 ed. published by Princeton University Press, which was issued as v. 3 of Princeton monographs in art and archaeology. Bound with the author's Giovanni della Robbia. New York, 1972. Includes bibliographical references. [NB623.R72M3 1972] 73-164572 ISBN 0-87817-103-7
1. Robbia, Luca della, 1400?-1482. I. Series: Princeton monographs in art and archaeology, 3.

Robbins, Frances (Baker)

ROBBINS, Frances (Baker) 920.79
Small town widow. Philadelphia, Franklin Pub. Co. [1966] 184 p. illus. 21 cm. Autobiography. [CT275.R713A3] 66-24280
I. Title.

Robbins, Phyllis.

ROBBINS, Phyllis. 927.92
Maude Adams; an intimate portrait. New York, Putnam [1956] 306p. illus. 22cm. [PN2287.A4R6] 56-6625
I. Adams, Maude, 1872-1953. II. Title.

ROBBINS, Phyllis. 927.92
The young Maude Adams. Francestown, N. H., M. Jones Co. [c1959] 163p. illus. 21cm. [PN2287.A4R63] 59-15779
I. Adams, Maude, 1872-1953. II. Title. **BIP**

Robelais, Francois, 1490 (ca-1553

LEWIS, Dominic Bevan Wyndham, 1894- 847.32
Doctor Rabelais. New York, Sheed and Ward [1957] 274p. 22cm. Includes bibliography. [PQ1693.L4 1957a] 57-10186
1. Robelais, Francois, 1490 (ca-1553 I. Title.

Robert, Edward Bane, 1898-

THE Life and work of E. B. (Ted) Robert. 378.1'11'0924 B Baton Rouge, Bureau of Educational Materials and Research, Louisiana State University, 1972. xvii, 436 p. 24 cm. [LD3112.8.R6L53] 73-620670 8.50
1. Robert, Edward Bane, 1898- I. Louisiana. State University and Agricultural and Mechanical College. Bureau of Educational Materials and Research.

Robert, Frost, 1874-1963.

MERTINS, Marshall Louis, 1885- 811.52
Robert Frost; life and talks-walking. Norman, Univ. of Okla. Pr. [c.1965] xiii, 450p. illus., ports. 23cm. [PS3511.R94Z786] 65-11238 7.50
1. Robert, Frost, 1874-1963. I. Title. **BIP**

Robert-Houdin, Jean Eugene, 1805-1871

EDMONDS, I. G. 793.8'092'4 B
The magic man; the life of Robert-Houdin, by I. G. Edmonds. Nashville, T. Nelson [1972] 170 p. illus. 21 cm. A biography of the nineteenth-century Frenchman whose conjuring skill gained him the title of "father of modern magic." [GV1545.R7E3] 92 71-181679 ISBN 0-8407-6146-5
1. Robert-Houdin, Jean Eugene, 1805-1871—Juvenile literature. I. Title. **BIP**

ROBERT-HOUDIN, Jean Eugene 920.97938
Memoirs of Robert-Houdin. Tr. from French by Lascelles Wraxall. New introd., notes by Milbourne Christopher. Newly illus. with rare prints, playbills, documents from the Christopher Collection. New York, Dover [1964] xvi, 336p. illus., facsims., ports. 22cm. 64-15516 2.00 pap.,
I. Title.

ROBERT-HOUDIN, Jean Eugene, 1805-1871 920.97938
Memoirs of Robert-Houdin. Tr. from French by Lascelles Wraxall. New introd., notes by Milbourne Christopher. Newly illus. with rare prints, playbills and documents from the Christopher Collection [Gloucester, Mass., P. Smith, 1965, c.1964]

xvi, 336p. illus., facsims., ports. 22cm. (Dover bk. rebound) [GV1545.R7A4] 4.00
I. Title.

Robert-Houdin, Jean Eugene

ROBERT-HOUDIN, Jean Eugene 920.97938
Memoirs of Robert-Houdin. Tr. from French by Lascelles Wraxall. New introd., notes by Milbourne Christopher. Newly illus. with rare prints, playbills, documents from the Christopher Collection. New York, Dover [1964] xvi, 336p. illus., facsims., ports. 22cm. 64-15516 2.00 pap.,
I. Title.

ROBERT-HOUDIN, Jean Eugene, 1805-1871 920.97938
Memoirs of Robert-Houdin. Tr. from French by Lascelles Wraxall. New introd., notes by Milbourne Christopher. Newly illus. with rare prints, playbills and documents from the Christopher Collection [Gloucester, Mass., P. Smith, 1965, c.1964] xvi, 336p. illus., facsims., ports. 22cm. (Dover bk. rebound) [GV1545.R7A4] 4.00
I. Title.

Robert I, King of Scotland, 1274-1329.

BARROW, G. W. S. 941.1'02'0924
Robert Bruce and the community of the realm of Scotland / G. W. S. Barrow. 2d ed. Edinburgh : Edinburgh University Press, 1976, i.e.1977 xx, 502 p., [8] leaves of plates : ill. ; 18 cm. Includes index. Bibliography: p. [ix]-x. [DA783.4.B34 1976] 77-358763 ISBN 0-85224-307-3 pbk. : 5.00
1. Robert I, King of Scotland, 1274-1329. 2. Scotland—Kings and rulers—Biography. 3. Scotland—History—War of Independence, 1285-1371. I. Title.
Distributed by Edinburgh Univ. Press, c/o Biblio Distribution Ctr., 81 Adams Dr., Totowa, N.J. 07512 BIP

MACKENZIE, Agnes Mure, 1891-1955. 941.02
Robert Bruce, King of Scots. Freeport, N.Y., Books for Libraries Press [1970] xvi, 379 p. illus., plans. 23 cm. Reprint of the 1934 ed. Includes bibliographical references. [DA783.4.M25 1970] 78-128880
1. Robert I, King of Scotland, 1274-1329. 2. Scotland—History—War of Independence, 1285-1371. I. Title. BIP

SCOTT, Tom, 1918- 941'.02'0924 B
Tales of King Robert the Bruce; freely adapted from The Brus of John Barbour (14th century). Illustrated by Ewart Oakeshott. [1st ed. Oxford, New York] Pergamon Press [1969] v, 135 p. illus., coats of arms, ports. 23 cm. (The Pergamon English library. Scottish literature series) [DA783.4.S34 1969] 68-55564
1. Robert I, King of Scotland, 1274-1329. I. Barbour, John, d. 1395. The Bruce. II. Title. III. Series: The Pergamon English library

Robert I, King of Scotland, 1274-1329—Juvenile literature.

OLIVER, Jane, Pseud. 920
The young Robert Bruce. Illus. by William Randell. New York, Roy [1963,c.1962] 144p. 21cm. 62-18554 3.00 bds.,
1. Robert I, King of Scotland, 1274-1329—Juvenile literature. I. Title.

Roberts. Bartholomew. 1682?-1722.

RICHARDS, Stanley 364.1350924
Black Bart. Llandybie (Carms.), C. Davies. 1966. 121p. plates (incl. ports., maps) tables. 23cm. Bibl. [G537.R57R5] 66-74818 3.50 bds.,
1. Roberts. Bartholomew. 1682?-1722. I. Title.
Available from Verry, Mystic. Conn.

Roberts, Benjamin Titus, 1823-1893.

ZAHNISER, Clarence Howard. 922.773
Earnest Christian; ;life and works of Benjamin Titus Roberts. [n. p., 1957] 349 p. illus. 24 cm. [BX8419.R6Z2] 57-38376
1. Roberts, Benjamin Titus, 1823-1893. I. Title.

Roberts, Bill.

DODSON, Kenneth. 248'.24 B
From make-believe to reality: the Bill Roberts story. Old Tappan, N.J., F. H. Revell Co. [1973] 154 p. 21 cm. [BV4935.R57D62] 73-8802 ISBN 0-8007-0614-5 4.95
1. Roberts, Bill. 2. Conversion. I. Title.

Roberts, Cecil,

ROBERTS, Cecil, 1892- 928.2
One year of life; some autobiographical pages. New York, Macmillan [c1952] 309p. illus. 23cm. [PR6035.O5Z5 1952a] 53-11720
I. Title.

Roberts, Cecil E., 1919-

ROBERTS, Cecil E., 1919- 355.3'32'0924 B
A soldier from Texas / Cecil E. Roberts. Fort Worth : Branch-Smith, c1978. vi, 210 p. : ill. ; 23 cm. [U53.R59A37] 78-67480 ISBN 0-87706-104-1 : 12.50
1. Roberts, Cecil E., 1919- 2. United States. Army—Officers—Biography. 3. Soldiers—Texas—Biography. 4. Texas—Biography. I. Title. BIP

Roberts, Columbus, 1870-1950.

DOWELL, Spright. 923.373
Columbus Roberts: Christian steward extraordinary. Nashville, Broadman Press ['1951] 171 p. illus. 23 cm. [CT275.R722D6] 51-14710
1. Roberts, Columbus, 1870-1950. I. Title.

Roberts, David Correll.

ROBERTS, Nancy, 1924- 362.7'8'3
David. Text by Nancy Roberts. Photos. by Bruce Roberts. [Rev. ed.] Atlanta, John Knox Press [1974, c1968] 72 p. illus. 20 x 23 cm. Bibliography: p. 72. [HQ773.7.R6 1974] 74-3710 3.95 (pbk.)
1. Roberts, David Correll. 2. Mongolism—Personal narratives. I. Roberts, Bruce, 1930- illus. II. Title. BIP

Roberts, Elizabeth Madox, 1886-1941.

CAMPBELL, Harry Modean. 928.1
Elizabeth Madox Roberts, American novelist [by] Harry Modean Campbell and Ruel E. Foster. With a foreword by J. Donald Adams. [1st ed.] Norman, University of Oklahoma Press [1956] 283p. 28cm. [PS3535.O172Z59] 56-11237
1. Roberts, Elizabeth Madox, 1886-1941. I. Foster, Ruel Elton, 1916-joint author. II. Title.

CAMPBELL, Harry Modean. 928.1
Elizabeth Madox Roberts, American novelist [by] Harry Modean Campbell and Ruel E. Foster. With a foreword by J. Donald Adams. [1st ed.] Norman, University of Oklahoma Press [1956] 283 p. 23 cm. [PS3535.O172Z59] 56-11237
1. Roberts, Elizabeth Madox, 1886-1941. I. Foster, Ruel Elton, 1916- joint author. II. Title.

Roberts, Evelyn, 1917-

ROBERTS, Evelyn, 1917- 269'.2'0924 B
His darling wife, Evelyn : the autobiography of Mrs. Oral Roberts / by Evelyn Roberts. New York : Dial Press, 1976. x, 273 p., [8] leaves of plates : ill. ; 22 cm. "A Damascus House book." [BX8495.R52A3] 76-23429 ISBN 0-8037-3601-0 : 6.95
1. Roberts, Evelyn, 1917- 2. Roberts, Oral. I. Title.

ROBERTS, Evelyn, 1917- 269'.2'0924
His darling wife Evelyn : the autobiography of Mrs. Oral Roberts / by Evelyn Roberts. New York : Dell Pub. Co., 1978,c1976. 256p., 8 l. of plates : ill. ; 18 cm. (A Dell Book) [BX8495.R52A3] ISBN 0-440-13660-1 pbk. : 1.95
1. Roberts, Evelyn, 1917- 2. Roberts, Oral. I. Title.
L.C. card no. for 1976 Dial Press ed.:76-23429. BIP

ROBERTS, Evelyn, 1917- 269'.2'0924 B
His darling wife, Evelyn : the autobiography of Mrs. Oral Roberts / Evelyn Roberts. Boston : G. K. Hall, 1977, c1976. 418 p. ; 25 cm. Large print ed. [BX8495.R52A3 1977] 77-1416 ISBN 0-8161-6469-X lib.bdg. : 11.95
1. Roberts, Evelyn, 1917- 2. Roberts, Oral. 3. Methodist Church—Clergy—Biography. 4. Clergymen's wives—Oklahoma—Tulsa—Biography. 5. Tulsa, Okla.—Biography. 6. Clergy—Oklahoma—Tulsa—Biography. 7. Large type books. I. Title.

Roberts, Frank, 1882-1963.

ROBERTS, Joyce. 625.1'9
Steam in miniature : Frank Roberts and his garden railway / Joyce Roberts. Wellington : A. H. & A. W. Reed, 1976. 88 p. : ill. ; 27 cm. [TF197.R6] 77-350150 ISBN 0-589-00948-6
1. Roberts, Frank, 1882-1963. 2. Railroads—Models. 3. Locomotive engineers—New Zealand—Biography. I. Title. BIP

Roberts, Frederick Sleigh Roberts, 1st Earl, 1832-1914.

HANNAH, W. H. 355.3'31'0924 B
Bobs: Kipling's general; the life of Field-Marshal Roberts of Kandahar, VC, by W. H. Hannah. [Hamden, Conn.] Archon Books, 1972. 263 p. illus. 23 cm. Bibliography: p. 251-254. [DA68.32.R6H25 1972] 72-3642 ISBN 0-208-01139-0 12.00
1. Roberts, Frederick Sleigh Roberts, 1st Earl, 1832-1914. I. Title.

Roberts, Kenneth J.,

ROBERTS, Kenneth J., 1930- 271'.53'024 B
Playboy to priest [by] Kenneth J. Roberts. Staten Island, N.Y., Alba House [1971] ix, 290 p. 22 cm. [BX4705.R58A3] 78-169145 ISBN 0-8189-0234-5 4.95
I. Title. BIP

Roberts, Oral.

ROBERTS, Evelyn, 1917- 269'.2'0924 B
His darling wife, Evelyn : the autobiography of Mrs. Oral Roberts / Evelyn Roberts. Boston : G. K. Hall, 1977, c1976. 418 p. ; 25 cm. Large print ed. [BX8495.R52A3 1977] 77-1416 ISBN 0-8161-6469-X lib.bdg. : 11.95
1. Roberts, Evelyn, 1917- 2. Roberts, Oral. 3. Methodist Church—Clergy—Biography. 4. Clergymen's wives—Oklahoma—Tulsa—Biography. 5. Tulsa, Okla.—Biography. 6. Clergy—Oklahoma—Tulsa—Biography. 7. Large type books. I. Title.

ROBERTS, Oral. 269'.2'0924 B
The call; an autobiography. [1st ed.] Garden City, N.Y., Doubleday, 1972 [c1971] 216 p. 22 cm. [BV3785.R58A23] 79-139057 4.95
I. Title.

ROBERTS, Oral. v. 12
My twenty years of a miracle ministry. [Tulsa, Okla., 1967] 96 p. illus. (part col.) ports. (part col.) 28 cm. 68-62744
1. Roberts, Oral. 2. Evangelists—Correspondence, reminiscences, etc. I. Title.

ROBINSON, Wayne, 1937- 269'.2'0924 B
Oral : the warm, intimate, unauthorized portrait of a man of God / Wayne A. Robinson. Los Angeles : Acton House, c1976. xi, 154 p. ; 23 cm. [BX8495.R528R62] 76-151756 ISBN 0-89202-003-2 : 5.95
1. Roberts, Oral. 2. Methodist Church—Clergy—Biography. 3. Clergy—Oklahoma—Tulsa—Biography. 4. Tulsa, Okla.—Biography. I. Title.

Roberts, Oral.

ROBERTS, Oral. 269'.2'0924 B
The call; an autobiography. [1st ed.] Garden City, N.Y., Doubleday, 1972 [c1971] 216 p. 22 cm. [BV3785.R58A23] 79-139057 4.95
I. Title.

Roberts, Robert Richford, Bp., 1778-1843.

TIPPY, Worth Marion, 1867- 922.773
Frontier bishop; the life and times of Robert Richford Roberts. New York, Abingdon Press [1958] 207 p. illus. 23 cm. Includes bibliography. [BX8495.R53T5] 58-5394
1. Roberts, Robert Richford, Bp., 1778-1843. I. Title.

Roberts, Robert, 1905-1974.

ROBERTS, Robert, 1905-1974. 942.7'33'08230924 B
A ragged schooling : growing up in the classic slum / [by] Robert Roberts. Manchester : University Press, 1976. [8], 224 p. : ill. ; 21 cm. [CT788.R5213A37] 77-372996 ISBN 0-7190-0652-X : £3.75
1. Roberts, Robert, 1905-1974. 2. England—Biography. I. Title.

Roberts, Thomas Benton.

ROBERTS, Thomas Benton. 791.43'092'4 B
Roll 'em : behind the scenes in early motion picture days / by Thomas Benton Roberts. 1st ed. New York : Vantage Press, c1976. 118 p. : ill. ; 21 cm. [PN1998.A3R594] 76-371914 ISBN 0-533-01913-3 : 6.95
1. Roberts, Thomas Benton. 2. Moving-picture industry—United States—Biography. 3. Boats and boating in motion pictures. I. Title.

Robertson, Alice Mary, 1854-1931.

SPAULDING, Joe Powell. v. 12
The life of Alice Mary Robertson. [Norman, Okla., 1959] 220 l. Film reproduction. Positive. 66-52940
1. Robertson, Alice Mary, 1854-1931. I. Title.

Robertson, Dede.

ROBERTSON, Dede. 248'.2 B
My God will supply : how the Lord provides in times of shortage / Dede Robertson, with John Sherrill. Lincoln, Va. : Chosen Books ; Waco, Tex. : distributed by Word Books, c1979. 172 p. ; 22 cm. [BR1725.R616A35] 79-16126 ISBN 0-912376-48-1 : 5.95
1. Robertson, Dede. 2. Christian biography—United States. 3. Soybean as food. 4. Cookery (Soybeans) I. Sherrill, John, joint author. II. Title.

Robertson family.

ROBERTSON, Isobel. 929'.2'0968
Aberdeen to Overberg : the life & family of William Robertson / by Isobel Robertson. Constantia [South Africa : I. Robertson, c1976. 45 p. : ill. ; 28 cm. Includes bibliographical references and index. [CS1599.R6 1976] 77-360700 ISBN 0-620-02217-5

1. Robertson family. 2. South Africa—Genealogy. I. Title.

Robertson, Frederick Williams, 1819-1870.

ROBERTSON, Julian 929.2'0973
Hart, 1899-
The story of Frederick Williams Robertson and Charlotte (Reynolds) Hackett Robertson. [Salisbury, N.C. 1969] 17 p. map. 25 cm. Bibliography: p. 11-12. [CT275.R726R6] 77-93966
1. Robertson, Frederick Williams, 1819-1870. 2. Robertson, Charlotte Reynolds Hackett Robertson, 1826-1902. I. Title.

Robertson, George, 1825-1898.

HOLROYD, John. 655.4'24 B
George Robertson of Melbourne, 1825-1898; pioneer bookseller & publisher. [Melbourne] Robertson & Mullens [1968] 64 p. illus., facsim., port. 23 cm. Bibliographical footnotes. [Z542.3.R6H6] 73-386701 3.75
1. Robertson, George, 1825-1898.

Robertson, William Spence,

ROBERTSON, William 987'.04'0924 B
Spence, 1872-
The life of Miranda. New York, Cooper Square Publishers, 1969. 2 v. illus., maps, ports. 24 cm. (Library of Latin American history and culture) Reprint of the 1929 ed. Bibliography: v. 2, p. [257]-276. [F2323.M6R62 1969] 77-79203
I. Miranda, Francisco de, 1750-1816. II. Title. BIP

Robertson, William, 1721-1793.

STEWART, Dugald. 1753- 920.042
1828
Biographical memoir of Adam Smith. New York, Kelley, 1966. clxxvii, 338p. port. 24cm. (Adam Smith lib.; Reprints of economic classics) Reprint of v.10 of the author's Complete works (Edinburgh, 1858), which was first pub. in 1811 under title: Biographical memoirs of Adam Smith, LL. D., of William Robertson, D. D., and of Thomas Reid, D. D. [CT821.S7] 66-15560 12.50
1. Smith, Adam, 1723-1790. 2. Robertson, William, 1721-1793. 3. Reid, Thomas, 1710-1796. I. Title. BIP

Robertson, William, 1795-1890.

MCGILCHRIST, 929.2'0994
Stevenson.
William Robertson, Victorian pioneer 1837-1890 [Melbourne, The Author, 445 St. Kilda Road, 1968?] 52 p. fold. geneal. table. 26 cm. [CT2858.R6M3] 72-392408 unpriced
1. Robertson, William, 1795-1890.

Robeson, Paul, 1898-1976.

HOYT, Edwin Palmer. 790.2'0924 B
Paul Robeson, the American Othello [by] Edwin P. Hoyt. [1st ed.] Cleveland, World Pub. Co. [1967] ix, 228 p. 22 cm. Bibliographical footnotes. [ML420.R73H7] 67-25579
1. Robeson, Paul, 1898- I. Title: The American Othello.

HOYT, Edwin Palmer. 782.1'092'4
Paul Robeson, the American Othello [by] Edwin P. Hoyt. [1st ed.] Cleveland, World Pub. Co. [1967] ix, 228 p. 22 cm. Bibliographical footnotes. [ML420.R73H7] [790.2'0924 (B)] 67-25579
1. Robeson, Paul, 1898- I. Title. II. Title: The American Othello.

ROBESON, Paul, 301.451'96073
1898-
Here I stand. With a pref. by Lloyd L. Brown. Boston, Beacon Press [1971, c1958] xx, 119 p. 21 cm. [E185.97.R62 1971] 70-159847 ISBN 0-8070-6406-8 5.95
I. Title. BIP

ROBESON, Paul, 1898- 790.2'092'4
1976.
Paul Robeson speaks : writings, speeches, interviews, 1918-1974 / edited, with introd. and notes, by Philip S. Foner. Larchmont, N.Y. : Brunner/Mazel, [1978] p. cm. Includes index. Bibliography: p. [E185.97.R63] 78-17590 ISBN 0-87630-179-0 : 17.50
1. Robeson, Paul, 1898-1976. 2. Afro-Americans—Biography. 3. Afro-American arts—Collected works. 4. Afro-Americans—Civil rights—Collected works. 5. Afro-Americans—Politics and suffrage—Collected works. 6. Blacks—Civil rights—Collected works. I. Foner, Philip Sheldon, 1910- II. Title.
Publisher's address: 19 Union Square, New York, N.Y 10003

WRIGHT, Charles 331.88'092'4 B
H., 1918-
Robeson, labor's forgotten champion / Charles H. Wright. Detroit, Mich. : Balamp Pub., [1975] vii, 171 p. : port. ; 24 cm. Includes index. Bibliography: p. 153. [HD8073.R57W74] 74-79061 ISBN 0-913642-06-1 : 7.95
1. Robeson, Paul, 1898- 2. Labor and laboring classes—History. 3. Race discrimination. I. Title.

Robeson, Paul, 1898-1976—Addresses, essays, lectures.

BROWN, Lloyd Louis, 790.2'092'4 B
1913-
Paul Robeson rediscovered / by Lloyd L. Brown. New York : American Institute for Marxist Studies, 1976. 23 p. ; 29 cm. (Occasional paper - American Institute for Marxist Studies ; no. 19) Cover title. "Delivered April 22, 1976, at the National Conference on Paul Robeson, Purdue University, Indiana; under the auspices of the Africana Studies and Research Center." Includes bibliographical references. [E185.97.R633] 76-370705 1.00
1. Robeson, Paul, 1898-1976—Addresses, essays, lectures. 2. Afro-Americans—Biography—Addresses, essays, lectures. I. Title. II. Series: American Institute for Marxist Studies. Occasional paper ; no. 19. BIP

PAUL Robeson, the 790.2'092'4 B
great forerunner / the editors of Freedomways. New York : Dodd, Mead, c1978. x, 383 p., [16] leaves of plates : ill. ; 24 cm. Includes index. Bibliography: p. 329-371. [E185.97.R6475] 78-7917 ISBN 0-396-07545-2 : 12.95
1. Robeson, Paul, 1898-1976—Addresses, essays, lectures 2. Afro-Americans—Biography—Addresses, essays, lectures. I. Freedomways.

Robeson, Paul, 1898- —Juvenile literature.

DU BOIS, Shirley 790.2'0924 B
Graham, 1906-
Paul Robeson, citizen of the world, by Shirley Graham. New York, J. Messner [1971] 264 p. ports. 22 cm. Reprint of the 1946 ed. Bibliography: p. 259. Biography of the actor and singer recognized the world over for his interpretations of various operatic roles. [E185.97.R635 1971] 92 75-160421 ISBN 0-671-32464-0 4.95
1. Robeson, Paul, 1898- —Juvenile literature. I. Title.

DU BOIS, Shirley 790.2'092'4 B
Graham, 1906-
Paul Robeson, citizen of the world, by Shirley Graham. Foreword by Carl Van Doren. Westport, Conn., Negro Universities Press [1971, c1946] 264 p. ports. 23 cm. Bibliography: p. 259. A biography of the actor and singer recognized the world over for his interpretations of various operatic roles. [E185.97.R635 1971b] 92 75-152393 ISBN 0-8371-6055-3 11.00
1. Robeson, Paul, 1898- —Juvenile literature. I. Title.

GREENFIELD, Eloise. 790.2'0924 B
Paul Robeson. Illustrated by George Ford. New York, Crowell [1975] 32 p. illus. 24 cm. (Crowell biographies) A biography of the black man who became a famous singer, actor, and spokesman for equal rights for his people. [E185.97.R642 1975] 92 74-13663 ISBN 0-690-00552-0 4.50
1. Robeson, Paul, 1898- —Juvenile literature. I. Ford, George, fl. 1969- illus. II. Title.
Lib. bdg. 5.25, ISBN 0-690-00660-8. BIP

HAMILTON, Virginia. 790.2'092'4 B
Paul Robeson : the life and times of a free Black man / by Virginia Hamilton. 1st ed. New York : Harper & Row, [1974] xvi, 217 p., [4] leaves of plates : ill. ; 22 cm. Includes index. Bibliography: p. 205-209. A biography of the world famous actor and singer who lost much of his popularity when he became a champion of communism. [E185.97.R643 1974] 92 72-82892 ISBN 0-06-022188-7 : 5.95 ISBN 0-06-022189-5 lib.bdg. : 5.11
1. Robeson, Paul, 1898- —Juvenile literature. I. Title.

HAMILTON, Virginia. 790.2'92'4 B
Paul Robeson : the life and times of a free Black Man / by Virginia Hamilton 1st ed. New York : Dell Pub. Co., 1979, c1974 224p. ; 18 cm. (A Laurel Leaf Book) Bibliography p. 215-218 [E185.97R643 1974] ISBN 0-440-96806-2 pbk. : 1.50
1. Robeson, Paul, 1898-1976 — Juvenile literature. I. Title.
L.C. card no. for1974 Harper & Row ed.: 72-82892 BIP

Robespierre, Maximilien Marie Isidore de, 1758-1794.

BELLOC, Hilaire, 944.04'092'4 B
1870-1953.
Robespierre, a study. Freeport, N.Y., Books for Libraries Press [1972] p. Reprint of the 1901 ed. [DC146.R6B4 1972] 72-8441 ISBN 0-8369-6964-2
1. Robespierre, Maximilien Marie Isidore de, 1758-1794. BIP

EAGAN, James 944.04'092'4 B
Michael, 1909-
Maximilien Robespierre : nationalist dictator / by James Michael Eagan. New York : Octagon Books, 1978, c1938. 242 p. : 24 cm. Originally presented as the author' thesis, Columbia University. Reprint of the ed. published by Columbia University Press, New York, which was issued as no. 437 of Studies in history, economics and public law. Includes index. Bibliography: p. 221-231. [DC146.R6E2 1978] 78-16351 ISBN 0-374-92440-6 lib.bdg. : 12.00
1. Robespierre, Maximilien Marie Isadore de, 1758-1794. 2. Jacobins. 3. Statesmen—France—Biography. I. Series: Columbia studies in the social sciences ; v. 437.

GALLO, Max, 1932- 944.04'0924
Robespierre the incorruptible; a psycho-biography. Translated by Raymond Rudorff. [New York] Herder and Herder [1971] 336 p. 22 cm. Translation of Maximilien Robespierre, histoire d'une solitude. [DC146.R6G3513] 73-147034 8.50
1. Robespierre, Maximilien Marie Isidore de, 1758-1794. I. Title.

MATHIEZ, Albert, 944.04'0924
1874-1932.
The fall of Robespierre, and other essays. The young Robespierre.—Aigoin.—The supreme being.—Catherine Theot.—Herman.—Truchon.—Marcandier.—Fouquier-Tinville.—The 9th Thermidor.—Barere and Vadier.—Babeuf. New York, A. M. Kelley, 1968. xii, 249 p. port. 22 cm. (Reprints of economic classics) Reprint of 1927 ed. Translation of Autour de Robespierre. Bibliographical footnotes. [DC146.R6M3 1968] 68-55329
1. Robespierre, Maximilien Marie Isidore de, 1758-1794. 2. France—History—Revolution, 1789-1799. I. Title.

MATRAT, Jean. 944.04'1'0924 B
Robespierre : or, The tyranny of the majority / Jean Matrat ; translated by Alan Kendall, with Felix Brenner. New York : Scribner, [1975] 296 p. : ill. ; 25 cm. Includes index. [DC146.R6M3513] 74-16891 ISBN 0-684-14055-1 : 12.50
1. Robespierre, Maximilien Marie Isidore de, 1758-1794.

RUDE, George F. 944'.035'0924
E., comp.
Robespierre, edited by George Rude. Englewood Cliffs, N.J., Prentice-Hall [1967] vii, 181 p. 21 cm. (Great lives observed) (A Spectrum book.) "Bibliographical note": p. 179-181. [DC146.R6R8] 67-18696
1. Robespierre, Maximilien Marie Isidore de, 1758-1794.

RUDE, George F. 944.04'1'0924 B
E.
Robespierre : portrait of a Revolutionary Democrat / George Rude. New York : Viking Press, 1976, c1975. 254 p., [6] leaves of plates : ill. ; 25 cm. Includes index. Bibliography: p. 231-234. [DC146.R6R83 1976] 75-2448 ISBN 0-670-60128-4 : 12.50
1. Robespierre, Maximilien Marie Isidore de, 1758-1794. BIP

THOMPSON, James 944.04'0924 B
Matthew, 1878-1956.
Robespierre. [1st American ed.] New York, H Fertig, 1968. 2 v. illus., ports. 24 cm. Reprint of the 1935 ed. Contents.Contents.—v. 1. From the birth of Robespierre to the death of Louis XVI.—v. 2. From the death of Louis XVI to the death of Robespierre. Bibliography: v. 1, p. xv-lv. [DC146.R6T45 1968] 68-9587
1. Robespierre, Maxmilien Marie Isidore de, 1758-1794. 2. France—History—Revolution, 1789-1799. BIP

THOMPSON, James Matthew, v. 12
1878-1956.
Robespierre and the French Revolution. 1st Colliers Books ed. New York, N.Y., Collier Books [1962] 159 p. 18 cm. (Men and history) 63-75540
1. Robespierre, Maximilien Marie Isidore de, 1758-1794. 2. France — Hist. — Revolution, 1789-1794. I. Title. BIP

Robin, 1944-1975.

ROBIN, 1944-1975. 286'.1'0924 B
Don't bury me 'til I'm dead / Robin. Denver : Accent Books, c1977. 128 p. ; 21 cm. [BX6495.R655A32] 76-50299 ISBN 0 916406-61-X : 2.95
1. Robin, 1944-1975. 2. Baptists—Georgia—Biography. 3. Cancer—Biography. 4. Death. I. Title. BIP

Robins, Margaret Dreier.

DREIER, Mary E. 331.88'092'4 B
Margaret Dreier Robins : her life, letters, and work / by Mary E. Dreier. Washington : Zenger Pub. Co., 1975, c1950. p. cm. Reprint of the ed. published by Island Press Cooperative, New York. Includes indexes. [HD6095.R58D7 1975] 75-34239 ISBN 0-89201-016-9
1. Robins, Margaret (Dreier) 2. Women in trade-unions—United States—History.

DREIER, Mary E. 923.373
Margaret Dreier Robins, her life, letters and work. New York, Island Press Cooperative, 1950. xviii, 278 p. illus., ports. 25 cm. [HD6095.R58D7] 50-9743
1. Robins, Margaret Dreier.

Robinson, Alfred S., 1835 or 6-1878.

DEWITT, John Doyle, 737.4'0924 B
1902-
Alfred S. Robinson, Hartford numismatist, by J. Doyle DeWitt. [Hartford] Connecticut Historical Society, 1968. 28 p. illus. 20 cm. Bibliography: p. 28. [CJ62.R6D4] 78-11034
1. Robinson, Alfred S., 1835 or 6-1878.

Robinson, Brooks, 1937-

ZANGER, Jack. 796.3576'4'0924
The Brooks Robinson story. Illustrated with photos. New York, J. Messner [1967] 192 p. illus., ports. 22 cm. [GV865.R58Z3] 67-21612
1. Robinson, Brooks, 1937-

Robinson, Brooks, 1937—Juvenile literature.

BURCHARD, Marshall. 796.357'0924 B
Sports hero: Brooks Robinson, by Marshall and Sue Burchard. New York, Putnam [1972] 77 p. illus. 23 cm. On spine: Brooks Robinson: sports hero. An easy-to-read biography of the Baltimore Orioles' third baseman sometimes called Mr. Impossible. [GV865.R58B8 1972] 92 73-161920 3.69
1. Robinson, Brooks, 1937—Juvenile literature. I. Burchard, Sue, joint author. II. Title. III. Title: Brooks Robinson: sports hero.

Robinson, Charles, 1818-1894.

BLACKMAR, Frank Wilson, 1854-1931. 978.1'03'0924 B
The life of Charles Robinson, the first State Governor of Kansas. Freeport, N.Y., Books for Libraries Press [1971] 438 p. illus. 23 cm. Reprint of the 1901 ed. [F681.R66 1971] 70-169751 ISBN 0-8369-5971-X
1. Robinson, Charles, 1818-1894. 2. Kansas—History—1854-1861. I. Title. BIP

ROBINSON, Charles. 741.64'092'2
Charles & William Heath Robinson / edited by David Larkin ; introduction by Leo John De Freitas. London : Constable, 1976. [16] p., [80] p. of plates : chiefly col. ill. ; 31 cm. [NC978.5.R6L37 1976] 77-354820 ISBN 0-09-461480-6 : £4.95
1. Robinson, Charles. 2. Robinson, William Heath, 1872-1944. I. Robinson, William Heath, 1872-1944, joint author. II. Larkin, David.

WILSON, Don W. 978.1'03'0924 B
Governor Charles Robinson of Kansas / Don W. Wilson. Lawrence : University Press of Kansas, [1975] c1974. ix, 214 p. : port. ; 22 cm. Includes index. Bibliography: p. 192-205. [F685.R648 1975] 75-6875 ISBN 0-7006-0133-3 : 11.00
1. Robinson, Charles, 1818-1894. I. Title. BIP

Robinson, Dorothy Redus.

ROBINSON, Dorothy Redus. 371.1'0092'4 B
The bell rings at four : a Black teacher's chronicle of change / by Dorothy Redus Robinson. 1st ed. Austin, Tex. : Madrona Press, c1978. x, 142 p., [16] leaves of plates : ill. ; 24 cm. [LA2315.T42R627] 78-61472 ISBN 0-89052-024-0 : 11.00
1. Robinson, Dorothy Redus. 2. Afro-American teachers—Texas—Biography. 3. Afro-Americans—Education—Texas. I. Title. BIP

Robinson, Edward G., 1893-1973.

•HIRSCH, Foster. 791.43'028'0924 B
Edward G. Robinson. New York, Pyramid, [1975] 158 p. ill. 20 cm. (Pyramid illustrated history of the movies.) Includes index. "Films of Edward G. Robinson" p. 145-153. Bibliography: p. 143. [PN2287] 75-613 ISBN 0-515-03642-0 1.75 (pbk.)
1. Robinson, Edward G., 1893-1973. 2. Moving-pictures—Biography. 3. Moving picture actors and actresses. I. Sennett, Ted. ed. II. Title. BIP

ROBINSON, Edward G., 1893-1973. 791.43'028'0924 B
All my yesterdays; an autobiography [by] Edward G. Robinson, with Leonard Spigelgass. New York, Hawthorn Books [1973] 344 p. illus. 25 cm. [PN2287.R67A295] 73-5443 10.00
1. Robinson, Edward G., 1893-1973. I. Spigelgass, Leonard. II. Title.

ROBINSON, Edward G 1933- 927.92
My father, my son, an autobiography, by Edward G. Robinson, Jr., with William Dufty, based on an idea by N. Peter Dee. New York, F. Fell [1958] 316p. illus. 22cm. [PN2287.R67A3] 57-14113
1. Robinson, Edward G., 1898- I. Title.

ROBINSON, Edward G 1933- 927.92
My father, my son, an autobiography, by Edward G. Robinson, Jr., with William Dufty, based on an idea by N. Peter Dee. New York, F. Fell [1958] 316p. illus. 22cm. [PN2287.R67A3] 57-14113
1. Robinson, Edward G., 1898- I. Title.

Robinson, Edward, 1794-1863.

†HITCHCOCK, Roswell Dwight, 1817-1887. 285'.8'0924 B
The life, writings, and character of Edward Robinson / Henry Boynton Smith and Roswell D. Hitchcock. New York : Arno Press, 1977, [c1863]. 100 p. ; 21 cm. (America and the Holy Land) Reprint of the ed. published by A. D. F. Randolph, New York. [BX7260.R62H5 1977] 77-70744 ISBN 0-405-10290-9 : 12.00
1. Robinson, Edward, 1794-1863. 2. Congregationalists—United States—Biography. I. Smith, Henry Boynton, 1815-1877, joint author. II. Title. III. Series. BIP

Robinson, Edwin Arlington, 1869-1935.

COXE, Louis Osborne, 1918- 811.52
Edwin Arlington Robinson. Minneapolis, University of Minnesota Press [1962] 48 p. 21 cm. (University of Minnesota pamphlets on American writers, no. 17) Includes bibliography. [PS3535.O25Z63] 62-62785
1. Robinson, Edwin Arlington, 1869-1935.

FRANCHERE, Hoyt C. 811'.9'12 B
Edwin Arlington Robinson, by Hoyt. C. Franchere. New York, Twayne Publishers [1968] 161 p. 21 cm. (Twayne's United States authors series, 137) Includes bibliographical references. [PS3535.O25Z657] 68-24295
1. Robinson, Edwin Arlington, 1869-1935.

NEFF, Emery Edward, 1892- 811'.5'2
Edwin Arlington Robinson [by] Emery Neff. New York, Russell & Russell [1968, c1948] 286p. port. 23cm. Bibl. refs. [PS3535.O25Z74 1968] (B) 68-25046 10.00
1. Robinson, Edwin Arlington, 1869-1935. I. Title.

REDMAN, Ben Ray, 1896-1961. 811'.5'2
Edwin Arlington Robinson. New York, Haskell House Publishers [1974, c1926] p. Reprint of the ed. published by R. M. McBride, New York. [PS3535.O25Z8 1974] 74-1444 ISBN 0-8383-2045-7 9.95
1. Robinson, Edwin Arlington, 1869-1935. BIP

RICHARDS, Laura Elizabeth (Howe) 1850-1943. 811'.5'2 B
E. A. R. New York, Russell & Russell [1967, c1936] 61 p. port. 20 cm. [PS3535.O25Z82 1967] 66-27140
1. Robinson, Edwin Arlington, 1869-1935. I. Title.

ROBINSON, Edwin Arlington, 1869-1935. 811'.5'2 B
Untriangulated stars; letters of Edwin Arlington Robinson to Harry de Forest Smith, 1890-1905. Edited by Denham Sutcliffe. Westport, Conn., Greenwood Press [1971, c1947] xxvii, 348 p. facsims., ports. 23 cm. Includes bibliographical references. [PS3535.O25Z54 1971] 76-113064 ISBN 0-8371-4704-2
1. Smith, Harry de Forest, 1869-1943. II. Sutcliffe, Denham, 1913- ed. III. Title. BIP

ROBINSON, William Ronald. 811'.5'2
Edwin Arlington Robinson; a poetry of the act [by] W. R. Robinson. [Cleveland] Press of Western Reserve University, 1967. 183 p. 24 cm. Bibliographical references included in "Notes" (p. 167-177) [PS3535.O25Z83] 67-11484
1. Robinson, Edwin Arlington, 1869-1935.

SMITH, Chard Powers, 1894- 928.1
Where the light falls; a portrait of Edwin Arlington Robinson. New York, Macmillan [1965] xx, 420 p. illus., ports. 22 cm. Bibliographical references included in "Notes" (p. 391-408) [PS3535.O25Z85] 65-11479
1. Robinson, Edwin Arlington, 1869-1935. I. Title.

VAN DOREN, Mark, 1894-1972 811'.5'2 B
Edwin Arlington Robinson / by Mark Van Doren. New York : Haskell House, [1976] c1927. p. cm. Reprint of the ed. published by Literary Guild of America, New York. Bibliography: p. [PS3535.O25Z9 1976] 75-30816 ISBN 0-8383-2103-8 lib.bdg. : 9.95
1. Robinson, Edwin Arlington, 1869-1935. BIP

Robinson, Elsie Anne (LeBeau)

KNOX, Olive Elsie. 920.7
Mrs. Minister. Philadelphia, Westminster Press [1956] 190p. 21cm. [CT275.R735K6] 56-5248
1. Robinson, Elsie Anne (LeBeau) I. Title.

Robinson, Frank, 1935-

ROBINSON, Frank, 1935- 796.357'0924 B
My life is baseball, by Frank Robinson with Al Silverman [1st ed.] Garden City, N.Y., Doubleday, 1968. 225 p. ports. 22 cm. [GV865.R59A3] 67-22442
1. Robinson, Frank, 1935- 2. Baseball. I. Silverman, Al, joint author. II. Title.

ROBINSON, Frank, 1935- 796.357'092'4 B
My life is baseball / by Frank Robinson, with Al Silverman. Garden City, N.Y. : Doubleday, [1975] c1968. 237 p., [4] leaves of plates : ports. ; 22 cm. [GV865.R59A3 1975] 74-33224 ISBN 0-385-05709-1 : 6.95
1. Robinson, Frank, 1935- 2. Baseball. I. Silverman, Al, joint author. II. Title.

SCHNEIDER, Russell J. 796.357'092'4 B
Frank Robinson : Russell J. Schneider. by Russell J. Schneider. New York : Coward, McCann & Geoghegan, c1976. 245 p. : ill. ; 22 cm. [GV865.R59S36 1976] 75-43864 ISBN 0-698-10731-4 : 8.95
1. Robinson, Frank, 1935- 2. Baseball. 3. Baseball managing.

Robinson, Frank, 1935- —Juvenile literature.

HIRSHBERG, Albert, 1909-1973. 796.357'092'4 B
Frank Robinson; born leader. New York, Putnam [1973] 191 p. port. 22 cm. (Putnam sports shelf) A biography of baseball star Frank Robinson emphasizing his careers with the Cincinnati Reds and the Baltimore Orioles. [GV865.R59H57 1973] 92 72-94266 ISBN 0-399-20337-0 4.89
1. Robinson, Frank, 1935- —Juvenile literature. I. Title.

YOUNG, Bernice Elizabeth. 796.357'092'4 B
The picture story of Frank Robinson / by B. E. Young ; illustrated with photos. New York : J. Messner, [1975] 60 p. : ill. ; 23 cm. A brief biography of the baseball star who in 1974 became major league baseball's first black manager. [GV865.R59Y68] 92 75-2236 ISBN 0-671-32736-4 lib.bdg. : 5.29 ISBN 0-671-32737-2 pbk. : 1.95
1. Robinson, Frank, 1935- —Juvenile literature. 2. Baseball—Juvenile literature. I. Title.

Robinson, George K., 1819-1902.

GAINES, Charles Kelsey, 1854-1943. 378.1'011'0924 B
George K. Robinson, 1819-1902; a memoir. [Schenectady, N.Y., 1970] 8 p. port. 18 cm. Previously published in The Laurentian, v. 15, no. 2, Feb. 1902. [LD4817.S313R65 1970] 75-135503
1. Robinson, George K., 1819-1902.

ROBINSON, Henry Crabb, 1775-1867. 928.2
The diary of Henry Crabb Robinson: an abridgement; edited with an introduction by Derek Hudson. London, New York [etc.] Oxford U.P., 1967. xix, 348 p. front. (port.), plate (port.). 22 1/2 cm. Unabridged ed. originally published as Henry Crabb Robinson on books and their writers. London, Dent, 1938. Bibliography: p. 319-320. [PR5233.R2A83] 828'.7'08 67-86319
1. Authors—Correspondence, reminiscences, etc. 2. Great Britain.—Intellectual life—19th century. I. Hudson, Derek, ed. II. Title.

Robinson, Henry Crabb, 1775-1867.

MORLEY, Edith Julia, 1875- 828'.7'08
The life and times of Henry Crabb Robinson, by Edith J. Morley. New York, AMS Press [1970, c1966] ix, 212 p. illus., facsims., ports. 23 cm. Reprint of the 1935 ed. [PR5233.R2M7 1970] 71-115396
1. Robinson, Henry Crabb, 1775-1867. I. Title. BIP

Robinson, James Herman.

ROBINSON, James Herman. 922.573
Road without turning, the story of Reverend James H. Robinson; an autobiography. New York, Farrar, Straus [1950] 312 p. 21 cm. [BX9225.R715A3] 50-9789
I. Title.

Robinson, Jay, 1930-

ROBINSON, Jay, 1930- 248'.24 B
The comeback / Jay Robinson, as told to Jim Hardiman. Lincoln, Va. : Chosen Book ; Waco, Tex. : distributed by Word Books, c1979. 251 p. : ill. ; 24 cm. [BV4935.R573A32] 78-31489 ISBN 0-912376-45-7 : 59.50
1. Robinson, Jay, 1930- 2. Converts—United States—Biography. I. Hardiman, James W., joint author. II. Title. BIP

Robinson, Jill, 1936- —Biography.

ROBINSON, Jill, 1936- FIC
Bed/time/story. [1st ed.] New York, Random House [1974] 307 p. 22 cm. [PS3562.O2898Z52] 813'.5'4 B 74-8578 ISBN 0-394-48803-2 7.95
1. Robinson, Jill, 1936- —Biography. I. Title. BIP

Robinson, Joan G.

ROBINSON, Joan G. juv
Dear Teddy Robinson, written and illustrated by Joan G. Robinson. Baltimore, Penguin Books [1966, c1960] 105 p. illus. 20 cm. (Puffin books, PS272) [PZ8.9.R6De3] 66-31473
I. Title. BIP

Robinson, John Roosevelt,

ROBINSON, John 927.96537
Roosevelt, 1919-
Breakthrough to the big leagues; the story of Jackie Robinson, by Jackie Robinson and Alfred Duckett. New York, Harper & Row [1965] xiii, 178 p. ports. 22 cm. (A Breakthrough book) [GV865.R6A27] 64-19719
1. Duckett, Alfred. II. Title.

ROBINSON, John 927.96357
Roosevelt, 1919-1972.
Breakthrough to the big league; the story of Jackie Robinson, by Jackie Robinson and Alfred Duckett. New York, Harper & Row [1965] xiii, 178 p. ports. 22 cm. (A Breakthrough book) [GV865.R6A27] 64-19719
I. Duckett, Alfred. II. Title.

Robinson, John Roosevelt, 1919-1972.

MANN, Arthur William, 927.96357
1901-
The Jackie Robinson story. New York, F. J. Low Co. [1950] 120 p. ports. 19 cm. [GV865.R6M3] 50-4371
1. Robinson, John Roosevelt, I. Title.

MANN, Arthur William, 927.96357
1901-
The Jackie Robinson story. New York, Grosset & Dunlap [1951] 224 p. ports. 20 cm (The Big league baseball library) [GV865.R6M3 1951] 51-3786
1. Robinson, John Roosevelt, I. Title.

MANN, Arthur William, 927.96357
1901-
The Jackie Robinson story. New York, Grosset & Dunlap [1956] 253p. illus. 20cm. (The Big league baseball library) [GV865.R6M3 1956] 56-4193
1. Robinson, John Roosevelt, 1919- I. Title. II. Series.

ROBINSON, John 927.96537
Roosevelt, 1919-
Breakthrough to the big leagues; the story of Jackie Robinson, by Jackie Robinson and Alfred Duckett. New York, Harper & Row [1965] xiii, 178 p. ports. 22 cm. (A Breakthrough book) [GV865.R6A27] 64-19719
I. Duckett, Alfred. II. Title.

ROBINSON, John 927.96357
Roosevelt, 1919-1972.
Breakthrough to the big league; the story of Jackie Robinson, by Jackie Robinson and Alfred Duckett. New York, Harper & Row [1965] xiii, 178 p. ports. 22 cm. (A Breakthrough book) [GV865.R6A27] 64-19719
I. Duckett, Alfred. II. Title.

ROBINSON, John 796.357'092'4
Roosevelt, 1919-1972.
I never had it made, by Jackie Robinson as told to Alfred Duckett. New York, Putnam [1972] 287 p. 22 cm. [GV865.R6A29 1972] 75-175272 ISBN 0-399-11010-0 7.95
1. Negroes. I. Duckett, Alfred. II. Title.
BIP

ROBINSON, John 796.357'092'4
Roosevelt, 1919-1972.
I never had it made, by Jackie Robinson as told to Alfred Duckett. Greenwich, Conn., Fawcett [1974, c1972] 256 p. 18 cm. (Fawcett world library) [GV865.R6A29 1974] 75-175272 1.25 (pbk.)
1. Negroes. I. Duckett, Alfred. II. Title.

ROWAN, Carl Thomas. 927.96357
Wait till next year; the life story of Jackie Robinson, by Carl T. Rowan with Jackie Robinson. New York, Random House [1960] 339 p. illus. 24 cm. [GV865.R6R64] 60-5566
1. Robinson, John Roosevelt, 1919- I. Title.

SHAPIRO, Milton J. 927.96357
Jackie Robinson of the Brooklyn Dodgers. New York, J. Messner [1957] 190 p. illus. 22 cm. [GV865.R6S5] 57-11511
1. Robinson, John Roosevelt, 1910- I. Title.
BIP

SHAPIRO, Milton J. 927.96357
Jackie Robinson of the Brooklyn Dodgers. New York, J. Messner [1957] 190 p. illus. 22 cm. [GV865.R6S5] 57-11511
1. Robinson, John Roosevelt, 1919-

SHAPIRO, Milton 796.3576'4'0924
J.
Jackie Robinson of the Brooklyn Dodgers, by Milton J. Shapiro. [Rev.] New York, Messner [1966] 191 p. illus., ports. 22 cm. [GV865.R6S5 1966] 65-25300
1. Robinson, John Roosevelt, 1919-

SHAPIRO, Milton J. 796.357'092'4
Jackie Robinson of the Brooklyn Dodgers, by Milton J. Shapiro. New York, J. Messner [1973] 192 p. illus. 22 cm. [GV865.R6S5 1973] 73-154195 ISBN 0-671-32603-1 4.29
1. Robinson, John Roosevelt, 1919-1972. I. Title.

Robinson, John Roosevelt, 1919-1972—Juvenile literature.

ELDRED, Patricia 796.357'092'4 B
Mulrooney.
Jackie Robinson / written by Patricia Mulrooney Eldred ; illustrated by Harold Henriksen. Mankato, Minn. : Creative Education, [1976] p. cm. A biography of the first black man to play major league baseball, who devoted the last fifteen years of his life to bettering the conditions of his people. [GV865.R6E42] 76-5814 ISBN 0-87191-276-7
1. Robinson, John Roosevelt, 1919-1972—Juvenile literature. 2. Baseball—Juvenile literature. I. Henriksen, Harold. II. Title.

EPSTEIN, Samuel, 796.357'092'4 B
1909-
Jackie Robinson: baseball's gallant fighter, by Sam and Beryl Epstein. Illustrated by Victor Mays. Champaign, Ill., Garrard Pub. Co. [1974] 96 p. illus. (part col.) 24 cm. Brief biography of the baseball star who was the first black player to be accepted by a major league team. [GV865.R6E67] 92 74-4499 ISBN 0-8116-6668-9 4.25
1. Robinson, John Roosevelt, 1919-1972—Juvenile literature. 2. Baseball—Juvenile literature. I. Epstein, Beryl Williams, 1910- joint author. II. Mays, Victor, 1927- illus. III. Title.

JOHNSON, Spencer. 796.357'092'4 B
The value of courage : the story of Jackie Robinson / by Spencer Johnson ; illustrated by Pileggi. 1st ed. La Jolla, Calif. : Value Communications, c1977. 64 p. : col. ill.; 29 cm. (ValueTales) A biography, stressing the courage, of the first black player in professional baseball. [GV865.R6J64] 77-8865 ISBN 0-916392-12-0 : 4.95
1. Robinson, John Roosevelt, 1919-1972—Juvenile literature. 2. Baseball players—United States—Biography—Juvenile literature. I. Title.
BIP

OLSEN, James T. 796.357'092'4 B
Jackie Robinson; pro ball's first Black star, by James T. Olsen. Illustrated by Harold Henriksen. Mankato, Minn., Creative Education; distributed by Childrens Press, Chicago [1974] 29 p. illus. (part col.) 25 cm. (Creative's superstars) A biography of the Negro whose distinguished baseball career inspired blacks everywhere and whose "cool" on the playing field helped open the door to other black athletes. [GV865.R6O38] 92 73-12437 ISBN 0-87191-276-7 4.95
1. Robinson, John Roosevelt, 1919-1972—Juvenile literature. I. Henriksen, Harold, illus. II. Title.

RUDEEN, Kenneth. 920
Jackie Robinson. Illus. by Richard Cuffari. New York, Thomas Y. Crowell [1973, c.1971] 40 p. illus. (pt. col.) 20 x 22 cm. (Crowell Crocodile) (Crowell biographies) [GV865.R6R8] 75-139100 ISBN 0-690-00208-4 0.95 (pbk.)
1. Robinson, John Roosevelt, 1919-Juvenile literature. I. Cuffari, Richard, 1925- illus. II. Title.
BIP

Robinson, Nelson Lemuel, 1857-1944.

ROBINSON, Ernest 340'.092'4 B
Leffert, 1911-
Nelson Lemuel Robinson, 1857-1944 / by his son, Ernest Leffert Robinson. Schenectady, N.Y. : Robinson, c1977. 14 p. : port. ; 19 cm. [KF373.R554R6] 77-89143
1. Robinson, Nelson Lemuel, 1857-1944. 2. Lawyers—New York (State)—Biography. I. Title.

Robinson, Peter, b. 1821.

ROBINSON, Joe, 796.8'3'0922 B
1937-
Claret and cross-buttock, or, Rafferty's prize-fighters / [by] Joe Robinson. London : Allen and Unwin, 1976. 3-151 p., [4] p. of plates. : ill., ports. ; 23 cm. ist. by Allen & Unwin 198 Ash St. Reading, Mass 01867 [GV1131.R6] 77-354084 ISBN 0-04-920048-8 : 11.50
1. Robinson, Peter, b. 1821. 2. Raffety family. 3. Boxers (Sports)—Biography. I. Title. II. Series.

Robinson, Ray, 1920-

ROBINSON, Ray, 796.8'3'0924 B
May3,1920-
Sugar Ray [by] Sugar Ray Robinson with Dave Anderson. New York, Viking Press [1970] 376 p. 22 cm. [GV1132.R6A3] 69-18799 6.95
1. Boxing—Biography. I. Anderson, Dave, joint author. II. Title.

SCHOOR, Gene. 927.9683
Sugar Ray Robinson. New York, Greenberg [1951] 119 p. illus. 20 cm. [GV1132.R6S35] 51-12109
1. Robinson, Ray, 1920- I. Title.

Robinson, Renault.

†MCCLORY, Robert, 363.2'09773'11
1932-
The man who beat clout city / Robert McClory. 1st ed. Chicago : Swallow Press, c1977. ix, 224 p., [4] leaves of plates : ill. ; 23 cm. Includes index. [HV7911.R62M3] 77-88692 ISBN 0-8040-0777-2 : 9.95
1. Robinson, Renault. 2. Chicago—Police—Biography. 3. Discrimination in employment—Illinois—Chicago. I. Title.
BIP

[Robinson, Reuben]

[ROBINSON, Reuben] 1860- 922.773
1942
Sunshine and smiles, life story, flash lights, sayings and sermons by [Rev.] Bud Robinson [2d ed.] Niles, Mich., Newby Bk. Room, 563 No. Clark St. [1963] 191p. illus. 20cm. 1.50
I. Title.

Robinson, Robbie.

ROBINSON, Robbie, 942.082'092'4 B
1909-
Give it a bloody go, mate! / [by] Robbie Robinson. Adelaide : Rigby, 1976. 193 p. : ill. ; 19 cm. (Seal books) [CT788.R524A33 1976] 77-366984 ISBN 0-7270-0083-7 : 2.25
1. Robinson, Robbie. 2. England—Biography. I. Title.

Robinson, Robert, Sir, 1886-1975.

ROBINSON, Robert, 547'.0092'4 B
Sir, 1886-1975.
Memoirs of a minor prophet : 70 years of organic chemistry / Sir Robert Robinson. Amsterdam ; New York : Elsevier, 1976- v. : ill. ; 24 cm. Autobiographical. "List of original memoirs, scientific papers, some letters ... relevant to the content of this volume": v. 1, p. 240-252. [QD22.R63A35 1976] 76-473928 ISBN 0-444-41459-2 (American Elsevier) (v. 1) : 19.95
1. Robinson, Robert, Sir, 1886-1975. 2. Chemists—Biography. I. Title.

Robinson, Roland E.—Biography.

ROBINSON, Roland E. 821 B
The drift of things: an autobiography, 1914-52 [by] Roland Robinson. Melbourne, Macmillan of Australia, 1973. 481 p. 23 cm. [PR9619.3.R594Z52] 74-173888 ISBN 0-333-13943-7 9.50
1. Robinson, Roland E.—Biography. I. Title.

ROBINSON, Roland E. 821 B
The shift of sands : an autobiography, 1952-62 / [by] Roland Robinson. South Melbourne, Vic. : Macmillan, 1976. 375 p. ; 23 cm. [PR9619.3.R594Z525] 77-351066 ISBN 0-333-21002-6
1. Robinson, Roland E.—Biography. 2. Authors, Australian—20th century—Biography. I. Title.

Robinson, Virgil E

ROBINSON, Virgil E 920
Those adventurous years. Illustrated by Harry Baerg Nashville, Southern Pub. Association [c1959] 175p. illus. 22cm. Autobiographical. [CT275.R743A3] 60-917
I. Title.

Robinson, William Wilcox, 1891- —Bio-bibliography.

HICKS, Jimmie. 016.91794'03'5
W. W. Robinson; a biography and a bibliography. Foreword by Lawrence Clark Powell. Los Angeles, W. Ritchie Press, 1970. xi, 83 p. illus., ports. 25 cm. [E175.5.R7H5] 77-127647
1. Robinson, William Wilcox, 1891- —Bio-bibliography.

Robsky, Paul

ROBSKY, Paul 920.9
The last of the Untouchables [by] Oscar Fraley, Paul Robsky. New York, Popular Lib. [c.1962] 183p. (Popular Library eagle bks., G569) .35 pap.,
I. Fraley, Oscar, 1914- II. Title.

Robson, Elizabeth.

ROBSON, Elizabeth. 081
Seems but yesterday. Philadelphia, Dorrance [1972] 54 p. 22 cm. Autobiographical. [CT275.R745A3] 76-184134 ISBN 0-8059-1659-8 3.95
I. Title.

Rochambeau, Jean Baptiste Donatien de Vimeur, comte de, 1725-1807.

WHITRIDGE, Arnold, 1891- 355.3320924
Rochambeau, by Arnold Whitridge. New York, Macmillan [1965] 340 p. illus., maps, ports. 21 cm. Includes bibliographical references. [E265.R69] 65-21462
1. Rochambeau, Jean Baptiste Donatien de Vimeur, comte de, 1725-1807. I. U.S. — Hist. — Revolution — French participation. II. Title. BIP

Rochester, Devereaux.

ROCHESTER, Devereaux. 940.53'44
Full moon to France / Devereaux Rochester. 1st ed. New York : Harper & Row, c1977. 261 p. ; 22 cm. [D802.F8R5837 1977] 76-26250 ISBN 0-06-013586-7 : 8.95
1. Rochester, Devereaux. 2. World War, 1939-1945—Underground movements—France—Biography. 3. World War, 1939-1945—Personal narrative, American. 4. Guerillas—France—Biography. I. Title. BIP

Rochester, John Wilmot, 2d earl of, 1647-1680.

DOBREE, Bonamy, 1891- 821'.4 B
Rochester; a conversation between Sir George Etherege and Mr. Fitzjames. [Folcroft, Pa.] Folcroft Library Editions, 1973. p. Reprint of the 1926 ed. published by L. and V. Woolf, London, which was issued as no. 2 of The Hogarth essays. Second series. [DA447.R6D6 1973] 73-13531 6.50
1. Rochester, John Wilmot, 2d earl of, 1647-1680. 2. Etherege, George, Sir, 1635?-1691. 3. Berwick, James Fitz-James, 1st duke of, 1670-1734.

PINTO, Vivian de Sola, 1895- 821'.4 B
Rochester: portrait of a restoration poet. Freeport, N.Y., Books for Libraries Press [1971] xxii, 294 p. illus. 23 cm. Reprint of the 1935 ed. Bibliography: p. 265-268. [PR3669.R2P5 1971] 73-175707 ISBN 0-8369-6622-8
1. Rochester, John Wilmot, 2d Earl of, 1647-1680. I. Title.

Rock music.

*PATON, Tam. 784'.092'4 B
The Bay City Rollers. [by] Tam Paton with Michael Wale. [New York] Berkley Publishing Corp. [1975] 154 p. illus. 18 cm. [ML420] ISBN 0-425-03044-X 0.95 (pbk.)
1. Rock music. I. Wale, Michael, joint author. II. Title. BIP

Rock music—Bio-bibliography.

THE Age of rock "n" roll 784 S / edited by Phil Hardy and Dave Laing. St. Albans [Eng.] : Panther, 1976. 352 p. ; 18 cm. (The encyclopedia of rock ; v. 1) Includes index. [ML102.P66E55 vol. 1] 784 77-368390 ISBN 0-586-04267-9 : £0.95
1. Rock music—Bio-bibliography. 2. Rock music—Dictionaries. I. Hardy, Phil. II. Laing, Dave. III. Title. IV. Series.

THE Encyclopedia of rock / 784 edited by Phil Hardy and Dave Laing. St. Albans [Eng.] : Panther, 1976- v. ; 18 cm. Includes index. [ML102.P66E55] 77-368391 ISBN 0-586-04267-9 (v. 1) : £0.95 (v. 1)
1. Rock music—Bio-bibliography. 2. Rock Music—Dictionaries. I. Hardy, Phil. II. Laing, Dave.

NITE, Norm N. 784.0922
Rock on : the illustrated encyclopedia of rock n' roll; the solid gold years / Norm N. Nite; special introduction by Dick Clark New York : Popular Library ,1977 c1974 [unpaged] 676 p. : ill. ; 18 cm. [ML105.N49] ISBN 0-445-08556-8 pbk. : 2.95
1. Rock music—Bio-bibliography. I. Title.
L.C. card no. for 1974 T. Y. Crowell edition: 74-12247. BIP

Rock music—United States—History and criticism.

MARCUS, Greil. 784
Mystery train : images of America in rock 'n' roll music / Greil Marcus. 1st ed. New York : E. P. Dutton, 1975. xii, 275 p. ; 22 cm. Includes index. Discography: p. 213-268. [ML3561.R62M35] 74-20813 8.95
1. Rock music—United States—History and criticism. 2. United States—Popular culture. 3. Rock musicians—Biography. I. Title. BIP

Rock musicians.

ADLER, Bill, ed. 927.8
Love letters to the Beatles. Illustrated by Osborn. New York, Putnam [1964] 1 v. (unpaged illus. 15 cm. [ML286.5.A3] 64-24561
I. The Beatles. II. Title.

GURALNICK, Peter. 785.4'2'0922 B
Feel like going home; portraits in blues & rock n' roll. New York, Outerbridge & Dienstfrey [1971] 224 p. ports. 22 cm. "A Fusion book." Bibliography: p. [219]-222. [ML385.G95] 70-174733 ISBN 0-87690-046-5 6.95
1. Rock musicians. I. Title.

LYDON, Michael. 784'.0922 B
Rock folk; portraits from the rock'n' roll pantheon. New York, Dial Press, 1971. 200 p. illus., ports. 22 cm. [ML394.L96] 71-131179 6.95
1. Rock musicians. I. Title.

ORLOFF, Katherine. 784'.092'2
Rock 'n' roll woman / by Katherine Orloff. Los Angeles : Nash Pub., [1974]. 199 p. : ports. ; 28 cm. Interviews with Nicoel Barclay, Toni Brown, Rita Coolidge, and others. [ML3561.R62O7] 73-93974 ISBN 0-8402-8077-7 : 6.95
1. Rock musicians. 2. Women as musicians—United States. I. Title.

RIVELLI, Pauline, comp. 784'.0922 B
The rock giants. Edited by Pauline Rivelli and Robert Levin. New York, World Pub. Co. [1970] 125 p. ports. 22 cm. ([Jazz & pop book series]) [ML385.R592] 73-133475 5.95
1. Rock musicians. 2. Music, Popular (Songs, etc.)—History and criticism. I. Title.

Rock musicians—Biography.

DALTON, David. 784'.092'2 B
Rock 100 / David Dalton and Lenny Kaye New York : Grosset & Dunlap, c1977. 280 p. : ill. ; 28 cm. Includes index. [ML385.D24] 74-27945 ISBN 0-448-12228-6 : 17.95 ISBN 0-448-12240-5 pbk. : 8.95
1. Rock musicians—Biography. I. Kaye, Lenny, joint author. II. Title.

KATZ, Susan. 784'.092'2 B
Superwomen of rock / by Susan Katz. New York : Tempo Books, c1978. 134 p., [6] leaves of plates : ill. ; 18 cm. Contents.Contents.—Debby Boone.—Rita Coolidge.—Olivia Newton-John.—Linda Ronstadt.—Stevie Nicks.—Carly Simon. Includes discographies. [ML400.K33] 79-116055 ISBN 0-448-16254-7 pbk. : 1.50
1. Rock musicians—Biography. 2. Women singers—Biography. I. Title. BIP

ROCK life / 784'.092'2 B [editor and designer Gavin Petrie]. London ; New York : Hamlyn, 1974. 128 p. : ports. (some col.) ; 29 cm. [ML385.R73] 75-309706 ISBN 0-600-38708-9 : £1.95
1. Rock musicians—Biography. 2. Rock music—Great Britain—Addresses, essays, lectures. I. Petrie, Gavin.

SPITZ, Robert Stephen. 784'.092'2
The making of superstars : artists and executives of the rock music business / by Robert Stephen Spitz. 1st ed. Garden City, N.Y. : Anchor Press, 1978. xx, 325 p. ; 22 cm. Includes index. [ML385.S64] 76-56338 ISBN 0-385-12413-9 : 8.95
1. Rock musicians—Biography. 2. Music trade—United States. I. Title.

Rock musicians—United States—Biography.

MCCOLM, Bruce. 784'.092'2 B
Where have they gone? : rock'n'roll stars / by Bruce McColm & Doug Payne. New York : Tempo Books, c1979. 254 p. : ill. ; 18 cm. [ML400.M24] 79-114876 ISBN 0-448-17025-6 : 1.95
1. Rock musicians—United States—Biography. I. Payne, Doug, joint author. II. Title.

Rockefeller, Abby Greene (Aldrich)

CHASE, Mary Ellen, 1887- 920.7
Abby Aldrich Rockefeller. New York, Macmillan, 1950. 159 p. ports. 22 cm. [CT275.R747C48] 50-9582
1. Rockefeller, Abby Greene (Aldrich) I. Title.

ROCKEFELLER, Abby Greene (Aldrich) 920.7
Abby Aldrich Rockefeller's letters to her sister Lucy. New York, c1957. 328p. 24cm. [CT275.R747A42] 57-2277
I. Aldrich, Lucy Truman. II. Title.

Rockefeller, David, 1915-

HOFFMAN, William, 1937- 332.1'0924 B
David. New York, L. Stuart [1971] 192 p. 25 cm. [HG2463.R6H6] 76-124504 5.95
1. Rockefeller, David, 1915- 2. Chase Manhattan Bank, New York. I. Title.

Rockefeller family.

COLLIER, Peter. 973.9'092'2 B
The Rockefellers : by Peter Collier and David Horowitz. Peter Collier and David Horowitz. 1st ed. New York : Holt, Rinehart and Winston, c1976. 746 p., [16] leaves of plates : ill. ; 24 cm. Includes bibliographical references and index. [E747.C64] 75-5465 ISBN 0-03-008371-0 : 15.00
1. Rockefeller family. I. Horowitz, David, 1939- joint author. II. Title.

KUTZ, Myer. 361.7'4'0922
Rockefeller power. New York, Simon and Schuster [1974] 288 p. 22 cm. Bibliography: p. 269-274. [E747.K87] 73-21050 ISBN 0-671-21718-6 7.95
1. Rockefeller family. I. Title. BIP

MANCHESTER, William Raymond, 1922- 929.2
A Rockefeller family portrait, from John D. to Nelson. [1st ed.] Boston, Little, Brown [1959] 184 p. illus. 22 cm. [E747.M33] 59-8440
1. Rockefeller family.

MORRIS, Joe Alex, 1904- 923.373
Those Rockefeller brothers; an infromal biography of five extraoridinary young men. [1st ed.] New York, Harper [c1953] 275p. 22cm. [E747.M74] 52-11692
1. Rockefeller family. I. Title.

PYLE, Tom 923.373
Pocantico; fifty years on the Rockefeller domain. Observed by Tom Pyle and told to Beth Day. New York, Duell [dist. Meredith, c.1964] 240p. illus., geneal. table, col. map (on lining papers) ports. 24cm. [CS71R67] 64-24480 6.95 bds.,
1. Rockefeller family. I. Day, Beth (Feagles) 1924- II. Title.

SILVERBERG, Robert 929.2
The fabulous Rockefellers; a compelling, personalized account of one of America's first families. Derby, Conn., Monarch [1963] 157p. 19cm. (Select bks., K68) Bibl. 63-1101 .50 pap.,
1. Rockefeller family. I. Title.

Rockefeller, John Davison, 1839-1937.

ABELS, Jules, 1913- 923.373
The Rockefeller billions; the story of the world's most stupendous fortune. New York, Macmillan [1965] xiii, 386 p. illus., facsims., ports. 22 cm. Bibliography: p. 356-370. [HD2769.O4A62] 65-13877
1. Rockefeller, John Davison, 1839-1937. I. Title.

CARR, Albert H. Z. 923.373
John D. Rockefeller's secret weapon. [1st ed.] New York, McGraw-Hill [1962] 383 p. 22 cm. [CT275.R75C3] 62-10598
1. Rockefeller, John Davison, 1839-1937. 2. Union Tank Car Company. I. Title.

FLYNN, John Thomas, 1883-1964. 338.7'62'233820924 B
God's gold; the story of Rockefeller and his times. Westport, Conn., Greenwood Press [1971, c1932] ix, 520 p. illus. 23 cm. Bibliography: p. 489-508. [CT275.R75F6 1971] 78-138231 ISBN 0-8371-5588-6
1. Rockefeller, John Davison, 1839-1937. 2. Standard Oil Company. I. Title. BIP

IZANT, Grace (Goulder) 338.7'62'233820924 B
John D. Rockefeller; the Cleveland years, by Grace Goulder. [1st ed.] Cleveland, Western Reserve Historical Society, 1972 [c1973] xiii, 271 p. illus. 23 cm. (Western Reserve Historical Society publication no. 126) Bibliography: p. 256-262. [HD9570.R6I9] 72-92688 ISBN 0-911704-09-4 7.95
1. Rockefeller, John Davison, 1839-1937. I. Title. II. Series: Western Reserve Historical Society, Cleveland. Publication no. 126.

NEVINS, Allan, 1890- 923.373
John D. Rockefeller; a one-volume abridgement, by William Greenleaf, of Study in power. New York, Scribner [1959] 371 p. illus. 22 cm. [CT275.R75N45] 59-7202
1. Rockefeller, John Davison, 1839-1937.

NEVINS, Allan, 1890-1971. 923.373
Study in power: John D. Rockefeller, industrialist and philanthropist. New York, Scribner, 1953. 2 v. illus., ports., maps. 25 cm. Bibliographical references included in "Notes" (v. 1, p. 403-441; v. 2, p. 437-466) "Bibliography of official documents": v. 2, p. 483-484. [CT275.R75N42] 53-9394
1. Rockefeller, John Davison, 1839-1937. I. Title.

ROCKEFELLER, John Davison, 1839-1937. 338.7'62'233820924 B
Random reminiscences of men and events. New York, Arno Press, 1973 [c1909] ix, 188 p. 23 cm. (Big business: economic power in a free society) Reprint of the ed. published by Doubleday, Page, New York. [HD9570.R6A3 1973] 73-2533 ISBN 0-405-05111-5 10.00
1. Rockefeller, John Davison, 1839-1937. 2. Standard Oil Company. 3. Charity. I. Title. II. Series. BIP

Rockefeller, John Davison, 1839-1937 — Juvenile literature.

GILBERT, Miriam. j 92
Money and mud; the life of John D. Rockefeller. Montgomery, Ala., American Southern [1964] vii, 95 p. 23 cm. [CT275.R75G5] 64-7154
1. Rockefeller, John Davison, 1839-1937 — Juvenile literature. I. Title.

Rockefeller, John Davison, 1839-1937—Juvenile literature.

KURLAND, Gerald, 1942- 338.7'62'233820924 B
John D. Rockefeller, nineteenth century industrialist and oil baron. Charlotteville, N.Y., SamHar Press, 1972. 32 p. 22 cm. (Outstanding personalities, no. 35) Bibliography: p. 32. A biography of the self-made millionaire characterized as both a robber baron and the embodiment of the American dream, emphasizing his philanthropic projects. [CT275.R75K87] 92 72-75369 1.98
1. Rockefeller, John Davison, 1839-1937—Juvenile literature. I. Title.
Pap. .98, ISBN 0-87157-035-1

MYERS, Elisabeth P. 338.7'62'233820924 B
John D. Rockefeller, boy financier, by Elisabeth P. Myers. Illustrated by Al Fiorentino. Indianapolis, Bobbs-Merrill [1973] 200 p. illus. 20 cm. (Childhood of famous Americans) A biography concentrating on the childhood of the self-made millionaire emphasizing his business acumen and philanthropic projects. [HD9570.R6M93] 92 72-11687 2.95 (pbk.)
1. Rockefeller, John Davison, 1839-1937—Juvenile literature. I. Fiorentino, Al, illus.

Rockefeller, John Davison, 1874-

FOSDICK, Raymond Blaine, 1883- 923.373
John D. Rockefeller, Jr., a portrait. [1st ed.] New York, Harper [1956] ix, 477 p. illus., ports. 25 cm. "Sources and bibliography": p. 437-440. [HD2769.O4F6] 56-6436
1. Rockefeller, John Davison, 1874-

Rockefeller, John William.

ROCKEFELLER, John William. 929.2
The poor Rockefellers. New York, Vanguard Press [1962] 316p. 21cm. Autobiographical. [CT275.R753A3] 62-11220
I. Title.

Rockefeller, Michael Clark.

MACHLIN, Milton. 301.2'092'4 B
The search for Michael Rockefeller [by] Milt Machlin. New York, Putnam [1972] 256 p. illus. 23 cm. Bibliography: p. 249-250. [GN21.R58M3 1972] 72-175266 6.95
1. Rockefeller, Michael Clark. 2. New Guinea—Description and travel. 3. Ethnology—New Guinea. I. Title.

Rockefeller, Nelson Aldrich, 1908-1979.

DESMOND, James 923.273
Nelson Rockefeller; a political biography. New York Macmillan [c.1964] xv, 330p. 22cm. 64-11758 5.00
1. Rockefeller, Nelson Aldrich, 1908- I. Title.

GERVASI, Frank Henry, 1906- 923.273
The real Rockefeller; the story of the rise, decline and resurgence of the presidential aspirations of Nelson Rockefeller. New York, Atheneum [c.]1964. xii, 271p. 22cm. 64-14919 5.00
1. Rockefeller, Nelson Aldrich, 1908- I. Title.

KRAMER, Michael S. 973.925'092'4 B
"I never wanted to be vice-president of anything!" : An investigative biography of Nelson Rockefeller / Michael Kramer & Sam Roberts. New York : Basic Books, inc., c1976. xii, 420 p., [8] leaves of plates : ill. ; 24 cm. Includes bibliographical references and index. [E748.R673K72] 75-36380 ISBN 0-465-03194-3 : 12.50
1. Rockefeller, Nelson Aldrich, 1908- I. Roberts, Sam, 1947- joint author. II. Title.

MORRIS, Joe Alex, 1904- 923.273
Nelson Rockefeller, a biography. [1st ed.] New York, Harper [1960] 369 p. illus. 22 cm. [E748.R673M6] 60-7534
1. Rockefeller, Nelson Aldrich, 1908-

POLING, James. 923.273
The Rockefeller record; a political self-portrait. New York, Crowell [1960] 177 p. 21 cm. Includes bibliography. [E748.R673P6] 60-7927
1. Rockefeller, Nelson Aldrich, 1908- I. Rockefeller, Nelson Aldrich, 1908- II. Title.

RODGERS, William H. 353.9747030924
Rockefeller's follies; an unauthorized view of Nelson A. Rockefeller. New York, Stein & Day [c.1966] 224p. 22cm. [E748.R673R6] 66-24098 5.95 bds.,
1. Rockefeller, Nelson Aldrich, 1908- 2. Rockefeller family. 3. New York (State)—Pol. & govt.—1951- I. Title.

Rockefeller, Winthrop, 1912-

WARD, John L., 1930- 976.7'05'0924 B
The Arkansas Rockefeller / John L. Ward. Baton Rouge : Louisiana State University Press, c1977. p. cm. Includes index. Bibliography: p. [F415.3.R62W37] 75-5354 ISBN 0-8071-0253-9 : 14.95
1. Rockefeller, Winthrop, 1912- 2. Arkansas—Governors—Biography. 3. Arkansas—Politics and government—1951- I. Title. BIP

Rocketry—Biography.

STOIKO, Michael. 629.47'52'0922 B
Pioneers of rocketry / Michael Stoiko ; introd. by Frederick C. Durant III. New York : Hawthorn Books, [1974] xii, 129 p. : ill. ; 22 cm. Includes index. Bibliography: p. 121-122. [TL781.85.A1S76 1974] 73-14229 ISBN 0-8015-5876-X : 6.95
1. Rocketry—Biography. I. Title.

Rockfeller family.

MOSCOW, Alvin. 332'.092'2 B
The Rockefeleller inheritance / Alvin Moscow. 1st ed. Garden City, N.Y. : Doubleday, 1977. p. cm. Includes index. Bibliography: p. [HG172.A2M67] 73-81445 ISBN 0-385-08087-5 : 14.95
1. Rockfeller family. 2. Capitalists and financiers—United States—Biography. I. Title.

Rockford College, Rockford, Ill.—Biography.

A Power not of the present; 378.1'1'0977331 B biographical studies of eight men and women whose lives were linked with the story of Rockford College. Edited by Elizabeth M. Asprooth. [Rockford, Ill.] Rockford College Press, 1973. 126 p. illus. 27 cm. Includes bibliographical references. [LD7251.R6P68] 73-83807 3.00
1. Rockford College, Rockford, Ill.—Biography. I. Asprooth, Elizabeth M., ed.
Publisher's Address: 5050 E. State, Rockford, Ill. 61104.

Rockhill, William Woodville, 1854-1914.

VARG, Paul A 923.273
Open door diplomat; the life of W. W. Rockhill. Urbana, University of Illinois Press, 1952. ix, 141p. oport. 26cm. (Illinois studies in the social sciences, v. 33, no. 4) Bibliography: p. 133-136. [H31.I4 vol.33, no.4] 52-12402
1. Rockhill, William Woodville, 1854-1914. 2. U. S.—For. rel.—20th cent. 3. Eastern question (Far East) I. Title. II. Series: Illinois. University. Illinois studies in the social sciences, v. 33, no. 4 BIP

VARG, Paul A. 327'.2'0924 B
Open door diplomat : the life of W. W. Rockhill / Paul A. Varg. Westport, Conn. : Greenwood Press, 1974, c1952. xiii, 141 p., [1] leaf of plates : port. ; 23 cm. Reprint of the ed. published by the University of Illinois Press, Urbana, which was issued as vol. 33, no. 4, of Illinois studies in the social sciences. Includes index. Bibliography: p. 133-136. [E748.R674V37 1974] 74-20342 ISBN 0-8371-7858-4 : 10.75
1. Rockhill, William Woodville, 1854-1914. 2. United States—Foreign relations—20th century. 3. Eastern question (Far East) I. Title. II. Series: Illinois. University. Illinois studies in the social sciences ; v. 33, no. 4.

Rockingham, Charles Watson-Wentworth, 2d marquis of, 1730-1782.

HOFFMAN, Ross John Swartz, 1902- 942.07'2'0924
The marquis; a study of Lord Rockingham, 1730-1782 [by] Ross J. S. Hoffman. New York, Fordham University Press, 1973. xiii, 397 p. illus. 23 cm. Includes bibliographical references. [DA512.R6H63] 72-93944 ISBN 0-8232-0970-9 15.00
1. Rockingham, Charles Watson-Wentworth, 2d marquis of, 1730-1782. BIP

Rockne, Knute Kenneth, 1888-1931.

BRONDFIELD, Jerry, 1913- 796.33'2'0924 B
Rockne, the coach, the man, the legend / by Jerry Brondfield. New York : Random House, [1976] p. cm. [GV939.R6B67] 76-14175 ISBN 0-394-40145-X : 8.95
1. Rockne, Knute Kenneth, 1881-1931. 2. Football coaches—Biography. I. Title.

DALEY, Arthur 927.96
Knute Rockne, football wizard of Notre Dame. New York, J. P. Kenedy [c.1960] 191p. illus. 22cm. (American background books, 15) 60-13884 2.50
1. Rockne, Knute Kenneth, 1888-1931. I. Title.

LOVELACE, Delos Wheeler, 1894- v. 12
Rockne of Notre Dame. New York, G. P. Putnam [1965? c1931] 235 p illus., ports. 20 cm. 66-71936
1. Rockne, Knute Kenneth, 1888-1931. I. Title.

MCCALLUM, John Dennis, 1924- 796.33'2'0924 B
We remember Rockne / John D. McCallum & Paul Castner. Huntington, IN : Our Sunday Visitor, inc., c1975. 240 p., [16] leaves of plates : ill. ; 25 cm. [GV939.R6M32] 75-22587 ISBN 0-87973-882-0 : 7.95
1. Rockne, Knute Kenneth, 1888-1931. 2. Notre Dame, Ind. University—Football. 3. Football. I. Castner, Paul, joint author. II. Title.

WALLACE, Francis. 927.96
Knute Rockne. [1st ed.] Garden City, N.Y., Doubleday, 1960. 286 p. illus. 22 cm. [GV939.R6W3] 60-13749
1. Rockne, Knute Kenneth, 1888-1931. I. Title.

YOUNG, Eugene J., 1903- 927.96
With Rockne at Notre Dame [by] Scrapiron Young. New York, Putnam [1951] 312 p. illus. 22 cm. [GV939.R6Y6] 51-13480
1. Rockne, Knute Kenneth, 1888-1931. I. Title.

Rockne, Knute Kenneth, 1888-1931—Juvenile literature.

SULLIVAN, George, 1927- 796.332'0924 B
Knute Rockne; Notre Dame's football great. Illustrated by Dom Lupo. Champaign, Ill., Garrard Pub. Co. [1970] 96 p. illus., ports. 24 cm. (Americans all) A biography of the immigrant boy whose successful career as head coach of Nortre Dame's Fighting Irish led President Hoover to mourn his death as a national loss. [GV939.R6S9] 92 70-113837
1. Rockne, Knute Kenneth, 1888-1931—Juvenile literature. I. Lupo, Dom, illus. II. Title. BIP

Rockwell, Cleveland, 1837-1907.

STENZEL, Franz. 526.9'092'4 B
Cleveland Rockwell, scientist and artist, 1837-1907. Portland, Oregon Historical Society, 1972. 157 p. illus. (part col.) 22 x 28 cm. Includes reproductions of the artist's works. Includes bibliographical references. [TA533.R63S83] 72-80732 ISBN 0-87595-037-X
1. Rockwell, Cleveland, 1837-1907. I. Rockwell, Cleveland, 1837-1907.

Rockwell, Kathleen Eloisa, 1876-1957.

LUCIA, Ellis. 927.92
Klondike Kate; the life & legend of Kitty Rockwell, the Queen of the Yukon. New York, Hastings House [1962] 305 p. illus. 21 cm. Includes bibliography. [PN1967.L8] 62-10089
1. Rockwell, Kathleen Eloisa, 1876-1957. 2. Vaudeville—Yukon Territory.

Rockwell, Norman, 1894-

GUPTILL, Arthur Leighton, 1891-1956. 759.13
Norman Rockwell, illustrator. Pref. by Dorothy Canfield Fisher. Biographical introd. by Jack Alexander. [3d ed.] New York, Watson-Guptill Publications [1970] 208 p. illus. (part col.), plan, col. plates, ports. (part col.) 31 cm. [ND237.R68G8 1970] 75-125848 17.50
1. Rockwell, Norman, 1894-

ROCKWELL, Norman, 1894- 759.13
Norman Rockwell, artist and illustrator [by] Thomas S. Buechner. [1st ed.] New York, H. N. Abrams [1970] 328 p. illus. (part col.) 44 cm. [ND237.R68B8] 75-125785
I. Buechner, Thomas S. II. Title.

WALTON, Donald. 759.13 B
A Rockwell portrait : an intimate biography / by Donald Walton. Kansas City [Kan.] : Sheed Andrews and McMeel, c1978. p. cm. [ND237.R68W34] 78-13076 ISBN 0-8362-6602-1 : 12.95
1. Rockwell, Norman, 1894- 2. Painters—United States—Biography. I. Title. BIP

Rod, Edouard, 1857-1910.

LERNER, Michael G. 843'.8
Edouard Rod (1857-1910) : a portrait of the novelist and his times / by Michael G. Lerner. The Hague : Mouton, 1975. 272 p. ; 22 cm. (Studies in French literature ; 24) Includes index. Bibliography of works by and about E. Rod: p. [254]-264. [PQ2388.R4Z6] 75-331031 ISBN 90-279-3091-0 pbk. : 19.75
1. Rod, Edouard, 1857-1910
Distributed by Humanities Press Atlantic Highlands N.J. BIP

Rodeos—The West—Biography.

KARR, Lee. 791.8 B
Rope burns : a fair likeness of a few good cowboys who know the meaning of the words / by Lee and Lela Karr. San Angelo, Tex. : Newsfoto Pub. Co., c1975. 112 p. : chiefly ill. ; 29 cm. [GV1833.5.K37] 75-30379
1. Rodeos—The West—Biography. I. Karr, Lela. II. Title.

Rodgers, Dorothy F., 1909-

RODGERS, Dorothy F., 1909- 782.8'1'0924 B
A personal book / Dorothy Rodgers. 1st ed. New York : Harper & Row, c1977. xiii, 188 p. : ill. ; 22 cm. [CT275.R754A3] 76-26251 ISBN 0-06-013588-3 : 8.95
1. Rodgers, Dorothy F., 1909- 2. Rodgers, Richard, 1902- 3. United States—Biography. 4. Wives—United States—Biography. I. Title. BIP

Rodgers, H. J.

RODGERS, H. J. 770'.92'4
Twenty three years under a sky-light; or, Life and experiences of a photographer, by H. J. Rodgers. New York, Arno Press,

1973 [c1872] 235 p. illus. 21 cm. (The Literature of Photography) [TR140.R63A35 1973] 72-9233 ISBN 0-405-04938-2 14.00.
1. Title. II. Series. **BIP**

Rodgers, James Charles, 1897-1933.

PORTERFIELD, Nolan. 784'.092'4 B
Jimmie Rodgers : the life and times of America's blue yodeler. Urbana : University of Illinois Press, c1979. p. cm. (Music in American life) Includes index. Bibliography: p. [ML420.R753P7] 79-11959 ISBN 0-252-00750-6 : 10.00
1. Rodgers, James Charles, 1897-1933. 2. Country musicians—United States—Biography. **BIP**

RODGERS, Carrie Cecil Williamson. 784'.092'4 B
My husband, Jimmie Rodgers / [Mrs. Jimmie Rodgers]. [Nashville] : Country Music Foundation Press, c1975. xxiii, 264 p. : ill. ; 19 cm. Reprint of the 1935 ed. published by Southern Literary Institute, San Antonio; with a new introd. and chronology by Nolan Porterfield. [ML419.R6M8 1975] 75-330345
1. Rodgers, James Charles, 1897-1933. I. Title.

Rodgers, James Charles, 1897-1933—Juvenile literature.

KRISHEF, Robert K. 784'.092'4 B
Jimmie Rodgers / by Robert K. Krishef. Minneapolis : Lerner Publications Co., c1978. 62, [2] p. : ill. ; 21 cm. (Country music library) Includes index. Discography: p. [63] A biography of country music's first solo recording star, in whose brief career out tragically short by death he recorded 111 songs that sold twenty million records. [ML3930.R62K7] 92 77-90156 ISBN 0-8225-1404-4 lib.bdg. : 4.95
1. Rodgers, James Charles, 1897-1933—Juvenile literature. 2. Country musicians—United States—Biography—Juvenile literature. I. Title. **BIP**

Rodgers, John, 1773-1838.

PAULLIN, Charles Oscar, 1868or9-1944. 973.4'0924 B
Commodore John Rogers; captain, commodore, and senior officer of the American Navy, 1773-1838. Annapolis, U.S. Naval Institute [1967] 434 p. illus., facsims., ports. 25 cm. First published in 1910. Bibliography: p. 405-410. [E353.1.R7P28 1967] 66-25467
1. Rodgers, John, 1773-1838. 2. United States. Navy—History. I. Title.

Rodgers, John, 1812-1882.

JOHNSON, Robert Erwin. 973.5'0924
Rear Admiral John Rodgers, 1812-1882 Annapolis, U.S. Naval Inst. [1967] xiv, 426p. illus., ports. 25cm. Bibl. [E182.R68J6] (B) 66-25468 10.00
1. Rodgers, John, 1812-1882. I. Title.

Rodgers, John, 1812-1882—Juvenile literature.

WERSTEIN, Irving. 327.519'073
The trespassers; Korea, June 1871. Illustrated by Joseph Papin. [1st ed.] New York, Dutton [1969] 158 p. illus., map. 21 cm. Bibliography: p. 157-158. Describes the first encounter in 1871 between Korea and the United States when the latter attempted to negotiate a trade agreement. [E183.8.K7W4 1969] 78-81726 4.50
1. Rodgers, John, 1812-1882—Juvenile literature. 2. U.S.—Foreign relations—Korea—Juvenile literature. 3. Korea—Foreign relations—U.S.—Juvenile literature. I. Papin, Joseph, illus. II. Title.

Rodgers, Pepper, 1931-

RODGERS, Pepper, 1931- 796.33'2'0924 B
Pepper! : The autobiography of an unconventional coach / by Pepper Rodgers and Al Thomy. 1st ed. Garden City, N.Y. : Doubleday, 1976. 176 p., [4] leaves of plates : ill. ; 22 cm. [GV939.R62A36] 76-28559 ISBN 0-385-11667-5 : 7.95
1. Rodgers, Pepper, 1931- 2. Football coaches—United States—Biography. I. Thomy, Al, joint author. II. Title.

Rodgers, Richard, 1902-1979.

EWEN, David, 1907- 927.8
Richard Rodgers. [1st ed.] New York, Holt [1957] 378 p. illus. 22 cm. [ML410.R6315E9] 57-10418
1. Rodgers, Richard, 1902-

EWEN, David, 1907- 927.8
With a song in his heart; the story of Richard Rodgers. [1st ed.] New York, Holt, Rinehart and Winston [1963] 216 p. group ports. 22 cm. Bibliography: p. 207-209. [ML3930.R63E9] 63-17335
1. Rodgers, Richard, 1902- — Juvenile literature. I. Title.

GREEN, Stanley 927.8
The Rodgers and Hammerstein story. New York, John Day [c.1963] 187p. illus. 22cm. Bibl. 63-10221 4.50
1. Rodgers, Richard, 1902- 2. Hammerstein, Oscar, 1895-1960. I. Title.

GREEN, Stanley. 782.8'1'0922 B
The Rodgers and Hammerstein story. New York, J. Day Co. [1963] 187 p. illus. 22 cm. A dual biography of the men whose musical partnership gave America such productions as Oklahoma, Carousel, South Pacific, The King and I, and The Sound of Music. Includes a list of all the songs they wrote. [ML410.R6315G7] 92 AC 68
1. Rodgers, Richard, 1902- 2. Hammerstein, Oscar, 1895-1960. I. Title.

MARX, Samuel, 1902- 782.8'1'0922 B
Rodgers & Hart : bewitched, bothered, and bedeviled : an anecdotal account / by Samuel Marx and Jan Clayton. New York : Putnam, c1976. 287 p., [8] leaves of plates : ill. ; 24 cm. Includes index. [ML410.R6315M4] 76-12494 ISBN 0-399-11786-5 : 10.00
1. Rodgers, Richard, 1902- 2. Hart, Lorenz Milton, 1895-1943. I. Clayton, Jan, joint author. II. Title.

RODGERS, Richard, 1902- 782.8'1'0924 B
Musical stages : an autobiography / Richard Rodgers. 1st ed. New York : Random House, [1975] 341 p. : ill. ; 24 cm. Includes index. [ML410.R6315A3] 75-10259 10.00
1. Rodgers, Richard, 1902- 2. Composers—Correspondence, reminiscences, etc. I. Title. **BIP**

TAYLOR, Deems, 1885- 927.8
Some enchanted evenings; the story of Rodgers and Hammerstein. [1st ed.] New York, Harper [1953] 244p. illus. 24cm. [ML410.R6315T3] 53-7750
1. Rodgers, Richard, 1902- 2. Hammerstein, Oscar, 1895- I. Title.

TAYLOR, Deems, 1885-1966. 782.8'1'0922 B
Some enchanted evenings; the story of Rodgers and Hammerstein. Westport, Conn., Greenwood Press [1972, c1953] 244 p. illus. 22 cm. [ML410.R6315T3 1972] 73-138132 ISBN 0-8371-5414-6
1. Rodgers, Richard, 1902- 2. Hammerstein, Oscar, 1895-1960. I. Title.

Rodgers, William Robert, 1909-1969.

O'BRIEN, Darcy. 821'.9'12 B
W. R. Rodgers (1909-1969) Lewisburg, Bucknell University Press [1971, c1970] 103 p. 22 cm. (Irish writers series) [PR6035.O615Z8 1971] 70-124646 ISBN 0-8387-7750-3 4.50
1. Rodgers, William Robert, 1909-1969. **BIP**

Rodin, Auguste, 1840-1917.

CHAMPIGNEULLE, Bernard, 1896- v. 12
Rodin; translated from the French by J. Maxwell Brownjohn. New York, Abrams [1967] 287 p. 132 illus. (incl. 16 col.) 22 cm. 68-86251
1. Rodin, Auguste, 1840-1917. I. Title. **BIP**

DESCHARNES, Robert. 730'.924
Auguste Rodin [by] Robert Descharnes and Jean-Francois Chabrun. [English translation by Edita Lausanne] New York, Viking Press [1967] 277, [4] p. illus. (part col.), facsims., ports. 30 cm. (A Studio book) Bibliography: p. [278]-[281]. [NB553.R7D43] 67-31963
1. Rodin, Auguste, 1840-1917. I. Chabrun, Jean Francois, 1920- joint author.

ELSEN, Albert Edward, 1927- 730.924 (B)
Auguste Rodin: readings on his life and work [by] Albert Elsen. Englewood Cliffs, N.J., Prentice-Hall [1965] 185 p. illus. 22 cm. Bibliographical footnotes. [NB553.R7E36] 65-17532
1. Rodin, Auguste, 1840-1917. I. Title.

JIANU, Ionel. 730/.924
Rodin [par] Ionel Jianou, C. Goldscheider. Paris, Arted, 1967. 118p. plates. 28cm. Errata slip inserted. Issued in a case. Bibl. [NB553.R7J5] 67-107873 12.50
1. Rodin, Auguste, 1840-1917. I. Goldscheider, Cecile. II. Title.
American distributor: Tudor, New York.

RILKE, Rainer Maria, 1875-1926. 730'.92'4
Rodin. Translated by Jessie Lemont and Hans Trausil. With an introd. by Padraic Colum. New York, Haskell House, 1974. xvi, 62 p. illus. 24 cm. Translation of Auguste Rodin. Reprint of the 1946 ed. published by Grey Walls Press, London. [NB553.R7R65 1974] 74-6405 ISBN 0-8383-1913-0
1. Rodin, Auguste, 1840-1917.

RIPLEY, Elizabeth 730.924
Rodin; a biography. [1st ed.] Philadelphia, Lippincott [1966] 72p. illus., ports. 2mcm.7bBibl. [NB553.R7R68] 66-8225 3.75; 3.39 lib. ed.,
1. Rodin, Auguste, 1840-1917. I. Title.

RIPLEY, Elizabeth, 1906- 730.924
Rodin; a biography. [1st ed.] Philadelphia, Lippincott [1966] 72 p. illus., ports. 27 cm. Bibliography: p. 70. [NB553.R7R68] 66-8225
1. Rodin, Auguste, 1840-1917. I. Title.

SUTTON, Denys. 730.924
Triumphant satyr: the world of Auguste Rodin. [1st Amer. ed.] New York, Hawthorn Books [1967, c1966] 149 p. illus. (part col.) port. 26 cm. Bibliographical footnotes. [NB553.R7S8 1967] 66-20197
1. Rodin, Auguste, 1840-1917. I. Title.

SUTTON, Denys. 730.924
Triumphant satyr: the world of Auguste Rodin. [1st Amer. ed.] New York, Hawthorn Books [1967, c1966] 149 p. illus. (part col.) port. 26 cm. Bibliographical footnotes. [NB553.R7S8 1967] 66-20197
1. Rodin, Auguste, 1840-1917. I. Title.

TIREL, Marcelle. 730'.92'4
The last years of Rodin. Translated by R. Francis. Pref. by Judith Cladel. New York, Haskell House, 1974. 224 p. illus. 20 cm. Translation of Rodin intime; ou, L'envers d'une gloire. Reprint of the 1925 ed. published by R. M. McBride, New York. [NB553.R7T52 1974] 74-16282 ISBN 0-8383-1945-9
1. Rodin, Auguste, 1840-1917. I. Title. **BIP**

Rodney, George Brydges Rodney, Baron, 1719-1792.

HANNAY, David, 1853-1934. 359.3'3'10924 B
Rodney. With a new introd. and pref. by George Athan Billias. Boston, Gregg Press, 1972. viii, vi, 222 p. port. 23 cm. (The American Revolutionary series. British accounts of the American Revolution) Reprint of the 1891 ed. published by Macmillan, London. [DA87.1.R6H2 1972] 72-8678 ISBN 0-8398-0805-4 12.00
1. Rodney, George Brydges Rodney, Baron, 1719-1792. I. Series: British accounts of the American Revolution. **BIP**

MUNDY, Godfrey Basil, d.1848. 359.3'3'10924 B
The life and correspondence of the late Admiral Lord Rodney. With a new introd. and pref. by George Athan Billias. Boston, Gregg Press, 1972. 2 v. 23 cm. (The American Revolutionary series. British accounts of the American Revolution) Reprint of the 1830 ed. published by J. Murray, London. [DA87.1.R6M9 1972] 72-8677 ISBN 0-8398-1271-X 35.00 (Lib. ed.)
1. Rodney, George Brydges Rodney, Baron, 1719-1792. I. Series: British accounts of the American Revolution. **BIP**

Rodrigues, Joao, 1561 (ca.)-1634.

COOPER, Michael, S.J. 271'.53'024 B
Rodrigues the interpreter; an early Jesuit in Japan and China. [1st ed.] New York, Weatherhill [1974] 416 p. illus. 24 cm. Bibliography: p. 385-395. [BX4705.R619C66] 73-88466 ISBN 0-8348-0094-2 13.50
1. Rodrigues, Joao, 1561 (ca.)-1634. I. Title.

Rodrigues Lobo, Francisco, 17th cent.

PRETO-RODAS, Richard A. 869'.8'207
Francisco Rodrigues Lobo: dialogue and courtly lore in Renaissance Portugal, by Richard A. Preto-Rodas. Chapel Hill, University of North Carolina Press [1971] 189 p. 24 cm. (University of North Carolina. Studies in the Romance languages and literatures, no. 109) "Begun as a doctoral dissertation." Bibliography: p. [181]-189. [PQ9231.R7C7336] 72-181399
1. Rodrigues Lobo, Francisco, 17th cent. Carte na aldeia. 2. Dialogue. I. Title. II. Series: North Carolina. University. Studies in the Romance languages and literature, no. 109.

Roe, Edward Payson, 1838-1888.

ROE, Mary Abigail. v. 12
E. P. Roe; reminiscences of his life, by his sister. New York, Dodd, Mead, 1899. vi, 235 p. plates, ports. 20 cm. [PS2728.R6] 99-5733
1. Roe, Edward Payson, 1838-1888. I. Title.

Roe family.

PATNODE, Genevieve Carroll, 1908- 929'.2'0973
A privileged generation : dealing with the families of Roe, La Shure, Stape, Carroll, Rhoda, Rockefeller, Pratt / by Genevieve Carroll Patnode, as told by Lola Stape Carroll. Leesburg, Fla. : Patnode, c1975. 205, xx p. : ill. ; 29 cm. [CS71.S7926 1975] 75-19745
1. Roe family. 2. Stape family. 3. Carroll family. I. Carroll, Lola Stape, 1884-1967. II. Title.

Roe, John Septimus, 1797-1878.

MERCER, Frederick Royston 923.941
Amazing career; the story of Western Australia's first surveyor-general. Record comp. by F. R. Mercer. [New Rochelle, N.Y., Australian Bk. Ctr., 1965] New Rochelle, N.Y., Australian Bk. Ctr., 1965 180p. illus., facsim., ports. 19cm. [DU372.R6M4] 65-4219 6.00
1. Roe, John Septimus, 1797-1878. I. Title.

Roe, Thomas, Sir, 1581?-1644.

BROWN, Michael J., 1932- 942.05'5'0924 B
Itinerant ambassador; the life of Sir Thomas Roe, by Michael J. Brown. Lexington, University Press of Kentucky, 1970. xv, 302 p. ports. 23 cm. Bibliography: p. [279]-290. [D244.8.R6B7] 77-94064 ISBN 8-13-111927- 9.95
1. Roe, Thomas, Sir, 1581?-1644. I. Title. **BIP**

Roeben, Frederick B.

ROEBEN, Frederick B. 1878- 920
Lure of the sea. New York, Vantage Press [1950] 64 p. 22 cm. Autobiography. [CT275.R755A3] 51-9039
1. Title.

Roebling family.

SCHUYLER, Hamilton, 1862-1933. 624.5'092'2
The Roeblings; a century of engineers, bridge-builders and industrialists; the story of three generations of an illustrious family, 1831-1931. Princeton, Princeton University Press, 1931. New York, AMS Press [1972] xx, 424 p. illus. 23 cm. Includes bibliographies. [TA140.R7S4 1972] 77-175582 ISBN 0-404-05625-3
1. Roebling family. 2. Roebling, John Augustus, 1806-1869. 3. Roebling, Washington Augustus, 1837-1926. I. Title. BIP

Roebling, John Augustus, 1806-1869.

SCHUYLER, Hamilton, 1862-1933. 624.5'092'2
The Roeblings; a century of engineers, bridge-builders and industrialists; the story of three generations of an illustrious family, 1831-1931. Princeton, Princeton University Press, 1931. New York, AMS Press [1972] xx, 424 p. illus. 23 cm. Includes bibliographies. [TA140.R7S4 1972] 77-175582 ISBN 0-404-05625-3
1. Roebling family. 2. Roebling, John Augustus, 1806-1869. 3. Roebling, Washington Augustus, 1837-1926. I. Title. BIP

STEINMAN, David Barnard, 1886- 926.2
The builders of the bridge; the story of John Roebling and his son. [2d ed.] New York, Harcourt, Brace [1950] xi, 457 p. illus., ports. 25 cm. Bibliography: p. 421-445. [TA140.R7S8] 50-8862
1. Roebling, John August, 1805-1309 2. Roebling, Washington Augustus, 1837-1926. I. Title. BIP

STEINMAN, David Barnard, 1886-1960. 624.2'092'2 B
The builders of the bridge; the story of John Roebling and his son. New York, Arno Press, 1972 [c1950] xi, 457 p. illus. 23 cm. (Technology and society) Bibliography: p. 421-445. [TA140.R7S8 1972] 72-5074 ISBN 0-405-04724-X
1. Roebling, John Augustus, 1806-1869. 2. Roebling, Washington Augustus, 1837-1926. I. Title. II. Series.

STEINMAN, David Barnard, 1886-1960. 624.2'092'2 B
The builders of the bridge; the story of John Roebling and his son. New York, Arno Press, 1972 [c1950] xi, 457 p. illus. 23 cm. (Technology and society) Bibliography: p. 421-445. [TA140.R7S8 1972] 72-5074 ISBN 0-405-04724-X
1. Roebling, John Augustus, 1806-1869. 2. Roebling, Washington Augustus, 1837-1926. I. Title. II. Series.

Roebling, Washington Augustus, 1837-1926.

VEGLAHN, Nancy. JUV
The spider of Brooklyn Heights. New York, Scribner [1967] 180 p. illus., ports. 24 cm. Bibliography: p. 175-176. A biography of the civil engineer who, despite fourteen long years of problems, politics, and invalidism, carried out his father's design and dream to construct a suspension bridge across the East River connecting Brooklyn and Manhattan. [PZ4.V422Sp] 92 AC 67
1. Roebling, Washington Augustus, 1837-1926. 2. Roebling, John Augustus, 1805-1869. 3. New York (City)—Bridges—Brooklyn Bridge. I. Title. BIP

Roehenstart, Charles Edward Stuart, called count, 1784?-1854.

SHERBURN, George Wiles, 1884- 920.8
Roehenstart, a late Stuart pretender; being an account of the life of Charles Edward August Maximilien Stuart, Baron Korff, Count Roehenstart. Edinburgh, Oliver and Boyd [1960] 148 p. illus. 23 cm. [DA816.R6S5] 61-287
1. Roehenstart, Charles Edward Stuart, called count, 1784?-1854. I. Title.

Roerich, Nikolai Konstantinovich, 1874-1947.

PAELIAN, Garabed Hagop, 1880- 759.7 B
Nicholas Roerich / Garabed Paelian. Agoura, Calif. : Aquarian Educational Group, [1974] 96 p. : ports. ; 27 cm. Bibliography: p. 93-96. [ND699.R6P35] 74-11757 ISBN 0-911794-09-3 : 6.00
1. Roerich, Nikolai Konstantinovich, 1874-1947. BIP

Roethke, Theodore, 1908-1963.

MILLS, Ralph J. 791'.092'4
Theodore Roethke. Minneapolis, University of Minnesota Press; [distributed to high schools in the U.S. by McGraw-Hill, New York, 1963] 47 p. 21 cm. (University of Minnesota pamphlets on American writers, no. 30) Bibliography: p. 46-47. [PS3535.O39Z7] 63-64002
1. Roethke, Theodore, 1908-1963. I. Series: Minnesota. University. Pamphlets on American writers, no. 30 BIP

SEAGER, Allan, 1906-1968. 811'.5'4 B
The glass house; the life of Theodore Roethke. [1st ed.] New York, McGraw-Hill [1968] 301 p. 23 cm. Bibliographical footnotes. [PS3535.O39Z83] 68-15741
1. Roethke, Theodore, 1908-1963. I. Title.

Roff, Charles L., 1894-

ROFF, Charles L., 1894- 340'.092'4 B
A boom town lawyer in the Osage, 1919-1927 / by Charles L. Roff. Quanah, Tex. : Nortex Press, c1975. xii, 122 p. : ill. ; 22 cm. [KF373.R56A3] 76-351924
1. Roff, Charles L., 1894- 2. Osage Co., Okla.—History. I. Title. BIP

Roger II, King of Sicily, d. 1154.

CURTIS, Edmund, 1881-1943. 945.8'04'0924 B
Roger of Sicily and the Normans in lower Italy, 1016-1154. New York, Putnam, 1912. [New York, AMS Press, 1973] p. Original ed. issued in series: Heroes of the nations. [DG867.25.C87 1973] 70-180443 ISBN 0-404-56536-0 30.00
1. Roger II, King of Sicily, d. 1154. 2. Sicily—History—1016-1189. 3. Normans in Italy. I. Title. II. Series: Heroes of the nations. BIP

Roger of Salisbury, Bp. of Salisbury, 1065?-1139.

KEALEY, Edward J. 942.02'092'4 B
Roger of Salisbury, viceroy of England, by Edward J. Kealey. Berkeley, University of California Press, 1972. xvi, 312 p. 25 cm. Bibliography: p. 278-294. [DA199.R6K4] 78-92681 ISBN 0-520-01985-7 13.50
1. Roger of Salisbury, Bp. of Salisbury, 1065?-1139. 2. Great Britain—Politics and government—1066-1154. I. Title. BIP

Rogers, A. H.

ROGERS, A. H. 923.9
Western memories, the life of a farmer, stockraiser and housebuilder. New York, Exposition [c.1963] 85p. illus. 21cm. 2.75
I. Title.

Rogers, Carl Ransom, 1902-

EVANS, Richard Isadore, 1922- 150'.19'5
Carl Rogers : the man and his ideas / Richard I. Evans. 1st ed. New York : Dutton, 1975. lxxxviii, 195 p. ; 22 cm. (His Dialogues with notable contributors to personality theory ; v. 8) Includes index. Bibliography: p. [187]-190. [BF109.R63E9 1975] 74-23270 ISBN 0-525-07645-X : 10.95 pbk. : 3.95
1. Rogers, Carl Ransom, 1902- 2. Psychology. 3. Psychotherapy. BIP

KIRSCHENBAUM, Howard. 150'.19'2 B
On becoming Carl Rogers / by Howard Kirschenbaum. New York : Delacorte Press, c1979. xvii, 444 p., [4] leaves of plates : ill. ; 24 cm. Includes index. Bibliography: p. 435. [BF109.R63K57] 78-13308 ISBN 0-440-06707-3 : 12.95
1. Rogers, Carl Ransom, 1902- 2. Psychologists—United States—Biography. 3. Humanistic psychology. 4. Client-centered psychotherapy. I. Title. BIP

Rogers, Dale Evans.

ROGERS, Dale Evans. 209'.2'4 B
Trials, tears, and triumph / Dale Evans Rogers. Old Tappan, N.J. : F. H. Revell Co., c1977. 128 p., [4] leaves of plates : ill. ; 21 cm. [BR1725.R63A324] 76-51293 ISBN 0-8007-0847-4 : 4.95
1. Rogers, Dale Evans. 2. Christian biography—California. I. Title. BIP

Rogers, Earl, 1870-1922.

HYND, Alan, 1908- 923.473
Defenders of the damned. New York, A.S. Barnes [1960] 182 p. 22cm. [KF372.H9] 60-12187
1. Rogers, Earl, 1870-1922. 2. Darrow, Clarence Seward, 1857-1938. 3. Fallon, William Joseph, 1886-1927. I. Title.

Rogers, Henry C., 1914-

ROGERS, Henry C., 1914- 659.2'092'4
Walking the tightrope : the private confessions of a public relations man / by Henry C. Rogers. New York : Morrow, 1980. p. cm. [HM263.R567] 79-24454 ISBN 0-688-03589-2 : 10.95
1. Rogers, Henry C., 1914- 2. Public relations consultants—United States—Biography. 3. Press agents—United States—Biography. I. Title.

Rogers, Henry Huttleston, 1840-1909.

DIAS, Earl J. 338'.04'0924 B
Henry Huttleston Rogers, portrait of a "capitalist," by Earl J. Dias. Fairhaven, Mass., Millicent Library [1974] 190 p. illus. 24 cm. Bibliography: p. 185-190. [HD9570.R64D5] 74-82011
1. Rogers, Henry Huttleston, 1840-1909.

Rogers, Horatio.

ROGERS, Horatio. 940.4'81'73 B
The diary of an artillery scout / Horatio Rogers. North Andover, Mass. : Rogers, 1975. 268 p., [14] leaves of plates : ill. ; 26 cm. [D570.9.R58] 74-31941
1. Rogers, Horatio. 2. European War, 1914-1918—Personal narratives, American. I. Title.

Rogers, Hosea, 1811 or 12-1904.

TYLER, Polly, 1909- 926.238
Hosea Rogers, builder of boats. [Rochester, N.Y., Published for the author by ABC Print Shop, 1952] unpaged. illus. 24 cm. [VM140.R62T9] 52-34671
1. Rogers, Hosea, 1811 or 12-1904. I. Title.

Rogers, Jack Bartlett.

ROGERS, Jack Bartlett. 269'.2'0924 B
Confessions of a conservative Evangelical, by Jack Rogers. Philadelphia, Westminster Press [1974] 144 p. 20 cm. [BX9225.R73A33] 74-12249 ISBN 0-664-24996-5 2.65 (pbk.)
1. Rogers, Jack Bartlett. 2. Evangelicalism. I. Title. BIP

Rogers, James Harvey

JAMES Harvey Rogers, 1886-1939 in memoriam. 923.373
Stamford, Conn., The Overbrook Press, 1940. 34p. port. 24cm. Foreword signed: Arnold Wolfers. 'Four hundred and fifty copies have been printed at the Overbrook Press ... for private distribution.' [HB119.R6J3] 53-50579
1. Rogers, James Harvey 1886-1939. II. Wolfers, Arnold, 1892-
Contents omitted.

Rogers, John, Chippewa chief.

ROGERS, John, Chippewa chief. 970.3 B
Red world and white; memories of a Chippewa boyhood, by John Rogers (Chief Snow Cloud). Foreword by Joseph W. Whitecotton. [New ed.] Norman, University of Oklahoma Press [1974] xvii, 153 p. front. 19 cm. (The Civilization of the American Indian series) Published in 1957 under title: A Chippewa speaks. Includes bibliographical references. [E99.C6R633 1974] 72-9263 ISBN 0-8061-1069-4 4.95
1. Rogers, John, Chippewa chief. 2. Chippewa Indians. I. Title. BIP

Rogers, John, d. 1558.

SHELDY, Lonnie Royce, 1935- 623'.0924
John Rogers: Tudor military engineer. Oxford, Clarendon P., 1967. xi, 182 p. 29 plates, illus., facsims. maps, plans. 26 cm. Bibliography: p. 165-170. [UG128.R63S45] 68-79071 ISBN 0-19-821366-2 75/-
1. Rogers, John, d. 1558.

Rogers, John, 1829-1904.

WALLACE, David H. 730'.924
John Rogers; the people's sculptor, by David H. Wallace. [1st ed.] Middletown, Conn., Wesleyan University Press [1967] xv, 326 p. illus., facsims., ports. 27 cm. "Catalogue of the works of John Rogers": p. 171-280. [NB237.R65W3] 67-24107
1. Rogers, John, 1829-1904.

Rogers, John, 1890-

MORRIS, Cheryl Haun, 1947- 340'.092'4 B
The cutting edge : the life of John Rogers / by Cheryl Haun Morris. 1st ed. Norman : Published for the Oklahoma Heritage Association by the University of Oklahoma Press, c1976. xiv, 226 p. : ill. ; 22 cm. (Oklahoma trackmaker series ; [v. 3]) Includes index. Bibliography: p. 213-215. [KF373.R58M67] 75-37736 ISBN 0-8061-1329-4 : 7.75
1. Rogers, John, 1890- I. Title. II. Series. BIP

Rogers, Kenneth Paul.

ROGERS, Kenneth Paul. 364.1'53 B
For one sweet grape : the extraordinary memoir of a convicted rapist-murderer / Kenneth Paul Rogers. 1st ed. Chicago : Playboy Press, [1974] xxix, 224 p., [4] leaves of plates : ill. ; 22 cm. [HV6248.R65A34] 74-82484 ISBN 0-87223-419-3 : 8.50
1. Rogers, Kenneth Paul. 2. Crime and criminals—Illinois—Correspondence, reminiscences, etc. I. Title.

Rogers, Mary Joseph, 1882-1955.

LYONS, Jeanne Marie, 1904- 922.273
Maryknoll's first lady. New York, Dodd, Mead [1964] xi, 327 p. illus., ports. 24 cm. [BV2300.M45L9] 64-12763
1. Rogers, Mary Joseph, 1882-1955. 2. Maryknoll Sisters of St. Dominic. I. Title.

LYONS, Jenne Marie, 1904- 922.275
Maryknoll's first lady, by Sister Jeanne

Marie. Garden City, N.Y., Doubleday [1967, c.1964] 319p. 19cm. (Echo bk., E39) .95 pap.,
1. Rogers, Mary Joseph, 1882-1955. 2. Mary-knoll Sisters of St. Dominic. I. Title.

Rogers, Peter V.

ROGERS, Peter V. 282'.092'4 B
Tragedy is my parish : working for God in the streets of New Orleans / Peter V. Rogers. New York : Macmillan, c1979. xii, 159 p., [6] leaves of plates : ill. ; 22 cm. p. cm. Autobiography. [BX4705.R648A34 1979] 78-25896 ISBN 0-02-604390-4 : 7.95
1. Rogers, Peter V. 2. Catholic Church—Clergy—Biography. 3. Clergy—Louisiana—New Orleans—Biography. 4. New Orleans—Biography. 5. Chaplains, Police—Louisiana—New Orleans—Biography. I. Title. **BIP**

Rogers, Randolph, 1825-1892.

ROGERS, Millard F. 730'.924 B
Randolph Rogers; American sculptor in Rome [by] Millard F. Rogers, Jr. [Amherst] University of Massachusetts Press, 1971. xviii, 237 p. illus. 24 cm. Bibliography: p. [187]-192. [NB237.R66R6] 75-164439 17.50
1. Rogers, Randolph, 1825-1892. I. Title.

Rogers, Robert, 1731-1795—Juvenile literature.

GAUCH, Patricia Lee. 973.2'6'0924 B
The impossible Major Rogers / by Patricia Lee Gauch ; drawings by Robert Andrew Parker. New York : Putnam, c1977. 61 p. : ill. ; 24 cm. A biography of the man who gained fame as the leader of the bold "Rogers' Rangers" in the French and Indian War but whose later life was marred by a ruined reputation, imprisonment, and poverty. [E199.R74G38 1977] 92 76-51233 ISBN 0-399-20593-4 : 5.95
1. Rogers, Robert, 1731-1795—Juvenile literature. 2. United States—History—French and Indian War, 1755-1763—Juvenile literature. 3. Soldiers—United States—Biography—Juvenile literature. I. Parker, Robert Andrew. II. Title. **BIP**

Rogers, Roy, 1912-

RASKY, Frank. 927.92
Roy Rogers, king of the cowboys. New York, Messner [1955] 189p. illus. 22cm. Includes bibliography. [PN2287.R73R3] 55-9865
1. Rogers, Roy, 1911- I. Title.

ROGERS, Roy, 1912- 790.2'092'2 B
Happy trails : the story of Roy Rogers and Dale Evans / with Carlton Stowers. Waco, Tex. : Word Books, c1979. 213 p., [8] leaves of plates : ill. ; 23 cm. Filmography: p. 208-213. [PN2287.R73A34] 79-124891 ISBN 0-8499-0086-7 : 8.95
1. Rogers, Roy, 1912- 2. Rogers, Dale Evans. 3. Moving-picture actors and actresses—United States—Biography. I. Rogers, Dale Evans, joint author. II. Stowers, Carlton, joint author. III. Title. IV. Title: Story of Roy Rogers and Dale Evans.

Rogers, Roy, 1912- —Juvenile literature.

ROPER, William L. 791.43'0924 B
Roy Rogers, king of the cowboys, by William L. Roper. Minneapolis, Denison [1971] 182 p. illus., group ports. 22 cm. (Men of achievement series) Bibliography: p. 177-179. A biography of the man whose movie roles as a singing cowboy made him famous as the "King of the Cowboys." [PN2287.R73R6] 92 74-99271 ISBN 0-513-00587-0
1. Rogers, Roy, 1912- —Juvenile literature. I. Title.

Rogers, Will, 1879-1935.

ALWORTH, E. Paul, 1917- 791'.092'4
Will Rogers, by E. Paul Alworth. New York, Twayne Publishers [1974] 140 p. port. 22 cm. (Twayne's United States authors series, TUSAS 236) Bibliography: p. 131-135. [PN2287.R74A7] 73-16415 ISBN 0-8057-0634-8 5.50
1. Rogers, Will, 1879-1935. **BIP**

AXTELL, Margaret Shellabarger, 1893- 791'.092'4 B
Will Rogers rode the range. Phoenix [Ariz., Allied Printing, c1972] viii, 168 p. illus. 29 cm. Includes bibliographical references. [PN2287.R74A9] 73-153889
1. Rogers, Will, 1879-1935. I. Title.

CROY, Homer, 1883- 928.1
Our Will Rogers. [1st ed.] New York, Duell, Sloan and Pearce [1953] 377 p. 21 cm. [PN2287.R74C7] 53-10229
1. Rogers, Will, 1879-1935. I. Title.

DAY, Donald, 1899- 928.1
Will Rogers, a biography. New York, D. McKay Co. [1962] 370 p. illus. 22 cm. [PN2287.R74D3] 62-16719
1. Rogers, Will, 1879-1935.

GARST, Doris Shannon, 1899- 928.1
Will Rogers, immortal cowboy. Illustrated by Charles Gabriel. New York, Messner [1950] 174 p. illus. 22 cm. Bibliography: p. 169-170. [PN2287.R74G3] 50-7011
1. Rogers, Will, 1879-1935.

GARST, Doris Shannon, 1899- 791'.0924 B
Will Rogers, immortal cowboy. Illustrated by Charles Gabriel. New York, Messner [1950] 174 p. illus. 22 cm. Bibliography: p. 169-170. A biography of the cowboy, philosopher, stage and movie star, and humorist. [PN2287.R74G3] 92 AC 68
1. Rogers, Will, 1879-1935. I. Gabriel, Charles, illus. II. Title.

KETCHUM, Richard M., 1922- 791'.092'4 B
Will Rogers, his life and times, by Richard M. Ketchum. In co-operation with the Will Rogers Memorial Commission and staff of the Will Rogers Memorial, Claremore, Oklahoma. New York, American Heritage Pub. Co.; distribution by McGraw-Hill [1973] 415 p. illus. 26 cm. (An American heritage biography) [PN2287.R74K45] 73-8713 ISBN 0-07-034411-6 17.50
1. Rogers, Will, 1879-1935. I. Title.

ISBN 0-448-12362-2 : 12.95 ISBN 0-448-12359-2 pbk. : 6.95. ISBN 0-448-13384-9 lib.bdg. : 12.99
1. Rogers, Will, 1879-1935. 2. Entertainers—United States—Biography. 3. Humorists, American—Biography. I. Sterling, Bryan B. II. Title.

ROGERS, Will [William Penn Adair Rogers] 1879-1935 928.1
Autobiography; selected, ed. by Donald Day. Foreword by Bill and Jim Rogers. New York, Lnaer [1963, c.1921-1949] 351p. 18cm. (74-814) .75)ap.,
I. Day, Donald, 1899- ed. II. Title.

ROGERS, Will, 1879-1935 928.1
The autobiography of Will Rogers, edited by Donald Day. [New York] Avon [1975, c1949] 397 p. 18 cm. [PN2287.R74A3] ISBN 0-380-00213-2 1.50 (pbk.)
I. Day, Donald, ed. II. Title.
L.C. card no. for original ed.: 49-11206 **BIP**

ROGERS, Will, 1879-1935. 791'.092'4 B
The autobiography of Will Rogers / selected and edited by Donald Day ; with a foreword by Bill and Jim Rogers. New York : AMS Press, [1979] p. cm. Reprint of the 1949 ed. published by Houghton Mifflin, Boston. Includes index. [PN2287.R74A3 1979] 76-6592 ISBN 0-404-15293-7 : 34.50
1. Rogers, Will, 1879-1935. 2. Humorists, American—Biography. I. Day, Donald, 1899-

ROGERS, Will, 1879-1935. 791'.092'4 B
The Will Rogers scrapbook / selected and edited by Bryan B. Sterling. New York : Grosset & Dunlap, c1976. 190 p. : ill. ; 28 cm. Interviews with Joel McCrea and others by Bryan B. Sterling, p. [115]-187. Includes index. [PN2287.R74A37] 76-549

ROGERS, Will, 1879-1935 928.1
The autobiography of Will Rogers, edited by Donald Day. [New York] Avon [1975, c1949] 397 p. 18 cm. [PN2287.R74A3] ISBN 0-380-00213-2 1.50 (pbk.)
I. Day, Donald, ed. II. Title.
L.C. card no. for original ed.: 49-11206 **BIP**

ROGERS, Will [William Penn Adair Rogers] 1879-1935 928.1
Autobiography; selected, ed. by Donald Day. Foreword by Bill and Jim Rogers. New York, Lnaer [1963, c.1921-1949] 351p. 18cm. (74-814) .75)ap.,
I. Day, Donald, 1899- ed. II. Title.

Rogers, Will, 1879-1935—Juvenile literature.

BENNETT, Cathereen L. 791'.0924 B
Will Rogers; the cowboy who walked with kings [by] Cathereen L. Bennett. Minneapolis, Minn., Lerner Publications Co. [1971] 71 p. illus., ports. 23 cm. A biography of the cowboy who became one of America's noted humorists. [PN2287.R74B4] 92 71-128806 ISBN 0-8225-0704-8
1. Rogers, Will, 1879-1935—Juvenile literature. I. Title.

CAMPBELL, Chester W. 791'.092'4 B
Will Rogers / by C. W. Campbell. Minneapolis : Dillon Press, c1979. p. cm. (The Story of an American Indian ; 29) A biography of the Oklahoma cowboy of Indian descent who became a well-known star of stage and screen and a noted humorist. [PN2287.R74C3] 79-4058 ISBN 0-87518-177-5 : 5.95
1. Rogers, Will, 1879-1935—Juvenile literature. 2. Entertainers—United States—Biography—Juvenile literature. 3. Humorists, American—Biography—Juvenile literature. I. Title.

JOHNSON, Spencer. 791'.092'4 B
The value of humor : the story of Will Rogers / by Spencer Johnson ; illustrated by Steve Pileggi. 1st ed. La Jolla, Calif. : Value Communications, c1976. 64 p. : col. ill. ; 29 cm. (A Value tale) One in a series of works which demonstrate the importance of various values. In this work a biography of Will Rogers illustrates the value of humor. [PN2287.R74J6] 92 76-41782 ISBN 0-916392-05-8 : 4.95
1. Rogers, Will, 1879-1935—Juvenile literature. 2. Entertainers—United States—Biography—Juvenile literature. 3. Humorists, American—Biography—Juvenile literature. I. Pileggi, Steve. II. Title. **BIP**

MONTGOMERY, Elizabeth Rider. 791.43'028'0924 B
Will Rogers, cowboy philosopher. Illustrated by Victor Mays. Champaign, Ill., Garrard Pub. Co. [1970] 96 p. col. illus., ports. 24 cm. (Americans all) The life of the Oklahoma cowboy of Indian descent who became a well-known writer and comedian. [PN2287.R74M6] 92 79-115469 2.49
1. Rogers, Will, 1879-1935—Juvenile literature. I. Mays, Victor, 1927- illus. II. Title.

MUSSO, Louis. 791'.092'4 B
Will Rogers, America's cowboy philosopher. Compiled with the assistance of the research staff of SamHar Press. Charlotteville, N.Y., SamHar Press, 1974. p. cm. (Outstanding personalities, no. 74) Bibliography: p. [PN2287.R74M8] 74-14622 2.29; 0.98 (pbk.)
1. Rogers, Will, 1879-1935—Juvenile literature. **BIP**

RICHARDS, Kenneth G., 1926- 791'.0924 B
Will Rogers, by Kenneth G. Richards. Chicago, Childrens Press [1968] 94 p. illus., ports. 29 cm. (People of destiny: a humanities series) Bibliography: p. 90-91. A biography of America's "unofficial president" whose famous remark," ... I never met a man I didn't like," was prompted by the Russian, Leon Trotsky. [PN2287.R74R5] 68-31308
1. Rogers, Will, 1879-1935—Juvenile literature. I. Title.

WAYNE, Bennett. 793.8'092'4
The super showmen, edited with commentary by Bennett Wayne. Champaign, Ill., Garrard Pub. Co. [1974] 167 p. illus. 22 cm. (A Target book) Biographies of three men who achieved fame for their ability to entertain—one as a magician, one as a cowboy comedian and philosopher, and one as a producer of motion pictures and animated cartoons. [PN1583.A2W35] 920 74-2282 ISBN 0-8116-4909-1 4.75
1. Houdini, Harry, 1874-1926—Juvenile literature. 2. Rogers, Will, 1879-1935—Juvenile literature. 3. Disney, Walt, 1901-1966—Juvenile literature. I. Title. **BIP**

Rogers, Woodes, d. 1732.

CRUSOE'S captain; 923.242
being the life of Woodes Rogers, seaman, trader, colonial governor. London, Odhams Press [dist. Hollywood-by-the-Sea, Fla., Trasatlantic Arts, 1960] 240p. Includes bibliography. illus., maps 23cm. 60-51001 5.50
1. Rogers, Woodes, d. 1732. I. Little, Bryan D.G.

Roget, Peter Mark, 1779-1869.

EMBLEN, Donald Lewis, 1918- 432.1 B
Peter Mark Roget: the word and the man [by] D. L. Emblen. New York, Crowell [1970] xvi, 368 p. illus., facsims., geneal. tables, ports. 22 cm. "The published writings of Peter Mark Roget": p. [341]-350. Bibliography: p. [351]-358. [CT788.R534E42] 72-109902 10.00
1. Roget, Peter Mark, 1779-1869. I. Title.

Rohan, William Joseph(1886-

WILLIAM Joseph Rohan, v. 12
a constructor in the building of the Americas. [Minneapolis] Winston Bros. Company, 1957] 99 [2]p. illus. 25cm. Limited edition.
1. Rohan, William Joseph(1886- 2. Winston Bros. Company. I. Hawkins, William G

Rohenstart, Charles Edward Stuart, called count, 1784?-1854.

SHERBURN, George Wiley, 1884- 920.8
Roehenstart, a late Stuart pretender; being an account of the life of Charles Edward August Maximilien Stuart Baron Korff Count Roehenstart. [Chicago] Univ. of Chicago Press [1961, c.1960] 148p. illls. 60-8402 5.50
1. Rohenstart, Charles Edward Stuart, called count, 1784?-1854. I. Title.

Rohrs, Frederick W

ROHRS, Frederick W 1876- 920
Autobiography, with adventures, reminiscences, and memoirs. [1st ed.] New York, Pageant Press [1952] 57p. 21cm. [CT275.R764A3] 53-348
I. Title.

Rojas, Ricardo,

ROJAS, Ricardo, 1882-1957 980/.02/0924
San Martin, knight of the Andes. Tr. by Herschel Brickell, Carlos Videla. Introd., notes by Herschel Brickell. New York, Cooper Sq., 1967(c.1945] xiii, 370p. port. 24cm. (Lib. of Latin-Amer. hist. and culture) Tr. of El santo de la espada. [F2235.4.R852 1967] (B) 66-30783 7.50
I. San Martin, Jose de, 1778-1850. II. Title.

Roland de la Platiere, Marie Jeanne Phlipon, 1754-1793.

DOBSON, Austin, 1840-1921. 944.04'092'2 B
Four Frenchwomen. Freeport, N.Y., Books for Libraries Press [1972] p. (Essay index reprint series) Reprint of the 1923 ed., which was issued as no. 248 of The World's classics. Contents.Contents.—Mademoiselle de Corday.—Madame Roland.—The Princess de Lamballe.—Madame de Genlis. [DC145.D7 1972] 72-6853 ISBN 0-8369-7269-4
1. Corday d'Armont, Marie Anne Charlotte de, 1768-1793. 2. Roland de la Platiere, Marie Jeanne (Phlipon) 1754-1793. 3. Lamballe, Marie Therese Louise de Savoie-Carignan, princesse de, 1749-1792. 4. Genlis, Stephanie Felicite Ducrest de Saint-Aubin, comtesse de, afterwards marquise de Sillery, 1746-1830. I. Title. BIP

LE GUIN, Charles A 944.0430924 (B)
Roland de la Platiere; a public servant in the eighteenth century [by] Charles A. Le Guin. Philadelphia, American Philosophical Society, 1966. 129 p. 30 cm. (Transactions of the American Philosophical Society, new ser., v. 56, pt. 6) Bibliography: p. 125-127. [DC146.R7L43] 66-29492
1. Roland de la Platiere, Jean Marie, 1734-1793. I. Title. II. Series: American Philosophical Society, Philadelphia. Transactions, new ser., v. 56, pt. 6 BIP

ROLAND de la Platiere, Marie Jeanne Phlipon, 1754-1793. 944.04'1'0924 B
The private memoirs of Madame Roland / edited, with an introd. by Edward Gilpin Johnson. 2d ed. New York : AMS Press, [1976] p. cm. (Women of letters) Reprint of the 1901 ed. published by A. C. McClurg, Chicago. Includes index. [DC146.R7A26 1976] 78-37719 ISBN 0-404-56829-7 : 24.50
1. Roland de la Platiere, Marie Jeanne Phlipon, 1754-1793. 2. France—History—Revolution, 1789-1799—Personal narratives. I. Johnson, Edward Gilpin. BIP

Rolfe, Frederick William, 1860-1913.

SYMONS, Alphonse James Albert, 1900- v. 12
The quest for Corvo; an experiment in biography. Baltimore, Md., Penguin Books [1966] 297 p. 68-25793
1. Rolfe, Frederick William, 1860-1913. I. Title. BIP

SYMONS, Alphonse James Albert, 1900-1941. 928.2
The quest for Corvo. With an introd. by Julian Symons. East Lansing, Michigan State University Press [1955] vi, 314p. port. 22cm. [PR5236.R27Z8 1955] 55-11687
1. Rolfe, Frederick William, 1860-1913. I. Title.

WEEKS, Donald. 823'8 [B]
Corvo; "saint or madman?" New York, McGraw-Hill [1971] [450 p.] 23 cm. Bibl.: p. 427-437 [PR5236.R2729 1972] 72-1371 ISBN 0-07-068965-2 8.95
1. Rolfe, Frederick William, I. Title.

Rolfe, Frederick William, 1860-1913—Biography.

BENKOVITZ, Miriam J. 823'.8 B
Frederick Rolfe, Baron Corvo : a biography / Miriam J. Benkovitz. 1st American ed. New York : Putnam, 1977. xiii, 332 p., [8] leaves of plates : ill. ; 24 cm. Includes bibliographical references and index. [PR5236.R27Z58 1977] 77-3671 10.95
1. Rolfe, Frederick William, 1860-1913—Biography. 2. Authors, English—19th century—Biography. I. Title.

Rolfe, Frederick William, 1860-1913—Correspondence.

DIFFERENT aspects : 823'.8
Frederick William Rolfe & the Foreign Office : Venice. Edinburgh : Tragara Press, 1976. 36, [1] p. ; 23 cm. Limited ed. of 125 copies, no. 55. [PR5236.R27Z53 1976] 77-373027 ISBN 0-902616-30-7 : £6.50
1. Rolfe, Frederick William, 1860-1913—Correspondence. 2. Authors, English—20th century—Correspondence. I. Rolfe, Frederick William, 1860-1913.

Rolfsrud, Erling Nicolai, 1912- —Biography—Youth—Juvenile literature.

ROLFSRUD, Erling Nicolai, 1912- 92
The tiger-lily years / by Erling Nicolai Rolfsrud. Alexandria, Minn. : Lantern Books, 1975. 103 p. : port. ; 21 cm. Recalls life of young boy growing up in North Dakota during the 1920's. [PA3568.O538Z527] 75-28585
1. Rolfsrud, Erling Nicolai, 1912- —Biography—Youth—Juvenile literature. I. Title.

Rolland, Romain, 1866-1944.

ROLLAND, Romain, 1866-1944. 782.1'0924
Richard Strauss & Romain Rolland; correspondence. Together with fragments from the diary of Romain Rolland and other essays and an introd. by Gustave Samazeuilh. Edited and annotated with a pref. by Rollo Myers. Berkeley, University of California Press, 1968. xvi, 239 p. facsims., music. 21 cm. Includes bibliographical references. [ML410.S93A4783 1968b] 67-22769
I. Strauss, Richard, 1864-1949. II. Myers, Rollo H., ed.

STARR, William Thomas, 1910- 928.4
Romain Rolland and a world at war. Evanston, Ill., Northwestern University Press, 1956. xii, 223p. 24cm. (Northwestern University studies. Humanities series, no. 31) Bibliographical footnotes. [PQ2635.O5Z84] 56-1981
1. Rolland, Romain, 1866-1944. I. Title. II. Series. BIP

STARR, William Thomas, 1910- 848'.9'1209 B
Romain Rolland and a world at war. New York, AMS Press [1971, c1956] xii, 223 p. 23 cm. (Northwestern University studies in the humanities, no. 31) Includes bibliographical references. [PQ2635.O5Z84 1971] 72-128947 ISBN 0-404-50731-X
1. Rolland, Romain, 1866-1944. I. Title. II. Series: Northwestern University studies. Humanities series, no. 31

WILSON, Ronald Alfred. 848'.9'1209
The pre-war biographies of Romain Rolland and their place in his work and the period, by Ronald A. Wilson. Port Washington, N.Y., Kennikat Press [1972] 233, iv p. 23 cm. "In substance, a thesis submitted in 1937 to the University of St. Andrews in fulfilment of the conditions for the degree of Ph.D." "Appendix (p. [217]-221): Two letters from Romain Roland to the author." Reprint of the 1939 ed. Bibliography: p. [222]-233. [PQ2635.O5Z92 1972] 71-160786 ISBN 0-8046-1618-3
1. Rolland, Romain, 1866-1944. 2. Biography. I. Title. BIP

ZWEIG, Stefan, 1881-1942. 848'.9'1209 B
Romain Rolland; the man and his work. Translated from the original ms. by Eden and Cedar Paul. New York, B. Blom, 1972. x, 377 p. illus. 18 cm. Reprint of the 1921 ed. published by T. Seltzer, New York. Bibliography: p. [357]-370. [PQ2635.O5Z97 1972] 79-174836 12.50
1. Rolland, Romain, 1866-1944.

ZWEIG, Stefan, 1881-1942. 848'.9'1209 B
Romain Rolland: the man and his work. Translated from the original manuscript by Eden and Cedar Paul. New York, Haskell House, 1970. x, 377 p. facsims., ports. 23 cm. Reprint of the 1921 ed. Bibliography: p. [357]-370. [PQ2635.O5Z97 1970] 70-130266 ISBN 0-8383-1173-3
1. Rolland, Romain, 1866-1944. I. Title.

Rolland, Romain, 1866-1944—Correspondence.

ROMAIN Rolland and 848'.9'1209 B
Gandhi correspondence : letters, diary extracts, articles, etc. / foreword by Jawaharlal Nehru. New Delhi : Publications Division, Ministry of Information and Broadcasting, Govt. of India, 1976. xxviii, 607 p., [1] leaf of plates : ill. ; 22 cm. French text of Rolland's writings translated by R. A. Francis. Includes index. [PQ2635.O5Z53 1976] 76-905656 Rs25.00 ($7.50 U.S.)
1. Rolland, Romain, 1866-1944—Correspondence. 2. Gandhi, Mohandas Karamchand, 1869-1948. 3. Statesmen—India—Correspondence. 4. Authors, French—20th century—Correspondence. I. Francis, R. A.

Rolle, Richard, of Hampole, 1290?-1349.

COMPER, Frances Margaret Mary. 821'.1 B
The life of Richard Rolle, together with an edition of his English lyrics (now for the first time published), by Frances M. M. Comper. [Folcroft, Pa.] Folcroft Library Editions, 1973. p. Reprint of the 1928 ed. published by Dent, London. "List of the writings ascribed to Richard Rolle": Bibliography: [PR2136.C6 1973] 73-17225 30.00
1. Rolle, Richard, of Hampole, 1290?-1349. I. Rolle, Richard, of Hampole, 1290?-1349. II. Title. BIP

COMPER, Frances Margaret Mary. 821'.1 B
The life of Richard Rolle, together with an edition of his English lyrics (now for the first time published), by Frances M. M. Comper. New York, Barnes & Noble [1969] xx, 340 p. illus., facsims., maps. 23 cm. Title on spine: The life and lyrics of Richard Rolle. Reprint of the 1928 ed. "List of writings ascribed to Richard Rolle": p. 326-328. Bibliography: p. 320-325. [PR2136.C6 1969] 70-5925 9.00
1. Rolle, Richard, of Hampole, 1290-1349. I. Title.

HODGSON, Geraldine Emma, 1865-1937. 821'.1 B
The sanity of mysticism : a study of Richard Rolle / by Geraldine E. Hodgson. Folcroft, Pa. : Folcroft Library Editions, 1976. p. cm. Reprint of the 1926 ed. published by the Faith Press, London. [PR2136.H6 1976] 76-11826 ISBN 0-8414-4845-0 lib. bdg. : 20.00
1. Rolle, Richard, of Hampole, 1290?-1349. 2. Mysticism. I. Title.

Roller derbies—Biography.

MICHELSON, Herb. 796.2'1'0922
A very simple game; the story of roller derby. [Oakland, Calif.] Occasional Pub. Co. [1971] v, 210 p. illus., ports. 18 cm. [GV851.6.M5] 73-164685 2.50
1. Roller derbies—Biography. I. Title.

Rollin, Betty

†ROLLIN, Betty. 616.9'94
First, you cry / by Betty Rollin New York : New American Library, 1977, c1976 232p. ; 18 cm. (A Signet Book.) [RC280.B8R64] ISBN 0-451-08534-5 pbk. : 1.95
1. Rollin, Betty 2. Breast — Cancer — Biography. I. Title.
L.C. card no. for 1976 Lippincott ed.:76-1604. BIP

Rolls, Charles Stewart, 1877-1910.

MONTAGU, Edward John Barrington Douglas-Scott-Montagu, baron, 1926- 629.2222
Rolls of Rolls-Royce; a biography of the Hon. C. S. Rolls [by] Lord Montagu of Beaulieu. Research by Michael Sedgwick. South Brunswick [N. J.] Barnes [1967, c1966] xiii, 250 p. illus., ports. 22 cm. [TL140.R63M6 1967] 67-12837
1. Rolls, Charles Stewart, 1877-1910. I. Title.

MONTAGU of Beaulieu, Edward John Barrington Douglas-Scott-Montagu, Baron, 1926- 629.2222
Rolls of Rolls-Royce; a biography of the Hon. C. S. Rolls [by] Lord Montagu of Beaulieu. Research by Michael Sedgwick. South Brunswick [N.J.] Barnes [1967, c1966] xiii, 250 p. illus., ports. 22 cm. [TL140.R63M6 1967] 67-12837
1. Rolls, Charles Stewart, 1877-1910. I. Title.

ROWLAND, John, 1907- 629.2'0922 B
The Rolls-Royce men; the story of C. S. Rolls and Henry Royce. Illustrated by Martin Henley. New York, Roy Publishers [1970, c1969] 130 p. illus. 21 cm. The life of two Englishmen from very different backgrounds who combined skills to produce one of the most famous automobiles in the world. [TL140.R63R6] 920 72-99505 3.95
1. Rolls, Charles Stewart, 1877-1910. 2. Royce, Henry, Sir, bart., 1863-1933. I. Henley, Martin, illus. II. Title.

Roloff, Lester, 1918-

ROLOFF, Marie Brady. 269'.2'0924 B
Lester Roloff : living by faith / by Marie Brady Roloff. Nashville : Action Press, c1978. 192 p., [4] leaves of plates : ill. ; 21 cm. [BX6495.R664R64] 78-3654 ISBN 0-8407-9506-8 pbk. : 3.95
1. Roloff, Lester, 1918- 2. Baptists—Texas—Biography. 3. Evangelists—Texas—Biography. 4. Texas—Biography. BIP

Roman emperors.

SUETONIAS, Tranquillus c. 937.060922
The lives of the twelve Caesars. Tr. by Philemon Holland, rev. for the present ed., with an introd., by Moses Hadas. Illus. with paintings by Salvatore Fiume. New York, Heritage [dist. Dial, c.1965] xvii, 482p. illus. (pt. mounted col.) 26cm. [DG277.S7H6] 65-8689 6.95
1. Roman emperors. 2. Rome—Hist.—Empire, 30 B.C.-284 A.D. I. Hadas, Moses, 1900- ed. II. Holland, Philemon, 1552-1637, tr. III. Fiume, Salvatore, 1915- illus. IV. Title.

SUETONIUS Tranquillus, C v. 12
The lives of the twelve Caesars. An unexpurgated English version, edited with notes and an introduction by Joseph Gavorse. New York, Modern Library [c1959] 361 p. (The Modern Library of the world's best books) 63-69752
1. Roman emperors. 2. Rome — Hist. Empire, B.C. 30-A.D. 284. I. Gavorse, Joseph. II. Title.

SYME, Ronald, Sir, 1903- 937'.07'0922
Emperors and biography: studies in the 'Historia Augusta'. Oxford, Clarendon Press, 1971. ix, 306 p. 25 cm. Continuation of Ammianus and the Historia Augusta. Bibliography: p. [291]-295. [DG274.S9] 70-22066 ISBN 0-19-814357-5 £3.25
1. Scriptores historiae Augustae. 2. Roman emperors. 3. Rome—History—Empire, 30 B.C.-284 A.D. I. Title. BIP

Roman emperors—Biography.

LUDWIG, Charles, 1918- 937'.07'0922 B
Rulers of New Testament times / Charles Ludwig. Denver : Accent Books, c1976. 128 p. : ill. ; 19 cm. Bibliography: p. 127-128. [DG274.L8] 75-40910 ISBN 0-916406-15-6 pbk. : 2.25
1. Roman emperors—Biography. 2.

Palestine—Kings and rulers—Biography. I. Title. BIP

Roman empresses—Biography.

FERRERO, 937'.06'0922 B
Guglielmo, 1871-1942.
The most beautiful women in Imperial Rome / Guglielmo Ferrero. Albuquerque : Gloucester Art Press, [1978] p. cm. Reprinted from the Century illustrated monthly magazine, v. 82, no. 1-6, May-Oct. 1911 and published separately under title: The women of the Caesars. [DG274.3.F47 1978] 78-11351 ISBN 0-930582-05-5 : 37.50
1. Roman empresses—Biography. 2. Rome—Princes and princesses—Biography. 3. Women—Rome—Biography. I. Title.
Publisher's address : P.O. Box 4526, Albuquerque, NM 87106 BIP

Roman, LuLu.

ROMAN, LuLu. 248'.24 B
LuLu / LuLu Roman. Old Tappan, N.J. : F. H. Revell, c1978. 173 p. : ill. ; 22 cm. [BR1725.R65A34] 78-15510 ISBN 0-8007-0956-X : 6.95
1. Roman, LuLu. 2. Christian biogrphy—United States. 3. Entertainers—United States—Biography. I. Title. BIP

Romanian Americans—Biography.

ANDRONESCU, 920'.0092'59073
Serban.
Who's who in Romanian America / Serban C. Andronescu, compiler ; American Institute for Writing Research Corp., editor. New York : Andronescu-Wyndill, 1976. 188 p. ; 27 cm. [E184.R8A5] 77-368872
1. Romanian Americans—Biography. I. American Institute for Writing Research. II. Title. BIP

Romano, Jacques, 1864-1962.

SCHWARZ, Berthold 973.9'0924 B
Eric, 1924-
The Jacques Romano story. New York, University Books [1968] x, 243 p. facsim., ports. 22 cm. Bibliographical footnotes. [CS275.R6S3] 68-18753
1. Romano, Jacques, 1864-1962. I. Title.

Romano, Juanita Napoles.

ROMANO, Juanita 286'.7'0924 B
Napoles.
The wind blows free on Cupcake Hill. Mountain View, Calif., Pacific Press Pub. Association [1973] 112 p. 22 cm. (A Destiny book, D-141) The author recalls her childhood in Hawaii, her growing-up years in the Philippines as the daughter of Seventh Day Adventist missionaries, and her marriage and battle with disease in the United States. [BX6193.R65A37] 73-85875
1. Romano, Juanita Napoles. I. Title.

Romano, Umberto, 1906-

ROMANO, Umberto, 1906- 759.13
Great men / Umberto Romano. New York : Dial Press, 1979. p. cm. [ND1329.R63A4 1979] 79-4131 35.00
1. Romano, Umberto, 1906- 2. Biography—Portraits. I. Title.

Romanov, House of.

BERGAMINI, John D. 947
The tragic dynasty; a history of the Romanovs, by John D. Bergamini. New York, Putnam [1969] 512 p. illus., geneal. table, maps, ports. 24 cm. Bibliography: p. [491]-495. [DK37.8.R6B45] 68-15498 10.00
1. Romanov, House of. 2. Russia—Kings and rulers. I. Title.

MAZOUR, Anatole Gregory, 929.747
1900-
Rise and fall of the Romanovs. Princeton, N. J., Van Nostrand [1960] 192p. illus. 18cm. (An Anvil original, no. 50) [DK113.M32] 60-13460
1. Romanov, House of. I. Title. BIP

Romans, Bernard, ca. 1720-ca. 1784.

PHILLIPS, Philip 526'.092'4 B
Lee, 1857-1924.
Notes on the life and works of Bernard Romans / by P. Lee Phillips. A facsim. reproduction of the 1924 ed. / with an introd. and index by John D. Ware. Gainesville : University Presses of Florida, 1975. xcvii, 128, 10 p., [12] leaves of plates : maps ; 22 cm. (Bicentennial Floridiana facsimile series) Three hundred and twenty-five copies printed. No. 77. Reprint of the ed. published by the Florida State Historical Society, DeLand, as no. 2 of its Publications. "A University of Florida book." [GA407.R65P48 1924a] 74-20757 ISBN 0-8130-0413-6
1. Romans, Bernard, ca. 1720-ca. 1784. 2. Florida—Description and travel—To 1865. 3. United States—Maps—Bibliography. I. Ware, John D., 1913-1973. II. Title. III. Series: Florida State Historical Society. Publications ; no. 2. BIP

Romanticism—France.

KELLY, Linda, 1936- 200.19
The young romantics : Paris, 1827-37 / [by] Linda Kelly. London : Bodley Head, 1976. [11], 146 p., [16] p. of plates : ill., ports. ; 23 cm. Includes index. Bibliography: p. 139-141. [PQ287.K4 1976b] 76-359699 ISBN 0-370-10264-9 : £3.75
1. Romanticism—France. 2. Authors, French—Biography. 3. Paris—Intellectual life. I. Title.

KELLY, Linda, 1936- 840'.9'14
The young romantics : Victor Hugo, Sainte-Beuve, Vigny, Dumas, Musset, and George Sand and their friendships, feuds, and loves in the French romantic revolution / Linda Kelly. 1st American ed. New York : Random House, c1976. x, 180 p., [8] leaves of plates : ill. ; 25 cm. Includes index. Bibliography: p. 173-176. [PQ287.K4 1976] 76-8219 ISBN 0-394-48705-2 : 8.95
1. Romanticism—France. 2. Authors, French—Biography. 3. Paris—Intellectual life. I. Title.

Romanus I Lecapenus, co-emperor of the East, d.948.

RUNCIMAN, Steven, Sir 1903- v. 12
The emperor Romanus Lecapenus and his reign; a study of tenth-century Byzantium. Cambridge, University Press, 1963. vi, 275 p. fold. map, fold. geneal. table. 22 cm. "First printed 1929; reprinted 1963." Bibliography: p. [254]-261. 65-87833
1. Romanus I Lecapenus, co-emperor of the East, d.948. 2. Byzantine empire—Hist. I. Title.

Rome—Biog.

PLUTARCHUS 937.00922
Makers of Rome; nine lives by Plutarch: Coriolanus, Fabius Maximus, Marcellus, Cato the Elder, Tiberius, Gracchus, Gaius Gracchus, Sertorius, Brutus, Mark Antony. Tr., introd. by Ian Scott-Kilvert. Baltimore, Penguin [c.1965] 366p. maps. 19cm. (The Penguin classics, L158) [DG260.A1P53] 65-29726 1.65 pap.,
1. Rome—Biog. I. Scott-Kilvert, Ian, ed. and tr. II. Title.

Rome—Biography.

COOLIDGE, Olivia E. 920.038
Lives of famous Romans [by] Olivia Coolidge. Illustrated by Milton Johnson. Boston, Houghton Mifflin, 1965. 248 p. ports. 22 cm. Contents.Contents.—Cicero.—Caesar.—Augustus.—Vergil and Horace.—Nero and Seneca.—Trajan.—Hadrian.—Marcus Aurelius.—Diocletian.—Constantine. [DG203.C63] 65-19297
1. Rome—Biography. I. Title. BIP

DUGGAN, Alfred Leo, 1903- 923.137
Julius Caesar; a great life in brief. [1st ed.] New York, Knopf, 1955. 205 p. 19 cm. (Great lives in brief; a new series of biographies) [DG261.D77] 54-7217
I. Caesar, C. Julius.

GLOVER, Terrot Reaveley, 920.037
1869-1943.
Life and letters in the fourth century. New York, Russell & Russell [1968] xvi, 398 p. 22 cm. Reprint of the 1901 ed. Contents.Contents.—Ammianus Marcellinus.—Julian.—Quintus of Smyrna. —Ausonius.—Women pilgrims.—Symmachus.—Macrobius.—St. Augustine's Confessions.—Claudian.—Prudentius.—Sulpicius Severus.—Palladas.—Synesius.—Greek and early Christian novels. Bibliographical footnotes. [DG312.G5 1968] 68-10923
1. Rome—Biography. 2. Classical literature—History and criticism. I. Title. BIP

JONES, Arnold Hugh 920.037
Martin, 1904-
The prosopography of the later Roman Empire, by A. H. M. Jones, J. R. Martindale and J. Morris. Cambridge [Eng.] University Press, 1971- v. geneal. tables. 24 cm. Contents.Contents.—v. 1. A.D. 260-395. [DG203.5.J6] 77-118859 ISBN 0-521-07233-6(v.1)
1. Rome—Biography. 2. Names, Personal—Roman. I. Martindale, John Robert, joint author. II. Morris, J., joint author. III. Title.

PLUTARCHUS. 920'.037
Fall of the Roman Republic: Marius, Sulla, Crassus, Pompey, Caesar, Cicero: six lives; translated [from the Latin] by Rex Warner. Revised ed. with introductions and notes by Robin Seager. Harmondsworth, Penguin, 1972. 361 p. 18 cm. (Penguin classics) Includes bibliographical references. [DG260.A1P53 1972] 73-157637 ISBN 0-14-044084-4 £0.50
1. Rome—Biography. I. Warner, Rex, 1905- tr. II. Seager, Robin. III. Title.

PLUTARCHUS. 920.037
Lives of the noble Romans; a selection edited by Edmund Fuller. [New York] [Dell Pub. Co.] [1959] 383 p. 17 cm. (A Laurel classic, LC139) [DE7.P7F82] 60-22729
1. Rome—Biography. I. Fuller, Edmund, 1914- ed. II. Title.

Rome—History—Empire, 30 B.C.-284A.D.

BRAUER, George C. 937'.07'0922
The young emperors, Rome, A. D. 193-244 [by] George C. Bauer, Jr. New York, Crowell [1967] 241 p. illus. 24 cm. Bibliography: p. 228-233. [DG298.B7] 67-18524
1. Rome—History—Empire, 30 B.C.-284A.D. 2. Roman emperors. I. Title.

Rome—History—Flavians, 69-96—Biography.

MCDERMOTT, William 937'.06'0922 B
Coffman, 1907-
Roman portraits : the Flavian-Trajanic period / William C. McDermott, Anne E. Orentzel. Columbia : University of Missouri Press, 1979. p. cm. Includes index. Bibliography: p. [DG291.6.M32] 79-1559 ISBN 0-8262-0275-6 : 17.50
1. Rome—History—Flavians, 69-96—Biography. 2. Rome—History—Trajan, 98-117—Biography. 3. Statesmen—Rome—Biography. 4. Rome—Nobility—Biography. I. Orentzel, Anne E., 1948- joint author. II. Title. BIP

Rome—History—The five Julii, 30 B.C.-68 A.D.

TACITUS, Cornelius. 937.07
The annals of Tacitus; a new translation by D. R. Dudley. New York, New American Library [1966] 432 p. illus., geneal. table, maps. 18 cm. (A Mentor book, MQ 676) [DG207.T3D8] 66-26534
1. Rome—History—The five Julii, 30 B.C.-68 A.D. I. Dudley, Donald Reynolds, tr. II. Title. BIP

Rome—History—30 B.C. 476 A.D.

MARSH, Henry. 937'.06'0922 B
The Caesars; the Roman Empire and its rulers. New York, St. Martin's Press [1972, c1971] 208 p. 23 cm. Bibliography: p. [195]-197. [DG270.M37 1972] 72-79779 5.95
1. Rome—History—30 B.C. 476 A.D. 2. Roman emperors. I. Title.

Rominger, Carl Ludwig, 1820-1907.

WRIGHT, Jean Davies. 550'.92'4 B
That remarkable man Carl Ludwig Rominger, State geologist. [Ann Arbor] Museum of Paleontology, University of Michigan, 1973. 148 p. illus. 26 cm. (Papers on paleontology, no. 4) Cover title. Bibliography: p. 147-148. [QE22.R69W74] 73-174807
1. Rominger, Carl Ludwig, 1820-1907. 2. Geology—Michigan—History. I. Title. II. Series.

Rommel, Erwin, 1891-1944.

CHANDLER, David 940.54'23'0924 B
G.
Rommel : battles and campaigns / by David G. Chandler. New York : Mayflower Books, [1979] p. cm. [U55.R6C47] 78-31786 ISBN 0-8317-7477-0 : 14.95
1. Rommel, Erwin, 1891-1944. 2. Germany. Heer—Biography. 3. Marshals—Germany—Biography. 4. World War, 1939-1945—Campaigns. I. Title.

COCKRELL, Monroe 923.594
Fulkerson, 1884-
Erwin Johannes Eugen Rommel in Tennessee, Virginia, Gettysburg. [Evanston, Ill., 1951] 1 v. 28cm. [U55.R6C6] 53-28027
1. Rommel, Erwin, 1891-1944. I. Title.

DOUGLAS-HOME, 940.54'23'0924 B
Charles, 1937-
Rommel. New York, Saturday Review Press [1973] 224 p. illus. 26 cm. (Great commanders) Bibliography: p. 219. [U55.R6D68] 73-75720 ISBN 0-8415-0255-2 12.50
1. Rommel, Erwin, 1891-1944.

IRVING, David 940.54'23'0924 B
John Cawdell, 1938-
The trail of the fox / David Irving. 1st ed. New York : Dutton, c1977. viii, 496 p., [16] leaves of plates : ill. ; 25 cm. "Thomas Congdon books." Includes index. Bibliography: p. 461-472. [U55.R6178 1977] 77-24009 ISBN 0-525-22200-6 : 12.95
1. Rommel, Erwin, 1891-1944. 2. Marshals—Germany—Biography. I. Title. BIP

LEWIN, Ronald. 940.542'3'0924
Rommel as military commander. London, Batsford; Princeton, N. J., Van Nostrand, 1968. x, 262p. 27 plates, illus., plans (incl. 4 col.) ports. 24cm. [Military commanders ser.] Bibl. [U55.R6L4] (B) 68-138838 8.95
1. Rommel, Erwin, 1891-1944. I. Title.

SIBLEY, Roger. 940.54'23'0924 B
Rommel [by] R. Sibley/M. Fry. [New York, Ballantine Books, 1974] 160 p. illus. 21 cm. (Ballantine's illustrated history of the violent century. War leader book no. 27) Includes bibliographical references. [DD247.R57S5] 74-176228 2.00 (pbk.)
1. Rommel, Erwin, 1891-1944. I. Fry, Michael, joint author.

YOUNG, Desmond. 940.542'30924 B
Rommel, the desert fox. Foreword by Sir Claude Auchinleck. Large type ed. New York, Harper & Row [1967, c1950] xvii, 264 p. maps. 29 cm. [U55] 68-2341
1. Rommel, Erwin, 1891-1944. I. Title.

YOUNG, Desmond. 923.543
Rommel, the desert fox: foreword by Sir Claude Auchinleck. [1st American ed.] New York, Harper [1951, c1950] xvii, 264 p. ports., maps. 22 cm. [U55.R6Y6 1951] 51-9112
1. Rommel, Erwin, 1891-1944. BIP

Romney, George W., 1907-

ANGEL, D. Duane, 973.923'0924
1939-
Romney; a political biography, by D. Duane Angel. [1st ed.] New York, Exposition Press [1967] xiii, 266 p. 21 cm.

(An Exposition-banner book) Bibliography: p. [247]-259. [F570.R6A7] 67-26387
1. Romney, George W., 1907-

GOLLAN, Antoni E. 973.923'0924
Romney behind the image, by Antoni E. Gollan. Introd. by M. Stanton Evans. Arlington, Va., Crestwood Books [1967] 150 p. ports. 19 cm. Bibliography: p. 141-150. [F570.R6G6] 67-28135
1. Romney, George W., 1907- I. Title.

HARRIS, T. George, 1924- 973.923'0924 B
Romney's way; a man and an idea, by T. George Harris. Englewood Cliffs, N.J., Prentice-Hall [1968, c1967] xiv, 274 p. 22 cm. Bibliographical footnotes. [F570.R6H3] 68-13399
1. Romney, George W., 1907- I. Title.

MAHONEY, Tom. 926.58
The story of George Romney: builder, salesman, crusader. [1st ed.] New York, Harper [c1960] 275p. illus. 22cm. [HD9710.U54A657] 59-13284
1. Romney, George W., 1907- 2. American Motors Corporation. I. Title.

MAHONEY, Tom [John Thomas Mahoney] 926.58
The story of George Romney: builder, salesman, crusader. New York, Harper [c.1960] ix, 275p. (bibl notes: p.248-254) illus. 22cm. 59-13284 4.00
1. Romney, George W., 1907- 2. American Motors Corporation. I. Title.

MOLLENHOFF, Clark R. 973.923'0924 B
George Romney, Mormon in politics, by Clark R. Mollenhoff. [1st ed.] New York, Meredith Press [1968] viii, 360 p. 22 cm. Bibliography: p. 329. [F570.R6M6] 68-19030
1. Romney, George W., 1907-

PLAS, Gerald O. 973.923'0924
The Romney riddle, by Gerald O. Plas. Detroit, Berwyn Publishers [1967] 126 p. 18 cm. Bibliographical references included in "Notes" (p. 123-126) [F570.R6P55] 67-66243
1. Romney, George W., 1907- I. Title.

Romney, George, 1734-1802.

CHAMBERLAIN, Arthur Bensley. 759.2 B
George Romney, by Arthur B. Chamberlain. Freeport, N.Y., Books for Libraries Press [1971] xv, 418 p. illus., ports. 27 cm. Reprint of the 1910 ed. Bibliography: p. xv. [ND497.R7C4 1971] 70-157329 ISBN 0-8369-5789-X
1. Romney, George, 1734-1802. BIP

Romulo, Carlos Pena, 1899-

ROMULO, Carlos Pena, 1899- 923.2914
I walked with heroes. New York, Avon [c.1961] 253p. illus. (S-106) .60 pap.,
I. Title.

ROMULO, Carlos Pena, 1899- 923.2914
I walked with heroes. [1st ed.] New York, Holt, Rinehart and Winston [1961] 342 p. illus. 22 cm. [DS686.2.R6A3] 61-6405
I. Title.

WELLS, Evelyn 923.2914
Carlos P. Romulo: voice of freedom. New York, Funk & Wagnalls [c.1964] 180p. port. 22cm. 64-11124 3.50
1. Romulo, Carlos Pena, 1899- I. Title.

Romulo, Carlos Pena, 1899- —Juvenile literature.

DE LEEUW, Adele Louise, 1899- 959.9'04'0924 B
Carlos P. Romulo, the barefoot boy of diplomacy / by Adele deLeeuw. Philadelphia : Westminster Press, c1976. 175 p. : ill. ; 21 cm. Includes index. Bibliography: p. 169-170. A biography of the Filipino statesman who became the first non-American to win the Pulitzer prize, the President of the U.N. General Assembly, and a champion for Philippine independence and the rights of all minorities. [DS686.2.R6D4] 92 75-35834 ISBN 0-664-32583-1 : 6.95
1. Romulo, Carlos Pena, 1899- —Juvenile literature. I. Title.

Ronan, Mary, 1852-

RONAN, Mary, 1852- 978.6'02'0924 B
Frontier woman : the story of Mary Ronan as told to Margaret Ronan / edited by H. G. Merriam. [Missoula] : University of Montana, c1973. viii, 172 p., [4] leaves of plates : ill. ; 22 cm. (University of Montana publications in history) Includes bibliographical references. [F731.R57] 75-310321
1. Ronan, Mary, 1852- 2. Frontier and pioneer life—Montana. 3. Indians of North America—Montana. 4. Montana—History. I. Ronan, Margaret, 1883- II. Title. III. Series: Montana. University. Missoula. Publications in history.

Rondeau, Noah John,

RONDEAU, Noah John, 1883-1967. 799.29'24 B
Noah John Rondeau, Adirondack hermit [edited by] Maitland C. De Sormo. Saranac Lake, N.Y., North Country Books [1969] xvi, 204 p. illus., ports. 24 cm. Includes bibliographical references. [SK17.R6A3] 74-271766 6.00
I. De Sormo, Maitland C., ed. II. Title.

Roney, Frank, 1841-1925.

RONEY, Frank, 1841-1925. 331.88'092'4 B
Frank Roney : an autobiography / edited by Ira B. Cross. New York : Arno Press, 1977 p. cm. (The Irish-Americans) Reprint of the ed. published by University of California Press, Berkeley. [HD8073.R6A3 1976] 76-6363 ISBN 0-405-09355-1 : 37.00
1. Roney, Frank, 1841-1925. 2. Fenians (Society) 3. Labor and laboring classes—California—Biography. 4. Labor and laboring classes—United States—Biography. 5. Ireland—History—1837-1901. I. Cross, Ira Brown, 1880- II. Title. III. Series.

RONEY, Frank, 1841-1925. 331.88'092'4 B
Frank Roney : Irish rebel and California labor leader : an autobiography / edited by Ira B. Cross. New York : AMS Press, 1977. xxxvi, 573 p., [8] leaves of plates : ill. ; 23 cm. (The Labor movement in fiction and non-fiction) Reprint of the 1931 ed. published by the University of California Press, Berkeley. Includes index. [HD6509.R65A35 1977] 74-22758 ISBN 0-404-58511-6 : 36.75
1. Roney, Frank, 1841-1925. 2. Trade-unions—California—Officials and employees—Biography. 3. Fenians—Biography. I. Title. II. Series.

Ronk, Emma Rosalie (Reynolds)

RONK, Emma Rosalie (Reynolds) 1865- 920.7
Emma Rosalie; a story out of the yesterdays. [Des Moines? -- 1950] 150 p. illus., ports. 22 cm. [CT275.R775A3] 51-18137
I. Title. II. Title: Out of the yesterdays.

Ronne, Finn.

RONNE, Finn. 919.8'9'040924
Antarctica, my destiny / by Finn Ronne. New York : Hastings House, 1979. p. cm. Includes index. [G875.R66A32] 79-18037 ISBN 0-8038-0485-7 : 12.95
1. Ronne, Finn. 2. Antarctic regions. 3. Explores—United States—Biography. I. Title.

Ronsisvalle, Daniel.

HUIE, William Bradford, 1910- 289.9 B
It's me O Lord! / William Bradford Huie. Nashville : T. Nelson, c1979. 189 p., [4] leaves of plates : ill. ; 21 cm. [BX8762.Z8R653] 79-403 ISBN 0-8407-5141-9 7.95
1. Ronsisvalle, Daniel. 2. Pentecostal churches—Clergy—Biography. 3. Clergy—United States—Biography. I. Title. BIP

Ronstadt, Linda.

CLAIRE, Vivian. 784'.092'4 B
Linda Ronstadt / Vivian Claire. New York : Flash Books, c1978. 72 p. : ill. ; 26 cm. Discography: p. 71-72. A biography of a popular singer whose career has spanned a decade. [ML420.R8753C6] 92 77-88753 ISBN 0-8256-3918-2 : 3.95
1. Ronstadt, Linda. 2. Singers—United States—Biography. I. Title.
Publisher's address : 33 W. 60th St., New York, N. Y. 10023 BIP

†KANAKARIS, Richard. 784'.092'4 [B]
Linda Ronstadt, a portrait / by Richard Kanakaris. Los Angeles : L.A. Pop Pub., 1977. 79 leaves, [3] leaves of plates : ports. ; 29 cm. Discography: leaves 24-47. [ML420.R8753K3] 77-91926 4.00
1. Ronstadt, Linda. 2. Singers—United States—Biography.

MOORE, Mary Ellen. 784'.092'4 B
The Linda Ronstadt scrapbook / by Mary Ellen Moore ; [front cover photo by Steve Shapiro ; back cover photo by Charlyn Zlotnik]. New York : Sunridge Press, c1978. 121 p., [1] leaf of plates : ill. ; 28 cm. On cover: An illustrated biography. [ML420.R8753M6] 79-114698 ISBN 0-441-48410-7 : 5.95
1. Ronstadt, Linda. 2. Singers—United States—Biography.

Rontgen, Wilhelm Conrad, 1845-1923.

GREY, Vivian. 530'.092'4 B
Roentgen's revolution: the discovery of the X ray. [1st ed.] Boston, Little, Brown [1973] xiv, 144 p. port. 21 cm. The biography of the German physicist who accidentally discovered the x ray and won the Nobel Prize for physics in 1901. [QC16.R47G7] 92 73-3153 ISBN 0-316-32821-9 5.95
1. Rontgen, Wilhelm Conrad, 1845-1923—Juvenile literature. 2. X-rays—Juvenile literature. I. Title. BIP

Rontgen, Wulhelm Conrad, 1845-1923.

DIBNER, Bern. 539.7
Wilhelm Conrad Rontgen and the discovery of X rays. New York, F. Watts [1968] 149 p. illus., facsims., ports. 22 cm. (Immortals of science) Bibliographical footnotes. Covers observations and theories leading to Rontgen's work, biographical information about the German physicist, Rontgen's discovery and further research, and improvements and applications of the X ray after the appearance of Rontgen's papers. [QC16.R47D5] AC 68
1. Rontgen, Wilhelm Conrad, 1845-1923. 2. X rays. I. Title.

ESTERER, Arnulf K. 530'.0924 B
Discoverer of X-ray: Wilhelm Conrad Rontgen, by Arnulf K. Esterer. New York, J. Messner [1968] 191 p. 22 cm. Bibliography: p. [187] A biography of the European teacher and scientist who was awarded the first Nobel prize in physics for his discovery of X-rays. [QC16.R47E8] 92 AC 68
1. Rontgen, Wilhelm Conrad, 1845-1923. I. Title.

NITSKE, W. Robert. 530'.0924 B
The life of Wilhelm Conrad Rontgen, discoverer of the X ray, by W. Robert Nitske. Tucson, University of Arizona Press [1971] xi, 355 p. illus., facsims., geneal. table, map (on lining paper), ports. 24 cm. Includes three papers by W. C. Rontgen, A new kind of ray, preliminary communication; A new kind of ray, continuation; and Further observations on the properties of X rays, third communication (p. 310-336) Bibliography: p. 339-345. [QC16.R47N55] 79-125167 ISBN 0-8165-0259-5 8.50
1. Rontgen, Wilhelm Conrad, 1845-1923. I. Title.

Rood, John, 1902-

JOHN Rood's sculpture. 735.73
Translated from the German by Desmond and Louise Clayton. Minneapolis, University of Minnesota Press [1958] 112p. illus. (part col.) 28cm. Bibliography: p. 29. [NB237.R68S3] 927.3 A58
1. Rood, John, 1902- I. Schneider, Bruno F

Rookmaaker, Hendrik Roelof, 1922-1977.

MARTIN, Linette. 284'.2'0924 B
Hans Rookmaaker : a biography / Linette Martin. Downers Grove, Ill. : InterVarsity Press, c1979. 187 p. ; 21 cm. Includes index. Bibliography: p. 179-180. [BX9479.R66M37 1979] 79-2382 ISBN 0-87784-725-8 : 4.95
1. Rookmaaker, Hendrik Roelof, 1922-1977. 2. Reformed (Reformed Church) in the Netherlands—Biography. BIP

Rooseboom (Ship)

GIBSON, Walter, 1914- 940.548142
The boat; illustrated by John Groth. Boston, Houghton Mifflin, 1953 [c1952] 101 p. illus. 22 cm. Autobiographical. [D805.J3G5 1953] 53-5112
1. Rooseboom (Ship) 2. World War, 1939-1945—Prisoners and prisons, Japanese. I. Title.

Roosevelt, Eleanor (Roosevelt) 1884-1962.

BLASSINGAME, Wyatt. 973.917'0924 B
Eleanor Roosevelt. Illustrated by Paul Frame. New York, Putnam [1968, c1967] 64 p. col. illus. 23 cm. (A See and read beginning to read biography) A simple biography of the woman who spent most of her life helping others, telling of her marriage and her work while her husband was Governor of New York and President. [E807.1.R485] 92 AC 68
1. Roosevelt, Eleanor (Roosevelt) 1884-1962. I. Frame, Paul, illus. II. Title.

DAVIS, Kenneth Sydney, 1912- 973.917'092'4 B
Invincible summer : an intimate portrait of the Roosevelts, based on the recollections of Marion Dickerman / by Kenneth S. Davis. 1st ed. New York : Atheneum, 1974. ix, 176 p., [20] leaves of plates : ill. ; 27 cm. [E807.1.D4 1974] 73-80746 ISBN 0-689-10566-5 : 12.95
1. Roosevelt, Franklin Delano, Pres. U.S.,

1882-1945. 2. Roosevelt, Eleanor Roosevelt, 1884-1962. 3. Roosevelt family. I. Dickerman, Marion. II. Title.

DOUGLAS, Helen (Gahagan) 920.7
1900-
The Eleanor Roosevelt we remember. Pictures edited by Aaron J. Ezickson. New York, Hill and Wang [1963] 173 p. illus. 29 cm. [E807.1.R49] 63-13309
1. Roosevelt, Eleanor (Roosevelt) 1884-1962. I. Title.

EATON, Jeanette. 920.7
The story of Eleanor Roosevelt. Illustrated with photos. New York, Morrow, 1956. 251 p. illus. 22 cm. Includes bibliography. [E807.1.R5] 56-6740
1. Roosevelt, Eleanor Roosevelt, 1884-1962.

GOODSELL, Jane. 973.917'0924 B
Eleanor Roosevelt. Illustrated by Wendell Minor. New York, Crowell [1970] 38 p. col. illus., ports. (part col.) 24 cm. (A Crowell biography) An easy-to-read biography of the wife of the thirty-second President who devoted herself to helping underprivileged people all over the world. [E807.1.R523] 92 71-106573 3.75
1. Roosevelt, Eleanor (Roosevelt), 1884-1962—Juvenile literature. I. Minor, Wendell, illus. II. Title.

GUREWITSCH, A. 973.917'092'4 B
David.
Eleanor Roosevelt: her day; a personal album, by A. David Gurewitsch. With a special introd. commemorating the 25th anniversary of the Universal declaration of human rights by William Korey. Foreword by Franklin D. Roosevelt, Jr. New York, Interchange Foundation [1973] 160 p. illus. 28 cm. [E807.1.R527] 74-157849
1. Roosevelt, Eleanor Roosevelt, 1884-1962—Portraits, caricatures, etc. 2. United Nations. General Assembly. Universal declaration of human rights.

GUREWITSCH, A. 973.917'092'4 B
David.
Eleanor Roosevelt: her day; a personal album, by A. David Gurewitsch. With an introd. by William Korey and the full text of the Universal declaration of human rights. Foreword by Franklin D. Roosevelt, Jr. [New York] Quadrangle [1974] 160 p. ports. 29 cm. [E807.1.R527 1974] 73-90188 ISBN 0-8129-0447-8 7.95
1. Roosevelt, Eleanor Roosevelt, 1884-1962—Portraits, caricatures, etc. 2. United Nations. General Assembly. Universal declaration of human rights.

HAREVEN, Tamara 973.917'092'4 B
K.
Eleanor Roosevelt : an American conscience / by Tamara K. Hareven. New York : Da Capo Press, 1975. xx, 326 p., [8] leaves of plates : ill. ; 21 cm. (Franklin D. Roosevelt and the era of the New Deal) Reprint of the 1968 ed. published by Quadrangle Books, Chicago; with new introd. Includes bibliographical references and index. [E807.1.H3 1975] 74-26539 ISBN 0-306-70705-5 : 20.00
1. Roosevelt, Eleanor (Roosevelt) 1884-1962. I. Title. II. Series. BIP

HAREVEN, Tamara K. 973.917'0924 B
Eleanor Roosevelt: an American conscience, by Tamara K. Hareven. Chicago, Quadrangle Books [1968] xx, 326 p. ports. 22 cm. Bibliographical references included in "A note on sources" (p. [311]-317) [E807.1.H3] 68-10834
1. Roosevelt, Eleanor (Roosevelt) 1884-1962. I. Title.

HERSHAN, Stella K. 973.917'0924
A woman of quality, by Stella K. Hershan. New York, Crown Publishers [1970] 256 p. 24 cm. Includes bibliographical references. [E807.1.R532 1970] 72-127505 5.95
1. Roosevelt, Eleanor (Roosevelt) 1884-1962. I. Title.

HICKOK, Lorena A 920.7
Reluctant First Lady. New York, Dodd, Mead, 1962. 176p. illus. 21cm. [E807.1.R534] 62-14129
1. Roosevelt, Eleanor (Roosevelt) 1884- I. Title.

JOHNSON, George, 1917- 920.7
Eleanor Roosevelt; the compelling life story of one of the most famous women of our time. Derby, Conn., Monarch Books [1962] 142p. 19cm. (A Monarch books original biography) Monarch books, K61. [E807.1.R54] 62-2172
1. Roosevelt, Eleanor (Roosevelt) 1884- I. Title.

KEARNEY, James R. 973.917'0924 B
Anna Eleanor Roosevelt; the evolution of a reformer [by] James R. Kearney. Boston, Houghton Mifflin, 1968. xvi, 332 p. ports. 22 cm. Bibliography: p. 312-323. [E807.1.R545] 68-12780
1. Roosevelt, Eleanor (Roosevelt) 1884-1962.

LASH, Joseph 973.917'092'4 [B]
P., 1909-
Eleanor: the years alone. Foreword by Franklin Delano Roosevelt, Jr. [New York] New American Lib. [1973 c.1972] 390 p. photos., 18 cm. (A Signet Book) Continue the biography of Mrs. Roosevelt which began in the author's Eleanor and Franklin. Includes bibliographical references [E807.1.R574] 72-2674 1.95 (pbk.)
1. Roosevelt, Eleanor (Roosevelt) 1884-1962. I. Title. BIP

LASH, Joseph P., 973.917'0924 [B]
1909-
Eleanor and Franklin; the story of their relationship, based on Eleanor Roosevelt's private papers [by] Joseph P. Lash. Foreword by Arthur M. Schlesinger, Jr. Introd. by Franklin D. Roosevelt, Jr. [New York] New American Lib. [1973] 1020 p. photos. 18 cm. (A Signet Non-Fiction) [E807.1.R572] 72-152667 1.95 (pbk.)
1. Roosevelt, Eleanor (Roosevelt) 1884-1962. 2. Roosevelt, Franklin Delano, Pres. U.S. 1882-1945. I. Title. BIP

LASH, Joseph P 1909- 920.7
Eleanor Roosevelt; a friend's memoir [by] Joseph P. Lash. [1st ed.] Garden City, N.Y., Doubleday, 1964. ix, 374 p. 22 cm. [E807.1.R573] 64-13843
1. Roosevelt, Eleanor (Roosevelt) 1884-1962. I. Title.

MCKNOWN, Robin 920.7
Eleanor Roosevelt's world. New York, Grosset [c.1964] 93p. illus., ports. 26cm. 64-24424 2.50; 2.90 lib. ed.,
1. Roosevelt, Eleanor (Roosevelt) 1884-1962. I. Title.

MACLEISH, Archibald, 362.0924
1892-
The Eleanor Roosevelt story. Boston, Houghton [c.]1965. 101p. illus., facsims., ports. 27cm. Text and illus. from the motion picture: The Eleanor Roosevelt story. [E807.1.R577] 65-26267 5.00
1. Roosevelt, Eleanor (Roosevelt) 1884-1962. I. The Eleanor Roosevelt story (Motion picture) II. Title.

ROOSEVELT, Eleanor 920.7
(Roosevelt) 1884-
On my own. [1st ed.] New York, Harper [1958] xii, 241p. illus., ports. 25cm. [E807.1.R424] 57-8179
I. Title.

ROOSEVELT, Eleanor 920.7
Roosevelt, 1884-1962.
Autobiography. [1st ed.] New York, Harper [1961] 454 p. illus. 25 cm. [E807.1.R35] 61-12222

ROOSEVELT, 973.917'092'4 B
Eleanor Roosevelt, 1884-1962.
This I remember / by Eleanor Roosevelt. Westport, Conn. : Greenwood Press, 1975, c1949. x, 387 p., [12] leaves of plates : ill. ; 23 cm. Reprint of the ed. published by Harper, New York. Includes index. [E807.1.R428 1975] 74-11884 ISBN 0-8371-7702-2 lib.bdg. : 21.75
1. Roosevelt, Eleanor Roosevelt, 1884-1962. 2. Roosevelt, Franklin Delano, Pres. U.S., 1882-1945. 3. United States—Politics and government—1933-1945. I. Title. BIP

ROOSEVELT, Eleanor 920.7
(Roosevelt) [Anna Eleanor (Roosevelt) Roosevelt 1884-
This is my story. Garden City, N.Y., Doubleday [1961, c.1937] 270p. (Dolphin bk. c 264) .95 pap.,
I. Title.

ROOSEVELT, 973.917'092'4 B
Elliott, 1910-
Mother R. : Eleanor Roosevelt's untold story / by Elliott Roosevelt and James Brough. New York : Putnam, c1977. p. cm. Includes index. [E807.1.R48R66 1977] 77-7281 ISBN 0-399-11998-1 : 8.95
1. Roosevelt, Eleanor Roosevelt, 1884-1962. 2. Roosevelt family. 3. Roosevelt, Elliott, 1910- 4. Presidents—United States—Wives—Biography. I. Brough, James, 1918- joint author. II. Title. BIP

ROOSEVELT, Elliott, 973.9170924
1910-
A rendezvous with destiny : the Roosevelts of the White House / Elliott Roosevelt and James Brough New York : Dell ,1976 c1975 442 p. : ill. ; 18 cm. Includes index [E807.R634] pbk. : 1.95
1. Roosevelt, Franklin Delano, Pres. U.S., 1882-1945 2. Roosevelt, Eleanor, 1884-1962 3. Roosevelt, Elliott, 1910- I. Brough, James, 1918- , joint author II. Title.
L.C. card no. for 1975 Putnam edition: 75-21677. BIP

ROOSEVELT, Elliott, 973.9170924
1910-
A rendezvous with destiny : the Roosevelts of the White House / Elliott Roosevelt and James Brough New York : Dell ,1976 c1975 442 p. : ill. ; 18 cm. Includes index [E807.R634] pbk. : 1.95
1. Roosevelt, Franklin Delano, Pres. U.S., 1882-1945 2. Roosevelt, Eleanor, 1884-1962 3. Roosevelt, Elliott, 1910- I. Brough, James, 1918- , joint author II. Title.
L.C. card no. for 1975 Putnam edition: 75-21677. BIP

ROOSEVELT, 973.917'092'4 B
Elliott, 1910-
A rendezvous with destiny : the Roosevelts of the White House / by Elliott Roosevelt and James Brough. New York : Putnam, c1975. 446 p., [4] leaves of plates : ill. ; 22 cm. Includes index. [E807.R634 1975] 75-21677 ISBN 0-399-11545-5 : 10.00
1. Roosevelt, Franklin Delano, Pres. U.S., 1882-1945. 2. Roosevelt, Eleanor Roosevelt, 1884-1962. 3. Roosevelt, Elliott, 1910- I. Brough, James, 1918- joint author. II. Title.

ROOSEVELT, 973.917'092'4 B
Elliott, 1910-
A rendezvous with destiny : the Roosevelts of the White House / by Elliott Roosevelt and James Brough. New York : Putnam, c1975. 446 p., [4] leaves of plates : ill. ; 22 cm. Includes index. [E807.R634 1975] 75-21677 ISBN 0-399-11545-5 : 10.00
1. Roosevelt, Franklin Delano, Pres. U.S., 1882-1945. 2. Roosevelt, Eleanor Roosevelt, 1884-1962. 3. Roosevelt, Elliott, 1910- I. Brough, James, 1918- joint author. II. Title.

SANDIFER, Irene 973.917'092'4 B
Reiterman.
Mrs. Roosevelt as we knew her / by Irene Reiterman Sandifer. Silver Spring, Md. : Sandifer, [1975] 134 p., [1] leaf of plates : ill. ; 24 cm. [E807.1.S5776] 75-319622
1. Roosevelt, Eleanor Roosevelt, 1884-1962. 2. Sandifer, Irene Reiterman. I. Title.

STEINBERG, Alfred, 1917- 920.7
Eleanor Roosevelt. Illustrated by Andre Le Blanc. New York, Putnam [1959] 127 p. illus. 21 cm. (Lives to remember) [E807.1.R58] 59-6508
1. Roosevelt, Eleanor (Roosevelt) 1884- I. Title.

STEINBERG, Alfred, 1917- 920.7
Mrs. R., the life of Eleanor Roosevelt. New York, Putnam [1958] 384 p. illus. 22 cm. Includes bibliography. [E807.1.R59] 58-10758
1. Roosevelt, Eleanor (Roosevelt) 1884- I. Title.

WEEP no more, v. 12
my lady. 1956 ed. [Raleigh, N.C., Graphic Press] 1956 [c1950] 62p. 20cm.
1. Roosevelt, Eleanor (Roosevelt) 1884- 2. Southern States—Soc. condit. I. Debnam, Waldemar Eros, 1898-

Roosevelt, Eleanor (Roosevelt) 1884-1962—Juvenile Literature.

GILBERT, Miriam. j 92
Shy girl; the story of Eleanor Roosevelt, First Lady of the world. Illustrated by Herbert McClure. [1st ed.] Garden City, New York, Doubleday [1965] 144 p. illus. 22 cm. (Doubleday signal books) [E807.1.R52] 65-14021
1. Roosevelt, Eleanor (Roosevelt) 1884-1962 — Juvenile literature. I. Title.

HICKOK, Lorena A 920.7
The story of Eleanor Roosevelt. Illustrated by William Barss. New York, Grosset Dunlap [1959] 180p. illus. 22cm. (Signature books 48) [E807.1.R535] 59-12012
1. Roosevelt, Eleanor (Roosevelt) 1884- — Juvenile literature. I. Title.

Roosevelt, Eleanor (Roosevelt) 1884-1962—Portraits, Caricatures, etc.

HARRITY, Richard. 920.7
Eleanor Roosevelt: her life in pictures, by Richard Harrity and Ralph G. Martin. [1st ed.] New York, Duell, Sloan and Pearce [1958] 212p. illus. 26cm. [E807.1.R53] 58-12266
1. Roosevelt, Eleanor (Roosevelt)1884- — Portraits, caricatures, etc. I. Martin, Ralph G., 1920- joint author. II. Title.

Roosevelt family.

ROOSEVELT, 973.917'092'4 B
Elliott, 1910-
Mother R. : Eleanor Roosevelt's untold story / by Elliott Roosevelt and James Brough. New York : Putnam, c1977. p. cm. Includes index. [E807.1.R48R66 1977] 77-7281 ISBN 0-399-11998-1 : 8.95
1. Roosevelt, Eleanor Roosevelt, 1884-1962. 2. Roosevelt family. 3. Roosevelt, Elliott, 1910- 4. Presidents—United States—Wives—Biography. I. Brough, James, 1918- joint author. II. Title. BIP

Roosevelt, Franklin Delano, Pres. U.S., 1882-1945.

BISHOP, James 973.917'092'4 B
Alonzo, 1907-
FDR's last year, April 1944-April 1945, by Jim Bishop. New York, W. Morrow, 1974. xiv, 690 p. 24 cm. Bibliography: p. 671-674. [E807.B57] 74-7002 ISBN 0-688-00276-5 12.50
1. Roosevelt, Franklin Delano, Pres. U.S., 1882-1945. I. Title.

BOOS, John E. v. 12
The man who brought the New Deal; Franklin D. Roosevelt. Albany, 1960. 134 p. photographs. 23 cm. 64-8979
1. Roosevelt, Franklin Delano, Pres. U.S. 1882-1945. I. Title.

BURNS, James MacGregor 923.173
Roosevelt: the lion and the fox. New York Harcourt [1963, c.1956] 553p. illus. 21cm. (Harvest bk., HB57) Bibl. 2.45 pap.,
1. Roosevelt, Franklin Delano, Pres. U.S. 1882-1845 I. Title. BIP

BURNS, James 940.532'2'730924
MacGregor.
Roosevelt: the soldier of freedom. New York, Harcourt [1973, c.1970] xiv, 722 p. illus., ports. 21 cm. (Harvest Book, HB247) Bibl: p. 621-685. [E807.B386] 71-95877 ISBN 0-15-678875-6 pap., 4.45
1. Roosevelt, Franklin Delano, Pres. U.S., 1882-1945. 2. World War, 1939-1945—U.S. I. Title. BIP

BURNS, James MacGregor. 923.173
Roosevelt: the lion the fox. [1st ed.] New York, Harcourt, Brace [1956] 553p. illus. 23cm. [E807.B835] 56-7920
1. Roosevelt, Franklin Delano, Pres. U. S., 1882-1945. 2. U. S.—Pol. & govt.—1933-1945. I. Title.

DALL, Curtis B. 973.917'0924
FDR, my exploited father-in-law, by Curtis B. Dall. Tulsa, Okla., Christian Crusade Publications [1967] 192 p. 18 cm. [E807.1.D3] 68-2835
1. Roosevelt, Franklin Delano, Pres. U.S., 1882-1945. 2. Roosevelt family. I. Title.

DAVIS, Kenneth 973.917'092'4 B

Sydney, 1912-
FDR: the beckoning of destiny, 1882-1928; a history, by Kenneth S. Davis. New York, Putnam [1972] 936 p. 25 cm. Bibliography: p. [910]-919. [E807.D36 1972] 72-79519 ISBN 0-399-10998-6 15.00
1. Roosevelt, Franklin Delano, Pres. U.S., 1882-1945. I. Title.

DAVIS, Kenneth 973.917'092'4 B
Sydney, 1912-
Invincible summer : an intimate portrait of the Roosevelts, based on the recollections of Marion Dickerman / by Kenneth S. Davis. 1st ed. New York : Atheneum, 1974. ix, 176 p., [20] leaves of plates : ill. ; 27 cm. [E807.1.D4 1974] 73-80746 ISBN 0-689-10566-5 : 12.95
1. Roosevelt, Franklin Delano, Pres. U.S., 1882-1945. 2. Roosevelt, Eleanor Roosevelt, 1884-1962. 3. Roosevelt family. I. Dickerman, Marion. II. Title.

DIVINE, Robert 940.532'2'730924
A.
Roosevelt and World War II, by Robert A. Divine. Baltimore, Johns Hopkins Press [1969] x, 107 p. illus. 22 cm. (The Albert Shaw lectures in diplomatic history, 1968) Bibliographical footnotes. [E807.D57] 69-13655 5.95
1. Roosevelt, Franklin Delano, Pres. U.S., 1882-1945. 2. U.S.—Foreign relations—1933-1945—Addresses, essays, lectures. I. Title. II. Series: The Albert Shaw lectures on diplomatic history, 1968

FLYNN, John 973.917'0924 B
Thomas, 1883-1964.
Country squire in the White House. New York, Da Capo Press, 1972 [c1940] vi, 122 p. 22 cm. (Franklin D. Roosevelt and the era of the New Deal) [E807.F58 1972] 77-167846 ISBN 0-306-70324-6
1. Roosevelt, Franklin Delano, Pres. U.S., 1882-1945. 2. United States—Politics and government—1933-1945. I. Title. II. Series.
BIP

FRISCH, Morton J. 320.9'73'0917 B
Franklin D. Roosevelt; the contribution of the New Deal to American political thought and practice [by] Morton J. Frisch. New York, Twayne Publishers [1975, c1974] p. cm. (Twayne's world leaders series) Bibliography: p. [E806.F74] 74-14425 ISBN 0-8057-3708-1 6.95 (lib.bdg.)
1. Roosevelt, Franklin Delano, Pres. U.S., 1882-1945. 2. United States—Politics and government—1933-1945.

GIES, Joseph. 973.917'0924 B
Franklin D. Roosevelt; portrait of a President. Garden City, N.Y., Doubleday [1971] 233 p. illus., col. port. 27 cm. [E807.G5] 70-160870
1. Roosevelt, Franklin Delano, Pres. U.S., 1882-1945.

GOSNELL, Harold Foote, 923.173
1896-
Champion campaigner: Franklin D. Roosevelt. New York, Macmillan, 1952. 235 p. illus. 22 cm. [E807.G68] 52-4277
1. Roosevelt, Franklin Delano, Pres. U. S., 1882-1945. 2. Elections—U. S. I. Title.

GUNTHER, John, 1901 923.173
Roosevelt in retrospect, a profile in history. New York, Pyramid [1962, c.1950] 432p. (T715) Bibl. .75 pap.,
1. Roosevelt, Franklin Delano, Pres. U.S., 1882-1945. I. Title.

GUNTHER, John, 1901-1970. 923.173
Roosevelt in retrospect a profile in history. [1st ed.] New York, Harper [1950] xii, 410 p. 22 cm. Bibliography: p. 381-385. [E807.G85] 50-8078
1. Roosevelt, Franklin Delano, Pres. U.S., 1882-1945. I. Title.

HARRITY, Richard. 923.173
The human side of F. D. R. [by] Richard Harrity and Ralph G. Martin. [1st ed.] Human side of F D R New York, Duell, Sloan and Pearce [1960] 1 v. (chiefly illus.) 26 cm. [E807.H33] 59-12247
1. Roosevelt, Franklin Delano, Pres. U.S.—Portraits, caricatures, etc. I. Martin, Ralph G., 1920- joint author. II. Title.

HIEBERT, Roselyn. 973.917'0924 B
Franklin Delano Roosevelt; President for the people, by Roselyn and Ray Eldon Hiebert. New York, F. Watts [1968] 246 p. ports. 22 cm. (Immortals of history) Bibliography: p. 237-239. [E807.H52] 68-15570
1. Roosevelt, Franklin Delano, Pres. U.S., 1882-1945. I. Hiebert, Ray Eldon, joint author.

HILL, Charles 973.9170924 (B)
Peter.
Franklin Roosevelt, by C. P. Hill. London, Oxford U.P., 1966. 62 p. 8 plates (incl. ports.) 20 1/2 cm. (The Clarendon biographies) 9/6 Biliography: p. 58-59. [E807.H53] 66-70680
1. Roosevelt, Franklin Delano, Pres. U.S., 1882-1945. I. Title.

JOSEPHSON, Emanuel Mann, 923.173
1895-
The strange death of Franklin D. Roosevelt; history of the Roosevelt-Delano dynasty, America's royal family. [New and rev. ed] New York, Chedney Press [1959] 283p. illus. 22cm. [Blacked out American history series] [E807.J65 1959] 59-2419
1. Roosevelt, Franklin Delano, Pres. U. S., 1882-1945. 2. Roosevelt family. 3. Delano family. 4. U. S.— Pol. govt.—1933-1945. I. Title.

LASH, Joseph P., 940.53'2'0922 B
1909-
Roosevelt and Churchill, 1939-1941 : the partnership that saved the West / Joseph P. Lash. Franklin Center, Pa. : Franklin Library, 1976. xxix, 826 p., [12] leaves of plates : ill., maps ; 25 cm. Includes index. Bibliography: p. 723-725. [D753.L27 1976b] 77-366525
1. Roosevelt, Franklin Delano, Pres. U.S., 1882-1945. 2. Churchill, Winston Leonard Spencer, Sir, 1874-1965. 3. World War, 1939-1945—Diplomatic history. 4. World War, 1939-1945—United States. 5. World War, 1939-1945—Great Britain. I. Title.
BIP

LINDLEY, Ernest 973.9'092'4 B
Kidder, 1899-
Franklin D. Roosevelt; a career in progressive democracy, by Ernest K. Lindley. New York, Da Capo Press, 1974 [c1931] 366 p. port. 22 cm. (Franklin D. Roosevelt and the era of the New Deal) Reprint of the ed. published by Blue Ribbon Books, New York. [E807.L565 1974] 73-21771 ISBN 0-306-70634-2 15.00
1. Roosevelt, Franklin Delano, Pres. U.S., 1882-1945. I. Title. II. Series.

LIPPMAN, Theo. 973.917'092'4 B
The squire of Warm Springs : F.D.R. in Georgia, 1924-1945 / by Theo Lippman, Jr. 1st ed. New York : Playboy Press, c1977. p. cm. Includes bibliographical references and index. [E807.L58] 77-13016 1.00
1. Roosevelt, Franklin Delano, Pres., U.S., 1882-1945. 2. Warm Springs, Ga.—History. 3. United States—Economic policy—1933-1945. 4. Physically handicapped—United States. 5. Presidents—United States—Biography. I. Title.

LORANT, Stefan, 1901- 923.173
FDR; a pictorial biography. New York, Simon and Schuster, 1950. 159, [1] p. illus., ports., facsims. 31 cm. Bibliography: p. 159-[160] [E807.L78] 50-11066
1. Roosevelt, Franklin Delano, Pres U.S., 1882-1945. I. Title.

MCKOWN, Robin. 92
Roosevelt's America. New York, Grosset & Dunlap [1962] 92p. illus. 26cm. [E807.M218] 62-52040
1. Roosevelt, Franklin Delano, Pres. U. S.—Juvenile literature. I. Title.

MERRIAM, Eve, 1916- 923.173
The real book about Franklin D. Roosevelt; illustrated by Bette J. Davis. [1st ed.] Garden City., Garden City Books, by arrangement with F. Watts [New York, 1952] 191 p. illus. 21 cm. (Real books) [E807.M4] 52-7627
1. Roosevelet, Franklin Delano, Pres. U.S., 1882-1945. I. Title.

MERRIAM, Eve, 1916- 923.173
The real book about Franklin D. Roosevelt; illustrated by Bette J. Davis. [1st ed.] Garden City., Garden City Books, by arrangement with F. Watts [New York, 1952] 191 p. illus. 21 cm. (Real books) [E807.M4] 52-7627
1. Roosevelet, Franklin Delano, Pres. U.S., 1882-1945. I. Title.

MONTGOMERY, Mabel. 923.173
A courageous conquest; the life story of Franklin Delano Roosevelt. Edited by Henry I. Christ. New York, Globe Book Co. [1951] 191 p. illus., ports. 21 cm. [E807.M64] 51-1032
1. Roosevelt, Franklin Delano, Pres. U.S 1882-1945. I. Title.

MOONEY, Booth, 1912- 973.917'0922
Roosevelt and Rayburn; a political partnership. [1st ed.] Philadelphia, Lippincott [1971] x, 228 p. 22 cm. Bibliography: p. 219-222. [E806.M72] 73-141905 6.95
1. Roosevelt, Franklin Delano, Pres. U.S., 1882-1945. 2. Rayburn, Sam Taliaferro, 1882-1961. 3. United States—Politics and government—1933-1945.

NASH, Gerald D., 973.917'0924
comp.
Franklin Delano Roosevelt, edited by Gerald D. Nash. Englewood Cliffs, N.J., Prentice-Hall [1967] vi, 182 p. 21 cm. (Great lives observed) (A Spectrum book.) "Bibliographical note": p. 175-178. [E807.N27] 67-25929
1. Roosevelt, Franklin Delano, Pres. U.S., 1882-1945.

•PERKINS, Frances 923.173
The Roosevelt I knew. New York, Harper [1964, c.1946] 408p. port. 21cm. (Colophon bks., CN40) 1.95 pap.,
1. Roosevelt, Franklin Delano, Pres. U.S., 1882-1945. I. Title.

PERKINS, Frances 923.173
The Roosevelt I knew [Gloucester, Mass., P. Smith, 1965, c.1946] vi, 408p. port. 21cm. (Colophon bks., CN40 rebound) 4.00
1. Roosevelt, Franklin Delano, Pres. U.S., 1882-1945 I. Title.

ROLLINS, Alfred Brooks, 923.173
1921-
Roosevelt and Howe. New York, Knopf [c.]1962. 479p. illus. 22cm. Bibl. 62-15578 5.95
1. Roosevelt, Franklin Delano, Pres., U.S., 1882-1945. 2. Howe, Louis McHenry, 1871-1936. I. Title.

ROOSEVELT, Elliott, 973.9170924
1910-
A rendezvous with destiny : the Roosevelts of the White House / Elliott Roosevelt and James Brough New York : Dell ,1976 c1975 442 p. : ill. ; 18 cm. Includes index [E807.R634] pbk. : 1.95
1. Roosevelt, Franklin Delano, Pres. U.S., 1882-1945 2. Roosevelt, Eleanor, 1884-1962 3. Roosevelt, Elliott, 1910- I. Brough, James, 1918- , joint author II. Title.
L.C. card no. for 1975 Putnam edition: 75-21677. **BIP**

ROOSEVELT, Elliott, 973.9170924
1910-
A rendezvous with destiny : the Roosevelts of the White House / Elliott Roosevelt and James Brough New York : Dell ,1976 c1975 442 p. : ill. ; 18 cm. Includes index [E807.R634] pbk. : 1.95
1. Roosevelt, Franklin Delano, Pres. U.S., 1882-1945 2. Roosevelt, Eleanor, 1884-1962 3. Roosevelt, Elliott, 1910- I. Brough, James, 1918- , joint author II. Title.
L.C. card no. for 1975 Putnam edition: 75-21677. **BIP**

ROOSEVELT, 973.917'092'4 B
Elliott, 1910-
A rendezvous with destiny : the Roosevelts of the White House / by Elliott Roosevelt and James Brough. New York : Putnam, c1975. 446 p., [4] leaves of plates : ill. ; 22 cm. Includes index. [E807.R634 1975] 75-21677 ISBN 0-399-11545-5 : 10.00
1. Roosevelt, Franklin Delano, Pres. U.S., 1882-1945. 2. Roosevelt, Eleanor Roosevelt, 1884-1962. 3. Roosevelt, Elliott, 1910- I. Brough, James, 1918- joint author. II. Title.

ROOSEVELT, 973.917'092'4 B
Elliott, 1910-
A rendezvous with destiny : the Roosevelts of the White House / by Elliott Roosevelt and James Brough. New York : Putnam, c1975. 446 p., [4] leaves of plates : ill. ; 22 cm. Includes index. [E807.R634 1975] 75-21677 ISBN 0-399-11545-5 : 10.00
1. Roosevelt, Franklin Delano, Pres. U.S., 1882-1945. 2. Roosevelt, Eleanor Roosevelt, 1884-1962. 3. Roosevelt, Elliott, 1910- I. Brough, James, 1918- joint author. II. Title.

ROOSEVELT, 973.917'092'4 B
Elliott, 1910-
An untold story; the Roosevelts of Hyde Park, by Elliott Roosevelt and James Brough. New York, Putnam Sons [1973] 318 p. illus. 22 cm. [E807.R635] 72-97308 ISBN 0-399-11127-1 7.95
1. Roosevelt, Franklin Delano, Pres. U.S., 1882-1945. 2. Roosevelt, Eleanor (Roosevelt) 1884-1962. I. Brough, James, 1918- joint author. II. Title.

ROOSEVELT, 973.917'092'4 B
Elliott, 1910-
An untold story; the Roosevelts of Hyde Park, by Elliott Roosevelt and James Brough. [New York, Dell, 1974, c1973] 365 p. 18 cm. [E807.R635] 1.75 (pbk.)
1. Roosevelt, Franklin Delano, Pres. U.S., 1882-1945. 2. Roosevelt, Eleanor (Roosevelt) 1884-1962. I. Brough, James, 1918- joint author. II. Title.
L.C. card number for hardbound ed.: 72-97308. **BIP**

ROOSEVELT, 973.917'092'4 B
Franklin Delano, Pres. U.S., 1882-1945.
The F. D. R. memoirs, as written by Bernard Asbell. Introd. by Anna Roosevelt Halsted. [1st ed.] Garden City, N.Y., Doubleday, 1973. xvii, 461 p. 24 cm. Includes bibliographical references. [E807.R6482] 72-92189 ISBN 0-385-08414-5 10.00
1. Roosevelt, Franklin Delano, Pres. U.S., 1882-1945. 2. United States—Politics and government—1933-1945. I. Asbell, Bernard.

ROOSEVELT, Franklin 940.53'22
Delano, Pres. U.S., 1882-1945.
Roosevelt and Churchill, their secret wartime correspondence. Edited by Francis L. Loewenheim, Harold D. Langley [and] Manfred Jonas. [1st ed.] New York, Saturday Review Press, 1975. xvi, 805 p. illus. 24 cm. Bibliography: p. 751-760. [E807.A4 1975] 74-14854 ISBN 0-8415-0331-1
1. Roosevelt, Franklin Delano, Pres. U.S., 1882-1945. 2. Churchill, Winston Leonard Spencer, Sir, 1874-1965. I. Churchill, Winston Leonard Spencer, Sir, 1874-1965, joint author. II. Loewenheim, Francis L., ed. III. Langley, Harold D., ed. IV. Jonas, Manfred, ed. V. Title.

ROOSEVELT, Franklin 940.53'2
Delano, Pres. U.S., 1882-1945.
Wartime correspondence between President Roosevelt and Pope Pius XII : with an introd. & explanatory notes / by Myson C. Taylor. New York : Da Capo Press, 1975, c1947. xiii, 127 p. : ports. ; 23 cm. (Franklin D. Roosevelt and the era of the New Deal) Reprint of the ed. published by Macmillan, New York. [D753.R69 1975] 74-31356 ISBN 0-306-70709-8 : 15.00
1. Roosevelt, Franklin Delano, Pres. U.S., 1882-1945. 2. Pius XII, Pope, 1876-1958. 3. Catholic Church—Relations (diplomatic) with the United States. 4. World War, 1939-1945—United States. 5. United States—Foreign relations—Catholic Church. I. Pius XII, Pope, 1876-1958. II. Taylor, Myron Charles, 1874-1959. III. Title. IV. Series.

ROOSEVELT, Franklin 923.173
Delano, Pres. U.S., 1882-1945.
Franklin D. Roosevelt's own story, told in his own words from his private and public papers as selected by Donald Day. [1st rd.] Boston, Little, Brown 1951. 461 p. 23 cm. "Sources and acknowledgments": p. [443]-445. [E807.R6485] 51-13942
1. U.S. — Pol. & govt. — 1933-1945. I. Day, Donald, 1890- ed. II. Title.

ROOSEVELT, Franklin 923.173
Delano, Pres. U.S. 1882-1945.
Roosevelt and Daniels, a friendship in politics. Edited with an introd. by Carroll

Kilpatrick. Chapel Hill, University of North Carolina Press [1952] xvi, 226 p. 21 cm. [E807.R655] 52-10959
1. Roosevelt, Franklin Delano, Pres. U.S. 2. Daniels, Josephus, 1862-1948. I. Daniels, Josephus, 1882-1948. II. Title.

ROOSEVELT, James, 1907- 923.173
Affectionately, F. D. R.; a son's story of a lonely man, by James Roosevelt and Sidney Shalett. [1st ed.] New York, Harcourt, Brace [1959] 394p. illus. 23cm. Includes bibliography. [E807.R657] 59-10248
1. Roosevelt, Franklin Delano, Pres. U. S., 1882-1945. 2. Roosevelt family. I. Shalett, Sidney, joint author. II. Title.

ROOSEVELT, James, 973.917'092'4 B 1907-
Affectionately, F. D. R. : a son's story of a courageous man / by James Roosevelt and Sidney Shalett. Westport, Conn. : Greenwood Press, 1975, c1959. 352 p., [4] leaves of plates : ill. ; 22 cm. Reprint of the ed. published by George G. Harrap, London. Includes index. Bibliography: p. [333]-339. [E807.R657 1975] 75-22309 ISBN 0-8371-8329-4 lib.bdg. : 17.75
1. Roosevelt, Franklin Delano, Pres. U.S., 1882-1945. 2. Roosevelt, James, 1907- 3. Roosevelt family. I. Shalett, Sidney, joint author. II. Title.

ROSENAU, James N ed. 923.173
The Roosevelt treasury. [1st ed.] Garden City, N.Y., Doubleday, 1951. xvi, 461 p. 22 cm. Bibliography: p. 451-461. [E807.R687] 51-11311
1. Roosevelt, Franklin Delano, Pres. U.S., I. Title.

ROSENMAN, Samuel Irving, 973.917 1896-
Working with Roosevelt, by Samuel I. Rosenman. New York, Da Capo Press, 1972 [c1952] xiv, 560 p. illus. 22 cm. (Franklin D. Roosevelt and the era of the New Deal) [E807.R73 1972] 75-168391 ISBN 0-306-70328-9
1. Roosevelt, Franklin Delano, Pres. U.S., 1882-1945. 2. Authorship—Collaboration. I. Title. II. Series. **BIP**

ROSEVELT, James, 1907 927.173 joint author
Affectionately, F.D.R a son's story of a lonely man, by James Roosevelt. Sidney Shalett New York, Avon [1961 c1959] 319 p. illus. Bibli. (v2032)
1. Rosevelt, Franklin Delano, Pres. U.S 1882-1945. I. Shalett, Sidney II. Title.

SCHOOR, Gene. 923.173
The picture story of Franklin Delano Roosevelt. New York, Fell, 1950. 94 p. illus., ports., facsims. 24 cm. [E807.S3] 50-11389
1. Roosevelt, Franklin Delano, Pres. U.S. 1882-1945. I. Title.

THOMAS, Henry 923.173
Franklin Delano Roosevelt. New York, Putnam [c.1962] 191p. (Lives to remember) Bibl. 61-13595 2.95
1. Roosevelt, Franklin Delano, Pres. U.S., 1882-1945. I. Title.

THOMAS, Henry, 1886- 923.173
Franklin Delano Roosevelt. New York, Putnam [1962] 194 p. 21 cm. (Lives to remember) Includes bibliography. [E807.T4] 61-13595
1. Roosevelt, Franklin Delano, Pres. U.S., 1882-1945. I. Title.

TUGWELL, Rexford Guy, 923.173 1891-
The democractic Roosevelt; a biography of Franklin D. Roosevelt. [1st ed.] Garden City, N.Y., Doubleday, 1957. 712 p. illus., ports. 25 cm. Bibliography: p. 683-686. [E807.T76] 57-7290
1. Roosevelt, Franklin Delano, Pres. U.S., 1882-1945. I. Title.

TUGWELL, Rexford Guy, 923.173 1891-
The democratic Roosevelt; a biography of Franklin D. Roosevelt. [1st ed.] Garden City, N. Y., Doubleday, 1957. 712 p. illus., ports. 25 cm. Bibliography: p. 683-686. [E807.T76] 57-7290
1. Roosevelt, Franklin Delano, Pres. U.S., 1882-1945. I. Title.

TUGWELL, Rexford Guy, 973.9170924 1891-
F. D. R., architect of an era [by] Rexford G. Tugwell. New York, Macmillan [1967] xvii, 270 p. ports. 21 cm. Bibliography: p. 265-266. [E807.T763] 67-10481
1. Roosevelt, Franklin Delano, Pres. U.S., 1882-1945. 2. United States—Politics and government—1933-1945. 3. United States—Social policy. I. Title.

TUGWELL, Rexford 973.917'092'4 Guy, 1891-
In search of Roosevelt [by] Rexford G. Tugwell. Cambridge, Harvard University Press, 1972. ix, 313 p. 24 cm. Includes bibliographical references. [E807.T765] 72-76559 ISBN 0-674-44625-9
1. Roosevelt, Franklin Delano, Pres. U.S., 1882-1945. I. Title. **BIP**

WALKER, Turnley. 923.173
Roosevelt and the Warm Springs story. New York, Wyn [1953] 311 p. 22 cm. "A Story Press book." [E807.W3] 53-5431
1. Roosevelt, Franklin Delano, Pres. U.S., 1882-1945. 2. Georgia Warm Springs Foundation. I. Title.

WEINGAST, David Elliott, 923.173 1912-
Franklin D. Roosevelt, man of destiny. New York, J. Messner [1952] 184 p. illus. 22 cm. Bibliography: p. 178-180. [E807.W4] 52-9207
1. Roosevelt, Franklin Delano, Pres. U.S., 1882-1945. I. Title.

Roosevelt, Franklin Delano, Pres. U.S., 1882-1945—Addresses, essays, lectures.

KIMBALL, Warren F., comp. 327.73
Franklin D. Roosevelt and the world crisis, 1937-1945. Edited and with an introd. by Warren F. Kimball. Lexington, Mass., Heath [1973] xxii, 297 p. illus. 21 cm. (Problems in American civilization) Bibliography: p. 287-297. [E806.K55] 73-2764 ISBN 0-669-84947-2
1. Roosevelt, Franklin Delano, Pres. U.S., 1882-1945—Addresses, essays, lectures. 2. United States—Foreign relations—1933-1945—Addresses, essays, lectures. 3. World War, 1939-1945—United States—Addresses, essays, lectures. I. Title. II. Series. **BIP**

Roosevelt, Franklin Delano, Pres. U.S., 1882-1945—Anecdotes.

ROOSEVELT, Franklin 973.917'092'4 Delano, Pres. U.S., 1882-1945.
The sunny side of FDR. Compiled and edited by M. S. Venkataramani. [Athens] Ohio University Press [1973] 292 p. port. 24 cm. Includes bibliographical references. [E807.A25 1973] 75-181688 ISBN 0-8214-0107-6 12.50
1. Roosevelt, Franklin Delano, Pres. U.S., 1882-1945—Anecdotes. I. Venkataramani, M. S., 1925- ed. II. Title.

Roosevelt, Franklin Delano, Pres. U.S., 1882-1945—Juvenile literature.

BLASSINGAME, Wyatt 92
Franklin D. Roosevelt, four times President. Illus. by Al Fiorentino. Champaign, Ill., Garrard [c.1966] 80p. col. illus. 23cm. (Discovery bk.) [E807.B6] 66-10024 1.98
1. Roosevelt, Franklin Delano, Pres. U.S., 1882-1945—Juvenile literature. I. Title.

CAVANAH, Frances. 92
Triumphant adventure; the story of Franklin Delano Roosevelt. Illustrated by Jo Polseno. Chicago, Rand McNally [1964] 184 p. illus. 22 cm. [E807.C26] 64-14400
1. Roosevelt, Franklin Delano, Pres. U. S., 1882-1945—Juvenile literature. I. Title.

COOK, Fred J. 973.917'0924 B
Franklin D. Roosevelt: valiant leader, by Fred J. Cook. Illustrated by Steele Savage. New York, Putnam [1969, c1968] 95 p. illus. (part col.) 24 cm. (An American pioneer biography) The life of the thirty-second President whose three terms in office spanned the years of the Depression and the Second World War. [E807.C57] 92 68-24507 2.97
1. Roosevelt, Franklin Delano, Pres. U.S., 1882-1945—Juvenile literature. I. Savage, Steele, illus. II. Title.

FABER, Doris, 973.917'092'4 B 1924-
Franklin Delano Roosevelt. New York, Abelard-Schuman [1974, c1975] 128 p. illus. 22 cm. Bibliography: p. [126] A biography concentrating on the public career of the thirty-second President, who was elected four times. [E807.F25] 92 74-9708 ISBN 0-200-00142-6 (lib. bdg.) 6.95
1. Roosevelt, Franklin Delano, Pres. U.S., 1882-1945—Juvenile literature. I. Title.

GURNEY, Gene. 973.917'0924
FDR and Hyde Park, by Gene and Clare Gurney. With special photography by Harold Wise. New York, Watts [1970] 65 p. illus., coat of arms, plans, ports. 23 cm. Describes the life, career, and home, now an historic site, of the thirty-second President of the United States. [E807.G87] 92 70-115410
1. Roosevelt, Franklin Delano, Pres. U.S., 1882-1945—Juvenile literature. 2. Home of Franklin D. Roosevelt National Historic Site, Hyde Park, N.Y.—Juvenile literature. I. Gurney, Clare, joint author. II. Wise, Harold, illus. III. Title.

HICKOK, Lorena A. 920
The road to the White House; F.D.R.: the pre-presidential years. New York, Scholastic [1963, c.1962] 212p. 17cm. (T479) .45 pap.,
1. Roosevelt, Franklin Delano, Pres. U.S.—Juvenile literature. II. Title.

JOHNSON, Gerald White, 92 (J) 1890-
Franklin D. Roosevelt; portrait of a great man, by Gerald W. Johnson. Decorations by Leonard Everett Fisher. New York, W. Morrow, 1967. 192 p. ports. 25 cm. [E807.J58] 67-2744
1. Roosevelt, Franklin Delano, Pres. U.S., 1882-1945—Juvenile literature. **BIP**

KELLY, Regina (Zimmerman) 92 (J) 1898-
Franklin Delano Roosevelt [by] Regina Z. Kelly. Cover painting by Bill McKibbin. Chicago, Follett Pub. Co. [1966] 144 p. ports. 22 cm. (Library of American heroes) [E807.K4] 67-1746
1. Roosevelt, Franklin Delano, Pres. U.S., 1882-1945—Juvenile literature. I. Title.

PEARE, Catherine Owens 920
The FDR story. New York, Crowell [c.1962] 245p. illus. Bibl. 62-11003 3.75
1. Roosevelt, Franklin Delano, Pres. U. S., 1882-1945— Juvenile literature. I. Title.

PEARE, Catherine Owens 92
The FDR story. New York, Crowell [c.1962] 245p. illus. Bibl. 62-11003 3.75
1. Roosevelt, Franklin Delano, Pres. U. S., 1882-1945— Juvenile literature. I. Title. **BIP**

WISE, William 92
Franklin Delano Roosevelt. Illus. by Paul Frame. New York, Putnam [1967] 63p. col. illus. 23cm. (See & read beginning to read biog.) [E807.W59] 67-14813 2.36 lib. ed.,
1. Roosevelt, Franklin Delano, Pres. U.S., 1882-1945—Juvenile literature. I. Frame, Paul illus. II. Title.

Roosevelt, James, 1907-

ROOSEVELT, James, 973.917'092'4 B 1907-
Affectionately, F. D. R. : a son's story of a courageous man / by James Roosevelt and Sidney Shalett. Westport, Conn. : Greenwood Press, 1975, c1959. 352 p., [4] leaves of plates : ill. ; 22 cm. Reprint of the ed. published by George G. Harrap, London. Includes index. Bibliography: p. [333]-339. [E807.R657 1975] 75-22309 ISBN 0-8371-8329-4 lib.bdg. : 17.75
1. Roosevelt, Franklin Delano, Pres. U.S., 1882-1945. 2. Roosevelt, James, 1907- 3. Roosevelt family. I. Shalett, Sidney, joint author. II. Title.

Roosevelt-Rondon Scientific Expedition.

ROOSEVELT, Theodore, 418.1 Pres., U.S., 1858-1919.
Through the Brazilian wilderness. With illus. from photos. by Kermit Roosevelt and other members of the expedition. New York, Greenwood Press [1969] xiv, 374 p. illus., maps, ports. 23 cm. Reprint of the 1914 ed. [F2515.R78 1969] 68-55216
1. Roosevelt-Rondon Scientific Expedition. 2. Brazil—Description and travel. 3. Zoology—Brazil. 4. Roosevelt River. I. Title. **BIP**

Roosevelt, Sara (Delano) 1854-1941.

STEEHOLM, Clara. 920.7
The house at Hyde Park, by Clara and Hardy Steeholm; together with Sara Delano Roosevelt's Household book. New York, Viking Press, 1950. viii, 277 p. illus., ports., map (on lining papers) 22 cm. [E807.1.S75] 50-12746
1. Roosevelt, Sara (Delano) 1854-1941. 2. Roosevelt family. I. Roosevelt, Sara (Delano) 1854-1941. Household book. II. Steeholm, Hardy, joint author. III. Title.

Roosevelt, Theodore, Pres. U.S., 1858-1919.

ALFONSO, Oscar M. 973.91'1'0924
Theodore Roosevelt and the Philippines, 1897-1909, by Oscar M. Alfonso. [1st U.S. ed.] New York, Oriole Editions [1974, c1970] xiv, 227 p. 23 cm. Bibliography: p. 215-220. [E756.A67 1974] 73-85113 ISBN 0-88211-052-7 10.00
1. Roosevelt, Theodore, Pres. U.S., 1858-1919. 2. Philippine Islands—Politics and government—1898-1935. I. Title. **BIP**

BLACKBURN, Joyce. 92
Theodore Roosevelt: naturalist, statesman. Illustrated by David Cunningham. Grand Rapids, Zondervan Pub. House [1967] 151 p. illus., ports. 23 cm. (Her People you should know) A biography of a man whose dynamic personality and active life permitted him to accomplish much good for America's wildlife and statesmanship in the late nineteenth and early twentieth centuries. [E757.B645] AC 67
1. Roosevelt, Theodore, Pres. U.S., 1858-1919. I. Cunningham, David, illus. II. Title.

BLUM, John Morton, 1921- 923.173
The Republican Roosevelt. New preface by the author. New York, Atheneum, 1962 [c.1954] 170p. 19cm. (7) 1.25 pap.,
1. Roosevelt, Theodore, Pres. U.S., 1858-1919. 2. U.S.—Pol. & govt.—1901-1909. I. Title.

BLUM, John Morton, 1921- 823.173
The Republican Roosevelt. Cambridge, Harvard University Press, 1954. 170 p. 22 cm. [E757.B65] 54-5182
1. Roosevelt, Theodore, Pres. U.S., 1858-1919. 2. United States—Politics and government—1901-1909. I. Title. **BIP**

BLUM, John 973.91'1'0924 B Morton, 1921-
The Republican Roosevelt / by John Morton Blum. 2d ed. Cambridge, Mass. : Harvard University Press, 1977. xix, 170 p. ; 21 cm. (A Harvard paperback ; HP 114) Includes bibliographical references and index. [E757.B65 1977] 76-55513 ISBN 0-674-76301-7. ISBN 0-674-76302-5 pbk. : 2.95
1. Roosevelt, Theodore, Pres. U.S., 1858-1919. 2. Presidents—United States—Biography. 3. United States—Politics and government—1901-1909. I. Title.

BRADFORD, Gamaliel, 1863- 920.02 1932.
The quick and the dead. Port Washington, N.Y., Kennikat Press [1969, c1931] x, 282 p. ports. 22 cm. (Essay and general literature index reprint series) Contents.Contents.—Theodore Roosevelt.—Woodrow Wilson.—Thomas Alva Edison.—Henry Ford.—Nikolai Lenin.—Benito Mussolini.—Calvin Coolidge. Bibliographical references

included in "Notes" (p. [259]-[274]) [CT120.B65 1969] 70-85991
1. Roosevelt, Theodore, Pres. U.S., 1858-1919. 2. Wilson, Woodrow, Pres. U.S., 1856-1924. 3. Edison, Thomas Alva, 1847-1931. 4. Ford, Henry, 1863-1947. 5. Lenin, Vladimir Il'ich, 1870-1924. 6. Mussolini, Benito, 1883-1945. 7. Coolidge, Calvin, Pres. U.S., 1872-1933. I. Title.

BURTON, David Henry, 1925- 973.91'1'0924
Theodore Roosevelt and his English correspondents: a special relationship of friends [by] David H. Burton. Philadelphia, American Philosophical Society, 1973. 70 p. 30 cm. (Transactions of the American Philosophical Society, new ser., v. 63, pt. 2) Bibliography: p. 68. [E757.B972] 73-75473 ISBN 0-87169-632-0 3.50 (pbk)
1. Roosevelt, Theodore, Pres. U.S., 1858-1919. I. Title. II. Series: American Philosophical Society, Philadelphia. Transactions, new ser., v. 63, pt. 2.

BURTON, David Henry, 1925- 973.91'1'0924 B
Theodore Roosevelt: confident imperialist [by] David H. Burton. Philadelphia, University of Pennsylvania Press [1969, c1968] ix, 203 p. 24 cm. Bibliographical footnotes. [E756.B8] 68-9737 ISBN 8-12-275829-
1. Roosevelt, Theodore, Pres. U.S., 1858-1919. 2. U.S.—Foreign relations—1901-1909.

BUSCH, Noel Fairchild, 1906- 923.173
T.R.; the story of Theodore Roosevelt and his influence on our times. New York, Reynal, 1963. 346 p. illus. 22 cm. Includes bibliography. [E757.B98] 63-13223
1. Roosevelt, Theodore, Pres. U.S., 1858-1919.

BUSCH, Noel Fairchild, 1906- 923.173
T. R.; the story of Theodore Roosevelt and his influence on our times New York, Apollo [1965, c.1963] 346p. illus. 20cm. (A-114) Bibl. [E757.B98] 1.95 pap.,
1. Roosevelt, Theodore, Pres. U.S., 1858-1919. I. Title.

CADENHEAD, Ivie Edward, 1923- 973.91'1'0924 B
A life of Theodore Roosevelt, by I. E. Cadenhead, Jr. Woodbury, N.Y., Barron's Educational Series, inc., 1974. p. cm. (Shapers of history series) Bibliography: p. A biography of the twenty-sixth President of the United States and an introduction to the era he dominated. [E757.C14] 92 74-790 ISBN 0-8120-0462-0
1. Roosevelt, Theodore, Pres. U.S., 1858-1919. I. Title.

CADENHEAD, Ivie Edward, 1923- 973.91'1'0924 B
Theodore Roosevelt; the paradox of progressivism, by I. E. Cadenhead, Jr. Woodbury, N.Y., Barron's Educational Series, inc. [1974] x, 385 p. 19 cm. (Shapers of history series) Bibliography: p. [366]-370. A biography of the twenty-sixth President of the United States and an introduction to the era he dominated. [E757.C14] 92 74-790 ISBN 0-8120-0462-0 2.95 (pbk.)
1. Roosevelt, Theodore, Pres. U.S., 1858-1919. I. Title.

CHESSMAN, G. Wallace. 973.91'1'0924 B
Theodore Roosevelt and the politics of power [by] G. Wallace Chessman. Edited by Oscar Handlin. Boston, Little, Brown [1969] viii, 214 p. 21 cm. (The Library of American biography) "A note on the sources": p. [200]-204. [E757.C55] 68-20501 5.00
1. Roosevelt, Theodore, Pres. U.S., 1858-1919. I. Title. II. Series. **BIP**

CUTRIGHT, Paul Russell, 1897-- 923.173
Theodore Roosevelt, the naturalist. Foreword by Fairfield Osborn. [1st ed.] New York, Harper [1956] 297p. illus. 22cm. Includes bibliography. [QH31.R72C8] 56-6914
1. Roosevelt, Theodore, Pres. U. S., 1858—1919. I. Title.

FEUERLICHT, Roberta Strauss 973.910924(B)
Theodore Roosevelt; a concise biography. New York, Amer. R. D. M. [c.1966] 72p. ports. 21cm. (Study master pubn., 924) Bibl. [E757] 66-28703 1.00 pap.,
1. Roosevelt, Theodore, Theodore, Pres. U. S., 1858-1919. I. Title.

FOSTER, Genevieve (Stump) 1893- 973.91'1'0924 B
Theodore Roosevelt, an initial biography. New York, Scribner [1954] 106 p. illus. 20 cm. A sample biography of the New Yorker who became Governor of the State, Vice President under McKinley, and twenty-sixth President of the United States. [PZ7.F8138Th] 92 AC 68
1. Roosevelt, Theodore, Pres. U.S., 1858-1919. I. Title.

GARDNER, Joseph Lawrence, 1933- 973.91'1'0924 B
Departing glory; Theodore Roosevelt as ex-President [by] Joseph L. Gardner. New York, Scribner [1973] xv, 432 p. illus. 24 cm. Bibliography: p. 415-420. [E757.G29] 72-11116 ISBN 0-684-13300-8 12.50
1. Roosevelt, Theodore, Pres. U.S., 1858-1919. I. Title.

GATEWOOD, Willard B. 973.91'1'0924
Theodore Roosevelt and the art of controversy; episodes of the White House years [by] Willard B. Gatewood, Jr. Baton Rouge, Louisiana State University Press [1970] vii, 294 p. 24 cm. Includes bibliographical references. [E757.G37] 74-122354 ISBN 0-8071-0430-2 8.95
1. Roosevelt, Theodore, Pres. U.S., 1858-1919. I. Title.

GRAFF, Stewart. 920
Theodore Roosevelt's boys. Illustrated by William Hutchinson. Champaign, Ill., Garrard Pub. Co. [1967] 72 p. col. illus. 23 cm. (Tall tales) Accounts of several times at Sagamore Hill and in the White House when the Roosevelt children were entertained by their father, Theodore, or got into mischief by themselves. [E757.3.G7] AC 67
1. Roosevelt, Theodore, Pres. U.S., 1858-1919. 2. Roosevelt family. I. Hutchinson, William M., illus. II. Title. **BIP**

GRANTHAM, Dewey W., comp. 973.91'1'0924
Theodore Roosevelt. Edited by Dewey W. Grantham. Englewood Cliffs, N.J., Prentice-Hall [1971] ix, 181 p. 21 cm. (Great lives observed) (A Spectrum book.) Includes bibliographical references. [E757.G73] 74-126818 5.95
1. Roosevelt, Theodore, Pres. U.S., 1858-1919.

HAGEDORN, Hermann, 1882-1964. 923.173
The Roosevelt family of Sagamore Hill. New York, Macmillan, 1954. 435 p. illus. 22 cm. [E757.3.H3] 54-11834
1. Roosevelt, Theodore, Pres. U.S., 1858-1919. 2. Roosevelt family. I. Title. **BIP**

HARBAUGH, William Henry, 1920- 973.911
The life and times of Theodore Roosevelt. New, rev. ed. New York, Collier Books [1963] 540 p. 18 cm. "CS 5V." First published in 1961 under title: Power and responsibility. Includes bibliography. [E757.H28] 63-13342
1. Roosevelt, Theodore, Pres. U.S. 1858-1919. I. Title. **BIP**

HARBAUGH, William Henry, 1920- 973.91'1'0924 B
The life and times of Theodore Roosevelt / William H. Harbaugh. New, rev. ed. London ; New York : Oxford University Press, c1975. xiv, 542 p. ; 21 cm. (A Galaxy book ; GB 447) First published in 1961 under title: Power and responsibility. Includes bibliographical references and index. [E757.H28 1975b] 75-15474 ISBN 0-19-519822-0 : 4.95 (U.S.)
1. Roosevelt, Theodore, Pres. U.S., 1858-1919. I. Title.

HARBAUGH, William Henry, 1920- 973.911
Power and responsibility; the life and times of Theodore Roosevelt. New York, Farrar, Straus and Cudahy [1961] 568p. illus. 22cm. Includes bibliography. [E757.H28] 61-10128
1. Roosevelt, Theodore, Pres. U. S., 1858-1919. I. Title. **BIP**

HARBAUGH, William Henry, 1920- 973.91'1'0924 B
Power and responsibility : the life and times of Theodore Roosevelt / by William Henry Harbaugh. New York : Octagon Books, 1975, c1961. p. cm. Reprint of the ed. published by Farrar, Straus and Cudahy, New York. Includes index. Bibliography: p. [E757.H28 1975] 75-1054 ISBN 0-374-93660-9
1. Roosevelt, Theodore, Pres. U.S., 1838-1919. I. Title.

HARBAUGH, William Henry, 1920- 973.91'1'0924 B
Power and responsibility : the life and times of Theodore Roosevelt / by William Henry Harbaugh. New, rev. ed. New York : Octagon Books, 1975, c1963. 540 p. : port. ; 22 cm. Reprint of the ed. published by Farrar, Straus and Cudahy, New York. Includes index. Bibliography: p. 497-524. [E757.H28 1975] 75 7502 ISBN 0 374-93660-9 lib.bdg. : 22.50
1. Roosevelt, Theodore, Pres. U.S., 1838-1919. I. Title.

HOYT, Edwin Palmer. 92
Teddy Roosevelt in Africa [by] Edwin P. Hoyt. New York, Duell, Sloan and Pearce [1967, c1966] vii, 147 p. 21 cm. Describes Teddy Roosevelt's adventures on an African safari after his retirement from public office in 1909. [E757.H866] AC 66
1. Roosevelt, Theodore, Pres. U.S. 1858-1919. 2. Africa, East—Description and travel. I. Title.

JOHNSTON, William Davision. 923.173
T. R., champion of the strenuous life; a photographic biography of Theodore Roosevelt. New York, Farrar, Straus and Cudahy [1958] 141p. illus. 27cm. Includes bibliography. [E757.J6] 58-14286
1. Roosevelt, Theodore, Pres. U. S., 1858-1919. 2. Roosevelt, Theodore, Pres, U. S., 1858-1919— Portriats. I. Title.

JUDSON, Clara Ingram, 1879-1960. 923.173
Theodore Roosevelt, fighting patriot. Front. and pencil drawings by Lorence F. Bjorklund. Chicago, Wilcox and Follett Co. [1953] 218 p. illus. 25 cm. [E757.J8] 53-13004
1. Roosevelt, Theodore, Pres. U.S., 1858-1919.

KELLER, Morton, comp. 973.91'1'0924 (B)
Theodore Roosevelt; a profile. [1st ed.] New York, Hill and Wang [1967] xix, 194 p. 21 cm. (American profiles) Bibliography: p. 191-192. [E757.K27] 67-26854
1. Roosevelt, Theodore, Pres. U.S., 1858-1919. I. Title.

LORANT, Stefan, 1901- 923.173
The life and times of Theodore Roosevelt. [1st ed.] Garden City, N. Y., Doubleday [1959] 640 p. illus., ports., facsims. 28 cm. Bibliography: p. 635. [E757.L85] 58-10732
1. Roosevelt, Theodore, Pres. U.S., 1858-1919. 2. Roosevelt, Theodore, Pres. U.S., 1858-1919—Iconography.

MANNERS, William, 1907- 973.91'2'0922
TR and Will; a friendship that split the Republican Party. [1st ed.] New York, Harcourt, Brace & World [1969] xiv, 335 p. illus., ports. 25 cm. Bibliography: p. 317-320. [E757.M34] 69-14838
1. Roosevelt, Theodore, Pres. U.S., 1858-1919. 2. Taft, William Howard, Pres. U.S., 1857-1930. I. Title.

MARKS, Frederick W. 973.91'1'0924 B
Velvet on iron : the diplomacy of Theodore Roosevelt / Frederick W. Marks III. Lincoln : University of Nebraska Press, c1979. p. cm. Includes index. Bibliography: p. [E756.M37] 79-1216 ISBN 0-8032-3057-5 : 15.00
1. Roosevelt, Theodore, Pres. U.S., 1858-1919. 2. United States—Foreign relations—1901-1909. 3. Presidents—United States—Biography. I. Title. **BIP**

MOWRY, George Edwin, 1909- 923.173
Theodore Roosevelt and and the progressive movement. New York, Hill & Wang [1960, c.1946] 405p. illus., (American century ser., AC31) Bibl.: p.385-393 1.95 pap.,
1. Roosevelt, Theodore, pres. U. S., 1858-1919. 2. Progressive party. I. Title.

MOWRY, George Edwin, 1909- 923.173
Theodore Roosevelt and and the progressive movement. New York, Hill & Wang [1960, c.1946] 405p. illus., (American century ser., AC31) Bibl.: p.385-393 1.95 pap.,
1. Roosevelt, Theodore, pres. U. S., 1858-1919. 2. Progressive party. I. Title.

MOWRY, George Edwin, 1909- 923.173
Theodore Roosevelt and the progressive movement. New York, Hill and Wang [1960, c1946] 405 p. illus. 21 cm. (American century series, AC31) Includes bibliography. [E757] A62
1. Roosevelt, Theodore, Pres. U.S., 1858-1919. 2. Progressive Party (Founded 1912) I. Title.

NEU, Charles E. 327.52'073
An uncertain friendship: Theodore Roosevelt and Japan, 1906-1909 [by] Charles E. Neu. Cambridge, Mass., Harvard University Press, 1967. x, 347 p. 22 cm. Bibliography: p. [323]-333. [E183.8.J3N37] 67-27091
1. Roosevelt, Theodore, Pres. U.S., 1858-1919. 2. United States—Foreign relations—Japan. 3. Japan—Foreign relations—United States. I. Title.

PRINGLE, Henry Fowles, 1897- 923.173
Theodore Roosevelt, a biography. [Rev.] New York, Harcourt, Brace [c1956] 435p. 19cm. (A Harvest book, 15) [E757.P967] 56-13739
1. Roosevelt, Theodore, Pres. U. S., 1858-1919. I. Title.

PUTNAM, Carleton, 1901- 923.173
Theodore Roosevelt, a biography. New York, Scribner, 1958- v. illus., ports., maps. 24 cm. Contents.Contents.—v. 1. The formative years, 1858-1886. Bibliography: v. 1, p. 609-616. [E757.P968] 58-6735
1. Roosevelt, Theodore, Pres. U.S., 1858-1919.

RIIS, Jacob August, 1849-1914. 973.91'1'0924
Theodore Roosevelt, the citizen. New York, Outlook Co., 1904. St. Clair Shores, Mich., Scholarly Press, 1970. xii, 471 p. illus., ports. 22 cm. Bibliography: p. 457-464. [E757.R57 1970] 77-108531
1. Roosevelt, Theodore, Pres. U.S., 1858-1919. I. Title.

RIIS, Jacob August, 1849-1914. 973.91'1'0924
Theodore Roosevelt, the citizen. New York, AMS Press [1969] xii, 471 p. illus., ports. 23 cm. Reprint of the 1904 ed. "Books by Theodore Roosevelt": p. [455]-464. [E757.R57 1969] 71-101270
1. Roosevelt, Theodore, Pres. U.S., 1858-1919. I. Title. **BIP**

ROOSEVELT, Eleanor Butler (Alexander) 920.7
Day before yesterday; the reminiscences of Mrs. Theodore Roosevelt, Jr. [1st ed.] Garden City, N. Y., Doubleday [1959] 478p. illus. 25cm. [E748.R68R6] 59-8270
1. Roosevelt, Theodore, 1887-1944. I. Title.

ROOSEVELT, Nicholas, 1893- 973.91'1'0924
Theodore Roosevelt; the man as I knew him. New York, Dodd, Mead [1967] xiv, 205 p. illus., ports. 24 cm. Bibliographical references included in "Notes" (p. 191-194) [E757.R76] 67-13368
1. Roosevelt, Theodore, Pres. U.S., 1858-1919. 2. Roosevelt family.

ROOSEVELT, Theodore, Pres. U. S., 1858-1919. 923.173
Autobiography. Condensed from the original ed., supplemented by letters, speeches, and other writing, and edited with an introd. by Wayne Andrews. Centennial ed. New York, Scribner [1958] xi, 372p. 22cm. Bibliography:p. 359-362. [E757.R794] 58-11634
I. Title.

ROOSEVELT, Theodore, Pres. U.S., 1858-1919. 973.91'1'0924 B
The autobiography of Theodore Roosevelt : condensed from the original ed., supplemented by letters, speeches, and other writings, and edited with an introd. by Wayne Andrews. New York : Octagon Books, 1975, c1958. xi, 372 p. ; 23 cm. Reprint of the ed. published by Scribner, New York. Includes index. Bibliography: p. 359-362. [E757.R794 1975] 74-31391 ISBN 0-374-96910-8 : 14.50
1. Roosevelt, Theodore, Pres. U.S., 1858-1919.

ROOSEVELT, Theodore, Pres. U. S., 1858-1919. 923.173
Cowboys and kings; three great letters. With an introd. by Elting E. Morison. Cambridge, Harvard University Press, 1954. xii, 128p. illus., ports. 22cm. [E757.R7957] 54-9117
I. Hay, John, 1838-1905. II. Trevelyan, George Otto, bart., Sir 1838-1928. III. Gray, David, 1870- IV. Title.

ROOSEVELT, Theodore, Pres. U. S., 1858-1919. 923.173
Letters, selected and edited by Elting E. Morison; John M. Blum, associate editor, John J. Buckley, copy editor. Cambridge, Harvard University Press, 1951-54. 8 v. illus., ports. 25cm. Vols. 3-4: Hope W. Wigglesworth, assistant editor: Sylvia Rice, copy editor. Vols. 5-8: Alfred D. Chandler, Jr., assistant editor; Sylvia Rice, copy editor. Contents.v. 1-2. The years of preparation. 1868-1900.--v. 3-4. The Square Deal, 1901-1905.--v. 5-6. The Big Stick, 1905-1909.--v. 7-8. The days of Armageddon, 1909-1914. [E757.R7958] 51-10037
I. Title.

ROOSEVELT, Theodore, Pres. U.S., 1858-1919. 973.91'1'0922
Selections from the correspondence of Theodore Roosevelt and Henry Cabot Lodge, 1884-1918. Edited by Henry Cabot Lodge and Charles F. Redmond. New York, Da Capo Press, 1971 [c1925] 2 v. ports. 24 cm. [E757.R79588 1971] 72-146156 ISBN 0-306-70129-4
I. Lodge, Henry Cabot, 1850-1924. II. Title. **BIP**

ROOSEVELT, Theodore, Pres. U. S., 1858-1919. 923.173
The Theodore Roosevelt treasury; a self-portrait from his writings. Compiled and with an introd. by Hermann Hagedorn. New York, Putnam [1957] 342p. port. 25cm. [E660.R885] 57-11713
I. Hagedorn, Hermann, 1882- ed. II. Title.

ROOSEVELT, Theodore, Pres. U.S., 1858-1919. 923.173
Theodore Roosevelt's letters to his children. Edited by Joseph Bocklin [i.e. Bucklin] Bishop. With a prologue and epilogue by Elting E. Morison. [New York] New American Library [1964] xiii, 159 p. illus. 18 cm. (A Signet classic, CP241) Bibliography: p. 158-159. [E757.R79586] 64-57865
I. Bishop, Joseph Bucklin, 1847-1928, ed. II. Title. **BIP**

THOMPSON, Charles Willis, 1871-1946. 973.9'0922
Presidents I've known and two near Presidents. Freeport, N.Y., Books for Libraries Press [1970, c1956] 386 p. 23 cm. (Essay index reprint series) Contents.Contents.—Hanna-McKinley.—Bryan.—Roosevelt.—Taft.—Wilson.—Harding.—Coolidge. [E176.1.T45 1970] 71-93383
1. Hanna, Marcus Alonzo, 1837-1904. 2. McKinley, William, Pres. U.S., 1843-1901. 3. Bryan, William Jennings, 1860-1925. 4. Roosevelt, Theodore, Pres. U.S., 1858-1919. 5. Taft, William Howard, Pres. U.S., 1857-1930. 6. Wilson, Woodrow, Pres. U.S., 1856-1924. 7. Harding, Warren Gamaliel, Pres. U.S., 1865-1923. 8. Coolidge, Calvin, Pres. U.S., 1872-1933. I. Title. **BIP**

U.S. President, 1901-1909 (Roosevelt) 971.91'1'0924
Theodore Roosevelt, 1858-1919; chronology, documents, bibliographical aids. Edited by Gilbert J. Black. Dobbs Ferry, N.Y., Oceana Publications, 1969. 120 p. 24 cm. (Oceana Presidential chronology series, 8) Bibliography: p. 109-117. [E756.U68] 69-15392 4.00
1. Roosevelt, Theodore, Pres. U.S., 1858-1919. 2. U.S.—History—1901-1953—Sources. I. Black, Gilbert J., ed.

WILSON, Robert Lawrence, 1939- 973.91'1'0924 B
Theodore Roosevelt: outdoorsman, by R. L. Wilson. Political background by G. C. Wilson. [New York] Winchester Press [1971] ix, 278 p. illus., facsims., maps, ports. 26 cm. Bibliography: p. 227-238. [E757.W75] 76-127959 ISBN 0-87691-002-9 12.95
1. Roosevelt, Theodore, Pres. U.S., 1858-1919. I. Wilson, Gregory Curtin, joint author.

Roosevelt, Theodore, Pres. U.S., 1858-1919—Addresses, essays, lectures.

COLLIN, Richard H., comp. 973.91'1'0924
Theodore Roosevelt and reform politics. Edited and with an introd. by Richard H. Collin. Lexington, Mass., Heath [1972] xvi, 192 p. 21 cm. (Problems in American civilization) Bibliography: p. 190-192. [E756.C75] 74-176364 ISBN 0-669-73379-2
1. Roosevelt, Theodore, Pres. U.S., 1858-1919—Addresses, essays, lectures. 2. U.S.—Politics and government—1901-1909—Addresses, essays, lectures. 3. U.S.—Politics and government—1909-1913—Addresses, essays, lectures. I. Title. II. Series.

Roosevelt, Theodore, Pres. U.S., 1858-1919—Bibliography—Catalogs.

HARVARD University. Library. 016.97391'1'0924
Theodore Roosevelt collection; dictionary catalogue and shelflist. Cambridge, Mass., Distributed by the Harvard University Press, 1970. 5 v. 32 cm. [Z8757.3.H36] 72-127844 ISBN 0-674-87775-6
1. Roosevelt, Theodore, Pres. U.S., 1858-1919—Bibliography—Catalogs. I. Title.

Roosevelt, Theodore, Pres. U. S., 1858-1919—Juvenile fiction.

PARKS, Edd Winfield, 1906- 920
Teddy Roosevelt, all around boy. Illus. by Gray Morrow. Indianapolis, Bobbs [c.1961] 200p. col. illus. (Childhood of famous Americans) 60-7719 2.25
1. Roosevelt, Theodore, Pres. U. S., 1858-1919—Juvenile fiction. I. Title.

Roosevelt, Theodore, Pres. U.S., 1858-1919 — Juvenile literature.

BEACH, James Caleb v. 12
Theodore Roosevelt, man of action. Illus. by William Hutchinson. New York, Grosset [1962, c.]1960. 80p. col. illus. 23cm. (Garrard Discovery bk.) 92A62 1.00 lib. ed.,
1. Roosevelt, Theodore, Pres. U. S., 1858-1919—Juvenile literature. I. Title.

BEACH, James Caleb. j92
Theodore Roosevelt, man of action. Illustrated by William Hutchinson. New York, Grosset & Dunlap [1962] 1960. 80 p. illus. 23 cm. (A Discovery book) [[E757]] A62
1. Roosevelt, Theodore, Pres. U. S., 1858-1919—Juvenile literature. I. Title.

BEACH, James Caleb. 923.173
Theodore Roosevelt, man of action. Illustrated by William Hutchinson. Champaign, Ill., Garrard Press [1960] 80 p. illus. 23 cm. (A Discovery book) [E757.B38] 60-6469
1. Roosevelt, Theodore, Pres. U.S., 1858-1919—Juvenile literature.

BLACKBURN, Joyce. 92 (J)
Theodore Roosevelt: naturalist, statesman. Illustrated by David Cunningham. Grand Rapids, Zondervan Pub. House [1967] 151 p. illus., ports. 23 cm. (Her People you should know) [E757.B645] 67-25729
1. Roosevelt, Theodore, Pres. U.S., 1858-1919—Juvenile literature.

CAVANAH, Frances. 923.173
Adventure in courage; the story of Theodore Roosevelt. Illustrated by Grace Paull. Chicago, Rand McNally [1961] 111p. illus. 24cm. Includes bibliography. [E757.C36] 60-8261
1. Roosevelt, Theodore, Pres. U. S., 1858-1919—Juvenile literature. I. Title.

COOK, Fred J. 92
Theodore Roosevelt, rallying a free people. Illus. by Robert Boehmer. Chicago, Britannica Bks.,)div. of Ency. Britannica [1963, c.1961] 190p. col. illus. 22cm. (Britannica bkshelf.: Great lives for young Amers.) 2.36 lib. ed.,
1. Roosevelt, Theodore, Pres. U.S., 1858-1919—Juvenile literature. I. Title.

DE KAY, Ormonde. 92 (J)
Meet Theodore Roosevelt. Illustrated by Jack Davis. New York, Random House [1967] 86 p. col. illus., col. map (on lining papers) col. ports. 22 cm. (Step-up books) [E757.D34] 67-5175
1. Roosevelt, Theodore, Pres. U.S., 1858-1919—Juvenile literature. I. Title. **BIP**

GRAFF, Stewart. 920 (J)
Theodore Roosevelt's boys. Illustrated by William Hutchinson. Champaign, Ill., Garrard Pub. Co. [1967] 72 p. col. illus. 23 cm. (Tall tales) [E757.3.G7] 67-11115
1. Roosevelt, Theodore, Pres. U.S., 1858-1919—Juvenile literature. 2. Roosevelt family—Juvenile literature. I. Title.

HAGEDORN, Hermann, 1882-1964. 973.91'1'0924 B
The boys' life of Theodore Roosevelt. Illustrated with cartoons and reproductions of Theodore Roosevelt's own diaries. New York, Harper [1950] 386 p. illus. 20 cm. [E757.H141 1950] 68-4945
1. Roosevelt, Theodore, Pres. U.S., 1858-1919—Juvenile literature. I. Title.

HANCOCK, Sibyl. 973.91'1'0924 B
Theodore Roosevelt / by Sibyl Hancock ; illustrated by Joseph Ciardiello. New York : Putnam, c1978. 60 p. : ill. ; 23 cm. (A See and read biography) An easy-to-read biography of the twenty-sixth President of the United States. [E757.H22 1978] 92 77-22614 ISBN 0-399-61107-X lib.bdg. : 4.49
1. Roosevelt, Theodore, Pres. U.S., 1858-1919—Juvenile literature. 2. Presidents—United States—Biography—Juvenile literature. I. Ciardiello, Joseph. II. Title.

MOTHNER, Ira 973.9110924
Man of action; the life of Teddy Roosevelt. New York, Platt & Munk [c.1966] 88p. illus., ports. 27cm. [E757.M89] 66-5510 2.95 bds.,
1. Roosevelt, Theodore, Pres. U. S., 1858-1919—Juvenile literature. I. Title.

THOMAS, Henry, 1886- 923.173
Theodore Roosevelt. Illustrated by Albert Orbaan. New York, Putnam [1959] 128 p. illus. 21 cm. (Lives to remember) [E757.T46] 59-6509
1. Roosevelt, Theodore, Pres. U.S., 1858-1919 — Juvenile literature. I. Title.

Root, Elihu, 1845-1937.

JESSUP, Philip Caryl, 1897- 923.273
Elihu Root, by Philip C. Jessup. Hamden, Conn., Archon Books, 1964. 2 v. fronts., plates, ports., map, facsims. 25 cm. Map on lining-papers. Contents.Contents.—I. 1845-1909.—II. 1905-1937. "Sources and bibliography": v. 2, p. 507-520; "Chronological list of the principal public speeches and papers of Elihu Root": v. 2, p. 521-552. [E664.R7J5] 38-31598
1. Root, Elihu, 1845-1937.

Root, John Wellborn 1850-1891. aMielotz, Charles Frederick William, 1860- illus.

MONROE, Harriet, 1860- 1936 720.924
John Wellborn Root; a study of his life and work. With etchings, drawings by Charles F. W. Mielatz and facsimiles of designs by Mr. Root. Park Forest, Ill., Prairie Sch. Pr. [1966] xxii, 291p. illus. maps. port. 23cm. First pub. in 1896. [NA737.R6M6 1966] 66-29040 8.50
1. Root, John Wellborn 1850-1891. aMielotz, Charles Frederick William, 1860- illus. I. Title.

Roper, Leighton Parks,

ROPER, Leighton Parks, 1913- 332.1'0924 B
Old hundredth. [1st ed.] Norfolk, Va., Teagle & Little, 1971. v, 130 p. 24 cm. [CT275.R7814A3] 73-177910 5.00
I. Title.

Roper Margaret (More), 1505-1544.

REYNOLDS, Ernst Edwin, 1894- 920.7
Margaret Roper, eldest daughter of St. Thomas More. New York, P. J. Kenedy [c.1960] 149p. illus. 60-13955 3.95
1. Roper Margaret (More), 1505-1544. I. Title.

REYNOLDS, Ernest Edwin, 1894- 920.7
Margaret Roper, eldest daughter of St. Thomas More. New York, P.J. Kenedy [1960] 149p. illus. 23cm. [DA335.R6R4] 60-13955
1. Roper, Margaret (More) 1505-1544. I. Title.

Rorem, Ned, 1923-

ROREM, Ned, 1923- 780'.92'4 B
An absolute gift : a new diary / Ned Rorem. New York : Simon and Schuster, c1978. 286 p. ; 23 cm. Includes index. [ML410.R693A25] 77-18512 ISBN 0-671-22666-5 : 9.95
1. Rorem, Ned, 1923- 2. Composers—United States—Biography. I. Title. BIP

Rorer, Sarah Tyson Heston, 1849-1937.

WEIGLEY, Emma Seifrit. 081 S
Sarah Tyson Rorer : the nation's instructress in dietetics and cookery / Emma Seifrit Weigley. Philadelphia : American Philosophical Society, 1977. ix, 196 p. : ill. ; 24 cm. (Memoirs of the American Philosophical Society ; v. 119 ISSN 0065-9738s) Includes index.IBibliography: p. 185-190. [Q11.P612 vol. 119] [TX140.R68] 640'.92'4 B 77-2115 ISBN 0-87169-119-1 pbk. : 6.00
1. Rorer, Sarah Tyson Heston, 1849-1937. 2. Home economics—Biograhy. I. Series: American Philosophical Society, Philadelphia. Memoirs ; v. 119. BIP

Rorschach, Hermann, 1884-1922. Psychodiagnostics.

DR. Hermann Rorschach. v. 12
Psychodiagnostics. Bibliography. New York, Grune & Stratton [c1954] 64p. 25cm. 'The most important publications about the Rorschach test (until 1954)' A 56
1. Rorschach, Hermann, 1884-1922. Psychodiagnostics. 2. Rorschach test—Bibl.

Ros, Herbert Spencer, 1909-

ROS, Herbert Spencer, 1909- 327'.2'0924 B
It is so nice to remember : the recollections of an Italian diplomat / by Herbert Spencer Ros. 1st ed. New York : Vantage Press, c1978. 182 p. : ill. ; 21 cm. [DG575.R59A34] 78-106035 ISBN 0-533-03151-6 : 8.95
1. Ros, Herbert Spencer, 1909- 2. Italy—Foreign relations. 3. Diplomats—Italy—Biography. 4. Sinologists—Italy—Biography. I. Title.

Rosa of Lima, Saint, 1586-1617.

KAYE-SMITH, Sheila, 1887- 922.2
Quartet in heaven. [1st ed.] New York, Harper [1952] viii, 279 p. 22 cm. [BX4667.K3] 52-5455
1. Caterina da Genova, Saint, 1447-1510. 2. Connelly, Cornelia Augusta (Peacock) 1809-1879. 3. Rosa of Lima, Saint, 1586-1617. 4. Therese, Saint, 1873-1897. I. Title.
Contents Omitted.

KAYE-SMITH, Sheila, 1887-1956. 282'.0922 B
Quartet in heaven. Freeport, N.Y., Books for Libraries Press [1970, c1952] viii, 244 p. 23 cm. (Biography index reprint series) Contents.Contents.—The matrons: Caterina Fiesca Adorna. Cornelia Connelly.—The maidens: Isabella Rosa de Santa Maria de Flores. Therese Martin.—Some notes on the nature of sanctity. [BX4667.K3 1970] 75-136649
1. Caterina da Genova, Saint, 1447-1510. 2. Connelly, Cornelia Augusta (Peacock) 1809-1879. 3. Rosa, of Lima, Saint, 1586-1617. 4. Therese, Saint, 1873-1897. I. Title. BIP

KEYES, Frances Parkinson (Wheeler) 1885-1970. 922.285
The Rose and the Lily; the lives and times of two South American saints. [1st ed.] New York, Hawthorn Books [1961] 253 p. illus. 22 cm. Includes bibliography. [BX4700.R6K4] 61-6704
1. Rosa, of Lima, Saint, 1586-1617. 2. Paredes y Flores, Marians de Jesus, Saint, 1618-1645. I. Title.

MARY Alphonsus, Sister, O.SS.R. 271'.972'0924 B
St. Rose of Lima, patroness of the Americas. St. Louis, Herder [1968] xiii, 304 p. 21 cm. (Cross and crown series of spirituality, no. 36) [BX4700.R6M27] 68-8925 5.50
1. Rosa, of Lima, Saint, 1586-1617. I. Title. II. Series.

RICHARDSON, Mary Kathleen 922.285
Linda. Drawings by R. M. Sax. New York, Sheed &Ward [c.1960] (part col.) illus. 21cm. (A Patron saint book) 60-6287 2.00 bds.,
1. Rosa, of Lima, Saint, 1586-1617 I. Title.

ROBERTO, Brother, 1927- 922.285
The girl who laughed at Satan; a story of St. Rose of Lima. Illus. by Elaine Smith. Notre Dame, Ind., Dujarie Press [1956] 94p. illus. 24cm. [BX4700.R6R6] 56-42846
1. Rosa of Lima, Saint, 1586-1617. I. Title.

Rosa, of Lima, Saint, 1586-1617—Juvenile literature.

RICHARDSON, Mary Kathleen, 1903 922.285
Linda. Drawings by R. M. Sax. New York, Sheed & Ward [1960] unpaged. illus. 21cm. (A Patron saint book) [BX4700.R6R5] 60-6287
1. Rosa, of Lima, Saint, 1586-1617—Juvenile literature. I. Title.

Rosa, Salvatore, 1615-1673.

BOETZKES, Ottilie Gertrude 927.5
Salvator Rosa, seventeenth-century Italian painter, poet, and patriot. New York. Vantage Press [c.1960] 196p. illus. 21cm. 60-11700 3.95
1. Rosa, Salvator, 1615-1673. I. Title.

BOETZKES, Ottilie Gertrude. 927.5
Salvator Rosa, seventeenth-century Italian painter, poet, and patriot. [1st ed.] New York, Vantage Press [1960] 196p. illus. 21cm. [ND623.R7B6] 60-11700
1. Rosa, Salvatore, 1615-1673. I. Title.

Rosati, Joseph, Bp., 1789-1843.

EASTERLY, Frederick John, 1910- 282'.092'4 B
The life of Rt. Rev. Joseph Rosati, C.M., first bishop of St. Louis, 1789-1843. Washington, Catholic University of America Press, 1942. [New York, AMS Press, 1974] xi, 203 p. 23 cm. Reprint of the author's thesis, Catholic University of America, 1942, which was issued as v. 33 of the Catholic University of America. Studies in American church history. Bibliography: p. 191-197. [BX4705.R723E3 1974] 73-3587 ISBN 0-404-57783-0 9.00
1. Rosati, Joseph, Bp., 1789-1843. 2. Catholic Church in St. Louis—History. 3. St. Louis, Mo. (Archdiocese)—History. I. Series: Catholic University of America. Studies in American church history, v. 33.

Rose, Billy, 1899-1966.

CONRAD, Earl. 792'.0924 B
Billy Rose, Manhattan primitive. Cleveland, World Pub. Co. [1968] xvi, 272 p. ports. 22 cm. [PN2287.R756C6] 67-26957
1. Rose, Billy, 1899-1966.

GOTTLIEB, Polly Rose. 792'.0924 B
The nine lives of Billy Rose. New York, Crown Publishers [1968] 290 p. illus., ports. 24 cm. [PN2287.R756G6] 68-19200
1. Rose, Billy, 1899-1966. I. Title.

Rose, Donald Frank,

ROSE, Donald Frank, 1890- 818.5
Full house; illustrated by Jo Metzer. [1st ed.] Philadelphia, Lippincott [1951] 256 p. illus. 21 cm. Autobiographical. [CT275.R7824A3] 51-9876
I. Title.

Rose, Edward, fl.1811-1834.

FELTON, Harold W., 1902- 92
Edward Rose; Negro trail blazer, by Harold W. Felton. Illustrated with photos., prints of the period, and maps. New York, Dodd, Mead [1967] xvi, 111 p. illus., maps, ports. 22 cm. Bibliography: p. 106-108. Few biographical facts exist about Edward Rose, a guide of the Early West, yet historical chronicles show he was present at most of the major events that expanded the American frontier in the early 1800's. [F592.R6F4] AC 67
1. Rose, Edward, fl.1811-1834. I. Title. BIP

Rose, Ernestine Louise, 1810-1892.

EISEMAN, Alberta. 973'.04'924 B
Rebels and reformers : biographies of four Jewish Americans : Uriah Phillips Levy, Ernestine L. Rose, Louis D. Brandeis, Lillian D. Wald / by Alberta Eiseman ; illustrated by Herb Steinberg. 1st ed. Garden City, N.Y. : Zenith Books, 1976. 131 p. : ill. ; 22 cm. Includes index. Biographies of four Jewish Americans whose activities in women's rights, abolition, law, nursing, and the military contributed to the growth, development, and needed reform of the country. [E184.J5E34] 920 75-21224 ISBN 0-385-01588-7 : 4.95 ISBN 0-385-09662-3 pbk. : 2.50
1. Levy, Uriah Phillips, 1792-1862. 2. Rose, Ernestine Louise, 1810-1892. 3. Brandeis, Louis Dembitz, 1856-1941. 4. Wald, Lillian D., 1867-1940. 5. Jews in the United States. I. Steinberg, Herbert, 1928- II. Title.

SUHL, Yuri, 1908- 301.41'21'0924 B
Eloquent crusader: Ernestine Rose. New York, J. Messner [1970] 191 p. 22 cm. Bibliography: p. [184]-188. A biography of the woman whose life-long crusade for women's rights and other social reforms began at age sixteen when she went to court to prevent her marriage to a man she didn't love. [HQ1413.R6S9] 92 78-100560 3.50
1. Rose, Ernestine Louise, 1810-1892. I. Title.

Rose Hill, N.C.-Biography.

WOLCOTT, Reed M., 1944- 920'.0756'382
Rose Hill / Reed M. Wolcott. New York : Putnam, c1976. 381 p., [8] leaves of plates : ill. ; 24 cm. [F264.R67W64 1976] 76-7951 ISBN 0-399-11622-2 : 8.95
1. Rose Hill, N.C.—Biography. 2. Rose Hill, N.C.—Social life and customs. I. Title.

WOLCOTT, Reed M., 1944- 920'0756'382
Rose Hill / Reed M. Wolcott. New York : Harper and Row, 1977. 381p. : [8] leaves of plates ; 21 cm. (Harper Colophon Books) [F264.R67W64] ISBN 0-06-090577-8 pbk. : 4.95
1. Rose Hill, N.C.-Biography. 2. Rose Hill, N.C.-Soial life and customs. I. Title.
L.C. card no. for 1976 G.P. Putnam ed.:76-7951. BIP

Rose, Hilly.

ROSE, Hilly. 789.9'1 B
"But, that's not what I called about" / Hilly Rose. Chicago : Contemporary Books, c1978. 201 p., [8] leaves of plates : ill. ; 22 cm. Includes index. [PN1991.4.R6A33 1978] 77-91174 ISBN 0-8092-7624-0 : 7.95
1. Rose, Hilly. 2. Radio broadcasters—United States—Biography. I. Title.

Rose, Isaac P., 1815-1899.

MARSH, James B. 917.8'0092'4 B
Four years in the Rockies; or, The adventures of Isaac P. Rose, by James B. Marsh. New York, Arno Press, 1973. 262 p. 23 cm. (The Far Western frontier) Reprint of the 1884 ed. [F721.M38 1973] 72-9459 ISBN 0-405-04987-0 13.00
1. Rose, Isaac P., 1815-1899. 2. Frontier and pioneer life—Rocky Mountains. 3. Fur trade—Rocky Mountains. I. Title. II. Series.

MARSH, James B. 973'.04'97 S
Four years in the Rockies : or, The adventures of Isaac Rose / James B. Marsh. New York : Garland Pub., 1976. 262 p. : port. ; 23 cm. (The Garland library of narratives of North American Indian captivities ; v. 94) Reprint of the 1884 ed. printed by W. B. Thomas, New Castle, Pa. [E85.G2 vol. 94] [F721] 978'.02'0924 75-7120 ISBN 0-8240-1718-8 lib.bdg. : 21.00
1. Rose, Isaac P., 1815-1899. 2. Frontier and pioneer life Rocky Mountains. 3. Rocky Mountains—Description and travel. 4. Indians of North America—Captivities. I. Title. II. Series.

Rose, Joseph.

ROSEBROCK, Ellen Fletcher. 330.9'747'103
Farewell to old England : New York in Revolution / by Ellen F. Rosebrock. New York : South Street Seaport Museum, c1976. p. cm. Bibliography: p. [HC102.5.A2R675] 75-3941 ISBN 0-913344-21-4 pbk. : 1.95
1. Rose, Joseph. 2. Sears, Isaac, ca. 1730-1786. 3. Low, Isaac, 1735-1791. 4. New York (City)—Commerce—History. 5. New York (City)—History—Colonial period, ca. 1600-1775. I. Title.

Rose, Leonard John, 1827-1899.

ROSE, Leonard John, 1862- 920
L. J. Rose of Sunny Slope, 1827-1899, California pioneer, fruit grower, wine maker, horse breeder. San Marino, Calif., Huntington Library, 1959. 235p. 24cm. [CT275.R7826R6] 59-13180
1. Rose, Leonard John, 1827-1899. I. Title.

Rose, Mary Davies Swartz, 1874-1941.

EAGLES, Juanita Archibald, 1915- 613.2'092'4 B
Mary Swartz Rose, 1874-1941, pioneer in nutrition / Juanita Archibald Eagles, Orrea Florence Pye, Clara Mae Taylor. New York : Teachers College Press, c1979. xviii, 172 p. : ill. ; 24 cm. Includes index. "Publications of Mary Swartz Rose:" p. 152-161. [TX350.8.R67E18] 79-4342 ISBN 0-8077-2556-0 : 9.95
1. Rose, Mary Davies Swartz, 1874-1941. 2. Nutritionists—Biography. I. Pye, Orrea Florence, 1907- joint author. II. Taylor, Clara Mae, 1898- joint author. III. Title.

Rose, Pete, 1942-

ROSE, Pete, 1942- 796.357'092'4 B
Charlie Hustle / by Pete Rose, with Bob Hertzel. Englewood Cliffs, N.J. : Prentice-Hall, [1975] viii, 227 p., [8] leaves of plates : ill. ; 22 cm. "An Associated Features book." [GV865.R65A295] 75-5517 ISBN 0-13-448209-3 : 7.95
1. Rose, Pete, 1942- 2. Baseball. I. Hertzel, Bob, 1941- joint author. II. Title. BIP

ROSE, Pete, 1942- 796.357'0924 B
The Pete Rose story: an autobiography. Introd. by Joe Garagiola. New York, World [1970] 202 p. illus., ports. 22 cm. [GV865.R65A3 1970] 71-120126 6.95
1. Baseball—Biography. I. Title.

Rose, Pete, 1942- —Juvenile literature.

BRANDT, Keith, 1930- 796.357'092'4 B
Pete Rose, "Mr. 300" / by Keith Brandt. New York : Putnam, c1977. 123 p. : ill. ; 21 cm. (Putnam sport shelf) Includes index. A biography stressing the baseball career of the star player of the Cincinnati Reds. [GV865.R65B72 1977] 92 76-54137 ISBN 0-399-61071-5 lib. bdg. : 5.29
1. Rose, Pete, 1942- —Juvenile literature. 2. Baseball players—United States—Biography—Juvenile literature. I. Title.

BURCHARD, Marshall. 796.357'092'4 B
Sports hero, Pete Rose / by Marshall Burchard. New York : Putnam, [1976] p. cm. (The Sports hero biographies) A biography of the team captain of the Cincinnati Reds, whose skills helped the team to victory in the 1975 World Series, their first championship in thirty-five years. [GV865.R65B87] 76-25894 ISBN 0-399-61038-3 lib.bdg. : 4.99
1. Rose, Pete, 1942- —Juvenile literature. 2. Baseball—Juvenile literature. I. Title.

LIBBY, Bill. 796.357'092'4 B
Pete Rose: they call him Charlie Hustle. New York, Putnam [1972] 159 p. 21 cm. (Putnam sports shelf) A biography of the hometown boy who became a well-known player for the Cincinnati Reds. [GV865.R65L52 1972] 92 77-188720 ISBN 0-399-20283-8 4.29
1. Rose, Pete, 1942- —Juvenile literature.

ROSE, Pete, 1941- 796.357'.092'4 B
Pete Rose : my life in baseball / by Pete Rose ; conceived and produced by Whitehall, Hadlyme & Smith, inc. 1st ed. Garden City, N.Y. : Doubleday, c1979. 134 p. : ill. ; 22 cm. (An I want to know about book) Includes index. One of baseball's-greatest hitters talks about his life and career. [GV865.R65A299] 92 78-18144 ISBN 0-385-13639-0 : 6.95.
1. Rose, Pete, 1941- —Juvenile literature. 2. Baseball players—United States—Biography—Juvenile literature. I. Whitehall, Handlyme & Smith. II. Title. BIP

RUBIN, Bob. 796.357'092'4 B
Pete Rose / by Bob Rubin ; illustrated with photos. New York : Random House, [1975] 152 p. : ill. ; 22 cm. (Major league library) Includes index. A biography stressing the baseball career of the star outfielder of the Cincinnati Reds, Pete Rose. [GV865.R65R82] 92 74-24761 ISBN 0-394-83026-1 : 2.50 ISBN 0-394-93026-6 lib. bdg. : 3.69
1. Rose, Pete, 1942- —Juvenile literature. 2. Baseball—Juvenile literature. I. Title.

Rose, Robert, 1704-1751.

ROSE, Robert, 1704-1751. 283'.092'4 B
The diary of Robert Rose : a view of Virginia by a Scottish colonial parson, 1746-1751 / edited and annotated by Ralph Emmett Fall ; map prepared and drawn by Murray Fontaine Rose. Verona, Va. : McClure Press, 1977. xxii, 400 p. : ill. ; 24 cm. Includes bibliographical references and indexes. [BX5995.R65A33] 77-88039 15.00
1. Rose, Robert, 1704-1751. 2. Church of England—Clergy—Biography. 3. Clergy—Virginia—Biography. I. Fall, Ralph Emmett. II. Title.

Rose, Samuel B.,

ROSE, Samuel B., 1889-1964. 917.47'2'03
Letters of Samuel B. Rose. [Compiled by his sons, Frederick, Daniel, and Elihu; edited by Theodore Solotaroff. Hastings-on-Hudson, N.Y., Printed at the Morgan Press, 1968] 189 p. illus., facsims., port. 23 x 30 cm. [CT275.R7828A4] 68-7374

Rose, William John, 1885-1968.

ROSE, William John, 1885-1968. 943.8'007'2024 B
The Polish memoirs of William John Rose / edited by Daniel Stone. Toronto : University of Toronto Press, [1975] xxv, 248 p. : port. ; 24 cm. Includes bibliographical references and index. [DK4139.25.R67A34 1975] 74-79986 ISBN 0-8020-5306-8 : 17.50
1. Rose, William John, 1885-1968. 2. Poland—History—20th century. I. Title. BIP

Rosebery, Archibald Philip Primrose, 5th earl of, 1847-1929.

JAMES, Robert Rhodes, 1933- 923.242
Rosebery, a biography of Archibald Philip, fifth earl of Rosebery. [1st American ed.] New York, Macmillan [1964, c1963] xiv, 534 p. illus., ports., geneal. table. 21 cm. Bibliography: p. [517]-521. [DA564.R7J3 1964] 64-11769
1. Rosebery, Archibald Philip Primrose, 5th earl of, 1847-1929.

THOMPSON, Edward Raymond, 1872- 942.081'092'4 B
The man of promise, Lord Rosebery; a critical study, by E. T. Raymond (Edward Raymond Thompson) Freeport, N.Y., Books for Libraries Press [1972] 263 p. 22 cm. Reprint of the 1923 ed. [DA564.R7T52 1972] 72-1276 ISBN 0-8369-6834-4
1. Rosebery, Archibald Philip Primrose, 5th Earl of, 1847-1929. 2. Great Britain—Politics and government, 1837-1901. I. Title.

Roseboro', Viola.

GRAHAM, Jane Kirkland. 920.5
Viola, the duchess of New Dorp; a biography of Viola Roseboro'. [Danville? Ill., 1955] 2v. in 1. illus., ports. 23cm. Bibliographical footnotes. [PN4874.R59G7] 55-13808
1. Roseboro', Viola. I. Title.

Roseboro, John.

ROSEBORO, John. 796.357'092'4 [B]
Glory days with the Dodgers, and other days with others / John Roseboro, with Bill Libby. 1st ed. New York : Atheneum, 1978. x, 297 p., [5] leaves of plates : ill. ; 22 cm. [GV865.R66A34 1978] 77-23679 ISBN 0-689-10864-8 : 9.95
1. Roseboro, John. 2. Baseball players—United States—Biography. I. Libby, Bill, joint author. II. Title.

Rosecrans, William Starke, 1819-1898.

LAMERS, William Mathias, 1900- 923.573
The edge of glory; a biography of General William S. Rosecrans, U. S. A. [1st ed.] New York, Harcourt, Brace [1961] 499p. illus. 22cm. Includes bibliography. [E467.1.R7L3] 61-7688
1. Rosecrans, William Starke, 1819-1898. I. Title.

Rosen, Richard Dean,

ROSEN, Richard Dean, 1949- 818'.5'403
Me and my friends, we no longer profess any graces; a premature memoir. New York, Macmillan [1971] 189 p. 21 cm. [PS3568.O774Z5] 79-152816 4.94
I. Title.

Rosen, Samuel, 1897-

ROSEN, Samuel, 1897- 617.8'00924 B
The autobiography of Dr. Samuel Rosen. [1st ed.] New York, Knopf; [distributed by Random House] 1973. xiv, 268 p. illus. 22 cm. [RF38.R67A3] 72-11041 ISBN 0-394-44343-8 6.95
1. Rosen, Samuel, 1897- 2. Otolaryngologists—Correspondence, reminiscences, etc.

Rosenbach, Abraham Simon Wolf, 1876-1952.

WOLF, Edwin, 1911- 926.55
Rosenbach; a biography, by Edwin Wolf, 2nd, with John F. Fleming. [1st ed.] Cleveland, World Pub. Co. [1960] 616 p. illus. 25 cm. [Z473.R7W6] 60-15992
1. Rosenbach, Abraham Simon Wolf, 1876-1952. I. Title.

Rosenberg, Isaac, 1890-1918—Biography.

COHEN, Joseph, 1926- 821'.9'12 B
Journey to the trenches : the life of Isaac Rosenberg, 1890-1918 / Joseph Cohen. New York : Basic Books, c1975. xvi, 224 p., [8] leaves of plates : ill. ; 25 cm. Includes index. Bibliography: p. [209]-216. [PR6035.O67Z6 1975b] 74-14110 ISBN 0-465-03676-7 : 12.50
1. Rosenberg, Isaac, 1890-1918—Biography. I. Title. BIP

Rosenberger, Homer Tope,

ROSENBERGER, Homer Tope, 1908- 917.3
Adventures and philosophy of a Pennsylvania Dutchman; an autobiography in a broad setting. Bellefonte, Pennsylvania Heritage, inc., 1971. 665 p. illus. 24 cm. [CT275.R7845A3] 79-165295 15.00
I. Title. BIP

Rosenblatt, Samuel, 1902-

ROSENBLATT, Samuel, 1902- 296.6'1 B
The days of my years : an autobiography / by Samuel Rosenblatt. New York : Ktav Pub. House, 1976. 207 p., [7] leaves of plates : ill. ; 22 cm. [BM755.R565A33] 76-47616 ISBN 0-87068-494-9 : 10.00
1. Rosenblatt, Samuel, 1902- 2. Rabbis—United States—Biography. I. Title.

Rosenblum, Davida, 1927-

ROSENBLUM, Davida, 1927- 974.7'23'004924 B
Relatives / Davida Rosenblum. New York : Dial Press, c1979. ix, 210 p. ; 22 cm. [F129.B7R677] 79-15527 8.95
1. Rosenblum, Davida, 1927- 2. Jews in Brooklyn—Biography. 3. Brooklyn—Biography. 4. New York (City)—Biography. I. Title. BIP

Rosenbluth, Eli Yitzchak, 1919-1945.

ROSENBLUTH, Martin, 1886- 920
Eli, the story of his life November, 1919 - March, 1945 [New York, 1962?] 60 p. illus., ports. 24 cm. [CT275.R7846R6] 62-20969
1. Rosenbluth, Eli Yitzchak, 1919-1945. I. Title.

Rosenfeld, Jay C.

ROSENFELD, Stephen. 362.1'9'699409 B
The time of their dying / by Stephen S. Rosenfeld. 1st ed. New York : Norton, c1977. 189 p. ; 22 cm. [RC263.R639 1977] 77-23264 ISBN 0-393-08771-9 : 7.95
1. Rosenfeld, Jay C. 2. Rosenfeld, Elizabeth K., 1905 or 6-1976. 3. Cancer—Biography. I. Title. BIP

Rosenfeld, Paul, 1890-1946.

MELLQUIST, Jerome, ed. 780'.92'4 B
Paul Rosenfeld, voyager in the arts / edited by Jerome Mellquist and Lucie Wiese. New York : Octagon Books, 1977. p. cm. Reprint of the 1948 ed. published by Creative Age Press, New York. Bibliography: [ML55.R65M4 1977] 77-11646 ISBN 0-374-95561-1 lib.bdg. : 14.50
1. Rosenfeld, Paul, 1890-1946. 2. Music—Addresses, essays, lectures. I. Wiese, Lucie, joint ed. BIP

Rosenman, Samuel Irving, 1896-1973.

HAND, Samuel B., 1931- 973.917'092'4 B
Counsel and advise : a political biography of Samuel I. Roseman / Samuel B. Hand. New York : Garland Pub., 1979. x, 362 p. ; 21 cm. (Modern American history) Includes bibliographical references and index. [E748.R73H36] 78-62383 ISBN 0-8240-3632-8 : 20.00
1. Rosenman, Samuel Irving, 1896-1973. 2. United States—Politics and government—1933-1945. 3. United States—Politics and government—1945-1953. 4. New York (State)—Politics and government—1965-1950. 5. Presidents—United States—Staff—Biography. 6. Judges—New York (State)—Biography. I. Title.

Rosenstock, Fred, 1895—

BOWER, Donald E. 020'.75'0924 B
Fred Rosenstock : a legend in books & art / by Donald E. Bower ; foreword by Frank Waters. 1st ed. [Flagstaff, Ariz.] : Northland Press, c1976. xvii, 212 p. : ill. ; 26 cm. "Based on research and interviews conducted by Dr. S. Lyman Tyler." Includes bibliographies. [Z473.R73B68] 76-10419 12.50
1. Rosenstock, Fred, 1895- 2. Book industries and trade—Colorado—Denver—Biography. 3. Denver—Biography. I. Tyler, Samuel Lyman, 1920- BIP

Rosenthal, Leonard.

ROSENTHAL, Leonard. 923.844
The pearl and I 1st ed. New York, Vantage Press [1955] 223p. 21cm. Autobiographical. [HD9678.P4R6] 55-8626
I. Title.

Rosenwald, Julius, 1862-1932.

JARRETTE, Alfred Q. 362.7'4'0924 B
Julius Rosenwald, son of a Jewish immigrant, a builder of Sears, Roebuck and Company, benefactor of mankind : a biography documented / by Alfred Q. Jarrette. Greenville, S.C. : Southeastern University Press, [1975] 143 p. : ill. ; 21 cm. [HV28.R6J37] 75-319942
1. Rosenwald, Julius, 1862-1932.

Rosenzweig, Franz,

ROSENZWEIG, Franz, 1886-1929 922.96
Franz Rosenzweig: his life and thought, presented by Nahum N. Glatzer [2d., rev. ed.] New York, Schocken [1962, c.1953, 1961] 404p. illus. (SB21) Bibl. 2.25 pap.,
I. Glatzer, Nahum Norbert, 1903- ed. II. Title.

Rosetti, Dante Gabriel, 1828-1882—Biography.

ROSSETTI, William Michael, 1829-1919. 016.821'8
Bibliography of the works of Dante Gabriel Rossetti / by William Michael Rossetti. Philadelphia : R. West, 1978. 53 p. ; 22 cm. Reprint of the 1905 ed. published by Ellis, London. Includes index. [Z8759.8.R7 1978] [PR5247] 78-1532 ISBN 0-8492-2383-0 : 10.00
1. Rosetti, Dante Gabriel, 1828-1882—Biography. I. Title. BIP

Roseveare, Helen.

BURGESS, Alan. 266'.023'0924 B
Daylight must come; the story of a courageous woman doctor in the Congo. New York, Delacorte Press [1975, c1974] vi, 297 p. illus. 22 cm. [BV3625.C63R633 1975] 74-5479 ISBN 0-440-03365-9 6.95
1. Roseveare, Helen. I. Title.

BURGESS, Alan. 266'.023'0924 B
Daylight must come; the story of a courageous woman doctor in the Congo. New York, Delacorte Press [1975, c1974] vi, 297 p. illus. 22 cm. [BV3625.C63R633 1975] 74-5479 ISBN 0-440-03365-9 6.95
1. Roseveare, Helen. I. Title.

BURGESS, Alan. 266'.023'0924 B
Daylight must come : the story of a courageous woman doctor in the Congo / Alan Burgess. Boston : G. K. Hall, 1975, c1974. 520 p. ; 25 cm. Originally published under title: Hostage. Large print ed. [BV3625.C63R633 1975b] 75-6727 ISBN 0-8161-6281-6 lib.bdg. : 12.95
1. Roseveare, Helen. 2. Sight-saving books. I. Title.

BURGESS, Alan. 266'.023'0924 B
Daylight must come : the story of a courageous woman doctor in the Congo / Alan Burgess. Boston : G. K. Hall, 1975, c1974. 520 p. ; 25 cm. Originally published under title: Hostage. Large print ed. [BV3625.C63R633 1975b] 75-6727 ISBN 0-8161-6281-6 lib.bdg. : 12.95
1. Roseveare, Helen. 2. Sight-saving books. I. Title.

ROSEVEARE, Helen. 266'.0092'4 B
Living sacrifice / by Helen M. Roseveare. Chicago : Moody Press, 1979. p. cm. Bibliography: p. [BV3625.C63R6433] 79-14831 ISBN 0-8024-4943-3 pbk. : 3.95
1. Roseveare, Helen. 2. Missionaries—Zaire—Biography. 3. Missionaries—United States—Biography. I. Title.

Rosewall, Ken.

ROWLEY, Peter. 796.34'2'0924
Ken Rosewall : twenty years at the top / by Peter Rowley, with Ken Rosewall. New York : Putnam, c1976. 252 p., [4] leaves of plates : ill. ; 22 cm. Includes index. [GV994.R67R68 1976] 75-42773 ISBN 0-399-11683-4 : 7.95
1. Rosewall, Ken. 2. Tennis. I. Rosewall, Ken, joint author.

Rosmini Serbati, Antonio, 1797-1855.

LEETHAM, Claude Richard Harbord. 921.5
Rosmini: priest, philosopher, and patriot. With an introd. by Giuseppe Bozzetti. Baltimore, Helicon Press [1958] 508p. illus. 23cm. [B3646.L4 1958] 58-10748
1. Rosmini Serbati, Antonio, 1797-1855. I. Title.

LEETHAM, Claude Richard Harbord. v. 12
Rosmini, priest, philosopher and patriot. With an introd. by Giuseppe Bozzetti. [1st ed.] London, New York, Longmans, Green [1957] xxiii, 508p. port., map, facsim. 23cm. Bibliography: p. 483-485. A58
1. Rosmini Serbati, Antonio, 1797-1855. I. Title.

Ross, Betsy Griscom, 1752-1836.

†MORRIS, Robert, 1905- 929.9'0973
The truth about the American flag / Robert Morris. 1st ed. Beach Haven, N.J. : Wynnehaven Pub. Co., c1976. xvii, 82 p. : ill. ; 24 cm. Includes index. Bibliography: p. 68-70. [CR113.M525] 76-12730 10.80 pbk. : 7.65
1. Ross, Betsy Griscom, 1752-1836. 2. Flags—United States. I. Title. BIP

THOMPSON, Ray, 1905- 917.48'03'20924 B
Betsy Ross: last of Philadelphia's Free Quakers. [Fort Washington, Pa., Bicentennial Press, 1972] 112 p. illus. 25 cm. Cover title. Bibliography: p. 109-110. [E302.6.R77T45] 72-80306
1. Ross, Betsy (Griscom) 1752-1836.

Ross, Burt.

ROSS, Philip, 1939- 320.9'749'21 B
The bribe / Philip Ross. 1st ed. New York : Harper & Row, c1976. 196 p. : ill. ; 22 cm. [JS883.F7R67] 75-25063 ISBN 0-06-013658-8 : 10.00
1. Ross, Burt. 2. Corruption (in politics)—Fort Lee, N.J. 3. Fort Lee, N.J.—Politics and government. I. Title. BIP

Ross, Charles Brewster, b. 1870.

ZIEROLD, Norman J. 364.15'4'0924
Little Charley Ross; America's first kidnapping for ransom, by Norman Zierold. [1st ed.] Boston, Little, Brown [1967] 304 p. illus., ports. 22 cm. Bibliographical references included in "Acknowledgments" (p. [303]-304) [HV6603.R6Z5] 67-11232
1. Ross, Charles Brewster, b. 1870. I. Title.

Ross, Diana, 1944-

ELDRED, Patricia Mulrooney. 784'.092'4 B
Diana Ross / Text, Patricia Mulrooney Eldred ; ill., John Keely. Mankato, Minn. : Creative Education, [1975] p. cm. Bibliography: p. [ML3930.R67E4] 75-23005 ISBN 0-87191-462-X : 4.95
1. Ross, Diana, 1944- I. Keely, John. II. Title.

ITZKOWITZ, Leonore K., 1933- 784'.092'4 B
Diana Ross [by] Leonore K. Itzkowitz. [New York] Random House [1974] p. cm. A biography of the black singer whose portrayal of Billie Holiday made her a nominee for an Academy Award. [ML420.R879I9] 74-1206 ISBN 0-394-12310-7
1. Ross, Diana, 1944- I. Title.

Ross, Dorothy.

ROSS, Dorothy. 630.1
Stranger to the desert. New York, W. Funk [1959] 249 p. 22 cm. Autobiographical. [CT275.R789A3] 59-11832
I. Title.

Ross, Edward Alsworth, 1866-1951.

†ROSS, Edward Alsworth, 1866-1951. 301'.092'4
Seventy years of it : an autobiography / Edward Alsworth Ross. New York : Arno Press, 1977, c1936. ix, 341 p., [8] leaves of plates : ill. ; 23 cm. (The Academic profession) Reprint of the ed. published by D. Appleton-Century Co., New York. Includes index. [HM22.U6R6 1977] 76-55183 ISBN 0-405-10010-8 lib. bdg. : 20.00
1. Ross, Edward Alsworth, 1866-1951. 2. Sociologists—United States—Biography. I. Title. II. Series. BIP

Ross, Frederick G., 1858-1942.

ROSS, Frederick G., 1858-1942. 792'.028'0924 B
The actor from Point Arena : excerpts taken from the Memories of an old theatrical man / by Frederick G. Ross ; edited with a commentary by Travis Bogard. [Berkeley] : Friends of the Bancroft Library, University of California, 1977. 38 p., [5] leaves of plates : ill., map (on lining papers) ; 24 cm. (Series of keepsakes ; no. 25) Errata slip inserted. [PN2287.R758A32 1977] 77-71872
1. Ross, Frederick G., 1858-1942. 2. Actors—California—San Francisco—Biography. 3. San Francisco—Biography. I. Bogard, Travis. II. Title. III. Series: Friends of the Bancroft Library. Keepsakes ; no. 25.

Ross, Harold Wallace, 1892-1951.

GRANT, Jane. 071'.471'0924
Ross, the New Yorker, and me. [New York] Reynal [1968] 271 p. illus., ports. 22 cm. [PN4874.R65G7] 68-12154
1. Ross, Harold Wallace, 1892-1951. 2. The New Yorker (New York, 1925-) I. Title.

Ross, James Davidson.

ROSS, James Davidson. 616.994
Margaret. [1st American ed.] New York, Dutton, 1958. 191p. 20cm. The story of a young girl's heroic acceptance of pain and death. [CT788.M2165R6 1958] 58-7820
I. Title.

Ross, John, Cherokee chief, 1790-1866.

EATON, Rachel Caroline. 970'.004'97 B
John Ross and the Cherokee Indians / by Rachel Caroline Eaton. New York : AMS Press, [1978] p. cm. Originally presented as the author's thesis, University of Chicago, 1919. Reprint of a private ed. distributed in 1921 by the University of Chicago Libraries, Chicago. [E99.C5E16 1978] 76-43694 ISBN 0-404-15526-X : 18.00
1. Ross, John, Cherokee chief, 1790-1866. 2. Cherokee Inndians. 3. Cherokee Indians—Biography. 4. Indians of North America—Biography. I. Title. BIP

MOULTON, Gary E. 970'.004'97 B
John Ross, Cherokee Chief / Gary E. Moulton. Athens : University of Georgia Press, 1978,c1977. p. cm. Includes index. Bibliography: p. [E99.C5R825] 76-1146 ISBN 0-8203-0422-0 : 12.00
1. Ross, John, Cherokee Chief, 1790-1866. 2. Cherokee Indians—Biography. 3. Cherokee Indians—History. I. Title.

Ross, John, Cherokee chief, 1790-1866—Juvenile literature.

CLARK, Electa. 970.3 B
Cherokee chief; the life of John Ross. Illus. by John Wagner. [New York] Crowell-Collier Press [1970] 118 p. illus. 22 cm. Bibliography: p. [115]-116. A biography of the Cherokee chief who struggled to maintain his tribe's independence and rights to its homeland. [E90.R78C55] 92 72-112283
1. Ross, John, Cherokee chief, 1790-1866—Juvenile literature. I. Wagner, John, illus. II. Title.

HARRELL, Sara Gordon. 970'.004'97 B
John Ross / by Sara Gordon Harrell. Minneapolis : Dillon Press, c1979. 62 p. : ill. ; 24 cm. (The Story of an American Indian) A biography of the Cherokee chief who led his people for more than 40 years, first in an effort to keep their homeland, and later through their greatest trial when they were forced to go west by the United States government. [E99.C5R674] 92 78-21042 ISBN 0-87518-173-2 lib. bdg. : 5.95
1. Ross, John, Cherokee chief, 1790-1866—Juvenile literature. 2. Cherokee Indians—History—Juvenile literature. 3. Cherokee Indians—Biography—Juvenile literature. I. Title. BIP

Ross, John, Sir, 1777-1856.

DODGE, Ernest Stanley. 919.8 B
The Polar Rosses: John and James Clark Ross and their explorations, by Ernest S. Dodge. New York, Barnes & Noble Books [1973] 260 p. illus. 21 cm. (Great travellers) Bibliography: p. 249-251. [G635.R6D62 1973b] 73-168131 ISBN 0-06-491732-0 9.25
1. Ross, John, Sir, 1777-1856. 2. Ross, James Clark, Sir, 1800-1862. I. Title.

DODGE, Ernest Stanley. 919.8 B
The Polar Rosses: John and James Clark Ross and their explorations, by Ernest S. Dodge. London, Faber, 1973. 3-260, [8] p. illus., maps, ports. 21 cm. (Great travellers) Bibliography: p. 249-251. [G635.R6D62 1973] 73-161761 ISBN 0-571-08914-3
1. Ross, John, Sir, 1777-1856. 2. Ross, James Clark, Sir, 1800-1862. I. Title. Distributed by Barnes & Nobles, 9.25

Ross, Martin H., 1918-

ROSS, Martin H., 1918- 940.53'1503'924 B
Marrano / by Martin H. Ross. Boston : Branden Press, c1976. 89 p. ; 22 cm. Autobiographical. [DS135.A93R687] 77-358669 ISBN 0-8283-1666-X : 5.95
1. Ross, Martin H., 1918- 2. Jews in Austria—Biography. 3. United States—Emigration and immigration. 4. Austria—Biography. I. Title. BIP

Ross, Ronald,

ROWLAND, John, 1907- 926.1
The mosquito man; the story of Sir Ronald Ross. New York, Roy [1963, c.1958] 150p. illus. 21cm. 62-15633 3.25 bds.,
1. Ross, Ronald, Sir I. Title.

Ross, Xavier, Mother, 1813-1895.

GILMORE, Julia, Sister. 922.273
Come north! The life-story of Mother Xavier Ross, foundress of the Sisters of Charity of Leavenworth. Illus. by Patricia De Buck. New York, McMullen Books, 1951. 310 p. illus. 21 cm. [BX4705.R7252G5] 52-6153
1. Ross, Xavier, Mother, 1813-1895. 2. Sisters of Charity of Leavenworth (Kansas) I. Title.

Rossellini, Roberto, 1906-

GUARNER, Jose Luis. 791.43'023'0924
Roberto Rossellini. Translated by Elisabeth Cameron. [New York] Praeger [1970] 144 p. 18 cm. ([Praeger film library]) [PN1998.A3R66513] 77-99497 4.95
1. Rossellini, Roberto, 1906-

Rossello, Maria Giuseppa, Saint, 1811-1880.

BURTON, Katherine (Kurz) 922.245
Wheat for this planting; the biography of Saint Mary Joseph Rossello, foundress of the Daughters of Our Lady of Mercy. Milwaukee, Bruce Pub. Co. [c.1960] ix, 158p. illus. 22cm. (Catholic life publications) 60-50092 3.50
1. Rossello, Maria Giuseppa, Saint, 1811-1880. 2. Daughters of Our Lady of Mercy. I. Title.

BURTON, Katherine (Kurz) 1890- 922.245
Wheat for this planting; the biography of Saint Mary Joseph Rossello, foundress of the Daughters of Our Lady of Mercy. Milwaukee, Bruce Press [1960] 158p. illus. 22cm. (Catholic life publications) [DX4700.R67D8] 60 50092
1. Rossello, Maria Giuseppa, Saint, 1811-1880. 2. Daughters of Our Lady of Mercy. I. Title.

Rossetti, Christina Georgina, 1830-1894.

BELL, Mackenzie, 1856-1930. 821'.8 B
Christina Rossetti; a biographical and critical study. Boston, Roberts Bros., 1898. [New York, AMS Press, 1973] xvi, 405 p. illus. 19 cm. "Bibliography, by J. P. Anderson": p. [377]-390. [PR5238.B4 1973] 70-148747 ISBN 0-404-08724-8 12.50
1. Rossetti, Christina Georgina, 1830-1894. BIP

BIRKHEAD, Edith. 821'.8
Christina Rossetti & her poetry. London, G. G. Harrap. [New York, AMS Press, 1972] 126 p. port. 19 cm. (Poetry and life series) Reprint of the 1930 ed. Bibliography: p. 8. [PR5238.B5 1972] 75-148751 ISBN 0-404-52503-2 8.00
1. Rossetti, Christina Georgina, 1830-1894. I. Title. II. Series. BIP

PACKER, Lona Mosk 928.2
Christina Rossetti. Berkeley, Univ. of Calif. Pr. [c.]1963. xx, 459p. illus., ports. 24cm. Bibl. 63-21221 9.00
1. Rossetti, Christina Georgina, 1830-1894. I. Title. BIP

PACKER, Lona Mosk. 082 S
Christina Rossetti. Berkeley, University of California Press, 1963. xx, 459 p. illus., ports. 24 cm. Bibliography: p. 435-447. [PR5238.P3] 63-21221
1. Rossetti. Christina Georgina, 1830-1894. I. Title.

SAWTELL, Margaret. 821'.8 B
Christina Rossetti : her life and religion / by Margaret Sawtell. Norwood, Pa. : Norwood Editions, 1975. 160 p., [7] leaves of plates : ill. ; 23 cm. Reprint of the 1955 ed. published by A. R. Mowbray, London. [PR5238.S35 1975] 75-44047 ISBN 0-88305-732-8 lib. bdg. : 22.50
1. Rossetti, Christina Georgina, 1830-1894. BIP

SAWTELL, Margaret. 301.41'2'0924 B
Christina Rossetti; her life and religion. [Folcroft, Pa.] Folcroft Library Editions, 1973. p. Reprint of the 1955 ed. published by Mowbray, London. [PR5238.S35 1973] 73-12609 20.00
1. Rossetti, Christina Georgina, 1830-1894.

SHOVE, Fredegond. 821'.8 B
Christina Rossetti; a study. New York, Octagon Press, 1969. xvi, 120 p. 20 cm. Reprint of the 1931 ed. [PR5238.S5 1969] 75-96169
1. Rossetti, Christina Georgina, 1830-1894. BIP

STUART, Dorothy Margaret. 821'.8
Christina Rossetti. New York, Haskell House, 1971. viii, 200 p. 23 cm. Reprint of the 1930 ed. [PR5238.S7 1971] 74-160429 ISBN 0-8383-1299-3
1. Rossetti, Christina Georgina, 1830-1894. BIP

THOMAS, Eleanor Walter. v. 12
Christina Georgina Rossetti. New York, AMS Press, 1966 [c1931] viii, 229 p. front. (port.) 23 cm. 68-13499
1. Rossetti, Christina Georgina, 1830-1894. I. Title. BIP

Rossetti, Christina Georgina, 1830-1894—Biography.

†PROCTOR, Ellen A. 821'.8 B
A brief memoir of Christina G. Rossetti / by Ellen A. Proctor ; with a pref. by W. M. Rossetti. Folcroft, Pa. : Folcroft Library Editions, 1976. 84 p. : port. ; 22 cm. Reprint of the 1895 ed. published by S.P.C.K., London. [PR5238.P7 1976] 76-28360 ISBN 0-8414-6780-3 lib. bdg. : 10.00
1. Rossetti, Christina Georgina, 1830-1894—Biography. 2. Poets, English—19th century—Biography. I. Title. BIP

Rossetti, Dante Gabriel, 1828-1882.

ANGELI, Helen (Rossetti) 759.2 B
Dante Gabriel Rossetti: his friends and enemies. New York, B. Blom, 1972. xx, 291 p. ports. 21 cm. Reprint of the 1949 ed. [PR5246.A8 1972] 76-184272
1. Rossetti, Dante Gabriel, 1828-1882.

CAINE, Hall, Sir, 1858-1931. 759.2 B
Recollections of Rossetti. New York, Haskell House Publishers, 1973. ix, 259 p. 23 cm. Reprint of the 1928 ed. [PR5246.C4 1973] 72-6285 ISBN 0-8383-1634-4 11.95
1. Rossetti, Dante Gabriel, 1828-1882. I. Title. BIP

CARY, Elisabeth Luther, 1867-1936. 760'.092'4
The Rossettis : Dante Gabriel and Christina / by Elisabeth Luther Cary. New York : Haskell House, 1974. iv, 310 p. : port. ; 22 cm. Reprint of the 1900 ed. published by Putnam, New York. Includes index. "List of the more important writings of Dante Gabriel Rossetti": p. 277-281. [NX547.6.R67C37 1974] 74-30190 ISBN 0-8383-1943-2 : 17.95
1. Rossetti, Dante Gabriel, 1828-1882. 2. Rossetti, Christina Georgina, 1830-1894. 3. Preraphaelitism—England. I. Title.

DOUGHTY, Oswald 928.2
A Victorian romantic, Dante Gabriel Rossetti; 2nd ed. [New York, Oxford University Press 1960] 712p. plates, ports. 'Select bibliography': p.694-699 and Bibl. notes. 8.00
1. Rossetti, Dante Gabriel, 1828-1882. I. Title.

KNIGHT, Joseph, 1829-1907. 759.2 B
Life of Dante Gabriel Rossetti. Port Washington, N.Y., Kennikat Press [1972] 186, xix p. 21 cm. Reprint of the 1887 ed. "Bibliography, and catalogue of pictures, by John P. Anderson": p. [i]-xix. [PR5246.K5 1972] 73-160765 ISBN 0-8046-1586-1
1. Rossetti, Dante Gabriel, 1828-1882. I. Title. BIP

KNIGHT, Joseph, 1829-1907. 759.2 B
Life of Dante Gabriel Rossetti. Freeport, N.Y., Books for Libraries Press [1972] 186, xix p. 23 cm. Reprint of the 1887 ed., which was issued in series: Great writers. "Bibliography and catalogue of pictures, by John P. Anderson": p. [i]-xix. [PR5246.K5 1972b] 75-38359 ISBN 0-8369-6776-3
1. Rossetti, Dante Gabriel, 1828-1882. I. Title.

KNIGHT, Joseph, 1829-1907. 759.2 B
Life of Dante Gabriel Rossetti. [Folcroft, Pa.] Folcroft Library Editions, 1973. 186, xix p. 20 cm. Reprint of the 1887 ed. published by W. Scott, London, in series: Great writers. "Bibliography and catalogue of pictures, by J. P. Anderson" p.: [i]-xix. [PR5246.K5 1973] 73-12645 ISBN 0-8414-5454-X (lib. bdg.)
1. Rossetti, Dante Gabriel, 1828-1882. I. Title.

MEGROZ, Rodolphe Louis, 1891- 759.2 B
Dante Gabriel Rossetti; painter poet of heaven in earth, by R. L. Megroz. New York, Haskell House Publishers, 1971. xi, 339 p. illus. 23 cm. "First published 1929." Bibliography: p. 319-321. [PR5246.M4 1971] 74-173851 ISBN 0-8383-1336-1
1. Rossetti, Dante Gabriel, 1828-1882. BIP

NICOLL, John. 759.2 B
Dante Gabriel Rossetti / John Nicoll. 1st American ed. New York : Macmillan, 1976, c1975. 175 p. : ill. (some col.) ; 28 cm. Includes bibliographical references and index. [ND497.R8N52 1976] 75-23267 ISBN 0-02-589340-8 : 22.50
1. Rossetti, Dante Gabriel, 1828-1882. 2. Painters—Great Britain—Biography. I. Rossetti, Dante Gabriel, 1828-1882.

THE Owl and the Rossettis : 700'.92'2 B
letters of Charles A. Howell and Dante Gabriel, Christina, and William Michael Rossetti / edited, with an introd. by C. L. Cline. University Park : Pennsylvania State University Press, [1978] p. cm. Includes indexes. Bibliography: p. [ND497.R8A34] 77-88468 ISBN 0-271-00530-0 : 12.50
1. Rossetti, Dante Gabriel, 1828-1882. 2. Howell, Charles Augustus, d. 1890. 3. Painters—England—Correspondence. 4. Art dealers—England—Correspondence. 5. Preraphaelitism—England. 6. Poets, English—19th century—Correspondence. I. Cline, Clarence Lee. BIP

ROSSETTI, Dante Gabriel, 1828-1882. 759.2 B
Dante Gabriel Rossetti: his family-letters. With a memoir by William Michael Rossetti. [1st AMS ed.] New York, AMS Press [1970] 2 v. facsim., ports. 23 cm. Reprint of the 1895 ed. [PR5246.A43 1970] 70-130231 ISBN 0-404-05434-X
1. Rossetti, Dante Gabriel, 1828-1882. 2. Rossetti family. 3. Artists—Correspondence, reminiscences, etc. I. Rossetti, William Michael, 1829-1919, ed.

SCOTT, William Bell, 1811-1890. 821'.8 B
Autobiographical notes of the life of William Bell Scott ... and notices of his artistic and poetic circle of friends, 1830 to 1882. Edited by W. Minto. Illustrated by etchings by himself and reproductions of sketches by himself and friends. New York, AMS Press [1970] 2 v. illus., ports. 23 cm. Reprint of the 1892 ed. Includes bibliographical references. [PR5349.S2A8 1970] 70-128417
1. Rossetti, Dante Gabriel, 1828-1882. I. Minto, William, 1845-1893, ed. II. Title.

WAUGH, Evelyn, 1903-1966. 759.2
Rossetti, his life and works. [Folcroft, Pa.] Folcroft Library Editions, 1973. 232 p. illus. 23 cm. Reprint of the 1928 ed. published by Duckworth, London. [ND497.R8W3 1973] 72-6678 ISBN 0-8414-0141-1 15.00
1. Rossetti, Dante Gabriel, 1828-1882.

Rossetti, Dante Gabriel, 1828-1882—Correspondence.

ROSSETTI, Dante Gabriel, 1828-1882. 759.2 B
Dante Gabriel Rossetti and Jane Morris : their correspondence / edited with an introd. by John Bryson, in association with Janet Camp Troxell. Oxford [Eng.] : Clarendon Press, 1976. xx, 219 p. : ill. ; 25 cm. Includes index. [PR5246.A45] 76-378435 ISBN 0-19-812464-3 : 21.00
1. Rossetti, Dante Gabriel, 1828-1882—Correspondence. 2. Morris, Jane Burden. 3. Poets, English—19th century—Correspondence. I. Morris, Jane Burden. distributed by Oxford U Pr.

ROSSETTI, Dante Gabriel, 1828-1882. 821'.8 B
The letters of Dante Gabriel Rosetti to his publisher, F. S. Ellis / edited, with introduction and notes, by Oswald Doughty. Folcroft, Pa. : Folcroft Library Editions, 1977. xlviii, 150 p. : facsim. ; 26 cm. Reprint of the 1928 ed. published by the Scolartis Press, London. Includes bibliographical references and index. [PR5246.A44 1977] 77-651 ISBN 0-8414-3802-1 lib. bdg. : 25.00
1. Rossetti, Dante Gabriel, 1828-1882—Correspondence. 2. Ellis, Frederick Startridge, 1830-1901. 3. Poets, English—19th century—Correspondence. I. Doughty, Oswald. II. Title.

Rossetti family.

PACKER, Lona Mosk, ed. 928.2
The Rossetti-Macmillan letters; some 133 unpublished letters written to Alexander Macmillan, F. S. Ellis, and others, by Dante Gabriel, Christina, and William Michael Rossetti, 1861-1889. Edited with an introd. and notes by Lona Mosk Packer. Berkeley, University of California Press, 1963. xxi, 166 p. 22 cm. "Abbreviations" (Bibliographical): p. xix. [PR5236.R9A38] 63-21222
1. Rossetti family. 2. Macmillan, firm, publishers, London. I. Rossetti, Dante Gabriel, 1828-1882. II. Macmillan, Alexander, 1818-1896. III. Title. BIP

WALLER, Ross Douglas. 851'.7 B
The Rossetti family, 1824-1854, by R. D. Waller. [Manchester] Manchester University Press, 1932. St. Clair Shores, Mich., Scholarly Press, 1972. xii, 324 p. illus. 22 cm. Original ed. issued as no. 21 of Publications of the University of Manchester, English series, and as no. 217 of Publications of the University of Manchester. Bibliography: p. 298-302. [PR5236.R7W3 1972] 73-145352 ISBN 0-403-01261-9 19.50
1. Rossetti family. 2. Rossetti, Gabriele Pasquale Giuseppe, 1783-1854. I. Series: Victoria University of Manchester. Publications. English series, no. 21. II. Series: Victoria University of Manchester. Publications, no. 217.

WALLER, Ross Douglas. 700'.92'2 B
The Rossetti family, 1824-1854, by R.D. Waller [Folcroft, Pa] Folcroft Library Editions, 1973. p. Reprint of the 1932 ed. published by the University of Manchester Press, Manchester, which was issued as no. 217 of Publications of the University of Manchester and as no. 21 of Publications of the University of Manchester English series. Bibliography: p. [PR5236.R9W3 1973] 73-15815 ISBN 0-8414-9477-0 (lib. bdg.)
1. Rossetti family. 2. Rossetti, Gabriele Pasquale Giuseppe, 1783-1854. I. Series: Victoria University of Manchester. Publications, no. 217. II. Series: Victoria University of Manchester. Publications. English series, no. 21. BIP

WEINTRAUB, Stanley, 1929- 700'.92'2 B
Four Rossettis : a Victorian biography / Stanley Weintraub. New York : Weybright and Talley, c1976. p. cm. Includes bibliographical references and index. [PR5236.R9W4] 76-21341 ISBN 0-679-40136-9 : 15.00
1. Rossetti family. I. Title.

Rossetti, William Michael, 1829-1919.

ROSSETTI, William Michael, 1829-1919. 700'.92'4 B
The diary of W. M. Rossetti 1870-1873 / edited with an introd. and notes by Odette Bornand. Oxford [Eng.] : Clarendon Press, 1978 xxiii, 302 p., [1] leaf of plates : port. ; 22 cm. Includes bibliographical references and index. [PR5249.R2A799 1977] 78-312738 ISBN 0-19-812458-9 : 26.50
1. Rossetti, William Michael, 1829-1919. 2. Rossetti Family. 3. Critics—England—Biography. 4. Art critics—England—Biography. 5. Poets, English—19th century—Biography. I. Bornand, Odette. II. Title.
Distributed by Oxford University Press, NY

ROSSETTI, William Michael, 1829-1919, comp. 759.2 B
Rossetti papers 1862 to 1870; acompilation by William Michael Rossetti New York, AMS Press [1970] xxiii, 559 p. 23 cm. Reprint of the 1903 ed. Papers and correspondence of D. G., C. G. and W. M. Rossetti. [PR5236.R9A3 1970] 76-130238
I. Rossetti, Dante Gabriel, 1828-1882. II. Rossetti, Christina Georgina, 1830-1894. BIP

ROSSETTI, William Michael, 1829-1919. 700'.924 B
Some reminiscences of William Michael Rossetti. New York, AMS Press [1970] 2 v. (xviii, 578 p.) illus., facsims., ports. 23 cm. Reprint of the 1906 ed. [PR5249.R2A8 1970] 75-132386 ISBN 0-404-05440-4
I. Title.

Rossiiskaia sotsial-demokraticheskaia rabochaia partiia.

SHUKMAN, Harold. 947.084'1
Lenin and the Russian Revolution. [1st American ed.] New York, Putnam [1967, c1966] 224 p. 21 cm. Bibliography: p. [210]-212. [DK262.S48 1967a] 67-15120
1. Rossiiskaia sotsial-demokraticheskaia rabochaia partiia. 2. Lenin, Vladimir Il'ich, 1870-1924. 3. Revolutionists, Russian. 4. Russia—History—Revolution, 1917-1921. I. Title.

Rossini, Gioacchino Antonio, 1792-1868.

BEYLE, Marie Henri, 1783-1842. 782.1'0924 B
Life of Rossini, by Stendhal. New and rev. ed. Translated and annotated by Richard N. Coe. New York, Orion Press, 1970. xxiii, 566 p. facsim. 23 cm. Translation of Vie de Rossini. Bibliography: p. 482-485. [ML410.R8B513 1970] 71-121698 ISBN 0-670-42790-X 10.00
1. Rossini, Gioacchino Antonio, 1792-1868.

ROUAULT, Georges, 1871-1958. 759.4
Rouault. Text by Giuseppe Marchiori. New York, Reynal [1967] 34. [86] p. plates (part col.) 36 cm. Bibliography: p. 34. [ND553.R66M33] 67-31964
I. Marchiori, Giuseppe. II. Title.

ROUAULT, Georges, 1871-1958. 759.4
Rouault. Text and notes by Joshua Kind. New York, Tudor Pub. Co. [1969] 36 p., 92 col. plates. 18 cm. Bibliography: p. 15. [ND553.R66K5] 69-18395
I. Kind, Joshua.

VENTURI, Lionello, 1885-1961. 759.4
Rouault, biographical and critical study. Translated from the Italian by James Emmons. [New York] Skira [1959] 141 p. mounted col. illus. 19 cm. (The Taste of our time, v. 26) Bibliography: p. 127-129. [ND553.R66V433] 59-7253
1. Rouault, Georges, 1871-1958.

Rouget, Marie Melanie,

ROUGET, Marie Melanie, 1883-1967. 848'.9'1203
Notes for myself (Notes intimes) [by] Marie Noel. Translated from the French by Howard Sutton. With a foreword by Francois Mauriac. Ithaca, N.Y., Cornell University Press [1968] xvii, 272 p. 22 cm. [PQ2635.O927N63] 68-27327
I. Sutton, Howard, tr. II. Title.

Roumain, Jacques, 1907-1944.

FOWLER, Carolyn. 841
A knot in the thread : the life and work of Jacques Roumain / Carolyn Fowler. Washington : Howard University Press, 1977[i.e.1976] p. cm. Includes index. Bibliography: p. [PQ3949.R73Z66] 76-53817 ISBN 0-88258-057-4 : 9.95
1. Roumain, Jacques, 1907-1944. 2. Authors, Haitian—Biography. I. Title. BIP

Rounds, Sterling P.,

ROUNDS, Sterling P., 1828-1887. 917.7'04'3
Among the craft; notes by the way. Edited and annotated by James Eckman. Rochester, Minn., Doomsday Press [1968] xiii, 25 p. facsim., port. 21 cm. "A keepsake for the Heritage of the graphic arts lectures, to the memory of Paul A. Bennett, fourth lecture, seventh series." "Reprinted from Rounds' printers' cabinet 9: 1 & 4 (Oct.) 1865." [Z232.R76E2] 68-57707
I. Eckman, James Russell, 1908- ed. II. Title.

Rous, Peyton, 1879-1970.

A Notable career in finding out; Peyton Rous, 1879-1970. 610'.924 B New York, Rockefeller University Press, 1971. 47 p. illus., facsims., ports. 25 cm. ([Rockefeller University, New York] Occasional paper 16) Cover title: Peyton Rous. [R154.R76N6] 77-160731 ISBN 0-87470-016-7
1. Rous, Peyton, 1879-1970. I. Title. II. Series.

Rous, Stanley, Sir.

ROUS, Stanley, Sir. 796.33'4'0924 B
Football worlds : a lifetime in sport / Sir Stanley Rous ; with a foreword by Sir Walter Winterbottom. London ; Boston : Faber and Faber, 1978. 223 p., [8] leaves of plates : ill. ; 22 cm. [GV942.7.R66A33] 79-301459 ISBN 0-571-11194-7 : 13.95
1. Rous, Stanley, Sir. 2. Soccer referees—Great Britain—Biography. I. Title.

Rouso d'Eres, Charles Dennis, b. 1761.

ROUSO d'Eres, Charles Dennis, b.1761. 973'.04'97 S
Memoirs of Charles Dennis Rusoe D'Eres / Charles Rouso. New York : Garland Pub., 1977. vi, 176 p. ; 19 cm. (The Garland library of narratives of North American Indian captivities ; v. 25) Reprint of the 1800 ed. printed for and sold by H. Ranlett, Exeter, N.H, under title: Memoirs of Charles Dennis Rusoe D'Eres, a native of Canada. Issued with the reprint of the 1801 ed. of Owen, J. T. The life and travels of James Tudor Owen. New York, 1977, and with the reprint of the 1803 ed. of Weatherwise, J., pseud. An affecting account of the death of Polly and Hannah Watts. New York, 1977. [E85.G2 vol. 25] [E87] 813'.2 76-56355 ISBN 0-8240-1649-1 lib.bdg. : 25.00
1. Rouso d'Eres, Charles Dennis, b. 1761. 2. Indians of North America—Captivities. 3. Canada—Biography. I. Title. II. Series.

Rousseau family.

DENNIS, Inez Jane. v. 12
Rousseau biographies. [Cornwall Bridge? Conn.] 1965. 52 p. ports. 23 cm. 66-430
1. Rousseau family. I. Title.

Rousseau, Henri Jullen Felix, 1844-1910.

ALLEY, Ronald. 759.4 B
Portrait of a primitive : the art of Henri Rousseau / Ronald Alley. New York : Dutton, 1978. 80 p. : ill. (Some col.) ; 29 cm. Errata slip inserted. Bibliography: p. 6. [ND553.R67A84 1978] 78-55003 ISBN 0-7148-1825-9 : 12.95. ISBN 0-7148-1908-5 pbk. : 6.95
1. Rousseau, Henri Julien Felix, 1844-1910. 2. Primitivism in art—France. 3. Painters—France—Biography. I. Title. BIP

ROUSSEAU, Henri Julien Felix, 1844-1910. 759.4
Henri Rousseau (1844-1910) Text by Alfred Werner. New York, H. N. Abrams [1957] unpaged. illus. 17cm. (The Pocket library of great art, A30) An Abrams art book. [ND553.R67W4] 58-4698
I. Werner, Alfred, 1911- II. Title. III. Series.

SALMON, Andre, 1881- 759.4
Rousseau. [Translated from the French by Paul Colacicchi] New York, H. N. Abrams [1963] 87 p. illus. 19 cm. [ND553.R67S33] 63-8671
1. Rousseau, Henri Jullen Felix, 1844-1910. I. Title.

Rousseau, Jean Jacques, 1712-1778.

GUEHENNO, Jean, 1890- 194.0924
Jean-Jacques Rousseau; translated from the French by John and Doreen Weightman. London, Routledge & K. Paul; New York, Columbia U.P., 1966. 2 v. 22 1/2 cm. L5 (B66-15858) Originally published as Jean-Jacques. Paris, Gallimard, 1962. Contents.CONTENTS. -- v. 1. 1712-1758. -- v. 2. 1758-1778. [PQ2043.G813] 66-12112
1. Rousseau, Jean Jacques, 1712-1778. I. Title.

Rousseau, Jean Jacques, 1712-1778—Biography.

HAVENS, George Remington, 1890- 848'.5'09 B
Jean-Jacques Rousseau / by George R. Havens. Boston : Twayne, c1978. 140 p. ; 21 cm. (Twayne's world authors series ; TWAS 471 : France) Includes index. Bibliography: p. 131-135. [PQ2043.H38] 77-24169 ISBN 0-8057-6312-0 : 7.95
1. Rousseau, Jean Jacques, 1712-1778—Biography. 2. Authors, French—18th century—Biography.

Rousseau, Jean Jacques, 1712-1778—Biography—Character.

HUIZINGA, Jakob Herman, 1908- 848'.5'09 B
The making of a saint : the tragi-comedy of Jean-Jacques Rousseau / J. H. Huizinga. London : H. Hamilton, 1976. xvii, 284 p., [2] leaves of plates : ill. ; 25 cm. American ed. published under title: Rousseau, the self-made saint. Includes index. Bibliography: p. [278]-280. [PQ2043.H84 1976b] 76-370072 ISBN 0-241-89275-9 : £7.95
1. Rousseau, Jean Jacques, 1712-1778—Biography—Character. 2. Authors, French—18th century—Biography. I. Title.

HUIZINGA, Jakob Herman, 1908- 848'.5'09 B
Rousseau, the self-made saint / J. H. Huizinga. New York : Grossman Publishers, 1976, c1975. p. cm. Includes index. Bibliography: p. [PQ2043.H84 1976] 76-13909 ISBN 0-670-60913-7 : 12.95
1. Rousseau, Jean Jacques, 1712-1778—Biography—Character. I. Title.

Rousseau, Jean Jacques, 1712-1778—Chronology.

COURTOIS, Louis J. 848'.5'09
Chronologie critique de la vie et des ouvres de Jean-Jacques Rousseau, par Louis J. Courtois. New York, B. Franklin [1973] p. Reprint of the 1924 ed., which was issued as vol. 15 (1923) of Annales de la Societe Jean-Jacques Rousseau. Bibliography: p. [PQ2042.C6 1973] 72-87246 ISBN 0-8337-4058-X 22.50
1. Rousseau, Jean Jacques, 1712-1778—Chronology. I. Title. II. Series: Societe Jean-Jacques Rousseau, Geneva. Annales de la Societe Jean-Jacques Rousseau, v. 15.

Rousseau, Jean Jacques, 1712-1778—Juvenile literature.

WEBB, Robert N. 848'.5'09 B
Jean Jacques Rousseau, the father of romanticism, by Robert N. Webb. New York, F. Watts [1970] 116 p. illus., map. 22 cm. (Immortals of literature) A biography of the French writer and philosopher who influenced the romantic movement in literature and whose political ideas inspired the leaders of the French Revolution. [PQ2043.W4] 92 76-93947
1. Rousseau, Jean Jacques, 1712-1778—Juvenile literature. I. Title.

Rousseau, Jean Jacques, 1712-1778—Political science.

HALL, John Cecil. 320.1'1'0924
Rousseau; an introduction to his political philosophy [by] John C. Hall. Cambridge, Mass., Schenkman Pub. Co. [1973] 167 p. 21 cm. (Philosophers in perspective) Bibliography: p. 158-162. [JC179.R9H34 1973b] 72-91537 ISBN 0-87073-552-7
1. Rousseau, Jean Jacques, 1712-1778—Political science. I. Title.

Roussel, Albert Charles Paul, 1869-1937.

DEMUTH, Norman, 1898-1968. 780'.92'4 B
Albert Roussel : a study / by Norman Demuth. Westport, Conn. : Hyperion Press, 1979. p. cm. (Encore music editions) Reprint of the 1947 ed. published by United Music Publishers, London. Includes index. "Chronological list of works":p. [ML410.R88D4 1979] 78-66890 ISBN 0-88355-736-3 : 16.00
1. Roussel, Albert Charles Paul, 1869-1937. 2. Composers—France—Biography. BIP

Rovnianek, Peter Vitazoslav, 1867-1933.

PETER V. Rovnianek. v. 12
New York, 1957. 95p. port. 21cm. Text in Slovak, summary in English. Bibliography, p. 85.
1. Rovnianek, Peter Vitazoslav, 1867-1933. I. Bolecek, Vincent.

Rowan, Carl Thomas.

BYNUM, Lynn. 070'.92'4 B
Carl T. Rowan, journalist extraordinary / by Lynn Bynum. Bloomington : Afro-American Arts Institute, Indiana University, 1975. 35 p. : port. ; 23 cm. (Blacks in American journalism series ; 2) A shorter version of this paper was presented at the annual meeting of the Association for Education in Journalism held in San Diego, Aug. 1974. Bibliography: p. 32-35. [PN4874.R74B9] 75-332786 9.95
1. Rowan, Carl Thomas. I. Title. II. Series.

Rowden, Paul D.

CARTER, John T. 266.6'1'0924 B
Witness in Israel; the story of Paul Rowden [by] John T. Carter. Nashville, Broadman Press [1969] 64 p. illus., ports. 19 cm. [BV3202.R6C3] 69-19023
1. Rowden, Paul D. 2. Missions—Israel. I. Title. BIP

Rowe, Alick.

ROWE, Alick. 942.4'46
Boy at the Commercial / Alick Rowe. London ; Boston : Faber, 1978. 134 p. ; 23 cm. [DA690.H54R687] 78-309172 ISBN 0-571-10977-2 : 11.95
1. Rowe, Alick. 2. Hereford, Eng. Commercial Hotel. 3. Herford, Eng.—Biography. I. Title.
Distributed by Faber & Faber, Salem, NH BIP

Rowell, E. C., 1914-

POWERS, Ormund. 328.759'092'4 B
E. C., Mr. Speaker, E. C. Rowell / by Ormund Powers. Webster, Fla. : Board of Governors of the E. C. Rowell Public Library, c1977. xiii, 190 p., [8] leaves of plates : ports. ; 23 cm. [F316.23.R68P68] 77-78907
1. Rowell, E. C., 1914- 2. Florida—Politics and government—1951- 3. Legislators—Florida—Biography. I. Title.

Rowell, Newton Wesley, 1867-1941.

PRANG, M. E. 340'.092'4 B
N. W. Rowell, Ontario nationalist / Margaret Prang. Toronto ; Buffalo : University of Toronto Press, [1975] x, 553 p., [4] leaves of plates ; 24 cm. Includes bibliographical references and index. [LAW] 73-89843 ISBN 0-8020-5300-9 : 25.00
1. Rowell, Newton Wesley, 1867-1941.

Rowlandson, Mary White, ca. 1635-ca, 1678.

ROWLANDSON, Mary White, ca.1635-ca.1678. 973'.04'97 S
A true history of the captivity and restoration of Mrs. Mary Rowlandson / Mary Rowlandson. New York : Garland Pub., 1977. 46 p. ; 24 cm. (The Garland library of narratives of North American Indian captivities ; v. 1) Reprint of the 1682 London ed., originally printed under title: The soveraignty & goodness of God. Issued with the reprint of the 1697 ed. of Mather, C. Humiliations follow'd with deliverances. New York, 1977. [E85.G2 vol. 1] [E87] 974.4'3'020924[B 77-4652 ISBN 0-8240-1625-4 (Set) : lib.bdg. : 29.50
1. Rowlandson, Mary White, ca. 1635-ca, 1678. 2. Indians of North America—Captivities. 3. Lancaster, Mass.—History—Colonial period, ca. 1600-1775. 4. King Philip's War, 1675-1676. 5. Massachusetts—Biography. I. Title. II. Series.

Rowley family.

ROWLEY, Scott, 1878-1960. 929'.2'0973
The village of North Fairfield, Ohio, and a rolling stone : an autobiography / by Charles Scott Rowley, 1878-1960 ; edited with an introd., materials toward a genealogy of the Rowley family, and an index by Alexander G. Rose, III. Baltimore : [A. G. Rose], 1975. xii, 109 leaves ; 29

cm. (The Family document series) [CS71.R884 1975] 75-309310
1. Rowley family. 2. Rowley, Scott, 1878-1960. I. Rose, Alexander Grant, 1913- II. Title.

Rowse, Alfred Leslie,

ROWSE, Alfred Leslie, 1903- 928.2
A Cornishman at Oxford; the education of a Cornishman. London, J. Cape [Mystic, Conn., Verry, c.1965] 319p. port. 23cm. [PR6035.O84Z52] 65-1502 6.00
I. Title.

ROWSE, Alfred Leslie, 1903- 928.2
The Cornishman at Oxford, the education of a Cornishman [by] A. L. Rowse. London, J. Cape [1965] 319 p. port. 23 cm. Autobiographical. [PR6035.I84Z52] 65-1502
I. Title.

Rowse, Alfred Leslie, 1903- — Biography—Youth.

ROWSE, Alfred Leslie, 1903- 828'.9'1209 B
A Cornish childhood : autobiography of a Cornishman / by A. L. Rowse. New York : Clarkson N. Potter : distributed by Crown Publishers, c1979. p. cm. Includes index. [PR6035.O84Z5 1979] 79-14610 ISBN 0-517-53845-8 : 10.00
1. Rowse, Alfred Leslie, 1903- — Biography—Youth. 2. Authors, English—20th century—Biography. 3. Cornwall, Eng.—Social life and customs. I. Title. **BIP**

ROWSE, Alfred Leslie, 1903- 928.2
A Cornishman at Oxford; the education of a Cornishman. London, J. Cape [Mystic, Conn., Verry, c.1965] 319p. port. 23cm. [PR6035.O84Z52] 65-1502 6.00
I. Title.

ROWSE, Alfred Leslie, 1903- 928.2
The Cornishman at Oxford, the education of a Cornishman [by] A. L. Rowse. London, J. Cape [1965] 319 p. port. 23 cm. Autobiographical. [PR6035.I84Z52] 65-1502
I. Title.

Rowse, Alfred Leslie, 1903- — Journeys.

ROWSE, Alfred Leslie, 1903- 828'.9'12 B
A Cornishman abroad / A. L. Rowse. London : J. Cape, 1976. 318 p. : port. ; 22 cm. Includes index. [PR6035.O84Z517] 76-360339 ISBN 0-224-01244-4 : £5.95
1. Rowse, Alfred Leslie, 1903- —Journeys. 2. Rowse, Alfred Leslie, 1903- —Friends and associates. I. Title.

Roy, Manabendra Nath,

ROY, Manabendra Nath, 1893-1954 923.254
M. N. Roy's memoirs. [dist. New York, Paragon, 1964] dist. New York, Paragon, 1964 xiii, 627p. illus., ports. 22cm. Bibl. [DS481.R6A3] SA64 9.00
I. Title.

Royal Ballet.

ANTHONY, Gordon. 792.8'092'2 B
A camera at the ballet : pioneer dancers of the Royal Ballet / [by] Gordon Anthony. Newton Abbot; [North Pomfret, Vt]: David & Charles, 1975. 96 p. : ill., ports. ; 26 cm. [GV1785.A1A613] 75-324246 ISBN 0-7153-6717-X : 10.95
1. Royal Ballet. 2. Ballet—Biography. 3. Dancers—Biography. I. Title. **BIP**

Royal, Darrell.

BANKS, Jimmy, 1925- 796.33'2'0924 B
The Darrell Royal story. Austin, Tex., Shoal Creek Publishers [1973] 178 p. illus. 24 cm. [GV939.R69B36] 73-86926 ISBN 0-88319-016-8 5.95
1. Royal, Darrell. I. Title. **BIP**

Royal Institution of Great Britain, London.

JONES, Henry Bence, 1814-1873. 506'.241
The Royal Institution, its founder and its first professors / by Bence Jones. New York : Arno Press, 1975. x, 431 p. ; 21 cm. (History, philosophy, and sociology of science) Reprint of the 1871 ed. published by Longmans, Green, London. Includes index. [Q41.R88J7 1975] 74-26270 ISBN 0-405-06598-1 : 25.00
1. Royal Institution of Great Britain, London. 2. Rumford, Benjamin Thompson, Sir, count, 1753-1814. 3. Davy, Humphry, Sir, bart., 1778-1829. 4. Young, Thomas, 1773-1829. I. Title. II. Series.

Royall, Anne (Newport) 1769-1854.

JAMES, Bessie (Rowland) 1895- 070.5'092'4 B
Anne Royall's U.S.A. New Brunswick, N.J., Rutgers University Press [1972] vii, 447 p. illus. 24 cm. Includes bibliographical references. [E340.R88J3] 72-1796 ISBN 0-8135-0732-4 15.00
1. Royall, Anne (Newport) 1769-1854. I. Title.

PORTER, Sarah Harvey, 1856-1922. 917.3'04'50924 B
The life and times of Anne Royall. New York, Arno Press, 1972 [c1908] 298 p. 23 cm. (American women: images and realities) Reprint of the 1909 ed. [E340.R88P6 1972] 72-2619 ISBN 0-405-04472-0 13.00
1. Royall, Anne (Newport) 1769-1854. I. Title. II. Series.

Royce, Josiah, 1855-1916.

KUKLICK, Bruce, 1941- 191
Josiah Royce: an intellectual biography. Indianapolis, Bobbs-Merrill [1972] ix, 270 p. 22 cm. Includes bibliographical references. [B945.R64K84] 70-173980 12.50
1. Royce, Josiah, 1855-1916.

Royce, Sarah Bayliss.

ROYCE, Sarah Bayliss. 979.4 B
A frontier lady : recollections of the gold rush and early California / by Sarah Royce , with a foreword by Katharine Royce ; edited by Ralph Henry Gabriel. Lincoln : University of Nebraska Press, 1977, c1932. xiv, 144 p. : map ; 21 cm. "A Bison book." Reprint of the ed. published by Yale University Press, New Haven. [F865.R86 1977] 76-44263 ISBN 0-8032-0909-6 : 8.95
1. Royce, Sarah Bayliss. 2. California—Gold discoveries. 3. Overland journies to the Pacific. 4. Frontier and pioneer life—California. 5. Pioneers—California—Biography. I. Title.

Roycroft Shop, East Aurora, N.Y.—Collectibles.

HAMILTON, Charles Franklin, 1915- 700'.6'574796
Roycroft collectibles : including collector items related to Elbert Hubbard, founder of the Roycroft shops / Charles F. Hamilton. South Brunswick, N.J. : A. S. Barnes, c1980. p. cm. Includes index. [NK1149.R6H35] 78-75308 ISBN 0-498-01919-5 : 15.00
1. Roycroft Shop, East Aurora, N.Y.—Collectibles. 2. Hubbard, Elbert, 1856-1915—Collectibles. 3. Hubbard, Elbert, 1856-1915—Biography. 4. Authors, American—19th century—Biography. 5. Printers—United States—Biography. I. Title.

Rozen, Andrei Evgen'evich, baron, 1800-1884.

BARRATT, G. R. V. 947'.07'0924 B
The rebel on the bridge : a life of the Decembrist Baron Andrey Rozen, 1800-84 / Glynn Barratt. Athens : Ohio University Press, 1975. xvii, 310 p., [4] leaves of plates : ill. ; 25 cm. Includes index. Bibliography: p. [301]-305. [DK209.6.R69B37 1975] 75-21990 ISBN 0-8214-0217-X : 19.00
1. Rozen, Andrei Evgen'evich, baron, 1800-1884. I. Title. **BIP**

Rolvaag, Ole Edvart, 1876-1931.

REIGSTAD, Paul. 839.8'2'372 B
Rolvaag: his life and art. Lincoln, University of Nebraska Press [1972] xi, 160 p. illus. 23 cm. Bibliography: p. 151-156. [PT9150.R55Z84] 70-175804 ISBN 0-8032-0803-0 8.50
1. Rolvaag, Ole Edvart, 1876-1931. I. Title.

Rubel, Angela Ambrosia.

FOX, Ray Errol. 362.1'9'615509
Angela Ambrosia / by Ray Errol Fox. 1st ed. New York : Knopf, 1979. 178 p. ; 22 cm. [RC643.F67 1979] 78-20386 ISBN 0-394-50096-2 : 7.95
1. Rubel, Angela Ambrosia. 2. Leukemia—Biography. I. Title. **BIP**

Rubens, Sir Peter Paul, 1377-1640.

AVERMAETE, Roger, 1893- 759.9'493 B
Rubens and his times. Translated by Christine Trollope. [1st American ed.] South Brunswick [N.J.] A. S. Barnes [1968] 218 p. illus., facsims., ports. 22 cm. Translation of Rubens et son temps. [ND673.R9A973 1968] 68-27197 6.00
1. Rubens, Peter Paul, Sir, 1577-1640. I. Title.

BAUDOUIN, Frans. 759.9493 B
Pietro Pauolo Rubens / Frans Baudouin ; translated by Elsie Callander. New York : Abrams, 1977. 405 p. : ill. (some col.) ; 34 cm. Text in English. Includes bibliographical references and indexes. [ND673.R9B238 1977b] 77-82339 ISBN 0-8109-1586-3 : 60.00
1. Rubens, Peter Paul, Sir, 1577-1640. 2. Painters—Belgium—Biography.

BURCKHARDT, Jakob Christoph, 1818-1897. 927.5
Recollections of Rubens. [Edited, with an introd., by H. Gerson. Translation of Burckhardt's essay by Mary Hottinger. Translation of the selected letters by R. H. Boothroyd and I. Grafe] New York, Phaidon Publishers; distributed by Oxford University Press [1950] xi, 374, [1] p. 143 plates (part col.) 19 cm. "Selected letters of Rubens": p. [191]-249. Bibliography: p. [375] [ND673.R9B784] 50-9158
1. Rubens, Sir Peter Paul, 1377-1640. I. Title.

CABANNE, Pierre. 759.9493
Rubens. [Translated from the French by Oliver Bernard] New York, Tudor Pub. Co. [1967] 286 p. 146 illus. (part col.) 22 cm. (The World of art library) Bibliographical references included in "Text references" (p. 274-276) [ND673] 67-9555
1. Rubens, Peter Paul, Sir, 1577-1640.

GERSON, Noel Bertram, 1914- 759.9493 B
Peter Paul Rubens; a biography of a giant, by Samuel Edwards. New York, D. McKay Co. [1973] 250 p. 22 cm. Bibliography: p. 240. [ND673.R9G46] 72-95157 6.95
1. Rubens, Peter Paul, Sir, 1577-1640.

JAFFE, Andrew Michael. 759.9493 B
Rubens and Italy / Michael Jaffe. Ithaca, N.Y. : Cornell University Press, 1977. 128 p., [103] leaves of plates : ill. (some col.) ; 29 cm. Includes index. Bibliography: p. 121-123. [ND673.R9J27] 76-20065 ISBN 0-8014-1064-9 : 55.00
1. Rubens, Peter Paul, Sir, 1577-1640. 2. Mannerism (Art)—Italy. 3. Art, Italian. I. Rubens, Peter Paul, Sir, 1577-1640. II. Title. **BIP**

LEPORE, Mario, 1912- 759.9493 B
The life and times of Rubens; translated [from the Italian] by F. B. Sear. Feltham, New York, Hamlyn, 1970. 2-75 p. illus. (chiefly col.), ports. (chiefly col.). 30 cm. (Portraits of greatness) Illus. on lining papers. [ND673.R9L4513] 79-851769 ISBN 0-600-37511-0 21/-
1. Rubens, Peter Paul, Sir, 1577-1640. I. Title.

PUYVELDE, Leo van, 1882- 759.9493
Rubens. Paris, New-York, Elsevier, 1952. 238p. illus. (part mounted col.) 31cm. (Les Peintres flamands du xviie siecle) Bibliographical references included in 'Notes' (p. [198]-219) [ND673.R9P82] [ND673.R9P82] 927.5 53-1873 53-1873
1. Rubens, Peter Paul, Sir 1577-1640. I. Title. II. Series.

RIPLEY, Elizabeth. 927.5
Rubens, a biography. With drawings and paintings by Rubens. New York, Oxford University Press, 1957. 68, [3]p. illus. 27cm. Bibliography: p.[70] [ND673.R9R5] 57-11450
1. Rubens, Sir Peter Paul, 1577-1640. I. Title.

RIPLEY, Elizabeth, 1906- 927.5
Rubens, a biography. With drawings and paintings by Rubens. New York, Oxford University Press, 1957. 68 [3] p. illus. 27 cm. Bibliography: p. [70] [ND673.R9R5] 57-11450
1. Rubens, Peter Paul, 1577-1640.

RUBENS, Peter Paul, Sir 1577-1640. 759.9493
Peter Paul Rubens (1577-1640) Text by Julius S. Held. New York, H. N. Abrams in association with Pocket Books [1954] [74] p. 38 illus. (part col.) 18cm. (The Pocket library of great art, A 17) An Abrams art book. Bibliography: p. [74] [ND673.R9H46] 927.5 54-14561
I. Held, Julius Samuel, 1905- II. Title.

WEDGWOOD, Cecily Veronica, Dame, 1910- 759.9493 B
The political career of Peter Paul Rubens / C. V. Wedgwood. London : Thames and Hudson, c1975. 64 p. : ill. ; 22 cm. (Walter Neurath memorial lectures ; 7) Bibliography: p. 62. [ND673.R9W38] 76-365317 ISBN 0-500-55007-7 : 9.25
1. Rubens, Peter Paul, Sir, 1577-1640. 2. Flanders—Foreign relations. I. Title. II. Series.
Distributed by transatlantic Arts. **BIP**

Rubenstein, Richard L.

RUBENSTEIN, Richard L. 296.3'092'4 B
Power struggle [by] Richard L. Rubenstein. New York, Scribner [1974] x, 193 p. 24 cm. Autobiographical. [BM755.R83A36] 73-1354 ISBN 0-684-13757-7 7.95
1. Rubenstein, Richard L. I. Title.

Rubin, Reuven, 1893-

RUBIN, Reuven, 1893- 759.95694 B
My life, my art; an autobiography and selected paintings by Reuven Rubin. With an introd. by Haim Gamzu. New York, Funk & Wagnalls [1969] 227 p. plates (part col.), ports. 31 cm. (Sabra books) At head of title: Rubin. [ND979.R8A2] 74-82694 25.00

I. Title.

RUBIN, Reuven, 1893- 759.95694 B
Reuven Rubin, by Sarah Wilkinson. New York, H. N. Abrams [1974] 288 p. illus. (part col.) 28 cm. Bibliography: p. 283-287. [N7279.R82W54] 71-166215 ISBN 0-8109-0463-2
1. Rubin, Reuven, 1893- I. Wilkinson, Sarah.

Rubinstein, Anton, 1829-1894.

BOWEN, Catherine (Drinker) 927.8
1897-
Free artist; the story of Anton and Nicholas Rubinstein. Boston, Little [1961, c.1939] xi, 412p. illus., map, music, facsim. 'Catalogue of compositions by Anton Rubinstein, comp. by Otto E. Albrecht': p.375-387. (Atlantic Monthly Pr. bk.) Bibl. 61-14927 6.00
1. Rubinstein, Anton, 1829-1894. 2. Rubinstein, Nikolai, 1835-1881. I. Title.

RUBINSTEIN, Anton, 780'.92'4 B
1829-1894.
Autobiography of Anton Rubinstein, 1829-1889. Translated from the Russian by Aline Delano. St. Clair Shores, Mich., Scholarly Press, 1972. Translation of Avtobiograficheskiia vospominaniia. Reprint of the 1892 ed. [ML410.R89A32 1972] 72-11817
I. Title. BIP

RUBINSTEIN, Anton, 780'.924 B
1829-1894.
Autobiography of Anton Rubinstein, 1829-1889. Translated from the Russian by Aline Delano. New York, Haskell House Publishers, 1969. xii, 171 p. port. 23 cm. "First published 1890." Translation of Vospominaniia (romanized form) "Supplement: Rubinstein as a composer (p. [141]-163); Rubinstein as a pianist (p. 163-171)" [ML410.R89A32 1969] 68-25303
I. Delano, Aline P. (Kuzmishcheva) b. 1845, tr. II. Title.

Rubinstein, Artur, 1886-

FORSEE, Aylesa. 786.1'0924 B
Artur Rubinstein, king of the keyboard. New York, T. Y. Crowell Co. [1969] vii, 178 p. illus. 21 cm. A biography of the Polish pianist whose virtuosity has brought him world-wide fame. [ML417.R79F7] 92 69-11082 4.50
1. Rubinstein, Artur, 1886-

RUBINSTEIN, Artur, 786.1'092'4 B
1886-
My young years [by] Arthur Rubinstein. [1st ed.] New York, Knopf; [distributed by Random House] 1973. xi, 478, xiii p. illus. 25 cm. [ML417.R79A3] 70-171147 ISBN 0-394-46890-2 10.00
1. Musicians—Correspondence, reminiscences, etc. I. Title.

RUBINSTEIN, Artur, 786.1'092'4 B
1896-
My young years [by] Arthur Rubinstein. New York, Popular Library [1974, c1973] 511 p. illus. 18 cm. [ML417.R79A3] 1.75 (pbk.)
1. Musicians—Correspondence, reminiscences, etc. I. Title.
L.C. card number for original ed.: 70-171147 BIP

Rubinstein, Helena, 1870-1965.

O'HIGGINS, 338.7'66'8550924 B
Patrick.
Madame; an intimate biography of Helena Rubinstein [by] Patrick O'Higgins. New York, Viking Press [1971] 296 p. illus., ports. 25 cm. [TP983.A66R86 1971] 71-147394 ISBN 0-670-44530-4 7.95
1. Rubinstein, Helena, 1870-1965. I. Title.

Rubinstein, Helena, 1870-1965— Juvenile literature.

FABE, Maxene. 338.7'66'8550924 B
Beauty millionaire; the life of Helena Rubinstein. Illustrated with photos. New York, Crowell [1972] xi, 178 p. illus. 22 cm. (Women of America) Bibliography: p. [169]-171. A biography of the Polish woman who built a multi-million dollar business as one of the first mass-producers of cosmetics. [TP983.A66R84 1972] 92 72-78281 4.50
1. Rubinstein, Helena, 1870-1965— Juvenile literature. I. Title.

Rubinstein, Serge, 1908-1955.

SMITH, Gene 923.4173
The life and death of Serge Rubinstein. Garden City, N.Y., Doubleday [c.]1962. 284p. 62-7681 4.50
1. Rubinstein, Serge, 1908-1955. I. Title.

SMITH. GENE 923.4173
The life and death of Serge Rubinstein. [New York] Macfadden [1963, c.1962] 256p. 18cm. (MB 75-119) .75 pap.,
1. Rubinstein, Serge, 1908-1955. I. Title.

SMITH, Gene. 923
The life and death of Serge Rubinstein. [1st ed.] Garden City, N.Y., Doubleday, 1962. 284 p. 22 cm. [HG172.R8S5] 4173 62-7681
1. Rubinstein, Serge, 1908-1955. I. Title.

Ruby, Bob.

RUBY, Bob. 384.54'092'4 B
Ruby in the rough / by Bob Ruby. Gretna, La. : Pelican Pub. Co., 1976. 179 p. : ill. ; 23 cm. [PN1991.4.R8A37] 76-40031 ISBN 0-88289-099-9 : 8.95
1. Ruby, Bob. 2. Radio broadcasters—United States—Biography. I. Title. BIP

Ruby, Jack.

KANTOR, Seth. 364.1'523'0924
Who was Jack Ruby? / By Seth Kantor. [New York] : Everest House, c1978. xi, 242 p. ; 24 cm. Includes bibliographical references and index. [E842.9.K29] 78-54078 ISBN 0-89696-004-8 : 10.95
1. Kennedy, John Fitzgerald, Pres. U.S., 1917-1963—Assassination. 2. Ruby, Jack. 3. Oswald, Lee Harvey. 4. Crime and criminal—Texas—Dallas—Biography. 5. Dallas—Biography. I. Title. BIP

PABST, Ralph M., 364.1'523'0924 B
1920-
Plodding toward terror : a personal look at the Jack Ruby case / by Ralph M. Pabst. 1st ed. New York : Vantage Press, c1974. 174 p. ; 21 cm. Includes bibliographical references and index. [E842.9.P32] 75-314981 ISBN 0-533-01302-X : 5.95
1. Ruby, Jack. 2. Kennedy, John Fitzgerald, Pres. U.S., 1917-1963—Assassination. I. Title.

WILLS, Garry, 1934- 364.15'23 B
Jack Ruby [by] Garry Wills and Ovid Demaris. [New York] New American Library [1968] 266 p. 21 cm. [E842.9.W47] 67-29996
1. Ruby, Jack. I. Demaris, Ovid, joint author.

Ruddiman, Thomas, 1674-1757.

CHALMERS, George, 686.2'092'4 B
1742-1825.
The life of Thomas Ruddiman. New York, Garland Pub. Inc., 1974. 467 p. illus. 22 cm. (The English book trade, 1660-1853) Reprint of the 1794 ed. printed for J. Stockdale, London. Includes "anecdotes of Buchanan." "A chronological list of news papers [1640-1793]": p. 404-442. "A list of the books, which were printed by Thomas Ruddiman": p. 450-467. [Z720.R9C4 1974] 74-7446 ISBN 0-8240-0981-9
1. Ruddiman, Thomas, 1674-1757. 2. Buchanan, George, 1506-1582. 3. English newspapers—Bibliography. I. Title. II. Series.

Rude, Francois, 1784-1855.

HAMERTON, Philip 920'.044
Gilbert, 1834-1894.
Modern Frenchmen; five biographies. Freeport, N.Y., Books for Libraries Press [1972] xiv, 422 p. 22 cm. (Essay index reprint series) Reprint of the 1878 ed. Contents.Contents.—Victor Jacquemont.—Henri Perreyve.—Francois Rude.—Jean Jacques Ampere.—Henri Regnault. [CT1012.H3 1972] 72-4579 ISBN 0-8369-2947-0 14.50
1. Jacquemont, Victor, 1801-1832. 2. Perreyve, Henri, 1831-1865. 3. Rude, Francois, 1784-1855. 4. Ampere, Jean Jacques Antoine, 1800-1864. 5. Regnault, Henri, 1843-1871. I. Title. BIP

Rudensky, Red,

RUDENSKY, Red, 1898- 364.1'0924 B
The gonif ... Red Rudensky, by Morris (Red) Rudensky and Don Riley. Edited by John M. Sullivan, Jr. Blue Earth, Minn., Piper Co. [1970] 215 p. illus., facsims., ports. 23 cm. [HV6248.R78A3] 71-139587 7.95
I. Riley, Don, joint author. II. Title.

Rudolf, Crown Prince of Austria, 1858-1889.

BARKELEY, Richard. 923.2436
The road to Mayerling; life and death of Crown Prince Rudolph of Austria. New York, St. Martin's Press, 1958. 292 p. illus. 23 cm. [DB89.R8B3] 58-14865
1. Rudolf, Crown Prince of Austria, 1858-1889. I. Title.

Rudolf II, Emperor of Germany, 1552-1612.

EVANS, Robert 914.3'03'340924
John Weston.
Rudolf II and his world: a study in intellectual history, 1576-1612, by R.J.W. Evans. Oxford, Clarendon Press, 1973. xi, 323 p. illus. 24 cm. Bibliography: p. [299]-310. [DD187.E82 1973] 73-161974 ISBN 0-19-822516-4 £7.50 ($24.00 U.S.)
1. Rudolf II, Emperor of Germany, 1552-1612. 2. Bohemia—Intellectual life. 3. Holy Roman Empire—Intellectual life. I. Title.

HOLZER, Hans W., 1920- 540'.1 B
The alchemist : the secret magical life of Rudolf von Habsburg / by Hans Holzer. New York : Stein and Day, 1974. 192 p. ; 24 cm. Includes index. Bibliography: p. 187. [QD24.R8H63] 74-78542 ISBN 0-8128-1734-6 : 7.95
1. Rudolf II, Emperor of Germany, 1552-1612. I. Title.

Rudolph, Wilma, 1940- —Juvenile literature.

JACOBS, Linda. 796.4'2'0924 B
Wilma Rudolph : run for glory / by Linda Jacobs. St. Paul, Minn. : EMC Corp., [1975] p. cm. (Women who win 2) A biography of the woman who overcame crippling polio as a child to become the first woman to win three gold medals in track in a single Olympics. [GV697.R8J32] 92 74-31084 ISBN 0-88436-172-1 lib.bdg. : 4.95 ISBN 0-88436-173-X pbk. : 2.95
1. Rudolph, Wilma, 1940- —Juvenile literature. 2. Track-athletics for women—Juvenile literature. I. Title. BIP

Rudometkin, John, 1940-

FORD, Herbert. 796.32'3'0924 B
Rudo: the reckless Russian. Mountain View, Calif., Pacific Press Pub. Association [1970] 97 p. illus., ports. 22 cm. (A Destiny book D-131) [GV884.R8F6] 71-109260
1. Rudometkin, John, 1940- I. Title.

Ruebush family.

RUEBUSH, Glenn W. 929'.2'0973
Mary Ruebush, 1736-1815, and her family in Virginia / [Glenn W. Ruebush]. [Harrisonburg? Va. : s.n., 1956?] 29 leaves : ill. ; 29 cm. Caption title. Typescript. [CS71.R8883 1956] 75-308019
1. Ruebush family. I. Title.

Ruffin, Charles Edward.

WORTHINGTON, Anne, 286'.1'0924 B
1943-
Pop. Bowie, Md., Golden Triangle Pub. Co., 1972. 245 p. illus. 19 cm. [BX6495.R75W67] 76-188929 8.98
1. Ruffin, Charles Edward. I. Title.

Ruffin, Edmund,

RUFFIN, Edmund, 973.7'13'0924 B
1794-1865.
The diary of Edmund Ruffin. Edited, with an introd. and notes, by William Kauffman Scarborough. With a foreword by Avery Craven. Baton Rouge, Louisiana State University Press, 1972- v. illus. 25 cm. (The Library of Southern civilization) Contents.—v. 1. Toward independence, October 1856-April 1861. Includes bibliographical references. [F230.R9314] 75-165069 ISBN 0-8071-0948-7 20.00
I. Scarborough, William Kauffman, ed. II. Title.

Rugby football—Biog.

THOMAS, John Brinley 927.96333
George
Great contemporary players. London, S. Paul [dist. New Rochelle, N.Y., SportShelf, 1964, c.1963] 174p. ports. 22cm. 64-5502 5.75 bds.,
1. Rugby football—Biog. I. Title.

Ruggles, Ora, 1894-

CARLOVA, John 926.1
The healing heart, by John Carlova with Ora Ruggles. New York, Messner [c.1961] 256p. 61-10125 3.95
1. Ruggles, Ora, 1894- I. Title.

Ruggles, Samuel Bulkley, 1800-1881.

THOMPSON, Daniel 328.747'0924 B
Garrison Brinton, 1899-
Ruggles of New York; a life of Samuel B. Ruggles, by D. G. Brinton Thompson. New York, AMS Press [1968] 222 p. fold. map, ports. 23 cm. (Studies in history, economics, and public law, no. 524) Series statement also appears as: Columbia University studies in the social sciences, 524. Reprint of the 1946 ed. which was originally presented as the author's thesis, Columbia University. Bibliography: p. 207-214. [F128.44.R955T5 1968] 76-76651
1. Ruggles, Samuel Bulkley, 1800-1881. I. Title. II. Series: Columbia studies in the social sciences, no. 524. BIP

Ruiz-Arnau, Ramon, 1874-1934.

ARANA-SOTO, Salvador, 1908- v. 12
El doctor Ramon Ruiz Arnau / S. Arana Soto. 1. ed. San Juan de Puerto Rico : [s.n.], 1974. 96 p., [7] leaves of plates : ill. ; 22 cm. Spanish, English or French. Bibliography: p. 96. [R476.R8A7] 76-453421
1. Ruiz-Arnau, Ramon, 1874-1934. I. Title.

ARANA-SOTO, Salvador, 1908- v. 12
El doctor Ramon Ruiz Arnau / S. Arana Soto. 1. ed. San Juan de Puerto Rico : [s.n.], 1974. 96 p., [7] leaves of plates : ill. ; 22 cm. Spanish, English or French.

Bibliography: p. 96. [R476.R8A7] 76-453421
1. Ruiz-Arnau, Ramon, 1874-1934. I. Title.

Rumford, Benjamin Thomston, count, Sir; 1753-1814.

BRADLEY, Duane. 530.0924 B
Count Rumford. Princeton, N.J., Van Nostrand [1967] vii, 176 p. illus., ports. 21 cm. A biography of the talented American scientist and social reformer whose expatriation, animosity and dishonest dealings erased his name from prominence in history. [Q143.R8B68] 92 AC 68
1. Rumford, Benjamin Thompson, Sir, count, 1753-1814. I. Title.

BROWN, Sanborn Conner, 1913- 530'.092'4 B
Benjamin Thompson, Count Rumford / Sanborn C. Brown. Cambridge, Mass. : MIT Press, c1979. p. cm. Includes index. Bibliography: p. [Q143.R8B69] 79-9110 ISBN 0-262-02138-2 : 19.95
1. Rumford, Benjamin Thompson, Sir, Count, 1753-1814. 2. Scientists—Great Britain—Biography. BIP

BROWN, Sanborn Conner, 1913- 925
Count Rumford, physicist extraordinary. [1st ed.] Garden City, N.Y., Anchor Books, 1962. 178 p. illus. 18 cm. (Science study series, S28) Includes bibliography. [Q143.R8B7] 62-14130
1. Rumford, Benjamin Thompson, Sir, count, 1753-1814. BIP

ELLIS, George Edward, 1814-1894. 509'.2'4 B
Memoir of Sir Benjamin Thompson, count Rumford, with notices of his daughter, by George E. Ellis. With a new series introduction and a pref. by George Athan Billias. Boston, American Academy of Arts and Sciences. Boston, Gregg Press, 1972. p. (American Revolutionary series) Reprint of the 1871 ed. The original ed. was "published in connection with an edition of Rumford's complete works." [Q143.R8E4 1972] 72-8777 ISBN 0-8398-0457-1
1. Rumford, Benjamin Thompson, Sir, Count, 1753-1814. 2. Rumford, Sarah Thompson, Countess, 1774-1852. I. Title. II. Series.

LEHRBURGER, Egon, 1904- 925
An American in Europe; the life of Benjamin Thompson, Count Rumford, by Egon Larsen [pseud.] New York, Philosophical Library [1953] 224 p. illus., ports. 22 cm. 'Extracts from Rumford's essays':p. 175-215. Bibliography:p. 217-218. [Q143] 53-13519
1. Rumford, Benjamin Thompson, count,Sir 1753-1814. I. Title.

SPARROW, W. J. 509.24
Knight of the White Eagle, Sir Benjamin Thompson, Count Rumford of Woburn, Mass. New York, Crowell [1965, c.1964] 301p. illus., facsims., ports. 22cm. Bibl. [Q143.R8S65] 5.95
1. Rumford, Benjamin Thompson, count, Sir 1753-1814. I. Title. II. Title: Count Rumford of Woburn, Mass.

Rundstedt, Gerd von, 1875-1953.

KEEGAN, John, 1934- 355.3'31'0924 B
Rundstedt. [New York, Ballantine Books, 1974] 160 p. illus. 21 cm. (Ballantine's illustrated history of the violent century. War leader book no. 25) [DD247.R8K4] 74-170445 1.50 (pbk.)
1. Rundstedt, Gerd von, 1875-1953.

Runners (Sports)—United States—Biography.

MARKS, Rick. 796.4'26
More than a run / Rick Marks ; [photos., Dick Bonneau ... et al.]. Los Angeles : J. P. Tarcher ; New York : distributed by St. Martin's Press, c1978. 374 p., [2] leaves of plates : ill. ; 25 cm. [GV697.A1M32 1978] 78-62792 ISBN 0-87477-083-1 : 10.00
1. Runners (Sports)—United States—Biography. 2. Police—United States—Biography. I. Title. BIP

Running.

HIGDON, Hal. 796.4'26 B
On the run from dogs and people. Chicago, Regnery [1971] 239 p. 22 cm. [GV1061.H54] 78-143840 5.95
1. Running. I. Title. BIP

Running—Biography.

NELSON, Cordner. 796.4'26 B
Runners and races; 1500 m./mile [by] Cordner Nelson & Roberto Quercetani. [Los Altos, Calif.] Tafnews Press [1973] vi, 326 p. illus. 23 cm. [GV1061.N39 1973] 72-90579 ISBN 0-911520-40-6 6.50
*1. Running—Biography. I. Quercetani, Roberto L., 1922- joint author. II. Title.*BIP

Runyon, Damon, 1880-1946.

CLARK, Tom, 1941- 818'.5'209 B
The world of Damon Runyon / by Tom Clark. 1st ed. New York : Harper & Row, c1978. p. cm. Bibliography: p. [PS3535.U52Z6] 78-2122 ISBN 0-06-010771-5 : 10.00
1. Runyon, Damon, 1880-1946. 2. Authors, American—20th century—Biography. I. Title.

HOYT, Edwin Palmer. 928.1
A gentleman of Broadway [by] Edwin P. Hoyt. [1st ed.] Boston, Little, Brown [1964] 369 p. ports. 22 cm. Bibliographical references included in "Chapter notes" (p. [315]-333) "Runyon checklist": p. [335]-340. [PS3535.U52Z65] 64-21492
1. Runyon, Damon, 1880-1946. I. Title.

Ruotsalainen, Paavo, 1777-1852.

ARDEN, Gothard Everett, 1905- 922.448
Four northern lights; men who shaped Scandinavian churches, by G. Everett Arden. Illus. by Hordan Lang. Minneapolis, Augsburg Pub. House [1964] 165 p. ports. 21 cm. "Originally presented as a series of lectures in connection with the twenty-fourth Luther Academy, held at Wartburg Theological Seminary, Dubuque, Iowa, during the summer of 1963." Includes bibliographies. [BX8079.A7] 64-21502
1. Ruotsalainen, Paavo, 1777-1852. 2. Hauge, Hans Nielsen, 1771-1824. 3. Grundtvig, Nikolai Frederik Severin, 1783-1872. 4. Rosenius, Carl Olof, 1916-1868. I. Title.

Rupert, Prince, Count Palatine, 1619-1682.

MORRAH, Patrick. 941.06'2'0924 B
Prince Rupert of the Rhine / [by] Patrick Morrah. London : Constable, 1976. xiii, 480 p., leaf of plate, [16] p. of plates : ill., facsims., ports. (1 col.) ; 24 cm. Includes index. Bibliography: p. 455-464. [DA407.R9M67 1976] 77-355568 ISBN 0-09-460910-1 : £8.50
1. Rupert, Prince, Count Palatine, 1619-1682. 2. Great Britain—Princes and princesses—Biography. I. Title.

THOMSON, George Malcolm. 941.06'2'0924 B
Warrior prince : Prince Rupert of the Rhine / George Malcolm Thomson. London : Secker & Warburg, 1976. ix, 238 p., [4] leaves of plates : ill. ; 24 cm. Includes index. [DA407.R9T46 1976] 76-373796 ISBN 0-436-52047-8 : £5.90
1. Rupert, Prince, Count Palatine, 1619-1682. 2. Great Britain—Princes and princesses—Biography. I. Title.

Rusch, Paul, 1897-

HEMPHILL, Elizabeth Anne. 266.3'0924 B
The road to KEEP; the story of Paul Rusch in Japan. With a foreword by Edwin O. Reischauer. [1st ed.] New York, Walker/Weatherhill [1970, c1969] ix, 195 p. illus., ports. 24 cm. Bibliography: p. 190. [BV3457.R8H4 1970] 78-96053 4.95
1. Rusch, Paul, 1897- 2. Protestant Episcopal Church in the U.S.A.—Missions. 3. Missions—Japan. I. Title.

Ruse, James, 1760-1837?

TOLCHARD, Clifford, 1908- 994.4020924
The humble adventurer; the life and times of James Ruse, convict and farmer. [Melbourne] Landsdowne Pr. [dist. New Rochelle, N. Y., SportShelf, 1965] 134p. illus., facsims., port. 23cm. Bibl. [DU172.R85T6] 65-9837 7.00 bds.,
1. Ruse, James, 1760-1837? 2. New South Wales Hist. I. Title.

Rush, Benjamin,

RUSH, Benjamin, 1745-1813. 610'.924 B
The autobiography of Benjamin Rush; his Travels through life together with his Commonplace book for 1789-1813. Edited with introd. and notes by George W. Corner. Westport, Conn., Greenwood Press [1970, c1948] 399 p. illus., facsims., ports. 23 cm. Includes bibliographical references. [E302.6.R85R8 1970] 72-100241
I. Corner, George Washington, 1889- ed. II. Rush, Benjamin, 1745-1813. A memorial containing travels through life or sundry incidents...

Rush, Benjamin, 1745-1813.

BINGER, Carl Alfred Lanning, 1889- 610.69520924 (B)
Revolutionary doctor: Benjamin Rush, 1746-1813, by Carl Binger. [1st ed.] New York. Norton [1966] 326p. port. 25cm. Bibl. [R154.R9B5] 66-15315 7.95
1. Rush. Benjamin, 1745-1813. I. Title.

BLINDERMAN, Abraham, 1916- 370'.92'2
Three early champions of education : Benjamin Franklin, Benjamin Rush, and Noah Webster / by Abraham Blinderman. Bloomington, Ind. : Phi Delta Kappa Educational Foundation, c1976. 34 p. ; 18 cm. (Fastback - Phi Delta Kappa Educational Foundation ; 74) (Bicentennial series) [LA2311.B57] 76-362357 ISBN 0-87367-074-4 : 0.50
1. Franklin, Benjamin, 1706-1790. 2. Rush, Benjamin, 1745-1813. 3. Webster, Noah, 1758-1843. 4. Education—United States—History. I. Title. II. Series: Phi Delta Kappa. Educational Foundation. Fastback ; 74. BIP

D'ELIA, Donald J. 973.3'092'4 B
Benjamin Rush, philosopher of the American Revolution / Donald J. D'Elia. Philadelphia : American Philosophical Society, 1974. 113 p. ; 30 cm. (Transactions of the American Philosophical Society ; new ser., v. 64, pt. 5 ISSN 0065-9746) Includes index. Bibliography: p. 3. [E302.6.R85D44] 74-77911 ISBN 0-87169-645-2 pbk. : 5.00
1. Rush, Benjamin, 1745-1813. I. Series: American Philosophical Society, Philadelphia. Transactions ; new ser., v. 64, pt. 5.

HAWKE, David Freeman. 973.3'0924
Benjamin Rush; revolutionary gadfly. Indianapolis, Bobbs-Merrill [1971] x, 490 p. port. 24 cm. Bibliography: p. [399]-454. [E302.6.R85H3] 70-145859 15.00
1. Rush, Benjamin, 1745-1813.

NEILSON, Winthrop. 926.1
Verdict for the doctor; the case of Benjamin Rush, by Winthrop &Frances Neilson. New York, Hastings House [1958] 245p. illus. 24cm. [R154.R9N4] 58-9241
1. Rush, Benjamin, 1745-1813. 2. Cobbett, William, 1763-1835. I. Nellson, Frances Fullerton, joint author. II. Title.

RIEDMAN, Sarah Regal, 1902- 926.1
Benjamin Rush; physician, patriot, Founding Father [by] Sarah R. Riedman and Clarence C. Green. London, New York, Abelard-Schuman [1964] 253 p. illus., facsims., map, ports. 23 cm. [R154.R9R5] 64-22349
1. Rush, Benjamin, 1745-1813. I. Green, Clarence Corleon, joint author. II. Title.

RIEDMAN, Sarah Regel, 1902- 926.1
Benjamin Rush: physician, patriot, Founding Father [by] Sarah R. Riedman, Clarence C. Green. New York, Abelard [c.1964] 253p. illus., facsims., map, ports. 23cm. 64-22349 4.50
1. Rush, Benjamin, 1745-1813. I. Green, Clarence Corleon, joint author. II. Title.

RUSH, Benjamin, 1745-1813. 610'.924 B
The autobiography of Benjamin Rush; his Travels through life together with his Commonplace book for 1789-1813. Edited with introd. and notes by George W. Corner. Westport, Conn., Greenwood Press [1970, c1948] 399 p. illus., tacsims., ports. 23 cm. Includes bibliographical references. [E302.6.R85R8 1970] 72-100241
I. Corner, George Washington, 1889- ed. II. Rush, Benjamin, 1745-1813. A memorial containing travels through life or sundry incidents...

Rushmore, Jane Palen,

JOHNSON, Emily (Cooper) 922.8673
Under Quaker appointment: the life of Jane P. Rushmore. Philadelphia, University of Pennsylvania, 1953. 211p. illus. 21cm. [BX7795.R8J6] 53-10517
1. Rushmore, Jane Palen, I. Title.

Rusk, Claude Ewing, 1871-

RUSK, Claude Ewing, 1871- 796.5'22'0924 B
Tales of a western mountaineer / C. E. Rusk ; with a portrait of C. E. Rusk by Darryl Lloyd. Seattle : Mountaineers, c1978. xiv, xii, 309 p., [24] leaves of plates : ill. ; 22 cm. Reprint of the 1924 ed. published by Houghton Mifflin, Boston. Includes bibliographical references. [GV199.42.C37R87 1978] 78-54427 ISBN 0-916890-62-7 pbk. : 6.95
1. Rusk, Claude Ewing, 1871- 2. Mountaineering—Cascade Range. 3. Cascade Range—Description. 4. Mountaineers—United States—Biography I. Title. BIP

Rusk, Howard A.,

RUSK, Howard A., 1901- 610'.92'4 B
A world to care for; the autobiography of Howard A. Rusk, M.D. [1st ed.] New York, Random House [1972] xii, 307 p. 22 cm. Autobiographical. [R154.R92A3] 72-5263 ISBN 0-394-48198-4 7.95
I. Title.

Rusk, Thomas Jefferson, 1803-1857.

CLARKE, Mary (Whatley) 973.5'0924 B
Thomas J. Rusk, soldier, statesman, jurist. Austin, Jenkins Pub. Co., 1971. xv, 274 p. illus. 24 cm. Bibliography: p. 213-231. [F389.R95C55] 79-157043
1. Rusk, Thomas Jefferson, 1803-1857. I. Title.

HUSTON, Cleburne. 328.73'092'4 B
Towering Texan; a biography of Thomas J. Rusk. Waco, Tex., Texian Press, 1971. xi, 191 p. illus. 24 cm. Bibliography: p. 181-183. [F389.R95H9] 75-135345 7.50
1. Rusk, Thomas Jefferson, 1803 1857. I. Title. BIP

Ruskay, Sophie.

RUSKAY, Sophie. 813'.5'4 B
Horsecars and cobblestones. Illus. by Cecil B. Ruskay. [New ed.] South Brunswick, A. S. Barnes [1973, c1948] 240 p. illus. 22 cm. Autobiographical. [PS3568.U757Z52] 72-6376 ISBN 0-498-01301-4 4.95
1. Ruskay, Sophie. I. Title. BIP

Ruskin family.

RUSKIN, John James. 828'.8'09 B
The Ruskin family letters: the correspondence of John James Ruskin, his wife, and their son, John, 1801-1843. Edited by Van Akin Burd. Ithaca [N.Y.] Cornell University Press [1973] 2 v. (lviii, 792 p.) illus. 25 cm. Contents.Contents.—v. 1. 1801-1837.—v. 2. 1837-1843. Bibliography: p. 759-761. [PR5263.A46 1973] 72-13130 ISBN 0-8014-0725-7 35.00

1. Ruskin family. I. Ruskin, Margaret Cock, 1781-1871. II. Ruskin, John, 1819-1900. III. Burd, Van Akin, 1914- ed. IV. Title.

Ruskin, John, 1819-1900.

BELL, Quentin. 828'.8'09 B
Ruskin / Quentin Bell. 1st American ed. New York : G. Braziller, 1978. p. cm. Includes index. Bibliography: p. [PR5263.B38 1978] 77-6123 ISBN 0-8076-0876-9 : 8.95
1. Ruskin, John, 1819-1900. 2. Authors, English—19th century—Biography.

BENSON, Arthur Christopher, 1862-1925. 828'.8'09 B
Ruskin : a study in personality / by Arthur Christopher Benson. New York : Haskell House Publishers, [1977.] p. cm. Reprint of the 1911 ed. published by Smith, Elder, London. [PR5263.B4 1976] 76-26 ISBN 0-8383-1921-1 : 13.95
1. Ruskin, John, 1819-1900. BIP

BENSON, Arthur Christopher, 1862-1925. 828'.8'09 B
Ruskin; a study in personality. London, Smith, Elder, 1911. St. Clair Shores, Mich., Scholarly Press, 1973. p. Seven lectures originally delivered at Magdalene College, Cambridge, in 1910. [PR5263.B4 1973] 73-6985 ISBN 0-403-01757-2 19.50
1. Ruskin, John, 1819-1900. I. Title.

COOK, Edward Tyas, Sir, 1857-1919. 700'.924 B
The life of John Ruskin. New York, Haskell House Publishers, 1968. 2 v. illus., ports. 24 cm. Reprint of the 1911 ed. Contents.—v. 1. 1819-1860.—v. 2. 1860-1900. [PR5263.C7 1968] 68-24903
1. Ruskin, John, 1819-1900. I. Title.

CROW, Gerald H. 828'.8'09 B
Ruskin, by Gerald Crow. [Folcroft, Pa.] Folcroft Library Editions, 1973. 140 p. 24 cm. Reprint of the 1936 ed. published by Duckworth, London, in series: Great lives. Bibliography: p. 140. [PR5263.C8 1973] 73-19678 ISBN 0-8414-3530-8 (lib. bdg.)
1. Ruskin, John, 1819-1900. BIP

DOWNES, Robert Percival, 1842-1924. 828'.8'09 B
John Ruskin : a study / by R. P. Downes. Norwood, Pa. : Norwood Editions, 1976. p. cm. Reprint of the 1890 ed. published by A. W. Hall, London. [PR5263.D65 1976] 76-4490 ISBN 0-88305-493-0 : 15.00
1. Ruskin, John, 1819-1900. BIP

EARLAND, Ada. 828'.8'09 B
Ruskin and his circle. New York, AMS Press [1971] xi, 340 p. illus., ports. 18 cm. Reprint of the 1910 ed. Bibliography: p. 333-334. [PR5263.E2 1971] 71-129381 ISBN 0-404-02232-4
1. Ruskin, John, 1819-1900. I. Title. BIP

EVANS, Joan, 1893- 709'.24
John Ruskin. New York, Oxford University Press, 1954. 447p. illus., ports. 23cm. Bibliography: p. 424-430. [PR5263.E9] 54-12299
1. Ruskin, John, 1819-1900. I. Title. BIP

EVANS, Joan, 1893- 828'.8'09 B
John Ruskin. New York, Haskell House Publishers, 1970. 447 p. illus., ports. 23 cm. Bibliography: p. 424-430. [PR5263.E9 1970] 70-117998 ISBN 0-8383-1053-2
1. Ruskin, John, 1819-1900.

GEDDES, Patrick, Sir, 1854-1932. 330'.092'4 B
John Ruskin, economist. [Folcroft, Pa.] Folcroft Library Editions, 1973. 43 p. 23 cm. Reprint of the 1884 ed. published by W. Brown, Edinburgh, which was issued as no. 3 of the Round table series. Includes bibliographical references. [HB103.R8G4 1973] 73-318 ISBN 0-8414-1337-1 4.50
1. Ruskin, John, 1819-1900. 2. Economics—History—Great Britain. I. Title. II. Series: The Round table series, 3. BIP

HARRISON, Frederic, 1831-1923. 820*.9*092
John Ruskin. New York, Macmillan, 1902. Ann Arbor, Mich., Gryphon Books, 1971. vi, 216 p. 22 cm. (English men of letters) [PR5263.H3 1971] 72-78229
1. Ruskin, John, 1819-1900. BIP

HEWISON, Robert, 1943- 709'.2'4 B
John Ruskin : the argument of the eye / Robert Hewison. London : Thames and Hudson, c1976. 228 p. : ill. (some col.) ; 24 cm. Includes index. Bibliography: p. 219-223. [ND497.R88H48 1976c] 77-364352 ISBN 0-500-01148-6 : £7.50
1. Ruskin, John, 1819-1900. BIP

HEWISON, Robert, 1943- 709'.2'4 B
John Ruskin : the argument of the eye / Robert Hewison. Princeton, N.J. : Princeton University Press, c1976. 228 p. : ill. (some col.) ; 24 cm. Includes index. Bibliography: p. 219-223. [ND497.R88H48] 77-352685 ISBN 0-691-03890-2 : 15.00
1. Ruskin, John, 1819-1900.

LEON, Derrick, 1908-1944. 700'.924 B
Ruskin, the great Victorian. [Hamden, Conn.] Archon Books, 1969. xxvi, 595 p. ports. 23 cm. "First published in ... 1949." Bibliography: p. 583-586. [PR5263.L4 1969] 79-8514 12.00
1. Ruskin, John, 1819-1900. I. Title. BIP

MATHER, Marshall, 1851-1916. 828'.8'09
John Ruskin, his life and teaching. [5th ed.] London, New York, F. Warne, 1903. New York, Haskell House Publishers, 1972. xxvii, 184 p. port. 23 cm. "Popular edition." Bibliography: p. [171]-179. [PR5263.M3 1972] 72-881 ISBN 0-8383-1425-2
1. Ruskin, John, 1819-1900.

MATHER, Marshall, 1851-1916. 828'.8'09
John Ruskin: his life and teaching. 5th ed. [Folcroft, Pa.] Folcroft Library Editions [1973. xxvii, 184 p. port. 23 cm. Reprint of the 1903 ed. published by F. Warne, London and New York. Bibliography: p. [171]-179. [PR5263.M3 1973] 73-14927 9.75
1. Ruskin, John, 1819-1900. I. Title.

RUSKIN, John, 1819-1900. 828'.8'09 B
The Brantwood diary of John Ruskin, together with selected related letters and sketches of persons mentioned. Edited and annotated by Helen Gill Viljoen. New Haven, Yale University Press, 1971. xv, 632 p. illus. 25 cm. [PR5263.A13 1971] 72-99844 ISBN 0-300-01227-6 25.00
I. Title.

RUSKIN, John, 1819-1900. 928.2
Diaries. Selected and edited by Joan Evans and John Howard Whitehouse. Oxford, Clarendon Press, 1956- v. illus., port. 25cm. Contents.[1] 1835-1847. [PR5263.A15] 56-14657
I. Evans, Joan, 1893- ed. II. Whitehouse, John Howard, 1873- ed. III. Title.

RUSKIN, John, 1819-1900. 914.5'04'8
Ruskin in Italy: letters to his parents, 1845; edited by Harold I. Shapiro. Oxford, Clarendon Press, 1972. xxii, 263 p., [8] leaves. illus. 23 cm. Includes bibliographical references. [PR5263.A27 1972] 72-192985 ISBN 0-19-812441-4 £6.00 ($20.50 U.S.)
I. Shapiro, Harold I., ed. II. Title.

RUSKIN, John, 1819-1900. 928.2
Ruskin's letters from Venice, 1851-1852 By John Lewis Bradley. New Haven, Yale University Press, 1955. xx. 330p. illus. 24cm. (Yale studies in English, v. 129) The editor's thesis--Yale University.Without thesis statement. 'Daily letters from Ruskin to his father.' Bibliographical footnotes. [PR5263.A37] 55-9436
I. Ruskin, John James. II. Bradley, John Lewis, ed. III. Title. IV. Series.

SPIELMANN, Marion Harry, 1858-1948. 828'.8'09 B
John Ruskin; a sketch of his life, his work, and his opinions, with personal reminiscences. [Folcroft, Pa.] Folcroft Library Editions, 1973. p. Reprint of the 1900 ed. published by Cassell, London, New York. [PR5263.S66 1973] 73-15854 ISBN 0-8414-7681-0 (lib. bdg.)
1. Ruskin, John, 1819-1900. BIP

VILJOEN, Helen Gill. 928.2
Ruskin's Scottish heritage, a prelude. Urbana, University of Illinois Press, 1956. 284 p. illus., ports., facsims., geneal. table. 24 cm. Bibliography: p. [257]-266. [PR5263.V5] 56-8062
1. Ruskin, John, 1819-1900. I. Title.

WHITEHOUSE, John Howard, 1873- ed. 828'.8'09 B
Ruskin, prophet of the good life. Edited by J. Howard Whitehouse. [Folcroft, Pa.] Folcroft Library Editions, 1974. 30 p. 23 cm. "Tributes paid to Ruskin at a luncheon of the Ruskin Society in February 1948." Reprint of the 1948 ed. published by Oxford University Press, London. [PR5263.W458 1974] 73-16263 ISBN 0-8414-9491-6 (lib. bdg.)
1. Ruskin, John, 1819-1900. I. Title.

WILENSKI, Reginald Howard, 1887- 828'.8'09
John Ruskin; an introduction to further study of his life and work, by R. H. Wilenski. New York, Russell & Russell [1967] 406 p. ports. 22 cm. Reprint of the 1933 ed. Bibliographical footnotes. [PR5263.W476 1967] 66-27182
1. Ruskin, John, 1819-1900. I. Title. BIP

WILENSKI, Reginald Howard, 1887- 828'.8'09
John Ruskin; an introduction to further study of his life and work, by R. H. Wilenski. New York, Russell & Russell [1967] 406 p. ports. 22 cm. Reprint of the 1933 ed. Bibliographical footnotes. [PR5263.W476 1967] 66-27182
1. Ruskin, John, 1819-1900.

WILENSKI, Reginald Howard, 1887- 828'.8'09 B
John Ruskin; an introduction to further study of his life and work, by R. H. Wilenski. [Folcroft, Pa.] Folcroft Library Editions, 1974. p. cm. Reprint of the 1933 ed. published by Faber & Faber, London. [PR5263.W476 1974] 74-9725 35.00 (lib. bdg.).
1. Ruskin, John, 1819-1900.

WILENSKI, Reginald Howard, 1887- 828'.8'09 B
John Ruskin : an introduction to further study of his life and work / by R. H. Wilenski. New York : AMS Press, [1978] p. cm. Reprint of the 1933 ed. published by Faber & Faber, London. Includes index. [PR5263.W476 1978] 75-30042 ISBN 0-404-14046-7 : 28.50
1. Ruskin, John, 1819-1900. 2. Authors, English—19th century—Biography.

WINGATE, Ashmore Kyle Paterson, 1881- 828'.8'09 B
Life of John Ruskin, by Ashmore Wingate. [Folcroft, Pa.] Folcroft Library Editions, 1973. p. Reprint of the 1910 ed. published by Walter Scott Pub. Co., London, in series: Great writers. Bibliography: p. [PR5263.W5 1973] 73-12590 20.00
1. Ruskin, John, 1819-1900. I. Title.

Ruskin, John, 1819-1900—Aesthetics.

CONNER, Patrick, 1947- 709'.2'4 B
Savage Ruskin / Patrick Conner. Detroit : Wayne State University Press, 1979. xiv, 189 p. ; 23 cm. Includes index. Bibliography: p. 172-182. [PR5267.A35C65 1979] 78-17051 ISBN 0-8143-1619-0 : 14.95
1. Ruskin, John, 1819-1900—Aesthetics. 2. Authors, English—19th century—Biography. 3. Art critics—Great Britain—Biography. I. Title. BIP

Ruskin, John, 1819-1900—Biography.

LARG, David Glass. 828'.8'09 B
John Ruskin, by David Larg. New York, Haskell House Publishers, 1974. 151 p. 22 cm. Reprint of the 1933 ed. published by D. Appleton, New York, in series: Appleton biographies. [PR5263.L26 1974] 74-1447 ISBN 0-8383-2047-3
1. Ruskin, John, 1819-1900—Biography. I. Series: Appleton biographies.

LARG, David Glass. 828'.8'09 B
John Ruskin, by David Larg. [Folcroft, Pa.] Folcroft Library Editions, 1974. p. cm. Reprint of the 1933 ed. published by D. Appleton, New York, in series: Appleton biographies. [PR5263.L26 1974b] 74-11438 ISBN 0-8414-5735-2 12.50
1. Ruskin, John, 1819-1900—Biography. I. Series: Appleton biographies.

MASEFIELD, John, 1878-1967. 828'.8'09 B
John Ruskin / by John Masefield. Folcroft, Pa. : Folcroft Library Editions, 1977. p. cm. "Originally delivered by Mr. Masefield as a lecture at the Ruskin Centenary Exhibition held at the Royal Academy in the autumn of 1919." Reprint of the 1920 ed. printed by H. Whitehouse and E. Daws at the Yellowsands Press, Bembridge, Eng. [PR5263.M28 1977] 77-24663 ISBN 0-8414-6213-5 lib. bdg. : 10.00
1. Ruskin, John, 1819-1900—Biography. 2. Authors, English—19th century—Biography. I. Title.

Ruskin, John, 1819-1900—Biography—Marriage.

WHITEHOUSE, John Howard, 1873- 828'.8'09 B
Vindication of Ruskin / by J. Howard Whitehouse. Folcroft, Pa. : Folcroft Library Editions, 1977. p. cm. Reprint of the 1950 ed. published by Allen and Unwin, London. Includes bibliographies. [PR5263.W475 1977] 77-13453 ISBN 0-8414-9638-2 lib. bdg. : 12.50
1. Ruskin, John, 1819-1900—Biography—Marriage. 2. James, William Milburne, Sir, 1881- The order of release. 3. Authors, English—19th century—Biography. I. Title. BIP

Ruskin, John, 1819-1900—Correspondence.

RUSKIN, John, 1819-1900. 828'.8'09 B
The gulf of years : letters from John Ruskin to Kathleen Olander / commentary by Kathleen Prynne ; edited and with a pref. by Rayner Unwin. Westport, Conn. : Greenwood Press, 1978. 95, [1] p., [2] leaves of plates : ill. ; 23 cm. Reprint of the 1953 ed. published by Allen & Unwin, London. "A select, chronological list of Ruskin's most important works": p. [96]. [PR5263.A327 1978] 77-18837 ISBN 0-313-20188-9 lib.bdg. : 19.95
1. Ruskin, John, 1819-1900—Correspondence. 2. Prynne, Kathleen

Olander. 3. Authors, English—19th century—Correspondence. I. Prynne, Kathleen Olander. II. Unwin, Rayner. III. Title. **BIP**

RUSKIN, John, 1819- 1900. 828'.8'09 B
John Ruskin's letters to William Ward : with a short biography of William Ward / by William C. Ward ; and an introd. by Alfred Mansfield Brooks. Norwood, Pa. : Norwood Editions, 1976, c1922. p. cm. Reprint of the ed. published by Marshall Jones Co., Boston. [PR5263.A475 1976] 76-15200 ISBN 0-8482-0163-9 : 20.00
1. Ruskin, John, 1819-1900—Correspondence. 2. Ward, William, 1829-1908. I. Ward, William C. II. Title.

RUSKIN, John, 1819- 1900. 828'.8'09 B
John Ruskin's letters to William Ward / with a short biography of William Ward by William C. Ward ; and an introd. by Alfred Mansfield Brooks. Folcroft, Pa. : Folcroft Library Editions, 1974 [c1922] p. cm. Reprint of the ed. published by M. Jones Co., Boston. [PR5263.A475 1974] 74-20802 ISBN 0-8414-3219-8 lib. bdg. : 22.50
1. Ruskin, John, 1819-1900—Correspondence. 2. Ward, William, 1829-1908. I. Ward, William, 1829-1908. II. Ward, William C., ed. III. Title. **BIP**

RUSKIN, John, 1819- 1900. 828'.8'09 B
Letters of John Ruskin to Bernard Quaritch, 1867-1888 / edited by Charlotte Quaritch Wrentmore. Norwood, Pa. : Norwood Editions, 1976. p. cm. Reprint of the 1938 ed. published by B. Quaritch, London. [PR5263.A45 1976] 76-13479 ISBN 0-8482-2855-3 lib. bdg. : 15.00
1. Ruskin, John, 1819-1900—Correspondence. 2. Quaritch, Bernard, 1819-1899. I. Quaritch, Bernard, 1819-1899. II. Title. **BIP**

RUSKIN, John, 1819- 1900. 828'.8'09 B
Letters of John Ruskin to Bernard Quaritch, 1867-1888. Edited by Charlotte Quaritch Wrentmore. [Folcroft, Pa.] Folcroft Library Editions, 1974. vi, 125 p. facsim. 24 cm. Reprint of the 1938 ed. published by B. Quaritch, London. [PR5263.A45 1974] 74-13028 17.50
1. Ruskin, John, 1819-1900—Correspondence. 2. Quaritch, Bernard, 1819-1899. I. Quaritch, Bernard, 1819-1899. II. Wrentmore, Charlotte Quaritch, ed. III. Title.

Ruskin, John, 1819-1900—Homes and haunts.

SYMON, James David. 828'.8'09 B
John Ruskin, his homes and haunts / by James D. Symon ; with twelve drawings in crayon by W. B. Robinson and other ill. Folcroft, Pa. : Folcroft Library Editions, 1977. p. cm. Reprint of the ed. published by Dodge Pub. Co., New York. Includes index. [PR5263.S9 1977] 77-12821 ISBN 0-8414-7864-3 lib. bdg. : 12.50
1. Ruskin, John, 1819-1900—Homes and haunts. 2. Authors, English—19th century—Biography. I. Title.

Ruskin, John, 1819-1900—Homes and haunts—Coniston, Eng.

WHITEHOUSE, John Howard, 1873- 828'.8'09 B
Ruskin & Brantwood; an account of the exhibition rooms. [Folcroft, Pa.] Folcroft Library Editions, 1973. 43 p. illus. 24 cm. Reprint of the 1937 ed. printed at the University Press, Cambridge, and published by the Ruskin Society. [PR5263.W455 1973] 73-17088 10.00
1. Ruskin, John, 1819-1900—Homes and haunts—Coniston, Eng. 2. Ruskin, John, 1819-1900—Museums, relics, etc. I. Title.

Ruskin, John, 1819-1900—Relationship with women—Rose La Touche.

LA TOUCHE, Rose. 828'.8'09 B
John Ruskin and Rose La Touche : her unpublished diaries of 1861 and 1867 / introduced and edited by Van Akin Burd. Oxford : Clarendon Press ; New York : Oxford University Press, 1980. p. cm. Includes index. [PR5263.L33] 79-40389 ISBN 0-19-812633-6 : 19.95
1. Ruskin, John, 1819-1900—Relationship with women—Rose La Touche. 2. La Touche, Rose. 3. Authors, English—19th century—Biography. 4. Dublin—Biography. I. Burd, Van Akin, 1914- II. Title.

Russell, Agnes, 1866-1927.

RUSSELL, John M., 1903- 378.1'12'0924 B
The Agnes Russell story [by] John M. Russell. New York, Teachers College, Columbia University [1973] 43 p. port. 24 cm. [LA2317.R78R87] 74-154472
1. Russell, Agnes, 1866-1927. I. Title.

Russell, Beatrice

RUSSELL, Beatrice 920.7
Living in state. Pref. by Robert McClintock. [New York] Macfadden [1962, c.1959] 208p. (50-132) .50 pap.,
I. Title.

Russell, Bertrand Russell, 3d Earl, 1872-1970.

AYER, Alfred Jules, Sir, 1910- 192 B
Bertrand Russell [by] A. J. Ayer. New York, Viking Press [1972] xii, 168 p. 19 cm. (Modern masters) Bibliography: p. [159]-160. [B1649.R94A86] 76-181979 ISBN 0-670-15899-2 2.25 (pbk.)
1. Russell, Bertrand Russell, 3d Earl, 1872-1970.

BELL, David R. 192
Bertrand Russell, by David R. Bell. Valley Forge, Pa., Judson Press [1972] 64 p. 19 cm. (Makers of modern thought) Bibliography: p. 63-64. [B1649.R94B28] 71-182459 ISBN 0-8170-0557-9 1.50
1. Russell, Bertrand Russell, 3d Earl, 1872-1970.

BERTRAND Russell; philosopher of the century. 192
Essays in his honour edited by Ralph Schoenman. [1st American ed.] Boston, Little, Brown [1967, i.e. 1968] 326 p. 23 cm. "An Atlantic monthly press book." Contents.Contents.—Fifty years; 1916-1966, by C. Malleson.—An old friendship, by J. Trevelyan.—Fifty years' influence, by V. Purcell.—To oppose the stream, by I. F. Stone.—Civil disobedience and morals, by M. Scott.—Prophets and priests, by E. Fromm.—Would civilization survive a nuclear war? By L. Pauling.—The relevance of style, by A. Huxley.—A philosophical debt, by H. Read.—Some personal impressions of Russell as a philosopher. Some remarks on sense-perception. By C. D. Broad.—erception. By C. D. Broad.—Reflections of a physicist, by M. Born.—An early appreciation, by H. Reichenbach.—Rudolf Carnap: the cross currents, by M. Reichenbach.—Russell's concept of philosophy, by W. Bloch.—An appraisal of Bertrand Russell's philosophy, by A. J. Ayer.—Existence and description in formal logic, by D. Scott.—Mathematical logic: whaEssays in his honour edited by Ralph Schoenman. [1st American ed.] Boston, Little, Brown [1967, i.e. 1968] 326 p. 23 cm. "An Atlantic monthly press book." Contents.Contents.—Fifty years; 1916-1966, by C. Malleson.—An old fr
1. Russell, Bertrand Russell, 3d earl, 1877- I. Schoenman, Ralph, ed.

CLARK, Ronald William. 192 B
The life of Bertrand Russell / Ronald W. Clark. 1st American ed. New York : Knopf, 1976, c1975. 766 p., [16] leaves of plates : ports. ; 25 cm. Includes index. Bibliography: p. [654]-662. [B1649.R94C55 1976] 75-8226 ISBN 0-394-49059-2 : 17.50
1. Russell, Bertrand Russell, 3d Earl, 1872-1970. I. Title. **BIP**

CRAWSHAY-WILLIAMS, Rupert. 192 B
Russell remembered. London, New York, Oxford U.P., 1970. [7], 163 p., plate. port. 23 cm. Includes bibliographical references. [B1649.R94C7] 75-543158 ISBN 0-19-211197-3 40/-
1. Russell, Bertrand Russell, 3d Earl, 1872-1970. I. Title.

GOTTSCHALK, Herbert, 1919- 192
Bertrand Russell; a life. Translated from the German by Edward Fitzgerald. New York, Roy Publishers [1966, c1965] 128 p. port. 21 cm. Bibliographical footnotes. [B1649.R94G653 1966] 66-10773
1. Russell, Bertrand Russell, 3d earl, 1872-1970. **BIP**

HARDY, Godfrey Harold, 1877-1947. 323.44'5'0924 B
Bertrand Russell & Trinity / G. H. Hardy. New York : Arno Press, 1977. p. cm. (The Academic profession) Reprint of the 1942 ed. published by the University Press, Cambridge. [B1649.R94H3 1977] 76-56697 ISBN 0-405-10022-1 lib.bdg. : 10.00
1. Russell, Bertrand Russell, 3d Earl, 1872 1970. 2. Oxford University. Trinity College. 3. Philosophers—Great Britain—Biography. I. Title. II. Series.

RUSSELL, Bertrand, 3rd Earl, 1872- 828'.9'1203
The autobiography of Bertrand Russell, 1872-1914. [1st Amer. ed.] Boston, Little [1967] 356p. illus., facsim., ports. 24cm. Atlantic Monthly Pr. bk. [B1649.R94A32] 67-14453 7.95
I. Title.

RUSSELL, Bertrand Russell. 3rd. Earl, 1872- 828'9'1203
The autobiography of Bertrand Russell, 1914-1944. [1st Amer. ed.] Boston, Little, Brown [1967] v. illus., facsim., ports. 24cm. Atlantic monthly Pr. bk. [B1649.R94A32] 67-14453 8.95
I. Title.

RUSSELL, Bertrand Russell 3rd. Earl 1872- 828'.9'1203
The autobiography of Bertrand Russell; 1872-1914. New York, Bantam [1968,c.1967] 308p. ports. 18cm. (Q3694) [B1649.R94A32] 1.25 pap.,
I. Title.

RUSSELL, Bertrand Russell, 3rd Earl, 1872- 828'.9'1203
The autobiography of Bertrand Russell, 1872-1914. [1st American ed.] Boston, Little, Brown [1967] 356 p. illus., facsim., ports. 24 cm. "An Atlantic Monthly Press book." [B1649.R94A32] 67-14453
I. Title. **BIP**

TAIT, Katharine, 1923- 192
My Father, Bertrand Russell / Katharine Tait. 1st ed. New York : Harcourt Brace Jovanovich, [1975] xii, 211 p., [4] leaves of plates : ill ; 22 cm. Includes bibliographical references and index. [B1649.R94T34] 75-15719 ISBN 0-15-130432-7 : 8.95
1. Russell, Bertrand Russell, 3d Earl, 1872-1970. I. Title.

Russell, Cazzie L.

RUSSELL, Cazzie L. 796.32'3'0924
Me, Cazzie Russell [by] Cazzie L. Russell, Jr. Westwood, N. J., F. H. Revell Co. [1967] 122 p. illus., ports. 21 cm. [GV884.R8A3] 67-14778
I. Title.

RUSSELL, Cazzie L. 796.32'3'0924
Me, Cazzie Russell [by] Cazzie L. Russell, Jr. Westwood. N. J., Revell [1967] 122p. illus., ports. 21cm. [GV884.R8A3] 67-14778 3.50 bds.,
I. Title.

Russell, Charles Marion,

RUSSELL, Charles Marion, 1864-1926. 927.5
Paper talk; illustrated letters of Charles M. Russell. Introd. and commentary by Frederic G. Renner. Fort Worth, Tex., Amon Carter Museum of Western Art [1962] 120p. illus. (part col.) ports., facsims, 30cm. [ND237.R75A33] 62-12663
I. Renner, Frederic Gordon, 1897- II. Amon Carter Museum of Western Art, Fort Worth, Tex. III. Title.

Russell, Charles Marion, 1864-1826.

MCCRACKEN, Harold, 1894- 927.5
The Charles M. Russell book; the life and work of the cowboy artist. Garden City, N.Y., Doubleday, [1957] 236 p illus., col. plates, ports. 35 cm. Bibliographical references included in "Notes" (p. 232-233) [ND237.R75M3] 759.13 57-11431
1. Russell, Charles Marion, 1864-1826. 2. The West in art.

Russell, Charles Marion, 1864-1926.

GARST, Doris Shannon, 1899- 927.5
Cowboy-artist: Charles M. Russell. New York, Messner [1960] 192 p. 22 cm. Includes bibliography. [ND237.R75G3] 60-7057
1. Russell, Charles Marion, 1864-1926. I. Title.

Russell, Charles Marion, 1864-1926.

ADAMS, Ramon Frederick, 1889- v. 12
Charles M. Russell,the cowboy artist a biography by Ramon F. Adams and Homer E. Britzman, with bibliographical check list by Karl Yost. [3d. ed.]Pasadena, Calif., Trail's End Pub. Co. 350 p. illus., col. plates, ports. 24 cm. 68-64570
1. Russell, Charles Marion, 1864-1926. I. Britzman, Homer Elwood, 1901- joint author. II. Yost, Karl, 1911- III. Title.

GARST, Doris Shannon, 1899- 709'.24 B
Cowboy-artist: Charles M. Russell. New York, Messner [1960] 192 p. 22 cm. Includes bibliography. A biography of the painter and sculptor who spent his boyhood yearning to go west, fulfilled his own dream of illustrating the life of the cowboy, and finally won recognition for his realistic portrayal of the Old West. [ND237.R75G3] 92 AC 68
1. Russell, Charles Marion, 1864-1926. I. Title.

LINDERMAN, Frank Bird, 1868-1938. 927.5
Recollections of Charley Russell. Edited by H. G. Merriam, with drawings by Charley Russell. [1st ed.] Norman, University of Oklahoma Press [1963] xxxii, 148 p. illus. (part col.) ports. 23 cm. Bibliographical footnotes. [ND237.R75L5] 63-18074
1. Russell, Charles Marion, 1864-1926. I. Title. **BIP**

MCCRACKEN, Harold, 1894- 759.13
The Charles M. Russell book; the life and work of the cowboy artist. Garden City, N. Y., Doubleday, 1957. 236p. illus., col. plates, ports. 35cm. 'First edition after the limited edition of 250 copies.' Bibliographical references included in 'Notes' (p. 232-233) [ND237.R75M3] 927.5 57-11431
1. Russell, Charles Marion, 1864-1926. I. Title.

RENNER, Frederic Gordon, 1877- 709'.24
Charles Marion Russell; greatest of all western artists, by Frederic G. Renner. Washington, Potomac Corral, The Westerners, 1968. 24 p. illus., port. 23 cm. (The Great western series, no. 2) [ND237.R75R4] 68-26566
1. Russell, Charles Marion, 1864-1926.

RUSSELL, Austin, 1887- 759.13
C. M. R.: Charles M. Ressell, cowboy artist, a biography. New York, Twayne Publishers [1957] 247p. illus. 23cm. Includes bibliography. [ND237.R75R8] [ND237.R75R8] 927.5 57-2024 57-2024
1. Russell, Charles Marion, 1864-1926. I. Title.

RUSSELL, Austin, 1887- 759.13
C. M. R.: Charles M. Russell, cowboy artist, a biography. New York, Twayne Publishers [1957] 247p. illus. 23cm. Includes bibliography. [ND237.R75R8] 927.5 57-2024
1. Russell, Charles Marion, 1864-1926. I. Title.

RUSSELL, Charles Marion, 1864-1926. 927.5
Paper talk; illustrated letters of Charles M. Russell. Introd. and commentary by Frederic G. Renner. Fort Worth, Tex., Amon Carter Museum of Western Art [1962] 120p. illus. (part col.) ports., facsims, 30cm. [ND237.R75A33] 62-12663
I. Renner, Frederic Gordon, 1897- II. Amon Carter Museum of Western Art, Fort Worth, Tex. III. Title.

SHELTON, Lola 927.5
Charles Marion Russell; cowboy, artist, friend. New York, Dodd [c.]1962. 230p. illus. 24cm. Bibl. 61-15986 4.00
1. Russell, Charles Marion, 1864-1926. I. Title.

SHELTON, Lola. 927.5
Charles Marion Russell; cowboy, artist, friend New York Dodd, Mead, 1962. 230 p. illus. 24 cm. Includes bibliography. [ND237.R75S5] 61-15986
1. Russell, Charles Marion, 1864-1926. I. Title.

Russell, Daniel Lindsay, 1845-1908.

CROW, Jeffrey J. 975.6'04'0924 B
Maverick Republican in the Old North State : a political biography of Daniel L. Russell / Jeffrey J. Crow and Robert F. Durden. Baton Rouge : Louisiana State University Press, c1977. p. cm. (Southern biography series) Includes bibliographical references and index. [F259.R87C76] 77-3657 ISBN 0-8071-0291-1 : 14.95
1. Russell, Daniel Lindsay, 1845-1908. 2. North Carolina—Governors—Biography. 3. North Carolina—Politics and government—1865-1950. 4. Reconstruction—North Carolina. I. Durden, Robert Franklin, joint author. II. Title. III. Series. BIP

Russell, Dora Winifred Black Russell, Countess, 1894-

RUSSELL, Dora Winifred Black Russell, Countess, 1894- 301.41'2'0924 B
The tamarisk tree : my quest for liberty and love / by Dora Russell. 1st American ed. New York : Putnam, 1975. 304 p., [4] leaves of plates : ill. ; 25 cm. Includes index. [HQ1595.5.R85A36 1975] 75-18634 ISBN 0-399-11576-5 : 9.95
1. Russell, Dora Winifred Black Russell, Countess, 1894- 2. Russell, Bertrand Russell, 3d Earl, 1872-1970. 3. Feminism—Great Britain. I. Title.

Russell E.

RUSSELL E. 925.8
Belored professor life and times of William Dodge Frost. New York, Vantage qFrost, William Dodge, 1867-1957. 60-15570
I. Title.

Russell, Elbert,

RUSSELL, Elbert, 1871-1951. 922.8673
Elbert Russell, Quaker: an autobiography. Jackson, Jackson, Tenn., Friendly Press [1956] 376p. illus. 24cm. [BX7795.R83A3] 56-5957
I. Title.

Russell family.

THOMSON, Gladys Scott. 923.242
Life in a noble household, 1641-1700. With a foreword by G. M. Trevelyan. [Ann Arbor] University of Michigan Press [1959] 406 p. 21 cm. (Ann Arbor paperbacks, AA27) [DA377.2.R8T45 1959] 59-964
1. Russell family. 2. England—Soc. life & cust. 3. Home economics—Hist. 4. Prices—Gt. Brit.—Hist. 5. Bedford, William Russell, 1st duke of, 1613-1700. I. Title.

Russell, George William, Lord, 1790-1846.

BLAKISTON, Georgiana. 914.2'03'70924 B
Lord William Russell and his wife, 1815-1846. [Wilmington, Del.] Scholarly Resources [1973, c1972] xvii, 566 p. illus. 24 cm. Bibliography: p. 545-547. [DA46.R88B53 1973] 73-75710 ISBN 0-8420-1681-3 17.50
1. Russell, George William, Lord, 1790-1846. 2. Russell, Elizabeth Anne, Lady, 1793-1874. I. Title. BIP

Russell, George William, 1867-1935.

KAIN, Richard Morgan, 1908- 828'.8'09 B
George Russell (A. E.) / Richard M. Kain and James H. O'Brien. Lewisburg [Pa.] : Bucknell University Press, [1974] c1975. p. cm. (The Irish writers series) Bibliography: p. [PR6035.U7Z69 1975] 72-3252 ISBN 0-8387-1101-4 : 4.50 ISBN 0-8387-1206-1 pbk. : 1.95
1. Russell, George William, 1867-1935. I. O'Brien, James Howard, 1919- joint author.

MERCHANT, Francis. 928.2
A. E.: an Irish Promethean; a study of the contribution of George William Russell to world culture. Columbia, S. C., Benedict College Press, 1954. 242p. 23cm. Bibliography: p. 231-236. [PR6035.U7Z72] 54-31883
1. Russell, George William, 1867-1935. I. Title.

RUSSELL, George William, 1867-1935. 928.2
Letters from AE. Selected and edited by Alan Denson. With a foreword by Monk Gibbon. London, New York, Abelard-Schuman [1962, c1961] 288 p. illus. 23 cm. [PR6035.U7254 1962] 60-13700
I. Denson, Alan, ed.

Russell, George William, 1867-1935, Biography.

SUMMERFIELD, Henry. 828'.8'09 B
That myriad-minded man; a biography of Geroge William Russell "A. E.," 1867-1935. Totowa, N.J., Rowman and Littlefield [1974] p. Includes bibliographical references. [PR6035.U7Z83] 74-2161 ISBN 0-87471-536-9
1. Russell, George William, 1867-1935—Biography. I. Title.

Russell, James William.

RUSSELL, James William. 616.85'8'0924
The stranger in the mirror, by James William Russell as told to Edward R. Sammis. [1st ed.] New York, Harper & Row [1968] vi, 215 p. 21 cm. [CT275.R8825A3] 68-11743
I. Sammis, Edward R. II. Title.

Russell, John Peter, 1858-1930.

SALTER, Elizabeth, 1918- 759.994 B
The lost Impressionist : a biography of John Peter Russell / [by] Elizabeth Salter. London : Angus and Robertson, 1976. [11] , 209 p., [16] p. of plates : ill. (some col.), ports. ; 23 cm. Includes index. Bibliography: p. 205-206. [ND1105.R87S24] 76-363397 ISBN 0-207-95566-2 : £5.80
1. Russell, John Peter, 1858-1930. I. Title.

Russell, John Russell, 1st Earl, 1792-1878.

PREST, John M. 942.081'092'4 B
Lord John Russell [by] John Prest. Columbia, University of South Carolina Press [1972] xvi, 558 p. illus. 24 cm. Bibliography: [432]-442. [DA564.R8P73 1972b] 72-5340 ISBN 0-87249-269-9
1. Russell, John Russell, 1st Earl, 1792-1878. BIP

WALPOLE, Spencer, Sir, 1839-1907. 942.081'0924 B
The life of Lord John Russell. New York, Haskell House Publishers, 1969. 2 v. ports. 23 cm. Reprint of the 1889 ed. Bibliographical footnotes. [DA536.R9W2 1969] 68-25281
1. Russell, John Russell, 1st Earl, 1792-1878. I. Title.

WALPOLE, Spencer, Sir, 1839-1907. 942.081'0924 B
The life of Lord John Russell. New York, Greenwood Press [1968] 2 v. ports. 23 cm. Reprint of the 1889 ed. Bibliographical footnotes. [DA536.R9W2 1968] 68-31010
1. Russell, John Russell, 1st Earl, 1792-1878. I. Title. BIP

Russell, Lillian, 1861-1922.

O'CONNOR, Richard, 1915- 792'.028'0924 B
Duet in diamonds; the flamboyant saga of Lillian Russell and Diamond Jim Brady in America's gilded age, by John Burke. New York, Putnam [1972] 286 p. illus. 22 cm. Bibliography: p. 269-271. [PN2287.R83O25] 75-187133 7.95
1. Russell, Lillian, 1861-1922. 2. Brady, James Buchanan, 1856-1917. I. Title.

RATHER, Lois, 1905- 792'.028'0924
Two lilies in America: Lillian Russell and Lillie Langtry [by] Lois Rather. Oakland, Ca[lif.] Rather Press, 1973. 87 p. illus. 24 cm. Limited to 101 copies. No. 94. Includes bibliographical references. [PN2287.R83R3] 74-154264
1. Russell, Lillian, 1861-1922. 2. Langtry, Lillie, 1853-1929. I. Title.

Russell, Lucy (Phillips)

RUSSELL, Lucy (Phillips) 1862- 920.7
A rare pattern. Chapel Hill, University of North Carolina Press [1957] 185p. 23cm. Autobiographical. [CT275.R8845A3] 57-4591
I. Title.

Russell, Mary Baptist, 1829-1898.

MCARDLE, Mary Aurelia. 922.273
California's pioneer Sister of Mercy, Mother Mary Baptist Russell, 1829-1898. Fresno, Calif., Academy Library Guild, 1954. 204p. illus. 23cm. [BX4705.R74M3] 56-36570
1. Russell, Mary Baptist, 1829-1898. I. Title.

Russell, Robert

RUSSELL, Robert 920.936214
To catch an angel; adventures in the world I cannot see. New York, Popular Lib. [1963, c.1962] 206p. 18cm. (M2031) .60 pap.,
I. Title. BIP

RUSSELL, Robert, 1924- 920.936214
To catch an angel; adventures in the world I cannot see. New York, PopularLib. [1966, c.1962] 206p. 18cm (60-2124) .60 pap.,
I. Title.

RUSSELL, Robert, 1924- 920.936214
To catch an angel; adventures in the world I cannot see. New York, Vanguard Press [1962] 317 p. 22 cm. Autobiographical. [HV1792.R8A3] 62-11209
I. Title.

Russell, Rosalind.

RUSSELL, Rosalind. 791.43'028'0924 B
Life is a banquet / by Rosalind Russell and Chris Chase. 1st ed. New York : Random House, c1977. xxii, 260 p., [16] leaves of plates : ill. ; 24 cm. Includes index. [PN2287.R86A35] 77-6001 ISBN 0-394-42134-5 : 10.00
1. Russell, Rosalind. 2. Actors—United States—Biography. I. Chase, Chris, joint author. II. Title. BIP

Russell, William.

RUSSELL, William. 363.2'092'4 B
The experiences of a French detective officer / "Waters" (pseud. of William Russell). New York : Arno Press, 1976. 317 p. ; 21 cm. (Literature of mystery and detection) Reprint of the ed. published by W. Glaisher, London. [HV7911.R87A33 1976] 75-32779 ISBN 0-405-07907-9 : 17.00
1. Russell, William. 2. Detectives—France—Correspondence, reminiscences, etc. I. Title. II. Series.

Russell, William Felton,

RUSSELL, William Felton. 1934- 796.3230924
Go up for glory [by] Bill Russell, as told to William McSweeny [New York] Berkley [1966] 175p. 18cm. (Medallion bk., X1365) [GV885.R82] .60 pap.,
I. McSweeny, William Francis. II. McSweeny, William Francis. III. Title.

RUSSELL, William Felton, 1934- 796.3230924
Go up for glory, by Bill Russell, as told to William McSweeny. New York, Coward-McCann [1966] 224 p. illus., ports. 22 cm. Autobiographical. [GV885.R82] 66-14593
I. McSweeny, William Francis. II. Title. BIP

Russell, William Felton, 1934-

DEEGAN, Paul J., 1937- 796.32'3'0924 B
Bill Russell, by Paul J. Deegan. Illustrated by Harold Henriksen. Mankato, Minn., Creative Education; distributed by Childrens Press, Chicago [1973] c1974. 31 p. illus. (part col.) 25 cm. (Creative's superstars) "Prepared for the publisher by Amecus Street." Biography of an outstanding athlete, who gained fame as a basketball player with the Boston Celtics. [GV884.R86D43] 92 73-13749 ISBN 0-87191-281-3 4.95
1. Russell, William Felton, 1934- I. Henriksen, Harold, illus. II. Amecus Street, inc. III. Title. BIP

HIRSHBERG, Albert, 1909- 927.96323
Bill Russell of the Boston Celtics. New York, Messner [c.1963] 191p. ports. 22cm. 63-16788 3.25; 3.19 lib. ed. net,
1. Russell, William Felton, 1934- I. Title.

RUSSELL, William 796.3230924
Felton. 1934-
Go up for glory [by] Bill Russell, as told to William McSweeny [New York] Berkley [1966] 175p. 18cm. (Medallion bk., X1365) [GV885.R82] .60 pap.,
I. McSweeny, William Francis. II. McSweeny, William Francis. III. Title.

RUSSELL, William 796.3230924
Felton, 1934-
Go up for glory, by Bill Russell, as told to William McSweeny. New York, Coward-McCann [1966] 224 p. illus., ports. 22 cm. Autobiographical. [GV885.R82] 66-14593
I. McSweeny, William Francis. II. Title.
BIP

RUSSELL, William 796.32'3'0924 B
Felton, 1934-
Second wind : the memoirs of an opinionated man / Bill Russell and Taylor Branch. 1st ed. New York : Random House, c1979. 265 p. ; 22 cm. [GV884.R86A35] 79-4780 ISBN 0-394-50385-6 : 10.00
1. Russell, William Felton, 1934- 2. Boston Celtics (Basketball team) 3. Basketball players—United States—Biography. I. Branch, Taylor, joint author. II. Title. BIP

Russell, William Felton, 1934- — Juvenile literature.

KLEIN, Dave. 796.32'3'0922 B
Pro basketball's big men. Illustrated with photos. New York, Random House [1973] 151 p. illus. 22 cm. (Pro basketball library) Brief biographies of three prominent basketball stars renowned for their skill and height. [GV884.A1K56 1973] 920 73-6743 ISBN 0-394-82627-2 1.95
1. Russell, William Felton, 1934- — Juvenile literature. 2. Chamberlain, Wilton Norman, 1936- —Juvenile literature. 3. Abdul-Jabbar, Kareem, 1947- —Juvenile literature. 4. Basketball—Biography—Juvenile literature. I. Title.

Russia

BOURGEOIS, Charles, 1887- 922.247
A priest in Russia and the Baltic. With an introd. by Sir David Kelly, translated from the French by the Earl of Wicklow. Dublin, Clonmore and Reynolds [1953] 146p. illus. 20cm. [BX4705.B728A32] 55-16784
1. Russia—Church history—1917- I. Title.

KROPOTKIN, Petr 923.347
Alekseevich, kniaz, 1842-1921.
Memoirs of a revolutionist. Ed. by James Allen Rogers. Garden City, N. Y., Doubleday [c.]1962. 338p. (Anchor bks., A287) Bibl. 62-16035 1.45 pap.,
1. Russia—Pol. & govt. 2. Anarchism and anarchists. I. Title.

Russia—Biography.

BABEL', Isaak 928.917
Emmanuilovich, 1894-1941.
Isaac Babel: the lonely years, 1925-1939; unpublished stores and private correspondence. Translated from the Russian by Andrew R. MacAndrew and Max Hayward. Edited and with an introd. by Nathalie Babel. New York, Farrar, Straus [1964] xxviii, 402 p. illus., ports. 21 cm. [PG3476.B2A25] 64-22499
1. Title: The lonely years. I. Title.

BRYANT, Louise, 947.084'1'0922
1890-1936.
Mirrors of Moscow. With five illus. by Cesare. Westport, Conn., Hyperion Press [1973, c1923] 209 p. ports. 23 cm. Reprint of the ed. published by T. Seltzer, New York. [DK253.B7 1973] 73-834 ISBN 0-88355-030-X 12.75
1. Russia—Biography. 2. Russia—History—Revolution, 1917-1921. I. Title.
BIP

INSTITUT zur Erforschung 920.047
der UdSSR.
Biographic directory of the USSR, compiled by the Institute for the Study of the USSR, Munich, Germany. [General editor: Wladimir S. Merzalow] New York, Scarecrow Press, 1958. ix, 782p. 23cm. [DK268.A1I5] 58-7804
1. Russia Biog. I. Merisalov, V. S., ed. II. Title.

SIMMONDS, George W. 920.047
Soviet leaders, edited by George W. Simmonds. New York, T. Y. Crowell Co. [1967] x, 405 p. 24 cm. (A Crowell reference book) Includes bibliographies. [DK275.A1S5] 67-12409
1. Russia—Biography. I. Title.

Russia—Biography—Dictionaries.

INSTITUT zur Erforschung 920.047
der UdSSR.
Who was who in the USSR; a biographic directory containing 5,015 biographies of prominent Soviet historical personalities. Compiled by the Institute for the Study of the USSR, Munich, Germany. Edited by Heinrich E. Schulz, Paul K. Urban [and] Andrew I. Lebed. Metuchen, N.J., Scarecrow Press, 1972. 677 p. 28 cm. [CT1212.I57] 70-161563 ISBN 0-8108-0441-7
1. Russia—Biography—Dictionaries. I. Schulz, Heinrich E., ed. II. Urban, Paul K., ed. III. Lebed', Andrei, ed. IV. Title.

TELBERG, Ina, comp. 920.047
Who's who in Soviet social sciences, humanities, art and government. Compiled by Ina Telberg. [New York, Telberg Book Co., 1961] v. 147 l. 28 cm. "Based on the information in the 3rd edition of 'Malaia Sovetskaia entsiklopedia' Moscow, 1958-1961." [DK275.A1W5] 61-16892
1. Russia — Biog. — Dictionaries. I. Title.

WHO'S who in Soviet 920.047
social sciences, humanities, art and government. comp. by Ina Telberg. [New York, Telberg Bk. Co., c.1961] v 147p. 28cm. 'Based on the information in the 3rd edition of 'Malaia Sovetskaia entsiklopedia' Moscow, 1958-1961.' 61-16892 9.80 bds.,
1. Russia—Biog.—Dictionaries. I. Telberg, Ina, comp.

WHO'S who in the USSR. 920.047
1965-66 [Montreal] Intercontinental Bk. & Pub. Co. [New York, Scarecrow] 1966. 1189p. 21cm. Vs. for 1965/66 comp. by the Inst. for the Study of the USSR, Munich. A biog. dicty. containing 5.000 biogs of prominent personalities in the USSR. Eds.: 1965-66. Andrew I. Lebed; Heinrich E. Schulz, Stephen S. Taylor [DK275.A1W53] 62-6474 25.00
1. Russia—Biog.—Dictionaries. I. Institut zur Erforschung der UdSSR.

Russia—Court and courtiers.

IN the Russian style 390'.22'0947
/ edited by Jacqueline Onassis, with the cooperation of the Metropolitan Museum of Art ; introd. by Audrey Kennett ; designed by Bryant Holme. New York : Viking Press, 1976. 184 p. : ill. ; 29 cm. (A Studio book) Bibliography: p. 183. [DK32.3.I5 1976] 76-54159 ISBN 0-670-39696-6 : 14.95
1. Russia Court and courtiers. 2. Russia—Nobility. 3. Russia—Social life and customs. 4. Costume—Russia. 5. Russia—Kings and rulers—Biography. I. Onassis, Jacqueline Kennedy, 1929- II. New York (City). Metropolitan Museum of Art.

Russia—Description and travel.

HUME, George, 1836- 914.7'03'8
Thirty-five years in Russia. New York, Arno Press, 1971. xxiii, 319 p. illus., fold. map, ports. 24 cm. (Russia observed) Reprint of the 1914 ed. [DK26.H8 1971] 79-115548 ISBN 0-405-03082-7
1. Russia—Description and travel. I. Title.
BIP

LONDONDERRY, Frances 914.7'03'7
Anne Emily (Vane-Tempest) Vane, Marchioness of, 1800-1865.
Russian journal of Lady Londonderry, 1836-37, edited by W. A. L. Seaman and J. R. Sewell. London, J. Murray, 1973. [9], 185, [8] p. illus., 2 ports. 23 cm. Includes index. [DK26.L85 1973] 73-174468 ISBN 0-7195-2851-8
1. Russia—Description and travel. 2. Russia—Court and courtiers. I. Title.
Available from Transatlantic Arts, for 9.50.

Russia—Foreign relations—1894-1917.

KALMYKOV, Andrei 947.08'0924 B
Dmitrievich, 1870-1941.
Memoirs of a Russian diplomat; outposts of the Empire, 1893-1917, by Andrew D. Kalmykow. Edited by Alexandra Kalmykow. New Haven, Yale University Press, 1971. xv, 290 p. ports. 25 cm. (Yale Russian and East European studies, 10) [DK254.K176A3] 67-13440 ISBN 0-300-01201-2 12.50
1. Russia—Foreign relations—1894-1917. I. Title. II. Series. BIP

Russia—History—Nicholas I, 1825-1855.

DALLAS, George 947'.07'0924
Mifflin, 1792-1864.
Diary of George Mifflin Dallas, United States Minister to Russia, 1837-1839. New York, Arno Press, 1970 [c1892] 214 p. port. 23 cm. (Russia observed) [DK210.D33 1970] 70-115527 ISBN 0-405-03019-3
1. Russia—History—Nicholas I, 1825-1855. 2. Russia—Court and courtiers. I. Title.

Russia—History—Revolution, 1917-1921—Personal narratives.

GALITZINE, 914.7'03'841 B
Tatiana, princess, 1909-
The Russian Revolution; childhood recollections [by] Tatiana Galitzine. Princeton, N.J., c1972] 85 p. illus., ports. 23 cm. [DK265.7.G25] 72-263
1. Russia—History—Revolution, 1917-1921—Personal narratives. I. Title.

VRANGEL, Petr 923.547
Nikolaevich, baron, 1878-1928.
Always with honour; [memoirs of General Wrangel] With a foreword by Herbert Hoover. [1st ed.] New York, R. Speller, 1957. 356 p. illus. 22 cm. (Makers of history series) Translation of 3 ANHCKH; HOROP6 1916-HOROP. 1920 (transliterated: Zapiski; noiabr 1916-noiabr 1920) [DK254.V7A35] 57-11885
1. Russia — Hist. Revolution, 1917-1921 — Personal narratives. I. Title.

WILLIAMS, Albert 947.084'1'0924
Rhys, 1883-1962.
Through the Russian Revolution. With a biographical sketch of the author by Joshua Kunitz. New York, Monthly Review Press [1967] cxxii, 311 p. illus. (part col.) 22 cm. [DK265.W46 1967] 67-19257
1. Russia—History—Revolution, 1917-1921—Personal narratives. 2. Communism—Russia I. Kunitz, Joshua, 1896- II. Title. BIP

Russia—History—1613-1689.

GORDON, Patrick, 947'.04'0924 B
1635-1699.
Passages from the diary of General Patrick Gordon of Auchleuchries in the years 1635-1699. New York, Da Capo Press, 1968. xxxvi, 244 p. port. 26 cm. (A Da Capo Press reprint edition.) (Russia through European eyes, no. 3) Reprint of the 1859 ed. [DK114.5.G6A33 1968] 68-27012
1. Russia—History—1613-1689. 2. Russia—History—Peter I, 1689-1725. 3. Swedish-Polish War, 1655-1660. I. Title. II. Series.

Russia—Kings and rulers.

BASSECHES, Nikolaus. 923.247
Stalin; translated from the German by E. W. Dickes. [1st ed.] New York, Dutton, 1952. 384 p. 22 cm. [DK268.S8B278] 52-10440
I. Stalin, Iosif, 1879- II. Title.

HINGLEY, Ronald. 947 B
The tsars, 1533-1917. [1st American ed.] New York, Macmillan [1968] 320 p. illus. (part col.), facsims., maps, ports. (part col.) 26 cm. Bibliography: p. 309-313. [DK37.6.H54 1968] 68-24114
1. Russia—Kings and rulers. 2. Russia—History. I. Title.

SALTUS, Edgar Evertson, 1855- 947
1921.
The imperial orgy; an account of the tsars from the first to the last. New York, AMS Press [1970] ix, 237 p. illus., ports. 22 cm. Reprint of the 1920 ed. [DK37.6.S3 1970] 74-121357
1. Russia—Kings and rulers. 2. Russia—Courts and courtiers. I. Title. BIP

Russia—Politics and government.

KROPOTKIN, Petr 947.08'0924 B
Alekseevich, kniaz', 1842-1921.
Memoirs of a revolutionist, by Peter Kropotkin. With a new introd. and notes by Nicolas Walter. New York, Dover Publications [1971] xxxiv, 557 p., port. 22 cm. [HX915.K92 1971] 75-121700 ISBN 0-486-22485-6 4.00
1. Russia—Politics and government. 2. Anarchism and anarchists. I. Walter, Nicolas. II. Title.

KROPOTKIN, Petr 947'.08'0924 (B)
Alekseevich, kniaz, 1842-1921.
Memoirs of a revolutionist, Edited by James Allen Rogers. Gloucester, Mass., P. Smith, 1967 [c1962] xviii, 338 p. 21 cm. "Bibliography (of major works of Kropotkin in English)": p. [316] Bibliographical references included in "Notes" (p. [317]-332) [HX915.K92] 67-2480
1. Russian — Pol. & govt. 2. Anarchism and anarchists. I. Rogers, James Allen, 1929- ed. II. Title.

KROPOTKIN, Petr 947.08'0924 B
Alekseevich, Kniaz, 1842-1921.
Memoirs of a revolutionist. New York, Horizon Press [1968] xxxviii, 519 p. 2 ports. 24 cm. The 1899 ed., with Georg Brandes' introd., reprinted with a new foreword by Barnett Newman, a pref. by Paul Goodman, and an index. "[First] published in 'The Atlantic monthly' (September 1898, to September 1899), under the title, 'The autobiography of a revolutionist.'" [HX915.K92 1968] 68-54186 10.00
1. Russia—Politics and government. 2. Anarchism and anarchists. I. Title. BIP

Russia—Politics and government—1894-1917.

MILIUKOV, Pavel 947.08'0924
Nikolaevich, 1859-1943.
Political memoirs, 1905-1917, by Paul Miliukov. Edited by Arthur P. Mendel. Translated by Carl Goldberg Ann Arbor, University of Michigan Press [1967] xviii, 508 p. 24 cm. Translation of Vospominaniia (romanized form) [DK254.M52A313] 67-25341
1. Russia—Politics and government—1894-1917. I. Mendel, Arthur P., ed. II. Title.

TROTSKII, Lev 1879- 923.2
My life [Gloucester, Mass., P. Smith, 1965, c.1930, 1960] xxii, 599p. 21cm. (Universal lib. bk. rebound) Name orig.:Lev Davidovich Bronshtein [DK254.T6A48] 4.50
1. Russia—Pol. & govt.—1894-1917. 2. Russia—Pol. & govt.—1917- I. Title.

TROTSKII, Lev, 1879-1940. 923.247
My life. New York, Grosset & Dunlap [1960] 599 p. 21 cm. (The Universal library, UL-72) [DK254.T6A48] 60-2423
1. Russia — Pol. & govt. — 1894-1917. 2. Russia — Pol. & govt. — 1917- Name originally: Lev Davidovich Bronshtein. I. Title.

TROTSKII, Lev, 947.084'0924 B
1879-1940.
My life [by] Leon Trotsky. Gloucester, Mass., P. Smith, 1970 [c1960] xxii, 599 p. 21 cm. Translation of Moia zhizn' (romanized form) [DK254.T6A48 1970b] 72-20244
1. Russia—Politics and government—1894-1917. 2. Russia—Politics and government—1917- I. Title.

TROTSKII, Lev, 1879- 947.084'0924
1940.
My life [by] Leon Trotsky. New York, Grosset [1973, c.1960] 599 p. 21 cm. (Universal library, UL-77) First published in 1930. [DK254.T6A48 1960] 60-2423 ISBN 0-448-00072-5 pap., 3.85

1. Russia—Politics and government—1894-1917. 2. Russia—Politics and government, 1917- I. Title.

TROTSKII, Lev, 1879-1940. 947.084'0924 B
My life; an attempt at an autobiography [by] Leon Trotsky. With an introd. by Joseph Hansen. New York, Pathfinder Press, 1970. xxxvii, 602 p. 23 cm. (A Merit book) Translation of Moia zhizn' (romanized form) [DK254.T6A48 1970] 73-108715 12.50
1. Russia—Politics and government—1894-1917. 2. Russia—Politics and government—1917- I. Title.

WITTE, Sergei Ivl'evich, graf. 1849-1915 947.08'08'0924
The memoirs of Count Witte. Tr. from the orig. Russian manuscript and ed. by Abraham Yarmolinsky. New York, Fertig, 1967 [1921] xi, 445p. port. 24cm. (romanized: Vospominaniia) Selections tr from (B) 11.00
1. Russia—Pol. & govt.—1894-1917. I. Title.

WITTE, Sergei LUl'evich, graf, 1849-1915. 947.08'0924 (B)
The memoirs of Count Witte. Translated from the original Russian manuscript and edited by Abraham Yarmolinsky. New York, H.Fertig, 1967[1921] xi,445 p. port. 24 cm. Selections translated from Vospominaniia) [DK254.W5A5] 67-24601
1. Russian—Pol. & govt.—1894-1917. I. Yarmolinsky, Avrahm, 1890- ed. and tr. II. Title.

Russia—Politics and government—1953-

KIRK, Irina. 322.4'4'0947
Profiles in Russian resistance / Irina Kirk. New York : Quadrangle/New York Times Book Co., [1975] xix, 297 p. ; 22 cm. [DK274.K55 1975] 74-77945 ISBN 0-8129-0484-2 : 10.95
1. Russia—Politics and government—1953- 2. Dissenters—Russia—Interviews. I. Title. II. Title: Russian resistance. BIP

Russia, Pre-revolutionary—Biog.

LAMB, Harold, 1892- 923.247
Chief of the Cossacks. Illustrated by Robert Frankenberg. New York, Random House [1959] 184p. illus. 22cm. (World landmark books, W-39) [DK118.5.L3] 59-5521
I. Razin, Stepan Timofeevich, d. 1671. II. Title.

POLOVTSOVA, A.A., ed. 920.47
Russkii biograficheskii Slovar; izdan pod nabliudeniem predsiedatelia. I. Russkago Istoricheskago Obshchectva A.A. Poloutsova; 25 v. [Dist. New York, 17, Kraus Reprint Corp., 16 E. 46 St., 1963] 25v. (various p.) 26 cm. set, 775.00 pap., 725.00
1. Russia, Pre-revolutionary—Biog. I. Title.

RUSSKII Biografcheskii 920.47
Slovar'; Azbuchnyi Ukazatel'imen russkikh dieaiatelei russkago biograficheskago slovaria. New York, Kraus Reprint, 1963. 2v. in 1. 1336p. 58.50
1. Russia, Pre-revolutionary—Biog.

Russia—Social conditions.

PIROGOV, Peter, 1920- 914.7
Why I escaped; the story of Peter Pirogov. New York, Duell, Sloan and Pearce [1950] xi, 336 p. 22 cm. "Translator's preface" signed: Ada Siegel. [DK268.P5A3] 50-6282
1. Russia—Social conditions. 2. Russia—Economic conditions—1918-1945. 3. World War, 1939-1945—Personal narratives, Russian. I. Title.

Russia—Social life and customs.

ALMEDINGEN, Martha Edith, 1898- 823'.9'12
Fanny, by E. M. Almedingen; illustrated by Ian Ribbons. London, Oxford U.P., 1970. x, 166 p. illus. 23 cm. Based on the life of Frances Hermione de Poltoratzky. [CT1218.P59A3 1970b] 75-509468 ISBN 0-19-271317-5 18/-
1. Russia—Social life and customs. I. Poltoratzky, Frances Hermione de, 1850-1916. II. Ribbons, Ian, illus. III. Title.

ALMEDINGEN, Martha Edith, 1898- 914.7'03'80924
Fanny (Frances Hermione de Poltoratzky, 1850-1916) by E. M. Almedingen. Illustrated by Ian Ribbons. [1st American ed.] New York, Farrar, Straus & Giroux [1970] 226 p. illus. 21 cm. (An Ariel book) A compilation of the writings of Frances Poltoratsky, novelist and historian, which tell of her childhood in Russia, France, and England. [CT1218.P59A3 1970] 92 77-109563 3.95
1. Russia—Social life and customs. I. Poltoratzky, Frances Hermione de, 1850-1916. II. Ribbons, Ian, illus. III. Title.

AVINOV, Marie. 914.7'03'840924 B
Marie Avinov; pilgrimage through hell; an autobiography told by Paul Chavchavadze. Englewood Cliffs, N.J., Prentice-Hall [1968] 275 p. port. 24 cm. [DK268.A9A3] 68-27797 6.95
1. Russia—Social life and customs. I. Chavchavadze, Paul. II. Title.

MATTHEWS, Tanya Svetlova. 920.7
Journey between freedoms. Philadelphia, Westminster Press [1951] 281 p. 22 cm. First published in London in 1949 under title: Russian child and Russian wife. [DK267.M36 1951] 51-12739
1. Russia—Social life and customs. I. Title.

Russia (1923- U.S.S.R.) Armiia—Military life.

SOLOVIEV, Mikhail, 1908- 920.5
My nine lives in the Red Army. Translated by Harry C. Stevens. Introd. by Leslie C. Stevens. New York, D. McKay Co. [1955] 308 p. 21 cm. Translation of Zapiski sovetskogo voennogo korrespondenta (romanized) [PN5276.S6A32] 55-1458
1. Russia (1923- U.S.S.R.) Armiia—Military life. 2. War correspondents, Russian—Correspondence, reminiscences, etc. I. Title.

Russia (1923- U.S.S.R.) Komitet gosudarstvennoi bezopasnosti.

SIGL, Rupert, 1925- 327'.12'0924 B
In the claws of the KGB : memoirs of a double agent / Rupert Sigl. Philadelphia : Dorrance, c1978. 247 p. ; 22 cm. [HV8225.S5] 78-105791 ISBN 0-8059-2520-1 : 7.95
1. Russia (1923- U.S.S.R.) Komitet gosudarstvennoi bezopasnosti. 2. Sigl, Rupert, 1925- 3. Intelligence officers—Russia—Biography. I. Title.

Russia (1923- U.S.S.R) Armiia. General'nyi shtab.

SHTEMENKO, Sergei Matveevich. 940.54'21'0924 B
The last six months : Russia's final battles with Hitler's Armies in World War II / S. M. Shtemenko ; translated by Guy Daniels. 1st ed. Garden City, N.Y. : Doubleday, 1977. xi, 436 p., [17] leaves of plates : ill. ; 22 cm. Includes bibliographical references and index. [D764.S46677] 73-18779 ISBN 0-385-00368-4 : 10.00
1. Russia (1923- U.S.S.R) Armiia. General'nyi shtab. 2. Shtemenko, Sergei Matveeich. 3. World War, 1939-1945—Campaigns—Eastern. 4. World War, 1939-1945—Personal narratives, Russian. 5. Generals—Russia—Biography.

Russo, Leslie—Juvenile literature.

HANEY, Lynn. 796.4'1'0924 B
Perfect balance : the story of an elite gymnast / by Lynn Haney ; photos. by Bruce Curtis. New York : Putnam, c1979. 60 p. : ill. ; 28 cm. Follows the career of a young American gymnast as she prepares for the 1980 Olympics to be held in Moscow. Includes profiles of several other prominent figures in gymnastic competition. [GV460.2.R87H36] 92 78-11634 ISBN 0-399-20661-2 : 8.95
1. Russo, Leslie—Juvenile literature. 2. Gymnasts—United States—Biography—Juvenile literature. 3. Gymnastics—Juvenile literature. I. Curtis, Bruce. II. Title. BIP

Russwurm, John Brown, 1799-1851—Juvenile literature.

SAGARIN, Mary. 070'.924 B
John Brown Russwurm; the story of Freedom's journal, freedom's journey. With an introd. by Ernest Kaiser. New York, Lothrop, Lee & Shepard [1970] 160 p. illus., facsims., maps, ports. 22 cm. Bibliography: p. 155-156. A biography of the editor of the first black newspaper in America and governor of the first American colony of freed slaves in Liberia. [E185.97.R89S2] 92 73-101477 3.95
1. Russwurm, John Brown, 1799-1851—Juvenile literature. 2. Freedom's journal—Juvenile literature. I. Title.

Ruth (Biblical character)

GARDINER, George E. 222'.35'0924 B
The romance of Ruth / by George E. Gardiner. Grand Rapids : Kregel Publications, [1977] p. cm. [BS580.R8G37] 77-79187 ISBN 0-8254-2718-5 pbk. : 1.50
1. Bible. O.T.—Biography. 2. Ruth (Biblical character) I. Title. BIP

Ruth (Biblical character)—Juvenile literature.

GRIFFITHS, Kitty Anna. 222'.35'09505
Come, meet Ruth : the story of the book of Ruth / Kitty Anna Griffiths ; illustrated by "Willy". 1st Zondervan ed. Grand Rapids : Zondervan Pub. House, 1978, c1976. 95 p. : ill. ; 21 cm. (Come, meet series) Retells the story of Ruth which describes her devotion and commitment to God. [BS580.R8G74 1978] 78-16723 ISBN 0-310-25261-X : 1.95
1. Ruth (Biblical character)—Juvenile literature. 2. Bible. O.T.—Biography—Juvenile literature. 3. Bible stories, English—O.T. Ruth. I. Willy. II. Title.

Ruth, Charles.

RATH, Ida Ellen 923.973
The Rath trail; non-fiction biography of Charles Rath, Indian trader, merchant, buffalo hunter, hide buyer, railroad grader, and organizer of early day towns and trading posts, a friend of Kit Carson and the Bents, a maker of trails. Wichita 1, Kan., McCormick-Armstrong, 1501 East Douglas [c.1961] 204p. illus. 61-16115 5.00
1. Ruth, Charles. 2. Frontier and pioneer life—The West. I. Title.

Ruth, George Herman, 1894-1948.

CREAMER, Robert W. 796.357'092'4 B
Babe: the legend comes to life [by] Robert W. Creamer. New York, Simon and Schuster [1974] 443 p. illus. 23 cm. [GV865.R8C73] 74-3319 ISBN 0-671-21770-4 9.95
1. Ruth, George Herman, 1895-1948. 2. Baseball. I. Title.

CREAMER, Robert W. 796.357'092'4 B
Babe; the legend comes to life [by] Robert W. Creamer. New York, Pocket Books [1976 c1974] 452 p. 18 cm. [GV865.R8C73] ISBN 0-671-80393-X 2.50 (pbk.)
1. Ruth, George Herman, 1895-1948. 2. Baseball. I. Title.
L.C. card no. of 1974 Simon and Schuster edition: 74-3319.

DANIEL, Daniel Margowitz, 1890- 92
The real Babe Ruth. With anecdotes: I remember Ruth, by H. G. Salsinger. 2d ed. St. Louis, Mo., Sporting News, 1963. 162 p. illus., ports. 24 cm. [GV865.R8D33 1963] 63-24075
1. Ruth, George Herman, 1894-1948. I. Salsinger, Harry G., 1885- II. Title.

HASKINS, James, 1941- 796.357'092'2 B
Babe Ruth and Hank Aaron; the home run kings. Illustrated with photos. New York, Lothrop, Lee & Shepard [1974] 123 p. illus. 22 cm. A dual biography of Babe Ruth and Hank Aaron, from childhood to championship. Includes comparative statistics, batting averages, and famous games. [GV865.R8H37] 920 74-11018 ISBN 0-688-41654-3
1. Ruth, George Herman, 1895-1948. 2. Aaron, Henry, 1934- 3. Batting (Baseball) I. Title. BIP

MEANY, Thomas. 927.96357
Babe Ruth; the big moments of the big fellow. New York, Grosset & Dunlap [1951] 249 p. illus., ports. 20 cm. (The Big league baseball library) [GV865.R8M4] 51-3785
1. Ruth, George Herman, 1894-1948. I. Title.

RICHARDS, Kenneth G., 1926- 796.357'0924
Babe Ruth, by Kenneth Richards. Chicago, Childrens Press [1967] 95 p. illus., ports. 30 cm. (People of destiny: a humanities series) Bibliography: p. 92. [GV865.R8R5] 67-26872
1. Ruth, George Herman, 1895-1948. I. Title.

RICHARDS, Kenneth G., 1926- 796.357'0924 B
Babe Ruth, by Kenneth Richards. Chicago, Childrens Press [1967] 95 p. illus., ports. 30 cm. (People of destiny: a humanities series) Bibliography: p. 92. A biography of the Sultan of Swat, who hit 714 home runs during his illustrious baseball career with the New York Yankees. [GV865.R8R5] 92 AC 68
1. Ruth, George Herman, 1894-1948. I. Title.

RUTH, Claire (Merritt) 927.96357
The Babe and I [by] Mrs. Babe Ruth with Bill Slocum. illus. New York, Avon [1961, c.1959] 128p. (T-513) .35 pap.,
1. Ruth, George Herman, 1894-1958. I. Title.

RUTH, Claire Merritt. 927.96357
The Babe and I, by Mrs. Babe Ruth with Bill Slocum. Englewood Cliffs, N. J., Prentice-Hall [1959] 215 p. illus. 22 cm. [GV865.R8R8] 59-8029
1. Ruth, George Herman, 1894-1948. I. Title.

SMELSER, Marshall. 796.357'092'4 B
The life that Ruth built : a biography / by Marshall Smelser. New York : Quadrangle/New York Times Book Co., [1975] xiv, 592 p. : ill. ; 24 cm. Includes index. Bibliography: p. [569]-570. [GV865.R8S62 1975] 74-24295 ISBN 0-8129-0540-7 : 12.50
1. Ruth, George Herman, 1895-1948. 2. Baseball. I. Title. BIP

SMITH, Robert, 1905- 796.357'092'4
Babe Ruth's America. New York, Crowell [1974] 309 p. illus. 24 cm. [GV865.R8S64] 74-8737 ISBN 0-690-00502-4 10.00
1. Ruth, George Herman, 1895-1948. I. Title.

SOBOL, Ken. 796.357'092'4 [B]
Babe Ruth & the American dream. Introduction by Dick Schaap. New York, Ballantine [1974] 269 p. illus. 18 cm. Bibliography: p. 256-260. [GV865.R8S72] 74-9051 1.50 (pbk.)
1. Ruth, George Herman, 1895-1948. 2. Baseball. I. Title.

VAN RIPER, Guernsey, 1909- 927.96357
Babe Ruth, baseball boy. Illustrated by Seymour Fleishman. Indianapolis, Bobbs-Merrill [1959] 192 p. illus. 20 cm. (Childhood of famous Americans) [GV865.R8V3] 59-13992
1. Ruth, George Herman, 1894-1948. I. Title. II. Series.

VAN RIPER, Guernsey, 1909- 927.96357
Babe Ruth, baseball boy; illustrated by

William B. Ricketts. [1st ed.] Indianapolis, Bobbs-Merrill [1954] 192p. illus. 20cm. (The Childhood of famous Americans series [77]) [GV865.R8V3] 54-6066
1. Ruth, George Herman, 1894-1948. I. Title.

WAGENHEIM, Kal. 796.357'092'4 B
Babe Ruth; his life and legend. New York, Praeger Publishers [1974] x, 274 p. illus. 25 cm. [GV865.R8W3] 73-13049 ISBN 0-275-19980-0 7.95
1. Ruth, George Herman, 1895-1948. 2. Baseball. I. Title.

Ruth, George Herman, 1894-1948—Juvenile literature.

ALLEN, Lee, 1915- 796.3570924 B
Babe Ruth; his story in baseball. New York, Putnam [1966] 189 p. 22 cm. [GV865.R8A7] 66-14317
1. Ruth, George Herman, 1894-1948—Juvenile literature. I. Title.

FARR, Naunerle C. 796.357'0922 B
Babe Ruth ; Jackie Robinson / [written by Naunerle C. Farr]. West Haven, Conn. : Pendulum Press, c1979. 63 p. : ill. ; 21 cm. (Pendulum illustrated biography series : Sports) Babe Ruth illustrated by Tony Caravana; Jackie Robinson illustrated by Nardo Cruz. "A Vincent Fago production." Presents in comic strip form the lives and careers of two renowned baseball players. [GV865.A1F32] 920 79-83596 ISBN 0-88301-371-1 : 4.50 ISBN 0-88301-359-2 pbk. : 1.45
1. Ruth, George Herman, 1894-1948—Juvenile literature. 2. Robinson, John Roosevelt, 1919-1972—Juvenile literature. 3. Baseball players—United States—Biography—Juvenile literature. I. Caravana, Tony. II. Cruz, Nardo. III. Farr, Naunerle C. Jackie Robinson. 1979. IV. Title. V. Series. BIP

VERRAL, Charles Spain. 796.357'092'4 B
Babe Ruth, Sultan of Swat / by Charles Spain Verral. Champaign, Ill. : Garrard Pub. Co., c1976. 95 p. : ill. ; 24 cm. [GV865.R8V47] 75-38825 ISBN 0-8116-6679-4 lib.bdg. : 3.84
1. Ruth, George Herman, 1895-1948—Juvenile literature. 2. Baseball—Juvenile literature. I. Title.

Ruthenberg, Charles Emil, 1882-1927.

JOHNSON, Oakley C 1890- 923.273
The day is coming; life and work of Charles E. Ruthenberg, 1882-1927. New York, International Publishers [1958, c1957] 192p. 21cm. [HX84.R8J6] 57-14538
1. Ruthenberg, Charles Emil, 1882-1927. 2. Socialism in the U. S. 3. Communism—U. S. I. Title.

Rutherford, Ernest Rutherford, baron, 1871-1937.

ANDRADE, Edward Neville da Costa, 1887- 925.3
Rutherford and the nature of the atom. [1st ed.] Garden City, N.Y., Doubleday [1964] xix, 218 p. illus., ports. 19 cm. (Science study series, S35) [QC16.R8A5] 64-11734
1. Rutherford, Ernest Rutherford, baron, 1871-1937. I. Title. II. Series. BIP

BIRKS, J. B., ed. 925.3
Rutherford at Manchester. New York, Benhamin, 1963[c.1962] x, 364p. illus., ports., facsim. 23cm. Bibl. 63-4940 12.50
1. Rutherford, Ernest Ruthorford, Baron, 1871-1937. 2. Victoria University of Manchester. 3. Nuclear Physics—Addresses, essays, lectures. I. Title.

KELMAN, Peter. 539'.0924 B
Ernest Rutherford, architect of the atom, by Peter Kelman and A. Harris Stone. Illustrated by Henry Gorski. Englewood Cliffs, N.J., Prentice-Hall [1969] v, 72 p. illus., ports. 22 cm. (History of science series) The life and contributions of the scientist called the father of nuclear science for his development of the nuclear theory of the atom in 1911 and discovery of alpha and beta rays and protons. [QC16.R8K44] 92 68-13215 3.95
1. Rutherford, Ernest Rutherford, Baron, 1871-1937. I. Stone, A. Harris, joint author. II. Gorski, Henry, illus. III. Title.

MANN, Frederick George. 796.352'092'4 B
Lord Rutherford on the golf course / by Frederick George Mann. Cambridge : The author, 1976. [2], v, 33 p., [2] leaves of plates, [4] p. of plates : ill., facsims., ports. ; 24 cm. Bibliography: p. iv-v. [GV964.R87M36] 76-362444 ISBN 0-9504840-0-8 : £1.50
1. Rutherford, Ernest Rutherford, Baron, 1871-1937. 2. Golf. I. Title.

OLIPHANT, Mark, Sir, 1901- 539.7'092'4 B
Rutherford: recollections of the Cambridge days. Amsterdam, New York, Elsevier Pub. Co., 1972. xii, 162 p. 23 p. of photos. 23 cm. Includes bibliographical references. [QC16.R8O54] 70-180006 ISBN 0-444-40968-8 fl23.40
1. Rutherford, Ernest Rutherford, Baron, 1871-1937. BIP

RUTHERFORD and 530'.09'041
physics at the turn of the century / edited by Mario Bunge and William R. Shea. Kent, Eng. : Dawson : New York : Science History Publications, 1979. 184 p. : port. ; 24 cm. Includes bibliographical references. [QC7.5.R87 1979] 78-13986 ISBN 0-88202-184-2 : 20.00
1. Rutherford, Ernest Rutherford, baron, 1871-1937. 2. Physics—History—Addresses, essays, lectures. 3. Physicists—Great Britain—Biography. I. Bunge, Mario Augusto. II. Shea, William R.

Rutherford, Ernest Rutherford, baron, 1871-1937—Juvenile literature.

MCKNOWN, Robin 920
Giant of the atom: Ernest Rutherford. New York, Messner [c.1962] 191p. 22cm. Bibl. 62-16674 2.99
1. Rutherford, Ernest Rutherford, baron, 1871-1937—Juvenile I. Title.

MCKOWN, Robin. 92
Giant of the atom: Ernest Rutherford. New York, J. Messner [1962] 191p. 22cm. Includes bibliography. [QC16.R8M3] 62-16674
1. Rutherford, Ernest Rutherford, baron. 1871-1937—Juvenile literature. I. Title.

Rutherford, George Garfield, 1881-

*RUTHERFORD, George Garfield 926.4
The end of the rainbow: memoirs of an octogenarian. New York, Pageant [c.1964] 137p. 21cm. 3.00
I. Title.

RUTHERFORD, George Garfield, 1881-
The end of the rainbow; memoirs of an octogenarian. New York, Pageant Press [1964] 137 p. 21 cm. 66-9373
1. Rutherford, George Garfield, 1881- I. Title.

Rutherford, Johnny, 1938- —Juvenile literature.

HIGDON, Hal. 796.7'2'0924 B
Johnny Rutherford, Indy champ / by Hall Higdon. New York : Putnam, 1979. p. cm. (Sports shelf series) Includes index. A biography of the champion racing driver who after many tries won the Indianapolis 500 in 1976. [GV1032.R87H53] 92 78-24397 ISBN 0-399-61136-3 lib. bdg. : 5.95
1. Rutherford, Johnny, 1938- —Juvenile literature. 2. Indianapolis Speedway Race—Juvenile literature. 3. Automobile racing drivers—United States—Biography—Juvenile literature. I. Title.

Rutherford, Samuel,

RUTHERFORD, Samuel, 1600?-1661. 922.541
Letters; newly edited, and with an essay entitled "Rutherford today" by Frank E. Gaebelein. Also, Andrew A. Bonar's biographical sketch abridged. Chicago, Moody Press, 1951. 480 p. 23 cm. (The Wycliffe series of Christian classics.) [BX8915.R79 1951] 51-14637
I. Gaebelein, Frank Ely, 1890- ed. II. Title. III. Series.

Ruthven, Alexander Grant,

RUTHVEN, Alexander Grant, 1882- 923.773
Naturalist in two worlds; random recollections of a university president. Ann Arbor, Univ. of Mich. Pr. [c.1963] 162p. 23cm. 63-12742 5.00
I. Title.

RUTHVEN, Alexander Grant, 1882- 923.773
Naturalist in two worlds; random recollections of a university president. Ann Arbor, University of Michigan Press [1963] 162 p. 23 cm. [LD3275 1929.R8] 63-12742
I. Title.

Rutledge, Archibald Hamilton, 1883-1973—Biography.

RUTLEDGE, Irvine H. 811'.5'2 B
We called him Flintlock : a picture story of Archibald Rutledge, poet laureate of South Carolina / compiled by his son, Irvine H. Rutledge. Columbia, S.C. : R. L. Bryan Co., 1974. 68 p. : ill. ; 29 cm. [PS3535.U87Z85] 74-28947
1. Rutledge, Archibald Hamilton, 1883-1973—Biography. 2. Rutledge, Archibald Hamilton, 1883-1973—Portraits, etc. I. Title.

Rutledge, John, 1739-1800.

BARRY, Richard Hayes, 1881- 975.7'02'0924
Mr. Rutledge of South Carolina [by] Richard Barry. Freeport, N.Y., Books for Libraries Press [1971, c1942] ix, 430 p. facsims., port. 23 cm. Bibliography: p. 401-411. [E302.6.R89B3 1971] 71-146851 ISBN 0-8369-5618-4
1. Rutledge, John, 1739-1800. BIP

Ruyter, Michiel Adriaanszoon de, 1607-1676.

BLOK, Petrus Johannes, 1855-1929. 359.3'31'0924 B
The life of Admiral de Ruyter / by P. Blok ; translated from the Dutch by G. J. Renier. Westport, Conn. : Greenwood Press, 1975. 388 p., [6] leaves of plates : ill. ; 22 cm. Translation of Michiel Adriaanszoon de Ruyter. Reprint of the 1933 ed. published by E. Benn, London. [DJ136.R8B52 1975] 74-9393 ISBN 0-8371-7666-2 lib.bdg. : 20.00
1. Ruyter, Michiel Adriaanszoon de, 1607-1676. 2. Netherlands—History, Naval. I. Title. BIP

Ryall, Edward W., 1902-

RYALL, Edward W., 1902- 133.9'013 B
Born twice : total recall of a seventeenth-century life / by Edward W. Ryall ; with an introd. and appendix by Ian Stevenson. 1st U.S. ed. New York : Harper & Row, [1975] c1974. 214 p., [4] leaves of plates : ill. ; 22 cm. Includes index. [BL515.R9 1975] 74-20412 ISBN 0-06-013713-4 : 8.95
1. Ryall, Edward W., 1902- 2. Reincarnation. I. Title.

Ryan, Cornelius.

RYAN, Cornelius. 362.1'9'699463 B
A private battle / Cornelius Ryan and Kathryn Morgan Ryan. New York : Simon and Schuster, c1979. 448 p. ; 24 cm. [RC280.P7R93] 78-27037 ISBN 0-671-22594-4 : 11.95
1. Ryan, Cornelius. 2. Prostate gland—Cancer—Biography. 3. Journalists—United States—Biography. I. Ryan, Kathryn Morgan, joint author. II. Title. BIP

Ryan, Edward George, 1810-1880.

BEITZINGER, Alfons J 923.473
Edward G. Ryan: lion of the law. Madison, State Historical Society of Wisconsin, 1960. vi, 24)014p. illus.()0, ports. 20cm. (State street books, 2) Bibliography: p.202-208. 59-63607
1. Ryan, Edward George, 1810-1880. I. Title. BIP

Ryan, James H.

RYAN, James H. 618.9'2
Pablum, parents, & pandemonium : glimpses of a pediatrician's world / by James H. Ryan. New York : Crowell, [1975] viii, 291 p. ; 21 cm. Includes index. [RJ45.R96 1975] 74-26869 ISBN 0-690-00647-0 : 7.95
1. Ryan, James H. 2. Pediatrics. 3. Pediatricians—Correspondence, reminiscences, etc. I. Title.

Ryan, John Augustine, 1869-1945.

BRODERICK, Francis L. 922.273
Right Reverend New Dealer, John A. Ryan. New York, Macmillan [c.1963] 290p. illus. 25cm. Bibl. 62-19419 5.95
1. Ryan, John Augustine, 1869-1945. I. Title.

Ryan, John, 1925-

RYAN, John, 1925- 820'.9'941835 B
Remembering how we stood : Bohemian Dublin at the mid-century / John Ryan. New York : Taplinger, 1975. xiv, 168 p., [4] leaves of plates : ill. ; 23 cm. Includes index. [PR8729.R9] 75-8412 ISBN 0-8008-6770-X : 8.95
1. Ryan, John, 1925- 2. Authors, Irish—Biography. 3. Dublin—Intellectual life. 4. Literary landmarks—Dublin. I. Title. BIP

Ryan, Nolan—Juvenile literature.

*LIBBY, Bill. 796.357'092'2 B
Nolan Ryan; fireballer. New York, G. P. Putnam [1975] 160 p. 22 cm. Includes index. [GV865] 75-10437 ISBN 0-399-60951-2 5.29.
1. Ryan, Nolan—Juvenile literature. I. Title. BIP

Ryan, Nolan, 1947-

RYAN, Nolan, 1947- 796.357'092'4 B
The other game / Nolan Ryan, with Bill Libby. Waco, Tex. : Word Books, c1977. 216 p. : ill. ; 23 cm. [GV865.R9A36] 76-56485 6.95
1. Ryan, Nolan, 1947- 2. Baseball players—United States—Biography. I. Libby, Bill, joint author. II. Title.

Ryan, Thomas Joseph, 1876-1921.

MURPHY, D. J. 328'.94'0924 B
T. J. Ryan : a political biography / [by] D. J. Murphy. St. Lucia, Q. : University of Queensland Press, 1975. xvii, 596 p., 22 p. of plates : ill. ; 24 cm. Includes index. Bibliography: p. [527]-537. [DU272.R9M87] 76-362558 ISBN 0-7022-0992-9 : 26.45
1. Ryan, Thomas Joseph, 1876-1921. 2. Labor Party (Australia) 3. Queensland—Politics and government. I. Title.
Available from Technical Impex,Lawrence,Mass. BIP

Ryan, Thomas, 1827-1903.

RYAN, Thomas, 1827-1903. 787'.1'0924 B
Recollections of an old musician / by Thomas Ryan. New York : Da Capo Press, 1979. xvi, 274 p., [44] leaves of plates : ill. ; 23 cm. (Da Capo Press music reprint series) Reprint of the 1899 ed. published by Dutton, New York. [ML419.R98A3

1979] 78-31843 ISBN 0-306-79521-3 : 25.00
1. Ryan, Thomas, 1827-1903. 2. Musicians—United States—Biography. I. Title.

Ryan, Tubal Claude, 1898-

WAGNER, William, 1909- 629.13'00924 B
Ryan, the aviator; being the adventures & ventures of pioneer airman & businessman, T. Claude Ryan, by William Wagner, in collaboration with Lee Dye. New York, McGraw-Hill [1971] xi, 253 p. illus., facsims., ports. 28 cm. [TL540.R88W3] 71-132961 ISBN 0-07-067670-4
1. Ryan, Tubal Claude, 1898- 2. Ryan Aeronautical Company, San Diego, Calif. I. Title.

Ryckman, Harold.

RYCKMAN, Lucile Damon. 266'.7'97 B
Paid in full : the story of Harold Ryckman, missionary pioneer to Paraguay and Brazil / by Lucile Damon Ryckman. Winona Lake, Ind. : Light and Life Press, c1979. 128 p. : ill. ; 21 cm. [BV2853.P3R927] 79-112549 ISBN 0-89367-033-2 pbk. : 3.75
1. Ryckman, Harold. 2. Missionaries—Paraguay—Biography. 3. Missionaries—Brazil—Biography. 4. Missionaries—United States—Biography. I. Title.

Ryckmans, Pierre.

RYCKMANS, Pierre. 915.1'04'5
Chinese shadows / by Simon Leys [i.e. P. Ryckmans]. New York : Viking Press, 1977. xvii, 220 p. ; 22 cm. Translation of Ombres chinoises. Includes index. Bibliography: p. 212-214. [DS711.R9313 1977] 77-23175 ISBN 0-670-21918-5 : 10.00
1. Ryckmans, Pierre. 2. China—Description and travel—1949- I. Title.

Ryken, Theodore James, 1797-1871.

AUBERT, Brother. 189.4
March on! God will provide. Boston, E. L. Grimes Co. [1961] 196p. illus. 17cm. 'Synopsized version of a full-length biography of Theodore James Ryken ... not ready for publication.' [BX4705.R9A8] 61-46755
1. Ryken, Theodore James, 1797-1871. I. Title.

Ryle, John Charles, Bp. of Liverpool, 1816-1900.

TOON, Peter, 1939- 283'.092'4 B
John Charles Ryle : evangelical bishop / by Peter Toon and Michael Smout. Cambridge : J. Clarke, 1976. 123 p., plate : port. ; 24 cm. "Selected list of tracts and books by J. C. Ryle": p. 121. [BX5199.R9T66 1976b] 77-358597 ISBN 0-227-67826-5 : £3.75
1. Ryle, John Charles, Bp. of Liverpool, 1816-1900. 2. Church of England—Bishops—Biography. 3. Bishops—England—Biography. I. Smout, Michael, 1937- joint author.

Rymer, J. Sykes.

RYMER, J. Sykes. 133.9'092'4
Stepping stones : from orthodoxy to a new understanding / by A. Pilgrim (Rev. J. Sykes Rymer). [Onchan] : [Barbara M. Rymer], [1976] 152 p. : ports. ; 21 cm. [BF1283.R94A34] 77-369511 ISBN 0-9505509-0-6 : £1.30
1. Rymer, J. Sykes. 2. Spiritualists—England—Biography. I. A. Pilgrim. II. Title.

Ryun, Jim, 1947-

LAKE, John. 796.4'26'0924 B
Jim Ryun, master of the mile. New York, Random House [1968] viii, 174 p. illus. 22 cm. (Random House sports library, 1) Traces the track career of the boy who became the first high school student to run a four-minute mile and who at age nineteen had surpassed the achievements of all the milers in history. [GV1061.L25] 92 AC 68
1. Ryun, Jim, 1947- I. Title.

NELSON, Cordner. 796.4'26
The Jim Ryun story. Photos. by Rich Clarkson. Los Altos, Calif., Tafnews Press [1967] 272 p. illus., ports. 23 cm. [GV1061.N38] 67-13361
1. Ryun, Jim, 1947-

Saenz, Aaron.

HEFLEY, James C. 332'.0924 B
Aaron Saenz; Mexico's revolutionary capitalist, by James C. Hefley. Waco, Tex., Word Books [1970] 146 p. illus., ports. 23 cm. Bibliography: p. 139-142. [HC132.5.S3H4] 72-134252 3.95
1. Saenz, Aaron.

Saenz, Manuela, 1796-1859.

VON HAGEN, Victor Wolfgang, 1908- 920.7
The four seasons of Manuela, a biography; the love story of Manuela Saenz and Simon Bolivar. New York, Duell, Sloan and Pearce [1952] x, 320 p. col. port., maps (on lining papers) 25 cm. Bibliography: p. [301]-312. [F2235.S17V6] 52-5527
1. Saenz, Manuela, 1796-1859. 2. Bolivar, Simon, 1783-1830. I. Title.

Sanchez de Arevalo, Rodrigo, Bp., 1404-1470.

BUTLER, Geoffrey Gilbert, Sir, 1887- 341.1'1'094
Studies in statecraft: being chapters, biographical, and bibliographical, mainly on the sixteenth century. Port Washington, N.Y., Kennikat Press [1970] vi, 138 p. 22 cm. Reprint of the 1920 ed. Contents.Contents.—Bishop Roderick and Renaissance pacificism.—The French "civilians," Roman law, and the new monarchy.—William Postel; world peace through world power.—Sully and his grand design.—"The grand design" of Emerich Cruce.—Appendices: A. Passages quoted in Chapter I. B. A bibliography of Rodericus Sancius, Bishop of Calahorra (p. [108]-113). C. English version of passages quoted in Chapter II. D. A bibliography of William Postel (p. [117]-131) [D234.B8 1970] 79-110899 ISBN 0-8046-0882-2
1. Sanchez de Arevalo, Rodrigo, Bp., 1404-1470. 2. Postel, Guillaume, 1510-1581. 3. Sully, Maximilien de Bethune, duc de, 1559-1641. 4. Cruce, Emeric, 1590?-1648. 5. Europe—Politics and government—1517-1648. 6. Peace. I. Title.

Sanchez, Florencio, 1875-1910.

RICHARDSON, Ruth, 1894- 862
Florencio Sanchez and the Argentine theatre / by Ruth Richardson. New York : Gordon Press, 1975. 243 p. ; 24 cm. Reprint of the 1933 ed. published by the Instituto de las Espanas en los Estados Unidos, New York. Thesis—Columbia. Vita. Bibliography: p. 229-243. [PQ8519.S4Z8 1975] 74-20335 ISBN 0-87968-227-2 lib.bdg. : 34.95
1. Sanchez, Florencio, 1875-1910. I. Title. **BIP**

Sao Paulo, Brazil (City)—Juvenile literature.

ANDUJAR, Claudia. 918.1'6
A week in Bico's world: Brazil. Photos. by Claudia Andujar. Text by Seymour Reit. [New York] Crowell-Collier Press [1970] [48] p. illus. 27 cm. Bico, a boy of Sao Paulo, goes to school, shops with his mother, and visits a snake institute and his grandfather's farm. [F2651.S24A7] 72-112851 4.50
1. Sao Paulo, Brazil (City)—Juvenile literature. 2. Children in Sao Paulo, Brazil (City)—Juvenile literature. I. Reit, Seymour. II. Title.

Sevigne, Marie de Rabutin Chantal, marquise de, 1626-1696.

ALLENTUCH, Harriet Ray. 846'.4 B
Madame de Sevigne : a portrait in letters / by Harriet Ray Allentuch. Westport, Conn. : Greenwood Press, [1978] c1963. p. cm. Reprint of the ed. published by Johns Hopkins Press, Baltimore. Includes index. Bibliography: p. [PQ1925.A953 1978] 78-16378 ISBN 0-313-20537-X lib.bdg. : 18.00
1. Sevigne, Marie de Rabutin Chantal, marquise de, 1626-1696. 2. Authors, French—17th century—Biography.

BOISSIER, Gaston, 1823-1908. 846'.4 B
Madame de Sevigne. Translated by Henry Llewllyn Williams. Freeport, N.Y., Books for Libraries Press [1972] 154 p. front. 23 cm. Reprint of the 1887 ed. [PQ1925.B65 1972] 73-39192 ISBN 0-8369-6794-1
1. Sevigne, Marie (de Rabutin-Chantal) marquise de, 1626-1696. **BIP**

MEGAW, Arthur Stanley, 1872- 846'.4 B
Madame de Sevigne, her letters and her world / by Arthur Stanley [i.e. A. S. Megaw]. Folcroft, Pa. : Folcroft Library Editions, 1976. p. cm. Reprint of the 1946 ed. published by Eyre & Spottiswoode, London. Includes index. [PQ1925.M4 1976] 76-23333 ISBN 0-8414-7727-2 lib. bdg. : 27.50
1. Sevigne, Marie (de Rabutin-Chantal) marquise de, 1626-1696. I. Title. **BIP**

RITCHIE, Anne Isabella (Thackeray) Lady, 1837-1919. 846'.4 B
Madame de Sevigne. Philadelphia, Lippincott, 1881. [New York, AMS Press, 1973] xii, 181 p. 19 cm. Reprint of the ed., issued in series: Foreign classics for English readers. [PQ1925.R5 1973] 77-37716 ISBN 0-404-56809-2 10.00
1. Sevigne, Marie (de Rabutin-Chantal) marquise de, 1626-1696. I. Series: Foreign classics for English readers. **BIP**

Simi Island—Description and travel.

TRAVIS, William, 1924- 914.99'6 B
Interval on Symi. Boston, Gambit, 1971. 222 p. col. illus., maps (on lining papers) 22 cm. Autobiographical. 1970 ed. has title: Bus stop Symi. [DF901.S54T73] 75-118218 5.95
1. Simi Island—Description and travel. 2. Simi Island—History. I. Title.

Suleyman I, the Magnificent, Sultan of the Turks, 1494-1566.

MERRIMAN, Roger Bigelow, 1876-1945. 956.1'01'0924 B
Suleiman the Magnificent, 1520-1566. New York, Cooper Square Publishers, 1966 [c1944] viii, 325 p. illus., ports. 24 cm. "A portion of the material ... derived from an unfinished life of Suleiman the Magnificent which was written by ... Archibald Cary Coolidge in 1901-02." Includes bibliographical references. [DR506.M4 1966] 65-25497
1. Suleyman I, the Magnificent, Sultan of the Turks, 1494-1566. 2. Turkey—History—1453-1683. I. Coolidge, Archibald Cary, 1866-1928. II. Title. **BIP**

Suryamalla, 1815-1868.

SHARMA, Vishnu Datt. 891'.479'13
Surya Mall Mishran / by Vishnu Datt Sharma. New Delhi : Sahitya Akademi, 1976. 37, [2] p. ; 23 cm. (Makers of Indian literature) Bibliography: p. [39] [PK2708.9.S9Z88] 76-902936 Rs2.50
1. Suryamalla, 1815-1868. 2. Poets, Rajasthani—19th century—Biography.

Sa'eed, 1863-1942.

RASOOLI, Jay M 922
The life story of Dr. Sa'eed of Iran, Kurdish physician to princes and peasants, nobles and nomads, by Jay M. Rasooli and Cady H. Allen. Grand Rapids, Grand Rapids International Publications, 1957. 188p. illus. 23cm. [BV3217.S3R3] 57-13245
1. Sa'eed, 1863-1942. 2. Missions—Persia. I. Allen, Cady Hews, 1886- joint author. II. Title.

Saadiah ben Joseph, gaon, 892?-942.

MALTER, Henry, 1864-1925. 296.6'1'0924
Saadia Gaon; his life and works. New York, Hermon Press [1969] 446 p. 23 cm. "First Edition: New York, 1926." Bibliography: p. [303]-419. [BM755.S2M3 1969] 77-82475
1. Saadiah ben Joseph, gaon, 892?-942. 2. Saadiah ben Joseph, gaon, 892?-942—Bibliography.

Saadiah ben Joseph, gaon, 892?-942— Juvenile literature.

KLAPERMAN, Libby M. 922.96
The scholar-fighter; the story of Saadia Gaon. Drawings by Charles Walker. [New York] Jewish Pubn. Soc. [dist.] Farrar. 178). (Covenant bks., 13) 61-8472 2.95
1. Saadiah ben Joseph, gaon, 892?-942—Juvenile literature. I. Title.

Saadullah Khan.

SAADULLAH Khan. 954.9'205
East Pakistan to Bangla Desh / by Saadullah Khan. Lahore : Lahore Law Times Publications, 1975. iii, 204 p., maps ; 23 cm. Includes index. [DS388.S2] 75-930469 6.25
1. Saadullah Khan. 2. India-Pakistan Conflict, 1971—Personal narratives. I. Title.
Distributed by South Asia Books

Saarinen, Eero, 1910-1961—Bibliography.

KUHNER, Robert A. 016.3092'08 S
Eero Saarinen, his life and work / Robert A. Kuhner. Monticello, Ill. : Council of Planning Librarians, 1975. 73 p. ; 28 cm. (Exchange bibliography - Council of Planning Librarians ; 836) Cover title. Includes index. [Z5942.C68 no. 836] [Z8772.4] [NA737.S28] 016.72'0924 75-321300 pbk. : 7.50
1. Saarinen, Eero, 1910-1961—Bibliography. I. Title. II. Series: Council of Planning Librarians. Exchange bibliography ; 836.

Saavedra Fajardo, Diego de, 1584-1648.

DOWLING, John Clarkson, 1920- 868'.3'09
Diego de Saavedra Fajardo / by John Dowling. Boston : Twayne Publishers, c1977. 172 p. : port. ; 21 cm. (Twayne's world authors series ; TWAS 437 : Spain) Includes index. Bibliography: p. 145-157. [PQ6431.S13Z67] 76-56178 ISBN 0-8057-6200-0 lib.bdg. : 8.95
1. Saavedra Fajardo, Diego de, 1584-1648. 2. Authors, Spanish—17th century—Biography. **BIP**

Sabin, Florence Rena, 1871-1953.

BLUEMEL, Elinor. 926.1
Florence Sabin; Colorado woman of the century. Boulder, University of Colorado Press [1959] 238 p. illus. 21 cm. Includes bibliography. [R154.S115B55] 59-1235
1. Sabin, Florence Rena, 1871-1953. 2. Women physicians.

PHELAN, Mary Kay. 610'.924 B
Probing the unknown; the story of Dr. Florence Sabin. New York, Crowell [1969] x, 176 p. 22 cm. (Women of America) Bibliography: p. 163-168. [R154.S115P44] 77-78265 4.50
1. Sabin, Florence Rena, 1871-1953. I. Title. **BIP**

Sabin, Joseph, 1821-1881.

GOFF, Frederick Richmond, 1916- 010'.92'4
Joseph Sabin, bibliographer, 1821-1881 [by]Frederick R. Goff. Amsterdam, N. Israel [1963] 30 p. facsims., port. 21 cm. [Z1004.S3G6] 64-5838

1. Sabin, Joseph, 1821-1881. I. Title.

Sabinson, Harvey.

SABINSON, Harvey. 792'.092'4
Darling, you were wonderful / Harvey Sabinson. Chicago : H. Regnery, c1977. xviii, 205 p. ; 22 cm. Includes index. [PN1590.P7S2] 76-55659 ISBN 0-8092-7872-3 : 8.95
1. Sabinson, Harvey. 2. Press agents—United States—Biography. I. Title. **BIP**

Sacagawea, 1786-1884

BLASSINGAME, Wyatt. 92
Sacagawea, Indian guide. Illustrated by Edward Shenton. Champaign, Ill., Garrard Pub. Co. [1965] 80 p. col. illus., col. map. 23 cm. [F592.7.S12B5] 65-17170
1. Sacagawea, 1786-1884 — Juvenile literature. I. Title.

BLASSINGAME, Wyatt. 970.3 B
Sacagawea, Indian guide. Illustrated by Edward Shenton. Champaign, Ill., Garrard Pub. Co. [1965] 80 p. col. illus., col. map. 23 cm. A biography of the Indian girl who led the Lewis and Clark expedition on its journey westward. [F592.7.S12B5] 92 AC 68
1. Sacagawea, 1786-1844. I. Shenton, Edward, 1895- illus. II. Title.

BURT, Olive Wooley, 1894- 970'.004'97 B
Sacajawea / Olive Burt. New York : Watts, 1978. 57 p. : ill. ; 27 cm. (A Visual biography) Includes bibliographical references and index. A biography of the Shoshoni Indian woman who acted as an interpreter, nurse, and guide for the Lewis and Clark expedition. [F592.7.S123B87] 92 78-1572 ISBN 0-531-00975-0 lib. bdg. : 4.90
1. Sacagawea, 1786-1884—Juvenile literature. 2. Lewis and Clark Expedition—Juvenile literature. 3. Shoshoni Indians—Biography—Juvenile literature. 4. Scouts and scouting—The West—Biography—Juvenile literature. I. Title.

FRAZIER, Neta (Lohnes) 1890- 92 (J)
Sacajawea: the girl nobody knows. New York, D. McKay Co., 1967. 182 p. fold. map. 21 cm. A biography of the Shoshoni Indian woman who acted as guide and interpreter for Lewis and Clark on their expedition to the Pacific coast. [F592.7.S1224] AC 67
1. Sacagawea, 1786-1884. I. Title.

FRAZIER, Neta (Lohnes) 1890- 92 (J)
Sacajawea: the girl nobody knows. New York, D. McKay Co., 1967. 182 p. fold. map. 21 cm. Bibliography: p. 175-177. [F592.7.S1224] 67-21181
1. Sacagawea, 1786-1884—Juvenile literature. I. Title.

HOWARD, Harold P. 970.3 B
Sacajawea [by] Harold P. Howard. [1st ed.] Norman, University of Oklahoma Press [1971] xiii, 218 p. illus. 19 cm. Bibliography: p. 201-208. [F592.7.S1233] 70-160495 ISBN 0-8061-0967-X
1. Sacagawea, 1786-1884. 2. Lewis and Clark Expedition. I. Title. **BIP**

SKOLD, Betty Westrom. 970'.004'97
Sacagawea / by Betty Westrom Skold. Minneapolis : Dillon Press, c1977. 74 p. : ill. ; 24 cm. (The Story of an American Indian) A biography of the Shoshoni woman who acted as interpreter, intermediary, and guide to the Lewis and Clark expedition across Louisiana Purchase lands in 1804 and 1805. [F592.7.S1237] 92 76-30613 ISBN 0-87518-095-7 : 4.95
1. Sacagawea, 1786-1884—Juvenile literature. 2. Lewis and Clark Expedition—Juvenile literature. 3. Shoshoni Indians—Biography—Juvenile literature. **BIP**

VOIGHT, Virginia Frances. 92 (J)
Sacajawea. Illustrated by Erica Merkling. New York, Putnam [1967] 63 p. col. illus. 23 cm. (A See and read beginning to read biography) [F592.7.S1238] 67-24178
1. Sacagawea, 1786-1884—Juvenile literature. I. Title.

Sacco, Nicola, 1891-1927.

DOS PASSOS, John, 1896- 343'.5'23
Facing the chair; story of the Americanization of two foreignborn workmen. New York, Da Capo Press, 1970. 127 p. 24 cm. (A Da Capo Press reprint series.) (Civil liberties in American history) Reprint of the 1927 ed. [HX84.A2D6 1970] 72-104066
1. Sacco, Nicola, 1891-1927. 2. Vanzetti, Bartolomeo, 1888-1927. I. Title. II. Series. **BIP**

Sacco-Vanzetti case.

SACCO, Nicola, 1891-1927. 364.15'23'0922 B
The letters of Sacco and Vanzetti. Edited by Marion Danman Frankfurter and Gardner Jackson. New York, Octagon Books, 1971 [c1928] xi, 414 p. facsims., ports. 21 cm. [HV6248.S3A4 1971] 76-159224 ISBN 0-374-97003-3
1. Sacco-Vanzetti case. I. Vanzetti, Bartolomeo, 1888-1927. II. Title. **BIP**

Sacher-Masoch, Leopold, Ritter von. 1835-1895.

CLEUGH, James. 301.41'5 [B]
The first masochist; a biography of Leopold von Sacher-Masoch New York, Stein and Day [1967] 230 p. 22 cm. Bibliography: p. [209]-214. [PT2461.S3Z83] 67-15761
1. Sacher-Masoch, Leopold, Ritter von. 1835-1895. I. Title.

Sachs, Maurice,

SACHS, Maurice, 1906-1945 928.4
Witches' sabbath. Tr. from French by Richard Howard. New York, Stein & Day [c.1960, 1964] 315p. 25cm. 64-20174 7.50 bds.,
I. Title.

Sackheim, Maxwell, 1890-

SACKHEIM, Maxwell, 1890- 659.1'092'4 B
My first 65 years in advertising / by Maxwell Sackheim 1st ed. Blue Ridge Summit, Pa. : G/L Tab Books, 1975. 209 p. : ill. ; 22 cm. Includes bibliographical references and index. [HF5810.S23A35] 75-27359 ISBN 0-8306-5816-5 : 9.95. ISBN 0-8306-4816-X pbk. : 5.95
1. Sackheim, Maxwell, 1890- 2. Advertising—Personal narratives. I. Title.

Sackville, George Sackville Germain, 1st viscount, 1716-1785.

VALENTINE, Alan Chester, 1901- 923.542
Lord George Germain. [New York] Oxford [c.]1962. x, 534p. port. 23cm. Bibl. 62-51253 10.10
1. Sackville, George Sackville Germain, 1st viscount, 1716-1785. I. Title.

VALENTINE, Alan Chester, 1901- 923.542
Lord George Germain. Oxford [Eng.] Clarendon Press, 1962. x, 534 p. port. 23 cm. Bibliography: p. [506]-515. [DA483.S2V3] 62-51253
1. Sackville, George Sackville Germain, 1st viscount, 1716-1785. I. Title.

WILKINSON, Louis Umfreville, 1881-1966. 942.07'2'0924 B
Sackville of Drayton (Lord George Sackville till 1770, Lord George Germain, 1770-1782 [and] Viscount Sackville from 1782) by Louis Merlow Totowa, N.J., Rowman and Littlefield [1974] 300 p. illus. 22 cm. Reprint of the 1948 ed. published by Home & Van Thal, London. Bibliography: p. 290-295. [DA483.S2W5 1974] 73-5835 ISBN 0-87471-191-6
1. Sackville, George Sackville Germain, 1st Viscount, 1716-1785. I. Title.

Sackville, Victoria Josephine Sackville-West, Lady, 1862-1936.

ALSOP, Susan Mary. 823'.9'12 B
Lady Sackville : a biography / Susan Mary Alsop. 1st. ed. in the U.S.A. Garden City, N.Y. : Doubleday, 1978. x, 273 p., [12] leaves of plates : ill. ; 22 cm. Includes index. Bibliography: p. [255]-259. [CT788.S12A47 1978] 78-58351 ISBN 0-385-11379-X : 10.00
1. Sackville, Victoria Josephine Sackville-West, Lady, 1862-1936. 2. England—Biography. I. Title. **BIP**

Sackville-West, Victoria Mary, Hon., 1892-1962.

STEVENS, Michael. 821'.9'12 B
V. Sackville-West: a critical biography. New York, Scribners [1974] xvi, 192 p. illus. 24 cm. Originally presented as the author's thesis, Uppsala. Bibliography: p. 180-186. [PR6037.A35Z87 1974] 73-19357 ISBN 0-684-13677-5 7.95
1. Sackville-West, Victoria Mary, Hon., 1892-1962.

Sackville-West, Victoria Mary, Hon., 1892-1962—Biography.

NICOLSON, Nigel. 821'.9'12 B
Portrait of a marriage. [1st ed.] New York, Atheneum, 1973. xi, 249 p. illus. 25 cm. [PR6037.A35Z8] 73-80754 ISBN 0-689-10574-6 10.00
1. Sackville-West, Victoria Mary, Hon., 1892-1962—Biography. 2. Nicolson, Harold George, Sir, 1886-1968—Biography. I. Title. **BIP**

NICOLSON, Nigel. 821'.912 B
Portrait of a marriage / by Nigel Nicolson. 1st Atheneum paperback ed. New York : Atheneum, 1980, c1973. p. cm. Includes index. [PR6037.A35Z8 1980] 79-25497 ISBN 0-689-70597-2 : 6.95
1. Sackville-West, Victoria Mary, Hon., 1892-1962—Biography. 2. Sackville-West, Victoria Mary, Hon., 1892-1962—Relationship with women—Violet Keppel Trefusis. 3. Trefusis, Violet Keppel, 1894-1972—Biography. 4. Nicolson, Harold George, Hon., 1886-1968—Biography. 5. Authors, English—20th century—Biography. I. Title.

Sackville-West, Victoria Mary, Hon., 1892-1962—Relationship with women—Violet Keppel Trefusis.

NICOLSON, Nigel. 821'.912 B
Portrait of a marriage / by Nigel Nicolson. 1st Atheneum paperback ed. New York : Atheneum, 1980, c1973. p. cm. Includes index. [PR6037.A35Z8 1980] 79-25497 ISBN 0-689-70597-2 : 6.95
1. Sackville-West, Victoria Mary, Hon., 1892-1962—Biography. 2. Sackville-West, Victoria Mary, Hon., 1892-1962—Relationship with women—Violet Keppel Trefusis. 3. Trefusis, Violet Keppel, 1894-1972—Biography. 4. Nicolson, Harold George, Hon., 1886-1968—Biography. 5. Authors, English—20th century—Biography. I. Title.

Sacred Heart Church, Hebron, Neb.

A Bicentennial centennial history, Sacred Heart Church, Hebron, Nebraska, 1876-1976. 282'.782'335 Hebron, Neb. : Sacred Heart Church, c1976. vi, 205 p. : ill. ; 28 cm. Cover title: The bell of Sacred Heart Church. Includes index. [BX4603.H38S22] 76-24301
1. Sacred Heart Church, Hebron, Neb. 2. Hebron, Neb.—Biography. I. Title: The bell of Sacred Heart Church.

Sadat, Anwar, 1918-

NARAYAN, B. K. 962'.05'0924 B
Anwar el Sadat : man with a mission / B. K. Narayan. New Delhi : Vikas Pub. House, c1977. x, 162 p., [4] leaves of plates : ill. ; 22 cm. Includes index. Bibliography: p. [155] [DT107.828.S23N37] 77-900410 10.50.
1. Sadat, Anwar, 1918- 2. Egypt—Politics and government—1952- 3. Egypt—Presidents—Biography.
Dist. by International Pubns. Service, N.Y. **BIP**

SADAT, Anwar, 1918- 962'.05'0924 B
In search of identity : an autobiography / by Anwar el-Sadat. 1st ed. New York : Harper & Row, c1978. 360 p., [4] leaves of plates : ill. ; 24 cm. Includes index. [DT107.828.S23A33 1978] 77-3767 ISBN 0-06-013742-8 : 15.00
1. Sadat, Anwar, 1918- 2. Egypt—Presidents—Biography. I. Title. **BIP**

Sade, Donatien Alphonse Francois, comte, called Marquis de, 1740-1814—Biography.

DRUMMOND, Walter 928.4
Philosopher of evil. Evanston, Ill., Regnery [c.1962] 158p. 18cm. 62-53054 .50 pap.,
1. Sade, Donatien Alphonse Francois, comte, called marquis de, 1740-1814. I. Title.

GORER, Geoffrey, 1905- 843.5
The life and ideas of the Marquis de Sade. New York, Norton [c.1962-1963] 250p. 22cm. First ed. pub. in 1934 under title: The revolutionary ideas of the Marquis de Sade. 63-11684 5.00
1. Sade, Donatien Alphonse Francois, comte, called the marquis de, 1740-1814. I. Title. **BIP**

GORER, Geoffrey, 1905- 843'.5 B
The life and ideas of the Marquis de Sade / by Geoffrey Gorer. Westport, Conn. : Greenwood Press, 1978, c1963. 250 p. ; 23 cm. Reprint of the ed. published by Norton, New York. Includes bibliographical references. [PQ2063.S3G6 1978] 77-16240 ISBN 0-313-20023-8 lib.bdg. : 17.50
1. Sade, Donatien Alphonse Francois, comte, called Marquis de, 1740-1814. 2. Authors, French—18th century—Biography. I. Title.

HAYMAN, Ronald, 1932- 843'.6 B
De Sade : a critical biography / Ronald Hayman. 1st U.S. ed. New York : Crowell, c1978. xxviii, 253 p. ; 24 cm. Includes index. Bibliography: p. [239]-243. [PQ2063.S3H34 1978] 78-3170 ISBN 0-06-01448-1 : 12.95
1. Sade, Donatien Alphonse Francoise, comte, Called Marquis de, 1740-1814—Biography. 2. Authors, French—18th century—Biography. I. Title. **BIP**

KAFKA, Franz, 1883-1924 928.3
Letters to Milena. Ed. by Willi Haas; tr. by Tania and James Stern. New York, Schocken [1962, c.1953] 238p. 21cm. (SB24) 62-13139 1.75 pap.,
1. Authors—Correspondence, reminiscences, etc. I. Jesenska, Milena, 1896-1944. II. Title.

LELY, Gilbert. 843'.6 B
The Marquis de Sade; a biography. Translated by Alec Brown. New York, Grove Press [1970, c1961] 464 p. 18 cm. (An Evergreen black cat book, B-234) Translation of Vie du marquis de Sade. [PQ2063.S3L413 1970] 77-111003 1.95
1. Sade, Donatien Alphonse Francois, comte, called Marquis de, 1740-1814.

LELY, Gilbert. 928.4
The Marquis de Sade, a biography. Translated by Alec Brown. New York, Grove Press [1962, c1961] 464 p. 21 cm. Translation of Vie du marquis de Sade. [PQ2063.S3L413 1962] 62-17529
1. Sade, Donatien Alphonse Francois, comte, called Marquis de, 1740-1814. I. Title.

LENNIG, Walter. 843'.6 B
Portrait of De Sade; an illustrated biography. Translated by Sarah Twohig. [New York] Herder and Herder [1971] 174 p. illus., facsims., ports. 21 cm. Translation of Marquis de Sade in Selbstzeugnissen und Bilddokumenten. Bibliography: p. 173-174. [PQ2063.S3L4413] 70-150140 6.95

1. Sade, Donatien Alphonse Francois, comte, called Marquis de, 1740-1814.

THOMAS, Donald Serrell. 843'.6 B
The Marquis de Sade / Donald Thomas 1st ed. Boston : Little, Brown, c1976. p. cm. "A New York Graphic Society book." Bibliography: p. [PQ2063.S3T5 1976] 76-24868 ISBN 0-316-83490-4 : 12.50
1. Sade, Donatien Alphonse Francois, comte, called Marquis de, 1740-1814—Biography. **BIP**

Sadleir, Michael

SADLEIR, Michael 928.2
Trollope, a commentary [New York] Oxford [1961] 435p. (Oxford paperback no. 35) Bibl. 2.50 pap.,
I. Title. **BIP**

SADLEIR, Michael 928.2
Trollope, a commentary [New York] Oxford [1961] 435p. (Oxford paperback no. 35) Bibl. 2.50 pap.,
I. Title. **BIP**

Sadler, Barry.

SADLER, Barry. 355.00924
I'm a lucky one, by Barry Sadler with Tom Mahoney. New York, Macmillan [1967] 191 p. illus., ports. 22 cm. Autobiographical. [U55.S25A3] 67-15666
I. Mahoney, Tom. II. Title.

Sadler, Robert, 1911-

SADLER, Robert, 266'.022'0924 B
1911-
The emancipation of Robert Sadler / by Robert Sadler, with Marie Chapian. Minneapolis : Bethany Fellowship, [1975] 254 p. : ill. ; 23 cm. [BR1725.S22A33] 75-14063 ISBN 0-87123-132-8 : 5.95
1. Sadler, Robert, 1911- 2. Slavery in the United States—Personal narratives. I. Chapian, Marie, joint author. II. Title. **BIP**

Sadoleto, Jacopo, Cardinal, 1477-1547.

DOUGLAS, Richard M. 922.245
Jacopo Sadoleto, 1477-1547: humanist and reformer. Cambridge, Harvard University Press, 1959. xvi, 307 p. illus., port. 22 cm. Bibliography: p. 229-242. [BX4705.S13D6] 58-12965
1. Sadoleto, Jacopo, Cardinal, 1477-1547.

Sage, Henry Williams, 1814-1897.

GOODSTEIN, Anita Shafer 926.5
Biography of a businessman: Henry W. Sage, 1814-1897. Ithaca, N.Y., Cornell Univ. Pr. [c.1962] xi, 279p. ports., maps. 24cm. Bibl. 62-19172 5.75
1. Sage, Henry Williams, 1814-1897. I. Title. **BIP**

Sage, Russell, 1816-1906.

SARNOFF, Paul 923.373
Russell Sage, the money king. Obolensky [dist. Cleveland, World, c.1965] 398p. illus., facsims., map (on lining papers) ports. 24cm. Bibl. [HG172.S3S35] 65-18178 6.95
1. Sage, Russell, 1816-1906. I. Title.

Sai-chin-hua, 1874-1936.

DRUNKEN WHISKERS. 920.7
That Chinese woman; the life of Sai-Chin-Hua, 1874-1936. Translated from the Chinese by Henry McAleavy. Illus. by Jeanyee Wong. New York, Crowell [c.1959] xx, 243p. illus. 22cm. 60-6234 4.50
1. Sai-chin-hua, 1874-1936. I. Title.

Saint-Evremond, Charles de Marguetel de Saint-Denis,

SAINT-EVREMOND, 848'.4'09 B
Charles de Marguetel de Saint-Denis, seigneur de, 1613?-1703.
The letters of Saint Evremond. Edited with an introd. and notes by John Hayward. New York, B. Blom, 1972. lxii, 383 p. illus. 21 cm. Reprint of the 1930 ed. One hundred forty letters, most of which were printed by Des Maizeaux in his translation of Saint-Evremond's Works, 1728. Bibliography: p. xviii. [PQ1917.S5Z53 1972] 72-83506
I. Title. **BIP**

SAINT-EVREMOND, 848'.4'09 B
Charles de Marguetel de Saint-Denis, seigneur de, 1613?-1703.
The letters of Saint Evremond. Edited with an introd. and notes by John Hayward. Freeport, N.Y., Books for Libraries Press [1971] lxii, 383 p. illus., ports. 23 cm. Reprint of the 1930 ed. One hundred forty letters, most of which were printed by Des Maizeaux in his translation of Saint-Evremond's Works, 1728. The rest are translated here for the first time. Bibliography: p. xviii. [PQ1917.S5Z53 1971] 76-164624 ISBN 0-8369-5907-8
I. Title. **BIP**

Saint Augustine of Canterbury Parish, Hecker, Ill.

WITTENAUER, Josephine 282'.773'91
Carole.
History of Saint Augustine of Canterbury Parish, 1824-1974. Hecker, Ill. : St. Augustine of Canterbury Church, [1974] xxii, 194 p. : ill. ; 23 cm. Bibliography: p. 188-189. [BX4603.H4S248] 75-304583
1. Saint Augustine of Canterbury Parish, Hecker, Ill. 2. Hecker, Ill.—Biography. I. Title.

Saint Edward Church, Providence.

WALSH, Richard A. 282'.745'2
The centennial history of Saint Edward Church, Providence, Rhode Island, 1874-1974, by Richard A. Walsh. With an introd. by Louis E. Gelineau. [Providence? R.I., 1974] 242 p. illus. 24 cm. Bibliography: p. [240]-242. [BX4603.P7S258] 74-163508
1. Saint Edward Church, Providence. 2. Providence—Biography. I. Title.

Saint Exupery, Antoine de, 1900-1944.

BREAUX, Adele. 629.13'0924 B
Saint-Exupery in America, 1942-1943; a memoir Rutherford [N.J.] Fairleigh Dickinson University Press [1971] 166 p. illus., ports. 22 cm. [PQ2637.A274Z63] 70-99322 ISBN 0-8386-7610-3 6.75
1. Saint Exupery, Antoine de, 1900-1944. I. Title. **BIP**

MIGEO, Marcel. 928.4
Saint-Exupery. Translated from the French by Herma Briffault. [1st American ed.] New York, McGraw-Hill [1960] 330 p. illus. 22 cm. [TL540.S18M53] 60-9851
1. Saint Exupery, Antoine de, 1900-1944.

RUMBOLD, Richard. 629.13'0924
The winged life; a portrait of Antoine de Saint-Exupery, poet and airman, by Richard Rumbold and Lady Margaret Stewart. New York, D. McKay [1955] 224p. 21cm. Bibliography: p. 217-220. [TL540.S18R] A55
1. Saint Exupery, Antoine de, 1900-1944. I. Stewart, Lady Margaret, 1910- joint author. II. Title.

SMITH, Maxwell Austin, 928.4
1894-
Knight of the air; the life and works of Antoine de Saint-Exupery. [1st ed.] New York, Pageant Press [1956] 265 p. 21 cm. Includes bibliography. [TL540.S18S6] 56-8535
1. Saint Exupery, Antoine de, 1900-1944. I. Title.

Saint-Gaudens, Augustus, 1848-1907.

SAINT-GAUDENS, 730'.92'4 B
Augustus, 1848-1907.
The reminiscences of Augustus Saint-Gaudens / edited and amplified by Homer Saint-Gaudens. [New York : Garland Pub., 1976], c1913-. v. : ill. ; 19 cm. (The Art experience in late nineteenth-century America) Reprint of the ed. published by the Century Co., New York, with new introd. [NB237.S2A2 1976] 75-28890 ISBN 0-8240-2247-5 lib.bdg. : 50.00
1. Saint-Gaudens, Augustus, 1848-1907. 2. Sculptors—United States—Biography. I. Saint-Gaudens, Homer, 1880- II. Title. III. Series. **BIP**

THARP, Louise (Hall) 730'.924 B
1898-
Saint-Gaudens and the gilded era. [1st ed.] Boston, Little, Brown [1969] xii, 419 p. illus., ports. 24 cm. Bibliographical references included in "Notes" (p. [383]-398) [NB237.S2T5] 72-79372 8.50
1. Saint-Gaudens, Augustus, 1848-1907. I. Title.

Saint-Germain, comte de, d. 1784?

COOPER-OAKLEY, 133'.0924 B
Isabel.
The Comte de St. Germain; the secret of kings. New York, S. Weiser, 1970. xvi, 249 p. illus., facsims., port. 22 cm. Reprint of the 1912 ed. Bibliography: p. 243-249. [BF1598.S3C6 1970b] 72-132187 ISBN 0-87728-026-6 7.50
1. Saint-Germain, comte de, d. 1784?

COOPER-OAKLEY, 133'.0924 B
Isabel.
The Count of Saint Germain. Introd. by Paul M. Allen. Blauvelt, N.Y., R. Steiner Publications, 1970. viii, 248 p. 22 cm. First published in 1912 under title: The Comte de St. Germain, the secret of kings. Bibliography: p. 243-248. [BF1598.S3C6 1970] 70-137422 7.95
1. Saint-Germain, comte de, d. 1784?

Saint Joseph, Mother, 1756-1838.

MCMANAMA, Mary Fidelis 922.2493
[Secular name: Maude E. McManama] 1886-
Treasure in a field; the life of Venerable Mother St. Joseph, confoundress of the Sisters of Notre Dame de Namur, nee Viscountess Marie Louise Francoise Blin de Bourdon, heiress of the Barony de Fezaineourt. Milwaukee, Bruce Pub. Co. [c.1960] 215p. illus. 60-15480 3.95
1. Saint Joseph, Mother, 1756-1838. 2. Sisters of Notre Dame de Namur. I. Title.

Saint-Just. Louis Antoine de, 1767-1794.

BRUUN, Geoffrey, 944.0440924
1898-
Saint-Just. apostle of the terror. Hamden. Conn., Archon [dist. Shoe String] 1966 [c.1932] 168p. 21cm. Bibl. [DC146.S135B7] 66-16083 4.00
1. Saint-Just. Louis Antoine de, 1767-1794. 2. France—Hist.—Revolution. 1793-1794. I. Title. **BIP**

CURTIS, Eugene 944.04'4'0924
Newton, 1880-1944.
Saint-Just, colleague of Robespierre. New York, Octagon Books, 1973 [c1935] xi, 402 p. illus. 23 cm. Reprint of the ed. published by Columbia University Press, New York. Bibliography: p. 387-[394] [DC146.S135C8 1973] 73-14540 ISBN 0-374-92010-9 14.00
1. Saint-Just, Louis Antoine de, 1767-1794. 2. France—History—Revolution, 1793-1794. I. Title.

Saint Laurent, Yves.

MADSEN, Axel. 746.9'2'0924 B
Living for design : the Yves Saint Laurent story / Axel Madsen. New York : Delacorte Press, c1979. p. cm. Includes index. Bibliography: p. [TT505.S24M32] 79-13818 ISBN 0-440-05358-7 : 12.95
1. Saint Laurent, Yves. 2. Costume designers—France—Biography. I. Title.

Saint-Martin, Louis Claude de, 1743-1803.

WAITE, Arthur Edward, 1857- 194 B
1942.
The unknown philosopher; the life of Louis Claude de Saint-Martin and the substance of his transcendental doctrine. Blauvelt, N.Y., R. Steiner Publications, 1970. 464 p. 22 cm. Reprint of the 1901 ed., published under title: The life of Louis Claude de Saint-Martin. "Bibliography of the writings of Saint-Martin": p. 439-458. [B2145.Z7W2 1970] 70-130815 10.00
1. Saint-Martin, Louis Claude de, 1743-1803. I. Title.

Saint Mary's College, Notre Dame, Ind.

MADELEVA, Sister, 1887- 923.773
My first seventy years. New York, Macmillan, 1959. 172p. 22cm. [LD7251.N9417 1934] 59-6135
1. Saint Mary's College, Notre Dame, Ind. I. Title.

MADELEVA, M. [Secular 923.773
name: Mary Evaline Wolff] Sister 1887-
My first seventy years. New York, Macmillan [1962, c.1959] 191p. 18cm. (121) 1.45 pap.,
1. Saint Mary's College, Notre Dame, Ind. I. Title.

Saint, Nathanael, 1923-1956.

HITT, Russell T. 922.6866
Jungle Pilot, the life and witness of Nate Saint. Photos by Nate Saint, other missionaries and Cornell Capa. Grand Rapids, Mich., Zondervan Publishing House [1973, c1959] 263 p. illus. 18 cm. [BV2853.E3S3] pap. 1.25
1. Saint, Nathanael, 1923-1956. 2. Missions—Ecuador. I. Title.
L.C. card no. for original ed. 59-10335

Saint, Philip.

SAINT, Philip. 266'.0092'4
Amazing Saints, by Phil Saint. Plainfield, N.J., Logos International, 1972. vii, 211 p. illus. 21 cm. Autobiographical. [BV3785.S15A3] 71-124480 ISBN 0-912106-24-7 4.95
1. Saint, Philip. I. Title.

Saint-Saens, Camille, 1835-1921.

HERVEY, Arthur, 1855- 780'.924
1922.
Saint-Saens. Freeport, N.Y., Books for Libraries Press [1969] xv, 159 p. facsims., ports. 23 cm. (Select bibliographies reprint series) "First published 1922." Bibliography: p. 157-159. [ML410.S15H3 1969] 70-94271
1. Saint-Saens, Camille, 1835-1921. **BIP**

LYLE, Watson. 780'.924 B
Camille Saint-Saens, his life and art. With a pref. by Leff Pouishnoff. Westport, Conn., Greenwood Press [1970] 210 p. music, port. 23 cm. Reprint of the 1923 ed. Bibliography: p. 209-210. [ML410.S15L9 1970] 71-109776 ISBN 0-8371-4266-0
1. Saint-Saens, Camille, 1835-1921. **BIP**

SAINT-SAENS, Camille, 1835- 780
1921.
Musical memories. Translated by Edwin Gile Rich. New York, Da Capo Press, 1969. 282 p. illus., ports. 24 cm. (Da Capo Press music reprint series) Translation of Ecole buissonniere. Reprint of the 1919 ed. [ML60.S14R4 1969] 70-93980
1. Music—Addresses, essays, lectures. 2. Musicians—Correspondence, reminiscences, etc. **BIP**

Saint-Simon, Claude Henri, comte de, 1760-1825.

MANUEL, Frank Edward 921.4
The new world of Henri Saint-Simon. Notre Dame, Ind., Univ. of Notre Dame Pr., 1963 [c.1956, 1963] 433p. illus. 21cm. (ndp 28) Bibl. 2.25 pap.,
1. Saint-Simon, Claude Henri, comte de, 1760-1825. I. Title.

MANUEL, Frank Edward. 921.4
The new world of Henri Saint-Simon. Cambridge, Harvard University Press, 1956. xi, 433p. ports. 25cm. Bibliographical references included in 'Notes' (p. [369]-423) [HX265.S4M3] 56-6519
1. Saint-Simon, Claude Henri, comte de, 1760-1825. I. Title.

Saint-Simon, Louis Rouvroy, duc de, 1675-1755.

DE LEY, Herbert. 944'.033'0924
Saint-Simon memorialist : "Un enchainement si singulier ... " / Herbert De Ley. Urbana : University of Illinois Press, c1975. 153 p. ; 20 cm. (English series ; 2) Bibliography: p. [145]-149. [DC130.S2D44] 75-4491 6.00
1. Saint-Simon, Louis Rouvroy, duc de, 1675-1755. I. Title.

DE LEY HERBERT 944'.033'0924
Saint-Simon memorialist : "Un enchainement si singulier ... " / Herbert De Ley. Urbana : University of Illinois Press, c1975. 153 p. ; 20 cm. (English series ; 2) Bibliography: p. [145]-149. [DC130.S2D44] 75-4491 6.00
1. Saint-Simon, Louis Rouvroy, duc de, 1675-1755. I. Title.

Sainte-Beuve, Charles Augustin, 1804-1869.

HARPER, George McLean, 1863-1947. 848'.7'09 B
Charles-Augustin Sainte-Beuve. Freeport, N.Y., Books for Libraries Press [1970] 388 p. port. 23 cm. Reprint of the 1909 ed. Bibliography: p. 375-[381] [PQ2391.Z5H3 1970] 74-124237
1. Sainte-Beuve, Charles Augustin, 1804-1869. BIP

LEHMANN, Andrew George 928.4
Sainte-Beuve; a portrait of the critic, 1804-1842. [New York] Oxford,]c.]1962[ ] xvi, 430p. illus., Bibl. 62-2346 10.10
1. Sainte-Beuve, Charles Augustin, 1804-1869. I. Title.

LEHMANN, Andrew George. 928.4
Sainte-Beuve: a portrait of the critic, 1804-1842. Oxford, Clarendon Press, 1962. xvi, 430p. plates, ports. 23cm. 'Select biographical appendix': p.[401]-410. Bibliographical references included in 'Notes' Charles Augustin, 1804-1869. [PQ2391.Z5L25] 62-2346
I. Title.

LEHMANN, Arthur George. v. 12
Sainte-Beuve; a portrait of the critic, 1804-1842 [by] A. G. Lehmann. Oxford, Clarendon Press, 1962. xvi, 430 p. illus., ports. 22 cm. "Select list of the works of Sainte-Beuve": p. [xv]-xvi. "Select bibliographical appendix": p. [401]-410. Bibliographical footnotes. 65-73118
1. Sainte-Beuve, Charles Augustin, 1804-1869. I. Title.

Sainte-Beuve, Charles Augustin, 1804-1869—Biography.

NICOLSON, Harold George, Sir, 1886-1968. 848'.7'09 B
Sainte-Beuve / Harold Nicolson. Westport, Conn. : Greenwood Press, 1978. xi, 274 p., [8] leaves of plates : ill. ; 23 cm. Reprint of the 1957 ed. published by Constable, London. Includes index. [PQ2391.Z5N46 1978] 77-20072 ISBN 0-313-20013-0 lib.bdg. : 19.50
1. Sainte-Beuve, Charles Augustin, 1804-1869—Biography. 2. Authors, French—19th century—Biography.

Sainte-Beuve, Charles Augustine, 1804-1869.

NICOLSON, Harold George, Hon. 1886- 928.4
Sainte-Beuve. Garden City, N. Y., Doubleday [1957] 274p. illus. 22cm. Includes bibliography. [PQ2391.Z5N46 1957a] 57-10010
1. Sainte-Beuve, Charles Augustine, 1804-1869. I. Title. BIP

Saints.

ATTWATER, Donald, 1892- 922.22
Saints of the East. New York, P. J. Kenedy [1963] 190 p. illus. 22 cm. [BX393.A83] 63-11328
1. Saints. I. Title.

BRODRICK, James, 1891- 270 B
A procession of saints. Freeport, N.Y., Books for Libraries Press [1972, c1949] p. (Biography index reprint series) Includes bibliographical references. [BX4655.B7 1972] 72-5436 ISBN 0-8369-8134-0
1. Saints. I. Title. BIP

BROU, Alexandre, 1862- 922.22
Saint Madeleine Sophie Barat: her life of prayer and her teaching, based on unpublished documents. Tr. by Jane Wynne Saul. New York, Desclee, [1964] ix, 189p. port. 22cm. 64-12766 3.50
I. Title.

BROWN, Beverly Holladay, 1912- ed. and tr. 922.22
St. Francis texts [edited and translated by Raphael Brown, pseud. Chicago, Franciscan Herald Press] 1954- v. 16cm. [BX4700.F6B76] 54-2915
I. Francesco d'Assisi, Saint, 1182-1226. II. Title.

BURGHARDT, Walter J 248.0922 (B)
Saints and sanctity [by] Walter J. Burghardt. Englewood Cliffs, N.J., Prentice-Hall [1965] xiv, 239 p. illus. 22 cm. Bibliographical footnotes. [BX4655.2.B8] 65-8828
1. Saints. 2. Exempla. I. Title.

BUTLER, Alban, 1711-1773. 235.20922
Lives of the saints. Edited, rev., and supplemented by Herbert Thurston and Donald Attwater. Complete ed. [New York. P. J. Kenedy, 1965, c1963] 4 v. 24 cm. Includes bibliographies. [BX4654.B8] 67-5269
1. Saints. 2. Devotional calendars. I. Thurston, Herbert, 1856-1939. II. Attwater, Donald, 1892- III. Title. BIP

BUTLER, Alban, 1711-1773. 922.22
Lives of the saints; edited, rev., and supplemented by Herbert Thurston and Donald Attwater. Complete ed. New York, Kenedy [1956] 4 v. 24 cm. Includes bibliographical references. [BX4654.B8 1956] 56-5383
1. Saints. 2. Devotional calendars. I. Thurston, Herbert, 1856-1939. II. Attwater, Donald, 1892- III. Title.

BUTLER, Alban, 1711-1773. 922.22
Lives of the saints. Edited, rev., and supplemented by Herbert Thurston and Donald Attwater. Complete ed. [New York] [Kenedy] [1962] 4 v. 24 cm. Includes bibliographical references. [BX4654.B8 1962] 62-51171
1. Saints. 2. Devotional calendars. I. Thurston, Herbert, 1856-1939. II. Attwater, Donald, 1892- III. Title.

BUTLER, Alban, 1711-1773. 922.22
Lives of the saints, with reflections for every day in the year; compiled from the "Lives of the saints" by Alban Butler, with new saints and those whose feasts are special to the United States. New York, Benziger [1953] 390 p. 19 cm. [BX4654.B95 1953] 53-27731
1. Saints. 2. Calendars. I. Title.

CORLEY, Francis Joseph, 1909- 922.2
Wings of eagles; the Jesuit saints and blessed [by]Francis J. Corley, Robert J. Willmes [Reissue] Chicago, Loyopa Univ. Pr., 1965 [c.1941, 1965] xvii, 206p. 24cm. (Loyola request reprint ser.) Bibl. [BX4655.C6] 65-2581 3.50
1. Saints. 2. Jesuits—Biog. I. Willmes, Robert Joseph. 1909- joint author. II. Title. III. Title: Jesuit saints and blessed.

FARJEON, Eleanor, 1881-1965. 920
Ten saints. With illus. by Helen Sewell. [Catholic ed.] New York, H. Z. Walck [1958, c1936] 124 p. illus. 25 cm. Brief biographical sketches of Saints Christopher, Martin, Dorothea, Bridget, Patrick, Hubert, Giles, Simeon Stylites, Nicholas, and Francis. [BR1711.F3 1958] AC 68
1. Saints. I. Sewell, Helen, 1896-1957, illus. II. Title.

FOSTER, John, 1898- 922.1
Five minutes a saint. Richmond, Va., Knox [1964, c.1963] 112p. 19cm. 64-15239 1.25 pap.,
1. Saints. 2. Nicholas, Saint, Bp of Myra—Juvenile literature. I. Title.

GARRETT, Randall 922.22
A gallery of the saints. Derby, Conn., Monarch [c.1963] 238p. 19cm. (Monarch select bk. MS9) .75 pap.,
I. Title.

HARNEY, Martin Patrick, 1896- 922.22
Boother and sister saints. [1st ed.] Paterson, N. J., St. Anthony Guild Press [1957] 128p. 20cm. Includes bibliography. [BX4657.H3] 58-26550
1. Saints. I. Title.

HARTON, Sibyl, 1898- 922.22
Stars appearing; lives of sixty-eight saints of the Anglican calendar. New York, Morehouse-Gorham [1954] 237p. 19cm. [BR1710] 55-42
1. Saints. I. Title.

HAUGHTON, Rosemary 922.22
Six saints for parents. New York, Sheed [1963, c.1962] 249p. 22cm. 63-8538 3.95
1. Saints. I. Title.

JACOBUS de Varagine. 282'.092'2 B
The golden legend; or, Lives of the saints, as Englished by William Caxton. London, J. M. Dent, 1900-39. [v. 1, 1931. New York, AMS Press, 1973] 7 v. cm. Original ed. issued in series: The Temple classics. [BX4654.J33 1973] 76-170839 ISBN 0-404-06770-0 92.50
1. Saints. I. Caxton, William, ca. 1422-1491, tr. II. Title.

LEVY, Rosalie Marie, 1889- 922.22
Heavenly friends. [Boston] St. Paul Educations c1958] 484p. illus. 22cm. [BX4655.L4] 59-25199
1. Saints. I. Title.

LIPTAK, David Q 922.22
101 saints. Milwaukee, Bruce Pub. Co. [c1963] xvii, 170 p. 17 cm. "Sermonlike essays." Bibliography: p. xi-xii. [BX4657.L47] 63-21342
1. Saints. I. Title.

LIVES of saints, 922.22
with excerpts from their writings. New York, J. J. Crawley [1954- v. col. illus., col. ports. 22 cm. [BR1710.L52] 54-37560
1. Saints. 2. Religious literature (Selections: Extracts, etc.)

LIVES of saints. 922.22
with excerpts from their writings. Introd. by Father Thomas Plassmann; editorial supervision by Father Joseph Vann. Roslyn, N. Y., Published for the Classics Club by W. J. Black [1953] 426p. 20cm. [BR1710.L5] 54-17181
1. Saints. 2. Religio0s literature (Selections: Extracts, etc() I. Vann, Joseph, Father, 1907- ed.

LIVES of saints, with excerpts from their writings. 922.22
Introd. by Father Thomas Plassmann; editorial supervision by Father Joseph Vann. New York, J. J. Crawley [1954] xv, 527p. col. illus. 22cm. [BR1710.L5 1954] 54-37560
1. Saints. 2. Religious literature (Selections: Extracts, etc.) I. Vann, Joseph, Father. 1907- ed.

THE Lives of the saints 922.22
for every day of the year; a new, illustrated collection, offering the modern reader the inspiration and example of God's heroes through twenty centuries. Chicago, Catholic Press [1959] 3v. illus. 19cm. [BX4655.L5] 59-3270
1. Saints. 2. Devotional calendars—Catholic church

LUCAS, Barbara, 1911- v. 12
Great saints and saintly figures. With illus. by Anne Linton. [1st ed.] New York, Hawthorn Books [1963] 417-512 p. illus., ports. (part col.) 26 cm. (The New library of Catholic knowledge, v. 5) Bibliography: p. 512. 65-63879
1. Saints. 2. Christian biog. 3. Catholic Church — Biog. I. Title.

LUCE, Clare (Boothe) 1903- ed. 922.22
Saints for now. New York, Sheed & Ward, 1952. 312 p. illus. 22 cm. [BX4655.L8] 52-10608
1. Saints. I. Title.

LUCE, Clare (Boothe) 1903- ed. 922.22
Saints for now. New York, All Saints [1963, c.1952] 311p. illus. 17cm. (AS704) .75 pap.,
1. Saints. I. Title.

MAYNARD, Theodore, 1890- 922.22
Saints for our times. Garden City, N. Y., Image Books [1955, c1952] 304p. 18cm. (A Doubleday image book, D 12) [BX4651] 55-824
1. Saints. I. Title.

MAYNARD, Theodore, 1890-1956. 922.22
Saints for our times. New York, Appleton-Century-Crofts [1952] 296 p. 22 cm. [BX4651.M382] 52-6723
1. Saints. I. Title.

THE Month. 922.22
Saints and ourselves; personal studies. [1st] - ser. New York, P. J. Kenedy [1953- v. 23cm. 'First published in the Month.' Editor: v. 1- P. Caraman. [BX4657.M66] 53-11510
1. Saints. I. Caraman, Philip, 1911- ed. II. Title.

MURRAY, Desmond P 922.22
A saint of the week; short lives of English, Irish, Scottish, and universal saints taken from the calendar of saints, followed by practical lessons. Chicago, H. Regnery Co., 1955. 294p. illus. 22cm. [BX4655.M79] 55-13790
1. Saints. I. Title.

MURRAY, Verona. 920
The saint of the week [by] Sister M. Verona Murray. Illustrated by Harold Schmitz. Milwaukee, Bruce Pub. Co. [1966] viii, 158 p. illus. 22 cm. Brief sketches of the lives of twenty-nine saints, for inspirational reading during the weeks of the Catholic school year. [BX4658.M8] AC 67
1. Saints. I. Schmitz, Harold, illus. II. Title.

PAINTING, Norman. 922.22
Stories of the saints. Edited by Michael Day. With a foreword by Peggy Bacon. Chicago, Franciscan Herald Press [1958?] 185p. 19cm. [BR1710.P3] 58-14609
1. Saints. I. Title.

ROEDER, Helen, 1909- 922.22
Saints and their attributes; with a guide to localities and patronage. Chicago, H. Regnery Co. [1956, c1955] xxviii, 391p. illus. 18cm. Biblliography: p. xiv. [BX4661] 56-13630
1. Saints. 2. Patron saints. I. Title.

THE saints; 922.22
a concise biographical dictionary, edited by John Coulson. With an introd. by C.C. Martindale. 1st ed. New York, Hawthorn Books [1958] 496p. plates (part col.) 26cm. Bibliography: p. 489-491. [BX4655.S28] 58-5626
1. Saints. I. Coulson, John, 1919- ed.

SAINTS (The); 922.22
a concise biographical dictionary, ed. by John Coulson. Introd. by C. C. Martindale. New York, Guild [1966, c.1958] 496p. plates (pt. col.) 26cm. (Angelus bk., 31181) Bibl. [BX4655.S28] .95 pap.,
1. Saints. I. Coulson, John, 1919- ed.

SHARKEY, Donald C 1912- 922.22
Popular patron saints [by] Don Sharkey and Sister Loretta Clare. Milwaukee, Bruce Pub. Co. [1960] 283 p. 24 cm. [BR1710.S46] 60-7175
1. Saints. I. Felertag, Loretta Clare 1890- joint author. II. Title.

WALSH, William Thomas, 1891-1949 922.22
Saints in action. Garden City, N. Y., Hanover House [c.1961] 359p. Bibl. 61-12567 4.95
1. Saints. I. Title.

WALSH, William Thomas, 1891-1949. 922.22
Saints in action. [1st ed.] Garden City, N.Y., Hanover House, 1961. 359 p. 22 cm. [BX4655.2.W25] 61-12597
1. Saints. I. Title.

WARD, Maisie [full name: Mary Josephine Ward Sheed] 922.22
Saints who made history: the first five centuries. New York, Sheed and Ward [1960, c.1959] xiv, 377p. (6p. bibl.) 22cm. 60-7310 4.50 bds.,

1. Saints. I. Title.

Saints—Biog.

THE lives of the fathers, v. 12 martyrs, and other principal saints; compiled from original moments, and other authentic records; illustrated with the remarks of judicious modern critics and historians. New York, D. & J. Sadlier [n. d.] 4 v. illus. (Part Col.) 29cm. 'Published with the approbation of the Most Rev. John Hughes, Archbishop of New York.' Issued in 55 parts. Text within ornamental border.
1. Saints—Biog. I. Butler, Alban, 1711-1773.

*ONGARO, A. Cremonini 922.22
Saint Pancratius. Illus. by G. de Luca. Boston, Daughters of St. Paul, c.1964. 28p. col. illus. 21cm. (St. Paul eds.) .50;.35 pap.,
I. Title.

*PREMONT, Brother Jeremy 920
The cardinal said no: St. John Fisher, Valatie, N.Y., Holy Cross Pr. [c.1964] 140p. 22cm. 2.50
I. Title.

*PURCELL, Mary 922.22
The first Jesuit, St. Ignatius Loyola. Garden City, N.Y., Doubleday [1965] 433p. 18cm. (Image bk., D189) Bill. .35 pap.,
I. Title.

Saints, British.

WEBB, J. F. ed. and tr. 922.22
Lives of the saints. Tr., introd. by J. F. Webb. Baltimore, Penguin [c.1965] 206p. 19cm. (Penguin classics, L153) [BX4659.G7W43] 65-4003 .95 pap.,
1. Saints, British. I. Brendan, Saint. Legend. II. Beda Venerabilis, 673-735. Life of Cuthbert. III. Eddi, fl. 669. Life of Wilfrid. IV. Title. V. Title: V. Life of Cuthbert. VI. Title: Life of Wilfrid.
Contents omitted.

Saints—Calendar.

BITTLE, Berchmans, 1887- 922.22
A saint a day, according to the liturgical calendar of the church. Milwaukee, Bruce Pub. Co. [1958] 356p. 23cm. [BX4655.B5] 58-6926
1. Saints—Calendar. I. Title.

DAUGHTERS of St. Paul 922.2
Saints for young people for everyday of the year; v.2 [Boston] St. Paul Eds. [dist.] Author [c.1964] 337p. illus. ,pt. col.) ports. (pt. col.) 22cm. Contents.v.2. July-Dec. 63-19997 2.50 pap.,
1. Saints—Calendar. 2. Saints—Juvenile literature. I. Title.

ENGLEBERT, Omer, 1893- 922.22
The lives of the saints. Translated by Christopher and Anne Fremantle. New York, D. McKay Co. [1951] xi, 532 p. 23 cm. Translation of Les saints. [BX4655.E513] 51-11328
1. Saints—Calendar. I. Title.

Saints—Dictionaries.

ATTWATER, Donald, 1892- 922.22
A dictionary of saints; based on Butler's Lives of the saints, complete ed. New York, P. J. Kenedy [1958] vii, 280 p. front. 24 cm. "With each entry ... an index reference is given to the fuller treatment in 'Butler' [published in 1956]" [BX4654.B8 1958 Index] 58-12556
1. Saints—Dictionaries. I. Butler, Alban, 1711-1773. The lives of the saints. New York, 1956. II. Title.

ATTWATER, Donald, 1892- 235.20922
The Penguin dictionary of saints. Baltimore, Penguin Books [1965] 362 p. 19 cm. (Penguin reference books, R30) [BX4655.8.A8] 65-5009
1. Saints—Dictionaries. I. Title. II. Title: Dictionary of saints.

ATTWATER, Donald, 1892- 235.20922
The Penguin dictionary of saints [Magnolia, Mass., P. Smith, 1967, c.1965] 362p. 19cm. (Penguin ref. bk., R30 rebound) [BX4655.8.A8] 3.50
1. Saints—Dictionaries. I. Title. II. Title: Dictionry of saints.

ATTWATER, Donald, 235.20922
2)1892-
The Penguin dictionary of saints [Magnolia, Mass., P. Smith, 1967, c.1965] 362p. 19cm. (Penguin ref. bk., R30 rebound) [BX4655.8.A8] 3.50
1. Saints—Dictionaries. I. Title. II. Title: Dictionary of saints. BIP

SHARP, Mary 922.22
A traveller's guide to saints in Europe. London, H. Evelyn [dist. Wilkes-Barre, Pa., Dimension Bks., c.1964] xv, 251p. 23cm. Bibl. 64-7696 5.95 bds.,
1. Saints—Dictionaries. I. Title. II. Title: Saints in Europe.

Saints, English.

ALBERSTON, Clinton, 235'.2'0922
comp.
Anglo-Saxon saints and heroes [ed., tr. by] Clinton Albertson. [Bronx, N.Y.] Fordham [1967] xv, 347p. illus. 24cm. Bibl. [BX4659.G7A5] 67-16652 7.50
1. Saints, English. I. Title.
Contents omitted.

ALBERTSON, Clinton, 235.20922
comp.
Anglo-Sazon saints and heroes [ed., tr. by] Clinton Albertson. [Bronx, N.Y.] Fordham [1967] xv, 347p. illus. 24cm. Bibl. [BX4659.G7A5] 67-16652 7.50
1. Saints, English. I. Title.
Contents omitted.

KNOWLES, David [Secular 922.22
name: Michael Clive Knowles] 1896-
Saints and Scholars; twenty-five medieval portraits. [New York] Cambridge [c]1962. 207p., illus. 21 cm. 62-4142 3.95; pap., 1.65
1. Saints—Gt. Brit 2. Scholars, English. I. Title.

WEBB, J. F. ed. and tr. 922.22
Lives of the saints. Tr., introd. by J. F. Webb. Baltimore, Penguin [c.1965] 206p. 19cm. (Penguin classics, L153) [BX4659.G7W43] 65-4003 .95 pap.,
1. Saints, British. I. Brendan, Saint. Legend. II. Beda Venerabilis, 673-735. Life of Cuthbert. III. Eddi, fl. 669. Life of Wilfrid. IV. Title. V. Title: V. Life of Cuthbert. VI. Title: Life of Wilfrid.
Contents omitted.

Saints,Georgian.

LANG, David Marshall, 922.1479
ed. and tr.
Lives and legends of the Georgian saints, selected and translated from the original texts by David Marshall Lang. London, Allen & Unwin; New York, Macmillan [1956] 179p. illus. 20cm. (Ethical and religious classics of East and West, no. 15) Includes bibliography. [BX669.A1L3] 57-3831
1. Saints, Georgian. I. Title.

LANG, David Marshall, 922.1479
ed. and tr.
Lives and legends of the Georgian saints, selected and translated from the original texts by David Marshall Lang. London, Allen & Unwin; New York, Macmillan [1956] 179p. illus. 29cm. (Ethical and religious classics of East and West, no. 15) Includes bibliography. [BX669.A1L3] 57-3831
1. Saints,Georgian. I. Title.

Saints—Gt. Brit

KNOWLES, David [Secular 922.22
name: Michael Clive Knowles] 1896-
Saints and Scholars; twenty-five medieval portraits. [New York] Cambridge [c]1962. 207p., illus. 21 cm. 62-4142 3.95; pap., 1.65
1. Saints—Gt. Brit 2. Scholars, English. I. Title.

Saints, Irish.

CURTAYNE, Alice. 922.22
More tales of Irish saints. Illustrated by Brigid Rynne. New York, Sheed and Ward [1957] 139p. illus. 21cm. [BX4659.I7C79] 57-10187
1. Saints, Irish. I. Title. II. Title: Tales of Irish saints.

LYNCH, Patricia, 1898- 922.22
Knights of God stories of the irish saints Chicago, H. Regnery Co., 1955. 216p. 22cm. [BX4659.I7L9] 55-6413
1. Saints, Irish. I. Title.

Saints, Irish—Juvenile literature.

LYNCH, Patricia, 1898- 274.15 B
Knights of God; tales and legends of the Irish saints. Illustrated by Victor Ambrus. [1st ed.] New York, Holt, Rinehart and Winston [1969] xix, 219 p. illus. 24 cm. Contents.Contents.—Introduction.—Saint Ciaran, the first of them all.—Saint Patrick, the Roman slave.—Enda of Aran.—Saint Brigid, the light of Kildare.—Brendan the voyager.—Columcille, dove of the church.—Kevin of Glendalough.—Lawrence O'Toole, captive prince.—There were other saints.—List of books (p. 219) [BX4659.I7L9 1969] 920 69-11811 4.50
1. Saints, Irish—Juvenile literature. I. Ambrus, Victor G., illus. II. Title.

REILLY, Robert T. 922.22
Irish saints. Illus. by Harry Barton. New York, Farrar [c.1964] xvii, 172p. illus., map. 22cm. (Vision bk., 63) 64-19806 2.25
1. Saints, Irish—Juvenile literature I. Title.

REILLY, Robert T 922.22
Irish saints, by Robert T. Reilly. Illustrated by Harry Barton. New York, Vision Books [1964] xvii, 172 p. illus., map. 22 cm. "63." [BX4659.I7R4] 64-19806
1. Saints, Irish — Juvenile literature. I. Title.

REILLY, Robert T 922.22
Irish saints, by Robert T. Reilly. Illustrated by Harry Barton. New York, Vision Books [1964] xvii, 172 p. illus., map. 22 cm. "63." [BX4659.I7R4] 64-19806
1. Saints, Irish — Juvenile literature. I. Title.

Saints—Juvenile literature.

BEEBE, Catherine, 1898- 922.22
Saints for boys and girls; stories. Pictures by Robb Beebe. Milwaukee, Bruce Pub. Co. [1959] 147p. illus. 21cm. [BX4658.B43] 59-13571
1. Saints—Juvenile literature. I. Title.

BURTON, Doris. 922.22
The girls' book of saints. Illustrated by T. J. Bond. St. Louis, Herder [1958] 149p. illus. 23cm. [BX4658.B8 1958] 59-2322
1. Saints—Juvenile literature. 2. Saints, Women. I. Title.

CHADWICK, Enid M. 920
Saints who loved animals, written, illus. by Enid M. Chadwick. London. A. R. Mowbrav [dist. Westminster, Md., Canterbury, 1963, c.1962] 61p. 21cm. 63-802 1.95 bds.,
1. Saints—Juvenile literature. I. Title.

CONWAY, E. Carolyn 922.22
The little ways. Illustrated by Astrid Walford. Baltimore, Helicon Press, 1960 [ ] 114p. illus. 20cm. 6 -9509 2.50 bds.
1. Saints—Juvenile literature. I. Title.

COOK, Frederick. 922.22
Young girl of France, and other stories. Paterson, N.J., St. Anthony Guild Press, 1956. 118p. illus. 21cm. [BX4658.C57] 56-14269
1. Saints—Juvenile literature. I. Title.

COUSINS, Mary 922.22
More about the saints. Illustrated by Margery Gill. Westministerr, Md., Newman Press, 1960.[ ] 158p. illus. (part col.) 22cm. 60-16074 2.75 bds.,
1. Saints —Juvenile 9iterature. I. Title.

COUSINS, Mary 920
The saints in history. Illus. by Sally Mellersh. New York, Kenedy [1963, c.1962] 125p. illus. map. 3cm. 62-22117 2.95
1. Saints—Juvenile literature.s8 I. Title.

CRISS, Mildred, 1890- 922.22
A book of saints. New York, Dodd, Mead, 1956. 156 p. illus. 22 cm. [BX4658.C6] 56-6800
1. Saints—Juvenile literature. I. Title.

DANIEL-ROPS, Henry 922.22
Golden legend of young saints. New York, Kenedy [c.1960] 192p. illus. 22cm. 60-7790 2.95
I. Saints—Juvenile literature. II. Title.

DAUGHTERS of St. Paul. 920
57 stories of saints for boys and girls. Written and illustrated by the Daughters of Saint Paul. [Boston] St. Paul Editions [1963] 581 p. illus. 22 cm. [BX4658.D35] 63-19996
1. Saints — Juvenile literature. I. Title.

DAUGHTERS of St. Paul. 920
57 stories of saints for for boys and girls. Written, illus. by the Daughters of Saint Paul [Boston] St. Paul Eds. [dist. daughter of St. Paul.] c.1963] 581p. col. illus. 22cm. 63-19996 4.00 5.00 pap.,
1. Saints —Juvenile literature. I. Title.

FLAHIVE, Robert F. 922.22
Saints for Scouts. Milwaukee, Bruce Pub. Co., [c.1960] ix, 149p. illus. 22 cm. 60-10657 2.75
1. Saints—Juvenile literature. I. Title.

FLAHIVE, Robert F. 922.22
Saints for servers. Illus. by Arnie Kohn. Milwaukee, Bruce [c.1961] 62p. 61-17438 1.25
1. Saints—Juvenile literature. I. Title.

GALES, Louis A 1896- 922.22
A first book of saints for little Catholics; illustrated by Gertrude Elliott Espenscheid. St. Paul, Catechetical Guild Educational Society, c1954. unpaged. illus. 17cm. (First books for little Catholics) [BX4653.G3] 54-27105
1. Saints—Juvenile literature. I. Title.

HASKELL, Arnold Lionel, 922.22
1903-
Saints alive; a study of six saints for young people. With a foreword by Barbara Ward. New York Roy Publishers [1953] 148 p. illus. 20 cm. [BX4658.H28] 54-7908
1. Saints—Juvenile literature. I. Title.

MARY Cornelius, Sister, 922.22
1901-
Saints to know. Milwaukee, Bruce Pub. Co. [1954] 128p. illus. 23cm. [BX4658.M424] 54-10664
1. Saints—Juvenile literature. I. Title.

MOORE, Margaret R 922.22
Big saints, by Margaret and John Travers Moore. Illus. by Gedge Harmon. St. Meinrad, Ind., Grail [c1954] 77p. illus. 22cm. [BX4658.M6] 55-14066
1. Saints—Juvenile literature. I. Moore, John Travers, joint author. II. Title.

O'NEILL, Mary 920
Saints: adventures in courage. Illus. by Alex Ross. Garden City, N. Y., Doubleday [c.1963] 186p. col. illus. 29cm. 63-17278 4.95
1. Saints—Juvenile literature. I. Title.

O'NEILL, Mary (Le Duc) 1908- 920
Saints: adventures in courage. Illustrated by Alex Ross. [1st ed.] Garden City, N.Y., Doubleday [1963] 186 p. illus. 29 cm. [BX4658.O5] 63-17278
1. Saints — Juvenile literature. I. Title.

PETERS, Caroline 920
Lives of the saints, for boys and girls, Drawings by Mitzi Young. Paterson. N. J., St. Anthony Guild Pr [c.1966] vi, 130p. illus. 25cm. [BX4658.P4] 66-17973 3.00
1. Saints—Juvenile literature. I. Title.

PETERS, Caroline. 920
Lives of the saints, for boys and girls. Drawings by Mitzi Young. Paterson, N. J., St. Anthony Guild Press [1966] vi. 130 p. illus. 25 cm. [BX4658.P4] 66-17973
1. Saints—Juvenile literature. I. Title.

ROSES, Anthony. 920 (J)
The golden man. Illustrated by Mary Taylor. Westminster, Md., Newman Press [1955] 99p. illus. 19cm. Stories adapted from Legenda aurea by Jacobus de

Varagine. [BX4658.R6] 55-8662
1. Saints—Juvenile literature. I. Jacobus de Varagine. Legenda aurea. II. Title.

ROSS Williamson, Hugh, 922.22
1901-
The young people's book of saints; sixty-three saints of the Western church from the first to the twentieth century. Illustrated by Sheila Connelly. New York, Hawthorn Books. [1960] 239 p. illus. 22 cm. [BX4653.R65] 60-10338
1. Saints—Juvenile literature. I. Title.

THOMPSON, Blance Jennings, j922
1887-
Saints of the Byzantine world. Illustrated by Donald Bolognese. New York, Vision Books [1961] 192 p. illus. 22 cm. (Vision books, 52) [BX393.T48] 61-11325
1. Saints — Juvenile literature. I. Title.

THOMPSON, Blanche Jennings 922.22
When saints were young. Illustrated by John Lawn. New York, Farrar, Straus and Cudahy [c.1960] 188p. illus. 22cm. (Vision books, 46) 60-6139 1.95
1. Saints—Juvenile literature. I. Title.

THOMPSON, Blanche Jennings, 922
1887-
Saints of the Byzantine world. Illus. by Donald Bolognese. New York, Vision Bks. [dist. Farrar, c.1961] 192p. (Vision bks., 52) 61-11325 1.95
1. Saints—Juvenile literature. I. Title.

THOMPSON, Blanche 922.22
Jennings, 1887-
When saints were young. Illustrated by John Lawn. New York, Vision Books [1960] 188 p. illus. 22 cm. (Vision books, 46) [BX4658.T52] 60-6139
1. Saints — Juvenile literature. I. Title.

TWIGG-PORTER, George. 920 (J)
Caves, conversions, and creatures. [Boston] St. Paul Editions [1967] 74 p. illus. 19 cm. Bibliographical footnotes. [BX4658.T87] 67-29165
1. Saints—Juvenile literature. I. Title.

WEDGE, Florence. 922.22
Saints without wrinkles; thirteen saints for teen-agers. Pulaski, Wis., Franciscan Printery, 1956. 173 p. 22 cm. [BX4658.W4] 57-36861
1. Saints — Juvenile literature I. Title.

WEDGE, Florence. 920
Sixty shining halos. Pulaski, Wis., Franciscan Publishers [1963] 187 p. illus. 22 cm. [BX4658.W42] 63-10259
1. Saints — Juvenile literature. I. Title.

WINDHAM, Joan, 1904- 922.22
Saints upon a time; Illustrated by Kurt Werth. New York, Sheed and Ward [1956] 160 p. illus. 21 cm. [RX4658.W55] 56-6133
1. Saints — Juvenile literature. I. Title.

Saints, Norwegian.

UNDSET, Sigrid, 1882- 282'.0922
1949.
Saga of saints. Translated by E. C. Ramsden. Freeport, N.Y., Books for Libraries Press [1968, c1934] xii, 321 p. illus., map, ports. 22 cm. (Essay index reprint series) Translation of Norske helgener. Contents.Contents.—The coming of Christianity.—St. Sunniva and the Seljemen.—St. Olav, Norway's king to all eternity.—St. Hallvard.—St. Magnus, Earl of the Orkney Islands.—St. Eystein, Archbishop of Nidaros.—St. Thorfinn, Bishop of Hamar.—Father Karl Schilling, Barnabite. [BX4659.N8U7 1968] 68-22952
1. Saints, Norwegian. 2. Norway—Church history. I. Title.
BIP

Saints—Poetry.

METCALFE, James J 1906- 922.22
Poem portraits of the saints; lives of the saints in verse. [1st ed.] Garden City, N. Y., Hanover House [1956] 119p. 22cm. [BX4657.M4] 56-5589
1. Saints—Poetry. I. Title.

Saints, Russian.

GRUNWALD, Constantin de. 922.147
Saints of Russia. Translated by Roger Capel. New York, Macmillan, 1960. 180p. 22cm. Translation of Quand la Russie avait des saints. [BX596.G713 1960] 60-12977
1. Saints, Russian. I. Title.

Saints, Women.

FARLEY, Luke A., 1919 922.22
Saints for the modern woman, a united nations of holiness for the woman of today. Written, illus. by Luke A. Farley. 53Boston] St. Paul Eds. [dist. Daughters of St. Paul, c.1961] 276p. Bibl. 61-18635 3.95; 2.50 pap.,
1. Saints, women. I. Title.

MARTINDALE, Cyril Charlie, 922.22
1879-
The Queen's daughters, a study of women saints. New York, Sheed & Ward, 1951. 252 p. 22 cm. [BX4656.M43] 51-13726
1. Saints, Women. I. Title.

WINDHAM, Joan, 1904- 922.22
Sixty saints for girls; a Joan Windham omnibus. Illus. by Renee George. New York, Sheed [1962] 376p. illus. 22cm. 62-15288 3.95
1. Saints, Women. I. Title.

Saintsbury, George Edward Bateman, 1845-1933.

WEBSTER, Adam Blyth, 1882- 809 B
1956.
George Saintsbury / by A. Blyth Webster. Folcroft, Pa. : Folcroft Library Editions, 1977. 47 p., [2] leaves of plates : ports. ; 26 cm. Reprint of the 1933 ed. published by Oliver and Boyd, Edinburgh. Includes bibliographical references. [PR5295.W4 1977] 77-23018 ISBN 0-8414-9618-8 lib. bdg. : 10.00
1. Saintsbury, George Edward Bateman, 1845-1933. 2. Literary historians Great Britain—Biography.
BIP

Sakharov, Andrei Dmitrievich, 1921—

SAKHAROV, Andrei 323.4'0947 B
Dmitrievich, 1921-
Sakharov speaks [by] Andrei D. Sakharov. Edited and with a foreword by Harrison E. Salisbury. [1st ed.] New York, A. A. Knopf, 1974. vi, 245 p. 22 cm. [DK274.S277 1974] 73-21154 6.95
1. Sakharov, Andrei Dmitrievich, 1921- 2. Russia—Politics and government—1953- —Addresses, essays, lectures. 3. Civilization, Modern—1950- —Addresses, essays, lectures. I. Title.
BIP

Saladin, Sultan of Egypt and Syria. 1137-1193.

ABU Shamah, 'Abd al- 909.07
Rahman ibn Isma'il, 1203-1267.
Arabische Quellenbeitrage zur Geschichte der Kreuzzuge / ubers. u. hrsg. von E. P. Goergens. Machdr. d. Ausg. Berlin 1879. Bd. 1. Zur Geschichte Salah ad-din's. Hildesheim ; New York : Olms, 1975. xxiii, 295 p. ; 19 cm. No more published. Reprint of the ed. published by Weidmann'sche Buchhandlung. Includes bibliographical references. [D152.A2 1975] 76-459998 ISBN 3-487-05590-2 : DM49.80
1. Saladin, Sultan of Egypt and Syria, 1137-1193. 2. Crusades—Sources. I. Goergens, E. P. II. Title.

EHRENKREUTZ, 962'.02'0924 B
Andrew S.
Saladin [by] Andrew S. Ehrenkreutz. [1st ed.] Albany, State University of New York Press, 1972. 290 p. 24 cm. Bibliography: p. 263-273. [DS38.4.S24E34] 78-161443 ISBN 0-87395-095-X 10.00
1. Saladin, Sultan of Egypt and Syria, 1137-1193.
BIP

GIBB, Hamilton 956'.01'0924 B
Alexander Rosskeen, Sir, 1895-
The life of Saladin: from the works of 'Imad ad-Din and Baha' ad-Din, by Sir Hamilton Gibb. Oxford, Clarendon Press, 1973. [5], 76 p. 23 cm. "Based on a chapter contributed by the author to the History of the crusades (ed., K. Setton), first published by the University of Pennsylvania Press (2nd edn., 1969)...." Includes bibliographical references. [DS38.4.S2G52 1973] 73-164005 ISBN 0-19-821499-5 £1.50 ($5.00 U.S.)
1. Saladin, Sultan of Egypt and Syria, 1137-1193. I. al-Katib al-Isfahani, 'Imad al-Din Muhammad ibn Muhammad, 1125-1201. al-Barq al-Shami. II. Ibn Shaddad, Baha' al-Din Yusuf ibn Rafi', 1145-1234. al-Nawadir al-sultaniyah. III. Title.

HINDLEY, Geoffrey. 956'.01'0924 B
Saladin / Geoffrey Hindley. New York : Barnes & Noble Books, 1976. xv, 208 p., [7] leaves of plates : ill. ; 23 cm. Includes index. Bibliography: p. [198]-200. [DS38.4.S2H56] 76-12067 ISBN 0-06-492877-2 : 18.00
1. Saladin, Sultan of Egypt and Syria, 1137-1193. 2. Islamic Empire—History—750-1258.
BIP

HINDLEY, Geoffrey. 956'.01'0924 B
Saladin / [by] Geoffrey Hindley. London : Constable, 1976. xv, 208 p., leaf of plate, [12] p. of plates : ill., facsims. ; 22 cm. Includes index. Bibliography: p. [198]-200. [DS38.4.S2H56 1976b] 76-377372 ISBN 0-09-457790-0 : £4.95
1. Saladin, Sultan of Egypt and Syria, 1137-1193. 2. Islamic Empire—History—750-1258.

LANE-POOLE, 956'.01'0924 B
Stanley, 1854-1931.
Saladin and the fall of the Kingdom of Jerusalem / by Stanley Lane-Poole. New York : AMS Press, 1978. xxiv, 416 p., [31] leaves of plates (3 fold.) : ill. ; 19 cm. Reprint of the 1898 ed. published by Putnam, New York, which was issued as v. 24 of Heroes of the nations. Includes bibliographical references and index. [DS38.4.S2L36 1978] 73-14453 ISBN 0-404-58270-2 : 30.00
1. Saladin, Sultan of Egypt and Syria, 1137-1193. 2. Islamic Empire—History—750-1258. 3. Jerusalem—Latin Kingdom, 1099-1244. 4. Egypt—Kings and rulers—Biography. 5. Syria—Kings and rulers—Biography. I. Heroes of the nations. II. Title.
BIP

SLAUGHTER, Gertrude 923.1
Elizabeth (Taylor) 1870-
Saladin. 1138-1193 a biography. With drawings by Robert Hill Taylor. [1st ed.] New York, Exposition Press [1955] 304p. illus. 21cm. (A Banner book) [D198.4.S2S5] 55-10302
1. Saladin, Sultan of Egypt and Syria. 1137-1193. I. Title.

Salcedo, Manuel Maria de, d. 1813.

ALMARAZ, Felix 976.4'02'0924 B
Diaz, 1933-
Tragic cavalier; Governor Manuel Salcedo of Texas, 1808-1813, by Felix D. Almaraz, Jr. Austin, University of Texas Press [1971] xii, 206 p. 23 cm. Bibliography: p. [183]-189. [F389.A22] 75-165917 ISBN 0-292-70139-X 7.00
1. Salcedo, Manuel Maria de, d. 1813. 2. Texas—History—To 1846. I. Title.

Salel, Hugues, 1504 (ca.)-1553.

KALWIES, Howard H. 841'.3
Hugues Salel, his life and works / Howard H. Kalwies. Ann Arbor : University Microfilms International ; Normal, Ill. : Applied Literature Press, 1979. p. cm. (Monograph publishing : Imprint series) (ALP Medieval studies ; v. 4) Bibliography: p. [PQ1703.S43Z74] 79-27150 ISBN 0-8357-0500-5 : 20.75
1. Salel, Hugues, 1504 (ca.)-1553. 2. Poets, French—16th century—Biography. I. Title. II. Series.

Salem, Mass.—Hist.

BENTLEY, William, 1759- 922.8173
1819
The diary of William Bentley, D.d., pastor of East Church, Salem, Massachusetts[4v.] Gloucester, Mass., Peter Smith, 1962 4v. (various p.) illus., 21cm. Contents.v.1. 1784-1792.--v.2. 1793-1802.--v.3. 1803-1810.--v.4. 1811-1819, including subject index to volumes 1-4 Bibl. 63-1100 11.25;45.00 ea., set,
1. Salem, Mass.—Hist. 2. Salem, Mass, East Church. I. Essex Institute, Salem, Mass. II. Title.

Salem United Methodist Church, Honey Creek, Wis.

MUELLER, Erhart. 287'.6775'76
The history of the Salem Church of Honey Creek; 1844-1946, Salem Evangelical Church, 1946-1969, Salem Evangelical United Brethren Church, 1969, Salem United Methodist Church. [Honey Creek? Wis., 1969?] 153 p. illus. 22 cm. On cover: Salem Church, 1844-1969. [BX8481.H77S35] 74-152494
1. Salem United Methodist Church, Honey Creek, Wis. 2. Honey Creek, Wis.—Biography. I. Title.

Salesmen and salesmanship.

WHELESS, Malone, 1870- 926.588
By the sweat of my brow. [1st ed.] Richmond, Outlook Publishers [1953] 152p. 21cm. [HF5438.W5245] 53-11208
1. Salesmen and salesmanship. I. Title.

Salinger, Jerome David, 1919-

GRUNWALD, Henry Anatole, 813.54
ed.
Salinger; a critical and personal portrait. New York, Harper [1963, c.1962] 287p. 21cm. (Colophon bks., CN13) Bibl. 1.75 pap.,
1. Salinger, Jerome David, 1919- I. Title.

Salisbury, De Witt Clinton.

SALISBURY, Dc 977.5'83'030924
Witt Clinton.
Pages from the diaries of De Witt Clinton Salisbury, 19th century Wisconsin citizen, and Civil War soldier / selections and comments by Mildred Hansen Osgood. Wauwatosa, Wis : M. H. Osgood, [1974] 120, [3] p. : ill. ; 22 cm. Bibliography: p. [123] [CT275.S3117A33] 75-302475 3.00
1. Salisbury, De Witt Clinton. I. Osgood, Mildred Hansen, ed. II. Title: Pages from the diaries of De Witt Clinton Salisbury ...

Salisbury, Robert Arthur Talbot Gascoyne-Cecil, 3d Marquis of, 1830-1903.

TAYLOR, Robert G. 941.081'092'4 B
Lord Salisbury / Robert Taylor. New York : St. Martin's Press, 1975. 202 p. ; 23 cm. (British political biography) Includes index. Bibliography: p. [195]-197. [DA564.S2T39 1975b] 75-7711 12.95
1. Salisbury, Robert Arthur Talbot Gascoyne-Cecil, 3d Marquis of, 1830-1903.
BIP

Salisbury, Robert Cecil, 1st Earl of, 1563-1612.

CECIL, Algernon, 942.05'5'0924
1879-1953.
A life of Robert Cecil, First Earl of Salisbury. Westport, Conn., Greenwood Press [1971] xii, 406 p. illus., ports. 23 cm. Reprint of the 1915 ed. Includes bibliographical references. [DA358.S2C4 1971] 71-109717 ISBN 0-8371-4207-5
1. Salisbury, Robert Cecil, 1st Earl of, 1563-1612. I. Title.

Salish Indians.

POINT, Nicolas, 1799- 970.4'8
1868.
Wilderness kingdom, Indian life in the Rocky Mountains: 1840-1847; the journals & paintings of Nicolas Point. Translated and introduced by Joseph P. Donnelly. With an appreciation by John C. Ewers. [1st ed.] New York, Holt, Rinehart and Winston [1967] xiii, 274 p. illus. (part col.), facsims. (part col.), col. maps, col. ports. 32 cm. Bibliography: p. 273-274. [E78.N77P6] 67-19048
1. Salish Indians. 2. Skitswish Indians. 3. Siksika Indians. 4. Indians of North America—Missions. 5. Jesuits in the Northwest, Pacific. 6. Rocky Mountains. 7. Indians of North America—Pictorial works. I. Donnelly, Joseph P., tr. II. Title.

Salk, Jonas Edward, 1914-

CARTER, Richard, 1918- 615.372
Breakthrough: the saga of Jonas Salk New York, Pocket Bks. [1967, c.1965] 420p. 18cm. (95061) [RC180.6.C3] .95 pap.,
1. Salk, Jonas Edward, 1914- 2. Poliomyelitis vaccine. I. Title.

ROWLAND, John, 1907- 926.1
The polio man; the story of Dr. Jonas Salk. New York, Roy Publishers [1961, c1960] 128 p. illus. 21 cm. [R154.S225R6] 61-6398
1. Salk, Jonas, 1914- I. Title.

Saller, Alfred, 1870-1937.

ADLER, Alfred, 1870- 150'.19'5308 1937.
Superiority and social interest : a collection of later writings / Alfred Adler ; edited by Heinz L. Ansbacher and Rowena R. Ansbacher ; with a biographical essay by Carl Furtmuller. New York : Norton, 1979. p. cm. "Bibliography of Alfred Adler": p. [BF173.A548 1979] 78-27620 ISBN 0-393-00910-6 pbk. : 5.95
1. Saller, Alfred, 1870-1937. 2. Psychoanalysis. 3. Psychoanalysts—Austria—Biography. I. Ansbacher, Heinz Ludwig, 1904- II. Ansbacher, Rowena R. III. Title. BIP

Sallustius Crispus, C.

STORONI Mazzolani, 937'.007'2022 Lidia.
Empire without end / Lidia Storoni Mazzolani ; with a foreword by Mario Pei ; translated by Joan McConnell and Mario Pei. New York : Harcourt Brace Jovanovich, c1976. p. cm. "A Helen and Kurt Wolff book." Translation of L'impero senza fine. Includes index. Bibliography: p. [DG206.S3S7613] 76-20672 ISBN 0-15-128780-5 : 10.95
1. Sallustius Crispus, C. 2. Livius, Titus. 3. Tacitus, Cornelius. 4. Rome—Historiography. I. Title.

Salm-Salm, Agnes (Joy) prinzessin zu, 1884?-1912.

ARMS, Florence. 920.7
Bright morning. Boston, Bruce Humphries [1962] 136p. 21cm. [D400.S2A8] 62-8825
1. Salm-Salm, Agnes (Joy) prinzessin zu, 1884?-1912. I. Title.

Salmon canning industry—Oregon.

HUME, Robert Deniston, 926.6 1845-1908.
A pygmy monopolist; the life and doings of R. D. Hume, written by himself and dedicated to his neighbors. Edited with an introd. by Gordon B. Dodds. Madison, State Historical Society of Wisconsin for the Dept. of History, University of Wisconsin, 1961. vi, 87p. map. 23cm. 'Hume published his autobiography in his own newspaper, the Wedderburn (Oregon) Radium, from February, 1904, until June, 1906.' Bibliographical references included in 'Notes' (p. 85-87) [HD9469.S23O73] 61-63121
1. Salmon canning industry—Oregon. I. Dodds, Gordon Barlow, 1932- ed. II. Title.

Salmon, Thomas William, 1876-1927.

BOND, Earl Danford, 1879- 926.1
Thomas W. Salmon, psychiatrist, by Earl D. Bond, with the collaboration of Paul O. Komora. [1st ed.] New York, Norton [1950] 237 p. ports. 21 cm. "A bibliography of the writings of Thomas W. Salmon": p. 231-237. [R154.S23B6] 50-5964
1. Salmon, Thomas William, 1876-1927. I. Title.

Salomon, Haym, 1740-1785.

AMERICAN Jewish 973.3'092'4 B Historical Society.
Haym Salomon, a gentleman of precision and integrity. Waltham, Mass. : American Jewish Historical Society, c1976. 16 p. : ill. ; 28 cm. [E302.6.S17A82 1976] 76-380453
1. Salomon, Haym, 1740-1785. 2. United States—History—Revolution, 1775-1783—Biography. 3. Jews in the United States—Biography. I. Title.

HART, Charles Spencer. 920.073
General Washington's son of Israel and other forgotten heroes of history. Illustrated by Harold Von Schmidt. Freeport, N.Y., Books for Libraries Press [1969] 229 p. illus. 24 cm. (Essay index reprint series) Reprint of the 1937 ed. Contents.Contents.—Haym Salomon.—William Dawes.—Sam Davis.—Johnny Fitch.—Amerigo Vespucci.—John Peter Zenger.—Jean Ribaut.—Charles Goodyear.—J. A. MacGahan.—Squire Boone.—James Shields.—John Sevier. [E176.H328 1969] 70-90642
1. Salomon, Haym, 1740-1785. 2. U.S.—Biography. 3. U.S.—History. I. Title. BIP

Salomon, Haym, 1740-1785 — Juvenile literature.

KNIGHT, Vick. 973.3'092'4 B
Send for Haym Salomon! / By Vick Knight, Jr. ; illustrated by Joseph M. Henninger. 1st ed. Alhambra, Calif. : Haym Salomon Foundation, in collaboration with Borden Pub. Co., c1976. 96 p. : ill. ; 24 cm. Bibliography: p. 85-86. A biography of the Polish-born Jew who was responsible for raising most of the money needed to finance the American Revolution and later save the nation from collapse. [E302.6.S17K55] 92 76-4688 5.95
1. Salomon, Haym, 1740-1785—Juvenile literature. 2. United States—History—Revolution, 1775-1783—Biography—Juvenile literature. 3. Jews in the United States—Biography—Juvenile literature. I. Henninger, Joseph M., 1906- II. Title.

MILGRIM, Shirley 973.3'092'4 B Gorson.
Haym Salomon, liberty's son / Shirley Milgrim ; illustrated by Richard Fish. 1st ed. Philadelphia : Jewish Publication Society of America, c1975. 119 p. : ill. ; 24 cm. A biography of the Polish-born Jew who cast his lot with the American rebels, helping to finance the American Revolution and later to save the new nation from economic collapse. [E302.6.S17M52] 92 75-17349 ISBN 0-8276-0073-9 : 4.50
1. Salomon, Haym, 1740-1785—Juvenile literature. I. Fish, Richard G. II. Title.

MILGRIM, Shirley (Gorson) 92
Haym Salomon. Illustrated by Hans Zander. Chicago, Follett Pub. Co. [1966] 143 p. col. illus. 22 cm. (Library of American heroes) [E302.6.S17M5] 67-815
1. Salomon, Haym, 1740-1785 — Juvenile literature. I. Title.

Salomoni, Giacomo, 1231-1314.

DESMOND, Cecelia. 271'.2'00924 B
Blessed James Salomoni; patron of cancer patients apostle of the afflicted. [Boston] St. Paul Editions [1971] 76, [1] p. illus. 20 cm. Bibliography: p. [77] [BX4705.S142D4] 70-150719 2.00
1. Salomoni, Giacomo, 1231-1314. I. Title.

Salsbury, Clarence.

MEANS, Florence (Crannell) 926.1 1891-
Sagebrush surgeon. New York, Friendship Press [c1955] 166p. 21cm. [R154.S24M4] 55-5763
1. Salsbury, Clarence. I. Title.

Salt, Henry Stephens, 1851-1939.

HENDRICK, George. 823'.9'12
Henry Salt, humanitarian reformer and man of letters / George Hendrick ; with the special assistance of John F. Pontin. Urbana : University of Illinois Press, c1977. 228 p. ; 21 cm. Includes bibliographical references and index. [PR5299.S217Z7] 77-5142 ISBN 0-252-00611-9 : 6.95
1. Salt, Henry Stephens, 1851-1939. 2. Authors, English—19th century—Biography.

Salt, Titus, Sir, 1803-1876.

TITUS of 338.7'67'7310942817
Salts / [edited by Roger W. Suddards ; photographs by Martin White ; illustrations and drawings by Barrie Birch and Trevor Skempton]. Bradford : Watmoughs Ltd., 1976. 64 p. : ill. plan, port. ; 22 cm. Bibliography: p. 64. [TS1440.S34T57] 77-361700 ISBN 0-903775-05-0 : £0.90
1. Salt, Titus, Sir, 1803-1876. 2. Salts (Saltaire) Ltd. 3. Bradford, Eng. (Yorkshire)—Biography. 4. Textile industry—Great Britain—Biography. I. Suddards, Roger W.

Salter family.

SHEWMAKE, Oscar Land, 929'.2'0973 1882-
Gawin Lane Corbin Salter, a gentlemen and a scholar, 1814-1890. Richmond [1960] 106 p. illus. 24 cm. [CS71.S177 1960] 61-36021
1. Salter family. I. Title.

Saltonstall family.

MOODY, Robert Earle, 974.4 S 1901- comp.
The Saltonstall papers, 1607-1815. Selected and edited and with biographies often members of the Saltonstall family in six generations, by Robert E. Moody Boston, Massachusetts Historical Society, 1972-74. 2 v. illus. 26 cm. (Collections of the Massachusetts Historical Society, v. 80-81) Contents.Contents.—v. 1. 1607-1789.—v. 2. 1791-1815. Bibliography: v. 1, p. [558]-574. [F61.M41 vol. 80-81] [CS71.S179] 929'.2'0973 72-80205
1. Saltonstall family. 2. Massachusetts—History—Colonial period, ca. 1600-1775—Sources. 3. Massachusetts—History—1775-1865—Sources. I. Title. II. Series: Massachusetts Historical Society, Boston. Collections, v. 80-81. BIP

Saltus, Edgar Evertson, 1855-1921.

SALTUS, Marie (Giles) 813'.4 B
Edgar Saltus, the man, by Marie Saltus. New York, AMS Press [1970] xxiii, 324 p. illus., facsims., ports. 19 cm. Reprint of the 1925 ed. [PS2753.S3 1970] 71-125173
1. Saltus, Edgar Evertson, 1855-1921.

SALTUS, Marie (Giles) 813'.4 B
Edgar Saltus, the man, by Marie Saltus. Chicago, P. Covici, 1925. St. Clair Shores, Mich., Scholarly Press, 1970. xxiii, 324 p. facsims., ports. 22 cm. [PS2753.S3 1970b] 75-145279 ISBN 0-403-01194-9
1. Saltus, Edgar Evertson, 1855-1921.

Salutati, Coluccio, 1331-1406—Correspondence.

WITT, Ronald G. v. 12
Coluccio Salutati and his public letters / Ronald G. Witt. Geneve : Librairie Droz, 1976. xii, 112 p., [3] leaves of plates : ill. ; 26 cm. (Travaux d'humanisme et Renaissance ; 151) Includes bibliographical references and index. [PA8420.S15A328] 77-463485 64.00F
1. Salutati, Coluccio, 1331-1406—Correspondence. 2. Authors, Latin—Correspondence. I. Title.

Salvado, Rosendo, Bp., 1814-1900.

SALVADO, Rosendo, 266'.2'0924 B Bp., 1814-1900.
The Salvado memoirs : historical memoirs of Australia and particularly of the Benedictine mission of New Norcia and of the habits and customs of the Australian natives / by Dom Rosendo Salvado ; translated and edited by E. J. Stormon. Nedlands, W.A. : University of Western Australia Press, [1977.] xx, 300 p., [7] leaves of plates : ill. ; 25 cm. Aus Translation of Memorie Storiche dell' Australia. Sold by International Scholarly Book Services, Forest Grove, Or. Includes bibliographical references and index. [BV3667.S25A3513] 77-559483 ISBN 0-85564-114-2 : 23.00
1. Salvado, Rosendo, Bp., 1814-1900. 2. Missionaries—Australia—Western Australia—Biography. 3. Missionaries—Spain—Biography. 4. Missions to Australian aborigines—Australia—Western Australia. 5. Australian aborigines—Australia—Western Australia. 6. Western Australia. I. Title.
Distributed by ISBS. BIP

Salvation Army—Exeter, Eng.—Biography.

BRADDICK, Muriel. 362.4'092'4 B
Born for a purpose / [by] Muriel Braddick. St. Ives, Cornwall : United Writers Publications, 1976. 158 p. ; 22 cm. [BX9743.B845A33] 76-374950 ISBN 0-901976-34-2 : £1.95
1. Salvation Army—Exeter, Eng.—Biography. 2. Braddick, Muriel. 3. Church work with the handicapped. I. Title.

Salviati, Leonardo, 1540-1589.

BROWN, Peter 458'.0092'4 B Melville.
Lionardo Salviati : a critical biography / by Peter M. Brown. London ; New York : Oxford University Press, 1974. xvi, 291 p., [1] leaf of plates : ill. ; 22 cm. (Oxford modern languages and literature monographs) Includes index. Bibliography: p. [263]-281. [PQ4632.S7Z6] 74-189052 ISBN 0-19-815523-9 : 32.00
1. Salviati, Leonardo, 1540-1589.

Samaras, Lucas, 1936-

SAMARAS, Lucas, 1936- 709'.2'4
Lucas Samaras. Exhibition directed by Robert Doty. [New York] Whitney Museum of American Art [1972] [72] p. illus. (part col.) 29 cm. Catalog of the exhibition held Nov. 18, 1972-Jan. 7, 1973, at the Whitney Museum of American Art. Bibliography: p. [64]-[67] [N6537.S3D67] 72-87740
1. Samaras, Lucas, 1936- I. Doty, Robert M. II. Whitney Museum of American Art, New York.

Sample, Johnny.

SAMPLE, Johnny. 796.332'0924 B
Confessions of a dirty ballplayer, by Johnny Sample with Fred J. Hamilton and Sonny Schwartz. New York, Dial Press, 1970. vi, 343 p. illus., ports. 22 cm. [GV939.S16A3] 77-131167 6.95
I. Hamilton, Fred J., joint author. II. Schwartz, Sonny, joint author. III. Title.

Sample, Zola (Bellis)

SAMPLE, Zola (Bellis) 1900- 920
The house with the jillion memories; the story of a pioneer homestead in Oklahoma. [1st ed.] New York, Exposition Press [1957] 99p. 21cm. Autobiographical. [CT275.S313A3] 57-7662
I. Title.

Sampson, Arthur.

SAMPSON, Arthur. 927.96357
Ted Williams; a biography of The Kid. New York, Barnes [1950] vi, 180 p. illus., ports. 21 cm. (Most valuable player series) [GV865.W5S3] 50-7864
I. Williams, Theodore Samuel, 1918- II. Title.

Sampson, Patricia.

SAMPSON, Patricia. 131'.32
A star to steer by : success through positive experiencing / Patricia Sampson. New York : F. Fell Publishers, c1977. xiii, 151 p. ; 22 cm. [BJ1611.2.S23 1977] 77-18064 ISBN 0-8119-0301-X :
1. Sampson, Patricia. 2. Success. 3. Sales personnel—United States—Biography. 4. Success—Case studies. I. Title. BIP

Sampter, Jessie Ethel, 1883-1938.

STRAUSS, Bertha (Badt) 928.1
1885-
White fire; the life and works of Jessie Sampter. New York, Reconstructionist Press, 1956. 191 p. illus. 22 cm. [PS3537.A567Z9] 56-8436
1. Sampter, Jessie Ethel, 1883-1938. I. Title.

WHITE fire; the life and v. 12
works of Jessie Sampter. New York, The Reconstructionist press, 1956. 191p. illus., ports. 22cm.
1. Sampter, Jessie Ethel, 1883-1938. I. Strauss, Bertha (Badt), 1885-

Sampter, Jessie Ethel, 1883-1938—Biography.

STRAUSS, Bertha Badt, 811'.5'2 B
1885-
White fire : the life and works [of] Jessie Sampter / Bertha Badt-Strauss. New York : Arno Press, 1977 [c1956] 191 p., [6] leaves of plates : ill. ; 23 cm. (America and the Holy Land) Reprint of the ed. published by the Reconstructionist Press, New York. [PS3537.A567Z9 1977] 77-70663 ISBN 0-405-10224-0 : 15.00
1. Sampter, Jessie Ethel, 1883-1938—Biography. 2. Authors, American—20th century—Biography. I. Title. II. Series.

Sampurnanand,

SAMPURNANAND, 1891- 923.254
Memories and reflections. New York, Asia [dist. Taplinger, c.1962] 188p. illus. (front port.) 23cm. 62-4181 6.75
I. Title.

Samru Begam, 1750?-1836—Fiction.

CHATTERJEE, Vera. FIC
All this is ended : the life and times of H. H. the Begum Sumroo of Sardhana / Vera Chatterjee. New Delhi : Vikas, c1979. vii, 201 p. ; 19 cm. [PZ4.C4925Al] [PR9499.3.C467] 823 79-903884 ISBN 0-7069-0719-1 : 12.00
1. Samru Begam, 1750?-1836—Fiction. I. Title.
Distributed by Advent Books, 141 E. 44th St., Suite 809, NY, NY 10017

Samson, Judge of Israel—Juvenile literature.

ROSE, Anne K. 92 (J)
Samson and Delilah [by] Anne K. Rose. Illustrated by Richard Powers. New York, Lothrop, Lee & Shepherd [1968] 1 v. (unpaged) col. illus. 26 cm. [BS580.S15R62] 68-27713 3.50
1. Samson, Judge of Israel—Juvenile literature. I. Powers, Richard, illus. II. Title. BIP

WALSH, Bill. 221.9'24 B
The secret of Samson / by Bill Walsh ; with an afterword for parents and teachers by Andrew Greely. Kansas City [Kan.] : Sheed Andrews and McMeel, c1978. 77 p. : ill. ; 27 cm. (A Cartoon Bible story) [BS580.S15W34] 78-4938 ISBN 0-8362-4302-1 pbk. : 1.95
1. Samson, Judge of Israel—Juvenile literature. 2. Bible. O.T.—Biography—Juvenile literature. I. Title. BIP

Samudra Gupta, 4th cent.

GOKHALE, Balkrishna 923.154
Govind
Samudra Gupta: life and times. New York, Asia House.[dist.Taplinger, 1963,c.1962] 120p. 23cm. Bibl. 63-3160 6.50
1. Samudra Gupta, 4th cent. I. Title.

GOKHALE, Balkrishna 923.154
Govind.
Samudra Gupta: life and times. New York, Asia Pub. House [1962] 120 p. 23 cm. [DS451.9.S3G6] 63-3160
1. Samudra Gupta, 4th cent. I. Title.

Samuel, Judge of Israel—Juvenile literature.

WHALEY, Richie. 222'.43'09505
Samuel, prophet and judge / Richie Whaley ; illustrated by Dean Shelton. Nashville : Broadman Press, c1978. 48 p. : col ill. ; 24 cm. (Biblearn series) Tells of the Hebrew prophet, priest, judge, and ruler who selected Saul as the first king of Israel and chose David to succeed him. [BS580.S2W46] 78-317387 ISBN 0-8054-4242-1 : 3.95
1. Samuel, Judge of Israel—Juvenile literature. 2. Bible. O.T.—Biography—Juvenile literature. I. Shelton, Dean. II. Title.

Samuel, Maurice,

SAMUEL, Maurice, 1895- 922.96
The gentleman and the Jew. [1st ed.] New York, Knopf, 1950. viii, 325 p. 22 cm. Autobiographical. [BM755.S243A3] 50-9222
I. Title. BIP

SAMUEL, Maurice, 296'.092'4 B
1895-
The gentleman and the Jew. Westport, Conn., Greenwood Press [1972, c1950] viii, 325 p. 23 cm. Autobiographical. [BM755.S243A3 1972] 70-163541 ISBN 0-8371-6201-7 13.50
I. Title.

Samuel, Maurice, 1895-1972—Addresses, essays, lectures.

SAMUEL, Maurice, 1895- 922.96
The gentleman and the Jew. [1st ed.] New York, Knopf, 1950. viii, 325 p. 22 cm. Autobiographical [BM755.S243A3] 50-9222
I. Title. BIP

SAMUEL, Maurice, 296'.092'4 B
1895-
The gentleman and the Jew. Westport, Conn., Greenwood Press [1972, c1950] viii, 325 p. 23 cm. Autobiographical. [BM755.S243A3 1972] 70-163541 ISBN 0-8371-6201-7 13.50
I. Title.

SAMUEL, Maurice, 296'.092'4 B
1895-1972.
The gentleman and the Jew : twenty-five centuries of conflict in manners and morals / Maurice Samuel. New York : Behrman House, 1978. viii, 325 p. ; 22 cm. (A Jewish legacy book) Autobiographical. [BM755.S243A3 1977] 77-6666 ISBN 0-87441-264-1 : 4.95
1. Samuel, Maurice, 1895-1972—Addresses, essays, lectures. 2. Bible. O.T.—Criticism, interpretation, etc.—Addresses, essays, lectures. 3. Jews in the United States—Biography—Addresses, essays, lectures. 4. Judaism—20th century—Addresses, essays, lectures. 5. Zionism—Addresses, essays, lectures. I. Title.

SAMUEL, Maurice, 1895-1972. 081
The worlds of Maurice Samuel : selected writings / edited, and with an introd. by Milton Hindus ; foreword by Cynthia Ozick. 1st ed. Philadelphia : Jewish Publication Society of America, 1977. xxxii, 445 p. ; 25 cm. [DS151.S32A25 1977] 76-52669 ISBN 0-8276-0091-7 : 12.50
1. Samuel, Maurice, 1895-1972—Addresses, essays, lectures. 2. Zionists—United States—Biography—Addresses, essays, lectures. 3. Jews in the United States—Biography—Addresses, essays, lectures. 4. Judaism—Addresses, essays, lectures. 5. Yiddish literature—History and criticism—Addresses, essays, lectures. 6. Jews in literature—Addresses, essays, lectures. I. Title.

Samuel, Sigmund,

SAMUEL, Sigmund, 1867-1962 926.5
In return, the autobiography of Sigmund Samuel. [Toronto] Univ. of Toronto Pr. [1964] viii, 166p. illus., ports. 23cm. 64-56684 price unreported
I. Title.

SAMUEL, Sigmund, 1867-1962. 926.5
In return, the autobiography of Sigmund Samuel. [Toronto] University of Toronto Press [1963] viii, 166 p. illus., ports. 23 cm. [F1059.5.T68S15] 64-56684
I. Title.

Samuels, Thomas W., 1886-

SAMUELS, Thomas W., 340'.092'4 B
1886-
Lawyer in action / by Thomas W. Samuels. 1st ed. Hicksville, N.Y. : Exposition Press, [1975] c1974. 224 p., [4] leaves of plates : ill. ; 21 cm. Autobiography. [KF373.S18A33] 74-84432 ISBN 0-682-48089-4 : 8.00
1. Samuels, Thomas W., 1886- 2. Lawyers—Illinois—Correspondence, reminiscences, etc. 3. Illinois—History. I. Title.

San Diego Chargers (Football club)

MANDELL, 796.33'264'0979498
Arnold J., 1934-
The nightmare season / Arnold J. Mandell. 1st ed. New York : Random House, c1976. 216 p. ; 22 cm. [GV956.S29M36] 75-40569 ISBN 0-394-40252-9 : 8.95
1. San Diego Chargers (Football club) 2. Mandell, Arnold J., 1934- 3. Football—Biography. I. Title.

San Francisco—Biography.

BLOCK, Eugene B. 979.4'61'0099 B
The immortal San Franciscans for whom the streets were named, by Eugene B. Block. San Francisco, Chronicle Books [1971] xii, 244 p. illus., ports. 24 cm. [F869.S353A23] 72-161029 7.95
1. San Francisco—Biography. 2. San Francisco—Streets. 3. Street names. I Title.

COWAN, Robert Ernest, 920.079461
1862-1942.
The forgotten characters of old San Francisco. Ritchie [dist. Menlo Park, Calif. Lane, c.1938-1964] xi, 103p. illus. ports., facsims. 23cm. 64-3295 5.95
1. San Francisco—Biog. I. Bancroft, Anne. Brummer and Lazarus. II. Ballou, Addie Lucia, 1837- Personal recollections of Norton I. III. Title.
Contents omitted.

DEFORD, Miriam Allen, 920.0794'61
1888-
They were San Franciscans. Freeport, N.Y., Books for Libraries Press [1970, c1941] 327 p. ports. 23 cm. (Essay index reprint series) Contents.Contents.—The miser who brought the stars to earth: James Lick.—The spirit of '49: Sam Brannan.—Cabby to impresario: Tom Maguire.—America's Marx and his Bebel: Henry George and Kate Kennedy.—Reconstructed rebel: Asbury Harpending.—Lady fire buff: Lillie Hitchcock Coit. Chinese and dynamite: Dennis Kearney and Burnette Haskell.—Last of the Tolstoyans: Fremont Older.—Charlatan or dupe?: Albert Abrams.—The "Christ angel": Ella May Clemmons.—Gentleman Jim: James J. Corbett.—Laureate of Bohemia: George Sterling. [F869.S3D43 1970] 70-117781
1. San Francisco—Biography. I. Title.

San Francisco—Mayors—Biography.

HEINTZ, William 979.4'61'040922 B
F.
San Francisco's mayors, 1850-1880 : including a missing mayor discovery / by William F. Heintz; research assistance by Gladys C. Hansen Woodside, Calif. : G. Richards Publications, c1975. vi, 120 p. : ill. ; 28 cm. Includes index. Bibliography: p. 111-116. [F869.S353A24] 75-17094
1. San Francisco—Mayors—Biography. 2. San Francisco—History. I. Title.

San Martin, Jose de, 1778-1850.

THE Liberator 980'.02'0924 B
General San Martin : a bicentennial tribute, 1778-February 25-1978. Washington : General Secretariat, Organization of American States, [1978?] vii, 51 p., [1] leaf of plates : ill. ; 28 cm. Translation of El Libertador general San Martin. "78-XVIII-001-E." [F2235.4.L5213] 79-111962 2.00
1. San Martin, Jose de, 1778-1850. 2. Generals—South America—Biography. 3. Statesman—South America—Biography. 4. South America—Wars of Independence, 1806-1830. I. Organization of American States. General Secretariat.

METFORD, J C J 923.58
San Martin, the liberator. With a foreword by Sir Eugen Millington-Drake. New York, Philosophical Library [1950] xi, 154 p. port., maps. 23 cm. [F2235.4.M58] 51-1758
1. San Martin, Jose de, 1778-1850. I. Title. BIP

METFORD, J. C. J. 980'.03'0924 B
San Martin, the liberator, by J. C. J. Metford. Westport, Conn., Greenwood Press [1971] v, 154 p. 23 cm. Reprint of the 1950 ed. [F2235.4.M58 1971] 76-97386 ISBN 0-8371-3012-3
1. San Martin, Jose de, 1778-1850. I. Title.

San Martin, Jose de, 1778-1850 Juvenile literature.

RINK, Paul, 1912- 980'.02'0924 B
Soldier of the Andes: Jose de San Martin. New York, Messner [1971] 189 p. 22 cm. Bibliography: p. [183] A biography of the South American soldier who was one of the leaders in the struggle against Spanish domination in the early nineteenth-century. [F2235.4.R63] 92 76-140677 ISBN 0-671-32383-0 3.95
1. San Martin, Jose de, 1778-1850—Juvenile literature. I. Title.

San Saba Co., Tex.—Biography.

SLOAN, Jym A. 917.64'68 D
Old timers of Wallace Creek, by Jym A. Sloan. San Saba, Tex., c1958. 155 p. illus. 22 cm. [F392.S24S57] 73-161176
1. San Saba Co., Tex.—Biography. I. Title. II. Title: Wallace Creek.

Sanapia, 1895-

JONES, David E. 615'.89 B
Sanapia, Comanche medicine woman, by David E. Jones. New York, Holt, Rinehart and Winston [1972] xvii, 107 p. illus. 24 cm. (Case studies in cultural anthropology) Includes bibliographies. [E99.C85S25] 73-179548 ISBN 0-03-088456-X
1. Sanapia, 1895- 2. Comanche Indians. 3. Indians of North America—Great Plains—Medicine. I. Title. II. Series.

Sancho, Ignatius,

SANCHO, 914.2'03'730924 B
Ignatius, 1729-1780.
Letters of the late Ignatius Sancho, an African; with memoirs of his life by Joseph Jekyll. Freeport, N.Y., Books for Libraries Press, 1971. xvi, 310 p. illus., facsim., port. 23 cm. (The Black heritage library collection) "First published 1802." [CT788.S168A32 1971] 74-154080 ISBN 0-8369-8791-8
I. Jekyll, Joseph, 1754-1837. II. Title. III. Series. BIP

Sand, George, pseud. of Mme. Dudevant, 1804-1876.

CARO, Elme Marie, 1826- 843'.8 B
1887.
George Sand. Translated by Gustave Masson. Port Washington, N.Y., Kennikat Press [1970] 198 p. 22 cm. Reprint of the ed. published in London by G. Routledge in 1888. [PQ2412.C32 1970] 76-103173
1. Sand, George, pseud. of Mme. Dudevant, 1804-1876. BIP

DOUMIC, Rene, 1860- 843'.7 B
1937.
George Sand: some aspects of her life and writings. Translated by Alys Hallard. Port Washington, N.Y., Kennikat Press [1972] viii, 309 p. illus. 22 cm. Reprint of the 1910 ed. Includes bibliographical references. [PQ2412.D7 1972] 76-153902 ISBN 0-8046-1593-4

1. Sand, George, pseud. of Mme Dudevant, 1804-1876.

MAUROIS, Andre, 1885-1967 928.4
Lelia, the life of George Sand. Tr. from French by Gerard Hopkins. New York, Pyramid [1968,c.1953] 592p. illus., ports., facsim. 18cm. (V-1763) Bibl. [PQ2412.M313 1953a] 1.25 pap.,
1. Sand, George, pseud. of Mme. Dudevant, 1804-1876. I. Title.

WINEGARTEN, Renee. 843'.7 B
The double life of George Sand, woman and writer : a critical biography / by Renee Winegarten. New York : Basic Books, c1978. x, 339 p. ; 24 cm. Includes index. Bibliography: p. 321-331. [PQ2412.W5] 78-54501 ISBN 0-465-01683-9 : 15.00
1. Sand, George, pseud. of Mme. Dudevant, 1804-1876. 2. Novelists, French—19th century—Biography. I. Title.

Sand, George, pseud. of Mme. Dudevant, 1804-1876 - Biography.

BARRY, Joseph Amber, 1917- 843'.8 B
Infamous woman : the life of George Sand / Joseph Barry ; with the editorial collaboration of Liliane Lassen. 1st ed. Garden City, N.Y. : Doubleday, 1976. p. cm. Includes index. Bibliography: p. [PQ2413.B3] 76-5335 ISBN 0-385-06830-1 : 12.95
1. Sand, George, pseud. of Mme. Dudevant, 1804-1876—Biography. I. Title. BIP

BARRY, Joseph Amber, 1917- 843'.8
Infamous woman : the life of George Sand / Joseph Barry. Garden City : Anchor Press/Doubleday, 1978, c1976. xvi, 436p., [24] leaves of plates : photos. ; 24 cm. Includes index. Bibliography: p. [385]-423. [PQ2413.B3] [b ISBN 0-385-13366-9 pbk. : 5.95
1. Sand, George, pseud. of Mme. Dudevant, 1804-1876 — Biography. I. Title.
L.C. card no. for 1976 Doubleday ed.: 76-5335.

CATE, Curtis, 1924- 843'.7 B
George Sand : a biography / by Curtis Cate. Boston : Houghton Mifflin, 1975. xxxvi, 812 p., [8] leaves of plates : ill. ; 24 cm. Includes index. Bibliography: p. [787]-791. [PQ2413.C3] 75-8680 ISBN 0-395-19954-9 : 17.50
1. Sand, George, pseud. of Mme. Dudevant, 1804-1876—Biography. BIP

GERSON, Noel Bertram, 1914- 843'.7 B
George Sand; a biography of the first modern, liberated woman, by Samuel Edwards. New York, D. McKay [1972] 271 p. 22 cm. Bibliography: p. 263-264. [PQ2412.G4] 72-75462 6.95
1. Sand, George, 1804-1876—Biography.

JORDAN, Ruth. 843'.8 B
George Sand : a biographical portrait / Ruth Jordan. New York : Taplinger Pub. Co., 1976. xvi, 367 p., [7] leaves of plates : ill. ; 23 cm. Includes index. Bibliography: p. 357-360. [PQ2412.J6 1976b] 76-5190 ISBN 0-8008-3199-3 : 12.50
1. Sand, George, pseud. of Mme. Dudevant, 1804-1876—Biography. 2. Novelists, French—19th century—Biography. BIP

MAUROIS, Andre, 1885-1967. 843'.8 B
Lelia : the life of George Sand / Andre Maurois ; translated from the French by Gerard Hopkins. New York : Penguin Books, 1977, c1953. 592 p., [4] leaves of plates : ill. ; 19 cm. Reprint of the ed. published by Harper, New York. Includes index. Bibliography: p. 575-585. [PQ2412.M313 1977] 76-29029 ISBN 0-14-004354-3 pbk. : 2.95
1. Sand, George, pseud. of Mme. Dudevant, 1804-1876—Biography. 2. Authors, French—Biography. I. Title. BIP

MAUROIS, Andre, 1885-1967. 928.4
Lelia, the life of George Sand; translated from the French by Gerard Hopkins. New York, Harper [1953] 482 p. illus., ports. facsim. 25 cm. Bibliography: p. 471-478. [PQ2412.M313 1953a] 53-7740
1. Sand, George, pseud. of Mme. Dudevant, 1804-1876—Biography. I. Title.

SAND, George, pseud. of Mme. Dudevant, 1804-1876. 843'.8 B
The convent life of George Sand / translated and with an introd. by Maria Ellery MacKaye ; with a new chronology of George Sand's life and work. Chicago : Cassandra Editions, 1977. p. cm. Translation of a portion of the author's Histoire de ma vie. Reprint of the 1893 ed. published by Roberts, Boston. [PQ2412.A2E5 1977] 77-10534 ISBN 0-915864-38-X pbk. : 5.00. ISBN 0-915864-39-8 7.50
1. Sand, George, pseud. of Mme. Dudevant, 1804-1876—Biography. 2. Novelists, French—19th century—Biography. I. Title.

SAND, George, pseud. of Mme. Dudevant, 1804-1876. 843'.7 B
The intimate journal of George Sand / edited and translated by Marie Jenney Howe. New York : Gordon Press, 1976, c1929. p. cm. Translation of Journal intime. Reprint of the ed. published by Loring & Mussey, New York. [PQ2412.A2E5 1976] 76-10201 ISBN 0-87968-452-6 lib.bdg. : 34.95
1. Sand, George, pseud. of Mme. Dudevant, 1804-1876—Biography. I. Title. BIP

SAND, George, pseud. of Mme. Dudevant, 1804-1876. 843'.7 B
The intimate journal of George Sand / pref. by Aurore Sand ; translation and notes by Marie Jenney Howe. New York : Haskell House Publishers, 1976 198 p. ; 22 cm. Translation of Journal intime. Reprint of the 1929 ed. published by Williams & Norgate, London. [PQ2412.A2E5 1975] 75-20492 ISBN 0-8383-1939-4 lib.bdg. : 11.95
1. Sand, George, pseud. of Mme. Dudevant, 1804-1876—Biography. I. Title.

SAND, George, pseud. of Mme. Dudevant, 1804-1876. 843'.8 B
The intimate journal of George Sand / edited and translated by Marie Jenney Howe. Chicago : Cassandra Editions, 1977, c1929. p. cm. Translation of Journal intime. Reprint of the ed. published by John Day Co., New York. [PQ2412.A2E5 1977b] 77-18044 ISBN 0-915864-51-7 : 7.50. ISBN 0-915864-50-9 pbk. : 5.00
1. Sand, George, pseud. of Mme. Dudevant, 1804-1876—Biography. 2. Novelists, French—19th century—Biography. I. Howe, Marie Jenney. II. Title.

THOMAS, Bertha. 843.8 B
George Sand / by Bertha Thomas. New ed. Folcroft, Pa. : Folcroft Library Editions, 1977. p. cm. Reprint of the new ed., 1889 published by W. H. Allen, London, in series: Eminent women series. [PQ2412.T5 1977] 77-9346 ISBN 0-8414-8633-6 lib. bdg. : 25.00
1. Sand, George, pseud, of Mme Dudevant, 1804-1876—Biography. 2. Novelists, French—19th century—Biography. I. Series: Eminent women series. BIP

Sand, George, pseud. of Mme. Dudevant, 1804-1876—Bibliography.

SAND, George, pseud. of Mme. Dudevant, 1804-1876. 843'.7 B
My life / by George Sand ; translated from the French and adapted by Dan Hofstadter. 1st ed. New York : Harper & Row, c1979. viii, 246 p. ; 25 cm. Translation of Histoire de ma vie. Includes index. [PQ2412.A2E5 1979] 77-3770 ISBN 0-06-013766-5 : 15.00
1. Sand, George, pseud. of Mme. Dudevant, 1804-1876—Bibliography. 2. Novelists, French—19th century—Biography. I. Hofstadter, Dan. II. Title.

Sand, George pseud, of Mme Dudevant 1804-1876 Correspondence.

SAND, George, pseud. of Mme. Dudevant, 1804-1876. 843'.7 B
Letters of George Sand / selected and translated by Veronica Lucas ; with an introd. by Elizabeth Drew. New York : Gordon Press, 1976. p. cm. Reprint of the 1930 ed. published by G. Routledge, London. Includes index. Bibliography: p. [PQ2412.A3E5 1976] 76-10966 ISBN 0-87968-451-8 lib.bdg. : 39.95
1. Sand, George, 1804-1876—Correspondence. I. Lucas, Veronica. II. Title. BIP

Sand, George, pseud. of Mme. Dudevant, 1804-1876—Juvenile literature.

HOVEY, Tamara. 843'.8 B
A mind of her own : a life of the writer George Sand / by Tamara Hovey. 1st ed. New York : Harper & Row, c1977. xi, 211 p. : ill. ; 22 cm. Includes index. Bibliography: p. 204-206. A biography of the nineteenth-century French author who defied many social conventions in order to live and write as she wanted. [PQ2412.H58] 92 76-24310 ISBN 0-06-022616-1 : 7.95 ISBN 0-06-022617-X lib.bdg. : 7.89
1. Sand, George, pseud. of Mme. Dudevant, 1804-1876—Juvenile literature. 2. Novelists, French—19th century—Biography—Juvenile literature. I. Title. BIP

Sand, George, pseud. of Mme. Dudevant, 1804-1876 Relationship with men.

GRIBBLE, Francis Henry, 1862-1946. 843'.8 B
George Sand and her lovers / by Francis Gribble. A new ed. [Folcroft, Pa.] : Folcroft Library Editions, 1976. p. cm. Reprint of the ed. published by Dutton, New York. Includes index. [PQ2412.G7 1976] 76-44500 ISBN 0-8414-4504-4 lib. bdg. : 30.00
1. Sand, George, pseud, of Mme Dudevant, 1804-1876—Relationship withmen. 2. Novelists, French—Biography. I. Title. BIP

Sandburg, Carl, 1878-1967.

CALLAHAN, North. 811'.5'2 B
Carl Sandburg, Lincoln of our literature: a biography. New York, New York University Press, 1970. xv, 253 p. port. 24 cm. Includes bibliographical references. [PS3537.A618Z538] 76-92521 ISBN 0-8147-0069-1 6.95
1. Sandburg, Carl, 1878-1967.

CROWDER, Richard. 928.1
Carl Sandburg. New York, Twayne Publishers [1964] 176 p. 21 cm. (Twayne's United States authors series, 47) Bibliography: p. 163-168. [PS3537.A618Z555] 63-20606
1. Sandburg, Carl, 1878-

GOLDEN, Harry Lewis, 1902- 928.1
Carl Sandburg. [1st ed.] Cleveland, World Pub. Co. [1961] 287 p. illus. 22 cm. [PS3537.A618Z58] 61-6650
1. Sandburg, Carl, 1878-1967.

FRANCHERE, Ruth. 811'.5'2 B
Carl Sandburg, voice of the people. Illustrated by Victor Mays. Champaign, Ill., Garrard Pub. Co. [1970] 144 p. illus., ports. 22 cm. The life of the American poet, biographer, and collector of folk songs whose biography of Lincoln took twenty years of research and writing. [PS3537.A618Z575] 79-87312 ISBN 8-11-645053- 2.59
1. Sandburg, Carl, 1887-1967—Juvenile literature. I. Mays, Victor, 1927- illus. II. Title.

HAAS, Joseph, 1929- 811'.5'2 B
Carl Sandburg; a pictorial biography, by Joseph Haas and Gene Lovitz. New York, Putnam [1967] 222 p. illus., ports. 27 cm. Bibliography: p. 211-212. [PS3537.A618Z59] 67-19394
1. Sandburg, Carl, 1878-1967. I. Lovitz, Gene, joint author.

LONGO, Lucas. 811'.5'2
Carl Sandburg, poet and historian. Charlotteville, N.Y., SamHar Press, 1971. 30 p. 22 cm. (Outstanding personalities, no. 9) Bibliography: p. 28-30. [PS3537.A618Z75] 73-185665
1. Sandburg, Carl, 1878-1967.

MELIN, Grace Hathaway. 811'.5'2 B
Carl Sandburg; young singing poet. Illustrated by Robert Doremus. Indianapolis, Bobbs-Merrill Co. [1973] 200 p. illus. 20 cm. (Childhood of famous Americans) A biography stressing the childhood of the American poet Carl Sandburg. [PS3537.A618Z77] 92 72-11688 2.95
1. Sandburg, Carl, 1878-1967—Juvenile literature. I. Doremus, Robert, illus. II. Title.

ROGERS, William Garland, 1896- 811'.5'2 B
Carl Sandburg, yes; poet, historian, novelist, songster, by W. G. Rogers. Illustrated with photos. [1st ed.] New York, Harcourt Brace Jovanovich [1970] 212 p. illus., map, ports. 21 cm. Bibliography: p. 201-204. A biography of the well-known American poet who was born on "the wrong side of the tracks" in Galesburg, Illinois. [PS3537.A618Z86] 92 70-124844 ISBN 0-15-214470-6
1. Sandburg, Carl, 1878-1967—Juvenile literature. I. Title.

ZEHNPFENNIG, Gladys. 92
Carl Sandburg, poet and patriot. Minneapolis, T. S. Denison [1963] 265 p. 23 cm. (Denison's Men of achievement series) [PS3537.A618Z89] 63-14389
1. Sandburg, Carl, 1878- — Juvenile literature. I. Title.

ZEHNPFENNIG, Gladys 920
Carl Sandburg, poet and patriot. Minneapolis, Denison [c.1963] 265p. 23cm. (Denison's Men of achievement ser.) 63-14389 3.50
1. Sandburg, Carl, 1878- —Juvenile literature. I. Title.

Sandburg, Carl, 1878-1967 - Abraham Lincoln: the prairie years.

MACE, Ronald C. 973.7'0924(B)
Sandburg's Abraham Lincoln: the prairie years; a critical commentary, by Ronald C. Mace. New York, Monarch Pr. [c.1966]

96p. 22cm. (Monarch notes & study gds., 867-2) Bibl. [E457.3] 66-27325 1.00 pap., *1. Sandburg, Carl, 1878- Abraham Lincoln: the prairie years. I. Title.*

Sandburg, Carl, 1878-1967 — Portraits, etc.

PRATT, Harry Edward, 1901-1956, ed. 811'.5'2 B
A tribute to Carl Sandburg at seventy-five : [being a special edition of the Journal of the Illinois State Historical Society issued to commemorate the 75th birthday of a great American, January 6th, 1953] / edited by Harry E. Pratt. Darby, Pa. : Arden Library, 1978. p.p. 295-416 p. : ill. ; 26 cm. Reprint of the 1953 ed. published by Abraham Lincoln Book Shop, Chicago. Bibliography: p. 402-406. [PS3537.A618Z85 1978] 78-4063 ISBN 0-8495-4312-6 : 30.00
1. Sandburg, Carl, 1878-1967—Addresses, essays, lectures. 2. Authors, American—20th century—Biography. I. Illinois State Historical Society. Journal. II. Title.

SANDBERG, Carl, 1878- 928.1
Always the young strangers. New York, Harcourt, Brace [1952] 527 l. 28 cm. "An uncorrected advance copy." Autobiographical. [PS3537.A618Z5 1952] 52-11351
I. Title.

SANDBURG, Carl, 1878- 928.1
Always the young strangers. New York, Harcourt, Brace [1952] 527 l. 28cm. 'An uncorrected advance copy.' Autobiographical. [PS3537.A618Z5 1952] 53-9843
I. Title. BIP

SANDBURG, Carl, 1878-1967. 928.1
Always the young strangers. New York, Harcourt, Brace [1953] 445 p. ports. (on lining papers) 22 cm. Autobiographical. [PS3537.A618Z5 1953] 52-11351
I. Title.

SANDBURG, Carl, 1878-1967. 812'.5'4
The letters of Carl Sandburg. Edited by Herbert Mitgang. [1st ed.] New York, Harcourt, Brace & World [1968] xiv, 577 p. 24 cm. [PS3537.A618Z53] 68-12588
I. Mitgang, Herbert, ed. II. Title. BIP

SANDBURG, Carl, 1878-1967. 811'.5'2
Prairie-town boy = taken from Always the young strangers / Carl Sandburg ; illustrated by Joe Krush. New York : Harcourt Brace Jovanovich, [1977] c1955. p. cm. (A Voyager/HBJ book) [P] [PS3537.A618Z5 1977] 77-4647 ISBN 0-15-673700-0 pbk. : 1.75
1. Sandburg, Carl, 1878-1967—Biography. 2. Poets, American—20th century—Biography. I. Title.

SANDBURG, Helga. 811'.5'2 B
A great and glorious romance : the story of Carl Sandburg and Lilian Steichen / Helga Sandburg. 1st ed. New York : Harcourt Brace Jovanovich, [1978] 319 p., [8] leaves of plates : ill. ; 25 cm. [PS3537.A618Z865] 77-84394 ISBN 0-15-136894-5 : 12.95
1. Sandburg, Carl, 1878-1967—Biography. 2. Sandburg, Helga—Biography—Youth. 3. Authors, American—20th century—Biography. I. Title.

STEICHEN, Edward, 1879-ed. 811.52
Sandburg; photographers view Carl Sandburg, ed., introd., by Edward Steichen. [1st ed.] New York, Harcourt [1966] 112p. ports. 31cm. [PS3537.A618Z87] 65-19070 10.75
1. Sandburg, Carl, 1878- —Portraits, etc. I. Title.

STEICHEN, Paula. 811'.5'2
My Connemara. [1st ed.] New York, Harcourt, Brace & World [1969] 178 p. illus., ports. 23 cm. [PS3537.A618Z873] 69-14844
1. Sandburg, Carl, 1878-1967—Homes and haunts—Connemara. I. Title.

SUTTON, William Alfred, 1915- 811'.5'2 B
Carl Sandburg remembered / by William A. Sutton. Metuchen, N.J. : Scarecrow Press, 1979. vii, 304 p. : ports. ; 23 cm. Includes bibliographical references and index. [PS3537.A618Z874] 78-31298 ISBN 0-8108-1202-9 : 12.50
1. Sandburg, Carl, 1878-1967—Friends and associates—Addresses, essays, lectures. 2. Authors, American—20th century—Biography—Addresses, essays, lectures. I. Title. BIP

Sanders, Alex.

JOHNS, June. 133.4'0924
King of the witches; the world of Alex Sanders. With photos. by Jack Smith. [1st American ed.] New York, Coward-McCann [1970, c1969] 154 p. illus., ports. 22 cm. [BF1408.2.S25J6 1970] 77-104689 5.00
1. Sanders, Alex. I. Title.

Sanders, Donald G., 1899-

SANDERS, Donald G., 1899- 384.1'092'4 B
The brasspounder / D. G. Sanders. New York : Hawthorn Books, c1978. x, 195 p. : ill. ; 23 cm. Includes index. [TK5243.S26A32 1978] 77-72820 ISBN 0-8015-0881-9 : 8.95
1. Sanders, Donald G., 1899- 2. Telegraphers—Ohio—Biography. 3. Railroads—United States—History. I. Title. BIP

Sanders, George Douglas, 1933-

SANDERS, George Douglas, 1933- 796.352'092'4 B
Come swing with me; my life on and off the tour, by Doug Sanders with Larry Sheehan. [1st ed.] Garden City, N.Y. Doubleday, 1974. 272 p. illus. 22 cm. "A portion of chapter 6 of this book appeared originally in Golf digest in December 1973." [GV964.S28A32] 73-9174 ISBN 0-385-05631-1 7.95
1. Sanders, George Douglas, 1933- 2. Golf I. Sheehan, Larry, joint author. II. Title.

Sanders, George, 1906-

AHERNE, Brian. 791.43'028'0924 B
A dreadful man / Brian Aherne, assisted by George Sanders and Benita Hume. New York : Simon and Schuster, c1979. 224 p., [8] leaves of plates : ill. ; 23 cm. [PN2598.S33A63] 79-10513 ISBN 0-671-24797-2 : 9.95
1. Sanders, George, 1906- 2. Moving-picture actors and actresses—Great Britain—Biography. I. Sanders, George, 1906- II. Hume, Benita, 1906-1968. III. Title. BIP

SANDERS, George 927.92
Memoirs of a professional cad. New York, Putnam [c.1960] 192p. illus. 21cm. 59-11028 3.50
I. Title.

SANDERS, George, 1906- 927.92
Memoirs of a professional cad. New York, Avon [1961, c.1960] 191p. (G-1064) .50 pap.,
I. Title.

SANDERS, George, 1906- 927.92
Memoirs of a professional cad. New York, Putnam [1960] 192p. illus. 21cm. [PN2287.S27A3] 59-11028
I. Title.

Sanders, Harland.

SANDERS, Harland. 658.89'6413'650924 B
Life as I have known it has been finger lickin' good / Harland Sanders. Carol Stream, Ill. : Creation House, 1974. 144 p. : ill. ; 23 cm. [TX910.5.S25A33] 74-83059 ISBN 0-88419-053-6 : 5.95
1. Sanders, Harland. I. Title.

Sanders, James Edward,

SANDERS, James Edward, 1911- 828
The time of my life; an autobiography, by James Sanders. Illus. by author. [Auckland] Minerva [1967] Dist. by Sportself, New Rochelle, New York. 180p. illus. 23cm. [CT2888.S35A3] 68-102331 7.50
I. Title.

Sanderson, Derek.

ESKENAZI, Gerald. 796.9'62'0924 B
The Derek Sanderson nobody knows; at 26 the world's highest paid athlete. Chicago, Follett Pub. Co. [1973] 219 p. illus. 23 cm. [GV848.5.S25E84] 73-82200 ISBN 0-695-80424-3 6.95
1. Sanderson, Derek. I. Title.

Sandford, Christine (Lush)

SANDFORD, Christine (Lush) 963'.05'0924 B
The Lion of Judah hath prevailed, being the biography of His Imperial Majesty Haile Selassie I, by Christine Sandford. Illustrated with 16 pages of photos. Westport, Conn., Greenwood Press [1972] xi, 192 p. illus. 22 cm. Reprint of the 1955 ed. [DT387.7.S38 1972] 73-135611 ISBN 0-8371-5198-8
1. Haile Selassie I, Emperor of Ethiopia, 1891- II. Title.

Sandino, Augusto Cesar, 1895-1934.

IBARRA Grijalva, Domingo. 322.4'2'097285 B
The last night of General Augusto C. Sandino. Translated from the Spanish by Gloria Bonitz. [1st ed.] New York, Vantage Press [1973] 256 p. illus. 21 cm. Errata slip inserted. Translation of La ultima noche del general Augusto C. Sandino. [F1526.3.S243513] 73-169424 ISBN 0-533-00288-5 6.95
1. Sandino, Augusto Cesar, 1895-1934. 2. Nicaragua—History—1909-1937. I. Title.

Sandley, Elmer M.

ROOKSBY, Denis 926.25
The Sandley story. With foreword by Frederic Shaw. San Francisco, Hesperian House [25 California St. c.1960] 72p. illus. 23cm. 60-9985 2.95 pap.,
1. Sandley, Elmer M. 2. Sandley, Norman Kenneth. 3. Railroads, Narrow-gage—Dalles of the Wisconsin. I. Title.

Sandoval, Antonio.

CORRELL, J. Lee. 970.3'05 S
Sandoval—traitor or patriot? By J. Lee Correll. [Window Rock, Ariz.] Research Section, Navajo Parks and Recreation, The Navajo Tribe, 1970. 51 p. 22 cm. (Navajo historical publications. Biographical series, no. 1) Includes bibliographical references. [E99.N3N32 no. 1] 970.3 B 73-174268
1. Sandoval, Antonio. I. Title. II. Series.

Sandys, George, 1578-1644.

DAVIS, Richard Beale. 928.2
George Sandys, poet-adventurer; a study in Anglo-American culture in the seventeenth century. London, The Bodley Head; New York, Columbia University Press, 1955. London, The Bodley Head [1955] 320p. illus., ports. 23cm. Bibliography: p. 287-309. [PR2338.D3 1955] 55-7835
1. Sandys, George, 1578-1644. I. Title. II. Title: —Another issue.

Sanford, Agnes Mary (White)

SANFORD, Agnes Mary (White) 266'.5'10924 B
Sealed orders [by] Agnes Sanford. Plainfield, N.J., Logos International, 1972. 313 p. 25 cm. Autobiographical. [BR1725.S27A37] 72-76592 ISBN 0-912106-37-9 5.95
1. Sanford, Agnes Mary (White) I. Title.

Sanford, Charlotte, 1936-

SANFORD, Charlotte, 1936- 285'.1'0924 B
Second sight : a miraculous story of vision regained / Charlotte Sanford and Lester David. New York : M. Evans, c1979. 203 p. ; 22 cm. [BX9225.S278A36] 79-10282 ISBN 0-87131-287-5 : 7.95 7.95
1. Sanford, Charlotte, 1936- 2. Presbyterians—United States—Biography. 3. Blind—Biography. I. David, Lester, joint author. II. Title. BIP

Sanford family.

ROBB, Alex M. 929.2'0973
The Sanfords of Amsterdam; the biography of a family in Americana, by Alex M. Robb. New York, William-Frederick Press, 1969. 217 p. illus., ports. (part col.) 23 cm. [CS71.S223 1969] 68-20175 5.50
1. Sanford family. I. Title.

Sanford, Henry Shelton, 1823-1891.

MOLLOY, Leo Thomas, 1892- 923.273
Henry Shelton Sanford, 1823-1891; a biography. [1st ed. Derby, Conn., Priv. print.] 1952. 51p. illus. 24cm. [E415.9.S16M6] 55-58672
1. Sanford, Henry Shelton, 1823-1891. I. Title.

Sanford, John Elroy, 1922-

REDD Foxx, B. S 791'.092'4 B
(before Sanford) Joe X. Price. Chicago : Contemporary Books, c1979. ix, 144 p. ; 24 cm. Includes index. [PN2287.F634R4 1979] 78-21669 ISBN 0-8092-7856-1 : 8.95
1. Sanford, John Elroy, 1922- 2. Comedians—United States—Biography. I. Price, Joe X.

Sanford, Maria Louisa, 1836-1920— Juvenile literature.

HARTLEY, Lucie K. 378.1'2'0924 B
Maria Sanford, pioneer professor / by Lucie K. Hartley. Minneapolis : Dillon Press, c1976. p. cm. Biography of the first woman professor in the United States, Maria Louisa Sanford who devoted her life to education. [LD3346.S3H37] 92 76-10341 ISBN 0-87518-134-1 lib.bdg. : 5.95
1. Sanford, Maria Louisa, 1836-1920—Juvenile literature. I. Title. BIP

Sanford, Mollie Dorsey, 1838 or 9-1915.

SANFORD, Mollie Dorsey, 1838or9-1915. 978.2'02
Mollie : the journal of Mollie Dorsey Sanford in Nebraska and Colorado Territories, 1857-1866 / with an introd. and notes by Donald F. Danker. Lincoln :

University of Nebraska Press, 1976, c1959. ix, 199 p. ; 21 cm. "A Bison book." [F666.S36 1976] 75-8764 ISBN 0-8032-5826-7 pbk. : 2.95
1. Sanford, Mollie Dorsey, 1838 or 9-1915. 2. Frontier and pioneer life—Nebraska. 3. Frontier and pioneer life—Colorado. 4. Nebraska—History. 5. Colorado—History—To 1876. I. Title. **BIP**

Sanger, Frederick, 1918- —Juvenile literature.

SILVERSTEIN, Alvin. 574.1'92'0924 B
Frederick Sanger; the man who mapped out a chemical of life, by Alvin and Virginia Silverstein. Illustrated by Frank Vaughn. New York, John Day Co. [1969] 79 p. illus. 22 cm. (Great men of science) A biography of the biochemist awarded the Nobel Prize in Chemistry for determining the structure of the insulin molecule. [QD22.S2S5] 92 78-79100 3.49
1. Sanger, Frederick, 1918- —Juvenile literature. I. Silverstein, Virginia B., joint author. II. Vaughn, Frank, 1915- illus. III. Title.

Sanger, Margaret (Higgins) 1883-1966.

COIGNEY, Virginia. 613.94'3'0924 B
Margaret Sanger; rebel with a cause. [1st ed.] Garden City, N.Y., Doubleday [1969] 185, [2] p. 22 cm. Bibliography: p. [187] A biography of the woman who campaigned for the social rights of women and especially for the lawful provision of birth control information. [HQ764.S3C63] 92 69-15155 3.95
1. Sanger, Margaret (Higgins) 1883-1966. I. Title.

Sanger, Margaret (Higgins) 1883-1966—Juvenile literature.

LADER, Lawrence. 613.94'3'0924 B
Margaret Sanger; pioneer of birth control [by] Lawrence Lader [and] Milton Meltzer. Illustrated with photos. New York, Crowell [1969] xii, 174 p. illus., ports. 21 cm. (Women of America) Bibliography: p. 164-166. A biography of the woman who sacrificed her marriage, family life, and health to pioneer birth control education in the United States and abroad. [HQ764.S3L28] 92 72-81955 4.50
1. Sanger, Margaret (Higgins) 1883-1966—Juvenile literature. I. Meltzer, Milton, 1915- joint author. II. Title.

LADER, Lawrence. 613.94'3'0924[B] [92]
Margaret Sanger; pioneer of birth control [by] Lawrence Lader [and] Milton Meltzer. [New York] [Dell] [1974, c1969] 191 p. 18 cm. (Woman of America) Bibliography: p. [182]-184. Biography of the woman who sacrificed her marriage, family life & health to pioneer birth control education in the U.S. & abroad. [HQ764.S3L28] 0.95 (pbk.)
1. Sanger, Margaret (Higgins) 1883-1966—Juvenile literature. 2. (Sanger, Margaret (Higgins) 1883-1966] I. Meltzer, Milton, 1915- joint author. II. Title.
L.C. card number for hardcover ed.: 72-81955. **BIP**

Sanger, Margaret, 1879-1966.

DASH, Joan. 920.72
A life of one's own; three gifted women and the men they married. [1st ed.] New York, Harper & Row [1973] xx, 388 p. ports. 22 cm. Bibliography: p. [365]-369. [CT3260.D37 1973] 76-138717 ISBN 0-06-010949-1 10.00
1. Sanger, Margaret, 1879-1966. 2. Millay, Edna St. Vincent, 1892-1950. 3. Mayer, Maria (Goeppert) 1906-1972. I. Title.

DOUGLAS, Emily (Taft) 1899- 613.94'3'0924 B
Margaret Sanger; pioneer of the future. [1st ed.] New York, Holt, Rinehart and Winston [1969, c1970] viii, 274 p. illus., ports. 22 cm. Bibliography: p. [263]-264. [HQ764.S3D66] 72-80339 7.50
1. Sanger, Margaret, 1879-1966.

DOUGLAS, Emily Taft, 1899- 613.9'4'0924 B
Margaret Sanger, pioneer of the future / Emily Taft Douglas. Garrett Park, Md. : Garrett Park Press, c1975. viii, 298 p., [8] leaves of plates ; 22 cm. Includes index. Bibliography: p. [286]-288. [HQ764.S3D66 1975] 75-29862 ISBN 0-912048-75-1 : 8.50
1. Sanger, Margaret, 1879-1966. I. Title.

GRAY, Madeline. 613.9'4'0924 B
Margaret Sanger : a biography of the champion of birth control / by Madeline Gray. New York : R. Marek, c1978. p. cm. Includes index. [HQ764.S3G7] 78-13000 ISBN 0-399-90019-5 : 12.50
1. Sanger, Margaret, 1879-1966. 2. Birth control—United States—History. **BIP**

LADER, Lawrence. 926.13
The Margaret Sanger story and the fight for birth control. [1st ed.] Garden City, N.Y., Doubleday, 1955. 352 p. illus. 22 cm. [HQ764.S3L3] 55-5257
1. Sanger, Margaret, 1879-1966. 2. Birth control. **BIP**

LADER, Lawrence. 613.9'4'0924 B
The Margaret Sanger story and the fight for birth control. Westport, Conn., Greenwood Press [1975, c1955] 348 p. 22 cm. Reprint of the ed. published by Doubleday, Garden City, N.Y. Bibliography: p. 347-348. [HQ764.S3L3 1975] 73-11855 ISBN 0-8371-7076-1
1. Sanger, Margaret, 1879-1966. 2. Birth control. I. Title.

SANGER, Margaret, 1879-1966. 613.94'0924 B
Margaret Sanger; an autobiography. New York, Dover Publications [1971] 504 p. port. 22 cm. Reprint of the 1938 ed. [HQ764.S3A3 1971] 73-150807 ISBN 0-486-20470-7 3.95

SANGER, Margaret, 1879-1966. 613.94'3'0924
My fight for birth control. New York, Maxwell Reprint Co. [1969, c1931] vii, 360 p. illus., facsim., ports. 24 cm. [HQ766.5.U5S2 1969] 70-98265
1. Birth control—U.S. I. Title.

Sanger, Margaret, 1879-1966—Juvenile literature.

WERNER, Vivian L. 613.94'3'0924 B
Margaret Sanger: woman rebel, by Vivian Werner. [1st ed.] New York, Hawthorn Books [1970] 128 p. facsim., ports. 23 cm. The life of one of the first women to champion birth control and family planning. [HQ764.S3W45] 92 77-92638 4.95
1. Sanger, Margaret, 1879-1966—Juvenile literature. I. Title.

Sanguillen, Manny, 1944- —Juvenile literature.

COHEN, Joel H. 796.357'092'4 B
Manny Sanguillen, jolly Pirate / by Joel H. Cohen. New York : Putnam, c1975. 127 p. ; 21 cm. (Putnam sports shelf) Includes index. A biography of the Panamanian-born star of the Pittsburgh Pirates describing the day-to-day routine of baseball life. [GV865.S23C63 1975] 92 75-4426 ISBN 0-399-60952-0 lib. bdg. : 5.29
1. Sanguillen, Manny, 1944- —Juvenile literature. 2. Pittsburgh. Baseball club (National League)—Juvenile literature. 3. Baseball—Juvenile literature. I. Title.

Sani, Alberto.

BERENSON, Bernhard, 1865-1959. 730'.924
Alberto Sani, an artist out of his time. (Un artista fuori del suo tempo) Westport, Conn., Greenwood Press [1972] 115 p. illus. 23 cm. Reprint of the 1950 ed. English and Italian. [NB623.S32B47 1972] 70-138202 ISBN 0-8371-5555-X
1. Sani, Alberto.

Sankey, Ira David, 1840-1908.

SANKEY, Ira David, 1840-1908. 783.9
My life and the story of the Gospel hymns and of sacred songs and solos. With an introd. by Theodore L. Cuyler. Philadelphia, Sunday School Times Co., 1907. [New York, AMS Press, 1974] 410 p. illus. 19 cm. [BV330.S4A3 1974] 72-1682 ISBN 0-404-08332-3
1. Sankey, Ira David, 1840-1908. 2. Hymns, English—History and criticism. I. Title. **BIP**

Sansovino, Andrea, 1460-1529.

HUNTLEY, George Haydn, 1905- 730'.92'4 B
Andrea Sansovino, sculptor and architect of the Italian Renaissance, by G. Haydn Huntley. Westport, Conn., Greenwood Press [1971, c1935] xvi, 155 p. illus. 24 cm. Bibliography: p. [137]-143. [N6923.S34H8 1971] 78-138152 ISBN 0-8371-5609-2
1. Sansovino, Andrea, 1460-1529.

Santangel, Luis de, d. 1505.

KAYSERLING, Meyer, 1829-1905. 970'.01'504924
Christopher Columbus and the participation of the Jews in the Spanish and Portuguese discoveries / by M. Kayserling ; translated from the author's manuscript with his sanction and revision by Charles Gross. Folcroft, Pa. : Folcroft Library Editions, 1978, c1894. xv, 189 p. ; 24 cm. Reprint of the ed. published by Longmans, Green, New York. English, Spanish, and Latin. Includes bibliographical references and index. [E111.K23 1978] 78-26172 ISBN 0-8414-5478-7 lib. bdg. : 25.00
1. Colombo, Cristoforo—Relations with Jews. 2. Maranos. 3. Santangel, Luis de, d. 1505. 4. Santangel family. 5. America—Discovery and exploration—Spanish. 6. Jews in Spain—History. 7. Spain—History—Ferdinand Isabella, 1479-1516. I. Title. **BIP**

Santa Anna, Antonio Lopez de, Pres. Mexico, 1794?-1876.

CALLCOTT, Wilfrid Hardy, 1895- 923.172
Santa Anna; the story of an enigma who once was Mexico. Hamden, Conn., Archon Books, 1964 [c1963] xiv, 391 p. illus., ports. 22 cm. Bibliography: p. 370-381. [F1232.S2312 1964] 64-13173
1. Santa Anna, Antonio Lopez de, Pres. Mexico, 1794?-1876. 2. Mexico—History—1821-1861. **BIP**

JONES, Oakah L. 972 B
Santa Anna, by Oakah L. Jones, Jr. New York, Twayne Publishers [1968] 211 p. map. 22 cm. (Twayne's rulers and statesmen of the world series, 6) Includes bibliographies. [F1232.S23155] 67-28861
1. Santa Anna, Antonio Lopez de, Pres. Mexico, 1794?-1876.

Santa Barbara, Calif. — Hist.

STORKE, Thomas More, 1876- 920.5
California editor, by Thomas M. Strorke in collaboration with Walker A. Tompkins. Foreword by Earl Warren. Los Angeles, Westernlore Press, 1958. 489 p. illus. 22 cm. [PN4874.S73A3] 58-59853
1. Santa Barbara, Calif. — Hist. I. Title.

Santa Clara Valley—Biography.

RAMBO, F. Ralph. 917.94'73'0340922 B
Pioneer blue book of the old Santa Clara Valley [by] Ralph Rambo. [San Jose, Calif., Rosicrucian Press, 1973] 48 p. illus. 23 cm. Cover title. Bibliography: p. 45. [F868.S25R318] 73-180439
1. Santa Clara Valley—Biography. 2. Santa Clara Valley—History. I. Title.

Santa Rosa Co., Fla.—History.

WELLS, William James, 1899- 975.9'985'06 B
Pioneering in the panhandle : a look at selected events and families of South Santa Rosa County, Florida / by William James Wells. [s.l. : s.n.], c1976 (Fort Walton Beach, Fla. : Melvin Business Services) vi, 285 p., p. A-Z : ill. ; 21 cm. Includes bibliographical references and index. [F317.S4W44] 77-151923
1. Santa Rosa Co., Fla.—History. 2. Santa Rosa Co., Fla.—Biography. 3. Frontier and pioneer life—Florida—Santa Rosa Co. I. Title.

Santana, Carmen, 1932-

SHEEHAN, Susan. 362.5'092'6
A welfare mother / Susan Sheehan ; with an introd. by Michael Harrington. Boston : Houghton Mifflin, 1976. xiv, 109 p. ; 22 cm. [HV99.N59S47] 76-13439 ISBN 0-395-24505-2 : 6.95
1. Santana, Carmen, 1932- 2. Welfare recipients—New York (City)—Biography. 3. Puerto Ricans in New York (City) I. Title. **BIP**

SHEEHAN, Susan. 362.5'092'6
A welfare mother / by Susan Sheehan ; with an introduction by Michael Harrington. New York : New American Library, 1977,c1975. 144p. ; 18 cm. (A Mentor Book) [HV99.N59S47] ISBN 0-451-61563-8 pbk. : 1.50
1. Santana, Carmen,1932- 2. Welfare recipients-New York (City)-Biography. 3. Puerto Ricans in New York (City) I. Title.
L.C. card no. for 1976 Houghton Mifflin ed.: 76-13439.

Santayana, George, 1863-1952.

ARNETT, Willard Eugene, 1921- 191
George Santayana [by] Willard E. Arnett. New York, Washington Square Press [1968] 184 p. 18 cm. (The Great American thinkers series) Includes bibliographies. [B945.S24A78] 68-4624
1. Santayana, George, 1863-1952.

BUTLER, Richard, 1918- 921.1
The life and world of George Santayana. Chicago, H. Regnery Co. [1960] 205p. 28cm. [B945.S24B78] 60-7924
1. Santayana, George, 1863-1952. I. Title.

CORY, Daniel, 1904- 921.1
Santayana: the later years; a portrait with letters. New York, Braziller [c.1963] 330p. 24cm. Bibl. 63-19573 7.50
1. Santayana, George, 1863-1952. I. Title.

HOWGATE, George Washburne, 1903-1950. 191 B
George Santayana. New York, Russell & Russell [1971] viii, 363 p. 23 cm. "First published in 1938." Originally presented as the author's thesis, University of

Pennsylvania, 1933. Bibliography: p. 349-352. [B945.S24H6 1971] 73-102537
1. Santayana, George, 1863-1952. **BIP**

KIRKWOOD, Mossie May 921.1
(Waddington)
Santayana: saint of the imagination. [Toronto] University of Toronto Press, 1961. 240p. illus. 24cm. [B945.S24K54] 61-65164
1. Santayana, George, 1863-1952. I. Title.

LAMONT, Corliss, 1902- ed. 921.1
Dialogue on George Santayana [by] James Gutmann [and others] Edited by Corliss Lamont with the assistance of Mary Redmer. New York, Horizon Press, 1959. 115p. 21cm. [B945.S24L3] 59-14696
I. Santayana, George, 1863-1952. II. Gutmann, James, 1897- III. Title.

*SANTAYANA, George, 1863- 921.1
1952
Persons and places; the background of my life. New York, Scribners [1964, c.1944] 262p. 21cm. (SL94) 1.45 pap.,
I. Title.

SANTAYANA, George, 1863- 921.1
1952.
Persons and places. [Single-volume ed.] New York, Scribner [1963] 3 v. in 1. port. 22 cm. Contents.Contents.—v. 1. The background of my life.—v. 2. The middle span.—v. 3. My host the world. [B945.S24A3 1963] 63-17239
I. Title.

Santley, Charles, Sir, 1834-1922.

SANTLEY, Charles, 782.1'092'4 B
Sir, 1834-1922.
Reminiscences of my life / Charles Santley ; with a discography by W. R. Moran. New York : Arno Press, 1977. xiv, ii, 319 p., [4] leaves of plates : ill. ; 23 cm. (Opera biographies) Reprint of the 1909 ed. published by I. Pitman, London. Discography: pt. 2, p. i-ii. [ML420.S233A3 1977] 76-29967 ISBN 0-405-09706-9 : 21.00
1. Santley, Charles, Sir, 1834-1922. 2. Singers—Biography. I. Title.

Santo, Ron, 1940- —Juvenile literature.

BROSNAN, Jim. 796.357'092'4 B
Ron Santo, 3B / by Jim Brosnan New York : Putnam, [1974] 143 p. ; 21 cm. (Putnam sports shelf) Includes index. A biography of Ron Santo who has earned a living at the great American pastime as third baseman for the Chicago Cubs and the Chicago White Sox. [GV865.S26B76] 92 73-88520 ISBN 0-399-20385-0. ISBN 0-399-60875-3 lib. bdg. : 4.97
1. Santo, Ron, 1940- —Juvenile literature. 2. Baseball—Juvenile literature.

Santos-Dumont, Alberto, 1873-1932.

BROWN, Rose (Johnston) 926.29
1883-
Bicycle in the sky, the story of Alberto Santos-Dumont; illustrated by Ann Sayre Wiseman. New York, Scribner [1953] 183p. illus. 22cm. [TL540.S25B76] 53-8953
1. Santos-Dumont, Alberto, 1873-1962. I. Title.

SANTOS-DUMONT, 629.13'0092'4 B
Alberto, 1873-1932.
My airships; the story of my life. With a new introd. by Sir Peter Wykeham. New York, Dover Publications [1973] xviii, 122 p. 22 cm. Translation of Dans l'air. [TL540.S25A3 1973] 71-145992 ISBN 0-486-22122-9 2.50 (pbk.)
1. Santos-Dumont, Alberto, 1873-1932. 2. Air-ships. I. Title. **BIP**

WYKEHAM, Peter. 926.29
Santos-Dumont; a study in obsession, [1st American ed.] New York, Harcourt, Brace & World [1963, c1962] 278 p. illus. 21 cm. Includes bibliography. [TL540.S25W9 1963] 63-8088
1. Santos-Dumont, Alberto, 1873-1932. **BIP**

Santos, Eduardo, Pres. Colombia, 1888-

BUSHNELL, David, 327.73'0861
1923-
Eduardo Santos and the good neighbor, 1938-1942. Gainesville, University of Florida Press, 1967. 128 p. 23 cm. (Latin American monographs, 2d ser., no. 4) Bibliographical footnotes. [E183.8.C7B8] 67-65496
1. Santos, Eduardo, Pres. Colombia, 1888- 2. United States—Foreign relations—Columbia. 3. Colombia—Foreign relations—United States. I. Title. II. Series. **BIP**

Sanuki no Suke, b. ca. 1079—Diaries.

†SANUKI no Suke, 895.6'8'103
b.ca.1079.
The Emperor Horikawa diary = Sanuki no Suke nikki / by Fujiwara no Nagako ; translated with an introd. by Jennifer Brewster. Honolulu : University Press of Hawaii, c1977. xi, 155 p. ; 23 cm. Translation of Sanuki no Suke no nikki. Includes index. Bibliography: p. [PL789.S2Z52 1977] 77-89194 ISBN 0-8248-0605-0 : 14.00
1. Sanuki no Suke, b. ca. 1079—Diaries. 2. Horikawa, Emperor of Japan, 1079-1107. 3. Authors, Japanese—Biography. 4. Japan—Emperors—Biography. I. Title.

Sanz, Jose Laureano, marques de San Juan de Puerto Rico, 1819-1898.

GOMEZ Acevedo, Labor. 364.135
Sanz, promotor de la conciencia separatista en Puerto Rico / Labor Gomez Acevedo ; prologo por Manuel Ballesteros Gaibrois. 2. ed., corr. [Rio Piedras] : Editorial Universitaria, Universidad de Puerto Rico, 1974. 320 p. ; 18 cm. (Serie Humanidades) (Coleccion Uprex ; 35) Includes index. Bibliography: p. 311-320. [F1973.S34G6 1974] 76-457203
1. Sanz, Jose Laureano, marques de San Juan de Puerto Rico, 1819-1898. 2. Puerto Rico—Politics and government—To 1898. I. Title. **BIP**

Sarada Devi, 1853-1920.

NIKHILANANDA, Swami. 921.9
Holy mother; being the life the life of Sri Sarada Devi, wife of Sri Ramakrishna and helpmate in his mission. New York 28, Ramakrishna-Vivekananda ctr., 17 E. 94th St. [c.]1962. 334p. illus. 21cm. 62-13423 4.50
1. Sarada Devi, 1853-1920. I. Title.

Sarafian, Kevork Avedis,

SARAFIAN, Kevork Avedis, 923.77O
1889-
From immigrant to educator. New York, Vantage [c.1963] 294p. 21cm. 63-4028 4.95
I. Title.

Saran, Mary.

SARAN, Mary. 335'.0092'4 B
Never give up : memoirs / by Mary Saran ; foreword by Sir Arthur Lewis. London : Wolff, 1976. xiii, 145 p., [16] p. of plates : map, ports. ; 23 cm. Includes index. [HX40S2824A37 1976] 77-351865 ISBN 0-85496-257-3 : £3.95
1. Saran, Mary. 2. Socialists—Biography. I. Title.

Sargant, William Walters.

SARGANT, William 616.89'00924
Walters.
The unquiet mind; the autobiography of a physician in psychological medicine [by] William Sargant. With a pref. by D. Ewen Cameron. [1st American ed.] Boston, Little, Brown [1967] xxii, 240 p. port. 22 cm. Bibliography: p. 231-232. [R489.S13A3 1967] 67-23830
I. Title.

Sargeant, Genevieve (Gildersleeve)

HENDRICKSON, Albert L 922.673
1893-
Life in a floating city, by Albert L. Hendrickson. Nashville, Southern Pub. Association [1964] 166 p. illus. 21 cm. [BX6193.S3H4] 64-18174
1. Sargeant, Genevieve (Gildersleeve) I. Title.

Sargent, Charles Sprague, 1841-1927.

SUTTON, Stephanne 581'.0924 B
Barry.
Charles Sprague Sargent and the Arnold Arboretum [by] S. B. Sutton. Cambridge, Harvard University Press, 1970. xvii, 382 p. ports. 25 cm. Includes bibliographical references. [QK31.S15S9] 73-120322 ISBN 0-674-11181-8 10.00
1. Sargent, Charles Sprague, 1841-1927. 2. Harvard University. Arnold Arboretum. I. Title.

Sargent, John Singer, 1856-1925.

SARGENT'S Boston, 759.13
with an essay a biographical summary & a complete check list of Sargent's portraits. Boston, Museum of Fine Arts, 1956. 132p. illus. (part col.) ports. 26cm. 'Catalogue of a centennial exhibition, Sargent's Boston, January 3 to February 7, 1956':p. 67-75. [ND237.S3M3] [ND237.S3M3] 927.5 56-1995 56-1995
1. Sargent, John Singer, 1856-1925. 2. Paintings, American—Exhibitions. I. McKibbin, David. II. Boston, Museum of Fine Arts.

Sargent, Malcolm, Sir, 1895-1967.

REID, Charles, 1900- 785'.0924 B
Malcolm Sargent; a biography. New York, Taplinger Pub. Co. [1970, c1968] xiv, 491 p. illus., ports. 22 cm. [ML422.S324R4 1970] 72-109011 ISBN 0-8008-5080-7 12.00
1. Sargent, Malcolm, Sir, 1895-1967. **BIP**

Sargent, Peter.

SARGENT, Peter. 979.4'05'0924 B
Nature's child / by Peter Sargent. 1st ed. San Diego : Tofua Press, c1975. xii, 155 p. : ill. ; 22 cm. [CT275.S335A35] 75-11157 ISBN 0-914488-05-8 pbk. : 5.00
1. Sargent, Peter. I. Title.

Sargeson, Frank—Biography.

MCELDOWNEY, Dennis, 1926- 823 B
Frank Sargeson in his time / Dennis McEldowney. Dunedin : J. McIndoe, 1976. 72 p. : ill. ; 24 cm. Includes index. Bibliography: p. 68-69. [PR9639.3.S3Z78] 77-361792 ISBN 0-908565-18-6
1. Sargeson, Frank—Biography. 2. Authors, New Zealand—20th century—Biography. I. Title.

Sark—Hist.

HATHAWAY, Sibyl 923.24234
(Collings)
Dame of Sark, an autobiography. New York, Coward [1962, c.1961] 211p. illus. 62-7509 4.00
1. Sark—Hist. I. Title.

Sarmiento, Domingo Faustino, Pres. Argentine Republic, 1811-1888.

BUNKLEY, Allison 923.182
Williams.
The life of Sarmiento. Princeton, Princeton University Press, 1952. xv, 566 p. illus., ports., geneal. table. 23 cm. Bibliography: p. 521-548. [F2846.S25138] 52-8763
1. Sarmiento, Domingo Faustino, Pres. Argentine Republic, 1811-1888. I. Title.

CROWLEY, Frances 982'.05'0924 B
G.
Domingo Faustino Sarmiento, by Frances G. Crowley. New York, Twayne Publishers [1972] 188 p. 21 cm. (Twayne's world authors series, TWAS 156. Argentina) Bibliography: p. 170-180. [F2846.S26C7] 76-120505
1. Sarmiento, Domingo Faustino, Pres. Argentine Republic, 1811-1888. **BIP**

†PATTON, Elda 982.050924 B
Clayton, 1913-
Sarmiento in the United States / Elda Clayton Patton. Evansville, Ind. : University of Evansville Press, 1976. xiii, 192 p. : ill. ; 24 cm. Bibliography: p. 190-192. [F2846.S26P34] 76-7319 7.95
1. Sarmiento, Domingo Faustino, Pres Argentine Republic, 1811-1888. 2. United States—Relations (general) with the Argentine Republic. 3. Argentine Republic—Relations (general) with the United States. 4. United States—Description and travel—1865-1900. 5. Presidents—Argentine Republic—Biography. I. Title.

SARMIENTO, Domingo 327'.2'0924
Faustino, Pres. Arentine Republic 1811-1888.
Facundo. Selected and edited by Navier A. Fernande [and] Reginald F. Brown. Boston, Ginn [1960] 205p. illus. 22cm. First published in 1843 under title: Civilizacion barbarie. [F2846.S24743] 60-1818
1. Argentine Republic—Hist.—1817-1860. 2. Argentine Republic—Descr. & trav. 3. Quiroga, Juan Facundo, 1790-1837. I. Title.

Sarnoff, David, 1891-1971.

DREHER, 338.7'61'384540924 B
Carl, 1896-
Sarnoff, an American success / by Carl Dreher. New York : Quadrangle/New York Times Book Co., c1977. vi, 282 p. ; 24 cm. Includes index. [TK6545.S3D73 1977] 76-50818 ISBN 0-8129-0672-1 : 12.50
1. Sarnoff, David, 1891-1971. 2. Radio—United States—Biography. 3. Television—United States—Biography. I. Title. **BIP**

LYONS, Eugene, 1898- 621.380924
David Sarnoff, a biography. New York, Harper [c.1966] x, 372p. illus., ports. 25cm. [TK6545.S3L9] 66-10632 6.95
1. Sarnoff, David, 1891- I. Title.

LYONS, Eugene, 1898- 621.380924
David Sarnoff, a biography. [1st ed.] New York, Harper & Row [1966] x, 372 p. illus., ports. 25 cm. [TK6545.S3L9] 66-10632
1. Sarnoff, David, 1891- I. Title.

TEBBEL, John William, 923.873
1912-.
David Sarnoff: putting electrons to work. Chicago, Encyclopaedia Britannica Press [c1963] 191 p. ports. 22 cm. (Britannica bookshelf: Great lives) [TK7807.S3T4] 63-17606
1. Sarnoff, David, 1891- — Juvenile literature. I. Title.

Saroyan, William,

SAROYAN, William, 1908- 928.1
Here comes, there goes, you know who. New York, Simon and Schuster, 1961. 273 p. illus. 24 cm. Autobiography. [PS3537.A826Z53] 61-17926
I. Title.

SAROYAN, William, 813'.5'2 B
1908-
Places where I've done time. New York, Praeger [1972] 182 p. facsim. 22 cm. Autobiographical. [PS3537.A826Z532] 70-178227 6.95
I. Title. **BIP**

SAROYAN, William, 813'.5'2 [B]
1908-
Places where I've done time. [New York, Dell, 1973 c.1972] [182 p.] 21 cm. (A Delta Book) [PS3537.A826Z532] 2.25 (pbk.)
I. Title.
L.C. card no. for original ed.: 70-178227.

Saroyan, William, 1908- —Biography.

SAROYAN, William, 1908- 928.1
Here comes, there goes, you know who. New York, Simon and Schuster, 1961. 273

p. illus. 24 cm. Autobiography. [PS3537.A826Z53] 61-17926
I. Title.

SAROYAN, William, 1908- 813'.5'2 B
Places where I've done time. New York, Praeger [1972] 182 p. facsim. 22 cm. Autobiographical. [PS3537.A826Z532] 70-178227 6.95
I. Title. BIP

SAROYAN, William, 1908- 813'.5'2 [B]
Places where I've done time. [New York, Dell, 1973 c.1972] [182 p.] 21 cm. (A Delta Book) [PS3537.A826Z532] 2.25 (pbk.)
I. Title.
L.C. card no. for original ed.: 70-178227.

SAROYAN, William, 1908- 818'.5'209 B
Sons come and go, mothers hang in forever / William Saroyan. New York : McGraw-Hill, c1976. p. cm. [PS3537.A826Z543] 75-43520 ISBN 0-07-054748-3
1. Saroyan, William, 1908- —Biography. I. Title.

Saroyan, William, 1908- —Friends and associates.

SAROYAN, William, 1908- 818'.5'203 B
Chance meetings / William Saroyan. 1st ed. New York : Norton, c1978. 135 p. ; 22 cm. [PS3537.A826Z525 1978] 77-17505 ISBN 0-393-08809-X : 7.95
1. Saroyan, William, 1908- —Friends and associates. 2. Authors, American—20th century—Biography. I. Title. BIP

SAROYAN, William, 1908- 818'.5'203 B
Chance meetings / William Saroyan. Boston : G. K. Hall, 1978. 174 p. ; 24 cm. "Published in large print." [PS3537.A826Z525 1978b] 78-16096 ISBN 0-8161-6614-5 lib. bdg. : 8.95
1. Saroyan, William, 1908- —Friends and associates. 2. Authors, American—20th century—Biography. 3. Large type books. I. Title.

SAROYAN, William, 1908- 813'.5'2 B
Sons come and go, mothers hang in forever / William Saroyan ; illustrated by Al Hirschfeld. 1st ed. Franklin Center, Pa. : Franklin Library, 1976. 230 p. : ill. ; 23 cm. At head of title: The First Edition Society. [PS3537.A826Z543 1976b] 77-364308
1. Saroyan, William, 1908- —Friends and associates. 2. Authors, American—20th century—Biography. I. Title.

Sarpi, Paolo, 1552-1623.

LIEVSAY, John Leon. 282'.092'4 B
Venetian Phoenix: Paolo Sarpi and some of his English friends (1606-1700) Lawrence, University Press of Kansas [1973] 262 p. 23 cm. Bibliography: p. 235-250. [BX4705.S36L53] 73-6818 ISBN 0-7006-0108-2 11.00
1. Sarpi, Paolo, 1552-1623. I. Title.

Sarrail, Maurice Paul Emmanuel, 1856-1929.

TANENBAUM, Jan Karl, 1936- 320.9'44'081 B
General Maurice Sarrail, 1856-1929; the French Army and left-wing politics. Chapel Hill, University of North Carolina Press [1974] xii, 300 p. maps. 24 cm. An extensive revision of the author's thesis, University of California at Berkeley. Bibliography: p. 269-288. [DC373.S3T36 1974] 73-17109 ISBN 0-8078-1222-6 12.95
1. Sarrail, Maurice Paul Emmanuel, 1856-1929. 2. France—Politics and government—1914-1940.

Sarto, Andrea del, 1486-1531.

FREEDBERG, Syndey Joseph 759.5
Andrea del Sarto [v.2] Cambridge, Mass., Belknap Pr., Harvard, 1963. 302p. illus. 29cm. Contents.[2] Catalogue raisonne. Bibl. 63-17198 15.00
1. Sarto, Andrea del, 1486-1531. I. Title.

SHEARMAN, John K G 759.9493'2
Andrea del Sarto [by] John Shearman. Oxford, Clarendon Press, 1965. 2 v. (xi, 466 p.) 181 plates. 29 cm. Includes bibliographies. [ND623.S2S5] 65-22669
1. Sarto, Andrea del, 1486-1531. I. Title.

Sarton, May,

SARTON, May, 1912- 818'.5'203
I knew a phoenix; sketches for an autobiography. New York, W. W. Norton [1969, c1959] 222 p. illus. 22 cm. [PS3537.A832Z52 1969] 74-957 5.00
I. Title. BIP

SARTON, May, 1912- 818'.5'203 B
Journal of a solitude. [1st ed.] New York, Norton [1973] 208 p. illus. 21 cm. [PS3537.A832J68] 72-13464 ISBN 0-393-07474-9 6.95
I. Title. BIP

Sarton, May, 1912- —Diaries.

SARTON, May, 1912- 818'.5'203 B
The house by the sea : a journal / by May Sarton ; photos. by Beverly Hallam. 1st ed. New York : Norton, c1977. 287 p. : ill. ; 22 cm. [PS3537.A832Z518 1977] 77-7490 ISBN 0-393-07518-4 : 8.95
1. Sarton, May, 1912- —Diaries. 2. Authors, American—20th century—Biography. I. Title. BIP

SARTON, May, 1912- 818'.5'203
I knew a phoenix; sketches for an autobiography. New York, W. W. Norton [1969, c1959] 222 p. illus. 22 cm. [PS3537.A832Z52 1969] 74-957 5.00
I. Title. BIP

SARTON, May, 1912- 818'.5'203 B
Journal of a solitude. [1st ed.] New York, Norton [1973] 208 p. illus. 21 cm. [PS3537.A832J68] 72-13464 ISBN 0-393-07474-9 6.95
I. Title. BIP

Sartre, Jean Paul, 1905-

BARNES, Hazel Estella. 848'.9'1409
Sartre [by] Hazel E. Barnes. [1st ed.] Philadelphia, Lippincott [1973] 194 p. 22 cm. (Portraits) Bibliography: p. [188]-190. [PQ2637.A82Z554] 72-13764 ISBN 0-397-00750-7 6.95
1. Sartre, Jean Paul, 1905- BIP

SARTRE, Jean Paul, 1905- 848.914
The words. Translated from the French by Bernard Frechtman. New York, G. Braziller [1964] 255 p. 21 cm. Autobiographical. [PQ2637.A82Z513] 64-21764
I. Title. BIP

THODY, Philip Malcolm Waller, 1928- 848'.9'1409 B
Sartre: a biographical introduction [by] Philip Thody. New York, Scribner [1972, c1971] 160 p. 21 cm. Bibliography: p. [143]-146. [B2430.S34T48 1972] 72-174652 ISBN 0-684-12673-7 6.95
1. Sartre, Jean Paul, 1905-

Sartre, Jean Paul, 1905- —Interviews.

SARTRE, Jean Paul, 1905- 848'.9'1409 B
Sartre by himself : a film directed by Alexandre Astruc and Michel Contat with the participation of Simone de Beauvoir, Jacques-Larent Bost, Andre Gorz, Jean Pouillon / translation by Richard Seaver. New York : Urizen Books, c1978. p. cm. Translation of Sartre. "Transcript of the soundtrack of the film, with ... minor corrections." [PQ2637.A32Z52713] 78-19019 ISBN 0-916354-34-2 : 10.95. ISBN 0-916354-35-0 pbk. : 3.95
1. Sartre, Jean Paul, 1905- —Interviews. 2. Authors, French—20th century—Biography. I. Astruc, Alexandre. II. Contat, Michel. III. Sartre par lui-meme [Motion picture] IV. Title.

Sas-Jaworsky, Alexander,

CHOATE, Joe. 920
The best answer is America; a biography of Dr. Alexander Sas-Jaworsky. [1st ed.] New York, Vantage Press [1959] 200p. illus. 21cm. [CT275.S3363C5] 59-14971
1. Sas-Jaworsky, Alexander, 2. The 64,000 question (Television program) I. Title.

Sassall, John.

BERGER, John. 610'.924
A fortunate man; the story of a country doctory, by John Berger and Jean Mohr. London. Allen Lane the Penguin P., 1967. 158 p. illus. 21 1/2 cm. 30/- Illus. on endpapers. Bibliographical footnotes. [R489.S2B4] 67-94226
1. Sassall, John. I. Mohr, Jean, joint author. II. Title.

BERGER, John. 610'.924 B
A fortunate man; the story of a country doctor, by John Berger and Jean Mohr. [1st ed.] New York, Holt, Rinehart and Winston [1967] 157 p. illus. 22 cm. Bibliographical footnotes. [R489.S2B4] 67-14213
1. Sassall, John. I. Mohr, Jean, joint author. II. Title.

Sasthi Brata.

SASTHI Brata. 954.04'092'4 B
Traitor to India : a search for home / Sasthi Brata. London : P. Elek, 1976[i.e.1977] 159 p. ; 23 cm. [CT1508.S18A35] 76-382114 ISBN 0-236-40039-8 : 9.95
1. Sasthi Brata. 2. India—Biography. 3. East Indians in England—Biography. I. Title.
Distributed by P. Elek, Salem, New Hampshire

Sasthi Brata.

SASTHI BRATA. 915.4'03'40924 B
My God died young. [1st U.S. ed.] New York, Harper & Row [1968] 285 p. 22 cm. [CT1508.S18A3 1968b] 68-28188 4.95
I. Title.

Sastiri, Valangiman Sankaranarayana Srinivass, 1869-1946.

KOLANDA RAO, Pandurangi, 1889- 954.03'5
The Right Honourable V. S. Srinivasa Sastri, P. C., C. H., LL. D., p., LITT.: a political biography. Bombay,New York, Asia Pub. House [1963] xix,476 p.illus., ports., facsims. 23 cm. Bibliography:p. 463-464. [[DS481]] S A
1. Sastiri, Valangiman Sankaranarayana Srinivass, 1869-1946. I. Title.

Sastramidjoyo, Ali, 1930-

SASTROAMIDJOYO, Ali, 1903- 959.8'03'0924 B
Milestones on my journey : the memoirs of Ali Sastroamijoyo, Indonesian patriot and political leader / edited by C. L. M. Penders. St. Lucia, Q. : University of Queensland Press, 1979. xiii, 405 p., [4] leaves of plates : ill. ; 22 cm. (Sources of modern Indonesian history and politics) Distributed by Prentice-Hall International, Hemel Hempstead, Eng. Includes index. [DS644.1.S2A35] 79-317320 ISBN 0-7022-1206-7 : 36.25
1. Sastramidjoyo, Ali, 1930- 2. Indonesia—Politics and government—20th century. 3. Prime ministers—Indonesia—Biography. I. Penders, Christian Lambert Maria. II. Title. III. Series.
Dist. by TIC, Lawrence Mass.

Sastri, Valangiman Sankaranarayana Srinivass, 1869-1946.

KODANDA RAO, Pandurangi, 1889- 923.254
The Right Honourable V. S. Srinivasa Sastri, P. C., C. H., LL. D., P. LITT.;a political biography. New York, Asia Pub. House [1963] xix, 476 p. illus., ports, facsims. 23 cm. Bibliography: p. 463-464. [DS481.S35K6] 63-24912
1. Sastri, Valangiman Sankaranarayana Srinivass, 1869-1946. I. Title.

SASTRI, Valangiman Sankaranarayana Srinivasa, 1869-1946 923.254
Letters. Ed. by T. N. Jagadisan [2d ed.] New York, Asia Pub. [dist. Taplinger, 1964] xv, 377p. facsims., ports. 23cm. 64-5941 7.25
I. Jagadisan, T.N. ed. II. Title.

Satanta, Kiowa chief, d. 1878.

CROCCHIOLA, Stanley Francis Louis, 1908- 970.3 B
Satanta and the Kiowas [by] F. Stanley. [Borger, Tex., Jim Hess Printers, 1968] iv, 391 p. port. 23 cm. Bibliography: p. 363-377. [E99.K5S23] 68-7193
1. Satanta, Kiowa chief, d. 1878. 2. Kiowa Indians. I. Title.

Satchidananda, Swami.

WIENER, Sita. 294.5'61'0924 B
Swami Satchidananda; his biography. [1st ed.] San Francisco, Straight Arrow Books; [distributed by the World, New York, 1970] 194 p. illus., ports. 22 cm. [BL1175.S38W5] 70-141477 7.95
1. Satchidananda, Swami.

Sathya Sai Baba,

SCHULMAN, Arnold. 294.5'6'20924
Baba. New York, Pocket Bks. [1973, c.1971] 174 p. illus., maps. 18 cm. [BL1175.S385S38 1971] ISBN 0-671-78260-6 pap., 1.25
1. Sathya Sai Baba, I. Title. BIP

SCHULMAN, Arnold. 294.5'6'20924
Baba. New York, Viking Press [1971] 177 p. illus., map, ports. 22 cm. [BL1175.S385S38 1971] 77-151261 ISBN 0-670-14343-X 5.95
1. Sathya Sai Baba, 1926- I. Title.

Satie, Erik, 1866-1925.

HARDING, James. 786.1'092'4 B
Erik Satie / James Harding. New York : Praeger, 1975. p. cm. Includes index. Bibliography: p. [ML410.S196H3] 75-5829 ISBN 0-275-53720-X : 13.00
1. Satie, Erik, 1866-1925.

MYERS, Rollo H. 786.1'092'4 B
Erik Satie [by] Rollo H. Myers. St. Clair Shores, Mich., Scholarly Press, 1974. p. cm. Reprint of the 1948 ed. published by D. Dobson, London, in series: Contemporary composers. [ML410.S196M9 1974] 73-22300 ISBN 0-403-01628-2 9.50
1. Satie, Erik, 1866-1925. I. Title. II. Series: Contemporary composers.

MYERS, Rolloe H. 786.1'0924
Erik Satie [by] Rollo H. Myers [Magnolia, Mass., Peter Smith, 1968] 150p. illus., facsims., music, ports. 22cm. (Rebound ed. of the Dover paperback (T1093), an unabridged & slightly corrected repubn. of the work orig. pub. in London in 1948 by Denis Dobson) [ML410.S196 M9 1968] 4.00

1. Satie, Erik, 1866-1925. I. Title.

TEMPLIER, Pierre Daniel. 786.1'0924
Erik Satie. Translation by Elena L. French and David S. French. Cambridge, MIT Press [1969] xi, 127 p. illus., facsims., ports. 24 cm. Discography: p. [117]-127. [ML410.S196T43] 69-12760
1. Satie, Erik, 1866-1925. **BIP**

Satire, English.

VINES, Sherard, 1890- ed. 821'.9'1209
Georgian satirists / by Sherard Vines. Folcroft, Pa. : Folcroft Library Editions, 1977. 217 p. ; 23 cm. Reprint of the 1934 ed. published by Wishart, London. Contents.Contents.—Satires of the Georgian Era.—Edward Young.—Richard Savage.—Robert Dodsley.—Christopher Smart.—Charles Churchill.—Robert Lloyd.—Christopher Anstey. Bibliography: p. 215-217. [PR1195.S3V47 1977] 77-8077 ISBN 0-8414-9183-6 lib. bdg. : 25.00
1. Satire, English. 2. English poetry—18th century. 3. Satirists, English—Biography. I. Title. **BIP**

Satre, Ellen.

SATRE, Elizabeth Dahl. 248'.2 B
The story of Ellen : how love transforms a troubled child / Elizabeth Dahl Satre. Minneapolis : Augsburg Pub. House, c1979. 110 p. ; 20 cm. [BR1725.S3S27] 78-66952 ISBN 0-8066-1691-1 pbk. : 2.95
1. Satre, Ellen. 2. Christian biography—United States. 3. Problem children—United States—Biography. I. Title. **BIP**

Satterthwaite, Frank.

SATTERTHWAITE, Frank. 796.34'3
The three-wall nick and other angles : a squash autobiography / by Frank Satterthwaite. 1st ed. New York : Holt, Rinehart, and Winston, c1979. p. cm. [GV1003.62.S27A37] 78-14173 ISBN 0-03-016666-7
1. Satterthwaite, Frank. 2. Squash (Game) 3. Squash players—United States—Biography. I. Title.

Saturday Club, Boston.

HOWE, Mark Anthony De Wolfe, 1864-1960, ed. 920.0744'61
Later years of the Saturday Club, 1870-1920 Freeport, N.Y., Books for Libraries Press [1968] xvii, 427 p. ports. 22 cm. (Essay index reprint series) Reprint of the 1927 ed. [F73.1.S254 1968] 68-29217
1. Saturday Club, Boston. 2. Boston—Biography. 3. Authors, American. I. Title. **BIP**

Sauder, Dan E.,

SAUDER, Dan E., 1888- 380.5'0924 B
Wheelin' and dealin'; the memoirs of Dan E. Sauder. [North Newton, Kan., Mennonite Press, 1971] 112 p. illus. 24 cm. [HE5623.S26] 78-183376
I. Title.

Sauer, Burton P., ed.

CHAPMAN, Liddie (Hohensee) 1885- v. 12
The Mother Bird, an autobiography. Edited by Burton P. Sauer. Chicago, L. Arthur Associates [1962] 312 p. illus., ports. 21 cm. 63-50223
1. Sauer, Burton P., ed. I. Title.

Sauer, Hank, 1919-

HOFFMAN, John C 927.96357
Hank Sauer. New York, A. S. Barnes [1953] 182p. illus. 22cm. (Most valuable player series) [GV865.S3H6] 53-5577
1. Sauer, Hank, 1919- I. Title.

Sauerbruch, Ferdinand,

SAUERBRUCH, Ferdinand, 1875-1951. 926.1
Master surgeon. Translated by Fernand G. Renier and Anne Cliff. New York, Crowell [1954, c1953] 277 p. illus. 21 cm. Translation of Das War Mein Leben. [R512.S23A34 1954] 54-9772
I. Title.

Saugrain de Vigni, Antoine Francois, 1763-1820.

DICKS, Samuel E. 610'.92'4 B
Antoine Saugrain (1763-1820) : a French scientist on the American frontier / by Samuel E. Dicks. Emporia : School of Graduate and Professional Studies of the Emporia Kansas State College, 1976. 27 p. : ill. ; 23 cm. (The Emporia State research studies ; v. 25, no. 1) Includes bibliographical references. [R154.S26D5] 77-620913
1. Saugrain de Vigni, Antoine Francois, 1763-1820. 2. Physicians—Mississippi Valley—Biography. 3. Scientists—Mississippi Valley—Biography. I. Title. II. Series.

Saul, King of Israel—Juvenile literature.

MCCALL, Yvonne Holloway. 222'.43'0905
The angry king : 1 Samuel 18-2 Samuel 5 for children / written by Yvonne Holloway McCall ; illustrated by Jim Roberts. St. Louis : Concordia Pub. House, c1976. p. cm. (Arch books ; ser. 14) Retells in rhyme how David came to replace Saul as king of Israel with emphasis on the meaning of love, trust in God, and handling competition in a Christian way. [BS580.S3M3] 76-27365 ISBN 0-570-06110-5 pbk. : 0.59
1. Saul, King of Israel—Juvenile literature. 2. David, King of Israel—Juvenile literature. 3. Bible. O.T.—Biography—Juvenile literature. I. Roberts, Jim. II. Title.

Sauma, Rabban, d. 1293?

THE Monks of 281'.8'0922 B
Kublai Khan, Emperor of China; or, The history of the life and travels of Rabban Sawma, envoy and plenipotentiary of the Mongol khans to the kings of Europe, and Markos who as Mar Yahbh-Allaha III became Patriarch of the Nestorian Church in Asia. Translated from the Syriac by E. A. Wallis Budge. With 16 plates and 6 illus. in the text. London, Religious Tract Society, 1928. [New York, AMS Press, 1973] xvi, 335 p. illus. 23 cm. Translation of Yish'iata demar Yahbalaha vdelaban Sauma. Bibliography: p. [307]-313. [DS752.Y5513 1973] 71-38051 ISBN 0-404-56905-6 20.00
1. Sauma, Rabban, d. 1293? 2. Yabhalaha III, Patriarch of the Nestorians, 1244?-1317. 3. Voyages and travels. 4. Nestorians. I. Budge, Ernest Alfred Thompson Wallis, Sir, 1857-1934, tr.

Saunders, Albert Edward.

MACNAIR, John Van, 1915- 922.373
Chaplain on the waterfront; the story of Father Saunders. New York, Seabury [c.] 1963. 141p. 22cm. 63-19451 3.50
1. Saunders, Albert Edward. 2. Longshoremen—New York (City) I. Title.

Saunders, Charles, fl. 1763.

SAUNDERS, Charles, fl.1763. 973'.04'97 S
The horrid cruelty of the Indians / Charles Saunders. New York : Garland Pub., 1977. p. cm. (The Garland library of narratives of North American Indian captivities ; v. 10) Reprint of the 1763 ed. printed by T. Warren, Birmingham. Issued with the reprint of the 1764 ed. of Grace, H. The history of the life and sufferings of Henry Grace. New York, 1977. The reprint of the 1768 ed. of Adventure of a young English officer. New York, 1977. The reprint of the 1767 ed. of Hollister, I. A brief narration of the captivity of Isaac Hollister. New York, 1977. The reprint of the 1768 ed. of Henry, W. Account of the captivity of William Henry. New York, 1977. The reprint of the 1774 ed. of Smethurst, G. A narrative of an extraordinary escape. New York, 1977. [E85.G2 vol. 10] [E99.S35] 970'.004'97 77-875 lib. bdg. : 25.00
1. Saunders, Charles, fl. 1763. 2. Shawnee Indians—Captivities. 3. Indians of North America—Captivities. 4. United States—Biography. I. Title. II. Series.

Saunders, Joseph Benjamin, 1901-

SCOTT, Otto J. 338.2'7'2820924 B
The professional : a biography of J. B. Saunders / by Otto J. Scott. 1st ed. New York : Athenum, 1976. ix, 497 p., [13] leaves of plates : ill. ; 24 cm. Includes index. [HD9570.S28S37 1976] 76-11779 ISBN 0-689-10726-9 : 15.00
1. Saunders, Joseph Benjamin, 1901- 2. Petroleum industry and trade—United States—History. I. Title.

Saunders, Mary.

SAUNDERS, Mary. 979.5'03'0924
The Whitman massacre : a true story by a survivor of this terrible tragedy which took place in Oregon in 1847 / Mary Saunders. Fairfield, Wash. : Galleon Press, 1977. 56 p. ; 24 cm. [E83.84.S28 1977] 77-13101 ISBN 0-87770-188-1 : 5.50 ISBN 0-87770-189-X pbk. : 2.95
1. Saunders, Mary. 2. Whitman Massacre, 1847—Personal narratives. 3. Northwest, Pacific—Biography. I. Title.

Saunders, Philip K

SAUNDERS, Philip K 926.22
Dr. Panto Fogo, an autobiography. Englewood Cliffs, N.J., Prentice-Hall [1960] 276p. 22cm. [CT275.S3385.A3] 60-9278
I. Title.

Saunders, Reginald Walter, 1920-

GORDON, Harry, 1926- 923.594
The embarrassing Australian; the story of an aboriginal warrior. Melbourne, Lansdowne Pr. [dist. New Rochelle, N.Y., SportShelf, 1964] 172p. illus., ports. 23cm. 64-2783 6.00
1. Saunders, Reginald Walter, 1920- 2. Australia—Native races. I. Title.

Saunders, Stephen, 1820-1859.

MACDONALD, Robert S. 813.54
Write me at Lavaca; the story of Stephen Saunders, 1820-1859. Boston, Humphries [c.1964] 294p. illus., ports. 23cm. 64-14799 5.00 bds.,
1. Saunders, Stephen, 1820-1859. I. Title.

Saunders. William Oscar. 1881-1940.

SAUNDERS, Keith. 071.975614
The independent man: the story of W. O. Sunders and his delightfully different newspaper. [Washington, Saunders Press, 1962] 282p. illus. 23cm. [PN1874.S2SS3] 62-16359
1. Saunders. William Oscar. 1881-1940. 2. The Independent. Elizabeth City. N. C. I. Title.

SAUNDERS, William Keith. v. 12
The Independent man; the story of W. O. Saunders and his delightfully different newspaper. [Raleigh, Edwards & Broughton Co., c1962] xix, 282 p. port. 23 cm. Foreword by Harry Golden. 63-57748
1. Saunders, William Oscar, 1884-1940. 2. The Independent. 3. Elizabeth City, N. C.—History. I. Title.

Saussure, Ferdinand de, 1857-1913.

CULLER, Jonathan D. 410'.92'4
Ferdinand de Saussure / Jonathan Culler. New York : Penguin Books, 1977, c1976. xix, 140 p. ; 18 cm. (Penguin modern masters) Includes index. Bibliography: p. [133]-135. [P85.S18C8 1977] 76-25161 ISBN 0-14-004369-1 pbk. : 2.50
1. Saussure, Ferdinand de, 1857-1913. 2. Structural linguistics. 3. Semiotics. **BIP**

Sava, Saint, Abp. of Serbia, 1169-1237.

MATEJIC, Mateja. 282'.092'4 B
Biography of Saint Sava / Mateja Matejic. Columbus, Ohio : Kosovo Pub. Co., 1976. 128 p. : ill. ; 23 cm. Bibliography: p. 127-128. [BX719.S35M37] 77-366931
1. Sava, Saint, Abp. of Serbia, 1169-1237. 2. Christian saints—Serbia—Biography. I. Title.

NIKOLAJ, Bp. of Ohrid, 1880- 922.1497
The life of St. Sava. Libertyville, Ill., Serbian Eastern Orthodox Diocese for United States of America and Canada [1951] 233p. illus. 21cm. [BX719.S35N49] 51-35108
1. Sava, Saint, Abp., of Serbia, 1169-1237. I. Title.

Savage, Mary—Biography.

SAVAGE, Mary. 362.2'092'4 B
Addicted to suicide : a woman struggling to live / Mary Savage. Cambridge, Mass. : Schenkman Pub. Co., [1979] p. cm. Reprint, with new foreword and afterword, of the 1975 ed. published by Capra Press, Santa Barbara, Calif. [PS3569.A828Z463 1979] 79-4695 ISBN 0-87073-906-9 : 11.95 ISBN 0-87073-907-7 pbk. : 4.50
1. Savage, Mary—Biography. 2. Mental illness—Biography. 3. Authors, English.—20th century—Biography. I. Title. **BIP**

Savage, Richard, d. 1743.

MAKOWER, Stanley Victor. 821'.5 B
Richard Savage; a mystery in biography, by Stanley V. Makower. Port Washington, N.Y., Kennikat Press [1972] vii, 343 p. ports. 23 cm. Reprint of the 1909 ed. Bibliography: p. 328-332. [PR3671.S2M3 1972] 72-160770 ISBN 0-8046-1597-7
1. Savage, Richard, d. 1743. **BIP**

TRACY, Clarence Rupert. v. 12
The artificial bastard; a biography of Richard Savage. Cambridge, Harvard University Press, 1953. xvii, 164p. 24cm. Bibliographical footnotes. A54
1. Savage, Richard, d. 1743. I. Title.

Savala, Refugio.

SAVALA, Refugio. 970'.004'97
The autobiography of a Yaqui poet / by Refugio Savala ; edited by Kathleen M. Sands. Tucson : University of Arizona Press, [1979] p. cm. Includes index. Bibliography: p. [E99.Y3S28] 79-19817 ISBN 0-8165-0620-0 pbk. : 8.95
1. Savala, Refugio. 2. Yaqui Indians—Biography. I. Sands, Kathleen M. II. Title. **BIP**

Savaric de Mauleon, fl. 1180-1232.

CHAYTOR, Henry John, 1871-1954. 849'.1'2 B
Savaric de Mauleon, baron and troubadour. [Folcroft, Pa.] Folcroft Library Editions, 1973. xii, 96 p. illus. 23 cm. Reprint of the 1939 ed. published by the University Press, Cambridge. Bibliography: p. [xi]-xii. [PC3330.S35C5 1973] 73-19981 20.00
1. Savaric de Mauleon, fl. 1180-1232. 2. John, King of England, 1167?-1216. 3. Poitou—History.

Savelli, Troilo, d. 1592.

BIONDO, Giuseppe. 230'.2 S
A relation of the death of ... Troilo Savelli / [by] Giuseppe Biondo ; [and] Holy philosophy / [by] Guillaume Du Vair ; [translated from the French by J. H.]. Ilkley [etc.] : Scolar Press, 1976. 464 p. (in various pagings) ; 20 cm. (English recusant literature, 1558-1640 ; v. 293) (Series: Rogers, David Morrison, comp. English recusant literature, 1558-1640 ; v. 293.) Biondo's work reprinted from a copy in the library of Downside Abbey of the 1620 ed.; references: Allison and Rogers 112; STC 3134. Du Vair's work reprinted from

a copy in the library of Heythrop College of the 1636 ed.; reference: Allison and Rogers 290. [BX1750.A1E5 vol. 293] [BX4705.S367] 248'.246 B 77-356063 ISBN 0-85967-294-8 : £10.00
1. Savelli, Troilo, d. 1592. 2. Christian martyrs—Italy—Rome (City)—Biography. 3. Rome (City)—Biography. 4. Christian life—Catholic authors. I. Du Vair, Guillaume, 1556-1621. De la sainte philosophie. English. 1976. II. Title. III. Series.

Savio, Domenico, Saint, 1842-1857.

BOSCO, Giovanni, Saint, 1815-1888. 922.245
Life of Blessed Dominic Savio; slightly abridged from the Italian by Roderic Bright. Paterson, N. J., Salesiana Publishers [c1950] 155p. illus. 22cm. Translation of Vita del giovanetto Dom. Savio. [BX4700.S35B62] 55-36994
1. Savio, Domenico, Saint, 1842-1857. I. Title.

BOSCO, Giovanni, Saint, 1815-1888. 922.245
The life of Saint Dominic Savio. 1st American ed., complete and unabridged, translated from the 5th Italian ed., with introd. and notes, by Paul Aronica. Paterson, N. J., Salesiana Publishers, 1955. 112p. illus. 22cm. Translation of Vita del giovanetto Dom. Savio. [BX4700.S35B616] 56-4539
1. Savio, Domenico, Saint, 1842-1857. I. Title.

ERNEST, Brother, 1897- 922.245
A story of Saint Dominic Savio. Pictures by Carolyn Lee Jagodits. Notre Dame, Ind., Dujarie Press [c1957] unpaged. illus. 21cm. [BX4700.S35E7] 57-27079
1. Savic, Domenico, Saint, 1842-1857. I. Title.

Savio, Dominico, Saint, 1842-1857—Juvenile literature.

ROBERTO, Brother, 1927- 92
Boy in a hurry; a story of Saint Dominic Savio. Notre Dame, Ind., Dujarie Press [1966] 95 p. illus. 24 cm. [BX4700.S35R54] 66-12758
1. Savio, Domenico, Saint, 1842-1857 — Juvenile literature. I. Title.

ROBERTO, Brother, Brother, 1927- 92
Boy in a hurry; a story of Saint Dominic Savio. Notre Dame, Ind., Dujarie [c.1966] 95p. illus. 24cm. [BX4700.S35R54] 66-12758 2.25
1. Savio, Dominico, Saint, 1842-1857—Juvenile literature. I. Title.

Savonarola, Girolamo Maria Francesco Matteo, 1452-1498.

RENNER, R Richard, 1896- 282.0924
Savonarola, the first great Protestant, by R. Richard Renner. [1st ed.] New York, Greenwich Book Publishers [c1965] 153 p. 21 cm. Bibliography: p. 153. [DG737.97.R4] 65-24258
1. Savonarola, Girolamo Maria Francesco Matteo, 1452-1498. I. Title.

RENNER, Richard, M.D., 1896- 282.0924
Savonarola, the first great Protestant, by R. Richard Renner, M.D. New York, Greenwich Bk. Pubs., [282 7th Ave., 1966, c.1965] 153p. 21cm. Bibl. [DG737.97.R4] 65-24258 2.95
1. Savonarola, Girolamo Maria Francesco Matteo, 1452-1498. I. Title.

RIDOLFI, Roberto, 1895- 922.245
The life of Girolamo Savonarola. Translated from the Italian by Cecil Grayson. [1st American ed.] New York, Knopf, 1959. 325 p. illus. 24 cm. "The extensive documentation of the original has been omitted." [DG737.97.R533 1959] 58-9668
1. Savonarola, Girolamo Maria Francesco Matteo, 1452-1498. **BIP**

RIDOLFI, Roberto, 1899- 271'.2'00924 B
The life of Girolamo Savonarola / by Roberto Ridolfi ; translated from the Italian by Cecil Grayson. Westport, Conn. : Greenwood Press, 1976, c1959. x, 325 p., [1] leaf of plates : port. ; 24 cm. Reprint of the ed. published by Knopf, New York. Translation of Vita di Girolamo Savonarola. Includes index. [DG737.97.R533 1976] 76-8001 ISBN 0-8371-8873-3 lib.bdg. : 21.00
1. Savonarola, Girolamo Maria Francesco Matteo, 1452-1498.

ROEDER, Ralph, 1890- 920.045
The man of the Renaissance; four lawgivers: Savonarola, Machiavelli, Castiglione, Aretino. New York, Meridian Books [1958] 504 p. illus. 21 cm. (Meridian books, MG17) [DG533.R6 1958] 58-11929
1. Savonarola, Girolamo Maria Francesco Matteo, 1452-1498. 2. Machiavelli, Niccolo, 1469-1527. 3. Castiglione, Baldassare, conte, 1478-1529. 4. Aretino, Pietro, 1492-1556. 5. Renaissance—Italy. I. Title.

ROEDER, Ralph, 1890-1970. 945'.05'0922
The man of the Renaissance : four lawgivers, Savonarola, Machiavelli, Castiglione, Aretino / by Ralph Roeder. Clifton, N.J. : A. M. Kelley, 1975, c1933. p. cm. (Viking reprint editions) Reprint of the ed. published by Viking Press, New York. Bibliography: p. [DG533.R6 1975] 78-122059 ISBN 0-678-03171-1
1. Savonarolda, Girolamo Maria Francesco Matteo, 1452-1498. 2. Machiavelli, Niccolo, 1469-1527. 3. Gastiglione, Baldassare, conte, 1478-1529. 4. Aretino, Pietro, 1492-1556. 5. Renaissance—Italy. I. Title. **BIP**

VAN PAASSEN, Pierre, 1895- 922.245
A crown of fire; the life and times of Girolamo Savonarola. New York, Scribner [1960] 330 p. illus. 22 cm. [DG737.97.V34] 60-6335
1. Savonarola, Girolamo Maria Francesco Matteo, 1452-1498. I. Title.

VILLARI, Pasquale, 1827-1917. 271'.2'0924 B
Life and times of Girolamo Savonarola. Translated by Linda Villari. New York, Haskell House Publishers, 1969. 2 v. illus., facsim., plates, ports. 23 cm. Translation of La storia di Girolamo Savonarola e de suoi tempi. Reprint of the 1888 ed. Bibliographical footnotes. [DG737.97.V7 1969] 68-25276
1. Savonarola, Girolamo Maria Francesco Matteo, 1452-1498. I. Title. **BIP**

VILLARI, Pasquale, 1827-1917. 271'.2'024 B
Life and times of Girolamo Savonarola. Translated by Linda Villari. New York, Scribner and Welford, 1888. St. Clair Shores, Mich., Scholarly Press, 1972. 2 v. illus. 22 cm. Translation of La storia di Girolamo Savonarola e de suoi tempi. Includes bibliographical references. [DG737.97.V7 1972] 79-115284 ISBN 0-403-00265-6 25.00
1. Savonarola, Girolamo Maria Francesco Matteo, 1452-1498. I. Title.

WEINSTEIN, Donald, 1926- 236'.3
Savonarola and Florence; prophecy and patriotism in the Renaissance. Princeton, N.J., Princeton University Press, 1970. viii, 399 p. illus., port. 25 cm. Includes bibliographical references. [DG737.97.W4] 76-113013 13.50
1. Savonarola, Girolamo Maria Francesco Matteo, 1452-1498. 2. Florence—History—Prophecies. 3. Millennialism—Italy—Florence. I. Title. **BIP**

Savorgnan de Brazza, Pierre Paul Francoise Camille, Comte, 1852-1905.

WEST, Richard. 967
Congo. New York, Holt, Rinehart and Winston [1972] 304 p. illus. 22 cm. Bibliography: p. 271-278. [DT546.W453] 79-182765 ISBN 0-03-091391-8 7.95
1. Savorgnan de Brazza, Pierre Paul Francoise Camille, Comte, 1852-1905. 2. Africa, French-speaking Equatorial—Discovery and exploration. I. Title.

Savoy, House of.

KATZ, Robert, 1933- 945.09
The fall of the House of Savoy; a study in the relevance of the commonplace or the vulgarity of history. New York, Macmillan [1971] xxii, 439 p. illus., maps, ports. 24 cm. Bibliography: p. 417-425. [DG611.5.K36] 77-132870 12.50
1. Savoy, House of. I. Title.

Savundra, Emil.

CONNELL, Jon. 364.1'63'0924 B
Fraud : the amazing career of Dr. Savundra / Jon Connell and Douglas Sutherland. Briarcliff Manor, N.Y. : Stein and Day, 1979, c1978. p. cm. [HV6248.S365C65 1979] 78-66247 ISBN 0-8128-2602-7 : 12.95
1. Savundra, Emil. 2. Crime and criminals—Great Britain—Biography. 3. Swindlers and swindling—Great Britain—Biography. 4. Fraud. I. Sutherland, Douglas, joint author. II. Title.

Sawyer, Ruth, 1880-

HAVILAND, Virginia, 1911- 813.52 (B)
Ruth Sawyer. [1st American ed.] New York, H. Z. Walck [1965] 78 p. port. 19 cm. Bibliography: p. 73-78. [PS3537.A974Z6 1965] 65-24175
1. Sawyer, Ruth, 1880- I. Title.

Saxe, Maurice, comte de, 1696-1750.

LIDDELL HART, Basil Henry, 1895- 909'.00922
Great captains unveiled. by B. H. Liddell Hart. Freeport, N.Y., Bks. for Libs. Pr. [1967] 274p. maps. 22cm. (Essay index reprint ser.) Reprint of the 1928 ed. [D106.L5 1967] 67-23240 8.50
1. Jenghis Khan, 1162-1227. 2. Saxe, Maurice, comte de, 1696-1750. 3. Gusstaf Adolf, King of Sweden, 1594-1632. 4. Wallenstein, Alberecht Wenzel Eusebius von. Herzog zu Friendland. 1583-1634. 5. Wolfe, James, 1727-1759. I. Title.
Contents omitted.

WHITE, Jon Ewbank Manchip, 1924- 923.544
Marshal of France; the life and times of Maurice, comte de Saxe, 1696-1750. Chicago, Rand McNally [1962] xiv, 299 p. illus., ports., maps (1 fold.), geneal. tables. 26 cm. "Notes and references": p. 279-[287] Bibliography: p. 275-277. [DC135.S3W5] 62-51615
1. Saxe, Maurice, comte de, 1696-1750. 2. France—History—Military—1715-1789. I. Title.

Say, Thomas, 1787-1834.

WEISS, Harry Bischoff, 1883- 595.7'092'4 B
Thomas Say, early American naturalist / Harry B. Weiss and Grace M. Ziegler. New York : Arno Press, 1978. p. cm. (Biologists and their world) Reprint of the 1931 ed. published by Thomas, Springfield, Ill. Includes index. Bibliography: p. [QL31.S2W4 1978] 77-81137 ISBN 0-405-10737-4 : 18.00
1. Say, Thomas, 1787-1834. 2. Zoologists—United States—Biography. I. Weiss, Grace M., joint author. II. Title. III. Series.

Sayers, Dorothy Leigh, 1893-1957.

HITCHMAN, Janet. 823'.9'12 B
Such a strange lady : a biography of Dorothy L. Sayers / by Janet Hitchman. 1st U.S. ed. New York : Harper & Row, [1975] p. cm. "First published in England under the title Such a strange lady: an introduction to Dorothy L. Sayers (1893-1957)." "The works of Dorothy L. Sayers": p. [PR6037.A95Z7 1975b] 75-6340 ISBN 0-06-011903-9 : 8.95
1. Sayers, Dorothy Leigh, 1893-1957. I. Title. **BIP**

HONE, Ralph E. 823'.9'12 B
Dorothy L. Sayers : a literary biography / by Ralph E. Hone. Kent, Ohio : Kent State University Press, c1979. xvii, 217 p., [4] leaves of plates : ill. ; 24 cm. Includes bibliographical references and index. [PR6037.A95Z73] 79-9783 ISBN 0-87338-228-5 : 15.00
1. Sayers, Dorothy Leigh, 1893-1957. 2. Authors, English—20th century—Biography. **BIP**

TISCHLER, Nancy Marie Patterson. 823'.912 B
Dorothy L. Sayers, a pilgrim soul / Nancy M. Tischler. Atlanta : John Knox Press, c1979. p. cm. Includes index Bibliography: p. [PR6037.A95Z9] 79-87739 ISBN 0-8042-0882-4 : 7.95
1. Sayers, Dorothy Leigh, 1893-1957. 2. Authors, English—20th century—Biography. 3. Scholars—England—Biography. I. Title.

Sayers, Dorothy Leigh, 1893-1957—Biography.

DALE, Alzina Stone, 1931- 823'.9'12
Maker and craftsman : the story of Dorothy L. Sayers / by Alzina Stone Dale. Grand Rapids : Eerdmans, c1978. xiv, 158 p., [4] leaves of plates : ill. ; 22 cm. Recounts the life of the English author who created the urbane, aristocratic sleuth, Lord Peter Wimsey. [PR6037.A95Z63] 92 78-15640 ISBN 0-8028-1739-4 : 8.95
1. Sayers, Dorothy Leigh, 1893-1957—Biography. 2. Authors, English—20th century—Biography. I. Title.

Sayers, Gale,

SAYERS, Gale, 1943- 796.332'0924 B
I am third [by] Gale Sayers with Al Silverman. Introd. by Bill Cosby. New York, Viking Press [1970] xii, 238 p. illus., ports. 23 cm. [GV939.S23A3 1970] 70-119775 6.95
I. Silverman, Al, joint author. II. Title. **BIP**

Sayers, Peig.

SAYERS, Peig. 941.96
An old woman's reflections / Peig Sayers ; translated from the Irish by Seamus Ennis and introduced by W. R. Rogers. Oxford [Eng.] ; New York : Oxford University Press, 1978. xiv, 131 p. : map ; 20 cm. (Oxford paperbacks) Translation of Machtnamh seana mhna. Includes bibliographical references. [DA990.B65S33 1978] 77-30568 pbk. : 3.50
1. Sayers, Peig. 2. Blasket Islands, Ire.—Social life and customs. 3. Blasket Islands, Ire.—Biography. I. Title.

SAYERS, Peig. 914.19'6'0380924 B
Peig: the autobiography of Peig Sayers of the Great Blasket Island. Translated into English by Bryan MacMahon. Introd. by Eoin McKiernan. Illus. by Catriona O'Connor. [Syracuse, N.Y.] Syracuse University Press, 1974. 212 p. illus. 21 cm. [DA990.B65S4213 1974] 74-11721 ISBN 0-8156-0106-9 7.95
1. Sayers, Peig. 2. Blasket Islands, Ire. **BIP**

Sayre, Francis Bowes,

SAYRE, Francis Bowes, 1885- 923.273
Glad adventure. New York, Macmillan, 1957. 356p. illus. 22cm. Autobiography. [E748.S3A3] 57-7213
I. Title.

Sayre, Ruth Buxton, 1896-

MCDONALD, Julie. 301.41'2'0924 B
Ruth Buxton Sayre, first lady of the farm / Julie McDonald. 1st ed. Ames : Iowa State University Press, 1980. p. cm. Includes index. [HQ1413.S28M23] 79-17698 ISBN 0-8138-1260-7 : 8.95 8.95
1. Sayre, Ruth Buxton, 1896- 2. Farmers' wives—United States—Biography. I. Title.

Scala, Bartolommeo, 1430-1497.

BROWN, Alison, 1934- 445'.51'050924 B
Bartolomeo Scala, 1430-1497, Chancellor of Florence : the humanist as bureaucrat / Alison Brown. Princeton, N.J. : Princeton

University Press, c1979. xi, 366 p. : port. ; 25 cm. Includes index. Bibliography: p. 345-352. [DG737.58.S28B76] 78-70280 ISBN 0-691-05270-0 : 25.00
1. Scala, Bartolommeo, 1430-1497. 2. Florence—History—1421-1737. 3. Statesmen—Italy—Florence—Biography. 4. Florence—Biography.

Scalabrini, Giovanni Battista, Bp., 1839-1905.

CALIARO, Marco. 282'.092'4 B
John Baptist Scalabrini, apostle to emigrants / Marco Caliaro and Mario Francesconi ; [translation by Alba I. Zizzamia]. 1st ed. New York : Center for Migration Studies, 1977. xi, 555 p. : ill. ; 24 cm. Translation of L'apostolo degli emigranti. Includes indexes. Bibliography: p. 453-469. [BX4705.S38C313] 76-44922 ISBN 0--913256-24-2 : 15.00
1. Scalabrini, Giovanni Battista, Bp., 1839-1905. 2. Catholic Church—Bishops—Biography. 3. Bishops—Italy—Biography. 4. Church work with emigrants—Italy. I. Francesconi, Mario, joint author. II. Title.

FELICI, Icilio, 1892- 922.245
Father to the immigrants, the servant of God: John Baptist Scalabrini, Bishop of Piacenza. Translated by Carol Della Chiesa. New York, P. J. Kenedy [1955] 248p. illus. 22cm. Translation of G. B. Scalabrini, vescovo insigne. [BX4705.S38F415] 55-11371
1. Scalabrini, Giovanni Battista, Bp., 1839-1905. I. Title.

Scalia, Joni Lynn.

SCALIA, Joni Lynn. 617'.092'4 B
The cutting edge / Joni Lynn Scalia. New York : McGraw-Hill, c1978. 257 p. ; 24 cm. [R154.S352A32] 78-7626 ISBN 0-07-055019-0 : 10.95
1. Scalia, Joni Lynn. 2. Surgeons—California—Biography. I. Title. BIP

Scaliger, Julius Caesar, 1484-1558.

HALL, Vernon, 1913- 928.7
Life of Julius Caesar Scalinger (1484-1558) Philadelphia, American Philosophical Society, 1950. 85-170 p. ports. 30 cm. (Transactions of the American Philosophical Society, new ser., v. 40, pt. 2) "Iteferences": p. 163-165. [Q11.P6 n. s., vol. 40, pt. 2] 51-9008
1. Scaliger, Julius Caesar, 1484-1558. I. Title. II. Series: AmericanPhilosophical Society. Transactions, new ser., v. 40, pt. 2

Scannell, Dorothy.

SCANNELL, Dorothy. 942.1'3 B
Mother knew best : memoir of a London girlhood / by Dorothy Scannell. 1st American ed. [New York] : Pantheon Books, [1975] c1974. 182 p. ; 22 cm. [CT788.S25A35 1975] 74-26519 ISBN 0-394-49766-X
1. Scannell, Dorothy. I. Title.

Scarlatti, Domenico, 1685-1757.

KILPATRICK, Ralph. v. 12
Domenico Scarlatti. Princeton, Princeton University Press [1965] xviii, 481 p. plates, port. tables (1 fold.) 24 cm. 67-92960
1. Scarlatti, Domenico, 1685-1757. I. Title. BIP

SITWELL, Sacheverell, Sir, Bart., 1897- 780'.924 B
A background for Domenico Scarlatti, 1685-1757; written for his two hundred and fiftieth anniversary. Freeport, N.Y., Books for Libraries Press [1970] 168 p. port. 23 cm. "First published 1935." [ML410.S221S6 1970] 74-107832
1. Scarlatti, Domenico, 1685-1757. I. Title.

SITWELL, Sacheverell, Sir, bart., 1897- 780'.924 B
A background for Domenico Scarlatti, 1685-1757; written for his two hundred and fiftieth anniversary. Westport, Conn., Greenwood Press [1970] 168 p. port. 23 cm. Reprint of the 1935 ed. [ML410.S221S6 1970b] 74-109845 ISBN 0-8371-4335-7
1. Scarlatti, Domenico, 1685-1757. I. Title. BIP

Scarne, John

SCARNE, John 795.0924
The odds against me; an autobiography. New York, S. & S. [c.1966] 537p. illus., ports. 22cm. [GV1545.S28A3] 66-11313 6.95 bds.,
I. Title.

SCARNE, John. 795.0924 (B)
The odds against me; an autobiography. New York, Simon and Schuster [1966] 537 p. illus., ports. 22 cm. [GV1545.S28A3] 66-11313
I. Title.

Scarron, Paul, 1610-1660.

PHELPS, Naomi Forsythe. 928.4
The Queen's invalid; a biography of Paul Scarron. Baltimore, Johns Hopkins Press, 1951. 289 p. port. 23 cm. Bibliography: p. 281-284. [PQ1919.Z5P5] 51-5905
1. Scarron, Paul, 1610-1660. I. Title.

Schaaf, James Edward.

SCHAAF, James Edward. 973.921'092'4 B
Mamie Doud Eisenhower and her chicken farmer cousin. [Whitehouse Station, N.J., Printed by Wilkie Print., 1974] 75 p. illus. 24 cm. [E837.E4S32] 74-157039
1. Eisenhower, Mamie (Doud) 1896- 2. Schaaf, James Edward. 3. Doud family. 4. Schaaf family. I. Title.

Schacht, Alexander,

SCHACHT, Alexander, 1894- 927.96357
My own particular screwball, an informal autobiography, by Al Schacht. Edited by Ed Keys. [1st ed.] Garden City, N. Y., Doubleday, 1955. 254 p. 22 cm. [GV865.S35.A32] 55-6483
I. Title.

Schacht, Hjalmar Horace Greeley, 1877-1970.

SCHACHT, Hjalmar Horace Greeley, 1877-1970. 332.1'092'4 B
Confessions of "the Old Wizard" : the autobiography of Hjalmar Horace Greeley Schacht / translated by Diana Pyke. Westport, Conn. : Greenwood Press, 1974, c1955. xx, 484 p., [13] leaves of plates : ill. ; 22 cm. Translation of 76 Jahre meines Lebens. Reprint of the ed. published by Houghton Mifflin, Boston. Includes index. [DD247.S335A3513 1974] 74-15559 ISBN 0-8371-7827-4 : 23.25
1. Schacht, Hjalmar Horace Greeley, 1877-1970. 2. Finance—Germany. 3. Germany—Economic conditions—1918-1945. I. Title.

Schaefer, Jack Warner, 1907-

HASLAM, Gerald W. 813'.5'4 B
Jack Schaefer / by Gerald Haslam. Boise, Idaho : Boise State University, 1976c1975 46 p. ; 21 cm. (Boise State University Western writers series ; no. 20) Bibliography: p. 45-46. [PS3537.C223Z69] 75-29981 ISBN 0-88430-019-6 pbk. : 1.50
1. Schaefer, Jack Warner, 1907- 2. Authors, American—20th century—Biography. I. Series: Boise State University. Boise State University Western writers series ; no. 20. BIP

Schaeffer, Nathan Christ, 1849-1919.

KOCH, Charles Dison. 923.773
Nathan C. Schaeffer, educational philosopher. Harrisburg, Pa. [Telegraph Press] 1951. 307 p. illus. 22 cm. [LB875.S336K6] 52-18636
1. Schaeffer, Nathan Christ, 1849-1919. I. Title.

Schaffer, Dori, 1938-1963.

SCHAFFER, Dori, 1938-1963. 301.41'2'0924 B
Dear Deedee : from the diaries of Dori Schaffer / edited and annotated by Anne Schaffer. 1st ed. Secaucus, N.J. : L. Stuart, c1978. 222 p. ; 24 cm. [HQ1229.S33 1978] 78-13203 ISBN 0-8184-0271-7 : 10.00
1. Schaffer, Dori, 1938-1963. 2. Young women—United States—Biographies. I. Schaffer, Anne. II. Title.

Schalit, Moishe Aaron,

SCHALIT, Moishe Aaron, 1874- 926.1
Travelled roads; memoirs of a doctor who lived in the land of Israel. With a foreword by Julius Stone. New York, Abelard-Schuman [1954] 365 p. illus. 22 cm. [R644.P3S3] 54-10229
I. Title.

Scharff, Hanns J.

TOLIVER, Raymond F. 940.54'72'43
The interrogator : the story of Hanns J. Scharff, Luftwaffe's master interrogator / by Raymond F. Toliver, in collaboration with Hanns J. Scharff. Fallbrook, CA : Aero Publishers, c1978. p. cm. Includes index. [D805.G3T64] 78-10626 ISBN 0-8168-6470-5 : 12.95
1. Scharff, Hanns J. 2. World War, 1939-1945—Prisoners and prisons, German. 3. Intelligence officers—Germany—Biography. I. Scharff, Hanns J., joint author. II. Title.

Scharnhorst, Gerhard Johann David von,

FIEDLER, Siegfried. v. 12
Scharnhorst; Geist und Tat. Herford, Maximilian-Verlag [c1963] 266 p. illus., facsims., ports. 21 cm. Bibliography: p. 245-255.
1. Scharnhorst, Gerhard Johann David von, 1755-1813. I. Title.

Schary, Dore.

ZIMMER, Jill (Schary) 927.92
With a cast of thousands; a Hollywood childhood. Introd. by Leonard Spigelgass. Stein & Day [dist. Philadelphia, Lippincott, c.1963] 252p. 22cm. 63-18382 4.95 bds.,
1. Schary, Dore. 2. Actors. I. Title.

Schary, Dore—Biography.

SCHARY, Dore. 812'.5'4
Heyday : an autobiography / Dore Schary. 1st ed. Boston : Little, Brown, c1979. p. cm. Includes index. [PS3537.C253Z523] 79-91255 ISBN 0-316-77270-4 : 14.95
1. Schary, Dore—Biography. 2. Dramatists, American—20th century—Biography. 3. Moving-picture producers and directors—United States—Biography. I. Title. BIP

Scheckter, Jody.

SCHECKTER, Jody. 796.7'2'0924 B
Jody : an autobiography / [Jody Scheckter] . Johannesburg : Keartland (Hugh), 1976. 128 p. : ill. (some col.) ; 26 cm. [GV1032.S28A34 1976] 77-362984 ISBN 0-949997-23-4 : R9.00
1. Scheckter, Jody. 2. Automobile racing drivers—South Africa—Biography. I. Title. BIP

Schecter, Solomon, 1847-1915.

BENTWICH, Norman De Mattos, 1883- v. 12
Solomon Schechter, a biography. New York, Burning Bush Press [1964, c1938] xvi, 374 p. front., pl., ports., facsims. 22 cm. "Bibliography of the principal writings of Solomon Schechter": p. 351-352. NUC66
1. Schecter, Solomon, 1847-1915. I. Title.

Scheda, Otto, 1863-1932.

TIEDEMANN, Wilhelmina (Scheda) 1886- 927.8
A comet among the stars [by] Marion Knight [pseud. 1st ed.] New York, Pageant Press [1953] 75p. 21cm. [ML418.T55K5] 53-12320
1. Scheda, Otto, 1863-1932. I. Title.

Scheele, Karl Wilhelm, 1742-1786.

URDANG, Georg, 1882- 925.4
The apothecary chemist, Carl Wilhelm Scheele; a pictorial biography. [2d ed.] Madison, Wis., American Institute of the History of Pharmacy [1958] 66 p. illus. 28 cm. First ed. published in 1942 under title: Pictorial life history of the apothecary chemist. [QD22.S3U6] 58-4727
1. Scheele, Karl Wilhelm, 1742-1786. 2. Pharamcy — Hist. I. Title.

Scheer, George F.

BLIVEN, Bruce, 1916- 381'.45'0705730924 B
Book traveller / Bruce Bliven, Jr. New York : Dodd, Mead, 1975, c1973. 62 p. ; 21 cm. "The material in this book originally appeared in the New Yorker." [Z473.S35B5 1975] 74-97 ISBN 0-396-06951-7 : 4.95
1. Scheer, George F. 2. Booksellers and bookselling—Southern States. I. Title. BIP

Scheffer, Victor B.

SCHEFFER, Victor B. 599'.0092'4 B
Adventures of a zoologist / by Victor B. Scheffer. New York : Scribner, c1980. p. cm. Includes index. [QL31.S28A34] 79-27463 ISBN 0-684-16439-6 : 10.95
1. Scheffer, Victor B. 2. Zoologists—Washington (State)—Biography. I. Title. BIP

Scheffler, Johann, 1624-1677.

GODECKER, Mary Hilda, Sister, 1890- 831'.5
Angelus Silesius' personality through his Ecclesiologia. New York, AMS Press [1970, c1938] 92 p. 23 cm. (Catholic University of America. Studies in German, v. 10) Originally presented as the author's thesis, Catholic University of America, 1938. Bibliography: p. 89-92. [PT1791.S2Z84 1970] 76-140023 ISBN 0-404-50230-X
1. Scheffler, Johann, 1624-1677. 2. Scheffler, Johann, 1624-1677. Ecclesiologia. I. Title. II. Series.

Schembechler, Bo.

SCHEMBECHLER, Bo. 796.33'2'0924 B
Man in motion, by Joe Falls. Ann Arbor, Mich., School-Tech Press [1973] v, 252 p. illus. 24 cm. Cover title: Bo Schembechler: man in action. [GV939.S33A35] 73-85215 6.95
1. Schembechler, Bo. 2. Football coaching. I. Falls, Joe. II. Title.

Schenk von Stauffenberg, Klaus Philipp, Graf, 1907-1944.

GRABER, Gerry. 943.086'092'4 B
Stauffenberg. [New York, Ballantine Books, 1973] 158 p. illus. 21 cm. (Ballantine's illustrated history of the violent century. War leader book no. 21) [DD256.3.G66] 74-155461 ISBN 0-345-23501-0 1.50 (pbk.)
1. Schenk von Stauffenberg, Klaus Philipp, Graf, 1907-1944. 2. Anti-Nazi movement—Pictorial works.

KRAMARZ, Joachim, 1931- 364.13'1 B
Stauffenberg, the architect of the famous July 20th conspiracy to assassinate Hitler.

Translated from the German by R. H. Barry. Introd. by H. R. Trevor-Roper. [1st American ed.] New York, Macmillan [1967] 255 p. port. 21 cm. Translation of Claus Graf Stauffenberg. Bibliography: p. 208-213. [DD256.3.K6713] 67-25269
1. Schenk von Stauffenberg, Klaus Philipp, Graf, 1907-1944. 2. Hitler, Adolf, 1889-1945—Assassination attempt, July 20, 1944. I. Title.

Schervier, Franziska,

MAYNARD, Theodore, 1890- 922.243
Through my gift: the life of Frances Schervier. New York, P. J. Kenedy [1951] 318 p. port. 21 cm. "Bibliographical note": p. 315-318. [BX4705.S51M3] 51-11216
1. Schervier, Franziska, 2. Sisters of the Poor of St. Francis. I. Title.

Scheubel, Johann, 1494-1570.

DAY, Mary Sarilda, 1890- 510'.92'4 B
Scheubel as an algebraist; being a study of algebra in the middle of the sixteenth century, together with a translation of and a commentary upon an unpublished manuscript of Scheubel's now in the library of Columbia University, by Mary S. Day. New York, Bureau of Publications, Teachers College, Columbia University, 1926. [New York, AMS Press, 1972] 168 p. facsims. 22 cm. Reprint of the 1926 ed., issued in series: Teachers College, Columbia University. Contributions to education, no. 219. Originally presented as the author's thesis, Columbia. "Photographic copies of original Scheubel manuscript, with translation and notes": p. [27]-161. Includes bibliographical references. [QA29.S3D3 1972] 78-176708 ISBN 0-404-55219-6 10.00
1. Scheubel, Johann, 1494-1570. 2. Algebra—History. I. Title. II. Series: Columbia University. Teachers College. Contributions to education, no. 219.

Scheuring, Tom.

SCHEURING, Tom. 282'.092'2 B
Two for joy : spirit-led journey of a husband and wife through Jesus to the Father / by Tom and Lyn Scheuring. New York : Paulist Press, c1976. v, 183 p. : ill. ; 21 cm. [BX2350.2.S32] 76-28274 ISBN 0-8091-1985-4 pbk. : 4.95
1. Scheuring, Tom. 2. Scheuring, Lyn. 3. Spiritual life—Catholic authors. 4. Christian communities. 5. Catholics in the United States—Biography. I. Scheuring, Lyn, joint author. II. Title.

Schiano, Anthony.

SCHIANO, Anthony. 363.2'32 B
Solo; self-portrait of an undercover cop [by] Anthony Schiano with Anthony Burton. New York, Dodd, Mead [1973] vii, 247 p. 22 cm. [HV7911.S34A3] 73-9274 ISBN 0-396-06856-1 6.95
1. Schiano, Anthony. I. Burton, Anthony. II. Title.

SCHIANO, Anthony. 363.2'32 B
Solo; self-portrait of an undercover cop [by] Anthony Schiano with Anthony Burton. [New York] Warner Paperback Library [1974, c1973] 221 p. 18 cm. [HV7911.S34A3] 1.50 (pbk.)
1. Schiano, Anthony. I. Burton, Anthony. II. Title.
L.C. card number for original ed.: 73-9274.

Schiaparelli, Elsa.

SCHIAPARELLI, Elsa. 926.46
Shocking life. [1st ed.] New York, Dutton, 1954. 254 p. illus. 22 cm. Autobiography. [TT505.S3A3] 54-10918
I. Title.

Schick, Bela, 1877-

GRONOWICZ, Antoni, 1913- 926.1
Bela Schick and the world of children. New York, Abelard-Schuman [1954] 216p. illus. 22cm. [R154.S3535G7] 53-10941
1. Schick, Bela, 1877- I. Title.

Schick, Bela, 1877- —Juvenile literature.

NOBLE, Iris 920
Physician to the children: Dr. Bela Schick. New York, Messner [c.1963] 189p. 22cm. 63-16792 3.19 lib. ed.,
1. Schick, Bela, 1877- —Juvenile literature. I. Title.

Schield, Vern L.

SCHIELD, Vern L. 338.4'7'6292250924 B
Buffalo grass and bare feet : the story of an Iowa industrialist and his program of helping developing nations help themselves without becoming enslaved by our technology / Vern L. Schield. Corte Madera, Calif. : Omega Books, c1977. 65 p. : ill. ; 22 cm. [TS140.S34A35] 76-24107 ISBN 0-89353-024-7 pbk. : 3.50
1. Schield, Vern L. 2. Manufacturers—Iowa—Biography. 3. Tractors. 4. Underdeveloped areas—Technology. 5. Lime industry—Iowa. I. Title.

Schiemann, Theodor, 1847-1921.

MEYER, Klaus. v. 12
Theodor Schiemann als politischer Publizist. Frankfurt am Main, Rutten & Loening, 1956. 320p. port. 24cm. (Nord- und osteuropaische Geschichtsstudien, Bd. 1) 'Theodor Schiemann-Schriftenverzeichnis:' p. 271-299. 'Literaturnachweis': p. 300-313. A57
1. Schiemann, Theodor, 1847-1921. I. Title. II. Series.

Schiff, Dorothy.

POTTER, Jeffrey. 070.5'092'4 B
Men, money & magic : the story of Dorothy Schiff / by Jeffrey Potter. New York : Coward, McCann & Geoghegan, c1976. 352 p. : ill. ; 24 cm. Includes index. [PN4874.S33P6] 74-30608 ISBN 0-698-10666-0 : 10.95
1. Schiff, Dorothy. 2. Journalists—United States—Biography. I. Title. **BIP**

Schiff, Jacob Henry,

SCHIFF, Jacob Henry, 1847-1920. 332'.092'4 B
Jacob H. Schiff: his life and letters. [Edited] by Cyrus Adler. Freeport, N.Y., Books for Libraries Press [1972] 2 v. facsims. ports. 22 cm. "First published 1928." [CT275.S3442A2 1972] 72-1474 ISBN 0-8369-6818-2
I. Adler, Cyrus, 1863-1940, ed.

SCHIFF, Jacob Henry, 1847-1920. 332.6'0924 B
Jacob H. Schiff; his life and letters, by Cyrus Adler. Garden City, N.Y., Doubleday, Doran, 1928. Grosse Pointe, Mich., Scholarly Press, 1968. 2 v. illus. 23 cm. Bibliographical footnotes. [CT275.S3442A2 1968] 79-2273
I. Adler, Cyrus, 1863-1940, ed.

Schiffman, Steve.

SCHIFFMAN, Steve. 248'.246
Once a thief ... / Steve Schiffman. Old Tappan, N.J. : F. H. Revell Co., c1978. 63 p. ; 18 cm. (New life ventures) [BV4935.S35A34] 77-18711 ISBN 0-8007-9007-3 pbk. : 0.95
1. Schiffman, Steve. 2. Converts—United States—Biography. I. Title. **BIP**

Schildkraut, Rudolf.

SCHILDKRAUT, Joseph, 1896- 927.92
My father and I [by] Joseph Schildkraut, as told to Leo Lania [pseud.] New York, Viking Press, 1959. 246 p. illus. 22 cm. [PN2658.S33S3] 59-6738
1. Schildkraut, Rudolf. I. Herrmann, Lazar, 1896- II. Title.

Schiller, Johann Christoph Friedrich von, 1759-1805.

CARLYLE, Thomas, 1795-1881. 831'.6 B
The life of Friedrich Schiller; comprehending an examination of his works. New York, Scribner. St. Clair Shores, Mich., Scholarly Press, 1972. p. (The works of Thomas Carlyle, v. 25) Reprint of the 1901 ed. [PR4420.F72 vol. 25] [PT2482] 72-10638
1. Schiller, Johann Christoph Friedrich von, 1759-1805. I. Title.

CARLYLE, Thomas, 1795-1881. 824'.8 S
The life of Friedrich Schiller, comprehending an examination of his works. New York, AMS Press [1974] xiv, 357 p. illus. 23 cm. (The works of Thomas Carlyle, v. 25) (Series: Carlyle, Thomas, 1795-1881. Works. 1974. vol. 25.) Reprint of the 1899 ed. published by Chapman and Hall, London. [PR4420.F74 vol. 25] [PT2482] 831'.6 B 74-3193 ISBN 0-404-01435-6 17.50
1. Schiller, Johann Christoph Friedrich von, 1759-1805. I. Series.

DEWHURST, Kenneth. 610'.92'4
Friedrich Schiller, medicine, psychology and literature : with the first English edition of his complete medical and psychological writings / by Kenneth Dewhurst & Nigel Reeves. Berkeley : University of California Press, 1978. xii, 413 p., [5] leaves of plates : ill. ; 22 cm. Includes indexes. Bibliography: p. 373-393. [R512.S265D48] 76-14308 ISBN 0-520-03250-0 : 25.00
1. Schiller, Johann Christoph Friedrich von, 1759-1805. 2. Schiller, Johann Christoph Friedrich von, 1759-1805—Knowledge—Medicine. 3. Schiller, Johann Christoph Friedrich von, 1759-1805—Knowledge—Psychology. 4. Physicians—Germany—Biography. 5. Medicine—History—18th century. 6. Psychology—History—18th century. I. Reeves, Nigel, joint author. II. Schiller, Johann Cristoph Friedrich von, 1759-1805. Selections. III. Title. **BIP**

GARLAND, Henry Burnand. 832.63
Schiller. New York, McBride [1950] viii, 280 p. ports, map. facsims. 23 cm. Bibliography: p. 272-273. [PT2482.G3 1950] 928.3 50-8004
1. Schiller, Johann Christoph Friedrich von, 1759-1805. I. Title.

GARLAND, Henry Burnand. 831'.6 B
Schiller / by H. B. Garland. Westport, Conn. : Greenwood Press, 1976. viii, 280 p. [7] leaves of plates : ill. ; 23 cm. Reprint of the 1949 ed. published by Harrap, London. Includes index. Bibliography: p. 272-273. [PT2482.G3 1976] 76-39809 ISBN 0-8371-9084-3 lib. bdg. : 17.50
1. Schiller, Johann Christoph Friedrich von, 1759-1805. 2. Authors, German—18th century—Biography.

HEISELER, Bernt von, 1907- 928.3
Schiller. Translated and annotated by John Bednall. Philadelphia, Dufour Editions, 1963. 210 p. illus., ports. 23 cm. "Descriptive list of the principal plays": p. 198-203. "Select bibliography": p. 193. [PT2482.H383 1963] 63-20549
1. Schiller, Johann Christoph Friedrich von, 1759-1805.

SCHILLER w the ideal of freedom; a study of Schiller's philosophical works, with chapters on Kant. Harrogate, The Duchy Press, 1959. 121p. 23cm. v. 12
1. Schiller, Johann Christoph Friedrich von, 1759-1805. I. Miller, Ronald Duncan, 1915-

THOMAS, Calvin, 1854-1919. 831'.6 B
The life and works of Friedrich Schiller. New York, AMS Press [1970] xvi, 481 p. 23 cm. Reprint of the 1901 ed. "A survey of Schiller literature": p. 465-473. Includes bibliographical references. [PT2482.T4 1970] 73-119662 ISBN 0-404-063691-
1. Schiller, Johann Christoph Friedrich von, 1759-1805. I. Title. **BIP**

Schiller, Johann Christoph Friedrich von, 1759-1805—Knowledge—Medicine.

DEWHURST, Kenneth. 610'.92'4
Friedrich Schiller, medicine, psychology and literature : with the first English edition of his complete medical and psychological writings / by Kenneth Dewhurst & Nigel Reeves. Berkeley : University of California Press, 1978. xii, 413 p., [5] leaves of plates : ill. ; 22 cm. Includes indexes. Bibliography: p. 373-393. [R512.S265D48] 76-14308 ISBN 0-520-03250-0 : 25.00
1. Schiller, Johann Christoph Friedrich von, 1759-1805. 2. Schiller, Johann Christoph Friedrich von, 1759-1805—Knowledge—Medicine. 3. Schiller, Johann Christoph Friedrich von, 1759-1805—Knowledge—Psychology. 4. Physicians—Germany—Biography. 5. Medicine—History—18th century. 6. Psychology—History—18th century. I. Reeves, Nigel, joint author. II. Schiller, Johann Cristoph Friedrich von, 1759-1805. Selections. III. Title. **BIP**

Schillinger, Frances.

SCHILLINGER, Frances. 785'.092'4 B
Joseph Schillinger : memoir / by Frances Schillinger. New York : Da Capo Press, 1976, c1949. viii, 224 p., [4] leaves of plates : ill. ; 24 cm. (Da Capo Press music reprint series) Reprint of the ed. published by Greenberg, New York. [ML410.S258S3 1976] 76-7575 ISBN 0-306-70780-2 : 17.50
I. Schillinger, Joseph, 1895-1943. **BIP**

Schillinger, Joseph, 1895-1943.

SCHILLINGER, Frances. 785'.092'4 B
Joseph Schillinger; a memoir by his wife. Plainview, N.Y., Books for Libraries Press [1974, c1949] p. cm. (Biography index reprint series) [ML410.S258S3 1974] 74-633 ISBN 0-8369-4600-6 13.00
1. Schillinger, Joseph, 1895-1943.

SCHILLINGER, Frances. 785'.092'4 B
Joseph Schillinger : memoir / by Frances Schillinger. New York : Da Capo Press, 1976, c1949. viii, 224 p., [4] leaves of plates : ill. ; 24 cm. (Da Capo Press music reprint series) Reprint of the ed. published by Greenberg, New York. [ML410.S258S3 1976] 76-7575 ISBN 0-306-70780-2 : 17.50
I. Schillinger, Joseph, 1895-1943. **BIP**

Schimpf family.

SHIMP, Charles James, 1898- 929'.2'0973
Biographical sketches of the Schimpf family. 1st ed. [Speingfield? Ill.,] 1965. 194 p. 29 cm. Bibliography: p. 133-135. [CS71.S333] 65-69573
1. Schimpf family. I. Title.

Schindler, R. M., 1887-1953.

GEBHARD, David. 720'.924
Schindler. Pref. by Henry-Russell Hitchcock. New York, Viking Press [1972, c1971] 216 p. illus., plans. 22 cm. (A Studio book) Bibliography: p. 205-211. [NA737.S5G37 1972] 71-172899 ISBN 0-670-62063-7 7.95
1. Schindler, R. M., 1887-1953.

Schizophrenia.

*PLANTE, Elizabeth. 616.8982 B
Rene; the biography of a schizophrenic. Introduction by Abram Hoffer. [1st. ed.] New York, Vantage Press [1974] 37 p. 22 cm. [RC514] ISBN 0-533-01071-3 4.50
1. Schizophrenia. I. Title.

Schlegel, Friedrich von, 1772-1829.

FORSTMANN, Jack. 230'.092'4
A romantic triangle : Schleiermacher and early German romanticism / by Jack Forstman. Missoula, Mont. : Published by

Scholars Press for the American Academy of Religion, c1977. xiv, 122 p. ; 24 cm. (AAR studies i2 religion ; no. 13) Includes bibliographical references. [BX4827.S3F68] 76-55709 ISBN 0-89130-124-0 : 4.50
1. Schleiermacher, Friedrich Ernst Daniel, 1768-1834. 2. Schlegel, Friedrich von, 1772-1829. 3. Hardenberg, Friedrich, Freiherr von, 1772-1801. 4. Romanticism—Germany. I. Title. II. Series: American Academy of Religion. AAR studies in religion ; no. 13. **BIP**

Schleiermacher, Friedrich Ernst Daniel, 1768-1834.

FORSTMANN, Jack. 230'.092'4
A romantic triangle : Schleiermacher and early German romanticism / by Jack Forstman. Missoula, Mont. : Published by Scholars Press for the American Academy of Religion, c1977. xiv, 122 p. ; 24 cm. (AAR studies i2 religion ; no. 13) Includes bibliographical references. [BX4827.S3F68] 76-55709 ISBN 0-89130-124-0 : 4.50
1. Schleiermacher, Friedrich Ernst Daniel, 1768-1834. 2. Schlegel, Friedrich von, 1772-1829. 3. Hardenberg, Friedrich, Freiherr von, 1772-1801. 4. Romanticism—Germany. I. Title. II. Series: American Academy of Religion. AAR studies in religion ; no. 13. **BIP**

REDEKER, Martin, 1900- 193 B
Schleiermacher: life and thought. Translated by John Wallhausser. Philadelphia, Fortress Press [1973] 221 p. 20 cm. Translation of Friedrich Schleiermacher; Leben und Werk. Bibliography: p. 214-218. [BX4827.S3R413] 72-91526 ISBN 0-8006-0149-1 4.50
1. Schleiermacher, Friedrich Ernst Daniel, 1768-1834. I. Title.

STRAUSS, David Friedrich, 1808-1874. 232.9'01
The Christ of faith and the Jesus of history : a critique of Schleiermacher's Life and Jesus / by David Friedrich Strauss ; translated, edited, and with an introduction by Leander E. Keck. Philadelphia : Fortress Press, c1977. cxii, 169 p. ; 19 cm. (Lives of Jesus series) Translation of Der Christus des Glaubens und der Jesus der Geschichte. Bibliography: p. cvii-cxii. [BT301.S363S813] 75-37152 ISBN 0-8006-1273-6 pbk. : 9.95
1. Schleiermacher, Friedrich Ernst Daniel, 1768-1834. Das Leben Jesu. 2. Jesus Christ—Biography. I. Title.

SYKES, Stephen. 230'.0924 B
Friedrich Schleiermacher. Richmond, John Knox Press [1971] viii, 51, [1] p. 19 cm. (Makers of contemporary theology) Bibliography: p. [52] [BX4827.S3S85 1971] 75-158145 ISBN 0-8042-0556-6
1. Schleiermacher, Friedrich Ernst Daniel, 1768-1834. **BIP**

Schlemmer, Oskar, 1888-1943.

SCHLEMMER, Oskar, 1888-1943. 700'.92'4 B
The letters and diaries of Oskar Schlemmer. Selected and edited by Tut Schlemmer. Translated from the German by Krishna Winston. [1st ed.] Middletown, Conn., Wesleyan University Press [1972] xiii, 425 p. illus. 24 cm. Translation of his Briefe und Tagebucher. [ND588.S2818A3413] 77-184362 ISBN 0-8195-4047-1 19.95
1. Schlemmer, Oskar, 1888-1943. 2. Painters—Germany—Correspondence, reminiscences, etc. **BIP**

Schlesinger, Arthur Meier,

SCHLESINGER, Arthur Meier, 1888- 928
In retrospect: the history of a historian. New York, Harcourt [c.1963] viii, 212p. 21cm. 63-15318 4.50
I. Title.

SCHLESINGER, Arthur Meier, 1888- 928
In retrospect: the history of a historian. [1st ed.] New York, Harcourt, Brace & World [1963] viii, 212 p. 21 cm. [E175.5.S37A3] 63-15318
I. Title.

Schlesinger, Marian Cannon—Biography.

SCHLESINGER, Marian Cannon. 813'.5'4 B
Snatched from oblivion : a Cambridge memoir / Marian Cannon Schlesinger. 1st ed. Boston : Little, Brown, c1979. 243 p. : ill. ; 22 cm. [PS2789.S53Z474] 78-31944 ISBN 0-316-77348-4 : 8.95
1. Schlesinger, Marian Cannon—Biography. 2. Authors, American—20th century—Biography. I. Title. **BIP**

Schley, Winfield Scott, 1839-1911.

WEST, Richard Sedgewick, 1902- 359'.00922 B
Admirals of American empire; the combined story of George Dewey, Alfred Thayer Mahan, Winfield Scott Schley, and William Thomas Sampson, by Richard S. West, Jr. Westport, Conn., Greenwood Press [1971, c1948] 354 p. illus. 23 cm. Includes bibliographical references. [E182.W45 1971] 73-156216 ISBN 0-8371-6167-3
1. Dewey, George, 1837-1917. 2. Mahan, Alfred Thayer, 1840-1914. 3. Schley, Winfield Scott, 1839-1911. 4. Sampson, William Thomas, 1840-1902. 5. U.S.—History, Naval—To 1900. I. Title. **BIP**

Schliemann, Heinrich, 1822-1890.

BRACKEN, Arnold C. 930'.1'0924 B
The dream of Troy / Arnold C. Brackman. New York : Van Nostrand Reinhold Co., [1979] p. cm. Original ed. published in 1974 by Mason & Lipscomb, New York. Includes index. Bibliography: p. [DF212.S4B67 1979] 78-26810 ISBN 0-442-26098-9 pbk. : 6.95
1. Schliemann, Heinrich, 1822-1890. 2. Archaeologists Greece, Modern—Biography. 3. Archaeologists—Germany—Biography. I. Title.

BRAYMER, Marjorie 925.71
The walls of Windy Troy; a biography of Heinrich Schliemann. New York, Harcourt [1966, c.1960] 189p. illus. 20cm. (Voyager bk. AVB20) [DF212.S4B68] 60-6207 .60 pap.,
1. Schliemann, Heinrich, 1822-1890. I. Title. **BIP**

DEUEL, Leo. 930'.1'0924 B
The memoirs of Heinrich Schliemann : drawn from his autobiographical writings, letters, and excavation reports / edited, introduced, annotated, and, in part, translated from the German by Leo Deuel. 1st ed. New York : Harper & Row, c1976. p. cm. Includes index. Bibliography: p. [DF212.S4D48 1976] 74 15820 ISBN 0-06-011106-2 : 15.00
1. Schliemann, Heinrich, 1822-1890. I. Schliemann, Heinrich, 1822-1890. II. Title.

ELKIN, Sam. 913.03'1'0924 B
Search for a lost city; the quest of Heinrich Schliemann. New York, Putnam [1967] 96 p. illus., map. 21 cm. In order to fulfill a childhood dream, Heinrich Schliemann defied popular theories of his day, contradicted respected historians, gave up his successful business, and personally conducted a search for the ancient city of Troy. [DF212.S4E4] 92 AC 68
1. Schliemann, Heinrich, 1822-1890. I. Title.

PAYNE, Pierre Stephen Robert, 1911- 925.71
The gold of Troy; the story of Heinrich Schliemann and the buried cities of ancient Greece. New York, Funk & Wagnalls [1959] 273 p. illus. 22 cm. [DF212.S4P3] 58-11361
1. Schliemann, Heinrich, 1822-1890. I. Title.

POOLE. LVNN 913.0310922
One passion. two loves: the story of Heinrich and Sophia Schliemann. discoverers of Trov. by Lvnn and Gray Poole. New York. Crowell [1966] xv 299p. illus., facsims., map, plans, ports. 22cm. [DF212S4P6] 66-25434 6.95
1. Schliemann, Heinrich, 1822-1890. 2. Schliemann. Sophie (Kastromenos) I. Poole, Gray, joint author. II. Title.

Schliemann, Heinrich, 1822-1890—Juvenile literature.

HONOUR, Alan 925.71
The unlikely hero; Heinrich Schliemann's quest for Troy. Illustrated by Grisha Dotzenko. New York, Whittlesey House, McGraw-Hill [c.1960] 175p. lbibl.: p.172-173) illus. 21cm. 59-15880 3.00
1. Schliemann, Heinrich, 1822-1890—Juvenile literature. I. Title.

Schlosser, George, 1875-1936.

SCHERER, Frances Schlosser, 1912- 266'.7'60922 B
George and Mary Schlosser : ambassadors for Christ in China / by Frances Schlosser Scherer. Winona Lake, Ind. : Light and Life Press, c1976. xiv, 189 p. : ill. ; 21 cm. [BX8419.S35S34] 76-371953 3.95
1. Schlosser, George, 1875-1936. 2. Schlosser, Mary, 1885-1955. 3. Missionaries—United States—Biography. 4. Missionaries—China—Biography. I. Title: Ambassadors for Christ in China. **BIP**

Schmedding, Joseph, 1887-

SCHMEDDING, Joseph, 1887- 917.89 B
Cowboy and Indian trader. Introd. by Jack Schaefer. Albuquerque, University of New Mexico Press [1974, c1951] xi, 364 p. illus. 21 cm. (A Zia book) Reprint of the ed. published by Caxton Printers, Caldwell, Idaho; with new introd. [F595.S33 1974] 73-92994 ISBN 0-8263-0319-6 3.95 (pbk.)
1. Schmedding, Joseph, 1887- 2. Cowboys—The West. 3. The West—History—1848-1950. I. Title.

Schmeling, E. Marianne.

SCHMELING, Marianne. 940.54'82'43
Flee the wolf : the story of a family's miraculous journey to freedom / by Marianne Schmeling. Norfolk, Va. : Donning, c1978. 290 p., [2] leaves of plates : maps ; 22 cm. (The Unilaw Library series) [D811.5.S32] 78-24154 ISBN 0-915442-67-1 pbk. : 5.95
1. Schmeling, E. Marianne. 2. World War, 1939-1945—Personal narratives, German. 3. Children—Germany—Biography. I. Title.
Available in hardcover for 9.95

Schmelzenbach, Elmer, 1910-

SCHMELZENBACH, Elmer, 1910- 266'.99 B
Sons of Africa : stories from the life of Elmer Schmelzenbach / as told to Leslie Parrott. Kansas City, Mo : Beacon Hill Press of Kansas City, c1979. 217 p. : ill. ; 21 cm. [BV3625.S92S357] 79-122616 ISBN 0-8341-0601-9 : 9.95
1. Schmelzenbach, Elmer, 1910- 2. Missionaries—Swaziland—Biography. 3. Missionaries—United States—Biography. I. Parrott, Leslie, 1922- II. Title.

Schmid, Charles Howard.

GILMORE, John. 364.15'23' B
The Tucson murders; an account of multiple teen-age murder and the story of the accused Charles Howard Schmid, Jr. [Los Angeles? 1967] iii, 402 l. port. 30 cm. Cover title. [HV6534.T8G5] 67-4432
1. Schmid, Charles Howard. I. Title.

Schmidt, Karl Patterson, 1890-1957.

WRIGHT, Arthur Gilbert, 1909- 92
In the steps of the great American herpetologist, Karl Patterson Schmidt, by A. Gilbert Wright. Illus. by Matthew Kalmenoff. New York, M. Evans; distributed in association with Lippincott, Philadelphia [1967] 127 p. illus. 22 cm. ([In the steps of the great American naturalists]) Bibliography: p. 124-127. A biography of the American naturalist whose major interest was the study of reptiles and amphibians. Includes an appendix of nature projects for young naturalists interested in herpetology. [QL31.S33W7] AC 67
1. Schmidt, Karl Patterson, 1890-1957. I. Kalmenoff, Matthew, illus. II. Title. **BIP**

Schmidt, Karl Patterson, 1890-1957—Juvenile literature.

WRIGHT, Arthur Gilbert, 1909- 92
In the steps of the great American herpetologis, Karl Patterson Schmidt, by A. Gilbert Wright. Illus. by Matthew Kalmenoff. New York, M.Evans; dist. Lippincott, Philadelphia [1967] 127p. illus. 22cm. ([In the steps of the great American naturalists]) Bibl. [QL31.S33W7] 67-18531 3.95
1. Schmidt, Karl Patterson, 1890-1957—Juvenile literature. I. Title.

Schmidt, Mike, 1949- —Juvenile literature.

WRIGHT, Jim. 796.357'092'4 B
Mike Schmidt, baseball's young lion / by Jim Wright. New York : Putnam, c1979. 192 p. : ill. ; 21 cm. (Putnam sport shelf) Includes index. A biography of the Philadelphia Phillies player who, after being the worst hitter in the major leagues, becames home-run champion three years in a row. [GV865.S36W74 1979] 92 78-12671 ISBN 0-399-61132-0 lib.bdg. : 5.96
1. Schmidt, Mike, 1949- —Juvenile literature. 2. Philadelphia. Baseball club (National League)—Juvenile literature. 3. Baseball players—United States—Biography—Juvenile literature. I. Title.

Schmidtke, Ernst, 1908-

LINNETT, Arthur. 267'.15'0924 B
Radiant rebel : the story of Ernst Schmidtke / by Arthur Linnett. London : Salvationist, 1976. 97 p. ; 19 cm. [BX9743.S3L56] 77-366233 ISBN 0-85412-292-3
1. Schmidtke, Ernst, 1908- 2. Salvationists—Germany—Biography. 3. Missionaries—China—Biography. 4. Missionaries—Germany—Biography. I. Title.

Schmied, Francois Louis, 1873—

RITCHIE, Ward, 1905- 686.2'092'4 B
Francois-Louis Schmied, artist, engraver, printer : some memories and a bibliography / by Ward Ritchie. Tucson : Graduate Library School, University of Arizona, c1976. vi, 41 p. : ill. ; 22 cm. (Bibliographic papers ; no. 1) Bibliography: p. [29]-41. [Z232.S253R58] 76-374430
1. Schmied, Francois Louis, 1873- 2. Printers—France—Biography. 3. Illustrators—France—Biography. 4. Engravers—France—Biography. I. Title.

Schmitt, Gladys, 1909-1972—Biography—Addresses, essays, lectures.

I could be mute : 813'.5'2 B
the life and work of Gladys Schmitt / edited by Anita Brostoff. 1st ed. Pittsburgh : Carnegie-Mellon University Press, 1978. 176 p. : ill. ; 23 cm. (Carnegie series in English) ISSN 0069-0678) "Consider the giraffe [by] Gladys Schmitt": p. 167-176. Includes bibliographical references. [PS3537.C5253Z7] 78-59831 ISBN 0-915604-21-3 : 10.95
1. Schmitt, Gladys, 1909-1972—Biography—Addresses, essays, lectures. 2. Schmitt, Gladys, 1909-1972—Friends and associates—Addresses, essays, lectures. 3. American novelists—20th century—Biography. I. Brostoff, Anita. II. Schmitt, Gladys, 1909-1972. Consider the giraffe. 1978. III. Title. IV. Series.

Schmitz, John G., 1930-

SCHMITZ, John G., 1930- 328.73'092'4 B
Stranger in the arena / by John G. Schmitz. Santa Ana, Calif. : Rayline Print. Co., [1974] x, 322 p., [8] leaves of plates : ill. ; 22 cm. Includes index. [E840.8.S35A37] 74-195083
1. Schmitz, John G., 1930- 2. United States—Politics and government—1963-

1969. 3. United States—Politics and government—1969-1974. I. Title.

Schmitz, Ettore, 1861-1928.

FURBANK, Philip Nicholas 853.8
Italo Svevo; the man and the writer [by] P. N. Furbank. Berkeley, Univ. of Calif. Pr. [c.1966] xi, 232p. illus., ports. 23cm. Bibl. [PQ4841.C482Z65 1966a] 66-29426 6.00 bds.,
1. Schmit2, Ettore, 1861-1928. I. Title.

Schmucker, Samuel Simon, 1799-1873.

WENTZ, Abdel Ross, 1883- 284'.13
Pioneer in Christian unity: Samuel Simon Schmucker. Philadelphia, Fortress Press [1967] xi, 372 p. port. 24 cm. Bibliographical footnotes. "Published writings of Samuel Simon Schmucker, 1799-1873": p. 355-364. [BX8080.S3W4] 67-10596
1. Schmucker, Samuel Simon, 1799-1873. I. Title.

Schnabel, Artur, 1882-1951.

SAERCHINGER, Cesar, 1889- 786.1'092'4 B
Artur Schnabel, a biography. With a tribute by Clifford Curzon. Westport, Conn., Greenwood Press [1973, c1957] xxi, 354 p. illus. 21 cm. Reprint of the ed. published by Dodd, Mead, New York. Discography: p. 333-343. [ML417.S36S3 1973] 73-7101 ISBN 0-8371-6910-0 15.00
1. Schnabel, Artur, 1882-1951.

Schneider, Hans J., 1935-

SCHNEIDER, Hans J., 1935- 629.13'092'4 B
Flying to be free / by Hans J. Schneider ; illustrated by Roy S. Wathne. Ashland, Or. : World Wide Pub. Co., c1978. 256 p. ; 21 cm. [TL540.S34A33] 77-26614 ISBN 0-930294-13-0 pbk. : 7.95
1. Schneider, Hans J., 1935- 2. Converts. 3. Air pilots—Biography. I. Title. **BIP**

Schneider, Wilma.

SCHNEIDER, Wilma. 365'.66'0924 B
Woman on the gun wall / Wilma Schneider and Robert Hollis. Millbrae, Calif. : Les Femmes Pub., 1978. p. cm. [HV9475.C3S765] 77-90025 0-89087-931-1 pbk. : 4.95
1. Schneider, Wilma. 2. California. State Prison, San Quentin. 3. Prisons—California—Officials and employees—Biography. I. Hollis, Robert, 1943- joint author. II. Title.

Schnitzer, Eduard, known as Emin Pasha, 1840-1892.

BUEL, James William, 1849-1920. 916'.03
Heroes of the Dark Continent; a complete history of all the great explorations and discoveries in Africa, from the earliest ages to the present time. Freeport, N.Y., Books for Libraries Press, 1971 [c1889] 576 p. illus., maps (1 fold.), ports. 27 cm. (The Black heritage library collection) [DT3.B75] 73-138333 ISBN 0-8369-8725-X
1. Stanley, Henry Morton, Sir, 1841-1904. 2. Schnitzer, Eduard, known as Emin Pasha, 1840-1892. 3. Livingstone, David, 1813-1873. 4. Africa—Discovery and exploration. 5. Explorers. I. Title. II. Series.

LYLE-SMYTHE, Alan, 1914- 916.7'04 B
South from Khartoum; the story of Emin Pasha [by] Alan Caillou. Drawings by Ian Smythe. New York, Hawthorn Books [1974] 265 p. illus. 22 cm. Bibliography: p. 257. [DT363.L92 1974] 73-366 8.95
1. Schnitzer, Eduard, 1840-1892. I. Title.

Schnitzler, Arthur,

SCHNITZLER, Arthur, 1862-1931. 832'.9'12
The correspondence of Arthur Schnitzler and Raoul Auernheimer with Raoul Auernheimer's Aphorisms. Edited with introd. and notes by Donald G. Daviau and Jorun B. Johns. Chapel Hill, University of North Carolina Press, 1972. xi, 158 p. 23 cm. (University of North Carolina studies in the Germanic languages and literatures, no. 73) [PT2638.N5Z543 1972] 73-150319
I. Auernheimer, Raoul, 1876-1948. II. Daviau, Donald G., ed. III. Johns, Jorun B., ed. IV. Title. V. Series: North Carolina. University. Studies in the Germanic languages and literature, no. 73.

SCHNITZLER, Arthur, 1862-1931. 832'.9'12 B
My youth in Vienna. Foreword by Frederic Morton. Translated by Catherine Hutter. [1st ed.] New York, Holt, Rinehart and Winston [1970] xiv, 304 p. illus., ports. 24 cm. Translation of Jugend in Wien. Includes bibliographical references. [PT2638.N5Z8113] 70-117273 ISBN 0-03-083148-2 8.95
I. Title.

Schockemohle, Alwin, 1937—

KAISER, Ulrich, 1934- 636.1'0092'4 B
Alwin Schockemohle / by Ulrich Kaiser. 1st U.S. ed. Woodbury, N.Y. : Barron's, 1977. p. cm. Translation of Laute Gedanken des Alwin Schockemohle. [SF284.G4K3413] 77-81578 ISBN 0-8120-5186-6 : 9.95
1. Schockemohle, Alwin, 1937- 2. Horse breeding—Germany, West. 3. Horse breeders—Germany, West—Biography. **BIP**

Schoenberg, Arnold, 1874-1951.

ARMITAGE, Merle, 1893-1975, ed. 780'.92'4 B
Schoenberg : articles / by Arnold Schoenberg ... [et al.] ; foreword by Leopold Stokowski ; affirmations by Arnold Schoenberg ; a bibliography of Schoenberg works ; port. by Edward Weston and George Gershwin ; a self port. by Arnold Schoenberg ; candid camera photo. by Otto Rothschild and two ink drawings by Carlos Dyer. Westport, Conn. : Greenwood Press, 1977. p. cm. Reprint of the 1937 ed. published by Schirmer, New York. [ML410.S283A73 1977] 79-106709 ISBN 0-8371-3439-0 lib.bdg. : 14.75
1. Schonberg, Arnold, 1874-1951. I. Title.

MACDONALD, Malcolm, 1948- 780'.92'4 B
Schoenberg / [by] Malcolm MacDonald. London : Dent, 1976. xiv, 289 p., [8] p. of plates : ill., facsim., music, ports. ; 20 cm. (The Master musicians series) "Catalogue of works [of A. Schonberg]": p. 258-266. Includes index. Bibliography: p. 276-281. [ML410.S283M15] 77-359244 ISBN 0-460-03143-0 : £4.25. ISBN 0-460-02183-4 pbk.
1. Schonberg, Arnold, 1874-1951. 2. Composers—Biography. I. Title. II. Series.

NEWLIN, Dika, 1923- 780'.92'4 B
Schoenberg remembered : diaries and recollections, 1938-76 / Dika Newlin. New York : Pendragon Press, c1980. p. cm. [ML410.S283N5] 79-19128 18.95
1. Schoenberg, Arnold, 1874-1951. 2. Newlin, Dika, 1923- 3. Composers—United States—Biography. I. Title.

REICH, Willi, 1898- 780'.924 B
Schoenberg: a critical biography. Translated by Leo Black. New York, Pracger [1971] xi, 268 p. illus., facsims., ports. 23 cm. Translation of Arnold Schonberg, oder Der konservative Revolutionar. Bibliography: p. 253-255. [ML410.S283R43 1971b] 73-134527 12.50
1. Schonberg, Arnold, 1874-1951.

ROSEN, Charles, 1927- 780'.92'4 B
Schoenberg / Charles Rosen. London : Marion Boyars ; Distributed by Calder and Boyars, 1976. [1], 124 p. : music ; 23 cm. American ed. published under title: Arnold Schoenberg. Bibliography: p. 123-124. [ML410.S283R65 1976] 77-367202 ISBN 0-7145-2566-9 : £4.25
1. Schonberg, Arnold, 1874-1951. 2. Composers—Biography.

STUCKENSCHMIDT, Hans Heinz, 1901- 780'.92'4 B
Arnold Schoenberg / by H. H. Stuckenschmidt ; translated by Edith Temple Roberts and Humphrey Searle. Westport, Conn. : Greenwood Press, 1979, c1959. 168 p., [7] leaves of plates : ill. ; 22 cm. Reprint of the 1960 ed. published by Grove Press, New York. Includes index. "Works by Arnold Schoenberg:" p. 161-163. [ML410.S283S93 1979] 78-10237 ISBN 0-313-20762-3 lib.bdg. : 15.75
1. Schonberg, Arnold, 1874-1951. 2. Composers—Austria—Biography. **BIP**

Schoenberner, Franz,

SCHOENBERNER, Franz, 1892- 920.5
You still have your head; excursions from immobility. New York, Macmillan, 1957. 247p. 22cm. Autobiographical. [PN5213.S5A34] 57-8567
1. Title.

Schoendienst, Albert Fred, 1923-

HIRSHBERG, Albert, 1909- 927.96357
The man who fought back: Red Schoendienst. New York, J. Messner [1961] 192p. illus. 61-6372 2.95
1. Schoendienst, Albert Fred, 1923- I. Title.

Schoenstein, Paul.

SCHOENSTEIN, Ralph, 1933- 070'.92'4 B
Citizen Paul : a story of father & son / Ralph Schoenstein. 1st ed. New York : Farrar Straus Giroux, 1978. 156 p., [6] leaves of plates : ill. ; 21 cm. [PN4874.S333S3 1978] 78-17986 ISBN 0-374-12385-3 : 8.95
1. Schoenstein, Paul. 2. Schoenstein, Ralph, 1933- 3. Journalists—United States—Biography. I. Title. **BIP**

Scholars, American—Direct.

CATTELL, Jaques, 1904- ed. 923.773
Directory of American scholars, a biographical directory. 2d ed. Lancaster, Pa., Science Press, 1951. 1072 p. 26 cm. [LA2311.C32 1951] 51-8846
1. Scholars, American—Direct. 2. Educators, American—Direct. 3. U. S.—Biog. I. Title.

DIRECTORY of American scholars; a biographical directory, v.1. Ed. by Jacques Cattelll Pr. 4th ed. New York, Bowker [c.]1963. 335p. 29cm. (Pub. 1963 with coop. of Amer. Council of Learned Socs.) Contents.v.1. History. 57-9125 15.00 923.773
1. Scholars, American—Direct.

DIRECTORY of American scholars: a biographical directory; v.2. Ed. by the Jacques Cattell Pr. 4th ed. New York, Pub. with the cooperation of the Amer. Council of Learned Socs. [by] Bowker [c.]1964. v. 29cm. Contents.v.2. English, speech, and drama. 57-9125 15.00 923.773
1. Scholars, American—Direct.

DIRECTORY of American scholars: a biographical directory v.3. Ed. by the Jaques Cattell Pr. 4th ed. New York, Pub. with the Amer. Council of Learned Socs. [by] Bowker [c.1964] 279p. 29cm. Contents.v.3. Foreign languages, modern and classical.--Linguistics and philology. 57-9125 15.00 923.773
1. Scholars, American—Direct. I. Bowker (R. R.) Company, firm, publishers, New York.

Scholars—Directories.

INTERNATIONAL scholars directory. John Warwick Montgomery, general editor. Strasbourg, France, International Scholarly Publishers, 1973. xix, 288 p. 28 cm. Includes bibliographical references. [CT3990.A2I57] 72-93860 ISBN 0-913440-01-9 38.50 001.2'025
1. Scholars—Directories. I. Montgomery, John Warwick, ed.

Publisher's Address: 2045 Half Day Rd. Deerfield, Ill. 60015.

Scholem, Gershom Gerhard, 1897-

BIALE, David, 1949- 296.7'1 B
Gershom Scholem : Kabbalah and counter-history / David Biale. Cambridge, Mass. : Harvard University Press, 1979. vi, 279 p. : port. ; 25 cm. Includes index. Bibliography: p. [217]-226. [BM755.S295B5] 78-23620 ISBN 0-674-36330-2 : 16.50
1. Scholem, Gershom Gerhard, 1897- 2. Scholars, Jewish—Germany—Biography. 3. Scholars, Jewish—Israel—Biography. **BIP**

Schonberg, Arnold, 1874-1951.

PAYNE, Anthony. 780'.924
Schoenberg. London, New York [etc.] Oxford U. P., 1968. 61 p. music. 23 cm. (B 68-12831) (Oxford studies of composers, 5) 21/- "List of Schoenberg's principal works:" p. 8. [ML410.S283P38] 68-113265
1. Schonberg, Arnold, 1874-1951. I. Title. II. Series. **BIP**

SCHOENBERG, Arnold, 1874-1951 927.8
Letters. Selected. ed. by Erwin Stein. Tr. from German by Eithne Wilkins, Ernst Kaiser. New York, St Martin's [1965, c.1964] 309p. music, port, 24cm. [ML410.S283A42] 65-12618 8.75
1. Musicians—Correspondence, reminiscences, etc. I. Stein, Erwin, 1885- ed. II. Title.

SCHONBERG, Arnold, 1874-1951. 927.8
Letters. Selected and edited by Erwin Stein. Translated from the original German by Eithne Wilkins and Ernst Kaiser. New York, St. Martin's Press [1965, 1964] 309 p. music, port. 24 cm. First pub. in 1958 under title Arnold Schonberg: Ausgewahite Briefe. [ML410.S283A42] 65-12618
1. Musicians—Correspondence, reminiscences, etc. I. Stein, Erwin, 1885- ed. II. Title.

Schongauer, Martin, 15th cent.

FLECHSIG, Eduard, 1864- 709'.2'4
Martin Schongauer. Strasbourg, P. H. Heitz, 1951. 410 p. 41 plates (incl. port.) 24 cm. [NE654.S5F55] A52
1. Schongauer, Martin, 15th cent. I. Title.

Schoolcraft, Henry Rowe, 1793-1864.

SCHOOLCRAFT, Henry Rowe, 1793-1864. 977'.004'97
Personal memoirs of a residence of thirty years with the Indian tribes on the American frontiers / Henry R. Schoolcraft. New York : AMS Press, 1978. xlviii, 703 p. : port. ; 23 cm. Reprint of the 1851 ed. published by Lippincott, Grambo, Philadelphia. [E77.S43 1978] 74-9021 ISBN 0-404-11899-2 : 37.50
1. Schoolcraft, Henry Rowe, 1793-1864. 2. Indians of North America. 3. Northwest, Old—Description and travel. 4. United States—History—1815-1861. I. Title. **BIP**

Schooley, Frank Budd, 1905-

SCHOOLEY, Frank Budd, 1905- 242'.4
Spiritual traveler / by Frank Budd Schooley. [Dallas? Pa.] : Schooley, 1976. 319 p. : ill. ; 24 cm. Includes index. [F159.D14S36] 76-365508
1. Schooley, Frank Budd, 1905- 2. Dallas, Pa.—History—Miscellanea. 3. Meditations. I. Title.

Schoonover, Frank Earle, 1877-1972.

SCHOONOVER, Frank Earle, 1877-1972. 760'.092'4 B
Frank Schoonover, illustrator of the North American frontier / by Cortlandt Schoonover. New York : Watson-Guptill Publications, 1976. p. cm. Includes index. [ND237.S4338S37] 76-16509 ISBN 0-8230-4655-9 : 35.00

1. Schoonover, Frank Earle, 1877-1972. 2. Indians of North American—Pictorial works. 3. The West in art. 4. Indians of North America—Canada, Northern—Pictorial works. 5. Canada, Northern, in art. I. Schoonover, Cortlandt. II. Title.

Schoor, Gene.

SCHOOR, Gene 927.96357
Casey Stengel, baseball's greatest manager, by Gene Schoor, Henry Gilfond. New York, Messner [1961, c.1958, 1961] 186p. front port. 61-3127 2.95
I. Title.

SCHOOR, Gene. 927.96357
Jackie Robinson, baseball hero. New York, Putnam [1958] 187p. 21cm. [GV865.R6S3] 58-7454
I. Robinson, John Rooseuett, 1919- II. Title.

Schopenhauer, Arthur, 1788-1860.

GARDINER, Patrick 193
Schopenhauer. Baltimore, Penguin [c.1963] 312p. 18cm. (Pelican bks., A614) 63-5710 1.65 pap.,
1. Schopenhauer, Arthur, 1788-1860. I. Title.

GARDINER, Patrick 193
Schopenhauer [Gloucester, Mass., P. Smith, 1964, c.1963] 312p. 19cm. (Pelican bk., A164 rebound) Bibl. 3.75
1. Schopenhauer, Arthur, 1788-1860. I. Title.

MCGILL, Vivian Jerauld, 193 B
1897-
Schopenhauer: pessimist and pagan, by V. J. McGill. New York, Haskell House, 1971. 312 p. illus., ports. 23 cm. Reprint of 1931 ed. Bibliography: p. 307-308. [B3147.M3 1971] 77-159487 ISBN 0-8383-1258-6
1. Schopenhauer, Arthur, 1788-1860. I. Title.

NIETZSCHE, Friedrich v. 12
Wilhelm, 1844-1900.
Schopenhauer as educator. Translated by James W. Hillesheim and Malcolm B. Simpson. Introd. by Eliseo Vivas. Chicago, Regenery [1965] xx, 115 p. 17 cm. (Gateway editions, 6092) Translation of Schopenhauer als erzicher. [B3149.E3N53] 65-16282
*1. Schopenhauer, Arthur, 1788-1860. 2. Education. I. Vivas, Eliseo, ed. II. Title.*BIP

Schorr, Daniel.

SCHORR, Daniel. 070'.92'4 [B]
Cleaning the air / Daniel Schorr. New York : Berkley Mcdallion Books, 1978, c1977 367p. : photos ; 18 cm. (A Berkley book) [PN4874.S335A33] ISBN 0-425-03903-X pbk. : 2.75
1. Schorr, Daniel. 2. Journalists — United States — Biography. I. Title.
L.C. card no. for 1977 Houghton Mifflin ed.:77-22014.

SCHORR, Daniel. 070'.92'4 B
Clearing the air / Daniel Schorr. Boston : Houghton Mifflin, 1977. xii, 333 p., [8] leaves of plates : ill. ; 24 cm. Includes bibliographical references and index. [PN4874.S335A33] 77-22014 ISBN 0-395-25721-2 : 10.95
1. Schorr, Daniel. 2. Journalists—United States—Biography. I. Title. BIP

Schoultz, Nils Gustaf von, 1807-1838.

PIPPING, Ella. 971.03'8'0924 B
Soldier of fortune; the story of a nineteenth century adventurer. Translated from the Swedish by Naomi Walford. Boston, Gambit, 1971. 192 p. illus. 22 cm. Translation of En orons legionar. Bibliography: p. 187-189. [CT1222.S3P513 1971] 70-107405 ISBN 0-87645-050-8 5.95
1. Schoultz, Nils Gustaf von, 1807-1838. I. Title. BIP

Schroder-Devrient, Wilhelmine,

PAULINE: memoirs of 782.1'0924 B
a singer (Aus den Memoiren einer Saengerin) Translated from the German. Los Angeles, Holloway House Pub. Co. [1967] 312 p. 18 cm. (Holloway House publication HH-146) "An original Holloway House edition." Pretended autobiography of Wilhelmine Schroder-Devrient. Cf. H. Hayn. Bibliotheca Germanorum erotica et curiosa. [ML420.S38A83 1967] 67-27018
I. Schroder-Devrient, Wilhelmine, 1804-1860. II. Title: Memoirs of a singer. III. Title: Aus den Memoiren einer Sangerin. English

Schrank, Robert.

SCHRANK, Robert. 301.44'42'0973
Ten thousand working days / Robert Schrank. Cambridge, Mass. : MIT Press, c1978. xiv, 243, [2] p. ; 24 cm. Bibliography: p. [245] [HD8073.S34A37] 77-14521 ISBN 0-262-19169-5 : 12.50
1. Schrank, Robert. 2. Labor and laboring classes—United States—Biography. I. Title. BIP

Schreiber, Charlotte Elizabeth Bertie Guest, Lady, 1812-1895.

SCHREIBER, 914.2'03'810924
Charlotte Elizabeth Bertie Guest, Lady, 1812-1895.
Lady Charlotte Schreiber: extracts from her journal, 1853-1891. Edited by the Earl of Bessborough. Westport, Conn., Greenwood Press [1974] xv, 212 p. illus. 22 cm. "In continuation of the diaries of Lady Charlotte Guest." Reprint of the 1952 ed. published by J. Murray, London. [DA565.S34A32 1974] 74-5926 ISBN 0-8371-7524-0
1. Schreiber, Charlotte Elizabeth Bertie Guest, Lady, 1812-1895.

Schreiner, Olive, 1855-1920—Correspondence.

CRONWRIGHT-SCHREINER, 828 B
Samuel Cron, 1863-1936.
The life of Olive Schreiner. New York, Haskell House Publishers, 1973. xlv, 414 p. illus. 23 cm. Reprint of the 1924 ed. [PR5299.S4Z6 1973] 72-2122 ISBN 0-8383-1461-9 19.95
I. Schreiner, Olive, 1855-1920. BIP

SCHREINER, Olive, 1855- 828 B
1920.
The letters of Olive Schreiner, 1876-1920 / edited by S. C. Cronwright-Schreiner. Westport, Conn : Hyperion Press, 1976. xiii, 410 p., [8] leaves of plates : ill. ; 23 cm. (Pioneers of the woman's movement) Reprint of the 1924 ed. published by T. F. Unwin, London. Includes index. [PR9369.2.S37Z53 1976] 74-33937 ISBN 0-88355-259-0 : 26.50
1. Schreiner, Olive, 1855-1920—Correspondence. I. Title. BIP

Schreyvogel, Charles, 1861-1912.

HORAN, James David, 1914- 759.13
The life and art of Charles Schreyvogel, painter-historian of the Indian-fighting army of the American West [by] James D. Horan. New York, Crown Publishers [1969] 62 p. illus., facsims., 91 plates (incl. ports.; part col.), ports. 32 x 41 cm. Includes bibliographical references. [ND237.S4345H6 1969] 70-93400 25.00
1. Schreyvogel, Charles, 1861-1912. I. Title.

Schroder, Fred.

†EASTON, Robert 909.81'092'4 B
Olney.
Guns, gold, and caravans : the life of Fred Schroder, the last frontiersman and soldier of fortune in the Far West, Far North, and Far East / by Robert Easton. Santa Barbara, Calif. : Capra Press, 1977. p. cm. Includes index. Bibliography: p. [CT275.S3455E2] 77-25022 ISBN 0-88496-122-2 : 12.95
1. Schroder, Fred. 2. Pioneers—United States—Biography. 3. Soldiers of fortune—Biography. I. Title.

Schroeder, Theodore Albert, 1864-1953—Bibliography.

MCCOY, Ralph 016.9173'03'910924
Edward, 1915-
Theodore Schroeder, a cold enthusiast; a bibliography, compiled by Ralph E. McCoy. Carbondale, Libraries, Southern Illinois University, 1973. vii, 86 p. 28 cm. (Bibliographic contributions, no. 8) [Z8796.M32] 73-180241
1. Schroeder, Theodore Albert, 1864-1953—Bibliography. I. Title. II. Series: Southern Illinois University. University Libraries. Bibliographic contributions, no. 8.

Schubert, Franz Peter, 1797-1828.

AUSTIN, George 780'.92'4 B
Lowell, 1849-1893.
The life of Franz Schubert / by George Lowell Austin. New York : AMS Press, 1980. p. cm. Reprint of the 1873 ed. published by Shepard and Gill, Boston. [ML410.S3A9 1980] 74-27330 ISBN 0-404-12856-4 : 17.50
1. Schubert, Franz Peter, 1797-1828. 2. Composers—Austria—Biography. I. Title. BIP

BARNE, Kitty, 1883- 927.8
Introducing Schubert. With drawings by J. J. Crockford. New York, Roy Publishers [1957] 68p. illus. 19cm. [ML3930.S38B3] 57-10087
1. Schubert Franz Peter. 1797-1828. 2. Music—Juvenile literature. I. Title.

BIE, Oskar, 1864-1938. 780'.924 B
Schubert, the man. Freeport, N.Y., Books for Libraries Press [1970] xvii, 215 p. illus., facsims., music, ports. 23 cm. "First published 1928." Translation of Franz Schubert, sein Leben und sein Werk. [ML410.S3B53 1970] 77-107794
1. Schubert, Franz Peter, 1797-1828 BIP

BIE, Oskar, 1864-1938. 780'.924 B
Schubert, the man [by] Oscar Bie. Westport, Conn., Greenwood Press [1971] xvii, 215 p. illus., facsims., music, ports. 23 cm. Reprint of the 1928 ed. Translation of Franz Schubert, sein Leben und sein Werk. [ML410.S3B53 1971] 76-109710 ISBN 0-8371-4201-6
1. Schubert, Franz Peter, 1797-1828.

BROWN, Maurice John Edwin 780.924
Essays on Schubert. London, Macmillan: New York, St. Martin's [c.]1966. xii, 315p. front., illus. (music) 14plates (incl. ports.) facsims. 23cm. [ML410.S3B67] 65-22791 10.00
1. Schubert, Franz Peter, 1797-1828. I. Title. BIP

BROWN, Maurice John 780'.92'4 B
Edwin.
Schubert : a critical biography / by Maurice J. E. Brown. New York : Da Capo Press, 1977, c1958. xi, 414 p., [7] leaves of plates : ill. ; 23 cm. (Da Capo Press music reprint series) Reprint of the ed. published by Macmillan, London. Includes index. 77-4160 ISBN 0-306-77409-7 : 19.50
1. Schubert, Franz Peter, 1797-1828. 2. Composers—Austria—Biography. BIP

DEUTSCH, Otto Erich, 1883- v. 12
1945, ed.
Schubert; die Dokumente seines Lebens. Kassel, New York, Barenreiter, 1964. xix, 684 p. 25 cm. (Schubert, Franz. Neue Ausgabe siimtiicher Werke. Ser. 8: Suppl., Bd. 5) Bibliography: p. 615-618. 65-85029 MN
1. Schubert, Franz Peter, 1797-1828. I. Title. II. Series. III. Series: Schubert, Franz Peter, 1797-1828. [Works] Neue Ausgabe samtlicher Werke. Ser. 8: Suppl., Bd. 5

DEUTSCH, Otto Erich, 780'.92'4 B
1883-1967.
Schubert : a documentary biography = being an English version of Franz Schubert : die Dokumente seines Lebens / by Otto Erich Deutsch ; translated by Eric Blom ; rev. and augm., with a commentary by the author. New York : Da Capo Press, 1977, c1946. xxxii, 1039 p., [19] leaves of plates : ill. ; 23 cm. (Da Capo Press music reprint series) Reprint of the ed. published by Dent, London. Includes bibliographical references and index. [ML410.S3D52 1977] 77-5499 ISBN 0-306-77420-8 lib.bdg. : 19.50
1. Schubert, Franz Peter, 1797-1828. 2. Composers—Austria—Biography.

EINSTEIN, Alfred, 1880- 927.8
Schubert; a musical portrait. New York, Oxford University Press, 1951. ix, 343 p. music. 22 cm. "Index of works, excluding songs": p. 325-330. "List of songs": p. 331-343. [ML410.S3E5] 51-578
1. Schubert, Franz Peter, 1797-1828. I. Title.

FISCHER-DIESKAU, 784'.3'00924
Dietrich, 1925-
Schubert : a biographical study of his songs / Dietrich Fischer-Dieskau ; translated and edited by Kenneth S. Whitton. London : Cassell, 1976. 331 p. ; 22 cm. Translation of Auf den Spuren der Schubert-Lieder. Includes indexes. Bibliography: p. 319-320. [ML410.S3F573 1976] 76-377917 ISBN 0-304-29002-5 : £5.95
1. Schubert, Franz Peter, 1797-1828. 2. Schubert, Franz Peter, 1797-1828. Songs. 3. Composers—Austria—Biography.

FISCHER-DIESKAU, 784'.3'00924
Dietrich, 1925-
Schubert's songs : a biographical study / by Dietrich Fischer-Dieskau ; translated from the German by Kenneth S. Whitton. 1st American ed. New York : Knopf, 1977, c1976. 233 p. ; 22 cm. 1976 ed. published under title: Schubert, a biographical study of his songs. Translation of Auf den Spuren der Schubert-Lieder. Includes indexes. Bibliography: p. 319-320. [ML410.S3F573 1977] 76-45385 ISBN 0-394-48048-1 : 12.50
1. Schubert, Franz Peter, 1797-1828. 2. Schubert, Franz Peter, 1797-1828. Songs. 3. Composers—Austria—Biography. BIP

FLOWER, Newman [Walter 927.8
Newman Flower] 1879-
Franz Schubert, the man and his cirle. New and rev. ed. London, Cassell [dist., Chester Springs, Pa., Dufour, 1964, c.1949] x, 262p. plates, ports., music. 26cm. Bibl. 49-6788 4.95
1. Schubert, Franz Peter, 1797-1828. I. Title.

GAL, Hans, 1890- 780'.92'4
Franz Schubert and the essence of melody / Hans Gal ; [translated by the author]. New York : Crescendo Pub., 1977, c1974. 205 p. : music ; 23 cm. Translation of Franz Schubert; oder, Die Melodie. Includes index. Bibliography: p. [195] [ML410.S3G23 1977] 77-153168 ISBN 0-87597-114-8 : 8.95
1. Schubert, Franz Peter, 1797-1828. 2. Composers—Austria—Biography. I. Title. BIP

HUTCHINGS, Arthur, 1906- 927.8
Schubert. [3d ed.] London, J. M. Dent; New York, Farrar, Strauss, and Cudahy [1956] vi, 233p. illus., ports., facsim., music. 19cm. (The Master musicians, new ser.) [ML410.S3H82 1956] 57-391
1. Schubert, Franz Peter, 1797-1828. I. Title. II. Series.

KOBALD, Karl, 1876- 780'.924 B
Franz Schubert and his times. Translated from the German by Beatrice Marshall. Port Washington, N.Y., Kennikat Press [1970] ix, 277 p. illus., ports. 22 cm. "First published in 1928." Translation of Franz Schubert und seine Zeit. [ML410.S3K65 1970] 70-102840 ISBN 0-8046-0756-7
1. Schubert, Franz Peter, 1797-1828. 2. Music—Vienna—History and criticism. 3. Vienna—Intellectual life. I. Marshall, Beatrice, tr. II. Title. BIP

KREISSLE von 780'.92'4 B
Hallborn, Heinrich, d.1869-
The life of Franz Schubert. Translated from the German by Arthur Duke Coleridge. With an appendix by George Grove. New York, Vienna House, 1972. 2 v. music. 20 cm. [ML410.S3K83 1972] 73-163791 ISBN 0-8443-0000-4 (v. 1)
1. Schubert, Franz Peter, 1797-1828. BIP

PEYSER, Herbert Francis, 927.8
1886-
Schubert and his work. New York, Grosset & Dunlap [1950] v. 58 p. illus., ports., facsims. 18 cm. "Complete list of recordings by the Philharmonic-Symphony

Society of New York": p. 55-58. [ML410.S3P35 1950] 50-11824
1. Schubert, Franz Peter, 1797-1828. 2. Orchestral music — Discography. I. Title.

REED, John. 780'.92'4 B
Schubert: the final years. New York, St.Martin's Press [1972] 280 p. illus. 23 cm. Includes bibliographical references. [ML410.S3R27 1972b] 72-85509 15.00
1. Schubert, Franz Peter, 1797-1828.

REED, John. 780'.92'4 B
Schubert / John Reed. London : Faber, 1978. 106 p. : ill. ; 23 cm. (The Great composers) Includes index. Bibliography: p. 96. [ML410.S3R26] 78-314683 ISBN 0-571-10327-8 : 7.95
1. Schubert, Franz Peter, 1797-1828. 2. Composers—Austria—Biography.
Distributed by Faber & Faber, Salem, NH BIP

SCHNEIDER, Marcel 927.8
Schubert. Translated by Elizabeth Poston. New York, Grove Press [1960, c.1959] 191p. (Bibliography: p. 177. Discography: p. 185-190.) illus., ports., music. 18cm. (Evergreen profile book 4) 59-6057 1.25 pap.,
1. Schubert, Franz Peter, 1797-1828. I. Title.

SCHNEIDER, Marcel, 780'.92'4 B
1913-
Schubert / Marcel Schneider ; translated by Elizabeth Poston. Westport, Conn. : Greenwood Press, 1975, c1959. 191 p. : ill. ; 20 cm. Reprint of the ed. published by Grove Press, New York, which was issued as no. 4 of Evergreen profile books. Bibliography: p. 177. [ML410.S3S2922 1975] 75-28926 ISBN 0-8371-8472-X lib.bdg. : 15.00
1. Schubert, Franz Peter, 1797-1828. BIP

WECHSBERG, Joseph, 780'.92'4 B
1907-
Schubert : his life, his work, his time / Joseph Wechsberg. New York : Rizzoli, 1977. 224 p. : ill. (some col.) ; 26 cm. Includes index. Bibliography: p. 220. [ML410.S3W17] 77-77677 ISBN 0-8478-0122-5 : 18.50
1. Schubert, Franz Peter, 1797-1828. 2. Composers—Austria—Biography.

Schubert, Franz Peter, 1797-1828—Juvenile literature.

GOFFSTEIN, M. B. 780'.92'4 B
A little Schubert. Story and pictures by M. B. Goffstein. Record by Peter Schaaf. [1st ed.] New York, Harper & Row [1972] [32] p. illus. and phonodisc (1 s., 6 in., 33 1/3 rpm.) in pocket 19 cm. Living in a bare room in Vienna, short, fat Franz Schubert wrote music and danced to keep warm. "Record of five of the twelve dances called 'Noble waltzes' that Franz Schubert wrote," Peter Schaaf, pianist. [ML3930.S38G6] 92 72-79899 ISBN 0-06-022026-0 3.95
1. Schubert, Franz Peter, 1797-1828—Juvenile literature. I. Title. BIP

Schulze, Gene.

SCHULZE, Gene. 610'.92'4 B
Yesterday's seasons : memories of a rural medical practice / by Gene Schulze. New York : Hawthorne Books, c1978. 288 p. ; 24 cm. [R154.S3536A33] 78-53481 ISBN 0-8015-0301-9 : 10.95
1. Schulze, Gene. 2. Physicians (General practice)—Texas—Schulenburg—Biography. 3. Medicine, Rural—Texas—Schulenburg. 4. Schulenburg, Tex.—Biography. I. Title.

Schumacher, Claire W.

SCHUMACHER, Claire W. 977.5'11
The Whiteside Island story : Emerald Isle of St. Louis Bay / by Claire W. Schumacher. 1st ed. [Duluth? Minn.] : Schumacher, [1974] 61 p. : ill. ; 22 cm. Bibliography: p. 60. [F587.D8S38] 74-29021
1. Schumacher, Claire W. 2. Clough Island, Wis.—History. I. Title.

Schumacher, Kurt,

EDINGER, Lewis Joachim, 923.243
1922-
Kurt Schumacher; a study in personality and political behavior [by] Lewis J. Edinger. Stanford, Calif., Stanford University Press, 1965. Bibliographical references included in "Notes" (p. [347]-367) Bibliography: p. [369]-381. [DD259.7S4E3] 65-12731
1. Schumacher, Kurt, I. Title. BIP

Schuman, William Howard, 1910-

SCHREIBER, Flora Rheta. 927.8
William Schuman, by Flora Rheta Schreiber and VincentPersichetti. New York, G. Schirmer [1954] iv, 139p. illus., ports., music. 22cm. 'List of works': p. 126-130, 133. 'List of records': p.131-132. Bibliography:p.134. [ML410.S386S3] 54-14322
1. Schuman, William Howard, 1910- 2. Schuman, William Howard, 1910- — Discography. I. Persichetti, Vincent, 1915- II. Title.

Schumann, Clara Josephine Wieck, 1819-1896.

DUNLOP, Agnes Mary 780'.922 B
Robertson.
Duet; the story of Clara and Robert Schumann, by Elisabeth Kyle. [1st ed.] New York, Holt, Rinehart and Winston [1968] 213 p. 22 cm. A biography of the famous musical couple which concentrates on the dramatic early days of their relationship. [ML3925.S318D85] 92 AC 68
1. Schumann, Clara Josephine (Wieck) 1819-1896. 2. Schumann, Robert Alexander, 1810-1956. I. Kyle, Elizabeth, pseud. II. Title.

LITZMANN, Berthold, 786.1'072'4 B
1857-1926.
Clara Schumann : an artist's life, based on material found in diaries and letters / by Berthold Litzmann ; translated and abridged from the 4th ed. by Grace E. Hadow ; with a new introd. by Elaine Brody. New York : Da Capo Press, 1979. p. cm. (Da Capo Press music reprint series) Reprint of the 1913 ed. published by Macmillan, London. [ML417.S4L72 1979] 79-20823 ISBN 0-306-79582-5 : 59.50 set
1. Schumann, Clara Josephine Wieck, 1819-1896. 2. Pianists—Germany—Biography.

SCHUMANN, Clara 786.1'092'4 B
Josephine (Wieck) 1819-1896.
Letters of Clara Schumann and Johannes Brahms, 1853-1896. Edited by Berthold Litzmann. New York, Vienna House [1971] 2 v. music. 23 cm. Reprint of the 1927 ed. [ML417.S4A43 1971] 77-163792 ISBN 0-8443-0018-7 (v. 1)
I. Brahms, Johannes, 1833-1897. II. Litzmann, Berthold, 1857-1926, ed. BIP

SCHUMANN, Clara 786.1'092'4 B
Josephine Wieck, 1819-1896.
Letters of Clara Schumann and Johannes Brahms, 1853-1896 / edited by Berthold Litzmann. Westport, Conn. : Hyperion Press, 1979. p. cm. (Encore music editions) Reprint of the 1927 ed. published by Longmans, Green, New York. [ML417.S4A43 1979] 78-67985 ISBN 0-88355-761-4 : 39.50
1. Schumann, Clara Josephine Wieck, 1819-1896. 2. Brahms, Johannes, 1833-1897. 3. Pianists—Germany—Correspondence. 4. Composers—Germany—Correspondence. I. Brahms, Johannes, 1833-1897. II. Litzmann, Berthold, 1857-1926.

SPAETH, Sigmund Gottfried, 927.8
1885-1965.
Dedication, the love story of Clara and Robert Schumann. New York, Holt [1950] xii, 180 p. 22 cm. "Recorded works of Schumann": p. 167-171. Bibliography: p. 172-173. [ML417.S4S7] 50-6819
1. Schumann, Clara Josephine Wieck, 1819-1896. 2. Schumann, Robert Alexander, 1810-1856. 3. Schumann, Robert Alexander, 1810-1856—Discography. I. Title.

Schumann, Clara Josephine Wieck, 1819-1896—Fiction.

WHITE, Hilda. 927.8
Song without end; the love story of Clara and Robert Schumann. [1st ed.] New York, Dutton, 1959. 300 p. 21 cm. [ML3925.S32W5] 59-11503
1. Schumann, Clara Josephine Wieck, 1819-1896—Fiction. 2. Schumann, Robert Alexander, 1810-1856—Fiction. 3. Musical fiction. I. Title.

Schumann family.

SCHUMANN, Eugenie, 780'.92'2 B
1851-1938.
Memoirs of Eugenie Schumann / translated by Marie Busch. Westport, Conn. : Hyperion Press, 1979. p. cm. (Encore music editions) Translation of Erinnerungen. Reprint of the 1927 ed. published by W. Heinemann, London. [ML410.S4S332 1979] 78-67986 ISBN 0-88355-762-2 : 23.50
1. Schumann family. 2. Brahms, Johannes, 1833-1897. 3. Musicians—Germany—Biography. BIP

SCHUMANN, Eugenie, 1851- 780'.922
1938.
The Schumanns and Johannes Brahms; the memoirs of Eugenie Schumann. Freeport, N.Y., Books for Libraries Press [1970] xi, 217 p. illus., ports. 22 cm. Translation of Erinnerungen. Reprint of the 1927 ed. [ML410.S4S332 1970] 75-124256
1. Schumann family. 2. Brahms, Johannes, 1833-1897. I. Title.

Schumann-Heink, Ernestine, 1861-1936.

†LAWTON, Mary. 782.1'092'4 B
Schumann-Heink, the last of the titans / Mary Lawton ; with a discography by W. R. Moran. New York : Arno Press, 1977, [c1928] 390, [30] p., [4] leaves of plates : ill. ; 23 cm. (Opera biographies) Reprint of the ed. published by Macmillan, New York. Discography: p. [391]-[417]. [ML420.S39L2 1977] 76-29945 28.00
1. Schumann-Heink, Ernestine, 1861-1936. 2. Singers—Biography. I. Title.

Schumann, Robert Alexander, 1810-1856.

ABRAHAM, Gerald Ernest 927.8
Heal, 1904- ed.
Schumann; a symposium. London, New York, Oxford University Press, 1952. vi, 319 p. music. 22 cm. [ML410.S4A6317] 52-7806
1. Schumann, Robert Alexander, 1810-1856. I. Title.
Contents Omitted. BIP

ABRAHAM, Gerald 780'.92'4 B
Ernest Heal, 1904-
Schumann : a symposium / edited by Gerald Abraham. Westport, Conn. : Greenwood Press, 1977. vi, 319 p. : music ; 23 cm. Reprint of the 1952 ed. published by Oxford University Press, London. Bibliography: p. [301]-308. [ML410.S4A6317 1977] 77-8051 ISBN 0-8371-9050-9 : 19.00
1. Schumann, Robert Alexander, 1810-1856. 2. Composers—Germany—Biography.
Contents omitted

BASCH, Victor, 1863- 780'.924 B
1944.
Schumann, a life of suffering. Translated from the French by Catherine Alison Phillips. Freeport, N.Y., Books for Libraries Press [1970] vii, 243, xi p. illus., ports. 23 cm. "First published 1931." Translation of La vie douloureuse de Schumann. [ML410.S4B193 1970] 76-107791
1. Schumann, Robert Alexander, 1810-1856. BIP

BEDFORD, Herbert, 780'.924 B
1867-1945.
Robert Schumann, his life and work. Westport, Conn., Greenwood Press [1971] x, 270 p. 23 cm. "Originally published in 1925 and 1933." [ML410.S4B42 1971] 70-106712 ISBN 0-8371-3442-0
1. Schumann, Robert Alexander, 1810-1856.

BOUCOURECHLIEU, Andre 927.8
Schumann. Translated from French by Arthur Boyars. New York, Grove Press (1959) 192 p. discography: pp. 190-192 illus. ports, facisms, music, 18 cm. Bibliography p. 184 59-6060 1.35
1. Schumann, Robert, Alexander, 1810-1856 I. Title.

BOUCOURECHLIEV, Andre 927.8
Schumann. Translated [from the French] by Arthur Boyars. New York, Grove Press [1959] 192p. Bibliography: p. 184. Discography: p. 190-192. illus. ports., facsims., music. 18cm. (Evergreen profile book 2) 59-6060 1.35 pap.,
1. Schumann, Robert Alexander, 1810-1856. I. Title.

BOUCOURECHLIEV, 780'.92'4 B
Andre.
Schumann / Andre Boucourechliev ; translated by Arthur Boyars. Westport, Conn. : Greenwood Press, 1976, c1959. 192 p. : ill. ; 20 cm. Reprint of the ed. published by Grove Press, New York, which was issued as no. 2 of Evergreen profile books. Bibliography: p. 184. [ML410.S4B772 1976] 75-28923 ISBN 0-8371-8475-4 lib.bdg. : 19.75
1. Schumann, Robert Alexander, 1810-1856.

BRION, Marcel, 1895- 784'.092'4
Schumann & the romantic age; translated by Geoffrey Sainsbury. New York, Macmillan [1956] viii, 371p. ports. 22cm. Translation of Schumann et l'ame romantique. [ML410.S4B] A57
1. Schumann, Robert Alexander, 1810-1856. 2. Romanticism in music. I. Title.

CHISSELL, Joan 927.8
Schumann. New York, Collier [1962] 282p. 18cm. (Gt. composers ser., BS151V) Bibl. 1.50 pap.,
1. Schumann, Robert Alexander, 1810-1856 I. Title. BIP

FULLER-MAITLAND, John 780'.924 B
Alexander, 1856-1936.
Robert Schumann, 1810-1856, by J. A. Fuller-Maitland. Foreword by Francesco Berger. Port Washington, N.Y., Kennikat Press [1970] viii, 150 p. port. 19 cm. "First published in 1913." [ML410.S4F95 1970] 73-102841
1. Schumann, Robert Alexander, 1810-1856. BIP

METZGER, Michael M. 438.6'42
Clara and Robert Schumann [by] Michael M. Metzger [and] Erika A. Metzger. Boston, H. Mifflin Co. [1967] 75 p. illus., facsims. (incl. music), ports. 22 cm. (German cultural readers) [ML410.S4M513] 67-1314

1. Schumann, Robert Alexander, 1810-1856. 2. Schumann, Clara Josephine (Wieck), 1819-1896. I. Metzger, Erika A., joint author. II. Title.

SCHAUFFLER, Robert Haven, 1879-1945 927.8
Florestan; the life and work of Robert Schuman [Gloucester, Mass., P. Smith, 1963, c.1945] 574p. ports., music. 21cm. (Dover bk. T132 rebound) Bibl. 4.25
1. Schumann, Robert Alexander, 1810-1856. 2. Schumann, Clara Josephine (Wieck) 1819-1896. I. Title.

SCHUMANN. v. 12
[2.ed.] London, Dent.; New York, Farrar, Strauss and Cudahy [1956] xi, 275p. illus., ports., facsim., music. 19cm. (The Master musicians, New ser.) Bibliography, p. 262-264.
1. Schumann, Robert Alexander, 1810-1856. I. Chissell, Joan.

SCHUMANN. [2. ed.] v. 12
London, Dent; New York, Farrar, Strauss and Cudahy [1956] xi, 275p. illus., ports., facsim., music. 19cm. (The Master musicians, New ser.) Bibliography, p. 262-264.
1. Schumann, Robert Alexander, 1810-1856. I. Chissell, Joan.

SCHUMANN, Robert Alexander, 1810-1856. 780'.924
Early letters of Robert Schumann, originally published by his wife. Translated by May Herbert. London, G. Bell, 1888; Republished. St. Clair Shores, Mich., Scholarly Press, 1970. xii, 307 p. 21 cm. Translation of Jugendbriefe. [ML410.S4A37 1970] 73-107190

SCHUMANN, Robert Alexander, 1810-1856 780'.924 B
The letters of Robert Schumann, selected and edited by Karl Storck. Translated by Hannah Bryant. [New York] B. Blom [1971] xviii, 299 p. ports. 21 cm. Reprint of the 1907 ed. [ML410.S4A375 1971] 79-173122
I. Storck, Karl G. L., 1873-1920, ed. **BIP**

SPAETH, Sigmund Gottfried, 1885-1965. 927.8
Dedication, the love story of Clara and Robert Schumann. New York, Holt [1950] xii, 180 p. 22 cm. "Recorded works of Schumann": p. 167-171. Bibliography: p. 172-173. [ML417.S4S7] 50-6819
1. Schumann, Clara Josephine Wieck, 1819-1896. 2. Schumann, Robert Alexander, 1810-1856. 3. Schumann, Robert Alexander, 1810-1856—Discography. I. Title.

WALKER, Alan, writer on music. 780.924 [B]
Robert Schumann: the man and his music; edited by Alan Walker; [contributors] Frank Cooper [and others]. New York, Barnes & Noble, [1974, c1972] xi, 489 p. illus. 24 cm. Bibliography: p. 442-445 [ML410.S4W18] 73-156256 ISBN 0-06-497367-0 15.00
1. Schumann, Robert Alexander, 1810-1856. I. Cooper, Frank, 1938- II. Title. **BIP**

WASIELEWSKI, Wilhelm Joseph von, 1822-1896. 780'.92'4 B
Life of Robert Schumann / by Joseph Wilhelm von Wasielewski ; translated by A. L. Alger ; with new introd. by Leon Plantinga. Detroit : Information Coordinators, 1975. viii, 275 p. ; 20 cm. (Detroit reprints in music) Reprint of the 1871 ed. published by O. Ditson, Boston. "Letters for 1833-1852": p. 195-253. [ML410.S4W213 1975] 74-75897 ISBN 0-911772-71-5 : 12.00
1. Schumann, Robert Alexander, 1810-1856. **BIP**

WHEELER, Opal. v. 12
Robert Schumann and mascot Ziff; illus. by Christine Price. [1st ed.] New York, E. P. Dutton [1963, 1947] 167 p. illus. 25cm. Includes music. "Fifth printing." 68-26067
1. Schumann, Robert Alexander, 1810-1856. 2. Music—Juvenile literature. I. Price, Christine, illus. II. Title.

Schumann, Robert Alexander, 1810-1856—Aesthetics.

BROWN, Thomas Alan. 780.1
The aesthetics of Robert Schumann. New York, Philosophical Library [1968] 207 p. facsims., music. 22 cm. Bibliography: p. 199-207. [ML410.S4B86] 67-29200
1. Schumann, Robert Alexander, 1810-1856—Aesthetics. 2. Schumann, Robert Alexander, 1810-1856. Works, piano. I. Title. **BIP**

Schumpeter, Joseph Alola, 1883-1950.

HARRIS, Seymour Edwin, 1897- ed. 923.373
Schumpeter, social scientist. Cambridge, Harvard University Press, 1951. x, 142 p. ports. 29 cm. "Published under the auspices of the Review of economics and statistics. Of the twenty essays included ... fifteen were published in the May 1951 issue." Bibliographical footnotes. [HB119.S35H3] 51-7762
1. Schumpeter, Joseph Alola, 1883-1950. I. Title. **BIP**

Schurz, Carl, 1829-1906.

FUESS, Claude Moore, 1885-1963. 923.273
Carl Schurz, reformer; 1829-1906. Port Washington, N. Y., Kennikat Press [1963] 421 p. illus., ports. 22 cm. "Selected bibliography": p. 395-401. [E664.S39F92 1963] 63-20588
1. Schurz, Carl, 1829-1906.

SCHURZ, Carl, 1829-1906. 923.273
Autobiography; an abridgment in one volume by Wayne Andrews. With an introd. by Allan Nevins. New York, Scribner [1961] 331p. 24cm. 'An abridgement ... of The reminiscences of Carl Schurz, originally published in three volumes, 1906-1908.' [E664.S39A337] 61-6900
I. Title.

SCHURZ, Carl, 1829-1906. 973.8'0924
Intimate letters of Carl Schurz, 1841-1869. Translated and edited by Joseph Schafer. New York, Da Capo, 1970 [c1929] xx, 491 p. illus., ports. 24 cm. Originally published as v. 30 of the Collections of the State Historical Society of Wisconsin. [E664.S39A43 1970] 73-106989 ISBN 3-06-718766-
I. Title. **BIP**

TERZIAN, James P 973.80924
Defender of human rights: Carl Schurz, by James P. Terzian. New York, J. Messner [1965] 192 p. 22 cm. Bibliography: p. 187. [E664.S39T4] 65-22250
1. Schurz, Carl, 1829-1906. I. Title.

Schurz, Carl, 1829-1906—Juvenile literature.

TUTT, Clara Little, 923.273
Carl Schurz, patriot. Illus. by Marjorie O'Brien-Rapaport. Madison, State Historical Society of Wisconsin. [c.] 1960 107p. illus. 20cm. 60-62505 3.00
1. Schurz, Carl, 1829-1906—Juvenile literature. I. Title.

Schutz, Heinrich, 1585-1672.

MOSER, Hans Joachim, 1889- 927.8
Heinrich Schutz; his life and work. Tr. from 2nd rev. [German] ed. by Carl F. Pfatteicher. St. Louis [Mo.] Concordia Publishing House [1960, c.1959] xxvi, 740p. illus., col. port., 25cm. Bibl. A60 15.00
1. Schutz, Heinrich, 1585-1672. I. Title.

MOSER, Hans Joachim, 1889- 783'.0924 (B)
Heinrich Schutz; a short account of his life and works. Translated and edited by Derek McCulloch. New York, St. Martin's Press [1967] 120 p. map, music, port. 23 cm. Originally published under title Kleines Heinrich-Schutz-Buch. Discography: p. 111-116. [ML410.S35M652 1967b] 67-25262
1. Schutz, Heinrich, 1585-1672. I. Title.

Schuyler, Catalina (Schuyler) 1701-1779?

GRANT, Anne (MacVicar) 1755-1838. 917.47 B
Memoirs of an American lady, with sketches of manners and scenes in America as they existed previous to the Revolution. With unpublished letters and a memoir of Mrs. Grant by James Grant Wilson. Freeport, N.Y., Books for Libraries Press [1972] xxxviii, 307, 300 p. illus. 23 cm. Reprint of the 1901 ed. List of author's works: p. 287-288 (3d group) [F122.G7 1972] 77-38354 ISBN 0-8369-6771-2
1. Schuyler, Catalina (Schuyler) 1701-1779? 2. New York (State)—Social life and customs—Colonial period, ca. 1600-1775. 3. Indians of North America. I. Wilson, James Grant, 1832-1914. II. Title. **BIP**

Schuyler, George Samuel, 1895

SCHUYLER, George Samuel, 1895- 070.10924 (B)
Black and conservative; the autobiography of George S. Schuyler. New Rochelle, N. Y., Arlington House [1966] 362 p. 22 cm. [PN4874.S35A3] 66-23140
1. Title. I. Title.

Schuyler, Philip John, 1733-1804.

GERLACH, Don R., 1932- 923.573
Philip Schuyler and the American Revolution in New York, 1733-1777. Lincoln, University of Nebraska Press, 1964. xxi, 358 p. illus., ports., map. 24 cm. Bibliography: p. 332-344. [E207.S3G4] 64-11354
1. Schuyler, Philip John, 1733-1804. 2. New York (State)—Politics and government—Colonial period. 3. New York (State)—Politics and government—Revolution I. Title.

GERLACH, Don R., 1932- 973.4'1'0924 B
Philip Schuyler and the growth of New York, 1733-1804, by Don R. Gerlach Albany, Office of State History, 1968. iii, 48, [1] p. illus. 22 cm. Bibliography: p. 48-[49] [E207.S3G42] 70-625894
1. Schuyler, Philip John, 1733-1804. 2. New York (State)—History. I. New York (State). Office of State History. II. Title.

LOSSING, Benson John, 1813-1891. 973.4'1'0924 B
The life and times of Philip Schuyler. New York, Da Capo Press, 1973- [c1872] v. 22 cm. (The Era of the American Revolution) [E207.S3L822] 78-167944 ISBN 0-306-70533-8 37.50 (2 vol.)
1. Schuyler, Philip John, 1733-1804. **BIP**

TUCKERMAN, Bayard, 1855-1923. 973.4'1'0924 B
Life of General Philip Schuyler, 1733-1804. Freeport, N.Y., Books for Libraries Press [1969] 277 p. illus., map, port. 23 cm. (Select bibliographies reprint series) Reprint of the 1903 ed. [E207.S3T8 1969] 71-95081 ISBN 0-8369-5031-3
1. Schuyler, Philip John, 1733-1804. I. Title.

Schwab, Charles M., 1862-1939.

HESSEN, Robert, 1936- 338.7'66'910924 B
Steel titan : the life of Charles M. Schwab / Robert Hessen. New York : Oxford University Press, 1975. xvi, 350 p., [4] leaves of plates : ill. ; 24 cm. Includes bibliographical references and index. [HD9520.S3H48] 75-10175 14.95
1. Schwab, Charles M., 1862-1939. I. Title. **BIP**

Schwalm, Vernon Franklin,

SCHWALM, Vernon Franklin, 1887- 923.773
Otho Winger eighteen seventy-seven-nineteen forty-six Elgin, Ill., Brothren Pub. House [1952] 295 p. illus. 21 cm. [LD3181.M517 1911a] 52-37998
I. Winger, Otho, 1877-1940. II. Title.

Schwartz, Delmore, 1913-1966.

ATLAS, James. 811'.5'2 B
Delmore Schwartz : the life of an American poet / by James Atlas. New York : Farrar, Straus and Giroux, [1977] p. cm. "Works by Delmore Schwartz": p. [PS3537.C79Z56] 77-23852 ISBN 0-374-13761-7 : 15.00
1. Schwartz, Delmore, 1913-1966. 2. Poets, American—20th century—Biography. **BIP**

Schwartz, Harold.

SCHWARTZ, Harold. 923.673
Samuel Gridley Howe, social reformer, 1801-1876. Cambridge, Harvard University Press, 1956. viii, 348p. 22cm. (Harvard historical studies, v. 67) Bibliographical footnotes. [HV1624.H7S35] 56-11286
1. Howe, Samuel Gridley, 1801-1876. II. Title. III. Series.

Schwartz, Helene E.

SCHWARTZ, Helene E. 340'.092'4 B
Lawyering / Helene E. Schwartz. New York : Farrar, Straus and Giroux, 1976. x, 308 p. ; 22 cm. [KF373.S346A32] 75-22451 ISBN 0-374-18422-4 : 10.00
1. Schwartz, Helene E. 2. Women lawyers—United States—Correspondence, reminiscences, etc. I. Title. **BIP**

Schwartz, Samuel,

SCHWARTZ, Samuel, 1880?- 922.96
Tell thy children; the autobiography of an American rabbi. Foreword by Leonard J. Mervis. [1st ed.] New York, Exposition Press [1959] 98p. illus. 21cm. [BM755.S36A3] 59-3892
I. Title.

Schwarzenberg, Felix, Furst zu, 1800-1852.

SCHWARZENBERG, Adolph. v. 12
Prince Felix zu Schwarzenberg, prime minister of Austria, 1848-1852, by Adolph Schwarzenberg. New York, AMS Press, 1966. xviii, 244 p. ports. First published 1946. Bibliography: p. [221]-229. 68-18962
1. Schwarzenberg, Felix, Furst zu, 1800-1852. 2. Austria—Hist.—1848-1866. 3. Austria—Pol. & govt.—1848-1866. I. Title. **BIP**

Schwarzenegger, Arnold.

SCHWARZENEGGER, Arnold. 646.7'5
Arnold : the education of a bodybuilder / Arnold Schwarzenegger, with Douglas Kent Hall. New York : Simon and Schuster, c1977. 256 p. : ill. ; 25 cm. [GV460.2.S38A32] 77-22558 ISBN 0-671-22879-X : 9.95
1. Schwarzenegger, Arnold. 2. Weight lifters—Biography. 3. Exercise. 4. Muscle strength. I. Hall, Douglas Kent, joint author. II. Title. **BIP**

Schwarzkopf, Vergil,

SCHWARZKOPF, Vergil, 1896- 637'.0924 B
The game of life, an autobiography. [La Grange Park? Ill., 1969] xxxi, 388 p. illus., ports. 23 cm. [S417.S33A3] 70-10725
I. Title.

Schwed, Fred.

SCHWED, Fred. 818.5
The pleasure was all mine; the journal of an undisappointed man. With drawings by Walt Kelly. New York, Simon and Schuster [1951] viii, 260p. illus. 21cm. [CT275.S3474A3] 51-10973
I. Title.

Schweiker, Richard Schultz, 1926-

LANDES, Burton R., 1921- 328.73'092'4 B
The making of a Senator, 1974 : a biography of Richard S. Schweiker / Burton R Landes Trappe, [Pa.] : Landes, c1976. iv, 100 p. ; 19 cm. "A study of the international press and other media in the shaping of public opinion: the Sarah Churchill cause": p. [69]-99. Includes bibliographical references. [E840.8.S37L36] 75-7003 ISBN 0-584-55922-4 : 7.95
1. Schweiker, Richard Schultz, 1926- 2. Churchill, Sarah, 1914- I. Landes, Burton R., 1921- A study of the international press and other media in the shaping of public opinion. 1976. II. Title.

Schweitzer, Albert, 1875-1965.

ALBERT Schweitzer, prophet of freedom. [Evanston, Ill.] 1957. 52p. illus. 22cm. Cover title. v. 12
1. Schweitzer, Albert, 1875- I. Phillips, Herbert M 1910-

ANDERSON, Erica 922.443
Ablbert Schweitzer's gift of friendship. New York, Harper [c.1964] viii, 152p. illus., ports. 24cm. 64-19496 4.95
1. Schweitzer, Albert, 1875- I. Title.

ANDERSON, Erica 922.443
Albert Schweitzer. Philadelphia, Chilton Co. [c.1961] 122p illus. (Meet your great contemporaries series, 633) 1.00 pap.,
1. Schweitzer, Albert, 1875- I. Title.

ANDERSON, Erica. 922.443
Albert Schweitzer. [1st ed.] Philadelphia, Chilton Co., Book Division [1961] 122p. illus. 21cm. (Meet your great contemporaries series, 633) [CT1098.S45A62] 61-9023
1. Schweitzer, Albert, 1875- I. Title.

BERRILL, Jacquelyn 922.443
Albert Schweitzer: man of mercy. Illus. with drawings by the author and with photos. 90th birthday ed. New York, Dodd [1965] 202p. illus., ports. 21cm. [CT1098.S45B4] 65-2217 3.25
1. Schweitzer, Albert, 1875- I. Title.

BERRILL, Jacquelyn. 922.443
Albert Schweitzer, man of mercy; illustrated with drawings bythe author and with photos. New York, Dodd, Mead [1956] 200p. illus. 21cm. [CT1098.S45B4] 56-5188
1. Schweitzer, Albert, 1875- I. Title.

BRABAZON, James. 266'.025'0924 B
Albert Schweitzer : a biography / by James Brabazon. New York : Putnam, [1975] 509 p., [8] leaves of plates : ill. ; 24 cm. Includes index. Bibliography: p. 485-488. [CT1098.S45B7 1975] 74-30545 ISBN 0-399-11421-1 : 12.50
1. Schweitzer, Albert, 1875-1965. I. Title.
BIP

BRABAZON, James. 266'.025'0924 B
Albert Schweitzer : a biography / James Brabazon. London : Gollancz, 1976. 509 p., [16] p. of plates : ill., plan, ports. ; 24 cm. Includes index. [CT1018.S45B72 1976] 76-383118 ISBN 0-575-02035-0 : £6.95
1. Schweitzer, Albert, 1875-1965. 2. Missionaries, Medical—Gabon—Biography. 3. Theologians—Europe—Biography. 4. Musicians—Europe—Biography.

COUSINS, Norman. 922.443
Dr. Schweitzer of Lambarene. With photos. by Clara Urquhart. New York, Harper [1960] 254 p. illus. 22 cm. [CT1098.S45C6] 60-9134
1. Schweitzer, Albert, 1875-1965. BIP

COUSINS, Norman. 266'.025'092'4 B
Dr. Schweitzer of Lambarene. With photos. by Clara Urquhart. Westport, Conn., Greenwood Press [1973, c1960] 254 p. illus. 22 cm. Reprint of the ed. published by Harper, New York. [CT1098.S45C6 1973] 73-7075 ISBN 0-8371-6902-X 12.50
1. Schweitzer, Albert, 1875-1965. I. Title.

DANIEL, Anita. 922.443
The story of Albert Schweitzer. Illustrated with photos. by Erica Anderson, and drawings by W. T. Mars. New York, Random House [1957] 179 p. illus. 22 cm. (World landmark books, W-33) [CT1098.S45D3] 57-7517
1. Schweitzer, Albert, 1875-1965.

FRANCK, Frederick, 1909- 266'.025'0924 B
Days with Albert Schweitzer; a Lambarene landscape. Illustrated by the author. Westport, Conn., Greenwood Press [1974, c1959] xii, 178 p. illus. 22 cm. Reprint of the ed. published by Holt, Rinehart and Winston, New York. [CT1098.S45F68 1974] 73-22636 ISBN 0-8371-7341-8 9.50
1. Schweitzer, Albert, 1875-1965. I. Title.
BIP

GOLLOMB, Joseph, 1881- v. 12
Albert Schweitzer: genius in the jungle. New York, Vanguard Press [1965? c1949] 249, [2] p. First published in this edition 1965? 67-88735
1. Schweitzer, Albert, 1875-1965. I. Title.
BIP

GREENE, Jay Elihu, 1914- ed. 920.02
Four complete biographies. New York, Globe Book Co. [1962] 750p. illus. 22cm. [CT106.G652] 62-5357
1. Churchill, Winston Leonard Spencer, Sir 1874- 2. Keller, Helen Adams, 1880- 3. Schweitzer, Albert, 1875- 4. Barnum, Phineas Taylor, 1810-1891. I. Title.
Contents omitted.

HAGEDORN, Hermann, 1882- 922.443
Albert Schweitzer; prophet in the wilderness. New rev. ed. New York, Collier Bks. [c.1947-1962] Previous eds. pub. under title: Prophet in the wilderness 61-18561 .95 pap.,
1. Schweitzer, Albert, 1875- I. Title.

HAGEDORN, Hermann, 1882- 922.443
Albert Schweitzer; prophet in the wilderness. New rev ed. New York, Collier Books [1962] 224p. 19cm. (Collier books, AS150) Previous editions published under title: Prophet in the wilderness. [CT1098.S45H3 1962] 61-18561
1. Schweitzer, Albert, 1875- I. Title.

HAGEDORN, Hermann, 1882- 922.443
Prophet in the wilderness; the story of Albert Schweitzer. Rev. ed. New York, Macmillan, 1954. 240p. illus. 21cm. [CT1098.S45H3 1954] 54-13060
1. Schweitzer, Albert, 1875- I. Title.

HASSOLD, Ernest Christopher, 1896- 266'.025'0924
Albert Schweitzer, E. R. Hagemann, editor. [Louisville, Ky., University of Louisville, 1969] [33] p. facsims., ports. 22 x 28 cm. "The occasion for this symposium, December 6, 1965, was to commemorate Albert Schweitzer (1875-1965) as part of the faculty lectures in the humanities at the University of Louisville." Contents.Contents.—Schweitzer's philosophy of culture, by E. C. Hassold.—Schweitzer and Indian philosophy, by D. P. Patnaik.—Schweitzer, the musician/personal recollections, by G. Herz. Includes bibliographical references. [CT1098.S45H35] 79-230389
1. Schweitzer, Albert, 1875-1965. I. Hagemann, Edward R., ed. II. Louisville, Ky. University. III. Patnaik, Deba Prasad. Schweitzer and Indian philosophy. 1969. IV. Herz, Gerhard, 1911- Schweitzer, the musican/personal recollections. 1969.

IM Lande Albert Schweitzers; meine besuche in Lambarene. Hamburg, Broschek [1958] 70p. plates, ports. 20cm. v. 12
1. Schweitzer, Albert, 1875- 2. Missions, Medical—Africa, West. I. Italiaander, Rolf, 1913-

JOY, Charles Rhind, 1885- 922.443
The Africa of Albert Schweitzer [by] Charles R. Joy & Melvin Arnold. Photos. by Charles R. Joy. New [i. e. 2d] ed., rev. London, A. & C. Black; New York, Harper [1958] 159p. illus. 24cm. [BV3625.G315S35 1958] 59-1239
1. Schweitzer, Albert. 1875- 2. Missions, Medical — Gabon. 3. Lambarene Gabon. I. Arnold, Melvin, joint author. II. Title.

JUNGK, Robert, 1913- 922.443
Albert Schweitzer; the story of his life, by Jean Pierhal [pseud.] New York, Philosophical Library [c1957] 100 p. illus. 23 cm. "A version of [the author's] Albert Schweitzer; das Leben eines guten Menschen." [CT1098.S45.J83] 57-13702
1. Schweitzer, Albert, 1875- I. Title.

KRAUS, Oskar, 1872-1942 922.443
Albert Schweitzer; his work and his philosophy [tr. from German by E. G. McColman] Introd. by A. D. Lindsay. London, A. & C. Black [Chester Springs, Pa., Dufour, 1966] x, 75p. front. (port.) 22cm. First pub. in the Jahrbuch fur charakterologie. Bibl. [CT1098.S45K72] A44 2.50
1. Schweitzer, Albert, 1875- I. McCalman, E. G., tr. II. Title.

MCKNIGHT, Gerald. 922.443
Verdict on Schweitzer, the man behind the legend of Lambarene. New York, John Day Co. [1964] 254 p. illus., plan, ports. 23 cm. Bibliography: p. 247. [CT1098.S45M24 1964a] 64-20467
1. Schweitzer, Albert, 1875-1965. I. Title.

MANTON, Jo, 1919- 922.443
The story of Albert Schweitzer. Illustrated by Astrid Walford. New York, Abelard-Schuman [1955] 223 p. illus. 22 cm. [CT1098.S45M3 1955a] 55-8542
1. Schweitzer, Albert, 1875-1965.

MARSHALL, George. 266'.025'0924 B
Schweitzer a biography [by] George Marshall and David Poling. New York, Pillar Books [1975 c1971] 346 p., illus. 18 cm. Includes index. [CT1098.S45M34] 71-130888 ISBN 0-89129-020-6 1.95 (pbk.)
1. Schweitzer, Albert, 1875-1965. I. Poling, David, joint author II. Title.

MARSHALL, George N. 362.10924
An understanding of Albert Schweitzer. New York, Philosophical Lib. [c.1966] 180p. illus., ports. 22cm. Bibl. [BV3625.G3S43] 65-28763 4.00
1. Schweitzer, Albert, 1875-1965. I. Title.

MONTAGUE, Joseph Franklin, 1893- 362.10924
The why of Albert Schweitzer; an appraisal in depth of the career of an extraordinary man of medicine. [1st ed.] New York, Hawthorn Books [1965] 312 p. illus., ports. 22 cm. "For those interested in further reading": p. 301-304. [CT1098.S45M6] 65-22911
1. Schweitzer, Albert, 1875-1965. I. Title.

OSTERGAARD-CHRISTENSEN, Lavrids, 1896- 922.443
At work with Albert Schweitzer. Tr. from Danish by F. H. Lyon. Boston, Beacon [c.1962] 117p. illus. 21cm. 61-5345 3.50
1. Schweitzer, Albert, 1875- I. Title.

OSTERGAARD, Christensen, Lavrids, 1896- 922.443
At work with Albert Schweitzer. Translated from the Danish by F. H. Lyon. Boston, Beacon Press [1962] 117p. illus. 21cm. Translation of Dansk laege hos Albert Schweitzer. [CT1098.S45O43 1962] 61-4345
1. Schweitzer, Albert, 1875- I. Title.

PAYNE, Pierre Stephen Robert, 1911- 922.443
The three worlds of Albert Schweitzer. New York, T. Nelson [1957] 252p. 21cm. [CT1098.S45P3] 57-11896
1. Schweitzer, Albert, 1875- I. Title.

PAYNE, Pierre Stephen Robert, 1911- 922.443
The three worlds of Albert Schweitzer. Bloomington, Indiana Univ. Press [1961, c.1957] 252p. (Midland bk. MB29) 1.75 pap.,
1. Schweitzer, Albert, 1875- I. Title.

PHILLIPS, Herbert M 1910- 922.443
Safari of discovery; the universe of Albert Schweitzer. New York, Twayne Publishers [1958] 271p. illus. 23cm. [CT1098.S45P47] 58-14291
1. Schweitzer, Albert, 1875- I. Title.

PICHT, Werner Robert Valentin, 1887- 922.443
The life and thought of Albert Schweitzer. Tr. from German by Edward Fitzgerald. New York, Harper [1965, c.1960, 1964] 288p. ports. 22cm. Bibl. [CT1098.S45P493] 65-10373 6.50
1. Schweitzer, Alb ert, I. Title.

PICHT, Werner Robert Valentin, 1887- 922.443
The life and thought of Albert Schweitzer. Tr. from German by Edward Fitzgerald. New York, Harper [1965, c.1960, 1964] 288p. ports. 22cm. Bibl. [CT1098.S45P493] 65-10373 6.50
1. Schweitzer, Alb ert, I. Title.

PIERHAL, Jean. 922.443
Albert Schweitzer; the story of his life. New York, Philosophical Library [c1957] 160p. illus. 23cm. [CT1098.S45P513] 57-13702
1. Schweitzer, Albert, 1875- I. Title.

RATTER, Magnus C. 922.443
Albert Schweitzer, life and message. Boston, Beacon Press, 1950. 214 p. group port. 20 cm. [CT1098.S45R3 1950] 50-5266
1. Schweitzer, Albert, 1875-1965.

RICHARDS, Kenneth G., 1926- 266'.025'0924 B
Albert Schweitzer, by Kenneth G. Richards. Chicago, Childrens Press [1968] 94 p. illus. 29 cm. (People of destiny: a humanities series) Bibliography: p. 90-91. Photographs, drawings, and text trace the life of the famous doctor whose dedicated service to suffering humanity in French Equatorial Africa made him a living symbol of his own philosophy of reverence for life. [CT1098.S45R5] 92 AC 68
1. Schweitzer, Albert, 1875-1965. I. Title.

SCHWEITZER, Albert, 1875- 922.443
Memoirs of childhood and youth. Tr. by C.T. Campion. New York, Macmillan [1963] 124p. 18cm. (133) .95 pap.,
I. Title.

SCHWEITZER, Albert, 1875- 922.443
Pilgrimage to humanity. Tr. [from German] by Walter E. Stuermann [ed. by Rudolf Grabs] New York, Philosophical Lib. [c.1961] 107p. Bibl. 61-15250 3.75
I. Title.

SCHWEITZER, Albert, 1875-1965. 266'.025'0924 B
Albert Schweitzer: reverence for life; the inspiring words of a great humanitarian. With a forword [sic] by Norman Cousins. Selected by Peter Seymour. Illustrated by Walter Scott. [Kansas City, Mo., Hallmark Cards, inc., c1971] 62 p. illus. 20 cm. (Hallmark editions) [CT1098.S45A27] 71-147796 ISBN 0-87529-203-8 2.50
I. Title: Reverence for life.

SCHWEITZER, Albert, 1875-1965. 786'.0924 B
Music in the life of Albert Schweitzer; with selections from his writings by Charles R. Joy. Freeport, N.Y., Books for Libraries Press [1971, c1951] xvii, 300 p. illus., ports. 23 cm. (Essay index reprint series) [ML416.S33A3 1971] 76-117840 ISBN 0-8369-2200-X
I. Title.

SCHWEITZER, Albert, 1875-1965. 266'.025'0924
My life and thought: an autobiography [by] Albert Schweitzer; translated [from the German] by C. T. Campion. London, Allen & Unwin, 1966. 225 p. 18 1/2 cm. 8/6 (B 66-24082) Translation of Aus meinem Leben und Denken. Bibliographical footnotes. [CT1098.S45A282] 67-105402
I. Title.

SEAVER, George, 1890- 922.443
Albert Schweitzer, the man and his mind. Rev. ed. New York, Harper [1956, c1955] ix, 370p. illus., ports. 24cm. [CT1098.S45S35 1956] 56-2431
1. Schweitzer, Albert, 1875- I. Title.

SEAVER, George, 1890- 922.443

Albert Schweitzer, the man and his mind. Rev. ed. New York, Harper [1956, c1955] ix, 370p. illus., ports. 24cm. [CT1098.S45S35 1956] 56-2431
1. Schweitzer, Albert, 1875- I. Title.

THE three worlds of Albert v. 12 Schweitzer [by] Robert Payne. Edinburgh, New York, T. Nelson [c1957] 252p. 21cm.
1. Schweitzer, Albert, 1875- I. Payne, Pierre Stephen Robert, 1911-

THE three worlds of Albert v. 12 Schweitzer. Bloomington, Indiana University Press [1961] 252p. 21cm. (Midland book, MB29)
1. Schweitzer, Albert, 1875- I. Payne, Pierre Stephen Robert, 1911-

TO Dr. Albert 922.443 Schweitzer; a festchrift commemorating his 80th birthday from a few of his friends. Evanston, Ill., 1955. 178p. 22cm. Edited by H. A. Jack. [CT1098.S45T6] 55-2440
1. Schweitzer, Albert, 1875- I. Jack, Homer Alexander, ed.
Contents omitted.

[ZOTTMANN, Thomas Michael] 92 1915-
Albert Schweitzer [by] M. Z. Thomas. Tr. [from German] by James Thin. Richmond, Va., John Knox Pr. [1965] 166p. illus., port. 21cm. [CT1098.S45Z63] 65-13917 2.50 bds.,
1. Schweitzer, Albert, 1875-1965. I. Title.

Schweitzer, Albert, 1875-1965—Juvenile literature.

ATWOOD, Ann. 113
For all that lives / by Ann Atwood and Erica Anderson ; with the words of Albert Schweitzer. New York : Scribner, [1975] [32] p. : col. ill. ; 21 x 27 cm. The meaning of life and man's alienation from himself and his natural environment is examined in brief selections, illustrated with photographs, from the works of Albert Schweitzer. [B3329.S54A86] 74-7809 ISBN 0-684-14001-2 lib. bdg. : 6.95
1. Schweitzer, Albert, 1875-1965—Juvenile literature. 2. Life—Juvenile literature. I. Anderson, Erica, joint author. II. Schweitzer, Albert, 1875-1965. III. Title.

FRANCK, Frederick 922.443 [Sigfred]
My friend in Africa, written and illustrated by Frederick Franck. Indianapolis, Bobbs-Merrill [c.1960] 94p. col. illus. 24cm. 60-7166 2.95 half cloth,
1. Schweitzer, Albert—Juvenile literature. I. Title.

JOHNSON, Spencer. 266'.025'0924 B
The value of dedication : the story of Albert Schweitzer / by Spencer Johnson. 1st ed. La Jolla, Calif. : Value Communications, c1979. p. cm. (ValueTales) Presents a biography of Albert Schweitzer who based his philosophy on what he called "reverence for life" and dedicated his life to serving humanity. [CT1018.S45J63] 92 79-21805 ISBN 0-916392-44-9 : 5.95
1. Schweitzer, Albert, 1875-1965—Juvenile literature. 2. Missionaries, Medical—Gabon—Biography—Juvenile literature. 3. Theologians—Europe—Biography—Juvenile literature. 4. Musicians—Europe—Biography—Juvenile literature. 5. Altruism—Juvenile literature. I. Title. BIP

MERRETT, John. 92
The true story of Albert Schweitzer, humanitarian. [American ed.] Chicago, Childrens Press [1964] 143 p. col. illus. 23 cm. First published in London in 1961 under title: The true book about Albert Schweitzer. [CT1098.S45M4] 64-12906
1. Schweitzer, Albert, 1875- — Juvenile literature. I. Title.

MERRETT, John. 92
The true story of Albert Schweitzer, humanitarian. [American ed.] Chicago, Childrens Press [1964] 143 p. col. illus. 23 cm. First published in London in 1961 under title: The true book about Albert Schweitzer. [CT1098.S45M4] 64-12906
1. Schweitzer, Albert, 1875- — Juvenile literature. I. Title.

MONTGOMERY, 266'.025'0924 B Elizabeth Rider.
Albert Schweitzer, great humanitarian. Illustrated by William Hutchinson. Champaign, Ill., Garrard Pub. Co. [1971] 144 p. illus., ports. 22 cm. ([A People in the arts and sciences book]) A biography of the musician, minister, and teacher who gave up a comfortable teaching career to become a missionary doctor in the African jungle. [CT1098.S45M63] 92 70-132035 ISBN 0-8116-4510-X 2.59
1. Schweitzer, Albert, 1875-1965—Juvenile literature. I. Hutchinson, William M., illus. II. Title.

MERRETT, John 922.443
The true book about Albert Schweitzer. Illus. by N. G. Wilson [dist. New Rochelle, N.Y., Sport Shelf c.1960] 141p. 61-520 2.75
1. Schweitzer, Albert, 1875- —Juvenile literature. I. Title.

MERRETT, John 920
The true story of Albert Schweitzer, humanitarian. Chicago, Childrens [c.1960, 1964] 143p. col. illus. 23cm. First pub. in London in 1961 under title: The true book about Albert Schweitzer. 64-12906 3.50; 2.63 lib. ed.,
1. Schweitzer, Albert, 1875- —Juvenile literature. I. Title.

SINGER, Kurt D., 1911- 920
Dr. Albert Schweitzer, medical missionary; a biographical sketch of a man who has dedicated his life to others. By Kurt Singer, Jane Sherrod. Minneapolis, Denison [1963, c.1962] 163p. 23cm. (Denison's men of achievement ser.) 62-22148 3.00
1. Schweitzer, Albert, 1875- —Juvenile literature. I. Sherrod, Jane, joint author. II. Title.

Schwerdtfeger, Johann Samuel William, 1734-1803.

SCHWERDTFEGER, Hazel Mae 922.471
Memoirs of Reverend J. Samuel Schwerdtfeger, 'the Saint of St. Lawrence Seaway,' first pastor of Upper Canada's first Protestant church, U. E. Loyalist and Lutheran patriarch of America. Carlton [dist. Comet, c.]1961. 84p. illus. (Reflection bk.) 61-16227 2.50
1. Schwerdtfeger, Johann Samuel William, 1734-1803. I. Title.

Schwerin, Doris.

SCHWERIN, 362.1'9'6994490924 B Doris.
Diary of a pigeon watcher / by Doris Schwerin. New York : Morrow, 1976. 288 p. ; 22 cm. Autobiographical. [ML410.S433A3] 75-38849 ISBN 0-688-03019-X : 8.95
1. Schwerin, Doris. I. Title. BIP

Schwiefert, Peter, 1917-1945.

SCHWIEFERT, Peter, 940.54'81 1917-1945.
The bird has no wings : letters of Peter edited by Claude Lanzmann ; translated by Barbara Lucas. New York : St. Martin's Press, c1976. 180 p., [4] leaves of plates : ill. ; 22 cm. Translation of L'oiseau n'a plus d'ailes. [D810.J4S3713] 75-34438 7.95
1. Schwiefert, Peter, 1917-1945. 2. World War, 1939-1945—Personal narratives, Jewish. 3. Jews in Germany—Persecutions. 4. Germany—History—1933-1945. I. Title.

Schwiering, Conrad, 1916-

WAKEFIELD, Robert. 759.13 B
Schwiering and the West. [1st ed. Aberdeen, S.D., North Plains Press, 1973] xvii, 207 p. illus. (part col.) 32 cm. [ND237.S4363W34] 73-77752 ISBN 0-87970-128-5 25.00
1. Schwiering, Conrad, 1916- 2. The West in art. I. Title. BIP

Schwinn, Monika, 1942-

SCHWINN, Monika, 1942- 959.704'37
We came to help / Monika Schwinn & Bernhard Diehl ; translated from the German by Jan van Heurck ; foreword by Benjamin H. Purcell. 1st ed. New York : Harcourt Brace Jovanovich, c1976. xi, 258 p. : ill. ; 22 cm. Translation of Eine Handvoll Menschlichkeit. "A Helen and Kurt Wolff book." [DS559.5.S3813] 76-13882 8.95
1. Schwinn, Monika, 1942- 2. Diehl, Bernhard, 1946- 3. Vietnamese Conflict, 1961-1975—Prisoners and prisons, North Vietnamese. 4. Vietnamese Conflict, 1961-1975—Personal narratives, German. I. Diehl, Bernhard, 1946- joint author. II. Title. BIP

Science—Biography.

DARMSTAEDTER, Ludwig, 509.22 1846-1927.
Naturforscher und Erfinder; biographische Miniaturen. Bielefeld, Velhagen & Klasing, 1926. New York, Johnson Reprint Corp., 1966 [1926] 182 p. illus., ports. 23 cm. (The Sources of science, no. 26) [Q141.D28 1966] 66-7097
1. Science — Biog. I. Title.

*MEREDITH. NICOLETE 925
Men of science, by Nicolete Meredith, Jean Shirley. Illus. by Ray Johnson. New York, Guild [1966] 142p. illus. 17cm. (Crusader bk. for young people, 31408) .50 pap.,
1. Science—Biography. I. Title.

Science—Early works to 1800.

CLAYTON, John, 1657-1725 509.24
The Reverend John Clayton, a parson with a scientific mind; his scientific writings and other related papers Ed., with a short biographical sketch, by Edmund Berkeley, Dorothy Smith Berkeley. Charlottesville, Pub. for the Va. Hist. Soc. [by] Univ. Pr. of Va. [c.]1965. 1xiii, 170p. plates. 26cm. (Va. Hist. Soc. documents, v. 6) Title. (Series: Virginia Historical Society, Richmond. Documents, v. 6) Bibl. [Q155.C5] 65-23459 6.50
1. Science—Early works to 1800. I. Berkeley, Edmund, ed. II. Berkeley, Dorothy Smith, ed. III. Title. IV. Series.

CLAYTON, John, 1657-1725. 509.24
The Reverend John Clayton, a parson with a scientific mind: his scientific writings and other related papers. Edited, with a short biographical sketch, by Edmund Berkeley [and] Dorothy Smith Berkeley. Charlottesville, Published for the Virginia Historical Society [by] University Press of Virginia, 1965. lxiii, 170 p. plates. 26 cm. (Virginia Historical Society documents v. 6) Bibliography: p. 151-158. [Q155.C5] 65-23459
1. Science — Early works to 1800. I. Berkeley, Edmund, ed. II. Berkeley, Dorothy Smith, ed. III. Title. IV. Series. V. Series: Virginia Historical Society, Richmond. Documents, v. 6

Science—Addresses, essays, lectures.

COMPTON, Arthur Holly, 1892- 500 1962.
The cosmos of Arthur Holly Compton. Edited by Marjorie Johnston, with an introd. by Vannevar Bush. [1st ed.] New York, Knopf, 1967 [i.e. 1968] xx, 468, xv p. 25 cm. Bibliographical references included in "Notes" (p. 423-448). "Scientific bibliography": p. 459-468. [Q171.C7617] 66-11343
1. Science—Addresses, essays, lectures. I. Title.

Science fiction, American—Bio-bibliography.

REGINALD, R. 016.823'0876
Science fiction and fantasy literature : a checklist, 1700-1947 . with Contemporary science fiction authors II / R. Reginald. Detroit : Gale Research Co., 1978 p. cm. The 1st ed. of v. 2 was published separately under title: Contemporary science fiction authors. Includes indexes. [Z1231.F4R42] [PS374.S35] 76-46130 45.00
1. Science fiction, American—Bio-bibliography. 2. Science fiction, English—Bio-bibliography. 3. Fantastic literature—Bibliography. 4. Authors, American—20th century—Biography. 5. Authors, English—20th century—Biography. I. Reginald, R. Contemporary science fiction authors. 1979. II. Title.

Science fiction—Bio-bibliography.

ASH, Brian. 809'.3'876 B
Who's who in science fiction / Brian Ash. New York : Taplinger Pub. Co., 1976. 219, [1] p. ; 23 cm. Bibliography: p. 217-[220] [PN3448.S45A83 1976] 76-11667 ISBN 0-8008-8274-1 : 8.95
1. Science fiction—Bio-bibliography. I. Title.

ASH, Brian. 809'.3'876
Who's who in science fiction / [by] Brian Ash. London : Elm Tree Books, 1976. 220 p. ; 23 cm. Bibliography: p. 217-[220] [PN3448.S45A83 1976b] 77-361941 ISBN 0-241-89383-6 : £3.95
1. Science fiction—Bio-bibliography. I. Title. BIP

Science—History.

KULJIAN, Harry A. 500
Universe and its man [by] Harry A. Kuljian. New York, T & T Publishing [1970] 207 p. illus., ports. 25 cm. Bibliography: p. 123. [Q125.K78] 70-96768 7.95
1. Science—History. 2. Scientists—Biography. I. Title.

Science—Social aspects—United States.

GOODELL, Rae. 509'.2'2
The visible scientists / Rae Goodell. 1st ed. Boston : Little, Brown, c1977. viii, 242 p. ; 22 cm. Based on the author's thesis. Includes bibliographical references and index. [Q175.52.U5G66] 77-350 ISBN 0-316-32000-5 : 10.00
1. Science—Social aspects—United States. 2. Technology—Social aspects—United States. 3. Scientists—United States. I. Title.

Scientists.

ANDREW, Warren, 1910- 509.22
One world of science; personal visits to men of research in many lands. iSpringfield, Ill., Thomas [1966] x, 271p. illus., ports. 24cm. (Amer. lect. ser., pubn. no. 650 Amer. lects., in the hist. of med. and sci.) [Q141.A62] 66-14252 8.75
1. Scientists. I. Title.

BIXBY, William. 925
Great experimenters. New York, McKay, 1964. x, 182 p. ports. 21 cm. [Q141.B54] 64-19408
1. Scientists. I. Title.

BURLINGAME, Roger [William Roger Burlingame] 1889- 925
Scientists behind the inventors. New York, Avon [1961, c.1948-1960] 128p. (F-113) Bibl. .40 pap.,
1. Scientists. 2. Inventors. I. Title.

BUSHER, Herbert Henry, M.D. 509.22
Scientific man; meddler, manipulator, or manager of evolution. New York, Fell [c.1966] 191p. 22cm. [Q141.B9] 66-17334 3.50 bds.,
1. Scientists. 2. Science as a profession. I. Title.

CANE, Philip 925
Giants of science. Illus. by Samuel Nisenson. New York, Pyramid [1962, c.1959] 288p., 18cm. (Worlds of sci., WS7) .75 pap.,
1. Scientists. I. Title.

CANE, Philip. 925
Giants of science. Illustrated by Samuel Nisenson. New York, Grosset & Dunlap [1959] 159p. illus., ports., diagrs. 20cm. [Q141.C13] 59-16432
1. Scientists. I. Title.

DREYER, John Louis Emil, 1852-1926 925.2
Tycho Brahe; a picture of scientific life and work in the sixteenth century. New York, Dover [1963] xvi, 405p. illus. 22cm. (T1057) Bibl. 63-19506 2.00 pap.,
I. Brahe, Tyge, 1546-1601. II. Title. **BIP**

GREENE, Jay Elihu, 1914- ed. 925
100 great scientists. Editor, Jay E. Greene. Authors: Murray Bromberg and others special contributors. John J. Carlin and Anne M. Newman. New York, Washington Square Press [1964] xii, 498 p. illus. 18 cm. Includes bibliographies. [Q141.G77] 64-4051
1. Scientists. I. Title.

HOWARD, Arthur Vyvyan. 925
Chambers's dictionary of scientists. New York, Dutton [1951] vi p., 500 columns. ports. 23 cm. [Q141.H69] 51-11762
1. Scientists. I. Title.

HYLANDER, Clarence John, 1897- 920
American scientists; pioneer teachers and specialists, by Clarence J. Hylander. Abridged ed. New York, Macmillan [1968, c1935] viii, 134 p. ports. 21 cm. "The first twelve chapters of the 1935 edition in their entirety." The work and discoveries of sixteen early American scientists including Benjamin Franklin, John James Audubon, Louis Agassiz, Luther Burbank and others. [Q141.H9 1968] AC 68
1. Scientists. I. Title.

MCGRAW-HILL encyclopedia of science and technology. 509.22
McGraw-Hill modern men of science, 426 leading contemporary scientists, presented by the editors of the McGraw-Hill encyclopedia of science and technology. New York, McGraw-Hill [1966-68] 2 v. illus., ports. 27 cm. Subtitle varies slightly in v. 2. [Q141.M15] 66-14808
1. Scientists. I. Title. II. Title: Modern men of science.

MCGRAW-HILL modern men of science; 509.22 426 leading contemporary scientists, presented by the eds. of the McGraw-Hill encyclopedia of science and technology. New York, McGraw. v. illus., ports. 26cm. Ed.-in-chief, v. 1 J. E. Greene; v. 2. W. H. Crouse. Subtitle varies: v. 2- 420 more leading contemporary scientists. V. 2. carries table of contents for both vs. [Q141.M15] 66-14808 19.50
1. Scientists. I. Greene, Jay Elihu, 1914- ed. II. Crouse, William H. ed. III. Title: Modern men of science.

MAKERS of modern science; 925
a twentieth century library trilogy. New York, Scribner, 1953. 124, 132 134 p. illus. 22 cm. (Twentieth century library) Contents.Contents—Charles Darwin, by P. B. Sears.—Sigmund Freud, by G. Zilboorg.—Albert Einstein, by L. Infeld. Includes bibliographies. [Q141.M24] 53-6238
1. Scientists. I. Sears, Paul Bigelow, 1891- Charles Darwin. II. Zilboorg, Gregory, 1890- Sigmund Freud. III. Infeld, Leopold, 1898- Albert Einstein.

NEWTON, Isaac, Sir 1642-1727 925.3
Correspondence, v. 3. Ed. by H. W. Turnbull. [New York] Cambridge Publisjed for the Royal Society. [c.]1961[ ] 445p. illus. 29cm. Contents.v. 3. 1688-1694. Bibl. 59-65134 25.00
1. Scientists—Correspondence, reminscences, etc. I. Turnbull, Herbert Western, 1885- ed. II. Title.

NEWTON, Isaac, Sir 1642-1727. 925.3
Correspondence, Edited by H. W. Turnbull. Cambridge [Eng.] Published for the Royal Society at the University Press,

1959- v. illus., port., facsims. 29cm. Includes bibliographical references. Contents.v. 1. 1661-1675. [QC16.N7A4] 59-65134
1. Scientists—Correspondence, reminiscences, etc. I. Turnbull, Herbert Westren, 1885- ed. II. Title.

NEWTON, Issac, Sir 1642-1727 925.3
Correspondence. Ed. by H. W. Turnbull Cambridge [Eng.] Pub. for the Royal Soc. at the Univ. Pr., [1967] v. illus., port., facsims. 29cm. Contents.v.4 1694-1709, ed. by J. F. Scott. [QC16.N7A4] 59-65134 38.50
1. Scientists — Correspondence, reminiscences, etc. I. turbull, Herbert Western, 1885- ed. II. Title.

PAYNE, Alma Smith. 509
Partners in science. Illustrated by Polly Bolian. Cleveland, World Pub. Co. [1968] 224 p. illus., ports. 21 cm. Includes bibliographies. Eight examples from different fields of science of men and women who worked together, as brother and sister, father and daughter, or man and wife, to contribute to scientific knowledge. Includes the Curies, the Herschels, the Szent-Gyorgyis, the Wrights, and others. [Q141.P39] AC 68
1. Scientists. I. Bolian, Polly, illus. II. Title.

SCHNITTKIND, Henry Thomas, 1888- 925
Living biographies of great scientists, by Henry Thomas [pseud.]and Dana Lee Thomas [pseud.] Garden City, N.Y., Perma Giants [1950, c1941] viii, 314 p. 22 cm. [Q141.S3 1950] 51-20939
1. Scientists. I. Schnittkind, Dana Arnold, 1918- joint author. II. Title.

SCIENTIFIC American. 925
Lives in science. New York, Simon and Schuster [1957] 274p. illus. 20cm. Includes bibliography. [Q141.S37] 57-7950
1. Scientists. I. Title. **BIP**

SCIENTIFIC American. v. 12
Lives in science. New York, Simon and Schuster [1963, c1957] xiv, 273 p. illus. (A scientific American book; an Essandess paperback) Bibliography: p. 270-273. 66-49697
1. Scientists. I. Title.

SIEDEL, Frank. 920
Pioneers in science [by] Frank and James M. Siedel. Introd. by Leonard Carmichael. Boston, Houghton Mifflin [1968] 160 p. ports. 27 cm. Bibliography: p. 154-158. Brief sketches of the lives and principal achievements of important scientists from the time of Aristotle to the present day. [Q141.S48] AC 68
1. Scientists. I. Siedel, James M., joint author. II. Gorka, Ted, illus. III. Sorisky, Michael, illus. IV. Title.

STEVENS, William Oliver, 1878- 925
Famous men of science; illustrated with photos. New York, Dodd, Mead, 1952. 164 p. illus. 23 cm. (Famous biographies for young people) [Q141.S78] 52-8988
1. Scientists. I. Title.

SULLIVAN, Navin 920
Pioneer germ fighters. Illus. by Eric Fraser. New York, Atheneum [c.]1962. 164p. 24cm. Bibl. 62-10255 3.75
1. Scientists—Juvenile literature. 2. Bacteriologists—Juvenile literaure. I. Title. II. Title: Germ fighters.

SULLIVAN, Navin 920
Pioneer germ fighters. Illus. by Eric Fraser. New York, Scholastic [1963, c.1962] 122p. illus. 20cm. (TX449) Bibl. .35 pap.,
1. Scientists—Juvenile literature. 2. Bacteriologists—Juvenile literature. I. Title. II. Title: Germ fighters.

SULLIVAN, Navin. j920
Pioneer germ fighters. Illustrated by Eric Fraser. [1st ed.] New York, Atheneum, 1962. 164 p. illus. 24 cm. Includes bibliography. [Q141.S83] 62-10255
1. Scientist—Juvenile literature. 2. Bacteriologists—Juvenile literature. I. Title.

THOMAS, Henry, 1886- 925
Living biographies of great scientists, by Henry Thomas and Dana Lee Thomas. Garden City, N.Y., Garden City Books [1959] 314 p. 22 cm. [Q141.S3 1959] 59-2816
1. Scientists. I. Title.

Scientists, American.

NATIONAL Academy of Sciences, Washington, D. C. 925
Biographical memoirs. v. 39. Washington, 1967- v. ports. 24cm. [Q141.N2] 5-26629 5.00
1. Scientists, American. I. Title.
Currently published for them by Columbia Univ. Pr., New York.

YOST, Edna, 1889- 926
Modern Americans in science and technology. New York, Dodd, Mead [1962] 175 p. illus. 21 cm. (Makers of our modern world books) Revision, with additions, of the work first published in 1941 under title: Modern Americans in science and invention. [Q141.Y64] 62-20016
1. Scientists, American. 2. Investors. I. Title.

Scientists, American—Direct.

AMERICAN men of science: 925
a biographical directory. 11th ed. New York, Bowker. 1967. v. 28cm. [Q141.A47] 6-7326 25.00
1. Scientists, American—Direct. I. Cattell (Jaques) Press, Tempe, Ariz.
Contents Omitted.

AMERICAN men of science: 925
a biographical dictionary. 11th ed. New York, Bowker, 1967. v. 28cm. Contents.v. 4. L-O: physical and biological sciences [Q141.A47] 6-7326 25.00
1. Scientists —American—Direct. I. Cattell (Jaques) Press, Tempe, Ariz.

AMERICAN men of science: 925
a biographical directory; supplement 1. Ed. by the Jaques Cattell Pr. 11th ed. New York, Bowker, 1966. x, 154p. 28cm. [Q141.A47] 6-7326 10.00 pap.,
1. Scientists, American—Direct. I. Cattell, (Jaques) Press, Tempe, Ariz.
Contents omitted.

AMERICAN men of science; 925
a biographical directory. 11th ed. New York, Bowker, 1967. v. 28cm. Ed. 196- by the Jaques Cattell Pr. Tempe, Ariz. [Q141.A47] 6-7326 Suppl. 2, 15.00; Suppl. 3, pap., 15.00
1. Scientists—American —Direct. I. Cattell (Jaques) Press, Tempe, Ariz.
Contents omitted.

AMERICAN men of science: 925
a biographical directory [v.3] 11th ed. Ed. by the Jaques Cattell Pr. New York, Bowker [c.]1966. x, 2015-2956p. 29cm. Contents.v.3. The physical and biological sciences. H-K. [Q141.A47] 6-7326 25.00
1. Scientists, American—Direct. I. Cattell (Jaques) Press, Tempe, Ariz.

AMERICAN men of science; 925
a biographical directory. 11th ed. New York, Bowker, 1968. v. 29cm. Ed. 1968 Jaques Cattell Pr., Tempe, Ariz. [Q141.A47] 6-7326 20.00
1. Scientists, American—Direct. I. Cattell (Jaques) Press, Tempe, Ariz. II. Bowker (R. R.) Company, firm, publishers, New York.
Contents Omitted.

AMERICAN men of science: 925
a biographical directory [v. 1-2] 11th ed. Ed. by the Jaques Cattell Pr. New York, Bowker [c.]1965. 2v. (x, x, 2013p.) 29cm. Contents.v.1-2gThe physical and biological sciences. [Q141.A47] 6-7326 25.00ea.,
1. Scientists, American—Direct. I. Cattell (Jacques) Press, Tempe, Ariz. II. .1. A-C—v.2. D-G.

AMERICAN men of science: 925
a biographical directory. 11th ed. New York, Bowker, 1967. v. 28cm. Ed. 196- Jaques Cattell Pr., Tempe, Ariz. kv.5. P-Sr: physical and biological sciences. [Q141.A47] 6-7326 25.00
1. Scientists—American—Direct. I. Cattell (Jaques) Press, Tempe, Ariz. II. Boker (R. R.) Company, firm, publishers, New York.

AMERICAN men of science; 925
a biographical dictionary;v.4, supplement 2. 11th ed. New York, Bowker, 1967. v. 28cm. Contents.v.4. The physical and biological sciences Suppl. 2. cumulates data in Supplement 1, and provides new info. on A-G and some late H-K biogs [Q141.A47] 6-7326 15.00
1. Scientists—American—Direct. I. Cattell, (Jaques) Press, Tempe, Ariz.

AMERICAN men of science; 925
a biographical dictonary. Tempe, Ariz. Jaques Cattell Pr. v. 26-29cm. Orig. pub. by Science Pr., Lancaster, Pa. in 1906. Ed. by the Jaques Cattell Pr. Orig. issued in 3 vols. [Q141.A47] 6-7326 25.00 2 v., ea.,
1. Scientists, American—Direct. I. Cattell, James McKeen, 1860-1944, ed. II. Cattell, Jaques, 1902- ed.
Order from Bowker, New York.

AMERICAN men of science; 925
a biographical directory, ed. by Jaques Cattell. 10th ed. Tempe, Arizona, Jaques Cattell Pub. Co., Arizona State University, Annex 15 [c.]1960. p.1127-2284. 29cm. Editor: 1960-38, J. McK. Cattell (with D. R. Brimhall, 1921, J. Cattell, 1927-38)--1944- J. Cattell. Beginning with 9th ed., issued in 3 volumes: v.1. Physical sciences v.2. Biologigal sciences v.3. Social sciences. Contents of this volume--The physical and biological sciences, F-K. 6-7326 25.00 buck.,
1. Scientists, American—Direct. I. Cattell, James McKeen, 1860-1944, ed. II. Cattell, Jaques, 1904- ed.

Scientists—Biographies.

ARAGO, Dominique Francois Jean, 1786-1853. 509'.22 B
Biographies of distinguished scientific men. Translated by W. H. Smyth, Baden Powell and Robert Grant. Freeport, N.Y., Books for Libraries Press [1972] 2 v. 23 cm. (Essay index reprint series) Reprint of the 1859 ed. Contents.Contents.—1st ser. The history of my youth.—Bailly.—Herschel.—Laplace.—Joseph Fourier. 2d ser. Carnot.—Malus.—Frensel.—Thomas Young.—James Watt. [Q141.A65 1972] 72-39662 ISBN 0-8369-2737-0
1. Scientists—Biographies. I. Title. **BIP**

Scientists—Biography.

ASIMOV, Isaac, 1920- 925
Asimov's biographical encyclopedia of science and technology; the living stories of more than 1000 great scientists from the age of Greece to the space age,

chronologically arranged. [1st ed.] Garden City, Doubleday, 1964. x, 662 p. ports. 25 cm. [Q141.A74] 64-16199
1. Scientists—Biography. I. Title: Biographical encyclopedia of science and technology. BIP

ASIMOV, Isaac, 1920- 509'.2'2 B
Asimov's biographical encyclopedia of science and technology; the lives and achievements of 1195 great scientists from ancient times to the present, chronologically arranged. New rev. ed. Garden City, N.Y., Doubleday, 1972. xxviii, 805 p. ports. 24 cm. [Q141.A74 1972] 78-139003 12.95
1. Scientists—Biography. I. Title: Biographical encyclopedia of science and technology.

BOLTON, Sarah Elizabeth Mary 925
(Knowele 1841-1916.
Famous men of science. T0)rev. by Barbara Lovett Cline. tFamous men of science. Rev. by Barbara Lovett Cline. c326p. 61-6133 3.50
1. Scientists—Biog. I. Title.

BOLTON, Sarah (Knowles) 1841- 925
1916.
Famous men of science. Rev. by Barbara Lovett Cline. [4th ed.] New York, Crowell [1961, c1960] 326p. 21cm. [Q141.B7 1961] 61-6133
1. Scientists—Biog. I. Title.

BRIDGES, Thomas Charles, 509'.22
1868-
Master minds of modern science, by T. C. Bridges and H. Hessell Tiltman. Freeport, N.Y., Books for Libraries Press [1969] 278 p. illus., ports. 23 cm. (Essay index reprint series.) Reprint of the 1931 ed. [Q141.B83 1969] 68-57307
1. Scientists—Biography. I. Tiltman, Hubert Hessell, 1897- joint author. II. Title. BIP

DEFRIES, Amelia 509'.22 B
Dorothy, 1882-
Pioneers of science; seven pictures of struggle and victory. Freeport, N.Y., Books for Libraries Press [1970] 189 p. illus. 22 cm. (Essay index reprint series) Reprint of the 1928 ed. Contents.Contents.—Sir Jagadis Bose, F.R.S.—Patrick Geddes.—Victor Branford, M.A.—Nicholas Roerich.—Sir Francis Bacon, Viscount Verulam.—Sir Humphrey Davy, F.R.S.—Michael Faraday, F.R.S. Includes bibliographical references. [Q141.D37 1970] 74-117782
1. Scientists—Biography. I. Title.

GUMPERT, Martin, 1897- 509'.22
1955.
Trail-blazers of science; life stories of some half-forgotten pioneers of modern research. Translated from the German by Edwin L. Shuman. Freeport, N.Y., Books for Libraries Press [1968] viii, 306 p. 22 cm. (Essay index reprint series) Reprint of the 1936 ed. Translation of Das leben fur die idee. Bibliographical footnotes. [Q141.G94 1968] 68-29212
1. Scientists—Biography. 2. Science—History. I. Title. BIP

HALACY, Daniel Stephen, 1919- 920
They gave their names to science, by D. S. Halacy, Jr. New York, Putnam [1967] 159 p. facsims., ports. 21 cm. Brief sketches of ten men who developed important scientific theories and inventions: Ernst Mach and his number, Gergor Mendel and his laws, Christian Johann Doppler and his number, Gregor Mendel and his laws, Christian Johann Doppler and his effect, Hans Geiger and his radiation counter, Nicholas Sadi Carnot and thermodynamics, Gustave, Gaspard de Coriolis and his force, Andrija Mohorovicic and the Moho, James Van Allen and the radiation belts, Rudolph Mossbauer and nuclear resonance, Alfred Noble and his prize. [Q141.H22] AC 67
1. Scientists—Biography. I. Title.

HAMMOND, D. B. 509'.22 B
Stories of scientific discovery, by D. B. Hammond. Freeport, N.Y., Books for Libraries Press [1969] vii, 199 p. ports. 23 cm. (Essay index reprint series) Reprint of the 1923 ed. Contents.Contents.—Priestley and Lavoisier and the chemical revolution.—The life and adventures of Benjamin Thompson, Count Rumford.—William Herschel and the discovery of the planet Uranus.—Fabre, poet of science.—Faraday and his electrical discoveries.—The Curies and the discovery of radium.—Darwin and Wallace and the evolutionary theory.—Pasteur and his work on germs and inoculations. [Q141.H25 1969] 74-76901
1. Scientists—Biography. 2. Science—History. I. Title. BIP

HART, Ivor Blashka, 1889- 509'.22
Makers of science; mathematics, physics, astronomy, by Ivor B. Hart. With an introd. by Charles Singer. Freeport, N.Y., Books for Libraries Press [1968] 320 p. illus., maps, ports. 22 cm. (Essay index reprint series) Reprint of the 1923 ed. Bibliography: p. [315]-316. [Q141.H3 1968] 68-8469
1. Scientists—Biography. 2. Science—History. I. Title.

JONES, Bessie Judith 509.22
(Zaban) ed.
The golden age of science; thirty portraits of the giants of 19th-century science, by their scientific contemporaries. Ed. by Bessie Zaban Jones, introd. by Everett Mendelsohn. New York, S. & S. in coop. with the Smithsonian Instn., Washington [c.1966] xxx, iii,, 659p. 22cm. Bibl. [Q141.J68] 66-20254 12.00
1. Scientists— Biog. I. Title.

JONES, Bessie Judity 509.22
(Zaban) ed.
The golden age of science; thirty portraits of the giants of 19th-century science, by their scientific contemporaries. Edited by Bessie Zaban Jones, with an introd. by Everett Mendelsohn. New York, Simon and Schuster, in cooperation with the Smithsonian Institution, Washington [c1966] xxx, iii, 659 p. 22 cm. Bibliographical footnotes. [Q141.J68] 66-20254
1. Scientists—Biog. I. Title.

LATE seventeenth century 509'.22
scientists. Editor: Donald Hutchings. [1st ed.] Oxford, New York, Pergamon Press [1969] xi, 183 p. illus. 21 cm. (The Commonwealth and international library. Education and education research) Contents.Contents.—Robert Boyle, 1627-1691, by D. C. Firth.—Marcello Malpighi, 1628-1694, by J. S. Wilkie.—Christopher Wren, 1632-1723, by A. J. Pacey.—Christiaan Huygens, 1629-1695, by D. E. Newbold.—Robert Hooke, 1635-1703, by D. C. Goodman.—Isaac Newton, 1642-1727, by D. W. Hutchings. Includes bibliographies. [Q141.L37 1969] 68-57233 ISBN 0-08-013359-2
1. Scientists—Biography. I. Hutchings, Donald William, ed. BIP

LENARD, Philipp Eduard 509'.22 B
Anton, 1862-1947.
Great men of science; a history of scientific progress. Translated from the 2d German ed. by H. Stafford Hatfield, with a pref. by E. N. da C. Andrade. Freeport, N.Y., Books for Libraries Press [1970] xx, 389 p. ports. 23 cm. (Essay index reprint series) Reprint of the 1933 ed. Translation of Grosse naturforscher. Includes bibliographical references. [Q141.L62 1970] 74-105026
1. Scientists—Biography. 2. Science—History. I. Title. BIP

MCSPADDEN, Joseph Walker, 925
1874-
How they blazed the way; Men who have advanced civilization. New York; Dodd, Mead, 1960[c.1939, 1960] 284p. illus. 60-50230 4.00
1. Scientists—Biog. 2. Inventors. I. Title.

MID-NINETEENTH-CENTURY 509'.22 B
scientists. Edited by John North. [1st ed.] Oxford, New York, Pergamon Press [1969] x, 190 p. illus. 20 cm. (Science and society, v. 4) (The Commonwealth and international library. Liberal studies division.) Contents.Contents.—Charles Babbage, by D. Nudds.—Charles Darwin, by J. North.—James Prescott Joule, by R. Fox.—Hugh Powell, James Smith and Andrew Ross; makers of microscopes, by G. Turner.—Joseph Lister, by E. Best.—W. H. Perkin, by D. Veal. [Q141.M43 1969] 68-55957
1. Scientists—Biography. I. North, John David, ed.

OLBY, Robert Cecil, ed. 509.22
Late eighteenth century European scientists, edited by R. C. Olby. [1st ed.] Oxford, New York, Pergamon Press [1966] 209 p. illus. 20 cm. (The Commonwealth and international library. Liberal studies division. Science and society, v. 2) [Q141.O4 1966] 66-23853
1. Scientists—Biography. I. Title.

SIEDEL, Frank. 509'.22
Pioneers in science [by] Frank and James M. Siedel. Introd. by Leonard Carmichael. Boston, Houghton Mifflin [1968] 160 p. ports. 27 cm. Bibliography: p. 154-158. [Q141.S48] 67-25974
1. Scientists—Biography. I. Siedel, James M., joint author. II. Title.

WALSH, James Joseph, 509'.22
1865-1942.
Catholic churchmen in science; sketches of the lives of Catholic ecclesiastics who were among the great founders in science. 1st-ser. Freeport, N. Y., Books for Libraries Press [1966- v. 1, 1968] v. ports. 19-22 cm. (Essay index reprint series) Reprint of the 1906-17 ed. [Q141.W24] 67-22126
1. Scientists—Biog. 2. Religion and science—1900-1925. 3. Catholics. I. Title.

WALSH, James Joseph, 509'.22
1865-1942.
Catholic churchmen in science; sketches of the lives of Catholic ecclesiastics who were among the great founders in science. 1st-ser. Freeport, N.Y., Books for Libraries Press [1966- ; v. 1, 1968] v. ports. 19-22 cm. (Essay index reprint series) Reprint of the 1906-17 ed. [Q141.W24] 67-22126
1. Scientists—Biography. 2. Religion and science—1900-1925. 3. Catholics. I. Title.

WALTZ, George H 1906- 925
What makes a scientist? [1st ed.] Garden City, N.Y., Doubleday, 1959. 142 p. illus. 22 cm. Includes bibliography. [Q141.W27] 59-12656
1. Scientists — Biog. I. Title.

WERNER, Vivian L. 509'.22
Scientist versus society / Vivian Werner. New York : Hawthorn Books, c1975. 160 p. ; 22 cm. Includes index. Bibliography: p. 151-153. [Q141.W5 1975] 74-33589 ISBN 0-8015-6586-3 : 6.95
1. Scientists—Biography. 2. Science—Social aspects. I. Title.

WILSON, Grove, 1883- 509'.2'2 B
1954.
The human side of science. Freeport, N.Y., Books for Libraries Press [1972] x, 397 p. illus. 22 cm. (Essay index reprint series) Reprint of the 1929 ed. Bibliography: p. 391-397. [Q141.W65 1972] 72-1286 ISBN 0-8369-2877-6 16.50
1. Scientists—Biography. 2. Science—History. I. Title. BIP

Scientists—Biography—Dictionaries.

DICTIONARY of 509'.22 B
scientific biography. Charles Coulston Gillispie, editor-in-chief. New York, Scribner [1970- v. illus. 29 cm. "Published under the auspices of the American Council of Learned Societies." Includes bibliographies. [Q141.D5] 69-18090 ISBN 0-684-10114-9 (v. 3) 35.00 per vol.
1. Scientists—Biography—Dictionaries. I. Gillispie, Charles Coulston, ed. II. American Council of Learned Societies Devoted to Humanistic Studies. BIP

WILLIAMS, Trevor 509'.22 B
Illtyd.
A biographical dictionary of scientists, edited by Trevor I. Williams. [New York] Wiley-Interscience [1969] xi, 592 p. 25 cm. [Q141.W62 1969b] 69-19757
1. Scientists—Biography—Dictionaries. I. Title.

WILLIAMS, Trevor 509'.2'2 B
Illtyd.
A biographical dictionary of scientists, edited by Trevor I. Williams. Assistant editor: Sonia Withers. 2d ed. New York, Wiley [1974] xv, 641 p. 25 cm. "A Halsted Press book." [Q141.W62 1974] 74-12374 ISBN 0-470-94681-4 17.95
1. Scientists—Biography—Dictionaries. I. Title.

Scientists—Biography—Directories.

WORLD who's who in 509'.22
science: a biographical dictionary of notable scientists from antiquity to the present. Editor: Allen G. Debus. Associate editors: Ronald S. Calinger [and] Edward J. Collins. Managing editor: Stephen J. Kennedy. 1st ed. Chicago, Marquis-Who's Who, inc. [1968] xvi, 1855 p. 28 cm. (Marquis biographical library) Bibliography: p. xi. [Q141.W7] 68-56149 ISBN 0-8379-1001-3
1. Scientists—Biography—Directories. I. Debus, Allen G., ed. II. Marquis-Who's Who, inc.

Scientists—Biography—Juvenile literature.

BETHELL, Jean. JUV
The how and why wonder book of famous scientists. Illustrated by Jo Kotula. Editorial production: Donald D. Wolf. [Deluxe ed.] New York, Grosset & Dunlap [1964] 48 p. illus. (part col) ports. (part col.) 29 cm. "4048." [PZ10.B2952256Ho] 920 64-14934
1. Scientists — Biog. — Juvenile literature. I. Title.

HOLMES, Edward, 509'.2'2
fl.1969-
Great men of science / [authors, Edward Holmes, Christopher Maynard ; editor, Jennifer L. Justice ; ill., Oliver Frey]. New York : Warwick Press, 1979, c1975. 48 p. : ill. (some col.) ; 28 cm. (Modern knowledge library) Includes index. Presents a history of science through the lives and work of scientists from the days of ancient Sumeria and Egypt to the present day. [Q141.H63 1979] 78-68533 ISBN 0-531-09150-3 lib. bdg. : 6.90
1. Scientists—Biography—Juvenile literature. 2. Science—History—Juvenile literature. I. Maynard, Christopher, joint author. II. Justice, Jennifer L. III. Frey, Oliver. IV. Title. BIP

LEIPOLD, L Edmond, 1902- 509'.22
Famous scientists and astronauts, by L. Edmond Leipold. Minneapolis, T. S. Denison [1967] 80 p. 25 cm. (His Famous American heroes and leaders series) [Q141.L52] 67-28677
1. Scientists—Biog.—Juvenile literature. 2. Inventors—Biog.—Juvenile literature. 3. Astronauts—Biog.—Juvenile literature. I. Title.

SOOTIN, Harry 925
12 pioneers of science. New York, Vanguaro Press [c.1960] 254p. illus. Bibl. 60-15074 3.00
1. Scientists—Biog.—Juvenile literature. 2. Science—Juvenile literature. I. Title.

Scientists, British.

HOLMYARD, Eric John, 1891- 925
British scientists. New York, Philosophical Library [1951] 88 p. illus. 19 cm. [Q141.H64 1951a] 51-13955
1. Scientists, British. I. Title.

Scientists—Europe—Biography.

TURKEVICH, John, 1907- 509'.22
Prominent scientists of continental Europe. Compiled by John Turkevich and Ludmilla B. Turkevich. New York, American Elsevier Pub. Co., 1968. 204 p. 27 cm. [Q141.T82] 68-19786 ISBN 0-444-00046-1
1. Scientists—Europe—Biography. 2. Scientists—Europe—Directories. I. Turkevich, Ludmilla Buketoff, joint author. II. Title.

Scientists—Gt. Brit.—Biography.

CROWTHER, James Gerald, 509'.22 B
1899-
Scientific types [by] J. G. Crowther. [Chester Springs, Pa.] Dufour [1970, c1968] 408 p. illus., ports. 23 cm. Bibliography: p. 393-399. [Q141.C715 1970] 76-91453 10.00

1. Scientists—Gt. Brit.—Biography. I. Title.

SOME nineteenth century British scientists. 509'.22 B Edited by R. Harre. [1st ed.] Oxford, New York, Pergamon Press [1969] viii, 259 p. illus., map, port. 20 cm. (The Commonwealth and international library. Liberal studies division. Science and society, v. 5) Contents.Contents.—Sir Charles Wyville Thomson, 1820-1882, and Sir James Murray, 1841-1914; the Challenger Expedition, by L. Leyton.—Arthur Cayley, 1821-1895, by J. North.—Sir Francis Galton, 1822-1910, by R. W. Morgan.—William Thomson, Lord Kelvin, 1824-1907, by C. Watson.—Sir Norman Lockyer, 1836-1920, by J. North.—Sidney Gilchrist Thomas, 1850-1885, by P. Hibbard.—Sir William Ramsay, 1852-1916, by D. Knight. Includes bibliographical references. [Q141.S567 1969] 69-19088
1. Scientists—Gt. Brit.—Biography. I. Harre, Romano, ed.

Scientists—Russia—Biography.

PARRY, Albert, 1901- 509'.2'2 B
The Russian scientist. New York, Macmillan [1973] 196 p. illus. 24 cm. (Russia old and new series) Bibliography: p. 183-186. [Q141.P37] 72-92454 6.95
1. Scientists—Russia—Biography. 2. Science—History—Russia. I. Title. II. Series. **BIP**

Scientists, Russian.

RUBY, Lawrence. v. 12
Who's who in Soviet nuclear science, compiled by Lawrence Ruby and Joan Hurst, March 1960. Berkeley, University of California, Lawrence Radiation Laboratory, 1960. 120 p. 28 cm. (UCRL-9173)
1. Scientists, Russian. I. Hurst, Joan. II. California. University. Lawrence Radiation Laboratory, Livermore. III. Title.

TURKEVICH, John, 1907- 925
Soviet men of science; academicians and corresponding members of the Academy of Sciences of the USSR. With J. Blanshei [others] Princeton, N.J., Van Nostrand [c.1963] 441p. 23cm. 63-24873 12.00
1. Scientists, Russian. I. Title.

TURKEVICH, John, 1907- 509'.2'2
Soviet men of science : academicians and corresponding members of the Academy of Sciences of the USSR / by John Turkevich ; with editorial assistance of J. Blanshei ... [et al.]. Westport, Conn. : Greenwood Press, 1975, c1963. 441 p. ; 22 cm. Reprint of the ed. published by Van Nostrand, Princeton, N.J. Includes bibliographies. [Q141.T83 1975] 75-19267 ISBN 0-8371-8246-8 lib.bdg. : 20.00
1. Scientists—Russia. I. Title.

WHO s who in Soviet science and technology. 925 Comp. by Ina Telberg. [2d ed., rev., enl. by Antania Dimiriev, V. G. Telberg] New York, Telberg, c.1964, vi, 301 1. 28cm. 64-13006 16.00 bds.,
1. Scientists, Ruesian. 2. Techonologists, Russian. I. Telberg, Ina, comp. II. Title: Soviet sicence and technology.

Scientists—United States.

HARRIS, Jonathan. 509'.22 B
Scientists in the shaping of America. Menlo Park, Calif., Addison-Wesley Pub. Co. [1971] 142 p. illus. 21 cm. (Specialized studies in American history series) Bibliography: p. 127-130. [Q141.H293] 76-31011
1. Scientists—United States. 2. Science—History—United States. I. Title.

POOLE, Lynn. 925
Scientists who work with astronauts, by Lynn and Gray Poole. With a foreword by Hugh L. Dryden. New York, Dodd, Mead [1964] xvi, 172 p. ports. 21 cm. (Makers of our modern world books) [Q141.P66] 64-15368
1. Scientists—U.S. 2. U.S. National Aeronautics and Space Administration—Officials and employees. I. Poole, Gray, joint author. II. Title.

Scientists—United States—Biography.

ELLIOTT, Clark A. 509'.2'2 B
Biographical dictionary of American science : the seventeenth through the nineteenth centuries / Clark A. Elliott ; consultant editors, Sally Gregory Kohlstedt ... [et. al.]. Westport, Conn. : Greenwood Press, 1979. xvii, 360 p. ; 29 cm. "A retrospective companion to American men of science." Includes bibliographical references and index. [Q141.E37] 78-4292 ISBN 0-313-20419-5 : 45.00
1. Scientists—United States—Biography. I. American men of science. II. Title. **BIP**

WHO was who in American history-science and technology : 509'.2'2 B a component of who's who in American history. 76 Bicentennial ed. Chicago : Marquis Who's Who, c1976. xiii, 688 p. ; 27 cm. [Q149.U5W5] 76-5763 ISBN 0-8379-3601-2 : 47.50
1. Scientists—United States—Biography. 2. Engineers—United States—Biography. 3. United States—History—20th century. I. Marquis Who's Who, inc.

YOUMANS, William Jay, 1838-1901. 509'.2'2 B
Pioneers of science in America / edited and rev. by William Jay Youmans. New York : Arno Press, 1978 [c1896] p. cm. (Biologists and their world) Reprint of the ed. published by D. Appleton, New York. [Q141.Y67 1978] 77-83845 ISBN 0-405-10743-9 : 35.00
1. Scientists—United States—Biography. I. Title. II. Series.

Scientists—United States—Biography—Juvenile literature.

†EMBERLIN, Diane. 509'.2'2 B
Science / by Diane Emberlin. Minneapolis : Dillon Press, c1977. 158, [1] p. : ill. ; 22 cm. (Contributions of women) Bibliography: p. [1]. Brief biographies of women who have made outstanding contributions to science: Annie Cannon, Lillian Gilbreth, Margaret Mead, Rachel Carson, Ruth Patrick, and Eugenie Clark. [Q141.E43] 920 76-30621 ISBN 0-87518-136-8 : 6.95
1. Scientists—United States—Biography—Juvenile literature. 2. Women scientists—United States—Biography—Juvenile literature. I. Title.

SIGNIFICANT American scientists. 509'.2'2 B Chicago : Childrens Press, [1976] p. cm. Includes index. Brief biographies of 166 American scientists arranged alphabetically within broad chronological periods of American history. [Q141.S485] 920 75-20680 ISBN 0-516-05310-8 : 6.95
1. Scientists—United States—Biography—Juvenile literature. I. Title: Scientists.

Scipio Aemilianus Africanus minor, Publius Cornelius.

ASTIN, A. E. 937'.05'0924 B
Scipio Aemilianus, by A. E. Astin. Oxford, Clarendon P., 1967. xiii, 374 p. diagr. 24 1/2 cm. Bibliography: p. [358]-364. [DG253.S4A8] 67-82263
1. Scipio Aemilianus Africanus minor, Publius Cornelius.

Scipio, Lynn Adolphus,

SCIPIO, Lynn Adolphus, 1876- 926.2
My thirty years in Turkey. Rindge, N. H., R. R. Smith, 1955. 364p. 23cm. [TA140.S35A3] 55-9048
I. Title.

Scobey, Bob, 1916-1963.

†SCOBEY, Jan. 785.06'72'0924 B
Jan Scobey presents He rambled! 'til cancer cut him down : Bob Scobey, Dixieland jazz musician and bandleader, 1916-1963. 1st ed. Northridge, Calif. : Pal Pub., 1976. 344 p. : ill. ; 29 cm. Continued by Cancer? what can you do! Includes index. [ML419.S35S4] 76-54444 ISBN 0-918104-01-7 : 30.00
1. Scobey, Bob, 1916-1963. 2. Jazz musicians—United States—Biography. I. Title. II. Title: He rambled! 'til cancer cut him down.

Scoggins, Thomas Barnes, 1873—

THOMAS Barnes Scoggins, v. 12 a man of fortitude and integrity. Sewanee, Tenn., The University of the South Press, 1958. 145p. plates. 22cm. 'Limited Edition.'
1. Scoggins, Thomas Barnes, 1873— 2. Scoggins family. I. Scoggins, Ethel McWhirter.

Scolnick, Sylvan.

ADLEMAN, Robert H., 1919- 364.1'63'0924 B
Alias Big Cherry: the confessions of a master criminal [by] Robert H. Adleman. New York, Dial Press, 1973. 334 p. 24 cm. [HV6248.S39A4] 73-4751 7.95
1. Scolnick, Sylvan. I. Title.

Scopes, John Thomas.

IPSEN, D. C. 345'.73'0288 B
Eye of the whirlwind: the story of John Scopes [by] D. C. Ipsen. Drawings by Richard Cuffari. [Reading, Mass.] Addison-Wesley [1973] 159 p. illus. 21 cm. "An Addisonian Press book." Recounts the life of John Thomas Scopes and his trial of 1925 which tested the right of a teacher to teach evolution. [KF224.S3I7] 92 72-4777 ISBN 0-201-03172-8 4.25
1. Scopes, John Thomas. 2. Evolution—Juvenile literature. I. Cuffari, Richard, 1925- illus. II. Title.

SCOPES, John Thomas. 343'.3
Center of the storm; memoirs of John T. Scopes [by] John T. Scopes and James Presley. [1st ed.] New York, Holt, Rinehart and Winston [1967] vi, 277 p. 22 cm. [LAW] 66-22204
1. Evolution. I. Presley, James. II. Title.

Scotland—Descr. & trav.

BENJAMIN Franklin in Scotland and Ireland, v. 12 1759 and 1771. Philadelphia, University of Pennsylvania Press; London, Oxford University Press, 1956. 229p. illus. 24cm. (Franklin miscellany, v. 2) 'Notes': p. 211-225.qFranklin, Benjamin, 1706-1790.
1. Scotland—Descr. & trav. 2. Dublin—Descr. I. Nolan, James Bennett, 1877-

Scotland—Biography.

DONALDSON, Gordon. 941'.00992
Who's who in Scottish history [by] Gordon Donaldson and Robert S. Morpeth. New York, Barnes & Noble Books [1973, i.e.1974] xx, 254 p. illus. 23 cm. Includes bibliographical references. [DA758.D66 1973b] 74-180274 ISBN 0-06-491739-8 13.00
1. Scotland—Biography. 2. Scotland—History. I. Morpeth, Robert S., joint author. II. Title. **BIP**

EARNSHAW, John. 914.12'5
Thomas Muir, Scottish martyr; some account of his exile to New South Wales. his adventurous escape in 1796 across the Pacific to California, and thence, by way of New Spain, to France. Cremorne, N.S.W., Stone Copying Co., 1959. 84 p. illus. 26 cm. [CT828.M78E2] 65-66585
I. Title.

KNIGHT, William Angus, 1836-1916. 920'.041
Some nineteenth century Scotsmen; being personal recollections. Edinburgh, Oliphant, Anderson & Ferrier, 1903. [Folcroft, Pa.] Folcroft Library Editions, 1973. p. [CT822.K64 1973] 73-4424 35.00
1. Scotland—Biography. I. Title.

LANG, Theo. 920.041
Great men of Scotland. New York, Roy Publishers [1958?] 128 p. illus. 19 cm. [DA758.L3 1958] 58-7715
1. Scotland—Biography. I. Title.

WATT, Donald Elmslie Robertson. 920'.0411
A biographical dictionary of Scottish graduates to A.D. 1410 / by D. E. R. Watt. Oxford : Clarendon Press, 1977. xlii, 607 p. ; 24 cm. Revision and expansion of the author's thesis, Oxford University. Includes index. [CT813.W37 1977] 78-325348 ISBN 0-19-822447-8 : 66.00
1. Scotland—Biography. I. Title.
Distributed by Oxford University Press, New York, NY **BIP**

Scotland—Church history—Dictionaries.

TOWILL, Edwin Sprott. 274.11
People and places in the story of the Scottish Church / [by] Edwin Sprott Towill ; illustrated by Colin Gibson. Edinburgh : St. Andrew Press, 1976. xix, 99 p. : ill., ports. ; 24 cm. [BR781.T68] 77-367785 ISBN 0-7152-0322-3 : £3.25. pbk.
1. Scotland—Church history—Dictionaries. 2. Christian biography—Scotland. I. Title.

Scotland—History—Mary Stuart, 1542-1567.

MELVILLE, James, Sir, 1535-1617. 941.06
Memoirs of his own life by Sir James Melville of Halhill. M.D.XLIX.-M.D.XCIII. From the original manuscript. Edinburgh, 1827. [New York, AMS Press, 1973] xxviii, 420, xvii p. 24 cm. Edited by T. Thomson. Original ed. issued as no. 18 of Bannatyne Club Publications. [DA785.M532] 74-172724 ISBN 0-404-52718-3 27.00
1. Scotland—History—Mary Stuart, 1542-1567. 2. Scotland—History—James VI, 1567-1625. I. Series: Bannatyne Club, Edinburgh. Publications, no. 18.

Scotland—Kings and rulers.

ANDERSON, Marjorie Ogilvie. 929.7'2
Kings and kingship in early Scotland [by] Marjorie O. Anderson. Totowa, N.J., Rowman and Littlefield [1974] xviii, 310 p. illus. 24 cm. Includes bibliographical references. [DA758.2.A65 1974] 73-8637 ISBN 0-87471-204-1 13.50
1. Scotland—Kings and rulers. 2. Scotland—History—To 1057. I. Title. **BIP**

BINGHAM, Caroline, 1938- 941.1'00992 B
The kings & queens of Scotland / Caroline Bingham. New York : Taplinger Pub. Co., 1976. xi, 182 p., [10] leaves of plates : ill. ; 23 cm. Includes index. Bibliography: p. 171-174. [DA758.2.B56 1976] 75-29950 ISBN 0-8008-4477-7 : 9.95
1. Scotland—Kings and rulers. 2. Scotland—History. I. Title. **BIP**

Scott, Bill, 1898-

GOULD, Ed. 971.1'34 B
The lighthouse philosopher : the adventures of Bill Scott / by Ed Gould. Saanichton, B.C. ; Seattle : Hancock House, c1976. 262 p., [24] leaves of plates : ill. ; 23 cm. [CT310.S36G68] 77-378993 ISBN 0-919654-68-1 : 9.95
1. Scott, Bill, 1898- 2. Intellectuals—Canada—Biography. I. Title.

Scott Co., Ind.—Biography.

†PERRIN, William Henry, d.1892? 920'.0772'183
1889 biographical and historical souvenir, Scott County, Indiana / by W.H. Perrin. Knightstown, Ind. : The Bookmark, 1977. 76 p. in various pagings ; 24 cm. Contains several parts of the work published in 1889 under title: Biographical and historical souvenir for the counties of Clark, Crawford, Harrison, Floyd, Jefferson, Jennings, Scott, and Washington, Indiana. Includes index. [F532.S35P47 1977] 78-103275 3.80
1. Scott Co., Ind.—Biography. 2. Scott Co., Ind.—History. I. Title. II. Title: Biographical and historical souvenir for the counties of Clark, Crawford, Harrison, Floyd, Jefferson, Jennings, Scott, and Washington, Indiana.

Scott Co., Va.—History.

†ADDINGTON, Robert Milford, 1867- 975.5'732
History of Scott County, Virginia / by Robert M. Addington. Baltimore : Regional Pub. Co., 1977. xiv, 364 p. : ill. ; 23 cm. Reprint of the 1932 ed. priv. print. by Kingsport Press, Kingsport, Tenn. Includes index. [F232.S3A3 1977] [f] 76-44246 ISBN 0-8063-8008-X 17.50
1. Scott Co., Va.—History. 2. Scott Co., Va.—Biography. I. Title. BIP

Scott, David, 1806-1849.

SCOTT, William Bell, 1811-1890. 759.941
Memoir of David Scott, R.S.A. : containing his journal in Italy, notes on art, and other papers / by William B. Scott. New York : AMS Press, [1975] p. cm. Reprint of the 1850 ed. published by A. & C. Black, Edinburgh. [ND497.S4S5 1975] 70-144685 ISBN 0-404-05646-6 : 24.50
1. Scott, David, 1806-1849. I. Title.

Scott family.

LOCKHART, Charlotte Sophia (Scott) 1799-1837. 828'.7'09 B
Letters, hitherto unpublished, written by members of Sir Walter Scott's family to their old governess. Edited, with an introd. and notes, by the Warden of Wadham College, Oxford. London, E. G. Richards, 1905. [Folcroft, Pa.] Folcroft Library Editions, 1973. p. "Of the forty-seven letters [to Miss Millar] twenty-eight were written by Charlotte Sophia Scott ... twelve by Anne Scott." [PR5335.L6 1973] 73-4625 ISBN 0-8414-2662-7 (lib. bdg.)
1. Scott family. I. Scott, Anne, 1803-1833. II. Wright-Henderson, Patrick Arkley, 1841-1922, ed. III. Millar, Miss, d. 1860? IV. Title. BIP

SCOTT, George Clytus, 1928- 929'.2'0973
One Scott family history / compiled by George Clytus Scott. Newport Beach, Calif. : Scott, c1976. 118, [7] p., [3] leaves of plates : ill. ; 28 cm. Includes index. Bibliography: p. [120] [CS71.S43 1976] 76-360160
1. Scott family. 2. United States—Genealogy. I. Title.

Scott, George Gilbert, Sir, 1811-1878.

SCOTT, George Gilbert, Sir, 1811-1878. 720'.92'4 B
Personal and professional recollections / by George Gilbert Scott ; edited by his son, G. Gilbert Scott ; with an introd. by John Williams Burgon. New York : Da Capo Press, 1977. xx, 436 p., [1] leaf of plates : port. ; 23 cm. (A Da Capo Press reprint series in architecture and decorative arts) Reprint of the 1879 ed. published by S. Low, Marston, Searle & Rivington, London. [NA997.S4A25 1977] 77-1202 ISBN 0-306-70873-6 : 27.50
1. Scott, George Gilbert, Sir, 1811-1878. 2. Architects—England—Biography. BIP

Scott, Jacob Richardson,

SCOTT, Jacob Richardson, 1815-1861. 922.673
To Thee this temple; the life, diary, and friends of Jacob Richardson Scott, 1815-1861, by Elizabeth Hayward and Roscoe Ellis Scott. Chester, Pa., American Baptist Historical Society, 1955. xiii, 405p. illus., port., facsims. 28cm. From family papers in the possession of the author's grandson, Roscoe Ellis Scott. Bibliography: p.379-380. [BX6495.S39A3] 55-18762
I. Hayward, Elizabeth (McCoy) 1901- ed. II. Scott, Roscoe Ellis, 1887- ed. III. Title.

Scott, John, 1632-1704.

MOWRER, Lilian (Thomson) 920
The indomitable John Scott: citizen of Long Island, 1632-1704. Pref. by Harold Hume. New York, Farrar, Straus and Cudahy [c.1960] xviii, 438p. Bibl.: p.411-428 22cm. 60-12983 6.50
1. Scott, John, 1632-1704. I. Title.

MOWRER, Lilian (Thomson) 920
The indomitable John Scott: citizen of Long Island, 1632-1704. Pref. by Harold Hume. New York, Farrar, Straus and Cudahy [1960] 438p. 22cm. Includes bibliography. [F127.L8S42] 60-12983
1. Scott, John, 1632-1704. I. Title.

MOWRER, Lilian (Thomson) 920
The indomitable John Scott. Scott: citizen of Long Island, 1632-1704. Pref. by Harold Hume. New York, Farrar, Straus and Cudahy [c.1960] xviii, 438p. Bibl.: p.411-1-428 428 22cm. 60-12983 6.50
1. Scott, John, 1632-1704. I. Title.

Scott, Joseph William, 1867-1918.

IVES, Edward D. 784'.092'4 B
Joe Scott, the woodsman-songmaker / Edward D. Ives. Urbana : University of Illinois Press, c1978. p. cm. (Music in American life) Includes index. Bibliography: p. [ML410.S436419] 78-8149 ISBN 0-252-00683-6 : 22.50
1. Scott, Joseph William, 1867-1918. 2. Composers—Maine—Biography. 3. Lumbermen—Maine—Biography. 4. Lumbermen—Songs and music. I. Title.

Scott, Marion duPont.

STRINE, Gerald. 636.1'0092'4 B
Montpelier : the recollections of Marion duPont Scott / as told to Gerald Strine. New York : Scribner, c1976. 219 p. : ill. ; 28 x 36 cm. [SF336.S36S83] 76-45809 ISBN 0-684-14798-X : 50.00
1. Scott, Marion duPont. 2. Horsemen—Virginia—Orange Co.—Biography. 3. Montpelier, Va.—History. I. Title.

Scott, Mary.

SCOTT, Mary, 1888- 828
Days that have been; an autobiography. Auckland, Blackwood & J. Paul, 1966. 207p. illus., map, ports. 23cm. [PR6069.C595Z5] 66-9123 4.50 bds.,
I. Title.
Available from Tri-Ocean. San Francisco.

THOMPSON, Phyllis. 362.8
The midnight patrol : the story of a Salvation Army lass who patrolled the dark streets of London's West End on a midnight mission of mercy / by Phyllis Thompson. U.S. ed. New York : Hawthorn Books, 1975, c1974 155, [2] p. ; 22 cm. Bibliography: p. [157] [HQ358.L8T46 1974b] 75-5031 ISBN 0-8015-5030-0 : 4.95
1. Scott, Mary. 2. Salvation Army. 3. Prostitution London. I. Title.

Scott, Orange,

SCOTT, Orange, 1800-1847. 287'.0924 B
The life of Rev. Orange Scott: In two parts. By Lucius C. Matlack. Freeport, N.Y., Books for Libraries Press, 1971. 307 p. port. 23 cm. (The Black heritage library collection) Reprint of the 1847-48 ed. Each part has special t.p. [BX8495.S37A3 1971] 70-138343 ISBN 0-8369-8735-7
I. Matlack, Lucius C., ed. II. Title. III Series.

Scott, Peter,

SCOTT, Peter, 1909- 925.7
The eye of the wind. Boston, Houghton Mifflin, 1961. 679p. illus. 23cm. Autobiography. [SK17.S27A3] 61-5377
I. Title.

Scott, Robert Falcon, 1868-1912.

BRENT, Peter Ludwig. 919.89'040924 B
Captain Scott and the Antarctic tragedy [by] Peter Brent. New York, Saturday Review Press [1974] 223 p. illus. 26 cm. Bibliography: p. 217. [G875.S35B66 1974b] 73-75732 12.50
1. Scott, Robert Falcon, 1868-1912. I. Title.

HUXLEY, Elspeth Joscelin Grant, 1907- 919.8'9'040924 B
Scott of the Antarctic / Elspeth Huxley. 1st American ed. New York : Atheneum, 1978, c1977. xiv, 303 p., [8] leaves of plates : ill. ; 24 cm. Includes index. Bibliography: [289]-290. [G875.S35H88 1978] 77-23662 ISBN 0-689-10861-3 : 12.95
1. Scott, Robert Falcon, 1868-1912. 2. Explorers—England—Biography. 3. Antarctic regions. I. Title. BIP

LUDLAM, Harry. 919.9040924 (B)
Captain Scott; the full story. London, New York, W. Foulsham [1965] 239 p. illus., maps, ports. 23 cm. [GS75.S35L8] 66-6781
1. Scott, Robert Falcon, 1868-1912. I. Title.

Scott, Robert Falcon, 1868-1912 — Juvenile literature.

BIXBY, William. 919.89'04 B
Robert Scott, Antarctic pioneer. Illustrated with photos. by members of the British Antarctic Expedition and original sketches by Edward A. Wilson. [1st ed.] Philadelphia, Lippincott [1970] 143 p. illus., maps, ports. 21 cm. A biography stressing the Antarctic expeditions of the explorer who lost his life while returning as loser from the race to the South Pole. [G875.S35B5] 92 71-117244 4.50
1. Scott, Robert Falcon, 1868-1912—Juvenile literature. I. Wilson, Edward Adrian, 1872-1912, illus. II. Title.

BRISTOW, Ioan. 919.89'040924 B
A world explorer: Robert Falcon Scott. Illustrated by William Hutchinson. Champaign, Ill., Garrard Pub. Co. [1972] 96 p. illus. (part col.) 24 cm. (World explorer books) A biography of the English explorer who lost his life in the race with Amundsen to the South Pole. [G875.S35B68] 72-182269 ISBN 0-8116-6468-6 2.79
1. Scott, Robert Falcon, 1868-1912—Juvenile literature. I. Hutchinson, William M., illus. II. Title.

WOOD, William Hollingsworth, 1914- j92
The true story of Captain Scott at the South Pole, by Will Holwood [pseud. American ed.] Chicago, Childrens Press [1964] 141 p. col. illus. 23 cm. First published in London in 1954 under title: The true book about Captain Scott. [G875.S35W6] 64-12904
1. Scott, Robert Falcon, 1868-1912 — Juvenile literature. I. Title.

Scott, Robert Lee, 1908—

SCOTT, Robert Lee, 1908- 358.41'3'310924
God is still my co-pilot. With a foreword by Strom Thurmond. Phoenix, Ariz., Augury Press, 1967. x, 276 p. ports. 23 cm. Memoirs. [U53.S37A3] 67-26200
I. Title.

SCOTT, Robert Lee, 1908- 926.2913
Tiger in the sky. New York, Ballantine Books [1959] 142p. 18cm. (Ballantine books, 306K) [TL540.S38A33] 59-10036
I. Title.

SCOTT, Robert Lee, 1908- 358.41'3'310924
God is still my co-pilot. With a foreword by Strom Thurmond. Phoenix, Ariz., Augury Press, 1967. x, 276 p. ports. 23 cm. Memoirs. [U53.S37A3] 67-26200
I. Title.

Scott, Robert Walter, 1929-

ROBERTS, Nancy, 1924- 975.6'04'0924
The Governor. Text by Nancy Roberts. Photos by Bruce Roberts. [1st ed.] Charlotte [N.C.] McNally and Loftin, 1972. 141 p. illus. 32 cm. [F260.S36R6] 72-77736 5.95
1. Scott, Robert Walter, 1929- I. Roberts, Bruce, 1930- II. Title.

Scott, Sheila.

SCOTT, Sheila. 629.13'092'4 B
Barefoot in the sky; an autobiography. Foreword and postscript by Philip K. Chapman. New York, Macmillan [1974, c1973] xv, 256 p. illus. 21 cm. Originally published under title: On top of the world. [TL540.S39A33] 73-8350 ISBN 0-02-608660-3 7.95
1. Scott, Sheila. I. Title.

Scott, Walter Dill, 1869-

JACOBSON, Jacob Zavel, 1900- 923.773
Scott of Northwestern; the life story of a pioneer in psychology and education. Chicago, L. Mariano [1951] 198 p. illus. 22 cm. [LD4045 1920.J3] 51-12199
1. Scott, Walter Dill, 1869- I. Title.

Scott, Walter Lee,

SCOTT, Walter Lee, 1882- 979.5'04'0924 B
Pan bred 'n jerky, by Walter L. Scott. Introd. by E. R. Jackman. Caldwell, Idaho, Caxton Printers, 1968. 174 p. illus., ports. 21 cm. Autobiographical. [CT275.S354A3] 68-15027
I. Title.

Scott, Walter, Sir, bart., 1771-1832.

CLARK, Arthur Melville, 1895- 823'.7
Sir Walter Scott: the formative years. New York, Barnes & Noble, 1970 [c1969] xvi, 322 p. ports. 23 cm. Includes bibliographical references. [PR5332.C5 1970] 70-13566 ISBN 3-89039-705- 8.00
I. Scott, Walter, Sir, Bart., 1771-1832.

DAICHES, David, 1912- 828'.7'09 B
Sir Walter Scott and his world. New York, Viking Press [1971] 143 p. illus., facsims., ports. 24 cm. (A Studio book) Bibliography: p. 129. [PR5332.D3] 75-150356 ISBN 0-670-64725-X 7.95
1. Scott, Walter, Sir, bart., 1771-1832. 2. Scotland—Description and travel. I. Title.

ELTON, Oliver, 1861-1945. 828'.7'09
Sir Walter Scott. [Folcroft, Pa.] Folcroft Library Editions, 1971. 96 p. 24 cm. Reprint of the 1924 ed. [PR5341.E4 1971] 72-193214
1. Scott, Walter, Sir, bart., 1771-1832.

GLEIG, George Robert, 1796-1888. 828'.7'09 B
The life of Sir Walter Scott. [Folcroft, Pa.] Folcroft Library Editions, 1973. viii, 134 p. illus. 24 cm. Reprint of the 1871 ed. published by A. & C. Black, Edinburgh, which was reprinted with corrections and additions from The Quarterly Review. [PR5335.G5 1973] 73-7579
1. Scott, Walter, Sir, bart., 1771-1832. I. Title.

GRIERSON, Herbert John Clifford, Sir, 1866-1960. 828'.7'09 B
Sir Walter Scott, bart. [Folcroft, Pa.] Folcroft Press, 1970. xii, 320 p. port. 24 cm. Reprint of the 1938 ed. Includes bibliographical references. [PR5332.G73 1970] 72-193213
1. Scott, Walter, Sir, bart., 1771-1832.

GRIERSON, Herbert John Clifford, Sir, 1866-1960. 828'.7'09 B
Sir Walter Scott, Bart. New York, Columbia University Press, 1938. [New York, AMS Press, 1973] xii, 320 p. port. 23 cm. Includes bibliographical references. [PR5332.G73 1973] 76-153326 ISBN 0-404-02914-0 12.50
1. Scott, Walter, Sir, bart., 1771-1832.

GWYNN, Stephen Lucius, 1846-1950. 828'.7'09 B
The life of Sir Walter Scott. Freeport, N.Y., Books for Libraries Press [1972] p. Reprint of the 1930 ed. [PR5332.G8 1972] 72-7031 ISBN 0-8369-6939-1
1. Scott, Walter, Sir, bart., 1771-1832.

HUDSON, William Henry, 1862-1918. 828'.7'09 B
Sir Walter Scott. London, Sands, 1901. [Folcroft, Pa.] Folcroft Library Editions, 1972. x, 304 p. port. 24 cm. [PR5332.H7 1972] 72-6573 ISBN 0-8414-0125-X (lib. bdg.)
1. Scott, Walter, Sir, bart., 1771-1832.

JENKS, Tudor, 1857-1922. 828'.7'09
In the days of Scott. [Folcroft, Pa.] Folcroft Library Editions, 1974. p. cm. Reprint of the 1906 ed. published by A. S. Barnes, New York, in series: Lives of great writers. Bibliography: p. [PR5332.J4 1974] 74-13033 ISBN 0-8414-5302-0 (lib. bdg.)
1. Scott, Walter, Sir, bart., 1771-1832. I. Title. II. Series: Lives of great writers.

JOHNSON, Edgar. 828'.7'09
Sir Walter Scott; the great unknown. [New York] Macmillan [1970] 2 v. (xxvi, 1397 p.) illus., plan, ports. 24 cm. Bibliography: v. 2, p. [1339]-1351. [PR5332.J6] 75-84431 20.00
1. Scott, Walter, Sir, Bart., 1771-1832.

MORGAN, Arthur Eustace, 1886- 821'.7
Scott & his poetry, by A. E. Morgan. London, G. G. Harrap, 1912. [New York, AMS Press, 1972] 180, [1] p. port. 19 cm. (Poetry and life series) Bibliography: p. [181] [PR5332.M7 1972] 79-120980 ISBN 0-404-52526-1 8.00
1. Scott, Walter, Sir, Bart., 1771-1832. I. Title. II. Series.

MORGAN, Arthur Eustace, 1886- 821'.7
Scott & his poetry, by A. E. Morgan. [Folcroft, Pa.] Folcroft Press [1969] 180, [1] p. port. 23 cm. Reprint of the 1915 ed., which was issued as no. 12 of the Poetry and life series. Bibliography: p. [181] [PR5332.M7 1969] 72-194972
1. Scott, Walter, Sir, bart., 1771-1832. I. Title. II. Series: Poetry and life series, no. 12. **BIP**

SCHULTZ, Pearle Henriksen. 828'.7'09
Sir Walter Scott: Wizard of the North. New York, Vanguard Press [1967] 212 p. illus., facsim., ports. 24 cm. Bibliography: p. [211]-212. [PR5332.S3 1967] 66-28884
1. Scott, Walter, Sir, bart., 1771-1832. I. Title.

SCOTT, Walter, Sir, bart., 1771-1832. 828'.7'03 B
The journal of Sir Walter Scott. Edited by W. E. K. Anderson. Oxford, Clarendon Press, 1972. xlvi, 812 p. illus. 24 cm. Includes bibliographical references. [PR5334.A2 1972] 72-188235 ISBN 0-19-812438-4 £12.50
I. Anderson, W. E. K., ed. **BIP**

SCOTT, Walter, Sir, Bart., 1771-1832. 828'.7'03 B
The journal of Sir Walter Scott; from the original manuscript at Abbotsford. New York, B. Franklin [1970] 2 v. illus., facsims., fold. map, ports. 23 cm. (Essays in literature and criticism, 82) (Burt Franklin research and source works series, 535.) Reprint of the 1890 ed. Pref. signed: D. D. [i.e. David Douglas] [PR5334.A2 1970] 73-123604
I. Douglas, David, 1823-1916, ed.

SCOTT, Walter, Sir, bart., 1771-1832. 828'.7'09
The letters of Sir Walter Scott. Edited by H. J. C. Grierson. Assisted by Davidson Cook, W. M. Parker and others. London, Constable, 1932-37. [New York, AMS Press, 1971] 12 v. 23 cm. "Centenary edition." Includes bibliographical references. [PR5334.A6 1971] 72-144431 ISBN 0-404-05650-4
I. Grierson, Herbert John Clifford, Sir, 1866- ed. II. Cook, Davidson, 1874-1941, ed. III. Parker, William Mathie, 1891- ed. **BIP**

Scott, Walter, Sir, bart., 1771-1832—Friends and associates.

CROCKETT, William Shillinglaw, 1866-1945. 828'.7'09 B
Sir Walter Scott / by W. S. Crockett and James L. Caw. Norwood, Pa. : Norwood Editions, 1976. p. cm. Reprint of the 1903 ed. published by Hodder and Stoughton, London, in series: The Bookman biographies. [PR5338.C7 1976] 76-4076 ISBN 0-88305-331-4 lib. bdg. : 5.50
1. Scott, Walter, Sir, bart., 1771-1832—Homes and haunts. 2. Scott, Walter, Sir, bart., 1771-1832—Portraits, etc. I. Caw, James Lewis, Sir, 1864-1950, joint author. II. Series: The Bookman biographies.

FRASER, George M., 1862- 828'.7'09 B
Sir Walter Scott and the Aberdonians / by G. M. Fraser. Folcroft, Pa. : Folcroft Library Editions, 1976. p. cm. Reprint of the 1908 ed. published by W. Smith, Aberdeen. [PR5338.F7 1976] 76-44855 ISBN 0-8414-4182-0 lib. bdg. : 8.50
1. Scott, Walter, Sir, bart., 1771-1832—Friends and associates. 2. Lockhart, John Gibson, 1794-1854. Life of Sir Walter Scott. 3. Novelists, Scottish—Biography. 4. Aberdeen, Scot.—Biography. I. Title. **BIP**

Scott, Walter, Sir, bart., 1771-1832.—Homes and haunts.

CROCKETT, William Shillinglaw, 1866-1945. 828'.7'09 B
Sir Walter Scott, by W. S. Crockett and James L. Caw. [Folcroft, Pa.] Folcroft Library Editions, 1973. iv, 44 p. illus. 29 cm. Original ed. issued in series: The Bookman biographies. Contents.Contents.—Crockett, W. S. Sir Walter Scott: some of his homes and haunts.—Caw, J. S. The portraits of Sir Walter Scott.—Biographical note. [PR5338.C7 1973] 72-12503 ISBN 0-8414-0931-5 (lib. bdg.)
1. Scott, Walter, Sir, bart., 1771-1832.—Homes and haunts. 2. Scott, Walter, Sir, bart., 1771-1832.—Portraits, etc. I. Caw, James Lewis, Sir, 1864- II. Title. III. Series: The Bookman biographies.

Scott, Walter, Sir, bart., 1771-1832—Biography.

ALLAN, George, 1806-1835. 828'.7'09 B
Life of Sir Walter Scott, baronet; with critical notices of his writings. [Folcroft, Pa.] Folcroft Library Editions, 1974. p. According to the Edinburgh University Library and British Museum catalogues, this was begun by W. Weir and completed by G. Allan. Reprint of the 1834 ed. published by T. Ireland, Edinburgh. [PR5332.A5 1974] 74-9795 45.00 (lib. bdg.).
1. Scott, Walter, Sir, bart., 1771-1832—Biography. I. Weir, William, 1802-1858. II. Title.

CARSWELL, Donald, 1882-1940. 828'.7'09
Scott and his circle. Freeport, N.Y., Books for Libraries Press [1971] vii, 299 p. ports. 23 cm. Reprint of the 1930 ed. published by Doubleday, Doran, Garden City, N.Y. London ed. (J. Murray, 1930) has title: Sir Walter. Bibliography: p. 297-299. [PR5332.C3 1971] 72-175692 ISBN 0-8369-6607-4
1. Scott, Walter, Sir, bart., 1771-1832—Biography. 2. Authors, English—19th century—Biography. I. Title. **BIP**

CARSWELL, Donald, 1882-1940. 828'.7'09
Sir Walter: a four-part study in biography (Scott, Hogg, Lockhart, Joanna Baillie). New York, Haskell House Publishers, 1971. ix, 292 p. ports. 23 cm. Reprint of the 1930 London ed. American ed. (Garden City, N.Y., Doubleday, Doran, 1930) has title: Scott and his circle. Bibliography: p. 287-289. [PR5332.C3 1971b] 70-176490 ISBN 0-8383-1365-5
1. Scott, Walter, Sir, Bart., 1771-1832—Biography. 2. Authors, English—19th century—Biography. I. Title.

CARSWELL, Donald, 1882-1940. 828'.7'09 B
Sir Walter: a four-part study in biography (Scott, Hogg, Lockhart, Joanna Baillie) [Folcroft, Pa.] Folcroft Library Editions, 1973. p. cm. Reprint of the 1930 ed. published by J. Murray, London; American ed. originally published in 1930 under: Scott and his circle. Bibliography: p. [PR5332.C3 1973] 73-20091 ISBN 0-8414-3532-4 (lib. bdg.)
1. Scott, Walter, Sir, Bart., 1771-1832—Biography. 2. Hogg, James, 1770-1835—Biography. 3. Lockhart, John Gibson, 1794-1854—Biography. 4. Baillie, Joanna, 1762-1851—Biography. I. Title.

CARSWELL, Donald, 1882-1940. 828'.7'09 B
Sir Walter: a four-part study in biography (Scott, Hogg, Lockhart, Joanna Baillie). [Folcroft, Pa.] Folcroft Library Editions, 1974, [i.e.1975] ix, 292 p. illus. 23 cm. Reprint of the 1930 ed. published by J. Murray, London. American ed. has title: Scott and his circle. Bibliography: p. 287-289. [PR5332.C3 1974] 74-984 11.75
1. Scott, Walter, Sir, bart., 1771-1832—Biography. 2. Authors, English—19th century—Biography. I. Title.

[GILLIES, Robert Pearse] 1788-1858. 828'.7'09 B
Recollections of Sir Walter Scott, bart. [Folcroft, Pa.] Folcroft Library Editions, 1973. p. Reprint of the 1837 ed. published by J. Fraser, London. [PR5332.G53 1973] 73-8885 ISBN 0-8414-2040-8
1. Scott, Walter, Sir, bart., 1771-1832—Biography. I. Title. **BIP**

[GILLIES, Robert Pearse] 1788-1858. 828'.7'09 B
Recollections of Sir Walter Scott, bart. [Folcroft, Pa.] Folcroft Library Editions, 1973, [i.e.1974] p. Reprint of the 1837 ed. published by J. Fraser, London. [PR5332.G53 1973] 73-8885 ISBN 0-8414-2040-8 25.00 (lib. bdg.).
1. Scott, Walter, Sir, bart., 1771-1832—Biography. I. Title.

GLEIG, George Robert, 1796-1888. 828'.7'09 B
The life of Sir Walter Scott. [Folcroft, Pa.] Folcroft Library Editions, 1973. viii, 134 p. illus. 24 cm. Reprint of the 1871 ed. published by A. & C. Black, Edinburgh, which was reprinted with corrections and additions from The Quarterly Review. [PR5335.G5 1973] 73-7579 ISBN 0-8414-2034-3 (lib. bdg.)
1. Scott, Walter, Sir, bart., 1771-1832—Biography. I. Title.

GLEIG, George Robert, 1796-1888. 821'.7 B
The life of Sir Walter Scott / by G. R. Gleig. [Norwood, Pa.] : Norwood Editions, 1976. p. cm. Reprint of the 1871 ed. published by A. & C. Black, Edinburgh, which was reprinted with corrections and additions from the Quarterly review. [PR5335.G5 1976] 76-6458 ISBN 0-8482-0859-5 : 15.00
1. Scott, Walter, Sir, bart., 1771-1832—Biography. I. Title.

GRIERSON, Herbert John Clifford, Sir, 1866-1960. 828'.7'09 B
Sir Walter Scott, bart. / by Sir Herbert J. C. Grierson. Norwood, Pa. : Norwood Editions, 1975. p. cm. Reprint of the 1938 ed. published by Columbia University Press, New York. Includes bibliographical references and index. [PR5332.G73 1975] 75-29372 ISBN 0-88305-881-2 : 25.00
1. Scott, Walter, Sir, bart., 1771-1832—Biography. **BIP**

HOGG, James, 1770-1835. 828'.7'09 B
Domestic manners of Sir Walter Scott / by James Hogg ; with Memoir of the Ettrick Shepherd by J. E. H. Thomson. Norwood, Pa. : Norwood Editions, 1975. 124 p. : ill. ; 23 cm. Reprint of the 1909 ed. published by E. MacKay, Stirling. Includes index. [PR5335.H58 1975] 75-31972 ISBN 0-88305-269-5 : 20.00
1. Scott, Walter, Sir, bart., 1771-1832—Biography. 2. Hogg, James, 1770-1835—Biography. I. Thomson, John Ebenezer Honeyman, 1841-1923. Memoir of the Ettrick Shepherd. 1975. II. Title. **BIP**

HUTTON, Richard Holt, 1826-1897. 828'.7'09 B
Sir Walter Scott. [Folcroft, Pa.] Folcroft Library Editions, 1973. p. Reprint of the 1909 ed. published by Macmillan, London, in series: English men of letters. [PR5332.H8 1973] 73-11307 12.00
1. Scott, Walter, Sir, bart., 1771-1832—Biography.

HUTTON, Richard Holt, 1826-1897. 821'.7 B
Sir Walter Scott. New York, AMS Press [1968] viii, 177 p. 22 cm. (English men of letters) Abridged from Lockhart's Life of Walter Scott, Edinburgh, 1839. Bibliographical footnotes. [PR5332.H8 1968] 68-58381
1. Scott, Walter, Sir, Bart., 1771-1832—Biography. I. Lockhart, John Gibson, 1794-1854.

IRVING, Washington, 1783-1859. 818'.2'07
The Crayon miscellany. New York, Putnam. [New York, AMS Press, 1973] 459 p. illus. 18 cm. (The works of Washington Irving, v. 8) At head of title: Hudson edition. "The author's revised edition." Reprint of the 1889 ed. [PS2060.A1 1973] 73-8784 ISBN 0-404-03518-3 20.00
1. Scott, Walter, Sir, bart., 1771-1832—Biography. 2. Byron, George Gordon Noel Byron, baron, 1788-1824. 3. The West—Description and travel—To 1848. I. Title.

THE life of Sir Walter Scott. v. 12
Introduction by W. M. Parker. New York, Dutton [1957] xvi, 675p. (Everyman's library. Biography, 39) 'First published in this edition 1906; reprinted 1957.' Bibliography: p. xvi.
1. Scott, Sir Walter, bart., 1771-1832. I. Lockhart, John Gibson, 1794-1854.

NORGATE, Gerald Le Grys, 1866- 821'.7 B
The life of Sir Walter Scott / by G. Le Grys Norgate. New York : Haskell House Publishers, 1974. viii, 365 p. : ill. ; 22 cm. Reprint of the 1906 ed. published by Methuen, London. Includes index. [PR5332.N6 1974] 74-30271 ISBN 0-8383-1927-0 : 21.95
1. Scott, Walter, Sir, bart., 1771-1832—Biography. I. Title.

NORGATE, Gerald Le Grys, 1866- 828'.7'09 B
The life of Sir Walter Scott, by G. Le Grys Norgate. With 53 illus. by Jenny Wylie. [Folcroft, Pa.] Folcroft Library Editions, 1973. p. cm. Reprint of the 1906 ed. published by Methuen, London. [PR5332.N6 1973] 73-18308 30.00
1. Scott, Walter, Sir, bart., 1771-1832—Biography. I. Title. BIP

PALGRAVE, Francis Turner, 1824-1897. 828'.7'09 B
Life of Sir Walter Scott, with remarks upon his writings. With an essay on Scott, by David Masson, and Dryburgh Abbey: a poem [by Charles Swain] [Folcroft, Pa.] Folcroft Library Editions, 1973. p. At head of title: A centennial offering, 1771-1871. Reprint of the 1871 ed. published by Porter & Coates, Philadelphia. [PR5335.P3 1973] 73-13530 ISBN 0-8414-6710-2 (lib. bdg.)
1. Scott, Walter, Sir, bart., 1771-1832—Biography. I. Masson, David, 1822-1907. II. Swain, Charles, 1801-1874. Dryburgh Abbey. 1973. III. Title.

PALGRAVE, Francis Turner, 1824-1897. 828'.7'09
Life of Sir Walter Scott : with remarks upon his writings / by Francis Turner Palgrave ; with an essay on Scott by David Masson ; and Dryburgh Abbey, a poem, by Charles Swain. Norwood, Pa. : Norwood Editions, 1976. p. cm. At head of title: A centennial offering, 1771-1871. Reprint of the 1871 ed. published by Porter & Coates, Philadelphia. [PR5335.P3 1976] 76-10192 ISBN 0-8482-2075-7 : 12.50
1. Scott, Walter, Sir, bart., 1771-1832—Biography. I. Masson, David, 1822-1907. II. Swain, Charles, 1801-1874 Dryburgh Abbey. 1976. III. Title.

PEARSON, Hesketh, 1887- 928.2
Sir Walter Scott, his life and personality. New York, Harper [1954] 295p. illus. 22cm. London ed. (Methuen) has title: Walter Scott, his life and personality. [PR5332.P4 1954a] 54-8982
1. Scott, Walter, Bart, Sir 1771-1832. I. Title.

SCOTT, Walter, Sir, bart., 1771-1832. 828'.7'09 B
Some unpublished letters of Sir Walter Scott, from the collection in the Brotherton library, compiled by J. Alexander Symington. [Folcroft, Pa.] Folcroft Library Editions, 1973. p. Reprint of the 1932 ed. published by B. Blackwell, Oxford, in series: Brotherton library publications. Bibliography: p. [PR5334.A68 1973] 73-11308 5.00
1. Scott, Walter, Sir, bart., 1771-1832—Biography. I. Symington, John Alexander, ed. II. Title. III. Series: Leeds, Eng. University. Brotherton library. Brotherton library publications.

WOOD, James, Rev. 828'.7'09 B
The life of Sir Walter Scott, bart.; a sketch. [Folcroft, Pa.] Folcroft Library Editions, 1973. p. Reprint of the 1886 ed. published by Ballantyne, Hanson, Edinburgh. [PR5332.W6 1973] 73-14866 6.50
1. Scott, Walter, Sir, bart., 1771-1832—Biography. I. Title.

WRIGHT, Sydney Fowler, 1874- 828'.7'09
The life of Sir Walter Scott, by S. Fowler Wright. New York, Haskell House, 1971. 739 p. 23 cm. Reprint of the 1932 ed. [PR5332.W7 1971] 70-176493 ISBN 0-8383-1361-2
1. Scott, Walter, Sir, bart., 1771-1832—Biography.

WRIGHT, Sydney Fowler, 1874-1967. 821'.7 B
The life of Sir Walter Scott. 1st ed. [Folcroft, Pa.] Folcroft Library Editions, 1973. 739 p. 21 cm. Reprint of the 1932 ed. published by the Poetry League, London, in 1932. [PR5332.W7 1973] 73-18341 29.75
1. Scott, Walter, Sir, bart., 1771-1832—Biography. I. Title.

WRIGHT, Sydney Fowler, 1874-1967. 821'.7 B
The life of Sir Walter Scott. 1st ed. [Folcroft, Pa.] Folcroft Library Editions, 1973. 739 p. 21 cm. Reprint of the 1932 ed. published by the Poetry League, London, in 1932. [PR5332.W7 1973] 73-18341 ISBN 0-8414-9503-3 (lib. bdg.)
1. Scott, Walter, Sir, bart., 1771-1832—Biography. I. Title.

YONGE, Charles Duke, 1812-1891. 828'.7'09 B
Life and writings of Sir Walter Scott. [Folcroft, Pa.] Folcroft Library Editions, 1973. p. Reprint of an undated ed. published by W. Scott Pub. Co., London, New York, in series: Great writers. Also published in 1888 under title: Life of Sir Walter Scott. Bibliography: p. [PR5332.Y6 1973] 73-12872 17.50
1. Scott, Walter, Sir, bart., 1771-1832—Biography.

YONGE, Charles Duke, 1812-1891. 828'.7'09 B
Life of Sir Walter Scott. [Folcroft, Pa.] Folcroft Library Editions, 1974. p. cm. Reprint of the 1888 ed. published by W. Scott, London, in series: Great writers. "Bibliography by John P. Anderson:" p. [PR5332.Y6 1974] 74-14533 17.50 (lib. bdg.).
1. Scott, Walter, Sir, bart., 1771-1832—Biography. I. Anderson, John Parker, 1841- II. Title. BIP

Scott, Walter, Sir, bart., 1771-1832—Correspondence.

SCOTT, Walter, Sir, bart., 1771-1832. 828'.7'09
The letters of Sir Walter Scott. Edited by H. J. C. Grierson. Assisted by Davidson Cook, W. M. Parker and others. London, Constable, 1932-37. [New York, AMS Press, 1971] 12 v. 23 cm. "Centenary edition." Contents.Contents.—v. 1. 1787-1807.—v. 2. 1808-1811.—v. 3. 1811-1814.—v. 4. 1815-1817.—v. 5. 1817-1819.—v. 6. 1819-1821.—v. 7. 1821-1823.—v. 8. 1823-1825.—v. 9. 1825-1826.—v. 10. 1826-1828.—v. 11. 1828-1831.—v. 12. 1831-1832, and appendices of early letters. Includes bibliographical references. [PR5334.A6 1971] 72-144431 ISBN 0-404-05650-4
I. Grierson, Herbert John Clifford, Sir, 1866- ed. II. Cook, Davidson, 1874-1941, ed. III. Parker, William Mathie, 1891- ed. BIP

SCOTT, Walter, Sir, bart., 1771-1832. 828'.7'09 B
The letters of Sir Walter Scott and Charles Kirkpatrick Sharpe to Robert Chambers, 1821-45 : with original memoranda of Sir Walter Scott : printed from manuscripts in the possession of C. E. S. Chambers, Edinburgh. Norwood, Pa. : Norwood Editions, 1975. 80 p., [3] leaves of plates : ports. ; 23 cm. Reprint of the 1904 ed. published by W. & R. Chambers, Edinburgh. [PR5334.A6 1975] 75-38749 ISBN 0-88305-949-5 : 15.00
1. Scott, Walter, Sir, bart., 1771-1832—Correspondence. 2. Sharpe, Charles Kirkpatrick, 1781?-1851. 3. Chambers, Robert, 1802-1871—Correspondence. I. Sharpe, Charles Kirkpatrick, 1781?-1851. II. Chambers, Robert, 1802-1871. III. Title. BIP

Scott, Walter, Sir, bart., 1771-1832—Friends and associates.

THE Ballantyne-Lockhart controversy, 1838-1839. 828'.7'09 B New York, Garland Pub. Inc., 1974. 88, 122, 125, 97 p. 22 cm. (The English book trade, 1660-1853) Reprint of Refutation of the mistatements and calumnies contained in Mr Lockhart's Life of Sir Walter Scott, bart., respecting the Messrs Ballantyne, by the trustees and son of the late Mr James Ballantyne, first published in 1838 by Longman, Orme, Brown, Green, and Longmans, London; of The Ballantyne-humbug handled, in a letter to Sir Adam Fergusson, by J. G. Lockhart, first published in 1839 by R. Cadell, Edinburgh; and of Reply to Mr Lockhart's pamphlet, entitled, "The Ballantyne-humbug handled," by the authors of a Refutation of the mistatements and calumnies contained in Mr Lockhart's Life of Sir Walter Scott, bart., respecting the Messrs Ballantyne, first published in 1839 by Longman, Orme, Brown, Green, and Longmans, London. [PR5338.B35 1974] 74-13211 ISBN 0-8240-0986-X
1. Scott, Walter, Sir, bart., 1771-1832—Friends and associates. 2. Ballantyne, James, 1772-1833. 3. Ballantyne, John, 1774-1821. 4. Lockhart, John Gibson, 1794-1854. Life of Sir Walter Scott. 5. Lockhart, John Gibson, 1794-1854. The Ballantyne-humbug handled. I. Lockhart, John Gibson, 1794-1854. The Ballantyne-humbug handled. 1974. II. Refutation of the mistatements and calumnies contained in Mr Lockhart's Life of Sir Walter Scott, bart., respecting the Messrs. Ballantyne. 1974. III. Reply to Mr. Lockhart's pamphlet, entitled, "The Ballantyne-humbug handled." 1974. IV. Title. V. Series.

QUAYLE, Eric. 828'.7'09 B
The ruin of Sir Walter Scott. [1st American ed.] New York, C. N. Potter; distributed by Crown Publishers [1969, c1968] 290 p. illus., facsims., ports. 22 cm. Bibliography: p. 281. [PR5338.Q3 1969] 78-75128 6.00
1. Scott, Walter, Sir, bart., 1771-1832—Friends and associates. 2. Edinburgh—Intellectual life. I. Title.

Scott, Walter, Sir, bart., 1771-1832—Relationship with women.

SCOTT, Adam, fl.1896. 828'.7'09 B
The story of Sir Walter Scott's first love. With illustrative passages from his life and works, and portraits of Sir Walter and Lady Scott, and of Sir William and Lady Forbes. Edinburgh, Macniven and Wallace, 1896. New York, Haskell House Publishers [1972] 192 p. ports. 23 cm. [PR5336.S3 1972] 72-2013 ISBN 0-8383-1450-3
1. Scott, Walter, Sir, bart., 1771-1832—Relationship with women. 2. Forbes, Williamina (Stuart) Lady, d. 1810. I. Title.

Scott, William Anderson, 1813-1885.

DRURY, Clifford Merrill, 1897- 285'.10924 B
William Anderson Scott, "no ordinary man." Glendale, Calif., H. Clark Co. 1967. 352 p. illus. ports. 25 cm. Bibliography: p. [344]-345. [BX9225.S34D7] 67-22431
1. Scott, William Anderson, 1813-1885.

Scott, Winfield Townley, 1910-1968.

DONALDSON, Scott. 811'.5'2 B
Poet in America: Winfield Townley Scott. Austin, University of Texas Press [1972] xiii, 400 p. ports. 23 cm. Bibliography: p. [379]-388. [PS3537.C943Z65] 75-38568 ISBN 0-292-76400-6
1. Scott, Winfield Townley, 1910-1968. I. Title.

Scott, Winfield, 1786-1866.

ELLIOTT, Charles Winslow, 1887- 973.5'092'4 B
Winfield Scott / Charles Winslow Elliott. New York : Arno Press, 1979. p. cm. (American military experience) Reprint of the 1937 ed. published by Macmillan, New York. Includes index. Bibliography: p. [E403.1.S4E6 1979] 78-22379 ISBN 0-405-11856-2 : 50.00
1. Scott, Winfield, 1786-1866. 2. United States—History—War with Mexico, 1845-1848. 3. Generals—United States—Biography.

GENERAL Scott and his staff: 973.6'23'0922 comprising memoirs of Generals Scott, Twiggs, Smith, Quitman, Shields, Pillow, Lane, Cadwalader, Patterson and Pierce; Colonels Childs, Riley, Harney, and Butler, and other distinguished officers attached to General Scott's army ... Compiled from public documents and private correspondence. Freeport, N.Y., Books for Libraries Press [1970] 11-224 p. illus., ports. 23 cm. "First published 1848." [E403.G32 1970] 77-109626
1. Scott, Winfield, 1786-1866. 2. U.S.—History—War with Mexico, 1845-1848—Biography.

SMITH, Arthur Douglas Howden, 1887-1945. 973.6'092'4 B
Old Fuss and Feathers; the life and exploits of Lt.-General Winfield Scott. Freeport, N.Y., Books for Libraries Press [1972] p. Reprint of the 1937 ed. [E403.1.S4S6 1972] 72-8465 ISBN 0-8369-6990-1
1. Scott, Winfield, 1786-1866. I. Title.

Scottish poetry.

ROSS, John Dawson, 1853-1939. 811'.008
Scottish poets in America, with biographical and critical notices. New York, B. Blom, 1972. 218 p. port. 21 cm. Reprint of the 1889 ed. [PR8693.A3R6 1972] 72-80502
1. Scottish poetry. 2. Poets, Scottish—Biography. 3. Scotch in America. I. Title.

Scovel, Myra

SCOVEL, Myra 920.7
The Chinese ginger jars [by] Myra Scovel with Nelle Keys Bell. New York, Harper & Row [c.1962] 189p. map. 22cm. 62-7299 3.75 bds.,
I. Title.

SCOVEL, Myra. 266'.5'7320924
The Chinese ginger jars [by] Myra Scovel with Nelle Keys Bell. [1st ed.] New York, Harper [1962] 189p. 22cm. Autobiographical. [BV3427.S38A3] 62-7299
I. Title.

SCOVEL, Myra. 818'.5'403
The happiest summer. Illustrated by Susan Perl. [1st ed.] New York, Harper & Row [1971] 117 p. illus. 22 cm. Autobiographical. [PS3537.C95Z52] 76-160633 4.95
I. Perl, Susan, illus. II. Title.

SCOVEL, Myra. 818'.5'403
To lay a hearth. [1st ed.] New York, Harper & Row [1968] 148 p. illus. 22 cm. Autobiographical. [PS3537.C95Z5] 68-17581
I. Title.

Screven, William, 1629?-1713.

BAKER, Robert Andrew 286.1320924
The first Southern Baptists. Nashville, Broadman [c.1966] 80p. 21cm. (Broadman hist. monograph) Bibl. [BX6495.S4B3] 66-10663 1.25 pap.,
1. Screven, William, 1629?-1713. 2. Charleston, S. C. First Baptist Church. I. Title.

BAKER, Robert Andrew. 286.1320924 (B)
The first Southern Baptists [by] Robert A. Baker. Nashville, Broadman Press [c1966] 80 p. 21 cm. (A Broadman historical monograph) Bibliographical references included in "Notes" (p. 69-80) [BX6495.S4B3] 66-10663
1. Screven, William, 1629?-1713. 2. Charleston, S.C. First Baptist Church. I. Title.

Scribe, Augustin Eugene, 1791-1861.

ARVIN, Neil Cole, 1889- 842'.7
Eugene Scribe and the French theatre, 1815-1860. New York, B. Blom [1967] xi, 268 p. port. 23 cm. First published in 1924. Appendices (p. 235-258): A. The Dentu edition of the complete works of Eugene Scribe (Paris, 1875).—B. List of books and articles relating to Scribe, the French drama, and Parisian theatres. [PQ2425.Z5A7 1967] 67-18422
1. Scribe, Augustin Eugene, 1791-1861. 2. French drama—19th century—History and criticism. I. Title. BIP

Scribner, Lucy Skidmore, 1853-1931.

BARRETT, Gurnee 378.1'011'0924 B
Hinman, 1887-1969.
Lucy Skidmore Scribner; a memoir. Saratoga Springs, N.Y., Skidmore College [1971] 64 p. illus., ports. 22 cm. [LD7251.S3613S33 1971] 79-289222
1. Scribner, Lucy Skidmore, 1853-1931. 2. Skidmore College, Saratoga Springs, N.Y.—History.

Scripps, Edward Wyllis, 1854-1926.

COCHRAN, Negley 070.5'092'4 B
Dakin, 1863-1941.
E. W. Scripps. Westport, Conn., Greenwood Press [1972, c1961] x, 315 p. illus. 22 cm. [PN4874.S37C6 1972] 73-38128 ISBN 0-8371-6326-9 14.00
1. Scripps, Edward Wyllis, 1854-1926. **BIP**

GARDNER, Gilson, 070.4'0924 B
1869-1935.
Lusty Scripps; the life of E. W. Scripps (1854-1926) New York, Vanguard Press, 1932. St. Clair Shores, Mich., Scholarly Press, 1971. xv, 274 p. port. 22 cm. [PN4874.S37G3 1971] 75-145035 ISBN 0-403-00981-2
1. Scripps, Edward Wyllis, 1854-1926. I. Title. **BIP**

SCRIPPS, Edward Wyllis, 070'.924
1854-1926.
Damned old crank; a self-portrait of E. W. Scripps drawn from his unpublished writings. Edited by Charles R. McCabe. Westport, Conn., Greenwood Press [1971, c1951] xvii, 259 p. port. 23 cm. [PN4874.S37A3 1971] 77-156209 ISBN 0-8371-6159-2
1. Journalists—Correspondence, reminiscences, etc. I. Title.

Scripps, Ellen Browning, 1836-1932.

BRITT, Albert, 1874- 920.5
Ellen Browning Scripps, journalist and idealist. [New York]. Oxford, Printed for Scripps College at the Univ. Press, 1960[ ] 134p. 61-4015 3.75
1. Scripps, Ellen Browning, 1836-1932. I. Title.

CLARKSON, Edward Dessau. 920.5
Ellen Browning Scripps; a biography. La Jolla, Calif., c1958. 123 l. illus. 29cm. Includes bibliography. [PN4874.S38C5] 59-19260
1. Scripps, Ellen Browning, 1836- 1932. I. Title.

HEPNER, Frances 070'.924 B
Parnell (Keating)
Ellen Browning Scripps; her life and times, by Frances K. Hepner. [San Diego?] Friends of the Library, San Diego State College, 1966. v, 39 p. 23 cm. Bibliography: p. 39. [PN4874.S38H4] 76-266893
1. Scripps, Ellen Browning, 1836-1932. I. Title.

Scriptores historiae Augustae.

SYME, Ronald, Sir, 937'.07'0922
1903-
Emperors and biography: studies in the 'Historia Augusta'. Oxford, Clarendon Press, 1971. ix, 306 p. 25 cm. Continuation of Ammianus and the Historia Augusta. Bibliography: p. [291]-295. [DG274.S9] 70-22066 ISBN 0-19-814357-5 £3.25
1. Scriptores historiae Augustae. 2. Roman emperors. 3. Rome—History—Empire, 30 B.C.-284 A.D. I. Title. **BIP**

Scuba diving.

GOTT, Jim. 797.2'3 B
Amphibian : the adventures of a professional diver / by Jim Gott, with Norman Lewis Smith. 1st ed. New York : Playboy Press, [1976] 204 p. : ill. ; 22 cm. [VM989.G67] 75-45072 ISBN 0-87223-462-2 : 8.95
1. Scuba diving. I. Smith, Norman Lewis, joint author. II. Title.

Scudery, Madeleine de, 1607-1701.

ARONSON, Nicole. 843'.4 B
Mademoiselle de Scudery / by Nicole Aronson ; translated by Stuart R. Aronson. Boston : Twayne Publishers, c1978. 178 p. : port. ; 21 cm. (Twayne's world author series ; TWAS 441 : France) Includes index. Bibliography: p. 171-174. [PQ1922.Z5A83] 78-1413 ISBN 0-8057-6278-7 lib. bdg. : 9.95
1. Scudery, Madeleine de, 1607-1701. 2. Authors, French—17th century—Biography. I. Title. **BIP**

MCDOUGALL, Dorothy. 843'.4 B
Madeleine de Scudery; her romantic life and death. New York, B. Blom, 1972. xii, 321 p. illus. 21 cm. Reprint of the 1938 ed. Bibliography: p. 311-313. [PQ1922.Z5M25 1972] 72-80149
1. Scudery, Madeleine de, 1607-1701. 2. Salons. 3. Precieuses. **BIP**

Scudder, Ida Sophia, 1870-

WILSON, Dorothy Clarke. 926.1
Dr. Ida; the story of Dr. Ida Scudder of Vellore. [1st ed.] New York, McGraw-Hill [1959] 358 p. illus. 21 cm. [BV3269.S356W5] 59-14469
1. Scudder, Ida Sophia, 1870- 2. Missions, Medical—India. I. Title.

Scullin, J. H. 1876-1953

*ROBERTSON, John. 329.009'2 B
J. H. Scullin; a political biography. s.l. University of Western Australia [1975 c1974] xii, 495 p. ill. ports. 25 cm. Includes index. Bibliography: p. 481-483. [JA98] ISBN 0-85564-074-X
1. Scullin, J. H. 1876-1953 2. Australia—Politics and Government. I. Title.
Distributed by Int'l Scholarly Book Services for 30.50. **BIP**

Scully, Frank,

SCULLY, Frank, 1892- 928.1
Cross my heart. New York, Greenberg [1955] 378p. illus. 22cm. Autobiographical. [PS3537.C976Z5] 55-10963
I. Title.

SCULLY, Frank, 1892- 928.1
This gay knight: an autobiography of a modern chevalier. With an introd. by Dale Francis. Cover illus. by Bill Little-john. [1st ed.] Philadelphia, Chilton Co., Book Division [1962] 232p. illus. 21cm. [PS3537.C976Z53] 62-18032
I. Title.

SCULLY, Frank [Francis 928.1
Joseph Xavier Scully] 1892-
This gay knight; an autobiography of a modern chevalier. Intro. by Dale Francis. Cover illus. by Bill Littlejohn. Philadelphia, Chilton [c.1962] 232p. illus. 21cm. 62-18032 4.95
I. Title.

Scully, William, 1821-1906.

SOCOLOFSKY, Homer 333.5'4'0924 B
Edward, 1922-
Landlord William Scully / Homer E. Socolofsky. Lawrence : The Regents Press of Kansas, c1979. xiii, 182 p. : ill. ; 24 cm. Includes index. Bibliography: p. 155-156. [HD210.M53S386] 78-31477 ISBN 0-7006-0189-9 lib.bdg. : 14.00
1. Scully, William, 1821-1906. 2. Businessmen—Middle West—Biography. 3. Landlord and tenant—Middle West—History. I. Title. **BIP**

Sculptors, American.

MCSPADDEN, Joseph 730'.922 B
Walker, 1874-
Famous sculptors of America, by J. Walker McSpadden. Freeport, N.Y., Books for Libraries Press [1968] xv, 377 p. illus., ports. 22 cm. (Essay index reprint series) Reprint of the 1924 ed. Bibliography: p. 369-377. [NB236.M3 1968] 68-57331
1. Sculptors, American. 2. Sculpture, American. I. Title. **BIP**

TURNBULL, Grace Hill, 1880- 927.3
Chips from my chisel, an autobiography. Rindge, N. H., R. R. Smith, 1953. 256p. illus. 25cm. [NB237.T8A3] 53-12776
I. Title.

Sculptors, British—Correspondence, reminiscences, etc.

WOOLNER, Thomas, 1825- 730'.924 B
1892.
Thomas Woolner, R.A., sculptor and poet; his life in letters. Written by his daughter Amy Woolner. New York, AMS Press [1971] xviii, 352 p. illus., ports. 23 cm. Reprint of the 1917 ed. "List of writings": p. 346. [NB497.W7A3 1971] 70-158614 ISBN 0-404-07030-2
1. Sculptors, British—Correspondence, reminiscences, etc. I. Woolner, Amy. **BIP**

Sculptors—Dictionaries.

NEW dictionary of modern 730'.922
sculpture. General editor: Robert Maillard. [Translated from the French by Bettina Wadia] New York, Tudor Pub. Co. [1971] 328 p. illus. 24 cm. Translation of Nouveau dictionnaire de la sculpture moderne, first published in 1960 under title: Dictionnaire de la sculpture moderne. [NB50.N6813] 70-153118 ISBN 0-8148-0479-9
1. Sculptors—Dictionaries. I. Maillard, Robert, ed. **BIP**

Sculptors, French—Correspondence, reminiscences, etc.

LIPCHITZ, Jacques, 730'.92'4 B
1891-
My life in sculpture, by Jacques Lipchitz with H. H. Arnason. New York, Viking Press [1972] xxxiv, 249 p. illus. 22 cm. (The Documents of 20th-century art) "Lipschitz: a documentary review, by Bernard Karpel": p. [233]-249. [NB553.L55A8 1972] 77-184539 ISBN 0-670-50000-3 10.00
1. Sculptors, French—Correspondence, reminiscences, etc. I. Arnason, H. Harvard. II. Title. III. Series. **BIP**

Sea Islands, S.C.

TOWNE, Laura Matilda, 917.57'99
1825-1901.
Letters and diary of Laura M. Towne; written from the Sea Islands of South Carolina, 1862-1884; edited by Rupert Sargent Holland. New York, Negro Universities Press [1969] xviii, 310 p. illus., port. 23 cm. "Originally published in 1912." [E185.93.S7T7 1969] 70-97415
1. Sea Islands, S.C. 2. Freedmen in South Carolina. I. Holland, Rupert Sargent, 1878-1952, ed. **BIP**

Seaborn, Mildred Grace (Marley) d. 1954.

SEABORN, Garland Jackson. v. 12
God gave me an angel. [1st ed.] New York, Vantage Press [1962] 152 p. 21 cm. 65-35326
1. Seaborn, Mildred Grace (Marley) d. 1954. I. Title.

Seabrook, William Buehler, 1887-

WORTHINGTON, Marjorie 818.52
[Muir] 1900-
The strange world of Willie Seabrook. New York, Harcourt [c.1966] 249, [1] p. 21 cm. Bibl. [CT275.S4W6] 66-12378 4.75
1. Seabrook, William Buehler, 1887- I. Title.

WORTHINGTON, Marjorie 818.52
(Muir) 1900-
The strange world of Willie Seabrook [by] Marjorie Worthington. [1st ed.] New York, Harcourt, Brace & World [1966] 249, [1] p. 21 cm. Autobiographical. "Books by William B. Seabrook"; p. [250] [CT275.S4W6] 66-12378
1. Seabrook, William Buehler, 1887- I. Title.

Seabury, Samuel, Bp., 1729-1796.

STEINER, Bruce E. 283'.092'4 B
Samuel Seabury, 1729-1796; a study in the High Church tradition [by bruce E. Steiner] [Athens] Ohio University Press [1972, c1971] xiii, 508 p. illus. 22 cm. Bibliography: p. 464-482. [BX5995.S3S73] 78-181686 ISBN 0-8214-0098-3 13.50
1. Seabury, Samuel, Bp., 1729-1796. **BIP**

THOMS, Herbert, 1885- 922.373
Samuel Seabury; priest and physician, Bishop of Connecticut. Hamden, Conn., Shoe String, 1963[c.1962] 166p. illus. 22cm. 63-12263 4.95
1. Seabury, Samuel, Bp., 1729-1796. I. Title. **BIP**

Seabury, Samuel, 1873-1958.

MITGANG, Herbert. 923.473
The man who rode the tiger; the life and times of Judge Samuel Seabury. [1st ed.] Philadelphia, Lippincott [1963] 380 p. illus. 24cm. (Legal studies of the William Nelson Cromwell Foundation) [KF373.S4M58] 63-8895
1. Seabury, Samuel, 1873-1958. I. Title.

MITGANG, Herbert. 347'.73'24 B
The man who rode the tiger : the life of Judge Samuel Seabury and the story of the greatest investigation of city corruption in this century / by Herbert Mitgang. New York : Norton, 1979, c1963. p. cm. Originally published in 1970 by Viking, New York. [KF373.S4M58 1979] 79-912 ISBN 0-393-00922-X pbk. : 5.95
1. Seabury, Samuel, 1873-1958. 2. Judges—New York (City)—Biography. 3. New York (City)—Politics and government—1898-1951. I. Title.

Seafaring life.

CLEAVES, Emery N. 910'.41'0924 B
Sea fever; the making of a sailor, by Emery N. Cleaves. Boston, Houghton Mifflin, 1972. x, 283 p. map (on lining papers) 22 cm. Autobiography. [G530.C6217] 74-177538 ISBN 0-395-13643-1 6.95
1. Seafaring life. I. Title.

GARRISON, James Holley, 923.573
1801-1842.
Behold me once more; the confessions of James Holley Garrison, brother of William Lloyd Garrison. Edited by Walter McIntosh Merrill. Boston, Houghton Mifflin, 1954. ix, 146 p. illus., facsim. 22 cm. Bibliographical references included in "Notes" (p. [131]-138) [G549.G32] 54-5700
1. Seafaring life. I. Merrill, Walter McIntosh, ed. II. Title.

HOLMES, James William, 910'.45
b.1855.
Voyaging; fifty years on the seven seas in sail [by] James William Holmes. Edited by Nora Coughlan. Foreword by John Masefield. New York, Dodd, Mead [1972, c1965] 206 p. illus. 23 cm. Autobiographical. [G530.H65 1972] 70-181823 ISBN 0-396-06497-3 8.95
1. Seafaring life. 2. Voyages and travels. 3. Clipper-ships. I. Coughlan, Nora, ed. II. Title.

SARGENT, Henry Jackson, 910.4'5
1834-1862.
The captain of the Phantom; the story of Henry Jackson Sargent, Jr., 1834-1862, as revealed in family letters. Foreword by Daniel Sargent. Mystic, Conn., Marine Historical Association, 1967. xviii, 72 p. illus., facsims., port. 26 cm. Bibliography: p. 71-72. [G540.A1S2 1967] 67-7998
1. Seafaring life. I. Title.

THOMAS, Lowell 923.543
Count Luckner the sea devil, by Lowell Thomas, Felix von Luckner. New York, Popular Lib. [1962, c.1927] 221p. (SP155) .50 pap.,
I. Title.

WILLIAMS, Frederick, 910'.09'163
1800-1877.
The voyages of Frederick Williams. Edited by Eleanor P. Cross. [Chesapeake, Va.] Norfolk County Historical Society of Chesapeake, Virginia, 1972. 183 p. illus. 24 cm. [G530.W7233 1972] 72-171278

1. Seafaring life. I. Title.

Seafaring life—Juvenile literature.

HEATTER, Basil, 1918- 910.4'5'0922
The sea dreamers. Illustrated by Raymond Burns. New York, Farrar, Straus & Giroux [1968] viii, 165 p. illus., maps. 22 cm. (An Ariel book) Contents.Contents.—Old Josh: Joshua Slocum.—The iron man: Howard Blackburn.—Venturesome Voss and the Tilikum: John Claus Voss.—The fearless Frenchman: Alain Gerbault.—Indestructible Pidgeon: Harry Pidgeon.—Robinson and Etera: William Albert Robinson.—Dwight and Timi: Dwight Long.—... and later.—Afterword. [G540.A1H4] 68-13676
1. Seafaring life—Juvenile literature. I. Title.

Seale, Albert B.

SEALE, Albert B. 362.1'9'699424 [B]
Behold the sun / by Albert B. Seale, with insightful commentaries by Cleta (Puddin') Seale. Houston, Tex. : D. Armstrong Co., c1977. 142 p. : ill. ; 23 cm. [RC280.L8S4] 77-74169 ISBN 0-918464-06-4 pbk. : 3.95
1. Seale, Albert B. 2. Lungs—Cancer—Biography. I. Seale, Cleta, joint author. II. Title. BIP

Seale, Bobby, 1936-

SEALE, Bobby, 1936- 322.4'2'0924 B
A lonely rage : the autobiography of Bobby Seale / foreword by James Baldwin. New York : Times Books, c1978. x, 238 p. ; 25 cm. [E185.97.S4A33 1978] 77-79046 ISBN 0-8129-0715-9 : 12.50
1. Seale, Bobby, 1936- 2. Black Panther Party. 3. Afro-Americans—Biography. I. Title. BIP

Sealy, Devro.

SEALY, Shirley. 289.3'3 B
Forever after / Shirley Sealy. Salt Lake City : Deseret Book Co., 1979. 137 p., [1] leaf of plates : port. ; 24 cm. [BX8695.S32S42] 79-17933 ISBN 0-87747-779-5 : 5.95
1. Sealy, Gayle Burch. 2. Sealy, Devro. 3. Sealy, Shirley. 4. Mormons and Mormonism in Utah—Biography. 5. Toxemia of pregnancy—Biography. I. Title. BIP

Sealy, Gayle Burch.

SEALY, Shirley. 289.3'3 B
Forever after / Shirley Sealy. Salt Lake City : Deseret Book Co., 1979. 137 p., [1] leaf of plates : port. ; 24 cm. [BX8695.S32S42] 79-17933 ISBN 0-87747-779-5 : 5.95
1. Sealy, Gayle Burch. 2. Sealy, Devro. 3. Sealy, Shirley. 4. Mormons and Mormonism in Utah—Biography. 5. Toxemia of pregnancy—Biography. I. Title. BIP

Seaman, SylviaS.

SEAMAN, Sylvia S. 973'.04'924 B
How to be a Jewish grandmother / Sylvia S. Seaman. 1st ed. Garden City, N.Y. : Doubleday, 1979. xii, 191 p. : ill. ; 17 cm. [E184.J5S397] 78-22646 ISBN 0-385-15205-1 : 6.95
1. Seaman, SylviaS. 2. Jews in the United States—Anecdotes, facetiae, satire, etc. 3. Grandmothers—Anecdotes, facetiae, satire, etc. 4. United States—Biography—Anecdotes, facetiae, satire, etc. I. Title. BIP

Searcy, Harvey B.,

SEARCY, Harvey B., M.D. 926.1
We used what we had. Northport, Ala., Colonial Pr. [c.1962] 102p. 2.00
I. Title.

SEARCY, Harvey B 1884- 926.1
We used what we had. Northport, Ala., Colonial Press [1962] 102p. illus. 20cm. Autobiographical. [R154.S3547A3] 62-5520
I. Title.

Seargeant, Helen (Humphreys)

SEARGEANT, Helen (Humphreys) 920.7
House by the Buckeye Road. San Antonio, Naylor Co. [1960] 210p. illus. 22cm. Autobiographical. [CT275.S42A3] 60-8225
I. Title.

Searls, Niles, 1825-1907.

SEARLS, Niles, 1825-1907. 385'.0973
Coast to coast by railroad: the journey of Niles Searls—May, 1869. Edited by Frances G. Long. [Enl. ed. Cornwallville, N.Y.] Hope Farm Press & Book Shop [1972] 18 p. illus. 23 cm. Reprint of an article, first published in the New York State Historical Association's New York State history, July 1969, to which has been appended 2 letters by Searls brother-in-law and wife, A. C. Niles and Mary C. Niles Searls, to their sister, Cornelia D. Niles. [TF23.6.S42 1972] 73-153692
1. Searls, Niles, 1825-1907. 2. Railroads—The West—History. 3. Pacific railroads—Early projects. I. Title.

Sears, Isaac, ca. 1730-1786.

ROSEBROCK, Ellen Fletcher. 330.9'747'103
Farewell to old England : New York in Revolution / by Ellen F. Rosebrock. New York : South Street Seaport Museum, c1976. p. cm. Bibliography: p. [HC102.5.A2R675] 75-3941 ISBN 0-913344-21-4 pbk. : 1.95
1. Rose, Joseph. 2. Sears, Isaac, ca. 1730-1786. 3. Low, Isaac, 1735-1791. 4. New York (City)—Commerce—History. 5. New York (City)—History—Colonial period, ca. 1600-1775. I. Title.

Sears, Jesse Brundage,

SEARS, Jesse Brundage, 1876- 923.773
Jesse Brundage Sears: an autobiography. Palo Alto, Calif., 1959. 194p. illus. 24cm. Includes bibliography. [LB875.S37A3] 59-13066
I. Title.

Sears, Joseph, 1843-1912.

KILNER, Colleen Browne. 917.73'1 B
Joseph Sears and his Kenilworth; the dreamer and the dream. [1st ed.] Kenilworth, Ill., Kenilworth Historical Society [1969] xix, 333, xxi-xxxix p. illus., facsims., ports. 25 cm. Cover title: Kenilworth. [F549.K35K5] 71 95266 6.50
1. Sears, Joseph, 1843-1912. 2. Kenilworth, Ill.—History. I. Title.

Searson, Louis Arthur, 1879-

SEARSON, Louis Arthur, 1879- v. 12
Horse-back auditor, my life from nothing to the eighties. [Columbia, S.C., 1962] 112 p. illus., ports. 24 cm. At head of title: "experto crede". 66-90188
1. Searson, Louis Arthur, 1879- I. Title.

Seaton, Elizabeth Ann, 1774-1821.

DAUGHTERS of St. Paul. 271.91024 B
Mother Seton : wife, mother, educator, foundress, saint : profile by the Daughters of St. Paul, based on "Elizabeth Seton" by Msgr. Joseph Bardi. Spiritual gems of Mother Seton. Boston : St. Paul Editions, 1975. 140 p. : ill. ; 22 cm. [BX4705.S57D3 1975] 75-6861 3.95 pbk. : 2.95
1. Seaton, Elizabeth Ann, 1774-1821. I. Bardi, Giuseppe, Mons. Elisabetta Anna Seton. II. Seton, Elizabeth Ann, 1774-1821. Spiritual gems. 1975. III. Title.

Seaton, Grace Mary.

SEATON, Grace Mary. 914.3'155'0384
A double life in the Kaiser's capital. Canaan, N.H., Phoenix Pub. [1973] vii, 121 p. 24 cm. [DD866.S4] 73-82977 ISBN 0-914016-00-8 5.95
1. Seaton, Grace Mary. 2. Berlin—Social life and customs. 3. Americans in Berlin. I. Title.

Seaton, William Winston, 1785-1866.

SEATON, Josephine, b.1822. 070'.924 B
William Winston Seaton of the National intelligencer. [New York] Arno [1970, c1871] 385 p. 23 cm. (The American journalists) [PN4874.S4S4 1970] 70-125714 ISBN 0-405-01695-6
1. Seaton, William Winston, 1785-1866. BIP

Seattle, Chief of the Suquamish and allied tribes, d. 1866.

METCALFE, James Vernon. 970.3 B
Chief Seattle. Watercolor illus. by Bernie Webber. [Seattle, Wash., Catholic Northwest Progress Publication, 1970?] 15 p. illus. 28 cm. Bibliography: p. 15. [E99.S85M47] 73-153347
1. Seattle, Chief of the Suquamish and allied tribes, d. 1866.

Seattle, Chief of the Suquamish and allied tribes, d. 1866—Juvenile literature.

BORING, Mel, 1939- 970'.004'97 B
Sealth / by Mel Boring. Minneapolis : Dillon Press, c1978. p. cm. A biography of the Indian chief,leader of the tribes of the Puget Sound area in the first half of the nineteenth century. [E99.S85B67] 77 25470 ISBN 0-87518-155-4 : 5.95
1. Seattle, Chief of the Suquamish and allied tribes, d. 1866—Juvenile literature. 2. Suquamish Indians—Biography—Juvenile literature. I. Title. BIP

MONTGOMERY, Elizabeth Rider. 92
Chief Seattle: great statesman. Illustrated by Russ Hoover. Champaign, Ill., Garrard Pub. Co. [1966] 80 p. col. illus. 23 cm. (Garrard Indian books) [E90.S4M6] 66-10081
1. Seattle, chief of the Suquamish and allied tribes, d. 1866—Juvenile literature.

Seaver, Tom, 1944-

COHEN, Joel H. 796.357'092'4 B
Inside corner; talks with Tom Seaver. Edited by Joel H. Cohen. [1st ed.] New York, Atheneum, 1974. 246 p. illus. 22 cm. [GV865.S4C63 1974] 73-91636 ISBN 0-689-10600-9 7.95
1. Seaver, Tom, 1944- 2. Baseball. I. Title.

*DEVANEY, John 796'.357'092'4 [B]
Tom Seaver. New York, Popular Library [1974] 254 p. 18 cm. [GV865] 1.50 (pbk.)
1. Seaver, Tom, 1944- 2. New York (City) Baseball Club. (National League, Mets) I. Title. BIP

SEAVER, Tom, 1944- comp. 796.357'092'2 B
How I would pitch to Babe Ruth, by Tom Seaver with Norman Lewis Smith. [Chicago] Playboy Press [1975, c1974] xix, 268 p. 18 cm. [GV865.A1537] 1.50 (pbk.)
1. Baseball—Biography. 2. Pitching (Baseball) 3. Batting (Baseball) I. Smith, Norman Lewis, joint comp. II. Title.

SEAVER, Tom, 1944- comp. 796.357'092'2 B
How I would pitch to Babe Ruth; Seaver vs. the sluggers. Written and edited by Tom Seaver, with Norman Lewis Smith. [1st ed. Chicago] Playboy Press [1974] xix, 268 p. illus. 22 cm. [GV865.A1S37] 73-91660 ISBN 0-87223-405-3 8.50
1. Baseball—Biography. 2. Pitching (Baseball) 3. Batting (Baseball) I. Smith, Norman Lewis, joint comp. II. Title.

SEAVER, Tom, 1944- 796.357'0924
The perfect game; Tom Seaver and the Mets, by Tom Seaver. With Dick Schaap. [1st ed.] New York, Dutton, 1970. 189 p. illus., ports. 22 cm. (A Maddick manuscripts book) [GV865.S4A3 1970] 75-113455 5.95
1. Seaver, Tom, 1944- 2. New York (City). Baseball club (National League, Mets) I. Schaap, Richard, 1934- II. Title.

Seaver, Tom, 1944- —Juvenile literature.

BELSKY, Dick. 796.357'092'4 B
Tom Seaver : baseball's superstar / Dick Belsky. New York : McKay, c1977. p. cm. A biography of a star pitcher for the Cincinnati Reds. [GV865.S4B44] 92 77-5234 ISBN 0-679-20427-X : 6.95
1. Seaver, Tom, 1944- —Juvenile literature. 2. Baseball players—United States—Biography—Juvenile literature. I. Title.

BURCHARD, Marshall. 796.357'092'4 B
Sports star: Tom Seaver [by] Marshall and Sue Burchard. Illustrated with photos. and with drawings by Paul Frame. [1st ed.] New York, Harcourt Brace Jovanovich [1974] 63 p. illus. 21 cm. A brief biography of pitcher Tom Seaver, who was instrumental in reversing the New York Mets losing streak and helping them become the National League champions. [GV865.S4B87] 92 74-7265 ISBN 0-15-277996-5
1. Seaver, Tom, 1944- —Juvenile literature. 2. Baseball—Juvenile literature. I. Burchard, S. H., joint author. II. Frame, Paul, illus. III. Title.

DEEGAN, Paul J., 1937- 796.357'092'4 B
Tom Seaver, by Paul J. Deegan. Illustrated by Harold Henriksen. [Mankato, Minn., Creative Education; distributed by Childrens Press, Chicago [1973] 1974. 30 p. illus. (part col.) 25 cm. (Creative's superstars) "Prepared for the publisher by Amecus Street." A biography of the New York Mets' pitcher, famous for his fastball. [GV865.S4D43] 92 73-13650 ISBN 0-87191-280-5 4.95
1. Seaver, Tom, 1944- —Juvenile literature. I. Henriksen, Harold, illus. II. Amecus Street, inc. III. Title.

DRUCKER, Malka. 796.357'092'4 B
Tom Seaver : portrait of a pitcher / by Malka Drucker, with Tom Seaver ; introd. by Tom Seaver. New York : Holiday House, c1978. 160 p. : ill. ; 24 cm. Includes index. A biography of the only major league pitcher to have 200 or more strikeouts in nine consecutive seasons. [GV865.S4D78] 92 77-17519 ISBN 0-8234-0322-X : 7.95
1. Seaver, Tom, 1944- —Juvenile literature. 2. Baseball players—United States—Biography—Juvenile literature. I. Seaver, Tom, 1944- joint author. II. Title. BIP

SULLIVAN, George, 1927- 796.357'0924 B
Tom Seaver of the Mets. New York, Putnam [1971] 159 p. 21 cm. (Putnam sports shelf) A biography of the major league baseball pitcher who played an important role in helping the New York Mets win the 1969 World Championship. [GV865.S4S9] 92 73-142464 3.86
1. Seaver, Tom, 1944- —Juvenile literature. 2. New York (City). Baseball Club (National League, Mets)—Juvenile literature. I. Title.

Sebastian, Fannie B

SEBASTIAN, Fannie B 920
One of ten, by Fannie B. Sebastian. Boston, Christopher Pub. House [1965] 185 p. 21 cm. [CT275.S426A3] 65-21525
I. Title.

Sebastian, Saint.

ROBERTO, Brother, 1927- 922.244
The soldier died twice; a story of St. Sebastian. Illus. by Elaine Shears. Notre Dame, Ind., Dujarie Press [1955] 94p. illus. 24cm. [BR1720.S3R6] 55-33456
1. Sebastian, Saint. I. Title.

Sechenov, Ivan Mikhailovich, 1829-1905.

SECHENOV, Ivan Mikhailovich, 1828-1905 926.1
Autobiographical notes. Ed. of English tr.: Donald B. Lindsley. Tr. from Russian by Kristan Hanes. Washington, D.C., Maer. Inst. of Biological Scis., c.1965. xiii, 174p. illus., port. 24cm. (Russian monographs on brain and behavior, 2) Added t.p. is an English tr. of the 1952 Russian t.p. Supported by U.S. Public Health Serv. grant NB-02347. Bibl. [R534.S4A313] 65-16726 4.00
I. Lindsley, Donald Benjamin, 1907- ed. II. Title. III. Series.

SECHENOV, Ivan Mikhailovich, 1829-1905. 150'.8
I. M. Sechenov: biographical sketch and essays. New York, Arno Press, 1973. xxxvi, [337]-489 p. illus. 24 cm. (Classics in psychology) Essays from the author's Selected works, Moscow, 1935. Contents.Contents.—Shaternikov, M. N. The life of I. M. Sechenov.—Sechenov, I. M. Who must investigate the problems of psychology, and how.—Sechenov, I. M. Impressions and reality.—Sechenov, I. M. The elements of thought. [BF121.S42 1973] 73-3028 ISBN 0-405-05161-1 10.00
1. Sechenov, Ivan Mikhailovich, 1829-1905. 2. Psychology. I. Title. II. Series.
Contents omitted.

SECHENOV, Ivan Mikhailovich, 1828-1905 926.1
Autobiographical notes. Ed. of English tr.: Donald B. Lindsley. Tr. from Russian by Kristan Hanes. Washington, D.C., Maer. Inst. of Biological Scis., c.1965. xiii, 174p. illus., port. 24cm. (Russian monographs on brain and behavior, 2) Added t.p. is an English tr. of the 1952 Russian t.p. Supported by U.S. Public Health Serv. grant NB-02347. Bibl. [R534.S4A313] 65-16726 4.00
I. Lindsley, Donald Benjamin, 1907- ed. II. Title. III. Series.

Secombe, Harry.

SECOMBE, Harry. 823'.9'14 B
Goon for lunch / Harry Secombe. New York : St. Martin's Press, 1976, c1975. 175 p. : ill. ; 21 cm. [PN2598.S43A3] 75-24747 7.95
1. Secombe, Harry. 2. Comedians—Great Britain—Correspondence, reminiscences, etc. I. Title.
Contents omitted. BIP

Securities fraud—Canada.

FLEMMING, Marlis. 364.1'63'0924 B
Under protective surveillance / Marlis Flemming. Toronto : McClelland and Stewart, c1976. 317 p. ; 22 cm. [HV6771.C2F53] 77-356050 ISBN 0-7710-3156-4 : 10.95
1. Securities fraud—Canada. 2. Swindlers and swindling—Canada—Biography. I. Title.
Distributed by J. B. Lippincott Philadelphia, PA 19105

Securities, Privately placed—U.S.

GOLDBERG, Stuart Charles. 346'.73'092
Private placements and restricted securities. New York, C. Boardman Co. [1971] 1 v. (various pagings) 26 cm. (Securities law series, v. 2) Includes bibliographical references. [KF1439.G64] 70-163723 ISBN 0-87632-078-7
1. Securities, Privately placed—U.S. I. Title. BIP

Sedgewick, Theodore, 1746-1813.

WELCH, Richard E. 923.273
Theodore Sedgwick, Federalist; a political portrait, by Richard E. Welch, Jr. [1st ed.] Middletown, Conn., Wesleyan University Press [1965] viii, 276 p. port. 24 cm. Bibliography: p. 255-268. [E302.6.S4W4] 65-14054
1. Sedgewick, Theodore, 1746-1813.

Sedgwick, Ellery,

SEDGWICK, Ellery, 1872-1960. 070.4'1'0924
The happy profession. Westport, Conn., Greenwood Press [1972, c1946] x, 343 p. 22 cm. Autobiographical. [PN4874.S42A3 1972] 78-152604 ISBN 0-8371-6039-1
I. Title. BIP

Sedley, Charles, Sir, bart., 1639?-1701.

PINTO, Vivian de Sola, 1895- 821'.4 B
Sir Charles Sedley, 1639-1701; a study in the life and literature of the Restoration, by V. De Sola Pinto. New York, AMS Press [1969] xi, 400 p. 23 cm. Reprint of the 1927 ed. Bibliography: p. 363-388. [PR3671.S4P5 1969] 76-85904
1. Sedley, Charles, Sir, bart., 1639?-1701.

PINTO, Vivian de Sola, 1895- 822'.4 B
Sir Charles Sedley, 1639-1701; a study in the life and literature of the Restoration, by V. de Sola Pinto. [Folcroft, Pa.] Folcroft Library Editions, 1973. p. Reprint of the 1927 ed. published by Constable, London. Bibliography: p. [PR3671.S4P5 1973] 73-12776 19.25
1. Sedley, Charles, Sir, bart., 1639?-1701.

Seel, David John, 1925-

SEEL, David John, 1925- 266'.025'0924
Challenge and crisis in missionary medicine / by David J. Seel. Pasadena, Calif. : William Carey Library, [1979] p. cm. Includes bibliographical references. [R722.32.S4A33] 79-16015 ISBN 0-87808-172-0 pbk. : 3.95
1. Seel, David John, 1925- 2. Missionaries, Medical—Korea—Biography. 3. Missions, Medical. I. Title. BIP

Seelos, Franz Xaver, 1819-1867.

CURLEY, Michael Joseph, 1900- 282'.0924 B
Cheerful ascetic: the life of Francis Xavier Seelos, C.SS.R., by Michael J. Curley. New Orleans, Redemptorist Fathers, 1969. ix, 436 p. illus., ports. 24 cm. Bibliography: p. [405]-420. [BX4705.S517C85] 76-12639
1. Seelos, Franz Xaver, 1819-1867. I. Title.

Segal, Harry, 1899-

SEGAL, Hyman R 927.96
They called him Champ; the story of Champ Segal and his fabulous era. [1st ed.] New York, Citadel Press [1959] 480p. illus. 22cm. [CT275.C4285S4] 59-14766
1. Segal, Harry, 1899- I. Title.

Segal, Patrick, 1948-

SEGAL, Patrick, 1948- 910'.41
The man who walked in his head / by Patrick Segal ; translated from the French by John Stephens. New York : Morrow, 1980. p. cm. Translation of L'homme qui marchait dans sa tete. [RC406.P3S4313] 79-21426 ISBN 0-688-03529-9 : 9.95
1. Segal, Patrick, 1948- 2. Paraplegics—France—Biography. I. Title. BIP

Seghers, Charles Jean, Abp., 1839-1886—Juvenile literature.

BETZ, Eva (Kelly) 1897- 92
Apostle of the ice and snow; a life of Bishop Charles Seghers. Valatie, N.Y., Holy Cross Pr. [c.1964] 126p. illus. 23cm. [BX4705.S52B4] 64-8535 2.50
1. Seghers, Charles Jean, Abp., 1839-1886—Juvenile literature. I. Title.

BOSCO, Antoinette 922.271
Charles John Seghers, pioneer in Alaska; illustrated by Matthew Kalmenoff. New York, P. J. Kenedy [c.1960] 190p. 22cm. (American background books, 16) (Bibl. notes:p.185-186) 60-14643 2.50
1. Seghers, Charles Jean, Abp., 1839-1886—Juvenile literature. I. Title.

BOSCO, Antoinette, 1928- 922.271
Charles John Seghers, pioneer in Alaska; illustrated by Matthew Kalmenoff. New York, P. J. Kenedy [1960] 190p. illus. 22cm. (American background books, 16) [BX4705.S52B6] 60-14643
1. Seghers, Charles Jean, Abp., 1839-1886—Juvenile literature. I. Title.

Seghers, Hercules, 17th cent.

HERCULES Seghers. 759.9492
[Chicago] University of Chicago Press [1953] ix, 149p. illus., 111plates. 31cm. Bibliography: p. 135-138. [ND653.S4C6] [ND653.S4C6] 927.5 53-12895 53-12895
1. Seghers, Hercules, 17th cent. I. Collins, Leo C
BIP

Sego, James, 1927-

SEGO, James, 1927- 783.8'092'4 B
Sego / by James Sego, with Robert Paul Lamb. Plainfield, N.J. : Logos International, c1977. xii, 156 p., [3] leaves of plates : ill. ; 21 cm. [ML420.S45A3] 77-83855 ISBN 0-88270-247-5 pbk. : 2.95
1. Sego, James, 1927- 2. Gospel musicians—United States—Biography. I. Lamb, Robert Paul, joint author. BIP

Segovia, Andres, 1893—

SEGOVIA, Andres, 1893- 787'.61'0924 B
Andres Segovia : an autobiography of the years 1893-1920 / translated by W. F. O'Brien. New York : Macmillan, 1976. p. cm. [ML419.S4A39] 76-42291 ISBN 0-02-609080-5 : 10.95
1. Segovia, Andres, 1893- 2. Guitarists—Spain—Biography.

Segye Kidokkyo T'ongil Sillyong Hyophoe.

SONTAG, Frederick. 289.9 B
Sun Myung Moon and the Unification Church / Frederick Sontag. Nashville, Tenn. : Abingdon Press, c1977. 224 p. : ill. ; 23 cm. Bibliography: p. 217-224. [BX9750.S4S66] 77-9075 ISBN 0-687-40622-6 : 8.95
1. Segye Kidokkyo T'ongil Sillyong Hyophoe. 2. Moon, Sun Myung. I. Title.

Seidensticker, Edward G., 1921-

SEIDENSTICKER, Edward G., 1921- 895.6'3'1 B
Genji days / Edward G. Seidensticker. 1st ed. Tokyo ; New York : Kodansha International, 1977. 225 p. ; 22 cm. [PL713.S38A38] 76-44157 ISBN 0-87011-296-1 : 15.00
1. Seidensticker, Edward G., 1921- 2. Murasaki Shikibu, b. 798? Genji monogatari. 3. Critics—United States—Biograhy. 4. Translators—United States—Biography. I. Title. BIP

Seidman, Phillip Kenneth, 1907-

SEIDMAN, Phillip Kenneth, 1907- 976.8'19
The man who likes Memphis : a memoir of forty years passed by / P. K. Seidman as told to James Cortese ; designed & illustrated by Leonard Crook. [College Station, Pa.] : Carnation Press, c1975. 110 p. : ill. ; 24 cm. Includes index. [F444.M5S44] 76-358478
1. Seidman, Phillip Kenneth, 1907- 2. Memphis—Biography. I. Cortese, James. II. Title.

Seil, Noland Blair, 1894-1968.

HAYS, Robert G. 070.4'092'4 B
Country editor: influence of a weekly newspaper, by Robert G. Hays. Danville, Ill., Interstate Printers & Publishers [1974] x, 83 p. port. 23 cm. Based on the author's master's thesis, Southern Illinois University, Carbondale. Bibliography: p. 77-78. [PN4874.S423H3 1974] 73-87423 3.00 (pbk.)
1. Seil, Noland Blair, 1894-1968. 2. Mercury-Independent. 3. Grayville, Ill.—Biography. I. Title.

Sekaquaptewa, Helen,

SEKAQUAPTEWA, Helen, 1898- 970.3
Me and mine; the life story of Helen Sekaquaptewa, as told to Louise Udall. Illustrated by Phillip Sekaquaptewa. Tuscon, University of Arizona Press [1969] 262 p. illus., map (on lining papers), port. 20 cm. [E90.S45A3] 68-54714 4.95
I. Udall, Louise. II. Title.

Sekowski, Jozef, 1800-1858. (Series: California. University. University of California publications in modern philology, v.73)

PEDROTTI, Louis 928.917
Jozef-Julian Sekowski; the genesis of a literary alien. Berkeley, Univ. of Calif. Pr. [c.]1965. viii, 223p. facsims. 24cm. (Univ. of Calif. pubns. in mod. philology, v.73] [PB13.C3 vol. 73] 65-63974 5.00 pap.,
1. Sekowski, Jozef, 1800-1858. (Series: California. University. University of California publications in modern philology, v.73) I. Title.

Selby, Hazel Barrington.

SELBY, Hazel Barrington. 817.54
Home to my mountains. Princeton, N. J., Van Nostrand [1962] 255 p. 20 cm. Autobiographical. [PS3537.E3595Z52 1962] 62-51511
I. Title.

Seldes, Marian.

SELDES, Marian. 792'.028'0924 B
The bright lights : a theatre life / Marian Seldes. Boston : Houghton Mifflin, 1978. vii, 280 p. : ill. ; 22 cm. [PN2287.S346A32] 78-17221 ISBN 0-395-26481-2 : 10.00
1. Seldes, Marian. 2. Actors—United States—Biography. I. Title. BIP

Self, James Cuthbert, 1876-1955.

ROBINSON, George Oscar, 1907- 338.4767721
The character of quality; the story of Greenwood Mills, a distinguished name in textiles, by G. O. Robinson. [Greenwood? S.C., 1964] xiii, 159 p. illus., facsim., map, ports. (part col.) 24 cm. [HD9879.G74R6] 65-44645
1. Self, James Cuthbert, 1876-1955. 2. Greenwood Mills, Greenwood, S.C. I. Title.

Self-portraits, American—Exhibitions.

VAN DEVANTER, Ann C. 757'.3'0973
American self-portraits, 1670-1973. Introd. and [exhibition] catalogue by Ann C. Van Devanter and Alfred V. Frankenstein with the assistance of Shirley S. Simpson. [Washington] International Exhibitions Foundation, 1974. 247 p. illus. 28 cm. Exhibition held at the National Portrait Gallery and the Indianapolis Museum of Art. Bibliography: p. 234-244. [ND1311.V36] 73-93138
1. Self-portraits, American—Exhibitions. I. Frankenstein, Alfred Victor, 1906- joint author. II. International Exhibitions Foundation. III. National Portrait Gallery, Washington, D.C. IV. Indianapolis Museum of Art. V. Title.

Selkirk, Alexander, 1676-1721.

BALLARD, Martin. 910.4'5'0924 B
The monarch of Juan Fernandez. Illustrated by A. R. Whitear. New York, Scribner [1968, c1967] 192 p. illus., map. 22 cm. Bibliography: p. 192. A biography of the man whose experiences as a castaway on a desert island in the Pacific inspired Defoe's Robinson Crusoe. [G530.S42B3] 92 AC 68
1. Selkirk, Alexander, 1676-1721. I. Whitear, A. R., illus. II. Title.

Selkirk, Alexander, 1676-1721—Juvenile literature.

BALLARD, Martin. 983'.2 B
The monarch of Juan Fernandez. Illustrated by A. R. Whitear. New York, Scribner [1968, c1967] 192 p. illus., map. 22 cm. Bibliography: p. 192. [G530.S42B3] 68-29361 3.95
1. Selkirk, Alexander, 1676-1721—Juvenile literature. I. Title.

MCREYNOLDS, Ginny. 910'.92
Alone on a desert island / Ginny McReynolds ; ill., Charles Shaw. Milwaukee : Raintree Publishers, c1980. p. cm. A biography of the man whose experiences as a castaway on a desert island in the Pacific inspired Defoe's Robinson Crusoe. [G530.S42M32] 92 79-22144 ISBN 0-8172-1571-9 (lib. bdg.) : 7.99
1. Selkirk, Alexander, 1676-1721—Juvenile literature. 2. Adventure and adventurers—England—Biography—Juvenile literature. I. Shaw, Charles, 1941- II. Title. BIP

Selkirk, Thomas Douglas,

GRAY, John Morgan 923.971
Lord Selkirk of Red River East lansing, mich mich state univ pr. 1964 [c]1963 xvii, 388 p. illus., geneal table, maps, ports bibli. 6410159 6.50
1. Selkirk, Thomas Douglas, 5th earl of 2. Red River Settlement. I. Title. BIP

Sell, Henry Blackman.

LECKIE, Janet T. 070.4'0924 B
A talent for living; the story of Henry Sell, an American original. New York, Hawthorn Books [1970] viii, 278 p. illus., ports. 24 cm. [CT275.S4296L4] 70-123480 12.95
1. Sell, Henry Blackman. I. Title.

Sellers, Peter, 1925-

EVANS, Peter, 1933- 791.43'028'0924
Peter Sellers; the mask behind the mask. Englewood Cliffs, N.J., Prentice-Hall [1968] 249 p. ports. 22 cm. [PN2598.S44E9] 68-30815 6.95
1. Sellers, Peter, 1925-

Selman, John Henry, 1839-1896.

METZ, Leon Claire 978.020924
John Selman, Texas gunfighter. New York, Hastings [c.1966] 254p. illus., ports. 21cm. Bibl. [F391.S48M4] 66-18351 6.95
1. Selman, John Henry, 1839-1896. I. Title.

METZ, Leon Claire. 978.020924 (B)
John Selman, Texas gunfighter. New York, Hastings House [1966] 254 p. illus., ports. 21 cm. Bibliography: p. 235-243. [F391.S48M4] 66-18351
1. Selman, John Henry, 1839-1896. I. Title.

Selmier, Dean.

SELMIER, Dean. 364.1'523
Blow away / Dean Selmier, and Mark Kram. New York : Viking Press, 1979. xiii, 273 p. ; 24 cm. [HV6248.S428A33 1979] 0924 78-12299 ISBN 0-670-17447-5 : 9.95
1. Selmier, Dean. 2. Crime and criminals—United States—Biography. I. Kram, Mark, joint author. II. Title. BIP

Selormey, Francis,

SELORMEY, Francis, 1927- 916.67'03'030924
The narrow path; an African childhood. New York, Praeger [1966] 183 p. 21 cm. [CT2508.S4A3 1966] 66-16927
I. Title.

Seltzer, Thomas.

LAWRENCE, David Herbert, 1885-1930. 823'.9'12 B
Letters to Thomas and Adele Seltzer / D. H. Lawrence ; edited by Gerald M. Lacy. Santa Barbara, CA: Black Sparrow Press, 1976. xiv, 284 p. : ill. ; 24 cm. Bibliography: p. 283-284. [PR6023.A93Z5354 1976] 76-10782 ISBN 0-87685-224-X : 14.00. ISBN 0-87685-225-8 pbk. : 4.00
1. Lawrence, David Herbert, 1885-1930—Correspondence. 2. Seltzer, Thomas. 3. Seltzer, Adele Szold, 1876- 4. Authors, English—20th century—Correspondence. I. Seltzer, Thomas. II. Seltzer, Adele Szold, 1876- III. Lacy, Gerald M. IV. Title. BIP

Selwyn, George Augustus, 1719-1791.

SHERWIN, Oscar, 1902- 914.2
A gentleman of wit and fashion; the extraordinary life and times of George Selwyn. New York, Twayne [1964, c.1963] 351p. illus., ports. 22cm. Bibl. 63-17406 6.00
1. Selwyn, George Augustus, 1719-1791. I. Title.

Selye, Hans, 1907-

REFLECTIONS on biologic research. 574'.0922 Compiled and edited by Giulio Gabbiani. St. Louis, W. H. Green [1967] xii, 244 p. illus., ports. 24 cm. "An anthology of autobiographic sketches, dedicated to Hans Selye on the occasion of his sixtieth birthday." Includes bibliographies. [QH26.R4] 67-26012
1. Selye, Hans, 1907- 2. Biologists—Correspondence, reminiscences, etc. 3. Biological research Addresses, essays, lectures. I. Selye, Hans, 1907- II. Gabbiani, Giulio, comp.

SELYE, Hans, 1907- 610'.92'4
The stress of my life : a scientist's memoirs / Hans Selye. 2d ed. New York : Van Nostrand Reinhold, [1979] p. cm. Includes index. [R464.S4A3 1979] 78-21278 ISBN 0-442-27659-1 : 10.95
1. Selye, Hans, 1907- 2. Medical scientists—Quebec (Province)—Montreal—Biography. 3. Stress (Physiology) I. Title. BIP

Selznick, David O., 1902-1965.

BOWERS, Ronald L. 791.43'0232'0924 B
The Selznick players / Ronald Bowers ; editorial assistant, C. Leigh Hibbard Church. South Brunswick : A. S. Barnes, c1976. 255 p. : ill. ; 29 cm. Includes index. Bibliography: p. 246. [PN1998.A2B628] 74-9278 ISBN 0-498-01375-8 : 15.00
1. Selznick, David O., 1902-1965. 2. Moving-picture actors and actresses—United States—Biography. I. Title. BIP

THOMAS, Bob, 1922- 791.43'0232'0924 B
Selznick. [1st ed.] Garden City, N.Y., Doubleday, 1970. 381 p. illus., ports. 25 cm. Includes bibliographical references. [PN1998.A3S4] 78-97696 7.95
1. Selznick, David, 1902-1965. I. Title. BIP

Semantics.

PEIRCE, Charles Santiago Sanders, 1839-1914. 921.1
Letters to Lady Welby, edited by Irwin C. Lieb. New Haven, Published by Whitlock for the Graduate Philosophy Club of Yale University, 1953. 55p. 23cm. [B945.P44A48] 53-30053
1. Semantics. I. Welby-Gregory, Hon. Victoria Alexandrina Maria Louisa (Stuart-Wortley) Lady, 1837-1912. II. Title.

Sembrich, Marcella, 1858-1935.

OWEN, Harry Goddard, 1905- 927.8
A recollection of Marcella Sembrich. [Bolton, N.Y.] Marcella Sembrich Memorial Association [1950] 77 p. illus., ports. 24 cm. [ML420.S47093] 50-35363
1. Sembrich, Marcella, 1858-1935. I. Title.

Semmelweis, Ignac Fulop, 1818-1865.

DESTOUCHES, Louis Ferdinand, 1894-1961. 844'.9'12
Mea culpa & The life and work of Semmelweis / Louis-Ferdinand Celine [i.e. L. F. Destouches] ; translated from the French (with an introd.) by Robert Allerton Parker. New York : H. Fertig, 1979, c1937. Reprint of the 1st edition by Little, Brown, Boston. [PQ2607.E834M393 1979] 79-13296 16.50
1. Semmelweis, Ignac Fulop, 1818-1865. 2. Communism—Russia. 3. Obstetricians—Hungary—Biography. I. Title.

RICH, Josephine. 926.1
The doctor who saved babies, Ignaz Philipp Semmelweis. New York, J. Messner [1961] 192 p. 22 cm. Includes bibliography. [R502.S5R5] 61-14759
1. Semmelweis, Ignac Fulop, 1818-1865. I. Title.

Semmes, Raphael, 1809-1877—Juvenile literature. (Series)

DALY, Robert Welter, 1916- 923.573
Raphael Semmes, Confederate admiral, by Robert W. Daly, Illus. by James J. Fox. New York, P.J. Kennedy, [1965] 191p. illus. 22cm. (Amer. background bks., 30) [E467.1.S47D3] 65-15456 2.50
1. Semmes, Raphael, 1809-1877—Juvenile literature. (Series) I. Title.

DAVIS, Evangeline. 973.7570924
Rebel raider; a biography of Admiral Semmes [by] Evangeline & Burke Davis. [1st ed.] Philadelphia, Lippincott [1966] 149 p. illus., map, ports. 22 cm. [E467.1.S47D38] 66-8186
1. Semmes, Raphael, 1809-1877—Juvenile literature. I. Davis, Burke, joint author. II. Title. BIP

Sempangi, F. Kefa.

SEMPANGI, F. Kefa. 289.9 B
A distant grief / F. Kefa Sempangi, with Barbara R. Thompson. Glendale, Calif. : GL Regal Books, c1979. 192 p. ; 21 cm. Includes bibliographical references. [BX9375.R438S45] 79-50394 ISBN 0-8307-0684-4 (pbk.) : 3.95
1. Sempangi, F. Kefa. 2. Redeemed Church of Uganda—Clergy—Biography. 3. Clergy—Uganda—Biography. I. Thompson, Barbara R., joint author. II. Title. BIP

Semple, Eugene, 1840-1908.

HYNDING, Alan, 1938- 979.5'04'0924 B
The public life of Eugene Semple, promoter and politician of the Pacific Northwest. Seattle, University of Washington Press [1973] xiv, 195 p. illus. 23 cm. Originally presented as the author's thesis, University of Washington. Bibliography: p. 175-183. [F891.H96 1973] 73-9903 ISBN 0-295-95288-1 10.00
1. Semple, Eugene, 1840-1908. I. Title.

Semprun, Jorge—Biography—Political career.

SEMPRUN, Jorge 843'.9'14
The autobiography of Federico Sanchez and the Communist underground in Spain / Jorge Semprun ; translated by Helen Lane. New York : Karz Publishers, c1979. 271 p. ; 22 cm. Translation of Autobiografia de Federico Sanchez. [PQ6669.E5117Z46313] 79-19605 ISBN 0-918294-05-3 : 19.95
1. Semprun, Jorge—Biography—Political career. 2. Authors, Spanish—20th century—Biography. 3. Communist—Spain—Biography. 4. Spain—Politics and government—1939-1975. I. Title. BIP

Sen, Keshab Chandra, 1838-1884.

MULLER, Friedrich Max, 1823-1900. 294.5'562'0924 B
Keshub Chunder Sen / F. Max Mueller ; edited by Nanda Mookerjee. Calcutta : S. Gupta, 1976. ii, xvii, 117 p. ; 23 cm. Includes bibliographical references. [BL1265.S4M84 1976] 76-904243 Rs10.00 ($2.00 U.S.)
1. Sen, Keshab Chandra, 1838-1884. 2. Brahma-samaj—Biography. I. Mookerjee, Nanda. II. Title. BIP

Senac, Felix, 1815-1866.

RAPIER, Regina. 973.7'86'0924' B
Felix Senac: saga of Felix Senac; being the legend and biography of a Confederate agent in Europe. Atlanta, [1972] 216 p. illus. 24 cm. (Bulletin of art and history, v. 11, no. 1) Bibliography: p. 205-208. [E608.S46R36] 72-169316 ISBN 0-9600584-1-9 10.00
1. Senac, Felix, 1815-1866. 2. United States—History—Civil War—Secret service—Confederate States. I. Title. II. Title: Saga of Felix Senac. III. Series.

Senapati, Fakir Mohan, 1843-1918—Biography.

MANSINHA, Mayadhar. 891'.45 B
Fakirmohan Senapati / Mayadhar Mansinha. New Delhi : Sahitya Akademi, 1976. 86 p. ; 23 cm. (Makers of Indian literature) [PK2579.S4Z727] 77-900629 Rs2.50
1. Senapati, Fakir Mohan, 1843-1918—Biography. 2. Authors, Oriya—19th century—Biography.

Sencourt, Robert,

SENCOURT, Robert, 1890- 821'.9'12 [B]
T. S. Eliot, a memoir. Edited by Donald Adamson. [New York] [Dell] [1973, c.1971] xiv, 266 p. illus. 20 cm. (Delta Book) Bibliographical references. [PS3509.L43Z8638 1971] pap., 2.65
I. Eliot, Thomas Stearns, 1888-1965.

Sendak, Maurice—Interviews.

SMITH, Jeffrey Jon. 741'.092'4 B
A conversation with Maurice Sendak / Jeffrey Jon Smith. [Elmhurst? Ill.] : Smith, [1974] [15] p. (incl. cover) : ill. ; 15 x 22 cm. Cover title. "Based on a transcript of a phone conversation ... taped on August 27, 1974." [PS3569.E6Z85] 75-305049
1. Sendak, Maurice—Interviews. I. Sendak, Maurice. II. Title.

Senger, Valentin.

SENGER, Valentin. 943'.41 B
No. 12 Kaiserhofstrasse / Valentin Senger ; translated by Ralph Manheim. 1st ed. New York : E. P. Dutton, c1979. p. cm. Translation of Kaiserhofstrasse 12. [DS135.G5S46713] 79-15084 ISBN 0-525-13816-1 : 10.00
1. Senger, Valentin. 2. Jews in Frankfurt am Main—Biography. 3. Jews in Germany—History—1933-1945. 4. Frankfurt am Main—Biography. I. Title.

Senior, Nassau William, 1790-1864.

LEVY, Samuel Leon, 1886- 330'.0924 B
Nassau W. Senior, 1790-1864, critical essayist, classical economist and adviser of governments [by] S. Leon Levy. [New ed.] New York, A. M. Kelley [1970] 336 p. port. 26 cm. 1943 ed. published under title: Nassau W. Senior, the prophet of modern capitalism. Includes bibliographical references. "Works of N. W. Senior": p. 281-285. [HC255.L54 1970] 67-30861
1. Senior, Nassau William, 1790-1864. 2. Gt. Brit.—Economic conditions—19th century. I. Title.

Sennett, Mack, 1880-1960.

*FOWLER, Gene, 1890-1960. 791.43'0233'0924 [B]
Father goose. [New York] Avon [1974, c1961] 288 p. 18 cm. [PN1998] 1.95 (pbk.)
1. Sennett, Mack. I. Title. BIP

LAHUE, Kalton C. 791.43'52
Mack Sennett's Keystone: the man, the myth, and the comedies [by] Kalton C. Lahue. South Brunswick, A. S. Barnes [1971] 315 p. illus. 26 cm. [PN1998.A3S434] 78-146763 ISBN 0-498-07461-7 10.00
1. Sennett, Mack, 1880-1960. 2. Keystone Film Company. I. Title.

Sephardim—U.S.—Biography.

BIRMINGHAM, Stephen. 920.073
The grandees; America's Sephardic elite. [1st ed.] New York, Harper & Row [1971] xiii, 368 p. illus., fold. geneal. table, ports. 25 cm. Bibliography: p. 355-357. [E184.J5B552 1971] 70-95942 10.00
1. Sephardim—U.S.—Biography. 2. Jews in the United States—Biography. I. Title.

Sequoya, Cherokee Indian, 1770?-1843. Fiction.

SEQUOYAH: leader of the v. 12
Cherokees. Illustrated by Bob Riger. Eau Claire, Wis., E. M. Hale [1956] 180p. illus. 22cm. (Landmark books [65]) 'Special edition ... printed and distributed by arrangement with ... Randon House, New York.'
1. Sequoya, Cherokee Indian, 1770?-1843. Fiction. I. Marriott, Alice Lee, 1910- II. Series.

Sequoyah, 1770?-1843.

FOSTER, George 970'.004'97 B
Everett, 1849-
Se-quo-yah, the American Cadmus and modern Moses / by Geo. E. Foster. New York : AMS Press, 1979. xviii, 244 p., [6] leaves of plates : ill. ; 19 cm. Reprint of the 1885 ed. published by the Office of the Indian Rights Association, Philadelphia. Includes index. [E99.C5S383 1979] 76-43709 23.50
1. Sequoyah, 1770?-1843. 2. Cherokee Indians—Biography. 3. Cherokee Indians. 4. Cherokee language—Alphabet. I. Title. BIP

Sequoyah, 1770?-1843—Juvenile literature.

CAMPBELL, Chester W. 970.3 B
Sequoyah, by C. W. Campbell. Minneapolis, Dillon Press [1973] 74 p. illus. 24 cm. (The Story of an American Indian) A biography of Sequoyah, inventor of a writing system for the Cherokee language. [E99.C5S382] 92 72-91159 ISBN 0-87518-057-4 3.95
1. Sequoyah, 1770?-1843—Juvenile literature. BIP

HUNT, Bernice Kohn. 497.5 B
The story of Sequoyah; talking leaves. Illustrated by Valli. [1st ed. New York, Hawthorn Books, 1969] [32] p. illus. (part col.) 24 x 26 cm. Published under the author's earlier name: Bernice Kohn. Summarizes the life of Sequoyah, the Cherokee warrior, who devised a written language for his people. [E99.C5H85 1969] 92 70-75190 4.25
1. Sequoyah, 1770?-1843—Juvenile literature. 2. Cherokee Indians—Biography. 3. Indians of North America—Biography. I. Van de Bovenkamp, Valli, illus. II. Title. III. Title: Talking leaves.

PATTERSON, Lillie. 970.3 B
Sequoyah : the Cherokee who captured words / by Lillie Patterson ; illustrated by Herman B. Vestal. Champaign, Ill. : Garrard Pub. Co., [1975] 80 p. : col. ill. ; 23 cm. A biography of the Cherokee Indian who did what white scholars said could not be done when he invented a syllabary for writing the Cherokee language. [E99.C5S386] 92 74-20966 ISBN 0-8116-6612-3 lib.bdg. : 3.12
1. Sequoyah, 1770?-1843—Juvenile literature. I. Vestal, Herman B., ill. II. Title. BIP

RADFORD, Ruby Lorraine, 497'.5 B
1891-
Sequoya, by Ruby L. Radford. Illustrated by Unada. New York, Putnam [1969] [59] p. col. illus. 23 cm. (A See and read beginning to read biography) A brief biography of the lame Cherokee who fulfilled his desire to help his people by inventing an alphabet for the Cherokee language. [E99.C5R19] 92 68-24542 2.52
1. Sequoyah, 1770?-1843—Juvenile literature. I. Unada, illus. II. Title.

Serafim, Saint, 1759-1833.

ZANDER, Valentine. 281.9'092'4 B
St. Seraphim of Sarov / Valentine Zander ; translated by Sister Gabriel Anne ; introd. by Boris Bobrinskoy. Crestwood, N.Y. : St. Vladimir's Seminary Press, 1975. p. cm. German translation has title: Seraphim von Sarow. Bibliography: p. [BX597.S37Z33 1975] 75-42136 ISBN 0-913836-28-1 : 4.95
1. Serafim, Saint, 1759-1833. I. Title. BIP

Serbia—History—Insurrection, 1804-1813.

NENADOVIC, Matija, 949.7'1 B
1777-1854.
The memoirs of Prota Matija Nenadovic. Edited and translated from the Serbian by Lovett F. Edwards. Oxford, Clarendon Press, 1969. xlvii, 227 p. port. maps. 23 cm. Translation of Memoari. [DR340.3.N4A313 1969] 71-439874 ISBN 1-9821476-6- unpriced
1. Serbia—History—Insurrection, 1804-1813. I. Edwards, Lovett Fielding, ed. II. Title. BIP

Sereni, Enzo, 1905-1944.

BONDY, Ruth. 956.94'001'0924 B
The emissary : a life of Enzo Sereni / Ruth Bondy ; translated from the Hebrew by Shlomo Katz ; with an afterword by Golda Meir. 1st American ed. Boston : Little, Brown, c1977. xi, 265 p., [4] leaves of plates : ill. ; 22 cm. Slightly abridged translation of ha-Shaliah. "An Atlantic Monthly Press book." Includes bibliographical references and index. [DS151.S4B6613 1977] 77-6754 ISBN 0-316-10130-3 : 8.95
1. Sereni, Enzo, 1905-1944. 2. Zionists—Italy—Biography. 3. Giv'at Brenner, Israel—Biography. I. Title. BIP

Serger, Frederick,

SERGER, Frederick, 1889- 759.13
Frederick Serger: life & work. Text by George Stiles. Photography by O. E. Nelson. New York, Schoeman Galleries, 1962. 151 p. illus. (part col.) ports. 26 cm. [ND237.S439S7] 62-21417
I. Stiles, George Edward, 1914- II. Title.

Serios, Ted.

EISENBUD, Jule. 133.8'0924
The world of Ted Serios; "thoughtographic" studies of an extraordinary mind. New York, Morrow, 1967. 367 p. illus., ports. 25 cm. Bibliography: p. [349]-357. [BF1027.S46E35] 66-27951
1. Serios, Ted. 2. Thought-transference. I. Title. II. Title: "Thoughtographic" studies.

Sermons, American.

CHAPPELL, Clovis 225.92'2
Gillham, 1882-
Men that count, by Clovis G. Chappell. Grand Rapids, Baker Book House [1967] 164 p. 20 cm. (Ministers paperback library) Reprint of the 1929 ed. Sermons. Contents.Contents.—Needless poverty: James.—Worry and its cure: Paul.—All things new: Paul.—A great believer: Paul.—At the cross: Paul.—A successful service: Peter.—Kept: Peter.—A pilgrim's progress: the man born blind.—The glory of the ordinary: Andrew.—A fighter: Zacchaeus.—A woman's revengc: John the Baptist.—A beautiful vocation: Onesiphorus.—Making life count: author of Hebrews.—A wholehearted saint: Caleb.—Mr. Sorrowful: Jabez.—The spoiled dream: Jeremiah. [BS571.5.C46 1967] 67-18173
1. Bible—Biography. 2. Sermons, American. I. Title. BIP

Serpico, Frank.

MAAS, Peter, 1929- 363.2'092'4 B
Serpico [by] Peter Maas. New York, Viking Press [1973] 314 p. illus. 23 cm. [HV7911.S4M3] 72-79002 ISBN 0-670-63498-0 7.95
1. Serpico, Frank. 2. New York (City)—Police. I. Title.

MAAS, Peter, 1929- 363.2'092' [B]
Serpico, by Peter Maas. New York, Bantam Books [1974, c.1973] 314 p. 18 cm. [HV7911.S4M3] 1.75 (pbk.)
1. Serpico, Frank. 2. New York (City)—Police. I. Title.
L.C. card no. for the hardbound edition: 72-79002. BIP

Serra, Junipero, 1713-1784.

AINSWORTH, Katherine, 282'.0924 B
1908-
In the shade of the juniper tree; a life of Fray Junipero Serra [by] Katherine Ainsworth and Edward M. Ainsworth. With a pref. by Salvador Garcia. [1st ed.] Garden City, N.Y., Doubleday, 1970. xii, 199 p. 22 cm. Bibliography: p. [189]-190. [F864.S417] 76-98541 5.95
1. Serra, Junipero, 1713-1784. I. Ainsworth, Edward Maddin, 1902-1968, joint author. II. Title.

BOLTON, Ivy May, 1879- 922.2
Father Junipero Serra; illustrated by Robert Burns. New York, Messner 1952 160 p. illus. 22 cm. Bibliography: p. 156-157. [F864.S418] 52-9144
1. Serra, Junipero, 1713-1784.

BOWDEN, Dina Moore. 271'.3'024 B
Junipero Serra in his native isle (1713-1749) / text, Dina Moore Bowden ; photos., Stefan Laszlo ; drawings, Xam. Palma [Majorca] : s.n., 1976. 170 p. : ill. ; 30 cm. Includes bibliographical references. [F864.S44B68] 77-372391 ISBN 8-440-01725-1
1. Serra, Junipero, 1713-1784. 2. Majorca—Church history. 3. Franciscans—Balearic Islands—Majorca—Biography. I. Laszlo, Stefan. II. Title.

ENGLEBERT, Omer, 1893- 922.2
The last of the conquistadors, Junipero Serra, 1713-1784. Translated from the French by Katherine Woods. [1st ed.] New York, Harcourt, Brace [1956] 368 p. illus. 25 cm. Includes bibliography. [F864.S442] 56-7917
1. Serra, Junipero, 1713-1784. I. Title.

ENGLEBERT, Omer, 282'.092'4 B
1893-
The last of the conquistadors, Junipero Serra, 1713-1784. Translated from the French by Katherine Woods. Westport, Conn., Greenwood Press [1974, c1956] ix, 368 p. illus. 23 cm. Reprint of the ed. published by Harcourt, Brace, New York. Bibliography: p. 355-359. [F864.S442 1974] 74-5924 ISBN 0-8371-7523-2
1. Serra, Junipero, 1713-1784. I. Title. BIP

HABIG, Marion Alphonse, 922.246
1901-
Man of greatness; Father Junipero Serra, by Marion A. Habig and Francis Borgia Steck. Chicago, Franciscan Herald Press [1964] 172 p. illus., ports. 21 cm. Bibliography: p. 171-172. [F864.S464] 64-14251
1. Serra, Junipero, 1713-1784 I. Steck, Francis Borgia, 1884- joint author. II. Title.

KING, Kenneth Moffat. 922.2
Mission to paradise: the story of Junipero Serra and the missions of California. Chicago, Franciscan Herald Press [c1956] 190p. illus: 23cm. Includes bibliography. [F864] 57-3010
1. Serra, Junipero, 1713-1784. 2. Missions—California. I. Title.

MAYNARD, Theodore, 1890- 922.2
1956.
The long road of Father Serra. New York, Appleton-Century-Crofts [1954] 297 p. illus. 22 cm. [F864.S476] 54-6213
1. Serra, Junipero, fray, 1713-1784. I. Title.

PALOU, Francisco, 979.4020924
1723-1789.
La vida de Junipero Serra. Ann Arbor, University Microfilms [1966] 344 p. facsims., map, port. 22 cm. (March of America facsimile series, no. 49) Reproduction of the original ed., Mexico, 1787, with t. p. reading: Relacion historica de la vida y apostolicas tareas del venerable padre Fray Junipero Serra. [F864.S49 1787a] 66-26320
1. Serra, Junipero, 1713-1784. 2. Missions—California. 3. Franciscans in California. 4. California—History—To 1846. I. Series.

PIRUS, Betty L. 266'.2'0924 B
Before I sleep / Betty L. Pirus. 1st ed. New York : Vantage Press, c1977. 206 p. ; 21 cm. Bibliography: p. 203-206. [F864.S535] 77-151737 ISBN 0-533-02580-X : 6.95
1. Serra, Junipero, 1713-1784. 2. Missions—California—History. 3. California—History—To 1846. 4. Franciscans—California—History. 5. Franciscans—California—Biography. I. Title.

REPPLIER, Agnes, 1855-1950 922.2
Junipero Serra, pioneer colonist of California, [by] Agnes Repplier. New York, All Saints Pr. [1962, c.1933] 184p. 17cm. (As.236) .50 pap.,
1. Serra, Junipero, Father, 1713-1784. 2. Missions—California. 3. Franciscans in California. 4. California—Hist.—To 1846. I. Title.

SERRA, Junipero, 266.2'0924 B
1713-1784.
Diario: the journal of Padre Serra, from Loreto, the capital of Baja California, to San Diego, capital of the new establishments of Alta California, in three months and three days, March 28 to July 1, 1769. A new grass roots translation by Ben F. Dixon. [2d ed.] San Diego, Calif., Don Diego's Libreria, 1967. xi, 116 p. illus., facsims., maps, ports. 22 cm. "The Song of Padre Serra" (unacc.) on inside front cover. Includes San Diego's water rights document. [F864.S393 1967] 71-276685 2.00
1. Missions—California—History—Sources. 2. Franciscans in California—History—Sources. I. Title.

WEBER, Francis J. 979.4'02'0924
The Golden State's religious pioneer [by] Francis J. Weber. Los Angeles, Dawson's Book Shop, 1974. 55 p. port. 19 cm. No. 34 of a limited ed. of 350 copies signed by the author. [F864.S544] 73-90827 6.50
1. Serra, Junipero, 1713-1784. I. Title.

WISE, Winifred Esther, 1906- 92
Fray Junipero Serra and the California conquest, by Winifred E. Wise. New York, Scribner [1967] 184 p. illus., facsims., maps, ports. 24 cm. Bibliography: p. 179-180. Biography of the well known Franciscan missionary who founded the first mission in Upper California and encouraged colonization of the West Coast. [F864.S545] AC 67
1. Serra, Junipero, 1713-1784. 2. California—History—to 1846. I. Title.

WOODGATE, Mildred 282.0924
Violet, 1904-
Junipera Serra, apostle of California, 1713-1784 by M. V. Woodgate. Westminster, Md., Newman [1966] 162p. illus. 27cm. Bibl. [F8.64.S546] 66-8807 3.95
1. Serra, Juniper, 1713-1784. I. Title.

Serra, Junipero, 1713-1784—Juvenile literature.

DEMAREST, Donald 92
The first Californian; the story of Fray Junipero Serra. Illus. by Joseph Romer. New York, Guild [1965, c.1963] 176p. illus. 18cm. (Turret bks., 31504) .50 pap.,
1. Serra, Junipero, 1713-1784—Juvenile literature. I. Title.

DEMAREST, Donald. 92
The first Californian; the story of Fray Junipero Serra. Illustrated by Joseph Romer. New York, Hawthorne Books [1963] 188 p. illus. (part col.) maps (part col.) 22 cm. (Credo books, 13) Bibliography: p. 181. 63-15104
1. Serra, Junipero, 1713-1784 — Juvenile literature. I. Title.

MARTINI, Teri. 922.2
Sandals on the golden highway; a life of Junipero Serra. Illus. by Nino Carbe. Paterson, N. J., St. Anthony Guild Press [1959] 139p. illus. 24cm. [F864.S475] 59-13344

1. Serra, Junipero, 1713-1784—Juvenile literature. I. Title.

Sert, Misia Godebska.

GOLD, Arthur. 944.08'092'4 B
Misia / by Arthur Gold and Robert Fizdale. 1st ed. New York : Knopf : distributed by Random House, 1979. p. cm. Includes index. Bibliography: p. [CT1018.S5G64 1979] 79-2223 ISBN 0-394-48710-9 : 15.95
1. Sert, Misia Godebska. 2. France—Biography. I. Fizdale, Robert, joint author. II. Title. **BIP**

SERT, Misia (Godebska) 920.7
Misia and the muses; the memoirs of Misia Sert. [Translation by Moura Budberg] With an appreciation by Jean Cocteau. New York, J. Day Co. [1953] 212p. illus. 22cm. 'First published in French in 1952 under the title: Misia.' [CT1018.S4A33 1953a] 53-12710
I. Title.

Servetus, Michael, 1509 or 11-1553.

BAINTON, Roland H. 922.8146
Hunted heretic; the life and death of Michael Servetus, 1511-1553. With a new foreword by the author. Boston, Beacon Press [c.1953, 1960] xiv, 270p. illus. 21cm. (Beacon ser. in liberal religion, no. 2) 1.75 pap.,
1. Servetus, Michael, 1509 or 11-1553. I. Title.

BAINTON, Roland Herbert, 1894- 922.8146
Hunted heretic; the life and death of Michael Servetus, 1511-1553. Boston, Beacon Press [1953] 270 p. illus. 22 cm. [BX9869.S4B3] 53-10320
1. Servetus, Michael, 1509 or 11-1553. I. Title. **BIP**

BAINTON, Ronald Herbert, 1894- 922.8146
Nunted heretic the life and death of Michael Servetus, 1511-1553. With a new foreword by the author. Boston, Beacon Press [1960] 270p. illus. 21cm. (Beacon series in liberal religion, LR2) Includes bibliography. [BX9869.S4B3 1960] 60-16079
1. Servetus, Michael, 1509 or 11-1553. I. Title.

FULTON, John Farquhar, 1899- 922.8146
Michael Servetus, humanist and martyr, with a bibliography of his works and census of known copies, by Madeline E. Stanton. New York, H. Reichner, 1953 [c1954] 98p. port., map, facsims. 23cm. (Historical Library, Yale Medical Library, and Dept. of the History of Medicine, Yale University. Publication no. 22) 'Selected source materials':p.98-95. [BX9869.S4F8] 54-14685
1. Servetus, Michael, 1509 or 11-1553. I. Stanton, Madeline Earle II. Title. III. Series: Yale University. School of mEdicine. Dept. of the History of Medicine. Publication no. 22

Service, Robert William, 1874-1958—Biography.

KLINCK, Carl Frederick, 1908- 811'.5'2 B
Robert W. Service : a biography / by Carl F. Klinck. New York : Dodd, Mead, [1976] p. cm. Bibliography: p. [PR6037.E72Z73] 76-22607 ISBN 0-396-07391-3 : 8.95
1. Service, Robert William, 1874-1958—Biography.

Service (Theology)

WASHBURN, Henry Bradford, 1869-1962. 261.8'3'0922
The religious motive in philanthropy: studies in biography. Freeport, N.Y., Books for Libraries Press [1970, c1931] 172 p. 23 cm. (Essay index reprint series) Contents.Contents.—Introduction.—Samuel Barnett. Vincent de Paul.—Francis of Assisi.—Jesus of Nazareth. [BT738.4.W36 1970] 72-105047 ISBN 8-369-16344-
1. Service (Theology) 2. Christian biography. I. Title.

Sessions, Kate Olivia, 1857-1940.

MACPHAIL, Elizabeth C. 635'.092'4 B
Kate Sessions : pioneer horticulturist / by Elizabeth C. MacPhail. San Diego, Calif. : San Diego Historical Society, 1976. vi, 153 p. : ill. ; 24 cm. Includes bibliographical references and index. [SB63.S47M3] 76-54013
1. Sessions, Kate Olivia, 1857-1940. 2. Horticulturists—California—San Diego. 3. San Diego, Calif.—Biography.

Sessoms, Frederick Douglas, 1879-

WILKERSON, Edward Lee. 926.1
Struggling to climb; a biography. [Cleveland! 1958] 115 p. illus 24 cm. [R154.S362W5] 58-12002
1. Sessoms, Frederick Douglas, 1879- I. Title.

Seton, Elizabeth Ann, Saint, 1774-1821.

CUSHING, Richard James, Cardinal, 1895- 922.273
Blessed Mother Seton. [Boston] St. Paul Editions [1963] 96, [61] p. illus. 22 cm. "Spiritual gems, written by Blessed Elizabeth Ann Seton": p. [55]-[97] "Pictorial biography of Blessed Mother Seton": p. [99]-[155] [BX4700.S4C8] 63-163333
1. Seton, Elizabeth Ann, 1774-1821. I. Seton, Elizabeth Ann, 1774-1821. II. Title.

CUSHING, Richard James, Cardinal, 1895- 922.273
Blessed Mother Seton. [Boston] St. Paul Editions [1963] 96, [61] p. illus. 22 cm. "Spiritual gems, written by Blessed Elizabeth Ann Seton": p. [55]-[97] "Pictorial biography of Blessed Mother Seton": p. [99]-[155] [BX4700.S4C8] 63-16333
1 Seton, Elizabeth Ann, 1774-1821. I. Seton, Elizabeth Ann, 1774-1821. II. Title.

DIRVIN, Joseph I. 922.273
Mrs. Seton, foundress of the American Sisters of Charity. New York, Farrar [c.1962] 498p. illus. 22cm. Bibl. 62-10503 6.95 bds.,
1. Seton, Elizabeth Ann, 1774-1821. 2. Sisters of Charity of St. Vincent de Paul. I. Title.

DIRVIN, Joseph I. 922.273
Mrs. Seton. Foreword by Francis Cardinal Spellman. Preface by Amleto Cardinal Cicognani [New York] Avon [1964, c.1962] 544p. 19cm. (N109) .95 pap.,
1. Seton, Elizabeth Ann; 1774-1821. 2. Sisters of Charity of St. Vincent de Paul. I. Title.

DIRVIN, Joseph I. 922.273
Mrs. Seton, foundress of the American Sisters of Charity. New York, Farrar, Straus and Giroux, 1962 498 p. illus. 22 cm. Includes bibliography. [BX4705.S57D5] 62-10503
1. Seton, Elizabeth Ann, 1774-1821. 2. Sisters of Charity of St. Vincent de Paul.

DIRVIN, Joseph I. 271'.91'024 B
Mrs. Seton, foundress of the American Sisters of Charity / Joseph I. Dirvin. New canonization ed. New York : Farrar, Straus and Giroux, 1975. xix, 498 p., [8] leaves of plates : ill. ; 21 cm. Includes index. Bibliography: p. [465]-469. [BX4705.S57D5 1975] 75-321767 ISBN 0-374-51255-8 : 4.95
1. Seton, Elizabeth Ann, 1774-1821. 2. Sisters of Charity of St. Vincent de Paul. I. Title.

DIRVIN, Joseph I. 922.273
Mrs. Seton, foundress of the American Sisters of Charity. New York, Farrar [c.1962] 498p. illus. 22cm. Bibl. 62-10503 6.95 bds.,
1. Seton, Elizabeth Ann, 1774-1821. 2. Sisters of Charity of St. Vincent de Paul. I. Title.

DIRVIN, Joseph I. 922.273
Mrs. Seton. Foreword by Francis Cardinal Spellman. Preface by Amleto Cardinal Cicognani [New York] Avon [1964, c.1962] 544p. 19cm. (N109) .95 pap.,
1. Seton, Elizabeth Ann; 1774-1821. 2. Sisters of Charity of St. Vincent de Paul. I. Title.

DIRVIN, Joseph I. 922.273
Mrs. Seton, foundress of the American Sisters of Charity. New York, Farrar, Straus and Giroux, 1962 498 p. illus. 22 cm. Includes bibliography. [BX4705.S57D5] 62-10503
1. Seton, Elizabeth Ann, 1774-1821. 2. Sisters of Charity of St. Vincent de Paul.

DIRVIN, Joseph I. 271'.91'024 B
Mrs. Seton, foundress of the American Sisters of Charity / Joseph I. Dirvin. New canonization ed. New York : Farrar, Straus and Giroux, 1975. xix, 498 p., [8] leaves of plates : ill. ; 21 cm. Includes index. Bibliography: p. [465]-469. [BX4705.S57D5 1975] 75-321767 ISBN 0-374-51255-8 : 4.95
1. Seton, Elizabeth Ann, 1774-1821. 2. Sisters of Charity of St. Vincent de Paul. I. Title.

ELIZABETH Seton's two Bibles, her notes and markings / 271'.91'024 B compiled and edited by Ellin M. Kelly. Huntington, Ind. : Our Sunday Visitor, c1977. 184 p. : ill. ; 21 cm. Includes bibliographical references and indexes. [BX4700.S4E43] 77-80539 ISBN 0-87973-741-7 pbk. : 3.95
1. Seton, Elizabeth Ann, Saint, 1774-1821. 2. Bible—Influence. 3. Christian saints—United States—Biography. I. Seton, Elizabeth Ann, Saint, 1774-1821. II. Kelly, Ellin M III. Bible. English. Douai. Selections. 1805.

*FEENEY, Leonard, 1897- 282'092'4 B
Elizabeth Seton: an American woman Huntington, In., Our Sunday Visitor [1975] 304 p. frontis. 18 cm. [BX4705.S] 75-21599 ISBN 0-87973-861-8 3.50 (pbk.)
1. Seton, Elizabeth Ann, 1774-1821. I. Title.

*FEENEY, Leonard, 1897- 282'092'4 B
Elizabeth Seton: an American woman Huntington, In., Our Sunday Visitor [1975] 304 p. frontis. 18 cm. [BX4705.S] 75-21599 ISBN 0-87973-861-8 3.50 (pbk.)
1. Seton, Elizabeth Ann, 1774-1821. I. Title.

LAVERTY, Rose Maria. 922.273
Loom of many threads; the English and French influences on the character of Elizabeth Ann Bayley Seton. New York, Paulist Press [c1958] 258p. illus. 22cm. Includes bibliography. [BX4705.S57L3] 59-7577
1. Seton, Elizabeth Ann, 1774-1821. I. Title.

LAVERTY, Rose Maria. 922.273
Loom of many threads; the English and French influences on the character of Elizabeth Ann Bayley Seton. New York, Paulist Press [c1958] 258p. illus. 22cm. Includes bibliography. [BX4705.S57L3] 59-7577
1. Seton, Elizabeth Ann, 1774-1821. I. Title.

MELVILLE, Annabelle (McConnell) 1910- 922.273
Elizabeth Bayley Seton, 1774-1821. New York, Scribner [c1960] 411p. illus. 22cm. Includes bibliography. [BX4705.S57M4 1960] 61-3468
1. Seton, Elizabeth Ann, 1774-1821. 2. Sisters of Charity of St. Vincent de Paul. I. Title. **BIP**

MELVILLE, Annabelle (McConnell) 1910- 922.273
Elizabeth Bayley Seton, 1774-1821 New York, Scribner, 1951. xvii, 411 p. illus. ports. 22 cm. Bibliography: p. 383-391. [BX4705.S57M4] 51-14503
1. Seton, Elizabeth Ann, Mother, 1774-1821. 2. Sisters of Charity of St. Vincent de Paul. I. Title.

MELVILLE, Annabelle McConnell, 1910- 271'.91'024 B
Elizabeth Bayley Seton, 1774-1821 / by Annabelle M. Melville. New York : Scribner, [1976] c1951. xix, 411 p., [4] leaves of plates : ill. ; 22 cm. "Hudson River editions." Includes index. Bibliography: p. 383-391. [BX4700.S4M44 1976] 76-8053 ISBN 0-684-14735-1 lib.bdg. : 12.50
1. Seton, Elizabeth Ann, Saint, 1774-1821. 2. Christian saints—United States—Biography.

MELVILLE, Annabelle (McConnell) 1910- 922.273
Elizabeth Bayley Seton, 1774-1821. New York, Scribner [c1960] 411p. illus. 22cm. Includes bibliography. [BX4705.S57M4 1960] 61-3468
1. Seton, Elizabeth Ann, 1774-1821. 2. Sisters of Charity of St. Vincent de Paul. I. Title. **BIP**

POWER-WATERS, Alma (Shelley) 1896- 922.273
Mother Seton and the Sisters of Charity Illustrated by John Lawn. New York, Vision Books [1957] 190p. illus. 22cm. (Vision books, 24) [BX4705.S57P67] 57-7699
1. Seton, Elizabeth Ann, 1774-1821. 2. Sisters of Charity of St. Vincent de Paul. I. Title.

POWER-WATERS, Alma (Shelley), 1896- 922.273
Mother Seton First American-born saint Revised edition. New York : Pocket Books [1976 c1957] viii, 182 p. : 18 cm. (Archway Paperback) Originally published under the title: Mother Seton and the Sisters of Charity. [BX4705.S57P67] ISBN 0-671-29785-6 pbk. : 1.25
1. Seton, Elizabeth Ann, 1774-1821 2. Sisters of Charity of St. Vincent de Paul. I. Title.
L.C. card no. for 1957 Vision Books edition: 57-7699. **BIP**

Seton, Elizabeth Ann, Saint, 1774-1821—Juvenile literature.

†HINDMAN, Jane F. 271'.91'024 B
Elizabeth Ann Seton, mother, teacher, saint for our time / by Jane F. Hindman. New York : Arena Lettres, c1976. vii, 82, [1] p. ; 18 cm. Bibliography: p. [83] A brief biography of the Catholic convert who founded a religious order and the first parochial school in the United States. She was proclaimed a saint in 1975. [BX4700.S4H56] 92 76-15327 pbk. : 1.50
1. Seton, Elizabeth Ann, Saint, 1774-1821—Juvenile literature. 2. Christian saints—United States—Biography—Juvenile literature. I. Title.

POWER-WATERS, Alma (Shelley) 1896- 920
Mother Seton and the Sisters of Charity. Condensed for very young readers from the original Vision book. Illus. by W. T. Mars. New York, Guild [dist. Golden c.1957, 1963] 76p. illus. (pt. col.) 24cm. (Jr. Vision bk.) 63-22935 2.50 bds.,
1. Seton, Elizabeth Ann, 1774-1821—Juvenile literature. 2. Sisters of Charity of St. Vincent de Paul—Juvenile literature. I. Title.

ROBERTO, Brother, 1927- 922.273
Please bring the children; a story of Mother Elizabeth Seton. Illus. by Carolyn Lee Jagodits. Notre Dame, Ind., Dujarie Press [1959] 94p. illus. 24cm. [BX4705.S57R6] 59-3312
1. Seton, Elizabeth Ann, 1774-1821—Juvenile literature. I. Title.

Seton, Ernest Thompson, 1860-1946.

SETON, Ernest Thompson, 1860-1946. 574'.092'4 B
Trail of an artist-naturalist : the autobiography of Ernest Thompson Seton. New York : Arno Press, 1978, c1940. p. cm. (Biologists and their world) Reprint of the ed. published by C. Scribner's Sons, New York. Includes index. [QH31.5.S48A36 1978] 77-81134 ISBN 0-405-10734-X : 27.00
1. Seton, Ernest Thompson, 1860-1946. 2. Naturalists—United States—Biography. I. Title. II. Series. BIP

SETON, Ernest Thompson, 1860-1946. 574
The worlds of Ernest Thompson Seton / edited by John G. Samson. New York : Knopf, 1976. p. cm. Includes index. Bibliography: p. [QH31.S48A37] .092'4[B 76-13711 ISBN 0-394-49547-0 : 25.00
1. Seton, Ernest Thompson, 1860-1946. 2. Naturalists—Correspondence, reminiscences, etc. BIP

WADLAND, John Henry. 574'.092'4 B
Ernest Thompson Seton : man in nature and the Progressive Era, 1880-1915 / John Henry Wadland. New York : Arno Press, 1978. xii, 528 p., [13] leaves of plates : ill. ; 24 cm. (Biologists and their world) Originally presented as the author's thesis, York University, Toronto, 1976. Bibliography: p. 462-528. [QH31.S48W33 1978] 77-81136 ISBN 0-405-10736-6 : 32.00
1. Seton, Ernest Thompson, 1860-1946. 2. Naturalists—United States—Biography. 3. Naturalists—Canada—Biography. I. Title. II. Series. BIP

Seton, Ernest Thompson, 1860-1946—Juvenile literature.

BLASSINGAME, Wyatt. 574'.0924 B
Ernest Thompson Seton, scout and naturalist. Illustrated by Frank Vaughn. Champaign, Ill., Garrard Pub. Co. [1971] 80 p. col. illus. 23 cm. (A Discovery book) An easy-to-read biography of the artist, naturalist, and conservationist who was one of the founders of the Boy Scouts of America. [QH31.S48B57] 92 76-148186 ISBN 0-8116-6305-1 2.59
1. Seton, Ernest Thompson, 1860-1946—Juvenile literature. I. Vaughn, Frank, 1915- illus. II. Title.

Seton, Marie.

SETON, Marie. 927.914
Sergei M. Eisenstein a biography. New York Grove Press [1960] 533 p. illus. 21 cm. (Evergreen E-251) [PN1998.A3E57 1960] 60-11107
I. Eisenstein, Sergei Mikhailovich, 1898-1948. II. Title.

Seurat, Georges Pierre, 1859-1891.

COURTHION, Pierre. 759.4
Georges Seurat. Text by Pierre Courthion. [Translated by Norbert Guterman. 1st ed.] New York, H. N. Abrams [1968] 160 p. illus. (part col.) 33 cm. (The Library of great painters) Bibliography: p. 160. [ND553.S5C643] 68-13066
1. Seurat, Georges Pierre, 1859-1891.

RUSSELL, John, 1919- 759.4
Seurat. New York, F. A. Praeger [1965] 286 p. illus. (part col.) 22 cm. (A Praeger world of art profile) Bibliography: p. 271. [ND553.S5R8] 65-20074
1. Seurat, Georges Pierre, 1859-1891. I. Title. BIP

Sevareid, Arnold Eric, 1912-

†SEVAREID, Arnold Eric, 1912- 973.9'092'2
Conversations with Eric Sevareid. Washington : Public Affairs Press, c1976. vi, 215 p. ; 23 cm. "Interviews with notable Americans: Walter Lippmann, William O. Douglas, Hugo Black, Dean Acheson, George Kennan, John McCloy, Robert Hutchins, Leo Rosten, Eric Hoffer, Mary Peabody, Marietta Tree, Frances Fitzgerald, Daniel Patrick Moynihan." [CT220.S48] 76-383346 ISBN 0-8183-0248-8 pbk. : 4.50
1. United States—Biography. 2. Interviews. I. Lippmann, Walter, 1889-1974. II. Title. BIP

SEVAREID, Arnold Eric, 1912- 070'.92'4 B
Not so wild a dream / Eric Sevareid ; with a new introd. by the author. New York : Atheneum, 1976. xxi, 522 p. ; 23 cm. Autobiography. Includes index. [PN4874.S43A3 1976] 76-11538 ISBN 0-689-10741-2 : 12.50
1. Sevareid, Arnold Eric, 1912- 2. Journalists—Correspondence, reminiscences, etc. 3. World War, 1939-1945—Personal narratives, American. I. Title. BIP

Seventh-Day Adventists— Doctrinal and controversial works.

FLECK, Alcyon Ruth 922.6728
A brand from the burning; a true story of the life of a Roman Catholic priest and of his conversion to the Seventh-Day Adventist Church where he is now a minister. Mountain View Calif., Pacific Press Pub. Association [c.1960] 183p. 23cm. 60-82992 4.50
1. Seventh-Day Adventists— Doctrinal and controversial works. 2. Catholic Church—Doctrinal and controversial works—Protestant authors, I. Title.

HOEN, Reu Everett, 1888- 922.673
The Creator and His workshop. Mountain View, Calif., Pacific Press Pub. Association [1951] ix, 176 p. 21 cm. [BX6154.H56] 51-4690
1. Seventh-Day Adventists—Doctrinal and controversial works. I. Title.

Seventh-Day Adventists—Biography.

OCHS, Daniel A., 1890- 286'.7'0922 B
The past and the presidents : biographies of the General Conference presidents / by Daniel A. Ochs and Grace Lillian Ochs. Nashville : Southern Pub. Association, [1974] 231 p. : ports. ; 21 cm. [BX6191.O26] 73-92699 ISBN 0-8127-0084-8 pbk. : 4.95
1. Seventh-Day Adventists—Biography. I. Ochs, Grace Lillian, joint author. II. Title.

WALL, Frank E., 1894-1972. 286'.7'0922 B
Uncertain journey : Adventist workers with a Mennonite heritage / Frank E. Wall and Ava C. Wall. Washington : Review and Herald Pub. Association, [1974] 160 p. ; 21 cm. Bibliography: p. 159-160. [BX6189.A1W34 1974] 74-196956 3.50
1. Seventh-Day Adventists—Biography. 2. Converts, Seventh-Day Adventist. 3. Mennonites—History. I. Wall, Ava C., joint author. II. Title.

WHY I joined ... 286'.7'0922 B
moving stories of changed lives, as told to Herbert E. Douglass. [Editor: Thomas A. Davis] Washington, Review and Herald Pub. Association [1974] 63 p. ports. 19 cm. [BX6191.W45] 74-78174
1. Seventh-Day Adventists—Biography. I. Douglass, Herbert E.

Seventh-Day Adventists—Missions.

HARE, Eric B. 266.6'7'0924 B
Fulton's footprints in Fiji [by] Eric B. Harc. Washington, Review and Herald Pub. Association [1969] 252 p. illus., map (on lining papers), ports. 22 cm. [BV3680.F6F8] 77-84993
1. Fulton, John Edwin, 1869-1945. 2. Seventh-Day Adventists—Missions. 3. Seventh-Day Adventists—Missions. 4. Missions—Fiji Islands. I. Title.

WESTPHAL, Barbara (Osborne) 266.6'7'0924 B
John, the intrepid, missionary on three continents, by Barbara Westphal. Washington, Review and Herald Pub. Association [1968] 188 p. 22 cm. [BV2831.W43] 68-22280
1. Seventh-Day Adventists—Missions. 2. Missions—Latin America. I. Title.

Seventh-Day Adventists—Zaire.

PIERSON, Robert H. 266'.6'767518
Angels over Elisabethville : a true story of God's providence in time of war / by Robert H. Pierson. Mountain View, Calif. : Pacific Press Pub. Association, c1975. 88 p. : ill. ; 22 cm. (A Destiny book ; D-150) [DT665.E4P53] 74-28684 ISBN pbk. : 2.95
1. Seventh-Day Adventists—Zaire. 2. Pierson, Robert H. 3. Lubumbashi—History. I. Title.

Severinus, Saint, d. 482.

EUGIPPIUS 281.40924
Leben des heiligen Severin. Ubersetzt von Carl Rodenberg. 3.,neubearb. Aufl. Leipzig, Verlag der Dykschen Buchhandlung [1884] . New York, Johnson Reprint [1965] 88p. 19cm. (Die Geschichtschreiber der deutschen Vorzeit. 2. Gesamtausg., Bd. 4) Tr. from T. Mommsen's ed. pub. in the Scriptores rerum Germanicarum in 1898 [BR1720.S4 E85 1965] 66-3872 Price unreported
1. Severinus, Saint, d. 482. I. Rodenberg, Carl, 1854-1926, ed. and tr. II. Title.

EUGIPPIUS 281.40924
The life of Saint Severin. Tr. by Ludwig Bieler with Ludmilla Krestan. Washington, Catholic Univ. of Amer. [c.1965] x, 139p. map. 22cm. (Fathers of the church, a new tr. v. 55) Bibl. [BR60.F3E853] 65-12908 4.40
1. Severinus, Saint, d. 482. I. Bieler, Ludwig, tr. II. Title. III. Series.

Severn, Arthur, 1842-1931.

BIRKENHEAD, Sheila (Berry) Smith, countess of 1913- 759.2
Illustrious friends; the story of Joseph Severn and his son Arthur. [New York] Reynal [dist. Morrow, 1966, c.1965] xiv, 393p. illus., ports. 25cm. Bibl. [ND497.S43B53] 66-2038 8.50
1. Severn, Arthur, 1842-1931. 2. Severn, Joseph, 1793-1879. I. Title.

Severn, Joseph, 1793-1879.

SHARP, William, 1855-1905. 759.2 B
The life and letters of Joseph Severn. London, S. Low, Marston, 1892. [New York, AMS Press, 1973] xix, 308 p. illus. 23 cm. [ND497.S43S5 1973] 70-175852 ISBN 0-404-07438-3 15.00
1. Severn, Joseph, 1793-1879. BIP

Severus Alexander, emperor of Rome, 208-235.

HOPKINS, Richard Valentine Nind, Sir 1880- v. 12
The life of Alexander Severus, by R. V. Nind Hopkins ... Cambridge [Eng.] The University press, 1907. xxp., 1 1., 280p. 20cm. (Half-title: Cambridge historical essays, no. XIV) The Prince consort prize, 1906. [DG304.H7] 9-30399
1. Severus Alexander, emperor of Rome, 208-235. 2. Rome —Hist.— Severus Alexander, 222-235. I. Title.

Severus, Lucius Septimus, Emperor of Rome, 146-211.

BIRLEY, Anthony Richard. 937'.07'0924 B
Septimius Severus; the African emperor [by] Anthony Birley. [1st ed. in the U.S. of America] Garden City, N.Y., Doubleday, 1972 [c1971] xiv, 398 p. illus. 22 cm. Bibliography: p. 361-375. [DG300.B57 1972] 70-116189 8.95
1. Severus, Lucius Septimius, Emperor of Rome, 146-211.

HASEBROEK, Johannes, 1893- 937'.07'0924 B
Untersuchungen zur Geschichte des Kaisers Septimius Severus / Johannes Hasebroek. New York : Arno Press, 1975. p. cm. (Roman history) Reprint of the 1921 ed. published by C. Winter, Heidelberg. [DG300.H3 1975] 75-7321 ISBN 0-405-07085-3
1. Severus, Lucius Septimus, Emperor of Rome, 146-211. 2. Rome—History—Lucius Septimus Severus, 193-211. I. Title. II. Series. BIP

PLATNAUER, Maurice. 937'.07'0924 B
The life and reign of the Emperor Lucius Septimius Severus. Westport, Conn., Greenwood Press [1970] vi, 221 p. 23 cm. Bibliography: p. [214]-218. [DG300.P7 1970] 79-109822
1. Severus, Lucius Septimius, Emperor of Rome, 146-211. 2. Rome—History—Lucius Septimius Severus, 193-211. BIP

Sevier, John, 1745-1815.

GILMORE, James Roberts, 1822-1903. 976.8'03 B
John Sevier as a commonwealth-builder; a sequel to The rearguard of the revolution, by James R. Gilmore (Edmund Kirke). Spartanburg, S.C., Reprint Co., 1974 [c1887] xvi, 321 p. map. 22 cm. Reprint of the 1898 ed. published by D. Appleton, New York. [E302.6.S45G4 1974] 73-23070 ISBN 0-87152-155-5 15.00
1. Sevier, John, 1745-1815. 2. Tennessee—History. I. Title.

Sevigne, Marie (de Rabutin Chantal) marquise de, 1626-1696.

ALLENTUCH, Harriet Ray. 846.4
Madame de Sevigne: a portrait in letters. Baltimore, Johns Hopkins Press [1963] xv, 219 p. 22 cm. Bibliography: p. 204-212. [PQ1925.A953] 63-22351
1. Sevigne, Marie (de Rabutin Chantal) marquise de, 1626-1696. I. Title. BIP

Sewall, Jonathan, 1728-1796.

BERKIN, Carol. 973.3'14'0924 B
Jonathan Sewall; odyssey of an American loyalist. New York, Columbia University Press, 1974. xi, 200 p. 22 cm. Originally presented as the author's thesis, Columbia University. Bibliography: p. [183]-196. [E278.S48B47 1974] 74-10795 ISBN 0-231-03851-8 10.95
1. Sewall, Jonathan, 1728-1796. 2. American loyalists.

Sewall, Samuel, 1652-1730.

CHAMBERLAIN, Nathan Henry, 1830(ca.)-1901. 974.4'02'924 (B)
Samuel Sewall and the world he lived in. 2d ed. New York, Russell & Russell [1967] 319 p. illus., facsim., ports. 22cm. Reprint of the 1897 ed. [F67.S52 1967] 66-24679
1. Sewall, Samuel, 1652-1730. I. Title. BIP

CHAMBERLAIN, Nathan Henry, 1830(ca.)-1901. 974.4'02'0924 B
Samuel Sewall and the world he lived in. 2d ed. New York, Russell & Russell [1967] 319 p. illus., facsim., ports. 22 cm. Reprint of the 1897 ed. [F67.S52 1967] 66-24679
1. Sewall, Samuel, 1652-1730. I. Title.

SEWALL, Samuel, 1652-1730. 974.4'02'0924
The diary of Samuel Sewall. Edited and abridged, with an introd. by Harvey Wish. New York, Putnam [1967] 189 p. 21 cm. Bibliographical references included in "Notes" (p. 181-189) [F67.S5162] 66-20302
1. Sewall, Samuel, 1652-1730. 2. Massachusetts—History—Colonial period, ca. 1600-1775—Sources. I. Wish, Harvey, 1909- ed. II. Title. BIP

WINSLOW, Ola Elizabeth. 923.473
Samuel Sewall of Boston. New York, Macmillan [c1964] vii. 235 p. illus., port., facsims, 22 cm. "Bibliographical note": p. 221-224. [F67.S547] 63-16140
1. Sewall, Samuel, 1652-1730. I. Title. BIP

Seward, Anna, 1742-1809.

ASHMUN, Margaret Eliza, 1875-1940. 821'.6 B
The singing swan; an account of Anna Seward and her acquaintance with Dr. Johnson, Boswell & others of their time. With a pref. by Frederick A. Pottle. New York, Greenwood Press [1968, c1931] xiv, 298 p. illus., ports. 23 cm. Bibliographical footnotes. [PR3671.S7Z6 1968] 68-57589

1. Seward, Anna, 1742-1809. I. Title. BIP

Seward, Anna, 1742-1809—Correspondence.

SEWARD, Anna, 1742-1809. 821'.6 B
Letters of Anna Seward written between the years 1784 and 1807. New York : AMS Press, 1975. 6 v. : ill. ; 19 cm. (Women of letters) Reprint of the 1811 ed. published by A. Constable, Edinburgh. Includes index. [PR3671.S7Z53 1975] 76-37721 ISBN 0-404-56840-8 : 165.00 (set)
1. Seward, Anna, 1742-1809—Correspondence. I. Title.

Seward, William Henry, 1801-1872.

BANCROFT, Frederic, 973.6'0924 B 1860-1945.
The life of William H. Seward. Gloucester, Mass., P. Smith, 1967 [c1899-1900] 2 v. ports. 21 cm. Bibliographical footnotes. [E415.9.S4B3 1967] 67-5001
1. Seward, William Henry, 1801-1872. I. Title. BIP

CONRAD, Earl. 923.273
The Governor and his lady; the story of William Henry Seward and his wife Frances. New York, Putnam [1960] 433 p. 22 cm. [E415.9.S4C6] 59-9841
1. Seward, William Henry, 1801-1872. 2. Seward, Frances Adeline Miller. I. Title.

LOTHROP, Thornton 973.6'0924 B Kirkland, 1830-1913.
William Henry Seward. Boston, Houghton, Mifflin. [New York, AMS Press, 1972] viii, 423 p. illus. 19 cm. (American statesmen, v. 27) Reprint of the 1899 ed. [E415.9.S4L6 1972] 77-128959 ISBN 0-404-50877-1
1. Seward, William Henry, 1801-1872. I. Title. II. Series.

VAN DEUSEN, Glyndon 973.7'0924 B Garlock, 1897-
William Henry Seward [by] Glyndon G. Van Deusen. New York, Oxford University Press, 1967. xi, 666 p. illus., ports. 24 cm. Bibliography: p. 635-648. [E415.9.S4V3] 67-28131
1. Seward, William Henry, 1801-1872.

Sex (Psychology)

BENGIS, Ingrid. 155.3
Combat in the erogenous zone. [1st ed.] New York, Knopf; [distributed by Random House] 1972. xviii, 260 p. 22 cm. Autobiographical. [BF692.B39] 72-2248 ISBN 0-394-47550-X 6.95
1. Sex (Psychology) 2. Lesbianism. I. Title.

Sexton, Anne—Correspondence.

SEXTON, Anne. 816'.5'4
Anne Sexton : a self-portrait in letters / edited by Linda Gray Sexton and Lois Ames. Boston : Houghton Mifflin, 1977. p. cm. Includes index. [PS3537.E915Z53 1977] 77-21355 ISBN 0-395-25727-1 : 12.95
1. Sexton, Anne—Correspondence. 2. Poets, American—20th century—Correspondence. I. Sexton, Linda Gray, 1953- II. Ames, Lois. BIP

Sexual deviation - Biography.

MCNEILL, 301.41'58'0924 Elizabeth.
Nine and a half weeks : a memoir of a love affair / Elizabeth McNeill. 1st ed. New York : Dutton, c1978. 131 p. ; 22 cm. "A Henry Robbins book." [HQ79.M26 1978] 77-12744 ISBN 0-525-16715-3 : 7.95
1. Sexual deviation—Biography. 2. Sadism—Biography. 3. Masochism—Biography. I. Title.

MCNEILL, 301.41'58'0924 Elizabeth.
Nine and a half weeks : a memoir of a love affair / Elizabeth McNeill. New York : Berkley Pub. Corp., 1979, c1978. 152p. ; 18 cm. (A Berkley Book) [HQ79.M26] ISBN 0-425-04032-1 pbk. : 2.25
1. Sexual deviation — Biography. 2. Sadism — Biography. 3. Masochism — Biography. I. Title.
L.C. card no. for 1978 Dutton ed.: 77-12744.

Seymour, Louis, 1832?-1915.

DUNHAM, Harvey Lesie 1887- 926.39
Adirondack French Louie; early life in the North Woods. Text illus. by Frank Devecis; chapter headings by the author. 96 reproductions from old photos. [Utien? N. Y.] 1952. 200 p. illus., ports., maps. 24 cm. [SK17.S45D8] 52-32851
1. Seymour, Louis, 1832?-1915. 2. Outdoor life—Adirondack Mountains. I. Title.

Sforza, Caterina,

BREISACH, Ernst. 945'.05'0924 (B)
Caterina Sforza, a Renaissance virago. Chicago, University of Chicago Press [1967] vi, 375 p. geneal. tables. port. 24 cm. Bibliographical references included in notes (p. 283-349). Bibliography: p. 350-360. [DG537.8.S3B7] 67-25511
1. Sforza, Caterina, I. Title. BIP

Shah 'Alam, Emperor of Hindustan, 1728-1806.

EDWARDES, 954'.029'0924 B Michael.
King of the world; the life and times of Shah Alam, Emperor of Hindustan. New York, Taplinger Pub. Co. [1971, c1970] vi, 278 p. map, col. port. 23 cm. Bibliography: p. 269-271. [DS470.S45E34 1971] 72-131025 ISBN 0-8008-4465-3 7.95
1. Shah 'Alam, Emperor of Hindustan, 1728-1806. I. Title.

Shabbethai Zebi, 1626 1676.

EVELYN, John, 1620- 296.6'1 B 1706.
The history of Sabatai Sevi, the suppos'd Messiah of the Jews (1669). Introd. by Christopher W. Grose. Los Angeles, William Andrews Clark Memorial Library, University of California, 1968. viii, [10], 41-111 p. 22 cm. (Augustan Reprint Society. Publication no. 131) Contains a reproduction of the author's note, "To the reader" and "The history of Sabatai Sevi, the pretended Messiah of the Jewes, in the year of our Lord, 1666. The third impostor" from his "The history of the three late famous impostors, viz. Padre Ottomano, Mahomed Bei, and Sabatai Sevi ... published in 1669. "Reproduced from a copy in the William Andrews Clark Memorial Library." [BM755.S45E92 1968] 68-66889
1. Shabbethai Zebi, 1626-1676. I. Title. II. Series.

SCHNUR, Harry C. 109'.22 B
Mystic rebels; Apollonius Tyaneus, Jan van Leyden, Sabbatai Zevi, Cagliostro, by Harry C. Schnur. Freeport, N.Y., Books for Libraries Press [1971, c1949] 316 p. illus. 23 cm. (Biography index reprint series) Includes bibliographical references. [BV5095.A1S3 1971] 74-179741 ISBN 0-8369-8109-X
1. Apollonius, of Tyana. 2. Beukelszoon, Jan, 1509?-1536. 3. Shabbethai Zebi, 1626-1676. 4. Cagliostro, Alessandro, conte di, 1743-1795. I. Title.

SCHOLEM, Gershom 296.6'1 B Gerhard, 1897-
Sabbatai Sevi; the mystical Messiah, 1626-1676. [Translated by R. J. Zwi Werblowsky. Princeton, N.J.] Princeton University Press [1973] xxvii, 1000 p. illus. 24 cm. (Bollingen series, 93) Rev. and augm. translation of Shabtai Tsevi veha-tenu'ah ha-shabta'it bi-yeme hayav. Bibliography: p. [931]-956. [BM199.S3S3713 1973] 75-166389 ISBN 0-691-09916-2 25.00
1. Shabbethai Zebi, 1626-1676. 2. Sabbathaians. I. Title. II. Series. BIP

Shabones, Potawatomi chief, 1775?-1859.

DOWD, James, 1937- 970'.004'97 B
Built like a bear : which is a descriptive name for one of the last great chiefs of the "Three Fires" in Illinois, Shabni (He Has Pawed Through) / James Dowd. Fairfield, Wash. : Ye Galleon Press, 1979. 197 p. : ill. ; 27 cm. Includes index. Bibliography: p. 184-190. [E99.P8S533] 79-11658 ISBN 0-87770-212-8 : 16.00
1. Shabones, Potawatomi chief, 1775?-1859. 2. Potawatomi Indians—History. 3. Potawatomie Indians—Biography. I. Title.

Shackelford, Otis M., 1871- — Biography.

SHACKELFORD, Otis M., 811'.4 B 1871-
Seeking the best; dedicated to the Negro youth. Kansas City, Mo., Burton Pub. Co., 1911. [New York, AMS Press, 1975] 181 p. port. 19 cm. Verse and prose. [PS3537.H12A525 1975] 73-18606 ISBN 0-404-11416-4 10.00
1. Shackelford, Otis M., 1871- — Biography. I. Title.

Shadwell, Thomas, 1642?-1692.

BORGMAN, Albert Stephens, 822'.4 1890-1954.
Thomas Shadwell; his life and comedies. New York, B. Blom, 1969. x, 269 p. 24 cm. Reprint of the 1928 ed. Bibliographical footnotes. [PR3671.S8B6 1969] 68-56540
1. Shadwell, Thomas, 1642?-1692. BIP

Shaffer, Cleve F.

SIVEL, Wenceslas Joseph 926.2 Henry, 1901-
Cleve Shaffer, the Leonardo da Vinci of the poor man; quasi a bibliography; by W.J. Sivel. 2d ed. [San Francisco] Regina Pr. & Pub. Co., 735 Geary [1964] 2v. (various p.) illus., facsims (music) maps, plans, ports. 28cm. [TA140.S46S5] 65-478 50.00 set,
1. Shaffer, Cleve F. I. Title.

Shaftesbury, Anthony Ashley Cooper, 1st Earl of, 1621-1683.

CHAPMAN, Hester 941.06'092'4 B W., 1899-1976.
Four fine gentlemen / Hester Chapman. Lincoln : University of Nebraska Press, 1978. 301 p., [4] leaves of plates : ports. ; 23 cm. Includes index. Bibliography: p. [289]-291. [DA377.3.C47 1977b] 77-20589 ISBN 0-8032-1401-4 : 12.50
1. Shaftesbury, Anthony Ashley Cooper, 1st Earl of, 1621-1683. 2. Temple, William, Sir, bart., 1628-1699. 3. Reresby, John, Sir, 2d bart., 1634-1689. 4. Shrewsbury, Charles Talbot, Duke of, 1660-1718. 5. Great Britain—History—17th century—Biography. 6. Statesmen—Great Britain—Biography. I. Title. BIP

HALEY, Kenneth 942.06'6'0924 Harold Dobson.
The first Earl of Shaftesbury, by K. H. D. Haley. Oxford, Clarendon P., 1968. xii, 767 p. plate, port. 24 cm. Bibliographical footnotes. [DA407.S5H3] 68-111124 ISBN 0-19-821369-7 £6/6/-
1. Shaftesbury, Anthony Ashley Cooper, 1st Earl of, 1621-1683. I. Title.

Shaftesbury, Anthony Ashley Cooper, 7th earl of, 1801-1885.

BATTISCOMBE, 362'.92'4 B Georgina.
Shaftesbury : the great reformer, 1801-1885 / by Georgina Battiscombe ; with an introd. by Elizabeth Longford. Illustrated with photos. 1st American ed. Boston : Houghton Mifflin, 1975, c1974. xviii, 365 p., [6] leaves of plates : ill. ; 25 cm. London ed. has title: Shaftesbury: a biography of the seventh Earl, 1801-1885. Includes index. Bibliography: p. [346]-349. [HV28.S46B37 1975] 74-32370 ISBN 0-395-19953-0 : 15.00
1. Shaftesbury, Anthony Ashley Cooper, 7th Earl of, 1801-1885. 2. Reformers—Biography. I. Title. BIP

BEST, Geoffrey Francis 923.642 Andrew
Shaftsburg. New York, Arco [c.1964] 139p. illus., ports. 23cm. (Makers of world hist. ser.) Bibl. 64-21652 3.95 bds.,
1. Shaftesbury, Anthony Ashley Cooper, 7th earl of, 1801-1885. I. Title.

BEST, Geoffrey Francis 923.642 Andrew.
Shaftesbury [by] G. F. A. Best. New York, Arco Pub. Co. [1964] 139 p. illus., ports. 23 cm. Bibliographical footnotes. [HV247.S5B4] 64-21652
1. Shaftesbury, Anthony Ashley Cooper, 7th earl of, 1801-1885. I. Title.

HAMMOND, John 362'.9'24 B Lawrence Le Breton, 1872-1949.
Lord Shaftesbury, by John L. Hammond and Barbara Hammond. Freeport, N.Y., Books for Libraries Press [1971] x, 313 p. 23 cm. (Makers of the nineteenth century) Reprint of the 1923 ed. Bibliography: p. [277]-280. [HV247.S5H3 1971] 70-169762 ISBN 0-8369-5982-5
1. Shaftesbury, Anthony Ashley Cooper, 7th Earl of, 1801-1885. I. Hammond, Barbara (Bradby) 1873-1962, joint author.

HAMMOND, John Lawrence 362'.924 Le Breton, 1872-1949.
Lord Shaftesbury [by] J. L. Hammond and Barbara Hammond. 4th ed. [Hamden, Conn.] Archon Books, 1969. ix, 323 p. port. 23 cm. This ed. was first published in 1936. Bibliography: p. [289]-290. [HV247.S5H3 1969b] 70-7504 ISBN 2-08-002154- 10.00
1. Shaftesbury, Anthony Ashley Cooper, 7th Earl of, 1801-1885. I. Hammond, Barbara (Bradby) 1873- joint author. BIP

Shahn, Ben, 1898-

RODMAN, Selden, 1909- 927.59
Portrait of the artist as an American; Ben Shahn: a biography with pictures. New York, Harper [1951] xiv, 180 p. illus. (part col.) ports. 26 cm. [ND237.S465R6] 51-13491
1. Shahn, Ben, 1898- I. Title.

Shaikewitz, Nahum Meir, 1849-1905—Biography.

ZUNSER, Miriam Shomer. 947'.652
Yesterday : a memoir of a Russian Jewish family / by Miriam Shomer Zunser ; as edited by her granddaughter Emily Wortis Leider. 1st ed. New York : Harper & Row, c1978. p. cm. [DS135.R93P56 1978] 78-2150 ISBN 0-06-012553-5 : 11.95
1. Bercinsky family. 2. Shaikewitz, Nahum Meir, 1849-1905—Biography. 3. Zunser, Miriam Shomer. 4. Jews in Pinsk, White Russia—Biography. 5. Authors, Yiddish—Biography. 6. Pinsk, White Russia—Biography. I. Leider, Emily Wortis. II. Title. BIP

Shakers.

EVANS, Frederick William, 289.8 1808-1893.
Shakers ; compendium of the origin, history, principles, rules and regulations, government, and doctrines of the United Society of Believers in Christ's Second Appearing ... / by F. W. Evans. 4th ed. New York : AMS Press, 1975. 190 p. ; 19 cm. (Communal societies in America) Reprint of the 1867 ed. published in New Lebanon, N.Y. Bibliography: p. [188]-190. [BX9771.E85 1975] 72-2985 ISBN 0-404-10747-8
1. Shakers. 2. Shakers—Biography. 3. Lee, Ann, 1736-1784. 4. Lee, William, 1740-1784. 5. Whittaker, James, 1751-1787. 6. Hocknell, John, 1723?-1799. 7. Meacham, Joseph, 1742-1796. 8. Wright, Lucy, 1760-1821. I. Title: Compendium of the origin, history, principles, rules and regulations, government, and doctrines of the United Society of Believers in Christ's Second Appearing. BIP

EVANS, Frederick William, 289.8 1808-1893.
Shakers; compendium of the origin, history, principles, rules and regulations, government, and doctrines of the United Society of Believers in Christ's Second Appearing. With biographies of Ann Lee, William Lee, Jas. Whittaker, J. Hocknell, J. Meacham, and Lucy Wright. New York, B. Franklin [1972] 184 p. 19 cm. (Burt

Franklin research and source work series. Philosophy & religious history monographs, 101) [BX9771.E85 1972] 72-75873 ISBN 0-8337-4091-1
1. Shakers. 2. Shakers—Biography.

Shakers—Biography.

EVANS, Frederick William, 1808-1893. 289.8
Shakers : compendium of the origin, history, principles, rules and regulations, government, and doctrines of the United Society of Believers in Christ's Second Appearing ... / by F. W. Evans. 4th ed. New York : AMS Press, 1975. 190 p. ; 19 cm. (Communal societies in America) Reprint of the 1867 ed. published in New Lebanon, N.Y. Bibliography: p. [188]-190. [BX9771.E85 1975] 72-2985 ISBN 0-404-10747-8
1. Shakers. 2. Shakers—Biography. 3. Lee, Ann, 1736-1784. 4. Lee, William, 1740-1784. 5. Whittaker, James, 1751-1787. 6. Hocknell, John, 1723?-1799. 7. Meacham, Joseph, 1742-1796. 8. Wright, Lucy, 1760-1821. I. Title: Compendium of the origin, history, principles, rules and regulations, government, and doctrines of the United Society of Believers in Christ's Second Appearing. BIP

Shakespear, William Henry I., 1878-1914.

WINSTONE, Harry Victor Frederick. 953'.04'0924 B
Captain Shakespear : a portrait / H. V. F. Winstone. London : J. Cape, 1976. 236 p., [8] leaves of plates : ill. ; 23 cm. Includes index. Bibliography: p. [225]-226. [DS243.S48W56] 76-366809 ISBN 0-224-01194-4 : £4.95
1. Shakespear, William Henry I., 1878-1914. 2. Arabia—History. I. Title.

WINSTONE, Harry Victor Frederick. 953'.04'0924 B
Captain Shakespear : a portrait / H. V. F. Winstone. New York : Quartet Books, [1978] p. cm. Includes index. Bibliography: p. [DS243.S48W56 1978] 78-2028 9.95
1. Shakespear, William Henry I., 1878-1914. 2. Arabia—History. 3. Soldiers—Great Britain—Biography. I. Title.
Distributed by Horizon Press, New York, NY

WINSTONE, Harry Victor Frederick. 953'.04'0924 B
Captain Shakespear : a portrait / [by] H. V. F. Winstone. [New ed.]. London ; New York : Quartet Books, 1978. 240 p., [8] p. of plates : ill., facsim., maps, ports. ; 20 cm. Includes index. Bibliography: p. [229]-230. [DS243.S48W56 1978b] 78-315739 ISBN 0-7043-3169-1 : 9.95
1. Shakespear, William Henry I., 1878-1914. 2. Arabia—History. 3. Soldiers—Great Britain—Biography. I. Title.
Dist. by Horizon Press, NY.

Shakespeare, William, 1564-1616.

ALEXANDER, Peter, 1893- 822.3'3 B
Shakespeare's life and art / by Peter Alexander. Westport, Conn. : Greenwood Press, 1979. vi, 247 p. ; 23 cm. Reprint of the 1961 ed. published by New York University Press, New York. Includes bibliographical references and index. [PR2894.A43 1979] 78-25749 ISBN 0-313-20666-X lib. bdg. : 19.25
1. Shakespeare, William, 1564-1616. 2. Dramatists, English—Early modern, 1500-1700—Biography. I. Title. BIP

ANSPACHER, Louis Kaufman, 1878-1947. 822.3'3
Shakespeare as poet and lover and the enigma of the sonnets. New York, Haskell House, 1973. 55 p. 22 cm. Reprint of the 1944 ed. published by Island Press, New York. [PR2848.A885 1973] 73-9528 ISBN 0-8383-1701-4 5.95
1. Shakespeare, William, 1564-1616. Sonnets. 2. Shakespeare, William, 1564-1616—Biography—London life. 3. Shakespeare, William, 1564-1616—Style. I. Title.

ARAGON, Louis, 1897- 741.9'46
Shakespeare [by] Aragon. [Illus. by] Picasso. [Translated from the French by Bernard Frechtman] New York, H. N. Abrams [1966] 124 p. illus. 48 cm. The text was originally a short story with title: Murmure. [NC248.P5A83] 65-21830
1. Shakespeare, William, 1564-1616. 2. Shakespeare, William, 1564-1616—Portraits, etc. I. Picasso, Pablo, 1881- II. Aragon, Louis, 1897- Murmure. III. Title. IV. Title: Murmure.

BENTLEY, Gerald Eades, 1901- 928.2
Shakespeare; a biographical handbook. New Haven [Conn.] Yale [1962, c.]1961. 256p. 21cm. (Yale Shakespeare supplements) Bibl. 1.45 pap.,
1. Shakespeare, William—Biog. I. Title. BIP

BLUMENTHAL, Walter Hart 928.2
The Mermaid myth; Shakespeare not among those present. [Hanovef, N. H.] Westholm Publications, 1959. 32p. 24cm. 59-65269 5.00, bds., lim. ed.
1. Shakespeare, William—Biog.—London life. 2. Shakespeare, William—Friends and associates. I. Title.

BRADBROOK, Muriel Clara. 822.3'3
Shakespeare : the poet in his world / M. C. Bradbrook. New York : Columbia University Press, 1978. ix, 272 p. ; 22 cm. Includes index. Bibliography: p. [253]-259. [PR2894.B69 1978] 78-7611 ISBN 0-231-04648-0 : 13.50
1. Shakespeare, William, 1564-1616. 2. Dramatists, English—Early modern, 1500-1700—Biography. BIP

BROWN, Ivor John Carnegie, 1891- 822.33
How Shakespeare spent the day [by] Ivor Brown. [1st American ed.] New York, Hill and Wang [1964, c1963] 237 p. 21 cm. Bibliography: p. 231. [PR2907.B7 1964] 64-14681
1. Shakespeare, William, 1564-1616. 2. Theater—London—History. I. Title.

BROWN, Ivor John Carnegie, 1891- v. 12
Shakespeare Special ed. New York Time, Inc. [1962] 393 p. geneal. table. 21 cm. (Time reading program) Bibliography: p. 381-382. 64-7989
1. Shakespeare, William-Biog. I. Title.

CHAMBERS, Edmond Kerchever 1866-1954. v. 12
A short life of Shakespeare, with the sources, abridged by Charles Williams from Sir Edmund Chamber's William Shakespeare: a study of facts and problems. Oxford, Clarendon Press [1956] 260 p. illus. 19 cm. First edition 1933. 66-31607
1. Shakespeare, William — Biog. 2. Shakespeare, William — Biog. — Sources. I. Williams, Charles, 1866-1945. II. Title.

CHAMBRUN, Clara (Longworth) comtesse de, 1873-1954. 822.33
Shakespeare: a portrait restored. New York, P. J. Kenedy [195-] 406p. illus. 26cm. 'Translation made by Clara Longworth, countess de Chambrun, of her Shakespeare retrouve.' [PR2896.C46] 57-6996
1. Shakespeare, William, 1564-1616. I. Title. BIP

CHUTE, Marchette Gaylord, 1909- v. 12
Shakespeare of London. New York, Dutton [1964] 397 p. map (on lining-papers) 23 cm. Anniversary ed., 1964. 66-13371
1. Shakespeare, William, 1564-1616. I. Title. BIP

DRINKWATER, John, 1882-1937. 822.3'3
Shakespeare. New York, Macmillan [1956?] 122p. port. 19cm. (Great lives. [1] 'Note on books': p. 121-122. [PR2894.D] A57
1. Shakespeare, William, 1564-1616. I. Title.

EAINES, Charles. 822.3'3
William Shakespeare and his plays. London, New York, Franklin Watts Ltd. [1971, c1968] vii, 181 p. 22 cm. ([Immortals of mankind]) Bibliography: p. 175-178. [PR2893.H3 1971] 75-874470 ISBN 0-85166-317-6 £1.25
1. Shakespeare, William, 1564-1616. I. Title.

FLEAY, Frederick Gard, 1831-1909. 822.3'3 B
A chronicle history of the life and work of William Shakespeare, player, poet, and playmaker. New York, AMS Press [1970] viii, 364 p. illus., port. 18 cm. Reprint of the 1886 ed. [PR2894.F5 1970] 70-130614 ISBN 0-404-02405-X
1. Shakespeare, William, 1564-1616. I. Title.

FRIPP, Edgar Innes, d.1931. v. 12
Shakespeare, man and artist. London, New York, Oxford university press [1964] 2 v. (939 p) illus., ports, maps, facsims. 23 cm. First published 1938. Bibliographical footnotes. 66-60489
1. Shakespeare, William — Biog. and personalia. 2. Shakespeare, William — Homes and Haunts. 3. Shakespeare, William — London of. 4. Shakespeare, — Friends and associates. I. Title.

FRYE, Roland Mushat. 822'.3'3
Shakespeare's life and times: a pictorial record. Princeton, N.J., Princeton University Press, 1967. 1 v. (unpaged) illus., ports. 29 cm. Bibliography. [PR2893.F7] 67-11031
1. Shakespeare, William, 1564-1616. 2. Shakespeare, William, 1564-1616—Contemporary England. I. Title. BIP

HALLIDAY, Frank Ernest, 1903- v. 12
The life of Shakespeare. Baltimore, Penguin Books [1963, c1961] 298 p. illus. 18 cm. (Pelican book, A642) American ediction (N.Y., T. Yoseloff) has title: Shakespeare. Includes bibliography. 64-43912
1. Shakespeare, William, 1564-1616. I. Title.

HALLIDAY, Frank Ernest, 1903- 822.33
Shakespeare, a pictorial biography. New York, T. Y. Crowell Co. [1956] 147p. illus. 25cm. (A Studio publication) [PR2894.H258] 928.2 57-821
1. Shakespeare, William—Biog. I. Title.

HALLIDAY, Frank Ernest, 1903- 928.2
Shakespeare. New York, T. Yoseloff [c.1961] 248p. illus. 25cm. Bibl. 61-9624 5.00
1. Shakespeare, William, 1564-1616. I. Title.

HALLIDAY, Frank Ernest, 1903- 928.2
Shakespeare. New York, T. Yoseloff [1961] 248 p. illus. 25 cm. London ed. (Duckworth) has title: The life of Shakespeare. Includes bibliography. [PR2894.H257] 61-9624
1. Shakespeare, William, 1564-1616. I. Title.

HALLIDAY, Frank Ernest, 1903- 928.2
Shakespeare, a pictorial biography, by F. E. Halliday [New ed.] New York, Viking [1964] 147p. illus., facsims., geneal. table. ports. (1 col.) 24cm. (Studio bk.) 64-3852 6.50
1. Shakespeare, William—Biog. I. Title.

HARBAGE, Alfred, 1901- 822.33
Conceptions of Shakespeare. Cambridge, Harvard University Press, 1966. viii, 164 p. 22 cm. Bibliographical references included in "Notes" (p. [149]-157) [PR2976.H3] 66-13180
1. Shakespeare, William, 1546-1616—Criticism and interpretation. 2. Shakespeare, William, 1564-1616—Biography. I. Title.

HAZLITT, William Carew, 1834-1913. 822.3'3
Shakespeare. [Folcroft, Pa.] Folcroft Library Editions, 1973. p. Reprint of the 1902 ed. published by B. Quaritch, London. [PR2894.H4 1973] 73-6584 ISBN 0-8414-2096-3 (lib. bdg.)
1. Shakespeare, William, 1564-1616—Biography. 2. Shakespeare, William, 1564-1616. Sonnets. 3. Shakespeare, William, 1564-1616—Friends and associates. I. Title.

HILL, Frank Ernest, 1888- 822.3'3
To meet Will Shakespeare. Illustrated by Addison Burbank. Freeport, N.Y., Books for Libraries Press [1970, c1949] xii, 481 p. illus. 23 cm. (Library of Shakespearean biography and criticism, ser. 3, pt. A) Bibliography: p. 435-436. [PR2894.H5 1970] 77-109650
1. Shakespeare, William, 1564-1616. I. Title. II. Series. BIP

HUGO, Victor Marie, comte, 1802-1885. 822.3'3
William Shakespeare. Translated by Melville B. Anderson. Freeport, N.Y., Books for Libraries Press [1970] xxiv, 424 p. 23 cm. (Library of Shakespearean biography and criticism, ser. 3, pt. A) "First published 1886." [PR2896.H7813 1970] 77-128888 ISBN 0-8369-5508-0
1. Shakespeare, William, 1564-1616. I. Title. II. Series.

KENNY, Thomas. 822.3'3
The life and genius of Shakespeare. London, Longman, Green, Longman, Roberts, and Green, 1864. [New York, AMS Press, 1973] viii, 414 p. illus. 23 cm. [PR2894.K4 1973] 75-171056 ISBN 0-404-03657-0 17.50
1. Shakespeare, William, 1564-1616. I. Title. BIP

KNIGHT, William Nicholas, 1939- 822.3'3
Shakespeare's hidden life: Shakespeare at the law, 1585-1595 [by] W. Nicholas Knight. New York, Mason & Lipscomb [1973] ix, 325 p. illus. 25 cm. Bibliography: p. [309]-320. [PR2894.K54] 73-84881 ISBN 0-88405-003-3 12.50
1. Shakespeare, William, 1564-1616. 2. Shakespeare, William, 1564-1616—Knowledge—Law. 3. Shakespeare, William, 1564-1616—Autographs. I. Title.

LAMBORN, Edmund Arnold Greening, 1877- v. 12
Shakespeare, the man and his stage, by E.A.G. Lamborn and G. B. Harrison. [Oxford, University Press, 1959] 128 p. illus. 19 cm. (World's manuals) First published 1923. 65-68446
1. Shakespeare, William — Biog. 2. Shakespeare, William — Stage history — To 1625. I. Title. II. Series.

MACARDLE, Dorothy, Margaret Callan, 1889- 822.33
Shakespeare, man and boy. Ed. by George Bott. London. Faber & Faber [New York, Hillary House, 1966, c.1961] 260p. illus. 21cm. [PR2895.M25] 62-5825 3.50
1. Shakespeare, William, 1564-1616. I. Title.

MCCURDY, Harold Grier, 1909- 822.33
The personality of Shakespeare; a venture in psychological method. New Haven, Yale University Press, 1953. xi, 248p. diagrs. 25cm. Bibliography: p. 231-234. [PR2909.M2] 53-7778
1. Shakespeare, William—Biog.—Character. 2. Shakespeare, William—Criticism and interpretation. I. Title. **BIP**

MACKENZIE, Barbara Alida. 821'.3
Shakespeare's sonnets, their relations to his life / by Barbara A. Mackenzie. 1st AMS ed. New York : AMS Press, 1978. x, 81 p. ; 19 cm. Reprint of the 1946 ed. published by M. Miller, Cape Town. Includes index. Bibliography: p. 80. [PR2848.M24 1978] 78-6965 ISBN 0-404-04135-3 : 9.50
1. Shakespeare, William, 1564-1616. Sonnets. 2. Shakespeare, William, 1564-1616—Friends and associates. 3. Sonnets, English—History and criticism. 4. Dramatists, English—Early modern, 1500-1700—Biography. I. Title.

MASSON, David, 1822-1907. 822.3'3 B
Shakespeare personally. Edited and arr. by Rosaline Masson. [Folcroft, Pa.] Folcroft Library Editions, 1974. p. cm. Reprint of the 1914 ed. published by Smith, Elder, London. [PR2894.M35 1974] 74-11143 22.50
1. Shakespeare, William, 1564-1616. 2. Shakespeare, William, 1564-1616—Biography—Character. I. Title. **BIP**

MAY, Robin. 822.3'3 B
Who was Shakespeare? : The man, the times, the works / Robin May. New York : St. Martin's Press, 1974. 143 p. : ill. ; 23 cm. Includes index. Bibliography: p. 137. [PR2894.M38 1974b] 74-81476 6.95
1. Shakespeare, William, 1564-1616. I. Title.

MENDILOW, Adam Abraham, 1909- 822'.3'3
The world & art of Shakespeare [by] A. A. Mendilow & Alice Shalvi. New York, D. Davey, 1967. viii, 285 p. 25 cm. [PR2893.M4 1967] 67-6655
1. Shakespeare, William, 1564-1616. I Shalvi, Alice, joint author. II. Title. **BIP**

MEURLING, Per. v. 12
Shakespeare. Stockholm, Wahlstrom & Widstrand [1952] 258p. illus., ports. 22cm. A52
1. Shakespeare, William, 1564-1616. I. Title.

MONTAGUE, William Kelly, 1892- 822.33
The man of Stratford--the real Shakespeare. New York, Vantage [1964, c.1963] 199p. illus. 22cm. Bibl. 64-2275 3.50
1. Shakespeare, William, 1564-1616. I. Title.

NOBLE, Iris. 92
William Shakespeare. New York, J. Messner [1961] 190p. 21cm. [PR2895.N6] 61-7995
1. Shakespeare, William—Juvenile literature. I. Title.

O'DONOVAN, Michael, 1903- v. 12
Shakespeare's progress [by] Frank O'Connor (pseud.] New York, Collier Books [1961, c1960] 192 p. 18 cm. (Collier books, BS 20) "Under the title The road to Stratford this book was published in somewhat different form in Great Britain in 1948." 65-22829
1. Shakespeare, William, 1564-1616. I. Title. II. Title: The road to Stratford.

PARROTT, Thomas Marc, 1866- 928.2
William Shakespeare, a handbook. Rev. ed. New York, Scribners [1961, c.1934, 1955] 266p. illus. (Scribner lib., SL42) Bibl. 1.45 pap.,
1. Shakespeare, William, 1564-1616. I. Title.

PARROTT, Thomas Marc, 1866-1960. 928.2
William Shakespeare, a handbook. Rev. ed. New York, Scribner [1955] 266 p. illus. 19 cm. Includes bibliography. [PR2894.P3 1955] 822.33 55-7294
1. Shakespeare, William, 1564-1616.

PEARSON, Hesketh [Edward Hesketh Gibbons Pearson] 928.2
A life of Shakespeare. With an anthology of Shakespeare's poetry. New York 22, Walker & Co. [75 E. 55 St., 1961] 239p. front., 61-7510 5.00
1. Shakespeare, William, 1564-1616. I. Title.

QUENNELL, Peter, 1905- 928.2
Shakespeare, a biography [New York] Avon [1964, c.1963] 384p. 18cm. (V2096) Bibl. .75 pap.,
1. Shakespeare, William, 1564-1616. I. Title.

QUENNELL, Peter, 1905- 928.2
Shakespeare, a biography. [1st ed.] Cleveland, World Pub. Co. [c1963] 352 p. illus., ports., facsims. 23 cm. Bibliography: p. 335-337. [PR2894.Q4] 63-8981
1. Shakespeare, William, 1564-1616. I. Title.

RIBNER, Irving. 822.3'3
William Shakespeare; an introduction to his life, times, and theatre. Waltham, Mass., Blaisdell Pub. Co. [1969] 280 p. illus. 21 cm. (A Blaisdell book in the humanities) Bibliography: p. 260-275. [PR2894.R5] 69-11170
1. Shakespeare, William, 1564-1616. I. Title.

ROSIGNOLI, Maria Pia. 822.3'3
The life and times of Shakespeare; text by Maria Pia Rosignoli, translator [from the Italian] Mary Kanani. London, New York [etc.] Hamlyn, 1968. 2-75 p. illus. (some col.), ports. (some col.), facsims. 30 cm. (Portraits of greatness) Col. illus. on lining papers. [PR2894.R6313] 74-401925 17/6
1. Shakespeare, William, 1564-1616. 2. Shakespeare, William, 1564-1616—Contemporary England. I. Title.

ROWSE, Alfred Leslie, 1903- 822.33
William Shakespeare, a biography. New York, Pocket Bks. [1965, c.1963] 511p. illus. 18cm. (Cardinal ed., 95014) Bibl. [PR2894.R68] .95 pap.,
1. Shakespeare, William, 1564-1616. I. Title.

ROWSE, Alfred Leslie, 1903- 822.33
William Shakespeare, a biography. [1st cd.] New York, Harper & Row [1963] xiv, 484 p. illus., ports., facsims. 24 cm. Bibliographical references included in "Notes" (p. 467-478) [PR2894.R68 1963a] 63-16517
1. Shakespeare, William, 1564-1616.

ROWSE, Alfred Leslie, 1903- 822.3'3
William Shakespeare, a biography. London, Macmillan, 1963. xiv, 484 p. illus., ports., map. 23 cm. Bibliographical references included in "Notes" (p. 467-478) [PR2894.R68] 63-25052
1. Shakespeare, William, 1564-1616. I. Title.

SCHELLING, Felix Emmanuel, 1858-1945. 822.3'3
Shakespeare biography and other papers, chiefly Elizabethan. Freeport, N.Y., Books for Libraries Press [1968] vii, 143 p. 22 cm. (Essay index reprint series) Reprint of the 1937 ed. Contents.Contents.—Shakespeare biography.—A negative of Shakespeare.—The return to Shakespearean orthodoxy.—Shakespeare our contemporary.—The land that the Puritans put behind them.—Memorial of Horace Howard Furness.—Shakespeare books in the library of the Furness Memorial.—Weir Mitchell, poet and novelist.—The study of literature.—Walls of brass: a fancy and a parallel. Bibliographical footnotes. [PR2890.S26 1968] 68-26473
1. Shakespeare, William, 1564-1616. I. Title. **BIP**

SHAKESPEARE. v. 12
London, Macmillan; New York, St. Martin' Press, 1957. 232p. 18cm. (Macmillan's pocket library)
1. Shakespeare, William—Biog. I. Raleigh, Walter Alexander, Sir 1861-1922.

SHAKESPEARE of London. v. 12
New York, Dutton. 1957. xii, 397p. map. (Dutton paperback everyman. D1) Bibliography: p.363-372.
1. Shakespeare, William, 1564-1616. I. Chute, Marchette Gaylord, 1909-

SISSON, Charles Jasper, 1885- v. 12
Shakespeare. London, New York, Published for the British Councilby Longmans, Green [1955] 50p. port. 22cm. (Bibliographical series of supplements to British book news, no. 58) Bibliography: p. 33-50. A55
1. Shakespeare, William, 1564-1616. I. Title. II. Series.

SISSON, Rosemary Anne. 928.2
The young Shakespeare; illustrated by Denise Brown. New York, Roy Publishers [1959] 160 p. illus. 21 cm. [PR2900.S5] 60-6950
1. Shakespeare, William — Juvenile literature. I. Title.

SPEAIGHT, Robert, 1904- 822.3'3
Shakespeare, the man and his achievement / Robert Speaight. New York : Stein and Day, [1977] p. cm. Includes index. Bibliography: p. [PR2894.S65] 76-12979 ISBN 0-8128-2097-5 : 15.00
1. Shakespeare, William, 1564-1616. I. Title.

WELLS, Stanley W., 1930- 822.3'3
Shakespeare : the writer and his work / by Stanley Wells. New York : Scribners, c1978. 104 p. : ill. ; 22 cm. Bibliography: p. 93-104. [PR2894.W44] 79-63320 ISBN 0-684-15983-X : 8.95 ISBN 0-684-15981 8 (pbk.) : 3.95
1. Shakespeare, William, 1564-1616. 2. Dramatists, English—Early modern, 1500-1700—Biography. **BIP**

WILSON, John Dover 822.33
The essential Shakespeare a biographical adventure. [New York] Cambridge University Press, 1960. viii, 148p. (bibl. notes: p. 146-148) illus. (front.) 19cm. 60-16128 1.25 pap.,
1. Shakespeare, William—Biog.—Character. 2. Shakespeare, William—Criticism and interpretation. I. Title.

WILSON, John Dover, 1881-1969. 822.3'3
The essential Shakespeare : a biographical adventure / by J. Dover. Wilson. Brooklyn : Haskell House, [1977] p. cm. Reprint of the 1952 ed. published by the University Press, Cambridge, England. Includes bibliographical references. [PR2894.W57 1977] 76-30694 lib.bdg. : 10.95
1. Shakespeare, William, 1564-1616. 2. Dramatists, English—Early modern, 1500-1700—Biography. I. Title.

Shakespeare, William, 1564-1616—Addresses, essays, lectures.

HEARN, Lafcadio, 1850-1904. 822.3'3
Lectures on Shakespeare / by Lafcadio Hearn ; edited by Iwao Inagaki. Folcroft, Pa. : Folcroft Library Editions, 1977. 128 p. ; 19 cm. Reprint of the 1931 ed. published by Hokuseido Press, Tokyo. Lectures delivered in 1899 at the Imperial University of Tokyo and first published in 1928. Colophon in Japanese at end. Includes index. [PR2890.H4 1977] 77-21975 ISBN 0-8414-5075-7 lib. bdg. : 15.00
1. Shakespeare, William, 1564-1616—Addresses, essays, lectures. 2. Dramatists, English—Early modern, 1500-1700—Biography—Addresses, essays, lectures. I. Title. **BIP**

Shakespeare, William, 1564-1616—Authorship.

ACHESON, Arthur, 1864-1930. 822.3'3
Shakespeare, Chapman and Sir Thomas More; providing a more definite basis for biography and criticism. New York, AMS Press [1970] v, 280 p. illus., facsim. 23 cm. Reprint of the 1931 ed. Contents.Contents.—Shakespeare as a serving man.—An unknown company identified.—Shakespeare and Pembroke's company.—Shakespeare, Chapman, and Sir Thomas More.—Greene's collaboration with Lodge and Nashe.—Stage history of Kyd and his plays.—Chapman as a pre-Shakespearean.—Peele's hand in Sir Thomas More. [PR2894.A25 1970] 72-113536 ISBN 0-404-00278-1
1. Shakespeare, William, 1564-1616—Biography—London life. 2. Shakespeare, William, 1564-1616—Authorship. 3. Chapman, George, 1559?-1634. 4. Sir Thomas More (Old play) 5. English drama—Early modern and Elizabethan, 1500-1600—History and criticism. I. Title.

EVANS, Alfred John, 1889- 822.3'3
Shakespeare's magic circle, by Alfred J. Evans. Freeport, N.Y., Books for Libraries Press [1970] 160 p. 23 cm. (Library of Shakespearean biography and criticism, ser. 3, pt. C) Reprint of the 1956 ed. Bibliography: p. 157. [PR2937.E85 1970] 72-128884
1. Shakespeare, William, 1564-1616—Authorship. 2. Shakespeare, William, 1564-1616—Friends and associates. I. Title. II. Series. **BIP**

Shakespeare, William, 1564-1616—Bibliography.

BROOKS, Alden 822.3'3 B
Will Shakspere, factotum and agent. New York, Round Table Press, 1937. [New York, AMS Press, 1974] 374 p. 23 cm. [PR2894.B77 1974] 77-39536 ISBN 0-404-01117-9 9.50
1. Shakespeare, William, 1564-1616—Dibliography.

SISSON, Charles Jasper, 1885- v. 12
Shakespeare. [rev.] London, New York, Published for the British Council and the National Book League by Longmans, Green [1959] 52 p. port. (Writers and their work no. 58) Bibliography: p. 36-52.
1. Shakespeare, William — Bibliography. I. Title.

Shakespeare, William, 1564-1616—Biography.

BAGEHOT, Walter, 1826-1877. 822.3'3
Shakespeare the man; an essay. New York, McClure, Phillips, 1901. [Folcroft, Pa.] Folcroft Library Editions, 1973. p. [PR2899.B26 1973] 73-4015 6.50
1. Shakespeare, William, 1564-1616—Biography. **BIP**

BAGEHOT, Walter, 1826-1877. 822.3'3
Shakespeare the man; an essay. [Folcroft, Pa.] Folcroft Library Editions, 1974. 48 p.

24 cm. Reprint of the 1901 ed. published by McClure, Phillips, New York. Includes bibliographical references. [PR2899.B26 1974] 73-4015 ISBN 0-8414-1765-2 (lib. bdg.)
1. Shakespeare, William, 1564-1616—Biography.

BOHN, Henry George, 1796-1884. 822.3'3 B
The Biography and bibliography of Shakespeare. [New York, AMS Press, 1972] xvi, 366, 2253-2368 p. illus. 19 cm. Reprint of the 1863 ed. Written for members of the Philobiblon Society. The bibliography has special t.p. [PR2894.B65 1972] 74-38033 ISBN 0-404-00920-4 12.50
1. Shakespeare, William, 1564-1616—Biography. 2. Shakespeare, William, 1564-1616—Bibliography. I. Philobiblon Society, London. BIP

BROWN, Charles Armitage, 1786-1842. 821'.3
Shakespeare's autobiographical poems. Being his sonnets clearly developed: with his character drawn chiefly from his works. London, J. Bohn, 1838. [New York, AMS Press, 1972] viii, 306 p. 18 cm. [PR2909.B7 1972] 76-39541 ISBN 0-404-01127-6 12.50
1. Shakespeare, William, 1564-1616—Biography. 2. Shakespeare, William, 1564-1616. Sonnets. I. Title.

CALMOUR, Alfred Cecil, 1857?-1912. 822.3'3
Fact and fiction about Shakespeare; with some account of the playhouses, players, and playwrights of his period. New York, AMS Press [1972] 112 p. illus. 19 cm. Reprint of the 1894 ed. [PR2894.C3 1972] 70-39876 ISBN 0-404-01365-1 22.50
1. Shakespeare, William, 1564-1616—Biography. 2. Shakespeare, William, 1564-1616—Stage history—To 1625. I. Title.

CLARK, Cumberland, 1862- 822.3'3 B
Shakespeare & Dickens; a lecture as delivered to the Dickens Fellowship, Shakespeare Reading Society, etc., London, and the Shakespeare Club, Stratford-on-Avon. New York, Haskell House, 1973. 39 p. 23 cm. Reprint of the 1918 ed. [PR2899.C52 1973] 73-9794 ISBN 0-8383-1703-0 5.95
1. Shakespeare, William, 1564-1616—Biography. 2. Dickens, Charles, 1812-1870—Biography. I. Title.

DEQUINCEY, Thomas, 1785-1859. 809 B
Biographies of Shakspeare, Pope, Goethe, and Schiller, and on the policial parties of modern England. New York, AMS Press [1972] vii, 376 p. port. 19 cm. Reprint of the ed. issued in 1862 by A. and C. Black, Edinburgh, as: De Quincey's works, v. 15. [PN452.D4 1972] 75-164822 ISBN 0-404-02079-8 17.50
1. Shakespeare, William, 1564-1616—Biography. 2. Pope, Alexander, 1688-1744. 3. Goethe, Johann Wolfgang von, 1749-1832—Biography. 4. Schiller, Johann Christoph Friedrich von, 1759-1805—Biography. 5. Political parties—Great Britain.

DRAKE, Nathan, 1766-1836. 822.3'3
Shakespeare and his times; including the biography of the poet; criticisms on his genius and writings; a new chronology of his plays; a disquisition on the object of his sonnets; and a history of the manners, customs, amusements, superstitions, poetry, and elegant literature of his age. New York, B. Franklin [1969] 2 v. in 1. (xi, 660 p.) 24 cm. (Selected essays in literature & criticism, #20) (Burt Franklin Research & source works series, #332.) Reprint of the 1838 ed. Bibliographical footnotes. [PR2894.D73 1969] 68-58458
1. Shakespeare, William, 1564-1616—Biography. 2. Shakespeare, William, 1564-1616—Criticism and interpretation. 3. Shakespeare, William, 1564-1616—Contemporary England. 4. English literature—Early modern, 1500-1700—History and criticism. I. Title.

ELTON, Charles Isaac, 1839-1900. 822.3'3 B
William Shakespeare: his family and friends. Edited by A. Hamilton Thompson with a memoir of the author by Andrew Lang. London, J. Murray, 1904. [New York, AMS Press, 1972] 521 p. illus. 23 cm. [PR2894.E5 1972] 72-166025 ISBN 0-404-02324-X
1. Shakespeare, William, 1564-1616—Biography. BIP

ELZE, Karl, 1821-1889. 822.3'3 B
William Shakespeare, a literary biography. Translated by L. Dora Schmitz. London, G. Bell, 1888. [New York, AMS Press, 1973] 587 p. 23 cm. Original ed. issued in series: Bohn's standard library. Includes bibliographical references. [PR2897.E5 1973] 73-166028 25.00
1. Shakespeare, William, 1564-1616—Biography. I. Title.

FOX, Levi. 822.3'3
The Shakespeare book. Norwich, Jarrold [1969]. [32] p. illus. (some col.), facsims., geneal. table, ports. 25 cm. Illus. and map on lining papers. [PR2899.F63] 76-465060 ISBN 0-85306-171-8 5/-
1. Shakespeare, William, 1564-1616—Biography. 2. Shakespeare, William, 1564-1616—Museums, relics, etc. I. Title.

FURNIVALL, Frederick James, 1825-1910. 822.3'3
Shakespeare; life and work, by F. J. Furnivall & John Munro. London, New York, Cassell, 1908. [New York, AMS Press, 1971] 278 p. illus. 19 cm. Bibliography: p. 266-270. [PR2895.F8 1971] 77-168082 ISBN 0-404-02664-8
1. Shakespeare, William, 1564-1616—Biography. I. Munro, John James, joint author.

HALLIWELL-PHILLIPPS, James Orchard, 1820-1889. 822.3'3 B
Life of William Shakespeare. New York, AMS Press [1973] xvi, 336 p. illus. 23 cm. Reprint of the 1848 ed. published by J. R. Smith, London. [PR2894.H28 1973] 73-168223 ISBN 0-404-03065-3 15.00
1. Shakespeare, William, 1564-1616—Biography. BIP

HARRIS, Frank, 1855-1931. 822.3'3
The man Shakespeare and his tragic life-story. New York, Horizon Press [1969] xviii, 422 p. 25 cm. Reprint of the 1909 ed. [PR2909.H3 1969] 79-92712 10.00
1. Shakespeare, William, 1564-1616—Biography. I. Title.

HAZLITT, William Carew, 1834-1913. 822.3'3
Shakespeare. [Folcroft, Pa.] Folcroft Library Editions, 1973. p. Reprint of the 1902 ed. published by B. Quaritch, London. [PR2894.H4 1973] 73-6584 ISBN 0-8414-2096-3 (lib. bdg.)
1. Shakespeare, William, 1564-1616—Biography. 2. Shakespeare, William, 1564-1616. Sonnets. 3. Shakespeare, William, 1564-1616—Friends and associates. I. Title.

KNIGHT, Charles, 1791-1873. 822.3'3 B
William Shakspere; a biography. [New York, AMS Press, 1972] 544 p. illus. 24 cm. Reprint of the 1843 ed. Includes bibliographical references. [PR2894.K5 1972] 73-168057 ISBN 0-404-03734-8 25.00
1. Shakespeare, William, 1564-1616—Biography.

LAMBORN, Edmund Arnold Greening, 1877- 822.3'3 B
Shakespeare, the man and his stage / by E. A. G. Lamborn and G. B. Harrison. Brooklyn, N.Y. : Haskell House Pub., 1977. 128 p. : ill. ; 21 cm. Reprint of the 1924 ed. published by Oxford University Press, London. [PR2894.L3 1977] 76-30695 lib.bdg. : 10.95
1. Shakespeare, William, 1564-1616—Biography. 2. Shakespeare, William, 1564-1616—Stage history—To 1625. 3. Dramatists, English—Early modern, 1500-1700—Biography. I. Harrison, George Bagshawe, 1894- joint author. II. Title.

LEE, Sidney, Sir, 1859-1926. 822.3'3 B
A life of William Shakespeare. New York, Macmillan, 1903. St. Clair Shores, Mich., Scholarly Press [1971, c1898] xxv, 476 p. illus. 22 cm. Includes bibliographical references. [PR2894.L4 1971] 70-145137 ISBN 0-403-01069-1
1. Shakespeare, William, 1564-1616—Biography. 2. Shakespeare, William, 1564-1616—Bibliography. I. Title.

LEE, Sidney, Sir 1859-1926. 822.3'3 B
A life of William Shakespeare. New York, Dover Publications [1968] xxxix, 792 p. illus. 22 cm. "An unabridged and unaltered republication of the ... edition published ... in 1931." Includes bibliographical references. [PR2894.L4 1968] 68-28404 3.75
1. Shakespeare, William, 1564-1616—Biography. 2. Shakespeare, William, 1564-1616—Bibliography. I. Title. BIP

*MORRILL, Sibley S. 822.33
The trouble with Shakespeare, [by] Sibley S. Morrill. San Francisco, Cadleon Press [1974] 98 p. 22 cm. [PR2935] 73-88927 ISBN 0-9600310-4-9 3.95 (pbk.)
1. Shakespeare, William, 1564-1616-biography. I. Title.

NORMAN, Charles, 1904- v. 12
The playmaker of Avon. New York, D. McKay [1966, c1949] 155 p. illus. 20 cm. (Tartan books, 22) 68-102475
1. Shakespeare, William, 1564-1616—Biog. I. Title.

PAYNE, Pierre Stephen Robert, 1911- 822'.3'3
By me, William Shakespeare / by Robert Payne. 1st ed. New York : Everest House, 1980, c1979. p. cm. Includes index. Bibliography: p. [PR2894.P35 1980] 79-51203 ISBN 0-89696-064-1 : 14.95
1. Shakespeare, William, 1564-1616—Biography. 2. Dramatists, English—Early modern, 1500-1700—Biography. I. Title. BIP

RALEIGH, Walter Alexander, Sir, 1861-1922. 822.3'3 B
Shakespeare. New York, Macmillan Co., 1907. [New York, AMS Press, 1972] v, 233 p. 23 cm. Reprint of the 1907 ed. originally issued in the series: English men of letters. [PR2894.R3 1972] 74-182702 ISBN 0-404-05206-1
1. Shakespeare, William, 1564-1616—Biography.

REESE, Max Meredith. 928.2
Shakespeare, his world & his work. New York, St. Martin's Press, 1953. xiii,589 p. illus., map. 23 cm. Bibliography: p. 566-568. [PR2894.R4 1953a] 53-4011
1. Shakespeare, William, 1564-1616—Biography. 2. Shakespeare, William, 1564-1616—Contemporary England.

ROLFE, William James, 1827-1910. 822.3'3 B
A life of William Shakespeare. Boston, D. Estes, 1904. [New York, AMS Press, 1973] iii, 551 p. illus. 19 cm. Bibliography: p. 491-517. [PR2894.R6 1973] 70-174961 ISBN 0-404-05387-4 20.00
1. Shakespeare, William, 1564-1616—Biography. I. Title. BIP

ROLFE, William James, 1827-1910 928.2
Shakespeare the boy; with sketches of the home and school life, games and sports, manners, customs and folk-lore of the time [Reissue] New York, Ungar [1965] x, 251p. illus. 21cm. [PR2903.R6] 64-25562 4.50
1. Shakespeare, William, 1564-1616.—Biog.—Youth. I. Title.

ROWSE, Alfred Leslie, 1903- 822'.3'3 B
Shakespeare the Elizabethan / A. L. Rowse. New York : Putnam, c1977. 128 p. : ill. ; 29 cm. Includes index. [PR2894.R66 1977b] 76-44575 ISBN 0-399-11889-6 : 14.95
1. Shakespeare, William, 1564-1616—Biography. 2. Dramatists, English—Early modern, 1500-1700—Biography. I. Title.

ROWSE, Alfred Leslie, 1903- 822.3'3 B
Shakespeare the man [by] A. L. Rowse. [1st U.S. ed.] New York, Harper & Row [1973] xi, 284 p. illus. 22 cm. (A Cass Canfield book) [PR2894.R67 1973b] 72-10683 ISBN 0-06-013691-X 10.00
1. Shakespeare, William, 1564-1616—Biography. I. Title.

SCHOENBAUM, Samuel, 1927- 822.3'3 B
William Shakespeare : a compact documentary life / S. Schoenbaum. New York : Oxford University Press, 1977. xix, 376 p. : ill. ; 22 cm. Abridged ed. of William Shakespeare, a documentary life. Includes bibliographical references and index. [PR2894.S33 1977] 75-46358 ISBN 0-19-502211-4 : 12.50
1. Shakespeare, William, 1565-1616—Biography. 2. Dramatists, English—Early modern, 1500-1700—Biography. BIP

SHORE, William Teignmouth, 1865-1932. 822.3'3 B
Shakespeare's self. New York, Haskell House Publishers, 1971. 186 p. 23 cm. Reprint of the 1920 ed. [PR2894.S45 1971] 72-179265 ISBN 0-8383-1366-3
1. Shakespeare, William, 1564-1616—Biography. I. Title. BIP

SYMON, Josiah Henry, Sir, 1846-1934. 822.3'3
Shakespeare the Englishman. New York, Haskell House, 1971. xv, 231 p. port. 23 cm. Reprint of the 1929 ed. Contents.Contents.—Shakespeare at home.—Shakespeare the Englishman.—Shakespeare quotation. [PR2894.S9 1971] 77-155114 ISBN 0-8383-1288-8
1. Shakespeare, William, 1564-1616—Biography. 2. Shakespeare, William, 1564-1616—Quotations. I. Title. BIP

WAGENKNECHT, Edward Charles, 1900- 822.3'3
The personality of Shakespeare [by] Edward Wagenknecht. [1st ed.] Norman, University of Oklahoma Press [1972] ix, 190 p. 24 cm. Includes bibliographical references. [PR2909.W3] 72-868 ISBN 0-8061-1028-7 5.00
1. Shakespeare, William, 1564-1616—Biography. 2. Shakespeare, William, 1564-1616—Criticism and interpretation. I. Title. BIP

WILSON, John Anthony Burgess, 1917- 822.3'3
Shakespeare [by] Anthony Burgess. [1st American ed.] New York, Knopf, 1970. 272 p. illus., facsims., 48 col. plates (incl. coat of arms, ports.) 27 cm. Bibliography: p. [266] [PR2894.W568 1970] 73-112637 17.50
1. Shakespeare, William, 1564-1616—Biography. 2. Shakespeare, William, 1564-1616—Contemporary England.

WILSON, John Anthony Burgess, 1917- 822.3'3 B
Shakespeare / Anthony Burgess [i.e. J. A. B. Wilson]. Harmondsworth, Eng. ; Baltimore : Penguin Books, 1972[i.e.1977] c1970 272 p. : ill. (some col.) ; 25 cm. Includes index. Bibliography: p. [266] [PR2894.W568 1972] 77-365967 ISBN 0-14-003441-2 pbk. : 4.95
1. Shakespeare, William, 1564-1616—Biography. 2. Shakespeare, William, 1564-1616—Contemporary England. 3. Dramatists, English—Early modern, 1500-1700—Biography.

Shakespeare, William, 1564-1616—Biography—Ancestry.

TANNENBAUM, Samuel Aaron, 1874?-1948. 822.3'3 B
The Shakspere coat-of-arms. New York, Printed and published for the author by the Tenny Press, 1908. [New York, AMS Press, 1974] 20 p. illus. 19 cm. [PR2901.T3 1974] 71-176453 ISBN 0-404-06336-5
1. Shakespeare, William, 1564-1616—Biography—Ancestry. 2. Shakespeare family. 3. Heraldry—Great Britain. I. Title. BIP

Shakespeare, William, 1564-1616—Biography—Character.

BAGEHOT, Walter, 1826-1877. 822.3'3
Shakespeare, the man; an essay. New York, AMS Press [1971] 48 p. 19 cm. Reprint of the 1901 ed. published in New York by the University Society. [PR2895.B3 1971] 71-126678 ISBN 0-404-00446-6
1. Shakespeare, William, 1564-1616—Biography—Character.

BEECHING, Henry Charles, 1859-1919. 822.3'3 B
The character of Shakespeare. [Folcroft, Pa.] Folcroft Library Editions, 1974. 23 p. 26 cm. Reprint of the 1917 ed. published by Oxford University Press, London, which was issued as the 1917 Annual Shakespeare lecture of the British Academy. Includes bibliographical references. [PR2899.B4 1974] 74-13418 ISBN 0-8414-3263-5 (lib. bdg.)
1. Shakespeare, William, 1564-1616—Biography—Character. I. Title. II. Series: British Academy, London (Founded 1901). Annual Shakespeare lecture, 1917. **BIP**

MCCURDY, Harold Grier, 1909- 822.33
The personality of Shakespeare; a venture in psychological method. New Haven, Yale University Press, 1953. xi, 248p. diagrs. 25cm. Bibliography: p. 231-234. [PR2909.M2] 53-7778
1. Shakespeare, William—Biog.—Character. 2. Shakespeare, William—Criticism and interpretation. I. Title. **BIP**

SMITH, Goldwin, 1823-1910. 822.3'3
Shakespeare, the man : an attempt to find traces of the dramatist's personal character in his dramas / by Goldwin Smith. Brooklyn : Haskell House, 1977. 77 p. : port. ; 21 cm. Reprint of the 1899 ed. published by G. N. Morang, Toronto. [PR2899.S5 1977] 76-30768 lib. bdg. : 8.95
1. Shakespeare, William, 1564-1616—Biography—Character. 2. Dramatists, English—Early modern, 1500-1700—Biography. I. Title.

WILSON, John Dover 822.33
The essential Shakespeare a biographical adventure. [New York] Cambridge University Press, 1960. viii, 148p. (bibl notes: p. 146-148) illus. (front.) 19cm. 60-16128 1.25 pap.,
1. Shakespeare, William—Biog.—Character. 2. Shakespeare, William—Criticism and interpretation. I. Title.

Shakespeare, William, 1564-1616—Biography—London life.

ACHESON, Arthur, 1864-1930. 822.3'3
Shakespeare, Chapman and Sir Thomas More; providing a more definite basis for biography and criticism. New York, AMS Press [1970] v, 280 p. illus., facsim. 23 cm. Reprint of the 1931 ed. Contents.Contents.—Shakespeare as a serving man.—An unknown company identified.—Shakespeare and Pembroke's company. Shakespeare, Chapman, and Sir Thomas More.—Greene's collaboration with Lodge and Nashe.—Stage history of Kyd and his plays.—Chapman as a pre-Shakespearean.—Peele's hand in Sir Thomas More. [PR2894.A25 1970] 72-113536 ISBN 0-404-00278-1
1. Shakespeare, William, 1564-1616—Biography—London life. 2. Shakespeare, William, 1564-1616—Authorship. 3. Chapman, George, 1559?-1634. 4. Sir Thomas More (Old play) 5. English drama—Early modern and Elizabethan, 1500-1600—History and criticism. I. Title.

ACHESON, Arthur, 1864-1930. 822.3'3 B
Shakespeare's lost years in London 1586-1592, giving new light on the pre-sonnet period; showing the inception of relations between Shakespeare and the Earl of Southampton and displaying John Florio as Sir John Falstaff. New York, Haskell House, 1971. vii, 261 p. 23 cm. Reprint of the 1920 ed. [PR2907.A4 1971] 79-152552 ISBN 0-8383-1235-7
1. Shakespeare, William, 1564-1616—Biography—London life. 2. Southampton, Henry Wriothesley, 3d Earl of, 1573-1624. 3. Florio, John, 1553?-1625. 4. Shakespeare, William, 1564-1616—Characters—Falstaff. I. Title.

ANSPACHER, Louis Kaufman, 1878-1947. 822.3'3
Shakespeare as poet and lover and the enigma of the sonnets. New York, Haskell House, 1973. 55 p. 22 cm. Reprint of the 1944 ed. published by Island Press, New York. [PR2848.A885 1973] 73-9528 ISBN 0-8383-1701-4 5.95
1. Shakespeare, William, 1564-1616. Sonnets. 2. Shakespeare, William, 1564-1616—Biography—London life. 3. Shakespeare, William, 1564-1616—Style. I. Title.

Shakespeare, William, 1564-1616—Biography—Marriage.

GRAY, Joseph William. 822.3'3 B
Shakespeare's marriage, his departure from Stratford and other incidents in his life. London, Chapman & Hall, 1905. [New York, AMS Press, 1973] xi, 285 p. facsims. 23 cm. Includes bibliographical references. [PR2905.G7 1973] 75-168182 ISBN 0-404-02894-2 15.00
1. Shakespeare, William, 1564-1616—Biography—Marriage. I. Title.

Shakespeare, William, 1564-1616—Biography—Sources.

BRINKWORTH, Edwin Robert Courtney. 822.3'3
Shakespeare and the Borvdy Court of Stratford, [by] E. R. C. Brinkworth; illustrated by Wendy Jones. Chichester, Phillimore, [1975 c1972] viii, 184 p. ill. fascisms, geneal table, map. 23 cm. Bibliography: p. 175 [PR2893.B68] ISBN 0-900592-82-6
1. Shakespeare, William, 1564-1616—Biography—Sources. 2. Shakespeare, William, 1564-1616—Homes and haunts—Stratford-upon-Avon. 3. Stratford-upon-Avon (Parish). Peculian Court. 4. Great Britain—Religion—17th century. I. Title. Distributed by Rowman and Littlefield for 11.00 L.C. card no. for original ed.: 73-166757

BROOKE, Charles Frederick Tucker, 1883-1946. 822.3'3
Shakespeare of Stratford; a handbook for students. Freeport, N.Y., Books for Libraries Press [1970, c1926] viii, 177 p. facsim. 23 cm. (Library of Shakespearean biography and criticism, ser. 3, pt. A) Includes bibliographical references. [PR2893.B7 1970] 79-128883
1. Shakespeare, William, 1564-1616—Biography—Sources. 2. Shakespeare, William, 1564-1616. I. Title. II. Series.

BUTLER, Pierce, 1873- comp. 822.3'3
Materials for the life of Shakespeare. New York, AMS Press [1971] x, 200 p. 19 cm. Reprint of the 1930 ed. Bibliography: p. [191]-194. [PR2893.B8 1971] 71-113568 ISBN 0-404-01248-5
1. Shakespeare, William, 1564-1616—Biography—Sources. I. Title. **BIP**

CHAMBRUN, Clara (Longworth) comtesse de, 1873-1954. 822.3'3
Essential documents never yet presented in the Shakespeare case / Clara Longworth de Chambrun. Norwood, Pa. : Norwood Editions, 1975. 54 p., 7 leaves of plates : ill. ; 23 cm. Reprint of the 1934 ed. published by Delmas, Bordeaux [PR2893.C54 1975] 75-28395 ISBN 0-88305-129-X lib. bdg. : 10.00
1. Shakespeare, William, 1564-1616—Biography—Sources. I. Title.

DOWDALL, John, fl.1693. 822.3'3
Traditionary anecdotes of Shakespeare. Collected in Warwickshire, in the year MDCXCIII. London, T. Rodd, 1838. [New York, AMS Press, 1972] 19 p. 23 cm. Original MS. (1693) has title: Description of severall places in Warwickshire. [PR2903.D6 1972] 70-164782 ISBN 0-404-02165-4
1. Shakespeare, William, 1564-1616—Biography—Sources. 2. Warwickshire, Eng. I. Title. II. Title: Description of severall places in Warwickshire.

LAMBERT, Daniel Henry, 1852- 822.3'3
Cartae Shakespeareanae. Shakespeare documents; a chronological catalogue of extant evidence relating to the life and works of William Shakespeare, collated and chronologically arranged by D. H. Lambert. London, G. Bell, 1904. [New York, AMS Press, 1973] xxi, 107 p. illus. 19 cm. [PR2893.L3 1973] 77-171646 ISBN 0-404-03804-2 8.00
1. Shakespeare, William, 1564-1616—Biography—Sources. I. Title. II. Title: Shakespeare documents.

LEWIS, Benjamin Roland, 1884-1959. 822.3'3
The Shakespeare documents; facsimiles, transliterations, translations, & commentary. Westport, Conn., Greenwood Press [1969, c1940-41] 2 v. (xxiv, 631 p.) illus., coats of arms, facsims., geneal. tables, maps, ports. 37 cm. Includes bibliographies [PR2893.L47 1969] 68-8742 ISBN 0-8371-4622-4
1. Shakespeare, William, 1564-1616—Biography—Sources. 2. Shakespeare, William, 1564-1616—Bibliography. I. Title. **BIP**

SCHOENBAUM, Samuel, 1927- 822.3'3
William Shakespeare : a documentary life / S. Schoenbaum. Oxford : Clarendon Press, 1975. xix, 273 p., [7] fold. leaves : ill., facsims., map, ports. ; 37 cm. Ill. on lining papers. Includes bibliographical references and index. [PR2893.S3] 75-332641 ISBN 0-19-812046-X : 50.00 deluxe editon : 150.00
1. Shakespeare, William, 1564-1616—Biography—Sources. 2. Shakespeare, William, 1564-1616—Biography. Distributed by Oxford University Press **BIP**

Shakespeare, William, 1564-1616—Biography—Youth.

BRACEBRIDGE, Charles Holte, 1799-1872. 822.3'3 B
Shakespeare no deerstealer; or, A short account of Fulbroke Park, near Stratford-on-Avon. London, Printed by Harrison, 1862. [New York, AMS Press, 1972] 32 p. 23 cm. [PR2903.B7 1972] 76-39517 ISBN 0-404-00921-2 5.00
1. Shakespeare, William, 1564-1616—Biography—Youth. I. Title.

GRAY, Arthur, 1852-1940. 822.3'3
A chapter in the early life of Shakespeare; Polesworth in Arden. New York, AMS Press [1969, c1926] ix, 122 p. illus., map. 19 cm. Includes bibliographical references. [PR2903.G65 1969] 72-130620
1. Shakespeare, William, 1564-1616—Biography—Youth. 2. Polesworth, Eng.—History. I. Title. **BIP**

KEEN, Alan. 822.3'3
The annotator; the pursuit of an Elizabethan reader of Halle's Chronicle involving some surmises about the early life of William Shakespeare, by Alan Keen & Roger Lubbock. With geneal. tables by Norman Long-Brown & Frances Keen. [1st AMS ed.] London, Putnam, 1954. [New York, AMS Press, 1971] xiii, 216 p. illus. 23 cm. Includes bibliographical references. [PR2903.K4 1971] 76-153334 ISBN 0-404-03641-4
1. Shakespeare, William, 1564-1616—Biography—Youth. 2. Shakespeare, William, 1564-1616—Sources. 3. Hall, Edward, d. 1547. The union of the two noble and illustre famelies of Lancastre & Yorke. I. Lubbock, Roger, joint author. II. Title.

POHL, Frederick Julius, 1889- 822.3'3 B
Like to the lark; the early years of Shakespeare, by Frederick J. Pohl. New York, C. N. Potter; distributed by Crown Publishers [1972] viii, 195 p. illus. 24 cm. Bibliography: p. 177-187. [PR2903.P65 1972b] 70-187512 7.95
1. Shakespeare, William, 1564-1616—Biography—Youth. 2. Shakespeare, William, 1564-1616—Biography—London life. I. Title.

ROLFE, William James, 1827-1910. 822.3'3
Shakespeare the boy; with sketches of the home and school life, the games and sports, the manners, customs and folk-lore of the time. A new ed. with forty-one illus. and a new index of plays and passages referred to. New York, Haskell House, 1971. viii, 256 p. illus. 23 cm. Reprint of the 1896 ed. [PR2903.R6 1971] 78-128411 ISBN 0-8383-1103-2
1. Shakespeare, William, 1564-1616—Biography—Youth. I. Title.

Shakespeare, William, 1564-1616—Characters.

HUDSON, Henry Norman, 1814-1886. 822.3'3
Shakespeare: his life, art, and characters. 4th ed., rev. [Folcroft, Pa.] Folcroft Library Editions, 1973. 2 v. 22 cm. Reprint of the 1895 ed. published by Ginn, Boston. [PR2989.H8 1973b] 73-15886 ISBN 0-8414-4783-7 (lib. bdg.)
1. Shakespeare, William, 1564-1616—Characters. 2. Shakespeare, William, 1564-1616. 3. English drama—Early modern and Elizabethan, 1500-1600—History and criticism. I. Title.

Shakespeare, William, 1564-1616—Contemporaries.

SWINBURNE, Algernon Charles, 1837-1969. 822'.3'09
Contemporaries of Shakespeare. Edited by Edmund Gosse and Thomas James Wise. [Folcroft, Pa.] Folcroft Press, 1970. xii, 308 p. 24 cm. Reprint of the 1919 ed. Contents.Contents.—Introduction, by E. Gosse.—Christopher Marlowe in relation to Greene, Peele, and Lodge.—George Chapman.—The earlier plays of Beaumont and Fletcher.—Philip Massinger.—John Day.—Robert Davenport.—Thomas Nabbes.—Richard Brome.—James Shirley. [PR421.S8 1970] 72-187514
1. Shakespeare, William, 1564-1616—Contemporaries. 2. English drama—Early modern and Elizabethan, 1500-1600—History and criticism. I. Gosse, Edmund William, 1849-1928, ed. II. Wise, Thomas James, 1859-1937, ed. III. Title. **BIP**

Shakespeare, William, 1564-1616—Contemporary England.

ROWSE, Alfred Leslie, 1903- 309.1'42'055
The case books of Simon Forman : sex and society in Shakespeare's age / [by] A. L. Rowse. London : Pan Books, 1976. 320 p. ; 20 cm. (Picador) Originally published under title: Simon Forman. Includes bibliographical references and index. [PR2910.R76 1976] 77-370736 ISBN 0-330-24784-0 : £1.25
1. Shakespeare, William, 1564-1616—Contemporary England. 2. Forman, Simon, 1552-1616. 3. Shakespeare, William, 1564-1616—Contemporaries. 4. England—Social life and customs—16th century. 5. Physicians—England—Biography. I. Title.

SULLIVAN, Walter J. 828'.3'09
Shakespeare: his times and his problems, by Walter Sullivan. Glen Rock, N.J., Paulist Press [1968] ix, 118 p. 19 cm. (Deus books) Bibliography: p. [105] [PR2910.S9] 68-54525 0.95
1. Shakespeare, William, 1564-1616—Contemporary England. 2. Shakespeare, William, 1564-1616—Authorship. I. Title.

Shakespeare, William, 1564-1616—Criticism and interpretation.

COLLINS, John Churton, 1848-1908. 822.3'3
Studies in Shakespeare. Westminster, A. Constable, 1904. [New York, AMS Press, 1973] xv, 380 p. 19 cm. [PR2976.C56 1973] 72-944 ISBN 0-404-01637-5 12.50
1. Shakespeare, William, 1564-1616—Criticism and interpretation. 2. Shakespeare, William, 1564-1616—Knowledge and learning. I. Title. Contents omitted.

DRAKE, Nathan, 1766-1836. 822.3'3
Shakespeare and his times; including the biography of the poet; criticisms on his genius and writings; a new chronology of his plays; a disquisition on the object of his sonnets; and a history of the manners, customs, amusements, superstitions, poetry, and elegant literature of his age. New York, B. Franklin [1969] 2 v. in 1. (xi, 660 p.) 24 cm. (Selected essays in literature & criticism, #20) (Burt Franklin Research & source works series, #332.) Reprint of the 1838 ed. Bibliographical footnotes. [PR2894.D73 1969] 68-58458
1. Shakespeare, William, 1564-1616—Biography. 2. Shakespeare, William, 1564-1616—Criticism and interpretation. 3. Shakespeare, William, 1564-1616—

Contemporary England. 4. English literature—Early modern, 1500-1700—History and criticism. I. Title.

SPENCER, Hazelton, 1893-1944. 822.3'3
The art and life of William Shakespeare. New York, Barnes & Noble [1970, c1940] xx, 495 p. illus., facsims., map, music, ports. 23 cm. Bibliography: p. 419-475. [PR2894.S67 1970] 70-15623 12.50
1. Shakespeare, William, 1564-1616—Criticism and interpretation. 2. Shakespeare, William, 1564-1616—Stage history. 3. Shakespeare, William, 1564-1616—Biography. I. Title.

Shakespeare, William, 1564-1616—Dictionaries, indexes, etc.

MAY, Robin. 822.3'3
Who's who in Shakespeare. With a foreword by Judi Dench. New York, Taplinger Pub. co. [1973, c1972] x, 189 p. 21 cm. [PR2892.M397 1973] 73-5334 ISBN 0-8008-8269-5 6.50
1. Shakespeare, William, 1564-1616—Dictionaries, indexes, etc. 2. Shakespeare, William, 1564-1616—Characters. I. Title.

WELLS, Stanley W., 1930- 822.3'3
Shakespeare, an illustrated dictionary / Stanley Wells. London : Kaye & Ward ; New York ; Oxford University Press, 1978. vii, 216 p. : ill. ; 23 cm. Includes index. Bibliography: p. 215-216. [PR2892.W44 1978] 77-18370 ISBN 0-19-520054-3 (Oxford) : 9.95
1. Shakespeare, William, 1564-1616—Dictionaries, indexes, etc. 2. Dramatists, English—Early modern, 1500-1700—Biography. I. Title.

BARNARD, Etwell Augustine Bracher. 822.3'3
New links with Shakespeare, by E. A. B. Barnard. Cambridge [Eng.] University Press, 1930. [New York, AMS Press, 1973] xiv, 135 p. illus. 23 cm. [PR2911.B3 1973b] 73-153301 ISBN 0-404-00655-8 10.00
1. Shakespeare, William, 1564-1616—Friends and associates. I. Title.

BARNARD, Etwell Augustine Bracher. 822.3'3
New links with Shakespeare. [Folcroft, Pa.] Folcroft Library Editions, 1973. p. Reprint of the 1930 ed. published by the University Press, Cambridge, Eng. [PR2911.B3 1973] 73-13844 ISBN 0-8414-3245-7 (lib. bdg.)
1. Shakespeare, William, 1564-1616—Friends and associates. I. Title.

FRIPP, Edgar Innes, d.1931. 822.3'3
Master Richard Quyny, bailiff of Stratford-upon-Avon and friend of William Shakespeare. [London] Oxford University Press, 1924. [New York, AMS Press, 1974] 215 p. illus. 18 cm. [PR2912.Q5F7 1974] 74-153320 ISBN 0-404-02621-4
1. Shakespeare, William, 1564-1616—Friends and associates. 2. Quiney, Richard, d. 1602. I. Title.

Shakespeare, William, 1564-1616—Friends and associates.

HOTSON, Leslie, 1897- 822.3'3
I, William Shakespeare, do appoint Thomas Russell, Esquire ... Freeport, N.Y., Books for Libraries Press [1970] 296 p. illus., facsims., 2 fold. geneal. tables, maps, ports. 23 cm. (Library of Shakespearean biography and criticism, ser. 3, pt. A) Reprint of the 1937 ed. [PR2911.H6 1970] 70-109651
1. Shakespeare, William, 1564-1616—Friends and associates. 2. Russell, Thomas, 1570-1634. I. Title. II. Series. BIP

Shakespeare, William—Homes and haunts—Stratford-upon-Avon.

ECCLES, Mark Williams 928.2
Shakespeare in Warwickshire. Madison, Univ. of Wisconsin Press [c.]1961. vi, 182p. illus., maps. Bibl. 61-5900 4.50
1. Shakespeare, William—Homes and haunts—Stratford-upon-Avon. 2. Shakespeare, William—Biog. I. Title. BIP

BRINKWORTH, Edwin Robert Courtney. 822.3'3
Shakespeare and the Borvdy Court of Stratford, [by] E. R. C. Brinkworth; illustrated by Wendy Jones. Chichester, Phillimore, [1975 c1972] viii, 184 p. ill. fascisms, geneal table, map. 23 cm. Bibliography: p. 175 [PR2893.B68] ISBN 0-900592-82-6
1. Shakespeare, William, 1564-1616—Biography—Sources. 2. Shakespeare, William, 1564-1616—Homes and haunts—Stratford-upon-Avon. 3. Stratford-upon-Avon (Parish). Peculian Court. 4. Great Britain—Religion—17th century. I. Title.
Distributed by Rowman and Littlefield for 11.00 L.C. card no. for original ed.: 73-166757

WISE, John Richard de Capel, 1831-1890. 822.3'3
Shakspere, his birthplace and its neighbourhood / by John R. Wise ; illustrated by W. J. Linton. New York : AMS Press, 1976. 164 p. : ill. ; 19 cm. Reprint of the 1861 ed. published by Smith, Elder, London. Includes index. [PR2916.W6 1976] 76-178313 ISBN 0-404-07003-5 : 7.50
1. Shakespeare, William, 1564-1616—Homes and haunts—Stratford-upon-Avon. 2. Stratford-upon-Avon—History. I. Title. BIP

Shakespeare, William, 1564-1616—Knowledge—Book arts and sciences.

JAGGARD, William, 1868-1947. 822.3'3
Shakespeare once a printer and bookman : lecture one of the twelfth series of printing trade lectures at Stationers Hall, London, E. C., Friday, twentieth October MCMXXXIII / by W. Jaggard. Norwood, Pa. : Norwood Editions, 1976. p. cm. Reprint of the 1934 ed. published by Shakespeare Press, Stratford-on-Avon. [PR3036.J3 1976] 76-8259 ISBN 0-8482-1255-X lib. bdg. : 7.50
1. Shakespeare, William, 1564-1616—Knowledge—Book arts and sciences. 2. Shakespeare, William, 1564-1616—Biography—London life. I. Title.

Shakespeare, William, 1564-1616—Knowledge—Law.

KNIGHT, William Nicholas, 1939- 822.3'3
Shakespeare's hidden life: Shakespeare at the law, 1585-1595 [by] W. Nicholas Knight. New York, Mason & Lipscomb [1973] xi, 325 p. illus. 25 cm. Bibliography: p. [309]-320. [PR2894.K54] 73-84881 ISBN 0-88405-003-3 12.50
1. Shakespeare, William, 1564-1616. 2. Shakespeare, William, 1564-1616—Knowledge—Law. 3. Shakespeare, William, 1564-1616—Autographs. I. Title.

Shakespeare, William, 1564-1616—Knowledge—Music.

WILSON, Christopher, 1874-1919. 822.3'3 B
Shakespeare and music / by Christopher Wilson. New York : Da Capo Press, 1977. xiii, 170 p., [1] leaf of plates : ill. ; 23 cm. (Da Capo Press music reprint series) Reprint of the 1922 ed. published by The Stage Office, London. Includes index. [ML80.S5W4 1977] 76-58560 ISBN 0-306-70868-X : 14.95
1. Shakespeare, William, 1564-1616—Knowledge—Music. 2. Music and literature. I. Title. BIP

Shakespeare, William, 1564-1616—Knowledge—Printing.

JAGGARD, William, 1868-1947. 822.3'3
Shakespeare once a printer and bookman. New York, Haskell House Publishers, 1972. 34 p. illus. 29 cm. Lecture one of the twelfth series of printing trade lectures at Stationers' Hall, London, E.C., Friday, twentieth October, MCMXXXIII. With five hundred supporting quotations. Reprint of the 1934 ed. [PR3036.J3 1972] 70-181003 ISBN 0-8383-1372-8
1. Shakespeare, William, 1564-1616—Knowledge—Printing. 2. Shakespeare, William, 1564-1616—Biography—London life. I. Title.

JAGGARD, William, 1868-1947. 822.3'3
Shakespeare once a printer and bookman. [Folcroft, Pa.] Folcroft Library Editions, 1973. p. Lecture one of the twelfth series of printing trade lectures at Stationers' Hall, London, E. C., Friday, twentieth October, MCMXXXIII. With five hundred supporting quotations. Reprint of the 1934 ed. published by Shakespeare Press, Stratford-on-Avon. [PR3036.J3 1973] 73-11106 10.00
1. Shakespeare, William, 1564-1616—Knowledge—Printing. 2. Shakespeare, William, 1564-1616—Biography—London life. I. Title. BIP

Shakespeare, William, 1564-1616.—Relationship with women.

BROWN, Ivor John Carnegie, 1891- 822.3'3
The women in Shakespeare's life [by] Ivor Brown. [1st American ed.] New York, Coward-McCann [1969] 224 p. 22 cm. Bibliography: p. 216-217. [PR2905.B7 1969] 68-23378 5.95
1. Shakespeare, William, 1564-1616.—Relationship with women. I. Title.

HUTCHESON, William J. Fraser. 822.3'3
Shakespeare's other Anne; a short account of the life and works of Anne Whately or Beck, a sister of the Order of St. Clare, who nearly married William Shakespeare in November 1582 A.D., by W. J. Fraser Hutcheson. New York, Haskell House, 1974. 128 p. illus. 23 cm. Reprint of the 1950 ed., published by MacLellan, Glasgow. [PR2905.H8 1974] 74-1149 ISBN 0-8383-1793-6 12.95 (lib. bdg.).
1. Shakespeare, William, 1564-1616—Relationship with women. 2. Whately, Anne, 1561?-1600? I. Title.

Shakespeare, William, 1564-1616—Sources.

KEEN, Alan. 822.3'3
The annotator; the pursuit of an Elizabethan reader of Halle's Chronicle involving some surmises about the early life of William Shakespeare, by Alan Keen & Roger Lubbock. With geneal. tables by Norman Long-Brown & Frances Keen. [1st AMS ed.] London, Putnam, 1954. [New York, AMS Press, 1971] xiii, 216 p. illus. 23 cm. Includes bibliographical references. [PR2903.K4 1971] 76-153334 ISBN 0-404-03641-4
1. Shakespeare, William, 1564-1616—Biography—Youth. 2. Shakespeare, William, 1564-1616—Sources. 3. Hall, Edward, d. 1547. The union of the two noble and illustre famelies of Lancastre & Yorke. I. Lubbock, Roger, joint author. II. Title.

Shakespeare, William, 1564-1616—Stage history.

DARLINGTON, Anne Charlotte. 133.8'0922
Shakespeare and the changing stage. [Charlottesville 1964] 55 p. 23 cm. Bibliographical footnotes. [PR3091.D28] 65-6822
1. Shakespeare, William, 1564-1616 —Stage history. I. Title.

GREBANIER, Bernard D. N., 1903- 791'.092'2
Then came each actor : Shakespearean actors, great and otherwise, including players and princes, rogues, vagabonds and actors motley, from Will Kempe to Olivier and Gielgud and after / Bernard Grebanier. New York : McKay, [1975] xii, 626 p., [16] leaves of plates : ill. ; 24 cm. Includes index. Bibliography: p. 539-552. [PR3112.G73] 74-82983 ISBN 0-679-50507-5 : 19.95
1. Shakespeare, William, 1564-1616—Stage history. 2. Actors—Biography. I. Title.

SPENCER, Hazelton, 1893-1944. 822.3'3
The art and life of William Shakespeare. New York, Barnes & Noble [1970, c1940] xx, 495 p. illus., facsims., map, music, ports. 23 cm. Bibliography: p. 419-475. [PR2894.S67 1970] 70-15623 12.50
1. Shakespeare, William, 1564-1616—Criticism and interpretation. 2. Shakespeare, William, 1564-1616—Stage history. 3. Shakespeare, William, 1564-1616—Biography. I. Title.

Shakespeare, William, 1564-1616—Stage history—U.S.

DUNN, Esther Cloudman, 1891- 792'.028'0922
Shakespeare in America. New York, B. Blom, 1968. xiii, 310 p. illus., port. 24 cm. Reprint of the 1939 ed. [PR3105.D8 1968] 68-21212
1. Shakespeare, William, 1564-1616—Stage history—U.S. 2. Theater—United States. 3. United States—Intellectual life. I. Title.

Shakespeare, William, 1564-1616—Technique.

TURNBULL, Harold George Dalway. 809.2
Shakespeare and Ibsen, by H. G. Dalway Turnbull. New York, Haskell House, 1971. 23 p. 23 cm. Reprint of the 1926 ed. [PR2995.T8 1971] 72-117586 ISBN 0-8383-1019-2
1. Shakespeare, William, 1564-1616—Technique. 2. Ibsen, Henrik, 1828-1906. 3. Literature, Comparative—English and Norwegian. 4. Literature, Comparative—Norwegian and English. I. Title. BIP

Shakespeare, William, 1564-1616—Tomb.

INGLEBY, Clement Mansfield, 1823-1886. 822.3'3
Shakespeare's bones : the proposal to disinter them, considered in relation to their possible bearing on his portraiture : illustrated by instances of visits of the living to the dead / by C. M. Ingleby. Norwood, Pa. : Norwood Editions, 1976. p. cm. Reprint of the 1883 ed. published by Trubner, London. Bibliography: p. [PR2908.I6 1976] 76-8276 ISBN 0-8482-1153-7 lib. bdg. : 8.50
1. Shakespeare, William, 1564-1616—Tomb. 2. Schiller, Johann Christoph Friedrich von, 1795-1805—Biography—Last years and death. 3. Exhumation. I. Title.

Shaklee, Forrest Clell.

SPUNT, Georges. 615'.534'0924 B
When nature speaks : the life of Forrest C. Shaklee, Sr. / by Georges Spunt. New York : F. Fell Publishers, c1977. 226 p. : ill. ; 22 cm. [RZ232.S5S68 1977] 77-9916 ISBN 0-8119-0279-X : 8.95
1. Shaklee, Forrest Clell. 2. Shaklee Corporation—History. 3. Chiropractors—California—Biography. I. Title.

Shamanism—Korea—Case studies.

HARVEY, Youngsook Kim.
Six Korean women : the socialization of shamans / Youngsook Kim Harvey. St. Paul : West Pub. Co., c1979. p. cm. (Monograph - The American Ethnological Society ; 65) Includes index. Bibliography: p. [BL2370.S5H36] 78-27500 ISBN 0-8299-0243-0 : 10.95
1. Shamanism—Korea—Case studies. 2. Women—Korea—Biography. I. Title. II. Series: American Ethnological Society. Monographs ; 65. BIP

Shame.

THE Naked therapist : a collection of embarrassments / Sheldon Kopp and others. San Diego : EdITS, 1976. xi, 244 p. ; 24 cm. Bibliography: p. 243-244. [BF575.S45N34] 76-17989 ISBN 0-912736-18-6 : 8.95 616.8'914'0922
1. Shame. 2. Embarrassment. 3. Psychologists—Biography. I. Kopp, Sheldon B., 1929-

Shanahan, Louise, joint author.

RUE, James J. 301.42'7
Daddy's girl, mama's boy / by James J. Rue and Louise Shanahan. Indianapolis : Bobbs-Merrill, [1978] p. cm. [HQ755.R85] 77-15435 ISBN 0-672-52348-5 : 8.95
1. Shanahan, Louise, joint author. 2. Mothers and sons. 3. Fathers and daughters. 4. Oedipus complex. I. Title. BIP

Shand, Jimmy.

PHILLIPS, David, 1914- 786.9'7'0924 B
Jimmy Shand / by David Phillips. Dundee : D. Winter and Son, Ltd, 1976. 166 p., [32] p. of plates : ill., ports. ; 22 cm. Discography: p. 132-143. [ML422.S515P5] 77-361726 ISBN 0-902804-05-7 : £3.50
1. Shand, Jimmy. 2. Musicians—Scotland—Biography.

Shankly, Bill.

SHANKLY, Bill. 796.33'4'0924 B
Shankly / Bill Shankly. London : Barker, 1976. 48, 182 p., [6] leaves of plates : ports. ; 23 cm. [GV942.7.S44A36] 76-378868 ISBN 0-213-16603-8 : £3.95
1. Shankly, Bill. 2. Soccer players—Great Britain—Biography.

Shannon, George, 1786 or 7-1836. — Juvenile literature.

EIFERT, Virginia Louise (Snider) 1911- 92
George Shannon, young explorer with Lewis and Clark. Illustrated by Manning de V. Lee. New York, Dodd, Mead [1963] vii, 275 p. illus. 22 cm. Bibliography: p. 271. [F592.7.E5] 63-16270
1. Shannon, George, 1786 or 7-1836. — Juvenile literature. 2. Lewis and Clark Expedition — Juvenile literature. I. Title.

Shantz, Bobby, 1925-

DELANEY, Ed. 927.96357
Bobby Shantz. New York, A. S. Barnes [1953] 150p. illus. 21cm. (Most valuable player series) [GV865.S45D4] 53-5575
1. Shantz, Bobby, 1925- I. Title.

SHANTZ, Bobby, 1925- 927.96357
The story of Bobby Shantz, as told to Ralph Bernstein. [1st ed.] Philadelphia, Lippincott [1953] 190p. illus. 21cm. [GV865.S45A3] 52-13736
I. Bernstein, Ralph, 1921- II. Title.

Sharaff, Irene.

SHARAFF, Irene. 746.9'2'0924 B
Broadway & Hollywood : costumes designed by Irene Sharaff / Irene Sharaff. New York : Van Nostrand Reinhold Co., 1976. 136 p. : ill. (some col.) ; 24 cm. Includes index. [TT505.S5A33] 75-43903 ISBN 0-442-27527-7 : 12.50
1. Sharaff, Irene. 2. Costume design. I. Title.

Shareshull, Sir William, 1289 (ca.)-1370.

PUTNAM, Bertha Haven, 1872- 923.442
The place in legal history of Sir William Shareshull, Chief Justice of the King's Bench, 1350-1361; a study of judicial & administrative methods in the reign of Edward III. Cambridge [Eng.] University Press, 1950. xviii, 328 p. maps, geneal. tables. 23 cm. (Cambridge studies in English legal history) Bibliography: p. [xv]-xviii. 51-1955
1. Shareshull, Sir William, 1289 (ca.)-1370. I. Title. II. Series.

Sharett, Moshe, 1894-1965.

ROSENSAFT, Menachem Z. 956.94050924 B
Moshe Sharett, statesman of Israel [by] Menachem Z. Rosensaft. New York, Shengold Publishers [1966] 64 p. illus., facsims., ports. 24 cm. [DS126.6.S4R63] 66-25854
1. Sharett, Moshe, 1894-1965. I. Title.

Sharian, Bedros, 1892?

*SHARIAN, Bedros M. 1892?- v. 12 B
I love America; Missionary address and my experiences here and there, [by] Bedros M. Sharian Sr. 1st. ed. New York, Vantage [1974] 64 p. 22 cm. [BV4501.2] 248 ISBN 0-533-01044-6 3.95
1. Sharian, Bedros, 1892? 2. Christian life. I. Title.

Sharif, Omar, 1932-

SHARIF, Omar, 1932- 791.43'028'0924 B
The eternal male / by Omar Sharif, with Marie-Therese Guinchard ; translated from the French by Martin Sokolinsky. Garden City, N.Y. : Doubleday, 1977. p. cm. Translation of L'eternel masculin. [PN2978.S5A3213] 77-89418 ISBN 0-385-12541-0 : 7.95
1. Sharif, Omar, 1932- 2. Moving-picture actors and actresses—Egypt—Biography. I. Guinchard, Marie Therese, joint author. II. Title. BIP

Sharman, William Tecumseh, 1820-1891.

LEWIS, Lloyd, 1891-1949. 923.573
Sherman, fighting prophet. Illustrated with reproductions of maps, engravings, and photos. With a new appraisal by Bruce Catton. New York, Harcourt, Brace [1958] xviii, 690p. illus., ports., maps. 25cm. Bibliography: p.655-689. [E467.1.S55L48 1958] 58-14960
1. Sharman, William Tecumseh, 1820-1891. I. Title.

Sharon, Mary Bruce, 1878-1961.

SHARON, Mary Bruce, 1878-1961. 759.13 B
Scenes from childhood / by Mary Bruce Sharon. 1st ed. New York : Dutton, [1978] p. cm. [ND237.S467A2 1978] 78-4939 ISBN 0-525-38820-6 : 6.95
1. Sharon, Mary Bruce, 1878-1961. 2. Painters—United States—Biography. I. Title. BIP

Sharon, William, 1821-1885.

KRONINGER, Robert Henry. 347.9
Sarah & the Senator, by Robert H. Kroninger. Berkeley, Calif., Howell-North, 1964. 253 p. illus., facsims., ports. 24 cm 64-7522
1. Sharon, William, 1821-1885. 2. Terry, Sarah Althea (Hill) I. Title.

Sharp, Cecil James, 1859-1924.

FOX-STRANGWAYS, Arthur Henry, 1859- 927.8
Cecil Sharp, by A. H. Fox Strangways and Maud Karpeles. 2d ed. London, New York, Oxford University Press, 1955. 225p. illus. 23cm. [ML423.S53F6 1955] 55-13787
1. Sharp, Cecil James, 1859-1924. I. Karpeles, Maud, joint author. II. Title.

KARPELES, Maud. 784.4942
Cecil Sharp: his life and work. [Chicago] Univ. of Chicago Pr. [1967] xii, 228p. illus., facsim., ports. 23cm. Rev. and rewriting of Cecil Sharp, by A. H. Fox-Strangways, Maud Karpeles. Bibl. [ML423] (B) 67-24299 5.95
1. Sharp, Cecil James, 1859-1924. I. Fox-Strangways, Arthur Henry, 1859-1948. Cecil Sharp. II. Title.

Sharp, Granville, 1735-1813.

LASCELLES, Edward Charles Ponsonby, 1884- 326'.0924
Granville Sharp and the freedom of slaves in England. New York, Negro Universities Press [1969] viii, 151 p. ports. 23 cm. Reprint of the 1928 ed. Bibliography: p. [147]-148. [HT1162.L3 1969] 74-97372
1. Sharp, Granville, 1735-1813. 2. Slavery in Great Britain—Anti-slavery movements. 3. Slave-trade—Gt. Brit. I. Title. BIP

STUART, Charles, 1783?-1865. 322.4'4'0924 B
A memoir of Granville Sharp, to which is added Sharp's "Law of passive obedience," and an extract from his "Law of retribution." Westport, Conn., Negro Universities Press [1970] 4, 156 p. illus. 23 cm. Reprint of the 1836 ed. [HT1162.S85 1970] 78-111589 ISBN 0-8371-4615-1
1. Sharp, Granville, 1735-1813. 2. Slavery in Great Britain—Anti-slavery movements. 3. Slave-trade—Great Britain. I. Sharp, Granville, 1735-1813. Law of passive obedience. 1970. II. Title.

Sharp, John Kean, 1892-

SHARP, John Kean, 1892- 282'.092'4 B
An old priest remembers, 1892-1978 / John K. Sharp. 2d enl. ed. Hicksville, N.Y. : Exposition Press, c1978. 216 p. ; 24 cm. [BX4705.S5847A35 1978] 78-69764 ISBN 0-682-49183-7 : 10.00
1. Sharp, John Kean, 1892- 2. Catholic Church—Clergy—Biography. 3. Clergy United States—Biography.

Sharp, Katharine Lucinda, 1865-1914.

GROTZINGER, Laurel Ann 020.924
The power and the dignity; librarianship and Katharine Sharp. New York, Scarecrow, 1966[c.1965] 331p. 22cm. Bibl. [Z720.S5G7] 66-13735 8.00
1. Sharp, Katharine Lucinda, 1865-1914. I. Title.

Sharp, Robert L.

SHARP, Robert L. 917.91'57
Big outfit; ranching on the Baca Float [by] Robert L. Sharp. Illus. by Elaine Cummings. Tucson, University of Arizona Press [1974] x, 157 p. illus. 23 cm. [F819.B32S52] 74-75821 ISBN 0-8165-0409-1 3.95 (pbk.)
1. Sharp, Robert L. 2. Baca Float Ranch, Ariz. 3. Ranch life—Arizona. I. Title.

Sharpe, Andrew E.

ANDREW, Margaret Jean, 1887- 917.13'58'0330924 B
The life of one man, 1917-1965, by Margaret Joan Andrew pseud. Belleville, Ont., Author, 11- Stanley St. 1966?] [4] p. ports. 23 cm. "Written in honour of Centennial Year, 1967." Cover title. [CT275.S442A67] 70-398951 unpriced
1. Sharpe, Andrew E. I. Title.

Sharpe, Charles Kirkpatrick, 1781?-1851.

SCOTT, Walter, Sir, bart., 1771-1832. 828'.7'09 B
The letters of Sir Walter Scott and Charles Kirkpatrick Sharpe to Robert Chambers, 1821-45 : with original memoranda of Sir Walter Scott : printed from manuscripts in the possession of C. E. S. Chambers, Edinburgh. Norwood, Pa. : Norwood Editions, 1975. 80 p., [3] leaves of plates : ports. ; 23 cm. Reprint of the 1904 ed. published by W. & R. Chambers, Edinburgh. [PR5334.A6 1975] 75-38749 ISBN 0-88305-949-5 : 15.00
1. Scott, Walter, Sir, bart., 1771-1832—Correspondence. 2. Sharpe, Charles Kirkpatrick, 1781?-1851. 3. Chambers, Robert, 1802-1871—Correspondence. I. Sharpe, Charles Kirkpatrick, 1781?-1851. II. Chambers, Robert, 1802-1871. III. Title. BIP

Sharpe, William,

SHARPE, William, 1882-1951. 926.1
Brain surgeon; the autobiography of William Sharpe. New York, Viking Press, 1952. 271 p. 22 cm. [R154.S367A3] 52-12763
I. Title.

Shastri, Lal Bahadur, 1904-1966.

GUPTA, Ram Chandra. 954.04'0924(B)
Lal Bahadur Shastri, the man and his ideas; an analysis of his socio-political and economic ideas. [1st ed.] Delhi, Sterling Pubs. [1966] xvi, 156p. illus., port. 22cm. Bibl. [DS481.S48G82] SA67 6.00
1. Shastri, Lala Bahadur, 1904-1966: I. Title.
American distributor: Verry, Mystic, Conn.

MANKEKAR, D. R. 954.04
Lal Bahadur, a political biography. Bombay, Popular Prakashan [dist. New York, Heinman, 1965] vi, 168p. group ports. 23cm. [DS481.S48M3] SA 65 4.50
1. Shastri. Lal Bahadur, 1904- I. Title.

Shattuck, Arthur, 1881-1951.

SHATTUCK, Arthur, 1881-1951. 927.8
Memoirs. Edited by S.F. Shattuck. With an account of his career by Willard Luedtke. Neenah, Wis., 1961. 247 p. illus. 27 cm. [ML417.S36A3] 61-36322
1. Shattuck, Arthur, 1881-1951. 2. Musicians — Correspondence, reminiscences, etc. I. Title.

Shattuck, Frederick Cheever, 1847-1929.

SHATTUCK, George Cheever, 1879- comp. 610'.924
Frederick Cheever Shattuck, M. D., 1847-1929; a memoir. With a chapter by James Howard Means. [Boston, 1967] xii, 327 p. ports. 21 cm. Cover title: A memoir of Frederick Cheever Shattuck. Bibliographical footnotes. [R154.S3685S47] 68-520
1. Shattuck, Frederick Cheever, 1847-1929. I. Title. II. Title: A memoir of Frederick Cheever Shattuck.

SHATTUCK, George Cheever, 1879- comp. 610'.924
Frederick Cheever Shattuck, M.D., 1847-1929; a memoir. With a chapter by James Howard Means. [Boston, 1967] xii, 327 p. ports. 21 cm. Cover title: A memoir of Frederick Cheever Shattuck. Bibliographical footnotes. [R154.S3685S47] 68-520
1. Shattuck, Frederick Cheever, 1847-1929. I. Title: A memoir of Frederick Cheever Shattuck

Shaw, Albert, 1857-1947.

GRAYBAR, Lloyd J. 070.4'092'4 B
Albert Shaw of the Review of reviews, an intellectual biography [by] Lloyd J. Graybar. [Lexington] University Press of Kentucky [1974] xiii, 229 p. illus. 24 cm. Bibliography: p. [205]-220. [PN4874.S45G7] 73-80464 ISBN 0-8131-1300-8 12.50
1. Shaw, Albert, 1857-1947. 2. Review of reviews and world's work. 3. United States—Politics and government—1901-1953. I. Title. BIP

Shaw, Artie, 1910-

SHAW, Artie, 1910- 788'.62'0924 B
The trouble with Cinderella : an outline of identity / Artie Shaw, with new introd. by the author. 1st Da Capo paperback ed. New York : Da Capo Press, 1979, c1952. xviii, 394 p., [3] leaves of plates : ill. ; 21 cm. (A Da Capo paperback) Autobiographical. Reprint of the ed. published by Farrar, Straus, and Young, New York. [ML410.S498A3 1979] 78-20839 ISBN 0-306-80091-8 pbk. : 6.95
1. Shaw, Artie, 1910- 2. Jazz musicians—United States—Biography. I. Title.

SHAW, Artie, 1911- 927.8
The trouble with Cinderella; an outline of identity. New York, Collier [1963, c.1952] 352p. 18cm. (AS540) .95 pap.,
1. Musicians—Correspondence, reminiscences, etc. I. Title.

SHAW, Artie, 1911- 927.8
The trouble with Cinderella; an outline of identity. New York, Farrar, Straus and Young [1952] 394 p. 22 cm. Autobiographical. [ML410.S498A3] 52-10229
1. Musicians—Correspondence, reminiscences, etc. I. Title.

Shaw, Bertha M C

SHAW, Bertha M C 923.771
Broken theads; memories of a northern Ontario school-teacher. [1st ed.] New York, Exposition Press [1955] 153p. 21cm. [CT310.S4A3] 55-11832
I. Title.

Shaw, Charlotte Frances Payne-Townshend.

DUNBAR, Janet 920.7
Mrs. G. B. S.; a portrait. New York, Harper [c.1963] 303p. illus. 22cm. 62-20109 5.95
1. Shaw, Charlotte Frances Payne-Townshend. 2. Shaw, George Bernard, 1856-1950. I. Title.

DUNBAR, Janet. 920.7
Mrs. G.B.S.; a portrait. [1st ed.] New York, Harper & Row [1963] 303 p. illus. 22 cm. [PR5366.D8] 62-20109
1. Shaw. Charlotte Frances Payne-Townshend. 2. Shaw, George Bernard. 1856-1950. I. Title.

Shaw, Elizabeth Cooper, 1794-1877.

DURACK, Mary. 994.1'02'0924 B
To be heirs forever / [by] Mary Durack. London : Constable, 1976. 286 p., [12] p. of plates, [2] leaves of plates (1 fold.) : ill., facsim., geneal. table, maps, ports. ; 23 cm. Includes index. Bibliography: p. [269]-271. [DU372.S53D87 1976] 77-367070 ISBN 0-09-461100-9 : £4.95
1. Shaw, Elizabeth Cooper, 1794-1877. 2. Shaw, William, 1788-1862. 3. Frontier and pioneer life—Australia—Western Australia. 4. Pioneers—Australia—Western Australia—Biography. 5. Western Australia—History. I. Title.

Shaw family.

HARRIS, Nathaniel. 929'.2'09415
The Shaws : the family of George Bernard Shaw / [by] Nathaniel Harris ; illustrated by Andrew Farmer. London : Dent, 1977. 63 p. : ill., ports. ; 23 cm. (Families in history series) Bibliography: p. 63. [PR5366.H353] 77-367098 ISBN 0-460-06735-4 : 5.95
1. Shaw family. 2. Shaw, George Bernard, 1856-1950—Biography—Youth. 3. Dramatists, Irish—19th century—Biography. I. Title.
Dist. by Rowman and Littlefield, Totowa, N J.

Shaw, George Bernard,

SHAW, George Bernard, 822'.9'12 B
1856-1950.
Shaw; an autobiography, selected from his writings by Stanley Weintraub. New York, Weybright and Talley [1969-70] 2 v. illus., ports. 25 cm. Contents.—[1] 1856-1898.—v. 2. 1898-1950. Includes bibliographies. [PR5366.A5 1969] 74-84621 10.00
I. Weintraub, Stanley, 1929- comp. II. Title.

SHAW, George Bernard, 1856- 928.1
1950.
To a young actress: the letters of Bernard Shaw to Molly Tompkins; the correspondence between Bernard Shaw and an American artist from 1921 through 1949. Edited and with an introd. by Peter Tompkins. [1st ed.] New York, C.N. Potter [1960] 192 p. illus., ports. 31 cm. Most of the letters are facsim. reproductions. [PR5366.A48 1960] 60-89262
I. Tompkins, Molly (Arthur) II. Thompkins, Peter, ed. III. Title.

Shaw, George Bernard, 1856-1950.

BENTLEY, Eric Russell, 928.2
1916-
Bernard Shaw. 1836-1950. Amended ed. Norfolk, Conn., New Directions Books [1957] 256p. 19cm. (The Makers of modern literature) [PR5367.B4 1957] 56-13364
1. Shaw, George Bernard, 1836-1950. I. Title.

BENTLEY, Eric Russell, 928.2
1916-
Bernard shaw, 1856-1950 Amended ed. [New York, New Directions Books, 1957] 256p. 19cm. (A New Directions paperbook, no. 59) [PR5367] 57-1459
1. Shaw, George Bernard, 1856-1950. I. Title.

BENTLEY, Eric Russell, 928.2
1916-
Bernard Shaw. 1856-1950. Amended ed. Norfolk, Conn., New Directions Books [1957] 256p. 19cm. (The Makers of modern literature) [PR5367.B4 1957] 56-13364
1. Shaw, George Bernard, 1856-1950. I. Title.

BROWN, Ivor John 822.912
Carnegie, 1891-
Shaw in his time [New York] Nelson [1966, c.1965] 212p. illus., ports. 23cm. Bibl. [PR5366.B7] 66-31903 6.00 bds.,
1. Shaw, George Bernard, 1856-1950. I. Title. **BIP**

BROWN, Ivor John 822'.9'12 B
Carnegie, 1891-
Shaw in his time / Ivor Brown. Westport, Conn. : Greenwood Press, 1979, c1965. p. cm. Reprint of the 1967 issue of the ed. published by Nelson, London and Camden, N.J. Includes index. Bibliography: p. [PR5366.B7 1979] 79-17319 ISBN 0-313-21999-0 : 19.75
1. Shaw, George Bernard, 1856-1950. 2. Dramatists, English—20th century—Biography. I. Title.

BURTON, Richard, 822'.9'12 B
1861-1940.
Bernard Shaw, the man and the mask / by Richard Burton. Norwood, Pa. : Norwood Editions, 1975 [c1916] viii, 305 p. ; 23 cm. Reprint of the ed. published by H. Holt, New York. Includes index. Bibliography: p. 295-296. [PR5366.B8 1975] 75-40453 ISBN 0-88305-969-X lib. bdg. : 22.50
1. Shaw, George Bernard, 1856-1950. I. Title.

CHAPPELOW, Allan. 822'.9'12 B
Shaw—"the Chucker-Out"; a biographical exposition and critique, and a companion to and commentary on "Shaw the villager". Foreword by Vera Brittain. New York, AMS Press [1971, c1969] xx, 558 p. illus. 24 cm. [PR5367.C49 1971] 74-152559 ISBN 0-404-08359-5 15.00
1. Shaw, George Bernard, 1856-1950. I. Title.

CHAPPELOW, Allan, ed. 928.2
Shaw the villager and human being, a biographical sympoisum, assembled, narrated by Allan Chappelow. Foreword by Sybil Thrndike. New York, Macmillan, 1962[c. 1961] xxvi, 354p. illus. 24cm. 62-51710 10.00
1. Shaw, George Bernard, 1856-1950. I. Title.

CHESTERTON, Gilbert Keith, 928.2
1874-1936.
George Bernard Shaw. New York, Hill and Wang, 1956. 190 p. 19 cm. (Dramabooks, D3) [PR5367] 56-19717
1. Shaw, George Bernard, 1856-1950.

COOLIDGE, Olivia E. 822'.9'12 B
George Bernard Shaw, by Olivia Coolidge. Boston, Houghton Mifflin, 1968. 226, [1] p. illus., ports. 22 cm. Bibliography: p. [227] A biography of the Irish playwright and leader of the Fabian Society, examining his contribution to changing social values in the nineteenth and twentieth centuries and to the history of drama. [PR5366.C64] 92 AC 68
1. Shaw, George Bernard, 1856-1950. I. Title.

CROUCH, A. P. 822'.9'12
Mr. G. B. Shaw : a sketch (strictly unauthorised) / by A. P. Crouch. Folcroft, Pa. : Folcroft Library Editions, 1975. 23 p. ; 23 cm. Reprint of the 1932 ed. published by H. Cleaver, Bath, Eng. [PR5366.C7 1975] 75-17983 ISBN 0-8414-3625-8 lib. bdg. : 10.00
1. Shaw, George Bernard, 1856-1950.

DERVIN, Daniel, 1935- 822'.9'12
Bernard Shaw : a psychological study / Daniel Dervin. Lewisburg : Bucknell University Press, [1975] 350 p. ; 22 cm. Includes index. Bibliography: p. 338-345. [PR5366.D48] 73-8301 ISBN 0-8387-1418-8 : 15.00
1. Shaw, George Bernard, 1856-1950. **BIP**

DU CANN, Charles Garfield 928.2
Lott, 1889-
The loves of George Bernard Shaw. New York, Funk & Wagnalls [1963] x, 300 p. illus., ports. 22 cm. [PR5368.W6D8] 63-18913
1. Shaw, George Bernard, 1856-1950. I. Title.

ERVINE, St. John Greer, 928.2
1883-
Bernard Shaw: his life, work, and friends. New York, Morrow, 1956. 628p. illus. 23cm. [PR5366.E7 1956a] 56-9717
1. Shaw, George Bernard, 1836-1930. I. Title.

G. B. S. 90; aspects 822'.9'12 B
of Bernard Shaw's life and work [by] Max Beerbohm [and others] Edited by S. Winsten New York, Haskell House [1974] p. cm. [PR5366.G2 1974] 74-16305 16.95 (lib. bdg.).
1. Shaw, George Bernard, 1865-1950. I. Winsten, Stephen, ed.

HAMON, Augustin 822'.9'12
Frederic, 1862-
The twentieth century Moliere : Bernard Shaw / by Augustin Hamon ; translated from the French by Eden and Cedar Paul. Norwood, Pa. : Norwood Editions, 1976. 322 p. ; 23 cm. Translation of Le Moliere du xxe siecle. Reprint of the 1916 ed. published by F. A. Stokes, New York. Includes bibliographical references. [PR5366.H313 1976] 76-8543 ISBN 0-8482-1007-7 : 27.50
1. Shaw, George Bernard, 1856-1950. I. Title. **BIP**

HENDERSON, Archibald, 1877- 928.2
George Bernard Shaw: man of the century. New York, Appleton-Century- Crofts [1956] xxxii, 969p. illus., ports., facsims. 25cm. Bibliographical footnotes. [PR5366.H43] 56-12110
1. Shaw, George Bernard, 1856-1950. I. Title.

HENDERSON, Archibald, 822'.9'12 B
1877-1963.
George Bernard Shaw: man of the century. New York, Da Capo Press, 1972 [c1956] 2 v. (xxviii, 969 p.) illus. 23 cm. Includes bibliographical references. [PR5366.H43 1972] 79-87485 ISBN 0-306-71491-4
1. Shaw, George Bernard, 1856-1950.

IRVINE, William, 1906- 928.2
The universe of G. B. S. New York, Whittlesey House [1949] x, 439p. port. 24cm. Bibliography: p. 417-425. [PR5366.I7] 49-11656
1. Shaw, George Bernard, 1856-1950. I. Title. **BIP**

JACKSON, Holbrook, 822'.9'12
1874-1948.
Bernard Shaw. 2d ed. Freeport, N.Y., Books for Libraries Press [1970] 240 p. 23 cm. Reprint of the 1909 ed. [PR5366.J3 1970] 71-124239 ISBN 8-369-54270-
1. Shaw, George Bernard, 1856-1950.

MACCARTHY, Desmond, 822'.9'12
Sir, 1878-1952.
Shaw. [Folcroft, Pa.] Folcroft Library Editions, 1973. ix, 217 p. 26 cm. Reprint of the 1951 ed. published by MacGibbon & Kee. London. [PR5367.M28 1973] 73-3385 ISBN 0-8414-2340-7 15.00 (lib. ed.)
1. Shaw, George Bernard, 1856-1950. **BIP**

MINNEY, Rubeigh James, 822'.9'12
1895-
Recollections of George Bernard Shaw [by] R. J. Minney. Englewood Cliffs, N.J., Prentice-Hall [1969] vii, 211 p. port. 24 cm. [PR5366.M53 1969] 69-19110 7.95
1. Shaw, George Bernard, 1856-1950. I. Title.

OHMANN, Richard Malin. 828.912
Shaw; the style and the man. Middletown, Conn., Wesleyan Univ. Pr. [c.1962] 200p. illus. 22cm. 62-18343 5.00
1. Shaw, George Bernard, 1856-1950. I. Title.

OHMANN, Richard Malin. 828.912
Shaw; the style and the man. [1st ed.] Middletown, Conn., Wesleyan University Press [1962] 200p. illus. 22cm. [PR5366.O45] 62-18343
1. Shaw, George Bernard, 1856-1950. I. Title.

OWEN, Harold, 1872-1930. 940.3'1
Common sense about the Shaw / by Harold Owen. Norwood, Pa. : Norwood Editions, 1976. p. cm. Reprint of the 1915 ed. published by G. Allen & Unwin, London. [D523.S447O9 1976] 76-10990 ISBN 0-8482-2004-8 : 15.00
1. Shaw, George Bernard, 1856-1950. Common sense about the war. 2. European War, 1914-1918. I. Title. **BIP**

PALMER, John Leslie, 822'.9'12 B
1885-1944.
Bernard Shaw : an epitaph / by John Palmer. Norwood, Pa. : Norwood Editions, 1976. p. cm. Reprint of the 1915 ed. published by Grant Richards, London. [PR5366.P27 1976] 76-9066 ISBN 0-8482-2053-6 : 7.50
1. Shaw, George Bernard, 1856-1950. **BIP**

PALMER, John Leslie, 822'.9'12
1885-1944.
George Bernard Shaw, harlequin or patriot? [Folcroft, Pa.] Folcroft Library Editions, 1973 [c1915] 81 p. port. 24 cm. Reprint of the ed. published by The Century Co., New York. [PR5366.P3 1973] 72-12904 ISBN 0-8414-1009-7 (lib. bdg.)
1. Shaw, George Bernard, 1856-1950. I. Title.

PALMER, John Leslie, 822'.9'12
1885-1944.
George Bernard Shaw, harlequin or patriot? [Folcroft, Pa.] Folcroft Library Editions, 1973 [c1915] 81 p. port. 24 cm. Reprint of the ed. published by The Century Co., New York. [PR5366.P3 1973] 72-12904 5.00 (lib. bdg.).
1. Shaw, George Bernard, 1856-1950. I. Title.

PATCH, Blanche Eliza, 1878- 928.2
Thirty years with G. B. S. New York, Dodd, Mead, 1951. 316 p. group port. 21 cm. [PR5366.P33 1951a] 51-10302
1. Shaw, George Bernard, 1856-1950. I. Title. **BIP**

PEARSON, Hesketh, 1887- 928.2
G.B.S., a full length portrait, and A postscript. New York, Harper [1952] 381, 120 p. illus. 22 cm. "G. B. S. A full length portrait is published in England under the title of Bernard Shaw: his life and personality." [PR5366.P4 1952] 52-5464
1. Shaw, George Bernard, 1856-1960. I. Title.

PEARSON, Hesketh, 1887- 928.2
George Bernard Shaw: his life and personality. New York, Atheneum, 1963. 480 p. 19 cm. (Atheneum paperbacks, 36) First published in London in 1942 under title: Bernard Shaw: his life and personality. [PR5366.P4] 63-4164
1. Shaw, George Bernard, 1856-1950. I. Title. **BIP**

PEARSON, Hesketh [Edward 928.2
Hesketh Gibbons Person] 1887-
George Bernard Shaw, his life and personaality. New York, Atheneum, 1963 [c.1942-1963] 480p. 19cm. (36) 1.95 pap.,
1. Shaw, George Bernard, 1856-1950. I. Title.

RATTRAY, Robert 822'.9'12 B
Fleming, 1886-
Bernard Shaw : a chronicle / R. F. Rattray ; with photos. by Therese Bonney. New

York : Haskell House, 1974, [i.e.1975] 347 p., [1] leaf of plates : ill. ; 22 cm. Reprint of the 1941 ed. published by Leagrave Press, Luton, Eng. Includes bibliographical references and indexes. [PR5366.R3 1974] 74-30342 ISBN 0-8383-1892-4 : 16.95
1. Shaw, George Bernard, 1856-1950. I. Title. **BIP**

RATTRAY, Robert Fleming, 1886- 928.2
Bernard Shaw; a chronicle. With photos. by Therese Bonney. New York, Roy Publishers [c1951] 347 p. ports., facsim. 22 cm. Bibliographical footnotes. [PR5366.R3 1951a] 52-6229
1. Shaw, George Bernard, 1856-1950. I. Title.

RIDER, Dan, 1869- 822'.9'12 B
Adventures with Bernard Shaw. [Folcroft, Pa.] Folcroft Library Editions, 1974. 36 p. illus. 26 cm. Reprint of the 1907 ed. published by Morley and Mitchell, London. [PR5366.R5 1974] 73-17091 ISBN 0-8414-7266-1 (lib. bdg.)
1. Shaw, George Bernard, 1856-1950. I. Title. **BIP**

ROSSET, B. C. 928.2
Shaw of Dublin; the formative years [by] B. C. Rosset. University Park, Pennsylvania State University Press, 1964. xxiv, 388 p. illus., facsims., map (on lining paper) plan (on lining paper) ports. 24 cm. Bibliography: p. 359-364. [PR5366.R6] 63-18892
1. Shaw, George Bernard, 1856-1950. I. Title.

SHANKS, Edward, 1892-1953. 822'.9'12 B
Bernard Shaw. [Folcroft, Pa.] Folcroft Library Editions, 1974. p. cm. Reprint of the 1924 ed. published by Nisbet, London, in series: Writers of the day. Bibliography: p. [PR5366.S5 1974b] 74-17486 9.75
1. Shaw, George Bernard, 1856-1950. **BIP**

SHENFIELD, Margaret 928.2
Bernard Shaw; a pictorial biography. New York, Viking [c.1962] 144p. illus. 24cm. (Studio bk.) 61-15435 5.95
1. Shaw, George Bernard, 1856-1950. I. Title.

SHENFIELD, Margaret. 928.2
Bernard Shaw; a pictorial biography. New York, Viking Press [1962] 144 p. illus. 24 cm. (A Studio book) [PR5366.S58] 61-15435
1. Shaw, George Bernard, 1856-1950 I. Title.

SMITH, Joseph Percy, 1914- 822.912 B
The unrepentant pilgrim; a study of the development of Bernard Shaw [by] J. Percy Smith. Boston, Houghton Mifflin, 1965. x, 274 p. 22 cm. Bibliographical footnotes. [PR5366.S62] 65-16950
1. Shaw, George Bernard, 1856-1950. I. Title.

TOMPKINS, Peter, ed. 928.2
Shaw and Molly Tompkins in their own words. New York, Potter [1962, c.1961] 287p. illus. 23cm. 61-15116 4.95
I. Shaw, George Bernard, 1856-1950. II. Tompkins, Molly (Arthur) III. Title.

TOMPKINS, Peter, ed. 928.2
Shaw and Molly Tompkins in their own words. New York, C. N. Potter [1962, c1961] 287 p. illus. 23 cm. [PR5366.T55 1962] 61-15116
I. Shaw, George Bernard, 1856-1950 II. Tompkins, Molly (Arthur) III. Title.

USSHER, Arland. v. 12
Three great Irishmen; Shaw, Yeats, Joyce, with portraits by Augustus John. [New York] The New American Library [1957] 127 p. ports. 18 cm. (A Mentor book, MD 205)
1. Shaw, George Bernard, 1856-1950. 2. Yeats, William Butler, 1865-1939. 3. Joyce, James, 1882-1941. I. Title. **BIP**

WEINTRAUB, Stanley, 1929- 822'.9'12 B
Journey to heartbreak; the crucible years of Bernard Shaw, 1914-1918. New York, Weybright and Talley [1971] xi, 368 p. 22 cm. Includes bibliographical references. [PR5366.W4] 76-149002 8.95
1. Shaw, George Bernard, 1856-1950. I. Title.

WILLIAMSON, Audrey May, 1913- 828.912
Bernard Shaw; man and writer. New York, Crowell-Collier [1963] 224p. 22cm. 63-11106 4.95
1. Shaw, George Bernard, 1856-1950. I. Title.

WINSTEN, Stephen. 928.2
Jesting apostle; the private life of Bernard Shaw. [1st ed.] New York, Dutton, 1957 [c1956] 231 p. illus. 24 cm. [PR5366.W52 1957] 57-5352
1. Shaw, George Bernard, 1856-1950. I. Title.

WINSTEN, Stephen. 928.2
Jesting apostle; the private life of Bernard Shaw. [1st ed.] New York, Dutton, 1957 [c1956] 231 p. illus. 24 cm. [PR5366.W52 1957] 57-5352
1. Shaw, George Bernard, 1856-1950. I. Title.

Shaw, George Bernard, 1856-1950.

HENDERSON, Archibald, 1877- 928.2
George Bernard Shaw: man of the century. [De luxe 1st ed.] New York, Appleton-Century-Crofts [1956] 2 v. [xxviii, 969 p.) illus., ports., facsims. 25 cm. "Limited to 100 sets, each autographed by the author ... Number 96." Bibliographical footnotes. [PR5366.H43 1956a] 56-14612
1. Shaw, George Bernard, 1856-1950.

Shaw, George Bernard, 1856-1950—Addresses, essays, lectures.

HENDERSON, Archibald, 1877-1963. 822'.9'12 B
George Bernard Shaw : man of the century / by Archibald Henderson. Folcroft, Pa. : Folcroft Library Editions, 1977. p. cm. "A lecture delivered under the auspices of the Gertrude Clarke Whittall Poetry and Literature Fund in the Coolidge Auditorium, Library of Congress, November 19, 1956." Reprint of the 1957 ed. published by the Reference Dept. of the Library of Congress, Washington, D.C. [PR5366.H433 1977] 77-12479 ISBN 0-8414-4957-0 : 7.50
1. Shaw, George Bernard, 1856-1950—Addresses, essays, lectures. 2. Dramatists, English—20th century—Biography—Addresses, essays, lectures.

Shaw, George Bernard, 1856-1950—Biography.

ESDAILE, Ernest, 1860- 822'.9'12 B
Bernard Shaw's postscript to fame / by Ernest Esdaile. [Folcroft, Pa.] : Folcroft Library Editions, 1974. p. cm. Reprint of the 1942 ed. published by Quality Press, London. [PR5366.E8 1974] 74 23948 ISBN 0-8414-3955-9 : 7.50
1. Shaw, George Bernard, 1856-1950—Biography. I. Title.

HACKETT, J. P. 822'.9'12 B
Shaw, George versus Bernard, by J. P. Hackett. [Folcroft, Pa.] Folcroft Library Editions, 1974. p. cm. Reprint of the 1937 ed. published by Sheed & Ward, London. [PR5366.H2 1974] 74-16314 12.50
1. Shaw, George Bernard, 1856-1950—Biography. I. Title. **BIP**

SHAW, George Bernard, 1856-1950. 822'.9'12 B
Shaw; an autobiography, selected from his writings by Stanley Weintraub. New York, Weybright and Talley [1969-70] 2 v. illus., ports. 25 cm. Contents.Contents.—[1] 1856-1898.—v. 2. 1898-1950. Includes bibliographies. [PR5366.A5 1969] 74-84621 10.00
I. Weintraub, Stanley, 1929- comp. II. Title.

SHAW, George Bernard, 1856-1950. 822'.9'12 B
Table-talk of G. B. S. Conversations on things in general between Bernard Shaw and his biographer, by Archibald Henderson. New York, Haskell House Publishers, 1974. ix, 191 p. 22 cm. Reprint of the 1925 ed. published by Chapman and Hall, London. [PR5365.T3 1974] 74-16315 ISBN 0-8383-1890-8
1. Table-talk. I. Henderson, Archibald, 1877-1963. II. Title.

SHAW, George Bernard, 1856-1950. 928.1
To a young actress: the letters of Bernard Shaw to Molly Tompkins; the correspondence between Bernard Shaw and an American artist from 1921 through 1949. Edited and with an introd. by Peter Tompkins. [1st ed.] New York, C.N. Potter [1960] 192 p. illus., ports. 31 cm. Most of the letters are facsim. reproductions. [PR5366.A48 1960] 60-8926
I. Tompkins, Molly (Arthur) II. Thompkins, Peter, ed. III. Title.

Shaw, George Bernard, 1856-1950—Books and reading—Addresses, essays, lectures.

LAURENCE, Dan H. 822'.9'12 B
Shaw, books, and libraries / Dan H. Laurence. [Austin] : Humanities Research Center, University of Texas at Austin, 1977,c1976 28 p. ; 23 cm. (Bibliographical monograph series ; no. 9) [PR5366.L38 1976] 76-620048 ISBN 0-87959-022-X : 5.95
1. Shaw, George Bernard, 1856-1950—Books and reading—Addresses, essays, lectures. 2. Dramatists, English—20th century—Biography—Addresses, essays, lectures. I. Title. II. Series. **BIP**

Shaw, George Bernard, 1856-1950—Congresses.

THE Genius of Shaw : 822'.9'12
a symposium / edited by Michael Holroyd. 1st American ed. New York : Holt, Rinehart and Winston, 1979. p. cm. [PR5366.G4 1979] 78-31306 ISBN 0-03-043541-2 : 18.95
1. Shaw, George Bernard, 1856-1950—Congresses. 2. Dramatists, English—20th century—Biography—Congresses. I. Holroyd, Michael.

Shaw, George Bernard, 1856-1950—Dictionaries, indexes, etc.

HARTNOLL, Phyllis. 822'.9'12
Who's who in Shaw / Phyllis Hartnoll. New York : Taplinger Pub. Co., 1975. 246 p. ; 21 cm. [PR5366.H36 1975] 74-21719 ISBN 0-8008-8270-9 : 8.95
1. Shaw, George Bernard, 1856-1950—Dictionaries, indexes, etc. 2. Shaw, George Bernard, 1856-1950—Characters. I. Title. **BIP**

Shaw, George Bernard, 1856-1950—Relationship with women—Florence Farr.

JOHNSON, Josephine. 822'.9'12 B
Florence Farr : Bernard Shaw's "new woman" / Josephine Johnson. Totowa, N.J. : Rowman and Littlefield, 1975. xiv, 222 p., [8] leaves of plates : ill. ; 23 cm. Includes bibliographical references and index. [PR5366.J64] 75-329754 ISBN 0-87471-707-8 : 12.50
1. Shaw, George Bernard, 1856-1950—Relationship with women—Florence Farr. 2. Emery, Florence Farr, d. 1917. I. Title. **BIP**

Shaw, George Bernard, 1856-1950—Religion and ethics.

BARR, Alan P. 822'.9'12 B
Victorian stage pulpiteer: Bernard Shaw's crusade [by] Alan P. Barr. Athens, University of Georgia Press [1974, c1973] xiv, 188 p. 24 cm. Bibliography: p. 172-182. [PR5368.R4B3] 70-190046 8.50
1. Shaw, George Bernard, 1856-1950—Religion and ethics. I. Title.

Shaw, Lemuel, 1781-1861.

CHASE, Frederic Hathaway, 1870-1948. 347'.744'0350924
Lemuel Shaw, chief justice of the Supreme Court of Massachusetts, 1830-1860. Freeport, N.Y., Books for Libraries Press [1973] p. Reprint of the 1918 ed. [KF368.S42C5 1973] 72-10665 ISBN 0-8369-7104-3
1. Shaw, Lemuel, 1781-1861.

Shaw, Nate.

SHAW, Nate. 917.61'4'0360924 B
All God's dangers; the life of Nate Shaw [compiled by] Theodore Rosengarten. [1st ed.] New York, Knopf; [distributed by Random House] 1974. xxv, 561, xii p. map. 25 cm. [HD1478.U6S5 1974] 74-8269 ISBN 0-394-49084-3
1. Shaw, Nate. 2. Share-cropping—Personal narratives. 3. Negroes—Alabama. I. Rosengarten, Theodore. **BIP**

Shaw, Robert Lawson, 1916-

MUSSULMAN, Joseph A. 785'.092'4 B
Dear people ... Robert Shaw / Joseph A. Mussulman. Bloomington : Indiana University Press, c1979. p. cm. Includes index. Discography: p. [ML422.S52M9] 78-20401 12.50
1. Shaw, Robert Lawson, 1916- 2. Conductors (Music)—United States—Biography. I. Title.

Shaw, Wilbur,

SHAW, Wilbur, 1902-1954. 927.967
Gentlemen, start your engines. New York, Coward-McCann [1955] 320 p. illus. 22 cm. Autobiography. [GV1029.S43] 55-8980
I. Title.

Shawn, Ted, 1891-1972.

TERRY, Walter. 793.3'2'0924 B
Ted Shawn, father of American dance : a biography / by Walter Terry. New York : Dial Press, 1976. 186 p., [8] leaves of plates : ill. ; 24 cm. Includes index. [GV1785.S5T47] 76-13200 ISBN 0-8037-8557-7 : 10.00
1. Shawn, Ted, 1891-1972. 2. Dancing.

Shcharansky, Avital.

SHCHARANSKY, Avital. 325'.247'095694 B
Next year in Jerusalem / by Avital Shcharansky ; with Ilana Ben-Josef ; translated from the Russian by Stefani Hoffman. 1st ed. New York : William Morrow, 1979. 189 p. : ill. ; 22 cm. [JV8749.P3S555] 79-17494 ISBN 0-688-03552-3 : 9.95
1. Shcharansky, Avital. 2. Shcharansky, Anatoly. 3. Israel—Emigration and immigration—Biography. 4. Jews in Russia—Biography. 5. Jews in Russia—Persecutions. 6. Russia—Emigration and immigration—Biography. I. Ben-Josef, Ilana, joint author. II. Title. **BIP**

Shearer, Moira, 1926-

CROWLE, Eileen Georgina Beatrice, 1903- 927.933
Moira Shearer, portrait of a dancer [by] Pigeon Crowle [pseud.] New York, Pitman Pub. Corp. [1950?] 80p. 47 plates (incl. ports.) 26cm. [GV1785.S54C7 1950] 50-7957
1. Shearer, Moira, 1926- I. Title.

Shears, Sarah.

SHEARS, Sarah. 914.22'3'03830924 B
A village girl; memoirs of a Kentish childhood. Introd. by R. F. Delderfield. New York, Simon and Schuster [1972, c1971] 256 p. 22 cm. Originally published under title: Tapioca for tea. [PR6069.H3955Z5 1972] 73-179580 ISBN 0-671-21058-0 6.95
1. Shears, Sarah. I. Title.

Shears, Sarah—Biography.

SHEARS, Sarah. 362.7'1 B
Other people's children / [by] Sarah Shears. London ; Salem. N.H. : Elek, 1978.

[2], 153 p. ; 23 cm. [PR6069.H3955Z473] 79-307806 ISBN 0-236-40117-3 : 8.95
1. Shears, Sarah—Biography. 2. Authors, English—20th century—Biography. 3. Baby sitters—Biography. I. Title.
Distributed by MerrimackBook Services, Salem, NH BIP

Sheean, Vincent, 1899-

SHEEAN, Vincent, 1899- 780'.07 B
First and last love / Vincent Sheean. Westport, Conn. : Greenwood Press, 1979, c1956. 305 p. ; 24 cm. Reprint of the ed. published by Random House, New York. Includes index. [ML429.S45A3 1979] 78-26964 ISBN 0-313-20549-3 lib. bdg. : 21.00
1. Sheean, Vincent, 1899- 2. Musicians—United States—Biography. 3. Journalists—United States—Biography. I. Title. BIP

SHEEAN, Vincent, 1899- 927.8
Oscar Hammerstein I the life and exploits of an impresario. With a pref. by Oscar Hammerstein II New York, Simon and Schuster, 1956. 363p. illus. 23cm. [ML429.H25S5] 56-7495
1. Hammerstein, Oscar, 1847-1919. II. Title.

SHEEAN, Vincent, 1899- 070'.924
Personal history. With a new introd. by the author. 1969 ed. Boston, Houghton Mifflin, 1969. xvii, 403 p. 22 cm. First published in 1935. Published also under title: In search of history. [PN4874.S46A3 1969] 73-2896 6.95
I. Title.

Sheehan, George.

SHEEHAN, George. 796.4'26 B
Running and being : the total experience / George A. Sheehan ; drawings by Nora Sheehan. New York : Simon and Schuster, c1978. 256 p. : ill. ; 25 cm. [GV697.S53A35] 77-18271 ISBN 0-671-22713-0 : 8.95
1. Sheehan, George. 2. Track and field athletes—United States—Biography. 3. Running. 4. Physical fitness. I. Title.

Sheeler, Charles, 1883-1965.

SHEELER, Charles, 1883-1965. 759.13
Charles Sheeler / Martin Friedman. New York : Watson-Guptill Publications, 1975. 224 p. : ill. (some col.) ; 31 cm. Includes index. Bibliography: p. 220-222. [ND237.S47F74 1975] 75-6524 ISBN 0-8230-4799-7 : 29.95
1. Sheeler, Charles, 1883-1965. I. Friedman, Martin L.

Sheen, Fulton John, Bp., 1895-1980.

CONNIFF, James C G 922.273
The Bishop Sheen story. Greenwich, Conn., Fawcett Publications, c1953. 32p. illus. 29cm. [BX4705.S612C6] 53-4243
1. Sheen, Fulton John, Bp., I. Title.

NOONAN, Daniel P. 282'.0924
Missionary with a mike: the Bishop Sheen story, by D. P. Noonan. [1st ed.] New York, Pageant Press [1968] 213 p. 21 cm. [BX4705.S612N6] 68-17834
1. Sheen, Fulton John, Bp., 1895- I. Title.

NOONAN, Daniel P. 282'.0924 [B]
The passion of Fulton Sheen, by D. P. Noonan. New York, Pyramid Books [1975, c1972] 156 p. illus. 18 cm. [BX4705.S612N63] 70-173885 ISBN 0-515-03658-7 1.25 (pbk.)
1. Sheen, Fulton John, Bp., 1895- I. Title. BIP

Sheetz, Ann Kindig.

SHEETZ, Ann Kindig. 248'.2 B
Born again, but still wet behind the ears / Ann Kindig Sheets. 1st ed. Chappaqua, N.Y. : Christian Herald Books, c1979. 160 p. ; 21 cm. [BR1725.S454A33] 78-64839 ISBN 0-915684-43-8 : 6.95
1. Sheetz, Ann Kindig. 2. Christian biography—United States. 3. Christian life—1960- I. Title. BIP

Sheffey, Robert Sayers, 1820-1902.

*CARR, Jess. 920
The saint of the wilderness: a biographical novel depicting the life and works of Robert Sayers Sheffey Radford, Va., Commonwealth Press [1974] 441 p. frontispiece 23 cm. [CT275] 74-77781 8.95
1. Sheffey, Robert Sayers, 1820-1902 I. Title.

STORY of the life of Robert Sayers Sheffey, v. 12 a courier of the long trail - God's gentleman -a man of prayer and unshaken faith. [Bluefield, Va., 195-?] 173p. ports. 23cm.
1. Sheffey, Robert Sayers, 1820-1902. 2. Mehodism. I. Barbery, Willard Sanders. BIP

Sheikh, Bilquis.

SHEIKH, Bilquis. 248'.246'0924 B
I dared to call him Father / Bilquis Sheikh, with Richard Schneider. [Lincoln, Va.] : Chosen Books ; Waco, Tex. : distributed by Word Books, c1978. 173 p. ; 23 cm. [BV2626.4.S53A33] 77-15603 ISBN 0-912376-22-8 : 7.95
1. Sheikh, Bilquis. 2. Converts from Islam—Biography. I. Schneider, Richard, 1922- II. Title. BIP

Sheil, Bernard James, Bp.

TREAT, Roger L 922.273
Bishop Sheil and the CYO. New York, Messner [1951] 211 p. illus. 22 cm. [BX4705.S613T7] 51-14642
1. Sheil, Bernard James, Bp. 2. Catholic Youth Organization of the Archdiocese of Chicago. I. Title.

Shelby Co., Ill.—Biography.

MIDDLESWORTH, Grace H. 917.73'798'03922 B
Excerpts of Shelby County, Illinois, history biographies, compiled by Grace Middlesworth. [Decatur, Ill., Decatur Genealogical Society] 1969. 79 p. 28 cm. [F547.S6M49] 73-171366
1. Shelby Co., Ill.—Biography. I. Title.

Shelby, Isaac, 1750-1826.

WROBEL, Sylvia. 976.9'03'0924 B
Isaac Shelby: Kentucky's first Governor and hero of three wars [by] Sylvia Wrobel and George Grider. Danville, Ky., Cumberland Press [1974] iv, 153 p. illus. 23 cm. Bibliography: p. 146-153. [F455.S57] 74-162986
1. Shelby, Isaac, 1750-1826. I. Grider, George, 1914- joint author.

Shelby, Joseph Orville, 1830-1897.

O'FLAHERTY, Daniel. 923.573
General Jo Shelby, undefeated rebel. Chapel Hill, University of North Carolina Press [1954] xiv, 437 p. map, port. 24 cm. Bibliography: p. 403-422. [E467.1.S53O3] 54-9545
1. Shelby, Joseph Orville, 1830-1897. I. Title.

Sheldon, Asa Goodell, b.

SHELDON, Asa Goodell, b. 1788. 926.373
Life of Asa G. Sheldon: Wilmington farmer. [Wilmington? Mass.] Friends of the Wilmington Public Library [1959] 374 p. 17 cm. [CT275.S462A3 1959] 59-37844
I. Title.

Sheldon, Donald Edward, 1921-

GREINER, James. 629.13'092'4 B
Wager with the wind; the Don Sheldon story. Foreword by Bradford Washburn. Illustrated with photos. Chicago, Rand McNally [1974] 256 p. illus. 24 cm. Bibliography: p. 251. A biography of the Alaskan bush pilot emphasizing his thirty-three year flying career and his contribution to the development of bush aviation. [TL540.S455G73] 92 74-16323 ISBN 0-528-81856-2 8.95
1. Sheldon, Donald Edward, 1921- 2. Aeronautics—Alaska—History. 3. Alaska—History. I. Title.

Sheldon, Edward Brewster, 1886-1946.

BARNES, Eric Wollencott. 928.1
The man who lived twice: the biography of Edward Sheldon, with an introductory chapter by Anne Morrow Lindbergh. New York, Scribner [1956] 367 p. illus. 24 cm. [PS3537.H62Z7] 56-9882
1. Sheldon, Edward Brewster, 1886-1946. I. Title.

Sheldon, Isaac, ca. 1629-1708.

HUNT, Charlotte Alling. 929'.0973
Isaac Sheldon of Windsor, Conn. [Worcester? Mass., 1967?] 9 l. map. 28 cm. Bibliography: leaf 9. [CT275.S4622H8] 74-5701
1. Sheldon, Isaac, ca. 1629-1708.

Shellabarger, Samuel, 1817-1896.

KINNISON, William A. 340.0924
Hon. Samuel Shellabarger (1817-1896), lawyer, jurist, legislator, by William A. Kinnison. [Springfield, Ohio] Clark County Hist. Soc., 1966. 61p. illus., facsims., port. 23cm. Bibl. 66-7685 1.00
1. Shellabarger, Samuel, 1817-1896. I. Clark County (Ohio) Historical Society. II. Title.
00 W. Main St., Springfield Ohio 45504

Shelley, Harriet Westbrook, d. 1816.

BOAS, Louise Schutz. 928.2
Harriet Shelley; five long years. London, New York, Oxford University Press, 1962. 237 p. illus. 23 cm. Includes bibliography. [PR5432.B6] 62-1224
1. Shelley, Harriet Westbrook, d. 1816. 2. Shelley, Percy Bysshe, 1792-1822. BIP

Shelley, Mary Wollstonecraft Godwin, 1797-1851.

SHELLEY, Mary Wollstonecraft (Godwin) 1797-1851. 928.2
My best Mary; the selected letters of Mary Wollstonecraft Shelley. Edited and with an introd. by Muriel Spark & Derek Stanford. New York, Roy Publishers [1953] 240p. port. 23cm. Bibliography: p.239-240. [PR5398] 53-9781
I. Title.

SHELLEY, Mary Wollstonecraft (Godwin) 1797-1851. 823'.7 B
My best Mary; the selected letters of Mary Wollstonecraft Shelley. Edited and with an introd. by Muriel Spark and Derek Stanford. [Folcroft, Pa.] Folcroft Library Editions, 1972. 240 p. port. 26 cm. "Limited to 150 copies." Reprint of the 1953 ed. Bibliography: p. 239-240. [PR5398.A43 1972] 72-189741
I. Spark, Muriel, ed. II. Stanford, Derek, ed. III. Title.

SHELLEY, Mary Wollstonecraft (Godwin) 1797-1861. 823'.7 B
Letters of Mary W. Shelley (mostly unpublished) with introd. and notes by Henry H. Harper. [Folcroft, Pa.] Folcroft Library Editions, 1972. 191 p. 24 cm. Reprint of the 1918 ed. [PR5398.A4 1972] 72-8901 25.00
I. Harper, Henry Howard, 1871- ed. BIP

BIGLAND, Eileen. 928.2
Mary Shelley. New York, Appleton-Century-Crofts [1959] 275 p. 22 cm. Includes bibliography. [PR5398.B5 1959a] 59-11977
1. Shelley, Mary Wollstonecraft Godwin, 1797-1851. BIP

CHURCH, Richard, 1893- 823'.7 B
Mary Shelley. Freeport, N.Y., Books for Libraries Press [1972] p. Reprint of the 1928 ed., issued in series: Representative women. Bibliography: p. [PR5398.C5 1972] 72-7188 ISBN 0-8369-6925-1
1. Shelley, Mary Wollstonecraft (Godwin) 1797-1851. I. Series: Representative women (New York) BIP

FLORESCU, Radu R. N. 823'.7
In search of Frankenstein / Radu Florescu ; with contributions by Alan Barbour & Matei Cazacu. Boston : New York Graphic Society, [1975] p. cm. Filmography: p. [PR5397.F73F6] 74-22502 ISBN 0-8212-0614-1 : 9.95
1. Shelley, Mary Wollstonecraft Godwin, 1797-1851. Frankenstein. 2. Shelley, Mary Wollstonecraft Godwin, 1797-1851—Biography. 3. Shelley, Percy Bysshe, 1792-1822—Biography. 4. Shelley, Mary Wollstonecraft Godwin, 1797-1851—Adaptations. I. Barbour, Alan G., joint author. II. Cazacu, Matei, joint author. III. Title.

GERSON, Noel Bertram, 1914- 823'.7 B
Daughter of earth and water; a biography of Mary Wollstonecraft Shelley [by] Noel B. Gerson. New York, Morrow, 1973. 280 p. front. 22 cm. Bibliography: p. 272-273. [PR5398.G4 1973] 76-182976 6.95
1. Shelley, Mary Wollstonecraft (Godwin) 1797-1851. I. Title.

GRYLLS, Rosalie Glynn, 1905- 828'.6'09 B
Mary Shelley; a biography, by R. Glynn Grylls. New York, Haskell House, 1969. xvi, 345 p. ports. 23 cm. Reprint of the 1938 ed. Bibliography: p. [330]-331. [PR5398.G7 1969] 76-95428 ISBN 0-8383-0978-X
1. Shelley, Mary Wollstonecraft (Godwin), Mrs., 1797-1851—Biography.

LEIGHTON, Margaret (Carver) 823'.7 B
Shelley's Mary; a life of Mary Godwin Shelley [by] Margaret Leighton. New York, Farrar, Straus and Giroux [1973] 234 p. 21 cm. Bibliography: p. 225-226. [PR5398.L4] 73-82693 ISBN 0-374-36779-5 5.95
1. Shelley, Mary Wollstonecraft (Godwin) 1797-1851. I. Title. BIP

MARSHALL, Florence A. (Thomas) 1843-1922. 823'.7 B
The life & letters of Mary Wollstonecraft Shelley, by Mrs. Julian Marshall. New York, Haskell House, 1970. 2 v. port. 22 cm. Reprint of the 1889 ed. [PR5398.M2 1970] 70-115181
1. Shelley, Mary Wollstonecraft (Godwin) 1797-1851.

ROSSETTI, Lucy Madox (Brown) 1843-1894. 823'.7 B
Mrs. Shelley. Folcroft, Pa., Folcroft Press [1969] viii, 238 p. 23 cm. Reprint of the 1890 ed., issued in series: Eminent women series. [PR5398.R6 1969] 72-194772
1. Shelley, Mary Wollstonecraft (Godwin) 1797-1851. I. Series: Eminent women series.

SPARK, Muriel. 823'.7 B
Child of light : a reassessment of Mary Wollstonecraft Shelley / by Muriel Spark. Folcroft, Pa. : Folcroft Library Editions, 1976, i.e.1977 xii, 235 p. : port. ; 23 cm. Reprint of the 1951 ed. published by Tower Bridge Publications, Hadleigh, Essex, Eng. Includes index. Bibliography: p. 231. [PR5398.S6 1976] 76-47464 ISBN 0-8414-7807-4 lib. bdg. : 25.00
1. Shelley, Mary Wollstonecraft (Godwin)

1797-1851. 2. Authors, English—19th century—Biography. I. Title.

Shelley, Mary Wollstonecraft Godwin, 1797-1851—Biography.

CHURCH, Richard, 1893- 823'.7 B
Mary Shelley / by Richard Church. Norwood, Pa. : Norwood Editions, 1975. 91, [4] p. : port. ; 23 cm. Reprint of the 1928 ed. published by G. Howe, London in the series: Representative women. "Books by Mary Shelley": p. [92] [PR5398.C5 1975] 75-28269 ISBN 0-88305-134-6 : 15.00
1. Shelley, Mary Wollstonecraft Godwin, 1797-1851—Biography. I. Series: Representative women (London)

DUNN, Jane. 823'.7 B
Moon in eclipse : a life of Mary Shelley / Jane Dunn. New York : St. Martin's Press, 1978. 374 p., [4] leaves of plates : ill. ; 22 cm. Includes index. Bibliography: p. [355]-357. [PR5398.D85] 78-850 ISBN 0-312-54692-0 : 14.50
1. Shelley, Mary Wollstonecraft Godwin, 1797-1851—Biography. 2. Authors, English—19th century—Biography. I. Title. BIP

FLORESCU, Radu R. N. 823'.7
In search of Frankenstein / Radu Florescu ; with contributions by Alan Barbour & Matei Cazacu. Boston : New York Graphic Society, [1975] p. cm. Filmography: p. [PR5397.F73F6] 74-22502 ISBN 0-8212-0614-1 : 9.95
1. Shelley, Mary Wollstonecraft Godwin, 1797-1851. Frankenstein. 2. Shelley, Mary Wollstonecraft Godwin, 1797 1851 Biography. 3. Shelley, Percy Bysshe, 1792-1822—Biography. 4. Shelley, Mary Wollstonecraft Godwin, 1797-1851—Adaptations. I. Barbour, Alan G., joint author. II. Cazacu, Matei, joint author. III. Title.

GRYLLS, Rosalie Glynn, 1905- 823'.7 B
Mary Shelley; a biography, by R. Glynn Grylls. [Folcroft, Pa.] Folcroft Library Editions, 1974. xvi, 345 p. illus. 23 cm. Reprint of the 1938 ed. published by Oxford University Press, London. Bibliography: p. [330]-331. [PR5398.G7 1974] 74-12163 ISBN 0-8414-4535-4 (lib. bdg.)
1. Shelley, Mary Wollstonecraft (Godwin) 1797-1851—Biography. BIP

ROSSETTI, Lucy Madox Brown, 1843-1894. 823'.7 B
Mrs. Shelley / by Lucy Madox Rossetti. Norwood, Pa. : Norwood Editions, 1975. viii, 238 p. ; 23 cm. Reprint of the 1890 ed. published by W. H. Allen, London, in series: Eminent women series. [PR5398.R6 1975] 75 34126 ISBN 0 88305-567-8 lib. bdg. : 25.00
1. Shelley, Mary Wollstonecraft Godwin, 1797-1851—Biography. I. Series: Eminent women series.

Shelley, Mary Wollstonecraft Godwin, 1797-1851—Biography—Juvenile literature.

HARRIS, Janet. 823'.7 B
The woman who created Frankenstein : a portrait of Mary Shelley / by Janet Harris. 1st ed. New York : Harper & Row, c1979. p. cm. Includes index. Bibliography: p. A biography of the 19th-century woman who wrote the first work of science fiction. [PR5398.H3] 92 78-19481 ISBN 0-06-022228-X : 7.95 ISBN 0-06-022229-8 lib. bdg. : 7.89
1. Shelley, Mary Wollstonecraft Godwin, 1797-1851—Biography—Juvenile literature. 2. Shelley, Mary Wollstonecraft Godwin, 1797-1851. 3. Authors, English—19th century—Biography—Juvenile literature. I. Title. BIP

Shelley, Mary Wollstonecraft Godwin, 1797-1851—Correspondence.

SHELLEY, Mary Wollstonecraft Godwin, 1797-1851. 823'.7 B
Letters of Mary W. Shelley (mostly unpublished) : with introduction and notes / by Henry H. Harper. Norwood, Pa. : Norwood Editions, 1976. 191 p. ; 23 cm. Reprint of the 1918 ed. printed only for members of the Bibliophile Society, Boston. [PR5398.A4 1976] 76-8529 ISBN 0-8482-1010-7 : 25.00
1. Shelley, Mary Wollstonecraft Godwin, 1797-1851—Correspondence.

SHELLEY, Mary Wollstonecraft (Godwin) 1797-1851. 928.2
My best Mary; the selected letters of Mary Wollstonecraft Shelley. Edited and with an introd. by Muriel Spark & Derek Stanford. New York, Roy Publishers [1953] 240p. port. 23cm. Bibliography: p.239-240. [PR5398] 53-9781
I. Title.

SHELLEY, Mary Wollstonecraft (Godwin) 1797-1861. 823'.7 B
Letters of Mary W. Shelley (mostly unpublished) with introd. and notes by Henry H. Harper. [Folcroft, Pa.] Folcroft Library Editions, 1972. 191 p. 24 cm. Reprint of the 1918 ed. [PR5398.A4 1972] 72-8901 25.00
I. Harper, Henry Howard, 1871- ed. BIP

SHELLEY, Mary Wollstonecraft (Godwin) 1797-1851. 823'.7 B
My best Mary; the selected letters of Mary Wollstonecraft Shelley. Edited and with an introd. by Muriel Spark and Derek Stanford. [Folcroft, Pa.] Folcroft Library Editions, 1972. 240 p. port. 26 cm. "Limited to 150 copies." Reprint of the 1953 ed. Bibliography: p. 239-240. [PR5398.A43 1972] 72-189741
I. Spark, Muriel, ed. II. Stanford, Derek, ed. III. Title.

Shelley, Percy Bysshe, 1792-1822.

BLUNDEN, Edmund Charles, 1896- 821'.7 B
Shelley, a life story, by Edmund Blunden. [Folcroft, Pa.] Folcroft Library Editions, 1973 [c1946] p. Reprint of the ed. published by Collins, London. [PR5431.B5 1973] 73-16265 20.00
1. Shelley, Percy Bysshe, 1792-1822. BIP

BLUNDEN, Edmund Charles, 1896- ed. 821'.7'09 B
Shelley and Keats, as they struck their contemporaries; notes, partly from manuscript sources, edited by Edmund Blunden. [Folcroft, Pa.] Folcroft Library Editions, 1974. 94 p. 23 cm. Reprint of the 1925 ed. published by C. W. Beaumont, London. [PR5431.B53 1974] 74-16306 ISBN 0-8414-9878-4 (lib. bdg.)
1. Shelley, Percy Bysshe, 1792-1822. 2. Keats, John, 1795-1821. I. Title.

BLUNDEN, Edmund Charles, 1896- 928.2
Shelly, a life story [Rev. ed.] New York, Oxford [1965] ix, 310p. 20cm. (95) First pub. in London in 1946. [PR5431.B5] 2.95 pap.,
1. Shelley, Percy Bysshe, 1792-1822. I. Title.

CAMERON, Kenneth Neill, comp. 821'.7 B
Romantic rebels; essays on Shelley and his circle. Cambridge, Harvard University Press, 1973. vi, 320 p. 24 cm. Essays originally published in v. 1-4 of Shelley and his circle. [PR5431.C28 1973] 72-97087 ISBN 0-674-77937-1 7.95
1. Shelley, Percy Bysshe, 1792-1822. 2. Authors, English—19th century—Biography. 3. Authors—Correspondence, reminiscences, etc. I. Carl H. Pforzheimer Library, New York. Shelley and his circle, 1773-1822. II. Title.
Contents omitted. BIP

CAMERON, Kenneth Neill. 821'.7 B
Shelley: the golden years. Cambridge, Harvard University Press, 1974. x, 669 p. 26 cm. Continuation of the author's The young Shelley. Includes bibliographical references. [PR5431.C29] 73-80566 ISBN 0-674-03160-1 20.00
1. Shelley, Percy Bysshe, 1792-1822. I. Title.

CAMERON, Kenneth Neill 928.2
The young Shelley; genesis of radical New York, Collier [1962, c.1950] 480 p. (Bs46) Bibli. pap. 1.50
1. Shelley, Percy Bysshe, 1792-1822. I. Title.

CAMERON, Kenneth Neill. 928.2
The young Shelley; genesis of a radical. New York, Macmillan, 1950. xii, 437 p. 22 cm. Bibliographical references included in "Notes" (p. [289]-412) [PR5432.C3 1962] 50-14819
1. Shelley, Percy Bysshe, 1792-1822. I. Title. BIP

CARL H. Pforzheimer Library, New York. 928.2
Shelley and his circle, 1773-1822. Edited by Kenneth Neill Cameron Cambridge, Harvard University Press, 1961- v. illus., ports., maps, facsims. 29 cm. "A complete edition of the manuscripts in the Shelley and his circle collection." Includes bibliographical references. [PR5431.A33] 60-5393
1. Shelley, Percy Bysshe, 1792-1822. 2. Authors, English. 3. Authors—Correspondence, reminiscences, etc. I. Cameron, Kenneth Neill, ed. II. Title.

CARPENTER, Edward, 1844-1929. 821'.7
The psychology of the poet Shelley, by Edward Carpenter and George Barnefield. London, Allen & Unwin. New York, Haskell House Publishers, 1972. 126 p. 23 cm. Reprint of the 1925 ed. Bibliography: p. 126-[127] [PR5431.C33 1972] 72-1334 ISBN 0-8383-1431-7
1. Shelley, Percy Bysshe, 1792-1822. I. Barnard, Guy Christian, 1896- II. Title. BIP

CLUTTON-BROCK, Arthur, 1868-1924. 821'.7 B
Shelley, the man and the poet. 2d and rev. ed. Freeport, N.Y., Books for Libraries Press [1973] p. Reprint of the 1923 ed. [PR5431.C5 1973] 72-10618 ISBN 0-8369-7106-X
1. Shelley, Percy Bysshe, 1792-1822. BIP

DOWDEN, Edward, 1843-1913. 821'.7
Letters about Shelley, interchanged by three friends—Edward Dowden, Richard Garnett, and Wm. Michael Rossetti. Edited, with an introd. by R. S. Garnett. [Folcroft, Pa.] Folcroft Library Editions, 1973. p. Reprint of the 1917 ed. published by Hodder and Stoughton, London and New York. [PR5431.D5 1973] 73-15900 ISBN 0-8414-4475-7 (lib. bdg.)
1. Shelley, Percy Bysshe, 1792-1822. I. Garnett, Richard, 1835-1906. II. Rossetti, William Michael, 1829-1919. III. Title. BIP

DOWDEN, Edward, 1843-1913. 821'.7 B
Letters about Shelley, interchanged by three friends—Edward Dowden, Richard Garnett and Wm. Michael Rossetti. Edited, with an introd., by R. S. Garnett. New York, AMS Press [1971] 271 p. 23 cm. Reprint of the 1917 ed. [PR5431.D5 1971] 77-168058 ISBN 0-404-05444-7 12.50
1. Shelley, Percy Bysshe, 1792-1822. I. Garnett, Richard, 1835-1906. II. Rossetti, William Michael, 1829-1919. III. Title. BIP

EDMUNDS, Edward William. 821'.7
Shelley & his poetry, by E. W. Edmunds. London, G. G. Harrap, 1912. [New York, AMS Press, 1972] 144 p. port. 19 cm. (Poetry and life) Bibliography: p. [145] [PR5431.E4 1972] 78-120961 ISBN 0-404-52511-3 8.00
1. Shelley, Percy Bysshe, 1792-1822. I. Title. II. Series. BIP

EDMUNDS, Edward William. 821'.7 B
Shelley & his poetry / by E. W. Edmunds. Brooklyn : Haskell House Publishers, 1977. 143 p. : port. ; 21 cm. Reprint of the 1923 ed. published by Harrap, London, in the series Poetry & life. Bibliography: p. 8. [PR5431.E4 1977] 76-52970 ISBN 0-8383-2124-0 lib. bdg. : 10.95
1. Shelley, Percy Bysshe, 1792-1822. 2. Poets, English—19th century—Biography. I. Title.

GRABO, Carl Henry, 1881- 821'.7 B
Shelley's eccentricities [by] Carl H. Grabo. [Folcroft, Pa.] Folcroft Library Editions, 1973. p. Reprint of the 1950 ed. published by the University of New Mexico Albuquerque, which was issued as no. 5 of the University of New Mexico publications in language and literature. [PR5431.G66 1973] 73-7623 ISBN 0-8414-2030-0
1. Shelley, Percy Bysshe, 1792-1822. I. Title. II. Series: New Mexico. University. University of New Mexico publications in language and literature, no. 5. BIP

GRAHAM, William. 821'.7'09 B
Last links with Byron, Shelley, and Keats. Folcroft, Pa., Folcroft Press [1969] xx, 121 p. 23 cm. Reprint of the 1898 ed. [PR457.G7 1969] 72-196918
1. Byron, George Gordon Noel Byron, Baron, 1788-1824. 2. Shelley, Percy Bysshe, 1792-1822. 3. Keats, John, 1795-1821. I. Title. BIP

KING-HELE, Desmond, 1927- 821.7
Shelley, the man and the poet. New York, T. Yoseloff [1960] 390 p. 24 cm. [PR5431.K5] 60-13136
1. Shelley, Percy Bysshe, 1792-1822.

MEDWIN, Thomas, 1788-1869. 821'.7
The life of Percy Bysshe Shelley. A new ed. printed from a copy copiously amended and extended by the author and left unpublished at his death. With an introd. and commentary by H. Buxton Forman. [Folcroft, Pa.] Folcroft Library Editions, 1973. Reprint of the 1913 ed. published by Oxford University Press, London, New York. Bibliography: p. [PR5431.M43 1973] 73-11336 ISBN 0-8414-5964-9 (lib. bdg.)
1. Shelley, Percy Bysshe, 1792-1822. I. Title.

PECK, Walter Edwin, 1891-1954. 821'.7 B
Shelley, his life and work. [Folcroft, Pa.] Folcroft Library Editions, 1973 [c1927] p. Reprint of the ed. published by Houghton, Mifflin, Boston. Contents.Contents.—v. 1. 1792-1817.—v. 2. 1817-1822. [PR5431.P45 1973] 73-15726 38.00
1. Shelley, Percy Bysshe, 1798-1822. I. Title.

PECK, Walter Edwin, 1891-1954. 821'.7 B
Shelley, his life and work. New York, B. Franklin [1969] 2 v. illus., ports. 24 cm. (Essays in literature and criticism 26) (Burt Franklin bibliography & references series, 271.) Reprint of the 1927 ed. Contents.Contents.—v. 1. 1792-1817.—v. 2. 1817-1822. Bibliographical footnotes. [PR5431] 69-18610
1. Shelley, Percy Bysshe, 1792-1822. I. Title.

REIMAN, Donald H. 821'.7' B
Percy Bysshe Shelley, by Donald H. Reiman. New York, Twayne Publishers [1969] 188 p. 22 cm. (Twayne's English authors series, 81) Bibliography: p. 173-178. [PR5431.R4] 76-81503
1. Shelley, Percy Bysshe, 1792-1822. I. Title. BIP

ROE, Ivan. 928.2
Shelley, the last phase. New York, Roy Publishers [1955] 256p. illus. 22cm. Includes bibliography. [PR5431] 55-5925
1. Shelley, Percy Byashe, 1792-1822. I. Title.

ROE, Ivan. 821'.7 B
Shelley, the last phase. [Folcroft, Pa.] Folcroft Library Editions, 1973. p. Reprint of the 1953 ed. published by Hutchinson, London. Bibliography: p. [PR5432.R6 1973] 73-11377 7.00
1. Shelley, Percy Bysshe, 1792-1822. BIP

ROE, Ivan. 821'.7 B
Shelley, the last phase. New York, Cooper Square Publishers, 1973. 256 p. illus. 22 cm. Reprint of the 1953 ed. published by Hutchinson, London. Bibliography: p. 247-248. [PR5431.R6 1973] 72-97078 ISBN 0-8154-0464-6 7.50 (Lib. ed.)
1. Shelley, Percy Bysshe, 1792-1822.

ROSSETTI, William Michael, 1829-1919. 821'.7 B
A memoir of Shelley (with a fresh preface)

London, Printed for the Shelley Society by R. Clay, 1886. [New York, AMS Press, 1971] viii, 154 p. port. 19 cm. Includes bibliographical references. [PR5431.R68 1971] 71-144680 ISBN 0-404-05427-7
1. Shelley, Percy Bysshe, 1792-1822. **BIP**

SHARP, William, 1855-1905. 821'.7
Life of Percy Bysshe Shelley. Port Washington, N.Y., Kennikat Press [1972] 201, xxvii p. 21 cm. Reprint of the 1887 ed., issued in the series: Great writers. "Bibliography, by John P. Anderson": p. [i] -xxvii. [PR5431.S5 1972] 73-160781 ISBN 0-8046-1613-2
1. Shelley, Percy Bysshe, 1792-1822. I. Title.

SHELLEY, Percy Bysshe, 1792-1822. 821'.7 B
Letters from Percy Bysshe Shelley to Elizabeth Hitchener. With an introd. and notes. Freeport, N.Y., Books for Libraries Press [1973] p. Reprint of the 1908 ed. [PR5431.A362 1973] 73-2720 ISBN 0-8369-7169-8
1. Shelley, Percy Bysshe, 1792-1822. 2. Hitchener, Elizabeth. I. Hitchener, Elizabeth. II. Title.

SMITH, George Barnett, 1841-1909. 821'.7
Shelley; a critical biography. [Folcroft, Pa.] Folcroft Library Editions, 1974. p. cm. Reprint of the 1877 ed. published by D. Douglas, Edinburgh. [PR5431.S75 1974b] 74-9793 ISBN 0-8414-7768-X (lib. bdg.)
1. Shelley, Percy Bysshe, 1792-1822. **BIP**

SPENDER, Stephen, 1909- v. 12
Shelley. London, New York, Published for the British Council by Longmans, en [1952] 56p. port. 22cm. (Bibliographical series of supplements to British book news, no. 29) Bibliography: p. 47-56. A54
1. Shelley, Percy Bysshe, 1792-1822. I. Title. II. Series.

SYMONDS, John Addington, 1840-1893. 821'.7 B
Shelley. New York, AMS Press [1968] x, 197 p. 22 cm. (English men of letters) Bibliography: p. [ix]-x. [PR5431.S85 1968] 68-58400
1. Shelley, Percy Bysshe, 1792-1822. I. Title.

THOMPSON, Francis, 1859-1907. 821'.7
Shelley. With an introd. by George Wyndham. [Folcroft, Pa.] Folcroft Library Editions, 1973. p. Reprint of the 1909 ed. published by Burns and Oates, London. [PR5438.T5 1973] 73-15597 7.50
1. Shelley, Percy Bysshe, 1792-1822.

WATERLOW, Sydney Philip Perigal, Sir, 1878-1944. 821'.7
Shelley. [Folcroft, Pa.] Folcroft Library Editions, 1973. 94 p. port. 18 cm. Reprint of the 1913 ed. published by T. C. & E. J. Jack, London. Bibliography: p. 90-91. [PR5431.W3 1973] 73-15662 4.50 (Lib. bdg.)
1. Shelley, Percy Bysshe, 1792-1822.

WHITE, Newman Ivey, 1892-1948. 821'.7 B
Shelley. New York, Octagon Books, [1972 i.e. 1973] 2 v. illus. 24 cm. Includes bibliographical references. [PR5431.W5 1972] 72-7385 ISBN 0-374-98426-3 65.00
1. Shelley, Percy Bysshe, 1792-1822. **BIP**

WILLIAMS, Edward Ellerker, 1793-1822. 821'.7'09 B
Journal of Edward Ellerker Williams, companion of Shelley and Byron in 1821. With an introd. by Richard Garnett. [Folcroft, Pa.] Folcroft Library Editions, 1970. 67 p. illus. 23 cm. "Limited to 150 copies." Reprint of the 1902 ed. [CT788.W755A32 1970] 72-192065
1. Shelley, Percy Bysshe, 1782-1822. 2. Byron, George Gordon Noel Byron, Baron, 1788-1824. **BIP**

Shelley, Percy Bysshe,

SHELLEY, Percy Bysshe, 1792-1822. 928.2
Letters. Edited by Frederick L. Jones. Oxford, Clarendon Press, 1964. 2 v. 23 cm. "Shelley's reading": v. 2, p. 467-488. Bibliographical footnotes. Contents.Contents.—v. 1. Shelley in England.—v. 2. Shelley in Italy. [PR5431.A3 1964] 64-1836
I. Jones, Frederick Lafayette, 1901- ed.

Shelley, Percy Bysshe, 1792-1822.—Juvenile literature.

RUSH, Philip 920
The young Shelley. Illus. by Anne Linton New York, Roy [1962, c.1961] 135p. illus. 21cm. (Young biographies ser.) 62-9028 3.00
1. Shelley, Percy Bysshe, 1792-1822.—Juvenile literature. I. Title.

Shelley, Percy Bysshe, 1792-1822—Addresses, essays, lectures.

†PEACOCK, Thomas Love, 1785-1866. 808.1
Peacock's Four ages of poetry ; Shelley's Defence of poetry ; Browning's Essay on Shelley / edited by H. F. B. Brett-Smith. Folcroft, Pa. : Folcroft Library Editions, 1977. xxxiii, 112 p. ; 23 cm. Reprint of the 1921 ed. published by B. Blackwell, Oxford, which was issued as no. 3 of The Percy reprints. Bibliography: p. xxvii-xxxiii. [PN1055.P384 1977] 77-27644 ISBN 0-8414-0697-9 lib. bdg. : 15.00
1. Shelley, Percy Bysshe, 1792-1822—Addresses, essays, lectures. 2. Poetry—Addresses, essays, lectures. 3. Poets, English—19th century—Biography—Addresses, essays, lectures. I. Shelley, Percy Bysshe, 1792-1822. Defence of poetry. 1977. II. Browning, Robert, 1812-1889. An essay on Shelley. 1977. III. Title. IV. Title: Four ages of poetry. V. Series: The Percy reprints ; no. 3.

ROGERS, Neville, comp. 821'.7'09 B
Keats, Shelley & Rome : an illustrated miscellany / compiled by Neville Rogers ; postscript by Earl Wavell. New York : Haskell House Publishers, [1976, i.e.1975] p. cm. Reprint of the 1949 ed. publshed by C. Johnson, London. [PR4836.R53 1976] 75-22076 ISBN 0-8383-2080-5 lib.bdg. : 9.95
1. Keats, John, 1795-1821—Addresses, essays, lectures. 2. Shelley, Percy Bysshe, 1792-1822—Addresses, essays, lectures. 3. Keats Shelley Memorial Association. 4. Literary landmarks—Rome (City) I. Title. Contents omitted.

Shelley, Percy Bysshe, 1792-1822—Biography.

BAILEY, Ruth. 821'.7 B
Shelley. [Folcroft, Pa.] Folcroft Library Editions, 1974. 143 p. 22 cm. Reprint of the 1934 ed. published by Duckworth, London, which was issued as no. 39 of Great lives. Includes bibliographical references. [PR5431.B3 1974] 74-1442 ISBN 0-8414-9910-1 (lib. bdg.)
1. Shelley, Percy Bysshe, 1792-1822—Biography.

FLORESCU, Radu R. N. 823'.7
In search of Frankenstein / Radu Florescu ; with contributions by Alan Barbour & Matei Cazacu. Boston : New York Graphic Society, [1975] p. cm. Filmography: p. [PR5397.F73F6] 74-22502 ISBN 0-8212-0614-1 : 9.95
1. Shelley, Mary Wollstonecraft Godwin, 1797-1851. Frankenstein. 2. Shelley, Mary Wollstonecraft Godwin, 1797-1851—Biography. 3. Shelley, Percy Bysshe, 1792-1822—Biography. 4. Shelley, Mary Wollstonecraft Godwin, 1797-1851—Adaptations. I. Barbour, Alan G., joint author. II. Cazacu, Matei, joint author. III. Title.

HOGG, Thomas Jefferson, 1792-1862. 821'.7 B
The life of Percy Bysshe Shelley. With an introd. by Edward Dowden. London, G. Routledge; New York, E. P. Dutton, 1906. St. Clair Shores, Mich., Scholarly Press, 1970. xx, 585 p. 21 cm. First published in 1858. [PR5431.H6 1970] 76-145089 ISBN 0-403-00754-2
1. Shelley, Percy Bysshe, 1792-1822—Biography.

HOLMES, Richard, 1945- 821'.7 B
Shelley : the pursuit / Richard Holmes. 1st American ed. New York : E. P. Dutton, 1975, c1974. xiii, 829 p., [12] leaves of plates : ill. ; 24 cm. Includes index. Bibliography: p. 736-738. [PR5431.H65 1975] 74-24372 ISBN 0-525-20287-0 : 22.50
1. Shelley, Percy Bysshe, 1792-1822—Biography.

MEDWIN, Thomas, 1788-1869. 821'.7 B
The life of Percy Bysshe Shelley. A new ed. printed from a copy copiously amended and extended by the author and left unpublished at his death. With an introd. and commentary by H. Buxton Forman, London, Humphrey Milford, Oxford University Press, 1913. St. Clair Shores, Mich., Scholarly Press, 1971. xxxii, 542 p. facsim., ports. 22 cm. "An annotated list of books brought out by Thomas Medwin": p. 487-505. [PR5431.M43 1971] 71-145172 ISBN 0-403-01100-0
1. Shelley, Percy Bysshe, 1792-1822—Biography. I. Forman, Harry Buxton, 1842-1917. II. Title.

PEACOCK, Thomas Love, 1785-1866. 821'.7 B
Peacock's memoirs of Shelley : with Shelley's letters to Peacock / edited by H. F. B. Brett-Smith. Folcroft, Pa. : Folcroft Library Editions, 1977. p. cm. Reprint of the 1909 ed. published by H. Frowde, London. [PR5431.P4 1977] 77-8470 ISBN 0-8414-9941-1 (lib. bdg.): 25.00
1. Shelley, Percy Bysshe, 1792-1822—Biography. 2. Shelley, Percy Bysshe, 1792-1822—Correspondence. 3. Peacock, Thomas Love, 1785-1866—Correspondence. 4. Authors, English—19th century—Correspondence. 5. Authors, English—19th century—Biography. I. Shelley, Percy Bysshe, 1792-1822. II. Brett-Smith, Herbert Francis Brett. III. Title.

SHARP, William, 1855-1905. 821'.7 B
Life of Percy Bysshe Shelley. [Folcroft, Pa.] Folcroft Library Editions, 1973. p. cm. Reprint of the 1887 ed. published by W. Scott, London, in series: Great writers. "Bibliography, by John P. Anderson": p. [PR5431.S5 1973] 73-19907 9.50
1. Shelley, Percy Bysshe, 1792-1822—Biography. **BIP**

Shelley, Percy Bysshe, 1792-1822—Biography—Character.

ULLMAN, James Ramsey, 1907-1971. 821'.7 B
Mad Shelley. New York, Gordian Press, 1975 [c1930] 120 p. 24 cm. Reprint of the ed. published by the Princeton University Press, Princeton. [PR5431.U6 1975] 74-18406 ISBN 0-87752-178-6
1. Shelley, Percy Bysshe, 1792-1822—Biography—Character. I. Title. **BIP**

Shelley, Percy Bysshe, 1792-1822—Biography—Descendants.

ROLLESTON, Maud. 821'.7 B
Talks with Lady Shelley / Maud Rolleston. Folcroft, Pa. : Folcroft Library Editions, 1977. 137 p., [1] leaf of plates : port. ; 23 cm. Reprint of the 1925 ed. published by G. G. Harrap, London. [PR5431.R66 1977] 77-8171 ISBN 0-8414-7306-4 lib. bdg. : 20.00
1. Shelley, Percy Bysshe, 1792-1822—Biography—Descendants. 2. Shelley, Jane Gibson, Lady, d. 1899. 3. Wives—England—Biography. I. Shelley, Jane Gibson, Lady, d. 1899. II. Title.

ROLLESTON, Maud. 821'.7 B
Talks with Lady Shelley / Maud Rolleston. Folcroft, Pa. : Folcroft Library Editions, 1977. 137 p., [1] leaf of plates : port. ; 23 cm. Reprint of the 1925 ed. published by G. G. Harrap, London. [PR5431.R66 1977] 77-8171 ISBN 0-8414-7306-4 lib. bdg. : 20.00
1. Shelley, Percy Bysshe, 1792-1822—Biography—Descendants. 2. Shelley, Jane Gibson, Lady, d. 1899. 3. Wives—England—Biography. I. Shelley, Jane Gibson, Lady, d. 1899. II. Title. **BIP**

Shelley, Percy Bysshe, 1792-1822—Biography—Last years.

TRELAWNY, Edward John, 1792-1881. 821'.7'09 B
Recollections of the last days of Shelley and Byron. With introd. by Edward Dowden. Freeport, N.Y., Books for Libraries Press [1971] xxii, 201 p. illus., ports. 23 cm. Reprint of the 1906 ed. [PR5671.T5A7 1971] 72-160998 ISBN 0-8369-5866-7
1. Shelley, Percy Bysshe, 1792-1822—Biography—Last years. 2. Byron, George Gordon Noel Byron, Baron, 1788-1824. I. Title. **BIP**

Shelley, Percy Bysshe, 1792-1822—Biography—Last years and death.

BIAGI, Guido, 1855-1925. 821'.7 B
The last days of Percy Bysshe Shelley : new details from unpublished documents / by Guido Biagi. Folcroft, Pa. : Folcroft Library Editions, 1976. p. cm. Translation of Gli ultimi giorni di Percy Bysshe Shelley. Reprint of the 1898 ed. published by T. F. Unwin, London. [PR5432.B53E5 1976] 76-17878 ISBN 0-8414-3344-5 lib. bdg. : 20.00
1. Shelley, Percy Bysshe, 1792-1822—Biography—Last years and death. I. Title.

Shelley, Percy Bysshe, 1792-1822—Biography—Marriage.

BOAS, Louise Schutz. 821'.7 B
Harriet Shelley : five long years / Louise Schutz Boas. Westport, Conn. : Greenwood Press, 1979, c1962. xi, 237 p. : ill. ; 23 cm. Reprint of the ed. published by Oxford University Press, London, New York. Includes index. Bibliography: p. 227-230. [PR5432.B6 1979] 78-12350 ISBN 0-313-21143-4 lib bdg : 20.00
1. Shelley, Percy Bysshe, 1792-1822—Biography—Marriage. 2. Shelly, Harriet Westbrook, d. 1816. 3. Poets, English—19th century—Biography. 4. Wives—England—Biography.

GODWIN, William, 1756-1836. 821'.7 B
The elopement of Percy Bysshe Shelley and Mary Wollstonecraft Godwin / as narrated by William Godwin ; with commentary by H. Buxton Forman. Folcroft, Pa. : Folcroft Library Editions, 1977. 24 p. ; 26 cm. Reprint of the 1911 ed. which was priv. print. for W. K. Bixby, Boston. [PR5432.G6 1977] 77-1972 ISBN 0-8414-4300-9 lib. bdg. : 8.50
1. Shelley, Percy Bysshe, 1792-1822—Biography—Marriage. 2. Shelley, Mary Wollstonecraft (Godwin) 1797-1851—Biography—Marriage. 3. Authors, English—19th century—Biography. I. Forman, Harry Buxton, 1842-1914. II. Title.

Shelley, Percy Bysshe, 1792-1822—Biography—Youth.

HOGG, Thomas Jefferson, 1792-1862. 821'.7 B
Shelley at Oxford. With an introd. by R. A. Streatfeild. [Folcroft, Pa.] Folcroft Library Editions, 1974. p. cm. Reprint of the 1904 ed. published by Methuen, London. [PR5432.H6 1974] 74-17483 ISBN 0-8414-4881-7 (lib. bdg.)
1. Shelley, Percy Bysshe, 1792-1822—Biography—Youth. I. Title.

MACCARTHY, Denis Florence, 1817-1882. 821'.7 B
Shelley's early life from original sources, with curious incidents, letters, and writings, now first published or collected / by Denis Florence MacCarthy. Folcroft, Pa. : Folcroft Library Editions, 1976. p. cm. Reprint of the 1872 ed. published by J. C. Hotten, London. [PR5432.M2 1976] 76-18865 ISBN 0-8414-6076-0 lib. bdg. : 40.00
1. Shelley, Percy Bysshe, 1792-1822—Biography—Youth. I. Title: Shelley's early life from original sources ... **BIP**

Shelley, Percy Bysshe, 1792-1822—Correspondence.

HITCHENER, Elizabeth. 821.7 B
Letters of Elizabeth Hitchener to Percy Bysshe Shelley. Folcroft, Pa. : Folcroft Library Editions, 1977. p. cm. Reprint of the 1926 ed. printed by the Pynson Printers for C. H. Pforzheimer, New York. [PR5431.A362 1977] 77-23115 ISBN 0-8414-7787-6 lib. bdg. : 10.00

1. Shelley, Percy Bysshe, 1792-1822—Correspondence. 2. Hitchener, Elizabeth. 3. Poets, English—19th century—Correspondence. 4. Teachers—Great Britain—Correspondence. I. Shelley, Percy Bysshe, 1792-1822. **BIP**

PEACOCK, Thomas Love, 1785-1866. 821'.7 B
Peacock's memoirs of Shelley : with Shelley's letters to Peacock / edited by H. F. B. Brett-Smith. Folcroft, Pa. : Folcroft Library Editions, 1977. p. cm. Reprint of the 1909 ed. published by H. Frowde, London. [PR5431.P4 1977] 77-8470 ISBN 0-8414-9941-1 (lib. bdg.): 25.00
1. Shelley, Percy Bysshe, 1792-1822—Biography. 2. Shelley, Percy Bysshe, 1792-1822—Correspondence. 3. Peacock, Thomas Love, 1785-1866—Correspondence. 4. Authors, English—19th century—Correspondence. 5. Authors, English—19th century—Biography. I. Shelley, Percy Bysshe, 1792-1822. II. Brett-Smith, Herbert Francis Brett. III. Title.

SHELLEY, Percy Bysshe, 1792-1822. 928.2
Letters. Edited by Frederick L. Jones. Oxford, Clarendon Press, 1964. 2 v. 23 cm. "Shelley's reading": v. 2, p. 467-488. Bibliographical footnotes. Contents.Contents.—v. 1. Shelley in England.—v. 2. Shelley in Italy. [PR5431.A3 1964] 64-1836
I. Jones, Frederick Lafayette, 1901- ed.

SHELLEY, Percy Bysshe, 1792-1822. 821'.7
Letters from Percy Bysshe Shelley to Jane Clairmont. Folcroft, Pa. : Folcroft Library Editions, 1977. viii, 104 p. ; 22 cm. Reprint of the privately printed, London, 1889 ed. [PR5431.A359 1977] 77-1985 ISBN 0-8414-7682-9 lib. bdg. : 20.00
1. Shelley, Percy Bysshe, 1792-1822—Correspondence. 2. Clairmont, Clara Mary Jane, 1798-1879. 3. Poets, English—19th century—Correspondence. I. Clairmont, Clara Mary Jane, 1798-1879. II. Title. **BIP**

SHELLEY, Percy Bysshe, 1792-1822. 821'.7 B
New Shelley letters / edited by W. S. Scott. Westport, Conn. : Hyperion Press, 1979. 169 p., [3] leaves of plates : ill. ; 22 cm. Reprint of the 1948 ed. published by Bodley Head, London. [PR5431.A354 1979] 78-59041 ISBN 0-88355-713-4 : lib.bdg. : 16.00
1. Shelley, Percy Bysshe, 1792-1822—Correspondence. 2. Hogg, Thomas Jefferson, 1792-1862—Correspondence. 3. Authors, English—19th century—Correspondence. I. Scott, Walter Sidney, 1900- II. Title. **BIP**

SHELLEY, Percy Bysshe, 1792-1822. 821'.7 B
Shelley at Oxford : the early correspondence of P. B. Shelley with his friend T. J. Hogg, together with letters of Mary Shelley and T. L. Peacock and a hitherto unpublished prose fragment by Shelley / edited by Walter Sidney Scott. Folcroft, Pa. : Folcroft Library Editions, 1974. 79 p. : ports. ; 27 cm. Reprint of the 1944 ed. published by the Golden Cockerel Press, London. Includes bibliographical references. [PR5431.A363 1974] 74-32409 ISBN 0-8414-7836-8 lib. bdg. : 15.00
1. Shelley, Percy Bysshe, 1792-1822—Correspondence. 2. Hogg, Thomas Jefferson, 1792-1862. 3. Authors, English—Correspondence, reminiscences, etc. I. Hogg, Thomas Jefferson, 1792-1862. II. Shelley, Mary Wollstonecraft Godwin, 1797-1851. III. Peacock, Thomas Love, 1785-1866. IV. Scott, Walter Sidney, 1900- ed. V. Title.

SHELLEY, Percy Bysshe, 1792-1822. 821'.7 B
Shelley's lost letters to Harriet. Edited with an introd. by Leslie Hotson. [Folcroft, Pa.] Folcroft Library Editions, 1974. 89 p. 23 cm. Reprint of the 1930 ed. published by Faber & Faber, London. [PR5431.A366 1974b] 74-16312 ISBN 0-8414-4858-2 (lib. bdg.)
1. Shelley, Percy Bysshe, 1792-1822—Correspondence. 2. Shelley, Harriet Westbrook, d. 1816. I. Shelley, Harriet Westbrook, d. 1816. II. Title.

SHELLEY, Percy Bysshe, 1792-1822. 821'.7 B
Shelley's lost letters to Harriet. Edited with an introd. by Leslie Hotson. New York, Haskell House [1974] p. cm. Reprint of the 1930 ed. published by Faber & Faber, London. [PR5431.A366 1974] 74-7113 ISBN 0-8383-1925-4 9.95
1. Shelley, Percy Bysshe, 1792-1822—Correspondence. 2. Shelley, Harriet Westbrook, d. 1816. I. Shelley, Harriet Westbrook, d. 1816. II. Title. **BIP**

Shelley, Percy Bysshe, 1792-1822—Criticism and interpretation.

TODHUNTER, John, 1839-1916. 821'.7
A study of Shelley. Folcroft, Pa., Folcroft Press [1969] vi, 293 p. 24 cm. Reprint of the 1880 ed. [PR5438.T6 1969] 72-191240
1. Shelley, Percy Bysshe, 1792-1822—Criticism and interpretation. I. Title.

Shelley, Percy Bysshe, 1792-1822—Friends and associates.

ANGELI, Helen (Rossetti) 821'.7 B
Shelley and his friends in Italy. With sixteen illus. by Maxwell Armfield. New York, Haskell House, 1973. xiii, 326 p. illus. 23 cm. Reprint of the 1911 ed. [PR5432.A5 1973] 72-3197 ISBN 0-8383-1539-9 15.95 (Lib. bdg.)
1. Shelley, Percy Bysshe, 1792-1822—Friends and associates. I. Title. **BIP**

CLARKE, Isabel Constance. 821'.7'09 B
Shelley and Byron, a tragic friendship, by Isabel C. Clarke. New York, Haskell House, 1971. 324 p. illus., ports. 24 cm. Reprint of the 1934 ed. Bibliography: p. 313. [PR5433.C55 1971] 74-118006 ISBN 0-8383-1062-1
1. Shelley, Percy Bysshe, 1792-1822—Friends and associates. 2. Byron, George Gordon Noel Byron, Baron, 1788-1824—Friends and associates. I. Title.

Shelley, Percy Bysshe, 1792-1822—Political and social views.

CAMERON, Kenneth Neill. 821'.7 B
The young Shelley; genesis of a radical. New York, Octagon Books, 1973 [c1950] xii, 437 p. 23 cm. Reprint of the ed. published by Macmillan, New York. Includes bibliographical references. [PR5432.C3 1973] 73-8660 ISBN 0-374-91255-6 15.00 (lib. bdg.)
1. Shelley, Percy Bysshe, 1792-1822—Political and social views. I. Title.

Shelley, Percy Bysshe, 1792-1822—Relationship with women.

GRIBBLE, Francis Henry, 1862-1946. 821'.7 B
The romantic life of Shelley and the sequel. New York, Haskell House Publishers, 1972. 387 p. port. 23 cm. Reprint of the 1911 ed. [PR5432.G7 1972] 72-3624 ISBN 0-8383-1566-6
1. Shelley, Percy Bysshe, 1792-1822—Relationship with women. 2. Shelley, Mary Wollstonecraft (Godwin) 1797-1851. I. Title. **BIP**

Shelnick, Thomas.

SHELNICK, Thomas. 627.720924
Above and below, by Tom Shelnick, with Ray Cristina. [1st ed.] Garden City, N. Y., Doubleday, 1965. 192 p. illus., ports. 22 cm. Autobiographical. [VM980.S5A3] 65-22574
I. Cristina, Raymond J. II. Title.

Shelton, Elwood, 1926-1975.

SHELTON, Barbara. 248'.86'0924
Woody / Barbara Shelton, with Bob Terrell. Chappaqua, N.Y. : Christian Herald Books, 1979. p. cm. [RC406.A24S53] 79-50949 ISBN 0-915684-52-7 pbk. : 4.95
1. Shelton, Elwood, 1926-1975. 2. Amyotrophic lateral sclerosis—Biography. 3. Christian life—1960- I. Terrell, Bob, joint author. II. Title. **BIP**

Shen, Fu,

SHEN, Fu, 1763-ca.1808 759.951
Chapters from a floating life; the autobiography of a Chinese artist. Translated from the Chinese by Shirley M. Black. Poems by Tu Fu and Li Po, translated by S. M. B. London, New York, Oxford University Press, 1960[ ] 108p. 8 ptes. 60-4904 3.75
I. Title.

Shenstone, William, 1714-1763.

HAZELTINE, Alice Isabel, 1862-1922. 821'.5
A study of William Shenstone and of his critics : with fifteen of his unpublished poems and five of his unpublished Latin inscriptions / Alice I. Hazeltine. Norwood, Pa. : Norwood Editions, 1976 [c1918] 94 p. ; 26 cm. Reprint of the ed. published by G. Banta Pub. Co., Menasha, Wis. Originally presented as the author's thesis (M.A.), Wellesley, 1913. Bibliography:p. [90]-94. [PR3677.H3 1976] 76-13618 ISBN 0-8482-1031-X lib. bdg. : 7.50
1. Shenstone, William, 1714-1763. I. Title.

HUMPHREYS, Arthur Raleigh. 821'.5 B
William Shenstone : an eighteenth-century portrait / by A. R. Humphreys. New York : AMS Press, 1976. 135 p. : port. ; 19 cm. Reprint of the 1937 ed. published by the University Press, Cambridge, Eng. Includes index. [PR3677.H8 1976] 75-41146 ISBN 0-404-14673-2 : 8.50
1. Shenstone, William, 1714-1763. **BIP**

Shenstone, William, 1714-1763—Correspondence.

SHENSTONE, William, 1714-1763. 821'.5 B
The letters of William Shenstone / arranged and edited with introd., notes, and index by Marjorie Williams. 1st AMS ed. New York : AMS Press, 1979. xxvii, 700 p. : ill. ; 23 cm. Reprint of the 1939 ed. published by B. Blackwell, Oxford. Includes index. [PR3677.A83 1979] 75-41250 ISBN 0-404-14601-5 : 34.00
1. Shenstone, William, 1714-1763—Correspondence. 2. Poets, English—18th century—Correspondence. I. Williams, Marjorie. II. Title. **BIP**

Shepard, Alan Barlett, 1923- —Juvenile literature.

SMAUS, Jewel (Spangler) 920
America's first spaceman [by] Jewel Spangler Smaus, Charles B. Spangler. Garden City, N.Y., Doubleday [1961, c.1962] 159p. illus. 62-7569 2.50
1. Shepard, Alan Barlett, 1923- —Juvenile literature. 2. Project Mercury—Juvenile literature. I. Spangler, Charles B., joint author. II. Title.

Shepard, Alan Bartlett, 1923-

WESTMAN, Paul. 629.4'092'4 B
Alan Shepard, first American in space / by Paul Westman. Minneapolis : Dillon Press, c1979. p. cm. (Taking part ; 2) Traces the life of the first American in space from his New England boyhood to his walk on the moon. [TL789.85.S5W47] 92 79-19866 ISBN 0-87518-184-8 : 6.95
1. Shepard, Alan Bartlett, 1923- 2. Astronauts—United States—Biography—Juvenile literature. I. Title. **BIP**

Shepard, Ernest Howard,

SHEPARD, Ernest Howard, 1879- 927.41
Drawn from life. New York, Dutton [1962, c1961] 217 p. illus. 22 cm. Autobiography. [NC242.S47A28 1962] 63-1603
I. Title.

SHEPARD, Ernest Howard, 1879-. 927.41
Drawn from memory. Philadelphia, Lippincott [1957] 190 p. illus. 22 cm. Autobiographical. [NC242.S47A3] 57-13370
I. Title.

Shepard, Helen Miller Gould, 1868-1938.

SETON, Celeste Andrews. 923.673
Helen Gould was my mother-in-law, by Celeste Andrews Seton, as told to Clark Andrews. New York, Crowell [1953] 277 p. illus. 21 cm. [CT275.S472S4] 53-8438
1. Shepard, Helen Miller Gould, 1868-1938. I. Andrews, Clark. II. Title.

Shepard, Martin, 1934-

SHEPARD, Martin, 1934- 616.8'9'00924
Memoirs of a defrocked psychoanalyst = originally published under the title A psychiatrist's head / by Martin Shepard. Sagaponack, N.Y. : Permanent Press, c1978. x, 269 p. ; 23 cm. [RC339.52.S48A33 1978] 78-58461 ISBN 0-932966-00-4 : 9.95
1. Shepard, Martin, 1934- 2. Psychoanalysts—United States—Biography. I. Title. II. Title: A psychiatrist's head.
Publisher's address: P.O. Box 43, Sagaponack, NJ 01962

Shepard, Thomas,

SHEPARD, Thomas, 1605-1649. 285'.9'0924 B
God's plot; the paradoxes of Puritan piety; being The autobiography & journal of Thomas Shepard. Edited with an introd. by Michael McGiffert. [Amherst] University of Massachusetts Press, 1972. vii, 252 p. 24 cm. (The Commonwealth series [v. 1]) Bibliography: p. [239]-241. [BX7260.S53A32] 71-181364 ISBN 0 87023-100-6 12.00
I. Shepard, Thomas, 1605-1649. The autobiography. 1972. II. Shepard, Thomas, 1605-1649. The journal. 1972. III. Title. IV. Series: The Commonwealth series (Amherst, Mass.) v. 1.

Shepherd, David, 1931-

SHEPHERD, David, 1931- 759.2 B
The man who loves giants : an artist among elephants and engines : David Shepherd's autobiography. New York : Scribner, c1975. 164 p. : ill. (some col.) ; 24 cm. [ND497.S46A25 1975b] 75-21663 ISBN 0-684-14509-X : 12.50
1. Shepherd, David, 1931- 2. Painters—Great Britain—Correspondence, reminiscences, etc. I. Title.

Shepherd, Holley M

SHEPHERD, Holley M 012
A bio-bibliography of John Thomas McNeill. Cambridge, Mass., Anover-Harvard Theological Library, 1960. 46 p. port. 23 cm. [Z8537.23.S45] 62-4482
I. McNeill, John Thomas, 1885 Bio-bibl. II. Title.

Shepherd, Mont.—Biography.

"LEST we forget ..." : 978.6'39
Shepherd, Montana / compiled by the Shepherd Historical Book Committee, Luella DeVries ... [et al.]. ; edited by R. H. Scherger ; cover design by Phil Bett ; artwork by Ben Gillet. 1st ed. [s.l.] : Frontier Press, c1976. 286 p. (p. 278-286 blank for "Notes") : ill. ; 28 cm. Includes index. [F739.S46L47] 76-368558
1. Shepherd, Mont.—Biography. 2. Shepherd, Mont.—History. I. DeVries, Luella. II. Scherger, R. H. III. Shepherd Historical Book Committee.

Sheppard, Jack, 1702-1724.

HIBBERT, Christopher, 1924- 923.4142
The road to Tyburn; the story of Jack Sheppard and the eighteenth century underworld. London, New York, Longmans, Green [1957] 163p. illus. 23cm. [HV6248.S56H5 1957] 57-3066
1. Sheppard(Jack, 1702-1724. I. Title.

HIBBERT, Christopher, 1924- 923.4142
The road to Tyburn; the story of Jack Sheppard and the eighteenth-century

London underworld. [1st American ed.] Cleveland, World Pub. Co. [1957] 251 p. illus. 22 cm. [HV6248.S56H5 1957a] 57-10935
1. Sheppard, Jack, 1702-1724. I. Title.

Sheppard, Moses.

FORBUSH, Bliss, 1896- 361'.02'0924 B
Moses Sheppard: Quaker philanthropist of Baltimore. With a foreword by Kenneth O. Walker. Philadelphia, Lippincott [1968] 317 p. illus., facsim., port. 22 cm. Bibliographical references included in "Notes" (p. 262-303) [HV28.S48F6] 68-28870
1. Sheppard, Moses.

Sheppard, Samuel H

SHEPPARD, Samuel H 340.0924
Endure and conquer [by] Sam Sheppard. [1st ed.] Cleveland, World Pub. Co. [1966] x, 329 p. 24 cm. Autobiographical. [343.522] 66-29489
I. Title.

Sheraton Corporation of America.

HENDERSON, Ernest 926.4794
The world of 'Mr. Sheraton.' New York, David McKay Co. [c.1960] 277p. 21cm. 60-7116 4.50
1. Sheraton Corporation of America. I. Title.

HENDERSON, Ernest, 1897- 926.4794
The world of 'Mr. Sheraton.' New York, D. McKay Co. [1960] 277p. 21cm. Autobiographical. [TX910.5.H4A3] 60-7116
1. Sheraton Corporation of America. I. Title.

Sherbondy, James Bryan, 1919-1969.

†WILLIAMSON, John Harvey, 1937- 365'.6'0924 B
The gray walls of hell : the legend of Jim Sherbondy, a true story / John H. Williamson. Pueblo, Colo. : Nationwide Press, c1976. 372 p., [4] leaves of plates : ill. ; 18 cm. [HV9468.S47W54] 76-11567 ISBN 0-917188-03-9 : 2.45
1. Sherbondy, James Bryan, 1919-1969. 2. Prisoners—Colorado—Biography. 3. Crime and criminals—Colorado—Biography. I. Title.

Sherbrooke, Robert Lowe, Viscount, 1811-1892.

WINTER, James, 1925- 941.081'092'4 B
Robert Lowe / James Winter. Toronto ; Buffalo : University of Toronto Press, c1976. xiv, 368 p., [4] leaves of plates : ill. ; 25 cm. Includes index. Bibliography: p. [349]-358. [DA565.S5W56] 75-43814 ISBN 0-8020-5323-8 : 17.50
1. Sherbrooke, Robert Lowe, Viscount, 1811-1892. 2. Great Britain—Politics and government—1837-1901. **BIP**

Sheridan, Clare Consuelo Frewen, 1885-1970—Biography.

LESLIE, Anita. 730'.92'4 B
Clare Sheridan / Anita Leslie. 1st ed. Garden City, N.Y. : Doubleday, 1977. xv, 318 p., [8] leaves of plates : ill. ; 22 cm. Includes index. [PR6037.H465Z7 1977] 76-23773 ISBN 0-385-06745-3 : 10.00
1. Sheridan, Clare Consuelo Frewen, 1885-1970—Biography. 2. Authors, English—20th century—Biography. 3. Artists—Great Britain—Biography. **BIP**

Sheridan, Philip Henry, 1831-1888.

FROST, Lawrence A. 973.73'0924 B
The Phil Sheridan album; a pictorial biography of Phillip Henry Sheridan, by Lawrence A. Frost. [1st ed.] Seattle, Superior Pub. Co. [1968] 173 p. illus., facsims., ports. 28 cm. Bibliography: p. 166-168. [E467.1.S54F7] 68-26749 12.95
1. Sheridan, Philip Henry, 1831-1888. I. Title.

O'CONNOR, Richard, 1915- 923.573
Sheridan, the inevitable. Maps by Wilson R. Springer. [1st ed.] Indianapolis, Bobbs-Merrill [1953] 400 p. illus., ports., maps. 23 cm. "Notes on sources": p. 361-391. [E467.1.S54O3] 53-5847
1. Sheridan, Philip Henry, 1831-1888.

RISTER, Carl Coke, 1889-1955. 973.8'092'4 B
Border command; General Phil Sheridan in the West. Westport, Conn., Greenwood Press [1974, c1944] xii, 244 p. illus. 22 cm. Reprint of the ed. published by University of Oklahoma Press, Norman. Bibliography: p. 226-235. [E467.1.S54R5 1974] 73-16950 ISBN 0-8371-7244-6
1. Sheridan, Philip Henry, 1831-1888. 2. The West—History—1848-1950. 3. Indians of North America—Wars, 1866-1895. I. Title.

Sheridan, Philip Henry, 1831-1888—Juvenile literature.

LOMASK, Milton. 923.573
General Phil Sheridan and the Union Cavalry. Illustrated by Jo Polseno. New York, P. J. Kenedy [1959] 178p. illus. 22cm. (American background books) [E467.1.S54L6] 59-12923
1. Sheridan, Philip Henry, 1831-1888—Juvenile literature. I. Title.

[REEDER, Russell Potter] 920
Sheridan, the general who wasn't afriad to take a chance, by Red Reeder. New York, Duell [dist. Meredith, c.1962] 238p. illus. 21cm. 62-8510 3.95
1. Sheridan, Philip Henry, 1831-1888—Juvenile literature. I. Title.

REEDER, Russell Potter. 92
Sheridan, the general who wasn't afraid to take a chance, by Red Reeder. [1st ed.] New York, Duell, Sloan and Pearce [1962] 238p. illus. 21cm. Includes bibliography. [E467.1.S54R4] 62-8510
1. Sheridan, Philip Henry, 1831-1888—Juvenile literature. I. Title.

Sheridan, Philip Henry, 1831-1888 — Juvenile literature.

ORBAAN, Albert. 92
Forked lightning, the story of General Philip H. Sheridan, written and illustrated by Albert Orbaan. New York, Hawthorn Books [1964] 189 p. illus. (part col.) 22 cm. (Credo books) [E467.1.S5407] 64-11241
1. Sheridan, Philip Henry, 1831-1888 — Juvenile literature. I. Title.

Sheridan, Richard Brinsley Butler, 1751-1816.

BINGHAM, Madeleine, Baroness Clanmorris. 822'.6 B
Sheridan: the track of a comet. New York, St. Martin's Press [1972] 383 p. illus. 22 cm. Bibliography: p. 372-374. [PR3683.B5 1972] 72-78178 12.50
1. Sheridan, Richard Brinsley Butler, 1751-1816. I. Title.

COVE, Joseph Walter, 1891- 822'.6 B
Sheridan [by] Lewis Gibbs. Port Washington, N.Y., Kennikat Press [1970] vii, 280 p. illus., ports. 22 cm. Reprint of the 1947 ed. Bibliography: p. 273-274. [PR3683.C6 1970] 75-103189
1. Sheridan, Richard Brinsley Butler, 1751-1816.

DURANT, Jack Davis, 1930- 822'.6 B
Richard Brinsley Sheridan / by Jack D. Durant. Boston : Twayne Publishers, [1975] 166 p. : port. ; 22 cm. (Twayne's English authors series ; TEAS 183) Includes index. Bibliography: p. 157-160. [PR3683.D87] 75-1094 ISBN 0-8057-6650-2 lib.bdg. : 7.95
1. Sheridan, Richard Brinsley Butler, 1751-1816. **BIP**

FOSS, Kenelm. 822'.6 B
Here lies Richard Brinsley Sheridan. [Folcroft, Pa.] Folcroft Library Editions, 1973. 390 p. ports. 26 cm. Reprint of the 1940 ed. Bibliography: p. [380] [PR3683.F6 1973] 72-13661 20.00 (lib. bdg.).
1. Sheridan, Richard Brinsley Butler, 1751-1816. I. Title.

FOSS, Kenelm. 822'.6 B
Here lies Richard Brinsley Sheridan. Freeport, N.Y., Books for Libraries Press [1973] p. Reprint of the 1940 ed. published by Dutton, New York. Bibliography: [PR3683.F6 1973b] 73-6602 ISBN 0-518-19044-7
1. Sheridan, Richard Brinsley Butler, 1751-1816. I. Title. **BIP**

LEFANU, Elizabeth (Sheridan) 1758-1837 920.7
Betsy Sheridan's journal; letters from Sheridan's sister, 1784-1786, and 1788-1790. Edited by William LeFanu. New Brunswick., N. J., Rutgers University Press 223p. illus. 60-51922 4.50
1. Sheridan, Richard Brinsley Butler, 1751-1816. I. LeFanu, William Richard, 1904- ed. II. Title.

MEMOIRS of the life of the Rt. Hon. Richard Brinsley Sheridan. New York, Redfield, 1958. 2v. port. 20cm. v. 12
1. Sheridan, Richard Brinsley Butler, 1751-1816. I. Moore, Thomas, 1779-1852. **BIP**

MOORE, Thomas, 1779-1852. 822'.6 B
Memoirs of the life of the Rt. Hon. Richard Brinsley Sheridan. New York, Greenwood Press [1968] 2 v. port. 23 cm. Reprint of the 1858 ed. On spine: Life of Sheridan. Bibliographical footnotes. [PR3683.M6 1968] 69-14001
1. Sheridan, Richard Brinsley Butler, 1751-1816. I. Title. II. Title: Life of Sheridan.

OLIPHANT, Margaret Oliphant (Wilson) 1828-1897. 822'.6 B
Sheridan. New York, AMS Press [1968] vi, 210 p. 22 cm. (English men of letters) [PR3683.O5 1968] 68-58392
1. Sheridan, Richard Brinsley Butler, 1731-1816.

OLIVER, Robert Tarbell, 1909- 942.07'3'0922
Four who spoke out: Burke, Fox, Sheridan, Pitt, by Robert T. Oliver. Freeport, N.Y., Books for Libraries Press [1969, c1946] x, 196 p. 23 cm. (Biography index reprint series) Bibliography: p. 184-196. [DA522.A1O55 1969] 75-101831
1. Burke, Edmund, 1729?-1797. 2. Fox, Charles James, 1749-1806. 3. Sheridan, Richard Brinsley Butler, 1751-1816. 4. Pitt, William, 1759-1806. 5. Orators, English. I. Title.

SANDERS, Lloyd Charles, 1857- 822'.6 B
Life of Richard Brinsley Sheridan. [Folcroft, Pa.] Folcroft Library Editions, 1974. p. cm. Reprint of the 1890 ed. published by W. Scott, London, in series: Great writers. Bibliography: p. [PR3683.S3 1974] 74-16492 17.50
1. Sheridan, Richard Brinsley Butler, 1751-1816. **BIP**

SHERWIN, Oscar, 1902- 928.2
Uncorking old sherry; the life and times of Richard Brinsley Sheridan. New York, Twayne Publishers [1960] 352 p. illus. 24 cm. Includes bibliography. [PR3683.S63] 60-12916
1. Sheridan, Richard Brinsley Butler, 1751-1816. I. Title.

Sheridan, Richard Brinsley Butler, 1751-1816—Biography.

DARLINGTON, William Aubrey, 1890- 822'.6 B
Sheridan, by W. A. Darlington. New York, Haskell House, 1974. 144 p. 22 cm. Reprint of the 1933 ed. published by Duckworth, London, which was issued as no. 15 of Great lives. Bibliography: p. 144. [PR3683.D3 1974] 74-7188 ISBN 0-8383-1926-2
1. Sheridan, Richard Brinsley Butler, 1751-1816—Biography.

DARLINGTON, William Aubrey, 1890- 822'.6 B
Sheridan, by W. A. Darlington. [Folcroft, Pa.] Folcroft Library Editions, 1974. p. cm. Reprint of the 1933 ed. published by Macmillan, New York, which was issued as Great lives, 15. Bibliography: p. [PR3683.D3 1974b] 74-12265 ISBN 0-8414-3775-0 (lib. bdg.)
1. Sheridan, Richard Brinsley Butler, 1751-1816—Biography. **BIP**

MOORE, Thomas, 1779-1852. 822'.6 B
Memoirs of the life of the Right Honourable Richard Brinsley Sheridan. 5th ed. London, Printed for Longman, Rees, Orme, Brown, and Green, 1826. Grosse Pointe, Mich., Scholarly Press, 1968. 2 v. port. 23 cm. Title on spine: The life of Sheridan. Bibliographical footnotes. [PR3683.M6 1968b] 77-5489
1. Sheridan, Richard Brinsley Butler, 1751-1816—Biography. I. Title. II. Title: The life of Sheridan. **BIP**

MOORE, Thomas, 1779-1852. 822'.6 B
Memoirs of the life of the Rt. Hon. Richard Brinsley Sheridan. Freeport, N.Y., Books for Libraries Press [1971] 2 v. port. 23 cm. Reprint of the 1858 ed. [PR3683.M6 1971] 79-152997 ISBN 0-8369-5749-0
1. Sheridan, Richard Brinsley Butler, 1751-1816—Biography. I. Title.

Sheridan, Richard Brinsley Butler, 1751-1816—Biography—Political career.

SADLEIR, Michael, 1888-1952. 822'.6 B
The political career of Richard Brinsley Sheridan; (the Stanhope essay for 1912). Followed by some hitherto unpublished letters of Mrs. Sheridan. [Folcroft, Pa.] Folcroft Library Editions, 1974. p. cm. Reprint of the 1912 ed. published by H. Blackwell, Oxford. [PR3683.S25 1974] 74-18272 12.50
1. Sheridan, Richard Brinsley Butler, 1751-1816—Biography—Political career. I. Sheridan, Elizabeth Ann Linley, 1754-1792. II. Title. III. Series: Stanhope essay, 1912.

Sherman, Allan,

SHERMAN, Allan, 1924-1973. 791.45023 B
A gift of laughter; the autobiography of Allan Sherman. [1st ed.] New York, Atheneum Publishers, 1965. x, 335 p. 22 cm. [PN1992.4.S5Z5] 65-15918
I. Title.

Sherman, Diane Finn.

SHERMAN, Diane Finn. 973.921'0924 B
The boy from Abilene; the story of Dwight D. Eisenhower, by Diane Sherman. Philadelphia, Westminster Press [1968] 159 p. illus., ports. 22 cm. Bibliography: p. 153. A biography of the World War II general who later became thirty-fourth President of the United States. [E836.S5] 92 AC 68
I. Title.

Sherman, John, 1823-1900.

BURTON, Theodore Elijah, 1851-1929. 973.8'0924 B
John Sherman. Boston, Houghton, Mifflin. [New York, AMS Press, 1972] vi, 449 p. illus. 19 cm. (American statesmen, v. 33) Reprint of the 1906 ed. [E664.S57B9 1972] 76-128948 ISBN 0-404-50883-9
1. Sherman, John, 1823-1900. I. Title. II. Series. **BIP**

SHERMAN, John, 1823-1900. 973.8'0924 B
Recollections of forty years in the House, Senate, and Cabinet; an autobiography. New York, Greenwood Press, 1968 [c1895] 2 v. (xviii, 1239 p.) illus. 24 cm. [E664.S57A3 1968] 68-28647
1. U.S.—Politics and government—19th century. I. Title.

Sherman, Oger, 1839-1897.

DESTLER, Chester McArthur, 1904- 338.272820924 (B)
Roger Sherman and the independent oil men. Ithaca, N.Y., Cornell University

Press [1967] ix, 305 p. map. 23 cm. Bibliography: p. 283-287. [HD9570.S46D4] 67-13466
1. Sherman, Oger, 1839-1897. 2. Standard Oil Company. 3. Petroleum industry and trade — U.S. I. Title. BIP

Sherman, Roger, 1721-1793.

BOARDMAN, Roger 973.3'0924 B
Sherman.
Roger Sherman, signer and statesman. New York, Da Capo Press, 1971 [c1938] vii, 396 p. 23 cm. (The Era of the American Revolution) Bibliography: p. 361-373. [E302.6.S5B6 1971] 75-168671 ISBN 0-306-70412-9
1. Sherman, Roger, 1721-1793.

Sherman, Sidney, 1805-1873.

BATE, Walter 976.4'05'0924 B
Nathaniel, 1893-
General Sidney Sherman, Texas soldier, statesman, and builder / by W. N. Bate. 1st ed. Waco : Texian Press, 1974. xii, 304 p. : ill. ; 24 cm. Includes index. Bibliography: p. 294-297. [F391.B288] 74-76248 10.00
1. Sherman, Sidney, 1805-1873. I. Title.

Sherman, Steve, 1938-

SHERMAN, Steve, 1938- 917.4
Appalachian odyssey : walking the trail from Georgia to Maine / by Steve Sherman and Julia Older ; with a foreword by Edward Abbey. Brattleboro, Vt. : S. Greene Press, c1977. xvi, 248 p. : ill. ; 22 cm. Includes index. Bibliography: p. 240-241. [GV199.42.A68S53] 76-50269 ISBN 0-8289-0294-1 : 10.50. ISBN 0-8289-0295-X pbk. : 6.95
1. Sherman, Steve, 1938- 2. Appalachian Trail. 3. Appalachian Mountains—Description and travel. 4. Backpacking—Appalachian Mountains. I. Older, Julia, 1941- joint author. II. Title. BIP

Sherman, Stuart Pratt, 1881-1926.

ZEITLIN, Jacob, 1883-1937. 809 B
Life and letters of Stuart P. Sherman, by Jacob Zeitlin and Homer Woodbridge. Freeport, N.Y., Books for Libraries Press [1971] 2 v. (xiv, 880 p.) illus., ports. 23 cm. Bibliography: v. 2, p. 801-860. [PS3537.H775Z9 1971] 74-150207 ISBN 0-8369-5720-2
1. Sherman, Stuart Pratt, 1881-1926. I. Woodbridge, Homer Edwards, 1882- joint author. II. Sherman, Stuart Pratt, 1881-1926. Correspondence. 1971. III. Title. BIP

Sherman, Thomas Ewing, 1856-1933.

DURKIN, Joseph Thomas, 922.273
1903-
General Sherman's son. New York, Farrar, Straus and Cudahy [1959] 276 p. illus. 22 cm. [BX4705.S6143D8] 59-6064
1. Sherman, Thomas Ewing, 1856-1933. I. Title.

Sherman, William Tecumseh, 1820-1891.

ATHEARN, Robert G. 923.573
William Tecumseh Sherman and the settlement of the West. [1st ed.] Norman, University of Oklahoma Press [1956] xix, 371 p. illus., ports., maps. 25 cm. Bibliography: p. 351-361. [E467.1.S55A8] 56-11229
1. Sherman, William Tecumseh, 1820-1891. 2. The West—History—1848-1950. I. Title.

CLARKE, Dwight 332.1'0924
Lancelot, 1885-
William Tecumseh Sherman: gold rush banker, by Dwight L. Clarke. San Francisco, California Historical Society, 1969. xviii, 446 p. illus., map (on lining papers), ports. 24 cm. (California Historical Society. Special publication no. 45) Includes extensive quotations from the letters of W. T. Sherman to H. S. Turner. Bibliography: p. 425-428. [HG2613.S5C46] 70-92033 9.95
1. Sherman, William Tecumseh, 1820-1891. 2. Banks and banking—San Francisco—History. 3. California—Gold discoveries. I. Sherman, William Tecumseh, 1820-1891. II. Turner, Henry Smith, 1811-1881.

GRAVES, Charles 355.3'3'31'0924 B
Parlin, 1911-
William Tecumseh Sherman; champion of the Union, by Charles P. Graves. Illustrated by Pers Crowell. Champaign, Ill., Garrard Pub. Co. [1968] 112 p. illus., maps, ports. 24 cm. A biography of "Uncle Billy" Sherman whose conquering of Atlanta and Savannah broke the back of the Confederacy and heralded an end to the war. [E467.1.S55Gr7] 92 AC 68
1. Sherman, William Tecumseh, 1820-1891. I. Crowell, Pers, illus. II. Title.

LIDDELL HART, Basil Henry 923.573
Sherman: soldier, realist, American. New York, Praeger [1960, c.1958] viii, 456p. (Bibl.: p. 432-441) port. front., maps 21cm. (Praeger paperback PPS 18) 1.95 pap.,
1. Sherman, William Tecumseh, 1820-1891. 2. U. S.—Hist.— Civil War—Campaigns and battles. I. Title.

LIDDELL HART, Basil 923.573
Henry, 1895-
Sherman: soldier, realist, American. New York, Praeger [1958] 456p. illus. 25cm. (Books that matter) Includes bibliography. [E467.1.S55L713 1958] 58-3318
1. Sherman, William Tecumseh, 1820-1891. 2. U. S.—Hist.— Civil War—Campaigns and battles. I. Title.

MERRILL, James M. 355.3'31'0924 B
William Tecumseh Sherman, by James M. Merrill. Chicago, Rand McNally [1971] 445 p. illus., ports. 24 cm. Bibliography: p. 413-431. [E467.1.S55M4] 78-153112 10.00
1. Sherman, William Tecumseh, 1820-1891.

SHERMAN, William 923.573
Tecumseh, 1820-1891.
Memoirs of General William T. Sherman by himself. Foreword by B. H. Liddell Hart. Bloomington, Indiana University Press [1957] 405, 409 p. 21 cm. (Civil War centennial series) [E467.1.S55S52 1957] 57-10722
1. U.S. — Hist. — Civil War. I. Title.

SHERMAN, William 355.3'31'0924 B
Tecumseh, 1820-1891.
Memoirs of General William T. Sherman, by himself. Foreword by B. H. Liddell Hart. Westport, Conn., Greenwood Press [1972, c1957] 2 v in 1 22 cm. Original ed. issued in series: Civil War centennial series. [E467.1.S55S52 1972] 70-170607 ISBN 0-8371-6253-X 26.00
1. United States—History—Civil War. I. Series: Civil War centennial series.

SHERMAN, William 923.573
Tecumseh, 1820-1891.
Memoirs of General William T. Sherman by himself. Foreword by B. H. Liddell Hart. Bloomington, Indiana University Press [1957] 409p. 21cm. (Civil War centennial series) [E467.1.S55S52 1957] 57-10722
1. U. S.—Hist.—Civil War. I. Title. II. Series.

SHERMAN, William 973.7'0922
Tecumseh, 1820-1891.
The Sherman letters; correspondence between General Sherman and Senator Sherman from 1837 to 1891. Edited by Rachel Sherman Thorndike. New York, Da Capo Press, 1969. xiv, viii, 398 p. ports. 22 cm. (A Da Capo Press reprint series. The American scene; comments and commentators) Reprint of the 1894 ed. with a new foreword by John Y. Simon. [E415.7.S55 1969] 68-8693 15.00
1. United States—History—1849-1877—Sources. 2. United States—History—Civil War, 1861-1865—Sources. I. Sherman, John, 1823-1900. II. Thorndike, Rachel (Sherman) ed. III. Title.

WHEELER, Richard. 973.7
Sherman's march / Richard Wheeler. 1st ed. New York : Crowell, c1978. p. cm. Includes index. Bibliography: p. [E476.69.W47 1978] 78-3321 ISBN 0-690-01746-4 : 8.95
1. Sherman, William Tecumseh, 1820-1891. 2. Sherman's March to the Sea. 3. Sherman's March through the Carolinas. 4. Generals—United States—Biography. I. Title. BIP

WHEELER, Richard. 973.7'41 B
We knew William Tecumseh Sherman / Richard Wheeler. New York : Crowell, c1977. xiii, 130 p. : ill. ; 24 cm. Includes index. Bibliography: p. 123-125. [E467.1.S55W48 1977] 77-4334 ISBN 0-690-01535-6 : 7.95
1. Sherman, William Tecumseh, 1820-1891. 2. United States. Army—Biography. 3. United States—History—Civil War, 1861-1865—Campaigns and battles. 4. Generals—United States—Biography. I. Title. BIP

WILLIAMS, Thomas Harry, 923.573
1909-
McClellan, Sherman, and Grant. New Brunswick, N.J., Rutgers [c.1962] 113p. illus. 20cm. (Brown and Haley lectures, 1962) Bibl. 62-21246 3.50 bds.,
1. McClellan, George Brinton 1826-1885. 2. Sherman, William Tecumseh, 1820-1891. 3. Grant, Ulysses Simpson, Pres. U. S., 1822-1885. I. Title. BIP

WILLIAMS, Thomas 355.3'31'0922 B
Harry, 1909-
McClellan, Sherman, and Grant / T. Harry Williams. Westport, Conn. : Greenwood Press, 1976 [c1962] p. cm. Reprint of the ed. published by Rutgers University Press, New Brunswick, N.J., in series: The Brown & Haley lectures, 1962. Bibliography: p. [E467.W5 1976] 76-29654 ISBN 0-8371-9280-3 lib.bdg. : 10.75
1. McClellan, George Brinton, 1826-1885. 2. Sherman, William Tecumseh, 1820-1891. 3. Grant, Ulysses Simpson, Pres. U.S., 1822-1885. 4. Generals—United States—Biography. I. Title. II. Series: The Brown & Haley lectures ; 1962.

Sherman, William Tecumseh, 1820-1891—Juvenile literature.

BLASSINGAME, Wyatt. 973.7'0924 B
William Tecumseh Sherman, defender of the Union. Illustrated by Ron Lesser. Englewood Cliffs, N.J., Prentice-Hall [1970] 143 p. illus. 22 cm. (Hall of Fame books) "A Rutledge book." Bibliography: p. 143. A biography of General Sherman, commander of the Union troops, examining the controversial personality that still puzzles many historians and Civil War buffs. [E467.1.S55B55] 92 69-10332 4.50
1. Sherman, William Tecumseh, 1820-1891—Juvenile literature. I. Lesser, Ron, illus. II. Title. III. Series.

GRAVES, Charles Parlin, 92 (J)
1911-
William Tecumseh Sherman; champion of the Union by Charles P. Graves Illustrated by Pers Crowell. Champaign, Ill., Garrard Pub. Co. [1968] 112 p. illus., maps, ports. 24 cm. [E467.1.S55G7] 68-11350
1. Sherman, William Tecumseh, 1820-1891—Juvenile literature.

Sherman, 1961 or 2- —Juvenile literature.

SHERMAN, 301.45'19'51073024 B
1961or2-
Sherman; a Chinese-American child tells his story, by Joe Molnar. New York, F. Watts, 1973. [48] p. (chiefly illus.) 26 cm. "Based on tape recordings of conversations with Sherman." A ten-year-old Chinese-American boy living on Long Island describes his family life, his school, and his hobbies. [F127.L8S46] 72-13576 ISBN 0-531-02613-2 Library ed. 4.50.
1. Sherman, 1961 or 2- —Juvenile literature. I. Molnar, Joe. II. Title. III. Title: A Chinese-American child tells his story.

Shero, Fred.

RAPPEPORT, Rhoda. 796.9'62'0924 B
Fred Shero : a kaleidoscopic view of the Philadelphia Flyers' coach / by Rhoda Rappeport. New York : St. Martin's Press, [1977] p. cm. [GV942.7.S48R36] 77-76649 ISBN 0-312-30362-9 : 7.95
1. Shero, Fred. 2. Philadelphia Flyers (Hockey club) 3. Hockey coaches—United States—Biography. BIP

Sherrill, Henry Knox,

SHERRILL, Henry Knox, 922.373
Bp., 1890-
Among friends. [Autobiography. 1st ed.] Boston, Little, Brown [1962] 340 p. illus. 22 cm. [BX5995.S345A3] 62-17949
I. Title.

Sherrington, Charles Scott, Sir, 1857-1952.

BROWN, John Mason, 812'.5'2 B
1900-1969.
The worlds of Robert E. Sherwood : mirror to his times, 1869-1939 / John Mason Brown. Westport, Conn. : Greenwood Press, [1979] c1965. p. cm. Reprint of the 1st ed. published by Harper & Row, New York. Includes index. "Works of Robert E. Sherwood": p. [PS3537.H825Z63 1979] 78-27835 ISBN 0-313-20937-5 lib. bdg. : 27.50
1. Sherwood, Robert Emmett, 1896-1955—Biography. 2. Dramatists, American—20th century—Biography. I. Title.

GRANIT, Ragnar, 612.8'00924 B
1900-
Charles Scott Sherrington; an appraisal. [1st ed.] Garden City, N.Y., Doubleday, 1967. xii, 188 p. illus., ports. 22 cm. (British men of science) "Notes and references": p. [179]-182. [QP26.S48G7 1967] 67-10486
1. Sherrington, Charles Scott, Sir, 1857-1952. I. Title.

Sherwood, Mary Martha Butt, 1775-1851.

CUTT, Margaret Nancy. 823'.8 B
Mrs. Sherwood and her books for children : a study / by M. Nancy Cutt. London : Oxford University Press, 1974. xi, 157, [71] p. : ill., facsims., port. ; 20 cm. (The Juvenile library) Includes reprints of The little woodman and his dog Caesar originally published: London, Houlston, 1850 and Soffrona and her cat Muff originally published: Wellington, Salop, Houlston, 1828. Includes indexes. Bibliography: p. 115-150. [PR5449.S4Z63] 74-190129 ISBN 0-19-278010-7 : £2.30
1. Sherwood, Mary Martha Butt, 1775-1851. I. Sherwood, Mary Martha Butt, 1775-1851. The little woodman and his dog Caesar. 1974. II. Sherwood, Mary Martha Butt, 1775-1851. Soffrona and her cat Muff. 1974. III. Title.

Sherwood, Robert Emmett, 1896-1955.

BROWN, John Mason, 1900- 812.52
1969.
The worlds of Robert E. Sherwood; mirror to his times, 1896-1939. [1st ed.] New York, Harper & Row [1965] xviii, 409 p. illus., ports. 22 cm. Sequel: The ordeal of a playwright. "Works of Robert E. Sherwood": p. 387-390. [PS3537.H825Z63] 65-20424
1. Sherwood, Robert Emmett, 1896-1955. I. Title.

Sherwood, Robert Emmett, 1896-1955—Biography.

BROWN, John Mason, 812'.5'2 B
1900-1969.
The worlds of Robert E. Sherwood : mirror to his times, 1869-1939 / John Mason Brown. Westport, Conn. : Greenwood Press, [1979] c1965. p. cm. Reprint of the 1st ed. published by Harper & Row, New York. Includes index. "Works of Robert E. Sherwood": p. [PS3537.H825Z63 1979] 78-27835 ISBN 0-313-20937-5 lib. bdg. : 27.50
1. Sherwood, Robert Emmett, 1896-1955—Biography. 2. Dramatists, American—20th century—Biography. I. Title.

Sherwood, Ruth,

SHERWOOD, Ruth, 1890- 927.3
Carving his own destiny; the story of Albin Polasek. Chicago, R. F. Seymour [1954]

466p. illus. 25cm. [NB237.P6S45] 55-18870
I. Polasek, Albin, 1879- II. Title.

Sherwood, Samuel, 1779-1862.

CROCKER, J. DeReu, comp. 973.5'1'0924
Letters and journals of Samuel and Laura Sherwood, 1813-1823. Edited by J. D. Crocker. Delhi, N.Y., 1967. 23 p. illus. 23 cm. [F123.S452C76] 75-303714
1. Sherwood, Samuel, 1779-1862. 2. Sherwood, Laura. I. Sherwood, Samuel, 1779-1862. II. Sherwood, Laura. III. Title.

Shev, Edward E.

SHEV, Edward E. 362.8
Good cops, bad cops : memoirs of a police psychiatrist / Edward E. Shev and Jeremy Joan Hewes. San Francisco : San Francisco Book Co., 1977. p. cm. Includes index. Bibliography: p. [HV7936.P75S483] 77-10 ISBN 0-913374-69-5 : 8.95
1. Shev, Edward E. 2. Police psychiatrists—United States—Biography. I. Hewes, Jeremy Joan, joint author. II. Title. BIP

Shick, Maete (Gordon)

SHICK, Maete (Gordon) 1885- 920.7
The burden and the trophy, an autobiography. Translated from the Yiddish by Mary J. Reuben. [1st ed.] New York, Pageant Press [1957] 209p. 21cm. [CT275.S4858A32] 57-9939
I. Title.

Shields, Brooke, 1965-

SHIELDS, Brooke, 1965- 659.1'52 B
The Brooke book / by Brooke Shields. New York : Pocket Books, c1978. ca. 150 p. : ill. ; 27 cm. "A Wallaby book." [HD6073.M77S53] 78-103748 ISBN 0-671-79018-8 pbk. : 3.95
1. Shields, Brooke, 1965- 2. Models, Fashion—Biography—Pictorial works. I. Title. BIP

Shields, Frederic James,

SHIELDS, Frederic James, 1833-1911. 759.2
The life and letters of Frederic Shields. Edited by Ernestine Mills. London, New York, Longmans, Green, 1912. [New York, AMS Press, 1972] xiv, 368 p. illus. 23 cm. [N6797.S5A3 1972] 76-148281 ISBN 0-404-04344-5
I. Mills, Ernestine (Bell) ed. II. Title. BIP

Shiff, Dorothy.

POTTER, Jeffrey. 070.5'092'4
Men, money & magic : the story of Dorothy Schiff / by Jeffrey Potter. New York : New American Library, 1977,c1976. 337[8]p. : ill. ; 18 cm. (A Signet Book) Includes index. [PN4874.S33P6] ISBN 0-451-07691-5 pbk. : 2.25
1. Shiff, Dorothy. 2. Journalists-United States-Biography. I. Title.
L.C. card no. for 1976 Coward McCann & Geoghegan ed.:74-30608.

Shingarev, Andrei Ivanovich, 1869-1918.

SHINGAREV, Andrei Ivanovich, 1869-1918. 947.084'1'0924
The Shingarev diary : how it was : the Peter and Paul Fortress, 27-XI-17-5-1-18 / A. I. Shingarev ; translated by Felicity Ashbee and Irina Tidmarsh. Royal Oak, MI : Strathcona Pub. Co., 1978. 120 p. ; 20 cm. Translation of Kak eto bylo. [DK254.S487A3413] 79-111447 11.50
1. Shingarev, Andrei Ivanovich, 1869-1918. 2. Russia—History—Revolution, 1917-1921—Personal narratives. 3. Political prisoners—Russia—Biography. I. Title: How it was.
Pub. address : Box 350, Royal Oak MI 48068

Shinn, Everett, 1876-1953.

DESHAZO, Edith. 759.13 B
Everett Shinn, 1876-1953, a figure in his time / by Edith DeShazo ; research assistant, Richard Shaw. 1st ed. New York : C. N. Potter : distributed by Crown Publishers, [1974] xvii, 236 p., [8] leaves of plates: ill. (some col.) ; 29 cm. Includes index. Bibliography: p. 227-230. [N6537.S53D47 1974] 74-77561 ISBN 0-517-51490-7 : 15.00
1. Shinn, Everett, 1876-1953.

Shinn, George.

SHINN, George. 650'.1
Good morning, Lord! / George Shinn. New York : Hawthorn Books, c1977. vii, 130 p. ; 22 cm. [HF5500.3.U54S53 1977] 76-5716 ISBN 0-8015-5769-0 : 6.95
1. Shinn, George. 2. Executives—United States—Biography. 3. Success. 4. Christian life—1960- I. Title. BIP

Shinran, 1173-1263.

KIKUMURA, Norihiko. 294.3'63 B
Shinran: his life and thought. Los Angeles, Nembutsu Press [1972] 192 p. 23 cm. Translation of Shinran. [BQ8749.S557K513] 70-172538 4.95
1. Shinran, 1173-1263.

Shipherd, Henry Robinson.

SHIPHERD, Henry Robinson. 920.4
A story of a bookman, a biographical essay. [1st ed.] New York, Exposition Press [1955] 96p. illus. 21cm. [Z743.S45] 55-12134
I. Title.

Shipley, Maynard, 1872-1964.

DE FORD, Miriam Allen, 1888- 920
Up-hill all the way; the life of Maynard Shipley. Yellow Springs, Ohio, Antioch Press [1956] 255p. illus. 24cm. [CT275.S48814D4] 56-6505
1. Shipley, Maynard, 1872-1964. I. Title.

Shipmasters—Juvenile literature.

SCOTT, Marcia. 910'.45'0922 B
Daring sea captains. Minneapolis, Lerner Publications Co. [1973] 79 p. illus. 22 cm. (A Pull ahead book) Biographical sketches of nine famous seamen: William Bligh, Horatio Nelson, Joshua Slocum, Ernest Shackleton, John F. Kennedy, Thor Heyerdahl, Jacques-Yves Cousteau, William R. Anderson, and Robin Lee Graham. [G175.S38] 920 72-3592 ISBN 0-8225-0465-0 3.95
1. Shipmasters—Juvenile literature. 2. Seamen—Juvenile literature. I. Title. BIP

Shipp, Ellis (Reymonds)

SHIPP, Ellis (Reymonds) 1847-1939. 926.1
The early autobiography and diary of Ellis Reynolds Shipp, M. D. Compiled and edited by her daughter Ellis Shipp Musser. With a foreword by Ellis Shipp Musser. [Salt Lake City] c1962. 202 p. illus. 19 cm. [R154.S158A3] 62-6768
I. Title.

Shipp, Nelson McLester, 1892-

SHIPP, Nelson McLester, 1892- 070.4'092'4 B
A vagabond newsman, by Nelson Shipp. Atlanta, Cherokee Pub. Co., 1974. 230 p. illus. 24 cm. Autobiography. [PN4874.S477A3] 74-79230 ISBN 0-87797-029-7 5.95
1. Shipp, Nelson McLester, 1892- I. Title. BIP

Shippen family.

LIVINGSTON, Anne Home (Shippen) 1763-1841. 917.48'11'0330924
Nancy Shippen, her journal book; the international romance of a young lady of fashion of colonial Philadelphia with letters to her and about her. Compiled and edited by Ethel Armes. New York, B. Blom, 1968. 348 p. illus., facsims., ports. 24 cm. Reprint of the 1935 ed. Bibliography: p. 317-[321] [E302.6.L67L6 1968] 68-21204
1. Shippen family. 2. Livingston family. I. Armes, Ethel Marie, ed. II. Title.

Shipstad, Eddie, 1907- —Juvenile literature.

LEIPOLD, L. Edmond, 1902- 796.9'1'0924 B
Eddie Shipstad, Ice Follies star, by L. E. Leipold. Minneapolis, Denison [1971] 162 p. illus., ports. 22 cm. (Men of achievement series) A biography of one of the founders, stars, and producers of the well-known Ice Follies. [GV850.S48L4] 92 74-118160 ISBN 0-513-01101-3
1. Shipstad, Eddie, 1907- —Juvenile literature. I. Title.

Shipton, Eric Earle,

SHIPTON, Eric Earle, 1907- 796.5'22'0924 B
That untravelled world: an autobiography, by Eric Shipton. Line illus. by Biro. New York, Scribner [1970, c1969] 286 p. illus., maps, ports. 22 cm. [G512.S45A3 1969b] 76-108129 6.95
I. Title.

Shiras, George, 1832-1924.

SHIRAS, George, 1839-1942. 923.473
Justice George Shiras, Jr., of Pittsburgh, Associate Justice of the United States Supreme Court, 1892-1903; a chronicle of his family, life, and times, by George Shiras, 3rd. Edited and completed, 1953, by Winfield Shiras. [Pittsburgh] University of Pittsburgh Press [1953] xx, 256p. illus., ports. 24cm. 53-5386
1. Shiras, George, 1832-1924. I. Shiras, Winfield. II. Title.

Shirer, William Lawrence, 1904-

SHIRER, William Lawrence, 1904- 940.54'81'73
Berlin diary : the journal of a foreign correspondent 1934-1941 / William L. Shirer. Harmondsworth, Eng. ; New York : Penguin Books, 1979, c1941. viii, 627 p. ; 20 cm. Reprint of the 1st ed. published in 1941 by Knopf, New York. Includes index. [D811.5.S5 1979] 79-11580 ISBN 0-14-005182-1 pbk. : 4.95
1. Shirer, William Lawrence, 1904- 2. World War, 1939-1945—Personal narratives, American. 3. World War, 1939-1945—Germany. 4. Europe—Politics and government—1918-1945. 5. Germany—Politics and government—1933-1945. 6. Journalists—United States—Biography. I. Title. BIP

Shirer, William Lawrence, 1904- —Biography.

SHIRER, William Lawrence, 1904- 070'.92'4 B
20th century journey : a memoir of a life and the times / by William L. Shirer. New York : Simon and Schuster, c1976- v. : ill. ; 24 cm. Includes index. Contents.Contents.—[1] The start, 1904-1930. [PS3537.H913Z52] 75-41417 ISBN 0-671-22195-7(v.1) : 11.95
1. Shirer, William Lawrence, 1904- —Biography. I. Title.

Shirley, James, 1596-1666.

NASON, Arthur Huntington, 1877-1944. 822'.4 B
James Shirley, dramatist; a biographical and critical study. New York, B. Blom [1967] 471 p. facsims., ports. 20 cm. Reprint of the 1915 ed. Bibliography: p. 401-459. [PR3146.N3 1967] 67-23860
1. Shirley, James, 1596-1666. BIP

Shirley, William, 1694-1771.

SCHUTZ, John A. 923.242
William Shirley, King's Governor of Massachusetts. Chapel Hill, Pub. for the Inst. of Early Amer. Hist. and Culture at Williamsburg, Va., by the Univ. of N. C. Pr. [c.1961] 292p. illus. Bibl. 61-66445 6.00
1. Shirley, William, 1694-1771. I. Title. BIP

SCHUTZ, John A 923.242
William Shirley, King's Governor of Massachusetts. Chapel Hill, Published for the Institute of Early American History and Culture at Williamsburg, Va., by the University of North Carolina Press [1961] 292p. illus. 24cm. Includes bibliography. [E195.S553] 61-66145
1. Shirley, William, 1694—1771. I. Title.

Shirreff, Emily Anne Eliza, 1814-1897.

ELLSWORTH, Edward W. 301.41'2'0922 B
Liberators of the female mind : the Shirreff sisters, educational reform, and the women's movement / Edward W. Ellsworth. Westport, Conn. : Greenwood Press, 1979. xii, 345 p. ; 22 cm. (Contributions in women's studies ; no. 7) ISSN 0147-104X) Includes index. Bibliography: p. 321-329. [HQ1595.A3E44] 78-67910 ISBN 0-313-20644-9 lib. bdg. : 25.00
1. Shirreff, Emily Anne Eliza, 1814-1897. 2. Grey, Maria Georgina Shirreff. 3. Social reformers—Great Britain—Biography. 4. Education of women—Great Britain—History. 5. Feminism—Great Britain—History. I. Title. II. Series. BIP

Shivaji, Raja, 1627-1680.

VERMA, Virendra. 954.02'5'0924
Shivaji, a captain of war with a mission / by Virendra Verma. Poona : Youth Education Publications : distributors, Youth Book Agencies, 1976. iii, 93, [1] p., [3] leaves of plates : maps ; 22 cm. Bibliography: p. [94] [DS461.9.S5V44] 76-905100 Rs14.00 ($2.00 U.S.)
1. Shivaji, Raja, 1627-1680. 2. India—Kings and rulers—Biography. 3. India—History, Military. I. Title.

Shivers, Allan, 1907-

KINCH, Sam. 976.4'06'0924 B
Allan Shivers: the Pied Piper of Texas politics [by] Sam Kinch and Stuart Long. Austin, Tex., Shoal Creek Publishers [1974, c1973] xiv, 247 p. illus. 23 cm. [F391.S562K56 1974] 73-86925 ISBN 0-88319-017-6 6.95
1. Shivers, Allan, 1907- 2. Texas—Politics and government—1865-1950. 3. Texas—Politics and government—1951- I. Long, Stuart, joint author. BIP

Shivers, Clarence L., 1924-

HISTORICAL perspective of a great American : an Austin and Cloutier Associates reader / [illustrated by Clarence L. Shivers]. 1st print. ed. Suitland, Md. : Austin and Cloutier Associates, 1974. viii, 52 p. : group port. ; 23 cm. [E185.96.H57] 74-17791 973'.0992 B
1. Shivers, Clarence L., 1924- Historical perspective of a great American (Painting). 2. Negroes—Biography. I. Shivers, Clarence L., 1924. II. Austin and Cloutier Associates.

Shlissel'burgskaia tiur'ma.

FIGNER, Vera Nikolaevna, 1852-1942. 335.8'3'0924 B
Memoirs of a revolutionist. New York, Greenwood Press, 1968 [c1927] 318 p. illus., ports. 24 cm. Translation of Zapechatlennyi trud (romanized form) [HX914.F5 1968] 68-30820
1. Shlissel'burgskaia tiur'ma. 2. Socialism in Russia. I. Title. BIP

Shoemaker, Samuel Moor, 1893-1963.

HARRIS, Irving D. 283'.092'4 B
The breeze of the spirit : Sam Shoemaker and the story of Faith at work / Irving Harris. New York : Seabury Press, 1978. p. cm. "A Crossroad book."

[BX5995.S347H37] 78-18237 ISBN 0-8164-0399-6 : 8.95
1. Shoemaker, Samuel Moor, 1893-1963. 2. Protestant Episcopal Church in the U.S.A.—Clergy—Biography. 3. Clergy—United States—Biography. 4. Faith at work. I. Title. BIP

SHOEMAKER, Helen (Smith) 283'.0924 B
I stand by the door; the life of Sam Shoemaker [by] Helen Smith Shoemaker. [1st ed.] New York, Harper & Row [1967] xviii, 220, [2] p. 22 cm. "Books written by Dr. Samuel Moor Shoemaker": p. [222] [BX5995.S347S5] 66-20784
1. Shoemaker, Samuel Moor, 1893-1963. I. Title.

Shoemakers—Biography.

WINKS, William Edward, 1842- 685'.31'00922
Lives of illustrious shoemakers. Freeport, N.Y., Books for Libraries Press [1973] p. (Essays index reprint series) Reprint of the 1883 ed. [CT9730.S5W6 1973] 72-13185 ISBN 0-8369-8181-2
1. Shoemakers—Biography. I. Title.

Shoghi, effendi.

BACH, Marcus, 1906- 922.97
Shoghi Effendi; an appreciation. New York, Hawthorn Books [1958] unpaged. 24cm. [BP395.S5B2] 58-10095
1. Shoghi, effendi. I. Title.

Sholes, Christopher Latham, 1819-1890.

FOULKE, Arthur Toye 926.5
Mr. Typewriter; a biography of Christopher Latham Sholes. Boston, Christopher Pub. House [c.1961] 134p. illus. 61-9665 3.75
1. Sholes, Christopher Latham, 1819-1890. 2. Typewriter—Hist. I. Title.

Shooting.

WHELEN, Townsend, 1877-1961. 799.3 B
Mister Rifleman, by Townsend Whelen and Bradford Angier. Los Angeles, Petersen Pub. Co. [1965] 377 p. illus., ports. 29 cm. "The preponderance of this autobiography was written by Colonel Townsend Whelen before his death in 1961. Later portions were written ... by Bradford Angier ... The colonel's early published works appearing in this book are reproduced just as they were originally printed." [GV1157.W5A3] 65-16552
1. Shooting. 2. Rifles. I. Angier, Bradford. II. Title.

Shooting—Biography.

BAIRD, John D., 1928- 799.2
Who's who in buckskins. Edited by John D. Baird. 1st ed. Big Timber, Mont., Buckskin Press [1973] iv, 182 p. illus. 29 cm. [GV1157.A1B34] 73-166284 ISBN 0-912420-09-X 10.00
1. Shooting—Biography. 2. Muzzle-loading firearms—Societies, etc.—Directories. I. Title. II. Title: Buckskins.

Shope, Bob, 1903-

WHERE there's life, v. 12
there's Bob Hope; the hilarious life story of America's favorite funny man. [Los Angeles, Petersen pub. co., 1957] 96p. illus., ports. 28cm. Cover title.
1. Shope, Bob, 1903- I. Guild, Leo, 1911-

Shor, Bernard.

CONSIDINE, Robert Bernard, 1906- 647'.95'0924 B
Toots, by Bob Considine. [1st ed.] New York, Meredith Press [1969] ix, 214 p. illus., ports. 24 cm. [TX910.5.S55C6] 73-91865 ISBN 6-9683921-0- 6.95
1. Shor, Bernard. I. Title.

Shore, Dinah.

CASSIDAY, Bruce. 784'.092'4 B
Dinah! : A biography / by Bruce Cassiday. New York : F. Watts, 1979. p. cm. [ML420.S538C34] 79-17002 ISBN 0-531-09915-6 : 7.95
1. Shore, Dinah. 2. Singers—United States—Biography. I. Title. BIP

Shores, Louis, 1904-

SHORES, Louis, 1904- 020'.92'4 B
Quiet world : a librarian's crusade for destiny : the professional autobiography of Louis Shores. Hamden, Conn. : Linnet Books, 1975. 309 p. ; 24 cm. Includes index. [Z720.S53A35] 75-2220 ISBN 0-208-01477-2 : 15.00
1. Shores, Louis, 1904- I. Title.

Shoriki, Matsutaro, 1885-

UHLAN, Edward. 923.252
Shoriki: miracle man of Japan; a biography, by Edward Uhlan and Dana L. Thomas. Foreword by Bob Considine. [1st ed.] New York, Exposition Press [1957] 202p. illus. 21cm. (A Banner book) [DS885.5.S45U34] 57-9226
1. Shoriki, Matsutaro, 1885- I. Thomas, Dana Lee, 1918- joint author. II. Title.

Shorrosh, Anis.

HEFLEY, James C. 248'.246'094 B
The liberated Palestinian : the Anis Shorrosh story / James and Marti Hefley. Wheaton, Ill. : Victor Books, c1975. 172 p. : ill. ; 21 cm. [BV3785.S46H43] 75-36003 ISBN 0-88207-652-3 pbk. : 2.95
1. Shorrosh, Anis. I. Hefley, Marti, joint author. II. Title.

Short, Arthur Rendle.

THE Faith of a 617'.092'4 B
surgeon : belief and experience in the life of Arthur Rendle Short / edited by W. M. Capper and D. Johnson. Exeter : Paternoster Press, 1976. iv, 156 p. ; 22 cm. Bibliography: p. 154-156. [R489.S46F34] 77-362938 ISBN 0-85364-198-6 : £1.80
1. Short, Arthur Rendle. 2. Surgeons—England—Biography. 3. Plymouth Brethren Biography. I. Short, Arthur Rendle. II. Capper, W. Melville. III. Johnson, Douglas.

Short, Luke L., 1854-1893.

COX, William Robert, 1901- 923.973
Luke Short and his era. Garden City, N. Y., Doubleday [c. 1948, 1961] 214p. Bibl. 61-7641 3.50
1. Short, Luke L., 1854-1893. 2. Gambling—The West. 3. Frontier and pioneer life—The West. I. Title.

Shoshoni Indians.

WILSON, Elijah Nicholas, 1842-1915. 970.3
Among the Shoshones. Medford, Or., Pine Cone Publishers [1971] 222 p. port. 22 cm. Autobiographical. "Facsimile reprint of the ... first edition ... originally printed in 1910 and consisting of a mere 20 copies." Facsim. of original t.p. not included. [E99.S4W7 1971] 79-162829 9.00
1. Shoshoni Indians. 2. Frontier and pioneer life—The West. I. Title.

Shostakovich, Dmitrii Dmitrievich, 1906-1975.

MARTYNOV, Ivan Ivanovich. 780'.924 B
Dmitri Shostakovich, the man and his work [by] Ivan Martynov. Translated from the Russian by T. Guralsky. New York, Greenwood Press [1969, c1947] 197 p. port. 23 cm. "Works of Dmitri Shostakovich": p. 189-193. [ML410.S53M32 1969] 75-88903 ISBN 8-371-21000-
1. Shostakovich, Dmitrii Dmitrievich, 1906- BIP

SEROFF, Victor Ilyitch, 1902- 785'.0924 B
Dmitri Shostakovich; the life and background of a Soviet composer, by Victor Ilyich Seroff, in collaboration with Nadejda Galli-Shohat. Freeport, N.Y., Books for Libraries Press [1970, c1943] x, 260, vii p. illus., ports. 23 cm. [ML410.S53S4 1970] 73-126255
1. Shostakovich, Dmitrii Dmitrievich, 1906- I. Shohat, Nadejda (Kokaoulin) Galli, joint author. BIP

SHOSTAKOVICH, Dmitrii Dmitrievich, 1906-1975. 785'.092'4 B
Testimony : the memoirs of Dmitri Shostakovich / transcribed and edited by Solomon Volkov ; translated from the Russian by Antonina W. Bouis. New York : Harper & Row, 1979. p. cm. Includes index. [ML410.S53A3] 79-2236 ISBN 0-06-014476-9 : 15.00
1. Shostakovich, Dmitrii Dmitrievich, 1906-1975. 2. Composers—Russia—Biography. I. Volkov, Solomon. II. Title.

Shrewsbury, Elizabeth Hardwick Talbot, Countess of, 1520-1608.

DURANT, David N. 942.05'5'0924 B
Bess of Hardwick : portrait of an Elizabethan dynast / David N. Durant. 1st American ed. New York : Atheneum Publishers, 1978, c1977. xiii, 274 p., [4] leaves of plates : ill. ; 23 cm. Includes index. Bibliography: p. [253]-255. [DA358.S4D87 1978] 77-24459 ISBN 0-689-10835-4 : 10.95
1. Shrewsbury, Elizabeth Hardwick Talbot, Countess of, 1520-1608. 2. Great Britain—Nobility—Biography. 3. Great Britain—History—Elizabeth, 1558-1603. I. Title.

Shriman Narayan, 1912-

SHRIMAN Narayan, 1912- 320.9'54'7505
Those ten months: President's rule in Gujarat. Delhi, Vikas Pub. House [1973] vi, 204 p. illus. 23 cm. [DS485.G8S485] 73-900700
1. Shriman Narayan, 1912- 2. Gujarat—Politics and government. I. Title.
Distributed by Verry; 9.00

Shriver, Robert Sargent.

LISTON, Robert A 923.273
Sargent Shriver; a candid portrait, by Robert A. Liston. New York, Farrar, Straus [1964] 209 p. illus., ports. 21 cm. [E748.S47L5] 64-19741
1. Shriver, Robert Sargent. I. Title.

Shropshire, Courtney William, 1877-

LEONHART, James Chancellor, 1897- 366.8
The fabulous octogenarian: Courtney W. Shropshire, M.D., founder and first president of Civitan International. Baltimore, Redwood House [1962] 394 p. illus. 26 cm. [HS2705.C53L4] 61-11506
1. Shropshire, Courtney William, 1877- 2. Civitan International. I. Title.

Shtein, Leonid Zakharovich, 1934-1973.

KEENE, Raymond D. 794.1'59
Leonid Stein : master of attack / [by] Raymond D. Keene. London : Hale, 1976. 159 p. : ill., port. ; 23 cm. Includes index. [GV1439.S49K43 1976] 77-354199 ISBN 0-7091-5547-6 : £3.95
1. Shtein, Leonid Zakharovich, 1934-1973. 2. Chess players—Biography.

Shu, Ch'ing-ch'un, 1898-1966.

VOHRA, Ranbir. 895.1'3'5 B
Lao She and the Chinese Revolution. Cambridge, Mass., East Asian Research Center, Harvard University; distributed by Harvard University Press, 1974. 199 p. 26 cm. (Harvard East Asian monographs, 55) Bibliography: p. 187-192. [PL2804.C5Z94] 73-82346 ISBN 0-674-51075-5 4.50 (pbk.)
1. Shu, Ch'ing-ch'un, 1898-1966. I. Title. II. Series. BIP

Shubert, Lee, 1873?-1953.

STAGG, Jerry, 1916- 792'.0922 B
The brothers Shubert. New York, Random House [1968] xii, 431 p. illus., ports. 25 cm. [PN2266.S8] 68-28528 10.00
1. Shubert, Lee, 1873?-1953. 2. Shubert, Sam S., 1875-1905. 3. Shubert, Jacob J., 1878?-1963. 4. Theater—United States—History. I. Title.

Shubert, Sam S., 1875-1905.

STAGG, Jerry, 1916- 792'.0922 B
The brothers Shubert. New York, Random House [1968] xii, 431 p. illus., ports. 25 cm. [PN2266.S8] 68-28528 10.00
1. Shubert, Lee, 1873?-1953. 2. Shubert, Sam S., 1875-1905. 3. Shubert, Jacob J., 1878?-1963. 4. Theater—United States—History. I. Title.

Shula, Don, 1930-—Juvenile literature.

SMITH, Jay H. 796.33'2'0924 B
Don Shula, by Jay H. Smith. Illustrated by Harold Henriksen. Mankato, Minn., Creative Education [1974] p. cm. A biography of the man who at age thirty-three became the youngest head coach in the NFL and later led the Miami Dolphins to two consecutive Super Bowl victories. [GV939.S46S58] 74-16346 ISBN 0-87191-383-6 4.95 (lib. bdg.).
1. Shula, Don, 1930-—Juvenile literature. 2. Football—Juvenile literature. 3. Football coaching—Juvenile literature. I. Henriksen, Harold, illus. II. Title.

Shultz, Gladys Denny

SHULTZ, Gladys Denny 927.84
Jenny Lind: the Swedish nightingale. Philadelphia, Lippincott [c.1962] 345p. 22cm. 62-10537 6.50 bds.,
I. Title.

Shultze, David,

SHULTZE, David, 1717-1797. 925.269
Journals and papers, translated and edited by Andrew S. Berky. ,531st ed.] Pennsburg, Pa., Schwenkfelder Library, 1952-53. 2v. maps., facsims. 25cm. Contents.v. 1. 1726-1760.--v. 2. 1761-1797. [BX9749.S47] 52-14356
I. Title.

Shumway, Nina Paul.

SHUMWAY, Nina Paul. 979.4'97 B
Your desert and mine / Nina Paul Shumway ; with an introd. by Harold O. Weight. Palm Springs, Calif : ETC Publications, 1979. p. cm. [F868.R6S48 1979] 78-32023 15.00
1. Shumway, Nina Paul. 2. Paul family. 3. Coachella Valley, Calif. — Biography. 4. Coachella Valley, Calif. — History. 5. Date — California — Coachella Valley. I. Title. BIP

Sibelius, Jean, 1865-1957.

EKMAN, Karl, 1895- 780'.92'4 B
Jean Sibelius, his life and personality. Translated from the Finnish by Edward Birse, with a foreword by Ernest Newman. Westport, Conn., Greenwood Press [1972, c1938] xxiii, 298, x p. illus. 22 cm. "List of Jean Sibelius's works": p. 269-296.

[ML410.S54E43 1972] 75-152594 ISBN 0-8371-6027-8
1. Sibelius, Jean, 1865-1957.

GRAY, Cecil, 1895-1951. 780'.92'4
Sibelius / by Cecil Gray. Westport, Conn. : Hyperion Press, 1979. ix, 223, [1] p. : port. ; 22 cm. (Encore music editions) Reprint of the 1931 ed. published by Oxford University Press, London. "Complete list of works": p. 206-224. [ML410.S54G7 1979] 78-66986 ISBN 0-88355-743-6 : 19.00
1. Sibelius, Jean, 1865-1957. 2. Composers—Finland—Biography.

JOHNSON, Harold Edgar, 1915- 780'.92'4 B
Jean Sibelius / by Harold E. Johnson. Westport, Conn. : Greenwood Press, 1978, c1959. xviii, xi, 287 p., [6] leaves of plates : ill. ; 23 cm. Reprint of the ed. published by Knopf, New York. Includes index. "Complete list of compositions and arrangements by Jean Sibelius": p. 241-277. [ML410.S54J6 1978] 78-5506 ISBN 0-313-20470-5 lib. bdg. : 15.00
1. Sibelius, Jean, 1865-1957. 2. Composers—Finland—Biography. BIP

LAYTON, Robert 780.924
Sibelius. London, J. M. Dent; New York, Farrar [1965] xi, 210p. illus., facsim., music, ports. 20cm. (Master musicians ser.) Bibl. [ML410.S54L35] 65-9788 4.95
1. Sibelius, Jean, 1865-1957. I. Title. BIP

LAYTON, Robert. 780'.924 B
Sibelius and his world. New York, Viking Press [1970] 120 p. illus., facsims., plates, ports. 24 cm. (A Studio book) [ML410.S54L352] 72-92799 6.95
1. Sibelius, Jean, 1865-1957. I. Title.

LEVAS, Santeri. 780'.92'4 B
Sibelius; a personal portrait. Translated by Percy M. Young. [1st American ed.] Lewisburg [Pa.] Bucknell University Press [1973, c1972] xxiii, 165 p. illus. 22 cm. Abridged translation of Jean Sibelius; muistelmia suuresta ihmisesta. "List of works": p. [136]-151. [ML410.S54L453 1973] 73-11556 ISBN 0-8387-1411-0 8.00
1. Sibelius, Jean, 1865-1957. I. Title.

RINGBOM, Nils Eric. 780'.92'4 B
Jean Sibelius : a master and his work / by Nils Eric Ringbom ; translated from the Swedish by G. I. C. de Courcy. Westport, Conn. : Greenwood Press, 1977. p. cm. Reprint of the 1954 ed. published by University of Oklahoma Press, Norman. Includes index. "Complete list of works": p. [ML410.S54R52 1977] 77-14425 ISBN 0-8371-9840-2 lib.bdg. : 15.00
1. Sibelius, Jean, 1865-1957. 2. Composers—Finnland—Biography. BIP

TAWASTSTJERNA, Erik. 780'.92'4 B
Sibelius / Erik Tawaststjerna ; translated by Robert Layton. London : Faber, 1976- v. : ill. ; 24 cm. Contents.Contents.—v. 1. 1865-1905. Includes bibliographies and indexes. [ML410.S54T2932] 76-380800 ISBN 0-571-08832-5 : £12.50
1. Sibelius, Jean, 1865-1957. 2. Composers—Finland—Biography. BIP

TAWASTSTJERNA, Erik. 780'.92'4 B
Sibelius / by Erik Tawaststjerna ; translated by Robert Layton. Berkeley : University of California Press, 1976- v. : ill. ; 25 cm. Includes indexes. Contents.Contents.—v. 1. 1865-1905. Bibliography: v. 1, p. 295. [ML410.S54T293] 75-13147 ISBN 0-520-03014-1 : 30.00
1. Sibelius, Jean, 1865-1957. 2. Composers—Finland—Biography.

Siberia—Description and travel.

HAUTZIG, Esther (Rudomin) 915.7'3
The endless steppe; growing up in Siberia, by Esther Hautzig. New York, T. Y. Crowell Co. [1968] 243 p. 21 cm. Autobiographical. [PS3558.A77Z5] 68-13582
1. Siberia—Description and travel. I. Title.

HAUTZIG, Esther (Rudomin) 915.7
The endless steppe; growing up in Siberia, by Esther Hautzig. New York, T. Y. Crowell Co. [1968] 243 p. 21 cm. During World War II, when she was eleven years old, the author and her family were arrested in Poland by the Russians as political enemies and exiled to Siberia. She recounts here the trials of the following five years spent on the harsh Asian steppe. [PS3558.A77Z5] AC 68
1. Siberia—Description and travel. I. Title. BIP

Sibley, Antoinette.

SPATT, Leslie E. 792.8'092'2 B
Sibley & Dowell / photos. by Leslie Spatt ; text by Nicholas Dromgoole. London : Collins, 1976. 223 p. : chiefly ill. ; 29 cm. [GV1785.S554S6] 77-351990 ISBN 0-00-211047-4 : £9.50
1. Sibley, Antoinette. 2. Dowell, Anthony. 3. Dancers—Biography. I. Dromgoole, Nicholas. II. Title.

Sibley, George.

SIBLEY, George. 973.9'092'4 B
Part of a winter / by George Sibley. New York : Harmony Books, [1978] p. cm. [CT275.S514A35 1978] 78-5647 ISBN 0-517-53469-X : 10.00
1. Sibley, George. 2. United States—Biography. I. Title.

Sibthorp, Richard Waldo, 1792-1879.

SYKES, Christopher, 1907- 922.242
Two studies in virtue. [1st American ed.] New York, Knopf, 1953. 256p. illus. 22cm. [BX4705.S62S9 1953a] 53-6864
1. Sibthorp, Richard Waldo, 1792-1879. 2. Catholic Church in England. 3. Zionism—Hist. I. Title.

Sick—Psychology.

MEDICAL encounters 362.1'092'6 : the experience of illness and treatment / edited by Alan Davis and Gordon Horobin. New York : St. Martin's Press, 1977. 223 p. ; 23 cm. Includes bibliographical references. [R726.5.M42 1977b] 76-44646 16.95
1. Sick—Psychology. 2. Social medicine. 3. Sick—Biography. 4. Sociologists—Biography. I. Davis, Alan G. II. Horobin, Gordon. BIP

Sickert, Walter, 1860-1942.

LILLY, Marjorie. 759.2
Sickert; the painter and his circle. [1st U.S. ed.] Park Ridge, N.J., Noyes Press [1973, c1971] 176 p. illus. 26 cm. [ND497.S48L5 1973] 72-86251 ISBN 0-8155-5014-6 14.00
1. Sickert, Walter, 1860-1942. I. Title.

SICKERT, Walter Richard, 1860-1942 759.2
Sickert. [by] Lillian Browse. London, Hart-Davis [dist. Chester Springs, Pa., Dufour, 1965, c.1960] 124p. illus., plates (pt. col.) 30cm. Bibl. [ND497.S48B7] 60-50038 12.50
I. Browse, Lillian. II. Title.

SUTTON, Denys. 759.2 B
Walter Sickert : a biography / [by] Denys Sutton. London : Joseph, 1976. 272 p., leaf of plate, [24] p. of plates : ill., ports. ; 24 cm. Includes index. Bibliography: p. 252-262. [ND497.S48S97 1976] 76-373164 ISBN 0-7181-1436-1 : £10.50
1. Sickert, Walter, 1860-1942. 2. Painters—Great Britain—Biography. BIP

Sickles, Daniel Edgar, 1819-1914.

SWANBERG, W. A., 1907- 923.573
Sickles the incredible. New York, Scribner, 1956. xii, 433 p. illus., ports., map. 24 cm. Bibliography: p. 419-423. [E467.S57S83] 56-5668
1. Sickles, Daniel Edgar, 1819-1914.

Siddons, Sarah (Kemble) 1755-1831.

ANDREWS, Charles Freer, 1871-1940. 266'.7'0924 B
John White of Mashonaland. New York, Negro Universities Press [1969] 316 p. 23 cm. Reprint of the 1935 ed. [BV3625.M3A6 1969] 79-91660 ISBN 0-8371-2070-5
1. White, John, 1866 (Jan. 6)-1933. BIP

DE LA TORRE, Lillian, 1902- 927.92
The actress; being the story of Sarah Siddons, showing how she began as a strolling player, how her stage lover won her heart and hand, how she struggled for fame and fortune and how she became queen of the London stage. New York, T. Nelson [1957] 223p. illus. 21cm. [PN2598.S5D4] 57-10020
1. Siddons, Sarah (Kemble) 1755-1831. I. Title.

FFRENCH, Yvonne. 792'.028'0924 B
Mrs. Siddons, tragic actress / Yvonne Ffrench. Westport, Conn. : Hyperion Press, [1979] p. cm. Reprint of the 1954 ed. published by D. Verschoyle, London. Bibliography: p. [PN2598.S5F4 1979] 78-13858 ISBN 0-88355-791-6 : 23.50
1. Siddons, Sarah (Kemble), 1755-1831. 2. Actors—Great Britain—Biography. I. Title.

FFRENCH, Yvonne. 920.72'094
Six great Englishwomen : Queen Elizabeth I, Sarah Siddons, Charlotte Bronte, Florence Nightingale, Queen Victoria, Gertrude Bell / by Yvonne Ffrench. Folcroft, Pa. : Folcroft Library Editions, 1976. p. cm. Reprint of the 1953 ed. published by Hamilton, London. [DA28.7.F42 1976] 76-10646 ISBN 0-8414-4219-3 lib. bdg. : 17.50
1. Elizabeth, Queen of England, 1533-1603. 2. Siddons, Sarah Kemble, 1755-1831. 3. Bronte, Charlotte, 1816-1855. 4. Nightingale, Florence, 1820-1910. 5. Victoria, Queen of Great Britain, 1819-1901. 6. Bell, Gertrude Lowthian, 1868-1926. I. Title.

FITZGERALD, Percy Hetherington, 1834-1925. 792'.028'0922 B
The Kembles; an account of the Kemble family, including the lives of Mrs. Siddons, and her brother, John Philip Kemble. New York, B. Blom, 1969- v. ports. 21 cm. Reprint of the 1871 ed. [PN2598.K38F5 1969] 73-89712
1. Kemble, John Philip, 1757-1823. 2. Siddons, Sarah (Kemble) 1755-1831. 3. Kemble family. I. Title.

HAYCRAFT, Molly (Costain) 1911- 927.92
First lady of the theatre: Sarah Siddons (July 5, 1755-June 8, 1831) New York, Messner [1958] 192p. 22cm. [PN2598.S5H3] 56-6017
1. Siddons Sarah (Kemble) 1755-1831. I. Title.

JONSON, Marian. 792'.028'0924 B
A troubled grandeur; the story of England's great actress, Sarah Siddons. [1st ed.] Boston, Little, Brown [1972] xiii, 238 p. illus. 21 cm. Bibliography: p. 237-238. [PN2598.S5J6] 72-182250
1. Siddons, Sarah (Kemble) 1755-1831. I. Title.

MANVELL, Roger, 1909- 792'.028'0924 B
Sarah Siddons: portrait of an actress. [1st American ed.] New York, Putnam [1971, c1970] xii, 385 p. illus., facsims., geneal. table, ports. 22 cm. Bibliography: p. 366-370. [PN2598.S5M28 1971] 76-105596 7.95
1. Siddons, Sarah (Kemble) 1755-1831.

PARSONS, Florence Mary (Wilson) 1864-1934. 792'.028'0924 B
The incomparable Siddons, by Mrs. Clement Parsons. New York, B. Blom [1969] xi, [v], 298 p. illus., facsims., geneal. table, ports. 24 cm. Reprint of the 1909 ed. Bibliography: p. [xiv]-[xvi] [PN2598.S5P3 1969] 77-84847
1. Siddons, Sarah (Kemble) 1755-1831. I. Title. BIP

PARSONS, Florence Mary (Wilson) 1864-1934. 792'.028'0924 B
The incomparable Siddons, by Mrs. Clement Parsons. Freeport, N.Y., Books for Libraries Press [1970] xix, 298 p. illus., facsims., geneal. table, ports. 23 cm. Reprint of the 1909 ed. Bibliography: p. xv-xvii. [PN2598.S5P3 1970] 74-107824
1. Siddons, Sarah (Kemble) 1755-1831. I. Title.

Sidnet, Philip, Sir 1554-1586

WALLACE, Malcolm William, 1873- 828'.3'09 (B)
The life of Sir Philip Sidney. New York, Octagon, 1967. 428p. facsim., general. table. 24cm. Reprint or the 1915 ed Bibl. [DA358.S5W3 1967] 67-18790 9.50
1. Sidnet, Philip, Sir 1554-1586 I. Title.
Oricinally published by Cambridge Univ. Pr. BIP

Sidney family.

COLLINS, Arthur, 1682?-1760, ed. 942.06
Letters and memorials of state in the reigns of Queen Mary, Queen Elizabeth, King James, King Charles the First, part of the reign of King Charles the Second, and Oliver's usurpation ... London, Printed for T. Osborne, 1746. [New York, AMS Press, 1973] 2 v. port. 27 cm. [DA350.C7 1973] 72-997 ISBN 0-404-01631-6 18.50
1. Sidney family. 2. Great Britain—History—Elizabeth, 1558-1603—Sources. 3. Great Britain—History—Early Stuarts, 1603-1649—Sources. 4. Great Britain—History—Commonwealth and Protectorate, 1649-1660—Sources. I. Title. BIP

Sidney, Philip, Sir, 1554-1586.

ADDLESHAW, Percy, 1866-1916. 821'.3 B
Sir Philip Sidney. Port Washington, N.Y., Kennikat Press [1970] xii, 381 p. ports. 22 cm. Reprint of the 1909 ed. [DA358.S5A4 1970] 77-113304
1. Sidney, Philip, Sir, 1554-1586.

BOAS, Frederick Samuel, 1862- 928.2
Sir Philip Sidney, representative Elizabethan; his life and writings. London, Staples Press distributed in U. S. A. by J. de Graff, New York [1956] 204p. illus. 23cm. [PR2343.B6 1956] 56-769
1. Sidney, Philip, Sir 1554-1586. I. Title.

BOAS, Frederick Samuel, 1862- 928.2
Sir Philip Sidney, representative Elizabethan; his life and writings, London, Staples Press distributed in U. S. A. by J. de Graff. New York [1956] 204p. illus. 23cm. [PR2343.B6 1956] 56-769
1. Sidney, Philip, Sir 1554-1586. I. Title.

BOAS, Frederick Samuel, 1862-1957. 821'.3 B
Sir Philip Sidney, representative Elizabethan; his life and writings. [Folcroft, Pa.] Folcroft Library Editions, 1974. p. Reprint of the 1955 ed. published by Staples Press, London. Includes bibliographical references. [PR2343.B6 1974] 74-5387 ISBN 0-8414-3153-1 (lib. bdg.)
1. Sidney, Philip, Sir, 1554-1586. I. Title. BIP

HAMILTON, A. C. 821'.3 B
Sir Philip Sidney : a study of his life and works / by A. C. Hamilton. Cambridge [Eng.] ; New York : Cambridge University Press, 1977. viii, 216 p. ; 22 cm. Includes index. Bibliography: p. [209]-211. [PR2343.H3] 76-47410 ISBN 0-521-21423-8 : 14.95
1. Sidney, Philip, Sir, 1554-1586. 2. Authors, English—Early modern, 1500-1700—Biography.

HOWELL, Roger. 828'.3'09 B
Sir Philip Sidney, the Shepherd Knight. [1st American ed.] Boston, Little, Brown [1968] viii, 308 p. port. 22 cm. "References": p. [271]-299. [DA358.S5H68 1968b] 68-24236
1. Sidney, Philip, Sir, 1554-1586. I. Title.

KELLOGG, Elizabeth Rockey, 1870- 928.2
Sir Philip Sidney: impressions of a remarkable character. Cincinnati, Priv. print. [by] the C. J. Krehbiel Co. [1960] 124p. 17cm. [DA358.S5K4] 60-322459
1. Sidney, Sir Philip, 1554-1586. I. Title.

LLOYD, Julius, 1830-1892. 821'.3 B
The life of Sir Philip Sidney. [Folcroft, Pa.] Folcroft Library Editions, 1974. p. cm. Reprint of the 1862 ed. published by Longman, Green, Longman, Roberts, and Green, London. [DA358.S5L7 1974] 74-10802 24.00
1. Sidney, Philip, Sir, 1554-1586. I. Title. BIP

OSBORN, James Marshall. 942.05'5'0924 B
Young Philip Sidney, 1572-1577 [by James M. Osborn] New Haven, Published for the Elizabethan Club [by] Yale University Press, 1972. xxiv, 565 p. illus. 25 cm. (The Elizabethan Club series, 5) Includes bibliographical references. [DA358.S5O8 1972] 77-151584 ISBN 0-300-01443-0 25.00
1. Sidney, Philip, Sir, 1554-1586. I. Title. II. Series. BIP

SYMONDS, John Addington, 1840-1893. 821'.3 B
Sir Philip Sidney. New York, AMS Press [1968] viii, 200 p. 22 cm. (English men of letters) [PR2343.S8 1968b] 68-58401
1. Sidney,Philip, Sir, 1554-1586.

SYMONDS, John Addington, 1840-1893 828'.3'09
Sir Philip Sidney. London. Macmillan [1886] Detroit, Gale, 1968. vii, 205p. 23cm. (Gale lib. of lives & letters: British writers ser.) Bibl. [PR2343.S8 1968] (B) 67-23878 7.80
1. Sidney, Sir Philip, 1554-1586. I. Title.

WARREN, Clarence Henry, 1895- 828'.3'09 B
Sir Philip Sidney; a study in conflict, by C. Henry Warren. New York, Haskell House, 1967. ix, 240 p. illus., ports. 23 cm. Reprint of the 1936 ed. [PR2343.W3 1967] 67-30823
1. Sidney, Philip, Sir, 1554-1586. BIP

WILSON, Mona, 1872- 942.05'5'0924 B
Sir Philip Sidney. [Folcroft, Pa.] Folcroft Library Editions, 1971. 328 p. illus. 23 cm. 150 copies printed. Reprint of the 1950 ed. Bibliography: p. 287-320. [DA358.S5W5 1971] 72-187163
1. Sidney, Philip, Sir, 1554-1586. BIP

Sidney, Philip, Sir, 1554-1586—Biography.

BROOKE, Fulke Greville, Baron, 1554-1628. 821'.3
Sir Fulke Greville's Life of Sir Philip Sidney, etc. : first published 1652 / with an introd. by Nowell Smith. Folcroft, Pa. : Folcroft Library Editions, 1977. xxv, 279 p. ; 23 cm. Reprint of the 1907 ed. published by Clarendon Press, Oxford, in series: Tudor & Stuart library. [PR2343.B7 1977] 77-4734 ISBN 0-8414-4427-7 lib. bdg. : 25.00
1. Sidney, Philip, Sir, 1554-1586—Biography. 2. Authors, English—Early modern, 1500-1700—Biography. I. Title. II. Title: Life of Sir Philip Sidney.

Siedliska, Maria Franciszka, Mother, 1842-1902.

BURTON, Katherine (Kurz), 1890- 922.273
Where there is love; the life of Mother Mary Frances Siedliska of Jesus the Good Shepherd. New York, Kenedy [1951] 200 p. illus. 21 cm. [BX4705.S624B8] 51-14256
1. Siedliska, Maria Franciszka, Mother, 1842-1902. I. Title.

Siegel, Benjamin, 1906-1947.

JENNINGS, Dean Southern, 1905- 364.14'3
We only kill each other; the life and bad times of Bugsy Siegel, by Dean Jennings. Englewood Cliffs, N.J., Prentice-Hall [1967] 253 p. illus. 24 cm. [HV6248.S5619J4] 67-26867
1. Siegel, Benjamin, 1906-1947. I. Title.

Siegel, Martin.

SIEGEL, Martin. 296.6'1 B
Amen: the diary of Rabbi Martin Siegel. Edited by Mel Ziegler. New York [Maddick Manuscripts; distributed by] World Pub. Co. [1971] xi, 276 p. 22 cm. [BM755.S528A3] 73-142133 6.95
I. Title.

Siemens, William, Sir, 1816-1896.

JEANS, William T. 669'.142'0922 B
The creators of the age of steel, by W. T. Jeans. Freeport, New York, Books for Libraries Press [1973] p. (Essay index reprint series) "First published 1854." Contents.Contents.—Introduction.—Sir Henry Bessemer.—Sir William Siemens.—Sir Joseph Whitworth.—Sir John Brown.—Mr. S. G. Thomas.—Mr. G. J. Snelus. [TN139.J45 1973] 73-1583 ISBN 0-518-10054-5
1. Bessemer, Henry, Sir, 1813-1898. 2. Siemens, William, Sir, 1816-1896. 3. Whitworth, Joseph, Sir, 1803-1887. 4. Brown, John, Sir, 1816-1896. 5. Thomas, Sidney Gilchrist, 1850-1885. 6. Snelus, George James, 1837-1906. 7. Steel—History. 8. Inventors. I. Title.

Sienkiewicz, Henryk, 1846-1916.

COLEMAN, Arthur Prudden, 1897- 927.92
Wanderers twain; Modjeska and Sienkiewicz: a view from California, by Arthur Prudden Coleman and Marion Moore Coleman. Cheshire, Conn. Cherry Hill-Books, 1964. ix, 111 p. illus., ports. 23 cm. [PN2618.M6C58] 63-20948
1. Sienkiewicz, Henryk, 1846-1916. 2. Modjeska, Helena, 1840-1909. I. Coleman, Marion (Moore) 1900- joint author. II. Title.

Sierra Nevada Mountains.

CLYDE, Norman. 796.5'22'0924 B
Norman Clyde of the Sierra Nevada; rambles through the range of light; 29 essays on the mountains. Foreword by Francis Farquhar; prologue by Jules Eichorn. With a long letter from Smoke Blanchard. [San Francisco] Scrimshaw Press, 1971. 172 p. illus. 23 cm. [F868.S5C55] 71-183953 ISBN 0-912020-19-9 (pbk)
1. Sierra Nevada Mountains. 2. Mountaineering. I. Title.

Sieyes, Emanuel Joseph, comte, 1748-1836.

VAN DEUSEN, Glyndon Garlock, 1897- 944.04'0924
Sieyes: his life and his nationalism, by Glyndon G. Van Deusen. New York, AMS Press [1970] 170 p. 23 cm. (Studies in history, economics, and public law, no. 362) Reprint of the 1932 ed. Bibliography: p. 157-167. [DC146.S5V3 1970] 68-58632
1. Sieyes, Emanuel Joseph, comte, 1748-1836. 2. France—Politics and government—1774-1793. 3. France—Politics and government—1789-1815. 4. Nationalism—France. I. Title. II. Series: Columbia studies in the social sciences, no. 362

Siffert, Jo, 1936-1971.

DESCHENAUX, Jacques. 796.7'2'0924 B
Jo Siffert. London, W. Kimber [1972] 208 p. illus. 23 cm. Stamped on t.p.: Distributed in the United States by Motorbooks International. [GV1032.S56D47 1972] 73-160780 ISBN 0-7183-0402-0 8.95
1. Siffert, Jo, 1936-1971. BIP

Signoret, Simone, 1921-

SIGNORET, Simone, 1921- 791.43'028'0924 B
Nostalgia isn't what it used to be / Simone Signoret. 1st ed. New York : Harper & Row, c1978. p. cm. Translation of La nostalgie n'est plus ce qu'elle etait. [PN2638.S47A3413 1978] 77-3773 ISBN 0-06-013986-2 : 12.50
1. Signoret, Simone, 1921- 2. Actors—France—Biography. I. Title. BIP

SIGNORET, Simone, 1921- 791.43'028'0924 B
Nostalgia isn't what it used to be / Simone Signoret. Harmondsworth, Eng. ; New York : Penguin Books, 1979. 464 p. ; 19 cm. Translation of La nostalgie n'est plus ce qu'elle etait. Includes index. [PN2638.S47A3413 1979] 78-27395 ISBN 0-14-005181-3 pbk. : 4.95
1. Signoret, Simone, 1921- 2. Actors—France—Biography. I. Title.

Sihler, Wilhelm, 1801-1885.

SPITZ, Lewis William, 1922- 284'.1'0924 B
Life in two worlds; biography of William Sihler, by Lewis W. Spitz. Saint Louis, Concordia Pub. House [1968] 199 p. 21 cm. Bibliographical references included in "Notes" (p. 178-191) [BX8080.S38S6] 68-13364
1. Sihler, Wilhelm, 1801-1885. I. Title.

Siksika Indians.

MY life as an Indian. v. 12
New York, Fawcett [1956, c1935] 204p. (Premier book s 25)
1. Siksika Indians. 2. Indians of North America—Social life & customs. I. Schultz, James Willard, 1859- BIP

SCHULTZ, James Willard, 1859-1947. 970.3 D
My life as an Indian. Greenwich, Conn., Fawcett Publications [1968, c1935] 204 p. 18 cm. (A Fawcett premier book, T386) [E99.S54S3 1968] 68-5778 0.75
1. Siksika Indians. 2. Indians of North America—Social life and customs. I. Title.

Silber, Jules Crawford.

SETH, Ronald. 940.4'8'7430924
The spy who never was caught. [1st American ed.] New York, Hawthorn Books [1967] 240 p. 22 cm. First published in 1966 under title: The spy who wasn't caught. [D639.S7S5] 66-22318
1. Silber, Jules Crawford. 2. European War, 1914-1918—Secret service—Germany. I. Title.

Silhouettes—United States.

CARRICK, Alice Van Leer, 1875- 741.7'0973
A history of American silhouettes; a collector's guide, 1790-1840 Rutland, Vt., C. E. Tuttle [1968] xx, 205 p. illus., facsims., ports. 24 cm. Reprint of the 1928 ed. published under title: Shades of our ancestors. Bibliography: p. 193-194. [NC910.C3 1968] 68-21119
1. Silhouettes—United States. 2. United States—Biography—Portraits. 3. Artists, American. I. Title. II. Title: American silhouettes.

Silkorsky, Igor Ivan, 1889-1972 Juvenile Literature

DELEAR, Frank J. 629.13'00924 B
Igor Sikorsky; his three careers in aviation, by Frank J. Delear. Foreword by James H. Doolittle. New York, Dodd, Mead [1969] xi, 272 p. illus. 24 cm. A biography of the aeronautical engineer whose achievements include the multi-motored airplane and the practical helicopter. [TL540.S54D45] 79-82620 4.95
1. Sikorsky, Igor Ivan, 1889- —Juvenile literature. 2. Sikorsky, Igor Ivan, 1889- BIP

DELEAR, Frank J. 629.13'0092'4 B
Igor Sikorsky, his three careers in aviation / by Frank J. Delear ; foreword by James H. Doolittle. Rev. ed. New York : Dodd, Mead, c1976. xi, 290 p. : ill. ; 24 cm. Includes index. A biography of the aeronautical engineer whose achievements include the multi-motored airplane and the helicopter. [TL540.S54D45 1976] 92 75-38370 ISBN 0-396-07282-8 : 5.25
1. Sikorsky, Igor Ivan, 1889-1972—Juvenile literature. I. Title.

Silliman, Benjamin, 1779-1864.

FULTON, John Farquhar, 1899-1960. 509'.24
Benjamin Silliman, 1779-1864; pathfinder in American science, by John F. Fulton and Elizabeth H. Thomson. New York, Greenwood Press, 1968 [c1947] ix, 294 p. illus., facsims., ports. 22 cm. Bibliography: p. 279-284. [Q143.S56F8 1968] (B) 69-10095
1. Silliman, Benjamin, 1779-1864. I. Thomson, Elizabeth Harriet, 1907- joint author.

PARSONS, Francis, 1871-1937. 378.746'8 B
Six men of Yale. Foreword by Charles Seymour. Freeport, N.Y., Books for Libraries Press [1971, c1939] xii, 145 p. ports. 23 cm. (Essay index reprint series) Contents.Contents.—Elisha Williams, 1694-1755.—Ezra Stiles, 1727-1795.—The young Silliman in Nelson's England, 1805-1806.—Edward J. Phelps, 1822-1900.—The second President Dwight, 1828-1916.—Henry Augustin Beer, 1847-1926. [LD6319.P3 1971] 72-156702 ISBN 0-8369-2329-4
1. Williams, Elisha, 1694-1775. 2. Stiles, Ezra, 1727-1795. 3. Silliman, Benjamin, 1779-1864. 4. Phelps, Edward John, 1822-1900. 5. Dwight, Timothy, 1828-1916. 6. Beers, Henry Augustin, 1847-1926. I. Title. BIP

Sillman, Leonard Dexter

SILLMAN, Leonard Dexter 927.92
Here lies Leonard Sillman, Straightened out at last; an autobiography, [1st ed.] New York, Citadel Press [1959] 377 p. illus. 22 cm. [PN2287.S38A3] 59-14761
I. Title.

Sills, Beverly.

SILLS, Beverly. 782.1'092'4 B
Bubbles : a self-portrait / by Beverly Sills. Indianapolis : Bobbs-Merrill, 1976. p. cm. [ML420.S562A3] 76-11606 ISBN 0-672-52268-3 : 12.50
1. Sills, Beverly. 2. Singers United States—Biography. I. Title. BIP

Sills, Kenneth Charles Morton, 1879-1954.

BROWN, Herbert Ross, 1902- 923.773
Sills of Bowdoin; the life of Kenneth Charles Morton Sills, 1879-1954. New York, Columbia University Press, 1964. xii, 440 p. illus., ports. 24 cm. [LD552.71918.B7] 64-14657
1. Sills, Kenneth Charles Morton, 1879-1954. 2. Bowdoin College. I. Title.

Silva, Vicente, (ca.) 1845-1893.

BACA, Carlos C. de. 364.15'0924 B
Vicente Silva, the terror of Las Vegas, by Carlos C. de Baca. [Truchas, N.M.] Tate Gallery, 1968. 48 p. port. 24 cm. [F801.S5B4] 68-5101
1. Silva, Vicente, (ca.) 1845-1893. 2. Brigands and robbers—New Mexico.

Silver City, S.D.—History.

BURKE, Florence, 1889- 978.3'93 B
Silver City : one hundred years of Black Hills history, 1876-1976 / Florence Burke. [Silver City, S.D. : Burke, c1977] 130 p. : ill. ; 22 cm. Cover title. [F659.S58B87] 77-153662
1. Silver City, S.D.—History. 2. Silver City, S.D.—Biography. I. Title.

Silvers, Phil, 1911-

SILVERS, Phil, 1911- 791'.092'4 B
The man who was Billko : the autobiography of Phil Silvers / with Robert Saffron. London ; New York : W. H. Allen, 1974. [9], 276 p., [24] p. of plates : ill., ports. ; 24 cm. American ed. published in 1973 under title: This laugh is on me : the Phil Silvers story. [PN2287.S384A326 1974] 75-312116
1. Silvers, Phil, 1911- I. Saffron, Robert, joint author. II. Title.

SILVERS, Phil, 1911- 790'.092'4 B
This laugh is on me: the Phil Silvers story, by Phil Silvers with Robert Saffron. Englewood Cliffs, N.J., Prentice-Hall [1973] 276 p. illus. 24 cm. [PN2287.S384A326] 73-11052 ISBN 0-13-919100-3 7.95
1. Silvers, Phil, 1911- I. Saffron, Robert, joint author. II. Title.

Silversmiths, American—Cincinnati.

BECKMAN, Elizabeth D. 739.2'092'2
An in-depth study of the Cincinnati silversmiths, jewelers, watch and clockmakers, through 1850, also listing the more prominent men in these trades from 1851 until 1900 / by Elizabeth D. Beckman. Cincinnati : B.B. & Co., c1975. xvi, 168 p. : ill. ; 27 cm. Includes index. Bibliography: p. 156-160. [NK7112.B42] 75-24983
1. Silversmiths, American—Cincinnati. 2. Jewelers—Cincinnati. 3. Clock and watch makers—Cincinnati. I. Title: An in-depth study of the Cincinnati silversmiths, jewelers ... II. Title: Cincinnati silversmiths, jewelers, watch and clockmakers.

Simcox, Edith Jemima—Relationship with women—George Eliot.

MCKENZIE, K. A. 070'.92 B
Edith Simcox and George Eliot / by K. A. McKenzie ; with an introd. by Gordon S. Haight. Westport, Conn. : Greenwood Press, 1978, c1961. xviii, 146 p. ; 23 cm. Reprint of the ed. published by Oxford University Press, London. Includes index. Bibliography: p. [140]-142. [PR5452.S27Z75 1978] 78-1538 ISBN 0-313-20269-9 : 14.00
1. Simcox, Edith Jemima—Relationship with women—George Eliot. 2. Eliot, George, pseud, i.e. Marian Evans, afterwards Cross, 1819-1880—Friends and associates. 3. Authors, English—19th century—Biography. BIP

Simenon, Georges,

SIMENON, Georges, 1903- 848'.9'1203 B
When I was old. Translated by Helen Eustis. [1st ed.] New York, Harcourt Brace Jovanovich [1971] 343 p. illus., ports. 22 cm. "A Helen and Kurt Wolff book." Autobiographical. Translation of Quand j'etais vieux. [PQ2637.I53Z513] 70-153690 ISBN 0-15-195950-1
I. Title. BIP

Simeon, Charles, 1759-1836.

HOPKINS, Hugh Alexander Evan. 283'.092'4 B
Charles Simeon of Cambridge / Hugh Evan Hopkins. [Grand Rapids, Mich.] : W. B. Eerdmans Pub. Co., 1977. 236 p. : ill. (on lining paper) ; 25 cm. Includes bibliographical references and index. [BX5199.S55H66 1977] 77-153375 ISBN 0-8028-3498-1 : 7.95
1. Simeon, Charles, 1759-1836. 2. Church of England—Clergy—Biography. 3. Clergy—England—Cambridge—Biography. 4. Cambridge, Eng.—Biography. I. Title. BIP

Simkins, Francis Butler, 1897-1966.

FRANCIS Butler 975'.0072'024 B
Simkins, 1897-1966, historian of the South. Columbia, S.C., printed by the State Printing Co. [1967?] 85 p. illus., ports. 23 cm. [E175.5.S5F7] 74-11790
1. Simkins, Francis Butler, 1897-1966.

Simmons, Edward, 1852-

SIMMONS, Edward, 1852- 759.13 B
From seven to seventy : memories of a painter and a Yankee / by Edward Simmons ; with an interruption by Oliver Herford. New York : Garland Pub., 1976, c1922. p. cm. (The Art experience in late nineteenth-century America) Reprint of the ed. published by Harper, New York. [ND237.S55A23 1976] 75-28891 ISBN 0-8240-2248-3 lib.bdg. : 25.00
1. Simmons, Edward, 1852- 2. Painters—United States—Biography. I. Title. II. Series.

Simms, Eric.

SIMMS, Eric. 500.9'2'4 B
Birds of the air : the autobiography of a naturalist and broadcaster / [by] Eric Simms. London : Hutchinson, 1976. 192 p., [16] p. of plates : ill., ports. ; 23 cm. Includes index. [QH31.S57A3] 76-374310 ISBN 0-09-126070-1 : 9.95
1. Simms, Eric. 2. Naturalists—Great Britain—Biography. I. Title.
Distributed by Hutchinson, Salem, New Hampshire

Simms, William Gilmore, 1806-1870.

SIMMS, William Gilmore, 1806-1870. 928.1
Letters; collected and edited by Mary C. Simms Oliphant, Alfred Taylor Odell [and] T. C. Duncan Eaves. Introd. by Donald Davidson. Biographical sketch by Alexander S. Salley. Columbia, University of South Carolina Press, 1952-56. 5v. illus. ports. maps. 24cm. Contents.v. 1. 1830-1844.--v. 2. 1845-1849.--v. 3. 1850-1857.--v. 4. 1858-1866.--v. 5. 1867-1870. Index. volumes I-v. Bibliographical footnotes. [PS2853.A4 1952] 52-2352
I. Title.

TRENT, William Peterfield, 1862-1939. 818'.3'09 B
William Gilmore Simms. New York, Haskell House, 1968. viii, 351 p. port. 23 cm. Reprint of the 1892 ed. Bibliography: p. [333]-342. [PS2853.T7 1968] 68-24944
1. Simms, William Gilmore, 1806-1870. BIP

TRENT, William Peterfield, 1862-1939. 818'.3'09 B
William Gilmore Simms. New York, Greenwood Press [1969] viii, 351 p. port. 23 cm. (American men of letters) Reprint of the 1892 ed. Bibliography: p. 334-342. [PS2853.T7 1969] 69-14122
1. Simms, William Gilmore, 1806-1870. I. Title. II. Series.

Simon, Carly.

*SIMON, Carly 784'.092'4
Carly Simon complete [by Peter - and] Carly Simon New York, Alfred A. Knopt/Warner Bros. Publications, 1975. 228 p. ports. (some col.), music, 30 cm. [ML3930.] 75-10582 ISBN 0-394-48753-2 15.00.
1. Simon, Carly. I. Simon, Peter joint author. II. Title.
Pbk. 9.95; 0-394-70625-0. BIP

Simon, Carly—Juvenile literature.

MORSE, Charles. 784'.092'4 B
Carly Simon. Text: Charles and Ann Morse. Illus.: Dick Brude. Mankato, Minn., Creative Education; [distributed by Childrens Press, Chicago, 1974, c1975] 31 p. illus. (part col.) 25 cm. (Rock 'n pop stars) A biography stressing the musical career of composer-folk singer Carly Simon. [ML3930.S55M7] 92 74-14550 ISBN 0-87191-393-3
1. Simon, Carly—Juvenile literature. I. Morse, Ann, joint author. II. Brude, Dick, illus. III. Title. BIP

Simon, Ernest Darwin Simon, baron, 1879-1960.

STOCKS, Mary Danvers (Brinton) 1891- 820'.9'0091
Ernest Simon of Manchester, by Mary Stocks. [Manchester] Manchester University Press [1963] viii, 181 p. illus., ports. 23 cm. Bibliography: p. 175-176. [DA566.9.S49S8] 64-55536
1. Simon, Ernest Darwin Simon, baron, 1879-1960. I. Title.

Simon, Francis Eugene, Sir 1893-1956.

ARMS, Nancy 530.0924
A prophet in two countries; the life of F. E. Simon Pergamon [c.1966] Long Island City, N.Y. Pergamon c.1966 viii, 171p. illus., ports. 20cm. (Commonwealth and intl. lib. Hist. div. Biog. sect.) [QC16.S5A7] 65-28551 2.45 pap.,
1. Simon, Francis Eugene, Sir 1893-1956. I. Title.

Simon. John, Sir 1816-1904.

LAMBERT, Royston 923.942
Sir John Simon, 1816-1904, and English social administration. London. MacGibbon & Kee, [New York, Humanities. 1966, c.1963] 669p. port. 23cm. Bibl. [HV28.S56L3] 10.00 bds.,
1. Simon. John, Sir 1816-1904. 2. Public welfare—Gt. Brit. 3. Hygiene, Public—Gt. Brit. I. Title.

Simons, Algie Martin, 1870-1950.

KREUTER, Kent, 1932- 335.5'0924 B
An American dissenter; the life of Algie Martin Simons, 1870-1950 [by] Kent & Gretchen Kreuter. Lexington, University of Kentucky Press, 1969. xii, 236 p. illus., ports. 25 cm. Includes bibliographical references. [HX84.S53K7] 68-55042 7.50
1. Simons, Algie Martin, 1870-1950. I. Kreuter, Gretchen, joint author. II. Title. BIP

Simons family.

SIMONS, Robert Bentham, 1888- 929'.2'0973
Thomas Grange Simons III, his forebears and elations. Thomas Grange Simons the third Charleston, 1954. 211p. illus. 24cm. [CS71.S588 1954] 56-3193
1. Simons family. 2. U. S.—Geneal. I. Title.

Simpson, Alyse.

SIMPSON, Alyse. 920.7
I threw a rose into the sea. Decorations by Rus Anderson. New York, J. Day Co. [1955] 247 p. illus. 21 cm. Autobiographical. [CT1398.S55A3 1955a] 55-9937
I. Title.

Simpson, Cedric Keith.

SIMPSON, Cedric Keith. 614'.1'0924 B
Forty years of murder : an autobiography / Keith Simpson. 1st U.S. ed. New York : Scribner, 1979, c1978. 328 p., [12] leaves of plates : ill. ; 23 cm. Includes index. [RA1025.S5A33 1979] 79-64357 ISBN 0-684-16334-9 : 12.95
1. Simpson, Cedric Keith. 2. Forensic pathologists—England—Biography. 3. Forensic pathology—Case studies. 4. Homicide investigation—Great Britain—Case studies. I. Title.

Simpson, James Young, Sir, bart., 1811-1870.

ROWLAND, John, 1907- 926.1
The chloroform man; the story of Sir James Simpson. New York, Roy Publishers [1962,c1961] 136 p. illus. 20 cm. [R489.S6R6 1962] 62-13286
1. Simpson, James Young, Sir, bart., 1811-1870. I. Title.

Simpson, Margaret Massie, 1913-

SIMPSON, Margaret Massie, 1913- 248'.86'0924 B
Coping with cancer / Margaret Simpson, with Francis A. Martin. Nashville : Broadman Press, 1977c1976 154 p. ; 19 cm. [RC280.B8S52] 76-21475 ISBN 0-8054-5245-1 pbk. : 2.50
1. Simpson, Margaret Massie, 1913- 2. Breast—Cancer—Biography. I. Martin, Francis A., joint author. II. Title. BIP

Simpson, Matthew, Bp., 1811-1884.

CLARK, Robert Donald, 1910- 922.773
The life of Matthew Simpson. New York, Macmillan, 1956. xi, 344 p. 22 cm. Bibliographical references included in "Notes" (p. 307-333) [BX8495.S55C55] 56-13618
1. Simpson, Matthew, Bp., 1811-1884.

Simpson, O. J., 1947—

BAKER, Jim, 1941- 796.33'2'0924 B
O. J. Simpson's most memorable games / Jim Baker. New York : Putnam, c1978. 288 p. : ill. ; 24 cm. [GV939.S47B34 1978] 78-1304 ISBN 0-399-12108-0 : 8.95
1. Simpson, O. J., 1947- 2. Football players—United States—Biography. I. Title. BIP

*DEVANEY, John. 796'.33'20924 [B]
O. J. Simpson: football's greatest runner. [New York] Warner Paperback Library [1974] 223 p. 18 cm. [GV939] 1.50 (pbk.)
1. Simpson, O. J. I. Title.

FOX, Larry. 796.33'2'0924 B
The O. J. Simpson story : born to run / Larry Fox ; introd. by Weeb Ewbank. New York : Dodd, Mead, [1974] ix, 173 p., [8] leaves of plates : ports. ; 22 cm. Traces the progression of running back O. J. Simpson from the ghetto to the gridiron. [GV939.S47F68] 92 74-7769 ISBN 0-396-07009-4 : 6.95
1. Simpson, O. J., 1947- 2. Football. I. Title. II. Title: Born to run. BIP

Simpson, O. J., 1947- —Juvenile literature.

BELSKY, Dick. 796.33'2'0924 B
The Juice : football's superstar, O. J. Simpson / Dick Belsky. New York : H. Z. Walck, c1977. 58 p. : ill. ; 22 cm. A biography of the 1968 Heisman trophy winner who is an NFL record-setting running back. [GV939.S47B44] 92 77-564 ISBN 0-8098-0005-5 : 5.95
1. Simpson, O. J., 1947- —Juvenile literature. 2. Football players—United States—Biography—Juvenile literature. I. Title. BIP

BURCHARD, Marshall. 796.33'2'0924 B
Sports hero, O. J. Simpson / by Marshall and Sue Burchard. New York : Putnam, [1975] 95 p. : ill. ; 23 cm. (The Sports hero biographies) An easy-to-read biography of the record-setting running back and 1968 winner of the Heisman trophy. [GV939.S47B87 1975] 92 74-21082 ISBN 0-399-60940-7 lib. bdg. : 4.69
1. Simpson, O. J., 1947- —Juvenile literature. 2. Football—Juvenile literature. I. Burchard, S. H., joint author. II. Title.

DEEGAN, Paul J., 1937- 796.33'2'0924 B
O. J. Simpson, by Paul J. Deegan. Illustrated by Harold Henriksen. Mankato, Minn., Creative Education; distributed by Childrens Press, Chicago [1974] 29 p. illus. (part col.) 25 cm. (Creative's superstars) A biography of the record-setting running back and 1968 winner of the Heisman

trophy. [GV939.S47D43] 92 73-17056 ISBN 0-87191-312-7 4.95 (lib. bdg.)
1. Simpson, O. J., 1947- —Juvenile literature. I. Henriksen, Harold, illus. II. Title.

HILL, Ray. 796.33'2'0924 B
O. J. Simpson / by Ray Hill. New York : Random House, [1975] 153 p. : ill. ; 22 cm. (The Punt, pass, and kick library ; 23) Includes index. A biography of O. J. Simpson, running back of the Buffalo Bills in the National Football League. [GV939.S47H54] 92 75-8080 ISBN 0-394-83061-X : 2.50 ISBN 0-394-93061-4 lib.bdg. : 3.69
1. Simpson, O. J., 1947- —Juvenile literature. 2. Football—Juvenile literature. I. Title. **BIP**

JAMESON, Jon. 796.33'2'0924 B
The picture life of O. J. Simpson / by Jon Jameson. New York : F. Watts, 1977, c1976. [47] p. : ill. ; 22 cm. A biography of the prominent football player with the Buffalo Bills who broke existing running and touchdown records. [GV939.S47J35 1977] 92 76-50103 ISBN 0-531-01270-0 lib. bdg. : 4.47
1. Simpson, O. J., 1947- —Juvenile literature. 2. Football players—United States—Biography—Juvenile literature. I. Title. **BIP**

LIBBY, Bill. 796.33'2'0924 B
O. J.: the story of football's fabulous O. J. Simpson. New York, Putnam [1974] 192 p. 22 cm. (Putnam sports shelf) Traces the football career of the winner of the Heisman Trophy and college and professional Player of the Year awards who has set many rushing records. [GV939.S47L42 1974] 92 73-88519 ISBN 0-399-20384-2 4.89
1. Simpson, O. J.—Juvenile literature. 2. Football—Juvenile literature. I. Title.

YOUNG, Andrew 796.332'0922 B
Sturgeon Nash, 1919-
Black champions of the gridiron: O. J. Simpson and Leroy Keyes, by A. S. Doc Young. [1st ed.] New York, Harcourt, Brace & World [1969] 120 p. illus., ports. 22 cm. (Curriculum-related books) Relates the backgrounds of two well-known players in college football - Simpson and Keyes - describing in depth their games of 1968. [GV939.S47Y6] 920 76-88110 3.50
1. Simpson, O. J.—Juvenile literature. 2. Keyes, Leroy—Juvenile literature. I. Title. **BIP**

Sims, George Madison, 1875-1961.

SIMS, Vilda (Barker) v. 12
It takes time to grow; a biography of George Madison Sims, Superintendent of Schools, Port Arthur, Texas. Port Arthur, Hinds [1963] 68 p. illus., port. 65-58785
1. Sims, George Madison, 1875-1961. 2. Port Arthur, Texas — Public schools. I. Title.

Sims, James Marion,

SIMS, James Marion, 617'.0924 B
1813-1883.
The story of my life, by J. Marion Sims. With a new preface by C. Lee Buxton. New York, Da Capo Press, 1968. xi, 471 p. 21 cm. (A Da Capo Press reprint ed.) Unabridged republication of 1st ed., published 1884. List of writings by J. M. Sims: p. 459-463. [R154.S5A3 1968] 68-29603
I. Title.

Sims, James Marion, 1813-1883.

HARRIS, Seale, 1870- 926.1
Woman's surgeon; the life story of J. Marion Sims, by Seale Harris, with the collaboration of Frances Williams Browin. New York, Macmillan, 1950. xx, 432 p. illus., ports., facsims. 22 cm. Bibliography: p. [393]-413. [RG76.S5H3] 50-7607
1. Sims, James Marion, 1813-1883. 2. Brooklyn. Woman's Hospital. I. Title.

MARR, James Pratt, 1898- 926.1
Pioneer surgeons of the Woman's Hospital; the lives of Sims, Emmet, Peaslee, and Thomas. Philadelphia, F. A. Davis Co., 1957. 148p. illus. 24cm. Includes bibliography. [RA982.N5W64] 57-8716
1. Sims, James Marlon, 1813-1883. 2. Emmet, Thomas Addis, 1828-1919. 3. Penslee, Edmund Randolph, 1814-1878. 4. Thomas, Theodore Gallard, 1832-1903. 5. New York. Woman's Hospital in the State of New York. I. Title.

SIMS, James Marion, 617'.0924 B
1813-1883.
The story of my life, by J. Marion Sims. With a new preface by C. Lee Buxton. New York, Da Capo Press, 1968. xi, 471 p. 21 cm. (A Da Capo Press reprint ed.) Unabridged republication of 1st ed., published 1884. List of writings by J. M. Sims: p. 459-463. [R154.S5A3 1968] 68-29603
I. Title.

Sims, William Sowden, 1858-1936.

MORISON, Elting 359.3'31'0924 B
Elmore.
Admiral Sims and the modern American Navy [by] Elting E. Morison. New York, Russell & Russell [1968, c1942] xiv, 547 p. illus., ports. 24 cm. Bibliography: p. 535-[540] [E748.S52M6 1968] 68-10932
1. Sims, William Sowden, 1858-1936. 2. United States—History, Naval—20th century. I. Title. **BIP**

Siniavskii, Andrei Donat'evich, 1925—

LOURIE, Richard, 891.7'8'4409 B
1940-
Letters to the future : an approach to Sinyavsky Tertz / Richard Lourie. Ithaca : Cornell University Press, 1975. 221 p. ; 21 cm. Includes index. Bibliography: p. [212]-217. [PG3476.S539Z75] 74-10413 ISBN 0-8014-0890-3 : 8.95
1. Siniavskii, Andrei Donat'evich, 1925- I. Title. **BIP**

Sinan, Koca, mimar, 1490-1588.

STRATTON, Arthur. 720'.924
Sinan. New York, Scribner [1971, c1972] 299 p. illus. 24 cm. Bibliography: p. [283]-285. [NA1373.S5S8] 70-162777 ISBN 0-684-12582-X 12.95
1. Sinan, Koca, mimar, 1490-1588.

Sinatra, Frank, 1917-

DOUGLAS-HOME, Robin 927.8
Sinatra. New York, Grosset [1963, c.1962] 64p. illus. 26cm. 63-18970 1.95
1. Sinatra, Frank, I. Title.

LONSTEIN, Albert I. 784'.0924 B
The compleat Sinatra; disgography [sic] filmography, television appearances, motion picture appearances, radio appearances, concert appearances, stage appearances, by Albert I. Lonstein [and] Vito R. Marino. [Ellenville, N.Y., Cameron Publications, c1970] xv, 383 p. illus. 26 cm. Includes bibliographies. [ML420.S565L6] 77-170787
1. Sinatra, Frank, 1917- 2. Sinatra, Frank, 1917- —Discography. I. Marino, Vito R., joint author. II. Title.

*SCIACCA, Tony. 784'.092'4 B
Sinatra. New York, Pinnacle Books [1976] 248 p. ill. 18 cm. [ML420] ISBN 0-523-00847-3 1.75 (pbk.)
1. Sinatra, Frank, 1917- I. Title.

WILSON, Earl, 1907- 790.2'092'4
Sinatra : an unauthorized biography / by Earl Wilson. New York : New American Library, 1977,c1976. 361,[8]p. : ill. ; 18 cm. (A Signet Book) [ML420.S565W5] ISBN 0-451-07487-4 pbk. : 2.25
1. Sinatra, Frank, 1917- I. Title.
L.C. card no. for 1976 Macmillan ed.: 75-44193. **BIP**

Sinatra, Frank, 1917- —juvenile literature.

TAYLOR, Paula. 784'.092'4 B
Frank Sinatra / text, Paula Taylor ; ill., John Keely. Mankato, Minn. : Creative Education, [1975] p. cm. Bibliography: p. A biography of the singer and actor whose highly successful thirty-year career made him a famous and controversial millionaire. [ML3930.S58T4] 92 75-22028 ISBN 0-87191-460-3 lib.bdg. : 4.95
1. Sinatra, Frank, 1917- —juvenile literature. I. Keely, John. II. Title. **BIP**

Sinclair, May.

BOLL, Theophilus 823'.9'12 B
Ernest Martin, 1902-
Miss May Sinclair: novelist; a biographical and critical introduction, by Theophilus E. M. Boll. Rutherford [N.J.] Fairleigh Dickinson University Press [1973] 332 p. illus. 25 cm. Bibliography: p. 317-321. [PR6037.I73Z58 1973] 72-414 ISBN 0-8386-1156-7 18.00
1. Sinclair, May.

Sinclair, Robert A.

SINCLAIR, Robert 386'.5'0924 B
A., 1898-
Winds over Lake Huron : chronicles in the life of a Great Lakes mariner / Robert A. Sinclair. 1st ed. Hicksville, N.Y. : Exposition Press, c1977. xi, 147 p., [4] leaves of plates : ill. ; 22 cm. Includes index. Bibliography: p. 145-146. [VK140.S36A33] 77-355850 ISBN 0-682-48709-0 : 7.50
1. Sinclair, Robert A. 2. Shipmasters—Ontario—Biography. 3. Great Lakes—Navigation—History. I. Title. **BIP**

Sinclair, Upton Beall, 1878-1968.

DELL, Floyd, 1887- 813'.5'2 B
1969.
Upton Sinclair; a study in social protest. New York, AMS Press [1970, c1927] 194 p. port. 23 cm. Bibliography: p. 189-191. [PS3537.I85Z6 1970] 73-133826 ISBN 0-404-02076-3
1. Sinclair, Upton Beall, 1878-1968.

HARRIS, Leon. 813'.5'2 B
Upton Sinclair, American rebel / by Leon Harris. New York : Crowell, [1975] x, 435 p., [11] leaves of plates : ill. ; 24 cm. Includes index. Bibliography: p. 411-413. [PS3537.I85Z64] 74-23582 ISBN 0-690-00671-3 : 12.95
1. Sinclair, Upton Beall, 1878-1968. I. Title.

SINCLAIR, Mary Craig 928.1
(Kimbrough)
Southern belle. With a foreword by Upton Sinclair. Memorial ed., with pref. and additions. Phoenix, Ariz., Sinclair Press, c1962. 407 p. illus. 23 cm. Autobiography. [PS3537.I 847Z5 1962] 62-13777
1. Sinclair, Upton Beall, 1878- I. Title.

SINCLAIR, Upton Beall 928.1
My lifetime in letters. Columbia, University of Missouri Press [c.1960] xxi, 412p. port. 24cm. 59-14141 6.50
1. Authors—Correspondence, reminiscences, etc. I. Title. **BIP**

SINCLAIR, Upton Beall. 813'.5'2
1878-1968.
American outpost; a book of reminiscences. Port Washington, N.Y., Kennikat Press [1969, c1932] 380 p. port. 21 cm. [PS3537.I85Z5 1969] 76-93072
I. Title.

SINCLAIR, Upton Beall, 813'.5'2
1878-1968.
American outpost; a book of reminiscences. Port Washington, N.Y., Kennikat Press [1969, c1932] 380 p. port. 21 cm. [PS3537.I85Z5 1969] 76-93072
I. Title.

SINCLAIR, Upton Beall, 928.1
1878-1968.
Autobiography. [1st ed.] New York, Harcourt, Brace & World [1962] 342 p. illus. 22 cm. [PS3537.I85Z517] 62-19592

SINCLAIR, Upton Beall, 928.1
1878-1968.
Autobiography. [1st ed.] New York, Harcourt, Brace & World [1962] 342 p. illus. 22 cm. [PS3537.I85Z517] 62-19592

SINCLAIR, Mary Craig 928.1
(Kimbrough)
Southern belle. With a foreword by Upton Sinclair. New York, Crown Publishers [1957] 407 p. illus. 22 cm. Autobiography. [PS3537.I 847Z5] 57-12824
1. Sinclair, Upton Beall, 1878- I. Title.

SINGLAIR, Mary Craig 928.1
(Kimbrough)
Southern belle. Foreword by Upton Sinclair. Memorial ed., with pref. and additions. Phoenix, Ariz., Sinclair Pr., P.O. Box 2503, c.1957, 1962 407p. illus. 23cm. 62-13777 5.95
1. Sinclair, Upton Beall, 1878- I. Title.

UPTON Sinclair; 813'.5'2
biographical and critical opinions. [Folcroft, Pa.] Folcroft Library Editions, 1972. 32 p. port. 24 cm. Reprint of the 1923 ed. "Limited to 150 copies." [PS3537.I85Z9 1972] 72-188929
1. Sinclair, Upton Beall, 1878-1968.

Sinclair, Upton Beall, 1878-1968—Bibliography.

GAER, Joseph, 1897- 016.813'5'2
ed.
Upton Sinclair; bibliography and biographical data. New York, B. Franklin [1971] 54 p. 24 cm. (Burt Franklin bibliography & reference series, 439. Essays in literature and criticism, 169) Reprint of the 1935 ed., which was issued as Monograph 6 of the California Literary Research Project. [Z8819.5.G18 1971] 79-156117 ISBN 0-8337-1262-4
1. Sinclair, Upton Beall, 1878-1968—Bibliography. 2. Sinclair, Upton Beall, 1878-1968. I. Series: California Literary Research Project. Monograph, 6

Siney, John, 1831-1880.

PINKOWSKI, Edward, 1916- 926.22
John Siney, the miners martyr. Philadelphia, Sunshine Pr., 1300 Cypress St. [c.]1963. 335p. illus. 22cm. Bibl. 63-18405 6.00
1. Siney, John, 1831-1880. I. Title.

Singer, Isaac Bashevis,

SINGER, Isaac 892.49'3'3 B
Bashevis, 1904-
A day of pleasure; stories of a boy growing up in Warsaw. With photos. by Roman Vishniac. New York, Farrar, Straus and Giroux [1969] 227 p. illus., ports. 20 cm. Autobiographical. Nineteen autobiographical stories about the author's childhood in Poland from 1908 to 1918. [PJ5129.S49L52 1969] 70-95461 4.50
I. Title. **BIP**

Singer, Isaac Bashevis, 1904- —Biography.

BRANDON, Ruth. 338.7'68'17677
A capitalist romance : Singer and the sewing machine / by Ruth Brandon. 1st ed. Philadelphia : Lippincott, c1977. xiii, 244 p., [8] leaves of plates : ill. ; 24 cm. Includes index. Bibliography: p. 233-236. [TJ140.S59B7] 76-55725 ISBN 0-397-01196-2 : 12.95
1. Singer, Isaac. 2. Sewing-machine industry—United States—History. 3. Inventors—United States—Biography. I. Title.

KRESH, Paul. 839'.09'33 B
Isaac Bashevis Singer, the magician of West 86th Street : a biography / by Paul Kresh. New York : Dial Press, c1979. xx, 441 p., [8] leaves of plates : ill. ; 23 cm. Includes index. Bibliography: p. [421]-427. [PJ5129.S49Z74] 79-18589 ISBN 0-8037-3696-7 : 14.95
1. Singer, Isaac Bashevis, 1904- —Biography. 2. Authors, Yiddish—United States—Biography. I. Title.

Singer, Isaac Bashevis, 1904- — Biography—Youth.

SINGER, Isaac 892.49'3'3 B
Bashevis, 1904-
A day of pleasure; stories of a boy growing up in Warsaw. With photos. by Roman Vishniac. New York, Farrar, Straus and Giroux [1969] 227 p. illus., ports. 20 cm. Autobiographical. Nineteen autobiographical stories about the author's childhood in Poland from 1908 to 1918. [PJ5129.S49L52 1969] 70-95461 4.50
I. Title. **BIP**

SINGER, Isaac 839'.09'33 B
Bashevis, 1904-
A little boy in search of God : mysticism in a personal light / Isaac Bashevis Singer and [illustrated by] Ira Moskowitz. 1st ed. Garden City, N.Y. : Doubleday, 1976. xii, 209 p., [8] leaves of plates : ill. ; 27 cm. [PJ5129.S49Z524] 75-6078 ISBN 0-385-06653-8 : 17.95
1. Singer, Isaac Bashevis, 1904- — Biography—Youth. 2. Singer, Isaac Bashevis, 1904- —Religion and ethics. 3. Authors, Yiddish—Biography. I. Moskowitz, Ira. II. Title. **BIP**

SINGER, Isaac 839'.09'33 B
Bashevis, 1904-
A young man in search of love / Isaac Bashevis Singer ; paintings aand drawings by Raphael Soyer. 1st. ed. Garden City, N.Y. : Doubleday, 1978. 177 p., [4] leaves of plates : ill. ; 25 cm. [PJ5129.S49Z528] 77-2538 ISBN 0-385-12357-4 : 12.95
1. Singer, Isaac Bashevis, 1904- — Biography—Youth. 2. Authors, Yiddish— Biography. I. Title.

Singers.

BRADDON, Russell Reading 927.8
Joan Sutherland. New York, St. Martin s [c.1962] 256p. illus. 22cm. oan, 1926- 62-16181 5.00
I. Title. II. Series.

CLAYTON, Ellen 782.1'0922 B
Creathorne, 1834-1900.
Queens of song; being memoirs of some of the most celebrated female vocalists who have performed on the lyric stage from the earliest days of opera to the present time. To which is added a chronological list of all the operas that have been performed in Europe. Freeport, N.Y., Books for Libraries Press [1972] 543 p. ports. 23 cm. (Essay index reprint series) Reprint of the 1865 ed. Bibliography: p. [xiii]-xiv. [ML400.C51 1972] 77-38713 ISBN 0-8369-2640-4
1. Singers. 2. Opera—Europe. I. Title. **BIP**

DAVIDSON, Gladys. 927.8
A treasury of opera biography. New York, Citadel Press [c1955] 352p. illus. 22cm. Includes bibliography. [ML400.D32] 55-11856
1. Singers. I. Title.

KLEIN, Hermann, 1856-1934. 927.8
Great women-singers of my time. With a foreword by Ernest Newman. New York, E. P. Dutton, 1931. 244 p. 16 port. 21 cm. [ML400.K63] A 31
1. Singers. I. Title.

MATZ, Mary Jane. 927.8
Opera stars in the sun; intimate glimpses of Metropolitan personalities. With a foreword by Milton Cross. Illus. by Susan Perl. New York, Farrar, Straus & Cudahy [1955] 349p. illus. 22cm. [ML400.M37] 55-10782
1. Singers. I. Title.

MILLER, Basil William, 927.8
1897-
Ten singers who became famous. Grand Rapids, Zondervan Pub. House [1954] 87p. illus. 20cm. [ML400.M6] 55-228
1. Singers. I. Title.

ROSENTHAL, Harold D. 784.0922
Great singers of today [by] Harold Rosenthal. London, Calder & Boyars, 1966. 212p. front., illus. (ports.) 29cm. [ML400.R79] 66-70785 12.00
1. Singers. I. Title.
Distributor: Hillary House, New York.

ULRICH, Hormer, 1906- 927.8
Famous women singers. New York, Dodd, Mead, 1953. 127p. illus. 23cm. (Famous biographies for young people) [ML400.U4] 53-5098
1. Singers. I. Title.

Singers, American.

MOORE, Thurston, ed. 927.8
Scrapbook of hillbilly and western stars. Special section starring sacred singers. Edited by Thurston Moore; assistant editor, Leslie Norman. Drawings by M. Smith. Cincinnati, Artist Publications, c1953. unpaged. illus. 21x28cm. [ML400.M78] 54-32393
1. Singers, American. I. Title.

Singers, American—Biography.

PLEASANTS, Henry. 784'.092'2 B
The great American popular singers. New York, Simon and Schuster [1974] 384 p. ports. 24 cm. [ML400.P647] 73-16878 ISBN 0-671-21681-3 9.95
1. Singers, American—Biography. 2. Music, Popular (Songs, etc.)—United States—History and criticism. I. Title. **BIP**

Singers, American—Juvenile literature.

SURGE, Frank. 784'.0922
Singers of the blues. Minneapolis, Lerner Publications Co. [1969] 63 p. illus., ports. 21 cm. (A Pull ahead book) Brief biographies of seventeen singers and musicians who helped develop the blues style and became legendary performers during their lifetime. [ML3930.A2S9] 920 68-30570
1. Singers, American—Juvenile literature. 2. Jazz musicians—Juvenile literature. I. Title. **BIP**

Singers—Biography.

BRESLIN, Herbert 782.1'092'2 B
H., comp.
The tenors. Edited by Herbert H. Breslin. New York, Macmillan Pub. Co. [1974] xv, 203 p. illus. 21 cm. Contents.Contents.— Bender, W. Richard Tucker.—Ardoin, J. Jon Vickers.—Downs, J. Franco Corelli.— Rich, A. Placido Domingo.—Rubin, S. E. Luciano Pavarotti. [ML400.B745T4] 74-11332 ISBN 0-02-515000-6 7.95
1. Singers—Biography. I. Title.
Contents omitted.

EDWARDS, Henry 782.1'092'2 B
Sutherland, 1828-1906.
The prima donna : her history and surroundings from the seventeenth to the nineteenth century / by H. Sutherland Edwards. New York : Da Capo Press, 1978. 2 v. ; 23 cm. (Da Capo Press music reprints series) Reprint of the 1888 ed. published by Remington, London. Includes indexes. [ML400.E28 1978] 77-17875 ISBN 0-306-77536-0 lib.bdg. : 42.50
1. Singers—Biography. 2. Opera. I. Title.

FERRIS, George 784'.092'2 B
Titus, b.1840.
Great singers. Freeport, N.Y., Books for Libraries Press [1972] 2 v. 22 cm. (Essay index reprint series) Originally published 1879-1881, New York. Contents.Contents.—1st ser. Faustina Bordoni. Catarina Gabrielli. Sophie Arnould. Elizabeth Billington and her contemporaries. Angelica Catalani. Ciuditta Pasta. Henrietta Sontag.—2d ser. Maria Felicia Malibran. Wilhelmina Schroder-Dervient. Giulia Grisi. Pauline Viardot. Fanny Persiani. Marietta Alboni. Jenny Lind. Sophie Cruvelli. Theresa Titiens. [ML400.F39 1972] 72-6821 ISBN 0-8369-7259-7 (v. 1)
1. Singers—Biography. I. Title.

KLEIN, Hermann, 1856- 782'.0922
1934.
Great women-singers of my time, by Herman Klein. With a foreword by Ernest Newman. Freeport, N.Y., Books for Libraries Press [1968] vi, 244 p. illus. 22 cm. (Essays index reprint series) [ML400.K63 1968] 68-16943
1. Singers—Biography. I. Title. **BIP**

KUTSCH, K. J. 784'.0922 B
A concise biographical dictionary of singers; from the beginning of recorded sound to the present, by K. J. Kutsch and Leo Riemens. Translated from German, expanded and annotated by Harry Earl Jones. [1st American ed.] Philadelphia, Chilton Book Co. [1969] xxiv, 487 p. 21 cm. Translation of Unvergangliche Stimmen: Kleines Sangerlexikon. [ML400.K9813 1969] 79-94106
1. Singers—Biography. I. Riemens, Leo, joint author. II. Title.

LAHEE, Henry 782.1'092'2 B
Charles, 1856-1953.
Famous singers of today and yesterday / by Henry C. Lahee. Boston : Longwood Press, 1978. p. cm. Reprint of the 1898 ed. published by L. C. Page, Boston. "Chronological table of famous singers": p. [ML400.L18 1978] 78-13904 ISBN 0-89341-438-7 lib.bdg. : 35.00
1. Singers—Biography. I. Title. **BIP**

MATZ, Mary Jane. 782.1'092'2 B
Opera stars in the sun; intimate glimpses of Metropolitan personalities. With a foreword by Milton Cross. Illus. by Susan Perl. Westport, Conn., Greenwood Press [1973, c1955] xiv, 349 p. illus. 22 cm. Reprint of the ed. published by Farrar, Straus & Cudahy, New York, and sponsored by the Metropolitan Opera Guild. [ML400.M37 1973] 73-2642 ISBN 0-8371-6813-9 15.00
1. Singers—Biography. I. Metropolitan Opera Guild. II. Title.

PLEASANTS, Henry. 782.0922
The great singers; from the dawn of opera to our own time. New York, Simon and Schuster [1966] 382 p. illus., music, ports. 24 cm. Bibliography: p. 361-365. [ML400.P65] 66-20250
1. Singers—Biography. I. Title.

ROGERS, Francis, 782.1'092'2 B
1870-1951.
Some famous singers of the 19th century / Francis Rogers. New York : Arno Press, 1977 [c1914] 128 p., [10] leaves of plates : ill. ; 21 cm. (Opera biographies) Reprint of the ed. published by H. W. Gray, New York. Contents.Contents.—The two Manuel Garcias.—Maria and Pauline Garcia.—Catalani and Pasta.—Luigi Lablache.—Three tenors (Rubini, Nourrit, Duprez)—Sontag and Lind.—Grisi, Mario and Tamburini.—Some conclusions. [ML400.R75 1977] 76-29963 ISBN 0-405-09703-4 lib.bdg. : 11.00
1. Singers—Biography. I. Title.
Contents omitted **BIP**

ROSENTHAL, Harold 782.1'092'2 B
D.
Great singers of today / Harold Rosenthal. New York : Arno Press, 1977, c1966. 212 p. : ill. ; 29 cm. (Opera biographies) Reprint of the ed. published by Calder & Boyars, London. [ML400.R775 1977] 76-29964 ISBN 0-405-09704-2 : 16.00
1. Singers—Biography. I. Title. **BIP**

Singers—Correspondence, reminiscences, etc.

ALDA, Frances. 782.1'0924 B
Men, women, and tenors. New York, AMS Press [1971] 307 p. illus., ports. 23 cm. Reprint of the 1937 ed. [ML420.A56A3 1971] 75-149653 ISBN 0-404-00306-0
1. Singers—Correspondence, reminiscences, etc. 2. Opera—New York (City) 3. Singers. I. Title.

LEHMANN, Lotte. 782.1'0924 B
Midway in my song; the autobiography of Lotte Lehmann. Westport, Conn., Greenwood Press [1970] ix, 250 p. illus., ports. 23 cm. Reprint of the 1938 ed. London ed. (K. Paul, Trench, Trubner) has title: Wings of song. Translation of Anfang und Aufstieg. [ML420.L33A33 1970b] 70-109765 ISBN 0-8371-4255-5
1. Singers—Correspondence, reminiscences, etc. I. Title.

RIDDLE, Almeda. 784'.0924
A singer and her songs; Almeda Riddle's book of ballads. Edited by Roger D. Abrahams. Music editor, George Foss. Baton Rouge, Louisiana State University Press, 1970. xi, 191 p. illus., music, ports. 25 cm. Autobiographical. [ML420.R53A3] 77-122352 ISBN 0-8071-0021-8 8.50
1. Singers—Correspondence, reminiscences, etc. 2. Ballads, American— History and criticism. I. Abrahams, Roger D., ed. II. Title. **BIP**

SHALIAPIN, Fedor 782.1'0924 B
Ivanovich, 1873-1938.
Man and mask; forty years in the life of a singer, by Feodor Chaliapin. Translated from the French for the first time by Phyllis Megroz. Westport, Conn., Greenwood Press [1970] xxvi, 358 p. illus., ports. 23 cm. Reprint of the 1932 ed. Translation of Maska i dusha (romanized form) [ML420.S53A312] 70-109841 ISBN 0-8371-4332-2
1. Singers—Correspondence, reminiscences, etc. I. Title.

Singers, English—Biography.

BROOK, Donald. 784'.0922 B
Singers of today. Freeport, N.Y., Books for Libraries Press [1971, c1969] 226 p. ports. 23 cm. (Biography index reprint series) [ML400.B88 1971] 70-160917 ISBN 0-8369-8080-8
1. Singers, English—Biography. I. Title. **BIP**

Singers—United States—Biography.

BALLIETT, Whitney. 784'.092'2 B
American singers / Whitney Balliett. New York : Oxford University Press, 1979. x, 178 p. ; 22 cm. "A group of portraits of leading American popular and jazz singers." [ML400.B25] 78-21545 ISBN 0-19-502524-5 : 10.00
1. Singers—United States—Biography. 2. Jazz musicians—United States—Biography. I. Title. **BIP**

Singh, Bakht.

SMITH, Daniel, 1915?- 922.342
Bakht Singh of India, a prophet of God. Foreword by H. Enoch. Introd. by Robert V. Finlay. Washington, International Students Press [1959] 87 p. illus., ports. 22 cm. [BV3269.S5S6] 67-4582
1. Singh, Bakht. 2. Evangelistic work — India. 3. Missions — India. I. Title.

Singh, Sundar, 1889-

DAVEY, Cyril James 922
The story of Sadhu Sundar Singh, the yellow robe. Chicago, Moody [1964] 158p. 18cm. (86) .59 pap.,
1. Singh, Sundar, 1889- I. Title.

DAVEY, Cyril James. 922
The story of Sadhu Sundar Singh, the yellow robe. Chicago, Moody [1964] 158p. 18 cm. (86) pap., .59
1. Singh, Sundar, 1889- I. Title.

LYNCH-WATSON, 266'.023'0924 B
Janet.
The saffron robe : a life of Sadhu Sundar Singh / by Janet Lynch-Watson. Grand Rapids, Mich. : Zondervan Pub. House, 1976, c1975. 157 p. ; 18 cm. Reprint of the ed. published by Hodder and Stoughton, London, in series: Hodder Christian paperbacks. [BV5095.S5L9 1976] 76-44813 pbk. : 1.75
1. Singh, Sundar, 1889- 2. Christian biography—India. I. Title.

Singleton, George A.

SINGLETON, George A. 922.773
The autobiography of George A. Singleton, Boston, Forum [c.1964] 272p. illus., ports. 22cm. 64-56507 5.00
I. Title.

Singleton, John Wesley.

HUGHES, Mary Kent. 926.1
Pioneer doctor; a biography of John Singleton. Melbourne, Oxford University Press, 1950. 163 p. illus. 22 cm. [R674.S5H8] 51-37569
1. Singleton, John Wesley. I. Title.

KENT HUGHES, Mary Ethel 926.1
Josephine (Cantwell) Thornton.
Pioneer doctor; a biography of John Singleton. Melbourne, Oxford University Press, 1950. 163p. illus. 22cm. [R674.S5K4] 51-37569

1. Singleton, John Wesley. I. Title.

Sinkler family.

SINKLER, Louise E. 917.3'03'91
Leaves folded down, by Louise E. Sinkler. Wayne, Pa., Haverford House, 1971. 216 p. illus. 27 cm. Autobiographical. [CS71.S6167 1971] 72-176079
1. Sinkler family. 2. Elkins family. I. Title.

Sirhan, Sirhan Bishara, 1944-

KAISER, Robert Blair. 364.15'24'0924
"R. F. K. must die!" A history of the Robert Kennedy assassination and its aftermath. [1st ed.] New York, Dutton, 1970. 634 p. facsims. 25 cm. [E840.8.K4K3 1970] 74-86074 9.95
1. Sirhan, Sirhan Bishara, 1944- 2. Kennedy, Robert F., 1925-1968—Assassination. I. Title.

Siringo, Charles A., 1855-1928.

APPLEMAN, Roy Edgar. 364.12'0924 B
Charlie Siringo, cowboy detective, by Roy E. Appleman. Washington, Potomac Corral, The Westerners, 1968. 19 p. ports. 23 cm. (The Great western series, no. 3) Bibliography: p. 18. [PS3537.I89Z56] 68-58272
1. Siringo, Charles A., 1855-1928. I. Title.

SIRINGO, Charles A., 1855-1928. 976.4'06'0924 B
A Texas cowboy : or, Fifteen years on the hurricane deck of a Spanish pony, taken from real life / by Charles A. Siringo ; with bibliographical study & introd. by J. Frank Dobie, including addenda to the 1886 ed. ; and drawings by Tom Lea. Lincoln : University of Nebraska Press, c1979. xl, 216 p. : ill. ; 21 cm. "A Bison book." "Bibliography of Siringo's writings": p. xxxvii-xl. [F391.S624A37 1979] 79-63094 ISBN 0-8032-9111-6 pbk. : 4.25
1. Siringo, Charles A., 1855-1928. 2. Frontier and pioneer life—Texas. 3. Cowboys—Texas—Biography. 4. Texas—History—1846-1950. 5. Texas—Biography. I. Title.

Sirk, Douglas, 1900

STERN, Michael, 1946- 791.43'0233'0924
Douglas Sirk / Michael Stern. Boston : Twayne Publishers, 1979. p. cm. (Twayne's theatrical arts series) Includes index. Bibliography: p. [PN1998.A3S54536] 79-13126 ISBN 0-8057-9269-4 : 9.95
1. Sirk, Douglas, 1900- BIP

Sissle, Noble, 1889-

KIMBALL, Robert. 782.8'1'0922 B
Reminiscing with Sissle and Blake, by Robert Kimball and William Bolcom. New York, Viking Press [1973] 254 p. illus. 29 cm. "Appendixes ... An attempt to catalogue the immense output of Sissle and Blake, as a team, separately, and as collaborators with other writers.": p. 240-254. [ML3556.K55] 72-91100 ISBN 0-670-59388-5 12.95
1. Sissle, Noble, 1889- 2. Blake, Eubie, 1883- 3. Negro musicians. I. Bolcom, William, joint author. II. Title. BIP

Sita Ram Pandey,

SITA Ram Pandey, b.1797. 355.3'32'0924 B
From sepoy to subedar; being the life and adventures of Subedar Sita Ram, a native officer of the Bengal Army written and related by himself. Edited by James Lunt. Translated and first published by Lieutenant-Colonel Norgate, Bengal Staff Corps at Lahore, 1873. Illustrated by Frank Wilson. [Hamden, Conn.] Archon Books, 1970. xxix, 186 p. illus., maps. 24 cm. [U55.S45A313 1970c] 73-19501
I. Lunt, James D., 1917- ed. II. Norgate, James Thomas, 1824-1894, tr. III. Wilson, Frank, 1901- illus. IV. Title. BIP

Sitenhop, Yente (Glaser)

BUKSBAZEN, Lydia (Sitenhof) 1908- 922.96
They looked for a city. Philadelphia, Friends of Israel Missionary and Relief Society [1955] 216p. illus. 20cm. [BV2622.S5B8] 56-17705
1. Sitenhop, Yente (Glaser) 2. Sitenhof, Benjamin. I. Title. BIP

Sites, David Eston,

SITES, David Eston, 1888- 917.3'03'90924 B
My first eighty years. Philadelphia, Dorrance [1970] 145 p. 22 cm. [CT275.S5218A3] 73-106351
I. Title.

Sitte, Willi.

SITTE, Willi. 741.973
Willi Sitte : Gemalde und Zeichnungen, 1950-1974 : [Ausstellung] Kunstverein in Hamburg, 12. April bis 18. Mai 1975. Hamburg : Kunstverein, [1975?] 108 p. : ill. (some col.) ; 24 cm. Bibliography: p. 101-103. [ND588.S474K86] 75-510364
1. Sitte, Willi. I. Kunstverein in Hamburg.

Sitting Bull, Dakota Chief, 1831-1890.

ADAMS, Alexander B. 970.3 B
Sitting Bull; an epic of the plains, by Alexander B. Adams. New York, Putnam Sons [1973] 446 p. illus. 22 cm. Bibliography: p. 423-431. [E99.D1S56] 72-79517 ISBN 0-399-10986-2 9.95
1. Sitting Bull, Dakota Chief, 1831-1890. 2. Teton Indians—Wars.

JOHNSON, Dorothy M. 970.3 B
Warrior for a lost nation: a biography of Sitting Bull, by Dorothy M. Johnson. With Sitting Bull's own pictographs. Philadelphia, Westminster Press [1969] 173 p. illus., port. 23 cm. Bibliography: p. 163-165. A biography of the warrior, prophet, and chief of the Sioux tribes who led his people's resistance to the advancing white man during the second half of the nineteenth century. [E99.D1J56] 92 69-12298 3.95
1. Sitting Bull, Dakota chief, 1831-1890. I. Title.

O'CONNOR, Richard, 1915- 970.3 B
Sitting Bull, war chief of the Sioux. Illustrated by Eric von Schmidt. New York, McGraw-Hill [1968] 144 p. illus. 21 cm. A biography of the Sioux chief who led the Indians at Custer's Last Stand, but who was also a man of mercy, wisdom, and pride seeking a peaceful existence for his people. [E99.D1O25] 92 AC 68
1. Sitting Bull, Dakota chief, 1831-1890. I. Von Schmidt, Eric, illus. II. Title.

VESTAL, Stanley, 1887- 970.2
Sitting Bull, champion of the Sioux; a biography. [New ed.] Norman, University of Oklahoma Press [1957] 349 p. illus. 24 cm. (The Civilization of the American Indian series) Includes bibliography. [E99.D1S627 1957] 57-5961
1. Sitting Bull, Dakota chief, 1831-1890. BIP

WHITTAKER, Jane. 970.3 B
Patriots of the plains: Sitting Bull, Crazy Horse, Chief Joseph. New York, Scholastic Book Services [1973] 128 p. illus. 21 cm. (Firebird books) [E99.D1W85] 72-90573 1.24 (pbk.)
1. Sitting Bull, Dakota chief, 1831-1890. 2. Crazy Horse, Oglala Indian, 1842 (ca.)-1877. 3. Joseph, Nez Perce chief, 1840-1904. I. Title.
Library binding; 2.79.

Sitting Bull, Dakota Chief, 1831-1890—Juvenile literature.

ANDERSON, LaVere. 970.3 B
Sitting Bull, great Sioux chief. Illustrated by Cary. Champaign, Ill., Garrard Pub. Co. [1970] 80 p. col. illus., map. 23 cm. A biography of the Sioux chief who was both feared and respected for his attempts to win peace and justice for his people. [E99.D1A5] 92 70-120462 2.39
1. Sitting Bull, Dakota chief, 1831-1890—Juvenile literature. I. Cary, illus. II. Title. BIP

FRONVAL, George. 973.8'0924 B
Sitting Bull, the great Sioux chief; illustrated by Jean Marcellin [translated from the French] Feltham, Odhams, 1968. 5-68 p. col. illus. 31 cm. Col. illus. on lining papers. A biography of the Sioux medicine man and chief who devoted his life to maintaining the rights of the Indian people. [E99.D1S60453] 92 75-480517 16/-
1. Sitting Bull, Dakota chief, 1831-1890—Juvenile literature. I. Marcellin, Jean, illus. II. Title.

KNOOP, Faith Yingling. 970.3 B
Sitting Bull. Minneapolis, Dillon Press [1974] 74 p. illus. 23 cm. (The Story of an American Indian) Running title: The story of Sitting Bull. A biography of the medicine man, artist, singer, storyteller, and warrior who was the only man ever to be chief of all the Plains Sioux. [E99.D1K58] 92 74-12015 ISBN 0-87518-065-5
1. Sitting Bull, Dakota chief, 1831-1890—Juvenile literature. I. Title. II. Title: The story of Sitting Bull. BIP

MAY, Julian. 970.3 B
Sitting Bull, chief of the Sioux. Illustrated by Phero Thomas. Mankato, Minn., Creative Educational Society [1973] [38] p. illus. 24 cm. (Personal close-up books) A brief biography of the Sioux Indian who defeated Custer at Big Horn and who led his people to Canada in search of safety and food. [E99.D1M45] 92 72-89462 ISBN 0-87191-221-X 4.95 (lib. bdg.)
1. Sitting Bull, Dakota chief, 1831-1890—Juvenile literature. I. Thomas, Phero, illus. II. Title.

O'CONNOR, Richard, 1915- 92 (J)
Sitting Bull, war chief of the Sioux. Illustrated by Eric von Schmidt. New York, McGraw-Hill [1968] 144 p. illus. 21 cm. [E99.D1O25] 68-13523
1. Sitting Bull, Dakota chief, 1811-1890—Juvenile literature.

Sitwell, Constance Talbot, 1887- —Diaries.

SITWELL, Constance Talbot, 1887- 828'.9'1209 B
Bounteous days / Constance Sitwell ; with an introd. by James Pope Hennessy. London : C. Woolf, c1976. 73 p., [1] leaf of plates : ill. ; 22 cm. [PR6037.I788Z52] 77-360682 ISBN 0-900821-32-9 : £2.50
1. Sitwell, Constance Talbot, 1887- —Diaries. 2. Authors, English—20th century—Biography. I. Title.

Sitwell, Edith, Dame, 1887-1964.

LEHMANN, John, 1907- 820.9'009'12
A nest of tigers; the Sitwells in their times. [1st Amer. ed.] Boston, Little, Brown [1968] x, 294p. illus., ports. 22cm. Atlantic Monthly Pr. bk. Bibl. [PR6037.I79L4 1968b] (B) 68-24243 6.95
1. Sitwell, Dame Edith, 1887-1964. 2. Sitwell, Sir Osbert, bart., 1892- 3. Sitwell, Sacheverell, 1897- I. Title.

LINDSAY, Jack, 1900- 809.1
Meetings with poets; memories of Dylan Thomas, Edith Sitwell, Louis Aragon, Paul Eluard, Tristan Tzara. [1st American ed.] New York, Ungar [1969, c1968] viii, 245 p. 23 cm. [PR6037.I8Z66 1969] 73-81572 ISBN 0-8044-2526-4 6.00
1. Sitwell, Edith, Dame, 1887-1964. 2. Poets—Biography. I. Title.

LINDSAY, Jack, 1900- 809.1
Meetings with poets; memories of Dylan Thomas, Edith Sitwell, Louis Aragon, Paul Eluard, Tristan Tzara. [1st American ed.] New York, Ungar [1969, c1968] viii, 245 p. 23 cm. [PR6037.I8Z66 1969] 73-81572 ISBN 0-8044-2526-4 6.00
1. Sitwell, Edith, Dame, 1887-1964. 2. Poets—Biography. I. Title.

MEGROZ, Rodolphe Louis, 1891- 820.9'009'12
The three Sitwells; a biographical and critical study, by R. L. Megroz. London, Richards Press, 1927. St. Clair Shores, Mich., Scholarly Press, 1971. 333 p. 22 cm. Bibliography: p. 333. [PR6037.I79M4 1971] 79-145174 ISBN 0-403-01102-7
1. Sitwell, Edith, Dame, 1887-1964. 2. Sitwell, Osbert, Sir, bart., 1892-1969. 3. Sitwell, Sacheverell, Sir, bart., 1897- I. Title.

MEGROZ, Rodolphe Louis, 1891- 820.9'009'12
The three Sitwells; a biographical and critical study, by R. L. Megroz. London, Richards Press, 1927. St. Clair Shores, Mich., Scholarly Press, 1971. 333 p. 22 cm. Bibliography: p. 333. [PR6037.I79M4 1971] 79-145174 ISBN 0-403-01102-7
1. Sitwell, Edith, Dame, 1887-1964. 2. Sitwell, Osbert, Sir, bart., 1892-1969. 3. Sitwell, Sacheverell, Sir, bart., 1897- I. Title.

MEGROZ, Rodolphe Louis, 1891- 828'.9'1209
The three Sitwells; a biographical and critical study, by R. L. Megroz. Port Washington, N.Y., Kennikat Press [1969] 333 p. 21 cm. Reprint of the 1927 ed. "Bibliographical list of books by the Sitwells": p. 333. [PR6037.I79M4 1969] 68-26215
1. Sitwell, Edith, Dame, 1887-1964. 2. Sitwell, Osbert, Sir, bart., 1892-1969. 3. Sitwell, Sacheverell, Sir, bart, 1897- I. Title. BIP

MEGROZ, Rodolphe Louis, 1891- 828'.9'1209
The three Sitwells; a biographical and critical study, by R. L. Megroz. Port Washington, N.Y., Kennikat Press [1969] 333 p. 21 cm. Reprint of the 1927 ed. "Bibliographical list of books by the Sitwells": p. 333. [PR6037.I79M4 1969] 68-26215
1. Sitwell, Edith, Dame, 1887-1964. 2. Sitwell, Osbert, Sir, bart., 1892-1969. 3. Sitwell, Sacheverell, Sir, bart, 1897- I. Title. BIP

PEARSON, John, 1930- 820'.9'00912 B
The Sitwells : a family's biography / John Pearson. 1st American ed. New York : Harcourt Brace Jovanovich, 1979, c1978. 534 p., [10] leaves of plates : ill. ; 24 cm. Originally published under the title: Facades. Includes index. Bibliography: p. [509]-521. [PR6037.I8Z73 1979] 78-22268 ISBN 0-15-182703-6 : 15.00
1. Sitwell, Edith, Dame, 1887-1964—Biography. 2. Sitwell, Osbert, Sir, bart., 1892-1969—Biography. 3. Sitwell, Sacheverall, Sir, bart., 1897- —Biography. 4. Authors, English—20th century—Biography. I. Title. BIP

SITWELL, Dame Edith, 1887-1964 928.2
Taken care of: the autobiography of Edith Sitwell 1st Amer. ed. New York, Atheneum [c.]1965. xii, 239p. illus., ports. 25cm. Bibl. [PR6037.I8Z5] 65-10912 5.95
I. Title.

SITWELL, Edith, Dame 1887-1964. 928.2
Taken care of: the autobiography of Edith Sitwell. [1st American ed.] New York, Atheneum, 1965. xii, 239 p. illus., ports. 25 cm. "Books by Edith Sitwell": p. 231-[232] [PR6037.I 8Z5] 65-10912
I. Title.

Sitwell, Edith, Dame, 1887-1964—Biography.

PEARSON, John, 1930- 820'.9'00912 B
The Sitwells : a family's biography / John Pearson. 1st American ed. New York : Harcourt Brace Jovanovich, 1979, c1978. 534 p., [10] leaves of plates : ill. ; 24 cm. Originally published under the title: Facades. Includes index. Bibliography: p. [509]-521. [PR6037.I8Z73 1979] 78-22268 ISBN 0-15-182703-6 : 15.00
1. Sitwell, Edith, Dame, 1887-1964—Biography. 2. Sitwell, Osbert, Sir, bart., 1892-1969—Biography. 3. Sitwell, Sacheverall, Sir, bart., 1897- —Biography. 4. Authors, English—20th century—Biography. I. Title. BIP

Sitwell family.

SITLWELL, Osbert, Sir, bart., 1892- 928.2
Left hand, right hand! Boston, Atlantic-Little [1964, c.1943, 1944] xvi, 327[1]p. 20cm. (48) 2.25 pap.,
1. Sitwell family. I. Title.

SITWELL, Osbert, Sir, bart., 1892- 928.2
Left hand, right hand! [Gloucester, mMss., P. Smith, 1965, c.1943, 1944] xvi, 327p. 20cm. (Atlantic-Little bk. rebound) [PR6037.I82Z5] 4.25
1. Sitwell family. I. Title.

Sitwell, George Reresby, Sir Bart., 1860-1943.

SITWELL, Osbert, bart. [Francis Osbert Sacheverell Sitwell] Sir 1892- 928.2
Tales my father taught me; an evocation of extravagant episodes. Boston, Atlantic-Little [c.1957-1962] 206p. illus. 22cm. 62-9554 4.75
1. Sitwell, George Reresby, bart., Sir 1860-1943. I. Title.

Sitwell, Osbert, Sir, bart., 1892-1969.

LEHMANN, John, 1907- 820.9'009'12
A nest of tigers; the Sitwells in their times. [1st Amer. ed.] Boston, Little, Brown [1968] x, 294p. illus., ports. 22cm. Atlantic Monthly Pr. bk. Bibl. [PR6037.I79L4 1968b] (B) 68-24243 6.95
1. Sitwell, Dame Edith, 1887-1964. 2. Sitwell, Sir Osbert, bart., 1892- 3. Sitwell, Sacheverall, 1897- I. Title.

MEGROZ, Rodolphe Louis, 1891- 820.9'009'12
The three Sitwells; a biographical and critical study, by R. L. Megroz. London, Richards Press, 1927. St. Clair Shores, Mich., Scholarly Press, 1971. 333 p. 22 cm. Bibliography: p. 333. [PR6037.I79M4 1971] 79-145174 ISBN 0-403-01102-7
1. Sitwell, Edith, Dame, 1887-1964. 2. Sitwell, Osbert, Sir, bart., 1892-1969. 3. Sitwell, Sacheverall, Sir, bart., 1897- I. Title.

MEGROZ, Rodolphe Louis, 1891- 828'.9'1209
The three Sitwells; a biographical and critical study, by R. L. Megroz. Port Washington, N.Y., Kennikat Press [1969] 333 p. 21 cm. Reprint of the 1927 ed. "Bibliographical list of books by the Sitwells": p. 333. [PR6037.I79M4 1969] 68-26215
1. Sitwell, Edith, Dame, 1887-1964. 2. Sitwell, Osbert, Sir, bart., 1892-1969. 3. Sitwell, Sacheverell, Sir, bart, 1897- I. Title. BIP

SITWELL, Osbert, bart., Sir 1892- 928.2
Noble essences, a book of characters. New York, Grosset & Dunlap [1957, c1950] 356p. 21cm. (Grosset's universal library, UL14) The final vol. of the autobiography. Earlier vols. were Left hand. right hand! The scarlet tree, Great morning and Laughter in the next room. [PR6037] 57-13643
1. Authors, English. 2. Authors—Correspondence, reminiscences. etc. I. Title.

SITWELL, Osbert, Sir, bart., 1892-1969. 828'.9'1209 B
Great morning! Westport, Conn., Greenwood Press [1972, c1947] xv, 360 p. 22 cm. A continuation of the autobiographies, Left hand, right hand! and The scarlet tree. [PR6037.I83Z514 1972] 79-156212 ISBN 0-8371-6162-2 15.25
I. Title. BIP

SITWELL, Osbert, Sir, bart., 1892-1969. 828'.9'1209 B
Laughter in the next room. Westport, Conn., Greenwood Press [1972, c1948] 400 p. 23 cm. A continuation of the autobiographies, Left hand, right hand! The scarlet tree, and Great morning! [PR6037.I83Z515 1972] 79-152607 ISBN 0-8371-6042-1 16.25
I. Title. BIP

SITWELL, Osbert, Sir, bart., 1892-1969. 828'.9'1209 B
Noble essences; a book of characters. Westport, Conn., Greenwood Press [1972, c1950] 356 p. 23 cm. Includes bibliographical references. [PR6037.I83Z517 1972] 72-152608 ISBN 0-8371-6043-X 15.25
I. Title.

*SITWELL, Sir Osbert, bart, 1892- 928.2
Left hand, right hand! Gloucester, Mass., Peter Smith, 1972. xvi, 327 p. 21 cm. This is the first of a series of family memoirs including The scarlet tree, Great morning and Laughter in the next room. [PR6037.] 5.50
I. Title. BIP

SITWELL, Sir Osbert, bart., 1892- 928.2
Noble essences; a book of characters. [1st ed.] Boston, Little, Brown, 1950. 356 p. 23 cm. "An Atlantic Monthly Press book." The final vol. of the autobiography. Earlier vols. were Left hand, right hand! The scarlet tree, Great morning, and Laughter in the next room. Full name: Sir Francis Osbert Sacheverell Sitwell, bart. [PR6037.I 83Z517] 50-9728
I. Title.

SITWELL, Sir Osbert, bart. 1892- 928.2
Noble essences a book of characters. New York, Grosset & Dunlap [1957, c1950] 356 p. 21 cm. (Grosset's universal library, UL14) The final vol. of the autobiography.Earlier vols. were Left hand, right hand! The scarlet tree, Great morning and Laughter in the next room. [[PR6037)] 57-13643
1. Authors, English. 2. Authors — Correspondence, reminiscences, etc. I. Title.

Sitwell, Osbert, Sir, bart., 1892-1969—Biography.

PEARSON, John, 1930- 820'.9'00912 B
The Sitwells : a family's biography / John Pearson. 1st American ed. New York : Harcourt Brace Jovanovich, 1979, c1978. 534 p., [10] leaves of plates : ill. ; 24 cm. Originally published under the title: Facades. Includes index. Bibliography: p. [509]-521. [PR6037.I8Z73 1979] 78-22268 ISBN 0-15-182703-6 : 15.00
1. Sitwell, Edith, Dame, 1887-1964—Biography. 2. Sitwell, Osbert, Sir, bart., 1892-1969—Biography. 3. Sitwell, Sacheverall, Sir, bart., 1897- —Biography. 4. Authors, English—20th century—Biography. I. Title. BIP

SITWELL, Osbert, Sir, bart., 1892-1969. 828'.9'1203 B
Queen Mary and others. New York, John Day Co. [1975, c1974] 171 p. illus. 22 cm. [PR6037.I83Q4 1975] 74-9361 ISBN 0-381-98279-3
1. Sitwell, Osbert, Sir, bart., 1892-1969—Biography. I. Title.

Sitwell, Sacheverell, Sir, bart., 1897-1969.

SITWELL, Sacheverell, Sir, bart., 1897-1969. 828'.9'1203 B
All summer in a day; an autobiographical fantasia, by Sacheverell Sitwell. London, Duckworth, 1926. St. Clair Shores, Mich., Scholarly Press, 1973. p. [PR6037.I85Z5 1973] 77-145302 ISBN 0-403-01214-7 14.50
1. Sitwell, Sacheverell, Sir, bart., 1897-1969. I. Title.

Siwundhla, Alice Princess (Msumba)

SIWUNDHLA, Alice Princess (Msumba) 920
Alice Princess; an autobiography [Pref. by Ralph Edwards. Omaha, Neb., Pacific Pr., c.1965] vii, 166p. illus., ports. 23cm. [CT1968.S55A3] 65-25620 2.95
I. Title.

SIWUNDHLA, Alice Princess (Msumba) 920
My two worlds. Mountain View, Calif., Pacific Press Pub. Association [1971] 198 p. illus., ports. 23 cm. [CT1968.S55A33] 79-155491
I. Title.

Sizemore, Chris Costner.

SIZEMORE, Chris Costner. 616.8'523 B
I'm Eve / Chris Costner Sizemore and Elen Sain Pittillo. 1st ed. Garden City, N.Y. : Doubleday, 1977. xiii, 461 p., [6] leaves of plates : ill. ; 22 cm. Autobiographical. [RC569.5.M8S59] 76-42396 ISBN 0-385-12062-1 : 10.00
1. Sizemore, Chris Costner. 2. Multiple personality—Biography. I. Pittillo, Elen Sain, joint author. II. Title. BIP

Skarstedt, Ernst Teofil, 1857-1929.

LINDQUIST, Emory Kempton, 1908- 301.451395073 S
An immigrant's American odyssey : a biography of Ernst Skarstedt / by Emory Lindquist. Rock Island, Ill. : Augustana Historical Society, [1974] xi, 240 p., [5] leaves of plates : ill. ; 25 cm. (Augustana Historical Society publication ; no. 24) Includes index. Bibliography: p. [233]-235. [F536.A96 vol. 24] [PN4874.S518] 070.4'092'4 B 74-21137 ISBN 0-910184-24-0 : 5.95
1. Skarstedt, Ernst Teofil, 1857-1929. I. Title. II. Series: Augustana Historical Society, Rock Island, Ill. Publication ; no. 24. BIP

Skaters—Biography—Juvenile literature.

LITSKY, Frank. 796.9'1'0922 B
Winners on the ice / by Frank Litsky. New York : F. Watts, 1979. 42 p. : ill. ; 23 cm. (A Picture life book) Biographical sketches of eight athletes who worked to become skating champions. [GV850.A2L57] 920 78-23454 ISBN 0-531-02291-9 lib. bdg. : 5.45
1. Skaters—Biography—Juvenile literature. I. Title. BIP

Skattebol, Olaf, 1847-1930.

SKATTEBoL, Olaf, 1847-1930. 284'.1'0924 B
Translation of extracts of biographical notes, memories from childhood, youth, etc. / written by Olaf Skattebol ; [translated by Enevold F. Schroder]. Oslo : Enevold F. Schroder, 1976] 25 leaves ; 30 cm. Cover title. [BX8080.S396A3513] 76-381853
1. Skattebol, Olaf, 1847-1930. 2. Lutheran Church—Clergy—Biography. 3. Clergy—Norway—Biography. I. Title.

Skelton, John, 1460?-1529.

EDWARDS, H. L. R. 821'.2 B
Skelton, the life and times of an early Tudor poet, by H. L. R. Edwards. Freeport, N.Y., Books for Libraries Press [1971] 325 p. 23 cm. (Library of Old English and medieval literature) Reprint of the 1949 ed. Includes bibliographical references. [PR2348.E4 1971] 77-148879 ISBN 0-8369-5673-7
1. Skelton, John, 1460?-1529. I. Title. BIP

†LLOYD, Leslie John. 821'.2 B
John Skelton : a sketch of his life and writings / by L. J. Lloyd. Folcroft, Pa. : Folcroft Library Editions, 1976. 152 p. ; 26 cm. Reprint of the 1938 ed. published by B. Blackwell, Oxford. Includes bibliographical references and index. [PR2348.L5 1976] 76-26921 ISBN 0-8414-5804-9 lib. bdg. : 25.00
1. Skelton, John, 1460?-1529. 2. Poets, English—Early modern, 1500-1700—Biography. BIP

LLOYD, Leslie John. 821'.2
John Skelton; a sketch of his life and writings, by L. J. Lloyd. New York, Russell & Russell [1969] 152 p. facsim. 23 cm. Reprint of the 1938 ed., with a new pref. by the author. [PR2348.L5 1969] 78-80954
1. Skelton, John, 1460?-1529.

POLLET, Maurice. 821'.2 B
John Skelton; poet of Tudor England. Translated by John Warrington. Lewisburg, [Pa.] Bucknell University Press [1971, c1962] xviii, 302 p. facsims., ports. 23 cm. Originally presented as the author's thesis, Paris. Bibliography: p. 263-285. [PR2348.P613] 73-124443 ISBN 0-8387-7737-6 10.00
1. Skelton, John, 1460?-1529.

Skelton, Marvin L.

SKELTON, Marvin L. 940.54'49'73
Memoirs of a World War II pilot / by Marvin L. Skelton. Manhattan, Kan. : Military Affairs/Aerospace Historian, c1978. ca. 450 p. in various pagings : ill. ; 29 cm. (Military affairs/Aerospace historian instant publishing series)

[D811.S538] 79-110605 ISBN 0-89126-064-1 : 25.00
1. Skelton, Marvin L. 2. United States. Army Air Forces—Biography. 3. World War, 1939-1945—Personal narratives, American. 4. Flight training—United States. 5. Air pilots, Military—United States—Biography. I. Title. II. Series: MA/AH instant publishing series. **BIP**

Skelton, Richard Bernard, 1913-

MARX, Arthur, 1921- 791'.092'4 B
Red Skelton / Arthur Marx. 1st ed. New York : Dutton, c1979. 325 p., [7] leaves of plates : ill. ; 22 cm. Includes index. Bibliography: p. 315. [PN2287.S395M3 1979] 79-10455 12.95
1. Skelton, Richard Bernard, 1913- 2. Comedians—United States—Biography. **BIP**

Ski racing—Biography—Juvenile literature.

EDWARDS, Harvey. 796.9'3'0922
Skiing to win. Illustrated with photos. [1st ed.] New York, Harcourt Brace Jovanovich [1973] 95 p. illus. 24 cm. Describes major competition skiing events throughout the world including biographies of international skiing champions and a special section on ski touring. [GV854.2.A1E37] 920 73-5239 ISBN 0-15-275400-8 5.95
1. Ski racing—Biography—Juvenile literature. 2. Cross-country skiing—Juvenile literature. I. Title. **BIP**

Skiers—Biography—Juvenile literature.

FRY, John, 1930- 796.9'3'0922 B
Winners on the ski slopes / by John Fry. New York : F. Watts, 1979. 48 p. : ill. ; 22 cm. (A Picture life book) Contents.Contents.—Jean-CLaude Killy.—Suzy Chaffee.—Sylvain Saudan.—Barbara Ann Cochran.—Bill Koch.—Nancy Greene.—Steve McKinney. [GV854.2.A1F79] 920 78-16443 ISBN 0-531-02292-7 lib. bdg. : 5.45
1. Skiers—Biography—Juvenile literature. I. Title. **BIP**

†WALTER, Claire. 796.9'3'0922 B
Skiing / by Claire Walter ; illustrated with photos. New York : Harvey House, c1977. 62 p. : ill. ; 23 cm. (Women in sports) Biographies of outstanding women skiers, Barbara Ann Cochran, Annemarie Moser Procll, Cindy Nelson, and Jana Hlavaty. Also includes a chapter about freestyle skiing, a new form of competition. [GV854.2.A1W34 1977] 920 77-80616 ISBN 0-8178-5612-9 lib.bdg. : 4.97
1. Skiers—Biography—Juvenile literature. 2. Athletes, Women—Biography—Juvenile literature. I. Title. II. Series.

Skin diving.

HASS, Hans. 797.2'3'0924 B
Challenging the deep. Translated by Ewald Osers. New York, W. Morrow [1973] 266 p. illus.(part col.) 25 cm. Translation of In unberuhrte Tiefen. Autobiographical. [GV840.S78H3313] 72-8443 ISBN 0-688-00140-8 11.95
1. Skin diving. 2. Marine biology. I. Title.

†HAUSER, Hillary. 797.2'3 B
Scuba diving / by Hillary Hauser. New York : Harvey House, c1976. 79 p. : ill. ; 23 cm. (Women in sports) Introduces five women who have successfully pursued diving careers. [GV840.S78H36 1976] 920 75-29590 ISBN 0-8178-5452-5 lib.bdg. : 4.97
1. Skin diving. 2. Women divers—Biography. 3. Divers—Biography. I. Title. II. Series.

Skinner, Burrhus Frederic, 1904-

EVANS, Richard Isadore, 150'.924
1922-
B. F. Skinner; the man and his ideas [by] Richard I. Evans. [1st ed.] New York, Dutton, 1968. xiv, 140 p. 19 cm. (His Dialogues with notable contributors to personality theory, v. 4) Bibliography: p. [131]-134. [BF109.S55E9] 68-28886 4.50
1. Skinner, Burrhus Frederic, 1904- 2. Psychology. I. Title.

FESTSCHRIFT for B. F. 156'.3'15
Skinner. Edited by P. B. Dews. New York, Appleton-Century-Crofts [1970] x, 413 p. illus., port. 26 cm. (Century psychology series) Includes bibliographies. [BF319.5.O6F47] 76-133193 6.95
1. Skinner, Burrhus Frederic, 1904- 2. Operant conditioning. I. Dews, P. B., 1922- ed. II. Skinner, Burrhus Frederic, 1904- **BIP**

SKINNER, 150'.19'4340924 B
Burrhus Frederic, 1904-
Particulars of my life / B. F. Skinner. New York : McGraw-Hill, 1977, c1976. p. cm. [BF109.S55A33 1977] 76-30414 ISBN 0-07-057897-4 pbk. : 3.95
1. Skinner, Burrhus Frederic, 1904- 2. Psychologists—Biography. I. Title. **BIP**

SKINNER, 150'.19'4340924 B
Burrhus Frederic, 1904-
The shaping of a behaviorist : part two of an autobiography / B. F. Skinner. 1st ed. New York : Knopf : distributed by Random House, 1979. 373 p., [4] leaves of plates : ill. ; 25 cm. Continues Particulars of my life. Includes bibliographical references. [BF109.S55A332 1979] 78-20620 ISBN 0-394-50581-6. : 12.95
1. Skinner, Burrhus Frederic, 1904- 2. Psychologists—United States—Biography. I. Skinner, Burrhus Frederic, 1904- Particulars of my life. II. Title.

WEIGEL, John A. 150'.19'4340924 B
B. F. Skinner / by John A. Weigel. Boston : Twayne Publishers, c1977. 125 p. : port. ; 21 cm. (Twayne's world leaders series ; TWLS 63) Includes index. Bibliography: p. 114-121. [BF109.S55W44] 77-1673 ISBN 0-8057-7713-X lib.bdg. : 7.50
1. Skinner, Burrhus Frederic, 1904- 2. Psychologists—United States—Biography. 3. Behaviorism. I. Title. **BIP**

Skippon, Philip, d. 1660

PHILLIPS, Cecil 942.06'3'0922 B
Ernest Lucas, 1898-
Cromwell's captains, by Cecil E. Lucas Phillips. Freeport, N.Y., Books for Libraries Press [1972] ix, 426 p. illus. 23 cm. Reprint of the 1938 ed. Bibliography: p. 399. [DA419.A1P45 1972] 73-37908 ISBN 0-8369-6746-1
1. Hampden, John, 1594-1643. 2. Skippon, Philip, d. 1660. 3. Blake, Robert, 1598-1657. 4. Lambert, John, 1619-1684. 5. Great Britain—History—Puritan Revolution, 1642-1660. I. Title. **BIP**

Skirving, Adam, 1719-1803.

CLUBBE, John, comp. 824'.8 B
Two reminiscences of Thomas Carlyle. Durham, N.C., Duke University Press, 1974. xiv, 145 p. illus. 25 cm. Contents.Contents.—Althaus, F. Thomas Carlyle: a biographical and literary portrait, with Thomas Carlyle's notes.—Reminiscence of Adam and Archibald Skirving. Includes bibliographical references. [PR4433.C54] 73-81497 ISBN 0-8223-0307-8 6.75
1. Carlyle, Thomas, 1795-1881—Biography. 2. Carlyle, Thomas, 1795-1881—Friends and associates. 3. Skirving, Adam, 1719-1803. 4. Skirving, Archibald, 1749-1819. I. Althaus, Friedrich, 1829-1897. Thomas Carlyle: a biographical and literary portrait, with Thomas Carlyle's notes. 1974. II. Carlyle, Thomas, 1795-1881. Reminiscence of Adam and Archibald Skirving. 1974. III. Title. **BIP**

Skis and skiing—Biography.

TOBIN, John C. 796.9'3'0924 B
The fall line; a skier's journal, by John C. Tobin. [1st ed.] New York, Meredith Press [1969] xi, 272 p. illus., ports. 24 cm. [GV854.2.T6A3] 78-93839 7.95
1. Skis and skiing—Biography. I. Title.

Sklovsky, Max, 1878-1967.

COVICH, Edith 621'.092'4 B
Sklovsky, 1907-
Max. Chicago, S. Brent, 1974. xviii, 268 p. illus. 24 cm. Includes bibliographical references. [TL140.S58C68] 73-90749 8.95
1. Sklovsky, Max, 1878-1967. I. Title.

Publisher's address: 670 North Michigan Avenue, Chicago, Ill. 60611.

Skriabin, Aleksandr Nikolaevich, 1872-1915.

BOWERS, Faubion, 786.1'0924 B
1917-
Scriabin: a biography of the Russian composers, 1871-1915 Tokyo, Palo Alto [Calif.] Kodansha International [1969] 2 v. illus., facsims., music, ports. 22 cm. [ML410.S5988B7] 69-16374 unpriced
1. Skriabin, Aleksandr Nikolaevich, 1872-1915.

HULL, Arthur 786.1'0924 B
Eaglefield, 1876-1928.
A great Russian tone-poet: Scriabin. New York, AMS Press [1970] viii, 304 p. music, ports. 19 cm. "Reprinted from the edition of 1918, New York." [ML410.S5988H9 1970] 79-126653 ISBN 0-404-03383-0
1. Skriabin, Aleksandr Nikolaevich, 1872-1915. I. Title.

SWAN, Alfred Julius, 786.1'0924 B
1890-
Scriabin, by Alfred J. Swan. New York, Da Capo Press, 1969. 119 p. 21 cm. (Da Capo Press music reprint series) Bibliography: p. [112] [ML410.S5988S9 1969] 75-76423
1. Skriabin, Aleksandr Nikolaevich, 1872-1915.

SWAN, Alfred Julius, 786.1'0924 B
1890-
Scriabin, by Alfred J. Swan. Westport, Conn., Greenwood Press [1970] 119 p. 23 cm. Reprint of the 1923 ed. Bibliography: p. [112] [ML410.S5988S9 1970] 76-109859
1. Skriabin, Aleksandr Nikolaevich, 1872-1915. **BIP**

Skripnikova, Aida Mikhailovna, 1942—

AIDA of Leningrad: 272 B
the story of Aida Skripnikova; edited by Xenia Howard-Johnston and Michael Bourdeaux. [Reading, Eng.] Gateway Outreach [1972] [8], 121 p. port. 23 cm. [BX6495.S52A75 1972] 73-160416 ISBN 0-901644-09-9 £1.50
1. Skripnikova, Aida Mikhailovna, 1942- 2. Persecution—Russia. I. Howard-Johnston, Xenia, ed. II. Bourdeaux, Michael, ed.

Skuthorpe, Lance, 1870-1958.

POLLARD, Jack 927.982
The roughrider; the story of Lance Skuthorpe. Melbourne, Lansdowne Pr. [dist. New Rochelle, N.Y.,SportShelf, 1964] 161p. illus., ports. 22cm. 64-3247 6.00 bds.,
1. Skuthorpe, Lance, 1870-1958. I. Title.

Slansky, Rudolf.

LONDON, Artur 364.13'1'0924 B
Gerard.
The confession [by] Artur London. Translated by Alastair Hamilton. New York, Morrow, 1970. xix, 442 p. 22 cm. French translation has title: L'Aveu. [DB215.5.L613] 70-136267 7.95
1. Slansky, Rudolf. 2. Clementis, Vladimir, 1902-1952. 3. Czechoslovak Republic—Politics and government—1945- 4. Trials (Political crimes and offenses)—Czechoslovak Republic. I. Title. **BIP**

Slade, Joseph Alfred, 1829-1864.

MCCLERNAN, John B. 978'.02'0924 B
Slade's Wells Fargo colt : historical notes / John B. McClernan ; ill. by J. P. Kelley. 1st ed. Hicksville, N.Y. : Exposition Press, c1977. 73 p. : ill. ; 24 cm. Includes index. Bibliography: p. 65-69. [F596.M125] 77-155145 ISBN 0-682-48925-5 : 5.00
1. Slade, Joseph Alfred, 1829-1864. 2. Frontier and pioneer life—The West. 3. Colt revolver. 4. Outlaws—Illinois—Carlyle—Biography. 5. Carlyle, Ill.—Biography. I. Title.

Slapgard, Astrid Hamnes, 1903-1976—Biography.

SLAPGARD, Astrid Hamnes, v. 12
1903-1976.
Langs livsvegen / Astrid og Bjarne Slapgard. Trondheim : Rune, 1976. 88 p. : ill. ; 27 cm. [PT9086.S396Z52] 77-475024 ISBN 8-252-30115-0 : kr60.00
1. Slapgard, Astrid Hamnes, 1903-1976—Biography. 2. Slapgard, Bjarne, 1901- —Biography. I. Slapgard, Bjarne, 1901- joint author. II. Title.

Slater, Jim, 1929-

RAW, Charles. 338.7'61'3326320941
A financial phenomenon : an investigation of the rise and fall of the Slater Walker empire / by Charles Raw. 1st U.S. ed. New York : Harper & Row, 1978, c1977. 389 p. ; 23 cm. Inlcudes index. [HG4530.R38 1977b] 77-17675 ISBN 0-06-013506-9 : 12.95
1. Slater, Walker Securities, Ltd. 2. Slater, Jim, 1929- 3. Walker, Peter Edward, 1932- 4. Capitalists and financiers—Great Britain—Biography. I. Title. **BIP**

Slater, Samuel, 1768-1835.

CAMERON, Edward Hugh 926.7
Samuel Slater, father of American manufacturers. [Freeport, Me.] B. Wheelwright Co. [c.1960] xvip. 206p. Bibl.: p.203-206. illus. 24cm. (American saga series) 60-10076 4.00
1. Slater, Samuel, 1768-1835. 2. Cotton trade—U. S. 3. Cotton manufacture—U. S. I. Title.

MINER, Lewis S. 677'.21'0924 B
Industrial genius Samuel Slater, by Lewis S. Miner. New York, J. Messner [1968] 186 p. 22 cm. Bibliography: p. 179. A biography of the Englishman who, concerned over the heavy human toll the Industrial Revolution was taking in England, left for America despite laws trying to keep textile workers from emigrating, and established the American textile industry. [HD9860.S5M5] 92 AC 68
1. Slater, Samuel, 1768-1835. I. Title.

WHITE, George 677'.21'0924
Savage, 1784-1850.
Memoir of Samuel Slater, the father of American manufactures; connected with a history of the rise and progress of the cotton manufacture in England and America. New York, A. M. Kelley, 1967. 448 p. illus., facsim., ports. 23 cm. (Library of early American business and industry, 4) (Reprints of economic classics) Reprint of the 1836 ed. [TS1570.S5W5 1967] 66-18322
1. Slater, Samuel, 1768-1835. 2. Cotton manufacture. I. Title.

Slater, Walker Securities, Ltd.

RAW, Charles. 338.7'61'3326320941
A financial phenomenon : an investigation of the rise and fall of the Slater Walker empire / by Charles Raw. 1st U.S. ed. New York : Harper & Row, 1978, c1977. 389 p. ; 23 cm. Inlcudes index. [HG4530.R38 1977b] 77-17675 ISBN 0-06-013506-9 : 12.95
1. Slater, Walker Securities, Ltd. 2. Slater, Jim, 1929- 3. Walker, Peter Edward, 1932- 4. Capitalists and financiers—Great Britain—Biography. I. Title. **BIP**

Slatin, Rudolf Carl, Freiherr von, 1857-1932.

BROOK-SHEPHERD, 355.3'32'0924 B
Gordon, 1918-
Between two flags; the life of Baron Sir Rudolf von Slatin Pasha, GCVO, KCMG, CB. [1st American ed.] New York, Putnam [1973, c1972] xvii, 366 p. illus. 22 cm. Includes bibliographical references. [DT108.05.S6B76 1973] 72-87605 ISBN 0-399-11061-5 8.95
1. Slatin, Rudolf Carl, Freiherr von, 1857-1932. I. Title.

HILL, Richard Leslie 923.2436
Slatin Pasha [New York] Oxford [c.]1965.

vii, 163p. facsim., maps., ports. 23cm. Bibl. [DT108.05.S6H5] 65-22879 4.00
1. Slatin, Rudolf Carl, Freiherr von, 1857-1932. I. Title.

Slattery, Sarah Lawrence,

SLATTERY, Sarah Lawrence, 1879- 248.2'5'0924 B
I choose. Winchester, Mass., University Press, 1969. 161 p. illus., ports. 23 cm. Autobiography. [CT275.S5228A3] 72-93891 4.95
I. Title.

Slave-trade.

CONNEAU, Theophile. 382'.44'0924 B
Adventures of an African slaver; an account of the life of Captain Theodore Canot, trader in gold, ivory, and slaves on the coast of Guinea. Written out and edited from the captain's journals, memoranda, and conversations by Brantz Mayer. With an introd. by Malcolm Cowley. New York, Dover Publications [1969] xvii, 448 p. illus. 21 cm. (Black rediscovery) "First published in 1854 under title: Captain Canot." [HT1322.C58 1969] 77-92390 3.50
1. Slave-trade. I. Mayer, Brantz, 1809-1879. II. Title.

Slave-trade—United States.

DRAKE, Philip. 382'.44'0924 B
Revelations of a slave smuggler: being the autobiography of Capt. Rich'd [i.e. Philip] Drake, an African trader for fifty years—from 1807 to 1857; during which period he was concerned in the transportation of half a million Blacks from African coasts to America. With a pref. by his executor, Henry Byrd West. New foreword by Blyden Jackson. Northbrook, Ill., Metro Books, 1972. xi, 100 p. illus. 23 cm. Reprint of the 1860 ed., with a new foreword. [HT1322.D7 1972] 74-99369 ISBN 0-8411-0040-3
1. Slave-trade—United States. I. Title.

Slavery in the United States—Alabama.

WILLIAMS, James, 1805- 301.45'22'0924 B
Narrative of James Williams, an American slave, who was for several years a driver on a cotton plantation in Alabama. [Philadelphia, Rhistoric Publications, 1969] xxiii, 108 p. 22 cm. (Rhistoric publication no. 245.) (Afro-American history series) Cover title. Reprint of the 1838 ed., with "James Williams and the controversial slave narrative 1838; introduction, by Maxwell Whiteman" added. [E444.W743 1969] 73-77082
1. Slavery in the United States—Alabama. I. Title. II. Series.

Slavery in the United States—Anti-slavery movements.

CHITTENDEN, Elizabeth F. 322.4'4'0973
Profiles in Black and white; stories of men and women who fought against slavery, by Elizabeth F. Chittenden. New York, Scribner [1973] x, 182 p. illus. 22 cm. [E449.C544 1973] 920 73-2929 ISBN 0-684-13387-3 5.95
1. Slavery in the United States—Anti-slavery movements. 2. Abolitionists. 3. Negroes—Biography. I. Title.
Contents omitted.

CONWAY, Moncure Daniel, 1832-1907. 288'.0924 B
Autobiography; memories and experiences of Moncure Daniel Conway. New York, Da Capo Press, 1970 [c1904] 2 v. illus., facsims., ports. 24 cm. [BX9869.C8A3 1970] 76-87495
1. Slavery in the United States—Anti-slavery movements.

CONWAY, Moncure Daniel, 1832-1907. 288'.0924 B
Autobiography: memories and experiences of Moncure Daniel Conway. New York, Negro Universities Press [1969] 2 v. illus., facsims., ports. 22 cm. Reprint of the 1904 ed. [BX9869.C8A3 1969] 71-88405
1. Slavery in the United States—Anti-slavery movements.

DOUGLASS, Frederick, 1817?-1895. 973.8'0924 B
From slave to statesman: the life and times of Frederick Douglass, written by himself. Specially abridged by Glenn Munson. [New York] Noble and Noble [1972] 231 p. 18 cm. (A Falcon book) Abridgement of The life and times of Frederick Douglass, which was originally published in 1892 as an enlargement of the Author's autobiography: My bondage and my freedom. [E449.D7382 1972] 70-38825
1. Slavery in the United States—Anti-slavery movements. 2. Slavery in the United States—Maryland. I. Munson, Glenn. II. Title.

DOUGLASS, Frederick, 1817?-1895. 326'.0924 B
Life and times of Frederick Douglass. Edited and abridged by Genevieve S. Gray. Illustrated by Scott Duncan. New York, Grosset & Dunlap [1970] viii, 181 p. illus. 24 cm. Abridged ed. of the author's autobiography as enlarged from his: My bondage and my freedom. [E449.D7382] 79-86689 4.50
1. Slavery in the United States—Anti-slavery movements. 2. Slavery in the United States—Maryland. I. Gray, Genevieve S., ed. II. Title.

DOUGLASS, Frederick, 1817?-1895. 326'.0924 B
Life and times of Frederick Douglass. Adapted by Barbara Ritchie. New York, Crowell [1966] viii, 210 p. 21 cm. Shortened version, adapted from the 2d rev. ed. of the authors's autobiography: Life and times, published in 1892, as enlarged from his My bondage and my freedom, 1855. [E449.D744 1966] 66-7048
1. Slavery in the United States—Anti-slavery movements. 2. Slavery in the United States—Maryland. I. Ritchie, Barbara. BIP

DOUGLASS, Frederick, 1817?-1895 923.673
The life and writings of Frederick Douglass [by] Philip S. Foner. New York, Intl. Pubs. [1967,c.1950] 4v. ports. 21cm. (New world paperbacks, NW-73-6) Contents.1. Early years, 1817-1849.--2. Pre-Civil War decade, 1850-1860.--3. The Civil War, 1861-1865.--4. Reconstruction and after. Bibl. [E449.D736] 50-7654 12.50 pap., bxd. set,
1. Slavery in the U. S.—Anti-slavery movements. I. Foner, Philip Sheldon, 1910- II. Title.

DOUGLASS, Frederick, 1817?-1895 973.71'14'0924
My bondage and my freedom. New York, Arno Pr., 1968. 464p. illus., port. 21cm. (Amer. Negro, his hist. & lit.) Reprint of the 1855 ed. [E449.D738 1968] 68-28994 14.50
1. Slavery in the U.S.—Anti-slavery movements. 2. Slavery in the U.S.—Maryland. I. Title. II. Series. BIP

DOUGLASS, Frederick, 1817?-1895. 973.71'14'0924
My bondage and my freedom. New York, Arno Press, 1968. 464 p. illus., port. 21 cm. (The American Negro, his history and literature) Reprint of the 1855 ed. [E449.D738] 68-28994
1. Slavery in the U.S.—Anti-slavery movements. 2. Slavery in the U.S.—Maryland. I. Title. II. Series. BIP

DOUGLASS, Frederick, 1817?-1895. 326.0924 B
My bondage and my freedom. Chicago, Johnson Pub. Co., 1970. xii, 370 p. illus., port. 24 cm. (Ebony classics) Reprint of the 1855 ed. [E449.D738 1970] 70-102981 7.95
1. Slavery in the United States—Anti-slavery movements. 2. Slavery in the United States—Maryland. I. Title.

DOUGLASS, Frederick, 1817?-1895. 326'.0924 B
My bondage and my freedom. New York, Arno Press, 1968. 464 p. illus., port. 21 cm. (The American Negro, his history and literature) Reprint of the 1855 ed. [E449.D738 1968] 68-28994
1. Slavery in the United States—Anti-slavery movements. 2. Slavery in the United States—Maryland. I. Title. II. Series.

DOUGLASS, Frederick, 1817?-1895. 301.45'22'0924
My bondage and my freedom. With a new introd. by Philip S. Foner. New York, Dover Publications [1969] xiii, 464 p. illus., port. 21 cm. (Black rediscovery) "Unabridged and unaltered republication of the work first published in 1855." [E449.D738 1969] 73-92688 3.50
1. Slavery in the United States—Anti-slavery movements. 2. Slavery in the United States—Maryland. I. Title.

MATHEWS, Edward, b.1812. 322'.4
The autobiography of the Rev. E. Mathews, the "Father Dickson" of Mrs. Stowe's Dred; also a description of the influence of the slave-party over the American Presidents, and the rise and progress of the anti-slavery reform. With a pref. by Handel Cossham. Miami, Fla., Mnemosyne Pub. Co. [1969] xii, 444 p. port. 23 cm. Reprint of the 1867 ed. [F449.M37 1969] 79-89392
1. Slavery in the United States—Anti-slavery movements. I. Title. BIP

WARD, Samuel Ringgold, b.1817. 326'.0924
Autobiography of a fugitive Negro. New York, Arno Press, 1968. xii, 412 p. port. 18 cm. (The American Negro, his history and literature) Reprint of the 1855 ed. [E449.W27 1968] 68-29022
1. Slavery in the United States—Anti-slavery movements. I. Title. II. Series. BIP

WARD, Samuel Ringgold, b.1817. 326'.0924 B
Autobiography of a fugitive Negro; his anti-slavery labors in the United States, Canada & England. Chicago, Johnson Pub. Co., 1970. xvi, 277 p. 24 cm. (Ebony classics) Reprint of the 1855 ed. [E449.W27 1970] 77-102980 4.95
1. Slavery in the United States—Anti-slavery movements. I. Title. II. Series.

Slavery in the United States—Anti-slavery movements—Biography.

PEASE, Jane H. 322.4'4'0973
Bound with them in chains; a biographical history of the antislavery movement [by] Jane H. Pease and William H. Pease. Westport, Conn., Greenwood Press [1972] xvii, 334 p. 22 cm. (Contributions in American history, no. 18) Bibliography: p. 319-325. [E449.P37] 74-175612 ISBN 0-8371-6265-3 12.50
1. Slavery in the United States—Anti-slavery movements—Biography. 2. Abolitionists—Biography. I. Pease, William Henry, 1924- joint author. II. Title. BIP

Slavery in the United States—Anti-slavery movements—Collected works.

DOUGLASS, Frederick, 1817?-1895. 322.4'4'0924
The life and writings of Frederick Douglass, [ed. by] Philip S. Foner. New York: International Publishers, [1950-1975] 5 v.; 21 cm. Contents.Contents:—1. Early years, 1817-1849.—2. Pre-Civil War decade, 1850-1860.—3. The Civil War, 1861-1865.—4. Reconstruction and after.—5. Supplementary volume, 1844-1860. Includes bibliographical references and index. [E449.D736] 50-7654
1. Slavery in the United States—Anti-slavery movements—Collected works. I. Foner, Philip Sheldon, 1910- ed.
V. 5, 1975, is available for 15.00, ISBN 0-7178-0453-4; pbk. 5.95, ISBN 0-7178-0454-2. BIP

Slavery in the United States—Condition of slaves.

ALBERT, Octavia Victoria (Rogers), 1853-1889? 301.44'93'0973
The house of bondage; or, Charlotte Brooks and other slaves, by Mrs. Octavia V. Rogers Albert. Freeport, N.Y., Books for Libraries Press, 1972 [c1890] xiv, 161 p. port. 23 cm. (The Black heritage library collection) [E444.A33 1972] 70-37580 ISBN 0-8369-8956-2
1. Slavery in the United States—Condition of slaves. 2. Negroes. I. Title. II. Series.

YETMAN, Norman R., 1938- comp. 301.45'22'0922
Life under the "peculiar institution"; selections from the Slave Narrative Collection [Library of Congress. Selected by] Norman R. Yetman. New York, Holt, Rinehart and Winston [1970] xi, 368 p. illus., facsim. 24 cm. Includes bibliographical references. [E444.Y4] 70-114673 ISBN 0-03-081424-3
1. Slavery in the United States—Condition of slaves. 2. Slavery in the United States—Personal narratives. I. Title.

Slavery in the United States—Connecticut.

MARS, James, b.1790. 301.45'22'0924 B
Life of James Mars, a slave born and sold in Connecticut, written by himself. 6th ed. [Philadelphia, Rhistoric Publications, 1969] 38 p. 21 cm. (Afro-American history series) (Rhistoric publication no. 225.) Cover title. Reprint of the 1868 ed. [E444.M362 1969b] 79-77062
1. Slavery in the United States—Connecticut. I. Title. BIP

MARS, James, b.1790. 301.45'22'0924 B
Life of James Mars, a slave, born and sold in Connecticut. 8th ed. Hartford, Press of Case, Lockwood, 1869. Miami, Fla., Mnemosyne Pub. Co. [1969] 38 p. 23 cm. Reprint of the 1869 ed. [E444.M362 1969] 76-89394
1. Slavery in the United States—Connecticut. I. Title.

Slavery in the United States—Controversial literature.

WOOLMAN, John, 1720-1772. 289.6'0924 B
The journal and major essays of John Woolman. Edited by Phillips P. Moulton. New York, Oxford University Press, 1971. xviii, 336 p. 24 cm. (A Library of Protestant thought) Contents.Contents.—The journal of John Woolman.—Major essays of John Woolman: Introduction to the essays. Some considerations on the keeping of Negroes. Considerations on keeping Negroes, part second. A plea for the poor. Bibliography: p. 315-318. [BX7795.W7A3 1971b] 71-171970 10.50
1. Slavery in the United States—Controversial literature. 2. Poor. I. Title. II. Series.

Slavery in the United States—Fugitive slaves.

FOUR fugitive slave narratives. 301.45'22'0922 B
With introductions by Robin W. Winks [and others] Reading, Mass., Addison-Wesley Pub. Co. [1969] 1 v. (various pagings) 22 cm. Contents.Contents.—An autobiography of the Reverend Josiah Henson.—Narrative of William W. Brown, a fugitive slave.—Twenty-two years a slave, and forty years a freeman, by A. Steward.—The refugee: a North-side view of slavery, by B. Drew. [E450.F75] 70-75213
1. Slavery in the United States—Fugitive slaves. I. Winks, Robin W. II. Henson, Josiah, 1789-1883. An autobiography of the Reverend Josiah Henson. III. Brown, William Wells, 1815-1884. Narrative of William W. Brown, a fugitive slave. IV. Steward, Austin, 1794-1860. Twenty-two years a slave, and forty years a freeman. V. Drew, Benjamin. The refugee: a north-side view of slavery. BIP

LOGUEN, Jermain Wesley, 1814-1872. 301.45'22'0924 B
The Rev. J. W. Loguen, as a slave and as a freeman; a narrative of real life. New York, Negro Universities Press [1968] 444 p. port. 22 cm. Reprint of the 1859 ed. [E444.L83 1968] 68-55898
1. Slavery in the United States—Fugitive slaves. 2. Slavery in the United States—Anti-slavery movements. 3. Underground railroad.

Slavery in the United States—Kentucky.

BIBB, Henry, b.1815. 301.45'22'0924 B
Narrative of the life and adventures of Henry Bibb, an American slave. Written by himself. With an introd. by Lucius C. Matlack. 3d stereotype ed. New York, Negro Universities Press [1969] xiv, 204 p. illus., port. 23 cm. Reprint of the 1850 ed. [E444.B58 1969b] 76-84686
1. Slavery in the United States—Kentucky. I. Title.

BIBB, Henry, b.1815. 301.45'22'0924 B
Narrative of the life and adventures of Henry Bibb, an American slave. With an introd. by Lucius C. Matlack. 3d stereotype ed. [Philadephia, Rhistoric Publications, 1969] x, 207 p. illus., port. 23 cm. (Rhistoric publication no. 204.) (Afro-American history series) Reprint of the 1850 ed., with a new introd. by M. Whiteman. Includes bibliographical references. [E444.B58 1969c] 70-77041
1. Slavery in the United States—Kentucky. I. Title. II. Series.

BIBB, Henry, b.1815. 301.45'22'0924 B
Narrative of the life and adventures of Henry Bibb, an American slave, written by himself. With an introd. by Lucius C. Matlack. 3d stereotype ed. New York, 1850. Miami, Fla., Mnemosyne Pub. Co. [1969] 207 p. illus., port. 23 cm. [E444.B58 1969] 70-89423
1. Slavery in the United States—Kentucky. I. Title. **BIP**

BROWNE, Martha (Griffith) Mrs., d.1906. 301.45'22'0924 B
Autobiography of a female slave. New York, Redfield, 1857. Miami, Fla., Mnemosyne Pub. Co. [1969] 401 p. 23 cm. [E444.B887 1969] 79-89412
1. Slavery in the United States—Kentucky. I. Title.

BROWNE, Martha (Griffith) d.1906. 301.44'93'0924 B
Autobiography of a female slave [by] Mattie Griffiths. New York, Redfield, 1857. Detroit, Negro History Press [1971?] 401 p. 23 cm. [E444.B887 1971] 71-92430
1. Slavery in the United States—Kentucky. I. Title. **BIP**

BROWNE, Martha (Griffith) d.1906. 301.45'22 B
Autobiography of a female slave. New York, Negro Universities Press [1969] 401 p. 23 cm. Reprint of the 1857 ed. [E444.B887 1969b] 71-92745 ISBN 8-371-21949-
1. Slavery in the United States—Kentucky. I. Title. **BIP**

Slavery in the United States—Maryland.

BALL, Charles, Negro slave. 301.44'93 B
Fifty years in chains. With a new introd. by Philip S. Foner. New York, Dover Publications [1970] xi, xii, 517 p. 21 cm. (Black rediscovery) Reprint of the 1837 ed. published under title: Slavery in the United States. [E444.B18 1970] 74-104979 ISBN 0-486-22462-7 3.75
1. Slavery in the United States—Maryland. 2. Slavery in the United States—South Carolina. 3. Slavery in the United States—Georgia. I. Title. II. Series. **BIP**

BALL, Charles, Negro slave. 301.44'93
Fifty years in chains; or, The life of an American slave. New York, H. Dayton, 1859. Detroit, Negro History Press [1971?] 430 p. 23 cm. Prepared by a Mr. Fisher from the verbal narrative of Ball, a slave. Originally published under title: Slavery in the United States. [E444.B18 1971] 78-92413
1. Slavery in the United States—Maryland. 2. Slavery in the United States—South Carolina. 3. Slavery in the United States—Georgia. I. Fisher, , of Lewistown? Pa. II. Title. III. Title: The life of an American slave. **BIP**

BALL, Charles, Negro slave. 301.45'22'0924 B
Fifty years in chains; or, The life of an American slave. New York, Dayton & Asher, 1858. Miami, Fla., Mnemosyne Pub. Co. [1969] 430 p. 23 cm. Prepared by a Mr. Fisher from the verbal narrative of Ball, a slave. Earlier editions published under title: Slavery in the United States. [E444.B18 1969b] 70-89426
1. Slavery in the United States—Maryland. 2. Slavery in the United States—South Carolina. 3. Slavery in the United States—Georgia. I. Fisher, , of Lewistown? Pa. II. Title. III. Title: The life of an American slave.

BALL, Charles, Negro slave. 301.45'22'0924 B
Slavery in the United States: a narrative of the life and adventures of Charles Ball, a black man ... New York, Negro Universities Press [1969] 517 p. 18 cm. Prepared by a Mr. Fisher from the verbal narrative of Ball. Reprint of the 1837 ed. [E444.B18 1969] 68-55869
1. Slavery in the United States—Maryland. 2. Slavery in the United States—South Carolina. 3. Slavery in the United States—Georgia. I. Fisher, of Lewistown? Pa. II. Title.

DOUGLASS, Frederick, 1817?-1895 326.92
Narrative of the life of Frederick Douglass, an American slave, written by himself. New York, New Amer. Lib. [1968, 1960] xviii, 126p. 18cm. (Signet bk., D3434) [E449.D74905] .50 pap.,
1. Slavery in the U. S.—Maryland. I. Title.

DOUGLASS, Frederick, 1817?-1895. 326.92
Narrative of the life of Frederick Douglass, an American slave, written by himself. Edited by Benjamin Quarles. Cambridge, Mass., Belknap Press, 1960. xxvi, 163 p. port., map. 22 cm. (The John Harvard library) [E449.D74905] 59-11516
1. Slavery in the United States—Maryland. I. Title. II. Series.

DOUGLASS, Frederick [Name orig.: Frederick Augustus Washington Bailey] 1817?-1895 326.92
Narrative of the life of Frederick Douglass, an American slave, written by himself. Garden City, N.Y., Doubleday [1963] 124p. facsimile t.p. 18cm. (Dolphin bk., C419) .95 pap.,
1. Slavery in the U.S.—Maryland. I. Title.

DOUGLASS, Frederick, [Name orig.: Frederick Augustus Washington Bailey] 1817?-1895 326.92
Narrative of the life of Frederick Douglass, an American slave. Written by himself. Ed. by Benjamin Quarles. Cambridge, Mass., Belknap Pr. of Harvard, 1967[c.1960] xxvi, 163p. map. 21cm. (John Harvard lib., JHL15) [E449.D74905] 59-11616 1.45 pap.,
1. Slavery in the U.S.—Maryland. I. Title. II. Series.

GREEN, William, slave. 301.45'22'0924 B
Narrative of events in the life of William Green (formerly a slave), written by himself. [Philadelphia, Rhistoric Publications, 1969] 23 p. 21 cm. (Afro-American history series) (Rhistoric publication no. 219.) Cover title. Reprint of the 1853 ed. [E444.G79 1969] 76-77056
1. Slavery in the United States—Maryland. I. Title.

THOMPSON, John, b.1812. 301.45'22'0924 B
The life of John Thompson, a fugitive slave; containing his history of 25 years in bondage, and his providential escape, written by himself. New York, Negro Universities Press [1968] vi, [13], 143 p. 22 cm. Reprint of the 1856 ed. [E444.T47 1968] 68-55920
1. Slavery in the United States—Maryland. I. Title.

Slavery in the United States—Missouri.

BROWN, William Wells, 1815-1884. 301.45'22'0924
Narrative of William W. Brown, a fugitive slave. Boston, Anti-slavery Office, 1847. New York, Johnson Reprint Corp. [1970] 110 p. port. 19 cm. (Series in American studies) [E444.B88 1970] 70-18940
1. Slavery in the United States—Missouri.

BRUCE, Henry Clay, 1836-1902. 301.45'22'09778
The new man. Twenty-nine years a slave; twenty-nine years a free man: recollections. New York, Negro Universities Press [1969] 176 p. port. 23 cm. Reprint of the 1895 ed. [E444.B9 1969b] 77-94474
1. Slavery in the United States—Missouri. I. Title.

Slavery in the United States—Personal narratives.

BONTEMPS, Arna Wendell, 1902-, comp. 301.45'22'0922 B
Great slave narratives. Selected and introduced by Arna Bontemps. Boston, Beacon Press [1969] xix, 331 p. 21 cm. Contents.—The slave narrative; an American genre, by A. Bontemps.—The life of Olaudah Equiano, or Gustavus Vassa, the African, written by himself.—The fugitive blacksmith; or, Events in the history of James W. C. Pennington, pastor of a Presbyterian church, New York, formerly a slave in the State of Maryland.—Running a thousand miles for freedom; or, The escape of William and Ellen Craft from slavery. [E444.B67] 77-84792 7.50
1. Slavery in the United States—Personal narratives. I. Title. **BIP**

BROWN, John, fl.1854. 301.44'93'0924 B
Slave life in Georgia; a narrative of the life of John Brown. Edited by L. A. Chamerovzow. Freeport, N.Y., Books for Libraries Press, 1971. ii, 250 p. port. 23 cm. (The Black heritage library collection) Reprint of the 1855 ed. [E444.B87 1971] 77-168512 ISBN 0-8369-8865-5
1. Slavery in the United States—Personal narratives. I. Title. II. Series.

CHAPMAN, Abraham, comp. 917.3'06'96073
Steal away; stories of the runaway slaves. New York, Praeger [1971] xi, 196 p. illus. 22 cm. Includes bibliographical references. [E444.C4 1971] 79-126775 6.95
1. Slavery in the United States—Personal narratives. I. Title.

FISK University, Nashville. Social Science Institute. 973
Unwritten history of slavery; autobiographical accounts of Negro ex-slaves. Washington, Microcard Editions, 1968. vi, 160 p. 27 cm. "Interviews ... conducted during 1929 and 1930 by Mrs. Ophelia Settle Egypt." [E444.F5 1968] 68-58168
1. Slavery in the United States—Personal narratives. I. Title.

FIVE Black lives; 301.44'93'0922 B
the autobiographies of Venture Smith, James Mars, William Grimes, the Rev. G. W. Offley, [and] James L. Smith. Introd. by Arna Bontemps. [1st ed.] Middletown, Conn., Wesleyan University Press [1971] x, 240 p. 24 cm. (Documents of Black Connecticut) A collection of narratives originally published separately, 1855-97. Each part has also special t.p. [E444.F49] 74-108647 ISBN 0-8195-4036-6 9.95
1. Slavery in the United States—Personal narratives. I. Title. II. Series.

MASON, Isaac, 1822- 301.451'96'024 B
Life of Isaac Mason as a slave. Worcester, Mass., 1893. Miami, Fla., Mnemosyne Pub. Co. [1969] 74 p. port. 23 cm. [E444.M39A3] 72-89393
1. Slavery in the United States—Personal narratives. I. Title. **BIP**

NICHOLS, Charles Harold, comp. 301.45'19'6073022 B
Black men in chains; narratives by escaped slaves. Edited by Charles H. Nichols. [1st ed.] New York, L. Hill [1972] 319 p. 22 cm. Contents.Contents.—Gustavus Vassa.—Nat Turner.—Moses Roper.—Frederick Douglass.—Lunsford Lane.—Moses Grandy.—William Wells Brown.—James W. C. Pennington.—Henry "Box" Brown.—Solomon Northup.—John Thompson.—Josiah Henson.—William and Ellen Craft.—Harriet Jacobs.—Israel Campbell.—William Parker.—Bibliography (p. [317]-319) [E450.N62 1972] 72-78320 ISBN 0-88208-003-2 7.95
1. Slavery in the United States—Personal narratives. I. Title. **BIP**

PENNINGTON, James W. C. 301.44'93'0924 B
The fugitive blacksmith; or, Events in the history of James W. C. Pennington. 3d ed. Westport, Conn., Negro Universities Press [1971] xix, 84 p. 23 cm. Reprint of the 1850 ed. [E450.P42 1971] 68-55906 ISBN 0-8371-4848-0
1. Slavery in the United States—Personal narratives. 2. Slavery in the United States—Fugitive slaves. I. Title.

WEEVILS in the wheat : 301.44'93'09755
interviews with Virginia Ex-slaves / edited by Charles L. Perdue, Jr., Thomas E. Barden, and Robert K. Phillips. Charlottesville : University Press of Virginia, 1976. xlv, 405 p. : ill. ; 24 cm. A collection of interviews of former slaves, conducted by the Virginia Federal Writers' Project in 1936 and 1937. Bibliography: p. [391]-394. [E444.V57] 75-17699 ISBN 0-8139-0596-6
1. Slavery in the United States—Personal narratives. 2. Slavery in the United States—Virginia. I. Perdue, Charles L., 1930- II. Barden, Thomas E. III. Phillips, Robert K. IV. Federal Writers' Project. Virginia.

YETMAN, Norman R., 1938- comp. 301.44'93'0973
Voices from slavery / edited by Norman R. Yetman. Huntington, N.Y. : R. E. Krieger Pub. Co., 1976. p. cm. Selections from the Slave Narrative Collection of the Federal Writers' Project. Reprint of the 1970 ed. published by Holt, Rinehart and Winston, New York. [E444.Y42 1976] 75-31798 ISBN 0-88275-364-9 : 12.50
1. Slavery in the United States Personal narratives. I. Federal Writers' Project. Slave narratives. 1976. II. Title.

Slavery in the United States—South Carolina.

ROPER, Moses. 301.45'22'075
A narrative of the adventures and escape of Moses Roper from American slavery. With a pref., by T. Price. New York, Negro Universities Press [1970] xii, 108 p. illus. 23 cm. Title on spine: Adventures and escape of Moses Roper. Reprint of 2d ed., published 1838. [E444.R785 1970] 75-100302
1. Slavery in the United States—South Carolina. I. Title.

Slavery in the United States—Virginia.

BROWN, Henry Box, b.1816. 301.45'22'0924 B
Narrative of Henry Box Brown, who escaped from slavery enclosed in a box 3 feet long and 2 wide, written from a statement of facts made by himself. With remarks upon the remedy for slavery by Charles Stearns. [Philadelphia, Rhistoric Publications, 1969] x, 90 p. illus., port. 21 cm. (Afro-American history series) (Rhistoric publication no. 205.) Cover title. Reprint of the 1849 ed., with "Henry Box Brown; a bibliographical note, by Maxwell Whiteman" added. [E450.B873 1969] 74-77042
1. Slavery in the United States—Virginia. I. Stearns, Charles. II. Title.

SMITH, James Lindsay. 301.451'96'024 B
Autobiography of James L. Smith; including also reminiscences of slave life, recollections of the war, education of freedmen, causes of the exodus, etc. Norwich [Conn.] Press of the Bulletin Co., 1881. Miami, Fla., Mnemosyne Pub. Co. [1969] xiii, 150 p. illus., port. 23 cm. [E444.S65 1969] 76-89430
1. Slavery in the United States—Virginia. 2. Freedmen. I. Title.

STEWARD, Austin, 1794-1860. 301.44'93
Twenty-two years a slave and forty years a freeman. With an introd. by Jane H. Pease and William H. Pease. Reading, Mass., Addison-Wesley Pub. Co. [1969] xv, 221

p. 21 cm. (Addison-Wesley's fugitive slave narratives, 3) Reprint of the 1857 ed. [E444.S845 1969] 69-10344
1. Slavery in the United States—Virginia. 2. Wilberforce Negro Colony, Middlesex County, Ont. I. Title. BIP

Slavery—Justification.

FAUST, Drew Gilpin. 001.2'0975
A sacred circle : the dilemma of the intellectual in the Old South, 1840-1860 / Drew Gilpin Faust. Baltimore : Johns Hopkins University Press, c1977. xii, 189 p. : ill. ; 24 cm. Includes bibliographical references and index. [E449.F2] 77-4547 ISBN 0-8018-1967-9 : 11.00
1. Slavery—Justification. 2. Southern States—Intellectual life. 3. Intellectuals—Southern States—Biography. I. Title. BIP

Slaves—United States—Biography.

THE American slave 301.45'19'6073 : a composite autobiography : supplement, series 2 / edited by George P. Rawick. Westport, Conn. : Greenwood Press, 1979. p. cm. (Contributions in Afro-American and African Studies ; no. 49) ISSN 0069-9624) Contents.Contents.—v. 1. Alabama, Arizona, Arkansas, District of Columbia, Florida, Georgia, Indiana, Kansas, Maryland, Nebraska, New York, North Carolina, Oklahoma, Rhode Island, South Carolina, Washington narratives.—v. 2-10. Texas narratives. [E444.A45 suppl. 2] 79-12456 ISBN 0-313-21423-9 : 315.00
1. Slaves—United States—Biography. 2. Slavery in the United States. I. Rawick, George P., 1929- II. Title. III. Series. BIP

THE American slave 301.45'196073 : a composite autobiography : supplement, series 1 / George P. Rawick, general editor ; Jan Hillegas, Ken Lawrence, editors. Westport, Conn. : Greenwood Pub. Co., [1978- 12 v. ; 27 cm. (Contributions in Afro-American and African studies ; no. 35) ISSN 0069-9624) Contents.Contents.—v. 1. Alabama narratives.—v. 2. Arkansas, Colorado, Minnesota, Missouri, and Oregon and Washington narratives.—v. 3. Georgia narratives, part 1.—v. 4. Georgia narratives, part 2.—v. 5. Indiana and Ohio narratives.—v. 6. Mississippi narratives, part 1.—v. 7. Mississippi narratives, part 2.—v. 8. Mississippi narratives, part 3.—v. 9. Mississippi narratives, part 4.—v. 10. Mississippi narratives, part 5.—v. 11. North Carolina and South Carolina narratives.—v. 12. Oklahoma narratives. [E444.A45 suppl. 1] 77-88899 ISBN 0-8371-9756-2 lib.bdg. : 325.00(12 vol.set)
1. Slaves—United States—Biography. 2. Slavery in the United States. I. Rawick, George P., 1929- II. Hillegas, Jan. III. Lawrence, Kenan Barrett, 1907- IV. Title. V. Series.

Sleeman, William Henry, Sir, 1789-1856.

SLEEMAN, William 915.4'03'30924 Henry, Sir, 1789-1856.
Rambles and recollections of an Indian official, by Sir W. H. Sleeman. Revised annotated edition by Vincent A. Smith. Karachi, Oxford University Press [1973] xxxvii, 667 p. map (fold. at end) 19 cm. (Oxford in Asia historical reprints) First published in 1844. Bibliography of the author's writings: p. [xxxi]-xxxvii. [DS412.S63 1973] 73-930306
1. Sleeman, William Henry, Sir, 1789-1856. 2. India—Description and travel—1762-1858. I. Smith, Vincent Arthur, 1848-1920. II. Title.
Distributed by Oxford University Press, N.Y., 6.00. BIP

Slessor, Kenneth, 1901-1971.

JAFFA, Herbert C. 821 B
Kenneth Slessor, by Herbert C. Jaffa. New York, Twayne Publishers [1971] 169 p. 21 cm. (Twayne's world authors series, TWAS 145. Australia) Bibliography: p. 157-163. [PR6037.L4Z7] 73-120507
1. Slessor, Kenneth, 1901- BIP

STEWART, Douglas Alexander, 821 B 1913-
A man of Sydney : an appreciation of Kenneth Slessor / Douglas Stewart. Melbourne : Nelson, 1977. xiv, 191 p., [8] leaves of plates : ill. ; 22 cm. Includes index. Bibliography: p. 176-185. [PR9619.3.S534Z9] 77-377871 ISBN 0-17-005149-8
1. Slessor, Kenneth, 1901-1971. 2. Poets, Australian—20th century—Biography. I. Title.

Slessor, Mary Mitchell, 1848-1915.

MILLER, Basil William, 922.566 1897-
Mary Slessor, missionary heroine. Grand Rapids,Mich., Zondervan [1965, c.1946] 132p. 21cm. [BV625.N6S64] 46-17815 1.00 pap.,
1. Slessor, Mary Mitchell, 1848-1915. I. Title.

SYME, Ronald, 1910- 266.54669
Nigerian pioneer; the story of Mary Slessor. Illustrated by Jacqueline Tomes. New York, Morrow, 1964. 189 p. illus. 21 cm. Bibliography: p. 13-14. [BV3625.N6S65] 64-15170
1. Slessor, Mary Mitchell, 1848-1915. 2. Missions—Calabar, Nigeria. I. Title.

YOUNG-O'BRIEN, Albert 922.566 Hayward, 1898-
She had a magic; the story of Mary Slessor, by Brian O'Brien [pseud.] [1st ed.] New York, Dutton, 1959 [c1958] 281 p. illus. 21 cm. [BV3625.N6S66] 59-5779
1. Slessor, Mary Mitchell, 1848-1915. I. Title.

Sletten, Harvey M., 1912—

SLETTEN, Harvey M., 978.4'34 B 1912-
Growing up on Bald Hill Creek / Harvey M. Sletten. 1st ed. Ames : Iowa State University Press, 1977. p. cm. [F644.H36S587] 77-23848 ISBN 0-8138-0080-3 : 6.95
1. Sletten, Harvey M., 1912- 2. Hannaford, N.D.—Biography. 3. Hannaford, N.D.—History. I. Title. BIP

Sleyman, Albert A., 1882-

†SLEYMAN, 973'.04'9275692 B Albert A., 1882-
The basket boy : the challenge and the man / Albert A. Sleyman. New York : William-Frederick Press, 1977. 131 p., [3] leaves of plates : ill. ; 23 cm. [CT275.S52315A32] 77-88613 ISBN 0-87164-036-8 : 7.50
1. Sleyman, Albert A., 1882- 2. United States—Biography. I. Title.

Slezak, Leo, 1874-1946.

SLEZAK, Leo, 1874- 782.1'092'4 B 1946.
Song of motley / Leo Slezak. New York : Arno Press, 1977. 302 p., [7] leaves of plates : ill ; 23 cm. (Opera biographies) Translation of Meine samtlichen Werke and Der Wortbruch. Reprint of the 1938 ed. published by W. Hodge, London. [ML420.S66A313 1977] 76-29968 ISBN 0-405-09707-7 : 18.00
1. Slezak, Leo, 1874-1946. 2. Singers—Czechoslovakia—Biography. I. Slezak, Leo, 1874-1946. Der Wortbruch. English. 1977. II. Title.

SLEZAK, Walter, 1902- 927.92
What time's the next swan? By Walter Slezak as told to Smith-Corona model 88E. Garden City, N. Y., Doubleday, c.1962. 227p. illus. 22cm. 62-17357 4.50
1. Slezak, Leo, 1874-1946. I. Title.

Slichter, Charles Sumner, 1864-1946.

INGRAHAM, Mark Hoyt, 510'.92'4 B 1896-
Charles Sumner Slichter; the golden vector [by] Mark H. Ingraham. Madison, University of Wisconsin Press [1972] xiii, 316 p. illus. 24 cm. [QA29.S62715] 79-176412 ISBN 0-299-06060-8
1. Slichter, Charles Sumner, 1864-1946. BIP

Slick, Grace.

ROWERS, Barbara. 784'.092'4 B
Grace Slick : the biography / Barbara Rowes. Garden City, N.Y. : Doubleday, 1980. p. cm. [ML420.S6625R7] 78-22351 ISBN 0-385-13390-1 : 10.95
1. Slick, Grace. 2. Rock musicians—United States—Biography. BIP

Slim, William Slim, 1st Viscount, 1891-1970.

CALVERT, Michael. 355.3'31'0924 B
Slim. [New York] B[allantine] B[ooks, 1973] 160 p. illus. 22 cm. (Ballantine's illustrated history of the violent century. War leader book no. 12) Bibliography: p. 160. [DA69.3.S55C34] 73-156329 ISBN 0-345-02681-0 1.00
1. Slim, William Slim, 1st Viscount, 1891-

LEWIN, Ronald. 940.54'25'0924 B
Slim, the standardbearer : a biography of Field-Marshal the Viscount Slim, KG, GCB, GCMG, GCVO, GBE, DSO, MC / by Ronald Lewin. Hamden, Conn. : Archon Books, c1976. xv, 350 p., [8] leaves of plates : ill. ; 24 cm. Includes index. Bibliography: p. 331-333. [DA69.3.S55L48 1976] 77-353858 ISBN 0-208-01637-6 : 15.00
1. Slim, William Slim, 1st Viscount, 1891-1970. 2. Great Britain. Army—Biography. 3. Generals—Great Britain—Biography. I. Title.

SLIM, William Slim, 355.3'31'0924 1st Viscount, 1891-
Unofficial history [by] Sir William Slim. Westport, Conn., Greenwood Press [1974, c1959] ix, 242 p. maps. 22 cm. Reprint of the 1962 ed. published by McKay, New York. [DA69.3.S55A3 1974] 74-71 ISBN 0-8371-7363-9 12.00
1. Slim, William Slim, 1st Viscount, 1891- I. Title.

Sliney, Eleanor (Mathews)

SLINEY, Eleanor (Mathews) 920.7
Forward ho! New York, Vantage Press [c.1960] 332p. illus. 21cm. 60-1503 3.95
I. Title.

Sloan, Ethel B.

SLOAN, Ethel B. 994.4
A Kangaroo in the kitchen / by E. B. Sloan. Indianapolis : Bobbs-Merrill, [1978] p. cm. [DU178.S547] 77-15437 ISBN 0-672-52378-7 : 7.95
1. Sloan, Ethel B. 2. Sydney—Social life and customs. 3. Americans in Sydney—Biography. I. Title.

Sloan, John, 1871-1951.

BROOKS, Van Wyck, 1886- 759.13
John Sloan; a painter's life. [1st ed.] New York, Dutton, 1955. 246p. illus. 23cm. [ND237.S57B7] 927.5 55-5350
1. Sloan, John, I. Title.

JOHN Sloan. [759.13]
New York, Published for the Whitney Museum of American Art by the Macmillan Co., 1952. 80 p. illus. 26 cm. Includes bibliography. [ND237.S57G6] 927.5 52-7168
1. Sloan, John, 1871-1951. I. Goodrich, Lloyd, 1897-

ST. John, Bruce. 760'.0924
John Sloan. New York, Praeger [1971] 156 p. illus. (part col.), ports. (part col.) 27 cm. (American art & artists) Bibliography: p. 150-152. [N6537.S57S3] 74-117478 15.00
1. Sloan, John, 1871-1951. I. Title. II. Series.

SCOTT, David W., 1916- 759.13
John Sloan / by David Scott. New York : Watson-Guptill, 1975. 223 p. : ill. (some col.) ; 32 cm. Includes index. Bibliography: p. 215-219. [ND237.S57S36] 75-6694 ISBN 0-8230-4869-1 : 25.00
1. Sloan, John, 1871-1951. I. Sloan, John, 1871-1951.

Sloane, Eric.

SLOANE, Eric. 741'.092'4 B
Legacy / by Eric Sloane. 1st ed. New York : Crowell, c1979. 77 p. : ill. ; 26 cm. "A Funk and Wagnalls book." [CT275.S52352A33] 78-22455 ISBN 0-308-10351-3 : 9.95
1. Sloane, Eric. 2. United States—Biography. 3. United States—Civilization. I. Title.

Sloane, Winifred Margaret Riley, 1904-1975.

SLOANE, Eugene 977.1'52'0924 B Hulse, 1902-
Walter Riley's daughter : a biography of Winifred Margaret Riley Sloane / by Eugene H. Sloane. Bay Ridge, Md. : Owl Press, 1976. x, 169 p., [1] leaf of plates : ill. ; 21 cm. [CT275.S52353S58] 76-44929 6.00
1. Sloane, Winifred Margaret Riley, 1904-1975. 2. United States—Biography. I. Title.

Slocum, Frances, 1773-1847.

MEGINNESS, John Franklin, 970.3 B 1827-1899.
Biography of Frances Slocum, the lost sister of Wyoming. New York, Arno Press, 1974 [c1890] 238, iv, 8 p. illus. 24 cm. (Women in America: from colonial times to the 20th century) Reprint of the 1891 ed. printed by Heller Bros.' Printing House, Williamsport, Pa. Bibliography: p. [235]-238. [E87.S612 1974] 74-3963 ISBN 0-405-06112-9
1. Slocum, Frances, 1773-1847. 2. Indians of North America—Captivities. I. Title. II. Series.

Slocum, Joshua, b. 1844.

JOYCE, Jessie (Slocum) 926.56
Joshua Slocum, sailor; a biography written by Beth Day, from the story told by his daughter Jessie Slocum Joyce. Illustrated by Walter F. Buehr. Boston, Houghton Mifflin, 1953. 248p. illus. 22cm. [VK140.S6J6] 52-11456
1. Slocum, Joshua, b. 1844. I. Day, Beth Feagles, 1924- II. Title.

SLOCUM, Victor. 926.56
Capt. Joshua Slocum; the life and voyages of America's best known sailor. New York, Sheridan House [1950] 384 p. illus., ports., maps. 24 cm. [VK140.S6S6] 50-6422
1. Slocum, Joshua, b. 1844. 2. Voyages and travels. I. Title.

TELLER, Walter Magnes. 910.4'1 B
Joshua Slocum [by] Walter Teller. [Extensively rev. and augm. ed.] New Brunswick, N.J., Rutgers University Press [1971] xviii, 253 p. illus. 25 cm. 1956 ed. published under title: The search for Captain Slocum. [VK140.S6T4 1971] 71-163954 ISBN 0-8135-0700-6 9.00
1. Slocum, Joshua, b. 1844. BIP

TELLER, Walter Magnes. 926.56
The search for Captain Slocum, a biography. New York, Scribner [1956] 258 p. illus. 22 cm. [VK140.S6T4] 56-9879
1. Slocum, Joshua, b. 1844. I. Title.

TELLER, Walter Magnes. 926.56
The search for Captain Slocum, a biography. New York, Scribner [1956] 253 p. illus. 22 cm. [VK140.S6T4] 56-9879
1. Slocum, Joshua, b. 1844.

Slonaker, Arthur Gordon.

SLONAKER, Arthur 378.1'11'0924 B Gordon.
Recollections and reflections of a college dean : including a brief history of the 103rd Barrage Balloon Battery / by Arthur Gordon Slonaker. Parsons, West Va., : McClain Print. Co., 1975. x, 218 p. : ill. ; 23 cm. Includes index. [LD5929.5.P6S56] 74-15998 ISBN 0-87012-197-9 : 8.00
1. Slonaker, Arthur Gordon. 2. United States. Army. 103d Antiaircraft Baloon Battery VLA Separate—History. I. Title.
Available from the author, 150 S. Mineral St., Keyser, WV 26726.

Slone, Verne Mae, 1914-

SLONE, Verna Mae, 1914- 976.9'165'040924 B
What my heart wants to tell / Verna Mae Slone. Washington : New Republic Books, 1979. xiii, 143 p., [4] leaves of plates : ill. ; 22 cm. Includes index. [F457.K5S58] 78-31688 ISBN 0-915220-47-4 : 8.95
1. Slone, Verne Mae, 1914- 2. Sloan family. 3. Knott Co., Ky.—Biography. 4. Knott Co., Ky.—Social life and customs. I. Title. **BIP**

Sloop, Mary T. Martin,

SLOOP, Mary T. Martin, 1873- 926.1
Miracle in the hills, by Mary T. Martin Sloop, with Le Gette Blythe. New York, McGraw-Hill [1953] 232 p. illus. 21 cm. Autobiographical. [R154.S515A3] 52-13467
I. Title.

Slope Co., N.D.—Biography.

SLOPE saga. 978.4'93'030922 B
[Amidon, N.D. : Slope Saga Committee, c1976] 1178 p. : ill. ; 29 cm. Cover title. Includes index. [F642.S6S55] 77-150491
1. Slope Co., N.D.—Biography. 2. Slope Co., N.D.—Genealogy. 3. Slope Co., N.D.—History. I. Slope Saga Committee.

Slovik, Edward Donald, 1920-1945.

HUIE, William Bradford, 1910- 355.1'33'0924 B
The execution of Private Slovik. New York, Delacorte Press [1970] viii, 230 p. 21 cm. [KF7652.S5H8 1970] 71-130041 1.95
1. Slovik, Edward Donald, 1920-1945. 2. Desertion, Military—U.S. I. Title.

Slye, Maud, 1879-1954.

MCCOY, Joseph J., 1917- 616.9'94'0420924 B
The cancer lady : Maud Slye and her hereditary studies / by J. J. McCoy. 1st ed. Nashville : T. Nelson, c1977. p. cm. Includes index. [RC268.4.M3] 77-12571 ISBN 0-8407-6552-5 : 6.95
1. Slye, Maud, 1879-1954. 2. Cancer—Genetic aspects. 3. Cancer research—United States—History. 4. Zoologists—United States—Biography. I. Title.

Small, Albion Woodbury, 1854-1926.

CHRISTAKES, George. 301'.092'4 B
Albion W. Small / by George Christakes. Boston : Twayne Publishers, c1978. 152 p. ; 22 cm. (Twayne's world leaders series ; TWLS 68) A revised and enlarged version of the author's thesis, Kansas State University, 1973. Includes index. Bibliography: p. 138-148. [HM22.U6S4833 1978] 77-5799 ISBN 0-8057-7718-0 : 10.95
1. Small, Albion Woodbury, 1854-1926. 2. Sociologists—United States—Biography. 3. Sociology—United States—History. **BIP**

DIBBLE, Vernon K. 301'.092'4 B
The legacy of Albion Small / Vernon K. Dibble. Chicago : University of Chicago Press, 1975. x, 255 p. ; 22 cm. (The Heritage of sociology) Includes bibliographical references and index. [HM22.U6S484] 74-16686 ISBN 0-226-14520-4 lib.bdg. : 15.00
1. Small, Albion Woodbury, 1854-1926. 2. Sociologists—Biography. I. Title. **BIP**

Smalley, George Washburn, 1833-1916.

MATHEWS, Joseph James, 1908- 070.4'092'4
George W. Smalley, forty years a foreign correspondent, by Joseph J. Mathews. Chapel Hill, University of North Carolina Press [1973] x, 229 p. illus. 23 cm. Includes bibliographical references. [PN4874.S52M3] 72-87496 ISBN 0-8078-1205-6 10.95.
1. Smalley, George Washburn, 1833-1916. I. Title.

Smalls, Robert, 1839-1915.

CRISTIANI, Leon, 1879- 922.22
Saint Bernadette. [Translated by Patrick O'Shaughnessy] Staten Island, N.Y. Alba House [1965] 181 p. 20 cm. [BX4700.S65C73] 65-15727
1. 1. Soubrious, Bernadette, Saint, 1844-1879. I. Title.

STERLING, Dorothy, 1913- 923.273
Captain of the Planter; the story of Robert Smalls. Illustrated by Ernest Crichlow. [1st ed.] Garden City, N.Y., Doubleday, 1958. 264 p. illus. 22 cm. Includes bibliography. [E185.97.S6S8] 58-5582
1. Smalls, Robert, 1839-1915. I. Title. **BIP**

STERLING, Philip. 920
Four took freedom; the lives of Harriet Tubman, Frederick Douglass, Robert Smalls, and Blanche K. Bruce [by] Philip Sterling and Rayford Logan. Illustrated by Charles White. [1st ed.] Garden City, N.Y., Doubleday, 1967. 116 p. illus., ports. 21 cm. (Zenith books, Z10) Biographical portraits of four famous Negro Americans who escaped the slavery into which they were born to further the fight for freedom and equality. [E185.96.S78] AC 67
1. Tubman, Harriet (Ross) 1815?-1913. 2. Douglass, Frederick, 1817?-1895. 3. Smalls, Robert, 1839-1915. 4. Bruce, Blanche Kelso, 1841-1898. 5. Negroes—Biography. I. Logan, Rayford Whittlingham, 1897- joint author. II. White, Charles, illus. III. Title. **BIP**

Smalls, Robert, 1839-1915—Juvenile literature.

MERIWETHER, Louise. 301.44'93'0924 B
The freedom ship of Robert Smalls. Illustrated by Lee Jack Morton. Englewood Cliffs, N.J., Prentice-Hall [1971] [32] p. illus. (part col.) 25 cm. A brief biography of the slave who escaped to freedom with his family and other runaway slaves on a captured Confederate gunboat. [E185.97.S6M4] 92 76-160258 ISBN 0-13-331082-5 4.50
1. Smalls, Robert, 1839-1915—Juvenile literature. I. Morton, Lee Jack, illus. II. Title. **BIP**

Smart, Christopher, 1722-1771.

ANDERSON, Frances E. 821'.6
Christopher Smart, by Frances E. Anderson. New York, Twayne Publishers [1974] 139 p. 20 cm. (Twayne's English authors series, TEAS 161) Bibliography: p. 130-136. [PR3687.S7Z57 1974] 73-15943 ISBN 0-8057-1502-9 5.50
1. Smart, Christopher, 1722-1771. **BIP**

DEVLIN, Christopher 821.6
Poor Kit Smart. Carbondale, Southern Ill. Univ. Pr. [1962, c.1961] 200p. Bibl. 62-8208 4.25 bds.,
1. Smart, Christopher, 1722-1771. I. Title.

SHERBO, Arthur, 1918- 821'.6 B
Christopher Smart, scholar of the university. [East Lansing] Michigan State University Press, 1967. 303 p. port. 24 cm. "Books in use at Cambridge about the year 1730, for arithmetic, algebra, geometry, physics, mechanics, and hydrostatics.": p. 273-277. Bibliographical references included in "Notes" (p. 277-285) [PR3687.S7Z8] 67-12575
1. Smart, Christopher, 1722-1771. I. Title.

Smart, John, 1741-1811.

FOSKETT, Daphne 927.5
John Smart: the man and his miniatures. New York, October House, [1965, c.1964] xviii, 100 p. geneal, tables (Fold.), plates (pt. col.) 21 cm. Collectors guidebks.) Bibl. [ND1337.G8S63] 65-11509 7.50 bds.,
1. Smart, John, 1741-1811. I. Title. **BIP**

***Smelley, Susan B.**

*SMELLEY, Susan B. 920.72
Susan's autobiography. New York, Carlton [1968] 61p. 21cm. (Hearthstone bk.) 2.00
I. Title.

Smet, Eugenie Marie Josephe, 1825-1871.

BUEHRIE, Marie Cecilia. 1887- 922.244
I am on fire: Blessed Mary of Providence, foundress of the Helpers of the Holy Souls, 1825-1871. Milwaukee, Bruce Press [1963] 264 p. illus. 23 cm. (Catholic life publications) [BX4367.Z8S4] 63-4805
1. Smet, Eugenie Marie Josephe, 1825-1871. 2. Helpers of the Holy Souls. I. Title.

BUEHRLE, Marie Cecilia, 1887- 922.244
I am on fire: Blessed Mary of Providence, foundress of the Helpers of the Holy Souls, 1825-1871. Milwaukee, Bruce [dist. Chicago, Helpers of the Holy Souls, 303 W. Barry, c1963. 264p. illus. 23cm. (Catholic life pubns.) 63-4805 3.95
1. Smet, Eugenie Marie Josephe, 1825-1871. 2. Helpers of the Holy Souls I. Title.

Smet, Pierre Jean de, 1801-1873.

HOPKINS, J G E 922.278
Black robe peacemaker, Pierre de Smet. Illustrated by W. N. Wilson. New York, P. J. Kenedy [1958] 188p. illus. 22cm. (American background books [8]) [F591.S632] 58-11453
1. Smet, Pierre Jean de, 1801-1873. 2. Indians of North America—Missions. I. Title.

SANDBERG, Harold William, 1902- 922.278
Black-robed Samson; the story of Peter de Smet, S.J., the apostle of the Indians. Illustrated by Paul A. Grout. [St. Meinrad, Ind., 1952] 75 p. illus. 22 cm. "A Grail publication." [F591.S644] 52-12081
1. Smet, Pierre Jean de, 1801-1873. I. Title.

TERRELL, John Upton, 1900- 922.278
Black robe; the life of Pierre-Jean de Smet, missionary, explorer & pioneer. [1st ed.] Garden City, N.Y., Doubleday, 1964. 381 p. maps (on lining papers) 22 cm. [F591.S647] 64-19231
1. Smet, Pierre Jean de, 1801-1873. I. Title.

Smet, Pierre Jean de, 1801-1873 — Juvenile literature.

BALTHAZOR, Thomas. 92
An apostle in the Rockies; a story of Father De Smet, s. j. Notre Dame. Ind., Dujarie Press [1961] 143p. illus. 22cm. [F591.S6315] 61 59639
1. Smet. Pierre Jean de, 1891-1873—Juvenile literature. 2. Indians of North America—Missions—Juvenile literature. I. Title.

HOPKINS, Joseph G E 922.278
Black robe peacemaker, Pierre de Smet. Illustrated by W. N. Wilson. New York, P.J. Kenedy [1958] 188 p. illus. 22 cm. (American background books [8]) [F591.S632] 58-11453
1. Smet, Pierre Jean de, 1801-1873 — Juvenile literature. 2. Indians of North America — Missions — Juvenile literature. I. Title.

Smethurst, Gamaliel.

SMETHURST, Gamaliel. 973'.04'97 S
A narrative of an extraordinary escape / Gamaliel Smethurst. New York : Garland Pub., 1977. 48 p. ; 23 cm. (The Garland library of narratives of North American Indian captivities ; v. 10) Issued with the reprint of the 1764 ed. of Saunders, C. The horrid cruelty of the Indians. New York, 1977. Reprint of the 1774 ed. printed for the author, London. [E85.G2 vol. 10] [E99.M6] 971.5'01 75-7030 ISBN 0-8240-1634-3 : part of 7 vol. set : 29.50 (set)
1. Smethurst, Gamaliel. 2. Micmac Indians. 3. New Brunswick—Description and travel. 4. Maritime Provinces—Description and travel. 5. Maritime Provinces—Biography. I. Title. II. Series.

Smit, Erasmus.

SMIT, Erasmus. 266'.4'20924 B
The diary of Erasmus Smit. Edited by H. F. Schoon. Translated by W. G. A. Mears. Cape Town, C. Struik, 1972. x, 186 p. illus. 22 cm. Translation of Uit het dagboek van Erasmus Smit. [BX9595.S63S613] 72-189813 ISBN 0-86977-013-6 10.00
I. Title.
Available from Verry. **BIP**

Smith, Abraham.

JANSEN, William Hugh. 398.2'2'0973
Abraham "Oregon" Smith : pioneer, folk hero, and tale-teller / William Hugh Jansen. New York : Arno Press, 1977. p. cm. (International folklore) Reprint of the author's thesis—Indiana University, 1949. [GR105.J35 1977] 77-70602 ISBN 0-405-10101-5 lib.bdg. : 22.00
1. Smith, Abraham. 2. Storytellers—United States—Biography. 3. Tales, American. I. Title. II. Series.

Smith, Adam, 1723-1790.

DANKERT, Clyde Edward, 1901- 330'.092'4 B
Adam Smith : man of letters and economist / Clyde E. Dankert. 1st ed. Hicksville, N.Y. : Exposition Press, [1974] ix, 297 p. ; 22 cm. (An Exposition-university book) Includes bibliographical references and index. [HB103.S6D35] 74-80675 ISBN 0-682-48020-7 . 10.00
1. Smith, Adam, 1723-1790. **BIP**

HIRST, Francis Wrigley, 1873-1953. 330.15'3'0924 B
Adam Smith. Freeport, N.Y., Books for Libraries Press [1973] p. Reprint of the 1904 ed. published by Macmillan, London, which was issued in series: English men of letters. [HB103.S6H6 1973] 73-5998 ISBN 0-518-19048-X
1. Smith, Adam, 1723-1790. **BIP**

HIRST, Francis Wrigley, 1873-1953. 330.15'3'0924 B
Adam Smith / by Francis W. Hirst. Folcroft, Pa. : Folcroft Library Editions, 1977. p. cm. Reprint of the 1904 ed. published by Macmillan, New York, in series: English men of letters. Includes index. [HB103.S6H6 1977] 77-3413 ISBN 0-8414-4801-9 lib. bdg. : 22.50
1. Smith, Adam, 1723-1790. 2. Economists—Great Britain—Biography.

RAE, John, 1845-1915 330.1220924
Life of Adam Smith. With an introd.: 'Guide to John Rae's Life of Adam Smith' by Jacob Viner. New York, A. M. Kelley [c.]1965. 145p. xv, 449p. 24cm. (Reprints of econ. classics) Bibl. [HB103.S6R2] 63-23522 20.00
1. Smith, Adam, 1723-1790. I. Viner, Jacob, 1892- II. Title.

SCOTT, William Robert, 1868-1940 330.1220924
Adam Smith as student and professor. NewYork, Kelley, 1965. xxiii, 445p. illus., facsims. 27cm. (Adam Smith Lib. Reprints of economic classics.) Orig. ed. Pub. 1937. With unpub. docts., including pts. of the Edinburgh lectures, a draft of The wealth of nations, extracts from the muniments of the University of Glasgow, and correspondence. Bibl. [HB103.S6S35] 65-26379 15.00
1. Smith, Adam, 1723-1790. I. Title. **BIP**

SMITH, Adam, 1723-1790. 330'.092'4 B
The correspondence of Adam Smith / edited by Ernest Campbell Mossner and Ian Simpson Ross. Oxford [Eng.] ; New York : Clarendon Press, 1977. xxx, 441 p. ; 24 cm. (The Glasgow edition of the works and correspondence of Adam Smith ; v. 6) Includes bibliographical references and indexes. [HB103.S6A47] 77-374053 ISBN 0-19-828185-4 : 33.00 (U.S.)
1. Smith, Adam, 1723-1790. I. Mossner, Ernest Campbell, 1907- II. Ross, Ian Simpson. III. Title. IV. Series.
Distributed by Oxford University Press New York.

STEWART, Dugald. 1753-1828 920.042
Biographical memoir of Adam Smith. New York, Kelley, 1966. clxxvii, 338p. port. 24cm. (Adam Smith lib.; Reprints of economic classics) Reprint of v.10 of the author's Complete works (Edinburgh, 1858), which was first pub. in 1811 under title: Biographical memoirs of Adam Smith, LL. D., of William Robertson, D. D., and of Thomas Reid, D. D. [CT821.S7] 66-15560 12.50
1. Smith, Adam, 1723-1790. 2. Robertson, William, 1721-1793. 3. Reid, Thomas, 1710-1796. I. Title. BIP

WEST, E. G. 330'.0924 B
Adam Smith, by E. G. West. New Rochelle, N.Y., Arlington House [1969] 221 p. 22 cm. (Architects of freedom series) Bibliographical references included in "Notes" (p. [207]-211) Bibliography: p. [213]-215. [HB103.S6W4] 69-16949 5.00
1. Smith, Adam, 1723-1790. BIP

WEST, E. G. 330.1'53 B
Adam Smith : the man and his works / E. G. West. Indianapolis : Liberty Press, c1976. 254 p. ; 22 cm. Includes indexes. Bibliography: p. [243]-247. [HB103.S6W42] 76-9436 ISBN 0-913966-06-1 : 6.95. ISBN 0-913966-07-X pbk. : 1.45
1. Smith, Adam, 1723-1790. 2. Economists, British—Biography. I. Title.

Smith, Adam, 1723-1790—Juvenile literature.

PIKE, Edgar Royston, 1896- 330.1530924 B
Adam Smith, father of the science of economics, by E. Royston Pike. [1st American ed.] New York, Hawthorn Books [1966, c1965] 128 p. 22 cm. ([Hawthorn Junior biographies]) [HB103.S6P5 1966] 66-15364
1. Smith, Adam, 1723-1790—Juvenile literature.

Smith, Albert E.

SMITH, Albert E. 927.7
Two reels and a crank, by Albert E. Smith in collaboration with Phil A. Koury. [1st ed.] Garden City, N. y., Doubleday, 1952. 285 p. illus., ports. 22 cm. Autobiographical. [TR849.S5A3] 52-11617
I. Title.

Smith, Alfred Emanuel, 1873-1944.

HANDLIN, Oscar, 1915- 923.273
Al Smith and his America. [1st ed.] Boston, Little, Brown [1958] 207 p. 21 cm. (The Library of American biography) Includes bibliography. [E748.S63H16] 57-6446
1. Smith, Alfred Emanuel, 1873-1944. I. Title. BIP

JOSEPHSON, Matthew, 1899- 973.91'5'0924 B
Al Smith: hero of the cities; a political portrait drawing on the papers of Frances Perkins [by] Matthew and Hannah Josephson. Boston, Houghton Mifflin, 1969. xx, 505 p. ports. 22 cm. Bibliography: p. [485]-491. [E748.S63J6] 73-79391 7.95
1. Smith, Alfred Emanuel, 1873-1944. I. Josephson, Hannah (Geffen) joint author. II. Perkins, Frances, 1882-1965.

O'CONNOR, Richard, 1915- 973.9150924 B
The first hurrah; a biography of Alfred E. Smith. New York, Putnam [1970] 318 p. ports. 22 cm. Bibliography: p. 304-305. [E748.S63O25] 70-97091 6.95
1. Smith, Alfred Emanuel, 1873-1944. I. Title.

PRINGLE, Henry Fowles, 1897-1958. 973.91'5'0924 B
Alfred E. Smith; a critical study. With a port. front. by Wilfred Jones. [1st AMS ed.] New York, AMS Press [1970] 402 p. 23 cm. Reprint of the 1927 ed. [E748.S63P9 1970] 75-101271
1. Smith, Alfred Emanuel, 1873-1944. BIP

WARNER, Emily (Smith) 923.273
The happy warrior; a biography of my father Alfred E. Smith[by] Emily Smith Warner with Hawthorne Daniel. [1st ed.] Garden City, N. Y., Doubleday 1956. 320p. illus. 22cm. [E748.S63W3] 56-9408
1. Smith, Alfred Emanuel, 1873-1944. I. Title.

WARNER, Emily (Smith) 923.273
The happy warrior; a biography of my father Alfred E. Smith [by] Emily Smith Warner with Hawthorne Daniel. [1st ed.] Garden City, N.Y., Doubleday, 1956. 320 p. illus. 22 cm. [E748.S63W3] 56-99408
1. Smith, Alfred Emanuel, 1873-1944. I. Title.

Smith, Alice Ravenel Huger, 1876-

ALICE Ravenel Huger Smith of Charleston, South Carolina; 759.13 an appreciation, on the occasion of her eightieth birthday, from her friends. Charleston, Privately published by her friends, 1956. 59p. 2 mounted illus. (1 col.) port. 24cm. [ND1839.S53A65] [ND1839.S53A65] 927.5 56-4870 56-4870
1. Smith, Alice Ravenel Huger, 1876-

Smith, Angie Frank, 1889-1962.

SPELLMAN, Norman W., 1928- 287'.6'0924
Growing a soul : the story of A. Frank Smith / Norman W. Spellman. Dallas : SMU Press, c1979. xiii, 513 p., [8] leaves of plates ; ill. ; 24 cm. Includes bibliographical references and index. [BX8495.S574S63] 78-20876 ISBN 0-87074-171-3 : 15.00
1. Smith, Angie Frank, 1889-1962. 2. Methodist Church—Bishops—Biography. 3. Bishops—Texas—Biography. 4. Texas—Biography. I. Title. BIP

Smith, Apollos Austin, 1825-1912.

COLLINS, Geraldine. 917.4753
The biography and funny sayings of Paul Smith, by Geraldine Collins. Paul Smiths, N.Y., Paul Smith's College [1965] 55 p. illus., ports. 24 cm. Cover title: Paul Smith. [F127.A2S58] 65-4773
1. Smith, Apollos Austin, 1825-1912. 2. Adirondack Mountains. I. Title.

Smith, Arthur James Marshall, 1902-

FERNS, John, 1940- 811'.5'2 B
A. J. M. Smith / by John Ferns. Boston : Twayne Publishers, 1979. 148 p. : port. ; 21 cm. (Twayne's world authors series ; TWAS 535 : Canada) Includes index. Bibliography: p. 136-141. [PR9199.3.S55147Z65] 78-27486 ISBN 0-8057-6377-5 : 14.95
1. Smith, Arthur James Marshall, 1902- 2. Authors, Canadian—20th century—Biography. BIP

Smith, Arthur Wincester, 1855-1944.

SULZBY, James Frederick, 1905- 976.1'98'050924
Arthur W. Smith, a Birmingham pioneer, 1855-1944. [Birmingham? Ala., 1961] 88 p. illus. 22 cm. [F334.B6S58] 61-10438
1. Smith, Arthur Wincester, 1855-1944. I. Title.

Smith, Bessie, 1898-1937.

ALBERTSON, Chris. 784'.092'4 B
Bessie. New York, Stein and Day [1972] 253 p. illus. 24 cm. "Selected discography": p. 239-242. [ML420.S667A7] 79-163353 ISBN 0-8128-1406-1 7.95
1. Smith, Bessie, 1898?-1937. I. Title. BIP

*ALBERTSON, Chris comp. 784.7'56
Bessie Smith: empress of the blues, compilation and biography by Chris Albertson, notes on Bessie Smith's singing style by Gunther Schuller, Musical arrangements by George N. Terry, edited by Clifford Richter New York, Schirmer Books [1975] Collier Macmillan, 143 p. music, 28 cm. [M1671] 74-78745 7.95 (pbk.)
1. Smith, Bessie, 1894-1937. 2. Blues (songs, etc.) I. Schuller, Gunther joint comp. II. Title. BIP

OLIVER, Paul. 927.8
Bessie Smith. New York, Barnes [1961, c1959] 82 p. illus. 21 cm. (Kings of jazz) A Perpetua book, P-4031. [ML420.S667O4 1961] 60-16821
1. Smith, Bessie, 1898-1937. 2. Jazz music. BIP

Smith, Bessie, 1898-1937—Juvenile literature

MOORE, Carman 784'.0924 [B]
Somebody's angel child; the story of Bessie Smith. [New York, Dell, 1975, c1969] 126 p. 18 cm. (Laurel-leaf library) (Women in America) Discography: [p. 118]-120. The life of the Negro singer who flourished in the twenties and was known as the Queen of the blues. [ML3930.S67M7] [92] 0.95 (pbk.)
1. Smith, Bessie, 1898-1937—Juvenile literature I. Title.
L.C. card number for original ed.: 77-94797 BIP

*Smith, Billie

*SMITH, Billie 920.7
Blood is thicker. New York, Carlton [c.1963] 159p. 21cm. (Reflection bk.) 2.75
I. Title.

Smith, Charles Henry,

SMITH, Charles Henry, 1875-1948 922.87
Mennonite country boy; the early years of C. Henry Smith. Newton, Kan., Faith & Life [c.1962] 261p. illus. (Mennonite hist. ser.) Bibl. 62-2760 4.00
I. Title.

Smith, Clark Ashton, 1893-1963.

CHALKER, Jack L. ed. v. 12
In memorian Clark Ashton Smith. With an introd. by Ray Bradbury. Illus. by David Prosser and Harry Warren Douthwaite. Baltimore, 1963. 97 p. illus. 28 cm. (Anthem fantasy library) Includes selections from Smith's prose and poetry. 65-31457
1. Smith, Clark Ashton, 1893-1963. I. Smith, Clark Ashton, 1893-1963. II. Title.

Smith, Clinton Lafayette.

SMITH, Clinton Lafayette. 973'.04'97 S
The boy captives : (Clinton and Jeff Smith) / [as told to] J. Marvin Hunter. New York : Garland Pub., 1976 [c1927] p. cm. (The Garland library of narratives of North American Indian captivities ; v. 110) Reprint of the ed. published by Frontier times, Bandera, Tex. [E85.G2 vol. 110] [E99.C85] 970'.004'97 B 75-7138 ISBN 0-8240-1734-X lib.bdg. : 21.00
1. Smith, Clinton Lafayette. 2. Smith, Jefferson Davis. 3. Comanche Indians—Captivities. 4. Apache Indians—Captivities. 5. Indians of North America—Captivities. I. Smith, Jefferson Davis, joint author. II. Hunter, John Marvin, 1880-1957. III. Title. IV. Series.

Smith Co., Tex. — Biog.

JOHNSON, Sidney Smith, 1840- v. 12
Some biographies of old settlers; historical personal and reminiscent. Vol. I. Tyler, Tex., 1900. [Tyler, Smith County Historical Society, 1965] iii, 400 p. illus., ports. 23 cm. No more published. 66-84764
1. Smith Co., Tex. — Biog. 2. Smith Co., Tex. — Hist. I. Title.

Smith, Coho, 1826-1914.

SMITH, Coho, 1826-1914. 976.4'05'0924
Cohographs / by Coho ; researched and edited by Iva Roe Logan. Fort Worth, Tex. : Branch-Smith, c1976. xix, 179 p. : ill. ; 23 cm. Includes bibliographical references and index. [F391.S63 1976] 76-21605 15.00
1. Smith, Coho, 1826-1914. 2. Frontier and pioneer life—Texas. 3. Pioneers—Texas—Biography. I. Title. BIP

Smith, Cornelius Cole, 1869-1936.

†SMITH, Cornelius Cole, 1913- 355.3'38'0924 B
Don't settle for second : life and times of Cornelius C. Smith / Cornelius C. Smith, Jr. ; with ill. by the author. San Rafael, Calif. : Presidio Press, 1976c1977 xvii, 229 p., [4] leaves of plates : ill. ; 24 cm. Includes index. Bibliography: p. 217-219. [E181.S55S5] 76-52040 ISBN 0-89141-007-4 : 14.95
1. Smith, Cornelius Cole, 1869-1936. 2. United States. Army—Biography. 3. Soldiers—United States—Biography. I. Title.

Smith, Daisy, 1891-1972.

HOPE Evangeline. 266'.0092'4 B
Daisy : the fascinating story of Daisy Smith, wife of Dr. Oswald J. Smith, missionary, statesman, and founder of the Peoples Church, Toronto / Hope Evangeline. Grand Rapids : Baker Book House, c1978. xiii, 247 p., [8] leaves of plates : ill. ; 21 cm. [BX9225.S477H66] 78-103025 ISBN 0-8010-3328-4 : 6.95
1. Smith, Daisy, 1891-1972. 2. Toronto. Peoples Church. 3. Smith, Oswald J. 4. Presbyterians—Canada—Biography. I. Title.

Smith, Daniel, 1748-1818.

DURHAM, Walter T., 1924- 328.73'092'4 B
Daniel Smith : frontier statesman / Walter T. Durham. Gallatin, Tenn. : Sumner County Library Board, c1976. xiv, 318 p., [8] leaves of plates : ill. ; 24 cm. Includes index. Bibliography: p. 266-271. [E340.S54D87] 76-18671 10.95
1. Smith, Daniel, 1748-1818. 2. Legislators—United States—Biography. 3. Tennessee—Biography.

Smith, Datus Clifford,

SMITH, Datus Clifford, 1907- 070.5'092'4
Journey with joy; letters from Datus C. Smith, Jr. Edited by his wife. Princeton, N.J., Published privately at the Sign of al Kalbu al Kabir al Aswad, 1972. 140 p. illus. 23 cm. [Z473.S588] 72-76765
I. Smith, Dorothy Hunt, ed. II. Title.

Smith, David,

SMITH, David, 1906-1965. 720'.924
David Smith, by David Smith; text and photos. by the author. Ed. by Cleve Gray. New York, Holt [1972] 176 p. illus. (pt. col.) facsims. port. 28 cm. (Holt pbk., 38) Bibl. [NB237.S567G7] 68-18582 ISBN 0-03-091563-5 pap., 9.95
I. Gray, Cleve, ed. II. Title.

Smith, David H., 1921-

SMITH, David H., 1921- 286'.1'0924 B
Remember the good times / David H. Smith. Nashville, Tenn. : Broadman Press, c1978. 128 p. : ill. ; 20 cm. [BX6495.S538A37] 78-66817 ISBN 0-8054-5704-6 pbk. : 2.95
1. Smith, David H., 1921- 2. Baptists—United States—Biography. I. Title. BIP

Smith, David, 1753- 1835.

MCBEE, May (Wilson) 923.973
The life and times of David Smith; patriot, pioneer, and Indian fighter. [Kansas City? Mo., 1959] 84p. 28cm. Includes bibliography. [F396.M22] 59-48881
1. Smith, David, 1753- 1835. 2. Frontier and pioneer life—Southwest, Old. I. Title.

Smith, E. D.

SMITH, E. D. 940.54'25
Battle for Burma / E. D. Smith. New York : Holmes & Meier Publishers, 1979. 190 p.,

[8] leaves of plates : ill. ; 24 cm. Includes index. Bibliography: p. [182]-183. [D767.6.S6 1979] 78-25679 ISBN 0-8419-0468-5 : 17.50
1. Smith, E. D. 2. World War, 1939-1945—Campaigns—Burma. 3. World War, 1939-1945—Personal narratives, English. 4. Burma—History—Japanese occupation, 1942-1945. 5. Soldiers—Great Britain—Biography. I. Title. **BIP**

Smith, Earl R.,

SMITH, Earl R., 1882-1967. 917.94
The days of my years; the autobiography of an average American. Portland, Oregon Historical Society, 1968. xiv, 314 p. illus., ports. 22 cm. [CT275.S5267A3] 68-64777
I. Title.

Smith, Edgar, 1934-

SMITH, Edgar, 1934- 345'.73'02523
Getting out. New York, Coward, McCann & Geoghegan [1973] 271 p. 22 cm. Includes bibliographical references. [HV9468.S65A33 1973] 72-76671 ISBN 0-698-10453-6 7.95
1. Smith, Edgar, 1934- I. Title.

Smith, Edward Elmer, 1890-1965.

ELLIK, Ron, 1938- 813.52
The universes of E. E. Smith, by Ron Ellik and Bill Evans. Introd. by James H. Schmitz. Bibliography by Al Lewis. Illus. by Bjo. [1st ed.] Chicago, Advent Publishers, 1966. 272 p. illus. 23 cm. Bibliography: p. [255]-263. [PS3537.M349Z6] 66-9092
1. Smith, Edward Elmer, 1890-1965. I. Evans, William Harrington, 1921- II. Title. **BIP**

Smith, Elbert A

SMITH, Elbert A 1871-1959. 922.8373
Brother Elbert; the life of Elbert A. Smith, 1871-1959, rev. and enl. from his autobiography On memory's beam. Independence, Mo., Herald House, 1959. 438 p. illus. 21 cm. [BX8678.S57A3 1959] 60-17896
I. Title.

Smith, Emma,

SMITH, Emma, pseud. 920.7
A Cornish waif's story, an autobiography. With a foreword by A. L. Rowse. [1st American ed.] New York, Dutton [1956] 192 p. 22 cm. [PR6037.M423Z5 1956] 56-5256
I. Title.

Smith, Erastus Almon, 1818-1907.

SMITH, Ernest Almon. 920
Middle River homestead. [Des Moines? 1955] 290p. 23cm. [CT275.S529S58] 56-28408
1. Smith, Erastus Almon, 1818-1907. I. Title.

Smith, Ethel (Sabin)

SMITH, Ethel (Sabin) 1887- 917.75
A furrow deep and true. [1st ed.] New York, W.W. Norton [1964] 224 p. 22 cm. Autobiographical. [CT275.S532A3] 64-13995
I. Title.

Smith family.

KEEFER, Estella Blanche (Keller) 1908- 929'.2'0973
The Smith family, Godfried, 1789-1958; historical, pictorial, biographical of the Schmidt, Smith family. [Franklin? Pa., 1958] 130p. illus. 28cm. [CS71.S643 1958a] 59-20368
1. Smith family. I. Title.

Smith family (Aaron Stuart Smith, fl. 1858)

SMITH, Charles Daniel, 1879- 929'.2'0973
A family biography; the story of Edward Willis & Jonnie Robertson Smith and their ten children. [n.p., c1954] 354p. illus. 27cm. [CS71.S643 1954a] 55-25883
1. Smith family (Aaron Stuart Smith, fl. 1858) I. Title.

Smith, Florence Blake

SMITH, Florence Blake 920.7
Cow chips 'n' cactus; The homestead in Wyoming. New York, Pageant [c.1962] 118p. 21cm. 2.50
I. Title.

Smith, Frank Eugene, 1856-1935.

HENDRICKSON, Hazel Parker (Smith) 1894- 926.213
The Smith family Robinson; memoris of the life of a San Francisco family, but more essentially the role played by Frank E. Smith in the early days of electricity in San Francisco and San Jose, California. [Davis? Calif., 1953] 160p. illus. 29cm. [CT275.S538H4] 53-30338
1. Smith, Frank Eugene, 1856-1935. I. Title.

Smith, Frank Leslie, 1867-

WOODDY, Carroll Hill. 320.9'773'04
The case of Frank L. Smith; a study in representative government. New York, Arno Press, 1974 [c1931] ix, 393 p. illus. 23 cm. (Politics and people: the ordeal of self-government in America) Reprint of the ed. published by University of Chicago Press, Chicago. Includes bibliographical references. [F546.S58W66 1974] 73-19187 ISBN 0-405-05907-8 21.00
1. Smith, Frank Leslie, 1867- 2. Illinois—Politics and government—1865-1950. 3. Corruption (in politics)—Illinois. I. Title. II. Series. **BIP**

Smith, George Gordon, 1905-1970.

LUCAS, Norman. 364.12'092'4 B
Spycatcher: a biography of Detective-Superintendent George Gordon Smith. London, New York, W. H. Allen, 1973. ix, 179, [8] p. illus., facsims., ports. 23 cm. [HV7911.S57L8] 73-159276 ISBN 0-491-00624-1 £2.75
1. Smith, George Gordon, 1905-1970. I. Title.

***Smith, George H.**

*SMITH, George H. 973.920924
Who is Ronald Reagan? New York, Pyramid [c.1968] 173p. 18cm. (T-1793) (B) .75 pap.,
I. Title.

Smith, George, 1808-1899.

SMITH, Alice Elizabeth, 1896- 332.60924
George Smith's money: a Scottish investor in America. Madison, State Hist. Soc. of Wis. [c.] 1966. vii, 197p. illus., ports. 23cm. Bibl. [HG172S6S6] 66-63001 4.50
1. Smith, George, 1808-1899. I. Title. **BIP**

Smith, Gerrit, 1797-1874.

FROTHINGHAM, Octavius Brooks, 1822-1895. 361'.924 B
Gerrit Smith; a biography. New York, Negro Universities Press [1969] 381 p. illus., port. 23 cm. Reprint of the 1878 ed. [E415.9.S64F9 1969] 74-98720
1. Smith, Gerrit, 1797-1874. **BIP**

HARLOW, Ralph Volney, 1884-1956. 361'.92'4 B
Gerrit Smith, philanthropist and reformer. New York, Russell & Russell [1972, c1939] 501 p. 25 cm. [HV28.S63H3 1972] 74-173547
1. Smith, Gerrit, 1797-1874.

Smith, Goldwin, 1823-1910.

WALLACE, Elisabeth. 920.5
Goldwin Smith, Victorian liberal. [Toronto] University of Toronto Press [1957] 297p. illus. 24cm. [CT788.S592W3] 57-2984
1. Smith, Goldwin, 1823-1910. I. Title.

WALLACE, Elisabeth. 920.5
Goldwin Smith, Victorian liberal. [Toronto] University of Toronto Press [1957] 297 p. illus. 24 cm. [CT788.S592W3] 57-2984
1. Smith, Goldwin, 1823-1910. I. Title.

Smith, Harry D.

SMITH, Harry D. 381 B
Through dirty windows / by Harry D. Smith. Windsor, N.S. : Lancelot Press, 1976. 84 p. : ill. ; 21 cm. [HD8107.S54A37] 77-351845 ISBN 0-88999-050-6
1. Smith, Harry D. 2. Clayton & Sons, Halifax, N.S. 3. Clerks (Retail trade)—Nova Scotia—Halifax—Biography. I. Title.

Smith, Hoke, 1855-1931.

GRANTHAM, Dewey W. 923.273
Hoke Smith and the politics of the New South. Baton Rouge, Louisiana State University Press, 1958. 396 p. ports. 24 cm. (Southern biography series) "Critical essay on authorities": p. 372-377. Bibliographical footnotes. [E748.S663G7] 58-9209
1. Smith, Hoke, 1855-1931. I. Series. **BIP**

Smith, Hyrum, 1800-1844.

CORBETT, Pearson Harris, 1900- 922.8373
Hyrum Smith, patriarch. Salt Lake City, Deseret [c.1963] 472p. illus. 24cm. Bibl. 63-1781 3.95
1. Smith, Hyrum, 1800-1844. I. Title. **BIP**

Smith, Ian Douglas, 1919-

JOYCE, Peter, 1935- 968.9'1'040924 B
Anatomy of a rebel: Smith of Rhodesia: a biography. New Rochelle, N.Y., Arlington House [1975, c1974] p. cm. [DT962.76.S64J69 1975] 74-18265 ISBN 0-87000-305-4
1. Smith, Ian Douglas, 1919- I. Title.

Smith, James Lindsay.

SMITH, James Lindsay. 301.451'96'024 B
Autobiography of James L. Smith; including also reminiscences of slave life, recollections of the war, education of freedmen, causes of the exodus, etc. Norwich [Conn.] Press of the Bulletin Co., 1881. Miami, Fla., Mnemosyne Pub. Co. [1969] xiii, 150 p. illus., port. 23 cm. [E444.S65 1969] 76-89430
1. Slavery in the United States—Virginia. 2. Freedmen. I. Title.

SMITH, James Lindsay. 301.45'19'6073024 B
Autobiography of James L. Smith : including also, reminiscences of slave life, recollections of the war, education of freedmen, causes of the exodus, etc. Norwich : Society of the Founders of Norwich, Connecticut, c1976. viii, 150 p. : ill. ; 22 cm. Reprint, with new introd., of the 1881 ed. published by Press of the Bulletin Co., Norwich, Conn. [E444.S65 1976] 76-20957
1. Smith, James Lindsay. 2. Slaves—Virginia—Biography. 3. Freedmen. 4. Virginia—Biography. I. Title.

Smith, James Monroe, 1839-1915.

COULTER, Ellis Merton, 1890- 926.3
James Monroe Smith; Georgia planter, before death and after. Athens, Univ. of Georgia Press [c.1961] 294p. illus. 25cm. Bibl. 61-9793 5.00
1. Smith, James Monroe, 1839-1915. I. Title.

Smith, James, 1737-1812.

NYE, Wilbur Sturtevant, 1898- 973.2'7'0924 B
James Smith: early Cumberland Valley patriot, by Wilbur S. Nye. Carlisle, Pa., Cumberland County Historical Society, 1969. 34 p. facsim., fold. map. 23 cm. Includes bibliographical references. [E195.S746] 74-14402
1. Smith, James, 1737-1812.

Smith, Jedediah Strong, 1799-1831.

BURT, Olive (Woolley) 1894- 978'.02'0924 B
Jed Smith, young western explorer, by Olive W. Burt. Illustrated by James Ponter. Indianapolis, Bobbs-Merrill [1963] 200 p. illus. 20 cm. (Childhood of famous Americans) Emphasizes the boyhood of the man who fulfilled his dream of exploring the vast, unknown areas of the West. [PZ7.B9456Jc] 92 AC 68
1. Smith, Jedediah Strong, 1799-1831. I. Ponter, James, illus. II. Title.

LATHAM, Frank Brown, 1910- 978'.02'0924 B
Jed Smith, trailblazer and trapper [by] Frank B. Latham. Illustrated by William Hutchinson. Champaign, Ill., Garrard Pub. Co. [1968] 80 p. col. illus. 23 cm. (A Discovery book) A brief biography of the man who grew up in the East, became a trapper, and fulfilled his dream of exploring areas of the American West which had been just white space on a map. [PZ7.L345Je5] 92 AC 68
1. Smith, Jedediah Strong, 1799-1831. I. Hutchinson, William, illus. II. Title.

MORGAN, Dale Lowell, 1914- 923.973
Jedediah Smith and the opening of the West. [1st ed.] Indianapolis, Bobbs-Merrill [1953] 458 p. illus., ports., map. 23 cm. Bibliographical references included in "Notes" (p. 371-438) [F592.S653] 53-10550
1. Smith, Jedediah Strong, 1799-1831. 2. Fur trade—The West. 3. The West—Discovery and exploration.

NEIHARDT, John Gneisenau, 1881- 917.8
The splendid wayfaring; the story of the exploits and adventures of Jedediah Smith and his comrades, the Ashley-Henry men, discoverers and explorers of the great central route from the Missouri River to the Pacific Ocean, 1822-1831 [by] John G. Neihardt. Lincoln, University of Nebraska Press [1970, c1920] ix, 290 p. map. 21 cm. "A Bison book." Bibliography: p. 288-290. [F592.N39 1970] 71-116054 1.80
1. Smith, Jedediah Strong, 1799-1831. 2. The West—Discovery and exploration. 3. Overland journeys to the Pacific. I. Title.

PHILLIPS, Fred M. 979'.02
Desert people and mountain men : exploration of the Great Basin, 1824-1865 / Fred M. Phillips. Bishop, Calif. : Chalfant Press, c1977. 62 p. : ill. ; 23 cm. Bibliography: p. 62. [F592.P47] 77-2335 ISBN 0-912494-25-5 pbk. : 3.95
1. Fremont, John Charles, 1813-1890. 2. Ogden, Peter Skene, 1790-1854. 3. Smith, Jedediah Strong, 1799-1831. 4. Walker, Joseph Reddeford, 1798-1876. 5. Great Basin—Discovery and exploration. 6. Explorers—Great Basin—Biography. 7. Indians of North America—Great Basin. I. Title. **BIP**

SULLIVAN, Maurice S., 1893-1935. 978'.02'0924 B
Jedediah Smith, trader and trail breaker. Foreword and notes by Rufus Rockwell Wilson. Illustrated by Howard Simon. New York, Press of the Pioneers, 1936. Millwood, N.Y., Kraus Reprint Co., 1973. xiii, 233 p. illus. 24 cm. [F592.S657 1973] 72-13825 10.00
1. Smith, Jedediah Strong, 1799-1831. 2. The West—History—To 1848. **BIP**

Smith, Jedediah Strong, 1799-1831—Juvenile literature.

MILLER, Helen Markley. 978'.02'0924 B
Jedediah Smith on the far frontier. Illustrated by Ted A. Xaras. New York,

Putnam [1971] 95 p. illus. 24 cm. (An American hero biography) A biography of the nineteenth-century trapper and explorer who earned his reputation on the western frontier. [F592.S6516 1971] 92 74-111529 3.64
1. Smith, Jedediah Strong, 1799-1831—Juvenile literature. I. Xaras, Theodore A., illus. II. Title. **BIP**

MORGAN, Dale Lowell, 1914- 923.973
Jedediah Smith and the opening of the West. Lincoln, Univ. of Neb. Pr. [1964, c.1953] 458p. illus., ports., map (fold.) 21cm. (BB134) 1.85 pap.,
1. Smith, Jedediah, 1799-1831. 2. Fur trade—The West. 3. The West—Disc. & explor. I. Title.

MORGAN, Dale Lowell, 1914- 923.973
Jedediah Smith and the opening of the West [Gloucester, Mass., P. Smith. 1964, c.1953] 458p. illus., port., map. 21cm. (Univ. of Neb. bk. rebound) Bibl. 4.00
1. Smith. Jedediah, 1799-1831. 2. Fur trade—The West. 3. The West. disc explor. I. Title. **BIP**

Smith, Jesse Guy, 1885-

SMITH, Jewell (Howell) v. 12
Dr. Jesse Guy Smith. [Commerce, Tex., Printed by students of East Texas State College Print. Dept., 1958?] 49 p. ports. 28 cm.
1. Smith, Jesse Guy, 1885- I. Title.

Smith, Jessie Willcox, 1863-1935.

SCHNESSEL, S. Michael. 741.9'73 B
Jessie Willcox Smith / S. Michael Schnessel. New York : Crowell, [1977] 224 p. : ill. (some col.) ; 29 cm. Includes bibliographical references and index. [NC975.5.S64S36] 77-3530 ISBN 0-690-01493-7 : 22.95
1. Smith, Jessie Willcox, 1863-1935. **BIP**

Smith, John, 1580-1631.

ASHTON, John, b.1834. 973.2'1'0924
The adventures and discoveries of Captain John Smith sometime president of Virginia, and admiral of New England. London, New York, Cassell, 1883. Detroit, Singing Tree Press, 1969. xx, 309 p. illus., maps, ports. 23 cm. Title on spine: The adventures of Captain John Smith. [F229.S714 1969] 76-78108
1. Smith, John, 1580-1631. 2. Virginia—History—Colonial period, ca. 1600-1775. I. Title. II. Title: The adventures of Captain John Smith.

BARBOUR, Philip L. 923.9
The three worlds of Captain John Smith, by Philip L. Barbour. Boston, Houghton Mifflin, 1964. xix, 553 p. illus., geneal. tables, maps, ports. 22 cm. Bibliography: p. [493]-527. [F229.S7145] 64-10543
1. Smith, John, 1580-1631. I. Title.

GERSON, Noel Bertram, 1914- 973.2'1'0924 B
The glorious scoundrel : a biography of Captain John Smith / by Noel B. Gerson. New York : Dodd, Mead, c1978. 251 p. : ill. ; 22 cm. Includes index. Bibliography: p. 241-243. [F229.S7G47] 78-1357 ISBN 0-396-07518-5 : 7.95
1. Smith, John, 1580-1631. 2. Explorers—Great Britain—Biography. 3. Jamestown, Va.—History. I. Title. **BIP**

[GERSON, Noel Bertram] 1914- 973.210924(B)
The great rogue; a biography of Captain John Smith, by Paul Lewis. New York, McKay [1966] x, 306p. 21cm. Bibl. [F229.S7178] 66-19261 5.95
1. Smith, John, 1580-1631. I. Title.

HENDERSON, Brantley, 1884- 923.9
Being the story of fabulous John Smith, Virginia's first explorer and author. Richmond, Printed by Whittet and Shepperson [c1956] 106p. illus. 21cm. Includes bibliography. [F229.S7195] 57-1337
1. Smith, John, 1580-1631. 2. mith. I. Title.

HENDERSON, Brantley 1884- 923.9
Being the story of fabulous John Smith, Virginia's first explorer and author. Richmond, Printed by Whittet and Shepperson [c1956] 106p. illus. 21cm. Includes bibliography. [F229.S7195] 57-1337
1. Smith, John, 1580-1631. I. Title. II. Title: Fabulous John Smith.

LEIGHTON, Margaret (Carver). 923.9
The sword and the compass; the far-flung adventures of Captain John Smith. Illustrated by James Leighton. Boston, Houghton Mifflin, 1951. 264 p. illus. 22 cm. [F229.S734] 51-11810
1. Smith, John, 1580-1631. I. Title.

PAINE, Lauran. 975.5'01'0924
Captain John Smith and the Jamestown story. New York, Hippocrene Books [1973] 206 p. illus. 23 cm. Bibliography: p. 200-201. [F229.S7385 1973b] 73-81582 ISBN 0-88254-171-4 6.95
1. Smith, John, 1580-1631. 2. Jamestown, Va.—History. I. Title.

SMITH, Bradford, 1909- 923.9
Captain John Smith, his life & legend. [1st ed.] Philadelphia, Lippincott [1953] 375p. port. 22cm. 'Captain John Smith's Hungary and Transyivania,' by L. P. Striker: p. 311-342. 'List of sources used by Smith in The generall historie': p. 348-350. bBibliographical references: p. 351-363. [F229.S7475] 53-8918
1. Smith, John, 1580-1631. I. Title.

SMITH, John, 1580-1631. 975.5'02'0924
Captain John Smith's America; selections from his writings. Edited by John Lankford. [1st ed.] New York, Harper & Row [1967] xviii, 195 p. 21 cm. (Harper torchbooks. The University library, TB3078) (American perspectives) "Selections included in this volume are from The generall historie, of 1624 and the Advertisements for the unexperienced planters of New England, of 1631, edited by Edward Arber and contained in his Travels and works of Captain John Smith, published ... in 1910." Bibliographical footnotes. [F229.S595] 67-11606
1. Virginia—History—Colonial period, ca. 1600-1775. 2. Virginia—Description and travel. 3. Indians of North America—Virginia. 4. New England—History—Colonial period, ca. 1600-1775. I. Lankford, John, ed. II. Title.

SYME, Ronald, 1910- 923.9
John Smith of Virginia; illustrated by William Stobbs. New York, Morrow, 1954. 192 p. illus. 21 cm. [Morrow junior books] [F229.S749 1954] 54-5521
1. Smith, John, 1580-1631. **BIP**

VAUGHAN, Alden T., 1929- 975.5'01'0924 B
American genesis : Captain John Smith and the founding of Virginia / Alden T. Vaughan ; edited by Oscar Handlin. Boston : Little, Brown, [1975] ix, 207 p. : ill. ; 20 cm. (The Library of American biography) Includes index. Bibliography: p. [191]-200. [F229.S7495] 74-5914 6.95 pbk. : 2.95
1. Smith, John, 1580-1631. 2. Virginia—History—Colonial period, ca. 1600-1775. I. Title. II. Series. **BIP**

WHARTON, Henry, 1664-1695. 923.9
The life of John Smith, English soldier. Translated from the Latin manuscript with an essay on Captain John Smith in seventeenth-century literature by Laura Polanyi Striker. Chapel Hill, Published for the Virginia Historial Society by the University of North Carolina Press [1957] 101 p. illus., ports., facsims. 24 cm. Bibliographical footnotes. [F229.S7W4] 57-13884
1. Smith, John, 1580-1631. I. Striker, Laura Polanyi. Captain John Smith in seventeenth century literature. II. Virginia Historial Society, Richmond. III. Title.

WHARTON, Henry, 1664-1695. 923.9
The life of John Smith, English soldier. Translated from the Latin manuscript with an essay on Captain John Smith in seventeenth-century literature by Laura Polanyi Striker. Chapel Hill, Published for the Virginia Historical Society by the University of North Carolina Press [1957] 101 p. illus., ports., facsims. 24 cm. Bibliographical footnotes. [F229.S7W4] 57-13884
1. Smith, John, 1580-1631. I. Striker, Laura Polanyi. Captain John Smith in seventeenth century literature. II. Virginia Historical Society, Richmond.

Smith, John, 1580-1631—Juvenile literature.

KURTZ, Henry Ira. 973.2'1'0924 B
Captain John Smith / Henry Ira Kurtz. New York : Watts, 1976. 57 p. : ill. ; 26 cm. (A Visual biography) Includes index. Bibliography: p. 54. A biography of John Smith including his life before he voyaged to Virginia, but with special emphasis on his exploits in North America. [F229.S73] 92 75-20148 ISBN 0-531-01105-4 lib.bdg. : 4.90
1. Smith, John, 1580-1631—Juvenile literature. I. Title. **BIP**

SYME, Ronald, 1910- 923.9
John Smith of Virginia. Illustrated by William Stobbs. New York, Morrow, 1954. 192 p. illus. 21 cm. [F229.S749] 54-5521
1. Smith, John, 1580-1631 — Juvenile literature. Full name: Neville Ronald Syme. I. Title.

Smith, John, 1790-1824.

NORTHCOTT, William Cecil, 1902- 322.4'4'0924 B
Slavery's martyr : John Smith of Demerara and the emancipation movement, 1817-24 / [by] Cecil Northcott. London : Epworth Press, 1976. 136 p. : facsims., maps ; 22 cm. Includes index. Bibliography: p. 131-133. [HT1029.S55N67 1976] 77-360969 ISBN 0-7162-0269-7 : £1.50
1. Smith, John, 1790-1824. 2. Abolitionists—Biography. 3. Slavery in Guyana. 4. Slavery in Great Britain—Anti-slavery movements. I. Title.

Smith, Joseph,

SMITH, Joseph, 1832-1914. 922.8373
Joseph Smith III and the Restoration. Edited by his daughter, Mary Audentia Smith Anderson and condensed by his granddaughter, Bertha Audentia Anderson Hulmes. Independence, Mo., Herald House [1952] 639 p. port. 23 cm. Condensed from the author's Memoirs which were published serially in the Saints' herald, Nov. 6, 1934-July 31, 1937. [BX8695.S6A3] 52-4972
I. Anderson, Mary Audentia (Smith) 1872- ed. II. Hulmes, Bertha Audentia (Anderson) 1892- III. Title.

Smith, Joseph Fielding, 1876-

HESLOP, J. M. 289.3'3'0924 B
Joseph Fielding Smith; a prophet among the people [by] J. M. Heslop and Dell R. Van Orden. Salt Lake City, Deseret Book Co., 1971. xi, 171 p. ports. 24 cm. [BX8695.S63H48] 77-175121 ISBN 0-87747-454-0 3.95
1. Smith, Joseph Fielding, 1876- I. Van Orden, Dell R., joint author.

MCCONKIE, Joseph F. 289.3'3 B
True and faithful; the life story of Joseph Fielding Smith [by] Joseph F. McConkie. Salt Lake City, Utah, Bookcraft, 1971. 102 p. illus. 24 cm. Includes bibliographical references. [BX8695.S64M25] 76-175137
1. Smith, Joseph Fielding, 1876- I. Title.

SMITH, Joseph Fielding, 1913- 289.3'3 B
The life of Joseph Fielding Smith, tenth President of the Church of Jesus Christ of the Latter-day Saints [by] Joseph Fielding Smith, Jr. and John J. Stewart. Salt Lake City, Deseret Book Co., 1972. xvi, 404 p. illus. 24 cm. Bibliography: p. [389]-392. [BX8695.S64S6] 72-90344 ISBN 0-87747-484-2 4.95
1. Smith, Joseph Fielding, 1876- I. Stewart, John J., joint author. II. Title.

Smith, Joseph Lindon, 1863-1950.

SMITH, Corinna Haven (Putnam) 920.7
Interesting people; eighty years with the great and near-great, by Corinna Lindon Smith. [1st ed.] Norman, University of Oklahoma Press [1962] 456 p. illus. 24 cm. [ND237.S6S5] 62-11273
1. Smith, Joseph Lindon, 1863-1950. I. Title. **BIP**

SMITH, Corinna (Putnam) 920.7
Interesting people; eighty years with the great and near-great, by Corinna Lindon Smith. Norman, Univ. of Okla. Pr. [c.1962] 456p. illus. 24cm. 62-11273 5.95
1. Smith, Joseph Lindon, 1863-1950. I. Title.

Smith, Joseph Russell, 1874-

ROWLEY, Virginia M., 1926- 910
J. Russell Smith, geographer, educator, and conservationist. Philadelphia, Univ. of Pa. Pr. [c.1964] 247p. port. 22cm. Bibl. 64-17757 6.00
1. Smith, Joseph Russell, 1874- I. Title. **BIP**

ROWLEY, Virginia M 1926- 910
J. Russell Smith, geographer, educator, and conservationist, by Virginia M. Rowley. Philadelphia, University of Pennsylvania Press [1964] 247 p. port. 22 cm. Bibliography: p. 218-242. [G69.S6R6] 64-17757
1. Smith, Joseph Russell, 1874- I. Title.

Smith, Joseph, 1805-1844.

ANDERSON, Richard Lloyd. 289.3'092'4 B
Joseph Smith's New England heritage; influences of grandfathers Solomon Mack and Asael Smith. Salt Lake City, Desert Book Co., 1971. xix, 230 p. illus. 24 cm. Bibliography: p. [225]-227. [BX8695.S6A68] 74-186263 ISBN 0-87747-460-5 4.95
1. Smith, Joseph, 1805-1844. 2. Smith family. I. Title.

ANDRUS, Hyrum Leslie, 1924- 922.8373
Joseph Smith, the man and the seer. Salt Lake City, Deseret Book Co., [1960] 144p. illus. 24cm. Includes bibliography. [BX8695.S6A72] 60-42656
1. Smith, Joseph. 1805-1844. I. Title.

ANDRUS, Hyrum Leslie, 1924- 922.8373
Joseph Smith, the man and the seer. Salt Lake City, Deseret Book Co. [c.1960] 144p. illus. (part col.) 60-42656 2.50
1. Smith, Joseph, 1805-1844. I. Title. **BIP**

BRODIE, Fawn (McKay) 1915- 289.3'0924 B
No man knows my history; the life of Joseph Smith, the Mormon prophet, by Fawn M. Brodie. 2d ed., rev. and enl. New York, Knopf, 1971. xiii, 499, xx p. illus., map, ports. 22 cm. Bibliography: p. 490-499. [BX8695.S6B7 1971] 71-136333 ISBN 0-394-46967-4 10.00
1. Smith, Joseph, 1805-1844. I. Title.

CHEVILLE, Roy Arthur, 1897- 289.3'092'2 B
Joseph and Emma Smith, companions for seventeen and a half years, 1827-1844 / by Roy A. Cheville. Independence, Mo. : Herald Pub. House, c1977. 206 p. ; 21 cm. [BX8695.S6C53] 76-44549 ISBN 0-8309-0174-4 : 8.00
1. Smith, Joseph, 1805-1844. 2. Smith, Emma Hale. 3. Mormons and Mormonism—Biography. I. Title.

CROWTHER, Duane S 922.8373
The prophecies of Joseph Smith. Salt Lake City, Bookcraft, 1963. 413 p. illus., ports., maps. 24 cm. [BX8695.S6C7] 64-3499
1. Smith, Joseph, 1805-1844. I. Title.

ETZENHOUSER, Rudolph, 1856- 289.3'22
From Palmyra, New York, 1830, to Independence, Missouri, 1894. Independence, Mo., Ensign Pub. House, 1894. [New York, AMS Press, 1971] 444 p. 22 cm. The Book unsealed, rev. and enl., which was first published in 1892, forms part one of this work. [BX8627.E78

1971] 73-134393 ISBN 0-404-08435-4 17.50
1. Smith, Joseph, 1805-1844. 2. Book of Mormon. 3. Mormons and Mormonism—Doctrinal and controversial works. I. Title.

GIBBONS, Francis M., 1921- 289.3'092'4 B
Joseph Smith, martyr, prophet of God / Francis M. Gibbons. Salt Lake City : Deseret Book Co., 1977. ix, 377 p. ; 23 cm. Includes index. Bibliography: p. 366-368. [BX8695.S6G52] 77-2019 ISBN 0-87747-637-3 : 6.95
1. Smith, Joseph, 1805-1844. 2. Mormons and Mormonism in the United States—Biography. 3. Mormons and Mormonism—History. I. Title.

HARTSHORN, Leon R. 289.3'0924 B
Joseph Smith: prophet of the restoration, by Leon R. Hartshorn. Salt Lake City, Deseret Book Co., 1970. 124 p. 24 cm. Includes bibliographic references. [BX8695.S6H32] 71-130321 ISBN 0-87747-372-2 3.95
1. Smith, Joseph, 1805-1844.

HILL, Donna. 289.3'092'4 B
Joseph Smith, the first Mormon / by Donna Hill. 1st ed. Garden City, N.Y. : Doubleday, 1977. xviii, 527 p., [8] leaves of plates : ill. ; 25 cm. Includes index. Bibliography: p. [495]-513. [BX8695.S6H54] 73-15345 ISBN 0-385-00804-X : 12.50
1. Smith, Joseph, 1805-1844. 2. Mormons and Mormonism—Biography. I. Title.

JACKSON, Ronald Vern. 289.3'092'4 B
The seer, Joseph Smith, his education from the Most High / by Ronald Vern Jackson. 3d ed., expanded and bound. Salt Lake City : Hawkes Pub. Inc., c1977. 248 p. : ill. ; 23 cm. Includes bibliographical references. [BX8695.S6J25 1977] 77-77303 ISBN 0-89036-088-X : 3.95
1. Smith, Joseph, 1805-1844. 2. Mormons and Mormonism in the United States—Biography. I. Title.
Publisher's address 3775 S. 500W. Box 15711, Salt Lake City, UT 84115

THE life of Joseph Smith, the prophet. v. 12
By George Q. Cannon. Salt Lake City, Utah, Deseret Book Company, 1958. 562p. 2 ports.
1. Smith, Joseph, 1805-1844. I. Cannon, George Quayle, 1827-1901.

NEELEY, Deta Petersen. 922.8373
A child's story of the prophet Joseph Smith, by Deta Petersen Neeley and Nathan Glen Neeley. Salt Lake City, Deserat News Press, 1958. 164p. illus. 20cm. [BX8695.S6N4] 59-21394
1. Smith, Joseph, 1805-1844 I. Neeley, Nathan Glen, joint author. II. Title.

SMITH, Lucy (Mack) 1776-1855. 922.8373
History of Joseph Smith, by his mother, Lucy Mack Smith. With notes and comments by Preston Nibley. Salt Lake City, Bookcraft, 1958. 355 p. illus. 24 cm. "Originally entitled The history of Mother Smith, by Herself," and first published in 1843. [BX8695.S6S63 1958] 61-21185
1. Smith, Joseph, 1805-1844. I. Title.

STEWART, John J v. 12
Joseph Smith, the Mormon prophet, by John J. Stewart. Salt Lake City, Mercury Pub. Co. [c1966] 257 p. illus. 68-6683
1. Smith, Joseph, 1805-1844. 2. Mormons and mormonism. I. Title.

STEWART, John J 922.8373
Joseph Smith, democracy's unknown prophet. Salt Lake City, Merenry Pub. Co. [1960] 119 p. illus. 16 cm. [BX8695.S6S8] 60-34862
1. Smith, Joseph, 1805-1844. I. Title. II. Title: Democracy's unknown prophet.

WIDTSOE, John Andreas, 1872- 922.S373
Joseph Smith; seeker after truth, prophet of God. Salt Lake City, Deseret News Press, 1951. x, 385 p. illus., ports. 24 cm. "A chrouology featuring political highlights in the career of Joseph Smith . . . by Dr. G. Homer Durham": p. [361]-370. bibliography: p. [371]-375. [BXS695.S6W52] 52-31355
1. Smith, Joseph, 1805-1844. I. Title.

WIDTSOE, John Andreas, 1872-1952. v. 12
Joseph Smith; seeker after truth, prophet of God. Salt Lake City, Bookcraft, 1957. x, 385 p. illus., ports. 24 cm. "A chronology featuring political highlights in the career of Joseph Smith ... by G. Homer Durham": p. [361]-370. Bibliography: p. [371]-375. 67-72928
1. Smith, Joseph, 1805-1844. I. Title.

Smith, Joseph, 1805-1844—Chronology.

CONKLING, J. Christopher, 1949- 289.3'092'4 B
A Joseph Smith chronology / J. Christopher Conking ; prepared for BEI Productions, inc. Salt Lake City : Deseret Book Company, 1979. ix, 276 p. : map ; 25 cm. Includes index. Bibliography: p. 253-266. [BX8695.S6C64] 79-896 ISBN 0-87747-734-5 : 7.95
1. Smith, Joseph, 1805-1844—Chronology. 2. Mormons and Mormonism in the United States—Biography. I. BEI Productions. II. Title. **BIP**

Smith, Joseph, 1805-1844—Collected works.

ANDRUS, Hyrum Leslie, 1924- comp. 289.3'092'4 B
They knew the prophet. Compiled by Hyrum L. Andrus and Helen Mae Andrus. Salt Lake City, Bookcraft [1974] xii, 207 p. 24 cm. [BX8695.S6A73] 74-75538 ISBN 0-88494-210-4
1. Smith, Joseph, 1805-1844—Collected works. I. Andrus, Helen Mae, joint comp. II. Title.

Smith, Joseph, 1805-1844—Family.

SMITH, Henry Allen, 1907- 922.8373
The day they martyred the prophet, a historical narrative. Salt Lake City, Bookcraft [c1963] 279 p. illus., port. 24 cm. [BX8695.S6S57] 64-3694
1. Smith, Joseph, 1805-1884.. 2. Smith, Hyrum, 1800-1844. I. Title.

SMITH, Lucy (Mack) 1776-1855. 289.3'0922 B
Biographical sketches of Joseph Smith, the prophet. New York, Arno Press, 1969. 282 p. 23 cm. (Religion in America) Reprint of the 1908 ed. [BX8695.S6S6 1969] 73-83439
1. Smith, Joseph, 1805-1844—Family. 2. Mack family. I. Title.

Smith, Junius, 1780-1853.

POND, Edgar LeRoy, 1883- 387.2'43'0924 B
Junius Smith; a biography of the father of the Atlantic liner, by E. LeRoy Pond. Freeport, N.Y., Books for Libraries Press [1971] ix, 292 p. port. 23 cm. Reprint of the 1927 ed. Bibliography: p. 281-286. [CT275.S549P6 1971] 75-179535 ISBN 0-8369-6664-3
1. Smith, Junius, 1780-1853. **BIP**

Smith, Leo, 1881-1952.

LEO Smith, v. 12
a biographical sketch. [Toronto] University of Toronto Press [c1956] ix, 53p. illus. 21cm. 'Works by Leo Smith': p. [49]-53.
1. Smith, Leo, 1881-1952. I. MoCarthy, Pearl.

LEO Smith, a biographical sketch. v. 12
[Toronto] University of Toronto Press [c1956] ix, 53p. illus. 21cm. 'Works by Leo Smith': p. [49]-53.
1. Smith, Leo, 1881-1952. I. McCarthy, Pearl.

Smith, Logan Pearsall, 1865-1946.

GATHORNE-HARDY, Robert, 1902- 928.2
Recollections of Logan Pearsall Smith; the story of a friendship. New York, Macmillan, 1950 ['1949] xi, 259 p. col. front. 22 cm. [PR6037.M5Z7 1950] 50-7048
1. Smith, Logan Pearsall, 1865-1946. I. Title.

Smith, Malcolm, 1938-

†SMITH, Malcolm, 1938- 269'.2'0924 B
Follow me! : The apprenticing of disciples / Malcolm Smith. Plainfield, N.J. : Logos International, c1976. 168 p. ; 22 cm. [DR1725.S54A33] 76-41065 5.95. pbk. : 5.95
1. Smith, Malcolm, 1938- 2. Clergy—New Jersey—Biography. 3. Christian life—1960- I. Title.

SMITH, Malcolm, 1938- 248'.3
How I learned to meditate / Malcolm Smith. Plainfield, N.J. : Logos International, c1977. viii, 127 p. ; 21 cm. [BX8762.Z8S637] 77-18482 ISBN 0-88270-253-X pbk. : 2.95
1. Smith, Malcolm, 1938- 2. Pentecostals—Clergy—Biography. 3. Clergy—United States—Biography. 4. Clergy—England—Biography. 5. Meditation. I. Title. **BIP**

Smith, Margaret

SMITH, Margaret 796.3420924
The Margaret Smith story [by] Margaret Smith, as told to Don Lawrence. London, S. Paul [dist. New Rochelle, N.Y., SportShelf, c.1965] 192p. illus., ports 22cm. [GV994.S6A3] 65-28643 5.75 bds.,
I. Lawrence, Don II. Title.

Smith, Margaret (Chase) 1898-

GRAHAM, Frank, 1925- 923.273
Margaret Chase Smith; woman of courage. New York, John Day Co. [1964] 188 p. ports. 21 cm. Bibliographical references included in preface. [E748.S667G7] 64-15625
1. Smith, Margaret (Chase) 1898- I. Title.

SMITH, Margaret 796.3420924
The Margaret Smith story [by] Margaret Smith, as told to Don Lawrence. London, S. Paul [dist. New Rochelle, N.Y., SportShelf, c.1965] 192p. illus., ports 22cm. [GV994.S6A3] 65-28643 5.75 bds.,
I. Lawrence, Don II. Title.

Smith, Margaret (Chase) 1898- — Juvenile literature.

FLEMING, Alice (Mulcahey) 1928- 973.92'0924 B
The Senator from Maine: Margaret Chase Smith, by Alice Fleming. New York, Crowell [1969] 136 p. 22 cm. (Women of America) A biography of the only women to serve in both houses of Congress and the first to be elected to four terms in the Senate. [E748.S667F55] 92 69-18665 3.95
1. Smith, Margaret (Chase) 1898- — Juvenile literature. I. Title. **BIP**

Smith, Mary.

THE Captivity and sufferings of Mary Smith. 973'.04'97 S
New York : Garland Pub., 1979 24 p. : ill. ; 23 cm. (The Garland library of narratives of North American Indian captivities ; v. 33) Issued with the reprint of the 1813 ed. of U.S. War Dept. Message from the President relative to murders committed by the Indians. New York, 1978. Reprint of the 1815 ed. printed by L. Scott, Providence, R.I., under title: An affecting narrative of the captivity and sufferings of Mrs. Mary Smith. [E85.G2 vol. 33] [E99.K4] 970'.004'97 78-6003 ISBN 0-8240-1657-2 : 29.50
1. Smith, Mary. 2. Kickapoo Indians—Captivities. 3. Indians of North America—Southern States—Captivities. 4. Southern States—Biography. I. Title.

SMITH, Mary. 973'.04'97 S
Savage barbarism. New York : Garland Pub., 1978 [1] fold. leaf ; 19 cm. (The Garland library of narratives of North American Indian captivities ; v. 27) Reprinted from Connecticut centinel, v. 32, Nov. 12, 1805. Issued with the reprint of the 1807 ed. of Bartlett, J. A narrative of the captivity of Joseph Bartlett among the French and Indians. New York, 1978; the reprint of the 1808 ed. of Horrid murder by the Indians. New York, 1978; the reprint of the 1927 ed. of Webster, I. A narrative of the captivity of Isaac Webster. New York, 1978; and with the reprint of the 1809 ed. of White, K. A narrative of the life, occurrences, vicissitudes, and present situation of K. White. New York, 1978. [E85.G2 vol. 27] [E87.S663] 976.3'004'97 78-15911 ISBN 0-8240-1651-3 : 33.00
1. Smith, Mary. 2. Indians of North America—Louisiana—Captivities. 3. Louisiana—Biography. I. Title. II. Series.

Smith, Mary (Bailey) 1809 or 10-1841.

SMITH, Ruby Kate, 1888- 922.8373
Mary Bailey. Salt Lake City, Deseret Book Co., 1954. 112p. illus. 24cm. [BX8695.S68S5] 54-25713
1. Smith, Mary (Bailey) 1809 or 10-1841. I. Title.

Smith, Matthew,

SMITH, Matthew, 1879-1959 759.12
Matthew Smith. London, Allen & Unwin [dist. Hollywood-by-the-Sea, Fla., Transatlantic, 1963, c.1962] [22]p. 52 col. plates. 31cm. 62-51568 15.75
I. Title.

Smith, Oswald J.

HALL, Douglas, 1929- 269'.2'0924 B
Not made for defeat; the authorized biography of Oswald J. Smith. With a foreword by Billy Graham and an introd. by John Wesley White. Grand Rapids, Zondervan [1969] 192 p. illus. 21 cm. [BX9225.S54H3] 77-81068
1. Smith, Oswald J. I. Title.

Smith, Parker F., 1943-

SMITH, Parker F., 1943- 959.704'38
Exile's odyssey : the memoirs of an American deserter / Parker F. Smith. Cranbury, N.J. : A. S. Barnes, 1980. p. cm. Includes bibliographical references and index. [DS559.8.D4S65] 78-75338 ISBN 0-498-02382-6 : 12.00
1. Smith, Parker F., 1943- 2. Vietnamese Conflict, 1961-1975—Desertions—United States. 3. Deserters, Military—United States—Biography. 4. Deserters, Military—Sweden—Biography. I. Title. **BIP**

Smith, Patsy Adam

SMITH, Patsy Adam 920.7
Hear the train blow; an Australian childhood. Sydney, Ure Smith [San Francisco, Tri-Ocean Bks., 1965, c.1964] 222p. 21cm. [CT2808.S6A3] 65-1487 3.50 bds.,
I. Title.

Smith, Preston, 1912-

CONN, Jerry Douglas. 320.9'764'060924 B
Preston Smith; the making of a Texas Governor. Austin, Jenkins Pub. Co., 1972. 173 p. illus. 24 cm. Bibliography: p. [171]-173. [F391.2.S6C6] 72-185281 6.95
1. Smith, Preston, 1912- 2. Texas—Politics and government—1951- **BIP**

Smith, Robert C., 1892-

SMITH, Robert C., 1892- 974.8'11'040924
After many days / by R. C. Smith. Boston : Branden Press, c1976. 97 p. ; 23 cm. [F158.5.S4] 76-8606 ISBN 0-8283-1664-3 : 7.50
1. Smith, Robert C., 1892- 2. Philadelphia—Biography. I. Title. **BIP**

Smith, Robert Metcalf, 1884- The Shelley legend.

WHITE, Newman Ivey, 1892- 1948. 928.2
An examination of The Shelley legend, by Newman I. White, Frederick K. Jones [and] Kenneth N. Cameron. Philadelphia, University of Pennsylvania Press, 1951. x, 114 p. 23 cm. Contents.Contents.--Introduction--The Shelley legend examined, by N.I. White.--The Shelley legend, by F.L. Jones.--A new Shelley legend, by K.N. Cameron. Bibliographical footnotes. [PR5431.S76W5] 51-12162
1. Smith, Robert Metcalf, 1884- The Shelley legend. I. Jones, Frederick Lafayette, 1901- II. Title.

Smith, Robert S., 1906-

SMITH, Robert S., 1906- 617'.092'4
Doctors and patients / by Robert S. Smith. Boise, Idaho : Syms-York Co., c1976. ix, 163 p., [14] leaves of plates : ill. ; 22 cm. [R154.S63A327] 76-24511 8.00
1. Smith, Robert S., 1906- 2. Surgeons—Idaho—Boise—Biography. 3. Boise, Idaho—Biography. 4. Physician and patient. I. Title.

SMITH, Robert S., 1906- 617'.092'4 B
Idaho surgeon : an autobiography / by Robert S. Smith. Boise, Idaho : Syms-York, 1974. viii, 151 p., [21] leaves of plates : ill. ; 22 cm. Bibliography: p. 149-151. [R154.S63A33] 74-84639 7.00
1. Smith, Robert S., 1906- 2. Surgeons—Correspondence, reminiscences, etc. I. Title.

Smith, Robyn Caroline—Juvenile literature.

JACOBS, Linda. 798'.4'00924 B
Robyn Smith : in silks / by Linda Jacobs ; photos. by Jeffrey E. Blackman. St. Paul : EMC Corp., 1976. 38 p. : ill. ; 23 cm. (Women who win ; 4) A biography of the young woman who in searching for something special to do with her life turned to horse racing, thus becoming one of the first female jockeys. [SF336.S62J3] 92 76-8489 ISBN 0-88436-234-5 lib.bdg.: 4.95 ISBN 0-88436-235-3 pbk. :
1. Smith, Robyn Caroline—Juvenile literature. 2. Jockeys—United States—Biography—Juvenile literature. I. Blackman, Jeffrey E. II. Title. BIP

Smith, Rodney, 1860-1947.

LAZELL, David. 269'.2'0924[B]
Gipsy Smith: from the forest I came. Chicago, Moody [1973, c.1970] 256 p. illus., ports. 18 cm. First published in London under title: From the forest I came: the story of Gipsy Rodney Smith. [BV3785] ISBN 0-8024-2959-9 pap., 0.95
1. Smith, Rodney, 1860-1947. I. Title. II. Title: From the forest I came.
L.C. card no. for the London edition: 74-516965.

Smith, Russell, 1812-1898.

LEWIS, Virginia Elnora, 1907- 759.13
Russell Smith, romantic realist. [Pittsburgh] University of Pittsburgh Press [1957, c1956] xix, 348p. plates, ports. 24cm. Bibliography: p. 327-333. [ND237.S632L4] [ND237.S632L4] 927.5 56-6427 56-6427
1. Smith, Russell, 1812-1898. I. Title.

Smith, Sam G., 1794-1835.

SMITH, Jonathan Kennon. 976.8'04'0924 B
General Samuel G. Smith. [Memphis, 1968] 31 l. facsim. 28 cm. Includes bibliographical references. [F436.S66S5] 75-838
1. Smith, Sam G., 1794-1835.

Smith, Samuel, 1752-1839.

CASSELL, Frank A., 1941- 328.73'0924 B
Merchant Congressman in the young Republic: Samuel Smith of Maryland, 1752-1839 [by] Frank A. Cassell. Madison, University of Wisconsin Press [1971] xiii, 283 p. illus. 24 cm. Bibliography: p. 267-271. [E302.6.S575C3] 79-157390 ISBN 0-299-06000-4
1. Smith, Samuel, 1752-1839. I. Title. BIP

Smith, Sarah Hathaway Bixby, 1871-1935.

SMITH, Sarah Hathaway Bixby, 1871-1935. 979.4'93'040924 B
Adobe days, being the truthful narrative of the events in the life of a California girl on a sheep ranch and in El Pueblo de Nuestra Senora de Los Angeles while it was yet a small and humble town ... / by Sarah Bixby Smith ; introd. by Robert Ernest Cowan. 4th ed., rev. Fresno, Calif. : Valley Publishers, 1974. xvi, 142 p., [5] leaves of plates : ill. ; 24 cm. Includes index. [F869.L85S58 1974] 74-196029 7.95
1. Smith, Sarah Hathaway Bixby, 1871-1935. 2. Frontier and pioneer life—California—Los Angeles. 3. Los Angeles—History. I. Title: Adobe days ...

Smith, Seba,

SMITH, Seba, 1792-1868. 818'.3'07
The life and writings of Major Jack Downing, of Downingville, away down East in the State of Maine. Written by himself. Boston, Lilly, Wait, Colman & Holden, 1833. [New York, AMS Press, 1973] 260 p. illus. 19 cm. [PS2876.L68 1973] 71-164785 ISBN 0-404-02168-9
I. Title.

Smith, St. Clair W., 1844-1909.

WILSON, Ealon V. 286'.63 B
The colorful and eventful life of St. Clair W. Smith, nineteenth century trail-blazer, western frontier missionary, Christian college founder-president, preacher and educator, by Ealon V. Wilson. With accounts of ancestors, contemporaries and descendants across the land, from Kentucky and Tennessee to Texas, New Mexico, California, etc. [Limited 1st ed.] Memphis, 1967. 46 p. illus. 21 cm. [BX6793.S63W55] 74-166166
1. Smith, St. Clair W., 1844-1909. 2. Smith family. I. Title.

Smith, Stan.

SMITH, Stan. 796.34'2'0924 B
It's more than just a game / Stan Smith. Old Tappan, N.J. : F. H. Revell Co., c1977. p. cm. (New life ventures) [GV994.S63A35] 77-14287 ISBN 0-8007-9002-2 : pbk. : 0.95
1. Smith, Stan. 2. Tennis players—United States—Biography. 3. Religion and sports. I. Title. BIP

Smith, Stan—Juvenile literature.

HASEGAWA, Sam. 796.34'2'0924 B
Stan Smith / by Sam Hasegawa ; illustrated by Fred Singler. Mankato, Minn. : Creative Education, [1975] p. cm. A biography of tennis star Stan Smith, who ranked number one in 1972. [GV994.S63H37] 92 75-23448 ISBN 0-87191-474-3 : 4.95
1. Smith, Stan—Juvenile literature. 2. Tennis—Juvenile literature. I. Singler, Fred. II. Title.

Smith, Susy.

SMITH, Susy. 133.9'0924 B
Confessions of a psychic. New York, Macmillan [1971] 315 p. illus., ports. 21 cm. Autobiographical. [BF1283.S62A3] 78-156993 6.95
I. Title. BIP

SMITH, Susy. 248'.246'0924 B
The conversion of a psychic / by Susy Smith. 1st ed. Garden City, N.Y. : Doubleday, 1978. 127, [2] p. ; 22 cm. Bibliography: p. [129]. [BV4935.S65A33] 76-50790 ISBN 0-385-12638-7 : 5.95
1. Smith, Susy. 2. Converts—Arizona—Tucson—Biography. 3. Pentecostals—Arizona—Tucson—Biography. 4. Tucson, Ariz.—Biography. I. Title. BIP

Smith, Sydney, 1771-1845.

BULLETT, Gerald William, 1894-1958. 824.7 B
Sydney Smith; a biography & a selection. Westport, Conn., Greenwood Press [1971] 316 p. port. 23 cm. Reprint of the 1951 ed. [BX5199.S73B84 1971] 77-138578 ISBN 0-8371-5777-3
1. Smith, Sydney, 1771-1845.

PEARSON, Hesketh, 1887-1964. 824'.7 B
The Smith of Smiths: being the life, wit, and humour of Sydney Smith. With an introd. by G. K. Chesterton. New York, Harper, 1934. St. Clair Shores, Mich., Scholarly Press, 1971. 336 p. 21 cm. Bibliography: p. 327-329. [PR5458.P4 1971] 73-145230 ISBN 0-403-01146-9
1. Smith, Sydney, 1771-1845. I. Title.

RUSSELL, George William Erskine, 1853-1919. 824'.7 B
Sydney Smith. New York, Macmillan, 1905. Ann Arbor, Mich., Gryphon Books, 1971. vii, 242 p. 22 cm. (English men of letters) [PR5458.R8 1971] 79-156929
1. Smith, Sydney, 1771-1845. BIP

SMITH, Sydney, 1771-1845. 928.2
Selected letters; edited by Nowell C. Smith. London, New York, Oxford University Press [1956] 353 p. 16 cm. (The World's classics, 548) [PR5458.A3 1956] 56-2412
1. Smith, Nowell Charles, 1871- ed. II. Title.

Smith T, John, 1770-1836.

HIGGINBOTHAM, Valle. 977.8'6'030924 B
John Smith T, Missouri pioneer. [Potosi, Mo., Printed by Independent-Journal, 1968] 56 p. illus., map, ports. 22 cm. [F466.S645H5] 70-500
1. Smith T, John, 1770-1836. 2. Frontier and pioneer life—Missouri. I. Title.

Smith, Thomas James, 1840-1870 — Juvenile literature.

WERSTEIN, Irving. 923.573
Marshal without a gun: Tom Smith. New York, J. Messner [1959] 192 p. 22 cm. Includes bibliography [F689.A2S55] 59-12768
1. Smith, Thomas James, 1840-1870 — Juvenile literature. 2. Crime and criminals — Kansas-Abilene. I. Title.

Smith, Thomas Long, 1801-1866.

TEMPLETON, Sardis W 1890-. 917.90924 (B)
The lame captain; the life and adventures of Pegleg Smith, by Sardis W. Templeton. Los Angeles, Westernlore Press, 1965. c.239 p. ports. 21 cm. (Great West and Indian series, 28) Bibliography: p. [229]-236. [F592.S664T4] 65-21223
1. Smith, Thomas Long, 1801-1866. 2. Frontier and pioneer life — The West. I. Title. II. Series.

Smith, Thomas, Sir 1513-1577.

DEWAR, Mary 923.242
Sir Thomas Smith, a Tudor intellectual in office [London] Univ. of London, Athlone Pr. [dist, New York, Oxford, c.]1964. ix, 222p. port. 23cm. Bibl. 64-7112 5.60
1. Smith, Thomas, Sir 1513-1577. I. Title.

STRYPE, John, 1643-1737. 942.05'3'0924 B
The life of the learned Sir Thomas Smith, kt., D.C.L.; principal Secretary of State to King Edward the Sixth, and Queen Elizabeth. New ed., with correction and additions by the author. New York, B. Franklin Reprints [1974] xix, 286 p. illus. 23 cm. (Burt Franklin research & source works series. Philosophy & religious history monographs, 144) Reprint of the "new edition," 1820, published at the Clarendon Press, Oxford. [DA358.S6S9 1974] 73-23077 ISBN 0-8337-3447-4 17.50
1. Smith, Thomas, Sir, 1513-1577. I. Title.

Smith, Thomas Vernor,

SMITH, Thomas Vernor, 1890- 923.773
A non-existent man, an autobiography. Austin, University of Texas Press [1962] 280 p. illus. 24 cm. [CT275.S557A3] 62-9796
I. Title.

Smith, Venture, 1729?-1805—Juvenile literature.

ZAGOREN, Ruby. 301.45'22 B
Venture for freedom; the true story of an African Yankee. With woodcuts by Ann Grifalconi. Cleveland, World Pub. Co. [1969] 125 p. illus. 22 cm. Adapted from A narrative of the life and adventures of Venture, a native of Africa, by Venture Smith. Only seven years old when captured by enemy tribesmen, the son of a West African tribal king related in his old age the biography on which this account of his capture, slavery, and successful struggle for freedom is based. [E444.Z3] 92 69-13062 3.95
1. Smith, Venture, 1729?-1805—Juvenile literature. 2. Slavery in the United States—Connecticut—Juvenile literature. I. Smith, Venture, 1729?-1805. A narrative of the life and adventures of Venture, a native of Africa. II. Grifalconi, Ann, illus. III. Title.

Smith, Walter George, 1854-1924.

BRYSON, Thomas A., 1931- 340'.092'4 B
Walter George Smith / Thomas A. Bryson. Washington : Catholic University of America Press, 1977. xiii, 225 p. : port. ; 24 cm. Includes index. Bibliography: p. 205-213. [KF373.S58B78] 77-9967 ISBN 0-8132-0539-5 : 13.95
1. Smith, Walter George, 1854-1924. 2. Lawyers—Pennsylvania—Philadelphia—Biography. 3. Politicians—Pennsylvania—Philadelphia—Biography. BIP

Smith, Wilbur Moorehead,

SMITH, Wilbur Moorehead, 1894- 285'.131'0924 B
Before I forget, by Wilbur M. Smith. Chicago, Moody Press [1971] 304 p. 24

cm. Autobiographical. [BR1725.S552A3] 79-155684 5.95
I. Title.

Smith, William Ward, 1893-1968.

SMITH, William Ward, 1893-1968. 301.41'792'4
A letter from my father : the strange, intimate correspondence of W. Ward Smith to his son Page Smith / edited by Page Smith. New York : Morrow, 1976. 472 p., [17] leaves of plates : ill. ; 24 cm. [HQ462.S54 1976] 75-31859 ISBN 0-688-03003-3 : 15.00
1. Smith, William Ward, 1893-1968. 2. Erotic literature. I. Smith, Page. II. Title.

Smith, William, 1727-1803.

JONES, Thomas Firth, 1934- 378.1'11'0924 B
A pair of lawn sleeves; a biography of William Smith (1727-1803) [1st ed.] Philadelphia, Chilton Book Co. [1972] 210 p. illus. 21 cm. Bibliography: p. [202]-205. [LD4525 1755.J6] 77-184137 ISBN 0-8019-5653-6
1. Smith, William, 1727-1803. I. Title.

SMITH, Horace Wemyss, 1825-1891. 378.1'11'0924 B
Life and correspondence of the Rev. William Smith, D.D. New York, Arno Press, 1972 [c1878] 2 v. in 1. ports. 24 cm. (Religion in America, series II) [LD4525 1755.S62] 79-38786 ISBN 0-405-04084-9
1. Smith, William, 1727-1803. 2. Pennsylvania. University. 3. Washington College, Chestertown, Md. I. Title. BIP

Smith, William, 1728-1793.

UPTON, Leslie Francis Stokes. 974.7'02'0924 B
The loyal Whig: William Smith of New York & Quebec [by] L. F. S. Upton. [Toronto] University of Toronto Press [1969] ix, 250 p. 24 cm. Bibliography: p. 225-237. [F122.S66U6] 73-389703 8.50
1. Smith, William, 1728-1793. I. Title.

Smith, William, 1769-1839.

PHILLIPS, John, 1800-1874. 551.7'0092'4 B
Memoirs of William Smith / John Phillips. New York : Arno Press, 1978. viii, 150 p., [4] leaves of plates : ill. ; 23 cm. (History of geology) Reprint of the 1844 ed. published by J. Murray, London. [QE22.S6P47 1978] 77-6535 ISBN 0-405-10455-3 : 12.00
1. Smith, William, 1769-1839. 2. Geologists—Great Britain—Biography. I. Title. II. Series. BIP

Smith, Willie, 1897-1973.

SMITH, Willie, 1897-1973. 786.1'092'4 B
Music on my mind : the memoirs of an American pianist / by Willie the Lion Smith with George Hoefer ; foreword by Duke Ellington ; new introd. by John S. Wilson. 1st paperback ed. New York : Da Capo Press, 1978. xvi, 318 p. ; 22 cm. (A Da Capo paperback) Reprint of the 1964 ed. published by Doubleday, New York. Discography: p. 302-311. [ML417.S675A3 1978] 78-17246 ISBN 0-306-80087-X pbk. : 6.95
1. Smith, Willie, 1897-1973. 2. Pianists—United States—Biography. 3. Jazz musicians—United States—Biography. I. Hoefer, George. II. Title.

Smollett, Tobias George, 1721-1771.

[BENJAMIN, Lewis Saul] 1874-1932 828.609
The life and letters of Tobias Smollett (1721-1771) by Lewis Melville [pseud.] Port Washington, N. Y., Kennikat [1966] xv. 319p. illus., facsim., ports 22cm. First pub. in 1927 Bibl. [PR3696.B4] 65-27123 8.50
1. Smollett, Tobias George, 1721-1771. I. Title.

HANNAY, David, 1853-1934. 823'.6 B
Life and writings of Tobias George Smollett. Freeport, N.Y., Books for Libraries Press [1971] 163, x p. 23 cm. Reprint of the 1887 ed., published under title: Life of Tobias George Smollett. Bibliography: p. [i]-x. [PR3696.H2 1971] 74-154151 ISBN 0-8369-5767-9
1. Smollett, Tobias George, 1721-1771. I. Title. BIP

HANNAY, David, 1853-1934. 823'.6 B
Life of Tobias George Smollett. [Folcroft, Pa.] Folcroft Library Editions, 1973. p. Reprint of the 1887 ed. published by W. Scott, London, in series: Great writers. Bibliography: p. [PR3696.H2 1973] 73-16120 7.95
1. Smollett, Tobias George, 1721-1771. BIP

KNAPP, Lewis Mansfield 928.2
Tobias Smollett, doctor of men and manners. New York, Russell & Russell, 1963[c.1949] xiii, 362p. plates. 23cm. Bibl. 63-8366 7.50
1. Smollett, Tobias George, 1721-1771. I. Title.

SMEATON, William Henry Oliphant, 1856-1914. 823'.6
Tobias Smollett, by Oliphant Smeaton. Edinburgh, Oliphant, Anderson & Ferrier. [Folcroft, Pa.] Folcroft Library Editions, 1973. p. Reprint of the 1897 ed., issued in the Famous Scots series. [PR3696.S6 1973] 73-3431 ISBN 0-8414-7508-3
1 Smollett, Tobias George, 1721-1771. BIP

Smuts, Jan Christiaan, 1870-1950.

CRAFFORD, F. S. 968.05'0924 B
Jan Smuts: a biography [by] F. S. Crafford. New York, Greenwood Press, 1968 [c1943] xi, 322 p. illus. 24 cm. Bibliography: p. 300-306. [DT779.8.S6C7 1968] 69-10081
1. Smuts, Jan Christiaan, 1870-1950. BIP

HANCOCK, William Keith, 1898- 968'.05'0924 B
Smuts. Cambridge [Eng.] University Press, 1962-68. 2 v. ports., fold. maps (part col.), facsim. 24 cm. Contents.—1. The sanguine years, 1870-1919.—2. The fields of force, 1919-1950. Bibliography: v. 1, p. 562-593; v. 2, p. 530-566. [DT779.8.S6H28] 62-52102
1. Smuts, Jan Christiaan, 1870-1950.

JOSEPH, Joan. 968'.05'0924 B
South African statesman: Jan Christiaan Smuts. New York, J. Messner [1969] 189 p. 22 cm. Bibliography: p. 183-184. [DT779.8.S6J6] 72-79695 3.50
1. Smuts, Jan Christiaan, 1870-1950. I. Title.

SMUTS, Jan christian, 1912- 923.568
Jan Christian Smuts; a biography. New York, Morrow, 1952. xiv, 496 p. illus., ports, maps. 22 cm. Bibliography: p. 478-483. [DT779.8.S6S5] 52-10783
1. Smuts, Jan Christiaan, 1870-1950. I. Title.

SMUTS, Jan Christian, 1912- 968.05'092'4 B
Jan Christian Smuts; a biography. Westport, Conn., Greenwood Press [1973, c1952] xiv, 496 p. illus. 22 cm. Reprint of the ed. published by Morrow, New York. Bibliography: p. 478-483. [DT779.8.S6S5 1973] 73-13409 ISBN 0-8371-7059-1 19.25
1. Smuts, Jan Christiaan, 1870-1950.

Smyth, Andrew Farney, 1817-1879.

SEALE, William. 976.4
Texas riverman; the life and times of Captain Andrew Smyth. Austin, University of Texas Press [1966] xii, 181 p. illus., map, ports. 24 cm. Bibliography: p. [165]-169. [F392.J27S4] 65-27538
1. Smyth, Andrew Farney, 1817-1879. 2. Smyth family. 3. Jasper Co., Tex.—Social life and customs. 4. River life. I. Title. BIP

Smyth, Dame Ethel Mary, 1858-1944.

ST. JOHN, Christopher Marie. 927.8
Ethel Smyth, a biography, With additional chapters by V. Sackville-W5st and Kathleen Dale. London, New York, Longmans, Green [1959] 316p. illus. 23cm. [ML410.S66S3] 59-2151
1. Smyth, Dame Ethel Mary, 1858-1944. I. Title.

Smythe, Pete,

SMYTHE, Pete, 1911- 818'.5'403
Pete Smythe: big-city dropout. Boulder, Colo., Pruett Press [1968] 242 p. illus., ports. 23 cm. [PN1991.4.S6A3] 68-58130 5.50
I. Title.

Smythson, Robert, 1534 or 5-1614.

GIROUARD, Mark, 1931- 720'.924
Robert Smythson and the architecture of the Elizabethan era. South Brunswick [N.J.] Barnes [1967] 232 p. illus., plans. 26 cm. Bibliographical footnotes. [NA997.S6G5 1967] 67-13084
1. Smythson, Robert, 1534 or 5-1614. 2. Architecture—England. I. Title.

Snavely, Guy Everett,

SNAVELY, Guy Everett, 1881- 378.73
A search for excellence, memoirs of a college administrator. New York, Vantage [c.1964] 194p. 21cm. 64-3894 3.50
I. Title.

SNAVELY, Guy Everett, 1881- 378.73
A search for excellence, memoirs of a college administrator. [1st ed.] New York, Vantage Press [1964] 194 p. 21 cm. [LA2317.S63A3] 64-3894
I. Title.

Snedden, David Samuel, 1868-1951.

DROST, Walter H. 370'.924 B
David Snedden and education for social efficiency [by] Walter H. Drost. Madison, University of Wisconsin Press, 1967. ix, 242 p. 25 cm. Bibliographical references included in "Notes" (p. 201-220) [LB875.S55D7] 67-25945
1. Snedden, David Samuel, 1868-1951. I. Title. BIP

Snider, Edwin Donald, 1926-

WINEHOUSE, Irwin. 927.96357
The Duke Snider story. New York, J. Messner [1964] 191 p. illus. 22 cm. [GV865.S55W5] 64-11367
1. Snider, Edwin Donald, 1926- I. Title.

Snipes, Ben E., 1835-1906.

SHELLER, Roscoe. v. 12
Ben Snipes: Northwest cattle king. [3d ed.] Portland, Or., Binfords & Mort [1959, c1957] 205 p. illus., ports. 23 cm. 67-13830
1. Snipes, Ben E., 1835-1906. 2. Cattle trade. 3. Frontier and pioneer life—Northwest, Pacific. I. Title. BIP

SHELLER, Roscoe. 926.362
Ben Snipes: Northwest cattle king. [1st ed.] Portland, Or., Binfords & Mort [1957] 205 p. illus. 23 cm. [SF33.S6S5] 57-13209
1. Snipes, Ben E., 1835-1906. 2. Cattle trade. 3. Frontier and pioneer life—Northwest, Pacific.

Snook, John Alfred, 1770-1857.

BIOGRAPHY of John Alfred Snook. v. 12
Compiled by Mrs. Frank H. Brown. Elkhart, Indiana, 1961. 1v. e(various pagings) 29cm. Mimeograph typescripts.
1. Snook, John Alfred, 1770-1857. 2. Snook geneal. I. Brown, Mrs. Frank H comp.

Snow, Charles Percy, Sir 1905-

BOYTINCK, Paul W. 016.823'9'12
C. P. Snow, a bibliography : works by and about him complete with selected annotations / by Paul Boytinck. Folcroft, Pa. : Folcroft Library Editions, 1978. 144 p. ; 26 cm. Reprint of the 1977 ed. published by Norwood Editions, Norwood, Pa. [Z8823.37.B68 1978] [PR6037.N58] 78-1950 ISBN 0-8414-0160-8 lib. bdg. : 25.00
1. Snow, Charles Percy, Baron Snow, 1905- Biography. I. Title.

THALE, Jerome 823.912
C. P. Snow. New York, Scribners [c.1964, 1965] 160p. 22cm. Bibl. [PR6037.N58Z89] 65-13069 3.50 bds.,
1. Snow, Charles Percy, Sir 1905- I. Title.

Snow, Erastus, 1818-1888.

LARSON, Andrew Karl. 289.3'0924 B
Erastus Snow; the life of a missionary and pioneer for the early Mormon Church. Salt Lake City, University of Utah Press [1971] 814 p. illus., facsims., ports. 27 cm. (University of Utah publications in the American West, v. 5) Bibliography: p. [775]-787. [BX8695.S747L37] 75-634390 ISBN 0-87480-031-5
1. Snow, Erastus, 1818-1888. I. Series: Utah. University. Publications in the American West, v. 5.

Snow, Jimmy.

SNOW, Jimmy. 269'.2'0924 B
I cannot go back / Jimmy Snow, with Jim and Marti Hefley ; [introd. by Johnny Cash]. Plainfield, N.J. : Logos International, c1977. 157 p., [8] leaves of plates : ill. ; 21 cm. [BV3785.S62A34] 76-566691 ISBN 0-88270-193-2 : 5.95 ISBN 0-88270-194-0 pbk. : 2.95
1. Snow, Jimmy. 2. Evangclists—Tennessee—Nashville—Biography. 3. Assemblies of god, general council—Clergy—Biography. 4. Nashville—Biography. I. Hefley, James C., joint author. II. Hefley, Marti, joint author. III. Title. BIP

Snow, John Ben, 1883-1973.

SNOW, Vernon F., 1924- 070.5'092'4 B
JBS, the biography of John Ben Snow / by Vernon F. Snow. Syracuse, N.Y. : Snow, [1974] vii, 86 p. : ill. ; 23 cm. [SF336.S63S66] 74-10416 2.00
1. Snow, John Ben, 1883-1973. I. Title.

Snow, Lorenzo, 1814-1901.

ROMNEY, Thomas Cottam, 1876- 922.83
The life of Lorenzo Snow, fifth president of the Church of Jesus Christ of Latter-Day Saints. [Salt Lake City, S. U. P. Memorial Foundation, 1955] 485p. illus. 23cm. [BX8695.S75R6] 57-44586
1. Snow, Lorenzo, 1814-1901. I. Title.

Snow, Lorenzo. 1814-1901—Juvenile literature.

NEELEY, Deta Petersen. 289.3'0924 B
A child's story of the prophet Lorenzo Snow, by Deta Peterson [i.e. Petersen] Neeley, Nathan Glen Neeley, and Melba Jensen Priday. Salt Lake City, Deseret Book Co., 1968. 100 p. 20 cm. A biography of a convert to the Church of Jesus Christ of Latter-day Saints who served his Church as a missionary, as a state prisoner, and eventually as its President. [BX8695.S75N4] 92 70-4178 2.25
1. Snow, Lorenzo. 1814-1901—Juvenile literature. I. Neeley, Nathan Glen, joint author. II. Priday, Melba Jensen, joint author. III. Title.

Snow, Sir Charles Percy, 1905-

THALE, Jerome. 823.212
C. P. Snow. New York, Scribner [1965]

160 p. 22 cm. Bibliography: p. 154-160. [PR6037.N58Z89] 65-13069
1. Snow, Sir Charles Percy, 1905- . I. Title.

Snow, Wilbert, 1884-

SNOW, Wilbert, 1884- 813'.5'4 B
Codline's child; the autobiography of Wilbert Snow. [1st ed.] Middletown, Conn., Wesleyan University Press [1974] ix, 489 p. illus. 23 cm. Includes bibliographical references. [PS3537.N683Z5] 73-15008 ISBN 0-8195-4069-2 14.95
1. Snow, Wilbert, 1884- I. Title. BIP

Snowden, Edgar.

QUENZEL, Carrol Hunter, 1906- v. 12
Edgar Snowden, Sr., Virginia journalist & civic leader. Charlottesville, Bibliographical Society of the University of Virginia, 1954. 59p. 17cm. A55
1. Snowden, Edgar. 2. The Alexandria gazette. I. Title.

Snowden, James Henry, 1852-1936.

MCKINNEY, William Wilson, 1893- ed. 922.573
The incomparable James Henry Snowden: his life and achievements. Contributors: David E. Culley [and others] Pittsburgh, Davis & Warde, 1961. 221p. illus. 22cm. Includes bibliography. [BX9225.S6M3] 61-18433
1. Snowden, James Henry, 1852-1936. I. Title.

Snowdon, Anthony Armstrong-Jones, 1st Earl of, 1930-

HUTCHINSON, Roger. 941.085'092'2 B
A family affair : the British royal family, its scandals, its crises and what really happened when Margaret and Tony's marriage broke up / by Roger Hutchinson and Gary Kahn. New York : Two Continents/Bunch Books, c1977. p. cm. [DA585.A5M338] 77-83854 ISBN 0-8467-0389-0 : 8.95
1. Margaret, Princess of Great Britain, 1930- 2. Snowdon, Anthony Armstrong-Jones, 1st Earl of, 1930- 3. Windsor, House of. 4. Great Britain—Princes and princesses—Biography. I. Kahn, Gary, joint author. II. Title.

SNOWDON, Antony Armstrong-Jones, 1st Earl of, 1930- 770'.92'4 B
Snowdon, a photographic autobiography. New York : Times Books, [1979] p. cm. [TR140.S63A37 1979] 79-51441 ISBN 0-8129-0848-1 : 29.95
1. Snowdon, Antony Armstrong-Jones, 1st Earl of, 1930- 2. Photographers—Great Britain—Biography. I. Title.

Snyder, Grace (McCance)

SNYDER, Grace (McCance) 1882- 920.7
No time on my hands. by Grace Snyder, as told to Nellie Snyder Yost. Caldwell, Idaho, Caxton, [c]1963. 541p. illus. (pt. col.) ports, map (on lining papers) 24cm. 63-18182 8.95
I. Yost. Nellie Irene (Snyder) II. Title.

SNYDER, Grace (McCance) 1882- 920.7
No time on my hands, by Grace Snyder, as told to Nellie Snyder Yost. Caldwell, Idaho, Caxton Printers, 1963. 541 p. illus., ports., map (on lining papers) 24 cm. [CT275.S587A3] 63-18182
I. Yost, Nellie Irene (Snyder) II. Title.

Soane, John, Sir, 1753-1837.

DU PREY, Pierre de la Ruffiniere. 720'.92'4 B
John Soane's architectural education, 1753-80 / Pierre de la Ruffiniere du Prey. New York : Garland Pub., 1977, i.e.1978 xxxv, 565, 299 p. : ill. ; 22 cm. (Outstanding dissertations in the fine arts) Originally presented as the author's thesis, Princeton, 1972. Bibliography: p. 557-565. [NA997.S7D86 1977] 76-23615 ISBN 0-8240-2686-1 lib.bdg. : 62.50
1. Soane, John, Sir, 1753-1837. 2. Architects—Education—England. 3. Architects—England—Biography. I. Title. II. Series.

Sobhuza II, King of Swaziland, 1899-

KUPER, Hilda. 968'.3'00994
Sobhuza II, Ngwenyama and King of Swaziland / by Hilda Kuper. New York : Africana Pub. Co., 1978. p. cm. Includes index. Bibliography: p. [DT971.82.S55K86 1978] 78-2356 ISBN 0-8419-0383-2 : 30.00
1. Sobhuza II, King of Swaziland, 1899- 2. Swaziland—Kings and rulers—Biography. I. Title.

Soccer.

ELLIS, Arthur E 1914- 927.9633
Refereeing soccer round the world. New York, Barnes, 1955. 207p. illus. 22cm. Autobiographical. [GV943.E55] 55-3495
1. Soccer. I. Title.

TYLER, Martin. 796.33'4'09
Soccer : the world game / by Martin Tyler. New York : St. Martin's Press, [1978] p. cm. [GV943.T93] 78-2982 ISBN 0-312-73134-5 : 15.00
1. Soccer. 2. Soccer—History. 3. Soccer players—Biography. 4. Soccer—Rules. I. Title. BIP

Social medicine.

MEDICAL 362.1'092'2 B
sociologists at work / edited by Ray H. Elling and Magdalena Sokolowska. New Brunswick, N.J. : Transaction Books, c1977. p. cm. Includes bibliographical references and index. [RA418.M512] 76-6204 ISBN 0-87855-139-5 : 14.95
1. Social medicine. 2. Sociologists—Biography. I. Elling, Ray H., 1929- II. Sokolowska, Magdalena. BIP

Social psychology—Addresses, essays, lectures.

SCHELLENBERG, James A., 1932- 301.1'092'2
Masters of social psychology : Freud, Mead, Lewin, and Skinner / James A. Schellenberg. New York : Oxford University Press, 1978. x, 141 p. ; 22 cm. Includes index. Bibliography: p. [133]-136. [HM251.S2993] 77-9927 ISBN 0-19-502278-5 : 9.95 ISBN 0-19-502279-3 pbk. : 2.00
1. Social psychology—Addresses, essays, lectures. 2. Psychologists—Biography. I. Title. BIP

Social reformers—Gt. Brit.

MARTIN, Hugh, 1890- ed. 261.8'3'0922
Christian social reformers of the nineteenth century, by James Adderley [and others] Freeport, N.Y., Books for Libraries Press [1970] vi, 242 p. illus., ports. 23 cm. (Essay index reprint series) Reprint of the 1927 ed. Contents.Contents.—Introduction: The Christian social movement in the nineteenth century, by W. Temple.—John Howard, by S. K. Ruck.—William Wilberforce, by R. Coupland.—Anthony Ashley Cooper, by C. Smith.—Charles Dickens, by A. J. Carlyle.—Florence Nightingale, by M. Scharlieb.—John Malcolm Ludlow, by C. E. Raven.—William Morris, by H. Martin.—George Cadbury, by H. G. Wood.—Henry Scott Holland, by J. Adderley.—James Keir Hardie, by A. F. Brockway. [HN385.M3 1970] 70-107725
1. Social reformers—Gt. Brit. 2. Sociology, Christian. I. Adderley, James Granville, 1861-1942. II. Title. BIP

Social reformers—Russia.

HARE, Richard. 309.1'47
Portraits of Russian personalities between reform and Revolution / Richard Hare. Westport, Conn. : Greenwood Press, 1975, c1959. viii, 360 p., [8] leaves of plates : ports. ; 22 cm. Reprint of the ed. published by the Oxford University Press, London. Includes bibliographical references and index. [HN523.H27 1975] 75-3735 ISBN 0-8371-8063-5 : 18.75
1. Social reformers—Russia. 2. Russia—Social conditions. 3. Social sciences—History—Russia. I. Title. BIP

Social reformers—United States—Biography—Juvenile literature.

BRIN, Ruth Firestone. 301.24'2'0922 B
Social reform / by Ruth F. Brin. Minneapolis : Dillon Press, c1977. 158, [1] p. : ill. ; 23 cm. (Contributions of women) Bibliography: p. [159]. Biographies of American women whose activities in the area of social reform made a positive impact on our society. [HQ1412.B74] 920 77-9585 ISBN 0-87518-145-7 : 6.95
1. Social reformers—United States—Biography—Juvenile literature. 2. Women—United States—Biography—Juvenile literature. 3. Feminists—United States—Biography—Juvenile literature. I. Title.

SIGNIFICANT 301.24'2'0922 B
American social reformers and humanitarians. Chicago : Childrens Press, [1976] p. cm. Includes index. Brief biographies of 141 social reformers and humanitarians arranged in chronological-alphabetical order. [HN65.S56] 75-21596 6.95
1. Social reformers—United States—Biography—Juvenile literature. I. Title: Social reformers and humanitarians.

Social work with children—England.

SPARROW, Jane. 362.7'092'4 B
Diary of a student social worker / Jane Sparrow. London ; Boston : Routledge and Kegan Paul, 1978. xvi, 148 p. ; 23 cm. [HV751.A6S63] 77-30664 ISBN 0-7100-8857-4 11.50
1. Social work with children—England. I. Title. BIP

Social workers—Correspondence, reminiscences, etc.

BRAITHWAITE, Edward Ricardo. 362.7'0924
Paid servant, by E. R. Braithwaite. [1st U.S. ed.] New York, McGraw-Hill [1968, c1962] 219 p. 21 cm. Autobiographical. [HV250.L8B7 1968] 68-17502
1. Social workers—Correspondence, reminiscences, etc. 2. Child welfare—London. I. Title.

Socialism—Addresses, essays, lectures.

LUXEMBURG, Rosa, 1870-1919. 335.4'0924 B
Rosa Luxemburg speaks. Edited with an introd. by Mary-Alice Waters. New York, Pathfinder Press, 1970. 473 p. port. 23 cm. "A Merit book." [HX276.L8433] 76-119530 10.00
1. Socialism—Addresses, essays, lectures. 2. Socialism—Collected works. I. Title. BIP

Socialism—History.

TAYLOR, George Robert Stirling. 335'.00922 B
Leaders of socialism, past and present, by G. R. S. Taylor. Freeport, N.Y., Books for Libraries Press [1968] 125 p. 23 cm. (Essay index reprint series) Reprint of the 1910 ed. Contents.Contents.—On leaders and leadership.—Robert Owen.—Saint Simon.—Fourier.—Louis Blanc.—Ferdinand Lassalle.—Karl Marx.—H. M. Hyndman.—Sidney Webb.—J. Keir Hardie.—G. Bernard Shaw.—Jean Jaures.—William Morris.—Robert Blatchford. [HX23.T2 1968] 68-24857
1. Socialism—History. 2. Socialism in Great Britain. 3. Socialists. I. Title. BIP

Socialism in Great Britain.

BAX, Ernest Belfort, 1854-1926. 942.081'0924
Reminiscences and reflexions of a mid and late Victorian. New York, A. M. Kelley, 1967. 283 p. port. 22 cm. (Reprints of economic classics) Reprint of the 1918 ed. [DA560.B3] 67-27466
1. Socialism in Great Britain. 2. Gt. Brit. — Intellectual life — 19th cent. I. Title.

BAX, Ernest Belfort, 1854-1926 942.081'0924
Reminiscences and reflexions of a mid and late Victorian. New York, A. M. Kelley, 1967. 283p. port. 22cm. (Reprints of econ. classics) Reprint of the 1918 ed. [DA560.B3 1967] 67-27466 7.50
1. Socialism in Great Britain. 2. Gt. Brit.—Intellectual life—19th cent. I. Title. BIP

Socialism in the United States.

CANNON, James Patrick, 1890- 335'.0092'4 B
Letters from prison [by] James P. Cannon. [2d ed.] New York, Pathfinder Press [1973] xx, 362 p. illus. 22 cm. Letters addressed to Rose Karsner. [HX86.C159 1973] 73-79781 3.45 (pbk.)
1. Socialism in the United States. 2. Socialists—Correspondence, reminiscences, etc. I. Karsner, Rose. II. Title.

HOWE, Bertha Washburn, 1866- 335'.0973
An American century; the recollections of Bertha W. Howe, 1866-1966. Recorded and edited, and with a biographical introd., by Oakley C. Johnson. New York, Published for A.I.M.S. by Humanities Press, 1966. x, 142 p. ports. 22 cm. [HX84.H6A3] 66-27970
1. Socialism in the U.S. I. Johnson, Oakley C., 1890- II. American Institute for Marxist Studies. III. Title.

Socialist Party (U.S.)—Addresses, essays, lectures.

DEBS, Eugene Victor, 1855-1926. 335'.3'0924
Eugene V. Debs speaks. Edited by Jean Y. Tussey. With an introd. by James P. Cannon. New York, Pathfinder Press [1970] 320 p. illus., ports. 23 cm. "A Merit book." [HX84.D3A312] 72-108720 6.95
1. Socialist Party (U.S.)—Addresses, essays, lectures. 2. Industrial Workers of the World—Addresses, essays, lectures. 3. Socialism in the United States—Addresses, essays, lectures. BIP

Socialists—Great Britain—Biography.

WERSKEY, Gary. 335'.0092'2 B
The visible college : the collective biography of British scientific socialists of the 1930's / Gary Werskey. 1st ed. New York : Holt, Rinehart, and Winston, 1979. 376 p., [4] leaves of plates : ill. ; 22 cm. Includes bibliographical references and index. [HX243.W47 1979] 78-13167 ISBN 0-03-012261-9 : 10.00
1. Socialists—Great Britain—Biography. I. Title. BIP

Socialists, Jewish—Biography.

WISTRICH, Robert S., 1945- 335'.0092'2 B
Revolutionary Jews from Marx to Trotsky / Robert S. Wistrich ; with a foreword by James Joll. New York : Barnes & Noble Books, 1976. 254 p. : ill. ; 23 cm. Includes bibliographical references and index. [HX23.W57 1976] 76-372865 ISBN 0-06-497806-0 : 16.00
1. Socialists, Jewish—Biography. 2. Jews—Biography. I. Title. BIP

Socialists—Russia—Correspondence, reminiscences, etc.

BROIDO, Eva L'vovna, 1876- 335'.00924
Memoirs of a revolutionary [by] Eva Broido; translated [from the Russian] and edited by Vera Broido. London, New York [etc.] Oxford U.P., 1967. xii, 150 p. front.,

8 plates (incl. ports.). 22 1/2 cm. [HX312.B7] 67-93384
1. Socialists—Russia—Correspondence, reminiscences, etc. I. Broido, Vera, ed. and tr. II. Title.

Society of the Cincinnati.

MUZZEY, Artemas 973.3'0922
Bowers, 1802-1892.
Reminiscences and memorials of men of the Revolution and their families. Ann Arbor, Mich., Plutarch Press, 1971. xviii, 424 p. illus., map, ports. 22 cm. Reprint of the 1883 ed. [E206.M97 1971] 70-142542
1. Society of the Cincinnati. 2. United States—History—Revolution, 1775-1783—Biography. I. Title.

Society of the Descendants of the Colonial Clergy—Directories.

SOCIETY of the 369'.12
Descendants of the Colonial Clergy.
Pedigrees of descendants of the Colonial Clergy / [edited by Robert Glenn Thurtle, associate editor Lillian S. King]. [Lancaster, Mass.] : Society of the Descendants of the Colonial Clergy, 1976. xviii, 688 p. ; 24 cm. [CS42.S5968] 74-25967
1. Society of the Descendants of the Colonial Clergy—Directories. 2. Clergy—United States—Biography. 3. United States—Genealogy. I. Thurtle, Robert Glenn.

Sociologists.

HONIGSHEIM, Paul, 1885- 320'.0924
1963
On Max Weber. Tr. by Joan Rytina. New York, Free Pr. [1968] ix, 155p. 23cm. Bibl. ref. [HM22.G3W444] 67-63230 4.95
I. Weber, Max, 1864-1920. II. Title.

ODUM, Howard Washington, 923
1884-1954, ed.
American masters of social science; an approach to the study of the social sciences through a neglected field of biography, by Howard W. Odum [others] Port Washington, N. Y., Kennikat [1965, c.1927] vii, 411p. ports. 22cm. Bibl. [HM22.U604] 64-24463 12.50
1. Sociologists. 2. Historians, American. 3. Educators, American. I. Title.

Sociology—History.

MARTINDALE, Don 301'.092'2
Albert, 1915-
Prominent sociologists since World War II / Don Martindale. Columbus, Ohio : Merrill, [1975] ix, 158 p. ; 23 cm. Includes bibliographies and index. [HM19.M363] 74-76125 ISBN 0-675-08795-3 pbk. : 3.95
1. Sociology—History. 2. Sociologists—Biography. I. Title.

Socrates.

BRUN, Jean, professor. 921.9
Socrates. Translated by Douglas Scott. New York, Walker [1963, c1962] 120 p. 21 cm. (A Sun book, SB-12. Philosophy) [B317.B713 1963] 62-127440
1. Socrates.

CROSS, Robert Nicol, 1883- 183'.2
Socrates, the man and his mission, by R. Nicol Cross. Freeport, N.Y., Books for Libraries Press [1970] x, 344 p. 23 cm. Reprint of the 1914 ed. Includes bibliographical references. [B317.C76 1970] 70-130546
1. Socrates. 2. Philosophy, Ancient. I. Title.

LANG, Mabel L., 1917- 183'.2 B
Socrates in the Agora / [prepared by Mabel L. Lang]. Princeton, N.J. : American School of Classical Studies at Athens, 1978. [32] p. : ill. ; 22 cm. (Excavations of the Athenian Agora : picture book ; no. 17) [B316.L36] 78-103576 ISBN 0-87661-617-1 pbk. : 1.00
1. Socrates. 2. Athens. Agora. 3. Philosophers—Greece—Biography. I. Title. II. Series. BIP

MASON, Cora. 921.9
Socrates, the man who dared ask. Boston, Beacon Press [1953] 165 p. illus. 22 cm. [B316.M3] 53-10318
1. Socrates.

PLATO. 183'.2 B
The trial and death of Socrates; being the Euthyphron, Apology, Crito, and Phaedo of Plato. Translated into English by F. J. Church. Freeport, N.Y., Books for Libraries Press [1972] lxxxix, 213 p. 22 cm. "First published 1880." [B316.P8 1972] 72-4215 ISBN 0-8369-6891-3
1. Socrates. I. Church, Frederick John, 1854-1888, tr. II. Title.

STRAUSS, Leo 882.01
Socrates and Aristophanes. New York, Basic [c.1966] 321p. 25cm. Bibl. [PA3879.S78] 66-23380 8.50
1. Socrates. I. Aristophanes. II. Title. BIP

TAYLOR, Alfred Edward, 921.9
1869-1945.
Socrates. Garden City, N. Y., Doubleday, 1953. 189p. 18cm. (Doubleday anchor books, A9) [B316.T33 1953] 54-1131
1. Socrates. I. Title.

TAYLOR, Alfred Edward, 921.9
1869-1945.
Socrates. Garden City, N.Y., Doubleday, 1953. 189 p. 18 cm. (Doubleday anchor books, A 9) [B316.T33 1953] 54-1131
1. Socrates.

TAYLOR, Alfred Edward, 921.9
1869-1945.
Socrates. Boston, Beacon Press, 1951. 192 p. port. 19 cm. Bibliography: p. 185-186. [B316.T33 1951] 51-12869
1. Socrates. BIP

TAYLOR, Alfred Edward, 183'.2
1869-1945.
Socrates / by A. E. Taylor. Westport, Conn. : Hyperion Press, [1979] 189 p. ; 22 cm. Reprint of the 1951 ed. published by Beacon Press, Boston. Includes index. Bibliography: p. [175]-177. [B316.T33 1979] 78-59046 ISBN 0-88355-718-5 : 17.00
1. Socrates. 2. Philosophers—Greece—Biography.

WILSON, Pearl Cleveland, 183'.2 B
1882-
The living Socrates : the man who dared to question, as Plato knew him / Pearl Cleveland Wilson ; introd. by George N. Shuster ; drawings by Joseph Sheppard. 1st ed. Owings Mills, Md. : Stemmer House, 1975 xix, 122 p. : ill. ; 25 cm. "A Barbara Holdridge book." Bibliography: p. 122. [B316.W524] 75-25021 ISBN 0-916144-00-3 : 11.95
1. Socrates. I. Plato. Dialogues. English. Selections. II. Title. BIP

WINSPEAR, Alban Dewes 183.2
Who was Socrates? By Alban D. Winspear and Tom Silverberg. [2d ed., enl.] New York, Russell & Russell, 1960, [c.1939, 1960] 96p. (3p. bibl.) 22cm. 60-5340 3.00
1. Socrates. I. Silverberg, Thomas, joint author. II. Title.

Soderholm, Eric.

SODERHOLM, Eric. 796.357
Conditioning for baseball / Eric Soderholm. Winter Park, Fla. : Anna Pub., c1978. 128 p. : ill. ; 21 cm. (Physical fitness and sports medicine) Bibliography: p. 128. [GV875.6.S65] 77-93123 ISBN 0-89305-020-2 : 3.95
1. Soderholm, Eric. 2. Baseball—Training. 3. Baseball players—United States—Biography. I. Title. II. Series. BIP

Soergel, Mary.

SOERGEL, Mary. 248'.2
Sing a gentle breeze : a story of a disintegrating family seeking wholeness / Mary Soergel. Wheaton, Ill. : Tyndale House Publishers, 1977. 266 p. ; 21 cm. [BR1725.S65A37] 76-47301 ISBN 0-8423-5889-7 : 4.95
1. Soergel, Mary. 2. Christian biography—Wisconsin. I. Title.

Sokolow, Nahum, 1859-1936.

KLING, Simcha. 920.5
Nachum Sokolow, servant of his people. New York, Herzl Press [1960] 205p. 22cm. [DS151.S6K55] 60-50588
1. Sokolow, Nahum. 1859-1936. I. Title.

KLING, Smicha 920.5
Nachum Sokolow, servant of his people. New York, Herzl Press [c.1960] 205p. 22cm. 60-50588 3.50
1. Sokolow, Nahum, 1859-1936. I. Title.

Soland, Francisco, Saint, 1549-1610.

ROYER, Fanchon, 1902- 922.285
St. Francis Solanus, apostle to America. Paterson, N. J., St. Anthony Guild Press, 1955. 207p. illus. 23cm. Includes bibliography. [BX4700.S6R6] 55-14671
1. Soland, Francisco, Saint, 1549-1610. I. Title.

Solander, Daniel Charles, 1733-1782.

RAUSCHENBERG, Roy 500.9'0924 B
Anthony, 1929-
Daniel Carl Solander, naturalist on the "Endeavour." Philadelphia, American Philosophical Society, 1968. 66 p. 30 cm. (Transactions of the American Philosophical Society, new ser., v. 58, pt. 8) Bibliography: p. 59-63. [Q11.P6 n.s., vol. 58, pt. 8] 68-54560 2.50
1. Solander, Daniel Charles, 1733-1782. 2. Endeavour (Ship) I. Series: American Philosophical Society, Philadelphia. Transactions, new ser , v 58, pt. 8 BIP

Solano, Francisco, Saint, 1549-1610.

GREENE, Genard, 1921- 922.285
Above the wind's roar; a story of Saint Francis Solano. Illus. by Brother Bernard Howard. Notre Dame, Ind., Dujarie Press [1953] 95p. illus. 24cm. [BX4700.S6G7] 53-2905
1. Solano, Francisco, Saint, 1549-1610. I. Title.

Solar system.

SELVIN, David F. 331.88'0922
Champions of Labor, by David F. Selvin. London, New York [etc.] Abelard-Schuman [1967] 256 p. ports. 22 cm. "Some notes on further reading": p. 244-247. [HD8073.A1S4] 67-16836
1. Solar system. I. Title.

Soldiers.

DECKER, Frank Walker, 1921- 920
1945.
Into the East; the life of Lt. (jg) Frank Walker Decker, U. S. N. R., 1921-1945. Edited by Florence Boston Decker. Richmond, 1951. 125 p. illus. 22 cm. [CT275.D3254A3] 52-18609
I. Title.

DRAKE, Peter, 1671- 923.5415
ca.1753
Amiable renegade; the memoirs of Capt. Peter Drake, 1671-1753. Stanford, Calif., Stanford University Press, [c.]1960. xliii, 410p. illus., map, plan. 23cm. 60-9049 7.50
1. Soldiers. I. Title.

Soldiers of fortune.

GRANT, James, 1822-1887. 920'.042
British heroes in foreign wars; or, The cavaliers of fortune. Freeport, N.Y., Books for Libraries Press [1973] p. (Essay index reprint series) Reprint of the 1858 ed. published by G. Rutledge, London, New York. Contents.Contents.—Arthur Count de Lally, general of the troops of Louis XV, in India.—Colonel John Cameron, of the Gordon Highlanders, slain at Quatre Bras.—Admiral Sir Samuel Greig, "Father of the Russian Navy".—Ulysses Count Brown, marshal of the armies of Maria Theresa.—Marshal Lacy, the conqueror of the Crimea.—Count Lacy, marshal of the imperial armies.—Count Lacy, captain general of Catalonia.—Louis Lacy, mariscal de Campo and commander of Leon.—Colonel Butler, of the Irish Musketeers under the Emperor Ferdinand.—Marshal Clarke, Duc de Feltre, and governor of Vienna.—General Kilmaine, commander of Lombardy, and the Armee d'Angleterre.—Counts O'Reilly, O'Donnel, and the Irish in Spain.—Baron Loudon, marshal of the Austrian Army.—Count O'Reilly, chamberlain ofOBritish heroes in foreign wars; or, The cavaliers of fortune. Freeport, N.Y., Books for Libraries Press [1973] p. (Essay index reprint series) Reprint of the 1858 ed. published by G. Rutledge, London, New York. Contents.Contents.—Arthur Count de Lally, general of
1. Soldiers of fortune. 2. Great Britain—Biography. I. Title.

Soldiers of fortune—United States—Biography.

MALLIN, Jay. 355'.0092'2 B
Merc : American soldiers of fortune / by Jay Mallin and Robert K. Brown. New York : Macmillan, c1979. p. cm. [G539.M34] 79-20483 ISBN 0-02-579330-6 : 12.95
1. Soldiers of fortune—United States—Biography. I. Brown, Robert K., 1932- joint author. II. Title. BIP

Solie, Hans, 1880-

SOLIE, Olga (Wisner) 920
Deep roots; the story of Hans and Olga Solie, compiled and published for their loving children so that their descendants may enjoy in the printed word incidents and events they have experienced at first hand. [Everett? Wash.] 1958. 143 p. illus. 24 cm. "Compiled by Olga and the eldest daughter, Helen, with help from all the family." [CT275.S589A3] 59-41754
1. Solie, Hans, 1880- I. Title.

Solman, Joseph,

SOLMAN, Joseph, 1909- 759.13
Joseph Solman. Introd. by A. L. Chanin. New York, Crown [1966] 16 p. [127] p. of illus. (part col.) illus. 29 cm. [ND237.S6327A47] 66-15519
I. Title.

Solomon ben Isaac, called RaSHI, 1040-1105.

LIBER, Maurice, 1884- 296.6'1 B
Rashi. Translated from the French by Adele Szold. New York, Hermon Press, [1970] 278 p. illus., geneal. table, map. 24 cm. Reprint of the 1906 ed. Includes bibliographical references. [BM755.S6L5 1970] 70-136767 7.50
1. Solomon ben Isaac, called RaSHI, 1040-1105. I. Title.

Solomon, Brother, 1745-1792.

BATTERSBY, William John. 922.244
Brother Solomon, martyr of the French Revolution. New York, Macmillan [1960] vi, 181 p. plates, port., facsim. 23 cm. [BX4705.S669B] A63
1. Solomon, Brother, 1745-1792. 2. France — Hist. — Revolution. 3. France — Church history. I. Title.

Solomon, King of Israel.

FREEHOF, Lillian B (Simon) 221.92
1906-
Stories of King Solomon; illustrated by Seymour R. Kaplan. Philadelphia, Jewish Publication Society of America [c1955] 175p. illus. 28cm. [BS580.S6F7] 55-8423
1. Solomon, King of Israel. I. Title.

GAUBERT, Henri, 1895- 221.9'24 B
Solomon the magnificent. Translated by Lancelot Sheppard and A. Manson. New York, Hastings House [1970] xix, 191 p. illus. 20 cm. (The Bible in history, v. 5) "A Giniger book." Bibliography: p. 187-188. [BS580.S6G313 1970] 69-15815 ISBN 0-8038-6685-2 5.95
1. Solomon, King of Israel. I. Title. II. Series.

WILSON, Clifford A. 221.92'4
A greater than Solomon is here, by

Clifford Wilson. [Melbourne, Australian Institute of Archaeology in association with Word of Truth Productions, 1968] 40 p. 21 cm. (A Word of truth production) [BS580.S6W53] 78-467107 unpriced
1. Solomon, King of Israel. 2. Jesus Christ—Person and offices. I. Australian Institute of Archaeology. II. Title.

Solomon, Samuel Joseph, 1899-

HAGGERTY, James J., 1920- 387.7'092'4 B
Aviation's Mr. Sam / by James Haggerty Fallbrook, Calif. : Aero Publishers, c1974. 184 p. : ill. ; 24 cm. [TL540.S658H33] 74-78958 ISBN 0-8168-3100-9 : 9.95
1. Solomon, Samuel Joseph, 1899- 2. Aeronautics—United States—History. I. Title. BIP

Solomon, William, 1775-1854.

MILWARD, Burton. 917.69'47 B
William (King) Solomon, 1775-1854 / by Burton Milward Lexington : King Library Press, University of Kentucky, 1974. 30, A-G p. : col. port. ; 17 cm. "One hundred copies. 78." Includes bibliographical references. [F459.L6M54] 74-186428
1. Solomon, William, 1775-1854. 2. Lexington, Ky.—History.

Solon.

FREEMAN, Kathleen, 1897-1959. 938'.5'020924 B
The work and life of Solon, with a translation of his poems / Kathleen Freeman. New York : Arno Press, 1975. p. cm. (History of ideas in ancient Greece) Reprint of the 1926 ed. published by the University of Wales Press Board, Cardiff. Bibliography: p. [DF224.S7F7 1975] 75-13265 ISBN 0-405-07307-0 : 13.00
1. Solon. 2. Athens—Politics and government. I. Title. II. Series. BIP

Solzhenitsyn, Aleksandr Isaevich, 1918—

BURG, David. 891.7'8'4409 B
Solzhenitsyn [by] David Burg and George Feifer. New York, Stein and Day [1972] 371 p. illus. 24 cm. Bibliography: p. 355-356. [PG3488.O4Z59 1972] 78-150520 ISBN 0-8128-1375-8 10.00
1. Solzhenitsyn, Aleksandr Isaevich, 1918- I. Feifer, George, joint author.

LABEDZ, Leopold, comp. 891.7'8'4409 B
Solzhenitsyn; a documentary record. Edited and with an introd. by Leopold Labedz. [London] Allen Lane the Penguin Press [1970] xvi, 182 p. 23 cm. [PG3488.O4Z74 1970] 70-29426 ISBN 0-7139-0220-5 £1.50
1. Solzhenitsyn, Aleksandr Isaevich, 1918- 2. Censorship—Russia.

LABEDZ, Leopold, comp. 891.7'8'4409 B
Solzhenitsyn : a documentary record / edited and with an introduction by Leopold Labedz ; [translated from the Russian]. [2d ed.]. Harmondsworth ; Baltimore : Penguin, 1974. 387 p. ; 18 cm. Includes bibliographical references. [PG3488.O4Z74 1974] 74-186634 ISBN 0-14-003395-5 : £0.50
1. Solzhenitsyn, Aleksandr Isaevich, 1918- 2. Censorship—Russia.

LABEDZ, Leopold, comp. 891.7'8'4409 B
Solzhenitsyn; a documentary record, edited and with an introd. by Leopold Labedz. Enl. ed. with the Nobel lecture in literature. Bloomington, Indiana University Press [1973] 320 p. 20 cm. (A Midland book, MB-164) Includes bibliographical references. [PG3488.O4Z74 1973] 72-94815 ISBN 0-253-20164-0 3.50
1. Solzhenitsyn, Aleksandr Isaevich, 1918- 2. Censorship—Russia.

MEDVEDEV, Zhores Aleksandrovich. 891.7'8'4409
Ten years after Ivan Denisovich [by] Zhores A. Medvedev. Translated from the Russian by Hilary Sternberg. New York, Vintage Books [1974, c1973] xii, 211 p. 19 cm. Reprint of ed. published by Knopf. Translation of Desiat' let posle Odnogo dnia Ivana Denisovicha. [PG3488.O4Z77513 1975] 74-3433 ISBN 0-394-71112-2 0.95 (pbk.).
1. Solzhenitsyn, Aleksandr Isaevich, 1918- 2. Tvardovskii, Aleksandr Trifonovich, 1910-1971. 3. Russia—Intellectual life—1917- 4. Censorship—Russia. I. Title. BIP

Solzhenitsyn, Aleksandr Isaevich, 1918—Biography.

RESHETOVSKAIA, Natal'ia A., 1919- 891.7'8'4409 B
Sanya : my life with Aleksandr Solzhenitsyn / by Natalya A. Reshetovskaya ; translated from the Russian by Elena Ivanoff. English language ed. Indianapolis : Bobbs-Merrill Co., [1975] 284 p., [8] leaves of plates : ill. ; 24 cm. Includes index. [PG3488.O4Z85] 75-21147 ISBN 0-672-52088-5 : 8.95
1. Solzhenitsyn, Aleksandr Isaevich, 1918—Biography. 2. Reshetovskaia, Natal'ia A., 1919- I. Title.

SOLZHENITSYN, Aleksandr Isaevich, 1918- 891.7'8'4409 B
Solzhenitsyn: a pictorial autobiography. New York, Farrar, Straus and Giroux [1974] 88 p. illus. 22 cm. (Noonday, 484) Translation of a French collection entitled Soljenitsyne; includes complete text of the author's brief autobiography written for the Nobel Committee, and excerpts from his other writings. [PG3488.O4A24 1974] 74-7070 ISBN 0-374-51192-6
1. Solzhenitsyn, Aleksandr Isaevich, 1918—Biography. I. Title.

Solzhenitsyn, Aleksandr Isaevich, 1918—Friends and associates.

CARLISLE, Olga Andreyev. 891.7'344
In the secret circle / by Olga Calisle. 1st ed. New York : Holt, Rinehart and Winston, c1978. p. cm. [PG3488.O4Z593] 77-20015 ISBN 0-03-040696-X : 8.95
1. Solzhenitsyn, Aleksandr Isaevich, 1918—Friends and associates. 2. Carlisle, Olga Andreyev. 3. Authors, Russian—20th century—Biography. I. Title.

CARLISLE, Olga Andreyev. 070.5'73
Solzhenitsyn and the secret circle / Olga Carlisle. 1st ed. New York : Holt, Rinehart and Winston, c1978. 212 p. ; 22 cm. [PG3488.O4Z593] 77-20216 ISBN 0-03-040696-X : 8.95
1. Solzhenitsyn, Aleksandr Isaevich, 1918—Friends and associates. 2. Carlisle, Olga Andreyev. 3. Authors, Russian—20th century—Biography. I. Title. BIP

Solzhenitsyn, Aleksandr Isaevich, 1918- —Juvenile literature.

FINKE, Blythe Foote. 891.7'8'4409 B
Aleksandr Solzhenitsyn, beleaguered literary giant of the USSR. Charlotteville, N.Y., SamHar Press, 1973. 28 p. 22 cm. (Outstanding personalities, no. 60) Bibliography: p. 27-28. Biography of the Russian recipient of the 1970 Nobel Prize for literature whose writings have been largely suppressed in his own country. [PG3488.O4Z65] 92 73-77599 0.98 (pbk.)
1. Solzhenitsyn, Aleksandr Isaevich, 1918—Juvenile literature. I. Title. Library binding; 1.98. BIP

Somers, Harry Stuart, 1925-

CHERNEY, Brian. 780'.92'4 B
Harry Somers / Brian Cherney. Toronto ; Buffalo : University of Toronto Press, [1975] p. cm. (Canadian Composers; 1 ISSN 0316-1293) "Compositions by Harry Somers": p. Includes index. Discography: p. [ML410.S6864C5] 75-15845 ISBN 0-8020-5325-4 : 15.00
1. Somers, Harry Stuart, 1925- I. Title. II. Series. BIP

Somerset, Edward Seymour, 1st Duke of, 1506?-1552.

JORDAN, Wilbur Kitchener, 1902- 942.05'3
Edward VI: the young King; the protectorship of the Duke of Somerset, by W. K. Jordan. Cambridge, Mass., Belknap Press of Harvard University Press [1971, c1968] 544 p. 22 cm. Includes bibliographical references. [DA345.J6 1971] 70-30093 ISBN 0-674-23965-2 11.50
1. Somerset, Edward Seymour, 1st Duke of, 1506?-1552. 2. Gt. Brit.—History—Edward VI, 1547-1553.

Somerset, Frances (Howard) Carr, Countess of, 1593-1632

LE COMTE, Edward Semple, 1916- 942.06'1'0924 B
The notorious Lady Essex [by] Edward Le Comte. New York, Dial Press, 1969. ix, 251 p. illus., ports. 22 cm. "A note on authorities": p. 244-251. [DA391.1.S7L4] 68-9460 5.95
1. Somerset, Frances (Howard) Carr, Countess of, 1593-1632 2. Great Britain—Court and courtiers. I. Title.

Somerville, Mary Fairfax, 1780-1872.

SOMERVILLE, Mary Fairfax, 1780-1872. 500.2'092'4 B
Personal recollections, from early life to old age, of Mary Somerville ; with selections from her correspondence by her daughter Martha Somerville. New York : AMS Press, [1975] vi, 377 p. : port. ; 19 cm. (Women of letters) Reprint of the 1876 ed. published by Roberts Bros., Boston. [Q143.S7A33 1975] 73-37723 ISBN 0-404-56837-8 : 19.00
1. Somerville, Mary Fairfax, 1780-1872. I. Title. BIP

Sommer, Daniel,

SOMMER, Daniel, 1850-1940. 285'.8'0924 B
Daniel Sommer, 1850-1940; a biography. [Edited and] compiled by William E. Wallace. [Lufkin? Tex., 1969] 307 p. illus., ports. 22 cm. Based on The record of my life, by Daniel Sommer. [BX7077.Z8A3] 76-10389
I. Wallace, William Edwin, 1928- ed.

Somoza, Anastasio, Pres. Nicaragua, 1896-1956.

CRAWLEY, Eduardo D. 320.9'7285'05
Dictators never die : a portrait of Nicaragua and the Somoza dynasty / by Eduardo Crawley. New York : St. Martin's Press, 1979. xi, 180 p. : maps ; 23 cm. Bibliography: p. 170-171. [F1527.C7 1979] 78-31151 ISBN 0-312-20007-2 : 14.50
1. Somoza, Anastasio, Pres. Nicaragua, 1896-1956. 2. Nicaragua—Politics and government—1937- I. Title.

Son, Yang-won.

AN, Yong-jun. 275.19 B
The triumph of Pastor Son; from Korea ... a true story of faith under persecution [by] Yong Choon Ahn with Phyllis Thompson. Downers Grove, Ill., InterVarsity Press [1974, c1973] 96 p. 18 cm. [BX9225.S62A83 1974] 73-93140 ISBN 0-87784-555-7 1.50 (pbk.)
1. Son, Yang-won. I. Thompson, Phyllis, joint author. II. Title.

Sondheim, Stephen.

ZADAN, Craig. 782.8'1'0924 B
Sondheim & Co. New York, Macmillan [1974] 279 p. illus. 24 cm. [ML410.S6872Z2] 74-14997 ISBN 0-02-633380-5 9.95
1. Sondheim, Stephen. 2. Musical revue, comedy, etc. I. Title.

Sone, Monica Itoi, 1919-

SONE, Monica Itoi, 1919- 979.7'77'004956 B
Nisei daughter / by Monica Sone ; introd. by S. Frank Miyamoto. Seattle : University of Washington Press, [1979] c1953. p. cm. [F899.S49J376 1979] 79-4921 ISBN 0-295-95688-7 pbk. : 5.95
1. Sone, Monica Itoi, 1919- 2. Japanese Americans—Washington (State)—Seattle—Biography. 3. Japanese Americans—Evacuation and relocation, 1942-1945. 4. Seattle—Biography. I. Title. BIP

Sonfist, Alan.

SONFIST, Alan. 709'.2'4
Autobiography of Alan Sonfist : a self-presentation by Alan Sonfist published in connection with an exhibition of his works at the Herbert F. Johnson Museum of Art, Cornell University, March 19-May 4, 1975. [Ithaca, N.Y. : Herbert F. Johnson Museum of Art, Cornell University, c1975] [32] p. : ill. ; 22 x 28 cm. Includes bibliography. [N6537.S64A22] 75-12049
1. Sonfist, Alan. I. Herbert F. Johnson Museum of Art. II. Title.

Song, Ben.

SONG, Ben. 269'.2'0924 B
Born out of conflict; the autobiography of Ben Song as told to Cliff Christians. Foreword by Dale Evans Rogers. Grand Rapids, Zondervan Pub. House [1970] 141 p. illus., ports. 22 cm. [BV3785.S65A3] 79-106429 2.95
I. Christians, Clifford. II. Title.

Songs.

FINCK, Henry Theophilus, 1854-1926. 784'.3'00922 B
Songs and song writers. Freeport, N.Y., Books for Libraries Press [1973] p. Reprint of the 1900 ed., issued in series: The Music lover's library. [ML390.F49 1973] 72-12698 ISBN 0-8369-7135-3
1. Songs. 2. Composers—Biography. I. Title. BIP

Songs, French—To 1800.

ADAM DE LAHALLE, 1288. 784'.0924 [Works]
Oeuvres completes du trouvere Adam de la Halle, Poesies et musique. Publiees sous les auspices de la Societe des sciences, des lettres et des arts de Lille. par E. de Coussemaker. Paris, 1872. [Ridgewood, N. J., Gregg Pr., 1965, ie.1966] lxxiv, 440p. col. facsim. 25cm. Includes music. Bibl. [M3.A2 1872a] 67-3156 21.00
1. Songs, French—To 1800. I. Coussemaker, Edmond de, 1805-1876, ed. II. Title.

Sonnenfeld, John,

SONNENFELD, John, 1883- 926.691
Life on two horizons: from Bosnia to Missouri. 1st ed. New York, Vantage Press [1956] 154p. illus. 21cm. Autobiography. [CT275.S592A3] 56-7515
I. Title.

Sons of Liberty—Juvenile literature.

SUTTON, Felix. 973.3'0922
Sons of Liberty. Illustrated by Bill Barss. New York, J. Messner [1969] 90 p. illus. 22 cm. A brief summary of events leading to the Revolution and short biographies of five members of the Sons of Liberty who played major roles in the struggle for independence. Included are Samuel Adams, John Hancock, Patrick Henry, Paul Revere, and Joseph Warren. [E216.S8] 69-12118 ISBN 0-671-32123-4 3.95
1. Sons of Liberty—Juvenile literature. 2. United States—History—Revolution, 1775-1783—Biography—Juvenile literature. I. Barss, Bill, illus. II. Title. BIP

Sontag, Alan.

SONTAG, Alan. 795.4'15'0924 B
The bridge bum : my life and play / by Alan Sontag. New York : Morrow, 1977. 240 p. ; 22 cm. [GV1282.3.S624] 76-30723 ISBN 0-688-03197-8 : 8.95

1. Sontag, Alan. 2. Contract bridge. I. Title. BIP

Sontag, Henriette, contessa Rossi, 1806-1854.

RUSSELL, Frank 927.8
Queen of song; the life of Henrietta Sontag. New York, Exposition [c.1964] 282p. 21cm. Bibl. 64-3995 5.00
1. Sontag, Henriette, contessa Rossi, 1806-1854. I. Title.

Soper, Eileen L.

SOPER, Eileen L. 920.72
The leaves turn / [by] Eileen L. Soper ; with illustrations by Ione Todd. Dunedin : McIndoe, 1973. 85 p. : ill. ; 21 cm. [CT2888.S9A34] 75-300141 1.80
1. Soper, Eileen L. I. Title.

Sophia Dorothea, consort of George I, King of Great Britain, 1666-1726.

JORDAN, Ruth. 942.07'1'0924 B
Sophie Dorothea. New York, G. Braziller [1972, c1971] xii, 292 p. illus. 23 cm. Bibliography: p. 278-279. [DD491.H2753J67 1972] 73-178741 ISBN 0-8076-0626-X 7.95
1. Sophia Dorothea, consort of George I, King of Great Britain, 1666-1726. I. Title. BIP

MORAND, Paul, 943'.044'0924 B
1888-
The captive princess: Sophia Dorothea of Celle. Translated from the French by Anne-Marie Geoghegan. New York, American Heritage Press [1972] 261 p. 22 cm. Translation of Ci-git Sophie Dorothee de Celle. [DA501.A2M613] 75-39601 ISBN 0-07-043037-3 6.95
1. Sophia Dorothea, consort of George I, King of Great Britain, 1666-1726. I. Title.

Sophie, consort of Ernest Augustus, Elector of Hanover. 1630-1714.

CHAPMAN, Hester W., 1899- 920.02
Privileged persons; four seventeenth-century studies [by]Hester W. Chapman. New York, Revnal [1966 ie 1967] 319p. plates (ports.) general.tables 23 cm Bibl. [CT117.C5 1966a] 66-24558
1. Louis XIII. King of France, 1601-1643. 2. Sophie, consort of Ernest Augustus, Elector of Hanover. 1630-1714. 3. Mararin. Hortense (Mancini) de La Porte, duchess de. 1649-1699. 4. Ailesbury, Thomas Bruce, 2d earl of, 1656-1741. I. Title.
Contents omitted. BIP

Sophocles.

LETTERS, Francis Joseph 928.7
Henry.
The life and work of Sophocles. London, New York, Sheed and Ward [1953] 310p illus. 23cm. [PA4417.L4] 53-3355
1. Sophocles. I. Title.

Sophocles—Style.

EARP, Frank Russell, 882'.01
1871-1955.
The style of Sophocles. New York, Russell & Russell [1972] 177 p. 20 cm. Reprint of the 1944 ed. [PA4432.E3 1972] 78-173521
1. Sophocles—Style. I. Title.

Sopwith, Thomas Octave Murdoch, Sir, 1888-

ROBERTSON, 629.133'343'0924
Bruce.
Sopwith: the man and his aircraft; text compiled and written by Bruce Robertson; line tracings by W. F. Hepworth; based on original drawings by Peter G. Cooksley. Letchworth (Herts.), Air Review Ltd., 1970. 244 p. 2 plates; illus. (incl. 1 col.), col. coat of arms, ports. 29 cm. [TL540.S66R6] 70-84076 ISBN 0-900435-15-1 £4.00
1. Sopwith, Thomas Octave Murdoch, Sir, 1888- 2. Aeronautics—Gt. Brit.—History. I. Title.

Soraya,

SORAYA, Princess of Iran, 920.7
1932-
Soraya, the autobiography of Her Imperial Highness. Translated from the German by Constantine Fitzgibbon. [1st ed.] Garden City, N.Y., Doubleday, 1964 [c1963] 181 p. ports. (on lining papers) 22 cm. Translation of Soraya Esfandiary: uneine eigene Geschichte. [DS318.S6A313 1964] 64-19306
I. Title.

Sorby, Henry Clifton, 1826-1908.

HIGHAM, Norman 925.5
A very scientific gentleman the major achivements of Henry Clifton Sorby. Foreword by Cyril Stanley Smith. Oxford, Pergamon; New York, Macmillan [1964, c.1963] xiv, 160p. ports. 20cm. (Commonwealth and intl. lib. of sci., tech., engin. and liberal studies. Hist. of sci. and tech. div. v.2; 202) Bibl. 63-22388 4.50
1. Sorby, Henry Clifton, 1826-1908. I. Title. II. Series.

Sorel, Georges, 1847-1922.

MEISEL, James Hans, 1900- 923.344
The genesis of Georges Sorel, an account of his formative period followed by a study of his influence. Ann Arbor, Mich., G. Wahr Pub. Co., 1951. 320 p. 25 cm. Bibliography: p. 299-312. [HX263.S6M4] 52-8960
1. Sorel, Georges, 1847-1922. I. Title.

Sorge, Richard, 1895-1944.

DE TOLEDANO, 355.3'432'0924
Ralph, 1916-
Spies, dupes, and diplomats. New Rochelle, N.Y., Arlington House [1967] xii, 258 p. 21 cm. [UB271.R9D4 1967] 66-25070
1. Sorge, Richard, 1895-1944. 2. Espionage, Russian. I. Title.

MEISSNER, Hans Otto. 923.547
The man with three faces. New York, Rinehart [1956, c1955] 243 p. 22 cm. [UB271.R92S6] 55-11019
1. Sorge, Richard, 1895-1944. I. Title.

Sorley, Charles Hamilton, 1895-1915.

SWANN, Thomas Burnett 928.2
The ungirt runner: Charles Hamilton Sorley, poet of World War I [Hamden, Conn.] Archon [dist. Shoe String, c.1965.] 151p. ports. 24cm. Bibl. [PR6037.O7Z86] 65-16217 4.50
1. Sorley, Charles Hamilton, 1895-1915. I. Title.

Sorokin, Pitirim Aleksandrovich,

SOROKIN, Pitirim 923.747
Aleksandrovich, 1889-1968.
A long journey; the autobiography of Pitirim A. Sorokin. New Haven, Conn., College and University Press [1963] 327 p. 23 cm. [HM22.U6S58] 63-17365
I. Title. BIP

Sotatsu, d. 1643.

GRILLI, Elise. 759.952
Tawaraya Sotatsu (active early 17th century) Edited by Ichimatsu Tanaka; English text by Elise Grilli. [1st English ed.] Tokyo, Rutland, Vt., C. E. Tuttle Co. [1956] 86p. illus. (part col.) 18cm. (Kodansha library of Japanese art, no. 6) Title also in Japanese on t. p. 'For theJapanese-language edition ... Professor Ichimatsu Tanaka provided ... [the] text ... Though the present book contains the same selection and arrangement of plates as originally made by Professor Tanaka, with his approval I [i. e. Elise Grilli] have written an entirely new text.' Bibliography: p. 86. [ND1059.S6G7] 927.5 56-8491
1. Sotatsu, d. 1643. I. Tanaka, Ichimatsu, 1895- II. Title. III. Series.

Sothern, Georgia.

SOTHERN, Georgia. 792.7 B
Georgia: my life in burlesque. [New York] New American Library [1972] 351 p. illus. 18 cm. (A Signet book) [PN2287.S66A3] 73-154754 1.25
1. Sothern, Georgia. I. Title.

Soto, Hernando de, 1500 (ca.)-1542.

IRVING, Theodore, 1809- 975.9'01
1880.
The conquest of Florida under Hernando de Soto. London, E. Churton, 1835. [Fort Myers Beach, Fla., Island Press, c1973] 2 v. 20 cm. Compiled from La Florida del Inca of Garcilasso de la Vega, and the English translation of 1686 of the anonymous Relacam verdadeira. Cf. Sabin 35120. Facsim. ed. with new introd. by R. F. Schell. [E125.S717 1835a] 73-78181 10.00 (each).
1. Soto, Hernando de, 1500 (ca.)-1542. 2. Florida—History—To 1565. I. Title. BIP

MAYNARD, Theodore, 1890- 973.1'6
1956.
De Soto and the conquistadores. New York, AMS Press [1969] xiii, 297 p. illus., maps, ports. 23 cm. Reprint of the 1930 ed. Bibliography: p. 279-287. [E125.S7M47 1969] 78-100816
1. Soto, Hernando de, 1500 (ca.)-1542. 2. America—Discovery and exploration—Spanish. I. Title. BIP

SCHELL, Rolfe F. 975.901
De Soto didn't land at Tampa, by Rolfe F. Schell. Maps and cover design by the author. Ft. Myers Beach, Fla., Island Press [1966] 96 p. illus., facsims., maps, port. 23 cm. [E125.S7S3] 66-17798
1. Soto, Hernando de, 1500 (ca.)-1542. 2. Florida—History—Spanish exploration to 1565. I. Title. BIP

Soto, Hernando de, 1500(ca.)-1542—Juvenile literature.

EDUCATIONAL Research 973.1'6'0924
Council of America. Social Science Staff.
Explorers and discoverers, De Soto and people De Soto met / prepared by the Social Science Staff of the Educational Research Council of America ; [Kenneth L. Shipley, Edward T. Beyer, design and illustration]. Lerner-verified ed. 2. Boston : Allyn and Bacon, [1974] 59 p. : ill. (some col.) ; 21 cm. (Concepts and inquiry, the ERC social science program) Traces De Soto's journey from Florida to the Mississippi in search of gold and describes the Indian tribes he met along the way. [E125.S7E3 1974] 92 B 73-78342 pbk. : 1.76
1. Soto, Hernando de, 1500 (ca.)-1542—Juvenile literature. I. Shipley, Kenneth L., ill. II. Beyer, Edward T., ill. III. Title. IV. Title: De Soto and people De Soto met. V. Series: Concepts and inquiry, the Educational Research Council social science program.

EDUCATIONAL Research 372.8'9
Council of America. Social Science Staff.
Explorers and discoverers: DeSoto, and people DeSoto met. Boston, Allyn and Bacon [1970] 59 p. illus. (part col.) 21 cm. (Concepts and inquiry: the ERC social science program) Traces De Soto's journey from Florida to the Mississippi in search of gold and describes the Indian tribes he met along the way. [E125.S7E3] 92 78-97105
1. Soto, Hernando de, 1500(ca.)-1542—Juvenile literature. I. Title. II. Title: DeSoto, and people DeSoto met. III. Series: Concepts and inquiry: the Educational Research Council social science program

GRANT, Matthew G. 973.1'6'0924 B
De Soto, explorer of the Southeast [by] Matthew G. Grant. Illustrated by Harold Henriksen. [Mankato, Minn., Creative Education; distributed by Childrens Press, Chicago, 1974] 25 p. illus. (part col.) 25 cm. (His Gallery of great Americans series. Explorers of America) A biography of the wealthy Spanish explorer who became the first white man to cross the Mississippi. [E125.S7G73] 73-13917 ISBN 0-87191-283-X 3.95
1. Soto, Hernando de, 1500 (ca.)-1542—Juvenile literature. I. Henriksen, Harold, illus. II. Title.

POSTEN, Margaret L. 92 (J)
The gold seekers: the story of Hernando de Soto; the people and incidents in the life of one of Spain's most colorful conquistadores, by Margaret L. Posten. Minneapolis, T. S. Denison [1967] 45 p. illus. 25 cm. Bibliography: p. 45. [E125.S7P6] 67-19662
1. Soto, Hernando de, 1500 (ca.)-1542—Juvenile literature. I. Title.

Soto, Hernando de, 1500 (ca.)-1542—Poetry.

HEWITT, John Hill, 818'.3'03 B
1801-1890.
Shadows on the wall; or, Glimpses of the past ... Also the historical poem of De Soto; or, The conquest of Florida, and minor poems. New York, AMS Press [1971] 249 p. 19 cm. Reprint of the 1877 ed. [PS1924.H53S5 1971] 76-166200 ISBN 0-404-07225-9
1. Soto, Hernando de, 1500 (ca.)-1542—Poetry. 2. Baltimore—History. 3. U.S.—Biography. 4. Musicians—Baltimore. I. Title.

MONTGOMERY, 973.1'6'0924 B
Elizabeth Rider.
A world explorer: Hernando De Soto. Illustrated by Henry Gillette. Champaign, Ill., Garrard Pub. Co. [1964] 96 p. illus. (part col.) 24 cm. (World explorer books) A biography of the New World explorer who unsuccessfully sought gold in Florida and led the first expedition of white men across the Mississippi River. [E125.S7M6] 92 AC 68
1. Soto, Hernando de, 1500 (ca)-1542. I. Gillette, Henry S., illus. II. Title.

Soto, Jesus Raphael, 1923-

CLAY, Jean. 730'.92'4
Soto. New York, H. N. Abrams [1974] p. [NB439.S6C55] 74-8620 ISBN 0-8109-4421-9 7.50
1. Soto, Jesus Raphael, 1923- I. Soto, Jesus Raphael, 1923-

Soubirous, Bernadette, Saint, 1844-1879.

BLANTON, Margaret (Gray) 922.244
The miracle of Bernadette. Englewood Cliffs, N. J., Prentice-Hall [1958] 288p. illus. 22cm. First ed. published in 1939 under title: Bernadette of Lourdes. Includes bibliography. [BX4700.S65B5 1958] 58-7144
1. Soubirous, Bernadette, Saint, 1844-1879. I. Title.

KEYES, Frances Parkinson 922.244
(Wheeler) 1885-
Bernadette of Lourdes, shepherdess, Sister, and Saint, [Rev. version, with new material added. New York] J. Messner [1953] 152p. illus. 22cm. 'Originally issued under the title The sublime shepherdess.' [BX4700.S65K4 1953] 53-1047
1. Soubirous, Bernadette, Saint, 1844-1879. I. Title.

MATT, Leonard von 922.244
Bernadette of Lourdes [by] Leonard von Matt, Francis Trochu. [Tr. from German] New York, Universe [c.1963] 47p. 80 illus. (incl. ports., facsims.) 18cm. (Orbis bks., 4) Summary of St. Bernadette: a pictorial biography, by Leonard von Matt and Francis Trochu. 63-18345 1.75 pap.,
1. Soubirous, Bernadette, Saint. 1844-1879. 2. Lourdes—Descr.—Views. I. Trochu, Francis, 1877- II. Title.

MATT, Leonard von. 922.244
St. Bernadette; a pictorial biography, by Leonard von Matt and Francis Trochu. Translated from the French by Herbert Rees. Chicago, H. Regnery Co. [1957] 91p. illus. 25cm. [BX4700.S65M35] 57-2781
1. Soubirous, Bernadette, Saint, 1844-1879. 2. Lourdes— Descr.—Views. I. Trochu, Francis, 1877- joint author. II. Title.

PAULI, Hertha Ernestine, 922.244
1909-
Bernadette, Our Lady's little servant.

Illustrated by Georges Vaux. New York, Vision Books [1956] 187p. illus. 22cm. (Vision books, 5) [BX4700.S65P3] 56-5200
1. Soubirous, Bernadette, Saint, 1844-1879. I. Title.

PETITOT, Hyacinthe, 1870-1934. 922.244
Saint Bernadette, by Henri Petitot. Translated from the French. Chicago, H. Regnery Co., 1955. 130p. 18cm. (Angelus books) Translation of Histoire exacte de la vie interieure et religieuse de ste. Bernadette. [BX4700.S65P413] 55-4767
1. Soubirous, Bernadette, Saint, 1844-1879. I. Title.

PETITOT, Hyacinthe, 1870-1934. 922.244
The true story of Saint Bernadette. Translated by a Benedictine of Stanbrook Abbey. Westminster, Md., Newman Press [1950] viii, 195 p. 22 cm. Translation of Histoire exacte de la vie interieure et religieuse de ste Bernadette. [BX4700.S65P414] 51-3572
1. Soubirous, Bernadette, Saint, 1844-1879. I. Title.

ROSS WILLIAMSON, Hugh, 1901- 922.244
The challenge of Bernadette. Westminster, Md., Newman Press [1958] 101p. 23cm. [BX4700.S65R58] 58-13634
1. Soubrious, Bernadette, Saint, 1844-1879. I. Title.

ST. Bernadette; a pictorial biography, by Leonard von Matt and Francis Trochu. Translated from the French by Herbert Rees. London, New York, Longmans, Green [1957] 91p. illus. v. 12
1. Soubirous, Bernadette, Saint, 1844-1879. 2. Lourdes—Descr.—Views. I. Matt, Leonard von. II. Trochu, Francis, 1877- joint author.

SAINT-PIERRE, Michel de, 1916- 922.244
Bernadette and Lourdes. Translated from the French by Edward Fitzgerald. Garden City, N. Y., Image Books [1955, c1954] 266p. 18cm. (A Doubleday image book, D16) [BX4700] 55-805
1. Soubirous, Bernadette, Saint, 1844-1879. 2. Lourdes. I. Title.

TROCHU, Francis, 1877- 922.244
Saint Bernadette Soubirous, 1844-1879. Translated and adapted by John Joyce. [New York] Pantheon [1958, c1957] 400 p. illus. 22 cm. [BX4700.S65T683] 58-14803
1. Soubirous, Bernadette, Saint, 1844-1879. I. Title.

TROCHU, Francis, 1877- 922.244
Saint Bernadette Soubirous, 1844-1879. Translated and adapted by John Joyce. London, New York, Longmans, Green [1958, c1957] 400 p. illus. 23 cm. Includes bibliography. [BX4700.S65T683] 58-2886
1. Soubirous, Bernadette, Saint, 1844-1879 I. Title.

TROUNCER, Margaret (Lahey) 1906- 922.244
Saint Bernadette, the child and the nun. New York, Sheed and Ward [1958] 248 p. 22 cm. Includes bibliography. [BX4700.S65T7] 58-5881
1. Soubirous, Bernadette, Saint, 1844-1879. Full name: Margaret Duncan (Lahey) Trouncer. I. Title.

Soubirous, Bernadette, Saint, 1844-1879—Juvenile literature.

ROBERTO, Brother, 1927- 92
The girl and the grotto; a story of Saint Bernadette. Illus. by Carolyn Lee Jagodits. Notre Dame, Ind., Dujarie Press [1966] 94 p. illus. 24 cm. [BX4700.S65R53] 66-12689
1. Soubirous, Bernadette, Saint, 1844-1879 — Juvenile literature. I. Title.

ROBERTO, Brother, Brother 1927- 92
The girl and the grotto; a story of Saint Bernadette. Illus. by Carolyn Lee Jagodits. Notre Dame, Ind., Dujarie Pr. [c.1966] 94p. illus. 24cm. [BX4700.S65R53] 66-12689 2.25 bds.,
1. Soubirous, Bernadette, Saint, 1844-1879—Juvenile literature. I. Title.

Soulie, Frederic, 1800-1847.

MARCH, Harold, 1896- 843'.7
Frederic Soulie, novelist and dramatist of the romantic period. New Haven, Yale University Press, 1931. [New York, AMS Press, 1973] viii, 379 p. 23 cm. Original ed. issued as v. 3 of Yale Romanic studies. Originally presented as the author's thesis, Yale, 1929. Bibliography: p. [283]-334. [PQ2429.S5Z7 1973] 72-1725 ISBN 0-404-53203-9 15.00
1. Soulie, Frederic, 1800-1847. I. Title. II. Series: Yale Romanic studies, v. 3.

Sousa, John Philip, 1854-1932.

BERGER, Kenneth Walter, 1924- 927.8
The march king and his band; the story of John Philip Sousa. [1st ed.] New York, Exposition Press [1957] 95p. illus. 21cm. (An Exposition-Banner book) [ML410.S688B4] 57-14134
1. Sousa, John Philip, 1854-1932. I. Title.

BIERLEY, Paul E. 785'.092'4 B
John Philip Sousa; American phenomenon [by] Paul E. Bierley. New York, Appleton-Century-Crofts [1973] xxiii, 261 p. illus. 25 cm. Bibliography: p. 245-248. [ML410.S688B5] 73-1712 8.95
1. Sousa, John Philip, 1854-1932.

LINGG, Ann M. 927.8
John Philip Sousa. [1st ed.] New York, Holt [1954] 250 p. 22 cm. ([Holt musical biography series]) [ML410.S688L5] 54-5451
1. Sousa, John Philip, 1854-1932.

Sousa, John Philip, 1854-1932—Juvenile literature.

WEIL, Ann, 1908- 920
John Philip Sousa, marching boy. Illus. By Katherine Sampson. Indianapolis, Bobbs [1962, c.1959] 200p. col. illus. 20cm. (Childhood of famous Amers.) 2.25
1. Sousa, John Philip, 1854-1932—Juvenile literature. I. Title.

WEIL, Ann, 1908- 792.8'4
John Philip Sousa, marching boy. Illustrated by Katherine Sampson. Indianapolis, Bobbs-Merrill [1959] 192 p. illus. 20 cm. (Childhood of famous Americans) [ML3930.S76W4] [ML3930.S76W4] 792.8'4 59-12856 59-12856
1. Sousa, John Phillip, 1854-1932 — Juvenile literature. I. Title.

South Africa—Biography.

LEGUM, Colin. 301.451'96'068
The bitter choice: eight South Africans' resistance to tyranny [by] Colin and Margaret Legum. Cleveland, World Pub. Co. [1968] 207 p. ports. 24 cm. (Excalibur books) Bibliographical references included in "Acknowledgments" (p. 199-200) Describes the efforts of eight South Africans, both black and white, who have worked against apartheid. [DT779.8.A2L4 1968] 920 68-26980 4.50
1. South Africa—Biography. 2. South Africa—Race question. I. Legum, Margaret (Roberts) joint author. II. Title.

TABLER, Edward C. 920'.068
Pioneers of Natal and southeastern Africa, 1552-1878/ Edward C. Tabler. Cape Town : A. A. Balkema, 1977, c1976. 117 p. ; 25 cm. (South African biographical and historical studies ; 23) Includes index. Bibliography: p. 109-114. [CT1924.T3 1977] 78-304722 ISBN 0-86961-090-2 : 17.50
1. South Africa—Biography. 2. Pioneers—South Africa—Biography. I. Title. II. Series.
Distributed by International Scholarly Book Services Inc., Forest Grove, OR 97116

South Africa—Description and travel—1801-1900.

BORCHERDS, Petrus Borchardus, 1786-1858. 916.8'03'3
An auto-biographical memoir of Petrus Borchardus Borcherds, Esq. ... being a plain narrative of occurrences from early life to advanced age ... Freeport, N.Y., Books for Libraries Press, 1972. xxv, 500 p. illus. 22 cm. (The Black heritage library collection) Reprint of the 1861 ed. [DT844.2.B58A3 1972] 72-5526 ISBN 0-8369-9135-4
1. South Africa—Description and travel—1801-1900. I. Title. II. Series.

South America—Biography.

LANSING, Marion Florence, 1883- 980'.00922
Liberators and heroes of South America, by Marion Lansing. Illustrated by Paul Quinn. Freeport, N.Y., Books for Libraries Press [1971, c1940] xiv, 320 p. illus., fold. map, ports. 23 cm. (Essay index reprint series) [F2205.L33 1971] 76-156675 ISBN 0-8369-2321-9
1. South America—Biography. 2. Statesmen—South America—Biography. I. Title. BIP

ROJAS, Ricardo, 1882-1957 980/.02/0924
San Martin, knight of the Andes. Tr. by Herschel Brickell, Carlos Videla. Introd., notes by Herschel Brickell. New York, Cooper Sq., 1967(c.1945] xiii, 370p. port. 24cm. (Lib. of Latin-Amer. hist. and culture) Tr. of El santo de la espada. [F2235.4.R852 1967] (B) 66-30783 7.50
I. San Martin, Jose de, 1778-1850. II. Title.

South America—Description and travel.

GOODMAN, Edward Julius. 918'.04'0922 B
The explorers of South America, by Edward J. Goodman. New York, Macmillan [1972] viii, 408 p. illus. 24 cm. Bibliography: p. 381-397. [F2221.G6] 79-165567 15.00
1. South America—Description and travel. 2. America—Discovery and exploration. I. Title.

South Carolina—Biography.

HENNIG, Helen (Kohn) 920.0757
Great South Carolinians. Freeport, N.Y., Books for Libraries Press [1970- v. illus., ports. 23 cm. (Essay index reprint series) Reprint of the 1940-49 ed. Contents.Contents.—[1] From colonial days to the Confederate War. [F268.H532] 79-117806
1. South Carolina—Biography. 2. South Carolina—History. I. Title. BIP

South Carolina—Biography—Dictionaries.

GARLINGTON, J. C. 920'.0757
Men of the time; sketches of living notables. A biographical encyclopedia of contemporaneous South Carolina leaders, by J. C. Garlington. Spartanburg, S.C., Garlington Pub. Co., 1902. [Spartanburg, S.C., Reprint Co., 1972] iii, 467 p. ports. 23 cm. [F268.G37 1972] 74-187366 ISBN 0-87152-094-X
1. South Carolina—Biography—Dictionaries. I. Title.

South Carolina. General Assembly. House of Representatives—History—Collected works.

BIOGRAPHICAL directory of the South Carolina House of Representatives. Walter B. Edgar, editor; Inez Watson, research consultant. Columbia, University of South Carolina Press [1974- p. "Compiled under the direction of the House Research Committee." Contents.Contents.—v. 1. Faunt, J. S. R. and Rector, R. E., with Bowden, D. K. Session lists, 1692-1973. Includes bibliographical references. [JK4278.B56] 73-13630 25.00 328.757'092'2 B
1. South Carolina. General Assembly. House of Representatives—History—Collected works. 2. South Carolina. General Assembly. House of Representatives—Registers—Collected works. 3. South Carolina. General Assembly. House of Representatives—Biography—Collected works. I. Edgar, Walter B., 1943- ed. II. South Carolina. General Assembly. House of Representatives. Research Committee. BIP

South Carolina. General Assembly. House of Representatives—Registers—Collected works.

BIOGRAPHICAL directory of the South Carolina House of Representatives. Walter B. Edgar, editor; Inez Watson, research consultant. Columbia, University of South Carolina Press [1974- p. "Compiled under the direction of the House Research Committee." Contents.Contents.—v. 1. Faunt, J. S. R. and Rector, R. E., with Bowden, D. K. Session lists, 1692-1973. Includes bibliographical references. [JK4278.B56] 73-13630 25.00 328.757'092'2 B
1. South Carolina. General Assembly. House of Representatives—History—Collected works. 2. South Carolina. General Assembly. House of Representatives—Registers—Collected works. 3. South Carolina. General Assembly. House of Representatives—Biography—Collected works. I. Edgar, Walter B., 1943- ed. II. South Carolina. General Assembly. House of Representatives. Research Committee. BIP

South Carolina—History—Colonial period—Juvenile literature.

FEDERAL Writers' Project. South Carolina. 917.57'03'20922 B
Palmetto pioneers; six stories of early South Carolinians. [Spartanburg, S.C., Reprint Co., 1972] 81 p. illus. 23 cm. Reprint of the 1938 ed., issued in series: American guide series. "Sponsored by the Division of Adult Education, State Department of Education, South Carolina." Bibliography: p. 77-81. Accounts of six pioneers who helped lay the foundations for South Carolina: Jean Ribaut, Joseph West, Tuscarora Jack, Colonel William Rhett, Jean Louis Gibert, and Attakullakulla. [F272.F45 1972] 920 71-187376 ISBN 0-87152-104-0
1. South Carolina—History—Colonial period—Juvenile literature. 2. South Carolina—Biography—Juvenile literature. I. South Carolina. Dept. of Education. Division of Adult Education. II. Title. III. Series: American guide series.

South Dakota—Hist.

RIGGS, Theodore F., M.D. 923.9783
A log house was my home; South Dakota Stories for my two boys. New York, Exposition Press [c.1961] illus. 3.00
1. South Dakota—Hist. I. Title.

South Dakota. University. Dept. of Zoology.

CHURCHILL, Edward Perry, 1882- 925.9
Three thousand coyotes and I; memoirs of a zoology professor, State University of South Dakota. Vermillion, State University of South Dakota, 1962. 88 p. illus., ports. 21 cm. [QL31.C54A3] 64-64123
1. South Dakota. University. Dept. of Zoology. I. Title.

Southampton, Henry Wriothesley, 3d Earl of, 1573-1624.

ACHESON, Arthur, 1864-1930. 822.3'3 B
Shakespeare's lost years in London 1586-1592, giving new light on the pre-sonnet period; showing the inception of relations between Shakespeare and the Earl of Southampton and displaying John Florio as Sir John Falstaff. New York, Haskell House, 1971. vii, 261 p. 23 cm. Reprint of the 1920 ed. [PR2907.A4 1971] 79-152552 ISBN 0-8383-1235-7
1. Shakespeare, William, 1564-1616—

Biography—London life. 2. Southampton, Henry Wriothesley, 3d Earl of, 1573-1624. 3. Florio, John, 1553?-1625. 4. Shakespeare, William, 1564-1616—Characters—Falstaff. I. Title.

AKRIGG, G. P. V. 942.6'1'0924 B
Shakespeare and the Earl of Southampton [by] G. P. V. Akrigg. Cambridge, Harvard University Press, 1968. xvi, 280 p. illus., facsim., maps, ports. (part col.) 26 cm. Bibliographical footnotes. [DA391.1.S8A65 1968b] 68-31993 6.00
1. Southampton, Henry Wriothesley, 3d Earl of, 1573-1624. 2. Shakespeare, William, 1564-1616—Friends and associates. I. Title.

Southampton Insurrection, 1831-

TURNER, Nat, 1800?- 975.5'55'03 1831.
The confessions of Nat Turner; leader of the late insurrection in Southampton, Va. As fully and voluntarily made to Thos. C. [i.e. R.] Gray, in the prison where he was confined, and acknowledged by him to be such, when read before the court of Southampton, convened at Jerusalem, November 5, 1831, for his trial. Miami, Fla., Mnemosyne Pub. Inc., 1969. 12 p. 23 cm. Reprint of the 1861 ed. [F232.S7T9 1969] 70-79011
1. Southampton Insurrection, 1831- I. Gray, Thomas R. II. Title.

Southeastern Conference.

BOLTON, Clyde. 796.33'272'0975
Unforgettable days in Southern football / by Clyde Bolton. Huntsville, Ala. : Strode Publishers, [1974] 257 p. : ill. ; 24 cm. [GV958.5.S59B64] 74-15506 ISBN 0-87397-057-8 : 7.95
1. Southeastern Conference. 2. Football—Biography. I. Title.

Southern Baptist Convention—Biog.

ROUTH, Porter, 286'.132'0922 B 1911-
Chosen for leadership : sketches of 39 presidents of the Southern Baptist Convention / Porter Routh. Nashville : Broadman Press, c1976. 110 p. : ports. ; 19 cm. Published in 1953 under title: Meet the presidents. [BX6493.R68 1976] 76-14632 ISBN 0-8054-6529-4 pbk. : 2.50
1. Southern Baptist Convention—Biography. 2. Baptists—Biography. I. Title.

ROUTH, Porter, 1911- 922.673
Meet the presidents. Nashville, Broadman Press [1953] 98p. illus. 16cm. [BX6241.R68] 53-9909
1. Southern Baptist Convention—Biog. I. Title.

Southern Baptist Convention—History.

BURTON, Joe 286'.132'0924 B Wright, 1907-1976.
Road to recovery : Southern Baptist renewal following the Civil War, as seen especially in the work of I. T. Tichenor / Joe W. Burton. Nashville : Broadman Press, c1977. 168 p. ; 20 cm. Bibliography: p. 166-168. [BX6207.S68B87] 76-24062 ISBN 0-8054-6530-8 bds. : 6.95
1. Southern Baptist Convention—History. 2. Tichenor, Isaac Taylor, 1825-1902. 3. Baptists—Clergy—Biography. 4. Clergy—Georgia—Atlanta—Biography. 5. Atlanta—Biography. I. Title.

Southern States—Biog.—Dictionaries.

WHO'S who in the South 920.075
and Southwest. 8th Ed. [1963] Chicago, Marquis [c.1950-1963] 983p. 27cm. 50-58231 25.00
1. Southern States—Biog.—Dictionaries. 2. Southwest, New—Biog,— Dictionaries. 3. Washington, D.C.—Biog.—Dictionaries.

WHO'S who in the South 920.078
and Southwest; a biographical dictionary of noteworthy men and women of the Southern and Southwestern states. Chicago, Marquis--Who's Who 9th ed. [c.1950-1965] 1057p. 24cm. [F208.W64] 50-58231 26.00
1. Southern States—Biog.—Dictionaries. 2. Southwest, New—Biog.—Dictionaries.

WHO'S who in the South 920.075
and Southwest; a biographical dictionary of noteworthy men and women of the Southern and Southwestern states. 10th ed. Chicago, Marquis [1967] v. 27cm. annual. Issue for 1950 called 2d but is 1st under Marquis editorship [F208.W64] 50-58231 27.00
1. Southern states Biog. Dictionaries. 2. Southwest, New —Biog..—Dictionaries. 3. Washington, D.C.—Biog.—Dictionaries.

Southern States—Biography.

EGERTON, John. 920.075
A mind to stay here; profiles from the South. With photos. by Al Clayton. [New York] Macmillan [1970] 190 p. ports. 22 cm. Contents.Contents.—Will Campbell.—James McBride Dabbs.—John Lewis.—Howard (Buck) Kester.—Fannie Lou Hamer.—Lucius H. Pitts and U. W. Clemmon.—Sarah Patton Boyle.—John Howard Griffin.—Billie and De De Pierce.—The South: the same, only different. [F208.E35] 70-115298 5.95
1. Southern States—Biography. 2. Southern States—Race question. I. Title.

NORTH Carolina. East 917.5030922 Carolina College, Greenville, Dept. of History.
Essays in Southern biography. Greenville, 1965. vii, 166 p. 22 cm. (East Carolina College publications in history, v. 2) Bibliographical footnotes. [F208.N6 vol. 2] 65-65020
1. Southern States — Biog. I. Title. II. Series. III. Series: North Carolina. East Carolina College, Greenville. Publications in history, v. 2

ODUM, Howard 975'.04'0922 Washington, 1884-1954, ed
Southern pioneers in social interpretation. Freeport, N.Y., Bks. for Libs. Pr. [1967] vi, 221p. 22cm. (Essay index reprint ser.) Reprint of the 1925 ed. [F208.O27 1967] 67-23254 7.50
1. Southern States—Biog. I. Title.
Contents omitted. BIP

RAND, Clayton, 1891- 920.075
Sons of the South. Portraits by Dalton Shourds, Harry Coughlin [and] Constance Joan Naar. [1st ed.] New York, Holt, Rinehart and Winston [1961] 212p. illus. 29cm. [F208.R3] 61-8069
1. Southern States—Biog. 2. Southern States—Biog.— Portraits. I. Title.

RAND, Clayton [Thomas] 920.075 1891-
Sons of the South. Portraits by Dalton Shourds, Harry Coughlin, Constance Joan Naar. New York, Holt, Rinehart and Winston [c.1961] 212p. illus. 29cm. 61-8069 7.50
1. Southern States—Biog. 2. Southern States—Biog.— Portraits. I. Title.

Southern States—Genealogy.

ARMSTRONG, Zella, 929'.2'0973 comp.
Notable Southern families. Spartanburg, S.C., The Reprint Co., 1974 [c1918-33] p. cm. Vol. 5 by J. P. C. French and Z. Armstrong; v. 6 by J. P. C. French. Reprint of the ed. published by Lookout Pub. Co., Chattanooga, and King Print. Co., Bristol, Tenn. Contents.Contents.—v. 1. Armstrong. Banning. Blount. Brownlow. Calhoun. Dearderick. Gaines. Howard. Key. Luttrell. Lyle. McAdoo. McGhee. McMillan. Phinizy. Polk. Sevier. shields. Stone. Turnley. VanDyke.—v. 2. Bean. Boone. Borden. Bryan. Carter. Davis. Donaldson. Hardwick. Haywood. Holliday. Honningsworth. Houston. Johnston. Kelton. Magill. Rhea. Montgomery. Shelby. Vance. Wear. Williams.—v. 3. Armstrong, "Trooper." Cockrill. Duke. Elston. Lea. Park. Parkes. Tunnell.—v. 4. The Sevier family.—v. 5. The Crockett family and connecting lines.—v. 6. The Doak family. [CS69.A853] 74-885 ISBN 0-87152-146-6 (v. 1)
1. Southern States—Genealogy. I. Title. BIP

Southern States—Social life and customs.

LUMPKIN, Katharine Du 917.5'03 Pre, 1897-
The making of a Southerner. Westport, Conn., Greenwood Press [1971, c1946] 247 p. 23 cm. Autobiographical. Bibliography: p. 241-[248] [F215.L86 1971] 70-135602 ISBN 0-8371-5194-5
1. Southern States—Social life and customs. 2. Negroes—Southern States. I. Title. BIP

Southerne, Thomas, 1660-1746.

DODDS, John Wendell, 1902- 822'.5
Thomas Southerne, dramatist. [Hamden, Conn.] Archon Books, 1970 [c1933] iv, [3], 232 p. 23 cm. (Yale studies in English, v. 81) "Chronology of Southerne's plays": p. [vii] [PR3699.S3Z6 1970] 78-91179
1. Southerne, Thomas, 1660-1746. I. Title. II. Series. BIP

Southey, Robert, 1774-1843.

CURRY, Kenneth. 821'.7 B
Southey / by Kenneth Curry. London ; Boston : Routledge & K. Paul, 1975. xii, 191 p. ; 22 cm. (Routledge author guides) Includes index. Bibliography: p. 179-183. [PR5466.C8] 75-316716 ISBN 0-7100-8112-X : 15.50
1. Southey, Robert, 1774-1843.

DOWDEN, Edward, 1843- 821'.7 B 1913.
Southey. New York, AMS Press [1968] 199 p. 22 cm. (English men of letters) "Reprinted from the edition of 1888." [PR5466.D6 1968] 68-58377
1. Southey, Robert, 1774-1843.

HALLER, William, 1885- 826'.7 B
The early life of Robert Southey, 1774-1803. New York, Octagon Books, 1966 [c1917] ix, 353 p. 21 cm. (Columbia University studies in English and comparative literature) Reprint of the author's thesis, Columbia University. Includes bibliographies. [PR5466.H32 1966] 66-28369
1. Southey, Robert, 1774-1843. I. Title. BIP

SIMMONS, Jack, 1915- 826'.7 B
Southey. Port Washington, N.Y., Kennikat Press [1968] 256 p. geneal. table, port. 22 cm. Reprint of the 1945 ed. "List of Southey's works": p. 226-229. Bibliographical references included in "Notes" (p. 230-250) [PR5466.S5 1968] 68-16286
1. Southey, Robert, 1774-1843 BIP

SOUTHEY, Robert, 1774- 821'.7 B 1843.
The life and correspondence of Robert Southey. Edited by his son, Charles Cuthbert Southey. London, Longman, Brown, Green, and Longmans, 1849-50. St. Clair Shores, Mich., Scholarly Press [1969?] 6 v. illus., ports. 22 cm. "List of the publications of Robert Southey, Esq.": v. 6, p. [397]-402. [PR5466.A6 1969] 70-108540 ISBN 0-403-00232-X
I. Southey, Charles Cuthbert, 1819-1888, ed. II. Title.

SOUTHEY, Robert, 1774-1843 826.7
New letters of Robert Southey, 2v. Ed. by Kenneth Curry. New York, Columbia *c.] 1965. 2v. (xix, 552; 566p.) port., facsim. 24cm. Contents.v.1. 1792-1810.--v.2. 1811-1838. [PR5466.A63] 64-21080 20.00 set,
1. Curry, Kenneth, ed. I. Title.

Southey, Robert, 1774-1843—Correspondence.

SOUTHEY, Robert, 1774- 821'.7 B 1843.
Journals of a residence in Portugal, 1800-1801 and a visit to France, 1838 : supplemented by extracts from his correspondence / Robert Southey ; edited by Adolfo Cabral. Westport, Conn. : Greenwood Press, 1978, c1960. xxiii, 285 p., [7] leaves of plates : ill. ; 23 cm. Reprint of the ed. published by Clarendon Press, Oxford. Includes bibliographical references and index. [PR5466.A34 1978] 78-16176 ISBN 0-313-20590-6 : 25.00
1. Southey, Robert, 1774-1843—Diaries. 2. Southey, Robert, 1774-1843—Correspondence. 3. Southey, Robert, 1774-1843—Journeys. 4. Portugal—Description and travel. 5. France—Description and travel. 6. Authors, English—19th century—Biography. I. Cabral, Adolfo. II. Title.

SOUTHEY, Robert, 1774- 821'.7 1843.
Letters of Robert Southey : a selection / edited, with introd. and notes, by Maurice H. Fitzgerald. New York : AMS Press, 1977. p. cm. Reprint of the 1912 ed. published by H. Frowde, Oxford University Press, London, which was issued as no. 169 of the World's classics. [PR5466.A4 1977] 75-41260 26.50
1. Southey, Robert, 1774-1843—Correspondence. 2. Authors, English—19th century—Correspondence. I. FitzGerald, Maurice Henry, 1877-

SOUTHEY, Robert, 1774- 821'.7 B 1843.
The letters of Robert Southey to John May, 1797 to 1838 / edited with an introd. by Charles Ramos. Austin : Jenkins Pub. Co., 1976. xi, 323 p. ; 23 cm. Includes index. Bibliography: p. 311. [PR5466.A45 1976] 75-36519 14.95
1. Southey, Robert, 1774-1843—Correspondence. 2. May, John, 1775-1856. 3. Authors, English—19th century—Biography. I. May, John, 1775-1856. II. Title. BIP

SOUTHEY, Robert, 1774- 821'.7 B 1843.
The life and correspondence of Robert Southey. Edited by his son, Charles Cuthbert Southey. London, Longman, Brown, Green, and Longmans, 1849-50. St. Clair Shores, Mich., Scholarly Press [1969?] 6 v. illus., ports. 22 cm. "List of the publications of Robert Southey, Esq.": v. 6, p. [397]-402. [PR5466.A6 1969] 70-108540 ISBN 0-403-00232-X
I. Southey, Charles Cuthbert, 1819-1888, ed. II. Title.

Southey, Robert, 1774-1843—Diaries.

SOUTHEY, Robert, 1774- 821'.7 B 1843.
Journals of a residence in Portugal, 1800-1801 and a visit to France, 1838 : supplemented by extracts from his correspondence / Robert Southey ; edited by Adolfo Cabral. Westport, Conn. : Greenwood Press, 1978, c1960. xxiii, 285 p., [7] leaves of plates : ill. ; 23 cm. Reprint of the ed. published by Clarendon Press, Oxford. Includes bibliographical references and index. [PR5466.A34 1978] 78-16176 ISBN 0-313-20590-6 : 25.00
1. Southey, Robert, 1774-1843—Diaries. 2. Southey, Robert, 1774-1843—Correspondence. 3. Southey, Robert, 1774-1843—Journeys. 4. Portugal—Description and travel. 5. France—Description and travel. 6. Authors, English—19th century—Biography. I. Cabral, Adolfo. II. Title.

Southwell, Robert, 1561?-1595.

DEVLIN, Christopher. 928.2
The life of Robert Southwell, poet and martyr. New York, Farrar, Straus and Cudahy [1956] 367 p. illus. 23 cm. [PR2349.S5Z65] 56-4401
1. Southwell, Robert, 1561?-1595.

DEVLIN, Christopher. 821'.3 B
The life of Robert Southwell, poet and martyr. New York, Greenwood Press [1969] x, 367 p. 23 cm. Bibliographical references included in "Notes" (p. 339-359) [PR2349.S5Z65] 72-90498
1. Southwell, Robert, 1561?-1595. I. Title. BIP

JANELLE, Pierre. 821'.3 B
Robert Southwell, the writer; a study in religious inspiration. Mamaroneck, N.Y., P. P. Appel, 1971 [c1935] xi, 336 p. 24 cm. Bibliography: p. [306]-323. [PR2349.S5Z7 1971] 72-162495 ISBN 0-911858-18-0 10.00
1. Southwell, Robert, 1561?-1595. **BIP**

THE life of Robert v. 12
Southwell, poet and martyr. London, New York, Longmans, Green [1956] x, 367 p. geneal. tables. 23 cm. Includes bibliographical references.
1. Southwell, Robert, 1561?-1595. I. Devlin, Christopher.

MOSELEY, Daisy Haywood. 928.2
Blessed Robert Southwell. New York, Sheed & Ward [1957] 182p. 21cm. [BX4705.S688M6] 57-10188
1. Southwell, Robert, 1561?-1595. I. Title.

Southwest, New—Description and travel.

AUDUBON, John 917.9'04'4
Woodhouse, 1812-1862.
Audubon's western journal, 1849-1850; being the MS. record of a trip from New York to Texas, and an overland journey through Mexico and Arizona to the gold-fields of California. With biographical memoir by his daughter, Maria R. Audubon. Introd., notes, and index by Frank Heywood Hodder. Glorieta, N.M., Rio Grande Press [1969] 249 p. illus., map (in pocket) 24 cm. (A Rio Grande classic) Reprint of the 1906 ed. [F786.A9 1969] 78-76176
1. Southwest, New—Description and travel. 2. Mexico—Description and travel. 3. U.S.—Description and travel—1848-1865. 4. Overland journeys to the Pacific. 5. California—Gold discoveries. I. Audubon, Maria Rebecca, 1843-1925. II. Title.

Soutine, Haim, 1894-1943.

WERNER, Alfred, 1911- 759.4
Chaim Soutine / text by Alfred Werner. New York : H. N. Abrams, 1977. 167 p. : ill. (some col.) ; 34 cm. (The Library of great painters) Includes index. Bibliography: p. 163. [ND553.S7W4] 77-1249 ISBN 0-8109-0468-3 : 25.00
1. Soutine, Haim, 1894-1943. 2. Painters—France—Biography. I. Soutine, Haim, 1894-1943.

Souza, Alfredo Barbosa de, 1908-

CHRISTMAN, Don R. 922.681
Savage fire. Washington, D.C., Review & Herald [1964, c.1961] 144p. illus., ports. 22cm. Appeared serially in The Youth's instructor under the title: The story of wildfire. [BV2853.B7S6] 64-18170 3.50
1. Souza, Alfredo Barbosa de, 1908- 2. Pemphigus. I. Title.

Sowers, Ray V.

DAVIS, Dan A. 378.1'2'0975921 B
A teacher for all seasons; a biography of Ray V. Sowers [by] Dan A. Davis & Michael E. Duclos. DeLand, Fla., Dept. of Education, Stetson University, 1971. xv, 210 p. illus. 24 cm. Bibliography: p. 176-178. [LA2317.S64D3] 73-173911 5.50
1. Sowers, Ray V. I. Duclos, Michael E., joint author. II. Title.

Soyer, Raphael, 1899-

SOYER, Raphael, 1899- 759.13 B
Diary of an artist / by Raphael Soyer. Washington : New Republic Books, c1977. p. cm. [ND237.S636A226] 77-4798 ISBN 0-915220-29-6 : 15.00
1. Soyer, Raphael, 1899- 2. Painters—United States—Biography. I. Title. **BIP**

SOYER, Raphael, 1899- 759.13
Raphael Soyer, by Lloyd Goodrich. New York, H. N. Abrams [1972] 349 p. illus. (part col.) 39 cm. Bibliography: p. 339-342. [ND237.S636G62] 72-2169 ISBN 0-8109-0486-1 50.00
I. Goodrich, Lloyd, 1897-

Spaak, Paul Henri Charles, 1899-

HUIZINGA, Jakob Herman, 923.2493
1908-
Mr. Europe; a political biography of Paul Henri Spaak, by James H. Huizinga. New York, Praeger [1961] 248 p. 22 cm. (Books that matter) Includes bibliography. [DH689.S6H8] 61-14053
1. Spaak, Paul Henri Charles, 1899- I. Title.

Spaggiari, Albert.

SPAGGIARI, Albert. 364.1'55 B
Fric-frac : the great Riviera bank robbery / Albert Spaggiari ; translated from the French by Martin Sokolinsky ; illustrated with photos. and maps. Boston : Houghton Mifflin, 1979. viii, 261 p., [8] leaves of plates : ill. ; 22 cm. Translation of Les egouts du paradis. [HV6248.S6139A413] 79-416 ISBN 0-395-27764-7 : 8.95
1. Spaggiari, Albert. 2. Crime and criminals—France—Biography. 3. Bank robberies—France—Nice. I. Title.

Spahn, Warren Edward, 1921-

SHAPIRO, Milton J. 927.96357
The Warren Spahn story. New York, Messner [1958] 192 p. illus. 22 cm. [GV865.S6S5] 58-7258
1. Spahn, Warren E., 1921- I. Title.

SHAPIRO, Milton J. 927.96357
The Warren Spahn story. New York, J. Mexxner [1959] 191 p. ports. 22 cm. [GV865.S6S5 1959] 59-1048
1. Spahn, Warren Edward, 1921- I. Title.

SILVERMAN, Al. 796.3570924
Warren Spahn, immortal southpaw. New York, Bartholomew House [1961] 158 p. 18 cm. (Sport magazine library, no. 9) [GV865.S6S55] 61-65872
1. Spahn, Warren Edward, 1921- I. Title.

Spain—Pol. & govt.—20th cent.

IBARRURI, Dolores, 946.0810924
1895-
They shall not pass; the autobiography of La Pasionaria [by Dolores Ibarruri. [1st ed. New York] Intl. Pubs. [1966] 351p. map, ports. 2icm. Translation of El unico camino. [DP233.I213] 66-25065 5.95
1. Spain—Pol. & govt.—20th cent. 2. Communism—Spain. 3. Spain—Hist.—Civil War, 1936-1939. I. Title.

Spain—Biography.

AUB, Max, 1903- 927.5
Jusep Torres Campalans. Tr. from Spanish by Herbert Weinstock. Garden City, N.Y., Doubleday [c.]1962. 318p. illus. (pt. col.) 24cm. 62-15917 5.95
I. Title.

PULGAR, Fernando del, 946'.0092
1436?-1492.
Claros varones de Castilla [by] Fernando del Pulgar; a critical edition, with introduction and notes by Robert Brian Tate. Oxford, Clarendon Press, 1971. lxviii, 118 p. 23 cm. Text in Spanish; introd. and notes in English. Bibliography: p. [108]-114. [DP58.P8 1971] 248'.22'0924 78-575284 ISBN 0-19-815702-9 £2.90
1. Spain—Biography. I. Tate, Robert Brian, ed. II. Title. **BIP**

Spain—History—Alfonso XIII, 1886-1931.

PILAPIL, Vicente 946.08'0924 B
R., 1941-
Alfonso XIII, by Vicente R. Pilapil New York, Twayne Publishers [1969] 242 p. 21 cm. (Twayne's rulers and statesmen of the world series, 12) Bibliography: p. 225-235. [DP240.P65] 78-77035
1. Spain—History—Alfonso XIII, 1886-1931.

Spain—History—Civil War, 1936-1939—Personal narratives.

LERMA, Jose Larios 946.0810924
Fernandez de Villavicencio, dugue de
Combat over Spain; memoirs of a nationalist fighter pilot, 1936-1939, by Jose Larios, Marquis of Larios, Duke of Lerma. New York, Macmillan [c.1966] 308p. fold. map. 21cm. [DP269.9.L4] 66-12972 6.95
1. Spain—Hist.—Civil War, 1936-1939—Personal narratives. 2. Spain—Hist.—Civil War—Aerial operations. I. Title.

LERMA, Jose Larios 946.0810924
Fernandez de Villavicencio, duque de.
Combat over Spain; memoirs of a nationalist fighter pilot, 1936-1939, by Jose Larios, Marquis of Larios, Duke of Lerma. New York, Macmillan [1966] 308 p. fold. map. 21 cm. [DP269.9.L4] 66-12972
1. Spain — Hist. — Civil War, 1936-1939 — Personal narratives. 2. Spain — Hist. — Civil War — Aerial operations. I. Title.

SPERBER, Murray A., comp. 946.081
And I remember Spain; a Spanish Civil War anthology, edited by Murray A. Sperber. New York, Collier Books [1974] xxvi, 337 p. 21 cm. Bibliography: p. [335]-337. [DP269.9.S68 1974b] 74-2644 3.95
1. Spain—History—Civil War, 1936-1939—Personal narratives. 2. Spain—History—Civil War, 1936-1939—Addresses, essays, lectures. I. Title. **BIP**

Spalding, Albert, 1883-1953.

SPALDING, Albert, 787'.1'0924 B
1888-1953.
Rise to follow : an autobiography / by Albert Spalding. New York : Da Capo Press, 1977 [c1943] 328 p. : port. ; 23 cm. (Da Capo Press music reprint series) Reprint of the ed. published by H. Holt, New York. Includes index. [ML418.S7A2 1977] 77-5563 ISBN 0-306-77422-4 : 19.50
1. Spalding, Albert, 1883-1953. 2. Violinists, violoncellists, etc.—United States—Biography.

Spalding, Baird Thomas, 1857-1953.

RYMAN, Walter Ira David 920.9133
Bruton, 1907-
Baird T. Spalding as I knew him, by David Bruton [pseud. 1st ed.] San Pedro, Calif., Institute of Esoteric Philosophy [1954] 129p. illus. 23cm. [BF1997.S6R9] 54-14202
1. Spalding, Baird Thomas, 1857-1953. I. Title.

Spalding, John Lancaster, Abp., 1840-1916.

COSGROVE, John J. 922.273
Most Reverend John Lancaster Spalding, first bishop of Peoria. Mendota, Ill., Wayside Press, Wayside Publishing Division, 1501W. Washington Rd. c.1960. 160p. illus. 27cm. 60-51068 4.50
1. Spalding, John Lancaster, Abp., 1840-1916. I. Title.

ELLIS, John Tracy, 1905- 922.273
John Lancaster Spalding, first bishop of Peoria, American educator. Milwaukee, Bruce [1962, c.1961] 106p. illus. 19cm. (Gabriel Richard lect.) 62-12433 2.75
1. Spalding, John Lancaster, Abp., 1840-1916. I. Title.

SWEENEY, David Francis 282.0924
The life of John Lancaster Spalding, First Bishop of Peoria, 1840-1916. [New York] Herder & Herder [1966, c.1965] 384p. port. 22cm. (Makers of Amer. Catholicism, v.1) Bibl. [BX4705.S7S39] 65-13480 7.50
1. Spalding, John Lancaster, Abp., 1840-1916. I. Title.

Spalding, Martin John, Abp., 1810-1872.

SPALDING, Thomas W. 282'.092'4 B
Martin John Spalding: American churchman [by] Thomas W. Spalding. Washington, Catholic University of America Press [1973] xi, 373 p. 23 cm. Bibliography: p. 353-364. [BX4705.S73S64] 74-171040 12.00
1. Spalding, Martin John, Abp., 1810-1872.

Spalding, Samuel Charles,

SPALDING, Samuel 285'.092'4
Charles, 1878-
I've had me a time! With autobiographical sketch, selected poems, and sermons. Great Barrington, Mass., Friends of Gould Farm, 1961. 72 p. port. 21 cm. "Limited edition of not more than one thousand copies, the first two hundred and fifty of which, at least, are to be numbered and autographed ... no. [C30]" [BX9225.S63A3] 285'.2'0924 78-230256
I. Title.

Spallanzani, Lazzaro, 1729-1799—Juvenile literature.

EPSTEIN, Sam. 574'.092'4 B
Secret in a sealed bottle : Lazzaro Spallanzani's work with microbes / by Sam and Beryl Epstein ; illustrated by Jane Sterrett. New York : Coward, McCann & Geoghegan, c1979. 63 p. : ill. ; 21 cm. Bibliography: p. 63. A biography of the 18th century Italian whose experiments with microbes disproved the theory of spontaneous generation and provided a base for the work of future scientists. [QH31.S63E67 1979] 92 78-1494 ISBN 0-698-30700-3 lib.bdg. : 5.49
1. Spallanzani, Lazzaro, 1729-1799—Juvenile literature. 2. Spontaneous generation—Juvenile literature. 3. Biologists—Italy—Biography—Juvenile literature. I. Epstein, Beryl Williams, 1910- joint author. II. Sterrett, Jane. III. Title.

Spanier, Ginette

SPANIER, Ginette 926.4
It isn't all mink. New York, Random House [c.1960, 1959] xviii, 233p. illus. 21cm. 60-12134 3.95
I. Title.

SPANIER, Ginette 926.4
It isn't all mink. New York, Random House [c.1960, 1959] xviii, 233p. illus. 21cm. 60-12134 3.95
I. Title.

SPANIER, 940.53'1503'924 B
Ginette.
Long road to freedom : the story of her life under the German occupation / Ginette Spanier. London : R. Hale, 1976. 172 p. : map ; 23 cm. [D810.J4S63 1976] 76-366741 ISBN 0-7091-5592-1 : £3.80
1. Spanier, Ginette. 2. World War, 1939-1945—Personal narratives, Jewish. I. Title.

Spanish America — Biog.

BAILEY, Bernadine 923.28
(Freeman) 1901-
Famous Latin-American liberators; illustrated by Gerald McCann. New York, Dodd, Mead, 1960. 158p. illus. 22cm. (Famous biographies for young people) [F1407.B3] 60-11626
1. Spanish America—Biog. I. Title.

BAILEY, Bernardine 923.28
(Freeman)
Famous Latin-American liberators; illustrated by Gerald McCann. New York, Dodd, Mead [c.]1960. 158p. illus. 22cm. (Famous biographies for young people) 60-11626 3.00
1. Spanish America—Biog. I. Title.

SCHIRMER, Mathilda, ed. 920.08
Latin-American leaders. Illus. by Dirk Gringhuis. Chicago, Berkley-Cardy [1951] 185 p. illus. 21 cm. (American in action) Contents.CONTENTS. -- Miguel Hidalgo y Costilla, by C. Campbell. -- Francisco de

Miranda, by O. W. Burt. -- Jose de San Martin, by L. Res. -- Bernardo O'Higgins, by H. L. Gillum. -- Simon Bolivar, by E. Martens. -- Antonio Jose de Sucre, by W. B. Garrison. -- Jose Bonifacio de Andrada e Silva, by E. Sherman. -- Domingo Faustino Sarmiento, by E. S. Eells. -- Jose Marti, by A. M. Shields. -- Eloy Alfare, by M. M. Slappey. [F1407.S35] 51-9385
1. Spanish America — Biog. I. Title.

Spanish-Americans in the United States—Biography—Juvenile literature.

AXFORD, Roger W. 301.45'16'872073
Spanish-speaking heroes [by] Roger W. Axford. [Midland, Mich.] Pendell Pub. Co. [1973] xii, 85 p. illus. 24 cm. Brief biographies of twenty-three Spanish-speaking men and women who have achieved prominence in a variety of fields. [E184.S75A95] 920 B 72-78441 ISBN 0-87812-041-6 3.95
1. Spanish-Americans in the United States—Biography—Juvenile literature. I. Title. BIP

WHEELOCK, Warren H. 973'.04'68
Ilustres hispanos de los EE. UU. / Warren H. Wheelock ; adaptacion, J. O. "Rocky" Maynes ; consultantes, Jorge Valdivieso ... [et al.]. St. Paul, Minn. : EMC, 1976. p. cm. Translation of Hispanic heroes of the U.S.A. Contents.Contents.—1. Raul H. Castro, la adversidad es mi angel. Tommy Nnez, arbitro del NBA. ! Presentando a Vikki Carr!—2. Henry B. Gonzalez, mas justicia para todos. Trini Lopez, el ritmo latino. Edward Roybal, despierten al gigante dormido.—3. Carmen Rosa Mayri, para servir a las mujeres americanas. Roberto Clemente, la muerte de un hombre orgulloso. Jose Feliciano, una voz, una guitarra.—4. Tony Perez, el superestrella callado. Lee Trevino, el supermexicano. Jim Plunkett, no se retiro. [E184.S75W517] 920 76-2446
1. Spanish Americans in the United States—Biography—Juvenile literature. I. Maynes, J. O. II. Title.

Spanish Americans in Washington, D.C.—Biography.

WHO'S who among 920'.0092'680753
Latin Americans in Washington / [editor, Gabriel Mantilla]. Bicentennial ed. Kensington, Md. : Gama Enterprises, c1976. 352 p. : ill., ports. ; 29 cm. English and Spanish. Includes indexes. [F205.S75W46] 76-40557 29.95
1. Spanish Americans in Washington, D.C.—Biography. 2. Latin Americans in Washington, D.C.—Biography. I. Mantilla, Gabriel.

Spanish language — Chrestomathies and readers.

VASCONCELOS, 917.2'03'810924
Jose, 1882-1959.
Ulises criollo. Edited by Ronald Hilton, with notes and vocabulary by Robert B. O'Neil. Boston, Heath [1960] 214 p. 21 cm. Full name: Jose Vasconcelos Calderon. "The first volume of Vasconcelos' autobiography, which was published in 1935, relates the events of his life down to the death of Madero in 1913." [F1234.V27] 60-7496
1. Spanish language — Chrestomathies and readers. I. Title. II. Series.

Spanish Succession, War of, 1701-1714—Juvenile fiction.

FELTON, Ronald Oliver, 1909- JUV
Captain of dragoons [by] Ronald Welch [pseud.] Illustrated by William Stobbs. London, Oxford University Press, 1956. 216 p. illus. 22 cm. [PZ7.F3372Cap] fic 57-6484
1. Spanish Succession, War of, 1701-1714—Juvenile fiction. I. Title.

Sparkman, Ivo Hall.

SPARKMAN, Ivo Hall. 328.73'092'4
Journeys with the Senator / by Ivo Sparkman. Huntsville, Ala. : Strode Publishers, c1977. 216 p. : ill. ; 24 cm. Includes index. [E748.S737S68] 77-79834 ISBN 0-87397-129-9 : 12.95
1. Sparkman, John Jackson, 1899- 2. Sparkman, Ivo Hall. 3. United States. Congress. Senate—Biography. 4. Legislators—United States—Biography. 5. Legislators' wives—United States—Biography. I. Title. BIP

Sparkman, John Jackson, 1899-

SPARKMAN, Ivo Hall. 328.73'092'4
Journeys with the Senator / by Ivo Sparkman. Huntsville, Ala. : Strode Publishers, c1977. 216 p. : ill. ; 24 cm. Includes index. [E748.S737S68] 77-79834 ISBN 0-87397-129-9 : 12.95
1. Sparkman, John Jackson, 1899- 2. Sparkman, Ivo Hall. 3. United States. Congress. Senate—Biography. 4. Legislators—United States—Biography. 5. Legislators' wives—United States—Biography. I. Title. BIP

Sparks, Jared, 1789-1866.

ADAMS, Herbert Baxter, 973.072024
1850-1901.
The life and writings of Jared Sparks, comprising selections from his journals and correspondence. Freeport, N.Y., Books for Libraries Press [1970] 2 v. ports. 23 cm. Reprint of the 1893 ed. "Bibliography of the writings of Jared Sparks": v. 2, p. [596]-617. [E175.5.S68 1970] 76-119924
1. Sparks, Jared, 1789-1866.

Sparrow, Jane.

SPARROW, Jane. 362.7'32'0924 B
Diary of a delinquent episode / Jane Sparrow. London ; Boston : Routledge & Paul, 1976. x, 130 p. ; 24 cm. [HV7428.S577] 76-359321 ISBN 0-7100-8340-8 : £1.95
1. Sparrow, Jane. 2. Social workers—England—Correspondence, reminiscences, etc. 3. Delinquent girls—England. I. Title. BIP

SPARROW, Jane. 362.7'092'4 B
Diary of a student social worker / Jane Sparrow. London ; Boston : Routledge and Kegan Paul, 1978. xvi, 148 p. ; 23 cm. [HV751.A6S63] 77-30664 ISBN 0-7100-8857-4 11.50
1. Social work with children—England. I. Title. BIP

Spathares, Soterios Eugeniou.

SPATHARES, 791.5'3'0924 B
Soterios Eugeniou.
Behind the white screen / Sotiris Spatharis. New York : Red Dust, 1976. 150 p. : ill. ; 24 cm. Translation of Apomnemoneumata S. Spathare. The section entitled Memoirs translated by Mario Rinvolucri, and the section entitled The history and art of Karagiosis translated by Leslie Finer. [PN1982.S6A3] 77-350342 10.95
1. Spathares, Soterios Eugeniou. 2. Karagoz. 3. Puppeteers—Greece, Modern—Biography. I. Title. BIP

Spaugh, Herbert, 1896-

HARDING, Barbara. 284'.6'0924 B
The boy, the man, and the Bishop; a biography of the Everyday Counselor, Bishop Herbert Spaugh. [Charlotte, N.C., Barnhardt Brothers, 1970] 178 p. illus., ports. 22 cm. [BX8593.S63H3] 79-20294
1. Spaugh, Herbert, 1896- I. Title.

Spaulding, Frank Ellsworth,

SPAULDING, Frank 923.773
Ellsworth, 1866-
One school administrator's philosophy: its development. [1st ed.] New York, Exposition Press [1952] 352 p. 22 cm. "An Exposition-University book." Autobiography. [LA2317.S66A3] 52-6102
I. Title.

Speaker, Tris—Juvenile literature.

EPSTEIN, Samuel, 796.357'092'2
1909-
More stories of baseball champions: in the Hall of Fame, by Sam and Beryl Epstein. Illustrated by Victor Mays. Champaign, Ill., Garrard Pub. Co. [1973] 96 p. illus. (part col.) 24 cm. Traces the careers of three baseball stars elected to the Baseball Hall of Fame in 1937. [GV865.A1E59] 920 73-2941 2.98
1. Young, Denton True, 1867-1955—Juvenile literature. 2. Lajoie, Napoleon, 1875-1959—Juvenile literature. 3. Speaker, Tris—Juvenile literature. 4. Cooperstown, N.Y. National Baseball Hall of Fame and Museum—Juvenile literature. 5. Baseball—Biography—Juvenile literature. I. Epstein, Beryl (Williams) 1910- joint author. II. Mays, Victor, 1927- illus. III. Title.

Spears, Leo Leaston, 1894-

REX, Erna 926.1
The lengthening shadow; the story of Doctor Leo L. Spears. Denver, Golden Bell Pr., 2400 Curtis [c.1962] 281p. 23cm. (Prestige bk.) 62-51433 4.50
1. Spears, Leo Leaston, 1894- I. Title.

Special librarians—Directories.

A Biographical 026'.000922
directory of librarians in the field of Slavic and East European studies, compiled and edited by Peter A. Goy with the editorial assistance of Laurence H. Miller, for the Slavic and East European Subsection of the Association of College and Research Libraries. Chicago, American Library Association, 1967. xv, 80 p. 24 cm. [Z675.A2B5] 67-28101
1. Special librarians—Directories. I. Goy, Peter A., 1925- II. Association of College and Research Libraries. Slavic and East European Subsection.

Speck, Richard, 1941-

ALTMAN, Jack, 364.15'23'0924
1938-
Born to raise hell; the untold story of Richard Speck, by Jack Altman & Marvin Ziporyn. New York, Grove Press [1967] 255 p. facsims., ports. 24 cm. [HV6248.S614A73] 67-27330
1. Speck, Richard, 1941- I. Ziporyn, Marvin, 1923- II. Title.

Spector, Abraham, 1888-

SPECTOR, Abraham, 917.3'06'924 B
1888-
Avremele: pilgrim from Horodok. Translated from Yiddish by Louis Falstein. New York [i.e. Elizabeth, N.J., F. Spector] 1973. 250 p. port. 24 cm. Autobiography. [DS135.R95S658] 73-166240
1. Spector, Abraham, 1888- I. Title.

Speed, Grant, 1930

HEDGPETH, Don. 730'.92'4 B
From broncs to bronzes : the life and work of Grant Speed / by Don Hedgpeth ; with a foreword by William E. Burford. 1st ed. Flagstaff, Ariz. : Northland Press, 1979. viii, 109 p. : ill. ; 24 x 25 cm. [NB237.S577H42] 79-88620 ISBN 0-87358-211-X : 17.50 pbk. : 10.00
1. Speed, Grant, 1930- 2. Sculptors—Texas—Biography. 3. Cowboys in art. I. Title.

Speer, Robert Elliott, 1867-1947.

WHEELER, William 922.573
Reginald, 1889-
A man sent from God; a biography of Robert E. Speer. Introd. by John A. Mackay. [Westwood, N. J., Revell [1956] 333p. illus. 22cm. [BX9225.S643W45] 56-5242
1. Speer, Robert Elliott, 1867-1947. I. Title.

Spellman, Francis Joseph, Cardinal, 1889-1967.

GANNON, Robert Ignatius, 922.273
1893-
The Cardinal Spellman story. New York, Pocket Bks. [1963, c.1962] 579p. 18cm. (M-7510) .75 pap.,
1. Spellman, Francis Joseph, Cardinal, 1889- I. Title.

GANNON, Robert Ignatius, 922.273
1893-
The Cardinal Spellman story. [1st ed.] Garden City, N. Y., Doubleday, 1962. 477 p. illus. 24 cm. Includes bibliography. [BX4705.S74G3] 62-8395
1. Spellman, Francis Joseph, Cardinal, 1889-

GANNON, Robert Ignatius, v. 12
1893-
The Cardinal Spellman story. New York, Pocket Books [1963] x, 579 p. 18 cm. (Permabook edition. M7510) Bibliographical references included in "Notes" (p. 547-556) 64-24854
1. Spellman, Francis Joseph, Cardinal, 1889- I. Title. II. Series.

IN memoriam: 262'.135'0924
Francis Cardinal Spellman, Archbishop of New York. [New York] Society of the Friendly Sons of Saint Patrick in the City of New York, 1968. 59 p. ports. (part col.) 25 cm. [BX4705.S7415] 70-268394
1. Spellman, Francis Joseph, Cardinal, 1889-1967. I. Society of the Friendly Sons of St. Patrick in the City of New York.

STEIBEL, Warren. 262.1350924
Cardinal Spellman, the man. With an introd. by Francis Cardinal Spellman. [1st ed.] New York, Appleton-Century [1966] 121 p. illus., ports. 27 cm. Adapted from the ABC-Television documentary of Cardinal Spellman: the man. [BX4705.S74S7] 66-27903
1. Spellman, Francis Joseph, Cardinal, 1889- I. American Broadcasting Company. II. Title.

Spence, Catherine Helen, 1825-1910.

COOPER, Janet. 324'.3'0924 B
Catherine Spence. Melbourne, Oxford University Press, 1972. 30 p. ill. 19 cm. (Great Australians) Includes bibliographical references. [HQ1847.S6C66] 73-174329 ISBN 0-19-550424-0 0.70
1. Spence, Catherine Helen, 1825-1910.

Spence, Joseph, 1690-1768.

WRIGHT, Austin. 928.2
Joseph Spence: a critical biography. Chicago, University of Chicago Press [1950] ix, 264 p. 23 cm. Bibliographical references included in "Notes" (p. 201-253) [PR3699.S4Z9] 50-13115
1. Spence, Joseph, 1690-1768. I. Title.

Spence, Joseph, 1699-1768—Correspondence.

SPENCE, Joseph, 1699- 828'.5'07 B
1768.
Letters from the grand tour / Joseph Spence ; edited by Slava Klima. Montreal : McGill-Queen's University Press, 1975. xii, 496 p. ; 26 cm. Includes index. Bibliography: p. ix-x. [PR3699.S4Z53 1975] 73-79098 ISBN 0-7735-0090-1 : 25.00
1. Spence, Joseph, 1699-1768—Correspondence. 2. Spence, Joseph, 1699-1768—Journeys. I. Klima, Slava. II. Title. BIP

Spence, Thomas, 1750-1814.

DAVIDSON, John 330.1'0922
Morrison.
Concerning four precursors of Henry George and the single tax, as also the land gospel according to Winstanley "the Digger", by J. Morrison Davidson. Port Washington, N.Y., Kennikat Press [1971] 151 p. 21 cm. Half title: Four precursors of Henry George. Reprint of 1899 ed. [HD1313.D2 1971] 77-115317
1. Ogilvie, William, 1736-1819. 2. Spence, Thomas, 1750-1814. 3. Paine, Thomas,

1737-1809. 4. Dove, Patrick Edward, 1815-1873. 5. Winstanley, Gerrard, b. 1609. I. Title. II. Title: Four precursors of Henry George.

Spencer, Anne, 1882-1975.

GREENE, J. Lee, 1944- 811'.5'2
Time's unfading garden : Anne Spencer's life and poetry / J. Lee Greene. Baton Rouge : Louisiana State University, c1977. p. cm. Includes index. Bibliography: p. [PS3537.P444Z65] 77-5960 ISBN 0-8071-0294-6 : 10.95
1. Spencer, Anne, 1882-1975. 2. Poets, American—20th century—Biography. I. Spencer, Anne, 1882-1975. II. Title.

GREENE, J. Lee, 1944- 811'.5'2
Time's unfading garden : Anne Spencer's life and poetry / J. Lee Greene. Baton Rouge : Louisiana State University, c1977. p. cm. Includes index. Bibliography: p. [PS3537.P444Z65] 77-5960 ISBN 0-8071-0294-6 : 10.95
1. Spencer, Anne, 1882-1975. 2. Poets, American—20th century—Biography. I. Spencer, Anne, 1882-1975. II. Title. BIP

Spencer, Charlotte Louise (Loomis)

SPENCER, Charlotte Louise (Loomis) 1877- 920.7
Roses in December. Memoirs] Carlisle, Pa., Printed by Baker & Gussman, c1950. 236 p. illus., ports. 22 cm. [CT275.S623A3] 50-2552
I. Title.

Spencer, Chauncey E., 1906-

SPENCER, Chauncey E., 1906- 629.13'092'4 B
Who is Chauncey Spencer? / By Chauncey E. Spencer. 1st ed. Detroit : Broadside Press, c1975. 150 p., [8] leaves of plates : ill. ; 23 cm. Includes bibliographical references. [E185.97.S73A37] 75-324885 ISBN 0-910296-25-1 : 7.95
*1. Spencer, Chauncey E., 1906- I. Title.*BIP

Spencer, Herbert, 1820-1903.

THOMSON, John Arthur, Sir, 1861-1933. 192 B
Herbert Spencer / by J. Arthur Thomson. New York : AMS Press, 1976. ix, 284 p. : port. ; 19 cm. "EMS 1." Reprint of the 1906 ed. published by J. M. Dent, London, and Dutton, New York, in series: English men of science. Includes index. Bibliography: p. 281-282. [B1656.T5 1976] 79-177452 ISBN 0-404-07891-5 : 17.50
1. Spencer, Herbert, 1820-1903. I. Series: English men of science. BIP

Spencer, June Lydiard.

SPENCER, June Lydiard. 926.1
Lamp in the wilderness. [1st ed.] New York, Vantage Press [1955] 135 p. 22 cm. The author's experiences as a nurse at a Canadian outpost. [RT37.S6A3] 54-12645
I. Title.

Spencer, Oliver M., 1781-1838.

SPENCER, Oliver M., 1781-1838. 973'.04'97 S
Indian captivity / Oliver M. Spencer. New York : Garland Pub., 1975. p. cm. (The Garland library of narratives of North American Indian captivities ; v. 53) Reprint of the 1835 ed. published by B. Waugh and T. Mason, New York, for the Sunday School Union of the Methodist Episcopal Church. [E85.G2 vol. 53] [E99.M8] 977.1'004'97 75-7075 ISBN 0-8240-1677-7 lib.bdg. : 21.00
1. Spencer, Oliver M., 1781-1838. 2. Indians of North America—Captivities. 3. Mohawk Indians—Captivities. I. Title. II. Series.

Spencer, Robert Nelson, Bp., 1877-

BRISTOL, Lee Hastings, 1923- 922.373
Seed for a song. [1st ed.] Boston, Little, Brown [1958] 244 p. illus. 21 cm. [BX5995.S76B7] 58-6037
1. Spencer, Robert Nelson, Bp., 1877- I. Title.

Spencer, Stanley, Sir, 1891-1959.

CARLINE, Richard. 759.2 B
Stanley Spencer at war / Richard Carline. London ; Boston : Faber and Faber, 1978. 224 p. : ill. ; 23 cm. Includes bibliographical references and index. [ND497.S75C37] 79-300467 ISBN 0-571-11028-2 : 21.95
1. Spencer, Stanley, Sir, 1891-1959. 2. Painters—Great Britain—Biography. I. Title.
Dist. by merrimack, Salem, NH 03079
BIP

ROBINSON, Duncan. 759.2 B
Stanley Spencer, visions from a Berkshire village / Duncan Robinson. Oxford : Phaidon, 1979. 80 p. : ill. (some col.) ; 29 cm. Bibliography: p. 6. [ND497.S75R53 1979] 78-73501 ISBN 0-7148-1970-0 : 14.95
1. Spencer, Stanley, Sir, 1891-1959. 2. Painters—England—Biography. I. Title.
Dist. by Dutton; N.Y., N.Y.

STANLEY Spencer, the man 759.2 B
: correspondence and reminiscences / edited by John Rothenstein. Athens : Ohio University Press, 1979. 156 p., [8] leaves of plates : ill. ; 25 cm. Includes index. [ND497.S75A3 1979a] 79-63683 ISBN 0-8214-0431-8 : 18.00
1. Spencer, Stanley, Sir, 1891-1959. 2. Painters—England—Correspondence. 3. Painters—England—Biography. I. Spencer, Stanley, Sir, 1891-1959. II. Rothenstein, John Knewstub Maurice, Sir, 1901- BIP

Spender, Sir Percy Claude, 1897-

SPENDER, Jean, Lady. 327'.2'0924
Ambassador's wife. [Sydney] Angus & Robertson [1968] 207p. illus., ports. 23cm [D839.7.S6A3] 68-1160543 6.50
1. Spender, Sir Percy Claude, 1897- 2. Diplomats—Correspondence, reminiscences, etc. I. Title.
Order from Tri-Ocean, San Francisco.

Spender, Stephen, 1909-

SPENDER, Stephen, 1909- 928.2
World within world. [1st American ed.] New York, Harcourt Brace [1951] vii, 312 21 cm. Autobiography. Full name: Stephen Harold Spender. [PR6037.P47Z5 1951] 51-10107
I. Title.

SPENDER, Stephen, 1909- v. 12
World within world; the autobiography of Stephen Spender. Berkeley, University of California Press, 1966. 349 p. port. 67-57515
1. Spender, Stephen, 1909- I. Title.

SPENDER, Stephen, 1909- 928.2
World within world. [1st American ed.] New York, Harcourt Brace [1951] vii, 312 21 cm. Autobiography. Full name: Stephen Harold Spender. [PR6037.P47Z5 1951] 51-10107
I. Title.

Spengler, Lazarus, 1479-1534.

GRIMM, Harold John, 1901- 270.6'092'4 B
Lazarus Spengler : a lay leader of the Reformation / by Harold J. Grimm. Columbus : Ohio State University Press, [1978] p. cm. Includes index. Bibliography: p. [BR350.S67G74] 78-13508 ISBN 0-8142-0290-X : 15.00
1. Spengler, Lazarus, 1479-1534. 2. Reformation—Germany, West—Nuremberg—Biography. 3. Nuremberg—Biography. BIP

Spengler, Oswald, 1880-1936.

FENNELLY, John Fauntleroy, 1899- 901.9
Twilight of the evening lands; Oswald Spengler—a half century later [by] John F. Fennelly. New York, Brookdale Press, [1972] vii, 181 p. 23 cm. Bibliography: p. 177-178. [CB83.S66F46] 72-78519 ISBN 0-912650-01-X 5.95
1. Spengler, Oswald, 1880-1936. Der Untergang des Abendlandes. 2. Spengler, Oswald, 1880-1936. I. Title.

Spenser, Edmund, 1552?-1599.

CHURCH, Richard William, 1815-1890. 821'.3 B
Spenser. New York, AMS Press [1968] 181 p. 22 cm. (English men of letters) [PR2363.C5 1968b] 68-58372
1. Spenser, Edmund, 1552?-1599.

CHURCH, Richard William, 1815-1890. 821'.3 B
Spenser. London, Macmillan [1906] Detroit, Gale Research Co., 1968. 188 p. 23 cm. (The Gale library of lives and letters. British writers series) [PR2363.C5 1968] 67-23879
1. Spenser, Edmund, 1552?-1599.

CHURCH, Richard William, 1815-1890. 821'.3 B
Spenser. [Folcroft, Pa.] Folcroft Library Editions, 1973. p. Reprint of the 1894 ed. published by Macmillan, London and New York, in series: English men of letters. [PR2363.C5 1973] 73-10493 ISBN 0-8414-3402-6 (lib. bdg.)
1. Spenser, Edmund, 1552?-1599.

EDMUND Spenser and the v. 12
Faerie Queene. [Chicago] Univ. of Chicago Press [1959] xi, 193p. 20cm.
1. Spenser, Edmund, 1552?-1599. I. Bradner, Leicester. BIP

JONES, Harry Stuart Vedder, 1878-1942. 821'.3 B
Spenser's defense of Lord Grey / by H. S. V. Jones. New York : AMS Press, 1976. 75 p. ; 23 cm. Reprint of the 1919 ed. published by University of Illinois, Urbana, which was issued as v. 5, no. 3 of University of Illinois studies in language and literature. Includes bibliographical references and index. [PR2364.J55 1976] 73-170822 ISBN 0-404-03599-X : 5.00
1. Spenser, Edmund, 1552?-1599. 2. Grey de Wilton, Arthur Grey, 14th baron, 1536-1593. 3. Irish question. I. Title. II. Series: Illinois. University. Illinois studies in language and literature ; v. 5, no. 3. BIP

JUDSON, Alexander Corbin, 1883- 821'.3 B
The life of Edmund Spenser, by Alexander C. Judson. Baltimore, Johns Hopkins Press [1966, c1945] xii, 238 p. illus., facsim., map, plans, ports. 26 cm. (The works of Edmund Spenser. A variorum ed., edited by Edwin Greenlaw [and others] v. 11) Bibliography: p. 213-223. [PR2351.G65 1966, vol. 11] 67-9510
1. Spenser, Edmund, 1552?-1599. I. Title.

LEGOUIS, Emile Hyacinthe, 1861-1937. 821'.3
Spenser / by Emile Legouis. Folcroft, Pa. : Folcroft Library Editions, 1974. vii, 140 p. ; 25 cm. Reprint of the 1926 ed. published by J. M. Dent, London. [PR2363.L43 1974] 74-22128 ISBN 0-8414-5680-1 : lib. bdg.
1. Spenser, Edmund, 1552?-1599. BIP

SHIRE, Helena Mennie. 821'.3 B
A preface to Spenser / Helena Shire. London ; New York : Longman, 1978 p. cm. (Preface books) Includes index. Bibliography: p. [PR2363.S5] 76-23272 ISBN 0-582-31511-5 : 9.50 ISBN 0-582-31512-3 pbk. : 5.50
1. Spenser, Edmund, 1552?-1599. I. Title.
BIP

TUCKWELL, William, 1829-1919. 821'.3 B
Spenser. [Folcroft, Pa.] Folcroft Press [1970] 85 p. illus. 22 cm. Reprint of the 1906 ed., which was originally issued in series: Bell's miniature series of great writers. Bibliography: p. [81]-82. [PR2363.T8 1970] 72-191658
1. Spenser, Edmund, 1552?-1599. I. Series: Bell's miniature series of great writers. BIP

TUCKWELL, William, 1829-1919. 821'.3 B
Spenser / by W. Tuckwell. Norwood, Pa. : Norwood Editions, 1975. 85 p., [8] leaves of plates : ill. ; 21 cm. Reprint of the 1906 ed. published by G. Bell, London, in series: Bell's miniature series of great writers. Includes index. Bibliography: p. [81]-82. [PR2363.T8 1975] 75-34332 ISBN 0-88305-670-4 lib. bdg. : 10.00
1. Spenser, Edmund, 1552?-1599. I. Series: Bell's miniature series of great writers.

WATKINS, Walter Barker Critz, 1907-1957. v. 12
Shakespeare & Spenser. Cambridge, Mass., Walker-de Berry [1961] ix, 339 p. 21 cm. (A Boar's head book) "First edition as a Boar's Head Book, 1961." "References and comments": p. 310-330.
1. Spenser, Edmund, 1552?-1599. 2. Shakespeare, William — Criticism and interpretation. I. Title. BIP

WINBOLT, Samuel Edward, 1868-1944. 821'.3
Spenser & his poetry. London, G. G. Harrap, 1912. [New York, AMS Press, 1972] 157 p. port. 19 cm. (Poetry and life series) Includes bibliographical references. [PR2363.W45 1972] 70-120978 ISBN 0-404-52534-2 8.00
1. Spenser, Edmund, 1552?-1599. I. Title.
BIP

Speranskii, Mikhail Mikhailovich, graf, 1772-1839.

RAEFF, Marc. 947'.07'0924 B
Michael Speransky, statesman of imperial Russia, 1772-1839 / by Marc Raeff. Westport, Conn. : Hyperion Press, [1978] i.e. 1979. p. cm. Reprint of the 1957 ed. published by M. Nijhoff, The Hague. Includes index. Bibliography: p. [DK201.R3 1979] 78-59037 ISBN 0-88355-709-6 : lib.bdg. : 26.50
1. Speranskii, Mikhail Mikhailovich, graf, 1772-1839. 2. Russia—Politics and government—19th century. 3. Statesmen—Russia—Biography.

Sperry, Armstrong,

SPERRY, Armstrong, 1897- 923.942
Captain Cook explores the South Seas, written and illustrated by Armstrong Sperry. New York, Random House [1955] 184 p. illus. 22 cm. (World landmark books, W-19) [G246.C7S7] 55-5827
I. Title.

Sperry, Elmer Ambrose, 1860-1930.

HUGHES, Thomas Parke. 621.3'0924 B
Elmer Sperry; inventor and engineer. Baltimore, Johns Hopkins Press [1971] xvii, 348 p. illus., facsims., maps, ports. 26 cm. Bibliography: p. 341-342. [TA140.S68H79] 71-110373 ISBN 0-8018-1133-3 15.00
1. Sperry, Elmer Ambrose, 1860-1930.

Sperry, Lawrence Burst, 1892-1923.

DAVENPORT, William Wyatt. 629.13'0092'4 B
Gyro : the life and times of Lawrence Sperry / by William Wyatt Davenport. New York : Scribner, [1978] p. cm. Includes index. [TL540.S687D38] 78-17826 ISBN 0-684-15793-4 : 14.95 12.95
1. Sperry, Lawrence Burst, 1892-1923. 2. Aeronautics—United States—Biography. I. Title. BIP

Spies.

HALACY, Daniel Stephen, 1919- 335.3'43'0922
The master spy, by Dan Halacy. Drawings by Frederic Marvin. New York, McGraw [1968] 192p. illus., ports. 24cm. [UB270.H26] 68-17186 4.95; 4.46 lib. ed.
1. Spies. I. Title.

HALACY, Daniel Stephen, 1919- 355.3'43'0922
The master spy, by Dan Halacy. Drawings by Frederic Marvin. New York, McGraw-Hill [1968] 192 p. illus., ports. 24 cm. Contents.Contents.—Dr. Stieber; spymaster with 40,000 agents.—Captain Nathan Hale; America's first spy.—Widow Rose Greenhow; spy belle of Washington.—Mary Louvestre; the slave who spied for freedom.—Lieutenant Karl Lody; the agent who died in vain.—Mata Hari; she danced her way to a firing squad.—William Sebold; counter spy for the U.S.—Michel Hollard; the spy who saved London.—Rudolf Abel; Russia's master spy.—Stig Wennerstrom; Sweden's traitor spy.—Cicero; the spy nobody believed.—Dr. Richard Sorge; the romantic double agent. [UB270.H26] 68-17186 4.95
1. Spies. I. Title. **BIP**

SETH, Ronald. 327'.12'0922
Some of my favorite spies. [1st ed.] Philadelphia, Chilton Book Co. [1968] xii, 189 p. ports. 21 cm. Contents.Contents.—Sir Francis Walsingham.—Daniel Defoe.—Major Benjamin Tallmadge.—Belle Boyd.—Robert Baden-Powell.—Jules Silber.—Charles Lucieto.—Louise de Bettignies.—Alexander Foote.—Wing Commander Yeo-Thomas G. C.—Christine Granville G. M.—Gordon Lonsdale. [UB270.S439] 68-19180
1. Spies. I. Title.

Spies—Biography.

MACLEAN, Fitzroy, Sir, bart., 1911- 327'.12'0922 B
Take nine spies / Fitzroy Maclean. 1st American ed. New York : Atheneum, 1978. 341 p., [4] leaves of plates : ill. ; 24 cm. Bibliography: p. 340-341. [UB270.M28 1978] 77-15315 ISBN 0-689-10854-0 : 11.95
1. Spies—Biography. 2. Espionage—History. I. Title.

Spies—Juvenile literature.

SURGE, Frank. 355.3'432
Famous spies. Minneapolis, Lerner Publications Co. [1969] 63 p. illus., ports. 21 cm. (A Pull ahead book) Brief descriptions of the lives and exploits of fourteen spies from various historical periods and geographical areas. [UB270.5.S87] 920 68-30569
1. Spies—Juvenile literature. I. Title. **BIP**

Spike, Robert Warren.

SPIKE, Paul, 1947- 323.4'092'4 B
Photographs of my father. [1st ed.] New York, Knopf; [distributed by Random House] 1973. 259 p. illus. 22 cm. Autobiographical. [BX7260.S72A33 1973] 72-11042 ISBN 0-394-47334-5 6.95
1. Spike, Robert Warren. 2. Spike, Paul, 1947- I. Title.

Spilman, Bernard Washington, 1871-

GREEN, Charles Sylvester, 1900- 922.673
B. W. Spilman, the Sunday school man. Nashville, Broadman Press [1953] 154p. illus. 21cm. [BV1518.S6G7] 53-32887
1. Spilman, Bernard Washington, 1871- I. Title.

Spilsbury, Bernard Henry, Sir, 1879-1947.

BROWNE, Douglas Gordon, 1884- 926.1
The scalpel of Scotland Yard; the life of Sir Bernard Spilsbury, by Douglas G. Browne and E. V. Tullett. With a foreword by W. Bentley Purchase. [1st ed.] New York, Dutton, 1952. 503 p. illus. 22 cm. [RA1025.S6B7] 52-6314
1. Spilsbury, Bernard Henry, Sir, 1879-1947. 2. Evidence, Expert—Gt. Brit. 3. Trials (Murder)—Gt. Brit. I. Title.

Spinoza, Benedictus de 1632-1677.

BROWNE, Douglas Gordon, 1884- 614'.19'0924 B
Bernard Spilsbury : his life and cases / by Douglas G. Browne and E. V. Tullett ; with a foreword by W. Bentley Purchase. London ; New York : White Lion Publishers, 1976. 422 p., [31] p. of plates : ill., facsims., ports. ; 23 cm. Includes index. [RA1025.S6B68 1976] 76-377052 ISBN 0-85617-216-2 : £6.50
1. Spilsbury, Bernard Henry, Sir, 1877-1947. 2. Medical examiners (Law)—Great Britain—Biography. 3. Forensic pathology Cases, clinical reports, statistics. 4. Homicide investigation—Great Britain—Case studies. I. Tullett, Eric Vivian, joint author.

HAMPSHIRE, Stuart, 1914- 199.492
Spinoza. [dist. New York, Barnes & Noble, 1961[ ] 176p. 3.50
1. Spinoza, Benedictus de 1632-1677. I. Title.

ALLISON, Henry E. 199'.492 B
Benedict de Spinoza / by Henry E. Allison. Boston : Twayne Publishers, [1975] 239 p. : port. ; 21 cm. (Twayne's world authors series ; TWAS 351 : The Netherlands) Includes index. Bibliography: p. 229-232. [B3997.A44] 75-2059 ISBN 0-8057-2853-8 lib.bdg. : 8.50
1. Spinoza, Benedictus de, 1632-1677. **BIP**

CAIRD, John, 1820-1898. 199'.492
Spinoza. Freeport, N.Y., Books For Libraries Press [1971] 315 p. 23 cm. Reprint of the 1888 ed. Includes bibliographical references. [B3998.C3 1971] 75-164593 ISBN 0-8369-5877-2
1. Spinoza, Benedictus dc, 1632-1677.

HAMPSHIRE, Stuart, 1914- v. 12
Spinoza, [Reprinted with revisions. Harmondsworth, Middlesex] Penguin Books [1962] 237 p. 18 cm. (Pelican books, A253) Bibliographical preface: p. 9-[10] 64-17523
1. Spinoza, Benedictus de, 1632-1677. I. Title. II. Series.

JASPERS, Karl, 1883-1969. 199.492
Spinoza. Edited by Hannah Arendt. Translated by Ralph Manheim. New York, Harcourt Brace Jovanovich [1974, c1966] vi, 121 p. 21 cm. (A Harvest book, HB 290) "A Helen and Kurt Wolff book." Previously published as part of v. 2 of the author's The great philosophers, which is a translation of Die grossen Philosophen. Bibliography: p. 119-120. [B3998.J3713] 74-4336 2.75 (pbk.)
1. Spinoza, Benedictus de, 1632-1677.

LEVIN, Dan. 199'.492
Spinoza, the young thinker who destroyed the past. New York, Weybright and Talley [1970] 338 p. 24 cm. Includes bibliographical references. [B3998.L39 1970] 78-106032
1. Spinoza, Benedictus de, 1632-1677.

LUCAS, Jean Maximilien, d.1697, supposed author. 199'.492 B
The oldest biography of Spinoza, edited with translation, introd., annotations, etc., by A. Wolf. Port Washington, N.Y., Kennikat Press [1970] 196 p. illus., facsims., ports. 21 cm. Reprint of the 1927 ed. First published 1719 in the Nouvelles litteraires, vol. X, p. 40-74, under title: La vie de Spinosa. Authorship variously ascribed to J. M. Lucas and to D. de Saint-Glain. Bibliography: p. 36-37. [B3997.L813 1970] 75-103217
1. Spinoza, Benedictus de, 1632-1677. I. Saint-Glain, Dominique de, 17th cent., supposed author. II. Wolf, Abraham, 1876-1948, ed. III. Title. **BIP**

POLLOCK, Sir Frederick, bart., 1845-1937. 199.492
Spinoza: his life and philosophy. 2d ed. New York, American Scholar Publications, 1966. xxiv, 427 p. facsim. 24 cm. "The life of Spinoza, by Colerus" (p. [383]-418) is a reprint of the London ed. of 1706. with original t. p. reading: The life of Benedict de Spinosa, written by John Colerus ... Done out of French. London, Printed by D. L. and sold by Benj. Bragg ... 1706. [B3998.P7] 65-24240
1. Spinoza, Benedictus de, 1632-1677. I. Colerus, Johannes, 1647-1707. The life of Spinosa. II. Title.

ROTH, Leon, 1896-1963. 199'.492
Spinoza / by Leon Roth. Westport, Conn. : Hyperion Press, 1979. p. cm. Reprint of the 1954 issue of the 1929 ed. published by Allyn & Unwin, London. Includes index. Bibliography: p. [B3998.R58 1979] 78-14139 ISBN 0-88355-813-0 pbk. : 17.00
1. Spinoza, Benedictus de, 1632-1677. **BIP**

WIENPAHL, Paul. 199'.492
The radical Spinoza / Paul Wienpahl. New York : New York University Press, 1979. xiii, 281 p. ; 24 cm. Includes bibliographical references and index. [B3998.W63] 78-65448 ISBN 0-8147-9186-7 : 12.50
1. Spinoza, Benedictus de, 1632-1677. I. Title. **BIP**

WOLFSON, Abraham. 199'.492 B
Spinoza; a life of reason. 2d enl. ed. New York, Philosophical Library [1969] xvi, 347 p. illus., facsim., ports. 25 cm. Bibliography: p. 329-334. [B3997.W75 1969] 76-99305 6.00
1. Spinoza, Benedictus de, 1632-1677. **BIP**

Spiridonova, Mariia Aleksandrovna, 1885—

STEINBERG, Isaac Nachman, 1888-1957. 947.084'0924
Spiridonova, revolutionary terrorist, by Isaac Steinberg. Translated and edited by Gwenda David and Eric Mosbacher. With an introd. by Henry W. Nevinson. Freeport, N.Y., Books for Libraries Press [1971] xxii, 313 p. ports. 23 cm. [DK254.S58S75 1971] 72-150201 ISBN 0-8369-5714-8
1. Spiridonova, Mariia Aleksandrovna, 1885- 2. Partiia sotsialistov-revoliutsionerov. 3. Russia—History—Revolution, 1917-1921. 4. Siberia—Exiles. **BIP**

Spiritualism.

DELFORGE, Thomas 271.10924
Columba Marmion, servant of God. Tr. by Richard L. Stewart. St. Louis, B. Herder [1966, c.1965] viii, 71p. 19cm. Bibl. [BX4705.M411D4] 66-3546 1.50 pap.,
1. Marmion, Columba, Abbott, 1858-1923. II. Title.

GARRETT, Eileen Jeanette (Lyttle) 1893- 133.9'1'0924 B
Many voices; the autobiography of a medium, by Eileen J. Garrett. With an introd. by Allan Angoff. New York, Putnam [1968] 254 p. 22 cm. [BF1283.G29A3] 68-20947
1. Spiritualism. I. Title.

STEMMER, Charles C 1883- 920.91339
A brand from the burning, from the depths of despair to the gates of heaven. Boston, Christopher Pub. House [1959] 132 p. illus. 21 cm. Autobiographical. [BF1261.2.S77] 50-6923
1. Spiritualism. I. Title.

Spiritualism — Communications.

SVENDSEN, Ruth G v. 12
Cleopatra speaks; tells own story. Santa Clara, Calif. Williams pub. co. [1962] 208 p. illus. 22 cm. 63-78016
1. Spiritualism — Communications. I. Cleopatra, Queen of Egypt, d. 30 B.C. II. Title.

Spitz, Mark—Juvenile literature.

OLSEN, James T. 797.2'1'0924 B
Mark Spitz: the shark, by James T. Olsen. Illustrated by Harold Henriksen. Mankato, Minn., Creative Education; distributed by Childrens Press, Chicago [1974] 31 p. illus. (part col.) 25 cm. (Creative's superstars) Biography of the swimmer who won seven gold medals in the 1972 Olympics. [GV838.S68O47] 92 73-11018 ISBN 0-87191-264-3 4.95
1. Spitz, Mark—Juvenile literature. I. Henriksen, Harold, illus. II. Title.

TAYLOR, Paula. 797.2'1'0924 B
Mark Spitz / written by Paula Taylor ; illustrated by Harold Henriksen. Mankato, Minn. : Creative Education, [1976] p. cm. A biography of the Olympic swimming champion who has entered the world of entertainment due to his post-Olympic publicity. [GV838.S68T39] 92 76-5815 ISBN 0-87191-263-5 lib.bdg. : 4.95
1. Spitz, Mark—Juvenile literature. 2. Swimming—Juvenile literature. I. Henriksen, Harold. II. Title.

Spivey, Larry.

ROSENBERG, Philip, 1942- 364.1'57'0924 B
The Spivey assignment : a double agents' infiltration of the drug smuggling conspiracy / Philip Rosenberg. 1st ed. New York : Holt, Rinehart and Winston, c1979. vi, 313 p. ; 24 cm. [HV5805.S64R67] 79-10085 ISBN 0-03-044371-7 : 10.95
1. Spivey, Larry. 2. Narcotic enforcement agents—Georgia—Biography. 3. Undercover operations. 4. Smuggling—Georgia. I. Title.

Splaver, Sarah.

SPLAVER, Sarah. 362.1'9'6994490924
Your mind and breast diseases : a psychologist-breast cancer patient who did not have a mastectomy describes her experiences and discusses the relationships between the mind and breast diseases / by Sarah Splaver. New York : Veritas Press, c1978. 95 p. : port. ; 22 cm. [RC280.B8S59] 78-62152 ISBN 0-932208-00-2 : 7.95
1. Splaver, Sarah. 2. Breast—Cancer—Biography. I. Title.

Spofford, Ainsworth Rand, 1825-1908.

AINSWORTH Rand 020'.92'4 B
Spofford, bookman and librarian / edited by John Y. Cole. Littleton, Colo. : Libraries Unlimited, 1975. p. cm. (The Heritage of librarianship series ; no. 2) Includes index. Bibliography: p. [Z720.S76A6] 75-31517 ISBN 0-87287-117-7 lib.bdg. : 11.50
1. Spofford, Ainsworth Rand, 1825-1908. 2. United States. Library of Congress—History—Sources. I. Cole, John Young, 1940- II. Series.

Spooner, John Coit, 1843-1919.

FOWLER, Dorothy (Ganfield) 1902- 923.273
John Coit Spooner, defender of Presidents. New York, University Publishers [c.1961] 436p. illus. (front. port.) Bibl. 61-8735 6.00
1. Spooner, John Coit, 1843-1919. I. Title.

Sporting goods.

BEAN, Leon Leonwood, 1872- 923.873
My story; the autobiography of a down-East merchant. Freeport, Me., 1960. 163p. illus. 23cm. [HD9999.S92B4] 60-3771
1. Sporting goods. I. Title.

Sports—Addresses, essays, lectures—Juvenile literature.

GUTMAN, Bill. 796'.092'2 B
Great sports feats of the '70s / by Bill Gutman. New York : J. Messner, c1979. p. cm. Relates outstanding sports feats and profiles the athletes who achieved them. [GV707.G83] 79-15298 ISBN 0-671-32954-5 : 7.79
1. Sports—Addresses, essays, lectures—Juvenile literature. 2. Athletes—Biography—Addresses, essays, lectures—Juvenile literature. I. Title. **BIP**

Sports—Biography.

ASSOCIATED Press. 796'.092'2 B
The sports immortals. [By the Associated Press Sports Staff] Englewood Cliffs, N.J., Prentice-Hall [1972] 320 p. illus. 28 cm.

"A Rutledge book." [GV697.A1A64] 72-6900 ISBN 0-13-837740-5 12.95
1. Sports—Biography. I. Title.

SCHOOR, Gene. 920
Courage makes the champion. Foreword by Frank Gifford. Princeton, N.J., Van Nostrand [1967] vi, 142 p. illus., ports. 22 cm. Biographical sketches of thirteen men and one woman who fought physical handicap and injury to become successful sportsmen: Mordecai Brown, Ben Hogan, Ike Eisenhower, Lou Gehrig, Glenn Cunningham, Jackie Robinson, Gene Tunney, Lou Brissie, Babe Didrikson, Roy Campanella, Barney Ross, Red Schoendienst, Canada Lee, and John F. Kennedy. [GV707.S33] AC 68
1. Sports—Biography. I. Title.

SILVERMAN, Al. 796
Sports titans of the 20th century. New York, Putnam [1968] 224 p. ports. 21 cm. Brief biographies of twelve great athletes including Jim Thorpe and Babe Zaharias named the best man and woman athletes of the twentieth century. Includes also: Babe Ruth, Jack Dempsey, Jim Brown, Ty Cobb, Bob Cousy, Jesse Owens, Bill Tilden, Maurice Richard, Willie Mays, and Red Grange. [GV697.A1S5] AC 68
1. Sports—Biography. I. Title.

SMITH, Chet. 796'.09748'8
Pittsburgh and western Pennsylvania sports hall of fame; the story about the men and women who made us a great sports area. Written by Chet Smith. Edited and illustrated by Marty Wolfson. Pittsburgh, Wolfson Pub. Co. [1969] 142 p. illus., ports. 30 cm. [GV584.P4S6] 73-14241
1. Sports—Biography. 2. Sports—Pennsylvania. 3. Sports—Pittsburgh. I. Wolfson, Marty, illus. II. Title.

WOODWARD, Stanley, ed. 927.96
Who's who in sports. [New York, Dell Pub. Co.] v. ports. 28 cm. annual. Editor: S. Woodward. [GV697.A1W537] 51-30945
1. Sports—Biog. I. Title.

Sports—Biography—Juvenile literature.

*HOLLANDER, Phyllis. 796.3[B]
It's the final score that counts, edited by Phyllis and Zander Hollander. New York, Grosset & Dunlap [1973] 113 p. photos. 24 cm. (An Associated Features Book) (A Thistle Book) Brief biographies of eleven notable Americans who started in the world of sports. [GV865] [920] 72-94236 ISBN 0-448-26236-3 4.99
1. Sports—Biography—Juvenile literature. I. Hollander, Zander, joint author. II. Title.

LANE, Ken. 796'.092'2
Champions all; 12 stories of famous sports heroes. Compiled and edited by Ken Lane. Illustrated by Jack Hearne. Middletown, Conn., Xerox Education Publications [1972] 95 p. illus. 18 cm. (A Pal paperback, B6) [GV697.A1L26] 920 72-83369 0.75 (pbk)
1. Sports—Biography—Juvenile literature. 2. Athletes—Biography—Juvenile literature. I. Hearne, Jack, illus. II. Title.
Contents omitted.

MCADAM, Robert Everett, 1920- 796'.0922
Bull on ice! By Robert McAdam. Illus. by Pete Bentovoja. [Glendale, Calif.] Bowmar [1971] 62 p. illus. (part col.) 24 cm. (His Play the game, book 4) Recounts special moments and achievements in sports. Includes athletes Bobby Hull, Lee Trevino, Jesse Owens, Babe Zaharias, Lou Gehrig, Jim Thorpe, Fred Steinmark, and Knute Rockne. [GV697.A1M26 book 4] 920 70-165176
1. Sports—Biography—Juvenile literature. I. Bentovoja, Pete, illus. II. Title.

MCADAM, Robert Everett, 1920- 796'.0922
Chief Cloud of Dust, by Robert McAdam. Illus. by Pete Bentovoja. [Glendale, Calif.] Bowmar [1971] 63 p. illus. (part col.) 24 cm. (His Play the game, book 3) Summarizes special moments and achievements in sports. Includes athletes Billy Mills, Corny Warmerdam, Babe Ruth, Peggy Fleming, Glenn Cunningham, Roy Reigels, Arthur Ashe, and Sandy Koufax. [GV697.A1M26 book 3] 920 79-165173
1. Sports—Biography—Juvenile literature. I. Bentovoja, Pete, illus. II. Title.

MCADAM, Robert Everett, 1920- 796'.0922
Forty for sixty, by Robert McAdam. Illus. by Pete Bentovoja. [Glendale, Calif.] Bowmar [1971] 50 p. illus. (part col.) 24 cm. (His Play the game, book 1) Recounts special moments and achievements in the sports world. Includes athletes Joe Kapp, Wilma Rudolph, Bill Rohr, Eddie Arcaro, Mickey Mantle, Ricky McCormick, Bobby Richards, and Cliff Cushman. [GV697.A1M26 book 1] 920 76-165175
1. Sports—Biography—Juvenile literature. I. Bentovoja, Pete, illus. II. Title.

MCADAM, Robert Everett, 1920- 796*.092
Play the game, by Robert McAdam. [Glendale, Calif., Bowmar, 1971- v. illus. (part col.) 24 cm. Contents.Contents.—book 1. Forty for sixty.—book 2. Viva Gonzales!—book 3. Chief Cloud of Dust.—book 4. Bull on ice! Recounts special moments and achievements in sports focusing on the dedication, hard work, and sportsmanship manifested by great athletes. [GV697.A1M26] 72-29282
1. Sports—Biography—Juvenile literature. I. Title. **BIP**

MCADAM, Robert Everett, 1920- 796'.0922
Viva Gonzales! By Robert McAdam. Illus. by Pete Bentovoja. [Glendale, Calif.] Bowmar [1971] 63 p. illus. (part col.) 24 cm. (His Play the game, book 2) Summarizes special moments and achievements in sports. Includes athletes Pancho Gonzales, Charlie Green, George Mikan, Vicki Smith, Willie Davis, Van Nelson, Monty Stratton, and Joe Louis. [GV697.A1M26 book 2] 920 72-165174
1. Sports—Biography—Juvenile literature. I. Bentovoja, Pete, illus. II. Title.

SILVERMAN, Al. 796'.0922 B
More sports titans of the 20th century. New York, Putnam [1969] 224 p. ports. 21 cm. (Putnam sports shelf) Contents.Contents.—Joe Louis.—Stan Musial.—George Mikan.—Walter Johnson.—Ben Hogan.—Eddie Shore.—Paavo Nurmi.—Johnny Weissmuller.—Gordie Howe.—Helen Wills.—Bob Mathias.—Bobby Jones.—Warren Spahn. [GV697.A1S49 1969] 920 76-77770 3.64
1. Sports—Biography—Juvenile literature. I. Title.

SILVERMAN, Al. 796'.0922
Sports titans of the 20th century. New York, Putnam [1968] 224 p. ports. 21 cm. Contents.Contents.—Jim Thorpe.—Babe Ruth.—Jack Dempsey.—Jim Brown.—Ty Cobb.—Bob Cousy.—Jesse Owens.—Bill Tilden.—Maurice Richard.—Babe Didrikson Zaharias.—Willie Mays.—Red Grange. [GV697.A1S5] 68-15080
1. Sports—Biography—Juvenile literature. I. Title.

Sports—Biography—Miscellanea.

PRETNER, Lee. 796
Pro sports trivia / Lee Pretner. New York : Watts, 1975, c1974. 159 p. : ill. ; 23 cm. Updated version of the ed. published by Stadia Sports Pub., New York. [GV697.A1P74 1975] 74-34548 ISBN 0-531-01091-0 : 5.95
1. Sports—Biography—Miscellanea. 2. Athletes—Biography—Miscellanea. I. Title. **BIP**

Sports journalism.

RUSSELL, Fred, 1906- 920.5
Bury me in an old press box; good times and life of a sportswriter. New York, Barnes [1957] 235p. illus. 22cm. [PN4784.J6R8] 57-12528
1. Sports journalism. 2. Journalists—Correspondence, reminiscences, etc. I. Title.

Sports—Juvenile literature.

CHALMERS, Robert Erskine Shaw. 796'.0922
The world of sport, by R. E. S. Chalmers, Joan Chalmers. London, New York [etc.] McGraw-Hill, 1968. 68 p. illus., ports. 22 cm. (Our world) Includes bibliographies. Profiles of five English champions and how they trained and played to win: Stanley Matthews—football; Angela Mortimer—tennis; Jim Clark—auto racing; Herb Elliott—running; and Garfield Sobers—cricket. [GV697.A1C5] 920 70-416110 10/6
1. Sports—Juvenile literature. 2. Sports—Biography. I. Chalmers, Joan, joint author. II. Title.

SCHOOR, Gene. 796'.0922
Courage makes the champion. Foreword by Frank Gifford. Princeton, N.J., Van Nostrand [1967] vi, 142 p. illus., ports. 22 cm. [GV707.S33] 67-27990
1. Sports—Juvenile literature. I. Title.
Contents omitted.

SCHOOR, Gene. 796'.0922
Courage makes the champion. Foreword by Frank Gifford. Princeton, N.J., Van Nostrand [1967] vi, 142 p. illus., ports. 22 cm. Contents.Contents.—Three fingers: Mordecai Brown.—The bantam from Texas: Ben Hogan.—The courage of the boy: Ike Eisenhower.—Pride of the Yankees: Lou Gehrig.—Run, run, run: Glenn Cunningham.—He broke the line: Jackie Robinson.—The champ who was different: Gene Tunney.—Big-league pitcher: Lou Brissie.—All-American woman: Babe Didrikson.—Hero of the Dodgers: Roy Campanella.—The fighting marine: Barney Ross.—They called him Red: Red Schoendienst.—Fighter in the footlights: Canada Lee.—One more profile in courage: John F. Kennedy. [GV707.S33] 67-27990
1. Sports—Juvenile literature. I. Title.

Sports stories.

SMITH, Walter Wellesley, 1905- 796'.08
Strawberries in the wintertime; the sporting world of Red Smith. [New York] Quadrangle/New York Times Book Co. [1974] viii, 340 p. 25 cm. [GV707.S64 1974] 73-90170 ISBN 0-8129-0422-2 9.95
1. Sports stories. I. Title.

Sports team owners—United States—Biography.

KOWET, Don. 338.4'77960922 B
The rich who own sports / Don Kowet. 1st ed. New York : Random House, c1977. ix, 271 p. ; 22 cm. [GV719.A2K68] 76-53483 ISBN 0-394-49561-6 : 8.95
1. Sports team owners—United States—Biography. I. Title. **BIP**

Sports—Virginia—History.

GOLDBLATT, Abe, 1915- 796'.09755
The great and the near-great : a century of sports in Virginia / by Abe Goldblatt and Robert W. Wentz, Jr. Norfolk : Donning, [1976] p. cm. [GV584.V8G64] 76-28315 ISBN 0-915442-07-8 : 14.95
1. Sports—Virginia—History. 2. Athletes—Virginia—History. I. Wentz, Robert W., 1932- joint author. II. Title. **BIP**

Sportswriters—United States—Biography.

NO cheering in the press box. 070.4'49'7960922 Recorded and edited by Jerome Holtzman. [1st ed.] New York, Holt, Rinehart and Winston [1974] xii, 287 p. 24 cm. Interviews with 18 sports writers, 1971-73. [GV719.A2N62] 73-12859 ISBN 0-03-012236-8 7.95
1. Sportswriters—United States—Biography. I. Holtzman, Jerome.

Spotswood, Alexander, 1676-1740.

DODSON, Leonidas. 975.5'02'0924
Alexander Spotswood, Governor of Colonial Virginia, 1710-1722. New York, AMS Press [1969] x, 323 p. port. 23 cm. Reprint of the 1932 ed. Bibliography: p. 310-315. [F229.S774 1969] 76-91784
1. Spotswood, Alexander, 1676-1740. 2. Virginia—History—Colonial period, ca. 1600-1775. I. Title.

Sprague, Catherine Jane (Chase) 1840-1899.

ROSS, Ishbel, 1897- 920.7
Proud Kate, portrait of an ambitious woman. [1st ed.] New York, Harper [c1953] 309p. illus. 22cm. [E415.9.S76R6] 51-11952
1. Sprague, Catherine Jane (Chase) 1840-1899. I. Title.

Sprague, Charles Ezra, 1842-1912.

MANN, Helen Scott. 330'.092'4 B
Charles Ezra Sprague / Helen Scott Mann. New York : Arno Press, 1978 [c1931] 67 p., [8] leaves of plates : ill. ; 24 cm. (The Development of contemporary accounting thought) Reprint of the ed. published by New York University, New York. [CT275.S627M3 1978] 77-87277 ISBN 0-405-10905-9 lib bdg : 12.00 12.00
1. Sprague, Charles Ezra, 1842-1912. 2. United States—Biography. I. Title. II. Series. **BIP**

Spreckels, Claus, 1828-1908.

ADLER, Jacob, 1913- 338.17360924 (B)
Claus Spreckels; the sugar king in Hawaii. Illustrated by Joseph Feher. Honolulu, University of Hawaii Press, 1966. 339 p. illus., ports. 24 cm. Bibliographical references included in "Notes" (p. 287-327) [HD9118.H25A6] 65-28712
1. Spreckels, Claus, 1828-1908. 2. Sugar growing — Hawaii. 3. Hawaii — Pol. & govt. I. Title.

Spreckelsen, Margrit von.

SPRECKELSEN, Margrit von. 741.943
Margrit v. Spreckelsen : Olbilder, Zeichnungen : [Ausstellung in der Galerie Brockstedt, Hamburg, Feb.-Marx 1975 : Katalog]. Hamburg : Galerie Brockstedt, [1975?] [8] p., [16] leaves of plates : ill. (some col.) ; 12 x 21 cm. [ND588.S615G35] 75-504831
1. Spreckelsen, Margrit von. I. Galerie Brockstedt. II. Title.

Springer, Helen Emily (Chairman) 1868-1949.

SPRINGER, John McKendree, Bp., 1873- 922.773
I love the trail: a sketch of the life of Helen Emily Springer. Publisher's agencies: Congo Book Concern, Nashville [etc. Nashville? 1952] 176 p. illus. 24 cm. [BV3505.S6S6] 52-27463
1. Springer, Helen Emily (Chairman) 1868-1949. I. Title.

Springsteen, Bruce.

GAMBACCINI, Peter. 784'.092'4 B
Bruce Springsteen / Peter Gambaccini. New York : Quick Fox, c1979. 127 p. : ill. ; 26 cm. Discography: p. [125]-127. A biography highlighting the career of the well-known rock musician. [ML420.S77G3] 92 78-68486 ISBN 0-8256-3935-2 pbk. : 4.95
1. Springsteen, Bruce. 2. Rock musicians—United States—Biography. I. Title. **BIP**

MARSH, Dave. 784'.092'4 B
Born to run : the Bruce Springsteen story / by Dave Marsh ; [cover photo by Lynn Goldsmith]. 1st ed. Garden City, N.Y. : Dolphin Books, 1979. 176 p. : ill. ; 28 cm. "The songs": p. 166-169. "A Delilah book." A biography highlighting the career of the well-known rock musician. [ML420.S77M33] 92 79-52514 ISBN 0-385-15443-7 : 7.95
1. Sprinsteen, Bruce. 2. Rock musicians—United States—Biography. I. Title. **BIP**

Sproul, Robert Gordon, 1891-

PETTITT, George Albert, 1901- 378.7940924
Twenty-eight years in the life of a university president, by George A. Pettitt. Foreword by Clark Kerr. [Berkeley] University of California, 1966. 254 p. illus., ports. 27 cm."public addresses [of R. G. Sproul]":p. 177-254. [LD7551930.P4] 66-63430
1. Sproul, Robert Gordon, 1891- 2. California. [university. I. Title.

Spruance, Raymond Ames, 1886-1969.

BUELL, Thomas B. 940.54'5'0924 B
The quiet warrior: a biography of Admiral Raymond A. Spruance, by Thomas B. Buell. [1st ed.] Boston, Little, Brown [1974] xviii, 486 p. illus. 24 cm. Bibliography: p. [441]-473. [V63.S68B8] 74-1181 ISBN 0-316-11470-7 15.00
1. Spruance, Raymond Ames, 1886-1969. I. Title.

Spry, William, 1864-1929.

ROPER, William L. 979.2'03'0924
William Spry: man of firmness, Governor of Utah, by William L. Roper and Leonard J. Arrington. Salt Lake City, University of Utah Press, 1971. xv, 236 p. illus., ports. 24 cm. (University of Utah publications in the American West, v. 6) Includes bibliographical references. [F826.S68R6] 70-634772 ISBN 0-87480-079-X
1. Spry, William, 1864-1929. 2. Utah—Politics and government. I. Arrington, Leonard J., joint author. II. Series: Utah. University. Publications in the American West, v. 6

Sptisbury, Sir Bernard Henry, 1877-1947.

BROWNE, Douglas Gordon, 1884- 926.1
Bernard Spilsbury, his life and cases, by Douglas G. Browne and E. V. Tullett. With a foreword by W. Bentley Purchase. [Harmondsworth, Middlesex] Penguin Books [1955] 408p. 18cm. (Penguin books, 1092) [RA1025.S6B68 1955] 56-35627
1. Sptisbury, Sir Bernard Henry, 1877-1947. I. Tullett, Eric Vivian, joint author. II. Title.

*DAY, Richard Ellsworth 251.'0092'4
The shadow of the broad brim : the life story of Charles Hadden Spurgeon, heir of the Puritans. Grand Rapids : Baker Book House, 1976c1934. 236p. : ill., ports. ; 20 cm. [BX6495.S7.] [B] ISBN 0-8010-2855-8 pbk. : 3.95.
1. Spurgeon, Charles Haddon, 1834-1892. 2. Preaching. I. Title.

Spurgeon, Charles Haddon, 1834-1892.

*DAY, Richard Ellsworth 251.'0092'4
The shadow of the broad brim : the life story of Charles Hadden Spurgeon, heir of the Puritans. Grand Rapids : Baker Book House, 1976c1934. 236p. : ill., ports. ; 20 cm. [BX6495.S7.] [B] ISBN 0-8010-2855-8 pbk. : 3.95.
1. Spurgeon, Charles Haddon, 1834-1892. 2. Preaching. I. Title.

BACON, Ernest Wallace. 253.7'0924 (B)
Spurgeon, heir of the Puritans [by] Ernest W. Bacon. [1st U. S. A. ed.] Grand Rapids, Mich., W. B. Eerdmans Pub. Co. [1968, 1967] 184 p. port. 23 cm. Bibliography: p. 178-179. [BX6495.S7B3] 67-30115
1. Spurgeon, Charles Haddon, 1834-1892. I. Title.

BACON, Ernest Wallace. 253.7'0924
Spurgeon, heir of the Puritans [by] Ernest W. Bacon. [1st U.S.A. ed.] Grand Rapids, Mich., Eerdmans [1968, c1967] 184p. port. 23cm. Bibl. [BX6495.S7B3] (B) 67-30115 3.95
1. Spurgeon, Charles Haddon, 1834-1892. I. Title.

FULLERTON, William Young, 1857-1932. 253.70924 B
Charles Haddon Spurgeon; a biography. Chicago, Moody Press [1966] 283 p. 23 cm. (The Tyndale series of great biographies) "First published, 1920." [BX6495.S7F8 1966] 66-8933
1. Spurgeon, Charles Haddon, 1834-1892. I. Title. II. Series.

Spurgeon family.

SPURGEON, Bee Dee Abbott. 929.2'0973
The Spurgeon story [by] Richard Bertrand Dimmitt, as told by Bee Dee Abbott Spurgeon, Santa Ana, California, 1971. [Orange, Calif., Orange County Public Library, 1971] [36] p. illus. 22 cm. [CS71.S7716 1971] 70-184659
1. Spurgeon family. I. Dimmitt, Richard Bertrand.

Spurling, Richard G., 1858-1935.

MARSHALL, June Glover. 289.9 B
A biographical sketch of Richard G. Spurling, Jr. / by June Glover Marshall. Cleveland, Tenn. : Pathway Press, [1974] 29 p. : port. ; 16 cm. [BX7020.Z8S685] 74-27630
1. Spurling, Richard G., 1858-1935. I. Title.

Spurrier, Steve,

SPURRIER, Steve, 1945- 796.332'0924
It's always too soon to quit; the Steve Spurrier story, as told to Mel Larson. Grand Rapids, Zondervan [1968] 157 p. illus., ports. 21 cm. [GV939.S65A3] 68-27464 3.95
I. Larson, Melvin Gunnard, 1916- II. Title.

Squanto, Wampanoag Indian, d. 1622.

BULLA, Clyde Robert. 970.3 B
Squanto, friend of the white men. Illustrated by Peter Burchard. New York, Crowell [1954] 160 p. illus. 22 cm. A biography of the Indian who went to London with some of the first English explorers, was sold into slavery in Spain, and finally returned to America where he befriended the Pilgrims when they landed. [PZ7.B912Sq] 92 AC 68
1. Squanto, Wampanoag Indian, d. 1622. I. Burchard, Peter, illus. II. Title.

STEVENSON, Augusta. 970.3'0924 B
Squanto, young Indian hunter. Illustrated by Nathan Goldstein. Indianapolis, Bobbs-Merrill [1962] 200 p. illus. 20 cm. (Childhood of famous Americans) The boyhood of the Wampanoag Indian who lived for a time in England and then returned to New England where he helped the Pilgrim settlers in Plymouth. [PZ7.S8467Sq] 92 AC 68
1. Squanto, Wampanoag Indian, d. 1622. I. Goldstein, Nathan, illus. II. Title.

Squanto, Wampanoag Indian, d. 1622 — Juvenile literature.

GRANT, Matthew G. 970.3 B
Squanto: the Indian who saved the Pilgrims [by] Matthew G. Grant. Illustrated by John Nelson and Harold Henriksen. [Mankato, Minn., Creative Education; distributed by Childrens Press, Chicago 1974] 30 p. illus. (part col.) 25 cm. (His Gallery of great American series. Indians of America) A biography of the Wampanoag Indian whose experiences at the hands of early English explorers later enabled him to help the struggling Plymouth colony. [E99.W2S63] 92 73-12813 ISBN 0-87191-270-8 3.95
1. Squanto, Wampanoag Indian, d. 1622—Juvenile literature. I. Nelson, John, 1928- illus. II. Henriksen, Harold, illus. III. Title.

ZINER, Feenie. 973.8'0924
Dark pilgrim; the story of Squanto. [1st ed.] Philadelphia, Chilton Books [1965] vii, 158 p. 21 cm. Bibliography: p. 150-154. [E90.S77Z5] 65-20900
1. Squanto, Wampanoag Indian, d. 1622 — Juvenile literature. I. Title.

Squibb, Edward Robinson, 1819-1900.

BLOCHMAN, Lawrence Goldtree, 1900- 926.1
Doctor Squibb; the life and times of a rugged idealist. New York, Simon and Schuster, 1958. 371 p. illus. 22 cm. [R154.S73B55] 58-11805
1. Squibb, Edward Robinson, 1819-1900.

Squire, John Collings, Sir 1884-1958.

HOWARTH, Patrick 928.2
Squire, most generous of men. London, Hutchinson. [Chester Springs, Pa., Dufour, 1964, c.1963] 307p. port. 22cm. Bibl. 64-41737 6.00
1. Squire, John Collings, Sir 1884-1958. I. Title.

Srivastava, Dhanpat Rai, 1881-1936.

GOPAL, Madan. 891.4'3'36
Munshi Premchand; a literary biography. Bombay, New York Asia Pub. House [1964] xvi, 462 p. illus. facsims., ports. 23 cm. [PK2097.S7Z69 1964] SA 65
1. Srivastava, Dhanpet Ral, 1881-1936. I. Title. BIP

GOPAL, Madan 928.9143
Munshi Premchand; a literary biography. New York, Asia Pub. [dist. Taplinger, c.1964] xvi, 462p. illus., facsims., ports. 23cm. [PK2097.S7Z69] SA65 13.75
1. Srivastava, Dhanpat Rai, 1881-1936. I. Title.

SWAN, Robert O. 891.4'3'36 B
Munshi Premchand of Lamhi village, by Robert O. Swan. Durham, N.C., Duke University Press, 1969. ix, 149 p. 25 cm. (Publication series of the Program in Comparative Studies on Southern Asia, no. 3) Bibliography: p. 142-146. [PK2098.S7Z93] 77-80813 6.00
1. Srivastava, Dhanpat Rai, 1881-1936. I. Title. II. Series: Duke University, Durham, N.C. Commonwealth-Studies Center. Program in Comparative Studies on Southern Asia. Publication series, no. 3 BIP

St. Albans, Suzanne Marie Adele Beauclerk, Duchess of.

ST Albans, Suzanne Marie Adele Beauclerk, Duchess of. 944'.941 B
The road to Bordeaux / the Duchess of St Albans. London : W. H. Allen, 1976. 146 p. : [4] leaves of plates ; 22 cm. [CT788.S13A37] 76-371414 ISBN 0-491-01685-9 : £3.95
1. St. Albans, Suzanne Marie Adele Beauclerk, Duchess of. 2. England—Biography. 3. France—Biography. I. Title.

St. Aldwyn, Michael Edwayd Hicks-Beach, 1st earl, 1837-1916.

HARRIS, Frank, 1855-1931. 920.042
Contemporary portraits (third series). New York, Greenwood Press [1969] viii, 233 p. illus., ports. 23 cm. Reprint of the 1920 ed. Contents.Contents.—H. G. Wells.—Upton Sinclair.—John Galsworthy.—Cunninghame Graham.—Gilbert K. Chesterton.—Arthur Symons.—Winston Churchill.—Russel Wallace.—Thomas Huxley.—Louis Wilkinson.—W. L. George.—Gaudier-Brzeska.—Earl St. Aldwyn.—Augustus John.—Coventry Patmore.—Walt Whitman. [PN761.H23 1969] 79-95103 ISBN 8-371-25774-
1. Gaudier-Brzeska, Henri, 1891-1915. 2. St. Aldwyn, Michael Edwayd Hicks-Beach, 1st earl, 1837-1916. 3. John, Augustus Edwin, 1878- 4. Authors, English. 5. Authors, American. I. Title.

St. Charles Parish, La.—Genealogy.

CONRAD, Glenn R. 929'.3763'33
St. Charles : abstracts of the civil records of St. Charles Parish, 1700-1803 / Glenn R. Conrad. Lafayette, La. : University of Southwestern Louisiana, 1974. xi, 544 p. ; 29 cm. (The USL history series ; [7]) Includes index. [F377.S124C66] 74-189424 17.50
1. St. Charles Parish, La.—Genealogy. 2. St. Charles Parish, La.—History—Sources. I. Title. II. Series: Louisiana. University of Southwestern Louisiana, Lafayette. The U.S.L. history series ; 7.

St. Croix, Virgin Islands—Social life and customs.

HAWES, Elizabeth, 1903- 917.297
But say it politely. [1st ed.] Boston, Little, Brown, 1951. 257 p. 22 cm. Autobiographical. [F2096.H3] 51-14096
1. St. Croix, Virgin Islands—Social life and customs. I. Title.

St. Denis, Louis Juchereau, Chevalier de, 1676-1744.

PHARES, Ross. 923.973
Cavalier in the wilderness; the story of the explorer and trader Louis Juchereau de St. Denis. Baton Rouge, Louisiana State University Press [1952] ix, 276 p. illus. 22 cm. Bibliography: p. [267]-271. [F372.S3P5] 52-7747
1. St. Denis, Louis Juchereau, Chevalier de, 1676-1744. 2. Louisiana—History—Colonial period. 3. Texas—History—To 1846. I. Title.

PHARES, Ross. 976.3'01'0924
Cavalier in the wilderness; the story of the explorer and trader Louis Juchereau de St. Denis. Gloucester, Mass., Peter Smith, 1970 [c1952] ix, 276 p. illus. 22 cm. Bibliography: p. [267]-271. [F372.S3P5 1970] 70-23753
1. St. Denis, Louis Juchereau, chevalier de, 1676-1744. 2. Louisiana—History—To 1803. 3. Texas—History To 1846. I. Title. BIP

St. Denis, Ruth, 1880-

ST. Denis, Ruth, 1880-1968. 793.3'0924 B
Ruth St. Denis, an unfinished life; an autobiography. Brooklyn [Dance Horizons, 1969, c1939] 391 p. illus., ports. 21 cm. (Dance horizons series, 30) [GV1785.S3A3 1969] 71-77182 ISBN 0-87127-030-7 5.95
I. Title.

TERRY, Walter. 793.3'2'0924 B
Miss Ruth; the "more living life" of Ruth St. Denis. New York, Dodd, Mead [1969] xi, 206 p. illus., ports. 22 cm. [GV1785.S3T4] 70-91280 6.95
1. St. Denis, Ruth, 1880- I. Title. BIP

St. Elizabeth's School, Wakpala, S. D.

CHAPMAN, William McKissack, 1905- 377.60924
Remember the wind; a prairie memoir [by] William McK. Chapman. With drawings by Douglas Gorsline. [1st ed.] Philadelphia, Lippincott [1965] 239 p. map (on lining papers) 22 cm. Includes an Episcopal hymn in Dakota, with music. [E97.6.S15C5] 65-17476
1. St. Elizabeth's School, Wakpala, S. D. 2. Dakota Indians. I. Title.

St. Ignatius Church, Hickory, Md.

JOERNDT, Clarence V., 1898- 282'.752'74
St. Ignatius, Hickory, and its missions, by Clarence V. Joerndt. [Baltimore, Printed by Publication Press, 1972] xii, 536 p. illus. 24 cm. Includes bibliographical references. [BX4603.H52S344] 72-92408 11.00
1. St. Ignatius Church, Hickory, Md. 2. Hickory, Md.—Biography. I. Title.

St. Innocent, Olga, marquise de.

ST. Innocent, Olga, marquise de. 914 B
Olga; the memoirs of Olga, la marquise de St. Innocent. New York, Walker [1974] 266 p. illus. 24 cm. [CT3150.S24A36] 72-95779 ISBN 0-8027-0414-X 9.95

1. St. Innocent, Olga, marquise de. I. Title.

St. John, Harold, 1876-1957.

ST. JOHN, Patrica Mary, 1920- 922.642
Harold St. John, a portrait by his daughter. New York, Loizeaux [1962, c.1961] 182p. illus. 19cm. 62-3910 3.25 bds.,
1. St. John, Harold, 1876-1957. I. Title.

ST. JOHN, Patricia Mary, 1920- 922
Harold St. John, a portrait by his daughter. New York, Loizeaux Bros, [c1961] 182p. illus. 19cm. [BV3705.S3S3] 62-3910
1. St. John, Harold, 1876-1957. I. Title.

St. John, Robert,

ST. JOHN, Robert, 1902- 922.96
Tongue of the prophets; the life story of Eliezer Ben Yehuda. [1st ed.] Garden City, N. Y., Doubleday, 1952. 377 p. 22 cm. [DS151.B4S3] 52-5233
I. Ben-Yehudah, Eliezer, 1858-1922. II. Title.

St. Johns, Adela (Rogers)

ST. Johns, Adela (Rogers) 070'.924
The honeycomb. [1st ed.] Garden City, N.Y., Doubleday, 1969. 598 p. illus., ports. 25 cm. Autobiography. [PS3537.A278Z5] 69-15885 8.95
I. Title. BIP

St. Johns, Adela Rogers - Biography.

ST. Johns, Adela Rogers. 812'.5'2 B
Love, laughter, and tears : my Hollywood story / Adela Rogers St. Johns. 1st ed. Garden City, N.Y. : Doubleday, 1978. xii, 342 p., [8] leaves of plates : ill. ; 22 cm. [PS3537.A278Z52] 76-50786 10.00
1. St. Johns, Adela Rogers—Biography. 2. Authors, American—20th century—Biography. 3. Moving-picture actors and actresses—United States—Anecdotes, facetiae, satire, etc. I. Title.

ST. Johns, Adela Rogers. 812'.5'2 B
Love, laughter, and tears : my Hollywood story / by Adela Rogers St. Johns. New York : New American Library, 1979, c1978. 325p. : ill. ; 18 cm. (A Signet book) [PS3537.A278Z52] ISBN 0-451-08752-6 pbk. : 2.50
1. St. Johns, Adela Rogers — Biography. 2. Authors, American — 20th century — Biography. 3. Moving-picture actors and actresses — United States — Anecdotes, facetiae, satire, etc. I. Title.
L.C. card no. for 1978 Doubleday ed.: 76-50786.

St. Laurent, Louis Stephen, 1882-

THOMSON, Dale C. 971.06'3'0924 B
Louis St. Laurent, Canadian [by] Dale C. Thomson. New York, St. Martin's Press, 1968 [c1967] x, 564 p. illus., ports. 23 cm. Bibliography: p. 543-552. [F1034.3.S2T48] 68-11107
1. St. Laurent, Louis Stephen, 1882-

St. Louis—Soc. life & cust.

PROETZ, Arthur Walter, 1888- 581'.0924
I remember you, St. Louis. With a foreword by Edgar C. Taylor. [1st ed.] Saint Louis, Zimmerman-Petty Co. [1963] 227 p. illus., ports., facsims 21 cm. "Most of this book first appeared as a series of articles in the St. Louis post-dispatch [between September 1962 and May 1963]" [F474.S2P7] 63-23572
1. St. Louis—Soc. life & cust. I. St. Louis post-dispatch. II. Title.

St. Louis. Baseball club (National league)

DEVANEY, John. 796.357'0922
The greatest Cardinals of them all. New York, Putnam [1968] 223 p. ports. 22 cm. [GV865.A1D4] 68-15045 3.49
1. St. Louis, Baseball club (National league) 2. Baseball—Biography. I. Title.

DEVANEY, John. 796.357
The greatest Cardinals of them all. New York, Putnam [1968] 223 p. ports. 22 cm. Brief descriptions of the careers of the Saint Louis Cardinals' greatest players, like Leo Durocher, Dizzy Dean, and Stan Musial, give behind-the-scene glimpses of the team's "Gas House" baseball style. [GV865.A1D4] AC 68
1. St. Louis. Baseball club (National league) 2. Baseball—Biography. I. Title.

St. Louis Blues (Hockey team)

FISCHLER, Stan. 796.9'62'0977866
Garry Unger and the battling Blues / by Stan Fischler. New York : Dodd, Mead, c1976. ix, 213 p., [8] leaves of plates : ill. ; 22 cm. [GV848.S32F56] 76-49993 ISBN 0-396-07388-3 : 7.95
1. St. Louis Blues (Hockey team) 2. Unger, Garry, 1947- 3. Hockey players—United States—Biography. I. Title. BIP

St. Louis Board of Education.

*ST. Louis Board of Education. 920.073 B
Mini-sketches of great Americans; with original drawings by young artists. New York, Pocket Books [1974, c1972] 272 p. illus. 18 cm. (Washington Square Press book) [CT211] ISBN 0-671-47917-2 0.95 (pbk.)
I. Title.

St. Louis Cardinals (Football team)

BURNES, Robert Liston, 1914- 796.33'264'0977866
Big Red : story of the football Cardinals / Robert L. Burnes ; foreword by Larry Wilson. Saint Charles, Mo. : Piraeus Publishers, 1975. xii, 243 p. : ill. ; 24 cm. Includes index. [GV956.S27B87] 75-11160 ISBN 0-913656-05-4
1. St. Louis Cardinals (Football team) 2. Football—Biography. I. Title. BIP

St. Vincent, John Jervis, earl, 1735-1823.

BERCKMAN, Evelyn 923.542
Nelson's dear lord; a portrait of St. Vincent. London, Macmillan [dist. New York, St. Martins, 1964, c.]1962. 274p. illus. 23cm. Bibl. 62-52383 6.95
1. St. Vincent, John Jervis, earl, 1735-1823. I. Title.

JAMES, William milburne, Sir 1881- 923.542
Old Oak; the life of John Jervis, Earl of St. Vincent. London, New York, Longmans, Green [1950] ix, 230 p. ports., maps. 22 cm. [DA87.1.S2J3] 51-1712
1. St. Vincent. John Jervis, earl, 1735-1823. I. Title.

Stabler, Ken—Juvenile literature.

FEINBERG, William H. 796.33'2'0924 B 92
Ken Stabler / by William H. Feinberg ; photos. by Bruce Curtis. Mankato, Minn. : Creative Education : Chicago : distributed by Childrens Press, c1978. 31 p. : col. ill. ; 25 cm. (Creative Education sports superstars) A biography of the left-handed quarterback who led the Oakland Raiders to the 1976 Super Bowl. [GV939.S68F44] 77-25128 ISBN 0-87191-670-3 lib.bdg. : 4.95
1. Stabler, Ken—Juvenile literature. 2. Football players—United States—Biography—Juvenile literaure. 3. Oakland Raiders (Football club)—Juvenile literature. I. Curtis, Bruce. II. Title. BIP

LIBBY, Bill. 796.33'2'0924 B
Ken Stabler : southpaw passer / by Bill Libby. New York : Putnam, c1977. 128 p. : ill. ; 21 cm. (Putnam sports shelf) Includes index. A biography of southpaw Ken Stabler who has become an outstanding professional football quarterback. [GV939.S68L52 1977] 92 76-23468 ISBN 0-399-61056-1 lib. bdg. : 5.29
1. Stabler, Ken—Juvenile literature. 2. Football—Juvenile literature. I. Title. BIP

Stacey, Edward George.

LIFELINES : 971.4'66
the Stacey letters, 1836-1858 / edited by Jane Vansittart. New York : Taplinger Pub. Co., 1976. x, 180 p., [2] leaves of plates : ill. ; 23 cm. [F1054.5.S55L53 1976] 76-362 ISBN 0-8008-4841-1 : 8.95
1. Stacey, Edward George. 2. Stacey, George, 1805-1862. 3. Sherbrooke, Quebec—Biography. 4. Pioneers—Quebec (Province)—Sherbrooke—Biography. I. Stacey, Edward George. II. Vansittart, Jane. BIP

Stacey, John F.

STACEY, John F. 917.12'1
To Alaska for gold [by] John F. Stacey. Fairfield, Wash., Ye Galleon Press, 1973. 69 p. illus. 25 cm. 300 copies. Reprint of the ed. originally published about 1916. [F931.S785 1973] 73-7598 ISBN 0-87770-096-6
1. Stacey, John F. 2. Klondike gold fields. I. Title. BIP

Stack, Robert, 1919-

STACK, Robert, 1919- 791.43'028'0924 B
Straight shooting / by Robert Stack with Mark Evans ; designed by Jack Meserole. New York : Macmillan, c1980. p. cm. [PN2287.S665A37] 79-26305 ISBN 0-02-613320-2 : 8.95
1. Stack, Robert, 1919- 2. Moving-picture actors and actresses—United States—Biography. I. Evans, Mark, joint author. II. Title. BIP

Stack, Walter, 1907-

BISHOP, Bob, 1949- 796.4'26 B
The running saga of Walter Stack / Bob Bishop. Millbrae, Calif. : Celestial Arts, c1978. 109 p. : ill. ; 22 cm. [GV697.S67B57] 78-54481 ISBN 0-89087-226-0 pbk. : 4.95
1. Stack, Walter, 1907- 2. Track and field athletes—United States—Biography. 3. Marathon running. I. Title. BIP

Stackhouse, Russell Orr, 1932-1954.

STACKHOUSE, Mildred (Orr) 920
God's plan for Russ; a mother's story of her gifted son's life. [1st ed.] New York, Exposition Press [1956] 98 p. 21 cm. [CT275.S636S8] 56-10977
1. Stackhouse, Russell Orr, 1932-1954. I. Title.

Stael, Nicolas de, 1914-1955.

STAEL, Nicolas de, 1914-1955. 759.4 B
Nicolas de Stael / by Guy Dumur ; translated by Fintan O'Connell ; photography by Henry B. Beville ... [et al.]. New York : Crown Publishers, c1976. p. cm. [ND553.S8D8413] 76-27652 ISBN 0-517-52611-5 : 4.95
1. Stael, Nicolas de, 1914-1955. 2. Painters—France—Biography. I. Dumur, Guy, 1921- II. Title.

Stael-Holstein, Anne Louise Germaine Necker, baronne de, 1766-1817.

ANDREWS, Wayne. 928.4
Germaine; a portrait of Madame de Stael. [1st ed.] New York, Atheneum, 1963. viii, 237 p. port. 24 cm. Bibliography: p. 223-229. [DC146.S7A66] 63-17856
1. Stael-Holstein, Anne Louise Germaine (Necker) Baronne de, 1766-1817. I. Title.

HEROLD, J Christopher. v. 12
Mistress to an age; a life of Madame de Stael. [Indianapolis] Charter Books [1962, c1958] viii, 500 p. 21 cm. 67-92254
1. Stael-Holstein, Anne Louise Germaine (Necker baronne de, 1766-1817. I. Title. BIP

HEROLD, J. Christopher. 928.4
Mistress to an age; a life of Madame de Stael. [1st ed.] Indianapolis, Bobbs-Merrill Co. [1958] 500 p. illus. 22 cm. Includes bibliography. [DC146.S7H44] 58-12385
1. Stael-Holstein, Anne Louise Germaine (Necker) baronne de, 1766-1817. I. Title.

HEROLD, J. Christopher. 944.04'092'4 B
Mistress to an age : a life of Madame de Stael / by J. Christopher Herold. New York : Harmony Books, [1979] c1958. p. cm. Includes index. Bibliography: p. [DC146.S7H44 1979] 78-26555 ISBN 0-517-53783-4 pbk. : 6.95
1. Stael-Holstein, Anne Louise Germaine Necker, baronne de, 1766-1817. 2. France—Biography. I. Title.

HEROLD, J. Christopher. 944.04'092'4 B
Mistress to an age : a life of Madame de Stael / by J. Christopher Herold. Westport, Conn. : Greenwood Press, 1975, c1958. viii, 500 p., [7] leaves of plates : ill. ; 22 cm. Reprint of the ed. published by Bobbs-Merrill, Indianapolis. Includes index. Bibliography: p. 477-486. [DC146.S7H44 1975] 75-18399 ISBN 0-8371-8339-1 : 23.25
1. Stael-Holstein, Anne Louise Germaine (Necker) baronne de, 1766-1817. I. Title.

HEROLD, J. Christopher. 928.4
Mistress to an age; a life of Madame de Stael. [1st ed.] Indianapolis, Bobbs-Merrill Co. [1958] 500 p. illus. 22 cm. Includes bibliography. [DC146.S7H44] 58-12385
1. Stael-Holstein, Anne Louise Germaine (Necker) baronne de, 1766-1817. I. Title.

HEROLD, J. Christopher. 944.04'092'4 B
Mistress to an age : a life of Madame de Stael / by J. Christopher Herold. Westport, Conn. : Greenwood Press, 1975, c1958. viii, 500 p., [7] leaves of plat : ill. ; 22 cm. Reprint of the ed. published by Bobbs-Merrill, Indianapolis. Includes index. Bibliography: p. 477-486. [DC146.S7H44 1975] 75-18399 ISBN 0-8371-8339-1 : 23.25
1. Stael-Holstein, Anne Louise Germaine (Necker) baronne de, 1766-1817. I. Title.

LEXAILLANT, Maurice, 1883- 928.4
The passionate exiles; Madame de Stael and Madame Recamjer. Translated from the French by Malcolm Barnes. New York, Farrar, Straus and Cudahy [1958] 334p. 22cm. Translation of Une amitie amoureuse. Includes bibliography. [PQ2431.L13] 58-8551
*1. Stael Holstein, Anne Eouise Germaine (Necker) reader-check validity card update -cards punched out *48 (Bernard) 1777 1849. I. Title.*

LEVAILLANT, Maurice, 1883-1961. 944.05'0922 B
The passionate exiles; Madame de Stael and Madame Recamier. Translated from the French by Malcolm Barnes. Freeport, N.Y., Books for Libraries Press [1971, c1958] xvii, 354 p. illus., ports. 23 cm. (Biography index reprint series) Translation of Une amitie amoureuse. Bibliography: p. 351-354. [PQ2431.L43 1971] 73-160923 ISBN 0-8369-8086-7
1. Stael-Holstein, Anne Louise Germaine (Necker) baronne de, 1766-1817. 2. Recamier, Jeanne Francoise Julie Adelaide (Bernard) 1777-1849. I. Title. BIP

LEVAILLANT, Maurice, 1883-1961. 944.05'0922 B
The passionate exiles; Madame de Stael and Madame Recamier. Translated from the French by Malcolm Barnes. Freeport, N.Y., Books for Libraries Press [1971, c1958] xvii, 354 p. illus., ports. 23 cm. (Biography index reprint series) Translation

of Une amitie amoureuse. Bibliography: p. 351-354. [PQ2431.L43 1971] 73-160923 ISBN 0-8369-8086-7
1. Stael-Holstein, Anne Louise Germaine (Necker) baronne de, 1766-1817. 2. Recamier, Jeanne Francoise Julie Adelaide (Bernard) 1777-1849. I. Title. **BIP**

STAEL-HOLSTEIN, Anne 846'.6
Louise Germaine (Necker), baronne de, 1766-1817.
De Stael-Du Pont letters; correspondence of Madame de Stael and Pierre Samuel Du Pont de Nemours and of other members of the Necker and Du Pont families. Edited and translated by James F. Marshall. Madison, University of Wisconsin Press, 1968. xxvii, 400 p. facsims., ports. 25 cm. English and French. [PQ2431.Z5A22] 68-9020 12.50
1. Du Pont de Nemours, Pierre Samuel, 1739-1817. II. Marshall, James Fred, 1912- ed. III. Title.

WEST, Anthony, 1914- 840'.9' B
Mortal wounds. New York, McGraw Hill [1973] x, 371 p. 24 cm. Bibliography: p. [365]-371. [PQ149.W4] 72-10469 ISBN 0-07-069475-3 10.00
1. Stael-Holstein, Anne Louise Germaine (Necker) baronnede, 1766-1817. 2. Charriere, Isabella Agneta (van Tuyll) de, d. 1805. 3. Sand, George, pseud. of Mme. Dudevant, 1804-1876. I. Title.

STAEL-HOLSTEIN, Anne 846'.6
Louise Germaine (Necker), baronne de, 1766-1817.
De Stael-Du Pont letters; correspondence of Madame de Stael and Pierre Samuel Du Pont de Nemours and of other members of the Necker and Du Pont families. Edited and translated by James F. Marshall. Madison, University of Wisconsin Press, 1968. xxvii, 400 p. facsims., ports. 25 cm. English and French. [PQ2431.Z5A22] 68-9020 12.50
I. Du Pont de Nemours, Pierre Samuel, 1739-1817. II. Marshall, James Fred, 1912- ed. III. Title.

Stagaard, George Hansen.

STAGAARD, George 209'.2'4 B
Hansen.
Pursuer or pursued [incidents from my life, by George Hansen Stagaard as told through P. P. W. New York, Loizeaux Bros., 1954?] 31 p. 17 cm. (Treasury of truth, no. 200) Cover title. [BR1725.S73A33] 75-304115
1. Stagaard, George Hansen. I. P. P. W. II. W., P. P. III. Title. IV. Series.

Stage lighting.

ROSENTHAL, Jean, 1912- 792'.025 B
The magic of light: the craft and career of Jean Rosenthal, pioneer in lighting for the modern stage [by] Jean Rosenthal and Lael Wertenbaker. Illus. by Marion Kinsella. [1st ed.] Boston, Little, Brown [1972] ix, 256 p. illus. 27 cm. Bibliography: p. 249-250. [PN2091.E4R68] 72-6465 ISBN 0-316-93120-9 15.00
1. Stage lighting. I. Wertenbaker, Lael Tucker, 1909- joint author. II. Title. **BIP**

Stagg, Amos Alonzo, 1862-1965.

CONSIDINE, Robert Bernard, 927.96
1906-
The unreconstructed amateur; a pictorial biography of Amos Alonzo Stagg. Illus. by Ray Sullivan. Ed. by Ralph Cahn. Amos Alonzo Stagg Found. [dist. Palo Alto, Calif., Stacey's, 2575 Hanover St., c.1962] 154p. illus. 29cm. 62-51941 7.50
1. Stagg, Amos Alonzo, 1862- I. Title.

LUCIA, Ellis. 796.332'0924 B
Mr. Football: Amos Alonzo Stagg. South Brunswick, A. S. Barnes [1970] 283 p. illus., ports. 22 cm. Bibliography: p. 271-273. [GV939.S7L8] 76-88283 7.50
1. Stagg, Amos Alonzo, 1862-1965. I. Title.

Stagg, Harry P., 1898-

O'BRIEN, Bonnie 286'.1'0924 B
Ball.
Harry P. Stagg : Christian statesman / Bonnie Ball O'Brien. Nashville : Broadman Press, c1976. 190 p. : ill. ; 21 cm. Bibliography: p. 190. [BX6495.S744O25] 76-18622 ISBN 0-8054-7215-0 pbk. : 3.00
1. Stagg, Harry P., 1898- 2. Baptists—Clergy—Biography. 3. Clergy—New Mexico—Biography.

Stagg, Henry, 1861-1954.

CARRUTH, Gertrude 976.4'06'0924
(Stagg)
Papa was in a hurry. San Antonio, Naylor Co. [1967] xi, 107 p. illus. 22 cm. [CT275.S645C3] 66-28868
1. Stagg, Henry, 1861-1954. I. Title.

Stahl, Ana Christina (Carlsen)

WESTPHAL, Barbara Osborne 922.685
Ana Stahl of the Andes and Amazon. Illustrated by Vernon Nye. Mountain View, Calif., Pacific Press Pub. Association [c.1960] viii, 127p. illus. 23cm. 60-16412 3.00
1. Stahl, Ana Christina (Carlsen) 2. Missions—Peru. I. Title.

Stainback, Berry.

STAINBACK, Berry. 796.332'64'0922
Football stars. New York, Pyramid Books [etc.] v. illus, ports. 18 cm. annual. Each vol. carries also in the title the year of issue, i.e., Football stars of 1967. [GV939.A1S72] 66-9834
I. Title.

Stainislaus, Sister, 1863-1949.

DOHERTY, Edward Joseph, 926.1
1890-
A nun with a gun, Sister Stanislaus, a biography. Milwaukee, Bruce Pub. Co. [c.1960] viii, 194p. 22cm. 60-15477 3.50
1. Stainislaus, Sister, 1863-1949. I. Title.

Stalin, Iosif, 1879-1953.

ADAMS, Arthur E. 947.084'2'0924 B
Stalin and his times [by] Arthur E. Adams. New York, Holt, Rinehart and Winston [1972] x, 243 p. illus. 21 cm. (Berkshire studies in history) Bibliography: p. 222-232. [DK268.S8A55] 70-183627 ISBN 0-03-085094-0
1. Stalin, Iosif, 1879-1953. 2. Russia—History—1925-1953. I. Title. **BIP**

ARCHER, Jules. 947.08420924
Man of steel, Joseph Stalin. New York, J. Messner [1965] 191 p. 22 cm. Bibliography: p. 179-181. [DK268.S8A72] 65-21606
1. Stalin, Iosif, 1879-1953. I. Title.

DEUTSCHER, Isaac 923.247
Stalin, a political biography New York, Vintage Books [c.1949, 1960] xxii, 600p. 19cm. (Vintage Russian Library R-1003) 1.65 pap.,
1. Stalin, Iosif, 1879-1953. I. Title.

DEUTSCHER, Isaac, 947.084'2'0924
1907-
Stalin; a political biography, 2d ed. New York, Oxford University Press, 1967 [c1966] xvi, 6 d. p. illus., ports. 22 cm. Bibliography: p. [631]-636. [DK268.S8D48 1967] 67-4373
1. Stalin, Iosif, 1879-1953. I. Title.

DEUTSCHER, 947.08420924 (B)
Isaac, 1907-
Stalin: a political biography, Revised ed. Harmondsworth, Penguin, 1966. 648 p. 18 1/2 cm. (Political leaders of the twentieth century) 10/6 Pelican book. A757. [DK268.S8D48 1966] 66-72866
1. Stalin, Iosif, 1870-1953. I. Title.

DEUTSCHER, Isaac, 947.084'2'0924
1907-1967.
Stalin; a political biography. 2d ed. New York, Oxford University Press, 1967, [c1966] xvi, 661 p. illus., ports. 22 cm. Bibliography: p. [631]-636. [DK268.S8D48 1967] 67-4373
1. Stalin, Iosif, 1879-1953. **BIP**

DEUTSCHER, Isaac, 327'.2'0924
1907-1967.
Stalin: a political biography [by] I. Deutscher. 2nd ed. London, New York [etc.] Oxford U. P., 1967. xix, 681 p. 15 plates (incl. ports. facsim.) 23 cm. 63/- (B 67-16686) Bibliography: p. 631-636. [DK268.S8D48] [947.084'2'0924] 67-97902
1. Stalin, Iosif, 1879-1953. I. Title.

DEUTSCHER, 947.084'2'0924 (B)
Issac, 1907-
Stalin: a political biography [by] I. Deutscher. 2nd ed. London, New York [etc.] Oxford U.P., 1967. xix, 661 p. 15 plates (incl. ports., facsim.) 22 1/2 cm. 63/ Bibliography: p. 631-636. [DK268.S8D48 1967b] 67-97902
1. Stalin, Iosif, 1879-1953. I. Title.

FELDMAN, A. Bronson 923.247
Stalin: red lord of Russia, 1879-1953. Philadelphia, Mercury Bks., 1512 Walnut St. [c.1962] 253p. 18cm. (Mod. biog. ser., MB102) 62-5024 .75 pap.,
1. Stalin, Iosif, 1879-1953. I. Title.

FISCHER, Louis, 1896- 923.247
The life and death of Stalin. [1st ed.] New York, Harper [1952] 272 p. illus. 22 cm. [DK268.S8F58] 52-5433
1. Stalin, Iosif, 1879- 2. Russia—Hist.—1917- I. Title.

GRAHAM, Stephen, 947.084'2'0924
1884-
Stalin; an impartial study of the life and work of Joseph Stalin. Port Washington, N.Y., Kennikat Press [1970] viii, 148 p. port. 21 cm. Reprint of the 1931 ed. Bibliography: p. 143. [DK268.S8 1970] 73-112803
1. Stalin, Iosif, 1879-1953.

HINGLEY, Ronald. 947.084'2'0924
Joseph Stalin: man and legend. New York, McGraw-Hill [1974] xxi, 482 p. illus. 25 cm. Bibliography: p. 454-468. [DK268.S8H56] 74-991 ISBN 0-07-028943-3 15.00
1. Stalin, Iosif, 1879-1953. 2. Russia—History—1925-1953. I. Title.

HUTTON, J. Bernard, 923.247
pseud.
Stalin, the miraculous Georgian. Pref. by Sir Robert Bruce Lockhart. London, N. Spearman [1961] 375p. illus. 23cm. [DK268.S8 H89] 62-5243 8.75 bds.,
1. Stalin, Iosif, 1879-1953. I. Title.
American distributor: Intl. Pubns. Serv., New York

HYDE, Harford 947.084'2'0924 [B]
Montgomery, 1907-
Stalin, the history of a dictator [by] H. Montgomery Hyde. New York, Popular Library [1974, c1971] 679 p. illus. 18 cm. Bibliography: p. 617-629. [DK268.S8H92 1974] 71-164541 1.95 (pbk.)
1. Stalin, Iosif, 1879-1953 2. Russia—Politics and government—1917-1936. 3. Russia—Politics and government—1936-1953. I. Title.

KROTKOV, 947.084'2092'4 B
IUrii, 1917-
The red monarch : scenes from the life of Stalin / Yuri Krotkov ; translated by Tanya E. Mairs ; edited by Carol Houck Smith. 1st ed. New York : Norton, c1979. 253 p. : port. ; 22 cm. [DK268.S8K7413 1979] 78-12127 ISBN 0-393-08836-7 : 10.95
1. Stalin, Iosif, 1879-1953. 2. Heads of state—Russia—Biography. I. Smith, Carol Houck. II. Title. **BIP**

LEVINE, Isaac Don, 1892- 923.247
Stalin's great secret. New York, Coward-McCann [1956] 126p. illus. 20cm. 'Author's postscript': 21. inserted. [DK268.S8L43] 56-10359
1. Stalin, Iosif, 1879-1953. I. Title.

MCNEAL, Robert 016.94708420924
Hatch, 1930-
Stalin's works; an annotated bibliography, comp. by Robert H. McNeal. [Stanford, Calif.] Hoover Instn. on War, Revolution, & Peace, Stanford Univ., 1967. xi, 197p. 26cm. (Hoover Instn. bibl. ser., 26) Bibl. [Z8833.5.M25] 67-15063 5.00
1. Stalin, Iosif, 1870-1953—Bibl. I. Title. II. Series: Stanford University. Hoover Institution on War, Revolution, and Peace. Bibliographical series, 26

PALEY, Alan L. 947.084'2'0924 B
Stalin, the iron-fisted dictator of Russia, by Alan L. Paley. Charlotteville, N.Y., SamHar Press, 1971. 32 p. 22 cm. (Outstanding personalities, no. 7) Bibliography: p. 31-32. [DK268.S8P288] 76-185663
1. Stalin, Iosif, 1879-1953. 2. Russia—History—20th century. I. Title.

PAYNE, Pierre 947.08420924
Stephen Robert, 1911-
The rise and fall of Stalin, by Robert Payne. [New York] Avon [1966, c.1965] 864p. illus. 18cm. (D2) Bibl. [DK268.S8P37] 1.65 pap.,
1. Stalin, Iosif, 1879-1953. I. Title.

RANDALL, Francis 947.08420924
Ballard, 1931-
Stalin's Russia; an historical reconsideration [by] Francis B. Randall. New York, Free Press [1965] 328 p. port. 22 cm. (Historical reconsiderations series) Bibliography: p. 311-317. [DK268.S8R33] 65-18559
1. Stalin, Iosif, 1879-1953. 2. Russia—Politics and government—1936-1953. I. Title. II. Series.

RIGBY, Thomas 947.08420924 B
Henry Richard.
Stalin, edited by T. H. Rigby. Englewood Cliffs, N.J., Prentice-Hall [1966] vii, 182 p. 21 cm. (Great lives observed) (A Spectrum book) "Bibliographical note": p. 179-182. [DK268.S8R524] 66-16348
1. Stalin, Iosif, 1879-1953.

SEATON, Albert, 355.4'3'00924 B
1921-
Stalin as warlord / Albert Seaton. London : Batsford, 1976. 312 p., [8] leaves of plates : ill., maps ; 24 cm. Includes index. Bibliography: p. [294]-300. [DK268.S8S35] 76-365433 ISBN 0-7134-3078-8 : £5.95
1. Stalin, Iosif, 1879-1953. 2. Russia (1923-U.S.S.R.) Armiia. 3. Russia—History, Military—1917- I. Title.

SMITH, Edward Ellis. 947.08'0924
The young Stalin; the early years of an elusive revolutionary. New York, Farrar, Straus and Giroux [1967] ix, 470 p. illus. 23 cm. Bibliography: p. [423]-443. [DK268.S8S52] 67-26488
1. Stalin, Iosif, 1879-1953. I. Title.

SVANIDZE, Budu. 923.247
My uncle, Joseph Stalin; translated and with a pref. by Waverley Root. Introd. by Gregory Bessedovsky. New York, Putnam [c1953] 235p. illus. 21cm. Published in London in 1952 under title: My Uncle Joe. [DK268.S8S8] 52-11030
1. Stalin, Iosif, 1879- I. Title.

TREMAIN, Rose. 947.084'2'0924 B
Stalin / Rose Tremain. New York : Ballantine Books, 1975. 159 p. : ill. ; 21 cm. (War leader book ; no. 31) (Ballantine's illustrated history of the violent century) Bibliography: p. 151. [DK268.S8T66] 75-319618 ISBN 0-345-24391-9 : 2.00
1. Stalin Iosif, 1879-1953. 2. Russia—History—20th century.

TUCKER, Robert 947.084'2'0924 B
C.
Stalin as revolutionary, 1879-1929; a study in history and personality [by] Robert C. Tucker. [1st ed.] New York, Norton [1973] xx, 519 p. illus. 24 cm. Bibliography: p. [494]-504. [DK268.S8T85 1973] 73-6541 ISBN 0-393-05487-X 14.95
1. Stalin, Iosif, 1879-1953. I. Title. **BIP**

ULAM, Adam 947.084'2'0924 B
Bruno, 1922-
Stalin; the man and his era [by] Adam B. Ulam. New York, Viking Press [1973] 760 p. 24 cm. Includes bibliographical references. [DK268.S8U4 1973] 73-6226 ISBN 0-670-66683-1 12.95
1. Stalin, Iosif, 1879-1953. 2. Russia—History—1925-1953. I. Title.

WARTH, Robert D. 947.084'2'0924 B
Joseph Stalin, by Robert D. Warth. New York, Twayne Publishers [1969] 176 p. 22 cm. (Twayne's rulers and statesmen of the world series, TROW 10) Includes bibliographical references. [DK268.S8W3] 70-77033
1. Stalin, Iosif, 1879-1953. I. Title. BIP

Stalin, Iosif, 1879-1953—Juvenile literature.

BLASSINGAME, Wyatt. 947.084'2'0924 B
Joseph Stalin and Communist Russia. Champaign, Ill., Garrard Pub. Co. [1971] 175 p. illus. 22 cm. (A Century book) A biography of the Russian revolutionary who became leader of the Soviet government in 1924 and remained in power until his death in 1953. [DK268.S8B52] 92 70-153153 ISBN 0-8116-4753-6 3.32
1. Stalin, Iosif, 1879-1953—Juvenile literature. 2. Russia—History—1917- —Juvenile literature. I. Title. BIP

LIVERSIDGE, Douglas, 1913- 947.084'2'0924 B
Joseph Stalin. London, New York, Franklin Watts Ltd., 1969. [4], 188 p. 4 plates, map, ports. 23 cm. (Immortals of history) [DK268.S8L54 1969b] 76-31003 ISBN 0-85166-301-X £1.25
1. Stalin, Iosif, 1879-1953—Juvenile literature. I. Title.

LIVERSIDGE, Douglas, 1913- 947.084'2'0924 B
Joseph Stalin. New York, Watts [1969] 188 p. illus., map, ports. 22 cm. (Immortals of history) A biography of the son of a Georgian shoemaker who rose from bitter poverty to rule as terrorist dictator of Communist Russia for twenty-four years. [DK268.S8L54] 92 69-15882
1. Stalin, Iosif, 1879-1953—Juvenile literature. I. Title.

Stallings, Laurence, 1894-1968.

BRITTAIN, Joan T., 1928- 813'.5'2 B
Laurence Stallings / by Joan T. Brittain. Boston : Twayne Publishers, [1975] 128 p. : port. ; 22 cm. (Twayne's United States authors series ; TUSAS 250) Includes index. Bibliography: p. 123-126. [PS3537.T164Z59] 74-23831 ISBN 0-8057-0686-0 lib.bdg. : 6.95
1. Stallings, Laurence, 1894-1968. BIP

Stallone, Sylvester—Juvenile literature.

SIMPSON, Janice Claire. 791.43'028'0924 B
Sylvester Stallone : going the distance / by Janice Simpson. St. Paul : EMC Corp., 1978. p. cm. (Headliners II) Highlights the life and career of the writer and star of the movie "Rocky" which was named best movie of the year. [PN2287.S667S5] 78-18845 ISBN 0-88436-436-4 : 5.95 ISBN 0-88436-437-2 pbk. : 2.95
1. Stallone, Sylvester—Juvenile literature. 2. Moving-picture actors and actresses—United States—Biography—Juvenile literature. I. Title. II. Series. BIP

Stambolov, Stefan Nikolov, 1854-1895.

BEAMAN, Ardern George Hulme, 1857-1929. 949.77'02'0924 B
M. Stambuloff. Freeport, N.Y., Books for Libraries Press [1972] 240 p. ports. 22 cm. Reprint of the 1895 ed. [DR85.5.S7B4 1972] 72-5471 ISBN 0-8369-6896-4
1. Stambolov, Stefan Nikolov, 1854-1895. 2. Bulgaria—History—1878-1944. BIP

Stammers, Gerald,

STAMMERS, Gerald, 1890- 914.2'03'820924 B
I remember. Norwich, (5 Patricia Rd.), [Gerald Stammers], 1971. 64 p. illus., ports. 25 cm. [CT788.S696A3] 72-185506 ISBN 0-9501281-1-2 £0.50
I. Title.

Stamps, Ellen de Kroon, 1940-

STAMPS, Ellen de Kroon, 1940- 269'.2'0922 B
My years with Corrie / Ellen de Kroon Stamps. Old Tappan, N.J. : F. H. Revell Co., c1978. 128 p. ; 22 cm. [BR1725.S733A35] 78-13979 ISBN 0-8007-0957-8 : 5.95
1. Stamps, Ellen de Kroon, 1940- 2. Ten Boom, Corrie. 3. Christian biography—United States. I. Title. BIP

Stanchfield, Wilma.

STANCHFIELD, Wilma. 248'.24 B
Struck by lightning, then by love / Wilma Stanchfield, with Helen Kooiman Hosier. Nashville : T. Nelson, c1979. 180 p. ; 21 cm. [BV4935.S66A37] 79-13763 ISBN 0-8407-5690-9 : 4.95
1. Stanchfield, Wilma. 2. Converts—United States—Biography. I. Hosier, Helen Kooiman, joint author. II. Title.

Standing Bear, Luther, Dakota chief, 1868-1939.

STANDING BEAR, Luther, Dakota chief, 1868-1939. 978.3'9'00497 B
My people, the Sioux / by Luther Standing Bear ; edited by E. A. Brininstool ; with an introd. by Richard N. Ellis. Lincoln : University of Nebraska Press, 1975. xx, 288 p. ; 21 cm. Reprint of the 1928 ed. published by Houghton Mifflin, Boston; with new introd. "A Bison book." Includes bibliographical references. [E99.D1S73 1975] 74-77394 ISBN 0-8032-5793-7 pbk. : 3.95
1. Standing Bear, Luther, Dakota chief, 1868-1939. 2. Dakota Indians. 3. Indians of North America—Great Plains—Social life and customs. I. Title. BIP

Standish, Myles, 1584?-1656.

STEVENSON, Augusta. 973.2'2'0924 B
Myles Standish, adventurous boy. Illustrated by Hazel Hoecker. Indianapolis, Bobbs-Merrill [1962] 200 p. illus. 20 cm. (Childhood of famous Americans) The boyhood of the Englishman, a Separatist, who helped the Pilgrims establish the first English colony in America, at Plymouth. [PZ7.S8467My4] 92 AC 68
1. Standish, Myles, 1584?-1656. I. Hoecker, Hazel, illus. II. Title.

Stanfield, Robert, 1914-

HALIBURTON, Ed D. 320'.92'4 B
My years with Stanfield, by E. D. Haliburton. Windsor, N.S., Lancelot Press [1972] 116 p. illus. 21 cm. [F1038.S74H34] 73-330978
1. Stanfield, Robert, 1914- 2. Nova Scotia—Politics and government. I. Title.

Stanford, Charles Villiers, Sir, 1852-1924.

PORTE, John Fielder. 780'.92'4 B
Sir Charles V. Stanford / by John F. Porte. New York : Da Capo Press, 1976. 154 p., [1] leaf of plates : ill. ; 23 cm. (Da Capo Press music reprint series) Reprint of the 1921 ed. published by K. Paul, Trench, Trubner, London. [MT92.S8P6 1976] 76-12570 ISBN 0-306-70790X : 15.00
1. Stanford, Charles Villiers, Sir, 1852-1924. Works. BIP

Stanford, Jane Lathrop, 1828-1905.

NAGEL, Gunther W. 378.794'73 B
Jane Stanford, her life and letters / by Gunther W. Nagel. Stanford, Calif. : Stanford Alumni Association, c1975. x, 179 p., [4] leaves of plates : ill. ; 24 cm. Bibliography: p. 178-179. [LD3024.5.S7N33] 75-31393 ISBN 0-916318-00-1. ISBN 0-916318-01-X pbk.
1. Stanford, Jane Lathrop, 1828-1905. I. Stanford, Jane Lathrop, 1828-1905. Jane Stanford, her life and letters. II. Title.

Stanford, Leland, 1824-1893.

BANCROFT, Hubert Howe, 1832-1918. 923.373
History of the life of Leland Stanford, a character study. [1st Calif. ed.] Oakland, Calif., Biobooks, 1952. vii, 235p. ports. 27cm. (Great American statesmen, no. 3) California relations, 34. This work, which was omitted from the author's Chronicles of the builders of the commonwealth, for which it was originally prepared, is now published for the first time. The ms. was found complete in the Huncroft Library of the University of California. [E664.S78B3] 53-652
1. Stanford, Leland, 1824-1893. I. Title.

HOYT, Edwin Palmer. 979.4'04'0924 B
Leland Stanford, by Edwin P. Hoyt. London, New York [etc.] Abelard-Schuman [1967] 160 p. illus., ports. 22 cm. Bibliography: p. 155. A biography of the innkeeper's son who became Governor of California, builder of a great railroad, United States Senator, and founder of Stanford University. [E664.S78H6] 92 AC 68
1. Stanford, Leland, 1824-1893. I. Title.

TUTOROW, Norman E. 979.4'04'0924 B
Leland Stanford: man of many careers [by] Norman E. Tutorow. Menlo Park, Calif., Pacific Coast Publishers [1971] xiii, 317 p. illus., ports. 24 cm. Bibliography: p. 297-312. [E664.S78T8] 79-129813 9.95
1. Stanford, Leland, 1824-1893. I. Title.

Stanford, Leland, 1824-1893—Juvenile literature.

HOYT, Edwin Palmer. 979.4'04'0924
Leland Stanford, by Edwin P. Hoyt. London, New York, Abelard [1967] 160p. illus., facsims., map, group ports. 22cm. Bibl. [E664.S78H6] (B) 67-18119 4.50
1. Stanford, Leland, 1824-1893—Juvenile literature. I. Title.

Stanford, Sally.

STANFORD, Sally. 301.415 B
The lady of the house; the autobiography of Sally Stanford. New York, Putnam [1966] 255 p. 22 cm. [HQ144.S75] 66-14341
I. Title.

Stanford, University. School of Medicine—Biography.

NAGEL, Gunther W. 610'.922 B
A Stanford heritage; sketches of ten teacher-physicians whose standards of excellence became the hallmark of a School of Medicine, by Gunther W. Nagel. Stanford, Calif., Stanford Medical Alumni Association [1970] 113 p. illus., ports. 26 cm. Contents.Contents.—David Starr Jordan.—William Ophuls.—Ray Lyman Wilbur.—Albion Walter Hewlett.—Stanley Stillman.—Emmet Rixford.—Robert Reid Newell.—Arthur L. Bloomfield.—Ludwig A. Emge.—Harold K. Faber. [R747.S75N3] 75-114854
1. Stanford, University. School of Medicine—Biography. I. Title.

Stanhope, Hester Lucy, Lady, 1776-1839.

SYMONDS, Emily Morse, d.1936. 920.042
Little memoirs of the nineteenth century. Freeport, N.Y., Books for Libraries Press [1969] ix, 375 p. ports. 23 cm. (Essay index reprint series) Reprint of the 1902 ed. Contents.Contents.—Benjamin Robert Haydon.—Lady Morgan (Sydney Owenson)—Nathaniel Parker Willis.—Lady Hester Stanhope.—Prince Puckler-Muskau in England.—William and Mary Howitt. [DA531.1.S9 1969] 70-86787 ISBN 8-369-11970-
1. Puckler-Muskau, Hermann Ludwig Heinrich, furst von, 1785-1871. 2. Morgan, Sydney (Owenson) lady, 1783?-1859. 3. Haydon, Benjamin Robert, 1786-1846. 4. Willis, Nathaniel Parker, 1806-1867. 5. Stanhope, Hester Lucy, Lady, 1776-1839. 6. Howitt, William, 1792-1879. 7. Howitt, Mary (Botham) 1799-1888. I. Title. BIP

LESLIE, Doris. 915.69 [B]
The desert queen. New York, Popular Library [1973, c.1972] 240 p. 18 cm. [DA536.S8L47] 0.95 (pbk.)
1. Stanhope, Lady Hester Lucy, 1776-1839. I. Title.
L.C. card no. for the hardbound (London) edition: 72-186934.

Stanislaus, Sister, 1863-1949.

LANCASTER, Vincentine. 922.244
Katie Malone, in religion Sister Stanislaus; a biography. St. Louis, Marillac Provincial House [1963?] viii, 83 p. illus., ports. 17 cm. [BX4705.S795L3] 67-38551
1. Stanislaus, Sister, 1863-1949. I. Title.

Stanislavskii, Konstantin Sergeevich, 1863-1938.

GORCHAKOV, Nikolai Mikhailovich. 927.92
Stanislavsky directs. Translation by Miriam Goldina. Virginia Stevens, translation editor. Foreword by Norris Houghton. New York, Funk & Wagnalls [1954] 402 p. 22 cm. Translation of Rezhisserskie uroki K. S. Stanislavskogo. [PN2728.S78G613] 54-9737
1. Stanislavskii, Konstantin Sergeevich, 1863-1938. I. Title. BIP

GORCHAKOV, Nikolai Mikhailovich. 792'.028'0924
Stanislavsky directs, by Nikolai M. Gorchakov. Translation by Miriam Goldina. Virginia Stevens, translation editor. Foreword by Norris Houghton. Westport, Conn., Greenwood Press [1974, c1954] x, 402 p. 23 cm. Translation of Rezhisserskie uroki K. S. Stanislavskogo. Reprint of the 1968 ed., published by Minerva Press, New York. [PN2728.S78G613 1974] 73-15243 ISBN 0-8371-7164-4
1. Stanislavskii, Konstantin Sergeevich, 1863-1938. I. Title.

MAGARSHACK, David. 792'.028'0924 B
Stanislavsky : a life / David Magarshack. Westport, Conn. : Greenwood Press, 1975. vii, 416 p.,[6] leaves of plates : ill. ; 23 cm. Reprint of the 1950 ed. published by Macgibbon & Kee, London; with new appendix. Includes index. [PN2728.S78M33 1975] 74-2558 ISBN 0-8371-7416-3 lib.bdg. : 22.00
1. Stanislavskii, Konstantin Sergeevich, 1863-1938. 2. Moscow. Moskovskii khudozhestvennyi akademicheskii teatr. I. Title.

Stanislaw Kostka, Saint, 1550-1568.

KERNS, Joseph E 922.2438
Portrait of a champion; a life of St. Stanley Kostka. Westminster, Md., Newman Press, 1957. 278p. 23cm. Includes bibliography. [BX4700.S7K4] 57-8613
1. Stanislaw Kostka, Saint, 1550-1568. I. Title.

UMINSKI, Sigmund H. 282'.0924 B
No greater love; a story of Saint Stanislaus Kostka, by Sigmund H. Uminski. With a foreword by John Cardinal Krol. New York, Polish Publication Society of America [1969] xv, 57 p. illus. 23 cm. (Saints who made history) [BX4700.S7U4] 70-97138 3.00
1. StanisOaw Kostka, Saint, 1550-1568. I. Title.

Stanislaw Kostka, Saint, 1550-1568 — Juvenile literature.

SIGISMUND, Brother, Brother 92
The lad who hiked to heaven; a story of Saint Stanislaus Kostka. Illus. by Carolyn Lee Jagodits. Rev. Notre Dame, Ind., Dujarie Pr., 1966 [c.1945, 1966] 93p. illus. 24cm. [BX4700.S7S5] 66-12691 2.25
1. Stanislaw Kostka, Saint, 1550-1568 — Juvenile literature. I. Title.

Stanley, Arthur Penrhyn, 1815-1881.

DARK, Sidney, 1874- 283'.0922
1947.
Five Deans: John Colet, John Donne, Jonathan Swift, Arthur Penrhyn Stanley, William Ralph Inge. Freeport, N.Y., Books for Libraries Press [1969] 255 p. 23 cm. (Essay index reprint series) Reprint of the 1928 ed. [BX5197.D25 1969b] 71-93332
1. Colet, John, 1467?-1519. 2. Donne, John, 1573-1631. 3. Swift, Jonathan, 1667-1745. 4. Stanley, Arthur Penrhyn, 1815-1881. 5. Inge, William Ralph, 1860-1954. I. Title.

DARK, Sidney, 1874- 283'.0922
1947.
Five Deans: John Colet, John Donne, Jonathan Swift, Arthur Penrhyn Stanley, William Ralph Inge. Port Washington, N.Y., Kennikat Press [1969] 255 p. 21 cm. (Essay and general literature index reprint series) Reprint of the 1928 ed. [BX5197.D25 1969] 70-86011
1. Colet, John, 1467?-1519. 2. Donne, John, 1573-1631. 3. Swift, Jonathan, 1667-1745. 4. Stanley, Arthur Penrhyn, 1815-1881. 5. Inge, William Ralph, 1860-1954. I. Title.

Stanley-Brown, Mary Garfield, b. 1867.

FEIS, Ruth Stanley-Brown. 92
Mollie Garfield in the White House. Chicago, Rand McNally [1963] 128 p. illus., ports. 22 cm. [E687.F4] 63-12329
1. Stanley-Brown, Mary Garfield, b. 1867. 2. Garfield, James Abram, Pres. U.S., 1831-1881. 3. Garfield family.

Stanley, Clarence Ballard, 1889-1969.

CARRAWAY, W. B. 286'.1'0924 B
Mr. Benevolence of Association Baptists; a biography of Clarence Ballard Stanley, by W. B. Carraway. [Texarkana, Ark., 1974] 100 p. illus. 23 cm. [BX6495.S755C37] 74-80033
1. Stanley, Clarence Ballard, 1889-1969. I. Title.

Stanley, Francis Edgar, 1849-1918—Juvenile literature.

JACKSON, Robert B. 629.22'92
The steam cars of the Stanley twins, by Robert B. Jackson. New York, H. Z. Walck [1969] 59 p. illus., ports. 23 cm. Describes the building and performance of the "teakettle on wheels" constructed at the turn of the twentieth century by the Stanley twins. [TL200.J3] 70-82674 3.75
1. Stanley, Francis Edgar, 1849-1918—Juvenile literature. 2. Stanley, Freelan Oscar, 1849-1940—Juvenile literature. 3. Automobiles, Steam—Juvenile literature. I. Title.

Stanley, Henry Morton, Sir, 1841-1904.

ANSTRUTHER, Ian. 923.942
Dr. Livingstone, I presume? [1st American ed.] New York, Dutton, 1957 [c1956] 207 p. illus. 22 cm. Published in London in 1956 under title: I presume. [DT351.S9A6 1957] 57-5333
1. Stanley, Henry Morton, Sir, 1841-1904. 2. Livingstone, David, 1813-1873.

BENET, Laura. 923.942
Stanley, invincible explorer. Illustrated with photos. New York, Dodd, mead, 1955. 299p. illus. 21cm. [DT351.S9B4] 55-5155
1. Stanley, Henry Morton, Sir 1841-1904. I. Title.

BUEL, James William, 916'.03
1849-1920.
Heroes of the Dark Continent; a complete history of all the great explorations and discoveries in Africa, from the earliest ages to the present time. Freeport, N.Y., Books for Libraries Press, 1971 [c1889] 576 p. illus., maps (1 fold.), ports. 27 cm. (The Black heritage library collection) [DT3.B75] 73-138333 ISBN 0-8369-8725-X
1. Stanley, Henry Morton, Sir, 1841-1904. 2. Schnitzer, Eduard, known as Emin Pasha, 1840-1892. 3. Livingstone, David, 1813-1873. 4. Africa—Discovery and exploration. 5. Explorers. I. Title. II. Series.

FARWELL, Byron. 916.7'04 B
The man who presumed; a biography of Henry M. Stanley. Westport, Conn., Greenwood Press [1974, c1957] ix, 334 p. 23 cm. Reprint of the ed. published by H. Holt, New York. Bibliography: p. 321-326. [DT351.S9F3 1974] 73-15205 ISBN 0-8371-7160-1 15.25
1. Stanley, Henry Morton, Sir, 1841-1904. I. Title.

FEATHER, A. G. 916.7
Stanley's story; or, Through the wilds of Africa; a thrilling narrative of his remarkable adventures, terrible experiences, wonderful discoveries and amazing achievements in the Dark Continent ... From information, data, and the official reports of Henry M. Stanley, by A. G. Feather. Chicago, Afro-Am Press, 1969. xx, 533 p. illus. 22 cm. Reprint of the 1890 ed. [DT351.F28 1969] 77-99411
1. Stanley, Henry Morton, Sir, 1841-1904. 2. Livingstone, David, 1813-1873. 3. Africa, Central—Description and travel. I. Title.

SMITH, Fredrika 916.7'04'0924 B
Shumway.
Stanley, African explorer. Illustrated by Charles Moser. [Chicago] Rand McNally [1968] 240 p. illus., map (on lining papers), ports. 22 cm. A biography of the boy, disowned by his family, whose wanderings eventually led him to international fame as the man who found Livingstone and explored the heart of Africa. [DT351.S9S62] 92 AC 68
1. Stanley, Henry Morton, Sir, 1841-1904. I. Moser, Charles, illus. II. Title.

STANLEY, Henry Morton, 916.7'04 B
Sir, 1841-1904.
The autobiography of Sir Henry Morton Stanley. Edited by his wife, Dorothy Stanley. New York, Greenwood Press [1969] xvii, 551 p. illus., facsims., map, ports. 24 cm. Reprint of the 1909 ed. "Books written by Henry M. Stanley": p. [541]. [DT351.S6A3 1969] 69-14097
I. Title.

Stanley, Henry Morton, Sir, 1841-1904—Juvenile literature.

ALTER, Robert Edmond. 910.09'42
Henry M. Stanley, the man from Africa. New York, Putnam [1967] 159 p. 22 cm. Bibliography: p. 154-155. [DT351.S9A48] 67-24135
1. Stanley, Henry Morton, Sir, 1841-1904—Juvenile literature.

EDUCATIONAL Research 916.704 B
Council of America. Social Science Staff.
Explorers and discoverers: Stanley and Livingstone, and people Stanley and Livingstone met. Boston, Allyn and Bacon [1970] 60 p. illus. (part col.), ports. (part col.) 21 cm. (Concepts and inquiry: the ERC social science program) An easy-to-read account of the work and travels of the English missionary, Dr. Livingstone, and his famous meeting with the journalist, Stanley. Also describes the subsequent voyages and discoveries made by Stanley. [DT351.S9E3] 920 77-97110
1. Stanley, Henry Morton, Sir, 1841-1904—Juvenile literature. 2. Livingstone, David, 1813-1873—Juvenile literature. I. Title. II. Title: Stanley and Livingstone, and people Stanley and Livingstone met. III. Series: Concepts and inquiry: the Educational Research Council social science program

GRAVES, Charles 916.7'04 B
Parlin, 1911-
A world explorer: Henry Morton Stanley, by Charles P. Graves. Illustrated by Nathan Goldstein. Champaign, Ill., Garrard Pub. Co. [1967] 96 p. col. illus., col. maps (on lining papers) 24 cm. (World explorer books) A biography of the journalist and explorer who not only found Dr. Livingstone but made many other important discoveries in Africa on subsequent journeys. [DT351.S9G7] 92 67-10038 2.19
1. Stanley, Henry Morton, Sir, 1841-1904—Juvenile literature. I. Goldstein, Nathan, illus. II. Title.

SMITH, Fredrika Shumway. 92 (J)
Stanley, African explorer. Illustrated by Charles Moser. [Chicago] Rand McNally [1968] 240 p. illus., map (on lining papers), ports. 22 cm. [DT351.S9S62] 68-14560
1. Stanley, Henry Morton, Sir, 1841-1904—Juvenile literature. I. Title.

WALTERS, Helen B j92
Henry Stanley & his secret key. St. Louis, Bethany Press [1963] 103 p. 21 cm. [DT351.S9W26] 63-17871
1. Stanley, Sir Henry Morton, 1841-1904 — Juvenile literature. I. Title.

Stanley, Sir Henry Morton. 1841-1904.

ALTER, Robert Edmond. 910.09'42
Henry M. Stanley, the man from Africa. New York, Putnam [1967] 159 p. 22 cm. Bibliography: p. 154-155. [DT351.S9A48] 67-24135
1. Stanley, Sir Henry Morton, I. Title.

ANSTRUTHER, Ian. 923.942
Dr. L Livingstone. Ippresume; [1st American ed.] New York, Dutton. 1957 [c1956] 207p. illus. 22cm. Published in London in 1956 under title: I presume. [DT351.S9A6 1957] 57-5333
1. Stanley, Sir Henry Morton. 1841-1904. 2. Livingstone, David. 1813-1873. I. Title.

HALL, Richard 916.7'04'0924 B
Seymour, 1925-
Stanley : an adventurer explored / Richard Hall. 1st American ed. Boston : Houghton Mifflin, 1975, c1974. 400 p. : ill. ; 24 cm. Includes indexes. Bibliography: p. 370-388. [DT351.S9H27 1975] 74-30393 ISBN 0-395-19426-1 : 12.50
1. Stanley, Henry Morton, Sir, 1844-1904.

STANLEY, sir Henry 916.7'03
Morton, 1841-1904.
Through the dark continent; or, The sources of the Nile around the great lakes of equatorial Africa and down the Livingstone River to the Atlantic Ocean. New York, Greenwood Press [1969] 2 v. illus. 24 cm. Reprint of the 1878 ed. [DT351.S83 1969] 68-55223
1. Africa, Central—Description and travel. I. Title.

Stanley, William, 1858-1916.

HAWKINS, Laurence Ashley, 926.213
1877-
William Stanley (1858-1916) his life and work. New York, Newcomen Society in North America, 1951. 52 p. illus. 23 cm. [TK140.S75H3] 52-1266
1. Stanley, William, 1858-1916. I. Title.

Stanmore, Arthur Hamilton-Gordon, baron, 1829-1912.

CHAPMAN, James Keith, 325'.31'096
1919-
The career of Arthur Hamilton Gordon, first Lord Stanmore, 1829-1912 [by] J. K. Chapman. [Toronto] University of Toronto Press [1964] vii, 387 p. illus., ports. 24 cm. Bibliography: p. [373]-377. [DA17.S7C5] 65-2477
1. Stanmore, Arthur Hamilton-Gordon, baron, 1829-1912. 2. Gt. Brit. — Colonies — Administration. I. Title.

Stans, Maurice H., 1908-

STANS, Maurice H., 364.1'32'0973
1908-
The terrors of justice : the untold side of Watergate / Maurice H. Stans. 1st ed. New York : Everest House, c1978. xii, 478 p. ; 24 cm. Includes bibliographical references and index. [E860.S8 1978] 78-57417 ISBN 0-89696-020-X : 10.95
1. Stans, Maurice H., 1908- 2. Watergate Affair, 1972- —Personal narratives. 3. Cabinet officers—United States—Biography. I. Title.

Stanton, Edwin McMasters, 1814-1869.

FLOWER, Frank 973.7'092'4 B
Abial, 1854-1911.
Edwin McMasters Stanton, the autocrat of rebellion, emancipation, and reconstruction. Akron, Ohio, Saalfield Pub. Co., 1905. [New York, AMS Press, 1973] 425 p. illus. 23 cm. [E467.1.S8F62 1973] 78-169090 ISBN 0-404-04590-1 18.00
1. Stanton, Edwin McMasters, 1814-1869.

PRATT, Fletcher, 1897- 923.273
1956.
Stanton, Lincoln's Secretary of War. [1st ed.] New York, Norton [1953] xiii, 520 p. port., maps. 22 cm. [E467.1.S8P7] 53-12171
1. Stanton, Edwin McMasters, 1814-1869. 2. U.S.—History—Civil War, 1861-1865.
BIP

THOMAS, Benjamin Platt, 923.273
1902-1956.
Stanton: the life and times of Lincoln's Secretary of War [by] Benjamin P. Thomas and Harold M. Hyman. [1st ed.] New York, Knopf, 1962. xvii, 642. xii p. illus., ports., facsim. 25 cm. Bibliographical footnotes. [E467.1.S8T45] 61-17829
1. Stanton, Edwin McMasters, 1814-1869. I. Title.

THOMAS, Benjamin Platt, 923.273
1902-1956.
Stanton, the life and times of Lincoln's Secretary of War [by] Benjamin P. Thomas and Harold M. Hyman. [1st ed.] New York, Knopf, 1962. xvii, 642, xii p. illus., ports., facsim. 25 cm. Bibliographical footnotes. [E467.1.S8T45] 61-17829
1. Stanton, Edwin McMasters, 1814-1869. I. Hyman, Harold Melvin, 1924- joint author.

Stanton, Elizabeth (Cady) 1815-1902.

LUTZ, Alma. 324'.3'0924 B
Created equal; a biography of Elizabeth Cady Stanton, 1815-1902. New York, Octagon Books, 1974 [c1940] xi, 345 p. illus. 23 cm. Reprint of the ed. published by the J. Day Co., New York. Bibliography: p. 327-330. [JK1899.S7L88 1974] 74-6500 ISBN 0-374-95167-5 14.00
1. Stanton, Elizabeth Cady, 1815-1902. 2. Women—Rights of women. I. Title.
BIP

OAKLEY, Mary Ann B. 324'.3'0924 B
Elizabeth Cady Stanton [by] Mary Ann B. Oakley. [1st ed. Old Westbury, N.Y.] Feminist Press, 1972. 148, [7] p. port. 18 cm. (Feminist Press biography, no. 2) Bibliography: p. [149] [HQ1413.S67O15] 72-80249 ISBN 0-912670-03-7 1.50
1. Stanton, Elizabeth (Cady) 1815-1902.
BIP

STANTON, Elizabeth 324'.3'0924 B
(Cady) 1815-1902.
Eighty years and more; reminiscences,

1815-1897. With a new introd. by Gail Parker. New York, Schocken Books [1971] xx, 474 p. ports. 21 cm. (Studies in the life of women) Reprint of the 1898 ed. Includes bibliographical references. [JK1899.S7A3 1971] 75-162284 ISBN 0-8052-0324-9 (pbk) 3.95
I. Title. BIP

STANTON, Elizabeth (Cady) 1815-1902. 324.3'0924 B
Eighty years and more (1815-1897); reminiscences of Elizabeth Lady Stanton. [New York] Source Book Press [1970] ix, 474 p. ports. 22 cm. Reprint of the 1898 ed. [JK1899.S7A3 1970] 76-133997 ISBN 0-87681-082-2
I. Title.

STANTON, Elizabeth (Cady) 1815-1902. 324'.3'0924 B
Eighty years and more; reminiscences, 1815-1897. With a new introd. by Gail Parker. New York, Schocken Books [1971] xx, 474 p. ports. 21 cm. (Studies in the life of women) Reprint of the 1898 ed. Includes bibliographical references. [JK1899.S7A3 1971] 75-162284 ISBN 0-8052-0324-9 (pbk) 3.95
I. Title. BIP

STANTON, Elizabeth (Cady) 1815-1902. 324.3'0924 B
Eighty years and more (1815-1897); reminiscences of Elizabeth Lady Stanton. [New York] Source Book Press [1970] ix, 474 p. ports. 22 cm. Reprint of the 1898 ed. [JK1899.S7A3 1970] 76-133997 ISBN 0-87681-082-2
I. Title.

STANTON, Elizabeth (Cady) 1815-1902. 324'.3'0924 B
Elizabeth Cady Stanton. Edited by Theodore Stanton and Harriot Stanton Blatch. New York, Arno, 1969. 2 v. illus., ports. 23 cm. Bibliographical footnotes. [JK1899.S7A4 1969] 77-79183
I. Stanton, Theodore, 1851-1925, ed. II. Blatch, Harriot (Stanton) 1856-1940, ed.

STANTON, Elizabeth (Cady) 1815-1902. 324'.3'0924 B
Elizabeth Cady Stanton. Edited by Theodore Stanton and Harriot Stanton Blatch. New York, Arno, 1969. 2 v. illus., ports. 23 cm. Bibliographical footnotes. [JK1899.S7A4 1969] 77-79183
I. Stanton, Theodore, 1851-1925, ed. II. Blatch, Harriot (Stanton) 1856-1940, ed.

WISE, Winifred Esther 920.7
Rebel in petticoats; the life of Elizabeth Cady Stanton. Philadelphia, Chilton Co., [c.1960] vii, 204p. (2p. bibl.) 22cm. 60-8103 2.95
1. Stanton, Elizabeth (Cady) 1815-1902. I. Title.

WISE, Winifred Esther, 1906- 920.7
Rebel in petticoats; the life of Elizabeth Cady Stanton. [1st ed.] Philadelphia, Chilton Co., Book Division [1960] 204 p. 22 cm. Includes bibliographies. [JK1899.S7W5] 60-8103
1. Stanton, Elizabeth (Cady) 1815-1902. I. Title.

Stanton, Elizabeth (Cady) 1815-1902- Juvenile literature

CLARKE, Mary Stetson. 324'.3'0924 B
Bloomers and ballots; Elizabeth Cady Stanton and women's rights. [1st ed.] New York, Viking Press [1972] 223 p. port. 25 cm. A biography of one of the early leaders of the women's rights movement and first public proponent of suffrage for women. [HQ1413.S67C5] 72-80523 ISBN 0-670-17437-8 6.50
1. Stanton, Elizabeth (Cady) 1815-1902—Juvenile literature. 2. Woman—Rights of women—Juvenile literature. I. Title. BIP

FABER, Doris, 1924- 324'.3'0924 B
Oh, Lizzie! The life of Elizabeth Cady Stanton. New York, Lothrop, Lee & Shepard [1972] 159 p. illus. 22 cm. Bibliography: p. [155]-156. A biography of a nineteenth-century pioneer in the women's rights movement. [JK1899.S7F33] 92 79-177322 4.95
1. Stanton, Elizabeth (Cady) 1815-1902—Juvenile literature. I. Title. BIP

FABER, Doris, 1924- 324'.3'0924 [B]
Oh, Lizzie! The life of Elizabeth Cady Stanton. New York, Pocket Books [1974, c1972] 175 p. illus. 18 cm. (An Archway paperback) Summary: The biography of a 19th century pioneer in the women's rights movement. [JK1899.S7F33] [92] ISBN 0-671-29617-5. 0.75 (pbk.)
1. Stanton, Elizabeth (Cady) 1815-1902- Juvenile literature I. Title.
L.C. card number for original ed.: 79-177322.

SALSINI, Barbara. 324'.3'0924 B
Elizabeth Stanton, a leader of the women's suffrage movement. Charlotteville, N.Y., SamHar Press, 1973. 31, [1] p. 22 cm. (Outstanding personalities, no. 54) Bibliography: p. 31-[32] A biography of the nineteenth-century pioneer in the struggle for women's rights. [HQ1413.S67S3] 92 72-89214 ISBN 0-87157-547-7 1.98 (lib. bdg.)
1. Stanton, Elizabeth (Cady) 1815-1902—Juvenile literature. 2. Woman—Suffrage—United States—Juvenile literature. 3. Woman—Rights of women—Juvenile literature. I. Title.
Pbk. 0.98; ISBN 0-87157-547-5

Stanton, Jim.

DAY, Beth (Feagles) 1924- 799.2774446
Grizzlies in their back yard. New York, Messner [1956] 224p. 22cm. Story of Jim and Laurette Station's life in the Great North Woods of British Columbia. [SK33.D3] 56-11466
1. Stanton, Jim. 2. Stanton, Laurette (De Nourde) 3. Hunting—British Columbia. 4. Outdoor life. I. Title.

Stanwyck, Barbara, 1907-

SMITH, Ella. 791.43'028'0924
Starring Miss Barbara Stanwyck. New York, Crown Publishers [1973, c1974] 340 p. illus. 28 cm. [PN2287.S67S6] 73-82944 ISBN 0-517-50602-5 10.00
1. Stanwyck, Barbara, 1907- I. Title.

*VERMILYE, Jerry. 791.43'028'0924 B
Barbara Stanwyck. New York, Pyramid, [1975] 159 p. ill. 20 cm. (Pyramid illustrated history of the movies.) Includes index. "Films of Barbara Stanwyck" p. 143-152. Bibliography: p. 141-142. [PN2287] 74-24838 ISBN 0-515-03641-2 1.75 (pbk.)
1. Stanwyck, Barbara, 1907- 2. Moving-pictures—Biography. 3. Moving picture actors and actresses. I. Sennett, Ted ed. II. Title. BIP

Stape family.

PATNODE, Genevieve Carroll, 1908- 929'.2'0973
A privileged generation : dealing with the families of Roe, La Shure, Stape, Carroll, Rhoda, Rockefeller, Pratt / by Genevieve Carroll Patnode, as told by Lola Stape Carroll. Leesburg, Fla. : Patnode, c1975. 205, xx p. : ill. ; 29 cm. [CS71.S7926 1975] 75-19745
1. Roe family. 2. Stape family. 3. Carroll family. I. Carroll, Lola Stape, 1884-1967. II. Title.

Stargell, Willie, 1941-

STARGELL, Willie, 1941- 796.357'092'4 B
Out of left field : Willie Stargell and the Pittsburgh Pirates / [photos. by] Bob Adelman and [interviews taped and edited by] Susan Hall. 1st ed. New York : Two Continents Pub. Group, c1976. 223 p. : ill. ; 21 x 24 cm. (A Prairie House book) [GV865.S76A36] 75-43477 ISBN 0-8467-0127-8 : 10.95
1. Stargell, Willie, 1941- 2. Pittsburgh. Baseball club (National League) 3. Baseball players—United States—Biography. I. Adelman, Bob. II. Hall, Susan. III. Title.

Stargell, Willie, 1941- —Juvenile literature.

LIBBY, Bill. 796.357'092'4 B
Willie Stargell, baseball slugger. New York, Putnam [1973] 159 p. port. 22 cm. (Putnam sports shelf) A biography of a Pittsburgh Pirate famous for his home runs. [GV865.S76L5 1973] 92 72-94265 ISBN 0-399-20334-6 4.69
1. Stargell, Willie, 1941- —Juvenile literature. I. Title.

Stark, Elizabeth, 1737-1814—Juvenile literature.

TARDIFF, Olive, 1916- 973.3'15'0420924 B
Molly Stark, woman of the Revolution / by Olive Tardiff ;ill. by Allen Moyler. Canaan. N.H. : Phoenix Pub., c1976. vii, 71 p. : ill. ; 23 cm. Includes index. A biography of Molly Stark who lived in New England during the American Revolution. [E263.M4T17] 92 75-12182 ISBN 0-914016-26-1 : 4.95
1. Stark, Elizabeth, 1737-1814—Juvenile literature. I. Moyler, Allen. II. Title.

Stark, John, 1728-1822.

STARK, Caleb, 1804-1864. 973.3'3'0922 B
Memoir and official correspondence of Gen. John Stark, with notices of several other officers of the Revolution. Also a bibliography of Capt. Phine[h]as Stevens and of Col. Robert Rogers, with an account of his services in America during the "Seven years' war." With a new introd. and pref. by George Athan Billias. Boston, Gregg Press, 1972 [c1860] x, 495 p. 23 cm. (The American Revolutionary series. American and French accounts of the American Revolution) Reprint of the ed. published by G. P. Lyon, Concord, N.H. Contents.Contents.—Memoir of General John Stark.—Correspondence (p. [107]-317)—General Jacob Bailey.—General Joseph Cilley.—Colonel Marinus Willef.—Major Caleb Stark.—Captain Phinehas Stevens.—Colonel Robert Rogers.—Thomas Barnside. [E207.S79S7 1972] 72-8760 ISBN 0-8398-1884-X 18.50 (Lib. ed.)
1. Stark, John, 1728-1822. 2. Stevens, Phinehas, 1707-1756. 3. Rogers, Robert, 1727-1800. 4. United States—History—Revolution—Biography. I. Stark, John, 1728-1822. Correspondence. 1972. II. Title. III. Series: American and French accounts of the American Revolution.

Stark, John, 1728-1822—Juvenile literature.

RICHMOND, Robert P. 973.3'3'0924 B
John Stark, freedom fighter / by Robert P. Richmond. 1st ed. Waterbury, Conn. : Dale Books, 1976. 82 p. : port. ; 23 cm. A biography of John Stark, a general in the American army during the Revolutionary War. [E207.S79R5] 92 75-46140 5.95 pbk. : 2.95
1. Stark, John, 1728-1822—Juvenile literature. I. Title. BIP

Starkie, Enid.

RICHARDSON, Joanna. 378.1'2'0924 B
Enid Starkie. [1st American ed.] New York, Macmillan [1974, c1973] 306 p. illus. 22 cm. Includes bibliographical references. [PQ67.S7R5 1974] 73-10563 7.95
1. Starkie, Enid. BIP

Starkie, Walter Fitzwilliam,

STARKIE, Walter Fitzwilliam, 1894- 928.2
Scholars and gypsies, an autobiography. Berkeley, University of California Press, 1963. xi, 324 p. 23 cm. [CT808.S8A3] 63-22845
I. Title.

Starkweather, Charles.

ALLEN, William, 1940- 364.1'523'0924 B
Starkweather : a chronicle of mass murder in the fifties / William Allen. Boston : Houghton Mifflin, 1976. p. cm. [HV6248.S6274A44] 75-42125 ISBN 0-395-24077-8 : 8.95
1. Starkweather, Charles. 2. Murder—Nebraska. I. Title.

ALLEN, William 1940- 364.1'523'0924
Starkweather : the story of a mass murder / byWilliam Allen. New York : Avon Books, 1977,c1976. 205,[16]p . : ill. ; 18 cm. [HV6248.S6274A44] ISBN 0-380-00973-0 pbk. : 1.75
1. Starkweather, Charles. 2. Murder-Nebraska. I. Title.
L.C. card no. for 1976 Houghton Mifflin ed.:75-42125

Starlight, Captain, 1837-1899.

MCCARTHY, Patrick Hubert. 364.1'55'0924 B
Starlight: the man and the myth [by] P. H. McCarthy. Melbourne, Hawthorne Press, 1972. 143 p. 23 cm. Includes bibliographical references. [DU115.M23] 73-158528 ISBN 0-7256-0063-2 5.95
1. Starlight, Captain, 1837-1899. 2. Browne, Thomas Alexander, 1826-1915. Robbery under arms. 3. Bush-rangers. I. Title.

Starr, Bart, 1934—

*DEVANEY, John 796.3320924
Bart Starr. New York, Scholastic [1967] 143-p. illus. 18cm. (TK1098) .50 pap.,
1. Starr, Bart, 1934- 2. Green Bay Packers. I. Title.

SCHOOR, Gene. 796.33'2'0924 B
Bart Starr : a biography / Gene Schoor. 1st ed. Garden City, N.Y. : Doubleday, c1977. 211 p., [8] leaves of plates : ill. ; 22 cm. [GV939.S73S33] 76-56332 ISBN 0-385-11694-2 : 6.95. ISBN 0-385-11695-0 lib.bdg. : 7.00
1. Starr, Bart—Juvenile literature. 2. Green Bay, Wis. Football club (National League)—Juvenile literature. 3. Football players—United States—Biography—Juvenile literature. I. Title. BIP

SULLIVAN, George, 1927- 796.332'0924 B
Bart Starr, the cool quarterback. New York, Putnam [1970] 192 p. illus. 22 cm. (Putnam sports shelf) A biography concentrating on the football career of the Green Bay Packer who has "quarterbacked more winning games than any other player in the history of pro football." [GV939.S73S8 1970] 92 73-113520 3.86
1. Starr, Bart. I. Title.

Starr, Belle (Shirley) 1848-1889.

BREIHAN, Carl W., 1915- 364.15'5'0922 B
The bandit Belle, by Carl W. Breihan with Charles A. Rosamond. [1st ed.] Seattle, Hangman Press [1970] 144 p. illus., facsims., ports. 27 cm. On spine: The bandit Belle and other tales. "Thrilling events; life of Henry Starr" (facsimile copy): p. [43]-[94] Bibliography: p. 140. [F594.S8B7] 76-127305
1. Starr, Belle (Shirley) 1848-1889. 2. Starr, Henry, 1873-1921. 3. Brigands and robbers. I. Rosamond, Charles A., joint author. II. Starr, Henry, 1873-1921. Thrilling events. 1970. III. Title.

HICKS, Edwin P. 923.4173
Belle Starr and her Pearl. Foreword by Homer Croy. Little Rock, Ark. [C. A. Harper] 1963. 183p. illus. 24cm. 63-1652 apply
1. Starr, Belle (Shirley) 1848-1889. 2. Starr, Pearl, 1867-1925. I. Title.

SCOTT, Jennette S 923.973
Belle Starr in velvet, by Kenneth D. Scott, as told by Jennette S. Scott. Tahlequah, Okla., Pan Press [c1963] 255 p. illus., ports. 22 cm. [F594.S8S3] 64-1089
1. Starr, Belle (Shirley) 1848-1889. I. Scott, Kenneth D. II. Title.

Starr, Blaze.

STARR, Blaze. 792.7 B
Blaze Starr; my life as told to Huey Perry. Afterword by Lora Fleming. New York, Praeger [1974] 210 p. 21 cm. [PN1949.S7S8] 73-9392 6.95
1. Starr, Blaze. I. Perry, Huey.

Starr, Cornelius Vander, 1892-1968.

WRITING Services Company. 368'.00924 B
Cornelius Vander Starr, 1892-1968. Prepared by Writing Services Company [New York? 1970] 51 p. illus. (part col.), ports. 28 cm. Includes reminiscences about C. V. Starr by his friends. [HG8952.S7W7] 70-98952
1. Starr, Cornelius Vander, 1892-1968.

Starr, James Harper, 1809- 1890.

CRAVENS, John Nathan, 1912- 923.273
James Harper Starr, financier of the Republic of Texas. Austin, Daughters of the Republic of Texas, 1950. xiv, 194p. illus. ports., map (on lining papers) facsims. 24cm. Bibliography: p. 187-194. [F390.S794C7] 57-17207
1. Starr, James Harper, 1809- 1890. I. Title.

Starr, Myra Belle (Shirley) 1846-1889.

FOX, Richard Kyle, 1846-1922. v. 12
Bella Starr, the bandit queen, or the female Jesse James. A full and authentic history of the dashing female highwayman, with copious extracts from her journal. Handsomely and profusely illustrated. New York, Richard K. Fox, pub., 1889, Austin, Tex., Steck Co. [1960] 64 p. illus. 23 cm. At head of title: A facsimile reproduction. "1960 facsimile reproduction of the first edition with preface, photographs, and Elizabeth Rice Bauknight illustrations added." 64-29088
1. Starr, Myra Belle (Shirley) 1846-1889. I. Title.

Starrett, Vincent, 1886-

RUBER, Peter A. 818'.5'209
The last bookman; a journey into the life & times of Vincent Starrett, author, journalist, bibliophile, by Peter Ruber. With an unorthodox introd. by the late Christopher Morley and a chronicle of friendship & tribute through poetry & prose by Franklin P. Adams [and others. 1st ed. New York, Candlelight Press, 1968] 115 p. illus., ports. 32 cm. "A bibliographical checklist: the writings of Vincent Starrett, by Esther Longfellow": p. 110-112. [PS3537.T246Z8] 72-44 10.00
1. Starrett, Vincent, 1886- I. Title.

STARRETT, Vincent, 1886- 818.5209 B
Born in a bookshop; chapters from the Chicago renascence. [1st ed.] Norman, University of Oklahoma Press [1965] ix, 325 p. illus., ports. 23 cm. [PS3537.T246Z5] 65-24204
I. Title.

Statelessness.

DAVIS, Garry [Sol Gareth Davis] 1921- 920
The world is my country; autobiography. New York, Putnam [c.1961] 254p. illus. 61-8341 4.50
1. Statelessness. I. Title.

Staten Island Zoo—Juvenile literature.

ZAPPLER, Georg. 596'.0074'04726
Behind the scenes at the zoo / Georg Zappler. 1st ed. Garden City, N.Y. : Doubleday, c1977. 89 p. : ill. ; 25 cm. The former director of the Staten Island Zoo recalls many daily occurrences and innovations at the zoo. [QL76.5.U62N489] 76-42418 ISBN 0-385-09515-5 : 5.95.
1. Staten Island Zoo—Juvenile literature. 2. Zappler, Georg—Juvenile literature. 3. Zoologists—United States—Biography—Juvenile literature. I. Title.

Statesmen.

BERNARDY, Francoise de. 923.244
Son of Talleyrand; the life of Comte Charles de Flahaut, 1785-1870. Translated by Lucy Norton. [1st American ed.] New York, Putnam [1957, c1956] 320p. illus. 22cm. Translation of Auguste Charles Joseph, comte de, 1785-1870. [DC255.F5B413] 57-13712
I. Title.

GRANT, Neil. 909.82'092'2 B
World leaders of today. London, New York, F. Watts, 1972. [8], 310 p. ports. 24 cm. [D412.6.G68] 73-152399 ISBN 0-85166-458-X £2.75
1. Statesmen. 2. Biography—20th century. I. Title.

HARDEN, Maximilian, 1861-1927. 920.02
I meet my contemporaries. Translated from the German by William C. Lawton. With an introd. by James W. Gerard. Freeport, N.Y., Books for Libraries Press [1968] vi, 287 p. 23 cm. (Essay index reprint series) Reprint of the 1925 ed. Contents.Contents.—Maximilian Harden.—Woodrow Wilson.—Lloyd George.—Clemenceau.—The Hindenburg myth.—Stinnes.—King Peter of Serbia.—Lenin.—Sarah Bernhardt.—Bonaparte in adversity. [D412.H3 1968] 68-57319
1. Statesmen. 2. Europe—Biography. I. Title. BIP

KENWORTHY, Leonard Stout, 1912- 923.2
Leaders of new nations. Illustrated by Samuel Kweskin. [1st ed.] Garden City, N.Y., Doubleday, 1959. 336 p. illus. 22 cm. [D839.5.K4] 59-12634
1. Statesmen. I. Title.

KENWORTHY, Leonard Stout, 1912- 920.02
Leaders of new nations [by] Leonard S. Kenworthy and Erma Ferrari. Illustrated by Michael Lowenbein. Garden City, N.Y., Doubleday [1968] 373 p. illus., map (on lining papers) ports. 22 cm. Contents.Contents.—Nyerere of Tanzania.—Kenyatta of Kenya.—Balewa of Nigeria. Nkrumah of Ghana.—Senghor of Senegal.—Mohammed v of Morocco.—Bourguiba of Tunisia. —Nasser of the United Arab Republic.—Ben-Gurion of Israel.—Hussein of Jordan.—Jinnah of Pakistan.—Nehru of India.—U Nu of Burma.—Rahman of Malaysia.—Sukarno of Indonesia.—Magsaysay of the Philippines. [D839.5.K4 1968] 67-19096
1. Statesmen. I. Ferrari, Erma Paul, joint author. II. Title.

KENWORTHY, Leonard Stout, 1912- 920
Leaders of new nations [by] Leonard S. Kenworthy and Erma Ferrari. Illustrated by Michael Lowenbein. Garden City, N.Y., Doubleday [1968] 373 p. illus., map (on lining papers) ports. 22 cm. Brief sketches of sixteen emergent nations and their leaders: Nyerere of Tanzania, Kenyatta of Kenya, Balewa of Nigeria, Nkrumah of Ghana, Senghor of Senegal, Mohammed v of Morocco, Bourguiba of Tunisia, Nasser of the United Arab Republic, Ben-Gurion of Israel, Hussein of Jordan, Jinnah of Pakistan, Nehru of India, U Nu of Burma, Rahman of Malaysia, Sukarno of Indonesia, and Magsaysay of the Philippines. [D839.5.K4 1968] AC 68
1. Statesmen. I. Ferrari, Erma Paul, joint author. II. Lowenbein, Michael, illus. III. Title.

LENGYEL, Emil, 1895- 923.1
From prison to power. Chicago, Follett Pub. Co., 1964. 360 p. ports. 24 cm. [D839.5.L4] 64-15330
1. Statesmen. I. Title.

LUDWIG, Emil, 1881-1948. 920.04
Nine etched from life; Nansen, Masaryk, Briand, Rathenau, Motta, Lloyd George, Venizelos, Mussolini, Stalin. Freeport, N.Y., Books for Libraries Press [1969] xiv, 383 p. 23 cm. (Essay index reprint series) Reprint of the 1934 ed. Translation of Fuhrer Europas. [D412.6.L8 1969] 70-90658 ISBN 0-8369-1225-X
1. Statesmen. 2. Europe—Politics and government—1918-1945. I. Title.

MARTIN, William, 1888-1934. 940.3'0922
Statesmen of the war in retrospect, 1918-1928. Freeport, N.Y., Books for Libraries Press [1970] xiii, 329 p. ports. 22 cm. (Essay index reprint series) "First published 1928." Contents.Contents.—William II.—Francis-Joseph.—Nicholas II.—Pachitch.—Von Bethmann-Hollweg.—Count Tisza.—Poincare.—Lord Grey.—Cardinal Mercier.—Baron Sonnino.—Venizelos.—Jon Bratiano.—Asquith.—Briand.—Hoover.—Gustave Ador.—President Wilson.—Colonel House.—Count Czernin.—President Masaryk and Dr. Benes.—Pilsudski and Paderewski.—Lloyd George.—Clemenceau. [D507.M35 1970b] 75-105029
1. Statesmen. 2. European War, 1914-1918—Biography. I. Title. BIP

PORTRAITS in power / 920'.02
edited by Jeremy Murray-Brown. New York : Times Books, [1979] p. cm. [D445.P65] 79-51439 ISBN 0-8129-0846-5 : 14.95
1. Statesmen. 2. Power (Social sciences)—Case studies. 3. History, Modern—20th century. I. Murray-Brown, Jeremy, 1932- BIP

SFORZA, Carlo, Conte, 1872-1952. 327'.2'0922
Makers of modern Europe; portraits and personel impressions and recollections. Freeport, N.Y., Books for Libraries Press [1969, c1930] 420 p. illus., ports. 23 cm. (Essay index reprint series) [D412.S4 1969] 68-57338
1. Statesmen. 2. Europe—Biography. I. Title.

STERLING Publishing Company, inc., New York. 923.2
Picture book of new world leaders prepared by the editors of Sterling. New York [1962] 64 p. illus. 26 cm. (Visual history series) [D839.5.S73] 61-15800
1. Statesmen. I. Title. II. Title: New world leaders.

STERLING Publishing Company, inc., New York. 923.2
Picture book of new world leaders, prepared by the eds. of Sterling. New York, Author [c.1962] 64p. illus. 26cm. (Visual hist. ser.) 61-15860 1.00 pap.,
1. Statesmen. I. Title. II. Title: New world leaders.

VALENTI, Jack. 920.02
The bitter taste of glory. New York, World Pub. Co. [1971] xiii, 170 p. 22 cm. Bibliography: p. 165-167. [D108.V33] 78-145837 5.95
1. Statesmen. I. Title.

WEBB, Robert N. 923.1
Leaders of our time; series 2. New York, Watts [c.1965] v, 152p. ports. 25cm. [D412.6.W4] 65-12124 3.95; 2.96 lib. ed.,
1. Statesmen. I. Title.
Contents omitted.

WEBB, Robert N. 909.8260922
Leaders of our time; series 3, by Robert N. Webb. New York, Watts [1966] 116p. ports. 25cm. [D412.6W42] 66-6803 3.95; 2.96 lib. ed.,
1. Statesmen. 2. Biography—20th cent. I. Title.
Contents omitted.

WEBB, Robert N. 909.8260922
Leaders of our time series 3 by Robert N. Webb. New York, F. Watts [1966] 116 p. ports. 24 cm. Contents.Contents.—Leonid Ilyich Brezhnev and Aleksei Nikolayevich Kosygin.—Arthur J. Goldberg.—Hubert Horatio Humphrey.—Robert Francis Kennedy.—Mohammad Ayub Khan.—John V. Lindsay.—Thurgood Marshall.—Robert S. McNamara.—Lester Bowles Pearson.—Walter Reuther.—George Wilcken Romney. [D412.6.W42] 66-6803
1. Statesmen. 2. Biography—20th century. I. Title.

WEBB, Robert N 923.1
Leaders of our time: series 1. New York, F. Watts [1964] vii, 150 p. ports 25 cm. Contents.CONTENTS. -- Konrad Adenauer. -- David Ben-Gurion. -- Fidel Castro. -- Charles de Gaulle. -- John F. Kennedy. -- Nikita Khrushchev. -- Harold Macmillan. -- Mao Tse-tung. -- Gamal Abdel Nasser. -- Jawaharial Nehru. -- Kwame Nkrumah. -- U Thant. [D412.6.W4] 64-12124
1. Statesmen. I. Title.

WHIBLEY, Charles, 1859-1930. 920.02
Political portraits. Port Washington, N.Y., Kennikat Press [1970] 327 p. 19 cm. Reprint of the 1917 ed. Contents.Contents.—Thomas Wolsey, Minister of War.—Shakespeare, patriot and Tory.—Edward Hyde, Earl of Clarendon.—Gilbert Burnet.—The Duke of Newcastle.—The crowned philosopher.—Charles James Fox.—A famous tsar.—Talleyrand.—Metternich.—Napoleon Vituperator.—Lord Melbourne.—Sir James Graham.—The corn laws: a group.—The Eighth Duke of Devonshire. [D108.W5 1970b] 70-112821
1. Statesmen. I. Title. BIP

WHIBLEY, Charles, 1859-1930. 940.2'0922
Political portraits, first series. Freeport, N.Y., Books for Libraries Press [1970] 327 p. 23 cm. (Essay index reprint series) "First published 1917." Contents.Contents.—Thomas Wolsey, Minister of War.—Shakespeare, patriot and Tory.—Edward Hyde, Earl of Clarendon.—Gilbert Burnet.—The Duke of Newcastle.—The crowned philosopher.—Charles James Fox.—A famous tsar.—Talleyrand.—Metternich.—Napoleon vituperator.—Lord Melbourne.—Sir James Graham.—The corn laws: a group.—The eighth Duke of Devonshire. [D108.W5 1970] 74-105050
1. Statesmen. I. Title.

Statesmen, American—Juvenile literature.

LAWSON, Don 923.273
Famous American political families. New York, Abelard [c.1965] 253p. ports. 22cm. Bibl. [E176.L43] 65-12121 4.50
1. Statesmen, American—Juvenile literature. I. Title.

Statesmen, American—Dictionaries.

BIOGRAPHICAL directory of the United States executive branch, 1774-1971. 973'.099
Robert Sobel, editor in chief. Westport, Conn., Greenwood Pub. Co. [1971] x, 491 p. 24 cm. [E176.B575] 78-133495 ISBN 0-8371-5173-2
1. Statesmen, American—Dictionaries. 2. U.S.—Officials and employees—Biography—Dictionaries. I. Sobel, Robert, 1931 (Feb. 19)- ed. BIP

Statesmen as authors—United States.

JENKINS, Starr, 1925- 973'.0992
Profiles of creative political leaders : American statesmen who were great writers / by Starr Jenkins. Ardmore, Pa. : Whitmore Pub. Co., [1975] 249 p. : ports. ; 22 cm. Bibliography: p. 244-249. [E176.J46] 73-94209 ISBN 0-87426-034-5 : 7.95
1. Statesmen as authors—United States. I. Title.

JENKINS, Starr, 1925- 973'.0992
Profiles of creative political leaders : American statesmen who were great writers / by Starr Jenkins. Ardmore, Pa. : Whitmore Pub. Co., [1975] 249 p. : ports. ; 22 cm. Bibliography: p. 244-249. [E176.J46] 73-94209 ISBN 0-87426-034-5 : 7.95
1. Statesmen as authors—United States. I. Title.

Statesmen—Australia—Biography.

HARRIS, Maxwell 329'.0092'2 B
Henley, 1921-
Sir Henry, Bjelke, Don baby and friends. Contributors: Ian Baker [and others] Edited by Max Harris [and] Geoffrey Dutton. Melbourne, Sun Books [1971] vi, 210 p. 19 cm. [DU117.2.A2H37] 72-185515 ISBN 0-7251-0130-X 1.95
1. Statesmen—Australia—Biography. 2. Australia—Politics and government—1945- I. Dutton, Geoffrey, joint author. II. Baker, Ian. III. Title.

Statesmen—Biography.

JENKINS, Roy. 909.82'092'2 B
Nine men of power / Roy Jenkins. New York : British Book Centre, [1975], c1974. p. cm. Essays first appeared in the London Times between 1970 and 1973. Includes index. [D412.6.J46 1975] 75-22022 ISBN 0-8277-4465-X : 17.95
1. Statesmen—Biography. 2. Biography—20th century. I. Title. BIP

Statesmen, British.

BAGEHOT, Walter, 942.081'0922
1826-1877.
Biographical studies. Edited by Richard Holt Hutton. New York, AMS Press [1970] vi, 368 p. 23 cm. Reprint of the 1881 ed. Contents.Contents.—The character of Sir Robert Peel.—Lord Brougham.—Mr. Gladstone.—William Pitt.—Bolingbrooke as a statesman.—Sir George Cornewall Lewis.—Adam Smith as a person.—Lord Althorp and the Reform act of 1832.—The Prince consort.—What Lord Lyndhurst really was.—The tribute at Hereford to Sir G. C. Lewis.—Mr. Cobden.—Lord Palmerston.—The Earl of Clarendon.—Mr. Lowe as Chancellor of the Exchequer.—Monsieur Guizot.—Professor Cairnes.—Mr. Disraeli as a member of the House of Commons. [DA531.2.B3 1970] 75-111469
1. Statesmen, British. I. Title. BIP

BAGEHOT, Walter, 942.081'092'2 B
1826-1877.
Biographical studies. Edited by Richard Holt Hutton. 2d ed. London, Longmans, Green, 1889. St. Clair Shores, Mich., Scholarly Press, 1972. p. Contents.Contents.—The character of Sir Robert Peel.—Lord Brougham.—Mr. Gladstone.—William Pitt.—Bolingbroke as a statesman.—Sir George Cornewall Lewis.—Adam Smith as a person.—Lord Althorp and the Reform act of 1832.—The Prince Consort.—What Lord Lyndhurst really was.—The tribute at Hereford to Sir G. C. Lewis.—Mr. Cobden.—Lord Palmerston.—The Earl of Clarendon.—Mr. Lowe as Chancellor of the Exchequer.—Monsieur Guizot.—Professor Cairnes.—Mr. Disraeli as a member of the House of Commons. [DA531.2.B3 1972] 70-144862 ISBN 0-403-00850-6
1. Statesmen, British. I. Title.

CECIL, Algernon, 1879- 354.42'061
1953.
British foreign secretaries 1807-1916; studies in personality and policy. Port Washington, N.Y., Kennikat Press [1971] ix, 378 p. 22 cm. Originally published in 1927. Includes bibliographical references. [DA531.2.C4 1971] 70-118463 ISBN 0-8046-1212-9
1. Statesmen, British. 2. Gt. Brit.—Foreign relations—19th century. 3. Gt. Brit.—Foreign relations—1901-1910. I. Title.

INNES, Arthur Donald, 942.05'0922
1863-1938.
Ten Tudor statesmen. [New ed.] Port Washington, N.Y., Kennikat Press [1971] 295 p. 22 cm. Reprint of the 1934 ed. Contents.Contents.—Henry VII.—Cardinal Wolsey.—Sir Thomas More.—Thomas Cromwell.—Henry VIII.—Protector Somerset.—Archbishop Cranmer.—William Cecil, Lord Burghley.—Sir Francis Walsingham.—Sir Walter Raleigh. [DA317.2.I5 1971] 79-118479
1. Statesmen, British. 2. Gt. Brit.—History—Tudors, 1485-1603. I. Title. BIP

MALCOLM, Ian Zachary, 328.42'0922
Sir 1868-
Vacant thrones; a volume of political portraits, by Sir Ian Malcolm. Freeport, N.Y., Books for Libs. Pr. [1967] xv, 204p. ports. 22cm. (Essay index reprint ser.) First pub. 1931. [DA566.9.A1M35 1967] 67-28760 8.50
1. Statesmen, British. 2. Gt. Brit. Parliament—Biog. I. Title.

Statesmen—Great Britain.

BEGBIE, Harold, 328'.42'0922
1871-1929.
The windows of Westminster. Freeport, N.Y., Books for Libraries Press [1970] xxiii, 193 p. ports. 23 cm. (Essay index reprint series) London ed., published in 1924, has title: The conservative mind. Contents.Contents.—Mr. Stanley Baldwin.—Sir Robert Horne.—Mr. Edward Wood.—Mr. Neville Chamberlain.—The Duke of Northumberland.—Sir Philip Lloyd-Greame.—Sir Douglas Hogg.—Captain Algernon Fitzroy.—Sir William Joynson-Hicks.—Mr. Oliver Stanley. [DA566.9.A1B4 1970] 77-104993 ISBN 0-8369-1447-3
1. Statesmen—Great Britain. 2. Great Britain—Politics and government—1910-1936. I. Title.

BOLTON, Sarah 942.081'0922 B
(Knowles) 1841-1916.
Famous English statesmen of Queen Victoria's reign. Freeport, N.Y., Books for Libraries Press [1972] 460 p. ports. 23 cm. (Essay index reprint series) Reprint of the 1891 ed. Contents.Contents.—Sir Robert Peel.—Lord Palmerston.—Lord Shaftesbury.—John Bright.—William Edward Forster.—Lord Beaconsfield.—Henry Fawcett.—William Ewart Gladstone. [DA531.2.B6 1972] 78-39705
1. Statesmen—Great Britain. 2. Great Britain—History—Victoria, 1831-1901. I. Title.

FARROW, John Neville 923.242
Villiers, 1904-
The story of Thomas More. Garden City, N.Y., Doubleday [1968,c.1954] 198 p. 18cm. (Image D236) [DA334.M8F33] .95 pap.,
I. More, Thomas, Sir 1478-1535. II. Title.

Statesmen—Great Britain—Biography.

REID, Wemyss, 942.081'092'2 B
Sir, 1842-1905.
Politicians of today, by T. Wemyss Reid. [1st ed. reprinted, with a new introduction by E. J. Feuchtwanger. Richmond, Surrey, Richmond Publishing Co., 1972. 5, iii-xi, 290, [3], 289 p. 18 cm. Reprint of 1st ed. originally published in two vols, London, Griffith and Farran, 1880. [DA562.R4 1972] 73-169643 ISBN 0-85546-166-7 £4.10
1. Statesmen—Great Britain—Biography. 2. Statesmen—Biography. 3. Great Britain—Politics and government—1837-1901. I. Title.

Statesmen—Juvenile literature.

DONOVAN, Frank Robert, 923.2
1906-
Famous twentieth century leaders. New York, Dodd, Mead [1964] 160 p. ports. 22 cm. (Famous biographies for young people) [D412.6.D6] 64-15367
1. Statesmen — Juvenile literature. I. Title.

WEBB, Robert N. 920.02
Leaders of our time: series 4, by Robert N. Webb. New York, Watts [1969] viii, 117 p. ports. 25 cm. Contents.Contents.—Moshe Dayan.—Indira Nehru Gandhi.—Ho Chi Minh.—Kurt Georg Kiesinger and Willy Brandt.—Eugene Joseph McCarthy.—Richard Milhous Nixon.—Eisaku Sato.—Nguyen Van Thieu and Nguyen Cao Ky.—Whitney M. Young, Jr. [D412.6.W422] 920 70-77242 3.95
1. Statesmen—Juvenile literature. 2. Biography—20th century—Juvenile literature. I. Title.

Statesmen—Latin America.

LATIN American government 920'.08 *leaders.* 2d ed. / edited by David William Foster. Tempe : Center for Latin American Studies, Arizona State University, 1975. viii, 135 p. ; 23 cm. [F1407.L37 1975] 75-15809 ISBN 0-87918-021-8
1. Statesmen—Latin America. 2. Latin America—Biography. I. Foster, David William. II. Arizona. State University, Tempe. Center for Latin American Studies.

Statesmen—Mental health.

LEE, Russel V. 616.8'9'09
The menace of madness in high places / Russel V. Lee. Corte Madera, Calif. : Omega Books, c1977. 204 p. ; 23 cm. Bibliography: p. 196-204. [RC451.4.S64L43] 76-47744 ISBN 0-89353-022-0 : 6.50
1. Statesmen—Mental health. 2. Mental illness—Biography. I. Title.

Statesmen—Mexico—Biography.

CAMP, Roderic Ai. 920'.072
Mexican political biographies, 1935-1975 / Roderic Ai Camp Tucson : University of Arizona Press, c1976. xxvii, 488 p. ; 24 cm. Bibliography: p. 463-468. [F1235.5.A2C35] 74-29361 ISBN 0-8165-0582-9 : 27.50 ISBN 0-8165-0496-2 pbk. : 8.95 8.95
1. Statesmen—Mexico—Biography. 2. Mexico—Biography. I. Title. BIP

Statesmen—New Zealand—Biography.

SCHOLEFIELD, Guy 993.1'0092'2 B
Hardy, 1877-1963.
Notable New Zealand statesmen; twelve prime ministers. Foreword by Peter Fraser. Freeport, N.Y., Books for Libraries Press [1972, c1947] 197 p. ports. 22 cm. (Biography index reprint series) Contents.Contents.—James Edward Fitzgerald.—Henry Sewell.—Sir William Fox.—Sir Edward Stafford.—Alfred Domett.—Sir Frederick Weld.—George Marsden Waterhouse.—Sir Julius Vogel.—Sir Harry Atkinson.—Sir George Grey.—John Ballance.—Richard John Seddon. [DU422.A2S36 1972] 72-5588 ISBN 0-8369-8139-1
1. Statesmen—New Zealand—Biography. I. Title. BIP

Statesmen—Rome.

OMAN, Charles 937'.02'0922
William Chadwick, Sir, 1860-1946.
Seven Roman Statesmen of the later republic: The Gracchi. Sulla. Crassus. Cato. Pompey. Caesar. Freeport, N.Y., Books for Libraries Press [1971] v, 348 p. illus., ports. 23 cm. (Essay index reprint series) Reprint of the 1902 ed. [DG260.A1O5 1971] 75-156699 ISBN 0-8369-2288-3
1. Statesmen—Rome. 2. Rome—History—Republic, 265-30 B.C. I. Title.

Statesmen's families—United States.

MACPHERSON, Myra. 329'.00973
The power lovers : an intimate look at politics and marriage / Myra MacPherson. New York : Putnam, c1975. 446 p. ; 23 cm. [E840.6.M33 1975] 75-18581 ISBN 0-399-11495-5 : 10.00
1. Statesmen's families—United States. 2. Statesmen's wives—United States. I. Title. BIP

Statesmen, South Asian.

HANNA, Willard Anderson, 923.159
1911-
Eight nation makers; Southeast Asia's charismatic statesmen, by Willard A. Hanna. New York, St. Martin's Press [1964] vii, 307 p. 22 cm. Bibliography: p. 295-296. [DS510.H3] 64-7585
1. Statesmen, South Asian. I. Title.

Statesmen—United States.

CURRENT, Richard Nelson. 923.273
Secretary Stimson, a study in statecraft. New Brunswick, Rutgers University Press, 1954. 272 p. 22 cm. [E748.S883C8] 54-6835
I. Stimson, Henry Lewis, 1867-1950. II. Title. BIP

CURRENT, Richard Nelson. 923.273
Secretary Stimson, a study in statecraft. New Brunswick, Rutgers University Press, 1954. 272 p. 22 cm. [E748.S883C8] 54-6835
I. Stimson, Henry Lewis, 1867-1950. II. Title. BIP

DONOVAN, Frank Robert. 973.30922
1906-
The women in their lives; the distaff side of the Founding Fathers. by Frank Donovan. New York, Dodd, [1966] 339p. ports. 22cm. [E302.5.D6] 66-23216 5.00
1. Statesmen, American. 2. U. S.—Hist.—Revolution—Biog. 3. Women in the U. S.—Biog. I. Title.
Contents omitted.

FORNEY, John Wien, 973.6'0922
1817-1881.
Anecdotes of public men. New York, Da Capo Press, 1970. 2 v. 23 cm. "This Da Capo Press edition ... is an unabridged republication of the first edition published in New York in 1873 and 1881." [E176.F68] 70-87540 ISBN 0-306-71456-6
1. Statesmen—United States. I. Title. BIP

HANSON, Galen 172.0922
Candles in conscience; ventures in the statecraft of rigor and restraint. Detroit, Harlo [1965] 123p. 23cm. Bibl. [E176.H28] 65-22816 price unreported
1. Statesmen, American. 2. Conscience. 3. Political ethics. I. Title.

LOWRY, Edward George, 973'.099
1876-1943.
Washington close-ups; intimate views of some public figures. Freeport, N.Y., Books for Libraries Press [1971] 275 p. ports. 23 cm. (Essay index reprint series) Reprint of the 1921 ed. [E747.L8 1971] 70-142656 ISBN 0-8369-2057-0
1. Statesmen—United States. 2. United States—Politics and government—1901-1953. I. Title.

LUCAS, Russell H., 973.91'0922 B
comp.
Outstanding American statesmen; lectures by William Henry Harbaugh [and others] Edited by Russell H. Lucas. Cambridge, Mass., Schenkman Pub. Co. [1970] viii, 84 p. 21 cm. "These papers were originally lectures arranged by the Society of Mayflower Descendants in Michigan for delivery at consecutive annual meetings of the society from November 1965 to November 1968 inclusive." Contents.Contents.—Theodore Roosevelt, by W. H. Harbaugh.—Woodrow Wilson and American traditions, by A. S. Link.—Franklin D. Roosevelt: the quest for security, by F. Freidel.—Dwight D. Eisenhower—the training and the tasks, by A. D. Chandler, Jr. [E176.1.L898] 70-118577
1. Statesmen—United States. 2. Presidents—United States—Biography. I. Title.

MACARTNEY, Clarence Edward 973
Noble, 1879-1957.
Men who missed it; great Americans who missed the White House. Freeport, N.Y., Books for Libraries Press [1970] 122 p. ports. 23 cm. (Essay index reprint series) Reprint of the 1940 ed. Contents.Contents.—Aaron Burr.—Henry Clay.—John C. Calhoun.—Daniel Webster.—William H. Seward.—Salmon P. Chase.—Stephan A. Douglas.—General George B. McClellan.—Horace Greeley.—Samuel J. Tilden.—James G. Blaine.—Robert M. La Follette.—William Jennings Bryan.—Charles Evans Hughes. [E176.M106 1970] 76-128274 ISBN 0-8369-1835-5
1. Statesmen—United States. 2. United States—Biography. I. Title.

MARTIN, John 973.921'0921'4 [B]
Bartlow.
Adlai Stevenson and the world : the life of Adlai E. Stevenson / John Bartlow Martin. Garden City, N.Y. : Anchor Books, 1978, c1977. 946p. : ill. ; 24 cm. Includes bibliographical references and index. [E748.S84M36] ISBN 0-385-12649-2 pbk. : 7.95
I. Title.
L.C. card no. for 1977 Doubleday ed.: 76-23781. BIP

STEVENS, William Oliver, 1878- 923.273
Famous American statesmen. New York, Dodd, Mead, 1953. 147p. illus. 23cm. (Famous bibographies for young people) [E176.S838] 52-12953
1. Statesmen, American. I. Title. BIP

*STONE, Irving 923.273
They also ran. New York, Pyramid [1964, c.1943-1964] 484p. 18cm. (T-1014) .75 pap.,
I. Title. BIP

TANSILL, Charles Callan, 1890- 923.273
The secret loves of the Founding Fathers; the romantic side of George Washington, Thomas Jefferson, Benjamin Franklin, Gouverneur Morris [and] Alexander Hamilton. New York, Devin-Adair Co. [1964] xviii, 235 p. ports. 21 cm. Bibliography: p. 219-224. [E302.5.T3] 64-22784
1. Statesmen—United States. 2. United States—History—Revolution, 1775-1783—Biography. I. Title.

THOMAS, Henry, 1886- 973'.099
Living biographies of American statesmen, by Henry Thomas and Dana Lee Thomas (Henry Thomas Schnittkind and Dana Arnold Schnittkind) Illus. by Gordon Ross. Freeport, N.Y., Books for Libraries Press [1971, c1942] viii, 323 p. illus. 23 cm. (Essay index reprint series) [E176.T54 1971] 78-167412 ISBN 0-8369-2473-8
1. Statesmen—United States. 2. United States—Biography. I. Thomas, Dana Lee, 1918- joint author. II. Title.

TUCKER, Ray Thomas, 1893- 973
The mirrors of 1932. With 10 cartoons by Cesare. Freeport, N.Y., Books for Libraries Press [1970] 247 p. ports. 23 cm. (Essay index reprint series) Originally published in 1931. [E747.T933] 78-121508
1. Statesmen, American. 2. Washington, D.C.—Biography. 3. U.S.—Politics and government—1919-1933. I. Cesare, Oscar Edward, 1885-1948, illus. II. Title.

Statesmen—United States—Biography—Juvenile literature.

SIGNIFICANT American 920'.073
government leaders. Chicago : Childrens Press, [1976] p. cm. Includes index. Brief biographies of 139 government leaders arranged in chronological-alphabetical order. [E176.8.S53] 920 75-20685 ISBN 0-516-05314-0 : 9.25
1. Statesmen United States—Biography—Juvenile literature. I. Title: Government leaders.

Statisticians.

BUGDALE, Madge. 311'.0924
My statistics are vital: life and work as a statistician. Reading, Educational Explorers, 1969. 118 p. illus., map. 21 cm. (My life and my work series) [HA23.D78A3] 75-386285 21/-
1. Statisticians. I. Title.

Statler, Ellsworth Milton.

JARMAN, Rufus. 647.94
A bed for the night; the story of the Wheeling bellboy, E. M. Statler, and his remarkable hotels. [1st ed.] New York, Harper [1952] 309 p. illus. 22 cm. [TX910.5.S7J3] 52-5452
1. Statler, Ellsworth Milton. 2. Hotels—Statler Company, Inc. I. Title.

MILLER, Floyd. 647'.94'0924 B
Statler, America's extraordinary hotelman. New York, Statler Foundation [1968] viii, 240 p. illus., ports. 22 cm. Bibliography: p. 235-236. [TX910.5.S7M5] 68-20407
1. Statler, Ellsworth Milton. I. Title. II. Title: America's extraordinary hotelman.

Staubach, Roger, 1942-

*BURCHARD, Marshall. 796.33'2'0924 [B]
Sports hero: Roger Staubach, by Marshall and Sue Burchard. New York, Putnam [1973] 94 p. photos 22 cm. (Sports hero series) [GV939] ISBN 0-399-60829-X. 3.86 (lib. bdg.)
1. Staubach, Roger, 1942- I. Burchard, Sue, joint author. II. Title.

STAUBACH, Roger, 1942- 796.33'2'0924 B
Staubach : first down, lifetime to go / Roger Staubach ; with Sam Blair and Bob St. John. Waco, Tex. : Word Books, [1974] 304 p. : ill. ; 23 cm. [GV939.S733A37] 74-81607 8.95
1. Staubach, Roger, 1942- 2. Football. I. Blair, Sam, 1932- II. St. John, Bob. III. Title. BIP

STAUBACH, Roger, 1942- 796.33'2'0924 B
Staubach : first down, lifetime to go / Roger Staubach ; with Sam Blair and Bob St. John. Waco, Tex. : Word Books, [1974] 304 p. : ill. ; 23 cm. [GV939.S733A37] 74-81607 8.95
1. Staubach, Roger, 1942- 2. Football. I. Blair, Sam, 1932- II. St. John, Bob. III. Title. BIP

STAUBACH, Roger, 1942- 796.3320924
Staubach : first down, lifetime to go Roger Staubach with Sam Blair and Bob St. John. New York : Avon Books ,1976 c1974. xiii, 306 p. : ill. ; 18 cm. [GV939.S733S37] ISBN 0-380-00806-8 pbk. : 1.75
1. Staubach, Roger, 1942- 2. Football. I. Blair, Sam, 1932- , joint author. II. St. John, Bob. III. Title.
L.C. card no. for 1974 Word Books edition: 74-81607.

STAUBACH, Roger, 1942- 796.3320924
Staubach : first down, lifetime to go Roger Staubach with Sam Blair and Bob St. John. New York : Avon Books ,1976 c1974. xiii, 306 p. : ill. ; 18 cm. [GV939.S733S37] ISBN 0-380-00806-8 pbk. : 1.75
1. Staubach, Roger, 1942- 2. Football. I. Blair, Sam, 1932- , joint author. II. St. John, Bob. III. Title.
L.C. card no. for 1974 Word Books edition: 74-81607.

Staubach, Roger, 1942-—Juvenile literature.

SMITH, Jay H. 796.33'2'0924 B
Roger Staubach, by Jay H. Smith. Illustrated by Harold Henriksen. Mankato, Minn., Creative Education [1974] p. cm. Traces Roger Staubach's rise to number one quarterback of the Dallas Cowboys after joining the team as a twenty-seven year-old rookie following four years in Vietnam. [GV939.S733S63] 92 74-13134 ISBN 0-87191-378-X 4.95 (lib. bdg.).
1. Staubach, Roger, 1942-—Juvenile literature. 2. Football—Juvenile literature. I. Henriksen, Harold, illus. II. Title. BIP

SULLIVAN, George, 1927- 796.33'2'0924 B
Roger Staubach, a special kind of quarterback / by George Sullivan. New York : Putnam, [1974] 158 p. ; 21 cm. (Putnam sports shelf) Includes index. A biography of the football star who became the Dallas Cowboys' starting quarterback despite a four-year military break between his college and professional careers. [GV939.S733S94 1974] 92 74-78901 ISBN 0-399-60910-5 lib. bdg. : 4.97
1. Staubach, Roger, 1942- —Juvenile literature. 2. Football—Juvenile literature. I. Title.

Staverman, F. H.,

STAVERMAN, F. H., 1874- 818.5403
Wooden Head: a story of nine decades in the Dutch East Indies, Holland, the United States, and Canada, by F. H. Staverman. [1st ed.] New York, Exposition [1966] 199p. 21cm. Autobiographical. [CT1158.S7A3] 66-6710 5.00
I. Title.

Stevenson, Robert Louis,

STEVENSON, Robert Louis, 1850-1894. 928.2
RLS Stevenson's letters to Charles Baxter. Edited by De Lancey Ferguson and Marshall Waingrow. New Haven, Yale University Press, 1956. xxvi, 385p. illus., port., facsims. 24cm. [PR5493.A3 1956] 56-7119
I. Baxter, Charles, 1848-1919. II. Ferguson, John De Lancy, 1888- ed. III. Waingrow, Marshall, ed. IV. Title.

Stead, Eugene A.—Addresses, essays, lectures.

STEAD, Eugene A. 610'.92'4
E. A. Stead, Jr. : what this patient needs is a doctor / edited by Galen S. Wagner, Bess Cebe, Marvin P. Rozear. Durham, N.C. : Carolina Academic Press, c1978. xii, 244 p. : ill. ; 24 cm. Includes bibliographies. [R117.S797] 77-88666 ISBN 0-89089-080-3 : 12.95
1. Stead, Eugene A.—Addresses, essays, lectures. 2. Duke University, Durham, N.C. School of Medicine—History—Addresses, essays, lectures. 3. Medicine—Quotations, maxims, etc. 4. Physicians—North Carolina—Durham—Biography—Addresses, essays, lectures. I. Wagner, Galen S. II. Cebe, Bess. III. Rozear, Marvin P. IV. Title.

Stead, William Thomas, 1849-1912.

WHYTE, Frederic, 1867-1941. 070.4'1'0924 B
The life of W. T. Stead. With a new introd. for the Garland ed. by Cynthia F. Behrman. New York, Garland Pub., 1971. 2 v. illus. 22 cm. (The Garland library of war and peace) Originally published in 1925. Includes bibliographical references. [PN5123.S7W6 1971] 77-147461 ISBN 0-8240-0320-9
1. Stead, William Thomas, 1849-1912. I. Title. II. Series. BIP

Stearns, George Luther, 1809-1867.

STEARNS, Frank Preston, 1846-1917. 322'.4 B
The life and public services of George Luther Stearns. New York, Arno Press, 1969. 401 p. illus., ports. 23 cm. (The Anti-slavery crusade in America) Reprint of the 1907 ed. Includes bibliographical references. [E415.9.S79S7 1969] 70-82224
1. Stearns, George Luther, 1809-1867. 2. Slavery in the United States—Anti-slavery movements. 3. U.S.—Politics and government—1849-1877. I. Title. II. Series. BIP

Stebbins, Catherine L.

STEBBINS, Catherine L. 922.244
Here I shall finish my voyage! Omena, Mich., Solle's Press [c.1960] 28p. illus., map 23cm. 1.75 pap.,
I. Title.

Stedman, John Gabriel, 1744-1797.

COLLIS, Louise. 988.3010924 B
Soldier in paradise; the life of Captain John Stedman, 1744-1797. [1st American ed.] New York, Harcourt, Brace & World [1966, c1965] 230 p. illus. 21 cm. [F2423.S7C6 1966] 66-19484
1. Stedman, John Gabriel, 1744-1797. 2. Surinam. I. Title.

Steelberg, Wesley Rowland.

SUMRALL, Lester Frank, 1913- 922.89
'All for Jesus'; the life story of Wesley Rowland Steelberg. Springfield, Mo., Gospel Pub. House [1955] 260p. illus. 20cm. [BX6198.A7S8] 56-17683
1. Steelberg, Wesley Rowland. I. Title.

Steele, Frederick, 1819-1868—Manuscripts—Exhibitions.

PALMER, Patricia J. 355.3'32'0924 B
Frederick Steele: forgotten general [by Patricia J. Palmer. Stanford Calif., 1971] 20 p. illus. 23 cm. "Published on the occasion of an exhibit of his papers [at] the Stanford University Libraries, October 1971." Includes bibliographical references. [E467.1.S845P34] 74-157745
1. Steele, Frederick, 1819-1868—Manuscripts—Exhibitions. I. Stanford University. Libraries.

Steele, Jennie Koons, 1870-1955.

STEELE, Jennie Koons, 1870-1955. 973.91'092'2 B
I remember ... / by Jennie Koons Steele ; edited by Marion Davault Steele ; with letters to and from Richard St. Clair Steele, 1888 to 1907. 1st ed. New York : Vantage Press, c1977. 357 p., [1] leaf of plates : ill. ; 21 cm. [CT275.S6748A34] 77-356872 ISBN 0-533-02198-7 : 8.95
1. Steele, Jennie Koons, 1870-1955. 2. Steele, Richard St. Clair, 1870-1938. 3. United States—Biography. I. Steele, Richard St. Clair, 1870-1938. II. Steele, Marion D., 1908- III. Title.

Steele, Richard, Sir, 1672-1729.

AITKEN, George Atherton, 1860-1917. 792'.09421'32
The life of Richard Steele. New York, Greenwood Press, 1968. 2 v. illus., geneal. table, ports. 23 cm. Reprint of the 1889 ed. "Music for Steele's songs": v. 2, p. [369]-386. Bibliography: v. 2, p. [387]-428. [PR3706.A7 1968] 68-30994
1. Steele, Richard, Sir, 1672-1729. I. Title.

AITKEN, George Atherton, 1860-1917. 824'.5 B
The life of Richard Steele. New York, Haskell House, 1968. 2 v. ports. 24 cm. Reprint of the 1889 ed. "Haskell House catalogue item #152." "Music for Steele's songs": v. 2, p. [369]-386. Bibliography: v. 2, p. [369]-428. [PR3706.A7 1968b] 68-24893
1. Steele, Richard, Sir, 1672-1729. I. Title. BIP

CONNELY, Willard, 1888- 824'.5 B
Sir Richard Steele. Port Washington, N.Y., Kennikat Press [1967, c1934] 462 p. illus., facsim., ports. 23 cm. Bibliographical references included in "Notes" (p. 435-453) [PR3706.C6 1967] 67-27588
1. Steele, Richard, Sir, 1672-1729. BIP

LOFTIS, John Clyde, 1919- 792'.09421'32
Steele at Drury Lane, by John Loftis. Westport, Conn., Greenwood Press [1973, c1952] 260 p. 22 cm. Originally presented as the author's thesis, Princeton. Includes bibliographical references. [PR3706.L6 1973] 72-6925 ISBN 0-8371-6302-4 11.50
1. Steele, Richard, Sir, 1672-1729. 2. London. Drury Lane Theatre. I. Title. BIP

MONTGOMERY, Henry Riddell, 1818-1904. 824'.5 B
Memoirs of the life and writings of Sir Richard Steele, soldier, dramatist, essayist, and patriot, with his correspondence, and notices of his contemporaries, the wits and statesmen of Queen Anne's time. New York, Haskell House, 1971. 2 v. ports. 23 cm. Reprint of the 1865 ed. [PR3706.M6 1971] 76-128570 ISBN 0-8383-0903-8
1. Steele, Richard, Sir, 1672-1729. I. Title.

STEELE, Richard, Sir, 1672-1729. 824'.5 B
The letters of Richard Steele. Selected and collated with the original mss., with an introd. by R. Brimley Johnson. [Folcroft, Pa.] Folcroft Library Editions, 1973. p. Reprint of the 1927 ed. published by J. Lane, London and Dodd, Mead, New York. [PR3706.A45 1973] 73-12601 ISBN 0-8414-5250-4 (lib. bdg.)
1. Steele, Richard, Sir, 1672-1729.

WINTON, Calhoun. 928.2
Captain Steele; the early career of Richard Steele. [Baltimore] Johns Hopkins Press [1964] ix, 225 p. 21 cm. Bibliographical footnotes. [PR3706.W5] 64-16314
1. Steele, Richard, Sir, 1672-1729. I. Title. BIP

WINTON, Calhoun. 824'.5 B
Sir Richard Steel, M.P.: the later career. Baltimore, Johns Hopkins Press [1970] xiv, 265 p. illus., ports. 22 cm. Includes bibliographical references. [PR3706.W54] 75-112616 9.00
1. Steele, Richard, Sir, 1672-1729.

Steele, Samuel Benfield, Sir, 1849-1919.

STEWART, Robert. 363.2'092'4 B
Sam Steele, lion of the frontier / Robert Stewart. 1st ed. Toronto : Doubleday Canada ; New York : Doubleday, 1979. p. cm. Includes index. Bibliography: p. [HV7911.S77S73] 77-27718 ISBN 0-385-13598-X : 10.95
1. Steele, Samuel Benfield, Sir, 1849-1919. 2. Canada. Royal Canadian Mounted Police. 3. Police—Canada—Biography. I. Title.

Steenson, Nellie Cline.

STEENSON, Nellie Cline. 917.81'49'0330924
The Jayhawkers; stories and memoirs of the early days in western Kansas. [1st ed.] New York, Exposition Press [1967] 136 p. illus., ports. 21 cm. (An Exposition-Lochinvar book) [CT275.S6755A3] 67-26398
I. Title.

STEENSON, Nellie Cline. 917.81'49'0330924
The Jayhawkers; stories and memoirs of the early days in western Kansas. [1st ed.] New York, Exposition Press [1967] 136 p. illus., ports. 21 cm. (An Exposition-Lochinvar book) [CT275.S6755A3] 67-26398
I. Title.

Steere, Richard, 1643-1721.

WHARTON, Donald P. 811'.1 B
Richard Steere : Colonial merchant poet / by Donald P. Wharton. University Park : Pennsylvania State University Press, c1979. x, 87 p. ; 23 cm. (The Pennsylvania State University studies ; no. 44) Bibliography: p. [ix]-x. [PS843.S74Z95] 78-68169 pbk. : 3.95
1. Steere, Richard, 1643-1721. 2. Poets, American—Colonial period, ca. 1600-1775—Biography. 3. Merchants—United States—Biography. I. Series: Pennsylvania. State University. The Pennsylvania State University studies ; no. 44. BIP

Stefan, Ross, 1934-

GOODMAN, John K. 759.13 B
Ross Stefan, an impressionistic painter of the contemporary Southwest / by John K. Goodman ; with a foreword by Clay Lockett. 1st ed. [Flagstaff, Ariz.] : Northland Press, c1977. xii, 91 p. : ill. (some col.) ; 31 cm. [ND237.S6825G66] 77-79013 ISBN 0-87358-168-7 : 25.00
1. Stefan, Ross, 1934- 2. Painters—United States—Biography. 3. Southwest, New, in art. 4. Indians of North America—Southwest, New—Pictorial works.

Stefan, Verena, 1947- —Biography.

STEFAN, Verena, 1947- 301.41'2'0924 B
Shedding / Verena Stefan ; translated by Johanna Moore and Beth Weckmueller. New York: Daughters Pub. Co., 1978. 118 p. ; 22 cm. Translation of Hautungen. [PT2681.T3566Z51513] 77-94979 ISBN 0-913780-22-7 : 5.00
1. Stefan, Verena, 1947- —Biography. 2. Authors, German—20th century—Biography. I. Title. BIP

Stefansson, Vilhjalmur, 1879-1962.

BERRY, Erick, 1892- 919.8 B
Mr. Arctic; an account of Vilhjalmur Stefansson, by Erick Berry. New York, D. McKay Co., 1966. 185 p. illus., map, ports. 21 cm. Bibliography: p. 181. [G635.S7B4] 66-12128
1. Stefansson, Vilhjalmur, 1879-1962. I. Title.

DIUBALDO, Richard J. 971.9'9'020924 B
Stefansson and the Canadian Arctic / Richard J. Diubaldo. Montreal : McGill-Queen's University Press, c1978. xii, 274 p., [4] leaves of plates : ill. ; 25 cm. Includes index. Bibliography: p. 255-270. [F1090.5.D58] 79-304078 ISBN 0-7735-0324-2 : 18.95
1. Stefansson, Vilhjalmur, 1879-1962. 2. Canada, Northern—Discovery and exploration. 3. Explorers—Canada—Biography. I. Title.
Distributed by McGill-Queen's University Press, Irvington, NY BIP

STEFANSSON, Vilhjalmur, 1879-1962. 923.973
Discovery; the autobiography of Vilhjalmur Stefansson. [1st ed.] New York, McGraw-Hill [1964] viii, 411 p. illus., ports. 22 cm. [G635.S7A3 1964] 64-16477
1. Arctic regions. I. Title.

Stefansson, Vilhjalmur, 1879-1962—Juvenile literature.

MYERS, Hortense 92
Vilhjalmur Stefansson, young Arctic explorer, by Hortense Myers, Ruth Burnett. Indianapolis, Bobbs [c.1966] 200p. col. illus. 20cm. (Childhood of famous Amers.) Bibl. [G635.S7M9] 66-18418 2.25
1. Stefansson, Vilhjalmur, 1879-1962—Juvenile literature. I. Burnett, Ruth, joint author. II. Title.

MYERS, Hortense. 92
Vilhjalmur Stefansson, young Arctic explorer, by Hortense Myers and Ruth Burnett. Indianapolis, Bobbs-Merrill [1966] 200 p. col. illus. 20 cm. (Childhood of famous Americans) Bibliography: p. 198. [G635.S7M9] 66-18418
1. Stefansson, Vilhjalmur, 1879-1962 — Juvenile literature. I. Burnett, Ruth, joint author. II. Title.

Stefanyk, Vasyl' Semenovych, 1871-1936.

STRUK, D. S. 891.7'9'32
A study of Vasyl' Stefanyk: the pain at the heart of existence [by] D. S. Struk. With foreword by G. S. N. Luckyj. [Littleton, Colo.] Ukrainian Academic Press, 1973. 200 p. 24 cm. Appendix (p. 142-188):—Stefanyk, V. S. Novellas in translation: "Loss." "A stone cross." "Suicide." "Sons." "Children's adventure." "All alone." "The agony." "The thief." "Sin." "Les' family." "News." "Mother." "The pious woman."—Bibliography (p. 189-196) [PG3948.S78Z86] 72-89110 ISBN 0-87287-056-1 8.50
1. Stefanyk, Vasyl' Semenovych, 1871-1936. I. Stefanyk, Vasyl' Semenovych, 1871-1936. II. Title.
Publishers address: Box 263, Littleton, Colo. 80120. BIP

Steffanides, George F.

STEFFANIDES, George F. 301.45'18'93073 B
America, the land of my dreams : the odyssey of a Greek immigrant / by George F. Steffanides. Fitchburg, Mass. : Steffanides, 1974. vi, 216 p. : ill. ; 24 cm. Bibliography: p. 216. [LA2317.S8152] 75-303197 6.95
1. Steffanides, George F. 2. Greeks in the United States. 3. Education—United States. 4. United States—Social life and customs. I. Title.

Steffens, Joseph Lincoln, 1866-1936.

KAPLAN, Justin. 070.4'092'4 B
Lincoln Steffens; a biography. New York, Simon and Schuster [1974] 380 p. illus. 25 cm. Includes bibliographical references. [PN4874.S68K3] 73-15486 ISBN 0-671-21592-2 10.00
1. Steffens, Joseph Lincoln, 1866-1936.

PALERMO, Patrick F. 070.4'092'4 B
Lincoln Steffens / by Patrick F. Palermo. Boston : Twayne Publishers, c1978. p. cm. (Twayne's United States authors series ; TUSAS 320) Includes index. Bibliography: p. [PN4874.S68P34] 78-17800 ISBN 0-8057-7253-7 lib. bdg. : 9.50
1. Steffens, Joseph Lincoln, 1866-1936. 2. Journalists—United States—Biography. BIP

STEFFENS, Joseph Lincoln, 1866-1936. 920.5
The autobiography of Lincoln Steffens. New York, Grosset & Dunlap [1957, c1931] 884p. illus. 22cm. (Biographies of distinction) [PN4874] 57-652
1. Journalists—Correspondence, reminiscences, etc. I. Title.

STEFFENS, Joseph Lincoln, 1866-1936. 070'.92'4
The autobiography of Lincoln Steffens. New York, Harcourt, Brace & World [1968, c1958] 2 v. (x, 884 p.) illus., facsims. 21 cm. "A Harvest book." [PN4874.S68A3 1968] 68-5917
1. Journalists—Correspondence, reminiscences, etc.

STEFFENS, Joseph Lincoln, 1866-1936. 070.4'092'4
The letters of Lincoln Steffens / edited with introductory notes by Ella Winter and Granville Hicks ; with a memorandum by Carl Sandburg. Westport, Conn. : Greenwood Press, 1974, c1938. 2 v. (xxiv, 1072 p., [32] leaves of plates) : ill. ; 23 cm. Reprint of the ed. published by Harcourt, Brace, New York. Includes index. Contents.Contents.—v. 1. 1889-1919.—v. 2. 1920-1936. Bibliography: p. 1053-1058. [PN4874.S68A4 1974] 74-11989 ISBN 0-8371-7710-3
1. Steffens, Joseph Lincoln, 1866-1936. BIP

STINSON, Robert, 1941- 070.4'092'4 B
Lincoln Steffens / Robert Stinson. New York : F. Ungar Pub. Co., c1979. p. cm. (Modern literature monographs) Includes index. Bibliography: p. [PN4874.S68S7] 79-4831 ISBN 0-8044-2829-8 : 8.95
1. Steffens, Joseph Lincoln, 1866-1936. 2. Journalists—United States—Biography.

Stehling, Kurt R.

STEHLING, Kurt R. 629.13'09
Bags up! : Great ballon adventures / Kurt R. Stehling. 1st ed. Chicago : Playboy Press, c1975. 253, [2] p. : ill. ; 24 cm. Bibliography: p. [255] [TL620.A1S83] 75-17268 ISBN 0-87223-442-8
1. Stehling, Kurt R. 2. Balloon ascensions. I. Title.

*Steiger, Brad

*STEIGER, Brad 792.0924
Valentino [by] Brad Steiger, Chaw Mank. Illus. with photographs from Valentino's private scrapbooks [New York] Macfadden [c.1966] 192p. illus. 18cm. (75-171) .75 pap.,
I. Title.

Steimer, C. H.

STEIMER, C. H. 920
One man's story. New York, Vantage [1962, c.1960] 64p. 2.50 bds.,
I. Title.

Stein, Benjamin, 1944- —Diaries.

STEIN, Benjamin, 1944- 818'.5'403
Dreemz / Benjamin Stein. 1st ed. New York : Harper & Row, c1978. 212 p. ; 22 cm. [PS3569.T36Z466 1978] 77-15900 ISBN 0-06-014071-2 : 8.95
1. Stein, Benjamin, 1944- —Diaries. 2. Authors, American—20th century—Biography. I. Title. BIP

Stein, David.

STEIN, Anne-Marie. 751.5'8'0924 B
Three Picassos before breakfast; memoirs of an art forger's wife, by Anne-Marie Stein, as told to George Carpozi, Jr. New York, Hawthorn Books [1973] 192 p. illus. 25 cm. [ND553.S855S83 1973] 72-7784 6.95
1. Stein, David. 2. Forgery of works of art. I. Carpozi, George. II. Title.

Stein, Edith, 1891-1942.

BORDEAUX, Henry, 1870- 922.243
Edith Stein: thoughts on her life and times. Translated by Donald and Idella Gallagher. Milwaukee, Bruce Pub. Co. [c1959] 87p. 22cm. Translation of La vie pathetique d'edith Stein. Includes bibliography. [BX4705.S814B63] 59-14276
1. Stein, Edith, 1891-1942. I. Title.

FABREGUES, Jean de 248.2460924
Edith Stein. [Tr. from French by Donald M. Antoine] Staten Island, N.Y., Alba [c.1965] 138p. 20cm. [BX4705.S814F313] 65-25849 2.95
1. Stein, Edith, 1891-1942. 2. Converts, Catholic. I. Title.

FABREGUES, Jean de. 248.2460924
Edith Stein. [Translated from the French by Donald M. Antoine] Staten Island, N.Y., Alba House [1965] 138 p. 20 cm. Translation of La conversion d'Edith Stein. [BX4705.S814F313] 65-25849
1. Stein, Edith, 1891-1942. 2. Converts, Catholic. I. Title.

GRAEF, Hilda C 922.243
The scholar and the cross; the life and work of Edith Stein. Westminster, Md., Newman Press, 1955. 234p. illus. 22cm. [BX4705.S814G7] 54-12447
1. Stein, Edith, 1891-1942. I. Title.

GRAEF, Hilda C 922.243
The scholar and the cross; the life and work of Edith Stein. London, New York, Longmans, Green [1955] 234p. illus. 23cm. [BX4705.S814G7 1955a] 55-2959
1. Stein, Edith, 1891-1942. I. Title.

ROBERTO, Brother, 1927- 922.243
The broken lamp; a story of Edith Stein. Illus. by Anthony Joyce. Notre Dame, Ind., Dujarie Press [1957] 94p. illus. 24cm. [BX4705.S814R6] 58-290
1. Stein, Edith, 1891-1942. I. Title.

Stein, Gertrude, 1874-1946.

BRINNIN, John Malcolm, 1916- 928.1
The third rose; Gertrude Stein and her world. [1st ed.] Boston, Little, Brown [1959] 427p. illus. 22cm. [PS3537.T323Z57] 59-13732
1. Stein, Gertrude, 1874-1946. I. Title.

BRINNIN, John Malcolm, 1916- 928.1
The third rose; Gertrude Stein and her world. New York, Grove Press [1961,c.1959] 427p. illus. (Evergreen, E-278) Bibl. 2.95 pap.,
1. Stein, Gertrude, 1874-1946. I. Title.

BRINNIN, John Malcolm, 1916- 928.1
The third rose; Gertrude Stein and her world. Gloucester, Mass., Peter Smith, 1968 [c.1959] xviii, 427p. ports. 21cm. Orig. pub. by Little, Brown in 1959. Bibl. [PS3537.T323 Z57] 7.50
1. Stein, Gertrude, 1874-1946. I. Title. BIP

BRINNIN, John Malcolm, 1916- 818'.5'209 B
The third rose; Gertrude Stein and her world. Gloucester, Mass., P. Smith, 1968 [c1959] xviii, 427 p. illus. 21 cm. "A selected bibliography of the works of Gertrude Stein": p. 411-413. [PS3537.T323Z57 1968] 68-7882
1. Stein, Gertrude, 1874-1946 I. Title.

GREENFELD, Howard. 818'.5'209 B
Gertrude Stein; a biography. [1st ed.] New York, Crown Publishers [1973] 151 p. illus. 24 cm. Bibliography: p. 145-146. [PS3537.T323Z62] 72-92385 ISBN 0-517-50260-7 5.95

1. Stein, Gertrude, 1874-1946.

MELLOW, James R. 818'.5'209 B
Charmed circle: Gertrude Stein & company [by] James R. Mellow. New York, Praeger [1974] 528 p. 24 cm. Bibliography: p. [507]-514. [PS3537.T323Z72] 73-7473 12.50
1. Stein, Gertrude, 1874-1946. I. Title.

ROGERS, William Garland, 928.1
1896
When this you see remember me, Gertrude stein in person. Bobbs [dist.] new york, mac fadden [1964, c1948] vii, 247 p. port. 21 cm. (Charter book 150)
1. Stein, Gertrude, 1874-1946. I. Title. BIP

ROGERS, William 818'.5'209 B
Garland, 1896-
When this you see remember me; Gertrude Stein in person, by W. G. Rogers. Westport, Conn., Greenwood Press [1971, c1948] vii, 247 p. port. 23 cm. [PS3537.T323Z8 1971] 72-139145 ISBN 0-8371-5761-7
1. Stein, Gertrude, 1874-1946. I. Title.

*SIMON, Linda, comp. 813
Gertrude Stein; a composite portrait, edited by Linda Simon. [New York] Avon [1974] 192 p. illus. 18 cm. (Discus books.) [PS3537.T323] 74-19905 ISBN 0-380-00169-1 1.65 (pbk.)
1. Stein, Gertrude, 1874-1946. I. Title. BIP

SPRIGGE, Elizabeth, 1900- 928.1
Gertrude Stein; her life and work. New York, Harper [1957] 277 p. illus. 25 cm. [PS3537.T323Z825] 56-12229
1. Stein, Gertrude, 1874-1946. I. Title.

SPRIGGE, Elizabeth, 1900- 928.1
Gertrude Stein: her life and work. New York, Harper [1957] 277 p. illus. 25 cm. [PS3537.T323Z825] 56-12229
1. Stein, Gertrude, 1874-1946.

STEIN, Gertrude, 818'.5'209 B
1874-1946.
Everybody's autobiography. New York, Vintage Books [1973, c1937] 328 p. 19 cm. [PS3537.T323Z53 1973] 72-8694 1.95
I. Title. BIP

STEIN, Gertrude, 818'.5'209 B
1874-1946.
Everybody's autobiography. New York, Cooper Square Publishers, 1971 [c1937] 318 p. illus., ports. 22 cm. [PS3537.T323Z53 1971] 70-159032 ISBN 0-8154-0386-0 10.00
I. Title.

STEWART, Allegra. 818'.5'209
Gertrude Stein and the present. Cambridge, Harvard University Press, 1967. ix, 223 p. 22 cm. Bibliographical footnotes. [PS3537.T323Z827] 67-20884
1. Stein, Gertrude, 1874-1946. I. Title.

STEWART, Allegra. 818'.5'209
Gertrude Stein and the present. Cambridge, Harvard University Press, 1967. ix, 223 p. 22 cm. Bibliographical footnotes. [PS3537.T323Z827] 67-20884
1. Stein, Gertrude, 1874-1946. I. Title. BIP

SUTHERLAND, Donald. 810.81
Gertrude Stein, a biography of her work. New Haven, Yale University Press, 1951. 218 p. 21 cm. [PS3537.T323Z83] 51-12323
1. Stein, Gertrude, 1874-1946. I. Title.

THE third rose; v. 12
Gertrude Stein and her world. New York, Grove Press [1961] 427p. illus. 22cm. (Evergreen, E-278)
1. Stein, Gertrude, 1874-1946. I. Brinnin, John Malcolm, 1916-

TOKLAS, Alice B. 818'.5'209 B
Staying on alone; letters of Alice B. Toklas. Edited by Edward Burns. With an introd. by Gilbert A. Harrison. New York, Liveright [1973] xxii, 426 p. illus. 24 cm. [PS3537.T323Z84] 73-82424 ISBN 0-87140-569-5 11.95
1. Stein, Gertrude, 1874-1946. 2. Toklas, Alice B. I. Title.

WILSON, Ellen Janet 818'.5'209 B
(Cameron)
They named me Gertrude Stein [by] Ellen Wilson. New York, Farrar, Straus and Giroux [1973] ix, 133 p. illus. 24 cm. Bibliography: p. 125-128. [PS3537.T323Z93] 73-76223 ISBN 0-374-37467-8 5.50
1. Stein, Gertrude, 1874-1946. I. Title. BIP

Stein, Gertrude, 1874-1946—Bibliography.

†SAWYER, Julian. 016.818'5'209
Gertrude Stein, a bibliography / by Julian Sawyer. Folcroft, Pa. : Folcroft Library Editions, 1976, c1940. 162 p. ; 26 cm. Reprint of the ed. published by Arrow Editions, New York. Includes index. [Z8838.9.S7S3 1976] [PS3537.T323] 76-41818 ISBN 0-8414-7777-9 lib. bdg. : 30.00
1. Stein, Gertrude, 1874-1946—Bibliography.

WILSON, Robert 016.818'5'209
Alfred Jump, 1922-
Gertrude Stein: a bibliography, compiled by Robert A. Wilson. New York, Phoenix Bookshop, 1974. xii, 227 p. 24 cm. (The Phoenix bibliographies, 7) [Z8838.9.W54] 73-85937 15.00
1. Stein, Gertrude, 1874-1946—Bibliography. I. Title.
Publishers address: 18 Cornelia Street, New York, 10014.

Stein, Gertrude, 1874-1946—Biography.

HOBHOUSE, Janet, 818'.5'209 B
1948-
Everybody who was anybody : a biography of Gertrude Stein / Janet Hobhouse. 1st American ed. New York : Putnam, 1975. xii, 244 p. : ill. ; 26 cm. Includes index. "Principal works of Gertrude Stein": p. vi-vii. [PS3537.T323Z647 1975] 75-10844 ISBN 0-399-11605-2 : 17.50
1. Stein, Gertrude, 1874-1946—Biography. I. Title. BIP

TOKLAS, Alice B. 818'.5'209 B
Staying on alone; letters of Alice B. Toklas. Edited by Edward Burns. With an introd. by Gilbert A. Harrison. New York, Vintage Books [1975, c1973] p. Reprint of the ed. published by Liveright, New York. [PS3537.T323Z84 1975] 74-5055 2.95 (pbk.)
1. Stein, Gertrude, 1874-1946—Biography. 2. Toklas, Alice B.—Correspondence. I. Title.

Stein, Gertrude, 1874-1946—Juvenile literature.

ROGERS, William 818'.5'209 B
Garland, 1896-
Gertrude Stein is Gertrude Stein is Gertrude Stein: her life and work, by W. G. Rogers. Illustrated with photos. New York, Crowell [1973] xiv, 237 p. illus. 21 cm. (Women of America) Bibliography. p. 223-227. A biography of the American author and art collector who was a prominent figure on the literary scene in early twentieth century Paris. [PS3537.T323Z795] 92 72-7555 ISBN 0-690-32585-1 4.50
1. Stein, Gertrude, 1874-1946—Juvenile literature. I. Title.

Stein, Gertrude, 1874-1946—Relationship with women.

SIMON, Linda, 1946- 818'.5'209 B
The biography of Alice B. Toklas / by Linda Simon. 1st ed. Garden City, N.Y. : Doubleday, 1977. x, 324 p., [12] leaves of plates : ill. ; 24 cm. Includes index. Bibliography: p. 301-313. [PS3537.T323Z823] 76-23798 ISBN 0-385-08140-5 : 10.00
1. Stein, Gertrude, 1874-1946—Relationship with women. 2. Toklas, Alice B. 3. Stein, Gertrude, 1874-1946—Friends and associates. 4. Paris—Intellectual life. 5. Authors, American—20th century—Biography. I. Title. BIP

Stein, Heinrich Friedrich Karl, Freiherr vom und zum, 1757-1831.

RAACK, R. C. 943.060924
The fall of Stein. Cambridge, Mass., Harvard [c.]1965. xi, 217p. 21cm. (Harvard historical monographs, 58) Bibl. [DD416.S8R24] 65-19828 6.50
1. Stein, Heinrich Friedrich Karl, Freiherr vom und zum, 1757-1831. 2. Prussia—Pol. & govt.—1806-1848. I. Title. II. Series. BIP

SEELEY, John 943'.06'0924 B
Robert, Sir, 1834-1895.
Life and times of Stein; or, Germany and Prussia in the Napoleonic age. New York, Haskell House Publishers, 1969. 3 v. maps, ports. 23 cm. Reprint of the 1878 ed. Includes bibliographical references. [DD416.S8S4 1969] 68-26368 ISBN 0-8383-0179-7
1. Stein, Heinrich Friedrich Karl, Freiherr vom und zum, 1757-1831. 2. Prussia—History—Frederick William III, 1797-1840. 3. Europe—History—1789-1900. 4. Europe—Politics and government—1789-1900. I. Title.

SEELEY, John 943'.06'0924 B
Robert, Sir, 1834-1895.
Life and times of Stein; or, Germany and Prussia in the Napoleonic age. Cambridge [Eng.] University Press, 1878. St. Clair Shores, Mich., Scholarly Press [1969] 3 v. maps, ports. 22 cm. Includes bibliographical references. [DD416.S8S4 1969b] 72-108538 ISBN 0-403-00231-1
1. Stein, Heinrich Friedrich Karl, Freiherr vom und zum, 1757-1831. 2. Prussia—History—Frederick William III, 1797-1840. 3. Europe—History—1789-1900. 4. Europe—Politics and government—1789-1900. I. Title.

SEELEY, John 943'.06'0924 B
Robert, Sir, 1834-1895.
Life and times of Stein; or, Germany and Prussia in the Napoleonic age. New York, Greenwood Press, 1968. 3 v. maps, ports. 22 cm. Reprint of the 1878 ed. Contents.Contents.—v. 1. 1757-1807.—v. 2. 1800-1812—v. 3. 1813-1831. Bibliography: v. 1, p. ix-xv. [DD416.S8S4 1968] 68-23324
1. Stein, Heinrich Friedrich Karl, Freiherr vom und zum, 1757-1831. 2. Prussia—History—Frederick William III, 1797-1840. 3. Europe—History—1789-1900. 4. Europe—Politics and government—1789-1900. I. Title. BIP

Stein, Judith Beck, 1925-

STEIN, Judith 320.9'73'0924 B
Beck, 1925-
The journal of Judith Beck Stein. Washington, Columbia Journal, inc., 1973. xv, 170 p. illus. 23 cm. [CT275.S6758A34] 73-179228
1. Stein, Judith Beck, 1925- I. Title.

Stein, Leo,

STEIN, Leo, 1872-1947. 928.1
Journey into the self, being the letters, papers & journals of Leo Stein, edited by Edmund Fuller. Introd. by Van Wyck Brooks. New York, Crown Publishers [1950] xiv, 331 p. illus., ports. 24 cm. [PS3537.T3232Z52] 50-8701
I. Fuller, Edmund, 1914- ed. II. Title.

Stein, Mark Aurel, Sir, 1862-1943.

MIRSKY, 939'.6'007202 B
Jeannette, 1903-
Sir Aurel Stein, archaeological explorer / Jeannette Mirsky. Chicago : University of Chicago Press, 1977. xiii, 585 p., [8] leaves of plates : ill. ; 24 cm. Includes bibliographical references and index. [DS785.S84M57] 76-17703 ISBN 0-226-53176-7 : 17.50
1. Stein, Mark Aurel, Sir, 1862-1943. 2. Archaeologists—Asia, Central—Biography. I. Title.

Steinbeck, John, 1902-1968.

LISCA, Peter. 813.5
The wide world of John Steinbeck. New Brunswick, N.J., Rutgers University Press, 1958. 326 p. 22 cm. Includes bibliography. [PS3537.T3234Z72] 57-10965
1. Steinbeck, John, 1902- I. Title.

STEINBECK Conference, 813'.5'2
Corvallis, Or., 1970.
Steinbeck: the man and his work; proceedings. Edited by Richard Astro and Tetsumaro Hayashi. Corvallis, Oregon State University Press [1971] ix, 183 p. ports. 23 cm. "Sponsored by Oregon State and Ball State Universities." Includes bibliographical references. [PS3537.T3234Z87 1970] 76-632782 ISBN 0-87071-443-0 5.00
1. Steinbeck, John, 1902-1968. I. Astro, Richard, ed. II. Hayashi, Tetsumaro, ed. III. Oregon. State University, Corvallis. IV. Indiana. Ball State University, Muncie.

Steinbeck, John, 1902-1968—Biography.

GANNETT, Lewis Stiles, 813'.5'2 B
1891-1966.
John Steinbeck, personal and bibliographical notes / by Lewis Gannett. Brooklyn : Haskell House Publishers, 1978, c1939 p. cm. [PS3537.T3234Z7 1977] 77-10503 ISBN 0-8383-2213-1 lib.bdg. : 9.95
1. Steinbeck, John, 1902-1968—Biography. 2. Novelists, American—20th century—Biography. I. Title.

KIERNAN, Thomas. 813'.5'2 B
The intricate music : a biography of John Steinbeck / Thomas Kiernan. 1st ed. Boston : Little, Brown, c1979. xvii, 331 p. : port ; 24 cm. "The works of John Steinbeck" : p. [318]-319. [PS3537.T3234Z716] 79-12595 ISBN 0-316-49202-7 : 12.50
1. Steinbeck, John, 1902-1968—Biography. 2. Authors, American—20th century—Biography. I. Title. BIP

Steinbeck, John, 1902-1968—Biography—Youth.

BENNETT, Robert. 813'.5'2 B
The wrath of John Steinbeck; or, St. John goes to church. With a foreword by Lawrence Clark Powell. Illustrated by Artemis. [Folcroft, Pa.] Folcroft Library Editions, 1974 [c1939] p. Reprint of the ed. published by the Albertson Press, Los Angeles. [PS3537.T3234Z6 1974] 74-3126 5.00
1. Steinbeck, John, 1902-1968—Biography—Youth. 2. Steinbeck, John, 1902-1968—Anecdotes. I. Title. II. Title: St. John goes to church.

BENNETT, Robert. 813'.5'2 B
The wrath of John Steinbeck : or, St. John goes to church / by Robert Bennett ; with a foreword by Lawrence Clark Powell ; illustrated by Artemis. Darby, Pa. : Arden Library, 1978 [c1939] p. cm. Reprint of the ed. published by Albertson Press, Los Angeles. [PS3537.T3234Z6 1978] 78-6903 ISBN 0-8495-0331-0 : 6.50
1. Steinbeck, John, 1902-1968—Biography—Youth. 2. Steinbeck, John, 1902-1968—Anecdotes. 3. Authors, American—20th century—Biography. I. Title.

Steinbeck, John, 1902-1968—Correspondence.

STEINBECK, John, 1902- 813'.5'2
1968.
Steinbeck : a life in letters / edited by Elaine Steinbeck and Robert Wallsten. New York : Viking Press, 1975. xv, 906 p. : port. ; 25 cm. Includes index. [PS3537.T3234Z53 1975] 75-15756 ISBN 0-670-66962-8 : 15.00
1. Steinbeck, John, 1902-1968—Correspondence. BIP

STEINBECK, John, 1902- 813'.5'2 B
1968.
Steinbeck : a life in letters / edited by Elaine Steinbeck and Robert Wallsten. New York : Penguin Books, 1976, c1975. xv, 908 p. : ill. ; 20 cm. Includes index. [PS3537.T3234Z53 1976] 76-18821 ISBN 0-14-004288-1 pbk. : 5.95
1. Steinbeck, John, 1902-1968—Correspondence.

Steinbeck, John, 1902-1968—Friends and associates.

ASTRO, Richard. 813'.5'2 B
John Steinbeck and Edward F. Ricketts: the shaping of a novelist. Minneapolis, University of Minnesota Press [1973, i.e.

1974] xii, 259 p. illus. 23 cm. Includes bibliographical references. [PS3537.T3234Z58] 73-87252 ISBN 0-8166-0704-4 12.95
1. Steinbeck, John, 1902-1968—Friends and associates. 2. Ricketts, Edward Flanders, 1896-1948. I. Title.

THE Outer shores 917.9'04'30924 / edited by Joel W. Hedgpeth. Eureka, Calif. : Mad River Press, c1978- v. : ill. ; 22 cm. Contents.Contents.—pt. 1. Ed Ricketts and John Steinbeck explore the Pacific Coast. Bibliography: v. 1, p. 127-128. [PS3537.T3234Z783] 79-107397 ISBN 0-916422-13-5 pbk. : 7.95
1. Steinbeck, John, 1902-1968—Friends and associates. 2. Ricketts, Edward Flanders, 1896-1948. 3. Pacific coast—Description and travel. 4. Novelists, American—20th century—Biography. 5. Marine biologists—United States—Biography. I. Hedgpeth, Joel Walker, 1911- II. Ricketts, Edward Flanders, 1896-1948. III. Steinbeck, John, 1902-1968.

Steinbeck, John, 1902-1968—Juvenile literature.

O'CONNOR, Richard, 1915- 813'.5'2 B
John Steinbeck. New York, McGraw-Hill [1970] 128 p. port. 21 cm. (American writers series) Includes bibliographies. A biography of the California-born author whose many works won him the Nobel Prize for Literature in 1962. [PS3537.T3234Z78] 92 79-107450 4.95
1. Steinbeck, John, 1902-1968—Juvenile literature. I. Title.

Steinberg, Alfred,

STEINBERG, Alfred, 1917- 923.973
Admiral Richard E., Byrd. Illustrated by Charles Beck. New York, Putnam [1960] 128 p. illus. 21 cm. (Lives to remember) [G585.B8S8] 60-6914
I. Byrd, Richard Evelyn. 1888-1957 —Juvenile literature. II. Title.

Steinberg, Milton, 1903-1950.

NOVECK, Simon. 296.6'1'0924 B
Milton Steinberg : portrait of a rabbi / by Simon Noveck. New York : Ktav Pub. House, c1978. xii, 353 p., [8] leaves of plates : ill. ; 24 cm. Includes index. Bibliography: p. 330-337. [BM755.S67N68] 77-25943 ISBN 0-87068-444-2 : 12.50
1. Steinberg, Milton, 1903-1950. 2. Rabbis—United States—Biography. BIP

Steiner, Ralph, 1899-

STEINER, Ralph, 1899- 770'.92'4 B
A point of view / Ralph Steiner. 1st ed. Middletown, Conn. : Wesleyan University Press, c1978. xii, 144 p. : ill. ; 27 cm. [TR140.S683A34] 77-20513 ISBN 0-8195-5019-1 : 20.00
1. Steiner, Ralph, 1899- 2. Photographers—United States—Biography. I. Title. BIP

Steiner, Rolf, 1933-

STEINER, Rolf, 1933- 355'.0092'4 B
The last adventurer / Rolf Steiner, with the collaboration of Yves-Guy Berges ; translated by Steve Cox. 1st English language ed. Boston : Little, Brown, c1978. viii, 275 p. ; 22 cm. Translation of Carre rouge. [DT515.9.E3S7713] 77-19070 ISBN 0-316-81239-0 : 8.95
1. Steiner, Rolf, 1933- 2. France. Armee. Legion etrangere. 3. Nigeria—History—Civil War, 1967-1970—Personal narratives. 4. Guerrillas—Sudan. 5. Soldiers of fortune—Nigeria—Biography. 6. Soldiers of fortune—Sudan—Biography. I. Berges, Yves Guy. II. Title.

Steiner, Rudolf, 1861-1925.

SHEPHERD, Arthur Pearce, 1885- v. 12
A scientist of the invisible; an introduction to the life and work of Rudolf Steiner. New York, British book centre, 1959. 221 p. illus. 20 cm.
1. Steiner, Rudolf, 1861 — 1925. I. Title.

STEINER, Rudolf, 1861-1925. 921.3
The course of my life. Rev. translation by the authorized translator, Olin D. Wannamaker. New York, Anthroposophic Press, 1951. 376 p. illus. 24 cm. [BP595.S895A32] 51-7011
I. Title.

STEINER, Rudolf, 1861-1925. 193 B
The course of my life. Rev. translation by the authorized translator, Olin D. Wannamaker. [2d ed.] New York, Anthroposophic Press [1970, c1951] 358 p. ports. 25 cm. Translation of Mein Lebensgang. [BP595.S854883 1970] 78-121898

WACHSMUTH, Guenther, 1893- 921.3
The life and work of Rudolf Steiner from the turn of the century to his death. Translated by Olin D. Wannamaker and Reginald E. Raab. 2d ed., supplemented and expanded, of the volume published in 1941 under the title Die Geburt der Geisteswissenshaft (The birth of spiritual science) New York, Whittier Books [1955] 594p. illus. 25cm. [BP595.S895W35] 55-14834
1. Steiner, Rudolf, 1861-1925. 2. Anthroposophy. I. Title.

Steinhaus, Edward Arthur, 1914-1969.

STEINHAUS, Edward Arthur, 1914-1969. 595.7'02
Disease in a minor chord : being a semihistorical and semibiographical account of a period in science when one could be happily yet seriously concerned with the diseases of lowly animals without backbones, especially the insects / Edward A. Steinhaus. Columbus : Ohio State University Press, [1975] xviii, 488 p. ; 24 cm. Includes indexes. Bibliography: p. [433]-467. [SB942.S75 1975] 75-4527 ISBN 0-8142-0218-7 : 20.00
1. Steinhaus, Edward Arthur, 1914-1969. 2. Insects—Diseases. 3. Insects—Diseases—Research—History. I. Title. BIP

Steinke, Bettina, 1913-

HEDGPETH, Don. 759.13 B
Bettina : portraying life in art / by Don Hedgpeth ; with a foreword by Eric Sloane. 1st ed. Flagstaff [Ariz.] : Northland Press, c1978. xvii, 155 p., [1] leaf of plates : ill. (some col.) ; 28 cm. [ND1329.S66H42] 77-93516 ISBN 0-87358-169-5 : 35.00
1. Steinke, Bettina, 1913- 2. Portrait painters—United States—Biography. I. Title. BIP

Steinman, David Barnard, 1886-

RATIGAN, William. 926.24
Highways over broad waters; life and times of David B. Steinman, bridgebuilder. [1st ed.] Grand Rapids, Eerdmans [1959] 359p. illus. 23cm. (His Great Lakes panorama) Includes bibliography. [TG140.S73R3] 59-12936
1. Steinman, David Barnard, 1886- I. Title.

Steinman, Philip,

STEINMAN, Philip, 1876- 920
Beechwood Flats. [1st ed.] New York, Vantage Press [1960] 205 p. illus. 21 cm. Autobiographical. [CT275.S6775A3] 60-50173
I. Title.

Steinman, Philip, III

STEINMAN, Philip, III 920
Beechwood Flats. New York, Vantage Press [c.1960] 205p. illus. 21cm. 60-50173 3.50 bds.,
I. Title.

Steinmetz, Charles Proteus, 1865-1923.

†GARLIN, Sender. 335'.0092'4 B
Charles P. Steinmetz, scientist and socialist (1865-1923), including the complete Steinmetz-Lenin correspondence / by Sender Garlin. New York : American Institute for Marxist Studies, c1977. i, 42 p., [1] leaf of plates : port. ; 29 cm. (Occasional paper - American Institute for Marxist Studies ; no. 22) Cover title. Bibliography: p. 40-42. [TK140.S77G37] 77-371979 pbk. : 1.50
1. Steinmetz, Charles Proteus, 1865-1923. 2. Electric engineers—United States—Biography. 3. Socialists—United States—Biography. I. Title. II. Series: American Institute for Marxist Studies. Occasional papers ; no. 22.

LAVINE, Sigmund A 926.213
Steinmetz, maker of lightning; illustrated with photos. New York, Dodd, Mead, 1955. 241p. illus. 22cm. [TK140.S77L3] 55-5852
1. Steinmetz, Charles Proteus, I. Title.

MARKEY, Dorothy. 926.213
The little giant of Schenectady, a story of Charles Steinmetz; illustrated by E. Harper Johnson. [1st ed.] New York, Aladdin Books, 1956. 191p. illus. 21cm. (American heritage series) [TK140.S77M3] 56-5478
1. Steinmetz, Charles Proteus, 1865-1923. I. Title.

MILLER, John Anderson, 1895- 926.213
Modern Jupiter; the story of Charles Proteus Steinmetz. New York, American Society of Mechanical Engineers [1958] 228p. illus. 22cm. [TK140.S77M5] 59-168
1. Steinmetz, Charles Proteus, 1805-1923. I. Title.

THOMAS, Henry 926.213
Charles Steinmetz; illustrated by Charles Beck. New, York, Putnam [c.1959] 126p. illus. 21cm. (Lives to remember) 59-13608 2.50
1. Steinmetz, Charles Proteus, 1865-1923. I. Title.

THOMAS, Henry, 1886- 926.213
Charles Steinmetz; illustrated by Charles Beck. New York, Putnam [1959] 126 p. illus. 21 cm. (Lives to remember) [TK140.S77T4] 59-13608
1. Steinmetz, Charles Proteus, 1865-1923. I. Title.

Steinmetz, Charles Proteus, 1865-1923—Juvenile literature.

[BEST, Allena (Champlin)] 1892- 92
Charles Proteus Steinmetz, wizard of electricity, by Erick Berry [pseud.] Illus. by John Martinez. New York, Macmillan [c.1966] 41p. col. illus. 25cm. (Sci. story lib.) [TH140.S77B45] 65-20202 2.95; 3.24 lib. ed.,
1. Steinmetz, Charles Proteus, 1865-1923—Juvenile literature. I. Martinez, John, illustrator. II. Title.

GUY, Anne (Welsh) 92
Steinmetz, wizard of light. Illus. by Leonard Rosoman. New York, Knopf [c. 1965] 104, iii p. illus. 22cm. [TK140.S77G8] 65-21565 3.50; 3.99 lib. ed.,
1. Steinmetz, Charles Proteus, 1865-1923—Juvenile literature. I. Title.

MILLER, Floyd. 92
The electrical genius of Liberty Hall: Charles Proteus Steinmetz. Foreword by Clyde Wagoner. New York, McGraw-Hill [1962] 126p. illus. 21cm. [TK140.S77M47] 62-19159
1. Steinmetz, Charles Proteus, 1865-1923—Juvenile literature. I. Title.

SEYMOUR, Alta Halverson, 1893- 621.3'0924 [B]
Charles Steinmetz. Illustrated by Huntley Brown. Chicago, Follett Pub. Co. [1966] 144 p. col. illus. 22 cm. (Library of American heroes) [TK140.S77S3] 65-14469
1. Steinmetz, Charles Proteus, 1865-1923—Juvenile literature.

Stekel, Wilhelm,

STEKEL, Wilhelm, 1868-1940. [921.36]
Autobiography. The life story of a pioneer psychoanalyst, edited by Emil A. Gutheil, with an introd. by Hilda Stekel. New York, Liveright [1950] 293 p. ports, facsims. 22 cm. [BF109.S75A3] [926.1] 50-7284
I. Gutheil, Emil Arthur, 1899- ed. II. Title.

Steller, Georg Wilhelm, 1709-1746.

BELL, Margaret Elizabeth, 1898- 925.7
Touched with fire; Alaska's George William Steller. Maps by Bob Ritter. New York, Morrow, 1960. 189 p. illus. 22 cm. [G226.S8B4] 60-10065
1. Steller, Georg Wilhelm, 1709-1746. I. Title.

SUTTON, Ann. 919.8
Steller of the North, by Ann and Myron Sutton. Illustrated by Leonard Everett Fisher. Chicago, Rand McNally [1961] 231 p. illus. 22 cm. [G226.S8S85] 61-6846
1. Steller, Georg Wilhelm, 1700-1746. I. Sutton, Myron. joint author. II. Title.

SUTTON, Ann, 1923- 919.8
Steller of the North, by Ann and Myron Sutton. Illustrated by Leonard Everett Fisher. Chicago, Rand McNally [1961] 231 p. illus. 22 cm. [G226.S8S85] 61-6846
1. Steller, Georg Wilhelm, 1709-1746. I. Sutton, Myron, joint author.

Steloff, Frances, 1887-

ROGERS, William Garland, 1896- 920.4
Wise men fish here; the story of Frances Steloff and the Gotham Book Mart. New York, Harcourt [c.1965] x, 246p. illus., ports. 21cm. [Z473.G63R6] 64-18293 5.95
1. Steloff, Frances, 1887- 2. Gotham Book Mart, New York. I. Title.

Stelzle, Charles,

STELZLE, Charles, 1869-1941. 309.1'747'1 B
A son of the Bowery; the life story of an East Side American. Freeport, N.Y., Books for Libraries Press [1971] 335 p. port. 23 cm. Reprint of the 1926 ed. [HM22.U6S7 1971] 74-179540 ISBN 0-8369-6669-4
I. Title. BIP

Stengel, Casey.

ALLEN, Maury, 1932- 796.357'092'4 B
You could look it up : the life of Casey Stengel / Maury Allen. New York : Times Books, c1979. p. cm. Includes index. [GV865.S8A63 1979] 79-51424 ISBN 0-8129-0830-9 : 10.95
1. Stengel, Casey. 2. New York (City). Baseball club (American League) 3. Baseball managers—United States—Biography. I. Stengel, Casey. II. Title. BIP

DURSO, Joseph. 796.3576'4'0924
Casey; the life and legend of Charles Dillon Stengel. Englewood Cliffs, N. J., Prentice-Hall [1967] ix, 211 p. illus., ports. 24 cm. [GV865.S8D8] 67-13566
1. Stengel, Casey. I. Title.

MACLEAN, Norman. 796.357'092'4 B
Casey Stengel / by Norman MacLean. New York : Drake Publishers, [1976] p.

cm. [GV865.S8M3] 75-36157 ISBN 0-8473-1068-X : 9.95
1. Stengel, Casey. 2. Baseball.

STENGEL, Casey. 927.96357
Casey at the bat; the story of my life in baseball as told to Harry T. Taxton. New York, Random House [1962] 354 p. illus. 21 cm. [GV865.S8A3] 62-8465
1. Baseball — Hist. I. Paxton, Harry T. II. Title.

Stengel, Casey—Juvenile literature.

VERRAL, Charles Spain. 796.357'64'0924 B
Casey Stengel, baseball's great manager / by Charles Spain Verral. Champaign, Ill. : Garrard Pub. Co., c1978. 93 p. : ill. ; 24 cm. A biography of the personal and professional life of Charles Dillon Stengel following his career through minor and major league play and his forty years as a team manager. [GV865.S8V47] 92 78-6894 ISBN 0-8116-6683-2 lib. bdg. : 4.78
1. Stengel, Casey—Juvenile literature. 2. Baseball managers—United States—Biography—Juvenile literature. I. Title.

Stengel, Charles Dillon.

GRAHAM, Frank, 1925- 927.96357
Casey Stengel, his half-century in baseball. New York, J. Day Co. [1958] 192 p. illus. 21 cm. [GV865.S8G7] 58-9706
1. Stengel, Charles Dillon.

SCHOOR, Gene. 927.96357
Casey Stengel, baseball's greatest manager, by Gene Schoor with Henry Gilfond. New York, J. Messner [1953] 185 p. illus. 22 cm. [GV865.S8S3] 53-10513
1. Stengel, Charles Dillon.

Steno, Nicolaus, Bp., 1638-1686.

CIONI, Aaffaello 922.2489
Niles Stensen, scientist-bishop. Tr. [from Italian] by Genevieve M. Camera. Pref. by John LaFarge. New York, Kenedy [c.1962] 192p. 22cm. 62-16530 3.95
1. Steno, Nicolaus, Bp., 1638-1686. I. Title.

Stensby, Yngvar,

STENSBY, Yngvar, 1914- 818.5
Imperfections of a preacher's kid. [1st ed.] New York, Pageant Press [1952] 129p. 21cm. Autobiography. [CT275.S68A3] 53-380
I. Title.

Stephen, James Fitzjames, Sir, bart., 1829-1894.

STEPHEN, Leslie, Sir, 1832-1904. 347'.42'03534 B
The life of Sir James Fitzjames Stephen, bart., K.C.S.I., a judge of the High Court of Justice, by his brother Leslie Stephen. South Hackensack, N.J., Rothman Reprints, 1972. x, 504 p. ports. 23 cm. Reprint of the 1895 ed. Bibliography: p. [483]-486. [KD631.S7S74 1972] 75-190291
1. Stephen, James Fitzjames, Sir, bart., 1829-1894.

Stephen, King of England, 1097?-1154.

APPLEBY, John Tate, 1907- 942.02'4'0924 B
The troubled reign of King Stephen, by John T. Appleby. New York, Barnes & Noble, 1970 [c1969] 218 p. 23 cm. Bibliography: p. 208-211. [DA198.5.A8 1970] 79-12566
1. Stephen, King of England, 1097?-1154. I. Title.

DAVID, Ralph H. C. 942.02'4'094 B
King Stephen, 1135-1154 / R. H. C. Davis. London : Longman, c1977. p. cm. Includes bibliographical references and index. [DA198.5.D3 1977] 77-4291 ISBN 0-582-48727-7 pbk. : 6.50
1. Stephen, King of England, 1097?-1154. 2. Great Britain—History—Stephen, 1135-1154. 3. Great Britain—Kings and rulers—Biography. I. Title.
Distributed by Longman N.Y.

DAVID, Ralph H. C. 942.02'4'094 B
King Stephen, 1135-1154 / R. H. C. Davis. London : Longman, c1977. p. cm. Includes bibliographical references and index. [DA198.5.D3 1977] 77-4291 ISBN 0-582-48727-7 pbk. : 6.50
1. Stephen, King of England, 1097?-1154. 2. Great Britain—History—Stephen, 1135-1154. 3. Great Britain—Kings and rulers—Biography. I. Title.
Distributed by Longman N.Y.

DAVIS, Ralph H. C. 942.02'4'0924
King Stephen, 1135-1154 [by] R. H. C. Davis. Berkeley, Univ. of Calif. Pr., 1967. 156p. illus., geneal. table, maps. 23cm. Bibl. [DA198.5.D3] 67-17539 5.00
1. Stephen, King of England, 1097?-1154. 2. Gt. Brit.—Hist.— Stephen, 1135-1154. I. Title.

DAVIS, Ralph H. C. 942.02'4'0924
King Stephen, 1135-1154 [by] R. H. C. Davis. Berkeley, University of California Press, 1967. 156 p. illus., geneal. table, maps. 23 cm. Includes bibliographical references. [DA198.5.D3] 67-17539
1. Stephen, King of England, 1097?-1154. 2. Gt. Brit. — Hist. — Stephen, 1135-1154. I. Title. BIP

Stephen, Leslie, Sir, 1832-1904.

†ANNAN, Noel Gilroy Annan, Baron, 1916- 828'.8'09 B
Leslie Stephen / Noel Gilroy Annan. New York : Arno Press, 1977. 342 p. ; 23 cm. (The Academic profession) Reprint of the 1952 ed. published by Harvard University Press, Cambridge. Includes bibliographical references and index. [PR5473.S6A88 1977b] 76-55199 ISBN 0-405-10028-0 lib. bdg. : 20.00
1. Stephen, Leslie, Sir, 1832-1904. 2. Authors, English—19th century—Biography. I. Title. II. Series.

ANNAN, Noel Gilroy Annan, Baron, 1916- 828'.8'09 B
Leslie Stephen, his thought and character in relation to his time / by Noel Gilroy Annan. New York : AMS Press, 1977 i.e. 1976 p. cm. Reprint of the 1951 ed. published by MacGibbon & Kee, London. Includes index. Bibliography: p. [PR5473.S6A88 1977] 75-30015 ISBN 0-404-14021-1 : 23.00
1. Stephen, Leslie, Sir, 1832-1904. 2. Authors, English—19th century—Biography. I. Title. BIP

COURTNEY, Janet Elizabeth Hogarth, 1865- 192 B
Freethinkers of the nineteenth century / by Janet E. Courtney. Norwood, Pa. : Norwood Editions, 1976. p. cm. Reprint of the 1920 ed. published by Chapman & Hall, London. Contents.Contents.—Frederick Denison Maurice.—Mathew Arnold.—Charles Bradlaugh.—Thomas Henry Huxley.—Leslie Stephen.—Harriet Martineau.—Charles Kingsley. [B1569.C6 1976] 76-17266 ISBN 0-8482-0386-0 : 25.00
1. Maurice, Frederick Denison, 1805-1872. 2. Arnold, Matthew, 1822-1888—Religion and ethics. 3. Bradlaugh, Charles, 1833-1891. 4. Huxley, Thomas Henry, 1825-1895. 5. Stephen, Leslie, Sir, 1832-1904. 6. Martineau, Harriet, 1802-1876. 7. Kingsley, Charles, 1819-1875. I. Title. BIP

MAITLAND, Frederic William, 1850-1906 828'.8'08
The life and letters of Leslie Stephen. London, Duckworth; Detroit, Gale, 1968. viii, 509p. 5 ports. 22cm. (Gale lib. of lives & letters: British writers ser.) Bibl. [PR5473.S6M3 1968] 67-23873 7.80
1. Stephen, Sir Leslie, 1832-1904. I. Title. BIP

Stephens, Alexander Hamilton, 1812-1883.

JOHNSTON, Richard Malcolm, 1822-1898. 973.7'13'0924 B
Life of Alexander H. Stephens, by Richard Malcolm Johnston and William Hand Browne. Freeport, N.Y., Books for Libraries Press [1971] 619 p. 23 cm. Reprint of the 1878 ed. [E467.1.S85J75 1971] 71-179526 ISBN 0-8369-6655-4
1. Stephens, Alexander Hamilton, 1812-1883. I. Browne, William Hand, 1828-1912, joint author. BIP

STEPHENS, Alexander Hamilton, 1812-1883. 973.77'2'0924
Recollections of Alexander H. Stephens; his diary kept when a prisoner at Fort Warren, Boston Harbour, 1865. Edited with an introd. by Myrta Lockett Avary. New York, Da Capo Press, 1971 [c1910] xiii, 572 p. port. 24 cm. [E467.1.S85S85 1971] 76-124914 ISBN 0-306-71984-3
1. United States—History—Civil War, 1861-1865—Prisoners and prisons. 2. Fort Warren. I. Avary, Myrta (Lockett), ed. II. Title.

VON ABELE, Rudolph Radama, 1922- 973.7'13'0924 B
Alexander H. Stephens, a biography, by Rudolph von Abele. Westport, Conn., Negro Universities Press [1971, c1946] xiii, 337, x p. ports. 23 cm. Originally presented as the author's thesis, Columbia, 1946. Bibliography: p. [328]-337. [E467.1.S85V6 1971] 74-135614 ISBN 0-8371-5201-1
1. Stephens, Alexander Hamilton, 1812-1883. I. Title.

Stephens, Charles Asbury, 1844-1931.

HARRIS, Louise. 813'.5'2
A chuckle and a laugh; a tale of the C. A. Stephens Collection. Providence, C. A. Stephens Collection, Brown University [1967] 182 p. illus., ports. 24 cm. [PS2919.S32Z6] 67-4789
1. Stephens, Charles Asbury, 1844-1931. I. Title.

STEPHENS, Charles Asbury, 1844-1931. 570'.1
Natural salvation : the message of science / Charles Asbury Stephens ; with two biographical essays by Gerald J. Gruman. New York : Arno Press, 1977, [c1905] p. 332-336, 184 p. : ports. ; 24 cm. (The Literature of death and dying) Reprint of the ed. published by The Laboratory, Norway Lake, Me. The two essays by Gruman are reprinted from v. 254, no. 14 of the New England journal of medicine and v. 14, no. 5 of Geriatrics, respectively. [QH331.S8 1977] 76-19588 ISBN 0-405-09583-X lib.bdg. 14.00
1. Stephens, Charles Asbury, 1844-1931. 2. Biology—Philosophy. 3. Life (Biology) 4. Physicians—United States—Biography. I. Title. II. Series.

†WHITNEY, Ronald G. 813'.5'2 B
The world of C. A. Stephens / by Ronald G. Whitney. Springfield, Mass. : Waynor Pub. Co., c1976. xiii, 199 p., [1] leaf of plates : ill. ; 28 cm. Includes bibliographical references. [PS3537.T3533Z9] 76-8714 ISBN 0-917070-01-1 pbk. : 9.95
1. Stephens, Charles Asbury, 1844-1931—Biography. 2. Authors, American—20th century—Biography. I. Title. BIP

Stephens, Charlotte, 1854-1951.

TERRY, Adolphine (Fletcher) 1882- 371.1'0092'4 B
Charlotte Stephens. Little Rock's first Black teacher. Little Rock, Academic Press of Arkansas [1973] 129 p. illus. 23 cm. [LA2317.S82T47] 73-91596 5.00
1. Stephens, Charlotte, 1854-1951. I. Title. Publisher's address: 300 Spring Bldg., Little Rock, Ark. 72201.

Stephens, James, 1825-1901.

RYAN, Desmond. 941.5'8'0924 B
The Fenian chief: a biography of James Stephens; with an introductory memoir by Patrick Lynch. Dublin, Sydney, Gill & Son, 1967. xxv, 390 p. 23 cm. Includes bibliographical references. [DA958.S7R9] 68-107897 45/-
1. Stephens, James, 1825-1901. I. Title. BIP

Stephens, John Lloyd, 1805-1852—Juvenile literature.

O'CONNOR, Richard, 1915- 913.03'1'0924 B
John Lloyd Stephens: explorer of lost worlds. Illustrated by Victor Lazzaro. New York, McGraw-Hill [1968] 126 p. illus. 21 cm. [F1435.S86O27] 68-27510 4.95
1. Stephens, John Lloyd, 1805-1852—Juvenile literature.

Stephens, Win, 1886- —Juvenile literature.

LEIPOLD, L. Edmond, 1902- 338.4'7'62920924 B
Win Stephens, business and civic leader, by L. E. Leipold. Minneapolis, T. S. Denison [1969] 216 p. illus., ports. 22 cm. (Men of achievement series) A biography of a prominent civic leader of Minneapolis, Minnesota. [HC102.5.S75L45] 92 72-89472
1. Stephens, Win, 1886- —Juvenile literature. I. Title.

Stephenson, George, 1781-1848.

ROBBINS, Michael 385.0922
George and Robert Stephenson. [New York] Oxford [c.] 1966. 64p. 8 plates (incl. ports., map5, facsim.) 21cm. (Clarendon biogs.) Maps on endpapers. Bibl. [TF140.S73R56] 66-71668 1.55 bds.,
1. Stephenson, George, 1781-1848. 2. Stephenson, Robert, 1803-1859. I. Title.

ROBBINS, Michael. 385.0922
George and Robert Stephenson. London, Oxford U.P., 1966. 64 p. 8 plates (incl. ports., maps, facsim.) 20 1/2 cm. (The Clarendon biographies) 9/6 Maps on endpapers. Bibliography: p. [63] [TF140.S73R56] 66-71668
1. Stephenson, George, 1781-1848. 2. Stephenson, Robert, 1803-1858. I. Title.

ROLT, Lionel Thomas Caswell, 1910- 385'.0922 B
George and Robert Stephenson : the railway revolution / L. T. C. Rolt ; with drawings and maps by Kenneth Lindley. Westport, Conn. : Greenwood Press, 1977. p. cm. Reprint of the 1960 ed. published by Longmans, London. Includes index. Bibliography: p. [TF140.S73R6 1977] 77-22800 ISBN 0-8371-9747-3 lib.bdg. : 23.00
1. Stephenson, George, 1781-1848. 2. Stephenson, Robert, 1803-1859. 3. Railroad engineers—England—Biography. I. Title. BIP

SMILES, Samuel, 1812-1904. 385'.0924 B
The life of George Stephenson, railway engineer. 5th ed., rev., with additions. Ann Arbor, Mich., Plutarch Press, 1971. xvi, 557 p. ports. 22 cm. Reprint of the 1858 ed. [TJ140.S8S6 1971] 74-142562
1. Stephenson, George, 1781-1848. 2. Railroads—Gt. Brit.—History. 3. Locomotives—History. I. Title.

Stephenson, William Samuel, Sir, 1896-

STEVENSON, William, 1925- 940.54'86'0924 B
A man called Intrepid : the secret war / William Stevenson. 1st ed. New York : Harcourt Brace Jovanovich, c1976. xxv, 486 p., [16] leaves of plates : ill. ; 24 cm. Includes index. [D810.S8S85] 75-30730 ISBN 0-15-156795-6 : 12.95
1. Stephenson, William Samuel, Sir, 1896- 2. World War, 1939-1945—Secret service. I. Title. BIP

Stepinac, Aloysius, Cardinal, 1898-1960.

RAYMOND, Father, 1903- 262'.135'0924 B
The man for this moment [by] M. Raymond. Staten Island, N.Y., Alba House [1971] xvii, 345 p. illus. 22 cm. Half-title: The life and death of Aloysius Cardinal Stepinac. [BX4705.S823R39] 77-169142 ISBN 0-8189-0220-5 6.95
1. Stepinac, Aloysius, Cardinal, 1898-1960. I. Title. II. Title: The life and death of Aloysius Cardinal Stepinac.

Sterling, Chandler W., Bp., 1911-

STERLING, Chandler W., Bp., 1911- 283'.092'4 B
Beyond this land of whoa, by Chandler W. Sterling. Philadelphia, United Church Press [1973] 141 p. 22 cm. "A Pilgrim Press book." [BX5995.S786A32] 73-5904 ISBN 0-8298-0261-4 4.95
1. Sterling, Chandler W., Bp., 1911- I. Title.

Sterling County, Tex.—History.

MILLING around 976.4'871 B
Sterling County : a history of Sterling County / edited by Beverly Daniels ; cover and sketches by Johnny Hughes. Canyon, Tex. : Staked Plains Press, c1976. 382 p. : ill. ; 29 cm. Bibliography: p. 381-382. [F392.S8M54] 77-150835
1. Sterling County, Tex.—History. 2. Sterling County, Tex.—Biography. 3. Sterling County, Tex.—Genealogy. I. Daniels, Beverly.

Sterling, George, 1869-1926.

WALKER, Franklin Dickerson, 1900- 811'.5'2 B
The seacoast of Bohemia, by Franklin Walker. New and enl. ed. Santa Barbara [Calif.] Peregrine Smith, 1973. vii, 127 p. illus. 26 cm. [PS3537.T42Z95 1973] 73-175538 ISBN 0-87905-008-X 10.00
1. Sterling, George, 1869-1926. 2. Authors, American—Carmel, California. 3. Carmel, California. I. Title.

Sterling, John, 1806-1844.

CARLYLE, Thomas, 1795-1881. 824'.8 B
The life of John Sterling. New York, Scribner. St. Clair Shores, Mich., Scholarly Press, 1972. p. (The works of Thomas Carlyle, v. 11) Reprint of the 1900 ed. [PR4420.F2 vol. 11] [PR5473.S8] 72-10639
1. Sterling, John, 1806-1844. I. Title. BIP

CARLYLE, Thomas, 1795-1881. 928.2
The life of John Sterling [and] Latter-day pamphlets. Boston, D. Estes [19--] iv, 455 p. plate, ports. 20 cm. (Illustrated cabinet edition) [[PR5473]] A 62
1. Sterling, John, 2. Social problems. 3. Gt. Brit—Soc. condit. I. Title. II. Title: Latter-day pamphlets.

Sterling, John, 1806-1844—Biography.

CARLYLE, Thomas, 1795-1881. 824'.8 S
The life of John Sterling. New York, AMS Press [1974] xi, 280 p. illus. 23 cm. (The works of Thomas Carlyle, v. 11) (Series: Carlyle, Thomas, 1795-1881. Works. 1974. vol. 11.) Reprint of the 1897 ed. published by Chapman and Hall, London. Includes bibliographical references. [PR4420.F74 vol. 11] [PR5473.S8] 824'.8 B 74-3166 ISBN 0-404-01421-6 17.50
1. Sterling, John, 1806-1844—Biography. I. Series.

Stern, Edith, 1952-

STERN, Aaron. 371.9'5'0924 B
The making of a genius. [Miami, Fla.] Hurricane House Publishers [1971] x, 172 p. 23 cm. [BF416.S73S73] 70-181866
1. Stern, Edith, 1952- 2. Genius—Case studies. I. Title. BIP

Stern, Herbert Jay, 1936-

HOFFMAN, Paul, 1934- 345'.73'01
Tiger in the court; Herbert J. Stern: the U.S. attorney who prosecuted 8 mayors, 2 secretaries of state, 2 state treasurers, 2 powerful political bosses, 1 U.S. Congressman ... and 64 other public officials. [1st ed. Chicago, Playboy Press, 1973] 290 p. 22 cm. Bibliography: p. [287]-290. [KF373.S7H6] 73-84926 8.50
1. Stern, Herbert Jay, 1936- I. Title.

Stern, Susan, 1943-

STERN, Susan, 1943- 322.4'2'0924
With the Weathermen : the personal journal of a revolutionary woman / Susan Stern. 1st ed. New York : Doubleday, 1975. 374 p., [6] leaves of plates : ill. ; 22 cm. [HQ1413.S68A36] 73-10819 ISBN 0-385-08070-0 : 8.95
1. Stern, Susan, 1943- 2. Weatherman (Organization) 3. Youth—United States—Political activity. 4. Feminism—United States. I. Title.

Stern, William,

STERN, William, 1907- 927.914
The taste of ashes; an autobiography by Bill Stern, with Oscar Fraley. [1st ed.] New York, Holt [1959] 218 p. illus. 23 cm. [PN1991.4.S83A3] 59-12903
I. Title.

STERN, William, 1907- 927.914
The taste of ashes; an autobiography by Bill Stern, with Oscar Fraley. [1st ed.] New York, Holt [1959] 218 p. illus. 23 cm. [PN1991.4.S83A3] 59-12903
I. Title.

Sternberg, Cecilia.

STERNBERG, Cecilia. 940.55'092'4 B
The journey / Cecilia Sternberg. New York : Dial Press, 1977. 576 p., [4] leaves of plates : ill. ; 24 cm. Includes index. [CT1495.S76A34 1977] 77-14691 ISBN 0-8037-4270-3 : 12.50
1. Sternberg, Cecilia. 2. Europe—Nobility—Biography. I. Title.

Sternberg, George Miller, 1838-1915.

GIBSON, John Mendinghall. 926.1
Soldier in white; the life of General George Miller Sternberg. Durham, N.C., Duke University Press, 1958. 277 p. illus. 24 cm. [R154.S8G5] 58-9388
1. Sternberg, George Miller, 1838-1915. I. Title. BIP

Sterne, Laurence, 1713-1768.

BRISSENDEN, R F v. 12
Samuel Richardson, by R. F. Brissenden. Henry Fielding, by John Butt. Laurence Sterne, by D. W. Jefferson. Tobias Smollett, by Laurence Brander. Lincoln, University of Nebraska Press [c1965] 146 p. ports. 21 cm. (British writers and their work, no. 6) A Bison book, BB455. Includes bibliographies. 68-107263
1. Richardson, Samuel, 2. Fielding, Henry, 3. Sterne, Laurence, 4. Smollett, Tobias George, I. Butt, John Everett, 1906-1965. Henry Fielding. II. Jefferson, Douglas William, 1912- Laurence Sterne. III. Brander, Laurence, 1903- Tobias Smollett. IV. Title. V. Series.

CONNELY, Willard, 1888- 823'.6 B
Laurence Sterne as Yorick / Willard Connely. Westport, Conn. : Greenwood Press, 1979. 240 p., [3] leaves of plates : ill. ; 22 cm. Reprint of the 1958 ed. published by Bodley Head, London. [PR3716.C6 1979] 79-17312 ISBN 0-313-22000-X lib. bdg. : 19.00
1. Sterne, Laurence, 1713-1768. 2. Novelists, English—18th century—Biography. I. Title. BIP

CROSS, Wilbur Lucius, 1862- v. 12
The life and times of Laurence Sterne, 3d ed., with alterations and additions. New Haven, Yale University Press; London, H. Milford, Oxford university press, 1929. [n.p.] Russell & Russell, 1967. xxvi, 670 p. Bibliography: p. 596-632. 68-91767
1. Sterne, Laurence, 1713-1768. I. Title. BIP

CROSS, Wilbur Lucius, 1862-1948. 823'.6 B
The life and times of Laurence Sterne. New York, Russell & Russell [1967, c1929] xxvi, 670 p. illus. 22 cm. Reprint of the 3d ed. Bibliography: p. [596]-632. [PR3716.C7 1967] 66-27187
1. Sterne, Laurence, 1713-1768. I. Title.

FROE, Arie de. 823'.6
Laurence Sterne and his novels studied in the light of modern psychology, by A. de Froe. Folcroft, Pa., Folcroft Press [1969] 234 p. port. 26 cm. Reprint of the 1925 ed. Bibliography: p. [232]-234. [PR3716.F7 1969] 72-193729
1. Sterne, Laurence, 1713-1768. 2. Psychology. I. Title.

PIPER, William Bowman, 1927- 823.6
Laurence Sterne. New York, Twayne Publishers [1966, c1965] 138 p. 21 cm. (Twayne's English authors series, TEAS26) Bibliography: p. 131-136. [PR3716.P55 1966] 65-24396
1. Sterne, Laurence, 1713-1768.

QUENNELL, Peter, 1905- 920.042
Four portraits; studies of the eighteenth century. [Rev.ed.] Hamden, Conn., Archon [dist. Shoe String c.1965] 256p. illus., ports. 22cm. First ed. pub. in 1945 under title: The profane virtues. [DA506.A1Q4] 65-21845 6.00
1. Boswell, James 1740-1795. 2. Gibbon, Edward, 1737-1794. 3. Sterne, Laurence, 1713-1768. 4. Wilkes, John, 1727-1797. I. Title.
Contents omitted.

QUENNELL, Peter, 1905- 920.042
Four portraits; studies of the eighteenth century, [Rev. ed.] Hamden, Conn., Archon Books, 1965. 256 p. illus., ports. 22 cm. First ed. published in 1945 under title: The profane virtues. Contents.James Boswell,--Edward Gibbon.--Laurence Sterne.--John Wilkes. [DA506.A1Q4] 65-21845
1. Boswell, James, 1740-1795. 2. Gibbon, Edward, 1737-1794 3. Sterne, Laurence, 1713-1768. 4. Wilkes, John, 1727-1797. I. Title. BIP

QUENNELL, Peter, 1905- 920'.041
The profane virtues : for studies of the eighteenth century / Peter Quennell. Westport, Conn. : Greenwood Press, 1979, c1945. 220 p., [8] leaves of plates : ill. ; 23 cm. Reprint of the ed. published by Viking, New York. Contents.Contents.—James Boswell.—Edward Gibbon.—Laurence Sterne.—John Wilkes. [DA506.A1Q4 1979] 78-11551 ISBN 0-313-21039-X lib. bdg. : 18.75
1. Boswell, James, 1740-1795. 2. Gibbon, Edward, 1737-1794. 3. Sterne, Laurence, 1713-1768. 4. Wilkes, John, 1727-1797. 5. Great Britain—Biography. I. Title.

STERNE, Laurence, 1713-1768 928.2
Letters of Laurence Sterne; ed. by Lewis Perry Curtis Oxford, Clarendon Pr. [New York, Oxford, 1966] xxxiv, 495p. front., plates, ports., fold. map, fold. plan, facsim. 23cm. Includes Sterne's 'Memoirs of the life and family of the late Rev. Mr. Laurence Sterne' and letters relating to Sterne and his family [PR3716.A35] 35-6762 8.80
I. Curtis, Lewis Perry, 1900- ed. II. Title.

STERNEIANA. 823'.6
New York, Garland Pub., 1974- p. cm. (The Life & times of seven major British writers) [PR3716.S85] 74-14955 22.00
1. Sterne, Laurence, 1713-1768. BIP

THOMSON, David, 1941- 823'.6 B
Wild excursions; the life and fiction of Laurence Sterne. New York, McGraw-Hill [1972] 325 p. illus. 23 cm. Bibliography: p. [293]-296. [PR3716.T5 1972b] 76-39750 ISBN 0-07-064510-8 8.95
1. Sterne, Laurence, 1713-1768. I. Title.

TRAILL, Henry Duff, 1842-1900. 823.6 B
Sterne. New York, AMS Press [1968] viii, 176 p. 22 cm. (English men of letters) [PR3716.T7 1968] 68-58403
1. Sterne, Laurence, 1713-1768. BIP

Sterne, Laurence, 1713-1768—Biography.

CASH, Arthur Hill. 823'.6 B
Laurence Sterne, the early & middle years / [by] Arthur H. Cash. London : Methuen, 1975. xxvii, 333 p., leaf of plate, [12] p. of plates : ill., geneal. table, ports. (1 col.) ; 25 cm. Ill. on lining papers. Distributed in the USA by Harper & Row, Barnes & Noble Import Division, N.Y. Bibliography: p. xix-xxiv. [PR3716.C29 1975] 75-328064 ISBN 0-416-82210-X : 37.50
1. Sterne, Laurence, 1713-1768—Biography. I. Title.

HARTLEY, Lodwick Charles, 1906- 823'.6 B
Laurence Sterne; a biographical essay, by Lodwick Hartley. Chapel Hill, University of North Carolina Press [1968] xii, 302 p. 21 cm. (Chapel Hill books, 29) 1943 edition published under title: This is Lorence. Bibliography: p. 291-[294] [PR3716.H36 1968] 68-63753 2.45
1. Sterne, Laurence, 1713-1768—Biography.

SHAW, Margaret Renee Bryers. 823'.6 B
Laurence Sterne: the making of a humorist, 1713-1762, by Margaret R. B. Shaw. [Folcroft, Pa.] Folcroft Press, 1970. xiv, 274 p. port. 26 cm. Reprint of the 1957 ed. "Limited to 150 copies." [PR3716.S45 1970] 72-194378
1. Sterne, Laurence, 1713-1768—Biography. I. Title.

Stetser, Carol.

STETSER, Carol. 779'.092'4
Continuum : an autobiography at thirty / Carol Stetser. Oatman, Ariz. : Padma Press, c1979. [60] p. ; 27 cm. Photographs. [TR654.S764] 78-70872 ISBN 0-917960-03-3 : 9.95
1. Stetser, Carol. 2. Photography, Artistic. I. Title. BIP

Stettinius, Edward Reilly, 1865-1925.

FORBES, John Douglas, 1910- 332.1'092'4 B
Stettinius, Sr.: portrait of a Morgan partner. Charlottesville, University Press of Virginia [1974] xii, 244 p. port. 25 cm. Bibliography: p. [233]-234. [HG2463.S64F67] 73-89906 ISBN 0-8139-0517-6 12.00
1. Stettinius, Edward Reilly, 1865-1925. 2. Morgan (J. P.) and Company. I. Title.

Stettinius, Edward Reilly, 1900-1949.

STETTINIUS, Edward Reilly, 1900-1949. 973.917'092'4
The diaries of Edward R. Stettinius, Jr., 1943-1946. Edited by Thomas M. Campbell and George C. Herring. New York, New Viewpoints, 1975. xxviii, 544 p. illus. 21 cm. Includes bibliographical references. [E748.S836A33] 74-9660 ISBN 0-531-05362-8 12.50
1. Stettinius, Edward Reilly, 1900-1949. I. Campbell, Thomas M., ed. II. Herring, George C., 1936- ed.
Pbk. 5.95; ISBN 0-531-05570-1

Steuben, Friedrich Wilhelm Ludolf Gerhard Augustin, baron von, 1730-1794.

PALMER, John McAuley, 1870-1955 973.330924
General von Steuben. Port Washington, N. Y., Kennikat [1966, c.1937] 434p. maps, ports. 22cm. Bibl. [E207.S8P3 1966] 66-25936 12.50
1. Steuben, Friedrich Wilhelm Ludolf Gerhard Augustin, baron von, 1730-1794. I. Title. BIP

PALMER, John McAuley, 1870-1955. 973.330924
General von Steuben. Port Washington, N.Y., Kennikat Press [1966, c1937] 434 p. maps, ports. 22 cm. Bibliography: p. [419]-423. [E207.S8P3] 66-25936

1. Steuben, Friedrich Wilheim Ludolf Gerhard Augustin, baron von, 1730-1794. I. Title.

Steuber, Roy Edward, 1892-1954.

BURKE, Frank. 926.5
The Roy Stueber story; biography of an Arkansas business builder. [1st ed.] New York, Vantage Press [1955] 72p. illus. 21cm. [HC102.5.S8B8] 55-8398
1. Steuber, Roy Edward, 1892-1954. I. Title.

Steuck, Judy.

STEUCK, Jeanine. 615.9'1 B
Good morning, Judy! / Jeanine Steuck. Minneapolis : Augsburg Pub. House, c1978. 140 p. ; 21 cm. [RA1247.C17S73] 78-52173 ISBN 0-8066-1652-0 : 6.95
1. Steuck, Judy. 2. Carbon monoxide—Toxicology—Biography. 3. Coma—Biography. I. Title. **BIP**

Steuer, Max, 1871-1940.

BOYER, Richard Owen, 1903- 923.473
Max Steuer; magician of the law, by Richard O. Boyer. New York, Greenberg [1932] vii p., 1l., 11-223p. 21cm. 32-8039
1. Steuer, Max, 1871-1940. I. Title.

Steunenberg, Frank, 1861-1905.

STEUNENBERG, Frank W 923.273
Greater love. Mountain View, Calif., Pacific Press Pub. Association [1952] 79p. illus. 19cm. [F746.S82] 52-11281
1. Steunenberg, Frank, 1861-1905. 2. Horsley, Albert E., 1866- I. Title.

Steurt, Marjorie Rankin.

STEURT, Marjorie Rankin. 266'.5'10924 B
Broken bits of old China. [1st ed.] Nashville, T. Nelson [1973] 152 p. 21 cm. Autobiographical. [BV3427.S814A3] 72-12986 ISBN 0-8407-6262-3 4.95
I. Title.

Steven, Norma.

STEVEN, Norma. 248'.833
Please, can I come home? No, you can't come home! Old Tappan, N.J., F. H. Revell Co. [1973] 126 p. illus. 19 cm. Exchange of letters between the author and her daughter Wendy. [BJ1681.S73] 73-6794 ISBN 0-8007-0619-6 1.95 (pbk.)
1. Steven, Norma. 2. Steven, Wendy. 3. Young women—Conduct of life. I. Steven, Wendy. II. Title.

Stevens, David Harrison, 1884-

STEVENS, David Harrison, 1884- 361.7'6'0924 B
A time of humanities : an oral history : recollections of David H. Stevens as director in the Division of the Humanities, Rockefeller Foundation, 1930-50, as narrated to Robert E. Gard by David H. Stevens / edited by Robert E. Yahnke and an essay What are the humanities? / By David H. Stevens. 1st ed. Madison : Wisconsin Academy of Sciences, Arts and Letters, c1976. ix, 151 p. : ill. ; 23 cm. "Titles of David H. Stevens": p. 141. Includes bibliographical index. [CT275.S6915A35] 76-22968 ISBN 0-88361-042-6 : 5.95
1. Stevens, David Harrison, 1884- 2. Scholars—United States—Biography. 3. Humanities. I. Gard, Robert Edward. II. Title.

Stevens family.

WOOD, Marie (Stevens) Walker, 1883- 929.2
Stevens-Davis and allied families; a memorial volume of history, biography, and genealogy. Macon, Ga., 1957. xi, 474 p. illus., maps, coats of arms, geneal. tables. 25 cm. "150 copies...printed for private circulation." Bibliography: p. 459-460. [CS71.S844 1957] 57-12341
1. Stevens family. 2. Davis family. 3. U.S. — Geneal. I. Title.

Stevens, Henry Herbert, 1878-1973.

WILBUR, J. Richard H. 328.71'092'4 B
H. H. Stevens, 1878-1973 / Richard Wilbur. Toronto : University of Toronto Press, c1977. xi, 244 p. ; 21 cm. (Canadian biographical studies) Includes bibliographical references and index. [F1034.S732W54] 78-309235 ISBN 0-8020-3339-3 : 9.50
1. Stevens, Henry Herbert, 1878-1973. 2. Politicians—Canada—Biography. 3. Canada—Politics and government—1914- **BIP**

Stevens, Isaac Ingalls, 1818-1862.

HAZARD, Joseph Taylor, 1879- 917.8
Companion of adventure; a biography of Isaac Ingalls Stevens, first governor of Washington Territory. Portland, Or., Binfords & Mort [1952] 238 p. illus. 22 cm. [F880.S845H3] 52-12976
1. Stevens, Isaac Ingalls, 1818-1862. 2. Northwest, Pacific—Hist. I. Title.

RICHARDS, Kent D., 1938- 979.7'03'0924 B
Isaac I. Stevens : young man in a hurry / Kent D. Richards. Provo, Utah : Brigham Young University Press, [1979] p. cm. Includes bibliographical references and index. [F880.S843R5] 79-13637 ISBN 0-8425-1697-2 : 15.95
1. Stevens, Isaac Ingalls, 1818-1862. 2. Pacific coast Indians, Wars with, 1847-1865. 3. Oregon—History—To 1859. 4. Washington (State)—History—To 1889. 5. Washington (State)—Governors—Biography. 6. Generals—United States—Biography. **BIP**

Stevens, John, 1749-1838.

TURNBULL, Archibald Douglas. 623.82'4'0924 B
John Stevens; an American record. Freeport, N.Y., Books for Libraries Press [1972] p. Reprint of the 1928 ed. [VM140.S7T8 1972] 72-8425 ISBN 0-8369-6994-4
1. Stevens, John, 1749-1838.

Stevens, Phinehas, 1707-1756.

STARK, Caleb, 1804-1864. 973.3'3'0922 B
Memoir and official correspondence of Gen. John Stark, with notices of several other officers of the Revolution. Also a bibliography of Capt. Phine[h]as Stevens and of Col. Robert Rogers, with an account of his services in America during the "Seven years' war." With a new introd. and pref. by George Athan Billias. Boston, Gregg Press, 1972 [c1860] x, 495 p. 23 cm. (The American Revolutionary series. American and French accounts of the American Revolution) Reprint of the ed. published by G. P. Lyon, Concord, N.H. Contents.Contents.—Memoir of General John Stark.—Correspondence (p. [107]-317)—General Jacob Bailey.—General Joseph Cilley.—Colonel Marinus Willef.—Major Caleb Stark.—Captain Phinehas Stevens.—Colonel Robert Rogers.—Thomas Barnside. [E207.S79S7 1972] 72-8760 ISBN 0-8398-1884-X 18.50 (Lib. ed.)
1. Stark, John, 1728-1822. 2. Stevens, Phinehas, 1707-1756. 3. Rogers, Robert, 1727-1800. 4. United States—History—Revolution—Biography. I. Stark, John, 1728-1822. Correspondence. 1972. II. Title. III. Series: American and French accounts of the American Revolution.

Stevens, Rise, 1913—

CRICHTON, Kyle Samuel, 1896- 927.8
Subway to the Met: Rise Stevens' story. [1st ed.] Garden City, N. Y., Doubleday, 1959. 240 p. illus. 22 cm. [ML420.S84C7] 59-11586
1. Stevens, Rise, 1913- I. Title.

Stevens, Thaddeus, 1792-1868.

BRODIE, Fawn (McKay) 1915- 923.273
Thaddeus Stevens, scourge of the South. [1st ed.] New York, Norton [1959] 448 p. illus. 24 cm. Includes bibliography. [E415.9.S84B7] 59-9236
1. Stevens, Thaddeus, 1792-1868. **BIP**

CALLENDER, Edward Belcher, 1851-1917. 973.6'092'4 B
Thaddeus Stevens: commoner. Boston, A. Williams, 1882. [New York, AMS Press, 1972] 210 p. 19 cm. [E415.9.S84C15 1972] 70-39881 ISBN 0-404-00011-8
1. Stevens, Thaddeus, 1792-1868. **BIP**

KORNGOLD, Ralph, 1886- 923.273
Thaddeus Stevens; a being darkly wise and rudely great. [1st ed.] New York, Harcourt, Brace [1955] xiv, 460 p. 24 cm. Bibliography: p. 447-452. [E415.9.S84K6] 55-9381
1. Stevens, Thaddeus, 1792-1868.

MCCALL, Samuel Walker, 1851-1923. 973.6'0924 B
Thaddeus Stevens. Boston, Houghton, Mifflin. [New York, AMS Press, 1972] vi, 369 p. illus. 18 cm. (American statesmen, v. 31) Reprint of the 1899 ed. [E415.9.S84M12 1972] 78-128951 ISBN 0-404-50881-2
1. Stevens, Thaddeus, 1792-1868. I. Title. II. Series. **BIP**

WOODLEY, Thomas Frederick, 1894- 973.60924 B
Great leveler; the life of Thaddeus Stevens. Freeport, N.Y., Books for Libraries Press [1969] 474 p. illus., facsims., ports. 23 cm. (Select bibliographies reprint series) First ed., 1934, has title: Thaddeus Stevens. Reprint of the 1937 ed. Bibliography: p. 437-452. "References": p. 453-460. [E415.9.S84W86 1969] 71-99675
1. Stevens, Thaddeus, 1792-1868. I. Title.

Stevens, Thaddeus, 1792 1868—Juvenile literature.

BUCKMASTER, Henrietta, pseud. 328.73'09'22 B
The fighting Congressmen: Thaddeus Stephens, Hiram Revels, James Rapier, Blanche K. Bruce. [New York] Scholastic Book Services [1971] 111 p. illus., facsims., ports. 21 cm. (Firebird books) Brief biographies of one white and three black congressmen active in the struggle to assure the rights of black people during the Reconstruction. [E663.B9] 920 75-131370
1. Stevens, Thaddeus, 1792-1868—Juvenile literature. 2. Revels, Hiram Rhoades, 1827?-1901—Juvenile literature. 3. Rapier, James T., 1839-1883—Juvenile literature. 4. Bruce, Blanche Kelso, 1841-1898—Juvenile literature. I. Title.

MELTZER, Milton, 1915- 973.6'0924
Thaddeus Stevens and the fight for Negro rights. New York, Crowell [1967] xii, 231 p. 21 cm. Bibliography: p. 221-224. [E415.9.S84M4] 67-1862
1. Stevens, Thaddeus, 1792-1868—Juvenile literature. 2. Negroes—Civil rights—Juvenile literature. I. Title.

Stevens, Thomas, 1828-1888.

BAKER, Wilma (Sinclair) Le Van. 927.4552
The silk pictures of Thomas Stevens; a biography of the Coventry weaver and his contribution to the art of weaving, with an illustrated catalogue of his work. [1st ed.] New York, Exposition Press [1957] 147p. illus. (part col.) ports. 24cm. [NK8998.S8B3] 57-9216
1. Stevens, Thomas, 1828-1888. 2. Slik. 3. Textile design. I. Title.

Stevens, Wallace, 1879-1955.

BROWN, Ashley, 1923- ed. 811'.5'2 B
The achievement of Wallace Stevens, edited by Ashley Brown and Robert S. Haller. New York, Gordian Press, 1973 [c1062] 287 p. 23 cm. Bibliography: p. 271-287. [PS3537.T4753Z62 1973] 73-5858 ISBN 0-87752-161-1 9.00
1. Stevens, Wallace, 1879-1955. I. Haller, Robert S., 1933- joint ed. II. Title. **BIP**

BUTTEL, Robert. 811'.5'2
Wallace Stevens: the making of Harmonium. Princeton, N.J., Princeton University Press, 1967. xv, 269 p. 23 cm. Bibliographical footnotes. [PS3537.T4753Z622] 66-17699
1. Stevens, Wallace, 1879-1955. Harmonium.

KERMODE, Frank 811.52
Wallace Stevens. New York, Grove Press [1961, c.1960] 134p. (Evergreen pilot books, EP4) Bibl. 61-6598 1.25 pap.,
1. Stevens, Wallace, 1879-1955. I. Title. **BIP**

TINDALL, William York, 1903- 811.52
Wallace Stevens. Minneapolis, University of Minnesota Press [1961] 47 p. 21 cm. (University of Minnesota pamphlets on American writers, no. 11) Includes bibliography. [PS3537.T4753Z77 1961] 61-62618
1. Stevens, Wallace, 1879-1955.

Stevens, Wallace, 1879-1955—Addresses, essays, lectures.

WALLACE Stevens : 811'.5'2
a celebration / edited by Frank Doggett and Robert Buttel. Princeton, N.J. : Princeton University Press, 1979, c1980. p. cm. Bibliography: p. [PS3537.T4753Z84] 79-18877 ISBN 0-691-06414-8 : 22.50
1. Stevens, Wallace, 1879-1955—Addresses, essays, lectures. 2. Poets, American—20th century—Biography—Addresses, essays, lectures. I. Doggett, Frank A. II. Buttel, Robert. **BIP**

Stevens, Wallace, 1879-1955—Biography—Youth.

STEVENS, Holly Bright. 811'.5'2 B
Souvenirs and prophecies : the young Wallace Stevens / Holly Stevens. 1st ed. New York : Knopf, 1977, c1976. vii, 288 p. ; 23 cm. An account of Stevens' early life, incorporating his journal and other writings. Includes bibliographical references and index. [PS3537.T4753Z7673 1977] 76-13733 ISBN 0-394-48715-X : 12.50
1. Stevens, Wallace, 1879-1955—Biography—Youth. I. Stevens, Wallace, 1879-1955. II. Title. **BIP**

Stevens, Wallace, 1879-1955—Criticism and interpretation.

STERN, Herbert J. 811.52
Wallace Stevens: art of uncertainty, by Herbert J. Stern. Ann Arbor, University of Michigan Press [1966] x, 206 p. 22 cm. Bibliography: p. 194-199. Bibliographical references included in "Notes" (p. 163-193) [PS3537.T4753Z767] 66-17024
1. Stevens, Wallace, 1879-1955—Criticism and interpretation. I. Title: Art of uncertainty.

SUKENICK, Ronald. 811'.5'2
Wallace Stevens. musing the obscure; readings and interpretation, and a guide to the collected poetry. New York, New York University Press, 1967. xvii, 234 p. 22 cm. Bibliography: p. 233-234. [PS3537.T4753Z768] 67-25041
1. Stevens, Wallace, 1879-1955—Criticism and interpretation.

Stevens, Wallace, 1879-1955—Exhibitions.

HENRY E. Huntington Library and Art Gallery, San Marino, Calif. 811'.5'2 B
Thirteen ways of looking at Wallace Stevens : a special exhibition. [San Marino, Calif.] : Huntington Library/Art Gallery/Botanical Gardens, c1975. [16] p. : ill. ; 27 cm. Cover title. Catalog of an exhibition held in 1975. [PS3537.T4753Z657 1975] 75-325364
1. Stevens, Wallace, 1879-1955—Exhibitions. 2. Stevens, Wallace, 1879-1955—Archives. I. Title.

Stevens. William Bagshaw,

STEVENS. WILLIAM BAGSHAW, 922.342
1756-1800
The journal of the Rev. William Bagshaw Stevens, ed. by Georgina Galbraith [New York] Oxford [c. 1965] xxvii, 550p. fold. geneal. table. map, port. 23cm. Bibl. [PR3717.S24Z5] 65-8452 10.10
1. Title.

Stevenson, Adlai Ewing, 1900-1965.

BROWN, Stuart Gerry, 1911- 973.92
Adlai E. Stevenson, a short biography: the conscience of the country. Woodbury, N.Y., Barron's [c.1965] viii, 216p. illus., ports. 21cm. Bibl. [E748.S84B7] 65-25681 3.25; .95 pap.,
1. Stevenson, Adlai Ewing, 1900-1965. I. Title.

BROWN, Stuart Gerry, 973.92 B
1912-
Adlai E. Stevenson, a short biography; the conscience of the country. Woodbury, N.Y., Barron's Woodbury Press [1965] viii, 216 p. illus., ports. 21 cm. Bibliography: p. 216. [E748.S84B7] 65-25681
1. Stevenson, Adlai Ewing, 1900-1965. I. Title.

BUSCH, Noel Fairchild, 923.273
1906-
Adlai E. Stevenson of Illinois, a portrait. New York, Farrar, Straus & Young [1952] 238 p. illus. 22 cm. [F546.S8B8] 52-11089
1. Stevenson, Adlai Ewing, 1900-1965.

DAVIS, John William, 973.9'0924
1873-1955.
The argument of an appeal in Goodrich, Herbert Funk, 1889-1962. A case on appeal ... [4th ed.] Philadelphia, Joint Committee on Continuing Legal Education of the American Law Institute and the American Bar Association [1967]n3 New York, Putnam [1967] 543 p. illus., ports. 25 cm. 1957 ed. published under title: A prophet in his own country: the triumphs and defeats of Adlai E. Stevenson. Bibliography: p. 525-528. [E748,S84D3] 67-15107
1. Stevenson, Adlai Ewing, 1900-1965. I. Davis, Kenneth Sydney, 1912- II. Title. III. Title: The politics of honor.

DAVIS, Kenneth Sydney, 973.90924
1912-
The politics of honor: a biography of Adlai E. Stevenson, by Kenneth S. Davis. New York, Putnam [1967] 543 p. illus., ports. 25 cm. 1957 ed. published under title: A prophet in his own country; the triumphs and defeats of Adlai E. Stevenson. Bibliography: p. 525-528. [E748.S84D3 1967] 67-15107
1. Stevenson, Adlai Ewing, 1900-1965. I. Title.

DAVIS, Kenneth Sydney, 923.273
1912-
A prophet in his own country; the triumphs and defeats of Adlai E. Stevenson. [1st ed.] Garden City, N. Y., Doubleday, 1957. 510 p. 22 cm. [F546.S8D3] 57-5784
1. Stevenson, Adlai Ewing, 1900-1965. I. Title.

DOYLE, Edward P., ed. 973.90924
As we knew Adlai; the Stevenson story by twenty-two friends, ed. & pref. by Edward P. Doyle. Foreword by Adlai E. Stevenson III. New York, Harper [c.1966] xii, 288p. ports. 22cm. [E748.S84D6] 66-16630 6.95
1. Stevenson, Adlai Ewing, 1900-1965. I. Title.

HARRIS, Patricia. 977.3'04'0924 B
Adlai, the Springfield years / by Patricia Harris. Nashville : Aurora Publishers, [1975] 194 p., [4] leaves of plates : ill. ; 24 cm. Includes index. [E748.S84H27] 73-76522 ISBN 0-87695-167-1 : 7.95
1. Stevenson, Adlai Ewing, 1900-1965. I. Title. **BIP**

HAYMAN, LeRoy 973.90924
American ambassador to the world: Adlai Stevenson. London, New York, Abelard [1966] 190p. illus., ports. 22cm. Bibl. [E748.S84H3] 66-14122 4.00
1. Stevenson, Adlai Ewing, 1900-1965. I. Title.

IVES, Elizabeth 975.6'04'0924 B
(Stevenson) 1897-
Back to beginnings; Adlai E. Stevenson and North Carolina [by] Elizabeth S. Ives and Sam Ragan. [Charlotte, N.C., 1969] 56 p. geneal. tables, ports. 19 x 22 cm. [E748.S8419] 76-21155 4.50
1. Stevenson, Adlai Ewing, 1900-1965. I. Ragan, Samuel Talmadge, 1915- joint author. II. Title.

IVES, Elizabeth 923.273
Stevenson, 1897-
My brother Adlai, by Elizabeth Stevenson Ives and Hildegarde Dolson. New York, Morrow, 1956. 308 p. illus. 22 cm. [F546.S8188] 56-7134
1. Stevenson, Adlai Ewing, 1900-1965. I. Dolson, Hildegarde, joint author. II. Title.

LEVINE, Israel E. 92
Spokesman for the free world: Adlai E. Stevenson, by I. E. Levine. New York, J. Messner [1967] 191 p. 22 cm. Bibliography: p. 183-184. A biography of an admirable statesman remembered more for his ideals than for the offices he held. His career dedicated to public service, included being Governor of Illinois, twice Presidential candidate, and Ambassador to the United Nations. [E748.S84L4] AC 67
1. Stevenson, Adlai Ewing, 1900-1965. I. Title.

MARTIN, John Bartlow, 923.273
1915-
Adlai Stevenson. [1st ed.] New York, Harper [1952] 175 p. 22 cm. [F546.S8M37] 52-9759
1. Stevenson, Adlai Ewing, 1900-1965.

MARTIN, John 973.921'092'4 B
Bartlow, 1915-
Adlai Stevenson and the world : the life of Adlai E. Stevenson / John Bartlow Martin. 1st ed. Garden City, N.Y. : Doubleday, 1977. 946 p., [8] leaves of plates : ill. ; 24 cm. Includes index. [E748.S84M36] 76-23781 ISBN 0-385-12179-2 : 15.00
1. Stevenson, Adlai Ewing, 1900-1965. 2. Statesmen—United States—Biography. 3. United States—Politics and government—1953-1961. 4. United States—Foreign relations—1961-1963. 5. United States—Foreign relations—1963-1965. I. Title.

MARTIN, John 973.921'092'4 B
Bartlow, 1915-
Adlai Stevenson of Illinois : the life of Adlai E. Stevenson / John Bartlow Martin. 1st ed. Garden City, N.Y. : Doubleday, 1976. ix, 828 p., [12] leaves of plates : ill. ; 25 cm. Includes bibliographical references and index. [E748.S84M37] 75-21237 ISBN 0-385-07010-1 : 14.95
1. Stevenson, Adlai Ewing, 1900-1965. I. Title. **BIP**

MARTIN, John 973.921'092'4 B
Bartlow, 1915-
Adlai Stevenson of Illinois : the life of Adlai E. Stevenson / John Bartlow Martin. Garden City, N.Y. : Anchor Press / Doubleday, 1977c1976. ix, 828p., [12] leaves of plates : ill. ; 24 cm. (Anchor Books) Includes bibliographical references and index. [E748.S84M37] ISBN 0-385-12648-4 pbk. : 6.95
1. Stevenson, Adlai Ewing,1900-1965. I. Title.
L.C. card no. for 1976 Doubleday ed.:75-21237.

MULLER, Herbert 973.9'0924 B
Joseph, 1905-
Adlai Stevenson; a study in values [by] Herbert J. Muller. [1st ed.] New York, Harper & Row [1967] xiii, 338 p. group port. 22 cm. [E748.S84M8] 67-22503
1. Stevenson, Adlai Ewing, 1900-1965.

ROSS, Lillian 973.920924
Adlai Stevenson. Philadelphia, Lippincott, 1966 [c.1965, 1966] 58p. illus., ports. 22cm. [E748.S84R6] 66-13367 2.95 bds.,
1. Stevenson, Adlai Ewing, 1900-1965. I. Title.

SEVERN, William 973.90924
Adlai Stevenson, citizen of the world, by Bill Severn. New York, McKay [c.1966] 184p. ports. 22cm. Bibl. [E748.S84S4] 66-18739 3.95
1. Stevenson, Adlai Ewing, 1900-1965. I. Title.

STEVENSON, Adlai Ewing, 920'.073
1835-1914.
Something of men I have known, with some papers of a general nature, political, historical, and retrospective. Freeport, N.Y., Books for Libraries Press [1972] p. Reprint of the 1909 ed. [E661.S84 1972] 72-8417 ISBN 0-8369-6992-8
1. United States—Politics and government—1865-1933. 2. United States—Biography. I. Title.

STEVENSON, Adlai Ewing, 973.90924
1900-1965.
Adlai Stevenson's public years, with text text from his speeches and writings, ed. by Jill Kneerim. Photos. by Cornell Capa, John Fell Stevenson, Inge Morath. Pref. by Walter Lippmann. New York, Grossman [c.]1966. 160p. illus., ports. 29cm. [E743.S765] 66-19525 8.95
1. U.S.—Pol. & govt.—1945- —Addresses, essays, lectures. 2. U.S.—For. rel.—1945- —Addresses, essays, lectures. I. Kneerim, Jill, ed. II. Title.

STEVENSON, Adlai 818'.5'408
Ewing, 1900-1965.
Letters from Choate, by Adlai E. Stevenson, II. Wallingford, Conn., Andrew Mellon Library, Choate School, 1968. 31 p. facsim., ports. 26 cm. [E748.S84A4] 68-4266
I. Title.

WARD, Martha Eads. 92
Adlai Stevenson, young ambassador. Illustrated by Nathan Goldstein. Indianapolis, Bobbs-Merrill [1967] 200 p. col. illus. 20 cm. (Childhood of famous Americans) Biography of Adlai Stevenson, statesman, scholar, and ambassador to the United Nations. [E748.S84W3] AC 67
1. Stevenson, Adlai Ewing, 1900-1965. I. Goldstein, Nathan, illus. II. Title.

WHITMAN, Alden Rogers, 973.92
1913-
Portrait--Adlai E. Stevenson: politician, diplomat, friend, by Alden Whitman and The New York Times. New York, Harper [c.1948-1965] ix, 289p. ports. 25cm. [E748.S84W47] 65-27638 5.95
1. Stevenson, Adlai Ewing, 1900-1965. I. New York times. II. Title.

Stevenson, Adlai Ewing. 1900-1965 — Juvenile literature.

LEVINE, Israel E. 973.9'0924 (B)
Spokesman for the free world; Adlai E. Stevenson, by I. E. Levine. New York, J. Messner [1967] 191 p. 22 cm. Bibliography: p. 183-184. [E748.S84L4] 67-3082
1. Stevenson, Adlai Ewing. 1900-1965 —, Juvenile literature. I. Title.

LEVINE, Israel E. 973.9'0924 B
Spokesman for the free world: Adlai E. Stevenson, by I. E. Levine. New York, J. Messner [1967] 191 p. 22 cm. Bibliography: p. 183-184. [E748.S84L4] 67-3082
1. Stevenson, Adlai Ewing, 1900-1965— Juvenile literature. I. Title.

WARD, Martha Eads. 92
Adlai Stevenson, young ambassador. Illustrated by Nathan Goldstein. Indianapolis, Bobbs-Merrill [1967] 200 p. col. illus. 20 cm. (Childhood of famous Americans) [E748.S84W3] 67-17737
1. Stevenson, Adlai Ewing, 1900-1965 — Juvenile literature. I. Title.

Stevenson, Adlai Ewing, 1900-1965— Quotations.

STEVENSON, Adlai 973.921'092'4
Ewing, 1900-1965.
Stevenson / Grace and David Darling, editors. Chicago : Contemporary Books, [1977] p. cm. [E742.5.S75 1977] 77-75727 ISBN 0-8092-7873-1 : 7.95
1. Stevenson, Adlai Ewing, 1900-1965— Quotations. I. Darling, Grace, 1922- II. Darling, David, 1923-

Stevenson, Fanny (Van de Grift) 1840-1914.

MACKAY, Margaret 823'.8 B
(Mackprang) 1907-
The violent friend; the story of Mrs. Robert Louis Stevenson, by Margaret Mackay. [1st ed.] Garden City, N.Y., Doubleday, 1968. ix, 566 p. illus., ports. (part col.) 24 cm. Bibliography: p. [544]-549. [PR5499.S1Z7] 64-13869
1. Stevenson, Fanny (Van de Grift) 1840-1914. 2. Stevenson, Robert Louis, 1850-1894. I. Title.

Stevenson, Robert Louis, 1850-1894.

BAILEY, Alice Cooper 823.8
To remember Robert Louis Stevenson. New York, McKay [c.]1966. vii, 87p. illus., facsims., ports. 22cm. [PR5493.B18] 66-12547 3.25
1. Stevenson, Robert Louis, 1850-1894. I. Title.

BALFOUR, Graham, Sir, 823'.8 B
1859-1929.
The life of Robert Louis Stevenson. New York, Scribner, 1901. Grosse Pointe, Mich., Scholarly Press, 1968. 2 v. fold. map., ports. 23 cm. "Chronological list of the writings of Robert Louis Stevenson": v. 2, p. 248-261. Bibliographical footnotes. [PR5493.B2 1968] 73-3152
1. Stevenson, Robert Louis, 1850-1894. I. Title. **BIP**

BUTTS, Dennis, 1932- 828.809
R. L. Stevenson. [1st American ed.] New York, H. Z. Walck [1966] 72 p. port. 19 cm. On cover: Robert Louis Stevenson. Bibliographical footnotes. "A Stevenson book list": p. 67-69. "A select list of American editions": p. 70-72. [PR5493.B8 1966a] 66-31351
1. Stevenson, Robert Louis, 1850-1894.

CALDWELL, Elisie (Noble) 928.2
Last witness for Robert Louis Stevenson. Norman, University of Oklahoma Press [c.1960] xiv, 384p. illus. 22cm. 60-7734 5.00
1. Stevenson, Robert Louis, 1850-1894. I. Field, Isobel (Osboune) II. Title. **BIP**

CALDWELL, Elsie (Noble) 928.2
1882-
Last witness for Robert Louis Stevenson. Norman, University of Oklahoma Press [1960] 384 p. illus. 22 cm. [PR5493.C27] 60-7731
1. Stevenson, Robert Louis, 1850-1894. I. Field, Isobel (Osbourne) II. Title.

CHESTERTON, Gilbert Keith, 928.2
1874-1936.
Robert Louis Stevenson. New York, Sheed and Ward 1955 [c1928] 175 p. 20 cm. (New World Chesterton) [PR5493.C5 1955] 55-7484
1. Stevenson, Robert Louis, 1850-1894.

CARRE, Jean Marie, 828'.8'09 B
1887-1958.
The frail warrior: a life of Robert Louis Stevenson. Translated from the French by Eleanor Hard. Westport, Conn., Greenwood Press [1973, c1930] xii, 297 p. 22 cm. Translation of La vie de Robert Louis Stevenson. Reprint of the ed. published by Coward-McCann, New York. [PR5493.C32 1973] 70-148633 ISBN 0-8371-5995-4 12.75
1. Stevenson, Robert Louis, 1850-1894. I. Title.

CLARKE, W. E. 828'.8'09 B
Reminiscences of Robert Louis Stevenson. [Folcroft, Pa.] Folcroft Library Editions, 1973. p. [PR5495.C55 1973] 73-561 ISBN 0-8414-1552-8
1. Stevenson, Robert Louis, 1850-1894. I. Title. **BIP**

CRUSE, Amy, 1870- 828'.8'09 B
Robert Louis Stevenson. [Folcroft, Pa.]

Folcroft Library Editions, 1973 [c1915] p. Reprint of the ed. published by F. A. Stokes, New York. [PR5493.C7 1973] 73-12592 ISBN 0-8414-3447-6 (lib. bdg.)
1. Stevenson, Robert Louis, 1850-1894.

DARK, Sidney, 1874- 828'.8'09 B
1947.
Robert Louis Stevenson. New York, Haskell House Publishers, 1971. vii, 310 p. 23 cm. Reprint of the 1931 ed. Includes bibliographical references. [PR5493.D3 1971] 76-173849 ISBN 0-8383-1343-4
1. Stevenson, Robert Louis, 1850-1894.

DARK, Sidney, 1874- 828'.8'09 B
1947.
Robert Louis Stevenson. London, Hodder and Stoughton. [Folcroft, Pa.] Folcroft Library Editions, 1972. p. Reprint of the 1931 ed. [PR5493.D3 1972] 72-8910 ISBN 0-8414-0437-2 (lib. bdg.)
1. Stevenson, Robert Louis, 1850-1894.

ELLISON, Joseph Waldo, 928.2
1890-
Tusitala of the South Seas; the story of Robert Louis Stevenson's life in the South Pacific. New York, Hastings House [1953] 297 p. 25 cm. [PR5495.E57] 53-7850
1. Stevenson, Robert Louis, 1850-1894. 2. Samoan Islands. I. Title.

ELWIN, Malcolm, 1902- 828'.8'09 B
The strange case of Robert Louis Stevenson. New York, Russell & Russell [1971] xv, 256 p. ports. 23 cm. Reprint of the 1950 ed. [PR5493.E55 1971] 72-152537
1. Stevenson, Robert Louis, 1850-1894. I. Title. BIP

FINLAY, Ian 823.8
The young Robert Louis Stevenson. Illus. by William Randell. New York, Roy [1966, c.1965] 124p. illus. 21cm. [PR5494.F5] 65-22985 3.25 bds.,
1. Stevenson, Robert Louis, 1850-1894—Juvenile literature. I. Title.

FURNAS, Joseph Chamberlain, 928.2
1905-
Voyage to windward; the life of Robert Louis Stevenson. New York, Apollo Eds. [1962, c.1951] x, 566p. 20cm. (A-55) Bibl. 2.50 pap.,
1. Stevenson, Robert Louis, 1850-1894. I. Title.

FURNAS, Joseph Chamberlain, 928.2
1905-
Voyage to windward; the life of Robert Louis Stevenson. New York, Sloane [1951] x, 566 p. illus., ports. 22 cm. Bibliography: p. 473-492. [PR5493.F8] 51-12678
1. Stevenson, Robert Louis, 1850-1894. I. Title.

GWYNN, Stephen 828'.8'09 B
Lucius, 1864-1950.
Robert Louis Stevenson. [Folcroft, Pa.] Folcroft Library Editions, 1973. p. Reprint of the 1939 ed. published by Macmillan, London, in series: English men of letters. [PR5493.G9 1973] 73-12597 20.00
1. Stevenson, Robert Louis, 1850-1894. BIP

HINKLEY, Laura L. 928.2
The Stevensons: Louis and Fanny. New York, Hastings House [1950] vii, 360 p. 20 cm. Bibliography: p. 345-348. [PR5495.H5] 50-9588
1. Stevenson, Robert Louis, 1850-1894. 2. Stevenson, Fanny Van de Grift, 1840-1914.

MCGAW, Martha Mary, Sister. 928.2
Stevenson in Hawaii. Honolulu, University of Hawaii Press, 1950. xviii, 182 p. illus., ports., maps. 24 cm. Bibliography: p. [161]-170. [PR5495.M3] 51-290
1. Stevenson, Robert Louis, I. Title. BIP

MASSON, Rosaline 828'.8'09 B
Orme.
Robert Louis Stevenson. [Folcroft, Pa.] Folcroft Library Editions, 1973. 94 p. port. 19 cm. Reprint of the 1920 ed. published by T. C. & E. C. Jack, London, in series: The People's books. Bibliography: p. 91. [PR5493.M34 1973] 73-12875 ISBN 0-8414-6004-3 (lib. bdg.)
1. Stevenson, Robert Louis, 1850-1894. BIP

NAKAJIMA, Atsushi, 1909- 823.8
1942.
Light, wind, and dreams; an interpretation of the life and mind of Robert Louis Stevenson. Tr. by Akira Miwa. [Tokyo] Hokuseido Pr. [dist. Austin, Tex., Perkins Oriental, 1964, c.1962] xxiv, 183p. illus., ports., maps. 19cm. 63-714 2.75 pap.,
1. Stevenson, Robert Louis, 1850-1894—Fiction. I. Title.

PEARE, Catherine Owens. 928.2
Robert Louis Stevenson: his life. Illustrated by Margaret Ayer. [1st ed.] New York, Holt [1955] 128 p. illus. 21 cm. [PR5493.P4] 55-10574
1. Stevenson, Robert Louis, 1850-1894.

PEARE, Catherine 828'.8'09 B
Owens.
Robert Louis Stevenson: his life. Illustrated by Margaret Ayer. [1st ed.] New York, Holt [1955] 128 p. illus. 21 cm. A biography of Robert Louis Stevenson who was well-launched on his writing career at age twenty-three, but it was not until the publication of Treasure Island that he became a popular, sought-after writer. [PR5493.P4] 92 AC 68
1. Stevenson, Robert Louis, 1850-1894. I. Ayer, Margaret, illus. II. Title.

RATHER, Lois, 1905- 828'.8'09 B
Stevenson's silver ship; biography of the "Casco". Oakland, Rather Press [1973] 74 p. 4 plates (incl. ports.) 22 cm. No. 41 of 100 copies. [PR5495.R3] 73-163389
1. Stevenson, Robert Louis, 1850-1894. 2. Casco (Yacht) I. Title.

STCVENSON, Robert Louis, 928.2
1850-1894.
RLS Stevenson's letters to Charles Baxter. Edited by De Lancey Ferguson and Marshall Waingrow. New Haven, Yale University Press, 1956. xxvi, 385p. illus., port., facsims. 24cm. [PR5493.A3 1956] 56-7119
I. Baxter, Charles, 1848-1919. II. Ferguson, John De Lancy, 1888- ed. III. Waingrow, Marshall, ed. IV. Title.

STERN, Gladys Bronwyn, 928.2
1890-
Robert Louis Stevenson, the man who wrote "Treasure Island": a biography. Illus. by Federico Castellon. New York, Macmillan, 1954. 142 p. illus. 22 cm. "Published in England under the title He wrote Treasure Island." [PR5493.S68 1954a] 54-13125
1. Stevenson, Robert Louis, 1850-1894.

STEVENSON, Robert 828'.8'09 B
Louis, 1850-1894.
The letters of Robert Louis Stevenson. Edited by Sidney Colvin. A new ed. rearranged in four volumes with 150 new letters. New York, Greenwood Press [1969] 4 v. 23 cm. At head of title: Biographical edition. Reprint of the 1911 ed. Contents.Contents.—v. 1. 1868-1880: Scotland, France, California.—v. 2. 1880-1887: Alps and Highlands, Hyeres, Bournemouth.—v. 3. 1887-1891: The Adirondacks, Pacific voyages, First year at Vailima.—v. 4. 1891-1894: Second, third, and fourth years at Vailima, the end. [PR5493.A3 1969b] 69-14101 ISBN 0-8371-1440-3
I. Colvin, Sidney, Sir, 1845-1927, ed. II. Title.

STEVENSON, Robert Louis, 928.2
1850-1894.
RLS: Stevenson's letters to Charles Baxter. Edited by De Lancey Ferguson and Marshall Waingrow. New Haven, Yale University Press, 1956. xxvi, 385 p. illus., port., facsims. 24 cm. [PR5493.A3] 56-7119
I. Baxter, Charles, 1848-1919 II. Ferguson, John De Lancey, 1888- ed. III. Waingrow, Marshall, ed. IV. Title.

STEVENSON, Robert 828'.8'09 B
Louis, 1850-1894.
RLS; Stevenson's letters to Charles Baxter. Edited by DeLancey Ferguson and Marshall Waingrow. Port Washington, N.Y., Kennikat Press [1973, c1956] xxvi, 385 p. illus. 24 cm. Includes bibliographical references. [PR5493.A3 1973] 72-85294 ISBN 0-8046-1723-6 17.50
I. Baxter, Charles, 1848-1919. II. Ferguson, John DeLancey, 1888- ed. III. Waingrow, Marshall, ed. IV. Title.

STEVENSON, Robert Louis, 826'.8
1850-1894.
Vailima letters; being correspondence addressed by Robert Louis Stevenson to Sidney Colvin, November 1890-October 1894. New York, Greenwood Press [1969] 2 v. ports. 23 cm. Edited by Sidney Colvin. Reprint of the 1895 ed. [PR5493.A35 1969] 69-14102
I. Colvin, Sidney, Sir, 1845-1927. II. Title.

WOOD, James Playsted, 1905- 823.8
The lantern beare; a life of Robert Louis Stevenson. Illus. by Saul Lambert. [New York] Pantheon [c.1965] 182p. illus. 22cm. (Pantheon portrait) Bibl. [PR5493.W6] 65-20665 3.75; 3.49 lib. ed.,
1. Stevenson, Robert Louis, 1850-1894. I. Title.

WOOD, James Playsted, 823.8 (B)
1905-
The lantern bearer; a life of Robert Louis Stevenson. Illustrated by Saul Lambert. [New York] Pantheon Books [1965] 182 p. illus. 22 cm. (A Pantheon portrait) Bibliography: p. 181-182. [PR5493.W6] 65-20665
1. Stevenson, Robert Louis, 1850-1894. I. Title.

WILKIE, Katharine Elliott, 920
1904-
Robert Louis Stevenson: storyteller and adventurer. Ill. by Anthony D'Adamo, iBoston, Houghton [c.1961] 189p. illus. (Piper.bks.) 61-5344 2.24; 1.76 piper ed.,
1. Stevenson, Robert Louis, 1850-1894—Juvenile literature. I. Title.

WILKIE, Katharine Elliott, j92
1904-
Robert Louis Stevenson: storyteller and adventurer. Illustrated by Anthony D'Adamo. Boston, Houghton Mifflin [1961] 189 p. illus. 22 cm. (Piper books) [PR5493.W5] 61-5344
1. Stevenson, Robert Louis, 1850-1894 — Juvenile literature. I. Title.

Stevenson, Robert Louis, 1850-1894—Biography.

BINDING, Paul. 828'.8'09 B
Robert Louis Stevenson / Paul Binding ; illustrated by Robin Jacques. London : Oxford University Press, 1974. [7], 206 p. : ill., ports ; 23 cm. Bibliography: p. 206. [PR5493.B47] 75-305161 ISBN 0-19-273133-5 : £2.00
1. Stevenson, Robert Louis, 1850-1894—Biography.

CARRE, Jean Marie, 828'.8'09 B
1887-1958.
Robert Louis Stevenson; the frail warrior. Translated from the French by Eleanor Hard. Freeport, N.Y., Books for Libraries Press [1971] xii, 297 p. 23 cm. Reprint of the 1930 ed. Translation of La vie de Robert Louis Stevenson. [PR5493.C32 1971] 78-165619 ISBN 0-8369-5926-4
1. Stevenson, Robert Louis, 1850-1894—Biography.

DAICHES, David, 1912- 828'.8'09 B
Robert Louis Stevenson and his world. London, Thames and Hudson [1973] 128 p. illus. 24 cm. Bibliography: p. 118. [PR5493.D22] 73-179615 ISBN 0-500-13045-0
1. Stevenson, Robert Louis, 1850-1894—Biography. I. Title.
Distributed by Transatlantic Arts; 8.75. BIP

HELLMAN, George 828'.8'09 B
Sidney, 1878-1958.
The true Stevenson; a study in clarification. New York, Haskell House Publishers, 1972. xiv, 253 p. illus. 23 cm. [PR5493.H4 1972] 72-1318 ISBN 0-8383-1443-0 12.95
1. Stevenson, Robert Louis, 1850-1894—Biography. I. Title.

POPE-HENNESSY, James. 828'.8'09
Robert Louis Stevenson / James Pope Hennessy. New York : Simon and Schuster, [1975] c1974. 320 p., [8] leaves of plates : ill. ; 22 cm. Includes index. Bibliography: p. 310-312. [PR5493.P6 1975] 74-23350 ISBN 0-671-21973-1 lib.bdg. : 9.95
1. Stevenson, Robert Louis, 1850-1894—Biography.

RICE, Edward. 828'.8'09 B
Journey to Upolu; Robert Louis Stevenson, Victorian rebel. New York, Dodd, Mead [1974] xi, 145 p. illus. 25 cm. [PR5493.R5] 73-21164 ISBN 0-396-06933-9 6.95
1. Stevenson, Robert Louis, 1850-1894—Biography. I. Title.

SIMPSON, Evelyn 828'.8'09 B
Blantyre, 1856-1920.
Robert Louis Stevenson / by E. Blantyre Simpson. Folcroft, Pa. : Folcroft Library Editions, 1977. p. cm. Reprint of the 1906 ed. published by T. N. Foulis, Edinburgh, which was issued as no. 2 of the Spirit of the age series. [PR5493.S5 1977] 77-10079 ISBN 0-8414-7875-9 lib. bdg. : 10.00
1. Stevenson, Robert Louis, 1850-1894—Biography. 2. Authors, Scottish—19th century—Biography. I. Title. II. Series: Spirit of the age series ; no. 2. BIP

SMITH, Janet Adam. 828'.8'09 B
R. L. Stevenson / by Janet Adam Smith. Folcroft, Pa. : Folcroft Library Editions, 1977. 144 p. ; 23 cm. Reprint of the 1937 ed. published by Duckworth, London, in series: Great lives. Includes bibliographical references. [PR5493.S6 1977] 77-9276 ISBN 0-8414-7856-2 lib. bdg. : 12.50
1. Stevenson, Robert Louis, 1850-1894—Biography. 2. Authors, Scottish—19th century—Biography. BIP

Stevenson, Robert Louis, 1850-1894—Biography—Juvenile literature.

GROVER, Eulalie Osgood, 1873- 828'.8'09 B
Robert Louis Stevenson, teller of tales. Illustrated by Marc Simont. New York, Dodd, Mead, 1940. Detroit, Gale Research Co., 1975. x, 265 p. illus. 22 cm. Bibliography: p. 263-265. A biography of the Scottish author of such well-known works as Kidnapped and Treasure Island. [PR5493.G7 1975] 92 71-164308 ISBN 0-8103-4080-1 11.00
1. Stevenson, Robert Louis, 1850-1894—Biography—Juvenile literature. I. Simont, Marc, illus. II. Title.
Pbk. 5.95; ISBN 0-275-85080-3. BIP

Stevenson, Robert Louis, 1850-1894—Homes and haunts—Edinburgh.

MCLAREN, Moray. 828'.8'09 B
Stevenson and Edinburgh; a centenary study. [Folcroft, Pa.] Folcroft Library Editions, 1974. p. cm. Reprint of the 1950 ed. published by Chapman & Hall, London. [PR5494.M35 1974b] 74-8356 12.50
1. Stevenson, Robert Louis, 1850-1894—Homes and haunts—Edinburgh.

Stevenson, Robert Louis, 1850-1894—Homes and haunts—Hawaii.

MCGAW, Martha Mary, Sister. 828'.8'09 B
Stevenson in Hawaii / Martha Mary McGaw. Westport, Conn. : Greenwood Press, 1978, c1950. xviii, 182 p. : ill. ; 23 cm. Reprint of the ed. published by University of Hawaii, Press, Honolulu. Includes index. Bibliography: p. [161]-170. [PR5495.M3 1978] 77-13757 ISBN 0-8371-9864-X lib.bdg. : 16.25
1. Stevenson, Robert Louis, 1850-1894—Homes and haunts—Hawaii. 2. Authors, Scottish—19th century—Biography. 3. Hawaii—Descripion and travel—To 1950. I. Title.

Stevenson, Robert Louis, 1850-1894—Homes and haunts—Pacific Islands (Ter.)

JOHNSTONE, Arthur. 828'.8'09 B
Recollections of Robert Louis Stevenson in the Pacific / by Arthur Johnstone. Folcroft, Pa. : Folcroft Library Editions, 1974. p. cm. Reprint of the 1905 ed. published by Chatto & Windus, London. [PR5495.J6 1974] 74-23652 ISBN 0-8414-5324-1 lib. bdg. : 25.00
1. Stevenson, Robert Louis, 1850-1894—Homes and haunts—Pacific Islands (Ter.) I. Title. BIP

Stevenson, Robert Louis, 1850-1894—Homes and haunts—Scotland—Leith Valley.

GEDDIE, John, 1848-1937. 914.13'2'0481
The home country of R. L. Stevenson : being the Valley of the Water of Leith from source to sea / by John Geddie ; illustrated by Joseph Brown ; port., from photos., by A. Roche. Folcroft, Pa. : Folcroft Library Editions, 1977. p. cm. Reprint of the 1898 ed. published by W. H. White, Edinburgh. Includes index. [PR5494.G4 1977] 77-10929 ISBN 0-8414-4457-9 lib. bdg. : 30.00
1. Stevenson, Robert Louis, 1850-1894—Homes and haunts—Scotland—Leith Valley. 2. Leith Valley, Scot.—History. 3. Authors, Scottish—19th century—Biography. I. Title.

GEDDIE, John, 1848-1937. 914.13'2'0481
The home country of R. L. Stevenson : being the Valley of the Water of Leith from source to sea / by John Geddie ; illustrated by Joseph Brown ; port., from photos., by A. Roche. Folcroft, Pa. : Folcroft Library Editions, 1977. p. cm. Reprint of the 1898 ed. published by W. H. White, Edinburgh. Includes index. [PR5494.G4 1977] 77-10929 ISBN 0-8414-4457-9 lib. bdg. : 30.00
1. Stevenson, Robert Louis, 1850-1894—Homes and haunts—Scotland—Leith Valley. 2. Leith Valley, Scot.—History. 3. Authors, Scottish—19th century—Biography. I. Title.

Stevenson, Robert Louis 1850-1894—Journeys—France—Cevennes Mountains.

STEVENSON, Robert Louis, 1850-1894. 914.4'8'0481
The Cevennes journal : notes on a journey through the French highlands / by Robert Louis Stevenson ; edited by Gordon Golding ; notes by Jacques Blondel, Gordon Golding, Jacques Poujol. Edinburgh : Mainstream Publishing ; New York : Taplinger Publishing, 1978. 159 p., 8 p. of plates : ill. ; 23 cm. Continuation of Travels with a donkey in the Cevennes. Includes bibliographical references. [PR5488.T8 1978] 78-67825 ISBN 0-8008-1414-2 (Taplinger) : 11.95
1. Stevenson, Robert Louis 1850-1894—Journeys—France—Cevennes Mountains. 2. Cevennes Mountains—Description and travel. 3. Authors, Scottish—19th century—Biography. I. Golding, Gordon. II. Blondel, Jacques. III. Poujol, Jacques. IV. Title.

Stevenson, William, 1768-1857.

VERNON, Walter N. 922.773
William Stevenson, riding preacher. Dallas, Southern Methodist Univ. Pr. [c.]1964. xiii, 78p. illus., facsims. 23cm. Bibl. [BX8495.S767V4] 65-1232 1.45 pap.,
1. Stevenson, William, 1768-1857. I. Title.

VERNON, Walter N 922.773
William Stevenson, Riding preacher [by] Walter N. Vernon. Dallas, Southern Methodist University Press, 1964. xiii, 78 p. illus., facsims. 23 cm. Bibliographical references included in "Notes" (p. 67-73) [BX8495.S767V4] 65-1232
1. Stevenson, William, 1768-1857. I. Title. BIP

Stevenson, Yvonne, 1915-

STEVENSON, Yvonne, 1915- 616.8'9'00924 B
The hot-house plant : the autobiography of a young girl / Yvonne Stevenson. London : Elek, 1976. xvi, 190 p. ; 23 cm. [BF109.S77A33 1976] 77-355272 ISBN 0-301-73101-2 : 9.95 ISBN 0-301-73102-0 pbk. : 5.95
1. Stevenson, Yvonne, 1915- 2. Psychologists—Biography. I. Title.
Distributed by P.Elek, Salem, NH

Stewart, Alexander Peter, 1821-1908.

WINGFIELD, Marshall, 1893- 923.573
General A. P. Stewart, his life and letters. Memphis, West Tennessee Historical Society, 1954. 259p. illus. 24cm. [E467.1.S863W5] 54-11115
1. Stewart, Alexander Peter, 1821-1908. I. Title.

Stewart, Donald Ogden, 1894- —Biography.

STEWART, Donald Ogden, 1894- 818'.5'209 B
By a stroke of luck : an autobiography / by Donald Ogden Stewart. New York : Paddington Press/Two Continents Pub. Group, [1975] p. cm. [PS3537.T485Z52] 75-11172 ISBN 0-8467-0063-8 : 10.95
1. Stewart, Donald Ogden, 1894- —Biography. I. Title.

Stewart, Douglas Alexander, 1913-

KEESING, Nancy. 821
Douglas Stewart. [2nd ed.] Melbourne, New York, Oxford University Press [1969] 48 p. 22 cm. (Australian writers and their work) Bibliography: p. 45-46. [PR6037.T463Z75 1969] 76-489602 1.00
1. Stewart, Douglas Alexander, 1913- I. Title.

Stewart, Dresden Blake, 1881-

JARCHOW, Merrill E., 1910- 712'.092'4 B
In search of fulfillment : episodes in the life of D. Blake Stewart / by Merrill E. Jarchow. [St. Paul] : North Central Pub. Co., 1974. ix, 86 p. : ill. ; 22 cm. [SB470.S67J37] 74-19986
1. Stewart, Dresden Blake, 1881- 2. Carleton College, Northfield, Minn. I. Title.

Stewart, Eliza (Daniel) 1816-1908.

BING, S. Louise. 178'.1'0924 B
The uncrowned queen of the temperance world [by S. Louise Bing. Charleston, W. Va., Printed by Jarrett Print. Co., 1967] 55 p. illus., ports. 22 cm. [HV5232.S7B5] 68-129
1. Stewart, Eliza (Daniel) 1816-1908. I. Title.

Stewart family.

DICKERSON, Florence (Smith) 1893- 929.2
The James Stewart family of early Augusta County, Virginia, and descendants, 1740-1960, by Florence S. Dickerson. [Parsons? W.Va., 1966] 318 p. illus, col. coat of arms, ports. 22 cm. [CS71.S93 1966] 66-27493
1. Stewart family. I. Title.

Stewart, Jackie.

THE Exciting world of Jackie Stewart. 796.7'2'0924 B Glasgow [etc.] : Collins [for the Scottish Educational Trust], 1974. 88 p. : ill. (some col.), ports. (some col.) ; 26 cm. [GV1032.S74E92] 74-192694 ISBN 0-00-106182-8 : 6.95
1. Stewart, Jackie. 2. Automobile racing.
Distributed by World Pub. Co. New York.

STEWART, Jackie. 796.7'2
Faster! A racer's diary, by Jackie Stewart and Peter Manso. New York, Farrar, Straus and Giroux [1972] 239 p. illus. 22 cm. [GV1032.S74A25 1972] 72-76337 ISBN 0-374-15370-1 7.95
1. Automobile racing. I. Manso, Peter, joint author. II. Title.

Stewart, James, 1908-

*HANNA, David. 791.43'028'0924 B
Four giants of the West. New York, Belmont Tower [1976] 223 p. ill. 18 cm. [PN2287] 1.50 (pbk.)
1. Fonda, Henry, 1905- 2. Stewart, James, 1908- 3. Wayne, John, 1907- 4. Cooper, Gary, 1901-1961. I. Title.

Stewart, John L., 1907-

STEWART, John L., 1907- 378.1'2'0924 B
Yesterday was tomorrow : autobiography of John L. Stewart. [Durham? N.C.] : Stewart, 1976. xii, 621 p. ; 23 cm. [LA2317.S83A35] 76-42836 ISBN 0-917798-01-5
1. Stewart, John L., 1907- 2. Teachers—United States—Biography. I. Title.

Stewart, Margaret (Ross) Evans,

STEWART, Margaret (Ross) Evans, 1874- 926.1
From dugout to hilltop. Culver City, Calif., Murray & Gee, 1951. 233 p. 23 cm. Autobiography. [R154.S8343A3] 51-13030
I. Title.

Stewart, William,

STEWART, William, 1881- 922.773
Mindful of man; the chronicle of an octogenarian Methodist minister. Farmington, Mo., 1964. xiii, 139 p. illus., ports. 24 cm. [BX8495.S764A3] 65-1230
I. Title.

Stewart, William George Drummond, bart., Sir 1768-1871.

PORTER, Mae Reed 923.973
Scotsman in buckskin; Sir William Drummond Stewart and the Rocky Mountain fur trade, by Mae Reed Porter, Odessa Davenport. New York, Hastings [c1963] 306p. illus. 21cm. Bibl. 63-13562 5.95
1. Stewart, William George Drummond, bart., Sir 1768-1871. 2. Fur trade—The West. I. Davenport, Odessa, joint author. II. Title.

Stewart, William Morris, 1827-1909.

HERMANN, Ruth. 979.3'02'0924 B
Gold and silver colossus : William Morris Stewart and his southern bride / Ruth Hermann. Sparks, Nev. : Dave's Print. & Pub., c1975. xxv, 430 p. : ill. ; 24 cm. Includes index. Bibliography: p. 381-403. [E664.S838H47] 75-24137 11.50
1. Stewart, William Morris, 1827-1909. 2. California—Gold discoveries. 3. Silver mines and mining—Nevada. 4. Nevada—History. I. Title.

***Stibbs, Alan M.**

*STIBBS, Alan M. 221.92
God's friend, studies in the life of Abraham. Chicago, Inter-Varsity [1964] 88p. 19cm. .75 pap.,
I. Title.

Stickney, Trumbull, 1874-1904.

WHITTLE, Amberys R. 811'.4
Trumbull Stickney [by] Amberys R. Whittle. Lewisburg [Pa.] Bucknell University Press [1973] 164 p. 22 cm. Bibliography: p. 149-155. [PS3537.T525Z95] 72-425 ISBN 0-8387-1154-5 8.75
1. Stickney, Trumbull, 1874-1904. BIP

Stieber, Wilhelm, 1818-1882.

STIEBER, Wilhelm, 1818-1882. 327'.12'0924 B
The chancellor's spy : memoirs of the founder of modern espionage / by Wilhelm J. C. E. Stieber ; translated from the German by Jan Van Heurch. 1st ed. New York : Grove Press : distributed by Random House, 1979. p. cm. Translation of Spion des Kanzlers. [DD205.S74A3713] 79-52090 ISBN 0-394-50869-6 : 12.50
1. Stieber, Wilhelm, 1818-1882. 2. Bismarck, Otto, Furst von, 1815-1898. 3. Spies—Germany—Biography. 4. Germany—Politics and government—1871-1888. I. Title.

Stieglitz, Alfred, 1864-1946.

NORMAN, Dorothy, 1905- 779'.092'4 B
Alfred Stieglitz: an American seer. [1st ed.] New York, Random House [1973] 253 p. illus. 31 cm. "An Aperture book." Bibliography: p. 243-249. [TR140.S7N59] 74-529 ISBN 0-394-48809-1 35.00
1. Stieglitz, Alfred, 1864-1946. I. Stieglitz, Alfred, 1864-1946.

SELIGMANN, Herbert Jacob, 1891- 779.0924
Alfred Stieglitz talking; notes on some of his conversations, 1925-1931. Foreword by Herbert J. Seligmann. New Haven [Conn.] Yale University Library, [c.]1966. ix, 149p. 24cm. [TR140.S7S4] 66-21942 7.50
1. Stieglitz, Alfred, 1864-1946. 2. Artists—Correspondence, reminiscences, etc. I. Stieglitz, Alfred, 1864-1946. II. Title.

Stieglitz, Alfred, 1864-1946—Art patronage.

HOMER, William Innes. 709'.73
Stieglitz and the American avant-garde / William Innes Homer. 1st ed. Boston : New York Graphics Society, c1977. p. cm. Bibliography: p. [N5220.S858H65 1977] 76-50068 ISBN 0-8212-0676-1 : 17.50
1. Stieglitz, Alfred, 1864-1946—Art patronage. 2. Art, American. 3. Art,

Modern—20th century—United States. 4. Photography, Artistic. 5. Artists—United States—Biography. I. Title.

Stikker, Dirk U.

STIKKER, Dirk U. 355.031 B
Men of responsibility; a memoir, by Dirk U. Stikker. [1st ed.] New York, Harper & Row [1966] xii, 418 p. ports. 22 cm. [D839.7.S7A3] 66-10639
I. Title.

Stiles, Ezra, 1727-1795.

MORGAN, Edmund Sears. 923.773
The gentle Puritan; a life of Ezra Stiles, 1727-1795. Published for the Institute of Early American History and Culture, Williamsburg, Va. New Haven, Yale University Press, 1962. ix, 490p. plates, ports., maps. 25cm. Bibliographical footnotes. [LD6330 1778.M6] 62-8257
1. Stiles, Ezra, 1727-1795. I. Title.

PARSONS, Francis, 1871-1937. 378.746'8 B
Six men of Yale. Foreword by Charles Seymour. Freeport, N.Y., Books for Libraries Press [1971, c1939] xii, 145 p. ports. 23 cm. (Essay index reprint series) Contents.Contents.—Elisha Williams, 1694-1755.—Ezra Stiles, 1727-1795.—The young Silliman in Nelson's England, 1805-1806.—Edward J. Phelps, 1822-1900.—The second President Dwight, 1828-1916.—Henry Augustin Beer, 1847-1926. [LD6319.P3 1971] 72-156702 ISBN 0-8369-2329-4
1. Williams, Elisha, 1694-1775. 2. Stiles, Ezra, 1727-1795. 3. Silliman, Benjamin, 1779-1864. 4. Phelps, Edward John, 1822-1900. 5. Dwight, Timothy, 1828-1916. 6. Beers, Henry Augustin, 1847-1926. I. Title.
BIP

Stiles, James Esmond, 1889-

UHLAN, Edward 920.5
Dynamo Jim Stiles, pioneer of progress; the story of a newspaper publisher who built a country and a legend. Foreword by Kent Cooper. Appreciation by Cranston Williams. 1st Ed. New York, Exposition Press [1959] 392 p. illus. 25 cm. [PN4874.S688U5] 59-4177
1. Stiles, James Esmond, 1889- I. Title.

STILL, James, 1812-1885. 616'.00924 B
Early recollections and life of Dr. James Still. Freeport, N.Y., Books for Libraries Press, 1971. 274 p. port. 23 cm. (The Black heritage library collection) Reprint of the 1877 ed. [E185.97.S85 1971] 72-164394 ISBN 0-8369-8853-1
I. Title. II. Series.

Still, James, 1812-1885.

STILL, James, 1812-1885. 616'.0092'4
Early recollections and life of Dr. James Still. Westport, Conn., Negro Universities Press [1970] 274 p. port. 23 cm. Reprint of the 1877 ed. [E185.97.S85 1970] 72-107522 ISBN 0-8371-3769-1
I. Title. BIP

STILL, James, 1812-1885. 616'.00924 B
Early recollections and life of Dr. James Still. Freeport, N.Y., Books for Libraries Press, 1971. 274 p. port. 23 cm. (The Black heritage library collection) Reprint of the 1877 ed. [E185.97.S85 1971] 72-164394 ISBN 0-8369-8853-1
I. Title. II. Series.

STILL, James, 1812-1885. 616'.0092'4 B
Early recollections and life of Dr. James Still, 1812-1885. New Brunswick, N.J., Rutgers University Press [1973, c1877] ix, 274 p. illus. 20 cm. Reprint of the ed. published by Lippincott, Philadelphia, with a new historical sketch by M. Cridland. [R154.S8348A33 1973] 73-14624 ISBN 0-8135-0769-3 7.50
1. Still, James, 1812-1885. 2. Negro physicians—Correspondence, reminiscences, etc. I. Title.

Still, Peter—Juvenile literature.

MANN, Peggy. 301.44'93'0924 B
The Man who bought himself : the story of Peter Still / by Peggy Mann and Vivian W. Siegal. New York : Macmillan, [1975] 215 p. : map ; 22 cm. Bibliography: p. 211-215. The life of the black man who was kidnapped and sold into slavery as a child and managed, after much effort, to buy his freedom and that of his wife and children. [E444.S849] 92 75-15514 ISBN 0-02-762220-7 : 6.95
1. Still, Peter—Juvenile literature. 2. Slavery in the United States—Juvenile literature. I. Siegal, Vivian W., joint author. II. Title. BIP

Stillman, Charles Kirtland, 1879-1938.

DICKERMAN, Marion. 917.46'5 B
The three founders: Dr. Charles Kirtland Stillman, Carl C. Cutler [and] Edward Eugene Bradley. With a foreword by Philip R. Mallory. [Mystic, Conn.] Marine Historical Association, 1965. 42 p. illus., ports. 23 cm. Cover title: The three founders of Mystic Seaport. [F104.M99D5] 71-17343
1. Mystic Seaport, Mystic, Conn. 2. Stillman, Charles Kirtland, 1879-1938. 3. Cutler, Carl C., 1878-1966. 4. Bradley, Edward Eugene, 1857-1938. I. Marine Historical Association. II. Title.

Stillman, James, 1850-1918.

BURR, Anna Robeson Brown, 1873-1941. 332.1'092'4 B
The portrait of a banker, James Stillman / Anna Robeson Burr. New York : Arno Press, 1975 [c1927] ix, 370 p., [18] leaves of plates : ill. ; 23 cm. (Wall Street and the security markets) Reprint of the ed. published by Duffield, New York. Includes index. [HG2463.S7B8 1975] 75-2624 ISBN 0-405-06950-2 : 25.00
1. Stillman, James, 1850-1918. 2. Bankers—United States—Biography. I. Title. II. Series.

Stillwell, Margaret Bingham, 1887-

STILLWELL, Margaret Bingham, 1887- 020'.92'4 B
Librarians are human; memories in and out of the rare-book world, 1907-1970. Boston [The Colonial Society of Massachusetts] 1973. xiv, 401 p. illus. 24 cm. [Z720.S833A3] 73-85910 ISBN 0-87451-091-0 20.00
1. Stillwell, Margaret Bingham, 1887- 2. Librarians—Correspondence, reminiscences, etc. 3. Bibliography—Rare books. I. Title.
Distributed by the University Press of New England.

Stilwell, Arthur Edward, 1861-1928.

BRYANT, Keith L. 385'.0924 B
Arthur E. Stilwell, promoter with a hunch [by] Keith M. Bryant, Jr. Nashville, Vanderbilt University Press, 1971. xi, 256 p. illus., port. 24 cm. Includes bibliographical references. [HE2754.S8B76] 78-170282 ISBN 0-8265-1173-2
1. Stilwell, Arthur Edward, 1861-1928. I. Title. BIP

Stilwell, Joseph Warren, 1883-1946.

LIANG, Chin-Tung, 1890- 951.04'2'0924
General Stilwell in China, 1942-1944: the full story. [Jamaica, N.Y., St. John's University Press, 1972] xviii, 321 p. illus. 24 cm. (Asia in the modern world series, no. 12) Bibliography: p. 297-307. [E745.S68L5] 72-78177 ISBN 0-87075-063-1
1. Stilwell, Joseph Warren, 1883-1946. 2. United States—Foreign relations—China. 3. China—Foreign relations—United States. 4. World War, 1939-1945—China. I. Title. II. Series: Asia in the modern world, no. 12.

ROONEY, Douglas David. 940.542'5
Stilwell [by] D. D. Rooney. [New York, Ballantine Books, 1971] 160 p. illus., maps, ports. 21 cm. (Ballantine's illustrated history of the violent century. War leader book no. 4) Cover title. Bibliography: p. 160. [D767.6.R66] 71-25335 ISBN 0-345-02261-0 1.00
1. Stilwell, Joseph Warren, 1883-1946. 2. World War, 1939-1945—Campaigns—Burma. 3. World War, 1939-1945—China.

TUCHMAN, Barbara (Wertheim) 951.04'2'0924 B
Stilwell and the American experience in China, 1911-45 [by] Barbara W. Tuchman. New York, Macmillan [1970] xv, 621 p. illus., maps, ports. 24 cm. Bibliography: p. 541-552. [E745.S68T8] 77-135647 10.00
1. Stilwell, Joseph Warren, 1883-1946. 2. U.S.—Foreign relations—China. 3. China—Foreign relations—U.S. 4 World War, 1939-1945—China. I. Title. BIP

Stimson, Henry Lewis, 1867-1950.

CURRENT, Richard Nelson. 973.9'0924
Secretary Stimson, a study in statecraft [by] Richard N. Current, with a new introd. by the author. [Hamden, Conn.] Archon Books, 1970 [c1954] xxxv, 272 p. 22 cm. Bibliography: p. 253-256. [E748.S883C8 1970] 71-114419
1. Stimson, Henry Lewis, 1867-1950. I. Title.

MORISON, Elting Elmore 923.273
Turmoil and tradition; a study of the life and times of Henry L. Stimson. New York, Atheneum, 1964 [c.1960] 565p. 18cm. (A51) Bibl. 2.45 pap.,
1. Stimson, Henry Lewis, 1867-1950. I. Title.

MORISON, Elting Elmore. 923.273
Turmoil and tradition; a study of the life and times of Henry L. Stimson. Boston, Houghton Mifflin, 1960. 686 p. illus. 22 cm. Includes bibliography. [E748.S883M6] 60-10132
1. Stimson, Henry Lewis, 1867-1950. I. Title.

STIMSON, Henry Lewis, 1867-1950. 973.91'0924 B
On active service in peace and war, by Henry L. Stimson and McGeorge Bundy. New York, Octagon Books, 1971 [c1948] xxii, 698 p. port. 25 cm. "About one fifth of the material in this book was published serially [in the Ladies home journal] under the title of Time of peril." [E748.S883A3 1971] 79-159230 ISBN 0-374-97627-9
1. U.S.—Politics and government—1901-1953. 2. U.S.—Foreign relations—20th century. I. Bundy, McGeorge. II. Title. BIP

Stirling, Alfred Thorpe, 1902-

STIRLING, Alfred Thorpe, 1902- 327'.2'0924
On the fringe of diplomacy, by Alfred Stirling. Melbourne, Hawthorn Press, 1973. 213 p. 23 cm. English, French, or Italian. [D413.S77A36] 73-179114 ISBN 0-7256-0102-7 9.95
1. Stirling, Alfred Thorpe, 1902- I. Title.

Stirling, Amiria Manutahi.

STIRLING, Amiria Manutahi. 993.1'1'004994 B
Amiria : the life story of a Maori woman / Amiria Manutahi Stirling ; as told to Anne Salmond. Wellington : A. H. & A. W. Reed, 1976. xii, 184 p. : ill. ; 26 cm. Includes index. Bibliography: p. 179-180. [DU422.82.S8A32] 77-367371 ISBN 0-589-00978-8
1. Stirling, Amiria Manutahi. 2. Maoris—Biography. I. Salmond, Anne. II. Title. BIP

Stirling, Leader.

STIRLING, Leader. 362.1'092'4 B
Tanzanian doctor / by Leader Stirling ; with an introd. by Julius K. Nyerere. Montreal : McGill-Queen's University Press, 1977. 138 p. : ill. ; 23 cm. [R722.32.S74A33 1977] 78-316167 ISBN 0-7735-0305-6 : 10.95
1. Stirling, Leader. 2. Missionaries, Medical—Tanzania—Biography. 3. Legislators—Tanzania—Biography. 4. Health-officers—Tanzania—Biography. 5. Public health—Tanzania—History. I. Title.
Distributed by University of Toronto Press, Buffalo, New York BIP

Stobo, Robert, 1727-1770.

ALBERTS, Robert C. 923.573
The most extraordinary adventures of Major Robert Stobo. Illus. with photos. and maps drawn by Samuel Hanks Bryant. Boston, Houghton, 1965[c.1963, 1965] x, 423p. illus., maps, plans, ports. 22cm. Bibl. [E199.S86A6] 65-10675 6.95
1. Stobo, Robert, 1727-1770. 2. U.S.—Hist.—French and Indian War, 1755-1763. I. Title.

Stock, Joseph Whiting, 1815-1855.

STOCK, Joseph Whiting, 1815-1855. 759.13 B
The paintings and the journal of Joseph Whiting Stock / edited by Juliette Tomlinson ; with a checklist of his works compiled by Kate Steinway. Middletown, Conn. : Wesleyan University Press, [1976] p. cm. Includes index. Bibliography: p. [ND1329.S69A25] 76-7189 ISBN 0-8195-4098-6 : 30.00
1. Stock, Joseph Whiting, 1815-1855. 2. Portrait-painters—United States—Correspondence, reminiscences, etc. 3. Primitivism in art—United States. I. Tomlinson, Juliette, 1921- II. Title.

Stock, Nelly (Weeton)

STOCK, Nelly (Weeton) b.1776. 914.27'2'03730924 B
Miss Weeton's journal of a governess. New introd. by J. J. Bagley. New York, A. M. Kelley, 1969. 2 v. illus., map. 23 cm. Reprint of the 1936-39 ed. with title: Miss Weeton: journal of a governess. Contents.Contents.—v. 1. 1807-1811.—v. 2. 1811-1825. Bibliographical footnotes. [CT788.S77A352] 68-27857
I. Title.

Stockard, Virginia Alice (Cottey) 1848-1940.

TROESCH, Helen De Rusha. 923.773
The life of Virginia Alice Cottey Stockard. [Nevada? Mo., 1955] 298p. illus., ports. 22cm. [LD7251.N25T7] 56-15673
1. Stockard, Virginia Alice (Cottey) 1848-1940. 2. Cottey College, Nevada, Mo.—Hist. I. Title.

Stockhausen, Karlheinz, 1928-

WORNER, Karl Heinrich, 1910-1969. 785'.092'4
Stockhausen; life and work. Introduced, translated, and edited by Bill Hopkins. [Rev. ed.] Berkeley, University of California Press, 1973. 270 p. illus. 23 cm. German ed. published in 1963 under title: Karlheinz Stockhausen. [ML410.S858W62] 76-174460 ISBN 0-520-02143-6 10.95
1. Stockhausen, Karlheinz, 1928- I. Hopkins, Bill, ed.

Stockmar, Christian Friedrich, Freiherr von, 1787-1863.

COLSON, Percy, 1873-1952. 920.71
Their ruling passions. Foreword by James Laver. Freeport, N.Y., Books for Libraries Press [1970] 221 p. illus., ports. 24 cm. (Biography index reprint series) Reprint of the 1949 ed. Contents.Contents.—Baron Stockmar, a study in wire-pulling.—Lord George Gordon, a study in fanaticism.—Dr. Samuel Parr, a study in egoism.—Joseph Nollekens, a study in avarice.—The young Disraeli, a study in ambition.

Includes bibliographies. [DA531.2.C78 1970] 70-136645
1. Stockmar, Christian Friedrich, Freiherr von, 1787-1863. 2. Gordon, George, Lord, 1751-1793. 3. Parr, Samuel, 1747-1825. 4. Nollekens, Joseph, 1737-1823. 5. Beaconsfield, Benjamin Disraeli, 1st Earl of, 1804-1881. I. Title. BIP

Stockton, Frank Richard, 1834-1902.

GRIFFIN, Martin Ignatius Joseph, 1906- 813.4
Frank R. Stockton; a critical biography. Port Washington, N. Y., Kennikat [1965, c.1939] 178 p. facsim., port. 22 cm. Bibl. [PS2928.G7] 65-18606 6.00
1. Stockton, Frank Richard, 1834-1902. I. Title. BIP

Stockton, Marcellus Lowry,

STOCKTON, Marcellus Lowry, Brig. Gen. 1893- 355.3320924
A general's story. New York, Vantage [c.1965] 248p. 21cm [CT275.S787A3] 65-8588 3.95 bds.,
I. Title.

STOCKTON, Marcellus Lowry, 1893- 355.3320924
A general's story [by] M. L. Stockton. [1st ed.) New York, Vantage Press [1965] 248 p. 21 cm. [CT275.S787A3] 65-8588
I. Title.

Stoddard, Herbert L.

STODDARD, Herbert L. 500.9 B
Memoirs of a naturalist [by] Herbert L. Stoddard, Sr. [1st ed.] Norman, University of Oklahoma Press [1969] xix, 303 p. illus. (part col.), ports. 23 cm. "Bibliography of writings by Herbert L. Stoddard, Sr.": p. 285-288. [QH31.S66A3] 69-16713
I. Title. BIP

Stoddard, Seneca Ray, 1844-1917.

DE SORMO, Maitland C. 770'.92'4 B
Seneca Ray Stoddard; versatile camera-artist, by Maitland C. De Sormo. Saranac Lake, N.Y., Adirondack Yesteryears [1972] 190 p. illus. 27 cm. [TR140.S73D47] 72-90586 10.50
1. Stoddard, Seneca Ray, 1844-1917. I. Title. BIP

Stoessinger, John George.

STOESSINGER, John George. 320'.092'4 B
Night journey : a story of survival and deliverance / John G. Stoessinger. 1st ed. Chicago : Playboy Press ; New York : trade distribution by Simon and Schuster, c1978. 216 p. ; 21 cm. [JA93.S85A35] 78-15265 ISBN 0-87223-512-2 : 9.95
1. Stoessinger, John George. 2. Political scientists—United States—Biography. I. Title.

Stoker, Bram, 1847-1912.

FARSON, Daniel, 1927- 823'.8 B
The man who wrote Dracula : a biography of Bram Stoker / Daniel Farson. New York : St. Martin's Press, 1976, c1975. 240 p., [4] leaves of plates : ill. ; 23 cm. Includes index. [PR6037.T617Z64 1976] 76-2657 8.95
1. Stoker, Bram, 1847-1912. 2. Authors, English—19th century—Biography. I. Title.

Stokes, Carl.

STOKES, Carl. 320.9'771'3204 B
Promises of power; a political autobiography, by Carl B. Stokes. New York, Simon and Schuster [1973] 288 p. 22 cm. [F499.C653S86] 73-3783 ISBN 0-671-21602-3 7.95
1. Stokes, Carl. 2. Cleveland—Politics and government. I. Title.

Stolypin, Petr Arkad'evich, 1862-1911.

BOCK, Maria (Stolypina) 1885- 947.08'0924 B
Reminiscences of my father Peter A. Stolypin, by Maria Petrovna von Bock. Translated and edited by Margaret Patoski. Metuchen, N.J., Scarecrow Press, 1970. xv, 321 p. ports. 22 cm. Translation of Vospominaniia o moem ottse P. A. Stolypine (romanized form) [DK254.S595B613] 75-16442
1. Stolypin, Petr Arkad'evich, 1862-1911. I. Title.

Stone, Annie, 1854-1877.

RUSSELL, Traylor. 345'.764'02523
The Diamond Bessie murder and the Rothschild trials. [1st ed.] Mount Pleasant, Tex. [1971] iv, 183 p. illus. 23 cm. Bibliography: p. 183. [HV6534.J4R9] 72-179519
1. Stone, Annie, 1854-1877. 2. Rothschild, Abraham, b. 1853. 3. Trials (Murder)—Jefferson, Tex. I. Title.

Stone, Barton Warren, 1772-1844.

WEST, William Garrett. 922.673
Barton Warren Stone; early American advocate of Christian unity. Nashville, Disciples of Christ Historical Society, 1954. xvi, 245p. port. 25cm. Bibliography:p. 227-237. [BX7343.S8W4] 54-12928
1. Stone, Barton Warren, 1772-1844. I. Title.

Stone, Elizabeth (Hickok) 1801-1895.

MUMEY, Nolie, 1891- 923.9
The saga of 'Auntie' Stone and her cabin: Elizabeth Hickok Robbins Stone (1801-1895) a pioneer woman who built and owned the first dwelling, operated the first hotel. built the first flour mill, and erected the first brick kiln in the city of Fort Collins, Colorado. Centenary ed. Boulder, Colo., Johnson Pub. Co., 1964. xix, 128p. illus. (pt. col.) facsim., geneal. table, ports. 31cm. Bibl. 64-54971 10.00. lim. ed.
1. Stone, Elizabeth (Hickok) 1801-1895. 2. Fort Collins. Colo.—Hist. I. Keays, Elizabeth (Parke) 1830-1922. II. Title.

Stone, Harlan Fiske, 1872-1946.

MASON, Alpheus Thomas, 1899- 923.473
Harlan Fiske Stone: pillar of the law. New York, Viking Press, 1956. xiii, 914p. illus. ports. 25cm. 'Bibliographic notes':p. 813-873. 'Note on Stone's legal writings': p. 888-891. 56-10404
1. Stone, Harlan Flake, 1872-1946. I. Title.

MASON, Alpheus Thomas, 1899- 347.99'73
Harlan Fiske Stone; pillar of the law. [Hamden, Conn.] Archon Books, 1968 [c1956] xiii, 914 p. illus., ports. 23 cm. Bibliography: p. 813-873. "Note on Stone's legal writings": p. 888-891. [KF8745.S8M3 1968] 68-21687
1. Stone, Harlan Fiske, 1872-1946.

MASON, Alpheus Thomas, 1899- 923.473
Harlan Fiske Stone& pillar of the law. New York, Viking Press, 1956. xiii, 914p. illus., ports. 25cm. 'Bibliographic notes': p. 813-878. 'Note on Stone's legal writings': p. 888-891. 56-10404
1. Stone, Harlan Flake, 1872-1946. I. Title.

*Stone, Irving

*STONE, Irving, ed. 927
Michelangelo, sculptor; an autobiography through letters. Ed. by Irving and Jean Stone. New York, New Amer. Lib. [1964, c.1962] 256p. ports. 18cm. (Signet T2462) .75. pap.,
I. Title.

*STONE, Irving 923.273
They also ran. New York, Pyramid [1964, c.1943-1964] 484p. 18cm. (T-1014) .75 pap.,
I. Title. BIP

Stone, Lucy, 1818-1893.

HAYS, Elinor Rice. 923.273
Morning star; a biography of Lucy Stone, 1818-1893. [1st ed.] New York, Harcourt, Brace & World [1961] 339 p. illus. 22 cm. Includes bibliography. [JK1899.S8H3] 61-12349
1. Stone, Lucy, 1818-1893. I. Title.

HAYS, Elinor Rice. 323.4'092'4 B
Morning star : a biography of Lucy Stone, 1818-1893 / Elinor Rice Hays. New York : Octagon Books, 1978, c1961. p. cm. Reprint of the ed. published by Harcourt, Brace & World, New York. Includes index. Bibliography: p. [JK1899.S8H3 1978] 78-16976 lib.bdg. : 17.50
1. Stone, Lucy, 1818-1893. 2. Women—United States—Biography. 3. Women—Suffrage—United States—History. I. Title.

Stone, Melville Elijah,

STONE, Melville Elijah, 1848-1929. 070.9'24
Fifty years a journalist. Half-tone illus. from photos. Line cuts by Paul Brown. New York, Greenwood Press, 1968 [c1921] xiv, 371 p. illus. 24 cm. [PN4874.S7A3 1968] 69-10161
I. Title. BIP

STONE, Melville Elijah, 1848-1929. 070.9'24 B
Fifty years a journalist. Half-tone illus. from photos. Line cuts by Paul Brown. Freeport, N.Y., Books for Libraries Press [1970] xiv, 371 p. illus., facsims., ports. 23 cm. Reprint of the 1921 ed. [PN4874.S7A3 1970] 76-124259
I. Title.

Stone, William Joel, 1848-1918.

TOWNE, Ruth Warner, 1917- 328.73'092'4 B
Senator William J. Stone and the politics of compromise / Ruth Warner Towne. Port Washington, N.Y. : Kennikat Press, 1979. p. cm. (Political science series) (National university publications) Includes index. Bibliography: p. [E664.S87T68] 79-521 ISBN 0-8046-9232-7 : 12.50
1. Stone, William Joel, 1848-1918. 2. United States. Congress. Senate—Biography. 3. United States—Politics and government—1865-1933. 4. European War, 1914-1918—United States. 5. Legislators—United States—Biography. I. Title. BIP

*Stoneman, Mary E.

*STONEMAN, Mary E. 920.72
Pioneering. New York, Pageant [c.1965] 97p. 21cm. 2.75
I. Title.

Stopes, Marie Charlotte Carmichael, 1880-1958.

BRIANT, Keith Rutherford 925.6
Passionate paradox; the life of Marie Stopes. New York, Norton [c.1962] 285p. illus. 22cm. 62-10094 5.00
1. Stopes, Marie Charlotte Carmichael, 1880-1958. I. Title.

HALL, Ruth, 1933- 613.9'4'0924 B
Passionate crusader : the life of Marie Stopes / Ruth Hall. 1st American ed. New York : Harcourt Brace Jovanovich, c1977. 351 p., [6] leaves of plates : ill. ; 25 cm. Includes index. Bibliography : p. [341]-344. [HQ764.S7H35 1977] 77-73054 ISBN 0-15-171288-3 : 14.95
1. Stopes, Marie Charlotte Carmichael, 1880-1958. 2. Feminists—Great Britain—Biography. 3. Birth control. 4. Marriage. I. Title. BIP

Stopp, Elisabeth, ed. and tr.

SALES, Francois de Saint, Bp. of Geneva, 1567-1622. 922.244
Selected letters. Translated with an introd. by Elisabeth Stopp. New York, Harper [1960] 318p. Bibl.: p.307-313. port., facsims. 21cm. (Classics of the contemplative life) 60-15274 5.00
1. Stopp, Elisabeth, ed. and tr. I. Title.

Storey, Del.

STOREY, Del. 269'.2'0924 B
Collision course / by Del Storey, with Laura Watson. Plainfield, N.J. : Logos International, c1977. xiv, 123 p. ; 21 cm. [BR1725.S825A34] 77-71143 ISBN 0-88270-230-0 pbk. : 2.95
1. Storey, Del. 2. Clergy—United States—Biography. I. Watson, Laura, joint author. II. Title. BIP

Storey, Moorfield, 1845-1929.

HOWE, Mark Antony De Wolfe, 1864-1960. 340'.092'4 B
Portrait of an Independent, Moorfield Storey, 1845-1929. Freeport, N.Y., Books for Libraries Press [1971] iii, 383 p. illus. 23 cm. Reprint of the 1932 ed. Bibliography: p. [363]-[371] [KF368.S75H68 1971] 76-37346 ISBN 0-8369-6693-7
1. Storey, Moorfield, 1845-1929. I. Title.

Storey, Wilbur F., 1819-1884.

WALSH, Justin E. 070.9'24 B
To print the news and raise hell! A biography of Wilbur F. Storey, by Justin E. Walsh. Chapel Hill, University of North Carolina Press [1968] ix, 303 p. illus. 24 cm. "Publication of this book was sponsored by the American Association for State and Local History, Nashville, Tennessee." Bibliography: p. 282-292. [PN4874.S72W3] 68-25913 7.50
1. Storey, Wilbur F., 1819-1884. I. Title.

Stormalong, Alfred Bulltop.

MALCOLMSON, Anne (Burnett) 1919- JUV
Mister Stormalong, by Anne Malcolmson and Dell J. McCormick. Illustrated by Joshua Tolford. Boston, Houghton Mifflin, 1952. 136 p. illus. 24 cm. Full name: Anne Elizabeth (Burnett) Malcolmson. [PZ8.1.M293Mi] fic 52-7196
1. Stormalong, Alfred Bulltop. I. Title.

Stormalong, Alfred Bulltop—Juvenile literature.

FELTON, Harold W., 1902- JUV
True tall tales of Stormalong; sailor of the seven seas, by Harold W. Felton. Illustrated by Joan Sandin. Englewood Cliffs, N.J., Prentice-Hall [1968] 64 p. illus. (part col.) 24 cm. The many tall tales about Stormalong are combined to form the seaman's life story. [PZ8.1.F27Tr] 813 398.22 68-22880 4.95
1. Stormalong, Alfred Bulltop—Juvenile literature. I. Sandin, Joan, illus. II. Title.

Storr, Paul, 1771-1844.

PENZER, Norman Mosley, 1892- 739.2'092'4
Paul Storr, 1771-1844, silversmith and goldsmith, [by] N. M. Penzer. Feltham, New York, Spring Books, 1971 [c1954] 5-292 p. illus., facsim., geneal. tables, maps, port. 31 cm. Originally published in 1954 under title: Paul Storr, the last of the goldsmiths. Includes bibliographical references and index. [NK7198.S85P4 1971] 73-169542 ISBN 0-600-37960-4 £4.25
1. Storr, Paul, 1771-1844.

Storrs, Ronald, Sir, 1881-1955.

STORRS, Ronald, Sir, 1881-1955. 325'.342'0924 B
The memoirs of Sir Ronald Storrs. New York, Arno Press, 1972 [c1937] xvii, 563 p. illus. 24 cm. (World affairs: national and international viewpoints) [D469.G7S75 1972] 72-4302 ISBN 0-405-04593-X
1. Storrs, Ronald, Sir, 1881- 2. Eastern question. I. Title. II. Series.

STORRS, Ronald, 325'.342'0924 B
Sir, 1881-1955.
The memoirs of Sir Ronald Storrs. [New York, AMS Press, 1973] xvii, 563 p. illus. 23 cm. Reprint of the 1937 ed. published by Putnam, New York. Includes bibliographical references. [D469.G7S75 1973] 77-180678 ISBN 0-404-56337-6 32.50
1. Storrs, Ronald, Sir, 1881-1955. 2. Eastern question. I. Title. BIP

Story, Joseph, 1779-1845.

DUNNE, Gerald T. 347'.7326'34 B
Justice Joseph Story and the rise of the Supreme Court [by] Gerald T. Dunne. New York, Simon and Schuster [1971, c1970] 458 p. port. 22 cm. Bibliography: p. 435-444. [KF8745.S83D84] 70-139620 ISBN 0-671-20665-6 12.95
1. Story, Joseph, 1779-1845. I. Title.

STORY, Joseph, 1779-1845. 923.473
Joseph Story; a collection of writings by and about an eminen: American jurist. Selected and edited by Mortimer D. Schwartz and John C. Hogan. New York, Oceana Publications, 1959. 228 p. 23 cm. Prose and Oems. 59-8603
I. Title.

STORY, William 347'.73'2634 B
Wetmore, 1819-1895.
Life and letters of Joseph Story, associate justice of the Supreme Court of the United States, and Dane professor of law at Harvard University. Edited by William W. Story. Freeport, N.Y., Books for Libraries Press [1971] 2 v. port. 23 cm. Reprint of the 1851 ed. [KF8745.S83S8 1971] 75-175710 ISBN 0-8369-6625-2
1. Story, Joseph, 1779-1845. I. Title.

Story, Thomas, 1662-1742.

DALGLISH, Doris N. 289.6'0922
People called Quakers, by Doris N. Dalglish. Freeport, N.Y., Books for Libraries Press [1969] 169 p. 23 cm. (Essay index reprint series) Reprint of the 1938 ed. Contents.Contents.—The first Quaker poet.—An American saint.—A digression on women and the eighteenth century.—A neighbour of Wordsworth.—A friend from France.—Convert and critic. [BX7791.D3 1969] 78-90628
1. Story, Thomas, 1662-1742. 2. Woolman, John, 1720-1772. 3. Wilkinson, Thomas, 1751-1836. 4. Grellet, Stephen, 1773-1855. 5. Stephen, Caroline Emelia, 1834-1909. 6. Friends, Society of—Biography. I. Title.

Story, William Wetmore, 1819-1895.

JAMES, Henry, 1843-1916. 927.3
William Wetmore Story and his friends; from letters, diaries, and recollections. New York, Grove Press [1957?] 2v. in 1. 22cm. [NB237.S7J3] 57-5157
1. Story, William Wetmore, 1819-1895. I. Title.

Stosch, Albrecht von, 1818-1896.

HOLLYDAY, Frederic B M 923.243
Bismarck's rival; a political biography of general and admiral Albrecht von Stosch. Durham, N. C., Duke University Press, 1960. x, 316p. port. 25cm. (Duke historical publications) Bibliography: p. [287]-299. [DD219.S74H6] 60-7077
1. Stosch, Albrecht von, 1818-1896. I. Title. BIP

HOLLYDAY, Frederic 943.08'092'4 B
B. M.
Bismarck's rival : a political biography of General and Admiral Albrecht von Stosch / Frederic B. M. Hollyday. Westport, Conn. : Greenwood Press, 1976, c1960. x, 316 p. : port. ; 23 cm. Reprint of the ed. published by Duke University Press, Durham, issued in series: Duke historical publications. Includes index. Bibliography: p. [287]-299. [DD219.S74H6 1976] 75-40917 ISBN 0-8371-8686-2
1. Stosch, Albrecht von, 1818-1896. I. Title. II. Series: Duke historical publications.

*Stoudt, John Joseph,

*STOUDT, John Joseph, 230'.0924
1911-
Jacob Boehme: His life and thought. Foreword by Paul Tillich. New York, Seabury [1968, c. 1957] 317p. 20cm. (SP 46) Orig. pub. under the title Sunrise to eternity. Bibl. 2.75 pap.,
I. Title.

Stoughton, Bradley, 1873-1959.

DOAN, Gilbert 669'00924 (B)
Everett, 1897-
Bradley Stoughton; mankind was my business [by] Gilbert E. Doan. [Metals Park, Ohio, American Society for Metals, 1967] 116 p. illus., ports. 24 cm. Includes bibliographical references. [TN140.S77D6] 67-30985
1. Stoughton, Bradley, 1873-1959. I. Title.

Stoughton, Wis.—Biography.

FROST blossoms : 977.5'83
yarns and impressions of Stoughton and regional life and adventures / by members of the Stoughton Regional Writers' Association, inc. ; edited by Robert E. Gard and Joan Sullivan, assisted by Rita Quale and Irving Quale ; decoration by Rita Quale ; cover by Denise Sullivan. [Madison] : University of Wisconsin Extension, c1978. 133 p. : ill. ; 28 cm. (Homeplace book) [F589.S8F76] 78-64445 4.95
1. Stoughton, Wis.—Biography. 2. Stoughton region, Wis.—Biography. I. Gard, Robert Edward. II. Sullivan, Joan. III. Stoughton Regional Writers' Association.

Stout, Hosea, 1810-1889.

STOUT, Hosea, 1810-1889. v. 12
Autobiography of Hosea Stout, 1810-1844. Edited by Reed A. Stout. [Salt Lake City, Utah State Historical Society] 1962. 88 p. illus., port. 24 cm. Reprinted from v. 30, 1962, Utah historical quarterly. 66-68326
1. Utah — Hist. — Sources. 2. Mormons and Mormonism — Hist. — Sources. I. Stout, Reed A., ed. II. Title.

STOUT, Wayne Dunham, 923.273
1894-
Hosea Stout, Utah's pioneer statesman. Salt Lake City, c1953. 304p. illus. 24cm. [F826.S77S7] 53-40550
1. Stout, Hosea, 1810-1889. 2. Mormons and Mormonism. I. Title.

Stout, Rex, 1886-1975—Biography.

BARING-GOULD, William 813'.5'2
Stuart, 1913-
Nero Wolfe of West Thirty-fifth Street; the life and times of America's largest private detective, by William S. Baring-Gould. New York, Viking Press [1969] xviii, 203 p. 23 cm. [PS3537.T73Z58 1969] 68-29055 5.50
1. Stout, Rex, 1886- I. Title.

MCALEER, John J. 813'.5'2 B
Rex Stout : a biography / John McAleer ; with a foreword by P. G. Wodehouse. 1st ed. Boston : Little, Brown, c1977. xvi, 621 p., [8] leaves of plates : ill. ; 24 cm. Includes index. "A Rex Stout checklist": p. [581]-591. [PS3537.T733Z78] 77-24896 ISBN 0-316-55340-9 : 15.00
1. Stout, Rex, 1886-1975—Biography. 2. Novelists, American—20th century—Biography. BIP

Stout, William,

STOUT, William, 658.8'0924 (B)
1665-1752
The autobiography of William Stout of Lancaster, 1665-1752, ed. by J. D. Marshall for the William Stout Tercentenary Study Group. Manchester, Manchester U. P.; New York, Barnes &Noble, 1967. viii, 311p. front. port.), plate (diagr.), 2 maps, tables. 23cm. Bibl. [CT788.S8A3 1967] 67-75652 9.00
I. Marshall, John Duncan, ed. II. Title.

Stovall, Emmett.

STOVALL, Emmett. 629.13'023
In the face of the sun, by Emmett Stovall, with R. E. Simon, Jr. [Chicago, Childrens Press, 1970] 64 p. illus., ports. 19 cm. (An Open door book) Autobiographical. A black man relates the obstacles he encountered in learning to fly and starting his own airline because no existing airline would hire a black pilot. [TL540.S833A3] 92 77-101731
I. Simon, Richard Edward, 1945- joint author. II. Title.

Stover, Elisha Terrill, 1920-1944.

STOVER, Elisha 940.54'49'73
Terrill, 1920-1944.
The saga of Smokey Stover / by E. T. Stover and Clark G. Reynolds. Charleston, S.C. : Tradd Street Press, 1978. vii, 119 p. : ill. ; 22 cm. Includes bibliographical references. [D790.S94] 78-64485 6.00
1. Stover, Elisha Terrill, 1920-1944. 2. United States. Navy—Biography. 3. World War, 1939-1945—Aerial operations, American. 4. World War, 1939-1945—Personal narratives, American. 5. World War, 1939-1945—Pacific Ocean. 6. Fighter pilots—United States—Biography. I. Reynolds, Clark G., joint author. II. Title. Publisher's address: 38 Tradd St., Charleston, SC 29401

Stover (Russell) Candies.

STOVER, Clara (Lewis) 926.641
The life of Russell Stover, an American success story, by Clar Stover with Phil A. Koury. New York, Random House [1958, 1957] 242 p. illus. 21 cm. [HD9999.C735S72] 57-14793
1. Stover (Russell) Candies. 2. Stover, Russell, 1888-1954. I. Title.

Stowe, Harriet Elizabeth Beecher, 1811-1896.

ADAMS, John R., 1900- 813.3
Harriet Beecher Stowe. Coll. & Univ. Pr. [dist.] New York, Grosset [1964, c.1963] 172p. 21cm. (Twayne's United States authors ser., 42) Bibl. 1.95 pap.,
1. Stowe, Harriet Elizabeth (Beecher) 1811-1806. I. Title.

ADAMS, John R., 1900- 813.3
Harriet Beecher Stowe. New York, Twayne [1964, c.1963] 172p. 21cm. (Twayne's U. S. authors sers., 42) Bibl. 63-17370 3.50 bds.,
1. Stowe, Harriet Elizabeth (Beecher) 1811-1896. I. Title.

FIELDS, Annie (Adams) 818'.3'09 B
1834-1915.
Life and letters of Harriet Beecher Stowe. Detroit, Gale Research Co., 1970. 406 p. 22 cm. Reprint of the 1897 ed. [PS2956.F5 1970] 77-102057
1. Stowe, Harriet Elizabeth (Beecher) 1811-1896. BIP

GILBERTSON, 818'.3'09 (B)
Catherine (Peebles) 1890-
Harriet Beecher Stowe, by Catherine Gilbertson. Port Washington, N.Y., Kennikat Press [1968, c1937] xii, 330 p. illus., ports. 23 cm. [PS2956.G5 1968] 67-27599
1. Stowe, Harriet Elizabeth (Beecher) 1811-1896. I. Title.

HARRIET Beecher 818/.3/09
Stowe, by Catherine Gilbertson. Port Washington, N. Y., Kennikat [1968,c.1937] xii, 330p. illus., ports. 23cm. [PS2956.G5 1968] (B) 67-27599 10.00
1. Stowe, Harriet Elizabeth (Beecher) 1811-1896. I. Gilbertson, Catherine (Peebles), 1890-

JOHNSTON, Johanna. 928.1
Runaway to heaven; the story of Harriet Beecher Stowe. [1st ed.] Garden City, N. Y., Doubleday, 1963. 490 p. illus. 22 cm. Includes bibliography. [PS2956.J6] 63-12167
1. Stowe, Harriet Elizabeth (Beecher) 1811-1896. I. Title.

MACKAY, Charles, 1814- 821'.7 B
1889.
Medora Leigh; a history and an autobiography. Edited by Charles Mackay. With an introd., and a commentary on the charges brought against Lord Byron by Mrs. Beecher Stowe. London, R. Bentley, 1869. [New York, AMS Press, 1973] 280 p. 19 cm. On spine: WOL. [PR4382.M3 1973] 78-37700 ISBN 0-404-56759-2 14.00
1. Byron, George Gordon Noel Byron, Baron, 1788-1824. 2. Stowe, Harriet Elizabeth (Beecher) 1811-1896. 3. Byron, Anne Isabella (Milbanke) Byron, Baroness, 1792-1860. 4. Leigh, Elizabeth Medora, 1814-1849. I. Leigh, Elizabeth Medora, 1814-1849. II. Title. BIP

MOERS, Ellen, 1928- 813'.3
Harriet Beecher Stowe and American literature / Ellen Moers. Hartford, Conn. : Stowe-Day Foundation, 1978. 47 p. ; ill ; 24 cm. Includes bibliographical references. [PS2956.M6] 78-4149 ISBN 0-917482-15-8 pbk. : 4.00
1. Stowe, Harriet Elizabeth Beecher, 1811-1896—Addresses, essays, lectures. 2. Stowe, Harriet Elizabeth Beecher, 1811-1896. Uncle Tom's cabin. 3. Clemens, Samuel Langhorne, 1835-1910—Addresses, essays, lectures. 4. Slavery in the United States in literature—Addresses, essays, lectures. 5. American fiction—19th century—History and criticism—Addresses, essays, lectures. 6. Authors, American—19th century—Biography—Addresses, essays, lectures. I. Title. BIP

STOWE, Harriet 818'.3'08
Elizabeth Beecher, 1811-1896.
Life of Harriet Beecher Stowe, compiled from her letters and journals by her son, Charles Edward Stowe. Detroit, Gale Research Co., 1967. xii, 530 p. illus., facsims., ports. 22 cm. (The Gale library of lives and letters. American writers series) Title page includes original imprint: Boston, Houghton, Mifflin, 1889. [PS2956.A4 1967] 67-23881
I. Stowe, Charles Edward, 1850- comp. II. Title. BIP

STOWE, Harriet 818'.3'08
Elizabeth Beecher, 1811-1896.
Life of Harriet Beecher Stowe, compiled from her letters and journals by her son, Charles Edward Stowe. Detroit, Gale Research Co., 1967. xii, 530 p. illus., facsims., ports. 22 cm. (The Gale library of lives and letters. American writers series) Title page includes original imprint: Boston, Houghton, Mifflin, 1889. [PS2956.A4 1967] 67-23881
1. Stowe, Charles Edward, 1850- comp. II. Title. BIP

WAGENKNECHT, Edward 928.1
Charles, 1900-
Harriet Beecher Stowe; the known and the unknown [by] Edward Wagenknecht. New York, Oxford University Press, 1965. 267 p. port. 21 cm. Bibliography: p. 253-258. [PS2956.W3] 65-15615
1. Stowe, Harriet Elizabeth Beecher, 1811-1896.

WILSON, Robert 818'.3'09 B
Forrest, 1883-1942.
Crusader in crinoline; the life of Harriet Beecher Stowe. Westport, Conn., Greenwood Press [1972, c1941] 706 p. illus. 23 cm. Bibliography: p. 643-657. [PS2956.W5 1972] 70-159717 ISBN 0-8371-6191-6
1. Stowe, Harriet Elizabeth (Beecher) 1811-1896. I. Title. BIP

WISE, Winifred Esther, 928.1
1906-
Harriet Beecher Stowe, woman with a cause woman with a cause. New York, Putnam [c.1965] 190p. 21cm. (Lives to remember) Bibl. [PS2956.W55] 65-133097 3.29 lib. ed.,
1. Stowe, Harriet Elizabeth (Beecher) 1811-1896. 2. Juvenile literature. I. Title.

Stowe, Harriet Elizabeth Beecher, 1811-1896—Addresses, essays, lectures.

MOERS, Ellen, 1928- 813'.3
Harriet Beecher Stowe and American literature / Ellen Moers. Hartford, Conn. : Stowe-Day Foundation, 1978. 47 p. : ill. ; 24 cm. Includes bibliographical references. [PS2956.M6] 78-4149 ISBN 0-917482-15-8 pbk. : 4.00
1. Stowe, Harriet Elizabeth Beecher, 1811-1896—Addresses, essays, lectures. 2. Stowe, Harriet Elizabeth Beecher, 1811-1896. Uncle Tom's cabin. 3. Clemens, Samuel Langhorne, 1835-1910—Addresses, essays, lectures. 4. Slavery in the United States in literature—Addresses, essays, lectures. 5. American fiction—19th century—History and criticism—Addresses, essays, lectures. 6. Authors, American—19th century—Biography—Addresses, essays, lectures. I. Title. BIP

Stowe, Harriet Elizabeth Beecher, 1811-1896—Biography.

GERSON, Noel Bertram, 818'.3'09 B
1914-
Harriet Beecher Stowe : a biography / by Noel B. Gerson. New York : Praeger Publishers, 1976. 218 p. ; 22 cm. Includes index. Bibliography: p. 211-212. [PS2956.G4] 75-4151 ISBN 0-275-34070-8 : 8.95
1. Stowe, Harriet Elizabeth Beecher, 1811-1896—Biography. 2. Authors, American—19th century—Biography.

Stowe, Harriet Elizabeth Beecher, 1811-1896—Biography—Juvenile literature.

HOOKER, Gloria, 1930- 818'.3'09 B
I shall not live in vain : the biography of Harriet Beecher Stowe, the New England author whose book changed attitudes about slavery / written by Gloria Hooker ; illustrated by Michael Hackett. St. Louis : Concordia Pub. House, c1978. 118 p. : ill. ; 24 cm. (Greatness with faith) A biography of the American author whose novel, "Uncle Tom's Cabin," attacked slavery in the United States. [PS2956.H65] 92 78-252 ISBN 0-570-07875-X : 4.95. ISBN 0-570-07880-6 pbk. : 2.95
1. Stowe, Harriet Elizabeth Beecher, 1811-1896—Biography—Juvenile literature. 2. Authors, American—19th century—Biography—Juvenile literature. I. Hackett, Michael. II. Title. III. Series.

Stowe, Harriet Elizabeth Beecher, 1811-1896—Juvenile literature.

JOHNSTON, Johanna. 818'.3'09 W
Harriet and the runaway book : the story of Harriet Beecher Stowe and Uncle Tom cabin / Johanna Johnston ; ill. by Ronald Himlaer. 1st ed. New York : Harper & Row, c1977. 80 p. : ill. ; 24 cm. A biography of the woman who wrote Uncle Tom's Cabin, stressing the experiences and impressions which caused her to write the famous book denouncing slavery. [PS2956.J59 1977 92] 76-24305 ISBN 0-06-022839-3 : 5.95 ISBN 0-06-022840-7 lib.bdg. : 5.79
1. Stowe, Harriet Elizabeth Beecher, 1811-1896—Juvenile literature. 2. Authors, American—19th century—Biography—Juvenile literature. 3. Slavery in the United States—Juvenile literature. I. Himler, Ronald. II. Title.

JOHNSTON, Johanna. 818'.3'09 W
Harriet and the runaway book : the story of Harriet Beecher Stowe and Uncle Tom cabin / Johanna Johnston ; ill. by Ronald Himlaer. 1st ed. New York : Harper & Row, c1977. 80 p. : ill. ; 24 cm. A biography of the woman who wrote Uncle Tom's Cabin, stressing the experiences and impressions which caused her to write the famous book denouncing slavery. [PS2956.J59 1977 92] 76-24305 ISBN 0-06-022839-3 : 5.95 ISBN 0-06-022840-7 lib.bdg. : 5.79
1. Stowe, Harriet Elizabeth Beecher, 1811-1896—Juvenile literature. 2. Authors, American—19th century—Biography—Juvenile literature. 3. Slavery in the United States—Juvenile literature. I. Himler, Ronald. II. Title. BIP

ROUVEROL, Jean. 818'.3'09 B
Harriet Beecher Stowe: woman crusader. Illustrated by Charles Brey. New York, Putnam [1968] 95 p. col. illus. 24 cm. (An American pioneer biography) A biography of the quiet woman who, according to Lincoln, started the Civil War by writing Uncle Tom's Cabin, the novel that made her America's first famous woman author. [PS2956.R6] 92 68-24544 2.97
1. Stowe, Harriet Elizabeth (Beecher) 1811-1896—Juvenile literature. I. Brey, Charles, illus. II. Title.

Strachan, John, Bp., 1778-1867.

HENDERSON, John L. H. 283'.0924 B
John Strachan, 1778-1867 [by] J. L. H. Henderson. [Toronto] University of Toronto Press [1969] 112 p. 21 cm. (Canadian biographical studies) Includes bibliographical references. [BX5620.S75H4] 70-408188 4.50
1. Strachan, John, Bp., 1778-1867. BIP

Strachan, Robert Kenneth, 1910-1965.

ELLIOT, 266'.023'0924 B
Elisabeth.
Who shall ascend; the life of R. Kenneth Strachan of Costa Rica. [1st ed.] New York, Harper & Row [1968] xii, 171 p. map (on lining paper), ports. 22 cm. [BV2843.C7S75] 68-11732
1. Strachan, Robert Kenneth, 1910-1965. 2. Missions—Costa Rica. I. Title.

ROBERTS, W. 266'.023'0924 B
Dayton.
Strachan of Costa Rica; missionary insights and strategies, by W. Dayton Roberts. Grand Rapids [1971] 187 p. 21 cm. (Christian world mission books) [BV2843.C7S78] 78-163657 2.95
1. Strachan, Robert Kenneth, 1910-1965. I. Title.

Strachey, Giles Lytton, 1880-1932.

BEERBOHM, Max, 828'.9'1209 B
Sir, 1872-1956.
Lytton Strachey. New York, Haskell House [1974] p. cm. Reprint of the 1943 ed. published by University Press, Cambridge, Eng., in series: Rede lecture. [PR6037.T73Z56 1974] 74-7186 ISBN 0-8383-1936-X 7.95 (lib. bdg.).
1. Strachey, Giles Lytton, 1880-1932. I. Series: Rede lecture. BIP

CLEMENS, Cyril, 828'.9'1209 B
1902-
Lytton Strachey. Foreword by Andre Maurois. With a brief pedigree by Sir Charles Strachey. [Folcroft, Pa.] Folcroft Library Editions, 1973. 19 p. 29 cm. Reprint of the 1942 ed. published by International Mark Twain Society, Webster Groves, Mo., which was issued as no. 11 of the Society's Biographical series. Bibliography: p. 18-19. [PR6037.T73Z63 1973] 73-15585 ISBN 0-8414-3476-X (lib. bdg.)
1. Strachey, Giles Lytton, 1880-1932. I. Series: International Mark Twain Society. Biographical series, no. 11. BIP

HOLROYD, Michael. 828'.9'1209 B
Lytton Strachey; a critical biography. [1st ed.] New York, Holt, Rinehart and Winston [1968, c1967] 2 v. illus. (part col.), ports. 25 cm. Contents.Contents.—v. 1. The unknown years, 1880-1910.—v. 2. The years of achievement, 1910-1932. Bibliography: v. 2, p. [721]-728. [PR6037.T73Z69 1968] 68-10061
1. Strachey, Giles Lytton, 1880-1932.

SANDERS, Charles Richard, 928.2
1904-
Lytton Strachey, his mind and art. New Haven, Yale University Press, 1957. 381 p. illus. 24 cm. Includes bibliography. [PR6037.T73Z8] 57-10155
1. Strachey, Giles Lytton, 1880-1932. BIP

STRACHEY, Giles 828'.9'1209 B
Lytton, 1880-1932.
Lytton Strachey by himself; a self-portrait. Edited and introd. by Michael Holroyd. [1st ed.] New York, Holt, Rinehart and Winston [1971] vi, 184 p. 22 cm. [PR6037.T73Z5 1971] 70-138875 ISBN 0-03-085995-6 5.95
I. Title.

WOOLF, Virginia (Stephen) 928.2
1882-1941.
Letters: Virginia Woolf & Lytton Strachey. Edited by Leonard Woolf & James Strachey. [1st American ed.] New York, Harcourt, Brace [c1956] vii, 166p. 21cm. 'Chronological bibliography of the books of Virginia Woolf': p. [viii] 'Chronological bibliography of the books of Lytton Strachey': p. [ix] [PR6045.O72Z53 1956a] 56-11962
1. Strachey, Giles Lytton, 1880-1932. I. Title.

Strachey, Giles Lytton, 1880-1932—Biography.

HOLROYD, Michael. 828'.9'1209 B
Lytton Strachey: a biography. Revised ed. Harmondsworth, Penguin, 1971. 1144 p., 8 plates. illus., facsim., ports. 18 cm. Previously published as the biographical material in Lytton Strachey: a critical biography, London, Heinemann, 1967-68. Bibliography: p. 1079-1087. [PR6037.T73Z692] 72-175874 ISBN 0-14-003198-7 £1.00 ($3.95 U.S.)
1. Strachey, Giles Lytton, 1880-1932—Biography. I. Holroyd, Michael. Lytton Strachey: a critical biography.

Strachey, John, 1901-1963.

THOMAS, Hugh, 1931- 320'.92'4 B
John Strachey. [1st U.S. ed.] New York, Harper & Row [1973] 319 p. 22 cm. Includes bibliographical references. [HX243.S86T56] 73-4129 ISBN 0-06-014271-5 8.50
1. Strachey, John, 1901-1963.

*Strachey, Lytton

*STRACHEY, Lytton 942.0810924
Queen Victoria. New York, Harcourt [1966, c. 1921] 311p. 18cm. (Harbracepaperback lib., HPL 7) .75 pap., *I. Title.*

Strachey, William, 1572?-1621.

CULLIFORD, S. G. 914.203610924
William Strachey, 1572-1621. Charlottesville, Univ. Pr. of Va. [c.1965] 224p. 23cm. Bibl. [DA391.1.S88C84] 65-19394 4.50
1. Strachey, William, 1572?-1621. I. Title.

CULLIFORD, S. G. 914.203610924 B
William Strachey, 1572-1621 [by S.G Culliford Charlottesville, University Press of Virginia [1965] 224 p. 23 cm. Based on the author's thesis, University of London. Bibliography: p. [190]-218. [DA391.1.S88C84] 65-19394
1. Strachey, William, 1572?-1621. I. Title.

Stradivari, Antonio, 1644-1737.

HENLEY, William 787.1
Antonio Stradivari, master luthier, Cremona, Italy, 1644-1737; his life and instruments. Rev., ed. by C. Woodcock. Brighton, Sussex, Eng., Amati Pub. ltd. [dist. New York, Heinman, 1962] 98p. illus., facsims. 24cm. 62-3737 20.00
1. Stradivari, Antonio, d. 1737. 2. Violin—Hist. I. Woodcock, C., ed. II. Title.

HILL, William Henry, 1857-1927. 787.12
Antonio Stradivari, his life and work, 1644-1737, by W. Henry Hill, Arthur F. Hill, and Alfred E. Hill. With a new introd. by Sydney Beck and new supplementary indexes by Rembert Wurlitzer. New York, Dover Publications [1963] xxiv, 314 p. illus., plates, facsims. 21 cm. (American Musicological Society—Music Library Association. Reprint series) [ML424.S8H62 1963] 63-17904
1. Stradivari, Antonio, d. 1737. I. Hill, Arthur Frederick, 1860-1939, joint author. II. Hill, Alfred Ebsworth, 1862-1940, joint author. III. Title. IV. Series. BIP

*JONES, George R. 787'12 [B]
Antonio Stradivari and his craft; a story of the master's life. Drawings by Marge Opitz Burridge. New York, Vantage [1973] 133 p. illus. 21 cm. Bibliography: p. 132. [ML424] ISBN 0-533-00501-9 5.95
1. Stradivari, Antonio, 1644-1737. I. Title.

JONES, George Roberts, 1883- 787'.1'0924 B
Antonio Stradivari and his craft; a story of the master's life, by George R Jones. Drawings by Marge Opitz Burridge. [1st ed.] New York, Vantage Press [1973] 133 p. illus. 21 cm. Bibliography: p. 132. A biography of the seventeenth-century Italian craftsman considered one of the finest violin makers of all time. [ML3930.S82J6] 92 73-173502 ISBN 0-533-00501-9 5.95
1. Stradivari, Antonio, d. 1737—Juvenile literature. I. Burridge, Marge Opitz, illus. II. Title.

Stafford, John Conrad, 1756-1840.

THE Life of John Conrad Shafford. 973'.04'97 S
Conrad Shafford. New York : Garland Pub., inc., 1977. 24 p. : ill. ; 24 cm. (The Garland library of narratives of North American Indian captivities ; v. 56) Issued with Wunderbare Flucht von Wilden, New York, 1977. Reprint of the 1840 ed. published by C. L. Carpenter, New York under title: Narrative of the extraordinary life of John Conrad Shafford, known by many by the name of the Dutch hermit. [E85.G2 vol. 56] [E87.S47] 971.4'02'0924 75-33258 ISBN 0-8240-1680-7 lib.bdg. : 21.00
1. Strafford, John Conrad, 1756-1840. 2. Indians of North America—Captivities. I. Series.

Strafford, Thomas Wentworth, 1st Earl of, 1593-1641.

TRAILL, Henry Duff, 1842-1900. 942.06'2'0924 B
Lord Strafford. Freeport, N.Y., Books for Libraries Press [1970] vii, 206 p. port. 23 cm. Reprint of the 1889 ed. [DA396.S8T7 1970] 70-137386
1. Strafford, Thomas Wentworth, 1st Earl of, 1593-1641. I. Title. BIP

WEDGWOOD, Cicely Veronica, Dame, 1910- 942.06'2'0924 B
Strafford, 1593-1641, by C. V. Wedgwood. Westport, Conn., Greenwood Press [1970] 366 p. ports. 23 cm. Reprint of the 1935 ed. Bibliography: p. 355-358. [DA396.S8W4 1970] 76-110882 ISBN 0-8371-4566-X
1. Strafford, Thomas Wentworth, 1st Earl of, 1593-1641. 2. Gt. Brit.—History—Charles I, 1625-1649.

Strahan, William, 1715-1785.

COCHRANE, James Aikman 920.4
Dr. Johnson's printer; the life of William Strahan. Cambridge, Mass., Harvard [c.] 1964. xiii, 225p. illus., facsims., geneal. table, port. 23cm. Bibl. [Z232.S887C6] 65-7048 6.00
1. Strahan, William, 1715-1785. I. Title.

COCHRANE, James Aikman. 926.55
Dr. Johnson's printer; the life of William Strahan, by J. A. Cochrane. London, Routledge & K. Paul [1964] xiii, 225 p. facsims., geneal, table, port. 23 cm. Bibliographical footnotes. [Z232.S887C6 1964a] 65-68018
1. Strahan, William, 1715-1785. I. Title.

COCHRANE, James Aikman. 920.4
Dr. Johnson's printer; the life of William Strahan, by J. A. Cochrane. Cambridge, Harvard University Press, 1964. xiii, 225 p. illus., facsims., geneal, table, port. 23 cm. Bibliographical footnotes. [Z232.S887C6] 65-7048
1. Strahan, William, 1715-1785. I. Title.

Straight, Willard Dickerman, 1880-1918.

CROLY, Herbert David, 1869-1930. 327'.2'0924 B
Willard Straight. Freeport, N.Y., Books for Libraries Press [1973] p. Reprint of the 1924 ed. [CT275.S878C7 1973] 72-10626 ISBN 0-8369-7107-8
1. Straight, Willard Dickerman, 1880-1918.

Strain, Samuel Frederick, 1895-

STRAIN, Samuel Frederick, 1895- 610'.92'4 B
From the Nolichucky to Memphis : reminiscences of a Tennessee doctor / by Samuel Frederick Strain . with a foreword by Eldon Roark. Memphis : Memphis State University Press, c1979. xiii, 232 p. : ill. ; 24 cm. (20th Century reminiscence series) Includes index. [R154.S853A34] 79-129552 ISBN 0-87870-064-1 : 12.95
1. Strain, Samuel Frederick, 1895- 2. Tennessee Valley Authority—Officials and employees—Biography. 3. Internists—Tennessee—Biography. I. Title. II. Series. BIP

Strait, Clifford Norman, 1902-

STRAIT, Clifford Norman, 1902- 917.47'03'40924 B
My short trip through time. [Canandaigua, N.Y.] 1968. 188 l. illus., ports. 29 cm. Autobiographical. [CT275.S8785A35] 74-173005
1. Strait, Clifford Norman, 1902- I. Title.

Strait, Treva Adams, 1909- —Juvenile literature.

STRAIT, Treva Adams, 1909- 978.2'03'0924 B
The price of free land / by Treva Adams Strait. Philadelphia : Lippincott, c1979. 96 p. : ill. ; 24 cm. The author relates her family's experiences as homesteaders in western Nebraska in 1914. [F666.3.S78] 78-24287 ISBN 0-397-31836-7 : 6.95
1. Strait, Treva Adams, 1909- —Juvenile literature. 2. Nebraska—Biography—Juvenile literature. 3. Frontier and pioneer life—Nebraska—Juvenile literature. 4. Nebraska—History—Juvenile literature. 5. Pioneers—Nebraska—Biography—Juvenile literature. I. Title. BIP

Strakhov, Nikolai Nikolaevich, 1828-1896.

GERSTEIN, Linda, 1938- 197 B
Nikolai Strakhov. Cambridge, Harvard University Press, 1971. xi, 237 p. port. 24 cm. (Russian Research Center studies, 65) Bibliography: p. 221-228. [PG2947.S7G4] 79-139720 ISBN 0-674-62475-0 8.50
1. Strakhov, Nikolai Nikolaevich, 1828-1896. I. Series: Harvard University. Russian Research Center. Studies, 65 BIP

Strambi, Vincenzo Maria, Saint, 1745-1824.

GRASHOFF, Raphael. 922.245
"I'll not be a traitor!" The story of the Passionist bishop, St. Vincent Mary Strambi. St. Meinrad, Ind., The Grail ['1951] 68 p. illus. 20 cm. [BX4700.S77G7] 52-6865
1. Strambi, Vincenzo Maria, Saint, 1745-1824. I. Title.

Stranahan, Frank, Mrs., 1881-

BURGHARD, August, 1901- 975.9'35'060924 B
Mrs. Frank Stranahan, pioneer. [Fort Lauderdale, Fla.] Historical Society of Fort Lauderdale [1968] [48] p. illus., ports. 22 cm. Cover title: Watchie-esta/hutrie (The little white mother) [F319.F7B8] 79-75226
1. Stranahan, Frank, Mrs., 1881- 2. Fort Lauderdale, Fla. I. Historical Society of Fort Lauderdale. II. Title: Watchie-esta/hutrie (The little white mother)

Strang, James Jesse, 1813-1856.

FITZPATRICK, Doyle C. 289.3'0924 B
The King Strang story; a vindication of James J. Strang, the Beaver Island Mormon King, by Doyle C. Fitzpatrick. [1st ed.] Lansing, Mich., National Heritage, 1970. xxviii, 289 p. illus., facsims., geneal. table, map (on lining papers), ports. 24 cm. [BX8680.S88S84] 70-140603 7.95
1. Strang, James Jesse, 1813-1856. 2. Beaver Island, Mich.—History I. Title.

STRANG, James Jesse, 1813-1856 922.8373
Diary. Deciphered, transcribed, introduced, and annotated by Mark A. Strang. Foreword by Russel B. Nye. [East Lansing] Michigan State Univ. Press [c.1961] xlv, 78p. front. port. Bibl. 60-16420 3.75
I. Title.

WEEKS, Robert Percy, 1915- 289.3'0924 B
King Strang; a biography of James Jesse Strang, by Robert P. Weeks. Ann Arbor [Mich.] Five Wives Press, 1971. vi, 82 p. facsim. 22 cm. Bibliography: p. 80-82. [BX8680.S88S88] 73-25917
1. Strang, James Jesse, 1813-1856. I. Title.

Strange, Ian J.

STRANGE, Ian J. 333.9'5'099711 B
The Bird Man : an autobiography / Ian Strange. London : Gordon & Cremonesi, c1976. 182 p., [14] leaves of plates : ill, maps (on lining papers) ; 27 cm. Includes index. [QL31.S78A33] 77-360205 ISBN 0-86033-015-X : £6.90 ($16.95 U.S.)
1. Strange, Ian J. 2. Ornithologists—Falkland Islands—Biography. 3. Wildlife conservation—Falkland Islands. I. Title.

Stratford de Redcliffe, Stratford Canning, 1st Viscount, 1786-1880.

LANE-POOLE, Stanley, 1854-1931. 327'.2'0924 B
The life of the Right Honourable Stratford Canning, Viscount Stratford de Redcliffe : from his memoirs and private and official papers / by Stanley Lane-Poole. New York : AMS Press, 1976. 2 v. ; ill. ; 23 cm. Reprint of the 1888 ed. published by Longmans, Green, London. Includes index. [DA536.S89L36 1976] 73-171653 ISBN 0-404-07387-5 : 70.00 (2 vol set)
1. Stratford de Redcliffe, Stratford Canning, 1st Viscount, 1786-1880. 2. Great Britain—Foreign relations—19th century. I. Title. BIP

Stratton, Charles Sherwood, 1838-1883.

DESMOND, Alice (Curtis) 1897- 925.738
Barnum presents General Tom Thumb. New York, Macmillan, 1954. [GN69.5.S9D4] 54-8544
1. Stratton, Charles Sherwood, 1838-1883. I. 0pc236p. illus. 22cm. II. Title.

FITZSIMONS, Raymund. 791.1'0924
Barnum in London. New York, St. Martin's Press [1970] 179 p. plates, ports. 23 cm. Bibliography: p. 170-173. [GV1811.B3F53 1970] 73-106205 6.95
1. Barnum, Phineas Taylor, 1810-1891. 2. Stratton, Charles Sherwood, 1838-1883. 3. Haydon, Benjamin Robert, 1786-1846. I. Title.

HUNT, Mabel Leigh, 1892- v. 12
"Have you seen Tom Thumb?" Illus. by Fritz Eichenberg. Philadelphia, Lippincott [196-? c1942] 259 p. illus. The life and carrer of Charles Stratton from the moment when P. T. Barnum discovered him in his Bridgeport home at five years old. Tom Thumb was a midget, but not a dwarf. His career, from 1842 to 1883, is a success story. Sources found most useful: p. 13. 67-96340
1. Stratton, Charles Sherwood, 1838-1883. I. Title. II. Title: Tom Thumb.

†ROMAINE, Mertie E., 1893- 573.8 B
General Tom Thumb and his lady / by Mertie E. Romaine. 1st ed. Taunton, Mass. : W. S. Sullwold Pub., c1976. 94 p. : ill. ; 24 cm. Bibliography: p. 94. [GN69.52.S83R65] 76-53594 ISBN 0-88492-018-6 : 5.95 ISBN 0-88492-019-4 pbk. : 2.95
1. Stratton, Charles Sherwood, 1838-1883. 2. Thumb, Tom, Mrs., 1841-1919. 3. Dwarfs—Biography. BIP

Stratton, Richard A., 1931-

BLAKEY, Scott. 959.704'37
Prisoner at war : the survival of Commander Richard A. Stratton / Scott Blakey. 1st ed. Garden City, N.Y. : Anchor Press/Doubleday, 1978. viii, 397 p. ; 22 cm. Includes index. Bibliography: p. 385-388. [DS559.4.B56] 77-92208 ISBN 0-385-12905-X : 10.00
1. Stratton, Richard A., 1931- 2. Vietnamese Conflict, 1961-1975—Prisoners and prisons, North Vietnamese. 3. Prisoners of War, American—Biography. I. Title. BIP

BLAKEY, Scott. 959.704'37
Prisoner at war : the survival of Commander Richard A. Stratton / Scott Blakey. New York : Penguin Books, 1979, c1978. viii, 397 p., [4] leaves of plates : ill. ; 18 cm. Includes index. Bibliography: p. 385-388. [DS559.4.B56 1979] 79-13708 ISBN 0-14-005225-9 pbk. : 2.95
1. Stratton, Richard A., 1931- 2. Vietnamese Conflict, 1961-1975—Prisoners and prisons, North Vietnamese. 3. Prisoners of War—United States—Biography. 4. Prisoners of War—Vietnam

(Democratic Republic, 1946-)—Biography. I. Title.

Stratton, Samuel Studdiford, 1916-

CROSS, Wilbur. 923.273
Samuel S. Stratton; a story of political gumption. New York, J. H. Heineman [1964] ix, 161 p. illus., ports. 22 cm. (The Future makers) [E748.S885C7] 64-22743
1. Stratton, Samuel Studdiford, 1916- I. Title. II. Series. BIP

Straus, Dorothea—Biography.

STRAUS, Dorothea. 813'.5'4 B
Palaces and prisons / Dorothea Straus. Boston : Houghton Mifflin, c1976. 209 p. ; 22 cm. [PS3569.T6918Z52 1976] 76-26102 ISBN 0-395-24671-7 : 7.95
1. Straus, Dorothea—Biography. 2. Authors, American—20th century—Biography. I. Title. BIP

Straus, Jesse Isidor, 1872-1936.

KAUFFMAN, Reginald Wright, 1877-1959. 327'.2'0924 B
Jesse Isidor Straus: a biographical portrait. New York, 1973. 376 p. illus. 24 cm. [HF3023.S85K38 1973] 72-96010
1. Straus, Jesse Isidor, 1872-1936.

Straus, Oscar, 1870-1954.

GRUN, Bernard, 1901- 927.8
Prince of Vienna; the life, the times, and the melodies of Oscar Straus. [1st American ed.] New York, Putnam [1957, c1955] 224p. illus. 23cm. [ML410] 57-6726
1. Straus, Oscar, 1870-1954. I. Title.

Strauss, David Friedrich, 1808-1874.

CROMWELL, Richard S. 230'.092'4 B
David Friedrich Strauss and his place in modern thought, by Richard S. Cromwell. Foreword by Wilhelm Pauck. Fair Lawn, N.J., R. E. Burdick [1974] 232 p. 23 cm. "A Carl Hermann Voss book." Bibliography: p. 219-224. [BX4827.S8C76 1974] 73-88620 ISBN 0-913638-05-6 12.50
1. Strauss, David Friedrich, 1808-1874. I. Title. BIP

HARRIS, Horton. 230'.092'4 B
David Friedrich Strauss and his theology. Cambridge [Eng.] University Press, 1973. xv, 301 p. illus. 22 cm. (Monograph supplements to the Scottish journal of theology) Bibliography: p. 295-298. [BX4827.S8H33] 72-93137 ISBN 0-521-20139-X
1. Strauss, David Friedrich, 1808-1874. I. Title. II. Series: Scottish journal of theology. Monograph supplements.
Distributed by Cambridge University Press, New York, 16.00.

Strauss, Eduard, 1835-1916.

PASTENE, Jerome. 927.8
Three-quarter time; the life and music of the Strauss family of Vienna. [1st ed.] New York, Abelard Press [1951] 307 p. illus., ports., music. 25 cm. "Selected recordings of Strauss compositions": p. 262-279. "A catalogue by opus numbers of the compositions of Johann Strauss I, Johann Strauss II, Josef Strauss [and] Edward Strauss": p. 280-305. bibliography: p. 306-307. [ML410.S89P3] 51-11219
1. Strauss, Johann, 1804-1849. 2. Strauss, Johann, 1825-1899. 3. Strauss, Joseph, 1827-1870. 4. Strauss, Eduard, 1835-1916. 5. Strauss family (Musicians)—Discography. I. Title.

Strauss family (Musicians)

PASTENE, Jerome. 785.4'1'0922 B
Three-quarter time; the life and music of the Strauss family of Vienna. Westport, Conn., Greenwood Press [1971, c1951] 307 p. illus. 23 cm. Bibliography: p. 306-307. [ML410.S89P3 1971] 76-91768 ISBN 0-8371-3991-0
1. Strauss family (Musicians) I. Title. BIP

WECHSBERG, Joseph, 1907- 785.4'1'0922 B
The waltz emperors; the life and times and music of the Strauss family. [1st ed.] New York, Putnam [1973] 272 p. illus. 26 cm. [ML410.S92W4] 73-78610 ISBN 0-399-11167-0 15.00
1. Strauss family. I. Title.

Strauss, Helen M.

STRAUSS, Helen M. 070.5'2'0924 B
A talent for luck : an autobiography / Helen M. Strauss. 1st ed. New York : Random House, c1979. 309 p. ; 24 cm. Includes index. [PN149.9.S75A37] 78-21804 ISBN 0-394-50428-3 : 12.95 12.95
1. Strauss, Helen M. 2. Literary agents—United States—Biography. I. Title.

Strauss, Johann, 1804-1849.

PASTENE, Jerome. 927.8
Three-quarter time; the life and music of the Strauss family of Vienna. [1st ed.] New York, Abelard Press [1951] 307 p. illus., ports., music. 25 cm. "Selected recordings of Strauss compositions": p. 262-279. "A catalogue by opus numbers of the compositions of Johann Strauss I, Johann Strauss II, Josef Strauss [and] Edward Strauss": p. 280-305. bibliography: p. 306-307. [ML410.S89P3] 51-11219
1. Strauss, Johann, 1804-1849. 2. Strauss, Johann, 1825-1899. 3. Strauss, Joseph, 1827-1870. 4. Strauss, Eduard, 1835-1916. 5. Strauss family (Musicians)—Discography. I. Title.

Strauss, Johann, 1825-1899.

FANTEL, Hans. 785.41'0922 B
The waltz kings; Johann Strauss, father & son, and their romantic age. New York, W. Morrow, 1972. 246 p. illus. 22 cm. "Published in Great Britain in 1971 under the title Johann Strauss: father and son, and their era." Bibliography: p. 223-227. [ML410.S91F3 1972] 71-151920 6.95
1. Strauss, Johann, 1825-1899. 2. Strauss, Johann, 1804-1849. I. Title.

GARTENBERG, Egon. 785.4'1'0924 B
Johann Strauss; the end of an era. University Park, Pennsylvania State University Press [1974] p. [ML410.S91G3] 73-15682 ISBN 0-271-01131-9 12.75
1. Strauss, Johann, 1825-1899. I. Title. BIP

GARTENBERG, Egon. 785.4'1'0924 B
Johann Strauss; the end of an era. University Park, Pennsylvania State University Press [1974] xiii, 360 p. illus. 24 cm. Bibliography: p. 345-349. [ML410.S91G3] 73-15682 ISBN 0-271-01131-9
1. Strauss, Johann, 1825-1899. I. Title.

GARTENBERG, Egon. 785.4'1'0924 B
Johann Strauss : the end of an era / Egon Gartenberg. New York : Da Capo Press, 1979, c1974. p. cm. (A Da Capo paperback) Reprint of the ed. published by Pennsylvania State University Press, University Park. [ML410.G91G3 1979] 78-20841 ISBN 0-306-80098-5 pbk. : 6.95
1. Strauss, Johann, 1825-1899. 2. Composers—Austria—Biography.

PASTENE, Jerome. 927.8
Three-quarter time; the life and music of the Strauss family of Vienna. [1st ed.] New York, Abelard Press [1951] 307 p. illus., ports., music. 25 cm. "Selected recordings of Strauss compositions": p. 262-279. "A catalogue by opus numbers of the compositions of Johann Strauss I, Johann Strauss II, Josef Strauss [and] Edward Strauss": p. 280-305. bibliography: p. 306-307. [ML410.S89P3] 51-11219
1. Strauss, Johann, 1804-1849. 2. Strauss, Johann, 1825-1899. 3. Strauss, Joseph, 1827-1870. 4. Strauss, Eduard, 1835-1916. 5. Strauss family (Musicians)—Discography. I. Title.

Strauss, Joseph, 1827-1870.

PASTENE, Jerome. 927.8
Three-quarter time; the life and music of the Strauss family of Vienna. [1st ed.] New York, Abelard Press [1951] 307 p. illus., ports., music. 25 cm. "Selected recordings of Strauss compositions": p. 262-279. "A catalogue by opus numbers of the compositions of Johann Strauss I, Johann Strauss II, Josef Strauss [and] Edward Strauss": p. 280-305. bibliography: p. 306-307. [ML410.S89P3] 51-11219
1. Strauss, Johann, 1804-1849. 2. Strauss, Johann, 1825-1899. 3. Strauss, Joseph, 1827-1870. 4. Strauss, Eduard, 1835-1916. 5. Strauss family (Musicians)—Discography. I. Title.

Strauss, Ray, 1886-1977.

STRAUSS, Ray, 1886-1977. 977.3'31 B
As it was told to me / by my grandfather Ray Strauss and my grandmother Sarah Strauss ; edited by David Patton and Cheryl Glasgow. Rockford, Ill. : Elysian Fields Pub., c1978. vii, 189 p. : ill. ; 22 cm. On cover: The Strauss tapes. [F549.R7S77 1978] 77-95394 pbk. : 6.95
1. Strauss, Ray, 1886-1977. 2. Strauss, Sarah, 1890- 3. Rockford, Ill.—Biography. I. Strauss, Sarah, 1890- joint author. II. Patton, David. III. Glasgow, Cheryl. IV. Title.
Publisher's address : 1603 Burton St., Rockford, IL 61103

Strauss, Richard, 1864-1949.

DEL MAR, Norman Rene, 1919- 927.8
Richard Strauss: a critical commetary on his life and works. v.1. London, Rarrie and Rockliff [dist. New York, Free Pr., 1963, c.1960] 462p. ports., music. 23cm. Bibl. 12.50
1. Strauss, Richard, 1864-1949. I. Title.

DEL MAR, Norman Rene, 1919- v. 12
Richard Strauss: a critical commentary on his life and works. New York, Free Press of Glencoe [1962]- v. ports., music. 23 cm. Includes lists of compositions. Bibliography: v. 1, p. [442]-444. 64-37548
1. Strauss, Richard, 1864-1949. I. Title.

DEL MAR, Norman Rene, 1919- 780'.924 B
Richard Strauss; a critical commentary on his life and works, by Norman Del Mar. Philadelphia, Chilton Book Co. [1969, v. 1, c1962] 2 v. illus., music, ports. 23 cm. Includes lists of compositions. Bibliography: v. 1, p. 442-444. [ML410.S93D4 1969] 69-11425 12.50 (v. 1)
1. Strauss, Richard, 1864-1949.

KENNEDY, Michael, 1926- 780'.92'4 B
Richard Strauss / by Michael Kennedy. London : Dent, 1976. xii, 274 p., [8] p. of plates : ill., music, ports. ; 20 cm. (The Master musicians series) Includes index. "Catalogue of works": p. 241-253. [ML410.S93K45] 76-368326 ISBN 0-460-03148-1 : 8.50 pbk.
1. Strauss, Richard, 1864-1949. 2. Composers—Germany—Biography. I. Title. II. Series.
Distributed by Rowman & Littlefield. BIP

KRAUSE, Ernst, writer on music. 780'.924
Richard Strauss, the man and his work. Boston, Crescendo Pub. Co. [1969] 587 p. illus., facsims., ports. 22 cm. Bibliography: p. 561-[562] [ML410.S93K73 1969] 78-77591 10.00
1. Strauss, Richard, 1864-1949.

MASON, Daniel Gregory, 1873-1953. 780'.92'2 B
Contemporary composers. New York, Macmillan Co., 1918. [New York, AMS Press, 1973] xi, 290 p. illus. 19 cm. Contents.Contents.—Introduction: Democracy and music.—Richard Strauss.—Sir Edward Elgar.—Claude Debussy.—Vincent d'Indy.—Music in America. [ML390.M383 1973] 72-1726 ISBN 0-404-08327-7 13.00
1. Strauss, Richard, 1864-1949. 2. Elgar, Edward William, Sir, 1857-1934. 3. Debussy, Claude, 1862-1918. 4. Indy, Vincent d', 1851-1931. 5. Music—History and criticism—19th century. I. Title. BIP

NEWMAN, Ernest, 1868-1959. 780'.924 B
Richard Strauss. With a personal note by Alfred Kalisch. Westport, Conn., Greenwood Press [1970] xxi, 144 p. illus., music, ports. 23 cm. Reprint of the 1908 ed. [ML410.S93N38 1970] 79-109806
1. Strauss, Richard, 1864-1949. BIP

STRAUSS, Richard, 1864-1949. 780'.8
Recollections and reflections. Edited by Willi Schuh. English translation by L. J. Lawrence. Westport, Conn., Greenwood Press [1974, c1953] p. cm. Translation of Betrachtungen und Erinnerungen. Reprint of the ed. published by Boosey & Hawkes, London, New York. Bibliography: p. [ML410.S93A372 1974] 74-72 ISBN 0-8371-7366-3 11.00
1. Strauss, Richard, 1864-1949. 2. Musicians—Correspondence, reminiscences, etc.

STRAUSS, Richard, 1864-1949. 927.8
A working friendship; the correspondence between Richard Strauss and Hugo von Hofmannsthal. Translated by Hanns Hammelmann and Ewald Osers. Introd. by Edward Sackville-West. New York, Random House [1961] xx, 558 p. illus., ports., facsims. 24 cm. [ML410.S93A453] 61-13839
I. Hofmannsthal, Hugo Hoffmann, Edler von, 1874-1929. II. Title.

STRAUSS, Richard, 1864-1949 927.8
A working friendship; the correspondence between Richard Strauss and Hugo von Hofmannsthal. Translated by Hanns Hammelmann and Ewald Osers. Introd. by Edward Sackville-West. New York, Vienna House, [1974, c1961] xx, 558 p. ports., facsims. 21 cm. [ML410.S93A453] 61-13839 ISBN 0-8443-0050-0 5.95 (pbk.)
I. Hofmannsthal, Hugo Hofmann, Edler von, 1874-1929 II. Title.

Strausz-Hupe, Robert,

STRAUSZ-HUPE, Robert, 1903- 973.9170924
In my time. [1st ed.] New York, W. W. Norton [1965] 284 p. 22 cm. Autobiographical. [D15.S85A3] 65-18022
I. Title.

Stravinskii, Igor' Fedorovich, 1882-1971.

CORLE, Edwin, 1906-1956, comp. 780'.924
Igor Stravinsky. Edited by Edwin Corle. Freeport, N.Y., Books for Libraries Press [1969, c1949] 245 p. illus. (part col.), ports. 24 cm. (Essay index reprint series) "A Merle Armitage book." "Contains five of the critiques from the 1936 volume [ed. by Merle Armitage]" [ML410.S932C77 1969] 77-84295
1. Stravinskii, Igor Fedorovich, 1882- I. Armitage, Merle, 1893-

CRAFT, Robert. 780'.924 B
Stravinsky; chronicle of a friendship, 1948-1971. [1st ed.] New York, A. A. Knopf, 1972. xvi, 424, xvi p. illus. 25 cm. [ML410.S932C8] 79-173776 ISBN 0-394-

47612-3 12.50
1. Stravinskii, Igor' Fedorovich, 1882-1971. BIP

CRAFT, Robert. 780'.92'4 B
Stravinsky; chronicle of a friendship, 1948-1971. New York, Vintage Books [1973 c1972] xvi, 424, xvi p. illus. 21 cm. [ML410.S932C8 1973] 73-4719 ISBN 0-394-71949-2 3.95 (pbk.)
1. Stravinskii, Igor' Fedorovich, 1882-1971.

DE LERMA, Dominique-Rene. 016.78'092'4
Igor Fedorovitch Stravinsky, 1882-1971; a practical guide to publications of his music by Dominique-Rene de Lerma assisted by Thomas J. Ahrens. [1st ed. Kent, Ohio] Kent State University Press [1974] x, 158 p. port. 22 cm. [ML134.S96D44] 74-79152 ISBN 0-87338-158-0 7.50
1. Stravinskii, Igor' Fedorovich, 1882-1971—Bibliography. I. Ahrens, Thomas J., joint author.

DOBRIN, Arnold. 780'.924 B
Igor Stravinsky, his life and times. New York, T. Y. Crowell Co. [1970] vii, 197 p. illus., ports. 21 cm. [ML3930.S86D6] 77-101924 4.50
1. Stravinskii, Igor' Fedorovich, 1882- — Juvenile literature.

HORGAN, Paul, 1903- 780'.92'4 B
Encounters with Stravinsky; a personal record. New York, Farrar Straus and Giroux [1972] x, 299 p. illus. 22 cm. Bibliography: p. 287-[288] [ML410.S932H67] 78-183238 ISBN 0-374-14828-7 7.95
1. Stravinskii, Igor' Fedorovich, 1882-1971. I. Title.

LANG, Paul Henry, 1901- 780.92
Stravinsky; a new appraisal of his work. With a complete list of works. New York, W. W. Norton [1963] 121 p. illus. 20 cm. (The Norton library, N199) [ML410.S932L3] 63-1337
1. Stravinskii, Igor' Fedorovich, 1882-1971. 2. Stravinskii, Igor' Fedorovich, 1882-1971—Bibliography.

LIBMAN, Lillian. 780'.92'4 B
And music at the close: Stravinsky's last years, a personal memoir. [1st ed.] New York, W. W. Norton [1972] 400 p. illus. 22 cm. [ML410.S932L44] 72-4499 ISBN 0-393-02113-0 9.95
1. Stravinskii, Igor' Fedorovich, 1882-1971. I. Title.

ROUTH, Francis. 780'.92'4
Stravinsky / by Francis Routh. London : Dent, 1977 ix, 202 p., [8] p. of plates : music, ports. ; 20 cm. (The Master musicians series) "Catalogue of works": p. 168-178. Includes index. Bibliography: p. 188-191. [ML410.S932R6] 76-358160 ISBN 0-87471-841-4 : 9.50
1. Stravinskii, Igor' Fedorovich, 1882-1971. I. Title. II. Series.
Distributed by Roman and Littlefield,N.J.

SIOHAN, Robert, 1894- 780'.92'4 B
Stravinsky. Translated by Eric Walter White. New York, Grossman Publishers, 1970 [c1965] 180 p. illus. 22 cm. (Library of composers, 2) [ML410.S932S573 1970] 76-94088 ISBN 0-670-67808-2 7.95
1. Stravinskii, Igor' Fedorovich, 1882-1971. I. Title. II. Series.

STRAVINSKII, Ignor' Fedrovich, 1882- 927.8
Expositions and developments [by] Igor Stravinsky, Robert Craft. Garden City, N. Y., Doubleday, 1962[c.1959-1962] 192p. illus. 61-12588 4.95
1. Musicians—Correspondence, reminiscences etc. I. Craft, Robert. II. Title.

STRAVINSKII, Igor Fedorovich, 1882- 927.8
Conversations with Igor Stravinsky [by] Igor Stravinsky and Robert Craft. [1st ed.] Garden City, N.Y., Doubleday, 1959. 162 p. illus. 22 cm. [ML410.S932A33] 59-6375
1. Music. 2. Craft, Robert. I. Title.

STRAVINSKII, Igor' Fedorovich, 1882-1971 927.8
Conversations with Igor Stravinsky [by] Igor Stravinsky and Robert Craft. [1st ed.] Garden City, N. Y., Doubleday, 1959. 162 p. illus. 22 cm. [ML410.S932A33] 59-6375
1. Music. I. Craft, Robert. II. Title.

STRAVINSKII, Igor Fedorovich, 1882-1971. 927.8
Dialogues and a diary [by] Igor Stravinsky and Robert Craft. [1st ed.] Garden City, N. Y., Doubleday, 1963. 279 p. group ports. 22 cm. [ML410.S932A335] 63-20511
1. Music. I. Craft, Robert. II. Title.

STRAVINSKII, Igor Fedorovich, 1882- 784'.092'4
Igor Stravinsky, an autobiography. New York, Norton [1962, 1936] 176 p. 20 cm. (The Norton Library, N161) Translation of Chroniques de ma vie. [ML410.S] A63 *I. Title.*

STRAVINSKII, Igor Fedorovich, 1882- 784'.092'4
Igor Stravinsky, an autobiography. New York, Norton [1962, 1936] 176 p. 20 cm. (The Norton Library, N161) Translation of Chroniques de ma vie. [ML410.S] A63 *I. Title.*

STRAVINSKII, Igor' Fedorovich, 1882-1971. 927.8
Memories and commentaries [by] Igor Stravinsky and Robert Craft. [1st ed.] Garden City, N. Y., Doubleday, 1960 [c1958] 167 p. illus. 22 cm. [ML410.S932A35] 60-10684
1. Music. I. Craft, Robert. II. Title.

STRAVINSKII, Igor Fedorovich, 1882- 927.8
Stravinsky: an autobiography [Tr. from French] New York, Norton [1962, c.1936] 176p. 20cm. (N161) 1.45 pap.,
I. Title.

STRAVINSKII, Igor Fedorovich, 1882- 927.8
Stravinsky: an autobiography [Tr. from French] New York, Norton [1962, c.1936] 176p. 20cm. (N161) 1.45 pap.,
I. Title.

STRAVINSKY, Vera. 780'.92'4 B
Stravinsky in pictures and documents / by Vera Stravinsky and Robert Craft. New York : Simon and Schuster, c1978. p. cm. Includes index. Bibliography: p. [ML410.S932S787] 78-15375 ISBN 0-671-24382-9 : 25.00
1. Stravinskii, Igor Fedorovich, 1882-1971. 2. Composers Biography. I. Craft, Robert, joint author. II. Title.

STRAWINSKY, Theodore, 1907- 927.8
The message of Igor Strawinsky; translated from the original French text by Robert Craft and Andre Marion. London, New York, Boosey & Hawkes [1953] 57p. illus. 20cm. [ML410 S932S82 1953] 53-4061
1. Stravinskil, Igor Fedorovich, 1882- I. Title.

VLAD, Roman, 1919- 780'.924
Stravinsky; translated from the Italian by Frederick and Ann Fuller. 2nd ed. London, New York [etc.] Oxford U.P., 1967. [vii], 264 p. plate, music. 23 cm. Bibliography: p. [257]-258. [ML410.S932V52 1967] 68-71387 42/-
1. Stravinskii, Igor' Fedorovich, 1882-

VLAD, Roman, 1919- 780'.92'4 B
Stravinsky / Roman Vlad ; translated from the Italian by Frederick Fuller. 3d ed. London ; New York : Oxford University Press, 1978. viii, 288 p. : music ; 23 cm. Translation of Strawinsky. Includes indexes. Bibliography: p. [281]-284. [ML410.S932V52 1978] 79-309066 ISBN 0-19-315444-7 : 14.95
1. Stravinskii, Igor' Fedorovich, 1882-1971. 2. Composers—Biography. I. Title.

VLAD, Roman, 1919- 780.92
Stravinsky, Translated by Frederick and Ann Fulton. London, New York, Oxford University Press, 1960. 232 p. port., music, 23 cm. Bibliography: p. [225]-226. [ML410.S932V52] 60-50776
1. Stravinskii, Igor Fedorovich, 1882- I. Title.

VLAD, Roman, 1919- 780'.924
Stravinsky; translated from the Italian by Frederick and Ann Fuller. 2nd ed. London, New York [etc.] Oxford U. P., 1967. [vii], 264 p. plate, music. 23 cm. 42/-(B68-00408) Bibliography; p. [257]-258. [ML410.S932V52 1967] 68-71387
1. Stravinskiy, Igor'Fedorovich, 1882- I. Title.

WHITE, Eric Walter. 780'.92'4
Stravinsky : a critical survey / Eric Walter White. Westport, Conn. : Greenwood Press, 1979. p. cm. Reprint of the 1948 ed. published by Philosophical Library, New York. Includes index. Bibliography: p. [ML410.S932W45 1979] 79-9863 ISBN 0-313-21463-8 : 18.25
1. Stravinskii, Igor' Fedorovich, 1882-1971. 2. Stravinskii, Igor' Fedorovich, 1882-1971—Discography. 3. Composers—Biography.

WHITE, Eric Walter, 1905- 780.924
Stravinsky: the composer and his works. Berkeley, University of California Press, 1966. xv, 608 p. facsims., music, ports. 26 cm. "Register of works": p. 125-506. Bibliography: p. 575-582. [ML410.S932W47] 66-27667
1. Stravinskii, Igor' Fedorovich, 1882- BIP

Streatfeild, Noel.

STREATFEILD, Noel. 828.912
A vicarage family, an autobiographical story. Illustrated by Charles Mozley. New York, F. Watts, 1963. ix, 245 p. illus. 25 cm. [PR6037.T77Z5 1963] 63-21029
I. Title.

Street, George Edmund, 1824-1881.

STREET, Arthur Edmund, 1855- 720'.92'4 B
Memoir of George Edmund Street, R.A., 1824-1881. New York, B. Blom, 1972. 441 p. port. 21 cm. Reprint of the 1888 ed. Includes lectures given before students of the Royal Academy in the spring of 1881. [NA997.S8S8 1972] 70-173141
1. Street, George Edmund, 1824-1881. 2. Architecture—Addresses, essays, lectures. BIP

Street, James Howell, 1903-1954.

STREET, James Howell, 1903-1954. 975'.004'96073
Look away! : A Dixie notebook / by James H. Street. Westport, Conn. : Greenwood Press, 1977, c1936. ix, 241 p. ; 22 cm. Reprint of the ed. published by Viking Press, New York. [E185.6.S79 1977] 75-142924 ISBN 0-8371-5950-4 lib.bdg. : 15.00
1. Street, James Howell, 1903-1954. 2. Southern States—Race relations—Addresses, essays, lectures. 3. Afro-Americans—Southern States—Addresses, essays, lectures. 4. Lynching—Addresses, essays, lectures. 5. Mississippi—Biography. I. Title.

Street, Jessie Mary Grey Lillingston, Lady, 1889-

SEKULESS, Peter. 335'.0092'4 B
Jessie Street, a rewarding but unrewarded life / Peter Sekuless. St. Lucia [Australia] : University of Queensland Press ; Hemel Hempstead, Eng. : distributed by Prentice-Hall International, c1978. xiv, 218 p. : ill. ; 23 cm. Includes index. Bibliography: p. [211]-213. [HQ1822.S76S44] 79-309995 ISBN 0-7022-1227-X : 8.50
1. Street, Jessie Mary Grey Lillingston, Lady, 1889- 2. Feminists—Australia—Biography. 3. Socialists—Australia—Biography. I. Title.
Dist. by Technical Impex Corp. 5 South Union St., lawrence MA 01843

Street names—Colorado—Fort Collins.

TRESNER, Charlene, 1918- 978.8'68'0922 B
Streets of Fort Collins / by Charlene Tresner. [Fort Collins? Colo.] : McMillen Pub. Co., c1977. 30 p. : ill. ; 26 cm. Bibliography: p. 30. [F784.F56T73] 77-150350
1. Street names—Colorado—Fort Collins. 2. Fort Collins, Colo.—Streets. 3. Fort Collins, Colo.—Biography. 4. Pioneers—Colorado—Fort Collins—Biography. I. Title.

Streeter, Fred.

HENNIG, Frank. 635'.092'4 B
"Cheerio Frank, cheerio everybody" : the gardening world of Fred Streeter / by Frank Hennig ; line drawings by Barbara Law. London : Angus and Robertson, 1976. vii, 181 p. : ill. ; 23 cm. [SB63.S77H46] 77-355400 ISBN 0-207-95711-8 : £3.80
1. Streeter, Fred. 2. Gardeners—England—Biography. 3. Radio broadcasters—England—Biography. I. Title.

Streeton, Arthur, Sir, 1867-1943.

GALBALLY, Ann. 709'.24
Arthur Streeton. [Melbourne] Lansdowne [1969] 87 p. illus., 32 col. plates. 27 cm. (Australian art library) Bibliography: p. 87. [ND1105.S7G3] 73-467371 8.50
1. Streeton, Arthur, Sir, 1867-1943. I. Title.

GALBALLY, Ann. 759.994
Arthur Streeton. Melbourne, New York, Oxford University Press, 1972. 30 p. illus. 19 cm. (Great Australians) Bibliography: p. 30. [ND1105.S7G32] 73-158518 ISBN 0-19-550415-1 0.70
1. Streeton, Arthur, Sir, 1867-1943.

Streisand, Barbra.

*BLACK, Jonathan. 790.2'092'4
Streisand. New York: Leisure Books, [1975] 187 p.: illus.; 18 cm. [ML420.] 1.50 (pbk.)
1. Streisand, Barbra. I. Title. BIP

BRADY, Frank, 1934- 784'.092'4 B
Barbra Streisand : an illustrated biography / by Frank Brady. New York : Grosset & Dunlap, c1979. 151 p. : ill. ; 28 cm. [ML420.S915B7] 78-73322 ISBN 0-448-16534-1 : 7.95
1. Streisand, Barbra. 2. Singers—United States—Biography.

ELDRED, Patricia Mulrooney. 790.2'092'4 B
Barbra Streisand / text, Patricia Mulrooney Eldred ; ill., John Keely. Mankato, Minn. : Creative Education, [1975] p. cm. Bibliography: p. A brief biography concentrating on the career of the well-known singer and movie star. [ML3930.S88E4] 92 75-20385 ISBN 0-87191-459-X lib.bdg. : 4.95
1. Streisand, Barbra—Juvenile literature. I. Keely, John. II. Title.

JORDAN, Rene. 790.2'092'4 B
The greatest star : the Barbra Streisand story, an unauthorized biography / by Rene Jordan. New York : Putnam, c1975. 253 p. ; 22 cm. [ML420.S915J67] 75-15471 ISBN 0-399-11597-8 : 7.95
1. Streisand, Barbra. I. Title.

JORDAN, Rene. 790.2'092'4 B
The greatest star : the Barbra Streisand story, an unauthorized biography / Rene Jordan. New York : Berkley Pub. Corp. : distributed by Putnam, 1977c1975. 242p. ; 18 cm. (A Berkley Medallion Book) [ML420.S915J67] ISBN 0-425-03355-4 pbk. : 1.75
1. Streisand, Barbra. I. Title.
L.C. card no. for 1975 Putnam ed. 75-15471.

Stresemann, Gustav, 1878-1929.

TURNER, Henry Ashby. 943.085'092'4
Stresemann and the politics of the Weimar Republic / by Henry Ashby Turner, Jr. Westport, Conn. : Greenwood Press, 1979, c1963. v, 287 p. ; 23 cm. Reprint of the ed. published by Princeton University Press, Princeton, N.J. Includes index. Bibliography: p. 269-276. [DD231.S83T87 1979] 78-26856 ISBN 0-313-20900-6 : 22.50
1. Stresemann, Gustav, 1878-1929. 2. Statesmen—Germany—Biography. 3. Germany—Politics and government—1918-1933. I. Title. BIP

Stribling, Thomas Sigismund, 1881-1965.

ECKLEY, Wilton. 813'.5'2 B
T. S. Stribling / by Wilton Eckley. Boston : Twayne Publishers, [1975] 127 p. ; 21 cm. (Twayne's United States authors series ; TUSAS 255) Includes index. Bibliography: p. 119-122. [PS3537.T836Z66] 75-1096 ISBN 0-8057-7151-4 lib.bdg. : 6.95
1. Stribling, Thomas Sigismund, 1881-1965. I. Title. BIP

Stribling, Young.

JONES, Jimmy, 1906- 796.8'3'0924 B
King of the canebrakes. [1st ed.] Macon, Ga., Southern Press [1969] 127 p. illus., ports. 22 cm. [GV1132.S7J6] 72-78411 4.95
1. Stribling, Young. I. Title.

Strickland, Henry Benjamin, 1884-1944.

FOSTER, John J., 1912- 282'.0924 B
A priest for all men; the life of Henry B. Strickland, by John J. Foster. Lebanon, Penn., Holy Name Society, Assumption B.V.M. Church [1971] 160 p. illus., facsim., ports. 23 cm. Bibliography: p. 160. [BX4705.S8433F68] 77-158664 3.00
1. Strickland, Henry Benjamin, 1884-1944. I. Title.

Strickland, William, 1787-1854.

GILCHRIST, Agnes Eleanor (Addison) 1907- 720'.924 B
William Strickland, architect and engineer, 1788-1854, by Agnes Addison Gilchrist. enl.ed. New York, Da Capo Press, 1969. 1 v. (various pagings) illus., plans, ports. 29 cm. (A Da Capo Press reprint edition) "An unabridged republication of the first edition, published in ... 1950 ... It includes as a supplement three articles about Strickland prepared by Mrs. Gilchrist [and first published in 1953-54]" Includes bibliographical references. [NA737.S68G5 1969] 69-13714 20.00
1. Strickland, William, 1787-1854. 2. Architecture—U.S. BIP

Strickler, Daniel Bursk,

STRICKLER, Daniel Bursk, 1897- 355.3'31'0924 B
The memoirs of Lieutenant Governor, Lieutenant General Daniel Bursk Strickler. Lancaster, Pa., 1972. 277 p. port. 24 cm. Edition limited to 200 copies. [U53.S76A33] 72-75181

Stricklin, Al, 1908-

STRICKLIN, Al, 1908- 785'.092'4 B
My years with Bob Wills / by Al Stricklin, with John McConal. San Antonio, Tex. : Naylor Co., c1976. xiv, 153 p., [5] leaves of plates : ill. ; 22 cm. [ML417.S92A3] 76-7228 ISBN 0-8111-0603-9 : 8.95
1. Stricklin, Al, 1908- 2. Wills, Bob, 1905-1975. 3. Country musicians—Correspondence, reminiscences, etc. I. McConal, Jon, 1937- joint author. II. Title.

Strindberg, August, 1849-1912.

CAMPBELL, George Archibald, 1900- 839.7'2'6 B
Strindberg, by G. A. Campbell. New York, Haskell House, 1971. 143, [1] p. 23 cm. (Great lives [20]) Reprint of the 1933 ed. Bibliography: p. [144] [PT9815.C3 1971] 71-163501 ISBN 0-8383-1320-5
1. Strindberg, August, 1849-1912.

CAMPBELL, George Archibald, 1900- 839.7'2'6 B
Strindberg, by G. A. Campbell. [Folcroft, Pa.] Folcroft Library Editions, 1973. p. Reprint of the 1933 ed. published by Macmillan, New York, in series: Great lives. Bibliography: p. [PT9815.C3 1973] 73-7815 ISBN 0-8414-3370-4 (lib. bdg.)
1. Strindberg, August, 1849-1912. BIP

JASPERS, Karl, 1883-1969. 616.8'982'09 B
Strindberg and Van Gogh : an attempt of a pathographic analysis with reference to parallel cases of Swedenborg and Holderlin / Karl Jaspers ; translated by Oskar Grunow and David Woloshin. Tucson, Ariz. : University of Arizona Press, [1977] p. cm. Translation of Strindberg und Van Gogh. Includes index. Bibliography: p. [PT9815.J313 1977] 77-9394 ISBN 0-8165-0608-6 : 12.50. ISBN 0-8165-0434-2 pbk. : 4.95
1. Strindberg, August, 1849-1912. 2. Gogh, Vincent van, 1853-1890. 3. Swedenborg, Emanuel, 1688-1772. 4. Holderlin, Friedrich, 1770-1843. 5. Psychology, Pathological—Cases, clinical reports, statistics. I. Title.

JOHNSON, Walter Gilbert, 1905- 839.7'2'6 B
August Strindberg / Walter Johnson. Boston : Twayne Publishers, c1976. 221 p. : port. ; 21 cm. (Twayne's world authors series ; TWAS 410 : Sweden) Includes index. Bibliography: p. 207-215. [PT9815.J6] 76-17910 ISBN 0-8057-6250-7 lib.bdg. 8.50
1. Strindberg, August, 1849-1912.

LAMM, Martin, 1880-1950. 839.7'2'6 B
August Strindberg. Translated and edited by Harry G. Carlson. New York, B. Blom, 1971. xxi, 561 p. 26 cm. Translated from the 1948 rev. ed. Bibliography: p. 541-546. [PT9816.L27213] 69-16323
1. Strindberg, August, 1849-1912. BIP

LIND-AF-HAGEBY, Lizzy, 1878- 839.7'2'6
August Strindberg; a study, by L. Lind-af-Hageby. Introductory note by Robert Loraine. Port Washington, N.Y., Kennikat Press [1970] 87 p. port. 19 cm. "Comprising a lecture delivered before the Anglo-Swedish Society on December 6th, 1927 ..." [PT9815.L48 1970] 76-103201
1. Strindberg, August, 1849-1912. I. Anglo-Swedish Society.

MCGILL, Vivian Jerauld, 1897- 928.397
August Strindberg, the bedeviled viking [Reissue] New York, Russell & Russell, 1965[c.1930] 459p. plates, ports. 22cm. Bibl. [PT9815.M3] 65-13933 8.50
1. Strindberg, August, 1849-1912. I. Title.

MORTENSEN, Brita M. E. 928.397
Strindberg; an introduction to his life and work, by Brita M. E. Mortensen, Brian W. Downs [New York] Cambridge 1965. 233p. 21cm. Bibl. [PT9815.M63] 1.75 pap.,
1. Strindberg, August, 1849-1912. I. Downs, brian Westerdale, 1893- II. Title.

MORTENSEN, Brita M. E. 928.397
Strindberg; an introduction to his life and work, by Brita M. E. Mortensen, Brian W. Downs [Reissue, New York] Cambridge, 1966. London. H. Hamilton [Chester Springs. Pa., Dufour, 1966, c.1961] xi, [1], 233p. port. 22cm. 209p. illus. 23cm. Bibl. [PT9815.M63] [PQ2367.M94Z57] 928.4 50-5053 62-495 3.75 5.00 bds.,
1. Strindberg, August, 1849-1912. 2. Murger, Henri, 1822-1861. 3. Bohemianism. I. Downs, Brian n3 II. Baldick, Robert III. Title. IV. Title: The first Bohemian;

SPRIGGE, Elizabeth, 1900- 839.7'2'6
The strange life of August Strindberg. New York, Russell & Russell [1972, c1949] ix, 246 p. ports. 22 cm. Bibliography: p. 236-237. [PT9815.S6 1972] 75-186704
1. Strindberg, August, 1849-1912. I. Title. BIP

STRINDBERG, August, 1849-1912. 839.7'2'6
The Cloister. Edited by C. G. Bjurstrom. Translated and with a commentary and notes by Mary Sandbach. [1st American ed.] New York, Hill and Wang [1969] 160 p. 23 cm. Translation of Klostret. [PT9814.K513 1969b] 69-16839 5.00
I. Bjurstrom, Carl Gustaf, 1919- ed. II. Title.

STRINDBERG, August, 1849-1912. 843
The confession of a fool. Translated by Ellie Schleussner. Covent Garden, S. Swift, 1912. New York, Haskell House, 1972. vi, 319 p. 23 cm. Translation of Le plaidoyer d'un fou. [PT9814.P513 1972] 79-39042 ISBN 0-8383-1397-3 11.95
I. Schleussner, Ellie, tr. II. Title. BIP

STRINDBERG, August, 1849-1912. 839.7'2'6 B
Legends; autobiographical sketches. New York, Haskell House Publishers 1973. 245 p. 23 cm. Reprint of the 1912 ed. Translation of Legender. [PT9814.L3813 1973] 72-2120 ISBN 0-8383-1479-1 10.95 (lib. bdg.)
I. Title.

STRINDBERG, August, 1849-1912. 928.397
Letters of Strindberg to Harriet Bosse. Edited and translated by Arvid Paulson. New York, T. Nelson [1959] 194 p. 22 cm. [PT9814.Z6B633] 59-10864
I. Bosse, Harriet Sofle, 1878- II. Title.

UDDGREN, Carl Gustaf, 1865-1927. 839.7'2'6 B
Strindberg the man, by Gustaf Uddgren. Translated from the Swedish by Axel Johan Uppvall. New York, Haskell House Publishers, 1972. 165 p. 23 cm. Bibliography: p. 161-165. [PT9815.U313 1972] 74-39416 ISBN 0-8383-1401-5
1. Strindberg, August, 1849-1912. I. Title. BIP

UPPVALL, Axel Johan, 1872- 839.7'2'6
August Strindberg; a psychoanalytic study with special reference to the Oedipus complex. New York, Haskell House Publishers, 1970. 95 p. 22 cm. Reprint of the 1920 ed. Thesis—Clark University. Bibliography: p. 91-95. [PT9815.U58 1970] 79-117593
1. Strindberg, August, 1849-1912. 2. Psychoanalysis. BIP

Strindberg, August, 1849-1912—Diaries.

STRINDBERG, August, 1849-1912. 839.7'26 B
Inferno and From an occult diary / August Strindberg ; selected by Torsten Eklund ; translated with an introd. by Mary Sandbach. Harmondsworth, Eng. ; New York : Penguin Books, 1979. 431 p. ; 18 cm. (Penguin classics) Includes bibliographical references. [PT9804.S2 1979] 79-322108 ISBN 0-14-044364-9 pbk. : 4.95
1. Strindberg, August, 1849-1912—Diaries. 2. Authors, Swedish—19th century—Biography. I. Eklund, Torsten, 1900- II. Sandbach, Mary. III. Strindberg, August, 1849-1912. Ockulta dagboken. English. Selections. 1979. IV. Title: Inferno.

Stritch, Samuel Alphonsus, Cardinal, 1887-1958.

BUEHRLE, Marie Cecilia, 1887- 922.273
The Cardinal Stritch story. Milwaukee, Bruce Pub. Co. [1959] 197p. illus. 22cm. [BX4705.S844B8] 59-12941
1. Stritch, Samuel Alphonsus, Cardinal, 1887-1958. I. Title.

Strober, Gerald.

STROBER, Gerald. 269'.2'0924 [B]
Billy Graham : His life and faith / Gerald Strober. New York : Pocket Books, 1978. 158p. ; 18 cm. [BV3785.G69S86] ISBN 0-671-81890-2 pbk. : 1.95
I. Title.
L.C. card no. for 1977 Word Books ed.: 76-56484. BIP

Strode, Hudson, 1892-

STRODE, Hudson, 1892- 973.9'092'4 B
The eleventh house : memoirs / Hudson Strode. 1st ed. New York : Harcourt Brace Jovanovich, [1975] 312 p. ; 24 cm. [D15.S89A33] 74-34266 ISBN 0-15-128230-7 : 10.95
1. Strode, Hudson, 1892- I. Title.

Stromberg, Leonard, 1871-1941.

STROMBECK, Rita. 839.7'3'6
Leonard Stromberg, a Swedish-American writer / Rita Strombeck. New York : Arno Press, 1979. p. cm. (Scandinavians in America) A revision of the author's thesis, University of Chicago, 1975. Bibliography: p. [PT9995.S7Z88 1979] 78-15848 ISBN 0-405-11660-8 : 22.00
1. Stromberg, Leonard, 1871-1941. 2. Authors, American—20th century—Biography. 3. Swedish Americans—Biography. I. Title. II. Series.

Strom, Erling, 1897-

STROM, Erling, 1897- 796.9'3'0924 B
Pioneers on skis / Erling Strom ; with an introd. by Lowell Thomas. 1st ed. Central Valley, N.Y. : Smith Clove Press, c1977. xi, 239 p. : ill. ; 22 cm. Autobiographical. [GV854.2.S85A36] 76-44187 9.50
1. Strom, Erling, 1897- 2. Skiers—Biography. 3. Cross-country skiing. I. Title.
Publishers address Central Valley, N.Y. 10917

Strong, Benjamin, 1872-1928.

CHANDLER, Lester Vernon, 1905- 332.1'1'0924 B
Benjamin Strong, central banker / Lester V. Chandler. New York : Arno Press, 1978 i.e. 1979, c1958. x, 495 p. : port. ; 24 cm. (International finance) Reprint of the ed. published by Brookings Institution, Washington. Includes index. [HG2563.S85C45 1979] 78-3903 ISBN 0-405-11216-5 : 12.00
1. Strong, Benjamin, 1872-1928. 2. Bankers—United States—Biography. 3. Federal Reserve banks—History. 4. Banks and banking, Central—History. 5. International finance—History. I. Title. II. Series: International financc (New York, 1979-)

Strong, George Templeton, 1820-1875.

STRONG, George Templeton, 1820-1875. 974.71
Diary; edited by Allan Nevins and Milton Halsey Thomas. New York, Macmillan, 1952. 4 v. illus., ports., facsims. 25 cm. Contents.Contents.—1. Young man in

New York, 1835-1849.—2. The turbulent fifties. 1850-1859.—3. The Civil War, 1860-1865.—4. Post-war years, 1865-1875. [E415.9.S86A3] 52-11147
1. Strong, George Templeton, 1820-1875. 2. United States—Politics and government—19th century. 3. New York (City)—Social life and customs. 4. United States—History—Civil War, 1861-1865—Personal narratives.

STRONG, George 917.47'1'0330924 B
Templeton, 1820-1875.
The diary of George Templeton Strong. Edited by Allan Nevins and Milton Halsey Thomas. New York, Octagon Books, 1974 [c1952] 4 v. illus. 24 cm. Reprint of the ed. published by Macmillan, New York. Contents.—1. Young man in New York, 1835-1849. 2. The turbulent fifties, 1850-1859. 3. The Civil War, 1860-1865.—4. Post-war years, 1865-1875. [E415.9.S86A3 1974] 73-21615 ISBN 0-374-96094-1 90.00 (4 vols.)
1. Strong, George Templeton, 1820-1875. 2. United States—Politics and government—19th century. 3. New York (City)—Social life and customs. 4. United States—History—Civil War, 1861-1865—Personal narratives. I. Title.
Contents omitted.

Strong, Hannah K. Russell.

WILLIAMS, Viva. 728'.092'4 B
Hannah K. [1st ed.] Lewiston, Idaho [1972] 80 p. illus. 24 cm. [CT275.S88216W53] 72-75165
1. Strong, Hannah K. Russell. I. Title.

Strong, June.

STRONG, June. 248'.833 B
Journal of a happy woman. Nashville, Southern Pub. Association [1973] 160 p. 23 cm. Includes bibliographical references. [BX6193.S77A3] 73-80238 ISBN 0-8127-0072-4 4.95
1. Strong, June. I. Title.

Strong, Kendrick.

STRONG, Kendrick. 922.573
Sagebrush circuit. New York, Macmillan, 1950. ix, 194 p. 21 cm. Full name: John Kendrick Strong. [BX7260.S85A3] 50-14969
I. Title.

Strong, Moses McCure, 1810-1894.

DUCKETT, Kenneth W 923.273
Frontiersman of fortune: Moses M. Strong of Mineral Point. [Madison] State Historical Society of Wisconsin [1955] xii, 253p. illus. ports. 24cm. Bibliographical references included in 'Notes to the text'(p. 199-227) 'Bibliographical essay': p. 231-237. [F586.S87D8] 55-1795
1. Strong, Moses McCure, 1810-1894. I. Title.

Strossmayer, Josip Juraj, Bp., 1815-1905.

SIVRIC, Ivo. 262'.5'20924 B
Bishop J. G. Strossmayer; new light on Vatican I. Chicago, Franciscan Herald Press [1974, i.e.1975] p. [BX4705.S845S56] 73-22014 ISBN 0-8199-0491-0 8.95
1. Strossmayer, Josip Juraj, Bp., 1815-1905. 2. Vatican Council, 1869-1870. BIP

Strother, David Hunter, 1816-188.

EBY, Cecil D., Jr. 927.4
'Porte Crayon': the life of David Hunter Strother. Chapel Hill, University of North Carolina Press [c.1960]Cxi, 258p. illus., ports. 'Published and unpublished writings of David Hunter Strother'; p.[227]-231. 'Journals, correspondence and Sketchbook of David Hunter Strother': p.[232]-238. Bibliography: p.[239]-251. 60-16921 5.00
1. Strother, David Hunter, 1816-188. I. Title.

EBY, Cecil D. 741'.092'4 B
"Porte Crayon": the life of David Hunter Strother, by Cecil D. Eby, Jr. Westport, Conn., Greenwood Press [1973] xi, 258 p. illus. 22 cm. Reprint of the 1960 ed. Bibliography: p. [239]-251. [E175.5.S87E2 1973] 72-11235 ISBN 0-8371-6638-1 12.00
1. Strother, David Hunter, 1816-1888. I. Title.

Stroud, Robert.

BIRDMAN of Alcatraz; v. 12
the story of Robert Stroud. With a special note to the second Signet ed. [New York] The New American Library [1962] 224 p. 19 cm. (A Signet book) 64-26980
1. Stroud, Robert. 2. U.S. Penitentiary, Alcatraz Island, Calif.

GADDIS, Thomas E. 923.4173
Birdman of Alcatraz; the story of Robert Stroud. New York, Random House [1955] 334 p. 21 cm. [HV9474.A4G3] 55-8147
1. Stroud, Robert. 2. U.S. Penitentiary, Alcatraz Island, Calif. I. Title.

GADDIS, Thomas E. 923.4173
Birdman of Alcatraz; the story of Robert Stroud. With a special note to the Signal ed. [New York] New Amer. Lib. [c.1955-1962] 224p. 17cm. (Signet bk., P2092) .60 pap.,
1. Stroud, Robert. 2. U. S. Penitentiary, Alcatraz Island, Calif. I. Title.

GADDIS, Thomas E v. 12
Birdman of Alcatraz; the story of Robert Stroud. With a special note to the second Signet ed. [New York] The New American Library [1962] 224 p. 19 cm. (A Signet book) 64-26980
1. Stroud, Robert. 2. U.S. Penitentiary, Alcatraz Island, Calif. I. Title.

Structural steel workers—United States—Personal narratives.

CHERRY, Mike, 331.7'69'3710924 B
1934-
On high steel; the education of an ironworker. New York, Ballantine Books [1975, c1974] xv, 235 p. 18 cm. [HD8039.B82U6 1975] 74-77935 ISBN 0-345-24580-6 1.50 (pbk.)
1. Structural steel workers—United States—Personal narratives. I. Title. BIP

Strunk, William Oliver, 1901-

POWERS, Harold, comp. 780.9
Studies in music history; essays for Oliver Strunk. Princeton, N.J., Princeton University Press, 1968. x, 527 p. facsims., music, ports. 25 cm. "Bibliography of the writings of Oliver Strunk": p. 511-517. [ML3797.1.P69S9] 67-21028 17.50
1. Strunk, William Oliver, 1901- 2. Musicology—Addresses, essays, lectures. I. Strunk, William Oliver, 1901- II. Title. BIP

Struss, Karl, 1886-

STRUSS, Karl, 1886- 779'.092'4
Karl Struss, man with a camera : the artist-photographer in New York and Hollywood ... Cranbrook Academy of Art/Museum ... [et al.] / [exhibition organized, and catalogue prepared, researched, written, and edited by Susan and John Harvith]. Bloomfield Hills, Mich. : The Museum, c1976. viii, 104 p. : ill. ; 26 cm. Bibliography: p. 103-104. [TR647.S88A44] 76-1404
1. Struss, Karl, 1886- 2. Photography, Artistic—Exhibitions. 3. Cinematographers—Correspondence, reminiscences, etc. I. Harvith, Susan. II. Harvith, John. III. Cranbrook Academy of Art, Bloomfield Hills, Mich. Museum. IV. Title.

Stuart Brent: Books and Records, Chicago.

BRENT, Stuart. 920.4
The Seven Stairs. Boston, Houghton Mifflin, 1962. 205p. 21cm. Autobiographical. [Z473.B795A3] 62-8119
1. Stuart Brent: Books and Records, Chicago. I. Title. BIP

BRENT, Stuart. 920.4
The seven stairs. Chicago, O'hara, [1973, c1962] xii, 222 p. 21 cm. Name originally: Stuart Brodsky. [Z473.B795A3] 73-4748 3.50 (pbk.)
1. Stuart Brent: Books and Records, Chicago. I. Title.

Stuart, Daniel, 1766-1846.

LETTERS from the Lake 821'.7'09 B
poets, Samuel Taylor Coleridge, William Wordsworth, Robert Southey to Daniel Stuart, editor of the Morning post and the Courier, 1800-1838. [Folcroft, Pa.] Folcroft Library Editions, 1974. p. cm. Reprint of the 1889 ed. printed by West, Newman, London. [PR1346.L4 1974] 74-6116 ISBN 0-8414-7749-3 (lib. bdg.)
1. Stuart, Daniel, 1766-1846. 2. Lake poets—Correspondence, reminiscences, etc. I. Coleridge, Samuel Taylor, 1772-1834. II. Wordsworth, William, 1770-1850. III. Southey, Robert, 1774-1843. IV. Stuart, Daniel, 1766-1846. BIP

Stuart, Elbridge Amos, 1856-1944.

MARSHALL, James 338.7'63'70924 B
Leslie, 1891-
Elbridge A. Stuart, founder of Carnation Company [by] James Marshall. Los Angeles, Carnation Co. [1970] viii, 257 p. illus., ports. 27 cm. [HD9282.U6C3 1970] 71-270807
1. Stuart, Elbridge Amos, 1856-1944. 2. Carnation Company.

Stuart, Eleanor (Calvert) Custis, d. 1811.

TORBERT, Alice (Coyle) 920.7
Eleanor Calvert and her circle. New York, William-Frederick Press, 1950. 150 p. geneal. table. 23 cm. "Published under the auspices of the National Society of the Colonial Dames of America in the District of Columbia." Bibliography: p. 129-130. [F230.S88T6] 50-4270
1. Stuart, Eleanor (Calvert) Custis, d. 1811. 2. Washington family. I. Title.

Stuart family (David Stewart, 1746-1817)

HEISER, Ellinor (Stewart) 920.7
Days gone by. Baltimore, 1953. 98p. illus. 24cm. [CT275.H52A3 1953] 54-16672
1. Stuart family (David Stewart, 1746-1817) I. Title.

HEISER, Ellinor (Stewart) 920.7
Days gone by. Baltimore, 1953. 98p. illus. 24cm. [CT275.H52A3 1953] 54-16672
1. Stuart family (David Stewart, 1746-1817) I. Title.

Stuart, Francis, 1902-

NATTERSTAD, J. H., 823'.9'12 B
1938-
Francis Stuart [by] J. H. Natterstad. Lewisburg [Pa.] Bucknell University Press [1974] 88 p. 21 cm. (The Irish writers series) Bibliography: p. 86-88. [PR6037.T875Z8 1974] 70-168817 ISBN 0-8387-7895-X 4.50
1. Stuart, Francis, 1902-
Pbk. 1.95; ISBN 0-8387-7979-4. BIP

Stuart, Gilbert, 1755-1828.

FLEXNER, James Thomas, 927.5
1908-
Gilbert Stuart; a great life in brief. [1st ed.] New York, Knopf, 1955. 197p. 23cm. (Great lives in brief; a new series of biographies) [ND237.S8F5] [ND237.S8F5] 759.13 55-6218 55-6218
1. Stuart, Gilbert, 1755-1828. I. Title.

MASON, George Champlin, 759.13 B
1820-1894.
The life and works of Gilbert Stuart. With selections from Stuart's portraits reproduced on steel and by photogravure. New York, B. Franklin Reprints [1974] x, 286 p. ports. 26 cm. (Burt Franklin research & source works series. Art history & reference series, 48) Reprint of the 1879 ed. published by Scribner, New York. [ND1329.S7M37 1974] 72-82298 ISBN 0-8337-5236-7
1. Stuart, Gilbert, 1755-1828. 2. Portraits—Catalogs. I. Title.

MOUNT, Charles Merrill. 927.5
Gilbert Stuart, a biography. [1st ed.] New York, W. W. Norton [1964] 384 p. illus., ports. 25 cm. "The works of Gilbert Stuart": p. [357]-379. Bibliographical references included in "Notes" (p. [333]-356) [ND237.S8M65] 63-15881
1. Stuart, Gilbert, 1755-1828.

Stuart, Granville, 1834-1918.

STUART, 978.6'02'0924 B
Granville, 1834-1918.
Pioneering in Montana : the making of a state, 1864-1887 / by Granville Stuart ; edited by Paul C. Phillips. Lincoln : University of Nebraska Press, 1977, c1925. 265 p. ; 21 cm. Reprint of v. 2 of Forty years on the frontier published by A. H. Clark, Cleveland, which was issued as no. 2 of Early western journals. Includes index. [F731.S912 1977b] 77-7651 ISBN 0-8032-0933-9 : 12.50 pbk. : 3.50
1. Stuart, Granville, 1834-1918. 2. Frontier and pioneer life—Montana. 3. Ranch life—Montana. 4. Indians of North America—Montana. 5. Pioneers—Montana—Biography. 6. Ranchers—Montana—Biography. 7. Montana—Biography. I. Title. II. Series: Early western journals ; no. 2. BIP

STUART, Granville, 978'.02'0924 B
1834-1918.
Prospecting for gold from Dogtown to Virginia City, 1852-1864 / by Granville Stuart ; edited by Paul C. Phillips. Lincoln : University of Nebraska Press, [1977] c1925. 272 p. : ill. ; 21 cm. Reprint of v. 1 of Forty years on the frontier ... published by A. H. Clark Co., Cleveland, which was issued as no. 2 of Early western journals. [F731.S912 1977] 77-7244 ISBN 0-8032-0932-0 : 12.50 pbk. : 3.50
1. Stuart, Granville, 1834-1918. 2. Montana—Gold discoveries. 3. Overland journeys to the Pacific. 4. Pioneers—Montana—Biography. I. Title. II. Series: Early western journals ; no. 2.

Stuart, James Ewell Brown, 1833-1864.

DAVIS, Burke. 923.573
Jeb Stuart, the last cavalier. With maps by Rafael D. Palacios. New York, Rinehart [1957] 462 p. illus., ports., maps. 24 cm. Bibliographical references included in "Notes" (p. 422-439) Bibliography: p. 443-448. [E467.1.S9D3] 57-9912
1. Stuart, James Ewell Brown, 1833-1864.

Stuart, Jesse, 1907-

BLAIR, Everetta Love. 818'.5'2'09
Jesse Stuart; his life and works. [1st ed.] Columbia, University of South Carolina Press, 1967. xxiv, 288 p. port. 23 cm.

Based on the author's thesis, University of South Carolina. Bibliography: p. 267-279. [PS3537.T92516Z58] 67-25915
1. Stuart, Jesse, 1907-

FOSTER, Ruel Elton, 1916- 818'.5'209
Jesse Stuart, by Ruel E. Foster. New York, Twayne Publishers [1968] 168 p. 21 cm. (Twayne's United States authors series, 140) Bibliography: P. 160-161. [PS3537.T92516Z7] 68-24298
1. Stuart, Jesse, 1907- BIP

PENNINGTON, Lee. 813'.5'2
The dark hills of Jesse Stuart; a consideration of symbolism and vision in the novels of Jesse Stuart. Cincinnati, Harvest Press [1967] iv, 166 p. illus. 23 cm. "Author's edition, limited to 500 copies." "Chronological list of Jesse Stuart's published books": p. 161-163. Bibliography: p. 165-166. Bibliographical references included in "Footnotes" (p. 155-159) [PS3537.T92516Z8] 67-31659
1. Stuart, Jesse, 1907-

STUART, Jesse, 1907- 818'.5'209 B
Beyond dark hills, a personal story. With six woodcuts by Ishmael. New York, McGraw-Hill [1972, c1938] xvi, 328 p. illus. 21 cm. [PS3537.T92516Z52 1972] 74-38932 ISBN 0-07-062204-3
I. Title.

STUART, Jesse, 1907- 371.1'00924 B
To teach, to love. New York, World Pub. Co. [1970] 317 p. 22 cm. [LA2311.S76] 79-88596 5.95
I. Title. BIP

STUART, Jesse, 1907- 371.1'00924 [B]
To teach, to love. Baltimore, Penguin Books [1973 c.1970] 315 p. 18 cm. [LA2311.S76] ISBN 0-14-003763-2 1.50 (pbk)
I. Title.
L.C. number for original ed.: 79-88596.

Stuart, Jesse, 1907——Biography—Teaching career.

STUART, Jesse, 1907- 928.1
The thread that runs so true. New York, Scribner [1958] 293 p. 22 cm. Autobiography. [PS3537.T92516Z5 1958] 58-12517
1. Stuart, Jesse, 1907- —Biography—Teaching career. I. Title.

STUART, Jesse, 1907- 371.1'0092'4 B
The thread that runs so true / Jesse Stuart ; with essays by Thomas D. Clark and Wilma Dykeman ; [illustrated by Barbara McCord]. Special ed. commemorating the centennial of Eastern Kentucky University. Lexington : University Press of Kentucky, [1974] xxxi, 313 p. : ill. ; 24 cm. Autobiography. [PS3537.T92516Z5 1974] 74-7883 ISBN 0-8131-1320-2 : 8.50
1. Stuart, Jesse, 1907—Biography—Teaching career. I. Title.

Stuart, Jesse, 1907- —Biography.

STUART, Jesse, 1907- 818'.5'209 B
The kingdom within : a spiritual autobiography / by Jesse Stuart. New York : McGraw-Hill, c1979. 168 p., [1] leaf of plates : fronts. ; 21 cm. [PS3537.T92516Z523] 78-26481 ISBN 0-07-062224-8 : 7.95
1. Stuart, Jesse, 1907- —Biography. 2. Authors, American—20th century—Biography. I. Title. BIP

Stuart, Jesse, 1907- —Homes and haunts—Kentucky.

STUART, Jesse, 1907- 818'.5'209 B
My world / Jesse Stuart. Lexington : University Press of Kentucky, c1975. 95 p. : map (on lining paper) ; 22 cm. (The Kentucky bicentennial bookshelf) [PS3537.T92516Z524] 75-3552 ISBN 0-8131-0211-1 : 3.95
1. Stuart, Jesse, 1907- —Homes and haunts—Kentucky. 2. Kentucky—Description and travel. I. Title. II. Series. BIP

Stubbs, Thomas, 1808-1877.

STUBBS, Thomas, 1808-1877. 968.04'092'4 B
The Reminiscences of Thomas Stubbs, including Men I have known / edited by W. A. Maxwell and R. T. McGeogh. Cape Town : Balkema (A. A.) ; for Rhodes University, Grahamstown, 1978. xvi, 302 p. : ill., fold. map ; 24 cm. (The Graham's Town series ; 4) Includes index. Bibliography: p. 226-228. [CT1929.S78A37 1978] 79-302307 ISBN 0-86961-092-9 : 18.75
1. Stubbs, Thomas, 1808-1877. 2. South Africa—Biography. I. Maxwell, Winifred A. II. McGeogh, R. T. III. Stubbs, Thomas, 1808-1877. Men I have known. 1978. IV. Title. V. Series.
Distributed by Merrimack Book Service, Inc, Salem NH

Stuck, Hudson, 1863-1920—Juvenile literature.

HERRON, Edward Albert, 1912- 922.373
Conqueror of Mount McKinley: Hudson Stuck. New York, J. Messner [1964] 191 p. 22 cm. Bibliography: p. 181. [F909.S93H4] 64-11818
1. Stuck, Hudson, 1863-1920—Juvenile literature. I. Title.

Student, Kurt.

FARRAR-HOCKLEY, Anthony H., 1924- 940.54'13'43 B
Student [by] Anthony Farrar-Hockley. [New York, Ballantine Books, 1973] 158, [2] p. illus. 21 cm. (Ballantine's illustrated history of the violent century. War leader book no. 15) Bibliography: p. [160] [UG635.G3S853] 73-154519 ISBN 0-345-02699-3 1.00 (pbk.)
1. Student, Kurt.

Student Nonviolent Coordinating Committee.

SELLERS, Cleveland, 1944- 322.4'4'0924 B
The river of no return; the autobiography of a Black militant and the life and death of SNCC, by Cleveland Sellers, with Robert Terrell. New York, Morrow, 1973. 279 p. 22 cm. [E185.97.S44A37] 72-108 7.95
1. Student Nonviolent Coordinating Committee. I. Terrell, Robert L. II. Title.

Students.

TRAHEY, Jane. 818.54
Life with Mother Superior. New York, Farrar, Straus and Cudahy [1962] 210 p. illus. 21 cm. Autobiographical. [LC485.T7] 62-16278
1. Students. I. Title. BIP

Stuhldreher, Harry Augustus.

STUHLDREHER, Mary A. 927.9633
Many a Saturday afternoon. New York, McKay [c.1964] 233p. 22cm. 64-17346 4.50
1. Stuhldreher, Harry Augustus. 2. Football coaching. I. Title.

Stump Family.

STUMP, Thurman, 1913- 929'.2'0973
Michael Stump, Sr. of Virginia, 1709-1768: a treatise on the origin and ancestry with surname armouals. Michael Stump, Senior of Virginia seventeen o nine-seventeen sixty eight Parsons, W.Va., McClain Print Co., 1975 xi, 239 p. ill., coats of arms; 23 cm. Includes index. Bibliography: p. 221-224. [CS71.59337] 73-93200 ISBN 0-87012-191-X 30.00
1. Stump Family. I. Title.

Stunt flying.

DWIGGINS, Don. 797.5'4'0922
The barnstormers; flying daredevils of the roaring twenties. New York, Grosset & Dunlap [1968] 151 p. illus., facsims., ports. 24 cm. (Adventures in flight) Bibliography: p. [145] [TL711.S8D9] 68-29963 4.50
1. Stunt flying. I. Title.

Stunt men—Correspondence, reminiscences, etc.

FROBOESS, Harry. 927.92
The reminiscing champ; a world-famous stunt man tells his story. [1st ed.] New York, Pageant Press [1953] 141p. illus. 21cm. [PN1995.F75] 53-8801
1. Stunt men—Correspondence, reminiscences, etc. I. Title.

Stunt men and women—United States—Biography—Juvenile literature.

WILSON, Lionel. 791.43'028'0922
The first stunt stars of Hollywood / by Lionel Wilson. New York : C.P.I. ; Morristown, N.J. : distributor, Silver Burdett Co., c1978. 47 p. : ill. ; 24 cm. Describes the careers and daring exploits of some of the first stunt men and women in the movies. [PN1995.9.S7W48] 920 B 78-14465 ISBN 0-89547-048-9 : 5.58
1. Stunt men and women—United States—Biography—Juvenile literature. I. Title.
Distributed by Silver Burdell, Morristown, NJ 07960 BIP

Sturges, Preston, 1898-1959.

*URSINI, James 791.43'028'0924 [B]
The fabulous life & times of Preston Sturges; an American dreamer. New York, Curtis Books [1973] 240 p. 18 cm. (The Curtis Film Series) Bibliography: p. 211-213. [PN2287] 1.50 (pbk)
1. Sturges, Preston, 1898-1959. I. Title.

Sturgis family.

PRUETT, Dorothy Sturgis, 1916- 929'.2'0973
Cousins by the dozens : Sturgis, Thrasher, Carlton, Mitchell, Branch : supplement / compiled by Dorothy Sturgis Pruett. Original ed. Macon, Ga. : Pruett, c1978- v. : ill. ; 23 cm. Includes index. [CS71.S935 1978] 78-106708 price unreported
1. Sturgis family. 2. Thrasher family. 3. Carlton family. I. Title.

Sturgis, Margie.

STURGIS, Margie. 364.6'2'0924 B
Let the record show : memoirs of a parole board member / Margie Sturgis. 1st ed. Hicksville, N.Y. : Exposition Press, c1978. 109 p. ; 21 cm. [HV9305.13S85] 78-302322 ISBN 0-682-48991-3 : 5.50
1. Sturgis, Margie. 2. Correctional personnel—Illinois—Biography. 3. Parole—Illinois. I. Title. BIP

Sturt, Charles, 1795-1869.

CUMPSTON, John Howard Lidgett, 1880- 923.594
Charles Sturt; his life and journeys of exploration. Melbourne, Georgian House [1951] 195 p. illus. 22 cm. [DU114.S8C8] 52-26271
1. Sturt, Charles, 1795-1869. I. Title.

Stutchbury, Oliver Piers.

STUTCHBURY, Oliver Piers. 941.085'092'4 B
Too much government? : a political Aeneid / [by] Oliver Stutchbury. Ipswich : Boydell Press, 1977. 128 p. ; 23 cm. [HC256.6.S78] 77-376837 £3.50
1. Stutchbury, Oliver Piers. 2. Great Britain—Economic policy—1945- 3. Politicians—Great Britain—Biography. I. Title.

Stuyvesant, Peter, 1592-1672.

CROUSE, Anna Erskine. 923.273
Peter Stuyvesant of old New York, by Anna & Russel Crouse; illustrated by Jo Spier. New York, Random House [1954] 184 p. illus. 22 cm. (Landmark books [43]) [F122.1.S922] 54-5161
1. Stuyvesant, Peter, 1592-1672. I. Crouse, Russel, 1893- joint author.

EERDMANS, Martha. 923.273
Pieter Stuyvesant, an historical documentation; compiled upon request of the Provincial Government of Friesland in commemoration of the Pieter Stuyvesant Festival at Wolvega, Friesland, July 12-16, 1955. Grand Rapids, Eerdmans, 1957. 78 p. illus., ports., facsims. 25 cm. Bibliography: 75-78. [F122.1.S923] 57-13734
1. Stuyvesant, Peter, 1592-1672.

KESSLER, Henry Howard, 1896- 923.273
Peter Stuyvesant and his New York, by Henry H. Kessler and Eugene Rachlis. New York, Random House [1959] 309p. illus. 22cm. Includes bibliography. [F128.4.S8K4] 59-5711
1. Stuyvesant, Peter, 1592-1672. 2. New York (City)—Hist.—Colonial period. I. Rachlis, Eugene, joint author. II. Title.

KESSLER, Henry Howard, 1896- 923.273
Peter Stuyvesant and his New York, by Henry H. Kessler and Eugene Rachlis. New York, Random House [1959] 309p. illus. 22cm. Includes bibliography. [F128.4.S8K4] 59-5711
1. Stuyvesant, Peter, 1592-1672. 2. New York (City)—Hist.—Colonial period. I. Rachlis, Eugene, joint author. II. Title.

Stuyvesant, Peter, 1592-1672—Juvenile literature.

DE LEEUW, Adele Louise, 1899- 974.7'02'0924 B
A colony leader: Peter Stuyvesant. Illustrated by Vincent Colabella. Champaign, Ill., Garrard Pub. Co. [1970] 64 p. col. illus., col. map., port. 24 cm. A biography showing the importance of Peter Stuyvesant's leadership to the growth of New Amsterdam. [F122.1.S9245] 92 73-90817 2.39
1. Stuyvesant, Peter, 1592-1672—Juvenile literature. I. Colabella, Vincent, illus. II. Title.

Stylianou, Demetrios, 1904-

OLIVER, Bernard J 371.920924
Demetrios discovered America; life and work of Dr. Demetrios Stylianou, a pioneer in care and treatment of the mentally retarded, by Bernard J. Oliver, Jr. Foreword by Edmund G. Brown. [1st ed.] Santa Ana, Calif., Pioneer Press, 1965. 164 p. 22 cm. [HV894.O4] 65-28311
1. Stylianou, Demetrios, 1904- 2. Mentally handicapped children — Care and treatment. I. Title.

Styne, Jule, 1905-

TAYLOR, Theodore, 1922- 784'.092'4 B
Jule : the story of composer Jule Styne / Theodore Taylor. 1st ed. New York : Random House, c1979. 293 p., [4] leaves of plates : ill. ; 24 cm. [ML410.S9426T4] 77-90294 ISBN 0-394-41296-6 : 10.95
1. Styne, Jule, 1905- 2. Composers—United States—Biography. I. Title. BIP

Su. Ch o. 498-546.

CHOU SHU. ENGLISH. SELECTIONS. 913.31
Biography of Su Ch'o [Chou shu, chuan 23] Translated and annotated by Chauncey S. Goodrich. Berkeley, University of California Press, 1953. 116p. 24cm. hinese dynastic histories translations, no. 3) (Institute of East Asiatic Studies, University of California. Based on the editor's thesis (M. A.)--University of California. The Chou shu was compliled under the direction of Ling-hu Te-fen. Bibliography: p. 112-116. [DS741.C3 no. 3] A53
1. Su. Ch o. 498-546. I. Goodrich, Chauncey Shafter, ed. and tr. II. Ling-hu,

Te-fen, 583-666. III. Title. IV. Series: California. University. Institute of East Asiatic Studies. Chinese dyanstic histories translations, no. 3

Su, Hsuan-ying, 1884-1918.

LIU, Wu-chi, 1907- 895.1'1'4 B
Su Man-shu. New York, Twayne [1972] 173 p. geneal. table. 21 cm. (Twayne's world authors series, TWAS 191: China) Bibliography: p. 153-156. [PL2724.U2Z7] 70-120494
1. Su, Hsuan-ying, 1884-1918.

Su, Shih, 1036-1101.

LIN, Yutang, 1895- 895.1'1'4 B
The gay genius; the life and times of Su Tungpo. Westport, Conn., Greenwood Press [1971, c1947] xi, 427 p. illus., facsim., map, ports. 23 cm. Bibliography: p. 399-413. [PL2685.Z5L48 1971] 71-112327 ISBN 0-8371-4715-8
1. Su, Shih, 1036-1101. I. Title. **BIP**

Subconsciousness.

SHALVEY, Thomas, 1937- 301.2'092'4
Claude Levi-Strauss : social psychotherapy and the collective unconscious / Thomas Shalvey. Amherst : University of Massachusetts Press, 1979. xii, 180 p. ; ill. ; 24 cm. Includes index. Bibliography: p. [172]-177. [GN21.L4S5] 78-19695 ISBN 0-87023-260-6 lib. bdg. : 12.50
1. Subconsciousness. **BIP**

Sublette, Andrew Whitley, 1808-1853.

NUNIS, Doyce Blackman. 923.973
Andrew Sublette, Rocky Mountain prince, 1808-1853. Los Angeles, Dawson's Book Shop, 1960. 123p. illus., port. 23cm. '330 copies printed.' Bibliographical footnotes. [F592.S85N8] 60-2531
1. Sublette, Andrew Whitley, 1808-1853. 2. Frontier and pioneer life—The West. 3. Sublette family. I. Title.

Sublette, William Lewis, 1799?-1845.

SUNDER, John Edward. 923.973
Bill Sublette, mountain man. [1st ed.] Norman, University of Oklahoma Press [1959] 279 p. illus. 24 cm. Includes bibliography. [F592.S86S8] 59-7492
1. Sublette, William Lewis, 1799?-1845. **BIP**

Subrahmanya Bharati, C., 1882-1921.

ROY, Kuldip K. 894'.811'15
Subramanya Bharati, by Kuldip K. Roy. New York, Twayne Publishers [1974] p. cm. (Twayne's world authors series, TWAS 325) Bibliography: p. [PL4758.9.S8437Z85] 74-6411 ISBN 0-8057-2153-3 7.95
1. Subrahmanya Bharati, C., 1882-1921

Success.

BROUSCH, John J., 1912- 158.1
John J. Brousch, conqueror of adversity; an autobiography. Minneapolis, Dension [1966] 307p. 23cm. (Men of achievement ser.) [CT275.B760A3] 66-23730 3.95
1. Success. 2. Labor and laboring classes—U. S.—1914- I. Title.

PONDER, Catherine. 222'.11'0922 B
The millionaires of Genesis, their prosperity secrets for you! / Catherine Ponder. Marina del Rey, Ca. : DeVorss, c1976. 178 p. ; 21 cm. (Her The Millionaires of the Bible) [BJ1611.2.P626] 76-19843 ISBN 0-87516-215-0 pbk. : 3.95
1. Bible. O.T.—Biography. 2. Success. 3. Patriarchs (Bible)—Biography. I. Title.

Success—Biography.

FIRESTONE, Ross. 650'.1'0922
The success trip / [by] Ross Firestone. Chicago : Playboy Press, 1977,c1976. 298p. ; 18 cm. Includes index. [HF5386.F4154] pbk. : 1.75
1. Success-Biography. I. Title.

L.C. card no. for 1976 hardcover ed.:76-15224.

FIRESTONE, Ross. 650'.1'0922 B
The success trip—how they made it, how they feel about it / by Ross Firestone. 1st ed. Chicago : Playboy Press, c1976. xiii, 298 p. ; 25 cm. Includes index. [HF5386.F4154] 76-15224 ISBN 0-87223-451-7 : 10.95
1. Success—Biography. I. Title.

Suckow, Ruth, 1892-1960.

KISSANE, Leedice McAnelly. 813'.5'2
Ruth Suckow. New York, Twayne Publishers [1969] 175 p. 22 cm. (Twayne's United States authors series, TUSAS 142) Bibliography: p. 166-173. [PS3537.U34Z8] 68-24300
1. Suckow, Ruth, 1892-1960. **BIP**

Sudan—Biog.

HILL, Richard Leslie. 920.0624
A biographical dictionary of the Sudan [by] Richard Hill 2nd ed. London, Cass, 1967, Oxford, Clarendon Pr., 1951. 409p. 23cm. Previous ed. pub. as A biographical dictionary of the Anglo-Egyptian Sudan. [DT108.05.A2H5 1967] 67-94080 14.50
1. Sudan—Biog. I. Title.
Distributed by Barnes & Noble, New York.

Sudan, Egyptian—Biog.

HILL, Richard Leslie. 920.0624
A biographical dictionary of the Anglo-Egyptian Sudan. Oxford, Clarendon Press, 1951. xvi, 391 p. 23 cm. [DT108.05.A2H5] 52-2206
1. Sudan, Egyptian—Biog. I. Title.

Sudan—History—1862-1899.

GORDON, Charles George, 1833-1885. 962.4'03'0924 B
Colonel Gordon in Central Africa, 1874-1879. With a portrait and map of the country, prepared under Colonel Gordon's supervision from original letters and documents. Edited by George Birkbeck Hill. 4th ed. London, T. De La Rue, 1885. New York, Kraus Reprint Co., 1969. xvi, 456 p. facsim., map, ports. 24 cm. [DT108.2.G66 1969] 72-99599
1. Sudan—History—1862-1899. I. Hill, George Birkbeck Norman, 1835-1903, ed. II. Title. **BIP**

Sudek, Josef, 1896-1976.

SUDEK, Josef, 1896-1976. 770'.92'4 B
Sudek / Sonja Bullaty. 1st ed. New York : C. N. Potter : distributed by Crown Publishers, c1978. 189 p. : chiefly ill. ; 29 cm. Bibliography: p. 188-189. [TR140.S737A34 1978] 78-17573 ISBN 0-517-53865-2 : 45.00
1. Sudek, Josef, 1896-1976. 2. Photography, Artistic. 3. Photographers—Czechoslovakia—Prague—Biography. I Bullaty, Sonja.

Suenens, Leon Joseph, Cardinal, 1904-

HAMILTON, Elizabeth, 1906- 262'.135'0924 B
Suenens : a portrait / Elizabeth Hamilton. 1st ed. in the U.S. of America. Garden City, N.Y. : Doubleday, 1975. 283 p. ; 22 cm. Includes index. [BX4705.S8684H35 1975] 74-32571 ISBN 0-385-09907-X : 7.95
1. Suenens, Leon Joseph, Cardinal, 1904-

Suffolk, Katharine (Willoughby) Brandon, duchess of, 1519-1580.

READ, Evelyn 920.7
My Lady Suffolk; a portrait of Catherine Willoughby, duchess of Suffolk. New York, Knopf, 1963[c.1962] 204p. illus. 22cm. Orig. pub. in England as Catherine, duchess of Suffolk. Bibl. 63-11109 5.00
1. Suffolk, Katharine (Willoughby) Brandon, duchess of, 1519-1580. 2. Gt. Brit.—Hist.—Tudors—1485-1603 I. Title.

Sufism—Biography.

IBN al-'Arabi, 1165-1240. 297'.4
Sufis of Andalusia; the Ruh al-quds and al-Durrah al-fakhirah of Ibn 'Arabi. Translated with introd. and notes by R. W. J. Austin. With a foreword by Martin Lings. Berkeley, University of California Press [1972, c1971] 173 p. illus. 23 cm. Translation of the biographical portion of [Ruh al-Quds (romanized form)] and of extracts from [al-Durrah al-fakhirah (romanized form)]. Bibliography: p. 161-162. [BP189.4.I13 1972] 77-165230 ISBN 0-520-01999-7 8.75
1. Sufism—Biography. 2. Muslims in Spain—Biography. I. Ibn al-'Arabi, 1165-1240. al-Durrah al-fakhirah. English. Selections. 1972. II. Title.

Suger, Abbot of Saint Denis, 1081-1151.

ROCKWELL, Anne F. 282'.0924 B
Glass, stones & crown; the Abbe Suger and the building of St. Denis [by] Anne Rockwell. [1st ed.] New York, Atheneum, 1968. 80 p. illus. 25 cm. The life and accomplishments of the religious leader who used his power to unite nobles and peasants under the King of the Franks, and helped begin the powerful French empire of the twelfth century. His rebuilding of St. Denis established the Gothic design in church architecture. [DC89.7.S8R6] 92 AC 68
1. Suger, Abbot of Saint Denis, 1081-1151. 2. Saint-Denis, France (Benedictine abbey) I. Title.

Suger, Abbot of Saint Denis, 1081-1151—Juvenile literature.

ROCKWELL, Anne F. 271'.1'0924' B
Glass, stones & crown; the Abbe Suger and the building of St. Denis [by] Anne Rockwell. [1st ed.] New York, Atheneum, 1968. 80 p. illus. 25 cm. [DC89.7.S8R6] 68-12241
1. Suger, Abbot of Saint Denis, 1081-1151—Juvenile literature. 2. Saint-Denis, France (Benedictine abbey)—Juvenile literature. I. Title.

Suhrie, Ambrose Leo,

SUHRIE, Ambrose Leo, 1876- 923.773
Teacher of teachers. Rindge, N. H., R. R. Smith, 1955. 418 p. illus. 23 cm. Autobiography. [LB875.S885A3] 55-9050
I. Title.

Suhaili (Ketch)

KNOX-JOHNSTON, Robin. 910.4'5
A world of my own; the single-handed, non-stop circumnavigation of the world in Suhaili. New York, Morrow, 1970 [c1969] xii, 240 p. illus., chart, facsims., maps. 22 cm. Part of the illustrative matter is colored. [G420.K6] 70-93845 6.95
1. Suhaili (Ketch) 2. Voyages around the world—1951- I. Title.

Suicide.

PORTWOOD, Doris. 364.1'522
Common-sense suicide : the final right / Doris Portwood. New York : Dodd, Mead, c1978. 142 p. ; 22 cm. Bibliography: p. 139-142. [HV6545.P66] 78-959 ISBN 0-8361-1849-9 : pbk. : 4.95
1. Suicide. 2. Aged. I. Title.

Sukarno, Pres. Indonesia, 1901-1970.

ADAMS, Cindy (Heller) 991'.03'0924
My friend the dictator, by Cindy Adams. Indianapolis, Bobbs-Merrill [1967] vi, 312 p. illus., ports. 22 cm. [DS644.1.S8A65] 67-27230
1. Sukarno, Pres. Indonesia, 1901-1970. I. Title.

DAHM, Bernhard. 991'.03'0924 B
Sukarno and the struggle for Indonesian independence. Translated from the German by Mary F. Somers Heidhues. Ithaca, [N.Y.] Cornell University Press [1969] xvii, 374 p. maps. 24 cm. "Revised and updated edition of Sukarnos Kampf um Indonesiens Unabhangigkeit." Bibliography: p. 354-370. [DS644.1.S8D283] 69-18356 15.00
1. Sukarno, Pres. Indonesia, 1901- I. Title. **BIP**

LEGGE, John David. 959.8'03'0924 B
Sukarno; a political biography [by] J. D. Legge. New York, Praeger [1972] ix, 431 p. 23 cm. Includes bibliographical references. [DS644.1.S8L4] 77-181868 10.95
1. Sukarno, Pres. Indonesia, 1901-1970. 2. Indonesia—Politics and government—20th century.

*PENDERS, C. L. M. 923.1598
The life and times of Sukarno. [by] C. L. M. Penders. Teaneck, N.J., Fairleigh Dickinson Univ. Press 1974 xi, 224 p. illus. 24 cm. Bibliography: p. 215-218. [DS644.S8] 74-369 ISBN 0-8386-1546-5 12.50
1. Sukarno-President of Indonesia, 1901-. I. Title. **BIP**

SUKARNO, Pres. Indonesia, 1901- 354.91030924
Sukarno; an autobiography, as told to Cindy Adams. Indianapolis, Bobbs [c.1965] x, 324p. ports. 24cm. [DS644.1.S8A3] 65-26511 6.00
1. Adams, Cindy (Heller) II. Title.

SUKARNO, Pres. Indonesia, 1901-1970. 354.91030924 B
Sukarno; an autobiography, as told to Cindy Adams. Indianapolis, Bobbs-Merrill [1965] x, 324 p. ports. 24 cm. [DS644.1.S8A3] 65-26511
I. Adams, Cindy Heller.

Suliman I, the Magnificent, Sultan of the Turks, 1494-1566.

LAMB, Harold, 1892-1962. 923.1496
Suleiman, the Magnificent, Sultan of the East. [1st ed.] Garden City, N. Y., Doubleday, 1951. ix, 370 p. front. 22 cm. Bibliographical references included in "Acknowledgment": p. 350-355. [DR506.L3] 51-9932
1. Suliman I, the Magnificent, Sultan of the Turks, 1494-1566.

Sulla, Lucius Cornelius.

BAKER, George Philip, 1879-1951. 937'.05'0924 B
Sulla the fortunate: the great dictator; being an essay on politics in the form of a historical biography. New York, Barnes & Noble [1967] 320 p. illus., geneal. tables, maps. 23 cm. First published 1927. [DG256.7.B3 1967] 67-8849

*1. Sulla, Lucius Cornelius. 2. Rome—History—Republic, 265-30 B.C. I. Title.*BIP

Sullivan, Andrew.

SULLIVAN, Andrew. 917.62'21 B
Yesterdays, by Sullivan A. <Andrew Sullivan> Brooklyn, N.Y., T. Gaus' Sons [1974] x, 118 p. 24 cm. Autobiographical. [CT275.S924A37] 74-75847
1. Sullivan, Andrew. I. Title.

Sullivan, Arthur Seymour, Sir, 1842-1900.

FINDON, Benjamin William, 1859-1943. 780'.92'4 B
Sir Arthur Sullivan, his life and music / by B. W. Findon. New York : AMS Press, 1976. viii, 214 p. : port. ; 18 cm. Reprint of the 1904 ed. published by Nisbet, London. "Complete list of Sir Arthur Sullivan's work": p. 204-214. [ML410.S95F5 1976] 74-24084 ISBN 0-404-12913-7 : 15.00
1. Sullivan, Arthur Seymour, Sir, 1842-1900. 2. Composers—England—Biography.

LAWRENCE, Arthur, 1870- 780'.924 B
Sir Arthur Sullivan; life story, letters, and reminiscences. With critique by B. W. Findon, and bibliography by Wilfrid Bendall. New York, Haskell House Publishers, 1973. 8, xii, 340 p. illus. 23 cm. Reprint of the 1899 ed. published by J. Bowden, London. "Appendix, comprising a complete list of Sir Arthur Sullivan's work, compiled by Wilfrid Bendall": p. [329]-340. [ML410.S95L3 1973] 72-3244 ISBN 0-8383-1522-4 15.95
1. Sullivan, Arthur Seymour, Sir, 1842-1900. I. Title.

SULLIVAN. HERBERT 927.8
Sir Arthur Sullivan; his life, letters & diaries, by Herbert Sullivan. Newman Flower. [2d ed.] London, Cassell [Chester Springs. Pa., Dufour. 1966] ix. 306p. ports., facsims. 24cm. Bibl. [ML410.S95S95] 54-27545 3.50
1. Sullivan, Arthur Seymour, Sir 1842-1900. 2. Musicians—Correspondence, reminiscences, etc. I. Flower, Newman, Sir 1879- joint author. II. Title.

YOUNG, Percy Marshall, 1912- 780'.924 B
Sir Arthur Sullivan [by] Percy M. Young. New York, W. W. Norton [1972, c1971] xiii, 304 p. illus. 25 cm. List of musical works: p. 271-285. [ML410.S95Y7 1972] 72-176486 12.50
1. Sullivan, Arthur Seymour, Sir, 1842-1900.

Sullivan, Arthur Seymour, Sir, 1842-1900—Exhibitions.

ALLEN, Reginald. 782.8'1'0924 B
Sir Arthur Sullivan : composer & personage / by Reginald Allen, in collaboration with Gale R. D'Luhy. New York : Pierpont Morgan Library, [1975] xxviii, 215 p. : ill., facsims. ; 28 cm. Catalog of an exhibition held at the Morgan Library, 13 Feb. to 20 Apr. 1975. Includes index. Bibliography: p. 207-208. [ML141.N4S84] 74-31986 ISBN 0-87598-049-X : 15.00
1. Sullivan, Arthur Seymour, Sir, 1842-1900—Exhibitions. 2. Sullivan, Arthur Seymour, Sir, 1842-1900—Bibliography—Catalogs. I. D'Luhy, Gale R., joint author. II. Pierpont Morgan Library, New York. BIP

Sullivan, Frank,

SULLIVAN, Frank, 1892- 818'.5'209
Frank Sullivan through the looking glass; a collection of his letters and pieces with an introd. by Marc Connelly. Edited, with an afterword, by George Oppenheimer. [1st ed.] Garden City, N.Y., Doubleday, 1970. xvi, 267 p. 22 cm. [PS3537.U47Z5] 72-111180 5.95
I. Oppenheimer, George, ed. II. Title.

Sullivan, Harry Stack, 1892-1949.

CHAPMAN, Arthur Harry, 1924- 150'.19'57
Harry Stack Sullivan : his life and his work / by A. H. Chapman. New York : Putnam, c1976. 280 p. ; 22 cm. Includes index. Bibliography: p. 267-270. [RC339.52.S87C47 1976] 75-42926 ISBN 0-399-11734-2 : 8.95
1. Sullivan, Harry Stack, 1892-1949. BIP

Sullivan, John Lawrence, 1858-1918.

FLEISCHER, Nathaniel S. 927.9683
John L. Sullivan, champion of champions. New York, Putnam [1951] xiii, 242 p. illus., ports. 22 cm. [GV1132.S95F63] 51-10380
1. Sullivan, John Lawrence, 1858-1918.

Sullivan, John Lawrence, 1858-1918—Juvenile literature.

HOFF, Sydney, 1912- 796.8'3'0922 B
Gentleman Jim and the great John L. / story and pictures by Syd Hoff. New York : Coward, McCann & Geoghegan, c1977. 47 p. : col. ill. ; 23 cm. (A Break-of-day book) Briefly recounts the events of the 1892 boxing match between heavyweight champion John L. Sullivan and challenger "Gentleman Jim" Corbett. [GV1132.S95H63 1977] 920 77-175 ISBN 0-698-30669-4 lib. bdg. : 4.69
1. Sullivan, John Lawrence, 1858-1918—Juvenile literature. 2. Corbett, James John, 1866-1933—Juvenile literature. 3. Boxers (Sports)—United States—Biography—Juvenile literature. I. Title. BIP

Sullivan, John William Navin

SULLIVAN, John William Navin 927.8
Beethoven; his spiritual development. New York, Vintage Books 1960[c.1927] viii, 173p. 19cm. K-100) 1.10 pap.,
I. Beethoven, Ludwig, Van. 1770-1827. II. Title. BIP

Sullivan, John, 1740-1795.

MCKONE, Frank E. 973.3'3'0924 B
General Sullivan : New Hampshire patriot / by Frank E. McKone. 1st ed. New York : Vantage Press, c1977- v. : ill. ; 22 cm. Bibliography: v. 1, p. 431-434. [E207.S9M3] 77-153943 ISBN 0-533-02684-9 : 9.00
1. Sullivan, John, 1740-1795. 2. United States. Army. Continental Army—Biography. 3. Generals—United States—Biography. 4. United States—History—Revolution, 1775-1783—Campaigns and battles. I. Title. BIP

WHITTEMORE, Charles Park, 1921- 923.573
A general of the Revolution, John Sullivan of New Hampshire. New York, Columbia University Press, 1961. viii, 317 p. port., maps. 25 cm. Revision of a doctoral dissertation issued in microfilm form in 1958 under title: New Hampshire's John Sullivan. Bibliography: p. [293]-305. Bibliographical references included in "Notes" (p. [231]-290) [E207.S9W5 1961] 61-11754
1. Sullivan, John, 1740-1795. 2. U.S. — Hist. — Revolution — Campaigns and battles. I. Title.

Sullivan, Louis Henry, 1856-1924.

CONNELY, Willard, 1888- 720.973
Louis Sullivan as he lived; the shaping of American architecture, a biography. New York, Horizon Press, 1960. 322 p. illus. 25 cm. Includes bibliography. [NA737.S9C6] 60-8160
1. Sullivan, Louis Henry, 1856-1924. 2. Architecture—U.S.

MORRISON, Hugh Sinclair, 1905- 927.2
Louis Sullivan, prophet of modern architecture. New York, Norton [1962, c.1935] 317p. illus. 20cm. (Norton lib., N116) Bibl. 1.95 pap.,
1. Sullivan, Louis Henry, 1856-1924. I. Title. BIP

MORRISON, Hugh Sinclair, 1905- v. 12
Louis Sullivan, prophet of modern architecture. New York, W. W. Norton [1962, c1935] 317 p. illus. 20 cm. (Norton library, N116) Includes bibliographies. 63-62195
1. Sullivan, Louis Henry, 1856-1924. 2. Architecture — U.S. I. Title.

MORRISON, Hugh Sinclair, 1905- 720'.924 B
Louis Sullivan, prophet of modern architecture, by Hugh Morrison. Westport, Conn., Greenwood Press [1971, c1935] 391 p. illus. 23 cm. "Dankmar Adler, a biographical sketch": p. 283-293. Includes bibliographies. [NA737.S9M6 1971] 78-139141 ISBN 0-8371-5757-9
1. Sullivan, Louis Henri, 1856-1924. 2. Adler, Dankmar, 1844-1900. 3. Architecture—United States.

PAUL, Sherman. 927.2
Louis Sullivan, an architect in American thought. Englewood Cliffs, N. J., Prentice [c.1962] 176p. illus. 21cm. (Spectrum bk., S47) Bibl. 62-19991 4.75 1.95 pap.,
1. Sullivan, Louis Henry,1856-1924. I. Title.

Sullivan, Louis Henri, 1856-1924—Juvenile literature.

KAUFMAN, Mervyn D. 720'.924 B
Father of skyscrapers; a biography of Louis Sullivan, by Mervyn Kaufman. [1st ed.] Boston, Little, Brown [1969] x, 171 p. illus., ports. 24 cm. A biography of the architect who helped lead the revolt against the established European school of architecture in America. [NA737.S9K3] 92 77-77450 4.95
1. Sullivan, Louis Henri, 1856-1924—Juvenile literature. I. Title.

Sullivan, Michael, 1948-1972.

SULLIVAN, James E. P., comp. 916.78'26'0440924
Love, Mike : the story of Michael Sullivan, buried on Kilimanjaro / [compiled] by James E. P. Sullivan and Charles Stough. [Kettering, Ohio] : J. E. P. Sullivan, [1974] 96 p. : ill. ; 21 cm. [CT275.S937S92] 75-305514
1. Sullivan, Michael, 1948-1972. 2. Sullivan, James E. P. 3. Kilimanjaro. I. Stough, Charles, joint comp. II. Title.

Sullivan, Tom, 1947- —Juvenile literature.

GILL, Derek L. T. 784'.092'4 B
Tom Sullivan : adventures in darkness / Derek L. T. Gill. New York : McKay, c1976. p. cm. A biography of the singer and television entertainer who has been blind from birth. [ML3930.S97G5] 92 76-13405 ISBN 0-679-20377-X : 7.95
1. Sullivan, Tom, 1947- —Juvenile literature. 2. Musicians, Blind—United States—Biography—Juvenile literature. I. Title.

GILL, Derek L.T. 784'092'4
Tom Sullivan's adventures in darkness / Derek L.T. Gill. New York : New American Library, 1977,c1976. 148p. : ill. ; 18 cm. (A Signet Book) A biography of the singer and television entertainer who has been blind from birth. [ML3930.S97G5] ISBN 0-451-07698-2 pbk. : 1.50
1. Sullivan, Tom,1947-Juvenile literature. 2. Musicians, Blind-United States-Biography-Juvenile literature. I. Title. II. Title: Adventures in darkness.
L.C. card no. for c1976 D. McKay ed.:76-13405. BIP

Sullivan, William Laurence, 1872-1935.

RATTE, John,(1936- 282'.0922
Three modernists; Alfred Loisy, George Tyrrell, William L. Sullivan. New York, Sheed [1967] viii. 370p. 22cm. Bibl. [BX1396.R3] 67-13763 6.95
1. Loisy, Alfred Firmin, 2. Sullivan, William Laurence, 1872-1935. 3. Tyrell, George, 1861-1909. 4. Modernism—Catholic Church. I. Title.

SULLIVAN, William Laurence, 1872-1935 282.0924
Under orders; the autobiography of William Laurence Sullivan. Boston, Beacon [1966, c1944] 200p. port. 21cm. Bibl. [BX9869.S8A3 1966] 66-23781 4.50 bds.,
I. Title.

Sully, Alfred, 1821-1879.

SULLY, Langdon. 355.3'31'0924 B
No tears for the general; the life of Alfred Sully, 1821-1879. Foreword by Ray Allen Billington. Palo Alto, Calif., American West Pub. Co. [1974] 255 p. illus. 24 cm. (Western biography series) Bibliography: p. 247-250. [E415.9.S89S94] 73-90794 ISBN 0-910118-33-7 9.95
1. Sully, Alfred, 1821-1879. I. Title.

Sully, Maximilien de Bethune, duc de, 1559-1641.

BUTLER, Geoffrey Gilbert, Sir, 1887- 341.1'1'094
Studies in statecraft: being chapters, biographical, and bibliographical, mainly on the sixteenth century. Port Washington, N.Y., Kennikat Press [1970] vi, 138 p. 22 cm. Reprint of the 1920 ed. Contents.Contents.—Bishop Roderick and Renaissance pacificism.—The French "civilians," Roman law, and the new monarchy.—William Postel; world peace through world power.—Sully and his grand design.—"The grand design" of Emerich Cruce.—Appendices: A. Passages quoted in Chapter I. B. A bibliography of Rodericus Sancius, Bishop of Calahorra (p. [108]-113). C. English version of passages quoted in Chapter II. D. A bibliography of William Postel (p. [117]-131) [D234.B8 1970] 79-110899 ISBN 0-8046-0882-2
1. Sanchez de Arevalo, Rodrigo, Bp., 1404-1470. 2. Postel, Guillaume, 1510-1581. 3. Sully, Maximilien de Bethune, duc de, 1559-1641. 4. Cruce, Emeric, 1590?-1648. 5. Europe—Politics and government—1517-1648. 6. Peace. I. Title.

Sully, Thomas, 1783-1872.

BIDDLE, Edward. 759.13 B
The life and works of Thomas Sully, by Edward Biddle and Mantle Fielding. New York, Kennedy Graphics, 1970. viii, 411 p. illus., facsim., ports. 27 cm. (Library of American art) Reprint of the 1921 ed. [ND237.S9B5 1970] 74-77716
1. Sully, Thomas, 1783-1872. I. Fielding, Mantle, 1865-1941, joint author. II. Title. BIP

Sully, Va.

GAMBLE, Robert S. 917.55'291
Sully, the biography of a house [by] Robert S. Gamble. Chantilly, Va., Sully Foundation, 1973. x, 228 p. illus. 27 cm. Bibliography: p. 222-224. [F232.F2G34] 73-91381 7.50
1. Sully, Va. I. Title.

Sulzberger, Cyrus Leo, 1912-

SULZBERGER, Cyrus Leo, 1912- 070'.924
A long row of candles; memoirs and diaries, 1934-1954 [by] C. L. Sulzberger. [New York] Macmillan [1969] xvi, 1061 p. illus., facsims., ports. 24 cm. Sequel: The last of the giants. [PN4874.S786A3] 69-10642

1. Journalists—Correspondence, reminiscences, etc. I. Title.

SULZBERGER, Cyrus 070'.92'4 B
Leo, 1912-
Seven continents and forty years / C. L. Sulzberger. New York : Quadrangle/New York Times Book Co., c1977. p. cm. Autobiographical. Includes index. [PN4874.S786A37] 76-9705 ISBN 0-8129-0655-1 : 15.00
1. Sulzberger, Cyrus Leo, 1912- 2. Journalists—United States—Biography. 3. World politics—1945- I. Title.

Sulzberger, Marina.

SULZBERGER, Marina. 909.82 B
Marina (in her own words) / [edited by] C. L. Sulzberger. New York : Crown Publishers, c1978. p. cm. Includes index. [CT275.S954 1978] 78-7926 ISBN 0-517-53375-8 : 122.95
1. Sulzberger, Marina. 2. Sulzberger, Cyrus Leo, 1912- 3. United States—Biography. I. Sulzberger, Cyrus Leo, 1912- II. Title.

Summerhayes, Martha, 1846-1911.

SUMMERHAYES, Martha, 979.1'04
1846-1911.
Vanished Arizona : recollections of the Army life of a New England woman / Martha Summerhayes ; introd. by Dan L. Thrapp. Lincoln : University of Nebraska Press, c1979. xxvi, 307 p. : ill. ; 21 cm. Reprint of the 2d ed. (1911) published by Salem Press, Salem, Mass. [F811.S95 1979] 78-26814 ISBN 0-8032-4106-2: 15.00 ISBN 0-8032-9105-1 pbk. : 4.95
1. Summerhayes, Martha, 1846-1911. 2. United States. Army—Military life. 3. Arizona—Description and travel. 4. Arizona—Biography. I. Title. BIP

Summerhill School, Leiston, Eng.

NEILL, Alexander 371.2'012'0924
Sutherland, 1883-
Neill! Neill! Orange peel! An autobiography, by A. S. Neill. New York, Hart Pub. Co. [1972] 538 p. illus. 24 cm. [LF795.L692953N38] 76-180998 ISBN 0-8055-1042-7 10.00
1. Summerhill School, Leiston, Eng. I. Title.

Summers, Eliza Ann, 1844-1900.

SUMMERS, Eliza Ann, 975.7'99
1844-1900.
"Dear Sister" : letters written on Hilton Head Island, 1867 / Josephine W. Martin, editor. Beaufort, S.C. : Beauford Book Co., 1978, c1977 xxxi, 133 p. : ill. ; 24 cm. Letters written by Eliza Ann Summers. Includes bibliographical references and index. [F277.B3S95 1977] 77-93718 7.95
1. Summers, Eliza Ann, 1844-1900. 2. Hilton Head Island—History—Sources. 3. Afro-Americans—South Carolina—Hilton Head Island—History—Sources. 4. Hilton Head Island—Biography. I. Martin, Josephine W. II. Title.

Sumner, Charles, 1811-1874.

DONALD, David Herbert, 923.273
1920-
Charles Sumner and the coming of the Civil War. [1st ed.] New York, Knopf, 1960. 392 p. illus. 25 cm. Includes bibliography. [E415.9.S9D6] 60-9144
1. Sumner, Charles, 1811-1874. BIP

DONALD, David Herbert, 973.7'0924
1920-
Charles Sumner and the rights of man, by David Donald. [1st ed.] New York, Knopf, 1970. xxiv, 595, xxxix p. illus., ports. 25 cm. Includes bibliographical references. [E415.9.S9D62 1970] 70-23393 15.00
1. Sumner, Charles, 1811-1874. 2. United States—Politics and government—Civil War, 1861-1865. 3. United States—Politics and government—1865-1877. I. Title. BIP

PIERCE, Edward 973.7'0924 B
Lillie, 1829-1897.
Memoir and letters of Charles Sumner. New York, Arno Press, 1969. 4 v. illus., ports. 23 cm. (The Anti-slavery crusade in America) Vols. 1 and 2 reprinted from the 1877 ed.; v. 3 and 4 reprinted from the 2d ed., 1894. Contents.Contents.—v. 1. 1811-1838.—v. 2. 1838-1845.—v. 3. 1845-1860.—v. 4. 1860-1874. [E415.9.S9P63] 72-82211
1. Sumner, Charles, 1811-1874. I. Sumner, Charles, 1811-1874. II. Title. III. Series. BIP

SCHURZ, Carl, 1829-1906. 923.273
Charles Sumner, an essay; edited by Arthur Reed Hogue. Urbana, University of Illinois Press, 1951. 152 p. port., facsim. 22 cm. [E415.9.S9S28] 51-1560
1. Sumner, Charles, 1811-1874. I. Hogue, Arthur Reed, ed. II. Title. BIP

STOREY, Moorfield, 973.6'0924 B
1845-1929.
Charles Sumner. New York, Russell & Russell [1970] 466 p. 20 cm. Reprint of the 1900 ed. [E415.9.S9S8 1970] 77-81478
1. Sumner, Charles, 1811-1874. BIP

STOREY, Moorfield, 973.7'0924 B
1845-1929.
Charles Sumner. Boston, Houghton, Mifflin. [New York, AMS Press, 1972] 466 p. illus. 18 cm. (American statesmen, v. 30) Reprint of the 1900 ed. [E415.9.S9S8 1972] 76-128956 ISBN 0-404-50880-4
1. Sumner, Charles, 1811-1874. I. Title. II. Series.

Sumner Co., Kan.—History.

FREEMAN, George D. 978.1'87
Midnight and noonday : or, The incidental history of southern Kansas and the Indiana Territory : Bi-centennial edition / by G. D. Freeman. [s.l.] : Sumner County Historical Society, [1976] 410 p., [14] leaves of plates : ill. ; 23 cm. Reprint, with additional material, of the 1892 ed. published by G. D. Freeman, Caldwell, Kan. [F687.S9F73 1976] 76-15496
1. Sumner Co., Kan.—History. 2. Caldwell, Kan.—History. 3. Crime and criminals—Kansas—Biography. I. Title. II. Title: The incidental history of southern Kansas and the Indiana Territory.

Sumner, Edwin Vose, 1797-1863.

CROCCHIOLA, 355.3'31'0924 B
Stanley Francis Louis, 1908-
E. V. Sumner; Major-General United States Army, 1797-1863, by F. Stanley. [Borger, Tex., Printed: J. Hess Printers, c1968] vi, 382 p. port. 23 cm. Bibliography: p. 345-363. [U53.S8C7] 79-19252
1. Sumner, Edwin Vose, 1797-1863.

Sumner, John Daniel.

SUMNER, John Daniel. 783.7 B
J. D. Sumner: Gospel music is my life [by] Bob Terrell. Nashville, Impact Books [1971] 208 p. illus. 22 cm. [ML420.S953A3] 77-182384 3.95
I. Terrell, Bob. II. Title: Gospel music is my life.

Sumpter, Jesse 1827-1910.

SUMPTER, Jesse, 917.64'435' B
1827-1910.
Paso del Aguila : a chronicle of frontier days on the Texas border as recorded in the memoirs of Jesse Sumpter / compiled by Harry Warren ; with Harry Warren of the Rio Grande by J. Frank Dobie ; edited and annotated by Ben E. Pingenot. Austin : Encino Press, c1969. xxv, 152 p. : ill., maps (on lining papers) ; 24 cm. Includes index. Bibliography: p. 119-130. [F394.E13S95 1969] 74-193264
1. Sumpter, Jesse 1827-1910. 2. Eagle Pass, Tex.—History. 3. Frontier and pioneer life—Texas. I. Warren, Harry, b. 1859. II. Pingenot, Ben E., ed.

Sumrall, Lester Frank, 1913-

SUMRALL, Lester 269'.2'0924 B
Frank, 1913-
Run with the vision / Lester Sumrall, with J. Stephen Conn. Plainfield, N.J. : Logos International, c1977. vi, 161 p., [3] leaves of plates : ill. ; 21 cm. [BV3785.S78A37] 77-87596 pbk. : 2.95
1. Sumrall, Lester Frank, 1913- 2. Evangelists—United States—Biography. I. Conn, J. Stephen, joint author. II. Title. BIP

Sumter, Thomas, 1734-1832.

BASS, Robert Duncan. 923.573
Gamecock; the life and campaigns of General Thomas Sumter. [1st ed.] New York, Holt, Rinehart and Winston [1961] 289 p. illus. 22 cm. Includes bibliography. [E207.S95B3] 61-10732
1. Sumter, Thomas, 1734-1832. I. Title.

Sun, Ch'ing-ling (Sung) 1890-

HAHN, Emily, 1905- 951.04'2'0922
The Soong sisters. Westport, Conn., Greenwood Press [1970, c1941] xxi, 349 p. ports. 23 cm. [DS778.A1H3 1970] 78-110041
1. Kung, Ai-ling (Sung) 1888- 2. Sun, Ch'ing-ling (Sung) 1890- 3. Chiang, Mei-ling (Sung) 1897- I. Title. BIP

Sun, Ch'ing-ling Sung, 1890- — Juvenile literature.

EUNSON, Roby. 951.04'092'2
The Soong sisters / by Roby Eunson. New York : Franklin Watts, 1975. 136 p. : ill. ; 24 cm. Includes index. Bibliography: p. 131-132. A biography of the three sisters who as Mrs. H. H. Kung, Mme Sun Yat-sen, and Mme Chiang Kai-shek exerted more influence upon United States policy toward China than almost "any other person or persons in this century." [DS778.K778E9] 920 75-5952 ISBN 0-531-02835-6 lib.bdg. : 5.90
1. Kung, Ai-ling Sung, 1888- —Juvenile literature. 2. Sun, Ch'ing-ling Sung, 1890- —Juvenile literature. 3. Chiang, Mei-ling Sung, 1897- —Juvenile literature. I. Title.

Sun Valley, Idaho—History.

OPPENHEIMER, Doug. 979.6'32
Sun Valley : a biography / by Doug Oppenheimer & Jim Poore. Boise, Idaho : Beatty Books, c1976. 185 p. : ill. ; 21 x 24 cm. [F754.S96O66] 76-27113 ISBN 0-916238-04-0 : 12.95. ISBN 0-916238-02-4 pbk. : 7.95
1. Sun Valley, Idaho—History. 2. Skis and skiing—Idaho—Sun Valley. I. Poore, Jim, joint author. II. Title. BIP

Sun, Yat-sen, 1866-1925.

BRUCE, Robert, 951.04'1'0924 B
1911-
Sun Yat-sen, by R. Bruce. London, Oxford U.P., 1969. 64 p. 8 plates, illus., facsims., map, ports. 21 cm. (The Clarendon biographies) Bibliography: p. 63. [DS777.B75] 70-418205 9/6
1. Sun, Yat-sen, 1866-1925.

BUCK, Pearl 923.151
(Sydenstricker) 1892-
The man who changed China: the story of Sun Yat-sen; illustrated by Fred Castellon. New York, Random House [1953] 185 p. illus. 22 cm. (World landmark books, W-9) [DS777.B8] 53-6263
1. Sun, Yat-sen, 1866-1925. I. Title. BIP

ESTERER, Arnulf 951.04'1'0924 B
K.
Sun Yat-Sen: China's great champion [by] Arnulf K. and Louise A. Esterer. New York, J. Messner [1970] 189 p. 22 cm. Bibliography: p. 185. A biography of the Chinese leader who dedicated his life to abolishing the Manchu dynasty and uniting China. [DS777.E8] 92 76-123172 3.50
1. Sun, Yat-sen, 1866-1925. I. Esterer, Louise A., joint author. II. Title.

LENG, Shao Chuan, 951.04'1'0924
1921-
Sun Yat-sen and communism / by Shao Chuan Leng and Norman D. Palmer. Westport, Conn. : Greenwood Press, 1976 [c1960] p. cm. Reprint of the 1961 ed. published by Thames and Hudson, London, which was issued as no. 10 of The Foreign Policy Research Institute series. Includes index. Bibliography: p. [DS777.L4 1976] 75-27683 ISBN 0-8371-8455-X lib.bdg. : 15.00
1. Sun, Yat-sen, 1866-1925. 2. Communism—China. I. Palmer, Norman Dunbar, joint author. II. Title. III. Series: The Foreign Policy Research Institute series ; no. 10.

LINEBARGER, Paul 951.04'1'0924 B
Myron Wentworth, 1871-1939.
Sun Yat Sen and the Chinese Republic. [1st AMS ed.] New York, AMS Press [1969] xviii, 371 p. illus. 23 cm. Reprint of the 1925 ed. [DS777.L5 1969] 70-96469
1. Sun, Yat-sen, 1866-1925. 2. China—History—1912-1937. I. Title. BIP

MARTIN, Bernard, 951.04'0924 B
1897-
Strange vigour; a biography of Sun Yat-sen. Port Washington, N.Y., Kennikat Press [1970] xii, 248 p. port. 22 cm. Originally published in 1944. Includes bibliographical references. [DS777.M3 1970] 74-112814
1. Sun, Yat-sen, 1866-1925. 2. China—History—Revolution, 1911-1912. 3. China—History—Republic, 1912-1949. I. Title. BIP

NEWMAN, John Henry, 922.242
Cardinal, 1801-1890.
Apologia pro vita sua. Edited with an introd. and note by A. Dwight Culler. Boston, Houghton Mifflin [1956] 384p. 21cm. (Riverside editions, B10) [BX4705.N5A3 1956] 56-2548
1. Catholic Church—Doctrinal and controversial works—Catholl authors. I. Title.

SCHIFFRIN, Harold 951.04'1'0924 B
Z.
Sun Yat-sen and the origins of the Chinese revolution [by] Harold Z. Schiffrin. Berkeley, University of California Press, 1968. xv, 412 p. maps, ports. 24 cm. (Center for Chinese Studies. Publications) Bibliography: p. [379]-393. [DS777.S32] 68-26530 9.50
1. Sun, Yat-sen, 1866-1925. I. Title. II. Series: California. University. Center for Chinese Studies. Publications BIP

SHARMAN, Lyon, 1872-1957 923.151
Sun Yat-sen, his life and its meaning; a critical biography. Hamden, Conn., Archon [dist. Shoe String 1965, c.1934] xvii, 418p. port. 21cm. Unaltered, unabridged ed. Bibl. [DS777.S5] 65-19600 11.50
1. Sun, Yet-sen, 1866-1925. 2. Chung-kuo kuo min tang. 3. China—Hist.—Revolution, 1911-1912. 4. China—Hist.—Republic, 1912-1949. I. Title.

SHARMAN, Lyon, 951.04'1'0924 B
1872-1957.
Sun Yat-sen; his life and its meaning; a critical biography. Stanford, Calif., Stanford University Press [1968, c1934] xxi, 420 p. 23 cm. Bibliography: p. 395-405. [DS777.S5 1968] 68-17141
1. Sun, Yat-sen, 1866-1925. 2. Chung-Kuo Kuo min tang. 3. China—History—Revolution, 1911-1912. 4. China—History—Republic, 1912-1949. BIP

SPENCER, Cornelia, 951.4'1'0924 B
1899-
Sun Yat-sen, founder of the Chinese Republic. New York, John Day Co. [1967] 191 p. illus. 21 cm. Bibliography: p. [181]-184. Biography of the leader of the revolution of 1911 which overthrew the Manchu dynasty and established China as a republic. [DS777.S64] 92 67-23529
1. Sun, Yat-sen, 1866-1925. I. Title.

WILBUR, Clarence 951.04'1'0924 B
Martin, 1908-
Sun Yat-sen, frustrated patriot / C. Martin Wilbur. New York : Columbia University Press, 1976. p. cm. Includes index. Bibliography: p. [DS777.A595W55] 76-18200 ISBN 0-231-04036-9 : 15.00
1. Sun, Yat-sen, 1866-1925. I. Title.

WILLIAM, Maurice. 951.04'1'0924
Sun Yat-sen versus communism : new evidence establishing China's right to the support of democratic nations / by Maurice William. Westport, Conn. : Hyperion Press, 1974. p. cm. Reprint of the 1932 ed. published by William & Wilkins, Baltimore. Includes index. [DS777.W5 1974] 74-10104 ISBN 0-88355-169-1

1. Sun Yat-sen, 1866-1925. 2. William, Maurice. The social interpretation of history. 3. Communism. I. Title.

YAUKEY, Grace 951.4'1'0924 (B) (Sydenstricker) 1899-
Sun Yat-sen, founder of the Chinese Republic [by] Cornelia Spencer. New York, John Day Co. [1967] 191 p. illus. 21 cm. Bibliography: p. [181]-184. [DS777.Y38] 67-23529
1. Sun, Yat-sen, 1866-1925. I. Title.

Sun, Yat-sen, 1866-1925—Addresses, essays, lectures.

SUN Yat-sen and 951.04'1'0924
China / edited by Paul K. T. Sih. Jamaica, N.Y. : St. John's University Press, [1974] x, 176 p. ; 18 cm. (Asia in the modern world series ; no. 15) Papers presented at the 15th annual conference of the American Association of Teachers of Chinese Language and Culture. "A preliminary bibliography of English-language biographies of Dr. Sun Yat-sen and translations of his writings, compiled by John T. Ma": p. 165-176. Includes bibliographical references. [DS777.S87] 74-19368 ISBN 0-87075-100-X pbk. : 2.95
1. Sun, Yat-sen, 1866-1925—Addresses, essays, lectures. I. Sih, Paul Kwang Tsien, 1909- ed. II. American Association of Teachers of Chinese Language and Culture. III. Series: Asia in the modern world ; no. 15.

Sunday, William Ashley, 1862-1935.

MCLOUGHLIN, William Gerald. 922
Billy Sunday was his real name. [Chicago] University of Chicago Press [1955] 324 p. illus. 24 cm. [BV3783.S8M35] 55-5138
1. Sunday, William Ashley, 1862-1935. I. Title.

THOMAS, Lee, 1918- 922
The Billy Sunday story: the life and times of William Ashley Sunday; an authorized biography. Grand Rapids, Zondervan Pub. House [1961] 256 p. illus. 23 cm. [BV3785.S8T5] 61-14864
1. Sunday, William Ashley, 1862-1935. I. Title.

THOMAS, Lee [Obra Lee Thomas] 922
The Billy Sunday story; the life and times of William Ashley Sunday; an authorized biography. Grand Rapids, Zondercan Pub. House [c.1961] 256p. illus. 61-14864 3.95
1. Sunday, William Ashley, 1862-1935. I. Title.

Sunderland, Robert Spencer, 2d Earl of, 1640-1702.

KENYON, John Philipps, 923.242 1927-
Robert Spencer, earl of Sunderland, 1641-1702. London, New York, Longmans, Green [1958] 396 p. illus. 23 cm. [DA437.S8K4 1958] 58-59402
1. Sunderland, Robert Spencer, 2d earl of, 1640-1702.

KENYON, John 941.06'6'0924 Philipps, 1927-
Robert Spencer, Earl of Sunderland, 1641-1702 / J. P. Kenyon. Westport, Conn. : Greenwood Press, 1975, c1958. xii, 396 p., [3] leaves of plates : ports. ; 22 cm. Reprint of the ed. published by Longmans, London, New York. Includes bibliographical references and index. [DA437.S8K4 1975] 75-8480 ISBN 0-8371-8150-X
1. Sunderland, Robert Spencer, 2d Earl of, 1640-1702. BIP

Supervielle, Jules,

SUPERVIELLE, Jules, 841'.9'12 1884-1960.
Supervielle. Translated from the French by Teo Savory. Santa Barbara [Calif.] Unicorn Press, 1967. 51 p. port. 18 cm. (Unicorn French series) Poems. English and French. [PQ2637.U6S813] 67-9100
I. Savory, Teo, tr.

Surfing—Biography—Juvenile literature.

OLNEY, Ross 797.1'72'0922 B Robert, 1929-
Kings of the surf, by Ross R. Olney and Richard W. Graham. New York, Putnam's Sons [1969] 192 p. illus. 22 cm. (Putnam sports shelf) Brief biographies of twenty well-known surfers explain the technique and terminology of one of the "fastest growing participant sports." [GV840.S8O38 1969] 920 78-77768 3.64
1. Surfing—Biography—Juvenile literature. I. Graham, Richard W., joint author. II. Title.

Surgeons—Correspondence, reminiscences, etc.

GAMSU, David, 1904- 617'.0924
Adventures of a South African brain surgeon. [Johannesburg] H. Keartland [1967] [x] 286p. 22cm. [R654.G3A3] 68-73218 7.95 bds.,
1. Surgeons—Correspondence, reminiscences, etc. I. Title.
American distributor: Tri-Ocean, San Francisco.

PARE, Ambroise, 1510?-1590. 926.1
The apologie and treatise of Ambroise Pare, containing the voyages made into divers places, with many of his writings upon surgery. Edited and with an introd. by Geoffrey Keynes. Chicago, University of Chicago Press [1952] xxii, [1]. 227 p. illus., ports. 22 cm. (The Classics of science) Bibliography: p. [xxiii] [R507.P3A3 1952] 52-10208
1. Surgeons — Correspondence, reminiscences, etc. 2. Surgery — Early works to 1800. I. Title. II. Series.

PARE, Ambroise, 1510- 617.0924 1590
The apologie and treatise of Ambroise Pare, containing the voyages made into divers places with many of his writings upon surgery. Ed., introd. by Geoffrey Kevnes [Magnolia, Mass., Peter Smith. 1968] xxii. [1] 227p. illus., ports. 22cm. (Dover bk., T1902 rebound) Repubn. of the ed. pub. by the Univ. of Chicago Pr. in 1952. Bibl. [R507.P3A3 1968] 7.50
1. Surgeons—Correspondence, reminiscences, etc. 2. Surgery—Early works to 1800. I. Title.

PARE, Ambroise, 1510?- 617'.0924 1590.
The apologie and treatise of Ambroise Pare, containing the voyages made into divers places with many of his writings upon surgery. Edited and with an introd. by Geoffrey Keynes. New York, Dover Publications [1968] xxii, [1] 227 p. illus., ports. 22 cm. A republication of the ed. published by the University of Chicago Press in 1952. Bibliography: p. [xxiii] [R507.P3A3 1968] 68-14763
1. Surgeons—Correspondence, reminiscences, etc. 2. Surgery—Early works to 1800. I. Title.

STONE, Harvey Brinton, 926.1 1882-
As a man thinketh; a surgeon thinks out loud. Baltimore, 1956. 188p. 24cm. [R154.S844A3] 57-451
1. Surgeons—Correspondence, reminiscences, etc. I. Title.

STONE, Harvey Brinton, 926.1 1882-
As a man thinketh; a surgeon thinks out loud. Baltimore, 1956. 188 p. 24 cm. [R154.S844A3] 57-451
1. Surgeons — Correspondence, reminiscences, etc. I. Title.

Surgery—History.

PARE, Ambroise, 617'.0924 B 1510?-1590.
Life and times of Ambroise Pare, 1510-1590, with a new translation of his Apology and an account of his journeys in divers places, by Francis R. Packard. New York, B. Blom, 1971. xii, 297 p. illus., 2 fold. maps. 21 cm. Translation of A. Pare's Apologie, et traite contenant les voyages faits en divers lieux, together with F. R. Packard's essay on Life and times of Ambroise Pare. [R507.P3A3 1971] 79-160607
1. Surgery—History. 2. France—History—16th century. I. Packard, Francis Randolph, 1870-1950, ed. II. Title.

Surgery, Plastic.

MALTZ, Maxwell, 1899- 926.1
Doctor Pygmalion, the autobiography of a plastic surgeon. New York, Crowell [1953] 261 p. 21 cm. [R154.M292A3] 53-10709
1. Surgery, Plastic. I. Title.

MALTZ, Maxwell, 1899- 926.1
Doctor Pygmalion, the autobiography of a plastic surgeon. Foreword by Melvin Powers. Hollywood, Calif., Wilshire, 1968 [c.1953] 261p. 21cm. [R154.M292A3] 2.00 pap.,
1. Surgery, Plastic. I. Title.

Surratt, Mary Eugenia (Jenkins) 1820-1865.

DE WITT, David Miller, 973.7'0924 1837-1912.
The judicial murder of Mary E. Surratt. Baltimore, J. Murphy, 1895. St. Clair Shores, Mich., Scholarly Press, 1970. vi, 259 p. 22 cm. [E457.5.S985D4 1970] 71-108472
1. Surratt, Mary Eugenia (Jenkins) 1820-1865. 2. Lincoln, Abraham, Pres. U.S., 1809-1865—Assassination. I. Title. BIP

Surrey, Henry Howard, Earl of, 1517?-1547.

CASADY, Edwin. v. 12
Henry Howard, Earl of Surrey. New York, Modern Language Association of America, 1938; New York, Kraus Reprint Corp., 1966. xii, 257 p. 23 cm. (Modern Language Association of America. Revolving fund series, 8) Reprint of 1938 edition. 68-93525
1. Surrey, Henry Howard, earl of, I. Title. II. Series.

CHAPMAN, Hester W., 1899- 928.2
Two Tudor portraits: Henry Howard, earl of Surrey and Lady Katherine Grey. [1st American ed.] Boston, Little, Brown [1963, c1960] 252 p. illus. 22 cm. Includes bibliography. [PR2373.C5 1963] 63-14602
1. Surrey, Henry Howard, Earl of, 1517?-1547. 2. Hertford, Catherine Grey Seymour, countess of, 1538?-1568. Hertford Catherine Grey Seymour 1538 1568 I. Title.

Surtees, Robert Smith, 1805-1864.

WATSON, Frederick, 1885- 823'.8 B 1935.
Robert Smith Surtees : a critical study / by Frederick Watson. Norwood, Pa. : Norwood Editions, 1976. 291 p., [6] leaves of plates : ill. ; 23 cm. Reprint of the 1933 ed. published by G. G. Harrap, London. Includes index. Bibliography: p. 274-280. [PR5499.S4Z86 1976] 76-46286 ISBN 0-8482-2953-3 lib. bdg. : 27.50
1. Surtees, Robert Smith, 1805-1864. 2. Novelists, English—19th century—Biography. BIP

Surtees, Robert Smith, 1805-1864—Biography.

SURTEES, Robert Smith, 823'.8 1805-1864.
Robert Smith Surtees (creator of "Jorrocks") 1803-1864, by himself and E. D. Cuming. New York, Scribner, 1924. Detroit, Gale Research Co., 1974. p. cm. [PR5499.S4Z5 1974] 74-13897 ISBN 0-8103-4069-0
1. Surtees, Robert Smith, 1805-1864—Biography. I. Cuming, Edward William Dirom, 1862-1941, joint author.

Susan (Name)—Juvenile literature.

GLAZER, Tom. 929.4
All about your name, Susan : Susie, Susanna, Suzanne, Sue / by Tom Glazer ; illustrated by Demi. 1st ed. Garden City, N.Y. : Doubleday, c1978. 45 p. : ill. ; 22 cm. A collection of facts about people, places, and things which bear or have borne, the name of Susan. [CS2391.S94G57] 77-15156 ISBN 0-385-06579-5 : 4.95. ISBN 0-385-06643-0 lib.bdg. : 5.90
1. Susan (Name)—Juvenile literature. 2. Biography—Miscellanea—Juvenile literature. I. Hitz, Demi. II. Title.

Susann, Jacqueline—Biography.

VENTURA, Jeffrey. 813'.5'4 B
The Jacqueline Susann story / Jeffrey Ventura. New York : Award Books, 1975. 170 p., [4] leaves of plates : ports. ; 18 cm. (An Award biography) [PS3569.U75Z93] 75-328031 pbk. : 1.50
1. Susann, Jacqueline—Biography. I. Title.

Susce, Andrew J., 1906-

HAYES, John 364.1'067'09748 Phillip, 1949-
Lonely fighter : one man's battle with the government of the United States / by John P. Hayes. 1st ed. Secaucus, N.J. : L. Stuart, c1979. 208 p., [4] leaves of plates : ill. ; 24 cm. [HJ5018.S92H39] 78-27094 ISBN 0-8184-0270-9 : 10.00
1. Susce, Andrew J., 1906- 2. United States. Internal Revenue Service—Officials and employees—Biography. 3. Corruption (in politics)—Pennsylvania. 4. Organized crime—Pennsylvania. I. Title.

Sustar, Bob R., 1938-1975.

†SUSTAR, Bob R., 1938- 248'.86 1975.
Yet will I serve Him / Bob R. Sustar, as told to Hoyt E. Stone. Cleveland, Tenn. : Pathway Press, c1976. 105 p. : port. ; 18 cm. Autobiography. [RC280.L9S85 1976] 76-1683 ISBN 0-87148-931-7 pbk. : 1.95
1. Sustar, Bob R., 1938-1975. 2. Lymphoma—Biography. I. Stone, Hoyt E., joint author. II. Title.

Sutcliffe, Frank, 1853-1941.

HILEY, Michael. 770'.92'4 B
Frank Sutcliffe, photographer of Whitby / Michael Hiley. Boston : D. R. Godine, c1974. 224 p. : ill. ; 30 cm. (Godine photographic monographs) Includes bibliographical references and index. [TR140.S74H55 1974b] 74-81519 ISBN 0-87923-105-X : 27.50
1. Sutcliffe, Frank, 1853-1941. 2. Photography, Artistic. I. Title.

Sutcliffe, Joseph Richard, 1897-

†SUTCLIFFE, 371.2'012'0924 B Joseph Richard, 1897-
Why be a headmaster? / J. R. Sutcliffe. Carlton, Australia : Melbourne University Press ; Forest Grove, Or. : International Scholarly Book Services, 1977. viii, 170 p., [2] leaves of plates : ill. ; 22 cm. [LA2394.S87A38] 78-308389 ISBN 0-522-84117-1 : 16.50
1. Sutcliffe, Joseph Richard, 1897- 2. School superintendents and principals—Australia—Biography. I. Title. BIP

Sutherland, George, 1862-1942.

PASCHAL, Joel 347.99'24 B Francis.
Mr. Justice Sutherland, a man against the State. New York, Greenwood Press [1969, c1951] xii, 267 p. port. 23 cm. Includes bibliographical references. [KF8745.S88P3 1969] 77-88917 ISBN 0-8371-2517-0
1. Sutherland, George, 1862-1942. I. Title.

Sutherland, Joan, 1926-

BRADDON, Russell. 927.8
Joan Sutherland. New York, St. Martin's Press [1962] 256p. illus. 22cm. [ML420.S96B7] 62-16181
1. Sutherland, Joan, 1926- I. Title.

Sutherland, John Bain, 1889-1948.

SCOTT, Harry G 927.9633
Jock Sutherland: architect of men; a

biography. Foreword by Grantland Rice. [1st ed.] New York, Exposition Press [1954] 298p. illus. 22cm. [GV939.S8S3] 54-9996
1. Sutherland, John Bain, 1889-1948. I. Title.

Sutherland, Norman Stuart.

SUTHERLAND, Norman Stuart. 616.8'9'00924 B
Breakdown / by N. S. Sutherland. New York : Stein and Day, [1976] p. cm. [RC464.S93A33] 75-37980 ISBN 0-8128-1941-1 : 8.95
1. Sutherland, Norman Stuart. 2. Mental illness—Personal narratives. 3. Psychotherapy. I. Title. **BIP**

SUTHERLAND, Norman Stuart. 616.8'9'00924 B
Breakdown : a personal crisis and a medical dilemma / [by] Stuart Sutherland. London : Weidenfeld and Nicolson, 1976. x, 276 p. ; 23 cm. Includes bibliographical references and indexes. [RC480.5.S84 1976] 77-359209 ISBN 0-297-77217-1 : £5.25
1. Sutherland, Norman Stuart. 2. Psychotherapy—Evaluation. 3. Mental illness—Biography. I. Title.

Sutro, Adolph Heinrich Joseph, 1830-1898.

STEWART, Robert Ernest, Jr. 926.22
Adolph Sutro, a biography, by Robert E. Stewart, Jr., Mary Frances Stewart. Berkeley, Calif., Howell-North [c.]1962. 243p. illus. 24cm. Bibl. 62-16167 6.00
1. Sutro, Adolph Heinrich Joseph, 1830-1898. I. Stewart, Mary Frances, joint author. II. Title.

Sutter, John Augustus, 1803-1880.

CLAIRMONTE, Glenn. 923.873
John Sutter of California. Decorations by L. Vosburgh. New York, Nelson [1954] 185p. illus. 21cm. [F865.S9476] 54-9878
1. Sutter, John Augustus, 1803-1880. I. Title.

DANA, Julian, 1907- 979.4'03'0924 B
Sutter of California; a biography. New York, Press of the Pioneers, 1934. St. Clair Shores, Mich., Scholarly Press, 1972. x, 423 p. illus. 22 cm. [F865.S948 1972] 76-144964 ISBN 0-403-00933-2
1. Sutter, John Augustus, 1803-1880. I. Title.

DANA, Julian, 1907- 979.4'03'0924 B
Sutter of California, a biography. Westport, Conn., Greenwood Press [1974] p. cm. Reprint of the 1934 ed. published by the Press of the Pioneers, New York. Bibliography: p. [F865.S948 1974] 74-11308 ISBN 0-8371-7644-1 19.50
1. Sutter, John Augustus, 1803-1880. I. Title. **BIP**

DILLON, Richard H. 979.4'03'0924 B
Fool's gold; the decline and fall of Captain John Sutter of California, by Richard Dillon. New York, Coward-McCann [1967] 380 p. illus., maps, ports. 22 cm. "Bibliographical reprise": p. 357-363. [F865.S94834] 67-21511
1. Sutter, John Augustus, 1803-1880. I. Title.

ZOLLINGER, James Peter, 1896- 979.4'54'030924 B
Sutter; the man and his empire, by J. Peter Zollinger. Gloucester, Mass., P. Smith, 1967 [c1939] xv, 374 p. illus., ports. 21 cm. Bibliography: p. 353-363. [F865.S976 1967] 67-8106
1. Sutter, John Augustus, 1803-1880. I. Title.

Sutter, John Augustus, 1803-1880 — Juvenile literature.

BOOTH, Edwin. j 92
John Sutter, Californian. Illustrated by Gerald McCann. [1st ed.] Indianapolis, Bobbs-Merrill [1963] 191 p. illus. 22 cm. [F865.S942] 63-11654
1. Sutter, John Augustus, 1803-1880 — Juvenile literature. I. Title.

Suttle, John William, 1872-

WASHBURN, Willard Wyan, 1912- v. 12
Brother John's Canaan in Carolina. [Salisbury, N.C., Printed by Rowan Printing Co., 1958] 335 p. plates, ports. 23 cm.
1. Suttle, John William, 1872- I. Title.

Suttner, Bertha Felicie Sophie (Kinsky) Freifrau von, 1843-1914.

KEMPF, Beatrix. 327'.172'0924 B
Woman for peace; the life of Bertha von Suttner. Translated from the German, by R. W. Last. [1st U.S. ed.] Park Ridge, N.J., Noyes Press [1973, c1972] viii, 200 p. 23 cm. Translation of Bertha von Suttner: das Lebensbild einer grossen Frau. "Bibliography of Bertha Suttner's writings": p. [190]-192. [JX1962.S8K413 1973] 72-87475 ISBN 0-8155-5013-8 8.95
1. Suttner, Bertha Felicie Sophie (Kinsky) Freifrau von, 1843-1914. I. Title. **BIP**

LENGYEL, Emil, 1895- 327'.172'0924 B
And all her paths were peace / Emil Lengyel. 1st ed. Nashville : T. Nelson, [1975] p.m. [JX1962.S8L45 1975] 75-19293 ISBN 0-8407-6450-2 : 6.50
1. Suttner, Bertha Felice Sophie Kinsky, Freifrau von, 1843-1914. I. Title.

PAULI, Hertha Ernestine, 1909- 928.3
Cry of the heart; the story of Bertha von Suttner. Translated by Richard and Clara Winston. New York, I. Washburn [1957] 210p. 21cm. [JX1962.S8P33] 57-6608
1. Suttner, Bertha Felicie Sophie (Kinsky) Freifrau von, 1843-1914. I. Title.

SUTTNER, Bertha Felicie Sophie (Kinsky) Freifrau von, 1843-1914. 327'.172
Memoirs of Bertha von Suttner; the records of an eventful life. With a new introd. for the Garland ed. by Irwin Abrams. New York, Garland Pub., 1972 [c1910] 2 v. port. 22 cm. (The Garland library of war and peace) [JX1962.S8A313 1972] 75-147458 ISBN 0-8240-0317-9
1. Peace. I. Title. II. Series.

Sutton, Ralph, 1922-

SHACTER, James D. 786.2'1'0924 B
Piano man : the story of Ralph Sutton / by James D. Shacter. Chicago : Jaynar Press, [1975] 244 p., [16] leaves of plates : ill. ; 22 cm. Includes index. Discography: p. 209-238. [ML417.S95S5] 74-33922 7.95
1. Sutton, Ralph, 1922- I. Title.

Sutton, William Francis.

SUTTON, William Francis. 923.4173
I, Willie Sutton, by Quentin Reynolds. New York, Farrar, Straus and Young [1953] 273p. 22cm. William Sutton's life story as told to Quentin Reynolds. [HV6248.S7A3] 53-7054
I. Reynolds, Quentin James, 1902- II. Title.

Sutzkever, Abraham, 1913- —Criticism and interpretation.

LEFTWICH, Joseph, 1892- 839'.09'13 B
Abraham Sutzkever: partisan poet. New York, T. Yoseloff [1971] 188 p. ports. 22 cm. [PJ5129.S86Z7] 75-146765 ISBN 0-498-07861-2 5.50
1. Sutzkever, Abraham, 1913- —Criticism and interpretation.

Suvorov, Aleksandr Vasil'evich, kniaz Italiiskii, 1729?-1800.

LA VERNE, Leger Marie Philippe Tranchant, comte de 1769-1815. 355.3'31'0924
The life of Field Marshal Souvarof; with reflections upon the principal events, political and military, connected with the history of Russia, during part of the eighteenth century, by L. M. P. de Laverne ... Translated from the French. Baltimore, E. J. Coale New York, Eastburn, Kirk, & co. [etc., etc.] 1814. viip., 1 l. [11]-305p. 23cm. [DK169.S8L2] 15-25124
1. Suvorov. Aleksandr Vasil'evich, kniaz' Italliskil, 1729?-1800. 2. Russia—Hist.—Catherine II, 1762-1796. I. Title.

LONGWORTH, Philip, 1933- 947.060924 (B)
The art of victory; the life and achievements of Field-Marshal Suvorov, 1729-1800. [1st ed.] New York, Holt, Rinehart and Winston [1966, c1965] 350 p. illus., maps, ports. 23 cm. Bibliography: p. [321]-334 [DK169.S8L75 1966] 66-11253
1. Suvorov, Aleksandr Vasil'evich, kniaz Italiiskii, 1729?-1800. I. Title.

Suzman, Helen.

STRANGWAYES-BOOTH, Joanna. 329.9'68 B
A cricket in the thorn tree : Helen Suzman and the Progressive Party of South Africa / Joanna Strangwayes-Booth. Bloomington : Indiana University Press, c1976. 320 p., [4] leaves of plates : ill. ; 23 cm. Includes index. Bibliography: p. 281-283. [DT779.95.S95S85 1976b] 76-486 ISBN 0-253-31483-6 : 12.50
1. Suzman, Helen. 2. Progressive Party of South Africa. 3. South Africa—Politics and government—1961- 4. Legislators—South Africa—Biography. I. Title. **BIP**

Suzuki, Shin'ichi, 1898-

HONDA, Masaaki, 1914- 780'.77
Suzuki changed my life / by Masaaki Honda. Evanston, Ill. : Summy-Birchard Co., c1976. p. cm. [ML418.S83H6] 76-10130 ISBN 0-87487-084-4
1. Suzuki, Shin'ichi, 1898- I. Title. **BIP**

Swaggi, Vincent Norfior, 1914-

KLOCKARS, Carl B. 364.1'62 B
The professional fence [by] Carl B. Klockars. New York, Free Press [1974] xii, 242 p. 22 cm. Originally presented as the author's thesis, University of Pennsylvania. Bibliography: p. 227-232. [HV6248.S75K56 1974] 74-483 ISBN 0-02-917560-7 8.95
1. Swaggi, Vincent Norfior, 1914- 2. Receiving stolen goods—United States. 3. Crime and criminals—United States—Biography. I. Title. **BIP**

Swaim, William, 1802-1835.

ARNETT, Ethel Stephens 920.5
William Swaim, fighting editor; the story of O. Henry's grandfather. Greensboro, N.C., Piedmont Pr. [dist. Straughans' Bk. Shop, c.]1963. 401p. illus. 24cm. Bibl. 63-11676 6.95
1. Swaim, William, 1802-1835. I. Title.

ARNETT, Ethel Stephens 070'.92'4
William Swaim, fighting editor; the story of O. Henry's grandfather. [1st ed.] Greensboro, N.C., Piedmont Press, 1963. 401 p. illus. 24 cm. Includes bibliography. [PN4874.S79A8] 63-11676
1. Swaim, William, 1802-1835. I. Title. **BIP**

Swain, Clara A., 1834-1910.

WILSON, Dorothy Clarke. 266.7'6'0924
Palace of healing; the story of Dr. Clara Swain, first woman missionary doctor, and the hospital she founded. [1st ed.] New York, McGraw-Hill [1968] x, 245 p. 22 cm. [R608.S92W5] 68-22771
1. Swain, Clara A., 1834-1910. 2. Clara Swain Hospital. I. Title.

Swain, David Lowry, 1801-1868— Juvenile literature.

CAMP, Cordelia, 1889- 923.2756
David Lowry Swain, Governor and university president. Asheville, N.C., Stephens Press, 1963. 64 p. illus., maps (on p. [2]-[3] of cover) ports. 23 cm. Bibliography: p. 62. [F258.S95] 64-5809
1. Swain, David Lowry, 1801-1868—Juvenile literature. I. Title.

Swanson, Gloria.

CARR, Larry. 791.43'028'0922
Four fabulous faces : Swanson, Garbo, Crawford, Dietrich / Larry Carr. New York : Penguin Books, 1978. 492 p. : ill. ; 28 cm. Reprint of the 1970 ed. published by Arlington House, New Rochelle, N.Y. [PN1998.A2C34 1978] 78-18862 ISBN 0-14-004988-6 : 12.95
1. Garbo, Greta, 1905- 2. Swanson, Gloria. 3. Crawford, Joan, 1908-1977. 4. Dietrich, Marlene, 1905- 5. Moving-picture actors and actresses—United States—Biography. I. Title. **BIP**

HUDSON, Richard M. 791.43'028'0924
Gloria Swanson, [by] Richard M. Hudson and Raymond Lee. South Brunswick, A. S. Barnes [1970] 269 p. illus., ports. 27 cm. Consists of a short biography and synopses of 66 movies. [PN2287.S9H8] 75-88280 8.50
1. Swanson, Gloria. I. Lee, Raymond, joint author.

Swarthout, Glendon Fred— Biography—Youth.

SWARTHOUT, Glendon Fred. 813'.5'2
The melodeon / Glendon Swarthout ; ill. by Richard Cuffari. 1st ed. New York : Doubleday, 1977. 129 p. : ill. ; 22 cm. Autobiographical. [PS3537.W3743Z52] 77-70983 ISBN 0-385-06163-3 : 6.95
1. Swarthout, Glendon Fred—Biography—Youth. 2. Novelists, American—20th century—Biography. I. Title. **BIP**

SWARTHOUT, Glendon Fred. 813'.5'2 B
The melodeon / Glendon Swarthout. Boston : G. K. Hall, 1978, c1977. 159 p. ; 24 cm. Large print ed. Autobiographical. [PS3537.W3743Z52 1978] 77-27879 ISBN 0-8161-6549-1 lib.bdg. : 8.95
1. Swarthout, Glendon Fred—Biography—Youth. 2. Novelists, American—20th century—Biography. 3. Large type books. I. Title.

Swartz, Joel,

SWARTZ, Joel, 1827-1914. 922.473
A short story of a long life; an autobiography. Written for the family, 1904. Edited and published by Philip Allen Swartz. [1st ed.] Poughkeepsie, N.Y. [1960] 224 p. illus. 23 cm. [BX7260.S875A3] 61-24999
I. Title.

Swedenborg, Emanuel, 1688-1772.

BEAMAN, Edmund Addison, b.1811. 289.4'0924 B
Swedenborg and the new age; or, "The Holy City New Jerusalem," ... New York, AMS Press [1971] 225 p. 22 cm. Reprint of the 1881 ed. [BX8748.B36 1971] 77-134422 ISBN 0-404-08458-3 10.00
1. Swedenborg, Emanuel, 1688-1772. I. Title. II. Title: The Holy City New Jerusalem.

JASPERS, Karl, 1883-1969. 616.8'982'09 B
Strindberg and Van Gogh : an attempt of a pathographic analysis with reference to parallel cases of Swedenborg and Holderlin / Karl Jaspers ; translated by Oskar Grunow and David Woloshin. Tucson, Ariz. : University of Arizona Press, [1977] p. cm. Translation of Strindberg und Van Gogh. Includes index. Bibliography: p. [PT9815.J313 1977] 77-9394 ISBN 0-8165-0608-6 : 12.50. ISBN 0-8165-0434-2 pbk. : 4.95
1. Strindberg, August, 1849-1912. 2. Gogh, Vincent van, 1853-1890. 3. Swedenborg, Emanuel, 1688-1772. 4. Holderlin, Friedrich, 1770-1843. 5. Psychology, Pathological—Cases, clinical reports, statistics. I. Title.

JONSSON, Inge. 289.4'0924
Emanuel Swedenborg. Translated from the Swedish by Catherine Djurklou. New York, Twayne Publishers [1971] 224 p. 21 cm. (Twayne's world authors series. Sweden, TWAS 127) Bibliography: 213-220. [BX8748.J64] 72-120397
1. Swedenborg, Emanuel, 1688-1772.

SIGSTEDT, Cyriel 289.4'0924 B
Sigrid (Ljungberg Odhner)
The Swedenborg epic; the life and works of Emanuel Swedenborg, by Cyriel Odhner Sigstedt. New York, Bookman Associates, 1952. New York, AMS Press, 1971] xvii, 517 p. illus. 23 cm. (Communal societies in America) Includes bibliographical references. [BX8748.S53 1971] 78-137269 ISBN 0-404-05999-6
1. Swedenborg, Emanuel, 1688-1772. I. Title.

SIGSTEDT, Cyriel Sigrid 922.84
(Ljungberg Odhner)
The Swedenborg epic; the life and works of Emanuel Swedenborg. New York, Bookman Associates, 1952. xvii, 517p. illus., ports., map (on lining papers) 14cm. List of works: p. 499-501. Bibliographical references included in Notes and references (p. 445-482) [BX8748.S53] 53-5811
1. Swedenborg, Emanuel, 1688-1772. I. Title.

TOKSVIG, Signe, 1891- 198'.5 B
Emanuel Swedenborg: scientist and mystic. Freeport, N.Y., Books for Libraries Press [1972, c1948] 389 p. ports. 22 cm. (Biography index reprint series) Includes bibliographical references. [BX8748.T65 1972] 72-5447 ISBN 0-8369-8140-5
1. Swedenborg, Emanuel, 1688-1772. **BIP**

TROBRIDGE, George, 1851- 922.84
1909.
Swedenborg, life and teaching. New York, Swedenborg Foundation, 1962. 298 p. illus. 20 cm. "Fifth reprint of the 1935 (fourth) edition of the Swedenborg Society of London." First published in 1907 under title: Emanuel Swedenborg, his life, teachings, and influence. [BX8748.T8 1962] 62-53182
1. Swedenborg, Emanuel, 1688-1772.

Swedish Americans.

BENSON, Adolph 917.3'09'74397
Burnett, 1881- ed.
Swedes in America, 1638-1938, edited by Adolph B. Benson and Naboth Hedin. New York, Haskell House Publishers, 1969. 614 p. illus. 24 cm. "Published for the Swedish American Tercentenary Association." Reprint of the 1938 ed. Includes bibliographical references. [E184.S23B33 1969] 73-98681 ISBN 0-8383-0326-9
1. Swedish Americans. 2. Swedes in the United States—Biography. I. Hedin, Naboth, 1884- joint ed. II. Swedish American Tercentenary Association. III. Title.

Sweeney, Zachary Taylor, 1849-1926.

MCALLISTER, Lester 286'.6'0924(B)
G.
Z. T. Sweeney: preacher and peacemaker, by Lester G. McAllister. St. Louis, Christian Board of Publication [1968] 128 p. port. 23 cm. Bibliography: p. 123-124. [BX7343.S94M3] 68-5649
1. Sweeney, Zachary Taylor, 1849-1926.

Sweeny, Charles, 1849-1916.

FAHEY, John. 979.6'91
The ballyhoo bonanza; Charles Sweeny and the Idaho mines. Seattle, University of Washington Press [1971] xiii, 288 p. illus. 24 cm. [F752.S5F3] 68-11046 10.00
1. Sweeny, Charles, 1849-1916. 2. Gold mines and mining—Coeur d'Alene Mountains, Idaho and Mont. I. Title. **BIP**

Sweet, George Cook, 1877-1953.

WHITE, Lillian C 923.573
Pioneer and patriot; George Cook Sweet, commander, u.S.N., 1877-1953; a biography, by Lillian C. White. Delray Beach, Fla., Southern Pub. Co., 1963. 172 p. illus., ports. 22 cm. Bibliography: p. 172. [E182.S98W5] 64-4394
1. Sweet, George Cook, 1877-1953. I. Title.

Sweeten, Jess, 1905-

LINDQUIST, Allan Sigvard 923.573
Jess Sweeten, Texas lawman. San Antonio, Tex., Naylor [c.1961] 221p. illus. 61-16730 4.95
1. Sweeten, Jess, 1905- 2. Crime and criminals—Henderson Co., Tex. I. Title.

Swenson, Birger, 1895-

SWENSON, Birger, 973'.04'395 S
1895-
My story : immigrant, executive, traveler / by Birger Swenson. Rock Island, Ill. : Augustana Historical Society, 1979. xi, 250 p. : ill. ; 25 cm. (Publication - Augustana Historical Society ; no. 27) [F536.A96 no. 27] [Z473.S955] 070.5'092'4 B 79-50724 ISBN 0-910184-27-5 : 7.50
1. Swenson, Birger, 1895- 2. Religious literature—Publication and distribution—Illinois. 3. Publishers and publishing—Illinois—Biography. 4. Lutherans—Illinois—Biography. 5. Swedes in Illinois—Biography. I. Title. II. Series: Augustana Historical Society, Rock Island, Ill. Publication ; no. 27.

Swensson, Carl Aaron, 1857-1904.

PEARSON, Daniel 973'.04'395 S
Merle.
The Americanization of Carl Aaron Swensson / by Daniel Merle Pearson. Rock Island, Ill. : Augustana Historical Society, c1977. xviii, 169 p. : ill. ; 25 cm. (Publication - Augustana Historical Society ; no. 25) Includes index. Bibliography: p. 161-165. [F536.A96 no. 25] [F686] 328.781'092'4 B 77-151736 5.95
1. Swensson, Carl Aaron, 1857-1904. 2. Swedish Americans—Kansas—History. 3. Kansas—Politics and government—1865-1950. 4. Politicians—Kansas—Biography. I. Title. II. Series: Augustana Historical Society, Rock Island, Ill. Publications ; no. 25.

Swerdfeger, Catherine German, 1857-

MEREDITH, Grace E. 973'.04'97 S
Girl captives of the Cheyennes / Grace E. Meredith. New York : Garland Pub., 1977. xv, 123 p., [12] leaves of plates : ill. ; 23 cm. (The Garland library of narratives of North American Indian captivities ; v. 109) Based on the personal recollections of Catherine German Swerdfeger. Reprint of the 1927 ed. published by Gem Pub. Co., Los Angeles. Issued with the reprint of the 1930 ed. of Frazier, J. Narrative of the captivity of Mrs. Jane Frazier. New York, 1977. The reprint of the 1931 ed. of History of the captivity of David Boyd. New York, 1977. The reprint of the 1932 ed. of Illsley, C. P. The Means massacre. New York, 1977. The reprint of the 1938 ed. of King, T. Narrative of Titus King. New York, 1977. [E85.G2 vol. 109] [E99.C53] 970'.004'97 76-30393 ISBN 0-8240-1733-1(set) lib.bdg. : 25.00
1. Swerdfeger, Catherine German, 1857- 2. German family. 3. Cheyenne Indians—Captivities. 4. Indians of North America—Captivities. 5. Kansas—Biography. I. Swerdfeger, Catherine German, 1857- II. Title. III. Series.

Swieson, Eddy, 1932-

SWIESON, Eddy, 285'.131'0924 B
1932-
When the angels laughed / Eddy Swieson tells his story with Howard Norton. Plainfield, N.J. : Logos International, c1977. x, 126 p., [3] leaves of plates : ill. ; 21 cm. [BX9225.S93A36] 77-20584 ISBN 0-88270-264-5 pbk. : 2.95
1. Swieson, Eddy, 1932- 2. Presbyterian Church—Clergy—Biography. 3. Clergy—United States—Biography. I. Norton, Howard Melvin, joint author. II. Title. **BIP**

Swift, Gustavus Franklin, 1839-1903.

NEYHART, Louise 923.873
(Albright)
Giant of the yards; illustrated by Frederick T. Chapman. Boston, Houghton Mifflin, 1952. 218 p. illus. 24 cm. [HD9419.S72N4] 52-5908
1. Swift, Gustavus Franklin, 1839-1903. 2. Swift and Company. I. Title.

Swift, Joan,

SWIFT, Joan, 1926- 811'.5'4
This element : poems / by Joan Swift. New York : AMS Press, 1975, c1965. 41 p. ; 20 cm. Reprint of the ed. published by A. Swallow, Denver, in series: New poetry series. [PS3569.W5T5 1975] 71-179830 ISBN 0-404-56030-X : 12.50
I. Title.

Swift, Jonathan, 1667-1745.

COLLINS, John 828'.5'09 B
Churton, 1848-1908.
Jonathan Swift; a biographical and critical study. [Folcroft, Pa.] Folcroft Library Editions, 1970. xvi, 280 p. 23 cm. Reprint of the 1893 ed. "Limited to 150 copies." Includes bibliographical references. [PR3726.C6 1970] 72-195913
1. Swift, Jonathan, 1667-1745. **BIP**

CRAIK, Henry, Sir, 1846- 827'.5 B
1927.
The life of Jonathan Swift. 2d ed. New York, B. Franklin [1969] 2 v. ports. 19 cm. (Essays in literature and criticism, 31) (Burt Franklin: Research and source works series, 379) Reprint of the 1894 ed. Bibliographical footnotes. [PR3726.C8 1969] 74-82016
1. Swift, Jonathan, 1667-1745. I. Title. **BIP**

DARK, Sidney, 1874- 283'.0922
1947.
Five Deans: John Colet, John Donne, Jonathan Swift, Arthur Penrhyn Stanley, William Ralph Inge. Freeport, N.Y., Books for Libraries Press [1969] 255 p. 23 cm. (Essay index reprint series) Reprint of the 1928 ed. [BX5197.D25 1969b] 71-93332
1. Colet, John, 1467?-1519. 2. Donne, John, 1573-1631. 3. Swift, Jonathan, 1667-1745. 4. Stanley, Arthur Penrhyn, 1815-1881. 5. Inge, William Ralph, 1860-1954. I. Title.

DARK, Sidney, 1874- 283'.0922
1947.
Five Deans: John Colet, John Donne, Jonathan Swift, Arthur Penrhyn Stanley, William Ralph Inge. Port Washington, N.Y., Kennikat Press [1969] 255 p. 21 cm. (Essay and general literature index reprint series) Reprint of the 1928 ed. [BX5197.D25 1969] 70-86011
1. Colet, John, 1467?-1519. 2. Donne, John, 1573-1631. 3. Swift, Jonathan, 1667-1745. 4. Stanley, Arthur Penrhyn, 1815-1881. 5. Inge, William Ralph, 1860-1954. I. Title.

DOORN, Cornelis van. 928.2
An investigation into the character of Jonathan Swift. New York, Haskell House, 1966. 151 p. port. 24 cm. Reprint of the 1931 ed. Proefschrift--Amsterdam, 1931. Bibliography: p. 149-151. [PR3726.D6] 68-714
1. Swift, Jonathan, 1667-1745. I. Title. **BIP**

EHRENPREIS, Irvin, 1920- 827'.5
The personality of Jonathan Swift. New York, Barnes & Noble [1969] 179 p. 23 cm. Reprint of the 1958 ed. Includes bibliographical references. [PR3726.E35 1969] 74-9613
1. Swift, Jonathan, 1667-1745. I. Title.

EHRENPREIS, Irvin, 1920- 828.5
Swift: the man, his works, and the age. Cambridge, Harvard, 1967 v. 23cm. Contents.v.2. Dr. Swift. Bibl. [PR3726.E37] 62-51793 17.50
1. Swift, Jonathan, 1667-1745. I. Title.

EHRENPREIS, Irvin, 1920- 828.5
Swift: the man, his works, and the age Cambridge, Harvard University Press, 1962- v. 23 cm. Contents.—v. 1. Mr. Swift and his contemporaries. Bibliography: v. 1, p. 288-294. [PR3726.E37] 62-51793
1. Swift, Jonathan, 1667-1745.

EWALD, William Bragg, 827'.5
1925-
The masks of Jonathan Swift. New York, Russell & Russell [1967, c1954] 203 p. 23 cm. Bibliography: p. [191]-197. [PR3726.E9 1967] 66-27067
1. Swift, Jonathan, 1667-1745. I. Title. **BIP**

GREENACRE, Phyllis. 928.2
Swift and Carroll; a psychoanalytic study of two lives. New York, International Universities Press [1955] 306p. illus. 23cm. [PR3726.G7] 55-8236
1. Swift, Jonathan, 1667-1745. 2. Dodgson, Charles Lutwidge, 1832-1898. I. Title. **BIP**

JACKSON, Robert Wyse. 828'.5'08 B
Jonathan Swift, dean and pastor. Freeport, N.Y., Books for Libraries Press [1970] viii, 185 p. illus., facsim., ports. 23 cm. Reprint of the 1939 ed. Includes bibliographical references. [PR3726.J3 1970] 78-137380
1. Swift, Jonathan, 1667-1745.

JACKSON, Robert Wyse. 828'.5'09 B
Jonathan Swift, dean and pastor / by Robert Wyse Jackson. Folcroft, Pa. : Folcroft Library Editions, 1974. x, 185 p., [8] leaves of plates : ill. ; 24 cm. Reprint of the 1939 ed. published by the Society for Promoting Christian Knowledge, London. Includes index. Bibliography: p. 176-179. [PR3726.J3 1974] 74-28423 ISBN 0-8414-5333-0 lib.bdg. : 12.50
1. Swift, Jonathan, 1667-1745. I. Title.

JACKSON, Robert Wyse. 828'.5'09 B
Jonathan Swift, dean and pastor / by Robert Wyse Jackson. Folcroft, Pa. : Folcroft Library Editions, 1974. x, 185 p., [8] leaves of plates : ill. ; 24 cm. Reprint of the 1939 ed. published by the Society for Promoting Christian Knowledge, London. Includes index. Bibliography: p. 176-179. [PR3726.J3 1974] 74-28423 ISBN 0-8414-5333-0 lib. bdg. : 12.50
1. Swift, Jonathan, 1667-1745. I. Title.

JEFFARES, Alexander 828'.5'09
Norman.
Jonathan Swift / by A. Norman Jeffares ; edited by Ian Scott-Kilvert. Harlow [Eng.] : Published for the British Council by Longman Group, 1976. 56 p. ; 22 cm. (Writers & their work ; 248) Bibliography: p. 46-56. [PR3727.J38] 76-371023 ISBN 0-582-01248-1
1. Swift, Jonathan, 1667-1745. 2. Authors, English—18th century—Biography. I. Title. II. Series.

JOHNSTON, Denis [William 928.2
Denis Johnston]
In search of Swift. Dublin, Hodges Figgis [dist., New York, Barnes & Noble]1959 [i.e., 1960] xii, 240p. (bibl. notes: p. 225-231) illus. 26cm. 59-51839 7.50 bds.,
1. Swift, Jonathan, 1667-1745. I. Title.

KING, Richard Ashe, 828'.5'09
1839-1932.
Swift in Ireland. New York, Haskell House Publishers, 1971. 204 p. illus. 23 cm. Reprint of 1895 ed. [PR3727.K5 1971] 79-171231 ISBN 0-8383-1338-8
1. Swift, Jonathan, 1667-1745. 2. Ireland—Politics and government—18th century. I. Title. **BIP**

LANDA, Louis A 1902- 928.2
Swift and the Church of Ireland. Oxford, Clarendon Press, 1954. xvi, 206p. 23cm. Bibliographical footnotes. [PR3726.L3] A55
1. Swift, Jonathan, 1667-1745. 2. Church of Ireland—Hist. I. Title. **BIP**

LEBROCQUY, Sybil 928.2
Cadenus; a reassessment in the light of new evidence of the relationships between Swift, Stella and Vanessa. Dublin, Dolmen Pr. [dist. Chester Springs, Pa., Dufour, 1964, c.1962] 160p. illus. 21cm. Bibl. [PR3726.L37] 63-453 3.95 bds.,
1. Swift, Jonathan, 1667-1745. 2. Johnson, Esther, 1681-1728. 3. Vanhomrigh, Esther, 1690-1723. I. Title.

MURRY, John Middleton, 928.2
1889-
Jonathan Swift, a critical biography. New York, Noon-day Press, 1955. 506p. illus. 22cm. [PR3726.M8 1955] 55-12009
1. Swift, Jonathan, 1667-1745. I. Title.

MURRY, John Middleton, 1889-1957. 828'.5'09
Jonathan Swift; a critical biography. New York, Farrar, Straus and Giroux [1967, c1955] 508 p. port. 21 cm. "Notes and references": p. 485-494. [PR3726.M8 1967] 67-3425
1. Swift, Jonathan, 1667-1745.

NEWMAN, Bertram, 1886- 828'.5'09 B
Jonathan Swift. London, G. Allen & Unwin Ltd. [Folcroft, Pa.] Folcroft Library Editions, 1972. p. Reprint of the 1937 ed. Bibliography: p. [PR3726.N4 1972] 72-10252 ISBN 0-8414-0687-1 (lib. bdg.)
1. Swift, Jonathan, 1667-1745. **BIP**

NEWMAN, Bertram, 1886- 828'.5'09 B
Jonathan Swift / by Bertram Newman. Norwood, Pa. : Norwood Editions, 1975. 432 p. ; 23 cm. Reprint of the 1937 ed. published by G. Allen & Unwin, London. Includes index. Bibliography: p. [397]-402. [PR3726.N4 1975] 75-33782 ISBN 0-88305-455-8 lib. bdg. : 30.00
1. Swift, Jonathan, 1667-1745.

QUINTANA, Ricardo. 928.2
The mind and art of Jonathan Swift. London, Oxford University Press, 1953. xvi, 400p. 22cm. 'First published in 1936. Reprinted with additional notes and bibliography in 1953.' Bibliography: p. [365]-380. [PR3726.Q] A54
1. Swift, Jonathan, 1667-1743. I. Title.

QUINTANA, Ricardo. 827.52
Swift: an introduction. London, New York, Oxford University Press, 1955. 204 p. 22 cm. Includes bibliography. [PR3726.Q53] 55-1158
1. Swift, Jonathan, 1667-1745. **BIP**

QUINTANA, Ricardo Beckwith 928.2
The mind and art of Jonathan Swift. Gloucester, Mass., P. Smith, 1965. xvi, 400p. 21cm. First pub. in 1936 by Oxford. Bibl. [PR3726.Q5] 6.00
1. Swift, Jonathan, 1667-1745. I. Title. **BIP**

SHERIDAN, Thomas, 1719-1788. 828'.5'09 B
The life of the Rev. Dr. Jonathan Swift, Dean of St. Patrick's, Dublin. [Folcroft, Pa.] Folcroft Library Editions, 1972. p. Reprint of the 1785 ed. [PR3726.S43 1972] 72-8021 ISBN 0-8414-0291-4 (lib. bdg.)
1. Swift, Jonathan, 1667-1745. I. Title.

SMITH, Sophie Shilleto. 828'.5'09 B
Dean Swift. [Folcroft, Pa.] Folcroft Library Editions, 1973. xi, 340 p. illus. 24 cm. Reprint of the 1910 ed. published by Putnam, New York. Bibliography: p. 331-335. [PR3726.S5 1972] 72-10251 ISBN 0-8414-0695-2 (lib. bdg.)
1. Swift, Jonathan, 1667-1745. I. Title. **BIP**

STEPHEN, Leslie, Sir, 1832-1904. 827'.5
Swift. New York, AMS Press [1968] x, 209 p. 22 cm. (English men of letters) Reprint of the 1889 ed. Bibliographical footnotes. [PR3726.S7 1968b] 68-58399
1. Swift, Jonathan, 1667-1745.

SWIFT, Deane, 1707-1783. 828'.5'09 S
An essay upon the life, writings, and character of Dr. Jonathan Swift (1755) by Deane Swift. A letter to Dean Swift on his Essay (1755) by Patrick Delany. New York, Garland Pub., 1974. 375, 53, 31 p. 22 cm. (The Life & times of seven major British writers. Swiftiana, 14) Reprint of 2 works, the 1st printed for C. Bathurst, London; the 2d printed by W. Reeve, London. [PR3726.S95 vol. 14] 828'.5'09 B 74-14988 ISBN 0-8240-1275-5
1. Swift, Jonathan, 1667-1745. 2. Swift, Deane, 1707-1783. An essay upon the life, writings, and character of Dr. Jonathan Swift. I. Delany, Patrick, 1685?-1768. A letter to Dean Swift on his Essay. 1974. II. Title. III. Title: A letter to Dean Swift on his Essay. IV. Series: Swiftiana, 14.

SWIFT, Jonathan, 1667-1745. 828'.5'09 B
The letters of Jonathan Swift to Charles Ford. Edited by David Nichol Smith. Folcroft, Pa., Folcroft Press [1969] xlvii, 260 p. 25 cm. Contents.Contents.—Letters of Swift and Ford.—Poems among Ford's papers.—Fragment of a pamphlet.—Letters to Ford from Gay, Pope and Parnell, Bolingbroke, and the Duchess of Ormond. [PR3726.A63 1969] 72-196548
I. Ford, Charles, 1682-1743. **BIP**

ULMAN, Craig Hawkins. 828'.5'09 B
Satire and the correspondence of Swift. Cambridge, Mass., Harvard University Press, 1973. 53 p. 19 cm. (The LeBaron Russell Briggs prize honors essays in English, 1972) Bibliography: p. 43-47. [PR3728.S2U4] 72-95457 ISBN 0-674-78976-8 2.50 (pbk.)
1. Swift, Jonathan, 1667-1745. 2. Satire. I. Title. II. Series. **BIP**

VANDOREN, Carl Clinton, 1885-1950 928.2
Swift Port Washingston, N.Y., Kennikat 279 p. ports. 23 cm 64-22538 7.50
1. Swift, Jonathan, 1667-1745 I. Title.

VAN DOREN, Carl Clinton, 1885-1950. 828'.5'09 B
Swift / by Carl Van Doren. New York : AMS Press, 1979 [c1930] p. cm. Reprint of the ed. published by Viking Press, New York. Includes index. Bibliography: p. [PR3726.V3 1979] 76-12127 ISBN 0-404-15239-2 : 26.50 26.50
1. Swift, Jonathan, 1667-1745. 2. Authors, Irish—18th century—Biography.

Swift, Jonathan, 1667-1745—Biography.

ACWORTH, Bernard. 828'.5'09 B
Swift / Bernard Acworth. Folcroft, Pa. : Folcroft Library Editions, 1978. xix, 250 p., [8] leaves of plates : ill. ; 26 cm. Reprint of the 1947 ed. published by Eyre & Spottiswoode, London. Includes index. [PR3726.A58 1978] 78-20836 ISBN 0-8414-2911-1 lib. bdg. : 30.00
1. Swift, Jonathan, 1667-1745—Biography. 2. Authors, Irish—18th century—Biography.

FORSTER, John, 1812-1876. 828'.5'09 B
The life of Jonathan Swift. Volume the first, 1667-1711. [Folcroft, Pa.] Folcroft Library Editions, 1974. p. cm. Reprint of the 1875 ed. published by J. Murray, London. No more published. [PR3726.F7 1974] 74-9746 ISBN 0-8414-4199-5 (lib. bdg.)
1. Swift, Jonathan, 1667-1745—Biography. I. Title.

FORSTER, John, 1812-1876. 828'.5'09 B
The life of Jonathan Swift. Volume the first, 1667-1711. [Folcroft, Pa.] Folcroft Library Editions, 1974. p. cm. Reprint of the 1875 ed. published by J. Murray, London. No more published. [PR3726.F7 1974] 74-9746 4.00 (lib. bdg.).
1. Swift, Jonathan, 1667-1745—Biography. I. Title.

HAY, James, 1838-1904. 828'.5'09 B
Swift; the mystery of his life and love. [Folcroft, Pa.] Folcroft Library Editions, 1972. xvi, 361 p. 24 cm. Reprint of the 1891 ed. [PR3726.H3 1972] 72-6144 ISBN 0-8414-0075-X
1. Swift, Jonathan, 1667-1745—Biography. **BIP**

MURRY, John Middleton, 1889-1957. 928.2
Jonathan Swift, a critical biography. New York, Noonday Press, 1955. 508 p. illus. 22 cm. [PR3726.M8 1955] 55-12009
1. Swift, Jonathan, 1667-1745—Biography.

QUINTANA, Ricardo. 828'.5'09
Swift : an introduction / by Ricardo Quintana. Westport, Conn. : Greenwood Press, 1979. p. cm. Reprint of the 1955 ed. published by Oxford University Press, London. Includes index. Bibliography: p. [PR3726.Q53 1979] 79-17607 ISBN 0-313-22052-2 lib. bdg. : 16.75
1. Swift, Jonathan, 1667-1745—Biography. 2. Authors, English—18th century—Biography. I. Title.

ROWSE, Alfred Leslie, 1903- 828'.5'09 B
Jonathan Swift / A. L. Rowse. New York : Scribner, c1975. 240 p. : ill. ; 24 cm. Includes index. Bibliography: p. 232-233. [PR3726.R75 1975] 75-37779 ISBN 0-684-14561-8 : 10.00
1. Swift, Jonathan, 1667-1745—Biography.

SHERIDAN, Thomas, 1719-1788. 828'.5'09 S
The life of the Rev. Dr. Jonathan Swift (1784) / by Thomas Sheridan. New York : Garland Pub., 1974. 568 p. : front. ; 22 cm. (The Life & times of seven major British writers) (Swiftiana ; 15) Reprint of the ed. printed for C. Bathurst et al., London. [PR3726.S95 vol. 15] 828'.5'09 B 74-23741 ISBN 0-8240-1276-3
1. Swift, Jonathan, 1667-1745—Biography. I. Title. II. Series.

THREE biographical pamphlets, 1745-1758. 828'.5'09 B
New York : Garland Pub., 1975. 209 p. ; 23 cm. (The Life & times of seven major British writers) (Swiftiana ; 13) Reprint of the 1755 ed. of An account of the life of the Reverend Jonathan Swift, D.D., by John Hawkesworth which appeared in v. 1 of The works of Jonathan Swift, D.D., printed for C. Bathurst, et. al., London; of the 1758 ed. of The life of Dr. Jonathan Swift by W. H. Dilworth, printed for G. Wright, London; and of the 1745 ed. of An authentic copy of the last will and testament of the Reverend Dr. Swift, printed in Dublin, reprinted in London and sold by J. Oldcastle. [PR3726.S95 vol. 13] [PR3726] 75-28165 ISBN 0-8240-1274-7 lib.bdg. : 28.00
1. Swift, Jonathan, 1667-1745—Biography. 2. Swift, Jonathan, 1667-1745—Parodies, travesties, etc. I. Hawkesworth, John, 1715?-1773. An account of the life of the Reverend Jonathan Swift, D.D. 1975. II. Dilworth, W. H. The life of Dr. Jonathan Swift. 1975. III. An Authentic copy of the last will and testament of the Reverend Dr. Swift. 1975. IV. Title. V. Series.

Swift, Jonathan, 1667-1745—Correspondence.

SWIFT, Jonathan, 1667-1745. 823'.5
Journal to Stella / Jonathan Swift ; edited by Harold Williams. New York : Barnes & Noble Books, 1975. 2 v. (lxii, 801 p.), [7] leaves of plates : ill. ; 20 cm. Reprint of the 1948 ed. published by Clarendon Press, Oxford. Includes bibliographical references and index. [PR3726.A43 1975] 75-320303 32.00(set)
1. Swift, Jonathan, 1667-1745—Correspondence. 2. Johnson, Esther, 1681-1728. I. Title. **BIP**

SWIFT, Jonathan, 1667-1745. 828'.5'09 B
The letters of Jonathan Swift to Charles Ford. Edited by David Nichol Smith. Folcroft, Pa., Folcroft Press [1969] xlvii, 260 p. 25 cm. Contents.Contents. Letters of Swift and Ford.—Poems among Ford's papers.—Fragment of a pamphlet.—Letters to Ford from Gay, Pope and Parnell, Bolingbroke, and the Duchess of Ormond. [PR3726.A63 1969] 72-196548
I. Ford, Charles, 1682-1743. **BIP**

[VANHOMRIGH, Esther] 1690-1723. 828'.5'09 B
Vanessa and her correspondence with Jonathan Swift. The letters edited for the first time from the originals, with an introd. by A. Martin Freeman. [Folcroft, Pa.] Folcroft Library Editions, 1974. 216 p. facsims. 23 cm. Reprint of the 1921 ed. published by Selwyn & Blount, London. Contents.Contents.—The correspondence of Swift and Vanessa.—Cadenus and Vanessa, and other documents.—Miscellaneous letters. [PR3726.A48 1974] 74-9722 ISBN 0-8414-4206-1 (lib. bdg.)
1. Swift, Jonathan, 1667-1745—Correspondence. 2. Vanhomrigh, Esther, 1690-1723. I. Swift, Jonathan, 1667-1745. II. Title. **BIP**

Swift, Jonathan, 1667-1745, in fiction, drama, poetry, etc.

SMEDLEY, Jonathan, 1671-1729. 828'.5'09 S
Gulliveriana, 1728 New York, Garland Pub., 1974. p. cm. (The Life & times of seven major British writers. Swiftiana, 8) Reprint of the ed. printed for J. Roberts, London. [PR3726.S95 vol. 8] [PR3687.S75] 828'.5'09 74-17378 ISBN 0-8240-1269-0 22.00
1. Swift, Jonathan, 1667-1745, in fiction, drama, poetry, etc. 2. Pope, Alexander, 1688-1744, in fiction, drama, poetry, etc. 3. Swift, Jonathan, 1667-1745. Miscellanies in prose and verse. I. Title. II. Series: Swiftiana, 8. **BIP**

Swift, Lucius Burrie, 1844-1929.

FOULKE, William Dudley, 1848-1935, ed. 973.8'0924 B
Lucius B. Swift; a biography. Freeport, N.Y., Books for Libraries Press [1971] vi, 153 p. ports. 23 cm Reprint of the 1930 ed. Includes bibliographical references. [JK693.S8F6 1971] 77-164600 ISBN 0-8369-5884-5
1. Swift, Lucius Burrie, 1844-1929. 2. Civil service reform. 3. Liberty.

Swig, Benjamin H., 1893-

BLUM, Walter. 917.3'03'910924 B
Benjamin H. Swig; the measure of a man. San Francisco, 1968. 80 p. col. illus., ports. 27 cm. [CT275.S9872B55] 68-57033
1. Swig, Benjamin H., 1893-

Swilling, Jack, 1830-1878.

MYERS, John Myers, 1906- FIC
I, Jack Swilling, founder of Phoenix, Arizona. New New York, Hastings House [c.1961] 308p. 61-7202 5.95
1. Swilling, Jack, 1830 1878. I. Title.

Swinburne, Algernon Charles, 1837-1909.

CASSIDY, John A. 821.8
Algernon C. Swinburne, by John A. Cassidy. New York, Twayne Publishers [1964] 186 p. 22 cm. (Twayne's English authors series, 10) Bibliography: p. 171-177. [PR5513.C3] 64-19035
1. Swinburne, Algernon Charles, 1837-1909. **BIP**

CHEW, Samuel Claggett, 1888-1960 821.8
Swinburne. Hamden, Conn., Archon [dist. Shoe String] 1966[c.1929] viii, 335p. illus., facsim., ports. 22cm. Bibl. [PR5513.C5] 66-15385 8.00
1. Swinburne, Algernon Charles, 1837-1909. I. Title.

GOSSE, Edmund William, Sir, 1849-1928. 821'.8 B
The life of Algernon Charles Swinburne. [Folcroft, Pa.] Folcroft Library Editions, 1973. p. Reprint of the 1917 ed. published by Macmillan, London. [PR5513.G59 1973] 73-13987
1. Swinburne, Algernon Charles, 1837-1909. I. Title.

GOSSE, Edmund William, Sir, 1849-1928. 821'.8
Swinburne; an essay written in 1875 and now first printed. [Folcroft, Pa.] Folcroft Library Editions, 1973. vi, 81 p. 24 cm. Reprint of the 1925 ed., printed for private circulation. [PR5513.G64 1973] 73-7959 10.00 (lib. bdg.)
1. Swinburne, Algernon Charles, 1837-1909. **BIP**

GOSSE, Edmund William, Sir, 1849-1928. 821'.8
Swinburne; an essay written in 1875 and now first printed. [Folcroft, Pa.] Folcroft Library Editions, 1973. vi, 81 p. 24 cm. Reprint of the 1925 ed., printed for private circulation. [PR5513.G64 1973] 73-7959 ISBN 0-8414-2036-X (lib. bdg.)
1. Swinburne, Algernon Charles, 1837-1909.

HARE, Humphrey. 821'.8 B
Swinburne, a biographical approach. Port Washington, N.Y., Kennikat Press [1970] xv, 216 p. ports. 22 cm. Reprint of the 1949 ed. Bibliography: p. 206-207. [PR5513.H3 1970] 74-113314
1. Swinburne, Algernon Charles, 1837-1909.

KERNAHAN, Coulson, 1858-1943. 821'.8 B
Swinburne as I knew him : with some unpublished letters from the poet to his cousin the Hon. Lady Henniker Heaton / by Coulson Kernahan. Folcroft, Pa. : Folcroft Library Editions, 1976. p. cm. Reprint of the 1919 ed. published by J. Lane, London. [PR5513.K4 1976] 76-17889 ISBN 0-8414-5517-1 lib. bdg. : 17.50
1. Swinburne, Algernon Charles, 1837-1909. I. Title.

LAFOURCADE, Georges. 821.8
Swinburne; a literary biography. New York, Russell & Russell [1967] xiv, 314 p. illus., facsim., ports. 23 cm. Reprint of the 1932 ed. "Bibliographical note": p. 304-307. [PR5513.L34] 66-24720
1. Swinburne, Algernon Charles, 1837-1909. I. Title. **BIP**

LAFOURCADE, Georges. 821.8
Swinburne: a literary biography New York, Russell & Russell [1967] xiv, 314 p. illus., facsim., ports. 23 cm. Reprint of the 1932 ed. "Bibliographical note": p. 304-307. [PR5513.L34 1967] 66-24720
1. Swinburne, Algernon Charles, 1837-1909. I. Title.

LAFOURCADE, Georges. 821.8
Swinburne: a literary biography New York, Russell & Russell [1967] xiv, 314 p. illus., facsim., ports. 23 cm. Reprint of the 1932 ed. "Bibliographical note": p. 304-307. [PR5513.L34 1967] 66-24720
1. Swinburne, Algernon Charles, 1837-1909. I. Title.

LAFOURCADE, Georges. 821'.8 B
Swinburne, a literary biography. [Folcroft, Pa.] Folcroft Library Editions, 1973. p. Reprint of the 1932 ed. published by G. Bell, London. Bibliography: p. [PR5513.L34 1973] 73-12878 ISBN 0-8414-5658-5 (lib. bdg.)
1. Swinburne, Algernon Charles, 1837-1909. I. Title.

NICOLSON, Harold George, Sir, 1886-1968. 821'.8
Swinburne. [Unaltered and unabridged ed. Hamden, Conn.] Archon Books, 1969 [c1926] viii, 207 p. 19 cm. Bibliography: p. 202-203. [PR5513.N5 1969] 69-19218
1. Swinburne, Algernon Charles, 1837-1909.

SWINBURNE, Algernon Charles, 1837-1909. 821'.8 B
The boyhood of Algernon Charles Swinburne; personal recollections by his cousin Mrs. Disney Leith, with extracts from some of his private letters. [Folcroft, Pa.] Folcroft Library Editions, 1973. p. Reprint of the 1917 ed. published by Chatto & Windus, London. "Extracts from the private letters of Algernon Charles Swinburne: p. [PR5513.A34 1973] 73-15519 22.50
1. Swinburne, Algernon Charles, 1837-1909. I. Leith, Mary Charlotte Julia (Gordon) II. Title. **BIP**

SWINBURNE, Algernon Charles, 1837-1909. 928.2
Letters. Edited by Cecil Y. Lang. New Haven, Yale University Press, 1959-62. 6 v. ports., facsims. 25 cm. Contents.v. 1. 1854-1869. -- v. 2. 1869-1875. -- v. 3. 1875-1877. -- v. 4. 1877-1882. -- v. 5. 1883-1800. -- v. 6. 1890-1909. Bibliographical footnotes. [PR5513.A32] 59-12698
I. Lang, Cecil Y. ed. II. Title.

WOODBERRY, George Edward, 1855-1930. 821'.8
Swinburne. [Folcroft, Pa.] Folcroft Library Editions, 1973, [i.e. 1974] p. Reprint of the ed. published by Macmillan, New York. [PR5514.W6 1973] 73-15594 5.00 (lib. bdg.).
1. Swinburne, Algernon Charles, 1837-1909.

Swinburne, Algernon Charles, 1837-1909—Biography.

FULLER, Jean Overton. 801.9
Swinburne; a biography. New York, Schocken Books [1971, c1968] 317 p. ports. 23 cm. First published in 1968 under title: Swinburne: a critical biography. Bibliography: p. 301-309. [PR5513.F8 1971] 79-146790 ISBN 0-8052-3388-1 8.00
1. Swinburne, Algernon Charles, 1837-1909—Biography. **BIP**

HENDERSON, Philip, 1906- 821'.8
Swinburne; portrait of a poet. [1st American ed.] New York, Macmillan [1974] xiii, 305 p. illus. 24 cm. Includes bibliographical references. [PR5513.H38] 74-478 ISBN 0-02-550960-8 10.95
1. Swinburne, Algernon Charles, 1837-1909—Biography. **BIP**

THOMAS, Donald Serrell. 821'.8 B
Swinburne, the poet in his world / Donald Thomas. 1st American ed. New York : Oxford University Press, 1979. 256 p., [4] leaves of plates : ill. ; 23 cm. Includes index. Bibliography: p. [241]-245. [PR5513.T4 1979] 78-74626 ISBN 0-19-520136-1 : 12.95
1. Swinburne, Algernon Charles, 1837-1909—Biography. 2. Authors, English—19th century—Biography. I. Title.

Swindlers and swindling—Biography.

WADE, Carlson. 364.1'63'0922 B
Great hoaxes and famous imposters / by Carlson Wade. Middle Village, N.Y. : Jonathan David Publishers, [1975] p. cm. [HV6245.W33] 75-14072 ISBN 0-8246-0200-5 : 9.95
1. Swindlers and swindling—Biography. 2. Impostors and imposture—Biography. I. Title. **BIP**

Swinfen, Averil Eady, Baroness Swinfen.

SWINFEN, Averil Eady, Baroness Swinfen. 636.1'8
Donkeys galore / by Averil Swinfen. Newton Abbot ; North Pomfret, Vt. : David and Charles, 1976. 136 p. : ill., ports. ; 23 cm. Includes index. [SF361.S95] 76-2883 ISBN 0-7153-7150-9 : 9.95
1. Swinfen, Averil Eady, Baroness Swinfen. 2. Donkeys—Legends and stories. 3. Donkey breeders—Ireland—Spanish Point—Biography. 4. Spanish Point, Ire.—Biography. I. Title. **BIP**

Swingle, Wilbur Willis, 1891-

W.W. Swingle, teacher and investigator; a symposium: four decades of American endocrinology, with particular reference to the works of W. W. Swingle, Princeton University, April, 1959. A tribute by his former associates and graduate students. [Elliott J. Collins, editor. Princeton? N.J., 1959] x, 70 p. ports, facsims, 26 cm. Includes bibliographies. [QP26.S85W2 1959] 59-44101 926.1
1. Swingle, Wilbur Willis, 1891-

Swinnerton, Frank Arthur, 1884-

BENNETT, Arnold, 1867-1931. 823'.9'12 B
Frank Swinnerton; personal sketches by Arnold Bennett, H. G. Wells [and] Grant M. Overton. Together with notes and comments on the novels of Frank Swinnerton. Plainview, N.Y., Books for Libraries Press [1974, c1920] p. cm. (The collected works of Arnold Bennett) Reprint of the ed. published by G. H. Doran Co., New York. [PR6037.W85Z6 1974] 74-5433 ISBN 0-518-19099-4
1. Swinnerton, Frank Arthur, 1884- I. Wells, Herbert George, 1866-1946. II. Overton, Grant Martin, 1887-1930. **BIP**

Swinton, John, 1829-1901.

GARLIN, Sender. 070'.92'4 B
John Swinton, American radical, 1829-1901 : including the full text of his interview with Karl Marx in 1880 / by Sender Garlin. New York : American Institute for Marxist Studies, 1976. 47 p. ; 28 cm. (Occasional papers - American Institute for Marxist Studies ; no. 20) Bibliography: p. 45-47. [HD8073.S84G37] 76-381714 pbk. : 1.50
1. Swinton, John, 1829-1901. 2. Journalists—United States—Biography. 3. Journalism, Labor—United States—History. I. Title. II. Series: American Institute for Marxist Studies. Occasional papers ; no. 20.

Swisher, Peter N., 1944-

SWISHER, Peter N., 1944- 959.704'38
A Vietnam diary / by Peter N. Swisher ; [ill. by Gene L. Adrean]. Richmond : Hesperia Publications, c1975. [71] p. : ill. ; 20 cm. [DS559.5.S95] 75-15211
1. Swisher, Peter N., 1944- 2. Vietnamese Conflict, 1961-1975—Personal narratives, American. I. Title.

Swisshelm, Jane Grey Cannon, 1815-1884.

SWISSHELM, Jane Grey Cannon, 1815-1884. 081
Crusader and feminist : letters of Jane Grey Swisshelm, 1858-1865 / edited with an introd. and notes by Arthur J. Larsen. Westport, Conn. : Hyperion Press, 1976, c1934. p. cm. (Pioneers of the woman's movement) Reprint of the ed. published by the Minnesota Historical Society, which was issued in its Publications series, and as v. 2 in its Narratives and documents series. [E501.S92 1976] 74-33957 ISBN 0-88355-276-0 : 25.00
1. Swisshelm, Jane Grey Cannon, 1815-1884. 2. United States—History—Civil War, 1861-1865—Personal narratives. 3. Washington, D.C.—History—Civil War, 1861-1865—Sources. 4. Minnesota—Description and travel—1858-1950. I. Title. II. Series: Minnesota Historical Society. Narratives and documents ; v. 2. III. Series: Minnesota Historical Society. Publications. **BIP**

WALKER, Peter, 1931- 322.4'4'0922 B
Moral choices : memory, desire, and imagination in nineteenth-century American abolition / Peter Walker. Baton Rouge : Louisiana State University Press, c1978. p. cm. Includes index. Bibliography: p. [E449.W185] 78-5922 24.95
1. Conway, Moncure Daniel, 1832-1907. 2. Swisshelm, Jane Grey Cannon, 1815-1884. 3. Douglass, Frederick, 1817(?)-1895. 4. Abolitionists—United States—Biography. 5. Slavery in the United States—Anti-slavery movements. I. Title. **BIP**

Switzerland—Biog.—Dictionaries.

WHO'S who in Switzerland, including the Principality of Lichtenstein, 1966-1967. A biographical dictionary containing about 3900 biographies of prominent people in and of Switzerland (including the Principality of Lichtenstein) Geneva, Nagel Pubs. [1966] 21cm. [DQ52.W5] 52-39693 22.00 920.0494
1. Switzerland—Biog.—Dictionaries. 2. Liechtenstein, Principality of—Biog.—Dictionaries.
Distributed by Intl. Pubns. Serv., New York.

WHO'S who in Switzerland, including the Principality of Liechtenstein, 1964-1965. A biog. dicty. containing about 3500 biogs. of prominent people in and out of Switzerland, including the Principality of Liechtenstein. Geneva, Nagel [New York, 10010, Intl. Bk. & Pub. Co., 257 Park Ave. South [1965, c.1964] xiv, 676p. 21cm. [DQ52.W5] 52-39693 16.00 920.0494
1. Switzerland—Biog.—Dictionaries. 2. Liechtenstein, Principality of—Biog.—Dictionaries.

Swope family.

MCLACHLAN, Winifred Morse. 929.2'0973
Jost Schwab and Jacob Schwob, Swope pioneers of early Lancaster County, Pennsylvania. Salt Lake City, 1969. 41 p. illus., geneal. table. 22 cm. [CS71.S988 1969] 74-7844
1. Swope family. I. Title.

Swope, Gerard, 1872-1957.

LOTH, David Goldsmith, 1899- 338.7'62'130924 B
Swope of G.E. / David Loth. New York : Arno Press, 1976, c1958. p. cm. (Companies and men, business enterprise in America) Reprint of the ed. published by Simon and Schuster, New York. [HD9695.U52L68 1976] 75-41769 ISBN 0-405-08084-0
1. Swope, Gerard, 1872-1957. 2. General Electric Company. I. Title. II. Series.

Swope, Herbert Bayard, 1882-1958.

LEWIS, Alfred Allan. 070.5'0924 B
Top of the world : Herbert Bayard Swope and the golden age of American journalism / by Alfred Allan Lewis. Indianapolis : Bobbs-Merrill, [1977] p. cm. Includes index. Bibliography: p. [PN4874.S796L4] 76-45577 ISBN 0-672-51858-9 : 15.00
1. Swope, Herbert Bayard, 1882-1958. 2. Journalists—United States—Biography. I. Title.

Sykes, Norman, 1897-1961.

BEZZANT, James Stanley, 1897- v. 12
The Very Reverend Norman Sykes, 1897-1961, by J. S. Bezzant. London, Oxford University Press [1962?] [417]-428 p. illus. 23 cm. Reprinted from the Proceedings of the British Academy, v. 47. Cover title. NUC66
1. Sykes, Norman, 1897-1961. I. Title.

Sylvester, Albert James, 1889-

SYLVESTER, Albert James, 1889- 941.083'092'4 B
Life with Lloyd George : the diary of A. J. Sylvester, 1931-45 / edited by Colin Cross. New York : Barnes & Noble, 1975. 351 p., [4] leaves of plates : ill. ; 23 cm. Includes index. [DA566.9.S85A33] 74-26182 ISBN 0-06-496251-2 : 23.50
1. Sylvester, Albert James, 1889- 2. Lloyd George, David Lloyd, 1st Earl, 1863-1945. I. Title.

Sylvester II, pope, d. 1003.

THE peasant boy who became Pope: story of Gerbert. London, New York, Abelard-Schuman [1958] xi, 179p. 16 plates. 20cm. v. 12
1. Sylvester II, pope, d. 1003. I. Lattin, Harriet (Pratt) 1898-

Sylvis, William H.,

SYLVIS, William H., 1828-1869 331.88'0924
The life, speeches, labors, & essays of William H. Sylvis, by his brother, James C. Sylvis. New York, Kelley, 1968. 456p. port. 20cm. (Lib. of Amer. labor hist.)

Reprints of econ. classics. Reprint of the 1872 ed. [HD8072.S97 1968] 66-21693 12.50
I. Sylvis, James C. ed. II. Title.

Syme, Ronald,

SYME, Ronald, 1910- 923.9469
Vasco da Gama, sailor toward the sunrise. Illustrated by William Stobbs. New York, Morrow, 1959. 95 p. illus. 22 cm. [G286.G2S9] 59-5018
I. Gama, Vasco da, 1469-1524. II. Title.

Symington, William Stuart, 1901-

WELLMAN, Paul Iselin, 923.273
1898-1966.
Stuart Symington; portrait of a man with a mission. [1st ed.] Garden City, N. Y., Doubleday, 1960. 283 p. 22 cm. [E748.S95W4] 60-6174
I. Symington, William Stuart, 1901-

Symonds, John Addington, 1840-1893.

GROSSKURTH, Phyllis. 928.2
The woeful Victorian; a biography of John Addington Symonds. [1st ed.] New York, Holt, Rinehart and Winston [1965, c1964] x, 370 p. illus., ports. 22 cm. First published in 1964 under title: John Addington Symonds. Bibliographical references included in "Notes" (p. 329-355) Bibliography: p. 357-361. [PR5523.G7 1965] 65-14446
I. Symonds, John Addington, 1840-1893. I. Title.

SYMONDS, John Addington, 826'.8
1840-1893.
The letters of John Addington Symonds. Edited by Herbert M. Schueller & Robert L. Peters. Detroit, Wayne State University Press, 1967-69. 3 v. illus., facsims., ports. 24 cm. Contents.Contents.—v. 1. 1844-1868.—v. 2 1869-1884.—v. 3 1885-1893. Includes bibliographical references. [PR5523.A46] 67-11765
I. Schueller, Herbert M., comp. II. Peters, Robert Louis, 1924- comp. III. Title. BIP

Symonds, John Addington, 1840-1893—Biography.

GROSSKURTH, Phyllis. 828'.8'09 B
John Addington Symonds : a biography / Phyllis Grosskurth. New York : Arno Press, 1975, c1964. x, 370 p., [8] leaves of plates : ill. ; 23 cm. (Homosexuality) Reprint of the ed. published by Longmans, London. Includes index. Bibliography: p. 357-361. [PR5523.G7 1975] 75-12322 ISBN 0-405-07356-9 : 20.00
I. Symonds, John Addington, 1840-1893—Biography. I. Title. II. Series. BIP

Symons, Arthur, 1865-1945.

LHOMBREAUD, Roger, 1922- 928.2
Arthur Symons, a critical biography [Chester Springs, Pa.] Dufour, 1964[c.1963] 333p. illus., facsims., ports. 22cm. Bibl. [PR5528] 64-25452 7.50
I. Symons, Arthur, 1865-1945. I. Title.

Symons, Arthur, 1865-1945—Friends and associates.

SYMONS, Arthur, 1865- 821'.8 B
1945.
The memoirs of Arthur Symons : life and art in the 1890s / edited by Karl Beckson. University Park : Pennsylvania State University Press, c1977. 284 p. : port. ; 24 cm. Includes bibliographical references and index. [PR5528.A42 1977] 76-42229 ISBN 0-271-01244-7 : 14.50
1. Symons, Arthur, 1865-1945—Friends and associates. 2. Authors, English—19th century—Biography. 3. Europe—Intellectual life.

Symphony.

WEINGARTNER, 785.1'1'0922 B
Felix, 1863-1942.
The symphony writers since Beethoven. From the German by Arthur Bles. With notice of the author's own No. 5 symphony by D. C. Parker added to this issue. Westport, Conn., Greenwood Press [1971] vii, 168 p. ports. 23 cm. Reprint of the 1925 ed. Translation of Die Symphonie nach Beethoven. [ML1255.W425 1971] 77-109878 ISBN 0-8371-4369-1
1. Symphony. I. Title. BIP

Synanon Foundation.

AUSTIN, Barbara Leslie. 362.2'93
Sad nun at Synanon. [1st ed.] New York, Holt, Rinehart and Winston [1970]. 186 p. 22 cm. Autobiographical. [HV5800.S93A9] 70-102150 ISBN 0-308-44932- 5.95
1. Synanon Foundation. I. Title. BIP

Synge, John Millington, 1871-1909.

GERSTENBERGER, Donna 822.912
Lorine.
John Millington Synge, by Donna Gerstenberger. New York, Twayne Publishers [1965, c1964] 157 p. 21 cm. (Twayne's Engfish authors series, 12) Bibliography: p. 142-152. [PR5534.G4 1965] 64-8332
1. Synge, John Millington, 1871-1909. BIP

GREENE, David Herbert, 928.2
1913-
J. M. Synge, 1871-1909, by David H. Greene and Edward M. Stephens. New York, Macmillan, 1959. 321 p. illus. 22 cm. Includes bibliography. [PR5533.G7] 59-7443
1. Synge, John Millington, 1871-1909. I. Stephens, Edward M., joint author.

SKELTON, Robin. 822'.9'12
J. M. Synge. Lewisburg [Pa.] Bucknell University Press [1972] 89 p. 21 cm. (The Irish writers series) Bibliography: p. 86-89. [PR5533.S48] 75-126277 ISBN 0-8387-7769-4 4.50
1. Synge, John Millington, 1871-1909. BIP

SKELTON, Robin. 822'.9'12 B
J. M. Synge and his world. New York, Viking Press [1971] 144 p. illus., facsims., map, ports. 24 cm. (A Studio book) Bibliography: p. 140. [PR5533.S5] 75-142147 ISBN 0-670-40729-1 7.95
1. Synge, John Millington, 1871-1909. I. Title.

SYNGE, John Millington, 1871- 822
1909.
The autobiography of J. M. Synge, constructed from the manuscripts by Alan Price. Chester Springs, Pa. Dufour Editions [1966, c1965] 46 p. illus. 25 cm. Contents.Contents.—Introduction, by A. Price.—The autobiography of J. M. Synge.—Photographs by J. M. Synge.—Synge and the photography of his time, by P. J. Pocock.—Bibliography (p. 46) [PR5533.A4P7] 64-25501
I. Price, Alan Frederick, ed.

SYNGE, John 822'.9'12 B
Millington, 1871-1909.
Letters to Molly; John Millington Synge to Maire O'Neill, 1906-1909. Edited by Ann Saddlemyer. Cambridge, Mass., Belknap Press of Harvard University Press, 1971. xxxii, 330 p. illus., facsims., map, ports. 24 cm. [PR5533.A46O5] 75-143231 ISBN 0-674-52834-4 11.00
I. O'Neill, Maire, 1887-1952. II. Saddlemyer, Ann, ed. III. Title. BIP

THORNTON, Weldon. 822'.9'12
J. M. Synge and the Western mind / Weldon Thornton. New York : Harper & Row, 1979. p. cm. (Irish literary studies ; 4) Includes index. Bibliography: p. [PR5533.T55 1979] 78-13301 ISBN 0-06-496879-0 : 22.50
1. Synge, John Millington, 1871-1909. 2. Authors, Irish—19th century—Biography. I. Title. II. Series. BIP

Synge, John Millington, 1871-1909—Biography.

[MASEFIELD, John], 822'.9'12 B
1878-1967.
John M. Synge : a few personal recollections with biographical notes. Folcroft, Pa. : Folcroft Library Editions, 1977. 32 p. ; 24 cm. Reprint of the 1916 ed. published by Garden City Press, Letchworth, Eng. [PR5533.M3 1977] 77-6709 ISBN 0-8414-1726-1 lib. bdg. : 10.00
1. Synge, John Millington, 1871-1909—Biography. 2. Authors, Irish—20th century—Biography. BIP

STEPHENS, Edward M. 822'.9'12 B
My uncle John; Edward Stephens's life of J. M. Synge. Edited by Andrew Carpenter. London, Oxford University Press, 1974. xv, 222 p. illus. 23 cm. Includes bibliographical references. [PR5533.S73] 74-176630 ISBN 0-19-211718-1
1. Synge, John Millington, 1871-1909—Biography. I. Title.
Distributed by Oxford University Press, New York, 10.00.

Synge, John Millington, 1871-1909—Biography—Addresses, essays, lectures.

J. M. Synge : 822'.9'12 B
interviews and recollections / edited by E. H. Mikhail ; foreword by Robin Skelton. New York : Barnes & Noble, 1977. p. cm. Includes index. [PR5533.J18 1977] 75-43223 ISBN 0-06-494817-X : 21.50
1. Synge, John Millington, 1871-1909—Biography—Addresses, essays, lectures. 2. Dramatists, Irish—19th century—Biography—Addresses, essays, lectures. I. Mikhail, E. H. BIP

Syrian Americans—Texas.

INSTITUTE of 976.4'004'9275692 B
Texan Cultures.
The Syrian and Lebanese Texans. [San Antonio] : University of Texas at San Antonio, Institute of Texan Cultures, [1974] 32 p. : ill. ; 22 x 28 cm. (The Texians and the Texans) Cover title. [F395.S98157 1974] 75-62150
1. Syrian Americans—Texas. 2. Lebanese Americans—Texas. 3. Texas—Biography. I. Title. II. Series.

Syrkin, Nachman, 1868-1924.

SYRKIN, Marie, 1900- 923.25694
Nachman Syrkin, Socialist Zionist; a biographical memoir. Selected essays. New York, Herzl Press, 1961 [c.1960] 332p. (Front. port.) 60-53236 5.00
1. Syrkin, Nachman, 1868-1924. I. Title.

SYRKIN, Marie, 1900- 923.25694
Nachman Syrkin, Socialist Zionist; a biographical memoir [and] selected essays. New York Herzl Press, 1961 [1960] 332 p. illus. 22 cm. [S151.S87S9] 60-53236
1. Syrkin, Nachman, 1868-1924. I. Title.

Szechenyi, Istvan, grof, 1791-1860.

BARANY, George, 943.9'1'040924 B
1922-
Stephen Szechenyi and the awakening of Hungarian nationalism, 1791-1841. Princeton, N.J., Princeton University Press, 1968. xviii, 487 p. illus., facsims., ports. 25 cm. A revision of the author's thesis, University of Colorado. Bibliographical footnotes. [DB933.3.S8B3 1968] 68-20865 15.00
1. Szechenyi, Istvan, grof, 1791-1860. 2. Nationalism—Hungary. I. Title.

Szenes, Hannah,

SZENES, 940.54'86'420924 B
Hannah, 1921-1944.
Hannah Senesh, her life & diary. Introd. by Abba Eban. New York, Schocken Books [1972] ix, 257 p. illus. 24 cm. Translation of Hanah Senesh. [CT1919.P38S9413 1972] 77-179076 ISBN 0-8052-3443-8 6.95
I. Title. BIP

Szenes, Hannah, 1921-1944.

MASTERS, 940.54'86'420924
Anthony, 1940-
The summer that bled; the biography of Hannah Senesh. New York, St. Martin's Press [1972, i.e. 1973] 349 p. illus. 22 cm. Bibliography: p. 339. [CT1919.P38S945 1972b] 72-88429 7.95
1. Szenes, Hannah, 1921-1944. 2. Holocaust, Jewish (1939-1945)—Hungary. I. Title.

MASTERS, 940.54'86'420924 B
Anthony, 1940-
The summer that bled; the biography of Hannah Senesh. New York, Pocket Books [1974, c1973] 338 p. illus. 18 cm. (A Washington Square Press book) Bibliography: p. 327. [CT1919.P38S945 1974] ISBN 0-671-48652-7. 1.65 (pbk.)
1. Szenes, Hannah, 1921-1944. 2. Holocaust, Jewish (1939-1945)—Hungary. I. Title.
L.C. card number for original ed.: 72-88429.

SZENES, 940.54'86'420924 B
Hannah, 1921-1944.
Hannah Senesh, her life & diary. Introd. by Abba Eban. New York, Schocken Books [1972] ix, 257 p. illus. 24 cm. Translation of Hanah Senesh. [CT1919.P38S9413 1972] 77-179076 ISBN 0-8052-3443-8 6.95
I. Title. BIP

Szlgeti, Joseph, 1892-1973.

SZIGETI, Joseph, 787'.1'0924 B
1892-1973.
With strings attached : reminiscences and reflections / by Joseph Szigeti. New York : Da Capo Press, 1979, c1947. xiii, 341, xvii, p., [8] leaves of plates : ill. ; 22 cm. (Da Capo Press music reprint series) Reprint of the ed. published by A. A. Knopf, New York. Includes index. Discography: p. 335-341. [ML418.S9A3 1979] 79-11318 ISBN 0-306-79567-1 : 22.50
1. Szigeti, Joseph, 1892-1973. 2. Violinists, violoncellists, etc.—Biography. I. Title. BIP

Szold, Henrietta, 1860-1945.

DASH, Joan. 956.94'001'0924 B
Summoned to Jerusalem : the life of Henrietta Szold / by Joan Dash. New York : Harper & Row, c1979. p. cm. Includes index. Bibliography: p. [DS151.S9D37 1979] 76-26217 ISBN 0-06-010963-7 : 15.00
1. Szold, Henrietta, 1860-1945. 2. Zionists—Biography. I. Title. BIP

FINEMAN, Irving, 1893- 923.25693
Woman of valor; the life of Henrietta Szold, 1860-1945. New York, Simon and Schuster, 1961. 448 p. ports. 22 cm. [DS151.S9F5] 61-15119
1. Szold, Henrietta, 1860-1945. I. Title.

LOWENTHAL, Marvin, 1890-1969. 956.94'001'0924 B
Henrietta Szold, life and letters. Westport, Conn., Greenwood Press [1974, c1942] p. cm. Reprint of the ed. published by Viking Press, New York. [DS151.S9L6 1974] 72-595 ISBN 0-8371-5998-9 14.50 (lib. bdg.).
1. Szold, Henrietta, 1860-1945. I. Szold, Henrietta, 1860-1945.

Taha Husayn, 1889-1973—Biography.

TAHA Husayn, 1889-1973. 892'.7'8509 B
A passage to France : the third volume of the autobiography of Taha Husain / translated from the Arabic by Kenneth Cragg. Leiden : E. J. Brill, 1976. xv, 165 p. ; 21 cm. (Arabic translation series ; v. 4) Translation of vol. 3 of al-Ayyam. Includes index. [PJ7864.A35Z513 1976] 77-456820 ISBN 9-00-404726-3
1. Taha Husayn, 1889-1973—Biography. 2. Authors, Arab—Egypt—Biography. I. Cragg, Kenneth. II. Title. III. Series.

T'ang T'ai-tsung, Emperor of China, 597-649.

FITZGERALD, Charles Patrick, 1902- 951'.01'0924 B
Son of heaven [a biography of Li Shih-Min, founder of the T'ang dynasty, by C. P. Fitzgerald] New York, AMS Press [1971] ix, 232 p. illus., geneal. table, maps, plans, port. 23 cm. Reprint of the 1933 ed. Includes bibliographical references. [DS749.3.F5 1971] 74-136382 ISBN 0-404-02404-1
1. T'ang T'ai-tsung, Emperor of China, 597-649. I. Title. **BIP**

Tapies Puig, Antonio, 1923—

TAPIES Puig, Antonio, 1923- 709'.2'4 B
Tapies / Roland Penrose. New York : Rizzoli, 1978. 278 p. : ill. (some col.) ; 25 cm. Bibliography: p. 263-270. [N7113.T3A4 1978] 77-88715 ISBN 0-8478-0155-1 : 25.00
1. Tapies Puig, Antonio, 1923- 2. Artists—Spain—Biography. I. Penrose, Roland, Sir.

Tojo, Hideki, 1884-1948.

BROWNE, Courtney, 1915- 952.03'0924 B
Tojo: the last Banzai. [1st ed.] New York, Holt, Rinehart and Winston [1967] viii, 260 p. illus., ports. 22 cm. Bibliography: p. 250-253. [DS890.T57B7] 67-12904
1. Tojo, Hideki, 1884-1948.

BUTOW, Robert Joseph Charles, 1924- 952.03'0924 B
Tojo and the coming of the war [by] Robert J. C. Butow. Stanford, Calif., Stanford University Press [1969, c1961] 584 p. illus., ports. 25 cm. Bibliography: p. 545-562. [DS890.T57B8 1969] 73-93492 16.50
1. Tojo, Hideki, 1884-1948. 2. World War, 1939-1945—Japan. I. Title. **BIP**

COOX, Alvin D. 952.03'3'0924 B
Tojo / Alvin D. Coox. New York : Ballantine Books, 1975. 160 p. : ill. ; 21 cm. (Ballantine's illustrated history of the violent century ; war leader book no. 38) Bibliography: p. 160. [DS890.T57C66] 75-323607 ISBN 0-345-24292-0 pbk. : 2.00
1. Tojo, Hideki, 1884-1948. 2. World War, 1939-1945—Japan.

Tabb, John Banister,

TABB, John Banister, 1845-1909. 928.1
Letters -- grave and gay, and other prose. Edited with introd. and notes by Francis E. Litz. Washington, Catholic University of America Press, 1950. xix, 266 p. illus. 23 cm. Bibliography: p. 261-262. [PS2968.A4 1950] A 50
I. Litz, Francis Edwards Aloysius, 1892- ed. II. Title.

Tabb, John Banister, 1845-1909—Juv. lit.

THE rambling rebel; v. 12
a story of John Banister Tabb. Illus. by Carolyn Lee Jagodits. Notre Dame, Ind., Dujarie [1961] 94p. illus. 24cm.
1. Tabb, John Banister, 1845-1909— Juv. lit. I. Roberto, Brother, 1927-

Taber, Gladys Bagg, 1899- —Biography.

TABER, Gladys Bagg, 1899- 818'.5'209 B
Harvest of yesterdays / Gladys Taber ; drawings by Pamela Johnson. 1st ed. Philadelphia : Lippincott, c1976. 224 p. : ill. ; 22 cm. Autobiographical. [PS3539.A136Z52] 75-44003 ISBN 0-397-01133-4 : 7.95
1. Taber, Gladys Bagg, 1899- —Biography. I. Title. **BIP**

TABER, Gladys Bagg, 1899- 818'.5'209 B
Harvest of yesterdays / Gladys Taber ; drawings by Pamela Johnson. Boston : G. K. Hall, 1976. xiii, 357 p. ; 24 cm. "Published in large print." Autobiographical. [PS3539.A136Z52 1976b] 76-26061 ISBN 0-8161-6405-3 : 10.95
1. Taber, Gladys Bagg, 1899- —Biography. 2. Authors, American—20th century—Biography. 3. Sight-savings books. I. Title.

Table-talk.

SHAW, George Bernard, 1856-1950. 822'.9'12 B
Table-talk of G. B. S. Conversations on things in general between Bernard Shaw and his biographer, by Archibald Henderson. New York, Haskell House Publishers, 1974. ix, 191 p. 22 cm. Reprint of the 1925 ed. published by Chapman and Hall, London. [PR5365.T3 1974] 74-16315 ISBN 0-8383-1890-8
1. Table-talk. I. Henderson, Archibald, 1877-1963. II. Title.

Tabor, Elizabeth Bonduel (McCourt) Doe, d. 1955.

BANCROFT, Caroline. 920.7
Photo story of the Matchless Mine and Baby Doe Tabor. [Denver, Golden Press, 1953] unpaged (chiefly illus.) 22cm. [CT275.T145B27] 53-10689
1. Tabor, Elizabeth Bonduel (McCourt) Doe, d. 1955. I. Title. II. Title: Matchless Mine and Baby Doe Tabor.

BANCROFT, Caroline. 920.7
Silver queen, the fabulous story of Baby Doe Tabor. Denver, Golden Press, Denver News Co., distributors, 1950. 76 p. 22 cm. [CT275.T145B3] 50-4168
1. Tabor, Elizabeth Bonduel (McCourt) Doe, d. 1965. I. Title. **BIP**

BANCROFT, Caroline. 920.7
Silver queen, the fabulous story of Baby Doe Tabor. [Rewritten, illustrated ed.] Denver, Golden Press, 1955. 80p. illus. 22cm. [CT275.T145B3 1955] 55-36242
1. Tabor, Elizabeth Bonduel (McCourt) Doe, d. 1955. I. Title.

O'CONNOR, Richard, 1915- 917.88'83'0330924 B
The legend of Baby Doe; the life and times of the Silver Queen of the West, by John Burke. New York, Putnam [1974] 273 p. illus. 22 cm. Bibliography: p. [264]-265. [CT275.T145O25] 73-87179 ISBN 0-399-11249-9 7.95
1. Tabor, Elizabeth Bonduel McCourt Doe, d. 1935. I. Title.

Tabor, Horace Austin Warner, 1830-1899.

SMITH, Duane A. 328.73'092'4 B
Horace Tabor: his life and the legend [by] Duane A. Smith. Boulder, Colorado Associated University Press [1973] xiv, 395 p. illus. 23 cm. Bibliography: p. 369-387. [F781.T322S63] 72-91068 ISBN 0-87081-045-6 12.50
1. Tabor, Horace Austin Warner, 1830-1899. I. Title.

Tabouis, Genevieve R., 1892—

TABOUIS, Genevieve R., 1892- 070'.92'4 B
They called me Cassandra, by Genevieve Tabouis. New York, Da Capo Press, 1973 [c1942] xii, 436 p. 22 cm. (Europe 1815-1945) Translation of Ils l'ont appelee Cassandre. [D413.T3A3 1973] 76-172178 ISBN 0-306-70298-3 15.00
1. Tabouis, Genevieve R., 1892- I. Title. II. Series. **BIP**

Tacitus, Cornelius.

MENDELL, Clarence Whittlesey, 1883- 878.6
Tacitus, the man and his work. New Haven, Yale University Press, 1957. vii, 397 p. 23 cm. Bibliography: p. 379-385. [PA6716.M4] 57-10152
1. Tacitus, Cornelius.

SYME, Ronald, 1910- 878.6
Tacitus. Oxford, Clarendon Press, 1958. 2 v. (xii, 856 p.) 24 cm. Bibliography: v. 2, p. [809]-823. [PA6716.S9] A58
1. Tacitus, Cornelius. I. Title.

Taft, Robert Alphonso, 1889-1953.

HARNSBERGER, Caroline Thomas, 1902- 923.273
A man of courage, Robert A. Taft. Foreword by Lloyd Bowers Taft. Chicago, Wilcox and Follett [1952] 370 p. illus. 23 cm. (Living American statesmen series) [E748.T2H26] 52-1590
1. Taft, Robert Alphonso, 1889- 2. U. S.—Pol. & govt.—1933-1945. 3. U. S.—Pol. & govt.—1945- I. Title.

KIRK, Russell. 328.73'0924
The political principles of Robert A. Taft, by Russell Kirk & James McClellan. New York, Fleet Press Corp. [1967] x, 213 p. 22 cm. "A project of the Robert A. Taft Institute of Government." Includes bibliographies. [E748.T2K5] 67-24073
1. Taft, Robert Alphonso, 1889-1953. I. McClellan, James, 1937- joint author. II. Robert A. Taft Institute of Government. III. Title. **BIP**

PATTERSON, James T. 328.73'092'4 B
Mr. Republican; a biography of Robert A. Taft [by] James T. Patterson. Boston, Houghton Mifflin, 1972. xvi, 749 p. illus. 24 cm. Bibliography: p. [621]-646. [E748.T2P37] 72-516 ISBN 0-395-13938-4 12.50
1. Taft, Robert Alphonso, 1889-1953. I. Title.

ROBBINS, Jhan. 923.273
Eight weeks to live; the last chapter in the life of Senator Robert A. Taft, by Jhan and June Robbins. [1st ed.] Garden City, N.Y., Doubleday, 1954. 23 p. illus. 22 cm. [E748.T2R6] 54-8110
1. Taft, Robert Alphonso, 1889-1953. I. Robbins, June, joint author. II. Title.

ROBBINS, Phyllis. 923.273
Robert A. Taft, boy and man. Cambridge, Mass., Dresser, Chapman & Grimes [1963] 288 p. illus. 22 cm. Includes bibliography. [E748.T2R62] 63-12109
1. Taft, Robert Alphonso, 1889-1953.

WHITE, William Smith. 923.273
The Taft story. [1st ed.] New York, Harper [1954] 288 p. illus. 22 cm. [E748.T2W5] 54-6035
1. Taft, Robert Alphonso, 1889-1953. I. Title.

Taft, William Howard, Pres. U.S., 1857-1930.

BUTT, Archibald Willingham, 1865-1912. 973.91'1'0924
Taft and Roosevelt; the intimate letters of Archie Butt, military aide. Port Washington, N.Y., Kennikat Press [1971] 2 v. (xxiv, 862 p.) port. 23 cm. (Kennikat Press scholarly reprints. Series in American history and culture in the twentieth century) [E748.B94A4 1971] 71-137968 ISBN 0-8046-1425-3
1. Taft, William Howard, Pres. U.S., 1857-1930. 2. Roosevelt, Theodore, Pres. U.S., 1858-1919. 3. Washington, D.C.—Social life and customs.

COLETTA, Paolo Enrico, 1916- 973.91'2'0924 B
The Presidency of William Howard Taft, by Paolo E. Coletta. Lawrence, University Press of Kansas [1973] ix, 306 p. 24 cm. (American Presidency series) Includes bibliographical references. [E761.C64] 72-92564 ISBN 0-7006-0096-5 10.00
1. Taft, William Howard, Pres. U.S., 1857-1930. 2. United States—Politics and government—1909-1913. I. Title. II. Series. **BIP**

MASON, Alpheus Thomas, 1899- 347.9973
William Howard Taft, Chief Justice. new York, S. ; S. [c.1964, 1965] 354p. port. 23cm. Bibl. 65-11166 6.50
1. Taft, William Howard, Pres. U.S., 1857-1930. I. Title.

MASON, Alpheus Thomas, 1899- 347.9973
William Howard Taft, Chief Justice. New York, Simon and Schuster [1965] 354 p. port. 23 cm. Includes bibliographical references. [KF8745.T27M3] 65-11166
1. Taft, William Howard, Pres. U.S., 1857-1930.

MINGER, Ralph Eldin, 1925- 327.73
William Howard Taft and United States foreign policy : the apprenticeship years, 1900-1908 / Ralph Eldin Minger. Urbana : University of Illinois Press, [1975] xii, 241 p. ; 24 cm. Includes index. Bibliography: p. 217-238. [E756.M56] 75-6691 ISBN 0-252-00427-2 : 9.50
1. Taft, William Howard, Pres. U.S., 1857-1930. 2. United States—Foreign relations—1901-1909. I. Title. **BIP**

PRINGLE, Henry Fowles, 1897-1958 923.173
The life and times of William Howard Taft, a biography [2v. Unaltered, unabridged ed.] Hamden, Conn., Archon [dist. Shoe String] 1964[c.1939] 2v. (xii, 1106p.) illus., ports. facsims. 23cm. Bibl. 64-13175 22.50 set.,
1. Taft, William Howard, Pres. U.S., 1857-1930. I. Title.

TAFT, William Howard, Pres. U.S., 1857-1930. 973.91'2'0924
William Howard Taft, 1857-1930; chronology, documents, bibliographical aids. Edited by Gilbert J. Black. Dobbs Ferry, N.Y., Oceana Publications, 1970. 89 p. 24 cm. (Oceana presidential chronology series) Bibliography: p. 83-87. [E761.B55] 70-116059 ISBN 0-379-12080-1
1. U.S.—History—1901-1953. I. Black, Gilbert J., ed. II. U.S. President, 1909-1913 (Taft)

THOMPSON, Charles Willis, 1871-1946. 973.9'0922
Presidents I've known and two near Presidents. Freeport, N.Y., Books for Libraries Press [1970, c1956] 386 p. 23 cm. (Essay index reprint series) Contents.Contents.—Hanna-McKinley.—Bryan.—Roosevelt.—Taft.—Wilson.—Harding.—Coolidge. [E176.1.T45 1970] 71-93383
1. Hanna, Marcus Alonzo, 1837-1904. 2. McKinley, William, Pres. U.S., 1843-1901. 3. Bryan, William Jennings, 1860-1925. 4. Roosevelt, Theodore, Pres. U.S., 1858-1919. 5. Taft, William Howard, Pres. U.S., 1857-1930. 6. Wilson, Woodrow, Pres. U.S., 1856-1924. 7. Harding, Warren Gamaliel, Pres. U.S., 1865-1923. 8. Coolidge, Calvin, Pres. U.S., 1872-1933. I. Title. **BIP**

Taft, William Howard, Pres. U.S., 1857-1930—Juvenile literature.

MYERS, Elisabeth P. 973.91'2'0924 B
William Howard Taft [by] Elisabeth P. Myers. Chicago, Reilly & Lee [1970] 168 p. illus., ports. 21 cm. Bibliography: p. 163-164. A biography of the twenty-seventh President whose main ambition was actually to be Chief Justice of the Supreme Court. [E762.M9] 92 72-105126 4.95
1. Taft, William Howard, Pres. U.S., 1857-1930—Juvenile literature. I. Title. **BIP**

SEVERN, William. 973.91'2'0924 B
William Howard Taft, the President who became Chief Justice, by Bill Severn. Drawings by Rus Anderson. New York, McKay [1970] 220 p. 21 cm. Bibliography: p. 215. A biography of the man whose many public offices included the two highest in the United States—President and Chief Justice. [E762.S48] 92 72-101963 4.95
1. Taft, William Howard, Pres. U.S., 1857-1930—Juvenile literature. I. Title.

Tagilacozzi, Gaspare, 1545-1599.

GNUDI, Martha (Teach), 1908- 926.1
The life and times of Gaspare Tagliacozzi, surgeon of Bologna, 1545-1599. With a documented study of the scientific and cultural life of Bologna in the sixteenth cenutry, by Martha Teach Gnudi and Jerome Pierce Webster. Pref. by Arturo Castiglioni. New York, H. Reichner [1950] xxii, 538 p. illus., ports., facsims. 28 cm. Bibliography: p. [491]-514. [R147.T3G6] 51-2026
1. Tagilacozzi, Gaspare, 1545-1599. 2. Surgery, Plastic—Hist. I. Webster, Jerome Pierce. joint author. II. Title.

Tagore, Rabindranath, Sir, 1861-1941.

KHANOLKAR, G. D. 928.914
The lute and the plough; a life of Rabindranath Tagore. Tr. [from Marathi] by Thomas Gay. Bombay, Book Ctr. [New York, Hillary House, 1966, c1963] xii, 376p. ports. 23cm. Bibl. [PK1718.T24Z693] SA 63 8.00
1. Tagore, Rabindranath, Sir 1861-1941. I. Title.

KRIPALANI, Krishna, 1907- 928.9144
Rabindranath Tagore; a biography New York, Grove [c.1962] 417p. illus. 23cm. Bibl. 61-11776 8.75
1. Tagore, Sir Rabindranath, 1861-1941. I. Title.

KRIPALANI, Krishna, 1907- 891.44'1'5 B
Rabindranath Tagore; a biography. New York, Oxford University Press, 1962. 417 p. illus., facsims., ports. 23 cm. Bibliography: p. [401]-406. [PK1725.K7] 73-9708
1. Tagore, Rabindranath, Sir, 1861-1941.

RHYS, Ernest, 1859-1946. 891.44'1'5 B
Rabindranath Tagore: a biographical study. New York, Macmillan Co., 1915. New York, Haskell House Publishers, 1970. xvii, 157 p. illus., facsims., ports. 23 cm. [PK1725.R5 1970] 78-133286 ISBN 8-383-11857-
1. Tagore, Rabindranath, Sir, 1861-1941.

ROY, Basanta Koomar. 891'.44'14 B
Rabindranath Tagore, the man and his poetry / by Basanta Koomar Roy ; with an introd. by Hamilton W. Mabie. Folcroft, Pa. : Folcroft Library Editions, 1977 [c1915] p. cm. Reprint of the ed. published by Dodd, Mead, New York. Bibliography: p. [PK1725.R63 1977] 77-8084 ISBN 0-8414-7330-7 lib. bdg. : 25.00
1. Tagore, Rabindranath, Sir, 1861-1941. 2. Authors, Bengali—20th century—Biography. BIP

THOMPSON, Edward John, 1886-1946. 891'.44'14 B
Rabindranath Tagore : poet and dramatist / by Edward Thompson. New York : Haskell House, 1974. xii, 330 p., [1] leaf of plates : ill. ; 21 cm. Reprint of the 1948 ed. published by Oxford University Press, London. Includes bibliographical references index. [PK1725.T53 1974] 74-30343 ISBN 0-8383-1982-3 : 15.95
1. Tagore, Rabindranath, Sir, 1861-1941. BIP

THOMPSON, Edward John, 1886-1946. 891'.44'14 B
Rabindranath Tagore, his life and work. 2d ed. New York, Haskell House [1974] p. Reprint of the 1928 ed. published by Association Press, Calcutta, and Oxford University Press, London, New York, which was issued in The Heritage of India series. [PK1725.T5 1974] 74-7119 ISBN 0-8383-1980-7 15.95 (lib. bdg.).
1. Tagore, Rabindranath, Sir, 1861-1941. I. Title.

THOMPSON, Edward John, 1886-1946. 891'.44'14 B
Rabindranath Tagore, poet and dramatist / by Edward Thompson. Westport, Conn. : Greenwood Press, 1975, c1948. xii, 330 p., [1] leaf of plates : ill. ; 22 cm. Reprint of the ed. published by Oxford University Press, London. [PK1725.T53 1975b] 75-3743 ISBN 0-8371-8065-1 : 17.50
1. Tagore, Rabindranath, Sir, 1861-1941. I. Title.

Tagore, Rabindranath, Sir, 1861-1941—Biography.

SINGH, Durlab. 891'.44'14 B
The sentinel of the East, a biographical study of Rabindra Nath Tagore. Foreword: Sir P. C. Ray. New York, Haskell House, 1974. 155, iii p. 20 cm. Reprint of the 1941 ed. published by Hero Publications, Lahore. [PK1725.S48 1974] 74-7099 ISBN 0-8383-1975-0
1. Tagore, Rabindranath, Sir, 1861-1941—Biography. I. Title.

TAGORE, Rabindranath, Sir, 1861-1941. 891'.44'14 B
The diary of a westward voyage / by Rabindranath Tagore ; translated by Indu Dutt from the original Bengali Pashchim yatrir diary. Westport, Conn. : Greenwood Press, 1975, c1962. 137 p. ; 22 cm. Translation of Pascima yatrira dayari. Reprint of the ed. published by Asia Pub. House, Bombay, New York. [PK1725.A4313 1975] 74-27392 ISBN 0-8371-7904-1 : 9.75.
1. Tagore, Rabindranath, Sir, 1861-1941—Biography. I. Title. BIP

TAGORE, Rathindranath, 1888-1961. 891'.44'14 B
On the edges of time / Rathindranath Tagore. Westport, Conn. : Greenwood Press, 1978, c1958. 191 p., [6] leaves of plates : ill. ; 22 cm. Reprint of the ed. published by Orient Longsmans, Bombay. Includes index. [PK1725.T3 1978] 78-10671 ISBN 0-313-20760-7 lib.bdg. : 17.75
1. Tagore, Rabindranath, Sir, 1861-1941—Biography. 2. Authors, Bengali—20th century—Biography. I. Title. BIP

Tagore, Rabindranath, Sir, 1861-1941—Journeys—Canada.

MAHALANOBIS, Prasanta Chandra, 1893-1972. 891'.44'14
Rabindranath Tagore's visit to Canada / by P. C. Mahalanobis. Brooklyn, N.Y. : Haskell House Pub., 1977. 73 p. ; 28 cm. On spine: Rabinadranath Tagore's visit to Canada and Japan. Reprint of the 1929 ed. published in Calcutta, which was issued as Bulletin no. 14 of Visva-Bharati. [PK1725.M282 1977] 76-52432 lib. bdg. : 9.95
1. Tagore, Rabindranath, Sir, 1861-1941—Journeys—Canada. 2. Canada—Description and travel—1867-1950. 3. Authors, Bengali—20th century—Biography. I. Title. II. Series: Visva-Bharati. Bulletin — Visva-Bharati ; no. 14. BIP

Tague, Lowry

TAGUE, Lowry 927
Divine Frequency, the memoirs of Lowry Tague. New York, Exposition [1963, c.1962] 88p. 21cm. 3.00
I. Title.

Tahara, Yoneko.

TAHARA, Yoneko. 248'.246'0924 B
Yoneko, daughter of happiness / by Yoneko Tahara ; as told to Bernard Palmer. Chicago : Moody Press, c1976. 173 p. ; 22 cm. [BV4935.T28A38] 76-19009 ISBN 0-8024-9811-6 : 5.95
1. Tahara, Yoneko. 2. Conversion. I. Palmer, Bernard Alvin, 1914- II. Title.

Taigi, Anna Maria, 1769-1837.

BESSIERES, Albert, 1877- 922.245
Wife, mother, and mystic (blessed Anna-Maria Taigi) Translated by Stephen Rigby; edited by Douglas Newton. Westminster, Md., Newman Press [1952] 256p. illus. 19cm. Translation of La bienheureuse Anna Maria Taigi. [BX4705.T25B43] 52-13325
1. Taigi, Anna Maria, 1769-1837. I. Title.

Tait family.

TAIT, Viola, 1912- 338.7'61'792
A family of brothers: the Taits and J. C. Williamson; a theatre history. Melbourne, Heinemann [1970] 303 p. illus., ports. 25 cm. [PN1583.T3T3] 70-129922 ISBN 0-85561-011-5
1. Tait family. 2. Williamson, James Cassius, 1845-1913. 3. Performing arts—Australia—History. I. Title.

Taiwan—Politics and government.

PENG, Ming-min. 951'.249'050924 B
A taste of freedom; memoirs of a Formosan independence leader. [1st ed.] New York, Holt, Rinehart and Winston [1972] xvi, 270 p. 22 cm. Autobiography. [DS895.F75P45] 79-182773 ISBN 0-03-091388-8 6.95
1. Taiwan—Politics and government. I. Title.

Takahashi, Shixu (Higuchi)

HULL, Eleanor (Means) 325.2520973
Suddenly the sun; a biography of Shizuko Takahashi. New York, Friendship Press [1957] 130p. 21cm. [E184.J3T3] 57-11363
1. Takahashi, Shixu (Higuchi) 2. Japanese in the U. S. I. Title.

Talbot, Catherine, 1721-1770.

CARTER, Elizabeth, 1717-1806. 821'.6 B
A series of letters between Mrs. Elizabeth Carter and Miss Catherine Talbot. New York, AMS Press [1974] p. cm. Reprint of the 1809 ed. published by F. C. and J. Rivington, London, under title: A series of letters between Mrs. Elizabeth Carter and Miss Catherine Talbot, from the year 1741 to 1770, to which are added Letters from Mrs. Elizabeth Carter to Mrs. Vesey, between the years 1763 and 1787; published from the original manuscripts in the possession of the Rev. Montagu Pennington. [PR3339.C4A83 1974] 73-20330 20.50
1. Carter, Elizabeth, 1717-1806. 2. Talbot, Catherine, 1721-1770. 3. Vesey, Elizabeth (Vesey) 1715?-1791. I. Talbot, Catherine, 1721-1770. II. Vesey, Elizabeth (Vesey) 1715?-1791.
Four volume set 80.00. BIP

Talbot, Ethelbert, Bp., 1848-1928.

BARNES, Calvin Rankin, 1891- 922.373
Ethelbert Talbot, 1848-1928, missionary bishop, diocesan bishop, presiding bishop. Philadelphia, Church Historicl Society [1955] 51p. illus:, ports. 23cm. (Church Historical Society. Publication no. 41) 'Reprinted from Historical magazine, volume xxiv (1955) pages 141-185. [BX5995.T22B3] 55-4033
1. Talbot, Ethelbert, Bp., 1848-1928. I. Title.

Talbot, Godfrey Walker.

TALBOT, Godfrey Walker. 070.4'092'4 B
Permission to speak / [by] Godfrey Talbot. London : Hutchinson, 1976. 190 p., [12] p. of plates : ill., facsims., ports. ; 23 cm. Includes index. [PN5123.A27A295] 77-352987 ISBN 0-09-127250-5 : £3.95
1. Talbot, Godfrey Walker. 2. Journalists—Great Britain—Biography. 3. Radio journalism—Great Britain. I. Title.

Talbot, Louis Thompson, 1889-1976.

TALBOT, Carol. 269'.2'0924 B
For this I was born / by Carol Talbot. Chicago : Moody Press, c1977. p. cm. Bibliography & filmography: p. [BR1725.T23T34] 77-10537 ISBN 0-8024-2822-3 pbk. : 4.95
1. Talbot, Louis Thompson, 1889-1976. 2. Clergy—United States—Biography. I. Title. BIP

Talbot, Matthew, 1856-1925.

DOHERTY, Edward Joseph, 1890- 922.2415
Matt Talbot. Milwaukee, Bruce Pub. Co. [1953] 200p. 21cm. [BX4705.T27D55] 53-11076
1. Talbot, Matthew, 1856-1925. I. Title.

ERNEST, Brother, 1897- 922.2415
Through the dark night, a story of Matt Talbot. Illus. by Brother Bernard Howard. Notre Dame, Ind., Dujarie Press [1952] 88 p. illus. 24 cm. [BX4705.T27E7] 52-39270
1. Talbot, Matthew, 1856-1925. I. Title.

GOLLAND TRINDADE, Henrique Heitor, Bp., 1897- 922.2415
Matt Talbot, worker and penitent; his life as seen through Franciscan eyes. Translated from the Portuguese by Conall O'Leary. Paterson, N. J., St. Anthony Guild Press, 1953 [i. e. 1954] 126p. illus. 20cm. [BX4705.T27G7] 54-24800
1. Talbot, Matthew, 1856-1925. I. Title.

PURCELL, Mary. 922.2415
Matt Talbot and his times; with a foreword by Richard J. Cushing. Archbishop of Boston. [1st American ed.] Westminster, Md., Newman Press, 1955. 278p. illus. 20cm. [BX4705.T27P8] 55-7054
1. Talbot, Matthew, 1856-1925. I. Title.

PURCELL, Mary, 1906- 282'.092'4 B
Matt Talbot and his times / by Mary Purcell ; with a foreword by Dermot Ryan. Rev. ed. Chicago : Franciscan Herald Press, [1977] p. cm. [BX4705.T27P8 1977] 77-3556 ISBN 0-8199-0657-3 : 4.95
1. Talbot, Matthew, 1856-1925. 2. Catholics in Dublin—Biography. 3. Dublin—Biography. I. Title.

Talbot, Thomas, 1771-1853.

ERMATINGER, Edward, 1797-1876. 917.13 B
Life of Colonel Talbot and the Talbot settlement. With a new introd. by James J. Talman. Belleville, Ont., Mika Silk Screening, 1972. iv, 230 p. 23 cm. Reprint of the 1859 ed. published by A. McLachlin's Home Journal Office, St. Thomas, Ont. [F1059.5.P8E7 1972] 73-169745 ISBN 0-919302-19-X
1. Talbot, Thomas, 1771-1853. 2. Port Talbot, Ont. 3. Ontario—Biography I. Title.

Talbot, William Henry Fox, 1800-1877.

ARNOLD, Harry John Philip, 1932- 770'.92'4 B
William Henry Fox Talbot : pioneer of photography and man of science / [by] H. J. P. Arnold. London : Hutchinson, 1977. 383 p., leaf of plate, [48] p. of plates : ill. (some col.), col. coat of arms, facsims., geneal. tables, ports. (some col.) ; 26 cm. Includes bibliographies and index. [TR140.T3A76] 78-320092 ISBN 0-09-129600-5 : 31.95
1. Talbot, William Henry Fox, 1800-1877. 2. Photographers—England—Biography.
Distributed by Merrimack Book Service BIP

BUCKLAND, Gail. 770'.92'4 B
Fox Talbot and the invention of photography / Gail Buckland. New York : Camera/Graphic Press, [1978] p. cm. Includes bibliographical references and index. [TR140.T3B8] 78-4405 ISBN 0-918696-07-0 : 37.50
1. Talbot, William Henry Fox, 1800-1877. 2. Photography—History. 3. Photographers—England—Biography. I. Title. BIP

HANNAVY, John. 770'.92'4 B
Fox Talbot : an illustrated life of William

Henry Fox Talbot, "Father of modern photography," 1800-1877 / John Hannavy. Princes Risborough : Shire Publications, 1976. 48 p. : ill., facsims., ports. ; 21 cm. (Lifelines ; 38) Includes index. Bibliography: p. 46. [TR140.T3H36] 76-383859 ISBN 0-85263-319-X : £0.60
1. Talbot, William Henry Fox, 1800-1877. 2. Photographers—England—Biography.

TALBOT, William Henry Fox, 1800-1877. 779'.092'4
William H. Fox Talbot, inventor of the negative-positive process [by] Andre Jammes. [English translation by Maureen Oberli-Turner] New York, Macmillan [1973] 96 p. plates. 28 cm. (Photography: men and movements, v. 2) Includes bibliographical references. [TR651.T3413] 73-10789 10.95
1. Talbot, William Henry Fox, 1800-1877. 2. Photography, Artistic. 3. Calotype. I. Jammes, Andre.

Tallchief, Maria.

MAYNARD, Olga. 927.928
Bird of fire, the story of Maria Tallchief. New York, Dodd, Mead, 1961. 201 p. illus. 22 cm. [GV1785.T32M3] 61-15629
1. Tallchief, Maria. I. Title.

MYERS, Elisabeth P. 792.82'0924 B
Maria Tallchief: America's prima ballerina, by Elisabeth P. Myers. New York, Grosset & Dunlap [1967, c1966] 175 p. illus. 22 cm. "A Rutledge book." [GV1785.T32M9] 67-3305
1. Tallchief, Maria. I. Title.

MYERS, Elisabeth P. 92
Maria Tallchief: America's prima ballerina, by Elisabeth P. Myers. New York, Grosset & Dunlap [1967, c1966] 175 p. illus. 22 cm. "A Rutledge book." Biography of America's first prima ballerina who danced with the Ballet Russe and achieved world fame for her roles in Firebird and The Nutcracker. [GV1785.T32M9] AC 66
1. Tallchief, Maria. I. Title.

Tallchief, Maria—Juvenile literature.

DE LEEUW, Adele Louise, 1899- 792.8'0924 B
Maria Tallchief: American ballerina. Illustrated by Russell Hoover. Champaign, Ill., Garrard Pub. Co. [1971] 144 p. illus., port. 22 cm. A biography of the Osage Indian who became one of America's foremost ballerinas. [GV1785.T32D4] 92 78-126417 ISBN 0-8116-4508-8
1. Tallchief, Maria—Juvenile literature. I. Hoover, Russell, illus. II. Title.

GRIDLEY, Marion Eleanor, 1906- 792.8'2'0924 B
Maria Tallchief, by Marion E. Gridley. Minneapolis, Dillon Press [1973] 74 p. illus. 24 cm. (The Story of an American Indian) A biography of the Osage Indian girl who became a world-renowned ballerina. [GV1785.T32G74] 92 73-8382 ISBN 0-87518-060-4 4.95
1. Tallchief, Maria—Juvenile literature. I. Title. II. Series. BIP

TOBIAS, Tobi. 792.8'0924 B
Maria Tallchief. Illustrated by Michael Hampshire. New York, Crowell [1970] 32 p. illus. (part col.) 24 cm. (A Crowell biography.) A biography of the Osage Indian girl from Oklahoma who became one of America's greatest ballerinas. [GV1785.T32T6 1970] 92 77-87159 3.75
1. Tallchief, Maria—Juvenile literature. I. Hampshire, Michael, illus. II. Title. BIP

Talleyrand-Perigord, Catherine Noel (Worlee) princesse de Benevent, 1762-1835.

BERNARD, Jack F. 944.04'092'4 B
Talleyrand; a biography, by J. F. Bernard. New York, Putnam [1973] 653 p. illus. 25 cm. Bibliography: p. 621-638. [DC255.T3B37 1973] 72-85242 ISBN 0-399-11022-4 12.95
1. Talleyrand-Perigord, Charles Maurice de, prince de Benevent, 1754-1838. BIP

COOPER, Duff, 1st viscount Norwich of Aldwich 1890-1954 923.244
Talleyrand London, Cape [dist. Mystic, Conn., Verry, 1964] 339p. ports. 23cm. (Bedford hist. ser., 6) Bibl. A48 6.00
1. Talleyrand-Perigord, Charles Maurice de, prince de Benevent, 1754-1838 I. Title. II. Series.

DODD, Anna Bowman (Blake) 1855-1929. 944.04'092'4 B
Talleyrand; the training of a statesman, 1754-1838. Freeport, N.Y., Books for Libraries Press [1973] p. Reprint of the 1927 ed. published by Putnam, New York. Bibliography: p. [DC255.T3D6 1973] 73-4492 ISBN 0-518-19027-7
1. Talleyrand-Perigord, Charles Mauricede, prince de Benevent, 1754-1838. 2. France—History—1789-1815. I. Title.

GREENBAUM, Louis S., 1930- 322'.1'0924
Talleyrand, statesman-priest; the agent-general of the clergy and the Church of France at the end of the Old Regime, by Louis S. Greenbaum. Washington, Catholic University of America Press, 1970. vii, 293 p. port. 24 cm. Bibliography: p. 258-282. [DC255.T3G7] 76-101408 ISBN 8-13-204978- 12.50
1. Talleyrand-Perigord, Charles Maurice de, prince de Benevent, 1754-1838. 2. Catholic Church in France—History.

JOELSON, Annette, 1903- 920.7
Courtesan princess; Catherine Grand, princesse de Talleyrand. [1st ed.] Philadelphia, Chilton Books [c1965] xi, 279 p. 21 cm. Bibliography: p. 269-271. [DC255.T28J6 1965] 65-12060
1. Talleyrand-Perigord, Catherine Noel (Worlee) princesse de Benevent, 1762-1835. I. Title.

KOMROFF, Manuel, 1890- 944.06'3'0922
Talleyrand. New York, J. Messner [1965] 190 p. 22 cm. Bibliography: p. 183-184. [DC255.T3K6] 923 65-12954
1. Talleyrand-Perigord, Charles Maurice de, Rince de Benevent, 1754-1838. I. Title.

ORIEUX, Jean, 1907- 944.04'092'4 B
Talleyrand; the art of survival. Translated from the French by Patricia Wolf. [1st American ed.] New York, Knopf, 1974. xii, 677, xxiii p. illus. 25 cm. Bibliography: p. [665]-677. [DC255.T3O7513 1974] 73-8989 ISBN 0-394-47299-3 12.95
1. Talleyrand-Perigord, Charles Maurice de, prince de Benevent, 1754-1838. BIP

Talleyrand-Perigord, Charles Maurice de, prince de Benevent, 1754-1838.

BERNARDY, Francoise de 944.060924
Talleyrand's last duchess. Tr. from French by Derek Coltman. New York, Stein & Day [c.1965, 1966] 348p. illus., ports. 22cm. Bibl. [DC255.T3B393] 66-14951 6.50 bds.,
1. Talleyrand-Perigord, Charles Maurice de, prince de Benevent, 1754-1838. 2. Talleyrand-Perigord, Dorothee (von Biron) duchess de, 1793-1862. I. Title.

BERNARDY, Francoise de. 944.060924 (B)
Talleyrand's last duchess. Translated from the French by Derek Coltman. New York, Stein and Day [1966] 348 p. illus., ports. 22 cm. Translation of the author's Le dernier amour de Talleyrand. Bibliography: p. 343-348. [DC255.T3B393] 66-14951
1. Talleyrand-Perigord, Charles Maurice de, prince de Benevent, 1754-1838. 2. Talleyrand-Perigord, Dorothee (von Biron) duchess de, 1793-1862. I. Title.

BRINTON, Clarence Cranc, 1898- 923.244
The lives of Talleyrand. New York, Norton [1963, c.1936] 316p. 20cm. (Norton Lib., N188) At head of title: Crane Brinton. Bibl. 1.65 pap.,
1. Talleyrand-Perigord, Charles Maurice de, Prince de Benevent, 1754-1838. I. Title. BIP

COOPER, Duff, 1st viscount Norwich, 1890-1954. 944.04'0924 (B)
Talleyrand. Stanford, Calif., Stanford University Press [1967, c1932] 399 p. port. 23 cm. "Bibliography and notes": p. 377-389. [DC255.T3C75] 67-29332
1. Talleyrand-Perigord, Charles Maurice de, prince de Benevent, 1754-1838. I. Title.

COOPER, Duff, 1st viscount Norwich, 1890-1954. 944.04'0924 B
Talleyrand. Stanford, Calif., Stanford University Press [1967, c1932] 399 p. port. 23 cm. "Bibliography and notes": p. 377-389. [DC255.T3C75 1967] 67-29332
1. Talleyrand-Perigord, Charles Maurice de, prince de Benevent, 1754-1838.

KOMROFF, Manuel, 1890- 923.244
Talleyrand. New York, Messner [c.1965] 190p. 22cm. Bibl. [DC255.T3K6] 65-12954 3.19 lib. ed.
1. Talleyrand-Perigord, Charles Maurice de, prince de Benevent, 1754-1838. I. Title.

TALLEYRAND-PERIGORD, Charles Maurice de, prince de Benevent, 1754-1838. 944.04'092'4 B
Memoirs of the Prince de Talleyrand. Edited, with a pref. and notes, by the duc de Broglie. Translated by Raphael Ledos de Beaufort. With an introd. by Whitelaw Reid. New York, Putnam, 1891. [New York, AMS Press, 1973] 5 v. illus. 22 cm. Vol. 3-5 translated by Mrs. Angus Hall. Includes bibliographical references. [DC255.T3A222] 78-176452 ISBN 0-404-07510-X 75.00
1. France—History—1789-1900. BIP

Talleyrand-Perigord, Dorothee (von Biron) duchesse de, 1793-1862.

ZIEGLER, Philip 920.7
The Duchess of Dino. New York, John Day [1963, c.1962] 381p. illus. 23cm. Bibl. 63-7961 5.95
1. Talleyrand-Perigord, Dorothee (von Biron) duchesse de, 1793-1862. I. Title.

Talleyrand-Perigord, Elie de, Cardinal, 1301-1364.

ZACOUR, Norman P. 922.244
Talleyrand, the cardinal of Perigord, 1301-1364. Philadelphia, American Philosophical Society [c.]1960. 83p. Bibl. footnotes. illus. 30cm. (Transactions of the American Philosophical Society, new ser., v. 50, p.7) 60-13624 2.00 pap.,
1. Talleyrand-Perigord, Elie de, Cardinal, 1301-1364. I. Title. II. Series: American Philosophical Society, Philadelphia. Transactions, new ser., v. 50, pt. 7

ZACOUR, Norman P 922.244
Talleyrand, the cardinal of Perigord-1301-1364. Philadelphia, American Philosophical Society, 1960. 83 p. illus. 30 cm. (Transactions of the American Philosophical Society, new ser., v. 50, pt. 7) Bibliographical footnotes. [Q11.P6 vol. 50, pt. 7] 60-13624
1. Talleyrand-Perigord, Elle de, Cardinal, 1301-1364 I. Title. II. Title: (Series: American Philosophical Society, Philadelphia. Transactions, new ser., v. 50, pt. 7)

Tallis, Thomas, 1505 (ca.)-1585.

DOE, Paul. 784'.092'4
Tallis. London, New York [etc.] Oxford U. P., 1968. 71 p. music. 23 cm. (Oxford studies of composers, 4) 21/- (B68-12832) Bibliography: p. 65. "List of works": p. 66-71. [ML410.]
1. Tallis, Thomas, 1505 (ca.)-1585. I. Title. II. Title: 147D6 III. Series. BIP

DOE, Paul. 783'.092'4 B
Tallis / Paul Doe. 2d ed. London ; New York : Oxford University Press, 1976. 71 p. ; 22 cm. (Oxford studies of composers ; 4) Music. "List of works": p. 66-71. [ML410.T147D6 1976] 76-361379 ISBN 0-19-314122-1 : 5.50
1. Tallis, Thomas, 1505 (ca.)-1585. I. Title. II. Series.

DOE, Paul. 783.'0924
Tallis. 2nd ed. London ; New York : Oxford University Press, 1976c1968. 71p. : music ; 22 cm. (Oxford studies of composers ; 4) Bibliography: p. 65. [ML410.T147D6] ISBN 0-19-314122-1 pbk. : 5.50
1. Tallis, Thomas, 1505(ca.)-1585. I. Title. II. Series.
L. C. card no. for 1st ed.68-118001.

Talma, Francois Joseph, 1763-1826.

COLLINS, Herbert F. 927.92
Talma, a biography of an actor. New York, Hill &Wang [c.1964] 407p. illus., facsim., ports. 23cm. Bibl. 64-15379 7.95
1. Talma, Francois Joseph, 1763-1826. I. Title.

COLLINS, Herbert F 927.92
Talma, a biography of an actor, by Herbert F. Collins. [1st American ed.] New York, Hill and Wang [1964] 407 p. illus., facsim., ports. 23 cm. "List of parts created by Talma from 1788 to 1826": p. 384-387. Bibliography: p. 389-393. [PN2638.T3C6 1964] 64-15379
1. Talma, Francois Joseph, 1763-1826. I. Title.

Talmadge, Constance, 1900-

LOOS, Anita, 1894- 791.43'028'0922 B
The Talmadge girls : a memoir / by Anita Loos. New York : Viking Press, 1978. 204 p. : ill. ; 22 cm. [PN2287.T14L6] 78-15449 ISBN 0-670-69302-2 : 12.50
1. Talmadge, Constance, 1900- 2. Talmadge, Norma, 1897- 3. Moving-picture actors and actresses—United States—Biography. I. Title.

LOOS, Anita, 1894- 791.43'028'0922 B
The Talmadge girls : a memoir / by Anita Loos. New York : Viking Press, [1978] p. cm. [PN2287.T14L6] 76-15449 ISBN 0-670-69302-2 : 10.00
1. Talmadge, Constance, 1900- 2. Talmadge, Norma, 1897- 3. Moving-picture actors and actresses—United States—Biography. I. Title.

Talmadge, Eugene, 1884-1946.

ANDERSON, William, 1941- 975.8'04'0924 B
The wild man from Sugar Creek : the political career of Eugene Talmadge / William Anderson. Baton Rouge : Louisiana State University Press, [1975] xviii, 268 p., [7] leaves of plates : ill. ; 24 cm. Includes index. Bibliography: p. 255-262. [F291.T3A52] 74-82002 ISBN 0-8071-0088-9 : 11.95
1. Talmadge, Eugene, 1884-1946. I. Title. BIP

Talmage, James Edward, 1862-1933.

TALMAGE, John R., 1911- 289.3'3 B
The Talmage story; life of James E. Talmage - educator, scientist, apostle [by] John R. Talmage. Salt Lake City, Bookcraft, 1972. 246 p. illus. 24 cm. [BX8695.T25T34] 77-189831
1. Talmage, James Edward, 1862-1933. I. Title.

Tamarack sentinel.

CHAPIN, Earl V. 920.5
Long Wednesdays. New York, Abelard Press [1953] 268 p. 22 cm. Autobiographical. [PN4874.C46A3] 53-8363
1. Tamarack sentinel. 2. Journalists—Correspondence, reminiscences, etc. I. Title.

Tamarin, Alfred H.

TAMARIN, Alfred H. 730'.924 B
The autobiography of Benvenuto Cellini, edited by Alfred Tamarin. Abridged and adapted from the translation by John Addington Symonds. [New York] Macmillan [1969] x, 164 p. illus. 26 cm. [NB623.C3S45 1969] 69-11591
1. Symonds, John Addington, 1840-1893, tr. II. Cellini, Benvenuto, 1500-1571. The autobiography.

Tamburi Cemil, 1871?-1915?

SIEGLIN, Angelika. 784'.092'4
Untersuchungen zur Kompositionstechnik in den Pesrev des Tanburi Cemil Bey / Angelika Sieglin. Hamburg : Verlag der Musikalienhandlung K. D. Wagner, 1975. 130 p. : music ; 21 cm. (Beitrage zur Ethnomusikologie ; Bd. 5) Bibliography: p. 97-99. [ML410.T16S57] 75-517272 ISBN 3-921029-24-4
1. Tamburi Cemil, 1871?-1915? I. Title. II. Series.

Tamiris, Helen, 1905-1966.

SCHLUNDT, Christena L. 793.3'092'4
Tamiris: a chronicle of her dance career, 1927-1955, by Christena L. Schlundt. New York, New York Public Library, 1972. 94 p. illus. 26 cm. [GV1785.T37S34] 72-86181 ISBN 0-87104-233-9
1. Tamiris, Helen, 1905-1966. I. Title.

Tancred, 1075 (ca.)-1112.

NICHOLSON, Robert Lawrence, 1908. 956'.01'0924
Tancred : a study of his career and work in their relation to the first Crusade and the establishment of the Latin states in Syria and Palestine / by Robert Lawrence Nicholson. 1st AMS ed. New York : AMS Press, 1978, c1940. 240 p. ; 23 cm. Originally presented as the author's thesis, University of Chicago, 1938. Reprint of the private ed. distributed by the University of Chicago Libraries, Chicago. Bibliography: p. 229-236. [D181.T3N5 1978] 79-29847 ISBN 0-404-15425-5 : 22.50
1. Tancred, 1075 (ca.)-1112. 2. Crusades—First, 1096-1099. 3. Syria—History. 4. Palestine—History—638-1917. 5. Crusades—Biography.

Tandy, James Napper, 1737-1803.

COUGHLAN, Rupert J. 941.8'35'0730924 B
Napper Tandy / Rupert J. Coughlan. Dublin : Anvil Books, 1976. xii, 276 p., [4] leaves of plates : ill. ; 23 cm. Includes index. Bibliography: p. 261-264. [DA995.D75T363 1976] 77-366017 ISBN 0-900068-34-5 : £6.50
1. Tandy, James Napper, 1737-1803. 2. Dublin—Biography. 3. Soldiers—Biography. **BIP**

Taney, Roger Brooke, 1777-1864.

LEWIS, Walker. 347.9924 (B)
Without fear or favor; a biography of Chief Justice Roger Brooke Taney. Boston, Houghton Mifflin, 1965. viii, 556 p. port. 22 cm. Bibliography: p. [539]-546. 65-18490
1. Taney, Roger Brooke, 1777-1864. I. Title.

SCHUMACHER, Alvin J. 923.473
Thunder on Capitol Hill; the life of Chief Justice Roger B. Taney. Illus. by Dirk Gringhuis. Milwaukee, Bruce [c.1964] vii, 160p. port. 22cm. 64-243971 3.25
1. Taney, Roger Brooke, 1777-1864. I. Title.

SMITH, Charles William, 1904- 347'.73'2634 B
Roger B. Taney: Jacksonian jurist, by Charles W. Smith, Jr. New York, Da Capo Press, 1973 [c1936] xi, 242 p. 22 cm. (Da Capo Press reprints in American constitutional and legal history) Originally presented as the author's thesis, University of Wisconsin, 1934. Bibliography: p. 215-238. [KF8745.T3S6 1973] 72-8802 10.00
1. Taney, Roger Brooke, 1777-1864. 2. State rights. 3. Sovereignty. 4. State, The. 5. Democracy. I. Title.

STEINER, Bernard Christian, 1867-1926. 347'.7326'34 B
Life of Roger Brooke Taney, Chief Justice of the United States Supreme Court. Westport, Conn., Greenwood Press [1970] 553 p. ports. 23 cm. Reprint of the 1922 ed. Includes bibliographical references. [E340.T2S8 1970] 74-109853 ISBN 0-8371-4344-6
1. Taney, Roger Brooke, 1777-1864. I. Title. **BIP**

SWISHER, Carl Brent, 1897- 923.473
Roger B. Taney. Hamden, Conn., Archon Bks. [dist. Shoe String] 1961 [c.1935] 608p. illus. 61-4990 12.50
1. Taney, Roger Brooke, 1777-1864. I. Title.

TYLER, Samuel, 1809-1877. 347'.73'2634 B
Memoir of Roger Brooke Taney. New York, Da Capo Press, 1970 [c1872] 659 p. port. 24 cm. Reprint of the ed. published by J. Murphy, Baltimore. [KF8745.T3T9 1970] 78-87703 ISBN 0-306-71688-7
1. Taney, Roger Brooke, 1777-1864. I. Title.

Tang (Ship)

O'KANE, Richard H., 1911- 940.54'51
Clear the bridge! : The war patrols of the U.S.S. Tang / by Richard H. O'Kane. Chicago : Rand McNally, c1977. 480 p. : ill. ; 24 cm. Includes index. [D783.5.T35O38] 77-7158 ISBN 0-528-81058-8 : 10.00
1. Tang (Ship) 2. O'Kane, Richard H., 1911- 3. United States. Navy—Biography. 4. World War, 1939-1945—Naval operations—Submarine. 5. World War, 1939-1945—Pacific Ocean. 6. World War, 1939-1945—Naval operations, American. 7. World War, 1939-1945—Personal narratives, American. 8. Seamen—United States—Biography. I. Title. **BIP**

Tange, Kenzo, 1913-

ALTHERR, Alfred, 1911- 720.922
Three Japanese architects. Drei japanische Architekten; Mayekawa, Tange, Sakakura. [English version by D. Q. Stephenson] New York, Architectural Book Pub. Co. [1968] 179 p. illus., plans. 23 x 29 cm. English and German. [NA1559.M3A78 1968] 68-5228
1. Maekawa, Kunio, 1905- 2. Tange, Kenzo, 1913- 3. Sakakura, Junzo. 4. Architecture, Modern—20th century—Japan. I. Title. II. Title: Drei japanische Architekten.

Tankard, John, 1752-1836.

FITZHUGH, Georgianna (Tankard) 929'.2'0973
The life of Dr. John Tankard, by Georgianna Fitzhugh. Onancock, Va., Eastern Shore of Virginia Historical Society, 1965. 130 p. illus., fold. geneal. tables, ports. 23 cm. 200 copies. First published in 1907. [CS71.T165 1965] 66-57742
1. Tankard, John, 1752-1836. 2. Tankard family. I. Title.

Tannahill, Robert, 1774-1810—Addresses, essays, lectures.

DOUGLAS, George Brisbane, Sir, bart., 1856-1935. 821'.7 B
James Hogg. [Folcroft, Pa.] Folcroft Library Editions, 1974. 154 p. 23 cm. Contains also brief essays on Robert Tannahill, William Motherwell, and William Thom. Reprint of the 1899 ed. published by O. Anderson & Ferrier, Edinburgh, issued in series: Famous Scots series. Includes bibliographical references. [PR4792.D6 1974] 74-10889 ISBN 0-8414-3762-9 (lib. bdg.)
1. Hogg, James, 1770-1835—Biography. 2. Tannahill, Robert, 1774-1810—Addresses, essays, lectures. 3. Motherwell, William, 1797-1835—Addresses, essays, lectures. 4. Thom, William, 1798?-1848—Addresses, essays, lectures. **BIP**

Tannenberg, David.

ARMSTRONG, William Howard, 1932- 786.6'3
Organs for America; the life and work of David Tannenberg, by William H. Armstrong. Philadelphia, University of Pennsylvania Press, 1967. xvi, 154 p. 21 plates (part col., incl. facsims.) 23 cm. Bibliography: p. 135-145. Discography: p. 145. [ML424.T35A85] 67-26221
1. Tannenberg, David. 2. Organs—United States. I. Title. **BIP**

Tanner, Annie Clark, 1864-1941.

TANNER, Annie Clark, 1864-1941. 289.3'092'4 B
A mormon mother; an autobiography. [1st rev. ed.] [Salt Lake City] Tanner Trust Fund, University of Utah Library [1973] xxix, 346 p. 23 cm. (Utah, the Mormons, and the West) [BX8695.T27A33 1973] 73-86679 10.00
1. Tanner, Annie Clark, 1864-1941. I. Title. II. Series.

Tanner, Cora English.

TRUTTER, John Thomas. 977.3'04'0922 B
The Governor takes a bride : the celebrated marriage of Cora English and John R. Tanner, Governor of Illinois (1897-1901) / by John Thomas Trutter and Edith English Trutter. Carbondale : Published for the Illinois State Historical Society [by] Southern Illinois University Press, c1977. 82 p. : ill. ; 21 cm. [F546.T152T78] 77-7643 ISBN 0-8093-0824-X : 4.95. pbk. : 3.95
1. Tanner, Cora English. 2. Tanner, John Riley, 1844-1901. 3. Illinois—Governors—Wives—Biography. 4. Illinois—Governors—Biography. I. Trutter, Edith English, joint author. II. Title. **BIP**

Tanner, Eliza Ellen Parkinson, 1857-1930.

TANNER, George Shepherd, 1897- v. 12
Henry Martin Tanner, Joseph City, Arizona pioneer, born June 11, 1852, San Bernardino, California; died March 21, 1935, Gilbert, Arizona, by George S. Tanner. [n.p.] 1964. 140 p. 28 cm. 66-63206
1. Tanner, Henry Martin, 1852-1935. 2. Tanner, Eliza Ellen Parkinson, 1857-1930. 3. Tanner, Emma Ellen Stapley, 1862-1933. I. Title.

Tanner, Henry Martin, 1852-1935.

TANNER, George Shepherd, 1897- v. 12
Henry Martin Tanner, Joseph City, Arizona pioneer, born June 11, 1852, San Bernardino, California; died March 21, 1935, Gilbert, Arizona, by George S. Tanner. [n.p.] 1964. 140 p. 28 cm. 66-63206
1. Tanner, Henry Martin, 1852-1935. 2. Tanner, Eliza Ellen Parkinson, 1857-1930. 3. Tanner, Emma Ellen Stapley, 1862-1933. I. Title.

Tanner, Henry Ossawa, 1859-1937.

MATHEWS, Marcia M. 759.13 B
Henry Ossawa Tanner, American artist [by] Marcia M. Mathews. Chicago, University of Chicago Press [1969] xvii, 261 p. illus. (part col.), ports. 23 cm. (Negro American biographies and autobiographies) Bibliographical footnotes. [ND237.T33M3] 69-19279
1. Tanner, Henry Ossawa, 1859-1937. I. Title. II. Series.

Tanner, John, 1780?-1847.

O MEARA, Walter. 923.973
The last portage. Illustrated by William Hofmann. Boston, Houghton Mifflin, 1962. 289p. illus. 23cm. Includes bibliography. [E87.T16O56] 62-11486
1. Tanner, John, 1780?-1847. 2. Indians of North America—Captivities. I. Title.

O'MEARA, Walter Andrew 923.973
The last portage. Illus. by William Hofmann. Boston, Houghton [c.]1962. 289p. 23cm. Bibl. 62-11486 5.00
1. Tanner, John, 1780?-1847. 2. Indians of North America—Captivities. I. Title.

TANNER, John, 1780?-1847. 973'.04'97 S
A narrative of the captivity and adventures of John Tanner (U.S. interpreter at the Saut de Ste. Marie) during thirty years residence among the Indians in the interior of North America / edited by Edwin James. New York : Garland Pub., 1975. p. cm. (The Garland library of narratives of North American Indian captivities ; v. 46) Reprint of the 1830 ed. published by G. & C. H. Carvell, New York. [E85.G2 vol. 46] [E87] 977.4'004'97 75-7068 ISBN 0-8240-1670-X lib.bdg. : 21.00
1. Tanner, John, 1780?-1847. 2. Indians of North America—Captivities. 3. Ottawa Indians. 4. Chippewa Indians. 5. Indians of North America—Languages. I. James, Edwin, 1797-1861. II. Title. III. Title: A narrative of the captivity and adventures of John Tanner ... IV. Series. **BIP**

Tanner, Simpson Bobo, 1853-1924.

JOHNSON, Gerald White, 1890- 926.772
The making of a southern industrialist; a biographical study of Simpson Bobo Tanner. Chapel Hill, University of North Carolina Press [1952] 84 p. illus. 21 cm. [HD9880.T3J6] 52-14578
1. Tanner, Simpson Bobo, 1853-1924. I. Title.

Tantaquidgeon, Harold.

VOIGHT, Virginia Frances. 970.30924
Mohegan chief; the story of Harold Tantaquidgeon. New York, Funk & Wagnalls [1965] 192 p. illus. 22 cm. [E90.T16V6] 65-19347
1. Tantaquidgeon, Harold. 2. Mohegan Indians. I. Title.

VOIGHT, Virginia Frances 970.30924
Mohegan chief; the story of Harold Tantaquidgeon. NewYork, Funk & Wagnalls [c.1965] 192p. illus. 22cm. [E90.T16V6] 65-19347 3.95
1. Tantaquidgeon, Harold. 2. Mohegan Indians. I. Title.

Tapia, Carlos, 1885-1945.

COLON, Ramon. 301.45'16'87295074710924 B
Carlos Tapia : a Puerto Rican hero in New York / by Ramon Colon. 1st ed. New York : Vantage Press, c1976. 89 p. : ill. ; 22 cm. [F129.B7T373] 77-353939 ISBN 0-533-02134-0 : 5.95
1. Tapia, Carlos, 1885-1945. 2. Puerto Ricans in Brooklyn—Biography. 3. Brooklyn—Biography.

Tapia, Gonzalo de, 1561?-1594.

SHIELS, William Eugene, 1897- 266'.272'1 B
Gonzalo de Tapia (1561-1594) : founder of the first permanent Jesuit mission in North America / W. Eugene Shiels. Westport, Conn. : Greenwood Press, 1978. ix, 198 p. : maps ; 22 cm. Reprint of the 1934 ed. published by the United States Catholic Historical Society, New York, which was issued as 14 of the Society's Monograph series. Includes index. Bibliography: p. 180-195. [F1219.3.M59T367 1978] 74-12835 ISBN 0-8371-7758-8 lib.bdg. : 15.50
1. Tapia, Gonzalo de, 1561?-1594. 2. Indians of Mexico—Missions. 3. Jesuits—Mexico—Biography. 4. Jesuits—Missions. I. Title. II. Series: United States Catholic Historical Society. Monograph series ; 14. **BIP**

Tappan, Arthur, 1786-1865.

TAPPAN, Lewis, 1788-1873. 326'.0924 B
The life of Arthur Tappan. Westport, Conn., Negro Universities Press [1970] 432 p. port. 23 cm. "Originally published in 1871." [E449.T16 1970b] 78-110017 ISBN 0-8371-4154-0
1. Tappan, Arthur, 1786-1865. 2. Slavery in the United States—Anti-slavery movements. I. Title. **BIP**

TAPPAN, Lewis, 1788-1873. 326'.0924 B
The life of Arthur Tappan. [New York] Arno [1970] 432 p. port. 23 cm. (The American journalists) Reprint of the 1870 ed. Includes bibliographical references. [E449.T16 1970] 75-125718 ISBN 0-405-01699-9
1. Tappan, Arthur, 1786-1865. 2. Slavery in the United States—Anti-slavery movements. I. Title.

WINTER, Rebecca J. 248'.5'0922 B
The night cometh : two wealthy evangelicals face the nation / Rebecca J. Winter. South Pasadena, Calif. : William Carey Library, c1977. xii, 84 p. ; 22 cm. Includes index. Bibliography: p. 78-80. [BR1643.A1W56] 77-87594 ISBN 0-87808-429-0 pbk. : 2.95
1. Tappan, Arthur, 1786-1865. 2. Tappan, Lewis, 1788-1873. 3. Evangelicalism—United States—Biography. 4. Philanthropists—United States—Biography. I. Title. BIP

Tapping, Minnie (Ellingson)

TAPPING, Minnie (Ellingson) 1867-1950. 920.7
Eighty years at the Gopher Hole; the saga of a Minnesota pioneer, 1867-1947. [1st ed.] New York, Exposition Press [1958] 228 p. 21 cm. [[CT275]] 58-719
I. Title.

Tarbell family.

THE Tarbells of Yankton : a family and a community, 1891-1932, presented in letters / arranged & edited, with comments & an afterword by Egbert S. Oliver. 1st ed. Portland, Or. : Hapi Press, 1978. vii, 514 p., [1] leaf of plates : ill. ; 22 cm. [F884.Y36T37] 78-59356 ISBN 0-913244-14-7 : 8.95 979.5'47
1. Tarbell family. 2. Yankton, Or.—Biography. I. Oliver, Egbert Samuel, 1902-
Publisher's address : 512 S.W. Maplecrest Dr., Portland, OR 97219

Tarbell, Ida Minerva, 1857-1944—Biography.

TARBELL, Ida Minerva, 1857-1944. 070'.92'4 B
All in the day's work : an autobiography / by Ida M. Tarbell. Washington : Zenger Pub. Co., 1975, c1939. p. cm. Reprint of the ed. published by Macmillan, New York. [PS3539.A58Z5 1975] 75-35979 ISBN 0-89201-013-4
1. Tarbell, Ida Minerva, 1857-1944—Biography. I. Title.

Tarbell, Ida Minerva, 1857-1944—Juvenile literature.

CONN, Frances G. 070'.92'4 B
Ida Tarbell, muckraker, by Frances G. Conn. [1st ed.] Nashville, T. Nelson [1972] 160 p. 21 cm. A biography of the woman who pioneered a new style of journalism in exposing the malpractices of the oil industry at the turn of the century. [PN4874.T23C6] 92 78-181678 ISBN 0-8407-6220-8
1. Tarbell, Ida Minerva, 1857-1944—Juvenile literature. I. Title.

FLEMING, Alice (Mulcahey) 1928- 070.9'2 B
Ida Tarbell; first of the muckrakers, by Alice Fleming. New York, Crowell [1971] 170 p. illus., ports. 21 cm. (Women of America) Bibliography: p. 163-164. A biography of the woman who pioneered a new style of journalism in exposing the malpractices of the oil industry at the turn of the century. [PN4874.T23F5] 92 76-139103 ISBN 0-690-42881-2 4.50
1. Tarbell, Ida Minerva, 1857-1944—Juvenile literature. I. Title.

Tardini, Domenico, Cardinal.

TARDINI, Domenico, Cardinal. 922.21
Memories of Pius XII. Translated by Rosmarie Goldie. Goldie. Westminster, Md., Newman [c.]1961. 175p. ports. (col.) 60-53377 2.75
I. Title.

Tarisio, Luigi, 1792-1854.

KLOBUCHAR, Jim. 796.33'20924
Tarkenton / by Jim Klobucher and Fran Tarkenton. New York : Harper and Row, 1977. xiii, 336p. : ill. ; 18 cm. (Perennial Library) [GV939.T3K56] ISBN 0-06-080425-4 pbk. : 1.95
1. Quarterback (Football)-Biography. I. Tarkenton, Francis A., joint author. II. Title.
L.C. card no. for 1976 Harper and Row ed.: 76-30426. BIP

SILVERMAN, William Alexander. 927.8
The violin hunter. With a foreword by Josef Gingold. New York, Day [1957] 256 p. 21 cm. [ML429.T3S5] 57-8238
1. Tarisio, Luigi, 1792-1854. I. Title.

Tarkenton, Francis A.

KLOBUCHAR, Jim. 796.33'2'0924 B
Tarkenton / by Jim Klobuchar and Fran Tarkenton. 1st ed. New York : Harper & Row, c1976. xii, 274 p., [8] leaves of plates : ill. ; 24 cm. Includes index. [GV939.T3K56 1976] 76-30426 ISBN 0-06-012412-1 : 8.95
1. Tarkenton, Francis A. 2. Quarterback (Football)—Biography. I. Tarkenton, Francis A., joint author.

TARKENTON, Francis A. 796.332'0924
Better scramble than lose, by Fran Tarkenton as told to Olsen. New York, Four Winds Press [1969] 126 p. illus., ports. 22 cm. Autobiographical. [GV939.T28A3] 73-81706 4.50
1. Football—Biography. I. Olsen, Jack. II. Title.

TARKENTON, Francis A. 796.332'64
Broken patterns; the education of a quarterback, by Fran Tarkenton, as told to Brock Yates. New York, Simon and Schuster [1971] 191 p. illus. 22 cm. [GV939.T3A27] 76-159137 ISBN 0-671-21053-X 5.95
I. Yates, Brock W. II. Title.

TARKENTON, Francis A. 796.332'64
Broken patterns; the education of a quarterback, by Fran Tarkenton, as told to Brock Yates. New York, Simon and Schuster [1971] 191 p. illus. 22 cm. [GV939.T3A27] 76-159137 ISBN 0-671-21053-X 5.95
I. Yates, Brock W. II. Title.

Tarkenton, Francis A.—Juvenile literature.

BRAUN, Thomas, 1944- 796.33'2'0924 B
Football's greatest passer, Fran Tarkenton / by Thomas Braun. [Mankato, Minn.] : Creative Education/Childrens Press, [c1977] 30 p. : ill. ; 19 cm. (The Allstars) A brief biography of the Minnesota Viking quarterback nicknamed "The Scrambler" for his style of playing. [GV939.T3B7] 92 76-44505 ISBN 0-87191-583-9 lib.bdg. : 4.95
1. Tarkenton, Francis A.—Juvenile literature. 2. Football players—United States—Biography—Juvenile literature. I. Title.

LIBBY, Bill. 796.332'0924
Fran Tarkenton: the scrambler. New York, Putnam [1970] 192 p. 21 cm. A biography of the football quarterback nicknamed "the Scrambler" for his style of playing. [GV939.T3L5 1970] 92 75-105648 3.64
1. Tarkenton, Francis A.—Juvenile literature. I. Title.

MAY, Julian. 796.33'2'0924 B
Fran Tarkenton, scrambling quarterback. Mankato, Minn., Crestwood House [1973] 47 p. illus. 24 cm. (Sports close-up books) A biography of a football player who has been star quarterback for the New York Giants and the Minnesota Vikings. [GV939.T3M38 1973] 92 73-80423 ISBN 0-913940-03-8
1. Tarkenton, Francis A.—Juvenile literature. I. Title.
Publisher's address: Box 423, 515 North Front Street, Mankato, Minn. 56001

SMITH, Jay H. 796.33'2'0924 B
Fran Tarkenton / written by Jay H. Smith ; illustrated by Harold Henriksen. Mankato, Minn. : Creative Education, [1976] p. cm. Traces the football career of the controversial quarterback of the Minnesota Vikings whose exciting running in emergencies has earned him the nickname "The Scrambler." [GV939.T3S64 1976] 92 76-25831 4.95
1. Tarkenton, Francis A.—Juvenile literature. 2. Football—Juvenile literature. I. Henriksen, Harold. BIP

Tarkington, Booth, 1869-1946.

FENNIMORE, Keith J. 813'.5'2
Booth Tarkington, by Keith J. Fennimore. New York, Twayne Publishers [1974] 167 p. 21 cm. (Twayne's United States authors series, TUSAS 238) Bibliography: p. 157-161. [PS2973.F4] 73-16403 ISBN 0-8057-0715-8 5.50
1. Tarkington, Booth, 1869-1946. BIP

WOODRESS, James Leslie. 928.1
Booth Tarkington, gentleman from Indiana. [1st ed.] Philadelphia, Lippincott [1955] 350 p. illus. 22 cm. Includes bibliography. [PS2973.W6] 55-6307
1. Tarkington, Booth, 1869-1946. BIP

WOODRESS, James Leslie. 813'.5'2 B
Booth Tarkington, gentleman from Indiana [by] James Woodress. New York, Greenwood Press [1969, c1955] 350 p. illus. 23 cm. "A bibliographical postscript": p. 319-342. [PS2973.W6 1969] 69-14155
1. Tarkington, Booth, 1869-1946.

Tarkington, Booth, 1869-1946—Biography.

TARKINGTON, Booth, 1869-1946. 813'.5'2 B
The world does move / by Booth Tarkington. Westport, Conn. : Greenwood Press, 1976. 294 p. ; 23 cm. Reprint of the 1928 ed. published by Doubleday, Doran, Garden City, N.Y. [PS2973.A4 1976] 76-8903 ISBN 0-8371-8876-8 lib. bdg. : 16.00
1. Tarkington, Booth, 1869-1946—Biography. I. Title. BIP

Tarleton, Sir Banastre, bart., 1754-1833.

BASS, Robert Duncan. 923.242
The green dragoon; the lives of Banastre Tarleton and Mary Robinson. [1st ed.] New York, Holt [1957] viii, 489p. illus., ports., maps. 25cm. Bibliography: p.455-469. [DA506.T3B3] 57-6183
1. Tarleton, Sir Banastre, bart., 1754-1833. 2. Robinson, Mary (Darby) 1758-1800. 3. Gt. Brit.—Soc. life & cust. I. Title.

Tarquinius Superbus, Lucius, fl. 534-510 B. C.

FRANZERO, Charles Marie, 1892- 923.137
The life and times of Tarquin the Etruscan. New York, John Day Co. [1961, c.1960] 254p. illus., Bibl., map 61-5692 4.50
1. Tarquinius Superbus, Lucius, fl. 534-510 B. C. I. Title.

Tarrants, Thomas A.

TARRANTS, Thomas A. 248'.2 B
The conversion of a Klansman : the story of a former Ku Klux Klan terrorist / Thomas A. Tarrants III. 1st ed. Garden City, N.Y. : Doubleday, 1979. x, 130 p. ; 22 cm. "A Doubleday-Galilee original." [BV4935.T37A33] 78-74713 ISBN 0-385-14926-3 : 7.95
1. Tarrants, Thomas A. 2. Ku Klux Klan (1915-) 3. Converts—United States—Biography. I. Title. BIP

Tarry, Ellen,

TARRY, Ellen, 1906- 920.5
The third door; the autobiography of an American Negro woman. New York, D. McKay Co. [1955] 304 p. 21 cm. [E185.97.T37A3] 55-14466
I. Title.

TARRY, Ellen, 1906- 920.5
The third door; the autobiography of an American Negro woman. New York, All Saints [dist.] Guild [c.1955, 1966] 304p. 21cm. (AS249) [E185.97.T37A3] .60 pap.,
I. Title.

TARRY, Ellen, 1906- 813'.5'4
The third door; the autobiography of an American Negro woman. Westport, Conn., Negro Universities Press [1971, c1955] ix, 304 p. 23 cm. [E185.97.T37A3 1971] 70-135613 ISBN 0-8371-5200-3
I. Title.

Tarthang Tulku.

ANNALS of the Nyingma lineage in America. [Berkeley, Calif.] : Dharma Pub., 1975- v. : ill. ; 28 cm. Contents.Contents.—v. 1. 1969-1975. [BQ7662.2.A56] 75-323606 ISBN 0-913546-23-2 294.3'923
1. Tarthang Tulku. 2. Rnin-ma-pa (Sect)—United States—History.

Tartini, Giuseppe, 1692-1770—Fiction.

SPALDING, Albert, 1888-- 788'.1'0924
A fiddle, a sword, and a lady' the romance of Giuseppe Tartini. [1st ed.] New York, Holt [1953] 338p. 22cm. [ML3925.T3S7] 53-5273
1. Tartini, Giuseppe, 1692-1770—Fiction. 2. Musical fiction. I. Title.

Tasman, Abel Janszoon, 1603?-1659.

SHARP, Andrew. 994'.01'0924
The voyages of Abel Janszoon Tasman. London, Clarendon Pr., 1968. xii, 375p. 21 plates illus., charts, facsims., maps. 23cm. Bibl. footnotes. [DU98.1.S5] (B) 68-134448 11.25
1. Tasman, Abel Janszoon, 1603?-1659. I. Title.
Available from Oxford Univ. Pr., New York. BIP

Tasso, Torquato, 1544-1595.

BOULTING, William. 851'.4 B
Tasso and his times. New York, Haskell House Publishers, 1968. xv, 314 p. illus., ports. 24 cm. Reprint of the 1907 ed. "List of authorities": p. 309-310. [PQ4646.B6 1968] 68-24953
1. Tasso, Torquato, 1544-1595. 2. Italy—Court and courtiers. I. Title. BIP

Tate, Allen, 1899-

BISHOP, Ferman. 818'.5'209
Allen Tate. New York, Twayne Publishers [1967] 172 p. 21 cm. (Twayne's United States authors series, 124) Bibliography: p. 161-165. [PS3539.A74Z63] 67-24765
1. Tate, Allen, 1899- I. Title. BIP

SQUIRES, James Radcliffe, 1917- 818'.5'209
Allen Tate; a literary biography [by] Radcliffe Squires. New York, Pegasus [1971] 231 p. 21 cm. (Pegasus American authors) Bibliography: p. 220-223. [PS3539.A74Z86] 75-128673 6.95
1. Tate, Allen, 1899-

Tate, Allen, 1899- —Biography.

TATE, Allen, 1899- 818'.5'209 B
Memoirs and opinions, 1926-1974 / Allen Tate. 1st ed. Chicago : Swallow Press, 1975. xi, 225 p. ; 23 cm. Includes index. [PS3539.A74Z52] 75-10757 ISBN 0-8040-0662-8 : 8.95
1. Tate, Allen, 1899- —Biography. 2. Authors—Correspondence, reminiscences, etc. 3. Literature—History and criticism—Addresses, essays, lectures. I. Title.

Tate, Maurice, 1895-1956.

BRODRIBB, Gerald. 796.358'092'4 B
Maurice Tate : a biography / Gerald Brodribb. London : London Magazine Editions, 1976. 215 p., [4] leaves of plates : ill. ; 23 cm. Includes bibliographical references and index. [GV915.T37B76] 76-363346 ISBN 0-904388-13-1 : £4.50
1. Tate, Maurice, 1895-1956. 2. Cricket.

Tate, Nahum, 1652-1715.

SPENCER, Christopher. 821'.4 B
Nahum Tate. New York, Twayne Publishers [1972] 184 p. 22 cm. (Twayne's English authors series, 126) Bibliography: p. 167-178. [PR3729.T115Z85] 76-152014
1. Tate, Nahum, 1652-1715. BIP

Tati, Jacques.

GILLIATT, Penelope. 791.43'0233'0924
Jacques Tati / Penelope Gilliatt. London : Woburn Press, 1976. 96 p. : ill. ; 21 cm. (The Entertainers) "The films of Jacques Tati": p. [92]-96. [PN1998.A3T33] 77-354109 ISBN 0-7130-0145-3 : £2.95
1. Tati, Jacques. 2. Moving-picture producers and directors—France—Biography. 3. Comedians—France—Biography. BIP

Tatishchev, Vasilii Nikitich, 1668-1750.

DANIELS, Rudolph L., 1945- 947'.06'0924
V. N. Tatishchev: guardian of the Petrine revolution [by] Rudolph L. Daniels. Philadelphia, Franklin Pub. Co. [1973] vii, 125 p. 24 cm. Bibliography: p. 117-125. [DK127.5.T3D3] 73-79746 8.95
1. Tatishchev, Vasilii Nikitich, 1668-1750. 2. Russia—History—1689-1800.

Taub, William L.

TAUB, William L. 973.92'092'4
Forces of power / by William L. Taub. New York : Grosset & Dunlap, c1979. 255 p., [4] leaves of plates : ill. ; 24 cm. Includes index. [CT275.T32A33] 78-68181 ISBN 0-448-15775-6 : 11.95
1. Taub, William L. 2. United States—Biography. I. Title. BIP

Tauber, Richard, 1891-1948.

CASTLE, Charles, 1939- 784'.0924 B
This was Richard Tauber [by] Charles Castle; in collaboration with Diana Napier Tauber. London, New York, W. H. Allen, 1971. 209 p., 33 plates. illus., facsims. (on lining papers), ports. 23 cm. [ML420.T126C4] 78-592703 ISBN 0-491-00117-7 £3.50
1. Tauber, Richard, 1891-1948. I. Tauber, Diana (Napier). II. Title.

Tauch, Waldine, 1892-

HUTSON, Alice, 1941- 730'.92'4 B
From chalk to bronze : a biography of Waldine Tauch / by Alice Hutson. 1st ed. Austin : Shoal Creek Publishers, c1978. p. cm. Includes index. Bibliography: p. [NB237.T38H87] 78-16000 ISBN 0-88319-037-0 : 15.00
1. Tauch, Waldine, 1892- 2. Sculptors—United States—Biography. I. Title.

Tauler, Johannes, 1300 (ca.)-1361.

CLARK, James Midgley, 1888-1961. 149'.3
The great German mystics: Eckhart, Tauler, and Suso. Folcroft, Pa., Folcroft Press [1969] vii, 121 p. 25 cm. Reprint of the 1949 ed., which was issued as no. 5 of Modern language studies. Bibliography: p. 110-117. [BV5077.G3C58 1969] 72-193479
1. Eckhart, Meister, d. 1327. 2. Tauler, Johannes, 1300 (ca.)-1361. 3. Suso, Heinrich, 1300?-1366. 4. Mysticism—Germany. I. Title.

Tausig, Karl, 1841-1871.

LENZ, Wilhelm von, 1808-1883. 786.1'092'2 B
The great piano virtuosos of our time, by W. von Lenz; this revised translation [from the German] edited by Philip Reder. London, New York, Regency Press, 1971. [7], 91 p. ports. 20 cm. Revised translation of Die grossen piano-virtuosen unserer zeit aus persönlicher bekanntschaft. [ML397.L57 1971] 72-190224 ISBN 0-7212-0138-5 £1.20
1. Liszt, Franz, 1811-1886. 2. Chopin, Fryderyk Franciszek, 1810-1849. 3. Tausig, Karl, 1841-1871. 4. Henselt, Adolf von, 1814-1889. I. Title. BIP

Taverner, John, 1495 (ca.)-1545.

JOSEPHSON, David S., 1942- 783'.026'0924 B
John Taverner, Tudor composer / by David S. Josephson. Ann Arbor : UMI Research Press, 1979. p. cm. (Studies in musicology series ; no. 6) Includes index. Bibliography: p. [ML410.T186J7] 79-12291 ISBN 0-8357-0990-6 : 27.95. ISBN 0-8357-0991-4 pbk. : 24.95
1. Taverner, John, 1495 (ca.)-1545. 2. Composers—England—Biography. I. Title. II. Series.

Tawes, Leonard S.,

TAWES, Leonard S., 1853-1932. 387.5'0924
Coasting Captain; journals of Captain Leonard S. Tawes, relating his career in Atlantic coastwise sailing craft from 1868 to 1922. Edited for the Museum by Robert H. Burgess. Newport News, Va., Mariners Museum, 1967. xix, 461 p. illus. (part col.), ports. 24 cm. (Museum publication no. 28) [VK140.T3A3] 67-17219
I. Burgess, Robert H., ed. II. Title. III. Series: Mariners' Museum, Newport News, Va Museum publication no. 28)

Tawil, Raymonda.

TAWIL, Raymonda. 956.94'004'927 B
My home, my prison / by Raymonda Tawil. 1st American ed. New York : Holt, Rinehart, and Winston, c1979. p. cm. [DS113.7.T38 1979] 79-10496 ISBN 0-03-049301-3. : 12.95
1. Tawil, Raymonda. 2. Palestinian Arabs—Israel—Biography. 3. Jordan (Territory under Israeli occupation, 1967-) 4. Jewish-Arab relation—1949- I. Title. BIP

Tawney, Richard Henry, 1880-1962.

TERRILL, Ross. 335'.0092'4 B
R. H. Tawney and his times; socialism as fellowship. Cambridge, Mass, Harvard University Press, 1973. x, 373 p. illus. 25 cm. Bibliography: p. 283-286. [HX243.T38T47] 72-83392 ISBN 0-674-74376-8 15.00
1. Tawney, Richard Henry, 1880-1962. 2. Tawney, Richard Henry, 1880-1962—Bibliography. I. Title. BIP

Taylor, Alfred Alexander, 1848-1931.

FAIN, Sara Pett. 923.273
"The fiddle and the bow." Boston, Christopher Pub. House [1952] 201 p. illus. 21 cm. [F436.T218F3] 52-7107
1. Taylor, Alfred Alexander, 1848-1931. 2. Taylor, Robert Love, 1850-1912. 3. Tennessee—Pol. & govt.—1865- I. Title.

Taylor, Bayard, 1825-1878.

SMYTH, Albert Henry, 1863-1907. 818'.3'09 B
Bayard Taylor. Detroit, Gale Research Co., 1970. vii, 320 p. port. 22 cm. "Facsimile reprint of the 1896 edition." Bibliography: p. [299]-307. [PS2993.S5 1896a] 75-99057
1. Taylor, Bayard, 1825-1878. BIP

Taylor, Catherine, 1914-

TAYLOR, Catherine, 1914- 968'.06
If courage goes : my twenty years in South African politics / Catherine Taylor. Johannesburg : Macmillan South Africa, 1976. 316 p., [4] leaves of plates : ill. ; 24 cm. [DT779.95.T38A34] 76-374843 ISBN 0-86954-027-0
1. Taylor, Catherine, 1914- 2. United Party (South Africa) 3. South Africa—Politics and government—1948-1961. 4. South Africa—Politics and government—1961- 5. Legislators—South Africa—Biography. I. Title.

Taylor, David, 1934-

TAYLOR, David, 1934- 636.089'092'4 [B]
Is there a doctor in the zoo? / David Taylor. New York : Bantam Books, 1979, c1978. 213p. ; 18 cm. [SF966.T37] ISBN 0-553-12003-4 pbk. : 2.25
1. Taylor, David, 1934- 2. Zoo animals — Diseases. 3. Veterinarians — Biography. I. Title.
L.C. card no. for 1978 Lippincott ed.: 78-2595. BIP

TAYLOR, David, 1934- 636.089'092'4 B
Is there a doctor in the zoo? / David Taylor ; with line drawings by Frankie Coventry 1st American ed. Philadelphia : Lippincott, c1978. 250 p. : ill. ; 22 cm. [SF996.T37] 78-2595 ISBN 0-397-01284-5 : 8.95
1. Taylor, David, 1934- 2. Zoo animals—Diseases. 3. Veterinarians—Biography. I. Title. BIP

TAYLOR, David, 1934- 636.089'092'4 B
Zoo vet : adventures of a wild animal doctor / David Taylor. 1st American ed. Philadelphia : Lippincott, c1977. 255 p. ; 22 cm. [SF996.T39 1977] 76-56834 ISBN 0-397-01203-9 : 8.95
1. Taylor, David, 1934- 2. Zoo animals—Diseases. 3. Veterinarians—Biography. I. Title. BIP

TAYLOR, David, 1934- 636.089'092'4 B
Zoo vet : adventures of a wild animal doctor / David Taylor 1st American ed. New York : Pocket Books, 1978, c1977. 202 p. : ill. ; 18 cm. (A Kangaroo Book) Contents.Contents [SF996.T39 1977] ISBN 0-440-19903-4 pbk. : 1.95
1. Taylor, david, 1934- 2. Zoo animals—Diseases. 3. Veterinarians—biography. I. Title.
L.C. card no. for 1977 Lippincott edition: 76-56834.

Taylor, Edward Plunkett, 1901-

ROHMER, Richard H. 338'.092'4 B
E. P. Taylor : the biography of Edward Plunket Taylor / Richard Rohmer. Toronto : McClelland and Stewart, c1978. 355 p. ; 24 cm. Includes index. [HC112.5.T38R64] 78-320220 ISBN 0-7710-7709-2 : 15.95
1. Taylor, Edward Plunkett, 1901- 2. Businessmen—Canada—Biography. 3. Capitalists and financiers—Canada—Biography.
Distributed by Harper & Row.

Taylor, Edward Robeson, 1838-1923.

JOHNSON, Kenneth M. 811'.4 B
The life and times of Edward Robeson Taylor, physician, lawyer, poet, and politician, by Kenneth M. Johnson. [San Francisco] Book Club of California, 1968. iii, 61 p. illus., facsims. ports. 25 cm. (Publication of the Book Club of California, no. 129) Bibliographical references included in "Notes" (p. 59-61) [PS3539.A89Z7] 77-6652
1. Taylor, Edward Robeson, 1838-1923. I. Title. II. Series: Book Club of California, San Francisco. Publication no. 129

Taylor, Edward, 1642-1729.

GRABO, Norman S. 922.573
Edward Taylor. New York, Twayne Publishers [1962, c1961] 192 p. 21 cm. (Twayne's United States authors series, 8) Includes bibliography. [BX7260.T28G7 1962] 61-15668
1. Taylor, Edward, 1642-1729. BIP

KELLER, Karl, 1933- 811'.1 B
The example of Edward Taylor / by Karl Keller. Amherst : University of Massachusetts Press, 1975. 319 p., [4] leaves of plates : ill. ; 24 cm. Includes bibliographical references and index. [PS850.T2Z74] 74-21240 ISBN 0-87023-174-X : 12.00
1. Taylor, Edward, 1642-1729. I. Title. BIP

Taylor, Edward, 1642-1729—Bibliography.

GEFVERT, Constance J. 016.285'9'0924
Edward Taylor; an annotated bibliography, 1668-1970, by Constance J. Gefvert. [1st ed. Kent, Ohio] Kent State University Press [1971] xxxiii, 83 p. 23 cm. (The Serif series: bibliographies and checklists, no. 19) [Z8861.4.G44] 70-144811 ISBN 0-87338-113-0 4.75
1. Taylor, Edward, 1642-1729—Bibliography. I. Title. II. Series.

Taylor, Elizabeth Rosemond, 1932-

ALLAN, John B. 927.92
Elizabeth Taylor; a fascinating story of America's most talented actress and the world's most beautiful woman. Derby, Conn., Monarch Books [c.1961] 139p. (K55) 61-2827 .35 pap.,
1. Taylor, Elizabeth Rosemond, 1932- I. Title.

DELL Publishing Company, inc., New York. 927.92
The life and loves of Liz Taylor, prepared by the publishers of Modern screen [and other publications] New York, '1952. 98 p. illus. 28 cm. [PN2287.T18D4] 52-42955
1. Taylor, Elizabeth Rosemond, 1932- I. Title.

MADDOX, Brenda. 791.43'028'0924 B
Who's afraid of Elizabeth Taylor? : A biography / by Brenda Maddox. New York : M. Evans ; Philadelphia : distributed by Lippincott, c1977. p. cm. Filmography: p. [PN2287.T18M3] 77-8798 ISBN 0-87131-243-3 : 8.95
1. Taylor, Elizabeth Rosemond, 1932- 2. Moving-picture actors and actresses—United States—Biography. I. Title.

RICE, Cy 927.92
Cleopatra in mink. New York, Paperback Lib. [c.1962] 160p. (Silver ed. 52-131) 62-2840 .50 pap.,
1. Taylor, Elizabeth Rosemond, 1932- I. Title.

SHEPPARD, Dick, 1933- 791.43'028'0924 B
Elizabeth: the life and career of Elizabeth Taylor. [1st ed.] Garden City, N.Y., Doubleday, 1974. xvii, 507 p. illus. 25 cm. Filmography: p. [469]-493. [PN2287.T18S5] 73-15366 ISBN 0-385-07348-8 12.50
1. Taylor, Elizabeth Rosemond, 1932- I. Title.

TAYLOR, Elizabeth Rosemond, 1932- 791.430280924
Elizabeth Taylor; an informal memoir. Photos. by Roddy McDowall, plus a collection from Elizabeth Taylor's family album. New York, Harper [c.1964, 1965]

177p. illus. ports. 22cm. [PN2287.T18A32] 65-26105 4.95
I. Title.

TAYLOR, Elizabeth Rosemond, 1932- 791.430280924
Elizabeth Taylor; an informal memoir, by Elizabeth Taylor. Photos. by Roddy McDowall, plus a collection from Elizabeth Taylor's family album. [New York] Avon [1967, c.1965] 208p. illus., ports. 18cm. (V2164) [PN2287.T18A32] .75 pap.,
I. Title.

WATERBURY, Ruth 927.92
Elizabeth Taylor. New York, Popular Lib. [1965, c.1964] 255p. 18cm. [PN2287.T18W3] .50 pap.,
1. Taylor, Elizabeth Rosemond, 1932- I. Title.

WATERBURY, Ruth. 927.92
Elizabeth Taylor. [1st ed.] New York, Appleton-Century [1964] 310 p. illus. ports. 22 cm. [PN2287.T18W3] 63-7418
1. Taylor, Elizabeth Rosemond, 1932- I. Title.

Taylor, Fred, 1884-

WHITEHEAD, Eric. 796.9'62'0924 B
Cyclone Taylor : a hockey legend / Eric Whitehead. 1st ed. Toronto : Doubleday Canada ; Garden City, N.Y. : Doubleday, 1977. 205 p., [6] leaves of plates : ill. ; 22 cm. [GV848.5.T39W48] 77-70902 ISBN 0-385-13063-5 : 7.95
1. Taylor, Fred, 1884- 2. Hockey players—Canada—Biography. I. Title.

Taylor, Frederick Winslow, 1856-1915.

COPLEY, Frank Barkley. 658.5'00924 B
Frederick W. Taylor, father of scientific management. New York, A. M. Kelley, 1969. 2 v. illus., ports. 23 cm. (Library of early American business and industry) (Reprints of economic classics.) Reprint of the 1923 ed. [T55.85.T38C6 1969] 68-55515
1. Taylor, Frederick Winslow, 1856-1915. 2. Industrial management. BIP

KAKAR, Sudhir. 658.5'00924 B
Frederick Taylor: a study in personality and innovation. Cambridge, Mass., MIT Press [1970] xi, 221 p. 21 cm. Includes bibliographical references. [T55.85.T38K3] 79-122260 6.95
1. Taylor, Frederick Winslow, 1856-1915. 2. Efficiency, Industrial.

TAYLOR Society, New York. 658.5'0092'4 B
Frederick Winslow Taylor: a memorial volume; being addresses delivered at the funeral of Frederick Winslow Taylor, Cedron, Indian Queen Lane, Germantown, Philadelphia, Pa., March 24, 1915; at a memorial meeting held under the auspices of the Society to Promote the Science of Management (now Taylor Society), University of Pennsylvania, Philadelphia, Pa., October 22, 1915; and at Mr. Taylor's home "Boxly," Chestnut Hill, Philadelphia, Pa., October 23, 1915. Easton [Pa.] Hive Pub. Co., 1972. vii, 108 p. port. 23 cm. (Hive management history series, no. 13) Reprint of the 1920 ed. published by Taylor Society, New York. [T55.85.T38T39 1972] 72-89987 ISBN 0-87960-013-6
1. Taylor, Frederick Winslow, 1856-1915. 2. Industrial engineering—Addresses, essays, lectures.

Taylor, George Braxton, 1860-1942—Juvenile literature.

MONSELL, Helen Albee, 1895- 92
The story of Cousin George. Illustrated by William Moyers. Birmingham, Ala., Woman's Missionary Union [1961] 122p. illus. 21cm. [BV3705.T3M6] 61-12680
1. Taylor, George Braxton, 1860-1942—Juvenile literature. I. Title.

Taylor, Glen Hearst, 1904-

TAYLOR, Glen Hearst, 1904- 328.73'092'4 B
The way it was with me / by Glen H. Taylor. 1st ed. Secaucus, N.J. : L. Stuart, c1979. 420 p. ; 24 cm. Includes index. [E748.T275A38 1979] 79-13549 ISBN 0-8184-0288-1 : 15.00
1. Taylor, Glen Hearst, 1904- 2. United States. Congress. Senate—Biography. 3. United States—Politics and government—1933-1945. 4. Idaho—Politics and government. 5. Legislators—United States—Biography. I. Title. BIP

Taylor, Graham, 1851-1938.

WADE, Louise C. 923.673
Graham Taylor, pioneer for social justice, 1851-1938. Chicago, Univ. of Chic. Pr. [c.1964] 268p. illus., ports. 25cm. Bibl. [HN80.C5W3] 64-24976 7.50
1. Taylor, Graham, 1851-1938. 2. Chicago—Soc. condit. I. Title.

Taylor, Hannis, 1851-1922.

MCWILLIAMS, Tennant S., 1943- 329'.0092'4 B
Hannis Taylor : the new Southerner as an American / Tennant S. McWilliams. University : University of Alabama Press, c1978. xi, 163 p. : ports. ; 22 cm. Includes index. Bibliography: p. 130-151. [E664.T17M3] 77-17124 ISBN 0-8173-5114-0 : 12.50
1. Taylor, Hannis, 1851-1922. 2. Politicians—United States—Biography. 3. United States—Politics and government—1865-1933. 4. United States—Foreign relations—1865-1921. BIP

Taylor, Henry, Sir, 1800-1886—Correspondence.

TAYLOR, Henry, Sir, 1800-1886. 821'.8 B
Correspondence of Henry Taylor. Edited by Edward Dowden. [Folcroft, Pa.] Folcroft Library Editions, 1974. p. cm. Reprint of the 1888 ed. published by Longmans, Green, London, New York. [PR5548.T8Z53 1974] 74-10771 ISBN 0-8414-3764-5 (lib. bdg.)
1. Taylor, Henry, Sir, 1800-1886—Correspondence. 2. Authors, English—Correspondence, reminiscences, etc.

Taylor, James Hudson, 1832-1905.

POLLOCK, John Charles 922.742
Hudson Taylor and Maria; pioneers in China. New York, McGraw [c.1962] 212p. Bibl. 61-17145 4.95 bds.,
1. Taylor, James Hudson, 1832-1905. 2. Taylor, Maria (Dyer) I. Title.

POLLOCK, John Charles 922.742
Hudson Taylor and Maria; pioneers in China. Grand Rapids, Mich., Zondervan [1967] 207p. 21cm. Bibl. [BV3427.T3P6] 1.95 pap.,
1. Taylor, James Hudson, 1832-1905. 2. Taylor, Maria (Dyer) I. Title.

TAYLOR, Frederick Howard 266.00924
J. Hudson Taylor; a biography. by Dr. and Mrs. Howard Taylor. Foreword by Arthur F. Glasser. Chicago, Moody [c.1965] xi, 366p. port. 23cm. (Tyndale ser. of great biogs.) [BV3427.T3T38] 66-32 4.95
1. Taylor, James Hudson, 1832-1905. 2. Missions—China. I. Taylor, Mary Geraldine (Guinness) joint author. II. Title.

TAYLOR, Frederick Howard. 266.00924 (B)
J. Hudson Taylor; a biography, by Dr. and Mrs. Howard Taylor. Foreword by Arthur F. Glasser. Chicago, Moody Press [1965] ix, 366 p. port. 23 cm. (The Tyndale series of great biographies) [BV3427.T3T38] 66-32
1. Taylor, James Hudson, 1832-1905. 2. Missions—China. I. Taylor, Mary Geraldine (Uginness) joint author. II. Title.

Taylor, Jeremy, Bp. of Down and Connor, 1613-1667.

GOOSE, Edmund William, Sir, 1849-1928. 283'.0924
Jeremy Taylor. New York, Greenwood Press, 1968 [c1904] xi, 234 p. 19 cm. [BX5199.T3G6 1968] (B) 68-28590
1. Taylor, Jeremy, Bp. of Down and Connor, 1613-1667.

ROSS Williamson, Hugh, 1901- 283'.092'4 B
Jeremy Taylor. [Folcroft, Pa.] Folcroft Library Editions, 1973. p. Reprint of the 1952 ed. published by Dobson, London, in series: A Pegasus biography. [BX5199.T3R65 1973] 73-15705 20.00
1. Taylor, Jeremy, Bp. of Down and Connor, 1613-1667. BIP

ROSS Williamson, Hugh, 1901- 283'.092'4 B
Jeremy Taylor / Hugh Ross Williamson. Norwood, Pa. : Norwood Editions, 1975. 179 p., [5] leaves of plates : ill. ; 24 cm. Reprint of the 1952 ed. published by D. Dobson, London, in series: A Pegasus biography. Includes index. Bibliography: p. 176. [BX5199.T3R65 1975] 75-31842 ISBN 0-88305-778-6 : 25.00
1. Taylor, Jeremy, Bp. of Down and Connor, 1613-1667.

STRANKS, Charles James. 283'.092'4 B
The life and writings of Jeremy Taylor, by C. J. Stranks. [Folcroft, Pa.] Folcroft Library Editions, 1973. p. Reprint of the 1952 ed. published by S.P.C.K., London, for the Church Historical Society. [BX5199.T3S8 1973] 73-11259 25.00
1. Taylor, Jeremy, Bp. of Down and Connor, 1613-1667. I. Church Historical Society (Gt. Brit.) II. Title. BIP

Taylor, John, 1580-1653.

NOTESTEIN, Wallace, 1878- 920.042
Four worthies: John Chamberlain, Anne Clifford, John Taylor, Oliver Heywood. New Haven, Yale University Press, 1957. 248p. illus. 21cm. [DA377.N6] 57-1426
1. Chamberlain, John, 1554?-1628. 2. Pembroke, Anne (Clifford) Herbert, countess of, 1590-1676. 3. Taylor, John, 1580-1653. 4. Heywood, Oliver, 1629-1702. I. Title.

Taylor, John, 1781-1864.

BLUNDEN, Edmund Charles, 1896-1974. 070.5'092'4 B
Keats's publisher; a memoir of John Taylor (1781-1864). Clifton [N.J.] A. M. Kelley, 1974. p. cm. (The English book trade, 13) Reprint of the 1936 ed. published by J. Cape, London. "John Taylor's writings": p. [Z325.T24B57 1974] 77-121320 ISBN 0-678-00683-0 11.50
1. Taylor, John, 1781-1864. 2. Keats, John, 1795-1821—Friends and associates. I. Title.

CHILCOTT, Tim. 070.5'092'4 B
A publisher and his circle: the life and work of John Taylor, Keat's publisher. London, Boston, Routledge and K. Paul, 1972. xi, 247 p. 23 cm. Bibliography: p. 232-241. [Z325.T24C45] 72-194396 ISBN 0-7100-7198-1 10.50
1. Taylor, John, 1781-1864. I. Title.

Taylor, John, 1808-1887.

ROBERTS, Brigham Henry, 1857-1933 922.8373
The life of John Taylor, third president of the Church of Jesus Christ of Latter-Day Saints. Salt Lake City, Bookcraft [1963] 499p. illus., ports. 24cm. 63-5946 price unreported
1. Taylor, John, 1808-1887. I. Title.

Taylor, John. 1808-1887—Juvenile literature.

NEELEY, Deta Petersen. 922.8373
A child's story of the prophet John Taylor, by Deta Petersen Neeley and Nathan Glen Neeley. Salt Lake City. Printed by the Deseret News Press, 1960. 140p. illus. 20cm. [BX8695.T3N4] 61-22320
1. Taylor, John. 1808-1887—Juvenile literature. I. Neeley, Nathan Glen, joint author. II. Title.

Taylor, Laurette, 1884-1946.

COURTNEY, Marguerite (Taylor) 1904- 927.92
Laurette. Introd. by Samuel Hopkins Adams. New York, Rinehart [1955] 433p. illus. 22cm. [PN2287.T25C6] 54-10448
1. Taylor, Laurette, 1884-1946. I. Title.

COURTNEY, Marguerite (Taylor) 1904- 792'.038'0924 (B)
Laurette, by Marguerite Courtney. With an introd. by Brooks Atkinson. New York, Atheneum, 1968. xiii, 445 p. ports. 22 cm. $7.95 Bibliographical footnotes. [PN2287.T25C6] 65-55413
1. Taylor, Laurette, 1884-1946. I. Title.

COURTNEY, Marguerite (Taylor) 1904- 792'.028'0924 B
Laurette, by Marguerite Courtney. With an introd. by Brooks Atkinson. New York, Atheneum, 1968. xiii, 445 p. ports. 22 cm. Bibliographical footnotes. [PN2287.T25C6 1968] 68-55413 7.95
1. Taylor, Laurette, 1884-1946. I. Title.

Taylor, Leslie Joseph Theodore, 1888-1927.

ANDERSON, Hugh. 364'.092'4
Larrikin crook; the rise and fall of Squizzy Taylor. [Milton, Q.] Jacaranda [1971] x, 220 p. illus., facsims., maps. 23 cm. [HV6248.T23A65] 72-177613 ISBN 0-7016-0370-4 4.50
1. Taylor, Leslie Joseph Theodore, 1888-1927. I. Title.

Taylor, Marshall William,

TAYLOR, Marshall William, 1878- 796.6 B
The fastest bicycle rider in the world; the story of a colored boy's indomitable courage and success against great odds. An autobiography by Marshall W. "Major" Taylor. Freeport, N.Y., Books for Libraries Press, 1971. 430 p. illus. 23 cm. (The Black heritage library collection) Reprint of the 1928 ed. [GV1051.T3A3 1971] 74-173618 ISBN 0-8369-8910-4
I. Title. II. Series.

Taylor, Maxwell Davenport,

TAYLOR, Maxwell Davenport, 1901- 355.3'31'0924 B
Swords and plowshares [by] Maxwell D. Taylor. [1st ed.] New York, W. W. Norton [1972] 434 p. illus. 25 cm. A memoir. [E745.T317 1972] 70-152677 ISBN 0-393-07460-9 10.00
I. Title.

Taylor, Moses.

HODAS, Daniel, 1927- 332'.092'4 B
The business career of Moses Taylor : merchant, finance capitalist, and industrialist / Daniel Hodas. New York : New York University Press, 1976. xvi, 356 p. : ill. ; 24 cm. Includes index. Bibliography: p. 339-345. [HC102.5.T29H63] 76-3288 ISBN 0-8147-3374-3 : 17.50
1. Taylor, Moses. I. Title. BIP

Taylor, Myron Charles, 1874-

MYRON C. Taylor, v. 12
an appreciation. [New York? 1956] 54p. port. 20cm. Introd. signed: Roger M. Blough.
1. Taylor, Myron Charles, 1874- I. [United States Steel Corporation]

UNITED States Steel Corporation. 923.373
Myron C. Taylor; an appreciation. [n.p. 1956] 54 p. illus. 21 cm. [HD9519.U6U67] 59-33712
I. Taylor, Myron Charles, 1874- II. Title.

Taylor, Nathaniel William, 1786-1858.

MEAD, Sidney Earl, 1904- 285'8'0924
Nathaniel William Taylor, 1786-1858; a Conneticut liberal [Hamden, Conn.] Archon, 1967 [c.1942] xi, 259p. 23cm. Bibl. [BX260.T32M35 1967] 67-15932 7.00
1. Taylor, Nathaniel William, 1786-1858. I. Title.

Taylor, Peter Hillsman, 1917-

GRIFFITH, Albert Joseph, 1932- 813'.5'4
Peter Taylor, by Albert J. Griffith. New York, Twayne Publishers [1970] 183 p. 21 cm. (Twayne's United States authors series, TUSAS 168) Bibliography: p. 168-175. [PS3539.A9633Z7] 70-110713
1. Taylor, Peter Hillsman, 1917-

Taylor, Rayard, 1825-1878.

CARY, Richard, 1909- 928.1
The genteel circle: Bayard Taylor and his New York friends. Ithaca, Cornell University Press, 1952. 44 p. 23 cm. (Cornell studies in American history, literature, andfolklore, no. 5) Bibliographical references included in "Notes" (p. 42-44) [E173.C7 no.5] 52-4453
1. Taylor, Rayard, 1825-1878. I. Title. II. Series: Cornell University. Cornell studies in American history, literature, and folklore, no. 5

Taylor, Robert, 1911-1969.

WAYNE, Jane Ellen. 791.43'028'0924 B
The life of Robert Taylor. [New York] Warner Paperback Library [1973] 349 p. illus. 18 cm. [PN2287.T27W3] 73-162044 ISBN 0-446-76103-6 1.25 (pbk.)
1. Taylor, Robert, 1911-1969.

Taylor, Susie King, b. 1848—Juvenile literature.

BOOKER, Simeon. 973.77'5'0924 B
Susie King Taylor, Civil War nurse. Illustrated by Harold James. New York, McGraw-Hill [1969] 127 p. illus. 22 cm. (McGraw-Hill Black legacy) "A Rutledge book." A biography of the woman who, during the Civil War, became the first Negro army nurse. [E621.T3B6] 92 72-77098
1. Taylor, Susie King, b. 1848—Juvenile literature. I. James, Harold, 1929- illus. II. Title. III. Series.

*Taylor, Willard H.

*TAYLOR, Willard H. 232.9
The story of our Saviour. Kansas City, Mo., Beacon Hill Pr. [c.1963] 138p.19cm. Bibl. 1.25 pap.,
I. Title.

Taylor, William,

TAYLOR, William, Bp., 1821-1902. 287'.6'0924 B
Story of my life. Edited by John Clark Ridpath. Illustrated by Frank Beard. Freeport, N.Y., Books for Libraries Press, 1972 [c1895] 2 v. (770 p.) illus. 28 cm. (The Black heritage library collection) [BX8495.T3A3 1972] 72-3999 ISBN 0-8369-9107-9 59.50
I. Title. II. Series.

Taylor, Zachary, Pres. U.S., 1784-1850.

DYER, Brainerd, 1901- 973.6'3'0924 (B)
Zachary Taylor. New York, Barnes & Noble [1967, c.1946] viii, 455p. illus., maps, ports. 22cm. (Southern biog. ser.) Bibl. [E422.D995 1967] 67-16626 10.00
1. Taylor, Zachary, Pres. U.S., 1784-1850. I. Title. II. Series.

FARRELL, John J., comp. 973.6'3'0922
Zachary Taylor 1784-1850 [and] Millard Fillmore 1800-1874; chronology, documents, bibliographical aids. Edited by John J. farrell Dobbs Ferry, N.Y., Oceana Publications, 1971. v, 118 p. 24 cm. [E421.F37] 78-116061 ISBN 0-379-12078-X
1. Taylor, Zachary, Pres. U.S., 1784-1850. 2. Fillmore, Millard, Pres. U.S., 1800-1874. 3. U.S.—Politics and government—1849-1853. I. Taylor, Zachary, Pres. U.S., 1784-1850. II. U.S. President, 1849-1850 (Taylor) III. U.S. President, 1850-1853 (Fillmore) **BIP**

HAMILTON, Holman. 973'.0992 B
The three Kentucky presidents—Lincoln, Taylor, Davis / Holman Hamilton. Lexington : University Press of Kentucky, c1978. xv, 69 , [1] p., [4] leaves of plates : ill. ; 21 cm. (The Kentucky Bicentennial bookshelf) Bibliography: p. 67-[70]. [E176.H248] 77-92922 ISBN 0-8131-0246-4 : 4.95
1. Lincoln, Abraham, Pres. U.S., 1809-1865. 2. Taylor, Zachary, Pres. U.S., 1784-1850. 3. Davis, Jefferson, 1808-1889. 4. Presidents—United States—Biography. 5. Kentucky—Biography. I. Title. II. Series.

HAMILTON, Holman 973.630924
Zachary Taylor. Hamden, Conn., Archon, 1966[c.1951] Contents.[1] Soldier of the Republic. [2] Soldier in the White house. [E422.H32] 66-25183
1. Taylor, Zachary, Pres. U. S., 1784-1850. I. Title. **BIP**

WILKIE, Katharine Elliott, 1904- 923.173
Zack Taylor, Young, Rough, and ready; illustrated by Syd Browne. [1st ed.] Indianapolis, Bobbs-Merrill [1952] 194p. illus. 20cm. (The Childhood of famous Americans series) [E422.W5] 52-5820
1. Taylor, Zachary, Pres. U. S., 1784-1850. I. Title.

Taylor, Zachary, Pres. U.S., 1784-1850—Juvenile literature.

HOYT, Edwin Palmer 973.630924
Zachary Taylor. Chicago, Reilly & Lee [c.1966] 162p. illus., ports. 21cm. (His President ser.) Bibl. [E422.H87] 66-15164 3.95
1. Taylor, Zachary, Pres. U.S., 1784-1850—Juvenile literature. I. Title.

MARTIN, Patricia Miles. 973.6'3'0924 B
Zachary Taylor. Illustrated by Tran Mawicke. New York, Putnam [1969] 62 p. illus. (part col.), col. map, port. 23 cm. (A see and read beginning to read biography) A biography of the general called "Old Rough and Ready" who became the twelfth President of the United States. [E422.M37 1969] 92 72-81659 2.68
1. Taylor, Zachary, Pres. U.S., 1784-1850—Juvenile literature. I. Mawicke, Tran, illus. **BIP**

YOUNG, Bob, 1916- 973.6'3'0924 B
Old Rough and Ready, Zachary Taylor [by] Bob and Jan Young. New York, J. Messner [1970] 191 p. 22 cm. Bibliography: p. 183. A biography of "Old Rough and Ready," hero of the Mexican War who became twelfth President of the United States. [E422.Y68 1970] 92 74-123169 3.50
1. Taylor, Zachary, Pres. U.S., 1784-1850—Juvenile literature. I. Young, Jan, 1919- joint author. II. Title.

Tchelitchew, Pavel, 1898-1957.

TYLER, Parker. 759.7
The divine comedy of Pavel Tchelitchew; a biography. New York, Fleet Pub. Corp. [1967] viii, 504 p. illus. (part col.) ports. 26 cm. Includes bibliographies. [ND699.T4T9] 66-25989
1. Tchelitchew, Pavel, 1898-1957. I. Title.

Te Kooti, 1830?-1893.

ROSS, W. Hugh 993.1020924 (B)
Te Kooti Rikirangi, general and prophet [by] W. Hugh Ross. Auckland [N.Z.] Collins; San Francisco, Tri-Ocean Books, 1966. 196 p. 22 cm. Bibliography: p. 195-196. [DU422.T4R6] 66-31838
1. Te Kooti, 1830?-1893. I. Title.

TE Kooti 793.102'092'4 B
Rikirangi te Turuki; an exhibition commemorating the life and deeds of an extraordinary man, designed and assembled by Frank Davis in conjunction with the Waikato Museum. Hamilton [1971?] [18] p. illus. 14 x 22 cm. [DU420.T38] 72-170955 0.25
1. Te Kooti, 1830?-1893. 2. New Zealand—History—1843-1870—Exhibitions. I. Davis, Frank. II. Waikato Museum.

Te Wiata, Inia, 1915-1971.

TE WIATA, Beryl Margaret McMillan. 782.1'092'4 B
Most happy fella : a biography of Inia Te Wiata / Beryl Te Wiata. Wellington : Reed, 1976. 307 p., [16] p. of plates : ill., ports. ; 23 cm. Includes index. [ML420.T38T5] 77-365009 ISBN 0-589-00954-0 : 7.95
1. Te Wiata, Inia, 1915-1971. 2. Singers—New Zealand—Biography. I. Title.

Teach, Edward, d. 1718.

LEE, Robert Earl, 1906- 364.1'35 B
Blackbeard the pirate : a reappraisal of his life and times / by Robert E. Lee. Winston-Salem, N.C. : J. F. Blair, [1974] viii, 264 p. : port. ; 24 cm. Includes index. Bibliography: p. [245]-255. [F257.T422L43] 74-75752 ISBN 0-910244-77-4 : 8.95
1. Teach, Edward, d. 1718. 2. Pirates. I. Title. **BIP**

PENDERED, Norman C. 364.1'35 B
Blackbeard : the fiercest pirate of all / by Norman C. Pendered. Manteo, N.C. : Times Print. Co., [1975] xii, 81 p. : ill. ; 18 cm. Bibliography: p. 77-78. A biography of the British pirate who terrorized the Virginia and Carolina coast in the early eighteenth century. [F257.T422P45] 92 75-5323 2.95
1. Teach, Edward, d. 1718. 2. Pirates. I. Title.

Teachers — Colorado.

DELTA Kappa Gamma Society. v. 12
[Biographies of pioneer women teachers of Colorado. Denver, 1956] 1 v. (various pagings) 28 cm. 64-36984
1. Teachers — Colorado. 2. Women in Colorado. 3. Colorado — Biog. I. Title.

Teachers Connecticut—Biography.

PIONEER women 371.1'009746 B
teachers of Connecticut, 1767-1970. [Edited by Helen M. Sheldrick. Hartford] Alpha Kappa State, Delta Kappa Gamma Society, International [1971] 149 p. map (on lining papers), ports. 25 cm. [LA2315.C6P5] 72-175124 5.00
1. Teachers—Connecticut—Biography. I. Sheldrick, Helen M., ed. II. Delta Kappa Gamma Society. Alpha Kappa State, Conn.

Teachers—Correspondence, reminiscences, etc.

BADRI, Babakr. 370'.924 B
The memoirs of Babikr Bedri; translated from the Arabic by Yousef Bedri and George Scott with an introduction by P. M. Holt. London, New York, Oxford U.P., 1969. xxii, 250 p. 2 plates (1 fold.)., maps, port. 23 cm. Translation of Tarikh hayati (romanized form) Bibliographical footnotes. [LA2389.B3A313] 70-434386 55/-
1. Teachers—Correspondence, reminiscences, etc. 2. Sudan—History—1820- I. Title. **BIP**

CATTELL, Ann, 1893- 923.773
Sixty miles north; saga of a country schoolteacher. New York, Comet Press Books [1953] 178p. 23cm. [LA2317.C38A3] 53-2751
1. Teachers—Correspondence, reminiscences, etc. I. Title.

DAVIS, Jehiel Shotwell, 1892- 923.773
A teacher's story, an autobiography. Boston, Christopher Pub. House [c.1961] 292p. illus. (front por.) 61-9663 4.00
I. Title.

DILLON, Elza E 1880- 923.773
My 66 years in the schoolroom. [1st ed.] New York, Pageant Press [1956] 140p. illus. 21cm. [LA2317.D54A35] 56-11389
1. Teachers—Correspondence, reminiscences, etc. I. Title.

HENDERSON, Harley A 372.110924
My little red schoolhouse, by Harley A. Henderson. Philadelphia, Dorrance [1966] 180 p. 20 cm. [LB1781.H4] 65-24608
1. Teachers — Correspondence, reminiscences, etc. I. Title.

NATHAN, Beatrice Stephens 923.773
Tales of a teacher. Chicago, H. Regnery Co., 1956. 302p. 22cm. Autobiographical. [LB1602.N3] 56-11657
1. Teachers—Correspondence, reminiscences, etc. I. Title.

NATHAN, Beatrice Stephens. 923.773
Tales of a teacher. Chicago, H. Regnery Co., 1956. 302 p. 22 cm. Autobiographical. [LB1602.N3] 56-11657
1. Teachers—Correspondence, reminiscences, etc. I. Title.

RASEY, Marie I 1887- 923.773
It takes time; an autobiography of the teaching profession. Foreword by Karen Horney. [1st ed.] New York, Harper [1953] 204p. 21cm. [LA2317.R28A3] 52-14110
1. Teachers—Correspondence, reminiscences, etc. I. Title.

ROUSCULP, Charles G. 373.1'100924 B
Chalk dust on my shoulder [by] Charles G. Rousculp. Line drawings by Donald Robison. Columbus, Ohio, C. E. Merrill [1969] xiii, 337 p. illus. 24 cm. [LA2317.R6A3] 69-16501 6.95
1. Teachers—Correspondence, reminiscences, etc. I. Title. **BIP**

Teachers—Europe—Biography.

LUTZ, Cora Elizabeth, 1906- 371.1'0092'2 B
Schoolmasters of the tenth century / Cora E. Lutz. Hamden, Conn. : Archon Books, 1977. xi, 202 p. : ill. ; 23 cm. Includes index. Bibliography: p. 189-195. [LA2371.L87] 76-29644 ISBN 0-208-01628-7 : 12.50
1. Teachers—Europe—Biography. 2. Education, Medieval. I. Title. **BIP**

Teachers—Illinois—Correspondence, reminiscences, etc.

HUMPHREY, Inez Faith. 371.1'00924 B
From the prairies to the mountains: memories, especially of Illinois and eastern Kentucky. [1st ed.] New York, Exposition Press [1968] 146 p. 21 cm. [LB1602.H8] 68-6048 5.00
1. Teachers—Illinois—Correspondence, reminiscences, etc. I. Title.

Teachers—North Dakota—Biography.

IN retrospect : 371.1'0092'2 B
teaching in North Dakota : recollections of retired teachers / compiler and editor, Marie Mynster Feidler ; drawings by Iletta Holman and Theresa Frederick. [Grand Forks] : North Dakota Retired Teachers Association, 1976. viii, 301 p. : ill. ; 23 cm. [LA2315.N9I5] 76-373117 4.50
1. Teachers—North Dakota—Biography. I.

Feidler, Marie Mynster. II. North Dakota Retired Teachers Association.

Teachers—Russia—Correspondence, reminiscences, etc.

VIGDOROVA, Frida Abramovna. 371.1'0092'4
Diary of a Russian schoolteacher, [by] F. Vigdorova. Translated from the Russian by Rose Prokofieva. Westport, Conn., Greenwood Press [1973] p. Translation of Moi klass. [LB1602.V513 1973] 73-7078 ISBN 0-8371-6909-7 11.25
1. Teachers—Russia—Correspondence, reminiscences, etc. 2. Education—Russia. I. Title. **BIP**

Teachers—Southern States—Correspondence, reminiscences, etc.

CULBERTSON, Manie. 371.1'0092'4
May I speak? Diary of a crossover teacher. Edited and introd. by Sue Eakin. Gretna [La.] Pelican Pub. Co., 1972. 156 p. 22 cm. [LA230.5.S6C84] 70-186542 ISBN 0-911116-59-1 4.95
1. Teachers—Southern States—Correspondence, reminiscences, etc. 2. Faculty integration—Southern States. I. Title. II. Title: A crossover teacher. **BIP**

Teachers—Wisconsin—Correspondence, reminiscences, etc.

GRUHLKE, Verna King, 1908- 371.1'00924
To hell with the kids! Milwaukee, Bruce Pub. Co. [1968] vi, 200 p. 22 cm. [LB1602.G78] 68-54985
1. Teachers—Wisconsin—Correspondence, reminiscences, etc. I. Title. **BIP**

Teaching.

ALCOTT, William Andrus, 1798-1859. 371.1'00924 B
Confessions of a school master. New York, Arno Press, 1969. xiv, 309 p. 23 cm. (American education: its men, ideas, and institutions) Reprint of the 1856 rev. ed. [LB1037.A3 1969] 77-89145
1. Teaching. 2. Teachers—Correspondence, reminiscences, etc. I. Title. II. Series. **BIP**

BRADFORD, Reed H. 371.1'001
A teacher's quest [by] Reed H. Bradford. [1st ed. Provo, Utah] Brigham Young University Press [1971] 77 p. illus. 23 cm. [BX8695.B65A3] 72-178774
1. Teaching. I. Title.

Teaching—Case studies.

JOHANSEN, Mary Lowry. 371.1'02'0924 B
All the way. Philadelphia, Dorrance [1973] 71 p. 22 cm. [LB885.J55] 73-84991 ISBN 0-8059-1892-2 4.95
1. Teaching—Case studies. I. Title.

Teagarden, Weldon Leo, 1905-1964.

SMITH, Jay D. 785'.092'4 B
Jack Teagarden : the story of a jazz maverick / by Jay D. Smith and Len Guttridge. New York : Da Capo Press, 1976. p. cm. (The Roots of jazz) Reprint of the ed. published by Cassell in London, 1960. Discography: p. [ML419.T25S6 1976] 76-6986 ISBN 0-306-70813-2 : 15.00
1. Teagarden, Weldon Leo, 1905-1964. I. Guttridge, Leonard F., joint author.

Teagle, Walter Clark, 1878-1962.

WALL, Bennett H. 338.7'66'550924 B
Teagle of Jersey Standard / Bennett H. Wall and George S. Gibb. New Orleans, La. : Tulane University, [1974] xxii, 386 p., [16] leaves of plates : ill. ; 24 cm. (History of business and business leaders series) Includes index. [HD9570.T4W34] 73-94124
1. Teagle, Walter Clark, 1878-1962. 2. Standard Oil Company. I. Gibb, George Sweet, 1916- joint author. II. Title. III. Series. **BIP**

Teague, Vera Snider, 1906-

TEAGUE, Vera Snider, 1906- 979.4'05'0924 B
Life with the old-timers / by Vera Snider Teague ; ill. by Don Raphael Madden. [s.l. : s.n.], c1977 (Ukiah, Calif. : Letter Shop) 256 p. : ill. ; 23 cm. [CT275.T38A34] 77-153810
1. Teague, Vera Snider, 1906- 2. California—Biography. I. Title.

Teale, Edwin Way, 1899-

DODD, Edward Howard, 1905- 925.7
Of nature, time, and Teale; a biographical sketch of Edwin Way Teale. New York, Dodd, Mead, 1960. 63 p. illus. 22 cm. [QH31.T4D6] 60-11016
1. Teale, Edwin Way, 1899- I. Title.

DODD, Edward Howard, 1905- 574.0924
Of nature, time, and Teale: a biographical sketch of Edwin Way Teale, by Edward H. Dodd, Jr. New York, Dodd, Mead [1966] 57 p. facsims., plates, ports. 22 cm. First published in 1960. "A bibliography of the books of Edwin Way Teale": p. 57. [QH31.T4D6 1966] 66-9484
1. Teale, Edwin Way, 1899- I. Title.

TEALE, Edwin Way, 1899- 925.7
Dune boy; the early years of a naturalist. Illustrated by Edward Shenton. Lone oak ed. New York, Dodd, Mead, 1957. 275p. illus. 22cm. [QH31.T4A3 1957] 57-14144
I. Title.

TEALE, Edwin Way, 1899- 925.7
Dune boy; the early years of a naturalist. Illustrated by Edward Shenton. Lone oak ed. New York, Dodd, Mead, 1957. 275 p. illus. 22 cm. [QH31.T4A3 1957] 57-14144
I. Title.

Teasdale, Sara, 1884-1933.

CARPENTER, Margaret Haley. 928.1
Sara Teasdale, a biography. [1st ed.] New York, Schulte Pub. Co., 1960. 377 p. illus. 22 cm. [PS3539.E15Z6] 60-9646
1. Teasdale, Sara, 1884-1933. **BIP**

Teasdale, Sara, 1884-1933—Biography.

CARPENTER, Margaret Haley. 811'.5'2 B
Sara Teasdale : a biography / by Margaret Haley Carpenter. Norfolk, Va. : Pentelic Press, c1977. xix, 377 p., [25] leaves of plates : ill. ; 23 cm. Includes index. Bibliography: p. 351-352. [PS3539.E15Z6 1977] 77-81159 ISBN 0-913110-03-5 : 14.95
1. Teasdale, Sara, 1884-1933—Biography. 2. Poets, American—20th century—Biography.

Tebaldi, Renata.

HARRIS, Kenn, 1947- 782.1'092'4 B
Renata Tebaldi. New York, Drake Publishers [1974] xiii, 161 p. ports. 24 cm. Discography: p. 155-161. [ML420.T28H3] 73-18069 ISBN 0-87749-597-1
1. Tebaldi, Renata.

HARRIS, Kenn, 1947- 782.1'092'4 B
Renata Tebaldi. New York, Drake Publishers [1974] xiii, 161 p. ports. 24 cm. Discography: p. 155-161. [ML420.T28H3] 73-18069 ISBN 0-87749-597-1
1. Tebaldi, Renata.

SEROFF, Victor Ilyitch, 1902- 927.8
Renata Tebaldi, the woman and the diva. New York, Appleton-Century-Crofts [c.1961] vii, 213p. ports. 61-7590 4.00
1. Tebaldi, Renata. I. Title. **BIP**

SEROFF, Victor Ilyitch, 1902- 927.8
Renata Tebaldi, the woman and the diva. New York, Appleton-Century-Crofts [c.1961] vii, 213p. ports. 61-7590 4.00
1. Tebaldi, Renata. I. Title. **BIP**

SEROFF, Victor Ilyitch, 1902- 782.1'0924 B
Renata Tebaldi, the woman and the diva [by] Victor Seroff. Freeport, N.Y., Books for Libraries Press [1970, c1961] viii, 213 p. illus., ports. 23 cm. (Biography index reprint series) Discography: p. [203]-210. [ML420.T28S5 1970] 70-136653
1. Tebaldi, Renata.

SEROFF, Victor Ilyitch, 1902- 782.1'0924 B
Renata Tebaldi, the woman and the diva [by] Victor Seroff. Freeport, N.Y., Books for Libraries Press [1970, c1961] viii, 213 p. illus., ports. 23 cm. (Biography index reprint series) Discography: p. [203]-210. [ML420.T28S5 1970] 70-136653
1. Tebaldi, Renata.

SEROFF, Victor Ilyitch, 1902- 927.8
Renata Tebaldi, the woman and the diva. New York, Appleton-Century-Crofts [1961] vii, 213 p. ports. 21 cm. "Operas and other works sung by Renata Tebaldi": p. [100]-202; "Discography of Renata Tebaldi recordings issued in the United States, compiled by George Jellinek": p. [108]=210. [ML420.T28S5] 61-7590
1. Tebaldi, Renata. I. Title.

SEROFF, Victor Ilyitch, 1902- 927.8
Renata Tebaldi, the woman and the diva. New York, Appleton-Century-Crofts [1961] vii, 213 p. ports. 21 cm. "Operas and other works sung by Renata Tebaldi": p. [100]-202; "Discography of Renata Tebaldi recordings issued in the United States, compiled by George Jellinek": p. [108]=210. [ML420.T28S5] 61-7590
1. Tebaldi, Renata. I. Title.

Tecumseh, Shawnee chief, 1768-1813.

COOKE, David Coxe, 1917- 970.3 B
Tecumseh, destiny's warrior [by] David C. Cooke. New York, Messner [1959] 192 p. 22 cm. Bibliography p. 185-6. A biography of the great Shawnee chief, orator, and statesman who, when peaceful means failed, allied many Indian tribes with the British in the War of 1812 in an attempt to prevent the Indian people's land from being usurped by the American Government. [E99.S35T116] 92 AC 68
1. Tecumseh, Shawnee Chief, 1768-1813. I. Title.

CREIGHTON, Luella Sanders Bruce, 1901- 92
Tecumseh: the story of the Shawnee chief, by Luella Bruce Creighton. Illustrated by William Lytle. New York, St. Martin's Press, 1965. 159 p. illus., maps. 22 cm. (Great stories of Canada, 30) [E99.S35C7] 65-20417
1. Tecumseh, Shawnee chief, 1766-1813. I. Title.

DRAKE, Benjamin, 1794-1841. 970.3'0924 B
Life of Tecumseh. New York, Arno Press, 1969. viii, 235 p. 23 cm. (Mass violence in America) Reprint of the 1841 ed. with a new introduction. 1841 and 1852 editions published under title: Life of Tecumseh and of his brother the prophet; with a historical sketch of the Shawanoe Indians. Includes bibliographical references. [E99.S35T12 1969] 75-90173
1. Tecumseh, Shawnee chief, 1768-1813. 2. Ellskwatawa, Shawnee prophet, 1775?-1834. 3. Shawnee Indians. I. Title. II. Series.

KLINCK, Carl Frederick, 1908- ed. 970.2
Tecumseh: fact and fiction in early records a book of primary source materials. Englewood Cliffs, N.J., Prentice-Hall [c.] 1961. 246p. illus. Bibl. 61-14702 2.25 pap.,
1. Tecumseh, Shawnee chief, 1768-1813. I. Title.

STEVENSON, Augusta. 970.3 B
Tecumseh, Shawnee boy. Illustrated by Vic Dowd. [Indianapolis, Bobbs-Merrill, 1962] 200 p. illus. 20 cm. (Childhood of famous Americans) The boyhood of the Shawnee Indian who worked to unite the various tribes against invasion by the white man. [PZ7.S8467Te3] 92 AC 68
1. Tecumseh, Shawnee chief, 1768-1813. I. Dowd, Victor, illus. II. Title.

TUCKER, Glenn. 970.2
Tecumseh; vision of glory. [1st ed.] Indianapolis, Bobbs-Merrill [1956] 399 p. 22 cm. Includes bibliography. [E99.S35T35] 56-8618
1. Tecumseh, Shawnee chief, 1768-1813. **BIP**

TUCKER, Glenn. 970.3 B
Tecumseh: vision of glory. New York, Russell & Russell [1973, c1956] 399 p. illus. 23 cm. Reprint of the ed. published by Bobbs-Merrill, Indianapolis. Bibliography: p. 366-381. [E99.S35T35 1973] 72-85011 ISBN 0-8462-1698-1 20.00
1. Tecumseh, Shawnee chief, 1768-1813.

Tecumseh, Shawnee chief, 1768-1813—Juvenile literature.

ICENHOWER, Joseph Bryan. 970.3 B
Tecumseh and the Indian confederation, 1811-1813: the Indian nations east of the Mississippi are defeated, by Joseph B. Icenhower. New York, F. Watts, 1975. 84 p. illus. 22 cm. (A Focus book) Bibliography: p. 77. Traces the events leading up to the defeat of Tecumseh's efforts to build a confederated Indian nation in the early 1800's. [E99.S35I27] 92 74-11353 ISBN 0-531-02780-5 3.45
1. Tecumseh, Shawnee chief, 1768-1813—Juvenile literature. 2. Indians of North America—Northwest, Old—Wars—Juvenile literature. I. Title. **BIP**

MCCAGUE, James. 970.3 B
Tecumseh, Shawnee warrior-statesman. Illustrated by Victor Dowd. Champaign, Ill., Garrard Pub. Co. [1970] 80 p. col. illus. 23 cm. The life of the Shawnee chief who vowed to avenge the loss of his Ohio homeland and fought with British forces in the War of 1812. [E99.S35T165] 92 73-83167 2.39
1. Tecumseh, Shawnee chief, 1768-1813—Juvenile literature. I. Dowd, Victor, illus. II. Title.

MCGOVERN, Ann. 973'.099 B
The defenders; Osceola, Tecumseh, Cochise. [New York] Scholastic Book Services [1970] 128 p. illus. (part col.), col. maps, ports. 21 cm. (Firebird books) Brief biographies of three Indian chiefs who struggled to save their people from the white man's oppression. [E99.S28O83] 920 75-116623
1. Osceola, Seminole chief, 1804-1838—Juvenile literature. 2. Tecumseh, Shawnee chief, 1768-1813—Juvenile literature. 3. Cochise, Apache chief, d. 1874—Juvenile literature. I. Title.

SCHRAFF, Anne E. 970'.004'97 B
Tecumseh / by Anne Schraff. Minneapolis : Dillon Press, c1979. 56 p. : ill. ; 24 cm. (The Story of an American Indian) A biography of the Shawnee warrior, orator, and leader who united a confederacy of Indians in an effort to save Indian land from the advance of white soldiers and settlers. [E99.S35T32] 92 78-13956 ISBN 0-87518-166-X : 5.95
1. Tecumseh, Shawnee chief, 1768-1813—Juvenile literature. 2. Shawnee Indians—Biography—Juvenile literature. 3. Indians

of North America—Ohio Valley—Biography—Juvenile literature. I. Title.

Tedyuskung, Delaware chief, d. 1763.

WALLACE, Anthony F. C., 1923- 970.3 B
King of the Delawares: Teedyuscung, 1700-1763, by Anthony F. C. Wallace. Freeport, N.Y., Books for Libraries Press [1970, c1949] xiii, 305 p. maps. 23 cm. Includes bibliographical references. [E99.D2T4 1970] 73-137387 ISBN 0-8369-5588-9
1. Tedyuskung, Delaware chief, d. 1763. 2. Delaware Indians. 3. Pennsylvania—History—Colonial period, ca. 1600-1775. I. Title.

Tegakoulta, Catharine, 1656-1680.

BUEHRLE, Marie Cecila, 1887- 970.2
Kateri of the Mohawks. Bruce paperback pub. in collaboration with All Saints. New York, [1962, c.1954] 202p. 16cm. (AS-231) .50 pap.,
1. Tegakoulta, Catharine, 1656-1680. I. Title.

Tegakouita. Catharine, 1656-1686—Juvenile literature.

STEPHENSON, Marion Bailey 922.273
Miracle of the Mohawks. New York, Pageant [1964] 96p. port. 21cm. Bibl. 64-16414 2.75
1. Tegakouita. Catharine, 1656-1686—Juvenile literature. I. Title.

Tegh Bahadur, 9th guru of the Sikhs, 1621-1675.

JOHAR, Surinder Singh. 294.6'61
Guru Tegh Bahadur : a biography / Surinder Singh Johar. New Delhi : Abhinav Publications, 1976 262 p., [1] leaf of plates : ill. ; 22 cm. Includes index. Bibliography: p. 245-249. [BL2017.9.T4J64] 75-908901 11.50
1. Tegh Bahadur, 9th guru of the Sikhs, 1621-1675. 2. Sikh gurus—Biography. I. Title.
Distributed by South Asia Books Columbia, Mo. BIP

Teilhard de Chardin, Pierre.

BARBOUR, George Brown, 1890- 925.72
In the field with Teilhard de Chardin [by] George B. Barbour. [New York] Herder and Herder [1965] 160 p. illus., ports. 22 cm. Bibliographical references included in "Notes" (p. 157-160) [QE707.T4B28] 65-13490
1. Teilhard de Chardin, Pierre. I. Title.

BARBOUR, George Brown, 1890- 925.72
In the field with Tielhard de Chardin [New York] Herder & Herder [c.1965] 160p. illus., ports. 22cm. Bibl. [QE707.T4D28] 65-13490 3.95
1. Teilhard de Chardin, Pierre. I. Title.

BRAYBROOKE, Neville, 1923- ed. 925.72
Teilhard de Chardin: pilgrim of the future. New York, Seabury [c.1964] 128p. 22cm. 64-19629 3.50
1. Teilhard de Chardin, Pierre. I. Title.

COFFY, Robert. 320.5310924
Teilhard de Chardin et le socialisme. Lyon, Chronique sociale de France, 1966. 176 p. col. plate. 18 cm. (Le Fond du probleme, 12) unpriced Illustrated cover. Bibliographical footnotes. [B2430.T374.C56] 67-67995
1. Teilhard de Chardin, Pierre. I. Title.

CORBISHLEY, Thomas. 230'.2'0924
The spirituality of Teilhard de Chardin. Paramus, N.J., Paulist Press [1971] 126 p. 18 cm. Includes bibliographical references. [B2430.T374C63 1971b] 72-78440 1.45
1. Teilhard de Chardin, Pierre. 2. Spirituality. I. Title.

CRISTIANI, Leon [Augustin Louis Leon Pierre Cristiani] 925.72
Pierre Teilhard de Chardin, his life and spirit by Nicolas Corte [pseud.] Translated [from the French] by Martin Jarrett-Kerr. New York, Macmillan [c.]1960. xx, 120p. illus. 22cm. 60-12446 3.25
1. Teilhard de Chardin, Pierre. I. Title.

CUENOT, Claude 925.72
Teilhard de Chardin; a biographical study. [Tr. from French by Vincent Colimore; ed. by Rene Hague] Helicon [dist. New York, Taplinger, c.1958, 1965] vi, 492p. illus., facsims., ports. 23cm. Bibl. [QE707.T4C813] 65-14382 9.75
1. Teilhard de Chardin, Pierre. I. Title.

CUENOT, Claude. 925.72
Teilhard de Chardin; a biographical study. [Translation by Vincent Colimore; edited by Rene Hague] Baltimore, Helicon [1965] vi, 492 p. illus., facsims., ports. 23 cm. "Bibliography of the works of Tellhard de Chardin": p. [409]-482. [QE707.T4C813] 65-14382
1. Teilhard de Chardin, Pierre. I. Title.

DETERRA, Helmut, 1900- 925.72
Memories of Teilhard de Chardin. Tr. from German by J. Maxwell Brownjohn. New York, Harper [1965, c.1962, 1964] 141p. 22cm. [QE707.T4D43] 65-10369 3.50
1. Teilhard de Chardin, Pierre. I. Title.

GRENET, Paul 560.10924
Teilhard de Chardin: the man and his theories. Tr. from French by R. A. Rudorff. [1st Amer. ed.] New York, Eriksson [dist. Hill & Wang, 1966, c.1961] 176p. illus., facsim., maps, ports. 24cm. (Profile in sci.) Bibl. [QE707.T4G713] 66-17489 5.00
1. Teilhard de Chardin, Pierre. I. Title.

GRENET, Paul Bernard. 560.10924 (B)
Teilhard de Chardin; the man and his theories. Translated from the French by R. A. Rudorff. [1st American ed.] New York, P. S. Eriksson [1966] New York, Harper & Row[1967] 176 p. illus., facsim., maps, ports. 24 cm. vii, 160 p. 22 cm. (A Profile in science) Bibliography: p, [170]-171. [QE707.T4G713] [B765.T54G783] 189.4 66-17489 66-11887
1. Teilhard de Chardin, Pierre. 2. Thomas Aquinas, Saint, 1225?-1274—Philosophy. I. Grenet, Paul Bernard. II. Title. III. Title: Thomism;

LUBAC, Henri de, 1896- 230.20924
Teilhard de Chardin: the man and his meaning. Tr. [from French] by Rene Hague. [1st Amer. ed.] New York, Hawthorn [c.1964, 1965] x, 203p. 22cm. Bibl. [B2430.T374L813] 65-22914 4.95
1. Teilhard de Chardin, Pierre. I. Title.

LUBAC, Henri de, 1896- 230.20924
Teilhard de Chardin the man and his meaning. Translated by Rene Hague, [1st American ed.] New York Hawthorn Books [1965] x, 203 p. 22 cm. Translation of La priere du Pere Teilhard de Chardin Bibliographical footnotes. [B2430.T374L813] 65-22914
1. Teilhard de Chardin, Pierre. I. Title.

LUBAC, Henri Henri de, 1896- 230'.2'0924
The religion of Teilhard de Chardin. Tr. by Rene Hague. New York, Desclee [1967] 380p. 22cm. Tr. of La pensee religieuse du pere Teilhard de Chardin. [B2430.T374L783 1967a] 67-17675 5.95
1. Teilhard de Chardin, Pierre. I. Title.

LUKAS, Mary, 1928- 194
Teilhard / by Mary Lukas and Ellen Lukas. 1st ed. Garden City, N.Y. : Doubleday, 1977. 360 p., [4] leaves of plates : ill. ; 22 cm. Includes bibliographical references and index. [B2430.T374L836] 74-33650 ISBN 0-385-02444-4 : 10.00
1. Teilhard de Chardin, Pierre. 2. Philosophers—France—Biography. I. Lukas, Ellen, 1933- joint author. II. Title. BIP

MARTIN, Maria Gratia. 248.4'8'20924
The spirituality of Teilhard de Chardin. Westminster, Md., Newman Press [1968] xii, 122 p. 21 cm. Bibliography: p. 119-122. [B2430.T374M27] 68-16674
1. Teilhard de Chardin, Pierre. I. Title.

RABUT, Olivier A 925.72
Teilhard de Chardin: a critical study. New York, Sheed and Ward [1961] 247p. 20cm. 'Originally published as Dialogue avec Teilhard de Chardin.' [QE707.T4R313] 61-11794
1. Teilhard de Chardin, Pierre. 2. Religion and science—1946- I. Title.

RAVEN, Charles Earle, 1885- 925.72
Teilhard de Chardin; scientist and seer. New York, Harper [1963, c.1962] 221p. 22cm. Bibl. 63-7982 4.00
1. Teilhard de Chardin, Pierre. I. Title.

SPEAIGHT, Robert, 1904- 560 B
The life of Teilhard de Chardin. [1st ed.] New York, Harper & Row [1967] 360 p. illus., maps, ports. 23 cm. London ed. (Collins) has title: Teilhard de Chardin: a biography. Bibliography: p. 339-340. [B2430.T374S73 1967b] 68-11729
1. Teilhard de Chardin, Pierre. I. Title.

SPEAIGHT, Robert, 1904- 230.2'0924
Teilhard de Chardin: re-mythologization; three papers on the thought of Teilhard de Chardin presented at a symposium at Seabury-Western Theological Seminary, Evanston, Illinois, September, 1968. By Robert Speaight, Robert V. Wilshire [and] J. V. Langmead Casserley. [Chicago, Argus Communications, 1970] 101 p. illus. 23 cm. (Peacock books) Cover title: Chardin: remytholi[sic]gization. Includes bibliographical references. [B2430.T374S75] 73-113275 2.45
1. Teilhard de Chardin, Pierre. I. Wilshire, Robert V. II. Casserley, Julian Victor Langmead, 1909- III. Title. IV. Title: Chardin: remytholi[sic]gization.

TEILHARD de Chardin, Pierre. 925.72
Letters from Egypt, 1905-1908. Pref. by Henri de Lubac [Tr. From French by Mary Ilford. New York] Herder & Herder [c.1965] 256p. 21cm. [QE707.T4A3953] 65-15702 4.95
I. Title.

TEILHARD de Chardin, Pierre. 271'.5'0924
Letters from Paris, 1912-1914. Introd. by Henri de Luba.(Annotation by Auguste Demoment and Henri de Lubac.(Translated by Michael Mazzarese [New York] Herder and Herder [1967] 157 p. 21 cm. Portion of the author's Lettres d'Hastings et de Paris, 1908-1914, published in 1965. Bibliographical footnotes. [B2430.T374A42] 67-17626
I. Lubac, Henri de, 1896- ed. II. Title.

TEILHARD de Chardin, Pierre. 940.4780924
The making of a mind; letters from a soldier-priest, 1914-1919. Tr. from French, Genese d'une pensee, by Rene Hague. New York, Harper [c.1961, 1965] 315p. map, port. 22cm. [QE707.T4A393] 65-20462 5.00
I. Title.

TEILHARD de Chardin, Pierre. 940.4780924
The making of a mind; letters from a soldier-priest, 1914-1919. Translated from the French, Genese d'une pensee, by Rene Hague. [1st ed.] New York, Harper & Row [1965] 315 p. map, port. 22 cm. [QE707.T4A393] 65-2046
I. Title.

TEILHARD de Chardin, Pierre. 940.4780924
The making of a mind; letters from a soldier-priest, 1914-1919. Translated from the French, Genese d'une pensee, by Rene Hague. [1st ed.] New York, Harper & Row [1965] 315 p. map, port. 22 cm. [QE707.T4A393] 65-2046
I. Title.

TEILHARD DE CHARDIN, Pierre. 925.72
Letters from Egypt, 1905-1908. Pref. by Henri de Lubac. [Translated by Mary Ilford. New York] Herder and Herder [1965] 256 p. 21 cm. [QE707.T4A3953] 65-15702
I. Title.

TOWERS, Bernard. 230.20924
Teilhard de Chardin. Richmond, Knox [1966] xi, 45p. 19cm. (Makers of contemp. theol.) Bibl. [B2430.T374T6] 66-15515 1.00 pap.,
1. Teilhard de Chardin, Pierre. I. Title. BIP

Teilhard de Chardin, Pierre—Juvenile literature.

SIMON, Charles May Hogue, 1897- 194 B
Faith has need of all the truth; a life of Pierre Teilhard de Chardin, by Charlie May Simon. [1st ed.] New York, Dutton [1974] 180 p. port. 22 cm. Bibliography: p. [171]-173. Biography of the paleontologist, priest, writer, and co-discoverer of Peking man who developed a theory claiming to unify cosmic evolution and Christianity. [B2430.T374S53] 92 73-16303 ISBN 0-525-29606-9 5.95
1. Teilhard de Chardin, Pierre—Juvenile literature. I. Title.

TeKooti, 1830-1893.

ROSS, W. Hugh 993.1020924
Te Kooti Rikirangi; general and prophet [by] W. Hugh Ross. Auckland [N.Z.] Collins; San Francisco, Tri-Ocean, 1966. 196p. 22cm. Bibl. [DU422.T4R6] 66-31838 5.00 bds.,
1. TeKooti, 1830-1893. I. Title.

Telemann, Georg Philipp, 1681-1767.

PETZOLDT, Richard, 1907- 780'.92'4 B
Georg Philipp Telemann. Translated by Horace Fitzpatrick. New York, Oxford University Press, 1974. xv, 255 p. illus. 22 cm. Bibliography: p. 223-224. [ML410.T26P5] 73-82633 ISBN 0-19-519722-4 7.50
1. Telemann, Georg Philipp, 1681-1767.

VALENTIN, Erich, 1906- 784'.092'4
Telemann in seiner Zeit; Versuch eines geistesgeschichtlichen Portrats Hamburg, H. Sikorski [1960] 51 p. 24 cm. (Veroffentlichungen der Hamburger Telemann-Gesellschaft, Heft 1) "Verzelchnis von Schallplatten mit Werken Georg Philipp Telemann": p. 51. Bibliography: p. 48. [ML410.T26V3] 60-26155
1. Telemann, Georg Philipp, 1681-1787. 2. (Series: Hamburger Telemann-Gesellschaft. Veroffentlichungen, Heft 1) I. Title.

Television broadcasting—Biog.

WHO'S who in TV 927.92
[New York] Dell [1967] v. ports. 18cm. annual. (9456) Orig. title: Who's who in TV & radio. 1967 ed. by R. H. Heller. [PN1991.1.W467] 52-24598 .60 pap.,
1. Television broadcasting—Biog.

Television personalities—United States—Biography.

MEYERS, Richard. 791.45'028'0922 B
Super TV stars / Richard Meyers. New York : Drake Publishers, 1977. 160 p. : ill. ; 29 cm. [PN1992.4.A2M48] 76-55091 ISBN 0-8473-1509-6 : 5.95
1. Television personalities—United States—Biography. 2. Television programs—United States. I. Title.

Telford, Thomas, 1757-1834.

BRACEGIRDLE, Brian. 624'.092'4 B
Thomas Telford [by] Brian Bracegirdle [and] Patricia H. Miles. Newton Abbot, David and Charles, 1973. 112 p. illus., maps, plans, port. 25 cm. (Great engineers and their works) Includes index. Bibliography: p. 110. [TA140.T3B7] 73-166607 ISBN 0-7153-5933-9
1. Telford, Thomas, 1757-1834. I. Miles, Patricia H., joint author.
Distributed by David & Charles, North Pomfret, Vermont, 9.95.

ROLT, Lionel Thomas Caswell, 1910- 926.2
Thomas Telford. London, New York, Longmans, Green [1958] 211p. illus. 23cm. Includes bibliography. [TA140.T3R6 1958] 58-3289
1. Telford, Thomas, 1757-1834. I. Title.

Teller, Edward, 1908-

BLUMBERG, Stanley A. 623.4'5119'0924 B
Energy and conflict : the life and times of Edward Teller / by Stanley A. Blumberg and Gwinn Owens. New York : Putnam, c1976. xvii, 492 p., [4] leaves of plates : ill. ; 23 cm. Includes bibliographical references and index. [QC16.T37B58 1976] 75-43812 ISBN 0-399-11551-X : 12.95
1. Teller, Edward, 1908- I. Owens, Gwinn, joint author. II. Title. BIP

Temecula—Biography.

HUDSON, Thomas, 1900- 917.94'97 B
They passed this way: biographical sketches; tales of historic Temecula Valley at the crossroads of California's southern immigrant trail [by Tom Hudson and Sam Hicks] Temecula, Calif., Laguna House [1970] 56 p. illus., maps. 22 cm. [F869.T43H8] 77-22218 1.00
1. Temecula—Biography. I. Hicks, Sam. II. Title.

Templars.

SIMON, Edith, 1917- 929.71
The piebald standard; a biography of the Knights Templars. [1st American ed.] Boston, Little, Brown [1959] 358 p. illus. 22 cm. [CR4743.S5 1959a] 59-11884
1. Templars. I. Title.

SIMON, Edith, 1917- 255'.79
The piebald standard : a biography of the Knights Templars / by Edith Simon. 1st AMS ed. New York : AMS Press, 1978, c1959. xi, 312 p., [8] leaves of plates : ill. ; 23 cm. Reprint of the ed. publishedby Cassell, London. Includes index. Bibliography: p. 301-302. [CR4743.S5 1978] 76-29836 ISBN 0-404-15419-0 : 32.00
1. Templars. I. Title.

Temple, Exra, 1865 or 6-1946.

DEN HARTOG, Egbert, 1892- 922.673
The tramp preacher. [New Sharan? Iowa, 1952, '1949] 214 p. illus. 20 cm. [BV3785.T36D4] 52-44002
1. Temple, Exra, 1865 or 6-1946. I. Title.

Temple, Shirley, 1928-

*BASINGER, Jeanine. 791.43'028'0922 B
Shirley Temple New York, Pyramid [1975] 160 p. illus. 20 cm. (Pyramid illustrated history of the movies) Bibliograpy: 146-147 [PN2287] ISBN 0-515-03643-9 1.75 (pbk.)
1. Temple, Shirley I. Title.

BURDICK, Loraine. 791.43'028'0924 B
The Shirley Temple scrapbook / by Loraine Burdick. Middle Village, N.Y. : Jonathan David Publishers, [1975] p. cm. [PN2287.T33B8] 74-31298 ISBN 0-8246-0197-1 : 12.95
1. Temple, Shirley, 1928- I. Title. BIP

EBY, Lois Christine, 1908- 927.92
Shirley Temple; the amazing story of the child actress who grew up to be America's fairy princess. Derby, Conn., Monarch [c.1962] 143p. 18cm. (Monarch original biog., K62) 62-5339 .35 pap.,
1. Temple, Shirley, 1928- I. Title.

WINDELER, Robert. 791.43'028'0924 B
The films of Shirley Temple / by Robert Windeler. 1st ed. Secaucus, N.J. : Citadel Press, c1978. 256 p. : ill. ; 29 cm. [PN2287.T33W48] 78-1408 ISBN 0-8065-0615-6 : 14.95
1. Temple, Shirley, 1928- 2. Moving-picture actors and actresses—United States—Biography. I. Title. BIP

WINDELER, Robert. 791.43'028'0924 B
Shirley Temple / Robert Windeler. London : W. H. Allen, 1976. 160 p., [24] p. of plates : ill., ports. ; 23 cm. Includes index. Filmography: p. 146-153. [PN2287.T33W5] 76-367534 ISBN 0-491-01524-0 : £3.50
1. Temple, Shirley, 1928-

Temple, William, Abp. of Canterbury, 1881-1944.

FLETCHER, Joseph Francis, 1905- 922.342
William Temple, twentieth-century Christian. New York, Seabury Press, 1963. 372 p. 21 cm. Includes bibliography. [BX5199.T42F5] 63-12587
1. Temple, William, Abp. of Canterbury, 1881-1944. I. Title.

IREMONGER, Frederic Athelwold, 1878- 922.342
William Temple, Archbishop of Canterbury; his life and letters. New york, Oxford [c.]1963. 292p. 20cm. (No. 59) Bibl. 1.85 pap.,
1. Temple, William, Abp. of Canterbury, 1881-1944. I. Title.

IREMONGER, Frederick Athelwold, 1878- 283'.092'4
William Temple, Archbishop of Canterbury; his life and letters Abridged ed. by D. C. Somervell. London, New York, Oxford University Press, 1963. 292 p. 20 cm. (Oxford AErbacks, no 59) [BX5199.T42I72] 64-1859
1. 1. Temple, William, Abp. of Canterbury, 1881-1944. I. Title.

Temple, William, Sir, bart., 1628-1699.

CHAPMAN, Hester W., 1899-1976. 941.06'092'4 B
Four fine gentlemen / Hester Chapman. Lincoln : University of Nebraska Press, 1978. 301 p., [4] leaves of plates : ports. ; 23 cm. Includes index. Bibliography: p. [289]-291. [DA377.3.C47 1977b] 77-20589 ISBN 0-8032-1401-4 : 12.50
1. Shaftesbury, Anthony Ashley Cooper, 1st Earl of, 1621-1683. 2. Temple, William, Sir, bart., 1628-1699. 3. Reresby, John, Sir, 2d bart., 1634-1689. 4. Shrewsbury, Charles Talbot, Duke of, 1660-1718. 5. Great Britain—History—17th century—Biography. 6. Statesmen—Great Britain—Biography. I. Title. BIP

STEENSMA, Robert C., 1930- 824'.4 B
Sir William Temple, by Robert C. Steensma. New York, Twayne Publishers [1970] 164 p. 21 cm. (Twayne's English authors series 109) Bibliography: p. 151-157. [PR3729.T2Z87] 70-120017
1. Temple, William, Sir, Bart., 1628-1699.

Ten Boom, Corrie.

TEN Boom, Corrie. 269'.2'0924 B
He sets the captive free / Corrie ten Boom. Old Tappan, N.J. : Revell, c1977. p. cm. (Her Jesus is victor) [BR1725.T35A33] 78-1503 ISBN 0-8007-0929-2 : 4.95
1. Ten Boom, Corrie. 2. Christian biography—Netherlands. 3. World War, 1939-1945—Personal narratives, Dutch. 4. Ravensbruck (Concentration camp) 5. Christian life—1960- I. Title. II. Series. BIP

TEN Boom, corrie 940.53'492
The hiding place, by Corrie ten Boom, with John and Elizabeth Sherrill. Boston, G. K. Hall, 1973 [c1971] 431 p. 25 cm. Autobiography. Large print ed. [D811.5.T427 1973] 73-10058 ISBN 0-8161-6138-0
1. Ten Boom, Corrie. 2. World War, 1939-1945—Personal narratives, Dutch. 3. Ravensbruck (Concentration camp) I. Sherrill, John L., joint author. II. Sherrill, Elizabeth, joint author. III. Title.

TEN BOOM, Corrie. 269'.2'0924 [B]
He sets the captive free / Corrie Ten Boom. Old Tappan, N.J. : Revell, 1978, c1977 93 p. ; 20 cm. (Her Jesus is victor) [BR1725.T35A33] 77-99134 ISBN 0-8007-0929-2 : 4.95
1. Ten Boom, Corrie. 2. Christian biography—Netherlands. 3. World War, 1939-1945—Personal narratives, Dutch. 4. Ravenbruck (Concentration camp) 5. Christian life—1960- I. Title. II. Series.

TEN BOOM, Corrie. 940.53'492
The hiding place, by Corrie ten Boom with John and Elizabeth Sherrill. Washington Depot, Conn., Chosen Books; [distributed by Revell, 1971] 219 p. 20 cm. [D811.5.T427 1971] 73-172389 2.95
1. Ten Boom, Corrie. 2. World War, 1939-1945—Personal narratives, Dutch. 3. Ravensbruck (Concentration camp) I. Sherrill, John L. II. Sherrill, Elizabeth. III. Title. BIP

Tendoy, Indian chief, 1834 (ca.)-1907.

CROWDER, David Lester. 970.3 b
Tendoy, chief of the Lemhis, by David L. Crowder. [Pocatello, Idaho] 1966. x, 120 l. illus., maps. ports. 28 cm. Thesis (M.A.)—Idaho State University. Bibliography: leaves [115]-120 . [E99.S4C7] 68-977
1. Tendoy, Indian chief, 1834 (ca.)-1907. 2. Shoshoni Indians—History. 3. Bannock Indians—History. 4. Lemhi Co., Idaho—History. BIP

Tene, Steve, 1949-

MAAS, Peter, 1929- 973'.04'91497
King of the gypsies / Peter Maas. London : Cape, 1976. xiii, 171 p., [6] p. of plates : ports. ; 23 cm. [DX127.T46M3 1976] 77-353764 ISBN 0-224-01252-5 : £3.50
1. Tene, Steve, 1949- 2. Gipsies—United States—Biography. I. Title.

MAAS, Peter, 1929- 973'.04'91497 B
King of the gypsies / Peter Maas. New York : Viking Press, 1975. 171 p., [3] leaves of plates : ill. ; 22 cm. [DX127.T46M3 1975] 75-20151 ISBN 0-670-41317-8 : 7.95
1. Tene, Steve, 1949- 2. Gipsies—United States. I. Title. BIP

Teniers, David, the Younger, 1610-1690.

DAVIDSON, Jane P. 759.9493 B
David Teniers the Younger / by Jane P. Davidson. Boulder, Colo. : Westview Press, [1979] p. cm. Includes index. Bibliography: p. [ND673.T3D38] 79-13221 ISBN 0-89158-564-8 lib. bdg. : 25.00
1. Teniers, David, the Younger, 1610-1690. 2. Painters—Belgium—Biography. I. Title. BIP

Tennessee — Biography.

ARMSTRONG, Zella. 973.3'4'0922 B
Some Tennessee heroes of the Revolution / compiled from pension statements by Zella Armstrong. 5 pts. in 1 v. Baltimore : Genealogical Pub. Co., 1975. 162 p. ; 23 cm. Reprint of the 1933-1944 editions published by Lookout Pub. Co., Chattanooga, which were issued as its Pamphlet no. 1-5. [F435.A74 1975] 75-21541 ISBN 0-8063-0684-X : 10.00
1. Tennessee—Biography. I. Title. II. Series: Lookout Publishing Company, Chattanooga, Tenn. Pamphlet ; no. 1-5. BIP

BASS, Frank Embrick, 1901- ed. v. 12
Who's who in Tennessee; a reference edition recording the biographies of contemporary leaders in Tennessee with special emphasis on their achievements in making the volunteer state one of America's greatest. Written and prepared under the supervision of Frank E. Bass. Hopkinsville, Ky., Historical Record Association, 1961. 774 p. illus. 27 cm.
1. Tennessee — Biography. I. Title.

CRUTCHFIELD, James Andrew, 1938- 920'.0768
Footprints across the pages of Tennessee history / compiled by James A. Crutchfield. Nashville : Williams Press, c1976. [109] p. : ports. ; 22 cm. Fifty-one capsule biographies of men and women of distinction from the state of Tennessee. [CT261.C78] 77-359433 8.95
1. Tennessee—Biography. I. Title.

TENNESSEE lives; 920.0768
the Volunteer State historical record. Written and prepared under the supervision of William T. Alderson. Assisted by an editorial advisory board composed of eminent Tennesseans. Hopkinsville, Ky., Historical Record Association, 1971. 448 p. ports. 27 cm. [F435.T36] 79-147231
1. Tennessee—Biography. I. Alderson, william Thomas, 1926- ed.

Tennessee. General Assembly—Biography.

MCBRIDE, Robert Martin, 1918- 328.768'092'2
Biographical directory of the Tennessee General Assembly / by Robert M. McBride and Dan M. Robison ; edited by Robert M. McBride. Nashville : Tennessee State Library and Archives, 1975- v. ; 26 cm. Includes index. Contents.Contents.—v. 1. 1796-1861. Bibliography: v. 1, p. 839-858. [JK5231 1975.M33] 76-350164
1. Tennessee. General Assembly—Biography. I. Robison, Daniel Merritt, joint author. II. Tennessee. State Library and Archives, Nashville. III. Title.

TENNESSEE. State Library and Archives, Nashville. 328.768'0922 B
Biographical directory: Tennessee General Assembly, 1796-1967; [preliminary sketches] Nashville [1968- v. 28 cm. Cover title. Contents.Contents.—v. [1] Robertson County.—v. 2. Lewis County, Perry County [and] Wayne County.—v. 3. Marshall County. [F435.T34] 68-65393
1. Tennessee. General Assembly—Biography. 2. Tennessee—Biography. I. Title.

Tennessee—Governors—Biography.

PHILLIPS, Margaret I. 976.8'00992 B
The Governors of Tennessee / by Margaret I. Phillips. Gretna, La. : Pelican Pub. Co., 1978. p. cm. (The Pelican

Governors series) Includes index. Bibliography: p. [F435.P48] 77-26845 ISBN 0-88289-169-3 : 12.95
1. Tennessee—Governors—Biography. I. Title. BIP

Tennessee—History.

CROCKETT, David, 1786-1836. 923.973
The adventures of Davy Crockett, told mostly by himself. With illus. by John W. Thomason, Jr. New York, Scribner [1955] 246 p. illus. 24 cm. Includes "Col. Crockett's exploits and adventures in Texas," a pseudo-autobiography generally ascribed to Richard Penn Smith. [F436.C87 1955] 55-12944
1. Tennessee—History. 2. Creek War, 1813-1814. 3. U.S.—Description and travel—1783-1848. 4. Texas—History—Revolution, 1835-1836. I. Smith, Richard Penn, 1799-1854, supposed author. Col. Crockett's exploits and adventures in Texas. II. Title.

CROCKETT, David, 1786-1836. 923.973
Davy Crockett's own story, as written by himself the autobiography of America's great folk hero Illustrated by Milton Glaser New York, Citadel Press [1955] 377 p. illus. 22 cm. 'Consists of . . . A narrative of the life of David Crockett . . . written by himself, published in 1834; An account of Col. Crockett's tour to the North and down East, published in 1834, and Col. Crockett's exploits and adventures in Texas, published posthumously in 1836.' 'Col. Crockett's exploits and adventures in Texas' is a pseudo-autobiography generally ascribed to Richard Penn Smith. [F436.C9] 55-10010
1. Tennessee-Hist. 2. Creek War, 1813-1814. 3. U. S.— Descr. & trav.—1783-1848. 4. Texas—Hist.—Revolution, 1835-1836. I. Smith, Richard Penn, 1799-1854. Col. Crockett s explots and adventures in Texas. II. Title.

CROCKETT, David, 1786-1836. 923.973
The life of Davy Crockett, by himself. To which is added an account of his glorious death at the Alamo while fighting in defense of Texan independence. [New York] New American Library [1955] 263 p. 18 cm. (A Signet book, S1214) 'Reprinted from the Keystone Publishing Company edition, published in Philadelphia in 1889. [F436.C939] 55-2913
1. Tennessee—Hist. 2. Creek War: 1813-1814. 3. U. S.—Descr. & trav.— 1783-1848. 4. Texas—Hist.—Revolution, 1835-1836. I. Title.

Tennessee—History—Addresses, essays, lectures.

DAVIS, Louise Littleton. 976.8
Frontier tales of Tennessee / Louise Littleton Davis. Gretna, La. : Pelican Pub. Co., 1976. ix, 190 p. ; 23 cm. Includes index. Bibliography: p. 180-186. [F436.D38] 76-18122 ISBN 0-88289-084-0 : 10.00
1. Tennessee—History—Addresses, essays, lectures. 2. Tennessee—Biography—Addresses, essays, lectures. 3. United States—Biography.—Addresses, essays, lectures. I. Title.
Contents omitted. BIP

Tennessee—Politics and government—1865-

HOOPER, Ben W., 1870-1957. 923.273
The unwanted boy; the autobiography of Governor Ben W. Hooper. Edited by Everett Robert Boyce. Knoxville, University of Tennessee Press, 1963. x, 258 p. plates, ports., facsims. 24 cm. Bibliography: p. [247]-251. [F436.H78 1963] 63-14135
1. Tennessee—Politics and government—1865- I. Title. BIP

Tennis.

LICHTENSTEIN, Grace. 796.34'2
A long way, baby; behind the scenes in women's pro tennis. Photography by Nancy Moran. New York, Morrow, 1974. 239 p. illus. 22 cm. [GV999.L52] 74-1166 ISBN 0-688-00263-3 6.95
1. Tennis. 2. Tennis—Biography. I. Title. BIP

Tennis—Biography.

JACOBS, Helen Hull, 1908- 796.34'2'0922 B
Gallery of champions. Freeport, N.Y., Books for Libraries Press [1970, c1949] viii, 224 p. illus., ports. 23 cm. (Biography index reprint series) Contents.Contents.—Suzanne Lenglen.—Helen Wills Roark.—Hilde Krahwinkel Sperling.—Alice Marble.—Dorothy Round Little.—Molla Bjurstedt Mallory.—Pauline Betz.—Simone Mathieu.—Cilli Aussem.—Sarah Palfrey Cooke.—Anita Lizana Ellis.—Louise Brough.—Margaret Osborne du Pont.—Betty Nuthall.—Margaret Scriven Vivien. [GV994.A1J2 1970] 71-136648 ISBN 8-369-80433-
1. Tennis—Biography. I. Title. BIP

SULLIVAN, George, 1927- 796.34'2'0922 B
Queens of the court / George Sullivan ; illustrated with photos. New York : Dodd, Mead, [1974] 111 p. : ill. ; 19 x 23 cm. Includes index. Brief biographies concentrating on the careers of six women tennis stars include: Margaret Court, Billie Jean King, Chris Evert, Evonne Goolagong, Rosemary Casals, and Virginia Wade. [GV994.A1S94] 920 74-3777 ISBN 0-396-06973-8 : 4.95
1. Tennis—Biography. I. Title. BIP

TINLING, Teddy 927.96342
White ladies [by] Teddy Tinling as told to Robert Oxby. Foreword by Ailsa Garland. London, S. Paul [dist. New Rochelle, N.Y., SportShelf, 1964, c.1963] 190p. ports. 22cm. 64-3318 5.75 bds.,
1. Tennis—Biog. I. Oxby, Robert. II. Title.

YOUNG, David, 1930- ed. 796.3420922
Points for victory. [London] Published for the Nestle Sports Foundation by S. Paul [1965] 128 p. ports. 25 cm. (The Nestle book of tennis, no. 3) Stamped on t.p.: Distributed by Sportshelf, New Rochelle, N.Y. [GV994.A1Y62] 66-722
1. Tennis — Biog. I. Title. II. Series.

Tennis—Biography—Juvenile literature.

HIGDON, Hal. 796.34'2'0922 B
Champions of the tennis court. Englewood Cliffs, N.J., Prentice-Hall [1971] ix, 60 p. illus., ports. 22 cm. Brief biographies of eleven champion tennis players: Bill Tilden, Suzanne Lenglen, Helen Wills, Don Budge, Billy Talbert, Jack Kramer, Pancho Gonzales, Maureen Connolly, Lew Hoad, Billie Jean King, and Arthur Ashe. [GV994.A1H5] 920 76-148490 ISBN 0-13-125419-7 3.95
1. Tennis—Biography—Juvenile literature. I. Title.

Tennis—History.

ALEXANDER, George E. 796.34'2'09
Lawn tennis : its founders & its early days / by George E. Alexander. Lynn, Mass. : H. O. Zimman, [1974] xv, 127 p., [8] leaves of plates : ill. ; 24 cm. Bibliography: p. 121-127. [GV993.A43] 74-195103
1. Tennis—History. 2. Tennis—Biography. I. Title.

JANOFF, Murray. 796.34'2'09
Game! Set! Match! [New York] Stadia Sports Pub. [1973] 160 p. illus. 20 cm. (Sport-spectrum classic) [GV993.J36] 73-75004 1.50
1. Tennis—History. 2. Tennis—Biography. I. Title.
Order from Dell.

WIND, Herbert Warren, 1918- 796.34'2
Game, set, and match ; the tennis boom of the 1960's and 70's / Herbert Warren Wind. 1st ed. New York : Dutton, c1979. xxiii, 229 p. ; 24 cm. "All the material ... originally appeared in The New Yorker in slightly different form." [GV995.W733 1979] 78-26895 12.95
1. Tennis—History. 2. Tennis players—Biography. I. Title.

Tennis—History—Juvenile literature.

COOK, Joseph J. 796.34'2'0922 B
Famous firsts in tennis / Joseph J. Cook. New York : Putnam, c1978. 63 p. : ill. ; 24 cm. (Famous firsts books) Includes index. Sketches the history of tennis and profiles some of its outstanding players through the years. [GV996.5.C66 1978] 920 77-21855 ISBN 0-399-61111-8 lib.bdg. : 4.49
1. Tennis—History—Juvenile literature. 2. Tennis players—Biography—Juvenile literature. I. Title. BIP

Tennis—Juvenile literature.

LAWRENCE, Andrew. 796.34'2'0922 B
Tennis : great stars, great moments / Andrew Lawrence. New York : Putnam, c1976. 127 p. ; 22 cm. (Putnam sports shelf) Includes index. Biographical sketches of twelve men and women who have provided great talent and great moments to tennis. [GV995.L4135 1976] 920 76-11008 lib. bdg. : 5.29. ISBN 0-399-61029-4 lib.bdg. : 5.29
1. Tennis—Juvenile literature. I. Title. BIP

Tennis players—Biography.

FRAYNE, Trent. 796.34'2'0922 B
Famous tennis players / by Trent Frayne. New York : Dodd, Mead, c1977. 192 p. : ill. ; 22 cm. Includes index. [GV994.A1F7] 77-6501 ISBN 0-396-07470-7 : 5.95
1. Tennis players—Biography. I. Title. BIP

TINLING, Teddy. 796.34'2'0922 B
Love and faults : personalities who have changed the history of tennis in my lifetime / by Ted Tinling, with Rod Humphries. New York : Crown Publishers, c1979. 314 p., [16] leaves of plates : ill. ; 24 cm. [GV994.A1T48 1979] 78-23276 ISBN 0-517-53305-7 : 10.95
1. Tennis players—Biography. I. Humphries, Rod, joint author. II. Title.

VINES, Ellsworth, 1911- 796.34'2'0922 B
Tennis : myth of the big game / by Ellsworth Vines and Gene Vier. New York : Viking Press, [1978] p. cm. "A Richard Seaver book." [GV994.A1V56 1978] 77-18544 ISBN 0-670-69665-X : 10.00
1. Tennis players—Biography. 2. Tennis. I. Vier, Gene, joint author. II. Title.

Tennis players—Biography—Juvenile literature.

GLICKMAN, William G. 796.34'2'0922 B
Winners on the tennis court / by William G. Glickman. New York : F. Watts, 1978. 48 p. : ill. ; 22 cm. (A Picture life book) Discusses the lives and careers of six young tennis champions. Included are Evonne Goolagong, Jimmy Connors, Bjorn Borg, Arthur Ashe, Chris Evert, and Billie Jean King. [GV994.A1G55] 920 77-21188 ISBN 0-531-02912-3 lib.bdg. : 4.90
1. Tennis players—Biography—Juvenile literature. I. Title. BIP

Tennis—United States—History.

JANOFF, Murray. 796.34'2'09
Tennis revolution / by Murray Janoff. New York : Stadia Sports Pub., 1974. 159 p., [2] leaves of plates : ill. ; 20 cm. (Sportscene ; v. 1, no. 3) [GV993.J37] 74-193270 pbk. : 1.50
1. Tennis—United States—History. 2. Tennis—Biography. I. Title.

Tennyson, Alfred Tennyson, Baron, 1809-1892.

BENSON, Arthur Christopher, 1862-1925. 821'.8 B
Alfred Tennyson. [Folcroft, Pa.] Folcroft Library Editions, 1973. p. Reprint of the 1905 ed. published by Methuen, London. [PR5581.B45 1973] 73-12616 10.00
1. Tennyson, Alfred Tennyson, Baron, 1809-1892. BIP

BENSON, Arthur Christopher, 1862-1925. 821'.8
Tennyson. 4th ed. Freeport, N.Y., Books for Libraries Press [1970] viii, 243 p. 23 cm. First published under the title: Alfred Tennyson. Reprint of the 1913 ed. [PR5581.B45 1970] 76-137369
1. Tennyson, Alfred Tennyson, Baron, 1809-1892.

BUCKLEY, Jerome Hamilton. v. 12
Tennyson; the growth of a poet. Boston, Houghton Mifflin [1965, c1960] 298 p. 22 cm. Includes bibliography 65-103049
1. Tennyson, Alfred Tennyson, baron, 1809-1892. I. Title. BIP

BUCKLEY, Jerome Hamilton. 821.8
Tennyson; the growth of a poet. Cambridge, Harvard University Press, 1960. 298 p. 22 cm. Includes bibliography. [PR5581.B8] 60-13298
1. Tennyson, Alfred Tennyson, baron, 1809-1892.

CHESTERTON, Gilbert Keith, 1873-1936. 821'.8 B
Tennyson, by G. K. Chesterton and Richard Garnett. London, Hodder and Stoughton, 1903. [Folcroft, Pa.] Folcroft Library Editions, 1972. p. [PR5581.C5 1972] 72-12905 ISBN 0-8414-1028-3 (lib. bdg.)
1. Tennyson, Alfred Tennyson, Baron, 1809-1892. I. Garnett, Richard, 1835-1906, joint author.

CUTHBERTSON, Evan J. 821'.8 B
Tennyson; the story of his life, by Evan J. Cuthbertson. [Folcroft, Pa.] Folcroft Library Editions, 1973. p. Reprint of the 1898 ed. published by W. & R. Chambers, London. [PR5581.C8 1973] 73-14566 15.00
1. Tennyson, Alfred Tennyson, Baron, 1809-1892.

CUTHBERTSON, Evan J. 821'.8 B
Tennyson; the story of his life, by Evan J. Cuthbertson. [Folcroft, Pa.] Folcroft Library Editions, 1973. 128 p. illus. 24 cm. Reprint of the 1898 ed. published by W. & R. Chambers, London. [PR5581.C8 1973] 73-14566 ISBN 0-8414-3472-7 (lib. bdg.)
1. Tennyson, Alfred Tennyson, Baron, 1809-1892.

CUTHBERTSON, Evan J. 821'.8 B
Tennyson : the story of his life / by Evan J. Cuthbertson. Norwood, Pa. : Norwood Editions, 1976. p. cm. Reprint of the 1898 ed. published by W. & R. Chambers, London. [PR5581.C8 1976] 76-1908 ISBN 0-88305-323-3 lib. bdg. : 12.50
1. Tennyson, Alfred Tennyson, Baron, 1809-1892.

FAUSSET, Hugh I'Anson, 1895- 821'.8 B
Tennyson; a modern portrait. New York, Russell & Russell [1968] 309 p. ports. 23 cm. Reprint of the 1923 ed. [PR5581.F3 1968] 68-11326
1. Tennyson, Alfred Tennyson, baron, 1809-1892. BIP

FIELDS, Annie (Adams) 1834-1915. 810.9'003
Authors and friends. New York, AMS Press [1969] 355 p ports., facsims. 23 cm. Reprint of the 1896 ed. Contents.—Longfellow: 1807-1882.—Glimpses of Emerson.—Oliver Wendell Holmes: personal recollections and unpublished letters.—Days with Mrs. Stowe.—Celia Thaxter.—Whittier: notes of his life and of his friendships.—Tennyson.—Lady Tennyson. [PS121.F5 1969b] 74-107343
1. Tennyson, Alfred Tennyson, Baron, 1809-1892. 2. Authors, American. I. Title.

FIELDS, Annie (Adams) 1834-1915. 810.9'003
Authors and friends. [6th ed.] Boston, Houghton, Mifflin, 1897 [c1896] Grosse Pointe, Mich., Scholarly Press, 1969. 355 p. 21 cm. Contents.Contents.—Longfellow: 1807-1882.—Glimpses of Emerson.—Oliver Wendell Holmes: personal recollections and unpublished letters.—Days with Mrs. Stowe.—Celia Thaxter.—Whittier: notes of his life and of his friendships.—Tennyson.—Lady Tennyson. [PS121.F5 1969] 76-4123
1. Tennyson, Alfred Tennyson, Baron, 1809-1892. 2. Authors, American. I. Title.

HORTON, Robert Forman, 1855-1934. 821'.8
Alfred Tennyson: a saintly life. New York, Haskell House Publishers, 1973. xi, 323 p. illus. 23 cm. Reprint of the 1900 ed. [PR5581.H6 1973] 72-10628 ISBN 0-8383-1687-5 14.95
1. Tennyson, Alfred Tennyson, Baron, 1809-1892. I. Title. BIP

HORTON, Robert Forman, 1855-1934. 821'.8
Alfred Tennyson, a saintly life. [Folcroft, Pa.] Folcroft Library Editions, 1973. xi, 323 p. port. 23 cm. Reprint of the 1900 ed. published by J. M. Dent, London, and E. P. Dutton, New York. [PR5581.H6 1973b] 73-11364 ISBN 0-8414-4722-5 (lib. bdg.)
1. Tennyson, Alfred Tennyson, baron, 1809-1892.

JENKINSON, Arthur. 821'.8 B
Alfred, Lord Tennyson, poet laureate; a brief study of his life and poetry. [Folcroft, Pa.] Folcroft Library Editions, 1974. x, 127 p. 24 cm. Reprint of the 1892 ed. published by J. Nisbet, London. Includes bibliographical references. [PR5581.J38 1974] 74-5005 ISBN 0-8414-5289-X (lib. bdg.)
1. Tennyson, Alfred Tennyson, Baron, 1802-1892. I. Title.

JOHNSON, Reginald Brimley, 1867-1932. 821'.8
Tennyson & his poetry. London, G. G. Harrap, 1917. [New York, AMS Press, 1972] 158, [1] p. port. 19 cm. (Poetry and life series) Bibliography: p. [159] [PR5581.J7 1972] 73-120976 ISBN 0-404-52524-5 8.00
1. Tennyson, Alfred Tennyson, Baron, 1809-1892. I. Title. II. Series. BIP

LANG, Andrew, 1844-1912. 821'.8 B
Alfred Tennyson. 2d ed. New York, AMS Press [1970] vi, 233 p. 23 cm. Reprint of the 1901 ed. Includes bibliographical references. [PR5588.L3 1970] 70-111615
1. Tennyson, Alfred Tennyson, baron, 1809-1892.

LANG, Andrew, 1844-1912. 821'.8 B
Alfred Tennyson. [Folcroft, Pa.] Folcroft Library Editions, 1973. p. Reprint of the 2d ed., published in 1901 by W. Blackwood, Edinburgh, in series: Modern English writers. Includes bibliographical references. [PR5588.L3 1973] 73-13762 ISBN 0-8414-5668-2 (lib. bdg.)
1. Tennyson, Alfred Tennyson, Baron, 1809-1892. I. Title. BIP

LOUNSBURY, Thomas Raynesford, 1838-1915. 928.2
The life and times of Tennyson, from 1809 to 1850. New York, Russell. 1962. 661p. 23cm. 61-17195 10.00
1. Tennyson, Alfred Tennyson, baron, 1809-1892. I. Title.

LYALL, Alfred Comyn, Sir, 1835-1911. 821'.8
Tennyson / by Sir Alfred Lyall. Brooklyn, N.Y. : Haskell House Pub., 1977. 200 p. ; 21 cm. Reprint of the 1914 ed. published by Macmillan, London, in series: English men of letters. Includes bibliography references and index. [PR5581.L8 1977] 76-53034 lib. bdg. : 11.95
1. Tennyson, Alfred Tennyson, Baron, 1809-1892. 2. Poets, English—19th century—Biography.

MOORE, John Murray. 821'.8
Three aspects of the late Alfred, Lord Tennyson. New York, Haskell House Publishers, 1972. 144 p. port. 23 cm. Reprint of the 1901 ed. [PR5581.M6 1972] 79-185968 ISBN 0-8383-1387-6
1. Tennyson, Alfred Tennyson, Baron, 1809-1892. I. Title.

MOORE, John Murray. 821'.8
Three aspects of the late Alfred, Lord Tennyson. [Folcroft, Pa.] Folcroft Library Editions, 1973, [i.e. 1974] p. Reprint of the 1901 ed. published by Marsden, Manchester. [PR5581.M6 1973] 73-13781 ISBN 0-8414-6020-5. 9.75
1. Tennyson, Alfred Tennyson, Baron, 1809-1892. I. Title. BIP

[NICOLL, William Robertson] Sir, 1851-1923. 821'.8 B
Alfred Tennyson; his life and works, by Walter E. Wace. [Folcroft, Pa.] Folcroft Library Editions, 1973. vii, 203 p. port. 23 cm. Reprint of the 1881 ed. published by Macniven and Wallace, Edinburgh. Bibliography: p. [176]-203. [PR5581.N5 1973] 73-18128 ISBN 0-8414-9507-6 (lib. bdg.)
1. Tennyson, Alfred Tennyson, Baron, 1809-1892.

NICOLSON, Harold George, Sir 1886 928.2
Tennyson, aspects of his life, character and poetry. Garden City, N.Y., Doubleday, 1962[c.1961] 339p. (Anchor bk., A284) 1.25 pap.,
1. Tennyson, Alfred Tennyson, baron 1809-1892. I. Title. BIP

NICOLSON, Harold George, Sir 1886- v. 12
Tennyson; aspects of his life, character & poetry. Garden City, N. Y., Doubleday, 1962. 339 p. 19 cm. (Doubleday anchor books, A 284) 63-34841
1. Tennyson, Alfred Tennyson, baron, 1809-1892. I. Title. II. Series.

NICOLSON, Harold George, Sir, 1886-1968. 821'.8 B
Tennyson; aspects of his life, character, and poetry. Freeport, N.Y., Books for Libraries Press [1972] ix, 308 p. 23 cm. Reprint of the 1923 ed. [PR5581.N53 1972] 72-12 ISBN 0-8369-9967-3
1. Tennyson, Alfred Tennyson, Baron, 1809-1892.

NICOLSON, Harold George, Sir, 1886-1968. 821'.8 B
Tennyson, aspects of his life, character and poetry. London, Constable. St. Clair Shores, Mich., Scholarly Press, 1970. viii, 309 p. 22 cm. Reprint of the 1949 ed.; first published in 1923. [PR5581.N53 1970] 74-145209 ISBN 0-403-00806-9
1. Tennyson, Alfred Tennyson, Baron, 1809-1892. I. Title.

NICOLSON, Harold George, Sir, 1886-1968. 821'.8 B
Tennyson: aspects of his life, character, and poetry. New York, Haskell House Publishers, 1973. viii, 309 p. 23 cm. Reprint of the 2d ed., which was first published in 1925. [PR5581.N53 1973] 72-2100 ISBN 0-8383-1458-9 11.95
1. Tennyson, Alfred Tennyson, Baron, 1809-1892.

PALMER, David John. 821'.8
Tennyson. Edited by D. J. Palmer. [Athens] Ohio University Press, 1973. xvi, 279 p. illus. 23 cm. (Writers and their background) Bibliography: p. [255]-265. [PR5588.P3] 72-95819 ISBN 0-8214-0116-5 10.00
1. Tennyson, Alfred Tennyson, Baron, 1809-1892.

RICHARDSON, Joanna. 821'.8 B
The pre-eminent Victorian; a study of Tennyson. Westport, Conn., Greenwood Press [1973, c1962] 313 p. port. 22 cm. Reprint of the ed. published by J. Cape, London. Bibliography: p. 297-306. [PR5581.R5 1973] 72-9727 ISBN 0-8371-6596-2 13.25
1. Tennyson, Alfred Tennyson, baron, 1809-1892. I. Title. BIP

RICKS, Christopher B. 821'.8
Tennyson [by] Christopher Ricks. New York, Macmillan [1972] xii, 349 p. 23 cm. (Masters of world literature series) Includes bibliographical references. [PR5581.R54] 76-165569 7.95
1. Tennyson, Alfred Tennyson, Baron, 1809-1892.

SIDGWICK, Arthur, 1840-1920. 821'.8 B
Tennyson. [Folcroft, Pa.] Folcroft Library Editions, 1973. 34 p. front. 23 cm. Reprint of the 1909 ed. published by Sidgwick and Jackson, London. Limited to 100 copies. [PR5588.S54 1973] 73-18305 4.50
1. Tennyson, Alfred Tennyson, Baron, 1809-1892.

TENNYSON, Charles, Sir, 1879- 821.8 B
Alfred Tennyson, by his grandson, Charles Tennyson. [Hamden, Conn.] Archon Books, 1968 [i.e. 1969, c1949] xv, 580 p. illus., ports. 23 cm. [PR5581.T38 1969] 74-2856 10.00
1. Tennyson, Alfred Tennyson, Baron, 1809-1892. BIP

TENNYSON, Emily Sellwood Tennyson, Baroness, 1813-1896. 821'.8 B
The letters of Emily Lady Tennyson. Edited with an introd. by James O. Hoge. University Park, Pennsylvania State University Press [1974] 404 p. illus. 24 cm. Bibliography: p. 377-379. [PR5581.A3 1974] 73-12629 ISBN 0-271-01123-8
1. Tennyson, Alfred Tennyson, Baron, 1809-1892. 2. Tennyson, Emily Sellwood Tennyson, Baroness, 1813-1896. I. Title. BIP

[TENNYSON, Hallam Tennyson, Baron] 1852-1928. 821'.8 B
Alfred Lord Tennyson; a memoir, by his son. Boston, Milford House [1973] 2 v. in 1. illus. 22 cm. Reprint of the 1897 ed. [PR5581.T4 1973] 77-165127 ISBN 0-87821-095-4 65.00
1. Tennyson, Alfred Tennyson, Baron, 1809-1892.

TENNYSON, Hallam Tennyson, Baron, 1852-1928. 821'.8 B
Alfred Lord Tennyson: a memoir, by his son. [Folcroft, Pa.] Folcroft Library Editions, 1973. p. Reprint of the 1906 ed. published by Macmillan, New York. [PR5581.T4 1973b] 73-11372 ISBN 0-8414-2689-9 (lib. bdg.)
1. Tennyson, Alfred Tennyson, Baron, 1809-1892.

TENNYSON, Hallam Tennyson, Baron, 1852-1928. 821'.8 B
Alfred Lord Tennyson; a memoir by his son. New York, Macmillan, 1897. St. Clair Shores, Mich., Scholarly Press, 1972. 2 v. illus. 22 cm. Includes bibliographical references. [PR5581.T4 1972] 71-115282 ISBN 0-403-00274-5 35.00
1. Tennyson, Alfred Tennyson, Baron, 1809-1892. I. Title. BIP

TENNYSON, Hallam Tennyson, baron, 1852-1928. 821'.8 B
Alfred Lord Tennyson; a memoir, by his son. New York, Greenwood Press [1969, c1897] 2 v. illus., geneal. table., ports. 23 cm. Bibliographical footnotes. [PR5581.T4 1969] 69-14111
1. Tennyson, Alfred Tennyson, baron, 1809-1892. I. Title.

TURNBULL, Arthur. 821'.8
Life and writings of Alfred, Lord Tennyson / by Arthur Turnbull. Folcroft, Pa. : Folcroft Library Editions, 1977. xi, 225 p. ; 23 cm. Reprint of the 1915 ed. published by the Walter Scott Pub. Co., London, in series: Great writers. Includes index. [PR5581.T8 1977] 77-22491 ISBN 0-8414-8636-0 lib. bdg. : 25.00
1. Tennyson, Alfred Tennyson, Baron, 1809-1892. 2. Poets, English—19th century—Biography. I. Title.

VAN DYKE, Henry, 1852-1933. 821.8
Studies in Tennyson. Port Washington, N.Y., Kennikat Press [1966, c1920] xi, 316 p. port. 19 cm. First published in 1889 under title: The poetry of Tennyson. "Chronology of Tennyson's life and works": p. [237]-273. [PR5588.V4 1966] 66-25949
1. Tennyson, Alfred Tennyson, baron, 1809-1892. I. Title. BIP

WALTERS, John Cuming. 821'.8 B
Tennyson: poet, philosopher, idealist; studies of the life, work, and teaching of the poet laureate. With a portrait on steel by Armytage after a photograph by Mrs. Cameron. New York, Haskell House, 1971. viii, 370 p. port. 23 cm. Includes bibliographical references. [PR5581.W3 1971] 70-153481 ISBN 0-8383-1238-1
1. Tennyson, Alfred Tennyson, Baron, 1809-1892.

WATSON, Aaron, 1850- 821'.8 B
Tennyson. [Folcroft, Pa.] Folcroft Library Editions, 1973. p. Reprint of the ed. published by T. C. & E. C. Jack, London. Bibliography: p. [PR5581.W47 1973] 73-13667 12.50
1. Tennyson, Alfred Tennyson, Baron, 1809-1892.

WATSON, Aaron, 1850- 821'.8 B
Tennyson. [Folcroft, Pa.] Folcroft Library Editions, 1974. 94 p. port. 23 cm. Reprint of the ed. published by T. C. & E. C. Jack, London. Includes bibliographical references. [PR5581.W47 1974] 73-13667 ISBN 0-8414-9406-1 (lib. bdg.)
1. Tennyson, Alfred Tennyson, Baron, 1809-1892.

Tennyson, Alfred Tennyson, Baron, 1809-1892—Biography.

HENDERSON, Philip. 821'.8 B
Tennyson, poet and prophet / Philip Henderson. London : Routledge & K. Paul, 1978. xix, 225 p., [7] leaves of plates : ill. ; 24 cm. Includes bibliographical references and index. [PR5581.H4] 78-307712 ISBN 0-7100-8776-4 : 16.95
1. Tennyson, Alfred Tennyson, Baron, 1809-1892—Biography. 2. Poets, Egnlsih—19th century—Biography. I. Title.
Distributed by Routledge Kegan Paul, Boston

Tennyson, Alfred Tennyson, Baron, 1809-1892—Friends and associates.

JENKINS, Elizabeth, 1907- 821'.8
Tennyson and Dr. Gully / Elizabeth Jenkins. Lincoln, Eng. : Tennyson Society, Tennyson Research Centre, 1974. 19 p. ; 23 cm. (Tennyson Society occasional papers ; no. 3) [PR5583.J4] 75-324929 ISBN 0-901958-12-3
1. Tennyson, Alfred Tennyson, Baron, 1809-1892—Friends and associates. 2. Gully, James Manby, 1808-1883. I. Title. II. Series: Tennyson Society, Lincoln, Eng. Tennyson Society occasional papers ; no. 3.

Tennyson, Alfred Tennyson, Baron, 1809-1892—Homes and haunts—England—Freshwater.

TENNYSON, Charles, Sir, 1879- 821'.8 B
Farringford : home of Alfred Lord Tennyson / by Charles Tennyson. Lincoln [Eng.] : Tennyson Society, Tennyson Research Centre, 1976. 24 p., [2] leaves of plates : ill. ; 23 cm. Tennyson, Alfred Tennyson, Baron, 1809-1892. [PR5584.T46] 77-370670 ISBN 0-901958-17-4
1. Tennyson, Alfred Tennyson, Baron, 1809-1892—Homes and haunts—England—Freshwater. 2. Freshwater, Eng. Farringford. I. Title.

Tennyson, Alfred Tennyson, Baron, 1809-1892—Homes and haunts—Somersby.

TENNYSON, Charles, Sir, 1879- 821'.8 B
Alfred Tennyson and Somersby / by Charles Tennyson. Rev. ed. Lincoln, Eng. : Tennyson Society, 1974. [16] p. : ill. ; 23 cm. [PR5584.T45 1974] 75-301733 ISBN 0-901958-11-5
1. Tennyson, Alfred Tennyson, Baron, 1809-1892—Homes and haunts—Somersby. 2. Somersby, Eng.—Description and travel. I. Title.

Tennyson, Alfred Tennyson, baron, 1890-1892—Juvenile literature.

HOPE, Charlotte 821.8
The young Tennyson. Illus. by William Randell. New York, Roy [1965, c.1964] 144p. illus. 21cm. [PR5582.H6] 65-188849 3.25 bds.,
1. Tennyson, Alfred Tennyson, baron, 1890-1892—Juvenile literature. I. Title.

Tennyson, Alfred Tennyson, Baron, 1809-1892—Religion and ethics.

SMYSER, William Emory, 1866-1935. 821'.8 B
Tennyson / by William Emory Smyser. Norwood, Pa. : Norwood Editions, 1976. p. cm. Reprint of the 1906 ed. published by Eaton & Mains, New York, issued in series: Modern poets and Christian teaching. Includes bibliographical references and index. [PR5592.R4S5 1976]

76-12988 ISBN 0-8482-2409-4 lib. bdg. : 25.00
1. Tennyson, Alfred Tennyson, Baron, 1809-1892—Religion and ethics. I. Series: Modern poets and Christian teaching.

Tennyson, Frederick, 1807-1898.

NICOLSON, Harold George, Sir, 1886-1968. 821'.8 B
Tennyson's two brothers. [Folcroft, Pa.] Folcroft Library Editions, 1973. p. Reprint of the 1947 ed. published by University Press, Cambridge, in series: Leslie Stephen lectures, 1947. [PR5599.T2Z75 1973] 73-13675 4.50
1. Tennyson, Frederick, 1807-1898. 2. Turner, Charles Tennyson, 1808-1879. I. Title. II. Series: Leslie Stephen lectures, 1947. BIP

Tennyson, Frederick, 1807-1898—Addresses, essays, lectures.

NICOLSON, Harold George, Sir, 1886-1968. 821'.8 B
Tennyson's two brothers / by Harold Nicolson. Norwood, Pa. : Norwood Editions, 1976. p. cm. Reprint of the 1947 ed. published at the University Press, Cambridge, which was issued as the 1947 Leslie Stephen lecture. [PR5599.T2Z75 1976] 76-10956 ISBN 0-8482-1910-4 lib. bdg. : 5.00
1. Tennyson, Frederick, 1807-1898—Addresses, essays, lectures. 2. Turner, Charles Tennyson, 1808-1879—Addresses, essays, lectures. I. Title. II. Series: Leslie Stephen lectures ; 1947.

Tenzing Norkey, 1914-

MALARTIC, Yves, 1910- 915.42
Tenzing of Everest. Translated from the French by Judith B. Heller. New York, Crown Publishers [1954] 285 p. illus. 22 cm. Translation of La conquete de l'Eversset par le Sherpa Tenzing. [DS486.E8M33] 54-12067
1. Tenzing Norkey, 1914- 2. Mount Everest Expedition, 1953. I. Title.

TENZING Norkey, 1914- 796.5'22'0924 B
After Everest : an autobiography / by Tenzing Norgay, Sherpa, as told to Malcolm Barnes. London : G. Allen & Unwin, 1977. 184 p., [12] leaves of plates : ill. (some col.) ; 23 cm. [GV199.92.T46] 77-365534 ISBN 0-04-920050-X : 11.50
1. Tenzing Norkey, 1914- 2. Mountaineers—Nepal—Biography. I. Barnes, Malcolm, 1909- II. Title.
Distributed by Allen and Unwin, 198 Ash St., Reading, MA 01867

Teresa,

TERESA, Saint, 1515-1582. 922.246
The letters of Saint Teresa of Jesus. Translated and edited by E. Allison Peers, from the critical ed. of P. Silverio de Santa Teresa. Westminster, Md., Newman Press [1950] 2 v. (xii, 1006 p.) 22 cm. [BX4700.T4A31] 52-8915
I. Title.

TERESA, Saint, 1515-1582. 922.246
The life of St. Teresa of Avila, including the relations of her spiritual state, written by herself. Translated from the Spanish by David Lewis. With an introd. by David Knowles. Westminster, Md., Newman Press [1962] 432 p. 20 cm. The Orchard books) [BX4700.T4A2 1962] 62-51605
I. Lewis, David, 1814-1895, tr. II. Title.

Teresa Margherita del Sacro Cuore di Gesu, Saint, 1747-1770.

TERESA MARGARET, Sister 922.245
God is love St. Teresa Margaret: her life. Milwaukee, Spiritual Life Pr., 1233 So. 45 St. [c.]1964. 168p. port. 23cm. 64-21566 1.95 pap.,
1. Teresa Margherita del Sacro Cuore di Gesu, Saint, 1747-1770. I. Title.

Teresa, Mother, 1910-

DOIG, Desmond. 266'.2'0924 B
Mother Teresa, her people and her work / Desmond Doig ; photos. by Raghu Rai ... [et al.]. 1st. U.S. ed. New York : Harper & Row, c1976. 175 p. : ill. (some col.) ; 25 cm. [BX4406.5.Z8D65 1976] 75-39857 ISBN 0-06-060560-X : 15.00
1. Teresa, Mother, 1910- I. Title.

MCGOVERN, James. 266'.2'0924 B
To give the love of Christ : a portrait of Mother Teresa and the Missionaries of Charity / by James McGovern. New York : Paulist Press, c1978. 109 p. ; 19 cm. (Emmaus books) [BX4705.T4455M32] 77-14832 ISBN 0-8091-2076-3 pbk. : 1.95
1. Teresa, Mother, 1910- 2. Missionaries of Charity—History 3. Nuns—India—Calcutta—Biography. 4. Calcutta—Biography. I. Title.

MUGGERIDGE, Malcolm, 1903- 266.2'0924 [B]
Something beautiful for God; Mother Teresa of Calcutta. New York, Ballantine [1973, c.1971] 156 p. illus. (1 col.) ports. 21 cm. [BX4406.5.Z8M8] ISBN 0-345-03276-4 2.00 (pbk.)
1. Teresa, Mother, 1910- 2. Missionaries of Charity. I. Title.
L.C. card no. for the hardbound ed.: 77155106. BIP

Teresa, Saint, 1515-1582.

AUCLAIR, Marcelle, 1899- 922.246
St. Teresa of Avila. Translation by Kathleen Pond; With a pref. by Andre Maurois. [New York] Pantheon [1953] 437p. illus. 22cm. Translation of La vie de sainte Therese d'Avila. [BX4700.T4A813] 53-6126
1. Teresa, Saint, 1515-1582. I. Title.

BEEVERS, John. 922.246
St. Teresa of Avila. [1st ed.] Garden City, N. Y., Hanover House [1961] 191p. 22cm. [BX4700.T4B37] 61-12492
1. Teresa, Saint, 1515-1582. I. Title.

BEEVERS, John Leonard 922.246
St. Teresa of Avila. Garden City, N.Y., Hanover House [c.1961] 191p. 61-12492 3.75
1. Teresa, Saint, 1515-1582. I. Title.

HAMILTON, Elizabeth, 1906- 922.246
Saint Teresa, a journey to Spain. New York, Scribner [1959] 192p. illus. 22cm. Includes bibliography. [BX4700.T4H3] 59-12684
1. Teresa, Saint, 1515-1582. I. Title.

KELLY, Joseph Patrick, 1902- 922.246
Meet Saint Teresa, an introduction to La Madre of Avila. New York, F. Pustet Co., 1958. 212p. illus. 21cm. Includes bibliography. [BX4700.T4K4] 58-49284
1. Teresa, Saint, 1515-1582. I. Title.

LOWRY, Walker. 271'.971'024 B
Teresa de Jesus : a secular appreciation / Walker Lowry. [New York : Lowry], 1977. 91 p. ; 27 cm. 125 copies. [BX4700.T4L68] 77-150320
1. Teresa, Saint, 1515-1582. 2. Christian saints—Spain—Avila—Biography. 3. Avila, Spain—Biography. I. Title.

NEVIN, Winifred. 922.246
Teresa of Avila, the woman. Milwaukee, Bruce Pub. Co. [1956] 169p. 22cm. [BX4700.T4N4] 56-7036
1. Teresa, Saint, 1515-1582. I. Title.

O'BRIEN, Kate, 1897- 922.246
Teresa of Avila. New York, Sheed & Ward [1951]wc96p. iii 19cm. (Personal portraits) [BX4700.T4O2] 51-13840
1. Teresa. Saint, 1515-1582. I. Title.

O'BRIEN, Kate, 1898- 922.246
Teresa of Avila. New York, Sheed & Ward [1951] 96 p. illus. 29 cm. (Personal portraits) [BX4700.T4O2] 51-13840
1. Teresa, Saint, 1515-1582. I. Title.

PAPASOGLI, Giorgio. 922.246
St. Teresa of Avila. Translated from the Italian by G. Anzilotto. New York, Society of St. Paul [c1959] 408p. illus. 22cm. Includes bibliography. [BX4700.T4P313] 58-12223
1. Teresa. Saint. 1515-1582. I. Title.

PEERS, Edgar Allison. 271.73
Handbook to the life and times of St. Teresa and St. John of the Cross. Westminster, Md., Newman Press [1954] vii, 277p. 23cm. Bibliographical footnotes. [BX3206] 54-10164
1. Teresa, Saint, 1515-1582. 2. Juan de la Cruz, Saint, 1542-1591. 3. Camelites—Hist. I. Title.

SCHMID, Evan 1920- 922.246
The eagle of Avila: a story of Saint Teresa, Illus. by Judith E. Quinn. Notre Dame, Dujarie Press [1956] 94p. illus. 24cm. [BX4700.T4S35] 56-23346
1. Teresa Saint, 1545-1582. I. Title.

TERESA, Saint, 1515-1582. 922.246
The letters of Saint Teresa of Jesus. Translated and edited by E. Allison Peers, from the critical ed. of P. Silverio de Santa Teresa. Westminster, Md., Newman Press [1950] 2 v. (xii, 1006 p.) 22 cm. [BX4700.T4A31] 52-8915
I. Title.

TERESA, Saint, 1515-1582. 922.246
The life of St. Teresa of Avila, including the relations of her spiritual state, written by herself. Translated from the Spanish by David Lewis. With an introd. by David Knowles. Westminster, Md., Newman Press [1962] 432 p. 20 cm. The Orchard books) [BX4700.T4A2 1962] 62-51605
I. Lewis, David, 1814-1895, tr. II. Title.

TERESA of Avila. v. 12
Translated by Kathleen Pond. With a preface by Andre Maurois. Garden City, N. Y., Image books (Doubleday co.) [1959, c1953] 480p. 18cm. (Image D79) Translation of La vie de Sainte Therese d' avila.
1. Teresa, Saint, 1515-1582. I. Auclair, Marcelle, 1899-

THOMAS, Father, ed. 922.246
St. Teresa of Avila studies in her life, doctrine, and times. Ed. by Father Thomas, Father Gabriel, Westminster, Md., Newman [1964] 249p. plates, ports. 23cm. Bibl. 64-969 4.75
1. Teresa, Saint. 1515-1582. 2. Mysticism—History of doctrines. I. Gabriele di Santa Maria Maddalena, Father Gabriel, joint ed. II. Title.

THOMAS, Father, ed. 922.246
St. Teresa of Avila; studies in her life, doctrine, and times. Edited by Father Thomas and Father Gabriel. Westminster, Md., Newman Press [1963] 249 p. plates, ports. 23 cm. Includes bibliographical references. [BX4700.T4T5] 64-969
1. Teresa, Saint, 1515-1582. 2. Mysticism — History of doctrines. I. Gabriele di Santa Maria Maddelena, Father, joint ed II. Title.

Teresa, Vincent Charles.

TERESA, Vincent Charles. 364.1'092'4 B
My life in the Mafia, by Vincent Teresa, with Thomas C. Renner. [1st ed.] Garden City, N.Y., Doubleday, 1973 x, 372 p. 22 cm. [HV6248.T27A3] 72-90972 ISBN 0-385-02718-4 8.95
1. Teresa, Vincent Charles. 2. Mafia. I. Renner, Thomas C., joint author. II. Title. BIP

Terhune, Albert Payson, 1872-1942.

UNKELBACH, Kurt. 813'.5'2 B
Albert Payson Terhune, the master of Sunnybank. New York, Charterhouse [1972] viii, 180 p. 22 cm. On spine: Albert Payson Terhune, a centennial biography. "The books of Albert Payson Terhune": p. 175-177. A biography of the author and dog-breeder who created many animal stories including "Lad:A Dog." [PS3539.E65Z9] 92 72-84215 4.95
1. Terhune, Albert Payson, 1872-1942. I. Title.

Terhune, Albert Payson, 1872-1942—Biography.

LITVAG, Irving. 813'.5'2 B
The master of Sunnybank, a biography of Albert Payson Terhune / Irving Litvag. 1st ed. New York : Harper & Row, c1977. x, 307 p., [4] leaves of plates : ill. ; 24 cm. Includes index. [PS3539.E65Z75] 76-10071 ISBN 0-06-126350-8 : 10.95
1. Terhune, Albert Payson, 1872-1942—Biography. 2. Authors, American—20th century—Biography. I. Title.

Terkel, Louis.

TERKEL, Louis. 070'.92'4 B
Talking to myself : a memoir of my times / Studs Terkel. 1st ed. New York : Pantheon Books, c1977. xiv, 316 p. ; 24 cm. [PN1990.72.T4A37] 76-54308 ISBN 0-394-41102-1 : 10.00
1. Terkel, Louis. 2. Broadcasters—United States—Biography. 3. Authors, American—20th century—Biography. BIP

TERKEL, Louis. 070'.92'4
Talking to myself : a memoir of my times / Studs Terkel 1st d. New York : Pocket Books, 1978,c1977. 323p. ; 18 cm. (A Kangaroo Book) [PN1990.72T4A37] ISBN 0-671-82054-0 pbk. : 2.50
1. Terkel, Louis. 2. Broadcasters-United States-Biography. 3. Authors, American-20th century-Biography. I. Title.
L.C. card no. for 1977 Pantheon d.. 76-54308.

Terrell, Mary (Church)

SHEPPERD, Gladys Byram. 923.673
Mary Church Terrell, respectable person. Baltimore, Human Relations Press 1959. 125 p. illus. 24 cm. Includes bibliography. [[E185.97.T17S48]] 60-1961
1. Terrell, Mary (Church) I. Title.

Terrell, Mary (Church) 1863-1954—Juvenile literature.

STERLING, Dorothy, 1913- 920.073
Lift every voice; the lives of Booker T. Washington, W. E. B. Du Bois, Mary Church Terrell, and James Weldon Johnson [by] Dorothy Sterling and Benjamin Quarles. Illustrated by Ernest Crichlow. [1st ed.] Garden City, N.Y., Doubleday, 1965. 116 p. illus., ports. 22 cm. (Zenith books) [E185.96.S77] 65-17237
1. Washington, Booker Taliaferro, 1859-1915—Juvenile literature. 2. Du Bois, William Edward Burghardt, 1868-1963—Juvenile literature. 3. Terrell, Mary (Church) 1863-1954—Juvenile literature. 4. Johnson, James Weldon, 1871-1938—Juvenile literature. I. Quarles, Benjamin, joint author. II. Title.

Terry, Alfred Howe, 1827-1890.

BAILEY, John W., 1934- 970'.004'97
Pacifying the plains : General Alfred Terry and the decline of the Sioux, 1866-1890 / John W. Bailey. Westport, Conn. : Greenwood Press, c1979. xiv, 236 p. : ill. : 27 cm. (Contributions in military history ; no. 17) ISSN 0084-9251) Includes index. Bibliography: p. [209]-226. [E99.D1B17] 78-19300 ISBN 0-313-20625-2 : 18.95
1. Terry, Alfred Howe, 1827-1890. 2. United States. Army—Biography. 3. Dakota Indians—Government relations—1869-1934. 4. Dakota Indians—Wars, 1866-1895. 5. Indians of North America—The West—Government relations—1869-1934. 6. Generals—United States—Biography. I. Title. II. Series. BIP

Terry, David Smith, 1823-1889.

BUCHANAN, Albert Russell, 1906- 923.273
David S. Terry of California, dueling judge. San Marino, Calif., Huntington Library, 1956. ix, 238p. 24cm. (Huntington Library publications) Bibliographical footnotes. [F864.T325] 56-10065
1. Terry, David Smith, 1823-1889. I. Title. II. Series: Henry E. Huntington Library and Art Gallery, San Marino, Calif. Huntington Library publications

WAGSTAFF, Alexander E., comp. 347'.794'03534 B
The life of David S. Terry, presenting an

authentic, impartial, and vivid history of his eventful life & tragic death, compiled and edited by A. E. Wagstaff. With a new introd.: Due process for the dead? by Eleazar Lipsky. South Hackensack, N.J., Rothman Reprints, 1971. 33, xvi, 15-526 p. illus., ports. 22 cm. Reprint of the 1892 ed., with a new introd. [KF368.T4W35 1971] 75-112407 ISBN 0-678-04541-0
1. Terry, David Smith, 1823-1889. I. Title.

Terry, Ellen, Dame, 1848-1928.

FECHER, 792'.028'0924 B
Constance, 1911-
Bright Star; a portrait of Ellen Terry. New York, Farrar, Straus & Girouz [1970] 236 p. illus., ports. 21 cm. (An Ariel book) Bibliography: p. [229]-230. [PN2598.T4F4] 70-125151 4.95
1. Terry, Ellen, Dame, 1848-1928. I. Title.

MANVELL, Roger, 1909- 792'.0924 B
Ellen Terry. [1st American ed.] New York, Putnam [1968] x, 390 p. illus., ports. 22 cm. Bibliography: p. [373]-375. [PN2598.T4M33 1968] 68-12102
1. Terry, Ellen, Dame, 1848-1928.

PRIDEAUX, Tom. 792'.028'0924 B
Love or nothing : the life and times of Ellen Terry / Tom Prideaux. New York : Scribner, [1975] x, 288 p., [8] leaves of plates : ill. ; 24 cm. Includes index. [PN2598.T4P7] 75-19175 ISBN 0-684-14380-1 : 10.00
1. Terry, Ellen, Dame, 1848-1928. I. Title.

TERRY, Ellen, 792'.028'0924 B
Dame, 1848-1928.
Ellen Terry's memoirs; with a pref., notes and additional biographical chapters, by Edith Craig and Christopher St. John. Westport, Conn., Greenwood Press [1970] xv, 367 p. illus., facsim., ports. 23 cm. Reprint of the 1932 ed. of Ellen Terry's autobiography, first published in 1908 under the title The story of my life. [PN2598.T4A3 1970] 77-100210 ISBN 0-8371-4039-0
1. Actresses—Correspondence, reminiscences, etc. I. Craig, Edith, 1869-1947. II. St. John, Christopher Marie.

TERRY, Ellen, 792'.028'0924 B
Dame, 1848-1928.
Ellen Terry's memoirs. With a pref., notes, and additional biographical chapters by Edith Craig and Christopher St. John. London, 1932. New York, B. Blom, 1969. xiii, 367 p. illus., facsims., ports. 24 cm. "A new edition of The story of my life, by Ellen Terry, London, 1908. With a collection of illustrations taken from the first limited edition of 1908." [PN2598.T4A3 1969] 74-77976
1. Actors—Correspondence, reminiscences, etc. I. Craig, Edith, 1869-1947. II. St. John, Christopher Marie. BIP

Terry family.

STEEN, 792'.028'0922 B
Marguerite.
A pride of Terrys : family saga / Marguerite Steen. Westport, Conn. : Greenwood Press, 1978, c1962. xvi, 412 p., [11] leaves of plates : ill. ; 24 cm. Reprint of the ed. published by Longmans, London. Includes index. Bibliography; p. xv-xvi. [PN2597.S8 1978] 77-18754 ISBN 0-313-20221-4 lib.bdg. : 21.50
1. Terry family. 2. Terry, Ellen, Dame, 1848-1928. 3. Theater—Great Britain—Biography. I. Title. BIP

Terry, Louisa (Ward), 1823-1897.

THARP, Louise (Hall) 929'.2'0973
1898-
Three saints and a sinner; Julia Ward Howe, Louisa, Annie, and Sam Ward. [1st ed.] Boston, Little, Brown [1956] 406 p. illus. 23 cm. Includes bibliography. [CS71.W26 1956] 56-10638
1. Howe, Julia (Ward) 1849-1910. 2. Terry, Louisa (Ward), 1823-1897. 3. Mailliard, Anne Eliza (Ward) 1824-1895. 4. Ward, Samuel, 1814-1884. I. Title.

THARP, Louise (Hall) 929'.2'0973
1898-
Three saints and a sinner: Julia Ward Howe, Louisa, Annie, Sam Ward. [1st ed.] Boston, Little, Brown [1956] 406 p. illus. 23 cm. Includes bibliography. [CS71.W26 1956] 56-10638
1. Howe, Julia (Ward) 1819-1910. 2. Terry, Louisa (Ward) 1823-1897. 3. Mailliard, Anne Eliza (Ward) 1824-1895. 4. Ward, Samuel, 1814-1884. I. Title.

Terry, Ronald.

TERRY, Ronald. 362.2'92'0926
The long suffering / by Ronald Terry. New York : Paulist Press, c1976. 77 p. ; 22 cm. [HV5060.T43] 75-32308 ISBN 0-8091-1914-5 pbk. : 3.95
1. Terry, Ronald. 2. Alcoholics—Biography. I. Title. BIP

Tertis, Lionel, 1876-

TERTIS, Lionel, 787'.2'0924 B
1876-1975.
My viola and I : a complete autobiography : with Beauty of tone in string playing and other essays / Lionel Tertis. 1st U.S. ed. Boston : Crescendo Pub. Co., 1975, c1974. xv, 184 p., [4] leaves of plates : ill., ports ; 23 cm. Includes index. "Works for viola solo": p. 171-174. [ML418.T47A36 1974b] 75-322775 ISBN 0-87597-098-2 : 8.75
1. Tertis, Lionel, 1876- 2. Violinists, violoncellists, etc.—Correspondence, reminiscences, etc. 3. Stringed instruments, Bowed—Instruction and study. I. Tertis, Lionel, 1876-1975. Beauty of tone in string playing. 1975. II. Title.

Tesla, Nikola, 1856-1943.

BECKHARD, Arthur J. 926.2
Electrical genius Nikola Tesla. New York, Messner [1959] 192 p. 22 cm. [TK140.T4B4] 59-7009
1. Tesla, Nikola, 1856-1943. I. Title.

BECKHARD, Arthur J. 621.3'0924 B
Electrical genius Nikola Tesla. New York, Messner [1959] 192 p. 22 cm. A biography of the electrical engineer whose inventions included an amplifier, an arc light, transformers, Tesla coils, rotating magnetic field motors for alternating current, and others. [TK140.T4B4] 92 AC 68
1. Tesla, Nikola, 1856-1943. I. Title.

HUNT, Inez. 926.2
Lightening in his hand; the life story of Nikola Tesla, by Inez Hunt and Wanetta W. Draper. Denver, Sage Books [1964] 269 p. illus., port. 23 cm. Bibliography: p. 250-263. [TK140.T4H8] 64-66184
1. Tesla, Nikola, 1856-1943. I. Draper, Wanetta W., joint author. II. Title.

HUNT, Inez 926.2
Lightning in his hand; the life story of Nikola Tesla, by Inez Hunt, Wanetta W. Draper. Denver, Sage [dist. Swallow, c.1964] 269p. illus., port. 23cm. Bibl. [TK140.T4H8] 64-66184 5.00
1. Tesla, Nikola, 1856-1943. I. Draper, Wanetta W., joint author. II. Title.

NIKOLA Tesla : 621.3'092'4 B
life and work of a genius / editorial board, Vojin Popovic ... [et al.]. Belgrade : Yugoslav Society for the Promotion of Scientific Knowledge Nikola Tesla, 1976. 107 p. : ports. ; 20 cm. Includes bibliographical references. [TK140.T4N48] 76-378419
1. Tesla, Nikola, 1856-1943. 2. Electric engineers—United States—Biography. 3. Electric engineering—History. I. Popovic, Vojin S.

WALTERS, Helen B. 926.2
Nikola Tesla, giant of electricity. Illus. by Leonard Everett Fisher. New York, Crowell [c.1961] 189p. illus. Bibl. 61-14531 3.50
1. Tesla, Nikola, 1856-1943. I. Title.

WALTERS, Helen B 926.2
Nikola Tesla, giant of electricity. Illustrated by Leonard Everett Fisher. New York, Crowell [1961] 180 p. illus. 21 cm. Includes bibliography. [TK140.T4W3] 61-14531
1. Tesla, Nikola, 1856-1943. I. Title.

Tester, M. H.

TESTER, M. H. 615'.852'0924 B
The healing touch [by] M. H. Tester. New York, Taplinger Pub. Co. [1970] 154 p. illus. 23 cm. [RZ408.T47A3 1970] 70-119621
I. Title. BIP

Tetrazzini, Lusia, 1871-1940.

TETRAZZINI, Luisa, 782.1'092'4 B
1871-1940.
My life of song / Luisa Tetrazzini. New York : Arno Press, 1977. 328 p., [8] leaves of plates : ill. ; 23 cm. (Opera biographies) Reprint of the 1921 ed. published by Cassell, London, New York. Includes index. [ML420.T36A3 1977] 76-29970 ISBN 0-405-09709-3 : 21.00
1. Tetrazzini, Lusia, 1871-1940. 2. Singers—Italy—Biography. I. Title. BIP

Tettemer, John Moyniahn, 1876-1949.

TETTEMER, John 271'.62'024 B
Moynihan, 1876-1949.
I was a monk; the autobiography of John Tettemer. Edited by Janet Mabie, with a foreword by Jean Burden and an introd. by John Burton. Wheaton, Ill. [Published by Pyramid Publications for the Theosophical Pub. House, 1974, c1951] 255 p. 18 cm. (Re-quest books) [BX4668.3.T47A34 1974] 73-89888 ISBN 0-8356-0300-8 1.25 (pbk.)
1. Tettemer, John Moyniahn, 1876-1949. I. Title.

Texas—Hist.—Sources.

HOUSTON, Samuel, 1793- 923.273
1863.
The autobiography of Sam Houston, edited by Donald Day & Harry Herbert Ullom. [1st ed.] Norman, University of Oklahoma Press [1954] xviii, 298p. illus., ports., maps. 25cm. Bibliography: p. 283-289. [F390.H8474] 54-10051
1. Texas—Hist.—Sources. I. Day, Donald, 1899- ed. II. Ullom, Harry Herbert, ed. III. Title.

Texas—Hist.—1846—

SHEFFY, Lester Fields. 923.373
The life and times of Timothy Dwight Hobart, 1855-1935. Colonization of West Texas. Canyon, Texas, Panhandle-Plains Historical Society, 1950. 322p. plates, ports., map (on lining papers) 24cm. Bibliography: p.[310]-313. [F391.H74S5] 54-38240
1. Texas—Hist.—1846- I. Hobart, Timothy Dwight, 1855-1935. II. Title. III. Title: Colonization of West Texas.

Texas—Biography.

BURNETT, Arthur 920.0764
Constant, 1885-
Yankees in the Republic of Texas; some notes on their origin and impact. Houston, Tex., Anson Jones Press for the Harris County Historical Society [1952] 62p. 24cm. [F389.B96] 53-18468
1. Texas-Biog. 2. New Englanders in Texas. I. Harris County Tex Historical Society. II. Title.

HEROES of Texas. 920.0764
Featuring oil portraits from the Summerfield G. Roberts collection. Introd. by Evelyn Oppenheimer. Dedication by Paul A. Loftin. Biographies by H. Bailey Carroll [and others] [1st ed.] Waco, Texian Press, 1964. xv, 142 p. illus., ports. (part col.) 29 cm. Portraits by Charles B. Normann. [F385.H4] 64-56351
1. Texas—Biography. 2. Texas—History—To 1846. I. Roberts, Summerfield G. II. Carroll, Horace Bailey, 1903- III. Normann, Charles B.

INSTITUTE of Texan 920'.0764
Cultures.
The Anglo-American Texans. [San Antonio] : University of Texas at San Antonio, Institute of Texan Cultures, [1975]. 32 p. : ill. ; 22 x 28 cm. (The Texians and the Texans) Cover title. [F385.I57 1975] 76-354177
1. Texas—Biography. 2. Texas—History. I. Title. II. Series.

INTERNATIONAL 920.0764
Biographical Research Corporation.
Who's who in Texas today. 1st- ed.; Austin, Pemberton Press. 1968 v. illus. (part col.) 26 cm. Vols. for 1968- prepared by the International Biographical Research Corporation. [F385.W55] 68-20724
1. Texas—Biog. I. Title.

OUTSTANDING young 976.4'0099'2 B
Texans / editor, Garland A. Smith, associate editor, Hugh Williamson ; field representative, Monroe Weyel. Austin, Tex. : Garland A. Smith Associates, c1976. 249 p. : ports. ; 29 cm. Includes index. [F385.O94] 75-39540
1. Texas—Biography. I. Smith, Garland A. II. Williamson, Hugh, 1907-

RICKARD, John Alison, 920.0764
1892-
Famous Texans. Dallas, B. Upshaw [1955] 367p. illus. 23cm. [F385.R5] 55-43958
1. Texas—Biog. I. Title.

WELCH, June Rayfield, 917.64'03
1927-
People and places in the Texas past / by June Rayfield Welch. Dallas : G. L. A. Press, 1974. viii, 233 p. : ill. ; 29 cm. Includes index. Bibliography: p. 217-226. [F385.W44] 74-19747 13.95
1. Texas—Biography. 2. Texas—History—Miscellanea. I. Title. BIP

WHO'S who in Texas 920.0764
today. 1st- ed.; 1968- Austin, Pemberton Pr. v. illus. (pt. col.) 26cm. Vols. for 1968- prepd. by the Intl. Biographical Res. Corp. [F385.W55] 68-20724 25.00
1. Texas—Biog. I. International Biographical Research Corporation.
Publisher's address: 1. Pemberton Pkway., Austin, Tex. 78703.

Texas—Biography—Juvenile literature.

ALLEN, Edward, 976.4'03'0922
1929-
Heroes of Texas. Illustrated by Paul Frame. New York, J. Messner [1970] 94 p. illus., ports. 22 cm. Contents.Contents.—Adventurous dreamer: Moses Austin.—The father of Texas: Stephen F. Austin.—The men of the Alamo: Travis, Bowie, Crockett.—General and statesman: Sam Houston.—Builder of a new nation: Mirabeau B. Lamar. [F385.A74] 920 72-102183 3.95
1. Texas—Biography—Juvenile literature. I. Frame, Paul, illus. II. Title.

KUBIAK, Daniel 976.4'04'0922
James
Ten tall Texans. San Antonio, Naylor [1967] xx, 132p. illus., ports. 22cm. [F385.K8] 67-17177 4.95
1. Texas—Biog.—Juvenile literature. I. Title.
Contents omitted.

KUBIAK, Daniel 976.4'04'0922
James.
Ten tall Texans. [Rev. and enl. ed.] San Antonio, Naylor Co. [1970] xx, 144 p. illus., ports. 22 cm. Contents.Contents.—Time and place.—Sam Houston.—Lorenzo de Zavala.—Stephen F. Austin.—Jose Antonio Navarro.—Ben Milam.—Andrea Castanon Candelaria.—David Crockett.—James (Jim) Bowie.—Juan N. Seguin.—William B. Travis.—Texans all.—Bibliography (p. 137-140) [F385.K8 1970] 920 70-10532 5.95
1. Texas—Biography—Juvenile literature. I. Title.

MCCALL, Edith S. 976.4'00922
Stalwart men of early Texas, by Edith McCall. Illustrated by Lou Aronson. Chicago, Childrens Press [1970] 127 p. illus. 21 cm. (Her Frontiers of America) Brief biographies of six men who explored and founded settlements in early Texas. Included are Cabeza de Vaca, Robert La Salle, and Moses Austin. [F385.M22] 920 78-101296
1. Texas—Biography—Juvenile literature. I. Aronson, Lou, illus. II. Title. BIP

Texas—Description and travel.

LUNDY, Benjamin, 1789-1839. 973.7114'0924 B
The life, travels, and opinions of Benjamin Lundy; including his journeys to Texas and Mexico, with a sketch of contemporary events, and a notice of the revolution in Hayti. Compiled under the direction and on behalf of his children [by Thomas Earle] New York, Negro Universities Press [1969] 316 p. map, port. 23 cm. Reprint of the 1847 ed. [E446.L955 1969] 70-92750
1. Texas—Description and travel. 2. Mexico—Description and travel. 3. Slavery in the United States—Anti-slavery movement. I. Earle, Thomas, 1796-1849, comp. II. Title.
BIP

LUNDY, Benjamin, 1789-1839. 973.71'14'0924 B
The life, travels and opinions of Benjamin Lundy, compiled by Thomas Earle, 1847. With the addition of his pamphlet The war in Texas [by a citizen of the United States] 1836. New York, A. M. Kelley, 1971. 316, 56 p. fold. map, port. 22 cm. (America through European eyes) [E446.L956 1971] 76-136302 ISBN 0-678-00809-4
1. Texas—Description and travel. 2. Mexico—Description and travel. 3. Slavery in the United States—Anti-slavery movements. 4. Texas—History—Revolution, 1835-1836. I. Earle, Thomas, 1796-1849, comp. II. A citizen of the United States. III. Title: The war in Texas.
BIP

Texas—Governors—Biography.

PHARES, Ross. 976.4'00992 B
The Governors of Texas / by Ross Phares. Gretna : Pelican Pub. Co., 1976. p. cm. (The Pelican governors series) Includes index. Bibliography: p. Short biographies with photos of all the governors of Texas during its French, Spanish, and Mexican periods, its interval as a Republic, and its statehood. [F385.P45] 920 76-7013 ISBN 0-88289-078-6 : 12.95
1. Texas—Governors—Biography. I. Title.
BIP

†WELCH, June Rayfield, 1927- 976.4'06'0922 B
The Texas governor / by June Rayfield Welch. Dallas : G.L.A. Press, c1977. viii, 198 p. : ill. ; 29 cm. Includes index. Bibliography: p. 187-191. [F385.W45] 77-93050 ISBN 0-912854-09-X : 13.95
1. Texas—Governors—Biography. I. Title.
Publisher's address : P.O. Box 5312, Irving, TX 75062
BIP

Texas—Governors—Wives—Biography.

FARRELL, Mary D. 976.4'0099'2 B
First ladies of Texas : the first one hundred years, 1836-1936 : a history / Mary D. Farrell and Elizabeth Silverthorne ; [sketches of first ladies by Marty Stephens] . Belton, Tex. : Stillhouse Hollow Publishers, c1976. xiv, 427 p. : ill. ; 23 cm. Bibliography: p. [401]-427. [F385.F35] 76-14700
1. Texas—Governors—Wives—Biography. I. Silverthorne, Elizabeth, joint author. II. Title.

Texas—History—To 1846.

ZUBER, William Physick, 1820-1913. 976.4'4'0924 B
My eighty years in Texas. Edited by Janis Boyle Mayfield. With notes and an introd. by Llerena Friend. Austin, University of Texas Press [1971] xvii, 285 p. port. 24 cm. (Personal narratives of the West) Compiled from the original ms. in the Texas State Archives. Appendices (p. 247-262):—A. An escape from the Alamo.—B. Historiography of the account of Moses Rose and the line that Travis drew, by Llerena Friend. "Bibliography, compiled by Llerena Friend": p. [263]-270. [F390.Z815 1971] 73-161971 ISBN 0-292-70050-4 7.50
1. Texas—History—To 1846. 2. Texas—History—1846-1865. I. Mayfield, Janis Boyle, ed. II. Title.
BIP

Texas Rangers.

PIKE, James, 1834-1867. 976.4'05'0924 B
Scout and ranger; being the personal adventures of James Pike of the Texas Rangers in 1859-60, reprinted from the ed. of 1865, with introd. and notes by Carl L. Cannon. New York, Da Capo Press, 1972 [c1932] xxviii, 164 p. illus. 22 cm. (Narratives of the trans-Mississippi frontier) (The American scene: comments and commentators) [F391.P63 1972] 74-39282 ISBN 0-306-70458-7
1. Texas Rangers. 2. Indians of North America—Wars—1815-1875. I. Title.

Texas Rangers—Biography.

RANGERS of Texas 976.4'04'0922
[by] Roger N. Conger [and others]. Foreword by Wilson E. Speir. Introd. by Rupert N. Richardson. Original paintings by David Sanders. [1st ed.] Waco, Tex., Texian Press, 1969. xxv, 159 p. illus., col. plates. 29 cm. [F391.R2] 75-98305 10.00
1. Texas Rangers—Biography. I. Conger, Roger Norman.

Texas—Social life and customs.

GROWING up in Texas; 917.64'03'60922
recollections of childhood, by Bertha McKee Dobie [and others] With woodcuts by Barbara Mathews Whitehead. [1st ed.] Austin, Encino Press, 1972. 153 p. illus. 24 cm. [F391.G86] 73-160697 7.95
1. Texas—Social life and customs. 2. Texas—Biography. I. Dobie, Bertha (McKee) 1890-

Texas. University at Arlington—Faculty.

ROBINSON, Duncan W. 378.1'2'0924 B
Duncan Robinson, Texas teacher & humanist : collected writings of Duncan Robinson, professor emeritus, University of Texas at Arlington / edited by Thomas Sutherland & Benjamin Capps. 1st ed. [Arlington] : University of Texas at Arlington, Dept. of English, c1976. xiii, 321 p. ; 24 cm. [LD5315.R6] 76-46649
1. Texas. University at Arlington—Faculty. 2. Robinson, Duncan W. 3. Educators—United States—Biography. I. Title.

Texas. University at Austin—Track-athletics.

STOWERS, Carlton. 796.4'2'0976431
Champions : University of Texas track and field / by Carlton Stowers and Wilbur Evans. Huntsville, Ala. : Strode Publishers, c1978. 415 p. : ill. ; 24 cm. [GV1060.62.T4S76] 77-79833 ISBN 0-87397-130-2 : 9.95
1. Texas. University at Austin—Track-athletics. 2. Track and field athletes—United States—Biography. I. Evans, Wilbur, 1913- joint author. II. Title.

Texas. Woman's university, Denton.

HUBBARD, Louis Herman, 1882- 923.773
Recollections of a Texas educator. Salado, Tex., Author, 1964. 287p. illus., facsim., ports. 25cm. Autobiographical. 64-56479 price unreported
1. Texas. Woman's university, Denton. I. Title.
BIP

Textile industry—United States—Biography.

LEADERS in the textile industry 338.4'7'67700922 B
/ Laurence A. Christiansen, Jr., editor, Richard G. Mansfield and Theodor V. Shumeyko, associate editors. New York : McGraw-Hill, c1978. p. cm. [HD9860.L4] 78-1676 ISBN 0-07-063721-0 : 35.00
1. Textile industry—United States—Biography. I. Christiansen, Laurence A. II. Mansfield, Richard G. III. Shumeyko, Theodor V.

Teyte, Maggie, Dame, 1888-1976.

O'CONNOR, Garry. 782.1'092'4 B
The pursuit of perfection : a life of Maggie Teyte / by Garry O'Connor. 1st American ed. New York : Atheneum, 1979. 327 p., [12] leaves of plates : ill. ; 25 cm. Discography: p. [300]-314. [ML420.T39O3 1979b] 78-20366 ISBN 0-689-10964-4 : 12.95
1. Teyte, Maggie, Dame, 1888-1976. 2. Teyte, Maggie, Dame, 1888-1976—Discography. 3. Singers—England—Biography. I. Title.
BIP

TEYTE, Maggie. 782.1'092'4 B
Star on the door / Maggie Teyte. New York : Arno Press, 1977, c1958. 192 p., [6] leaves of plates : ill. ; 24 cm. (Opera biographies) Reprint of the ed. published by Putnam, London. Discography: p. 188-192. [ML420.T39A3 1977] 76-29971 ISBN 0-405-09710-7 : 12.00
1. Teyte, Maggie. 2. Singers—England—Biography. I. Title.
BIP

Thacher, James, 1754-1844.

THACHER, James, 1754-1844. 973.33'7
Military journal of the American Revolution. [New York] New York times [1969] xiv, 538 p. illus., ports. 24 cm. (Eyewitness accounts of the American Revolution) Reprint of the 1862 ed. [E275.T3642] 74-79946
1. Thacher, James, 1754-1844. 2. Washington, George, Pres. U.S., 1732-1799. 3. United States—History—Revolution, 1775-1783—Personal narratives. 4. United States—History—Revolution, 1775-1783—Biography. I. Title. II. Series.
BIP

THACHER, James, 1754-1844. 973.3'3
Military journal of the American Revolution, from the commencement to the disbanding of the American Army; comprising a detailed account of the principal events and battles of the Revolution, with their exact dates, and a biographical sketch of the most prominent generals. To which is added the life of Washington, his farewell address, the Declaration of Independence, and the Constitution of the United States. Boston, Milford House [1974, c1861] p. First ed. published in 1823 under title: A military journal during the American Revolutionary War. Reprint of the 1862 ed. published by Hurlbut, Williams, Hartford. [E275.T3643] 67-307867 ISBN 0-87821-069-5 35.00
1. Thacher, James, 1754-1844. 2. Washington, George, Pres. U.S., 1732-1799. 3. United States—History—Revolution, 1775-1783—Personal narratives. 4. United States—History—Revolution, 1775-1783—Biography. I. Title.

Thackeray, William Makepeace, 1811-1863.

BENJAMIN, Lewis Saul, 1847-1932. 823'.8 B
William Makepeace Thackeray; a biography including hitherto uncollected letters & speeches & a bibliography of 1300 items, by Lewis Saul Benjamin (pseud. Lewis Melville). London, J. Lane, 1910. Grosse Pointe, Mich., Scholarly Press, 1968. 2 v. illus., facsims., ports. 23 cm. "The bibliography of William Makepeace Thackeray": v 2, p. [143]-347. [PR5631.B5 1968] 73-8577
1. Thackeray, William Makepeace, 1811-1863.
BIP

CHESTERTON, Gilbert Keith, 1874-1936. 823'.8 B
Thackeray, by G. K. Chesterton and Lewis Melville. London, Hodder and Stoughton, 1903. [Folcroft, Pa.] Folcroft Library Editions, 1974. iv, 40 p. illus. 29 cm. Reprint of the 1903 ed. published by Hodder and Stoughton, London. [PR5631.C5 1972] 72-12906 ISBN 0-8414-1025-9 (lib. bdg.)
1. Thackeray, William Makepeace, 1811-1863. I. Benjamin, Lewis Saul, 1874-1932, joint author.

CURLING, Audrey 92
The young Thackeray. Illus. by Denise Brown. New York, Roy [1966] 136p. illus. 21cm. [PR5631.C8] 66-22230 3.25 bds.,
1. Thackeray, William Makepeace, 1811-1863—Juvenile literature. I. Title.

ELWIN, Malcolm, 1902- 823.8
Thackeray, a personality. New York, Russell & Russell, 1966. 410 p. port. 23 cm. First published in 1932. Bibliography: p. 372-392. [PR5631.E5 1966] 66-15427
1. Thackeray, William Makepeace, 1811-1863. I. Title.

[GREGO, Joseph] 1843-1908, comp. 823'.8
Thackerayana; notes and anecdotes. Illustrated by hundreds of sketches by William Makepeace Thackeray, depicting humorous incidents in his school life, and favourite scenes and characters in the books of his every-day reading. A new ed. New York, Haskell House, 1971. xiv, 494 p. illus. 23 cm. Reprint of the 1901 ed. [PR5631.G7 1971] 71-137436 ISBN 0-8383-1191-1
1. Thackeray, William Makepeace, 1811-1863. I. Title.

GREIG, John Young Thomson, 1891- 823'.8
Thackeray; a reconsideration [by] J. Y. T. Greig. [Hamden, Conn.] Archon Books, 1967. vii, 215 p. 22 cm. Reprint of the 1950 ed. Bibliography: p. 191-194. [PR5631.G73 1967] 67-19515
1. Thackeray, William Makepeace, 1811-1863.
BIP

GULLIVER, Harold Strong, 1893- 823'.8
Thackeray's literary apprenticeship : a study of the early newspaper and magazine work of William Makepeace Thackeray, including previous unknown poems, humorous sketches, art criticism, and book reviews : making material additions to the Thackeray bibliography / by Harold Strong Gulliver. Folcroft, Pa. : Folcroft Library Editions, 1979 [c1934] p. cm. Reprint of the ed. printed by Southern Stationery and Print. Co., Valdosta, Ga. Originally presented as the author's thesis, Yale, 1930. Includes index. Bibliography: p. [PR5632.G8 1979] 79-23894 ISBN 0-8414-4631-8 (lib. bdg.) : 30.00
1. Thackeray, William Makepeace, 1811-1863. 2. Authors, English—19th century—Biography. I. Title.

MERIVALE, Herman Charles, 1839-1906. 823'.8 B
Life of W. M. Thackeray, by Herman Merivale and Frank T. Marzials. [Folcroft, Pa.] Folcroft Library Editions, 1973. p. Reprint of the 1891 ed. published by W. Scott, London, in series: Great writers.

[PR5631.M5 1973] 73-14525 ISBN 0-8414-6032-9 (lib. bdg.)
1. Thackeray, William Makepeace, 1811-1863. I. Marzials, Frank Thomas, 1840-1912, joint author. II. Title. BIP

RAY, Gordon Norton, 1915- 928.2
The buried life; a study of the relation between Thackeray's fiction and his personal history. London, Published for the Royal Society of Literature by Oxford University Press, 1952. vi, 148p. group port., geneal. table. 22cm. Bibliographical references included in 'Notes' (p. [128]-142) [PR5631.R3 1952a] 53-25502
1. Thackeray, William Makepeace, 1811-1863. I. Title.

RAY, Gordon Norton, 1915- 823'.8 B
The buried life; a study of the relation between Thackeray's fiction and his personal history, by Gordon N. Ray. New York, Haskell House, 1974. vi, 148 p. 22 cm. Reprint of the 1952 ed. published for the Royal Society of Literature by G. Cumberlege, Oxford University Press, London. Includes bibliographical references. [PR5631.R3 1974] 74-6372 ISBN 0-8383-1984-X
1. Thackeray, William Makepeace, 1811-1863. I. Title. BIP

RAY, Gordon Norton, 1915- 823'.8
The buried life; a study of the relation between Thackeray's fiction and his personal history, by Gordon N. Ray. [Folcroft, Pa.] Folcroft Library Editions, 1974. vi, 148 p. illus. 24 cm. Reprint of the 1952 ed. published for the Royal Society of Literature by Oxford University Press, London. Includes bibliographical references. [PR5631.R3 1974b] 74-11249 ISBN 0-8414-7323-4 (lib. bdg.)
1. Thackeray, William Makepeace, 1811-1863. I. Title.

RAY, Gordon Norton, 1915- 928.2
The buried life; a study of the relation between Thackeray's fiction and his personal history. Cambridge, Harvard University Press, 1952. vi, 148p. group port., geneal. table. 22 cm. Bibliographical references included in "Notes" (p. [128]-142) [PR5631.R3] 52-11301
1. Thackeray, William Makepeace, 1811-1863. I. Title.

RAY, Gordon Norton, 1915- 928.2
Thackeray. New York, McGraw-Hill [1955-58] 2 v. plates, ports, facsims., geneal. tables. 22 cm. Contents.Contents.—[1] The uses of adversity, 1811-1846.—[2] The age of wisdom, 1847-1863. Bibliographical references included in "Notes" (v. 1, p. 435-503; v. 2, p. 433-501) [PR5631.R33] 55-7282
1. Thackeray, William Makepeace, 1811-1863.

STEVENSON, Lionel, 1902- 823'.8 B
The showman of Vanity Fair; the life of William Makepeace Thackeray. New York, Russell & Russell [1968, c1947] 405 p. illus. 25 cm. [PR5631.S73 1968] 68-25050
1. Thackeray, William Makepeace, 1811-1863. I. Title. BIP

WHIBLEY, Charles, 1859- 823'.8
1930.
William Makepeace Thackeray. [Folcroft, Pa.] Folcroft Library Editions, 1973. p. Reprint of the 1903 ed. published by W. Blackwood, Edinburgh, issued in series: Modern English writers. [PR5631.W5 1973] 73-13951 20.00
1. Thackeray, William Makepeace, 1811-1863. BIP

WILLIAMS, Ioan M. 823'.8 B
Thackeray [by] Ioan M. Williams. New York, Arco [1969] 137 p. illus. 21 cm. (Arco literary critiques) Bibliography: p. 135. [PR5631.W55 1969] 78-78852 1.95
1. Thackeray, William Makepeace, 1811-1863. BIP

WILSON, James Grant, 823'.8 B
1832-1914.
Thackeray in the United States, 1852-3, 1855-6, including a record of a variety of Thackerayana, with six score illus. and a bibliography by Frederick S. Dickson. New York, Haskell House Publishers, 1970. 2 v. illus., facsims., ports. 23 cm. Reprint of the 1904 ed. "A bibliography of William Makepeace Thackeray in the United States": v. 2, p. [223]-399. [PR5632.W5 1970] 70-119439
1. Thackeray, William Makepeace, 1811-1863. I. Dickson, Frederick Stoever, 1850-1925. II. Title.

Thackeray, William Makepeace, 1811-1863—Anecdotes.

STODDARD, Richard Henry, 823'.8 B
1825-1903, ed.
Anecodte biographies of Thackeray and Dickens / edited by Richard Henry Stoddard. Folcroft, Pa. : Folcroft Library Editions, 1979. p. cm. Reprint of the 1875 ed. published by Scribner, Armstrong, New York, which was issued as no. 2 of the Bric-a-brac series. Includes index. [PR5631.S75 1979] 79-20240 ISBN 0-8414-8022-2 (lib. bdg.) : 30.00
1. Thackeray, William Makepeace, 1811-1863—Biography. 2. Dickens, Charles, 1812-1870—Biography. 3. Thackeray, William Makepeace, 1811-1863—Anecdotes. 4. Dickens, Charles, 1812-1870—Anecdotes. 5. Novelists, English—19th century—Biography. I. Title. II. Series: Bric-a-brac series ; 2.

Thackeray, William Makepeace, 1811-1863—Biography.

STODDARD, Richard Henry, 823'.8 B
1825-1903, ed.
Anecodte biographies of Thackeray and Dickens / edited by Richard Henry Stoddard. Folcroft, Pa. : Folcroft Library Editions, 1979. p. cm. Reprint of the 1875 ed. published by Scribner, Armstrong, New York, which was issued as no. 2 of the Bric-a-brac series. Includes index. [PR5631.S75 1979] 79-20240 ISBN 0-8414-8022-2 (lib. bdg.) : 30.00
1. Thackeray, William Makepeace, 1811-1863—Biography. 2. Dickens, Charles, 1812-1870—Biography. 3. Thackeray, William Makepeace, 1811-1863—Anecdotes. 4. Dickens, Charles, 1812-1870—Anecdotes. 5. Novelists, English—19th century—Biography. I. Title. II. Series: Bric-a-brac series ; 2.

Thackeray, William Makepeace, 1811-1863—Correspondence.

THACKERAY, William 823'.8 B
Makepeace, 1811-1863.
A collection of letters of W. M. Thackeray, 1847-1855. With ports. and reproductions of letters and drawings. 2d ed. New York, Haskell House, 1970. ix, 189 p. illus., facsims., ports. 24 cm. Reprint of the 1887 London ed. [PR5631.A3B7 1970] 77-129570 ISBN 0-8383-1154-7
I. Title. BIP

THACKERAY, William 823'.8 B
Makepeace, 1811-1863.
Some family letters of W. M. Thackeray, together with recollections by his kinswoman Blanche Warre Cornish. [Folcroft, Pa.] Folcroft Library Editions, 1974 [c1911] 76 p. port. 27 cm. Reprint of the ed. published by Houghton Mifflin, Boston. [PR5631.A3W3 1974] 74-6225 10.00 (lib. bdg.).
1. Thackeray, William Makepeace, 1811-1863—Correspondence. 2. Thackeray, William Makepeace, 1811-1863—Biography. I. Warre Cornish, Blanche Ritchie. II. Title.

Thackeray, William Makepeace, 1811-1863—Criticism and interpretation.

ENNIS, Lambert, 1906-1954. 823'.8
Thackeray: the sentimental cynic. New York, AMS Press [1970, c1950] vii, 233 p. 24 cm. (Northwestern University humanities series, v. 25) Includes bibliographical references. [PR5638.E5 1970] 77-128940 ISBN 0-404-50725-5
1. Thackeray, William Makepeace, 1811-1863—Criticism and interpretation. I. Title. II. Series: Northwestern University studies. Humanities series, v. 25

Thackeray, William Makepeace, 1811-1863—Homes and haunts.

CROWE, Eyre, 1824-1910. 823'.8 B
Thackeray's haunts and homes. [Folcroft, Pa.] Folcroft Library Editions, 1974. p. cm. Reprint of the 1897 ed. published by Smith, Elder, London. [PR5634.C8 1974] 74-2069 ISBN 0-8414-3542-1 (lib. bdg.)
1. Thackeray, William Makepeace, 1811-1863—Homes and haunts. I. Title. BIP

CROWE, Eyre, 1824-1910. 823'.8
Thackeray's haunts and homes / by Eyre Crowe. Norwood, Pa. : Norwood Editions, 1976 [c1897] ix, 82 p. : ill. ; 23 cm. Reprint of the ed. published by Smith, Elder, London. [PR5634.C8 1976] 76-1900 ISBN 0-88305-332-2 lib. bdg. : 10.00
1. Thackeray, William Makepeace, 1811-1863—Homes and haunts. I. Title.

Thailand—Soc. life & cust.

WOOD, William 915.9303030924
Alfred Rae, 1878-
Consul in paradise; sixty-nine years in Siam [by] W. A. R. Wood. [London] Souvenir Pr. [1965] xiii, 175p. illus., facsim., ports. 23cm. [DS568.W6] 66-6933 6.75 bds.,
1. Thailand—Soc. life & cust. 2. Diplomats—Correspondence, reminiscenes, etc. I. Title.
Available from Leisure Time Bks., New Rochelle, N.Y.

Thakombau, Chief of the Fiji Islands, 1817-1883.

WATERHOUSE, 996'.11'020924 B
Joseph.
The king and people of Fiji : containing a life of Thakombau, with notices of the Fijians, their manners, customs, and superstitions, previous to the great religious reformation in 1854 / by Joseph Waterhouse. New York : AMS Press, [1978] p. cm. Reprint of the 1866 ed. published by Wesleyan Conference Office, London. [DU600.T44W37 1978] 75-35162 ISBN 0-404-14176-5 : 36.00
1. Thakombau, Chief of the Fiji Islands, 1817-1883. 2. Fiji Islands—Kings and rulers—Biography. 3. Fiji Islands—History. I. Title.

Thalberg, Irving, 1899-1936.

THOMAS, Bob, 793'.0232'0924 B
1922-
Thalberg; life and legend. Garden City, N.Y., Doubleday, 1969. 415 p. illus., ports. 24 cm. Bibliography: p. [395]-397. [PN1998.A3T5] 69-10991 7.95
1. Thalberg, Irving, 1899-1936.

Thaler, Alwin, 1891-

THALER, Alwin, 378.1'2'0924 B
1891-
Ports and happy havens : an autobiography / by Alwin Thaler. Knoxville : Dept. of English, University of Tennessee, 1974. 297 p. ; 22 cm. [LA2317.T486A33] 76-620703
1. Thaler, Alwin, 1891- I. Title.

Thane, Elswyth, 1900- —Biography.

THANE, Elswyth, 1900- 813'.5'2 B
The strength of the hills / Elswyth Thane. Chappaqua, N.Y. : Christian Herald House, c1976. 219 p. : ill. ; 21 cm. Published in 1950 under title: Reluctant farmer. [PS3539.H143Z517 1976] 75-45861 ISBN 0-915684-06-3 : 6.95
1. Thane, Elswyth, 1900- —Biography. 2. Farmers—Vermont—Biography. I. Title. BIP

Thant, U, 1909-1974.

BINGHAM, June, 1919- 341.130924 B
U Thant; the search for peace. [1st ed.] New York, Knopf, 1966. xxii, 300, vii p. map, ports. 22 cm. Bibliography: p. 293-300. [D839.7.T5B5] 66-12397
1. Thant, U, 1909-

THANT, U, 1909- 341.23'3'0924 B
1974.
View from the UN / U Thant. 1st ed. Garden City, N.Y. : Doubleday, 1978. xix, 508 p. ; 22 cm. [D839.7.T5A35] 76-57517 ISBN 0-385-11541-5 : 10.00
1. Thant, U, 1909-1974. 2. United Nations—Biography. 3. Statesmen—Biography. I. Title.

Thatcher, Margaret.

MAYER, Allan J. 941.085'7'0924 B
Madam Prime Minister : Margaret Thatcher and her rise to power / Allan J. Mayer. New York : Newsweek Books, c1979. 223 p. : ill. ; 24 cm. [DA591.T47M39] 79-3025 ISBN 0-88225-285-2 : 8.95
1. Thatcher, Margaret. 2. Great Britain—Politics and government—1964- 3. Prime ministers—Great Britain—Biography. I. Title. BIP

Thatcher, Philip.

ARDELYAN, John W. 365'.6'0924 B
Convict's cry; a true story about one of the few who made it back, by John W. Ardelyan in cooperation with Norman B. Rohrer. Chicago, Moody Press [1970] 250 p. 22 cm. [HV6248.T35A7] 72-123155 3.95
1. Thatcher, Philip. I. Rohrer, Norman B. II. Title.

Thaxter, Celia (Laighton) 1835-1894.

THAXTER, Rosamond 920.7
Sandpiper; the life of Celia Thazter. [Sanbornville, N. H.] Wake-Brook [c.1962] 351p. illus. 22cm. 62-13418 5.00
1. Thaxter, Celia (Laighton) 1835-1894. I. Title.

THAXTER, Rosamond. 928.1
Sandpiper; the life & letters of Celia Thaxter, and her home on the Isles of Shoals, her family, friends & favorite poems. Rev. ed. Francestown, N.H., M. Jones Co. [1963] 283 p. illus. 22 cm. [PS3013.T45 1963] 63-5475
1. Thaxter, Celia (Laighton) 1835-1894. I. Title.

THAXTER, Rosamond 928
Sandpiper& the life & letters of Celia Thaxter, and her home on the Isles of Shoals, her family, friends & favorite poems. Rev. ed. Francestown, N.H., M. Jones Co. [c.1963] 283p. illus. map. (on lining pap.) 63-5475 5.00
1. Thaxter, Celia (Laighton) 1835-1894. I. Title.

Thayer, Abbott Handerson, 1840-1921.

WHITE, Nelson C 927.5
Abbott H. Thayer, painter and naturalist. [Hartford] Connecticut Printer, 1951. xxi, 277 p. ports., plates (part col.) 28 cm. Bibliography: p.265-269 [ND237.T5W5] 51-7151
1. Thayer, Abbott Handerson, 1840-1921. I. Title. BIP

Thayer, Gertrude Wheeler, d. 1964.

THAYER, Charles Wheeler, 818.5403
1910-
Muzzy, by Charles W. Thayer. [1st ed.] New York, Harper & Row [1966] x, 196 p. 22 cm. [CT275.T513T5] 66-16629
1. Thayer, Gertrude Wheeler, d. 1964. I. Title.

The Beatles.

DAVIES, Hunter, 1936- 780'.922
The Beatles; the authorized biography. [1st ed.] New York, McGraw-Hill Book Co.

[1968] x, 357 p. illus., facsims., ports. 23 cm. [ML286.5.D38] 68-9046
1. The Beatles.

DAVIES, Hunter, 1936- 784'.092'2 B
The Beatles / by Hunter Davies. Rev. ed. New York : McGraw-Hill, c1978. xvi, 381 p., [20] leaves of plates : ill. ; 24 cm. Discography: p. 354-381. [ML421.B4D38 1978] 77-25031 ISBN 0-07-015463-5 : 9.95
1. The Beatles. 2. Rock musicians—England—Biography.

DE BLASIO, Edward. 927.8
All about The Beatles. [New York, Macfadden-Bartell Corp., 1964] 96 p. illus., ports. 18 cm. (Macfadden books, 50-210) [ML286.5.D4] 65-4042
1. The Beatles. I. Title.

FAST, Julius, 1918- 780'.922
The Beatles; the real story. New York, G. P. Putnam's Sons [1968] 252 p. ports. 22 cm. [ML286.5.F38] 68-55025
1. The Beatles.

KAHN, Stephen, ed. 338.7'61'78910922
The Beatles! Publisher and editorial director: Stephen Kahn. Photography: Wide World Photos. New York, Beatle Pub. Corp., 1964. 65 p. illus. 28 cm. [ML286.5.B38] 64-5383 MN
1. The Beatles. I. Title.

LEAF, Earl 927.784
The original Beatles book; delicious insanity, where will it end? Los Angeles, Petersen, c.1964] 1v. (unpaged) illus. 28cm. (Petersen specialty pubn.) 64-6614 .50 pap.,
1. The Beatles. I. Title.

MCCABE, Peter, 1945- 784'.092'2 B
Apple to the core; the unmaking of the Beatles, by Peter McCabe and Robert D. Schonfeld. New York, Pocket Books [1972] 200 p. illus. 18 cm. [ML421.B4M2] 72-188717 ISBN 0-671-78172-3 1.25
1. The Beatles. I. Schonfeld, Robert D, joint author. II. Title.

NOEBEL, David A. 784'.092'2
The Beatles: a study in drugs, sex, and revolution, by David A. Noebel. Tulsa, Okla., Christian Crusade Publications, 1971, c1969. 64 p. 20 cm. "Fifth printing." Includes bibliographical references. [ML421.B4N6] 74-150845 1.00
1. The Beatles. I. Title.

SCADUTO, Anthony. 784'.0922
The Beatles. [New York] New American Library [1968] 157 p. illus., ports. 18 cm. (A Signet book) [ML286.5.S29] 71-203263 0.75
1. The Beatles.

SCHAFFNER, Nicholas, 1953- 784'.092'2
The Beatles forever / Nicholas Schaffner. Harrisburg, Pa. : Stackpole Co., c1977. 222 p., [2] leaves of plates : ill. ; 29 cm. Includes index. Bibliography: p. 215-217. [ML421.B4S28] 77-76774 ISBN 0-8117-0225-1 : 19.95
1. The Beatles. I. Title.
Available from Two Continents **BIP**

SCHAUMBURG, Ron. 784
Growing up with the Beatles : an illustrated tribute / by Ron Schaumburg. New York : Harcourt Brace Jovanovich, 1978. p. cm. (A Harvest/HBJ book) Reprint of the 1976 ed. published by Pyramid Books, New York. [ML421.B4S3 1978] 78-6374 ISBN 0-15-637387-4 pbk. : 5.95
1. The Beatles. 2. Rock musicians—England—Biography. I. Title.

SHEPHERD, Billy 927.8
The true story of The Beatles. Illus. by Bob Gibson.iNew York, Bantam [c.1964] 224p. illus., ports. 18cm. (Bantam extra HZ2850) 64-4459 .60 pap.,
1. The Beatles. I. Title.

YOUNG, Paul. 784'.092'2
The Lennon factor. New York, Stein and Day [1972] 1 v. (unpaged) 26 cm. [ML421.B4Y7] 73-186496 ISBN 0-8128-1465-7 3.95
1. The Beatles. 2. Popular culture. I. Title.

The Beatles—Discography.

CARR, Roy. 784'.092'2
The Beatles : an illustrated record / Roy Carr & Tony Tyler. New York : Harmony Books, [1975] 128 p. : ill. (some col.) ; 30 cm. [ML156.7.B4C34] 74-32652 ISBN 0-517-52045-1 : 6.95
1. The Beatles—Discography. 2. The Beatles—Chronology. I. Tyler, Tony, joint author. II. Title. **BIP**

The Beatles—Juvenile literature.

PIRMANTEN, Patricia. 784'.092'2 B
The Beatles. Illustrator: Dick Brude. Mankato, Minn., Creative Education [1974] p. cm. Offers individual biographical sketches of the four Beatles with emphasis on their collective careers. [ML3930.B39P6] 920 74-14656 ISBN 0-87191-398-4 4.95 (lib. bdg.)
1. The Beatles—Juvenile literature. I. Brude, Dick, illus. II. Title.

PIRMANTGEN, Patricia. 784'.092'2 B
The Beatles. Illus. : Dick Brude. Mankato, Minn., Creative Education; [distributed by Childrens Press, Chicago, 1974, c1975] 31 p. illus. (part col.) 25 cm. Offers individual biographical sketches of the four Beatles with emphasis on their collective careers. [ML3930.B39P6] 920 74-14656 ISBN 0-87191-398-4
1. The Beatles—Juvenile literature. I. Brude, Dick, illus. II. Title.

The Bee Gees.

GIBB, Barry. 784'.092'2 B
Bee Gees : the authorized biography / by Barry, Robin, and Maurice Gibb, as told to David Leaf. New York : distributed by Dell Pub., c1979. 157 p., [2] leaves of plates : ill. ; 28 cm. Includes discographies. A biography of the lives and careers of the Brothers Gibb, very successful rhythm and blues artists, with numerous black and white photographs. [ML421.B43G5] 920 78-74097 ISBN 0-440-04072-8 : 6.95
1. The Bee Gees. 2. Musicians—Biography. I. Gibb, Robin. II. Gibb, Maurice. III. Title.

*STEVENS, Kim. 784'.092'2 B
The Bee Gees : a photo bio / by Kim Stevens ; designed by Paul Gamarello. New York : Jove Pubns., 1979, c1978. 192p. : photos, : 18 cm. (A Jove/HBJ Book) [ML421] pbk. : 1.95
1. The Bee Gees. 2. Rock musicians — England — Biography. I. Title. **BIP**

STEVENS, Kim. 784'.092'2 B
The Bee Gees / Kim Stevens. New York : Quick Fox, c1978. 92 p. : ill. ; 26 cm. Discography: p. 88-92. Narrates the successful musical career of 3 British brothers whose fame as rock stars has lasted nearly 20 years. [ML421.B43S84] 920 78-56220 ISBN 0-8256-3923-9 pbk. : 3.95
1. The Bee Gees. 2. Rock musicians—Biography. I. Title.

The Capital times.

EVJUE, William Theodore, 1882- 070.9'24 B
A fighting editor [by William T. Evjue. 1st ed.] Madison, Wis., Printed by Wells Print. Co. [1968] xvi, 875 p. col. port. 23 cm. Autobiographical Includes bibliographical references. [PN4874.E8A3] 68-59389
1. The Capital times.

The Christophers, inc.

KELLER, James Gregory, 1900- 922.273
To light a candle; the autobiography of James Keller, founder of the Christophers. Garden City, N.Y. Doubleday [1965, c.1963] 233p. 18cm. (Echo bk., E5) [BX4705.K34A3] .85 pap.,
1. The Christophers, inc. I. Title.

KELLER, James Gregory, 1900- 922.273
To light a candle; the autobiography of James Keller, founder of the Christophers. Garden City, N.Y., Doubleday [c.]1963. 260p. 22cm. 62-15904 4.50
1. The Christophers, Inc. I. Title.

The Dial (Boston)

COOKE, George Willis, 1848-1923. 191
Memorabilia of the Transcendentalists in New England. Hartford, Transcendental Books [1973] 122 l. 29 cm. First published in 1902 under title: An historical and biographical introduction to accompany the Dial. [B905.C72 1973] 74-156816 12.50
1. The Dial (Boston) 2. Transcendentalism (New England)—Biography. I. Title.

The Doors.

JAHN, Mike. 784'.0922
Jim Morrison & The Doors; an unauthorized book. [New York] Grosset & Dunlap [1969] 95 p. illus. 22 cm. [ML400.J33] 71-84745 1.00
1. The Doors. I. Title.

The East—Biog.—Dictionaries.

BIOGRAPHICAL dictionary, v. 12
translated from the Arabic by Bn Mac Guckin de Slane. New York, Johnson Reprint Corp., 1842-71 [i.e. 1961] 4v. 29cm. English title preceded by title in Arabic.
1. The East—Biog.—Dictionaries. I. Ibn Khallikan, 1211-1282.

The Grateful Dead (Musical group)

HARRISON, Hank. 784'.06'5
The Dead book; a social history of the Grateful Dead. New York, Links [1973] 178 p. illus. 22 cm. and phonodisc (2 s. 7 in. 33 1/3 rpm.) [ML421.G72H4] 72-89537 ISBN 0-8256-3001-0 3.95
1. The Grateful Dead (Musical group) I. Title.

The Grossinger, Ferndale, N.Y.

GROSSINGER, Tania. 647'.94747'35
Growing up at Grossinger's. New York, David McKay [1975] 213 p. illus. 21 cm. [TX941.G75G76] 75-23234 ISBN 0-679-50570-9 8.95
1. The Grossinger, Ferndale, N.Y. 2. Grossinger, Tania. I. Title. **BIP**

(The Makers of Christendom)

TALBOT, Charles H ed. and tr. 922.1
The Anglo-Saxon missionaries in Germany; being the lives of S.S. Willibrord Boniface, Sturm, Leoba, and Lebuin, together with the Hodoeporicon of St. Willibald and a selection from the correspondence of St. Boniface New York, Sheed and Ward, 1954. xx, 234 p. 22 cm. Bibliography: p. xix-xx. [BR754.A1T3] 54-11139
1. (The Makers of Christendom) 2. Christian biography. 3. Germany-Church history. 4. Missions—Germany. I. Title.

The Petal paper.

EAST, P. D. 920.5
The magnolia jungle; the life, times, and education of a southern editor. New York, Simon and Schuster, 1960. 243 p. illus. 22 cm. [PN4874.E3A3] 60-10973
1. The Petal paper. 2. Afro-Americans—Segregation. I. Title.

The Rolling Stones.

CARR, Roy. 784'.092'2 B
The Rolling Stones : an illustrated record / by Roy Carr. New York : Harmony Books, c1976. p. cm. [ML421.R64C3] 76-10423 ISBN 0-517-52642-5 : 12.95
1. The Rolling Stones. I. Title.

DALTON, David. 784'.092'2 B
The Rolling Stones / edited by David Dalton. New York : Quick Fox, c1979. 126 p. : ill. ; 26 cm. Discography: p. 123-[127] [ML421.R64D3 1979] 78-68479 ISBN 0-8256-3929-8 pbk. : 4.95
1. The Rolling Stones. 2. Rock musicians—Biography.

ELMAN, Richard M. 784'.06'542
Uptight with the Stones; a novelist's report, by Richard Elman. New York, Scribner [1973] 119 p. illus. 23 cm. [ML421.R64E4] 72-11135 ISBN 0-684-13299-0 5.95
1. The Rolling Stones. I. Title.

GREENFIELD, Robert. 784'.092'2 B
S.T.P., a journey through America with The Rolling Stones. [1st ed.] New York, Saturday Review Press; [distributed by] E. P. Dutton, 1974. 337 p. illus. 21 cm. [ML421.R64G7] 73-16346 8.95
1. The Rolling Stones. I. Title.
Pbk., 3.95. **BIP**

JASPER, Tony. 784'.092'2 B
The Rolling Stones / [by] Tony Jasper. London : Octopus Books, 1976. 5-92 p. : ill. (some col.), ports. (some col.) ; 30 cm. [ML421.R64J4] 77-351443 ISBN 0-7064-0549-8 : £1.99
1. The Rolling Stones. 2. Rock musicians—England—Biography. I. Title.

PASCALL, Jeremy. 784'.092'2 B
The Rolling Stones / [written and edited by Jeremy Pascall]. London ; New York : Hamlyn, 1977. 96 p. : ill. (some col.), ports. (some col.) ; 31 cm. Ill. on lining papers. [ML421.R64P34] 77-374550 ISBN 0-600-37596-X : £1.99
1. The Rolling Stones. 2. Rock musicians—England—Biography. I. Title.

THE Rolling Stones. 927.8
Our own story, by the Rolling Stones, as we told it to Pete Goodman. Illus. by Bob Gibson. Toronto, New York, Bantam Books [1965, c1964] 187 p. illus., ports. 18 cm. A Bantam extra) [ML286.5.R64] 65-18171
I. Goodman, Pete. II. Title.

SANCHEZ, Tony. 784'.092'2 B
Up and down with The Rolling Stones / by Tony Sanchez. New York : W. Morrow, 1979. 309 p., [5] leaves of plates : ill. ; 24 cm. [ML421.R64S2] 79-15236 ISBN 0-688-03515-9 : 17.95 ISBN 0-688-08515-6 pbk. : 8.95
1. The Rolling Stones. 2. Rock musicians—England—Biography. I. Title. **BIP**

The Times, London—Indexes.

OBITUARIES from the 920'.02
Times, 1971-1975, including an index to all obituaries and tributes appearing in the Times during the years 1971-1975 / compiler, Frank C. Roberts. Reading, Eng. : Newspaper Archive Developments Lit. : Westport, Conn. : distributed in North America by Meekler Books, 1978. 647 p. : 31 cm. Includes index. [CT120.O17] 77-22500 ISBN 0-913672-18-1 lib.bdg. : 85.00
1. The Times, London—Indexes. 2. Obituaries. 3. Biography—20th century. 4. Obituaries—Indexes. I. Roberts, Frank C. II. The Times, London.

The West

BRONSON, Edgar Beecher, 1856-1917. 920.8
Reminiscences of a ranchman. Lincoln, Univ. of Neb. Pr. [c.]1962. 369p. 21cm. (Bison bk. BB127) Bibl. 62-8407 1.50 pap.,
1. The West—Soc. life & cust. 2. Dakota Indians. 3. Ranch life. I. Title. **BIP**

HUNTER, John Marvin, 1880-1957. 978.020922
The album of gunfighters, by J. Marvin Hunter and Noah H. Rose. Decorated and designed by Warren Hunter. [San Antonio? 1965] xi, 236 p. illus., ports. 31 cm. [F591.H935 1965] 66-3801
1. The West — Biog. — Portraits. 2. Outlaws. I. Rose, Noah Hamilton, 1874-1952. II. Title.

MERIWETHER, David, 1800-1892. 978.020924 (B)
My life in the mountains and on the plains; the newly discovered autobiography. Edited and with an introd. by Robert A. Griffen. [1st ed.] Norman, University of Oklahoma Press [1965] xxi, 301 p. illus., ports. 24 cm. (The American exploration and travel series [46]) Bibliography: p. 267-284. [F591.M4] 65-11240
1. The West — Hist. 2. Frontier and pioneer life — The West. 3. New Mexico — Pol. & govt. I. Griffen, Robert A., ed. II. Title. III. Series. BIP

The West—Biography.

BREIHAN, Carl W. 364.15'23'0922
Great gunfighters of the West / by Carl W. Breihan. New York : New American Library 1977c1971. 182p. : ill. ; 18 cm. rime and crimials-The West. (A Signet Brand Western.) [F594.B8051962] ISBN 0-451-07434-3 pbk. : 1.50.
1. The West-Biography. I. Title.
L.C. card no. for 1962 Naylor ed.:62-13063.

BREIHAN, Carl W., 1915- 920.02
Great gunfighters of the West. San Antonio, Naylor Co. [1962] 175 p. illus. 23 cm. [F594.B805 1962] 62-13063
1. The West—Biography. 2. Crime and criminals—The West. I. Title. BIP

BREIHAN, Carl W., 1915- 364.15'23'0922
Great gunfighters of the West [by] Carl W. Breihan. San Antonio, Naylor Co. [1971] xx, 207 p. illus. 22 cm. [F594.B805 1971] 77-30092 ISBN 0-8111-0289-0 5.95
1. The West—Biography. 2. Crime and criminals—The West. I. Title.

BROWN, Dee Alexander. 917.8'03'0922
The Westerners [by] Dee Brown. New York, Holt, Rinehart and Winston [1974] p. cm. Bibliography: p. [F591.B88] 73-15456 ISBN 0-03-088360-1 17.95
1. The West—Biography. 2. The West—History. 3. Indians of North America—The West. I. Title. BIP

BURT, Olive (Woolley) 1894- 920
Mountain men of the early West, by Olive W. Burt. Illustrated by Jules Gotlieb. [1st ed.] New York, Hawthorn Books [1967] 128 p. illus., ports. 23 cm. Bibliography: p. 121-122. Describes the hardship and humor in the lives of early American trappers and trailblazers John Colter, Manuel Lisa, Jedediah Strong Smith, Jim Bridger, Thomas ("Broken Hand") Fitzpatrick, Kit Carson, Ewing Young, and Joe Meek. [F597.B95] AC 68
1. The West—Biography. 2. Frontier and pioneer life—The West. 3. Fur trade—The West. I. Gotlieb, Jules, illus. II. Title.

BURT, Olive (Woolley) 1894- 920
Young wayfarers of the early West, by Olive W. Burt. Illustrated by Jules Gotlieb. [1st ed.] New York, Hawthorn Books [1968] 191 p. illus. 22 cm. Bibliography: p. 185-186. Brief biographies of ten teen-age boys and girls, famous and lesser-known, whose bravery and determination helped shape the American West. [F591.B92] AC 68
1. The West—Biography. I. Gotlieb, Jules, illus. II. Title.

COOLIDGE, Dane, 1873-1940. 920.078
Fighting men of the West. Freeport, N.Y., Books for Libraries Press [1968, c1932] 343 p. illus., ports. 22 cm. (Essay index reprint series) [F591.C78 1968] 68-24846
1. The West—Biography. 2. Texas Rangers. 3. Crime and criminals—The West. I. Title. BIP

FORBES, Bertie Charles, 1880-1954. 978'.0099 B
Men who are making the West. Freeport, N.Y., Books for Libraries Press [1972] 343 p. ports. 23 cm. (Essay index reprint series) Reprint of the 1923 ed. [F595.F68 1972] 72-330 ISBN 0-8369-2793-1
1. The West—Biography. 2. California—Biography. 3. Capitalists and financiers—The West. I. Title. BIP

MASTERSON, William Barclay, 1853-1921. 364.1'0922
Famous gunfighters of the Western frontier, by W. B. (Bat) Masterson (Bartholomew Masterson) Fort Davis, Tex., Frontier Book Co., 1968. 112 p., illus., ports. 21 cm. Contents.Contents.—Luke Short.—Bill Tilghman.—Ben Thompson.—Doc Holliday.—Wyatt Earp. [F591.M32] 73-7817
1. The West—Biography. I. Title. BIP

SCHAEFER, Jack Warner, 1907- 920.078
Heroes without glory; some goodmen of the old West. Boston, Houghton [c.]1965. xix, 323p. 22cm [F591.S33] 65-12485 5.95
1. The West—Biog. I. Title.

SCHOENBERGER, Dale T. 364.15'0922 B
The gunfighters, by Dale T. Schoenberger. Illustrated by Ernest L. Reedstrom. Caldwell, Idaho, Caxton Printers, 1971. xvi, 207 p. illus. 29 cm. Bibliography: p. [187]-198. [F594.S37] 70-123583 ISBN 0-87004-207-6 12.25
1. The West—Biography. 2. Crime and criminals—The West. I. Title. BIP

STECKMESSER, Kent Ladd, 1928- 920.078
The Western hero in history and legend. Norman, Univ. of Okla. Pr. [c.1965] xiii, 281 illus., ports. 23cm. Bibl. [F591.S8] 65-11226 5.95
1. The West—Biog. 2. Heroes in literature. I. Title.

THORP, Raymond W 1896- 927.993
Spirit Gun of the West; the story of Doc W. F. Carver: plainsman, trapper, buffalo hunter, medicine chief of the Santee Sioux, world's champion marksman, and originator of the American Wild West show. Glendale, Calif., A. H. Clark Co., 1957. 266 p. illus. 25 cm. [GV1811.C28T45] 57-4230
1. (Western frontiersmen series, 7) 2. Carver, William F., 1840-1927. I. Title.

VESTAL, Stanley, 1887- 917.8'03'20922
Mountain men, by Walter Stanley Campbell (Stanley Vestal, pseud.) Freeport, N.Y., Books for Libraries Press [1969, c1937] x, 296 p. illus., map (on lining papers), ports. 23 cm. (Essay index reprint series) Bibliography: p. 294-296. [F591.V47 1969] 77-99620
1. The West—Biography. 2. Fur trade—The West. 3. Frontier and pioneer life—The West. I. Title.

WALLIS, George A. 920'.078
Unforgettable men of the West. by George A. Wallis. Titusville, Fla., Viking Press [1974] 74 p. illus. 28 cm. [F595.W24] 74-4595 5.00
1. The West—Biography.
Contents omitted. BIP

WHO'S who in the West; 920.078
a biographical dictionary of noteworthy men and women of the Pacific coast and Western States. 8th ed. Chicago, Marquis [c.1949-1962] 806p. 27cm. 49-48186 25.00
1. The West—Biog.

WHO'S who in the West; 920.078
a biographical dictionary of noteworthy men and women of the Pacific coast and the Western States. 1949- Chicago, A. N. Marquis Co. v. 24 cm. Vols for 1949- published also under title Who's who on the Pacific coast. Supersedes in part Who's who in the South and Southwest, published by Larkin, Roosevelt & Larkin. [F595.W64] 49-48186
1. The West — Biog.

WHO'S who in the West (and Western Canada); 920.078
a biographical dictionary of noteworthy men and women of the Pacific Coastal and Western States and Western Canada. 10th ed. Chicago, Marquis [c.1966] 1002p. 27cm. Title and sub-title changed to accomodate wider geographical coverage 8th ed. title: Who's who in the West; a biogiographical dictionary of noteworthy men and women of the Pacific coast and Western States. 49-48186 27.00
1. The West—Biog.

WHO'S who of the Wild West, 978'.02'0922 B
a biographical guide to the American frontier from 1783 to 1890. Editor in charge: Robert A. Irwin. Chicago, Marquis-Who's Who [1969] 30 p. illus. (part col.) 26 cm. Includes bibliographies. [F596.W57] 75-15295
1. The West—Biography. 2. Frontier and pioneer life—The West. I. Irwin, Robert A., ed.

The West—Biography—Juvenile literature.

BLASSINGAME, Wyatt. 920
The Mountain Men, by Wyatt Blassingame & Richard Glendinning. New York, Watts [1962] 166p. 22cm. [F592.B59] 62-10376
1. The West—Biog.—Juvenile literature. 2. Frontier and pioneer life—The West—Juvenile literature. 3. Fur trade—The West—Juvenile literature. I. Glendinning. Richard, joint author. II. Title.

BURT, Olive (Wooley), 1894- 920
Mountain men of the early West, by Olive W. Burt. Illustrated by Jules Gotlieb. [1st ed.] New York, Hawthorn [1967] 128p. illus., ports, 23cm. Bibl. [F597.B95] 67-23995 3.95 lib. ed.,
1. The West—Biog.—Juvenile literature. 2. Frontier and pioneer life—The West—Juvenile literature. 3. Fur trade—The West—Juvenile literature. I. Title.

BURT, Olive (Woolley) 1894- 920 (J)
Young wayfarers of the early West, by Olive W. Burt. Illustrated by Jules Gotlieb. [1st ed.] New York, Hawthorn Books [1968] 191 p. illus. 22 cm. Bibliography: p. 185-186. [F591.B92] 68-27651 4.95
1. The West—Biography—Juvenile literature. I. Title.

SURGE, Frank. 978'.02'0922 B
Western lawmen. Minneapolis, Lerner Publications Co. [1969] 62 p. illus., ports. 21 cm. (A Pull ahead book) Brief biographies of some well-known lawmen and other personalities of the Old West whose characters and exploits have become legendary. [F591.S887] 920 68-30568
1. The West—Biography—Juvenile literature. 2. Peace officers—The West—Juvenile literature. I. Title. BIP

SURGE, Frank. 978.02'0922
Western outlaws. Minneapolis, Lerner Publications Co. [1969] 54 p. illus., ports. 21 cm. (A Pull ahead book) Vignettes of fourteen famous outlaws or gangs and their crimes and deaths. Includes Jesse James, The Reno Brothers, John Wesley Hardin, The Apache Kid, and Belle Starr. [F591.S89] 920 68-30567
1. The West—Biography—Juvenile literature. 2. Crime and criminals—The West—Juvenile literature. I. Title. BIP

YOUNG, Bob, 1916- 978'.00922
Seven faces West, by Bob and Jan Young. New York, J. Messner [1969] 191 p. 22 cm. Contents.Contents.—Hard riding captain: Juan de Anza (1735-1788).—In the spirit of martyrs: Jason Lee (1803-1845).—It is a pleasure to be rich: Leland Stanford (1824-1893).—Colossus of Nevada: William Stewart (1825-1909).—Man who matched the mountain: Adolph Sutro (1830-1898).—Fighting editor: William Byers (1831-1903).—King of the mountains: Clarence King (1842-1901).—Bibliography (p. 183-184). [F591.Y6] 920 B 75-79693 3.50
1. The West—Biography—Juvenile literature. I. Young, Jan, 1919- joint author. II. Title.

The West—Description and travel—To 1848.

LEONARD, Zenas, 1809-1857. 917.804
Narrative of the adventures of Zenas Leonard. Ann Arbor [Mich.] University Microfilms [1966] iv, 87 p. 24 cm. (March of America facsimile series no. 69) Original t.p. has imprint: Clearfield, Pa., D. W. Moore, 1839. [F592.L36 1839a] 66-26339
1. The West—Description and travel—To 1848. 2. Fur trade—The West. I. Title. II. Series. BIP

PIKE, Zebulon Montgomery, 1779-1813. 917.8'04'2
Zebulon Pike's Arkansaw journal: in search of the southern Louisiana Purchase boundary line (interpreted by his newly recovered maps). Edited, with bibliographical resume, 1800-1810, by Stephen Harding Hart and Archer Butler Hulbert. Westport, Conn., Greenwood Press [1972, c1932] xcvi, 200 p. illus. 22 cm. Original ed. issued as vol. 1 of Overland to the Pacific series. The journal is part of the author's An account of expeditions to the sources of the Mississippi. [F592.P638 1972] 72-138172 ISBN 0-8371-5629-7
1. The West—Description and travel—To 1848. 2. United States—Exploring expeditions. I. Hart, Stephen Harding, ed. II. Hulbert, Archer Butler, 1873-1933, ed. III. Title. IV. Title: Arkansaw journal. V. Series: Overland to the Pacific; the Charles B. Voorhis series, v. 1

RUXTON, George Frederick Augustus, 1820-1848. 978.020924
Mountain men; George Frederick Ruxton's first hand accounts of fur trappers and Indians in the Rockies. Edited and illustrated by Glen Rounds. New York, Holiday House [1966] 278 p. illus. 24 cm. "The first three chapters ... are from [the author's] Adventures in Mexico and the Rocky Mountains, published in 1848. The remainder ... is virtually the complete text of his Life in the Far West which first appeared as a magazine serial in 1848." [F592.R9835] 66-8006
1. The West—Description and travel—To 1848. 2. Frontier and pioneer life—The West. 3. Trapping. 4. Indians of North America—The West. I. Rounds, Glen, 1906- ed. and illus. II. Title.

The West in art.

SAMUELS, Peggy. 709'.2'2 B
The illustrated biographical encyclopedia of artists of the American West / Peggy and Harold Samuels. 1st ed. Garden City, N.Y. : Doubleday, 1976. p. cm. Includes index. Bibliography: p. [N8214.5.U6S25] 76-2816 ISBN 0-385-01730-8 : 25.00
1. The West in art. 2. Indians of North America—Pictorial works. 3. Artists—Biography. 4. Artists—United States—Biography. I. Samuels, Harold, joint author. II. Title. BIP

The West in art—Bibliography.

DYKES, Jefferson Chenowth, 1900- 016.741'092'2
Fifty great Western illustrators : a bibliographic checklist / by Jeff Dykes. [Flagstaff, Ariz.] : Northland Press, [1975] xiv, 457 p. : ill. (some col.) ; 30 cm. [Z5956.W45D94] [N8214.5.U6] 73-79780 ISBN 0-87358-114-8 : 35.00
1. The West in art—Bibliography. 2. Illustrators—United States—Bibliography. I. Title.

Theater as a profession.

SWEETING, Elizabeth Jane. 658'.91'792
Beginners please: working in the theatre, by Elizabeth Sweeting; with a foreword by Alan Bullock. Reading, Educational Explorers, 1971. 136 p., 8 plates. illus. 21 cm. (My life and my work series) Bibliography: p. [135]-136. [PN2598.S9A3] 76-866020 ISBN 0-85225-734-1 £1.50
1. Theater as a profession. I. Title.

Theater—Great Britain—Biography.

AGATE, James Evershed, 1877-1947, comp. 792'.028'0922
These were actors; extracts from a newspaper cutting book, 1811-1833, selected and annotated by James Agate. New York, B. Blom [1969] 150 p. illus., ports. 23 cm. "There is evidence ... that the collection is the work of ... James St. Aubyn, a barrister." Reprint of the 1943 ed. [PN2594.A4 1969] 72-91889
1. Theater—Gt. Brit. 2. English drama—19th century—History and criticism. 3. Actors, English. 4. Actresses, English. I. St. Aubyn, James. II. Title. BIP

WHO was who in the theatre, 1921-1976 792'.028'0922 B
biographical dictionary of actors, actresses, directors, playwrights, and producers of the English-speaking theatre / compiled from Who's who in theatre, volumes 1-5 (1912-1972 Detroit : Gale Research Co., c1978. p. cm. (An Omnigraphs book) (Gale composite biographical dictionary series ; no. 3) Includes index. [PN2597.W52] 78-

9634 ISBN 0-8103-0406-6 : 140.00 (4 vol. set)
1. Theater—Great Britain—Biography. 2. Theater—United States—Biography. I. Who's who in the theatre. II. Title. III. Series. IV. Series: An Omnigraphics book.

WHO'S who in the 927.92
theatre; a biographical record of the contemporary stage. Originally comp. by John Parker. 13th ed. Ed. by Freda Gaye. New York, Pitman [c.1961] 1594p. illus. 12-22402 20.00
1. Theater—Gt. Brit. 2. Actors, English. 3. Actors, American. 4. London, Theatres. 5. Theatres—New York (City) I. Parker, John, comp. II. Gaye, Freda, ed.

Theater—Great Britain—History.

BROWNE, Maurice, 1881- 927.92
1955.
Too late to lament; an autobiography. Bloomington, Indiana University Press, 1956. 403p. illus. 22cm. [PN2598] 56-12001
1. Theater—England—Hist. 2. Theater—U. S.—Hist. I. Title.

ENKVIST, Nils Erik. 822'.0092'7
Caricatures of Americans on the English stage prior to 1870. Port Washington, N.Y., Kennikat Press [1968] 168 p. front. 23 cm. Reprint of the 1951 ed. Bibliography: p. 159-162. [PN2594.E5 1968] 68-26273
1. Theater—Great Britain—History. 2. American wit and humor—History. 3. Americans in literature. I. Title. BIP

Theater—History.

CURTIS, Anthony. 791'.092'2 B
The rise and fall of the matinee idol; past deities of stage and screen, their roles, their magic, and their worshippers, edited by Anthony Curtis. Illus. consultants: Raymond Mander and Joe Mitchenson. New York, St. Martins Press [1974] 215 p. illus. 26 cm. [PN2189.C8 1974b] 73-86600 9.95
1. Theater—History. 2. Moving-pictures—History. 3. Actors—Biography. I. Title

Theater—New York (City)

GORDON, Max. 1892- 927.92
Max Gordon presents. With Lewis Funke. [New York] Geis, dist. Random [c.1963] vi, 314p. illus., ports. 22cm. 63-11412 4.95 bds.,
1. Theater—New York (City) I. Funke, Lewis, 1912- II. Title.

SOBEL, Bernard. 927.92
Broadway heartbeat: memoirs of a press agent. New York, Hermitage House, 1953. 352p. 22cm. [PN2287.S62A3] 53-12014
1. Theater—New York (City) I. Title.

Theater management—Biography.

THE Theatrical 658.1'594'0922
manager in England and America; player of a perilous game: Philip Henslowe, Tate Wilkinson, Stephen Price, Edwin Booth, Charles Wyndham. Edited by Joseph W. Donohue, Jr. Princeton, N.J., Princeton University Press, 1971. xii, 216 p. illus, facsims., ports. 23 cm. "The essays collected in this volume were originally delivered as lectures at Princeton University during the course of the 1969-70 academic year." Includes bibliographical references. [PN2597.T46] 72-154992 ISBN 0-691-06188-2 8.50
1. Theater management—Biography. I. Donohue, Joseph W., 1935- ed.

Theater—United States.

BISHOP, James Alonzo, 1907- 920.5
The Mark Hellinger story; a biography of Broadway and Hollywood. New York, Appleton-Century-Crofts [1952] 367 p. illus. 23 cm. [PN1998.A3H37] 52-13839
I. Hellinger. Mark, 1903-1947. II. Title.

DALRYMPLE, Jean. 927.92
September child; the story of Jean Dalrymple, by herself. New York, Dodd, Mead [1963] xvi, 318 p. illus., ports. 24 cm. [PN2287.D23A3] 63-13557
1. Theater—U.S. I. Title.

RICE, Elmer L 1892- 928.1
Minority report: an autobiography. New York, Simon and Schuster, 1963. 474 p. 22 cm. [PS3535.I 224Z5] 63-15364
1. Theater — U.S. I. Title.

RICE(ELMER L., 1892- 928.1
Minority report. an autobiography. New York, S. & S. [c.]1963. 473p. 22cm. 63-15364 6.50
1. Theater—U.S. I. Title.

STRANG, Lewis 782.8'1'0922 B
Clinton, 1869-1935.
Celebrated comedians of light opera and musical comedy in America. New York, B. Blom, 1972. 293 p. ports. 22 cm. Reprint of the 1901 ed. [ML400.S89 1972] 72-91574
1. Theater—United States. 2. Operetta—United States. 3. Comedians—United States. I. Title. BIP

WINTER, William, 792'.028'0922
1836-1917.
The wallet of time, containing personal, biographical, and critical reminiscence of the American theatre. New York, B. Blom [1969] 2 v. illus., ports. 24 cm. Reprint of the 1913 ed. [PN2285.W55 1969b] 79-83400
1. Theater—U.S. 2. Actors, American. I. Title.

WINTER, William, 792'.028'0922
1836-1917.
The wallet of time; containing personal, biographical, and critical reminiscence of the American theatre. Freeport, N.Y., Books for Libraries Press [1969] 2 v. ports. 23 cm. (Essay index reprint series) Reprint of the 1913 ed. [PN2285.W55 1969] 76-84347
1. Theater—U.S. 2. Actors, American. I. Title.

Theater—United States—Biography—Directories.

WEARING, J. P. 792'.0295
American and British theatrical biography : a directory / by J. P. Wearing. Metuchen, N.J. : Scarecrow Press, 1979. v, 1007 p. ; 23 cm. [PN2285.W42] 78-31162 ISBN 0-8108-1201-0 : 37.50
1. Theater—United States—Biography—Directories. 2. Theater—Great Britain—Biography—Directories. I. Title. BIP

Theatre Guild.

HELBURN, Theresa 927.92
A wayward quest; the autobiography of Theresa Helburn. Boston, Little, Brown [c.1960] 344p. illus. 22cm. 60-9333 5.00
1. Theatre Guild. 2. Theatre—U. S.—Hist. I. Title.

HELBURN, Theresa. 927.92
A wayward quest; the autobiography of Theresa Helburn. [1st ed.] Boston, Little, Brown [1960] 344p. illus. 22cm. [PN2287.H415A3] 60-9333
1. Theatre Guild. 2. Theater—U. S.—Hist. I. Title.

LANGNER, Lawrence, 1890 927.92
1962.
The magic curtain; the story of a life in two fields, theatre and invention, by the founder of the Theatre Guild. [1st ed.] New York, Dutton, 1951. x, 498 p. illus., ports. 25 cm. "A Story Press book." [PN2295.T5L3] 51-13798
1. Theatre Guild. 2. Theater—U.S.—History. I. Title.

Themistocles, ca. 524-ca. 459 B.C.

LENARDON, Robert 938'.03'0924 B
J., 1928-
The saga of Themistocles / Robert J. Lenardon. London : Thames & Hudson, c1978. 248 p., [8] leaves of plates : ill. ; 23 cm. (Aspects of Greek and Roman life) Includes indexes. Bibliography: p. 242-243. [DF228.T4L46] 78-311675 ISBN 0-500-40036-9 : 19.95
1. Themistocles, ca. 524-ca. 459 B.C. 2. Statesmen—Greece—Biography. 3. Generals—Greece—Biography. I. Title. II. Series.
Distributed by W. W. Norton, New York BIP

PODLECKI, Anthony 938'.03'0924 B
J.
The life of Themistocles : a critical survey of the literary and archaeological evidence / A. J. Podlecki. Montreal : McGill-Queen's University Press, 1975. xiii, 250 p., [4] leaves of plates : ill. ; 26 cm. Includes indexes. Bibliography: p. [209]-224. [DF228.T4P6] 73-93001 ISBN 0-7735-0185-1 : 18.00
1. Themistocles, ca. 524-ca. 459 B.C I. Title.
Distributed by McGill Queen's University Press Irvington, New York. BIP

Theobald, Abp. of Canterbury, d. 1161.

SALTMAN, Avrom. 282'.0924 B
Theobald, Archbishop of Canterbury. New York, Greenwood Press, 1969. xvi, 594 p. illus. 23 cm. (University of London historical studies, 2) Reprint of the 1956 ed. Part 2 (p. [179]-556): Introduction to the charters.—Texts of the charters.—Supplementary documents.—Manuscripts. [BX4705.T482S3 1969] 69-14068
1. Theobald, Abp. of Canterbury, d. 1161. 2. Gt. Brit.—Church history—Sources. I. Series: London. University. Historical studies, 2 BIP

Theodora, consort of Justinian I, Emperor of the East, d. 548.

DIEHL, Charles, 949.5'01'0924 B
1859-1944.
Theodora, Empress of Byzantium. Translated by Samuel R. Rosenbaum. New York, F. Ungar Pub. Co. [1972] xi, 204 p. illus. 22 cm. [DF572.5.D513] 75-189879 ISBN 0-8044-1230-8 7.00
1. Theodora, consort of Justinian I, Emperor of the East, d. 548. I. Title.

Theodorus Studita, Saint, 759?-826.

GARDNER, Alice, 281.9'092'4 B
1854-1927.
Theodore of Studium; his life and times. New York, B. Franklin Reprints [1974] xiii, 284 p. illus. 23 cm. (Burt Franklin research & source works series. Philosophy & religious history monographs, 151) Reprint of the 1905 ed. published by E. Arnold, London. "The published works of Theodore": p. 271-277. Includes bibliographical references. [BR1720.T38G3 1974] 72-82007 ISBN 0-8337-1280-2 12.00
1. Theodorus Studita, Saint, 759?-826. 2. Byzantine Empire—Politics and government.

Theologians.

HUNT, George Laird, comp. 230
Twelve makers of modern Protestant thought. Edited with introd. by George L. Hunt. New York, Association Press [1971] 140 p. 18 cm. 1958 ed. published under title: Ten makers of modern Protestant thought. Contents.Contents.—Albert Schweitzer, by H. A. Rodgers.—Walter Rauschenbusch, by R. T. Handy.—Soren Kierkegaard, by F. J. Denbeaux.—Karl Barth, by T. F. Torrance.—Reinhold Niebuhr, by C. Welch.—Paul Tillich, by R. C. Johnson.—Rudolph Bultmann, by C. Michalson.—Martin Buber, by W. E. Wiest.—Dietrich Bonhoeffer, by T. A. Gill.—Martin Heidegger, by J. Macquarrie.—Jurgen Moltmann, by D. L. Migliore.—Alfred North Whitehead, by J. B. Cobb, Jr. Includes bibliographical references. [BX4825.H8 1971] 70-152897 ISBN 0-8096-1824-9 2.25
1. Theologians. I. Title.

Theology—Collected works—Early church.

AMBROSIUS, Saint, 230.1'4'0924
Bp. of Milan.
Letters. Translated by Mary Melchior Beyenka. [Reprinted with corrections] Washington, Catholic University of America [1967, c1954] xix, 515 p. 22 cm. (The Fathers of the Church, a new translation, v. 26) Contents.Letters to emperors.--Letters to bishops.--Synodal letters.--Letters to Priests.--Letters to his sister.--Letters to layment. Bibliography: p. xiv. [BR60.F3A5612] 67-28583
1. Theology—Collected works—Early church. I. Title. II. Series.

Theology—Bibliography.

CENTER for Reformation 016.23
Research.
Evangelical theologians of Wurttemberg in the sixteenth century : a finding list of CRR holdings. St. Louis : Center for Reformation Research, 1975. 57 p. ; 22 cm. (Sixteenth century bibliography ; 3) [Z7751.C38 1975] [BR118] 76-355415 2.00
1. Theology—Bibliography. 2. Theologians—Wurttemberg—Biography. I. Title. II. Series.

Theology, Catholic—Bio-bibliography.

CENTER for 016.23'02'0922
Reformation Research.
Early sixteenth century Roman Catholic theologians and the German Reformation : a finding list of CRR holdings. Saint Louis : Center for Reformation Research, 1975, c1974. 55 p. ; 22 cm. (Sixteenth century bibliography ; 2) [Z7837.C45 1975] [BX1749] 75-315894
1. Theology, Catholic—Bio-bibliography. 2. Reformation—Germany—Bio-bibliography. I. Title. II. Series.

Theology—Collected works—Early church, ca. 30-600.

AMBROSIUS, Saint, 230.1'4'0924
Bp. of Milan.
Letters. Translated by Mary Melchior Beyenka. [Reprinted with corrections] Washington, Catholic University of America [1967, c1954] xix, 515 p. 22 cm. (The Fathers of the Church, a new translation v. 26) Contents.Contents.—Letters to emperors.—Letters to bishops.—Synodal letters.—Letters to Priests.—Letters to his sister.—Letters to laymen. Bibliography: p. xiv. [BR60.F3A5612] 67-28583
1. Theology—Collected works—Early church, ca. 30-600. I. Title. II. Series.

Theosophy—Addresses, essays, lectures.

JUDGE, William Quan, 1851- 191 B
1896.
William Quan Judge, 1851-1896; the life of a theosophical pioneer and some of his outstanding articles. Compilers Sven Eek and Boris de Zirkoff Wheaton, Ill., Theosophical Pub. House, 1969. 96 p. facsims., ports. 24 cm. List of writings of W. Q. Judge (p. 38-40) [BP525.J8 1969] 74-263250
1. Theosophy—Addresses, essays, lectures. I. Eek, Sven, 1900- comp. II. De Zirkoff, Boris, joint comp.

Theotocopuli, Dominico, called El Greco. d. 1614.

GUDIOL i Ricart, Josep. 759.6
Domenikos Theotokopoulos, El Greco, 1541-1614, by Jose Gudiol. Translated from the Spanish by Kenneth Lyons. New York, Viking Press, 1973. 374 p. illus. (part col.) 30 cm. Bibliography: p. 361-364. [ND813.T4G7813] 73-381 38.50
1. Theotocopuli, Domenico, called El Greco, d. 1614.

PUPPI, Lionello. 759.6
El Greco. [Tr. from Italian by Eva Pirie. 1st Amer. ed.] New York, Grosset [1967] 39, [78]p. illus. (pt. col.) 18cm.E(New Grosset art lib., 5) On cover: El Greco: the life and work of the artist. [ND813.T4P83 1967] 67-25789 1.25 pap.,
1. Theotocopuli, Dominico, called El Greco. d. 1614. I. Title.

THEOTOCOPULI, Dominico, 759.6
called El Greco, d. 1614
El Greco, by Andre Leclerc. New York, Crown [1965] 36p. (chiefly illus. (pt. col.) 18cm. (Little bks. on great artists) Biographical sketch in French, English, and German. [ND813.T4L38] 65-3291 .69 pap.,
I. Leclerc, Andre. II. Title.

Therese. Saint, 1873-1897.

COMBES, Andre, 1899- 922.244
St. Therese and suffering; the spirituality of St. Therese in its essence. Pref. by Vernon Johnson; translated from the French ed. by Philip E. Hallett. New York, P. J. Kenedy [1952, '1951] 133 p. 22 cm. Companion volume to The spirituality of St. Therese. Translation of part of Introduction a la spiritualite de sainte Therese de l'Enfant-Jesus. [BX4700.T5C725 1952] 52-9810
1. Therese. Saint, 1873-1897. I. Title.

Therese, Saint, 1873-1897.

ANTONELLIS, Costanzo J. 248.0924
A saint of ardent desires; meditations on the virtues of St. Therese of Lisieux. [Boston] St. Paul Eds. [dist. Daughters of St. Paul, c.1965] 212p. illus. 18cm. [BX4700.T5A78] 65-17556 3.00; 2.00
1. Therese, Saint, 1873-1897. I. Title.

BEEVERS, John. 922.244
Storm of glory : St. Therese of Lisieux / byJohn Beevers. Garden City, N.Y. : Image Books, 1977c1949. 196p. ; 18 cm. (A Doubleday Image Book) Originally published by Sheed & Ward. [BX4700.T5] ISBN 0-385-12617-4 pbk. : 1.95.
1. Therese, Saint, 1973-1897. I. Title.
L.C. card no. for 1955 Image Books Ed.:55-767.

BEEVERS, John. 922.244
Storm of glory: St. Therese of Lisieux. New York, Sheed & Ward, 1950. vii, 231 p. port. 21 cm. Erratum slip inserted Bibliography: p. 229-231. [BX4700.T5B37 1950] 56-2137
1. Therese, Saint, 1873-1897. I. Title.

BOYLE, John, 1922- 922.244
The little one; a story of St. Therese of the Child Jesus. Illus. by Nancy Langenbahn. Notre Dame, Ind., Dujarie Press [1954] 85p. illus. 24cm. [BX4700.T5B6] 54-3702
1. Therese, Saint, 1873-1897. I. Title.

BULGER, James E 1889- 922.244
Louis Martin's daughter. Milwaukee, Bruce Pub. Co. [1952] 161p. 21cm. [BX4700.T5B8] 53-181
1. Therese, Saint, 1873-1897. 2. Martin, Louis Joseph Aloys Stanislaus, 1823-1894. 3. Martin, Zelie Marie (Guerin) 1831-1877. I. Title.

CARBONEL, J 922.244
Little Therese; the life of Soeur Therese of Lisieux for children. Translated from the French by a religious of the Society of the Holy Child Jesus. Fresno, Calif., Academy Library Guild [1955] 195p. illus. 19cm. [BX4700] 56-2435
1. Therese, Saint, 1873-1897. I. Title.

COMBES, Andre, 1899- 922.244
The heart of Saint Therese; translated by a Carmelite nun. New York, Kenedy [1951] 196 p. 22 cm. Translation of L'amour de Jesus chex Sainte Therese de Lisieux. [BX4700.T5C723] 51-14066
1. Therese. Saint, 1873-1897. I. Title.

COMBES, Andre, 1899- 922.244
Saint Therese and her mission; the basic principles of Theresian spirituality. Translated by Alastair Guinan. New York, P. J. Kenedy [1955] 244p. 21cm. [BX4700.T5C737] 55-9611
1. Therese, Saint, 1873-1897. I. Title.

ERNEST, Brother, 1897- 922.244
A story of Saint Therese. Pictures by Sister M. John Vianney. Notre Dame, Ind., Dujarie Press [1957] unpaged. illus. 21cm. [BX4700.T5E7] 57-30284
1. Therese, Saint, 1873-1897. I. Title.

GUITTON, Jean. 922.244
The spiritual genius of St. Therese. Translated by a religious of the Retreat of the Sacred Heart. Westminster, Md., Newman Press, 1958. 51p. 19cm. (Doctrine and life) [BX4700.T5G83] 59-2067
1. Therese, Saint, 1873-1897. I. Title.

HAUGHTON, 271'.971'0924 (B)
Rosemary.
Therese Martin; the story of St. Therese of Lisieux. [Rev. Ed.] New York, Macmillan [1967] 218 p. illus., ports. 22 cm. [BX4700.T5H3] 67-21249
1. Therese, Saint, 1873-1897. I. Title.

HAUGHTON, Rosemary. 922.244
Therese Martin, written and illustrated by Rosemary Houghton. London, Longmans, Green Westminster, Md., Newman Press [1957] 277p. illus. 19cm. [BX4700.T5H3] 58-13638
1. Therese, Saint, 1873-1897. I. Title.

HAUGHTON, 271'.971'0924 B
Rosemary.
Therese Martin; the story of St. Therese of Lisieux. [Rev. ed.] New York, Macmillan [1967] 218 p. illus., ports. 22 cm. A biography of the French woman who entered the Carmelite order at the age of fifteen, died of tuberculosis at twenty-four, and was canonized in 1925. [BX4700.T5H3 1967] 92 AC 68
1. Therese, Saint, 1873-1897. I. Title.

KEYES, Frances Parkinson 922.244
(Wheeler)
Therese: saint of a little way. New rev. ed. New York, Hawthorn [c.1955,1962] 186p. illus. First pub. in 1937 under title: Written in heaven. Bibl. 62-8391 3.95
1. Therese, Saint, 1873-1897. I. Title.

KEYES, Frances Parkinson 922.244
(Wheeler) 1885-
Therese: saint of a little way. New and rev. ed. New York, Hawthorn Books [1962] 186p. illus. 22cm. First published in 1937 under title: Written in heaven. Includes bibliography. [BX4700.T5K4 1962] 62-8391
1. Therese, Saint, 1873-1897. I. Title.

LAVEILLE, Auguste Pierre, 922.244
1856-1928.
Life of the Little Flower St. Therese of Lisieux, according to the official documents of the Carmel of Lisieux. Translated by M. Fitzsimons. New York, McMullen Books, 1952. xiv, 376p. 22cm. Bibliographical footnotes. [BX4700.T5L334] 52-14392
1. Therese, Saint, I. Title.

PHILIPON, Marie Michel, 922.244
Father.
The message of Therese of Lisieux; translated by E. J. Ross. Westminster, Md., Newman Press, 1950. xv, 121 p. 18 cm. [BX4700.T5P513] 50-9053
1. Therese, Saint, 1873-1897. I. Title.

PHILIPON, Marie Michel, 922.244
1898-
The message of Therese of Lisieux; translated by E. J. Ross. Westminster, Md., Newman Press, 1950. xv, 121p. 18c4. [BX47.00.T5P513] 50-9053
1. Therese, Saint, 1873-1897. I. Title.

ROBO, Etienne. 922.244
Two-portraits of St. Teresa of Lisieux. [Rev. and enl.] Westminster, Md., Newman Press [1957] 238p. illus. 19cm. [BX4700.T5R6 1957] 57-14029
1. Therese, Saint. 1873-1897. I. Title.

ROBO, Etienne. 922.244
Two portraits of St. Therese of Lisieux. Chicago, Regnery [1955] 205p. illus. 19cm. [BX4700.T5R6] 55-13535
1. Therese, Saint, 1873-1897. I. Title.

SHERIDAN, Doris, 1905- 922.244
The whole world will love me; the life of Saint Therese of the Child Jesus and of the Holy Face. Emeric B. Scallan, editor. New York, William-Frederick Press, 1954. 337p. illus. 23cm. [BX4700.T5S4] 53-5666
1. Therese, Saint, 1873-1897. I. Title.

TERESA, Margaret 922.22
I choose all; a study of St. Therese of Lisieux and her spiritual doctrine. Westminster, Md., Newman [c.]1964. 252p. 23cm. Bibl. 64-57885 4.75
1. Therese, Saint, 1873-1897 I. Title.

TERESA, Margaret, Sister. 922.22
I choose all; a study of St. Therese of Lisieux and her spiritual doctrine. Westminster, Md., Newman Press, 1964. 252 p. 23 cm. Bibliography: p. [7]-[8] [BX4700.T4T4] 64-57885
1. Therese, Saint, I. Title.

THERESE, Saint, 1873- 922.244
1897.
Autobiography; the complete and authorized text of L'histoire d'une ame. Newly translated by Ronald Knox. With a foreword by Vernon Johnson. New York, Kenedy [1958] 320 p. illus., ports. 22 cm. [BX4700.T5A5 1958] 58-7325

THERESE, Saint, 1873- 922.244
1897.
The autobiography of St. Therese of Lisieux; the story of a soul. Newly translated, with an introd. by John Beevers. Garden City, N.Y., Image Books [1957] 159 p. 19 cm. (A Doubleday image book, D56) Translation of Histoire d'une ame. [BX4700.T5A5 1957] 57-10467
I. Title.

THERESE, Saint, 1873- 922.244
1897.
The story of a soul; the autobiography of Saint Therese of Lisieux. Edited by Mother Agnes of Jesus. Translated, with a critical pref., by Michael Day. [3d ed.] Westminster,Md., Newman Press [1957] 173 p. 19 cm. (Universe books) [BX4700.T5A5 1957a] 57-4180
I. Title.

THERESE, Saint, 271'.971'024 B
1873-1897.
Story of a soul : the autobiography of St. Therese of Lisieux ; a new translation from the original manuscripts by John Clarke. Washington : ICS Publications, 1975. xviii, 288 p., [4] leaves of plates : ill. ; 22 cm. Translation of Histoire d'une ame. Includes bibliographical references. [BX4700.T5A5 1975] 74-12777 3.95
1. Therese, Saint, 1873-1897. I. Title.

THERESE, Saint, 271'.971'024 B
1873-1897.
Story of a soul : the autobiography of St. Therese of Lisieux / a new translation from the original manuscripts by John Clarke. 2d ed. Washington : ICS Publications, 1976. xviii, 299 p., [4] leaves of plates : ill. ; 22 cm. Translation of Histoire d'une ame. Includes bibliographical references and index. [BX4700.T5A5 1976] 76-43620 ISBN 0-9600876-4-8 pbk. : 4.95
1. Therese, Saint, 1873-1897. 2. Christian saints—France—Lisieux—Biography. 3. Lisieux, France—Biography. I. Title.

THERESE, Saint, 1873- 922.244
1897.
The story of a soul; the autobiography of Saint Therese of Lisieux, in a new and rev. translation by Michael Day. With a foreword by Vernon Johnson. Westminster, Md., Newman Press, 1952. x. 208 p. 19 cm. [BX4700.T5A5] 52-9637
I. Title.

Therese, Saint, 1873-1897—Portraits.

JOHNSON, Vernon Cecil, 922.244
1886-
Spiritual childhood- a study of St. Teresa's teaching. New York, Sheed and Ward, 1954. 216p. 22cm. [BX4700.T5J6] 54-8061
I. Therese, Saint, 1873-1897. II. Title.

THE Photo album of St. 922.244
Therese of Lisieux. Commentary by Francois de Sainte-Marie, translated by Peter Thomas Rohrbach. New York, P. J. Kenedy [1962] 224p. illus., ports. 26cm. 'This authorized edition has been made from Le visage de Therese of Lisieux.' [BX4700.T5V543] 62-10909
1. Therese, Saint, 1873-1897—Portraits. I. Francois de Sainte Marle, Father.

PHOTO album of St. 922.244
Therese of Lisieux (The). Commentary by Francois de Sainte-Marie, tr. by Peter Thomas Rohrbach. New York, Kenedy [c.1961,1962] 224p. illus. 26cm. 62-10909 12.50
1. Therese, Saint, 1873-1897—Portraits. I. Francois de Sainte Marie Father.

Theta Delta Chi.

HACKETT, Norman, 378.1'98'55
1874-
Come my boys. [New York] Hackett Memorial Publication Fund, 1960. 420p. illus. 24cm. Autobiographical. [LJ75.T48H3] 60-42181
1. Theta Delta Chi. I. Title.

Thielicke, Helmut, 1908-

THIELICKE, Helmut, 1908- 916.7 B
African diary : my search for understanding / Helmut Thielicke. Waco, Tex. : Word Books, [1974] 213 p. ; 23 cm. Translation of So sah ich Afrika. [DT758.T4813] 74-78040 6.95
1. Thielicke, Helmut, 1908- 2. Africa, South—Description and travel—1966- 3. Mozambique—Description and travel. 4. Africa, East—Description and travel—1951- I. Title.

Thiers, Adolphe, 1797-1877.

†ALBRECHT-CARRIE, 944.07'092'4 B
Rene 1904-
Adolphe Theirs, or ; The triumph of the bourgeoisie / by Rene Albrecht-Carrie. Boston : G. K. Hall, c1977. 176 p. : port. ; 21 cm. (Twayne's world leaders series ; TWLS 67) Includes index. Bibliography: p. 171.173. [DC280.5.T5A67] 77-23494 ISBN 0-8057-7717-2 lib.bdg. : 9.95
1. Thiers, Adolphe, 1797-1877. 2. Statesmen—France—Biography.

ALLISON, John 944.06'3'0924
Maudgridge Snowden, 1888-1944.
Thiers and the French monarchy. [Hamden, Conn.] Archon Books, 1968. xi, 379 p. illus., ports. 22 cm. "An unaltered and unabridged [reprint of the 1926] edition." Bibliography: p. 362-372. [DC344.A7 1968] 68-21684
1. Thiers, Adolphe, 2. France—Pol. & govt.—1830-1848. I. Title. **BIP**

Thieves.

HAPGOOD, Hutchins, 1869- 364.16'2
1944.
The autobiography of a thief. Recorded by Hutchins Hapgood. New York, Fox, Duffield, 1903. New York, Johnson Reprint Corp., 1970. 349 p. 19 cm. (Rediscovering America) [HV6653.Z9H3 1970] 79-22256
1. Thieves. I. Title. **BIP**

Thille, Grace (Sharp)

THILLE, Grace (Sharp) 1875- 920.7
Day before yesterday. Santa Paula, Calif., 1952. 160p. illus. 22cm. Autobiographical. [CT275.T525A3] 54-3004
I. Title.

Thirion, Andre, 1907- —Biography.

THIRION, Andre, 322.4'2'0924 B
1907-
Revolutionaries without revolution. Translated by Joachim Neugroschel. [1st American ed.] New York, Macmillan [1975] viii, 499 p. illus. 24 cm. [PQ2639.H368Z513 1975] 74-9859 ISBN 0-02-617400-6 12.95
1. Thirion, Andre, 1907- —Biography. I. Title. **BIP**

Thirkell, Angela (Mackai) 1890-1961.

MCINNES, Graham 828.91403
The road to Gundagai. New York, London House [1966, c.1965] 285p illus., maps (pt. fold.) ports 23cm. Autobiographical. [PR6063.A24Z5] 66-17848 5.95 bds.,
1. Thirkell, Angela (Mackai) 1890-1961. I. Title. **BIP**

Thirty Years' War, 1618-1648—Biography.

CUST, Edward, Sir 940.2'4'0922 B
bart., 1794-1878.
Lives of the warriors of the Thirty Years' War; warriors of the seventeenth century. Freeport, N.Y., Books for Libraries Press [1972] 2 v. (xiv, 603 p.) 23 cm. (Essay index reprint series) Reprint of the 1865 ed. [D270.A2C8 1972] 75-38742 ISBN 0-8369-2643-9
1. Thirty Years' War, 1618-1648—Biography. I. Title. **BIP**

Thoma, Ludwig, 1867-1921.

STEINBRUCKNER, 838'.9'1209 B
Bruno Friedrich.
Ludwig Thoma / by Bruno F. Steinbruckner. Boston : Twayne Publishers, 1978. 155 p. : port. ; 21 cm. (Twayne's world authors series ; TWAS 494 : Germany) Includes indexes. Bibliography: p. [PT2642.H58Z798] 78-5282 ISBN 0-8057-6335-X lib. bdg. : 13.50
1. Thoma, Ludwig, 1867-1921. 2. Authors, German—20th century—Biography. I. Title. **BIP**

Thomapson,

SHEEAN, Vincent [James 928.1
Vincent Sheean] 1899-
Dorothy and Red. Greenwich, Conn., Fawcett [1964, c.1963] 320p. illus. 18cm. (Crest bk. T 776) .75 pap.,
1. Thomapson, I. Title.

Thomas a Becket, Saint, Abp. of Canterbury, 1118?-1170.

BENEDICT, Abbot 942.03'1'0924 B
of Peterborough, d.1193.
Benedicti Abbatis Petriburgensis de vita et miraculis S. Thomae Cantuar. The life and miracles of Saint Thomas of Canterbury, by the Rev. Dr. Giles. New York, B. Franklin [1967] 281 p. 23 cm. (Burt Franklin research & source works series, no. 154) Reprint of the 1850 ed., which was issued as publication 11 of the Caxton Society. Text in Latin; preface in English. [DA209.T4B36 1967] 72-185363
1. Thomas a Becket, Saint, Abp. of Canterbury, 1118?-1170. I. Title. II. Title: The life and miracles of Saint Thomas of Canterbury. III. Series: Caxton Society. Publications.

DUGGAN, Alfred Leo, 1903- 922.242
My life for my sheep. Illus. by George Hartmann. Garden City, N. Y., Image Books [1957, c1955] 318p. illus. 18cm. (A Doubleday image book, D53) [DA209.T4D78 1957] 57-3693
1. Thomas a Becket, Saint, Abp. of Canterbury, 1118?-1170. I. Title.

DUGGAN, Alfred Leo, 1903- 922.242
1964.
My life for my sheep. New York, Coward-McCann [1955] 341 p. illus. 23 cm. [DA209.T4D78] 55-10305
1. Thomas a Becket, Saint, Abp. of Canterbury, 1118?-1170. I. Title.

DUGGAN, Alfred Leo, 942.020924
1903-1964.
My life for my sheep. New York, Weybright and Talley [196-? c1955] 314 p. map. 22 cm. [DA209.T4D78] 68-12873
1. Thomas a Becket, Saint, Abp. of Canterbury, 1118?-1170. I. Title.

DUGGAN, Alfred Leo, 942.020924
1903-1964
My life for my sheep. New York, Weybright & Talley [19-? c1955] 314p. map. 2cm. [DA209.T4D78] 68-12873 6.50
1. Thomas a Becket, Saint, Abp. of Canterbury, 1118?-1170. I. Title.

SMALLEY, Beryl. 942.03'1'0924 B
The Becket conflict and the schools; a study of intellectuals in politics. Totowa, N.J., Rowman and Littlefield [1973] xiv, 257 p. 23 cm. Includes bibliographical references. [DA209.T4S6 1973] 72-14254 ISBN 0-87471-172-X 13.50
1. Thomas a Becket, Saint, Abp. of Canterbury, 1118?-1170. 2. Scholasticism. 3. England—Intellectual life—Medieval period, 1066-1485. I. Title.

WATT, Francis, 1849- 914.22'3
1927.
Canterbury pilgrims and their ways. [Folcroft, Pa.] Folcroft Library Editions, 1973. xiv, 288 p. illus. 26 cm. Reprint of the 1917 ed. published by Dodd, Mead, New York. [DA690.C3W3 1973] 73-4912 ISBN 0-8414-9353-7 22.50 (lib. ed.)
1. Thomas a Becket, Saint, Abp. of Canterbury, 1118?-1170. 2. Canterbury, Eng.—Description. 3. Pilgrims and pilgrimages—Canterbury, Eng. I. Title. **BIP**

WINSTON, Richard. 942.03'1'0924
Thomas Becket. [1st ed.] New York, Knopf, 1967. x, 413 p. illus. 25 cm. Bibliography: p. 407-413. [DA209.T4W5] 66-10752
1. Thomas a Becket, Saint, Abp. of Canterbury, 1118?-1170.

Thomas a Becket, Saint, Abp. of Canterbury, 1118?-1170—Juvenile literature.

CORFE, Thomas 942.03'1'0924 B
Howell.
Archbishop Thomas and King Henry II / Tom Corfe Cambridge ; New York : Cambridge University Press, 1975. 48 p. : ill., facsim., geneal. tables, maps, plans, ports. ; 21 x 22 cm. (Cambridge introduction to the history of mankind : Topic book) Discusses the events surrounding the murder of Thomas a Becket, the Archbishop of Canterbury, and the living conditions in England during the reign of Henry II. [DA209.T4C63] 920 74-14442 pbk. : 2.75
1. Thomas a Becket, Saint, Abp. of Canterbury, 1118?-1170—Juvenile literature. 2. Henry II, King of England, 1133-1189—Juvenile literature. I. Title.

Thomas a Kempis, 1380-1471.

DE MONTMORENCY, James 242'.1
Edward Geoffrey, 1866-1934.
Thomas a Kempis; his age and book. Port Washington, N.Y., Kennikat Press [1970] xxiii, 312 p. facsims. 22 cm. "First published in 1906." Contents.Contents.—Introduction.—List of manuscripts of the treatise "De imitatione Christi" in English libraries.—List of other manuscripts cited.—List of printed editions of the treatise "De imitatione Christi" cited.—The age of Thomas a Kempis.—Some fifteenth century manuscripts and editions of the Imitation. Master Walter Hilton and the authorship of the Imitation.—The structure of the Imitation.—The content of the Imitation.—Appendix I. "De meditatione cordis," by Jean le Charlier de Gerson, chancellor of Paris.—Appendix II. Extract from the "Garden of roses," by Thomas a Kempis. [BV4829.D4 1970] 73-103183
1. Thomas a Kempis, 1380-1471. 2. Imitatio Christi. I. Gerson, Joannes, 1363-1429. De meditatione cordis.

Thomas, Albert, 1821-1895.

NICHOLAS, Ann T. 301.45'22'0924 B
Albert, by Ann T. Nicholas. Philadelphia, Dorrance [1970] 41 p. illus. 22 cm. [E185.97.T48N5] 72-126540 ISBN 8-05-914773- 2.95
1. Thomas, Albert, 1821-1895. I. Title.

Thomas Aquinas, Saint, 1225?-1274.

BOURKE, Vernon Joseph, 922.22
1907-
Aquinas' search for wisdom [by] Vernon J. Bourke. Milwaukee, Bruce Pub. Co. [1965] x, 244 p. 23 cm. (Christian culture and philosophy series) Bibliographical footnotes. [BX4700.T6B6] 65-12046
1. Thomas Aquinas, Saint, 1225?-1274. I. Title. II. Series.

CHESTERTON, Gilbert 922.245
Keith, 1874-1936.
St. Thomas Aquinas. Garden City, N. Y., Image Books [1956] 198p. 18cm. (A Doubleday image book, D66) [BX4700.T6C5 1956] 56-5405
1. Thomas Aquinas, Saint, 1225?-1274. I. Title.

D'ARCY, Martin Cyril, 922.245
1888-
St. Thomas Aquinas. Dublin, Clonmore & Reynolds; [label: Westminster, Md., Newman Press, 1953] 220p. 22cm. First ed. published in 1930 under title: Thomas Aquians. [B765.T54D3 1953] 54-1170
1. Thomas Aquinas, Saint, 1225?-1274. I. Title.

GERMAIN, Brother, 1912- 922.245
Knight without armor, a story of St. Thomas Aquinas. Illus. by Bernard Howard. Notre Dame, Ind., Dujarie Press [1951] 88 p. illus. 24 cm. [BX4700.T6G4] 52-15610
1. Thomas Aquinas, Saint, 1225?-1274. I. Title.

GRABMANN, Martin, 1875- 922.245
The interior life of St. Thomas Aquinas, presented from his works and the acts of his canonization process; translated by Nicholas Ashenbrener. Milwaukee, Bruce [1951] 92 p. illus. 21 cm. [BX4700.T6G673] 51-7705
1. Thomas Aquinas, Saint, 1225?-1274. I. Title.

GRABMANN, Martin, 1875- 922.245
1949
Thomas Aquinas, his personality and thought. Authorized tr. [from German] by Virgil Michel. New York, Russel, 1963. 191p. 23cm. Bibl. 63-15160 6.00
1. Thomas Aquinas, Saint 1225? 1274. I. Michel, Virgil George, Father, 1890-1938, tr. II. Title.

MCINERNY, Ralph M. 230'.2'0924
St. Thomas Aquinas / by Ralph McInerny. Boston : Twayne Publishers, c1977. 197 p. : port. ; 21 cm. (Twayne's world authors series ; TWAS 408 : Italy) Includes index. Bibliography: p. 183-189. [B765.T54M244] 76-25959 ISBN 0-8057-6248-5 lib.bdg. : 8.95
1. Thomas Aquinas, Saint, 1225?-1274. **BIP**

MARITAIN, Jacques, 1882- 922.245
St. Thomas Aquinas. [Newly translated and rev. by Joseph W. Evans and Peter O'Reilly] New York, Meridian Books [1958] 281p. 19cm. (Merdian books, M55) Includes bibliography. [BX4700.T6M345] 57-10837
1. Thomas Aquinas, Saint, 1225?-1274. 2. Scholasticism. I. Title.

NEWLAND, Mary 271'.2'0924 B
(Reed)
St. Thomas Aquinas; a concise biography. Foreword by J. M. Donahue. New York, American R.D.M. Corp. [1967] 62 p. port. 21 cm. (A Study master publication, 961) Bibliography: p. 62. [BX4700.T6N4] 66-28705
1. Thomas Aquinas, Saint, 1225?-1274.

PETITOT, Hyacinthe, 1880- 189.4 B
1934.
The life and spirit of Thomas Aquinas [by] L. H. Petitot. Translated by Cyprian Burke. Chicago, Priory Press [1966] 174 p. 21 cm. Translation of Saint Thomas d'Aquin; la vocation, l'oeuvre, la vie spirituelle. Includes bibliographical references. [BX4700.T6P42] 66-24109
1. Thomas Aquinas, Saint, 1225?-1274. I. Title.

PIEPER, Josef, 1904- 922.245
Guide to Thomas Aquinas. Tr. from German by Richard and Clara Winston [New York] New Amer. Lib. [1964,c.1962] 160p. 18cm. (Mentor-omega MP 581) Bibl. .60 pap.,
1. Thomas Aquinas, Saint, 1225?-1274. I. Title.

PIEPER, Josef, 1904- 922.245
Guide to Thomas Aquinas. Translated from the German by Richard and Clara Winston. [New York] Pantheon Books [1962] 181p. 21cm. Includes bibliography. [BX4700.T6P53] 62-11079
1. Thomas Aquinas, Saint, 1225?-1274. I. Title.

WALZ, Angelus Maria, 922.245
Father, 1893-
Saint Thomas Aquinas, a biographical study. English translation by Father Sebastian Bullough. Westminister, Md., Newman Press, 1951. xi, 254 p. illus., map (on lining paper) 24 cm. Bibliography: p. 229-239. [BX4700.T6W313] 51-12488
1. Thomas Aquinas, Saint, 1225?-1274. I. Title.

WEISHEIPL, James A. 189'.4 B
Friar Thomas D'Aquino: his life, thought, and work [by] James A. Weisheipl. [1st ed.] Garden City, N.Y., Doubleday, 1974. xii, 464 p. port. 25 cm. Bibliography: p. [355]-410. [B765.T54W35] 73-80801 ISBN 0-385-01299-3 8.95
1. Thomas Aquinas, Saint, 1225?-1274. I. Title.

Thomas Aquinas, Saint, 1225?-1274—Juvenile literature.

PITTENGER, William 271'.2'0924 B
Norman, 1905-
Saint Thomas Aquinas; the angelic doctor, by Norman Pittenger. New York, F. Watts [1969] vii, 150 p. map. 22 cm. (Immortals of philosophy and religion) Bibliography: p. 146-148. A biography of the thirteenth-century philosopher best known for his ability to reconcile the basic principles of Christian and Aristotelian thought. [BX4700.T6P565] 92 77-79849
1. Thomas Aquinas, Saint, 1225?-1274—Juvenile literature. I. Title.

Thomas, Charles Spalding, 1849-1934.

THOMAS, Sewell, 1884- 923.273
Silhouettes of Charles S. Thomas, Colorado Governor and United States Senator. Caldwell, Idaho, Caxton Printers, 1959. xi, 228 p. illus., ports., facsims. 25 cm. [E664.T36T4] 59-7608
1. Thomas, Charles Spalding, 1849-1934. I. Title.

Thomas, Dylan, 1914-1953.

ACKERMAN, John 828.912
Dylan Thomas, his life and work. New York, Oxford [c.]1964. 201p. facsims., port. 23cm Bibl. [PR6039.H52Z55] 65-435 5.75
1. Thomas, Dylan, 1914-1953. I. Title.

ACKERMAN, John. 828.912
Dylan Thomas, his life and work. London, New York, Oxford University Press, 1964. 201 p. facsims., port. 23 cm. Bibliography: p. [191]-194. [PR6039.H52Z55] 65-435
1. Thomas, Dylan, 1914-1953.

BRINNIN, John Malcolm, 821.912
1916- ed.
A casebook of Dylan Thomas. New York, Crowell [1960] xiii, 322 p. 22 cm. Bibliography: p. 295-310. [PR6039.H52Z59] 60-9937
1. Thomas, Dylan, 1914-1953. I. Title.

BRINNIN, John Malcolm, 928.2
1916-
Dylan Thomas in America, an intimate journal. With photos. [1st ed.] Boston, Little, Brown [1955] 303p. illus. 21cm. (An Atlantic Monthly Press book) [PR6039.H52Z6] 55-10768
1. Thomas, Dylan, 1914-1953. I. Title.

DYLAN Thomas, v. 12
'dog among the fairies.' New York, John de Graff, 1956. 158p. 19cm.
1. Thomas, Dylan, 1914-1953. I. Treece, Henry, 1912-

DYLAN Thomas in America v. 12
an intimate journal. New York, Viking Press [1957] 303p. 20cm.

1. Thomas, Dylan, 1914-1953. I. Brinnin, John Malcom, 1916-

FITZ Gibbon, Constantine. 821.912 B
The life of Dylan Thomas. [1st American ed.] Boston, Little, Brown [1965] xi, 370 p. facsims., ports. 25 cm. "An Atlantic monthly press book." Includes bibliographical references. [PR6039.H52Z643 1965] 65-20748
1. Thomas, Dylan, 1914-1953. I. Title. **BIP**

FITZGIBBON, Constantine 821.912
The life of Dylan Thomas [1st Amer. ed.] Boston, Atlantic-Little [c.1965] xi, 370p. facsims., ports. 25cm. Bibl. [PR6039.H52Z643] 65-20748 7.95
1. Thomas, Dylan, 1914-1953. I. Title.

JONES, Thomas Henry, 1921- v. 12
Dylan Thomas [by] T. H. Jones. New York, Barnes & Noble [1966, c1963] 118 p. 18 cm. (Writers and critics) 67-42242
1. Thomas, Dylan, 1914-1953. I. Title.

READ, Bill, 1917- 928.2
The days of Dylan Thomas. Photos. by Rollie McKenna, others. New York, McGraw [1964] 184p. illus., facsims., maps (1 fold.) ports. 21cm. (McGraw paperbacks) Bibl. 64-16490 1.95 pap.,
1. Thomas, Dylan, 1914-1953. I. Title.

SINCLAIR, Andrew. 821'.9'12
Dylan Thomas no man more magical / by Andrew Sinclair. New York : Holt, Rinehart and Winston, [1975] p. cm. [PR6039.H52Z849] 75-5461 ISBN 0-03-014536-8 : 15.95
1. Thomas, Dylan, 1914-1953. I. Title.

STANFORD, Derek. v. 12
Dylan Thomas; a literary study. [2d paperbound ed.] New York, Citadel Press [1965, c1964] 212 p. 20 cm. 68-66034
1. Thomas, Dylan, 1914-1953. I. Title.

TEDLOCK, Ernest Warnock, 1910- ed. 821'.9'12 B
Dylan Thomas: the legend and the poet; a collection of biographical and critical essays, edited by E. W. Tedlock. Westport, Conn., Greenwood Press [1975, c1960] x, 283 p. 22 cm. Reprint of the ed. published by Heinemann, London. [PR6039.H52Z855 1975] 72-9050 ISBN 0-8371-6564-4
1. Thomas, Dylan, 1914-1953.

THOMAS, Caitlin. 928.2
Leftover life to kill. [1st American ed.] Boston, Little, Brown [1957] 262 p. 22 cm. Autobiographical. [PR6039.H52Z86 1957a] 57-11993
1. Thomas, Dylan, 1914-1953. I. Title.

THOMAS, Dylan, Full name: Dylan Mariais Thomas, 1914-1953. 928.2
Letters to Vernon Watkins. Edited with an introd. by Vernon Watkins. [New York] New Directions [1957] 145 p. illus. 21 cm. [PR6039.H52Z53] 57-13084
I. Watkins, Vernon Phillips, 1906- II. Title. **BIP**

TREECE, Henry, 1912- v. 12
Dylan Thomas, 'dog among the fairies. New York, John de Graff, 1956. 158 p. 19 cm.
1. Thomas, Dylan, 1914-1953. I. Title. **BIP**

Thomas, Dylan, 1914-1953 — Biography

FERRIS, Paul, 1929- 821'.9'12 B
Dylan Thomas / by Paul Ferris. New York : Dial Press, c1977. 399 p., [8] leaves of plates : ill. ; 24 cm. Includes index. Bibliography : p. [373]-375. [PR6039.H52Z637] 76-54936 ISBN 0-8037-1939-6 : 10.00
1. Thomas, Dylan, 1914-1953—Biography. 2. Authors, Welsh—20th century—Biography.

FERRIS, Paul, 1929- 821'.9'12 B
Dylan Thomas / Paul Ferris. Harmondsworth; New York : Penguin Books, 1978 c1977. xvii, 466p., 8 leaves of plates : ill ; 18 cm. Includes index. Bibliography: [415]-417 [PR6039.H52Z637] ISBN 0-14-00-4773-5 pbk. : 3.95
1. Thomas, Dylan, 1914-1953 — Biography 2. Authors Welsh — 20th century — Biography I. Title.
L.C. card no. for 1977 Dial Press ed., 76-54936

Thomas, Edward, 1878-1917.

ECKERT, Robert Paul, 1903- 821'.9'12 B
Edward Thomas : a biography and a bibliography / by Robert P. Eckert. Folcroft, PA : Folcroft Library Editions, 1978. xxi, 328 p. : port. ; 26 cm. Reprint of the 1937 ed. published by Dutton, New York. Includes index. [PR6039.H55Z7 1978] 78-2619 ISBN 0-8414-4040-9 lib. bdg. : 30.00
1. Thomas, Edward, 1878-1917. 2. Thomas, Edward, 1878-1917—Bibliography. 3. Authors, English—20th century—Biography. **BIP**

MARSH, Jan. 821'.9'12 B
Edward Thomas, a poet for his country / Jan Marsh. New York : Barnes & Noble Books, 1978. xiv, 225 p., [4] leaves of plates : ill. ; 24 cm. Includes index. Bibliography: p. [207]-208. [PR6039.H55Z75 1978b] 79-101450 ISBN 0-06-494563-4 : 23.50
1. Thomas, Edward, 1878-1917. 2. Authors, English—20th century—Biography. I. Title.

Thomas, Edward, 1878-1917—Biography.

THOMAS, Helen Noble. 821'.9'12 B
Time & again : memoirs and letters / [by] Helen Thomas ; edited by Myfanwy Thomas. Manchester : Carcanet New Press, 1978. 161 p., [8] p. of plates : ports. ; 23 cm. [PR6039.H55Z827] 78-325650 ISBN 0-85635-243-8 : 11.95
1. Thomas, Edward, 1878-1917—Biography. 2. Thomas, Helen Noble. 3. Authors, English—20th century—Biography. 4. Wives—England—Biography. I. Thomas, Myfanwy.
Distributed by Persea Books, 225 Lafayette St., New York, NY 10012 **BIP**

Thomas, George Henry, 1816-1870.

CLEAVES, Freeman, 1904- 973.7'3'0924 B
Rock of Chickamauga, the life of General George H. Thomas. Westport, Conn., Greenwood Press [1974, c1948] xi, 328 p. illus. 22 cm. Reprint of the ed. published by University of Oklahoma Press, Norman. Bibliography: p. 309-316. [E467.1.T4C6 1974] 73-8253 ISBN 0-8371-6973-9 15.00
1. Thomas, George Henry, 1816-1870. 2. United States—History—Civil War, 1861-1865—Campaigns and battles. I. Title. **BIP**

MCKINNEY, Francis F 1891- 923.573
Education in violence; the life of George H. Thomas and the history of the Army of the Cumberland. Detroit, Wayne State University Press, 1961. 530p. illus. 25cm. Includes bibliography. [E467.1.T4M17] 61-6040
1. Thomas, George Henry, 1816- 1870. 2. U. S. Army. Dept. of the Cumberland. 3. U. S.—Hist.—Civil War—Regimental histories—Dept. of the Cumberland. I. Title.

THOMAS, Wilbur D. 923.573
General George H. Thomas, the indomitable warrior, supreme in defense and in counterattack; a biography. New York, Exposition [c.1964] 649p. illus., map, plans, ports. 24cm. (Exposition-Lochinvar) Bibl. 64-6015 10.00
1. Thomas, George Henry, 1816-1870. I. Title.

Thomas, George, 1756?-1802.

HENNESSY, Maurice N. 954'.558'0310924 B
The Rajah from Tipperary [by] Maurice Hennessy. New York, St. Martin's Press [1972, c1971] xx, 183 p. illus. 23 cm. Bibliography: p. 178-179. [DS470.T4H44 1972] 72-77016
1. Thomas, George, 1756?-1802. 2. Haryana—History. I. Title.

Thomas, Helen, 1920-

THOMAS, Helen, 1920- 973'.0992 B
Dateline: White House Helen Thomas New York : Macmillan, 1975. xviii, 298 p., [4] leaves of plates : ill. ; 21 cm. Includes index. [PN4874T.424A33] 75-30625 ISBN 0-02-617620-3 : 10.95
1. Thomas, Helen, 1920- 2. Journalists—United States—Correspondence, reminiscences, etc. 3. United States—Politics and government—1945- 4. Presidents—United States—Biography. 5. Presidents—United States—Wives. I. Title.

Thomas, Isaiah, 1749-1831.

NICHOLS, Charles Lemuel, 1851-1929. 686'.20924
Isaiah Thomas, printer, writer & collector; a paper read April 12, 1911, before the Club of Odd Volumes. With a bibliography of the books printed by Isaiah Thomas. New York, B. Franklin [1971] 144 p. 24 cm. (Burt Franklin research & source works series, 438) (American classics in history and social science, 195) Reprint of the 1912 ed. Bibliography: p. [37]-133. [Z232.T4N53 1971] 70-165413 ISBN 0-8337-4301-5
1. Thomas, Isaiah, 1749-1831. I. Club of Odd Volumes, Boston.

Thomas, James Henry, 1874?-1949.

BLAXLAND, Gregory 923.242
J. H. Thomas, a life for unity. London, F. Muller New Rochelle, N. Y., SportShelf, c.1964 303p. illus., ports. 23cm. Bibl. 64-56807 9.50
1. Thomas, James Henry, 1874?-1949. I. Title.

Thomas, Jesse O.,

THOMAS, Jesse O., 1885- 973.9'0924 B
My story in black and white; the autobiography of Jesse O. Thomas. Foreword by Whitney M. Young, Jr. [1st ed.] New York, Exposition Press [1967] 300 p. 21 cm. (An Exposition-banner book) [E185.97.T49A3] 67-24271
I. Title.

Thomas, John Peyre, 1833-1912.

THOMAS, Albert Sidney, 1873-. 378.757'915
The career and character of Col. John Peyre Thomas, L.L.D., compiled by his son, Albert Sidney Thomas. [Columbus? S.C.] 1964. iii, 60 l. port. 29 cm. "Publications of Colonel Thomas": p. 46-48. [U430.S59] 65-3710
1. Thomas, John Peyre, 1833-1912. 2. The Citadel, the Military College of South Carolina, Charleston. I. Title.

Thomas, Joshua, 1776-1853.

WALLACE, Adam, 1825-1903 922.773
The parson of the islands; a biography of the Rev. Joshua Thomas; embracing sketches of his contemporaries, and remarkable camp meeting scenes, revival incidents, and reminiscences of the introduction of Methodism on the islands of the Chesapeake, and the Eastern Shores of Maryland and Virginia. Introd. by James A. Massey. Cambridge, Md., Tidewater Pubs. [dist Cornell Maritime] 1961. 312p. illus. Facsimile reprint of the Philadelphia ed. of 1861. 61-17566 3.95
1. Thomas, Joshua, 1776-1853. I. Title.

Thomas, Lowell

THOMAS, Lowell 923.543
Count Luckner the sea devil, by Lowell Thomas, Felix von Luckner. New York, Popular Lib. [1962, c.1927] 221p. (SP155) .50 pap.,
I. Title.

Thomas, Lowell Jackson, 1892-

BOWEN, Norman R., comp. 070.924
Lowell Thomas, the stranger everyone knows; America's most illustrious newsman as colleagues and others have seen him through the last five decades. Profiles by Russel Crouse [and others] Edited by Norman R. Bowen. Garden City, N.Y., Doubleday [1968] xx, 187 p. illus. (part col.), ports. (part col.) 24 cm. "Lowell Thomas' list of books": p. 186. [CT275.T554B6] 68-1418
1. Thomas, Lowell Jackson, 1892- I. Crouse, Russel, 1893-1966. II. Title.

THOMAS, Lowell Jackson, 1892- 070'.92'4 B
Good evening everybody : from Cripple Creek to Samarkand / by Lowell Thomas. New York : Morrow, 1976. 349 p., [16] leaves of plates : ill. ; 24 cm. Autobiography. [CT275.T554A34] 76-10668 ISBN 0-688-03068-8 : 12.50
1. Thomas, Lowell Jackson, 1892- I. Title. **BIP**

THOMAS, Lowell Jackson, 1892- 070'.92'4 B
So long until tomorrow : from Quaker Hill to Kathmandu / by Lowell Thomas. New York : Morrow, 1977. p. cm. Continues Good evening everybody. Autobiographical. [CT275.T554A35] 77-10541 ISBN 0-688-03236-2 : 10.95
1. Thomas, Lowell Jackson, 1892- 2. United States—Biography. I. Title.

THOMAS, Lowell Jackson, 1892- 920.02
The vital spark; 101 outstanding lives. Ports. by Louis Lupas. [1st ed.] Garden City, N.Y., Doubleday, 1959. 480 p. illus. 25 cm. Bibliography. [CT104.T537] 59-12649
I. Title.

Thomas, Lowell Jackson, 1892- — Juvenile literature.

COMFORT, Mildred Houghton, 1886- 920.5
Lowell Thomas, adventurer. Minneapolis, T. S. Denison [1965] 239 p. illus., ports. 22 cm. (Men of achievement series) [CT275.T554C6] 63-14387
1. Thomas, Lowell Jackson, 1892- — Juvenile literature. I. Title.

Thomas, Norman Mattoon, 1884-1968.

DURAM, James C., 1939- 335'.0092'4 B
Norman Thomas, by James C. Duram. New York, Twayne Publishers [1974] 176 p. port. 22 cm. (Twayne's United States authors series, TUSAS 234) Bibliography: p. 167-171. [HX84.T47D87] 73-15831 ISBN 0-8057-0727-1 5.50
1. Thomas, Norman Mattoon, 1884-1968. **BIP**

FLEISCHMAN, Harry. 923.273
Norman Thomas, a biography. New York, Norton [1964] 320 p. ports. 22 cm. "Selected works of Norman Thomas": p. 312-314. Bibliography: p. 311. [HX84.T47F55] 62-12282
1. Thomas, Norman Mattoon, 1884-1968.

FLEISCHMAN, Harry. 335'.00924 B
Norman Thomas; a biography: 1884-1968. With a new chapter The final years New York, Norton [1969] 346 p. illus., ports. 23 cm. Includes bibliographies. [HX84.T47F553] 74-78066 6.95
1. Thomas, Norman Mattoon, 1884-1968.

GORHAM, Charles Orson, 1911- 335'.00924 B
Leader at large; the long and fighting life of Norman Thomas [by] Charles Gorham. New York, Farrar, Straus & Giroux [1970] xii, 217 p. illus., facsim., ports. 21 cm. Bibliography: p. 205-208. [HX84.T47G63] 72-119548 4.95
1. Thomas, Norman Mattoon, 1884-1968. I. Title.

SEIDLER, Murray Benjamin, 1924- 923.273
Norman Thomas: respectable rebel. [Syracuse, N. Y.] Syracuse Univ. Pr. [c.] 1961. 368p. illus. Bibl. 61-13115 5.50
1. Thomas, Norman Mattoon, 1884- 2. Socialist Party (U. S.) 3. Socialism in the U. S. I. Title. BIP

SEIDLER, Murray Benjamin, 1924- 335'.00973
Norman Thomas: respectable rebel [by] Murray B. Seidler. [2d ed. Syracuse, N.Y.] Syracuse Univ. Pr. [1967] x, 394p. illus., ports. 21cm. (Men movements) Bibl. [HX84.T47S4 1967] 67-15881 7.00
1. Thomas, Norman Mattoon, 2. Socialist Party (U.S.) 3. Socialism in the U.S. I. Title. II. Series.

SEIDLER, Murray Benjamin, 1924- 923.273
Norman Thomas: respectable rebel. [Syracuse, N. Y.] Syracuse University Press, 1961. 368p. illus. 21cm. Includes bibliography. [HX84.T47S4] 61-13115
1. Thomas, Norman Mattoon, 1884- 2. Socialist Party (U. S.) 3. Socialism in the U. S. I. Title.

STEWARD, Dwight. 335'.0092'4 B
Mr. Socialism, being an account of Norman Thomas and his labors to keep America safe from socialism / by Dwight Steward. Secaucus, N.J. : L. Stuart, c1974. 223 p. ; 24 cm. [HX84.T47S84] 73-87815 ISBN 0-8184-0162-1 7.95
1. Thomas, Norman Mattoon, 1884-1968. 2. Socialism in the U.S. 3. U.S.—Politics and government—20th century. I. Title: Mr. Socialism, being an account of Norman Thomas ...

SWANBERG, W. A., 1907- 329'.81'00924 B
Norman Thomas, the last idealist / W. A. Swanberg. New York : Scribner, c1976. xii, 528 p., [17] leaves of plates : ill. ; 23 cm. Includes bibliographical references and index. [HX84.T47S9] 76-15591 ISBN 0-684-14768-8 : 15.00
1. Thomas, Norman Mattoon, 1884-1968. I. Title.

Thomas, Robert E., 1914-

JARMAN, Rufus. 338.7'62'10924 B
The energy merchant / by Rufus Jarman. 1st ed. New York : R. Rosen Press, 1977. 279 p. : ill. (some col.) ; 25 cm. [HD9579.P42T484] 77-154071 lib. bdg. 10.00
1. Thomas, Robert E., 1914- 2. Mapco—History. 3. Businessmen—United States—Biography. I. Title. BIP

Thomas, Sidney Gilchrist, 1850-1885.

JEANS, William T. 669'.142'0922 B
The creators of the age of steel, by W. T. Jeans. Freeport, New York, Books for Libraries Press [1973] p. (Essay index reprint series) "First published 1854." Contents.Contents.—Introduction.—Sir Henry Bessemer.—Sir William Siemens.—Sir Joseph Whitworth.—Sir John Brown.—Mr. S. G. Thomas.—Mr. G. J. Snelus. [TN139.J45 1973] 73-1583 ISBN 0-518-10054-5
1. Bessemer, Henry, Sir, 1813-1898. 2. Siemens, William, Sir, 1816-1896. 3. Whitworth, Joseph, Sir, 1803-1887. 4. Brown, John, Sir, 1816-1896. 5. Thomas, Sidney Gilchrist, 1850-1885. 6. Snelus, George James, 1837-1906. 7. Steel—History. 8. Inventors. I. Title.

Thomas, Tay.

†THOMAS, Tay. 283'.092'4 B
My war with worry / Tay Thomas. [Lincoln, Va.] : Chosen Books ; Waco Tex. : distributed by Word Books, c1977. 154 p. : ill. ; 23 cm. [BX5995.T4A33] 77-80669 6.95
1. Thomas, Tay. 2. Episcopalians—Biography. 3. Anchorage, Alaska—Earthquake, 1964—Personal narratives. 4. Pentecostalism. I. Title.

Thomas, Theodore, 1835-1905.

RUSSELL, Charles Edward, 1860-1941. 785'.0924 B
The American orchestra and Theodore Thomas. Westport, Conn., Greenwood Press [1971, c1927] xx, 344 p. illus. 23 cm. Includes bibliographical references. [ML1211.R88 1971] 76-139146 ISBN 0-8371-5762-5
1. Thomas, Theodore, 1835-1905. 2. Symphony orchestras—U.S. I. Title. BIP

THOMAS, Rose Fay, 1852-1929. 785'.092'4 B
Memoirs of Theodore Thomas. Freeport, N.Y., Books for Libraries Press [1971] xviii, 569 p. illus. 23 cm. Reprint of the 1911 ed. [ML422.T46A3 1971] 73-37356 ISBN 0-8369-6703-8
1. Thomas, Theodore, 1835-1905. BIP

Thomason, John William, 1893-1944.

WILLOCK, Roger. 923.573
Lone Star marine; a biography of the late Colonel John W. Thomason, Jr., U.S.M.C. Princeton, N. J. [1961] 195 p. illus. 25 cm. [E746.T5W5] 61-8032
1. Thomason, John William, 1893-1944. I. Title.

Thomes, William Henry, 1824-1895—Homes and haunts—California.

THOMES, William Henry, 1824-1895. 813'.4 B
Recollections of old times in California : or, California life in 1843 / by William Henry Thomes ; edited with an introd. by George R. Stewart. Berkeley : Friends of the Bancroft Library, University of California, 1974. 29 p., [6] leaves of plates : ill. ; 24 cm. (The series of keepsakes ; no. 22) [PS3030.T65Z525 1974] 74-79326
1. Thomes, William Henry, 1824-1895—Homes and haunts—California. I. Title. II. Title: California life in 1843. III. Series: Friends of the Bancroft Library. Keepsakes ; no. 22.

Thompson, Anna Young, 1851-1932.

KINNEAR, Elizabeth Kelsey. 266.5'1'0924 B
She sat where they sat; a memoir of Anna Young Thompson of Egypt. Grand Rapids, Eerdmans [1971] 112 p. port. 20 cm. (Christian world mission books) [BV3572.T87K55] 76-147363 2.45
1. Thompson, Anna Young, 1851-1932. I. Title.

Thompson, Benjamin, 1843-1884.

LIFE and adventures of Ben Thompson, the famous Texan. Including a detailed and authentic statement of his birth, history and adventures, by one who has known him since a child. Austin, The author, 1884. A facsim. ed. Austin, Steck Co., 1956. 229p. col. illus., port. 21cm. v. 12
1. Thompson, Benjamin, 1843-1884. I. Walton, William M

STREETER, Floyd Benjamin, 1888-1956. 927.95
Ben Thompson, man with a gun. With an introd. by William F. Kelleher. New York, F. Fell [1957] 217 p. illus. 22 cm. Includes bibliography. [CT275.T5736S7] 57-12115
1. Thompson, Benjamin, 1843-1884. I. Title.

WALTON, William M v. 12
Life and adventures of Ben Thompson, the famous Texan. Including a detailed and authentic statement of his birth, history and adventures, by one who has known him since a child. Austin, The author, 1884. A facsim. ed. Austin, Steck Co., 1956. 229 p. col. illus., port. 21 cm.
1. Thompson, Benjamin, 1843-1884. I. Title.

Thompson, Corrie—Juvenile literature.

THOMPSON, Corrie. 917.64'122
My beach buddies of bygone days; a book for children about the seashore of Texas. Edited by Edwin M. Eakin. Quanah, Tex., Nortex Press [1974] 91 p. illus. 26 cm. The author describes the seashore animals and other scenes and memories of her youth in Rockport, Texas. [F392.A6T47] 74-79251 ISBN 0-89015-060-5 4.95
1. Thompson, Corrie—Juvenile literature. 2. Aransas Bay, Tex.—Juvenile literature. 3. Seashore biology—Texas—Aransas Bay—Juvenile literature. 4. Rockport, Tex.—History—Juvenile literature. I. Title.

Thompson, Dorothy, 1893-1961.

SANDERS, Marion K. 070.4'092'4 B
Dorothy Thompson: a legend in her time [by] Marion K. Sanders. Illustrated with photos. and drawings. Boston, Houghton Mifflin, 1973. xv, 428 p. illus. 24 cm. Includes bibliographical references. [PN4874.T43S2] 72-9013 ISBN 0-395-15467-7 10.00
1. Thompson, Dorothy, 1893-1961.

SANDERS, Marion K. 070.4'092'4 B
Dorothy Thompson; a legend in her time [by] Marion K. Sanders. Illustrated with photographs and drawings. [New York] Avon [1974, c1973] 414 p. illus. 18 cm. Includes bibliographical references. [PN4874.T4352] ISBN 0-380-00019-9. 1.95 (pbk.)
1. Thompson, Dorothy, 1893-1961. I. Title. L.C. card number for original ed.: 72-9013. BIP

SHEEAN, Vincent, 1899- 928.1
Dorothy and Red. Boston, Houghton Mifflin, 1963. xii, 363 p. illus., ports., facsims. 22 cm. [PS3539.H649Z85] 63-21040
1. Thompson, Dorothy, 1894-1961. 2. Lewis, Sinclair, 1885-1951. I. Title.

Thompson, Ernest Trice, 1894-

THOMPSON, Ernest Trice, 1894- v. 12
Ernest Trice Thompson, an appreciation. Richmond, Va., Union Theological Seminary in Virginia, 1964. 52 p. illus. 26 cm. "Selections from the published works of ... Thompson" - p. 51-2.
1. Thompson, Ernest Trice, 1894- I. Title.

Thompson, Evelyn Wingo.

THOMPSON, Evelyn Wingo. 286.0924 (B)
Luther Rice: believer in tomorrow. Nashville, Broadman Press [c1967] 234 p. 22 cm. Bibliography: p. 226-228. [BX6495.R55T5] 67-10034
1. Rice, Luther, 1783-1836. II. Title.

Thompson family.

GOODSON, Nona Maughan, 1903- ed. 929'.2'0973
Life histories of George Thompson and Eliza Jane (Jennie) Sells and their descendants. Compiled by descendants, with notes of important events from 1957 to August 1962. [Provo, Utah, Dept. of Extension Publications, Brigham Young University, 1962] 165 p. 28 cm. [CS71.T47 1962] 63-5047
1. Thompson family. I. Title.

Thompson, Francis, 1859-1907.

LA GORCE, Agnes de. 821'.8 B
Francis Thompson. Translated from the French by H. F. Kynaston-Snell. [Folcroft, Pa.] Folcroft Library Editions, 1973. p. Translation of Francis Thompson et les poetes catholiques d'Angleterre. Reprint of the 1933 ed. published by Burns, Oates & Washbourne, London. [PR5651.L32 1973] 73-7773 ISBN 0-8414-1877-2 (lib. bdg.)
1. Thompson, Francis, 1859-1907. 2. English literature—Catholic authors—History and criticism. BIP

MEYNELL, Everard. 821'.8 B
The life of Francis Thompson. New York, Scribner, 1913. St. Clair Shores, Mich., Scholarly Press, 1971. xi, 360 p. illus., ports. 22 cm. [PR5651.M4 1971] 75-145181 ISBN 0-403-01107-8
1. Thompson, Francis, 1859-1907. I. Title. BIP

REID, John Cowie. 928.2
Francis Thompson, man and poet. Westminster, Md., Newman Press [1960, c1959] 232p. illus. 23cm. [PR5651.R4 1960] 60-1617
1. Thompson, Francis, 1859-1907. I. Title. BIP

THOMSON, John, 1871- 821'.8 B
Francis Thompson: poet and mystic. [3d enl. ed.] New York, Haskell House, 1974. 159 p. 20 cm. Reprint of the 1923 ed. published by Simpkin, Marshall, Hamilton, Kent, London. Includes bibliographical references. [PR5651.T5 1974] 74-7190 ISBN 0-8383-2014-7
1. Thompson, Francis, 1859-1907. BIP

THOMSON, John, 1871- 821'.8 B
Francis Thompson, the Preston-born poet; with notes on some of his works. [Folcroft, Pa.] Folcroft Library Editions, 1972. 78 p. illus. 24 cm. Reprint of the 1912 ed. [PR5651.T55 1972] 72-6663 ISBN 0-8414-0162-4
1. Thompson, Francis, 1859-1907. I. Title.

THOMSON, Paul van Kuykendall, 1916- 821'.8 B
Francis Thompson; a critical biography, by Paul van K. Thomson. New York, Gordian Press, 1973 c1972] 280 p. port. 23 cm. Reprint of the ed. published by Nelson, New York. Bibliography: p. [261]-266. [PR5651.T55 1973] 73-165666 ISBN 0-87752-155-7 8.50
1. Thompson, Francis, 1859-1907. Pbk. 2.50. BIP

WALSH, John, 1927- 821'.8 B
Strange harp, strange symphony; the life of Francis Thompson. [1st ed.] New York, Hawthorn Books [1967] xvi, 298 p. illus., facsims., ports. 24 cm. Bibliography: p. [282]-283. [PR5651.W3] 67-24650
1. Thompson, Francis, 1859-1907. I. Title.

Thompson, Goldianne Guyer,

THOMPSON, Goldianne Guyer, 1880- 917.8'03'2
Pioneer living with Mema; the autobiography of Goldianne (Guyer) Thompson. [1st ed.] Denver, Colo., Publishers Press, 1971. ix, 185 p. map (on cover), port. (on cover) 23 cm. [CT275.T57335A3] 78-168629 7.00
I. Title.

Thompson, James Harrison Wilson, b. 1906.

WARREN, William, 1930- 338.4'7'677390924
The legendary American; the remarkable career and strange disappearance of Jim Thompson. Boston, Houghton Mifflin, 1970. xi, 275 p. illus., map, ports. 22 cm. [CT275.T5734W3] 72-96065 5.95
1. Thompson, James Harrison Wilson, b. 1906. I. Title.

Thompson, James R., 1936-

HARTLEY, Robert E. 977.3'04'0924 B
Big Jim Thompson of Illinois / by Robert E. Hartley. Chicago : Rand McNally, 1979. p. cm. Includes index. [F546.4.T47H37] 79-19262 ISBN 0-528-81824-4 : 9.95
1. Thompson, James R., 1936- 2. Illinois—Politics and government—1951- 3. Illinois—Governors—Biography. I. Title. BIP

Thompson, John Albret, 1827-1876—Juvenile literature.

CASEWIT, Curtis W. 383'.143 B
The adventures of Snowshoe Thompson, by Curtis W. Casewit. Illustrated by Albert Orbaan. Editorial consultant; Edna B. Ziebold. New York, Putnam [1970] 126 p. illus., port. 23 cm. A biography of the man who fashioned the frontier's first skis to help him carry the mail over snowy mountain trails. [F864.T455C3 1970] 92 73-102395 3.64
1. Thompson, John Albret, 1827-1876—Juvenile literature. I. Orbaan, Albert, illus. II. Title.

Thompson, John Henry, 1861-1934.

HAYES, Jess G., 1901- 363.2'0924 B
Sheriff Thompson's day; turbulence in the Arizona Territory [by] Jess G. Hayes. Tucson, University of Arizona Press [1968] xiii, 190 p. illus. 20 cm. (Southwest chronicles) [F817.G5H33] 68-58321 4.95
1. Thompson, John Henry, 1861-1934. 2. Crime and criminals—Gila Co., Ariz. I. Title.

Thompson, Lorne F.

THOMPSON, Lorne F. 286'.1'0924 B
The raw edge of courage [by] Lorne F. Thompson. Grand Rapids, Baker Book House [1970] 199 p. 21 cm. Autobiographical. [BX6495.T44A3] 70-141553 3.95
I. Title.

Thompson, Maurice, 1844-1901.

SCHUMACHER, George A. 813'.4 B
Maurice Thompson; archer and author [by] George A. Schumacher. [1st ed.] New York, Vantage Press [1968] 205 p. ports. 21 cm. [PS3038.S3] 76-1357 3.95
1. Thompson, Maurice, 1844-1901.

Thompson, Meriwether Jeff, 1826-1876.

MONAGHAN, James, 1891- 973.742
Swamp Fox of the Confederacy; the life and military services of M. Jeff Thompson. [Limited ed.] Tuscaloosa, Ala., Confederate Pub. Co., 1956. 123p. illus. 22cm. (Confederate centennial studies, no. 2) Includes bibliography. [E467.1.T47M6] 56-58449
1. Thompson, Meriwether Jeff, 1826-1876. I. Title.

Thompson, Milton, 1875 or 6-1961.

THOMPSON, Maud. 920
My hero who gave his life to help others. [1st ed.] New York, Vantage Press [c1956] 65p. 21cm. [CT275.T5753T5] 56-11674
1. Thompson, Milton, 1875 or 6-1961. I. Title.

Thompson, Sir D'Arcy Wentworth, 1860-1948.

THOMPSON, Ruth D'Arcy, 1902- 925.7
D'Arcy Wentworth Thompson, the scholar-naturalist, 1860-1918, by his daughter. With a postscript by P. B. Medawar. London, New York Oxford University Press, 1958. 244 p. illus. 23 cm. [QH31.T48T48] 58-3021
1. Thompson, Sir D'Arcy Wentworth, 1860-1948. I. Title.

Thompson, William Hale, 1869-1944.

WENDT, Lloyd. 923.273
Big Bill of Chicago, by Lloyd Wendt and Herman Kogan. [1st ed.] Indianapolis, Bobbs-Merrill [1953] 384 p. illus. 23 cm. Includes bibliography. [F548.5.T476] 53-9862
1. Thompson, William Hale, 1869-1944. 2. Chicago—Politics and government. I. Kogan, Herman, joint author. II. Title.

Thompson, William Oxley, 1855-1933.

POLLARD, James Edward, 1894- 923.773
William Oxley Thompson, evangel of education. Columbus, Ohio State University, 1955. 303p. illus. 24cm. [LD4225 1899.P6] 56-62689
1. Thompson, William Oxley, 1855-1933. I. Title.

Thompson, Wilson,

THOMPSON, Wilson, 1788-1866. 286'.63'0924
The autobiography of Elder Wilson Thompson; his life, travels, and ministerial labors. Springfield, Ohio, E. T. Aleshire, 1962. 363 p. illus. 23 cm. [BX6793.T54A3] 63-1325
I. Title.

Thomson, Alexander, 1817-1875.

MCFADZEAN, Ronald. 720'.92'4 B
The life and work of Alexander Thomson / Ronald McFadzean. London ; Boston : Routledge & K. Paul, 1979. xvi, 304 p. : ill. ; 26 cm. Originally presented as the author's thesis, University of Sheffield. Includes index. Bibliography: p. 298-300. [NA997.T49M3 1979] 79-40136 ISBN 0-7100-0069-3 : 38.50
1. Thomson, Alexander, 1817-1875. 2. Architects—Scotland—Biography. I. Title. BIP

Thomson, Charles, 1729-1824.

HENDRICKS, James Edwin, 1935- 973.3'092'4 B
Charles Thomson and the making of a new nation, 1729-1824 / J. Edwin Hendricks. Rutherford, N.J. : Fairleigh Dickinson University Press, 1979. p. cm. Includes index. Bibliography: p. [E302.6.T48H4 1979] 77-74392 ISBN 0-8386-2072-8 : 15.00
1. Thomson, Charles, 1729-1824. 2. United States. Continental Congress—Biography. 3. United States—Politics and government—Revolution, 1775-1783. 4. United States—Politics and government—1783-1789. 5. Statesmen—United States—Biography. I. Title. BIP

Thomson, Clara Linklater.

THOMSON, Clara Linklater. 823'.6 B
Samuel Richardson; a biographical and critical study. Port Washington, N.Y., Kennikat Press [1970] viii, 308 p. illus., ports. 21 cm. Reprint of the 1900 ed. Bibliography: p. [292]-301. [PR3666.T5 1970] 74-103214
I. Richardson, Samuel, 1689-1761.

Thomson, David, 1914- —Biography.

THOMSON, David, 1914- 823'.9'14 B
Woodbrook / David Thomson. New York : Universe Books, 1976, c1974. 313 p. : maps (on lining papers) ; 22 cm. Autobiographical. Includes bibliographical references. [PR6070.H677Z52 1976] 75-34588 ISBN 0-87663-225-8 : 10.00
1. Thomson, David, 1914- —Biography. 2. Authors, Scottish—20th century—Biography. I. Title.

Thomson, Edward Deas, 1800-1879.

FOSTER, Stephen Glynn, 1948- 994.4'02'0924 B
Colonial improver : Edward Deas Thomson, 1800-1879 / S. G. Foster. Carlton [Australia] : Melbourne University Press ; Forest Grove, Or. : exclusive distributor, ISBS, 1978. xv, 209 p., [2] leaves of plates : ill. ; 23 cm. "Based on a thesis which was presented to the University of New England." Includes index. Bibliography: p. 187-201. [DU172.T45F67] 78-670160 ISBN 0-522-84136-8 : 19.95
1. Thomson, Edward Deas, 1800-1879. 2. New South Wales—Politics and government. 3. Colonial administrators—Australia—New South Wales—Biography. I. Title.

Thomson, Elihu, 1853-1937.

WOODBURY, David Oakes 926.2
Elihu Thomson, beloved scientist, 1853-1937; inventive genius, engineer, educator, pioneer of the electrical age. With appreciations by James R. Killian, Jr., and Owen D. Young. Boston, Museum of Science [dist. Cambridge, Mass., Harvard] [c.]1960 xv, 358p. Bibl.: p. 349. illus. 24cm. First published in 1944 under title: Beloved scientist; Elihu Thomson, a guiding spirit of the electrical age. 60-11802 6.00
1. Thomson, Elihu, 1853-1937. I. Title.

Thomson, James, 1834-1882.

DOBELL, Bertram, 1842-1914. 821'.8
The laureate of pessimism; a sketch of the life and character of James Thomson ("B.V.") Port Washington, N.Y., Kennikat Press [1970] iv, 64 p. 19 cm. Reprint of the 1910 ed. [PR5658.D6 1970] 77-105781
1. Thomson, James, 1834-1882. I. Title.

SALT, Henry Stephens, 1851-1939. 821'.8 B
The life of James Thomson ("B. V."), with a selection from his letters and a study of his writings. Port Washington, N.Y., Kennikat Press [1972] vi, 335 p. port. 21 cm. Reprint of the 1889 ed. Includes bibliographical references. [PR5658.S3 1972] 75-160779 ISBN 0-8046-1611-6
1. Thomson, James, 1834-1882. I. Title.

THOMSON, James, 1700-1748. 928.2
Letters and documents. Edited by Alan Dugald McKillop. Lawrence, University of Kansas Press, 1958. xi, 225 p. ports., facsim. 24 cm. [PR3733.A45 1958] 57-11249
I. Title.

Thomson of Fleet, Roy Herbert Thomson, baron, 1894.

BRADDON, Russell 072.0924
Roy Thomson of Fleet Street, New York, Walker [1966, c.1965] 396p. illus., ports. 24cm. Bibl. [PN4913.T45B7] 66-17222 7.50
1. Thomson of Fleet, Roy Herbert Thomson, baron, 1894. I. Title.

Thomson, Samuel,

THOMSON, Samuel, 1769-1843. 615'.537'0924 B
A narrative of the life and medical discoveries of Samuel Thomson; containing an account of his system of practice, and the manner of curing disease with vegetable medicine, upon a plan entirely new; to which is added an introduction to his New guide to health, or botanic family physician, containing the principles upon which the system is founded, with remarks on fevers, steaming, poison, &c. New York, Arno Press, 1972 [c1822] 180 p. 21 cm. (Medicine & society in America) Spine title: Life and medical discoveries of Samuel Thomson. [RV8.T47A3 1972] 79-180594 ISBN 0-405-03976-X
I. Title. II. Title: Life and medical discoveries of Samuel Thomson. III. Series.

Thomson, Sir Joseph John, 1856-1940.

THOMPSON, George Paget, Sir, 1892 925.3
J. J. Thomson and the Cavendish Laboratory in his day. Garden City, N.Y., Doubleday, 1965 [c.1964] xi, 186p. illus., ports. 21cm. (British men of sci.) [QC515.T53T4] 65-10821 4.95
1. Thomson, Sir Joseph John, 1856-1940. 2. Cambridge. University. Cavendish Laboratory. I. Title.

THOMSON, George Page Sir 1892- v. 12
J. J. Thomson, discoverer of the electron. Garden city, N. Y., Anchor Books, Doubleday [1966] xvi, 215 p. illus., ports. 18 cm. (Science study series, S48) Originally published under title: J. J. Thomson and the Cavendish Laboratory in his day. 67-65902
1. Thomson, Sir Joseph John, 1856-1940. I. Cambridge. University. Cavendish Laboratory. II. Title. III. Title: J. J. Thomson and the Cavendish Laboratory in his day.

THOMSON, George Paget, Sir 1892- 925.3
J. J. Thomson, discoverer of the electron. Garden City, N.Y., Doubleday [1966, c.1965] xi, 186p. illus., ports. 21cm. (Sci. study ser.) [QC515.T53T4 1965] 65-10821 1.45 pap.,
1. Thomson, Joseph John,Sir 1856-1940. 2. Cambridge. University. Cavendish Laboratory. I. Title.

THOMSON, George Paget, Sir, 1892- 530'.0924 B
J. J. Thomson discoverer of the electron. Garden City, N.Y., Anchor Books [1968, c1964] xvi, 215 p. illus., ports. 18 cm. (Science study series, S48) Published in 1964 under title: J. J. Thomson and the Cavendish Laboratory in his day. [QC515] 67-31925
1. Thomson, Joseph John, Sir, 1856-1940. 2. Cambridge. University. Cavendish Laboratory. I. Title. II. Series.

Thomson, Tom, 1877-1917.

DAVIES, Blodwen. 759.11 (B)
Tom Thomson; the story of a man who looked for beauty and for truth in the wilderness. Foreword by A.Y. Jackson. Sketches by Arthur Lismer. [Rev. memorial ed.] Vancouver, Mitchell Press [c1967] 102 p. illus., col. plates 26 cm. C68-1662 First published in 1935 under title: A study of Tom Thomson. [ND249.T5D3] 68-113509
1. Thomson, Tom, 1877-1917. I. Title.

Thomson, Virgil, 1896-

HOOVER, Kathleen O'Donnell. 927.8
Virgil Thomson: his life and music, by Kathleen Hoover and John Cage. New York, T. Yoseloff [1959] 288 p. illus. 25 cm. [ML410.T452H6] 58-12144
1. Thomson, Virgil, 1896- I. Cage, John.

HOOVER, Kathleen O'Donnell. 780'.924 B
Virgil Thomson: his life and music, by Kathleen Hoover and John Cage. Freeport, N.Y., Books for Libraries Press [1970, c1959] 288 p. illus., facsims., music, ports. 24 cm. [ML410.T452H6 1970] 70-119933
1. Thomson, Virgil, 1896- I. Cage, John, joint author.

THOMSON, Virgil, 1896- 780'.92'4 B
Virgil Thomson / by Virgil Thomson. New York : Da Capo Press [1977] c1966. 424, xiii p., [16] leaves of plates : ill. ; 22 cm. (A Da Capo paperback) Reprint of the ed. published by A. A. Knopf, New York. Includes index. [ML410.T452A3 1977] 77-23407 ISBN 0-306-80081-0 pbk. : 6.95
1. Thomson, Virgil, 1896- 2. Composers—United States—Biography. I. Title.

Thonga tribe.

CHITLANGOU, of the Khamban Clan, 1920- 916'.03'30924 B
Chitlangou, son of a chief, by Andre D. Clerc. Translated by Margaret A. Bryan. With a foreword by Alan Paton. Westport, Conn., Negro Universities Press [1971] 208 p. illus. 23 cm. "This story was told to the author by Chitlangou himself." Reprint of the 1950 ed. [DT458.C5 1971] 74-140805 ISBN 0-8371-5839-7
1. Thonga tribe. I. Clerc, Andre Daniel. BIP

Thorburn, Grant,

THORBURN, Grant, 1773-1863. 818'.3'03 B
Forty years' residence in America; or, The doctrine of a particular providence exemplified in the life of Grant Thorburn ... Freeport, N.Y., Books for Libraries Press [1969] 264 p. 23 cm. (Select bibliographies reprint series) Reprint of the 1834 ed. [PS3039.T9Z5 1969] 78-95080
I. Title.

Thore, Theophile Etienne Joseph, 1807-1869.

JOWELL, Frances 709'.2'4 B Suzman.
Thore-Burger and the art of the past / Frances Suzman Jowell. New York : Garland Pub., 1977. xxiii, 409 p., [24] leaves of plates : ill. ; 21 cm. (Outstanding dissertations in the fine arts) Originally presented as the author's thesis, Harvard, 1971. Bibliography: p. 394-406. [N7483.T53J68 1977] 76-23632 ISBN 0-8240-2701-9 lib.bdg. : 45.00
1. Thore, Theophile Etienne Joseph, 1807-1869. 2. Art historians—France—Biography. I. Title. II. Series.

JOWELL, Frances 709'.2'4 B Suzman.
Thore-Burger and the art of the past / Frances Suzman Jowell. New York : Garland Pub., 1977. xxiii, 409 p., [24] leaves of plates : ill. ; 21 cm. (Outstanding dissertations in the fine arts) Originally presented as the author's thesis, Harvard, 1971. Bibliography: p. 394-406. [N7483.T53J68 1977] 76-23632 ISBN 0-8240-2701-9 lib.bdg. : 45.00
1. Thore, Theophile Etienne Joseph, 1807-1869. 2. Art historians—France—Biography. I. Title. II. Series.

Thoreau family.

HOSMER, Horace, 1830- 818'.3'09 B 1894.
Remembrances of Concord and the Thoreaus : letters of Horace Hosmer to Dr. S. A. Jones / edited by George Hendrick. Urbana : University of Illinois Press, 1977. p. cm. Includes bibliographical references and index. [PS3053.H58 1977] 77-24232 ISBN 0-252-00660-7 : 10.00
1. Thoreau, Henry David, 1817-1862—Biography—Sources. 2. Thoreau family. 3. Hosmer, Horace, 1830-1894. 4. Jones, Samuel Arthur, 1834-1912—Correspondence. 5. Concord, Mass.—Social life and customs. 6. Authors, American—19th century—Correspondence. I. Jones, Samuel Arthur, 1834-1912. II. Hendrick, George. III. Title.

Thoreau, Henry David, 1817-1862.

ATKINSON, Justin 818'.3'09 Brooks, 1894-
Henry Thoreau, the cosmic yankee, by J. Brooks Atkinson. [Folcroft, Pa.] Folcroft Library Editions, 1973 [c1927] p. Reprint of the ed. published by A. A. Knopf, New York. [PS3053.A85 1973] 73-15993 12.50
1. Thoreau, Henry David, 1817-1862. **BIP**

ATKINSON, Justin 818'.3'09 B Brooks, 1894-
Henry Thoreau : the cosmic Yankee / by J. Brooks Atkinson. Norwood, Pa. : Norwood Editions, 1975 [c1927] 158 p., [1] leaf of plates : port. ; 23 cm. Reprint of the ed. published by Knopf, New York. [PS3053.A85 1975] 75-38879 ISBN 0-88305-034-X : 15.00
1. Thoreau, Henry David, 1817-1862.

ATKINSON, Justin 818'.3'09 Brooks, 1894-
Henry Thoreau, the cosmic Yankee, by J. Brooks Atkinson. [Folcroft, Pa.] Folcroft Library Editions, 1973 [c1927] 158 p. port. 23 cm. Reprint of the ed. published by A. A. Knopf, New York. [PS3053.A85 1973] 73-15993 ISBN 0-8414-2935-9 (lib. bdg.)
1. Thoreau, Henry David, 1817-1862.

CANBY, Henry Seidel, 1878- 928.1
Thoreau [Gloucester, Mass., Peter Smith, 1962 c.1939] 508p. (BeaconBP65 rebound) Bibl. 4.75
1. Thoreau, Henry David, 1817-1862. I. Title.

CANBY, Henry Seidel, 1878- 928.1
Thoreau. Boston, Beacon Press [1958, c1939] 508p. 28cm. (Beacon BP65) Includes bibliography. [PS3053.C3 1958] 58-44486
1. Thoreau, Henry David, 1817-1862. I. Title.

CANBY, Henry Seidel, 1878- 928.1 1961
Thoreau. Gloucester, Mass., P. Smith, 1965 [c.1939] xx, 508p. 21cm. Reprint of the 1939 ed. pub. by Houghton. Bibl. [PS3053.C3] 65-3466 5.00
1. Thoreau, Henry David, 1817-1862. I. Title.

CONDRY, William M 928.1
Thoreau. [New York] Philosophical Library [1954] 114p. illus. 21cm. Includes bibliography. [PS3053] 54-11703
1. Thoreau, Henry David, 1817-1862. I. Title.

DERLETH, August William, 928.1 1909-
Concord rebel; a life of Henry D. Thoreau. Philadelphia, Chilton [c.1962] 213p. illus. 22cm. 62-15166 3.50
1. Thoreau, Henry David, 1817-1862. I. Title.

EMERSON, Edward Waldo, 818'.3'09 1844-1930.
Henry Thoreau as remembered by a young friend. [Concord, Mass.] Thoreau Foundation, 1968. vii, 151 p. ports. 19 cm. Reprint of the 1917 ed. [PS3053.E45 1968] 68-19227
1. Thoreau, Henry David, 1817-1862. **BIP**

HARDING, Walter Roy, 818.309 B 1917-
The days of Henry Thoreau, by Walter Harding. [1st ed.] New York, Knopf, 1965. xvi, 472 p. illus., map, ports. 22 cm. Bibliography: p. 471-472. [PS3053.H3] 65-18766
1. Thoreau, Henry David, 1817-1862. I. Title.

HARDING, Walter Roy, 818'.3'09 B 1917- comp.
Henry David Thoreau; a profile. Edited by Walter Harding. [1st ed.] New York, Hill and Wang [1971] xxiii, 260 p. 21 cm. (American profiles) (American century series) Bibliography: p. 254-255. [B931.T44H37] 74-163577 ISBN 0-8090-0215-9 (pbk) 6.50
1. Thoreau, Henry David, 1817-1862.

HARDING, Walter Roy, 1917- 928.1 ed.
Thoreau, man of Concord. New York, Holt, Rinehart and Winston [1960] xx, 251p. port. 21cm. Bibliography: p. 245. [PS3053.H325] 60-14388
1. Thoreau, Henry David, 1817-1862. I. Title.

HARDING, Walter Roy, 1917- 928.1 ed.
Thoreau, man of Concord. New York, Holt, Rinehart and Winston [c.1960] xx, 251p. port. Bibl.: p. 245. 60-14388 2.00 pap.,
1. Thoreau, Henry David, 1817-1862. I. Title.

HOUGH, Henry Beetle, 1896- 928.1
Thoreau of Walden; the man and his eventful life. New York, Simon and Schuster, 1956. 275p. 22cm. [PS3053.H6] 56-6672
1. Thoreau, Henry David, 1817-1862. I. Title. **BIP**

HOUGH, Henry Beetle, 818'.3'09 B 1896-
Thoreau of Walden; the man and his eventful life. [Hamden, Conn.] Archon Books, 1970. viii, 275 p. 22 cm. Reprint of the 1956 ed. [PS3053.H6 1970] 77-103988
1. Thoreau, Henry David, 1817-1862. I. Title.

JAPP, Alexander Hay, 818'.3'09 B 1839-1905.
Thoreau : his life and aims / by H. A. Page [i.e. A. H. Japp]. Folcroft, Pa. : Folcroft Library Editions, 1976. p. cm. Reprint of the 1901 ed. published by Chatto & Windus, London. [PS3053.J3 1976] 76-28372 ISBN 0-8414-6778-1 lib. bdg. : 30.00
1. Thoreau, Henry David, 1817-1862.

JAPP, Alexander Hay, 818'.3'09 B 1839-1905.
Thoreau: his life and aims, by H. A. Page. Folcroft, Pa., Folcroft Press [1969] xi, 271 p. port. 23 cm. Reprint of the 1901 ed. [PS3053.J3 1969] 72-195011
1. Thoreau, Henry David, 1817-1862.

JAPP, Alexander Hay, 818'.3'09 B 1839-1905.
Thoreau: his life and aims; a study, by H. A. Page. London, Chatto and Windus, 1878. New York, Haskell House Publishers, 1972. xi, 271 p. illus. 23 cm. [PS3053.J3 1972] 72-3653 ISBN 0-8383-1585-2 11.95
1. Thoreau, Henry David, 1817-1862.

KRUTCH, Joseph Wood, 1893- 928.1
Henry David Thoreau [New York, Dell] 1965[c.1948] viii, 298p. 20cm. (Delta bk. 3852; Amer. men of letters ser.) [PS3053.K7] 1.95 pap.,
1. Thoreau, Henry David, 1817-1862. (Series) I. Title. **BIP**

KRUTCH, Joseph Wood, 818'.3'09 B 1893-1970.
Henry David Thoreau. Westport, Conn., Greenwood Press [1973, c1948] xii, 298 p. port. 22 cm. Original ed. issued in series: The American men of letters series. [PS3053.K7 1973] 72-9589 ISBN 0-8371-6587-3 13.00
1. Thoreau, Henry David, 1817-1862. I. Series: The American men of letters series.

LEBEAUX, Richard, 818'.3'09 [B] 1946-
Young man Thoreau / by Richard LeBeaux. New York : Harper & Row, 1978, c1977. 262p. ; 21 cm. (Harper Colophon books) Includes index. Bibliography: p[249]-255. [PS3053.L37] ISBN 0-06-090614-6 pbk. : 3.95
1. Thoreau, Henry David, 1817-1862 — Biography — Character. 2. Authors, American — 19th century — Biography. I. Title.
L.C. card no. for 1977 University of Massachusetts Press ed. : 76-44851. **BIP**

LONGSTRETH, Thomas Morris, 92 1886-
Henry Thoreau, American rebel. Illus. with photos. by Edwin Way Teale. New York, Dodd [c.1963] x, 204p. illus., port., maps. 21cm. Bibl. 63-18783 3.50
1. Thoreau, Henry David, 1817-1862—Juvenile literature. I. Title.

LONGSTRETH, Thomas Morris, j 92 1886-
Henry Thoreau, American rebel. Illustrated with photos. by Edwin Way Teale. New York, Dodd, Mead [1963] x, 204 p. illus., port., maps. 21 cm. Bibliography: p. 199. [PS3053.L6] 63-18783
1. Thoreau, Henry David, 1817-1862 — Juvenile literature. I. Title.

MARBLE, Annie (Russell) 818'.3'09 1864-1936.
Thoreau; his home, friends, and books. New York, AMS Press [1969] viii, 343 p. illus., ports. 23 cm. Reprint of the 1902 ed. [PS3053.M3 1969] 73-85906
1. Thoreau, Henry David, 1817-1862.

NORMAN, Charles, 1904- 928.1
To a different drum; the story of Henry David Thoreau. Pictures by Margaret Bloy Graham. [1st ed.] New York, Harper [1954] 113p. illus. 22cm. [PS3053.N6] 54-8977
1. Thoreau, Henry David, 1817-1862. I. Title.

NORTH, Sterling, 1906- 928.1
Thoreau of Walden Pond. Illustrated by Harve Stein. Boston, Houghton Mifflin, 1959. 183p. illus. 22cm. (North Star books [8]) [PS3053.N63] 59-5205
1. Thoreau, Henry David, 1817-1862—Juvenile literature. I. Title.

SALT, Henry Stephens, 818.309 1851-1939
Life of Henry David Thoreau. [Hamden, Conn.] Archon, 1968. 208. x p. 18cm. Reprint of 1896 ed. Bibl. [PS3053.S3 1968] 68-21692 5.75
1. Thoreau, Henry David, 1817-1862. I. Title. **BIP**

SEEFURTH, Nathaniel 818'.3'08 Henry.
Thoreau; a view from emeritus, by Nathaniel H. Seefurth. Chicago, Seefurth Foundation [1968] x, 65 p. 20 cm. [PS3053.S55] 68-56971
1. Thoreau, Henry David, 1817-1862. I. Title.

SOPHIA Thoreau's 928.1 *scrapbook,* from the collection of George L. Davenport, Jr., ed. by Walter Harding. Genesc)0eo, N.Y., Thoreau Soc. [c.]1964. 66p. facsims., ports. 28cm. (Thoreau Soc. Bklet. 20) Material by and about members of the Thoreau family, and other material collected by them. Reproduce,53s] only the manuscritp materials and the exceptionally rare printed materials. 64-6420 1.00 pap.,
1. Thoreau, Henry David, 1817-1862. 2. Thoreau family. I. Thoreau, Sophia E., 1876 d. II. Davenport, George L. III. Harding, Walter Roy, 1917- ed. IV. Series.

STERN, Philip Van 818'.3'09 B Doren, 1900-
Henry David Thoreau: writer and rebel. New York, Crowell [1972] vi, 183 p. 21 cm. Bibliography: p. 175-176. A biography of the poet, naturalist, and observer of mankind whose philosophy of passive resistance inspired such leaders as Gandhi and King. [PS3053.S78] 92 74-139108 ISBN 0-690-37715-0 4.50
1. Thoreau, Henry David, 1817-1862—Juvenile literature. I. Title.

THOREAU, Henry David, 1817- 928.1 1862.
Correspondence, edited by Walter Harding and Carl Bode. [New York] New York University Press, 1958. xxi, 665 p. port. 24 cm. [PS3053.A3 1958] 58-11447
1. Authors—Correspondence, reminiscences, etc.

THOREAU, Henry David, 974.2'72 1817-1862.
A week on the Concord and Merrimack Rivers / Henry David Thoreau ; with an introd. by Charles R. Anderson ; and ill. by R. J. Holden. Avon, Conn. : Limited Editions Club, 1975. xv, 327 p. : ill. ; 26 cm. [F72.M7T5 1975] 75-326258
1. Thoreau, Henry David, 1817-1862. 2. Merrimack River—Description and travel. 3. Concord River—Description and travel. I. Title. **BIP**

TOWARD the making of 818'.3'09 *Thoreau's modern reputation :* selected correspondence of S. A. Jones, A. W. Hosmer, H. S. Salt, H. G. O. Blake, and D. Ricketson / edited by Fritz Oehlschlaeger and George Hendrick. Urbana : University of Illinois Press, c1979. p. cm. Includes bibliographical references and index. [PS3053.T6] 79-12831 ISBN 0-252-00725-5 : 25.00
1. Thoreau, Henry David, 1817-1862. 2. Literary historians—United States—Correspondence. 3. Authors, American—19th century—Biography. I. Jones, Samuel Arthur, 1834-1912. II. Oehlschlaeger, Fritz. III. Hendrick, George.

WOOD, James Playsted, 818'.3'09 B 1905-
A hound, a bay horse, and a turtle-dove; a life of Thoreau for the young reader. Illus. by Douglas Gorsline. [New York] Pantheon Books [1963] xvi, 172, [3] p. illus. 22 cm. Bibliography: p. 175. A biography of a forthright individualist of nineteenth century America who lived his life as he saw fit, and bequeathed his ideas and ideals to all those who wished to follow him. [PS3053.W6] 92 AC 68
1. Thoreau, Henry David, 1817-1862. I. Gorsline, Douglas W., 1913- illus. II. Title.

WOOD, James Playsted, 1905- 928.1
A hound, a bay horse, and a turtle-dove; a life of Thoreau for the younger reader. Illus. by Douglas Gorsline. [New York] Pantheon Books [1963] xvi, 172, [3] p. illus. 22 cm. Bibliography: p. 175. [PS3053.W6] 63-15484
1. Thoreau, Henry David, 1817-1862 — Juvenile literature. I. Title.

Thoreau, Henry David, 1817-1862—Addresses, essays, lectures.

THOREAU, the cosmic 818'.3'09 *Yankee.* Folcroft, Pa. : Folcroft Library Editions, 1977. 40 p. : ports. ; 26 cm. Reprint of the 1946 ed. published by the Roman Forum, Los Angeles. [PS3053.T53

1977] 77-9275 ISBN 0-8414-7385-4 lib. bdg. : 10.00
1. Thoreau, Henry David, 1817-1862—Addresses, essays, lectures. 2. Authors, American—19th century—Biography—Addresses, essays, lectures. I. Ishill, Joseph.
Contents omitted

Thoreau, Henry David, 1817-1862—Biography—Character.

LEBEAUX, Richard, 1946- 818'.3'09 B
Young man Thoreau : Henry David Thoreau's pre-Walden life and writings / by Richard Lebeaux. [Amherst] : University of Massachusetts Press, 1977. p. cm. Includes index. Bibliography: p. [PS3053.L37] 76-44851 ISBN 0-87023-231-2 lib.bdg. : 12.50
1. Thoreau, Henry David, 1817-1862—Biography—Character. 2. Authors, American—19th century—Biography. I. Title.

Thoreau, Henry David, 1817-1862—Biography—Sources.

HOSMER, Horace, 1830-1894. 818'.3'09 B
Remembrances of Concord and the Thoreaus : letters of Horace Hosmer to Dr. S. A. Jones / edited by George Hendrick. Urbana : University of Illinois Press, 1977. p. cm. Includes bibliographical references and index. [PS3053.H58 1977] 77-24232 ISBN 0-252-00660-7 : 10.00
1. Thoreau, Henry David, 1817-1862—Biography—Sources. 2. Thoreau family. 3. Hosmer, Horace, 1830-1894. 4. Jones, Samuel Arthur, 1834-1912—Correspondence. 5. Concord, Mass.—Social life and customs. 6. Authors, American—19th century—Correspondence. I. Jones, Samuel Arthur, 1834-1912. II. Hendrick, George. III. Title.

Thoreau, Henry David, 1817-1862—Correspondence.

THOREAU, Henry David, 1817-1862. 818'.3'09 B
The correspondence of Henry David Thoreau. Edited by Walter Harding and Carl Bode. Westport, Conn., Greenwood Press [1974, c1958] xxi, 665 p. port. 23 cm. Reprint of the ed. published by New York University Press, New York. [PS3053.A3 1974] 73-16954 ISBN 0-8371-7247-0 24.00
1. Thoreau, Henry David, 1817-1862—Correspondence. 2. Authors, American—Correspondence, reminiscences, etc. I. Title. **BIP**

THOREAU, Henry David, 1817-1862. 818'.3'09 B
Letters to various persons / by Henry D. Thoreau. Folcroft, Pa. : Folcroft Library Editions, 1975. 229 p. ; 22 cm. Reprint of the 1877 ed. published by J. R. Osgood, Boston. [PS3053.A3 1975] 75-41323 ISBN 0-8414-8591-7 lib. bdg. : 12.50
1. Thoreau, Henry David, 1817-1862—Correspondence. I. Title. **BIP**

Thornburg, Miles O

THORNBURG, Miles O 1891- 926.5
The thread of my life. Charlotte [N.C.] W. Loftin [c1958] 157 p. illus. 23 cm. [CT275.T57725A3] 59-52467
I. Title.

Thorndike, Edward Lee, 1874-1949.

JONCICH, Geraldine M. 150'.924 B
The sane positivist; a biography of Edward L. Thorndike, by Geraldine Joncich. [1st ed.] Middletown, Conn., Wesleyan University Press [1968] 634 p. illus., ports. 24 cm. "An essay on sources": p. [592]-612. [BF109.T43J6] 68-27542 12.50
1. Thorndike, Edward Lee, 1874-1949. I. Title. **BIP**

Thorndike, Israel, 1755-1832.

FORBES, John Douglas, 1910- 923.373
Israel Thorndike, Federalist financier. [1st ed.] New York, Published for the Beverly Historical Society by Exposition Press [1953] 160p. illus. 21cm. 'Exposition-University book.' [HC102.5T45F6] 53-5629
1. Thorndike, Israel, 1755-1832. I. Title.

Thornton, Charles Bates, 1913-

LAY, Beirne, 1909- 338.8'6'0924
Someone has to make it happen; the inside story of Tex Thornton, the man who built Litton Industries. Foreword by James H. Doolittle. Englewood Cliffs, N.J., Prentice-Hall [1969] ix, 204 p. illus., ports. 24 cm. [HC102.5.T46L3] 74-75683 6.95
1. Thornton, Charles Bates, 1913- 2. Litton Industries, inc., Beverly Hills, Calif. I. Title.

Thornton, Marianne, 1797-1887.

FORSTER, Edward Morgan, 1879- 920.7
Marianne Thornton, a domestic biography, 1797-1887.[1st ed.] New York, Harcourt, Brace [1956] 337p. illus. 22cm. [CT788.T566F6] 56-6662
1. Thornton, Marianne, 1797-1887. I. Title.

FORSTER, Edward Morgan, 1879-1970. 914.2'03'80924 B
Marianne Thornton: a domestic biography, 1797-1887. New York, Harcourt Brace Jovanovich [1973, c1956] xii, 337 p. illus. 21 cm. (A Harvest book) [CT788.T566F6 1973] 73-154180 ISBN 0-15-657300-8 pap. 3.45
1. Thornton, Marianne, 1797-1887.

FORSTER, Edward Morgan, 1879-1970. 920.7
Marianne Thornton, 1797-1887; a domestic biography, by E. M. Forster. New York, Harcourt [1973, c.1956] xii, 337 p. illus. ports., geneal. 21 cm. (Harvest Book, HB248) [CT788.T566F6] 56-6662 pap., 3.45
1. Thornton, Marianne, 1797-1887. I. Title.

Thornwell, James Henley, 1812-1862.

PALMER, Benjamin Morgan, 1818-1902. 285'.1'0924 B
The life and letters of James Henley Thornwell. New York, Arno Press, 1969. xi, 614 p. port. 23 cm. (Religion in America) Reprint of the 1875 ed. [BX9225.T64P3 1969] 78-83432
1. Thornwell, James Henley, 1812-1862. I. Thornwell, James Henley, 1812-1862. II. Title.

Thorp, Nathan Howard, 1867-1940.

THORP, Nathan Howard, 1867-1940. 978'.02'0922 B
Pardner of the wind : story of the Southwestern cowboy / by N. Howard (Jack) Thorp, in collaboration with Neil M. Clark. Lincoln : University of Nebraska Press, 1977, c1945. p. cm. Reprint of the ed. published by Caxton Printers, Caldwell, Idaho. [F786.T47] 77-7243 ISBN 0-8032-0938-X : 14.50 ISBN 0-8032-5875-5 pbk. : 4.75
1. Thorp, Nathan Howard, 1867-1940. 2. Cowboys—Southwest, New—Biography. 3. Southwest, New—History. 4. Frontier and pioneer life—Southwest, New. I. Clark, Neil McCullough, 1890- joint author. II. Title.

Thorpe, Jim, 1888-1953.

GOBRECHT, Wilbur J. 796'.0924 B
Jim Thorpe, Carlisle Indian, by Wilbur J. Gobrecht. [Carlisle, Pa.] Cumberland County Historical Society [1969] 25 p. ports. 23 cm. Bibliography: p. 24-25. [GV697.T5G6] 77-281403
1. Thorpe, Jim, 1888-1953. I. Cumberland County Historical Society (Pa.) II. Title.

SCHOOR, Gene. 927.96
The Jim Thorpe story, America's greatest athlete, by Gene Schoor with Henry Gilfond. New York, Messner 1951 186 p. illus. 22 cm. [GV697.T5S4] 51-12790
1. Thorpe, Jim, 1888-1953.

WHEELER, Robert W., 1945- 796'.092'4 B
Jim Thorpe, world's greatest athlete / by Robert W. Wheeler. Rev. ed. Norman : University of Oklahoma Press, 1978. p. cm. Published in 1975 under title: Pathway to glory. Includes index. Bibliography: p. [GV697.T5W47 1978] 78-58080 ISBN 0-8061-1470-3 : 12.50
1. Thorpe, Jim, 1888-1953. 2. Athletes—United States—Biography. I. Title.

Thorpe, Jim, 1888-1953—Juvenile literature.

REISING, Robert. 796'.092'4 B
Jim Thorpe. Minneapolis, Dillon Press [1974] 58 p. illus. 23 cm. (The Story of an American Indian) A biography of the Oklahoma Indian who won fame for his all-around athletic excellence, but was plagued with personal difficulties throughout his life. [GV697.T5R44] 92 74-13150 ISBN 0-87518-076-0
1. Thorpe, Jim, 1888-1953—Juvenile literature. I. Title. **BIP**

SNOW, Donald Clifford, 1917- 796.332'0924 [B]
Jim Thorpe, by Thomas Fall. Illus. by John Gretzer. New York, T. Y. Crowell [1973, c.1970] 33 p. illus. (pt. col.) 23 cm. (Crowell crocodile) (Crowell biographies) An easy-to-read biography of the Oklahoma Indian who came to be considered "one of the world's finest all-round athletes." [GV939.T45S6] 72-94793 ISBN 0-690-46219-0 0.95 (pbk.)
1. Thorpe, Jim, 1888-1953—Juvenile literature. I. Gretzer, John, illus. II. Title. **BIP**

SULLIVAN, George, 1927- 796'.0924 B
Jim Thorpe, all-around athlete. Illustrated by Herman B. Vestal. Champaign, Ill., Garrard Pub. Co. [1971] 96 p. illus. (part col.), ports. 24 cm. (Americans all) A biography of the only athlete, an American Indian, to win both the pentathlon and the decathlon in the Olympics. [GV939.T45S9] 92 70-135180 ISBN 0-8116-4566-5 2.49
1. Thorpe, Jim, 1888-1953—Juvenile literature. I. Vestal, Herman B., illus. II. Title.

Thorpe, Thomas Bangs, 1815-1878.

RICKLES, Milton 928.1
Thomas Bangs Thorpe, humorist ofthe Old Osoutwest. Baton Rouge, La. State Univ. Pr. [c.]1962. 275p. illus. Bibl. 62-8018 5.00
1. Thorpe, Thomas Bangs, 1815-1878. I. Title.

Thorson, Ralph Edgar.

KEANE, Christopher. 364 B
The hunter / Christopher Keane. New York : Arbor House, c1976. x, 289 p. ; 22 cm. [HV6248.T48K4 1976] 76-8644 ISBN 0-87795-135-7 : 8.95
1. Thorson, Ralph Edgar. 2. Crime and criminals—United States—Biography. I. Title.

Thorwall, Axel Johnson, 1890-1960.

THORWALL, LaReau. 289.9'0924 B
And light new fires; the story of Axel Johnson Thorwall, an immigrant blacksmith who exchanged his forge for a frock coat, by LaReau Thorwall as told to Mel Larson. Foreword by John B. Anderson. Minneapolis, Free Church Publications [1969] 186 p. illus. 22 cm. [BX7548.Z8T48] 70-103414 4.95
1. Thorwall, Axel Johnson, 1890-1960. I. Larson, Melvin Gunnard, 1916- II. Title.

Thought and thinking.

MURRY, John Middleton, 1889-1957. 108
Heroes of thought. Freeport, N.Y., Books for Libraries Press [1971, c1938] xiii, 368 p. 23 cm. (Essay index reprint series) Contents.Contents.—Heaven and earth.—Chaucer.—Montaigne.—Shakespeare.—Oliver Cromwell.—John Milton.—Rousseau.—Goethe.—William Godwin.—Wordsworth.—Shelley.—Karl Marx.—William Morris. [CT104.M78 1971] 76-167389 ISBN 0-8369-2436-3
1. Thought and thinking. 2. Biography. I. Title. **BIP**

Thrall family.

PIOZZI, Hester Lynch Salusbury Thrale, 1741-1821. 828'.6'09 B
The Thrales of Streatham Park / [edited] by Mary Hyde. Cambridge : Harvard University Press, [1977] p. cm. Annotated journal of Hester Thrale. Includes index. [PR3619.P5A827 1977] 77-24922 ISBN 0-674-88746-8 : 15.00
1. Piozzi, Hester Lynch Salusbury Thrale, 1741-1821—Biography. 2. Thrall family. 3. Salusbury family. 4. England—Social life and customs—18th century. I. Hyde, Mary Morely Crapo. II. Title.

Thrasher, Anthony Apakark, 1937-

THRASHER, Anthony Apakark, 1937- 970'.004'97 B
Thrasher ... skid row eskimo / by Anthony Apakark Thrasher, in collaboration with Gerard Deagle and Alan Mettrick. Toronto : Griffin House, 1976. xi, 164 p. : ill. ; 22 cm. [E99.E7T53] 77-354380 ISBN 0-88760-082-4 : 8.95
1. Thrasher, Anthony Apakark, 1937- 2. Eskimos—Canada—Biography. 3. Eskimos—Canada—Social conditions. I. Deagle, Gerard, joint author. II. Mettrick, Alan, joint author. III. Title.

Thrasher family.

PRUETT, Dorothy Sturgis, 1916- 929'.2'0973
Cousins by the dozens : Sturgis, Thrasher, Carlton, Mitchell, Branch : supplement / compiled by Dorothy Sturgis Pruett. Original ed. Macon, Ga. : Pruett, c1978- v. : ill. ; 23 cm. Includes index. [CS71.S935 1978] 78-106708 price unreported
1. Sturgis family. 2. Thrasher family. 3. Carlton family. I. Title.

Thumb, Tom, Mrs., 1841-1919.

THUMB, Tom, Mrs., 1841-1919. 791.3'092'4 B
The autobiography of Mrs. Tom Thumb : (some of my life experiences) / by Countess M. Lavinia Magri, formerly Mrs. General Tom Thumb, with the assistance of Sylvester Bleeker ; edited and introduced by A. H. Saxon. Hamden, Conn. : Archon Books, 1979. 199 p., [8] leaves of plates : ill. ; 22 cm. (An Archon book on popular entertainments) Includes index. Bibliography: p. 191-193. [GV1811.T55A33] 78-26267 ISBN 0-208-01760-7 : 15.00
1. Thumb, Tom, Mrs., 1841-1919. 2. Circus performers—United States—Biography. I. Bleeker, Sylvester, joint author. II. Saxon, A. H. III. Series: Archon book on popular entertainments. **BIP**

Thurber, Charles S., 1864-

BLAISDELL, Ethel F. 922.773
And God caught an eel. New York, Coward-McCann [1954] 242 p. illus. 21 cm. [BV2678.T5B6] 54-10140
1. Thurber, Charles S., 1864- I. Title.

Thurber, James,

THURBER, James, 1894-1961. 741.5973
Thurber & company. Introd. by Helen Thurber. [1st ed.] New York, Harper & Row [1966] 208 p. (chiefly illus.) 27 cm. [NC1429.T53 1966] 64-18067
I. Thurber, Helen, comp. II. Title. **BIP**

Thurber, James, 1894-1961.

HOLMES, Charles Shiveley. 818'.5'209
The clocks of Columbus; the literary career of James Thurber [by] Charles S. Holmes.

[1st ed.] New York, Atheneum, 1972. xiv, 360 p. illus. 25 cm. Bibliography: p. [335]-339. [PS3539.H94Z7] 72-78287 10.00
1. Thurber, James, 1894-1961. I. Title. BIP

THURBER, James, 1894-1961. 818'.5'207
My life and hard times. With an introd. by John K. Hutchens. New York, Harper & Row [1973, c1933] 114 p. illus. 19 cm. (Perennial library, P 290) [PS3539.H94M87 1973] 73-161582 0.95 (pbk.)
1. Authors—Correspondence, reminiscences, etc. I. Title. BIP

THURBER, James, 1894-1961. 741.5973
Thurber & company. Introd. by Helen Thurber. [1st ed.] New York, Harper & Row [1966] 208 p. (chiefly illus.) 27 cm. [NC1429.T53 1966] 64-18067
I. Thurber, Helen, comp. II. Title. BIP

Thurber, James, 1894-1961—Biography.

BERNSTEIN, Burton. 818'.5'209 B
Thurber : a biography / by Burton Bernstein ; illustrated with drawings by James Thurber and photos. New York : Dodd, Mead, [1975] ix, 532 p., [16] leaves of plates : ill. ; 24 cm. Includes index. Bibliography: p. 517-520. [PS3539.H94Z57] 74-10004 ISBN 0-396-07027-2 : 15.00
1. Thurber, James, 1894-1961—Biography.

Thurman, Howard, 1899-

THURMAN, Howard, 1899- 280'.4 B
With head and heart ; the autobiography of Howard Thurman. 1st ed. New York : Harcourt Brace Jovanovich, c1979. p. cm. Includes index. [BX6495.T53A38] 79-1848 ISBN 0-15-142164-1 : 10.00
1. Thurman, Howard, 1899- 2. Baptists—Clergy—Biography. 3. Clergy—United States—Biography. I. Title.

YATES, Elizabeth, 1905- 922.89
Howard Thurman, portrait of a practical dreamer. New York, John Day Co. [1964] 249 p. port. 22 cm. "Chronological bibliography of works by Howard Thurman": p. 241-242. [BX6455.T5Y3] 64-14201
1. Thurman, Howard, 1899- I. Title.

YATES, Elizabeth, 1905- 922.89
Howard Thurman, portrait of a practical dreamer. New York, John Day Co. [1964] 249 p. port. 22 cm. "Chronological bibliography of works by Howard Thurman": p. 241-242. [BX6455.T5Y3] 64-14201
1. Thurman, Howard, 1899-

Thurman, Steve

THURMAN, Steve 923.4173
'Baby Face' Nelson. Derby, Conn., Monarch Bks. [c.1961] 139p. (MA 313) .35 pap.,
I. Title.

Thurmond, Strom, 1902-

LACHICOTTE, Alberta Morel. 973.90924
Rebel Senator: Strom Thurmond of South Carolina, by Alberta Lachicotte. New York, Devin-Adair Co. [1966] xi, 255 p. illus., ports. 21 cm. [E748.T58L3] 66-26024
1. Thurmond, Strom, 1902- I. Title.

Thurstan, Abp. of York, 1070 (ca.)-1140.

NICHOLL, Donald, 1923- 270.4
Thurstan, Archibishop of York, 1114-1140. York, Stonegate Pr., 1964. xi, 277p. 23cm. Bibl. [BR754.T57N5] 66-6700 7.00
1. Thurstan, Abp. of York, 1070 (ca.)-1140. I. Title.
American distributor: Dufour in Chester Springs, Pa.

Thurston. Herbert, 1856-1939.

CREHAN, Joseph. 922.242
Father Thurston; a memoir, with a bibliography of his writings. London, New York, Sheed and Ward [1952] 235 p. illus. 21 cm. [BX4705.T652C7] 52-3072
1. Thurston. Herbert, 1856-1939. I. Title.

Thurston, John Bates, Sir, 1836-1897.

SCARR, Deryck. 996'.11 B
The majesty of colour, a life of Sir John Bates Thurston. Canberra, Australian University Press, 1973- v. illus. 25 cm. Contents.Contents.—v. 1. I, the very bayonet. Bibliography: v. 1, p. 345-360. [DU600.T52S25] 74-170877
1. Thurston, John Bates, Sir, 1836-1897. 2. Fiji Islands—Politics and government. I. Title.
Distributed by International Scholarly Book Service; 18.05. ISBN 0-7081-0704-4 (vol I)

Thurston, Louis Leon,

WOOD, Dorothy (Adkins) 1912- v. 12
Louis Leon Turstone; creative thinker, dedicated teacher, eminent psychologist. [Princeton, N.J., Educational Testing Service, c1962] 68 p. illus., ports. "Bibliography of [Thurstone's] published works": p. [37]-68. 63-38092
1. Thurston, Louis Leon, 1887-1955. I. Title.

Tibbett, Lawrence, 1896-1960.

TIBBETT, Lawrence, 1896-1960. 782.1'092'4 B
The glory road / Lawrence Tibbett ; with a discography by W. R. Moran. New York : Arno Press, 1977. 70, xxii p., [10] leaves of plates : ill. ; 24 cm. (Opera biographies) Reprint of the 1933 ed. Discography: p. i-xii. [ML420.T52A3 1977] 76-29972 ISBN 0-405-09711-5 : 12.00
1. Tibbett, Lawrence, 1896-1960. 2. Singers—United States—Biography. I. Title.

Tibble, Anne (Northgrave)

TIBBLE, Anne (Northgrave) 820'.9 B
Greenhorn: a twentieth-century childhood [by] Anne Tibble; illustrated by Karen Heywood. London, Boston, Routledge and Kegan Paul, 1973. [7], 126 p. illus. 23 cm. [PR6039.I2Z52] 73-75946 ISBN 0-7100-7570-7 6.50
1. Tibble, Anne (Northgrave) I. Title. BIP

Tibble, Anne Northgrave—Biography.

TIBBLE, Anne Northgrave. 820'.9
One woman's story : an autobiography / Anne Tibble. London : P. Owen, 1976. 160 p. ; 22 cm. Includes bibliographical references. [PR6039.I2Z524] 76-375003 ISBN 0-7206-0154-1 : £3.95
1. Tibble, Anne Northgrave—Biography. 2. Authors, English—20th century—Biography. I. Title.

Tiberius, Emperor of Rome, 42 B.C.-37 A.D.

BAKER, George Philip, 1879-1951 937'.06'0924 (B)
Tiberius Caesar. New York, Barnes & Noble [1967] xi, 322p. illus., geneal. table., maps. 23cm. First pub. 1929. [DG282.B3 1967] 67-8848 7.50
1. Tiberius, Emperor of Rome, 42 B.C.—37 A. D. 2. Rome—Hist.— Augustus, 30 B. C.-14 A. D. 3. Rome—Hist.—Tiberius, 14-37. I. Title. BIP

LEVICK, Barbara Mary. 937'.07'0924 B
Tiberius the politician / Barbara Levick. London : Thames and Hudson, 1976. 328 p., [8] leaves of plates : ill. ; 22 cm. (Aspects of Greek and Roman life) Includes index. Bibliography: p. [295]-302. [DG282.L58 1976] 76-380263 ISBN 0-500-40029-6 : £9.50
1. Tiberius, Emperor of Rome, 42 B.C.-37 A.D. 2. Roman emperors—Biography. I. Title. II. Series.

MARANON, Gregorio, 1887- 923.137
Tiberius; the resentful Cabsar. With a foreword by Ronald Syme. [Translation by Warre Bradley Wells. 1st ed.] New York, Duell, Sloan and Pearce [c1956] 234p. 22cm. Includes bibliography. [DG282.M283] 57-7572
1. Tiberius, Emperor of Rome, 42 B. C.-37 A. D. I. Title.

MASON, Ernst. 923.137
Tiberius. New York, Ballantine Books [1960] 143p. 18cm. (Ballantine books, 361K) [DG282.M35] 60-568
1. Tiberius, Emperor of Rome, 42 B. C.-37 A. D. I. Title.

ROGERS, Robert Samuel, 1900- 937'.06
Studies in the reign of Tiberius; some imperial virtues of Tiberius and Drusus Julius Caesar. Westport, Conn., Greenwood Press [1972, c1943] ix, 181 p. illus. 22 cm. Bibliography: p. 157-161. [DG282.R6 1972] 77-152601 ISBN 0-8371-6036-7
1. Tiberius, Emperor of Rome, 42 B.C.-37. 2. Drusus Caesar, 13 (ca.) B.C.-23. 3. Rome—History—Tiberius, 14-37. I. Title.

SEAGER, Robin. 937'.07'0924 B
Tiberius. Berkeley, University of California Press, 1972. xviii, 300 p. illus. 24 cm. Bibliography: p. 281-287. [DG282.S43 1972b] 74-185511 ISBN 0-520-02212-2 12.95
1. Tiberius, Emperor of Rome, 42 B.C.-37 A.D. BIP

Ticknor, George, 1791-1871.

TYACK, David B. 917.44'03'3
George Ticknor and the Boston Brahmins [by] David B. Tyack. Cambridge, Mass., Harvard, 1967. x, 289p. illus., ports. 24cm. Bibl. [PS3064.T5Z92] 67-13255 6.95
1. Ticknor, George, 1791-1871. I. Title.

Tidd family.

LETTERS eighteen eleven to eighteen fifty-six Tidd, Lord, Henchman, Carret / [compiled by Margaret Garrison Phoutrides]. [Berkeley, Calif. : Phoutrides, 1955] 146 p. ; 28 cm. [CS71.T556 1955] 75-319464 929'.2'0973
1. Tidd family. 2. Lord family. 3. Carret family. I. Phoutrides, Margaret Garrison.

Tieck, Johann Ludwig, 1773-1853.

MATENKO, Percy, 1901- 928.3
Ludwig Tieck and America. Chapel Hill University of North Carolina Press [1954] 120p. 23cm. (University of North Carolina studies in Germanic languages and literatures, no. 12) [PD25.N6 no. 12] 54-62860
1. Tieck, Johann Ludwig, 1773-1853. 2. Literature, Comparative—German and American. 3. Literature, Comparative—American and German. I. Title. II. Series: North Carolina. University. Studies in the Germanic languages and literatures no. 12 BIP

TIECK, Johann Ludwig, 1773-1853. 838'.7'09 B
Letters of Ludwig Tieck, hitherto unpublished, 1792-1853, collected and edited by Edwin H. Zeydel, Percy Matenko [and] Robert Herndon Fife, with the co-operation of the Department of Germanic Languages, Columbia University. New York, Modern Language Association of America, 1937. Millwood, N.Y., Kraus Reprint Co., 1973. xxxi, 604 p. facsim. 24 cm. Original ed. issued in series: The Modern Language Association of America. General series. Bibliography: p. xxxi. [PT2539.A419 1973] 73-9682 ISBN 0-527-90100-8 20.00 (pbk)
1. Tieck, Johann Ludwig, 1773-1853. I. Zeydel, Edwin Hermann, 1893- ed. II. Matenko, Percy, 1901- ed. III. Fife, Robert Herndon, 1871-1958, ed. IV. Columbia University. Dept. of Germanic Languages and Literatures. V. Series: Modern Language Association of America. General series. BIP

Tiepolo, Giovanni Battista, 1696-1770.

G. B. Tiepolo, his life and work. New York, Phaidon Publishers; distributed by Garden City Books [1955] 152p. plates (part col.) 31cm. Translated from the Italian by Mr. and Mrs. Peter Murray. Bibliography: p. 141-142. [ND623.T5M72] 759.5 55-3929 927.5
1. Tiepolo, Giovanni Battista, 1696-1770. I. Morassi, Antonio, 1892-

KNOX, George. 769'.945'074011384
Etchings by the Tiepolos : Domenico Tiepolo's collection of the family etchings ... = Eaux-fortes des Tiepolo : recueil de Domenico Tiepolo rassemblant les eaux-fortes de sa famille ... / by George Knox ... with the assistance of Elaine Dee. Ottawa : National Gallery of Canada : obtainable from National Museums of Canada, 1976. 167 p. : ill. ; 23 cm. English and French. Catalogue of an exhibition held at the National Gallery of Canada. Includes index. Bibliography: p. 157-159. [NE2052.5.T5K68] 76-472661 ISBN 0-88884-289-9
1. Tiepolo, Giovanni Battista, 1696-1770. 2. Tiepolo, Giovanni Domenico, 1726?-1804. 3. Tiepolo, Lorenzo, b. 1736?-1776. I. Tiepolo, Giovanni Domenico, 1726?-1804. II. Dee, Elaine Evans, joint author. III. National Gallery of Canada. IV. Title. V. Title: Eaux-fortes des Tiepolo.

Tiepolo, Giovanni Domenico, 1726?-1804.

KNOX, George. 769'.945'074011384
Etchings by the Tiepolos : Domenico Tiepolo's collection of the family etchings ... = Eaux-fortes des Tiepolo : recueil de Domenico Tiepolo rassemblant les eaux-fortes de sa famille ... / by George Knox ... with the assistance of Elaine Dee. Ottawa : National Gallery of Canada : obtainable from National Museums of Canada, 1976. 167 p. : ill. ; 23 cm. English and French. Catalogue of an exhibition held at the National Gallery of Canada. Includes index. Bibliography: p. 157-159. [NE2052.5.T5K68] 76-472661 ISBN 0-88884-289-9
1. Tiepolo, Giovanni Battista, 1696-1770. 2. Tiepolo, Giovanni Domenico, 1726?-1804. 3. Tiepolo, Lorenzo, b. 1736?-1776. I. Tiepolo, Giovanni Domenico, 1726?-1804. II. Dee, Elaine Evans, joint author. III. National Gallery of Canada. IV. Title. V. Title: Eaux-fortes des Tiepolo.

Tierney, Gene.

TIERNEY, Gene. 791.43'028'0924 B
Self-portrait / Gene Tierney, with Mickey Herskowitz. 1st ed. New York : Wyden Books : trade distribution by Simon and Schuster, c1979. 264 p., [8] leaves of plates : ill. ; 24 cm. Filmography: p. [246]-264. [PN2287.T48A37] 78-26161 ISBN 0-88326-152-9 : 10.95
1. Tierney, Gene. 2. Moving-picture actors and actresses—United States—Biography. I. Herskowitz, Mickey, joint author. II. Title. BIP

Tiffany, Kathleen S.

TIFFANY, Kathleen S. 920
The story of St. Francis. Pictures by Johannes Troyer. New York, Golden Pr. [dist. Affiliated Pubs.] c.1961 unpaged. col. illus. (Guild Pr.; Catechetical guild bk., First bk. for little Catholics) .25 bds.,
I. Title.

Tiffany, Louis Comfort, 1848-1933.

KOCH, Robert, 1918- 748'.0924
Louis C. Tiffany, rebel in glass. 2d ed. New York, Crown Publishers [1966] 246 p. illus. (part col.) ports. 29 cm. Bibliography: p. 221-233. [NK5198.T5K6 1966] 67-5755
1. Tiffany, Louis Comfort, 1848-1933. I. Title.

WINTER, Henry. 748'.8
[The dynasty of Louis Comfort Tiffany; the final. Boston?, Mass., 1971] 280 p. illus. (part col.), coat of arms, facsims., ports. 29 cm. Title from dust jacket. [NK5198.T5W52] 77-24673
1. Tiffany, Louis Comfort, 1848-1933. I. Title.

Tigert, John James, 1882-1965.

OSBORN, George 370'.92'4 B
Coleman, 1904-
John James Tigert: American educator. Gainesville, The University Presses of Florida [1974] xvi, 544 p. illus. 24 cm. "A University of Florida book." Bibliography: p. [507]-534. [LA2317.T54O72] 74-6314 ISBN 0-8130-0498-5
1. Tigert, John James, 1882-1965.

Tikhon, Patriarch of Moscow and all Russia, 1865-1925.

SWAN, Jane. v. 12
A biography of Patriarch Tikhon. Jordanville, N. Y., Holy Trinity Monastery, 1964. 112 p. port. 68-17773
1. Tikhon, Patriarch of Moscow and all Russia, 1865-1925. I. Title.

Tikhon Zadonskii, Saint, Bp. of Voronezh, 1724-1783.

GORODETZKY, 281.9'092'4 B
Nadejda, 1904-
Saint Tikhon of Zadonsk, inspirer of Dostoevsky / by Nadejda Gorodetzky. Rev. ed. Crestwood, NY : St. Vladimir's Seminary Press, 1977. 318 p. ; 22 cm. Includes index. Bibliography: p. 275-295. [BX597.T53G67 1976] 76-49919 ISBN 0-913836-32-X pbk. : 6.95
1. Tikhon Zadonskii, Saint, Bp. of Voronezh, 1724-1783. 2. Christian saints—Russia—Biography. I. Title.

Tilak. Bal Gangadhar, 1856-1920.

RAM GOPAL, 1912- 320.0924
Lokamanya Tilak: a biography. [1st ed.] reprinted. London. Asia Pub., 1965[i.e.,1966] xi, 481p. front. (port.) 23cm. [DS479.1.T54R3 1966] 66-77379 9.75
1. Tilak. Bal Gangadhar, 1856-1920. I. Title.
Available from Taplinger, New York City.

Tilak, Lakshmibai (Gokhale)

TILAK, Lakshmibai (Gokhale) 922
1873-1936.
I follow after, an autobiography. Translated by E. Josephine Inkster. [Madras, New York] Indian Branch, Oxford University Press [1950] 353p. ports. 20cm. (Champak library) Translation of the first three parts of Smrti citrem, published in Marathi, 1964-37. Geneal. tables and map on lining paper. [BV3269.T57A38] 52-6050
I. Title.

Tilden, Samuel Jones, 1814-1886.

FLICK, Alexander 923.273
Clarence, 1869-1942.
Samuel Jones Tilden; a study in political sagacity, by Alexander Clarence Flick, assisted by Gustav S. Lobrano. Port Washington, N. Y., Kennikat Press [1963, c1939] 597 p. illus., ports. 22 cm. Bibliography: p. 535-553. [E415.9.T5F5 1963] 63-20591
1. Tilden, Samuel Jones, 1814-1886. 2. U.S.—Politics and government—1865-1900. BIP

FLICK, Alexander 973.8'0924 B
Clarence, 1869-1942.
Samuel Jones Tilden; a study in political sagacity, by Alexander Clarence Flick, assisted by Gustav S. Lobrano. Westport, Conn., Greenwood Press [1973, c1939] ix, 597 p. illus. 23 cm. Reprint of the ed. published by Dodd, Mead, New York, in series: American political leaders. Bibliography: p. 535-553. [E415.9.T5F5 1973] 73-7103 ISBN 0-8371-6912-7
1. Tilden, Samuel Jones, 1814-1886. 2. United States—Politics and government—1865-1900. I. Lobrano, Gustav Stubbs, joint author. II. Series: American political leaders.

TILDEN, Samuel 973.8'0924 B
Jones, 1814-1886.
Letters and literary memorials of Samuel J. Tilden. Edited by John Bigelow. Freeport, N.Y., Books for Libraries Press [1971] 2 v. (xxxi, 751 p.) 23 cm. Reprint of the 1908 ed. [E415.6.T59 1971b] 74-164629 ISBN 0-8369-5913-2
I. Bigelow, John, 1817-1911, ed. BIP

Tilden, William Tatem, 1893-1953.

DEFORD, Frank. 796.34'2'0924 B
Big Bill Tilden : the triumphs and the tragedy / by Frank Deford. New York : Simon and Schuster, c1976. 286 p., [8] leaves of plates : ill. ; 22 cm. "This work is an outgrowth of a two-part magazine series written by Mr. Deford for Sports illustrated (January 13, January 20, 1975)." Includes index. [GV994.T5D43 1976] 75-45011 ISBN 0-671-22254-6 : 8.95
1. Tilden, William Tatem, 1893-1953. 2. Tennis players—United States—Biography. I. Title.

Tilghman, William Matthew, 1854-1924.

MILLER, Floyd. 363.2'0924 B
Bill Tilghman; marshal of the last frontier. [1st ed.] Garden City, N.Y., Doubleday, 1968. x, 252 p. illus., map (on lining papers), ports. 22 cm. Bibliography: p. [241]-245. [F595.T5M5] 68-14218
1. Tilghman, William Matthew, 1854-1924.

MILLER, Floyd. 976.6'04'0924 B
Bill Tilghman; marshal of the last frontier. [1st ed.] Garden City, N.Y., Doubleday, 1968. x, 252 p. illus., map (on lining papers), ports. 22 cm. Bibliography: p. [241]-245. A biography of the man who became a legend in his lifetime as Marshal of the Oklahoma Territory. [F595.T5M5] 92 AC 68
1. Tilghman, William Matthew, 1854-1924. I. Title.

TILGHMAN, Zoe Agnes 923.573
(Stratton) 1880-
Marshal of the last frontier; life and services of William Matthew (Bill) Tilghman, for 50 years on of the greatest peace officers of the west Zoe A. Tilghman. [Rev. ed.] Glendale, Calif., A. H. Clark Co., 1964. 390 p. illus., map, ports. 25 cm. (Western frontiersmen series, 3) [F595.T5T5] 65-1979
1. Tilghman, William Matthew 2. Crime and criminals — The West. I. Title.

Tillamook Co., Or.—Biography.

TILLAMOOK memories; 917.95'44'03
places we love come back to us as sweet music. [Tillamook, Or., Tillamook Pioneer Association] c1972. 218 p. illus. 28 cm. [F882.T5T54] 72-92557
1. Tillamook Co., Or.—Biography. 2. Tillamook Co., Or.—History. 3. Tillamook, Or.—History.

Tillamook County, Ore.

HUCKLEBERRY, 917.95'44'0340924 B
E. R., 1894-
The adventures of Dr. Huckleberry: Tillamook County, Oregon, by E. R. Huckleberry. [Portland] Oregon Historical Society, 1970. viii, 272 p. illus., map, ports. 23 cm. [F882.T5H8] 70-129303 ISBN 0-87595-025-6
1. Tillamook County, Ore. 2. Lumbering—Oregon—Tillamook County. I. Title.

Tillamook Rock Light Station.

GIBBS, James Atwood, 623.894
1922-
Tillamook Light. Portland, Or., Binfords & Mort [1953] 188 p. illus. 23 cm. Autobiographical. [VK140.G5A3] 627.9 54-328
1. Tillamook Rock Light Station. I. Title. BIP

Tillich, Paul, 1886-1965.

FERRE, Nels Fredrick 230'.0924
Solomon, 1908-
Paul Tillich: retrospect and future. [Articles by] Nels F. S. Ferre [and others] Introd. by T. A. Kantonen. Nashville, Abingdon Press [1967, c1966] 63 p. 19 cm. "Reprinted from Religion in life, winter 1966." [BX4827.T53P3] 67-31858
1. Tillich, Paul, 1886-1965. I. Title. II. Title: Religion in life.

MAY, Rollo. 230'.092'4 B
Paulus; reminiscences of a friendship. [1st ed.] New York, Harper & Row [1973] vii, 113 p. 21 cm. Includes bibliographical references. [BX4827.T53M34] 72-78075 ISBN 0-06-065535-6 5.95
1. Tillich, Paul, 1886-1965. I. Title.

PAUCK, Wilhelm, 230'.092'4 B
1901-
Paul Tillich, his life & thought / Wilhelm & Marion Pauck. 1st ed. New York : Harper & Row, c1976- v. : ill. ; 22 cm. Contents.Contents.—v. 1. Life. Includes bibliographical references and index. [BX4827.T53P28 1976] 74-25709 ISBN 0-06-066474-6 (v. 1) : 15.00
1. Tillich, Paul, 1886-1965. 2. Theologians—United States—Biography. 3. Theologians—Germany—Biography. I. Pauck, Marion, joint author.

TAIT, Leslie Gordon, 230'.0924
1926-
The promise of Tillich, by L. Gordon Tait. [1st ed.] Philadelphia, Lippincott [1971] 127 p. 21 cm. (The Promise of theology) Bibliography: p. 123-127. [BX4827.T53T25] 79-146687 3.95
1. Tillich, Paul, 1886-1965. I. Title.

THOMAS, John Heywood 230.0924
Paul Tillich. [Amer. ed.] Richmond, Va., Knox [1966] 48p. 19cm. (Makers of contemp. theol.) 1st pub. in England by the Carey Kingsgate Pr., 1965. [BX4827.T53T49] 66-11072 1.00 pap.,
1. Tillich, Paul, 1886-1965. I. Title.

TILLICH, Hannah. 910'.4
From place to place : travels with Paul Tillich, travels without Paul Tillich / Hannah Tillich. New York : Stein and Day, 1976. 223 p. : ill. ; 24 cm. [BX4827.T53T52] 75-34490 ISBN 0-8128-1902-0 : 10.00
1. Tillich, Paul, 1886-1965. 2. Tillich, Hannah. 3. Theologians—United States—Biography. 4. Wives—United States—Biography. I. Title. BIP

TILLICH, Hannah. 230'.092'4 B
From time to time. New York, Stein and Day [1973] 252 p. 24 cm. [BX4827.T53T53] 73-79225 ISBN 0-8128-1626-9 7.95
1. Tillich, Paul, 1886-1965. I. Title.

TILLICH, Hannah. 230'.092'4 B
From time to time. New York, Stein and Day [1974 c1973] 252 p. 18 cm. [BX4827.T53T53] ISBN 0-8128-1742-7 1.95 (pbk.)
1. Tillich, Paul, 1886-1965. I. Title.
L.C. card no. for original edition: 73-79225 BIP

Tillman, Benjamin Ryan, 1847-1918.

SIMKINS, Francis Butler, 923.273
1898-
Pitchfork Ben Tillamn, South Carolinian. Gloucester, Mass., P. Smith, 1964[c.1944] xii, 577p. illus., facsim., ports. 21cm. (Southern biog. ser.) Bibl. [E664.T57S5] 65-1581 6.75
1. Tillman, Benjamin Ryan, 1847-1918. 2. South Carolina—Pol. & govt.—1865-1950. I. Title. II. Series.

Timoleon, 411 ca.-337 B.C.

TALBERT, R. J. A. 937.8
Timoleon and the revival of Greek Sicily, 344-317 B.C. / by R. J. A. Talbert. London ; New York : Cambridge University Press, 1974 [i.e. 1975] xii, 235 p. ; 23 cm. (Cambridge classical studies) Includes index. Bibliography: p. 209-229. [DF232.T55T34] 74-16854 ISBN 0-521-20419-4 : 15.00
1. Timoleon, 411 ca.-337 B.C. 2. Greece—History—To 146 B.C. 3. Sicily—History—To 800. 4. Greeks in Sicily. 5. Carthaginians—Sicily. I. Title. II. Series.

Timoshenko, Stephen,

TIMOSHENKO, Stephen, 620'.00924 B
1878-
As I remember; the autobiography of Stephen P. Timoshenko [by] Stephen P. Timoshenko. Translated from the Russian by Robert Addis. Princeton, N. J., Van Nostrand [1968] xvi, 430 p. illus., ports. 22 cm. Translation of (Vospominan-32ia) (romanized) "Principal writings of S. P. Timoshenko": p. 418-429. [TA140.T55A213] 67-18069
I. Title.

Timothy (Biblical character)—Juvenile literature.

CALDWELL, Louise. 227'.092'4 B
Timothy, young pastor / Louise Caldwell ; illustrated by Paul Karch. Nashville : Broadman Press, c1978. 48 p. : col. ill. ; 24 cm. (Biblearn series) Tells the story of the pastor and missionary who is thought to have been converted to Christianity by Paul. [BS2520.T5C34] 78-105195 ISBN 0-8054-4239-1 pbk. : 3.95
1. Bible. N.T.—Biography—Juvenile literature. 2. Timothy (Biblical character)—Juvenile literature. I. Karch, Paul. II. Title.

Timpson, John, 1928-

TIMPSON, John, 1928- 070'.92'4 B
Today and yesterday / John Timpson. London : G. Allen & Unwin, 1976. 158 p. : ill. ; 23 cm. Includes index. [PN5123.T4A3] 76-381574 ISBN 0-04-927008-7 : 9.50
1. Timpson, John, 1928- 2. Journalists—Great Britain—Biography. I. Title.
Distributed by Allen and Unwin, 198 Ash Street, Reading, MA.01867

Timrod, Henry, 1828-1867.

PARS, Edd Winfield, 1906- v. 12
Henry Timrod. New York, Twayne Publishers [1964] 158 p. Twayne's United States authors series, 4553) Bibliography: p. 146-149. 66-83825
1. Timrod, Henry, 1828-1867. I. Title. BIP

THOMPSON, Henry 811'.3 B
Tazewell, 1859-
Henry Timrod, Laureate of the Confederacy [by Henry T. Thompson] New York, AMS Press [1971] 147 p. illus., port. 23 cm. Reprint of the 1928 ed. Selections from the works of Timrod: p. 81-137. Includes bibliographical references. [PS3073.T4 1971] 77-144695 ISBN 0-404-06421-3
1. Timrod, Henry, 1828-1867. BIP

Tims, Margaret

TIMS, Margaret 923.673
Jane Addams of Hull House, 1860-1935, a centenary study. New York, Macmillan [c.]1961. 166p. (front. port.) 61-16149 4.25 bds.,
I. Title.

Timur, the Great, 1336-1405.

HOOKHAM, Hilda 950.2
Tamburlaine, the Conqueror. London, Hodder & Stoughton [dist. Mystic, Conn., Verry, 1964, c.1962] xv, 344p. illus. (pt.

col.) port., maps (pt. fold.) 23cm. Bibl. 63-25469 7.50
1. Timur, the Great. I. Title.

IBN 'Arabshah, 950'.2'0924 B
Ahmad ibn Muhammad, 1392-1450.
Tamerlane : or, Timur, the great amir / translated by J. H. Sanders from the Arabic life by Ahmed ibn Arabshah. Lahore : Progressive Books, 1976. xviii, 341 p. ; 23 cm. Reprint of the 1936 ed. published by Luzac, London. Translation of 'Aja'ib al-maqdur fi akhbar Timur. Includes index. [DS23.I213 1976] 76-930258 Rs60.00
1. Timur, the Great, 1336-1405. 2. Turks—Kings and rulers—Biography. I. Sanders, John Herne, 1888- II. Title. III. Title: Timur, The great amir.

Tinkerbelle (Sailboat)

MANRY, Robert, 1918- 910.453
Tinkerbelle. Drawings by Roy C. Hearn. [1st ed.] New York, Harper & Row [1966] 254 p. illus., fold. map. 22 cm. Autobiographical. [G530.M313] 66-15735
1. Tinkerbelle (Sailboat) 2. Voyages and travels.

Tinsley, William, 1804-1885.

FORBES, John Douglas, 1910- 927.2
Victorian architect; the life and work of William Tinsley. Bloomington, Indiana University Press, 1953. xiv, 153p. illus., ports., map. 25cm. 'Bibliographical note':p. 140-146. [NA737.T5F6] 53-10024
1. Tinsley, William, 1804-1885. I. Title.

Tiny Tim.

STEIN, Harry. 784'.092'4 B
Tiny Tim / by Harry Stein. 1st ed. Chicago : Playboy Press, c1976. 243 p., [4] leaves of plates : ill. ; 22 cm. [ML420.T553S7] 76-10329 ISBN 0-87223-455-X : 8.95
1. Tiny Tim.

THE True, fantastic 784'.0924
story of Tiny Tim. [Rochelle Larkin: editor. Barry Weiser photography. New York, Corncob, 1968] 74 p. ports. 28 cm. Cover title. [ML420.T553T8] 68-6536 0.50
1. Tiny Tim. I. Larkin, Rochelle, ed.

Tirrell, Mary Pierre.

TIRRELL, Mary Pierre. 922.246
Mary was her life; the story of a nun, Sister Maria Teresa Quevedo, 1930-1950. New York, Benziger Bros. [1960] 234 p. illus. 21 cm. Quevedo, Maria Teresa, 1930-1950. [BX4705.Q44T5] 60-9445
I. Title.

Titmus Optical Company, inc., Petersburg, Va.

TITMUS, Edward Hutson, 926.81
1877-
Looking through the lens. Petersburg, Va., 1953. 79p. illus. 20cm. Autobiographical. [HD9999.O64T5] 54-15655
1. Titmus Optical Company, inc., Petersburg, Va. I. Title.

Tito, Josip Broz, Pres. Yugoslavia, 1892-

ARCHER, Jules. 949.7'02'0924 B
Red rebel; Tito of Yugoslavia. New York, J. Messner [1968] 190 p. 22 cm. Bibliography: p. 181-182. [DR359.T5A75] 68-25097 3.50
1. Tito, Josip Broz, Pres. Yugoslavia, 1892- 2. Communism—Yugoslavia. I. Title.

AUTY, Phyllis. 949'.702'0924 B
Tito; a biography. New York, McGraw-Hill [1970] xiv, 343 p. illus., maps, ports. 23 cm. Bibliography: p. 321-329. [DR359.T5A9 1970b] 75-107283 8.50
1. Tito, Josip Broz, Pres. Yugoslavia, 1892-

AUTY, Phyllis. 949.7'02'0924 B
Tito. [New York, Ballantine Books, 1972] 160 p. illus. 21 cm. (Ballantine's illustrated history of the violent century. War leader book, no. 10) Bibliography: p. 160. [DR359.T5A89] 72-190010 1.00
1. Tito, Josip Broz, Pres. Yugoslavia, 1892-

AUTY, Phyllis. 949.7'02'0924 B
Tito : a biography / by Phyllis Auty. Revised ed. Harmondsworth : Penguin, 1974. 400 p., [8] p. of plates : ill., maps, ports. ; 19 cm. (Political leaders of the twentieth century) (Pelican books) Includes index. Bibliography: p. 376-385. [DR359.T5A89 1974] 75-314064 ISBN 0-14-021800-9 : £1.00
1. Tito, Josip Broz, Pres. Yugoslavia, 1892-

BILAINKIN, George, 1903- 923.5497
Tito. New York, Philosophical Library [1950] 287 p. ports. 19 cm. [DR359.T5B5 1950] 50-3607
1. Tito, Jonip Bros, known as, 1892- I. Title.

DEDIJER, Vladimir. 923.5497
Tito. New York, Simon and Schuster, 1953 [i. e. 1952] 443p. 22cm. [DR359.T5D4] 53-6161
1. Tito, Josip Broz, known as, 1892- I. Title. BIP

DEDIJER, 949.7'02'0924 B
Vladimir.
Tito. New York, Arno Press, 1972. vii, 443 p. 23 cm. (World affairs: national and international viewpoints) Reprint of the 1953 ed. [DR359.T5D4 1972] 72-4269 ISBN 0-405-04565-4 21.00
1. Tito, Josip Broz, Pres. Yugoslavia, 1892- I. Title. II. Series.

DRASKOVICH, Slobodan M 949.7
1910-
Tito, Moscow's Trojan horse. Chicago, H. Regnary Co., 1957. 357p. 22cm. [DR370.D72] 57-8121
1. Tito, Josip Broz, Pres. Yugoslavia, 1892- 2. Communism. I. Title.

MACLEAN, Fitzroy, Sir, 949.7
bart., 1911-
The heretic; the life and times of Josip Broz-Tito. [1st American ed.] New York, Harper [1957] 436 p. illus. 22 cm. London ed. (J. Cape) has title: Disputed barricade. [DR359.T5M25 1957a] 57-6130
1. Tito, Josip Broz, Pres. Yugoslavia, 1892- I. Title.

STANOJEVIC, Tihomir 923.1497
Tito, his life and work [by] Tihomir Stanojevic, Dragan Markovic [Tr. by Ivo Vidan] Zagreb, Stvarnost. [dist. New York, Vanous, 1964, c.1962] 1v. (unpaged) illus., facsims., ports. 34cm. (Political ser.) Bibl. 64-4825 25.00
1. Tito, Josip Broz, Pres. Yugoslavia, 1892- I. Markovic, Dragan, joint author. II. Title.

TITO; v. 12
the man who defied Hitler and Stalin. New York, Ballantine Books [1957] 424p. (Ballantine books, S 489 K) Original title: The Heretic.
1. Tito, Josip Broz, Pres. Yugoslovia, 1892- I. Maclean, Fitzroy, Sir bart., 1911-

Tito, Josip Broz, Pres. Yugoslavia, 1892- —Juvenile literature

FRANCHERE, Ruth. 949'.702'0924 B
Tito of Yugoslavia. [New York] Macmillan [1970] 184 p. illus., map, ports. 21 cm. Bibliography: p. 181. The life of the peasant boy who became the first President of Yugoslavia. [DR359.T5F7 1970] 92 70-117958
1. Tito, Josip Broz, Pres. Yugoslavia, 1892- —Juvenile literature I. Title.

Tittle, Ernest Fremont, 1885-1949.

MILLER, Robert 287'.1'0924 B
Moats.
How shall they hear without a preacher? The life of Ernest Fremont Tittle. Chapel Hill, University of North Carolina Press [1971] xii, 524 p. illus. 24 cm. Bibliography: p. [515]-518. [BX8495.T67M5] 74-149031 ISBN 0-8078-1173-4 12.50
1. Tittle, Ernest Fremont, 1885-1949. I. Title. BIP

Titus, Emperor of Rome, 40-81—Juvenile literature.

DESMOND, Alice 937'.07'0924 B
Curtis, 1897-
Titus of Rome / Alice Curtis Desmond. New York : Dodd, Mead, c1976. ix, 275 p., [16] leaves of plates : ill. ; 22 cm. Includes index. Bibliography: p. 261-266. A biography of the second Flavian emperor who was noted for his generosity and regard for the people's welfare. [DG290.D47] 92 75-38353 ISBN 0-396-07299-2 : 5.95
1. Titus, Emperor of Rome, 40-81—Juvenile literature. I. Title. BIP

Tizard, Sir Henry Thomas, 1885-1959.

CLARK, Ronald William. 925
Tizard [by] Ronald W. Clark. Cambridge, M.I.T. Press [1965] xvii, 458 p. illus., ports. 28 cm. Bibiliography: p. [437]-438. [Q143.T5C6] 65-12911
1. Tizard, Sir Henry Thomas, 1885-1959. 2. Science and state — Gt. Brit. I. Title.

Tiziano, Vecelli, 1477-1576.

BALLARIN, Alessandro. 759.5
Titian. [The life and work of the artist, illustrated with 80 full-color plates. Translated from the Italian by Pearl Sanders. 1st American ed.] New York, Grosset & Dunlap [1968] 40 p. illus., col. plates. 18 cm. (The New Grosset art library, 14) Bibliography: p. 35. [ND623.T7B313 1968b] 68-26685
1. Tiziano, Vecelli, 1477-1576 I. Tiziano, Vecelli, 1477-1576. II. Title.

BORTOLON, Liana. 759.5
The life and times of Titian; text by Liana Bortolon, translator [from the Italian] Clara Green. London, New York [etc.] Hamlyn, 1968. 75 p. illus. (some col.), facsims. 30 cm. (Portraits of greatness) Illus. on lining papers [ND623.T7B73] 70-396965 17/6
1. Tiziano Vecelli, 1477-1576. I. Title.

CECCHI, Dario, 1918- 759.5
Titian. Translated from the Italian by Nora Wydenbruck. New York, Farrar, Straus and Cudahy [1958] 232p. illus. 22cm. [ND623.T7C43] [ND623.T7C43] 927.5 58-5962 58-5962
1. Tiziano Vecelli, 1477-1576. I. Title.

CECCHI, Dario, 1918- 759.5
Titian. Translated from the Italian by Nora Wydenbruck. Freeport, N.Y., Books for Libraries Press [1973] (Biography index reprint series) Translation of Tiziano. Reprint of the 1958 ed. [ND623.T7C43 1973] 72-13188 ISBN 0-8369-8143-X
1. Tiziano, Vecelli, 1477-1576.

FISHER, M. Roy. 759.5 B
Titian's assistants during the later years / M. Roy Fisher. New York : Garland Pub., 1977. xxii, 148, 133 p. : ill. ; 21 cm. (Outstanding dissertations in the fine arts) Originally presented as the author's thesis, Harvard, 1958. Bibliography: p. 141-148. [ND623.T7F53 1977] 76-23618 ISBN 0-8240-2689-6 lib.bdg. : 40.00
1. Tiziano Vecelli, 1477-1576. 2. Apprentices—Italy—Venice—Biography. I. Title. II. Series. BIP

Tiziano Vecelli, 1477-1576—Juvenile literature.

RIPLEY, Elizabeth, 927.5'945
1906-
Titian, a biography. Philadelphia, Lippincott [1962] 68 p. illus. 27 cm. Includes bibliography. [ND623.T7R56] 62-13146
1. Tiziano Vecelli, 1477-1576—Juvenile literature.

Tkachev, Petr Nikitich, 1844-1886.

HARDY, Deborah, 322.4'2'0924 B
1927-
Petr Tkachev, the critic as Jacobin / Deborah Hardy. Seattle : University of Washington Press, c1977. xiii, 339 p. ; 21 cm. (Publications on Russia and Eastern Europe of the Institute for Comparative and Foreign Area Studies ; no. 8) Includes index. Bibliography: p. 315-329. [HX312.T55H37] 76-49170 ISBN 0-295-95547-3 : 12.50
1. Tkachev, Petr Nikitich, 1884-1886. 2. Revolutionists—Russia—Biography. I. Series: Washington (State). University. Institute for Comparative and Foreign Area Studies. Publications on Russia and Eastern Europe ; no. 8. BIP

WEEKS, Albert Loren, 335.4'0924
1929-
The first Bolshevik; a political biography of Peter Tkachev, by Albert L. Weeks. New York, New York University Press, 1968. xiv, 221 p. facsims., ports. 24 cm. "Tkachev's writings": p. 201-204. Bibliography: p. 205-212. [HX312.T55W4] 68-15336
1. Tkachev, Petr Nikitich, 1844-1886. I. Title. BIP

Tobin, James Edward, 1905-joint author.

DELANEY, John J. 922.2
Dictionary of Catholic biography [by] John J. Delaney, James Edward Tobin. Garden City, N. Y., Doubleday [c.1961] xi, 1245p. 27cm. [ith thumb-index, p19.95] 62-7620 18.50;
1. Tobin, James Edward, 1905-joint author. 2. Catholic Church—Biog.—Dictionaries. I. Title.

Tocqueville, Alexis Charles Henri Maurice Clerel de, 1805-1859.

MAYER, Jacob Peter 923.244
Alexis de Tocqueville; a biographical study in political science, with a new essay, 'Tocqueville after a Century.' [Tr. from the French by M. M. Bozman and C. Hahn.] New York, Harper [1939, c.1960] xv, 144p. (Bibl. notes: p. 131-141) front. 21cm. (Harper Torchbooks, TB014, The Academy Library) Original title: The prophet of the mass age. 1.35 pap.,
1. Tocqueville, Alexis Charles Henri Maurice Crerel de, 1805-1859. I. Bozman, Mildred Mary, tr. II. Hahn, C., joint tr. III. Title.

MAYER, Jacob Peter, 1903- 923.244
Alexis de Tocqueville; a biographical study in political science. With a new essay, Tocqueville after a century. New York,

Harper [1960] 144p. illus. 21cm. (Harper torchbooks, TB1014. The Academy library) [JC229.T8M35 1960] 60-3198
1. Tocqueville, Alexis Charles Henri Maurice Clerel de, 1805-1859. I. Title.

MAYER, Jacob Peter, 1903- 923.244
Alexis de Tocqueville; a biographical study in political science. With a new essay, Tocqueville after a century [Gloucester, Mass., Peter Smith, 1960] xv, 144p. front. (port.) 21cm. (Harper torchbooks, TB1014. The Academy library, rebound in cloth) 3.25
1. Tocqueville, Alexis Charles Henri Maurice Clerel de, 1805-1859. I. Title.

MAYER, Jacob Peter, 1903- 320'.0924(B)
Alexis de Tocqueville; a biographical study in political science [by] J. P. Mayer. New essay, 'Tocqueville after a century.' Gloucester, Mass., P. Smith, 1966[c.1960] xv, 144p. port. 21cm. First pub. in 1939 under title: Prophet of the mass age. Bibl. [JC229.T8M35 1966] 67-2454 3.75
1. Tocqueville, Alexis Charles Henri Maurice Clerel de, 1805-1859. I. Title. BIP

TOCQUEVILLE, Alexis Charles Henri Maurice Clerel de, 1805-1859. 944.07'0924
Correspondence and conversations of Alexis de Tocqueville with Nassau William Senior, from 1834 to 1859. Edited by M. C. M. Simpson. 2d ed. New York, A. M. Kelley, 1968. 2 v. in 1 22 cm. (Reprints of economic classics) Reprint of the 1872 ed. [DC255.T6A3 1968] 68-30544
I. Senior, Nassau William, 1790-1864. II. Simpson, Mary Charlotte Mair (Senior), ed. III. Title. BIP

TOCQUEVILLE, Alexis Charles Henri Maurice Clerel de, 1805-1859. 944.07
The recollections of Alexis de Tocqueville / translated by Alexander Teixeira de Mattos ; edited with many additions from the original text and an introd. by J. P. Mayer. Westport, Conn. : Greenwood Press, [1978] p. cm. Translation of Souvenirs d'Alexis de Tocqueville. Reprint of the 1949 ed. published by Columbia University Press, New York. Includes index. [DC270.T652 1978] 78-13685 ISBN 0 ISBN 0-313-21052-7 lib. bdg. 20.50
1. Tocqueville, Alexis Charles Henri Maurice Cherel de, 1805-1859. 2. France—History—February Revolution, 1848. 3. Historians—France—Biography. I. Mayer, Jacob Peter, 1903-

Todd, Michael, 1900-1958.

COHN, Art, 1909-1958. 927.914
The nine lives of Michael Todd. New York, Random House [1958] 396p. illus. 22cm. [PN1998.A3T6] 58-12335
1. Todd, Michael, 1900-1958. I. Title.

Todd, Robert M., 1897-

TODD, Robert M., 1897- 940.
Sopwith camel fighter ace / by Robert M. (Bob) Todd. Falls Church, VA : AJAY Enterprises, 1978. 112 p. : ill. ; 23 cm. [D640.T668] 49'730924 78-72947 pbk. : 6.95
1. Todd, Robert M., 1897- 2. United States. Army Air Forces. 17th Aero Squadron—Biography. 3. European War, 1914-1918—Personal narratives, American. 4. Fighter pilots—United States—Biography. I. Title. BIP

Toews, Katharina.

TOEWS, Susanna. 940.54'81'47
Trek to freedom : the escape of two sisters from South Russia during World War II / by Susanna Toews ; translated by Helen Megli. Winkler, Man. : Heritage Valley Publications, c1976. 43 p. : ill. ; 22 cm. [D805.R9T6613] 76-18416
1. Toews, Katharina. 2. Toews, Susanna. 3. World War, 1939-1945—Prisoners and prisons, Russian. 4. World War, 1939-1945—Personal narratives, Russian. 5. Germans in Russia—Biography. I. Title.

Tog-o, Heihachiro, count, 1848-1934.

BLOND, Georges. 923.552
Admiral Togo; translated by Edward Hyams. New York, Macmillan, 1960. 252 p. illus. 22 cm. [DS884.T6B553] 60-8592
1. Tog-o, Heihachiro, count, 1848-1934.

Toguri, Ikuko, 1916-

DUUS, Masayo, 1938- 940.54'889'520924
Tokyo Rose, orphan of the Pacific / Masayo Duus ; translated from the Japanese by Peter Duus ; introd. by Edwin O. Reischauer. 1st ed. Tokyo : Kodansha International ; New York : distributed in the United States through Harper & Row, 1979. xvii, 248 p. : ill. ; 25 cm. Translation of Tokyo Rozu. Includes bibliographical references and index. [CT275.T717D8813] 78-60968 ISBN 0-87011-354-2 : 12.95
1. Toguri, Ikuko, 1916- 2. United States—Biography. 3. Japanese Americans—Biography. 4. Trials (Treason)—California—San Francisco. I. Title.

Toio, Hideki. 1884-1948.

BROWNE, Courtney, 1915- 952.03'0924
Tojo: the last bonzai. London. Angus & Robertson, 1967. x. 245p. 12 plates (incl ports., facsims.). 23cm. Bibl. [DS890.T57B7 1967] (B) 68-103512 6.75
1. Toio, Hideki. 1884-1948. I. Title.
Distributed by TriOcean, San Francisco.

Toklas, Alice B.

SIMON, Linda, 1946- 818'.5'209 B
The biography of Alice B. Toklas / by Linda Simon. 1st ed. Garden City, N.Y. : Doubleday, 1977. x, 324 p., [12] leaves of plates : ill. ; 24 cm. Includes index. Bibliography: p. 301-313. [PS3537.T323Z823] 76-23798 ISBN 0-385-08140-5 : 10.00
1. Stein, Gertrude, 1874-1946—Relationship with women. 2. Toklas, Alice B. 3. Stein, Gertrude, 1874-1946—Friends and associates. 4. Paris—Intellectual life. 5. Authors, American—20th century—Biography. I. Title. BIP

STEIN, Gertrude, 1874-1946. 928.1
The autobiography of Alice B. Toklas. New York, Random House [1955, c1933] 252 p. 19 cm. (Modern library paperbacks, P12) The autobiography of Gertrude Stein written by herself as though it were the autobiography of her secretary, Alice B. Toklas. [PS3537] 55-5727
1. Toklas, Alice B. 2. Paris—Intellectual life. I. Title. BIP

Tokugawa, Ieyasu, 1543-1616.

SADLER, Arthur Lindsay, 1882- 952'.025'0924 B
The maker of modern Japan : the life of Tokugawa Ieyasu / A. L. Sadler. Rutland, Vt. : C. E. Tuttle Co., 1978. 429 p., [9] leaves of plates : ill. ; 19 cm. Includes index. Bibliography: p. [411]-412. [DS872.T6S25 1978] 78-54935 ISBN 0-8048-1297-7 : 7.50
1. Tokugawa, Ieyasu, 1543-1616. 2. Japan—History—Tokugawa period, 1600-1868. 3. Shoguns—Biography. I. Title. BIP

SADLER, Arthur Lindsay, 1882- 952'.025'0924 B
The maker of modern Japan : the life of Tokugawa Ieyasu / A. L. Sadler. New York : AMS Press, [1977] 429 p., [9] leaves of plates (1 fold.) : ill. ; 23 cm. Reprint of the 1937 ed. published by Allen & Unwin, London. Includes index. Bibliography: p. [411]-412. [DS872.T6S25 1977] 75-41238 ISBN 0-404-14595-7 : 27.50
1. Tokugawa, Ieyasu, 1543-1616. 2. Japan—History—Tokugawa period, 1600-1868. 3. Shoguns—Biography. I. Title.

Tolbert, William R., 1913-

PRESIDENTIAL papers: documents, diary, and record of activities of the Chief Executive; 966.6'203'0924 first year of the administration of President William R. Tolbert, Jr., July 23, 1971-July 31, 1972. Monrovia, Republic of Liberia, Executive Mansion [1972?] 574 p. illus. 26 cm. [DT636.T64P73] 74-168274
1. Tolbert, William R., 1913- 2. Liberia—Politics and government. I. Tolbert, William R., 1913-

Toles, E. B.

TOLES, E. B. 286'.1'0924 B
A layman shares Jesus / E. B. Toles ; [foreword by Grady Wilson]. Nashville : Broadman Press, c1979. 158 p. : ill. ; 21 cm. [BX6495.T58A35] 78-67925 ISBN 0-8054-5506-X pbk. : 3.95
1. Toles, E. B. 2. Baptists—Biography—United States. I. Title. BIP

Tolkien, John Ronald Reuel, 1892-1973.

EVANS, Robley. 828'.9'1209
J. R. R. Tolkien. New York, Warner Paperback Library [1972] 206 p. 18 cm. (Writers for the seventies) Bibliography: p. 203-204. [PR6039.O32Z64] 73-159496 ISBN 0-446-68988-2 1.50
1. Tolkien, John Ronald Reuel, 1892- BIP

THE Tolkien scrapbook / edited by Alida Becker. 828'.9'1209 B Philadelphia : Running Press, c1979. p. cm. Includes index. Bibliography: p. Includes folklore, songs, poems, and recipes of Middle Earth, a collection of articles about Tolkien and his works, a biography, reading list, and directory of national and international Tolkien and fantasy societies and publications. [PR6039.O32Z86] 92 79-11435 ISBN 0-89471-083-4 lib. bdg. : 15.90 ISBN 0-89471-082-6 pbk. : 7.95
1. Tolkien, John Ronald Reuel, 1892-1973. 2. Authors, English—20th century—Biography. I. Becker, Alida, 1948- BIP

Tolkien, John Ronald Reuel, 1892-1973—Addresses, essays, lectures.

THE Tolkien scrapbook / edited by Alida Becker ; ill. 828'.9'1209 B by Michael Green, col. ill. by Tim Kirk. New York : Grosset & Dunlap, c1978. 192 p., [4] leaves of plates : ill. (some col.) ; 28 cm. Bibliography: p. 180-190. [PR6039.O32Z86 1978] 78-65276 ISBN 0-448-16455-8 : 17.95
1. Tolkien, John Ronald Reuel, 1892-1973—Addresses, essays, lectures. 2. Authors, English—20th century—Biography—Addresses, essays, lectures. I. Becker, Alida, 1948-

Tolkien, John Ronald Reuel, 1892-1973—Biography.

CARPENTER, Humphrey. 828'.9'1209 B
Tolkien : a biography / by Humphrey Carpenter. Boston : Houghton Mifflin, 1977. 286 p., [8] leaves of plates : ill. ; 24 cm. Includes index. "The published writings of J. R. R. Tolkien": p. 268-275. [PR6039.O32Z62 1977] 77-9081 ISBN 0-395-25360-8 : 10.00
1. Tolkien, John Ronald Reuel, 1892-1973—Biography. 2. Authors, English—20th century—Biography. I. Title. BIP

GROTTA-KURSKA, Daniel, 1944- 828'.9'1209 B
J. R. R. Tolkien : architect of Middle Earth : a biography / by Daniel Grotta-Kurska ; edited by Frank Wilson. Philadelphia : Running Press, c1976. 165 p. ; 21 cm. Bibliography: p. 162-165. [PR6039.O32Z65 1976] 75-17046 ISBN 0-914294-29-6 lib. bdg. : 9.80. ISBN 0-914294-28-8 pbk. : 2.95
1. Tolkien, John Ronald Reuel, 1892-1973—Biography. 2. Authors, English—20th century—Biography.

GROTTA-KURSKA, Daniel, 1944- 828'.9
J.R.R. Tolkien architect of Middle Earth : a biography / by Daniel Grotta-Kurska ; edited by Frank Wilson. New York : Warner Books, 1977,c1976. 253p. ; 18 cm. Bibliography:p. 246-251. [PR6039.O32Z65 1976] ISBN 0-446-89410-9 pbk. : 1.95
1. Tolkien, John Ronald Reud, 1892-1973-Biography. 2. Authors, English-20th century-Biography. I. Title.
L.C. card no. for 1976 Running Press ed.:75-10746.

GROTTA-KURSKA, Daniel, 1944- 828'.9'1209 B
The biography of J. R. R. Tolkien : architect of Middle Earth / by Daniel Grotta. Philadelphia : Running Press, c1978. p. cm. Earlier (c1976) ed. published under title: J. R. R. Tolkien. Includes index. Bibliography: p. [PR6039.O32Z65 1978] 77-29209 ISBN 0-89471-034-6 lib. bdg. : 9.80. ISBN 0-89471-035-4 pbk. : 3.95
1. Tolkien, John Ronald Reuel, 1892-1973—Biography. 2. Authors, English—20th century—Biography. I. Title.

Tolkien, John Ronald Reuel, 1892-1973—Friends and associates.

CARPENTER, Humphrey. 823'.9'12 B
The inklings : C. S. Lewis, J. R. R. Tolkien, Charles Williams, and their friends / by Humphrey Carpenter. 1st American ed. Boston : Houghton Mifflin, 1978, c1979. xiv, 287 p., [8] leaves of : ill. ; 25 cm. Includes index. Bibliography: p. 260-265. [PR6023.E926Z613 1979] 78-26042 ISBN 0-395-27628-4 : 9.95
1. Lewis, Clive Staples, 1898-1963—Friends and associates. 2. Tolkien, John Ronald Reuel, 1892-1973—Friends and associates. 3. Williams, Charles, 1886-1945—Friends and associates. 4. Authors, English—20th century—Biography. 5. Oxford—Biography. 6. England—Intellectual life—20th century. I. Title.

Tolstaia, Sof'ia Andreevna (Bers) grafinia, 1844-1919.

ASQUITH, Cynthia Mary Evelyn (Charteris), Lady, 1887-1960. 891.7'3'3 B
Married to Tolstoy. New York, Greenwood Press [1969] 288 p. illus., facsim., geneal. table, ports. 23 cm. Reprint of the 1960 ed. Bibliography: p. [283] [PG3390.A8 1969] 69-13803
1. Tolstaia, Sof'ia Andreevna (Bers) grafinia, 1844-1919. 2. Tolstoi, Lev Nicholaevich, graf, 1828-1910. I. Title.

ASQUITH, Lady Cynthia Mary Evelyn (Charteris) 1887- 920.7
Married to Tolstoy. Boston, Houghton Mifflin, 1961 [c.1960] 288p. illus. 61-7607 5.00
1. Tolstaia, Sof'ia Andreevna (Bers) grafinia, 1844-1919. 2. Tolstoi, Lev Nikolaevich, graf, 1828-1910. I. Title. BIP

TOLSTAIA, Sof'ia Andreevna (Bers) grafinia, 1844-1919. 891.7'3'3 B
The countess Tolstoy's later diary, 1891-1897. Authorized translation from Russian, with an introd. by Alexander Werth Freeport, N.Y., Books for Libraries Press [1971] 267 p. 23 cm. [PG3385.T6213 1971] 72-175712 ISBN 0-8369-6627-9

Tolstoi, Lev Nikolaevich, graf, 1828-1910.

ABRAHAM, Gerald Ernest Heal, 1904- 891.7'3'3
Tolstoy, by Gerald Abraham. New York, Haskell House Publishers, 1974. 144 p. 22 cm. Reprint of the 1935 ed. published by Duckworth, London, which was issued as no. 47 of Great lives. Bibliography: p. [143]-144. [PG3385.A2 1974] 74-7018 ISBN 0-8383-1965-3
1. Tolstoi, Lev Nikolaevich, graf, 1828-1910.

CHERTKOV, Vladimir Grigor'evich, 1854-1936. 891.7'3'3 B
The last days of Tolstoy, by Vladimir

Tchertkoff. Translated from the Russian by Nathalie A. Duddington. London, W. Heinemann, 1922. Millwood, N.Y., Kraus Reprint Co., 1973. xxvi, 151 p. 24 cm. Translation of Ukhod Tolstogo. [PG3395.C513 1973] 73-9663 ISBN 0-527-16500-X 12.00
1. Tolstoi, Lev Nikolaevich, graf, 1828-1910. I. Title. **BIP**

DILLON, Emile Joseph, 891.7'3'3 B 1855-1933.
Count Leo Tolstoy; a new portrait. New York, Haskell House, 1972. 286 p. illus. 23 cm. Reprint of the 1933 ed. Includes bibliographical references. [PG3385.D5 1972] 72-700 ISBN 0-8383-1420-1 11.95
1. Tolstoi, Lev Nikolaevich, graf, 1828-1910.

GARNETT, Edward, 891.7'8'309 1868-1937.
Tolstoy; his life and writings. London, Constable, 1914. [Folcroft, Pa.] Folcroft Library Editions, 1973. p. Original ed. issued in series: Modern biographies. Bibliography: p. [PG3385.G3 1973] 73-923 ISBN 0-8414-2000-9 (lib. bdg.)
1. Tolstoi, Lev Nikolaevich, graf, 1828-1910. I. Title. II. Series: Modern biographies.

GARNETT, Edward, 891.7'3'3 B 1868-1937.
Tolstoy; his life and writings. New York, Haskell House [1974] p. cm. Reprint of the 1914 ed. published by Constable, London, and Houghton Mifflin, Boston, in series: Modern biographies. Bibliography: p. [PG3385.G3 1974] 74-7035 ISBN 0-8383-1970-X 9.95
1. Tolstoi, Lev Nikolaevich, graf, 1828-1910. I. Title. II. Series: Modern biographies.

HECHT, Leo. 891.7'3'3 B
Tolstoy the rebel / by Leo Hecht. With 39 rare & previously unpublished photos. of Tolstoy, his family & friends. New York : Revisionist Press, 1976. p. cm. Includes index. Bibliography: p. [PG3385.H37] 76-2557 ISBN 0-87700-222-3 lib.bdg. : 29.95
1. Tolstoi, Lev Nikolaevich, graf, 1828-1910. I. Title. **BIP**

HOFMANN, Modeste 1887- v. 12
By deeds of truth the life of Leo Tolstoy [by] Modest Hofmann and Andre Pierre. Translated from the French by Ruth Whipple Fermaud. London, New York B. Hanison [1959] 268 p. ports. Translation of La vie de Tolstoi. 64-72755
1. Tolstoi, Lev Nikolacvich, graf, 1828-1910. I. Pierre, Andre, joint author. II. Title.

HOFMANN, Modeste, 1887- 928.917
By deeds of truth; the life of Leo Tolstoy [by] Modest Hofmann and Andre Pierre. Translated from the French by Ruth Whipple Fermaud. New York, Orion Press; distributed by Crown Publishers [1958] 268 p. illus. 23 cm. Translation of La vie de Tolstoi. [PG3385.H613] 58-7919
1. Tolstoi, L ev Nikolaevich, graf, 1828-1910. I. Pierre, Andre, joint author. II. Title.

LESLIE, Shane, Sir, 920.042 bart., 1885-
Salutation to five. Freeport, N.Y., Books for Libraries Press [1970] v, 156 p. 23 cm. (Biography index reprint series) Reprint of the 1951 ed. Includes bibliographical references. [CT106.L4 1970] 75-126321 ISBN 8-369-80271-
1. Fitzherbert, Maria Anne (Smythe) 1756-1837. 2. Warre, Edmond, 1837-1920. 3. Butler, William Francis, Sir, 1838-1910. 4. Tolstoi, Lev Nikolaevich, graf, 1828-1910. 5. Sykes, Mark, Sir, bart., 1879-1919. I. Title.

MAUDE, Aylmer, 1858- 891.7'3'3 B 1938.
Leo Tolstoy / by Aylmer Maude. New York : Haskell House, 1975. x, 331 p. : port. ; 22 cm. Reprint of the 1918 ed. published by Methuen, London. Includes index. [PG3385.M294 1975] 75-20491 ISBN 0-8383-2001-5 : 15.95
1. Tolstoi, Lev Nikolaevich, graf, 1828-1910. I. Title. **BIP**

MAUDE, Aylmer, 1858- 891.7'3'3 B 1938.
Leo Tolstoy and his works. New York, Haskell House, 1974. 75, [1] p. illus. 20 cm. Reprint of the 1930 ed. published by G. Routledge, London. Bibliography: p. 74-[76] [PG3385.M295 1974] 74-6377 ISBN 0-8383-2009-0
1. Tolstoi, Lev Nikolaevich, 1828-1910. I. Title. **BIP**

MEREZHKOVSKII, 891.7'3'3 Dmitrii Sergeevich, 1865-1941.
Tolstoi as man and artist; with an essay on Dostoievski, by Dmitri Merejkowski. Westport, Conn., Greenwood Press [1970] 310 p. 23 cm. Reprint of the 1902 ed. Includes bibliographical references. [PG3385.M4 1970] 69-13996
1. Tolstoi, Lev Nikolaevich, graf, 1828-1910. 2. Dostoevskii, Fedor Mikhailovich, 1821-1881. I. Title.

MICEK, Eduard. 928.917
The real Tolstoy; impressions and evaluation. Austin, Tex., Czech Literary Society, c1958. 61p. 21cm. [PG3386.M5] 58-33005
1. Toustol, Lev Nikolaevich, fraf, 1828-1910. I. Title.

NAZAROFF, Alexander I. 891.7'3'3
Tolstoy, the inconstant genius; a biography, by Alexander I. Nazaroff. Freeport, N.Y., Books for Libraries Press [1971, c1929] 351 p. illus. 23 cm. Bibliography: p. 343-346. [PG3385.N3 1971] 72-175704 ISBN 0-8369-6619-8
1. Tolstoi, Lev Nikolaevich, graf, 1828-1910. I. Title.

ROLLAND, Romain, 891.7'3'3 B 1866-1944.
Tolstoy. Translated by Bernard Miall. Port Washington, N.Y., Kennikat Press [1972] 256 p. 22 cm. Reprint of the 1911 ed. Translation of La vie de Tolstoi. [PG3385.R6 1972] 74-160776 ISBN 0-8046-1608-6
1. Tolstoi, Lev Nikolaevich, 1828-1910.

ROLLAND, Romain, 891.7'3'3 B 1866-1944.
Tolstoy. Translated by Bernard Miall. With a new introd. for the Garland ed., by Esther Kingston-Mann. New York, Garland Pub., 1972 [c1911] 11, 321 p. 22 cm. (The Garland library of war and peace) Translation of La vie de Tolstoy. [PG3385.R6 1972b] 71-147457 ISBN 0-8240-0316-0
1. Tolstoy, Lev Nikolaevich, graf, 1828-1910. I. Title. II. Series.

SIMMONS, Ernest Joseph, 891.7'3'3 1903-1972.
Tolstoy, by Ernest J. Simmons. London, Boston, Routledge and K. Paul, 1973. xi, 260 p. 22 cm. (Routledge author guides) Bibliography: p. 249-253. [PG3385.S54 1973] 72-95126 ISBN 0-7100-7394-1 £3.50
1. Tolstoi, Lev Nikolaevich, Graf, 1828-1910.

STEINER, Edward Alfred, 891.7'3'3 1866-1956.
Tolstoy the man, by Edward A. Steiner. New York, Haskell House Publishers, 1969. xx, 310 p. illus., ports. 23 cm. Reprint of the 1909 ed. [PG3385.S82 1969] 70-92986
1. Tolstoi, Lev Nikolaevich, graf, 1828-1910. I. Title.

TOLSTAIA, Aleksandra 928.917 L'vovna, grafinia, 1884-
Tolstoy; a life of my father, by Alexandra Tolstoy. Translated from the Russian by Elizabeth Reynolds Hapgood. [1st ed.] New York, Harper [1953] 543 p. illus. 22 cm. [PG3385.T53] 53-7749
1. Tolstoi, Lev Nikolaevich, graf, 1828-1910.

TOLSTAIA, 891.7'3'3 B Aleksandra L'vovna, grafinia, 1884-
Tolstoy: a life of my father, by Alexandra Tolstoy. Translated from the Russian by Elizabeth Reynolds Hapgood. New York, Octagon Books, 1973 [c1953] ix, 543 p. illus. 23 cm. Translation of Otets. [PG3385.T53 1973] 73-3185 ISBN 0-374-97956-1 16.50
1. Tolstoi, Lev Nikolaevich, graf, 1828-1910. I. Title.

TOLSTOI. LEV NIKOLAEVICH, 928.917 graf.
Last diaries. Translated [from the Russian] by Lydia Weston-Kesich. Edited and with an introd. by Leon Stilman. New York, Capricorn Books [dist. Putnam, c.1960] 285p. 19cm. (A Putnam Capricorn book, CAP21) 60-6121 1.35 pap.,
I. Title.

TOLSTOI, Sergei L'vovich, 928.917 graf, 1863-1947.
Tolstoy remembered by his son. Translated from the Russian by Moura Budberg. [1st American ed.] New York, Atheneum, 1962 [c1961] 234 p. 22 cm. Translation of (transliterated: Ocherki bylogo) [PG3385.T853 1962] 62-9413
1. Tolstoi, Lev Nikolaevich, graf, 1828-1910. I. Title.

Tolstoi, Lev Nikolaevich, graf, 1828-1910—Biography.

CRANKSHAW, Edward. 891.7'3'3
Tolstoy; the making of a novelist. New York, Viking Press [1974] 276 p. illus. 27 cm. (A Studio book) Bibliography: p. 272-273. [PG3385.C67] 73-6078 ISBN 0-670-71861-0 16.95
1. Tolstoi, Lev Nikolaevich, graf, 1828-1910—Biography.

GOR'KII, Maksim, 891.7'8'309 B 1868-1936.
Reminiscences of Leo Nikolaevich Tolstoy / by Maxim Gorky ; authorized translation from the Russian by S. S. Koteliansky and Leonard Woolf. Folcroft, Pa. : Folcroft Library Editions, 1977 [c1920] 86 p. ; 23 cm. Translation of Vospominaniia o L've Nikolaeviche Tolstom. Reprint of the ed. published by B. W. Huebsch, New York. [PG3335.G162 1977] 77-23858 ISBN 0-8414-4455-2 lib. bdg. : 20.00
1. Tolstoi, Lev Nikolaevich, graf, 1828-1910—Biography. 2. Gor'kii, Maksim, 1868-1936—Biography. 3. Authors, Russian—19th century—Biography. I. Title.

MAUDE, Aylmer, 1858- 891.7'3'3 B 1938.
Leo Tolstoy and his works / by Aylmer Maude. Norwood, Pa. : Norwood Editions, 1976. 75 p., [1] leaf of plates : ill. ; 23 cm. Reprint of the 1930 ed. published by G. Routledge, London. Bibliography: p. 74-75. [PG3386.M368 1976] 76-2655 ISBN 0-88305-534-1 : 5.00
1. Tolstoi, Lev Nikolaevich, Graf, 1828-1910—Biography. I. Title.

MAUDE, Aylmer, 1858- 891.7'3'3 B 1938.
Leo Tolstoy and his works / by Aylmer Maude. Folcroft, Pa. : Folcroft Library Editions, 1975. 75 p. : ill. ; 23 cm. Reprint of the 1930 ed. published by G. Routledge, London. Bibliography: p. 74-75. [PG3386.M368 1975] 75-37637 ISBN 0-8414-6110-4 lib. bdg. : 6.00
1. Tolstoi, Lev Nikolaevich, graf, 1828-1910—Biography. I. Title.

SUKHOTINA, Tat'iana 891.7'3'3 L'vovna Tolstaia, 1864-1950.
Tolstoy remembered / by Tatyana Tolstoy ; translated from the French by Derek Coltman ; with an introd. and forewords by Daniel Gilles. New York : McGraw-Hill, c1977. 312 p., [8] leaves of plates : ill. ; 24 cm. Translation of Avec Leon Tolstoi. Includes index. [PG3385.S8813 1977] 77-16266 ISBN 0-07-064940-5 : 14.95
1. Tolstoi, Lev Nikolaevich, graf, 1828-1910—Biography. 2. Sukhotina, Tat'iana L'vovna Tolstaia, 1864-1950. 3. Authors, Russian—19th century—Biography. I. Title.

Tolstoi, Lev Nikolaevich, Graf, 1828-1910—Biography—Juvenile literature.

CARROLL, Sara Newton. 891.7'3'3 B
The search; a biography of Leo Tolstoy. Illus. by Stephen Gammell. [1st ed.] New York, Harper & Row [1973] 158 p. illus. 24 cm. Bibliography: p. 150-153. [PG3385.C3] 73-5481 ISBN 0-06-020952-6 5.95
1. Tolstoi, Lev Nikolaevich, Graf, 1828-1910—Biography—Juvenile literature. I. Gammell, Stephen, illus. II. Title.
Library ed. 5.79; ISBN 0-06-020953-4.

Tolstoi, Lev Nikolaevich, graf, 1828-1910—Biography—Last years.

BULGAKOV, Valentin 891.7'3'3 B Fedorovich, 1886-
The last year of Leo Tolstoy [by] V. F. Bulgakov. Translated from the Russian by Ann Dunnigan. With an introd. by George Steiner. New York, Dial Press, 1971. xxv, 235 p. port. 24 cm. Translation of U L. N. Tolstogo v posliednii god ego zhizni (romanized form) [PG3395.B7913] 73-131182 7.95
1. Tolstoi, Lev Nikolaevich, graf, 1828-1910—Biography—Last years. **BIP**

Tolstoi, Lev Nikolaevich, graf, 1828-1910—Biography—Last years and death.

TOLSTAIA, Sof'ia 891.73'3 Andreevna Bers, grafinia, 1844-1919.
The final struggle : being Countess Tolstoy's diary for 1910 : with extracts from Leo Tolstoy's diary of the same period / preface by S. L. Tolstoy, editor of the Russian ed. ; translated with an introd. by Aylmer Maude. New York : Octagon Books, 1980. p. cm. Translation of Dnevniki. Reprint of the 1936 ed. published by Oxford University Press, New York. Includes index. [PG3385.T6213 1980] 79-27574 20.00
1. Tolstoi, Lev Nikolaevich, graf, 1828-1910—Biography—Last years and death. 2. Tolstaia, Sof'ia Andreevna Bers, grafinia, 1844-1919. 3. Novelists, Russian—19th century—Biography. 4. Novelists, Russian—19th century—Wives—Biography. I. Tolstoi, Lev Nikolaevich, graf, 1828-1910. II. Maude, Aylmer, 1858-1938. III. Title.

Tolstoi, Lev Nikolaevich, graf, 1828-1910—Criticism and interpretation.

MAUDE, Aylmer, 1858- 891.7'3'3 1938.
Tolstoy and his problems; essays. 2d ed. New York, Haskell House, 1974. vii, 220 p. 21 cm. Reprint of the 1902 ed. published by G. Richards, London. Contents.Contents.—Leo Tolstoy: a short biography.—Tolstoy's teaching.—An introduction to "What is art."—Tolstoy's view of art.—How "Resurrection" was written.—Introduction to "The slavery of our times."—The Tsar's coronation.—Right and wrong.—War and patriotism.—Talks with Tolstoy. [PG3410.M3 1974] 74-7137 ISBN 0-8383-1999-8
1. Tolstoi, Lev Nikolaevich, graf, 1828-1910—Criticism and interpretation. I. Title.

Tolstoi, Lev. Nikolaevich, graf — Homes and haunts.

SUKHOTINA, Tat'iana 928.917 L'vovna (Tolstaia) 1864-1950.
The Tolstoy home; diaries of Tatiana Sukhotin-Tolstoy. Translated by Alec Brown. New York, Columbia University Press, 1951. 352 p; plates, ports, geneal. table. 23 cm; [[PG3401.S]] 51-8955
1. Tolstoi, Lev. Nikolaevich, graf — Homes and haunts. I. Title.

Tolton, Augustine, 1854-1897.

HEMESATH, Caroline. 282'.092'4 B
From slave to priest: a biography of the Rev. Augustine Tolton (1854-1897), first Afro-American priest of the United States. Chicago, Franciscan Herald Press [1973] xiii, 174 p. illus. 21 cm. Bibliography: p. [167]-169. [BX4705.T6813H4] 73-11113 ISBN 0-8199-0468-6 5.95
1. Tolton, Augustine, 1854-1897. I. Title.

Tom, John Nichols, 1799/-1838.

ROGERS, Philip G. 920.8
Battle in Bossenden Wood; the strange story of Sir William Courtenay. New York, Oxford [c.]1961[ ] 241p. illus. 61-19455 4.00
1. Tom, John Nichols, 1799/-1838. 2. Kent, Eng.—Hist. I. Title.

Toma, David.

*TOMA, David. 363.2'092'2 B
Toma, by David Toma with Michael Brett [New York, Dell, 1974] 269 p. 18 cm. [HV7911] 1.25 (pbk.)
1. Toma, David. I. Title.

TOMA, David. 363.2'092'4 B
Toma: the compassionate cop, by David Toma with Michael Brett. New York, Putnam [1973] 283 p. illus. 22 cm. [HV7911.T63A3 1973] 73-87178 ISBN 0-399-11277-4 6.95
1. Toma, David. 2. Police—Correspondence, reminiscences, etc. I. Tripp, Miles, 1923- joint author. II. Title.

Tomas de Villanueva, Saint, 1488-1555.

DUNSTAN, Brother, 1915- 922.246
The poor rich man; a story of St. Thomas of Villanova. Illus. by Judith E. Quinn. Notre Dame, Ind., Dujarie Press [1955] 93p. illus. 24cm. [BX4700.T7D8] 55-38173
1. Tomas de Villanueva, Saint, 1488-1555. I. Title.

Tombaugh, Clyde William, 1907-

RATH, Ida Ellen 920
Boy planet seeker. Dodge City [Kan.] Rollie Jack [c.1963] 108p. illus. 20cm. 63-3485 4.00
1. Tombaugh, Clyde William, 1907- I. Title.

RATH, Ida Ellen 925.2
The star that did not twinkle. San Antonio Naylor [c.1963] 134p.illus. 22cm. 63-13578 4.95
1. Tombaugh, Clyde William, 1907- I. Title.

RATH, Ida Ellen. 925.2
The star that did not twinkle. San Antonio, Tex., Naylor Co. [1963] 134 p. illus. 22 cm. [QB36.T6R3] 63013578
1. Tombaugh, Clyde William, 1907- I. Title.

Tombstone, Ariz.—Biography.

TRAYWICK, Ben T. 917.91'53 B
Tombstone's immortals, by Ben T. Traywick. [Tombstone? Ariz., 1973] 126 p. illus. 22 cm. [F819.T6T74] 73-176069
1. Tombstone, Ariz.—Biography. I. Title.

Tomkins, Leonora (Brooks)

TOMKINS, Leonora (Brooks) 920
1911-
My lovely days, by Leonora Tompkins. New York, Carlton Press [1966] 136 p. illus. ports. 21 cm. (A reflection book) Autobiographical. [CT3150.T6A3] 63-1161
I. Title.

Tomkins, Molly (Arthur)

TOMKINS, Molly (Arthur) 928.2
Shaw and Molly Tompkins in their own words. Edited by Peter Tompkins. New York, C. N. Potter [1962, c1961] 287 p. illus. 23 cm. Combination of narrative by Molly Tompkins and letters to her from G. B, Shaw. [PR5366.T55] 61-15116
I. Shaw, George Bernard, 1856-1960. II. Tompkins, Peter, ed. III. Title.

Tomkins, Thomas, 1575 (ca.)-1656.

STEVENS, Denis William, 927.8
1922-
Thomas Tankins 1572-1656. London, Macmillan; New York, St. Martin's Press, 1957. xi, 214 p. plate, facsims., geneal. tables, music. 23 cm. "List of works and their sources": p. 173-196. Bibliography: p. 197-201. "Discography": p. 203-204. [ML410.T65S8] 57-14152
1. Tomkins, Thomas, 1575 (ca.)-1656. I. Title.

STEVENS, Denis William, 927.8
1922-
Thomas Tomkins, 1572-1656. London, Macmillan; New York, St. Martin's Press, 1957. xi, 214p. plate, facsims., geneal. tables, music. 23cm. 'List of works and their sources : p. 173-196. Bibliography: p. 197-201. Discography : p. 203-204. [ML410.T65S8] 57-14152
1. Tomkins, Thomas, 1575 (ca.)-1656. I. Title. BIP

STEVENS, Denis William, 780'.924
1922-
Thomas Tomkins, 1572-1656, by Denis Stevens New York, Dover Publications [1967] xxi, 214 p. illus., facsims., geneal. tables, music. 22 cm. "This Dover edition is an unabridged and corrected republication of the work first published in 1957." "List of works and their sources": p. 173-196. Bibliography: p. 197-201. Discography: p. 203. [ML410.T65S8 1967] 66-25706
1. Tomkins, Thomas, 1575 (ca.)-1656.

Tomlinson, Henry Major,

TOMLINSON, Henry 828'.9'1209 B
Major, 1873-1958.
A mingled yarn; autobiographical sketches. Freeport, N.Y., Books for Libraries Press [1971, c1953] v, 172 p. port. 23 cm. (Essay index reprint series) [PR6039.O35M5 1971] 71-134146 ISBN 0-8369-2254-9
I. Title. BIP

Tomlinson, Monette Whaley

TOMLINSON, Monette 917.6428
Whaley
Crossroads cameos; charactor sketches. San Antonio, Tex., Naylor Co. [1964] 104 p. illus. 22 cm. Autobiographical. [CT275.T718A3] 64-60233
I. Title.

TOMLINSON, Monette 917.6428
Whaley
Crossroads cameos(character sketches. San Antonio, Tex., Naylor [c.1964] 104p. illus. 22cm. Autobiographical. [CT275.T718A3] 64-66223 2.95
I. Title.

Tommasini, Maria.

RICHARDSON, Mary 922.245
Kathleen, 1903-
To grow holy merrily; the life of Mother Tommasini. Fresno, Calif., Acad. Guild Pr. [1963,c.1960] 160p. 23cm. First pub. in London in 1960 under title: Tommasini. 63-12103 4.50
1. Tommasini, Maria. I. Title.

Tomo-chi-chi, d. 1739.

TODD, Helen, 1908- 970'.004'97 B
Tomochichi Indian friend of the Georgia Colony / by Helen Todd. Atlanta : Cherokee Pub. Co., 1977. xiii, 182 p. : ill. ; 19 cm. Includes index. Bibliography: p. 167-176. [E99.Y22T657] 77-75268 ISBN 0-87797-040-8 : 7.95
1. Tomo-chi-chi, d. 1739. 2. Yamassee Indians—Biography. 3. Greek Indians—History. 4. Oglethorpe, James Edward, 1696-1785. 5. Georgia—History—Colonial period, ca. 1600-1775. I. Title.

Tomo-chi-chi, Creed chief, d. 1739—Juvenile literature.

HARRELL, Sara 970'.004'97 B
Gordon.
Tomo-chi-chi / by Sara Gordon Harrell. Minneapolis : Dillon Press, c1977. p. cm. (The Story of an American Indian) A biography of the Creek Indian chief who did much to insure peaceful relations between the first English colonists in Georgia and the native Americans. [E99.C9T653] 92 77-8936 ISBN 0-87518-146-5 : 5.95
1. Tomo-chi-chi, Creed chief, d. 1739—Juvenile literature. 2. Creek Indians—Biography—Juvenile literature. BIP

Tompion, Thomas, 1639-1713.

SYMONDS, Robert Wemyss, 926;8111
1889-
Thomas Tompion, his life & work. London, New York, Batsford [1951] xvi, 320 p. illus. (part col.) ports. 30 cm. [NK7417.T6S8] 52-35554
1. Tompion, Thomas, 1639-1713. 2. Clocks and watches — England. I. Title.

SYMONDS, Robert 681'.11'0924
Wemyss, 1899-1958.
Thomas Tompion: his life and work [by] R. W. Symonds. London, New York, Spring Books, 1969. viii, 320 p., 3 plates (2 fold.). illus. (incl. 4 col.), facsims., map, ports. 30 cm. Includes bibliographical references. [NK7497.T6S9 1969] 72-522090 63/-
1. Tompion, Thomas, 1639-1713.

Tompkins, Daniel Augustus,

TOMPKINS, 338.1'7'3510924 B
Daniel Augustus, 1851-1914.
A builder of the New South; being the story of the life work of Daniel Augustus Tompkins, by George Tayloe Winston. Freeport, N.Y., Books for Libraries Press [1972] viii, 403 p. port. 23 cm. Reprint of the 1920 ed. [CT275.T72A3 1972] 75-38375 ISBN 0-8369-6792-5
I. Winston, George Tayloe, 1852- II. Title.

Tompkins, James J., 1870-

BOYLE, George, 1902- 922.271
Father Tompkins of Nova Scotia. New York, P. J. Kenedy [1953] 234p. illus. 21cm. [BX4705.T682B6] 53-9633
1. Tompkins, James J., 1870- I. Title.

Tompkins, Leonora (Brooke)

TOMPKINS, Leonora (Brooke) 920
1911-
My lovely days. New York, Carlton [c.1966] 136p. illus., ports. 21cm. (Reflection bk.) [CT3150.T6A3] 66-1161 3.50
I. Title.

Tompkins, Peter,

TOMPKINS, Peter, ed. 928.2
Shaw and Molly Tompkins in their own words. New York, Potter [1962, c.1961] 287p. illus. 23cm. 61-15116 4.95
I. Shaw, George Bernard, 1856-1950. II. Tompkins, Molly (Arthur) III. Title.

TOMPKINS, Peter, ed. 928.2
Shaw and Molly Tompkins in their own words. New York, C. N. Potter [1962, c1961] 287 p. illus. 23 cm. [PR5366.T55 1962] 61-15116
I. Shaw, George Bernard, 1856-1950 II. Tompkins, Molly (Arthur) III. Title.

Ton, Jill.

TON, Mary Ellen. 301.42'7
For the love of my daughter / Mary Ellen Ton. Elgin, Ill. : D. C. Cook Pub. Co., c1978. 153 p. ; 22 cm. [HQ798.T66T67] 77-87253 ISBN 0-89191-104-9 pbk. : 2.95
1. Ton, Jill. 2. Mother and daughters—Biography. 3. Runaway youth—United States—Biography. I. Title. BIP

Tone, Theobald Wolfe, 1763-1798.

MOLONY, John Chartres, 920.415
1877-
Ireland's tragic comedians. Freeport, N.Y., Books for Libraries Press [1970] ix, 313, [1] p. port. 23 cm. (Essay index reprint series) Reprint of the 1934 ed. "Bibliographical note": p. 313-[314] [DA948.6.A1M6 1970] 73-134117
1. Clare, John Fitzgibbon, 1st Earl of, 1749-1802. 2. Tone, Theobald Wolfe, 1763-1798. 3. Fitzgerald, Edward, Lord, 1763-1798. 4. Emmet, Robert, 1778-1803. I. Title. BIP

Tong, James.

BROWNING, Mary 266.2'0924 B
Carmel.
Think big; a partial biography of Reverend James Tong, S.J. [1st ed.] Owensboro, Ky., Printed by Winkler Print. Co., 1970. 109 p. illus., ports. 28 cm. [BV3269.T67B76] 76-134943
1. Tong, James. I. Title.

Tonson, Jacob, 1656?-1736.

GEDULD, Harry M. 655.4'24
Prince of publishers; a study of the work and career of Jacob Tonson [by] Harry M. Geduld. Bloomington, Indiana University Press, 1969. 245 p. illus., facsims., ports. 23 cm. (Indiana University humanities series, no. 66) Bibliographical references included in "Notes" (p. 203-235) [AS36.1385 no. 66] 68-64121 6.75
1. Tonson, Jacob, 1656?-1736. I. Title. II. Series: Indiana. University. Indiana University humanities series, no. 66

LYNCH, Kathleen 070.5'0924 B
Martha.
Jacob Tonson, Kit-Cat publisher, by Kathleen M. Lynch. [1st ed. Knoxville] University of Tennessee Press [1971] xii, 241 p. illus., geneal. table, ports. 23 cm. Bibliography: p. 219-224. [Z325.T6L95] 77-111046 ISBN 0-87049-122-9 9.75
1. Tonson, Jacob, 1656?-1736. BIP

Toobin, Jerome, 1922-

TOOBIN, Jerome, 782'.1092'4 B
1922-
Agitato : a trek through the musical jungle / Jerome Toobin. New York : Viking Press, 1975. 213 p. ; 22 cm. [ML429.T66A3] 74-6566 ISBN 0-670-11040-X : 7.95
1. Toobin, Jerome, 1922- 2. Symphony of the Air. I. Title.

Toole, John, 1815-1860.

O'NEAL, William Bainter 759.13
Primitive into painter; life and letters of John Toole. Charlottesville, University of Virginia Press [c.]1960. 113p. 12 plates. 31cm. Bibl.: p.104-105. 60-16871 10.00
1. Toole, John, 1815-1860. I. Title.

Toomay, Pat.

TOOMAY, Pat. 796.33'2'0924 B
The crunch / Pat Toomay. 1st ed. New York : Norton, [1975] 203 p., [8] leaves of plates : ill. ; 21 cm. [GV939.T66A33 1975] 75-15628 ISBN 0-393-08726-3 : 7.95
1. Toomay, Pat. 2. Football. I. Title. BIP

Toombs, Robert Augustus, 1810-1885.

PHILLIPS, Ulrich 973.71'3'0924 B
Bonnell, 1877-1934.
The life of Robert Toombs. New York, B. Franklin [1968] ix, 281 p. 23 cm. (Burt Franklin bibliography & reference series, 265) (American classics in history and social science, 73.) Reprint of the 1913 ed. Bibliographical footnotes. [E415.9.T6] [P5 1968] 69-18607
1. Toombs, Robert Augustus, 1810-1885. I. Title. BIP

THOMPSON, William 973.71'3'0924 B
Y.
Robert Toombs of Georgia, by William Y. Thompson. Baton Rouge, Louisiana State University Press, 1966. xiii, 281 p. illus.,

ports. 24 cm. (Southern biography series) "Critical essay on authorities": p. 261-270. [E415.9.T6T45] 66-25722
1. Toombs, Robert Augustus, 1810-1885. I. Title. II. Series.

Toperoff, Sam

TOPEROFF, Sam 818'.5'403
All the advantages. [1st ed.] Boston, Little [1967] 215p. 21cm. Atlantic Monthly Pr. bk. Autobiographical. [CT275.T724A3] 67-16706 4.95
I. Title.

Topp, Mildred (Spurrier)

TOPP, Mildred (Spurrier) 818.5 1897-
In the pink. Boston, Houghton Mifflin, 1950. 242 p. ports. (on lining papers) 22 cm. Autobiographical. Sequel to Smile please. [CT275.T725A28] 50-8823
I. Title.

Tordenskiold. Peter, 1690-1720.

ADAMSON, Hans Christian. 923.5489
Admiral Thunderbolt; the spectacular career of Peter Wessel, Norway's greatest sea hero, who in eight years of naval warfare sailed, shot, and stormed his way from sea cadet to vice admiral (A. D. 1711 to 1718) [1st ed.] Philadelphia, Chilton Co., Book Division [1959] 336 p. illus. 25 cm. [DL196.8.T6A62] 59-13580
1. Tordenskiold, Peter, 1690-1720. I. Title.

ADAMSON. HANS CHRISTIAN. 923.5489
Admiral Thunderbolt: the spectacular career of Peter Wessel. Norway's greatest sea hero, who in eight years of naval warfare sailed, shot, and stormed his way from sea cadet to vice admiral (A. D. 1711 to 1718) [1st ed.] Philadelphia, Chilton Co., Book Division [1959] 336p. illus. 25cm. [DL196.8.T6A62] 59-13580
1. Tordenskiold. Peter, 1690-1720. I. Title.

Tories, English.

KEBBEL, Thomas Edward, 329.9'42 1827-1917.
A history of Toryism. [1st ed. reprinted]; new introduction by E. J. Fouchtwanger. Richmond, Richmond Publishing Co. Ltd, 1972. [6], viii, 400 p. 19 cm. Reprint of 1st ed., London, W. H. Allen, 1886. [JN1129.T7K4 1972] 72-170726 ISBN 0-85546-168-3 £4.50
1. Tories, English. 2. Great Britain—Politics and government—19th century. 3. Statesmen—Great Britain. I. Title.

Tornay, Maurice, 1910-1949.

LOUP, Robert. 922.2515
Martyr in Tibet; the heroic life and death of Father Maurice Tornay, St. Bernard missionary to Tibet. Translated from the French by Charles Davenport. New York, D. McKay Co. [1956] 238p. illus. 21cm. [BV3427.T5L62] 56-14036
1. Tornay, Maurice, 1910-1949. 2. Missions Tibet. 3. Augustinian Canons. Congregation of the Great St Bernard. I. Title.

Toronto. Hockey Club (National League)

FISCHLER, Stan. 796.9'62'09713541
Make way for the Leafs : Toronto's comeback / by Stan Fischler. Scarborough, Ont. : Prentice-Hall of Canada, [1975?] 128 p. : chiefly ill. ; 28 cm. "A Stuart L. Daniels book." [GV848.T6F566] 74-9245 ISBN 0-13-545582-0 : 4.95
1. Toronto. Hockey Club (National League) 2. Hockey—Biography. I. Title.

Toronto. Peoples Church.

HOPE Evangeline. 266'.0092'4 B
Daisy : the fascinating story of Daisy Smith, wife of Dr. Oswald J. Smith, missionary, statesman, and founder of the Peoples Church, Toronto / Hope Evangeline. Grand Rapids : Baker Book House, c1978. xiii, 247 p., [8] leaves of plates : ill. ; 21 cm. [BX9225.S477H66] 78-103025 ISBN 0-8010-3328-4 : 6.95
1. Smith, Daisy, 1891-1972. 2. Toronto. Peoples Church. 3. Smith, Oswald J. 4. Presbyterians—Canada—Biography. I. Title.

Torreon, Mexico—Social life and customs.

JAMIESON, Tulitas, 1886- 917.2'1
Tulitas of Torreon; reminiscences of life in Mexico, by Tulitas Jamieson, as told to Evelyn Payne. El Paso, Texas Western Press, 1969. xvi, 146 p. illus., ports. 23 cm. [F1391.T7J3] 69-20291 5.00
1. Torreon, Mexico—Social life and customs. I. Payne, Evelyn, 1907- II. Title.

Torre, Pedro de la, b. ca. 1507.

LANNING, John Tate, 610'.92'4 B 1902-
Pedro de la Torre, doctor to conquerors. Baton Rouge, Louisiana State University Press [1974] xiv, 145 p. facsims. 23 cm. Bibliography: p. 138-140. [R558.T67L36] 73-83909 ISBN 0-8071-0064-1 7.50
1. Torre, Pedro de la, b. ca. 1507. 2. Medicine—Mexico—History. I. Title.

Torres, Manual J.

RETTIG, Richard 364.36'3'0924 B P.
Manny : a criminal-addict's story / Richard P. Rettig, Manual J. Torres, Gerald R. Garrett. Boston : Houghton Mifflin, c1977. 264 p. ; 22 cm. Bibliography: p. 257-264. [HV6248.T617R47] 76-14654 ISBN 0-395-24838-8 : 5.95
1. Torres, Manual J. 2. Crime and criminals—New York (City)—Biography. 3. Narcotic addicts—New York (City)—Biography. 4. Puerto Ricans in New York (City) I. Torres, Manual J., joint author. II. Garrett, Gerald R., joint author. III. Title. BIP

Torres Restrepo, Camilo.

BRODERICK, Walter 322.4'2'0924 B J., 1935-
Camilo Torres : a biography of the priest-guerrillero / Walter J. Broderick. 1st ed. New York : Doubleday, 1975. viii, 370 p., [8] leaves of plates : ill. ; 22 cm. Includes index. Bibliography: p. [341]-361. [F2278.T6B76] 73-15327 ISBN 0-385-08710-1 : 10.00
1. Torres Restrepo, Camilo. 2. Guerrillas—Colombia.

GUZMAN Campos, 986.1'063'0924 B German.
Camilo Torres, by German Guzman. Translated by John D. Ring. New York, Sheed and Ward [1969] vi, 310 p. 22 cm. Translation of El padre Camilo Torres. Bibliographical references included in "Notes" (p. 299-310) [F2278.T6G813] 69-16991 6.95
1. Torres Restrepo, Camilo.

Torres, Victor.

TORRES, Victor. 248'.2 B
Son of evil street / Victor Torres with Don Wilkerson. 2d ed. Minneapolis : Bethany Fellowship, 1977. 166 p. ; 18 cm. (Dimension books) [BV4935.T65A37 1977] 77-150672 ISBN 0-87123-516-1 pbk. : 1.95
1. Torres, Victor. 2. Narcotic addicts—New York (State)—Brooklyn—Biography. 3. Converts—New York (State)—Brooklyn—Biography. 4. Brooklyn—Biography. I. Wilkerson, Don, joint author. II. Title. BIP

Torrey, Charles Turner, 1813-1846.

LOVEJOY, Joseph 326'.0924 B Cammet, 1805-1871.
Memoir of Rev. Charles T. Torrey, who died in the penitentiary of Maryland, where he was confined for showing mercy to the poor. New York, Negro Universities Press [1969] viii, 364 p. port. 23 cm. Reprint of the 1847 ed. [E449.T69 1969] 76-92749
1. Torrey, Charles Turner, 1813-1846. I. Title.

Torrio, Johnny.

MCPHAUL, John J. 364.1'0924 B
Johnny Torrio; first of the gang lords [by] Jack McPhaul. New Rochelle, N.Y., Arlington House [1970] 489 p. illus., ports. 22 cm. Bibliography: p. [420]-423. [HV6248.T62M32] 71-115345 8.95
1. Torrio, Johnny.

Tors, Ivan.

TORS, Ivan. 591'.092'4
My life in the wild / Ivan Tors. Boston : Houghton Mifflin, 1979. vi, 209 p. : ill. ; 24 cm. [QL31.T59A37] 79-12252 ISBN 0-395-27766-3 : 10.95
1. Tors, Ivan. 2. Zoologists—United States—Biography. 3. Moving-picture producers and directors—United States—Biography. I. Title. BIP

Toscanini, Arturo, 1867-1957.

ANTEK, Samuel. 927.8
This was Toscanini. With photos. by Robert Hupka. Foreword by Marcia Davenport. New York, Vanguard Press [1963] 192 p. illus., ports., facsims., music. 32 cm. "The recorded repertoire of Arturo Toscanini": p. 186-192. [ML422.T67A75] 63-15196
1. Toscanini, Arturo, 1867-1957. 2. Toscanini, Arturo, 1867-1957—Discography. I. Hupka, Robert. II. Title. BIP

CHOTZINOFF, Samuel, 1889- 927.8 1964.
Toscanini: an intimate portrait. [1st ed.] New York,Knopf, 1956. 148 p. illus. 25 cm. "The first four parts of this book originally appeared in Holiday in slightly different form." [ML422.T67C38] 56-5784
1. Toscanini, Arturo, 1867-1957. BIP

CHOTZINOFF, Samuel, 785'.092'4 B 1889-1964.
Toscanini : an intimate portrait / by Samuel Chotzinoff. New York : Da Capo Press, 1976, c1956. 148 p., [2] leaves of plates : ports. ; 24 cm. (Da Capo Press music reprint series) Reprint of the ed. published by Knopf, New York. [ML422.T67C38 1976] 76-7576 ISBN 0-306-70777-2 : 15.00
1. Toscanini, Arturo, 1867-1957.

CHOTZINOFF, Samule, 1889- 927.8
Toscanini: an intimate portrait. [1st ed.] New York, Knopf, 1956. 148p illus. 25cm. 'The first four parts of this book originally appeared in Holiday in slightly different form.' [ML422.T67C38] 56-5784
1. Toscanini, Arturo, 1867- I. Title.

EWEN, David, 1907- 927.8
The story of Arturo Toscanini. Rev. and enl. ed. New York, Holt, Rinehart and Winston [1960, c1951] xviii, 142p. Bibl.: p. 125-126 illus. 22cm. 60-4144 3.00
1. Toscanini, Arturo, 1867-1957. 2. Toscanini, Arturo, 1867-1957—Discography. I. Title.

EWEN, David, 1907- 927.8
The story of Arturo Toscanini. [1st ed.] New York, Holt [1951] xviii, 142 p. port. 22 cm. [Holt musical biography series] "For further readings on Toscanini": p. 125-126. "A complete list of Toscanini recordings": p. 127-133. [ML422.T67E9] 51-1021
1. Toscanini, Arturo, 1867- 2. Toscanini, Arturo, 1867-—Discography.

GILMAN, Lawrence, 1878- 780'.15 1930.
Toscanini and great music. Freeport, N.Y., Books for Libraries Press [1972] p. (Essay index reprint series) Reprinted from the ed. of 1938, New York. [ML422.T67G5 1972] 72-6815 ISBN 0-8369-7253-8
1. Toscanini, Arturo, 1867-1957. 2. Music—Analysis, appreciation. I. Title.

HAGGIN, Bernard H., 1900- 927.8
Conversations with Toscanini. [1st ed.] Garden City, N. Y., Doubleday, 1959. 261 p. ports. 22 cm. Discography: p. 165-249. [ML422.T67H3] 59-6357
1. Toscanini, Arturo, 1867-1957. I. Title.

HAGGIN, Bernard H. 1900- 780.924
The Toscanini musicians knew [by] B. H. Haggin. New York, Horizon. 1967. 245p. music, ports. 24cm. [ML422.T67H32] 67-17782 7.50
1. Toscanini, Arturo, 1867-1957. I. Title.

MAREK, George 785'.092'4 B Richard, 1902-
Toscanini / George R. Marek. 1st ed. New York : Atheneum, 1975. xiv, 321 p., [10] leaves of plates : ill. ; 25 cm. Includes index. Bibliography: p. 302-304. [ML422.T67M29] 74-20356 ISBN 0-689-10655-6 : 12.95
1. Toscanini, Arturo, 1867-1957.

SACCHI, Filippo, 1887- 927.8
The magic baton; Toscanini's life for music. [Rev. and abridged by the author] New York, Putnam [1957] 224p. 23cm. Translation of Toscanini. [ML422.T67S32 1957a] 57-11716
1. Toscanini, Arturo, 1867-1957. I. Title.

TAUBMAN, Hyman Howard, 1907- 927.8
The maestro, the life of Arturo Toscanini. New York, Simon and Schuster, 1951. viii, 342 p. ports. 24 cm. [ML422.T67T3] 51-2529
1. Toscanini, Arturo, 1867- I. Title. BIP

TAUBMAN, Hyman 785'.092'4 B Howard, 1907-
The maestro : the life of Arturo Toscanini / by Howard Taubman. Westport, Conn. : Greenwood Press, [1977] c1951. viii, 342 p., [8] leaves of plates : ill. ; 22 cm. Reprint of the ed. published by Simon and Schuster, New York. Includes index. [ML422.T67T3 1977] 76-57171 ISBN 0-8371-9434-2 lib. bdg. 19.75
1. Toscanini, Arturo, 1867-1957. 2. Conductors (Music)—Biography. I. Title.

Toulouse-Lautrec Monfa, Henri Marie Raymond de, 1864-1901.

BOURET, Jean. 759.4
The life and work of Toulouse-Lautrec; court painter to the wicked. [Translated from the French by Daphne Woodward] New York, H. N. Abrams [1966] 270 p. illus. (part col.) facsims. ports. 21 cm. Translation of Toulouse-Lautrec. [ND553.T7B613] 66-13667
1. Toulouse-Lautrec Monfa, Henri Marie Raymond de, 1864-1901. I. Title.

COGNIAT, Raymond, 1896- 759.4
Lautrec. [Translated from the French by Anne Ross] New York, Crown Publishers [1966] 43 p. illus. (part col.) 19 cm. (Basic art library) [ND553.T7C543] 66-26178
1. Toulouse-Lautrec Monfa, Henri Marie Raymond de, 1864-1901.

HANSON, Lawrence. 759.4
The tragic life of Toulouise-Lautrec [by] Lawrence and Elisabeth Hanson. N[ew] Y[ork] Random House [1956] x, 277p. plates, ports. 24cm. Bibliography: p. 264-270. [ND553.T7H3] 927.5 56-5208
1. Toulouse-Lautrec Monfa, Henri Marie Raymond de, 1864-1901. I. Hanson, Elisabeth M., joint author. II. Title.

JEDLICKA, Gotthard, 1899- 759.4
Henri de Toulouse-Lautrec. [Tr.: Joan Erskine] New York, Barnes & Noble [1962, c.1961] 85p. illus. (pt. col.) 18cm. (Barnes & Noble art ser. 62-52815 .75 pap.,
1. Toulouse-Lautrec Monfa, Henri Marie Raymond de, 1864-1901. I. Title.

JULIEN, Edouard 759.4
Lautrec. [Translated from the French by Helen C. Slonim] New York, Crown Publishers, 1959 [ ] llus. (part mounted col.) col. plates. 29cm. 95p. b(bibl.) 59-65436 2.95 bds.,
1. Toulouse-Lautrec Monfa, Henri Marie Raymond de, 1864-1901. I. Title.

NEGRI, Renata. 760'.092'4
Toulouse-Lautrec / by Renata Negri. 1st U.S. ed. New York : Avenel Books ; distributed by Crown Publishers, 1979. p.

cm. [ND553.T7N3713 1979] 78-71514 ISBN 0-517-27792-1 pbk. : 4.98
1. Toulouse-Lautrec Monfa, Henri Marie Raymond de, 1864-1901. 2. Painters—France—Biography.

PERRUCHOT, Henri, 1917- 759.4
T-Lautrec. Tr. by Humphrey Hare. New York, Collier [1962, c.1958, 1960] 350p. illus. 18cm. (BS124Y) Bibl. 1.50 pap.,
1. Toulouse-Lautrec Monfa, Henri Marie Raymond de, 1864-1901. I. Title.

PERRUCHOT, Henri, 1917- 759.4
T-Lautrec. Translated by Humphrey Hare. [1st American ed.] Cleveland, World Pub. Co. [1961, c1960] 317 p. illus. 23 cm. (His Art and destiny) Translation of La vie de Toulouse Lautrec. Includes bibliography. [ND553.T7P413] 61-6334
1. Toulouse-Lautrec Monfa, Henri Marie Raymond de, 1864-1901.

THOMSON, Richard. 760'.092'4 B
Toulouse-Lautrec / Richard Thomson. 1st U.S. ed. New York : Two Continents, c1977. p. cm. (The Oresko art book series) Includes index. Bibliography: p. [ND553.T7T47 1977] 77-21483 ISBN 0-8467-0372-6 : 15.95 9.95
1. Toulouse-Lautrec Monfa, Henri Marie Raymond de, 1864-1901. 2. Painters—France—Biography. I. Title. II. Series.

TIETZE, Hans, 1880- 927.5
Toulouse Lautrec. [1st ed.] New York, Beechhurst Press [1953] 61, [2] p. illus. (part col.) port. 36 cm. Bibliography: p. [63] [ND553.T7T5] 53-13338
1. Toulouse-Lautrec Monfa, Henri Marie Raymond de, 1864-1901.

Toulouse-Lautrec Monfa, Henri Marie Raymond de, 1864-1901—Juvenile literature.

RABOFF, Ernest Lloyd. 759.4
Henri de Toulouse-Lautrec, by Ernest Raboff. Garden City, N.Y., Doubleday [1970] [31] p. illus. (part col.), ports. (part col.) 29 cm. (Art for children) (A Gemini-Smith book) A brief biographical sketch of the nineteenth-century artist accompanies examples and discussions of his works. [ND553.T7R3] 70-93207 3.95
1. Toulouse-Lautrec Monfa, Henri Marie Raymond de, 1864-1901—Juvenile literature. I. Title. BIP

Tourgee, Albion Winegar, 1838-1905.

DIBBLE, Roy Floyd, 1887-1929. 813'.4 B
Albion W. Tourgee. Port Washington, N.Y., Kennikat Press [1968, c1921] 160 p. 19 cm. Bibliography: p. 149-153. [PS3088.D5 1968] 68-16287
1. Tourgee, Albion Winegar, 1838-1905.

OLSEN, Otto H 813.4
Carpetbagger's crusade; the life of Albion Winegar Tourgee, by Otto H. Olsen. Baltimore, Johns Hopkins Press, 1965. xiv, 395 p. illus., facsims., ports. 24 cm. "Bibliography of Tourgee's writings": p. 355-362. "General bibliography": p. 363-382. [PS3088.05] 63-13522
1. Tourgee. Albion Winegar, 1838-1905 I. Title. BIP

Tournachon, Felix, 1820-1910.

TOURNACHON, Felix, 1820-1910. 779'.2'0924
Nadar / Nigel Gosling. London : Secker & Warburg, 1976. 298 p. : ill. ; 31 cm. Includes index. [TR681.F3T68 1976] 77-355116 ISBN 0-436-18610-1 : £9.75
1. Tournachon, Felix, 1820-1910. 2. Photography—Portraits. 3. France—Biography—Portraits. I. Gosling, Nigel.

TOURNACHON, Felix, 1820-1910. 779'.2'0924
Nadar / Nigel Gosling. 1st American ed. New York : Knopf : distributed by Random House, 1976. 298 p. : ill. ; 31 cm. Includes index. [TR681.F3T68 1976b] 76-27546 ISBN 0-394-41106-4 : 25.00
1. Tournachon, Felix, 1820-1910. 2. Photography—Portraits. 3. France—Biography—Portraits. 4. Photographers—France—Biography. I. Gosling, Nigel. II. Title.

Tousley, Clare M., 1889-

TOUSLEY, Clare M., 1889- 361'.92'4 B
Letter to Jeanie : highlights of sixty years with social work professionals and volunteers / Clare M. Tousley. New York : Family Service Association of America, c1976. xi, 74 p., [2] leaves of plates : ill. ; 21 cm. [HV28.T66A45 1976] 76-16430 ISBN 0-87304-144-5
1. Tousley, Clare M., 1889- 2. Social workers—United States—Biography. I. Title.

Toussaint Louverture, Francois Dominique, 1743-1803.

BEARD, John Relly, 1800-1876. 972.94'03'0924 B
The life of Toussaint L'Ouverture, the Negro patriot of Hayti: comprising an account of the struggle for liberty in the island, and a sketch of its history to the present period. Westport, Conn., Negro Universities Press [1970] xi, 335 p. illus., map. 23 cm. Reprint of the 1853 ed. [F1923.T7 1970] 75-109316
1. Toussaint Louverture, Francois Dominique, 1743-1803. 2. Haiti—History—Revolution, 1791-1804. I. Title.

KORNGOLD, Ralph, 1886- 972.94'03'0924 B
Citizen Toussaint / by Ralph Korngold. Westport, Conn. : Greenwood Press, 1979, c1944. xvii, 351 p. ; 23 cm. Reprint of the 1965 ed.published by Hill and Wang, New York. Includes index. Bibliography: p. [333]-351. [F1923.T69K67 1979] 78-21026 ISBN 0-313-20794-1 lib. bdg. : 22.50
1. Toussaint Louverture, Francois Dominique, 1743-1803. 2. Revolutionists—Haiti—Biography. 3. Generals—Haiti—Biography. 4. Haiti—History—Revolution, 1791-1804. I. Title.

KORNGOLD, Ralph, 1886- 923.27294
Citizen Toussaint. New York, Hill & Wang [1965, c.1944] xvii, 338p. 21cm. (H26) [F1923.T855] 65-17428 2.25 pap.,
1. Toussaint Louverture, Francois Dominique, 1743-1803. 2. Haiti—Hist.—Revolution, 1791-1804. I. Title. BIP

SCHERMAN, Katharine. 923.27294
The slave who freed Haiti; the story of Toussaint Louverture. Illustrated by Adolf Dehn. New York, Random House [1954] 182 p. illus. 22 cm. (World landmark books, W-15) [F1923.T915] 54-7006
1. Toussaint Louverture, Pierre Dominique, 1746?-1803. I. Title. BIP

Toussaint Louverture, Francois Dominique, 1743-1803—Juvenile literature.

GRIFFITHS, Ann. 972.94'03'0924 B
Black patriot and martyr; Toussaint of Haiti. New York, J. Messner [1970] 192 p. map. 22 cm. Bibliography: p. 184. Biography of the eighteenth-century Haitian who led the revolution against French domination in the Caribbean. [F1923.T824] 92 71-107396 3.50
1. Toussaint Louverture, Francois Dominique, 1743-1803—Juvenile literature. I. Title.

SYME, Ronald, 1910- 972.94'03'0924 B
Toussaint; the Black liberator. Illustrated by William Stobbs. New York, Morrow [1971] 191, [1] p. illus., ports. 21 cm. Bibliography: p. [192] A biography of the eighteenth-century slave who led his people in the struggle for an independent Haiti. [F1923.T952] 92 72-152072 4.50
1. Toussaint Louverture, Francois Dominique, 1743-1803—Juvenile literature. 2. Haiti—History—Revolution, 1791-1804—Juvenile literature. I. Stobbs, William, illus. II. Title. BIP

Toussaint, Pierre, 1766-1853?

LEE, Hannah Farnham (Sawyer) 1780-1865. 301.45'22 B
Memoir of Pierre Toussaint, born a slave in St. Domingo. Westport, Conn., Negro Universities Press [1970] 124 p. port. 23 cm. Reprint of the 1854 ed. [E185.97.T73 1970] 79-132072
1. Toussaint, Pierre, 1766-1853? I. Title. BIP

Toussaint, Pierre, 1766-1853?—Juvenile literature.

SHEEHAN, Arthur T. 920
Pierre Toussaint, pioneer in brotherhood [by] Arthur and Elizabethan Odell Sheehan. Illus. by Salem Tamer. New York, Kenedy [c.1963] 189p. illus. 22cm. (Amer. background bks. [24]) 63-11330 2.50
1. Toussaint, Pierre, 1766-1853?—Juvenile literature. I. Sheehan, Elizabeth Odell, 1919- joint author. II. Title.

Tovey, Donald Francis, Sir, 1875-1940.

GRIERSON, Mary. 927.8
Donald Francis Tovey; a biography based on letters. London, New York, Oxford University Press, 1952. xi, 337 p. ports., facsim. 23 cm. "List of books and compositions by Donald Tovey": p. 329-332. [ML410.T685G7] 52-8084
1. Tovey, Sir Donald Francis, 1875-1940. I. Title. BIP

GRIERSON, Mary. 780'.92'4 B
Donald Francis Tovey; a biography based on letters. Westport, Conn., Greenwood Press [1970] xi, 337 p. ports. 23 cm. "Originally published in 1952." "List of books and compositions by Donald Tovey": p. 329-332. [ML410.T685G7 1970] 70-104237 ISBN 0-8371-3935-X
1. Tovey, Donald Francis, Sir, 1875-1940.

Tovey, Doreen—Biography.

TOVEY, Doreen. 823'.9'14
Life with grandma / Doreen Tovey ; drawings by ffolkes. London : Elek Books, [1976?] c1964. 167 p. : ill. ; 23 cm. Place of publication covered by label: Paul Elek, inc., Salem, N.H. [PR6039.O75Z52 1976] 76-375514 ISBN 0-236-31146-8 : 7.95
1. Tovey, Doreen—Biography. 2. Authors, English—20th century—Biography. I. Title. BIP

Towle, Tony,

†TOWLE, Tony, 1939- 811'.5'4
Autobiography and other poems / Tony Towle. 1st ed. New York : SUN/Coach House South, 1977. p. cm. [PS3570.O9A95] 77-3591 ISBN 0-915342-18-9 pbk. : 2.95
I. Title. BIP

Towne, Carola,

TOWNE, Carola, 1897- 271'.979 B
Keys and pedals; an autobiography, by Sister M. Carola Towne, C.S.A. Philadelphia, Dorrance [1972] 173 p. 22 cm. [BX4705.T735A3] 72-81634 ISBN 0-8059-1719-5 4.95
I. Title.

Townsend, John Wilson, 1885-1968.

TOWNSEND, Dorothy Edwards, 1915- 976.9'007'2024
The life and works of John Wilson Townsend; Kentucky author and historian, 1885-1968. [1st ed.] Lexington, Ky., Printed by the Keystone Printery, 1972. 87 p. ports. 24 cm. "Antiquities at Idleberg [by A. Barbour] reprinted from the Knickerbocker magazine, April 1843": p. [55]-70. Includes bibliographical references. [E175.5.T58T6] 72-86082 4.95
1. Townsend, John Wilson, 1885-1968. I. Barbour, Ambrose, 1822-1852. Antiquities at Idleberg. 1972.

Townsend, Peter, 1914-

BARRYMAINE, Norman. 923.542
The Peter Townsend story. [1st ed.] New York, Dutton, 1958. 240p. illus. 21cm. [DA585.A5M3] 58-10823
1. Townsend, Peter, 1914- 2. Margaret, Princess of Great Britain, 1930- I. Title.

TOWNSEND, Peter, 1914- 941.085'092'4 B
Time and chance : an autobiography / Peter Townsend. New York : Methuen, c1978. 317 p., [8] leaves of plates : ill. ; 24 cm. Includes index. [CT788.T686A3 1978b] 78-61629 ISBN 0-458-93710-X : 10.95
1. Townsend, Peter, 1914- 2. England—Biography. I. Title.

Townsend, William Cameron, 1896-

HEFLEY, James C. 266'.023'0924 B
Uncle Cam : the story of William Cameron Townsend, founder of the Wycliffe Bible Translators and the Summer Institute of Linguistics / James & Marti Hefley ; photo editor, Cornell Capa. Waco, Tex. : Word Books, [1974] 272 p. : ports. ; 23 cm. [BV2372.T68H43] 73-91556 6.95
1. Townsend, William Cameron, 1896- 2. Wycliffe Bible Translators. 3. Summer Institute of Linguistics. I. Hefley, Marti, joint author. II. Title.

Townsend, William, 1909-1973.

TOWNSEND, William, 1909-1973. 759.2 B
The Townsend journals : an artist's record of his times, 1928-51 / edited by Andrew Forge. London : Tate Gallery Publications, 1976. 3-98 p. : ill., ports. ; 26 cm. Includes index. [ND497.T755A55 1976] 77-358156 ISBN 0-900874-97-X : £3.50
1. Townsend, William, 1909-1973. 2. Painters—Great Britain—Biography. 3. Great Britain—Social life and customs—20th century. I. Title.

Townshend, Charles, 1725-1767.

NAMIER, Lewis Bernstein Sir 923.242
Charles Townshend; his character & career. [New York] Cambridge, University Press, 1959[ ] 29p. (bibl. fo0tnotes) 19cm. (Leslie Stephen lecture, 1959) 59-65279 apply pap.,
1. Townshend, Charles, 1725-1767. I. Title.

NAMIER, Lewis Bernstein, Sir 1888-1960 923.242
Charles Townshend, by Sir Lewis Namier, John Brooke [New York] St Martin's [c.] 1964. vii, 198p. port. 23cm. Bibl. 64-16387 7.00
1. Townshend, Charles, 1725-1767. I. Brooke, John, joint author. II. Title.

NAMIER, Lewis Bernstein, sir 1888-1960. 923.242
Charles Townshend. by Sir Lewis Namier and John Brooke. [New York] St Martin's Press, 1964. vii, 198 p. port. 23 cm. "List of cooks by Sir Lewis Namier": p. [192]-198. Bibliographical footnotes. [DA501.T7N33] 64-16387
1. Townshend, Charles, 1725-1767. I. Brooks, John, joint author. II. Title.

Toyama, Kyuzo, 1868-1910.

WAKUKAWA, Seiei. v. 12
The life and times of Kyuzo Toyama, 1868-1910; a contribution to the history of modern Okinawa. Honolulu, Toyama-Kyuzo Memorial Committee, 1953. 271p. illus., ports. 20cm. Title from cover; title page and text in Japanese. 'Published in commemoration of the semicentennial of Okinawan immigrants in Hawaii, 1900-1950. [PL805.T6W3] 53-37926
1. Toyama, Kyuzo, 1868-1910. I. Title.

Toyama, Masakazu, 1848-1900.

HEARN, Lafcadio, 1850-1904. 813'.4 B
Letters / Lafcadio Hearn ; [editors, Hojin Yano, Tadanobu Kawai, Hiroyishi Kishimoto]. New York : AMS Press, 1975.

p. cm. Reprints of letters in the Tenri University Library, Tenri, Japan. Contents.Contents.—v. 1. To and from various persons.—v. 2. To and from B. H. Chamberlain. [PS1918.A45 1975] 75-25954 ISBN 0-404-13210-3 (v. 1)
1. Hearn, Lafcadio, 1850-1904—Correspondence. 2. Hearn, Lafcadio, 1850-1904—Manuscripts—Facsimiles. 3. Toyama, Masakazu, 1848-1900. 4. Chamberlain, Basil Hall, 1850-1935. I. Chamberlain, Basil Hall, 1850-1935.

Toynbee, Arnold Joseph, 1889-

SINGER, Charles Gregg, 1910- v. 12
Toynbee, by C. Gregg Singer. Philadelphia, Presbyterian and Reformed Pub. Co., 1965. 76 p. 23 cm. (International library of philosophy and theology. Modern thinkers series) Bibliography: p. [7] 67-59069
1. Toynbee, Arnold Joseph, 1889- I. Title. II. Series. **BIP**

Tozer, Aiden Wilson, 1897-1963.

FANT, David Jones, 1897- 922.89
A. W. Tozer, a twentieth century prophet. Harrisburg, Pa., Christian Pubns., 1522 N. Third St. [1964] 180p. port. 21cm. 64-21945 price unreported
1. Tozer, Aiden Wilson, 1897-1963. I. Title.

Tracey, Margot, 1907-

TRACEY, Margot, 1907- 947.084'1'0924
Red rose / Margot Tracey. Newton Abbot ; North Pomfret, Vt. : David & Charles, 1978. 230 p. : ill. ; 23 cm. [DK601.T72] 78-312165 ISBN 0-7153-7440-0 : 12.95
1. Tracey, Margot, 1907- 2. Moscow—Biography. 3. French in Moscow—Biography. I. Title. **BIP**

Trachtenberg, Susan.

TRACHTENBERG, Inge. 362.1'9'75540926
My daughter, my son / by Inge Trachtenberg ; with contributions by Susan Trachtenberg. New York : Summit Books, c1978. p. cm. Bibliography: p. [RJ456.C74T72] 78-16962 ISBN 0-671-40043-6 : 9.95
1. Trachtenberg, Susan. 2. Ulcerative colitis in children—Biography. 3. Ileostomy—Biography. I. Trachtenberg, Susan, joint author. II. Title. **BIP**

Track-athletics—Biography.

HANLEY, Reid M., 1945- 796.4'2'0922 B
Who's who in track and field [by] Reid M. Hanley. New Rochelle, N.Y., Arlington House [1973] 160 p. 25 cm. [GV697.A1H34] 73-11872 ISBN 0-87000-219-8 6.95
1. Track-athletics—Biography. I. Title. **BIP**

OWENS, Jesse, 1913- 796.4'26'0924 B
The Jesse Owens story, by Jesse Owens with Paul G. Neimark. New York, Putnam [1970] 109 p. 22 cm. The Negro athlete who won four gold medals in the 1936 Berlin Olympics tells his life story. [GV697.O9A3 1970] 92 72-90865 3.29
1. Track-athletics—Biography. 2. Track-athletics—Juvenile literature. I. Neimark, Paul G. **BIP**

Track-athletics—Biography—Juvenile literature.

DAVIS, Mac, 1905- 796.4'2'0922
Pacemakers in track and field. Illustrated by Sam Nisenson. Cleveland, World Pub. Co. [1968] 128 p. illus. 29 cm. "A Holly book." Brief biographies of thirty outstanding track performers including Paavo Nurmi, Jesse Owens, and Jim Thorpe. [GV697.A1D35] 920 68-13706
1. Track-athletics—Biography—Juvenile literature. I. Nisenson, Samuel, illus. II. Title.

Track-athletics for women.

GLEASNER, Diana C. 796.4'2'0922 B
Track and field / by Diana C. Gleasner ; illustrated with photos. New York : Harvey House, c1977. 77 p. : ill. ; 23 cm. (Women in sports) [GV1060.5.G56 1977] 76-55532 ISBN 0-8178-5602-1 lib.bdg. : 4.97
1. Track-athletics for women. 2. Track-athletics—North America—Biography. I. Title. II. Series.

Tracy, Benjamin Franklin, 1830-1915.

COOLING, B. Franklin. 353.7 B
Benjamin Franklin Tracy: father of the modern American fighting Navy, by Benjamin Franklin Cooling. [Hamden, Conn.] Archon Books, 1973. xvi, 211 p. illus. 22 cm. Bibliography: p. 189-202. [E664.T72C66] 73-6645 ISBN 0-208-01336-9 10.00
1. Tracy, Benjamin Franklin, 1830-1915. 2. United States. Navy—History. I. Title.

Tracy, Leighton Stanley, 1882-1942.

TRACY, Olive Gertrude, 1908- 922.654
Tracy Sahib of India. Kansas City, Mo. Beacon Hill Press [1954] 191p. illus. 20cm. [BV3269.T7T7] 54-1974
1. Tracy, Leighton Stanley, 1882-1942. I. Title.

Tracy, Spencer, 1900-1967.

KANIN, Garson, 1912- 791.43'028'0922
Tracy and Hepburn; an intimate memoir. New York, Viking Press [1971] x, 307 p. 22 cm. [PN2287.T7K27] 71-163875 ISBN 0-670-72293-6 7.95
1. Tracy, Spencer, 1900-1967. 2. Hepburn, Katharine, 1909- I. Title.

KANIN, Garson, 1912- 791.43'028'0922
Tracy and Hepburn; an intimate memoir. Boston, G. K. Hall, 1972 [c1971] 575 p. 25 cm. Large print ed. [PN2287.T7K27 1972] 72-1555 ISBN 0-8161-6031-7 12.95
1. Tracy, Spencer, 1900-1967. 2. Hepburn, Katharine, 1909- I. Title.

SWINDELL, Larry. 791.43'028.0924
Spencer Tracy a biography. New York New American Library [1972] 280 p. illus. ports. 18 cm. Chronology of films, p. 244-269 [PN2287.T759] 69-18516 0.95 (pbk)
1. Tracy, Spencer, 1900-1967. I. Title.

Trade-unions—United States—History.

MORTIMER, Wyndham, 1884-1966. 331.88'0924 B
Organize! My life as a union man. Edited by leo Fenster. Boston, Beacon Press [1971] xxvi, 274 p. illus., ports. 22 cm. [HD8073.M6A3 1971] 73-136233 ISBN 0-8070-5438-0 9.95
1. Trade-unions—United States—History. I. Title.

Trade-unions—United States—Officials and employees—Biography.

WHO'S who in labor. 331'.092'2 B
1st ed. New York : Arno Press, 1976. xxi, 807 p. ; 25 cm. Includes index. "Bibliography of labor periodicals": p. 743-754. [HD8073.A1W5] 75-7962 ISBN 0-405-06651-1 : 65.00
1. Trade-unions—United States—Officials and employees—Biography. 2. Labor and laboring classes—United States—Biography. 3. Trade-unions—United States—Directories. **BIP**

Trade-unions—United States—Officials and employees—Interviews—Bibliography.

PENNSYLVANIA. State University. Dept. of Labor Studies. 331.88'092'2 B
Collection of oral history interviews conducted by the Department of Labor Studies, The Pennsylvania State University, to August, 1973. [University Park, 1973?] 28 l. 28 cm. Caption title. Annotated directory. [Z7164.T7P45 1973] 74-185498
1. Trade-unions—United States—Officials and employees—Interviews—Bibliography. I. Title.

Traherne, Thomas, d. 1674.

STEWART, Stanley N. 821'.4
The expanded voice: the art of Thomas Traherne, by Stanley Stewart. San Marino, Calif., Huntington Library, 1970. ix, 235 p. 24 cm. Includes bibliographical references. [PR3736.T7S8] 71-111800 7.50
1. Traherne, Thomas, d. 1674. I. Title.

Tran Van Con, 1917—

TRAN Van Con, 1917- 959.7'04
Our endless war / Tran Van Don. San Raphael, Calif. : Presidio Press, c1978. p. cm. Includes index. [DS556.9.O94] 78-7914 ISBN 0-89141-019-8 : 12.95
1. Tran Van Con, 1917- 2. Vietnam—History—1945- 3. Generals—Vietnam—Biography. I. Title.

Transcendentalism (New England)—Biography.

COOKE, George Willis, 1848-1923. 191
Memorabilia of the Transcendentalists in New England. Hartford, Transcendental Books [1973] 122 l. 29 cm. First published in 1902 under title: An historical and biographical introduction to accompany the Dial. [B905.C72 1973] 74-156816 12.50
1. The Dial (Boston) 2. Transcendentalism (New England)—Biography. I. Title.

Transportation—U.S.—Biog.

TRANSPORT Publishers Corporation. 380.5'0922
Leading men in American transportation. New York, Transport Publishers Corp. [c1967] 164 p. 29 cm. [HE151.5.A21A] 68-4217
1. Transportation—U.S.—Biog. I. Title.

Transvaal—Politics and government—1880-1910.

GANDHI, Mohandas Karamchand, 1869-1948. 968'.204
Mahatma Gandhi at work; his own story continued. Edited by C. F. Andrews. Freeport, N.Y., Books for Libraries Press [1971] 407 p. illus. 23 cm. Reprint of the 1931 ed. Bibliography: p. 403-404. [DS481.G3A32 1971] 75-37343 ISBN 0 8369-6690-2
1. Transvaal—Politics and government—1880-1910. 2. East Indians in the Transvaal. I. Title. **BIP**

KRUGER, Stephanus Johannes Paulus, Pres. South African Republic, 1825-1904. 968'.2'040924
The memoirs of Paul Kruger, four times president of the South African republic, told by himself. New York, Negro Universities Press [1969] xiii, 444 p. illus., map, ports. 23 cm. Translation of Gedenkschriften. Reprint of the 1902 ed. [DT929.8.K8A27 1969] 77-84689
1. Transvaal—Politics and government—1880-1910.

KRUGER, Stephanus Johannes Paulus, Pres. South African Republic, 1825-1904. 968'.2'040924
The memoirs of Paul Kruger, four times President of the South African Republic. Port Washington, N.Y., Kennikat Press [1970] 2 v. (ix, 543 p.) map, ports. 22 cm. Translation of Lebenserinnerungen. Reprint of the 1902 ed. [DT929.8.K8A3414 1970] 70-112810 ISBN 8-04-610770-
1. Transvaal—Politics and government—1880-1910.

Transvestism.

THOMPSON, Charles John Samuel, 1862-1943. 301.41
The mysteries of sex : women who posed as men and men who impersonated women / by C. J. S. Thompson. New York : Causeway Books, [1974] 256 p., [8] leaves of plates. : ill. ; 24 cm. [HQ77.T5] 73-83733 7.95
1. Transvestism. 2. Impersonators, Male—Biography. 3. Impersonators, Female—Biography. I. Title.

Trantino, Tommy.

TRANTINO, Tommy, 1938- 818.5409 B
Lock the lock. New York, Bantam Books [1975 c1973] 181 p., illus. 18 cm. Autobiographical. [PS3570.R335Z52] 1.95 (pbk.)
1. Trantino, Tommy. I. Title.
L.C. card no. for original edition: 73-7305.

TRANTINO, Tommy, 1938- 818'.5'409 B
Lock the lock. [1st ed.] New York, Knopf, 1974 [c1973] vii, 170 p. illus. 24 cm. Autobiographical. [PS3570.R335Z52] 73-7305 ISBN 0-394-48885-7 6.95
1. Trantino, Tommy. I. Title.
Pbk. 1.95; ISBN 0-394-70985-3.

Trapnell, Garrett Brock, 1938-

ASINOF, Eliot, 1919- 364.1'62
The fox is crazy too : the true story of Garrett Trapnell, adventurer, skyjacker, bank robber, con man, lover / by Eliot Asinof. New York : Morrow, 1976. 308 p. ; 22 cm. [HV6248.T73A74] 75-17937 ISBN 0-688-02964-7 : 8.95
1. Trapnell, Garrett Brock, 1938- I. Title.

Trapp Family Singers.

TRAPP, Maria Augusta. 927.8
The story of the Trapp Family Singers. [New York] Dell [1960, c.1949] 352p. 17cm. (F106) .50 pap.,
1. Trapp Family Singers. 2. Musicians—Correspondence, reminiscences, etc. I. Title.

TRAPP, Maria Augusta. 927.8
The story of the Trapp Family Singers. Garden City, N.Y., Image Books [1957, c1949] 312 p. 18 cm. (A Doubleday image book, D46) [[ML400]] 57-477
1. Trapp Family Singers. 2. Musicians — Correspondence, reminiscences, etc. I. Title.

Trapp, Maria Augusta.

TRAPP, Maria Augusta. 784'.092'4 B
Maria, by Maria von Trapp. [1st ed.] Carol Stream, Ill., Creation House [1972] 203 p. illus. 23 cm. Autobiographical. [ML429.T7A3] 72-81112 5.95 202

Trasher, Lillian Hunt, 1887-

HOWELL, Beth Prim. 922
Lady on a donkey. [1st ed.] New York, Dutton, 1960. 224 p. illus. 21 cm. [HV1345.A82A84] 60-12101
1. Trasher, Lillian Hunt, 1887- 2. Assiut, Egypt. Orphanage. I. Title.

SUMRALL, Lester Frank, 1913- 922
Lillian Trasher, the Nile mother. Springfield, Mo., Gospel Pub. House [1951] xiii, 177 p. illus., ports., map. 20 cm. [BV3572.T7S8] 51-5459
1. Trasher, Lillian Hunt,1887- . I. Title.

Trasvina, Cesar—Juvenile literature.

RUIZ, Jesse N. 917.3'06'6872
El gran Cesar, by Jesse N. Ruiz. Menlo Park, Calif., Educational Consulting Associates [1973] 83 p. (chiefly illus.) 18 cm. Spanish and English. A young Californian of Mexican descent describes his home, family, school, daily activities, and cultural heritage. [E184.M5R84] 73-78219 2.95 (pbk.)
1. Trasvina, Cesar—Juvenile literature. 2. Mexican Americans—Juvenile literature. I. Title.

Publisher's address: Box 1057, Menlo Park, Calif. 94025.

Traubel, Helen.

TRAUBEL, Helen. 927.8
St. Louis woman. In collaboration with Richard G. Hubler. With an introd. by Vincent Sheean. [1st ed.] New York, Duell, Sloan and Pearce [1959] 296 p. illus. 21 cm. Autobiography. [ML420.T5A3] 59-5557
1. Musicians — Correspondence, reminiscences, etc. I. Title. BIP

TRAUBEL, Helen. 782.1'092'4 B
St. Louis woman / Helen Traubel, in collaboration with Richard G. Hubler. New York : Arno Press, 1977, c1959. xiv, 296 p., [2] leaves of plates : ill. ; 23 cm. (Opera biographies) Reprint of the ed. published by Duell, Sloan and Pearce, New York. [ML420.T75A3 1977] 76-29974 ISBN 0-405-09712-3 : 19.00
1. Traubel, Helen. 2. Singers—United States—Biography. I. Hubler, Richard Gibson, 1912- joint author. II. Title.

Traumatology—Biography.

CURRY, George J. 617.1'00922 B
Profiles in trauma, by George J. Curry, Isidore Cohn [and] Franklin V. Wade. Springfield, Ill., C. C. Thomas [1969] xxii, 262 p. ports. 24 cm. Bibliography: p. 262. [RD131.C87] 69-16878
1. Traumatology—Biography. 2. Surgeons—Biography. I. Cohn, Isidore, 1921- joint author. II. Wade, Franklin V., 1924- joint author. III. Title.

Travelers, Women.

MIDDLETON, Dorothy. 910.922
Victorian lady travellers. [1st ed.] New York, Dutton, 1965. xiii, 182 p. illus., map, ports. 22 cm. Bibliography: p. 177-178. [CT3203.M5 1965a] 65-19958
1. Travelers, Women. I. Title.

Travell, Janet,

TRAVELL, Janet, 1901- 610'.924 B
Office hours: day and night; the autobiography of Janet Travell, M.D. New York, World Pub. Co. [1968] xvi, 496 p. ports. 24 cm. (An NAL book) "Bibliography of writings by the author": p. 474-480. Bibliographical footnotes. [R154.T674A3] 68-57422 7.95
I. Title.

Traven, B.—Biography.

STONE, Judy, 1924- 813'.5'2 B
The mystery of B. Traven / Judy Stone. Los Altos, Calif. : W. Kaufmann, c1977. viii, 128 p. : port. ; 24 cm. Includes index. Bibliography: p. 123-128. [PT3919.T7Z89] 76-54942 ISBN 0-913232-32-7 : 6.95
1. Traven, B.—Biography. 2. Traven, B.—Interviews. 3. Authors, Mexican—20th century—Biography. 4. Authors, German—20th century—Biography. I. Title. BIP

Travers, Austin.

TRAVERS, Austin. 070.9'2'4 B
Stumbling blocks and stepping-stones : an autobiography / Austin Travers. Ilfracombe : Stockwell, 1976. 45 p. ; 18 cm. (A Pocket-book autobiography) [CT788.T715A37 1976] 77-363461 ISBN 0-7223-0913-9 : £0.75
1. Travers, Austin. 2. England—Biography. I. Title.

Travis, John Mastin,

TRAVIS, John Mastin, 1877- 610'.92'4
Of many, one; an autobiography. [1st ed.] Jacksonville, Tex., Kiely Print. Co., 1963. 114 p. illus., ports. 22 cm. [R154.T675A3] 73-207469
I. Title.

Travis, Richard Charles, 1886-1918.

GASSON, James Arthur 993.1'02'0924
Travis, V. C., by James Gasson. Wellington, Auckland [etc.] Reed [1966] 127p. illus., ports. 23cm. [DU422.T7G3] 67-85520 5.00 bds.,
1. Travis, Richard Charles, 1886-1918. I. Title.
American distributor: Tri-Ocean, San Francisco.

Travis, William Barret, 1809-1836.

MCCALEB, Walter Flavius, 1873- 923.273
William Barret Travis. San Antonio, Naylor Co. [1957] 96p. illus. 20cm. [F389.T7M3] 57-2849
1. Travis, William Barret, 1809-1836. 2. Texas—History, Juvenile. I. Title.

MCDONALD, Archie P. 976.4'03'0924 B
Travis / Archie P. McDonald. Austin, Tex. : Jenkins Pub. Co., 1976. 214 p. : ill. ; 23 cm. Includes index. Bibliography: p. 197-206. [F390.T75M3] 76-55914 12.50
1. Travis, William Barret, 1809-1836. 2. Texas—Militia—Biography. 3. Soldiers—Texas—Biography. 4. Alamo—Siege, 1836. BIP

TURNER, Martha Anne. 976.4'03'0924 B
William Barret Travis: his sword and his pen. [1st ed. Waco, Tex., Texian Press, 1972] xv, 318 p. illus. 26 cm. Includes bibliographical references. [F389.T7T87] 70-177901 12.00
1. Travis, William Barret, 1809-1836. 2. Texas—History—To 1846. 3. Alamo—Siege, 1836. I. Title.

Travolta, John, 1954-

MUNSHOWER, Suzanne L. 791'.092'4 B
John Travolta / by Suzanne Munshower ; edited by Barbara Williams Prabhu. New York : Grosset & Dunlap, 1979, c1978 92 p. : ill. ; 21 cm. Abridged from the author's John Travolta scrapbook. A biography of a young actor best known for his role in the television series "Welcome back, Kotter" and the movie "Saturday Night Fever." [PN2287.T73M81978] 78-59480 ISBN 0-448-26270-3 : 4.99
1. Travolta, John, 1954- 2. Travolta, John, 1954- 3. Actors—United States—Biography. 4. Actors and actresses. I. Prabhu, Barbara Williams. II. Title.

MUNSHOWER, Suzanne L. 791'.092'4 B
The John Travolta scrapbook : an illustrated biography / by Suzanne Munshower. New York : Sunridge Press, c1978. 121 p. : ill. ; 28 cm. "Adapted from [the author's] book Meet John Travolta." [PN2287.T73M8] 78-52375 ISBN 0-441-40632-7 : 4.95
1. Travolta, John, 1954- 2. Actors—United States—Biography. I. Munshower, Suzanne L. Meet John Travolta. II. Title.

Travolta, John, 1954- —Juvenile literature.

JACOBS, Linda. 791.45'028'0924 B
John Travolta : making an impact / by Linda Jacobs. St. Paul : EMC Corp., 1977. 38 p. : ill. ; 23 cm. (Center stage) A brief biography of the popular actor appearing in the television series "Welcome Back Kotter." [PN2287.T73J3] 92 77-24995 ISBN 0-88436-412-7 lib.bdg. : 4.95 ISBN 0-88436-413-5 pbk. : 2.95
1. Travolta, John, 1954- —Juvenile literature. 2. Actors—United States—Biography—Juvenile literature. I. Title. II. Series. BIP

Treadgold, Arthur Newton Christian, 1863-1951.

GREEN, Lewis, 1925- 971.9'1'020924 B
The gold hustlers / Lewis Green. Anchorage : Alaska Northwest Pub. Co., c1977. xv, 339 p. : ill. ; 22 cm. Includes index. Bibliography: p. [322]-329. [F1095.K5G73] 77-7341 ISBN 0-88240-0886-6 pbk. : 7.95
1. Treadgold, Arthur Newton Christian, 1863-1951. 2. Klondike gold fields. 3. Mining engineers—Yukon Territory—Biography. 4. Yukon Territory—Biography. I. Title. BIP

Trease, Geoffrey, 1909-—Biography.

TREASE, Geoffrey, 1909- 828'.9'1209 B
Laughter at the door : a continued autobiography / Geoffrey Trease. New York : St. Martin's Press, 1974. 186 p. ; 23 cm. "List of books by Geoffrey Trease": p. [185]-186. [PR6039.R33Z52 1974] 74-79598 8.95
1. Trease, Geoffrey, 1909-—Biography. I. Title.

Treasure-trove.

MARX, Robert F., 1933- 910.4'53
Always another adventure, by Robert F. Marx. Cleveland, World Pub. Co. [1967] 332 p. illus., ports. 22 cm. Autobiographical. [G530.M3137 1967] 67-24468
1. Treasure-trove. I. Title.

Treat, Robert, 1622-1710.

SCULLY, Charles Alison, 1887- 929.2
Robert Treat, 1622-1710. Philadelphia, 1959. 133 l. 29cm. Includes bibliography. [F97.T78S3] 59-3465
1. Treat, Robert, 1622-1710. 2. Treat family. I. Title.

Treblinka (Concentration camp)—Addresses, essays, lectures.

THE Death camp 940.53'1503'924
Treblinka : a documentary / edited by Alexander Donat ; [cover design by Eric Gluckman]. New York : Holocaust Library : [distributed by Schocken Books], c1979. 320 p. : ill. ; 22 cm. Bibliography: p. 320. [D805.P7D37] 79-53471 ISBN 0-89604-009-7 : 4.95
1. Treblinka (Concentration camp)—Addresses, essays, lectures. 2. Holocaust, Jewish (1939-1945)—Personal narratives. I. Donat, Alexander. BIP

Tree, Herbert Beerbohm, Sir, 1853-1917.

BINGHAM, Madeleine, Baroness Clanmorris. 792'.028'0924 B
The great lover : the life and art of Herbert Beerbohm Tree / Madeleine Bingham. 1st American ed. New York : Atheneum, 1979. viii, 293 p., [8] leaves of plates : ill. ; 23 cm. Includes index. Bibliography: p. [275]-277. [PN2598.T7B5 1979] 78-65197 ISBN 0-689-10950-4 : 11.95
1. Tree, Herbert Beerbohm, Sir, 1853-1917. 2. Actors—Great Britain—Biography. I. Title.

PEARSON, Hesketh, 1887- 927.92
Beerbohm Tree: his life and laughter. New York, Harper [c1956] 250p. illus. 22cm. [PN2598.T7P4 1956a] 55-10699
1. Tree, Herbert Beerbohm, Sir 1853-1917. I. Title.

PEARSON, Hesketh, 1887- 927.92
Beerbohm Tree: his life and laughter. New York, Harper [c1956] 250p. illus. 22cm. [PN2598.T7P4 1956a] 55-10699
1. Tree, Sir Herbert Beerbohm, 1853-1917. I. Title. BIP

PEARSON, Hesketh, 1887-1964. 792'.028'0924 B
Beerbohm Tree; his life and laughter. Westport, Conn., Greenwood Press [1971, c1956] 250 p. illus. 23 cm. Includes bibliographical references. [PN2598.T7P4 1971] 70-138123 ISBN 0-8371-5699-8
1. Tree, Herbert Beerbohm, Sir, 1853-1917. I. Title.

Trefusis, Violet Keppel, 1894-1972—Biography.

JULLIAN, Philippe. FIC
The other woman : a life of Violet Trefusis, including previously unpublished correspondence with Vita Sackville-West / Philippe Jullian and John Phillips. Boston : Houghton Mifflin, 1976. xii, 256 p., [6] leaves of plates : ill. ; 22 cm. Includes index. [PR6039.R39Z7] 823'.9'12 B 76-25141 ISBN 0-395-20539-5 : 10.00
1. Trefusis, Violet Keppel, 1894-1972—Biography. 2. Trefusis, Violet Keppel, 1894-1972—Correspondence. 3. Sackville-West, Victoria Mary, Hon., 1892-1962—Correspondence. I. Phillips, John, joint author. II. Sackville-West, Victoria Mary, Hon., 1892-1962. III. Trefusis, Violet Keppel, 1894-1972. The other woman. 1976. IV. Title.

NICOLSON, Nigel. 821'.912 B
Portrait of a marriage / by Nigel Nicolson. 1st Atheneum paperback ed. New York : Atheneum, 1980, c1973. p. cm. Includes index. [PR6037.A35Z8 1980] 79-25497 ISBN 0-689-70597-2 : 6.95
1. Sackville-West, Victoria Mary, Hon., 1892-1962—Biography. 2. Sackville-West, Victoria Mary, Hon., 1892-1962—Relationship with women—Violet Keppel Trefusis. 3. Trefusis, Violet Keppel, 1894-1972—Biography. 4. Nicolson, Harold George, Hon., 1886-1968—Biography. 5. Authors, English—20th century—Biography. I. Title.

Trefusis, Violet Keppel, 1894-1972—Correspondence.

JULLIAN, Philippe. FIC
The other woman : a life of Violet Trefusis, including previously unpublished correspondence with Vita Sackville-West / Philippe Jullian and John Phillips. Boston : Houghton Mifflin, 1976. xii, 256 p., [6] leaves of plates : ill. ; 22 cm. Includes index. [PR6039.R39Z7] 823'.9'12 B 76-25141 ISBN 0-395-20539-5 : 10.00
1. Trefusis, Violet Keppel, 1894-1972—Biography. 2. Trefusis, Violet Keppel, 1894-1972—Correspondence. 3. Sackville-West, Victoria Mary, Hon., 1892-1962—Correspondence. I. Phillips, John, joint author. II. Sackville-West, Victoria Mary, Hon., 1892-1962. III. Trefusis, Violet Keppel, 1894-1972. The other woman. 1976. IV. Title.

Tregian, Francis, 1548-1608.

BOYNA, Pearl Alexina. 922.242
Francis Tregian, Cornish recusant, by P. A. Boyan and G. R. Lamb. London, New York, Sheed and Ward [1955] 160p. illus. 21cm. Includes bibliography. [BX4705.T74B6] 55-4108
1. Tregian, Francis, 1548-1608. I. Lamb, George, Robert, joint author. II. Title.

Treitschke, Heinrich Gotthard von, 1834- 1896.

DORPALEN, Andreas. 943.08'3'0924 B
Heinrich von Treitschke. Port Washington, N.Y., Kennikat Press [1973, c1957] ix, 345 p. illus. 23 cm. Bibliography: p. 325-335. [DD219.T7D6 1973] 72-85312 ISBN 0-8046-1693-0 16.00
1. Treitschke, Heinrich Gotthard von, 1834-1896.

HEINRICH von 923.243
Treitschke. New Haven, Yale University Press, 1957. ix, 345p. port., map. 24cm. Bibliography: p. 325-335. [DD219.T7D6] [DD219.T7D6] 928.3 57-6337 57-6337
1. Treitschke, Heinrich Gotthard von, 1834- 1896. I. Palen, Andreas. BIP

Trelawny, Edward John, 1792-1881.

ARMSTRONG, Margaret Neilson, 1867-1944. 828'.7'09 B
Trelawny; a man's life. [Folcroft, Pa.] Folcroft Library Editions, 1973. p. Reprint of the 1941 ed. published by R. Hale,

London. [PR5671.T5A9 1973] 73-14577 ISBN 0-8414-2904-9 (lib. bdg.)
1. Trelawny, Edward John, 1792-1881. BIP

TRELAWNY, Edward John, 1792-1881. 828'.7'09 B
Letters of Edward John Trelawny. Edited, with a brief introd. and notes, by H. Buxton Forman. London, New York, H. Frowde, 1910. [New York, AMS Press, 1973] xxiv, 306 p. illus. 23 cm. [PR5671.T5A65 1973] 74-177570 ISBN 0-404-07439-1 14.00
1. Trelawny, Edward John, 1792-1881. I. Forman, Harry Buxton, 1842-1917, ed. BIP

Trelawny, Edward John, 1792-1881—Biography.

GERSON, Noel Bertram, 1914- 828'.7'09 B
Trelawny's world : a biography of Edward John Trelawny / Noel B. Gerson. 1st ed. Garden City, N.Y. : Doubleday, 1977. p. cm. Bibliography: p. [PR5671.T5G4] 76-56294 ISBN 0-385-02678-1 : 8.95
1. Trelawny, Edward John, 1792-1881—Biography. 2. Authors, English—19th century—Biography. I. Title. BIP

HILL, Anne, 1911- 828'.7'09 B
Trelawny's strange relations : an account of the domestic life of Edward John Trelawny's mother & sisters in Paris and London, 1818-1829 / by Anne Hill. Folcroft, Pa. : Folcroft Library Editions, 1977. 36 p. ; 26 cm. Reprint of the 1956 ed. published by Mill House Press, Stanford Dingley, Eng. Includes bibliographical references. [PR5671.T5H5 1977] 77-23561 ISBN 0-8414-4755-1 lib. bdg. : 10.00
1. Trelawny,Edward John, 1792-1881—Biography. 2. Trelawny family.

Tremlett, George.

*TREMLETT, George. 784'.092'4 B
The Rolling Stones. [New York] Warner Books [1975] 174 p. illus. 18 cm. [ML420] 1.25 (pbk.)
I. Title.

Tremlett, Rex.

TREMLETT, Rex. 926.22
Road to Ophir; the autobiography of a prospector. New York, Roy Publishers [1957] 190 p. illus. 22 cm. [[TN140]] 57-9917
I. Title.

Trenchard, Hugh Montague Trenchard, baron, 1873-1956.

BOYLE, Andrew, 1919- 923.542
Trenchard. New York, Norton [c.1962] 768p. illus. 24cm. Bibl. 62-52501 8.50
1. Trenchard, Hugh Montague Trenchard, baron, 1873-1956. I. Title.

Trendle, George W., 1884-

BICKEL, Mary E. 791.43'0232'0924 B
Geo. W. Trendle, creator and producer of: The Lone Ranger, The Green Hornet, Sgt. Preston of the Yukon, The American agent, and other successes. An authorized biography by Mary E. Bickel. [1st ed.] New York, Exposition Press [1971] 193 p. illus. 22 cm. (An Exposition-banner book) [PN1583.T7B5] 79-171704 ISBN 0-682-47348-0 5.00
1. Trendle, George W., 1884-

Trenholm, George Alfred, 1806-1876.

NEPVEUX, Ethel Trenholm Seabrook. 973.7'21'0924
George Alfred Trenholm; the company that went to war, 1861-1865. [Charleston, S.C., 1973] vii, 123 p. illus. 24 cm. Bibliography: p. 111-118. [E467.1.T7N46] 74-154359
1. Trenholm, George Alfred, 1806-1876.

Trepman, Paul.

TREPMAN, Paul. 940.53'1503'924
Among men and beasts / Paul Trepman ; translated from the Yiddish by Shoshana Perla and Gertrude Hirschler. South Brunswick, [N.J.] : A. S. Barnes, c1978. 229 p., [1] leaf of plates : ill. ; 22 cm. [D810.J4T6813] 77-89648 ISBN 0-498-02168-8 : 9.95
1. Trepman, Paul. 2. Holocaust, Jewish (1939-1945)—Poland—Personal narratives. 3. Jews in Poland—Biography. 4. Poland—Biography. I. Title. BIP

Trepper, Leopold, 1904-

TREPPER, Leopold, 1904- 940.54'86'0924
The great game : memoirs of the spy Hitler couldn't silence / Leopold Trepper. New York : McGraw-Hill, c1977. 442 p., [8] leaves of plates : ill. ; 24 cm. Translation of Le grand jeu. Includes index. [D810.S8T65713] 76-7537 ISBN 0-07-065146-9 : 12.95
1. Trepper, Leopold, 1904- 2. World War, 1939-1945—Secret service. I. Title.

Tretyak, Vladislav, 1952-

TRETYAK, Vladislav, 1952- 796.9'62'0924 B
The hockey I love / by Vladislav Tretyak, with V. Snegirev ; translated by Anatole Konstantin. 1st U.S. ed. Westport, Conn. : L. Hill, 1977. p. cm. [GV848.5.T73A3413 1977] 77-9486 ISBN 0-88208-080-6 : 6.95
1. Tretyak, Vladislav, 1952- 2. Hockey players—Russia—Biography. I. Snegirev, V., joint author. II. Title. BIP

Treudley, Mary Bosworth.

TREUDLEY, Mary Bosworth. 973.9'092'4 B
A fool for love of God / Mary Bosworth Treudley. [Winter Park, Fla. : Anna Pub.], c1978. ii, 130 p. ; 23 cm. [CT275.T8694A33] 78-52030 ISBN 0-89305-021-0 : 5.95
1. Treudley, Mary Bosworth. 2. United States—Biography. I. Title.

Treuer, Robert.

TREUER, Robert. 977.6'78 B
The tree farm / Robert Treuer ; drawings by Sandra Sandholm Reischel. 1st ed. Boston : Little, Brown, c1977. xi, 244 p. : ill. ; 22 cm. Autobiographical. [SD129.T74A35] 76-52959 ISBN 0-316-85273-2 : 7.95
1. Treuer, Robert. 2. Tree farms—Minnesota—Bemidji region 3. Bemidji region, Minn. Biography. 4. Country life—Minnesota—Bemidji region. I. Title. BIP

Trevellick, Richard F., d. 1895.

HICKS, Obadiah. 331.88'0924 B
Life of Richard F. Trevellick, the labor orator. New York, Arno, 1971. 226 p port. 21 cm. (American labor: from conspiracy to collective bargaining) Reprint of the 1896 ed. [HD6509.T7H5 1971] 77-156418 ISBN 0-405-02926-8
1. Trevellick, Richard F., d. 1895. I. Title. II. Series.

Trevelyan, Charles Philips, Sir, 1870-1958.

MORRIS, A. J. Anthony. 441.082'092'4 B
C. P. Trevelyan, 1870-1958 : portrait of a radical / A. J. A. Morris. New York : St. Martin's Press, 1979, c1977. 193 p., [5] leaves of plates : ports. ; 23 cm. Includes bibliographical references and index. [DA566.9.T7M67 1979] 78-13022 ISBN 0-312-11242-4 : 17.95
1. Trevelyan, Charles Philips, Sir, 1870-1958. 2. Great Britain—Politics and government—20th century. 3. Statesmen—Great Britain—Biography.

Trevelyan, George Otto, Sir, bart., 1838-1928.

CLARK, Perceval. 828'.8'09 B
Index to Trevelyan's Life and letters of Lord Macaulay, cabinet edition, 1878. [Folcroft, Pa.] Folcroft Library Editions, 1973. viii, 91 p. 26 cm. Reprint of the 1881 ed. published by Longmans, Green, London, which was issued as no. 6, 1879 of Index Society Publications. [DA3.M3T75 1973] 73-11257 17.50
1. Trevelyan, George Otto, Sir, bart., 1838-1928. Life and letters of Lord Macaulay—Indexes. I. Trevelyan, George Otto, Sir, bart., 1838-1928. Life and letters of Lord Macaulay. II. Title. III. Series: Index Society, London. Publications, no. 6, 1879.

CLARK, Perceval. 828'.8'09 B
Index to Trevelyan's Life and letters of Lord Macaulay, cabinet edition, 1878. [Folcroft, Pa.] Folcroft Library Editions, 1973. viii, 91 p. 26 cm. Reprint of the 1881 ed. published by Longmans, Green, London, which was issued as no. 6, 1879 of Index Society Publications. [DA3.M3T75 1973] 73-11257 ISBN 0-8414-3408-5 (lib. bdg.)
1. Trevelyan, George Otto, Sir, bart., 1838-1928. Life and letters of Lord Macaulay—Indexes. I. Trevelyan, George Otto, Sir, bart., 1838-1928. Life and letters of Lord Macaulay. II. Title. III. Series: Index Society, London. Publications, no. 6, 1879.

TREVELYAN, George Otto, Sir, bart., 1838-1928. 915.4'04'31
The competition wallah / by G. O. Trevelyan. New York : AMS Press, 1977. p. cm. Reprint of the 2d ed., with omissions and corrections, published in 1866 by Macmillan, London. [DS413.T815 1977] 75-41272 ISBN 0-404-14782-8 : 21.50
1. Trevelyan, George Otto, Sir, bart., 1838-1928. 2. India—Description and travel—1859-1900. I. Title. BIP

Trevelyan, Katharine,

TREVELYAN, Katharine, 1908- 942.3'74
Fool in love. London, Gollancz, 1962. 245 p. 23 cm. Autobiographical. [CT788.T784A3] 63-4837
I. Title.

TREVELYAN, Katharine, 1908- 920.7
Through mine own eyes; the autobiography of a natural mystic. New York, Holt [1963, c.1962] 243p. 22cm. First pub. in London in 1962 under title: Fool in love. 63-10204 4.50 bds.,
I. Title.

Trevelyan, Paulina Jermyn (Jermyn), lady, 1816 1866—Biography.

TREVELYAN, Raleigh. 820'.9 B
A pre-Raphaelite circle / by Raleigh Trevelyan. Totowa, N.J. : Rowman and Littlefield, 1978. 256 p., [2] leaves of plates : ill. ; 23 cm. Includes index. Bibliography: p. 248-252. [PR5674.T54Z9 1978b] 78-105621 ISBN 0-8476-6025-7 : 18.50
1. Trevelyan, Paulina Jermyn (Jermyn), lady, 1816-1866—Biography. 2. Authors, English—19th century—Biography. 3. Preraphaelites—England—Biography. I. Title. BIP

Trevino, Elizabeth Borton, 1904- —Biography.

TREVINO, Elizabeth Borton, 1904- 813'.5'2 B
The hearthstone of my heart / Elizabeth Borton de Trevino ; introduction by Margaret Cousins. 1st ed. Garden City, N.Y. : Doubleday, 1977. x, 225 p. ; 22 cm. [PS3539.R455Z516] 76-18340 ISBN 0-385-03550-0 : 7.95
1. Trevino, Elizabeth Borton, 1904- —Biography. 2. Authors, American—20th century—Biography. I. Title.

TREVINO, Elizabeth (Borton) 1904- 917.2'03'82
My heart lies south; the story of my Mexican marriage, with epilogue, by Elizabeth Borton de Trevino. New York, Crowell [1972] 252 p. ports. 21 cm. [F1210.T675 1972] 72-185629 ISBN 0-690-56905-X 5.95
1. Mexico—Social life and customs. I. Title.

Trevino, Lee—Juvenile literature.

JACKSON, Robert B. 796.352'092'4 B
Supermex; the Lee Trevino story, by Robert B. Jackson. Illustrated with photos. New York, H. Z. Walck [1973] 72 p. illus. 21 cm. A biography of the famous Mexican-American golfer concentrating on his professional career. [GV964.T73J32] 72-10652 ISBN 0-8098-2093-5 4.95
1. Trevino, Lee—Juvenile literature. I. Title.

MAY, Julian. 796.352'092'4 B
Lee Trevino, the golf explosion / by Julian May. Mankato, Minn. : Crestwood House, c1974. 48 p. : ill. ; 24 cm. (Sports close-up books) Biography of Lee Trevino, a Mexican American golfer who, combining skill and wit, has become a top winner on the professional golf circuit. [GV964.T73M38 1974] 92 74-82743 ISBN 0-913940-08-9
1. Trevino, Lee—Juvenile literature. 2. Golf—Juvenile literature. I. Title.

MORSE, Charles. 796.352'092'4 B
Lee Trevino, by Charles and Ann Morse. Illustrated by Harold Henriksen. Mankato, Minn., Amecus Street; [distributed by Childrens Press, Chicago, 1974] 31 p. col. illus. 25 cm. (Superstars) A biography of Lee Trevino, champion golfer who won three national championships in four weeks—the British, American, and Canadian. [GV964.T73M67] 92 74-2420 ISBN 0-87191-342-9 4.95 (lib. bdg.)
1. Trevino, Lee—Juvenile literature. 2. Golf—Juvenile literature. I. Morse, Ann, joint author. II. Henriksen, Harold, illus. III. Title. BIP

WHEELOCK, Warren. 973'.04'68 S
Tony Perez, the silent superstar ; Lee Trevino, Supermex ; Jim Plunkett, he didn't drop out / written by Warren H. Wheelock and J. O. "Rocky" Maynes, Jr. ; consultants, Jorge Vadivieso, Amalia Perez, Ruben A. Soruco B. St. Paul : EMC Corp., [1976] p. cm. (Their Hispanic heroes of the U.S.A. ; 4) Brief biographies of three Spanish Americans: a professional golfer, a major league baseball star, and a professional football quarterback. [E184.S75W5 vol. 4] [GV697.A1] 920'.0092'6373 75-40231 ISBN 0-88436-246-9. ISBN 0-88436-247-7 pbk.
1. Perez, Tony, 1942- —Juvenile literature. 2. Trevino, Lee—Juvenile literature. 3. Plunkett, Jim—Juvenile literature. I. Maynes, J. O., joint author II. Title. III. Title. Lee Trevino, Supermex. IV. Title: Jim Plunkett, he didn't drop out.

WHEELOCK, Warren H. 973'.04'68 S
Tony Perez, el superestrella callado. Lee Trevino, el supermexicano. Jim Plunkett, no se retiro / Warren H. Wheelock ; adaptacion, J. O. "Rocky" Maynes ; consultantes, Jorge Valdivieso [et al.]. St. Paul, Minn. : EMC, 1976. p. cm. (His Ilustres hispanos de los EE. UU. ; 4) Translation of Tony Perez, the silent superstar. Brief biographies of three Spanish Americans: a professional golfer, a major league baseball star, and a professional football quarterback. [E184.S75W517 vol. 4] [GV697.A1] 920'.0092'6873 920 76-2419 ISBN 0-88436-254-X. ISBN 0-88436-255-8 pbk.
1. Perez, Tony, 1942- —Juvenile literature. 2. Trevino, Lee—Juvenile literature. 3. Plunkett, Jim—Juvenile literature. I. Mayes, J. O. II. Title. III. Title: Lee Trevino, el supermexicano. IV. Title: Jim Plunkett, no se retiro.

Trevithick, Richard, 1771-1833.

ROLT, Lionel Thomas Caswell, 1910- 926.2
The Cornish giant; the story of Richard Trevithick, father of the steam locomotive. New York, St. Martin's [1962, c.1960] 160p. illus. 21cm. (front. port.) 62-7129 3.25
1. Trevithick, Richard, 1771-1833. I. Title.

Trexler, Samuel Geiss, 1877-1949.

DEVOL, Edmund. 922.473
Sword of the Spirit; a biography of Samuel Trexler. New York, Dodd, Mead, 1954. 298p. illus. 22cm. [BX8080.T7D4] 54-7087
1. Trexler, Samuel Geiss, 1877-1949. I. Title.

Trials—U.S.

NIZER, Louis, 1902- 340'.0924
The jury returns. New York, Pocket Bks. [1968,c.1965] 504p. 18cm. (12505) 1.25 pap.,
1. Trials—U.S. 2. Lawyers—U.S.—Correspondence, reminiscences, etc. I. Title.

NIZER, Louis, 1902- 340.0924
The jury returns. [1st ed.] Garden City, N.Y., Doubleday, 1966. 438 p. 25 cm. [KF220.N48 1966] 65-19910
1. Trials—United States. 2. Lawyers—United States—Correspondence, reminiscences, etc. I. Title.

Tribonianus, d. 545?

HONORE, Antony Maurice, 1921- 340.5'4'0924 B
Tribonian / Tony Honore. Ithaca, N.Y. : Cornell University Press, 1978. xvii, 314 p. ; 26 cm. Includes bibliographical references and index. [LAW] 77-79701 ISBN 0-8014-1148-3 : 37.50
1. Tribonianus, d. 545? 2. Lawyers—Byzantine Empire—Biography. 3. Roman law—History. 4. Byzantine Empire—History—Justinian I, 527-565. I. Title. BIP

Triebel, Frederick Ernst, 1865-1944.

COOLEY, Adelaide N. 730'.92'4 B
The monument maker : biography of Frederick Ernst Triebel / Adelaide N. Cooley. 1st ed. Hicksville, N.Y. : Exposition Press, c1978. 32 p., [12] leaves of plates : ill. ; 22 cm. Bibliography: p. 31-32. [NB237.T66C66] 78-103167 ISBN 0-682-49051-2 : 5.95
1. Triebel, Frederick Ernst, 1865-1944. 2. Sculptors—United States—Biography. I. Title. BIP

Trillin, Calvin.

TRILLIN, Calvin. 647'.9573
American fried; adventures of a happy eater. [1st ed.] Garden City, N.Y., Doubleday, 1974. 215 p. illus. 22 cm. [TX633.T74] 73-11637 ISBN 0-385-00440-0 6.95
1. Trillin, Calvin. 2. Dinners and dining—United States. 3. Restaurants, lunchrooms, etc.—United States. 4. Gastronomy. I. Title.

Trinity, Jersey. Jersey Zoological Park.

DURRELL, Gerald Malcolm, 1925- 591'.092'4 B
Catch me a Colobus [by] Gerald Durrell. Illustrated by Edward Mortelmans. New York, Viking Press [1972] 221 p. illus. 23 cm. [QL61.D87 1972] 72-83338 ISBN 0-670-20662-8 5.95
1. Trinity, Jersey. Jersey Zoological Park. 2. Wild animal collectors—Correspondence, reminiscences, etc. I. Title. BIP

DURRELL, Gerald Malcolm, 1925- 591'.092'4 B
Catch me a Colobus / Gerald Durrell ; illustrated by Edward Mortelmans. New York : Viking Press, [1976] c1972. p. cm. (A Viking compass book ; C624) [QL61.D87 1976] 75-41411 ISBN 0-670-20662-8. pbk. : 2.25
1. Trinity, Jersey. Jersey Zoological Park. 2. Wild animal collectors—Correspondence, reminiscenses, etc. I. Title.

Trinity United Methodist Church, Richland Center, Wis.

SCOTT, Margaret Helen. 287'.6775'75
Glory to Thy name; a story of a church. Richland Center, Wis., Richland County Publishers, 1973. 110, xiv p. illus. 26 cm. Bibliography: p. 107-110. [BX8481.R43T747] 73-76879
1. Trinity United Methodist Church, Richland Center, Wis. 2. Richland Center, Wis.—Biography. I. Title.

Tristan y Moscozo, Flore Celestine Therese Henriette, 1803-1844.

DESANTI, Dominique. 301.41'2'0924 B
A woman in revolt : a biography of Flora Tristan / by Dominique Desanti ; translated by Elizabeth Zelvin. New York : Crown Publishers, c1976. p. cm. Translation of Flora Tristan, la femme revoltee. [HQ1615.T7D4613 1976] 75-43739 ISBN 0-517-51878-3 : 9.95
1. Tristan y Moscozo, Flore Celestine Therese Henriette, 1803-1844. I. Title.

Trohan, Walter, 1903-

TROHAN, Walter, 1903- 070'.92'4
Political animals; memoirs of a sentimental cynic. [1st ed.] Garden City, N.Y., Doubleday, 1975. xiii, 411 p. 25 cm. [PN4874.T7A32] 74-2835 ISBN 0-385-01786-3
1. Trohan, Walter, 1903- 2. Journalists—Correspondence, reminiscences, etc. I. Title.

Trollope, Anthony, 1815-1882.

ESCOTT, Thomas Hay Sweet, 1844-1924. 823'.8
Anthony Trollope; his public services, private friends, and literary originals. Port Washington, N.Y., Kennikat Press [1967] xvi, 351 p. illus., port. 22 cm. Reprint of the 1913 ed. "A bibliography of the first editions of the works of Anthony Trollope, compiled by Margaret Lavington": p. [309] -336. [PR5686.E7 1967] 67-27595
1. Trollope, Anthony, 1815-1882. BIP

SADLEIR, Michael, 1888-1957. 823'.8 B
Trollope, a commentary / Michael Sadleir. New York : Octagon Books, 1975, c1927. 435 p. : port. ; 23 cm. Reprint of the rev. American ed. published in 1947 by Farrar, Straus, New York. Includes index. [PR5686.S3 1975] 75-11761 ISBN 0-374-97013-0 : 16.50
1. Trollope, Anthony, 1815-1882. 2. Trollope, Frances (Milton) 1780-1863.

SADLEIR, Michael, 1888-1957. 823'.8 B
Trollope, a commentary / Michael Sadleir. New York : Octagon Books, 1975, c1927. 435 p. : port. ; 23 cm. Reprint of the rev. American ed. published in 1947 by Farrar, Straus, New York. Includes index. [PR5686.S3 1975] 75-11761 ISBN 0-374-97013-0 : 16.50
1. Trollope, Anthony, 1815-1882. 2. Trollope, Frances (Milton) 1780-1863.

SNOW, Charles Percy, Baron Snow, 1905- 823'.8
Trollope, his life and art / C. P. Snow. New York : Scribner, c1975. 191 p., [12] leaves of plates : ill. (some col.) ; 26 cm. Includes bibliographical references and index. [PR5686.S5] 75-4088 ISBN 0-684-14401-8 : 14.95
1. Trollope, Anthony, 1815-1882. I. Title.

STEBBINS, Lucy (Poate) 1886- 823'.8 B
The Trollopes; the chronicle of a writing family, by Lucy Poate Stebbins and Richard Poate Stebbins. New York, AMS Press, 1966 [c1945] 394 p. ports. 23 cm. Bibliography: p. [343]-375. [PR5686.S8 1966] 71-182720
1. Trollope, Anthony, 1815-1882. 2. Trollope family. I. Stebbins, Richard Poate. 1913- joint author. II. Title.

TROLLOPE, Anthony, 1815-1882. 928.2
An autobiography. Garden City, N.Y., Doubleday [1960] 276p. (Dolphin bk., C128) .95 pap.,
I. Title.

*TROLLOPE, Anthony, 1815-1882. 928.2
An autobiography / by Anthony Trollope ; with an introd. by Bradford Allen Booth. Berkeley : University of California Press, 1978, c1947. xxii, 312p. ; 18 cm. Includes index. [PR5686.A5] ISBN 0-520-03722-7 pbk. : 3.95
I. Title.

TROLLOPE, Anthony, 1815-1882. 928.2
An autobiography. With a pref. by Frederick Page and illus. chosen by John Johnson. London, New York, Oxford University Press, 1950. xxvi, 411 p. illus. 21 cm. (The Oxford Trollope. Crown ed.) [PR5686.A5 1950] 51-5315

TROLLOPE, Anthony, 1815-1882. 928.2
Letters; edited by Bradford Allen Booth. London, New York, Oxford University Press, 1951. xxx, 519 p. 21 cm. [PR5686.A55 1951] 51-5349

Trollope, Anthony, 1815-1882—Biography.

TROLLOPE, Anthony, 1815-1882. 823'.8 B
An autobiography / edited by Michael Sadleir and Frederick Page ; with an introd. and notes by P. D. Edwards. Oxford ; New York : Oxford University Press, 1980. p. cm. (The World's classics) Includes index. Bibliography: p. [PR5686.A5 1980] 79-42710 ISBN 0-19-281509-1 pbk. : 4.95
1. Trollope, Anthony, 1815-1882—Biography. 2. Novelists, English—19th century—Biography. I. Sadleir, Michael, 1888-1957. II. Page, Frederick, 1879- III. Edwards, Peter David. IV. Title.

Trollope, Anthony, 1815-1882—Correspondence.

TROLLOPE, Anthony, 1815-1882. 928.2
Letters; edited by Bradford Allen Booth. London, New York, Oxford University Press, 1951. xxx, 519 p. 21 cm. [PR5686.A55 1951] 51-5349

TROLLOPE, Anthony, 1815-1882. 823'.8 B
The letters of Anthony Trollope / edited by Bradford Allen Booth. Westport, Conn. : Greenwood Press, 1979, c1951. xxx, 519 p. ; 23 cm. Reprint of the ed. published by Oxford University Press, London, New York. Includes bibliographical references and index. [PR5686.A55 1979] 78-12349 ISBN 0-313-21156-6 lib. bdg. : 31.00
1. Trollope, Anthony, 1815-1882—Correspondence. 2. Novelists, English—19th century—Correspondence. I. Booth, Bradford Allen, 1909- BIP

Trollope, Frances Milton, 1780-1863.

BIGLAND, Eileen. 928.2
The indomitable Mrs. Trollope. Philadelphia, Lippincott, 1954 [c1953] 255 p. illus. 21 cm. [PR5699.T3Z59 1954] 54-6102
1. Trollope, Frances Milton, 1780-1863. I. Title.

TROLLOPE, Frances Eleanor Ternan. 823'.7 B
Frances Trollope : her life and literary work from George III to Victoria / by her daughter-in-law Frances Eleanor Trollope. New York : AMS Press, 1975. 2 v. : ports. ; 19 cm. Reprint of the 1895 ed. published by R. Bently, London. Includes index. [PR5699.T3Z8 1975] 79-148318 32.00(2 vols set)
1. Trollope, Frances (Milton) 1780-1863.

Trollope, Frances Milton, 1780-1863—Biography.

HEINEMAN, Helen, 1936- 823'.7 B
Mrs. Trollope : the triumphant feminine in the nineteenth century / Helen Heineman. Athens : Ohio University Press, [1978] p. cm. Includes index. Bibliography: p. [PR5699.T3Z715] 78-9940 ISBN 0-8214-0354-0 : 15.00
1. Trollope, Frances Milton, 1780-1863—Biography. 2. Authors, English—19th century—Biography.

JOHNSTON, Johanna. 823'.7 B
The life, manners, and travels of Fanny Trollope : a biography / Johanna Johnston. New York : Hawthorn Books, c1978. x, 242 p., [3] leaves of plates : ill. ; 25 cm. Includes index. Bibliography: p. 229-231. [PR5699.T3Z74] 76-15422 ISBN 0-8015-2557-8 : 10.95
1. Trollope, Frances Milton, 1780-1863—Biography. 2. Authors, English—19th century—Biography. I. Title. BIP

Trosse, George, 1631-1713.

TROSSE, George, 1631-1713. 285'.092'4 B
The life of the Reverend Mr. George Trosse, written by himself, and published posthumously according to his Order in 1714. Edited by A. W. Brink. Montreal, McGill-Queen's University Press, 1974. xi, 140 p. port. 23 cm. Includes bibliographical references. [BX5207.T75A33 1974] 73-79097 ISBN 0-7735-0153-3 9.75
1. Trosse, George, 1631-1713. I. Brink, A. W., ed. II. Title.
Distributed by McGill Queens University Press, New York. BIP

Trotman, Dawson.

WALLIS, Ethel Emilia. 922
Lengthened cords; how Dawson Trotman, founder of the Navigators, also helped extend the world-wide outreach of the Wycliffe Bible Translators. [Glendale, Calif., Wycliffe Bible Translators, 1958] 127 p. illus. 22 cm. [BV3785.T7W2] 58-49551
1. Trotman, Dawson. I. Title.

WALLIS, Ethel Emily. 922
Lengthened cords; how Dawson Trotman, founder of the Navigators, also helped extend the world-wide outreach of the Wycliffe Bible Translators. [Glendale, Calif., Wycliffe Bible Translators, 1958] 127 p. illus. 22 cm. [BV3785.T7W2] 58-49551
1. Trotman, Dawson. I. Title.

Trotskii, Lev, 1879-1940.

ALI, Tariq. 947.084'.092'4 B
Trotsky for beginners / text by Tariq Ali ; ill. by Phil Evans. New York : Pantheon Books, 1980. p. cm. Bibliography: p. [DK254.T6A68] 79-1967 ISBN 0-394-50921-8 : 8.95
1. Trotskii, Lev, 1879-1940. 2. Revolutionists—Russia—Biography. 3. Communist—Russia—Biography. I. Title. BIP

CARMICHAEL, Joel. 947.084'092'4 B
Trotsky : an appreciation of his life / by Joel Carmichael. New York : St. Martin's, [1975] 512 p., [4] leaves of plates : ill. ; 25 cm. Includes index. Bibliography: p. [483]-488. [DK254.T6C37] 75-9471 15.00
1. Trotskii, Lev, 1879-1940.

DEUTSCHER, Isaac, 1907- 923.247
The prophet outcast: Trotsky, 1929-1940 London, New York, Oxford University Press, 1963. xv, 543 p. illus., ports., facsim. 23 cm. The 3d vol. of the author's trilogy, the 1st of which is The prophet armed: Trotsky, 1879-1921, the 2d of which is The prophet unarmed: Trotsky, 1921-1929. [DK254.T6D415] 63-24133
1. Trotskii, Lev, 1879-1940. I. Title.

*DEUTSCHER, Isaac, 1907- 923.247
Trotsky; 3v. New York, Random [1965, c.1954-1963] 3v. (various p.) 18cm. (Vintage Russian lib., V746/8) Contents.v.1. The prophet armed; Trotsky: 1879-1921.--v.2. The prophet unarmed; Trotsky: 1921-1929.--v.3. The prophet outcast; Trotsky: 1929-1940. Bibl. [DK254.T6] 2.45 pap., ea.,
1. Trotskii, Lev, 1879-1940. I. Title.

DEUTSCHER, Isaac, 947.084'092'4 B
1907-1967.
The prophet armed—Trotsky, 1879-1921 / Isaac Deutscher. London ; New York : Oxford University Press, [1980] c1954. p. cm. Includes index. Bibliography: p. [DK254.T6D4 1980] 80-67 ISBN 0-19-281064-2 pbk. : 7.95
1. Trotsii, Lev, 1879-1940. 2. Revolutionists—Russia—Biography. 3. Statesmen—Russia—Biography. I. Title.

DEUTSCHER, Isaac, 947'.084'0924 B
1907-1967.
The prophet outcast: Trotsky, 1924-1940. London, Oxford U.P., 1970. xiii, 543 p. 21 cm. (Oxford paperbacks, 229) Bibliography: p. [525]-532. [DK254.T6D415 1970] 71-852492 ISBN 0-19-281066-9 25/-
1. Trotskii, Lev, 1879-1940. I. Title.

DEUTSCHER, Isaac, 1907- 923.247
1967.
The prophet outcast: Trotsky, 1929-1940 London, New York, Oxford University Press, 1963. xv, 543 p. illus., ports., facsim. 23 cm. The 3d vol. of the author's trilogy, the 1st of which is The prophet armed: Trotsky, 1879-1921, the 2d of which is The prophet unarmed: Trotsky, 1921-1929. [DK254.T6D415] 63-24133
1. Trotskii, Lev, 1879-1940. I. Title.

DEUTSCHER, Isaac, 947.084'092'4 B
1907-1967.
The prophet outcast—Trotsky, 1929-1940 / Isaac Deutscher. London ; New York : Oxford University Press, [1980] c1963. p. cm. Includes index. Bibliography: p. [DK254.T6D415 1980] 80-90 ISBN 0-19-281066-9 pbk. : 7.95
1. Trotskii, Lev, 1879-1940. 2. Revolutionists—Russia—Biography. 3. Statesmen—Russia—Biography. I. Title.

DEUTSCHER, Isaac, 947.084'092'4 B
1907-1967.
The prophet unarmed—Trotsky, 1921-1929 / Isaac Deutscher. Oxford ; New York : Oxford University Press, [1980] c1979. p. cm. Includes index. Bibliography: p. [DK254.T6D42 1980] 80-79 ISBN 0-19-281065-0 pbk. : 7.95
1. Trotskii, Lev, 1879-1940. 2. Revolutionists—Russia—Biography. 3. Statesmen—Russia—Biography. I. Title.

EASTMAN, Max, 947.084'0924 B
1883-1969.
Leon Trotsky: the portrait of a youth. New York, AMS Press [1970] viii, 181 p. 19 cm. Reprint of the 1925 ed. [DK254.T6E3 1970] 73-124774
1. Trotskii, Lev, 1879-1940.

HOWE, Irving. 335.43'092'4 B
Leon Trotsky / Irving Howe. New York : Viking Press, 1978. viii, 214 p. ; 22 cm. Includes index. Bibliography: p. [199]-201. [HX312.T75H68 1978] 77-26978 ISBN 0-670-42372-6 : 7.95
1. Trotskii, Lev, 1879-1940. **BIP**

HOWE, Irving. 947.084'092'4 B
Leon Trotsky / Irving Howe. Harmondsworth, Eng. ; New York : Penguin Books, 1979, c1978. 214 p. ; 19 cm. (Penguin modern masters) Includes index. Bibliography: p. [199]-201. [DK254.T6H68 1979] 78-27407 ISBN 0-14-005002-7 pbk. : 2.95
1. Trotsii, Lev, 1879-1940. 2. Kommunisticheskaia partiia Sovetskogo Soiuza—Biography. 3. Revolutionists—Russia—Biography. 4. Communists—Russia—Biography.

LEON Trotsky: the 947.084'0924
man and his work. Reminiscences and appraisals, by Joseph Hansen [and others] New York, Merit Publishers [1969] 128 p. illus., ports. 28 cm. Contents.Contents.—The attempted assassination of Leon Trotsky, by J. Hansen.—To the memory of the old man, by J. P. Cannon.—With Trotsky to the end, by J. Hansen.—Trotsky's last battle against the revisionists, by J. Hansen.—How it happened, by N. S. Trotsky.—Father and son, by N. S. Trotsky.—Lev Davidovich, by J. van Heijenoort.—On the same plane as Marx, Engels and Lenin, by F. Dobbs.—A speech to the youth on Trotsky, by J. Hansen.—On some critics of Trotsky, by J. van Heijenoort.—Revolutionary teacher of the colonial peoples, by L. Fu-jen.—How the Fourth International was conceived, by J. van Heijenoort.—With Trotsky in Mexico, by C. Cornell.—Trotsky's struggle for the Fourth International, by J. G. Wright.—The man and his works, by E. Germain.—A fictionized version of the murder, by A. Rosmer.—Trotsky "psychoanalyzed", by J. Hansen.—Trotsky's place iReminiscences and appraisals, by Joseph Hansen [and others] New York, Merit Publishers [1969] 128 p. illus., ports. 28 cm. Contents.Contents.—The attempted assassination of Leon Trotsky, by J. Hansen.—To the memory of the old man, by J. P. Cannon.—With Trotsky to the end, by J. Hansen.—Trotsky's last battle against the revisionists, by J. Hansen.—How it happened, by N. S. Trotsky.—Father and son, by N. S. Trotsky.—Lev Davidovich, by J. va
1. Trotskii, Lev, 1879-1940. I. Hansen, Joseph.

PAYNE, Pierre 947.084'092'4 B
Stephen Robert, 1911-
The life and death of Trotsky / by Robert Payne. New York : McGraw-Hill, c1977. p. cm. Includes index. Bibliography: p. [DK254.T6P35] 77-7523 ISBN 0-07-048940-8 : 12.50
1. Trotskii, Lev, 1879-1940. 2. Revolutionists—Russia—Biography. 3. Communists—Russia—Biography. I. Title. **BIP**

SERGE, Victor, 947.084'092'4 B
1890-1947.
The life and death of Leon Trotsky / Victor Serge and Natalia Sedova Trotsky ; translated by Arnold J. Pomerans. New York : Basic Books, c1975. 296 p. ; 22 cm. Translation of Vie et mort de Trotsky. Includes bibliographical references and index. [DK254.T6S413] 75-3759 ISBN 0-465-03942-1 : 10.95
1. Trotskii, Lev, 1879-1940. I. Trotskaia, Nataliia Ivanovna Sedova, 1882-1962, joint author. II. Title.

SMITH, Irving H., 947.084'092'4 B
comp.
Trotsky. Edited by Irving H. Smith. Englewood Cliffs, N.J., Prentice-Hall [1973] vii, 181 p. 21 cm. (Great lives observed) (A Spectrum book) Bibliography: p. 177-178. [DK254.T6S54 1973] 73-3226 ISBN 0-13-930974-8 6.95
1. Trotskii, Lev, 1879-1940. I. Title.
pap. 2.45; ISBN 0-13-930066-7. **BIP**

TROTSKII, Lev 1879- 923.2
My life [Gloucester, Mass., P. Smith, 1965, c.1930, 1960] xxii, 599p. 21cm. (Universal lib. bk. rebound) Name orig.:Lev Davidovich Bronshtein [DK254.T6A48] 4.50
1. Russia—Pol. & govt.—1894-1917. 2. Russia—Pol. & govt.—1917- I. Title.

TROTSKII, Lev, 1879-1940. 923.247
Diary in exile, 1935. Translated from the Russian by Elena Zarudnaya. Cambridge, Harvard University Press, 1958. 218 p. illus. 22 cm. Name originally: Lev Davidovich Bronshtein. [DK254.T6A43] 58-13548
I. Title.

TROTSKII, Lev, 1879- 923.247
1940.
Diary in exile, 1935. Translated from the Russian by Elena Zarudnaya Cambridge, Harvard University Press, 1958. 218 p. illus. 22 cm. [DK254.T6A43] 58-13548
I. Title.

TROTSKII, Lev, 1879-1940. 923.247
My life. New York, Grosset & Dunlap [1960] 599 p. 21 cm. (The Universal library, UL-72) [DK254.T6A48] 60-2423
1. Russia — Pol. & govt. — 1894-1917. 2. Russia — Pol. & govt. — 1917- Name originally: Lev Davidovich Bronshtein. I. Title.

TROTSKII, Lev, 947.084'0924 B
1879-1940.
My life [by] Leon Trotsky. Gloucester, Mass., P. Smith, 1970 [c1960] xxii, 599 p. 21 cm. Translation of Moia zhizn' (romanized form) [DK254.T6A48 1970b] 72-20244
1. Russia—Politics and government—1894-1917. 2. Russia—Politics and government—1917- I. Title.

TROTSKII, Lev, 1879- 947.084'0924
1940.
My life [by] Leon Trotsky. New York, Grosset [1973, c.1960] 599 p. 21 cm. (Universal library, UL-77) First published in 1930. [DK254.T6A48 1960] 60-2423 ISBN 0-448-00072-5 pap., 3.85
1. Russia—Politics and government—1894-1917. 2. Russia—Politics and government, 1917- I. Title.

TROTSKII, Lev, 947.084'0924 B
1879-1940.
My life; an attempt at an autobiography [by] Leon Trotsky. With an introd. by Joseph Hansen. New York, Pathfinder Press, 1970. xxxvii, 602 p. 23 cm. (A Merit book) Translation of Moia zhizn' (romanized form) [DK254.T6A48 1970] 73-108715 12.50
1. Russia—Politics and government—1894-1917. 2. Russia—Politics and government—1917- I. Title.

TROTSKII, Lev, 335.43'092'2 B
1879-1940.
Portraits, political & personal / by Leon Trotsky ; [edited by George Breitman and George Saunders]. 1st ed. New York : Pathfinder Press, 1977. 237, [1] p. : ill. ; 23 cm. Includes index. Bibliography: p. [238] [HX23.T74 1977] 77-50342 ISBN 0-87348-503-3 : 11.00. ISBN 0-87348-504-1 pbk. : 2.95
1. Communists—Biography. 2. Communists—Russia—Biography. 3. Socialists—Biography. I. Breitman, George. II. Saunders, George, 1936- III. Title.

TROTSKII, Lev, 947.084'092'4 B
1879-1940.
Trotsky's Diary in exile, 1935 / translated from the Russian by Elena Zarudnaya ; with a foreword by Jean van Heijenoort. Cambridge, Mass. : Harvard University Press, 1976. xvii, 218 p., [5] leaves of plates : ill., facsims. ; 22 cm. Includes index. [DK254.T6A43 1976] 75-42972 ISBN 0-674-91006-0 : 10.00
1. Trotskii, Lev, 1879-1940. 2. Revolutionists—Russia—Biography. 3. Communists—Russia—Biography. I. Title. II. Title: Diary in exile, 1935.

VAN HEIJENOORT, 947.084'092'4 B
Jean, 1912-
With Trotsky in exile : from Prinkipo to Coyoacan / Jean van Heijenoort. Cambridge : Harvard University Press, 1978. ix, 164 p. : ill. ; 24 cm. Includes index. [DK254.T6V36] 78-935 ISBN 0-674-80255-1 : 12.50
1. Trotskii, Lev, 1879-1940. 2. Van Heijenoort, Jean, 1912- 3. Revolutionists—Russia—Biography. 4. Statesmen—Russia—Biography. 5. Secretaries—Biography. I. Title.

WARTH, Robert D. 947.084'092'4 B
Leon Trotsky / by Robert D. Warth. Boston : Twayne Publishers, c1977. 215 p. : port. ; 24 cm. (Twayne's world leaders series ; TWLS 63) Includes index. Bibliography: p. 201-206. [DK254.T6W37] 77-8944 ISBN 0-8057-7720-2 lib.bdg. : 8.95
1. Trotskii, Lev, 1879-1940. 2. Statesmen—Russia—Biography. 3. Revolutionists—Russia—Biography. I. Title. **BIP**

WOLFE, Bertram David, 923.247
1896-
Three who made a revolution, a biographical history. [4th rev. ed.] New York, Dial 1964 [c.1948, 1964] 661p. ports. 22cm. 48-8725 7.50
1. Lenin, Vladimir Il'ich, 1870-1924. 2. Trotski, Lev, 1879-1940. 3. Stalin, Iosif, 1879-1953. I. Title.

WOLFE, Bertram David, 947.08
1896-
Three who made a revolution; a biographical history. [4th rev. ed.] New York, Dial Press, 1964. viii, 659 p. ports. 22 cm. [DK254.L4W6 1964] 64-3227
1. Lenin, Vladimir Il'ich, 1870-1924. 2. Trotskii, Lev, 1879-1940. 3. Stalin, Iosif, 1879-1953. I. Title.

WOLFE, Bertram David, 947.080922
1896-
Three who made a revolution; a biographical history [by] Bertram D. Wolfe. With a new introd. by Allen Dulles. New York, Time, inc. [1964- ports. 21 cm. (Time reading program special edition) [DK254.L4W62] 66-1200
1. Lenin, Vladimir Il'ich, 1870-1924. 2. Trotskill, Lev, 1879-1940. 3. Stalin, Iosif, 1879-1953. I. Title.

WOLFE, Bertram David, 647.08
1896-
Three who made a revolution, a biographical history, by Bertram D. Wolfe. [4th rev. ed. New York, Dell Pub. & Co.] 1964. viii, 659 p. facsims, ports. 21 cm. (A Delta book) "8869" Bibliographical footnotes. [DK254.L4W6 1964a] 64-4595
1. Lenin, Vladimir Il'ich, 1870-1924. 2. Trotskii, Lev. 1879-1940. 3. Stalin, Iosif, 1879-1953. I. Title.

WOLFENSTEIN, E. Victor. 335.43
The revolutionary personality: Lenin, Trotsky, Gandhi, by E. Victor Wolfenstein. Princeton, N. J., [Published for the Princeton Center of International Studies by] Princeton University Press, 1967. x, 330 p. 33 cm. Bibliography: p. 319-325. [HX312.L36W6] 67-11035
1. Lenin, Vladimir Il'ich, 1870-1924. 2. Trotskii, Lev, 1879-1940. 3. Gandhi, Mohandas Karamchand, 1869-1948. 4. Revolutionists. I. Princeton University. Center of International Studies. II. Title.

WYNDHAM, Francis. 947.084'092'4 B
Trotsky; a documentary, by Francis Wyndham and David King. New York, Praeger [1972] 204 p. illus. 31 cm. Bibliography: p. 202. [DK254.T6W88] 73-189061 12.50
1. Trotskii, Lev, 1879-1940. I. King, David, 1943- joint author.

WYNDHAM, Francis. 947.084'092'4 B
Trotsky; a documentary, by Francis Wyndham and David King. New York, Praeger [1972] 204 p. illus. 31 cm. Bibliography: p. 202. [DK254.T6W88] 73-189061 12.50
1. Trotskii, Lev, 1879-1940. I. King, David, 1943- joint author.

Trotskii, Lev, 1879-1940—Assassination.

FOURTH 947.084'092'4 B
International
How the GPU murdered Trotsky / by the International Committee of the Fourth International. London : The Committee, 1976. 104] p. : ill., ports. ; 44 cm. On cover: Security and the Fourth International. "The indictment that remains unanswered": [4] p. laid in. [DK254.T6F68 1976] 77-354564 ISBN 0-902030-78-7 : £3.00
1. Trotskii, Lev, 1879-1940—Assassination. 2. Russia (1923- U.S.S.R.) Ob"edinennoe gosudarstvennoe politicheskoe upravlenie. 3. Revolutionists—Russia—Biography. 4. Communists—Russia—Biography. I. Title.

LEVINE, Isaac 364.1'524'0924 B
Don, 1892-
The mind of an assassin / Isaac Don Levine. Westport, Conn. : Greenwood Press, [1979] c1959. p. cm. Reprint of the ed. published by Farrar, Straus, and Cudahy. Includes bibliographical references and index. [DK254.T6L48 1979] 79-9939

ISBN 0-313-20972-3 : 20.00
1. Trotskii, Lev, 1879-1940—Assassination. 2. Mercader del Rio Hernandez, Jaime Ramon, 1914- 3. Assassins—Biography. I. Title.

Trotskii, Lev, 1879-1940—Juvenile literature.

ARCHER, Jules. 947.084'092'4 B
Trotsky, world revolutionary. New York, J. Messner [1973] 191 p. 22 cm. Bibliography: p. 181. A biography of Trotsky, leader of and inspiration for the 1905 and 1917 revolutions in Russia. [DK254.T6A85] 92 73-5381 ISBN 0-671-32615-5 5.25
1. Trotskii, Lev, 1879-1940—Juvenile literature. I. Title.
Library edition 4.79; ISBN 0-671-32616-3.

Trott zu Solz, Adam von, 1909-1944.

SYKES, Christopher, 1907- 943.086'0924 B
Tormented loyalty; the story of a German aristocrat who defied Hitler. [1st U.S. ed.] New York, Harper & Row [1969] 477 p. illus., ports. 22 cm. First published in London in 1968 under title: Troubled loyalty. Bibliographical footnotes. [DD247.T7S95 1969] 69-15266 8.95
1. Trott zu Solz, Adam von, 1909-1944. 2. Hitler, Adolf, 1889-1945—Assassination attempt, July 20, 1944. 3. Anti-Nazi movement. I. Title.

Trotter, Nathan, 1787-1853.

TOOKER, Elva. 923.873
Nathan Trotter, Philadelphia merchant, 1787-1853. Cambridge, Harvard University Press, 1955. xvii, 276 p. illus., ports., maps, facsim., geneal. tables, tables. 24cm. (Harvard studies in business history, 18) Includes bibliographical references. [HF3163.P5T7] 55-5064
1. Trotter, Nathan, 1787-1853. 2. Philadelphia—Comm. I. Title. II. Series. BIP

TOOKER, Elva. 380.1'092'4 B
Nathan Trotter, Philadelphia merchant, 1787-1853. New York, Arno Press, 1972 [c1955] xvii, 276 p. illus. 24 cm. (Technology and society) Original ed. issued as v. 18 of Harvard studies in business history. Includes bibliographical references. [HF3163.P5T7 1972] 72-5080 ISBN 0-405-04729-0
1. Trotter, Nathan, 1787-1853. 2. Philadelphia—Commerce. I. Title. II. Series. III. Series: Harvard studies in business history, 18.

Trotter, William Monroe, 1872-1934.

FOX, Stephen R. 323.1'19'6024 B
The guardian of Boston: William Monroe Trotter [by] Stephen R. Fox. [1st ed.] New York, Atheneum, 1970. ix, 307 p. 23 cm. (Studies in American Negro life) Bibliography: p. [283]-296. [E185.97.T75F6 1970] 78-108822 7.95
1. Trotter, William Monroe, 1872-1934. 2. Negroes—History—1877-1964. I. Title.

Trouppe, Quincy, 1912-

TROUPPE, Quincy, 1912- 796.357'092'4 B
20 years too soon / by Quincy Trouppe. 1st ed. Los Angeles : S and S Enterprises, c1977. 285 p. : ill. ; 23 cm. [GV865.T7A35] 77-73030 ISBN 0-930236-01-7 : 8.95
1. Trouppe, Quincy, 1912- 2. Baseball players—United States—Biography. I. Title.

Trowbridge, Charles Christopher, 1800-1883.

KILFOIL, Jack F. 332.1'092'4 B
C. C. Trowbridge, Detroit banker and Michigan land speculator, 1820-1845 / Jack F. Kilfoil. New York : Arno Press, 1979, c1969. vi, 258 p. ; 24 cm. (The Management of public lands in the United States) Originally presented as the author's thesis, Claremont Graduate School, 1969. Bibliography: p. 255-258. [HC102.5.T76K54 1979] 78-56680 ISBN 0-405-11337-4 : 21.00
1. Trowbridge, Charles Christopher, 1800-1883. 2. Businessmen—Michigan—Biography. 3. Bankers—Michigan—Biography. 4. Michigan—Economic conditions. 5. Michigan—History—To 1837. 6. Michigan—History—1837- I. Title. II. Series: Management of public lands in the United States.

Trubetskoi, Sergei Nikolaevich, kniaz', 1862-1905.

BOHACHEVSKY-CHOMIAK, Martha. 197'.2 B
Sergei N. Trubetskoi : an intellectual among the intelligentsia in prerevolutionary Russia / Martha Bohachevsky-Chomiak. Belmont, Mass. : Nordland Pub. Co., 1976. 310 p. ; 23 cm. Bibliography: p. 273-310. [DK254.T685B64] 75-27492 ISBN 0-913124-21-4 : 20.50
1. Trubetskoi, Sergei Nikolaevich, kniaz', 1862-1905. 2. Intellectuals—Russia—Biography. 3. Philosophers—Russia—Biography. 4. Russia—Intellectual life—1801-1917.

Trubetskoe, Nikolai Sergeevich, Khiaz', 1890-1938.

TRUBETSKOI, Nikolai Sergeevich, kniaz', 1890-1938. 409.2
N. S. Trubetzkoy's letters and notes / prepared for publication by Roman Jakobson, with the assistance of H. Baran, O. Ronen and Martha Taylor. Tha Hague ; Paris : Mouton, 1976 xxiii, 508 p., [7] leaves of plates : ill. ; 24 cm. (Janua linguarum : Series maior ; 47) Text in Russian with pref. and footnotes in English. Includes bibliographical references and indexes. [P85.T75A44 1975] 76-351846 ISBN 9-02-793181-X : 76.00
1. Trubetskoe, Nikolai Sergeevich, Khiaz', 1890-1938. 2. Jakobson, Roman, 1896- 3. Linguists—Correspondence, reminiscences, etc. I. Title. II. Series.
Distributed by Humanities

Trudeau, Edward Livingston, 1848-1915.

HARROD, Kathryn E 926.1
Man of courage; the story of Dr. Edward L. Trudeau. New York, J. Messner [1959] 192p. 22cm. Includes bibliography. [R154.T7H33] 59-12762
1. Trudeau, Edward Livingston, 1848-1915. I. Title.

Trudeau, Margaret, 1948-

TRUDEAU, Margaret, 1948- 971.06'44'0924 B
Beyond reason / Margaret Trudeau. New York : Paddington Press ; distributed by Grosset & Dunlap, c1979. 256 p., [16] leaves of plates : ill. ; 24 cm. Includes index. [CT310.T76A35] 78-26865 ISBN 0-448-23037-2 pbk. : 10.00
1. Trudeau, Margaret, 1948- 2. Trudeau, Pierre Elliott. 3. Canada—Biography. 4. Prime ministers' wives—Canada—Biography. I. Title. BIP

Trudeau, Pierre Elliott.

RADWANSKI, George. 971.06'44'0924 B
Trudeau / George Radwanski. New York : Taplinger Pub. Co., 1978. p. cm. Includes index. Bibliography: p. [F1034.3.T7R32 1978b] 78-67827 ISBN 0-8008-7897-3 : 14.95
1. Trudeau, Pierre Elliott. 2. Prime ministers—Canada—Biography. 3. Canada—Politics and government—1945- I. Title. BIP

Trueblood, David Elton, 1900-

TRUEBLOOD, David Elton, 1900- 289.6'092'4 B
While it is day; an autobiography [by] Elton Trueblood. [1st ed.] New York, Harper & Row [1974] xi, 170 p. 22 cm. [BX7795.T75A37] 73-18680 ISBN 0-06-068741-X 5.95
1. Trueblood, David Elton, 1900- I. Title.

Trueman, Freddie, 1931-

TRUEMAN, Freddie, 1931- 796.358'092'4 B
Ball of fire : an autobiography / [by] Fred Trueman. London : Dent, 1976. 191 p., [16] p. of plates : ill., facsim., ports. ; 23 cm. Includes index. [GV915.T7A29] 76-377425 ISBN 0-460-04304-8 : £3.95
1. Trueman, Freddie, 1931- 2. Cricket players—England—Biography. I. Title. BIP

Truett, George Washington, 1867-1944.

JAMES, Powhatan Wright, 1880- 922.673
George W. Truett, Biography, With an introd. by Douglas Southall Freeman. Memorial ed. Nashville, Broadman Press [1953] 311p. illus. 20cm. [BX6495.T7J3 1953] 53-7935
1. Truett, George Washington, 1867-1944. I. Title.

Truffaut, Francois.

WALL, James McKendree, 1928- 796.43'092'2
Three European directors: Francois Truffaut [by] James M. Wall. Fellini's film journey [by] Roger Ortmayer. Luis Bunuel and the death of God [by] Peter P. Schillaci. Edited by James M. Wall. Grand Rapids, Eerdmans [1973] 224 p. 21 cm. Includes bibliographies. [PN1998.A2W33] 72-84010 ISBN 0-8028-1504-9 3.95
1. Truffaut, Francois. 2. Fellini, Federico. 3. Bunuel, Luis, 1900- I. Ortmayer, Roger. II. Schillaci, Peter P., 1927- III. Title.

Trujillo Molina, Rafael Leonidas, Pres. Dominican Republic, 1891-1961.

CRASSWELLER, Robert D. 972.930530924 B
Trujillo; the life and times of a Caribbean dictator [by] Robert D. Crassweller. New York, Macmillan [1966] xii, 468 p. illus., map (on lining papers) ports. 22 cm. Bibliography: p. 451-459. [F1938.5.T7C7] 66-14689
1. Trujillo Molina, Rafael Leonidas, Pres. Dominican Republic, 1891-1961. I. Title.

ESPAILLAT, Arturo R. 923.17293
Trujillo: the last Caesar. Chicago, Regnery, 1963. xiv, 192p. 21cm. 63-21921 4.95
1. Trujillo Molina, Rafael Leonidas, Pres. Dominican Republic, 1891-1961. I. Title.

NANITA, Abelardo Rene. 923.17293
Trujillo; the biography of a great leader. [1st U. S. ed.] New York, Vantage Press [c1957] 222p. illus. 21cm. Translation of Trujillo de cuerpo entero. Includes bibliography. [F1938.5.T7N282 1957] 56-12781
1. Trujillo Molina, Rafael Leonidas, Pres. Dominican Republic, 1891- I. Title.

ORNES, Coiscou, German E. 923.17293
Trujillo: Little Caesar of the Caribbean. New York, Nelson [1958] 338 p. 24 cm. [F1938.5.T7O7] 58-9038
1. Trujillo Molina, Rafael Leonidas, Pres. Dominican Republic, 1891- I. Title.

ORNES Coiscou, German E. 923.17293
Trujillo: Little Caesar of the Caribbean. New York, Nelson [1958] 338 p. 24 cm. [F1938.5.T7O7] 58-9038
1. Trujillo Molina, Rafael Leonidas, Pres. Dominican Republic, 1891-1961.

Trujillo Molina, Rafael Leonidas, Pres. Dominican Republic, 1891-1961—Assassination.

DIEDERICH, Bernard. 972.93'054
Trujillo : the death of the goat / Bernard Diederich. 1st ed. Boston : Little, Brown, c1978. xxi, 264 p. : port. ; 21 cm. [F1938.5.T7D5] 78-4076 ISBN 0-316-18440-3 : 8.95
1. Trujillo Molina, Rafael Leonidas, Pres. Dominican Republic, 1891-1961—Assassination. 2. Dominican Republic—Presidents—Biography. 3. Dominican Republic—Politics and government—1930-1961. 4. Dominican Republic—Politics and government—1961- I. Title. BIP

Trullinger, Florence Wildman.

TRULLINGER, Florence Wildman. 917.4'03'40924 B
Part of my heart, by Florence W. Trullinger. Philadelphia, Dorrance [1970] vii, 122 p. 22 cm. [CT275.T876A3] 70-120296 3.95
I. Title.

Truman, Harry S., Pres. U.S., 1884-1972.

DANIELS, Jonathan, 1902- 923.173
The man of Independence. [1st ed.] Philadelphia, Lippincott [1950] 384 p. 22 cm. Bibliography: p. 371-373. [E814.D3] 50-9689
1. Truman, Harry S., Pres. U.S., 1884-1972. I. Title. BIP

DONOVAN, Robert J. 973.918'092'4
Conflict and crisis : the Presidency of Harry S. Truman, 1945-1948 / Robert J. Donovan. 1st ed. New York : Norton, c1977. xvii, 473 p., [8] leaves of plates : ill. ; 24 cm. Includes index. Bibliography: p. [442] [E813.D6 1977] 77-9584 ISBN 0-393-05636-8 : 14.95
1. Truman, Harry S., Pres., U.S., 1884-1972. 2. United States—Politics and government—1945-1953. 3. World politics—1945-1955. I. Title. BIP

GIES, Joseph. 973.918'0924 B
Harry S. Truman, a pictorial biography. [1st ed.] Garden City, N.Y., Doubleday, 1968. ix, 178 p. illus., facsim., ports. 27 cm. [E814.G5] 67-19087 6.95
1. Truman, Harry S., Pres. U.S., 1884-

GOSNELL, Harold Foote, 1896- 973.918'092'4 B
Truman's crises : a political biography of Harry S. Truman / Harold F. Gosnell. Westport, Conn. : Greenwood Press, 1980. p. cm. (Contributions in political science ; no. 33) ISSN 0147-1066) Includes index. Bibliography: p. [E814.G67] 79-7360 ISBN 0-313-21273-2 lib. bdg. : 35.00
1. Truman, Harry S., Pres., U.S., 1884-1972. 2. Missouri—Politics and government—1865-1950. 3. United States—Politics and government—1933-1945. 4. United States—Politics and government—1945-1953. 5. Presidents—United States—Biography. I. Title. II. Series. BIP

HARRY Truman: Mr. Citizen. C. H. Schrepfer, photographer. 973.918'092'4 B
Independence, Mo., Independence Press [1972] 33 p. (chiefly illus.) 26 cm. [E814.H34] 73-154178 ISBN 0-8309-0095-0
1. Truman, Harry S., Pres. U.S., 1884-1972. I. Schrepfer, C. H., illus.

HAYNES, Richard F. 973.918'092'4
The awesome power, Harry S. Truman as Commander in Chief [by] Richard F.

Haynes. Baton Rouge, Louisiana State University Press [1973] vii, 359 p. 24 cm. Bibliography: p. 335-345. [E813.H42] 73-81847 ISBN 0-8071-0054-4 12.95
1. Truman, Harry S., Pres. U.S., 1884-1972. 2. United States—Foreign relations—1945- I. Title.

HEDLEY, John Hollister. 973.918'092'4 B
Harry S. Truman, the 'little' man from Missouri / by John Hollister Hedley. Woodbury, N.Y. : Barron's Educational Series, c1977. p. cm. (Shapers of history series) Includes index. Bibliography: p. A biography of the thirty-third president who helped end World War II and established several programs to aid European recovery. [E814.H38] 76-54969 ISBN 0-8120-0518-X : 2.95
1. Truman, Harry S., Pres. U.S., 1884-1972. 2. Presidents—United States—Biography. 3. United States—Politics and government—1945-1953. 4. United States—Foreign relations—1945-1953. I. Title.

MARTIN, Ralph G., 1920- 923.173
President from Missouri: Harry S. Truman, by Ralph G. Martin. New York, J. Messner [1964] 191 p. 22 cm. Bibliography: p. 184. [E814.M35] 64-20154
1. Truman, Harry S., Pres. U.S., 1884-1972. I. Title.

MILLER, Merle, 1919- 973.918'092'4 B
Plain speaking; an oral biography of Harry S. Truman. New York, Berkley Pub. Corp.; distributed by Putnam [1974] 448 p. 24 cm. [E814.M54 1974] 73-87198 ISBN 0-399-11261-8 8.95
1. Truman, Harry S., Pres. U.S., 1884-1972. 2. United States—Politics and government—1945-1953. I. Title. **BIP**

MOLLMAN, John Peter, 1931- 973.918'0924(B)
Harry S. Truman; a biography, by Robert Owens. New York, Monarch Pr. [c.1966] 112p. 22cm. (Monarch notes &study gds., 894-6) [E814] 66-27335 1.00 pap.,
1. Truman, Harry S., Pres. U.S.,1884- I. Title.

ROBBINS, Charles. 973.918'092'4 B
Last of his kind : an informal portrait of Harry S. Truman / by Charles Robbins ; with photos. and captions by Bradley Smith. 1st ed. New York : Morrow, 1979. 159 p., [32] leaves of plates : ill. ; 24 cm. Includes index. [E814.R6] 79-1201 ISBN 0-688-03447-0 : 14.95
1. Truman, Harry S., Pres. U.S., 1884-1972. 2. Presidents—United States—Biography. I. Smith, Bradley. II. Title.

ROSS, Irwin. 329'.023'730918
The loneliest campaign : the Truman victory of 1948 / Irwin Ross. Westport, Conn. : Greenwood Press, 1977, c1968. viii, 304 p., [4] leaves of plates : ill. ; 23 cm. Reprint of the ed. published by the New American Library, New York. Includes bibliographical references and index. [E815.R6 1977] 75-22761 ISBN 0-8371-8353-7 lib.bdg. : 18.50
1. Truman, Harry S., Pres. U.S., 1884-1972. 2. Presidents—United States—Election—1948. I. Title. **BIP**

STEINBERG, Alfred, 1917- 923.173
The man from Missouri; the life and times of Harry S. Truman. New York, Putnam [1962] 447 p. 22 cm. Includes bibliography. [E814.S74] 62-8004
1. Truman, Harry S., Pres. U.S., 1884-1972. I. Title.

THOMSON, David S. 973.918'092'4 B
A pictorial biography: HST. Text by David S. Thomson. New York, Grosset & Dunlap [1973] 152 p. illus. 28 cm. [E814.T56 1973] 70-164475 ISBN 0-448-03141-8 2.95 (pbk.)
1. Truman, Harry S., Pres. U.S., 1884-1972. I. Title.

TRUMAN, Harry S., Pres. U.S., 1884- 973.918
Memoirs. [1st ed.] Garden City, N.Y., Doubleday, 1955-56. 2 v. 22 cm. Contents.Contents.—v. 1. Year of decisions.—v. 2. Years of trial and hope. [E814.T75] 55-10519
1. United States—Politics and government—1945- —Sources.

TRUMAN, Harry S., Pres. U.S., 1884- 923.173
Mr. Citizen. New York, Popular Lib. [1961, c.1953-1960] 238p. (Popular special SP92) .50 pap.,
1. U. S.—Pol. & govt.—1953- 2. U.S.—For. rel.—1953- I. Title.

TRUMAN, Harry S. Pres. U.S. 1884- 923.173
Mr. Citizen. [New York, Geis Associates; distributed by Random House [1960] 315 p. illus. 24 cm. Autobiographical. [ES14.A33] 60-10127
1. U.S. — Pol. & govt. — 1953- 2. U.S. — For. rel. — 1953- I. Title.

TRUMAN, Harry S., Pres. U.S., 1884-1972. 923.173
Mr. President; the first publication from the personal diaries, private letters, papers, and revealing interviews of Harry S. Truman, thirty-second President of the United States of America. By William Hillman. Pictures by Alfred Wagg. New York, Farrar, Straus and Young [1952] 253 p. illus. (some col.), ports. (some col.) 29 cm. [E814.T7] 52-6976
1. United States—Politics and government—1945- —Sources. I. Hillman, William, 1895- ed. II. Title.

TRUMAN, Margaret, 1924- 973.918'0924B
Harry S. Truman. New York, Pocket Books [1973] 660 p. illus. 18 cm. [E814.T8] ISBN 0-671-78647-4 1.95 (pbk.)
1. Truman, Harry S., Pres. U.S., 1884-1972. 2. United States—Politics and government-1945-1953. I. Title. L.C. card no. for hardbound edition: 73-170238.

WOLFSON, Victor. 973.9180924 (B)
The man who cared; a life of Harry S. Truman. [New York] Ariel Books [1966] 146 p. 22 cm. Bibliography: p. 145-146. [E814.W6] 65-19336
1. Truman, Harry S., Pres. U.S., 1884- — Juvenile literature. I. Title.

Truman, Harry S., Pres. U.S., 1884-1972—Juvenile Literature.

COLLINS, David R. 973.918'092'4 B
Harry S. Truman : people's President / by David R. Collins ; illustrated by Paul Frame. Champaign, Ill. : Garrard Pub. Co., [1975] 80 p. : col. ill. ; 23 cm. (A Discovery book) A brief biography of the "common man" from Missouri who became the thirty-third President of the United States. [E814.C64] 92 74-20965 ISBN 0-8116-6318-3
1. Truman, Harry S., Pres., U.S., 1884-1972—Juvenile literature. I. Frame, Paul, ill. II. Title. **BIP**

FABER, Doris, 1924- 973.918'092'4 B
Harry Truman. Illustrated with photos. New York, Abelard-Schuman [1973, c1972] 96 p. illus. 22 cm. Bibliography: p. 94. A biography of the farm boy from Missouri who became a Senator, Vice-President, and finally President of the United States. [E814.F3] 92 72-2076 ISBN 0-200-71905-X 4.95
1. Truman, Harry S., Pres. U.S., 1884- — Juvenile literature. **BIP**

HAYMAN, LeRoy. 973.918'0924 B
Harry S. Truman; a biography. New York, Crowell [1969] 182 p. 21 cm. Bibliography: p. 173-174. A biography of the United States President who made the decision to drop the atomic bomb on Japan in 1945 and whose Truman Doctrine and Marshall Plan have greatly affected United States foreign policy. [E814.H37] 92 75-81953 4.50
1. Truman, Harry S., Pres. U.S., 1884- — Juvenile literature. I. Title.

HUDSON, Wilma J. 973.918'092'4 B
Harry S. Truman; Missouri farm boy, by Wilma J. Hudson. Illustrated by Robert Doremus. Indianapolis, Bobbs-Merrill [1973] 200 p. col. illus. 20 cm. (Childhood of famous Americans) A biography stressing the childhood of the Missouri farm boy who became the thirty-third President. [E814.H82] 92 73-11788
1. Truman, Harry S., Pres. U.S., 1884-1972—Juvenile literature. I. Doremus, Robert, illus. II. Title.

KELTON, Nancy. 973.918'092'4 B
Harry Four Eyes / author, Nancy, Kelton. Milwaukee : Raintree Editions ; Chicago : distributed by Childrens Press, c1977. 31 p. : ill. ; 23 cm. Because of his glasses, the young Harry Truman is taunted by his friends who discover that poor vision doesn't hinder Harry's judgment nor his sense of fair play. [E.814.K44] 92 76-44244 ISBN 0-8172-0453-9 lib. bdg. : 4.95
1. Truman, Harry S., Pres. U.S., 1884-1972—Juvenile literature. 2. Presidents—United States—Biography—Juvenile literature. I. Title. **BIP**

*MIKLOWITZ, Gloria. 973.918'0924 B
Harry Truman. New York, G. P. Putnam [1975] [63 p] illus. 23 cm. (A See and Read Biography) [E814] 74-83008 ISBN 0-399-60918-0 3.96
1. Truman, Harry S., Pres. U.S., 1884-1972—Juvenile Literature. I. Scabrini, Janet, illus. II. Title.

RICHARDS, Kenneth G., 1926- 973.918'0924 B
Harry S. Truman, by Kenneth G. Richards. Chicago, Childrens Press [1968] 94 p. illus., ports. 29 cm. (People of destiny: a humanities series) Bibliography: p. 90-91. [E814.R45] 68-15563
1. Truman, Harry S., Pres. U.S., 1884- — Juvenile literature.

STEINBERG, Alfred, 1917- 92
Harry S. Truman. New York, G. P. Putnam [1963] 223 p. 21 cm. Includes bibliography. [E814.S73] 63-15554
1. Truman, Harry S., Pres. U.S., 1884- —Juvenile literature. I. Title.

Truman, Margaret,

TRUMAN, Margaret, 1924- 920.7
Souvenir, Margaret Truman's own story; by Margaret Truman, with Margaret Cousins. New York, McGraw-Hill [1956] 365 p. illus. 22 cm. [E814.1.T7] 56-8871
I. Title.

Trumble, David, 1867-

TRUMBLE, David, 1867- 971.3'03'0924 B
When I was a boy / David Trumble ; edited by Glen Ellis. [Don Mills, Ont.] : J. M. Dent & Sons (Canada), c1976. 107 p. : ill., ports. ; 22 cm. Text prepared from taped conversations with the author. [CT310.T78A35] 77-375642 ISBN 0-460-95815-1 : 7.95
1. Trumble, David, 1867- 2. Ontario—Biography. I. Title.

Trumbo, Dalton, 1905- —Biography.

COOK, Bruce, 1932- 813'.5'2
Dalton Trumbo / by Bruce Cook. New York : Scribner, c1977. 343 p., [8] leaves of plates : ill. ; 24 cm. Includes index. Bibliography: p. 324-326. [PS3539.R928Z62] 76-42141 ISBN 0-684-14750-5 : 12.50
1. Trumbo, Dalton, 1905- —Biography. 2. Authors, American—20th century—Biography. 3. Screen writers—United States—Biography.

Trumbull, John, 1750-1831.

COWIE, Alexander, 1896- 811'.2 B
John Trumbull, Connecticut wit. Westport, Conn., Greenwood Press [1972, c1936] xi, 230 p. port. 22 cm. Bibliography: p. [215]-223. [PS853.C6 1972] 72-4233 ISBN 0-8371-6094-4
1. Trumbull, John, 1750-1831. **BIP**

TRUMBULL, John, 1756-1843. 927.5
The autobiography of Colonel John Trumbull, patriotartist, 1756-1843; edited by Theodore Sizer. Containing a supplement to [the editor's] The works of Colonel John Trumbull. New Haven, Yale University Press, 1953. xxiii, 404p. ports. 24cm. Bibliographical footnotes. [ND237.T8A32] 53-7771
I. Sizer, Theodore, 1892- The works of Colonel John Trumbull. II. Title.

TRUMBULL, John, 1756-1843. 759.13
The autobiography of Colonel John Trumbull, patriot-artist, 1756-1843. Edited by Theodore Sizer. New York, Kennedy Graphics, 1970 [c1953] xxiii, 404 p. ports. 24 cm. (Library of American art) Contains a supplement to the editor's The works of Colonel John Trumbull. Includes bibliographical references. [ND237.T8A32 1970] 79-116912
I. Sizer, Theodore, 1892-1967. The works of Colonel John Trumbull.

Trumbull, Jonathan, 1710-1785.

WEAVER, Glenn. 923.273
Jonathan Trumbull, Connecticut's merchant magistrate, 1710-1785. Hartford, Connecticut Historical Society, 1956. 182 p. illus. 25 cm. "In its original form, this ... was a dissertation presented to ... Yale University." Includes bibliography. [E263.C5T9] 56-58343
1. Trumbull, Jonathan, 1710-1785. I. Title.

Trumbull, Lyman, 1813-1896.

KRUG, Mark M., 1915 973.7
Lyman Trumbull, conservative radical. New York, A. S. Barnes [c.1965] 370p. ports. 22cm. Bibl. [E415.9.T86K7] 64-16775 7.50
1. Trumbull, Lyman, 1813-1896. I. Title.

Truszkowska, Maria Angela, 1825-1899.

CEGIELKA, Francis A 922.2438
The pierced heart; the life of Mother Mary Angela Truszkowska, foundress of the Congregation of the Sisters of St. Felix (Felician Sisters) Milwaukee, Bruce Press [1955] 76p. illus. 21cm. (Catholic life publications) [BX4705.T794C4] 55-3134
1. Truszkowska, Maria Angela, 1825-1899. I. Title.

Truth, Sojourner, d. 1883.

BERNARD, Jacqueline. 326'.0924 B
Journey toward freedom; the story of Sojourner Truth. [1st ed.] New York, Norton [1967] xiv, 265 p. illus., ports. 24 cm. Bibliography: p. [255]-259. [E185.97.T82] 65-11012
1. Truth, Sojourner, d. 1883. I. Title.

BERNARD, Jacqueline. 301.44'93'0924 B
Journey toward freedom; the story of Sojourner Truth. [1st ed.] New York, Norton [1967] xiv, 265 p. illus., ports. 24 cm. Bibliography: p. [255]-259. Biography of Sojourner Truth, who was born into slavery, freed in 1827, and became famous for her courage, quick wit, and ready challenge as she campaigned for abolition and women's rights in New York and the Midwestern States [E185.97.T82] 92 AC 68
1. Truth, Sojourner, d. 1883. I. Title.

FAUSET, Arthur Huff, 1899- 326'.0924 B
Sojourner Truth; God's faithful pilgrim. New York, Russell & Russell [1971] viii, 187 p. port. 22 cm. Reprint of the 1938 ed. Bibliography: p. 181-182. [E185.97.T85 1971] 75-139920
1. Truth, Sojourner, d. 1883.

GILBERT, Olive. 326'.0924 B
Narrative of Sojourner Truth. New York, Arno Press, 1968. 320 p. illus., facsims., ports. 21 cm. (The American Negro, his history and literature) Reprint of the 1878 ed. "Book of life [by Frances W. Titus": p. [127]-320. [E185.97.T882] 68-29021
1. Truth, Sojourner, d. 1883. I. Titus, Frances W. II. Title. III. Series.

GILBERT, Olive. 326'.0924 B
Narrative of Sojourner Truth, a bondswoman of olden time, emancipated by the New York Legislature in the early part of the present century, with a history of her labors and correspondence drawn

from her Book of life. Chicago, Johnson Pub. Co., 1970. xv, 240 p. illus., facsims., ports. 24 cm. (Ebony classics) On cover: Sojourner Truth: narrative and Book of life. First published in 1850. "Book of life," by F. W. Titus: p. 99-240. [E185.97.T883] 72-102979 4.50
1. Truth, Sojourner, d. 1883. I. Titus, Frances W. II. Title. III. Series.

PAULI, Hertha Ernestine, 1909- 922
Her name was Sojourner Truth. [1st ed.] New York, Appleton-Century-Crofts [1962] 250 p. 21 cm. Includes bibliography. [E185.97.T87] 62-8494
1. Truth, Sojourner, d. 1883. I. Title. BIP

PAULI, Hertha Ernestine, 1909- 922
Her name was Sojourner Truth. New York : Avon Books, 1976c1962. 254p. ; 18 cm. Includes bibliography. [E185.97T89] ISBN 0-380-00719-3 pbk. : 1.50
1. Truth, Sojourner, d. 1883. I. Title.
L.C. no. of 1962 Appleton-Century-Crofts edition: 62-8494.

Truth, Sojourner, d. 1883—Juvenile literature.

MAY, Julian. 301.44'93'0924 B
Sojourner Truth: freedom-fighter. Illustrated by Phero Thomas. Mankato, Minn., Creative Educational Society; distributed exclusively by Childrens Press, Chicago, c1973. [39] p. illus. 24 cm. (Personal close-up books) A brief biography of the northern slave who became the first black woman to give anti-slavery lectures in the United States. [E185.97.T886] 92 74-166235 ISBN 0-87191-228-7 4.95 (lib. bdg.)
1. Truth, Sojourner, d. 1883—Juvenile literature. I. Thomas, Phero, illus. II. Title.

ORTIZ, Victoria, 1942- 301.44'93'0924 B
Sojourner Truth, a self-made woman. [1st ed.] Philadelphia, Lippincott [1974] 157 p. illus. 21 cm. A brief biography of the northern slave who after gaining her freedom became the first black woman to give antislavery lectures in the United States. [E185.97.T888] 92 73-22290 ISBN 0-397-31504-X 5.50
1. Truth, Sojourner, d. 1883—Juvenile literature.

PETERSON, Helen Stone. 301.44'93'0924 B
Sojourner Truth, fearless crusader. Illustrated by Victor Mays. Champaign, Ill., Garrard Pub. Co. [1972] 96 p. col. illus. 24 cm. (Americans all) A brief biography of the northern slave who became the first black woman to give antislavery lectures in the United States. [E185.97.T893] 92 70-182271 ISBN 0-8116-4574-6 2.79
1. Truth, Sojourner, d. 1883—Juvenile literature. I. Mays, Victor, 1927- illus. II. Title.

Truxtun, Thomas, 1755-1822.

FERGUSON, Eugene S 923.573
Truxtun of the Constellation; the life of Commodore Thomas Truxtun, U. S. Navy, 1755-1822. Baltimore, Johns Hopkins Press, 1956. 322p. illus. 22cm. Includes bibliography. [E182.T7F43] 56-11649
1. Truxtun, Thomas, 1755-1822. I. Constellation (Frigate) II. Title.

Truxtun, Thomas, 1755-1822—Juvenile literature.

GRANT, Bruce 923.573
Captain of the Constellation, Commodore Thomas Truxtun. Illustrated by Charles Beck. New York, Putnam [c.1960] 128p. illus. 21cm. (Lives to remember) 60-6875 2.50
1. Truxtun, Thomas, 1755-1822—Juvenile literature. 2. Constellation (Frigate)—Juvenile literature. I. Title.

Ts'ai, Yuan-p'ei, 1867-1940.

DUIKER, William J., 1932- 370'.92'4 B
Ts'ai Yuan-p'ei, educator of modern China / by William J. Duiker. University Park : Pennsylvania State University Press, [1977] p. cm. (The Pennsylvania State University studies ; no.) Includes bibliographical references. [LA2383.C52T753] 77-1748 ISBN 0-271-00504-1 pbk. : 3.95
1. Ts'ai, Yuan-p'ei, 1867-1940. 2. Ts'ai, Yuan-p'ei, 1867-1940—Knowledge—Education. 3. Educators—China—Biography. 4. Education—China—History. I. Series: Pennsylvania. State University. The Pennsylvania State University studies ; no.

DUIKER, William J., 1932- 370'.92'4 B
Ts'ai Yuan-p'ei, educator of modern China / by William J. Duiker. University Park : Pennsylvania State University Press, [1977] p. cm. (The Pennsylvania State University studies ; no.) Includes bibliographical references. [LA2383.C52T753] 77-1748 ISBN 0-271-00504-1 pbk. : 3.95
1. Ts'ai, Yuan-p'ei, 1867-1940. 2. Ts'ai, Yuan-p'ei, 1867-1940—Knowledge—Education. 3. Educators—China—Biography. 4. Education—China—History. I. Series: Pennsylvania. State University. The Pennsylvania State University studies ; no.

Ts'ao, Yin, 1658-1712.

SPENCE, Jonathan D. 951.030924
Ts'ao Yin and the K'ang-hsi Emperor; bondservant and master, by Jonathan D. Spence. New Haven, Yale University Press, 1966. xiv, 329 p. map. 24 cm. (Yale historical publications. Miscellany 85) Bibliography: p. 308-318. [DS754.4.T72S66] 66-21537
1. Ts'ao, Yin, 1658-1712. 2. Ch'ing Sheng-tsu, Emperor of China, 1654-1722. I. Title. II. Series.

Tsai, Christiana.

TSAI, Christiana. 248'.246
Christiana Tsai / by Christiana Tsai ; pictures by James N. Howard. Chicago : Moody Press, c1978. 188 p. : ill. ; 22 cm. Includes bibliographical references. [BR1725.T69A33] 77-25085 ISBN 0-8024-1422-2 pbk. : 3.50
1. Tsai, Christiana. 2. Christian biography—China. 3. Christian biography—Pennsylvania—Paradise. 4. Paradise, Pa.—Biography. 5. Malaria—Biography. I. Title. BIP

Tschichold, Jan, 1902-1974.

MCLEAN, Ruari. 686.2'2'0924 B
Jan Tschichold, typographer / Ruari McLean. 1st U.S. ed. Boston : D. R. Godine, 1975. 160 p. : ill. (some col.) ; 25 cm. Includes index. Bibliography: p. 120. [Z232.T863M3 1975b] 75-13029 ISBN 0-87923-160-2 : 22.50
1. Tschichold, Jan, 1902-1974.

Tschudi, Burckhardt, 1702-1773.

DALE, William. 786.2'3'0924 B
Tschudi, the harpsichord maker. Boston, Milford House [1973] xi, 81 p. illus. 22 cm. Reprint of the 1913 ed. published by Constable, London. [ML424.T8D2 1973] 73-11229 ISBN 0-87821-166-7 10.00 (lib. bdg.)
1. Tschudi, Burckhardt, 1702-1773. 2. Harpsichord. BIP

Tshombe, Moise.

BOUSCAREN, Anthony Trawick. 967.5'03'0924
Tshombe, by Anthony Bouscaren. Introd. by Daniel Lyons. New York, Twin Circle Pub. Co. [1967] iii, 154 p. 18 cm. Includes bibliographies. [DT663.T7B6] 67-66390
1. Tshombe, Moise. I. Title. BIP

Tsvetaeva, Marina Ivanovna Efron, 1892-1941—Biography—Addresses, essays, lectures.

TSVETAEVA, Marina Ivanovna Efron, 1892-1941. 891.78'4209
A captive spirit : selected prose / Marina Tsvetaeva ; editor and translator J. Marin King. Ann Arbor : Ardis Publishers, 1980. p. cm. Translated from the Russian. Includes bibliographical references and index. [PG3476.T75A25 1980] 80-11664 ISBN 0-88233-352-6 : 22.50
1. Tsvetaeva, Marina Ivanovna Efron, 1892-1941—Biography—Addresses, essays, lectures. 2. Voloshin, Maksimilian Aleksandrovich, 1877-1932—Addresses, essays, lectures. 3. Pushkin, Aleksandr Sergeevich, 1799-1837—Appreciation—Addresses, essays, lectures. 4. Poets, Russian—20th century—Biography—Addresses, essays, lectures. 5. Poets, Russian—19th century—Biography—Addresses, essays, lectures. I. King, J. Marin. II. Title. BIP

Tubbs, Frank Dean,

MAGOON, Charles Alden, 1883- 923.773
He dared to think; a biographical memorial to Frank Dean Tubbs, scientist, scholar, historian, theologian, teacher, and inspirer of men, 1864-1939. Manchester, Me., Falmouth Pub. House [1951] 208 p. illus. 21 cm. [LD331.B718T88] 52-18632
1. Tubbs, Frank Dean, I. Title.

Tuberculosis—Biography.

MOONEY, Elizabeth Comstock. 362.1'9'699509 B
In the shadow of the white plague : a memoir / by Elizabeth Mooney. 1st ed. New York : Crowell, c1979. 196 p. ; 21 cm. [RC312.M66] 78-3311 ISBN 0-690-01696-4 : 10.00
1. Tuberculosis—Biography. 2. Comstock, Bess. I. Title. BIP

Tubman, Harriet (Ross) 1815?-1913.

BRADFORD, Sarah Elizabeth (Hopkins) b.1818. 326.92
Harriet Tubman, the Moses of her people. New York, Corinth Books [1961] 149 p. illus. 19 cm. (The American experience series) First ed. published in 1869 under title: Scenes in the life of Harriet Tubman. "Reprint of the expanded second edition of 1886." [E444.T894] 61-8152
1. Tubman, Harriet (Ross) 1815?-1913. BIP

BRADFORD, Sarah Elizabeth (Hopkins) b.1818. 326'.0924 B
Scenes in the life of Harriet Tubman. Freeport, N.Y., Books for Libraries Press, 1971. 132 p. port. 23 cm. (The Black heritage library collection) Reprint of the 1869 ed. [E444.T894 1971] 70-154071 ISBN 0-8369-8782-9
1. Tubman, Harriet (Ross) 1815?-1913. I. Title. II. Series. BIP

BRADFORD, Sarah Elizabeth (Hopkins) b, 1818. 326.92
Harriet Tubman, the Moses of her people. Introd. by Butler A. Jones [Gloucester, Mass., Peter Smith, c.1961] 149p. illus. (Amer. experience ser.) First ed. pub. in 1869 under title: Scenes in the life of Harriet Tubman. 'Reprint of the expanded second ed. of 1886.' (Corinth bk. rebound) 3.25
1. Tubman, Harriet (Ross) 1815?-1913. I. Title.

EPSTEIN, Samuel, 1909- 301.44'93'0924 B
Harriet Tubman: guide to freedom, by Sam and Beryl Epstein. Illustrated by Paul Frame. Champaign, Ill., Garrard Pub. Co. [1968] 96 p. illus. (part col.), ports. 24 cm. (Americans all) A biography of Harriet Tubman stressing her fight for freedom and dedication to the task of freeing other Southern slaves. [E444.E6] 92 AC 68
1. Tubman, Harriet (Ross) 1815?-1913. I. Epstein, Beryl (Williams) 1910- joint author. II. Frame, Paul, illus. III. Title.

HUMPHREVILLE, Frances T., 1909- JUV
Harriet Tubman: flame of freedom [by] Frances T. Humphreville. Illustrated by David Hodges. Boston, Houghton Mifflin [1967] 189 p. col. illus., col. maps. 22 cm. (Piper books) Biography of the Negro woman who escaped from slavery and became a well known figure in the underground railroad as she personally conducted scores of slaves north to freedom. [PZ7.H893Har] 92 AC 67
1. Tubman, Harriet (Ross) 1815?-1913. I. Hodges, David, illus.

STERLING, Philip. 920
Four took freedom; the lives of Harriet Tubman, Frederick Douglass, Robert Smalls, and Blanche K. Bruce [by] Philip Sterling and Rayford Logan. Illustrated by Charles White. [1st ed.] Garden City, N.Y., Doubleday, 1967. 116 p. illus., ports. 21 cm. (Zenith books, Z10) Biographical portraits of four famous Negro Americans who escaped the slavery into which they were born to further the fight for freedom and equality. [E185.96.S78] AC 67
1. Tubman, Harriet (Ross) 1815?-1913. 2. Douglass, Frederick, 1817?-1895. 3. Smalls, Robert, 1839-1915. 4. Bruce, Blanche Kelso, 1841-1898. 5. Negroes—Biography. I. Logan, Rayford Whittlingham, 1897- joint author. II. White, Charles, illus. III. Title. BIP

Tubman, Harriet (Ross) 1815?-1913—Fiction.

HUMPHREVILLE, Frances T., 1909- JUV
Harriet Tubman: flame of freedom [by] Frances T. Humphreville. Illus. by David Hodges. Boston, Houghton [1967] 189p. col. illus., col. maps. 22cm. (Piper bks.) [PZ7.H893Har] 920 67-10459 2.20 pap.,
1. Tubman, Harriet (Ross) 1815?-1913—Juvenile fiction. I. Title.

PETRY, Ann (Lane) 1911- JUV
Harriet Tubman, conductor on the Underground Railroad. New York, Crowell [1955] 247 p. 21 cm. [PZ7.P4473Har] fic 55-9215
1. Tubman, Harriet (Ross) 1815?-1913—Fiction.

Tubman, Harriet (Ross) 1815?-1913—Juvenile literature.

*CHILDRESS, Alice. 812.54
When the rattlesnake sounds, drawings by Charles Lilly. New York, Coward, McCann & Geoghegan, [1975] 32 p. ill. 24 cm. A play about one summer in Harriet's life when she worked as a hotel laundress to raise money for the abolitionist cause. [PZ4] 75-10456 ISBN 0-698-20342-9 5.95.
1. Tubman, Harriet—Juvenile literature. I. Title.

GRANT, Matthew G. 301.44'93'0924 B
Harriet Tubman; black liberator [by] Matthew G. Grant. Illustrated by John Keely and Dick Brude. [Mankato, Minn., Creative Education; distributed by Childrens Press, Chicago, 1974] 29 p. illus. (part col.) 25 cm. (His Gallery of great Americans series. Women of America) A biography of the famous conductor on the Underground Railroad who worked to free her people before, during, and after the Civil War. [E444.T8974] 92 73-15849 ISBN 0-87191-309-7 3.95
1. Tubman, Harriet (Ross) 1815?-1913—Juvenile literature. I. Keely, John, illus. II. Brude, Dick, illus. III. Title.

JOHNSON, Ann Donegan. 301.44'93'0924 B
The value of helping : the story of Harriet Tubman / by Ann Donegan Johnson. 1st ed. La Jolla, Calif. : Value Communications, c1979. p. cm. (ValueTales) Describes the helpful work of Harriet Tubman in aiding slaves to flee the South, in assisting the Union army during the Civil War, and in establishing homes for the old and needy after the war. [E444.T82T63] 79-21652 ISBN 0-916392-41-4 lib. bdg. : 5.95
1. Tubman, Harriet Ross, 1815?-1913—Juvenile literature. 2. Underground railroads—Juvenile literature. 3. Slavery in the United States—Fugitive slaves—Juvenile literature. 4. Slaves—United States—Biography—Juvenile literature. 5. Afro-Americans—Biography—Juvenile literature. 6. Altruism—Juvenile literature. I. Title.

Distributed by Oak Tree Pubs., 11175 Flintkote Ave. Suite C, San Diego CA BIP

KELTON, Nancy. 301.44'93'0924 B
Rebel slave / author, Nancy Kelton ; illustrator, Peg Zych. Milwaukee : Raintree Editions ; Chicago : distributed by Childrens Press, c1977. 31 p. : ill. ; 23 cm. A biography of a young slave whose cruel experiences in the South lead her to seek freedom in the North for herself and others. [E444.T8976] 92 76-46446 ISBN 0-8172-0450-4 lib. bdg. : 4.95
1. Tubman, Harriet Ross, 1815?-1913—Juvenile literature. 2. Slaves—United States—Biography—Juvenile literature. I. Zych, Peg. II. Title. BIP

MCGOVERN, Ann. 92(J)
Runaway slave; the story of Harriet Tubman. Pictures by R. M. Powers. New York, Four Winds Press [1965] 1 v. (unpaged) illus. 16 x 22 cm. [E444.T898] 65-9611
1. Tubman, Harriet (Ross) 1815?-1913—Juvenile literature. I. Title.

Tubman, William Vacanarat Shadrach, Pres. Liberia, 1895-

LIBERIA. Dept. 966.6'203'0924 B
of Information and Cultural Affairs.
Liberia remembers; President Tubman's diamond jubilee, 1895-1970. Monrovia, 1971. 128 p. illus. 30 cm. [DT636.T8L53 1971] 74-152394
1. Tubman, William V. S., Pres. Liberia, 1895-1971. I. Title.

SMITH, Robert 966.6'2'2030924 B
A.
The judgment of history; William V. S. Tubman, a memoir, by Robert A. Smith. Monrovia, Liberia, Providence Publications [1971] iii, 80 l. 25 cm. (Liberian writers series, 16) [DT636.T8S57] 73-170293
1. Tubman, William V. S., Pres. Liberia, 1895-1971. I. Title. II. Series.

SMITH, Robert A. v. 12
The life and work of a great african president and statesman: William V. S. Tubman, President of Liberia. First publication anywhere. [Sinkor, Monrovia, Providence Publication, 1966] iii, 179 l. 28 cm. Mimeographed. Bibliographical footnotes. 67-65966
1. Tubman, William Vacanarat Shadrach, Pres. Liberia, 1895- 2. Liberia — Pol. & govt. I. Title.

SMITH, Robert A. 966.6'203'0924 B
William V. S. Tubman; the life and work of an African President and statesman, by Robert A. Smith. Monrovia, Liberia, Providence Publications [1971] ii, 168 l. 27 cm. (Liberian writers series, 12) [DT636.T8S6 1971] 73-170294
1. Tubman, William V. S., Pres. Liberia, 1895-1971. I. Title. II. Series.

SMITH, Robert A. 966.6'203'0924 B
William V. S. Tubman, 1895-1971; a profile of an African president & statesman, by Robert A. Smith Monrovia, Liberia, Providence Publications [1971] iv, 74 l. 26 cm. (Liberian writers series, 14) [DT636.T8S62] 72-196702
1. Tubman, William V. S., Pres. Liberia, 1895-1971. I. Title. II. Series.

Tucholsky, Kurt, 1890-1935.

POOR, Harold L. 837'.9'12 B
Kurt Tucholsky and the ordeal of Germany, 1914-1935 [by] Harold L. Poor. New York, Scribner [1968] xii, 285 p. illus., ports. 25 cm. Bibliography: p. 265-274. [PT2642.U4Z8] 68-17344 7.95
1. Tucholsky, Kurt, 1890-1935. I. Title.

Tuck, William M., 1896-

CRAWLEY, William 975.5'04'0924 B
Bryan, 1944-
Bill Tuck, a political life in Harry Byrd's Virginia / William Bryan Crawley, Jr. Charlottesville : University Press of Virginia, 1978. x, 281 p. : ill. ; 24 cm. Based on the author's thesis, University of Virginia. Includes index. Bibliography: p. [271]-273. [F231.T82C72] 78-16751 ISBN 0-8139-0766-7 : 14.95
1. Tuck, William M., 1896- 2. United States. Congress. House—Biography. 3. Virginia—Governors—Biography. 4. Virginia—Politics and government—1865-1950. 5. Legislators—United States—Biography. I. Title.

Tucker, Charles Lloyd, 1913-1971.

SMITH, Lois, 1941- 709'.2'4 B
The life and works of Charles Lloyd Tucker / by Lois Smith. [Hamilton?], Bermuda : Smith, [1976?]. 44 p., [2] leaves of plates : ill. (some col.) ; 23 cm. [N6615.B4T827] 77-358582
1. Tucker, Charles Lloyd, 1913-1971. 2. Artists—Bermuda—Biography. I. Title.

Tucker, Cornelia Dabney, 1881-

KITTEL, Mary Badham. 322'.4 B
The first Republican southern belle. [Fort Worth? Tex., 1969] xii, 83 p. ports. 24 cm. [CT275.T925K57] 73-6749
1. Tucker, Cornelia Dabney, 1881- I. Title.

Tucker, George, 1775-1861.

MCLEAN, Robert Colin. 921.1
George Tucker, moral philosopher and man of letters. Chapel Hill, University of North Carolina Press [1961] xiv, 265p. 24cm. Bibliography:p. [235]-251. [BJ354.T8M3] 61-3911
1. Tucker, George, 1775-1861. I. Title.

Tucker, Nathaniel Beverley, 1784-1851.

BRUGGER, Robert J. 975'.03'0924 B
Beverley Tucker : heart over head in the Old South / Robert J. Brugger. Baltimore : Johns Hopkins University Press, c1978. xvii, 294 p. : ill. ; 24 cm. (The Johns Hopkins University studies in historical and political science ; 96th ser., no. 2) Includes bibliographical references and index. [F230.T92B78] 77-16294 ISBN 0-8018-1982-2 : 15.00
1. Tucker, Nathaniel Beverley, 1784-1851. 2. Lawyers—Virginia—Biography. 3. Virginia—Biography. 4. Secession. 5. Slavery in the United States. I. Series: Johns Hopkins University. Studies in historical and political science ; 96th ser., no. 2.

Tucker, Preston, 1903-1956.

PEARSON, Charles T. 923.373
The indomitable Tin Goose; the true story of Preston Tucker and his car. New York, Abelard-Schuman [c.1960] 285p. illus. 22cm. 60-7214 4.95
1. Tucker, Preston, 1903-1956. 2. Tucker Corporation, Chicago. I. Title. BIP

PEARSON, Charles T. 923.373
The indomitable Tin Goose; the true story of Preston Tucker and his car. New York, Abelard-Schuman [c.1960] 285p. illus. 22cm. 60-7214 4.95
1. Tucker, Preston, 1903-1956. 2. Tucker Corporation, Chicago. I. Title. BIP

PEARSON, 338.7'62'92220924 B
Charles T.
The indomitable Tin Goose; the true story of Preston Tucker and his car [by] Pearson. Minneapolis, Motorbooks International Publishers & Wholesalers [1974, c1960] 285 p. illus. 25 cm. Reprint of the ed. published by Abelard-Schuman, London, New York. [HD9710.U54T86 1974] 74-18396 ISBN 0-87938-020-9 9.95.
1. Tucker, Preston, 1903-1956. 2. Tucker Corporation, Chicago. I. Title.

PEARSON, 338.7'62'92220924 B
Charles T.
The indomitable Tin Goose; the true story of Preston Tucker and his car [by] Pearson. Minneapolis, Motorbooks International Publishers & Wholesalers [1974, c1960] 285 p. illus. 25 cm. Reprint of the ed. published by Abelard-Schuman, London, New York. [HD9710.U54T86 1974] 74-18396 ISBN 0-87938-020-9 9.95.
1. Tucker, Preston, 1903-1956. 2. Tucker Corporation, Chicago. I. Title.

Tucker, Samuel, 1747-1833.

SMITH, Philip 359.3'32'0924 B
Chadwick Foster.
Captain Samuel Tucker (1747-1833), Continental Navy / Philip Chadwick Foster Smith; foreword by Robert G. Albion. Salem, Mass. : Essex Institute, 1976. xv, 115 p., [5] leaves of plates (1 fold.) : ill. ; 24 cm. "First published ... as volume 112, no. 3, of the [Essex] Institute's Historical collections." "Limited edition of 500 clothbound copies." Includes index. Bibliography: p. 107-110. [E207.T8S6] 76-17150 ISBN 0-88389-058-5 : 10.00
1. Tucker, Samuel, 1747-1833. 2. United States. Navy—Biography.

Tuckerman, Frederick Goddard, 1821-1873.

GOLDEN, Samuel A. 811.3
Frederick Goddard Tuckerman, by Samuel A. Golden. New York, Twayne Publishers [1966] 176 p. 21 cm. (Twayne's United States authors series, 104) Bibliography: p. 164-169. [PS3104.T5Z66 1966] 66-17065
1. Tuckerman, Frederick Goddard, 1821-1873. BIP

Tudor, House of.

MORRIS, 942.05'092'2 B
Christopher.
The Tudors / [by] Christopher Morris. Revised ed. London : Severn House : [Distributed by Hutchinson], 1976. 202 p. : ill., facsims., geneal. table, ports. ; 21 cm. Includes index. Bibliography: p. 186-189. [DA317.1.M65 1976] 76-381591 ISBN 0-7278-0116-3 : £5.00
1. Tudor, House of. 2. Great Britain—Kings and rulers—Biography. 3. Great Britain—History—Tudors, 1485-1603. I. Title. BIP

PLOWDEN, Alison. 929.7'2
The house of Tudor / Alison Plowden. New York : Stein and Day, [1976] p. cm. [DA317.1.P55] 76-6936 16.95
1. Tudor, House of. 2. Great Britain—Kings and rulers—Biography. I. Title. BIP

ROSS, Josephine. 942.04'092'2 B
The Tudors : Englands golden age / Josephine Ross. 1st American ed. New York : Putnam, 1979. 184 p. : ill. ; 31 cm. Includes index. Bibliography: p. 179. [DA317.1.R67 1979] 79-84036 ISBN 0-399-12417-9 : 15.95
1. Great Britain—Kings and rulers—Biography. 2. Great Britain—History—Tudors, 1485-1603. I. Title. BIP

Tudor, Tasha.

TUDOR, Bethany. 741'.092'4 B
Drawn from New England / by Bethany Tudor. New York : Collins, 1979. p. cm. [NC975.5.T82T82] 79-14230 ISBN 0-529-05531-7 : 10.95
1. Tudor, Tasha. 2. Illustrators—United States—Biography. I. Title.

Tugend, Frank C., 1892-1974.

JURY, Mark. 362.1'9'61360924
Gramp : photographs / by Mark Jury and Dan Jury ; narrative text by Mark Jury. New York : Penguin Books, [1977] p. cm. [R726.8.J87 1977] 77-2366 ISBN 0-14-004526-0 pbk. : 5.95
1. Tugend, Frank C., 1892-1974. 2. Terminal care. 3. Arteriosclerosis—Biography. I. Jury, Dan, joint author. II. Title.

JURY, Mark. 362.1'9'613600924 B
Gramp : photographs / by Mark Jury and Dan Jury ; narrative text by Mark Jury ; [family photos on p. 8 to 10 by Florence C. Tugend]. New York : Grossman Publishers, 1976. xiii, 152 p. : ill. ; 22 cm. [R726.8.J87] 75-35595 ISBN 0-670-00602-5 pbk. : 5.95
1. Tugend, Frank C., 1892-1974. 2. Terminal care. 3. Arteriosclerosis—Personal narratives. I. Jury, Dan, joint author. II. Title.

Tugwell, Rexford Guy,

TUGWELL, Rexford Guy, 923.273
1891-
The light of other days. [1st ed.] Garden City, N.Y., Doubleday, 1962. 404 p. 22 cm. Autobiographical. [H59.T8A3] 62-7690
I. Title.

Tulare Co., Calif.—History.

MITCHELL, Annie 917.94'86'03
Rosalind, 1906-
A modern history of Tulare County. Visalia, Calif., Limited Editions of Visalia [1974] 203 p. illus. 32 cm. Historical text by Annie R. Mitchell. A biographical section prepared by the members of the editorial staff of Limited Editions of Visalia. [F868.T8M58] 74-175879
1. Tulare Co., Calif.—History. 2. Tulare Co., Calif.—Biography. I. Limited Editions of Visalia. II. Title.

Tulloch, James Francis, b. 1848.

TULLOCH, James 979.7'74 B
Francis, b.1848.
The James Francis Tulloch diary, 1875-1910 : the true story of the ups and downs of James and Annie Tulloch and their nine children, all of whom were born and raised on Orcas Island in Washington State's San Juan Islands / compiled and edited by Gordon Keith. 1st ed. Portland, Or. : Binford & Mort, 1978. vii, 124 p., [1] leaf of plates : ill. ; 23 cm. Includes index. [F897.S2T84] 78-56345 ISBN 0-8323-0302-X : 7.95 ISBN 0-8323-0303-8 pbk. : 4.95
1. Tulloch, James Francis, b. 1848. 2. Tulloch family. 3. Orcas Island—Biography. I. Keith, Gordon. II. Title.

Tully, William, 1785-1859.

TULLY, William, 615'.092'4 B
1785-1859.
The journal of William Tully, professor of materia medica and therapeutics, Yale Medical Institution, 1829-1842 / Oliver S. Hayward and Elizabeth H. Thomson, editors ; with a foreword by John F. Fulton. New York : Science History Publications, 1977. p. cm. [RM88.T84 1977] 77-13727 ISBN 0-88202-175-3 : 15.00
1. Tully, William, 1785-1859. 2. Pharmacology. 3. Pharmacologists—Connecticut—Biography.

Tulman, David.

TULMAN, David. 943.9'04'0924 B
Going home / Victor David Tulman, in collaboration with Marcelle Routier ; translated from the French by Eileen Finletter. New York : Times Books, c1977. 302 p. ; 22 cm. Translation of Va-t'en! [DS135.H93T8413 1977] 77-79044 ISBN 0-8129-0701-9 : 10.00
1. Tulman, David. 2. Jews in Hungary—Biography. 3. Hungary—Biography. I. Routier, Marcelle, joint author. II. Title. BIP

Tung, Yueh, 1620-1686.

BRANDAUER, Frederick P. 895.1'3'4
Tung Yueh / by Frederick P. Brandauer. Boston : Twayne Publishers, 1978. p. cm. (Twayne's world authors series ; TWAS 498 : China) Includes index. Bibliography: p. [PL2698.T83H733] 78-19058 ISBN 0-8057-6339-2 lib. bdg. : 12.50
1. Tung, Yueh, 1620-1686. Hsi yu pu. 2. Tung, Yueh, 1620-1686. 3. Authors, Chinese—Biography. I. Title. BIP

Tunis, John Roberts,

TUNIS, John Roberts, 1889- 928.1
A measure of independence, by John R. Tunis. [1st ed.] New York, Atheneum, 1964. 307 p. 22 cm. Autobiographical [PS3539.U52M4] 64-14927
I. Title.

TUNIS, John Roberts, 1889- 808.83
Schoolboy Johnson. New York, W.

Morrow, 1958. 192 p. 21 cm. [Morrow junior books] [PZ.T8236Sc] 58-5728
I. Title.

Turberville, George, 1540?-1610?

HANKINS, John Erskine, 1905- 821'.3
The life and works of George Turbervile. [Folcroft, Pa.] Folcroft Library Editions, 1973. p. "The materials of this volume are in large measure drawn from my doctoral dissertation, submitted to the Yale University Graduate School [1929]" Reprint of the 1940 ed. published by University of Kansas, Lawrence, which was issued as no. 25 of Humanistic studies, University of Kansas publications. Includes bibliographical references. [PR2384.T5Z6 1973] 73-12648 20.00
1. Turberville, George, 1540?-1610? I. Series: Kansas. University. Humanistic studies, no. 25.

Turgenev, Ivan Sergeevich, 1818-1883.

FORD, Ford Madox, 1873-1939. v. 12
Portraits from life; memories and criticisms. Chicago, Regnery [1960, c1937] vii, 301 p. 17 cm. (A Gateway edition) "6059". 66-67809
1. Turgenev, Ivan Sergeevich, 1818-1883. 2. Authors, English. 3. Authors, American. I. Title.

LLOYD, John Arthur Thomas, 1870-1956. 891.7'3'3 B
Ivan Turgenev. Port Washington, N.Y., Kennikat Press [1972] 227 p. illus. 23 cm. Reprint of the 1942 ed. Bibliography: p. 224. [PG3435.L5 1972] 78-160769 ISBN 0-8046-1591-8
1. Turgenev, Ivan Sergeevich, 1818-1883. BIP

MAGARSHACK, David. 928.917
Turgenev, a life. New York, Grove Press [1954] 328p. illus. 23cm. [PG3435] 54-12099
1. Turgenev, Ivan Sergeevich, 1818-1883. I. Title.

PRITCHETT, Victor Sawden, 1900- 891.7'3'3 B
The gentle barbarian : the life and work of Turgenev / V. S. Pritchett. 1st ed. New York : Random House, c1977. xi, 243 p., 4 leaves of plates : ill. ; 25 cm. Includes bibliographical references. [PG3435.P7] 76-53457 ISBN 0-394-49730-9 : 10.00
1. Turgenev, Ivan Sergeevich, 1818-1883. 2. Authors, Russian—19th century—Biography. I. Title.

PRITCHETT, Victor Sawdon, 1900- 891.7'3'3 B
The gentle barbarian : the life and work of Turgenev / V. S. Pritchett. New York : Vintage Books, 1977. p. cm. [PG3435.P7 1978] 77-12555 ISBN 0-394-72526-3 : 10.00
1. Turgenev, Ivan Sergeevich, 1818-1883. 2. Authors, Russian—19th century—Biography. I. Title. BIP

TURGENEV, Ivan Sergeevich, 1818-1883. 928.917
Letters, a selection. Edited and translated from the Russian, French, and German originals by Edgar H. Lehrman. [1st ed.] New York, Knopf, 1961 [c1960] xxvi, 401, xvi p. ports., facsim. 21 cm. "Sources of letters": p. [369]-396. Bibliography: p. [397]-401. [PG3432 1961] 60-10817

TURGENEV, Ivan Sergeevich, 1818-1883. 928.917
Literary reminiscences and autobiographical fragments. Translated with an introd. by David Magarshack, and an essay on Turgenev by Edmund Wilson. New York, Farrar, Strauss and Cudahy [1958] 309 p. 22 cm. Translation of (translated: Literaturnye I zhitelskie vospominania) [PG3431.L5E5] 58-7839
1. Authors — Correspondence, reminiscences, etc. I. Title.

YARMOLINSKY, Avrahm, 1890- 928.917
Turgenev, the man, his art and his age. New York, Orion Press [1959] 406 p. illus. 22 cm. [PG3435.Y3 1959] 59-7894
1. Turngenev, Ivan Sergeevich, 1818-1883. I. Title. BIP

YARMOLINSKY, Avrahm, 1890- v. 12
Turgenev; the man, his art and his age. [1st Collier Books ed.] New York, Collier Books [1961, c1959] 384 p. 18 cm. (Collier Books, BS4) "Bibliographical note": p. 370-372. 63-39073
1. Turgenev, Ivan Sergeevich, 1818-1883. I. Title.

ZHITOVA, Varvara Nikolaevna (Bogdanovich) b. 1833. 920.7
The Turgenev family. [Translated by A. S. Mills] New York, Roy Publishers [1954?] 179p. 19cm. Translation of qTurgeneva, Varvara Petrovna,d. 1850. [PG3435] 54-10480
1. Turgenev, Ivan Sergeevich. 1818-1883. 2. Turgenev, Nikolai Sergeevich, 1816-1879. I. Title.

Turgenev, Ivan Sergeevich, 1818-1883—Biography.

SCHAPIRO, Leonard Bertram, 1908- 891.7'3'3 B
Turgenev, his life and times / Leonard Schapiro. 1st American ed. New York : Random House, c1978. xiii, 382 p., [8] leaves of plates : ill. ; 24 cm. Includes indexes. Bibliography: p. [333]-343. [PG3435.S3 1978] 78-5190 ISBN 0-394-49640-X : 15.95
1. Turgenev, Ivan Sergeevich, 1818-1883—Biography. 2. Authors, Russian—19th century—Biography. I. Title.

YARMOLINSKY, Avrahm, 1890- 891.7'3'3 B
Turgenev, the man, his art, and his age / Avrahm Yarmolinsky. New York : Octagon Books, 1977, c1959. 384 p. ; 23 cm. Reprint of the 1961 ed. published by Collier Books, New York. Includes index. Bibliography: p. 370-372. [PG3435.Y3 1977] 76-58465 ISBN 0-374-98832-3 lib.bdg. : 18.00
1. Turgenev, Ivan Sergeevich, 1818-1883—Biography. 2. Authors, Russian—19th century—Biography. I. Title.

Turgot, Anne Robert Jacques, baron de l'Aulne, 1727-1781.

DAKIN, Douglas 923.344
Turgot and the ancien regime in France. New York, Octagon, 1965. xi, 361p. map. port. 24cm. Orig. pub. 1939. Bibl. [DC137.5.T9D3] 65-16771 8.00
1. Turgot, Anne Robert Jacques, baron de l' Aulne, 1727-1781. 2. France—Pol. &govt.—1774-1793. 3. Finance, Public—France—To 1789. 4. Taxation—France—Hist. I. Title. BIP

SHEPHERD, Robert Perry, 1867- 330'.092'4 B
Turgot and the six edicts. New York, B. Franklin [1971] 213 p. 23 cm. (Burt Franklin research and source works series, 831. Selected essays in history, economics & social science, 301) Reprint of the 1903 ed. Bibliography: p. 210-213. [HB105.T8S5 1971] 75-157164 ISBN 0-8337-4392-9
1. Turgot, Anne Robert Jacques, baron de l'Aulne, 1727-1781. 2. France—History—Louis XVI, 1774-1793. I. Title. BIP

SHEPHERD, Robert Perry, 1867- 330'.0924 B
Turgot and the six edicts. [1st AMS ed.] New York, AMS Press [1970] 213 p. 23 cm. (Columbia University studies in the social sciences, 47) Reprint of the 1903 ed. Bibliography: p. 210-213. [HB105.T8S5 1970] 74-127448 ISBN 0-404-51047-7
1. Turgot, Anne Robert Jacques, baron de l'Aulne, 1727-1781. 2. France—History—Louis XVI, 1774-1793. I. Title. II. Series: Columbia studies in the social sciences, 47

Turkey—History—1878-1909.

PEARS, Edwin, Sir, 1835-1919. 956.1'01'0924 B
Forty years in Constantinople; the recollections of Sir Edwin Pears, 1873-1915. Freeport, N.Y., Books for Libraries Press [1971] xiii, 390 p. illus. 23 cm. Reprint of the 1916 ed. [DR568.8.P4A3 1971] 78-179533 ISBN 0-8369-6662-7
1. Turkey—History—1878-1909. 2. Turkey—History—Mohammed V, 1909-1918. I. Title. BIP

Turkey. Ordu—Political activity.

TAMKOC, Metin. 956.1'02'0922
The warrior diplomats : guardians of the national security and modernization of Turkey / Metin Tamkoc. Salt Lake City : University of Utah Press, c1976. xix, 394 p. : ill. ; 24 cm. Includes index. Bibliography: p. [363]-372. [DR590.T35] 73-93301 ISBN 0-87480-115-X : 12.00
1. Turkey. Ordu—Political activity. 2. Statesmen—Turkey—Biography. 3. Turkey—Politics and government—1918-1960. 4. Turkey—Politics and government—1960- I. Title.

Turkow-Kaminska, Ruth, 1920-

TURKOW-KAMINSKA, Ruth, 1920- 947.084'2'0924 B
I don't want to be brave anymore / Ruth Turkow-Kaminska. Washington : New Republic Books ; New York : distribution by Simon and Schuster, 1978. p. cm. [DS135.R95T877] 78-17417 ISBN 0-915220-42-3 : 10.00
1. Turkow-Kaminska, Ruth, 1920- 2. Jews in Russia—Biography. 3. Political prisoners—Russia—Biography. 4. Russia—Biography. I. Title. BIP

Turley, Bob.

SCHOOR, Gene. 927.96357
Bob Turley, fireball pitcher. New York, Putnam [1959] 192 p. 21 cm. [GV865.T8S35] 59-11449
1. Turley, Bob.

Turnbull, Bob, 1936-

STONE, Robert B. 269'.2'0924 B
Jesus has a man in Waikiki; the story of Bob Turnbull [by] Robert B. Stone. Old Tappan, N.J., F. H. Revell Co. [1973] 128 p. illus. 21 cm. [BV4447.S72] 73-3311 ISBN 0-8007-0599-8 1.95 (pbk)
1. Turnbull, Bob, 1936- 2. Church work with youth—Honolulu. I. Title.

Turnbull, Grace Hill,

TURNBULL, Grace Hill, 1880- 927.3
Chips from my chisel, an autobiography. Rindge, N. H., R. R. Smith, 1953. 256p. illus. 25cm. [NB237.T8A3] 53-12776
I. Title.

Turner, Amasa, 1800-1877.

BOETHEL, Paul Carl, 1904- 974'.06'0924
Colonel Amasa Turner, the gentleman from Lavaca and other captains at San Jacinto. Austin, Tex., Printed by Von Boeckmann-Jones [1963] 168 p. illus. 25 cm. Includes bibliography. [F391.T8B6] 63-30235
1. Turner, Amasa, 1800-1877. I. Title.

Turner, Dick, 1911-

TURNER, Dick, 1911- 971.9'3'030924 B
Wings of the north / [by Dick Turner]. Saanichton ; Seattle : Hancock House, 1977, c1976 288 p. : ill. ; 22 cm. [TL540.T89A3] 78-309704 ISBN 0-919654-61-4 : 10.95
1. Turner, Dick, 1911- 2. Air pilots—Canada—Biography. 3. South Nahanni Valley, N.W.T.—Description and travel. I. Title. BIP

Turner, Francis Charles

TURNER, Francis Charles 923.142
James II. London, Eyre & Spottiswoode [dist. Chester Springs, Pa., Dufour, 1965] 544p. ports. 23cm. Bibl. [DA450] 64-9349 6.95
I. James II, King of Great Britain, 1633-1701. II. Title.

Turner, Frederick Jackson, 1861-1932.

BENNETT, James D. 973'.07'2024 B
Frederick Jackson Turner / by James D. Bennett. Boston : Twayne Publishers, [1975] p. cm. (Twayne's United States authors series ; 254) Includes index. Bibliography: p. [E175.5.T83B46] 74-32112 ISBN 0-8057-7150-6 lib.bdg. : 7.50
1. Turner, Frederick Jackson, 1861-1932. BIP

BILLINGTON, Ray Allen, 1903- 973'.07'2024 B
Frederick Jackson Turner: historian, scholar, teacher. New York, Oxford University Press, 1973. x, 599 p. illus. 24 cm. Bibliography: p. 565-579. [E175.5.T83B49] 72-91005 ISBN 0-19-501609-2 17.50
1. Turner, Frederick Jackson, 1861-1932.

HOFSTADTER, Richard, 1916-1970. 973'.07'2022
The progressive historians—Turner, Beard, Parrington / Richard Hofstadter. Chicago : University of Chicago Press, 1979, c1968. p. cm. Reprint of the ed. published by Knopf, New York. Includes index. Bibliography: p. [E175.45.H6 1979] 79-12591 ISBN 0-226-34818-0 : 7.95
1. Turner, Frederick Jackson, 1861-1932. 2. Beard, Charles Austin, 1874-1948. 3. Parrington, Vernon Louis, 1871-1929. 4. Historians—United States—Biography. 5. United States—Historiography. I. Title.

TURNER, Frederick Jackson, 1861-1932. 973'.072'024
"Dear Lady": the letters of Frederick Jackson Turner and Alice Forbes Perkins Hooper, 1910-1932. Edited by Ray Allen Billington. With the collaboration of Walter Muir Whitehill. San Marino, Calif., Huntington Library, 1970. 487 p. illus., facsims., ports. 27 cm. Includes bibliographical references. [E175.5.T83A43 1970] 76-134261 10.00
I. Hooper, Alice Forbes Perkins, b. 1867. II. Billington, Ray Allen, 1903- ed. III. Title.

Turner, Frederick Jackson, 1861-1932—Addresses, essays, lectures.

JACOBS, Wilbur R. 973'.07'2022
Turner, Bolton, and Webb : three historians of the American frontier / Wilbur R. Jacobs, John W. Caughey, and Joe B. Frantz. Seattle : University of Washington Press, c1965, 1979 printing. xv, 113 p. : ill. ; 21 cm. "Second printing with new preface." "Lectures originally delivered at the 1963 meeting of the Western History Association." Includes bibliographies and index. [E175.45.J3 1965b] 79-129116 ISBN 0-295-95677-1 pbk. : 4.95
1. Turner, Frederick Jackson, 1861-1932—Addresses, essays, lectures. 2. Bolton, Herbert Eugene, 1870-1953—Addresses, essays, lectures. 3. Webb, Walter Prescott, 1888-1963—Addresses, essays, lectures. 4. Historians—United States—Biography—Addresses, essays, lectures. 5. The West—Historiography—Addresses, essays,

lectures. I. Caughey, John Walton, 1902- joint author. II. Frantz, Joe Bertram, 1917- joint author. III. Title. BIP

Turner, Gladys Davis, 1914-

CARTER, Mary Ellen. 133.8'092'4 [B]
My years with Edgar Cayce; the personal story of Gladys Davis Turner. [New York] Warner Paperback Library [1974, c1972] 158 p. 18 cm. [BF1027.C3C26] 78-175159 1.25 (pbk.)
1. Turner, Gladys Davis, 1914 2. Cayce, Edgar, 1877-1945. I. Title.

Turner, Glenn, 1935—

FRASCA, John. 650.1'0924 B
Con man or saint? [1st ed.] Anderson, S.C., Droke House; distributed by Grosset and Dunlop, New York [1969] 223 p. 24 cm. [HF5391.F585] 75-104056 4.95
1. Turner, Glenn, 1935- 2. Success. I. Title.

MAXA, Rudy. 364.1'63'0924
Dare to be great / Rudy Maxa. New York : Morrow, 1977. 256 p. : ill. ; 22 cm. Includes index. [HV6698.Z9T875] 76-27848 ISBN 0-688-03101-3 : 8.95
1. Turner, Glenn, 1935- 2. Fraud—United States—Case studies. 3. Swindlers and swindling—United States—Biography. I. Title. BIP

Turner, Harry Smith.

TURNER, Alice (Martin) 920
The tempest maker; the story of Harry Turner. With a memoir compiled from the writings of Harry Turner. [1st ed.] New York, Exposition Press [1955] 219p. 21cm. [CT275.T94T8] 55-11193
1. Turner, Harry Smith. I. Title.

Turner, Henry McNeal, Bp., 1834-1915.

PONTON, Mungo Melanchthon, 1860- 287'.6'0924 B
Life and times of Henry M. Turner; the antecedent and preliminary history of the life and times of Bishop H. M. Turner, his boyhood, education and public career, and his relation to his associates, colleagues and contemporaries, by M. M. Ponton. New York, Negro Universities Press [1970] 173 p. port. 23 cm. "Originally published in 1917." [E185.97.T94 1970] 70-109363
1. Turner, Henry McNeal, Bp., 1834-1915.

Turner, Jonathan Baldwin, 1805-1899.

CARRIEL, Mary (Turner) b. 1845 923.773
The life of Jonathan Baldwin Turner. [Centennial ed.] Urbana, Univ. of Ill., Pr. [c.1911, 1961] 267p. 61-14349 5.50
1. Turner, Jonathan Baldwin, 1805-1899. I. Title.

Turner, Joseph Mallord William, 1775-1851.

CAMBRIDGE. University. Fitzwilliam Museum. 759.2
J. M. W. Turner, R.A., 1775-1851 : a catalogue of drawings and watercolours in the Fitzwilliam Museum, Cambridge / Malcolm Cormack keeper of paintings and drawings Cambridge ; New York : Published for the Museum [by] Cambridge University Press, 1975. p. cm. (Fitzwilliam Museum catalogues) [NC242.T9C35 1975] 75-12158 ISBN 0-521-20955-2 : 14.95
1. Turner, Joseph Mallord William, 1775-1851. I. Turner, Joseph Mallord William, 1775-1851. II. Cormack, Malcolm. III. Series: Cambridge. University. Fitzwilliam Museum. Fitzwilliam Museum catalogues.

FINBERG, Alexander Joseph, 1866-1939. 759.2
The life of J. M. W. Turner, R. A. 2d ed., rev., with a supplement, by Hilda F. Finberg. Oxford [c.]1961[ ] xvi, 543p. illus. 25cm. Bibl. 61-4374 10.10
1. Turner, Joseph Mallord William, I. Title.

HERRMANN, Luke. 760'.0924
Ruskin and Turner; a study of Ruskin as a collector of Turner, based on his gifts to the University of Oxford; incorporating a catalogue raisonne of the Turner drawings in the Ashmolean Museum. New York, F. A. Praeger [1969, c1968] 108 p. 52 plates (4 col.) 26 cm. Bibliography: p. 17. [NC1115.T82H4 1969] 69-12954 11.50
1. Turner, Joseph Mallord William, 1775-1851. 2. Ruskin, John, 1819-1900—Art collections. I. Oxford. University. Ashmolean Museum. II. Title.

KITSON, Michael. 759.2
J. M. W. Turner [by] Michael Kitson. New York, Barnes & Noble [1964] 90 p. illus. (part col.) 18 cm. (Barnes & Noble art series, no. 618) [ND497.T8K5] 64-56938
1. Turner, Joseph Mallord William, 1775-1851. I. Title.

LINDSAY, Jack, 1900- 759.2
J. M. W. Turner: his life and work; a critical biography. [Greenwich, Conn.] N. Y. Graphic [1966] 275p. illus. (pt. col.) 25cm. Bibl. [ND497.T8L5 1966] 66-15798 12.50
1. Turner, Joseph Mallord William, 1775-1851. I. Title.

LINDSAY, Jack, 1900- 759.2
J. M. W. Turner: his life and work; a critical biography. [Greenwich, Con..] New York Graphic Society [1966] 275 p. illus. (part col.) 25 cm. Bibliography: p. 265-270. [ND497.T8L5 1966] 66-15798
1. Turner, Joseph Mallord William, 1775-1851.

LINDSAY, Jack, 1900- 759.2 B
J. M. W. Turner: his life and work; a critical biography. New York, Harper & Row [1971, c1966] 275 p. illus. 24 cm. (Icon editions, IN-4) Bibliography: p. 265-270. [ND497.T8L5 1971] 73-148425 ISBN 0-06-435350-8 3.95
1. Turner, Joseph Mallord William, 1775-1851.

REYNOLDS, Graham. 759.2 B
Turner. New York, H. N. Abrams [1969?] 216 p. illus. (part col.) 22 cm. Includes bibliographical references. [ND497.T8R4 1969b] 69-14192
1. Turner, Joseph Mallord William, 1775-1851. BIP

TURNER, Joseph Mallord William, 1775-1851. 759.2
J. M. W. Turner / text by John Walker. New York : H. N. Abrams, [1976] p. cm. (The Library of great painters) Includes index. Bibliography: p. [ND497.T8W34] 76-4090 ISBN 0-8109-0513-2 : 22.50
1. Turner, Joseph Mallord William, 1775-1851. I. Walker, John, Dec. 24, 1906-

Turner, Kay.

TURNER, Kay. 639'.9'0924 B
Serengeti home / by Kay Turner ; with a foreword by Bernhard Grzimek. New York : Dial Press, 1977. p. cm. Includes index. [SK255.T3T87] 77-3908 ISBN 0-8037-8173-3 : 9.95
1. Turner, Kay. 2. Game wardens—Tanzania—Serengeti Plain—Biography. 3. Serengeti Plain, Tanzania. I. Title. BIP

Turner, Lana, 1920-

BASINGER, Jeanine. 791.43'028'0924 B
Lana Turner / by Jeanine Basinger. New York : Pyramid Publications, 1976. 159 p. : ill. ; 20 cm. (A Pyramid illustrated history of the movies) "The films of Lana Turner": p. 147-152. Includes index. Bibliography: p. 146. [PN2287.T8B3] 76-46168 ISBN 0-515-04194-7 pbk. : 1.75
1. Turner, Lana, 1920- 2. Actors—United States—Biography. BIP

MORELLA, Joe. 791.43'028'0924
Lana: the public and private lives of Miss Turner [by] Joe Morella & Edward Z. Epstein. [1st ed.] New York, Citadel Press [1971] 297 p. illus. 22 cm. [PN2287.T8M6] 73-175829 ISBN 0-8065-0226-6 6.95
1. Turner, Lana, 1920- I. Epstein, Edward Z., joint author. II. Title.

Turner, Nat, 1800?-1831.

FONER, Eric, comp. 975.5'55'030924 B
Nat Turner. Englewood Cliffs, N.J., Prentice-Hall [1971] viii, 184 p. 22 cm. (Great lives observed) (A Spectrum book) Contents.Contents.—Nat Turner and the Southampton Insurrection: Contemporary accounts. Trial and execution. The confessions of Nat Turner.—Americans reaction to the insurrection. Virginia reactions. Southern reactions. The slaves and Nat Turner. Reactions in the North. The abolitionist response. The attack on the abolitionists. Virginians demand action by the State legislature. Nat Turner and the Virginia debate on slavery. Virginia and other states strengthen their slave codes. The attack on freedom of discussion, and emergence of the proslavery argument.—Nat Turner in history: John Brown and Nat Turner. Thomas Wentworth Higginson: this extraordinary man. The Civil War and slave rebellion. A pioneer Black historian and Nat Turner. Nat Turner remembered: the 1880s. William S. Drewry on Nat Turner, 1900. 1931: the 100th anniversary of the Turner insurrectionONat Turner. Englewood Cliffs, N.J., Prentice-Hall [1971] viii, 184 p. 22 cm. (Great lives observed) (A Spectrum book) Contents.Conten
1. Turner, Nat, 1800?-1831. 2. Southampton Insurrection, 1831. BIP

JOHNSON, Frank Roy, 1911- 975.5'55'030924
The Nat Turner story; history of the South's most important slave revolt, with new material provided by Black tradition and white tradition [by] F. Roy Johnson. Murfreesboro, N.C., Johnson Pub. Co. [1970] 240 p. illus., maps. 22 cm. Bibliography: p. 220-226. [F232.S7J62] 78-141637
1. Turner, Nat, 1800?-1831. 2. Southampton Insurrection, 1831. I. Title.

TURNER, Nat, 1800?-1831. 975.5'55'030924 B
The confession, trial, and execution of Nat Turner, the Negro insurrectionist : also, a list of persons murdered in the insurrection in Southampton County, Virginia, on the 21st and 22nd of August, 1831, with introductory remarks / by T. R. Gray. New York : AMS Press, 1975. 23 p. ; 23 cm. Reprint of the 1881 ed. published by J. B. Ege, Petersburg, Va. [F232.S7T9 1975] 71-177580 ISBN 0-404-00120-3 : 5.00
1. Turner, Nat, 1800?-1831. 2. Southampton Insurrection, 1831. I. Gray, Thomas R. II. Title. BIP

Turner, Nat, 1800?-1831—Juvenile literature.

GRIFFIN, Judith Berry. 975.5'55'030924 B
Nat Turner. Illustrated by Leo Carty. New York, Coward-McCann [1970] 62 p. illus. 22 cm. A biography of the Negro slave who believed he had been chosen by God to lead a rebellion that would free all slaves. [F232.S7G7 1970] 92 70-104391 3.69
1. Turner, Nat, 1800?-1831—Juvenile literature. I. Carty, Leo, illus. II. Title. BIP

WILSON, Ruth, 1919- 322.4'4'0922 B
Our blood and tears; black freedom fighters. New York, Putnam [1972] 192 p. 21 cm. Brief biographies of three nineteenth-century black men emphasizing their struggles to free their people from slavery. [E185.96.W58 1972] 920 70-185404 4.69
1. Bannecker, Benjamin, 1731-1806—Juvenile literature. 2. Turner, Nat, 1800?-1831—Juvenile literature. 3. Douglass, Frederick, 1817?-1895—Juvenile literature. I. Title. BIP

Turner, Reginald, 1809?-1938.

WEINTRAUB, Stanley, 1929- 823.912 (B)
Reggie; a portrait of Reginald Turner. New York, G. Braziller [1965] 293 p. illus., ports. 22 cm. "References": p. [279]-288. [PR6039.U69Z95] 65-19321
1. Turner, Reginald, 1809? 1938. I. Title. BIP

Turner, Taos Lee, 1972-

TURNER, Dean. 242
Krinkle nose : a prayer of thanks / by Dean Turner. Old Greenwich, Conn. : Devin-Adair Co., c1979. 92 p., [2] leaves of plates : ill. ; 24 cm. [BR1725.T77T87] 77-78424 ISBN 0-8159-6002-6 : 4.95
1. Turner, Taos Lee, 1972- 2. Turner, Dean. 3. Christian biography—United States. I. Title. BIP

Turner, Ted.

VAUGHAN, Roger. 623.88'092'4 B
Ted Turner / by Roger Vaughan. Boston : Sail Books, 1978. p. cm. Includes index. [GV812.5.T87V38] 78-64763 ISBN 0-914814-15-X : 10.95
1. Turner, Ted. 2. Seamen—United States—Biography. 3. America's Cup races. 4. Sports team owners—United States—Biography. I. Title.

Turner, Thomas Trussler, 1927-

DOWN, Goldie M. 286'.73 B
More lives than a cat / by Goldie M. Down. Nashville : Southern Pub. Association, c1979. p. cm. [BX6193.T87D68] 79-17814 ISBN 0-8127-0243-3 : 3.95
1. Turner, Thomas Trussler, 1927- 2. Seventh-Day Adventists—South Africa—Biography. 3. Clergy—South Africa—Biography. I. Title. BIP

Turner, William Ira,

TURNER, William Ira, 1898- 920
Lest any man should boast; an autobiography of a father of fifteen children, by William I. Turner, [1st ed.] New York, Greenwich Book Publishers [c1963] 103 p. 21 cm. [CT275.T956A3] 63-17386
I. Title.

Turow, Scott.

TUROW, Scott. 340'.07'3
One L / Scott Turow. New York : Putnam, c1977. 300 p. ; 23 cm. [KF373.T88A33] 76-57246 ISBN 0-399-11932-9 : 7.95
1. Turow, Scott. 2. Harvard University. Law School. 3. Law students—Massachusetts—Biography. I. Title.

TUROW, Scott. 340'.07'3
One L / Scott Turow. New York : Penguin Books, [1978] p. cm. [KF373.T88A33 1978] 78-9647 ISBN 0-14-004913-4 pbk. : 2.95
1. Turow, Scott. 2. Harvard University. Law School. 3. Law students—Massachusetts—Biography. I. Title. BIP

Turra, Mario, 1931-

TURRA, Mario, 1931- 940.53'161'0924 B
Mario / by Mario Turra. Acworth, Ga. : Names of Distinction, c1975. 174 p. : ill. ; 24 cm. [D811.5.T84] 75-33477 7.95
1. Turra, Mario, 1931- 2. World War, 1939-1945—Personal narratives, Italian. I. Title.

Tuskegee Institute.

WASHINGTON, Booker Taliaferro, 1859?-1915. 378'.00924 B
The story of my life and work. With an introd. by J. L. M. Curry. Copiously illustrated with photo-engravings, original pen drawings by Frank Beard. New York, Negro Universities Press [1969] 423 p. illus., ports. 23 cm. Reprint of the 1900 ed. [E185.97.W29 1969] 70-82473
1. Tuskegee Institute. I. Title. BIP

WASHINGTON, Booker Taliaferro, 1859?-1915. 923.773
Up from slavery, an autobiography. Garden City, N.Y., Doubleday, 1963. 243 p. illus. 22 cm. [E185.97.W3163] 63-3987

1. Tuskegee Institute. I. Title.

WASHINGTON, Booker Taliaferro, 1859?-1915 923.773
Up from slavery. Introd. by Louis Lomax [New York, Dell, 1965] 224p. 17cm. (Laurel-leaf lib., 9224) [E185.97.W3163] .45 pap.,
1. Tuskegee Institute. I. Title.

WASHINGTON, Booker Taliaferro, 1859?-1915. 301.451'96'024 B
Up from slavery. With an introd. by Booker T. Washington III and illus. by Denver Gillen. New York Limited Editions Club, 1970. xiv, 212 p. col. illus. 28 cm. [E185.97.W31642] 73-15841
1. Tuskegee Institute. I. Title. **BIP**

WASHINGTON, Booker Taliaferro, 1859?-1915. 923.773
Up from slavery; an autobiography. With illus. of the author and his environment, together with an introd. by Langston Hughes. New York, Dodd, Mead [1965] 212 p. illus., ports. 22 cm. (Great illustrated classics) [E185.97.W3164] 65-21868
1. Tuskegee Institute. I. Title.

Tuskegee Normal and Industrial Institute.

WASHINGTON, Booker Taliaferro, 1859?-1915 923.773
Up from slavery, an autobiography. New York, Bantam [1963, c.1900, 1901] 241p. 18cm. (Pathfinder Ed., HP16) .60 pap.,
1. Tuskegee Normal and Industrial Institute. I. Title.

Tutankhamen, King of Egypt.

CARTER, Michael. 913.32'03'10924
Tutankhamun, the golden monarch. [1st American ed.] New York, McKay [1972] 135 p. 21 cm. [DT87.5.C43 1972] 72-86137 4.95
1. Tutankhamen, King of Egypt.

DESROCHES-NOBLECOURT, Christiane, 1913- 913.2031
Tutankhamen; life and death of a Pharaoh.Pref. by Sarwat Okasha. Color-plate captions by A. Shoukry. [Tr. from French by Claude] Abridged ed. Garden City, N. Y., Doubleday, 1965 [c.1963, 1965] 222p. illus., map, 32 col. plates. 20cm. Bibl. [DT87.5.D4] 65-15744 2.95 pap.,
1. Tutankhamen, King of Egypt. I. Title.

DESROCHES-NOBLECOURT, Christiane, 1913- 932.010924
Tutankhamen : life and death of a pharoah / with 75 color photographs by F. L. Kenett ; preface by Sarwat Okashu ; notes on the color plates by A. Shoukry. Boston : New York Graphic Society [1976c1963] 312p. : ill. ; 25 cm. Includes index. Bibliography: p. 306-307. [DT87.5.D4] ISBN 0-8212-0695-8 pbk. : 8.95
1. Tutenkhamun, King of Egypt. I. Title.
L. C. card no. for original edition: 63-15145.

DESROCHES-NOBLECOURT, Christiane, 1913- 913.32031
Tutankhamen; life and death of a Pharaoh. Pref. by Sarwat Okasha. Color-plate captions by A. Shoukry. [Translated from the French by Claude] Abridged ed. Garden City, N.Y., Doubleday, 1965. 222 p. illus., map, 32 col. plates. 20 cm. Bibliography: p. 213-214. [DT87.5.D4 1965] 65-15744
1. Tutankhamen, King of Egypt. I. Title.

Tutankhamen, King of Egypt—Juvenile literature.

BRUCKNER, Karl, 1906- 923.132
The golden Pharaoh, Translated by France Lobb. New York] Pantheon Books [1959] 190p. illus. 22cm. [DT87.5.B713] 59-11963
1. Tutenkhamun, King of Egypt—Juvenile literature. 2. Tombs—Egypt—Juvenile literature. I. Title.

KNAPP, Ron. 932'.01'0924 B
Tutankhamun and the mysteries of ancient Egypt / by Ron Knapp ; illustrated with drawings by Becky Pobanz and with photos. New York : Messner, c1979. 96 p. : ill. ; 22 cm. Includes index. Describes the 1922 discovery of the treasure-laden tomb of Tutankhamen. Also discusses life in Egypt during the pharaoh's rule. [DT87.5.K57] 79-15504 ISBN 0-671-33036-5 lib. bdg. : 7.29
1. Tutankhamen, King of Egypt—Juvenile literature. 2. Egypt—Antiquities—Juvenile literature. 3. Pharoahs—Biography—Juvenile literature. I. Pobanz, Becky. II. Title. **BIP**

SCHLEIN, Miriam. 932'.01'0924 B
I, Tut : the boy who became pharaoh / by Miriam Schlein ; ill. by Erik Hilgerdt. New York : Four Winds Press, c1979. [48] p. : ill. (some col.) ; 27 cm. Bibliography: p. [48] The young pharaoh of Egypt tells about his life and times. [DT87.5.S3] 92 78-15603 ISBN 0-590-07571-3 : 7.95
1. Tutankhamen, King of Egypt—Juvenile literature. 2. Pharoahs—Biography—Juvenile literature. I. Hilgerdt, Erik. II. Title. **BIP**

Tutwiler, Julia Strudwick, 1841-1916.

PANNELL, Anne Gary. 923.773
Julia S. Tutwiler and social progress in Alabama [by] Anne Gary Pannell and Dorothea E. Wyatt. [University, Ala.] University of Alabama Press, 1961. 158p. illus. 21cm. Includes bibliography. [LB1822.L617 1888f] 60-11576
1. Tutwiler, Julia Strudwick, 1841-1916. I. Wyatt, Dorothea E., joint author. II. Title.

Twachtman, John Henry, 1853-1902.

TWACHTMAN, John Henry, 1853-1902. 759.13 B
John Twachtman / Richard J. Boyle. New York : Watson Guptill, [1979] p. cm. Includes index. Bibliography: p. [ND237.T85A4 1979] 79-12564 ISBN 0-8230-2569-1 : 20.00
1. Twachtman, John Henry, 1853-1902. 2. Painters—United States—Biography. I. Boyle, Richard J.

Tweed, William Marcy, 1823-1878.

HERSHKOWITZ, Leo. 974.7'1'040924 B
Tweed's New York : another look / Leo Hershkowitz. Garden City, N.Y. : Anchor Press/Doubleday, 1978. xx, 409 p., [8] leaves of plates : ill. ; 24 cm. Includes index. Bibliography: p. 381-391. [F128.47.H54 1978] 78-300384 ISBN 0-385-07665-7 : 6.95
1. Tweed, William Marcy, 1823-1878. 2. New York (City)—Politics and government—To 1898. 3. Politicians—New York (City)—Biography. 4. New York (City)—Biography. I. Title. **BIP**

Tweedy, Maureen.

TWEEDY, Maureen. 910'.92'4 B
A label round my neck / Maureen Tweedy. Lavenham, [Eng.] : T. Dalton, 1976. 194 p., [12] leaves of plates : ill. ; 23 cm. [DS10.T8] 76-376708 ISBN 0-900963-66-2 : £3.90
1. Tweedy, Maureen. 2. Asia—Description and travel—1951- I. Title.

Twentieth Century-Fox Film Corporation.

PARISH, James Robert. 791.43'028'0922 B
The Fox girls. New Rochelle, N.Y., Arlington House [1972, c1971] 722 p. illus. 26 cm. [PN1998.A2P39 1972] 73-154412 ISBN 0-87000-128-0 14.95
1. Twentieth Century-Fox Film Corporation. 2. Moving-picture actors and actresses—United States—Biography. I. Title.

Twichell, Joseph Hopkins, 1838-1918.

STRONG, Leah A 285.87463 (B)
Joseph Hopkins Twichell, Mark Twain's friend and pastor, by Leah A. Strong. Athens, University of Georgia Press [1966] x, 182 p. port. 25 cm. Bibliography: p. 172-179. [BX7260.T99S8] 66-23072
1. Twichell, Joseph Hopkins, 1838-1918. 2. Clemens, Samuel Langhorne, 1835-1910. I. Title. **BIP**

Twigg, Ena.

TWIGG, Ena. 133.9'1'0924 B
Ena Twigg: medium, by Ena Twigg, with Ruth Hagy Brod. Introd. by Mervyn Stockwood. New York, Hawthorn Books [1972] xviii, 297 p. 22 cm. [BF1283.T95A3 1972] 72-1970 6.95
1. Twigg, Ena. 2. Spiritualism. I. Brod, Ruth Hagy. II. Title.

TWIGG, Ena. 133.9'1'0924 B
Ena Twigg, medium, by Ena Twigg with Ruth Hagy Brod; introduction by Mervyn Stockwood. London, New York, W. H. Allen, 1973. xix, 295 p. 23 cm. [BF1283.T95A3 1973] 73-158703 ISBN 0-491-00903-8 £3.00
1. Twigg, Ena. 2. Spiritualism. I. Brod, Ruth Hagy. II. Title.

Twiggy.

WHITESIDE, Thomas, 1918- 659.15'2 B
Twiggy and Justin. New York, Farrar, Straus and Giroux [1968] 122 p. illus., ports. 21 cm. [HD6073.M72G77] 68-19009
1. Twiggy. 2. De Villeneuve, Justin. I. Title. **BIP**

Twitchell, Thomas Donn.

TWITCHELL, Thomas Donn. 285'.1'0924 B
"That they may be one" : convincing a puzzled world that God sent His Son / by Thomas Donn Twitchell. Plainfield, N.J. : Logos International, c1979. xii, 216 p. ; 21 cm. [BX9225.T84A36] 79-83792 ISBN 0-88270-360-9 pbk. : 3.95
1. Twitchell, Thomas Donn. 2. Presbyterian Church—Clergy—Biography. 3. Clergy—United States—Biography. 4. Christian union. I. Title.

Tyler, John, Pres. U.S., 1790-1862.

CHIDSEY, Donald Barr, 1902- 973.5'8'0924
And Tyler too / Donald Barr Chidsey. 1st ed. Nashville : T. Nelson, c1978. 158 p. ; 21 cm. Includes index. Bibliography: p. 139-151. [E397.C47] 78-807 ISBN 0-8407-6585-1 : 6.95
1. Tyler, John, Pres. U.S., 1790-1862. 2. Presidents—United States—Biography. 3. United States—Politics and government—1841-1845. I. Title. **BIP**

SEAGER, Robert, 1924- 923.173
And Tyler too; a biography of John & Julia Gardiner Tyler. [1st ed.] New York, McGraw-Hill [1963] xvii, 681 p. 22 cm. Bibliography: p. 647-654. [E397.S4] 63-14259
1. Tyler, John, Pres. U.S., 1790-1862. 2. Tyler, Julia Gardiner. I. Title.

TYLER, Lyon Gardiner, 1853-1935. 973.5'8
The letters and times of the Tylers. New York, Da Capo Press, 1970 [c1884-86] 3 v. illus., facsims., ports. 24 cm. [E397.T982] 71-75267
1. Tyler, John, Pres. U.S., 1790-1862. 2. Tyler family. 3. U.S.—Politics and government—1783-1865. I. Title. **BIP**

Tyler, Royall, 1757-1826.

TANSELLE, George Thomas, 1934- 818'.2'09
Royall Tyler [by] G. Thomas Tanselle. Cambridge, Harvard University Press, 1967. xvi, 281 p. illus., ports. 22 cm. Includes bibliographical references. [PS855.T7Z86] 67-12103
1. Tyler, Royall, 1757-1826. **BIP**

Tyndale, William, d.1536.

DE LEEUW, Cateau, 1903- 922.342
William Tyndale, martyr for the Bible. New York, Association Press [1955] 125p. illus. 20cm. (Heroes of God series) [BR350.T8D36] 55-7419
1. Tyndale, William, d.1536. I. Title.

MOZLEY, James Frederic, 1887- 283'.0924 B
William Tyndale, by J. F. Mozley. Westport, Conn., Greenwood Press [1971] ix, 364 p. illus., ports. 23 cm. Reprint of the 1937 ed. Bibliography: p. vii. [BR350.T8M6 1971] 70-109801 ISBN 0-8371-4292-X
1. Tyndale, William, d. 1536.

Tyndall, John,

TYNDALL, John, 1820-1893 925.3
Faraday as a discoverer. New York, Apollo Eds. [c.1961] 213p. illus. (A-20) 1.75 pap.,
I. Title.

Type and type-founding.

ZAPF, Hermann. 655.2'4
About alphabets; some marginal notes on type design. [Translated by Paul Standard. Rev. ed.] Cambridge, M.I.T. Press [1970] 142 p. illus., port. 19 cm. Autobiographical. Bibliography: p. 90-108. [Z250.A2Z36 1970] 72-110238
1. Type and type-founding. 2. Printing—Specimens. I. Title.

Type and type-founding—Italic type.

DREYFUS, John. 655.2
Italic quartet; a record of the collaboration between Harry Kessler, Edward Johnston, Emery Walker and Edward Prince in making the Cranach Press italic. Cambridge, University Printing House, 1966. vii, 50 p. illus., facsims., ports. 26 cm. Limited ed. of 500. "A note on sources" (p. 49-50) [Z250.5.I8D7] 79-366374
1. Type and type-founding—Italic type. 2. Type designers. I. Title.

Tytler, James, 1745-1805.

FERGUSSON, James, Sir, bart., 1904- 629.133'22'0924 B
Balloon Tytler [by] Sir James Fergusson of Kilkerran. London, Faber, 1972. 160, [2] p., [6] leaves. illus., ports. 23 cm. Bibliography: p. 155-157. [TL540.T93F47 1972] 72-171364 ISBN 0-571-09986-6
1. Tytler, James, 1745-1805. I. Title.
Distributed by Transatlantic 12.00. **BIP**

Tz'u-hsi, Empress Dowager of China, 1835-1908.

HALDANE, Charlotte (Franken) 1894-1969. 951'.03'0924 B
The last great Empress of China, by Charlotte Haldane. Indianapolis, Bobbs-Merrill [1966, c1965] 304 p. port. 23 cm. Bibliography: p. 278. [DS763.T8H3 1966] 66-28337
1. Tz'u-hsi, Empress dowager of China, 1835-1908. I. Title.

HUSSEY, Harry 923.151
Venerable ancestor; the life and times of Tz'u Hsi, 1835-1908, Empress of china. Garden City, N.Y. Doubleday [1960, c.1949] 391p. (Dolphin bk C157) 1.45 pap.,
1. Tz'u-hsi, Empress Dowager of China, 1835-1908. I. Title. **BIP**

HUSSEY, Harry. 951'.03'0924 B
Venerable ancestor; the life and times of Tz'u hsi, 1835-1908, Empress of China. Drawings by Shirley Wang. Westport, Conn., Greenwood Press [1970, c1949] xix, 354 p. illus., geneal. table. 23 cm. [DS763.T8H8 1970] 71-110042 ISBN 0-8371-4430-2
1. Tz'u-hsi, Empress dowager of China, 1835-1908. I. Title.

WU, Yung, 1865-1936. 951'.03'0924 B
The flight of an empress. Told by Wu Yung, whose other name is Yu-ch'uan,

transcribed by Liu K'un; translated and edited by Ida Pruitt. Introd. by Kenneth Scott Latourette. Westport, Conn., Hyperion Press [1973, c1936] xxiii, 222 p. illus. 23 cm. Translation of Keng tzu hsi shou ts'ung t'an. Reprint of the ed. published by Yale University Press, New Haven. [DS763.T8W813 1973] 73-902 ISBN 0-88355-098-9 14.50
1. Tz'u-hsi, Empress dowager of China, 1835-1908. 2. China—History—1900. 3. Boxers. I. Liu, K'un chin shih, 1903- II. Pruitt, Ida, tr. III. Title. BIP

U. S., see also United States

U.S.—Armed Forces—Negroes.

JOHNSON, Jesse J., 1914- 355.3'32'0924
Ebony brass: an autobiography of Negro frustration amid aspiration, by Jesse J. Johnson. New York, William-Frederick, 1967. c141p. 23cm. [U53.J6A3] 67-14249 4.95
1. U.S.—Armed Forces—Negroes. I. Title.

JOHNSON, Jesse J., 1914- 355.3'32'0924 B
Ebony brass; an autobiography of Negro frustration amid aspiration, by Jesse J. Johnson Hampton, Va., Distributed by J. J. Johnson [1970] 141 p. ports. 23 cm. [U53.J6A3 1970] 70-130353
1. U.S.—Armed Forces—Negroes. I. Title.

U. S.—Bio-bibl.

AUTHORS, American-- 20th cent. 810.9'005'2
Contemporary authors; a bio-bibliographical guide to current authors and their works. James M. Ethridge [and] Barbara Kopala, editors. 1st revision. Detroit, Gale Research Co. [1967- v. 26 cm. "[Vol. 1] represents a complete revision and a consolidation into one alphabet of biographical material which originally appeared in four separate quarterly issues of Contemporary authors, volumes 1, 2, 3, and 4. published in 1962 and 1963. The revised material is down to date, in most cases, through spring, 1967." [Z1224.C59] 67-9634
1. U. S.—Bio-bibl. I. Ethridge, James M., ed. II. Kopala, Barbara, ed. III. Gale Research Company. IV. Title.

CONTEMPORARY authors; 928.1
a bio-bibliographical guide to current authors and their works; v.4. Ed.: James M. Ethridge. Detroit, Gales Res. [c.1963] 289p. 26cm. 62-52046 10.00
1. U. S.— Bio-bibl. 2. Authors, American. I. Gale Research Company.

CONTEMPORARY authors; 928.1
a bio-bibliographical guide to current authors and their work; v.2. Ed.: James M Ethridge. Detroit, Gale Res. [c.1963] 240p. 27cm. quarterly. 62-52046 10.00
1. U.S.—Bio-bibl. 2. Authors, American. I. Gale Research Company

CONTEMPORARY authors; 928.1
the international bio-bibliographical guide to current authors and their works. v.1. Ed.: James M. Ethridge. Detroit, Gale Res. [c.]1962. 245p. 27cm. 62-52046 10.00
1. U S.—Bio bibl. 2. Authors, American. I. Gale Research Company.

CONTEMPORARY authors: 928.1
a biobibliographical guide to current authors and their works; v. 7-8. James M. Ethridge, ed. Detroit, Gale [1964, c.1963] 661p. 26cm. 62-52046 15.00
1. U.S.—Bio-Bibl. 2. Authors, American. I. Gale Research Company, II. Ethridge, James M., ed.

CONTEMPORARY authors: 928.1
a bio-bibliographical guide to current authors and their works; v.5-6. James M. Ethridge, ed. Detroit, Gale Res. [1964.c.1963] 497p. 26cm. 62-52046 15.00
1. U.S.— Bio-Bibl. 2. Authors, American. I. Gale Research Company. II. Ethridge, James M., ed.

CONTEMPORARY authors: 928.1
a bio-bibliographical guide e to current authors and their works; v.9-10. James M. Ethridge, ed. Detroit, Gale [c.1964] 481p. 27cm. 62-52046 price unreported
1. U.S.—Bio.—Bibl. 2. Authors, American. I. Gale Research Company. II. Ethridge, James M., ed.

CONTEMPORARY authors; 928.1
a biobibliographical guide to current authors and their works v.15-16. Detroit Gale [1966, i.e., 1967] v. 27cm. Eds.: 1967- J.M. Ethridge, B. Kopala. 62-52046 15.00
1. U.S.—Bio-Bibl. 2. Authors, American. I. Gale Research Company. II. Ethridge, James M., ed. III. Kopala, Barbara, joint ed.

CONTEMPORARY authors, 928.1
a bio-bibliographical guide to current authors and their works; v.11-12 [in 1v.] James M. Ethridge, Barbara Kopala, eds. Detroit, Mich., Gale [c.1965] 472p. 26cm. Contains cumulative index to vs. 1-12. 62-52046 15.00
1. U. S.—Bio.—Bibl. 2. Authors, American. I. Gale Research Company. II. Ethridge, James M., ed.

U.S.—Biography.

ADAMS, John Quincy, Pres. U. S., 1767-1848. 923.173
Diary, 1794-1845; American diplomacy and political, social, and intellectual life from Washington to Polk, Edited by Allan Nevins New York, Scribner, 1951. xxxv, 586 p. 25 cm. "A selection from 'The memoirs of John Quincy Adams, comprising portions of his diary from 1795 to 1848.'" [E377.A213] 51-10345
1. U. S.—Hist.—1783-1865. 2. U. S.—Pol. & govt.—1783-1865. 3. U. S.—For. rel.—1783-1865. I. Nevins, Allan, 1890- ed. II. Title.

BALLENTINE, George, b.1812? v. 12
Autobiography of an English soldier in the United States Army; Comprising observations and adventures in the States and Mexico. New York, Stringer & Townsend, 1853. Collation of the original: xii, 288 p. illus. (American culture series, 242: 7) Microfilm copy (positive) made in 1963 by University Microfilms, Ann Arbor, Mich.
1. U.S.—Hist.—War with Mexico, 1845-1848—Personal narratives. I. Title.

BOYER, Samuel Pellman, 1839-1875 926.1
Naval surgeon; the diary of Dr. Samuel Pellman Boyer [2v.] Ed. by Elinor Barnes, James A. Barnes. Introd. by Allan Nevins. Bloomington, Ind. Univ. Pr. [c.1963] 2v. (390; 279p.) illus., ports., maps, facsims. 24cm. Contents.[1] Blockading the South, 1862-1866.--[2] Revolt in Japan, 1868-1869. Bibl. 63-9723 10.00, 6.95; 15.00 v.1, v.2, set,
1. U.S.—Hist.—Civil War—Personal narratives. 2. U.S.—Hist.—Civil War—Blockade. 3. Japan—Hist.—Meiji period, 1867-1912. 4. East (Far East)—Descr. & trav. 5. U.S. Navy—Sanit. affairs. I. Title.

BOYER, Samuel Pellman, 1839-1875. 926.1
Naval surgeon; the diary of Dr. Samuel Pellman Boyer. Edited by Elinor Barnes and James A. Barnes. Introd. by Allan Nevins. Bloomington. Indiana University Press [1963] 2 v. illus., ports., maps, facsims. 24 cm. Contents.CONTENTS. -- [1] Blockading the South, 1862-1866. -- [2] Revolt in Japan, 1868-1869. Includes bibliographies. [E182.B7] 63-9723
1. U.S. — Hist. — Civil War — Personal narratives. 2. U.S. — Hist. — Civil War — Blockade. 3. Japan — Hist. — Meiji period, 1867-1912. 4. East (Far East) — Descr. & trav. 5. U.S. Navy — Saint. affairs. I. Title.

*CARY, Sturges F. 923.173
Arrow book of Presidents. Illus. by Leo Summers. New York, Scholastic Bk. [c.1965] 94p. 21cm. (TW 653) .45 pap.,
I. Title.

COY, Harold. 920
The first book of Presidents. Rev. ed. New York, F. Watts [1966] 65 p. illus., ports. 23 cm. Describes the general duties and responsibilities of the President and summarizes the careers of those who have held the office. [E176.1.C798 1966] AC 66
I. Title. BIP

HILF, Mary (Asia) 1874- 920.7
No time for tears, by Mary Asia Hilf, as told to Barbara Bourns. New York, Yoseloff [c.1964] 271p. 22cm. 64-13191 5.00
1. U.S.—Emig. & immig.—Personal narratives. I. Bourns, Barbara. II. Title.

HILF, Mary (Asia) 1874- 920.7
No time for tears, by Mary Asia Hilf, as told to Barbara Bourns. New York, T. Yoseloff [1964] 271 p. 22 cm. [E184.J5H57] 64-13191
1. U.S. — Emig. & immig. — Personal narratives. I. Bourns, Barbara. II. Title.

LEIPOLD, L. Edmond, 1902- 920
Explorers of our land, by L. Edmond Leipold. Minneapolis, Denison [1967] 72p. 25cm. (His Famous Amer. heroes and leaders ser.) [E179.5.L4] 67-22261 3.69
1. U.S.—Territorial expansion—Juvenile literature. 2. Explorers—Juvenile literature. 3. U.S.—Exploring expeditions—Juvenile literature. I. Title.

REEDER, Russell Potter 973.741
The Norther generals, by Red Reeder. Maps by Ned Glattauer. New York, Duell [dist. Meredith, 1964] xvi, 205p. ports., maps. 21cm. Bibl. 64-12455 4.50
1. U. S.—Hist.—Civil War—Biog.—Juvenile literature. 2. Generals—U. S.—Juvenile literature. 3. U. S.—Hist.—Civil War—Campaigns and battle—Juvenile literature. I. Title.

SEOANE, Consuelo Andrew, 1876 923.573
Beyond the ranges, by Consuelo Andrew Seoane as told to Robert L. Niemann. New York, R. Speller, [c.]1960. 256p. port. 60-9610 5.00
1. U. S.— History, Military. I. Niemann, Robert L. II. Title.

SHEEHAN, Donald Henry, 1917- 923.173
The American Presidency. [Prepared with the cooperation of the American Geographical Society] Garden City, N. Y., N. Doubleday [1957] 64p. illus. 21cm. (Know your America program) [E176.1.S536] 57-31312
1. U. S.—Presidents. 2. Presidents—U. S.—Portraits. I. American Geographical Society of New York. II. Title.

SOBOL, Donald J. 923.573
To flags flying. Pref. by Ralph Newman. Illus. by Jerry Robinson. New York, Platt & Munk [c.1960] 216p. illus. (part col.) 29cm. 60-12388 3.95 bds.,
1. U. S.—Hist.— Civil War—Biog.—Juvenile literature. I. Title.

STEINBERG, Alfred, 1917- 973'.0922
The first ten; the founding Presidents and their administrations. [1st ed.] Garden City, N.Y., Doubleday, 1967. ix, 493 p. 22 cm. Bibliography: p. [446]-483. [E301.S84] 67-11186
1. United States—Presidents. 2. United States—Politics and government—1783-1865. I. Title.

U.S.—Biography—Dictionaries.

AMERICAN Council of Learned Societies Devoted to Humanistic Studies. 920.073
Dictionary of American biography. New York, Scribner [1946? v. 26 cm. Edited by Allen Johnson and others. "Published under the auspices of the American Council of Learned Societies." Reprint of the original 20 vol. ed. published 1928-37 with supplementary v. 21-22 which were added in 1944 and 1958. "Volume 1 contains corrections of fact and additional data which have come to the attention of the editors from the first publication of the work up to the present." Vol. 11: Supplement 1, to Dec. 31, 1935. Supplement 2, to Dec. 31, 1940. [E176.D563] 60-2195
1. U.S. — Biog. — Dictionaries. I. Title. BIP

THE Biographical 920.073
encyclopedia of the United States. [1st ed. New York, Allied Publishers, 1968] 5 v. (1030 p.) illus., ports. 29 cm. [CT220.B5] 68-24277
1. United States—Biography—Dictionaries.

CONCISE Dictionary of 920.073
American biography. New York, Scribner [1964] viii, 1273 p. 26 cm. [E176.D564] 64-10623
1. U.S. — Biog. — Dictionaries. BIP

CONCISE Dictionary of 920'.073
American biography. 2d ed. New York : Scribner, c1977. xii, 1229 p. ; 19 cm. "Joseph G. E. Hopkins, editor." Edited under the sponsorship of the American Council of Learned Societies. [E176.D564 1977] 76-49520 ISBN 0-684-14877-3 : 40.00
1. United States—Biography—Dictionaries. I. American Council of Learned Societies Devoted to Humanistic Studies. II. Hopkins, Joseph G. E. III. Dictionary of American biography.

DRAKE, Francis Samuel, 1828-1885. 920.073
Dictionary of American biography, including men of the time; containing nearly ten thousand notices of persons of both sexes, of native and foreign birth, who have been remarkable, or prominently connected with the arts, sciences, literature, politics, or history, of the American continent ... Boston, J. R. Osgood, 1872. Ann Arbor, Mich., Gryphon Books, 1971. 2 v. (xvi, 1019 p.) 22 cm. [E176.D725 1971] 73-161186
1. U.S.—Biography—Dictionaries. 2. America—Biography—Dictionaries. I. Title.

DRAKE, Francis Samuel, 1828-1885 920'.073
Dictionary of American biography, including men of the time; containing nearly ten thousand notices of persons of both sexes, of native and foreign birth, who have been remarkable, or prominently connected with the arts, sciences, literature, politics, or history, of the American continent ... Boston, J. R. Osgood, 1872. Detroit, Gale Research Co., 1973. p. [CT213.D7 1973] 73-11061 42.50
1. United States—Biography—Dictionaries. 2. America—Biography—Dictionaries. I. Title.

GANNON, Francis Xavier. 920.073
Biographical dictionary of the left, by Francis X. Gannon. Belmont, Mass., American opinion [1968- v. 23 cm. (American opinion preview series) [E747.G3] 68-4923
1. United States—Biography—Dictionaries. I. Title.

GARRATY, John Arthur, 1920- 920'.073
Encyclopedia of American biography. John A. Garraty, editor. Jerome L. Sternstein, associate editor. [1st ed.] New York, Harper & Row [1974] xiv, 1241 p. 25 cm. [CT213.G37 1974] 74-1807 22.50
1. United States—Biography—Dictionaries. I. Sternstein, Jerome L., joint author. II. Title. BIP

HOUGH, Franklin Benjamin, 1822-1885. 920'.073
American biographical notes, being short

notices of deceased persons, chiefly those not included in Allen's or in Drake's biographical dictionaries, gathered from many sources. Albany, J. Munsell, 1875. Harrison, N.Y., Harbor Hill Books, 1974. p. cm. [CT213.H68 1974] 74-6218
1. United States—Biography—Dictionaries. I. Title. **BIP**

MORRIS, Richard Brandon, 1904- ed. 920.073
Four hundred notable Americans, edited by Richard B. Morris. Henry Steele Commager, Chief consultant editor. [1st perennial library ed., rev. and with a new introd.] New York, Harper & Row [1965] 279 p. 19 cm. (Perennial library P19) "Originally published as the biographical section of the Encyclopedia of American history, revised and enlarged edition ... 1961." [E176.M88] 65-14848
1. U.S. — Biog. — Dictionaries. I. Title.

OUTSTANDING young men in America. 1967. 920'.71'03
Montgomery Ala., Outstanding Young Americans, 1967. v. ports, 26 cm. annual. Title varies: 1967- Outstanding young men of America [E840.608] 65-3612 price unreported
1. U.S.—Biog.—Dictionaries. 2. Young men—Biog. I. Montgomery Ala. Junior Commerce

THE Twentieth century biographical dictionary of notable Americans. 920.073
Editor-in-chief: Rossiter Johnson. Managing editor: John Howard Brown. Boston, Biographical Society, 1904. Detroit, Gale Research Co., 1968. 10 v. illus., ports. 24 cm. "Corrected edition of a work previously published under the titles: The Cyclopaedia of American biography, 1897-1903, and Lamb's biographical dictionary of the United States, 1900-1903." [E176.C993] 68-19657
1. United States—Biography—Dictionaries. I. Johnson, Rossiter, 1840-1931, ed. II. Brown, John Howard, 1840-1917, ed. III. Title: The Cyclopaedia of American biography. **BIP**

VAN DOREN, Charles Lincoln, 1926- 920'.073
Webster's American biographies / Charles Van Doren, editor, Robert McHenry, associate editor. Springfield, Mass. : G. & C. Merriam Co., [1975] xii, 1233 p. ; 26 cm. [CT213.V36 1975] 75-9559 ISBN 0-87779-153-8 : 15.00
1. United States—Biography—Dictionaries. I. McHenry, Robert, joint author. II. Title.

VAN DOREN, Charles Lincoln, 1926- 920'.073
Webster's American biographies. Charles Van Doren, editor; Robert McHenry, associate editor. Springfield, Mass., G. & C. Merriam Co. [1974] xii, 1233 p. 26 cm. [CT213.V36] 74-6341 ISBN 0-87779-053-1 15.00
1. United States—Biography—Dictionaries. I. McHenry, Robert, joint author. II. Title.

WHO was who in America; 920.073
historical volume, 1607-1896. A component volume of Who's who in American history. A compilation of sketches of individuals, both of the United States of America and some other countries who have made contribution to, or whose activity was in some manner related to the history of the United States, from the founding of Jamestown Colony to the year of continuation by v.1 of Who was who. Chicago, Marquis [c.]1963. 670p. 27cm. (Who was who in Amer., 1.) 43-3789 price unreported
1. U.S.—Biog.—Dictionaries.

WHO'S who in America; 920.073
a biographical dictionary of notable living men and women. v. 31 (1960-1961); revised and reissued biennially. Chicago, A. N. Marquis Co. 3356p. 29cm. 4-16934 26.00
1. U.S.—Biog.—Dictionaries. I. Leonard, John William, 1849- ed. II. Marquis, Albert Nelson, d. 1943, ed.

WHO'S who in America. 920.073
v. 35. 1968-1969. Chicago, Marquis-Who's Who v. 20-31 cm. biennial. A biographical dictionary of notable living men and women (varies slightly) Component vol. of Who's who in American history, 1966-67- Founded 1899 by A. N. Marquis. Vols. 28-30 accompanied by separately pub. pts. with title: Indices and necrology. [E176. W642] 4-16934 price unreported
1. U. S.—Biog.—Dictionaries. I. Marquis, Albert Nelson, d. 1943. II. Who's who in American history.

WHO'S who in American history. 920.073
Who was who in America; a companion biographical reference work to Who's who in America. 1607/1896- Chicago, Marquis-Who's Who [etc.] v. 27 cm. Vol. for 1607/1896 called Historical volume, published in 1963; vols. for 1897/1942-1951/60 called v. 1-3, were published prior to this volume. "A component volume of Who's who in American history," 1607/1896- Subtitle varies slightly. [E176.W64] 43-3789
1. U.S. — Biog. — Dictionaries. I. Title.

WHO'S who in commerce and industry; 923.873
13th ed. Chicago, Marquis [c.1936-1963] 1464p. 27cm. (The Intl. business who's who) binnial, (irregular) Title varies 36-7601 26.00
1. U.S.—Biog.—Dictionaries. 2. Canada—Biog.—Dictionaries. 3. Capitalists and financiers—U.S. I. Institute for Research in Biography, inc.

WHO'S who in commerce and industry; 923.873
14th ed. Chicago, Marquis [c.1936-1965] xv, 1556p. 27cm. (The International business who's who) Founder in 1936 as who's who in commerce and industry. Title varies. 36-7601 27.50
1. U.S.—Biog.—Dictionaries. 2. Canada—Biog.—Dictionaries. 3. Capitalists and financiers—U.S. I. Institute for Research in Biography, Inc.

WHO'S who in the Midwest; 920.077
a biographical dictionary of noteworthy men and women of the Central and Midwestern States. 8th ed. Chicago, Marquis [c.1949-1963] 1032p. 27cm. 50-289 25.00
1. U. S.—Biog. —Dictionaries.

WHO'S who in the Midwest and Central Canada; 920.077
a biographical dictionary of noteworthy men and women of the Central and Midwestern states and Central Canada. 10th ed. Chicago, Marquis [c.1949-1966] 1117p. 27cm. 50-289 27.00
1. U.S.—Biog.—Dictionaries. 2. Canada—Biog.—Dictionaries.

WORLD who's who in commerce and industry. 923'.873
15th ed.; [1968/1969] Chicago, Marquis-Who's Who 1967. v. 21-27cm. biennial (irregular) The intl. busi. who s who. Title varies: 1936-59, Who's who in commerce and industry. Vs. for 1940/41, 1947-59 called Intl. ed. Vs. for 1936-38 pub. in New York by the Inst. For Res. in Biog., Inc. [HF3023.A2W5] 36-7601 27.00
1. U.S.—Biog.—Dictionaries. 2. Canada—Biog.— Dictionaries. 3. Capitalists and financiers—U.S. I. Institute for Research in Biography, Inc. II. Title: Who's who in commerce and industry.

U.S.—Biography—Juvenile literature.

BAILEY, Helen Miller 920
40 American biographies. General ed.: Lewis Paul Todd. Edit. consultantants Mabel B. Casner, Ralph H. Gabriel New York, Harcourt [c.1964] vi, 250p. 21cm. Bibl. 64-56614 2.40
1. U.S.—Biog.—Juvenile literature. I. Title.

BROWN, Ralph A. 973'.0992 B
Exploring with American heroes. General editor: Ralph Adams Brown. 2d ed. Chicago, Follett Pub. Co. [1973] 351 p. illus. (part col.) 27 cm. Traces the development of the United States through biographical profiles of well-known men and women in several fields. [E176.8.B76 1973] 920 73-160591 4.74
1. United States—Biography—Juvenile literature. I. Title.

CATHON, Laura E., comp. 920.073
For patriot dream, compiled by Laura E. Cathon [and] Thusnelda Schmidt. Drawings by Sarah Kurek. Nashville, Abingdon Press [1970] 206 p. illus. 24 cm. Excerpts from fictional and non-fictional accounts of events and people important in the founding and development of the United States. [E176.8.C34] 79-105062 ISBN 0-687-13292-4 4.95
1. United States—Biography—Juvenile literature. 2. United States—History—Anecdotes, facetiae, satire, etc.—Juvenile literature. I. Schmidt, Thusnelda, joint comp. II. Kurek, Sarah, illus. III. Title.

CLIFFORD, Harold Burton, 1893- 920.073
American leaders. [New York] American Book Co. [1953] 320p. illus. 21cm. Includes bibliography. [E178.3.C67] 53-6013
1. U.S.—Biog.—Juvenile literature. I. Title.

COTTLER, Joseph, 1899- 920.073
Champions of democracy. Freeport, N.Y., Books for Libraries Press [1970] 310 p. illus., ports. 23 cm. (Essay index reprint series) Reprint of the 1936 ed. Contents.Contents.—The voice in the wilderness, Roger Williams.—The arch-rebel, Thomas Jefferson.—Horace Mann takes the case.—The liberator, William Lloyd Garrison.—Susan Brownell Anthony vs. the United States.—The oracle of democracy, Charles William Eliot.—The printer and the riddle, Henry George.—Judge Holmes and the Constitution.—The grand old man of labor, Samuel Gompers.—Up from slavery, Booker T. Washington.—The good neighbor, Jane Addams.—The new freedom, Woodrow Wilson. [E176.C75 1970] 920 78-128229
1. U.S.—Biography—Juvenile literature. I. Title. **BIP**

DAUGHERTY, Sonia (Medvedeva) 1893- 973
Ten brave men; makers of the American way. With drawings by James Daugherty. [1st ed.] Philadelphia, Lippincott [1951] 152 p. illus. 22 cm. [E176.8.D3] 51-11163
1. United States—Biography Juvenile literature. I. Title.

DENNISTON, Elinore, 1900- 920
Famous makers of America, by Rae Foley [pseud.] New York, Dodd, Mead [1963] 154 p. illus. 22 cm. (Famous biographies for young people) [E176.8D45] 63-14157
1. U.S. — Biog. — Juvenile literature. I. Title.

DIKTY, T. E. 920
Every boy's book of American heroes. New York, Fell [c.1963] 188p. 22cm. (Fell's every boy's ser.) 63-14281 3.95
1. U.S.—Biog.—Juvenile literature. 2. Heroes—Juvenile literature. I. Title.

DIRKSEN, Everett McKinley. 920.073
Gallant men; stories of American adventure, by Everett McKinley Dirksen and H. Paul Jeffers. New York, McGraw-Hill [1967] 122 p. illus. 24 cm. "Based on Senator Dirksen's Capitol recording Gallant men, conceived and written by H. Paul Jeffers." Contents.Contents.—William Bradford, the shepherd boy who led the Pilgrims.—Samuel Adams, a man who made a revolution.—Doctor Warren and the Minutemen.—Jefferson and his Declaration.—Defenders of Fort McHenry.—General Warren of Little Round Top.—Mr. Lincoln goes to Gettysburg. —Lovely lady, holding the lamp.—Four gallant men: Alvin York, John F. Kennedy, Connie Charlton, Bill Carpenter.—John Glenn, voyager on a new sea.—Pledge of allegiance to the flag. [CT217.D5] 67-25348
1. United States—Biography—Juvenile literature. I. Jeffers, Harry Paul, 1934- Gallant men. II. Title.

DOUTY, Esther (Morris) 920.073
Under the new roof; five patriots of the young Republic. Chicago, Rand McNally [c.1965] 288p. ports. 22cm. [E176.8.D68] 65-18584 4.50
1. U.S.—Biog.—Juvenile literature. I. Title. Contents omitted.

FIEDLER, Jean 920
Great American heroes. Illus. by Raymond Burns. New York, Hart [1966] 192p. illus. 23cm. (Sunrise lib.) [E176.8F47] 66-15776 1.50; 3.29 bds. ,lib. ed.,
1. U. S.—Biog.—Juvenile literature. 2. Heroes—Juvenile literature. I. Burns, Raymond, illus. II. Title.

FISHER, Dorothea Frances Canfield, 1879-1958. 920.073
And long remember; some great Americans who have helped me. Illustrated by Ezra Jack Keats. New York, Whittlesey House [1959] 118 p. illus. 26 cm. [E176.8.F5] 59-11929
1. U.S.—Biography—Juvenile literature. I. Title.

FLEMING, Alice (Mulcahey) 1928- 920.073
Pioneers in print; adventures in courage, by Alice Fleming. Chicago, Reilly & Lee Books [1971] 130 p. illus. 24 cm. Bibliography: p. 129-130. Brief biographies of nine men and women whose printed works paved new roads in literature and journalism. [CT217.F57] 920 70-163277 5.95
1. U.S.—Biography—Juvenile literature. I. Title.

FOWLER, Mary Jane. 920 (J)
Great Americans [by] Mary Jane Fowler [and] Margaret Fisher. Grand Rapids, Fideler Co. [1968] 144 p. illus., ports. 28 cm. (American history and culture) [E176.8.F6 1968] 68-21255
1. United States—Biography—Juvenile literature. I. Hertel, Margaret (Fisher), joint author. II. Title.

GENG, Veronica. 920.073 B
Guess who? A cavalcade of famous Americans. Illustrated by Huntley Brown. New York, Platt & Munk [1969] [64] p. col. illus. 23 cm. Statements and illustrations give clues to the identity of sixty famous Americans. The reader turns the page for the answers and a capsule biography of each individual. [CT217.G4] 920 72-75889
1. U.S.—Biography—Juvenile literature. I. Brown, Huntley, illus. II. Title.

GRIFFITH, Ward. 920.073
Fifty famous Americans. Illustrated by Henry E. Vallely. Freeport, N.Y., Books for Libraries Press [1970, c1946] 236 p. illus., ports. 24 cm. (Biography index reprint series) Recounts briefly the careers of fifty famous Americans from various periods of national history. Includes statesmen, artists, musicians, soldiers, explorers, and inventors. [CT217.G7 1970] 920 79-117325 ISBN 0-8369-8017-4
1. United States—Biography—Juvenile literature. I. Vallely, Henry E., illus. II. Title. **BIP**

HAYNES, Samuel. 920
Trailblazers of America. Illustrated by Frank Nicholas. Racine, Wis., Whitman Pub. Co. [1961] 91p. illus. 24cm. (A Badger book) [E176.H395] 61-66723
1. U. S.— Biog.—Juvenile literature. I. Title.

HOYT, Edwin Palmer 920
The idea men. New York, Duell [dist. Meredith, c.1966] 192p. 21cm. [HC102.5.A2H65] 66-14960 3.95 bds.,
1. U. S.—Biog.—Juvenile literature. 2. Businessmen—U. S.—Juvenile literature. I. Title.

LEIPOLD, L. Edmond, 1902- 920'.073
Americans born abroad, by L. Edmond Leipold. Minneapolis, T. S. Denison [1973] 64 p. col. illus. 25 cm. (His Lives of great Americans) Contents.—John James Audubon.—Alexander Graham Bell.—William W. Mayo.—Hendrik Van Loon.—Knute Rockne. [CT217.L42] 920 70-190689 3.99 (Lib. Ed.)
1. United States—Biography—Juvenile literature. I. Title.

LEIPOLD, L Edmond, 1902- 920
Citizens born abroad, by L. Edmond Leipold. Minneapolis, Denison [1967] 73 p. 25 cm. (His Famous American heroes and leaders series) [CT217.L45] 67-22258
1. U. S.—Biog.—Juvenile literature. I. Title.

LEIPOLD, L. Edmond, 1902- 920.073
Crusaders for a cause, by L. Edmond Leipold. Minneapolis, Denison [1967] 76p. 25cm. (Famous Amer. heroes and leaders ser.) [CT217.L455] 67-26346 3.69
1. U.S.—Biog.—Juvenile literature. I. Title. Contents Omitted.

LEIPOLD, L. Edmond, 1902- 920
Founders of our cities, by L. Edmond Leipold. Minneapolis, Denison [1967] 71p. 25cm. (His Famous Amer. heroes and leaders ser.) [CT217.L47] 67-22259 3.69
1. U.S.—Biog.—Juvenile literature. 2. Cities and towns.—U.S.—Hist.—Juvenile Literature. I. Title.

LEIPOLD, L. Edmond, 1902- 920
Heroes in time of war, by L. Edmond Leipold. Minneapolis, Denison [1967] 82p. 25 cm. (His Famous Amer. heroes and leaders ser.) [E181.L48] 67-22260 3.69
1. U.S.—Biog Juvenile literature. 2. U.S.—History, Military—Juvenile literature. I. Title.

LEIPOLD, L. Edmond, 920'.073
1902-
Heroes of a different kind, by L. Edmond Leipold. Minneapolis, T. S. Denison [1973] 64 p. col. illus. 25 cm. (His Lives of great Americans) Contents.Contents.—Phillis Wheatley.—Jim Thorpe.—James Whitcomb Riley.—Thomas Alva Edison.—Walt Disney. [CT217.L49] 920 72-190687 ISBN 0-513-01238-9 3.99
1. United States—Biography—Juvenile literature. I. Title.

LEIPOLD, L. Edmond, 920'.073
1902-
Makers of a better America, by L. Edmond Leipold. Minneapolis, T. S. Denison [1972] 63 p. col. illus. 25 cm. (Lives of great Americans) Contents.Contents.—John Jacob Astor.—Horace Mann.—Clara Barton.—George Washington Carver.—Dr. Walter Reed. [CT217.L494] 920 75-190685
1. United States—Biography—Juvenile literature. I. Title. II. Series: Lives of great Americans (Minneapolis)

LEIPOLD, L. Edmond, 920'.073
1902-
They gave their lives, by L. Edmond Leipold. Minneapolis, Denison [1972] 64 p. col. illus. 25 cm. (Lives of great Americans) Brief biographies of five men who died serving their country: Elijah Lovejoy, Abraham Lincoln, George A. Custer, John F. Kennedy, and Martin Luther King. [E176.8.L44] 920 79-190686 ISBN 0-513-01237-0 3.99 (Lib. Ed.)
1. United States—Biography—Juvenile literature. I. Title. II. Series: Lives of great Americans (Minneapolis)

LOWENSTEIN, Evelyn. 920
Picture book of famous immigrants. [Prepared by Evelyn Lowenstein and others] New York, Sterling [1962] 64p. illus. 26cm. (Visual hist. ser.) 62-18641 1.00 pap.,
1. U. S.—Biog.—Juvenile literature. 2. U. S.—Emig. & immig.—Juvenile literature. I. Title. II. Title: Famous immigrants.

MCMILLEN, Wheeler, 1893- 920
Fifty useful Americans. New York, Putnam [1966, c.1965] 218p. 21cm. Bibl. [CT217.M19] 65-25612 3.95
1. U. S.—Biog.—Juvenile literature. I. Title.

MCNEER, May Yonge, 1902- 920
Give me freedom, Drawings by Lynd Ward. New York, Abingdon Press [1964] 128 p. illus., ports 25 cm. Contents.Contents.—To freedom's shore: William Penn.—Voice of the Revolution: Thomas Paine.—I take my stand: Elijah Parish Lovejoy.—As good as a boy: Elizabeth Cady Stanton.—The shoes of happiness: Edwin Markham—The Whole world in His hands: Marian Anderson.—A game called"X": Albert Einstein. [E176.8.M2] 64-10155
1. U.S.—Biography—Juvenile literature. 2. Liberty—Juvenile literature. I. Title.

MEYER, Edith Patterson 920.073
Champions of the four freedoms. Illus. by Eric von Schmidt. [1st ed.] Boston, Little [1966] xv, 301p. illus. 21cm. Bibl. [E176.M47] 66-17689 4.95
1. U. S.—Biog.—Juvenile literature. I. Title.

PIELMEIER, Mary Francis 920 (j)
Assisi, 1919-
The brave and the free [by] Sister M. Francis Assisi. [Boston] Ginn [1967] vi, 377 p. illus. (part col.) 24 cm. (Frontiers of freedom) [CT217.P5] 67-10329
1. United States—Biography—Juvenile literature. I. Title.

REINFELD, Fred, 1910- 920.073
The great dissenters, guardians of their country's laws and liberties. New rev., enlarged ed. New York, Bantam [c.1959, 1964] 175p. 18cm. (Pathfinder ed. HP76) [E339.R4] .60 pap.,
1. U. S.—Biog.—Juvenile literature. I. Title.

REINFELD, Fred, 1910- 920.073
1964.
The great dissenters; guardians of their country's laws and liberties. New, rev., enl. ed. New York, Bantam Books [1964] x, 178 p. 18 cm. (Bantam pathfinder editions, HP76) Bibliography: p. 173-175. [E339.R4] 65-2026
1. U.S. — Biog. — Juvenile literature. I. Title.

*ST. Louis Board of 920.073 B
Education.
Mini-sketches of great Americans; with original drawings by young artists. New York, Pocket Books [1974, c1972] 272 p. illus. 18 cm. (Washington Square Press book) [CT211] ISBN 0-671-47917-2 0.95 (pbk.)
I. Title.

SCHIRMER, Mathilda, ed. 920.073
Builders for progress. Illus. by Dirk Gringhuis. Chicago, Beckley-Cardy [1950] 180 p. illus. 21 cm. (Americans in action) [CT217.S35] 50-58137
1. U.S.—Biography—Juvenile literature. I. Title.

SOUTHWORTH, Gertrude (Van 920.073
Duyn) 1874-
Heroes of our America, by Gertrude Van Duyn Southworth and John Van Duyn Southworth; illustrated with original artwork by Malcolm Ware. Syracuse, N.Y., Iroquois Pub. Co. [1952] 408 p. illus. 22 cm. [CT217.S68] 52-4055
1. U.S. — Biography — Juvenile literature. I. Title.

†THE Spirit of '76 : 920'.073
a compilation of exemplary acts of conduct by American men and women throughout the first two-hundred years of United States history / general editor, Willard E. Rosenfeld; ill. by Howard Lindberg; design by Edward Olderen. Minneapolis : Denison, c1976. 605 p. : ill. ; 29 cm. "The stories ... are adapted from The spirit of '76, a series of radio programs produced and sponsored by the Union Oil Company of California." One-page biographical sketches of American men and women whose accomplishments exemplify the spirit of America. [CT217.S69] 76-366695 ISBN 0-513-01493-4 : 19.95
1. United States—Biography—Juvenile literature. I. Rosenfelt, Willard E. II. Lindberg, Howard E. III. Union Oil Company of California.

SPRIGGS, Elsie Helena. 920.07
Pioneers of the New World; stories of Christian founders of Canada and the U.S.A. Illustrated by H.W. Whanslaw. New York, Library Publishers [1952] 136p. illus. 19cm. Includes bibliography. [E176.S834] 52-148180
1. U. S.—Biog.—Juvenile literature. 2. Canada—Biog.—Juvenile literature. I. Title.

STRONG, Sydney Dix, 1860- 920.073
1938, ed.
What I owe to my father, by Jane Addams [and others] Edited by Sydney Strong. With an introd. by James E. West. Freeport, N.Y., Books for Libraries Press [1972] viii, 184 p. 23 cm. (Essay index reprint series) Reprint of the 1931 ed. Fourteen American men and women pay tribute to their fathers as an important influence in their lives. [CT215.S7 1972] 920 69-17590 ISBN 0-8369-2672-2
1. United States—Biography—Juvenile literature. 2. Fathers—Biography—Juvenile literature. I. Addams, Jane, 1860-1935. **BIP**

TAYLOR, L. B. 920'.073
Rescue! : True stories of heroism / By L. B. Taylor, Jr. ; illustrated by Michael Deas. New York : F. Watts, 1978. 87 p. : ill. ; 25 cm. Relates the exploits of teenagers who were awarded the Carnegie Hero Fund Commission's medal of honor for their heroic efforts at saving lives. [CT217.T37] 78-3665 ISBN 0-531-02223-4 : 5.90
1. United States—Biography—Juvenile literature. 2. Heroes—United States—Biography—Juvenile literature. 3. Youth—United States—Biography—Juvenile literature. I. Deas, Michael. II. Title.

TAYLOR, L.B. 920'.073
Rescue : true stories of heroism / by L. B. Taylor Jr. ; illustrated by Michael Deas. New York : Pocket Books, 1980, c1978. 119 p.; 18 cm. (An Archway Paperback) Relates the exploits of teenagers who were awarded the Carnegie Hero Fund Commission's medal of honor for their heroic efforts at saving lives. [CT217.T37] ISBN 0-671-29989-1 pbk. : 1.80
1. United States — Biography — Juvenile literature. 2. Heroes — United States — Biography — Juvenile literature. 3. Youth — United States -Biography -Juvenile literature I. Title.
L.C. card no. for 1978 F. Watts ed.: 78-3665 **BIP**

THOMAS, Eleanor, 1898- 920.073
Heroes, heroines, and holidays, by Eleanor Thomas and Mary G. Kelty. Freeport, N.Y., Books For Libraries Press [1971, c1952] vi, 248 p. illus., ports. 23 cm. (Biography index reprint series) Profiles of some of America's explorers, statesmen, inventors, naturalists, and suffragettes, explaining how some of these figures are responsible for holidays we now observe. [E176.T5 1971] 920 78-148228 ISBN 0-8369-8075-1
1. U.S.—Biography—Juvenile literature. 2. Holidays—U.S.—Juvenile literature. I. Kelty, Mary Gertrude, 1890-1964, joint author. II. Title.

WELCH, Helena 920
When they were children. Illus. by Don Fields. Nashville, Southern Pub. [1965] 136p. illus. 21cm. [CT107.W54] 65-10246 2.95
1. U. S.—Biog.—Juvenile literature. 2. Gt. Brit.—Biog.—Juvenile literature. I. Title.

WELCH, Helena 920
When they were children. Illus. by Don Fields. Nashville, Southern Pub. Assn. [1967, c.1965] 136p. illus. 21cm. (Summit bk.) [CT107.W54] 1.00 pap.,
1. U.S.—Biog.—Juvenile literature. 2. Gt. Brit.—Biog.—Juvenile literature. I. Title.

U.S.—Civilization—1945-

CLARK, John Pepper, 917.3'03'92
1935-
America, their America [by] J. P. Clark. New York, Africana Pub. Corp. [1969, c1964] 224 p. 19 cm. [E169.12.C53 1969] 79-80851 1.50
1. U.S.—Civilization—1945- 2. National characteristics, American. 3. Students, Foreign—Princeton, N.J. I. Title. **BIP**

U.S.—Civilization—1970-

MUNGO, Raymond, 917.3'03'924
1946-
Total Loss Farm; a year in the life. [1st ed.] New York, Dutton, 1970. 181 p. illus. 21 cm. Autobiographical. [E169.12.M84 1970] 73-125905 5.95
1. U.S.—Civilization—1970- 2. U.S.—Description and travel—1960- I. Title. **BIP**

U.S.—Diplomatic and consular service.

RUSSELL, Beatrice. 327.73
Living in state. Pref. by Robert McClintock. New York, D. McKay Co. [1959] 272 p. 21 cm. [D413.R8A3] 59-9554
1. U.S.—Diplomatic and consular service. 2. Diplomats—Correspondence, reminiscences, etc. I. Title.

U.S. Federal Bureau of Investigation.

COCHRAN, Louis, 1899- 364.120924
FBI man; a personal history. [1st ed.] New York, Duell, Sloan and Pearce [1966] xiii, 207 p. 22 cm. [HV7914.C65] 66-11057
1. U.S. Federal Bureau of Investigation. 2. Crime and criminals—U.S. I. Title.

PAYNE, Cril. 364.12'092'4 B
Deep cover : an FBI agent infiltrates the radical underground / by Cril Payne. New York : Newsweek Books, c1979. p. cm. [HV7911.P38A33] 79-51632 ISBN 0-88225-274-7 : 12.95
1. Payne, Cril. 2. U.S. Federal Bureau of Investigation—Officials and employees—Biography. 3. Weather Underground Organization. 4. Radicalism—United States. I. Title.

U.S.—Foreign relations—Gt. Brit.

WILLSON, Beckles, 327.73'042
1869-1942.
America's ambassadors to England, 1785-1928; a narrative of Anglo-American diplomatic relations. Freeport, N.Y., Books for Libraries Press [1969] xiv, 497 p. ports. 23 cm. (Essay index reprint series) Reprint of the 1968 ed. Includes bibliographical references. [E183.8.G7W65 1969] 70-93388
1. U.S.—Foreign relations—Gt. Brit. 2. Gt. Brit.—Foreign relations—U.S. 3. U.S.—Diplomatic and consular service—Gt. Brit. I. Title.

U.S.—History.

HASSLER, Warren W 923.573
Commanders of the Army of the Potomac. Baton Rouge, Louisiana State University Press [1962] 281p. illus. 24cm. Includes bibliography. [E470.2.H32] 62-11738
1. U. S. —Hist.—Civil War—Regimental histories—Army of the Potomac. 2. U. S.—Hist.—Civil War—Biog. 3. Generals—U. S. I. Title. **BIP**

MCGUIRE, Edna. 372.8'973
They made America great. New York, Macmillan [1971] vii, 296 p. illus. (part col.) col. maps. 24 cm. (Macmillan elementary history series) Divides American history into nine time periods stressing the contributions of various individuals to the history of each period. [E178.3.M159 1971] 920 76-29949
1. U.S.—History—Juvenile literature. I. Title.

MCGUIRE, Edna. 372.8'9'73
They made America great. Teacher's annotated ed. New York, Macmillan [1971] vii, 296, iv, 67 p. illus. (part col.), col. maps., ports. 24 cm. (Macmillan elementary history series) Teacher's manual (iv, 67 p.) at end. Bibliography: p. 64-67 (4th group) Divides American history into nine time periods, from the nation's founding to the space age, stressing the contributions of various individuals to the history of each period. [E178.3.M159 1971] 920 76-24567
1. U.S.—History—Juvenile literature. I. Title.

MOORE, Frank, 1828-1904. v. 12
Women of the war; their heroism and self-sacrifice, by Frank Moore. Hartford, Conn., S. S. Scranton and co., 1966. 596 p. 67-29687
1. U.S. — Hist. — Civil war — Women's work. 2. U.S. — Hist. — Civil war — Biography. I. Title.

NASH, Roderick. 973'.0992
From these beginnings ...; a biographical approach to American history. New York, Harper & Row [1973] 548 p. illus. 24 cm. Includes bibliographies. [E178.N18] 72-9395 ISBN 0-06-044725-7 6.95
1. United States—History. 2. United States—Biography. I. Title. **BIP**

NASH, Roderick. 973'.0992
From these beginnings ... : a biographical approach to American history / Roderick Nash. 2d ed. New York : Harper & Row, c1978. 2 v. : ill. ; 24 cm. Includes bibliographies and indexes. [E178.N18 1978] 77-17091 ISBN 0-06-044717-6 (v.1) pbk. : 7.95
1. United States—History. 2. United States—Biography. I. Title.

NICHOLAS, Edward, 1906- 973
The hours and the ages; a sequence of Americans. Port Washington, N.Y., Kennikat Press [1969, c1949] 304 p. 22 cm. (Essay and general literature index reprint series) [E178.N517 1969] 75-86050

1. U.S.—History. 2. U.S.—Biography. I. Title. BIP

SOBOL, Donald J 1924- 920.073
Lock, stock, and barrel, by Donald J. Sobol. Illustrated by Edward J. Smith. Philadelphia, Westminster Press [1965] 256 p. illus. 23 cm. Includes bibliographies. [E206.S7] 65-10364
1. U.S. — Hist. — Revolution — Biog. — Juvenile literature. I. Title.

U. S.—History—Revolution—Biography.

BAKELESS, John Edwin, 1894- 973.31'3'0922 B
Signers of the declaration [by] John and Katherine Bakeless. Boston, Houghton Mifflin, 1969. xiv, 300 p. 22 cm. Bibliography: p. [299]-300. [E221.B33] 69-14723 3.95
1. U.S. Declaration of Independence—Signers. I. Bakeless, Katherine (Little) 1895- joint author. II. Title. BIP

COOKE, Donald Ewin, 1916- 973.31'3'0922 B
Fathers of America's freedom; the story of the signers of the Declaration of Independence, by Donald E. Cooke. Port. illus. by Harry J. Schaare. [Maplewood, N.J.] Hammond [1969] 93 p. illus., facsims., maps, ports. 26 cm. (Profile series) Part of illustrative matter is colored. Bibliography: p. 92. Outlines the history of the Declaration of Independence and gives brief biographies of its fifty-six signers. [E221.C75] 920 70-76983
1. U.S. Declaration of Independence—Signers—Juvenile literature. I. Schaare, Harry J., illus. II. Title.

FEUERLICHT, Roberta Strauss. 973.31'3
A free people; the story of the Declaration of Independence and the men who wrote it. Illustrated by Jules Gotlieb. New York, Messner [1969] 96 p. illus., facsim., ports. 23 cm. Bibliography: p. 90. Describes the events leading to the Declaration of Independence and gives brief biographies of the five men responsible for writing the document: Thomas Jefferson, John Adams, Benjamin Franklin, Roger Sherman, and Robert R. Livingston. [E221.F44] 76-83358 3.95
1. U.S. Declaration of Independence—Juvenile literature. I. Gotlieb, Jules, illus. II. Title.

FINK, Sam. 973.31'3'0922 B
The fifty-six who signed. New York, McCall Pub. Co. [1971] 116 p. illus. 25 cm. [E221.F55 1971] 70-153185 ISBN 0-8415-2038-0 4.95
1. U.S. Declaration of independence—Signers—Portraits, caricatures, etc. I. Title.

HILLARD, Elias Brewster, 1825-1895. 973.3'0922
The last men of the Revolution; containing a photograph of each from life, accompanied by brief biographical sketches ... Edited by Wendell D. Garret. Introd. by Archibald MacLeish. [Barre, Mass.] Barre Publishers, 1968. 116 p. illus., ports. 24 cm. Reprint of the 1864 ed. Contents.Contents.—Samuel Downing.—Daniel Waldo.—Lemuel Cook.—Alexander Milliner.—William Hutchings.—Adam Link.—James Barham. [E206.H54 1968] 67-23658 6.95
1. U. S.—History—Revolution—Biography. I. Garrett, Wendell D., ed. II. Title.

LOSSING, Benson John, 1813-1891. 973.31'3'0922
Biographical sketches of the signers of the Declaration of American independence. The Declaration historically considered; and a sketch of the leading events connected with the adoption of the Articles of confederation and of the Federal Constitution. Glendale, N.Y., Benchmark Pub. Co., 1970. iv, 384 p. illus., ports. 23 cm. On spine: Lives of the signers. Reprint of the 1858 ed. [E221.L914 1970] 70-22618 8.50
1. U.S. Declaration of Independence. 2. U.S. Declaration of Independence—Signers. I. Title.

MCGEE, Dorothy Horton. 973.313
Famous signers of the Declaration; with photographic illus. New York, Dodd, Mead, 1955. 307p. illus. 22cm. (Famous biographies for young people) [E221.M15] 55-5860
1. U. S. Declaration of independence—Signers. I. Title.

MORRIS, Richard Brandon, 1904- 973.3'092'2 B
Seven who shaped our destiny; the Founding Fathers as revolutionaries [by] Richard B. Morris. [1st ed.] New York, Harper & Row [1973] 334 p. illus. 22 cm. (A Cass Canfield book) Includes bibliographical references. [E302.5.M67] 73-4111 ISBN 0-06-013078-4 8.95
1. United States—History—Revolution—Biography. 2. United States—History—Revolution—Causes. I. Title.

MORRIS, Richard Brandon, 1904- 973.3'092'2 B
Seven who shaped our destiny; the Founding Fathers as revolutionaries [by] Richard B. Morris. New York, Harper & Row [1976 c1973] 334 p. illus. 22 cm. (A Harper Colophon Book) Includes bibliographical references and index. [E302.5.M67] ISBN 0-06-090454-2 4.95 (pbk.)
1. United States—History—Revolution—Biography. 2. United States—History—Revolution—Causes. I. Title.
L.C. card no. for original edition: 73-4111. BIP

U.S. Congress. 328.73'0922 B
Biographical directory of the American Congress, 1774-1971, the Continental Congress, September 5, 1774, to October 21, 1788, and the Congress of the United States, from the First through the Ninety-first Congress, March 4, 1789, to January 3, 1971, inclusive. [Washington] U.S. Govt. Print. Off., 1971. 1972 p. 30 cm. (92d Congress, 1st session. Senate document no. 92-8) Lawrence F. Kennedy, chief compiler. [JK1010.A5 1971] 79-616224 15.75
1. U.S. Continental Congress—Biography. 2. U.S. Congress—Biography. 3. U.S.—Biography—Dictionaries. I. Kennedy, Lawrence F., comp. II. Title. III. Series: U.S. 92d Congress, 1st session, 1971. Senate. Document no. 92-8.

WHITNEY, David C 973.313
Founders of freedom in America; lives of the men who signed the Declaration of independence and so helped to establish the United States of America, by David C. Whitney. Coordinating editor, Thomas C. Jones; editor of prints and photos., Kathrine B. Sanforn. Political and philosophical origins of the Declaration of independence, by David S. Lovejoy. Chicago, J. G. Ferguson Pub. Co. [1964] 260 p. illus. (part col.) facsims., map, ports. (part col.) 29 cm. [E221.W57] 64-17918
1. U.S. Declaration of independence—Signers. I. Title.

WHITNEY, David C. 973.31'3'0922
Founders of freedom in America; lives of the men who signed the Declaration of independence and so helped to establish the United States of America. Chicago, Distributed by Encyclopaedia Britannica Educational Corp. [1971] 2 v. illus. (part col.), facsims., ports. (part col.) 29 cm. (American freedom library) Cover title: Signers of the Declaration of independence. A brief analysis of the political and philosophical origins of the Declaration of independence accompanies biographies of the fifty-six Signers. Also includes biographies of Patrick Henry and James Otis and an "Almanac of Independence." [E221.W57 1971] 920 79-24514
1. U.S. Declaration of independence—Signers. I. Title. II. Title: Signers of the Declaration of independence.

WILDMAN, Edwin, 1867-1932. 973.3'0922
The founders of America in the days of the revolution; the lives and deeds of the great patriots who gave this Nation its independence. Freeport, N. Y., Books for Libraries Press [1968] x, 326 p. illus., ports. 23 cm. (Essay index reprint series) Reprint of the 1924 ed. Bibliography: p. 319-321. [E302.5.W64 1968] 68-57344
1. U.S.—History—Revolution—Biography. I. Title.

U.S.—History—1783-1865.

THOMAS, Ebenezer Smith, 1775-1845. 917.3'03'3
Reminiscences of the last sixty-five years. [New York] Arno [1970] 300, 300 p. 23 cm. (The American journalists) Reprint of the 1840 ed. [E302.6.T4T4 1970] 79-125719 ISBN 0-405-01700-6
1. U.S.—History—1783-1865. 2. U.S.—Biography. I. Title. BIP

U.S.—History—1783-1865—Sources.

ADAMS, John Quincy, Pres. U.S., 1767-1848. 973.5'0924
Memoirs of John Quincy Adams, comprising portions of his diary from 1795 to 1848. Edited by Charles Francis Adams. Freeport, N.Y., Books for Libraries Press [1969] 12 v. ports. 24 cm. (Select bibliographies reprint series) Reprint of the 1874-77 ed. [E377.A2 1969] 71-85454
1. U.S.—History—1783-1865—Sources. 2. U.S.—Politics and government—1783-1865. 3. U.S.—Foreign relations—1783-1865. I. Adams, Charles Francis, 1807-1886, ed. II. Title. BIP

MADISON, James, Pres. U.S., 1751-1836. 016.9735'1'0924
Calendar of the correspondence of James Madison. New York, B. Franklin [1970] vii, 739, 70 p. 24 cm. (American classics in history & social sciences, 120) (Burt Franklin bibliography & reference series, 328.) Reprint of the 1894 ed., and index originally published in 1895. [E302.M16 1970] 73-119768
1. U.S.—History—1783-1865—Sources. I. Title. BIP

U.S.—History—1901-1953.

TAFT, William Howard, Pres. U.S., 1857-1930. 973.91'2'0924
William Howard Taft, 1857-1930; chronology, documents, bibliographical aids. Edited by Gilbert J. Black. Dobbs Ferry, N.Y., Oceana Publications, 1970. 89 p. 24 cm. (Oceana presidential chronology series) Bibliography: p. 83-87. [E761.B55] 70-116059 ISBN 0-379-12080-1
1. U.S.—History—1901-1953. I. Black, Gilbert J., ed. II. U.S. President, 1909-1913 (Taft)

U.S. Library of Congress—History.

COLE, John Young, 1940- 027.5'753 B
Ainsworth Spofford and the "National Library." [Washington?] 1971. xi, 154 l. 29 cm. Thesis—George Washington University. Bibliography: leaves 148-154. [Z733.U6C56] 78-29542
1. U.S. Library of Congress—History. 2. Spofford, Ainsworth Rand, 1825-1908. I. Title.

U.S. Marine Corps—Biog.

SCHUON, Karl 923.573
U.S. Marine Corps biographical dictionary; the corps' fighting men, what they did, where they served. New York, Watts [c.1963] vii, 278p. col. illus., ports. 25cm. 63-16921 10.00
1. U.S. Marine Corps—Biog. I. Title.

U.S. Marine Corps—History.

VANDEGRIFT, Alexander Archer, 1887- 923.573
Once a marine; the memoirs of General A. A. Vandegrift, United States Marine Corps, as told to Robert B. Asprey. [1st ed.] New York, Norton [1964] 338 p. illus., ports., maps. 22 cm. [E746.V3] 64-10576
1. U.S. Marine Corps — Hist. I. Asprey, Robert B. II. Title.

VANDEGRIFT, Alexander Archer, 1887- 923.573
Once a marine; the memoirs of General A. A. Vandegrift, United States Marine Corps, as told to Robert B. Asprey. [1st ed.] New York, Norton [1964] 338 p. illus., ports., maps. 22 cm. [E746.V3] 64-10576
1. U.S. Marine Corps—History. I. Asprey, Robert B. II. Title.

VANDERGRIFT, Archer A., Gen. 1887- 923.573
Once a marine; the memoirs of General A.A. Vandergrift. United States Marine Corps. as told to Robert B. Asprey. New York. Ballantine [1966, c.1964] ix. 348p. illus., maps. 18cm. (U6082) .75 pap.,
1. U.S. Marine Corps—Hist. I. Asprey, Robert B. II. Title.

U.S.—Military.

ANDERS, Curtis, 1927- 358.400922
Fighting airmen, by Curt Anders. New York, Putnam [1966] 287 p. 22 cm. Bibliography: p. 277-278. [UG633.A725] 66-15575
1. U.S. Air Force — Biog. 2. Air pilots — Biog. I. Title.

ANDERS, Curtis, 1927- 358.400922
Fighting airmen. New York, Putnam [c.1966] 287p. 22cm. Bibl. [UG633.A725] 66-15575 5.95
1. U.S. Air Force—Biog. 2. Air pilots—Biog. I. Title.

ARMY times, Washington, D.C. 923.573
Great American cavalrymen, by the editors of the Army times. New York, Dodd, Mead [1964] 159 p. illus., ports. 22 cm. [E181.A76] 64-19930
1. U.S. Army — Biog. — Juvenile literature. 2. U.S. Army. Cavalry — Hist. — Juvenile literature. 3. U.S. — History, Military — Juvenile literature. I. Title.

CLARK, Maurine Doran. 923.573
Captain's bride, general's lady; the memoirs of Mrs. Mark W. Clark. New York, McGraw-Hill [1956] 278 p. illus. 21 cm. [E745.C45A35] 56-8860
1. U.S. Army—Military life. 2. Clark, Mark Wayne, 1896- I. Title.

DUPRE, Flint O 923.573
U.S. Air Force biographical dictionary, by Flint O. DuPre. New York, F. Watts [1965] x. 273 p. 25 cm. U.S. Air Force -- Biog. [UG633.D8] 65-11718
I. Title.

LEMAY, Curtis E. 358.413320924 B
Mission with LeMay; my story, by Curtis E. LeMay with MacKinlay Kantor. [1st ed.] Garden City, N. Y., Doubleday, 1965. xiv, 581 p. illus., ports. 24 cm. [E745.L4A3] 65-19908
1. U.S. Army. Air Corps—History. 2. U.S. Air Force—History. I. Kantor, MacKinlay, 1904- II. Title.

MILLER, Ed Mack. 926.2913
Men of the contrail country. Englewood Cliffs, N.J., Prentice-Hall [1963] ix, 244 p. 22 cm. True stories of flyers and airmen of the 20th century. [UG633.M37] 63-18115
1. U.S. Air Force — Biog. 2. Air pilots — Biog. I. Title.

SAMFORD, Doris E. 355.3'48'0924
Ruffles and drums, by Doris Samford. Line drawings by Arminta Neal. Boulder, Colo., Printed by Pruett Pr. [c.1966] ix, 165p. illus., maps. 24cm. [UA565.W6S2] 66-30691 6.50
1. U. S. Army. Women's Army corps. I. Title.

SCOTT, Robert Lee, 1908- 923.573
Boring a hole in the sky; six million miles with a fighter pilot. New York, Random House [1961] 292 p. illus. 24 cm.

[E745.S2A3] 61-6259
1. U.S. Air Force—Officers—Correspondence, reminiscences, etc. I. Title.

U.S. Military Academy, West Point.

BAUMER, William Henry, 1909- 920.073
Not all warriors; portraits of 19th century West Pointers who gained fame in other than military fields, by William Baumer, Jr. Freeport, N.Y., Books for Libraries Press [1971] xii, 313 p. 23 cm. (Essay index reprint series) Reprint of the 1941 ed. Contents.Contents.—Benjamin Louis Eulalie de Bonneville, explorer.—Jefferson Davis, statesman.—Leonidas Polk, clergyman.—Edgar Allan Poe, author and poet.—Henry du Pont, business executive.—James McNeill Whistler, artist.—Horace Porter, diplomat.—Bibliography (p. 305-309) [CT219.B38 1971] 70-152156 ISBN 0-8369-2180-1
1. U.S. Military Academy, West Point. 2. U.S.—Biography. I. Title.

U.S. Military Academy, West Point—Biography.

REEDER, Russell Potter. 355'.0071'174731 B
Heroes and leaders of West Point, by Red Reeder. [1st ed.] New York, Nelson [1970] 192 p. illus., maps, ports. 23 cm. Bibliography: p. 187-190. [U410.M1A44] 76-123113
1. U.S. Military Academy, West Point—Biography. I. Title.

U.S. Navy—Biography.

HILL, Jam Dan, 1897- 923.573
Sea dogs of the sixties. Farragut and seven contemporaries. New York, A. S. Barnes [1961, c1935] xiv, 265 p. illus., ports., maps. 21 cm. (A Perpetua book) Bibliography: p. 253-255. [E467.H65 1961] 63-25222
1. U.S. Navy—Biography. 2. U.S.—History—Civil War—Biography. 3. U.S.—History—Civil War—Naval operations. I. Title.

HILL, Jim Dan, 1897- 923.573
Sea dogs of the sixties: Farragut and seven contemporaries. New York, A. S. Barnes, [1961, c1935] xiv, 265 p. illus., ports., maps. 21 cm. (A Perpetua book) Bibliography: p. 253-255. [E467.H65 1961] 63-25222
1. U.S. Navy — Biog. 2. U.S. — Hist. — Civil War — Biog. 3. U.S. — Hist. — Civil War — Naval operations. I. Title.

LEWIS, Charles Lee, 1886- 359.3'32'0922 B
Famous American naval officers. Rev. ed. Freeport, N.Y., Books for Libraries Press [1971, c1948] x, 444 p. illus., map, ports. 23 cm. (Essay index reprint series) Contents.Contents.—Paul Jones and the beginning of our Navy.—Stephen Decatur and the Barbary corsairs.—Isaac Hull and "Old Ironsides."—David Porter and the cruise of the Essex.—Oliver Hazard Perry and the war on the Great Lakes.—Thomas Macdonough and the battle of Lake Champlain.—Matthew Calbraith Perry and the awakening of Japan.—David Glasgow Farragut and the Civil War.—Alfred Thayer Mahan, the historian of sea power.—Robert Edwin Peary and naval exploration.—George Dewey and the war with Spain.—William Sowden Sims and our Navy in the First World War.—Ernest Joseph King and the Second World War.—Chester William Nimitz: naval commander in chief in the Pacific.—William Frederick Halsey: the fighting admiral.—Bibliography (p. 429-432) [E182.L57 1971] 76-142655 ISBN 0-8369-2170-4
1. U.S. Navy—Biography. 2. U.S. Navy—History. I. Title. BIP

SCORPION (Submarine) 359.3'1'0922 B
United States Ship Scorpion (SSN-589): in memoriam. [Washington, U.S. Govt. Print. Off., 1969] viii, 64 p. illus. (part col.), ports. 27 cm. [V62.S36] 78-602279
1. U.S. Navy—Biography. I. Title.

U. S. Navy—Biog.—Dictionaries.

SCHUON, Karl 923.573
U. S. Navy biographical dictionary. New York, Watts [1965, c.1964] 277p. 24cm. [E182.S45] 64-17396 15.00
1. U. S. Navy—Biog.—Dictionaries. I. Title.

U.S. Navy—Biography—Juvenile literature.

ICENHOWER, Joseph Bryan. 359.3'3'10922
American sea heroes, by Joseph Icenhower. Illus. by Jack Woodson. [Maplewood, N.J.] Hammond [1970] 93 p. illus. (part. col.), col. maps, col. plans, col. ports. 27 cm. Contents.Contents.—John Paul Jones.—Stephen Decatur.—David Porter.—James Lawrence.—Oliver Hazard Perry.—Thomas MacDonough.—Matthew Calbraith Perry.—William B. Cushing.—David Dixon Porter.—Franklin Buchanan.—David Glasgow Farragut.—George Dewey.—Robert E. Peary.—William S. Sims.—Richard E. Byrd.—Chester W. Nimitz.—Raymond A. Spruance.—William F. Halsey. [E182.I25] 920 73-120306 3.50
1. U.S. Navy—Biography—Juvenile literature. I. Woodson, Jack, illus. II. Title.

NAVY times. 359.0922
Great American naval heroes, by the editors of the Navy times. New York, Dodd, Mead [1965] x, 144 p.ports. 22 cm. [E182.N35] 65-23771
1. U.S. Navy — Biog. — Juvenile literature. I. Title.

U.S. Navy—Sea life.

GALLERY, Daniel V. 359.332 B
Eight bells, and all's well [by] Daniel V. Gallery. [1st ed.] New York, Norton [1965] 308 p. illus., ports. 22 cm. Autobiographical. [E182.G25] 65-18021
1. U.S. Navy—Sea life. I. Title.

U.S. — Officials and employees — Biog.

GREEN, William, 1938- 328.73'0924
The congressman. Photography by Dennis Brack. New York, McGraw-Hill [1969] 128 p. illus. 22 cm. (A Week with ... series) An autobiography. Pennsylvania Congressman William Green discusses his day-to-day activities on the House floor, in the office, in his congressional district, and with his family during a typical week. [E840.8.G7A3] 68 30972
1. U.S. Congress. House—Juvenile literature. 2. Legislators—U.S.—Juvenile literature. I. Brack, Dennis, illus. II. Title.

KUHN, Delia, ed. 923.573
Adventures in public service; the careers of eight honored men in the United States Government, by Howard Simons [and others] Edited by Delia and Ferdinand Kuhn. With an introd. by Robert F. Goheen. New York, Vanguard Press [c1963] xvi, 272 p. ports. 22 cm. [JK765.K8] 63-21855
1. U.S. — Officials and employees — Biog. 2. Rewards (Prizes, etc.) — U.S. I. Kuhn, Ferdinand, joint ed. II. Title.

U.S. Penitentiary, Alcatraz Island, Calif.

ELLIS, Steve. 365'.924 B
Alcatraz: number 1172. Los Angeles, Holloway House Pub. Co. [1969] 309 p. 18 cm. Autobiography. [HV9474.A4E55] 76-79889 0.95
1. U.S. Penitentiary, Alcatraz Island, Calif. I. Title.

U.S.—Politics and government—19th century.

SHERMAN, John, 1823-1900. 973.8'0924 B
Recollections of forty years in the House, Senate, and Cabinet; an autobiography. New York, Greenwood Press, 1968 [c1895] 2 v. (xviii, 1239 p.) illus. 24 cm. [E664.S57A3 1968] 68-28647
1. U.S.—Politics and government—19th century. I. Title.

U. S. Presidents—Portraits.

*EASTERWOOD, Birch D. 973'.0922
Pen renderings of the presidents. New York, Vantage [1968] 78p. 36 ports. 28cm. 3.50 bds.,
1. U. S. Presidents—Portraits. I. Title.

U.S.—Race question.

KING, Larry L. 301.451'96'073
Confessions of a white racist [by] Larry L. King. New York, Viking Press [1971] xviii, 173 p. 22 cm. [E185.61.K524 1971] 70-147391 ISBN 0-670-23715-9 5.95
1. U.S.—Race question. I. Title. BIP

LACY, Leslie Alexander. 323.2'0924 B
The rise and fall of a proper Negro; an autobiography. [New York] Macmillan [1970] viii, 244 p. 21 cm. [E185.97.L23A3] 71-95302
1. U.S.—Race question. I. Title. BIP

OWENS, Jesse, 1913- 301.451'96'0924
Blackthink; my life as black man and white man [by] Jesse Owens, with Paul G. Neimark. New York, Morrow, 1970. 215 p. 22 cm. [E185.61.O93] 73-106343 5.95
1. U.S.—Race question. 2. Negroes—Civil rights. I. Neimark, Paul G. II. Title.

U.S.—Social conditions—1960-

BERRIGAN, Daniel. 261.7
The dark night of resistance. [1st ed.] Garden City, N.Y., Doubleday, 1971. vi, 181 p. 22 cm. Contains personal narrative, poetry, and prose. [BX4705.B3845A29] 74-150282 5.95
1. U.S.—Social conditions—1960- 2. Government, Resistance to. I. Title.

DAVIDSON, Sara. 309.1'73'092
Loose change : three women of the sixties / Sara Davidson. 1st ed. Garden City, N.Y. : Doubleday, 1977. 367 p., [16] leaves of plates : ill. ; 22 cm. [HN65.D337] 76-2766 ISBN 0-385-03630-2 : 9.50
1. United States—Social conditions—1960- 2. Radicalism—United States. 3. College students—United States. 4. Young women—United States Biography. I. Title. BIP

U.S.—Social conditions—1960- —Addresses, essays, lectures.

FELDMAN, Saul D., comp. 309.1'73'092
Life styles : diversity in American society / edited by Saul D. Feldman, Gerald W. Thielbar. 2d ed. Boston : Little, Brown, [1975] xiii, 482 p. ; 24 cm. Includes bibliographical references. [HN59.F45 1975] 74-25678 pbk. : 6.95
1. United States—Social conditions—1960- —Addresses, essays, lectures. 2. United States—Social life and customs—1945- —Addresses, essays, lectures. I. Thielbar, Gerald W., joint comp. II. Title. BIP

FELDMAN, Saul D., comp. 309.1'73'092
Life styles; diversity in American society. Edited by Saul D. Feldman [and] Gerald W. Thielbar. Boston, Little, Brown [1971, c1972] xii, 383 p. 24 cm. Includes bibliographical references. [HN59.F45] 76-166968
1. U.S.—Social conditions—1960- —Addresses, essays, lectures. 2. U.S.—Social life and customs—1945- —Addresses, essays, lectures. I. Thielbar, Gerald W., joint comp. II. Title.

U.S. Supreme Court.

DUNHAM, Allison, ed. 923.473
Mr. Justice, ed. by Allison Dunham, Philip B. Kurland. Rev., enl. ed. Chicago, Univ. of Chic. Pr. [c.1956, 1964] xi, 344p. ports. 21cm. Bibl. 64-15821 7.50
1. U.S. Supreme Court. 2. Judges—U.S. I. Kurland, Philip B., joint ed. II. Title.

DUNHAM, Allison, ed. 923.473
Mr. Justice, ed. by Allison Dunham, Philip B. Kurland. Rev., enl. Chicago, Univ. of Chic. Pr. [c.1956, 1964] xi, 344p. ports. 21cm. Bibl. 64-15821 2.95 pap.,
1. U.S. Supreme Court. 2. Judges—U.S. I. Kurland, Philip B., joint ed. II. Title.
Contents omitted.

DUNHAM, Allison, ed. 923.473
Mr. Justice, edited by Allison Dunham & Philip B Kurland. [Chicago] University of Chicago Press [1956] xi, 241p. ports. 23cm. Includes bibliographical references. 56-10080
1. U. S. Supreme Court. 2. Judges—U. S. I. Kurland, Philip B., joint ed. II. Title.
Contents omitted

DUNHAM, Allison, ed. v. 12
Mr. Justice, edited by Allison Dunham & Philip B. Kurland. Rev. and enl. Chicago, University of Chicago Press [1964] xi, 344 p. ports. 21 cm. Contents.Contents. -- Mr. Chief Justice Marshall, by W.W. Crosskey. -- Mr. Chief Justice Taney, by C.B. Swisher. -- Mr. Justice Bradley, by C. Fairman. -- Mr. Justice Harlan, by A F. Westin. -- Mr. Justice Holmes, by F. Biddle. -- Mr. Chief Justice Hughes, by M.J. Pusey. -- Mr. Justice Brandeis, by P.A. Freund. -- Mr. Justice Sutherland, by J.F. Paschal. -- Mr. Chief Justice Stone, by A. Dunham. -- Mr. Justice Cardozo, by A.L. Kaufman. -- Mr. Justice Murphy, by J.P. Roche. -- Mr. Justice Rutledge, by J.P. Stevens. Includes bibliographical references. [923.473] 64-15821
1. U.S. Supreme Court 2. Judges — U.S. I. Kurland, Philip B., joint ed. II. Title.

U.S. Supreme Court—Biography.

ASCH, Sidney H. 347'.7326'34 B
The Supreme Court and its great justices [by] Sidney H. Asch. New York, Arco [1971] vi, 266 p. 23 cm. Bibliography: p. 253-254. [KF8744.A94] 74-125940 ISBN 0-668-02372-4 5.95
1. U.S. Supreme Court—Biography. I. Title. BIP

CAMPBELL, Tom Walter, 1874- 923.473
Four score forgotten men; sketches of the justices of the U. S. Supreme Court. Little Rock, Ark., Pioneer Pub. Co. [1950] v, 424 p. ports. 23 cm. 50-13923
1. U. S. Supreme Court—Biog. I. Title.

FRIEDMAN, Leon, comp. 347.99'22
The justices of the United States Supreme Court, 1789-1969, their lives and major opinions. Leon Friedman & Fred L. Israel, editors; with an introd. by Louis H. Pollak. New York, Chelsea House in association with Bowker, 1969. 4 v. (xxiv, 3373 p.) 25 cm. Includes bibliographies. [KF8744.F75]

69-13699
1. U.S. Supreme Court—Biography. I. Israel, Fred L., joint comp. II. Title.

UMBREIT, Kenneth Bernard. 347.99'22 B
Our eleven Chief Justices; a history of the Supreme Court in terms of their personalities. Port Washington, N.Y., Kennikat Press [1969, c1938] 2 v. (xiv, 539 p.) ports. 24 cm. (Essay and general literature index reprint series) Contents.Contents.—v. 1. John Jay. John Rutledge. Oliver Ellsworth. John Marshall. Roger Brooke Taney.—v. 2. Salmon Portland Chase. Morrison Remick Waite. Melville Weston Fuller. Edward Douglass White. William Howard Taft. Charles Evans Hughes. Bibliography (p. 502-517) [KF8744.U5 1969] 75-86069 ISBN 8-04-605939-
1. U.S. Supreme Court—Biography. I. Title. II. Title: Chief Justices. III. Title: A history of the Supreme Court.

Udden, Johan August, 1859-1932.

HEIMAN, Monica. 550'.92'4
Johan August Udden, a biography. [Kerrville? Tex., 1963] xv, 210 p. illus., ports., maps. 25 cm. Cover title: A pioneer geologist. No. 104 of 200 copies. Reproduced in full from thesis (M.A.), Sul Ross State College. Bibliography: p. [95]-99. "List of papers published by J. A. Udden": p. [201]-210. [QE22.U3I14] 63-53216
1. Udden, Johan August, 1859-1932. I. Title. II. Title: A pioneer geologist.

Uglow, Jim.

UGLOW, Jim. 910'.92'4 B
Sailorman : a barge-master's story / by Jim Uglow ; photographs collected by Tony Farnham. Greenwich : Conway Maritime Press, 1975. 163 p., leaf of plate, [16] p. of plates : ill., ports. ; 23 cm. [VK140.U35A33] 76-351613 ISBN 0-85177-085-1 : £3.60
1. Uglow, Jim. I. Title.

Uhlig, Theodor, 1822-1853.

WAGNER, Richard, 1813-1883. 782.1'092'4 B
Richard Wagner's letters to his Dresden friends, Tehodor Uhlig, Wilhelm Fischer, and Ferdinand Heine. Translated into English, with a pref. by J. S. Shedlock. And an etching of Wagner by C. W. Sherborn. New York, Vienna House [1972] xi, 512 p. port. 23 cm. "Originally published by Scribner and Welford, New York, 1890." [ML410.W1A38 1972] 72-163800 ISBN 0-8443-0006-3
1. Uhlig, Theodor, 1822-1853. 2. Fischer, Christian Wilhelm, 1789-1859. 3. Heine, Ferdinand. I. Shedlock, John South, 1843-1919, tr.

Ukrainka, Lesia, 1871-1913.

BIDA, Konstantyn. 891.79'8'309
Lesya Ukrainka; life and work by Constantine Bida. Selected works, translated by Vera Rich. [Toronto] Published for the Women's Council of the Ukrainian Canadian Committee by University of Toronto Press [1968] viii, 259 p. 24 cm. Bibliographical footnotes. [PG3948.U4Z675] 68-111130
1. Ukrainka, Lesia, 1871-1913. I. Ukrainka, Lesia, 1871-1913. II. Ukrainian Canadian Committee. Women's Council.

Ukrainian Americans—Biography.

UKRAINIANS in North America : 973'.04'91791 B a biographical directory of noteworthy men and women of Ukrainian origin in the United States and Canada / editor, Dmytro M. Shtohryn ; editorial board, Jurij Fedynskyj ... [et al.]. 1st ed. Champaign, Ill. : Association for the Advancement of Ukrainian Studies, 1975. xxiv, 424 p. ; 25 cm. Includes indexes. [E184.U5U486] 76-353106 ISBN 0-916332-01-2
1. Ukrainian Americans—Biography. 2. Ukrainians in Canada—Biography. I. Shtohryn, Dmytro M. II. Association for the Advancement of Ukrainian Studies.

Ulam, Stanislaw M.

ULAM, Stanislaw M. 510'.92'4 B
Adventures of a mathematician / S. M. Ulam. New York : Scribner, c1976. xi, 317 p., [11] leaves of plates : ill. ; 24 cm. Includes index. Bibliography: p. 307-308. [QA29.U4A33] 75-20133 ISBN 0-684-14391-7 : 14.95
1. Ulam, Stanislaw M. I. Title. BIP

Ulanova, Galina Sergeevna, 1910-

KAHN, Albert Eugene, 1912- 792.8'092'4 [B]
Days with Ulanova / by Albert E. Kahn ; with an introd. by Arnold L. Haskell. New York : Simon and Schuster, [1978] c1962. (A Fireside book) [GV1785.U4K3 1978] 78-14559 ISBN 0-671-24294-6 pbk. : 5.95
1. Ulanova, Galina Sergeevna, 1910- 2. Dancers—Biography. I. Title. BIP

Ulbricht, Walter, 1893-

STERN, Carola, pseud. 923.1431
Ulbricht: a political biography. [Translated and adapted for the English-language ed. by Abe Farbstein] New York, Praeger [1965] xi, 231 p. 22 cm. (Praeger publications in Russian history and world communism, no. 151) Bibliographical references included in "Notes" (p. 215-223) [DD261.7.U4S813] 65-15644
1. Ulbricht, Walter, 1893- I. Title.

STERN, Carola, pseud. 923.1431
Ulbricht: a political biography [Tr. from German, adapted for the Eng.-lang. ed. by Abe Farbstein] New York, Praeger [c.1965] xi, 231p. 22cm. (Praeger pubns. in Russian hist. and world communism, no. 151) Bibl. [DD261.7.U4S813] 65-15644 5.95
1. Ulbricht, Walter, I. Title.

Ullman, Liv.

GARFINKEL, Bernard Max, 1929- 791.43'028'0924 B
Liv Ullman / by Bernie Garfinkel. New York : Drake Publishers, [1975] p. cm. [PN2778.U5G3] 75-10763 ISBN 0-8473-1006-X : 9.95
1. Ullman, Liv.

OUTERBRIDGE, David. 791.43'028'0924 B
Without makeup, Liv Ullmann : a photo-biography / compiled by David E. Outerbridge. 1st ed. New York : W. Morrow, 1979. 160 p. : ill. ; 29 cm. [PN2768.U4O9] 79-451 ISBN 0-688-03441-1 : 15.00
1. Ullmann, Liv. 2. Actors—Norway—Interviews. 3. Actors—Norway—Biography. I. Ullmann, Liv. II. Title.

ULLMANN, Liv. 791.43'028'0924 B
Changing / by Liv Ullmann. 1st American ed. New York : Knopf, 1977. p. cm. Translation of Forandringen. [PN2768.U4A3213 1977] 76-13167 ISBN 0-394-41148-X : 8.95 signed,limited ed. : 25.00
1. Ullmann, Liv. 2. Actors—Norway—Biography. I. Title. BIP

Umano, 1828-1927.

MOWRER, Edgar Ansel, 1892- 327'.172'0924
Umano and the price of lasting peace, by Edgar Ansel Mowrer [and] Lilian T. Mowrer. New York, Philosophical Library [1973] x, 158 p. port. 23 cm. [JX1962.U5M68] 72-91111 ISBN 0-8022-2103-3 6.00
1. Umano, 1828-1927. 2. Peace. I. Mowrer, Lilian (Thomson), joint author. II. Title. BIP

Unamuno y Jugo, Miguel de, 1864-1936.

RUDD, Margaret Thomas 928.6
The lone heretic, a biography of Miguel de Unamuno y Jugo. Introd. by Federico de Onis. Austin, Univ. of Tex. Pr. [c.1963] 349p. illus. 24cm. Bibl. 63-7437 6.50
1. Unamuno y Jugo, Miguel de, 1864-1936. I. Title.

Unamuno y Jugo, Miguel de, 1864-1936—Biography.

RUDD, Margaret Thomas. 868'.6'209 B
The lone heretic : a biography of Miguel de Unamuno y Jugo / by Margaret Thomas Rudd ; introd. by Federico de Onis. New York : Gordian Press, 1975. p. cm. Reprint of the 1963 ed. published by University of Texas Press, Austin; with new pref. Includes index. Bibliography: p. [PQ6639.N3Z835 1975] 75-31688 ISBN 0-87752-181-6 : 12.50
1. Unamuno y Jugo, Miguel de, 1864-1936—Biography. I. Title.

RUDD, Margaret Thomas. 928.6
The lone heretic, a biography of Miguel de Unamuno y Jugo. Introd. by Federico de Onis. Austin, University of Texas Press [1963] 249 p. illus. 24 cm. Includes bibliography. [PQ6639.N3Z835] 63-7437
1. Unamuno y Jugo, Miguel de. 1864-1966. I. Title.

Uncas, Chief of the Mohegans—Juvenile literature.

VOIGHT, Virginia Frances. 970.2
Uncas, sachem of the Wolf People; the story of a great Indian chief. New York, Funk & Wagnalls [1963] 209 p. 22 cm. Includes bibliography. [E99.M83U53] 63-8872
1. Uncas, Chief of the Mohegans—Juvenile literature. I. Title.

Underground railroad.

COFFIN, Levi, 1798-1877. 973.71'15'0924 B
Reminiscences of Levi Coffin, the reputed president of the underground railroad. New York, A. M. Kelley, 1968. viii, 712 p. ports. 22 cm. (Reprints of economic classics) Reprint of the 1876 ed. [E450.C64 1968] 68-55510
1. Underground railroad. 2. Slavery in the United States—Fugitive slaves. 3. Slavery in the United States—Ohio. I. Title.

COFFIN, Levi, 1798-1877. 973.7'115'0924 B
Reminiscences of Levi Coffin, the reputed president of the underground railroad; being a brief history of the labors of a lifetime in behalf of the slave, with the stories of numerous fugitives, who gained their freedom through his instrumentality, and many other incidents. [1st AMS ed.] New York, AMS Press [1971] viii, 712 p. 23 cm. Reprint of the 1876 ed. [E450.C65 1971] 79-113578 ISBN 0-404-00143-2
1. Underground railroad. 2. Slavery in the United States—Fugitive slaves. 3. Slavery in the United States—Ohio. I. Title.

WILLIAMS, James, b.1825. 301.45'22'0924
Life and adventures of James Williams, a fugitive slave, with a full description of the Underground Railroad. 3d ed. San Francisco, Women's Union Print, 1874. [Saratoga, Calif., R. & E. Research Associates, 1969] 124 p. 22 cm. [E450.W72 1969] 79-86461
1. Underground railroad. 2. Slavery in the United States—Fugitive slaves.

Underground railroad—Pennsylvania.

SMEDLEY, Robert Clemens, 1832-1883. 974.8'1'03
History of the Underground Railroad in Chester and the neighboring counties of Pennsylvania. New York, Negro Universities Press [1968] 407 p. ports. 23 cm. Reprint of the 1883 ed. [E450.S63 1968] 68-55915
1. Underground railroad—Pennsylvania. 2. Chester Co., Pa.—Biography. I. Title. BIP

Underhill, Evelyn, 1875-1941.

ARMSTRONG, Christopher J. R., 1935- 248'.22'0924 B
Evelyn Underhill, 1875-1941 : an introduction to her life and writings / by Christopher J. R. Armstrong. Grand Rapids : Eerdmans, 1976, c1975. xxiii, 303 p. ; 22 cm. Includes index. Bibliography: p. 293-303. [BV5095.U5A75 1976] 75-33401 ISBN 0-8028-3474-4 : 7.95
1. Underhill, Evelyn, 1875-1941.

Undset, Sigrid, 1882-1949.

UNDSET, Sigrid, 1882-1949. 839.8'2'87203 B
Happy times in Norway / Sigrid Undset ; translated from the Norwegian by Joran Birkeland. Westport, Conn. : Greenwood Press, 1979, c1942. viii, 224 p. : ill. ; 24 cm. Reprint of the ed. published by Knopf, New York. Translation of Lykkelige dager. [PT8950.U5L8413 1979] 79-9997 ISBN 0-313-21267-8 lib. bdg. : 18.75
I. Title. BIP

WINSNES, Andreas Hofgaard, 1889- 928.3982
Sigrid Undset, a study in Christian realism. Translated by P. G. Foote. New York, Sheed and Ward, 1953. xi, 258 p. ports. 22 cm. "Translation of Sigrid Undsets' works in English": p. 251-252. [PT8950.U5Z953] 53-5581
1. Undset, Sigrid, 1882-1949. BIP

Unitarian Churches—Biog.

SCOTT, Clinton Lee 922.8173
These live tomorrow; twenty Unitarian Universalist biographies. Illus. by Robert MacLean. Boston, Beacon [1964] ix, 277p. ports. 21cm. 64-13537 price unreported
1. Unitarian Churches—Biog. 2. Universalist Church—Biog. I. Title.

Unitarian churches—Biography.

FRITCHMAN, Stephen Hole, 1902- 288'.0922
Men of liberty; ten Unitarian pioneers. With illus. by Hendrik Willem Van Loon. Port Washington, N.Y., Kennikat Press [1968, c1944] xi, 180 p. illus. 21 cm. (Essay and general literature index reprint series) Contents.Contents.—Michael Servetus.—Faustus Socinus.—Francis

David.—John Biddle.—Joseph Priestley.—Thomas Jefferson.—William Ellery Channing.—Ralph Waldo Emerson.—Theodore Parker.—Magnus Eiriksson. [BX9867.F7 1968] 68-15826
1. Unitarian churches—Biography. I. Title.

Unitas, John,

FITZGERALD, Edward E., 1919- 927.96332
Johnny Unitas; the amazing success story of Mr. Quarterback. New York, Nelson [c.1961] 151p. (Sport magazine library book) 61-10429 2.50 bds.,
1. Unitas, Johnny. I. Title.

GREENE, Lee. 927.96332
The Johnny Unitas story. New York, Putnam [1962] 183 p. illus. 21 cm. [GV939.U5G7] 61-13409
1. Unitas, Johnny. BIP

UNITAS, John, 1933- 796.332640924
Pro quarterback, my own story, by Johnny Unitas and Ed Fitzgerald. New York, Simon and Schuster [1965] 188 p. illus. 21 cm. [GV939.U5A3] 65-22266
I. Fitzgerald, Edward E., 1919- II. Title.

Unitas, John, 1933- —Juvenile literature.

MORSE, Charles. 796.33'2'0924 B
Johnny Unitas, by Charles and Ann Morse. Illustrated by Harold Henriksen. Mankato, Minn., Amecus Street; [distributed by Childrens Press, Chicago, 1974] 31 p. col. illus. 25 cm. (Superstars) A brief biography concentrating on the career of the quarterback who set several records including 290 touchdown passes. [GV939.U5M67] 92 74-745 ISBN 0-87191-346-1
1. Unitas, John, 1933- —Juvenile literature. I. Morse, Ann, joint author. II. Henriksen, Harold, illus. III. Title. BIP

United Church of Canada—Clergy—Correspondence, reminiscences, etc.

FALLIS, George Oliver. 922
A padre's pilgrimage. Toronto, Ryerson Press [1953] 166p. illus. 22cm. Autobiographical. [BX9883.F3A3] 54-24763
1. United Church of Canada—Clergy—Correspondence, reminiscences, etc. I. Title.

United Church of Christ—Clergy—Biography.

GARDNER, Carl, 1931- 341.23'3'0924 B
Andrew Young : a biography / by Carl Gardner. New York : Drake, [1978] p. cm. [E840.8.Y64G37] 77-88945 ISBN 0-8473-1700-5 : 9.95
1. Young, Andrew J., 1932- 2. United Church of Christ—Clergy—Biography. 3. United States. Congress. House—Biography. 4. Clergy—United States—Biography. 5. Legislators—United States—Biography. 6. Ambassadors—United States—Biography. BIP

United Confederate Veterans. Company B, Confederate Veterans of Nashville, Tenn.

UNITED Confederate Veterans. Company B, Confederate Veterans of Nashville, Tenn. 973.7'42'0922 B
Biographical sketches and pictures of Company B, Confederate Veterans of Nashville, Tenn. [Brentwood, Tenn. : B. P. Barnes, 1974?] 88 p. : ports. ; 18 cm. Reprint of the 1902 ed. printed by Foster & Webb, Nashville. [E483.1.T4U54 1974] 75-324022
1. United Confederate Veterans. Company B, Confederate Veterans of Nashville, Tenn. 2. Confederate States of America—Biography. 3. United States—History—Civil War, 1861-1865—Biography. I. Title.

United Lutheran Church in America. Board of Publication.

UNITED Lutheran Church in America. Board of Publication. 922.473
Mr. Protestant: an informal biography of Franklin Clark Fry. [Philadelphia? 1960] 76 p. ports. 21 cm. [BX8080.F74U5] 60-38562
I. Fry, Franklin Clark, 1900- II. Title.

United Mine Workers of America.

BROPHY, John 923.3173
A miner's life, an autobiography. Ed., supplemented by John O. P. Hall. Madison, Univ. of Wis. Pr. [c.] 1964. xv, 320p. facsim., map, ports. 25cm. Bibl. 64-17770 7.50
1. United Mine Workers of America. I. Title.

BROPHY, John. 923.3173
A miner's life, an autobiography. Edited and supplemented by John O. P. Hall. Madison, University of Wisconsin Press, 1964. xv, 320 p. facsim., map, ports. 25 cm. Bibliography: p. 306-307. [HD6509.B7A3] 64-17770
1. United Mine Workers of America. I. Title.

United Nations.

ASHER, Mildred Graves. 920.7
Saints alive! [1st ed.] New York, Vantage Press [1955] 264p. 21cm. [CT275.A836A3] 56-5498
1. United Nations. I. Title.

United Nations—Biog.

BURCKEL, Christian E. ed. 923
Who's who in the United Nations 1st-Yonkers-on-Hudson, N.Y., C.E. Burckel & Associates. 1951. v. ports. 23 cm. Editor: 1951- C.E. Burckel. [JZ1977.A1W5] 51-5415
1. United Nations—Biog. 2. International agencies—Biog. I. Title.

WHO'S who in the United Nations and related agencies. 341.23'092'2 B
1st ed. New York : Arno Press, 1975. xxxiii, 785 p. ; 24 cm. Includes index. [JX1977.W467] 75-4105 65.00
1. United Nations—Biography. 2. International agencies—Biography. BIP

United States.
See Also-U.S.

AARON, Daniel, 1912- 920.073
Men of good hope; a story of American progressives. New York, Oxford Univ. Press [1961, c.1951] xiv, 329p. Bibl. 1.95 pap.,
1. U. S.—Biog. I. Title. BIP

AMERICAN biographies; 920.073
a genealogical, historical and biographical cyclopedia, compiled by the Editorial Press Bureau, inc. Washington [1950- v. ports 28 cm. [CT220.A55] 51-372
1. U. S.—Biog. I. Editorial Press Bureau, inc., Washington, D. C.

BAILEY, Helen Miller 920
40 American biographies. General ed.: Lewis Paul Todd. Edit. consultantants Mabel B. Casner, Ralph H. Gabriel New York, Harcourt [c.1964] vi, 250p. 21cm. Bibl. 64-56614 2.40
1. U.S.—Biog.—Juvenile literature. I. Title.

BROOKS, Van Wyck, 1886- 920
Fenollosa and his circle; with other essays in biography. [1st ed.] New York, Dutton, 1962. 321p. 22cm. [E176.B88] 62-14709
1. U. S.—Biog. 2. Fenollosa, Ernest Francisco, 1853- 1908. I. Title.

CAREY, Mathew, 1760-1839. 070.5'0924 B
Autobiographical sketches. [New York] Arno [1970] xvi, 156 p. 23 cm. (The American journalists) Reprint of the 1829 ed. Original t.p.: Auto biographical sketches, in a series of letters, addressed to a friend. Vol. I. Containing a view of the rise and progress of the American system—the efforts made to secure its establishment—the causes which prevented its complete success, &c. No more published. [E338.C27 1970] 70-125683 ISBN 0-405-01660-3
1. U.S.—Politics and government—1815-1861. 2. Tariff—U.S.—History.

CHAMBERLAIN, Hope. 328.73'092'2
A minority of members: women in the U.S. Congress. New York, New American Library [1974, c1973] xiii, 391 p. 18 cm. (A Mentor book) [JK1030.A2C5] 2.25 (pbk.)
1. United States. 2. Congress—Biography. 3. Women in the United States—Biography. 4. Women and politics-United States—History. I. Title.
L.C. card number for original ed.: 73-191950.

CLAY, Henry, 1777-1852. 973.6'3'0924 B
The life and speeches of the Hon. Henry Clay. Compiled and edited by Daniel Mallory. Freeport, N.Y., Books for Libraries Press [1972] p. Reprint of the 1843 ed. [E337.8.C594] 72-8481 ISBN 0-8369-6983-9
1. United States—Politics and government—1815-1861. I. Mallory, Daniel, ed.

CLIFFORD, Harold Burton, 1893- 920.073
American leaders. [New York] American Book Co. [1953] 320p. illus. 21cm. Includes bibliography. [E178.3.C67] 53-6013
1. U.S.—Biog.—Juvenile literature. I. Title.

CURTIN, Andrew 920.073
Gallery of great Americans. Illus. by Ken Alexander. New York, Watts [1966, c.1965] viii, 102p. ports. 23cm. [E176.C9] 66-12637 2.95; 2.21 lib. ed.,
1. U.S.—Biog. I. Title.

DENNISTON, Elinore, 1900- 920
Famous makers of America, by Rae Foley [pseud.] New York, Dodd, Mead [1963] 154 p. illus. 22 cm. (Famous biographies for young people) [E176.8D45] 63-14157
1. U.S. — Biog. — Juvenile literature. I. Title.

DICTIONARY of American biography. 923.273
The American Plutarch; 18 lives selected from the Dictionary of American biography. Ed. by Edward T. James. Introd. by Howard Mumford Jones. New York, Scribners [c.1964] xxiii, 408p. 21cm. Bibl. 64-12033 2.50 pap.,
1. U. S.—Biog. 2. Statesmen, American. I. James, Edward T., ed. II. Title.

DIKTY, T. E. 920
Every boy's book of American heroes. New York, Fell [c.1963] 188p. 22cm. (Fell's every boy's ser.) 63-14281 3.95
1. U.S.—Biog.—Juvenile literature. 2. Heroes—Juvenile literature. I. Title.

DOUGLAS, Stephen Arnold, 1813-1861 923.273
Letters. Ed. by Robert W. Johannsen. Urbana, Univ. of Ill. Pr. [c.1961. xxxi, 558p. illus. 61-62768 10.00
1. U.S.—Pol. & govt.—1815-1861. I. Johannsen Robert Walter, 1925- ed. II. Title.

DOUGLAS, Stephen Arnold, 1813-1861 923.273
Letters. Ed. by Robert W. Johannsen. Urbana, Univ. of Ill. Pr. [c.1961. xxxi, 558p. illus. 61-62768 10.00
1. U.S.—Pol. & govt.—1815-1861. I. Johannsen Robert Walter, 1925- ed. II. Title.

DOUGLAS, Stephen Arnold, 1813-1861 923.273
Letters. Ed. by Robert W. Johannsen. Urbana, Univ. of Ill. Pr. [c.1961. xxxi, 558p. illus. 61-62768 10.00
1. U.S.—Pol. & govt.—1815-1861. I. Johannsen Robert Walter, 1925- ed. II. Title.

DOUTY, Esther (Morris) 920.073
Under the new roof; five patriots of the young Republic. Chicago, Rand McNally [c.1965] 288p. ports. 22cm. [E176.8.D68] 65-18584 4.50
1. U.S.—Biog.—Juvenile literature. I. Title.
Contents omitted.

EVENING Star, (The) Washington, D. C. 923.273
The New Frontiersmen; profiles of the men around Kennedy. Foreword by I. William Hill. Introd. by M. B. Schnapper. Washington, D. C., Public Affairs Press [c.1961] 254p. 61-11685 4.50
1. U. S.—Biog. 2. U. S.—Officials and employees. 3. U. S.—Pol. & govt.—1961- I. Title.

FIEDLER, Jean 920
Great American heroes. Illus. by Raymond Burns. New York, Hart [1966] 192p. illus. 23cm. (Sunrise lib.) [E176.8F47] 66-15776 1.50; 3.29 bds. ,lib. ed.,
1. U. S.—Biog.—Juvenile literature. 2. Heroes—Juvenile literature. I. Burns, Raymond, illus. II. Title.

FISHWICK, Marshall William. 920.073
American heroes, myth and reality. Introd. by Carl Carmer. Washington, Public Affairs Press [1954] 242p. 24cm. Includes bibliography. [E176.F53] 54-12693
1. U. S.—Biog. 2. Heroes. I. Title.

FRASER, Dorothy (McClure) 1913- 001.2
Under freedom's banner [by] Dorothy M. Fraser [and] Helen F. Yeager. Consultants: Evelyn R. Girardin [and] Forbes W. Williams. [New York] American Book Co. [1964] 378 p. illus. (part col.) 24 cm. (ABC history series) [E176.8.F7] 64-2184
1. U.S. — Biog. 2. U.S. — Hist. I. Yeager, Helen F., joint author. II. Title.

GARRATY, John Arthur, 1920- ed. 920.073
The unforgettable Americans. Developed as a project of the Society of American Historians, by Allan Nevins. Great Neck, N. Y., Channel Press [c.1960] vii, 338p. 24cm. 60-15694 6.00 half cloth,
1. U. S.—Biog. 2. Society of American Historians. I. Title.

GOEBEL, Edmund Joseph, 1896- 920.073
Builders of our country [by] Edmund J. Goebel, Thomas J. Quigley [and] John E. O'Loughlin. Chicago, Laidlaw Bros. ['1951] 384 p. illus. 22 cm. (Catholic school history series) [E178.3.G6] 52-1742
1. U. S.—Biog. 2. U. S.—History, Juvenile. I. Title.

**GREAT modern American short biographtes,* 920.073
ed., introd. by Joseph Mersand [New York, Dell, c.1966] 256p. 18cm. (Laurel-leaf lib., 3126) Bibl. .50 pap.,
1. U.S.—Biog. I. Mersand, Joseph, ed.

HAYNES, Samuel. 920
Trailblazers of America. Illustrated by Frank Nicholas. Racine, Wis., Whitman Pub. Co. [1961] 91p. illus. 24cm. (A Badger book) [E176.H395] 61-66723
1. U. S.— Biog.—Juvenile literature. I. Title.

HAZELTINE, Alice Isabel, 1878- comp. 920.073
We grew up in America; stories of American youth told by themselves. New York, Abingdon Press [1954] 240p. illus. 24cm. [E747.H3] 55-5052
1. U. S.—Biog. I. Title.

HEATH, Monroe, 1899- 920.073
Great Americans at a glance; [Portraits and biographies] Art [by] Robert Blanchard [and] Ricahrd Coyne. Rodwood City, Calif., Pacific Coast Publishers [1955- v. illus. 28cm. [E176.H46] 55-3513
1. U. S.—Biog. 2. U. S.—Biog.— Portraits. I. Title.

HEATH, Monroe [Charles Monroe Heath] 1899- 920.073
Great Americans at a glance; [portraits and biographies] Art [by] Robert Blanchard, Richard Coyne. Redwood City, Calif., Pacific Coast Pubs. [1963, c.1956] 34p.illus. 28cm. (Great Amers. ser.,v. 3) 55-3513 1.00 pap.,
1. U.S.—Biog. 2. U.S.—Biog. Portraits. I. Title.

HOYER, eva Hood. 920.073
Sixteen exceptional Americans; biographical sketches. [1st ed.] New York, Vantage Press [1959] 390p. illus: 21cm.
Includes bibliography. [E176.H895] 59-1113
1. U. S.—Biog. I. Title.

HOYT, Edwin Palmer 920
The idea men. New York, Duell [dist. Meredith, c.1966] 192p. 21cm. [HC102.5.A2H65] 66-14960 3.95 bds.,
1. U. S.—Biog.—Juvenile literature. 2. Businessmen—U. S.—Juvenile literature. I. Title.

HUNTER, Robert 973.6'0924 B
Mercer Taliaferro, 1809-1887.
Correspondence of Robert M. T. Hunter, 1826-1876. Edited by Charles Henry Ambler. New York, Da Capo Press, 1971. 383 p. 24 cm. (12th report of the Historical Manuscripts Commission) (The American scene) Reprint of the 1st ed. published in 1918 as v. 2 of the Annual report of the American Historical Association for the year 1916. [E415.9.H9A4 1971] 76-75307 ISBN 0-306-71257-1
1. U.S.—Politics and government—1815-1861. I. Ambler, Charles Henry, 1876-1957, ed. II. Series: American Historical Association. Historical Manuscripts Commission. Report of the Historical Manuscripts Commission, 12

JOHNSON, Gerald White, 920.073
1890-
The lunatic fringe. [1st ed.] Philadelphia, Lippincott [1957] 248p. 22cm. [E176.J6] 57-8949
1. U. S.—Biog. I. Title.

KORNITZER, Bela. 920.073
American fathers and sons. [1st ed. New York] Hermitage House [1952] 316 p. illus. 23 cm. [E747.K6] 52-9118
1. U. S.—Biog. I. Title.

LARDNER, Rex. 920.073
Ten heroes of twenties. New York, Putnam [1966] 255 p. 21 cm. Contents.Introduction. -- Babe Ruth, home run king. -- Ernest Hemingway, writer. -- Admiral Richard E. Byrd, polar explorer. -- Charles A. Lindbergh, aviator. -- J. Edgar Hoover, lawyer. -- George Gershwin, composer. [CT220.L3] 66-14327
1. U.S.= =Biog. I. Title.

LAW, Frederick Houk, 920.073
1871-
Great Americans. New York, Globe Book Co. [1953] 569p. illus. 21cm. [E176.L4] 53-4283
1. U. S.—Biog. I. Title.

LEIPOLD, L Edmond, 1902- 920
Citizens born abroad, by L. Edmond Leipold. Minneapolis, Denison [1967] 73 p. 25 cm. (His Famous American heroes and leaders series) [CT217.L45] 67-22258
1. U. S.—Biog.—Juvenile literature. I. Title.

LEIPOLD, L. Edmond, 1902- 920.073
Crusaders for a cause, by L. Edmond Leipold. Minneapolis, Denison [1967] 76p. 25cm. (Famous Amer. heroes and leaders ser.) [CT217.L455] 67-26346 3.69
1. U.S.—Biog.—Juvenile literature. I. Title.
Contents Omitted.

LEIPOLD, L. Edmond, 1902- 920
Founders of our cities, by L. Edmond Leipold. Minneapolis, Denison [1967] 71p. 25cm. (His Famous Amer. heroes and leaders ser.) [CT217.L47] 67-22259 3.69
1. U.S.—Biog.—Juvenile literature. 2. Cities and towns.—U.S.—Hist.—Juvenile Literature. I. Title.

LEIPOLD, L. Edmond, 1902- 920
Heroes in time of war, by L. Edmond Leipold. Minneapolis, Denison [1967] 82p. 25 cm. (His Famous Amer. heroes and leaders ser.) [E181.L48] 67-22260 3.69
1. U.S.—Biog. Juvenile literature. 2. U.S.—History, Military—Juvenile literature. I. Title.

LEVY, Louis S 1877-1952. 920.073
Yesterdays. New York, Library Publishers [1954] 353p. illus. 23cm. [E747.L4] 54-4877
1. U. S.—Biog. I. Title.

LOWENSTEIN, Evelyn. 920
Picture book of famous immigrants. [Prepared by Evelyn Lowenstein and others] New York, Sterling [1962] 64p. illus. 26cm. (Visual hist. ser.) 62-18641 1.00 pap.,
1. U. S.—Biog.—Juvenile literature. 2. U. S.—Emig. & immig.—Juvenile literature. I. Title. II. Title: Famous immigrants.

MCGOVERN, John Terence, 920.073
1876-
Diogenes discovers us. Freeport, N. Y., Books for Libraries Press [1967] 304 p. ports. 22 cm. (Essay index reprint series) Reprint of the 1933 ed. Contents.--Diogenes awakes.--Gilmour C. Doble.--Evert Jansen Wendell.--Lord Burghley.--George Herman Ruth.--Elizabeth Mills Reid.--Frank A. Hinkey.--Sir Thomas Lipton, Bart.--Lady Astor.--Edward Kimball Hall.--Devereux Milburn.--Willard Dickerman Straight.--Quentin Roosevelt, John Williams Overton, Hobart Baker.--Gertrude Vanderbilt Whitney.--Gustavus Town Kirby.--The conclusions of Diogenes. [CT215.M3] 67-26758
1. U. S.—Biog. I. Title. **BIP**

MCMILLEN, Wheeler, 1893- 920
Fifty useful Americans. New York, Putnam [1966, c.1965] 218p. 21cm. Bibl. [CT217.M19] 65-25612 3.95
1. U. S.—Biog.—Juvenile literature. I. Title.

MASON, Gabriel Richard, 920.073
ed.
Great American liberals. Boston, Starr King Press [1956] 177p. 22cm. [E176.M38] 56-10079
1. U. S.—Biog. I. Title. **BIP**

MEARS, Louise Wilhelmina, 920.073
1874-
They come and go, short biographies. Boston, Christopher Pub. House [1955] 122p. 21cm. [CT216.M4] 56-59021
1. U.S.—Biog. I. Title.

MEYER, Edith Patterson 920.073
Champions of the four freedoms. Illus. by Eric von Schmidt. [1st ed.] Boston, Little [1966] xv, 301p. illus. 21cm. Bibl. [E176.M47] 66-17689 4.95
1. U. S.—Biog.—Juvenile literature. I. Title.

MOTT, Frank Luther, 1886- 920.073
ed.
A gallery of Americans; an anthology of American biography and autobiography. [New York] New American Library [1951] 224 p. 19 cm. (A Mentor book, M61) [E176.M89] 51-3609
1. U.S. — Biog. I. Title.

NEW York University. Hall 920.073
of Fame.
The Hall of Fame for Great Americans at New York University: official handbook. Edited by Theodore Morello. Rev. ed. [New York] New York University Press, 1967. 210 p. illus., ports. 22 cm. First published in 1927 under title: Hand-book of the Hall of Fame, New York University. [LD3885.H3A5] 67-10691
1. U.S.—Biog. I. Morello, Theodore, ed. II. Title.

NYE, Russel Blaine, 1913- 920.073
A baker's dozen: thirteen unusual Americans. East Lansing, Michigan State University Press [1956] 300p. 22cm. Includes bibliography. [E176.N95] 56-11739
1. U.S.—Biog. I. Title. **BIP**

PADOVER, Saul Kussiel, 920.073
1905-
The genius of America; men whose ideas shaped our civilization. [1st ed.] New York, McGraw-Hill [1960] 369p. 22cm. Includes bibliography. [E176.P2] 60-14225
1. U. S.—Biog. 2. Philosophy, American. I. Title.

PATTERSON, Robert, 1899- 920.073
ed.
On our way; young pages from American autobiography [Reissue] Sel. by Robert Patterson, Mildred Mebel, Lawrence Hill. Illus. by Robert Patterson. New York, Holiday House [1965, c.1962] 372p. illus. 22cm. [CT217.P3] 52-13988 4.50
1. U.S.—Biog. I. Title.

PINKOWSKI, Edward, 1916- 920.073
Forgotten fathers. Ports. by Tec Kunda. Philadelphia, Sunshine Press [1953] 390p. illus. 23cm. Includes bibliography. [E176.P55] 54-2229
1. U. S.—Biog. I. Title.

REINFELD, Fred, 1910- 920.073
The great dissenters, guardians of their country's laws and liberties. New rev., enlarged ed. New York, Bantam [c.1959, 1964] 175p. 18cm. (Pathfinder ed. HP76) [E339.R4] .60 pap.,
1. U. S.—Biog.—Juvenile literature. I. Title.

REINFELD, Fred, 1910- 920.073
1964.
The great dissenters; guardians of their country's laws and liberties. New, rev., enl. ed. New York, Bantam Books [1964] x, 178 p. 18 cm. (Bantam pathfinder editions, HP76) Bibliography: p. 173-175. [E339.R4] 65-2026
1. U.S. — Biog. — Juvenile literature. I. Title.

ROSS, Robert S., 320.9'73'092
1940- comp.
Public choice and public policy; seven cases in American government. Edited by Robert S. Ross. Chicago, Markham Pub. Co. [1971] xii, 190 p. 24 cm. (Markham political science series) Contents.Contents.—The Presidency: Steel and the Presidency, by G. McConnell.—Congress: Senatorial discourtesy; the nomination of Francis X. Morrissey, by I. Schiffman.—The courts: New York apportionement acts and the courts, by C. B. T. Lee.—The bureaucracy: The politics of conservation; establishing the Redwood National Park, by D. M. Ogden, Jr.—Local government. The politics of school integration; two strategies for power, by B. E. Swanson.—Political parties: New politics and old pols; two case studies in insurgency, by L. Chester, G. Hodgson and B. Page.—Pressure groups: The National Association of Real Estate Boards and the ghetto system, by J. H. Denton. Includes bibliographical references. [JK271.R87] 75-163344 ISBN 0-8410-3054-5
1. U.S.—Politics and government—1945-—Case studies. I. Title.

SILVER, Lily Jay 920.073
Profiles in success; forty lives of achievement. Introd. by Carter Davidson. New York, Fountainhead [c.1965] xviii, 451p. ports. 24cm. [CT220.S54] 64-22452 10.00
1. U. S.—Biog. I. Title.

SILVER, Lily Jay. 920.073
Profiles in success; forty lives of achievement. Introd. by Carter Davidson. New York. Fountainhead Publishers [1965] xviii, 451 p. ports. 24 cm. [CT220.S54] 64-22452
1. U. S.—Biog. I. Title.

SPRIGGS, Elsie Helena. 920.07
Pioneers of the New World; stories of Christian founders of Canada and the U.S.A. Illustrated by H.W. Whanslaw. New York, Library Publishers [1952] 136p. illus. 19cm. Includes bibliography. [E176.S834] 52-14818
1. U. S.—Biog.—Juvenile literature. 2. Canada—Biog.—Juvenile literature. I. Title.

STEVENS, Theodore A 920.073
Anecdotes about 101 distinguished Americans, together with reproductions of "free franks" from the author's collection, by Theodore A. Stevens. [Columbus? Ohio, 1964] xiii, 264 p. illus., facsims., ports. 26 cm. Bibliography: p. 260. [E176.S837] 64-17827
1. U.S. — Biog. 2. Covers (Philately) 3. Franking privilege — U.S. I. Title.

TANNER, Louise (Stickney) 920.073
Here today . . . New York, Crowell [c.1959] 311p. (9p. bibl.) 21cm. 59-12498 4.50
1. U.S.—Biog. I. Title.

TANNER, Louise (Stickney) 920.073
Here today . . . [New York, Dell] 1963 [c.1959, 1963] 320p. 20cm. (Delta bk. 3591) 1.75 pap.,
1. U.S.—Biog. I. Title.

TAYLOR, Charles William, 920.073
1896-
Eminent Americans, 1952 San Francisco [1951, c1952] 634 p. ports. 28 cm. [E176.T28 1952] 52-432
1. U.S. — Biog. I. Title.

THEIS, Paul A., ed. 320'.0922
Who's who in American politics. 1st- ed.; New York, Bowker 1967-68 v. 20 cm. biennial. "A biographical directory of United States political leaders." Editors: 1967/68- P. A. Theis and E. L. Henshaw. [E176.W6424] 67-25024
1. U. S.—Biog. I. Henshaw, Edmund Lee, ed. II. Title.

THOMAS, Eleanor, 1898- 920.073
Heroes, heroines, and holidays, by Eleanor Thomas and Mary G. Kelty. Boston, Ginn [1952] 248 p. illus. 21 cm. [E176.T5] 52-4452
1. U.S. — Biog. 2. Holidays — U.S. I. Title. **BIP**

WEBSTER, Daniel, 1782- 973.5'0924
1852.
The letters of Daniel Webster, from documents owned principally by the New Hampshire Historical Society. Edited by C. H. Van Tyne. New York, McClure, Phillips, 1902. St. Clair Shores, Mich., Scholarly Press, 1970. xxii, 769 p. port. 22 cm. Includes letters written by and to Webster. Includes bibliographical references. [E337.8.W365 1970] 79-108553
1. U.S.—Politics and government—1815-1861. I. Van Tyne, Claude Halstead, 1869-1930, ed. II. Title.

WEED, Thurlow, 1797- 329'.00924 B
1882.
Life of Thurlow Weed. New York, Da Capo Press, 1970. 2 v. illus., ports. 24 cm. Reprint of the 1883-84 ed., originally published under title: Life of Thurlow Weed including his autobiography and a memoir. Contents.Contents.—v. 1. Autobiography of Thurlow Weed, edited by H. A. Weed.—v. 2. Memoir of Thurlow Weed, by T. W. Barnes. [E415.9.W39W33] 79-87686
1. U.S.—Politics and government—1815-1861. 2. New York (State)—Politics and government—1775-1865. I. Title. **BIP**

WELCH, Helena 920
When they were children. Illus. by Don Fields. Nashwille, Southern Pub. [1965] 136p. illus. 21cm. [CT107.W54] 65-10246 2.95
1. U. S.—Biog.—Juvenile literature. 2. Gt. Brit.—Biog.—Juvenile literature. I. Title.

WELCH, Helena 920
When they were children. Illus. by Don Fields. Nashville, Southern Pub. Assn. [1967, c.1965] 136p. illus. 21cm. (Summit bk.) [CT107.W54] 1.00 pap.,
1. U.S.—Biog.—Juvenile literature. 2. Gt. Brit.—Biog.—Juvenile literature. I. Title.

WHO'S who in America; 920.073
a biographical dict. of notable living men and women; v.33 (1964-1965) Rev. & reissued biennially. Chicago, Marquis [c.1899-1964] 287, xiii p. 28cm. 4-16934 29.50
1. U.S.—Biog. 2. Biography—Dictionaries.

WHO'S who in American 320'.0922
politics. 1st-ed.; 1967/68- New York, Bowker. 1967 v. 29cm. biennial. A biographical directory of United States political leaders. Eds.: 1967/68- P. A. Theis E. L. Henshaw [E176.W6424] 67-25024 25.00
1. U. S.—Biog. I. Theis, Paul A., ed. II. Henshaw, Edmund Lee, ed.

WHO'S who in the East [and 920.74
Eastern Canada]; a biographical dictionary of noteworthy men and women of the Middle Atlantic and Northeastern States. 9th ed. hicago, Marquis [c.1948-1963] 1100p. 27cm. Subtitlevaries slightly. First ed. pub. in Boston by Larkin, Roosevelt & Larkin. 43-18522 price unreported
1. U.S.—Biog. 2. New England—Biog. 3. Middle States—Biog.

United States—Armed Forces—Biography.

UNITED States. Dept. of the Army. 355.3'0922
"I am an American fighting man." [Washington, 1966] 1 v. (unpaged) illus. 27 cm. (Its Troop topics) "DA pam 360-225." Cover title. [U52.A52] 67-60132
1. United States—Armed Forces—Biography. I. Title.

United States—Armed Forces—Biography—Portraits.

CHASE, Joseph Cummings, 1878-1965. 355.3'3'0922
Speaking of heroes; portraits of the men of the A.E.F. from generals to privates both World Wars and Korea, the collection in the Smithsonian Institution painted by Joseph Cummings Chase. [Wauwatosa? Wis., c1972] 173 p. ports. 24 cm. [U52.C47 1972] 72-86479 10.00
1. United States—Armed Forces—Biography—Portraits. I. United States. National Museum. II. Title.

United States. Army Air Forces—Biography.

MUSCIANO, Walter A. 940.54'26'0922
Corsair aces / Walter A. Musciano. New York : Arco Pub. Co., [1978] p. cm. Bibliography: p. [D790.M83] 78-2452 ISBN 0-668-04597-3 : 9.95 ISBN 0-668-04600-7 pbk. : 5.95
1. United States. Army Air Forces—Biography. 2. World War, 1939-1945—Aerial operations, American. 3. Fighter pilots—United States—Biography. 4. Corsair (Fighter planes) I. Title.

United States. Army Air Forces. 5th Air Force—Biography.

†STAFFORD, Gene B. 940.54'49'730922
Aces of the Southwest Pacific / by Gene B. Stafford ; illustrated by Don Greer. Warren, Mich. : Squadron/Signal Publications, c1977. 64 p. : ill. ; 28 cm. [D790.S77] 77-156235 6.95
1. United States. Army Air Forces. 5th Air Force—Biography. 2. World War, 1939-1945—Aerial operations, American. 3. Fighter pilots—United States—Biography. 4. World War, 1939-1945—Pacific Ocean. I. Title.
Mail order address: Squadron Shop, 28107 John R., Madison Heights, MI 48071

United States. Army Air Forces. 9th Air Force.

KETCHUM, Carlton G., 1892- 940.54'49'73 B
The recollections of Colonel Retread, USAAF 1942-1945 / by Carlton G. Ketchum. 1st ed. Pittsburgh : Hart Books, c1976. 296 p. : ill. ; 24 cm. Autobiographical. [D790.K47] 76-29524 9.00
1. United States. Army Air Forces. 9th Air Force. 2. Ketchum, Carlton G., 1892- 3. United States. Army Air Forces—Biography. 4. World War, 1939-1945—Aerial operations, American. 5. World War, 1939-1945—Personal narratives, American. I. Title.

United States. Army—Biography.

BAIRD, John A., 1918- 973.7'41'0924 B
Profile of a hero : the story of Absalom Baird, his family, and the American military tradition / by John A. Baird, Jr. Philadelphia : Dorrance, c1977. xiii, 234 p., [6] leaves of plates (1 fold.) : ill. ; 22 cm. Includes index. Bibliography: p. 227-228. [E467.1.B15B34] 77-155112 ISBN 0-8059-2460-4 : 7.95
1. Baird, Absalom, 1824-1905. 2. United States. Army—Biography. 3. Baird family. 4. Generals—United States—Biography. 5. United States—History—Civil War, 1861-1865—Campaigns and battles. I. Title.

BILLIAS, George Athan, 1919- ed. 973.3'3'0922
George Washington's generals / edited by George Athan Billias. Westport, Conn. : Greenwood Press, 1980, c1964. p. cm. Reprint of the ed. published by Morrow, New York. Includes index. Bibliography: p. [E206.B5 1980] 79-28195 ISBN 0-313-22280-0 lib. bdg. : 25.00
1. United States. Army—Biography. 2. United States—History—Revolution, 1775-1783—Biography. 3. Generals—United States—Biography. I. Title.

GEER, Allen Morgan, 1840-1926. 973.7'81 B
The Civil War diary of Allen Morgan Geer, Twentieth Regiment, Illinois Volunteers / edited by Mary Ann Andersen. Denver : R. C. Appleman, c1977. xxii, 306 p., [2] leaves of plates : ill. ; 22 cm. Bibliography: p. [292]-306. [E505.5 20th.G43 1977] 77-3830 15.00
1. Illinois Infantry. 20th Regt., 1861-1865. 2. United States. Army—Biography. 3. Geer, Allen Morgan, 1840-1926. 4. United States—History—Civil War, 1861-1865—Regimental histories—Illinois Infantry—20th. 5. United States—History—Civil War, 1861-1865—Personal narratives. 6. Soldiers—United States—Biography. I. Title.

LONGACRE, Edward G., 1946- 973.7'3'0924 B
The man behind the guns : a biography of General Henry Jackson Hunt, Chief of Artillery, Army of the Potomac / by Edward G. Longacre. South Brunswick [N.J.] : A. S. Barnes, c1977. p. cm. Bibliography: p. [E467.1.H89L66] 76-10885 ISBN 0-498-01656-0 : 15.00
1. Hunt, Henry Jackson, 1819-1889. 2. United States. Army—Biography. 3. United States. Army. Army of the Potomac. 4. Generals—United States—Biography. 5. United States—History—Civil War, 1861-1865—Regimental histories—Army of the Potomac. I. Title.

MADIGAN, Thomas F., 1891-1936. 920'.073
A biographical index of American public men, classified and alphabetically arranged : a useful hand-book and check list for autograph collectors, librarians, etc. / by Thomas F. Madigan. Detroit : Gale Research Co., 1976 [i.e.1975] c1916. p. cm. Reprint of the ed. published by Madigan, New York. Includes index. [E176.M2 1976] 75-42085 11.00
1. United States. Army—Biography. 2. Statesmen—United States—Biography. 3. United States—Biography. I. Title.

WILLIAMSON, Porter B., 1916- 940.54'21'0924 B
I remember General Patton's principles / by Porter B. Williamson. Tucson, Ariz. : Management and Systems Consultants, c1979. 167 p., [8] leaves of plates : ill. ; 20 cm. [E745.P3W54] 77-70779 ISBN 0-918356-03-2 : 5.95
1. Patton, George Smith, 1885-1945. 2. United States. Army—Biography. 3. Williamson, Porter B., 1916- 4. Generals—United States—Biography. I. Title.

United States. Army—Biography—Addresses, essays, lectures.

RANK and file : 973.7'092'2 B
Civil War essays in honor of Bell Irvin Wiley / edited by James I. Robertson, Jr. and Richard M. McMurry. San Rafael, Calif. : Presidio Press, c1976. 164 p. ; 24 cm. "Bibliography of Bell Irvin Wiley," by J. P. Bloom: p. 157-164. [E467.R37] 76-48787 ISBN 0-89141-011-2 : 8.95
1. United States. Army—Biography—Addresses, essays, lectures. 2. Confederate States of America. Army—Biography—Addresses, essays, lectures. 3. Wiley, Bell Irvin, 1906- —Addresses, essays, lectures. 4. United States—History—Civil War, 1861-1865—Biography—Addresses, essays, lectures. 5. United States—Biography—Addresses, essays, lectures. 6. Historians—United States—Biography—Addresses, essays, lectures. I. Wiley, Bell Irvin, 1906- II. Robertson, James I. III. McMurry, Richard M.
Contents omitted

United States. Army—Biography—Juvenile literature.

SIGNIFICANT 355'.0092'2 B
American military leaders. Chicago : Childrens Press, c1976. p. cm. Includes index. Brief biographies of 152 important American military leaders arranged alphabetically within five chronological periods of American history. [E181.S53] 75-20682 ISBN 0-516-05316-7 : 6.95
1. United States. Army—Biography—Juvenile literature. 2. United States. Navy—Biography—Juvenile literature. 3. Indians of North America—Biography—Juvenile literature. I. Title: Military leaders.

United States. Army. Infantry—History.

WALTHALL, Melvin C., 1920- 940.54'12'73
"We can't all be heroes" : a history of the separate infantry regiments in World War II / by Melvin C. Walthall. [Chesterfield? Va.] : Walthall, [1974?] [100] leaves in various foliations : ill. ; 30 cm. [D769.2.W34] 74-299040
1. United States. Army. Infantry—History. 2. Walthall, Melvin C., 1920- 3. World War, 1939-1945—United States. 4. World War, 1939-1945—Personal narratives, American. I. Title.

United States. Army. Military Commission.

WEICHMANN, Louis J. 364.1'31'0973
True history of the assassination of Abraham Lincoln and of the Conspiracy of 1865 Louis J. Weichmann ; edited by Floyd E. Risvold. 1st ed. New York : Knopf, 1975. xxxii, 492, xvi p., [8] leaves of plates : ill. ; 25 cm. Includes 23 letters written by A. C. Richards to Weichmann from Apr. 1898 to Nov. 1901. Includes index. Bibliography: p. 461-463. [E457.5.W44] 74-21278 ISBN 0-394-49319-2 : 15.00
1. Lincoln, Abraham, Pres. U.S., 1809-1865—Assassination. 2. Booth, John Wilkes, 1838-1865. 3. United States. Army. Military Commission. Lincoln's assassins. 1865. 4. Weichmann, Louis J. I. Richards, A. C., d. 1907. II. Title.

WEICHMANN, Louis J. 973.7'092'4 B
A true history of the assassination of Abraham Lincoln and of the conspiracy of 1865 / Louis J. Weichmann ; edited by Floyd E. Risvold. New York : Vintage Books, 1977, c1975. xxx, 492, xvi p. ; 24 cm. Includes 23 letters written by A. C. Richards to L. J. Weichmann from Apr. 1898 to Nov. 1901. Includes index. Bibliography: p. 461-463. [E475.5.W44 1977] 76-41211 ISBN 0-394-72260-4 pbk. 5.95
1. Lincoln, Abraham, Pres. U.S., 1809-1865—Assassination. 2. Booth, John Wilkes, 1838-1865. 3. United States. Army. Military Commission. Lincoln's assassins. 1865. 4. Weichmann, Louis J. I. Richards, A. C., d. 1907. II. Title. BIP

United States. Army—Military life.

FARMER, James E., 1842or3-1932. 917.8'03'2
My life with the Army in the West; the memoirs of James E. Farmer, 1858-1898. Edited by Dale F. Giese. [1st ed.] Santa Fe [N.M.] Stagecoach Press [1967] 83 p. port. 18 cm. [F596.F23] 67-30402
1. United States. Army—Military life. 2. Frontier and pioneer life—The West. I. Giese, Dale F., ed. II. Title.

SUMMERHAYES, Martha, 1846-1911. 979.1'04'0924 B
Vanished Arizona : recollections of the Army life of a New England woman / by Martha Summerhayes. Glorieta, N.M. : Rio Grande Press, 1976 [c1911] p. cm. (A Rio Grande classic) Reprint of the 2d ed. published by the Salem Press Co., Salem, Mass.; with new 1976 publisher's pref. Includes index. [F811.S95 1976] 76-54922 ISBN 0-87380-120-2 lib.bdg. : 10.00
1. United States. Army—Military life. 2. Summerhayes, Martha, 1846-1911. 3. Arizona—Description and travel. 4. Southwest, New—Description and travel. 5. Indians of North America—Wars—1866-1895. 6. Army wives—Arizona—Biography. I. Title.

United States. Army Nurse Corps.

AYNES, Edith A., 1909- 355.3'45 B
From nightingale to eagle; an Army nurse's history [by] Edith A. Aynes. Englewood Cliffs, N.J., Prentice-Hall [1973] xxvi, 318 p. illus. 23 cm. Includes bibliographies. [RT41.A9] 72-13074 ISBN 0-13-332262-9 5.95 (pbk)
1. United States. Army Nurse Corps. 2. Nurses and nursing. I. Title.

United States. Army. Signal Corps. 833d Signal Service Company—History.

SHERWEN, Douglas S. 940.54'12'73
The Persian corridor : the little-known story of the Signal Corps in the Middle East during World War II / Douglas S. Sherwen. 1st ed. Hicksville, N.Y. : Exposition Press, c1979. 232 p. : ill. ; 21 cm. [D769.363 833d.S48] 79-50139 ISBN 0-682-49337-6 : 9.50
1. United States. Army. Signal Corps. 833d Signal Service Company—History. 2. World War, 1939-1945—Regimental histories—United States—Signal Corps. 833d Signal Service Company. 3. World War, 1939-1945—Personal narratives, American. 4. Sherwen, Douglas S. 5. World War, 1939-1945—Iran. 6. Iran—History—1909- 7. Soldiers—United States—Biography. I. Title. BIP

United States. Army—Surgeons—Biography—Juvenile literature.

EPSTEIN, Samuel, 1909- 612'.3
Dr. Beaumont and the man with a hole in his stomach / by Sam and Beryl Epstein ; illustrated by Joseph Scrofani. New York : Coward, McCann & Geoghegan, [1977] p. cm. (A Science discovery book) Bibliography: p. A biography of a curious physician and the unusual patient who enabled him to carry out experiments concerning digestion. [QP145.E67] 920 77-8236 ISBN 0-698-30680-5 lib. bdg. : 4.99
1. Beaumont, William, 1785-1853—Juvenile literature. 2. United States. Army—Surgeons—Biography—Juvenile literature. 3. St. Martin, Alexis, 1797?-1880—Juvenile literature. 4 Digestion Juvenile literature. 5. Fur traders—Canada—Biography—Juvenile literature. I. Epstein, Beryl Williams, 1910- joint author. II. Scrofani, Joseph. III. Title. BIP

United States. Army. 1st Ranger Batallion—History.

ALTIERI, James. 940.54'12'73
The spearheaders : a personal history of Darby's Rangers in World War II / by James Altieri. Washington : Zenger Pub. Co., [1979] p. cm. Reprint of the 1960 ed. published by Bobbs-Merrill, Indianapolis. [D769.31 1st.A44 1979] 79-18951 ISBN 0-89201-061-4 : 12.95
1. United States. Army. 1st Ranger Batallion—History. 2. United States. Army. 3d Ranger Batallion—History. 3. United States. Army. 4th Ranger Batallion—History. 4. Altieri, James. 5. World War, 1939-1945—Regimental histories—United States—1st Ranger Battalion. 6. World War, 1939-1945—Regimental histories—United States—3d Ranger Battalion. 7. World War, 1939-1945—Regimental histories—United States—4th Ranger Battalian. 8. World War, 1939-1945—Personal narratives, American. 9. World War, 1939-1945—Campaigns—Africa, North. 0. Soldiers—United States—Biography. I. Title.

United States. Army. 12th Artillery (Colored)

MARRS, Elijah 301.451'96'0924 B
P., 1840-
Life and history of the Rev. Elijah P. Marrs. Louisville, Ky., Bradley & Gilbert Co., 1885. Miami, Fla., Mnemosyne Pub. Co. [1969] 146 p. port. 23 cm. Running title: History of the Rev. E. P. Marrs. [E185.97.M36 1969] 70-89395
1. United States. Army. 12th Artillery (Colored) 2. Negroes—Kentucky. 3. United States—History—Civil War, 1861-1865—Personal narratives. I. Title. II. Title: History of the Rev. E. P. Marrs.

United States. Army. 2d Cavalry.

UTAH, fl.1858-1859. 973.6'8
To Utah with the Dragoons and glimpses of life in Arizona and California, 1858-1859 / edited by Harold D. Langley. Salt Lake City : University of Utah Press, c1974. xvi, 230 p. : ill. ; 24 cm. (University of Utah publications in the American West ; v. 11) "Letters originally appeared in the Philadelphia Daily evening bulletin during 1858-59." Includes index. Bibliography: p. 216-221. [F826.U7 1974] 73-80998 ISBN 0-87480-087-0
1. Utah Expedition, 1857-1858—Personal narratives. 2. United States. Army. 2d Cavalry. 3. Utah, fl. 1858-1859. 4. The West—Description and travel—1848-1860. I. Langley, Harold D. II. Title. III. Series: Utah. University. Publications in the American West ; v. 11.

United States. Army. 3d Ranger Batallion—History.

ALTIERI, James. 940.54'12'73
The spearheaders : a personal history of Darby's Rangers in World War II / by James Altieri. Washington : Zenger Pub. Co., [1979] p. cm. Reprint of the 1960 ed. published by Bobbs-Merrill, Indianapolis. [D769.31 1st.A44 1979] 79-18951 ISBN 0-89201-061-4 : 12.95
1. United States. Army. 1st Ranger Batallion—History. 2. United States. Army. 3d Ranger Batallion—History. 3. United States. Army. 4th Ranger Batallion—History. 4. Altieri, James. 5. World War, 1939-1945—Regimental histories—United States—1st Ranger Battalion. 6. World War, 1939-1945—Regimental histories—United States—3d Ranger Battalion. 7. World War, 1939-1945—Regimental histories—United States—4th Ranger Battalian. 8. World War, 1939-1945—Personal narratives, American. 9. World War, 1939-1945—Campaigns—Africa, North. 0. Soldiers—United States—Biography. I. Title.

United States. Army. 4th Armored Division—Biography.

FRANKEL, Nat. 940.54'12'73
Patton's best : an informal history of the 4th Armored Division / by Nat Frankel and Larry Smith. New York : Hawthorn Books, c1978. xi, 198 p., [11] leaves of plates : ill. ; 25 cm. Includes index. [D769.305 4th.F72] 77-79918 ISBN 0-8015-5797-6 : 9.95
1. United States. Army. 4th Armored Division—Biography. 2. Frankel, Nat. 3. World War, 1939-1945—Regimental histories—United States—4th Armored Division. 4. World War, 1939-1945—Personal narratives, American. 5. Soldiers—United States—Biography. I. Smith, Larry, 1940- joint author. II. Title.

United States. Army. 4th Ranger Batallion—History.

ALTIERI, James. 940.54'12'73
The spearheaders : a personal history of Darby's Rangers in World War II / by James Altieri. Washington : Zenger Pub. Co., [1979] p. cm. Reprint of the 1960 ed. published by Bobbs-Merrill, Indianapolis. [D769.31 1st.A44 1979] 79-18951 ISBN 0-89201-061-4 : 12.95
1. United States. Army. 1st Ranger Batallion—History. 2. United States. Army. 3d Ranger Batallion—History. 3. United States. Army. 4th Ranger Batallion—History. 4. Altieri, James. 5. World War, 1939-1945—Regimental histories—United States—1st Ranger Battalion. 6. World War, 1939-1945—Regimental histories—United States—3d Ranger Battalion. 7. World War, 1939-1945—Regimental histories—United States—4th Ranger Battalian. 8. World War, 1939-1945—Personal narratives, American. 9. World War, 1939-1945—Campaigns—Africa, North. 0. Soldiers—United States—Biography. I. Title.

United States—Biography.

ACTON, Jay. 920'.073
Mug shots; who's who in the new earth, by Jay Acton, Alan Le Mond [and] Parker Hodges. Photos. by Raeanne Rubenstein. New York, World Pub. [1972] 244 p. illus. 29 cm. "A Meridian book." [CT220.A27 1972] 77-174672 ISBN 0-529-04513-3 9.95
1. United States—Biography. I. Le Mond, Alan, joint author. II. Hodges, Parker, joint author. III. Title.

ADDAMS, Jane, 1860-1935. 920.073
The excellent becomes the permanent. Feeport, N.Y., Books for Libraries Press [1970] 162 p. 23 cm. (Essay index reprint series) Reprint of the 1932 ed. "Memorial addresses." Contents.Contents.—Introduction.—Jenny Dow Harvey.—Sarah Rozet Smith.—Henry Demarest Lloyd.—Alice Kellogg Tyler.—Gordon Dewey.—Judge Murray F. Tuley.—Joseph Tilton Bowen.—Mary Hawes Wilmarth.—Lydia Avery Coonley-Ward.—Canon Samuel A. Barnett.—(By way of an appendix) Early reactions to death. [CT219.A3 1970] 77-107680
1. U.S.—Biography. I. Title. BIP

*AGAN, Patrick. 790.2'092'2 B
Is that who I think it is? Vol. 2. New York, Ace Books [1975 c1974] 201 p. illus. 18 cm. Original title: Whatever happened to- [CT220] 1.25 (pbk.)
1. United States—Biography. 2. Performing arts—United States—Biography. I. Title.

ALLEN, Devere, 1891-1955, ed. 920.073
Adventurous Americans. Illustrated by Bernard Sanders. Freeport, N.Y., Books for Libraries Press [1971] ix, 346 p. ports. 23 cm. (Essay index reprint series) Reprint of the 1932 ed. [E176.A42 1971] 71-156604 ISBN 0-8369-2264-6
1. U.S.—Biography. I. Title. BIP

AMERICAN Academy of Arts and Letters. 700'.922
Commemorative tributes of the American Academy of Arts and Letters, 1905-1941. Freeport, N.Y., Books for Libraries Press [1968, c1942] 432 p. 22 cm. (Essay index reprint series) [AS36.A484A16] 68-20286
1. United States—Biography. 2. Authors, American. 3. Artists, American. I. Title.

AMERICAN bicentennial biographical album, 1776-1976 / edited by Janneyne Gnacinski and Christine Nowak. Baltimore : Gateway Press, 1976. 417 p. : 23 cm. Includes bibliographical references and index. [CT214.A44] 75-45820 16.00 920'.073
1. United States—Biography. I. Gnacinski, Janneyne Longley. II. Nowak, Christine.

AMERICAN biographical encyclopedia; profiles of prominent personalities. Phoenix, Ariz., P. W. Pollock [1967- v. ports. 32 cm. Contents.Contents.—v. 1. Arizona ed. [CT220.A53] 68-1722 920.073
1. United States—Biography. I. Pollock, Paul W.

ARCHER, Jules. 920.073
The unpopular ones. New York, Crowell-Collier Press [1968] 200 p. illus. 21 cm. (America in the making) Contents.Contents.—"Newe and dangerous opinions": Roger Williams.—Morning star of liberty: John Peter Zenger.—"Whether it be popular or unpopular": Thomas Paine.—The common scold: Anne Royall.—The beatnik of 1830: Joseph Palmer.—"Burn the Tribune! Hang Old Greeley!": Horace Greeley.—"I was not born to be forced": Henry David Thoreau.—The branded hand: Jonathan Walker.—"If the women mean to wear the pants": Amelia Jenks Bloomer.—"The minority are right!": Eugene Debs.—"I believe that men will see the truth": Woodrow Wilson.—First lady doctor in the West: Bethenia Owens.—"The law was wrong, not I": Margaret Sanger. —"The atomic clock ticks faster": J. Robert Oppenheimer.—"My God, I feel so alone!": J. William Fulbright.—Bibliography (p. [193]-195) [E176.A72] 68-20746
1. United States—Biography. 2. Reformers—Biography. I. Title.

BARTLETT, David Vandewater Golden, 1828-1912. 920.073
Modern agitators; or, Pen portraits of living American reformers, by David W. Bartlett. Freeport, N.Y., Books for Libraries Press, 1970. 396 p. illus. 23 cm. (The Black heritage library collection) Reprint of the 1854 ed. [E415.8.B28 1970] 70-133146 ISBN 0-8369-8702-0
1. U.S.—Biography. 2. Reformers. I. Title. II. Title: Pen portraits of living American reformers. III. Series. BIP

BEARD, Annie E. S., d.1930. 920.073
Our foreign-born citizens; rev. by William A. Fahey. New rev. [i. e. 5th] ed. New York, Crowell [1955] 308 p. 21 cm. [E176.B38 1955] 55-9203
1. U.S.—Biography. I. Title.

BEARD, Annie E. S., d.1930. 920.073 B
Our foreign-born citizens. 6th ed. New York, Crowell [1968] 276 p. 21 cm. Contents.Contents.—John James Audubon.—Andrew Carnegie.—John Muir.—Alexander Graham Bell.—Joseph Pulitzer.—Augustus St. Gaudens.—Samuel Gompers.—Felix Adler.—Ottmar Mergenthaler.—Charles Proteus Steinmetz.—Hideyo Noguchi.—Albert Einstein.—Hans Hofmann.—Walter Gropius.—Philip Murray.—Igor Sikorsky.—David Dubinsky.—Raymond Loewy.—Spyros Skouras.—Alfred Hitchcock.—Enrico Fermi.—W. H. Auden.—Erich Leinsdorf. [E176.B38 1968] 68-17083
1. United States—Biography. I. Title. BIP

BECKWITH, John A., ed. 920.073
Contemporary American biography, edited by John A. Beckwith and Geoffrey Coope. Freeport, N.Y., Books for Libraries Press [1971, c1941] viii, 347 p. 23 cm. (Essay index reprint series) Includes bibliographical references. [CT214.B4 1971] 77-142607 ISBN 0-8369-2483-5
1. United States—Biography. 2. Biography (as a literary form) I. Coope, Geoffrey, joint ed. II. Title. BIP

BISHOP, Joseph Bucklin, 1847-1928. 920.073
Notes and anecdotes of many years. Freeport, N.Y., Books for Libraries Press [1970] 236 p. port. 23 cm. (Essay index reprint series) Reprint of the 1925 ed. Contents.Contents.—A plea for anecdotage.—"The Tribune" and Horace Greeley.—The tragic Greeley campaign.—Two famous preachers.—John Hay.—Isaac H. Bromley—William Winter.—Edwin L. Godkin.—Theodore Roosevelt.—Friends of many kinds.—Maj.-Gen. George W. Goethals. [CT214.B5 1970] 78-128210
1. U.S.—Biography. I. Title. BIP

BLIVEN, Bruce, 1889- 920'.073
A mirror for greatness : six Americans / Bruce Bliven. New York : McGraw-Hill, [1975] 251 p. : ports. ; 21 cm. "Several of the chapters in this book are greatly expanded and rewritten versions of material that has appeared elsewhere." [E176.B59] 74-22221 ISBN 0-07-005904-7 : 7.95
1. United States—Biography. I. Title.

BLIVEN, Bruce, 1916- 920'.073
The finishing touch / Bruce Bliven, Jr. New York : Dodd, Mead, c1978. 215 p., [6] leaves of plates : ill. ; 22 cm. [CT220.B53] 78-1356 ISBN 0-396-07534-7 : 8.95
1. United States—Biography. I. Title. BIP

BOLTON, Sarah Knowles, 1841-1916. 920'.073
How success is won. Freeport, N.Y., Books for Libraries Press [1973] p. (Essay index reprint series) Reprint of the 1885 ed., which was issued as 3d ser. of Little biographies. Contents.Contents.—Peter Cooper.—John B. Gough.—John Greenleaf Whittier.—John Wanamaker.—Henry M. Stanley.—Johns Hopkins.—William M. Hunt.—Elias Howe, Jr.—Alexander H. Stephens.—Thomas A. Edison.—Dr. Wm. T. G. Morton.—Rev. John H. Vincent, D. D. [CT105.B63 1973] 72-10821 ISBN 0-8369-7209-0
1. United States—Biography. I. Title. II. Series: Little biographies. Boston, 1884- ser. 3.

BRADFORD, Gamaliel, 1863-1932. 920.073
American portraits 1875-1900. Port Washington, N.Y., Kennikat Press [1969, c1922] xii, 248 p. illus., ports. 22 cm. (Essay and general literature index reprint series) Bibliographical references included in "Notes" (p. 227-241) [CT219.B7 1969] 71-85994
1. U.S.—Biography. I. Title.

BRADFORD, Gamaliel, 1863-1932. 973
Damaged souls. Port Washington, N.Y., Kennikat Press [1969, c1923] xi, 276 p. 22 cm. (Essay and general literature index reprint series) Contents.Contents.—Damaged souls.—Benedict Arnold.—Thomas Paine.—Aaron Burr.—John Randolph of Roanoke.—John Brown.—Phineas Taylor Barnum.—Benjamin Franklin Butler. Bibliographical references included in "Notes" (p. 261-276) [E176.B8 1969] 77-85990
1. U.S.—Biography. I. Title.

BROWN, Charles Reynolds, 1862-1950. 920.073
They were giants. Freeport, N.Y., Books for Libraries Press [1968] vii, 279 p. 23 cm. (Essay index reprint series) Reprint of the 1934 ed. Contents.Contents.—Benjamin Franklin.—Horace Bushnell.—Anthony Trollope.—Peter Cooper.—Edward Everett Hale.—Silas Weir Witchell.—Phillips Brooks.—David Starr Jordan.—Washington Gladden.—Abraham Lincoln. [CT214.B7 1968] 68-54332
1. United States—Biography. 2. Biography. I. Title. BIP

BROWN, Rollo Walter, 1880-1956. 920.073
Lonely Americans. Freeport, N.Y., Books for Libraries Press [1970] 319 p. ports. 23 cm. (Essay index reprint series) Reprint of the 1929 ed. Contents.Contents.—An Olympian [Charles W. Eliot].—Whistler and America.—A listener to the winds [Edward MacDowell].—An adventurer out of the West [George Bellows].—A self-indulgent apostle [Charles Eliot Norton].—Cosmic prospector [Raphael Pumpelly].—A sublimated Puritan [Emily Dickenson] .—Lincoln the radical. [E176.B885 1970] 74-121452
1. U.S.—Biography. I. Title. BIP

BULLARD, John Morgan, 1890- 929'.2'0973
The Greens as I knew them, by John M. Bullard. New Bedford, Mass., 1964. x, 103 p. illus., ports. 24 cm. [CS71.G8] 65-3029
I. Title.

BUSCH, Niven, 1903- 917.3'03'910922
Twenty-one Americans; being profiles of some people famous in our time, together with silly pictures of them drawn by De Miskey. Freeport, N.Y., Books for Libraries Press [1970, c1930] vi, 332 p. illus. 23 cm. (Essay index reprint series) [E747.B97 1970] 72-99686
1. U.S.—Biography. I. Title.

CARROLL, Howard, 1854-1916. 920.073
Twelve Americans; their lives and times. Freeport, N.Y., Books for Libraries Press [1971] xii, 473 p. ports. 23 cm. (Essay index reprint series) Reprint of the 1883 ed. Contents.Contents.—Horatio Seymour.—Charles Francis Adams.—Peter Cooper.—Hannibal Hamlin.—John Gilbert.—Robert C. Schenck.—Frederick Douglass.—William Allen.—Allen G. Thurman.—Joseph Jefferson.—Elihu B. Washburne.—Alexander H. Stephens. [E176.C3 1971] 70-37154 ISBN 0-8369-2489-4
1. United States—Biography. 2. Statesmen—United States. I. Title. BIP

COLEMAN, McAlister, 1889- 920.073
Pioneers of freedom. With an introd. by Norman Thomas. Freeport, N.Y., Books

for Libraries Press [1968] vi, 222 p. 22 cm. (Essay index reprint series) Reprint of 1929 ed. Contents.Contents.—Thomas Paine.—Thomas Jefferson.—Francis Wright.—Wendell Phillips.—John P. Altgeld.—Henry George.—Samuel Gompers.—Eugene Debs.—John Mitchell.—Charles Steinmetz. [E176.C69 1968] 68-20292
1. United States—Biography. I. Title. **BIP**

CONGRESSIONAL Quarterly 320'.0922
Service, Washington, D.C.
Candidates 1968; the public records of twenty-five Americans prominently mentioned for the Presidency or Vice Presidency Washington, 1967. 130 p. ports. 28 cm. (Congressional Quarterly background) Includes bibliography. [E840.6.C6] 67-30436
1. United States.—Biography. I. Title.

CREEL, George, 1876-1953. 920.073
Sons of the eagle; soaring figures from America's past. Illustrated by Herbert Morton Stoops. Freeport, N.Y. Books for Libraries Press [1970, c1927] 321 p. illus. 23 cm. (Essay index reprint series) [E176.C85 1970] 79-117778
1. U.S.—Biography. I. Title.

DICTIONARY of American 920'.073
biography : supplement five, 1951-1955 : with an index guide to the supplements / John A. Garraty, editor. New York : Scribner, c1977. viii, 799 p. ; 26 cm. Includes index. [E176.D563 Suppl. 5] 77-2942 ISBN 0-684-15054-9 : 45.00
1. United States—Biography. I. Garraty, John Arthur, 1920-

DIEHL, Digby. 920'.073
Supertalk. [1st ed.] New York, Doubleday, 1974. ix, 293 p. ports. 22 cm. [CT220.D53] 73-83626 8.95
1. United States—Biography. 2. Interviews. I. Title.

EILLS, Nancy. 920'.073
Here lies America : a collection of notable graves / Nancy Eills and Parker Hayden. New York : Hawthorn Books, c1978. xii, 178 p. : ill. ; 28 cm. [CT215.E38 1978] 77-72815 ISBN 0-8015-3425-9 : pbk. : 6.95
1. United States—Biography. 2. Sepulchral monuments—United States. I. Hayden, Parker, joint author. II. Title.

EPSTEIN, Perle S. 920'.073
Individuals all [by] Perle Epstein. New York, Crowell-Collier Press [1972] 175 p. 22 cm. [CT215.E68] 72-77277 4.95
1. United States—Biography. I. Title. **BIP**

EVANS, Eva (Knox) 1905- 920
American biographies [by] Eva Knox Witte. New York, Holt, Rinehart and Winston [1968] 288 p. illus., ports. 25 cm. Biographical sketches of twenty-six famous Americans, stressing their most important accomplishments in the fields of law and government, civil rights, industry and labor, urban growth, education, arts, or science. Includes study questions, projects, and reading lists. [E176.8.E87] AC 68
1. United States—Biography. I. Title.

FABER, Harold. 920
American heroes of the 20th century, by Harold and Doris Faber. Illustrated with photos. New York, Random House [1967] 179 p. illus., ports. 29 cm. (A Landmark giant, 14) Bibliography: p. 176-177. Biographies of twenty Americans whose contributions to the modern world range from polar exploration and civil rights to war correspondence and photography. [CT217.F28] AC 67
1. United States—Biography. I. Faber, Doris, 1924- joint author. II. Title. **BIP**

FARIS, John Thomson, 920.073
1871-1949.
Men who conquered. Freeport, N.Y., Books for Libraries Press [1968] 185 p. 22 cm. (Essay index reprint series) Reprint of the 1922 ed. Bibliography: p. 184-185. [CT219.F3 1968] 68-55846
1. United States—Biography. I. Title. **BIP**

FARIS, John Thomson, 1871- 973
1949.
The romance of forgotten men. Freeport, N.Y., Books for Libraries Press [1969, c1928] xiv, 312 p. illus., ports. 23 cm. (Essay index reprint series) Bibliography: p. 297-300. [E176.F225 1969] 68-58787
1. U.S.—Biography. I. Title. **BIP**

FELTON, Bruce. 920'.073
Felton & Fowler's Famous Americans you never knew existed / Bruce Felton and Mark Fowler. New York : Stein and Day, 1979. p. cm. [CT215.F44 1979] 78-56944 ISBN 0-8128-2511-X : 9.95
1. United States—Biography. I. Fowler, Mark, joint author. II. Title. III. Title: Famous Americans you never knew existed. **BIP**

FISHWICK, Marshall 920'.073
William.
American heroes : myth and reality / by Marshall W. Fishwick ; introd. by Carl Carmer. Westport, Conn. : Greenwood Press, 1975, c1954. viii, 242 p. ; 22 cm. Reprint of the ed. published by Public Affairs Press, Washington. Includes bibliographical references and index. [E176.F53 1975] 72-10695 ISBN 0-8371-6610-1 lib.bdg. : 13.25
1. United States—Biography. 2. Heroes. I. Title.

FISHWICK, Marshall 920.073
William.
The hero, American style [by] Marshall Fishwick. New York, D. McKay Co. [1969] vii, 270 p. 21 cm. Bibliography: p. 261-264. Bibliographical footnotes. [E176.F535] 69-13472 5.95
1. U.S.—Biography. 2. Heroes. I. Title.

FITZPATRICK, James K. 920'.073 B
Builders of the American dream / James K. Fitzpatrick. New Rochelle, N.Y. : Arlington House, c1977. 374 p. : ports. ; 24 cm. Contents.Contents.—Daniel Boone, frontier hero.—George Washington, Founding Father.—Robert E. Lee, gentleman soldier.—Abraham Lincoln, one nation, under God, indivisible.—William Jennings Bryan, the great commoner.—Thomas Alva Edison, the wizard of Menlo Park.—Walter Reed, doctor in uniform.—Charles Lindbergh, the Spirit of St. Louis.—Will Rogers, cowboy philosopher.—George Herman Ruth, the Babe.—Eddie Rickenbacker, the ace.—Walt Disney, something wonderful.—Douglas MacArthur, duty, honor, country. [CT214.F57] 77-21479 ISBN 0-87000-381-X : 9.95
1. United States—Biography. I. Title.
Contents omitted **BIP**

FOWLER, Mary Jane. 372.8
Great Americans [by] Mary Jane Fowler [and] Margaret Fisher. Grand Rapids, Fideler Co. [1968] 144 p. illus., ports. 28 cm. (American history and culture) Social studies textbook with brief biographies of seventeen famous American authors, explorers, scientists, and politicians. Includes questions at the end of each chapter and a glossary. [E176.8.F6 1968] AC 68
1. United States—Biography. I. Hertel, Margaret (Fisher), joint author. II. Title.

GANNON, Francis Xavier. 920.73
Biographical dictionary of the Left, by Francis X. Gannon. Boston, Western Islands [1969- v. 22 cm. [E747.G32] 76-12821 8.00 (v. 1)
1. United States—Biography. I. Title. **BIP**

GEIST, Harold. 920'.073 B
From eminently disadvantaged to eminence. Compiled and edited by Harold Geist. St. Louis, Mo., W. H. Green [1973] xi, 109 p. ports. 24 cm. [CT220.G4] 78-176180
1. United States—Biography. I. Title. **BIP**

GEIST, Harold. 920'.073 B
From eminently disadvantaged to eminence. Compiled and edited by Harold Geist. St. Louis, Mo., W. H. Green [1973] xi, 109 p. ports. 24 cm. [CT220.G4] 78-176180 8.50
1. United States—Biography. I. Title.

GLASS, Willie 976.1'47'050924 B
Elmore.
Miss Willie : happenings of a happy family, 1816-1926 / by Willie Elmore Glass. Lineage ed. Essington, Pa. : Huntingdon Press, c1976. 419 p. : geneal. tables (on lining papers), ill. ; 27 cm. [CT275.G47A35] 77-356482
1. United States—Biography. 2. Elmore family. 3. Glass, Willie Elmore. I. Title.

GOODRICH, David L. 338'.0922 B
Horatio Alger is alive and well and living in America; success stories of the under-30 generation, by David L. Goodrich. [1st ed.] New York, Cowles Book Co. [1971] xix, 198 p. ports. 22 cm. [CT214.G66 1971] 72-146811 ISBN 0-402-12059-0 5.95
1. United States—Biography. 2. Success—Biography. I. Title.

GREAT American families 920'.073
/ Gore Vidal ... [et al.]. New York : Norton, 1977, c1975. 192 p. : ill. ; 29 cm. "First published (in part) in The Sunday times magazine, London." Includes index. [CT215.G73 1977] 77-372557 15.95
1. United States—Biography. 2. Upper classes—United States—Biography. I. Vidal, Gore, 1925- **BIP**

GROSS, Marthe. 920'.073
The possible dream; ten who dared. [1st ed.] Philadelphia, Chilton Book Co. [1970] 204 p. ports. 24 cm. Biographies of ten people who reached the top in their field: Arthur Ashe, Jr., Ralph Nader, Neil Simon, Mary Wells, James D. Watson, Edward Villella, Carl Stokes, Peggy Fleming, Bill Moyers, and Shirley Verrett. [CT220.G7 1970] 79-115686 ISBN 0-8019-5512-2
1. United States—Biography. I. Title.

GROSS, Theodore L., comp. 920.073
Representative men: cult heroes of our time, edited by Theodore L. Gross. New York, Free Press [1970] xiv, 531 p. 21 cm. [CT220.G73] 70-93112
1. U.S.—Biography. I. Title.

HART, Larry. 920.073
Did I wake you up? Schenectady, N.Y., Riedinger & Riedinger [1970] 215 p. ports. 24 cm. [CT220.H37 1970] 73-145762
1. U.S.—Biography. I. Title.

HIGGINSON, Thomas 920.073
Wentworth, 1823-1911.
Contemporaries. Upper Saddle River, N.J., Literature House [1970] 379 p. 23 cm. Reprint of the 1900 ed. Contents.Contents.—Ralph Waldo Emerson.—Amos Bronson Alcott.—Theodore Parker.—John Greenleaf Whittier.—Walt Whitman.—Sidney Lanier.—An evening with Mrs. Hawthorne.—Lydia Maria Child.—Helen Jackson ("H. H.")—John Holmes. Thaddeus William Harris.—A visit to John Brown's household in 1859.—William Lloyd Garrison.—Wendell Phillips.—Charles Sumner.—Dr. Howe's antislavery career.—Ulysses Simpson Grant.—The eccentricities of reformers.—The road to England. [PS1927.C65 1970] 79-104483
1. U.S.—Biography. I. Title. **BIP**

HIMBER, Charlotte. 920.073
Famous in their twenties. Freeport, N.Y., Books for Libraries Press [1970, c1942] xii, 128 p. 23 cm. (Essay index reprint series) Contents.Contents.—He sees by music, Alec Templeton.—From elocution to exploration, by Lowell Thomas.—All the world his stage, Norman Bel Geddes.—Heroine in shorts, Alice Marble.—We investigate the investigator, Samuel Untermyer.—They fight leprosy, the Buker twins.—"Remember the name", Leslie MacMitchell. Let my people go, Paul Robeson.—Lenses on the world, Margaret Bourke-White.—"The public likes his informality", the Reverend Daniel A. Poling.—"Textbook stuff". [CT220.H5 1970] 79-111837
1. U.S.—Biography. I. Title. **BIP**

HOLBROOK, Stewart Hall, 923.673
1893-
Dreamers of the American dream. [1st ed.] Garden City, N. Y., Doubleday, 1957. 369p. 25cm. (Mainstream of America series) Includes bibliography. [HN57.H55] 57-11424
1. U. S.—Biog. 2. Reformers. 3. U. S.—Soc. condit. I. Title.

HOLBROOK, Stewart Hall, 923.673
1893-1964.
Dreamers of the American dream. [1st ed.] Garden City, N.Y., Doubleday, 1957. 369 p. 25 cm. (Mainstream of America series) Includes bibliography. [HN57.H55] 57-11424
1. United States—Biography. 2. Social reformers—United States. 3. United States—Social conditions. I. Title. **BIP**

HUNTER, Thomas C. 920'.073
Beginnings / Thomas C. Hunter. 1st ed. New York : Crowell, c1978. viii, 254 p. : ports. ; 21 cm.. [CT220.H86 1978] 77-27831 ISBN 0-690-01687-5 : 9.95
1. United States—Biography. 2. Professions—United States. I. Title.

HUSBAND, Joseph, 1885- 920.073
1938.
Americans by adoption; brief biographies of great citizens born in foreign lands. With an introd. by William Allan Neilson. Freeport, N.Y., Books for Libraries Press [1969] xv, 153 p. illus., ports. 23 cm. (Essay index reprint series) Reprint of the 1920 ed. Contents.Contents.—Stephen Girard.—John Ericsson.—Louis Agassiz.—Carl Schurz.—Theodore Thomas.—Andrew Carnegie.—James J. Hill.—Augustus Saint-Gaudens.—Jacob A. Riis. [E176.H96 1969] 70-86763
1. U.S.—Biography. I. Title.

INSTITUTE for 917.3'03'90922
Religious and Social Studies, Jewish Theological Seminary of America.
Thirteen Americans: their spiritual autobiographies. Edited by Louis Finkelstein. Port Washington, N.Y., Kennikat Press [1969, c1953] xii, 296 p. 23 cm. (Essay and general literature index reprint series.) (Religion and civilization series) "Includes eleven lectures given at the Institute for Religious and Social Studies of the Jewish Theological Seminary of America during the winter of 1949-50." Contents.Contents.—Preface, by L. Finkelstein.—Clarence E. Pickett.—Ordway Tead.—Henry Norris Russell.—Edwin Grant Conklin.—Richard McKeon.—Erwin D. Canham.—Elbert D. Thomas.—Judith Berlin Lieberman.—Channing H. Tobias.—David de Sola Pool.—Basil O'Connor.—Willard L. Sperry.—Julian Morgenstern. Biographical sketches. Bibliographical footnotes. [E176.I5 1969] 68-26190
1. U.S.—Biography. 2. U.S.—Religion. I. Finkelstein, Louis, 1895- ed. II. Title. III. Series.

THE Intimate and 973.9'092'4 B
agonizing diary of a man who fell madly in love with a beautiful Catholic nun. Albuquerque, N.M. : Gloucester Art Press, [1979] 91 leaves, [9] leaves of plates : ill. ; 28 cm. [CT275.Z9I54] 79-4158 ISBN 0-930582-25-X : 19.75
1. United States—Biography.

JACQUES Cattell Press. 973
The big book of halls of fame in the United States and Canada / Jaques Cattell Press. New York : R. R. Bowker, 1977- p. cm. [CT215.J36] 77-82734 ISBN 0-8352-1039-1 : 63.80
1. United States—Biography. 2. Canada—Biography. 3. Biography. 4. Halls of fame—United States. 5. Halls of fame—Canada. I. Title.

JOHNSON, Gerald White, 920'.073
1890-
The lunatic fringe, by Gerald W. Johnson. Westport, Conn., Greenwood Press [1973, c1957] 248 p. 22 cm. [E176.J6 1973] 72-12626 ISBN 0-8371-6680-2
1. United States—Biography. I. Title. **BIP**

KAHN, Roger. 920'.073
How the weather was. [1st ed.] New York, Harper & Row [1973] xvi, 217 p. 22 cm. A selection of the author's profiles and articles from the world of sports, music, and literature. [CT220.K33] 73-4096 ISBN 0-06-012243-9 7.95
1. United States—Biography. I. Title.

KEARNY, Edward N. 973'.0992 B
Mavericks in American politics : eight men who forced the issues of their day / by Edward N. Kearny. Madison, Wis. : Mimir Publishers, c1976. 285 p. ; 24 cm. Includes bibliographical references and indexes. [E176.K36] 76-361531 8.95
1. United States—Biography. 2. United States—Politics and government. I. Title.

KETCHUM, Richard M., 920.073
1922-
Faces from the past [by] Richard M. Ketchum. New York, American Heritage Press [1970] 172 p. illus., ports. 26 cm. [E176.K47 1970] 70-108812 ISBN 0-8281-0092-6 6.95

1. United States—Biography. 2. Photography—Portraits. I. Title.

KIELL, Norman, ed. 920.073
Psychological studies of famous Americans: the Civil War era. New York, Twayne Publishers [1964] 302 p. 22 cm. Bibliography: p. 301-302. [E415.K5] 63-19366
1. United States—Biography. I. Title.

KOSTELANETZ, Richard. 920.073
Master minds; portraits of contemporary American artists and intellectuals. [New York] Macmillan [1969] xiii, 370 p. music. 22 cm. "Bibliographical essays": p. 336-359. [CT220.K67] 69-18246
1. U.S.—Biography. I. Title. **BIP**

LAMPARSKI, Richard. 920.073
Whatever became of ... ? Second series. New York, Crown Publishers [1968] 206 p. illus., ports. 24 cm. Based on the author's radio program, Whatever became of ... ? [CT220.L28 1968] 68-9092 4.95
1. United States—Biography. I. Title.

LAMPARSKI, Richard. 920.073
Whatever became of ...? Introd. by Cleveland Amory. New York, Crown Publishers [1966, c1967] 207 p. ports. 24 cm. Based on the author's radio program Whatever became of ...? —Jacket. [CT220.L28] 66-26180
1. United States—Biography. I. Title.

*LAMPARSKI, Richard. 920'.073
Whatever became of ...? Fourth series. New York, Crown Publishers [1973] 206 p. illus., ports. 24 cm. (Whatever became of series) [CT220] 72-96663 ISBN 0-517-50425-1 5.95
1. United States—Biography. I. Title. II. Title: Whatever became of ... (Radio program) III. Series.

LAMPARSKI, Richard. 790.20922
Whatever became of...? Fifth series. New York, Bantam Books [1975 c1974] 275 p. illus. 18 cm. [CT220.L284] 1.50 (pbk.)
1. United States—Biography. 2. Performing arts—United States—Biography. I. Title. L.C. card no. for original edition: 75-1372.

LAMPARSKI, Richard. 790.2'092'2 B
Whatever became of ... ? Fifth series / by Richard Lamparski. New York : Crown Publishers, [1975] c1974. 206 p. : ill. ; 24 cm. Includes index. [CT220.L285 1975] 75-1372 6.95
1. United States—Biography. 2. Performing arts—United States—Biography. I. Title.

LAMPARSKI, Richard. 790.2'092'2 B
Whatever became of ...? Fourth series. New York, Crown Publishers [1973] 206 p. illus. 24 cm. [CT220.L284 1973] 72-96665 ISBN 0-517-50425-1 5.95
1. United States—Biography. 2. Performing arts—United States—Biography. I. Title.

LAW, Frederick Houk, 1871-1957. 920.073
Modern great Americans; short biographies of twenty great Americans of modern times who won wide recognition for achievements in various types of activity. Freeport, N.Y., Books for Libraries Press [1969] viii, 314 p. ports. 23 cm. (Essay index reprint series) Reprint of the 1926 ed. Contents.Contents.—Alexander Graham Bell.—Luther Burbank.—John Burroughs.—Andrew Carnegie.—Alexis Carrel.—Samuel Langhorne Clemens.—Thomas Alva Edison.—George Washington Goethals.—William Crawford Gorgas.—Albert Abraham Michelson.—Robert Andrews Millikan.—Robert Edwin Peary.—John Joseph Pershing.—Theodore William Richards.—Theodore Roosevelt.—Elihu Root.—John Singer Sargent.—Henry Van Dyke.—Woodrow Wilson.—Wilbur and Orville Wright. [CT214.L3 1969] 72-99706
1. U.S.—Biography. I. Title.

LEIPOLD, L. Edmond, 1902- 920
Citizens born abroad, by L. Edmond Leipold. Minneapolis, Denison [1967] 73 p. 25 cm. (His Famous American heroes and leaders series) Sketches of eleven American immigrants who came to the United States for reasons as varied as the talents they later developed in their new home: William Worrall Mayo, Alexander Hamilton, Hendrik Van Loon, Alexander Graham Bell, Samuel Slater, Carl Schurz, Michael Pupin, John James Audubon, Knute Rockne, Ottmar Mergenthaler, and Thomas Cole. [CT217.L45] AC 68
1. United States—Biography. I. Title.

LEIPOLD, L. Edmond, 1902- 920
Crusaders for a cause, by L. Edmond Leipold. Minneapolis, T. S. Denison [1967] 76 p. 25 cm. (Famous American heroes and leaders series) Biographical sketches of ten Americans who made unique contributions to their nation: Elijah Lovejoy, Benjamin Franklin, John Chapman, Booker T. Washington, Daniel Webster, Horace Mann, Horace Greeley, Dr. Walter Reed, Dwight Moody, William Lloyd Garrison. [CT217.L455] AC 67
1. United States—Biography. I. Title.

LEIPOLD, L. Edmond, 1902- 920
Founders of our cities, by L. Edmond Leipold. Minneapolis, Denison [1967] 71 p. 25 cm. (His Famous American heroes and leaders series) Brief accounts of the founding and founders of ten American cities: Savannah, Philadelphia, Providence, Salt Lake City, Nininger, Baltimore, Boston, New York, the District of Columbia, and Jamestown. [CT217.L47] AC 68
1. United States—Biography. 2. Cities and towns—History. I. Title.

LEIPOLD, L. Edmond, 1902- 920
Heroes in time of war, by L. Edmond Leipold. Minneapolis, Denison [1967] 82 p. 25 cm. (His Famous American heroes and leaders series) Short biographies of ten American men whose leadership and courage in wartime contributed to the course of American history. [E181.L48] AC 67
1. United States—Biography. 2. United States—History, Military. I. Title.

LIPPMANN, Walter, 1889-1974. 920'.073
Public persons / Walter Lippmann ; edited by Gilbert A. Harrison. 1st ed. New York : Liveright, c1976. 189 p. ; 22 cm. [CT220.L56 1976] 76-23103 ISBN 0-87140-620-9 : 7.95
1. United States—Biography. I. Title. **BIP**

MCAULIFFE, Martin L. 920'.073
Profiles of excellence, by Martin L. McAuliffe, Jr. Introd. by Wallace B. Graves. [Evansville, Ind.] University of Evansville Press [1970?] 193 p. 22 cm. [CT220.M25] 72-180736
1. United States—Biography. I. Title.

MCCABE, James Dabney, 1842-1883. 920'.073
Great fortunes, and how they were made; or, The struggles and triumphs of our self-made men. Freeport, N.Y., Books for Libraries Press [1972] 633 p. illus. 22 cm. Reprint of the 1870 ed. [CT219.M2 1972] 70-37895 ISBN 0-8369-6732-1
1. United States—Biography. I. Title. **BIP**

MCKELVIE, Martha Groves. 920.073
Presidents, politicians, and people I have known. Philadelphia, Franklin Pub. Co. [1970?] xii, 171 p. facsims., ports. 24 cm. [E747.M27] 77-101601 5.95
1. United States—Biography. 2. Presidents—United States—Anecdotes, facetiae, satire, etc. I. Title.

MADISON, Charles Allan. 920.073
Critics & crusaders; a century of American protest. 2d ed. New York, Ungar [1959] 662 p. illus. 22 cm. Includes bibliography. [E176.M22 1959] 58-14283
1. U.S.—Biography. 2. Liberty. I. Title.

MALONE, Dumas, 1892- 920.073
Saints in action. Freeport, N.Y., Books for Libraries Press [1971] 178 p. 22 cm. (Essay index reprint series) Reprint of the 1939 ed. Includes bibliographical references. [E176.M26 1970] 70-142664 ISBN 0-8369-2062-7
1. U.S.—Biography. 2. Christian biography. I. Title.

MARCUS, Robert D., 1936- comp. 920'.0373
America personified; portraits from history. Robert D. Marcus [and] David Burner, editors. Combined ed. New York, St. Martin's Press [1974] 434 p. ports. 24 cm. [E176.M267 1974] 74-76210 5.95 (pbk.).
1. United States—Biography. I. Burner, David, 1937- joint comp. II. Title.

MARTIN, Thornton, 1901- 927.92
Pete Martin calls on ... by Pete Martin. New York, Simon and Schuster, 1962. 510p. 22cm. [PN2285.M35] 62-14279
I. Title.

MARTINEZ, Al. 920'.073
Rising voices : profiles of Hispano-American lives / by Al Martinez. New York : New American Library, 1974. xii, 210 p. : ports. ; 18 cm. (A Signet book) [CT220.M34] 74-189550 pbk. : 1.50 1.50
1. United States—Biography. I. Title.

MASON, Gabriel Richard, ed. 973'.099
Great American liberals. Freeport, N.Y., Books for Libraries Press [1971, c1956] viii, 177 p. 23 cm. (Essay index reprint series) [E176.M38 1971] 76-156691 ISBN 0-8369-2413-4
1. U.S.—Biography. I. Title.

MEN, women, and issues in American history / edited by Howard H. Quint and Milton Cantor. Homewood, Ill. : Dorsey Press, 1975- 2 v. ; 23 cm. (Dorsey series in history) [E176.M456] 74-24453 ISBN 0-256-01686-0(v.1) pbk. : 5.50 ISBN 0-256-01687-9(v.2) pbk. : 5.50 920'.073
1. United States—Biography. 2. United States—History—Addresses, essays, lectures. I. Quint, Howard H. II. Cantor, Milton. **BIP**

MERSAND, Joseph E., 1907- ed. 001.2
Great modern American short biographies, edited and introduced by Joseph Mersand. [New York, Dell Pub. Co., 1966] 256 p. 18 cm. (Laurel-leaf library) "3126." Cover title: Great American short biographies. Includes bibliographies. [E176.M46] 66-31554
1. United States—Biography. I. Title. II. Title: Great American short biographies.

MITCHELL, George, 1944- 920'.073
Yessir, I've been here a long time : the faces and words of Americans who have lived a century / George Mitchell. 1st ed. New York : Dutton, 1975. 124 p. : ill. ; 24 cm. [CT215.M57 1975] 75-16182 8.95
1. United States—Biography. 2. Centenarians—United States—Biography. 3. Interviews. I. Title.

MOLEY, Raymond, 1886- 973.0992 B
27 masters of politics, in a personal perspective Westport, Conn., Greenwood Press [1972, c1949] xii, 276 p. illus. 22 cm. Original ed. issued in series: A Newsweek book. [E747.M7 1972] 79-163546 ISBN 0-8371-6206-8
1. United States—Biography. 2. United States—Politics and government—1901-1953. I. Title.

NEIDLE, Cecyle S. 920'.073
Great immigrants, by Cecyle S. Neidle. New York, Twayne Publishers [1973] 295 p. 21 cm. (The Immigrant heritage of America series) [CT215.N45] 72-3234 7.95
1. United States—Biography. 2. United States—Emigration and immigration. I. Title.
Contents Omitted. **BIP**

NEW York University. Hall of Fame. 920.073
The Hall of Fame for Great Americans at New York University; official handbook. Edited by Theodore Morello. [New York] New York University Press, 1962. 192 p. illus., ports., diagr. 22 cm. Published in 1927-39 under title: Hand-book of the Hall of Fame, New York University. [LD3885.H3A5 1962] 61-18175
1. United States—Biography. I. Morello, Theodore, ed.

NEW York University. Hall of Fame. 920.073
The Hall of Fame for Great Americans at New York University; official handbook. Edited by Theodore Morello. Rev. ed. [New York] New York University Press, 1967. 210 p. illus., ports. 22 cm. Published in 1937-39 under title: Hand-book of the Hall of Fame, New York University. [LD3885.H3A5 1967] 67-10691
1. United States—Biography. I. Morello, Theodore, ed.

NEWS front. 926.5
The 50 great pioneers of American industry; the stories of Rockefeller, Swift, Edison, Woolworth, Squibb, Proctor, Sears, Otis, Singer, Carrier, and 40 other business leaders and courageous innovators whose activities founded major industries and shaped today's economy. By the editors of News front [and] Year. [Maplewood, N.J., C. S. Hammond, c1964] 207 p. illus., ports. 32 cm. [HC102.5.A2N43] 65-485
1. U.S. — Biog. 2. U.S — Indus. — Hist. I. Year. II. Title.

NEWS front The 50 great 926.5
pioneers of American industry; the stories of Rockefeller, Swift, Edison, Woolworth, Squibb, Proctor, Sears, Otis, Singer, Carrier, and 40 other business leaders and courageous innovators whose activities founded major industries and shaped today's economy. By eds. of News front [and] Year [Maplewood, N.J., Hammond, c.1964] 207p. illus., ports. 32cm. [HC102.5.A2N43] 65-485 10.00 bds.,
1. U.S.—Biog. 2. U.S.—Indus.—Hist. I. Year.

NYE, Russel Blaine, 1913- 920.073
A baker's dozen; thirteen unusual Americans, by Russel B. Nye. Westport, Conn., Greenwood Press [1974, c1956] xi, 300 p. 23 cm. Reprint of the ed. published by Michigan State University Press, East Lansing. [E176.N95 1974] 74-8067 ISBN 0-8371-7495-3
1. United States—Biography. I. Title.

PEDERSON, Kern O. 920'.073
Leaders of America : capsule biographies of over 260 famous personalities / by Kern Pederson. Waukesha, Wis. : Country beautiful, [1975] p. cm. Includes index. [E176.P36] 75-786 ISBN 0-87294-073-X : 25.00
1. United States—Biography. I. Title.

PIELMEIER, Mary Francis Assisi, 1919- 920
The brave and the free [by] Sister M. Francis Assisi. [Boston] Ginn [1967] vi, 377 p. illus. (part col.) 24 cm. (Frontiers of freedom) A textbook of American history told through biographical sketches of selected leaders in many fields. [CT217.P5] AC 67
1. United States—Biography. I. Title.

POLLITT, Basil Hubbard, 1896- 920
The life and loves of Baron Von Audax, some time private, corporal, 'tenny-anty,' and first lieutenant in the United States Marine Corps, as told to Basil H. Pollitt. New York, Vantage [c.1962] 200p. 21cm. 3.50 bds.,
I. Title.

PRESTON, Wheeler. 920'.073
American biographies. New York, Harper. Detroit, Gale Research Co., 1974. viii, 1147 p. 22 cm. Reprint of the 1940 ed. Includes bibliographies. [CT213.P7 1974] 73-10407 ISBN 0-8103-4054-2
1. United States—Biography. I. Title. **BIP**

PROCTER, Ben H 923.273
Not without honor; the life of John H. Reagan. Austin, University of Texas Press [1962] xii, 361 p. illus., ports. 24 cm. Bibliography: p. [303]-328. [E664.R29P7] 62-9791
I. Reagan, John Henninger. 1818-1905. II. Title.

ROBSKY, Paul 920.9
The last of the Untouchables [by] Oscar Fraley, Paul Robsky. New York, Popular Lib. [c.1962] 183p. (Popular Library eagle bks., G569) .35 pap.,
I. Fraley, Oscar, 1914- II. Title.

ROOT, Elihu, 1845-1937. 973'.0922
Men and policies; addresses. Collected and edited by Robert Bacon and James Brown Scott. Freeport, N.Y., Books for Libraries Press [1968] ix, 511 p. 24 cm. (Essay index reprint series) Reprint of the 1925 ed. [E742.R78 1968] 68-22942
1. United States—Biography. 2. Law—Addresses, essays, lectures. 3. European War, 1914-1918—Addresses, sermons, etc. 4. International relations—Addresses, essays, lectures. I. Bacon, Robert, 1860-1919. II. Scott, James Brown, 1866-1943, ed. III. Title. **BIP**

SCHECHTER, William. 973.92'0922
Countown '68; profiles for the Presidency. Introduction by Thurston B. Morton and John M. Bailey. New York, Fleet Press Corp. [1967] xi, 227 p. illus. 23 cm. [E840.6.S3] 67-24074
1. United States—Biography. I. Title.

SCHECHTER, William. 973.92'0922
Countdown '68; profiles for the Presidency. Introductions by Thurston B. Morton and John M. Bailey. New York, Fleet Press Corp. [1967] xi, 227 p. illus. 23 cm. [E840.6.S3] 67-24074
1. U. S—Biog. I. Title.

SEAGER, Allan, 1906-1968. 920'.073
They worked for a better world. Illustrated by Theodore Haupt. Freeport, N.Y., Books for Libraries Press [1973] p. (Essay index reprint series) Reprint of the 1939 ed. published by Macmillan, New York, which was issued as no. 4 of The Peoples library. [CT214.S4 1973] 73-5590 ISBN 0-518-10132-0
1. United States—Biography. I. Title.

SEITZ, Don Carlos, 1862-1935. 973'.0922
The "also rans"; great men who missed making the presidential goal. Freeport, N.Y., Books for Libraries Press [1968] xxiv, 356 p. illus., facsims., ports. 22 cm. (Essay index reprint series) Reprint of the 1928 ed. Contents.Contents.—Introduction: Our presidents.—Aaron Burr.—William H. Crawford.—John C. Calhoun.—Henry Clay.—Lewis Cass.—Daniel Webster.—Winfield Scott.—John C. Fremont.—Stephen A. Douglas.—William H. Seward.—George B. McClellan.—Horatio Seymour.—Horace Greeley.—Samuel J. Tilden.—Winfield Scott Hancock.—James G. Blaine.—Benjamin F. Butler.—William Jennings Bryan. [E176.S44 1968] 68-20332
1. United States—Biography. 2. United States—Politics and government. I. Title. II. Title: Presidential goal. BIP

†SEVAREID, Arnold Eric, 1912- 973.9'092'2
Conversations with Eric Sevareid. Washington : Public Affairs Press, c1976. vi, 215 p. ; 23 cm. "Interviews with notable Americans: Walter Lippmann, William O. Douglas, Hugo Black, Dean Acheson, George Kennan, John McCloy, Robert Hutchins, Leo Rosten, Eric Hoffer, Mary Peabody, Marietta Tree, Frances Fitzgerald, Daniel Patrick Moynihan." [CT220.S48] 76-383346 ISBN 0-8183-0248-8 pbk. : 4.50
1. United States—Biography. 2. Interviews. I. Lippmann, Walter, 1889-1974. II. Title. BIP

SHOOK, Robert L., 1938- 920'.073
Total commitment / by Robert L. Shook and Ron L. Bingaman. New York : F. Fell Publishers, [1975] p. cm. Bibliography: p. [CT220.S52 1975] 75-12690 ISBN 0-8119-0232-3 : 9.95
1. United States—Biography. I. Bingaman, Ron, joint author. II. Title. BIP

SMITH, Helen Ainslie. 920'.073
One hundred famous Americans. Freeport, N.Y., Books for Libraries Press [1972] viii, 566 p. illus. 24 cm. (Essay index reprint series) Reprint of the 1886 ed. [CT214.S57 1972] 72-5677 ISBN 0-8369-7286-4
1. United States—Biography. I. Title. BIP

SMITH, Seba, 1792-1868. 818'.3'07
The life and writings of Major Jack Downing, of Downingville, away down East in the State of Maine. Written by himself. Boston, Lilly, Wait, Colman & Holden, 1833. [New York, AMS Press, 1973] 260 p. illus. 19 cm. [PS2876.L68 1973] 71-164785 ISBN 0-404-02168-9
I. Title.

STEARNS, Frank Preston, 1846-1917. 920.073
Cambridge sketches. Freeport, N.Y., Books for Libraries Press [1968] 374 p. ports. 22 cm. (Essay index reprint series) Reprint of the 1905 ed. Contents.Contents.—The close of the war.—Francis J. Child.—Longfellow.—Lowell.—C. P. Cranch.—T. G. Appleton.—Doctor Holmes.—Frank Bird and the Bird Club.—Sumner.—Chevalier Howe.—The war governor.—The colored regiments.—Emerson's tribute to George L. Stearns.—Elizur Wright.—Dr. W. T. G. Morton.—Leaves from a Roman diary.—Centennial contributions. [E415.8.S79 1968] 68-24855
1. United States—Biography. 2. Cambridge, Mass.—Biography. I. Title. BIP

STONE, Irving, 1903- 920.073
They also ran; the story of the men who were defeated for the presidency [by] Irving Stone. Garden City, New York, Doubleday, Doran and Co., Inc., 1966. xi p., 2 l., 434 p. ports. 22 cm. Table on lining-papers. "Source notes": p. 407-419. "Selected bibliography": p. 421-422. [E176.S87 1945] 45-9342
1. U.S.—Biography. 2. U.S.—Politics and government. I. Title.

STONE, Irving, 1903- ed. 920.073
We speak for ourselves; a self portrait of America, edited and with an introd. by Irving Stone, with Richard Kennedy. [1st ed.] Garden City, N.Y., Doubleday, 1950. xvii, 462 p. 22 cm. [E176.S875] 50-9974
1. U.S.—Biography. I. Title.

STURGES, Clark. 917.3'03'920922
Witnesses. Berkeley, Glendessary Press [1974] 139 p. illus. 22 cm. [CT220.S85] 73-88640 ISBN 0-87709-221-4 3.50 (pbk.).
1. United States—Biography. I. Title. BIP

TAYLOR, Daniel R., comp. 301.15'43'20973
Voices above the crowd; life-styles of fifteen outstanding Americans [by] Daniel R. Taylor. Waco, Tex., Word Books [1970] 96 p. 20 cm. Includes bibliographical references. [CT216.T38 1970] 70-135116 2.95
1. U.S.—Biography. I. Title.

TELLER, Walter Magnes, comp. 920'.073
Twelve works of naive genius. Edited by Walter Teller. [1st ed.] New York, Harcourt, Brace, Jovanovich [1972] xiii, 306 p. illus. 22 cm. Contents.Contents.—A narrative of the sufferings of Seth Hubbell & family in his beginning a settlement in the town of Wolcott, in the state of Vermont, by S. Hubbell.—A narrative of the life and medical discoveries of the author, by S. Thomson.—Memoirs of the life and religious labors of Edward Hicks, late of Newtown, Bucks County, Pennsylvania, by E. Hicks.—My egotistigraphy, by C. Harding.—Incidents in the Life of a slave girl, by L. Brent.—Poor little hearts, by N. Luce.—Autobiography, by A. T. Still.—Six hundred dollars a year (Anonymous)—Journal written on bark Nautilus, 1869-1874, by L. P. Vincent Smith.—Voyage of the "Destroyer" from New York to Brazil, by J. Slocum.—Sketches of my life in the South, by J. Stroyer.—Paragraphs from the studio of a recluse. Some verses about his pictures. By A. P. Ryder. [CT214.T45] 72-78450 ISBN 0-OTwelve works
1. United States—Biography I. Title.

THOMAS, Cal. 920'.073
Public persons and private lives : intimate interviews / Cal Thomas. Waco, Tex. : Word Books, c1979. 168 p. : ill. ; 21 cm. [CT220.T48] 79-63942 ISBN 0-8499-2845-1 pbk : 5.95
1. United States—Biography. 2. Interviews. I. Title.

THOMAS, Henry, 1886- 920.073
Living biographies of famous Americans, by Henry Thomas and Dana Lee Thomas (Henry Thomas Schnittkind and Dana Arnold Schnittkind). Illus. by Gordon Ross. Freeport, N.Y., Books for Libraries Press [1972, c1946] viii, 307 p. illus. 23 cm. (Essay index reprint series) [E176.T55 1972] 71-167413 ISBN 0-8369-2624-2
1. United States—Biography. I. Thomas, Dana Lee, 1918- joint author. II. Title.

THWING, Charles Franklin, 1853-1937. 920.073
Friends of men; being a second series of Guides, philosophers, and friends. Freeport, N.Y., Books for Libraries Press [1968] xi, 479 p. 22 cm. (Essay index reprint series) Reprint of 1933 ed. Contents.Contents.—Phillips Brooks.—George Edward Woodberry.—Arthur James Balfour.—William Howard Taft.—Walter Hines Page.—Thomas Wentworth Higginson.—William Roscoe Thayer.—William Everett.—Talcott Williams.—Henry Theophilus Finck.—Francis Edward Clark.—Barrett Wendell.—Edward Williams Morley.—Haldane.—Henry Johnson.—Charles Albert Dickinson.—Theodore Chickering Williams.—Peabody and Bowen.—Charles Franklin Hoover.—Frank Emory Bunts.—John Phillips.—Carl August Hamann.—Raymond and Seelye.—Francis Amasa Walker.—William Pepper.—Edgar Fahs Smith.—Benjamin Ide Wheeler.—Woodrow Wilson.—David Starr Jordan. [CT119.T56 1968] 68-8500
1. U.S.—Biography. I. Title.

THWING, Charles Franklin, 1853-1937. 378.1'12'0922 B
Guides, philosophers, and friends; studies of college men. Freeport, N.Y., Books for Libraries Press [1971] x, 476 p. 23 cm. (Essay index reprint series) Reprint of the 1927 ed. [LA2311.T55 1971] 70-156723 ISBN 0-8369-2445-2
1. United States—Biography. 2. Educators—United States—Biography. I. Title. BIP

*TOVAR, Federico Ribes. 920'.073
100 biografias de Puertorriquenos ilustres [New York] Plus Ultra Educational Publishers [1973] 304 p. ports. 18 cm. [CT217.] 2.95 (pbk.)
1. United States—Biography. 2. Puerto Rico—Biography. I. Title.

VILLARD, Oswald Garrison, 1872-1949. 920.073
Prophets, true and false. Freeport, N.Y., Books for Libraries Press [1969] 355 p. 23 cm. (Essay index reprint series) Reprint of the 1928 ed. [E747.V54 1969] 75-93384 ISBN 0-8369-1386-8
1. United States—Biography. 2. Statesmen—United States. I. Title. BIP

VIORST, Milton. 973.92'0922
Hustlers and heroes; an American political panorama. New York, Simon and Schuster [1971] 382 p. 22 cm. [E840.6.V5] 70-156163 ISBN 0-671-20978-7 8.95
1. United States—Biography. 2. Statesmen—United States. I. Title.

WILSTACH, Paul, 1870-1952. 973.3'0922 B
Patriots off their pedestals. Freeport, N.Y., Books for Libraries Press [1970, c1927] 240 p. 23 cm. (Essay index reprint series) Contents.Contents.—The idea.—George Washington.—Benjamin Franklin.—Patrick Henry.—Alexander Hamilton.—John Adams.—Thomas Jefferson.—John Marshall.—James Madison. [E302.5.W74 1970] 78-117862 ISBN 0-8369-1738-3
1. United States—Biography. 2. Statesmen—United States. I. Title. BIP

WIN if you will; thirteen 920.71
winners show how. Personal accounts as told to Paul H. Dunn. With a foreword by Harold B. Lee. Salt Lake City, Utah, Bookcraft, 1972. xii, 257 p. illus. 24 cm. Contents.Contents.—Gene Fullmer, boxing champ.—Homer R. Warner, heart authority—medical computer innovator.—Don L. Lind, Ph.D. astronaut.—L. Jay Silvester, world-record discus thrower.—Billy Casper, golfer extraordinary.—Bernard F. Fisher, congressional medal of honor holder.—Harmon Killebrew, American League home run champion.—George Romney, top business and government administrator.—Bruno Gerzeli, international soccer star.—James A. Jensen, scientist explorer.—Vernon Law, Cy Young award winner.—G. Homer Durham, higher education's distinguished servant.—J. Willard Marriott, Washington's catering magnate. [CT220.W58] 72-75472
1. United States—Biography. I. Dunn, Paul H.

YOUNG, Valton Joseph. 923.273
The Speaker's agent. [1st ed.] New York, Vantage Press [1956] 83p. illus. 22cm. [E748.R24Y6] 55-11654
1. Rayburn. Sam Taliaferro, 1882- II. Title.

United States—Biography—Addresses, essays, lectures.

LIPPMANN, Walter, 1889- 320.9'73
Men of destiny. Introd. by Richard Lowitt. Drawings by Rollin Kirby. Seattle, University of Washington Press [1969, c1927] xxi, 244 p. illus. 23 cm. (Americana library) [E747.L76 1969] 71-9039
1. United States—Biography—Addresses, essays, lectures. 2. United States—Politics and government—1919-1933—Addresses, essays, lectures. I. Title. BIP

United States—Biography—Anecdotes, facetiae, satire, etc.

TYRRELL, R. Emmett. 920'.073
Public nuisances / R. Emmett Tyrrell, Jr. ; drawings by Elliot Banfield. New York : Basic Books, c1979. viii, 248 p. : ill. ; 22 cm. Includes index. [CT120.T96] 78-19940 ISBN 0-465-06772-7 : 11.95
1. United States—Biography—Anecdotes, facetiae, satire, etc. 2. Biography—20th century—Anecdotes, facetiae, satire, etc. I. Title.

United States—Biography—Bibliography.

DARGAN, Marion. 016.92'0073
Guide to American biography. Foreword by Dumas Malone. Westport, Conn., Greenwood Press [1973, c1949-52] 2 v. in 1 (viii, 510 p.) 22 cm. Reprint of the ed. published by the University of New Mexico Press, Albuquerque. Contents.Contents.—pt. 1. 1607-1815.—pt. 2. 1815-1933. [Z5305.U5D323] 73-13455 ISBN 0-8371-7134-2 18.75
1. United States—Biography—Bibliography. I. Title. BIP

United States—Biography—Indexes.

BIOGRAPHICAL 920'.073
dictionaries master index : supplement / edited by Miranda C. Herbert and Barbara McNeil. Detroit : Gale Research Co., 1979- p. cm. [Z5305.U5B56 Suppl.] [CT213] 79-22270 ISBN 0-8103-1082-1 : 60.00
1. United States—Biography—Indexes. 2. Canada—Biography—Indexes. I. Herbert, Miranda C. II. McNeil, Barbara.

BIOGRAPHICAL 920'.073
dictionaries master index / Dennis La Beau, Gary C. Tarbert, editors. 1st ed., 1975-1976. Detroit : Gale Research Co., [1975- v. ; 29 cm. Contents.Contents.—v. 1. A-F. [Z5305.U5B56] [CT213] 75-19059 ISBN 0-8103-1077-5 : 65.00
1. United States—Biography—Indexes. 2. Canada—Biography—Indexes. I. La Beau, Dennis. II. Tarbert, Gary C.

United States—Biography—Miscellanea.

BONKO, Larry, 1934- 920'.073
Sinners and show-offs / by Larry Bonko. Virginia Beach, Va. : Donning, [1975] 236 p., [8] leaves of plates : ill. ; 22 cm. [CT220.B58] 74-33670 ISBN 0-915442-01-9 : 6.95
1. United States—Biography—Miscellanea. I. Title. BIP

United States—Biography—Poetry.

MERRIAM, Eve, 1916- 811
Independent voices. Drawings by Arvis Stewart. New York, Atheneum, 1968. xi, 79 p. illus., ports. 22 cm. Pays tribute in verse to: Benjamin Franklin, Elizabeth Blackwell, Frederick Douglass, Henry Thoreau, Lucretia Mott, Ida B. Wells, and Fiorello H. La Guardia. [PZ8.3.M55187In] AC 68
1. United States—Biography—Poetry. I. Stewart, Arvis, illus. II. Title.

United States—Biography—Portraits.

SUMMERS, Ian. 920'.073
The yearbook book / by Ian Summers ; with a foreword by Jack Pontifell. 1st ed. New York : Ballantine Books, 1976. 152 p. : ill. ; 28 cm. Includes index. [CT220.S9] 75-44321 ISBN 0-345-24732-9 pbk. : 5.95
1. United States—Biography—Portraits. 2. High school students—United States—Biography—Portraits. I. Title. BIP

UNITED States news & world report. 920.073
Roster of eminence; 200 distinguished men and women who made news, 1949-1952, as published in U.S. news & world report. [Washington, 1953] 60p. ports. 28cm. [E813.U52] 53-2835
1. U.S.—Biog.—Portraits. I. Title.
. S. news & world report.

United States. Bureau of Refugees, Freedmen, and Abandoned Lands.

HOWARD, Oliver Otis, 1830-1909. 973.7'0924 B
Autobiography of Oliver Otis Howard, Major General, United States Army. Freeport, N.Y., Books for Libraries Press, 1971. 2 v. illus. 23 cm. (The Black heritage library collection) Reprint of the 1907 ed. [E467.1.H8A3 1971] 73-170699 ISBN 0-8369-8889-2
1. United States. Bureau of Refugees, Freedmen, and Abandoned Lands. 2. United States—History—Civil War, 1861-1865—Campaigns and battles. I. Title. II. Series.

United States. Central Intelligence Agency.

COLBY, William Egan, 1920- 327'.12'0924 B
Honorable men : my life in the CIA / William Colby and Peter Forbath. New York : Simon and Schuster, c1978. 493 p., [8] leaves of plates : ill. ; 24 cm. Includes index. [JK468.I6C59] 78-1525 ISBN 0-671-22875-7 : 10.95
1. United States. Central Intelligence Agency. 2. Colby, William Egan, 1920- 3. Intelligence officers—United States—Biography. I. Forbath, Peter, joint author. II. Title. BIP

PHILLIPS, David Atlee. 327'.12'0924 B
The night watch / David Atlee Phillips. 1st ed. New York : Atheneum, 1977. x, 309 p. ; 25 cm. Autobiographical. Includes index. [JK468.I6P54 1977] 76-11855 ISBN 0-689-10754-4 : 10.00
1. United States. Central Intelligence Agency. 2. Phillips, David Atlee. 3. Spies—Biography. 4. United States—Foreign relations—Latin America. 5. Latin America—Foreign relations—United States. I. Title. BIP

STOCKWELL, John, 1937- 967'.303
In search of enemies : a CIA story / John Stockwell. 1st ed. New York : Norton, c1978. 285 p. : ill. ; 25 cm. Includes index. [DT611.76.S76A34 1978] 78-104579 ISBN 0-393-05705-4 : 12.95
1. United States. Central Intelligence Agency. 2. Stockwell, John, 1937- 3. Angola—History—Revolution, 1961-1975—Personal narratives. 4. Angola—History—Revolution, 1961-1975—Foreign participation, American. 5. Spies—United States—Biography. 6. Spies—Angola—Biography. I. Title. BIP

United States. Civil Service Commission—Biography.

UNITED States. Civil Service Commission. Library. 353.001'092'2 B
Fifty United States Civil Service Commissioners; biographical sketch, biographical sources, writings. Washington, 1971. 275 p. 27 cm. Cover title. Includes bibliographies. [JK693.A2A5] 78-614566
1. United States. Civil Service Commission—Biography. I. Title.

United States—Civilization—To 1783.

†BRADLEY, Francis, 1903- 973'.0992
The American proposition : a new type of man / by Francis Bradley ; ill. by Jaquelin Taliafero Smith. New York : Moral Re-armament, 1977. ix, 175 p. : ill., map (on lining papers) ; 23 cm. Includes index. Bibliography: p. 139-154. [E162.B77] 77-10293 6.50
1. United States—Civilization—To 1783. 2. United States—Civilization—1783-1848. 3. Statesmen—United States—Biography. 4. Presidents—United States—Biography. 5. National characteristics, American. I. Title.
Publisher's Address: 124 East 40th St. Suite 702 New York, NY, 10016

United States—Civilization—1783-1865.

ELLIS, Joseph J. 920'.073
After the Revolution : profiles of early American culture / by Joseph J. Ellis. 1st ed. New York : Norton, c1979. p. cm. Includes bibliographical references and index. [E164.E4 1979] 79-16771 ISBN 0-393-01253-0 : 16.95
1. United States—Civilization—1783-1865. 2. Intellectuals—United States—Biography. I. Title. BIP

United States. Congress—Biography.

CHAMBERLIN, Hope. 328.73'092'2 B
A minority of members: women in the U.S. Congress. New York, Praeger Publishers [1973] ix, 374 p. 24 cm. [JK1030.A2C5] 73-151950
1. United States. Congress—Biography. 2. Women—United States—Biography. 3. Women in politics—United States—History. I. Title.

CONGRESSIONAL Quarterly, inc. 328.73'092'2 B
Members of Congress since 1789. Washington : Congressional Quarterly Inc., 1977. 181 p. ; 28 cm. [JK1010.C66 1977] 76-57729 ISBN 0-87187-105-X : 5.25
1. United States. Congress—Biography. 2. Legislators—United States—Biography. I. Title. BIP

LANMAN, Charles, 1819-1895. 920'.073
Biographical annals of the civil Government of the United States, during its first century : from original and official sources / by Charles Lanman. Detroit : Gale Research Co., 1975. p. cm. Reprint of the 1876 ed. published by J. Anglim, Washington, D.C. Includes indexes. [E176.L2918 1975] 68-30626 ISBN 0-8103-4300-2 : 27.00
1. United States. Congress—Biography. 2. United States—Biography. 3. United States—Registers. I. Title.

MOONEY, Booth, 1912- 923.273
Mr. Speaker; four men who shaped the United States House of Representatives. Chicago, Follett Pub Co. [1964] xi, 226 p. 24 cm. Contents.Contents.—The Speaker.—Star of the West: Henry Clay.—The Czar: Thomas B. Reed.—Uncle Joe: Joseph G. Cannon.—Man of the House: Sam Rayburn.—The Speakers of the House.—Bibliography (p. 217-219) [E176.M82] 64-23608
1. United States. Congress—Biography. 2. United States. Congress. House—Speaker. I. Title.

SALTER, John Thomas, 1898- ed. 973'.099 B
Public men in and out of office, edited by J. T. Salter. New York, Da Capo Press, 1972 [c1946] xx, 513 p. illus. 23 cm. (Franklin D. Roosevelt and the era of the New Deal) [E747.S3 1972] 76-39131 ISBN 0-306-70457-9
1. United States. Congress—Biography. 2. United States—Biography. 3. Statesmen, American. I. Title. II. Series. BIP

United States. Congress. House.

MILLER, William, 1909- 328.73'0924
Fishbait : the memoirs of the congressional doorkeeper / by William "Fishbait" Miller as told to Frances Spatz Leighton. Englewood Cliffs, N.J. : Prentice-Hall, c1977. ix, 389 p., [16] leaves of plates : ill. ; 24 cm. Includes index. [JK1319.M54] 76-58404 ISBN 0-13-320416-2 : 12.50
1. United States. Congress. House. 2. Miller, William M., 1909- 3. Legislators—United States. I. Leighton, Frances Spatz, joint author. II. Title. BIP

United States. Congress. House—Biography—Juvenile literature.

HASKINS, James, 1941- 973.92'092'4 B
Andrew Young, man with a mission / James Haskins. 1st ed. New York : Lothrop, Lee & Shepard Co., c1979. 192 p. : ill. ; 24 cm. Includes index. An account of the life of Andrew Young, including his activities as a clergyman, civil rights worker, legislator, and United States Ambassador to the United Nations. [E840.8.Y64H37] 79-1046 ISBN 0-688-41896-1 : 6.25 ISBN 0-688-51896-6 lib.bdg. : 6.00
1. Young, Andrew J., 1932- —Juvenile literature. 2. United States. Congress. House—Biography—Juvenile literature. 3. United Church of Christ—Clergy—Biography—Juvenile literature. 4. Ambassadors—United States—Biography—Juvenile literature. 5. Legislators—United States—Biography—Juvenile literature. 6. Clergy—United States—Biography—Juvenile literature.

United States Congress. Senate Biography.

BERMAN, Edgar. 973.923'092'4 B
Hubert : the triumph and tragedy of the Humphrey I knew / Edgar Berman. New York : Putnam, c1979. 300 p., [8] leaves of plates : ill. ; 24 cm. Includes index. [E748.H945B47 1979] 79-4259 ISBN 0-399-12314-8 : 10.95
1. Humphrey, Hubert Horatio, 1911-1978. 2. United States. Congress. Senate—Biography. 3. Berman, Edgar. 4. Vice-Presidents—United States—Biography. 5. Legislators—United States—Biography. I. Title. BIP

KENNEDY, John Fitzgerald, Pres. U.S., 1917-1963. 923.273
Profiles in courage; Young readers memorial ed., abridged. Special Memorial foreword by Robert F. Kennedy. Illus. by Emil Weiss. New York, Harper & Row [1964, c1961] xxxiii, 164 p. illus. 22 cm. [E176.K43 1964] 64-17696
1. United States. Congress. Senate—Biography. 2. Courage. I. Title. BIP

KENNEDY, John Fitzgerald, Pres. U.S., 1917-1963 923.273
Profiles in courage. Special foreword by Robert F. Kennedy. Memorial ed. New York, Watts [1965, c.1955, 1956] 319p. 29cm. (Keith Jennison bk.) Bibl. [E176.K4] 65-4480 6.95; 4.95 lib. ed.,
1. U.S. Congress. Senate—Biog. 2. Courage. I. Title.

KENNEDY, John Fitzgerald Pres. U. S., 1917- 923.273
Profiles in courage [1st ed.] New York, Harper [c1956] 266p. illus. 22cm. Includes bibliography. [K176.K4] 55-11279
1. U. S. Congress. senate—Biog. 2. Courage. I. Title.

KENNEDY, John Fitzgerald, Pres. U. S., 1917- 923.273
Profiles in courage. [Inaugural ed.] New York, Harper [1961] xiii, 266p. illus., ports., facisms. 22cm. Bibliography: p.249-261 [E176.K4 1961] 61-8730
1. U. S. Congress. Senate—Biog. 2. Courage. I. Title.

KENNEDY, John Fitzgerald, Pres. U.S., 1917-1963. 923.273
Profiles in courage. [Memorial ed.] New York, Harper & Row [c1964] 287 p. port. 24 cm. Bibliography: p. 269-281. [E176.K4 1964] 64-16194
1. U.S. Congress. Senate — Biog. 2. Courage. I. Title.

KENNEDY, John Fitzgerald, Pres. U.S., 1917-1963. 923.273
Profiles in courage. Special foreword by Robert F. Kennedy. Memorial ed. New York, F. Watts [c1964] 319 p. 29 cm. Bibliography: p. 305-319. [E176.K4 1964b] 65-4480
1. U.S. Congress. Senate — Biog. 2. Courage. I. Title.

KENNEDY, John Fitzgerald, Pres. U.S., 1917-1963. 923.273
Profiles in courage. Memorial ed. Special foreword by Robert F. Kennedy. New York, Harper [c.1955-1964] xvi, 238p. 19cm. (Perennial lib., P1) Bibl. 64-5396 .65 pap.,
1. U.S. Congress. Senate—Biog. 2. Courage. I. Title.

KENNEDY, John Fitzgerald, Pres. U. S., 1917-1963. 923.273
Profiles in courage; young readers edition, abridged. Illus. by Emil Weiss. [1st ed.] New York, Harper [1961] 164 p. illus. 22 cm. [E176.K43 1961] 61-10040
1. U. S. Congress. Senate—Biography. 2. Courage. I. Title.

KENNEDY, John Fitzgerald, Pres. U. S., 1917-1963. 923.273
Profiles in courage; young readers edition, abridged. Illus. by Emil Weiss. [1st ed.] New York, Harper [1961] 164 p. illus. 22 cm. [E176.K43 1961] 61-10040
1. U. S. Congress. Senate—Biography. 2. Courage. I. Title.

KENNEDY, John Fitzgerald, Pres. U.S., 1917-1963. 923.273
Profiles in courage. Memorial ed. Special foreword by Robert F. Kennedy. New York, Harper & Row [1964] xvi, 238 p. 19 cm. (Perennial library, P1) Bibliography: p. 221-232. [E176.K4 1964a] 64-5396
1. U.S. Congress. Senate — Biog. 2. Courage. I. Title.

KENNEDY, John Fitzgerald, Pres. U.S., 1917- 923.273
Profiles in courage. [Inaugural ed.] New York, Harper [c. 1955-1961] xiii, 266p. illus., ports. Bibl. 61-8730 3.95 half cloth,
1. U.S. Congress. Senate—Biog. 2. Courage I. Title.

STUART, Roger Winship 923.273
Meet the Senators. [New York, Macfadden, c.1963] 284p. illus., ports. 18cm. (Macfadden Capitol Hill bk., 75-124, Macfadden orig.) 63-25184 .75 pap.,
1. U.S. Congress. Senate—Biog. I. Title.

MCCAUGHEY, Elizabeth P., 1948- 973.3'092'4 B
From Loyalist to Founding Father : the political odyssey of William Samuel Johnson / Elizabeth P. McCaughey. New York : Columbia University Press, 1979. p. cm. Includes index. Bibliography: p. [E302.6.J7M3] 79-17042 ISBN 0-231-04506-9 : 22.50
1. Johnson, William Samuel, 1727-1819. 2. United States. Congress. Senate—Biography. 3. Columbia University—Presidents—Biography. 4. Connecticut—Politics and government—Colonial period, ca. 1600-1775. 5. United States—Politics and government—1783-1789. 6. Legislators—United States—Biography. 7. College presidents—United States—Biography. I. Title. BIP

TUCKER, Ray Thomas, 1893- 328.73'0922
Sons of the wild jackass, by Ray Tucker and Frederick R. Barkley. Cartoons by R. G. List. Introd. by Robert S. Maxwell. Seattle, University of Washington Press [1970, c1932] xxviii, 398 p. illus. 23 cm. (Americana library 17) [E747.T94 1970] 78-125180
1. United States. Congress. Senate—Biography. 2. Statesmen—United States. I. Barkley, Frederick Reuben, 1892- joint author. II. Title. BIP

TUCKER, Ray Thomas, 1893- 328.73'0922
Sons of the wild jackass, by Ray Tucker and Frederick R. Barkley. With fifteen

cartoons by R. G. List. Freeport, N.Y., Books for Libraries Press [1969] xii, 398 p. ports. 23 cm. (Essay index reprint series) Reprint of the 1932 ed. [E747.T94 1969] 70-99727 ISBN 0-8369-1385-X
1. United States. Congress. Senate—Biography. 2. Statesmen—United States. I. Barkley, Frederick Reuben, 1892- joint author. II. Title.

WELCH, June 328.73'092'2 B
Rayfield, 1927-
The Texas Senator / June Rayfield Welch. Dallas : G.L.A. Press, 1978. ix, 179 p. : ill. ; 29 cm. Includes index. Bibliography: p. 171-174. [F385.W46] 78-65161 13.95
1. United States. Congress. Senate—Biography. 2. Politicians—Texas—Biography. 3. Legislators—United States—Biography. 4. Texas—Biography. I. Title. BIP

United States. Congress. Senate. Select Committee on Presidential Campaign Activities.

DASH, Samuel. 364.1'32'0973
Chief counsel : inside the Ervin Committee—the untold story of Watergate / by Samuel Dash. 1st ed. New York : Random House, c1976. p. cm. [E860.D36] 76-14171 ISBN 0-394-40853-5 : 10.00
1. United States. Congress. Senate. Select Committee on Presidential Campaign Activities. 2. Dash, Samuel. 3. Watergate Affair, 1972- —Personal narratives. 4. Lawyers—Washington, D.C.—Biography. 5. Washington, D.C.—Biography. I. Title.

THOMPSON, Fred D. 364.1'32'0973
At that point in time : the story of the Senate Watergate Committee / Fred D. Thompson. New York : Quadrangle/New York Times Book Co., [1975] Includes index. [E860.T45] 74-24290 ISBN 0-8129-0536-9 : 9.95
1. United States. Congress. Senate. Select Committee on Presidential Campaign Activities. 2. Thompson, Fred D. 3. Watergate Affair, 1972- I. Title.

United States. Constitution—Signers.

MCGEE, Dorothy 342.73'0922
Horton.
Framers of the Constitution. New York, Dodd, Mead [1968] xvii, 394 p. facsim., ports. 21 cm. Bibliography: p. 381-388. [JK146.M279] 67-26154
1. United States. Constitution—Signers. I. Title.

UNITED States. 973.3'13'0922 B
National Park Service.
Signers of the Constitution : historic places commemorating the signing of the Constitution. Washington : U.S. Dept. of the Interior, National Park Service, 1976. p. cm. (The National survey of historic sites and buildings ; v. 19) Bibliography: p. [E302.5.U6 1976] 75-619382
1. United States. Constitution—Signers. 2. Historic sites—United States—Guide-books. I. Title. II. Series.

United States. Constitution—Signers—Biography.

MASON, Ed. 973.3'092'2 B
Signers of the Constitution / Ed Mason. Columbus, Ohio : Dispatch Print. Co., c1975. 191 p. : ill. ; 22 cm. (His Builders of a nation series ; book 2) [E302.5.M27] 75-40682
1. United States. Constitution—Signers—Biography. I. Title.

United States. Constitutional Convention, 1787.

LANSING, John, 1754- 342.73'02
1829.
The delegate from New York; or, Proceedings of the Federal Convention of 1787, from the notes of John Lansing, Jr. Edited by Joseph Reese Strayer. Port Washington, N.Y., Kennikat Press [1967, c1939] viii, 125 p. port. 21 cm. Bibliographical footnotes. [JK141 1967] 67-27618
1. United States. Constitutional Convention, 1787. I. Strayer, Joseph Reese, 1904- ed. II. Title.

United States. Continental Congress—Biography.

BIOGRAPHICAL 353.04'092'2 B
directory of the United States executive branch, 1774-1977 / Robert Sobel, editor in chief. Westport, Conn. : Greenwood Press, c1977. x, 503 p. ; 25 cm. Includes indexes. [E176.B576] 77-84 ISBN 0-8371-9527-6 lib.bdg. : 29.95
1. United States. Continental Congress—Biography. 2. Cabinet officers—United States—Biography. 3. Presidents—United States—Biography. 4. Vice-Presidents—United States—Biography. I. Sobel, Robert, 1931 (Feb. 19)-

JONES, Charles 975.8'03'0922 B
Colcock, 1831-1893.
Biographical sketches of the delegates from Georgia to the Continental Congress. Boston, Houghton, Mifflin, 1891. [Spartanburg, S.C., Reprint Co., 1972] x, 211 p. 23 cm. Includes bibliographical references. [E263.G3J7 1972] 74-187390 ISBN 0-87152-085-0
1. United States. Continental Congress—Biography. 2. Georgia—History—Revolution, 1775-1783. 3. Georgia—Biography. I. Title. BIP

UNITED States. Congress. 328.73
Biographical directory of the American Congress, 1774-1961: the Continental Congress, September 5, 1774, to October 21, 1788 and the Congress of the United States, from the First to the Eighty-sixth Congress, March 4, 1789, to January 3, 1961, inclusive. [Rev. ed. Washington] U.S. Govt. Print. Off., 1961. 1863 p. illus. 30 cm. (85th Cong., 2d sess. House document, no. 442) "This volume, compiled by Clifford P. Reynolds, publications technician of the [Joint] Committee [on Printing], is a revision of the Dictionary of the United States Congress and the general government, published in 1859 and again revised in 1869, by Charles Lanman; the Biographical annals of the civil government of the United States in 1876, by Joseph Lanman and James Anglin, and the Lanman edition of 1876 as corrected by Joseph M. Morrison in 1887; the Political register and congressional directory of 1878; by Ben: Perley Poore; the Biographical congressional directory of 1903, by O. M. Enyart; the BiogOBiographical directory of the American Congress, 1774-1961: the Continental Congress, September 5, 1774, to October 21, 1788 and the Congress of the United States, from the First to the E
1. United States. Continental Congress—Biography. 2. United States. Congress—Biography. 3. United States—Biography—Dictionaries. I. Reynolds, Clifford P. II. Title. III. Series: United States. 85th Cong., 2d sess., 1958. House. Document no. 442

United States. Declaration of Independence—Signers.

ARCHER, Jules. 973.3'13'0922 B
They made a revolution, 1776 / by Jules Archer. New York : St. Martin's Press, [1975] c1973. 175 p. ; 20 cm. [E221.A72 1975] 920 75-16211 6.95
1. United States. Declaration of independence—Signers. 2. United States—History—Revolution, 1775-1783—Biography. I. Title.
Contents omitted.

FEHRENBACH, T. R. 973.31'3'0922
Greatness to spare; the heroic sacrifices of the men who signed the Declaration of Independence [by] T. R. Fehrenbach. Princeton, N.J., Van Nostrand [1968] 247 p. 22 cm. [E221.F4] 68-30756 5.95
1. United States. Declaration of Independence—Signers. I. Title.

GOODRICH, Charles 973.3'13'0922 B
Augustus, 1790-1862.
Lives of the signers of the Declaration of independence : with a sketch of the life of Washington / by Charles A. Goodrich. Charlotteville, N.Y. : SamHar Press, [1976] p. cm. Reprint of the 1848 ed. published by H. E. Robins and Co., Hartford. [E221.G8637 1976] 75-16256 15.00 pbk. : 6.00
1. United States. Declaration of independence—Signers. 2. Washington, George, Pres. U.S., 1732-1799. I. Title.

United States. Declaration of independence—Signers—Biography.

PHYSICIAN signers 973.3'13'0922 B
of the Declaration of independence / George E. Gifford, Jr., editor. New York : Science History Publications, 1976. 163 p. : ill. ; 24 cm. Includes bibliographical references and index. [E221.P55] 76-17348 ISBN 0-88202-159-1 : 10.00
1. United States. Declaration of independence—Signers—Biography. 2. Physicians—United States—Biography. I. Gifford, George Edmund. BIP

United States. Department of State—Biography.

GRAEBNER, Norman 353.1'092'2 B
A., ed.
An uncertain tradition : American Secretaries of State in the twentieth century / edited by Norman A. Graebner. Westport, Conn. : Greenwood Press, [1980] c1961. p. cm. Reprint of the ed. published by McGraw-Hill, New York, in series: McGraw-Hill series in American history. Includes index. Bibliography: p. [E747.G68 1980] 79-26791 ISBN 0-313-22317-3 lib. bdg. : 25.00
1. United States. Department of State—Biography. 2. Cabinet officers—United States—Biography. 3. United States—Foreign relations—20th century. I. Title. BIP

HELLER, Dean, 1924- 973
Paths of diplomacy; America's Secretaries of State [by] Deane and David Heller. [1st ed.] Philadelphia, Lippincott [1967] 192 p. illus., ports. 25 cm. Describes the times and lives of twenty Secretaries of State whose decisions and courage helped guide the history of the United States and the world. An appendix includes brief portraits of other Secretaries, who served briefly or in less tumultuous times. [E183.7.H4] AC 67
1. United States. Dept. of State—Biography. 2. Statesmen. 3. United States.—Foreign relations. I. Heller, David, 1922, joint author. II. Title.

HELLER, Deane Fons, 973'.0922
1924-
Paths of diplomacy; America's Secretaries of State [by] Deane and David Heller. [1st ed.] Philadelphia, Lippincott [1967] 192 p. illus., ports. 25 cm. [E183.7.H4] 67-5010
1. United States. Dept. of State—Biography. 2. Statesmen, American. 3. United States—Foreign relations. I. Heller, David, 1922- joint author. II. Title.

United States. Dept. of the Interior—Biography.

TRANI, Eugene P. 353.3'092'2 B
The Secretaries of the Department of the Interior, 1849-1969 / by Eugene P. Trani. [Washington] : National Anthropological Archives, 1975. 307 p. ; 27 cm. Includes bibliographies and index. [JK868.T73] 75-602882
1. United States. Dept. of the Interior—Biography. 2. United States. Dept. of the Interior—History. I. Title.

United States—Description and travel—1783-1848.

CATHER, Thomas. 917.3
Voyage to America; the journals of Thomas Cather. Edited with an introd. by Thomas Yoseloff. Illustrated with contemporary drawings by Harry Tyler. Westport, Conn., Greenwood Press [1973, c1961] 176 p. illus. 22 cm. [E165.C37 1973] 72-11303 ISBN 0-8371-6650-0 9.75
1. United States—Description and travel—1783-1848. I. Title. BIP

CHATEAUBRIAND, 917.4'04'3
Francois Auguste Rene, vicomte de, 1768-1848.
Travels in America. Translated by Richard Switzer. Lexington, University of Kentucky Press, 1969. xxi, 224 p. illus., ports. 25 cm. Translation of Voyages en Amerique. Bibliography: p. [209]-210. [E164.C4983] 68-55043 7.95
1. U.S.—Description and travel—1783-1848. 2. Indians of North America. I. Title.

MACDONALD, Donald, 917.3'04'54 B
1791-1872.
The diaries of Donald Macdonald, 1824-1826. With an introd. by Caroline Dale Snedeker. Clifton [N.J.] A. M. Kelley, 1973. 147-379 p. 23 cm. (Reprints of economic classics) Reprint of the 1942 ed. published by the Indiana Historical Society, Indianapolis, which was issued as v. 14, no. 2 of its Publications. [E165.M13 1973] 72-77060 ISBN 0-678-00914-7 12.50
1. United States—Description and travel—1783-1848. 2. New Harmony, Ind.—History. I. Series: Indiana Historical Society. Publications, v. 14, no. 2. BIP

SCHULTZ, Christian. 917.3'04'48
Travels on an inland voyage through the States of New York, Pennsylvania, Virginia, Ohio, Kentucky, and Tennessee, and through the Territories of Indiana, Louisiana, Mississippi, and New-Orleans, performed in the years 1807 and 1808 ... Ridgewood, N.J., Gregg Press [1968] 2 v. in 1. illus., maps. 24 cm. Reprint of the 1810 ed., with a new introd. by T. D. Clark. [E164.S39 1968] 68-29285
1. U.S.—Description and travel—1783-1848. I. Title.

United States—Description and travel—1848-1865.

BODICHON, 917.3'03'680924 B
Barbara Leigh (Smith) 1827-1891.
An American diary, 1857-8. Edited from the manuscript by Joseph W. Reed, Jr. London, Routledge & K. Paul [1972] 198 p. ports. 23 cm. Bibliography: p. 185-186. [E166.B65 1972] 73-153582 ISBN 0-7100-7330-5 8.25
1. United States—Description and travel—1848-1865. I. Reed, Joseph W., ed. II. Title.
Distributed by Routledge & K. Paul Boston, Mass. BIP

United States—Economic conditions.

HUGHES, Jonathan R. T. 330.973
The vital few; American economic progress and its protagonists, by Jonathan Hughes. Boston, Houghton Mifflin, 1966 [c1965] vi, 504 p. 22 cm. "Bibliographical notes": p. [467]-477. [HC102.5.A2H8] 65-23202
1. United States—Economic conditions. 2. United States—Biography. I. Title. BIP

HUGHES, Jonathan R. T. 330.9'73
The vital few; American economic progress and its protagonists [by] Jonathan Hughes. London, New York, Oxford University Press [1973] xiv, 504 p. 20 cm. (A Galaxy book) Bibliography: p. [467]-477. [HC102.5.A2H8 1973] 73-78999 3.95 (U.S.)
1. United States—Economic conditions. 2. United States—Biography. I. Title.

United States Equestrian Team.

MILES, Hugh Tyler, 1943- 798'.24
Horse on course / Hugh Tyler Miles. South Brunswick, [N.J.] : A. S. Barnes, [1978] p. cm. [SF295.7.M54] 76-50208 ISBN 0-498-02034-7 : 15.00
1. United States Equestrian Team. 2. Plumb, John Michael. 3. Three-day event (Horsemanship) 4. Three-day event (Horsemanship)—United States. 5. Horsemen—United States—Biography. I. Title. BIP

United States. Federal Civil Defense Administration—Officials and employees—Biography.

HOWARD, Katherine 329'.0092'4 B
Graham, 1898-
With my shoes off / Katherine G. Howard. 1st ed. New York : Vantage Press, c1977. 347 p. : ill. ; 21 cm. [E748.H785A38] 77-74556 ISBN 0-533-02950-3 : 10.00
1. Howard, Katherine Graham, 1898- 2. United States. Federal Civil Defense

Administration—Officials and employees—Biography. 3. Republican Party. National Convention. 25th, Chicago, 1952. 4. Eisenhower, Dwight David, Pres. U.S., 1890-1969. 5. Presidents—United States—Election—1952. 6. United States—Civil defense. I. Title. BIP

United States—Foreign population—Juvenile literature.

RASKIN, Joseph. 917.3'03'2
The newcomers; ten tales of American immigrants [by] Joseph and Edith Raskin. Illustrated by Kurt Werth. New York, Lothrop, Lee & Shepard [1974] 126 p. illus. 22 cm. Ten true stories of emigrants from different countries and cultures who settled in colonial America. [E184.A1R35 1974] 920 74-2117 ISBN 0-688-41590-3 4.50
1. United States—Foreign population—Juvenile literature. 2. United States—Emigration and immigration—Juvenile literature. 3. United States—Biography—Juvenile literature. I. Raskin, Edith, joint author. II. Werth, Kurt, illus. III. Title. BIP

United States—Foreign relations—Germany.

WILSON, Hugh Robert, 943.086
1885-1946.
A career diplomat, the third chapter: the Third Reich. [Edited] by Hugh R. Wilson, Jr. Westport, Conn., Greenwood Press [1973, c1960] 112 p. port. 22 cm. Letters and diary excerpts. Bibliography: p. 112. [E183.8.G3W52 1973] 72-11747 ISBN 0-8371-6702-7 7.75
1. United States—Foreign relations—Germany. 2. Germany—Foreign relations—United States. 3. Germany—Politics and government—1933-1945. I. Wilson, Hugh Robert, ed. II. Title.

United States—Foreign relations—Japan.

GREW, Joseph Clark, 327.73'052
1880-1965.
Ten years in Japan, a contemporary record drawn from the diaries and private and official papers of Joseph C. Grew, United States ambassador to Japan, 1932-1942. Westport, Conn., Greenwood Press [1973, c1944] xii, 554 p. illus. 22 cm. [E183.8.J3G72 1973] 72-12556 ISBN 0-8371-6723-X 20.00
1. United States—Foreign relations—Japan. 2. Japan—Foreign relations—United States. 3. Japan—Politics and government—1912-1945. 4. World War, 1939-1945—Causes. I. Title. BIP

United States—History—Chronology.

WEBSTER'S guide to American 973
history; a chronological, geographical, and biographical survey and compendium. [Editors: Charles Van Doren and Robert McHenry] Springfield, Mass., G. & C. Merriam Co. [1971] 1428 p. illus., facsims., maps (part col.), ports. 24 cm. "A Merriam-Webster." [E174.5.W4] 76-24114 ISBN 0-87779-081-7
1. United States—History—Chronology. 2. United States—Biography. 3. United States—Historical geography—Maps. I. Van Doren, Charles Lincoln, 1926- ed. II. McHenry, Robert, ed.

United States—History—Civil War.

SHERMAN, William 923.573
Tecumseh, 1820-1891.
Memoirs of General William T. Sherman by himself. Foreword by B. H. Liddell Hart. Bloomington, Indiana University Press [1957] 405, 409 p. 21 cm. (Civil War centennial series) [E467.1.S55S52 1957] 57-10722
1. U.S. — Hist. — Civil War. I. Title.

SHERMAN, William 355.3'31'0924 B
Tecumseh, 1820-1891.
Memoirs of General William T. Sherman, by himself. Foreword by B. H. Liddell Hart. Westport, Conn., Greenwood Press [1972, c1957] 2 v in 1 22 cm. Original ed. issued in series: Civil War centennial series. [E467.1.S55S52 1972] 70-170607 ISBN 0-8371-6253-X 26.00
1. United States—History—Civil War. I. Series: Civil War centennial series.

SHERMAN, William 923.573
Tecumseh, 1820-1891.
Memoirs of General William T. Sherman by himself. Foreword by B. H. Liddell Hart. Bloomington, Indiana University Press [1957] 409p. 21cm. (Civil War centennial series) [E467.1.S55S52 1957] 57-10722
1. U. S.—Hist.—Civil War. I. Title. II. Series.

United States—History—Civil War—Secret service—Confederate States—Juvenile literature.

BAKELESS, 973.7'86'0922 B
Katherine (Little) 1895-
Confederate spy stories [by] Katherine and John Bakeless. [1st ed.] Philadelphia, Lippincott [1973] 159 p. map. 22 cm. Biographies of men and women who, for patriotic or mercenary reasons, engaged in espionage for the Confederacy. [E608.B14] 920 73-4984 ISBN 0-397-31230-X 4.95
1. United States—History—Civil War—Secret service—Confederate States—Juvenile literature. I. Bakeless, John Edwin, 1894- joint author. II. Title. BIP

United States—History—Civil War, 1861-1865—Biography.

BRADFORD, Gamaliel, 973.7'41'0922
1863-1932.
Union portraits. Freeport, N.Y., Books for Libraries Press [1968, c1916] xvi, 330 p. ports. 22 cm. (Essay index reprint series) Bibliography: p. [297]-298. [E467.B782 1968] 68-29194
1. United States—History—Civil War, 1861-1865—Biography. I. Title. BIP

BROCKETT, Linus 920'.073
Pierpont, 1820-1893.
Men of our day; or, Biographical sketches of patriots, orators, statesmen, generals, reformers, financiers and merchants, now on the stage of action... Freeport, N.Y., Books for Libraries Press [1973] p. (Essay index reprint series) Reprint of the 1872 ed. [E467.B84 1973] 73-1152 ISBN 0-518-10037-5
1. United States—History—Civil War—Biography. 2. United States—Biography. I. Title.

HOAR, Jay S., 973.7'4'0922 B
1933-
New England's last Civil War veterans / by Jay S. Hoar. Arlington, Tex. : Seacliff Press, 1976. ix, 195 p., [13] leaves of plates : ill. ; 23 cm. Includes index. Bibliography: p. 187-190. [E467.H7] 76-24491
1. United States—History—Civil War, 1861-1865—Biography. 2. United States—History—Civil War, 1861-1865—Registers, lists, etc. 3. New England—Biography. I. Title.

MITCHELL, Joseph 973.7'3'0922 B
Brady, 1915-
Military leaders in the Civil War [by] Joseph B. Mitchell. New York, Putnam [1972] 251 p. illus. 23 cm. Bibliography: p. 238. [E467.M68 1972] 76-189236 ISBN 0-399-10933-1 6.95
1. United States—History—Civil War—Biography. I. Title.

NUNN, William 973.7'464'0922
Curtis, 1908-
Ten Texans in gray. W. C. Nunn, editor. [Hillsboro, Tex., Hill Junior College Press, 1968] xii, 229 p. ports. 24 cm. Seminar papers written by selected graduate students in history at Texas Christian University. Contents.Contents.—John Robert Baylor, by A. Gilligan.—Edward Clark, by T. Larison.—Richard W. "Dick" Dowling, by J. Ward.—John Bell Hood, by H. B. Simpson.—Francis Richard Lubbock, by L. A. Adams.—John Bankhead Magruder, by T. Settles.—Pendleton Murrah, by L. Harper.—John H. Reagan, by S. W. Schuster.—Louis Trezevant Wigfall, by G. Wirsdorfer.—Bibliography (p. [195]-220). [E580.N8] 68-58539 6.00
1. United States—History—Civil War, 1861-1865—Biography. 2. Texas—Biography. I. Title.

RICHARDSON, Frank 920.073
Charles.
Five Civil War vignettes. Drawings by Charles Hargens with an assist in editing from Matthew Imrie. [New Hope] Pa., 1964. 55 p. illus. 23 cm. Bibliography: p. 54-55. [E468.9.R54] 65-2065
1. U.S. — Hist. — Civil War — Biog. I. Title.

ROBITSCHER, Jean. 973.7'0922
Notable man and women of the Civil War, by Jean Robitscher and Naomi Dank. [n.p.] Precision Pub. Co. [1970] 88 p. illus. 26 cm. "A Clear print book." On spine: The Civil War. Bibliography: p. 86-87. [E467.R6] 75-132544
1. United States—History—Civil War, 1861-1865—Biography. I. Dank, Naomi, joint author. II. Title. III. Title: The Civil War.

STEINER, Paul Eby, 973.7'4'0922
1902-
Medical-military portraits of Union and Confederate generals, by Paul E. Steiner. Philadelphia, Whitmore Pub. Co. [1968] vii, 342 p. ports. 25 cm. Includes bibliographical references. [E467.S8] 67-29633 6.00
1. United States—History—Civil War, 1861-1865—Biography. 2. Generals—United States. I. Title.

STOWE, Harriet 973.7'092'2 B
Elizabeth (Beecher) 1811-1896.
Men of our times; or, Leading patriots of the day. Being narratives of the lives and deeds of statesmen, generals, and orators, including biographical sketches and anecdotes ... Freeport, N.Y., Books for Libraries Press [1973] p. (Essay index reprint series) Reprint of the 1868 ed. [E467.S88 1973] 72-14145 ISBN 0-518-10026-X
1. United States—History—Civil War—Biography. 2. United States—Biography. I. Title. II. Title: Leading patriots of the day.

United States—History—Civil War, 1861-1865—Campaigns and battles.

DUKE, Basil Wilson, 973.7'0924
1838-1916.
Reminiscences of General Basil W. Duke. Freeport, N.Y., Books for Libraries Press [1969] xii, 512 p. port. 23 cm. (Select bibliographies reprint series) Reprint of the 1911 ed. [E470.D89 1969] 71-103650 ISBN 0-8369-5150-6
1. United States—History—Civil War, 1861-1865—Campaigns and battles. I. Title.

United States—History—Civil War, 1861-1865—Negroes—Juvenile literature.

STILLER, Richard. 973.7'092'2 B
The spy, the lady, the captain, and the colonel. [New York] Scholastic Book Services [1970] 127 p. illus. (part. col.) 21 cm. (Firebird books) Contents.Contents.—John Scobell; black spy for freedom.—Elizabeth Keckley; ex-slave in the White House.—Robert Smalls; the slave who stole a ship.—Thomas Wentworth Higginson; white colonel, black regiment. [E540.N3S83] 920 72-116625
1. United States—History—Civil War, 1861-1865—Negroes—Juvenile literature. 2. United States—History—Civil War, 1861-1865—Biography—Juvenile literature. I. Title.

United States—History—Civil War, 1861-1865—Personal narratives—Confederate side.

HOLMES, Sarah 917.63'03'0924 B
Katherine (Stone) 1841-1907.
Brokenburn; the journal of Kate Stone, 1861-1868. Edited by John Q. Anderson. Baton Rouge, Louisiana State University Press [1972] xxviii, 400 p. port. 23 cm. (Library of Southern civilization) Includes bibliographical references. [E487.H74 1972] 72-84122 ISBN 0-8071-0231-8 8.95
1. United States—History—Civil War, 1861-1865—Personal narratives—Confederate side. I. Title. BIP

United States—History—Civil War, 1861-1865—Prisoners and prisons.

STEPHENS, Alexander 973.77'2'0924
Hamilton, 1812-1883.
Recollections of Alexander H. Stephens; his diary kept when a prisoner at Fort Warren, Boston Harbour, 1865. Edited with an introd. by Myrta Lockett Avary. New York, Da Capo Press, 1971 [c1910] xiii, 572 p. port. 24 cm. [E467.1.S85S85 1971] 76-124914 ISBN 0-306-71984-3
1. United States—History—Civil War, 1861-1865—Prisoners and prisons. 2. Fort Warren. I. Avary, Myrta (Lockett), ed. II. Title.

United States—History—Civil War, 1861-1865—Sources.

LOUISIANA Historical 973.8'0924
Association.
Calendar of the Jefferson Davis postwar manuscripts. New York, B. Franklin [1970] ii l., 325 p. 29 cm. (American classics in history & social science, 121) (Burt Franklin bibliography & reference series, 329.) Reprint of the 1943 ed. Includes bibliographical references. [CD3047.L6 1970] 70-114342
1. United States—History—Civil War, 1861-1865—Sources. 2. Confederate States of America—History—Sources. 3. Manuscripts—United States—Catalogs. I. Davis, Jefferson, 1808-1889. II. Title.

United States—History—Colonial period, ca. 1600-1775—Biography.

BOLTON, Charles 973.2'092'2
Knowles, 1867-1950.
The founders : portraits of persons born abroad who came to the Colonies in North America before the year 1701, with an introduction, biographical outlines, and comments on the portraits / by Charles Knowles Bolton. Baltimore : Genealogical Pub. Co., 1976. 2 v. (vii, 1103 p.) : ports. ; 23 cm. Half-title: Portraits of the founders. Reprint of the 1919-1926 ed. published by the Boston Athenaeum as no. 6 of its Publications of the Robert Charles Billings Fund. Includes indexes. [E187.5.B69 1976] 75-29181 ISBN 0-8063-0692-0 : 38.50
1. United States—History—Colonial period, ca. 1600-1775—Biography. 2. Portraits, American. I. Title. II. Title: Portraits of the founders. III. Series: Boston Athenaeum. Robert Charles Billings Fund. Publications ; no. 6. BIP

GUMMERE, Richard Mott, 973.2'0922
1883-
Seven wise men of colonial America [by] Richard M. Gummere. Cambridge, Harvard University Press, 1967. xi, 114 p. 22 cm. Contents.—Hugh Jones.—Robert Calef.—Michael Wigglesworth.—Samuel Davies.—Henry Melchior Muhlenberg.—Benjamin Rush.—Thomas Paine. Bibliographical references included in "Notes" (p. 97-108) [E187.5.G8] 67-27084
1. United States—History—Colonial period, ca. 1600-1775—Biography. 2. United States—Civilization—Greek influences. 3. United States—Civilization—Roman influences. I. Title. BIP

MARTIN, Sheila W. 973.2'092'2 B
The colonial spirit / by Sheila W. Martin. Warminster, Pa. : Colonial Press, c1975. 103 p. : ill. ; 21 cm. Forty-three sketches about the people and life in the colonies during the period before and throughout the American Revolution. [E187.5.M3] 76-359609 1.95
1. United States—History—Colonial period, ca. 1600-1775—Biography. 2. United States—History—Revolution, 1775-1783—Biography. I. Title.

United States—History—Colonial period, ca. 1600-1775—Biography—Juvenile literature.

CARSE, Robert 1903- 920
The young colonials a history. Illus. by Gil Walker. Maps by Bob Ritter. New York, Norton [c.1963] 223p. 21cm. Bibl. 62-21516 3.50
1. U.S.—Hist.—Colonial period—Biog.—Juvenile literature. I. Title.

CARSE, Robert, 1903-. j920
The young colonials, a history. Illustrated by Gil Walker. Maps by Bob Ritter. [1st ed.] New York, Norton [1963] 223 p. illus. 21 cm. Includes bibliography. [E187.5.C2] 62-21516
1. U.S. — Hist. — Colonial period — Biog. — Juvenile literature. I. Title.

LEIPOLD, L. Edmond, 973.2'092'2 B 1902-
When our country was very young, by L. Edmond Leipold. Minneapolis, Denison [1972] 69 p. col. illus. 25 cm. (His Lives of great Americans) Brief biographies of five men and women who had prominent roles in early American history: Hernando DeSoto, John Smith, Pocahontas, Roger Williams, and William Penn. [E187.5.L45] 920 78-160734 ISBN 0-513-01162-5 (lib. bdg.) 3.99
1. United States—History—Colonial period, ca. 1600-1775—Biography—Juvenile literature. I. Title.

SIGNIFICANT 973.2'092'2 B
American colonial leaders. Chicago : Childrens Press, [1976] p. cm. Includes index. Brief biographies of 163 colonial leaders arranged alphabetically within chronological periods of colonial American history. [E187.5.S56] 920 75-20678 ISBN 0-516-05315-9 lib.bdg. : 9.25
1. United States—History—Colonial period, ca. 1600-1775—Biography—Juvenile literature. I. Title: Colonial leaders.

United States—History—Colonial period, ca. 1600-1775—Sources.

GAGE, Thomas, 1721-1787. 973.2
The correspondence of General Thomas Gage ... Compiled and edited by Clarence Edwin Carter. [Hamden, Conn.] Archon Books, 1969- v. 23 cm. Reprint of the 1931 ed. Contents.Contents.—v. 1. With the Secretaries of State, 1763-1775. Bibliographical footnotes. [E187.G14] 73-85914 ISBN 0-208-00812-8
1. United States—History—Colonial period, ca. 1600-1775—Sources. 2. Great Britain—Colonies—Administration—Sources. 3. United States—Politics and government—Colonial period, ca. 1600-1775. I. Carter, Clarence Edwin, 1881-1961, ed. II. Great Britain. Secretary of State for the Southern Dept. III. Great Britain. Secretary of State for the American or Colonial Dept. IV. Title.

United States—History—Constitutional period, 1789-1809—Sources.

WASHINGTON, George, 973.4'1'0924 Pres. U.S., 1732-1799.
George Washington, 1732-1799; chronology, documents, bibliographical aids. Edited by Howard F. Bremer. Dobbs Ferry, N.Y., Oceana Publications, 1967. 90 p. 24 cm. ([Oceana presidential chronology series, 1]) Bibliography: p. 81-87. [E312.B8] 67-20934
1. United States—History—Constitutional period, 1789-1809—Sources. I. Bremer, Howard F., ed. II. United States. President, 1789-1797 (Washington)

United States—History—Revolution, 1775-1783—Afro-Americans—Juvenile literature.

WINSLOW, Eugene. 973.3'092'2 B
Afro-Americans '76 : Black Americans in the founding of our nation / written and illustrated by Eugene Winslow. Chicago : Afro-Am Pub. Co., [1975] 80 p. : col. ill. ; 29 cm. Includes index. Bibliography: p. 79. Provides biographical sketches of Afro-Americans who contributed to the exploration, Revolution, and growth of the United States. [E269.N3W56] 75-23936 ISBN 0-910030-20-0. ISBN 0-910030-21-9 pbk.
1. United States—History—Revolution, 1775-1783—Afro-Americans—Juvenile literature. 2. Afro-Americans—Biography—Juvenile literature. 3. Slavery in the United States—Anti-Slavery movements—Juvenile literature. 4. Afro-Americans—Biography. 5. Slavery in the United States—Anti-slavery movements. I. Title.

United States—History—Revolution, 1775-1783—Anecdotes.

HARKNESS, David James, 973.3'0922 1913-
Forgotten heroes of the American Revolution, compiled by David J. Harkness. Knoxville [University of Tennessee] 1968. 16 p. 23 cm. (University of Tennessee extension series, v. 43, no. 1) [E296.H36] 74-629306
1. United States—History—Revolution, 1775-1783—Anecdotes. 2. United States—History—Revolution, 1775-1783—Biography. I. Title.

United States—History—Revolution, 1775-1783—Biography.

*ANTICAGLIA, 973.315042 Elizabeth.
Heroines of '76 New York, Walker and Co. [1975] xii, 112 p. 23 cm. Bibliography: p. 109-110. [E276] 74-24583 ISBN 0-8027-6210-7 6.95.
1. United States—History—Revolution, 1775-1783—Biography. 2. Women—United States—Biography. 3. Women soldiers. I. Title.
Library binding 6.83; ISBN: 0-8027-6209-3.

BILLIAS, George Athan, 973.33 1919- ed.
George Washington's generals. New York [Apollo Eds., 1966, c.1964] xvii, 327p. maps. 20cm. (A138) Bibl. 1.95 pap.,
1. U.S.—Hist.—Revolution—Biog. 2. Generals—U.S. 3. U.S. Army—Biog. I. Title.

BILLIAS, George Athan, 973.33 1919- ed.
George Washington's generals. New York, W. Morrow, 1964. xvii, 327 p. ports., maps 22 cm. Essays. Includes bibliographical references. [E206.B5] 64-12038
1. U.S.—Hist.—Revolution—Biog. 2. Generals—U.S. 3. U.S. Army—Biog. I. Title.
Contents Omitted

CALLAHAN, North. 974.6'03'0922
Connecticut's Revolutionary War leaders. Chester, Conn., Pequot Press, 1973. 52 p. ports. 23 cm. (Connecticut Bicentennial series, 3) Bibliography: p. 52. [E206.C34] 73-83251 ISBN 0-87106-120-1
1. United States—History—Revolution, 1775-1783 Biography. 2. Connecticut—History—Revolution, 1775-1783. 3. Connecticut—Biography. I. Title. II. Series.

COLONIAL Williamsburg, inc. 973.3
They gave us freedom; the American struggle for life, liberty, and the pursuit of happiness, as seen in portraits, sculptures, historical paintings and documents of the period: 1761-1789. [Williamsburg, Va.] Colonial Williamsburg and the College of William & Mary in Virginia [1951] 65 p. illus., ports., map (on lining papers) facsims. 29 cm. "Catalogue of the exhibition [held May-June 1951]": p. 61-65. [E302.5.C64] 51-5329
1. U. S.—Hist.—Revolution—Biog. I. William and Mary College. Williamsburg. Va. II. Title.

DAUGHTERS of the 973.3'092'2 B American Revolution. Pennsylvania. Pittsburgh Chapter. Bicentennial Committee.
Pittsburgh patriots / Bicentennial Committee, Pittsburgh Chapter, Daughters of the American Revolution. 1st ed. [Pittsburgh] : The Chapter, [1974] 78 p. : ill. ; 24 cm. Includes bibliographical references. [E206.D24 1974] 74-187917
1. United States—History—Revolution, 1775-1783—Biography. 2. Pittsburgh—Biography. I. Title.

DES COGNETS, Louis. 973.330922
Black sheep and heroes of the American Revolution, by Louis des Cognets, Jr. [Princeton, N.J., c1965] 386 p. 24 cm. Bibliography: p. 375. [E206.D39] 65-20610
1. U.S. — Hist. — Revolution — Biog. I. Title.

ELLET, Elizabeth 973.3'0922 B Fries (Lummis) 1818-1877.
The women of the American Revolution. 4th ed. New York, Haskell House, 1969. 3 v. ports. 23 cm. Reprint of the 1850 ed. Bibliographical footnotes. [E206.E45 1969] 68-31269 ISBN 0-8383-0197-5
1. United States—History—Revolution, 1775-1783—Biography. 2. Women—United States—Biography. I. Title.

THE face of liberty : 757'.9
founders of the United States / by James Thomas Flexner ; biographies of sitters and painters by Linda Bantel Samter ; in cooperation with the Amon Carter Museum of Western Art, Fort Worth, Texas. 1st ed. New York : Potter : distributed by Crown Publishers, c1975. x, 310 p. : ill. (some col.) ; 29 cm. Includes a catalog of an art exhibition held at Amon Carter Museum of Western Art, Fort Worth, Tex. Includes index. Bibliography: p. [288]-304. [E206.F32 1975] 75-30662 ISBN 0-517-52491-0 : 15.95
1. United States—History—Revolution, 1775-1783—Biography. 2. United States—History—Revolution, 1775-1783—Portraits—Exhibitions. 3. Portraits, American—Exhibitions. 4. Painters—United States—Biography. I. Flexner, James Thomas, 1908- II. Samter, Linda Bantel. III. Amon Carter Museum of Western Art, Fort Worth, Tex. **BIP**

HILLARD, Elias 973.3'0922 Brewster, 1825-1895.
The last men of the Revolution; containing a photograph of each from life, accompanied by brief biographical sketches ... Edited by Wendell D. Garret. Introd. by Archibald MacLeish. [Barre, Mass.] Barre Publishers, 1968. 116 p. illus., ports. 24 cm. Reprint of the 1864 ed. Contents.Contents.—Samuel Downing.—Daniel Waldo.—Lemuel Cook.—Alexander Milliner.—William Hutchings.—Adam Link.—James Barham. [E206.H54 1968] 67-23658 6.95
1. U. S.—History—Revolution—Biography. I. Garrett, Wendell D., ed. II. Title.

HOAGLAND, Stewart. 973.3'092'2 B
New Jersey historical profiles; Revolutionary times. Somerville, N.J., Somerset Press, 1973. xi, 141 p. illus. 22 cm. Bibliography: p. 141. [E206.H62] 74-155406
1. United States—History—Revolution, 1775-1783—Biography. 2. New Jersey—History—Revolution, 1775-1783. 3. New Jersey—Biography. I. Title.

ILLINOIS State 973.3'092'2 Genealogical Society.
Soldiers of the American Revolution buried in Illinois : a Bicentennial project of the Illinois State Genealogical Society. Springfield : The Society, 1976, c1975. 288 p. : ill. ; 24 cm. "Mrs. John S. Devanny, compiler." Includes indexes. Bibliography: p. 273-274. [E206.I44 1976] 76-354016
1. United States—History—Revolution, 1775-1783—Biography. 2. Illinois—Genealogy. 3. Registers of births, etc.—Illinois. I. Devanny, John S., Mrs. II. Title.

JUDSON, Levi 973.3'0922 B Carroll.
The sages and heroes of the American Revolution. Including the signers of the Declaration of Independence. Two hundred and forty three of the sages and heroes are presented in due form and many others are named incidentally, by L. Carroll Judson. Port Washington, N.Y., Kennikat Press [1970] 480 p. 24 cm. (Kennikat American bicentennial series) Reprint of the 1851 ed. [E206.J92 1970] 74-120881 ISBN 0-8046-1274-9
1. United States—History—Revolution, 1775-1783—Biography. I. Title.

MCCORMICK, Robert, 973.3 Rutherford, 1880-
The Founding Fathers; a series of addresses broadcast over WGN, WGNB, and the Mutual Broadcasting System. [Chicago, Chicago Tribune, 1951] c84 p. 24 cm. [E302.5.M15] 51-5174
1. U. S.—Hist.—Revolution—Biog. 2. Statesmen, American. I. Title.
Contents Omitted

MORRIS, Richard 973.3'092'2 B Brandon, 1904-
Seven who shaped our destiny; the Founding Fathers as revolutionaries [by] Richard B. Morris. [1st ed.] New York, Harper & Row [1973] 334 p. illus. 22 cm. (A Cass Canfield book) Includes bibliographical references. [E302.5.M67] 73-4111 ISBN 0-06-013078-4 8.95
1. United States—History—Revolution—Biography. 2. United States—History—Revolution—Causes. I. Title.

MORRIS, Richard 973.3'092'2 B Brandon, 1904-
Seven who shaped our destiny; the Founding Fathers as revolutionaries [by] Richard B. Morris. New York, Harper & Row [1976 c1973] 334 p. illus. 22 cm. (A Harper Colophon Book) Includes bibliographical references and index. [E302.5.M67] ISBN 0-06-090454-2 4.95 (pbk.)
1. United States—History—Revolution—Biography. 2. United States—History—Revolution—Causes. I. Title.
L.C. card no. for original edition: 73-4111. **BIP**

THE Patriots : 973.3'092'2 B
the American Revolution generation of genius / edited by Virginius Dabney ; introd. by Henry Steele Commager. 1st ed. New York : Atheneum, c1975. xii, 248 p. : ill. ; 30 cm. [E302.5.P37 1975] 75-13801 ISBN 0-689-10690-4 : 14.95
1. United States—History—Revolution, 1775-1783—Biography. 2. United States—Politics and government—Revolution, 1775-1783. I. Dabney, Virginius, 1901- **BIP**

SCHULTZ, Pearle 973.3'092'2 B Henriksen.
Generous strangers : six heroes of the American Revolution / by Pearle Henriksen Schultz. New York : Vanguard Press, c1975. xvii, 197 p., [4] leaves of plates : ill. ; 21 cm. Bibliography: p. 193-197. [E206.S38 1975] 70-134680 ISBN 0-8149-0673-7 : 6.95
1. United States—History—Revolution, 1775-1783—Biography. 2. United States—History—Revolution, 1775-1783—Foreign participation. I. Title.

SOMERVILLE, Mollie 973.3'15'042 B D.
Women and the American Revolution, compiled by Mollie Somerville. Illustrated by Alexia Scheffler Scott. [Washington] National Society, Daughters of the American Revolution, 1974. 67 p. illus. 21 x 23 cm. Includes bibliographical references. [E206.S76] 74-77229
1. United States—History—Revolution, 1775-1783—Biography. 2. United States History—Revolution, 1775-1783—Women. I. Title.

WILDMAN, Edwin, 1867- 973.3'0922 1932.
The founders of America in the days of the revolution; the lives and deeds of the great Patriots who gave this Nation its independence. Freeport, N.Y., Books for Libraries Press [1968] x, 326 p. illus., ports. 23 cm. (Essay index reprint series) Reprint of the 1924 ed. Bibliography: p. 319-321. [E302.5.W64 1968] 68-57344
1. United States—History—Revolution, 1775-1783—Biography. I. Title.

WUNDER, George, 973.3'092'2 B 1912-
Amateurs at arms / George Wunder. Harrisburg, Pa. : Stackpole Books, c1975. 96 p. : ill. ; 29 cm. (An Early American Society book) Includes index. [E206.W86] 75-28502 ISBN 0-8117-0096-8 : 9.95
1. United States—History—Revolution, 1775-1783—Biography. I. Title.

United States—History—Revolution, 1775-1783—Biography—Bibliography—Union lists.

WHITE, J. Todd. 016.9733'092'2 B
Fighters for independence : a guide to sources of biographical information on soldiers and sailors of the American

Revolution / edited by J. Todd White and Charles H. Lesser. Chicago : University of Chicago Press, 1977. xiv, 112 p. ; 24 cm. (Clements Library Bicentennial studies) Includes index. [Z1238.W45] [E206] 77-78068 ISBN 0-226-89498-3 lib.bdg. : 10.00
1. United States—History—Revolution, 1775-1783—Biography—Bibliography—Union lists. 2. United States—History—Revolution, 1775-1783—Sources—Bibliography—Union lists. 3. United States—Genealogy—Bibliography—Union lists. 4. Catalogs, Union—United States. I. Lesser, Charles H., joint author. II. Title. III. Series. **BIP**

United States—History—Revolution, 1775-1783—Biography—Juvenile literature.

DAVIS, Burke. 973.3'0922 B
Heroes of the American Revolution. Illustrated with photos., prints and maps. New York, Random House [1971] 146 p. illus., facsims., maps, ports. 27 cm. "A book for young Americans." Contents.Contents.—Paul Revere, spy and courier.—John Adams, mastermind of rebellion.—Henry Knox, selftaught master of artillery.—Thomas Jefferson, declarer of independence.—Thomas Paine, radical pamphleteer.—Benjamin Franklin, master of diplomacy.—Friedrich von Steuben, the drillmaster.—George Rogers Clark, conqueror of the West.—John Paul Jones, victor at sea.—Nathanael Greene, savior of the South.—George Washington, Commander in Chief. [E206.D27] 920 79-136587 ISBN 0-394-92152-6 (library ed.)
1. United States—History—Revolution, 1775-1783—Biography—Juvenile literature. I. Title. **BIP**

FISHER, Leonard Everett. 973.3'0922
Picture book of Revolutionary War heroes, written and illustrated by Leonard Everett Fisher. [Harrisburg, Pa.] Stackpole Books [1970] 62 p. col. illus., col. ports. 29 cm. "A Giniger book." Briefly recounts the heroic deeds of fifty men and women from the thirteen colonies and their foreign allies during the Revolutionary War. [E206.F57] 920 70-123405 ISBN 0-8117-1259-1 4.95
1. United States—History—Revolution, 1775-1783—Biography—Juvenile literature. I. Title.

HAYMAN, LeRoy. 973.3'0922 B
Leaders of the American Revolution. New York, Four Winds Press [1970] 190 p. illus., facsims., map, ports. 24 cm. Brief biographies of fourteen men who played leading roles in the American Revolution. [E206.H29] 920 79-124186 4.88
1. United States—History—Revolution, 1775-1783—Biography—Juvenile literature. I. Title. **BIP**

HIRSCH, S. Carl. 973.3'092'2 B
Famous American revolutionary war heroes, by S. Carl Hirsch. Line drawings by Lorence Bjorklund. Chicago, Rand McNally [1974] 93 p. illus. (part col.) 29 cm. From the Boston Massacre through the Battle of Yorktown, traces the wartime activities of eight Revolutionary War heroes central to the American cause. [E206.H57] 920 74-8469 ISBN 0-528-82467-8
1. United States—History—Revolution, 1775-1783—Biography—Juvenile literature. I. Bjorklund, Lorence F., illus. II. Title.

LEIPOLD, L. Edmond, 1902- 973.3'092'2
America becomes free, by L. Edmond Leipold. Minneapolis, Denison [1972] 60 p. col. illus. 25 cm. (Lives of great Americans) Brief biographies of five men and women who played a prominent role in the Revolution: George Washington, Benjamin Franklin, Nathan Hale, Molly Pitcher, and James Lawrence. [E206.L34] 920 74-174481 ISBN 0-513-01216-8
1. United States—History—Revolution, 1775-1783—Biography—Juvenile literature. I. Title. II. Series: Lives of great Americans (Minneapolis)

LONG, John Cuthbert, 1892- 973.3'0922
The young revolutionaries [by] J. C. Long. New York, John Day Co. [1968] 143 p. 23 cm. Bibliography: p. 141-143. Brief sketches of several young men and women—farm boys, aristocrats, and college students—who played important roles in the colonies' struggle for independence. [E206.L6] 920 68-24151 3.69
1. United States—History—Revolution, 1775-1783—Biography—Juvenile literature. I. Title.

MCGIFFIN, Lee. 920 (J)
Yankee Doodle Dandies; eight generals of the American Revolution. Illustrated by Donald Carrick. [1st ed.] New York, Dutton [1967] 160 p. 21 cm. Contents.Contents.—The men who fought.—Henry Lee.—John Glover.—Anthony Wayne.—Joshua Barney.—Francis Marion.—Nathaniel Greene.—Daniel Morgan.—Henry Knox.—Bibliography (p. 153-154) [E206.M12] 67-20130
1. United States—History—Revolution, 1775-1783—Biography—Juvenile literature. 2. Generals—United States—Juvenile literature. I. Title.

MYERS, J. Jay. 973.3'0922
The revolutionists [by] J. Jay Myers. New York, Washington Square Press [1971] xxvi, 182 p. illus., ports. 18 cm. Includes bibliographies. Brief biographies of ten men who helped conceive, finance, fight, and win the Revolution: Sam Adams, Crispus Attucks, John Adams, Patrick Henry, Thomas Jefferson, Benjamin Franklin, James Madison, Haym Salomon, John Glover, and George Washington. [E206.M99] 920 78-28683 ISBN 0-671-47855-9 0.95
1. United States—History—Revolution, 1775-1783—Biography—Juvenile literature. I. Title. **BIP**

REEDER, Russell Potter. 973.3'092'2 B
Bold leaders of the American Revolution, by Red Reeder. Maps by Samuel H. Bryant. [1st ed.] Boston, Little, Brown [1973] x, 226 p. maps. 22 cm. Bibliography: p. [213]-221. Capsule biographies of twelve prominent figures in the American Revolution: Ethan Allen, John Burgoyne, Thaddeus Kosciuszko, Benjamin Thompson, Charles Lee, Margaret Corbin, John Barry, George Rogers Clark, Marinus Willett, Anthony Wayne, Francis Marion, and Deborah Sampson. [E206.R43] 920 73-10288 5.95
1. United States—History—Revolution, 1775-1783—Biography—Juvenile literature. I. Title. **BIP**

United States—History—Revolution, 1775-1783—British forces.

BILLIAS, George Athan, 1919- 973.33'0922
George Washington's opponents: British generals and admirals in the American Revolution. New York, Morrow, 1969. xxvii, 362 p. illus., maps, ports. 22 cm. Essays. Contents.Contents.—Thomas Gage, by J. Shy.—William Howe, by M. A. Jones.—Henry Clinton, by W. B. Willcox.—Guy Carleton, by P. H. Smith.—John Burgoyne, by G. A. Billias.—Charles Lord Cornwallis, by H. F. Rankin.—Richard Lord Howe, by I. D. Gruber.—Arbuthnot, Gambier, and Graves, by W. B. Willcox.—Samuel Hood, by D. A. Baugh.—George Rodney, by C. Lloyd. Includes bibliographies. [E267.B56] 69-11350 7.50
1. United States—History—Revolution, 1775-1783—British forces. 2. Generals—Great Britain. 3. Admirals—Great Britain.

United States—History—Revolution, 1775-1783—British forces—Juvenile literature.

ALDERMAN, Clifford Lindsey. 973.3'41'0922
The royal opposition; the story of the British generals in the American Revolution. [New York] Crowell-Collier Press [1970] ix, 180 p. illus., ports. 21 cm. Bibliography: p. [175]-176. Analyzes the errors that contributed to the failure of six British generals to win the war with America, 1775-1783. [E267.A28] 73-119122 4.95
1. United States—History—Revolution, 1775-1783—British forces—Juvenile literature. 2. Generals—Great Britain—Juvenile literature. I. Title.

United States—History—Revolution, 1775-1783—Campaigns and battles.

HEATH, William, 1737-1814. 973.33'0924 B
Memoirs of Major General William Heath. [New York] New York times [1968, c1901] 401 p. ports. 23 cm. (Eyewitness accounts of the American Revolution) [E230.H442] 67-29034
1. United States—History—Revolution, 1775-1783—Campaigns and battles. 2. United States—History—Revolution, 1775-1783—Personal narratives. I. Title. II. Series.

HUDDLESTON, Joe D., 1937- 973.3'3
Colonial riflemen in the American Revolution / by Joe D. Huddleston. York, Pa. : G. Shumway, 1978. 70 p. : ill. ; 32 cm. (Longrifle series) Based on the author's thesis. Includes index. Bibliography: p. 68-69. [E230.H87] 76-14293 ISBN 0-87387-074-3 : 18.00
1. United States—History—Revolution, 1775-1783—Campaigns and battles. 2. United States—History—Revolution, 1775-1783—American forces. 3. Kentucky rifle. I. Title. **BIP**

United States—History—Revolution, 1775-1783—Naval operations.

JONES, John Paul, 1747-1792. 973.35'0924 B
Memoirs of Rear-Admiral Paul Jones, compiled from his original journals and correspondence. New York, Da Capo Press, 1972. 2 v. in 1. port. 23 cm. (The Era of the American Revolution) Reprint of the 1830 ed. [E207.J7A3 1972] 77-166333 ISBN 0-306-70247-9
1. United States—History—Revolution, 1775-1783—Naval operations.

United States—History—Revolution, 1775-1783—Personal narratives.

ADLUM, John, 1759-1836. 973.3'092'4
Memoirs of the life of John Adlum in the Revolutionary War. Edited with an introd. by Howard H. Peckham. Chicago, Published for the William L. Clements Library Associates by the Caxton Club, 1968. vii, 143 p. 19 cm. "The original manuscripts were presented to the William L. Clements Library in 1961 by James S. Schoff." [E275.A3A3] 68-25140
1. United States—History—Revolution, 1775-1783—Personal narratives. I. Peckham, Howard Henry, 1910- ed. II. Michigan. University. William L. Clements Library. III. Title.

BOUDINOT, Elias, 1740-1821. 973.3'0924 B
The life, public services, addresses, and letters of Elias Boudinot. Edited by J. J. Boudinot. New York, Da Capo Press, 1971 [c1896] 2 v. ports. 23 cm. (The Era of the American Revolution) Includes bibliographical references. [E302.6.B7A45 1971] 72-119059 ISBN 0-306-71946-0
1. United States—History—Revolution, 1775-1783—Personal narratives. 2. United States—History—Constitutional period, 1789-1809. I. Boudinot, Jane J., ed. II. Title.

BURR, Aaron, 1756-1836. 973.4'6'0924 B
Memoirs of Aaron Burr. With miscellaneous selections from his correspondence, by Matthew L. Davis. Freeport, N.Y., Books for Libraries Press [1970] 2 v. ports. 23 cm. Reprint of the 1836-37 ed. [E302.6.B9A34] 71-107798 ISBN 0-8369-5213-8
1. United States—History—Revolution, 1775-1783—Personal narratives. 2. United States—Politics and government—Constitutional period—1789-1809. 3. New York (State)—Politics and government—1775-1865. I. Davis, Matthew Livingston, 1773-1850.

DUBROS times : 973.3'44'10922 B
selected depositions of Maine Revolutionary War veterans / edited by Sylvia J. Sherman. Augusta : Maine State Archives, 1975. viii, 20 p. : ill. ; 26 cm. (Maine State Archives documentary publication ; no. 1) [E263.M4D82] 75-24772
1. United States—History—Revolution, 1775-1783—Personal narratives. 2. Maine—Biography. I. Sherman, Sylvia J. II. Series: Maine State Archives. Maine State Archives documentary publication ; no. 1.

SHERBURNE, Andrew, 1765-1831. 973.35'0924
Memoirs of Andrew Sherburne; a pensioner of the navy of the Revolution. Freeport, N.Y., Books for Libraries Press [1970] 262 p. 23 cm. Reprint of the 1828 ed. [E271.S53 1970] 71-133532 ISBN 0-8369-5564-1
1. United States—History—Revolution, 1775-1783—Personal narratives. 2. United States—History—Revolution, 1775-1783—Naval operations. **BIP**

United States—History—Revolution, 1775-1783—Personal narratives—British.

ANDRE, John, 1751-1780. 973.33'0924 B
Major Andre's journal. [New York] New York times [1968] 128 p. facsim., map, port. 23 cm. (Eyewitness accounts of the American Revolution) Reprint of the 1930 ed. "The ethics of Major Andre's mission [by C. D. Willcox]": p. 113-126. [E280.A5A22 1968] 67-29031
1. United States—History—Revolution, 1775-1783—Personal narratives—British. 2. United States—History—Revolution, 1775-1783—Campaigns and battles. I. Willcox, Cornelis DeWitt, 1861-1938. II. Title. III. Series. **BIP**

United States—History—Revolution, 1775-1783—Women.

ENGLE, Paul, 1908- 973.3'3'0922 B
Women the American Revolution / by Paul Engle. Chicago : Follett, c1976. xvii, 299 p. : ill. ; 24 cm. Includes index. Bibliography: p. 275-286. [E276.E5] 75-2933 ISBN 0-695-80604-1 : 9.95
1. United States—History—Revolution, 1775-1783—Women. 2. United States—History—Revolution, 1775-1783—Biography. I. Title.

EVANS, Elizabeth. 917.3'03'30922 B
Weathering the storm; women of the American Revolution. New York, Scribner [1975] 372 p. illus. 25 cm. Bibliography: p. 361-367. [E276.E93] 74-10524 ISBN 0-684-13953-7
1. United States—History—Revolution, 1775-1783—Women. 2. United States—History—Revolution, 1775-1783—Biography. I. Title. **BIP**

United States—History—Revolution, 1775-1785—Registers, lists, etc.

JULICH, Louise Milam. 973.3'6
Roster of Revolutionary soldiers and patriots in Alabama / Louise Milam Julich ; [Alabama Society] Daughters of the American Revolution. Montgomery, Ala. : Parchment Press, c1979. xii, 692 p. ; 29 cm. Includes bibliographical references and indexes. [E255.J84] 79-103918 ISBN 0-88428-045-4 : 25.00
1. United States—History—Revolution, 1775-1785—Registers, lists, etc. 2. Alabama—Genealogy. 3. Alabama—Biography. I. Daughters of the American Revolution. Alabama. II. Title. **BIP**

United States—History—Revolution, 1775-1789—Personal narratives.

BURR, Aaron, 1756-1836. 973.4'6'0924
Memoirs of Aaron Burr, with miscellaneous selections from his correspondence, by Matthew L. Davis. New York, Da Capo Press, 1971. 2 v. ports. 23 cm. (The Era of the American

Revolution) Reprint of the 1836-37 ed. [E302.6.B9A34 1971] 73-152836 ISBN 0-306-70139-1
1. United States—History—Revolution, 1775-1789—Personal narratives. 2. United States—Politics and government—Constitutional period, 1789-1809. 3. New York (State)—Politics and government—1775-1865. I. Davis, Matthew Livingston, 1773-1850.

United States—History—War of 1898—Naval operations.

DEWEY, George, 1837-1917. 973.8'95'0924 B
Autobiography of George Dewey, admiral of the Navy. New York, Scribner, 1913. St. Clair Shores, Mich., Scholarly Press, 1971. x, 337 p. 21 cm. [E714.6.D51A3 1971] 73-144974 ISBN 0-403-00942-1
1. United States—History—War of 1898—Naval operations. 2. Manila Bay, Battle of, 1898. 3. United States—History—Civil War, 1861-1865—Naval operations. BIP

United States—History—War with Mexico, 1845-1848—Juvenile literature.

SCHMIDT, James Norman, 1912- 973.6'23
The young generals, by James Norman. New York, Putnam [1968] 223 p. 22 cm. (American battles and campaigns) Describes one of the major campaigns of the Mexican War of 1845, the march from Veracruz to Mexico City, and the part played by participating officers such as Ulysses S. Grant, Robert E. Lee, and others who were to become prominent in the Civil War. [E404.S3] 68-24539 3.49
1. United States—History—War with Mexico, 1845-1848—Juvenile literature. 2. Generals—United States—Juvenile literature. I. Title.

United States—History—War with Mexico, 1845-1848—Personal narratives.

CLARK, Amasa Gleason, 1825-1927. 973.6'24'0924 B
Reminiscences of a centenarian, as told by Amasa Gleason Clark, veteran of the Mexican War, to Cora Tope Clark. San Antonio, Tex., Naylor Co. [1972] xiii, 84 p. illus. 21 cm. Compiled by Cora Tope Clark. Reprint of the 1930 ed. [E411.C55 1972] 73-182036 ISBN 0-8111-0439-7
1. United States—History War with Mexico, 1845-1848—Personal narratives. I. Title.

United States—History—1815-1861—Sources.

VAN BUREN, Martin, Pres. U.S. 1782-1862. 973.5'7'0924
Martin Van Buren, 1782-1862; chronology, documents, bibliographical aids. Edited by Irving J. Sloan. Dobbs Ferry, N.Y., Oceana Publications, 1969. 116 p. 24 cm. (Oceana presidential chronology series, 7) Bibliography: p. 109-113. [E386.S55] 69-15391 4.00
1. United States—History—1815-1861—Sources. I. Sloan, Irving J., ed. II. United States. President, 1837-1841 (Van Buren) BIP

United States—History—1849-1877—Sources.

SHERMAN, William Tecumseh, 1820-1891. 973.7'0922
The Sherman letters; correspondence between General Sherman and Senator Sherman from 1837 to 1891. Edited by Rachel Sherman Thorndike. New York, Da Capo Press, 1969. xiv, viii, 398 p. ports. 22 cm. (A Da Capo Press reprint series. The American scene; comments and commentators) Reprint of the 1894 ed. with a new foreword by John Y. Simon. [E415.7.S55 1969] 68-8693 15.00
1. United States—History—1849-1877—Sources. 2. United States—History—Civil War, 1861-1865—Sources. I. Sherman, John, 1823-1900. II. Thorndike, Rachel (Sherman) ed. III. Title.

United States—History—1865-1898—Sources.

HAYES, Rutherford Birchard, Pres. U.S., 1822-1893. 973.8'3'0924
Rutherford B. Hayes, 1822-1893; chronology, documents, bibliographical aids. Edited by Arthur Bishop Dobbs Ferry, N.Y., Oceana Publications, 1969. 90 p. 24 cm. (Oceana presidential chronology series, 12) Bibliography: p. 83-87. [E681.B59] 69-15394 3.00
1. United States—History—1865-1898—Sources. I. Bishop, Arthur, ed. II. United States President, 1877 1881 (Hayes) BIP

United States—History—1919-1933—Sources.

MORAN, Philip R., comp. 973.91'5'0924
Calvin Coolidge, 1872-1933; chronology, documents, bibliographical aids. Edited by Philip R. Moran. Dobbs Ferry, N.Y., Oceana Publications, 1970. 144 p. 24 cm. (Oceana presidential chronology series) Bibliography: p. 137-142. [E791.M6] 74-116060 ISBN 0-379-12079-8
1. U.S.—History—1919-1933—Sources. I. Coolidge, Calvin, Pres. U.S., 1872-1933. II. U.S. President, 1923-1929 (Coolidge)

MORAN, Philip R., comp. 973.91'4'0924
Warren G. Harding, 1865-1923: chronology, documents, bibliographical aids. Edited by Philip R. Moran. Dobbs Ferry, N.Y., Oceana Publications, 1970. 120 p. 24 cm. (Oceana presidential chronology series [14]) Bibliography: p. 115-119. [E785.M73] 78-95013 ISBN 0-379-12064-X 3.00
1. United States—History—1919-1933—Sources. I. Harding, Warren Gamaliel, Pres. U.S., 1865-1923. II. United States. President, 1921-1923 (Harding) III. Title. BIP

United States—History—1933-1945.

JOSEPHSON, Matthew, 1899- 973.9170924
Infidel in the temple; a memoir of the nineteen-thirties. [1st ed.] New York, Knopf, 1967. xvi, 513 p. 25 cm. Bibliographical footnotes. [E806.J66] 66-10030
1. United States—History—1933-1945. I. Title.

United States—History—1945-

NIXON, Richard Milhous, 1913- 973.92
Six crises. [1st ed.] Garden City, N.Y., Doubleday, 1962. 460 p. 24 cm. [E748.N5A3] 62-8074
1. United States—History—1945- I. Title. BIP

United States—History—1945- —Biography—Collected works.

†*POLITICAL profiles /* 920'.073
editor, Nelson Lichtenstein, associate editor, Eleanora W. Schoenebaum. New York : Facts on File, inc., c1976- v. ; 27 cm. Vol. [4]: associate editors: E. W. Schoenebaum and M. L. Levine. Contents.Contents.— —[3] The Kennedy years.—[4] The Johnson years. Includes bibliographies and indexes. [E840.6.P64] 76-20897 ISBN 0-87196-450-3 lib.bdg. : 45.00
1. United States—History—1945- —Biography—Collected works. 2. United States—Biography—Collected works. I. Lichtenstein, Nelson. II. Schoenebaum, Eleanora W. III. Levine, Michael L. IV. Facts on File, inc., New York.

United States. Library of Congress—Biography—Addresses, essays, lectures.

LIBRARIANS of Congress, 1802-1904. 020'.92'2 B
Washington : Library of Congress, 1977. p. cm. A collection of articles which first appeared in the Quarterly journal of the Library of Congress. [Z720.A4L52] 77-608073 ISBN 0-8444-0238-9
1. United States. Library of Congress—Biography—Addresses, essays, lectures. 2. Librarians—United States—Biography—Addresses, essays, lectures. I. United States. Library of Congress. II. United States. Library of Congress. Quarterly journal.

United States. Marine Corps—Biography.

CAPUTO, Philip. 959.704'38
A rumor of war / Philip Caputo. 1st ed. New York : Holt, Rinehart and Winston, c1977. xix, 346 p. ; 24 cm. Autobiographical. [DS559.5.C36] 76-29900 ISBN 0-03-017631-X : 10.95
1. United States. Marine Corps—Biography. 2. Caputo, Philip. 3. Vietnamese Conflict, 1961-1975—Personal narratives, American. 4. Soldiers—United States—Biography. I. Title. BIP

United States. Marine Corps Reserve—Biography.

FINNEY, Ben, 1900- 359.9'6'0924 B
Once a marine-always a marine / Ben Finney ; foreword by Lem Shepard. New York : Crown Publishers, 1977. 128 p. : ill. ; 24 cm. [VE25.F56A34 1977] 77-15629 ISBN 0-517-53275-1 : 6.95
1. Finney, Ben, 1900- 2. United States. Marine Corps Reserve—Biography. 3. United States. Marine Corps—History. 4. Soldiers—United States—Biography. I. Title. BIP

United States. Naval Reserve. Women's Reserve.

HANCOCK, Joy Bright, 1898- 359.3'48'0924 B
Lady in the Navy; a personal reminiscence. Annapolis, Md., Naval Institute Press [1972] xi, 289 p. illus. 23 cm. [VA390.H27] 76-189847 ISBN 0-87021-336-9 9.00
1. United States. Naval Reserve. Women's Reserve. I. Title.

United States. Navy—Aviation.

WILSON, Eugene Edward, 1887- 338.4'7'6291300924
Slipstream; the autobiography of an air craftsman, by Eugene E. Wilson. [3d ed. Palm Beach, Fla., Literary Investment Guild, 1967, c1965] xx, 366 p. 24 cm. [HD9711.U6W5 1967] 67-7562
1. United States. Navy—Aviation. I. Title.

United States. Navy—Biography.

ALDEN, Carroll Storrs, 1876- 359.3'3'10922 B
Makers of naval tradition, by Carroll Storrs Alden and Ralph Earle. Rev. and continued by Carroll Storrs Alden. Freeport, N.Y., Books for Libraries Press [1972] xiv, 378 p. illus. 23 cm. (Essay index reprint series) Reprint of the 1942 ed. [E182.A35 1972] 76-167303 ISBN 0-8369-2733-8
1. United States. Navy—Biography. I. Earle, Ralph, 1874-1939, joint author. II. Title. BIP

DECKER, Benton Weaver, 1899- 940.53'144'0952 B
Return of the black ships / by Benton Weaver Decker and Edwina Naylor Decker. 1st ed. New York : Vantage Press, c1978. x, 420 p. : ill. ; 21 cm. [DS889.15.D42] 79-106940 ISBN 0-533-03368-3 : 11.95
1. Decker, Benton Weaver, 1899- 2. United States. Navy—Biography. 3. United States. Navy—Foreign service—Japan—Biography. 4. Decker, Edwina Naylor. 5. Japan—History—Allied occupation, 1945-1952. 6. Admirals—United States—Biography. 7. Japan—Description and travel—1945- 8. Yokosuka, Japan—Description. I. Decker, Edwina Naylor, joint author. II. Title. BIP

WALDO, Samuel Putnam, 1780-1826. 973.35'0922
Biographical sketches of distinguished American naval heroes in the War of the Revolution, between the American Republic and the Kingdom of Great Britain; comprising sketches of Com. Nicholas Biddle, Com. John Paul Jones, Com. Edward Preble, and Com. Alexander Murray. With incidental allusions to other distinguished characters. Port Washington, N.Y., Kennikat Press [1970] x, 392 p. illus., ports. 22 cm. (Kennikat American bicentennial series) Half title: American naval heroes. Originally published in 1823. [E271.W16 1970] 73-120897 ISBN 0-8046-1290-0
1. United States. Navy—Biography. 2. United States—History—Revolution, 1775 1783—Naval operations. 3. United States—History—Revolution, 1775-1783—Biography. I. Title. II. Title: American naval heroes. BIP

United States. Navy—Foreign service—Japan—Biography.

DECKER, Benton Weaver, 1899- 940.53'144'0952 B
Return of the black ships / by Benton Weaver Decker and Edwina Naylor Decker. 1st ed. New York : Vantage Press, c1978. x, 420 p. : ill. ; 21 cm. [DS889.15.D42] 79-106940 ISBN 0-533-03368-3 : 11.95
1. Decker, Benton Weaver, 1899- 2. United States. Navy—Biography. 3. United States. Navy—Foreign service—Japan—Biography. 4. Decker, Edwina Naylor. 5. Japan—History—Allied occupation, 1945-1952. 6. Admirals—United States—Biography. 7. Japan—Description and travel—1945- 8. Yokosuka, Japan—Description. I. Decker, Edwina Naylor, joint author. II. Title. BIP

United States. Peace Corps—Ecuador—Personal narratives.

COWAN, Rachel. 309.2'235'0924 B
Growing up Yanqui / Rachel Cowan. New York : Viking Press, [1975] p. cm. Includes index. Bibliography: p. The author recounts her life as a Peace Corps volunteer in Ecuador, and other related experiences, describing how she changed from being a naive believer in United States foreign policy to a critic of it. [HC60.5.C695] 75-16334 ISBN 0-670-35597-6 : 6.95
1. United States. Peace Corps—Ecuador—Personal narratives. 2. Cowan, Rachel. 3. Cuba—Description and travel—1951- I. Title. BIP

United States. Penitentiary, Alcatraz Island, Calif.

GADDIS, Thomas E. 365'.6'0922 B
Unknown men of Alcatraz / by Thomas E. Gaddis ; ill. by Chris Edmiston. Portland, Or. : NewGate Pub. Co., c1977. iii, 168 p. : ill. ; 20 cm. [HV9468.G33] 77-81547
1. United States. Penitentiary, Alcatraz Island, Calif. 2. Prisoners—United States—Biography. I. Title.

United States—Politics and government.

BOUTWELL, George Sewall, 1818-1905. 974.4'03'0924
Reminiscences of sixty years in public affairs. New York, Greenwood Press, 1968, [c1902] 2 v. port. 24 cm. [E661.B76 1968] 68-28618
1. U.S.—Politics and government. I. Title. BIP

CHANDLER, David Leon. 975'.00992 B
The natural superiority of Southern politicians : a revisionist history / David Leon Chandler. 1st ed. Garden City, N.Y. : Doubleday, 1977. xii, 394 p., [8] leaves of plates : ill.; 22 cm. Includes index. [E183.C46] 75-21219 ISBN 0-385-03526-8 : 10.00
1. United States—Politics and government. 2. Statesmen—Southern States—Biography. 3. Southern States—Politics and government. I. Title.

HOFSTADTER, Richard, 1916-1970. 973
The American political tradition and the men who made it. New York, Vintage Books, 1954 [c1948] 381 p. 19 cm. (A

Vintage book, K9) Includes bibliography. [E178] 54-12054
1. United States—Politics and government. 2. United States—Biography. I. Title.

HOFSTADTER, Richard, 1916-1970. 973'.0992
The American political tradition and the men who made it. With a foreword by Christopher Lasch. New York, Knopf, 1973. xxxiii, 378, xix p. 22 cm. "Twenty-fifth anniversary edition." Bibliography: p. 349-378. [E183.H67 1973] 73-7291 ISBN 0-394-48880-6 7.95
1. United States—Politics and government. 2. United States—Biography. I. Title.

HOFSTADTER, Richard, 1916-1970. 320.9'73 B
The American political tradition and the men who made it. With a foreword by Christopher Lasch. New York, Vintage Books [1974, c1948] xl, 501, xxiv p. 18 cm. Reprint of the ed. published by Knopf, New York. Bibliography: p. 463-501. [E178.H727 1974] 73-20353 ISBN 0-394-70009-0 3.95 (pbk.)
1. United States—Politics and government. 2. United States—Biography. I. Title.

LA FOLLETTE, Robert Marion, 1855-1925 923.273
La Follette's autobiography; a personal narrative of political experiences. With a foreword by Allan Nevins. Madison, University of Wisconsin Press, 1960[c.1911-1960] 349p. illus. 60-50989 1.95 pap.,
1. U. S.—Pol. & govt. 2. Wisconsin—Pol. & govt.—1848-1950. 3. Presidents—U. S.—Election—1912. I. Title.

LAFOLLETTE, Robert Marion, 1855-1925 923.273
La Follette's autobiography; a personal narrative of political experiences. Forward by Allan Nevins. [Gloucester, Mass., P. Smith, 1966, c.1911, 1913] x 349p. illus. 22cm. (Univ. of Wis. Pr. bk. rebound) [E664.L16L16 1960] 4.00
1. U.S.—Pol. & govt. 2. Wisconsin—Pol. & govt.—1848-1950. 3. Presidents—U.S.—Election—1912. I. Title. BIP

SMITH, Alfred Emanuel, 1873-1944. 974.704
Alfred E. Smith; an anthology [edited by] Richard M. Lynch. [1st ed.] New York, Vantage Press [1967, c1966] 133 p. 22 cm. Includes bibliographical references. [E742.5.S6] 66-24843
1. United States—Politics and government. 2. New York (State)—Politics and government—1865-1950. I. Lynch, Richard M., ed.

United States—Politics and government—Civil War, 1861-1865.

BATES, Edward, 1793-1869. 973.71'0924
The diary of Edward Bates, 1859-1866. Edited by Howard K. Beale. New York, Da Capo Press, 1971. xvi, 685 p. 24 cm. Reprint of the 1933 ed. Originally published as Annual report of the American Historical Association for the year 1930, v. 4. [E415.9.B2A3 1971] 75-75304 ISBN 0-306-71260-1
1. United States—Politics and government—Civil War, 1861-1865. 2. Reconstruction—Missouri. I. Title.

WELLES, Gideon, 1802-1878. 923.273
Diary. Edited by Howard K. Beale, assisted by Alan W. Brownsword. With an introd. by Howard K. Beale and appendices drawn from Welles's correspondence. New York, W.W. Norton [1960] 3 v. ports. 25 cm. Contents.v. 1. 1861-March 30, 1864. -- v. 2. April 1, 1864-December 31, 1866. -- v. 3. January 1, 1867-June 6, 1869. [E468.W444] 60-6275
1. U.S. — Pol. & govt. — Civil War. 2. U.S. — Pol. & govt. — 1865-1869. 3. U.S. — Hist. — Civil War — Sources. 4. Reconstruction. I. Title.

United States—Politics and government—1783-1809—Sources.

JAY, John, 1745-1829. 973.3'0924
The correspondence and public papers of John Jay. Edited by Henry P. Johnston. New York, B. Franklin [1970] 4 v. 22 cm. (Burt Franklin research and source works series, 595. American classics in history & social science, 157) Reprint of the 1890-93 ed. Contents.—v. 1. 1763-1781.—v. 2. 1781-1782.—v. 3. 1782-1793.—v. 4. 1794-1826. Includes bibliographical references. [E302.J423] 73-140983 ISBN 0-8337-1847-9
1. United States—Politics and government—1783-1809—Sources. 2. United States—Politics and government—Revolution, 1775-1783—Sources. I. Johnston, Henry Phelps, 1842-1923, ed.

JAY, John, 1745-1829. 973.3'0924 B
The correspondence and public papers of John Jay, 1763-1826. Edited by Henry P. Johnston New York, Da Capo Press, 1971. 1 v. (various pagings) 29 cm. Reprint of the 1890-1893 ed. Includes bibliographical references. [E302.J423 1971] 69-16639 ISBN 0-306-71124-9
1. United States—Politics and government—1783-1809—Sources. 2. United States—Politics and government—Revolution, 1775-1783—Sources. I. Title. BIP

United States Politics And Government 1783-1865.

JEFFERSON, Thomas, Pres. U.S., 1743-1826. 016.9734'6'0924
Calendar of the correspondence of Thomas Jefferson. New York, B. Franklin [1970] 3 v. 24 cm. (Burt Franklin bibliography & reference series, 310) Reprint of the 1894-1903 ed. Contents.Contents.—pt. 1. Letters from Jefferson.—pt. 2. Letters to Jefferson.—pt. 3. Supplementary. [E302.J453] 74-109372
1. U.S.—Politics and government—1783-1865. I. Title. BIP

United States Politics And Government 1849-1877.

CLAY, Cassius Marcellus, 1810-1903. 973.6'0924 B
The life of Cassius Marcellus Clay; memoirs, writings, and speeches, showing his conduct in the overthrow of American slavery, the salvation of the Union, and the restoration of the autonomy of the States. [Vol. 1] New York, Negro Universities Press [1969] xiii, 600 p. illus., ports. 23 cm. Reprint of the 1886 ed. No more published. [E415.9.C55A3 1969] 75-89028
1. U.S.—Politics and government—1849-1877. I. Title.

WELLES, Gideon, 1802-1878. 923.273
Diary. Edited by Howard K. Beale, assisted by Alan W. Brownsword. With an introd. by Howard K. Beale and appendices drawn from Welles's correspondence. New York, W.W. Norton [1960] 3 v. ports. 25 cm. Contents.v. 1. 1861-March 30, 1864. -- v. 2. April 1, 1864-December 31, 1866. -- v. 3. January 1, 1867-June 6, 1869. [E468.W444] 60-6275
1. U.S. — Pol. & govt. — Civil War. 2. U.S. — Pol. & govt. — 1865-1869. 3. U.S. — Hist. — Civil War — Sources. 4. Reconstruction. I. Title.

United States Politics And Government 1865-1900.

CULLOM, Shelby Moore, 1829-1914. 328.73'0924 B
Fifty years of public service; personal recollections of Shelby M. Cullom. New York, Da Capo Press, 1969 [c1911] xi, 467 p. illus., ports. 24 cm. (A Da Capo Press reprint edition) [E661.C96 1969] 75-87504
1. U.S.—Politics and government—1865-1900. 2. Illinois—Politics and government—1865-1950. I. Title. BIP

United States—Politics and government—1865-1933.

STEVENSON, Adlai Ewing, 1835-1914. 920'.073
Something of men I have known, with some papers of a general nature, political, historical, and retrospective. Freeport, N.Y., Books for Libraries Press [1972] p. Reprint of the 1909 ed. [E661.S84 1972] 72-8417 ISBN 0-8369-6992-8
1. United States—Politics and government—1865-1933. 2. United States—Biography. I. Title.

United States—Politics and government—1877-1881.

HAYES, Rutherford Birchard, Pres. U.S., 1822-1893. 973.83
Hayes: the diary of a president 1875-1881, covering the disputed election, the end of reconstruction, and the beginning of civil service. Edited by T. Harry Williams. New York, D. McKay Co. [1964] xliv, 329 p. 21 cm. [E682.H48] 64-10784
1. United States—Politics and government—1877-1881. I. Williams, Thomas Harry, 1909- ed. II. Title: The diary of a president, 1875-1881.

United States Politics And Government 1901-1953.

HENDRICKS, Joseph Edward, 1903- 973.917'0924 (B)
Little Joe: my memories ... Kissimmee, Fla., Cody Publications [1966] 417 p. ports. 24 cm. [E748.H41513] 67-6456
1. U.S. — Pol. & govt. — 1933-1953. I. Title.

STIMSON, Henry Lewis, 1867-1950. 973.91'0924 B
On active service in peace and war, by Henry L. Stimson and McGeorge Bundy. New York, Octagon Books, 1971 [c1948] xxii, 698 p. port. 25 cm. "About one fifth of the material in this book was published serially [in the Ladies home journal] under the title of Time of peril." [E748.S883A3 1971] 79-159230 ISBN 0-374-97627-9
1. U.S.—Politics and government—1901-1953. 2. U.S.—Foreign relations—20th century. I. Bundy, McGeorge. II. Title. BIP

WILSON, Woodrow, Pres. U.S., 1856-1924. 923.173
Woodrow Wilson's own story, selected and edited by Donald Day. [1st ed.] Boston, Little, Brown [1952] 371 p. 23 cm. "Sources and acknowledgments": p. [359]-360. [E767.W833] 52-9078
1. U.S.—Pol. & govt.—1913-1921. I. Day, Donald, 1899- ed. II. Title.

United States—Politics and government—1933-1945.

FARLEY, James Aloysius, 1888- 320.9'73'0917 B
Behind the ballots; the personal history of a politician [by] James A. Farley. Westport, Conn., Greenwood Press [1972] 392 p. port. 23 cm. Reprint of the 1938 ed. [E748.F24A3 1972] 78-114521 ISBN 0-8371-4738-7
1. United States—Politics and government—1933-1945. 2. Politics, Practical. I. Title. BIP

FARLEY, James Aloysius, 1888- 320.9'73'0917 B
Behind the ballots; the personal history of a politician, by James A. Farley. New York, Da Capo Press, 1973 [c1938] 390 p. 22 cm. (Franklin D. Roosevelt and the era of the New Deal) [E748.F24A3 1973] 72-2370 ISBN 0-306-70475-7 15.00
1. United States—Politics and government—1933-1945. 2. Politics, Practical. I. Title. II. Series.

ROOSEVELT, Franklin Delano, Pres. U.S., 1882-1945. 973.917'0924 B
Franklin Delano Roosevelt, 1882-1945. Edited by Howard F. Bremer. Dobbs Ferry, N.Y., Oceana Publications, 1971. 220 p. 24 cm. ([The Presidential chronologies]) Bibliography: p. 205-216. [E742.5.R577] 71-116062 ISBN 0-379-12066-6 7.00
1. U.S.—Politics and government—1933-1945. I. U.S. President, 1933-1945 (Franklin D. Roosevelt) II. Bremer, Howard F., ed.

ROOSEVELT, Franklin Delano, Pres. U.S., 1882-1945. 923.173
Franklin D. Roosevelt's own story, told in his own words from his private and public papers as selected by Donald Day. [1st rd.] Boston, Little, Brown 1951. 461 p. 23 cm. "Sources and acknowledgements": p. [443]-445. [E807.R6485] 51-13942
1. U.S. — Pol. & govt. — 1933-1945. I. Day, Donald, 1890- ed. II. Title.

United States—Politics and government—1945-

ANDERSON, Clinton Presba, 1895- 973.917'0924 B
Outsider in the Senate; Senator Clinton Anderson's memoirs [by] Clinton P. Anderson with Milton Viorst. New York, World Pub. Co. [1970] viii, 328 p. illus., ports. 22 cm. [E840.8.A5A3] 73-137667 10.00
1. U.S.—Politics and government—1945- I. Viorst, Milton, joint author. II. Title.

DOUGLAS, Paul Howard, 1892- 328.73'092'4 B
In the fullness of time; the memoirs of Paul H. Douglas. [1st ed.] New York, Harcourt Brace Jovanovich [1972] xii, 642 p. illus. 24 cm. [E748.D68A3] 74-182327 ISBN 0-15-144376-9
1. United States—Politics and government—1945- I. Title. BIP

STEVENSON, Adlai Ewing, 1900-1965. 973.90924
Adlai Stevenson's public years, with text text from his speeches and writings, ed. by Jill Kneerim. Photos. by Cornell Capa, John Fell Stevenson, Inge Morath. Pref. by Walter Lippmann. New York, Grossman [c.]1966. 160p. illus., ports. 29cm. [E743.S765] 66-19525 8.95
1. U.S.—Pol. & govt.—1945- —Addresses, essays, lectures. 2. U.S.—For. rel.—1945- —Addresses, essays, lectures. I. Kneerim, Jill, ed. II. Title.

WHITE, William Smith. 973.9'0922 B
The responsibles [by] William S. White. [1st ed.] New York, Harper & Row [1971, c1972] 275 p. 22 cm. Contents.Contents.—The way they are.—Harry S. Truman.—Robert A. Taft.—Dwight D. Eisenhower.—John F. Kennedy.—Lyndon B. Johnson. [E743.W584 1972] 79-95990 ISBN 0-06-014619-2 7.95
1. U.S.—Politics and government—1945- 2. U.S.—Biography. I. Title.

United States—Politics and government—1945- —Sources.

TRUMAN, Harry S., Pres. U.S., 1884- 973.918
Memoirs. [1st ed.] Garden City, N.Y., Doubleday, 1955-56. 2 v. 22 cm. Contents.Contents.—v. 1. Year of decisions.—v. 2. Years of trial and hope. [E814.T75] 55-10519
1. United States—Politics and government—1945- —Sources.

TRUMAN, Harry S., Pres. U.S., 1884-1972. 923.173
Mr. President; the first publication from the personal diaries, private letters, papers, and revealing interviews of Harry S. Truman, thirty-second President of the United States of America. By William Hillman. Pictures by Alfred Wagg. New York, Farrar, Straus and Young [1952] 253 p. illus. (some col.), ports. (some col.) 29 cm. [E814.T7] 52-6976
1. United States—Politics and government—1945- —Sources. I. Hillman, William, 1895- ed. II. Title.

United States Politics And Government 1953-1961.

BROWN, John Mason, 1900-1969. 973'.099 B
Through these men; some aspects of our passing history. Freeport, N.Y., Books for Libraries Press [1972, c1956] ix, 302 p. 23 cm. (Essay index reprint series) [E835.B7 1972] 71-167318 ISBN 0-8369-2756-7
1. United States—Politics and

government—1953-1961. 2. United States—Biography. I. Title.

CHAMBERS, Whittaker. 320.9'24 B
Odyssey of a friend; Whittaker Chambers' letters to William F. Buckley, Jr., 1954-1961. Edited with notes by William F. Buckley, Jr. Foreword by Ralph de Toledano. New York, Putnam [1970, c1969] 303 p. 22 cm. Bibliographical footnotes. [E835.C45 1970] 70-88575 6.95
1. U.S.—Politics and government—1953-1961. I. Buckley, William Frank, 1925- ed. II. Title.

United States—Politics and government—1961-1963.

HELLER, Deane Fons, 353'.0922
1924-
The Kennedy Cabinet; America's men of destiny [by] Deane and David Heller. Foreword by A. S. Mike Monroney. Freeport, N.Y., Books for Libraries Press [1969, c1961] 159 p. 23 cm. (Biography index reprint series) [E841.H4 1969] 77-101829 ISBN 0-8369-8002-6
1. United States—Politics and government—1961-1963. 2. Cabinet officers—United States. 3. United States—Officials and employees. I. Heller, David, 1922- joint author. II. Title.

United States—Politics and government—1974- —Anecdotes, facetiae, satire, etc.

REEVES, Richard. 320.9'73'0925
Old faces of 1976 : a few thousand fairly well-chosen words on Jerry Ford, Nelson Rockefeller, Teddy Kennedy, George Wallace, Hubert Humphrey, Ronald Reagan, Ed Muskie, Scoop Jackson, George McGovern, Hugh Carey, Abe Beame, Jack Javits, Jerry Brown, and some other men you probably wouldn't want your daughter to marry / Richard Reeves. 1st ed. New York : Harper & Row, c1976. xix, 235 p. ; 22 cm. Includes index. [E865.R4 1976] 75-30343 ISBN 0-06-013526-3 : 10.00
1. United States—Politics and government—1974- —Anecdotes, facetiae, satire, etc. 2. United States—Politics and government—1969-1974—Anecdotes, facetiae, satire, etc. 3. Statesmen—United States—Anecdotes, facetiae, satire, etc. 4. Presidents—United States—Election—1976- —Anecdotes, facetiae, satire, etc. I. Title.

United States—Politics and government—20th century.

CELLER, Emanuel, 1888- 923.273
You never leave Brooklyn; the autobiography of Emanuel Celler. New York, J. Day Co. [1953] 280p. illus. 21cm. [E748.C4A3] 52-12683
1. U. S.—Pol. & govt.—20th cent. I. Title.

HAYS, Brooks. 973.91'0924
A hotbed of tranquility; my life in five worlds. With an appreciation by Donald G. Herzberg. New York, Macmillan [1968] xv, 238 p. 22 cm. [E748.H389A25] 68-15266
1. United States—Politics and government—20th century. 2. American wit and humor. I. Title.

HELLER, Deane, 1924- 923.273
The Kennedy Cabinet; America's men of destiny [by] Deane and David Heller. Foreword by A. S. Mike Monroney. Derby, Conn., Monarch Books [1961] 159p. 19cm. (A Monarch Americana book) [E841.H4] 61-19205
1. U. S.—Pol. & govt.—1961- 2. Cabinet officers—U. S. 3. U. S.—Officials and employees. I. Heller, David, 1922- joint author. II. Title.

JARRETT, Derek. 760'.092'4 B
The ingenious Mr Hogarth / Derek Jarrett. London : M. Joseph, 1976. 223 p., [12] leaves of plates : ill. ; 24 cm. Includes index. Bibliography: p. [214]-217. [ND497.H7J37] 76-380637 ISBN 0-7181-1489-2 : £7.00
1. Hogarth, William, 1697-1764. 2. Painters—Great Britain—Biography. I. Title.

MARSH, Benjamin Clarke, 923.273
1877-1952.
Lobbyist for the people; a record of fifty years. Washington, Public Affairs Press [1953] 224p. 21cm. Autobiographical. [F748.M34A3] 53-10837
1. U. S.—Pol. & govt.—20th cent. 2. People's Lobby. I. Title.

MARTIN, Joseph William, 923.273
1884-
My first fifty years in politics, as told to Robert J. Donovan. New York, McGraw-Hill [1960] 261p. illus. 22cm. [E748.M375A3] 60-15002
1. U. S.—Pol. & govt.—20th cent. I. Donovan, Robert J. II. Title.

MURPHY, John Francis, 353.03'13
1922(Aug.20)-
The pinnacle: the contemporary American Presidency [by] John F. Murphy. Philadelphia, Lippincott [1974] 215 p. 21 cm. (The Lippincott series in American government) Includes bibliographical references. [E743.M87] 74-3164 ISBN 0-397-47312-5 2.95 (pbk.).
1. United States—Politics and government—20th century. 2. Presidents—United States—Biography. I. Title.

ROBERTS, Charles 973.9230922
Wesley, 1916-
LBJ's inner circle, by Charles Roberts. With an introd. by Pierre Salinger. New York, Delacorte Press [1965] 223 p. illus., ports. 22 cm. [E846.R56] 65-21935
1. U.S. — Pol. & govt. — 1963- 2. U.S Executive Office of the President. 3. Cabinet officers — U.S. 4. Johnson, Lyndon Johnson, Pres. U.S., 1908- I. Title.

TRUMAN, Harry S., Pres. 923.173
U.S., 1884-
Mr. Citizen. New York, Popular Lib. [1961, c.1953-1960] 238p. (Popular special SP92) .50 pap.,
1. U. S.—Pol. & govt.—1953- 2. U.S.—For. rel.—1953- I. Title.

TRUMAN, Harry S. Pres. 923.173
U.S. 1884-
Mr. Citizen. [New York, Geis Associates; distributed by Random House [1960] 315 p. illus. 24 cm. Autobiographical. [ES14.A33] 60-10127
1. U.S. — Pol. & govt. — 1953- 2. U.S. — For. rel. — 1953- I. Title.

United States—Presidents—Biography.

THE Presidents and their wives : 973'.092'2 B
from George Washington to Gerald Rudolph Ford. Rev. Washington : National Souvenir Center, 1975. 71 p. : ports. ; 23 cm. Cover title. At head of title: Bi-centennial edition, 1776-1976. [E176.1.P92] 75-309314 2.00
1. United States—Presidents—Biography. 2. United States—Presidents—Wives—Biography.

United States. Quartermaster's Dept.—Biography.

KIEFFER, Chester 355.3'31'0924 B
L.
Maligned General : the biography of Thomas Sidney Jesup. San Rafael, Calif. : Presidio Press, c1979. xiii, 376 p. : ports. ; 24 cm. Includes index. Bibliography: p. 355-361. [U53.J47K53] 78-24028 ISBN 0-89141-027-9 : 16.95
1. Jesup, Thomas Sidney, 1788-1860. 2. United States. Quartermaster's Dept.—Biography. 3. United States. Army—History—19th century. 4. Generals—United States—Biography. I. Title.

United States—Social conditions.

DEUR, Lynne. 361'.92'2 B
Doers and dreamers; social reformers of the nineteenth century. Minneapolis, Lerner Publications Co. [1972] 88 p. illus. 22 cm. (A Pull ahead book) Brief biographies of fourteen nine-teenth-century men and women involved in such reform movements as women's rights, temperance, and the abolition of slavery. [HV27.D47] 920 79-128808 ISBN 0-8225-0462-6
1. United States—Social conditions. 2. United States—Biography—Juvenile literature. I. Title.

United States—Social conditions—1945-

LORBER, Richard, 1946- 309.1'73
The gap, by Richard Lorber and Ernest Fladell. [1st ed.] New York, McGraw-Hill [1968] 179 p. 21 cm. Autobiographical. [HN58.L65] 68-18550
1. United States—Social conditions—1945- 2. Conflict of generations. I. Fladell, Ernest, 1925- joint author. II. Title.

United States—Social life and customs—1865-1918.

CANBY, Henry Seidel, 917.3'03'8
1878-1961.
American memoir. New York, Greenwood Press, 1968 [c1947] x, 433 p. 24 cm. [PN4874.C23A3 1968] 68-54988
1. United States—Social life and customs—1865-1918. I. Title. **BIP**

United States—Social life and customs—1865-1918—Sources—Juvenile literature.

SCHWARTZ, Alvin, 1927- 973.8
When I grew up long ago : family living, going to school, games and parties, cures and deaths, a comet, a war, falling in love, and other things I remember : older people talk about the days when they were young / by Alvin Schwartz ; drawings by Harold Berson. Philadelphia : Lippincott, c1978. p. cm. Includes index. Bibliography: p. Brief statements from "older people" on such areas of their past lives as food, social life, music, holidays and health present glimpses of life in the United States during the 19th and 20th centuries. [E168.S417] 78-8719 ISBN 0-397-31726-3 : 9.95
1. United States—Social life and customs—1865-1918—Sources—Juvenile literature. 2. United States—Social life and customs—20th century—Sources—Juvenile literature. 3. United States—Biography—Juvenile literature. I. Berson, Harold. II. Title.

United States Steel Corporation.

UNITED States Steel 923.373
Corporation.
Myron C. Taylor; an appreciation. [n.p. 1956] 54 p. illus. 21 cm. [HD9519.U6U67] 59-33712
I. Taylor, Myron Charles, 1874- II. Title.

United States. Supreme Court.

WESTIN, Alan F., 347'.73'2634 B
ed.
An autobiography of the Supreme Court : off-the-bench commentary by the justices / edited and with an introd. by Alan F. Westin. Westport, Conn. : Greenwood Press, 1978, c1963. xii, 475 p. ; 24 cm. Reprint of the ed. published by Macmillan, New York. Includes bibliographical references. [KF8742.A5W48 1978] 78-5165 ISBN 0-313-20385-7 lib. bdg. : 29.75
1. United States. Supreme Court. I. Title. **BIP**

United States. Supreme Court—Biography.

BARNES, Catherine 347'.73'2634 B
A.
Men of the Supreme Court : profiles of the justices / by Catherine A. Barnes. New York : Facts on File, c1978. ix, 221 p. : ports. ; 26 cm. Includes index. Bibliography: p. 199-204. [KF8744.B34] 78-11633 ISBN 0-87196-459-7 : 20.00
1. United States. Supreme Court—Biography. 2. Judges—United States—Biography. I. Title. **BIP**

FLYNN, James J. 347.99'73 B
Famous justices of the Supreme Court, by James J. Flynn. New York, Dodd, Mead [1968] 157 p. illus., ports. 22 cm. (Famous biographies for young people) Bibliography: p. 153-154. [KF8744.F54] 68-14248
1. United States. Supreme Court—Biography. I. Title.

UNITED States. 347'.73'2634 B
Congress. Senate. Committee on the Judiciary.
The Supreme Court of the United States : hearings and reports on successful and unsuccessful nominations of Supreme Court Justices by the Senate Judiciary Committee, 1916-1972 / compiled by Roy M. Mersky, J. Myron Jacobstein. Buffalo : W. S. Hein, 1975. 11 v. in 12 ; 24 cm. Reprint of documents published by the U.S. Govt. Print. Off., Washington. Contents.Contents.—v. 1-3. Brandeis.—v. 4. Black, Reed, Frankfurter, Douglas, Murphy, Stone, Jackson.—v. 5. Clark, Minton, Warren.—v. 6. Harlan, Brennan, Whittaker, Stewart, White, Goldberg.—v. 7. Fortas, Marshall, Burger.—v. 8. Blackmun, Rehnquist, Powell.—v. 9. Parker, Fortas, Thornberry.—v. 9A. Fortas, Thornberry.—v. 10. Haynsworth.—v. 11. Carswell. Includes bibliographical references. [KF8744.J8] 75-13630
1. United States. Supreme Court—Biography. I. Mersky, Roy M. II. Jacobstein, J. Myron. III. Title.

United States. Supreme Court—History.

CARSON, Hampton 347'.73'2609
Lawrence, 1852-1929.
The history of the Supreme Court of the United States, with biographies of all the chief and associate justices. With ports. of the 58 judges, engraved by Max and Albert Rosenthal. New York, B. Franklin [1971] 2 v. (xii, 650 p.) ports. 24 cm. (Burt Franklin research & source works series, 887. American classics in history and social science, 223) Reprint of the 1902 ed. Includes bibliographical references. [KF8742.C3 1971] 77-172197 ISBN 0-8337-4506-9
1. United States. Supreme Court—History. 2. Judges—United States—Biography. I. Title.

United States. Supreme Court—Statistics.

BLAUSTEIN, Albert 347'.73'2634
P., 1921-
The first one hundred justices : statistical studies on the Supreme Court of the United States / by Albert P. Blaustein and Roy M. Mersky. Hamden, Conn. : Archon Books, 1978. 210 p. ; 24 cm. Includes index. Bibliography: p. 151-203. [KF8741.A152B6] 77-23543 ISBN 0-208-01290-7 : 17.50
1. United States. Supreme Court—Statistics. 2. Judges—United States—Biography. I. Mersky, Roy M., joint author. II. Title. **BIP**

United States. War Dept.—Biography.

WEBSTER'S American military biographies. 355'.0092'2 B
Springfield, Mass. : G. & C. Merriam Co., c1978. xi, 548 p. ; 26 cm. [U52.W4] 77-18688 ISBN 0-87779-063-9 : 12.95
1. United States. War Dept.—Biography. 2. United States. Dept. of Defense—Biography. 3. Soldiers—United States—Biography. 4. United States—History, Military—Chronology. I. Merriam (G. & C.) Company, publishers, Springfield, Mass.

United Steel Workers of America.

MCDONALD, David 331.881'72'0924 B
John, 1902-
Union man, by David J. McDonald. [1st ed.] New York, Dutton, 1969. 352 p. ports. 22 cm. Autobiographical. [HD8073.M2A3] 77-78947 7.95
1. United Steel Workers of America. 2. Strikes and lockouts—Steel industry—U.S. I. Title.

Universal Negro Improvement Association—Addresses, essays, lectures.

BURKETT, Randall K. 209'.73
Black redemption : churchmen speak for the Garvey movement / Randall K. Burkett. Philadelphia : Temple University Press, 1978. x, 197 p. : ports ; 22 cm. Includes bibliographical references. [BR563.N4B87] 77-81332 12.50
1. Universal Negro Improvement Association—Addresses, essays, lectures. 2.

Garvey, Marcus, 1887-1940—Addresses, essays, lectures. 3. Afro-Americans—Religion—Addresses, essays, lectures. 4. Afro-American clergy—Biography—Addresses, essays, lectures. I. Title. BIP

Unser, Bobby.

SCALZO, Joe. 796.7'2'0924 B
The Bobby Unser story / Joe Scalzo & Bobby Unser. 1st ed. Garden City, N.Y. : Doubleday, 1979. 203 p., [16] leaves of plates : ill. ; 22 cm. [GV1032.U57S27] 78-14689 ISBN 0-385-13436-3 : 10.00
1. Unser, Bobby. 2. Automobile racing drivers—United States—Biography. I. Unser, Bobby, joint author. II. Title. BIP

Unser, Bobby—Juvenile literature.

GILBERT, John, 1942- 796.7'2'0924 B
An interview with Bobby Unser / by John Gilbert ; photographs by Vernon J. Biever. Mankato, Minn. : Creative Education, c1977 31 p. : col. ill. ; 25 cm. ("Interviews") A brief biography of the race car driver who won the 1975 Indianapolis 500. [GV1032.U57G54] 92 76-42276 ISBN 0-87191-572-3 lib.bdg. 5.95
1. Unser, Bobby—Juvenile literature. 2. Automobile racing drivers—United States—Biography—Juvenile literature. I. Biever, Vernon J. II. Title. BIP

Untouchables.

HAZARI. 915.4'03'350924 B
Untouchable; the autobiography of an Indian outcaste. Introd. by Beatrice Pitney Lamb. New York, Praeger [1969, c1951] xvii, 198 p. 22 cm. First published in 1951 under title: I was an outcaste. A young Indian recounts his struggle to free himself from the restrictions of his caste. [DS422.C3H39 1969] 92 68-8902 5.95
1. Untouchables. 2. India—Social life and customs. I. Title.

Unwin, Sir Stanley

UNWIN, Sir Stanley 920.4
The truth about a publisher; an autobiographical record. New York, Macmillan [c.]1960. 455p. illus. 22cm. 60-10781 4.50
I. Title.

Unwin, Stanley, Sir,

UNWIN, Stanley, sir, 1884- 920.4
The truth about a publisher; an autobiographical record. New York, Macmillan, 1960. 455 p. illus. 22 cm. [Z325.U5A3] 60-10781
I. Title.

Updike, John.

HAMILTON, Alice. 813'.5'4
The elements of John Updike [by] Alice and Kenneth Hamilton. [Grand Rapids, Mich.] Eerdmans [1970] 267 p. 24 cm. Bibliography: p. 250-253. [PS3571.P4Z69] 70-88075 6.95
1. Updike, John. I. Hamilton, Kenneth, joint author. II. Title.

Upham, Charles Hazlitt, 1908-

SANDFORD, Kenneth 940.5481931
Mark of the lion; the story of Capt. Charles Upham, V.C. and Bar. New York, Popular Lib. [1964, c.1962] 288p. 18cm. (M2057) .60 pap.,
1. Upham, Charles Hazlitt, 1908- I. Title.

SANDFORD, Kenneth. 940.5481931
Mark of the lion, the story of Capt. Charles Upham, v. c. and bar. New York, I. Washburn [1963, c1962] 287 p. 21 cm. [DU422.U65S3] 63-10698
1. Upham, Charles Hazlitt, 1906- I. Title.

SANFORD, Kenneth 940.5481931
Mark of the lion, the story of Capt. Charles Upham, v. c. and bar. New York, Washburn [1963, c.1962] 287p. 21cm. 63-10698 3.95
1. Upham, Charles Hazlitt, 1908- I. Title.

Upjohn, Richard, 1802-1878.

UPJOHN, Everard Miller, 1903- 720'.924 B
Richard Upjohn, architect and churchman, by Everard M. Upjohn. New York, Da Capo Press, 1968 [c1939] xvii, 243 p. illus., plans, port. 24 cm. (Da Capo Press series in architecture and decorative art, v. 15) Bibliography: p. [227]-228. [NA737.U6U6 1968] 68-26119
1. Upjohn, Richard, 1802-1878. 2. Church architecture—United States.

Upper classes—United States.

AMORY, Cleveland. 917.3
Who killed society? [1st ed.] New York, Harper [1960] 599 p. illus. 22 cm. Includes bibliography. [E161.A4] 60-15314
1. Upper classes—United States. 2. United States—Social life and customs. 3. United States—Biography. I. Title.

Upshur, Abel Parker, 1790-1844.

HALL, Claude Hampton, 1922- 923.273
Abel Parker Upshur, conservative Virginian, 1790-1844. Madison, State Hist. Soc. of Wis. [1964, c.]1963. v, 271p. illus., ports., map. 23cm. Bibl. 64-63005 5.50
1. Upshur, Abel Parker, 1790-1844. 2. Virginia—Pol. & govt.—1775-1865. 3. U.S.—Pol. & govt.—1841-1845. I. Title. BIP

Upshur family.

UPSHAW, Sophie W., 1904- 929'.2'0973
Captain William Upshaw, gent., planter of Virginia : some of his Georgia descendants and allied families, Francis, Wright, MacAllen, Bardwell, Daves, Chalmers / compiled by Sophie W. Upshaw. Baltimore : Gateway Press, 1975. xii, 500 p., [14] leaves of plates (1 fold.) : ill. ; 24 cm. Includes index. [CS71.U68 1975] 75-27313
1. Upshur family. 2. Francis family. 3. Wright family. 4. Virginia—Genealogy. I. Title.

Urban, Georg,

URBAN, Georg, ed. 270.6'092'4
Philipp Melanchthon, 1497-1560; Gedenkschrift zum 400. Todestag des Reformators 19. April 1560/1560. 2. erweiterte Aufl. Bretten, Melanchthonverein, 1960. 224 p. illus., ports., facsims. 24 cm. Includes bibliographies. [BR335.U6] 61-42769
I. Melanchthon, Philipp, 1497-1560. II. Title.

Urban renewal—Massachusetts—Cambridge.

URBAN Land Institute. 309.2'62'097444
Cambridge Center : an evaluation of the redevelopment potential of Cambridge Center in the Kendall Square Urban Renewal Area for the Cambridge Redevelopment Authority, Cambridge Massachusetts, November 15-19, 1976 : a panel service report / by ULI-the Urban Land Institute. Washington : ULI, c1977. 42 p. : ill. ; 28 cm. [HT177.C27U7 1977] 77-151874
1. Urban renewal—Massachusetts—Cambridge. I. Cambridge, Mass. Redevelopment Authority. II. Title.

Urey, Harold Clayton, 1893- — Juvenile literature.

SILVERSTEIN, Alvin. 540'.924 B
Harold Urey; the man who explored from earth to moon [by] Alvin and Virginia Silverstein. Illustrated by Lee J. Ames. New York, J. Day Co. [1970, c1971] 79 p. illus., ports. 22 cm. (Great men of science) A biography of the chemist who was awarded the Nobel Prize in 1934 for the discovery of deuterium, a heavy hydrogen. [QD22.U75S57 1971] 92 74-125573
1. Urey, Harold Clayton, 1893- —Juvenile literature. I. Silverstein, Virginia B., joint author. II. Ames, Lee J., illus. III. Title.

Urquhart, David, 1805-1877.

ROBINSON, Gertrude. 327.42 B
David Urquhart; some chapters in the life of a Victorian knight errant of justice and liberty. New York, A. M. Kelley, 1970. xii, 328 p. illus., facsim., ports. 22 cm. (Reprints of economic classics) Reprint of the 1920 ed. [DA46.U8R6 1970] 78-110120
1. Urquhart, David, 1805-1877. BIP

Urquhart, Thomas, Sir, 1611-1660.

ROE, Frederick Charles, 1894- 828'.4'09
Sir Thomas Urquhart and Rabelais, by F. C. Roe. [Folcroft, Pa.] Folcroft Library Editions, 1973. 23 p. 26 cm. Reprint of the 1957 ed. published by Clarendon Press, Oxford, in series: The Taylorian lecture, 1957. Includes bibliographical references. [PR3736.U6R6 1973] 73-4484 4.00
1. Urquhart, Thomas, Sir, 1611-1660. 2. Rabelais, Francois, 1490 (ca.)-1553? I. Title. II. Series: The Taylorian lecture, 1957. BIP

Urrea, Teresa.

HOLDEN, William Curry, 1896- 972.08'1'0924 B
Teresita / William Curry Holden ; illustrated by Jose Cisneros. 1st ed. Owings Mills, Md. : Stemmer House Publishers, 1978. xviii, 235 p. : ill. ; 23 cm. "A Barbara Holdridge book." Bibliography: p. 235. [BF1283.U77H64 1978] 78-2321 ISBN 0-916144-24-0 : 14.95. ISBN 0-916144-25-9 pbk. : 8.95
1. Urrea, Teresa. 2. Healers—Mexico—Biography. 3. Psychical research—Biography. BIP

Ursua, Pedro de, d. 1561.

SIMON, Pedro, b.1565. 910'.9 S
The expedition of Pedro de Ursua & Lope de Aguirre in search of El Dorado and Omagua in 1560-1. Translated from Fray Pedro Simon's "Sixth historical notice of the conquest of tierra firme" by William Bollaert. With an introd. by Clements R. Markham. New York, B. Franklin [1971] liii, 237 p. fold. map. 23 cm. (Works issued by the Hakluyt Society, 1st ser., 28) Reprint of the 1861 ed. Translation of the 6th noticia of the Primera parte de las noticias historiales. [G161.H22 no. 28] [E125.A35] 981'.1'03 79-162707 ISBN 0-8337-3271-4
1. Ursua, Pedro de, d. 1561. 2. Aguirre, Lope de, d. 1561. 3. El Dorado. 4. Venezuela—History—1556-1772. I. Bollaert, William, 1807-1876, tr. II. Markham, Clements Robert, Sir, 1830-1916, ed. III. Series: Hakluyt Society. Works, no. 28. BIP

Uspenskii, Petr Dem'ianovich, 1878-1947—Addresses, essays, lectures.

USPENSKII, Petr Dem'ianovich, 1878-1947. 309.1'47'0841
Letters from Russia, 1919 / P. D. Ouspensky. London ; Boston : Routledge & K. Paul, 1978. ix, 59 p. : map ; 19 cm. [DK265.17.U75 1978] 79-306175 ISBN 0-7100-0077-4 pbk. : 6.95
1. Uspenskii, Petr Dem'ianovich, 1878-1947—Addresses, essays, lectures. 2. Russia—History—Revolution, 1917-1921—Personal narratives, Russian—Addresses, essays, lectures. 3. Russia—Social conditions—1917- —Addresses, essays, lectures. 4. Journalists—Russia—Biography—Addresses, essays, lectures. I. Title. BIP

Ussher, James, Abp. of Armagh, 1581-1656.

KNOX, R Buick. 283'.0924 (B)
James Ussher, Archbishop of Armagh, b R Buick Knox. Cardiff, University of Wales P., 1967. [7], 205 p. plate, port. 23 cm. 35/- (B 68-00565) Bibliography: p. 194-201. [BX5595.U8K5] 68-75114
1. Ussher, James, Abp. of Armagh, 1581-1656. I. Title.

KNOX, R. Buick. 283'.0924
James Ussher, Archbishop of Armagh, by R. Buick Knox. Cardiff, Univ. of Wales Pr., 1967. [7], 205p. plate, port. 23cm. Bibl. [BX5595.U8K5] (B) 68-75114 10.00
1. Ussher, James, Abp. of Armagh, 1581-1656. I. Title.
Distributed by Verry, Mystic, Conn.

Ussishkin, Menahem Mendel, 1863-1941.

KLING, Simcha. 923.25693
The mighty warrior; the life-story of Menachem Ussishkin. New York, J. David [1965] xi, 148 p. port. 22 cm. Bibliography: p. 145-148. [SD151.U75K58] 64-8424
1. Ussishkin, Menahem Mendel, 1863-1941. I. Title.

Ustinov, Peter—Biography.

USTINOV, Peter. 791'.092'4 B
Dear me / by Peter Ustinov. 1st ed. Boston : Little, Brown, c1977. p. cm. Autobiographical. "An Atlantic Monthly Press book." Includes index. [PR6041.S73Z514] 7-9021 ISBN 0-316-89051-0 : 14.95
1. Ustinov, Peter—Biography. 2. Authors, English—20th century—Biography. 3. Actors—Great Britain—Biography. I. Title. BIP

USTINOV, Peter. 791'.092'4 B
Dear me / Peter Ustinov. New York : Penguin Books, 1979, c1977. 348p., [12] leaves of plates : ill. ; 18 cm. Includes index. [PR6041.S73Z514] ISBN 0-14-004940-1 pbk. : 2.95
1. Ustinov, Peter — Biography. 2. Authors, English — 20th century — Biography. 3. Actors — Great Britain — Biography. I. Title.
L.C. card no. for 1977 Little Brown ed.: 77-9021.

Utah — Hist. — Sources.

STOUT, Hosea, 1810-1889. v. 12
Autobiography of Hosea Stout, 1810-1844. Edited by Reed A. Stout. [Salt Lake City, Utah State Historical Society] 1962. 88 p. illus., port. 24 cm. Reprinted from v. 30, 1962, Utah historical quarterly. 66-68326
1. Utah — Hist. — Sources. 2. Mormons and Mormonism — Hist. — Sources. I. Stout, Reed A., ed. II. Title.

Utah—Description and travel.

CHANDLESS, William. 917.8
A visit to Salt Lake; being a journey across the Plains and a residence in the Mormon settlements at Utah. New York, AMS Press [1971] xii, 346 p. 22 cm. Reprint of the 1857 ed. [F826.C45 1971] 76-134391 ISBN 0-404-08434-6 12.50
1. Utah—Description and travel. 2. Overland journeys to the Pacific. 3. Mormons and Mormonism. 4. Salt Lake City—Description. I. Title.

Utah Expedition, 1857-1858—Personal narratives.

UTAH, fl.1858-1859. 973.6'8
To Utah with the Dragoons and glimpses of life in Arizona and California, 1858-1859 / edited by Harold D. Langley. Salt Lake City : University of Utah Press, c1974. xvi, 230 p. : ill. ; 24 cm. (University of Utah publications in the American West ; v. 11) "Letters originally appeared in the Philadelphia Daily evening bulletin during 1858-59." Includes index. Bibliography: p. 216-221. [F826.U7 1974] 73-80998 ISBN 0-87480-087-0
1. Utah Expedition, 1857-1858—Personal narratives. 2. United States. Army. 2d Cavalry. 3. Utah, fl. 1858-1859. 4. The West—Description and travel—1848-1860. I. Langley, Harold D. II. Title. III. Series: Utah. University. Publications in the American West ; v. 11.

Utah—History.

HICKMAN, William A., 1815-1877or8. 289.3'0924 B
Brigham's destroying angel: being the life,

confession, and startling disclosures of the notorious Bill Hickman, the Danite chief of Utah. Written by himself, with explanatory notes by J. H. Beadle. Freeport, N.Y., Books for Libraries Press [1971] vii, 221 p. illus. 23 cm. Reprint of the 1904 ed. [F826.H63 1971] 74-165642 ISBN 0-8369-5951-5
1. Utah—History. 2. Mormons and Mormonism. I. Title.

RAWLINS, Joseph 923.273
Lafayette, 1850-1926.
'The unfavored few'; the autobiography of Joseph L. Rawlins, edited and amplified by Alta Rawlins Jensen. [n. p., 1956] 195p. illus. 21cm. [F826.R3] 59-33423
1. Utah—Hist. 2. Mormons and Mormonism in Utah. I. Title.

Utamaro, 1754 1806.

KITAGAWA Utamaro 761.283
(1753-1806) Text by Ichitaro Kondo; English adaptation by Charles S. Terry. [1st Eng. ed.] Tokyo, Rutland, Vt., C. E. Tuttle Co. [1956] 1v. (unpaged) illus (part col.) 18cm. (Kodansha library of Japanese art, no. 5) Title also in Japanese on t. p. Bibliography: [1] p. at end. [NE1325.U8K6] 927.6 56-8490
1. Utamaro, 1754 1806. I. Kondo, Ichitaro, 1910- II. Ferry, Charles S. III. Series.

Utica Normal and Industrial Institute, Utica Institute, Miss.

HOLTZCLAW, William 378'.00925 B
Henry, 1870?-
The Black man's burden. With an introd. by Booker T. Washington. New York, Negro Universities Press [1970] 232 p. illus., ports. 23 cm. Reprint of the 1915 ed. [E185.97.H75 1970] 76-100293
1. Utica Normal and Industrial Institute, Utica Institute, Miss. I. Title. BIP

HOLTZCLAW, William 378'.00924 B
Henry, 1870?-
The Black man's burden, by William H. Holtzclaw. With an introd. by Booker T. Washington. New York, Haskell House, 1971. 232 p. illus., ports. 23 cm. Reprint of the 1915 ed. [E185.97.H75 1970b] 70-154044 ISBN 0-8383-1277-2
1. Utica Normal and Industrial Institute, Utica Institute, Miss. I. Title.

Utley, Freda,

UTLEY, Freda, 1898- 335'.14'0924
Odyssey of a liberal; memoirs. Washington, Washington National Press [1970] vi, 319 p. 25 cm. Includes bibliographical references. [D15.U84A3] 68-8695 10.00
I. Title.

Utrillo, Maurice, 1883-1955.

COUGHLAN, Robert, 1914- 927.5
The wine of genius; a life of Maurice Utrillo. [1st ed.] New York, Harper [1951] 112 p. illus. 22 cm. [ND553.U7C64] 51-11895
1. Utrillo, Maurice, 1883-1955. I. Title.

DE POLNAY, Peter, 1906- 759.4 B
Enfant terrible; the life and world of Maurice Utrillo. [Rev. ed.] New York, Morrow, 1969. 249 p. illus., ports. 22 cm. First ed. published in 1967 under title: The world of Maurice Utrillo. Bibliography: p. [231]-232. [ND553.U7D4 1969] 73-79726 5.95
1. Utrillo, Maurice, 1883-1955. I. Title.

UTRILLO, Maurice, 1883- 927.5
1955.
Utrillo. [Text by Alfred Werner. New York, H. N. Abrams, 1953] 6 p. illus. 16 col. plates (incl. cover) 39 cm. (An Abrams art book) Cover title. "Collectors edition" - Copyright application. Published in 1962 under title: Maurice Utrillo. [ND553.U7W47 1953] 759.4 53-4264
I. Werner, Alfred, 1911-

Utter, Charles H., b. 1838.

SPRING, Agnes 917.8'03'20924 B
(Wright) 1894-
Colorado Charley, Wild Bill's pard. Boulder, Colo., Pruett Press, 1968. xvi, 144 p. illus. 23 cm. Bibliography: p. [129]-136. [F594.U8S6] 68-21780 6.50
1. Utter, Charles H., b. 1838. 2. Hickok, James Butler, 1837-1876. I. Title.

Uyesugi, Ruth Farlow.

UYESUGI, Ruth Farlow. 977.2'27 B
Don't cry, Chiisai, don't cry / Ruth Farlow Uyesugi. Paoli, Ind. : Stout's Print Shop, c1977. 149 p. ; 21 cm. [F534.P36U937] 77-151220
1. Uyesugi, Ruth Farlow. 2. Paoli, Ind.—Biography. 3. Japanese Americans—Indiana—Paoli—Biogrphy. 4. Interracial marriage—United States. I. Title.

Vazquez de Coronado, Francisco, 1510-1549.

DAY, Arthur Grove, 979.1'0924 B
1904-
Coronado and the discovery of the Southwest, by A. Grove Day. [1st ed.] New York, Meredith Press [1967] ix, 191 p. illus., maps, ports. 22 cm. [E125.V3D27] 67-20858
1. Vazquez de Coronado, Francisco, 1510-1549. 2. Southwest, New—History. I. Title.

Vazquez de Coronado, Francisco, 1510-1549—Juvenile literature.

GRANT, Matthew G. 973.1'6'0924 B
Coronado; explorer of the Southwest [by] Matthew G. Grant. Illustrated by Harold Henriksen. [Mankato, Minn., Creative Education; distributed by Childrens Press, Chicago, 1974] 26 p. illus. (part col.) 25 cm. (His Gallery of great Americans series. Explorers of America) A brief biography of the Spanish explorers who led an expedition into the American Southwest in search of Gran Quivira and the seven cities of Cibola. [E125.V3G72] 92 73-13957 ISBN 0-87191-285-6 3.95
1. Vazquez de Coronado, Francisco, 1510-1549—Juvenile literature. I. Henriksen, Harold, illus. II. Title.

JENSEN, Malcolm 979.1'01'0924 B
C.
Francisco Coronado [by] Malcolm C. Jensen. Illustrated with prints, maps, and photos. New York, Watts, 1974. 58 p. illus. 26 cm. (A Visual biography) Bibliography: p. 56. A biography of the Spanish explorer who in two years traveled over four thousand miles through the Southwest and Great Plains yet failed to find what he was searching for. [E125.V3J46] 92 73-12087 ISBN 0-531-00973-4 4.95
1. Vazquez de Coronado, Francisco, 1510-1549—Juvenile literature. I. Title. BIP

Velez de Escalante, Silvestre, fl. 1768-1779.

VELEZ de Escalante, 917.8
Silvestre, fl.1768-1779.
The Dominguez-Escalante journal : their expedition through Colorado, Utah, Arizona, and New Mexico in 1776 / translated by Angelico Chavez ; edited by Ted J. Warner. Provo, Utah : Brigham Young University Press, c1976. xix, 203 p. : ill. ; 28 cm. English and Spanish. Bibliography: p. 201-203. [F799.V4413 1976] 76-44561 ISBN 0-8425-0037-5 : 12.95
1. Escalante-Dominguez Expedition, 1776—Personal narratives. 2. Velez de Escalante, Silvestre, fl. 1768-1779. 3. Dominguez, Francisco Atanasio, fl. 1776. 4. Explorers—Spain—Biography. I. Title.

V-2 rocket.

HUZEL, Dieter K 926.23
Peenemunde to Canaveral, With an introd. by Werner von Braun. Englewood Cliffs, Prentice-Hall [1962] 247p. illus. 22cm. Autobiographical. [UG635.G3H8] 62-14015
1. V-2 rocket. 2. World War, 1939-1945—Personal narratives, German. 3. Rocketry—Hist. I. Title.

HUZEL, Dieter K. 926.23
Peenmunde to Canaveral. Introd. by Werner von Braun. Englewood Cliffs, Prentice [c.1962] 247p. illus. 22cm. 62-14015 4.95
1. V-2 rocket. 2. World War, 1939-1945—Personal narratives, German. 3. Rocketry—Hist. I. Title.

Vadim, Roger.

VADIM, Roger. 791.43'0233'0924 B
Memoirs of the devil / [by] Roger Vadim ; translated [from the French] by Peter Beglan. London : Hutchinson, 1976. 192 p., [16] p. of plates : ports. ; 23 cm. Autobiographical. Translation of Memoires du diable. Includes index. [PN1998.A3V2913 1976] 77-472245 ISBN 0-09-127670-5 : £3.95
1. Vadim, Roger. 2. Moving-picture producers and directors—France—Biography. I. Title. BIP

VADIM, Roger. 791.43'0233'0924 B
Memoirs of the Devil / Roger Vadim ; translated by Peter Beglan. 1st American ed. New York : Harcourt Brace Jovanovich, 1977, c1976. 187 p., [8] leaves of plates : ill. ; 22 cm. Translation of Memoires du diable. Autobiographical. Translation of Memoires du diable. [PN1998.A3V2913 1977] 76-27428 ISBN 0-15-111906-6 : 7.95
1. Vadim, Roger. 2. Moving-picture producers and directors—France—Biography. I. Title.

Vajda, Albert, 1919- —Biography.

VAJDA, Albert, 894'.511'33 B
1919-
Lend me an eye / Albert Vajda. New York : St. Martin's Press, 1975, c1974. 173 p. ; 23 cm. [PH3351.V18Z52 1975] 74-33914 7.95
1. Vajda, Albert, 1919- —Biography. I. Title. BIP

Vajiranana Varoros, Prince, Supreme Patriarch, 1859-1921.

VAJIRANANA 294.3'657'0924 B
Varoros, Prince, Supreme Patriarch, 1859-1921.
Autobiography, the life of Prince-Patriarch Vajirana of Siam, 1860-1921 / Prince Vajiranana-varorasa ; translated, edited, and introduced by Craig J. Reynolds. Athens : Ohio University Press, 1979. p. cm. (Southeast Asia translation series ; 3) [BQ994.A447A3513] 79-9725 ISBN 0-8214-0376-1 : 12.00
1. Vajiranana Varoros, Prince, Supreme Patriarch, 1859-1921. 2. Priests, Buddhist—Thailand—Biography. 3. Thailand—Princes and princesses—Biography. I. Reynolds, Craig J. II. Title. III. Series.

VAJIRANANA 294.3'657'0924 B
Varoros, Prince, Supreme Patriarch, 1859-1921.
Autobiography, the life of Prince-Patriarch Vajiranana of Siam, 1860-1921 / Prince Vajiranana-varorasa ; translated, edited, and introduced by Craig J. Reynolds. Athens : Ohio University Press, 1979. p. cm. (Southeast Asia translation series ; 3) [BQ994.A447A3513] 79-9725 ISBN 0-8214-0376-1 : 12.00 12.00 ISBN 0-8214-0408-3 (pbk.)
1. Vajiranana Varoros, Prince, Supreme Patriarch, 1859-1921. 2. Priests, Buddhist—Thailand—Biography. 3. Thailand—Princes and princesses—Biography. I. Reynolds, Craig J. II. Title. III. Series.

Valadon, Suzanne, 1865-1938.

STORM, John. 927.5
The Valadon drama; the life of Suzanne Valadon. [1st ed.] New York, Dutton, 1958. 271 p. illus. 22 cm. [ND553.V3S78] 58-9605
1. Valadon, Suzanne, 1865-1938. I. Title.

Valdes, Juan de, d. 1541.

LONGHURST, John Edward, 922.246
1918-
Erasmus and the Spanish Inquisition: the case of Juan de Valdes. Albuquerque, University of New Mexico Press, 1950. 114 p. 23 cm. (University of New Mexico publications in history. no. 1) Issued also as thesis, University of Michican, in microfilm form. Bibliography: p. 97-114. [BR350.V34L6 1950] 50-63470
1. Valdes, Juan de, d. 1541. 2. Erasmus, Desiderius, d. 1536. 3. Inquisition. Spain. I. Title. II. Series: New Mexico. University. University of New Mexico publications in history, no.1

Valdes Leal, Juan de, 1622-1690.

TRAPIER, Elizabeth [759.6] 927.5
Du Gue, 1893-
Valdes Leal, baroque concept of death and suffering in his paintings. New York, Hispanic Society of America, 1956. 49 p. illus. 23 cm. (Hispanic notes & monographs; essays, studies, and brief biographies) [ND813.V2T7] 56-14473
1. Valdes Leal, Juan de, 1622-1690. 2. Painting, Baroque. 3. Death — Art. I. Title.

Valdivia, Pedro de, 1500?-1554?

GRAHAM, Robert 983'.02'0924 B
Bontine Cunninghame, 1852-1936.
Pedro de Valdivia, conqueror of Chile. Boston, Milford House [1973] xiii, 227 p. port. 22 cm. Reprint of the 1926 ed. published by W. Heinemann, London. [F3091.V15 1973] 73-4895 ISBN 0-87821-134-9 25.00
1. Valdivia, Pedro de, 1500?-1554? 2. Chile—History—To 1565.

GRAHAM, Robert 983'.02'0924 B
Bontine Cunninghame, 1852-1936.
Pedro de Valdivia, conqueror of Chile. Westport, Conn., Greenwood Press [1974] xiii, 227 p. illus. 22 cm. Reprint of the 1926 ed. published by W. Heinemann, London. Includes bibliographical references. [F3091.V15 1974] 74-3619 ISBN 0-8371-7454-6
1. Valdivia, Pedro de, 1500?-1554? 2. Chile—History—To 1565. BIP

GRAHAM, Robert 983'.02'0924 B
Bontine Cunninghame, 1852-1936.
Pedro de Valdivia, conqueror of Chile. Westport, Conn., Greenwood Press [1974] xiii, 227 p. illus. 22 cm. Reprint of the 1926 ed. published by W. Heinemann, London. Includes bibliographical references. [F3091.V15 1974] 74-3619 ISBN 0-8371-7454-6 12.50
1. Valdivia, Pedro de, 1500?-1554? 2. Chile—History—To 1565.

GRAHAM, Robert 983'.02'0924 B
Bontine Cunninghame, 1852-1936.
Pedro de Valdivia, conqueror of Chile / by R. B. Cunninghame Graham. Boston : Longwood Press, 1977. p. cm. Reprint of the 1926 ed. published by W. Heinemann, London. Includes bibliographical references. [F3091.V144G7 1977] 77-88575 ISBN 0-89341-281-3 lib.bdg. : 25.00
1. Valdivia, Pedro de, 1500?-1554? 2. Chile—History—To 1565. 3. Chile—Governors—Biography. 4. Explorers—Chile—Biography. I. Title.

Vale, Roy Ewing, 1885-1959.

KISSINGER, Dorothy 285'.2'0924
May (Vale) 1916-
Say a good word; a biography of the Reverend Roy Ewing Vale, D. D., LL. D., moderator of the 156th General Assembly of the Presbyterian Church, U.S.A. [Mesa? Ariz., 1963] 243 p. port. 24 cm. [BX9225.V28K5] 63-25797
1. Vale, Roy Ewing, 1885-1959. I. Title.

Valentiner, Wilhelm Reinhold, 1880-1958.

STERNE, Margaret 069'.9'70924 B
Heiden, 1902-
The passionate eye : the life of William R. Valentiner / by Margaret Sterne. Detroit : Wayne State University Press, 1980. p. cm. Includes index. "Chronology and selected bibliography": p. [N560.V34S73] 79-24961 ISBN 0-8143-1631-X : 19.95
1. Valentiner, Wilhelm Reinhold, 1880-1958. 2. Detroit. Museum of Art. 3. Museum directors—United States—Biography. I. Title. BIP

Valentines, Va.—History.

WRIGHT, William 975.5'575
Robertson, 1930-
The Valentines, Virginia community / William R. Wright. [s.l. : s.n., c1976] 87 leaves : ill. ; 29 cm. [F234.V34W74] 76-29813
1. Valentines, Va.—History. 2. Valentines, Va.—Genealogy. 3. Valentines, Va.—Biography. I. Title.

Valentino, Rudolph, 1895-1926.

*BOTHAM, Noel. 791'.43'028'0924
Valentino : the love god / Noel Botham & Peter Donnelly. New York : Ace Books, 1977. 245p. : photos. ; 18 cm. (An Ace Book) [PN2287] ISBN 0-441-85906-2 pbk. : 1.95
1. Valentino, Rudolph, 1895-1926. I. Donnelly, Peter, joint author. II. Title. BIP

*MACKENZIE, 791'.43'028'0924
Norman A.
The magic of Rudolph Valentino [by] Norman A. MacKenzie. With a foreword by S. George Ullman. London, Research Pub. [1974] 210 p. illus. 23 cm. [PN2287] 0-7050
1. Valentino, Rudolph, 1895-1926 I. Title.
Distributed by International Publications Service, N.Y., for 10.00

OBERFIRST, Robert. 927.92
Rudolph Valentino : The man behind the myth / by Robert Oberfirst. New York : Berkley Pub. Corp., 1977,c19622. 252,[28] p. : ill. ; 18 cm. (A Berkley Medallion Book) [PN2287.V3O25] ISBN 0-425-03458-5 pbk. : 1.95
1. Valentino, Rudolph, 1895-1926. I. Title.
L.C. card for 1962 Citadel Press ed.:62-21008

OBERFIRST, Robert. 927.92
Rudolph Valentino, the man behind the myth. [1st ed.] New York, Citadel Press [1962] 320 p. illus. 22 cm. [PN2287.V3O25] 62-21008
1. Valentino, Rudolph, 1895-1926.

SCAGNETTI, 791.43'028'0924 B
Jack.
The intimate life of Rudolph Valentino / by Jack Scagnetti. Middle Village, N.Y. : Jonathan David Publishers, [1975] p. cm. [PN2287.V3S3] 74-31270 ISBN 0-8246-0197-1 : 12.95
1. Valentino, Rudolph, 1895-1926. I. Title. BIP

SHULMAN, Irving. 791.43'0924 B
Valentino. New York, Trident Press, 1967. xii, 499 p. illus., ports. 22 cm. [PN2287.V3S5] 66-12335
1. Valentino, Rudolph, 1895-1926. I. Title.

SHULMAN, Irving. 791.43'0924
Valentino. New York, Pocket Bks. [1968,c. 1967] x, 404p. illus. ports. 18cm. (77026) [PN2287.V3S5] (B) .95 pap.,
1. Valentino, Rudolph, 1895-1926. I. Title. BIP

*STEIGER, Brad. 791.43'0233'0924
Valentino. [New York] Manor Books [1975, c1966] 192 p. 18 cm. [PN1998] 1.50 (pbk.)
1. Valentino, Rudolf. I. Mank, Chaw joint author II. Title. BIP

WALKER, 791.43'028'0924 B
Alexander, film critic.
Rudolph Valentino / Alexander Walker. New York : Stein and Day, [1976] p. cm. [PN2287.V3W3 1976] 76-15174 ISBN 0-8128-2098-3 : 10.00
1. Valentino, Rudolph, 1895-1926. BIP

WALKER, 791.43'028'0924 B
Alexander, film critic.
Rudolph Valentino / by Alexander Walker. London : Elm Tree Books, 1976. 127 p. : ill., ports. ; 25 cm. Includes index. Bibliography: p. 124. [PN2287.V3W3 1976b] 76-376720 ISBN 0-241-89349-6 : £2.75
1. Valentino, Rudolph, 1895-1926. 2. Moving-picture actors and actresses—United States—Biography.

WALKER, 791.43'028'0924 B
Alexander, film critic.
Rudolph Valentino / Alexander Walker. Harmondsworth, Eng. ; New York : Penguin Books, 1977, c1976. 127 p. : ill. ; 23 cm. Includes index. Filmography: p. 121-123. [PN2287.V3W3 1977] 77-6460 ISBN 0-14-003615-6 pbk. : 2.95
1. Valentine, Rudolph, 1895-1926. 2. Moving-picture actors and actresses—United States—Biography.

Valery, Paul, 1871-1945.

MACKAY, Agnes Ethel. 841.912
The universal self; a study of Paul Valery. Toronto, University of Toronto Press [1961] 263p. illus. 23cm. Includes bibliography. [PQ2643.A26Z715] 61-65142
1. Valery, Paul, 1871-1945. I. Title.

WHITING, Charles G v. 12
Valery, jeune poete. [1 ed.] New Haven, Yale University Press, 1960. 154 p. 23 cm. At head of title: Institut d'etudes francaises de Yale University. [PZ2643.A26Z9] 60-50663
1. Valery, Paul, 1871-1945. I. Whiting, Charles G II. Title.

Valie, Jose Cecillo del, 1776-1834.

BUMGARTNER, Louis E. 923.2728
Jose del Valle of Central America. Durham, N.C., Duke University Press, 1963. 302 p. illus. 25 cm. Includes bibliography. [F1438.V175B8] 63-9007
1. Valie, Jose Cecillo del, 1776-1834. I. Title. BIP

Valla, Alene

VALLA, Alene 920.7
The secret diary of Lady Takayama. [dist. Los Angeles , Perkins Oriental Books, c.1961] 49p. illus., plates (part col.) 26cm. 7.50 lim. signed ed., bds.,
I. Title. II. Title: Lady Takayama, Secret diary of.

Valle-Inclan, Ramon del. 1870-1936—Bibl.

RUBIA BARCIA, Jose 016.86081
A biobibliography and iconography of Valle Inclan, 1866-1936. Berkeley, University of California Press, 1960. vii, 101p. illus., ports., facsims. 24cm. (University of California publications in modern philology, v. 59) 60-64047 2.00 pap.,
1. Valle-Inclan, Ramon del. 1870-1936—Bibl. 2. Valle-Inclan, Ramon del, 1870-1936—Portarits, caricatures, etc. I. Title. II. Series: California. University. University of California publications in modern philogy, v. 59

Valle, Jose Cecillo del. 1776-1834.

BUMGARTNER, Louis E. 923.2728
Jose del Valle of Central America. Durham, N. C., Duke [c.]1963. 302p. illus. 25cm. Bibl. 63-9007 8.75
1. Valle, Jose Cecillo del. 1776-1834. I. Title.

Valle, Juan del, Bp. of Popayan, fl. 1548-1560.

FRIEDE, Juan. 922.244
Vida y luchas de don Juan del Valle, primer obispo de Popayan y protector de indios estudio documental basado en investigaciones realizadas en los archivos de Colombia, Espana y el Vaticanno. Prologo del Dr. D. Manuel Gimenez Fernandez. Popayan [Colombia, Editorial Universidad] 1961. 270 p. 25 cm. Bibliographical references included in "Notas." [BX4705.V28F72] 63-39092
1. Valle, Juan del, Bp. of Popayan, fl. 1548-1560. I. Title.

Vallee, Rudy, 1901—

VALLEE, Rudy, 1901- 784'.092'4 B
Let the chips fall / Rudy Vallee. Harrisburg, Pa. : Stackpole Books, [1975] 320 p. : ill. ; 25 cm. Includes index. [ML419.V2A28] 75-17629 ISBN 0-8117-0947-7 : 8.95
1. Vallee, Rudy, 1901- 2. Musicians—Correspondence, reminiscences, etc. I. Title.

Valle y Caviedes, Juan del, 1652-1692.

KOLB, Glen L. 861.3
Juan del Valle y Caviedes; a study of the life, times, and poetry of a Spanish colonial satirist. New London, Connecticut College, [c.] 1959 viii, 68p. Bibliography: p.62-68. 24cm. (Connecticut College monograph no. 7) 59-14760 3.00; 2.00 bds., pap.,
1. Valle y Caviedes, Juan del, 1652-1692. I. Title. II. Series: Connecticut College for Women(New London. Connecticut College monograph no. 7

Vampatella, Philip Victor, 1940-

SULLIVAN, George 358.430924
Edward, 1927-
Philip Vampatella, fighter pilot; the complete life story of a college dropout who became one of the first aircraft carrier pilots to fly over Vietnam. New York, Nelson [c.1966] 127p. illus., ports. 22cm. (Champion bks. Rutledge bk.) [TL540.V32S9] 66-15985 2.95
1. Vampatella, Philip Victor, 1940- I. Title.

SULLIVAN, George, 358.430924
1927-
Philip Vampatella, fighter pilot; the complete life story of a college dropout who became one of the first aircraft carrier pilots to fly over Vietnam, by George Sullivan. Edinburgh, New York, T. Nelson [1966] 127 p. illus., ports. 22 cm. (Champion books) "A Rutledge book." [TL540.V32S9] 66-15985
1. Vampatella, Philip Victor, 1940- I. Title.

Van Alstyne, Frances Jane Crosby, 1820-1915.

LOVELAND, John. 811'.4 B
Blessed assurance : the life and hymns of Fanny J. Crosby / John Loveland. Nashville : Broadman Press, c1978. 223 p. : ill. ; 21 cm. Bibliography: p. 220-222. [PS3114.V43Z73] 77-78622 ISBN 0-8054-7220-7 pbk. : 3.95
1. Van Alstyne, Frances Jane Crosby, 1820-1915. 2. Poets, American—19th century—Biography. 3. Hymn writers—United States—Biography. 4. Methodists in the United States—Biography. I. Title. BIP

MILLER, Basil William, 928.1
1897-
Fanny Crosby: Singing I go. Grand Rapids, Zondervan Pub. House [1950] 119 p. 20 cm. [PS3114.V43Z74] 51-589
1. Van Alstyne, Frances Jane (Crosby) 1820-1915. I. Title.

Van Alstyne, Frances Jane Crosby, 1820-1915—Biography.

RUFFIN, Bernard, 1947- 811'.4 B
Fanny Crosby / by Bernard Ruffin. [Philadelphia] : United Church Press, c1976. 257 p. ; 22 cm. "A Pilgrim Press book." Includes bibliographical references. [PS3114.V43Z84] 75-45273 ISBN 0-8298-0290-8 8.00
1. Van Alstyne, Frances Jane Crosby, 1820-1915—Biography. I. Title. BIP

Van Anda, Carr Vattel, 1864-1945.

FINE, Barnett. 070'.924 B
A giant of the press: Carr Van Anda. With an epilogue by Robert W. Desmond. Oakland, Calif., Acme Books, 1968 [c1933] 104 p. illus., facsims., ports. 23 cm. Bibliography: p. 95-96. [PN4874.V26F5 1968] 68-55349 3.95
1. Van Anda, Carr Vattel, 1864-1945. 2. New York times. I. Title.

Van Arsdale, Tom, 1943-

VAN ARSDALE, Tom 796.32'3'0922
1943-
Our basketball lives, by Tom and Dick Van Arsdale, with Joel H. Cohen. New York, Putnam [1972, c1973] 223 p. 21 cm. (Putnam sports shelf) [GV884.V36A36 1973] 72-76738 ISBN 0-399-20305-2 4.89
1. Van Arsdale, Tom, 1943- 2. Van Arsdale, Dick, 1943- 3. Basketball—United States. I. Van Arsdale, Dick, 1943- joint author. II. Cohen, Joel H., joint author. III. Title. BIP

Van Briggle, Artus, 1869-1904.

BOGUE, Dorothy McGraw. 738.3'0924
The Van Briggle story. [Colorado Springs, Printed by Dentan-Berkeland Print. Co.] 1968. 53 p. illus., ports. 22 cm. Bibliography: p. 50-52. [NK4210.V35B6] 68-56344 2.00
1. Van Briggle, Artus, 1869-1904. I. Title.

Van Buren, Martin, Pres. U.S., 1782-1862.

ALEXANDER, Holmes 973.5'7'0924 B
Moss, 1906-
The American Talleyrand; the career and contemporaries of Martin Van Buren, eighth President, by Holmes Alexander. New York, Russell & Russell [1968, c1962] 430 p. illus., coat of arms, facsims., ports. 23 cm. Bibliography: p. 424-430. [E387.A55 1968] 68-10899
1. Van Buren, Martin, Pres. U.S., 1782-1862. 2. United States—Politics and government—1815-1861. I. Title. BIP

LYNCH, Denis 973.5'7'0924 B
Tilden.
An epoch and a man; Martin Van Buren and his times. Port Washington, N.Y., Kennikat Press [1971, c1929] 2 v. (566 p.) illus., ports. 23 cm. (Kennikat Press scholarly reprints. Series in American history and culture in the nineteenth century) Bibliography: p. 547-551. [E387.L98 1971] 73-137920 ISBN 0-8046-1485-7
1. Van Buren, Martin, Pres. U.S., 1782-1862. I. Title. BIP

SHEPARD, Edward 973.5'7'0924 B
Morse, 1850-1911.
Martin Van Buren. Boston, Houghton, Mifflin. [New York, AMS Press, 1972] (American statesmen, v. 18) Reprint of the 1899 ed. [E387.S59] 76-128964 ISBN 0-404-50868-5
1. Van Buren, Martin, Pres. U.S., 1782-1862. I. Title. II. Series. BIP

VAN BUREN, Martin, 973.5'7'0924 B
Pres. U.S., 1782-1862.
The autobiography of Martin Van Buren. Edited by John C. Fitzpatrick. New York, A. M. Kelley, 1969. 808 p. 24 cm. (Reprints of economic classics) "First published 1920." Bibliographical footnotes. [E387.V2 1969] 68-58656 ISBN 0-678-00531-1
1. Van Buren, Martin, Pres. U.S., 1782-1862. I. Fitzpatrick, John Clement, 1876-1940, ed. II. Title.

VAN BUREN, Martin, 973.5'7'0924 B
Pres. U.S., 1782-1862
The autobiography of Martin Van Buren. Edited by John C. Fitzpatrick. New York, Da Capo Press, 1973. 2 v. (808 p.) 23 cm. (The American scene: comments and commentators) Reprint of the 1920 ed., which was issued as v. 2 of the Annual report of the American Historical Association for the year 1918. Includes bibliographical references. [E387.A32 1973] 72-75314 ISBN 0-306-71275-X 35.00 (Lib. ed.)
1. Van Buren, Martin, Pres. U.S., 1782-1862. I. Fitzpatrick, John Clement, 1876-1940, ed. II. Series: American Historical Association. Annual report, 1918, v. 2.

VAN BUREN, Martin, Pres. U.S. 1782-1862. 973.5'7'0924
Martin Van Buren, 1782-1862; chronology, documents, bibliographical aids. Edited by Irving J. Sloan. Dobbs Ferry, N.Y., Oceana Publications, 1969. 116 p. 24 cm. (Oceana presidential chronology series, 7) Bibliography: p. 109-113. [E386.S55] 69-15391 4.00
1. United States—History—1815-1861—Sources. I. Sloan, Irving J., ed. II. United States. President, 1837-1841 (Van Buren) BIP

Van Buren, Martin, Pres. U.S., 1782-1862—Juvenile literature.

HOYT, Edwin Palmer 923.173
Martin Van Buren. Chicago, Reilly & Lee [c.]1964. 141p. port. 21cm. Bibl. 64-14604 3.95
1. Van Buren, Martin, Pres. U.S., 1782-1862—Juvenile literature. I. Title.

Van Campen, Moses, 1757-1849.

HUBBARD, John Niles, 1815-1897. 973.04'97 S
Sketches of the life and adventures of Moses Van Campen / John Niles Hubbard. New York : Garland Pub., 1977. 310 p. ; 19 cm. (The Garland library of narratives of North American Indian captivities ; v. 13) Reprint of the 1841 ed. printed by G. W. Stevens, Dansville, N.Y. under title: Sketches of the life and adventures of Moses Van Campen, a surviving officer of the Army of the Revolution. Issued with the reprint of the 1780? ed. of Van Campen, M. A narrative of the capture of certain Americans. New York, 1977. [E85.G2 vol. 13] [E275.V22] 973.3'8 B 75-7033 ISBN 0-8240-1637-8 : 25.00
1. Van Campen, Moses, 1757-1849. 2. United States. Army. Continental Army—Biography. 3. United States—History—Revolution, 1775-1783—Personal narratives. 4. Soldiers—United States—Biography. 5. Indians of North America—Captivities. I. Title. II. Series.

Van Cleef, Frank Chapman, 1881-

VAN CLEEF, Frank Chapman, 1881- 977.1'23'040924 B
Ninety-nine bottles : recollections and episodes since 1896 originating in Lorain County, Ohio / by Frank Chapman Van Cleef. Oberlin, Ohio : Oberlin Historical and Improvement Organization, 1976. 110 p. : ill. ; 23 cm. [CT275.V217A36] 75-330105 6.75
1. Van Cleef, Frank Chapman, 1881- I. Title.

Van Cleef, Monique.

*VAN CLEEF, Monique. 301.41'5
The house of pain: the strange world of Monique van Cleef, the queen of humiliation; an autobiography and a message to all human slaves by Monique van Cleef with William Waterman. New York, Bantam, [1975] 289 p. 18 cm. [HQ79] 1.95 (pbk.)
1. Van Cleef, Monique. 2. Sexual perversion. 3. Sadism. I. Title.

Van Cortlandt family.

CORRESPONDENCE of the Van Cortlandt family of Cortlandt Manor, 1800-1814 / edited by Jacob Judd. Tarrytown, N.Y. : Sleepy Hollow Restorations, c1978. lii, 778 p. : port. ; 22 cm. (The Van Cortlandt family papers ; v. 3) Includes bibliographical references and index. [CS71.V22175 1976, vol. 3] 929'.2'0973 78-16849 ISBN 0-912882-34-4 : 22.00 929'.2'0973 S
1. Van Cortlandt family. 2. Van Cortlandt, Philip, 1749-1831. 3. Van Cortlandt, Pierre, 1762-1848. I. Judd, Jacob, 1929- II. Title. III. Series. BIP

Van Cortlandt, Philip, 1749-1831.

CORRESPONDENCE of the Van Cortlandt family of Cortlandt Manor, 1748-1800 / compiled and edited by Jacob Judd. Tarrytown, N.Y. : Sleepy Hollow Restorations, c1977. lxi, 675 p. : ill. ; 22 cm. (Van Cortlandt family papers ; v. 2) Includes index. Bibliography: p. 625-652. [CS71.V22175 1976 vol. 2] [F123] 929'.2'0973 77-3281 ISBN 0-912882-29-8 : 19.00 929'.2'0973 S
1. Van Cortlandt, Pierre, 1721-1814. 2. Van Cortlandt, Philip, 1749-1831. 3. Van Cortlandt family. 4. New York (State)—Biography. I. Judd, Jacob, 1929- II. Series.

CORRESPONDENCE of the Van Cortlandt family of Cortlandt Manor, 1800-1814 / edited by Jacob Judd. Tarrytown, N.Y. : Sleepy Hollow Restorations, c1978. lii, 778 p. : port. ; 22 cm. (The Van Cortlandt family papers ; v. 3) Includes bibliographical references and index. [CS71.V22175 1976, vol. 3] 929'.2'0973 78-16849 ISBN 0-912882-34-4 : 22.00 929'.2'0973 S
1. Van Cortlandt family. 2. Van Cortlandt, Philip, 1749-1831. 3. Van Cortlandt, Pierre, 1762-1848. I. Judd, Jacob, 1929- II. Title. III. Series. BIP

Van Cortlandt, Pierre, 1721-1814.

CORRESPONDENCE of the Van Cortlandt family of Cortlandt Manor, 1748-1800 / compiled and edited by Jacob Judd. Tarrytown, N.Y. : Sleepy Hollow Restorations, c1977. lxi, 675 p. : ill. ; 22 cm. (Van Cortlandt family papers ; v. 2) Includes index. Bibliography: p. 625-652. [CS71.V22175 1976 vol. 2] [F123] 929'.2'0973 77-3281 ISBN 0-912882-29-8 : 19.00 929'.2'0973 S
1. Van Cortlandt, Pierre, 1721-1814. 2. Van Cortlandt, Philip, 1749-1831. 3. Van Cortlandt family. 4. New York (State)—Biography. I. Judd, Jacob, 1929- II. Series.

Van Court, Catharine.

VAN COURT, Catharine. 917.6226
The old house. Richmond, Dietz Press, 1950. xii, 137 p. illus. 24 cm. Autobiographical. [CT275.V22A3] 50-3756
I. Title.

Van De Linde, Gerard, 1840—

VAN DE LINDE, Gerard, 1840- 657'.092'4 B
Reminiscences / Gerard Van De Linde. New York : Arno Press, 1978. 434 p., [1] leaf of plates : port. ; 21 cm. (The Development of contemporary accounting thought) Reprint of the 1917 ed. published by Gee & Co., London. [HF5616.G7V36 1978] 77-87290 ISBN 0-405-10917-2 : 25.00
1. Van De Linde, Gerard, 1840- 2. Accounting—Great Britain—History. 3. Accountants—Great Britain—Biography. I. Title. II. Series.

Van Dellen, Idzerd.

VAN DELLEN, Idzerd. 922.573
In God's crucible, an autobiography. Grand Rapids, Baker Book House, 1950 134 p. 22 cm. [BX6843.V3A3] 50-37398
I. Title.

Van der Hurk, Pieter, 1911-

BROWNING, Norma Lee. 133.9'3'0924
Peter Hurkos : I have many lives / Norma Lee Browning. 1st ed. Garden City, N.Y. : Doubleday, 1976. 223 p. ; 22 cm. [BF1027.V3B69] 75-21213 ISBN 0-385-01508-9 : 6.95
1. Van der Hurk, Pieter, 1911- I. Title.

VAN DER HURK, Pieter, 1911- 920.91338
Psychic; the story of Peter Hurkos by Peter Hurkos [pseud.] Indianapolis, Bobbs-Merrill, [1961] 224 p. 22 cm. [BF1027.V3A3] 61-15545
I. Title.

[VAN DER HURK, Pieter] 1911- 920.91338
Psychic; the story of Peter Hurkos, by Peter Hurkos [pseud.] New York, Popular Lib. [1966, c.1961] 160p. 18cm. (60-2118) [BF1027.V3A3] .60 pap.,
I. Title.

Van der Kemp, Francis Adrian(1752-1829.

JACKSON, Harry F. 923
Scholar in the wilderness: Francis Adrian Van der Kemp. [Syracuse, N.Y.] Syracuse Univ. Pr. [c.]1963. xi, 356p. illus., ports. 22cm. Bibl. 63-19192 6.95
1. Van der Kemp, Francis Adrian(1752-1829. I. Title. BIP

Van der Post, Laurens.

VAN DER POST, Laurens. 916.89'7'042
Venture to the interior. Westport, Conn., Greenwood Press [1973, c1951] 253 p. maps. 22 cm. Reprint of the 1964 printing published by Morrow, New York. [DT862.V3 1973] 73-13411 ISBN 0-8371-7058-3
1. Van der Post, Laurens. 2. Malawi—Discovery and exploration. I. Title. BIP

Van Der Rhoer, Edward.

VANDERRHER, Edward. 940.54'86
Deadly magic / by Edward Van Der Rhoer. New York : Scribner, [1978] p. cm. [D810.C88V36] 78-17120 ISBN 0-684-15873-6 : 9.95
1. Van Der Rhoer, Edward. 2. United States. Office of Naval Communications—Biography. 3. World War, 1939-1945—Cryptography. 4. World War, 1939-1945—Personal narratives, American. 5. Seamen—United States—Biography. 6. World War, 1939-1945—United States. 7. World War, 1939-1945—Pacific Ocean. I. Title. BIP

Van der Spuy, Kenneth Reid,

VAN DER SPUY, Kenneth Reid, 1892- 355.3'32'0924
Chasing the wind [Cape Town] Books of Africa. 1966. 261p. illus., ports. 24cm. Autobiographical. [U55.V27A3] 67-8093 5.60 bds.,
I. Title.

Van DerZee, James—Juvenile literature.

HASKINS, James, 1941- 770'.92'4 B
James Van DerZee, the picture-takin' man / by Jim Haskins ; illustrated with Van Der Zee photos. New York : Dodd, Mead, c1979. 256 p. : ill. ; 24 cm. Includes index. A biography of the black photographer who has received acclaim for his prints of Harlem. [TR140.V37H37] 92 78-22431 ISBN 0-396-07678-5 : 8.95
1. Van DerZee, James—Juvenile literature. 2. Afro-American photographers—New York (City)—Biography—Juvenile literature.

Van Doren, Carl Clinton, 1885-1950—Biography.

VAN DOREN, Carl Clinton, 1885-1950. 809 B
Three worlds / by Carl Van Doren. Westport, Conn. : Greenwood Press, [1977] c1936. p. cm. Autobiography. Reprint of the 1st ed. published by Harper, New York. Includes index. [PS3543.A555Z5 1977] 77-14329 ISBN 0-8371-9831-3 lib.bdg. : 19.50
1. Van Doren, Carl Clinton, 1885-1950—Biography. 2. Authors, American—20th century—Biography. I. Title. BIP

Van Doren, Mark,

VAN DOREN, Mark, 1894- 928.1
Autobiography. [1st ed.] New York, Harcourt, Brace [1958] 371 p. illus. 22 cm. [PS3543.A557Z52] 58-10897
I. Title.

VAN DOREN, Mark, 1894- 811.5'2 B
Autobiography. New York, Greenwood Press [1968, c1958] 371 p. ports. 23 cm. [PS3543.A557Z52 1968] 68-30829

Van Dorn, Earl, 1820-1863.

HARTJE, Robert 973.73'013'0924 (B)
Van Dorn, the life and times of a Confederate general [by] Robert G. Hartje. [Nashville] Vanderbilt Univ. Pr., 1967. xiii, 359p. maps. port. 25cm. Bibl. [E467.1V2H3] 67-16280 8.95
1. Van Dorn, Earl, 1820-1863. I. Title.

Van Dyke, Henry, 1852-1933—Journeys—Palestine.

†VAN DYKE, Henry, 1852-1933. 915.694'04'40924 B
Out-of-doors in the Holy Land / Henry Van Dyke. New York : Arno Press, 1977, [c1908]. xii, 325 p., [12] leaves of plates : ill. ; 21 cm. (America and the Holy Land) Reprint of the ed. published by Scribner, New York. [DS107.3.V3 1977] 77-70751 ISBN 0-405-10297-6 : 20.00
1. Van Dyke, Henry, 1852-1933—Journeys—Palestine. 2. Palestine—Description and travel. 3. Authors, American—20th century—Biography. I. Title. II. Series.

Van Dyke, Woodbridge Strong, 1889-1943.

CANNOM, Robert C. 791.43'0233'0924 B
Van Dyke and the mythical city, Hollywood / Robert C. Cannom. New York : Garland Pub., 1977, [c1948]. 424 p., [16] leaves of plates : ill. ; 23 cm. (The Garland classics of film literature) Reprint of the 1948 ed. published by Murray & Gee, Culver City, Calif. [PN1998.A3V33 1977] 76-52096 ISBN 0-8240-2870-8 lib.bdg. : 17.00
1. Van Dyke, Woodbridge Strong, 1889-1943. 2. Moving-picture producers and directors—United States—Biography. I. Title. II. Series. BIP

Van Ess, Dorothy.

VAN ESS, Dorothy. 266'.5'7320924 B
Pioneers in the Arab world, by Dorothy F. Van Ess. Grand Rapids, W. B. Eerdmans Pub. Co. [1974] 188 p. illus. 21 cm. (The Historical series of the Reformed Church in America, no. 3) Bibliography: p. 187-188. [BV2626.V36A36] 74-14964 ISBN 0-8028-1585-5
1. Van Ess, Dorothy. 2. Van Ess, John, 1879- 3. Missions to Muslims—Basra. I. Title. II. Series: Reformed Church in America. The historical series, no. 3. BIP

Van Gogh, Vincent Willem, 1853-1890.

BURRA, Peter 759.9492
Van Gogh [by] Peter Burra. New York, Coller [1962] 127p. 18cm. (AS65Y) .95 pap.,
1. Van Gogh, Vincent Willem, 1853-1890. I. Title.

Van Hise, Charles Richard, 1857-1918.

VANCE, Maurice M. 923.773
Charles Richard Van Hise; scientist progressive. Madison, State Historical Society of Wisconsin, 1960. 246 p. illus. 23 cm. [LD6125 1903.V3] 60-63390
1. Van Hise, Charles Richard, 1857-1918. I. Title.

Van Horne, Harriet.

VAN HORNE, Harriet. 070.4'092'4
Never go anywhere without a pencil. New York, Putnam [1972] 313 p. 22 cm. [AC8.V144] 72-81457 ISBN 0-399-11038-0 7.95
I. Title.

Van Lew, Elizabeth—Juvenile literature.

NOLAN, Jeanette (Covert), 1896- 973.78'5'0924 B
Yankee spy, Elizabeth Van Lew. New York, J. Messner [1970] 190 p. 22 cm.

Bibliography: p. 182-183. A biography of the Virginia-born woman who served as a Union spy in Richmond throughout the Civil War. [E608.V34N6 1970] 92 79-123170 3.50
1. Van Lew, Elizabeth—Juvenile literature. I. Title.

Van Loon, Hendrik Willem, 1882-1944.

VAN LOON, Gerard 907.2'024 B
Willem, 1911-
The story of Hendrik Willem van Loon. [1st ed.] Philadelphia, Lippincott [1972] xi, 399 p. illus. 24 cm. Bibliography: p. 377-379. [D15.V27V35] 74-37131 ISBN 0-397-00844-9 10.00
1. Van Loon, Hendrik Willem, 1882-1944.

Van Orman, Ward Tunte, 1894-1978.

VAN ORMAN, Ward 629.13'092'4 B
Tunte, 1894-1978.
The wizard of the winds / by Ward T. Van Orman ; as told to Robert Hull ; [pen sketches, Patrick A. Dwyer]. Saint Cloud, Minn. : North Star Press, c1978. xvi, 278 p., [1] leaf of plates : ill. ; 23 cm. [TL620.V28A36] 78-106446 ISBN 0-87839-032-4 : 12.00
1. Van Orman, Ward Tunte, 1894-1978. 2. Balloonists—United States—Biography. I. Hull, Robert Charlton. II. Title. BIP

Van Orsdel, William Wesley, 1848-1919.

LIND, Robert W 242'.4
From the ground up; the story of 'Brother Van,' Montant pioneer minister, 1848-1919. [n. p., Treasure State Pub. Co., 1961] 182p. illus. 20cm. Includes bibliography. [BX8495.V2L5] 61-59891
1. Van Orsdel, William Wesley, 1848-1919. I. Title.

Van Paassen, Pierre,

VAN PAASSEN, Pierre, 1895- 818.52
To number our days. New York, Scribner [1964] 404 p. ports. 24 cm. Autobiographical. [D413.V35A39] 64-13633
I. Title.

Van Raalte, Albertus Christiaan, 1811-1876.

SCHOOLLAND, Marian M 922.573
1902-
The story of Van Raalte, "a man strong and of good courage." Grand Rapids, W. B. Eerdmans Pub. Co., 1951. 144 p. illus. 20 cm. [F575.D9S37] 52-9305
1. Van Raalte, Albertus Christiaan, 1811-1876. 2. Dutch in Michigan. 3. Reformed Church in Michigan. I. Title.

Van Sweringen, Mantis James, 1881-1935.

HAMPTON, Taylor, 1910- 385'.092'4
The fabulous Van Sweringens; empire building, 1915-1935, by Virginia Taylor Hampton. Winter Park Fla., 1965. vii, 391 1 illus., facsims. 30 cm. Typescript (carbon copy) Bibliography: leaves 387-391. [HE2754.V25H3] 65-29792
1. Van Sweringen, Mantis James, 1881-1935. 2. Van Sweringen, Oris Paxton, 1870-1936. I. Title.

Van Til, Cornelius, 1895-

RUSHDOONY, Rousas John 922.473
Van Til. Philadelphia, Presbyterian and Reformed Pub. Co., 1960. 51p. (International library of philosophy and theology. Modern thinkers series) Bibl. 60-6805 1.25 pap.,
1. Van Til, Cornelius, 1895- I. Title.

RUSHDOONY, Rousas John. v. 12
Van Til. Grand Rapids, Mich., Baker Book House, 1960. 51 p. 23 cm. (International library of philosophy and theology. Modern thinkers series) Includes bibliography. 68-81200
1. Van Til, Cornelius, 1895- I. Title. BIP

WHITE, William, 285'.731'0924 B
1934-
Van Til, defender of the faith : an authorized biography / William White, Jr. Nashville : T. Nelson Publishers, c1979. 233 p., [4] leaves of plates : ill. ; 21 cm. Includes bibliographical references. [BX9225.V37W47] 79-9732 ISBN 0-8407-5670-4 pbk. : 4.95
1. Van Til, Cornelius, 1895- 2. Theologians—United States—Biography. I. Title.

Van Vechten, Carl, 1880-1964.

KELLNER, Bruce. 813'.5'2 B
Carl Van Vechten and the irreverent decades. [1st ed.] Norman, University of Oklahoma Press [1968] xxii, 354 p. illus., ports. 24 cm. Bibliography: p. 317-329. [PS3543.A653Z77] 68-15683
1. Van Vechten, Carl, 1880-1964.

LEUDERS, Edward G 1923- v. 12
Carl Van Vechten. New York, Twayne Publishers [1965] 158 p. (Twayne's United States authors series, 74) Includes bibliography and chronology. 66-86277
1. Van Vechten, Carl, 1880- I. Title. BIP

Van Vogt, Alfred Elton, 1912- — Biography.

VAN VOGT, Alfred 813'.5'4 B
Elton, 1912-
Reflections of A. E. Van Vogt : the autobiography of a science fiction giant : with a complete bibliography. 1st ed. Lakemont, Ga. : Fictioneer Books, 1975. 136 p. : ill. ; 21 cm. Bibliography: p. [123]-136. [PS3543.A6546Z52] 73-94037 3.50
1. Van Vogt, Alfred Elton, 1912- —Biography. 2. Van Vogt, Alfred Elton, 1912- —Bibliography. I. Title.

Van Waters, Miriam.

ROWLES, Burton J 923.5
The lady at Box 99; the story of Miriam Van Waters. Greenwich, Conn., Seabury Press [1962] 367p. 22cm. [HV9468.V25] 62-9151
1. Van Waters, Miriam. I. Title.

Van Zeller, Hubert,

VAN ZELLER, Hubert, 282.0924
1905-
One foot in the cradle; an autobiography. NewYork, Holt [1966, c.1965] xi, 282p. illus., ports. 22cm. [BX4705.V33A3 1966] 66-22064 5.95
I. Title.

Vanamee, Mary de Peyster Rutgers McCrea (Conger)

VANAMEE, Mary de Peyster 922.342
Rutgers McCrea (Conger)
Vanamee, by Mary Conger Vanamee (Mrs. Parker Vanamee) [Oxford, 1956] 176 p. 23 cm. [BX5995.V32V3] 59-46552
I. Vanamee, Parker. II. Title.

Vanamee, parker, d. 1918.

VANAMEE, v. 12
by Mary Conger Vanamee (Mrs. Parker Vanamee) [Oxford, Eng. riv. print. by Mrs. H. H, Gretton, 1956] 176p. 23cm. 'Reprinted for private circulation in 1956.' Imprint on lablc mounted on p. 2 of cover, label headed Calvary Episcopal church, Burnt Hills, N. Y. War letters of Parker Vanamee, p. 106-176.
1. Vanamee, parker, d. 1918. 2. European war, 1914- 1918—Personal narratives, American. I. Vanamee, Mary de Peyster Rutgers McCrea (Conger)

VANAMEE, Mary de Peyster 922.342
Rutgers McCrea (Conger)
Vanamee, by Mary Conger Vanamee (Mrs. Parker Vanamee) [Oxford, 1956] 176 p. 23 cm. [BX5995.V32V3] 59-46552
I. Vanamee, Parker. II. Title.

Vanauken, Sheldon.

VANAUKEN, Sheldon. 248'.2'0924 B
A severe mercy / by Sheldon Vanauken. 1st U.S. ed. San Francisco : Harper & Row, c1977. p. cm. Includes index. [BX5995.V33A35 1977] 77-6161 ISBN 0-06-068821-1 : 6.95
1. Vanauken, Sheldon. 2. Lewis, Clive Staples, 1898-1963—Correspondence. 3. Anglicans—United States—Biography. 4. Anglicans—England—Biography. I. Title. BIP

Vanbrugh, John, Sir, 1664-1726.

DOBREE, Bonamy, 1891- 820.9'004
Essays in biography, 1680-1726 Freeport, N.Y., Books for Libraries Press [1967] x, 362 p. illus., ports. 21 cm. (Essay index reprint series) Reprint of the 1925 ed. Contents.Contents.—His Excellency, Sir George Etherege.—The architect of Blenheim, Sir John Vanbrugh.—The first Victorian, Joseph Addison.—Appendices: Godolphin's warrant to Vanbrugh. Mrs. Yarburgh. Secret. The Frenzy. Pope's letters.—Bibliography (p. [353]-357) [PR433.D6 1967] 67-23203
1. Etherege, George, Sir, 1635?-1691. 2. Vanbrugh, John, Sir, 1664-1726. 3. Addison, Joseph, 1672-1719. 4. Blenheim Palace. I. Title.

HUSEBOE, Arthur R., 822'.4 B
1931-
Sir John Vanbrugh / by Arthur R. Huseboe. Boston : Twayne Publishers, c1976. p. cm. (Twayne's English authors series ; TEAS 191) Includes index. Bibliography: p. [PR3738.H8] 76-18217 lib. bdg. : 7.95
1. Vanbrugh, John, Sir, 1664-1726. BIP

Vance, Zebulon Baird, 1830-1894.

SHIRLEY, Franklin Ray 923.273
Zebulon Vance, Tarheel spokesman. Charlotte [N.C.] McNally & Loftin [1963, c1962] 161p. 24cm. Bibl. 62-21046 3.50
1. Vance, Zebulon Baird, 1830-1894. I. Title.

TUCKER, Glenn 973.80924
Zeb Vance: champion of personal freedom. Indianapolis, Bobbs [1966, c.1965] viii, 564p. maps, port. 24cm. Bibl. [E664.V2T8] 65-26513 8.50
1. Vance, Zebulon Baird, 1830-1894. I. Title.

VANCE, Zebulon 973.8'0924 B
Baird, 1830-1894.
My beloved Zebulon; the correspondence of Zebulon Baird Vance and Harriett Newell Espy. Edited by Elizabeth Roberts Cannon. With an introd. by Frances Gray Patton. Chapel Hill, University of North Carolina Press [1971] xxv, 278 p. facsim., ports. 24 cm. [E664.V2A4] 72-132258 ISBN 0-8078-1157-2 10.00
I. Vance, Harriett Newell Espy, 1832-1878. II. Title.

Vance, Zebulon Baird, 1830-1894—Juvenile literature.

CAMP, Cordelia, 1889- 385.0924
Governor Vance; a life for young people. Asheville, N.C., Stephens Press [c1961] 58 p. illus., ports., map. 24 cm. Bibliography: p. 55-56. [E664.V2C3] 64-31014
1. Vance, Zebulon Baird, 1830-1894—Juvenile literature. I. Title.

Vancouver, George, 1757-1798.

ANDERSON, Bern. 910.0942
The life and voyages of Captain George Vancouver, surveyor of the sea. Toronto, University of Toronto Press [1966] xii, 274 p. illus., maps, port. 24 cm. (Canadian university paperbooks, 57) (C67-615) Includes account of Captain Vancouver's explorations along the Pacific Coast of Canada. "The original version of this study was submitted as a doctoral thesis: Harvard University." p. vi. First published Seattle, University of Washington Press, 1960, under title: Surveyor of the sea; the life and voyages of Captain George Vancouver. Bibliography: p. 259-266. [G246.V3A7 1966] 67-100187
1. Vancouver, George. 1757-1798. I. Title.

MCGUIRE, M. B. 910'.92'4 B
The Vancouver story / M. B. McGuire. 1st ed. New York : Vantage Press, c1977. 237 p. ; 21 cm. Includes index. Bibliography: p. 231-234. [G246.V3M23] 76-50943 ISBN 0-533-02667-9 : 8.95
1. Vancouver, George, 1757-1798. 2. Explorers—England—Biography. I. Title.

MEANY, Edmond Stephen, 979.77
1862-1935.
Vancouver's discovery of Puget Sound; portraits and biographies of the men honored in the naming of geographic features of northwestern America. Portland, Ore., Binfords & Mort, 1957 [c1935] 344, 44 p. illus. 25 cm. "A New Vancouver journal on the discovery of Puget Sound, by a member of the Chatham's crew. Edited by Edmond S. Meany. Seattle, 1915" (44 p.) has special t.p. [F897.P9M4 1957] 62-1648
1. Vancouver, George, 1757-1798. 2. Puget Sound. 3. Northwest coast of North America. 4. Nootka Sound.

Vancouver, George, 1757-1798—Juvenile literature.

SYME, Ronald, 1910- 910'.924
Vancouver; explorer of the Pacific coast. Illustrated by William Stobbs. New York, Morrow [1970] 96 p. illus. 22 cm. A biography of the English explorer whose four and a half year search for the legendary Northwest Passage produced charts and records that helped open up the Pacific Northwest. [G246.V3S9] 92 79-89463 3.75
1. Vancouver, George, 1757-1798—Juvenile literature. I. Stobbs, William, illus. II. Title.

Vandeman, Herbert A.

EDWARDS, Josephine 286'.73 B
Cunnington.
With an holy calling / by Josephine Cunnington Edwards. Mountain View, Calif. : Pacific Press Pub. Association, c1979. 124 p. ; 22 cm. (A Destiny book ; D-172) [BX6193.V36E38] 78-53671 ISBN 0-8163-0250-2 pbk. : 3.95
1. Vandeman, Herbert A. 2. Seventh-Day Adventists—United States—Biography. I. Title. BIP

Vandenberg, Arthur Hendrick, 1884-1951.

VANDENBERG, Arthur 973.917'092'4
Hendrick, 1884-1951.
The private papers of Senator Vandenberg / edited by Arthur H. Vandenberg, Jr. ; with the collaboration of Joe Alex Morris. Westport, Conn. : Greenwood Press, 1974, c1952. xxii, 599 p. [11] leaves of plates : ill. ; 22 cm. Reprint of the ed. published by Houghton Mifflin, Boston. Includes bibliographical references and index. [E742.5.V35 1974] 74-15561 ISBN 0-8371-7829-0 : 22.50
1. Vandenberg, Arthur Hendrick, 1884-1951. 2. United States—Politics and government—1945- —Sources. 3. United States—Foreign relations—1945- —Sources. I. Vandenberg, Arthur Hendrick, ed. II. Morris, Joe Alex, 1904- ed. III. Title. BIP

Vanderbilt, Cornelius, 1794-1877.

HOYT, Edwin Palmer. 923.373
Commodore Vanderbilt. Chicago, Reilly & Lee Co., 1962. 166p. illus. 21cm. Includes bibliography. [CT275.V23H6] 62-16398
1. Vanderbilt, Cornelius, 1794-1877. I. Title.

HOYT, Edwin Palmer 923.373
Commondore Vanderbilt. Chicago, Reilly & Lee [c.] 1962. 166p. illus. 21cm. Bibl. 62-16398 3.95
1. Vanderbilt, Cornelius, 1794-1877. I. Title.

LANE, Wheaton Joshua, 380.5 B
1902-
Commodore Vanderbilt; an epic of the steam age, by Wheaton J. Lane. New York, Knopf, 1942. [New York, Johnson Reprint Corp., 1973] xiv, 357, xii p. illus. 22 cm. (History of the American economy) Bibliography: p. [326]-357. [CT275.V23L3 1973] 73-247 ISBN 0-384-31275-6
1. Vanderbilt, Cornelius, 1794-1877. I. Title. BIP

MINNIGERODE, Meade, 650'.0922 B
1887-1967.
Certain rich men; Stephen Girard, John Jacob Astor, Jay Cooke, Daniel Drew, Cornelius Vanderbilt, Jay Gould, Jim Fisk. Freeport, N.Y., Books for Libraries Press [1970] xi, 210 p. illus., facsim., ports. 23 cm. (Essay index reprint series) Reprint of the 1927 ed. Bibliography: p. ix-xi. [CT219.M55 1970] 71-121489
1. Girard, Stephen, 1750-1831. 2. Astor, John Jacob, 1763-1848. 3. Cooke, Jay, 1821-1905. 4. Drew, Daniel, 1797-1879. 5. Vanderbilt, Cornelius, 1794-1877. 6. Gould, Jay, 1836-1892. 7. Fisk, James, 1835-1872. I. Title.

Vanderbilt, Cornelius, 1898-

VANDERBILT, Cornelius, 920.5
1898-
Man of the world; my life on five continents. New York, Crown Publishers [1959] 342 p. illus. 24 cm. [CT275.V232A3] 59-14035
I. Title.

VANDERBILT, Cornelius, 070'.92'4
1898-
Personal experiences of a cub reporter. New York, Beekman Publishers, 1974. ix, 212 p. 23 cm. (American newspapermen, 1790-1933) Reprint of the 1922 ed. published by G. Sully, New York. [PN4874.V3A3 1974] 74-569 ISBN 0-8464-0003-0 12.00
1. Vanderbilt, Cornelius, 1898- 2. Reporters and reporting. I. Title.

Vanderbilt family.

CROFFUT, William 380.5 B
Augustus, 1835-1915.
The Vanderbilts and the story of their fortune / William A. Croffut. New York : Arno Press, 1975, c1886. p. cm. (The Leisure class in America) Reprint of the ed. published by Belford, Clarke, Chicago. [CS71.V228 1975] 75-1837 ISBN 0-405-06906-5 : 20.00
1. Vanderbilt family. 2. Vanderbilt, Cornelius, 1794-1877. I. Title. II. Series.

HOYT, Edwin Palmer 929.2
The Vanderbilts and their fortunes. Garden City, N.Y., Doubleday [c.]1962. 434p. 25cm. Bibl. 62-7647 4.95
1. Vanderbilt family. I. Title.

HOYT, Edwin Palmer. 929'.2'0973
The Vanderbilts and their fortunes. [1st ed.] Garden City, N. Y., Doubleday, 1962. 434p. 25cm. [CS71.V228 1962] 62-7647
1. Vanderbilt family. I. Title.

Vanderbilt, Gloria, 1924-

VANDERBILT, Gloria, 700'.92'4 B
1924-
Woman to woman / Gloria Vanderbilt. 1st ed. Garden City, N.Y. : Doubleday, 1979. 305 p. : ill. ; 27 cm. [N6537.V33A2 1979] 77-25612 ISBN 0-385-13645-5 : 14.95
1. Vanderbilt, Gloria, 1924- 2. Artists—United States—Biography. I. Title. BIP

Vanderbuilt, Grace Wilson, 1870-1953.

VANDERBILT, Cornelius, 920.7
1898-
Queen of the Golden Age; the fabulous story of Grace Wilson Vanderbilt. New York, McGraw-Hill [1956] 311 p. illus. 22 cm. [CT275.V235V3] 56-11730
1. Vanderbuilt, Grace Wilson, 1870-1953. I. Title.

Vanderlyn, John, 1775-1852.

SCHOONMAKER, Marius, 1811- 927.5
1894.
John Vanderylyn, artist, 1775-1852; biography. Kingston, N.Y., Senate House Association, 1950. vi, 77 p. 24 cm. [ND237.V15S35] 50-31190
1. Vanderlyn, John, 1775-1852. I. Title.

Vanderveer, George Francis, 1875-1942.

HAWLEY, Lowell Stillwell. 923.473
Counsel for the damned; a biography of George Francis Vanderveer, by Lowell S. Hawley and Ralph Bushnell Potts. [1st ed.] Philadelphia, Lippincott [1953] 320p. 22cm. 53-8926
1. Vanderveer, George Francis, 1875-1942. 2. Trials—U. S. I. Potts, Ralph Bushnell, joint author. II. Title.

Vane, Henry, Sir, 1612?-1662.

ADAMSON, Jack H. 942.06'2'0924 B
Sir Harry Vane: his life and times (1613-1662), by J. H. Adamson and H. F. Folland. Boston, Gambit, 1973. 498 p. illus. 24 cm. Bibliography: p. [481]-489. [DA407.V2A65] 72-94005 ISBN 0-87645-064-8 10.00
1. Vane, Henry, Sir, 1612?-1662. I. Folland, H. F., 1906- joint author. II. Title.

IRELAND, William 942.06'2'0924 B
Wotherspoon, 1832-1909.
The life of Sir Henry Vane the younger, with a history of the events of his time. London, E. Nash, 1905. [New York, AMS Press, 1971] xv, 513 p. illus. 23 cm. [DA407.V216 1971] 70-137248 ISBN 0-404-03507-8 14.00
1. Vane, Henry, Sir, 1612?-1662. I. Title.

Vanier, George Philias,

VANIER, George 971.06'4'0924
Philias, 1888-1967.
Only to serve; selections from addresses of Governor-General Georges P. Vanier, edited by George Cowley and Michel Vanier. [Toronto] University of Toronto Press [1970] xx, 115 p. illus., ports. 24 cm. [F1034.3.V27A25 1970] 76-18789 6.50
I. Cowley, George, ed. II. Vanier, Michel, ed. III. Title.

Varconi, Victor, 1891-1976.

VARCONI, 791.43'028'0924 B
Victor, 1891-1976.
It's not enough to be Hungarian / by Victor Varconi and Ed Honeck. Denver : Graphic Impressions, c1976. 192 p. : ill. ; 24 cm. [PN2859.H86V3 1976] 76-20877 ISBN 0-914628-09-7 : 8.95
1. Varconi, Victor, 1891-1976. 2. Actors—Hungary—Biography. I. Honeck, Ed, joint author. II. Title. BIP

Vardaman, James Kimble, 1861-1930.

HOLMES, William 976.2'06'0924 B
F.
The White Chief: James Kimble Vardaman, by William F. Holmes. Baton Rouge, Louisiana State University Press [1970] xiii, 418 p. port. 24 cm. (Southern biography series) Includes bibliographical references. [E748.V24H6] 70-108201 10.95
1. Vardaman, James Kimble, 1861-1930. I. Title. II. Series.

Varela y Morales, Felix, 1788-1853.

MCCADDEN, Joseph 972.91'05'0924 B
James, 1898-
Father Varela; torch bearer from Cuba, by Joseph and Helen McCadden. New York, United States Catholic Historical Society, 1969. xviii, 194 p. 2 ports. 24 cm. (United States Catholic Historical Society. Monograph series, 27) Bibliography: p. 174-186. [F1783.V2546] 71-15050
1. Varela y Morales, Felix, 1788-1853. I. McCadden, Helen, joint author. II. Title. III. Series.

Varese, Edgard, 1883-1965.

OUELLETTE, Fernand. 780'.924 B
Edgard Varese. Translated from the French by Derek Coltman. New York, Orion Press [1968] ix, 270 p. illus., facsims., ports. 24 cm. Translation of Edgard Varese published in 1966. Bibliography: p. 244-262. [ML410.V27O83] 68-15461
1. Varese, Edgard, 1883-1965.

VARESE, Louise 785'.0924 B
(McCutcheon) 1890-
Varese; a looking-glass diary [by] Louise Varese. New York, Norton [1972- v. illus. 22 cm. Contents.Contents.—v. 1. 1883-1928. [ML410.V27V272] 74-139392 ISBN 0-393-07461-7 8.95
1. Varese, Edgard, 1883-1965.

Vargas, Getulio, Pres. Brazil, 1883-1954.

DULLES, John W. F. 981'.06'0924 B
Vargas of Brazil: a political biography, by John W. F. Dulles. Austin, University of Texas Press [1967] xiii, 395 p. illus., maps (part fold.), ports. 24 cm. Bibliography: p. [349]-368. [F2538.V33D8] 67-20502
1. Vargas, Getulio, Pres. Brazil, 1883-1954. 2. Brazil—Politics and government—1930-1954. I. Title. BIP

LEVINE, Robert M. 981.06'0924
The Vargas regime; the critical years, 1934-1938, by Robert M. Levine. New York, Columbia University Press, 1970. x, 270 p. map. 24 cm. Sponsored by the Institute of Latin American Studies of Columbia University. Bibliography: p. [237]-252. [F2538.V33L4] 78-115222 9.00
1. Vargas, Getulio, Pres. Brazil, 1883-1954. 2. Brazil—Politics and government—1930-1954. I. Columbia University. Institute of Latin American Studies. II. Title.

Varker, Philip J.

VARKER, Philip J 253.20924
The Lord will provide. Illus. by Robert L. Varker [Highland Park, N.J., Author, 228 Donlsn, c.1965] 170p. 23cm. Autobiographical. [BX8495.V34A3] 65-27994 1.95 pap.,
I. Title.

Varnhagen von Ense, Rahel Antonie Friederike Levin, 1771-1833.

ARENDT, Hannah. 838'.6'08 B
Rahel Varnhagen, the life of a Jewish woman. Translated by Richard and Clara Winston. Rev. ed. New York, Harcourt Brace Jovanovich [1974] xx, 236 p. port. 21 cm. Published in 1957 under title: Rahel Varnhagen, the life of a Jewess. Bibliography: p. 232-236. [PT2546.V22A913 1974] 74-6478 7.95
1. Varnhagen von Ense, Rahel Antonie Friederike Levin, 1771-1833. 2. Jews in Germany. BIP

KEY, Ellen Karolina 838'.6'08 B
Sofia, 1849-1926.
Rahel Varnhagen : a portrait / by Ellen Key ; translated from the Swedish by Arthur G. Chater ; with an introd. by Havelock Ellis. Westport, Conn. : Hyperion Press, 1976, c1913. xix, 312 p., [2] leaves of plates : ill. ; 22 cm. (Pioneers of the woman's movement) Reprint of the ed. published by G. P. Putnam, New York. Includes bibliographical references. [PT2546.V22K4 1976] 75-7680 ISBN 0-88355-351-1 : 21.00
1. Varnhagen von Ense, Rahel Antonie Frederike Levin, 1771-1833—Biography.

Vartan, of Armenia, Saint, d. 451.

BANKER, Marie Sarrafian. 922.1
St. Vartan: hero of Armenia; the story of Armenia's early struggle for freedom to worship Christ. New York, Exposition Press [1951] 164 p. illus. 22 cm. [BX129.V3B3] 51-14405
1. Vartan, of Armenia, Saint, d. 451. I. Title.

Vasari, Giorgia, 1511-1574.

BOASE, Thomas Sherrer 709'.2'4 B
Ross, 1898-1974.
Georgio Vasari : the man and the book / T. S. R. Boase. [Princeton, N.J.] : Princeton University Press, 19978,c1977 p. cm. (Bollingen series ; XXXV : 20) (The A. W. Mellon lectures in the fine arts ; 20) Based on 6 lectures given at the National Gallery of Art in Washington in Feb. and Mar. 1971. Includes index. Bibliography: p. [N7483.V37B6] 77-4763 ISBN 0-691-09905-7 : 22.50
1. Vasari, Giorgia, 1511-1574. 2. Art historians—Italy—Biography. I. Title. II. Series. III. Series: Bollingen series ; 35.

Vasconcelos, Jose, 1882-1959.

HADDOX, John Herbert, 199'.72
1929-
Vasconcelos of Mexico, philosopher and prophet, by John H. Haddox. Austin, University of Texas Press [1967] ix, 103 p. port. 21 cm. (Texas Pan-American series) Bibliography: p. [95]-99. [B1019.V34H3] 67-65612
1. Vasconcelos, Jose, 1882-1959. I. Title.

VASCONCELOS, Jose, 1882- 923.272
1959
A Mexican Ulysses, an autobiography. Tr. [from Spanish] abridged by W. Rex Crawford. Bloomington, Ind. Univ. Pr. [c.1963] 288p. 24cm. 63-9726 6.95
I. Title.

VASCONCELOS, Jose, 370'.92'4 B
1882-1959.
A Mexican Ulysses; an autobiography. Translated and abridged by W. Rex Crawford. Westport, Conn., Greenwood Press [1972, c1963] 288 p. 23 cm. An abridgement of the autobiographical series which consists of four volumes: Ulises criollo, La tormenta, El desastre, and El proconsulado. [F1234.V27162] 72-6215 ISBN 0-8371-6477-X 13.00
I. Crawford, William Rex, 1898- tr. II. Title.

VASCONCELOS, 917.2'03'810924
Jose, 1882-1959.
Ulises criollo. Edited by Ronald Hilton, with notes and vocabulary by Robert B. O'Neil. Boston, Heath [1960] 214 p. 21 cm. Full name: Jose Vasconcelos Calderon. "The first volume of Vasconcelos' autobiography, which was published in 1935, relates the events of his life down to the death of Madero in 1913." [F1234.V27] 60-7496
1. Spanish language — Chrestomathies and readers. I. Title. II. Series.

VASCONCELOS, Jose, 1882- 923.272
1959
A Mexican Ulysses, an autobiography. Tr. [from Spanish] abridged by W. Rex Crawford. Bloomington, Ind. Univ. Pr. [c.1963] 288p. 24cm. 63-9726 6.95
I. Title.

VASCONCELOS, Jose, 370'.92'4 B
1882-1959.
A Mexican Ulysses; an autobiography. Translated and abridged by W. Rex Crawford. Westport, Conn., Greenwood Press [1972, c1963] 288 p. 23 cm. An abridgement of the autobiographical series which consists of four volumes: Ulises criollo, La tormenta, El desastre, and El

proconsulado. [F1234.V27162] 72-6215 ISBN 0-8371-6477-X 13.00
1. Crawford, William Rex, 1898- tr. II. Title.

Vasquez, Tiburcio, 1835-1875.

BEERS, George A. 364.1'092'4 B
The California outlaw: Tiburcio Vasquez. Compiled by Robert Greenwood. New York, Arno Press, 1974 [c1960] 296 p. illus. 24 cm. (The Mexican American) First published in 1875 under title: Vasquez. Reprint of the ed. published by Talisman Press, Los Gatos, Calif. Bibliography: p. 59. [HV6452.C3V3 1974] 73-14203 ISBN 0-405-05677-X 16.00
1. Vasquez, Tiburcio, 1835-1875. I. Greenwood, Robert, comp. II. Title. III. Series.

BEERS, George A. 923.4173
The California outlaw: Tiburcio Vasquez. Compiled by Robert Greenwood. Including the rare contemporary account by George Beers. With numberous photos. and excerpts from contemporary newspapers. Los Gatos, Calif., Talisman Press, 1960. 296 p. ports., map (on lining papers) diagrs., facsims. 24 cm. Added t.p.: Vasquex; or, The hunted bandits of the San Joaquin. Containing thrilling scenes and incidents among the outlaws and desperadoes of southern California. With a full and accurate account of the capture, trial, and execution of the noted bandit. New York, R. M. De Witt, 1875. Bibliography: p. 58-59. [HV6452.C3V3 1960] 60-9511
1. Vasquez, Tiburcio, 1835-1875. I. Greenwood, Robert, comp. II. Title.

HOFFER, Dominga L. (Cervantes) 923.4173
Tiburcio Vasquez. Impressions by Gestetner completed. Puyallup, Wash., Historic Memories Pr., 1964. vi, 107p. illus., maps, ports. 28cm. 64-7965 price unreported
1. Vasquez, Tiburcio, 1835-1875. 2. Monterey, Calif.—Hist. 3. Spanish missions of California. I. Title.

RAMBO, F. Ralph. 364.1'0924 B
Trailing the California bandit, Tiburcio Vasquez, 1835-1875. Illus. and hand-lettered text by the author. [San Jose, Calif., Lithographed by Rosicrucian Press 1968] 40 p. illus., map, ports. 23 cm. (Pioneer series, no. 3) [HV6452.C3V3 1968] 76-3824
1. Vasquez, Tiburcio, 1835-1875. I. Title.

Vass, Winifred Kellersberger.

VASS, Winifred Kellersberger. 967.5'1'03
Thirty-one banana leaves / Winifred Kellersberger Vass. Atlanta : John Knox Press, [1975] p. cm. [BV4501.2.V36] 74-7617 ISBN 0-8042-2581-8 : 3.95
1. Vass, Winifred Kellersberger. 2. Meditations. 3. Zaire—Description and travel—1951- I. Title. **BIP**

Vatican Council, 2d—Biog.

NOVAK, Michael, ed. 922.2
The men who make the Council [vs. 7-12] Notre Dame, Ind., Univ. of Notre Dame Pr. [c.1964] 6v. (various p.) 18cm. Each v. has also special t.p. On cover: Critical portraits. [BX4664.2.N6] 64-7964 .75 pap.,
1. Vatican Council, 2d—Biog. 2. Cardinals. I. Title.
Contents omitted.

Vaughan, Alfred Jefferson, 1800-1871.

VAUGHAN, Jack C 923.573
Alfred Jefferson Vaughan; Virginian, Missourian and Californian. [Grand Prairie, Tex., 1960] 223 1. illus. 29 cm. (His American histories, v. 9) [E467.1.V28V3] 61-357
1. Vaughan, Alfred Jefferson, 1800-1871. 2. Virginia — Hist. — Civil War. 3. California — Surveys. 4. Indians of North America — Treaties; 1855. I. Title.

Vaughan, Alfred Jefferson, 1867-1942.

VAUGHAN, Jack C. 976'.04'0924 B
Blossom Chapline Vaughan (1877-1965) of Arkansas and Alfred Jefferson Vaughan, III (1867-1942) of Mississippi / by Jack Chapline Vaughan. Arlington, Tex. : Vaughan, [1975- v. : ill. ; 29 cm. (Vaughan's American histories ; v. 18-) Includes index. Bibliography: v. 1, p. 283-284. [F411.V38] 75-314320
1. Vaughan, Alfred Jefferson, 1867-1942. 2. Vaughan, Blossom Chapline, 1877-1965. 3. Vaughan family. 4. Chapline family. 5. United States—History—Civil War, 1861-1865—Campaigns and battles. I. Title: Blossom Chapline Vaughan (1877-1965) of Arkansas ...

Vaughan, Blossom Chapline, 1877-1965.

VAUGHAN, Jack C. 976'.04'0924 B
Blossom Chapline Vaughan (1877-1965) of Arkansas and Alfred Jefferson Vaughan, III (1867-1942) of Mississippi / by Jack Chapline Vaughan. Arlington, Tex. : Vaughan, [1975- v. : ill. ; 29 cm. (Vaughan's American histories ; v. 18-) Includes index. Bibliography: v. 1, p. 283-284. [F411.V38] 75-314320
1. Vaughan, Alfred Jefferson, 1867-1942. 2. Vaughan, Blossom Chapline, 1877-1965. 3. Vaughan family. 4. Chapline family. 5. United States—History—Civil War, 1861-1865—Campaigns and battles. I. Title: Blossom Chapline Vaughan (1877-1965) of Arkansas ...

Vaughan, Curry N.

VAUGHAN, Curry N. 285'.092'4 B
Battle-ground : a personal account of God's move upon the American military forces / by Curry N. Vaughan, Jr., with Bob Slosser. Plainfield, N.J. : Logos International, c1978. 193 p., [2] leaves of plates : ill. ; 20 cm. [BX9225.V39A33] 78-51865 ISBN 0-88270-301-3 : 2.95
1. Vaughan, Curry N. 2. Presbyterian Church—Clergy—Biography. 3. Chaplains, Military—United States—Biography. 4. Church work with military personnel. 5. Pentecostals—United States—Biography. I. Slosser, Bob, joint author. II. Title.

Vaughan family.

VAUGHAN, Jack C. 976'.04'0924 B
Blossom Chapline Vaughan (1877-1965) of Arkansas and Alfred Jefferson Vaughan, III (1867-1942) of Mississippi / by Jack Chapline Vaughan. Arlington, Tex. : Vaughan, [1975- v. : ill. ; 29 cm. (Vaughan's American histories ; v. 18-) Includes index. Bibliography: v. 1, p. 283-284. [F411.V38] 75-314320
1. Vaughan, Alfred Jefferson, 1867-1942. 2. Vaughan, Blossom Chapline, 1877-1965. 3. Vaughan family. 4. Chapline family. 5. United States—History—Civil War, 1861-1865—Campaigns and battles. I. Title: Blossom Chapline Vaughan (1877-1965) of Arkansas ...

Vaughan, George Lester.

VAUGHAN, George Lester. 630.11'24 B
The cotton renter's son, by G. L. Vaughan. Wolfe City, Tex., Henington Pub. Co. [1967] v, 195 p. illus., ports. 23 cm. [CT275.V445A3] 68-900
I. Title.

Vaughan, Henry, 1622-1695.

WILLY, Margaret. v. 12
Richard Crashaw, Henry Vaughan, Thomas Traherne. Lincoln, University of Nebraska Press [c1964] [87]-143 p. 21 cm. (British writers and their work, no. 4) A Bison book. 67-34369
1. Crashaw, Richard, 1613?-1649. 2. Vaughan, Henry, 1622-1695. 3. Traherne, Thomas, d. 1674. I. Title. II. Series.

Vaughan, Stephen, d. 1549.

RICHARDSON, Walter Cecil, 1902- 923.242
Stephen Vaughan, financial agent of Henry VIII; a study of financial relations with the Low Countries. Baton Rouge, Louisiana State University Press [1953] 102p. 23cm. (Louisiana State University studies. Social science series, no. 3) [HJ1003.V3R5] 53-3511
1. Vaughan, Stephen, d. 1549. 2. Finance, Public —gt. Brit.—To 1688. I. Title. II. Series.

Vaughan Williams, Ralph, 1872-1958.

DAY, James 927.8
Vaughan Williams. [New York, Farrar, c.1961] 228p. illus. (Master musicians ser.) Bibl. 61-65106 3.50
1. Vaughan Williams, Ralph, 1872-1958. I. Title.

FOSS, Hubert James, 1899-1953. 780'.92'4 B
Ralph Vaughan Williams; a study. Westport, Conn., Greenwood Press [1974] 219 p. port. 22 cm. Reprint of the 1950 ed. published by Harrap, London. Bibliography: p. 204-212. [ML410.V3F6 1974] 74-9042 ISBN 0-8371-7610-7
1. Vaughan Williams, Ralph, 1872-1958. **BIP**

PAKENHAM, Simona. v. 12
Ralph Vaughan Williams; a discovery of his music. London, Macmillan; New York, St. Martin's Press, 1957. ix, 205p. port. 23cm. Bibliography: p. 194. A59
1. Vaughan Williams, Ralph, 1872- I. Title.

RALPH Vaughan Williams; v. 12
a discovery of his music. London, New York, Macmillan, 1957. ix, 205p. port. 23cm.
1. Vaughan Williams, Ralph, 1872- I. Pakenham, Simona.

VAUGHAN WILLIAMS, Ursula. 927.8
R. V. W.; a biography of Ralph Vaughan Williams. London, New York, Oxford University Press, 1964. xiv, 448 p. facsim., music, ports. 23 cm. Bibliography: p. [xii]-xiv. [ML410.V3V4] 65-2154
1. Vaughan Williams, Ralph, 1872-1958. I. Title. **BIP**

Vaughan Williams, Ralph, 1872-1958—Iconography.

LUNN, John E. 780'.924 B
Ralph Vaughan Williams: a pictorial biography, [by] John E. Lunn and Ursula Vaughan Williams. London, New York, Oxford University Press, 1971. [6], 121 p. (chiefly illus., facsims., ports., music). 26 cm. Includes bibliographical references. [ML88.V39L85] 79-885544 ISBN 0-19-315420-X £3.30
1. Vaughan Williams, Ralph, 1872-1958—Iconography. I. Vaughan Williams, Ursula, joint author. **BIP**

Vaught, John,

VAUGHT, John, 1909- 796.332'0924 B
Rebel coach; my football family. Memphis, Memphis State University Press [1971] viii, 203 p. illus., ports. 24 cm. [GV939.V3A3] 78-171535 ISBN 0-87870-008-0 6.95
I. Title. **BIP**

Vaus, James Arthur.

VAUS, James Arthur. 362.7'092'4 B
The devil loves a shining mark; the story of my life [by] Jim Vaus with Julie Maxey. Waco, Tex., Word Books [1974] 157 p. illus. 23 cm. [HV6248.V37A325] 73-91555 5.95
1. Vaus, James Arthur. 2. Crime and criminals—Correspondence, reminiscences, etc. 3. Social workers—Correspondence, reminiscences, etc. I. Maxey, Julie. II. Title.

Veblen, Thorstein, 1857-1929.

DIGGINS, John P. 330'.092'4 B
The bard of savagery : Thorstein Veblen and modern social theory / John P. Diggins. New York : Seabury Press, 1978. xiii, 257 p. ; 24 cm. (A Continuum book) Includes bibliographical references and index. [HB119.V4D46] 77-13319 ISBN 0-8164-9323-5 : 14.95
1. Veblen, Thorstein, 1857-1929. 2. Social reformers—United States—Biography. 3. Economics—United States—History. 4. Social history. I. Title. **BIP**

DOWD, Douglas Fitzgerald, 1919- 330.1
Thorstein Veblen. New York, Washington Sq. [c.1964] xvii, 205p. 18cm. (Great Amer. thinkers ser. W880) Bibl. 64-56158 .60 pap.,
1. Veblen, Thorstein, 1857-1929. I. Title.

DUFFUS, Robert Luther, 1888- 330'.092'4 B
The innocents at Cedro; a memoir of Thorstein Veblen and some others, by Robert L. Duffus. With the advice and consent of William M. Duffus. Clifton [N.J.] A. M. Kelley, 1972. vi, 163 p. 22 cm. (Reprints of economic classics) Reprint of the 1944 ed. [HB119.V4D7 1972] 74-182193 ISBN 0-678-00885-X 8.50
1. Veblen, Thorstein, 1857-1929. I. Title. **BIP**

HOBSON, John Atkinson, 1858-1940. 330'.0924
Veblen. New York, A. M. Kelley, 1971. 227 p. 22 cm. (Reprints of economic classics) Reprint of the 1936 ed. [HB119.V4H6 1971] 79-158836 ISBN 0-678-00019-0
1. Veblen, Thorstein, 1857-1929. **BIP**

Veeck, Bill.

VEECK, Bill. 796.357
Veeck—as in wreck; the autobiography of Bill Veeck with Ed Linn. New York, Putnam [1962] 380 p. 22 cm. [GV865.V4A3] 62-10982

Vega Carpio, Lope Felix de, 1562-1635.

ASTRANA MARIN LUIS, 1889- 862.3
Lope de Vega. New York, Las Americas [1965] 383p. Facsims. 18cm. (Coleccion Z, no. 91-92) [PQ6469.A79] 65-5004 2.00 pap.,
1. Vega Carpio, Lope Felix de, 1562-1635. I. Title.

RENNERT, Hugo Albert, 1858-1927. 862'.3
The life of Lope de Vega, 1562-1635 New York, B. Blom, 1968. xiii, 587 p. port. 20 cm. Reprint of the 1904 ed. Bibliography: p. [417]-553. [PQ6469.R3 1968] 67-13337
1. Vega Carpio, Lope Felix de, 1562-1635. 2. Vega Carpio, Lope Felix de, 1562-1635—Bibliography. **BIP**

Vela, Maria.

VELA, Maria. 922.246
The third mystic of Avila; the self revelation of Maria Vela, a sixteenth century Spanish nun. Foreword and translation by Frances Parkinson Keyes. New York, Farrar, Straus and Cudahy [1960] 300 p. illus. 22 cm. Autograph by translator inside front cover. [BX4705.V427A3] 60-9735
I. Keyes, Frances Parkinson (Wheeler) 1885- II. Title.

Velarde, Pablita, 1918- —Juvenile literature.

NELSON, Mary Carroll. 759.13 B
Pablita Velarde. Minneapolis, Dillon Press [1971] 58 p. illus. 24 cm. A biography of a Pueblo Indian artist whose prize winning-work reflects the heritage of the American Indian. [E99.T35V45] 92 77-140992 ISBN 0-87518-037-X
1. Velarde, Pablita, 1918- —Juvenile literature. I. Title. **BIP**

Velazquez Cardenas y Leon, Joaquin, 1732-1786.

ENGSTRAND, Iris 972'.2'020924 B
Wilson.
Royal officer in Baja California, 1768-1770 : Joaquin Velazquez de Leon / by Iris Wilson Engstrand, drawings by Jean Noel Los Angeles : Dawson's Book Shop, 1976. 133 p., [4] leaves of plates : ill., maps (2 fold. in pocket) ; 22 cm. (Baja California trvels series ; 37) "500 copies printed." Includes index. Bibliography: p. 123-127. [F1246.E48] 75-43216 24.00
1. Velazquez Cardenas y Leon, Joaquin, 1732-1786. 2. Baja California—Description and travel. 3. Natural history—Mexico—Baja California. I. Title. II. Series.

Velazquez, Diego Rodriguez de Silva y, 1599-1660.

KAHR, Madlyn Millner. 759.6 B
Velazquez : the art of painting / Madlyn Millner Kahr. 1st ed. New York : Harper & Row, c1976. xii, 233 p. : ill. ; 24 cm. (Icon editions) Includes index. Bibliography: p. [221]-225. [ND813.V4K24 1976] 75-39563 ISBN 0-06-433575-5 : 12.50
1. Velazquez, Diego Rodriguez de Silva y, 1599-1660. 2. Painters—Spain—Biography. BIP

LAFUENTE Ferrari, Enrique. 759.6
Velazquez; biographical and critical study. Translated by James Emmons from the French version of the original Spanish. Lausanne] Skira; [distributed in the U.S. by World Pub. Co., Cleveland, 1960] 128 p. mounted col. illus., port. 19 cm. (The Taste of our time, v. 33) Bibliography: p. 117-[120] [ND813.V4L33] 60-8731
1. Velazquez, Diego Rodriguez de Silva y, 1599-1660.

MULLER, Joseph Emile. 759.6 B
Velazquez / Joseph-Emile Muller ; [translated from the French by Jane Brenton]. London : Thames and Hudson, 1976. 264 p. : ill. (some col.) ; 22 cm. Translation of Velazquez. Label mounted on t.p.: Transatlantic Arts, Levittown, N.Y. sole distributor for the U.S.A. Includes index. Bibliography: p. 251. [ND813.V4M7413 1976] 76-378650 ISBN 0-500-18152-7 : 12.95 ISBN 0-500-20147-1 pbk. : 6.95
1. Velazquez, Diego Rodriguez de Silva y, 1599-1660. 2. Painters—Spain—Biography.

RIPLEY, Elizabeth 759.6
Velazquez, a biography. Philadelphia, Lippincott [c.1965] 72p. illus. 27cm. Bibl. [ND813.V4R55] 65-21846 3.75; 3.69 lib. ed.,
1. Velazquez, Diego Rodriguez de Silva y, 1599-1660. I. Title.

RIPLEY, Elizabeth, 1906- 759.6
Velazquez, a biography. [1st ed.] Philadelphia, Lippincott [1965] 72 p. illus. 26 cm. Bibliography: p. 70. [ND813.V4R55] 65-21846
1. Velazquez, Diego Rodriguez de Silva y, 1599-1660. I. Title.

VELAZQUEZ, Diego Rodriguez 759.6
de Silva y 1599-1660
Velazquez, by Xavier de Salas. [New York] Phaidon dist. Greenwich, Conn., N. Y. Graphic [c.1962] 75p. 51 col. plates. 32cm. 62-51949 5.95
I. Salas, Xavier de. II. Title.

VELAZQUEZ, Diego 759.6
Rodriguez de Silva y, 1599-1660.
Velazquez. [Prepared under the direction of Alfred E. Herzer. Selection of the reproductions by F. J. Sanchez Canton. The introd. and interleaving texts were written by Jose Ortega y Gasset. Translation by C. David Ley] New York, Random House [1953] lxxxiii p. 105 plates (part col.) 29 cm. [ND813.V4O68] 53-9707
I. Ortega y Gasset, Jose, 1883-1955.

WHITE, Jon Ewbank 759.6 B
Manchip, 1924-
Diego Velazquez; painter and courtier, by Jon Manchip White. Chicago, Rand McNally [1969] xxiii, 180 p. illus., ports. (part col.) 23 cm. Bibliography: p. 173-174. [ND813.V4W6 1969b] 69-11132 6.95
1. Velazquez, Diego Rodriguez de Silva y, 1599-1660.

Velazquez, Diego Rodriguez de Silva y, 1599-1660—Juvenile literature.

RABOFF, Ernest Lloyd. 759.6
Diego Rodriguez de Silva y Velasquez, by Ernest Raboff. Edited by Bradley Smith. Garden City, N.Y., Doubleday [1970] [31] p. illus. (part col.), ports. (part col.) 29 cm. (Art for children) (A Gemini Smith book.) A brief biographical sketch of the sixteenth-century Spanish painter accompanies color reproductions and discussions of some of his works. [ND813.V18R3] 74-121783 3.95
1. Velazquez, Diego Rodriguez de Silva y, 1599-1660—Juvenile literature. I. Title.

Venard, Jean Theophane,

VENARD, Jean Theophane, 922.251
1829-1861.
A modern martyr, adapted by Edward A. McGurkin from the book of the same title by James Anthony Walsh. New York, McMullen Books [1952] 118p. 20cm. [BX4705.V43A29] 52-12881
I. McGurkin, Edward A., 1905- II. Walsh, James Anthony, Bp., 1867-1936, ed. III. Title.

Venard, Jean Theophane, 1829-1861.

GREENE, Genard, 1921- 922.251
The hour of the dragon; a story of Blessed Theophane Venard. Illus. by Carolyn Lee Jagodits. Notre Dame, Ind., Dujarie Press [1956] 96p. illus. 24cm. [BX4705.V43G7] 56-25345
1. Venard, Jean Theophane, 1829-1861. I. Title.

VENARD, Jean Theophane, 922.251
1829-1861.
A modern martyr, adapted by Edward A. McGurkin from the book of the same title by James Anthony Walsh. New York, McMullen Books [1952] 118p. 20cm. [BX4705.V43A29] 52-12881
I. McGurkin, Edward A., 1905- II. Walsh, James Anthony, Bp., 1867-1936, ed. III. Title.

Vendome Hotel, Boston.

SEARS, Clara Endicott, 920.02
1863-
Snapshots from old registers. Limited ed. [Boston? 1955] 329p. illus. 24cm. [CT106.S4] 55-38568
1. Vendome Hotel, Boston. 2. Biography. I. Title.

Venice—Biography.

OLIPHANT, Margaret 914.5'31 B
Oliphant (Wilson), 1828-1897.
The makers of Venice; doges, conquerors, painters, and men of letters. With illus. by R. R. Holmes. London, New York, Macmillan. [New York, AMS Press, 1972] xii, 410 p. illus. 23 cm. Reprint of the 1888 ed. [DG671.4.O44 1972] 77-173809 ISBN 0-404-04815-3 14.50
1. Venice—Biography. I. Title. BIP

Venice—History—1508-1797.

MASSON, Georgina. 301.41'54'0945
Courtesans of the Italian Renaissance / Georgina Masson. New York : St. Martin's Press, 1976, c1975. viii, 180 p., [8] leaves of plates : ill. ; 25 cm. Includes index. Bibliography: p. 169-171. [DG678.24.A1M37 1976] 76-11415 10.00
1. Venice—History—1508-1797. 2. Rome (City)—History—1420-1798. 3. Courtesans—Italy—Venice—Biography. 4. Courtesans—Italy—Rome (City)—Biography. I. Title. BIP

Venizelos, Eleutherios, 1864-1936.

BOX, Pelham Horton, 909.82 B
1898-1937.
Three master builders and another; studies in modern revolutionary and liberal statesmanship. With an introd. by Ernest Barker. Freeport, N.Y., Books for Libraries Press [1968] 395 p. ports. 22 cm. (Essay index reprint series) Reprint of the 1925 ed. Contents.Contents.—Nikolai Lenin.—Benito Mussolini.—Eleutherios Venizelos.—Woodrow Wilson. Includes bibliographies. [D412.6.B6 1968] 68-22904
1. Lenin, Vladimir Il'ich, 1870-1924. 2. Mussolini, Benito, 1883-1945. 3. Venizelos, Eleutherios, 1864-1936. 4. Wilson, Woodrow, Pres. U.S., 1856-1924. I. Title. BIP

Ventresca, Francesco,

VENTRESCA, Francesco, 923.773
1872-
Personal reminiscences; celebrating sixty years in America (1891-1951) [and] fifty-five years a teacher of foreign languages (1896-1951) 1st complete ed. [Western Springs? Ill.] 1951. 340 p. illus. 21 cm. First published in 1937 under title: Personal reminiscences of a naturalized American. [CT275.V52A3] 52-21915
I. Title.

Venturi, Ken.

VENTURI, Ken. 796.3520924
Comeback; the Ken Venturi story, by Ken Venturi with Oscar Fraley. [1st ed.] New York, Duell, Sloan and Pearce [1966] viii, 184 p. ports. 21 cm. [GV964.V4A3] 66-27905
I. Fraley, Oscar, 1914- II. Title.

Ver Mehr, John Leonard, ca. 1809-1886.

RIDOUT, Lionel 283'.092'2 B
Utley.
Renegade, outcast, and maverick: three Episcopal clergymen in the California gold rush, by Lionel U. Ridout. San Diego, University Press, San Diego State University, c1973. iii, 127 p. 24 cm. On spine: Pioneer clergy. Includes bibliographical references. [BX5990.R52] 74-180275
1. Leavenworth, Thaddeus, 1802-1893. 2. Ver Mehr, John Leonard, ca. 1809-1886. 3. Ewer, Ferdinand Cartwright, 1826-1883. I. Title. II. Title: Pioneer clergy.

Veracini, Francesco Maria, 1690-1768.

HILL, John Walter, 780'.92'4 B
1942-
The life and works of Francesco Maria Veracini / by John Walter Hill. Ann Arbor, Mich. : UMI Research Press, [1979] c1975. p. cm. (Studies in musicology series ; no. 3) Includes index. Bibliography: p. [ML410.V39H5] 79-20453 ISBN 0-8357-1000-9 : 52.95 ISBN 0-8357-1001-7 pbk. : 49.95
1. Veracini, Francesco Maria, 1690-1768. 2. Composers—Italy—Biography. I. Title. II. Series. BIP

Vercheres, Marie Magdelaine Jarret de, (afterwards Mme. Tarieu de la Perade) 1678-1747.—Juvenile literature.

BONING, Richard A. 970'.004'97 B
Soldier girl / Richard A. Boning ; illustrated by Joseph Forte. Baldwin, N.Y. : Dexter & Westbrook, c1975. 46 p. : col. ill. ; 24 cm. (The Incredible series) A fourteen-year-old girl leads a small band defending a fort against an Iroquois attack in New France, October, 1692. [E99.I7B66] 75-25470 ISBN 0-87966-110-0
1. Vercheres, Marie Magdelaine Jarret de, (afterwards Mme. Tarieu de la Perade) 1678-1747.—Juvenile literature. 2. Vercheres, Marie Magdelaine Jarret de, (afterwards Mme. Tarieu de la Perade) 1678-1747. 3. Iroquois Indians—Wars. 4. Iroquois Indians—Wars. I. Forte, Joseph. II. Title. BIP

Verdi, Giuseppe, 1813-1901.

CROWEST, Frederick 782.1'092'4 B
James, 1850-1927.
Verdi, man and musician : his biography with special reference to his English experiences / by Frederick J. Crowest. New York : AMS Press, 1978. xiv, 306 p., [4] leaves of plates : ports. ; 23 cm. Reprint of the 1897 ed. published by J. Milne, London. Includes index. Bibliography: p. [293]-300. [ML410.V4C9 1978] 74-24065 ISBN 0-404-12890-4 : 21.00
1. Verdi, Giuseppe, 1813-1901. 2. Composers—Italy—Biography. I. Title.

GATTI, Carlo, 1876- 927.8
Verdi, the man and his music. Translated from the Italian by Elisabeth Abbott. New York, Putnam [1955] 371 p. 22 cm. [ML410.V4G199] 55-5776
1. Verdi, Giuseppe, 1813-1901. I. Title.

HUME, Paul. 782.1'092'4 B
Verdi / by Paul Hume. 1st ed. New York : E. P. Dutton, c1977. p. cm. (The Metropolitan Opera Guild composer series) [ML410.V4H74] 77-5810 ISBN 0-525-22845-4 : 8.95
1. Verdi, Giuseppe, 1813-1901. 2. Composers—Italy—Biography. I. Series: Metropolitan Opera Guild. The Metropolitan Opera Guild composer series.

HUSSEY, Dyneley, 1893- 927.8
Verdi. New York, Collier [1962] 380p. music. 18cm. (Great composers ser., BS115X) Bibl. 1.50 pap.,
1. Verdi, Giuseppe, 1813-1901. I. Title. II. Series. BIP

HUSSEY, Dyneley, 1893-. v. 12
Verdi. [3d ed.] London, J. M. Dent; New York, Farrar, Straus and Cudahy [1963] xiii, 365 p. illus., ports., music. (The Master musicians series) Includes bibliography. 65-3232
1. Verdi, Giuseppe, 1813-1901. I. Title.

MARTIN, George Whitney. 927.8
Verdi; his music, life and times. Illustrated with drawings by Everett Raymond Kinstler, photos., maps, and Delfico cartoons. New York, Dodd, Mead, 1963. xxi, 633 p. illus. 24 cm. [ML410.V4M266] 63-15475
1. Verdi, Giuseppe, 1813-1901.

MARTIN, George 782.1'092'4 B
Whitney.
Verdi, his music, life, and times / by George Martin ; illustrated with drawings

by Everett Kinstler, photos., maps, and Delfico cartoons. New York : Da Capo Press, 1979, c1963. xxi, 633 p. : ill. ; 24 cm. (Da Capo Press music reprint series) Reprint of the ed. published by Dood, Mead, New York. Includes index. Bibliography: p. 602-608. [ML410.V4M266 1979] 78-31783 ISBN 0-306-79549-3 : 29.50
1. Verdi, Giuseppe, 1813-1901. 2. Composers—Italy—Biography.

PETIT, Pierre Yves Marie Camille, 1922- 780.924
Verdi. Tr. from French, by Patrick Bowles. London, J. Calder [New York, Hillary House, 1966] 192p. illus., facsims, music, ports. 21cm. (Illus. Calder bk. CB. 55) Bibl. [ML410.V4P273] 66-4819 4.00
1. Verdi. Giuseppe, 1813-1901. I. Title.

TOYE, Francis, 1883- 782.1'092'4 B
Giuseppe Verdi, his life and works. Introd. by Herbert Weinstock. New York, Vienna House, [1973 c1946] xxi, 414, xiv p. illus. 24 cm. Reprint of the ed. published by Knopf, New York. Bibliography: p. xvi-xvii. [ML410.V4T7 1972] 72-81577 ISBN 0-8443-0067-5 14.50
1. Verdi, Giuseppe, 1813-1901.

VERDI : 782.1'092'4 B
a documentary study / compiled, edited, and translated by William Weaver. [London] : Thames & Hudson, [1977] 256 p. : ill. (some col.) ; 31 cm. Includes index. [ML410.V4V29] 77-376231 ISBN 0-500-01184-2 : 37.50
1. Verdi, Giuseppe, 1813-1901. 2. Composers—Italy—Biography. I. Weaver, William, 1923-
Distributed by W.W. Norton. BIP

VERDI, Giuseppe, 1813-1901. 782.1'0924 B
Letters of Giuseppe Verdi; selected, translated, and edited by Charles Osborne. New York, Holt, Rinehart and Winston [1972, c1971] 280 p. ports. 24 cm. Selected principally from I copialettere. [ML410.V4A387 1972] 79-138896 ISBN 0-03-086007-5 7.95
I. Osborne, Charles, 1927- ed.

VERDI, Giuseppe, 1813-1901. 782.1'0924 B
Verdi, the man in his letters. As edited and selected by Franz Werfel and Paul Stefan. Translated by Edward Downes. Freeport, N.Y., Books for Libraries Press [1970] 469 p. illus., ports. 23 cm. Reprint of the 1942 ed. [ML410.V4A385 1970] 71-130565
I. Werfel, Franz V., 1890-1945, ed. II. Stefan-Gruenfeldt, Paul, 1879-1943, ed. III. Title.

VERDI, Giuseppe, 1813-1901. 782.1'092'4 B
Verdi, the man in his letters. As edited and selected by Franz Werfel and Paul Stefan. Translated by Edward Downes. New York, Vienna House [1973, c1942] 469 p. illus. 21 cm. [ML410.V4A385 1973] 73-86364 ISBN 0-8443-0088-8 5.45
1. Verdi, Giuseppe, 1813-1901. 2. Musicians—Correspondence, reminiscences, etc. I. Werfel, Franz V., 1890-1945, ed. II. Stefan-Gruenfeldt, Paul, 1879-1943, ed. III. Title.

WALKER, Frank, 1907- 927.8
The man Verdi. New York, Knopf, 1962. xiii, 526 p. plates. 25 cm. [ML410.V4W3] 62-8686
1. Verdi, Giuseppe, 1813-1901. I. Title. BIP

WECHSBERG, Joseph, 1907- 782.1'092'4 B
Verdi / Joseph Wechsberg. New York : Putnam, [1974]. 255 p. : ill. ; 26 cm. Includes index. [ML410.V4W37] 74-81703 ISBN 0-399-11409-2 : 15.00
1. Verdi, Giuseppe, 1813-1901.

YBARRA, Thomas Russell, 1880- 927.8
Verdi; miracle man of opera. [1st ed.] New York, Harcourt, Brace [1955] 312 p. 21 cm. [ML410.V4Y3] 55-6830
1. Verdi, Giuseppe, 1813-1901.

Verdi, Giuseppe, 1813-1901—Juvenile literature.

KAUFMANN, Helen (Loep) j92
Anvil chorus; the story of Giuseppe Verdi, by Helen L. Kaufmann. Illustrated by Vivian Berger. New York, Hawthorn Books [1964] 185 p. illus., mpa. 22 cm. (Credo books [22]) Bibliography: p. [179] [ML3930.V4K4] 64-21459
1. Verdi, Giuseppe, 1813-1901 — Juvenile literature. I. Title.

MALVERN, Gladys. 927.8
On golden wings; [the story of Giuseppe Verdi] Philadelphia, Macrae Smith [1960] 192p. 23cm. [ML3930.V4M23] 60-14033
1. Verdi, Giuseppe, 1813-1901—Juvenile literature. I. Title.

Vereide, Abraham, 1886-

GRUBB, Norman Percy, 1895- 207'.11
Modern viking; the story of Abraham Vereide, pioneer in Christian leadership. Grand Rapids, Zondervan Pub. House [1961] 205p. illus. 23cm. [BX6.8.V4G7] 61-16751
1. Vereide, Abraham, 1886- I. Title.

Verghese, Mary, 1925-

WILSON, Dorothy Clarke. 926.1
Take my hands; the remarkable story of Dr. Mary Verghese. New York, McGraw-Hill [1963] 216 p. 22 cm. [R608.V4W5] 62-22228
1. Verghese, Mary, 1925- I. Title.

WILSON, Dorothy Clarke. 926.1
Take my hands; the remarkable story of Dr. Mary Verghese. New York, McGraw-Hill [1963] 216 p. 22 cm. [R608.V4W5] 62-22228
1. Verghese, Mary, 1925- I. Title.

Vergilius Maro, Publius.

FRANK, Tenney, 1876-1939. 928.7
Vergil, a biography. New York, Russell & Russell, 1965 [c1922] vii, 200 p. 23 cm. Bibliographical footnotes. [PA6825.F75 1965] 65-13942
1. Vergilius Maro, Publius. I. Title.

HAECKER, Theodor, 1879-1945. 871.'01
Virgil, father of the West. Translated by A. W. Wheen. London, Sheed & Ward, 1934. New York, Johnson Reprint Corp. [1970] 120 p. 19 cm. (Essays in order, no. 14) Translation of Vergil, Vater des Abendlandes. [PA6825.H313 1970] 71-139394
1. Vergilius Maro, Publius. I. Title. II. Series.

HAECKER, Theodor, 1879-1945. 871'.01
Virgil, father of the West. Translated by A. W. Wheen. [Folcroft, Pa.] Folcroft Library Editions, 1973. p. Reprint of the 1934 ed. published by Sheed & Ward, London, which was issued as no. 14 of Essays in order. Translation of Vergil, Vater des Abendlandes. [PA6825.H313 1973] 73-6610 ISBN 0-8414-2090-4 (lib. bdg.)
1. Vergilius Maro, Publius. I. Title. BIP

WOODBERRY, George Edward, 1855-1930. 871'.01
Virgil. New York, Haskell House Publishers, 1972. 35 p. 23 cm. [PA6826.W6 1972] 72-3495 ISBN 0-8383-1564-X
1. Vergilius Maro, Publius. I. Title. BIP

Verlaine, Paul Marie, 1844-1896.

COULON, Marcel, 1873- 841'.8 B
Poet under Saturn; the tragedy of Verlaine. Translated and with an introd. by Edgell Rickword. Port Washington, N.Y., Kennikat Press [1970] 206 p. 22 cm. Translation of Verlaine, poete saturnien. Reprint of the 1932 ed. [PQ2464.C62 1970] 77-103176
1. Verlaine, Paul Marie, 1844-1896. I. Title. BIP

HANSON, Lawrence. 928.4
Verlaine: fool of God, by Lawrence and Elisabeth Hanson. New York, Random House [1957] 394p. illus. 22cm. Includes bibliography. [PQ2464.H3] 57-10048
1. Verlaine, Paul Marie, 1844-1896. I. Hanson, Elisabeth M., joint author. II. Title.

HANSON, Lawrence. 928.4
Verlaine: fool of God, by Lawrence and Elisabeth Hanson. New York, Random House [1957] 394p. illus. 22cm. Includes bibliography. [PQ2464.H3] 57-10048
1. Verlaine, Paul Marie, 1844-1896. I. Hanson, Elisabeth M., joint author. II. Title.

LEPELLETIER, Edmond Adolphe de Bouhelier, 1846-1913. 841'.8 B
Paul Verlaine, his life—his work. Translated by E. M. Lang. [1st AMS ed.] New York, AMS Press [1970] x, 463 p. facsim., ports. 23 cm. Reprint of the 1909 ed. [PQ2464.L42 1970] 79-128938
1. Verlaine, Paul Marie, 1844-1896.

RICHARDSON, Joanna. 841'.8 B
Verlaine. New York, Viking Press [1971] ix, 432 p. illus., ports. 22 cm. Bibliography: p. 405-418. [PQ2464.R5 1971b] 74-151882 ISBN 0-670-74518-9 10.00
1. Verlaine, Paul Marie, 1844-1896.

VERLAINE, Paul Marie, 1844-1896. 928.4
Confessions of a poet. Pref. by Martin L. Wolf. Translated from the French by Ruth Saltzman Wolf and Joanna Richardson. New York, Philosophical Liprary [1950] 192 p. ports., facsim. 23 cm. Translation of Confessions; notes autobiographiques. [PQ2464.A23] 50-9065
I. Title. BIP

Vermeer, Johannes, 1632-1675.

KILBRACKEN, John Raymond Godley, baron, 1920- 927.5
The master forger; the story of Han van Meegeren. New York, W. Funk [1951?] 223p. illus. 20cm. [ND653.M58K53 1951a] 51-7661
1. Meegeren, Han van, 1889-1947. 2. Vermeer, Johannes, 1632-1675. 3. Hooch, Pieter de, 17th cent. 4. Forgery of works of art. 5. Paintings—Expertising. I. Title.

Vermont. General Assembly. Senate.

SMALLWOOD, Frank. 328.743'092'4
Free and independent / Frank Smallwood. Brattleboro, Vt. : S. Greene Press, c1976. xvii, 235 p. ; 24 cm. Includes index. Bibliography: p. 229-230. [JK3076.S6] 75-41878 ISBN 0-8289-0272-0 : 7.95
1. Vermont. General Assembly. Senate. 2. Smallwood, Frank. 3. Legislators—Vermont—Correspondence, reminiscences, etc. I. Title. BIP

Vermont—Social life and customs.

WOLF, Marguerite Hurrey. 974.3
I'll take the back road / Marguerite Hurrey Wolf ; drawings by Robert MacLean. Brattleboro, Vt. : S. Greene Press, [1975] xii, 171 p. : ill. ; 24 cm. Published in 1965 under title: Anything can happen in Vermont. Essays. [F55.W6 1975] 74-27458 ISBN 0-8289-0244-5 : 7.95
1. Vermont—Social life and customs. 2. Vermont—Description and travel—1951- 3. Country life—Vermont. 4. Wolf, Marguerite Hurrey. I. Title. BIP

Vermuyden, Cornelius, Sir, 1590-1677.

KORTHALS-ALTES, J. 627'.5'0924 B
Sir Cornelius Vermuyden : the lifework of a great Anglo-Dutchman in land-reclamation and drainage / J. Korthals-Altes. New York : Arno Press, 1977. p. cm. (European business) Reprint of the 1925 ed. published by Williams & Norgate, London. [TC978.G7K67 1977] 76-29751 ISBN 0-405-09767-0 : 17.00
1. Vermuyden, Cornelius, Sir, 1590-1677. 2. Drainage—England. 3. Reclamation of land—England. I. Title. II. Series. BIP

Verne, Jules, 1828-1905.

ALLOTT, Kenneth. 843.8 B
Jules Verne. Port Washington, N.Y., Kennikat Press [1970] xvi, 283 p. illus., ports. 22 cm. Reprint of the 1954 ed. Bibliography: p. 270-274. [PQ2469.Z5A7 1970] 70-113305 ISBN 8-04-609926-
1. Verne, Jules, 1828-1905.

ALLOTTE DE LA FUYE, Marguerite (Pichelin) 1874- 928.4
Jules Verne, Translated by Erik de Mauny. 1st American ed.] New York, Coward-McCann [1956] 222p. 20cm. [PQ2469.Z5A72] 56-11213
1. Verne, Jules, 1828-1905. I. Title.

ALLOTTE DE LA FUYE, Marguerite (Pichelin) 1874 928.4
Jules Verne. Translated by Erik de Mauny. [1st American ed.] New York, Coward-McCann [1956] 222p. 20cm. [PQ2469.Z5A72] 56-11243
1. Verne, Jules, 1828-1905. I. Title.

BECKER, Beril 843.8 (B)
Jules Verne. New York, Putnam [1966] 224p. 22cm. (Lives to remember ser.) [PQ2469.Z5B4] 66-7065 3.29 lib. ed.,
1. Verne, Jules, 1828-1905. I. Title.

EVANS, Idrisyn Oliver, 1894- 843.8
Jules Verne and his work [by] I. O. Evans. [New York] Twayne Publishers [1966] 188 p. illus., ports. 22 cm. Bibliography: p. 173-181. [PQ2469.Z5E9 1966] 67-12
1. Verne, Jules, 1828-1905. I. Title. BIP

FREEDMAN, Russell 843.8
Jules Verne, portrait of a prophet. [New York] Holiday House [c.1965] 256p. illus., facsims., ports. 22cm. [PQ2469.Z5F75] 65-8238 3.95
1. Verne, Jules, 1828-1905. I. Title.

PEARE, Catherine Owens. 928.4
Jules Verne: his life. Illustrated by Margaret Ayer. [1st ed.] New York Holt [1956] 122p. illus. 21cm. [PQ2469.Z5P4] 56-6232
1. Verne, Jules, 1828-1905. I. Title.

Verne, Jules, 1828-1905—Biography.

COSTELLO, Peter. 843'.8 B
Jules Verne, inventor of science fiction / by Peter Costello. New York : Scribner, [1978] p. cm. Includes index. Bibliography: p. [PQ2469.Z5C66 1978] 78-57528 ISBN 0-684-15824-8 : 12.50
1. Verne, Jules, 1828-1905—Biography. 2. Novelists, French—19th century—Biography. I. Title.

JULES-VERNE, Jean, 1892- 843'.8 B
Jules Verne : a biography / by Jean Jules-Verne ; translated and adapted by Roger Greaves. New York : Taplinger Pub. Co., 1976. xii, 245 p., [12] leaves of plates : ill. ; 24 cm. "An Arnold Lent book." Includes index. Bibliography: p. 227-238. [PQ2469.Z5J7813] 73-16958 ISBN 0-8008-4439-4 : 10.95
1. Verne, Jules, 1828-1905—Biography.

JULES-VERNE, Jean, 1892- 843'.8 B
Jules Verne : a biography / by Jean Jules-Verne ; translated and adapted [from the French] by Roger Greaves. London : Macdonald and Jane's, 1976. x, 245 p., [24] p. of plates : ill., ports. ; 24 cm. Translation of Jules Verne. Includes index. Bibliography: p. 227-238. [PQ2469.Z5J7813] 76-382466 ISBN 0-356-08196-6 : £6.50
1. Verne, Jules, 1828-1905—Biography. 2. Novelists, French—19th century—Biography.

Verner, Elizabeth O'Neill, 1884-

BUSSMAN, Marlo Pease. 741'.0924 B
Born Charlestonian; the story of Elizabeth O'Neill Verner. [Columbia, S.C., Lithographed by State Print. Co., 1969] 120 p. illus. 29 cm. [NE2210.V4B8] 73-6146
1. Verner, Elizabeth O'Neill, 1884- I. Title.

Verney, Edmund, Sir 1590-1642.

VERNEY, Peter. 1930- 923.242
The standard bearer; the story of Sir Edmund Verney, knight-marshal to King Charles I. London, Hutchinson [1963, New York, Hillary House, 1966] 224p. illus., ports. (1 col.) geneal. tables. 24cm. Bibl. [DA396.V4V4] 66-50873 6.50
1. Verney, Edmund, Sir 1590-1642. 2. Gt. Brit.—Hist.—Charlesb1, 1625-1649. I. erney family. II. Title.

Vernon, Bob.

VERNON, Bob. 363.2'092'4 B
L.A. cop : peacemaker in blue / Bob Vernon. Nashville : Impact Books, c1977. 146 p. ; 21 cm. [HV7911.V44A34] 77-153978 ISBN 0-914850-43-1 pbk. : 2.50 ISBN 0-914850-17-2 : 4.95
1. Vernon, Bob. 2. Los Angeles—Police—Biography. 3. Police—Biography. I. Title.

Vernon, Edward, 1946-

VERNON, Edward. 610'.92'4 B
Practice makes perfect / Edward Vernon. New York : St. Martin's Press, c1977. 254 p. ; 22 cm. [R489.V47A35 1977] 77-10174 ISBN 0-312-63535-4 : 8.95
1. Vernon, Edward. 2. Physicians (General practice)—England—Midlands—Biography. I. Title. BIP

VERNON, Edward, 1946- 610'.92'4 B
Practice what you preach / Edward Vernon. New York : St. Martin's Press, c1978. 223 p. ; 22 cm. [R489.V47A36 1978] 78-19409 ISBN 0-312-63542-7 : 8.95
1. Vernon, Edward, 1946- 2. Physicians (General practice)—England—Midlands—Biography. I. Title. BIP

Verot, Augustine, Bp., 1804-1876.

GANNON, Michael V. 922.273
Rebel bishop: the life and era of Augustin Verot. Foreword by John TracyEllis. Milwaukee, Bruce [c.1964] xvii, 267p. illus., map, ports. 22cm. Bibl. 64-23895 4.95
1. Verot, Augustinc, Bp., 1804-1876. 2. St. Augustine (Diocese)—Hist. I. Title.

Verran, Roger, 1916-

VERRAN, Roger, 1916- 979.4'15
Can you survive your escape? : Life on California's north coast / Roger Verran ; [drawings by Nick Carter]. San Rafael, Calif. : Presidio Press, c1978. 142 p., [2] leaves of plates : ill. ; 24 cm. [F869.G83V47] 78-3461 ISBN 0-89141-037-6 : 8.95. ISBN 0-89141-066-X pbk. : 6.95
1. Verran, Roger, 1916- 2. Gualala, Calif.—Biography. 3. California—Description and travel—1951- 4. Seaside resorts—California. I. Title. BIP

Verrazzano

NEWCOMB, Covelle, 973.1'8'00924 B 1908-
Explorer with a heart; the story of Giovanni da Verrazzano. New York, D. McKay Co. [1969] xi, 242 p. 21 cm. A biography of the sixteenth-century navigator who searched for a route to Asia and who for years was confused with a pirate by a similar name. Bibliography: p. 233-242. [E133.V5N4] 092 4.50
1. Verrazzano 2. Verrazzano, Giovanni da, 1485?-1527—Juvenile literature. I. Title.

Verrazzano, Giovanni da, 1485?-1527—Juvenile literature.

NEWCOMB, Covelle, 973.1'8'0924 B 1908-
Explorer with a heart; the story of Giovanni da Verrazzano. New York, D. McKay Co. [1969] xi, 242 p. 21 cm. Bibliography: p. 233-242. A biography of the sixteenth-century navigator who searched for a route to Asia and who for years was confused with a pirate by a similar name. [E133.V5N4] 75-81902 4.50
1. Verrazzano, Giovanni da, 1485?-1527—Juvenile literature. I. Title.

SYME, Ronald, 973.1'8'0924 B 1910-
Verrazano, explorer of the Atlantic Coast. Illustrated by William Stobbs. New York, Morrow, 1973. 95, [1] p. illus. 23 cm. Bibliography: p. [96] A biography of the Italian who explored the Atlantic Coast from Cape Fear to Cape Breton discovering New York and Narragansett bays during his voyages. [E133.V5S9] 92 72-7130 3.95
1. Verrazzano, Giovanni da, 1485?-1527—Juvenile literature. 2. America—Discovery and exploration—French—Juvenile literature. I. Stobbs, William, illus. II. Title.
Library edition 3.78; ISBN 0-688-30056-1. BIP

Versalles, Zoilo, 1940-

TERZIAN, James P. 796.3576'4'0924
The kid from Cuba: Zoilo Versalles, by James Terzian. [1st ed.] Garden City, N.Y., Doubleday [1967] 142 p. illus., ports. 22 cm. (Doubleday signal books) [GV865.V47T4] 67-17271
1. Versalles, Zoilo, 1940- I. Title.

Verwoerd, Hendrik Frensch, 1901-1966.

HEPPLE, Alexander, 968/.05/0924 1904-
Verwoerd. Baltimore, Penguin [1967] 253p. 18cm. (Pol. leaders of the twentieth cent.) Pelican bk. A913 Bibl. [DT779.8.V4H4] (B) 67-108656 1.25 pap.,
1. Verwoerd, Hendrik Frensch, 1901-1966. I. Title.

HEPPLE, Alexander, 968'.05'0924 1904-
Verwoerd [Magnolia, Mass., Peter Smith, 1968, c.1967] 253p. 18cm. (Pelican bk., A913: Political leaders of the twentieth cent. rebound) Bibl. [DT779.8.V4H4] (B) 3.25
1. Verwoerd, Hendrik Frensch, 1901-1966. I. Title.

Very, Jones, 1813-1880.

BARTLETT, William Irving. 811'.3
Jones Very, Emerson's "brave saint." New York, Greenwood Press, 1968 [c1942] xv, 237 p. illus., facsims., ports. 24 cm. Bibliography: p. [209]-227. [PS3128.B3 1968] 68-29741
1. Very, Jones, 1813-1880. BIP

GITTLEMAN, Edwin. 811'.3
Jones Very: the effective years, 1833-1840. New York, Columbia University Press, 1967. xx, 436 p. 22 cm. Bibliography: p. 411-420. [PS3128.G5] 67-16202
1. Very, Jones, 1813-1880. I. Title. BIP

Vesalius, Andreas, 1514-1564.

FULTON, John Farquhar, 926.1 1899-
Vesalius four centuries later. Medicine in the eighteenth century. Lawrence, University of Kansas Press, 1950. 52 p. port. 22 cm. (Logan Clendening lectures on the history and philosophy of medicine. First series) [QM16.V5F8] 51-362
1. Vesalius, Andreas, 1514-1564. 2. Medicine—Hist. I. Title. II. Series.

TARSHIS, Jerome, 611'.00924 B 1936-
Andreas Vesalius; father of modern anatomy. New York, Dial Press [1969] 144 p. 22 cm. Bibliography: p. 136-137. [QM16.V5T3] 71-88649 3.95
1. Vesalius, Andreas, 1514-1564.

Vesalius, Andreas, 1514-1564—Bibl.

CUSHING, Harvey Williams, 012 1869-1939
A bio-bibliography of Andreas Versalius 2d ed. Hamden, Conn., Archon [dist. Shoe String] 1962. vii p., facsim. ([iii]-xxxviii, 222p. illus., ports., facsims.), [223]-264p. 26cm. Reproduced from the orig. ed. issued in 1943 by Schuman's, New York, as Pubn. no. 6, Historical Lib., Yale Medical Lib. 62-525286 22.50
1. Vesalius, Andreas, 1514 1564 Bibl. I. Title.

Vesco, Robert.

*DORMAN, Michael. 364.1630924
Vesco; the infernal money making machine. [New York] Berkley Pub. Co. [1975] vi, 248 p. 18 cm. (A Berkley medallion book) [HV6766] 02845-3 1.50 (pbk.)
1. Vesco, Robert I. Title.

HUTCHISON, Robert 364.1'63'0924 B A., 1938-
Vesco [by] Robert A. Hutchison. [New York] Avon [1976 c1974] 442 p. illus. 18 cm. [HV6766.V48H87] ISBN 0-380-00526-3 1.95 (pbk.)
1. Vesco, Robert. I. Title.
L.C. no. of original edition: 73-8399. BIP

HUTCHISON, 364.1'63'0924 [B] Robert A. 1938-
Vesco [by] Robert A. Hutchison. New York, Praeger [1974] 376 p. illus. 24 cm. [HV6766.V48H87] 73-8399 ISBN 0-275-19860-X 9.95
1. Vesco, Robert. I. Title.

Vesey, Denmark, 1769 (ca.)-1822—Juvenile literature.

SPENCER, Philip, 326'.092'2 B 1925-
3 against slavery: Denmark Vesey, William Lloyd Garrison, Frederick Douglass. [New York] Scholastic Book Services [1972] 128 p. illus. 21 cm. (Firebird biographies) (Firebird books) Brief biographies of three nineteenth-century men—two black, one white—who led the struggle for the abolition of slavery. [E449.S75617] 920 76-187885
1. Vesey, Denmark, 1769 (ca.)-1822—Juvenile literature. 2. Garrison, William Lloyd, 1805-1879—Juvenile literature. 3. Douglass, Frederick, 1817?-1895—Juvenile literature. I. Title.

Vespucci, Amerigo, 1451-1512.

ARCINIEGAS, German, 923.945 1900-
Amerigo and the New World; the life & times of Amerigo Vespucci. Translated from the Spanish by Harriet de Onis. [1st ed.] New York, Knopf, 1955. 322 p. illus. 22 cm. Includes bibliography. [E125.V5A65] 53-9487
1. Vespucci, Amerigo, 1451-1512. I. Title.

Vespucci, Amerigo, 1451-1512—Juvenile literature.

SYME, Ronald, 1910- 973.1'9 B
Amerigo Vespucci, scientist and sailor. Illustrated by William Stobbs. New York, W. Morrow [1969] 94 [1] p. illus., maps. 22 cm. Bibliography: p. [95] A biography of Amerigo Vespucci, whose discoveries of the American Continent remained unrecognized for many centuries. [E125.V5S9] 92 69-10483 3.50
1. Vespucci, Amerigo, 1451-1512—Juvenile literature. I. Stobbs, William, illus. II. Title.

Vestal, Stanley, 1887-1957.

TASSIN, Ray. 917.8'03'2072024 B
Stanley Vestal: champion of the Old West. Glendale, Calif., A. H. Clark Co., 1973. 299 p. ports. 25 cm. Bibliography: p. [279]-292. [E175.5.V38T37] 72-97805 ISBN 0-87062-105-X 11.00
1. Vestal, Stanley, 1887-1957.

Vester, Bertha Hedges Spafford, 1878-

†VESTER, Bertha 266'.023'095694 Hedges Spafford, 1878-
Our Jerusalem / Bertha Spafford Vester. New York : Arno Press, 1977, c1950. x, 332 p. ; 23 cm. (America and the Holy Land) Reprint of the ed. published by Doubleday, Garden City, N.J. [DS109.V3 1977] 77-70752 ISBN 0-405-10296-8 : 22.00
1. Vester, Bertha Hedges Spafford, 1878- 2. Jerusalem—Description. 3. Americans in Jerusalem—Biography. 4. Missionaries—United States—Biography. 5. Missionaries—Jerusalem—Biography. I. Title. II. Series.

Vestris, Lucia Elizabeth (Bartolozzi) 1797-1856.

PEARCE, Charles E. 792'.028'0924
Madame Vestris and her times, by Charles E. Pearce. New York, B. Blom [1969] 314 p. illus., ports. 24 cm. Reprint of the 1923 ed. [PN2598.V5P4 1969] 70-77975
1. Vestris, Lucia Elizabeth (Bartolozzi) 1797-1856. I. Title. BIP

Vetch, Samuel, 1668-1732.

WALLER, George Macgregor 923.273
Samuel Vetch, colonial enterpriser. Chapel Hill, Published for the Institute of Early American History and Culture at Williamsburg, Va. by University of North Carolina Press [c.1960] x, 311p. Includes bibliography. illus. 24cm. 60-10970 6.00
1. Vetch, Samuel, 1668-1732. I. Title.

WALLER, George Macgregor, 923.273 1919-
Samuel Vetch, colonial enterpriser. Chapel Hill, Published for the Institute of Early American History and Culture at Williamsburg, Va. by University of North Carolina Press [1960] 311 p. illus. 24 cm. Includes bibliography. [F1038.V57] 60-10970
1. Vetch, Samuel, 1668-1732. I. Title.

Vetenarians—Correspondence, reminiscences, etc.

HERRIOT, James. 636.089'092'4 [B]
All creatures great and small. New York, Bantam Books [1973, c.1972] 499 p. 18 cm. [SF613.H44A28] 1.75 (pbk.)
1. Vetenarians—Correspondence, reminiscences, etc. I. Title.
L.C. card no. for the hardbound edition: 72-79632. BIP

PRICE, Willet J., 636.089'092'4 B 1902-1972.
Boots and forceps [by] Willet J. Price, as told to Hazel Heckman. Drawings by Helen Hiatt Ames, Iowa State University Press, 1973. ix, 181 p. illus. 23 cm. [SF613.P7A3] 77-39465 ISBN 0-8138-0265-2 5.95
1. Veterinarians—Correspondence, reminiscences, etc. I. Heckman, Hazel. II. Title. BIP

YOUNKER, Lucas. 636.089'092'4 B
Animal doctor / Lucas Younker and John J. Fried. 1st ed. New York : Dutton, c1976. 247 p., [4] leaves of plates : ill. ; 22 cm. [SF613.Y68A32 1976] 76-15390 ISBN 0-8415-0466-0 : 9.95
1. Veterinarians—Correspondence, reminiscences, etc. I. Fried, John J., joint author. II. Title.
Distributed by Dutton BIP

Vetter, Hal

VETTER, Hal 920.7
Women of the swastika. Evanston, Ill., Regency [c.1963] 156p. 18cm. (RB 312) .50 pap.,
I. Title.

Vettori, Francesco, 1474-1539.

JONES, Rosemary Devonshire. 945'.06'0924 B
Francesco Vettori, Florentine citizen and Medici servant. London, Athlone Press, 1972. xi, 319 p. geneal. table. 23 cm. (University of London. Historical studies, 34) Distributed in the USA by Humanities Press, New York. Originally presented as the author's thesis, University of London, 1958. Bibliography: p. [301]-306. [DG738.14.V47J66 1972] 73-160329 ISBN 0-485-13134-X 18.25
1. Vettori, Francesco, 1474-1539. 2. Florence—Politics and government. I. Series: London. University. Historical studies, 34.

Vianney, Jean Baptiste Marie, Saint, 1786-1859.

BETZ, Eva (Kelly) 1897- 922.244
The man who fought the Devil; the Cure of Ars. Illus. by Kathleen Voute. Paterson, N. J., St. Anthony Guild Press [1958] 144p. illus. 20cm. [BX4700.V5B4] 59-20729
1. Vianney, Jean Baptiste Marie, Saint, 1786-1859. I. Title.

LA VARENDE, Jean de, 1887- 922.244
The Cure of Ars and his cross. Translated by Jane Wynne Saul. Photos. by J. A. Fortier. Designs by R. Galoyer. New York, Desclee Co. [1959] 221p. illus. 21cm. [BX4700.V5L353] 59-12544
1. Vianney, Jean Baptiste Marie, Saint, 1786-1859. I. Title.

LOMASK, Milton. 922.244
The Cure of Ars; the priest who outtalked the devil. Illustrated by Johannes Troyer. New York, Vision Books [1958] 190p. illus. 22cm. (Vision books, 36) [BX4700.V5L6] 58-6983
1. Vianney, Jean Baptiste Marie, Saint, 1786-1859. I. Title.

O'BRIEN, Bartholomew J 922.244
Secrets of a parish priest. [Chicago, J. S. Paluch Co., c1956] 121p. 18cm. (Lumen books, 540) Includes bibliography. [BX4700.V5O2] 57-31083
1. Vianney, Jean Bartiste Marie, Saint, 1786-1859. I. Title.

PAULUS, Brother, 1911- 922.244
Saint of the countryside; a story of Saint John Vianney. Illus. by Bernard Howard. Notre Dame, Ind., Dujarie Press [1951] 88 p. illus. 24 cm. [BX4700.V5P3] 52-16004
1. Vianney, Jean Baptiste Marie, Saint, 1786-1859. I. Title.

PEZERIL, Daniel 922.244
Blessed and poor; the spiritual odyssey of the Cure of Ars. Tr. [from French] by Pansy Pakenham. [New York] Pantheon [1961,c.1959] 255p. Bibl. 61-7453 4.00
1. Vianney, Jean Baptiste Marie, Saint, 1786-1859. I. Title.

SAINT-PIERRE, Michel de, 1916- 922.244
The remarkable Cure of Ars: the life and achievements of St. John Mary Vianney. Tr. [from French] by A. Angeline Bouchard. Garden City, N.Y., Doubleday, 1963[c.1958,1963] 230p. 22cm. 63-8738 3.95
1. Vianney, Jean Baptiste Marie, Saint, 1786-1859. I. Title.

TREECE, Henry, 1912- v. 12
Dylan Thomas, 'dog among the fairies. New York, John de Graff, 1956. 158 p. 19 cm.
1. Thomas, Dylan, 1914-1953. I. Title. BIP

TROCHU, Francis, 1877- 922.244
The cure d'Ars; a shorter biography. [Translation by Ronald Matthews] Westminster, Md., Newman Press [1955] 193p. illus. 20cm. Translation of L'admirable vie du cure d'Ars. [BX4700.V5T485] 55-8663
1. Vianney, Jean Baptiste Marie, Saint, 1786-1859. I. Title.

Vianney, Martin Gerard.

VIANNEY, Gina. 362.7'8'19699400924 B
Martin : the true story of a boy's fight against cancer / by Gina Vianney. Alton : Redemptorist Publications, 1974. 187 p. ; 18 cm. [RC281.C4V52] 75-594615 ISBN 0-85231-012-9 : £0.50
1. Vianney, Martin Gerard. 2. Tumors in children. 3. Cancer—Personal narratives. I. Title.

Viardot-Garcia, Pauline, 1821-1910.

FITZLYON, April 927.8
The price of genius; a life of Pauline Viardot. New York, Appleton-Century [dist. Meredith, 1965, c.1964] 520p. illus., geneal. table, ports. 21cm Bibl. [ML420.V36F6] 64-24474 5.95
1. Viardot-Garcia, Pauline, 1821-1910. I. Title.

Viaud, Julien, 1850-1923.

LERNER, Michael G. 843'.8 B
Pierre Loti, by Michael G. Lerner. New York, Twayne Publishers [1974] 172 p. port. 22 cm. (Twayne's world authors series, TWAS 285. France) Bibliography: p. 165-168. [PQ2472.Z8L44] 73-2368 ISBN 0-8057-2546-6
1. Viaud, Julien, 1850-1923. I. Title. BIP

Vice-Presidents.

FEERICK, John D. 920
The Vice-Presidents of the United States, by John D. and Emalie P. Feerick. New York, F. Watts [1967] 91 p. ports. 23 cm. An introduction to the office of Vice President, with brief sketches of the men who have assisted the President to date. [E176.F4] AC 67
1. Vice-Presidents. I. Feerick, Emalie P., joint author. II. Title. BIP

GRIFFITH, Winthrop. 923.273
Humphrey, a candid biography. New York, Morrow [1968, c.1965] xii, 337p. 20cm. [E748.H945G7] 65-14953 2.95 pap.,
I. Humphrey, Hubert Horatio, 1911- II. Title.

Vice-Presidents—U.S.—Biography.

BARZMAN, Sol. 973'.0992 B
Madmen and geniuses : the vice-presidents of the United States / Sol Barzman. Chicago : Follett, [1974] xi, 335 p. : ports. ; 24 cm. Includes index. Bibliography: p. 313-326. [E176.B28] 74-78583 ISBN 0-695-80487-1 : 8.95
1. Vice-Presidents—United States—Biography. I. Title.

LUCCHETTI, Anthony, 1924- 923.273
The Vice-Presidents of the United States, by John Prescott [pseud.] Portraits by Barbara Koski. New York, Comet Press Books, 1957. 54p. illus. 21cm. [E176.L9] 57-7021
1. Vice-Presidents—U. S.—Biog. I. Title.

VEXLER, Robert I. 973'.0992 B
The Vice-Presidents and Cabinet members : biographies arranged chronologically by Administration / by Robert I. Vexler. Dobbs Ferry, N.Y. : Oceana Publications, 1975. 2 v. (xix, 887 p.) ; 26 cm. Includes bibliographies and index. [E176.V48] 75-28085 ISBN 0-379-12089-5 (v. 1). ISBN 0-379-12090-9 (v. 2) : 50.00
1. Vice-Presidents—United States—Biography. 2. Cabinet officers—United States—Biography. 3. United States—Biography. I. Title.

YOUNG, Klyde H. 973 B
Heirs apparent; the Vice Presidents of the United States [by] Klyde Young and Lamar Middleton. Freeport, N.Y., Books for Libraries Press [1969, c1948] vi, 314 p. 23 cm. (Biography index reprint series) Bibliography: p. 305-306. [E176.Y7 1969] 70-101835
1. Vice-Presidents—U.S.—Biography. I. Middleton, Lamar, joint author. II. Title.

Vice-Presidents—U.S.—Biography—Juvenile literature.

ALVAREZ, Joseph A. 973 B
Vice-Presidents of destiny, by Joseph A. Alvarez. New York, Putnam [1969] 191 p. ports. 22 cm. Bibliography: p. 186-187. Brief biographies of eight Vice-Presidents who succeeded to the Presidency when the incumbent died in office. [E176.A45] 920 68-24498 3.64
1. Vice-Presidents—U.S.—Biography—Juvenile literature. I. Title. BIP

FEERICK, John D. 973'.0992 B
The first book of the Vice-Presidents of the United States / by John D. and Emalie P. Feerick. 3d ed. New York : Watts, c1977. p. cm. (A First book) Includes index. An introduction to the office of Vice-President, with brief sketches of the men who have filled that post from John Adams to Walter F. Mondale. [E176.8.F43 1977] 77-1454 ISBN 0-531-02907-7 lib.bdg. : 4.47
1. Vice-Presidents—United States—Biography—Juvenile literature. I. Feerick, Emalie P., joint author. II. Title.

FEERICK, John D. 920
The Vice-Presidents of the United States, by John D. & Emalie P. Feerick. Rev. ed. New York, F. Watts, 1973. 91 p. ports. 23 cm. (A First book) [E176.F4] 67-14514 ISBN 0-531-00659-X 3.95 (lib. ed.)
1. Vice-Presidents—U.S.—Biog.—Juvenile literature. I. Feerick, Emalie P., joint author. II. Title.

Vice-Presidents—United States—Anecdotes, facetiae, satire, etc.

CURTIS, Richard. 353'.0318'0207
Not exactly a crime; our vice presidents from Adams to Agnew, by Richard Curtis and Maggie Wells. New York, Dial Press, 1972. xii, 202 p. illus. 21 cm. [E176.C93] 79-37466
1. Vice-Presidents—United States—Anecdotes, facetiae, satire, etc. I. Wells, Maggie, joint author. II. Title.

Vicentino, Nicola, 1511-1572.

KAUFMANN, Henry William. 780.924
The life and works of Nicola Vicentino, 1511-c.1576. [n.p.] American Institute of Musicology, 1966. 241 p. facsim., music. 25 cm. (American Institute of Musicology. Musicological studies and documents, 11) Bibliography: p. 225-234. [ML410.V777K4] 66-5661
1. Vicentino, Nicola, 1511-1572. I. American Institute of Musicology. II. Title. III. Series. IV. Series: American Institue of Musicology. Studies and documents, 11

Vickrey, Robert, 1926-

VICKREY, Robert, 1926- 759.13 B
Robert Vickrey, artist at work / by Robert Vickrey. New York : Watson-Guptill, 1979. p. cm. Includes index. [ND237.V48A2 1979] 79-13352 ISBN 0-8230-4580-3 : 19.50
1. Vickrey, Robert, 1926- 2. Painters—United States—Biography. I. Title.

Vico, Giovanni Battista, 1668-1744.

ADAMS, Henry Packwood. 195
The life and writings of Giambattista Vico, by H. P. Adams. New York, Russell & Russell [1970] 236 p. 20 cm. Reprint of the 1935 ed. Includes bibliographical references. [B3583.A3 1970] 72-102463
1. Vico, Giovanni Battista, 1668-1744.

Victoria,

VICTORIA, Queen of Great Britain, 1819-1901. 923.142
Dearest child; letters between Queen Victoria and the Princess Royal, 1858-1861. Edited by Roger Fulford. New York, Holt, Rinehart and Winston [1965, c1964] x, 401 p. ports. 22 cm. [DA552.D4 1965] 65-14228
I. Victoria, consort of Frederick. II. German Emperor, 1840-1901. III. Fulford, Roger, 1902- ed. IV. Title.

Victoria, consort of Frederic III, German Emperor, 1840-1901

BARKELEY, Richard German Emporor 1840-1901 923.143
The Empress Frederick, daughter of Queen Victoria. With a foreword by G. P. Gooch. London, Macmillan; New York, St. Martin's Press, 1956. 321p. illus. 23cm. [DD224.9.B3] 56-4798
1. Victoria, consort of Frederic III, German Emperor, 1840-1901 I. Title.

BENNETT, Daphne. 943.08'4'0924 B
Vicky. New York, Popular Lib. [1973, c.1971] 511 p. illus., ports., geneal. 18 cm. Hardbound edition had title: Vicky: Princess Royal of England and German Empress. Bibliography: p. 491-497. [DD224.9B45 1972] 1.25 (pbk.)
1. Victoria, consort of Frederick III, German Emperor, 1840-1901. I. Title.
L.C. card no. for hardbound ed.: 74-145442.

BENNETT, Daphne. 943.08'4'0924 B
Vicky: Princess Royal of England and German Empress. [New York] St. Martin's Press [1972] 382 p. illus. 24 cm. Bibliography: p. 367-371. [DD224.9.B45 1972] 74-145442 10.00
1. Victoria, consort of Frederick III, German Emperor, 1840-1901. I. Title.

Victoria, Queen of Great Britain, 1819-1901.

ARONSON, Theo. 941.081'092'2
Victoria and Disraeli : the making of a romantic partnership / Theo Aronson. 1st American ed. New York : Macmillan, 1978, c1977. xii, 212 p., [4] leaves of plates : ill. ; 22 cm. Includes index. Bibliography: p. [203]-206. [DA554.A726 1978] 78-8181 ISBN 0-02-503490-1 : 9.95
1. Victoria, Queen of Great Britain, 1819-1901. 2. Beaconsfield, Benjamin Disraeli, 1st Earl of, 1804-1881. 3. Great Britain—Kings and rulers—Biography. 4. Prime ministers—Great Britain—Biography. I. Title. BIP

AUCHINCLOSS, Louis. 941.081'092'4 B
Persons of consequence : Queen Victoria and her circle / Louis Auchincloss. 1st American ed. New York : Random House, c1979. 208 p. : ill. ; 26 cm. Includes index. Bibliography: p. 201-203. [DA554.A92 1979] 78-26626 ISBN 0-394-50427-5 : 17.95
1. Victoria, Queen of Great Britain, 1819-1901. 2. Great Britain—Court and courtiers. 3. Great Britain—History—Victoria, 1837-1901. 4. Great Britain—Kings and rulers—Biography. I. Title. BIP

BAYNES, Dorothy Julia. 923.142
The youthful Queen Victoria; a discursive narrative, by Dormer Creston [pseud.] New York, Putnam [1952] xv, 428 p. illus., ports. 22 cm. Bibliography: p. 407-415. [DA554.B28 1952a] 52-9830
1. Victoria. Queen of Great Britain, 1819-1901. I. Title.

COLLIEU, E. G. 942.0810942
Queen Victoria [New York] Oxford [c.] 1965. 64p. illus., ports. 21cm. (Clarendon biog. 6) Bibl. [DA554.C58] 65-5295 1.40 bds.,
1. Victoria, Queen of Great Britain, 1819-1901. I. Title.

COLLIEU, E G 942.0810942 (B)
Queen Victoria, by E. G. Collieu. [London] Oxford University Press, 1965. 64 p. illus., ports. 21 cm. (The Clarendon biographies, 6) "Suggestions for further reading": p. [62] [DA554.C58] 65-5295
1. Victoria, Queen of Great Britain, 1819-1901. I. Title.

CULLEN, Tom A. 942.081'0924
The Empress Brown; The true story of a Victorian scandal, by Tom Cullen. Illustrated with photos. Boston, Houghton Mifflin, 1969. ix, 250 p. illus., ports. 22 cm. Bibliography: p. [231]-240. [DA555.C82 1969] 66-12066
1. Victoria, Queen of Great Britain, 1819-1901. 2. Brown, John, 1826-1883. I. Title.

DUFF, David, 1912- 942.081'092'2 B
Victoria and Albert. New York, Taplinger Pub. Co. [1972] 319 p. illus. 24 cm. Bibliography: p. 303-308. [DA554.D8 1972] 72-2203 ISBN 0-8008-7967-8 9.95
1. Victoria, Queen of Great Britain, 1819-1901. 2. Albert, Consort of Queen Victoria, 1819-1861. I. Title.

DUFF, David, 1912- 942.081'0924 B
Victoria travels; journeys of Queen Victoria between 1830 and 1900, with extracts from her journal. Illustrated with photos. from the private albums of the Queen's constant companions, H. R. H. Princess Beatrice and John Brown, her personal attendant, and contemporary drawings, paintings, and photos. from a variety of collections. New York, Taplinger [1971, c1970] 383 p. illus., map (on lining papers), ports. 26 cm. Includes bibliographical references. [DA555.D8 1971] 70-133434 ISBN 0-8008-7972-4 14.95
1. Victoria, Queen of Great Britain, 1819-1901. 2. Europe—Description and travel—1800-1918. I. Title. **BIP**

EPTON, Nina Consuelo. 942.081'0922 B
Victoria and her daughters [by] Nina Epton. New York, Norton [1971] 252 p. illus. 22 cm. Bibliography: p. 241-244. [DA554.E68 1971b] 70-162796 ISBN 0-393-05445-4 7.95
1. Victoria, Queen of Great Britain, 1819-1901. I. Title.

FFRENCH, Yvonne. 920.72'094
Six great Englishwomen : Queen Elizabeth I, Sarah Siddons, Charlotte Bronte, Florence Nightingale, Queen Victoria, Gertrude Bell / by Yvonne Ffrench. Folcroft, Pa. : Folcroft Library Editions, 1976. p. cm. Reprint of the 1953 ed. published by Hamilton, London. [DA28.7.F42 1976] 76-10646 ISBN 0-8414-4219-3 lib. bdg. : 17.50
1. Elizabeth, Queen of England, 1533-1603. 2. Siddons, Sarah Kemble, 1755-1831. 3. Bronte, Charlotte, 1816-1855. 4. Nightingale, Florence, 1820-1910. 5. Victoria, Queen of Great Britain, 1819-1901. 6. Bell, Gertrude Lowthian, 1868-1926. I. Title.

GERNSHEIM, Helmut, 1913- 923.142
Victoria R.: a biography with four hundred illustrations based on her personal photograph albums, by Helmut and Alison Gernsheim. [1st American ed.] New York, Putnam [1959] 307 p. illus. 29 cm. [DA555.G4 1959] 59-11013
1. Victoria, Queen of Great Britain, 1819-1901. I. Gersheim, Alison, joint author.

HAYCRAFT, Mary (Costain) 923.142
Queen Victoria, May 24, 1819-January 22, 1901. New York, Messner [1956] 191p. 22cm. [DA554.H37] 56-6788
1. Victoria, Queen of Great Britain, 1819-1901. I. Title.

HAYCRAFT, Molly (Costain) 1911- 923.142
Queen Victoria, May 24, 1819-January 22, 1901. New York, Messner [1956] 191p. 22cm. [DA554.H37] 56-6788
1. Victoria, Queen of Great Briatian, 1819-1901. I. Title.

LONGFORD, Elizabeth (Harman) Countess of Pakenham 1906- 923.142
Queen Victoria: born to succeed New York, Pyramid [1966, c.1965] 635p. illus. ports. 18cm. (V-1280) Bibl. [DA554.L6] 1.25 pap.,
1. Victoria, Queen of Great Britain, 1819-1901. I. Title.

LONGFORD, Elizabeth (Harman) Pakenham, countess of, 1906- 923.142
Queen Victoria: born to succeed, by Elizabeth Longford. 1st ed. New York, Harper & Row [1965, c1964] 635 p. illus., fold. geneal. table, ports. 25 cm. First published in London in 1964 under title: Victoria R.I. "Reference notes": p. 579-604. [DA554.L6 1965] 64-25117
1. Victoria, Queen of Great Britain, 1819-1901. I. Title.

LONGFORD, Elizabeth (Harman) Pakenham, countess of, 1906- 923.142
Queen Victoria; born to succeed, by Elizabeth Longford. New York, Harper & Row [1974, c1964] 635 p. photos. 18 cm. (Perennial library) First published in London in 1964 under title: Victoria R. I. Includes bibliographical references. [DA554.L6 1974] ISBN 0-06-080320-7. 1.95 (pbk.)
1. Victoria, Queen of Great Britain, 1819-1901. I. Title.
L.C. card number for hardbound ed.: 64-25117.

LONGFORD, Elizabeth (Harman) Pakenham, Countess of, 1906- 942.081'092'4 B
Victoria R. I. [by] Elizabeth Longford. Illustrated [1st U.S.] ed. New York, Harper & Row [1973] 287 p. illus. (part col.) 26 cm. Abridgment of Queen Victoria: born to succeed. [DA554.L6 1973] 73-2001 ISBN 0-06-012672-8 15.00
1. Victoria, Queen of Great Britain, 1819-1901. I. Title.

MALLET, Marie, Lady, 1862-1934. 942.081'0924
Life with Queen Victoria; Marie Mallet's letters from court, 1887-1901. Edited by Victor Mallet. Boston, Houghton Mifflin, 1968. xxiv, 245 p. illus. 23 cm. [DA559.5.M34] 68-21250 5.95
1. Victoria, Queen of Great Britain, 1819-1901. I. Mallet, Victor, Sir, 1893- ed. II. Title.

MARSHALL, Dorothy. 942.081'092'4 B
The life and times of Victoria. Introd. by Antonia Fraser. New York, Praeger [1974, c1972] 224 p. illus. 26 cm. Bibliography: p. 220-221. [DA554.M37 1974] 73-12971 10.95
1. Victoria, Queen of Great Britain, 1819-1901. I. Title.

RICHARDSON, Joanna. 941.081'092'2 B
Victoria and Albert / Joanna Richardson. New York : Quadrangle/The New York Times Book Co., c1977. 239 p. : ill. ; 25 cm. Includes index. Bibliography; p. 233. [DA554.R5 1977] 76-52822 ISBN 0-8129-0692-6 : 12.95
1. Victoria, Queen of Great Britain, 1819-1901. 2. Albert, Consort of Queen Victoria, 1819-1961. 3. Great Britain—Kings and rulers—Biography. 4. Great Britain—Princes and princesses—Biography. I. Title. **BIP**

STEVENSON, Sarah Coles, 1789-1848. 942.081
Victoria, Albert, and Mrs. Stevenson, edited by Edward Boykin. New York, Rinehart [1957] x, 309 p. illus., ports. 24 cm. "Letters of Sallie Coles Stevenson, written between 1836 and 1841 when her husband was Minister at the court of St. James." [DA559.5.S8A4] 57-5218
1. Victoria, Queen of Great Britain, 1819-1901. 2. Albert, consort of Queen Victoria, 1819-1861. 3. Gt. Brit.—Court and courtiers. I. Boykin, Edward Carrington, 1889- ed.

STRACHEY, Giles Lytton, 1880-1932. v. 12
Queen Victoria. [Text ed.] New York, Harcourt, Brace [1960, c1921] 434 p. 21 cm. (Harbrace modern classics) First issued in this series in 1949. Bibliography: p. 425-429.
1. Victoria, Queen of Great Britain, 1819-1901. I. Title.

STRACHEY, Giles Lytton, 1880-1932. 941.081'092'4 B
Queen Victoria / by Lytton Strachey. New York : Harcourt Brace Jovanovich, [1978] c1921. 434 p., 4 leaves of plates : ports. ; 21 cm. (A Harvest/HBJ book) Includes index. Bibliography: p. 425-429. [DA554.S7 1978] 77-92139 ISBN 0-15-676245-5 : 4.95
1. Victoria, Queen of Great Britain, 1819-1901. 2. Great Britain—Kings and rulers—Biography. 3. Great Britain—History—Victoria, 1837-1901. I. Title.

*STRACHEY, Lytton 942.0810924
Queen Victoria. New York, Harcourt [1966, c. 1921] 311p. 18cm. (Harbracepaperback lib., HPL 7) .75 pap.,
I. Title.

*STRACHEY, Lytton 942.0810924
Queen Victoria. New York, Harcourt [1966, c. 1921] 311p. 18cm. (Harbracepaperback lib., HPL 7) .75 pap.,
I. Title.

STREATFEILD, Noel. 942.081
Queen Victoria. Illustrated by Robert Frankenberg. New York, Random House [1958] 184 p. illus. 22 cm. (World landmark books, W-37) [DA554.S8] 58-6187
1. Victoria, Queen of Great Britain, 1819-1901.

STREATFEILD, Noel. 942.081'0924 B
Queen Victoria. Illustrated by Robert Frankenberg. New York, Random House [1958] 184 p. illus. 22 cm. (World landmark books, W-37) A biography of Victoria, whose mother was a Saxe-Coburg and whose father was a Hanover, and who herself was born and raised in Britain to become Queen of an Empire and image of an era. [DA554.S8] 92 AC 68
1. Victoria, Queen of Great Britain, 1819-1901. I. Frankenberg, Robert, illus. II. Title.

TISDALL, Evelyn Ernest Percy, 1907- 923.142
Queen Victoria's private life, 1837-1901. [1st American ed.] New York, John Day Co. [1962, c1961] 224 p. illus. 22 cm. [DA554.T5 1962] 62-7339
1. Victoria, Queen of Great Britain, 1819-1901. I. Title.

TISDALL, Evelyn Ernest Percy, 1907- 923.142
Queen Victoria's private life, 1837-1901 [1st American ed.] New York, John Day Co. [1962, c1961] 224 p. illus. 22 cm. [DA554.T6 1962] 62-7339
1. Victoria, Queen of Great Britain, 1819-1901.

VICTORIA, Queen of Great Britain, 1819-1901. 923.142
Dearest child; letters between Queen Victoria and the Princess Royal, 1858-1861. Edited by Roger Fulford. New York, Holt, Rinehart and Winston [1965, c1964] x, 401 p. ports. 22 cm. [DA552.D4 1965] 65-14228
I. Victoria, consort of Frederick. II. German Emperor, 1840-1901. III. Fulford, Roger, 1902- ed. IV. Title.

WOODHAM Smith, Cecil Blanche (Fitz Gerald), 1896- 942.081'092'4 B
Queen Victoria, from her birth to the death of the Prince Consort [by] Cecil Woodham-Smith. [1st American ed.] New York, Knopf; [distributed by Random House] 1972. xii, 486 p. illus. 25 cm. [DA554.W8 1972] 72-2235 ISBN 0-394-48245-X 10.00
1. Victoria, Queen of Great Britain, 1819-1901. 2. Great Britain—History—Victoria, 1837-1901.

Victoria, Queen of Great Britain, 1819-1901—Anniversaries, etc.—Addresses, essays, lectures.

QUEEN Victoria's Jubilees, 1887 & 1897. 941.081'092'4 B New York : Arco Pub. Co., [1978] p. cm. [DA555.Q35] 77-21832 ISBN 0-668-04402-0 : 15.00
1. Victoria, Queen of Great Britain, 1819-1901—Anniversaries, etc.—Addresses, essays, lectures. 2. Great Britain—Kings and rulers—Biography—Addresses, essays, lectures. 3. Great Britain—Social life and customs—19th century—Addresses, essays, lectures.

Victoria, Queen of Great Britain, 1819-1901—Juvenile literature.

BOOTH, Arthur Harold. j 92
The true story of Queen Victoria, British monarch, by Arthur H. Booth. Chicago, Childrens Press [1964] 143 p. col. illus., col. ports. 23 cm. On spine: Queen Victoria. [DA557.B6] 64-19878
1. Victoria, Queen of Great Britain, 1819-1901 — Juvenile literature. I. Title.

COOPER, Lettice Ulpha, 1897- 92
The young Victoria. Illus. by Denise Brown. New York, Roy [1962, c.1961] 144p. illus. 21cm. 62-9027 3.00
1. Victoria, Queen of Great Britain, 1819-1901—Juvenile literature. I. Title.

GLENDINNING, Sally. 942.081'0924 B
Queen Victoria; English empress. Champaign, Ill., Garrard Pub. Co. [1970] 176 p. illus., ports. 22 cm. (A Century book) The life of the nineteenth-century English monarch whose sixty-three year reign over one-quarter of the world's population covered a period of great industrial and social change. [DA557.G55] 92 71-116038 ISBN 8-11-647501- 2.98
1. Victoria, Queen of Great Britain, 1819-1901—Juvenile literature. I. Title.

GRANT, Neil. 942.081'0924 B
Victoria: Queen and Empress. New York, Watts [1970] ix, 233 p. illus., geneal. table, ports. 22 cm. (Immortals of history) Includes bibliographical references. A biography of Queen Victoria, ruler of the British Empire for sixty-three years. [DA557.G73] 92 73-121922
1. Victoria, Queen of Great Britain, 1819-1901—Juvenile literature. I. Title.

Victoria, Queen of Great Britain, 1819-1901—Personality.

HARDY, Alan. 941.081'092'4 B
Queen Victoria was amused / Alan Hardy. New York : Taplinger Pub. Co., 1977, c1976. x, 214 p., [6] leaves of plates : ill. ; 23 cm. Includes index. Bibliography: p. [203]-207. [DA555.H37 1977] 76-55035 ISBN 0-8008-6566-9 : 8.95
1. Victoria, Queen of Great Britain, 1819-1901—Personality. 2. Great Britain—Kings and rulers—Biography. I. Title. **BIP**

Victorio, Apache chief, d. 1881.

THRAPP, Dan L. 970.3 B
Victorio and the Mimbres Apaches [by] Dan L. Thrapp. [1st ed.] Norman, University of Oklahoma Press [1974] xix, 393 p. illus. 23 cm. (The Civilization of the American Indian series) Bibliography: p. 315-325. [E99.M63T47] 72-9269 ISBN 0-8061-1076-7 9.95
1. Victorio, Apache chief, d. 1881. 2. Mimbreno Indians. I. Title. II. Series. **BIP**

Vidocq, Eugene Francois, 1775-1857.

GERSON, Noel Bertram, 1914- 363.2'092'4 B
The Vidocq dossier : the story of the world's first detective / by Samuel Edwards [i.e. N. B. Gerson]. Boston : Houghton Mifflin, 1977. 191, [4] p. : port. ; 22 cm. Bibliography: p. [195] [HV7911.V5G47] 76-53777 ISBN 0-395-25176-1 : 7.95
1. Vidocq, Eugene Francois, 1775-1857. 2. Detectives—France—Biography.

STEAD, Philip John. 923.544
Vidocq, a biography. New York, Roy Publishers [1954?] 263p. illus. 22cm. [HV7911] 54-11166
1. Vidocq, Eugene Francois, 1775-1857. I. Title.

VIDOCQ, Eugene Francois, 1775-1857. 363.2'092'4 B
Memoirs of Vidocq / Eugene Francois Vidocq. New York : Arno Press, 1976. 2 v. : port. ; 21 cm. (Literature of mystery and detection) Translation of Memoires. Reprint of the 1828-29 ed. issued as v. 25-28 of Autobiography, a collection of the most instructive and amusing lives ever published. Vol. 1-2 printed for Hunt and Clarke, London; v. 3-4 published by Whittaker, Treacher, and Arnot, London. [HV7911.V4713 1976] 75-32789 ISBN 0-405-07903-6 : 60.00(4 vols.)
1. Vidocq, Eugene Francois, 1775-1857. 2. Police—France—Correspondence, reminiscences, etc. I. Title. II. Series. III. Series: Autobiography; a collection of the most instructive and amusing lives ever published ; v. 25-28.

Vidor, King Wallis, 1895-

VIDOR, King Wallis, 1895- 791.43'0233'0924
King Vidor on film making. New York,

McKay [1972] xi, 239 p. illus. 22 cm. [PN1998.A3V48 1972] 72-86969 6.95
1. Moving-pictures—Production and direction. I. Title.

VIDOR, King Wallis, 1895- 927.914
A tree is a tree. [1st ed.] New York, Harcourt, Brace [1953] 315p. illus. 21cm. Autobiography. [PN1998.A3V5] 53-9221
1. Moving-pictures—Hist. I. Title.

†VIDOR, King Wallis, 1895- 791.43'0233'0924 B
A tree is a tree / King Vidor. New York : Garland Pub., 1977, c1953. 315 p., [8] leaves of plates : ill. ; 23 cm. (The Garland classics of film literature) Reprint of the ed. published by Harcourt, Brace, New York; with additions to the filmography. Includes index. Filmography: p. [293]-[305] [PN1998.A3V48 1977] 76-52132 ISBN 0-8240-2896-1 : 14.00
1. Vidor, King Wallis, 1895- 2. Moving-picture producers and directors—United States—Biography. I. Title. II. Series.

Vieira da Silva, Marie Helena, 1908-

VIEIRA da Silva, Marie Helena, 1908- 759.4
Vieira da Silva : paintings, 1967-1971 : [exhibition, M. Knoedler & Co., inc., New York, May 4-June 5, 1971] / John Rewald. New York : M. Knoedler, c1971. 36 p. : ill. (some col.) ; 22 cm. [ND553.V53R48] 75-518484
1. Vieira da Silva, Marie Helena, 1908- I. Rewald, John, 1912- II. Knoedler (M.) and Company, inc.

Vienna. Spanische Reitschule.

PODHAJSKY, Alois. 798.20924 B
My dancing white horses. Translated by Frances Hogarth-Gaute. [1st ed.] New York, Holt, Rinehart and Winston [1965] 302 p. illus., ports. (part col.) 24 cm. Translation of Ein Leben fur die Lipizzaner. [SF309.P773 1965] 65-22462
1. Vienna. Spanische Reitschule. I. Title.

Viereck, George Sylvester, 1884-1962.

JOHNSON, Niel M. 301.15'4'0924 B
George Sylvester Viereck, German-American propagandist [by] Niel M. Johnson. Urbana, University of Illinois Press [1972] x, 282 p. illus. 24 cm. Bibliography: p. [265]-276. [PS3543.I32Z7] 70-173459 ISBN 0-252-00222-9 9.95
1. Viereck, George Sylvester, 1884-1962.

Viertel, Salka.

VIERTEL, Salka. 791'.0924
The kindness of strangers. [1st ed.] New York, Holt, Rinehart, and Winston [1969] 338 p. port. 22 cm. Autobiographical. [PN2287.V47A3] 69-11801 6.95
I. Title.

Vietnamese Conflict, 1961-1975—Biography.

KERRIGAN, Evans E. 959.7'0434'0922 B
The Medal of Honor in Vietnam, by Evans E. Kerrigan. [1st ed.] Noroton Heights, Conn., Medallic Pub. Co. [1971- v. ports. 23 cm. [DS557.A6315K45] 77-173048
1. Vietnamese Conflict, 1961-1975—Biography. 2. Medal of Honor. I. Title.

Vietnamese Conflict, 1961-1975—Personal narratives, American.

GLOECKNER, Fred. 959.704'37
A civilian doctor in Vietnam. Philadelphia, Winchell Co. [1972] 123 p. illus. 23 cm. [DS557.A69G56] 72-78348
1. Vietnamese Conflict, 1961-1975—Personal narratives, American. 2. Vietnamese Conflict, 1961-1975—Medical and sanitary affairs. I. Title.

Vietnamese Conflict, 1961-1975—Prisoners and prisons, North Vietnamese.

ROWAN, Stephen A., 1928- 959.704'37
They wouldn't let us die; the prisoners of war tell their story [by] Stephen A. Rowan. Middle Village, N.Y., J. David Publishers [1973] 252 p. 23 cm. [DS557.A675R67] 73-80414 ISBN 0-8246-0157-2
1. Vietnamese Conflict, 1961-1975—Prisoners and prisons, North Vietnamese. 2. Vietnamese Conflict, 1961-1975—Personal narratives, American. I. Title. **BIP**

SURVIVORS / 959.704'37
[edited] by Zalin Grant. 1st ed. New York : Norton, [1975] 345 p. ; 21 cm. [DS559.4.S9 1975] 75-17637 ISBN 0-393-08727-1 : 8.95
1. Vietnamese Conflict, 1961-1975—Prisoners and prisons, North Vietnamese. 2. Vietnamese Conflict, 1961-1975—Personal narratives, American. I. Grant, Zalin.

Vietnamese Conflict, 1961-1975—Prisoners and prisons, Viet Cong.

ROWE, James N., 1938- 959.7'04'37
Five years to freedom, by James N. Rowe. [1st ed.] Boston, Little, Brown [1971] 467 p. illus., facsims., map, ports. 22 cm. [DS557.A675R68] 70-128357 7.95
1. Vietnamese Conflict, 1961-1975—Prisoners and prisons, Viet Cong. 2. Vietnamese Conflict, 1961-1975—Personal narratives, American. I. Title.

Vigil, Donaciano, 1802-1877.

CROCCHIOLA, Stanley Francis Louis, 1908- 363.2'0924
Giant in Lilliput; the story of Donaciano Vigil, by F. Stanley [pseud. Pampa? Tex., Pampa Print Shop 1963] 219 p. 23 cm. [F801.V5C7] 63-23933
1. Vigil, Donaciano, 1802-1877. I. Title.

Vigo, Jean, 1905-1934.

GOMES, Paulo Emilio Salles, 1916- 791.43'0233'0924 B
Jean Vigo [by] P. E. Sailes Gomes. Berkeley, University of California Press [1971] 256 p. illus. 22 cm. Includes bibliographical references. [PN1998.A3V5413] 72-104102 ISBN 0-520-01676-9 8.95
1. Vigo, Jean, 1905-1934.

SMITH, John Milton. 791.43'023'0924 B
Jean Vigo [by] John M. Smith. [New York] Praeger [1972] 144 p. illus. 18 cm. Bibliography: p. 143-144. [PN1998.A3V547] 71-151833 6.95
1. Vigo, Jean, 1905-1934.

Viktoria Luise, Herzogin zu Braunschweig und Luneburg, 1892—

VIKTORIA Luise, Herzogin zu Braunschweig und Luneburg, 1892- 943.08'092'4 B
The Kaiser's daughter : memoirs of H. R. H. Viktoria Luise, Duchess of Brunswick and Luneburg, Princess of Prussia / translated and edited by Robert Vacha. 1st U.S. ed. Englewood Cliffs, N.J. : Prentice-Hall, c1977. xii, 276 p., [12] leaves of plates : ill. ; 25 cm. Translated, compiled, and edited from the author's Ein Leben als Tochter des Kaisers, Im Glanz der Krone, and Im Strom der Zeit. Includes index. [DD229.8.V5A2513 1977b] 77-79339 ISBN 0-13-514653-4 : 12.50
1. Viktoria Luise, Herzogin zu Braunschweig und Luneburg, 1892- 2. Germany—Princes and princesses—Biography. 3. Germany—History—20th century—Sources. I. Vacha, Robert. II. Title.

Vilas, William Freeman, 1840-1906.

MERRILL, Horace Samuel. 923.273
William Freeman Vilas, doctrinaire Democrat. Madison, State Historical Society of Wisconsin, 1954. vii, 310p. illus., ports. 24cm. Bibliographical references included in 'Notes to the text' (p. 263-295) Bibliography: p. 209-294. [E664.V6M4] 54-10806
1. Vilas, William Freeman, 1840-1906. I. Title.

Villa, Francisco, 1878-1923.

BRADDY, Haldeen, 1908- 972.08'1'0924 B
Cock of the walk; qui-qui-ri-qui! The legend of Pancho Villa. Port Washington, N.Y., Kennikat Press [1970] xiii, 174 p. illus., ports. 22 cm. Reprint of the 1955 ed., with a new pref. by the author. Bibliography: p. 169-174. [F1234.V678 1970] 79-85988
1. Villa, Francisco, 1878-1923. I. Title. II. Title: The legend of Pancho Villa.

BRADDY, Haldeen, 1908- 972.08'1'0924 B
The paradox of Pancho Villa / by Haldeen Braddy ; ill. by Manuel Acosta. El Paso : Texas Western Press, 1978. ix, 95 p., [2] leaves of plates : ill. ; 24 cm. Includes index. Bibliography: p. 90-92. [F1234.V63B72] 77-91577 ISBN 0-87404-059-0 : 10.00
1. Villa, Francisco, 1878-1923. 2. Revolutionists—Mexico—Biography. 3. Mexico—History—1910-1946. I. Title. **BIP**

GUZMAN, Martin Luis, 1887- 972.081
Memoirs of Pancho Villa. Translated by Virginia H. Taylor. Austin, University of Texas Press [1965] xii, 512 p. illus., fold. map, ports. 24 cm. (The Texas Pan-American series) "The Spanish version has been slightly condensed in translation." [F1234.V68453] 65-11146
1. Villa, Francisco, 1878-1923. I. Title. **BIP**

GUZMAN, Martin Luis, 1890- 972.081
Memoirs of Pancho Villa. Tr. by Virginia H. Tavlor. Austin, Univ. of Tex. Pr. [c.1965] xii, 512p. illus., fold. map, ports, 24cm. (Tex. Pan-Amer. ser.) Spanish version, orig. pub. in Mexico in 1951, has been somewhat condensed in translation. [F1234.V68453] 65-11146 8.50
1. Villa, Francisco, 1877-1923. I. Title.

LANSFORD, William Douglas. 972.080924
Pancho Villa. [1st ed.] Los Angeles, Sherbourne Press [1965] 283 p. illus., ports. 22 cm. Bibliography: p. 281-283. [F1234.V686] 65-23704
1. Villa, Francisco, 1878-1923. I. Title.

PINCHON, Edgcumb, 1883- 972.08'1'0924
Viva Villa! A recovery of the real Pancho Villa, peon, bandit, soldier, patriot. New York, Arno Press, 1970 [c1933] 383 p. illus., map (on lining papers), ports. 23 cm. (American imperialism) Includes bibliographical references. [F1234.V698 1970] 70-111729
1. Villa, Francisco, 1878-1923. 2. Mexico—History—1910-1946. I. Title. **BIP**

Villa, Francisco, 1878-1923—Anecdotes.

PANCHO Villa : 972.08'1'0924
intimate recollections by people who knew him / edited by Jessie Peterson and Thelma Knoles. New York : Hastings House, [1977] p. cm. Includes index. [F1234.V697] 77-12034 ISBN 0-8038-5819-1 : 12.95
1. Villa, Francisco, 1878-1923—Anecdotes. 2. Generals—Mexico—Anecdotes, facetiae, satire, etc. I. Peterson, Jessie. II. Knoles, Thelma. **BIP**

Villa, Francisco, 1878-1923—Juvenile literature.

ROUVEROL, Jean. 972.08'1'0924 B
Pancho Villa: a biography. [1st ed.] Garden City, N.Y., Doubleday [1972] 208 p. illus. 22 cm. Bibliography: p. [207]-208. A biography of the turn-of-the-century Mexican outlaw who helped overthrow the Diaz government in the Revolution of 1910. [F1234.V726 1972] 92 70-180104 ISBN 0-385-00638-1 4.50
1. Villa, Francisco, 1878-1923—Juvenile literature. I. Title.

Villano, Anthony.

VILLANO, Anthony. 364.12'092'4 B
Brick agent : inside the Mafia for the FBI / Anthony Villano, with Gerald Astor. New York : Quadrangle/New York Times Book Co., c1977. 228 p. ; 25 cm. [HV7911.V54A33 1977] 76-52818 ISBN 0-8129-0687-X : 10.00
1. Villano, Anthony. 2. United States. Federal Bureau of Investigation—Officials and employees—Biography. 3. Organized crime—New York (City) 4. Mafia. I. Astor, Gerald, 1926- joint author. II. Title. **BIP**

Villard, Oswald Garrison, 1872-1949.

HUMES, Dollena Joy, 1921- 920.5
Oswald Garrison Villard, liberal of the 1920's. [Syracuse, N. Y.] Syracuse University Press, 1960. 276p. illus. 21cm. (Men and movements series) Includes bibliography. [E664.V65H8] 60-15159
1. Villard, Oswald Garrison, 1872-1949. 2. Liberalism. 3. U. S.—Pol. & govt.—20th cent. I. Title.

HUMES, Dollena Joy, 1921- 920.5
Oswald Garrison Villard, liberal of the 1920's. [Syracuse, N.Y.] 0Syracuse University Press [c.]1960. 276p. illus. (Men and movements series) Bibl. notes: p.264-268 60-15159 4.50
1. Villard, Oswald Garrison, 1872-1949. 2. Liberalism. 3. U.S.—Pol. & govt.—20th cent. I. Title. **BIP**

HUMES, Dollena Joy, 1921- 973.91'092'4 B
Oswald Garrison Villard, liberal of the 1920's / D. Joy Humes. Westport, Conn. : Greenwood Press, 1977. p. cm. Reprint of the 1960 ed. published by Syracuse University Press, Syracuse, N.Y., which was issued in Men and movements series. Includes index. Bibliography: p. [E748.V53H85 1977] 77-23783 ISBN 0-8371-9752-X lib.bdg. : 19.00
1. Villard, Oswald Garrison, 1872-1949. 2. Liberalism—United States. 3. United States—Politics and government—1901-1953. 4. Intellectuals—United States—Biography. 5. Journalists—United States—Biography. I. Title. II. Series: Men and movements (Syracuse)

WRESZIN, Michael 920.5
Oswald Garrison Villard, pacifist at war. Bloomington, Ind. Univ. Pr. [c.1965] ix, 342p. port. 24cm. Bibl. [E664.V65W7] 65-11795 6.95
1. Villard, Oswald Garrison, 1872-1949. I. Title.

WRESZIN, Michael. 920.5
Oswald Garrison Villard, pacifist at war. Bloomington, Indiana University Press [1965] ix, 342 p. port. 24 cm. Bibliographical references included in "Notes" (p. 276-329) [E664.V65W7] 65-11795
1. Villard, Oswald Garrison, 1872-1949.

Villiard, Paul.

VILLIARD, Paul. 917.97'77 B
Growing pains; the autobiography of a young boy. New York, Funk & Wagnalls [1970] 180 p. 22 cm. [CT275.V563A3] 72-98524 6.95
I. Title.

Villiers de l'Isle-Adam, Jean Marie Mathias Philippe Auguste, comte de, 1838-1889.

CONROY, William Thomas. 848'.8'09 B
Villiers de l'Isle-Adam / by William T. Conroy, Jr. Boston : Twayne Publishers, 1978. 167 p. : port. ; 21 cm. (Twayne's world authors series ; TWAS 491 : France) Includes index. Bibliography: p. 159-162. [PQ2476.V4Z559] 78-1812 ISBN 0-8057-6332-5 lib. bdg. : 11.50
1. Villiers de l'Isle-Adam, Jean Marie

Mathias Philippe Auguste, comte de, 1838-1889. 2. Authors, French—19th century—Biography. **BIP**

Villodas, Ricardo de, 1849-1904.

BOWLES, Thomas A. 759.6 B
Ricardo de Villodas, 1846-1904 : collection, catalogue, and biography : inaugural exhibition, Huntsville Museum of Art, Von Braun Civic Center, March 15-30 April, 1975 / prepared by Thomas A. Bowles, III. [Huntsville, Ala.] . Huntsville Museum of Art, 1975. 39 p., [10] leaves of plates : ill. ; 25 cm. [ND813.V54B68] 75-312707
1. Villodas, Ricardo de, 1849-1904. I. Villodas, Ricardo de, 1846-1904. II. Huntsville Museum of Art.

Villon, Francois, b. 1431—Juvenile literature.

HOLBROOK, Sabra. 841'.2 B
A stranger in my land; a life of Francois Villon. New York, Farrar, Straus and Giroux [1972] 166 p. 24 cm. Bibliography: p. [157]-161. A biography with translations and analyses of some of the works of the fifteenth-century student rebel poet. [PQ1593.H6] 92 76-184702 ISBN 0-374-37276-4 4.95
1. Villon, Francois, b. 1431—Juvenile literature. I. Title. **BIP**

Vincent de Paul, Saint, 1576?-1660.

CALVET, Jean, 1874- 922.22
Saint Vincent de Paul. Translated by Lancelot C. Sheppard. New York, D. McKay [1951] 302p. 22cm. 'Bibliographical note': p. 296-298. [BX4700.V6C] A53
1. Vincent de Paul, Saint, 1576?-1660. I. Title.

CHAIGNE, Louis, 1899- 922.244
Saint Vincent de Paul. Tr. by Rosemary Sheed. New York, Macmillan, 1962 [c.1960,1962] 120p. 18cm. (Your name--your saint ser.) Bibl. 62-12422 2.50
1. Vincent de Paul, Saint, 1576?-1660. I. Title.

COSTE, Pierre 922.244
The life & works of Saint Vincent de Paul (Monsieur Vincent: le grand saint du grand siecle) Translated from the French by Joseph Leonard. Westminster, Md., Newman Press, 1952. 3 v. illus., ports., maps. 21 cm. Bibliography: v. 3, p. 499-522. [BX4700.V6C652] 52-9978
1. Vincent de Paul, Saint, 1576?-1660. I. Title.

CRISTIANI, Leon, 1879- 271'.79 B
Saint Vincent de Paul, 1581-1660 / by Leon Cristiani; translated by John R. Gregoli Boston : St. Paul Editions, c1977. p. cm. [BX4700.V6C7413] 77-4377 3.95 pbk. : 2.95
1. Vincent de Paul, Saint, 1581-1660. 2. Christian saints—France—Biography.

DANIEL-ROPS, Henry, 1901- 922.244 [RealnameHenryJulesCharlesPetiot]
Monsieur Vincent; the story of St. Vincent de Paul. Tr. from French by Julie Kernan. New York, Hawthorn Books [c.1961] 141p. illus. (part col.) 61-6711 3.95
1. Vincent de Paul, Saint, 1576?-1660. I. Title.

DELARUE, Jacques, 1914- 922.244
The holiness of Vincent de Paul. [English translation from the French by Suzanne Chapman] New York, P. J. Kenedy [c.1960] 132p. illus. 60-14108 3.50
1. Vincent de Paul, Saint, 1576?-1660. I. Title.

MATT, Leonard von 922.244
St. Vincent de Paul [by] Leonard von Matt and Louis Cognet. Translated from the French by Emma Craufurd. Chicago, H. Regnery Co., 1960[ ] 232p. (chiefly illus.) 25cm. 60-16335 7.00 bds.,
1. Vincent de Paul, Saint, 1576?-1660. I. Cognet, Louis, joint author. II. Title.

MAYNARD, Michel Ulysse, 922.244 1814-1893.
Virtues and spiritual doctrine of Saint Vincent de Paul. Rev. by Carlton A. Prindeville. St. Louis, Vincentian Foreign Mission Press [1961] 359p. 23vm. First published in French in 1864. [BX4700.V6M36 1961] 61-3733
1. Vincent de Paul, Saint, 1576?-1660. I. Title.

PURCELL, Mary 922.244
The world of Monsieur Vincent. New York, Scribners [c.1963] 243p. illus. 22cm. Bibl. 63-10449 4.50
1. Vincent de Paul, 1581-1660. I. Title.

ST. John's University, 922.244 Brooklyn
Saint Vincent de Paul, a tercentenary commemoration of his death. 1660-1960. Jamaica, N. Y., St. John's University Press [Grand Central and Utopia Parkways, c.1960] 108p. (bibl. footnotes) illus. 26cm. 'The Saint Vincent de Paul annual lectures, sponsored since 1948 by Saint John's University, Jamaica, New York.' 60-2148 3.95;1.95 pap.,
1. Vincent de Paul, Saint, 1576?-1660. I. Title.

ST. John's University, 922.244 New York.
Saint Vincent de Paul, a tercentenary commemoration of his death. 1660-1960. Jamaica, N. Y., St. John's University Press [1960] 108p. illus. 26cm. 'The Saint Vincent de Paul annual lectures, sponsored since 1948 by Saint John's University, Jamaica, New York.' Includes bibliography. [BX4700.V6S26] 60-2148
1. Vincent de Paul, Saint, 1576?-1660. I. Title.

ST. Vincent de Paul. v. 12
Jamaica, N. Y., St. John's University Press, 1961. x, 157p. 23cm. (Thought patterns, v. 9)
1. Vincent de Paul, Saint, 1576?-1660. I. Kovacs, Arpad Francis, 1898- ed.

WOODGATE, Mildred Violet, 922.244 1904-
Saint Vincent de Paul. Westminster, Md., Newman Press [1960, c1958] 136 p. 20 cm. [BX4700.V6W6] 60-3592
1. Vincent de Paul, Saint, 1576?-1660. I. Title.

Vincent de Paul, Saint, 1576?-1660—Juvenile literature.

HUBBARD, Margaret Ann 922.244
Vincent de Paul, Saint of charity. Illustrated by Harry Barton. New York, Farrar, Straus & Cudahy [c.1960] 190p. Bibl. p.11 illus. 22cm. (Vision books, 48) 60-10366 1.95
1. Vincent de Paul, Saint, 1576?-1660—Juvenile literature. I. Title.

HUBBARD, Margaret Ann, 922.244 1909-
Vinent de Paul, Saint of charity. Illustrated by Harry Barton. New York, Farrar, Straus & Cudahy [1960] 190p. illus. 22cm. (Vision books, 48) Includes bibliography. [BX4700.V6H8] 60-10366
1. Vincent de Paul, Saint, 1576 -1660 — Juvenile literature. I. Title.

LOMUPO, Robert. 922.244
Fire in his name, a life of St. Vincent de Paul. Illustrated by Cajetan Holland. Valatie, N.Y., Holy Cross Press, 1964. 128 p. illus. 23 cm. (Saints who changed history series) [BX4700.V6L6] 64-2855
1. Vincent de Paul, Saint, 1581-1660 — Juvenile literature. I. Title.

LOMUPO, Robert 922.244
Fire is his name; a life of St. Vincent de Paul. Illus. by Cajetan Holland. Valatie, N. Y., Holy Cross Pr. [c.]1964. 128p. illus. 23cm. (Saints who changed hist. ser.) 64-28552 2.50
1. Vincent de Paul, Saint, 1581-1660—Juvenile literature. I. Title.

Vincent, Leon Henry,

VINCENT, Leon 287'.6'0924 B Henry, 1859-1941.
John Heyl Vincent; a biographical sketch. Freeport, N.Y., Books for Libraries Press [1970] 319 p. port. 23 cm. Reprint of the 1925 ed. [BX8495.V5V5 1970] 71-124263 ISBN 8-369-54513-
I. Vincent, John Heyl, Bp., 1832-1920.

Vincentius Ferrerius, Saint, 1350 (ca.)-1419.

ALLIES, Mary Helen 282'.0922 B Agnes, 1852-1927.
Three Catholic reformers of the fifteenth century Freeport, N.Y., Books for Libraries Press [1972] xii, 235 p. 23 cm. (Essay index reprint series) Reprint of the 1878 ed. Includes bibliographical references. [BX1302.A63 1972] 73-38755 ISBN 0-8369-2633-1 9.75
1. Vincentius Ferrerius, Saint, 1350 (ca.)-1419. 2. Bernardino da Siena, Saint, 1380-1444. 3. Giovanni da Capistrano, Saint, 1385 or 6-1456. 4. Church history—15th century. I. Title. **BIP**

[MARY Catherine, Sister, 922.246 of the English Dominioan Congregation of Saint Catherine of Siena]
Angel of the judgement; a life of Vincent Ferrer, by S. M. C. Notre Dame, Ind., Ave Maria Press [1954] 234p. 24cm. [BX4700.V/M3] 54-5298
1. Vincentius Ferrerius, Saint, 1350 (ca.)-1419. I. Title.

ROBERTO, Brother, 1927- 922.246
The King's trumpeter; a story of Saint Vincent Ferrer. Illus. by Brother Eagan. Notre Dame, Ind., Dujarie Press [1957] 94p. illus. 24cm. [BX4700.V7R6] 58-257
1. Vincentius Ferrerius, Saint, 1850 (ca.)-1419. I. Title.

Vincenzo I Gonzaga, Duke of Mantua, 1562-1612.

BELLONCI, Maria. 923.245
A prince of Mantua; the life and times of Vincenzo Gonzaga. Translated from the Italian by Stuart Hood. [1st American ed.] New York, Harcourt, Brace [1956] 312 p. 22 cm. Translation of Il duca nel labirinto, the 3d section of the author's Segreti dei Gonzaga. [DG975.M3B434 1956a] 56-14102
1. Vincenzo I Gonzaga, Duke of Mantua, 1562-1612. I. Title.

Vinet, Alexandre Rodolphe, 1797-1847.

FUHRMANN, Paul Traugott, 201 1903-
Extraordinary Christianity; the life and thought of Alexander Vinet. Pref. by John T. McNeil. Philadelphia. Westminster [c.1964] 125p. 21cm. Bibl. 64-10520 3.00
1. Vinet, Alexandre Rodolphe, 1797-1847. I. Title.

Vining, Donald, 1917-

VINING, Donald, 301.41'57'0924 B 1917-
A gay diary / Donald Vining. 1st ed. New York : Pepys Press, c1979- v. : port. ; 23 cm. Includes index. Contents.Contents.—[1] 1933-1946. [HQ75.8.V56A38] 78-71282 ISBN 0-9602270-0-8 (v. 1) : 14.95 ISBN 0-9602270-1-6 pbk. : 9.95
1. Vining, Donald, 1917- 2. Homosexuals, Males—United States—Biography. I. Title. **BIP**

Vining, Elizabeth Gray, 1902- — Diaries.

VINING, Elizabeth Gray, 813'.5'2 1902-
Being seventy : the measure of a year / Elizabeth Gray Vining. 1st ed. New York : Viking Press, 1978. 194 p. ; 22 cm. [PS3572.I55Z464 1978] 77-25480 ISBN 0-670-15539-X : 10.00
1. Vining, Elizabeth Gray, 1902- —Diaries. 2. Authors, American—20th century—Biography. I. Title. **BIP**

VINING, Elizabeth Gray, 813'.5'2 1902-
Being seventy : the measure of a year / Elizabeth Gray Vining. Boston : G. K. Hall, 1979 289 p. ; 24 cm. "Published in large print." [PS3572.I55Z464 1978b] 78-11894 ISBN 0-8161-6623-4 : 10.95
1. Vining, Elizabeth Gray, 1902- —Diaries. 2. Authors, American—20th century—Biography. 3. Large type books. I. Title.

Vinplac, Lemuel,

VINPLAC, Lemuel, 1917- 920.9
Mr. Danger: the life and exploits of Lemuel Vinplac, G. C., C.S.I., as told to Herman J. McLatchy. New York, Pageant [c.1961] 224p. 3.00
I. McLatchy, Herman J. II. Title.

Vins, Georgii Petrovich, 1928—

VINS, Georgii Petrovich, 2.3092B 1928-
Testament from prison / Georgi Vins ; translated by Jane Ellis ; edited by Michael Bourdeaux. Elgin, Ill. : D. C. Cook Pub. Co., c1975. 283 p. ; 18 cm. [BX6495.V5A3713]
1. Vins, Georgii Petrovich, 1928- 2. Baptists in Russia—Biography. 3. Persecution—Russia. I. Title.

VINS, Georgii Petrovich, 914.3'1 1928-
Testament from prison / Georgi Vins ; translated by Jane Ellis ; edited by Michael Bourdeaux. Elgin, Ill. : D. C. Cook Pub. Co., c1975. 283 p. ; 18 cm. [BX6495.V5A3713] 75-18986 ISBN 0-912692-84-7 : 2.50
1. Vins, Georgii Petrovich, 1928- 2. Baptists in Russia—Biography. 3. Persecution—Russia. I. Title.

Vintners—California—Biography.

BENSON, Robert, 663'.22'0922 B 1942-
Great winemakers of California : conversations with Robert Benson / with a pref. by Andre Tchelistcheff. Santa Barbara, CA : Capra Press, 1977. p. cm. Includes index. [TP547.A1B46] 77-3888 ISBN 0-88496-107-9 : 15.00
1. Vintners—California—Biography. I. Title.

Vinton, Bobby.

VINTON, Bobby. 784'.092'4 B
The Polish prince / by Bobby Vinton, with Robert E. Burger. New York : M. Evans, c1978. p. cm. [ML420.V384A3] 78-15059 ISBN 0-87131-270-0 : 8.95
1. Vinton, Bobby. 2. Singers—United States—Biography. I. Burger, Robert E., joint author. II. Title. **BIP**

Violin makers.

BRINSER, Marlin. 787'.12'0922 B
Dictionary of twentieth century Italian violin makers / by Marlin Brinser. Irvington, N.J. : American Graphic, c1978. 111 p. ; 28 cm. [ML830.B74] 78-74638 ISBN 0-9602298-1-7 : 8.95
1. Violin makers. I. Title.

FAIRFIELD, John 787'.12'0922 B Houghton, 1899-
Known violin makers, by John H. Fairfield. [Athens, Ga., printed by Guest Printing Co., c1973] xiv, 201 p. 24 cm. Reprint of the 1942 ed. published by Bradford Press, New York. "Supplementary appendix concerning contemporary (1973) prices," by H. M. Chaitman: p. 193-201. [ML404.F2K6 1973] 74-158492
1. Violin makers. I. Title. **BIP**

STAINER, Cecie. 787'.12'0922 B
A dictionary of violin makers. Compiled from the best authorities by C. Stainer. Rev. ed. Boston, Milford House [1973] [6], 102 p. 22 cm. Reprint of the 1896 ed. published by Novello, Ewer, in series: Novello, Ewer and Co.'s music primers and educational series. Bibliography: 4th-5th prelim. pages. [ML802.S82 1973] 73-12274 ISBN 0-87821-162-4 10.00 (lib. bdg.)
1. Violin makers. I. Title.

Violin makers—Biography.

STAINER, Cecie. 787'.1'0922 B
A dictionary of violin makers / compiled from the best authorities by C. Stainer. Boston : Longwood Press, 1977. [6], 102 p. ; 22 cm. Reprint of the 1896 ed. published by Novello, Ewer, in series: Novello, Ewer and Co.'s music primers and educational series. Bibliography: p. [4]-[5] (1st group) [ML802.S82 1977] 77-75207 ISBN 0-89341-070-5 : 12.50
1. Violin makers—Biography. I. Title. **BIP**

Violinists, violoncellists, etc.—Biography.

CLARKE, A. Mason. 787'.0092'2 B
A biographical dictionary of fiddlers, including performers on the violoncello and double bass, past and present, containing a sketch of their artistic career. Together with notes of their compositions, &c. St. Clair Shores, Mich., Scholarly Press, 1972. 360 p. ports. 22 cm. Reprint of the 1895 ed. [ML105.C61 1972] 79-166225 ISBN 0-403-01351-8
1. Violinists, violoncellists, etc.—Biography. I. Title. **BIP**

FERRIS, George Titus, b.1840. 786.1'092'2 B
Great violinists and pianists. Freeport, N.Y., Books for Libraries Press [1972] p. (Essay index reprint series) Reprinted from the ed. of 1881, New York. [ML395.F39 1972] 72-6819 ISBN 0-8369-7257-0
1. Violinists, violoncellists, etc.—Biography. 2. Pianists—Biography. I. Title. **BIP**

FLESCH, Karl, 1873-1944. 787'.1'0924 B
The memoirs of Carl Flesch / translated by Hans Keller and edited by him in collaboration with C. F. Flesch ; foreword by Max Rostal. New York : Da Capo Press, 1979 [c1957] xiii, 393 p., [7] leaves of plates : ill. ; 23 cm. (Da Capo Press music reprint series) Reprint of the ed. published by Rockliff, London. Includes index. [ML418.F81A3 1979] 79-10071 ISBN 0-306-77574-3 : 25.00
1. Violinists, violoncellists, etc.—Biography. I. Title. **BIP**

LAHEE, Henry Charles, 1856-1953. 787'.1'0922 B
Famous violinists of today and yesterday / Henry C. Lahee. Boston : Longwood Press, 1977. p. cm. Reprint of the 1899 ed. published by L. C. Page, Boston. Includes index. [ML398.L18 1977] 77-75218 ISBN 0-89341-118-3 : 40.00
1. Violinists, violoncellists, etc.—Biography. I. Title. **BIP**

Violinists, violoncellists, etc.—Juvenile literature.

BURCH, Gladys, 1899- 787'.1'0922 B
Famous violinists for young people. Freeport, N.Y., Books for Libraries Press [1972, c1946] vii, 232 p. illus. 27 cm. (Biography index reprint series) A brief introduction to the violin—its history, construction, and music—accompanies biographies of fourteen famous violinists. [ML3930.A2B855 1972] 920 75-38316 ISBN 0-8369-8118-9
1. Violinists, violoncellists, etc.—Juvenile literature. I. Title. **BIP**

Virginia Anne Barge.

MORGAN-GRENVILLE, Gerald. 914.4'48'0483
Barging into southern France. Illustrated by the author. New York, Van Nostrand Reinhold Co. [1973, c1972] 239 p. illus. 23 cm. [GV836.M62 1972b] 72-13193 ISBN 0-442-25514-4 6.95
1. Virginia Anne (Barge) 2. France—Description and travel—1945- I. Title.

MORGAN-GRENVILLE, Gerard. 914.442
Barging into Burgundy / Gerard Morgan-Grenville ; illustrated by the author with nineteen drawings in pen and ink. Newton Abbot [Eng.] : David & Charles, [1975] 176 p. : ill. ; 23 cm. [GV836.M59] 74-19779 ISBN 0-7153-6834-6 : 12.95
1. Virginia Anne Barge. 2. France—Description and travel—1945- 3. Morgan-Grenville, Gerard. I. Title.
Distributed by David and Charles, North Pomfret, Vt.

Virginia—Biography.

BRUCE, Philip Alexander, 1856-1933. 973.2'0922 B
The Virginia Plutarch. New York, Russell & Russell [1971] 2 v. illus., fold. map, ports. 23 cm. Reprint of the 1929 ed. Contents.Contents.—I. The colonial and revolutionary eras.—II. The national era. [F225.B88 1971] 75-139474
1. Virginia—Biography. 2. Virginia—History. 3. U.S.—Biography. 4. U.S.—History. I. Title. **BIP**

CARTER, Landon 975.5020924
The diary of Colonel Landon Carter of Sabine Hall, 1752-1778; 2v. Ed., introd., by Jack P. Greene. Charlottesville, Pub. for the Virginia Hist. Soc. [by] the Univ. Pr. of Va. 1965. 2v. (xvi, 1204p.) illus., maps, ports. 26cm. (Va. Hist. Soc. Richmond Documents, v.4-5) [F229.C29] 64-19201 25.00 set,
1. Virginia—Hist.—Colonial period—Sources. 2. Virginia—Soc. life & cust.—Colonial period. I. Greene, Jack P., ed. II. Title. III. Series.

EDMUNDS, Pocahontas Wight. 920'.0755
Virginians out front. [1st ed.] Richmond, Whittet & Shepperson, 1972. x, 583 p. ports. 24 cm. Bibliography: p. [517]-566. [CT265.E34] 72-93198 15.00
1. Virginia—Biography. I. Title.

MEADE, William, Bp., 1789-1862 929.3
Old churches, ministers, and families of Virginia: 2v. Reprinted. with digested index and genealogical guide comp. by Jennings Cropper Wise. Baltimore, Genealogical. 1966. 2v. (various p.) 23cm. Orig. pub. in 1857 with an index composed in 1910. [F225.M4913] 65-28854 22.50
1. Virginia—Church history. 2. Virginia—Geneal. 3. Protestant Episcopal Church in the U. S. A.—Virginia. 4. Virginia—Hist.—Colonial period. I. Title.

MOORMAN, Fay, 1887- 917.55
My heart turns back; childhood memories of rural Virginia in the nineties. [1st ed.] New York, Exposition Press [c1964] 124 p. 21 cm. (An Exposition-Lochinvar book) Autobiographical. [CT275.M5942A3] 64-2779
1. Virginia — Soc. life & cust. I. Title.

MORTON, Richard Lee, 1889- ed. 920.0755
Virginia lives; the Old Dominion who's who. A reference edition recording the biographies of contemporary leaders in Virginia ... Written and prepared under the supervision of Richard Lee Morton. Hopkinsville, Ky., Historical Record Association, 1964. 1120 p. ports. 27 cm. [F225.V88] 64-7595
1. Virginia — Biog. I. Title. II. Title: The Old Dominion who's who.

SUTHERLAND, Elihu Jasper, 1886- 920.0755
Some Sandy Basin characters. Clintwood, Va., Author [c.]1962. 246p. illus. 22cm. Bibl. 62-44359 4.50
1. Virginia—Biog. 2. Virginia—Soc. life & cust. I. Title.

VIRGINIA. Convention, Richmond, 1861. 342'.755'020922
Biographical register of members: Virginia State Convention of 1861, first session, by William H. Gaines, Jr. Richmond, Virginia State Library, 1969. 87 p. 24 cm. Includes bibliographical references. [F230.A25 1861j] 74-628577
1. Virginia—Biography. I. Gaines, William Harris, 1918- II. Title.

VIRGINIA lives; 920.0755
the Old Dominion who's who. a reference edition recording the biographies of contemporary leaders in Virginia. Written, prepared under the supervision of Richard Lee Morton. Hopkinsville, Ky., Historical Record Assn., 1964. 1120p. ports. 27cm. 64-7595 19.00
1. Virginia—Biog. I. Morton, Richard Lee, 1889— ed. II. Title: The Old Dominion who's who.

WHO'S who in Virginia, 1974/75 920'.0755
: a composite of biographical sketches of outstanding men and women of the State of Virginia. 1st ed. Acworth, Ga. : Names of Distinction, inc., [1975] 320 p. : ports. ; 28 cm. [CT265.W48] 74-78233
1. Virginia—Biography. I. Names of Distinction, inc.

Virginia City, Nev.

WALDORF, John Taylor. 979.3'56'020924
A kid on the Comstock. Illustrated with the original cartoons by Herb Roth from "The Bulletin" and with biographical and background materials by Dolores Waldorf Bryant. [Berkeley, Calif.] Friends of the Bancroft Library, 1968. 92 p. illus. 29 cm. (Friends of the Bancroft Library. Keepsakes, no. 16) Bibliography: p. 89. [F849.V8W3] 68-64510
1. Virginia City, Nev. I. Roth, Herb, illus. II. Bryant, Dolores Waldorf. III. Title. IV. Series.

WALDORF, John Taylor. 917.93'56 B
A kid on the Comstock; reminiscences of a Virginia City childhood. Edited with introd. and commentary by Dolores Bryant Waldorf [i.e. Dolores Waldorf Bryant] Palo Alto, Calif., American West Pub. Co. [1970] 198 p. illus., ports. 24 cm. "Portions of this book were originally published by the Friends of the Bancroft Library as A kid on the Comstock (1968)" Bibliography: p. 192-193. [F849.V8W33] 73-108628 ISBN 0-910118-14-0 5.95
1. Virginia City, Nev. 2. Comstock lode, Nev. I. Bryant, Dolores Waldorf, ed. II. Title.

Virginia. Convention, 1788.

GRIGSBY, Hugh Blair, 1806-1881. 342'.73'02
The history of the Virginia Federal Convention of 1788. New York, Da Capo Press, 1969. 2 v. in 1. 24 cm. (A Da Capo Press reprint edition) Edited by R. A. Brock. Reprint of the 1890-91 ed. Includes bibliographical references. [JK3925 1788.G7] 70-75319
1. Virginia. Convention, 1788. 2. U.S. Constitution. 3. Virginia—Politics and government—1775-1865. 4. Virginia—Biography. I. Brock, Robert Alonzo, 1839-1914, ed. II. Title.

Virginia. General Assembly. Senate—Biog.

ROGERS, George Wesley. 923.273
Officers of the Senate of Virginia, 1776-1956. Richmond, 1959. ix, 144p. illus., ports., facsim. 24cm. [JK3976.R6] 59-12727
1. Virginia. General Assembly. Senate—Biog. 2. Virginia—Biog. I. Title.

Virginia—Governors.

LUTHER, Roslyn. 975.5'00992
Governors of Virginia, 1776-1974 / by Roslyn and Edwin C. Luther, III. Accomac, Va. : Eastern Shore news, 1974. iv, 124 p. : ill. ; 24 cm. Includes bibliographical references and index. [F225.L87] 74-187945
1. Virginia—Governors. I. Luther, Edwin C., joint author. II. Title.

Virginia—History—Colonial period, ca. 1600-1775.

SMITH, John, 1580-1631. 975.5'02'0924
Captain John Smith's America; selections from his writings. Edited by John Lankford. [1st ed.] New York, Harper & Row [1967] xviii, 195 p. 21 cm. (Harper torchbooks. The University library, TB3078) (American perspectives) "Selections included in this volume are from The generall historie, of 1624 and the Advertisements for the unexperienced planters of New England, of 1631, edited by Edward Arber and contained in his Travels and works of Captain John Smith, published ... in 1910." Bibliographical footnotes. [F229.S595] 67-11606
1. Virginia—History—Colonial period, ca. 1600-1775. 2. Virginia—Description and travel. 3. Indians of North America—Virginia. 4. New England—History—Colonial period, ca. 1600-1775. I. Lankford, John, ed. II. Title.

Virginia in literature.

ROSENBERGER, Francis Coleman, 1915- ed. 810'.8'0372
Virginia reader: a treasury of writings from the first voyages to the present, edited with an introd. and notes by Francis Coleman Rosenberger. New York, Octagon Books, 1972 [c1948] 576 p. 23 cm. [PS266.V5R6 1972] 77-159251 ISBN 0-374-96914-0
1. Virginia in literature. 2. American literature—Virginia. 3. Authors, American—Virginia—Biography. I. Title.

Virginia Infantry. 18th Regiment, 1861-1865.

IRBY, Richard. 975.5'04 B
The captain remembers : the papers of Captain Richard Irby / edited by Virginia Fitzgerald Jordan. [Blackstone, Va.] : Nottoway County Historical Association, 1975. 124 p., [1] leaf of plates : ill. ; 23 cm. [E581.5 18th.I72] 75-315869
1. Virginia Infantry. 18th Regiment, 1861-1865. 2. Irby, Richard. 3. United States—History—Civil War, 1861-1865—Regimental histories—Virginia Infantry—18th. 4. United States—History—Civil War, 1861-1865—Personal narratives—Confederate side. I. Title.

Virginia. Medical College, Richmond.

SANGER, William Thomas, 1885- 610'.7'11755451
As I remember, by William T. Sanger. [Richmond, Printed by Dietz Press] 1971 [c1972] ix, 194 p. ports. 24 cm. Includes bibliographical references. [R747.V723S36] 72-188916
1. Virginia. Medical College, Richmond. I. Title.

Virginia—Politics and government—Revolution, 1775-1783.

GRIGSBY, Hugh Blair, 1806-1881. 974.5'03'0922 B
The Virginia Convention of 1776. New York, Da Capo Press, 1969. 206 p. ports. 24 cm. (A Da Capo Press reprint edition) Reprint of the 1855 ed. Bibliographical footnotes. [E263.V8G8 1969] 75-75320
1. Virginia—Politics and government—Revolution, 1775-1783. 2. Virginia—Biography. I. Title. **BIP**

Virginia—Politics and government—1865-1950.

MILLER, Francis Pickens, 1895- 320.9'755
Man from the valley; memoirs of a 20th-century Virginian. Chapel Hill, University of North Carolina Press [1971] xvii, 253 p. illus., ports. 24 cm. [F231.M58] 71-132255 ISBN 0-8078-1161-0 8.75
1. Virginia—Politics and government—1865-1950. I. Title.

Virginia—Registers.

STANARD, William Glover, 1858-1933, comp. 929.3
The colonial Virginia register; a list of governors, councillors and other higher officials, and also of members of the House of Burgesses and revolutionary conventions of the colony of Virginia, compiled by William G. and Mary Newton Stanard. Baltimore, Genealogical Pub. Co., 1965. 249 p. 23 cm. "Originally published, Albany, 1902." [F229.S8 1965] 65-21922
1. Virginia—Registers. 2. Virginia—Biography. 3. Virginia—History—Colonial period—Sources. I. Stanard, Mary Mann Page Newton, 1865-1929, joint comp. II. Title.

Virginia, University—Biog.

CLEMONS, Harry, 1879- 378.755481
Notes on the professors for whom the University of Virginia halls and residence houses are named. Foreword by Edgar Finley Shannon, Jr. Charlottesville, Univ. of Va. Pr. [1962, c.1961] 143p. illus. 61-18456 3.00; 1.50 bds., pap.,
1. Virginia, University—Biog. I. Title.

Visalia, Calif.—Biography.

JOHNS, Sylvia K. 917.94'86
Like father-like son, by Sylvia K. Johns. Visalia, Calif., Josten's American Yearbook Co. [1971] 133 p. illus. 29 cm. "Compilation of sixty-one ... stories published in the Visalia Times-delta, May 1st through June 25th, 1970-71." [F869.V8J65] 75-182232 10.00
1. Visalia, Calif.—Biography. I. Title.

Visconti, Luchino, 1906-1976.

NOWELL-SMITH, Geoffrey. 791.43'0233'0924
Luchino Visconti. Garden City, N.Y., Doubleday, 1968. 192 p. illus., ports. 20 cm. (Cinema world, 3) [PN1998.A3V5855 1968] 68-12995
1. Visconti, Luchino, 1906- BIP

NOWELL-SMITH, Geoffrey. 791.43'0233'0924
Luchino Visconti. New York, Viking Press [1973,i.e. 1974] 220 p. illus. 20 cm. (Cinema one, 3) Filmography: p. 207-220. [PN1998.A3V5855 1973] 73-17729 ISBN 0-670-44426-X 6.95
1. Visconti, Luchino, 1906-
Pbk. 3.95; ISBN 0-670-01979-8.

STIRLING, Monica, 1916- 791.43'0233'0924 B
A screen of time : a study of Luchino Visconti / by Monica Stirling. 1st ed. New York : Harcourt Brace Jovanovich, c1979. 295 p., [16] leaves of plates : ill. ; 24 cm. "A Helen and Kurt Wolff book." Includes index. Bibliography: p. 279-281. [PN1998.A3V5865] 78-22273 14.95
1. Visconti, Luchino, 1906-1976. 2. Moving-picture producers and directors—Italy—Biography. 3. Moving-pictures—Italy. I. Title. BIP

Viscott, David S., 1938-

VISCOTT, David S., 1938- 616.8'9'00924 B
Dorchester boy; portrait of a psychiatrist as a very young man, by David S. Viscott. New York, Arbor House [1973] 250 p. 22 cm. Autobiographical. [RC339.52.V57A3] 73-82182 ISBN 0-87795-070-9 7.95
1. Viscott, David S., 1938- 2. Psychiatrists—United States—Correspondence, reminiscences, etc. I. Title.

Vitkauskas, Arejas.

VITKAUSKAS, Arejas. 920
An immigrant's story. New York, Philosophical Library [1956] 192 p. 21 cm. [CT275.V585A3] 56-13820
I. Title.

Vivaldi, Antonio, 1678-1741.

KOLNEDER, Walter. 780'.924 B
Antonio Vivaldi; his life and work. Translated by Bill Hopkins. Berkeley, University of California Press, 1970. x, 288 p. illus., facsims., music, ports. (part col.) 25 cm. Bibliography: p. 213-219. [ML410.V82K553] 71-101341 ISBN 0-520-01629-7 15.00
1. Vivaldi, Antonio, 1678-1741.

PINCHERLE, Marc, 1888- 927.8
Vivaldi, genius of the baroque. Tr. from French by Christopher Hatch. New York, Norton [c.1955-1962] 278p. illus. 22cm. (N168) Bibl. 1.65 pap.,
1. Vivaldi, Antonio, 1680 (ca.)-1741. I. Title.

PINCHERLE, Marc, 1888- 927.8
Vivaldi, genius of the baroque. Translated from the French by Christopher Hatch. [1st ed.] New York, W.W. Norton [1957] 278 p. illus. 22 cm. [ML410.V82P532] 57-11245
1. Vivaldi, Antonio, 1678-1741.

TALBOT, Michael. 780'.92'4 B
Vivaldi / Michael Talbot. London : Dent, 1978. 275 p., [4] leaves of plates : ill. ; 20 cm. (The Master musicians series) Includes music and indexes. Bibliography: p. 252-258. [ML410.V82T34] 79-302925 ISBN 0-460-03164-3 : 11.50
1. Vivaldi, Antonio, 1678-1741. 2. Composers—Italy—Biography. I. Title. II. Series.
Distributed by Biblio Distribution Centre, Totowa, NJ BIP

Vivas, Eliseo.

VIVAS, Eliseo. 191
Two roads to ignorance : a quasi biography / by Eliseo Vivas. Carbondale : Southern Illinois University Press, c1979. xiii, 304 p. ; 24 cm. Includes index. [B945.V54A36] 79-757 ISBN 0-8093-0916-5 : 15.00
1. Vivas, Eliseo. 2. Philosophers—United States—Biography. I. Title. BIP

Vivekananda, Swami, 1863-1902.

NIKHILANANDA, Swami. 921.9
Vivekananda, a biography. New York, Ramakrishna-Vivekananda Center, 1953. viii, 216 p. ports. 25 cm. [B133.V5N5] 53-7851
1. Vivekananda, Swami, 1863-1902.

REMINISCENCES of Swami Vivekananda, by his Eastern and Western admirers, Hollywood, Calif. 1961] [dist. by Vedanta Press 404p. illus. 3.50 61-65950 921.9
1. Vivekananda, Swami, 1863-1902.

Vives-Atsara, Jose, 1919—

WEST, Nancy Glass, 1940- 759.6 B
Jose Vives-Atsara, his life and his art / by Nancy Glass West Austin, Tex. : Shoal Creek Publishers, c1976. p. cm. Includes index. Bibliography: p. [ND813.V58W47] 76-47664 ISBN 0-88319-027-3 : 50.00
1. Vives-Atsara, Jose, 1919- 2. Painters—Spain—Biography.

Vizzini, Sal.

VIZZINI, Sal. 363.2'092'4 B
Vizzini: the secret lives of America's most successful undercover agent, by Sal Vizzini, with Oscar Fraley and Marshall Smith. New York, Arbor House [1972] 330 p. 22 cm. [HV7911.V5A3] 77-184886 ISBN 0-87795-050-4 8.95
I. Fraley, Oscar, 1914- II. Smith, Marshall, 1914- III. Title.

Vlad II, Dracul, Prince of Wallachia, d. ca. 1476.

FLORESCU, Radu R. N. 949.8'2'010924 B
Dracula; a biography of Vlad the Impaler, 1431-1476 [by] Radu Florescu and Raymond T. McNally. New York, Hawthorn Books [1973] x, 239 p. illus. 24 cm. Bibliography: p. 215-228. [DR240.5.V55F57] 73-364 7.95
1. Vlad II, Dracul, Prince of Wallachia, d. ca. 1476. I. McNally, Raymond T., 1931- joint author.

Vladimirov, Petr Parfenovich, 1905-1953.

VLADIMIROV, Petr Parfenovich, 1905-1953. 951.04'2'0924
The Vladimirov diaries : Yenan, China, 1942-1945 / Peter Vladimirov. 1st ed. Garden City, N.Y. : Doubleday, 1975. p. cm. Includes bibliographical references and index. [DS796.Y4V56 1975] 74-27591 ISBN 0-385-00928-3 : 10.95
1. Vladimirov, Petr Parfenovich, 1905-1953. 2. Yenan, China—History—Sources. 3. China—Foreign relations—Russia. 4. Russia—Foreign relations—China. I. Title.

Vlanney, Jean Baptisic Marie, Satint,

SHEPPARD, Lancelot Capel, 1906- 922.244
Portrait of a parish priest; St. John Vianney, the cure d'Ars. Westminster, Md., Newman Press [1958] 189 p. illus. 23 cm. [BX4700.V5S5] 58-13646
1. Vlanney, Jean Baptisic Marie, Satint, I. Title.

Vlasov, Andrei Andreevich, 1900-1946.

STEENBERG, Sven. 355.3'32'0924 B
Vlasov. Translated from the German by Abe Farbstein. [1st American ed.] New York, Knopf, 1970. vi, 230, ix p. ports. 22 cm. Translation of Wlassow: Verrater oder Patriot? Includes bibliographical references. [DK268.V56S713 1970] 69-11788 7.50
1. Vlasov, Andrei Andreevich, 1900-1946. 2. Russkaia osvoboditel'naia armiia. I. Title.

Vo-nguyen-Giap.

O'NEILL, Robert John. 959.7'04'0924 B
General Giap; politician and strategist [by] Robert J. O'Neill. [Melbourne] Cassell Australia [1969] xi, 219 p. illus., maps, ports. 23 cm. [U55.V6O5 1969b] 79-465460 5.50
1. Vo-nguyen-Giap. I. Title.

O'NEILL, Robert John. 959.7'04'0924 B
General Giap; politician and strategist [by] Robert J. O'Neill. New York, Praeger [1969] xi, 219 p. illus., maps, plans, ports. 22 cm. Bibliography: p. 206-211. [U55.G5O5 1969] 69-12713 6.95
1. Vo-nguyen-Giap. I. Title.

Vocations, Religious, for women.

THE mystery of my future life. Translated from the French by Sister Eugenia Logan, S. P. New York, Society of Saint Paul [c1956] 240p. 21cm. Bibliographical notes: p.[227]-238. v. 12
1. Vocations, Religious, for women. I. Delarhove, Jean. II. Logan, Eugenia.

Vogau, Boris Andreevich, 1894-1937.

RECK, Vera T. 891.7'3'42
Boris Pil'niak : a Soviet writer in conflict with the state / Vera T. Reck. Montreal : McGill, Queen's University Press, 1975. 243 p. ; 24 cm. Includes index. Bibliography: p. 230-236. [PG3476.V6Z85] 76-356287 ISBN 0-7735-0237-8 : 12.00 ISBN 0-7735-0248-3 pbk. :
1. Vogau, Boris Andreevich, 1894-1937. 2. Literature and state—Russia.
Distributed by McGill-Queen's University Press, Irvington, N.Y. BIP

Vogel, Traugott, 1930-

VOGEL, Traugott, 1930- 248'.246 B
Under the SS shadow / Traugott Vogel with Shirley Stephens. Nashville : Broadman Press, 1977c1976 192 p. : ill. ; 21 cm. [BX6495.V6A37] 76-27478 ISBN 0-8054-7216-9 : 6.95
1. Vogel, Traugott, 1930- 2. Baptists—Clergy—Biography. 3. Clergy—United States—Biography. 4. Converts—Germany—Biography. I. Stephens, Shirley, joint author. II. Title. BIP

Voinovich, Vladimir, 1932- — Biography.

VOINOVICH, Vladimir, 1932- 891.7'3'44 B
The Ivankiad : or, The tale of the writer Voinovich's installation in his new apartment / translated by David Lapeza. New York : Farrar, Straus and Giroux, 1977. ix, 131 p. ; 22 cm. Translation of Ivan'kiada, ili rasskaz o vselenii pisatelia Voinovicha v novuiu kvartiru. [PG3489.4.I53Z5213] 77-5642 ISBN 0-374-17845-3 : 8.95 ISBN 0-374-51398-8 pbk. : 2.95
1. Voinovich, Vladimir, 1932- —Biography. 2. Authors, Russian—20th century—Biography. I. Title.

Volker, William, 1859-1847.

CORNUELLE, Herbert C. 923.673
Mr. Anonymous, the story of William Volker. Caldwell, Idaho, Caxton Printers, 1951. 212 p. illus. 23 cm. [CT275.V59C6] 51-11808
1. Volker, William, 1859-1847. I. Title.

Vollard, Ambroise, 1867-1939.

VOLLARD, Ambroise, 1867-1939. 706'.5 B
Recollections of a picture dealer / Ambroise Vollard ; translated from the French by Violet M. Macdonald. New York : Dover Publications, 1978. 326 p., [18] leaves of plates : ill. ; 22 cm. Translation of Souvenirs d'un marchand de tableaux. Includes index. [N8660.V6A2 1978b] 77-88948 ISBN 0-486-23582-3 : 4.50
1. Vollard, Ambroise, 1867-1939. 2. Art dealers—France—Biography. I. Title. BIP

VOLLARD, Ambroise, 1867-1939. 706'.5 B
Recollections of a picture dealer / Ambroise Vollard ; with a new foreword by Una E. Johnson ; [translated from the French by Violet M. MacDonald]. New York : Hacker Art Books, 1978. xv, 326 p., [16] leaves of plates : ill. ; 25 cm. Translation of Souvenirs d'un marchand de tableaux. Includes index.. [N8660.V6A2 1978] 77-76778 ISBN 0-87817-218-1 : lib.bdg. : 30.00
1. Vollard, Ambroise, 1867-1939. 2. Art dealers—France—Biography. 3. Art—Collectors and collecting. 4. Art—Anecdotes, facetiae, satire, etc. I. Title.

Vollmer, August, 1876-1955.

PARKER, Alfred Eustace, 1899- 923.573
Crime fighter: August Vollmer. New York, Macmillan, 1961. 181p. 21cm. [HV7911.V6P3] 61-9078
1. Vollmer, August, 1876-1955. I. Title.

Voloshin, Maksimilian Aleksandrovich, 1877-1932—Addresses, essays, lectures.

TSVETAEVA, Marina Ivanovna Efron, 1892-1941. 891.78'4209
A captive spirit : selected prose / Marina Tsvetaeva ; editor and translator J. Marin King. Ann Arbor : Ardis Publishers, 1980. p. cm. Translated from the Russian. Includes bibliographical references and index. [PG3476.T75A25 1980] 80-11664 ISBN 0-88233-352-6 : 22.50
1. Tsvetaeva, Marina Ivanovna Efron, 1892-1941—Biography—Addresses, essays, lectures. 2. Voloshin, Maksimilian Aleksandrovich, 1877-1932—Addresses, essays, lectures. 3. Pushkin, Aleksandr Sergeevich, 1799-1837—Appreciation—Addresses, essays, lectures. 4. Poets, Russian—20th century—Biography—Addresses, essays, lectures. 5. Poets, Russian—19th century—Biography—

[illegible] ssays, lectures. I. King, J. [illegible] itle. BIP

[illegible]olpe, Robert, 1942-

ADAMS, Laurie. 364.1'62
Art cop Robert Volpe, art crime detective / by Laurie Adams. New York : Dodd, Mead, [1974] xi, 240 p., [4] leaves of plates : ill. ; 24 cm. Includes index. [N8795.5.V64A32] 74-15238 ISBN 0-396-07027-2 : 8.95
1. Volpe, Robert, 1942- 2. Art thefts—New York (City) I. Title.

Volta, Alessandro Giuseppe Antonio Anastasio, conte, 1745?-1827.

DIBNER, Bern 925.3
Alessandro Volta and the electric battery. New York, Watts [c.1964] 135p. illus., ports. 22cm. (Immortals of sci.) Includes a tr. of the author s On the electricity excited by the mere contact of conducting substances of different kind,' originally written in French with English title. First pub. in Royal Soc. of London, Philosophical transactions, 1800, pt. 2. 64-11915 2.95
1. Volta, Alessandro Giuseppe Antonio Anastasio, conte, 1745?-1827. I. Volta, Alessandro Giuseppe Antonio Anastasio, conte, 1745-1827. On the electricity excited by the mere contact of conducting substances of different kinds. II. Title.

Voltaire, Francois Marie Arouet de, 1694-1778.

ALDINGTON, Richard, 1892-1962. 848'.5'09 B
Voltaire / by Richard Aldington. Folcroft, Pa. : Folcroft Library Editions, 1977. p. cm. Reprint of the 1925 ed. published by G. Routledge, London, Dutton, New York, in series: The Republic of letters. Includes index. Bibliography: p. [PQ2099.A48 1977] 77-21922 ISBN 0-8414-1738-5 lib. bdg. : 25.00
1. Voltaire, Francois Marie Arouet de, 1694-1778. 2. Authors, French—18th century—Biography. I. Series: The Republic of letters.

BESTERMAN, Theodore, 1904- 848'.5'09 B
Voltaire. [1st American ed.] New York, Harcourt, Brace & World [1969] 637 p. illus. 22 cm. Includes bibliographical references. [PQ2099.B38] 75-78870 12.50
1. Voltaire, Francois Marie Arouet de, 1694-1778.

BESTERMAN, Theodore, 1904-1976. 848'.5'09 B
Voltaire / Theodore Besterman. 3d ed. Chicago : University of Chicago Press, 1977. 718 p., [20] leaves of plates : ill. (some col.) ; 23 cm. Includes bibliographical references and index. [PQ2099.B38 1976b] 77-152566 ISBN 0-226-04430-0 lib.bdg. : 25.00
1. Voltaire, Francois Marie Arouet de, 1694-1778. 2. Authors, French—18th century—Biography.

BRAILSFORD, Henry Noel, 1873-1958 928.4
Voltaire. New York, Oxford, 1963. 141p. 20cm. (Oxford paperbacks, no. 74) Bibl. 63-24199 1.50 pap.,
1. Voltaire, Francois Marie Arouet de, 1694-1778. I. Title.

BRANDES, Georg Morris Cohen, 1842-1927 928.4
Voltaire; 2v. [Tr. by Otto Kruger, Pierce Butler] New York, Ungar [1964] 2v. port. 22cm. 64-15687 15.00 set
1. Voltaire, Francois Marie Arouet de, 1694-1778. I. Title.

BRANDES, Georg Morris Cohen, 1842-1927 928.4
Voltaire. Tr., introd. by John Butt. Baltimore, Penguin [c.1964] 190p. 18cm. (Penguin classics, L126) .95 pap.,
1. Voltaire, Francois Marie Arouet de, 1694-1778. I. Title.

BRUMFITT, J. H. 901
Voltaire: historian, by J. H. Brumfitt. [1st ed. reprinted]; with new preface. London, Oxford University Press, 1970. x, 178 p. 23 cm. A shortened version of a doctoral thesis presented in the University of Oxford. Bibliography: p. [170]-173. [D15.V6B7 1970] 72-21651 ISBN 0-19-815704-5 £2.50
1. Voltaire, Francois Marie Arouet de, 1694-1778. I. Title.

CHASE, Cleveland Bruce, 1903- 848'.5'09 B
The young Voltaire, by Cleveland B. Chase. New York, Haskell House Publishers [1972, c1926] p. Bibliography: p. [PQ2102.C5 1972] 72-3493 ISBN 0-8383-1551-8
1. Voltaire, Francois Marie Arouet de, 1694-1778. I. Title. BIP

CHASE, Cleveland Bruce, 1903- 848'.5'09 B
The young Voltaire, by Cleveland B. Chase. Freeport, N.Y., Books for Libraries Press [1971] ix, 253 p. illus., ports. 23 cm. Bibliography: p. 241-247. [PQ2102.C5 1971] 79-160962 ISBN 0-8369-5830-6
1. Voltaire, Francois Marie Arouet de, 1694-1778. I. Title.

GOOCH, George Peabody, 1873- 923.147
Catherine the Great, and other studies. London, New York, Longmans, Green [1954] xi, 292p. ports. 23cm. [DK170.G65] 54-10190
1. Voltaire, Francois Marie Arouet de, 1694-1778. 2. Bismarck, Otto Furst von, 1815-1898. 3. Catharine II, Empress of Russia, 1729-1796. 4. France—Intellectual life. I. Title.

GOOCH, George Peabody, 1873- 920.02
Catherine the Great, and other studies [by] G. P. Gooch. Hamden, Conn. [dist. Shoe String] 1966. xi, 292p. ports. 22cm. First pub. in 1954. [DK170.G65] 66-18227 7.50
1. Catharine II, Empress of Russia. 1729-1796. 2. Voltaire, Francois Marie Arouet de, 1694-1778. 3. Bismarck, Otto, Furst von, 1815-1898. 4. France—Intellectual life. I. Title.

GROSS, Rebecca H. 928.4
Voltaire, noncomformist. New York, Philosophical [c.1965] 162p. 22cm. Bibl. [PQ2099.G75] 65-14264 4.50
1. Voltaire, Francois Marie Arouet de. 1694-1778. I. Title.

GROSS, Rebecca H 928.4
Voltaire, nonconformist, by Rebecca H. Gross. New York, Philosophical Library [1965] 162 p. 22 cm. Bibliography: p. 159-162. [PQ2099.G75] 65-14264
1. Voltaire, Francois Marie Arouet de, 1694-1778. I. Title.

HALL, Evelyn Beatrice, 1868-1919. 848'.5'09 B
The life of Voltaire, by S. G. Tallentyre. Freeport, N.Y., Books for Libraries Press [1972] 2 v. illus. 22 cm. Reprint of the 1903 ed. Includes bibliographical references. [PQ2099.H3 1972] 72-2504 ISBN 0-8369-6867-0 29.50
1. Voltaire, Francois Marie Arouet de, 1694-1778.

LANSON, Gustave, 1857-1934. 848.509
Voltaire. English translation by Robert A. Wagoner. With an introd. by Peter Gay. New York, Wiley [1966] xii, 258 p. ports. 22 cm. Bibliography: p. 246-247. [PQ2099.L313] 66-14137
1. Voltaire, Francois Marie Arovet de, 1694-1778. I. Wagoner, Robert A., tr.

MITFORD, Nancy, 1904- 928.4
Voltaire in love. 1st American ed. New York, Harper [1957] 320p. illus. 22cm. Includes bibliography. [PQ2103.D7M5 1957a] 58-5425
1. Voltaire, Francois Marie Arouet de, 1694-1778. 2. Du Chatelet-Lomont, Gabrielle Emilie (Le Tonneller de Breteuli) marquise, 1706-1749. I. Title.

MOREHOUSE, Andrew Richmond. 848'.5'09
Voltaire and Jean Meslier, by Andrew R. Morehouse. New Haven, Yale University Press, 1936. [New York, AMS Press, 1973] x, 158 p. 23 cm. Original ed. issued as no. 9 of the Yale Romanic studies. Bibliography: p. [153]-158. [PQ2130.M56 1973] 72-1716 ISBN 0-404-53209-8 7.00
1. Voltaire, Francois Marie Arouet de, 1694-1778. 2. Meslier, Jean, 1664-1729. I. Title. II. Series: Yale Romanic studies, no. 9. BIP

MORLEY, John Morley, Viscount, 1838-1923. 848'.5'09 B
Voltaire. New York, B. Franklin [1973] xiii, 365 p. 18 cm. (Burt Franklin research and source works series. Philosophy and religious history monographs, 130) Reprint of the 1923 ed. published by Macmillan, London. Includes bibliographical references. [PQ2099.M6 1973] 72-82326 ISBN 0-8337-4293-0
1. Voltaire, Francois Marie Arouet de, 1694-1778.

ORIEUX, Jean, 1907- 848'.5'09
Voltaire / by Jean Orieux ; translated from the original French by Barbara Bray and Helen R. Lane. 1st ed. Garden City, N.Y. : Doubleday, 1979. p. cm. Includes bibliographical references and index. [PQ2099.O713] 74-25095 ISBN 0-385-08567-2 : 15.95
1. Voltaire, Francois Marie Arouet de, 1694-1778. 2. Authors, French—18th century—Biography.

TORREY, Norman Lewis, 1894- 848'.5'09
The spirit of Voltaire [by] Norman L. Torrey. New York, Russell & Russell [1968] xiii, 314 p. illus., ports. 23 cm. Reprint of the 1938 ed. Bibliographical references included in "Notes" (p. 285-300) [PQ2099.T67 1968] 68-10948
1. Voltaire, Francois Marie Arouet de, 1694-1778. I. Title. BIP

VULLIAMY, Colwyn Edward, 1886- 848'.5'09 B
Voltaire, by C. E. Vulliamy. Port Washington, N.Y., Kennikat Press [1970] ix, 344 p. port. 22 cm. Reprint of the 1930 ed. [PQ2099.V8 1970] 76-113328
1. Voltaire, Francois Marie Arouet de, 1694-1778. BIP

WADE, Ira Owen, 1896- 194
Studies on Voltaire, with some unpublished papers of Mme. du Chatelet, by Ira O. Wade. New York, Russell & Russell [1967, c1947] ix, 244 p. 23 cm. Bibliographical footnotes. [B2177.W3 1967] 66-27196
1. Voltaire, Francois Marie Arouet de, 1694-1778. I. Du Chatelet-Lomont, Gabrielle Emilie (Le Tonnelier de Breteuil) marquise, 1706-1749. II. Title.

Voltaire, Francois Marie Arouet de, 1694-1778—Biography.

ALDRIDGE, Alfred Owen, 1915- 848'.5'09 B
Voltaire and the century of light / A. Owen Aldridge. Princeton, N.J. : Princeton University Press, [1975] p. cm. Includes index. Bibliography: p. [PQ2099.A5] 75-2978 ISBN 0-691-06287-0 : 20.00
1. Voltaire, Francois Marie Arouet de, 1694-1778—Biography. I. Title. BIP

HALL, Evelyn Beatrice, 1868-1919. 848'.5'09 B
The life of Voltaire / by S. G. Tallentyre [i.e. E. B. Hall]. 3d ed. Folcroft, Pa. : Folcroft Library Editions, 1975. p. cm. Reprint of the 1905 ed. published by Smith, Elder, London. Includes index. Bibliography: p. [PQ2099.H3 1975] 75-25996 ISBN 0-8414-7826-0 lib. bdg. 25.00
1. Voltaire, Francois Marie Arouet de, 1694-1778—Biography. I. Title. BIP

HEARSEY, John E. N. 848'.5'09 B
Voltaire / John E. N. Hearsey. New York : Barnes & Noble Books, 1976. xiv, 367 p., [5] leaves of plates : ill. ; 23 cm. Includes index. Bibliography: p. 355-356. [PQ2099.H49 1976b] 75-40527 ISBN 0-06-492780-6 : 18.50
1. Voltaire, Francois Marie Arouet de, 1694-1778—Biography. 2. Authors, French—18th century—Biography.

HEARSEY, John E. N. 848'.5'09 B
Voltaire / [by] John E. N. Hearsey. London : Constable, 1976. xiv, 367 p., leaf of plate, [8] p. of plates : ill., ports. ; 23 cm. Includes index. Bibliography: p. 355-356. [PQ2099.H49 1976] 76-363160 ISBN 0-09-460030-9 : £6.00
1. Voltaire, Francois Marie Arouet de, 1694-1778—Biography. 2. Authors, French—18th century—Biography.

Voltaire, Francois Marie Arouet de, 1694-1778—Correspondence.

VOLTAIRE, Francois Marie Arouet de, 1694-1778. 848'.5'09 B
The selected letters of Voltaire, edited and translated by Richard A. Brooks. New York, New York University Press, 1973. xxxvii, 349 p. 24 cm. [PQ2084.Z4B7 1973] 72-96429 ISBN 0-8147-0972-9
1. Voltaire, Francois Marie Arouet de, 1694-1778—Correspondence. I. Brooks, Richard A., 1931- ed. II. Title. BIP

VOLTAIRE, Francois Marie Arouet de, 1694-1778. 848'.5'09
Voltaire and Catherine the Great; selected correspondence. Translated, with commentary, notes and introd. by A. Lentin. With a foreword by Elizabeth Hill. Cambridge, Eng., Oriental Research Partners, 1974. 186 p. illus. 22 cm. Bibliography: p. 178-186. [PQ2084.C313 1974] 74-181322 £3.50 ($9.50 U.S.)
1. Voltaire, Francois Marie Arouet de, 1694-1778—Correspondence. 2. Catharine II, Empress of Russia, 1729-1796. I. Catharine II, Empress of Russia, 1729-1796. II. Lentin, Antony, ed. III. Title.

VOLTAIRE, Francois Marie Arouet de, 1694-1778. 848'.5'09 B
Voltaire in his letters; being a selection from his correspondence. Translated with a pref. and forewords by S. G. Tallentyre. Freeport, N.Y., Books for Libraries Press [1971] xxix, 270 p. ports. 23 cm. [PQ2084.Z4H3 1971] 77-150205 ISBN 0-8369-5718-0
I. Hall, Evelyn Beatrice, 1868-1919, tr. II. Title.

Voltaire, Francois Marie Arouet de, 1694-1778—Relationship with women.

MITFORD, Nancy, 1904- 848.509
Voltaire in love. New York, Greenwood Press [1969, c1957] 320 p. illus., ports. 23 cm. Bibliography: p. 305. [PQ2103.D7M5 1969] 77-88909
1. Voltaire, Francois Marie Arouet de, 1694-1778—Relationship with women. 2. Du Chatelet-Lomont, Gabrielle Emilie (Le Tonnelier de Breteuil) marquise, 1706-1749. I. Title. BIP

Von Berg, Charles L., 1835-1918.

HEERWAGEN, Paul K. 978'.02'0924 B
Indian scout, Western painter: Captain Charles L. Von Berg, by Paul K. Heerwagen. Little Rock, Ark., Pioneer Press [1969] vii, 119 p. ports. 23 cm. Bibliographical footnotes. [F594.V6H4] 75-92588 2.95
1. Von Berg, Charles L., 1835-1918. I. Title.

Von Braun, Wernher, 1912-

WALTERS, Helen B 926.2
Wernher Von Braun, rocket engineer, by Helen B. Walters. Introd. by Wernher Von Braun. New York, Macmillan [1964] x, 187 p. illus., ports. 22 cm. Bibliography p. 175-180. [TL781.85V6W3] 64-12177
1. Von Braun, Wernher, 1912- I. Title.

WALTERS, Helen B. 926.2
Wernher Von Braun, rocket engineer, by

Helen B. Walters. Introd. by Wernher Von Braun. New York, Macmillan [1964] x, 187 p. illus., ports. 22 cm. Bibliography: p. 175-180. [TL781.85.V6W3] 64-12177
1. Von Braun, Wernher, 1912- I. Title.

Von Braun, Wernher, 1912—Juvenile literature.

GOODRUM, John C. 629.4'0924 B
Wernher von Braun, space pioneer, by John C. Goodrum. [Huntsville, Ala.] Strode Publishers [1969] 166 p. illus., facsims., group ports. 22 cm. (Heroes of space series) A biography of the German rocket engineer responsible for the planning and execution of the Apollo program that put man on the moon. [TL781.85.V6G6] 92 78-94442
1. Von Braun, Wernher, 1912—Juvenile literature. I. Title.

Von Hagen, Victor Wolfgang,

VON HAGEN, Victor Wolfgang, 1908- 720.9'24
F. Catherwood, architect-explorer of two worlds. Introd. by Aldous Huxley. Barre, Mass., Barre, 1968 [c1967] xv, 60p. illus. 24cm. Bibl. [NA997.C33V57] 67-25571 6.95
I. Catherwood, Frederick. II. Title.

Von Herff, Ferdinand Ludwig, 1820-1912.

HERFF, Ferdinand Peter, 1883-1965. 610'.92'22 B
The doctors Herff: a three-generation memoir. Edited by Laura L. Barber. San Antonio, Trinity University Press, 1973. 2 v. (xiii, 519 p.) illus. 25 cm. Issued in a case. [R154.H377A35 1973] 78-128375 ISBN 0-911536-40-X 18.00
1. Von Herff, Ferdinand Ludwig, 1820-1912. 2. Herff, Adolph, 1858-1952. 3. Herff, Ferdinand Peter, 1883-1965. I. Title. BIP

Von Karman, Theodore, 1881-1963.

HALACY, Daniel Stephen, 1919- 001.'94
Father of supersonic flight, Theodor von Karman [by] D. S. Halacy, Jr. New York, Messner [1965] 192 p. 22 cm. Bibliography: p. 186. [TL789.85.V65H3] [629.1333490924] 65-21608
1. Von Karman, Theodore, 1881-1963. I. Title.

HALACY, Daniel Stephen, Jr. 1919- 629.1333490924
Father of supersonic flight, Theodor von Karman. New York, Messner [c.1965] 192p. 22cm. Bibl. [TD789.85.V65H3] 65-21608 3.25; 3.19 lib. ed.,
1. Von Karman, Theodore, 1881-1963. I. Title.

VON KARMAN, Theodore, 1881-1963. 629.1'0924
The wind and beyond; Theodore von Karman, pioneer in aviation and pathfinder in space, by Theodore von Karman with Lee Edson. [1st ed.] Boston, Little, Brown [1967] 376 p. illus., ports. 24 cm. Bibliography: p. [355]-361. [TL540.V67A3] 67-11227
I. Edson, Lee. II. Title.

Von Mises, Ludwig, 1881-1973.

VON MISES, Ludwig, 1881-1973. 330'.092'4 B
Ludwig von Mises, notes and recollections / foreword by Margit von Mises ; translation and postscript by Hans F. Sennholz. South Holland, Ill. : Libertarian Press, c1978. x, 181 p. : port. ; 24 cm. Includes bibliographical references and index. [HB101.V66A35] 76-29877 ISBN 0-910884-04-8 : 9.95
1. Von Mises, Ludwig, 1881-1973. 2. Economists—Austria—Biography. 3. Austrian school of economists. I. Sennholz, Hans F. II. Title.

VON MISES, Margit. 330'.092'4 B
My years with Ludwig von Mises / Margit von Mises. New Rochelle, N.Y. : Arlington House, c1976. 191 p. : ill. ; 24 cm. Includes bibliographical references. [HB101.V66V66] 76-40265 ISBN 0-87000-368-2 : 12.95
1. Von Mises, Ludwig, 1881-1973. 2. Economists—Biography. I. Title. BIP

Von Nosaack, Ann, 1947-

VON NOSSACK, Ann, 1947- 286'.73 B
Diary of another Ann / Ann Von Nossack. Washington : Review and Herald Pub. Association, [1979] p. cm. [BX6193.V66A33] 79-15691 pbk. : 3.95
1. Von Nosaack, Ann, 1947- 2. Seventh-Day Adventists—United States—Biography. I. Title.

Von Sternberg, Joseph,

CALIFORNIA. University. University at Los Angeles. Motion Picture Division. v. 12
Mr. Josef von Sternberg, compiled by G. Charles Essert. Los Angeles, 1965. 1 v. [unpaged] illus. (The Film in retrospect, v. 1, no. 2) 68-47647
1. Von Sternberg, Joseph, I. Essert, G. Charles. II. Title. III. Series.

VON STERNBERG, Josef, 1894- 927.9143
Fun in a Chinese laundry. New York, Macmillan [c.1965] 348p. illus., ports. 21cm. [PN1998.A3V6] 65-11574 6.95
I. Title.

Von Stroheim, Erich, 1885-1957.

CURTISS, Thomas Quinn. 791.43'0233'0924 B
Von Stroheim. New York, Vintage Books [1973] xxii, 357 p. illus. 19 cm. "Filmography": p. 345-355. [PN1998.A3V6424 1973] 72-8303 2.45 (pbk.)
1. Von Stroheim, Erich, 1885 1957. BIP

CURTISS, Thomas Quinn. 791.43'0233'0924 B
Von Stroheim. New York, Farrar, Straus and Giroux [1971] xxii, 357 p. illus. 24 cm. "Filmography": p. 345-355. [PN1998.A3V6424 1971] 78-143300 ISBN 0-374-28520-9 10.00
1. Von Stroheim, Erich, 1885-1957.

FINLER, Joel Waldo. 791.43'0233'0924
Stroheim [by] Joel W. Finler. [1st American ed. Berkeley] University of California Press [1968] 143 p. illus., ports. 18 cm. Bibliography: p. 143. [PN1998.A3V644 1968] 68-17757
1. Von Stroheim, Erich, 1885-1957. I. Title. BIP

NOBLE, Peter, 1917- 791.43'092'4 B
Hollywood scapegoat; the biography of Erich Von Stroheim. New York, Arno Press, 1972. xii, 246 p. illus. 24 cm. (The Arno Press cinema program. The Literature of cinema) Reprint of the 1950 ed. published by Fortune Press, London. Bibliography: p. 171-184. [PN1998.A3V65 1972] 70-169352 ISBN 0-405-03922-0
1. Von Stroheim, Erich, 1885-1957. I. Title. II. Series: The Arno Press cinema program. III. Series: The Literature of cinema. BIP

Vonier, Anscar, 1875-1938.

GRAF, Ernest, 1879- 922.242
Anscar Vonier, abbot of Buckfast, with some account of the restoration of the Abbey and its church. Westminster. Md., Newman Press [1957] 154p. illus. 22cm. [BX4705.V75G7] 57-11814
1. Vonier, Anscar, 1875-1938. I. Title.

Voorhis, Aurelius Lyman, 1841-1913.

VOORHIS, Horace Jeremiah, 1901- 973.7'81 B
The life and times of Aurelius Lyman Voorhis / Jerry Voorhis, Sr. 1st ed. New York : Vantage Press, c1976. xvii, 370 p. : ill. ; 21 cm. [F689.R8V66] 77-352331 ISBN 0-533-02351-3 : 8.50
1. Voorhis, Aurelius Lyman, 1841-1913. 2. United States. Army. 46th Regiment of Indiana Volunteers—Biography. 3. United States—History—Civil War, 1861-1865—Regimental histories—Indiana Volunteers—46th regt. 4. Russell, Kan.—Biography. I. Title.

Voorhis, Horace Jeremiah, 1901-

BULLOCK, Paul. 328.73'092'4 B
Jerry Voorhis, the idealist as politician / by Paul Bullock. 1st ed. New York : Vantage Press, c1978. xi, 364 p. : ports. ; 22 cm. Includes bibliographical references. [E748.V66B84] 78-109086 ISBN 0-533-03120-6 : 10.95
1. Voorhis, Horace Jeremiah, 1901- 2. United States. Congress. House—Biography. 3. Legislators—United States—Biography. 4. United States—Politics and government—1901-1953. 5. Cooperative societies—United States—History. I. Title.

Vorobev, Marevna, 1892—

VOROBEV, Marevna, 1892- 927.5
Life in two worlds. Tr. by Benet Nash. Pref. by Ossip Zadkine. NewYork, Abelard [c.1962] 309p. illus. 23cm. 62-11783 5.00
1. Artists—Correspondence, reminiscences, etc. I. Title.

VOROBEV, Marevna, 1892- 700'.944'361
Life with the painters of La Ruche [by] Marevna. [Translation from the original Russian by Natalia Heseltine. 1st American ed.] New York, Macmillan [1974] x, 213 p. illus. 22 cm. [ND553.V67A2413 1974] 73-10564 6.95
1. Vorobev, Marevna, 1892- 2. Painters—France—Correspondence, reminiscences, etc. I. Title. BIP

Vorse, Mary Marvin Heaton.

VORSE, Mary Marvin Heaton. 818'.5'209 B
Autobiography of an elderly woman. New York, Arno Press, 1974 [c1911] 269 p. 21 cm. (Women in America: from colonial times to the 20th century) Reprint of the ed. published by Houghton Mifflin, Boston. [PS3543.O88Z52 1974] 74-3977 ISBN 0-405-06125-0
1. Vorse, Mary Marvin Heaton. I. Title. II. Series. BIP

Vorster, Joe, 1887-1945.

PILLMAN, Naka. 730'.92'4 B
African portrait : the life and sculpture of Sister Joe Vorster / Naka Pillman. 1st ed. Johannesburg : H. Keartland, 1976. 128 p. : ill. ; 32 cm. [NB1096.V67P54] 77-366429 ISBN 0-949997-31-5
1. Vorster, Joe, 1887-1945. 2. Sculptors—South Africa—Biography. 3. Blacks in art. I. Vorster, Joe, 1887-1945. II. Title.

Voulkos, Peter.

SLIVKA, Rose. 730'.92'4 B
Peter Voulkos : a dialogue with clay / Rose Slivka. 1st ed. Boston : New York Graphic Society, c1978. xvii, 142 p., [12] leaves of plates : ill. ; 31 cm. Bibliography: p. 139-142. [NB237.V64S58 1978] 77-17166 27.50
1. Voulkos, Peter. 2. Sculptors—United States—Biography. I. Title. BIP

Voyages and travels.

BRUCE, Michael, Sir 923.242
No escape from adventure. New York, Hastings House [1955, c1954] 263p. illus. 22cm. Autobiography. Published in London in 1954 under title: Tramp royal. [G463.B89 1955] 55-7947
1. Voyages and travels. I. Title.

BRUCE, Michael, 1894- 923.242
Tramp royal. London, New York, Elek [1954] 263p. illus. 23cm. Autobiography. [G463.B89 1954] 55-15977
1. Voyages and travels. I. Title.

CLARK, Joseph L., 1870-1961. 910.4 B
Joseph L. Clark, 1870-1961: his autobiography. Edited by Adelle Rogers Clark. Wolfe City, Tex., Henington Pub. Co. [1967] 236 p. ports. 28 cm. [G463.C5914 1967] 68-1494
1. Voyages and travels. I. Clark, Adelle Rogers, ed.

CURLE, Richard, 1883- 824'.9'12
Caravansary and conversation; memories of places and persons. Freeport, N.Y., Books for Libraries Press [1971, c1937] x, 309 p. 23 cm. (Essay index reprint series) [PR6005.U7C3 1971] 73-134070 ISBN 0-8369-2151-8
1. Voyages and travels. 2. Authors—Correspondence, reminiscences, etc. I. Title.

DAVIS, Nathaniel Penistone, 1895- 353.008920924 B
Few dull moments; a foreign service career, by Nathaniel P. Davis. [Philadelphia, Dunlap Print. Co., 1967] 158 p. 24 cm. [G463.D325] 67-29789
1. Voyages and travels. 2. United States—Diplomatic and consular service. I. Title.

FANNING, Edmund, 1769-1841. 910'.45
Voyages to the South Seas, Indian and Pacific Oceans, China Sea, Northwest Coast, Feejee Islands, South Shetlands, &, &. Fairfield, Wash., Ye Galleon Press, 1970. 324 p. illus., facsims. 25 cm. Reprint of the 2d ed., 1838. Part of illustrative matter in pocket. First ed. published in 1833 under title: Voyages round the world; 1924 ed. published under title: Voyages and discoveries in the South Seas, 1792-1832. [G440.F3 1970b] 72-185919
1. Voyages and travels. 2. Voyages around the world. I. Title.

FARSON, Negley, 1890-1960. 910'.4
Wanderlust: the world of Negley Farson; compiled and introduced by Daniel Farson. London, New York, White Lion Publishers, 1972. [vi], ii-218 p. illus., facsim., ports. 22 cm. [G463.F37 1972] 73-155733 ISBN 0-85617-460-2 6.95 (lib. ed.)
1. Voyages and travels. I. Title.

POLO, Marco, 1254-1323? 910.4
The travels of Marco Polo, the Venetian. The translation of Marsden rev., with a selection of his notes. Edited by Thomas Wright. London, H. G. Bohn, 1854. New York, AMS Press [1968] xxviii, 508 p. 21 cm. Original ed. issued in series: Bohn's antiquarian library. [G370.P72 1968b] 68-57871
1. Voyages and travels. 2. Asia—Description and travel. 3. Mongols—History. I. Wright, Thomas, 1810-1877, ed. II. Marsden, William, 1754-1836, tr.

Voyages and travels—Juvenile literature.

HURDY, John Major. 910.4'5
Two years before the mast, by Richard Henry Dana. Abridged and adapted by John M. Hurdy. Illustrated by Dennis Dierks. Belmont, Calif., Fearon Publishers

[1971] 92 p. col. illus. 20 cm. (Pacemaker classics) A simplified edition of the work describing life at sea in the 1830's from the viewpoint of a common sailor in the American merchant service. [G540.D22H8] 75-158878
1. Voyages and travels—Juvenile literature. 2. Seafaring life—Juvenile literature. I. Dana, Richard Henry, 1815-1882. Two years before the mast. II. Dierks, Dennis A., illus. III. Title.

Voyages and travels—1951-

BENCHLEY, Peter. 910.41
Time and a ticket. Boston, Houghton Mifflin, 1964. xiii, 239 p. 21 cm. Autobiographical. [G464.B4] 64-18994
1. Voyages and travels—1951- I. Title.

BRACKEN, Peg. 910'.92'4 B
But I wouldn't have missed it for the world! The pleasures and perils of an unseasoned traveler. [1st ed.] New York, Harcourt Brace Jovanovich [1973] xiii, 270 p. 21 cm. [G464.B62] 73-8678 ISBN 0-15-114984-4 6.95
1. Voyages and travels—1951- I. Title.

BRACKEN, Peg. 910'.92'4 B
But I wouldn't have missed it for the world! The pleasures and perils of an unseasoned traveler. Greenwich, Conn., Fawcett [1974, c1973] 222 p. 18 cm. (A Fawcett crest book) [G464.B62] 1.25 (pbk.)
1. Voyages and travels—1951- I. Title.
L.C. card number for original ed.: 73-8678.

GUILLAIN, France. 910'.41
Call of the sea / France and Christian Guillain ; translated from the French by Caroline Hillier. 1st U.S. ed. New York : Harper & Row, c1976. 198 p., [8] leaves of plates : ill. ; 24 cm. Translation of Le bonheur sur la mer. [G530.G8913 1976] 75-23884 ISBN 0-06-011631-5 : 12.95
1. Voyages and travels—1951- 2. Seafaring life. 3. Guillain, France. I. Guillain, Christian, joint author. II. Title. **BIP**

HOYT, Jo Wasson. 353.008920924
For the love of Mike, by Jo Wasson Hoyt with Frank Graham, Jr. New York, Random House [1966] 210 p. 22 cm. Autobiographical. [G464.H75] 66-21467
1. Voyages and travels—1951- 2. U.S.—Diplomatic and consular service. I. Graham, Frank, 1925- II. Title.

RICE, Lillian L. 910.4
And I got caught in Cairo, by Lillian L. Rice. Philadelphia, Dorrance [1968] 74 p. 22 cm. Letters. [G464.R47] 68-54481 3.00
1. Voyages and travels—1951- I. Title.

TROOPER Tom, 1944- 910.4'1
Because it is mine, by Trooper Tom. [Forestville, Conn., 1969] 226 p. illus., maps, ports. 20 cm. Autobiographical. [G464.T74] 70-284036
1. Voyages and travels—1951- I. Title.

Voyages around the world.

LAPEROUSE, Jean Francois de Galaup, comte de, 1741-1788. 910'.924
Voyages and adventures of La Perouse. Translated from the French by Julius S. Gassner. Honolulu, Published for Friends of the Library of Hawaii [by] University of Hawaii Press, 1969. xix, 161 p. illus., map., port. 26 cm. Translated "from the fourteenth edition of the F. Valentin abridgment, Tours, 1875," of Voyage de Laperouse autour du monde. Includes bibliographical references. [G420.L222 1969] 68-13887 ISBN 0-87022-445-X 8.00
1. Voyages around the world. I. Title.

SILVERBERG, Robert. 910'.41
The longest voyage; circumnavigators in the age of discovery. Indianapolis, Bobbs-Merrill [1972] 536 p. illus. 24 cm. Bibliography: p. 509-512. [G420.A2S5] 69-13089 10.00
1. Voyages around the world. 2. Explorers. I. Title.

Voysey, Charles F. A., 1857-1941.

GEBHARD, David. 720'.92'4
Charles F. A. Voysey, architect / by David Gebhard. Los Angeles : Hennessey & Ingalls, 1975. vii, 184 p. : ill. ; 23 cm. (Architectural monographs ; 2) Includes bibliographies and index. [NA997.V6G38] 75-15870 ISBN 0-912158-54-9 : 12.95
1. Voysey, Charles F. A., 1857-1941. I. Title. **BIP**

Vrooman, Carl Schurz, 1872-1966.

CAVANAGH, Helen Marie, 1904- 973.91'092'4 B
Carl Schurz Vrooman : self styled "constructive conservative" / by Helen M. Cavanagh. [s.l. : s.n.], c1977 (Chicago : Lakeside Press) x, 631 p., [1] leaf of plates : ill. ; 25 cm. Includes index. Bibliography: p. 609-619. [E748.V76C38] 77-78277 15.95
1. Vrooman, Carl Schurz, 1872-1966. 2. Politicians—United States—Biography. 3. United States—Politics and government—1901-1953. 4. Agriculture and state—United States—History. 5. United States—Economic policy—To 1933. I. Title.

Vuillard, Edouard, 1868-1940.

NEW York. Museum of Modern Art. 759.4
Edouard Vuillard, by Andrew Carnduff Ritchie. The Museum of Modern Art, New York, in collaboration with the Cleveland Museum of Art. [New York, 1954] 104p. illus. (part col.) ports. (part col.) 26cm. [ND553.V9N4] [ND553.V9N4] 927.5 54-6136 54-6136
1. Vullard, Edouard, 1868-1940. 2. Paintings, French—Exhibitions. I. Ritchie, Andrew Carnduff. II. Cleveland Museum of Art. III. Title.
Contents omitted.

ROGER-MARX, Claude, 1888- 759.4 B
Vuillard, his life and work / by Claude Roger Marx ; [translated from the French by E. B. D'Auvergne]. New York : AMS Press, [1976] p. cm. Translation of Vuillard et son temps. Reprint of the 1946 ed. published by P. Elek, London. Bibliography: p. [ND553.V9R62 1976] 75-41229 ISBN 0-404-14718-6 : 25.00
1. Vuillard, Edouard, 1868-1940. 2. Painters—France—Biography. **BIP**

W., Bill.

THOMSEN, Robert. 362.2'92'0924 B
Bill W. / Robert Thomsen. 1st ed. New York : Harper & Row, [1975] 373 p. ; 22 cm. [HV5032.W19T45 1975] 74-1861 ISBN 0-06-014267-7 : 10.95
1. W., Bill. 2. Alcoholics Anonymous. **BIP**

Waas, Milton J

WAAS, Milton J 926.176
As it was. Philadelphia, Dorrance [1957] 125 p. 20 cm. [RK43.W2A3] 57-11236
I. Title.

Waddell, Hugh, 1734?-1773.

WADDELL, Alfred Moore, 1834-1912. 973.345'6 B
A colonial officer and his times, 1754-1773; a biographical sketch of Gen. Hugh Waddell. Spartanburg, S.C., The Reprint Co. [1973, c1885] 242 p. illus. 22 cm. Reprint of the 1890 ed. Includes bibliographical references. [F257.W25W32 1973] 73-2617 ISBN 0-87152-142-3 12.00
1. Waddell, Hugh, 1734?-1773. 2. Brunswick Co., N.C.—History. 3. North Carolina—History—Colonial period. I. Title. **BIP**

Waddell, William H.

WADDELL, William H. 636.089'092'4 B
People are the funniest animals / William H. Waddell IV. Philadelphia : Dorrance, c1978. ix, 329 p. : port. ; 22 cm. Autobiographical. [SF613.W23A36] 78-104785 ISBN 0-8059-2507-4 : 8.95
1. Waddell, William H. 2. Veterinarians—United States—Biography. 3. Afro-Americans in veterinary medicine. I. Title.

Wade, Benjamin Franklin, 1800-1878.

TREFOUSSE, Hans Louis 923.273
Benjamin Franklin Wade, radical Republican from Ohio. New York, Twayne [c.1963] 404p. illus. 22cm. Bibl. 63-11185 6.50
1. Wade, Benjamin Franklin, 1800-1878. I. Title. **BIP**

TREFOUSSE, Hans Louis. 923.273
Benjamin Franklin Wade, radical Republican from Ohio. New York, Twayne Publishers [1963] 404 p. illus. 22 cm. Includes bibliography. [E415.9.W16T7] 63-11185
1. Wade, Bejamin Franklin. 1800-1878. I. Title.

Wadekar, Ajit, 1941-

WADEKAR, Ajit, 1941- 796.358'092'4
My cricketing years [by] Ajit Wadekar, as told to K. N. Prabhu. Foreword by Vijay Merchant. Delhi, Vikas Pub. House [1973, i.e., 1974] x, 159 p. illus. 22 cm. [GV915.W27A35] 72-908460
1. Wadekar, Ajit, 1941- 2. Cricket. I. Prabhu, K. N. II. Title.
Distributed by International Publications Service; 4.95

Wadsworth, James Wolcott, 1877-1952.

FAUSOLD, Martin L., 1921- 328.73'092'4 B
James W. Wadsworth, Jr. : the gentleman from New York / Martin L. Fausold. 1st ed. Syracuse, N.Y. : Syracuse University Press, 1975. p. cm. Includes bibliographical references and index. [E664.W13F38] 75-6111 ISBN 0-8156-2171-X
1. Wadsworth, James Wolcott, 1877-1952. **BIP**

FAUSOLD, Martin L., 1921- 328.73'092'4 B
James W. Wadsworth, Jr. : the gentleman from New York / Martin L. Fausold. 1st ed. Syracuse, N.Y. : Syracuse University Press, 1975. xvi, 457 p. : ill. ; 23 cm. (A New York State study) Includes index. Bibliography: p. 421-430. [E664.W13F38] 75-6111 ISBN 0-8156-2171-X : 17.50
1. Wadsworth, James Wolcott, 1877-1952.

Waerenskjold, Elise Amalie Tvede, 1815-1895.

WaRENSKJOLD, Elise Amalie Tvede, 1815-1895. 976.4'277'050924 B
The lady with the pen : Elise Waerenskjold in Texas / edited by C. A. Clausen ; foreword by Theodore C. Blegen. New York : Arno Press, 1979, c1961. p. cm. (Scandinavians in America) Reprint of the ed. published by the Norewegian-American Historical Association as v. 6 of its Travel description series. Includes index. [F392.K25W338 1979] 78-15856 ISBN 0-405-11663-2 : 16.00
1. Waerenskjold, Elise Amalie Tvede, 1815-1895. 2. Norwegian Americans—Texas—Kaufman Co.—Biography. 3. Frontier and pionner life—Texas—Kaufman Co. 4. Kaufman Co., Tex.—Biography. I. Clausen, Clarence Arthur, 1896- II. Seres. III. Title. IV. Series. V. Series: Norwegian-American Historical Association. Travel and description series ; v. 6.

Wagenknecht, Edward Charles,

WAGENKNECHT, Edward Charles, 1900- 920'.00924 B
As far as yesterday; memories and reflections [by] Edward Wagenknecht. [1st ed.] Norman, University of Oklahoma Press [1968] vii, 224 p. 23 cm. Autobiographical. "A check list of the publications of Edward Wagenknecht": p. 209-217. [PS3545.A26Z5] 68-15690
I. Title. **BIP**

Wagenvoord, James.

WAGENVOORD, James. 974.7'1'04
City lives / written and photographed by James Wagenvoord. 1st ed. New York : Holt, Rinehart and Winston, c1976. 226 p. : ill. ; 26 cm. [F128.52.W38] 75-21492 ISBN 0-03-015131-7 : 12.95 pbk. : 7.95
1. Wagenvoord, James. 2. New York (City)—Description—1951- 3. New York (City)—Social conditions. I. Title. **BIP**

Wagner, Charles Ludwig.

WAGNER, Charles Ludwig. 782.1'092'4 B
Seeing stars / Charles L. Wagner. New York : Arno Press, 1977, c1940. ix, 403 p., [7] leaves of plates : ill. ; 23 cm. (Opera biographies) Reprint of the ed. published by Putnam, New York. Includes index. [ML429.W13A3 1977] 76-29976 ISBN 0-405-09714-X : 24.00
1. Wagner, Charles Ludwig. 2. Impressarios—United States—Biography. I. Title. **BIP**

Wagner, Harold A.

WAGNER, Harold A. 267'.39794'93
As I lived it : an autobiographical history of the YMCA of Los Angeles, 1925-1966 / by Harold A. Wagner. Glendale, Calif. : A. H. Clark Co., 1979. 332 p. : ill. ; 25 cm. Includes index. [BV1050.L67W33] 79-50564 ISBN 0-87062-129-7 : 10.00
1. YMCA of Los Angeles. 2. Wagner, Harold A. 3. Young Men's Christian Associations—Biography. I. Title. **BIP**

Wagner, Landsay—Juvenile literature.

JACOBS, Linda. 792'.028'0924 B
Lindsay Wagner, her own way / by Linda Jacobs. St. Paul : EMC Corp., 1977. p. cm. (Center stage) A biography of the star of the "Bionic Woman" television series. [PN2287.W23J3] 92 77-22955 ISBN 0-88436-414-3 lib.bdg. : 4.95 ISBN 0-88436-415-1 pbk. : 2.95
1. Wagner, Landsay—Juvenile literature. 2. Actors—United States—Biography—Juvenile literature. I. Title. II. Series.

JACOBS, Linda. 792'.028'0924 B
Lindsay Wagner, her own way / by Linda Jacobs. St. Paul : EMC Corp., 1977. p. cm. (Center stage) A biography of the star of the "Bionic Woman" television series. [PN2287.W23J3] 92 77-22955 ISBN 0-88436-414-3 lib.bdg. : 4.95 ISBN 0-88436-415-1 pbk. : 2.95
1. Wagner, Landsay—Juvenile literature. 2. Actors—United States—Biography—Juvenile literature. I. Title. II. Series.

Wagner, Minna (Planer) 1809-1886.

HARDING, Bertita (Leonarz) 927.8
Magic fire; scenes around Richard Wagner. [1st ed.] Indianapolis, Bobbs-Merrill [1953] 451p. illus. 23cm. [ML410.W19H3] 53-9860
1. Wagner, Richard, 1813-1883. 2. Wagner, Minna (Planer) 1809-1866. 3. Wesendonck, Mathilde (Luckemyer) 1828-1902. 4. Wagner, Cosima (Liszt) 1837-1930. I. Title.

WAGNER, Richard, 1813-1883. 782.1'092'4 B
Richard to Minna Wagner; letters to his first wife. Translated, prefaced, etc., by William Ashton Ellis. New York, Vienna House [1972] 2 v. (xviii, 812 p.) ports. 23 cm. Reprint of the 1909 ed. [ML410.W1A387 1972] 75-163797 ISBN 0-8443-0012-8 (v. 1)
1. Wagner, Minna (Planer) 1809-1886. I. Ellis, William Ashton, d. 1919, ed.

Wagner, Otto, 1841-1918.

GERETSEGGER, Heinz. 720'.924 B
Otto Wagner, 1841-1918; the expanding city, the beginning of modern architecture, by Heinz Geretsegger and Max Peintner. Associate author: Walter Pichler. Introd. by Richard Neutra. Translated by Gerald Onn. New York, Praeger [1970] 276 p. illus. (part col.), maps, ports. 29 cm.

Bibliography: p. 264-270. [NA1038.W3G43] 69-16757 25.00
1. Wagner, Otto, 1841-1918. I. Peintner, Max, joint author. II. Pichler, Walter, 1936- joint author.

GERETSEGGER, Heinz. 720'.92'4 B
Otto Wagner 1841-1918 : the expanding city, the beginning of modern architecture / by Heinz Geretsegger and Max Peintner ; associate author Walter Pichler ; introd. by Richard Neutra ; translated by Gerald Onn. English language ed. New York : Rizzoli, 1979. 272 p. : ill ; 28 cm. Includes index. Bibliography: p. 262-268. [NA1011.5.W3G413 1979] 78-68493 ISBN 0-8478-0217-5 pbk. : 19.95
1. Wagner, Otto, 1841-1918. I. Peintner, Max, joint author. II. Pichler, Walter, 1936- joint author. III. Title.

Wagner, Richard, 1813-1883.

BARTH, Herbert, 1910- 782.1'092'4 B
Wagner : a documentary study / compiled and edited by Herbert Barth, Dietrich Mack, Egon Voss ; pref. by Pierre Boulez. New York : Oxford University Press, 1975. 256 p. : ill., facsims., music (some col.) ; 31 cm. Translation of Wagner: sein Leben und seine Welt in zeitgenoss. Bildern u. Texten. Includes index. Bibliography: p. 251. [ML410.W1B1853 1975b] 75-4097 ISBN 0-19-519818-2 : 37.50
1. Wagner, Richard, 1813-1883. 2. Composers—Germany—Biography. I. Mack, Dietrich, joint author. II. Voss, Egon, joint author.

BEKKER, Paul, 1882-1937. 782.1'0924 B
Richard Wagner, his life in his work. Translated by M. M. Bozman. Westport, Conn., Greenwood Press [1971] vii, 522 p. port. 23 cm. Reprint of the 1931 ed. Translation of Wagner, das Leben im Werke. [ML410.W13B243 1971] 74-106713 ISBN 0-8371-3443-9
1. Wagner, Richard, 1813-1883. BIP

BEKKER, Paul, 1882-1937. 782.1'0924 B
Richard Wagner, his life in his work. Translated by M. M. Bozman. Freeport, N.Y., Books for Libraries Press [1970] vii, 522 p. port. 23 cm. "First published 1931." [ML410.W13B243 1970] 70-107792
1. Wagner, Richard, 1813-1883.

CLEATHER, Alice Leighton. 782.1'092'4
The ring of the Nibelung : an interpretaion of embodying Wagner's own explanations / by Alice Leighton Cleather and Basil Crump. 7th ed. Folcroft, Pa. : Folcroft Library Editions, 1977. vii, 164 p. : ill. ; 23 cm. Reprint of the 1924 ed. published by Methuen, London. [MT100.W25C6 1977] 77-18100 ISBN 0-8414-1844-6 lib. bdg. : 20.00
1. Wagner, Richard, 1813-1883. Der Ring des Nibelungen. I. Crump, Basil Woodward, 1866-1945, joint author. II. Title.

CULSHAW, John. 782.1'092'4
Wagner, the man and his music / John Culshaw ; picture editor, Gerald Fitzgerald. 1st ed. New York : E. P. Dutton, c1978. p. cm. (The Metropolitan Opera Guild composer series) Includes index. [ML410.W1C9] 78-842 ISBN 0-525-22960-4 : 8.95
1. Wagner, Richard, 1813-1883. I. Series: Metropolitan Opera Guild. The Metropolitan Opera Guild Composer series.

FINCK, Henry Theophilus, 1854-1926. 782.1'0924 B
Wagner and his works; the story of his life, with critical comments. New York, Haskell House, 1968. 2 v. ports. 23 cm. Reprint of the 1893 ed. Bibliographical footnotes. [ML410.W1F3 1968] 68-25287
1. Wagner, Richard, 1813-1883. I. Title.

GAL, Hans, 1890- 782.1'092'4 B
Richard Wagner / by Hans Gal ; translated by Hans-Hubert Shonzeler. New York : Stein and Day, [1976] p. cm. Includes index. Bibliography: p. [ML410.W1G143 1976] 75-37776 ISBN 0-8128-1942-X : 8.95
1. Wagner, Richard, 1813-1883.

GAL, Hans, 1890- 782.1'092'4 B
Richard Wagner / [by] Hans Gal ; translated [from the German] by Hans-Hubert Schonzeler. London : Gollancz, 1976. 224 p. : music ; 23 cm. Translation of Richard Wagner. Includes index. Bibliography: p. [211]-212. [ML410.W1G143 1976b] 76-363317 ISBN 0-575-01847-X : £5.50
1. Wagner, Richard, 1813-1883.

GARTEN, Hugh Frederick, 1904- 782.1'092'4
Wagner the dramatist / by H. F. Garten. Totowa, N.J. : Rowman and Littlefield, 1978, c1977. 159 p. : ill. ; 23 cm. Includes index. Bibliography: p. [151]-155. [ML410.W1G195 1978] 78-105857 ISBN 0-8476-6058-3 : 10.00
1. Wagner, Richard, 1813-1883. 2. Composers—Germany—Biography. I. Title. BIP

GLASENAPP, Carl Friedrich, 1847-1915. 782.1'092'4 B
Life of Richard Wagner / being an authorised English version by Wm. Ashton Ellis of C. F. Glasenapp's Das Leben Richard Wagners. New York : Da Capo Press, 1977- v. ; 22 cm. (Da Capo Press music reprint series) Vols. 4-6, with title: Life of Richard Wagner, by Wm. Ashton Ellis, are entirely the work of Ellis. Reprint of the 1900-1908 ed. published by K. Paul, Trench, Trubner, London. Includes bibliographical references and indexes. [ML410.W1G533 1977] 77-2022 ISBN 0-306-70883-3 : 32.50 (vol.3)
1. Wagner, Richard, 1813-1883. 2. Composers—Germany—Biography. I. Ellis, William Ashton, d. 1919.

GUTMAN, Robert W. 782'.1'0924 B
Richard Wagner; the man, his mind, and his music, by Robert W. Gutman. [1st ed.] New York, Harcourt, Brace & World [1968] xx, 490 p. 24 cm. Bibliography: p. 457-469. [ML410.W1G83] 67-20310
1. Wagner, Richard, 1813-1883. BIP

GUTMAN, Robert W. 782.1'092'4 B
Richard Wagner; the man, his mind, and his music [by] Robert W. Gutman. New York, Harcourt Brace Jovanovich [1974, c1968] xx, 490 p. illus. 21 cm. (A Harvest book, HB 272) Bibliography: p. 457-469. [ML410.W1G83 1974] 73-12381 ISBN 0-15-677610-3 4.50 (pbk.)
1. Wagner, Richard, 1813-1883.

GUTMAN. ROBERT W. 782'.1'0924
Richard Wagner: the man. his mind, and his music. by Robert W. Gutman. [1st ed.] New York, Harcourt. [1968] xx. 490p. 24 cm. Bibl. [ML410.W1G38] (B) 67-20310 12.50
1. Wagner, Richard, 1813-1883. I. Title.

HARDING, Bertita (Leonarz) 927.8
Magic fire; scenes around Richard Wagner. [1st ed.] Indianapolis, Bobbs-Merrill [1953] 451p illus. 22cm. [ML410.W19H3] 53-9860
1. Wagner, Richard, 1813-1883. 2. Wagner, Minna (Planer) 1809-1866. 3. Wesendonck, Mathilde (Luckemyer) 1828-1902. 4. Wagner, Cosima (Liszt) 1837-1930. I. Title.

HENDERSON, William James, 1855-1937. 782.1'0924 B
Richard Wagner, his life and his dramas. New York, AMS Press [1971] xiv, 504 p. music, port. 19 cm. Reprint of the 1923 ed. [ML410.W1H52 1971] 70-137240 ISBN 0-404-03239-7
1. Wagner, Richard, 1813-1883.

HUEFFER, Francis, 1845-1889. 782.1'0924
Richard Wagner and the music of the future; history and aesthetics, by Franz Hueffer. Freeport, N.Y., Books for Libraries Press [1971] v, 333 p. 23 cm. (Essay index reprint series) Reprint of the 1874 ed. Contents.Contents.—The drama: Richard Wagner.—The song: Franz Schubert. Robert Schumann. Robert Franz and Franz Liszt.—Appendix [An account of the festival at Bayreuth on the occasion of the foundation-stone of the Wagner theatre being laid] [ML390.H88 1971] 70-37122 ISBN 0-8369-2508-4
1. Wagner, Richard, 1813-1883. 2. Songs—History and criticism. 3. Music—History and criticism—19th century. 4. Music—Philosophy and aesthetics. I. Title.

JACOB, Walter. 784'.092'4
Richard Wagner; Leben und Werk. Hamburg, H. Sikorski [1958] 86p. illus. 18cm. (Kleine Musikbucherel, Bd. 12) [ML410.W1J16] 58-38288
1. Wagner, Richard, 1813-1883. I. Title.

JACOBS, Robert Louis 927.8
Wagner New York, Collier [1962] 253p. 18cm. (BS141V) Bibl. 1.50 pap.,
1. Wagner, Richard, 1813-1883. I. Title.

JACOBS, Robert Louis. v. 12
Wagner. [Rev. ed.] London, J. M. Dent; New York, Farrar, Straus and Giroux [1965] 278 p. illus. (music), plates. (The master musicians series) "Catalogue of works": p. 222-225. "Selected list of literary works": p. 240-242. Bibliography: p. 232-239. 66-48205
1. Wagner, Richard, 1813-1883. I. Title.

JACOBS, Robert Louis. v. 12
Wagner, by Robert L. Jacobs. New York, Collier Books [1962] 253 p. illus. (music) 18 cm. (Great composers series, BS 141 V) "First Collier Books edition, 1962." "Catalogue of works": p. 209-211. "Selected list of literary works": p. 224-225. Bibliography: p. 217-223. 65-78803
1. Wagner, Richard, 1813-1883. I. Title.

LANDRE, Willem, 1874-1944. v. 12
Richard Wagner. Hilversum, J. J. Lispet [195-?] 62 p. port. 19 cm. A 52
1. Wagner, Richard, 1813-1883. I. Title.

MAYER, Hans, Mar.19,1907- 782.1'092'4 B
Portrait of Wagner; an illustrated biography. Translated by Robert Nowell. [New York] Herder and Herder [1972] 175 p. illus., ports. 21 cm. Originally published as Richard Wagner in Selbstzeugnissen und Bilddokumenten, 1959. [ML410.W1M28 1972] 78-185748 6.95
1. Wagner, Richard, 1813-1883. 2. Wagner, Richard, 1813-1883—Iconography. I. Title.

NEUMANN, Angelo, 1838-1910. 782.1'092'4 B
Personal recollections of Wagner / by Angelo Neumann ; translated from the 4th German ed. by Edith Libermore. New York : Da Capo Press, 1976, c1908. iv, 329 p., [5] leaves of plates : ill. ; 23 cm. (The Lyric stage) Reprint of the ed. published by Holt, New York. Includes index. [ML410.W1N42 1976] 76-16506 ISBN 0-306-70843-4 : 22.50
1. Wagner, Richard, 1813-1883.

NEWMAN, Ernest, 1868-1959. 782.1'092'4 B
The life of Richard Wagner / Ernest Newman. Cambridge ; New York : Cambridge University Press, 1976, c1933-46. p. cm. Reprint of the ed. published by Knopf, New York. Contents.Contents.—v. 1. 1813-1848.—v. 2. 1848-1860.—v. 3. 1859-1866.—v. 4. 1866-1883. Includes bibliographies and indexes. [ML410.W1N532] 76-22682 ISBN 0-521-29094-5 : 7.95
1. Wagner, Richard, 1813-1883. BIP

NEWMAN, Ernest, 1868-1959. 927.8
Wagner as man and artist. New York, Vintage Books, 1960 [c.1924, 1952] xvii, 440p. (Bibl footnotes) illus. 19cm. (A Vintage book, V-107) 60-50078 1.65 pap.,
1. Wagner, Richard, 1813-1883. I. Title.

OSBORNE, Charles, 1927- 782.1'092'4 B
Wagner and his world / Charles Osborne. New York : C. Scribner's Sons, c1977. 128 p. : 142 ill. ; 25 cm. Includes index. Bibliography: p. 121. [ML410.W1O8] 76-56892 ISBN 0-684-14892-7 : 8.95
1. Wagner, Richard, 1813-1883. 2. Composers—Germany—Biography. I. Title.

PADMORE, Elaine. 782.1'092'4 B
Wagner. New York, T. Y. Crowell Co. [1973, c1971] 100 p. illus. 26 cm. (The Great composers) Bibliography: p. 95. Biography of a German musical genius who revolutionized opera and composed music notable for its drama and power. [ML410.W1P23 1972] 92 73-158698 ISBN 0-690-86511-2 4.95
1. Wagner, Richard, 1813-1883. I. Title.

PANOFSKY, Walter 927.8
Wagner; a pictorial biography. [Tr. from German by Richard Rickett] New York, Viking [1964, c.1963] 144p. illus., ports., facsims. (incl. music) 24cm. (Studio bk.) Bibl. 64-10447 6.50
1. Wagner, Richard—Iconography. I. Title.

POURTALES, Guy de, comte, 1881-1941. 782.1'0924 B
Richard Wagner; the story of an artist. Translated from the French by Lewis May. Westport, Conn., Greenwood Press [1972, c1932] xii, 409 p. illus. 23 cm. Bibliography: p. 387-388. [ML410.W1P73 1972] 76-138173 ISBN 0-8371-5630-0
1. Wagner, Richard, 1813-1883. BIP

STEARNS, Monroe. 782.1'0924 B
Richard Wagner; Titan of music. New York, F. Watts [1969] viii, 306 p. illus., ports. 22 cm. (Immortals of music) "Stories of Wagner's operas": p. [213]-286. Bibliography: p. 293-296. [ML410.W13S78] 69-12391
1. Wagner, Richard, 1813-1883. 2. Wagner, Richard, 1813-1883—Stories of operas.

STEIN, Jack Madison. 782.1'092'4
Richard Wagner & the synthesis of the arts, by Jack M. Stein. Westport, Conn., Greenwood Press [1973, c1960] 229 p. music. 22 cm. Reprint of the ed. published by Wayne State University Press, Detroit. Bibliography: p. [219]-222. [ML410.W1S83 1973] 73-1840 ISBN 0-8371-6806-6 10.50
1. Wagner, Richard, 1813-1883. 2. Music and literature. I. Title. BIP

TAYLOR, Ronald Jack, 1924- 782.1'092'4 B
Richard Wagner : his life, art and thought / Ronald Taylor. New York : Taplinger Pub. Co., 1979. 285 p., [8] leaves of plates : ill. ; 25 cm. "A Crescendo book." [ML410.W1T4] 78-63053 ISBN 0-8008-4792-X : 14.95
1. Wagner, Richard, 1813-1883. 2. Composers—Germany—Biography. BIP

TURNER, Walter James, 1889-1946. 782.1'092'4 B
Wagner / by W. J. Turner. Westport, Conn. : Greenwood Press, 1979. 143 p. : port. ; 23 cm. Reprint of the 1948 ed. published by A. A. Wun, New York. [ML410.W1T8 1979] 78-12226 ISBN 0-313-21084-5 lib. bdg. 13.75
1. Wagner, Richard, 1813-1883. 2. Composers—Germany—Biography. BIP

WAGNER, Cosima Liszt, 1837-1930. 782.1'092'4 B
Cosima Wagner's Diaries / edited and annotated by Martin Gregor-Dellin and Dietrich Mack ; translated and with an introd. by Geoffrey Skelton. New York : Harcourt Brace Jovanovich, 1978- p. cm. "A Helen and Kurt Wolff book." Contents.—v. 1. 1869-1877. Includes bibliographical references and indexes. [ML410.W11C5253 1978] 78-53919 ISBN 0-15-122635-0 : 29.95
1. Wagner, Richard, 1813-1883. 2. Wagner, Cosima Liszt, 1837-1930. 3. Composers—Germany—Biography. 4. Wives—Germany—Biography. I. Gregor-Dellin, Martin, 1926- II. Mack, Dietrich, 1940- III. Skelton, Geoffrey. BIP

WAGNER, Richard, 1813-1883. 782.1'0924
Correspondence of Wagner and Liszt. Translated into English, with a pref., by Francis Hueffer. New ed. rev., and furnished with an index, by W. Ashton Ellis. New York, Greenwood Press [1969] 2 v. port., music. 23 cm. Reprinted from the 1897 ed. Contents.Contents.—v. 1. 1841-1853.—v. 2. 1854-1861. [ML410.W1A365 1969b] 68-31009
I. Liszt, Franz, 1811-1886. BIP

WAGNER, Richard, 1813-1883. 782.1'0924
Correspondence of Wagner and Liszt. Translated into English with a pref. by Francis Hueffer. New ed. rev., and furnished with an index, by W. Ashton Ellis. New York, Haskell House, 1969. 2 v. 23 cm. "First published 1897." Contents.Contents.—1. 1841-1853.—2. 1854-1861. [ML410.W1A365 1969] 68-25304 ISBN 8-383-03161-

I. Liszt, Franz, 1811-1886. II. Hueffer, Francis, 1845-1889, tr. III. Ellis, William Ashton, d. 1919, ed.

WAGNER, Richard, 1813-1883. 782.1'092'4 B
Correspondence of Wagner and Liszt. Translated into English, with a pref. by Francis Hueffer. 2d ed., rev. by W. Ashton Ellis. New York, Vienna House [1973] 2 v. ports. 21 cm. Reprint of the 1897 ed. published by C. Scribner's Sons, New York. Contents.Contents.—v. 1. 1841-1853.—v. 2. 1854-1861. [ML410.W1A365 1973] 73-86923 ISBN 0-8443-0099-3 3.95 per vol.
I. Liszt, Franz, 1811-1886. II. Hueffer, Francis, 1845-1889, tr. III. Ellis, William Ashton, d. 1919, ed.

WAGNER, Richard, 1813-1883. 782.1'0924
Correspondence of Wagner and Liszt. Translated into English, with a pref., by Francis Hueffer. New ed. rev., and furnished with an index, by W. Ashton Ellis. New York, Greenwood Press [1969] 2 v. port., music. 23 cm. Reprinted from the 1897 ed. Contents.Contents.—v. 1. 1841-1853.—v. 2. 1854-1861. [ML410.W1A365 1969b] 68-31009
I. Liszt, Franz, 1811-1886. BIP

WAGNER, Richard, 1813-1883. 782.1'092'4 B
Letters of Richard Wagner; the Burrell collection. Edited with notes by John N. Burk. New York, Vienna House, 1973, c1950 x, 665 p. illus. 24 cm. [ML410.W1A3125 1972] 78-183325 ISBN 0-8443-0031-4 17.50
1. Wagner, Richard, 1813-1883. I. Burrell, Mary (Banks) d. 1898. BIP

WAGNER, Richard, 1813-1883. 782.1'092'4 B
My life. Authorized translation. St. Clair Shores, Mich., Scholarly Press, 1972. p. Reprint of the 1936 ed. [ML410.W1W146] 78-181292 ISBN 0-403-01715-7 44.50

WAGNER, Richard, 1813-1883. 782.1'092'4 B
My life. Authorized translation. St. Clair Shores, Mich., Scholarly Press, 1972. p. Reprint of the 1936 ed. [ML410.W1W146] 78-181292 ISBN 0-403-01715-7 44.50

WAGNER, Richard, 1813-1883 927.8
My Life. Authorized tr. from German. New York, Dodd. [1963, c.1911, 1939] 911p. 22cm. 63-10254 10.00
1. Wagner, Richard, 1813-1883. I. Title.

WAGNER, Richard, 1813-1883. 782.1'0924 B
Richard Wagner to Mathilde Wesendonck. Translated, prefaced, etc. by William Ashton Ellis. 2d ed. Boston, Milford House [1971] lxii, 386 p. illus. 23 cm. Reprint of the 1905 ed. [ML410.W1A392 1971] 76-86960 ISBN 0-87821-020-2
I. Wesendonck, Mathilde (Luckemeyer) 1828-1902. II. Ellis, William Ashton, d. 1919, ed.

WAGNER, Richard, 1813-1883. 782.1'092'4 B
Richard Wagner to Mathilde Wesendonck. Translated, prefaced, etc., by William Ashton Ellis. 2d ed. New York, Vienna House [1972] lxii, 386 p. illus. 23 cm. Reprint of the 1905 ed. [ML410.W1A392 1972] 74-163794 ISBN 0-8443-0010-1
I. Wesendonck, Mathilde (Luckemeyer) 1828-1902. II. Ellis, William Ashton, d. 1919, ed.

WAGNER, Richard, 1813-1883. 782.1'0924 B
Richard Wagner to Mathilde Wesendonck. Translated, prefaced, etc. by William Ashton Ellis. 2d ed. Boston, Milford House [1971] lxii, 386 p. illus. 23 cm. Reprint of the 1905 ed. [ML410.W1A392 1971] 76-86960 ISBN 0-87821-020-2
I. Wesendonck, Mathilde (Luckemeyer) 1828-1902. II. Ellis, William Ashton, d. 1919, ed.

WAGNER, Richard, 1813-1883. 782.1'092'4 B
Richard Wagner to Mathilde Wesendonck. Translated, prefaced, etc., by William Ashton Ellis. 2d ed. New York, Vienna House [1972] lxii, 386 p. illus. 23 cm. Reprint of the 1905 ed. [ML410.W1A392 1972] 74-163794 ISBN 0-8443-0010-1
I. Wesendonck, Mathilde (Luckemeyer) 1828-1902. II. Ellis, William Ashton, d. 1919, ed.

WHITE, Chappell. 780.924 B
An introduction to the life and works of Richard Wagner. Englewood Cliffs, N.J., Prentice-Hall [1967] iv, 186 p. music. 21 cm. Bibliography: p. 179-181. [ML410.W1W56] 67-12591
1. Wagner, Richard, 1813-1883. I. Title.

WHEELER, Opal. 927.8
Adventures of Richard Wagner. Illustrated by Floyd Webb. [1st ed.] New York, Dutton, 1960. 155 p. illus. 24 cm. [ML3930.W2W54] 60-6016
1. Wagner, Richard, 1813-1883. 2. Music—Juvenile literature.

Wagner, Richard, 1813-1883—Performances—Bayreuth, Ger. (City)

SKELTON, Geoffrey 780.924
Wagner at Bayreuth: experment and tradition. Foreword by Wieland Wagner. [1st Amer. ed.] New York, Braziller [c.1965] 239p. illus. (pt. col.), ports. 22cm. Bibl. [ML410.W2S55 1966a] 66-20191 6.50
1. Wagner, Richard, 1813-1883—Performances—Bayreuth, Ger. (City) 2. Bayreuth, Ger. (City) Festspiele. 3. Wagner family. I. Title.

SKELTON, Geoffrey. 780.924
Wagner at Bayreuth: experiment and tradition. Foreword by Wieland Wagner. [1st American ed.] New York, G. Braziller [c1965] 239 p. illus. (part col.), ports. 22 cm. Bibliography: p. 232-233. [ML410.W2S55 1966a] 66-20191
1. Wagner, Richard, 1813-1883 — Performances — Bayreuth, Ger. (City) 2. Bayreuth, Ger. (City) Festspiele. 3. Wagner family. I. Title.

Wagner, Robert Ferdinand, 1877—1953.

HUTHMACHER, J. Joseph. 973.91'0924
Senator Robert F. Wagner and the rise of urban liberalism [by] J. Joseph Huthmacher. [1st ed.] New York, Atheneum, 1968. xi, 362p. ports. 25cm. Bibl. [E748W2H8 1968] (B) 68-16869 10.00
1. Wagner, Robert Ferdinand, 1877—1953. I. Title.

Wailes, Benjamin Leonard Covington, 1797-1862.

SYDNOR, Charles Sackett, 1898- 917.62'2 B
A gentleman of the old Natchez region, Benjamin L. C. Wailes, by Charles S. Sydnor. Westport, Conn., Negro Universities Press [1970] xii, 337 p. maps, ports. 23 cm. Reprint of the 1938 ed. Bibliography: p. 307-326. [F341.W16 1970] 72-100312
1. Wailes, Benjamin Leonard Covington, 1797-1862. I. Title. BIP

Wain, John Barrington

WAIN, John Barrington 928.2
Sprightly running, part of an autobiography. New York, St. Martin's [1963, c.1962] 264p. 22cm. 63-9419 5.00 bds.,
I. Title.

Wainewright, Thomas Griffiths, 1794-1847.

NORMAN, Charles, 1904- 920.5
The genteel murderer. New York, Macmillan, 1956. 175p. illus. 22cm. [CT788.W28N6] 56-10628
1. Wainewright, Thomas Griffiths, 1794-1847. I. Title.

Wake, Nancy, 1917-

BRADDON, Russell. 940.53'44 B
Nancy Wake : the story of a very brave woman / Russell Braddon. London ; New York : White Lion Publishers, 1976. 287 p., [12] p. of plates : ill., facsims., map, ports. ; 21 cm. Includes index. [D802.F8B69 1976] 77-355558 ISBN 0-85617-436-X : £3.95
1. Wake, Nancy, 1917- 2. World War, 1939-1945—Underground movements—France—Biography. 3. Guerrillas—France—Biography.

Wake, William, Abp. of Canterbury, 1657-1737.

SYKES, Norman, 1897- 922.342
William Wake, Archbishop of Canterbury, 1657-1737. Cambridge [Eng.] University Press, 1957. 2 v. port., facsims. 24 cm. Bibliography: v. 2, p. 272-278. [BX5199.W216S9] 58-1230
1. Wake, William, of Canterbury, Abp. 1657-1737. I. Title.

WILLIAM Wake, v. 12
Archbishop of Canterbury, 1657- 1737. Cambridge [Eng.] University Press, 1957. 2 v. 23cm.
1. Wake, William, Abp. of Canterbury, 1657-1737. I. Sykes, Norman, 1897-

Wakefield, Dan.

WAKEFIELD, Dan. 070.440924
Between the lines; a reporter's personal journey through public events. [New York] New American Library [1966] xii, 274 p. 22 cm. Autobiographical. [AC8.W16] 66-18835
I. Title.

WAKEFIELD, Dan. 070.440924
Between the lines; a reporter's personal journey through public events. Boston, Little, Brown [1968,c.1966] 274p. 20cm. (Atlantic Monthly Pr. bk., 92) Autobiographical. [AC8.W16] 2.45 pap.,
I. Title.

Wakefield, Edward Gibbon, 1796-1862.

PHILIPP, June. 325'.394
A great view of things: Edward Gibbon Wakefield. [Melbourne, Thomas] Nelson [(Australia) 1971] xii, 113 p. illus., ports. 19 cm. (Nelson's Australasian paperbacks) Bibliography: p. 103-109. [JV1025.P5] 72-193823 ISBN 0-17-004896-9
1. Wakefield, Edward Gibbon, 1796-1862. 2. Great Britain—Colonies—Administration. 3. Australia—Colonization. I. Title.

Wakefield, Edward Jerningham, 1820-1876.

WAKEFIELD, Edward Jerningham, 1820-1876. 993.101
Adventure in New Zealand / [by] Edward Jerningham Wakefield ; an abridgement edited by Joan Stevens. Auckland : Golden Press, 1975,i.e. 1977 xx, 230 p., [16] p. of plates : ill., maps, ports. ; 23 cm. (New Zealand classics) Label mounted on t.p.: Transatlantic Arts, New York, sole distributor for the U.S.A. Reprint of the 1955 ed. published by Whitcombe and Tombs, London. Includes bibliographical references and index. [DU410.W34 1975] 77-355750 ISBN 0-85558-440-8 : 8.50
1. Wakefield, Edward Jerningham, 1820-1876. 2. New Zealand—Description and travel—to 1840. 3. Maoris. I. Title. BIP

Wakefield, Sarah F.

WAKEFIELD, Sarah F. 973'.04'97 S
Six weeks in the Sioux tepees / Sarah F. Wakefield. New York : Garland Pub., 1977. 63 p. ; 23 cm. (Garland library of narratives of North American Indian captivities ; v. 79) Reprint of the 2d ed. published in 1864 by Argus Book and Job Printing Office, Shakopee, Minn. Issued with the reprint of the 1864 ed. of Coleson, A. Miss Coleson's narrative. New York, 1977, with the reprint of the 1866 ed. of Hopkins, T. M. Reminiscences of Col. John Ketcham. New York, 1977, and with the reprint of the 1866 ed. of Gertrude Morgan. New York, 1977. [E85.G2 vol. 79] [E83.86] 970'.004'97 77-1397 ISBN 0-8240-1703-X lib.bdg. : 25.00
1. Wakefield, Sarah F. 2. Dakota Indians—Captivities. 3. Dakota Indians—Wars, 1862-1865. 4. Indians of North America—Captivities. 5. Minnesota—Biography. I. Title. II. Series. BIP

Wakeley, Margritte Fletcher (Hevry) 1850-ca. 1920.

WAKELEY, Maudine, 1891- 920.7
Aunt Marg, 'Little Mother of the Hills.' San Antonio, Naylor Co. [1954] 73p. illus. 22cm. [CT275.W227W3] 54-29033
1. Wakeley, Margritte Fletcher (Hevry) 1850-ca. 1920. I. Title.

Wakeman, Edgar, 1813-1875.

NEWELL, Gordon R 910.45
Paddlewheel pirate; the life and adventures of Captain Ned Wakeman. [1st ed.] New York, Dutton, 1959. 248p. illus. 21cm. [G530.W27N4] 59-10776
1. Wakeman, Edgar, 1813-1875. 2. New World (Steamboat) I. Title.

Wakley, Thomas, 1795-1862.

SPRIGGE, Samuel Squire, Sir, 1860-1937. 610'.92'4 B
The life and times of Thomas Wakley. With introd. by Charles G. Ronald. [Huntington, N.Y.] R. E. Krieger Pub. Co., 1974. xv, xix, 509 p. port. 25 cm. Facsim. reprint of the 1899 ed. published by Longmans, Green, London; with new introd. Includes bibliographical references. [R489.W2S7 1899a] 73-89696 ISBN 0-88275-134-4 17.50
1. Wakley, Thomas, 1795-1862. 2. The Lancet, London. 3. Medicine—Great Britain—History. I. Title.

Wald, Lillian D., 1867-1940—Juvenile literature.

BLOCK, Irvin. 610.73'0924 B
Neighbor to the world; the story of Lillian Wald. New York, [1969] viii, 181 p. illus., ports. 22 cm. (Women of America) Bibliography: p. [173] A biography of the nurse whose many campaigns, including her establishment of the settlement house on Henry Street in New York, introduced the concept of public health nursing to America. [RT37.W35B55] 92 79-81946 4.50
1. Wald, Lillian D., 1867-1940—Juvenile literature. I. Title.

ROGOW, Sally 92
Lillian Wald, the nurse in blue. Paintings by Itzhak Sankowsky. Philadelphia, Jewish Pubn. Soc. [c.]1966. vi, 145p. illus., port. 22cm. (Covenant bks., 19) Bibl. [HV28.W3R6] 66-11719 2.95
1. Wald, Lillian D., 1867-1940—Juvenile literature. I. Title.

Waldersee, Alfred Heinrich Karl Ludwig, Graf von, 1832-1904.

WALDERSEE, Alfred Heinrich Karl Ludwig, Graf von, 1832-1904. 355.3'31'0924 B
A field-marshal's memoirs : from the diary, correspondence, and reminiscences of Alfred, Count von Waldersee ... / condensed and translated by Frederic Whyte. Westport, Conn. : Greenwood Press, 1978. p. cm. Translation of Denkwurdigkeiten. Reprint of the 1924 ed. published by Hutchinson, London. [DD219.W3A3 1978] 72-136884 ISBN 0-8371-5326-3 lib.bdg. : 19.00
1. Waldersee, Alfred Heinrich Karl Ludwig, Graf von, 1832-1904. 2. Generals—Germany—Biography. 3. Germany—History—1871-1918—Sources. I. Whyte, Frederic, 1867-1941. II. Title. BIP

Waldersee, Marie Esther Lee, Grafin von, 1837 or 8- 1914.

SMITH, Alson Jesse. 920.7
A view of the Spree. New York, John Day Co. [1962] 305 p. illus. 22 cm. Includes bibliography. [DD219.W32S55] 62-7338
1. Waldersee, Marie Esther Lee, Grafin von, 1837 or 8- 1914. 2. Wilhelm II, German Emperor, 1859-1941. I. Title.

Waldman, Morris David,

WALDMAN, Morris David, 1879- 923.143
Sieg heil! the story of Adolf Hitler. Introd. by George N. Shuster. Dobbs Ferry, N.Y., Oceans. Publications, 1962. 318 p. 22 cm. [DD247.H5W28] 62-11854
I. Title.

Wales—Biography.

PUGHE, William Owen, 1759-1835. 936.2'00992 B
The Cambrian biography / William Owen Pughe. New York : Garland Pub. Co., 1979. p. cm. (Myth & romanticism) Reprint of the 1803 ed. printed for E. Williams, London. [DA716.A1P9 1979] 78-60896 ISBN 0-8240-3569-0 : 60.00
1. Wales—Biography. I. Title. II. Series: Myth and romanticism.

Wales, South—Description and travel.

MALKIN, Benjamin Heath, 1769-1842. 914.29
The scenery, antiquities and biography of South Wales, by B. H. Malkin. [1st ed. reprinted]; with a new foreword by T. T. Hopkins. Wakefield, S.R. Publishers, 1970. v, [3], vii, 636 p.; 13 plates (1 fold.): illus., map. 25 cm. Reprint of 1804 ed. [DA730.M25 1970] 76-862151 ISBN 0-85409-612-4 £6.30
1. Wales, South—Description and travel. I. Title.

Walewska, Maria Laczynska, 1789-1817.

SUTHERLAND, Christine. 944.05'092'4 B
Marie Walewska : Napoleon's great love / Christine Sutherland. New York : Vendome Press : distributed by Viking Press, 1979. 265 p., [2] leaves of plates : ill. ; 24 cm. Includes index. Bibliography: p. 251-258. [DC204.S94] 79-5092 ISBN 0-670-28473-4 : 9.95.
1. Walewska, Maria Laczynska, 1789-1817. 2. Napoleon I, Emperor of the French, 1769-1821—Relations with women. 3. Favorites, Royal—Biography—France.

Walker, Charles Thomas, 1858-1921.

FLOYD, Silas Xavier, 1869- 286'.133'0924 B
Life of Charles T. Walker ... With an introd. by Robert Stuart MacArthur. New York, Negro Universities Press [1969] 193 p. illus., ports. 23 cm. Reprint of the 1902 ed. [BX6455.W3F5 1969] 70-97423
1. Walker, Charles Thomas, 1858-1921. I. Title.

Walker, Danton.

WALKER, Danton. 920.5
Danton's inferno; the story of a columnist and how he grew. New York, Hastings House [1955] 312 p. illus. 21 cm. [PN4874.W26A3] 55-7903
I. Title.

Walker, David,

WALKER, David, 1806-1879. 923.473
The life and letters of Judge David Walker of Fayetteville ... Compiled and edited by W. J. Lemke. Fayetteville, Ark., Washington County Historical Society, 1957. 114 p. port. 27cm. "Besides Judge Walker's own letters, the current volume contains other material of historical value." [KF368.W3A32] 61-40674
I. Lemke, Walter, J., 1891- ed.

Walker, Ernest, 1870-1949.

DENEKE, Margaret. 927.8
Ernest Walker. London, New York, Oxford University Press, 1951. 144 p. illus. 21 cm. [ML410.W277D4] 51-8715
1. Walker, Ernest, 1870-1949. I. Title.

Walker, James John, 1881-1946.

FOWLER, Gene, 1890-1960. 974.7'1'040924 B
Beau James; the life & times of Jimmy Walker. Clifton, [N.J.] A. M. Kelley, 1973 [c1949] x, 389 p. ports. 23 cm. (Viking reprint editions) [F128.5.W22F68 1973] 70-122073 ISBN 0-678-03154-1
1. Walker, James John, 1881-1946. I. Title.

FOWLER, Gene, 1890-1960. 974.7'1'040924 B
Beau James; the life & times of Jimmy Walker. Clifton, [N.J.] A. M. Kelley, 1973 [c1949] x, 389 p. ports. 23 cm. (Viking reprint editions) [F128.5.W22F68 1973] 70-122073 ISBN 0-678-03154-1 15.00
1. Walker, James John, 1881-1946. I. Title.

WALSH, George, 1931- 974.7'1'040924 B
Gentleman Jimmy Walker, mayor of the jazz age. Foreword by Robert Moses. New York, Praeger [1974] xiii, 362 p. 25 cm. Bibliography: p. 343-347. [F128.5.W22W34] 74-7897 ISBN 0-275-50840-4 10.95
1. Walker, James John, 1881-1946. I. Title.

Walker, Jesse, 1766-1835.

PENNEWELL, Almer. 922.773
A voice in the wilderness; Jesse Walker, 'the Daniel Boone of Methodism.' Niles, Ill. [195-?] 192p. 23cm. Includes bibliography. [BX8495.W242P4] 60-45684
1. Walker, Jesse, 1766-1835. I. Title.

Walker, Jimmy—Juvenile literature.

JACOBS, Linda. 792.2'092'4 B
Jimmie Walker : funny is where it's at / by Linda Jacobs. St. Paul : EMC Corp., c1977. p. cm. (Center stage) A biography of a young Afro-American comic who coined the expression "dyn-o-mite" while working on his successful television series. [PN2287.W24J3] 77-24950 ISBN 0-88436-416-X lib.bdg. : 4.95 ISBN 0-88436-417-8 pbk. : 2.95
1. Walker, Jimmy—Juvenile literature. 2. Walker, Jimmy. 3. Comedians—United States—Biography—Juvenile literature. I. Title. II. Series. BIP

Walker, John, Dec. 24, 1906-

WALKER, John, Dec.24,1906- 069'.9'70924 B
Self-portrait with donors; confessions of an art collector. [1st ed.] Boston, Little, Brown [1974] xxvi, 320 p. illus. 24 cm. "An Atlantic Monthly Press book." [N856.W34] 74-9511 ISBN 0-316-91803-2
1. Walker, John, Dec. 24, 1906- 2. United States. National Gallery of Art. 3. Art—Collectors and collecting United States. I. Title. BIP

Walker, John Grimes, 1835-1907.

THOMAS, Frances P 923.573
Career of John Grimes Walker, U.S.N., 1835-1907. Boston, 1959. 174 p. 28 cm. [E182.W2T5] 59-48431
1. Walker, John Grimes, 1835-1907. I. Title.

Walker, Jonathan, 1799-1878.

WALKER, Jonathan, 1799-1878. 345'.73'0231
Trial and imprisonment of Jonathan Walker, at Pensacola, Florida, for aiding slaves to escape from bondage. A facsim. reproduction of the 1845 ed., with an introd. and index by Joe M. Richardson. Gainesville, University Presses of Florida, 1974 [i.e.1975] xcvi, 119, 8 p. illus. 19 cm. (Bicentennial Floridiana facsimile series) "A University of Florida book." Facsim. of the ed. published by the Anti-slavery Office, Boston. Includes bibliographical references. [E450.W15 1845a] 74-19173 ISBN 0-8130-0371-7 : 8.50
1. Walker, Jonathan, 1799-1878. 2. Slavery in the United States—Fugitive slaves. 3. Slavery in the United States—Florida. I. Title. II. Series. BIP

Walker, Maggie Lena—Juvenile literature.

BURT, Olive Wooley, 1894- 920.72'0973 B
Black women of valor, by Olive W. Burt. Illustrated by Paul Frame. New York, J. Messner [1974] 96 p. illus. 22 cm. Contents.Contents.—Juliette Derricotte.—Maggie Mitchell Walker.—Ida Wells Barnett.—Septima Poinsette Clark.—Other Black women of valor. [E185.96.B95] 920 74-7595 ISBN 0-671-32699-6 6.25
1. Derricotte, Juliette Aline, 1897-1931—Juvenile literature. 2. Walker, Maggie Lena—Juvenile literature. 3. Barnett, Ida B. Wells, 1862-1931—Juvenile literature. 4. Clark, Septima (Poinsette) 1898- Juvenile literature. I. Frame, Paul, illus. II. Title.
Library binding; 5.79, ISBN 0-671-32700-3. Contents omitted. BIP

Walker, Mary Edwards, 1832-1919.

SNYDER, Charles McCool 926.1
Dr. Mary Walker: the little lady in pants. New York, Vantage [c.1962] 166p. illus. 21cm. Bibl. 62-4753 3.95
1. Walker, Mary Edwards, 1832-1919. I. Title.

SNYDER, Charles McCool. 610'.92'4 B
Dr. Mary Walker: the little lady in pants. New York, Arno Press, 1974 [c1962] 166 p. illus. 23 cm. (Women in America: from colonial times to the 20th century) Reprint of the ed. published by Vantage Press, New York. [R154.W18S5 1974] 74-3973 ISBN 0-405-06122-6
1. Walker, Mary Edwards, 1832-1919. I. Title. II. Series.

Walker, Mary Edwards, 1832-1919—Juvenile literature.

HALL, Marjory, 1908- 610'.924 B
Quite contrary: Dr. Mary Edwards Walker. New York, Funk & Wagnalls [1970] 160 p. port. 22 cm. Bibiography: p. [159]-160. A biography of the woman who was among the first of her sex to become a doctor, serve in the Civil War, and champion a change in women's clothing. [R154.W18H3] 92 76-100652 4.95
1. Walker, Mary Edwards, 1832-1919—Juvenile literature. I. Title.

SNYDER, Charles McCool. 926.1
Dr. Mary Walker: the little lady in pants. [1st ed.] New York, Vantage Press [1962] 166 p. illus. 21 cm. [R154.W18S5] 62-4753
1. Walker, Mary Edwards, 1882-1919. I. Title.

Walker, Mary Hardway, 1848-1969.

EDWARDS, J. Loyd. 973'.04'96073 B
The ex-slave extra, the living voice and autobiography of an ex-slave in Bicentennial history : the saga of a centenarian in never too old, coming from slavery thru slums to celebrity / by J. Loyd Edwards, Jr. [Chattanooga, Tenn. : Help inc., Cosmopotitan Community Church], c1976. 10, 108 p., [8] leaves of plates : ill. ; 29 cm. [E185.97.W132E38] 77-371724 5.00
1. Walker, Mary Hardway, 1848-1969. 2. Afro-Americans—Biography. 3. Slaves—United States—Biography. 4. Afro-Americans—History. I. Title.

Walker, Mickey,

WALKER, Mickey, 1901- 927.9683
Mickey Walker, the Toy Bulldog, and his times, by Mickey Walker with Joe Reichler. New York, Random House [1961] 305 p. illus. 22 cm. [CT275.W2458A3] 61-6252
I. Reichler, Joe, joint author. II. Title.

WALKER, Mickey, 1901- 927.9683
The will to conquer. Hollywood, Calif., House-Warven [1953] 112p. 19cm. Autobiographical. [GV1132.W25A3] 53-7407
I. Title.

Walker, Robert James, 1801-1869.

BROWN, George Washington, 1820-1915. 320.9'781'020924
Reminiscences of Gov. R. J. Walker. Freeport, N.Y., Books For Libraries Press, 1972 [c1902] 204 p. ports. 23 cm. (Black heritage library collection) [F685.B873 1972] 79-38010 ISBN 0-8369-8978-3
1. Walker, Robert James, 1801-1869. 2. Kansas—Politics and government—1854-1861. I. Title. II. Series.

DODD, William Edward, 1869-1940. 973.6'1'0924
Robert J. Walker, imperialist. Gloucester, Mass., P. Smith, 1967 [c1914] 40 p. 18 cm. Bibliographical footnotes. [E415.9.W2D6 1967] 67-4527
1. Walker, Robert James, 1801-1869.

SHENTON, James Patrick, 1925- 923.273
Robert John Walker, a politician from Jackson to Lincoln. New York, Columbia. [c.]1961. 288p. illus. Bibl. 61-11283 6.00
1. Walker, Robert James, 1801-1869. I. Title.

Walker, Rollin Hough, 1865-1955.

QUIMBY, Chester Warren, 1891- 287.1'0924
Sojourner in two worlds; a memoir of Dr. Rollin Hough Walker, professor of English Bible at Ohio Wesleyan University, 1900-1936. Assembled, arranged, and edited by Chester Warren Quimby. [Long Beach? Miss.] 1967. 55 p. 28 cm. [BX8495.W2426Q5] 74-5874
1. Walker, Rollin Hough, 1865-1955. I. Title.

Walker, Samuel Hamilton, 1817-1847.

WALKER, Samuel Hamilton, 1817-1847. 976.4'04'0924 B
Samuel H. Walker's account of the Mier expedition / edited with an introd. by Marilyn McAdams Sibley. [Austin] : Texas State Historical Association, c1978. 110 p. : ill. ; 27 cm. Includes bibliographical references and index. [F390.W194 1978] 78-63306 ISBN 0-87611-040-5 : 10.50 ISBN 0-87611-038-3 collector's ed. : 50.00
1. Mier Expedition, 1842. 2. Walker, Samuel Hamilton, 1817-1847. 3. Texas Rangers—Biography. 4. Soldiers—Texas—Biography. I. Sibley, Marilyn McAdams. II. Texas State Historical Association. III. Title. IV. Title: The Mier expedition. BIP

Walker, Thomas Calhoun,

WALKER, Thomas Calhoun, 1862-1953. 923.473
The honey-pod tree; the life story of Thomas Calhoun Walker. New York, J. Day Co. [1958] 320 p. illus. 21 cm. [E185.97.W133A3] 58-10117
I. Title.

Walker, Tom, 1945-

WALKER, Tom, 1945- 979.8'3
We live in the Alaskan bush / Tom Walker ; sketches by Gretchen Walker. Anchorage : Alaska Northwest Pub. Co., c1977. vii, 135 p. : ill. ; 23 cm. [F912.M2A35] 77-17347 ISBN 0-88240-101-7 : 7.95
1. Walker, Tom, 1945- 2. McKinley, Mount, region, Alaska—Description and travel. 3. McKinley, Mount, region, Alaska—Biography. I. Title. BIP

Walker, Turnley.

WALKER, Turnley. 616.83
Journey together. New York, McKay [1951] 144 p. 21 cm. "A Story Press book." Autobiographical. [RJ496.P2W18] 51-13383

I. Title.

Walker, William, 1824-1860.

ABDULLAH, Achmed, 1881-1945. 909'.09'712420810922
Dreamers of empire, by Achmed Abdullah [and] T. Compton Pakenham. Illustrated by B. K. Morris. Freeport, N.Y. Books for Libraries Press [1968] xiv, 368 p. ports. 23 cm. (Essay index reprint series) Reprint of the 1929 ed. Contents.Contents.—Cecil John Rhodes.—Richard Francis Burton.—John Nicholson.—Henry Montgomery Lawrence.—William Walker.—Charles George Gordon. [DA531.1.A2 1968] 68-57300
1. Rhodes, Cecil John, 1853-1902. 2. Burton, Richard Francis, Sir, 1821-1890. 3. Nicholson, John, 1822-1857. 4. Lawrence, Henry Montgomery, Sir, 1806-1857. 5. Walker, William, 1824-1860. 6. Gordon, Charles George, 1833-1885. I. Pakenham, Thomas Compton, joint author. II. Title. BIP

CARR, Albert H. Z. 923.973
The world and William Walker. [1st ed.] New York, Harper & Row [1963] 289 p. illus. 22 cm. Includes bibliography. [F1526.27.W3C3] 63-16504
1. Walker, William, 1824-1860. I. Title. BIP

CARR, Albert H. Z. 972.8'5'040924 B
The world and William Walker / Albert Z. Carr. Westport, Conn. : Greenwood Press, 1975, c1963. viii, 289 p., [10] leaves of plates : ill. ; 22 cm. Reprint of the ed. published by Harper & Row, New York. Includes index. Bibliography: p. 275-280. [F1526.27.W3C3 1975] 75-18354 ISBN 0-8371-8328-6 lib.bdg. : 17.25
1. Walker, William, 1824-1860. I. Title.

GERSON, Noel Bertram, 1914- 972.85'04'0924 B
Sad swashbuckler : the life of William Walker / by Noel B. Gerson. 1st ed. Nashville : T. Nelson, c1976. 160 p. ; 21 cm. Includes index. Bibliography: p. 150. [F1526.27.W3G47] 76-2366 ISBN 0-8407-6483-9 : 6.95
1. Walker, William, 1824-1860. 2. Nicaragua—History—Filibuster War, 1855-1860 I. Title. BIP

ROSENGARTEN, Frederic. 972.85'04'0924 B
Freebooters must die! : The life and death of William Walker, the most notorious filibuster of the nineteenth century / by Frederic Rosengarten, Jr. Wayne, Pa. : Haverford House, c1976. xi, 226 p. : ill. ; 26 cm. Includes index. Bibliography: p. 218-221. [F1526.27.W3R67] 76-4274 ISBN 0-910702-01-2 : 12.95
1. Walker, William, 1824-1860. I. Title.

SCROGGS, William Oscar, 1879- 972.85'04'0924 B
Filibusters and financiers; the story of William Walker and his associates, by William O. Scroggs. New York, Russell & Russell [1969, c1916] ix, 408 p. maps, port. 23 cm. Bibliographical footnotes. [F1526.27.W3S3 1969] 72-83846
1. Walker, William, 1824-1860. 2. Nicaragua—History—Filibuster War, 1855-1860. 3. Filibusters. I. Title. BIP

Wall, Mervyn, 1908-

HOGAN, Robert Goode, 1930- 823'.9'12
Mervyn Wall [by] Robert Hogan. Lewisburg [Pa.] Bucknell University Press [1972] 75 p. 22 cm. (The Irish writers series) Bibliography: p. 74-75. [PR6045.A3255Z7] 72-175641 ISBN 0-8387-1065-4 4.50
1. Wall, Mervyn, 1908- BIP

Wallace, Alfred Russel, 1823-1913.

GEORGE, Wilma B. 925.7
Biologist philosopher: a study of the life and writings of Alfred Russel Wallace. London, New York, Abelard-Schuman [1964] x, 320 p. ports., maps. 28 cm. (The Life of science library, 43) Bibliography: p. 293-308. [QH31.W2G4] 64-12738
1. Wallace, Alfred Russel, 1823-1913. I. Title.

WALLACE, Alfred Russel, 1823-1913. 574'.092'4 B
Alfred Russel Wallace : letters and reminiscences / by James Marchant. New York : Arno Press, 1975, c1916. viii, 507 p. : port. ; 21 cm. (History, philosophy, and sociology of science) Reprint of the ed. published by Harper, New York. Includes bibliographical references. [QH31.W2A33 1975] 74-26273 ISBN 0-405-06601-5 : 29.00
1. Wallace, Alfred Russel, 1823-1913. 2. Naturalists—Correspondence, reminiscences, etc. I. Marchant, James, 1867-1956. II. Title. III. Series. BIP

WALLACE, Alfred Russel, 1823-1913. 574'.092'4
My life; a record of events and opinions. New York, Dodd, Mead, 1905. [New York, AMS Press, 1974] 2 v. illus. 23 cm. [QH31.W2W34 1974] 72-1668 ISBN 0-404-08184-3
1. Wallace, Alfred Russel, 1823-1913. I. Title.

Wallace, Alfred Russel, 1823-1913—Juvenile literature.

COTTLER, Joseph, 1899- 575.01620924
Alfred Wallace, explorer-naturalist. Illus. by John Kautmann. Boston, Little [c.1966] 212p. illus. 22cm. [QH31.W2C65] 65-18363 4.50
1. Wallace, Alfred Russel, 1823-1913—Juvenile literature. I. Title.

Wallace, Cornelia, 1939-

WALLACE, Cornelia, 1939- 976.1'06'0924 B
C'nelia / Cornelia Wallace. 1st ed. Philadelphia : A. J. Holman Co., c1976. 240 p. : ill. ; 24 cm. [F330.W28] 75-35835 ISBN 0-87981-047-5 : 7.95
1. Wallace, Cornelia, 1939- 2. Wallace, George Corley, 1919- I. Title. BIP

Wallace, David Richard, 1825-1911.

MOORE, Doris Dowdell. 616.89'17'0924 B
The biography of Doctor D. R. Wallace: pioneer physician, educator, philosopher, and author, the first eminent psychiatrist of Texas and the Southwest. Dallas, Timberlawn Foundation [1966] xiv, 182 p. illus., facsims., ports. 24 cm. Bibliography: p. 171-176. [R154.W185M6] 67-1185
1. Wallace, David Richard, 1825-1911. I. Title.

Wallace, Edgar, 1875-1932.

LANE, Margaret, 1907- 823.912
Edgar Wallace: the biography of a phenomenon. Introd. by Graham Greene. [Rev. ed.] London, H. Hamilton [New York, Hillary House, 1966, c.1938, 1964] xiv, 338p. illus., facsims., ports. 23cm. [PR6045] 65-29992 6.00 bds.,
1. Wallace, Edgar, 1875-1932. I. Title.

Wallace, Elizabeth,

WALLACE, Elizabeth, 1866- 923.773
The unending journey. Minneapolis, University of Minnesota Press [1952] 286 p. illus. 23 cm. Autobiography. [CT275.W2524A3] 52-5323
I. Title.

Wallace, George Corley, 1919-

DORMAN, Michael. 976.1'06'0924 B
The George Wallace myth / by Michael Dorman. Toronto ; New York : Bantam Books, 1976. 216 p. ; 18 cm. Includes index. Bibliography: p. 194-204. [F330.W3D67] 76-373594 ISBN 0-553-02836-7 pbk. : 1.75
1. Wallace, George Corley, 1919- 2. Alabama—Politics and government—1951- 3. Alabama—Governors—Biography. I. Title.

FRADY, Marshall. 976.1'06'0924 B
Wallace. New York, World Pub. Co. [1968] viii, 246 p. illus. 22 cm. [F330.W3F7] 68-31468
1. Wallace, George Corley, 1919- BIP

GEORGE Wallace; a rebel and his cause. 976.1'06'0924 [New York, Universal Publishing and Distributing Corp., 1968] 64 p. ports. 28 cm. [F330.W3G4] (B) 68-7655 1.00
1. Wallace, George Corley, 1919- 2. Presidents—United States—Election—1968.

JONES, William Grover. 976.1060924
The Wallace story, by Bill Jones. Northport, Ala., American Southern Pub. Co. [1966] 471 p. port. 23 cm. [F330.W3J6] 66-31685
1. Wallace, George Corley, 1919- 2. Alabama—Politics and government—1951- I. Title.

WALLACE, George Corley, 1919- 976.1'06'0924 B
Stand up for America / George C. Wallace. 1st ed. Garden City, N.Y. : Doubleday, 1976. 183 p., [8] leaves of plates : ill. ; 22 cm. Includes index. [F330.W3A35] 76-16263 ISBN 0-385-09411-6 : 7.95
1. Wallace, George Corley, 1919- 2. Alabama—Governors—Biography. I. Title.

Wallace, George Corley, 1919-—Juvenile literature.

KURLAND, Gerald, 1942- 976.1'06'0924 B
George Wallace, Southern governor and presidential candidate. Charlotteville, N.Y., SamHar Press, 1972. 32 p. 22 cm. (Outstanding personalities, no. 29) Bibliography: p. 32. A biography concentrating on the political career of the Alabama governor and his attempts to win support as a Presidential candidate. [F330.W3K87] 92 72-75368
1. Wallace, George Corley, 1919-—Juvenile literature. I. Title.

Wallace, George John, 1906-

WALLACE, George John, 1906- 598.2'092'4 B
My world of birds : memoirs of an ornithologist / by George J. Wallace. Philadelphia : Dorrance, c1979. xii, 345 p. : ill. ; 24 cm. Includes bibliographies. [QL31.W27A34] 78-67257 ISBN 0-8059-2586-4 : 10.00
1. Wallace, George John, 1906- 2. Birds. 3. Ornithologists—Vermont—Biography. 4. Ornithologists—Michigan—Biography. I. Title.

Wallace, Henry Agard, 1888-1965.

LORD, Russell, 1895-1964. 973'.0099
The Wallaces of Iowa. New York, Da Capo Press, 1972 [c1947] xiii, 615 p. illus. 23 cm. (Franklin D. Roosevelt and the era of the New Deal) Includes bibliographical references. [E748.W23L6 1972] 76-167843 ISBN 0-306-70325-4
1. Wallace, Henry Agard, 1888-1965. 2. Wallace, Henry Cantwell, 1866-1924. 3. Wallace, Henry, 1836-1916. I. Title. II. Series. BIP

MARKOWITZ, Norman D. 973.917'092'4 B
The rise and fall of the people's century: Henry A. Wallace and American liberalism, 1941-1948 [by] Norman D. Markowitz. New York, Free Press [1973] xi, 369 p. illus. 22 cm. Bibliography: p. [343]-360. [E748.W23M37] 72-86508 8.95
1. Wallace, Henry Agard, 1888-1965. 2. United States—Politics and government—1933-1945. 3. United States—Politics and government—1945- I. Title.

SCHAPSMEIER, Edward L. 973.917'0924
Prophet in politics: Henry A. Wallace and the war years, 1940-1965 [by] Edward L. and Frederick H. Schapsmeier. [1st ed.] Ames, Iowa State University Press [1971, c1970] xv, 268 p. illus., ports. 24 cm. Bibliography: p. 241-244. [E748.W23S32] 70-114795 ISBN 8-13-812953-
1. Wallace, Henry Agard, 1888-1965. I. Schapsmeier, Frederick H., joint author. II. Title.

WALLACE, Henry Agard, 1888-1965. 973.917'092'4 B
The price of vision; the diary of Henry A. Wallace, 1942-1946, edited and with an introd. by John Morton Blum. Boston, Houghton Mifflin, 1973. x, 707 p. 24 cm. [E748.W23A36 1973] 72-6806 ISBN 0-395-17121-0 15.00
1. Wallace, Henry Agard, 1888-1965. 2. United States—Politics and government—1933-1945. 3. United States—Politics and government—1945-1953. 4. United States—Foreign relations—1933-1945. 5. United States—Foreign relations—1945-1953. I. Blum, John Morton, 1921- ed. II. Title.

WALLACE, Henry Agard, 1888-1965. 973.917'092'4 B
The reminiscences of Henry Wallace / Henry Wallace. Glen Rock, N.J. : Microfilming Corp. of America, 1976. p. cm. (New York times oral history program) (Columbia University oral history collection ; pt. 3, no. 40) Includes indexes. [E748.W23W29] 76-12534 ISBN 0-667-00044-5
1. Wallace, Henry Agard, 1888-1965. 2. United States—Politics and government—1933-1945. 3. United States—Foreign relations—1945-1953. 4. Agriculture and state—United States. I. Title. II. Series.

WISE, James Waterman, 1901- 923.273
Meet Henry Wallace. New York, Boni and Gaer, 1948. 91 p. illus., ports. 28 cm. [E748.W23W5] 48-7915
1. Wallace, Henry Agard, 1888- 2. Campaign literature, 1948 — Progressive. I. Title.

Wallace, Henry Cantwell, 1866-1924.

LORD, Russell, 1895-1964. 973'.0099
The Wallaces of Iowa. New York, Da Capo Press, 1972 [c1947] xiii, 615 p. illus. 23 cm. (Franklin D. Roosevelt and the era of the New Deal) Includes bibliographical references. [E748.W23L6 1972] 76-167843 ISBN 0-306-70325-4
1. Wallace, Henry Agard, 1888-1965. 2. Wallace, Henry Cantwell, 1866-1924. 3. Wallace, Henry, 1836-1916. I. Title. II. Series. BIP

Wallace, Irving, 1916- —Biography.

LEVERENCE, John. 813'.5'4 B
Irving Wallace; a writer's profile. With an introd. by Jerome Weidman, an interview by Sam L. Grogg, Jr., and an afterword by Ray B. Browne. Bowling Green, Ohio, Popular Press, 1974. 454 p. illus. 24 cm. (Profiles in popular culture, no. 1) [PS3573.A426Z76] 73-93855 ISBN 0-87972-063-8 6.95
1. Wallace, Irving, 1916- —Biography. 2. Wallace, Irving, 1916- —Correspondence. I. Grogg, Sam L. II. Title. III. Series. BIP

Wallace, James, 1849-1939.

KAGIN, Edwin. 923.773
James Wallace of Macalester. With a foreword by his son, DeWitt Wallace. [1st ed.] Garden City, N. Y., Doubleday, 1957. 255p. illus. 21cm. [LD3141.M2217 1894] 57-8698
1. Wallace, James, 1849-1939. 2. Macalester College, St. Paul, Minn.—Hist. I. Title.

Wallace, Judith Gytha, 1932-

WALLACE, Judith Gytha, 1932- 994.4
Memories of a country childhood / [by] Judith Wallace. St. Lucia, Q. : University of Queensland Press, 1978. 138 p. : ill. ; 23 cm. [DU180.A7W348] 78-304539 ISBN 0-7022-1067-6 : 8.75
1. Wallace, Judith Gytha, 1932- 2. Country life—Australia—Armidale. 3. Armidale, Australia—Biography. I. Title. Available from Technical Impex Corp., Lawrence, MA 01843 BIP

Wallace, Lewis,

WALLACE, Lewis, 1827- 340'.092'4 1905.
Lew Wallace; an autobiography. New York, MSS Information Corp. [1972] p. Reprint of the 1906 ed. [E467.W2A34 1972] 72-8102 ISBN 0-8422-8121-5

Wallace, Lewis, 1827-1905 —Juvenile fiction.

SCHAAF, Martha E. 920
Lew Wallace, boy writer. Illus. by Frank Nicholas. Indianapolis, Bobbs [1962, c.1961] 200p. illus. (Childhood of famous Americans) 62-9256 2.25
1. Wallace, Lewis, 1827-1905 —Juvenile fiction. I. Title.

Wallace, Lurleen, 1926-1968.

SMITH, Anita. 976.1'06'0924 B
The intimate story of Lurleen Wallace; her crusade of courage. Edited by Ron Gibson. Montgomery, Ala., Communications Unlimited [1969] 120 p. illus. 22 cm. [F330.W33S6] 75-9005 1.50
1. Wallace, Lurleen, 1926-1968. I. Title.

Wallace, Norman Verschuer, 1897-

WALLACE, Norman 340'.092'4 B Verschuer, 1897-
Bush lawyer / [by] Norman Verschuer Wallace. Adelaide : Rigby, 1976. 181 p., [8] leaves of plates : ill. ; 22 cm. [LAW] 77-366707 ISBN 0-7270-0151-5
1. Wallace, Norman Verschuer, 1897- 2. Lawyers—South Australia—Biography. I. Title.

Wallace, Wendell.

WALLACE, Wendell. 269'.2'0924 B
Born to burn, by Wendell Wallace with Pat King. [Special Charisma ed.] Watchung, N.J., Charisma Books [1972, c1970] 103 p. ports. 18 cm. [BR1725.W29A32 1972] 77-131116 0.95
1. Wallace, Wendell. I. King, Pat, joint author. II. Title.

Wallace, William Alexander Anderson, 1817-1899.

DUVAL, John 917.640340924 Crittenden, 1816-1897
The adventures of Big-Foot Wallace. Ed. by Mable Major, Rebecca Smith Lee. Lincoln, Univ. of Neb. Pr. [1966, c.1936] xxxv. 353p. illus., ports. 21cm. (Bison bk. BB343) Bibl. [F390.W25 1966] 66-6906 1.80 pap.,
1. Wallace, William Alexander Anderson, 1817-1899. 2. Frontier and pioneer life—Texas. 3. Mier Expedition, 1842. I. Major, Mabel, 1894- ed. II. Lee, Rebecca Washington (Smith) 1894- ed. III. Title.

GARST, Doris Shannon, 923.973 1899-
Big Foot Wallace of the Texas Rangers; illustrated by Lee Ames. New York, Messner [1951] 183 p. illus. 22 cm. Includes bibliography. [F390.W254] 51-13105
1. Wallace, William Alexander Anderson, 1817-1899. 2. Frontier and pioneer life—Texas. I. Title.

GARST, Doris 917.64'03'40924 B Shannon, 1899-
Big Foot Wallace of the Texas Rangers; illustrated by Lee Ames. New York, Messner [1951] 183 p. illus. 22 cm. Bibliography: p. 179-180. The life of the Texas pioneer who fought for Texas against the Mexicans as a Texas Ranger, in the Army, and as leader of a company of volunteers protecting the frontier. [F390.W254] 92 AC 68
1. Wallace, William Alexander Anderson, 1817-1899. 2. Frontier and pioneer life—Texas. I. Ames, Lee J., illus. II. Title.

Wallace, William L., 1908-1951.

FLETCHER, Jesse C. 922.673
Bill Wallace of China. Nashville, Tenn., Broadman [1967, c.1963] 157p. 18cm. [BV3427.W3F5] 63-17522 1.25 pap.,
1. Wallace, William L., 1908-1951. I. Title.
BIP

Wallach family—Portraits.

NOREN, Catherine. 929'.2
The camera of my family / Catherine Hanf Noren. 1st ed. New York : Knopf : distributed by Random House, 1976. 240 p. : chiefly ill. ; 24 x 29 cm. [TR680.N68 1976] 75-36805 ISBN 0-394-48838-5 : 20.00
1. Wallach family—Portraits. 2. Photography—Portraits. I. Title. BIP

NOREN, Catherine. 779'.2'07401471
The camera of my family. [Catalogue of exhibition] April 11, 1973-September 3, 1973, Jewish Museum, New York. [New York, Jewish Museum, 1973] [12] p. illus. 24 cm. [TR680.N67] 73-78651
1. Wallach family—Portraits. 2. Photography—Portraits—Exhibitions. I. Jewish Theological Seminary of America. Jewish Museum. II. Title.

Wallenda, Karl.

MORRIS, Ron. 796.4'6'0924 B
Wallenda : a biography of Karl Wallenda / Ron Morris. Chatham, N.Y. : Sagarin Press, 1976. 182 p., [16] leaves of plates : ill. ; 23 cm. [GV1811.W18M67] 75-13390 ISBN 0-915298-04-X : 8.95
1. Wallenda, Karl. 2. Aerialists—Biography. I. Title. BIP

Wallenstein, Albrecht Wenzel Eusebius von, Herzog zu Friedland, 1583-1634.

LIDDELL HART, Basil 909'.00922 Henry, 1895-
Great captains unveiled. by B. H. Liddell Hart. Freeport, N.Y., Bks. for Libs. Pr. [1967] 274p. maps. 22cm. (Essay index reprint ser.) Reprint of the 1928 ed. [D106.L5 1967] 67-23240 8.50
1. Jenghis Khan, 1162-1227. 2. Saxe, Maurice, comte de, 1696-1750. 3. Gusstaf Adolf, King of Sweden, 1594-1632. 4. Wallenstein, Albrecht Wenzel Eusebius von. Herzog zu Friendland. 1583-1634. 5. Wolfe, James, 1727-1759. I. Title.
Contents omitted.

MANN, Golo, 1909- 943'.04'0924 B
Wallenstein, his life narrated / by Golo Mann ; translated by Charles Kessler. New York : Holt, Rinehart and Winston, 1976. p. cm. [D270.W19M313] 76-4721 ISBN 0-03-091884-7 : 20.00
1. Wallenstein, Albrecht Wenzel Eusebius von, Herzog zu Friedland, 1583-1634. I. Title.

MANN, Golo, 1909- 940.2'4'0924 B
Wallenstein, his life narrated / by Golo Mann ; translated by Charles Kessler. London : Deutsch, 1976. 909 p. ; 25 cm. Translation of Wallenstein, sein Leben erzahlt. Includes index. Bibliography: p. [885]-886. [D270.W19M313 1976b] 76-381965 ISBN 0-233-96813-X ; £10.50
1. Wallenstein, Albrecht Wenzel Eusebius von, Herzog zu Friedland, 1583-1634. 2. Generals—Austria—Biography. 3. Thirty Years' War, 1618-1648.

MITCHELL, John, 940.2'4'0924 B 1785-1859.
Life of Wallenstein, Duke of Friedland. New York, Greenwood Press [1968] xx, 368 p. port. 23 cm. (The West Point military library) Reprint of the 1837 ed. [D270.W19M6 1968] 68-54800
1. Wallenstein, Albrecht Wenzel Eusebius von, Herzog zu Friedland, 1583-1634. I. Title. BIP

Waller, Fats. 1904-1943.

KIRKEBY, W. T. Ed. 780.924
Ain't misbehavin'; the story of Fats Waller by Ed Kirkeby, with Duncan P. Schiedt, Sinclair Traill. New York, Dodd [1966] 248p. ports. 22cm. The music of Thomas 'Fats' Waller; a selective discography comp. by the 'Storyville Team':p. 233-248. [ML417.W15K6 1966a] 66-26667 5.00
1. Waller, Fats. 1904-1943. I. Schiedt, Duncan P., joint author. II. Traill, Sinclair, joint author. III. Title.

KIRKEBY, W. T. Ed. 780'.92'4 B
Ain't misbehavin' : the story of Fats Waller / Ed Kirkeby, in collaboration with Duncan P. Schiedt and Sinclair Traill. New York : Da Capo Press, 1975, c1966. 248 p., [8] leaves of plates : ill. ; 23 cm. Reprint of the ed. published by Dodd, Mead, New York. Discography: p. 233-248. [ML417.W15K6 1975] 75-14124 ISBN 0-306-80015-2 pbk. : 3.45 ISBN 0-306-70683-0 lib.bdg. : 12.95
1. Waller, Fats, 1904-1943. I. Schiedt, Duncan P., joint author. II. Traill, Sinclair, joint author. III. Title. BIP

VANCE, Joel B
Fats Waller, his life and times / Joel Vance New York : Berkley Publishing Corp., 1979, c1977 213p. ; 18 cm. Bibliography: p. 203-204 [ML417.W15V3.785.4'2'0924] ISBN 0-425-04065-8 pbk. : 2.25
1. Waller, Fats, 1904-1943 2. Jazz musicians — United States — Biography I. Title.
L.C. card no. for 1977 Contemporary Books ed.: 77-75853

VANCE, Joel. 785.4'2'0924 B
Fats Waller, his life and times / Joel Vance. Chicago : Contemporary Books, c1977. viii, 179 p., [4] leaves of plates : ill. ; 24 cm. Includes index. Bibliography: p. 171-172. [ML417.W15V3] 77-75853 ISBN 0-8092-8133-3 : 8.95
1. Waller, Fats, 1904-1943. 2. Jazz musicians—United States—Biography. I. Title.

WALLER, Maurice. 785.4'2'0924 B
Fats Waller / by Maurice Waller and Anthony Calabrese. New York : Schirmer Books, c1977. p. cm. Includes index. [ML417.W15W3] 77-5208 ISBN 0-02-872730-4 : 12.95
1. Waller, Fats, 1904-1943. 2. Jazz musicians—United States—Biography. I. Calabrese, Anthony, joint author. BIP

Waller, Fats, 1904-1943—Juvenile literature.

SILL, Harold D., 785.4'2'0924 B 1922-
Misbehavin' with Fats : a Toby Bradley adventure / by Harold D. Sill, Jr. ; drawings by Mike Eagle. Reading, Mass. : Addison-Wesley, c1978. 93 p. : ill. ; 22 cm. The life and music of Fats Waller as seen through the eyes of a young boy. [ML3930.W24S5] 92 77-10763 lib. bdg. : 5.95
1. Waller, Fats, 1904-1943—Juvenile literature. 2. Jazz musicians—United States—Biography—Juvenile literature. I. Eagle, Michael. II. Title.

Wallin, Bernice.

WALLIN, 616.9'94'490924 B Bernice.
I beat cancer / Bernice Wallin ; with Fred Wallin. Chicago : Contemporary Books, 1978. xi, 193 p. ; 22 cm. [RC280.B8W34] 77-83923 ISBN 0-8092-7736-0 : 8.95
1. Wallin, Bernice. 2. Breast—Cancer—Biography. I. Title. BIP

Wallis, Barnes Neville, 1887-

MORPURGO, J. E. 629.13'0092'4 B
Barnes Wallis, a biography, by J. E. Morpurgo. New York, St. Martin's Press [1972] xvi, 400 p. illus. 23 cm. Includes bibliographical references. [TL540.W27M67 1972b] 72-76794 10.95
1. Wallis, Barnes Neville, 1887-

Wallis, Hal B., 1899-

NEW York 016.79143'0232'0924 (City). Museum of Modern Art.
Hal B. Wallis, film producer. Edited by Adrienne Mancia. New York [1970] [23] p. illus. 28 cm. A program of selected films of Hal B. Wallis at the Museum of Modern Art, Nov. 18, 1970-Jan. 10, 1971. [PN1998.A3W255] 76-141631
1. Wallis, Hal B., 1899- 2. Moving-pictures—Exhibitions. I. Mancia, Adrienne, ed. II. Title.

Wallower, Lucille,

WALLOWER, 974.8'02'0924 B Lucille, 1910-
William Penn. Illustrated with drawings by Louis Cary and contemporary pictorial material. Chicago, Follett Pub. Co. [1968] 157, [3] p. illus., ports. 23 cm. (Library of American heros) Bibliography: p. [158] The life of the English gentleman who became a Quaker and established the colony of Pennsylvania as a peaceful settlement with religious freedom for all and friendly relations with the Indians. [F152.2.W25] 92 AC 68
I. Cary, Louis F., illus. II. Title.

Walls, Henry James.

WALLS, Henry James. 614'.19'0924
Scotland Yard scientist; my thirty years in forensic science [by] H. J. Walls. Foreword by Keith Simpson. New York, Taplinger Pub. Co. [1973, c1972] 208 p. illus. 21 cm. First published in London under title: Expert witness. [RA1025.W3A33 1973] 73-1763 ISBN 0-8008-7010-7 6.95
1. Walls, Henry James. 2. Medical jurisprudence—Great Britain. 3. Chemists—Correspondence, reminiscences, etc. I. Title. BIP

Walls, Josiah T., 1842-1905.

KLINGMAN, Peter 975.9'06'0924 B D., 1945-
Josiah Walls : Florida's Black Congressman of Reconstruction / Peter D. Klingman. Gainesville : University Presses of Florida, 1976. xi, 157 p. : port. ; 24 cm. "A University of Florida book." Includes index. Bibliography: p. 145-151. [E664.W19K54] 75-45206 ISBN 0-8130-0399-7 : 7.50
1. Walls, Josiah T., 1842-1905. 2. Negroes—History—1863-1877. 3. Negroes—Politics and suffrage. BIP

Walpole, Horace, 4th Earl of Oxford, 1717-1797.

DOBSON, Austin, 1840- 828'.6'09 B 1921.
Horace Walpole; a memoir. With an appendix of books printed at the Strawberry Hill Press. With illus. by Percy and Leon Moran. New York, Haskell House, 1971. 370 p. illus., plans. 23 cm. Reprint of the 1890 ed. [DA483.W2D6 1971] 72-160127 ISBN 0-8383-1267-5
1. Walpole, Horace, 4th Earl of Orford, 1717-1797.

GWYNN, Stephen Lucius, 828.609 B 1864-1950.
The life of Horace Walpole. New York, Haskell House, 1971. 285 p. illus., ports. 23 cm. Reprint of the 1932 ed. [DA483.W2G8 1971b] 76-160467 ISBN 0-8383-1302-7
1. Walpole, Horace, 4th Earl of Orford, 1717-1797. I. Title.

GWYNN, Stephen Lucius, 828'.609 B 1864-1950.
The life of Horace Walpole. Port Washington, N.Y., Kennikat Press [1972] 285 p. illus., ports. 22 cm. Reprint of the 1932 ed. [DA483.W2G8 1972] 79-153900 ISBN 0-8046-1599-3
1. Walpole, Horace, 4th Earl of Oxford, 1717-1797. I. Title.

GWYNN, Stephen 828'.6'09 B Lucius, 1864-1950.
The life of Horace Walpole. Freeport,

N.Y., Books for Libraries Press [1971] 285 p. illus., ports. 23 cm. Reprint of the 1932 ed. [DA483.W2G8 1971] 73-160974 ISBN 0-8369-5842-X
1. Walpole, Horace, 4th Earl of Orford, 1717-1797.

GWYNN, Stephen Lucius, 1864-1950. 828'.6'09 B
The life of Horace Walpole. [Folcroft, Pa.] Folcroft Library Editions, 1973. p. Reprint of the 1934 ed. published by T. Butterworth, London, in series: Keystone library. [DA483.W2G8 1973] 73-13908 9.75
1. Walpole, Horace, 4th Earl of Orford, 1717-1797. I. Title. II. Series: Keystone library. BIP

JUDD, Gerrit Parmele, 1915- 928.2
Horace Walpole's memoirs. College Univ. Pr. [dist. New York, Tawayne, 1962, c.1959] 119p. 21cm. (LI) Bibl., 1.25 pap.,
1. Walpole, Horace 4th earl of Orford, 1717-1797. I. Title.

JUDD, Gerrit Parmele, 1915- 928.2
Horace Walpole's memoirs. New York, Bookman Associates [1959] 119p. 23cm. Bibliographical references included in 'Notes' (p. 89-116) [DA483.W2J8] 59-14630
1. Walpole, Horace, 4th earl of Orford, 1717-1797. I. Title. BIP

JUDD, Gerritt Parmele 928.2
Horace Walpole's memoirs. New York, Bookman Associates [c.1959] 119p. Bibliographical references included in 'Notes' (p.89-116) 23cm. 59-14630 3.50
1. Walpole, Horace, 4th earl of Oxford, 1717-1797. I. Title.

KETTON-CREMER, Robert Wyndham, 1906- 828.609
Horace Walpole;. a biography, [1st Amer. ed.] Ithaca, N. Y., Cornell Univ. Pr. [1966, c.1964] xv, 317p. geneal. table, plates, ports. 23cm. Bibl. [DA483.W2K4] 66-11431 6.95
1. Walpole, Horace, 4th earl of Orford, 1717-1797. I. Title.

LEWIS, Wilmarth Sheldon, 1895- 020'.75
Collector's progress, by Wilmarth Lewis. Westport, Conn., Greenwood Press [1974, c1951] xix, 253, xiii p. illus. 22 cm. Reprint of the ed. published by A. A. Knopf, New York. [Z989.L5 1974] 73-16738 ISBN 0-8371-7219-5 14.25
1. Walpole, Horace, 4th Earl of Orford, 1717-1797. 2. Lewis, Wilmarth Sheldon, 1895- 3. Book collecting. I. Title. BIP

LEWIS, Wilmarth Sheldon, 1895- 928.2
Horace Walpole. [New York] Pantheon Books [1961, c.1960, 1961] xxvii, 215p. illus. 26cm. (N3llingen series, 35. The A. W. Mellon lectures in the fine arts, 9) Bibl. 61-4248 6.50
1. Walpole, Horace, 4th earl of Orford, 1717-1797. I. Title. II. Series: Bollingen series, 35 III. Series: The A. W. Mellon lectures in the fine arts, 9)

LEWIS, Wilmarth Sheldon, 1895- 928.2
Horace Walpole. [New York] Pantheon Books [1960] xxvii, 122p. illus., ports., facsims. 26cm. (Bollingen series, 35. The A. W. Mellon lectures in the fine arts, 9) Bibliographical footnotes. [PR3757.W2Z73] 61-7449
1. Walpole, Horace, 4th earl of Orford, 1717-1797. I. Title. II. Series: Bollingen series, 35. Series: The A. W. Mellon lectures in the fine arts, 9 BIP

LEWIS, Wilmarth Sheldon, 1895- 828'.6'09 B
Rescuing Horace Walpole / Wilmarth S. Lewis. New Haven : Yale University Press, 1978. p. cm. [DA483.W2L43] 78-7590 ISBN 0-300-02278-6 : 20.00.
1. Walpole, Horace, 4th Earl of Orford, 1717-1797. 2. Great Britain—Nobility—Biography. I. Title. BIP

WALPOLE, Horace 4th earl of Orford 1717-1797 928.2
The Yale edition of Horace Walpole's correspondence; vs. 32-34, ed. by W.S. Lewis. New Haven, Conn., Yale [c.1965] 3vs. (various p.) 26cm. Contents.vs. 32-34. Correspondence with the Countess of Upper Osory [bks. 1-3] [DA483.W2A12] 52-4945 17.50 ea.,
I. Title.

WALPOLE, Horace, 4th Earl of Orford, 1717-1797. 826'.6
Selected letters of Horace Walpole. Edited by W. S. Lewis. New Haven, Yale University Press, 1973. xix, 323 p. illus. 22 cm. [DA506.W2A4 1973] 72-91300 ISBN 0-300-01643-3 12.50
1. Walpole, Horace, 4th Earl of Orford, 1717-1797. I. Lewis, Wilmarth Sheldon, 1895- ed. BIP

WALPOLE, Horace, 4th Earl of Orford, 1717-1797. 828'.6'09
Some unpublished letters of Horace Walpole, ed. by Sir Spencer Walpole. With 2 photogravure portraits. [Folcroft, Pa.] Folcroft Library Editions, 1973. p. Reprint of the 1902 ed. published by Longmans, Green, London. [DA483.W2A56 1973] 73-14759 ISBN 0-8414-9438-X (lib. bdg.)
1. Walpole, Horace, 4th Earl of Orford, 1717-1797. I. Title.

Walpole, Hugh, Sir, 1884-1941—Biography.

HART-DAVIS, Rupert, Sir. 823'.912 B
Hugh Walpole : a biography / by Rupert Hart-Davis. Westport, Conn. : Greenwood Press, [1980] p. cm. Reprint of the 1st ed. published in 1952 by Macmillan, London. Includes index. Bibliography: p. [PR6045.A34Z58 1980] 79-26786 ISBN 0-313-22258-4 lib. bdg. : 37.00
1. Walpole, Hugh, Sir, 1884-1941—Biography. 2. Novelists, English—20th century—Biography.

HART-DAVIS, Rupert. v. 12
Hugh Walpole, a biography. [A remarkable portrait of a man, an epoch, and a society] New York, Harcourt, Brace & World [1962] xii, 467 p. illus. 21 cm. (Harvest book, HB 52) Bibliography: p. 448. 64-20729
1. Walpole, Sir Hugh, 1884-1941. I. Title.

Walpole, Robert, Earl of Oxford, 1676-1745.

DICKINSON, H. T. 942.071'092'4 B
Walpole and the Whig supremacy [by] H. T. Dickinson. London, English Universities Press, 1973. 205, [8] p. illus., ports. 23 cm. Includes index. Bibliography: p. 193-196. [DA501.W2D52] 74-150453 ISBN 0-340-11515-7
1. Walpole, Robert, Earl of Oxford, 1676-1745. 2. Great Britain—Politics and government—1714-1760. I. Title.
Distributed by Verry, 5.00. BIP

KEMP, Betty. 942.07'1'0924 B
Sir Robert Walpole / Betty Kemp ; introd. by A. J. P. Taylor. London : Weidenfeld and Nicholson, c1976. x, 147 p., [4] leaves of plates : ill. ; 23 cm. Includes index. Bibliography: p. 139-141. [DA501.W2K37] 76-365426 ISBN 0-297-77067-5 : £4.25
1. Walpole, Robert, Earl of Orford, 1676-1745. 2. Great Britain—Politics and government—1702-1714. 3. Great Britain—Politics and government—1714-1760. I. Title.

MORLEY, John Morley, Viscount, 1838-1923. 942.06'9'0924
Walpole. Westport, Conn., Greenwood Press [1971] vi, 251 p. 23 cm. Reprint of the 1889 ed. Includes bibliographical references. [DA501.W2M8 1971] 76-110858 ISBN 0-8371-4527-9
1. Walpole, Robert, Earl of Oxford, 1676-1745. BIP

PLUMB, John Harold, 1911- 923.242
Sir Robert Walpole, the making of a statesman. Boston, Houghton, Mifflin, 1956- v. illus. 22cm. [DA501.W2P52] 56-11765
1. Walpole, Robert, Earl of Oxford, 1676-1745. I. Title.

PLUMB, John Harold, 1911- 942.06'9'0924 B
Sir Robert Walpole [by] J. H. Plumb. Clifton [N.J.] A. M. Kelley, 1973- v. illus. 23 cm. (Houghton Mifflin reprint editions) Reprint of the 1956-61 ed. Contents.Contents.—1. The making of a statesman.—2. The king's minister. Includes bibliographical references. [DA501.W2P522] 72-128080 30.00 (2 vol. set)
1. Walpole, Robert, Earl of Orford, 1676-1745. BIP

WALPOLE, Horace, 4th Earl of Orford, 1717-1797. 942.07'3
The last journals of Horace Walpole during the reign of George III from 1771-1783. With notes by Dr. Doran. Edited with an introd. by A. Francis Steuart. London, New York, J. Lane, 1910. London, New York, J. Lane, 1910. [New York, AMS Press, 1973] 2 v. illus. 23 cm. [DA506.W2A154 1973] 71-177879 ISBN 0-404-06815-4 32.50 (set)
1. Great Britain—History—1760-1789. I. Title.

Walsh, David Ignatius, 1872-1947.

WAYMAN, Dorothy (Godfrey) 1893- 923.273
David I. Walsh, citizen-patriot. Milwaukee, Bruce Pub. Co. [1952] 366 p. illus. 23 cm. [F70.W2W39] 52-12759
1. Walsh, David Ignatius, 1872-1947. I. Title.

Walsh, Edmund Aloysius, 1885-1956.

GALLAGHER, Louis Joseph, 1885- 922.273
Edmund A. Walsh, S. J. a biography. New York, Benziger Bros. [1962]) 250 p. illus. 21 cm. [BX4705.W256G3] 63-2063
1. Walsh, Edmund Aloysius, 1885-1956. I. Title.

Walsh, James Edward, Bp., 1891-

KERRISON, Raymond 922.273
Bishop Walsh of Maryknoll, a biography. New York, Putnam [c.1962] 314p. 61-12733 4.95 bds.,
1. Walsh, James Edward, Bp., 1891- I. Title.

KERRISON, Raymond 922.273
Bishop Walsh of Maryknoll, a biography. New York, Lancer [1963, c.1962] 255p. 18cm. (73-413) .60 pap.,
1. Walsh, James Edward, Bp., 1891- I. Title.

Walsh, John C.

WALSH, John C. 282'.092'4 B
The day after Christmas / J. C. Walsh. [s.l. : s.n., c1976] 186 leaves ; 28 cm. "Number 9 of an edition limited to twenty copies." [BX4705.W2574A33] 77-152057
1. Walsh, John C. 2. Catholic Church—Clergy—Biography. 3. Clergy—United States—Biography. I. Title.

Walsh, Mary, Mother, 1850-1922.

BOARDMAN, Anne Cawley. 922.273
Such love is seldom; a biography of Mother Mary Walsh, O. P. [1st ed.] New York, Harper [1950] xiii, 236 p. illus., ports. 22 cm. [BX4705.W2575B6] 50-10800
1. Walsh, Mary, Mother, 1850-1922. 2. Sisters of the Order of St. Dominic, New York. I. Title.

Walsh, Raoul, 1892—

WALSH, Raoul, 1892- 791.43'0233'0924 B
Each man in his time; the life story of a director. New York, Farrar, Straus and Giroux [1974] 385 p. illus. 24 cm. [PN1998.A3W258 1974] 74-9721 ISBN 0-374-14553-9 8.95
1. Walsh, Raoul, 1892- I. Title.

Walter Carl Ferdinand Wilhelm, 1811-1887.

SPITZ, Lewis William, 1895- 922.473
The life of Dr. C. F. W. Walther. St. Louis, Concordia Pub. House, 1961. 117 p. illus. 21 cm. [BX8080.W3S7 1961] 61-18227
1. Walter Carl Ferdinand Wilhelm, 1811-1887. I. Title.

Walter Hoving Home.

HOBE, Laura. 248'.246 B
Try God / by Laura Hobe ; foreword by David Wilkerson. 1st ed. Garden City, N.Y. : Doubleday, 1977. 191 p. ; 22 cm. [BV4930.H6] 76-50771 ISBN 0-385-12443-0 : 6.50
1. Walter Hoving Home. 2. Converts—United States—Biography. 3. Church work with delinquent girls—New York (State)—Garrison. I. Title. BIP

HOBE, Laura. 248'.246 [B]
Try God / by Laura Hobe ; foreword by David Wilkerson. New York : Warner Books, 1978,c1977. 207p. ; 18 cm. [BV4930.H6] ISBN 0-446-89708-6 pbk. : 1.95
1. Walter Hoving Home. 2. Converts — United States — Biography. 3. Church work with delinquent girls — New York (State) — Garrison. I. Title.
L.C. card no. for 1977 Doubleday ed.: 76-50771.

Walterman, Eunice,

WALTERMAN, Eunice, 1912- 920.7
Don't call me Dad. [Kansas City, Kan.] c1950. 195 p. group ports., facsims. 22 cm. Autographical. [CT275.W259A3] 50-30140
I. Title.

Walters, Edith (Gardner)

WALTERS, Edith (Gardner) 1921- 920.8
Matin ("Star of Morning"); a spiritual autobiography. [1st ed.] New York, Greenwich Book Publishers [1960] 252 p. 21 cm. [BF1999.W23] 60-11838
I. Title. II. Title: Star of Morning.

Walters, Herbert Sanford, 1891-

HILL, Howard L v. 12
The Herbert Walters story [with] Part II, U.S. Senator from Tennessee, 1963-1964. Morristown, Tenn., Morristown Printing Co., 1966. 232, lxvii p. illus. 24 cm. 67-102425
1. Walters, Herbert Sanford, 1891- I. Title.

Walters, Vernon A.

WALTERS, Vernon A. 355.3'31'0924 B
Silent missions / Vernon A. Walters. 1st ed. Garden City, N.Y. : Doubleday, 1978. xi, 654 p., [12] leaves of plates : ill. ; 23 cm. Includes index. [E840.5.W34A37] 77-16853 ISBN 0-385-13500-9 : 12.95
1. Walters, Vernon A. 2. United States. Army—Biography. 3. Generals—United States—Biography. 4. World War, 1939-1945—Personal narratives, American. 5. United States—Foreign relations—1945- 6. Military attaches—United States—Biography. I. Title. BIP

Walther, Carl Ferdinand Wilhelm, 1811-1887.

SPITZ, Lewis William, 1895- 922.473
The life of Dr. C. F. W. Walther. St. Louis, Concordia [c.]1961. 117p. illus. 61-18227 2.50
1. Walther, Carl Ferdinand Wilhelm, 1811-1887. I. Title.

WALTHER, Carl Ferdinand Wilhelm, 1811-1887. 284.173'0924
Letters of C. F. W. Walther; a selection. Translated, edited, and with an introd. by Carl S. Meyer. Philadelphia, Fortress Press [1969] xii, 155 p. 21 cm. (Seminar editions) Bibliographical footnotes. [BX8080.W3A413] 72-84539 2.25
I. Title.

Walther von der Vogelweide, 12th cent.

SCHEIBE, Fred Karl, 1911- 831'.2
Walther von der Vogelweide, troubadour of the Middle Ages, his life and his reputation in the English-speaking countries. [1st ed.] New York, Vantage Press [1969] 137 p. 21 cm. Bibliography: p. 132-137. [PT1671.S35] 79-9144 3.50
1. Walther von der Vogelweide, 12th cent.

Waltmire, Baily, 1896-1962.

BRACE, Beverly Waltmire, 1924- 287'.632'0924 B
The Humboldt years, 1930-1939 / Beverly Waltmire Brace. Chicago : Adams Press, c1977. iv, 206 p. ; 22 cm. [BX8495.W2444B7] 77-154518 pbk. : 4.50
1. Waltmire, Baily, 1896-1962. 2. Methodist Church—Clergy—Biography. 3. Humboldt Park Community Methodist Episcopal Church, Chicago, Ill.—History. 4. Clergy—Illinois—Chicago—Biography. 5. Chicago—Biography. 6. Chicago—Church history. I. Title. BIP

Walton, Bill, 1952-

LIBBY, Bill. 796.32'363'0979494
The Walton gang. New York, Coward, McCann & Geoghegan [1974] 286 p. illus. 22 cm. [GV884.W3L52 1974] 73-78769 ISBN 0-698-10565-6 8.95
1. Walton, Bill, 1952- 2. California. University. University at Los Angeles—Basketball. I. Title. BIP

SCOTT, Jack, 1942- 796.32'3'0924 B
Bill Walton : on the road with the Portland Trail Blazers / Jack Scott. 1st ed. New York : Crowell, c1978. xxi, 294 p., [8] leaves of plates : ill. ; 24 cm. [GV884.W3S37 1978] 77-11569 ISBN 0-690-01694-8 : 10.95
1. Walton, Bill, 1952- 2. Basketball players—United States—Biography. BIP

Walton, Bill, 1952-—Juvenile literature.

BATSON, Larry, 1930- 796.32'3'0924 B
Bill Walton. Illustrated by Harold Henriksen. Mankato, Minn., Amecus Street; [distributed by Childrens Press, Chicago, 1974] 31 p. col. illus. 25 cm. (Superstars) A biography of Bill Walton, whose outstanding performance in college basketball at UCLA twice won him the nation's outstanding amateur athlete award. [GV884.W3B37] 92 74-16498 ISBN 0-87191-379-8 4.95
1. Walton, Bill, 1952- —Juvenile literature. 2. Basketball—Juvenile literature. I. Henriksen, Harold, illus. II. Title. BIP

BURCHARD, Marshall. 796.32'3'0924 B
Sports hero, Bill Walton / by Marshall Burchard. New York : Putnam, [1978] p. cm. (Sports hero biographies) A biography of the captain and center player of the champion Portland Trail Blazers basketball team. [GV884.W3B87] 92 78-17442 ISBN 0-399-61128-2 lib. bdg. : lib.bdg. : 5.49
1. Walton, Bill, 1952- —Juvenile literature. 2. Basketball players—United States—Biography—Juvenile literature. I. Title.

HAHN, James. 796.32'3'0924 B
Bill Walton : maverick cager / by James and Lynn Hahn. St. Paul : EMC Corp., 1978. p. cm. (Their Champions and challengers I) A biography of the controversial captain of the Portland Trail Blazers who has strong opinions about athletes' public and private lives. [GV884.W3H33] 92 78-9447 ISBN 0-88436-443-7 : 5.95
1. Walton, Bill, 1952-—Juvenile literature. 2. Basketball players—United States—Biography—Juvenile literature. I. Hahn, Lynn, joint author. II. Title. III. Series. BIP

STAMBLER, Irwin. 796.32'3'0924 B
Bill Walton, super center / by Irwin Stambler. New York : Putnam, c1976. 158 p. ; 21 cm. (Putnam sports shelf) Includes index. A biography of the basketball player whose performance at UCLA twice won him the nation's outstanding amateur athlete award. [GV884.W3S82 1976] 92 75-35931 ISBN 0-399-60980-6 lib. bdg. : 5.29
1. Walton, Bill, 1952- —Juvenile literature. 2. Basketball—Juvenile literature. I. Title.

Walton, Izaak, 1593-1683.

NOVARR, David. 928.2
The making of Walton's Lives. Ithaca, N. Y., Cornell University Press [1958] xvi, 527p. 25cm. (Cornell studies in English, v. 41) Bibliographical footnotes. [DA377.W27N6] 58-1012
1. Walton, Izaac, 1593-1683. The lives of Dr. John Donne, Sir Henry Wotton, Mr. Richard Hooker. Mr. George Herbert and Dr. RobertSanderson. I. Title. II. Series: Cornell University. Cornell studies in English, v.41 BIP

TEALE, William Henry, 1810-1878. 283'.092'2 B
Lives of English laymen, Lord Falkland, Izaak Walton, Robert Nelson. Freeport, N.Y., Books for Libraries Press [1972] p. (Essay index reprint series) Reprint of the 1842 ed. Includes bibliographical references. [CT781.T4 1972] 72-3363 ISBN 0-8369-2930-6
1. Falkland, Lucius Cary, 2d Viscount, 1610?-1643. 2. Walton, Izaak, 1593-1683. 3. Nelson, Robert, 1656-1715. I. Title.

Wanamaker, John, 1838-1922.

APPEL, Joseph Herbert, 1873- 381'.0924 B
The business biography of John Wanamaker, founder and builder; America's merchant pioneer from 1861 to 1922; with glimpses of Rodman Wanamaker and Thomas B. Wanamaker, by Joseph H. Appel. New York, AMS Press [1970] xxvi, 471 p. facsim., port. 23 cm. Reprint of the 1930 ed. [CT275.W272A7 1970] 70-101267
1. Wanamaker, John, 1838-1922. 2. Wanamaker, Rodman, 1863-1928. 3. Wanamaker, Thomas Brown, 1861-1908. I. Title.

GIBBONS, Herbert Adams, 1880-1934. 381'.0924 B
John Wanamaker. Port Washington, N.Y., Kennikat Press [1971, c1926] 2 v. illus., facsims., ports. 22 cm. (Kennikat series on American history and culture in the nineteenth century) Bibliography: v. 2, p. [467]-481. [E664.W24G4 1971] 70-137911 ISBN 0-8046-1479-2
1. Wanamaker, John, 1838-1922. BIP

Wanamaker, Rodman, 1863-1928.

APPEL, Joseph Herbert, 1873- 381'.0924 B
The business biography of John Wanamaker, founder and builder; America's merchant pioneer from 1861 to 1922; with glimpses of Rodman Wanamaker and Thomas B. Wanamaker, by Joseph H. Appel. New York, AMS Press [1970] xxvi, 471 p. facsim., port. 23 cm. Reprint of the 1930 ed. [CT275.W272A7 1970] 70-101267
1. Wanamaker, John, 1838-1922. 2. Wanamaker, Rodman, 1863-1928. 3. Wanamaker, Thomas Brown, 1861-1908. I. Title.

Wandering Jew.

VIERECK, George Sylvester, 1884- v. 12
My first two thousand years [by] George Sylvester Viereck and Paul Eldridge. Greenwich, Conn., Fawcett [1956] 287 p. (Crest book) 67-20837
1. Wandering Jew. I. Eldridge, Paul, 1888- joint author. II. Title.

VIERECK, George Sylvester, 1884- v. 12
My first two thousand years; the autobiography of the Wandering Jew [by] George Sylvester Viereck and Paul Eldridge. New York, Sheridan House, 1963. xiii p., 1 l., [9]-501, [1] p. 21 cm. 67-81134
1. Wandering Jew. I. Eldridge, Paul, 1888- joint author. II. Title.

Wang, An-shih, 1021-1086.

MESKILL, John Thomas, 1925- ed. 923.251
Wang An-shih, practical reformer? Boston, Heath [1963] 99p. 24cm. (Problems in Asian civilizations) Bibl. 63-12328 1.65 pap.,
1. Wang, An-shih, 1021-1086. 2. China—Pol. & govt.—Early to 1643. I. Title.

WILLIAMSON, Henry Raymond. 951'.02'0924 B
Wang An Shih ... a Chinese statesman and educationalist of the Sung Dynasty. Westport, Conn., Hyperion Press [1973] 2 v. 23 cm. Reprint of the 1935-37 ed. published by A. Probsthain, which was issued as v. 21-22 of Probsthain's oriental series. Originally presented as the author's thesis, University of London, 1931. Bibliography: v. 2, p. viii. [DS751.W35 1973] 73-901 ISBN 0-88355-096-2 (v. 1)
1. Wang, An-shih, 1021-1086. 2. China—Politics and government.

WILLIAMSON, Henry Raymond. 951'.02'0924 B
Wang An Shih ... a Chinese statesman and educationalist of the Sung Dynasty. Westport, Conn., Hyperion Press [1973] 2 v. 23 cm. Reprint of the 1935-37 ed. published by A. Probsthain, which was issued as v. 21-22 of Probsthain's oriental series. Originally presented as the author's thesis, University of London, 1931. Bibliography: v. 2, p. viii. [DS751.W35 1973] 73-901 ISBN 0-88355-095-4 37.50
1. Wang, An-shih, 1021-1086. 2. China—Politics and government.

Wang, Mang, d. 23.

PAN, Ku, 32-92. 931'.00994 B
Wang Mang : a translation of the official account of his rise to power as given in the History of the former Han dynasty / with introd. and notes [by] Clyde Bailey Sargent. Westport, Conn. : Hyperion Press, 1977. p. cm. (China studies) Translation of chapter 99 of Ch'ien Han shu, generally attributed to Pan Ku, but begun by his father, Pan Piao, and completed by his sister, Pan Chao. Reprint of the 1947 ed. published by Graphic Art Book Co., Shanghai. Originally presented as C. B. Sargent's thesis, Columbia. Bibliography: p. [DS748.16.W36P36213 1977] 75-39030 ISBN 0-88355-386-4 : 16.00
1. Wang, Mang, d. 23. 2. Statesmen—China—Biography. I. Pan, Piao, 3-54. II. Pan, Chao, 1st cent. III. Sargent, Clyde Bailey. IV. Series: China studies (Westport, Conn.).

Wang, Mary.

WANG, Mary. 275.1
The Chinese church that will not die [by] Mary Wang, with Gwen and Edward England. Wheaton, Ill., Tyndale House Publishers [1972] 201 p. illus. 18 cm. [BR1297.W28A3 1972] 79-188533 ISBN 0-8423-0235-2 1.25
1. Wang, Mary. 2. Christianity—China. 3. Persecution—China. I. England, Gwen, joint author. II. England, Edward O., joint author. III. Title.

Wang, Shou-jen, 1472-1528.

CHANG, Chai-sen, 1886- 181.11
Wang Yong-ming: idealist philosopher of sixteenth-century China, by Carsun Chang. Jamaica, N.Y., St John's Univ. Pr. [c.]1962 vi-102p. illus. 21cm. (Asian philosophical studies, no. 1) Bibl. 62-12341 2.50 pap.,
1. Wang, Shou-jen, 1472-1528. I. Title. II. Series.

War correspondents, American—Correspondence, reminiscences, etc.

CHAPELLE, Dickey. 920.5
What's a woman doing here? A reporter's report on herself. New York, Morrow, 1962 [c1961] 285 p. illus. 22 cm. [PN4874.C44A3] 62-7716
1. War correspondents, American—Correspondence, reminiscences, etc. I. Title.

Warbasse, James Peter,

WARBASSE, James Peter, 1866- 926.1
North Star; a contribution to autobiography. Falmouth, Mass., Kendall Press, 1958. 123 p. 24 cm. [R154.W19A33] 59-31083
I. Title.

WARBASSE, James Peter, 1866- 926.1
Three voyages; the story of an inquiring soul exploring his way through life and living it as he goes, being fragments of an autobiography. [Chicago] Cooperative League of the U. S. A. [1956] 274p. illus. 22cm [R154.W19A3] 56-35131
I. Title.

WARBASSE, James Peter, 1866- 926.1
Three voyages; the story of an inquiring soul exploring his way through life and living it as he goes, being fragments of an autobiography. [Chicago] Cooperative League of the U.S.A. [1956] 274 p. illus. 22 cm. [R154.W19A3] 56-35131
I. Title.

Warburg, Fredric, 1898-

WARBURG, Fredric, 1898- 070.5'092'4
All authors are equal : the publishing life of Fredric Warburg, 1936 1971. New York : St. Martin's Press, 1974, c1973. xii, 310 p., [3] leaves of plates : ill. ; 25 cm. Includes bibliographical references and index. [Z325.W29A298 1974] 74-78691 10.00
1. Warburg, Fredric, 1898- 2. Publishers and publishing—Great Britain—Correspondence, reminiscences, etc. I. Title.

WARBURG, Fredric, 1898- 926.55
An occupation for gentlemen. [1st American ed.] Boston, Houghton Mifflin, 1960 [c1959] 287 p. illus. 22 cm. Autobiographical. [Z325.W29A3 1960] 60-5220
1. Publishers and publishing—Gt. Brit. I. Title.

Warburg, James Paul,

WARBURG, James Paul, 1896- 923.273
The long road home; the autobiography of a maverick. [1st ed.] Garden City, N.Y., Doubleday, 1964. xvii, 314 p. illus., ports. 22 cm. Includes bibliographies. [E748.W258A3] 64-14277
I. Title.

Ward, Aaron Montgomery, 1844-1913.

AARON Montgomery Ward, 380.1
entrepreneur, environmentalist, consumerist. [Chicago, Montgomery Ward

& Co.? 1971] 1 case. 31 cm. Title from case. Consists of 4 illustrated brochures of various sizes fastened together, 1 of which includes a reproduction of Ward's 1st catalog page (1872); a book mark; and a reproduction of Ward's Catalogue no. 13, spring and summer, 1875 (72 p.) [HF5467.W3A25] 73-170438
1. Ward, Aaron Montgomery, 1844-1913. 2. Ward (Montgomery) and Company. I. Ward (Montgomery) and Company. Catalogue no. 13, spring and summer, 1875. 1971.

BAKER, Nina (Brown) 1888- 658.872
Big catalogue: the life of Aaron Montgomery Ward. Illustrated by Alan Moyler. [1st ed.] New York. Harcourt, Brace [1956] 115p. illus. 21cm. [HF5467.W3B3] 56-10736
1. Ward, Aaroa Montgomery, 1844-1913. 2. Ward (Montgomery) and 0Company. I. Title.

Ward, Andrew, 1946-

WARD, Andrew, 1946- 973.92'092'4 B
Fits and starts : the premature memoirs of Andrew Ward. 1st ed. Boston : Little, Brown, c1978. xi, 177 p. ; 22 cm. "An Atlantic Monthly Press book." [CT275.W27446A33] 77-18850 ISBN 0-316-92199-8 : 8.95
1. Ward, Andrew, 1946- 2. United States—Biography. I. Title.

Ward, Arland Langdon, 1885-1965.

HILL, Kate Adele, 1900- 630'.924 B
A. L. Ward-Texan, 1885-1965. [Waco, Tex., Printed by Texian Press, 1967] xi, 276 p. illus., ports. 24 cm. [S417.W37H5] 67-28922
1. Ward, Arland Langdon, 1885-1965.

Ward, Artemas, 1727-1800.

MARTYN, Charles, 1874- 973.3'0924 B
The life of Artemas Ward, the first Commander-in-Chief of the American Revolution. Port Washington, N.Y., Kennikat Press [1970] xiii, 334 p. illus., facsims., map, port. 22 cm. (Kennikat American bicentennial series) Reprint of the 1921 ed. Includes bibliographical references. [E207.W2M38 1970] 71-120883 ISBN 0-8046-1276-5
1. Ward, Artemas, 1727-1800. 2. United States—History—Revolution, 1775-1783—Campaigns and battles. 3. Massachusetts—History—Revolution, 1775-1783. I. Title.

Ward, Arthur Sarsfield, 1883-1959.

VAN ASH, Cay. 813'.5'2 B
Master of villainy; a biography of Sax Rohmer, by Cay Van Ash and Elizabeth Sax Rohmer. Edited, with foreword, notes, and bibliography, by Robert E. Briney. Bowling Green, Ohio, Bowling Green University Popular Press [1972] ix, 312 p. illus. 23 cm. "Chronological bibliography of the books of Sax Rohmer": p. 299-303. [PS3545.A653Z9] 76-186636
1. Ward, Arthur Sarsfield, 1883-1959. I. Rohmer, Elizabeth Sax, joint author. II. Title. BIP

Ward, C. M.

WEAD, Doug. 289.9 B
The C. M. Ward story, with Doug Wead. Harrison, Ark. : New Leaf Press, c1976. 255 p. ; 23 cm. Includes index. [BX6198.A78W43] 76-22267 ISBN 0-89221-022-2 : 5.95
1. Ward, C. M. 2. Assemblies of God, General Council—Clergy—Biography. 3. Clergy—United States—Biography. I. Ward, C. M. II. Title.

Ward family (John Ward, d. 1698)

WARD, Samuel, 1725-1776. 923.273
Correspondence of Governor Samuel Ward, May 1775-March 1776, with a biographical introd., based chiefly on the Ward papers covering the period 1725-1776, edited by Bernhard Knollenberg; and Genealogy of the Ward family: Thomas Ward, son of John, of Newport and some of his descendants, compiled by Clifford P. Monahon. Providence, Rhode Island Historical Society, 1952. ix, 254 p. 24 cm. Bibliography: p. 239-244. [E207.W26A4] 52-2486
1. Ward family (John Ward, d. 1698) I. Monahon, Clifford Philip, 1897- II. Rhode Island Historical Society. III. Title.

Ward, Joseph, 1838-1889.

JOSEPH Ward, the builder. v. 12
Sioux Falls, S. D. [c1957] 66p. 20cm.
1. Ward, Joseph, 1838-1889. 2. Dakota—History. I. Nordness, Reinhart L

Ward, Lemuel T.

BERKEY, Barry R. 745.59'3 B
Pioneer decoy carvers : a biography of Lemuel and Stephen Ward / Barry Robert Berkey, Velma Berkey, Richard Eric Berkey. Cambridge, Md. : Tidewater Publishers, 1977. p. cm. Includes index. Bibliography: p. [NK9797.B47] 77-13075 ISBN 0-87033-243-0 : 17.50
1. Ward, Lemuel T. 2. Ward, Stephen Wesley, 1895-1976. 3. Wood-carvers—United States—Biography. 4. Decoys (Hunting) I. Berkey, Velma A., joint author. II. Berkey, Richard, 1964- joint author. III. Title. BIP

Ward, Lester Frank, 1841-1913.

SCOTT, Clifford H. 301'.092'4 B
Lester Frank Ward / by Clifford H. Scott. Boston : Twayne Publishers, c1976. 192 p. : port. ; 21 cm. (Twayne's United States authors series ; TUSAS 275) Includes index. Bibliography: p. 183-189. [HM22.U6W35] 76-16539 ISBN 0-8057-7175-1 lib.bdg. 8.50
1. Ward, Lester Frank, 1841-1913. BIP

Ward, Maisie, 1889-

WARD, Maisie, 1889- 901.94'6 B
To and fro on the earth: the sequel to an autobiography. London, New York, Sheed and Ward, 1973, [i.e.1974] [5], 176 p. 23 cm. [BX4705.W287A29] 72-12475 ISBN 0-7220-7301-1 8.50
1. Ward, Maisie, 1889- I. Title.

WARD, Maisie, 1889- 920.4
Unfinished business. New York, Sheed and Ward [1964] viii, 374 p. 22 cm. Autobiography. [BX4705.W287A3] 64-19907
I. Title.

Ward, Mary Augusta Arnold, 1851-1920—Biography.

JONES, Enid Huws. 823'.8 B
Mrs Humphry Ward. New York, St. Martin's Press [1973] x, 179 p. illus. 23 cm. Bibliography: p. 174-177. [PR5716.J6 1973b] 73-80643 7.95
1. Ward, Mary Augusta Arnold, 1851-1920—Biography.

JONES, Enid Huws. 823'.8 B
Mrs Humphry Ward. London, Heinemann [1973] x, 179 p. illus. 22 cm. Bibliography: p. 174-177. [PR5716.J6 1973] 74-157255 ISBN 0-434-37730-9
1. Ward, Mary Augusta Arnold, 1851-1920—Biography.
Distributed by St. Martin Press, 7.95

Ward, Mary, 1585-1645.

MARY Oliver, Mother. 922.242
Mary Ward, 1585-1645. Introd. and epilogue by Maisie Ward. New York, Sheed and Ward [1959] 229p. 22cm. [BX4705.W29M34] 59-12092
1. Ward, Mary, 1585-1645. I. Title.

Ward, Nancy, d. 1822—Juvenile literature.

FELTON, Harold W., 1902- 973.3'092'4 B
Nancy Ward, Cherokee / Harold W. Felton ; illustrated by Carolyn Bertrand. New York : Dodd, Mead, [1975] 89 p. : ill. ; 24 cm. Includes index. A brief biography of the eighteenth-century Cherokee Indian woman who did much to help her own people and to assist the colonists in their fight for independence. [E99.C5W263] 92 74-25512 ISBN 0-396-07072-8 : 4.95
1. Ward, Nancy, d. 1822—Juvenile literature. I. Bertrand, Carolyn, ill. BIP

Ward, Rodger—Juvenile literature.

LIBBY, Bill. 796.7'2'0922 B
Superdrivers : three auto racing champions / by Bill Libby. Champaign, Ill. : Garrard Pub. Co., c1977. 96 p. : ill. ; 24 cm. Biographical sketches of three American racing car drivers: Rodger Ward, Lee Petty, and Don Garlits. [GV1032.A1L53] 920 76-47475 ISBN 0-8116-6681-6 lib.bdg. : 3.84
1. Ward, Rodger—Juvenile literature. 2. Petty, Lee—Juvenile literature. 3. Garlits, Don—Juvenile literature. 4. Automobile racing drivers—United States—Biography—Juvenile literature. I. Title. BIP

Ward, Samuel, 1814-1884.

STEELE, Robert V. P. 928.1
Sam Ward: king of the lobby. Boston, Houghton Mifflin, 1965. 533 p. illus., ports. 22 cm. Bibliography: p. [501]-517. [PS3144.W3Z89] 65-10327
1. Ward, Samuel, 1814-1884. I. Title.

THOMAS, Lately, pseud. 928.1
Sam Ward: king of the lobby. Boston, Houghton [c.]1965. 533p. illus., ports. 22cm. Bibl. [PS3144.W3Z89] 65-10327 6.95
1. Ward, Samuel, 1814-1884. I. Title.

Ward, Samuel, 1814-1884—Biography.

ELLIOTT, Maud Howe, 1854-1948. 327.73'07'8 B
Uncle Sam Ward and his circle / by Maud Howe Elliott. New York : Arno Press, 1975, c1938. p. cm. (The Leisure class in America) Reprint of the ed. published by Macmillan, New York. [PS3144.W3Z7 1975] 75-1844 ISBN 0-405-06912-X : 43.00
1. Ward, Samuel, 1814-1884—Biography. 2. Ward family. I. Title. II. Series. BIP

Ward, William George, 1812-1882.

WARD, Wilfrid Philip, 1856-1916. 282'.092'4 B
William George Ward and the Catholic revival / by Wilfrid Ward. 1st AMS ed. New York : AMS Press, 1978. xlvi, 468 p. : ill. ; 23 cm. Reprint of the 1893 ed. published by Macmillan, London, New York. Includes bibliographical references and index. [BX4705.W3W3 1978] 75-29626 ISBN 0-404-14042-4 : 31.50
1. Ward, William George, 1812-1882. 2. Catholics—England—Biography. 3. Converts, Catholic. I. Title. BIP

WARD, Wilfrid Philip, 1856-1916. 283'.092'4 B
William George Ward and the Oxford movement / by Wilfrid Ward. New York : AMS Press, 1977. xxix, 462 p. : ill. ; 23 cm. Reprint of the 1889 ed. published by Macmillan, London, New York. [BX4705.W3W35 1977] 75-29625 ISBN 0-404-14043-2 : 31.50
1. Ward, William George, 1812-1882. 2. Catholics in England—Biography. 3. Oxford movement. I. Title. BIP

Warde, Mary Francis Xavier, 1810?-1884.

HEALY, Kathleen. 271'.92'024 B
Frances Warde: American founder of the Sisters of Mercy. New York, Seabury Press [1973] x, 535 p. 21 cm. "A Crossroad book." Bibliography: p. 509-517. [BX4705.W32H42] 73-6433 ISBN 0-8164-1139-5 14.50
1. Warde, Mary Francis Xavier, 1810?-1884. 2. Sisters of Mercy.

Warde, Mary Francis Xavier, 1810 - 1884— Juvenile literature.

MARIE Christopher, Sister. 922.273
Frances Warde and the first Sisters of Mercy. Illustrated by John Lawn. New York, Farrar, Straus & Cudahy [1960] 189p. illus. 22cm. (Vision books, 47) [BX4705.W35M34] 60-10365
1. Warde, Mary Francis Xavier, 1810 - 1884— Juvenile literature. 2. Sisters of Mercy—Juvenile literature. I. Title.

Ware, Ella Kinney,

WARE, Ella Kinney, 1841-1931. 920.02
Reminiscences. Selected and compiled by Dorothy Hall. [1st ed.] New York, Printed by Comet Press [1967] 51 p. illus., ports. 24 cm. [CT275.W2813A3] 70-13976
I. Hall, Dorothy, comp. II. Title.

Ware, Harold M., 1890-1935.

HARRIS, Lement U., 1904- 338.1'092'4 B
Harold M. Ware, 1890-1935, agricultural pioneer, U.S.A. and U.S.S.R. / by Lement Harris. New York : American Institute for Marxist Studies, c1978. 72 p. ; 28 cm. (Occasional paper - American Institute for Marxist Studies ; no. 30) Cover title. Includes bibliographical references. [S417.W38H37] 78-106519 pbk. : 1.75
1. Ware, Harold M., 1890-1935. 2. Farmer—United States—Biography. 3. Farm mechanization—Russia—History. 4. Agriculture—United States—History. I. Title. II. Series: American Institute for Marxist Studies. Occasional papers ; no. 30.

Warfield, Bernis.

JOHNSON, Lois Pheips. 922.673
I'm gonna fly; the biography of Bernis Warfield. [1st ed.] Saint Paul, Macalester Park Pub. Co. [1959] 176p. 21cm. [BX6455.W34J6] 60-19260
1. Warfield, Bernis. I. Title.

Warfield, Frances,

WARFIELD, Frances, 1901- 920.96178
Keep listening. New York, Viking Press, 1957. 158 p. 22 cm. Autobiography. [HV2534.W3A32] 57-6431
I. Title.

Warfield, Sandra.

MCCRACKEN, James, 1927- 784'.0924 B
A star in the family; an autobiography in diary form, by James McCracken and Sandra Warfield. Edited by Robert Daley. New York, Coward McCann & Geoghegan [1971] 388 p. illus., ports. 22 cm. [ML400.M25A37] 70-136444 6.95
1. Warfield, Sandra. 2. Musicians—Correspondence, reminiscences, etc. I. Warfield, Sandra, joint author. II. Title.

Warfield, Wallis

WARFIELD, Wallis Duchess of Windsor 1896- 920.7
The heart has its reasons; the memoirs of the Duchess of Windsor. New York, D. McKay Co. [1956] 372p. illus. 22cm. [DA581.W5A3] 56-14107
I. Title.

Warhol, Andy, 1928-

COPLANS, John. 709'.24
Andy Warhol, by John Coplans with contributions by Jonas Mekas and Calvin Tomkins. [Greenwich, Conn.] New York Graphic Society [1970] 160 p. illus., plates (part col.) 29 cm. Bibliography: p. 157-160. [N6537.W28C6] 78-115841 10.00
1. Warhol, Andy, 1930- I. Mekas, Jonas. II. Tomkins, Calvin, 1925-

CRONE, Rainer, 1942- 759.13
Andy Warhol. [Translated from German by John William Gabriel.] New York, Praeger [1970] 331 p. illus. 29 cm. [N6537.W28C713 1970] 76-129866 22.95
1. Warhol, Andy, 1928-

KOCH, Stephen. 791.43'0233'0924
Stargazer; Andy Warhol's world and his films. New York, Praeger [1973] 155 p. illus. 24 cm. Filmography: p. 143-151. [PN1998.A3W277] 72-93433 8.95
1. Warhol, Andy, 1928- I. Title.

WARHOL, Andy, 1928- 700'.92'4 B
POPism : the Warhol '60s / by Andy Warhol and Pat Hackett. 1st ed. New York : Harcourt Brace Jovanovich, c1980. p. cm. Includes index. [NX512.W37A2 1980] 79-1851 ISBN 0-15-173095 : 14.95
1. Warhol, Andy, 1928- 2. Artists—United States—Biography. 3. Pop art—United States. I. Hackett, Pat, joint author. II. Title.

WILCOCK, John. 709'.24 B
The autobiography and sex life of Andy Warhol, by John Wilcock and a cast of thousands. Photos by Shunk-Kender except where indicated. New York, Other Scenes Inc. [1971] 1 v. (unpaged) illus., ports. 28 cm. [NX93.W37W5] 78-25787 5.00
1. Warhol, Andy, 1928- I. Title.

Warhol, Andy, 1928- —Exhibitions.

WARHOL, Andy, 1928- 759.13
Andy Warhol, portraits of the seventies / text by Robert Rosenblum. 1st ed. New York : Random House, c1979. p. cm. A catalog published to coincide with a major exhibition opening at the Whitney Museum, Nov. 20, 1979. [NE2237.5.W37A4 1979] 79-4852 ISBN 0-394-50656-1 : 15.00 ISBN 0-394-73738-5 pbk. : 8.95
1. Warhol, Andy, 1928- —Exhibitions. 2. Biography—20th century—Portraits—Exhibitions. I. Rosenblum, Robert. II. Whitney Museum of American Art, New York. III. Title.

Waring, George Edwin, 1833-1898.

MELOSI, Martin V., 628'.092'4 B
1947-
Pragmatic environmentalist, sanitary engineer George E. Waring, Jr / Martin V. Melosi. Washington : Public Works Historical Society, 1977. 30 p. : ill. ; 22 cm. (Essays in public works history ; essay no. 4) Includes bibliographical references. [TD140.W3M44] 77-154123
1. Waring, George Edwin, 1833-1898. I. Title. II. Series.

Warm Spring Apache Indians.

KAYWAYKLA, James, ca.1873- 970.3
1963.
In the days of Victorio; recollections of a Warm Springs Apache [by] Eve Ball. James Kaywaykla, narrator. Tucson, University of Arizona Press [1970] xv, 222 p. illus., maps, ports. 24cm. Bibliography: p. 211-217. [E99.W36K38 1970] 73-101103 6.50
1. Warm Spring Apache Indians. I. Ball, Eve. II. Title.

Warmer, Rose.

WARMER, Rose. 248'.246 B
The journey : the story of Rose Warmer's triumphant discovery / written by Myrna Grant. Wheaton, Ill. : Tyndale House Publishers, c1978. 207 p. ; 21 cm. [BV2623.W27A34] 78-58746 ISBN 0-8423-1970-0 pbk. : 4.95 4.95
1. Warmer, Rose. 2. Converts from Judaism—Biography. I. Grant, Myrna. II. Title.

Warner, Abraham Joseph, b. 1821.

WARNER, Abraham 283'.092'4 B
Joseph, b.1821.
The private journal of Abraham Joseph Warner; extracts from volumes I, III, and IV (4 November 1838 to 25 December 1864). Extracted by Herbert B. Enderton. [San Diego? Calif., 1973] ix, 319 p. illus. 23 cm. "Limited edition of two hundred copies." [BX5995.W346A33] 73-78433
1. Warner, Abraham Joseph, b. 1821. I. Enderton, Herbert B. II. Title.

Warner Brothers Pictures, inc.

MEYER, William 791.43'0233'0922 B
R., 1949-
The Warner Brothers directors : the hard-boiled, the comic, and the weepers / by William R. Meyer. New Rochelle, N.Y. : Arlington House, c1978. 381 p. : ill. ; 26 cm. Includes index. Includes filmographies. [PN1998.A2M398] 77-22194 ISBN 0-87000-397-6 : 20.00
1. Warner Brothers Pictures, inc. 2. Moving-picture producers and directors—United States—Biography. I. Title. BIP

Warner, Charles Dudley, 1829-1900.

FIELDS, Annie (Adams) 814'.4
1834-1915.
Charles Dudley Warner, by Mrs. James T. Fields. Freeport, N.Y., Books for Libraries Press [1972] 209 p. port. 22 cm. Reprint of the 1904 ed., issued in series: Contemporary men of letters series. [PS3153.F5 1972] 72-4187 ISBN 0-8369-6878-6
1. Warner, Charles Dudley, 1829-1900. I. Series: Contemporary men of letters series. BIP

WASHINGTON Irving. 813/.2
Port Washington, N.Y., Kennikat [1968.c1881] vi, 304p. 21cm [PS2081. W25 1968] (B) 67-27660 7.50
I. Warner, Charles Dudley, 1829-1900 II. Irving, Washington, 1783-1859.

Warner, Edith, 1891 or 2-1951.

CHURCH, Peggy Pond, 1903- 920.7
The house at Otowi Bridge; the story of Edith Warner and Los Alamos. Drawings by Connie Fox Boyd. [1st ed. Albuquerque] University of New Mexico Press [1960] 149p. illus. 25cm. [F804.L6W3] 60-13408
1. Warner, Edith, 1891 or 2-1951. 2. Los Alamos, N. M. I. Title.

Warner, Glenn Scobey, 1871-1954—Juvenile literature.

VAN RIPER, Guernsey, Jr. 920
1909-
Yea, coach! Three great football coaches. Illus. by Robert Doremus. Champaign, Ill., Garrard [c.1966] 94p. illus. (pt. col.) ports. 24cm. (Sports lib. bks.) [GV939.A1V3] 66-12389 2.19 bds.,
1. Warner, Glenn Scobey, 1871-1954—Juvenile literature. 2. Heisman, John William, 1869-1936—Juvenile literature. 3. Rockne, Knute Kenneth, 1888-1931—Juvenile literature. I. Title.

VAN Riper, Guernsey, 1909- j 920
Yea, coach! Three great football coaches. Illustrated by Robert Doremus. Champaign, Ill., Garrard Pub. Co. [1966] 94 p. illus. (part col.) ports. 24 cm. ([Sports library books]) [GV939.A1V3] 66-12389
1. Warner, Glenn Scobey, 1871-1954 — Juvenile literature. 2. Heisman, John William, 1869-1966 — Juvenile literature. 3. Rockne, Knute Kenneth, 1888-1931 — Juvenile literature. I. Title. BIP

Warner, Jack Leonard,

WARNER, Jack Leonard, 927.9143
1892-
My first hundred years in Hollywood [by] Jack L. Warner, with Dean Jennings. New York, Random House [1965] 331 p. illus., ports. 22 cm. Autobiographical. [PN1998.A3W3] 65-11267
I. Jennings, Dean Southern, 1905- II. Title.

Warner, Juan Jose, 1807-1893.

MORRISON, Lorrin 301.45'1'0979493
L
Warner, the man and the ranch. Illus., maps, and photos. (unless otherwise credited) by Carroll Spear Morrison. Los Angeles, 1962. 87p. illus. 26cm. Includes bibliography. [F868.S15W3] 61-18946
1. Warner, Juan Jose, 1807-1893. 2. Warner's Ranch, Calif. I. Title.

Warner, Langdon, 1881-1955.

BOWIE, Theodore 913.03'1'0924
Robert.
Langdon Warner through his letters, edited by Theodore Bowie. Bloomington, Indiana University Press, 1966. xii, 225 p. illus., map, ports. 23 cm. (Indiana University humanities series, no. 62) [AS36.I385 no. 62] 75-21668
1. Warner, Langdon, 1881-1955. I. Title. II. Series: Indiana. University. Indiana University humanities series, no. 62

BOWIE, Theodore Robert 709.24(B)
Langdon Warner through his letters, ed. by Theodore Bowie. Bloomington, Indiana Univ. Pr., 1966. xii. 225p. illus., map, ports. 23cm. [N8375.W35B6] 66-63378 6.75
1. Warner, Langdon, 1881-1955. I. Title.

Warner, Matt, 1864-1938.

SHELLER, Roscoe. v. 12
Bandit to lawman. Yakima, Wash., Franklin Press, 1966. x, 176 p. illus. 22 cm. 68-66101
1. Warner, Matt, 1864-1938. 2. Outlaws, 3. Crimes and criminals—The West. I. Title.

Warner, Ross T.,

WARNER, Ross T., 657.6'0924 B
1895-
Oklahoma boy; an autobiography [by] Ross T. Warner. [1st ed. Tulsa? Okla., 1968] 293 p. ports. 24 cm. [CT275.W2855A3] 68-24179
I. Title.

Warnke, Mike.

WARNKE, Mike. 248'.2'0924 B
Hitchhiking on Hope Street / Mike Warnke. 1st ed. Garden City, N.Y. : Doubleday, 1979. 112 p. ; 22 cm. "A Doubleday-Galilee original." [BV4935.W34A28] 78-73197 ISBN 0-385-14540-3 : 6.95
1. Warnke, Mike. 2. Converts—United States—Biography. 3. Christian life—1960- I. Title. BIP

Warnshuis, Abbe Livingston, 1877-1958.

GOODALL, Norman, v. 12
Christian ambassador; a life of A. Livingston Warnshuis... Manhasset, N. Y., Channel Press [c1963] xi, 174 p. 21 cm. 64-23148
1. Warnshuis, Abbe Livingston, 1877-1958. I. Title.

Warre, Edmond, 1837-1920.

LESLIE, Shane, Sir, 920.042
bart., 1885-
Salutation to five. Freeport, N.Y., Books for Libraries Press [1970] v, 156 p. 23 cm. (Biography index reprint series) Reprint of the 1951 ed. Includes bibliographical references. [CT106.L4 1970] 75-126321 ISBN 8-369-80271-
1. Fitzherbert, Maria Anne (Smythe) 1756-1837. 2. Warre, Edmond, 1837-1920. 3. Butler, William Francis, Sir, 1838-1910. 4. Tolstoi, Lev Nikolaevich, graf, 1828-1910. 5. Sykes, Mark, Sir, bart., 1879-1919. I. Title.

Warren, Althea Hester, 1886-1958.

BOAZ, Martha Terosse, 1913- 920.2
Fervent and full of gifts; the life of Althea Warren. New York, Scarecrow Press, 1961. 163p. illus. 22cm. [Z720.W3B6] 61-8719
1. Warren, Althea Hester, 1886-1958. I. Title.

Warren Co., Miss. — Hist. — Civil War.

GIBSON, James 929'.3762'26
Monroe, 1856-1930.
Memoirs of J. M. Gibson; terrors of the Civil War and Reconstruction days. Edited by James Gibson Alverson and James Gibson Alverson, Jr. [San Gabriel? Calif., 1966] 108 p. illus., coat of arms, maps, port. 23 cm. [F347.W29G5] 67-1420
1. Warren Co., Miss. — Hist. — Civil War. 2. Reconstruction — Mississippi. I. Alverson, James Gibson, 1904- ed. II. Alverson, James Gibson, 1933- ed. III. Title.

Warren, Earl, 1891-

KATCHER, Leo. 347.99'73 B
Earl Warren; a political biography. [1st ed.] New York, McGraw-Hill [1967] 502 p. 23 cm. Bibliography: p. 481-483. [KF8745.W3K3] 67-19902
1. Warren, Earl, 1891-

POLLACK, Jack 347'.73'2634 B
Harrison.
Earl Warren, the judge who changed America / Jack Harrison Pollack. Englewood Cliffs, N.J. : Prentice Hall, c1979. viii, 386 p., [4] leaves of plates : ill. ; 24 cm. Includes index. Bibliography: p. 370-375. [KF8745.W3P64] 78-24234 ISBN 0-13-222315-5 : 14.95
1. Warren, Earl, 1891-1974. 2. Judges—United States—Biography. I. Title.

SEVERN, William. 347'.7326'34 B
Mr. Chief Justice; Earl Warren, by Bill Severn. New York, D. McKay Co. [1968] 186 p. 21 cm. Bibliography: p. 179. A biography of the lawyer who became a Governor of California, a vice-presidential candidate, and finally, as Chief Justice of the Supreme Court, a defender of individual and civil liberties. [KF8745.W3S4] 92 AC 68
1. Warren, Earl, 1891- I. Title.

SEVERN, William. 347.99'73 B
Mr. Chief Justice; Earl Warren, by Bill Severn. New York, D. McKay Co. [1968] 186 p. 21 cm. Bibliography: p. 179. [KF8745.W3S4] 68-14123
1. Warren, Earl, 1891- I. Title.

WARREN, Earl, 347'.73'2634 B
1891-1974.
The memoirs of Earl Warren / by Earl Warren. 1st ed. Garden City, N.Y. : Doubleday, 1977. xii, 394 p., [12] leaves of plates : ill. ; 24 cm. Includes index. [KF8745.W3A35] 76-42842 10.00
1. Warren, Earl, 1891-1974. 2. Judges—United States—Biography.

WEAVER, John 347.99'73 (B)
Downing,
Warren: the man, the court, the era, by John D. Weaver. [1st ed.] Boston. Little, Brown [1967] 406p. port. 22cm. Bibl. [KF8745.W3W4] 67-18105 7.95
1. Warren, Earl, 1891- I. Title.

Warren, Fred D., 1873-

BREWER, George D. 070'.92'4 B
The fighting editor—Warren and the Appeal. New York, Beekman Publishers, 1974. 211 p. illus. 23 cm. (American newspapermen, 1790-1933) Reprint of the 1910 ed. published by G. D. Brewer, Girard, Kan. [HX84.W3B7 1974] 74-1499 ISBN 0-8464-0030-8 13.00
1. Warren, Fred D., 1873- 2. The American Freeman. 3. Socialism in the United States. I. Title. BIP

Warren, Harry, 1893-

THOMAS, Tony, 1927- 782.8'5'0924 B
Harry Warren and the Hollywood musical / by Tony Thomas ; foreword by Bing Crosby. Secaucus, N.J. : Citadel Press, [1975] 344 p. : ill. ; 31 cm. "The Harry Warren catalog": p. 331-341. [ML410.W2959T5] 74-29545 ISBN 0-8065-0468-4 : 17.95
1. Warren, Harry, 1893- 2. Moving-pictures, Musical—History and criticism. 3. Moving-picture music—Excerpts—Vocal scores with piano. 4. Music, Popular (Songs, etc.)—United States. I. Title.

THOMAS, Tony, 1927- 782.8'5'0924 B
Harry Warren and the Hollywood musical / by Tony Thomas ; foreword by Bing Crosby. Secaucus, N.J. : Citadel Press, [1975] 344 p. : ill. ; 31 cm. "The Harry Warren catalog": p. 331-341. [ML410.W2959T5] 74-29545 ISBN 0-8065-0468-4 : 17.95
1. Warren, Harry, 1893- 2. Moving-pictures, Musical—History and criticism. 3. Moving-picture music—Excerpts—Vocal scores with piano. 4. Music, Popular (Songs, etc.)—United States. I. Title. BIP

Warren, Ind. (Township)—Biog.

BRADY, Pearl (Schilling). 920.0772
History; Lowell District, Warren Township, Marion County, Indiana, 1822-1944. Indianapolis, Mail Print. Co., 1950. xi, 185 p. illus. 22 cm. [F534.W28B7] 52-33386
1. Warren, Ind. (Township)—Biog. I. Title.

Warren, Jonathan Mason, 1811-1867.

WARREN, Jonathan Mason, 1811-1867. 081 S
The Parisian education of an American surgeon : letters of Jonathan Mason Warren, 1832-1835 / with notes and introd. by Russell M. Jones. Philadelphia : American Philosophical Society, 1978. 266 p. : ill. ; 24 cm. (Memoirs of the American Philosophical Society ; v. 128 ISSN 0065-9738s) Letters to the author's father, J. C. Warren. Includes bibliographical references and index. [Q11.P612 vol. 128] [RD27.35.W37] 617'.092'4 B 78-56709 ISBN 0-87169-128-0 pbk. : 8.00
1. Warren, Jonathan Mason, 1811-1867. 2. Warren, John Collins, 1778-1856. 3. Surgeons—Massachusetts—Boston—Correspondence. 4. Surgery—France—Paris—History—19th century—Sources. I. Warren, John Collins, 1778-1856. II. Jones, Russell Moseley, 1927- III. Title. IV. Series: American Philosophical Society. Memoirs ; v. 128.

Warren, Joseph, 1741-1775.

CARY, John Henry, 1926- 923.273
Joseph Warren: physician, politician, patriot. Urbana, Univ. of Ill. Pr. [c.]1961. ix, 260p. p ix, 260p. front. por. Bibl. 61-62763 5.00
1. Warren, Joseph, 1741-1775. I. Title. BIP

FROTHINGHAM, Richard, 1812-1880. 973.3'0924
Life and times of Joseph Warren. New York, Da Capo Press, 1971. xix, 558 p. facsim., port. 24 cm. (The Era of the American Revolution) Reprint of the 1865 ed. Includes bibliographical references. [E263.M4W24 1971] 72-146148 ISBN 0-306-70133-2
1. Warren, Joseph, 1741-1775. BIP

TRUAX, Rhoda. 917'.00922 B
The doctors Warren of Boston; first family of surgery. Boston, Houghton Mifflin, 1968. xiii, 369 p. geneal. table (on lining papers) 22 cm. Bibliography: p. [355]-357. [R154.W274T7] 68-23435 7.95
1. Warren, Joseph, 1741-1775. 2. Warren family. I. Title.

Warren, Josiah, 1798-1874.

BAILIE, William. 322'.44'0924
Josiah Warren, the first American anarchist; a sociological study. Brooklyn, H. C. Roseman, 1971. xxxviii, 134 p. illus. 22 cm. Reprint of the 1906 ed. [HX843.B3 1971] 76-30668 ISBN 0-87700-024-7
1. Warren, Josiah, 1798-1874. I. Title. BIP

BAILIE, William. 335'.83'0924 B
Josiah Warren, the first American anarchist; a sociological study. New York, Arno Press, 1972 [c1906] xxxviii, 134 p. front. 23 cm. (The Right wing individualist tradition in America) [HX843.B3 1972] 78-172201 ISBN 0-405-00411-7
1. Warren, Josiah, 1798-1874. I. Title. II. Series.

Warren, Mercy (Otis) 1728-1814.

ANTHONY, Katharine 1877- 920.7
First lady of the Revolution: the life of Mercy Otis Warren. Garden City, N. Y., Doubleday, 1958. 258p. 22cm. Includes bibliography. [PS858.W8A85] 58.12030
1. Warren, Mercy (Otis) 1728-1814. I. Title.

BROWN, Alice, 1857-1948 811'.1
Mercy Warren. New York, Scribner, 1896. [Spartenburg, S.C., Reprint Co., 1968] xi, 316p. port. 22cm. (Women of colonial & Revolutionary times) Series: Massachusetts heritage series, no. 3) Mass. heritage ser., no. 3. [PS858.W8B7 1968] 67-30159 12.50
1. Warren, Mercy (Otis) 1728-1814. I. Title. II. Series. BIP

FRITZ, Jean. 973.3'092'2 B
Cast for a revolution; some American friends and enemies, 1728-1814. Boston, Houghton Mifflin, 1972. xii, 400 p. illus. 22 cm. Bibliography: p. [365]-380. [PS858.W8F7] 72-515 ISBN 0-395-13945-7 7.95
1. Warren, Mercy (Otis) 1728-1814. 2. United States—History—Revolution, 1775-1783—Biography. I. Title.

Warren, Peter, Sir, 1703-1752.

GWYN, Julian. 332 B
The enterprising admiral : the personal fortune of Admiral Sir Peter Warren / by Julian Gwyn. Montreal : McGill-Queen's University Press, 1974. xvi, 292 p., [8] leaves of plates : ill. ; 25 cm. Includes index. Bibliography: p. [261]-278. [HG172.W27G9] 74-75970 ISBN 0-7735-0170-3 : 16.00
1. Warren, Peter, Sir, 1703-1752. 2. Wealth—Great Britain—History. 3. Prize money—Great Britain—History. I. Title. Distributed by McGill Queens University Press New York. BIP

Warren, William Whipple, 1825-1853—Juvenile literature.

ANTELL, Will. 970.3 B
William Warren. Minneapolis, Dillon Pub. [1973] 56 p. illus. 23 cm. (The story of an American Indian) A biography of the Ojibway historian who was the only Indian representative elected to the Legislature of the Territory of Minnesota in 1850. [E99.C6A47] 92 72-91157 ISBN 0-87518-056-6 4.95
1. Warren, William Whipple, 1825-1853—Juvenile literature. 2. Chippewa Indians—Juvenile literature. I. Title. BIP

Warrender, Simon, 1922-

WARRENDER, Simon, 1922- 919.4'03'50924 B
Score of years. [Melbourne] Wren [1973] 255 p. illus. 22 cm. [CT2808.W37A33] 74-180020 ISBN 0-85885-101-6
1. Warrender, Simon, 1922- I. Title.

Warwick, Richard Neville, earl of, 1428-1471.

KENDALL, Paul Murray. 923.242
Warwick the kingmaker. [1st ed.] New York, Norton [1957] 408p. illus., ports., maps. geneal. table. 22cm. Bibliography: p. 373-376. Bibliographical references included in 'Notes to the text' (p. 376-394) [DA247.W25K4] 57-10000
1. Warwick, Richard Neville, earl of, 1428-1471. I. Title.

Warwick, Robert Rich, earl of, 1587-1658. T. Holland, Henry Rich, 1st earl of, 1590-1649.

BEATTY, John 0 Louis, 1922- 942.060922
Warwick and Holland; being the lives of Robertand Henry Rich. Denver, A. Swallow [c.1965] 262p. ports. 23cm. (Bks. of the Renaissance ser.) Bibl. [DA390.1.W3B4] 65-16523 6.50
1. Warwick, Robert Rich, earl of, 1587-1658. T. Holland, Henry Rich, 1st earl of, 1590-1649. I. Title.

Washburn, Israel, 1813-1883.

HUNT, Gaillard, 1862-1924, comp. 973.6'0922 B
Israel, Elihu and Cadwallader Washburn; a chapter in American biography. Freeport, N.Y., Books for Libraries Press [1971] vi, 397 p. illus. 23 cm. Reprint of the 1925 ed. [E664.W32H8 1971] 71-169765 ISBN 0-8369-5985-X
1. Washburn, Israel, 1813-1883. 2. Washburne, Elihu Benjamin, 1816-1887. 3. Washburn, Cadwallader Colden, 1818-1882.

HUNT, Gaillard, 1862-1924, comp. 973.7'0922 B
Israel, Elihu, and Cadwallader Washburn; a chapter in American biography. New York, Da Capo Press, 1969 [c1925] vi, 397 p. illus., ports. 24 cm. (The American scene: comments and commentators) (A Da Capo Press reprint series.) (A Da Capo Press reprint edition.) [E664.W32H8 1969] 71-87440
1. Washburn, Israel, 1813-1883. 2. Washburne, Elihu Benjamin, 1816-1887. 3. Washburn, Cadwallader Colden, 1818-1882.

Washburne, Elihu Benjamin, 1816-1887.

HUNT, Gaillard, 1862-1924, comp. 973.6'0922 B
Israel, Elihu and Cadwallader Washburn; a chapter in American biography. Freeport, N.Y., Books for Libraries Press [1971] vi, 397 p. illus. 23 cm. Reprint of the 1925 ed. [E664.W32H8 1971] 71-169765 ISBN 0-8369-5985-X
1. Washburn, Israel, 1813-1883. 2. Washburne, Elihu Benjamin, 1816-1887. 3. Washburn, Cadwallader Colden, 1818-1882.

HUNT, Gaillard, 1862-1924, comp. 973.7'0922 B
Israel, Elihu, and Cadwallader Washburn; a chapter in American biography. New York, Da Capo Press, 1969 [c1925] vi, 397 p. illus., ports. 24 cm. (The American scene: comments and commentators) (A Da Capo Press reprint series.) (A Da Capo Press reprint edition.) [E664.W32H8 1969] 71-87440
1. Washburn, Israel, 1813-1883. 2. Washburne, Elihu Benjamin, 1816-1887. 3. Washburn, Cadwallader Colden, 1818-1882.

Washington, Booker Taliaferro, 1859?-1915.

BONTEMPS, Arna Wendell, 1902- 378.1'11'0924 B
Young Booker; Booker T. Washington's early days, by Arna Bontemps. New York, Dodd, Mead [1972] 196 p. illus. 22 cm. Traces the events of his youth and early career that were the driving force behind Booker T. Washington's determination to help educate his people. [E185.97.W4B66] 92 72-3724 ISBN 0-396-06514-7 6.95
1. Washington, Booker Taliaferro, 1859-1915. I. Title.

DRINKER, Frederick E. 301.451'96'024
Booker T. Washington, the master mind of a child of slavery; a human interest story depicting the life achievements of a great leader of a rising race. New York, Negro Universities Press [1970] viii, 320 p. illus., ports. 23 cm. Subtitle varies. Reprint of the 1915 memorial ed. [E185.97.W17 1970] 77-100288
1. Washington, Booker Taliaferro, 1859?-1915. I. Title.

GRAHAM, Shirley. 923.773
Booker T. Washington, educator of hand, head, and heart. Front. and jacket by Donald W. Lambo. New York, Messner [1955] 192 p. illus. 22 cm. [E185.97.W226] 55-9855
1. Washington, Booker Taliaferro, 1859?-1915.

HARLAN, Louis R. 378.1'11'0924 B
Booker T. Washington : the making of a black leader, 1856-1901 / [by] Louis R. Harlan. London ; New York : Oxford University Press, 1975. [11], 379 p., [8] p. of plates : ill., ports. ; 21 cm. (A Galaxy book : 428) Includes bibliographical references and index. [E185.97.W4H37 1975] 75-329178 ISBN 0-19-501915-6 pbk. : 3.95
1. Washington, Booker Taliaferro, 1859?-1915. BIP

HAWKINS, Hugh, ed. 923.773
Booker T. Washington and his critics; the problem of Negro leadership. Boston, Heath [1962] 113 p. 24 cm. (Problems in American civilization) Includes bibliography. [E185.97.W235] 62-4235
1. Washington, Booker Taliaferro, 1859?-1915. 2. Negroes—Segregation.

MATHEWS, Basil Joseph, 1879-1951. 301.451'96'024
Booker T. Washington, educator and interracial interpreter. College Park, Md., McGrath Pub. Co. [1969, c1948] xvii, 350 p. illus., ports. 23 cm. Includes bibliographical references. [E185.97.W249 1969] 70-84104
1. Washington, Booker Taliaferro, 1859?-1915. I. Title.

SPENCER, Samuel R. 923.773
Booker T. Washington and the Negro's place in American life. [1st ed.] Boston, Little, Brown [1955] 212 p. 22 cm. (The Library of American biography) [E185.97.W272] 55-7476
1. Washington, Booker Taliaferro, 1859?-1915. 2. Negroes. BIP

STEVENSON, Augusta. 923
Booker T. Washington, ambitious boy. Illustrated by Charles V. John. [1st ed.] Indianapolis, Bobbs-Merrill [1950] 199 p. illus. 20 cm. (The Childhood of famous Americans series) [PZ7.S8467Bo] 50-14744
1. Washington, Booker Taliaferro, 1859?-1915.

STEVENSON, Augusta. 378.1'11'0924 B
Booker T. Washington, ambitious boy. Illustrated by Mel Bolden. Indianapolis, Bobbs-Merrill [1960] 192 p. illus. 20 cm. (Childhood of famous Americans) Concentrates on the boyhood of the man who started life as a slave and grew to become a great Negro educational leader and organizer of Tuskegee Institute. [PZ7.S8467Bo5] 92 AC 68
1. Washington, Booker Taliaferro, 1859?-1915. I. Bolden, Mel, illus. II. Title.

THORNBROUGH, Emma Lou, comp. 301.451'96'024
Booker T. Washington. Englewood Cliffs, N.J., Prentice-Hall [1969] vii, 184 p. 22 cm. (Great lives observed) (A Spectrum book.) "Bibliographical note": p. 178-182. [E185.97.W277] 69-15336 4.95
1. Washington, Booker Taliafero, 1859?-1915. BIP

WASHINGTON, Booker Taliaferro, 1859?-1915. 301.45'19'6073024
The Booker T. Washington papers. Louis R. Harlan, editor. Urbana, University of Illinois Press [1972- v. illus. 25 cm. Contents.Contents.—v. 1. The autobiographical writings.—v. 2. 1860-

89.—v. 3. 1889-95.—v. 4. 1895-98. Includes bibliographies. [E185.97.W274] 75-186345 ISBN 0-252-00242-3 (v. 1) 15.00 (v. 1-2) varies
1. Washington, Booker Taliaferro, 1859?-1915. 2. Negroes—History—Sources. BIP

WASHINGTON, 301.451'96'0924
Booker Taliaferro, 1859?-1915.
My larger education; being chapters from my experience. Miami, Fla., Mnemosyne Pub. Inc., 1969. viii, 313 p. illus. 23 cm. Reprint of the 1911 ed. [E185.97.W28 1969] 70-79019
1. Negroes. I. Title.

WASHINGTON, Booker 923.773
Taliaferro, 1859?-1915
Up from slavery. Introd. by Louis Lomax [New York, Dell, 1965] 224p. 17cm. (Laurel-leaf lib., 9224) [E185.97.W3163] .45 pap.,
1. Tuskegee Institute. I. Title.

WASHINGTON, Booker 923.773
Taliaferro, 1859?-1915
Up from slavery, an autobiography. New York, Bantam [1963, c.1900, 1901] 241p. 18cm. (Pathfinder Ed., HP16) .60 pap.,
1. Tuskegee Normal and Industrial Institute. I. Title.

WASHINGTON, Booker 923.773
Taliaferro, 1859?-1915.
Up from slavery; an autobiography. With illus. of the author and his environment, together with an introd. by Langston Hughes. New York, Dodd, Mead [1965] 212 p. illus., ports. 22 cm. (Great illustrated classics) [E185.97.W3164] 65-21868
1. Tuskegee Institute. I. Title.

*WASHINGTON, Booker 923.73
Taliaserro, 1859-1915
Up from slavery; an autobiography [Belmont, Mass.] Western Islands [1965, c.1900, 1901] 181p. 18cm. (Americanist lib., AL006) 1.00 pap.,
I. Title.

WEISBERGER, 378.1'11'0924 B
Bernard A., 1922-
Booker T. Washington, by Bernard A. Weisberger. New York, New American Library [1972] 142 p. 18 cm. (A Mentor book, MY1171) [E185.97.W4W45] 72-83404 1.25
1. Washington, Booker Taliaferro, 1859?-1915. BIP

WISE, William. 378.1'11'0924 B
Booker T. Washington. Illus. by Paul Frame. New York, Putnam [1968] 62 p. col. illus. 23 cm. (A see and read beginning to read biography) An easy-to-read biography of the man who was born a slave and through great effort became a renowned teacher. [E185.97.W54] 92 AC 68
1. Washington, Booker Taliaferro, 1859?-1915. I. Frame, Paul, illus. II. Title. BIP

Washington, Booker Taliaferro, 1859?-1915—Addresses, essays, lectures.

HAWKINS, Hugh, 378.1'11'0924 B
ed.
Booker T. Washington and his critics : Black leadership in crisis / edited and with an introd. by Hugh Hawkins. 2d ed. Lexington, Mass. : Heath, [1974] xvi, 208 p. : ports. ; 21 cm. (Problems in American civilization) Bibliography: p. 204-208. [E185.97.W4H38 1974] 74-4727 ISBN 0-669-87049-8 pbk. : 2.95
1. Washington, Booker Taliaferro, 1859?-1915—Addresses, essays, lectures. 2. Du Bois, William Edward Burghardt, 1868-1963—Addresses, essays, lectures. 3. Negroes—Segregation—Addresses, essays, lectures. 4. United States—Race question—Addresses, essays, lectures. I. Title. II. Series: Problems in American civilization.

Washington, Booker Taliaferro, 1859-1915—Juvenile literature.

STERLING, Dorothy, 1913- 920.073
Lift every voice; the lives of Booker T. Washington, W. E. B. Du Bois, Mary Church Terrell, and James Weldon Johnson [by] Dorothy Sterling and Benjamin Quarles. Illustrated by Ernest Crichlow. [1st ed.] Garden City, N.Y., Doubleday, 1965. 116 p. illus., ports. 22 cm. (Zenith books) [E185.96.S77] 65-17237
1. Washington, Booker Taliaferro, 1859-1915—Juvenile literature. 2. Du Bois, William Edward Burghardt, 1868-1963—Juvenile literature. 3. Terrell, Mary (Church) 1863-1954—Juvenile literature. 4. Johnson, James Weldon, 1871-1938—Juvenile literature. I. Quarles, Benjamin, joint author. II. Title.

STERLING, Dorothy, 1913- 920.073
Lift every voice; the lives of Booker T. Washington, W. E. B. Du Bois, Mary Church Terrell, and James Weldon Johnson [by] Dorothy Sterling and Benjamin Quarles. Illustrated by Ernest Crichlow. [1st ed.] Garden City, N.Y., Doubleday, 1965. 116 p. illus., ports. 22 cm. (Zenith books) [E185.96.S77] 65-17237
1. Washington, Booker Taliaferro, 1859-1915—Juvenile literature. 2. Du Bois, William Edward Burghardt, 1868-1963—Juvenile literature. 3. Terrell, Mary (Church) 1863-1954—Juvenile literature. 4. Johnson, James Weldon, 1871-1938—Juvenile literature. I. Quarles, Benjamin, joint author. II. Title.

Washington, D.C.—Biography.

LEAMER, Laurence. 920'.0753
Playing for keeps : in Washington / by Laurence Leamer ; photographs by Lynne Bundesen. New York : Dial Press, 1977. 417 p., [8] leaves of plates : ill. ; 24 cm. Bibliography: p. 409-417. [F200.2.L4] 77-72675 ISBN 0-8037-7064-2 : 10.00
1. Washington, D.C.—Biography. 2. United States—Politics and government—1945- I. Title.

PAST, present : 920'.0753
recording life stories of older people / [edited by] Sara Jenkins. Washington : St. Alban's Parish : may be ordered from the Publications Dept., National Council on Aging, c1978. 149 p. : ill. ; 21 cm. Bibliography: p. 147. [F193.P37] 78-61372 4.95
1. Washington, D.C.—Biography. 2. Washington, D.C.—Social life and customs. 3. Oral history. I. Jenkins, Sara. II. Washington, D.C. St. Albans Parish.

Washington, D.C.—Social life and customs.

CLAY-CLOPTON, 917.53'03'2
Virginia, 1825-1915.
A belle of the fifties; memoirs of Mrs. Clay of Alabama, covering social and political life in Washington and the South, 1853-1866. Put into narrative form by Ada Sterling. New York, Da Capo Press, 1969. xxii, 386 p. ports. 24 cm. (The American scene) (A Da Capo Press reprint series.) Reprint of the 1905 ed. [F213.C63 1969] 79-84187
1. Washington, D.C.—Social life and customs. 2. United States—History—Civil War, 1861-1865—Personal narratives—Confederate side. I. Sterling, Ada, d. 1939. ed. II. Title.

MADISON, Dolley 973.5'1'0924
(Payne) Todd, 1768-1849.
Memoirs and letters of Dolly Madison, wife of James Madison, President of the United States. Edited by her grand-niece. Port Washington, N.Y., Kennikat Press [1971] 210 p. 18 cm. (Kennikat Press scholarly reprints. Series in American history and culture in the nineteenth century.) First published in 1886. [E342.1.M18 1971] 70-137922
1. Washington, D.C.—Social life and customs. I. Cutts, Lucia Beverly, 1851- ed.

Washington, D.C. White House.

FIELDS, Alonzo 923.173
My 21 years in the White House. Greenwich, Conn. Fawcett [1961, c.1960] 144p. (Crest bk., d492) .50 pap.,
1. Washington, D.C. White House. 2. Washington, D.C.—Soc. life & cust. 3. Presidents—U.S.—Biog. 4. Presidents—U. S.—Wives. 5. Visits of state—U.S. I. Title.

FIELDS, Alonzo. 923.173
My 21 years in the White House. New York, Coward-McCann [1961] 223 p. 22 cm. [F204.W5F5] 61-15068
1. Washington, D. C. White House. 2. Washington, D. C.—Social life and customs. 3. Presidents—U.S.—Biography. 4. Presidents—U.S.—Wives. 5. Visits of state—U.S. I. Title.

FURMAN, Bess, 1894- 923.173
White House profile; a social history of the White House, its occupants and its festivities. [1st ed.] Indianapolis, Bobbs-Merrill '[1951] 368 p. illus. 23 cm. Bibliography: p. 345-356. [F204.W5F8] 51-14153
1. Washington, D. C. White House. 2. Presidents—U. S.—Biog. 3. Presidents—U. S.—Wives. 4. Washington, D. C.—Soc. life & cust. I. Title.

LEISH, Kenneth W. 917.53
The White House, by Kenneth W. Leish and the editors of the Newsweek Book Division. New York, Newsweek [1972] 170, [1] p. illus. (part col.) 30 cm. (Wonders of man) Bibliography: p. [171] [F204.W5L53] 72-178706 ISBN 0-88225-020-5
1. Washington, D.C. White House. 2. Presidents—United States—Biography. 3. Washington, D.C.—Social life and customs. I. Newsweek, inc. Book Division. II. Title. BIP

Washington, D.C. White House—Juvenile literature.

BOURNE, Miriam Anne. 973'.0992
White House children / by Miriam Anne Bourne ; illustrated by Gloria Kamen. New York : Random House, [1979] p. cm. (Step-up books) Describes the lives of the children and grandchildren of Presidents Washington, Lincoln, Theodore Roosevelt, Kennedy, and Carter. [E176.45.B68] 3.95 ISBN 0-394-94094-6 lib.bdg. : 3.99
1. Washington, D.C. White House—Juvenile literature. 2. Presidents—United States—Children—Biography—Juvenile literature. I. Kamen, Gloria. II. Title. BIP

CAVANAH, Frances. 923
They lived in the White House. With illus. by Clifford Schule. [2d ed.] Philadelphia, Macrae Smith Co. [1961] 197p. illus. 21cm. [F204.W5C33 1961] 61-66589
1. Washington, D. C. White House—Juvenile literature. 2. Presidents—U. S.—Children—Juvenile literature. I. Title.

CAVANAH, Frances. 923.173
They lived in the White House. With illus. by Clifford Schule. Philadelphia, Macrae Smith [1959] 191p. illus. 21cm. [F204.W5C33] 59-13259
1. Washington, D. C. White House—Juvenile literature. 2. Children—Anecdotes and sayings. 3. Presidents— U. S.—Children. I. Title.

LAWSON, Don 920
Young people in the White House. Illustrated by Elizabeth Donald. London, New York, Abelard- Schuman [1961] 160p. illus. 21cm. [F204.W5L38] 61-15715
1. Washington, D. C. White House — Juvenile literature. 2. Presidents—U. S.—Children—Juvenile literature. I. Title.

LAWSON, Don. 920.0753
Young people in the White House. Illustrated by Elizabeth Donald. Rev. ed. London, New York, Abelard-Schuman [1970] 176 p. illus. 21 cm. Bibliography: p. [169]-170. Anecdotes about sons, daughters, and other children related to Presidents, from John Adams to Richard Nixon, who spent time in the White House. [F204.W5L38 1970] 74-110580 ISBN 0-200-71685-9 4.50
1. Washington, D.C. White House—Juvenile literature. 2. Presidents—U.S.—Children—Juvenile literature. I. Donald, Elizabeth, illus. II. Title.

WILLIAMSON, Mary Lynn 923.173
(Harrison) 1850-
George Washington, soldier and statesman. Illus. by Stan Lilstrom. Chicago, Beckley-Cardy [1951] 191 p. illus.(part col.) map. 21 cm. A revision of the author's life of Washington, published in 1911. [E312.66.W57] 51-11303
1. Washington, George, Pres. U.S.—Juvenile literature. I. Title.

Washington family.

THANE, Elswyth, 973.4'1'0924
1900-
Mount Vernon family. New York, Crowell-Collier Press [1968] 152 p. illus., geneal. tables, ports. 21 cm. Bibliography: p. [148] Describes the lives and relationships of the various young people living in the George Washington household. [E312.19.T45] 920 68-23066
1. Washington family. I. Title. BIP

Washington, George, Pres. U.S., 1732-1799.

AULAIRE, Ingri (Mortenson) v. 12
d', 1904-
George Washington, by Ingri & Edgar Parin d'Aulaire. Garden City, N.Y., Doubleday [196-?] c1936. 60 p. illus. (part col.) 32 cm. 68-38352
1. Washington, George, Pres. U.S., 1732-1799. I. Aulaire, Edgar Parin d', 1898- joint author. II. Title.

BELLAMY, Francis Rufus, 923.173
1886-
The private life of George Washington. New York, Crowell, 1951. v, 409 p. 24 cm. Bibliography: p. 387-401. [E312.B45] 51-13923
1. Washington, George, Pres. U.S., 1732-1799. I. Title.

BORDEN, Morton, comp. 973.2'0924
George Washington. Englewood Cliffs, N.J., Prentice-Hall [1969] vi, 154 p. 21 cm. (Great lives observed) (A Spectrum book.) Bibliographical footnotes. [E312.B6] 74-90974 4.95
1. Washington, George, Pres. U.S., 1732-1799. I. Title.

CORBIN, John, 973.4'1'0924 B
1870-1959.
The unknown Washington; biographic origins of the Republic. Freeport, N.Y., Books for Libraries Press [1972] x, 454 p. 22 cm. Reprint of the 1930 ed. Bibliography: p. 431-439. [E312.C76 1972] 72-1273 ISBN 0-8369-6823-9 15.50
1. Washington, George, Pres. U.S., 1732-1799. 2. United States—Constitutional history. I. Title.

CUNLIFFE, Marcus. 923.173
George Washington, man and monument. [1st ed.] Boston, Little, Brown [1958] 234 p. illus. 22 cm. Includes bibliography. [E312.C88] 58-7859
1. Washington, George, Pres, U.S., 1732-1799.

CUNLIFFE, Marcus 923.173
[Falkner]
George Washington, man and monument. New York New American Library 1960, c.1958 192p. (bibl. p.179-184) 19cm. (Mentor bk. MD284) .50 pap.,
1. Washington, George, Pres. U.S., 1732-1799 I. Title.

DECATUR, Stephen, 973.4'1'0924 B
1886-
Private affairs of George Washington, from the records and accounts of Tobias Lear, Esquire, his secretary. New York, Da Capo Press, 1969 [c1933] xv, 356 p. illus. 24 cm. (The American scene: comments and commentators) Reprint of the ed. published by Hougton, Mifflin, Boston. Bibliography: p. 335-[337] [E312.29.D32 1969] 77-86596
1. Washington, George, Pres. U.S., 1732-1799. I. Lear, Tobias, 1762-1816. II. Title.

ELIOT, Charles 973'.0992 B
William, 1834-1926.
Four American leaders. [Folcroft, Pa.] Folcroft Library Editions, 1973. p. Reprint of the 1907 ed. published by P. Green, London. Contents.Contents.—Franklin.—Washington.—Channing.—Emerson. [E176.E42 1973] 73-14550 ISBN 0-8414-3916-8 (lib. bdg.)
1. Franklin, Benjamin, 1706-1790. 2. Washington, George, Pres. U.S., 1732-1799. 3. Channing, William Ellery, 1780-1842. 4. Emerson, Ralph Waldo, 1803-1882. I. Title. BIP

EMERY, Noemi, 973.4'1'0924 B
1938-
Washington : a biography / Noemie Emery. New York : Putnam, c1976. 432 p. ; 24 cm. Includes index. Bibliography: p. 415-421. [E312.E43 1976] 76-6529 ISBN 0-399-11617-6 : 12.95
1. Washington, George, Pres. U.S., 1732-1799. BIP

FITZPATRICK, John 973.4'1'0924 B
Clement, 1876-1940.
George Washington himself : a common-sense biography written from his manuscripts / by John C. Fitzpatrick. Westport, Conn. : Greenwood Press, 1975, c1933. p. cm. Reprint of the ed. published by Bobbs-Merrill, Indianapolis. Includes bibliographical references and index. [E312.F52 1975] 75-18398 ISBN 0-8371-8338-3 lib.bdg. : 23.75
1. Washington, George, Pres. U.S., 1732-1799. I. Title.

FLEMING, Thomas J. 973.4'1'0924 B
First in their hearts; a biography of George Washington [by] Thomas J. Fleming. Illustrated with photos. and engravings. [1st ed.] New York, W. W. Norton [1968] 136 p. illus., facsims., map, ports. 24 cm. Bibliography: p. 132-133. A biography of the surveyor, militia major, and aide to the British General Braddock, who became leader of the American forces during the Revolution and first President of the new nation. [E312.F55] 92 AC 68
1. Washington, George, Pres. U.S., 1732-1799. I. Title.

FLEXNER, James Thomas, 973.20924
1908-
George Washington: the forge of experience, 1732-1775. [1st ed.] Boston, Little [c.1965] x, 390p. illus., facsim., map (on lining papers) ports. 25cm. Bibl. [E312.2.F6] 65-21361 7.95
1. Washington, George, Pres. U. S., 1732-1799. I. Title.

FLEXNER, James 973.20924 B
Thomas, 1908-
George Washington: athe forge of experience, 1732-1775. [1st ed.] Boston, Little, Brown [1965] x, 390 p. illus., facsim., map (on lining papers) ports. 25 cm. ([His George Washington, v. 1]) "Source references": p. 361-377. [E312.2.F6] 65-21361
1. Washington, George, Pres. U.S., 1732-1799. I. Title.

FLEXNER, James 973.4'3'0924 B
Thomas, 1908-
George Washington: anguish and farewell (1793-1799) [1st ed.] Boston, Little, Brown [1972] xii, 554 p. illus. 25 cm. (His George Washington, v. 4) Bibliography: p. 509-516. [E312.29.F56] 72-6875 ISBN 0-316-28602-8 15.00
1. Washington, George, Pres. U.S., 1732-1799. I. Title.

FLEXNER, James 973.4'1'0924 B
Thomas, 1908-
Washington, the indispensable man. [1st ed.] Boston, Little, Brown [1974] xvii, 423 p. illus. 24 cm. Bibliography: p. 407-410. [E312.F556] 74-7235 ISBN 0-316-28605-2
1. Washington, George, Pres. U.S., 1732-1799. I. Title. BIP

FORD, Paul 973.4'1'0924 B
Leicester, 1865-1902.
The true George Washington. Freeport, N.Y., Books for Libraries Press [1971] 319 p. illus., facsims., ports. 23 cm. Reprint of the 1896 ed. [E312.F719 1971] 70-160973 ISBN 0-8369-5841-1
1. Washington, George, Pres. U.S., 1732-1799. BIP

FORD, Paul Leicester, 792'.0973
1865-1902.
Washington and the theatre. New York, B. Franklin [1970] 68 p. illus., facsims. 19 cm. (Burt Franklin research & source works series, 573. Theatre & drama series, 12) Reprint of the 1899 ed. Bound with Dunlap, William. Darby's return. New York, 1789. Includes bibliographical references. [E312.17.F67 1970] 77-130099 ISBN 0-8337-1204-7
1. Washington, George, Pres. U.S., 1732-1799. 2. Theater—U.S.—History. I. Title. BIP

FREEMAN, Douglas 923.173
Southall, 1886-1953.
George Washington, a biography. New York, Scribner, 1948-54. 6v. ports., maps, facsims. 24cm. Contents.v. 1-2. Young Washington.--v. 3. Pianter and patriot.--v. 4. Leader of the Revolution.--v. 5. Victory with the help of France--v. 6. Patriot and President. Includes bibliographies. [E312.F82] 48-8880
1. Washington, George, Pres. U. S., 1732-1799. I. Title. BIP

FREEMAN, Douglas 973.4'1'0924 B
Southall, 1886-1953.
George Washington, a biography / by Douglas Southall Freeman. Clifton, N.J. : A. M. Kelley, 1975- c1948- p. cm. (Scribner reprint editions) Reprint of the 1st ed. published by Scribner, New York. Contents.Contents.— —v. 2. Young Washington. —v. 6. Patriot and President. Includes bibliographies and indexes. [E312.F82 1975] 75-4504 ISBN 0-678-02828-1 (v. 2) ISBN 0-678-02834-6(7 vol. set) lib.bdg. : 150.00
1. Washington, George, Pres. U.S., 1732-1799. I. Title.

FREEMAN, Douglas 973.4'1'0924 B
Southall, 1886-1953.
Washington. New York, Scribner [1968] xvi, 780 p. facsims., maps, ports. 24 cm. "An abridgment in one volume, by Richard Harwell, of the seven-volume George Washington." [E312.F83] 68-17342 14.95
1. Washington, George, Pres. U.S., 1732-1799. I. Harwell, Richard Barksdale, ed.

FREEMAN, Douglas 975.5020924
Southall, 1886-1953.
Young Washington; a selection from George Washington, a biography. New York, Scribner [1966] xxviii, 298 p. illus., facsims., fold. map, ports. 24 cm. Includes bibliographical references. [E312.2.F7] 66-18541
1. Washington, George, Pres. U.S., 1732-1799. 2. Virginia—Social life and customs—Colonial period, ca. 1600-1775. I. Freeman, Douglas Southall, 1886-1953. George Washington. II. Title.

GLASS, Francis, 973.4'1'0924 B
1790-1824.
A composite translation of A life of George Washington in Latin prose / by Francis Glass ; edited with foreword and index by John Francis Latimer. [1st ed.] Washington : George Washington University, [1976] xxv, 125 p. ; 21 cm. Includes index. [E312.G5413 1976] 76-53286
1. Washington, George, Pres. U.S., 1732-1799. 2. Presidents—United States—Biography. I. Latimer, John Francis, 1903- II. Title.

GRAFF, Stewart. v. 12
George Washington, father of freedom. Illustrated by Robert Doremus. [New York, Dell Pub. Co., 1966, c1960] 80 p. illus. 20 cm. (A Discovery book) "A Dell Yearling book, 2858." 68-41756
1. Washington, George, Pres. U. S., 1732-1799. I. Title. BIP

*GRAFF, Stewart 92
George Washington: father of freedom. Illus. by Robert Doremus [New York, Dell, 1966, c.1960] 80p. illus. 20cm. (Discovery bk., Yearling bk., 2858) .50 pap.,
1. Washington, George, Pres., U.S., 1732-1799—Juvenile literature. I. Title.

GRIGGS, Edward Howard, 1868- 973
1951.
American statesmen; an interpretation of our history and heritage. Freeport, N.Y., Books for Libraries Press [1970] 364 p. 24 cm. (Essay index reprint series) Reprint of the 1927 ed. Contents.Contents.—Washington: the first American.—Franklin: the practical American.—Jefferson: the democratic American.—Hamilton and the making of our government.—Lee: the American warrior.—Lincoln: the prophetic American.—Bibliography: p. 348-355. [E176.G852 1970] 76-121474
1. Washington, George, Pres. U.S., 1732-1799. 2. Franklin, Benjamin, 1706-1790. 3. Jefferson, Thomas, Pres. U.S., 1743-1826. 4. Hamilton, Alexander, 1757-1804. 5. Lee, Robert Edward, 1807-1870. 6. Lincoln, Abraham, Pres. U.S., 1809-1865. 7. Statesmen, American. I. Title. BIP

IRVING, 973.4'1'0924 B
Washington, 1783-1859.
George Washington : a biography / by Washington Irving ; abridged and edited with an introd. by Charles Neider. 1st ed. Garden City, N.Y. : Doubleday, 1976. xlvii, 740 p., [4] leaves of plates : ill. ; 22 cm. Abridged ed. of the author's The life of George Washington originally published in 5 v. in 1856-1859. Includes index. [E312.I734 1976] 74-27449 ISBN 0-385-09929-0 : 9.95
1. Washington, George, Pres. U.S., 1732-1799. I. Neider, Charles, 1915-

IRVING, 973.4'1'0924 B
Washington, 1783-1859.
Life of George Washington. New York, Putnam. [New York, AMS Press, 1973] 5 v. illus. 19 cm. (The works of Washington Irving, v. 22-26) At head of title: Hudson edition. Reprint of the 1890 ed. [E312.I77 1973] 73-8731 20.00 ea.
1. Washington, George, Pres. U.S., 1732-1799. I. Title. BIP

IRVING, 973.4'1'0924 B
Washington, 1783-1859.
Life of George Washington / by Washington Irving ; edited and abridged by Jess Stein ; with an introd. by Richard B. Morris. Tarrytown, N.Y. : Sleepy Hollow Restorations, 1975. xxi, 721 p., [28] leaves of plates : ill. ; 25 cm. An abridgment of the 1855-59 ed. published by Putnam, New York. Includes index. [E312.I77 1975] 74-7845 ISBN 0-912882-18-2 : 19.95. ISBN 0-912882-19-0 pbk.
1. Washington, George, Pres. U.S., 1732-1799. I. Stein, Jess M. II. Title.

ISELY, Bliss, 1881- 923.173
The horseman of the Shenandoah; a biographical account of the early days of George Washington. Milwaukee, Bruce Pub. Co. [1962] 232 p. illus. 23 cm. [E312.2.I8] 62-15224
1. Washington, George, Pres. U.S., 1732-1799. I. Title.

JONES, Robert 973.4'1'0924 B
Francis, 1935-
George Washington / by Robert F. Jones. Boston : Twayne Publishers, 1979. p. cm. (Twayne's world leaders series ; TWLS 80) Includes index. Bibliography: p. [E312.J79] 79-16615 ISBN 0-8057-7726-1 : 11.95
1. Washington, George, Pres. U.S., 1732-1799. 2. Presidents—United States—Biography.

KETCHUM, Richard 973.4'1'0924 B
M., 1922-
The world of George Washington, by Richard M. Ketchum. New York, American Heritage Pub. Co.; book trade distribution by McGraw-Hill [1974] 275 p. illus. 35 cm. Issued in a case. [E312.K47 1974] 74-8020 ISBN 0-07-034409-4 50.00
1. Washington, George, Pres. U.S., 1732-1799. I. Title. BIP

KINNAIRD, Clark, 973.4'1'0924 (B)
1901-
George Washington, the pictorial biography. [1st ed.] New York, Hastings House [1967] vi, 265 p. illus., facsims., maps, plans, ports. 30 cm. Bibliography: p. 255-256. [E312.K56] 67-66398
1. Washington, George, Pres. U. S., 1732-1799. I. Title.

KINNAIRD, Clark, 973.4'1'0924 B
1901-
George Washington, the pictorial biography. [1st ed.] New York, Hastings House [1967] vi, 265 p. illus., facsims., maps, plans, ports. 30 cm. Bibliography: p. 255-256. [E312.K56] 67-66398
1. Washington, George, Pres. U.S., 1732-1799.

KNOLLENBERG, Bernhard, 923.173
1892-
George Washington, the Virginia period, 1732-1775. Durham, N.C., Duke Univ. Pr. [c.]1964. x, 238p. 23cm. Bibl. [E312.2.K56] 64-24989 4.50
1. Washington, George, Pres. U.S., 1732-1799. I. Title. BIP

KNOLLENBERG, Bernhard, 923.173
1892-1973.
George Washington, the Virginia period, 1732-1775. Durham, N. C., Duke University Press, 1964. x, 238 p. 23 cm. Bibliography: p. [197]-210. [E312.2.K56] 64-24989
1. Washington, George, Pres. U.S., 1732-1799. I. Title.

LARNED, Josephus 153.9'8'0922 B
Nelson, 1836-1913.
A study of greatness in men. Freeport, N.Y., Books for Libraries Press [1972] 303 p. 23 cm. (Essay index reprint series) Reprint of the 1911 ed. Contents.Contents.—What goes into the making of a great man?—Napoleon: a prodigy, without greatness.—Cromwell: imperfect in greatness.—Washington: impressive in greatness.—Lincoln: simplest in greatness. [BF412.L4 1972] 73-156677 ISBN 0-8369-2557-2
1. Napoleon I, Emperor of the French, 1769-1821. 2. Cromwell, Oliver, 1599-1658. 3. Washington, George, Pres. U.S., 1732-1799. 4. Lincoln, Abraham, Pres. U.S., 1809-1865—Addresses, essays, lectures. 5. Genius. I. Title. BIP

LITTLE, Shelby. v. 12
George Washington, [by] Shelby Little. New York, Capricorn Books, 1962. 489 p. 21 cm. Bibliography: p. 465-481. 66-35304
1. Washington, George, Pres. U.S., 1782-1799 I. Title.

LODGE, Henry 973.4'1'0924 B
Cabot, 1850-1924.
George Washington. Boston, Houghton, Mifflin. [New York, AMS Press, 1972] 2 v. illus. 18 cm. (American statesmen, v. 4-5) Reprint of the 1898 ed. [E312.L82 1972] 74-128969 ISBN 0-404-50890-1
1. Washington, George, Pres. U.S., 1732-1799. I. Title. II. Series.

LODGE, Henry 973.4'1'0924 B
Cabot, 1850-1924.
George Washington. New Rochelle, N.Y., Arlington House [1970] 349, 427 p. illus., ports. 21 cm. (Giants of America. The Founding Fathers) Originally published in 1889. Includes bibliographical references. [E312.L82 1970] 77-111220 ISBN 0-87000-092-6
1. Washington, George, Pres. U.S., 1732-1799.

LOWITZ, Sadyebeth. 973.4'1'0924 B
General George the Great; a really truly story, by Sadyebeth & Anson Lowitz. [Rev. ed.] Minneapolis, Lerner Publications Co. [1967, c1932] [58] p. illus. 19 x 22 cm. A brief biography of George Washington emphasizing his rise to Commander of the Colonial Troops and President of the United States. [E312.66] 92 AC 68
1. Washington, George, Pres. U.S., 1732-1799. I. Lowitz, Anson, joint author. II. Title.

MCDONALD, Forrest. 973.4'1'0924 B
The Presidency of George Washington. Lawrence, University Press of Kansas [1974] xi, 210 p. port. 23 cm. (American Presidency series) Bibliography: p. 187-199. [E311.M12] 73-11344 ISBN 0-7006-0110-4
1. Washington, George, Pres. U.S., 1732-1799. 2. United States—Politics and government—1789-1797. I. Title. II. Series. BIP

MCDONALD, Forrest. 973.4'1'0924 B
The Presidency of George Washington / by Forrest McDonald. New York : Norton, 1975, c1974. vii, 210 p. ; 20 cm. (The Norton library) Reprint of the ed. published by the University Press of Kansas, Lawrence, in the American Presidency series. Includes index. Bibliography: p. 193-199. [E311.M12

Eaton, Margaret L. (O'Neale) Timberlake, 1799(?)-1879. I. Title.

THANE, Elswyth 920.7
Washington's lady. New York, Dodd, Mead, 1960 [c.1954-1960] xiv, 368p. (4p. bibl note) illus. (col. front.) 22cm. 59-14718 5.00
1. Washington, Martha (Dandridge) Custis, 1731-1802- I. Title.

THANE, Elswyth, 1900- 920.7
Washington's lady. New York, Dodd, Mead, 1960. 368 p. illus. 22 cm. Includes bibliography. [E312.19.W95T48] 59-14718
1. Washington, Martha (Dandridge) Custis, 1731-1802. I. Title. BIP

THANE, Elswyth, 1900- 973.4'1'0924 B
Washington's lady / Elswyth Thane. Mettituck, N.Y. : Aeonian Press, [1976] c1960. p. cm. Reprint of the ed. published by Dodd, Mead, New York. Includes index. Bibliography: p. [E312.19.W95T48 1976] 76-46550 ISBN 0-88411-957-2 lib.bdg. : 6.95
1. Washington, Martha Dandridge Custis, 1731-1802. 2. Presidents—United States—Wives—Biography. I. Title.

WHARTON, Anne Hollingsworth, 1845-1928. 973.4'1'0924 (B)
Martha Washington. [Spartanburg, S. C., Reprint Co., 1967] xiv, 306 p. port. 22 cm. (Women of colonial and revolutionary times) Series: Virginia heritage series, no. 4) Virginia heritage series, no. 4. Title page includes original imprint: New York, Scribner, 1897. Bibliography: p. ix-x. [E312.19.W95W5 1967] 67-30158
1. Washington, Martha (Dandridge) Custis, 1731-1802. I. Title. II. Series.

Washington, Martha Dandridge Custis, 1731-1802—Juvenile literature.

ANDERSON, LaVere. 973.4'1'0924 B
Martha Washington: First Lady of the Land. Illustrated by Cary. Champaign, Ill., Garrard Pub. Co. [1973] 80 p. col. illus. 23 cm. (A Discovery book) An essay-to-read account of the public and private life of the Nation's first First Lady. [E312.19.A52] 92 72-5884 2.59
1. Washington, Martha (Dandridge) Custis, 1731-1802—Juvenile literature. I. Cary, Louis F., 1915- illus. II. Title.

WAYNE, Bennett. 973'.0992 B
Women in the White House / four first ladies / edited, with commentary by Bennett Wayne. Champaign, Ill. : Garrard Pub. Co., c1976. 168 p. : ill. ; 23 cm. (A Target book) Includes indexes. Brief biographies of Martha Washington, Abigail Adams, Dolly Madison, and Mary Lincoln. [E176.2.W38] 920 75-20388 ISBN 0-8116-4915-6 : 4.48
1. Washington, Martha Dandridge Custis, 1731-1802—Juvenile literature. 2. Adams, Abigail Smith, 1744-1818—Juvenile literature. 3. Madison, Dolley (Payne) Todd, 1768-1849—Juvenile literature. 4. Lincoln, Mary Todd, 1818-1882—Juvenile literature. I. Title. BIP

Washington, Mary (Ball) 1708-1789.

CONKLING, Margaret Cockburn, 1814-1890. 320.1'58
Memoirs of the mother and wife of Washington. New ed., rev. and enl. New York, Miller, Orton, 1857. 248p. port. 19cm. [E312.19.C76] 15-27859
1. Washington, Mary (Ball) 1708-1789. I. Washington, Martha (Dandridge) Custis, 1731-1802. II. Title.

DESMOND, Alice (Curtis) 1897- 920.7
George Washington's mother. Illus. with photos. Drawings, maps by the author. New York, Dodd [c.]1961. 235p. 61-10360 3.50
1. Washington, Mary (Ball) 1708-1789. I. Title.

Washington (State)—Historic houses, etc.

MCDONALD, Lucile Saunders, 1898- 979.7
Where the Washingtonians lived; interesting early homes and the people who built and lived in them. Photos. by Werner Lenggenhager. Text by Lucile McDonald. [1st ed.] Seattle, Superior Pub. Co. [1969] 224 p. illus. 28 cm. [F892.M3] 69-19754 12.95
1. Washington (State)—Historic houses, etc. 2. Washington (State)—Biography. I. Lenggenhager, Werner, illus. II. Title.

Wasson, Arthur Lee, 1869-

RICHARDSON, Rupert Norval, 1891- 926.36
Adventuring with a purpose; life story of Arthur Lee Wasson. San Antonio, Naylor Co. [1951] 114 p. illus. 22 cm. [CT275.W318R5] 51-12314
1. Wasson, Arthur Lee, 1869- I. Title.

Watanabe, Kiyoshi, 1890?-

NOLAN, Liam. 940.5472520924
Small man of Nanataki; the true story of a Japanese who risked his life to provide comfort for his enemies. Postscript by Sir Selwyn Selwyn-Clarke. New York : Dutton [c.]1966. ix, 161p. port. 22 cm. [CT1838.W33N6] 66-13656 3.95
1. Watanabe, Kiyoshi, 1890?- 2. World War, 1939-1945—Prisoners and prisons, Japanese. I. Title.

Watchorn, Robert,

WATCHORN, Robert, 1858-1944. 923.573
Autobiography. Edited by Herbert Faulkner West. Oklahoma City, Robert Watchorn Charities, 1958 [i.e. 1959] 218 p. illus. 24 cm. [JV6455.W43] 59-2769
I. Title.

Water-color painting, English—England—Scarborough.

BULLAMORE, Colin P. 759.28'47 B
Scarborough and Whitby watercolourists / by Colin P. Bullamore. [Whitby] : The author, 1976. 47 p., [8] p. of plates : ill., ports. ; 22 cm. Bibliography: p. 46-47. [ND1931.S33B84] 77-376062 ISBN 0-9504109-1-8
1. Water-color painting, English—England—Scarborough. 2. Water-color painting, English England—Whitby. 3. Scarborough, Eng. in art. 4. Whitby, Eng. in art. 5. Water-colorists—England—Biography. I. Title.

Water-colorists—Great Britain—Biography.

MALLALIEU, Huon. 759.941 B
The dictionary of British water-colour artists up to 1920 / H. L. Mallalieu. Woodbridge [Eng.] : Antique Collectors' Club, c1976. 298 p. ; 29 cm. [ND1928.M27] 77-353075 ISBN 0-902028-48-0 : £15.00
1. Water-colorists—Great Britain—Biography. I. Antique Collector's Club. II. Title. III. Title: British watercolour artists.

Waterbury, Ruth

WATERBURY, Ruth 927.92
Richard Burton. New York, Pyramid [c.1965] 171p. illus., ports. 18cm. [PN2598.B795W3] 65-2089 .60 pap.,
I. Title.

Waterfield, Lina (Duff-Gordon)

WATERFIELD, Lina (Duff-Gordon) 1874- 920.7
Castle in Italy; an autobiography. New York, Crowell [1962, c.1962] 277p. illus. 22cm. 62-18236 6.95
I. Title.

Waters, Ethel, 1900-1977.

DEKORTE, Juliann. 783.7'092'4 B
Finally home / by Juliann DeKorte. Old Tappan, N.J. : F. H. Revell Co., c1978. 128 p., [9] leaves of plates : ill. ; 22 cm. At head of title: Ethel Waters. [ML420.W24D4] 78-5697 ISBN 0-8007-0934-9 : 5.95
1. Waters, Ethel, 1900-1977. 2. Singers—United States—Biography. I. Title. BIP

WATERS, Ethel, 1900- v. 12
His eye is on the sparrow; an autobiography by Ethel Waters with Charles Samuels. New York, Bantam Books [1952; reprinted 1959] 278 p. 18 cm. (Bantam F 1976)
1. Musicians — Correspondence, reminiscences, etc. 2. Jazz music. I. Title.

WATERS, Ethel, 1900- 927.8
His eye is on the sparrow; an autobiography by Ethel Waters with Charles Samuels. New York, Pyramid [1967, c.1951] 278p. 18cm. (T-1613) [ML420.W24A3] .75 pap.,
1. Musicians—Correspondence, reminiscence etc. 2. Jazz music I. Title.

WATERS, Ethel, 1900- 927.8
His eye is on the sparrow; an autobiography by Ethel Waters with Charles Samuels. [1st ed.] Garden City, N.Y., Doubleday, 1951. 278 p. illus. 22 cm. [ML420.W24A3] 51-9726
1. Musicians—Correspondence, reminiscences, etc. 2. Jazz music. I. Title. BIP

WATERS, Ethel, 1900-1977. 783.7'092'4 B
His eye is on the sparrow : an autobiography / by Ethel Waters with Charles Samuels. Westport, Conn. : Greenwood Press, 1978, c1951. p. cm. Reprint of the ed. published by Doubleday, Garden City, N.Y. [ML420.W24A3 1978] 77-27496 lib.bdg. : 17.50
1. Waters, Ethel, 1900- 2. Singers—United States—Biography. I. Samuels, Charles. II. Title. BIP

Waters, Lance, 1895-

WATERS, Lance, 1895- 630'.92'4 B
Mostly a farmer : eighty years of living / by Lance Waters. Whatamongo Bay : Cape Catley, 1976. 193 p. : maps (on lining papers) ; 22 cm. [S417.W32A35] 77-375714 ISBN 0-908561-01-6 ; 8.75
1. Waters, Lance, 1895- 2. Farmers—New Zealand—Marlborough (Provincial District)—Biography. 3. Marlborough, N.Z. (Provincial District)—Biography. 4. Murchison, N.Z.—Biography. I. Title.

Waters, Wilburn, 1812-1879.

COALE, Charles B v. 12
The life and adventures of Wilburn Waters, the famous hunter and trapper of White Top Mountain, by Charles B. Coal printed in Richmond, Virginia 1878, reprinted by Rev. M. D. Hart, 1960. West Jefferson, N.C., 1960. 57 p. 23 cm. 64-61923
1. Waters, Wilburn, 1812-1879. 2. N.C. — Mountaineers. I. Title.

Watie, Stand, 1806-1871.

FRANKS, Kenny Arthur, 1945- 970.004'97 B
Stand Watie and the agony of the Cherokee Nation / by Kenny A. Franks. Memphis : Memphis State University Press, c1979. viii, 257 p. : ill. ; 24 cm. Based on the author's thesis, Oklahoma State University, 1973. Includes index. Bibliography: p. [241]-248. [E99.C5W433 1979] 79-124380 ISBN 0-87870-063-3 : 14.95
1. Watie, Stand, 1806-1871. 2. Cherokee Indians—Tribal government. 3. United States—History—Civil War, 1861-1865—Indian troops. 4. Cherokee Indians—Biography. I. Title. BIP

Watson, Elizabeth G.

WATSON, Elizabeth G. 289.6'092'4 B
Guests of my life / Elizabeth Watson ; ill. by Ann Mikolowski. Burnsville, NC : Celo Press, c1979. 189 p. : ports. ; 19 cm. Includes bibliographical references. [BX7795.W318A33] 79-52445 ISBN 0-914064-12-6 : 9.00 ISBN 0-914064-13-4 (pbk.) : 6.50
1. Watson, Elizabeth G. 2. Friends, Society of—United States—Biography. 3. Poetry—Influence. I. Title. BIP

Watson, Emile Emdon, 1885-

BANGERT, Herbert Daniel, 1889- 923.673
Career of Emile E. Watson, on the occasion of the 35th anniversary of his actuarial organization. Colmbus, Ohio [1954] 52p. illus. 23cm. [HD7125.B3] 54-
1. Watson, Emile Emdon, 1885- I. Title.

Watson family.

BREY, Jane W. T. 929.2
A Quaker saga; the Watsons of Strawberryhowe, the Wildmans, and other allied families from England's north counties and Lower Bucks County in Pennsylvania, by Jane W. T. Brey. Philadelphia, Dorrance [1967] xxvi, 646 p. illus., maps. 25 cm. Bibliographical footnotes. [CS71.W34 1967] 66-11051
1. Watson family. 2. Wildman family. 3. Friends, Society of. I. Title.

Watson, Frank, 1921-

WATSON, Frank, 1921- 365'.6'0924 B
Been there and back / by Frank Watson, with Peggy Hoffmann, Winston-Salem, N.C. : J. F. Blair, c1976. viii, 171 p. ; 23 cm. [HV9468.W36A33] 76-49968 ISBN 0-910244-91-X : 8.95. ISBN 0-910244-92-8 pbk. : 3.95
1. Watson, Frank, 1921- 2. Prisoners—North Carolina—Biography. I. Hoffmann, Margaret Jones, joint author. II. Title. BIP

Watson, James, 1799-1874.

LINTON, William James, 1812-1897. 323.44'5'0924
James Watson; a memoir of the days of the fight for a free press in England and of the agitation for the people's charter. New York, A. M. Kelley, 1971. 93 p. port. 22 cm. (The English book trade) Reprint of the 1880 ed. [DA565.W25L5 1971] 74-107903 ISBN 0-678-00631-8
1. Watson, James, 1799-1874.

Watson, John Broadus, 1878-1958.

COHEN, David, 1946- 150.19'432'0924 B
J. B. Watson, the founder of behaviourism : a biography / David Cohen. London ; Boston : Routledge & Kegan Paul, 1979. vi, 297 p. ; 24 cm. Includes index. Bibliography: p. 285-293. [BF109.W39C63] 79-40210 ISBN 0-7100-0054-5 : 20.00
1. Watson, John Broadus, 1878-1958. 2. Psychologists—United States—Biography. 3. Behaviorism (Psychology)—History. I. Title. BIP

Watson, R. R., 1900-

WATSON, R. R., 1900- 977.8'7
Boyhood days on an Ozark farm / by R. R. Watson. New Market, Iowa : College Hill Press, 1978. 166 p. : ill. ; 23 cm. [F472.O9W37] 78-12248 5.95
1. Watson, R. R., 1900- 2. Ozark Mountains—Biography. I. Title.

Watson, Thomas Edward, 1856-1922.

WOODWARD, Comer Vann, 1908- 923.273
Tom Watson: agrarian rebel. New York, Rinehart [1955, c1938] 518p. illus. 22cm. Includes bibliography. [E664] 55-6190
1. Watson, Thomas Edward, 1856-1922. I. Title. BIP

WOODWARD, Comer Vann, 1908- 923.273
Tom Watson, agrarian rebel [Gloucester,

Mass., P. Smith, 1964, c.1938] 518p. ports. 21cm. (Galaxy bk. rebound) Bibl. 4.50
1. Watson, Thomas Edward, 1856-1922. I. Title.

Watson, Thomas John, 1874-1956.

BALDEN, Thomas Graham. 926.5
The lengthening shadow; the life of Thomas J. Watson, by Thomas Graham Belden and Marva Robins Belden. [1st ed.] Boston, Little, Brown [1962] 332p. illus. 22cm. [HD9999.B94I52] 61-8065
1. Watson, Thomas John, 1874-1956. 2. International Business Machines Corporation. I. Belden, Marva Robins, joint author. II. Title.

BELDEN, Thomas Graham 926.5
The lengthening shadow; the life of Thomas J. Watson, by Thomas Graham Belden, Marva Robins Belden. Boston, Little [c.1962] 332p. illus. 22cm. Bibl. 61-8065 5.00
1. Watson, Thomas John, 1874-1956. 2. International Business Machines Corporation. I. Belden, Marva Robins, joint author. II. Title.

RODGERS, William H. 338.7'61'65180924
Think; a biography of the Watsons and IBM, by William Rodgers. New York, Stein and Day [1969] 320 p. illus., ports. 25 cm. Bibliography: p. 312-313. [HD9999.B94I54] 69-19394 ISBN 8-12-812263- 7.95
1. International Business Machines Corporation. 2. Watson, Thomas John, 1874-1956. 3. Watson, Thomas J., 1914- I. Title.

Watson-Watt, Robert Alexander, Sir, 1892-

ROWLAND, John, 1907- 926.2138
The radar man; the story of Sir Robert Watson-Watt. New York, Roy Publishers [1964] 143 p. illus. 21 cm. [TK6545.W3R6] 64-11821
1. Watson-Watt, Robert Alexander, Sir, 1892- I. Title.

Watt, James W., 1843-1944.

WATT, James W., 1843-1944. 979.7'03'0924 B
Journal of mule train packing in eastern Washington in the 1860's / James W. Watt. Fairfield, Wash. : Ye Galleon Press, 1978. 54 p. : ill. ; 27 cm. Originally published in the Washington historical quarterly, 1928-1929. Includes index. [F891.W47A35] 78-16012 ISBN 0-87770-205-5 : 9.95
1. Watt, James W., 1843-1944. 2. Pioneers—Washington (State)—Biography. 3. Muleteers—Washington (State)—Biography. 4. Washington (State)—History—To 1889. 5. Frontier and pioneer life—Washington (State). 6. Packing for shipment. 7. Washington (State)—Biography. I. Title. BIP

Watt, James, 1736-1819.

CROWTHER, James Gerald, 1899- 925
Scientists of the industrial revolution: Joseph Black, James Watt, Joseph Priestley [and] Henry Cavendish. Chester Springs. Pa., Dufour, 1963[c.1962] xii, 365p. ports. 23cm. Bibl. 63-21150 6.95
1. Black, Joseph, 1728-1799. 2. Watt, James, 1736-1819. 3. Priestley, Joseph, 1733-1804. 4. Cavendish, Henry, 1731-1810. I. Title.

DICKINSON, Henry Winram, 1870-1852. 621.1'0924 (B)
James Watt, craftsman & engineer. New York, A. M. Kelley. 1967. xvi, 207 p. illus., facsims., ports. 23 cm. (Reprints of economic classics) Reprint of the 1936 ed. Bibliography: p. [201]-202. [TA140.W3D52 1967] 67-27677
1. Watt, James, 1736-1819. 2. Steam-engines—Hist. I. Title. BIP

DICKINSON, Henry Winram, 1870-1952. 621.1'0924 B
James Watt, craftsman & engineer. New York, A. M. Kelley, 1967. xvi, 207 p. illus., facsims., ports. 23 cm. (Reprints of economic classics) Reprint of the 1936 ed. Bibliography: p. [201]-202. [TA140.W3D52 1967] 67-27677
1. Watt, James, 1736-1819. 2. Steam-engines—History.

HART, Ivor Blashka, 1889- 926.211
James Watt, pioneer of mechanical power. London, Weidenfeld & Nicholson [dist. New Rochelle, N.Y. SportShelf, 1964, c.1962] 128p. illus., port. 19cm. (Pathfinder biogs., 7) 64-4997 3.50 bds.,
1. Watt, James, 1736-1819. I. Title.

ROBINSON, Eric, 1924- comp. 621.1'0924 B
James Watt and the steam revolution; a documentary history, by Eric Robinson and A. E. Musson. New York, A. M. Kelley, 1969. ix, 228 p. illus., part col. facsims., ports. 26 cm. Bibliographical footnotes. [TA140.W3R57] 71-96795 ISBN 0-678-07756-8
1. Watt, James, 1736-1819. I. Musson, Albert Edward, 1920- joint comp. II. Title.

ROLT, Lionel Thomas Caswell, 1910- 926.2
James Watt. New York, Arco [1963c.1962] 144p. illus. 23cm. 63-17093 3.95
1. Watt, James, 1736-1819. I. Title.

Watt, James, 1736-1819—Juvenile literature.

CRANE, William Dwight 92
The man who transformed world: James Watt. New York, Messner [c.1963] u90p. 22cm. Bibl. 16785 325; 3.19 lib. ed.,
1. Watt, James, 1736-1819—Juvenile literature. I. Title.

CRANE, William Dwight. j 92
The man who transformed the world: James Watt. New York, Messner [1963] 190 p. 22 cm. Bibliography: p. 180-181. [TA140.W3C7] 63-16785
1. Watt, James 1736-1819—Juvenile literature. I. Title.

WEBB, Robert N. 621.1'092'4 B
James Watt: inventor of a steam engine, by Robert N. Webb. London, New York, Franklin Watts Ltd, 1972. vi, 118 p. illus., port. 23 cm. Bibliography: p. 113. A biography of the eighteenth-century Scottish inventor and engineer whose improved designs of the steam engine made its wide use possible. [TA140.W3W4 1972] 74-165795 ISBN 0-85166-219-6 £1.25
1. Watt, James, 1736-1819—Juvenile literature. I. Title.

WEBB, Robert N. 621.1'0924 B
James Wyatt, inventor of a steam engine, by Robert N. Webb. New York, F. Watts [1970] vi, 118 p. illus., ports. 22 cm. (Immortals of engineering) Bibliography: p. [113] A biography of the eighteenth-century Scottish inventor and engineer whose improved designs of the steam engine made its wide use possible. [TA140.W3W4] 92 74-93767
1. Watt, James, 1736-1819—Juvenile literature. I. Title.

Watt, Maud (Maloney)

ANDERSON, William Ashley. 917.12
Angel of Hudson Bay, the true story of Maud Watt. [1st ed.] New York, Dutton [1961] 217 p. illus. 21 cm. [F1054.5.R8A5] 61-6007
1. Watt, Maud (Maloney) 2. Frontier and pioneer life—Hudson Bay. 3. Indians of North America—Hudson Bay. 4. Rupert House, Que. I. Title.

Watteau, Jean Antoine, 1684-1721.

HUYGHE, Rene. 741.9'44
Watteau. [Translated by Barbara Bray] New York, G. Braziller [1970, c1968] 121 p. 58 illus. (part col.) 25 cm. (The Great draughtsmen) Translation of L'Univers de Watteau. [NC248.W3H813 1970] 75-97899 7.95
1. Watteau, Jean Antoine, 1684-1721. I. Title. BIP

SCHNEIDER, Pierre. 760'.0924
The world of Watteau, 1684-1721, by Pierre Schneier and the editors of Time-Life Books New York, Time, inc. [1967] 191 p. illus. (part col.) 31 cm. (Time-Life library of art) Bibliography: p. 185. [ND553.W3S35] 67-20332
1. Watteau, Jean Antoine, 1684-1721. 2. France—Social life and customs.—Pictorial works. I. Time-Life Books. II. Title. BIP

Watters, Pat.

WATTERS, Pat. 070.4'092'4 B
The angry middle-aged man / Pat Watters. New York : Grossman, 1976. p. cm. [PN4874.W295A3] 76-27763 ISBN 0-670-12684-5 : 7.95
1. Watters, Pat. 2. Journalists—United States—Biography. 3. United States—Social conditions—1960- I. Title.

Watterson, Henry, 1840-1921.

MARCOSSON, Isaac Frederick, 1876- 920.5
"Marse Henry", a biography of Henry Watterson. With a foreword by Arthur Krock. New York, Dodd, Mead [1951] xviii, 269 p. illus., ports. 22 cm. [PN4874.W3M3] 51-13630
1. Watterson, Henry, I. Title.

MARCOSSON, Isaac Frederick, 1876-1961. 070.4'1'0924 B
"Marse Henry"; a biography of Henry Watterson. With a foreword by Arthur Krock. Westport, Conn., Greenwood Press [1971, c1951] xviii, 269 p. illus. 23 cm. [PN4874.W3M3 1971] 74-156200 ISBN 0-8371-6150-9
1. Watterson, Henry, 1840-1921. I. Title.

WALL, Joseph Frazier. 920.5
Henry Watterson, reconstructed rebel. With an introd. by Alben W. Barkley. New York, Oxford University Press, 1956. 362 p. illus. 24 cm. [PN4874.W3W3 1956] 56-5672
1. Watterson, Henry, 1840-1921. I. Title.

WALL, Joseph Frazier. 920.5
Henry Watterson, reconstructed rebel. With an introd. by Alben W. Barkley. New York, Oxford University Press, 1956. 362p. illus. 24cm. [PN4874.W3W3 1956] 56-5672
1. Watterson, Henry, 1840-1921. I. Title.

WATTERSON, Henry, 1840-1921. 070.4'1'0924 B
"Marse Henry": an autobiography. New York, Beekman Publishers, 1974. 2 v. illus. 23 cm. (American newspapermen, 1790-1933) Reprint of the 1919 ed. published by G. H. Doran, New York. [E664.W34A35 1974] 74-503 ISBN 0-8464-0002-2 35.00 (2 vol. set)
1. Watterson, Henry, 1840-1921. I. Title.

Watts, Alan Wilson, 1915-1973.

HOYT, Edwin Palmer. 191 B
Alan Watts / David Stuart [i.e. E. P. Hoyt]. 1st ed. Radnor, Pa. : Chilton Book Co., c1976. xiii, 250 p. ; 22 cm. Includes index. [B945.W324H69 1976] 75-40066 ISBN 0-8019-5965-9
1. Watts, Alan Wilson, 1915-1973.

WATTS, Alan Wilson, 1915- 294.3'927'0924 B
In my own way; an autobiography, 1915-1965 [by] Alan Watts. [1st ed.] New York, Pantheon Books [1972] xii, 400 p. illus. 22 cm. [BL1473.W3A34] 72-3409 ISBN 0-394-46911-9 7.95
I. Title.

WATTS, Alan Wilson, 1915- 294.3'927'0924 B
In my own way; an autobiography, 1915-1965 [by] Alan Watts. New York, Vintage Books [1973, c1972] xi, 466 p. 18 cm. [BQ995.T8A33 1973] 73-5592 2.45
1. Watts, Alan Wilson, 1915- I. Title. BIP

Watts, Alaric Alexander, 1797-1864—Biography.

WATTS, Alaric Alfred, 1825-1901. 070'.92'4 B
Alaric Watts; a narrative of his life. London, R. Bentley, 1884. [New York, AMS Press, 1974] 2 v. ports. 19 cm. [PR5759.W4Z9 1974] 79-148326 ISBN 0-404-07495-2
1. Watts, Alaric Alexander, 1797-1864—Biography.

Watts-Dunton, Theodore, 1832-1914.

HAKE, Thomas, d.1917. 828'.8'09 B
The life and letters of Theodore Watts-Dunton, by Thomas Hake and Arthur Compton-Rickett. Including some personal reminiscences by Clara Watts-Dunton. With 16 illus. London, T. C. & E. C. Jack; New York, Putnam's Sons, 1916. [New York, Johnson Reprint Corp., 1972] 2 v. illus. 22 cm. (Belles lettres in English) [PR5763.H3 1972] 78-38688
1. Watts-Dunton, Theodore, 1832-1914. I. Compton-Rickett, Arthur, 1869-1937, joint author. II. Watts-Dunton, Clara Jane (Reich) BIP

Watts, George Frederick, 1817-1904.

BAYLISS, Wyke, Sir, 1835-1906. 759.2
Five great painters of the Victorian era: Leighton, Millais, Burne-Jones, Watts, Holman Hunt. New York, AMS Press [1971] vii, 159 p. illus., ports. 19 cm. Reprint of the 1902 ed. [ND467.B4 1971] 72-129384 ISBN 0-404-00696-5
1. Leighton, Frederic Leighton, Baron, 1830-1896. 2. Millais, John Everett, Sir, bart., 1829-1896. 3. Burne-Jones, Edward Coley, Sir, bart., 1833-1898. 4. Watts, George Frederick, 1817-1904. 5. Hunt, William Holman, 1827-1910.

EWING, Lucy Elizabeth Lee. 759.2
George Frederick Watts, Sandro Botticelli, Matthew Arnold, by Lucie Lee Ewing. [Folcroft, Pa.] Folcroft Library Editions, 1973 [c1904] 64 p. illus. 22 cm. Reprint of the ed. published by Grafton Press, New York. [ND497.W3E9 1973] 73-8983 15.00
1. Watts, George Frederick, 1817-1904. 2. Botticelli, Sandro, 1447?-1510. 3. Arnold, Matthew, 1822-1888. BIP

Wauchope, Andrew Gilbert, 1846-1899.

BAIRD, William, F.S.A. Scot. 355.3'31'0924 B
General Wauchope. 3d ed. Freeport, N.Y., Books for Libraries Press, 1972. 211 p. illus. 22 cm. (The Black heritage library collection) Reprint of the 1901 ed. [DA68.32.W3B2 1972] 72-4077 ISBN 0-8369-9094-3 13.25
1. Wauchope, Andrew Gilbert, 1846-1899. I. Title. II. Series. BIP

Wauchope, Gladys Mary,

WAUCHOPE, Gladys Mary, 1889- 610'.92'4
The story of a woman physician. With a foreword by Lord Brain. Bristol, J. Wright [distributed by the Williams & Wilkins Co., Baltimore] 1963. vii, 138 p. 24 cm. Autobiographical. Bibliography: p. 135-136. [R489.W39A3] 63-24255
I. Title.

Waugh, Alec [Alexander Raban Waugh]

WAUGH, Alec [Alexander Raban Waugh] 1898- 928.2
The early years of Alec Waugh. New

York, Farrar [1963, c.1962] 312p. front. port. 22cm. 63-6040 6.00
I. Title. BIP

Waugh, Evelyn, 1903-1966.

DONALDSON, Frances 828'.9'1209
(Lonsdale) Lady.
Evelyn Waugh; portrait of a country neighbour [by] Frances Donaldson. Philadelphia, Chilton [1968, c1967] xvii, 124 p. illus., facsims., ports. 23 cm. [PR6045.A97Z67 1968] 68-11545
1. Waugh, Evelyn, 1903-1966.

PHILLIPS, Gene D. 823'.9'12
Evelyn Waugh's officers, gentlemen, and rogues : the fact behind his fiction / Gene D. Phillips. Chicago : Nelson-Hall, c1975. p. cm. Includes index. Bibliography: p. [PR6045.A97Z75] 75-26546 ISBN 0-88229-172-6 : 8.95
1. Waugh, Evelyn, 1903-1966. I. Title. BIP

PRYCE-JONES, David, 823'.9'12 B
1936-
Evelyn Waugh and his world. Edited by David Pryce-Jones. [1st American ed.] Boston, Little, Brown [1973] viii, 248 p. illus. 26 cm. [PR6045.A97Z76 1973] 73-5746 12.95
1. Waugh, Evelyn, 1903-1966. I. Title. BIP

STOPP, Frederick J. 823.914
Evelyn Waugh, portrait of an artist. Boston, Little, Brown [1958] 254 p. illus. 23 cm. [PR6045.A97Z8 1958a] 59-5157
1. Waugh, Evelyn, 1903-1966.

WAUGH, Evelyn, 1903-1966. 928.2
A little learning; an autobiography: the early years. [1st American ed.] Boston, Little, Brown [1964] 234 p. illus., facsims., ports. 22 cm. [PR6045.A97Z5] 64-23290
I. Title.

WAUGH, Evelyn, 1903-1966. 916.7
Tourist in Africa / Evelyn Waugh. Westport, Conn. : Greenwood Press, 1977, c1960. 200 p., [6] leaves of plates : ill. ; 23 cm. Reprint of the 1st ed. published by Little, Brown, Boston. [DT365.2.W38 1977] 76-30533 ISBN 0-8371-9358-3 lib.bdg. : 15.50
1. Waugh, Evelyn, 1903-1966. 2. Africa, Eastern—Description and travel. 3. Africa, Southern—Description and travel. I. Title. BIP

Waugh, Evelyn, 1903-1966—Biography.

SYKES, Christopher, 823'.9'12 B
1907-
Evelyn Waugh : a biography / Christopher Sykes. 1st American ed. Boston : Little, Brown, [1975] xii, 462 p., [6] leaves of plates : ill. ; 24 cm. [PR6045.A97Z83 1975] 75-25721 ISBN 0-316-82600-6 : 12.50
1. Waugh, Evelyn, 1903-1966—Biography. BIP

Waugh, Evelyn, 1903-1966—Diaries.

WAUGH, Evelyn, 1903- 823'.9'12 B
1966.
The diaries of Evelyn Waugh / edited by Michael Davie. 1st ed. Boston : Little Brown, 1977,c1976 818 p. ; 25 cm. [PR6045.A97Z498 1976b] 77-153170 17.50
1. Waugh, Evelyn, 1903-1966—Diaries. 2. Authors, English—20th century—Biography. I. Title.

WAUGH, Evelyn, 1903- 823'.9'12 B
1966.
The diaries of Evelyn Waugh / edited by Michael Davie. London : Weidenfeld and Nicolson, 1976. [12], 814 p. : facsim. ; 25 cm. Includes index. [PR6045.A97Z498 1976] 77-352257 ISBN 0-297-77126-4 : £7.95
1. Waugh, Evelyn, 1903-1966—Diaries. 2. Authors, English—20th century—Biography. I. Davie, Michael. II. Title.

Waugh, Frederick Judd, 1861-1940.

HAVENS, George 759.13 B
Remington, 1890-
Frederick J. Waugh, American marine painter, by George R. Havens. Orono, University of Maine Press, 1969. xii, 361 p. illus. (part col.), ports. 24 cm. (University of Maine studies, no. 89) Includes bibliographical references. [ND237.W36H3] 70-7555 7.00
1. Waugh, Frederick Judd, 1861-1940. I. Series: Maine. University. University of Maine studies, no. 89

Wauneka, Annie—Juvenile literature.

NELSON, Mary Carroll. 970.3 B
Annie Wauneka. Minneapolis, Minn., Dillon Press [1972] 66 p. illus. 24 cm. (The Story of an American Indian) Biography of a Medal of Freedom winner who has spent her life improving the health and welfare of her fellow Navajos. [E99.N3N363] 92 72-86544 ISBN 0-87518-053-1 3.95
1. Wauneka, Annie—Juvenile literature. 2. Navaho Indians—Biography. I. Title.

Wavell, Archibald Percival Wavell, 1st Earl, 1883-1950.

[ROBERTSON, John Henry] 923.542
1909-
Wavell, scholar and soldier, by John Connell pseud. New York, Harcourt [1965, c.1964] 573p. illus., maps, ports. 24cm. Bibl. [DA69.3.W37R6] 65-14704 8.75
1. Wavell, Archibald Percival Wavell, 1st earl, 1883-1950. I. Title.

WAVELL, Archibald 325'.342'0954
Percival Wavell, 1st Earl, 1883-1950.
Wavell: the viceroy's journal; edited by Penderel Moon. London, Oxford University Press, 1973. xvi, 528, [25] p. illus., facsim., map (on lining papers), ports. 24 cm. Includes index. [DS481.W35A3 1973] 73-168584 ISBN 0-19-211723-8 £8.00
1. Wavell, Archibald Percival Wavell, 1st Earl, 1883-1950. 2. India—Politics and government—1919-1947. I. Moon, Penderel, 1905- ed. II. Title.

Waverley, John Anderson, 1st viscount, 1882-1958.

WHEELER-BENNETT, John 923.242
Wheeler, Sir 1902-
John Anderson, viscount Waverley. New York, St. Martin's [1963, c.]1962. xv, 430p. ports. 23cm. Bibl. 63-7 10.00
1. Waverley, John Anderson, 1st viscount, 1882-1958. I. Title.

Wax modellers—Biography—Dictionaries.

PYKE, E. J. 736'.93'0922
A biographical dictionary of wax modellers [by] E. J. Pyke. Oxford, Clarendon Press, 1973. lxvi, 216, [79] p. illus. 24 cm. Includes index. Bibliography: p. 164-186. [NK9580.P94] 73-174552 ISBN 0-19-817194-3
1. Wax modellers—Biography—Dictionaries. I. Title.
Distributed by Oxford University Press, N.Y., 64.00; Library binding 50.56.

Wayland, Julius Augustus, 1854-1912.

WAYLAND, Julius 335'.0092'4
Augustus, 1854-1912.
Leaves of life : a story of twenty years of socialist agitation / by J. A. Wayland. Westport, Conn. : Hyperion Press, 1975, c1912. p. cm. (The Radical tradition in America) Reprint of the ed. published by Appeal to reason, Girard, Kan. [HX84.W4A34 1975] 75-350 ISBN 0-88355-253-1 : 18.75
1. Wayland, Julius Augustus, 1854-1912. 2. Socialism. I. Title.

Wayman, John Hudson, 1820-1867.

WAYMAN, John Hudson, 917.8'04'2
1820-1867.
A doctor on the California trail; the diary of Dr. John Hudson Wayman from Cambridge City, Indiana, to the gold fields in 1852. Edited by Edgeley Woodman Todd. Denver, Old West Pub. Co. [1971] xv, 136 p. illus. 29 cm. Bibliography: p. 125-131. [R154.W298A33] 72-162933 ISBN 0-912094-16-8
1. Wayman, John Hudson, 1820-1867. 2. Overland journeys to the Pacific. I. Title.

Wayne, Anthony, 1745-1796.

STEVENSON, 973.3'44'0924 B
Augusta.
Anthony Wayne, daring boy. [Illustrated by Gray Morrow] Indianapolis, Bobbs-Merrill [1962] 200 p. illus. 20 cm. (Childhood of famous Americans) The childhood of the courageous American officer in the Revolution who was the hero of the recapture of Stony Point and wintered at Valley Forge. [PZ7.S8467Ap5] a92 AC 68
1. Wayne, Anthony, 1745-1796. I. Morrow, Gray, illus. II. Title.

STILLE, Charles 973.3'44'0924 B
Janeway, 1819-1899.
Major-General Anthony Wayne and the Pennsylvania line in the Continental Army. Port Washington, N.Y., Kennikat Press [1968] x, 441 p. illus., port. 25 cm. Reprint of the 1893 ed. [E207.W35S8 1968] 68-26268
1. Wayne, Anthony, 1745-1796. 2. Pennsylvania—History—Revolution, 1775-1783. 3. United States—History—Revolution, 1775-1783—Regimental histories—Pennsylvania. I. Title. BIP

WILDES, Harry 973.3'44'0924 B
Emerson, 1890-
Anthony Wayne, trouble shooter of the American Revolution. Westport, Conn., Greenwood Press [1970, c1941] xii, 514 p. maps, port. 23 cm. Bibliography: p. 489-501. [E207.W35W5 1970] 70-106701 ISBN 0-8371-3383-1
1. Wayne, Anthony, 1745-1796. BIP

Wayne, Anthony, 1745-1796—Juvenile literature.

DELEEUW, Adele 973.3'44'0924 B
Louise, 1899-
Anthony Wayne: Washington's general, by Adele and Cateau deLeeuw. Illustrated by Andrew Snyder. Philadelphia, Westminster Press [1974] 143 p. illus. 22 cm. A biography of the Revolutionary War general renowned for his military skill and his courage and daring. [E207.W35D38] 92 74-1130 ISBN 0-664-32547-5
1. Wayne, Anthony, 1745-1796—Juvenile literature. I. DeLeeuw, Cateau, 1903- joint author. II. Snyder, Andrew, illus. III. Title. BIP

WELLS, Robert W. 973.3440924 B
"Mad Anthony" Wayne, by Bob Wells. New York, Putnam [1970] 192 p. 22 cm. (Lives to remember) A biography of one of the youngest American generals in the Revolutionary War. [E207.W35W4 1970] 92 71-92824 3.64
1. Wayne, Anthony, 1745-1796—Juvenile literature. I. Title.

Wayne, James Moore, 1790-1867.

LAWRENCE, 347'.7326'340924 B
Alexander A., 1906-
James Moore Wayne, Southern unionist [by] Alexander A. Lawrence. Westport, Conn., Greenwood Press [1970, c1943] xx, 250 p. ports. 23 cm. Includes bibliographical references. [E340.W3L3 1970] 75-135511 ISBN 0-8371-5177-5
1. Wayne, James Moore, 1790-1867. BIP

Wayne, John, 1907-1979.

BOSWELL, John, 791.43'028'0924 B
1945-
Duke : the John Wayne album :the legend of our time / John Boswell & Jay David ; foreword by Richard Schickel. 1st ed. New York : Ballantine Books, 1979. 160 p., [4] leaves of plates : ill. ; 28 cm. [PN2287.W454B6] 79-2470 ISBN 0-345-28088-1 : 8.95
1. Wayne, John, 1907- 2. Moving-picture actors and actresses—United States—Biography. I. Fisher, David, 1946- joint author.

CARPOZI, George. 791.43'028'0924
The John Wayne story / by George Carpozi, Jr. New Rochelle, N.Y. : Arlington House, c1979. p. cm. Includes index. "A John Wayne filmography": p. [PN2287.W454C3 1979] 79-18667 ISBN 0-87000-171-X : 10.95
1. Wayne, John, 1907- 2. Moving-picture actors and actresses—United States—Biography. I. Title. BIP

*HANNA, David. 791.43'028'0924 B
Four giants of the West. New York, Belmont Tower [1976] 223 p. ill. 18 cm. [PN2287] 1.50 (pbk.)
1. Fonda, Henry, 1905- 2. Stewart, James, 1908- 3. Wayne, John, 1907- 4. Cooper, Gary, 1901-1961. I. Title.

†*JOHN Wayne.* 791.43'028'0924 B
[Sherman Oaks, CA : E-Go Enterprises, 1976] 66 p. : ill. ; 28 cm. (E-GO collectors series ; no. 4) Cover title. [PN2287.W454J6] 77-375417 1.00
1. Wayne, John, 1907- 2. Moving-picture actors and actresses—United States—Biography.
Publisher's address : 13510, Ventura Blvd., Sherman Oaks, Calif.

PAIGE, David. 791.43'028'0924 B
John Wayne / written by David Paige ; designed by Gene Kohler. [Mankato, Minn.] : Creative Education, [c1977] 31 p. : ill. ; 25 cm. (Stars of stage and screen) A brief biography concentrating on the career of one of the most famous stars in the history of films. [PN2287.W454P3] 92 76-28996 ISBN 0-87191-551-0 lib.bdg. 4.95
1. Wayne, John, 1907- —Juvenile literature. 2. Moving-picture actors and actresses—United States—Biography—Juvenile literature. I. Title. BIP

TOMKIES, Mike. 791.43'028'0924 B
Duke: the story of John Wayne. Chicago, Regnery [1971] 149 p. ports. 22 cm. "A John Wayne filmography": p. [145]-149. [PN2287.W454T6] 71-143841 5.95
1. Wayne, John, 1907- I. Title.

ZOLOTOW, 791.43'028'0924 B
Maurice, 1913-
Shooting star; a biography of John Wayne. New York, Simon and Schuster [1974] 416 p. illus. 23 cm. [PN2287.W36Z6] 73-20549 ISBN 0-671-21686-4 9.95
1. Wayne, John, 1907- I. Title. BIP

Weafer, Eugene Clyde.

WEAFER, Elizabeth (Boyd) 923.773
1924-
Baaltie, life and legend. San Antonio, Naylor [c.1964] x, 134p. 22cm. 64-18679 4.95
1. Weafer, Eugene Clyde. I. Title.

WEAFER, Elizabeth (Boyd) 923.773
1924-
Baaltie, life and legend, by Elizabeth Weafer. San Antonio, Naylor Co. [1964] x, 134 p. 22 cm. [CT275.W346W4] 64-18679
1. Weafer, Eugene Clyde. I. Title.

Weage, Arthur Deane, 1934-1954.

WEAGE, Avery D. 920
Broken blossoms; the story of our son Art. Philadelphia, Dorrance [1958] 116 p. illus. 20 cm. [CT275.W347W4] 58-6881
1. Weage, Arthur Deane, 1934-1954. I. Title.

Wearin, Otha Donner, 1903-

WEARIN, Otha 328.73'092'4 B
Donner, 1903-
Country roads to Washington / Otha D. Wearin. Des Moines : Wallace Homestead Co., c1976 181 p. : ill. ; 24 cm. Autobiographical. Includes index. [E748.W42A33] 77-356166 9.95
1. Wearin, Otha Donner, 1903- 2. Legislators—United States—Biography. 3.

Agriculture and state—United States. I. Title.

Weatherford, Willis Duke, 1875-

DYKEMAN, Wilma. 378.00924
Prophet of plenty; the first ninety years of W. D. Weatherford. [1st ed.] Knoxville, University of Tennessee Press [1966] x, 263 p. port. 23 cm. Bibliography: p. 242-255. [CT275.W348D9] 66-26067
1. Weatherford, Willis Duke, 1875- 2. Appalachian region. 3. Education—Southern States. 4. Southern States—Race question. I. Title.

Weatherhead, Leslie Dixon, 1893-

WEATHERHEAD, Andrew Kingsley, 1923- 287'.1'0924 B
Leslie Weatherhead : a personal portrait / A. Kingsley Weatherhead. Nashville : Abingdon, [1975] 269 p. : port. ; 23 cm. [BX8495.W329W4] 75-17574 ISBN 0-687-21375-4 : 7.95
1. Weatherhead, Leslie Dixon, 1893- BIP

Weatherly, Edward Christopher, 1855-1934—Archives.

COLORADO. University. Libraries. Western Historical Collections. 011
Guide to the Edward Christopher Weatherly papers, 1890-1936 / compiled by Doris Mitterling ; edited by John A. Brennan. Boulder : Western Historical Collections, University of Colorado Libraries, 1975. v, 60 p. ; 28 cm. Includes index. [Z6611.E5C64 1975] [TN24.C6] 75-623676
1. Weatherly, Edward Christopher, 1855-1934—Archives. 2. Colorado. University. Libraries. I. Mitterling, Doris. II. Title.

Weaver, Benjamin Witwer, 1853-1928.

WENGER, Eli D. 289.7'748'15
The Weaverland Mennonites, 1766-1968, including a biography of Bishop Benjamin W. Weaver with excerpts from his diary, by Eli D. Wenger. Transcript of the Weaverland Mennonite cemeteries, by George G. Sauder. [Adamstown, Pa., Printed by Ensinger Print. Service] 1968. 363 p. illus., plan, ports. 24 cm. [BX8143.W3W35] 78-261963
1. Weaver, Benjamin Witwer, 1853-1928. 2. Mennonite Church. Lancaster County Conference. I. Sauder, George G. Transcript of the Weaverland Mennonite cemeteries. 1968. II. Title. III. Title: Transcript of the Weaverland Mennonite cemeteries.

Weaver, George Sumner,

WEAVER, George Sumner, 1818-1908. 288'.092'4
Autobiography; a sketch of a busy life, 1914. [Schenectady, N.Y., E. L. Robinson, 1965] 121 p. facsim., port. 23 cm. 125 copies printed. [BX9969.W4A3] 64-41427
I. Title.

Weaver, Harriet Shaw.

LIDDERDALE, Jane. 070.5'0924 B
Dear Miss Weaver: Harriet Shaw Weaver, 1876-1961 [by] Jane Lidderdale & Mary Nicholson. New York, Viking Press [1970] 509 p. illus., facsims., ports. 25 cm. Includes bibliographical references. [Z325.W4L54 1970b] 70-124320 ISBN 0-670-26084-3 15.00
1. Weaver, Harriet Shaw. 2. Joyce, James, 1882-1941. I. Crawford, Mary, 1912- joint author. II. Title.

Weaver, James Baird, 1833-1912.

HAYNES, Frederick Emory, 1868- 973.8'092'4 B
James Baird Weaver / Frederick Emory Haynes. New York : Arno Press, 1975. p. cm. (The Mid-American frontier) Reprint of the 1919 ed. published by the State Historical Society of Iowa, Iowa City, issued in series: Iowa biographical series. Includes bibliographical references. [E664.W36H4 1975] 75-102 ISBN 0-405-06870-0 : 29.00
1. Weaver, James Baird, 1833-1912. I. Title. II. Series. III. Series: Iowa biographical series. BIP

Weaver, Samuel Pool,

WEAVER, Samuel Pool, 1882- 923.473
Autobiography of a Pennsylvania Dutchman. New York, Vantage Press [1953] 228 p. illus. 23 cm. [CT275.W35A3] 53-5692
I. Title.

Webb and Knapp, Inc., New York.

ZECKENDORF, William, 1905- 333.3'3'0924
The autobiography of William Zeckendorf, with Edward McCreary. [1st ed.] New York, Holt, Rinehart and Winston [1970] viii, 312 p. illus., facsims., map, ports. 24 cm. [HD205 1970.Z4] ISBN 0-03-084494-0 7.95
1. Webb and Knapp, Inc., New York. I. McCreary, Edward A.

Webb, Beatrice Potter, 1858-1943.

MACKENZIE, Jeanne. 335'.14'0922 B
A Victorian courtship : the story of Beatrice Potter and Sidney Webb / Jeanne MacKenzie. 1st American ed. New York : Oxford University Press, 1979. 148 p., [4] leaves of plates : ill. ; 23 cm. Includes index. [HX243.W4M33 1979] 79-121382 ISBN 0-19-520166-3 : 10.95
1. Webb, Beatrice Potter, 1858-1943. 2. Passfield, Sidney James Webb, Baron, 1859-1947. 3. Socialists—Great Britain—Biography. I. Title. BIP

MUGGERIDGE, Kitty. 330'.0924 B
Beatrice Webb; a life, 1858-1943 [by] Kitty Muggeridge & Ruth Adam. [1st American ed.] New York, Knopf, 1968 [c1967] 271 p. illus., ports. 22 cm. Bibliography: p. 269-271. [HX243.W4M8 1968] 68-12664
1. Webb, Beatrice (Potter) 1858-1943. I. Adam, Ruth, joint author.

WEBB, Beatrice (Potter) 1858-1943. 923.342
Diaries, edited by Margaret I. Cole, with an introd. by Lord Beveridge. London, New York, Longmans, Green [1952- v. ports. 23cm. Contents.[1] 1912-1924.--[2] 1924-1932. [HX246.W33] 50-11654
1. Gt. Brit.— Pol. & govt.—1910-1936. I. Title.

WEBB, Beatrice (Potter) 1858-1943. 923.342
Diaries, 1912-1924, edited by Margaret I. Cole with an introd. by Lord Beveridge. London, New York, Longmans, Green [1952] xxvi, 272 p. ports. 22 cm. [HX246.W33] 52-11654
1. Gt. Brit. — Pol. & govt. — 1910-1936. I. Title.

WEBB, Beatrice Potter, 1858-1943. 335'.14'0924 B
My apprenticeship / by Beatrice Webb. New York : AMS Press, [1977]. xii, 442 p., [7] leaves of plates : ill. ; 23 cm. Reprint of the 1926 ed. published by Longmans, Green, New York. Includes index. [HX243.W385 1977] 75-30041 ISBN 0-404-14045-9 : 27.50
1. Webb, Beatrice Potter, 1858-1943. 2. Socialists—Great Britain—Biography. I. Title. BIP

Webb, Catherine J.

WEBB, Catherine J. 979.4'37 B
Growing up in Nevada City / by Catherine J. Webb ; graphics by Cathy Harder. 1st ed. Berkeley, Calif. : Type-Ink-Berkeley, c1975. p. 123-252 : ill. ; 29 cm. "Part II." A continuation of the author's Family history of California. [F869.N4W424] 75-44738
1. Webb, Catherine J. 2. Nevada City, Calif.—Biography. I. Title.

Webb, Conrade, 1778-1842.

HASTINGS, William Thomson, 1881- 929.2
Conrade Webb of Hampstead. Providence, Brown University Press, 1958. xiv, 102p. illus., ports., map, facsims., plan. 23cm. Bibliographical footnotes. [CT275.W352H3] 58-7622
1. Webb, Conrade, 1778-1842. I. Title. BIP

Webb, Hanor A., 1888-

SHAPIRO, Jacob W 925
Growth of a philosophy: Hanor A. Webb. Nashville, Bureau of Publications, George Peabody College for Teachers, 1963. x, 436 p. ports. 22 cm. Includes bibliographical references. [Q143.W4S5] 63-18478
1. Webb, Hanor A., 1888- I. Title.

SHAPIRO, Jacob W. 925
Growth of a philosophy: Hanor A. Webb. Nashville, bur. of Pubns., George Peabody Coll. for Teachers [c.]1963. x, 436p. ports. 22cm. Bibl. 63-18478 4.00 2.50 pap.,
1. Webb, Hanor A., 1888- I. Title.

Webb, James Watson, 1802-1884.

CROUTHAMEL, James L., 1931- 070'.924 B
James Watson Webb; a biography, by James L. Crouthamel. [1st ed.] Middletown, Conn., Wesleyan University Press [1969] x, 262 p. port. 24 cm. Includes bibliographical references. [E415.9.W37C7] 70-82536 10.00
1. Webb, James Watson, 1802-1884.

Webb, Mary Gladys Meredith, 1881-1927.

COLES, Gladys Mary. 823'.9'12 B
The flower of light : a biography of Mary Webb / Gladys Mary Coles. London : Duckworth, 1979. xxi, 352 p., [6] leaves of plates : ill. ; 23 cm. Includes index. Bibliography: p. [335]-341. [PR6045.E2Z6 1978] 78-323267 ISBN 0-7156-1120-8 : 13.95
1. Webb, Mary Gladys Meredith, 1881-1927. 2. Novelists, English—20th century—Biography. I. Title.
Distributed by Biblio Distribution Centre, Box 327, Totowa, NJ 07511 BIP

Webb, Matthew, 1848-1883.

JARVIS, Margaret A. 797.2'1
Captain Webb and 100 years of Channel swimming / Margaret A. Jarvis. Newton Abbot ; North Pomfret, Vt. : David & Charles, c1975. 64 p. : ill. ; 25 cm. [GV838.W42J37] 75-14 ISBN 0-7153-6995-4 : 7.95
1. Webb, Matthew, 1848-1883. 2. Swimming. 3. English Channel. I. Title.

Webb, Robert N

WEBB, Robert N 92
Gregor Mendel and heredity. New York, F. Watts [c1963] 114 p. illus. 22 cm. (Immortals of science) Mendel, Gregor, 1822-1881 -- Juvenile literature. [QH31.M45W4] 63-16918
I. Title.

Webb School, Bell Buckle, Tenn.—History.

MCMILLIN, Laurence. 373.1'2'0924
The schoolmaker; Sawney Webb and the Bell Buckle story. Chapel Hill, University of North Carolina Press [1971] xxiii, 186 p. illus., facsims. (on lining papers), ports. 24 cm. [LD7501.B35M3] 72-144336 ISBN 0-8078-1163-7 7.95
1. Webb School, Bell Buckle, Tenn.—History. 2. Webb, William Robert, 1842-1926. I. Title. BIP

Webb, Sheyann.

WEBB, Sheyann. 301.45'19'6073022 B
Selma, Lord, Selma : girlhood memories of the civil-rights movement / by Sheyann Webb & Rachel West Nelson, as told to Frank Sikora. University : University of Alabama Press, [1980] p. cm. [F334.S4W4] 79-19327 ISBN 0-8173-0031-7 : 8.95
1. Webb, Sheyann. 2. Nelson, Rachel West. 3. Afro-Americans—Civil rights—Alabama—Selma. 4. Selma, Ala.—Race relations. 5. Afro-Americans—Alabama—Selma—Biography. I. Nelson, Rachel West, joint author. II. Sikora, Frank, 1936- III. Title.

Webb, Walter Prescott, 1888-1963.

FURMAN, Necah Stewart. 907'.202'4 B
Walter Prescott Webb : his life and impact / Necah Stewart Furman. 1st ed. Albuquerque : University of New Mexico Press, c1976. xiv, 222 p., [4] leaves of plates : ill. ; 24 cm. Includes index. Bibliography: p. 211-215. [E175.5.W4F87] 75-40834 ISBN 0-8263-0412-5 : 12.00
1. Webb, Walter Prescott, 1888-1963. BIP

RUNDELL, Walter. 979.1'072'024
Walter Prescott Webb. Austin, Tex., Steck-Vaughn Co. [1971] ii, 43 p. 21 cm. (Southwest writers series, no. 37) Bibliography: p. 37-43. [E175.5.W4R8] 70-138525 ISBN 0-8114-3907-0
1. Webb, Walter Prescott, 1888-1963. I. Title. II. Series.

TOBIN, Gregory M., 1936- 978'.007'2024 B
The making of a history : Walter Prescott Webb and The Great Plains / Gregory M. Tobin. Austin : University of Texas Press, c1976. xix, 184 p. : ill. ; 24 cm. Originally presented as the author's thesis, University of Texas at Austin, 1972. Includes index. Bibliography: p. [159]-176. [E175.5.W4T62 1976] 76-3120 ISBN 0-292-75029-3 : 10.95
1. Webb, Walter Prescott, 1888-1963. 2. Webb, Walter Prescott, 1888-1963. The Great Plains. 3. Great Plains—History. 4. Mississippi Valley—History. 5. Historians—United States—Biography. I. Title. BIP

Weber, Joseph Francis, 1865-1935.

WEBER, Francis J. 189.4
Mayor of Indianapolis : Father Joseph F. Weber / [written by Francis J. Weber]. Worcester [Mass.] : Achille J. St. Onge, 1975. 26 p. : port. ; 74 mm. 300 copies. [BX4705.W395W4] 73-90828
1. Weber, Joseph Francis, 1865-1935. 2. Indianapolis—Flood, 1913. 3. Bibliography—Microscopic and miniature editions—Specimens. I. Title.

Weber, Karl Maria Friedrich Ernst, Freiherr von, 1786-1826.

SAUNDERS, William, 1877- 780'.924 B
Weber. With a new bibliography compiled by Frederick Freedman. New York, Da Capo Press, 1970. ix, 348 p. illus., music, ports. 23 cm. (Da Capo Press music reprint series) Reprint of the 1940 ed. Bibliography: p. 295-348. [ML410.W3S18 1970] 69-11670
1. Weber, Karl Maria Friedrich Ernst, Freiherr von, 1786-1826.

WARRACK, John Hamilton, 1928- 780'.92'4 B
Carl Maria von Weber / John Warrack. 2d ed. Cambridge ; New York : Cambridge University Press, c1976. p. cm. Includes index. "List of works": p. [ML410.W3W26 1976] 76-26655 ISBN 0-521-21354-1 : 29.50 ISBN 0-521-29121-6 pbk. :
1. Weber, Karl Maria Friedrich Ernst, Freiherr von, 1786-1826. 2. Compoers—Germany—Biography. BIP

WARRACK, John Hamilton, 1928- 780.924 B
Carl Marie von Weber, by John Warrack. [1st American ed.] New York, Macmillan Co. [1968] 377 p. illus., music, ports. 25 cm. Bibliographical footnotes. [ML410.W3W26] 67-31200
1. Weber, Karl Maria Friedrich Ernst, Freiherr von, 1786-1826.

WEBER in London, 1826 780'.92'4 B
/ edited by David Reynolds .... London : Wolff, 1976. 56 p. : ill., facsims., maps, music, ports. ; 21 x 27 cm. "Selections from Weber's letters to his wife, translated by Noel Currer-Briggs, and from the writings of his contemporaries; London in 1826, by Hermione Hobhouse; Weber's legacy, by John Warrack." Bibliography: p. 5. [ML410.W3W45] 76-376627 ISBN 0-85496-403-7 : £1.95
1. Weber, Karl Maria Friedrich Ernst, Freiherr von, 1786-1826. 2. Composers—England—London—Correspondence. I. Reynolds, David.

WEBER, Max Maria, Freiherr von, 1822-1881. 780'.924 B
Carl Maria von Weber; the life of an artist. From the German of his son, Baron Max Maria von Weber, by J. Palgrave Simpson. New York, Greenwood Press [1969] 2 v. 23 cm. Reprint of the 1865 ed. [ML410.W3W32 1969] 68-31013
1. Weber, Karl Maria Friedrich Ernst, Freiherr von, 1786-1826. **BIP**

WEBER, Max Maria, Freiherr von, 1822-1881. 780.924 B
Carl Maria von Weber; the life of an artist. From the German of his son, Baron Max Maria von Weber, by J. Palgrave Simpson. New York, Haskell House, 1968. 2 v. port. 23 cm. "First published 1865." [ML410.W3W32 1968] 68-25305
1. Weber, Karl Maria Friedrich Ernst, Freiherr von, 1786-1826.

Weber, Karl Maria Friedrick Ernst, Freiherr von, 1786-1826 — Juvenile literature.

ROBERTO, Brother, 1927-- 92
No more shall I wander; a story of Carl Maria von Weber. Illus. by Carolyn Lee Jagodits. Notre Dame, Ind., Dujarie Press [1962] 95 p. illus. 24 cm. [ML3930.W35R6] 63-1249
1. Weber, Karl Maria Friedrick Ernst, Freiherr von, 1786-1826 — Juvenile literature. I. Title.

Weber, Max, 1864-1920.

BENDIX, Reinhard. 923.343
Max Weber : an intellectual portrait / Reinhard Bendix ; with an introduction to the new edition by Guenther Roth. Berkeley, CA : University of California Press, 1977. li, 522p. ; 21 cm. [HM22.G3W42] ISBN 0-520-03194-6 pbk. : 6.95
1 Weber, Max, 1864-1920. I. Title.

BENDIX, Reinhard. 923.343
Max Weber; an intellectual portrait. [1st ed.] Garden City, N. Y., Doubleday, 1960. 480 p. 22 cm. [HM22.G3W42] 60-5953
1. Weber, Max, 1864-1920. **BIP**

DRONBERGER, Ilse. 320.9'24
The political thought of Max Weber; in quest of statesmanship. New York, Appleton-Century-Crofts [1971] xv, 436 p. port. 25 cm. Includes bibliographical references. [JC263.W42D7] 70-133904 ISBN 0-390-27384-8
1. Weber, Max, 1864-1920. 2. Germany—Politics and government—1871-1918. I. Title. **BIP**

WEBER, Marianne Schnitger, 1870-1954. 301'.092'4 B
Max Weber : a biography / Marianne Weber ; translated from the German and edited by Harry Zohn. New York : Wiley, [1975] xiv, 719 p. : ill. ; 23 cm. "A Wiley-Interscience publication." Includes bibliographical references and index. [HB107.W4W413 1975] 74-23904 ISBN 0-471-92333-8 : 19.95
1. Weber, Max, 1864-1920. **BIP**

L.C. card no. for 1960 Doubleday ed.: 60-5953.

Weber, Max, 1881-1961.

WEBER, Max, 1881-1961. 759.13
Max Weber. Text by Alfred Werner. New York, Abrams [1975] 200 p. illus. (part col.) 28 cm. Bibliography: p. [198] [ND237.W37W47] 74-9808 ISBN 0-8109-0540-X 37.50
1. Weber, Max, 1881-1961. I. Werner, Alfred, 1911-

Weber, Nancy, 1942-

WEBER, Nancy, 1942- 818.5'409
The life swap. [New York, Dell, 1975, c1974 254 p. 18 cm. [CT275.W353A34] 1.75 (pbk.)
1. Weber, Nancy, 1942- I. Title.
L.C. card number for original ed.: 74-3458

WEBER, Nancy, 1942- 818'.5'409
The life swap. New York, Dial Press, 1974. 262 p. 24 cm. Autobiographical. [CT275.W353A34] 74-3458 ISBN 0-8037-6783-8 6.95
1. Weber, Nancy, 1942- I. Title.

Webern, Anton von, 1883-1945.

MOLDENHAUER, Hans. 780'.92'4 B
Anton von Webern, a chronicle of his life and work / Hans Moldenhauer and Rosaleen Moldenhauer. 1st American ed. New York : Knopf : distributed by Random House, 1979, c1978. 803 p., [8] leaves of plates : ill. ; 25 cm. Includes index. Bibliography: p. [757]-773. [ML410.W33M55 1979] 77-20370 ISBN 0-394-47237-3 20.00
1. Webern, Anton von, 1883-1945. 2. Composers—Austria—Biography. I. Moldenhauer, Rosaleen.

Webster, Daniel, 1782-1852.

BARTLETT, Irving H. 973.5'092'4 B
Daniel Webster / Irving H. Bartlett 1st ed. New York : Norton, c1978. xii, 333 p. : ill. ; 24 cm. Includes bibliographical references and index. [E340.W4B26 1978] 77-27542 ISBN 0-393-07524-9 : 12.95
1. Webster, Daniel, 1782-1852. 2. Legislators—United States—Biography 3. United States—Politics and government—1783-1865.

BAXTER, Maurice Glen, 1920- 347.9973
Daniel Webster & the Supreme Court [by] Maurice G. Baxter. [Amherst] University of Massachusetts Press, 1966. ix, 265 p. 24 cm. Bibliography: p. 253-260. [KF8748.B3] 66-28116
1. Webster, Daniel, 1782-1852. 2. United States. Supreme Court. I. Title. **BIP**

COURNOS, Helen Sybil Norton (Kestner) 1893- 923.273
Candidate for truth: the story of Daniel Webster, by Sybil Norton [pseud.] and John Cournos. Illustrated by Rus Anderson. [1st ed.] New York, Holt [1953] 176p. illus. 21cm. [E340.W4C77] 53-8970
1. Webster, Daniel, 1782-1852. I. Cournos, John, 1881- joint author. II. Title.

CURRENT, Richard Nelson 923.273
Daniel Webster and the rise of national conservatism. Boston, Little [1962, c.1955] 215p. 20cm. (Lib. of Amer. biog. 4.) Bibl. 1.65 pap.,
1. Webster, Daniel, 1782-1852. I. Title. **BIP**

CURRENT, Richard Nelson. 923.273
Daniel Webster and the rise of national conservatism. 1st ed. Boston, Little, Brown 1955 215p. 21 cm. (The Library of American biography) Includes bibliography. [E340.W4C87] 55-7468
1. Webster, Daniel 1867-1852 I. Title.

FUESS, Claude Moore, 1885-1963 923.273
Daniel Webster. [2v.] Hamden, Conn. Archton [dist.Shoe String] 1963[c.1930,1958] 2v.(398;465p.)illus., ports., fascisms. 24cm. Contents.v.1. 1782-1830.--v.2. 1830-1852. Bibl. 63-17434 20.00 set,
1. Webster, Daniel, 1782-1852. I. Title.

FUESS, Claude Moore, 1885-1963. 973.5'0924 B
Daniel Webster. New York, Da Capo Press, 1968 [c1930] 2 v. illus., facsims., ports. 24 cm. (The American scene) (A Da Capo Press reprint edition.) Contents.Contents.—v. 1. 1782-1830.—v. 2. 1830-1852. Bibliography: p. [419]-430. [E340.W4F955 1968] 68-8722 35.00
1. Webster, Daniel, 1782-1852.

LODGE, Henry Cabot, 1850-1924. 973.5'0924 B
Daniel Webster. Boston, Houghton, Mifflin. [New York, AMS Press, 1972] viii, 378 p. illus. 19 cm. (American statesmen, v. 21) Reprint of the 1899 ed. [E340.W4L82 1972] 71-128960 ISBN 0-404-50871-5
1. Webster, Daniel, 1782-1852. I. Title. II. Series.

STEINBERG, Alfred, 1917- 923.273
Daniel Webster. Illustrated by Leonard Vosburgh. New York, Putnam, [1959] 128 p. illus. 21 cm. (Lives to remember) [E340.W4S84] 59-9449
1. Webster, Daniel, 1782-1832 — Juvenile literature. I. Title.

WEBSTER, Daniel, 1782-1852. 973.5'0924
The letters of Daniel Webster, from documents owned principally by the New Hampshire Historical Society. Edited by C. H. Van Tyne. New York, McClure, Phillips, 1902. St. Clair Shores, Mich., Scholarly Press, 1970. xxii, 769 p. port. 22 cm. Includes letters written by and to Webster. Includes bibliographical references. [E337.8.W365 1970] 79-108553
1. U.S.—Politics and government—1815-1861. I. Van Tyne, Claude Halstead, 1869-1930, ed. II. Title.

WEBSTER, Daniel, 1782-1852. 973.5'0924 B
Speak for yourself, Daniel; a life of Webster in his own words. Edited and arr. by Walker Lewis. Boston, Houghton Mifflin, 1969. xix, 505 p. illus., facsims., ports. 22 cm. "Notes and sources": p. 468-494. [E340.W4A13] 69-12574 8.95
I. Lewis, Walker, ed. II. Title.

Webster, John, 1580?-1625?

HENDERSON, Philip, 1906- v. 12
Christopher Marlowe. Lincoln, Univ. of Nebraska Press [1966] 182 p. illus. 67-101088
1. Marlowe, Christopher, 1564-1593. 2. Jonson, Ben, 1572-1637. 3. Webster, John, 1580?-1625? 4. Ford, John, 1586-ca. 1640. I. Title. II. Title: Ben Jonson III. Title: John Webster IV. Title: John Ford

JUMP, John Davies, 1913- 821.3
The white devil and The Duchess of Malfi (John Webster) [by] John D. Jump. New York, Barnes & Noble [1966] vii, 71 p. 19 cm. (Notes on English literature, 20) Bibliography: p. 69. [PR3187.J8] 67-10
1. Webster, John, 1580?-1625? The Duchess of Malfi. 2. Webster, John, 1580?-1625? The white devil. I. Title.

WEBSTER, John, 1580?-1625? 922.3
The tragedy of the Duchess of Malfi, [New Ed.] New York, Washington Square Press [1959] xxix, 124 p. illus. 17 cm. (A Folger Library general reader's edition) A Washington Square Press book, W-101. [PR3184.D8 1959] 59-4357
I. Title. II. Title: The Duchess of Malfi.

Webster, Margaret,

WEBSTER, Margaret, 1905- 792'.0233'0924 B
Don't put your daughter on the stage. [1st ed.] New York, Knopf, 1972. xix, 379, xi p. illus. 25 cm. Autobiography. [PN2287.W4555A3] 72-2135 ISBN 0-394-47603-4 10.00
I. Title.

Webster, Nesta Helen.

WEBSTER, Nesta Helen. 928.2
Spacious days; an autobiography. London, New York Hutchinson [1950?] 196 p. illus., ports. 24 cm. Errata ship inserted. [CT788.W397A3] 51-29087
I. Title.

Webster, Noah, 1758-1843.

BELOK, Michael. 370'.8 S
Noah Webster revisited, by Michael V. Belok Tempe, Bureau of Educational Research and Services, Arizona State University, 1973. 32 p. 23 cm. (Arizona State University. Bureau of Educational Research and Services. Research and services bulletin no. 32) Bibliography: p. 29-31. [LB5.A73 no. 32] [PE64.W5] 423'.092'4 B 74-622345
1. Webster, Noah, 1758-1843. I. Title. II Series: Arizona. State University, Tempe. Bureau of Educational Research and Services. Research and services bulletin no. 32.

FORD, Emily Ellsworth (Fowler) 1826-1893, comp. 423'.0924 B
Notes on the life of Noah Webster. Edited by Emily Ellsworth Ford Skeel. New York, B. Franklin [1971] 2 v. illus., ports. 19 cm. (Burt Franklin research and source works series, 660. American classics in history and social science, 172) Reprint of the 1912 ed. Includes bibliographies. [PE64.W5F7 1971] 74-150160 ISBN 0-8337-1196-2
1. Webster, Noah, 1758-1843. I. Title. **BIP**

GRANFIELD, Marcella A 924.2
Meet Dr. Webster, by Marcella A. Granfield. [1st ed.] New York, Vantage Press [1965] 78 p. 21 cm. [PE64.W5G7] 65-2044
1. Webster, Noah, 1758-1843. I. Title.

MORGAN, John Smith, 1921- 423'.092'4 B
Noah Webster / John S. Morgan. 1st ed. New York : Mason/Charter, 1975. vii, 216 p. : port. ; 24 cm. Includes index. Bibliography: p. 206-210. [PE64.W5M67] 75-5883 ISBN 0-88405-108-0 : 8.95
1. Webster, Noah, 1758-1843.

SCUDDER, Horace Elisha, 1838-1902. 423'.0924
Noah Webster. 6th ed. Ann Arbor, Mich., Plutarch Press, 1971. vi, 302 p. 22 cm. (American men of letters) "Facsimile reprint of the 1886 edition." [PE64.W5S4 1883a] 71-99056
1. Webster, Noah, 1758-1843. I. Title. II. Series. **BIP**

SHOEMAKER, Ervin C 1890- v. 12
Noah Webster, pioneer of learning. New York, AMS Press, 1966. x, 347 p. front. (port.), illus., plates. 24 cm. Originally published in 1936. 68-27433
1. Webster, Noah, 1758-1843. 2. Education. I. Title.

WARFEL, Harry Redcay, 1899- 423'.0924 B
Noah Webster, schoolmaster to America,

by Harry R. Warfel. New York, Octagon Books, 1966 [c1936] xii, 460 p. illus., facsims., ports. 24 cm. "Sources and bibliography": p. [439]-449. [PE64.W5W3 1966] 66-28378
1. Webster, Noah, 1758-1843.

WEBSTER, Noah, 1758-1843. 924.2
Letters: edited with an introd. by Harry R. Warfel. New York, Library Publishers [1953] xivl. 562p. 24cm. [PE64.W5A4] 53-4192
I. Title.

Webster-Smith, Irene, 1888-

HITT, Russell T. 266.0924 B
Sensei; the life story of Irene Webster-Smith [by] Russell T. Hitt. [1st ed.] New York, Harper & Row [1965] 240 p. illus., ports. 22 cm. (Harper jungle missionary classics) [BV3457.W4H5] 65-20452
1. Webster-Smith, Irene, 1888- 2. Missions—Japan. I. Title.

HITT, Russell T. 266.0924
Sensie; the life story of Irene Webster-Smith. New York, Harper [c.1965] 240p. illus., ports. 22cm. (Harper jungle missionary classics) [BV3457.WH5] 65-20452 3.95 bds.,
1. Webster-Smith, Irene, 1888- 2. Missions—Japan. I. Title.

Wechsberg, Joseph, 1907-

WECHSBERG, Joseph, 1907- 787'.1'0924 B
Looking for a bluebird. Illustrated by F. Strobel. Westport, Conn., Greenwood Press [1974, c1945] 210 p. illus. 23 cm. Reprint of the ed. published by Houghton Mifflin, Boston. [ML418.W3A3 1974] 73-16801 ISBN 0-8371-7234-9 10.75
1. Wechsberg, Joseph, 1907- 2. Musicians—Correspondence, reminiscences, etc. I. Title. **BIP**

WECHSBERG, Joseph, 1907- 787'.1'0924 B
The Vienna I knew : memories of a European childhood / Joseph Wechsberg. 1st ed. Garden City, N.Y. : Doubleday, 1979. 263 p. ; 22 cm. [DB844.W4A38] 78-22540 ISBN 0-385-12674-3 : 10.95
1. Wechsberg, Joseph, 1907- 2. Vienna—Biography. I. Title.

Weckesser, Henry Jacob, 1836-1911.

WHALEY, Miriam (Weckesser) 1916- ed. 929.2
The life and times of Henry Weckesser. [n.p., 1959] 84 p. illus. 23 cm. [CT275.W36W4] 59-11331
1. Weckesser, Henry Jacob, 1836-1911. I. Title.

Wedel, Werner H. O 1903

CHRISEMER, Edgar T. 266.40924
The Werner Wedel story, by Edgar T. Chrisemer. Boston, Branden Pr. [1966] 86p. 23cm. [BV3427.W4C5] 66-18428 3.00
1. Wedel, Werner H. O 1903 I. Title.

*Wedgwood, Cicely Veronica,

WEDGWOOD, Cicely Veronica, 1910- 923.244
Richelieu and the French monarchy New, rev. ed. New York, Collier Books [1962] 155 p. 18 cm. (Men and history, BS130V) Includes bibliography. [DC123.9.R5W4 1962] 62-19197
I. Richelieu, Armand Jean du Plessis, Cardinal, duc de, 1585-1642 II. Title. **BIP**

*WEDGWOOD, Cicely Veronica, 1910- 949.2'03'0924
William the Silent, William of Nassau, Prince of Orange, 1533-1584 by C. V. Wegwood. New York, Norton [1968] 256p. 20cm. (N185) (B) 1.95 pap.,
I. Title.

Wedgwood, Josiah, 1730-1795.

BURTON, Anthony. 738.3'7 B
Josiah Wedgwood / Anthony Burton. New York : Stein and Day, [1976] p. cm. Includes index. Bibliography: p. [NK4210.W4B87] 76-6989 ISBN 0-8128-1907-1
1. Wedgwood, Josiah, 1730-1795. **BIP**

METEYARD, Eliza, 1816-1879. 738.3'7 B
The life of Josiah Wedgwood. New York, A. M. Kelley, 1971. 2 v. illus. 24 cm. (Reprints of economic classics) Reprint of the 1865-1866 ed. Includes bibliographical references. [NK4210.W4M6 1971] 78-183175 ISBN 0-678-00890-6
1. Wedgwood, Josiah, 1730-1795. 2. Wedgwood ware. 3. Pottery—England. I. Title.

SMILES, Samuel, 1812-1904. 738.3'7 B
Josiah Wedgwood, F.R.S., his personal history. Ann Arbor, Mich., Plutarch Press, 1971. xi, 304 p. 22 cm. Reprint of the 1894 ed. [NK4210.W4S7 1971] 71-141603
1. Wedgwood, Josiah, 1730-1795. 2. Wedgwood ware.

Weed, Thurlow, 1797-1882.

VAN DEUSEN, Glyndon Garlock, 1897- 329'.00924 B
Thurlow Weed, wizard of the lobby, by Glyndon G. Van Deusen. New York, Da Capo Press, 1969 [c1947] xiv, 403 p. facsims., ports. 24 cm. (The American scene) (A Da Capo Press reprint series.) Bibliography: p. [387]-393. [E415.9.W39V3 1969] 73-87698
1. Weed, Thurlow, 1797-1882. I. Title.

WEED, Thurlow, 1797-1882. 329'.00924 B
Life of Thurlow Weed. New York, Da Capo Press, 1970. 2 v. illus., ports. 24 cm. Reprint of the 1883-84 ed., originally published under title: Life of Thurlow Weed including his autobiography and a memoir. Contents.Contents.—v. 1. Autobiography of Thurlow Weed, edited by H. A. Weed.—v. 2. Memoir of Thurlow Weed, by T. W. Barnes. [E415.9.W39W33] 79-87686
1. U.S.—Politics and government—1815-1861. 2. New York (State)—Politics and government—1775-1865. I. Title. **BIP**

Weedon, George, 1734-1793.

WARD, Harry M. 081 S
Duty, honor, or country : General George Weedon and the American Revolution / Harry M. Ward. Philadelphia : American Philosophical Society, 1979. xi, 297 p. : ill. ; 24 cm. (Memoirs of the American Philosophical Society ; v. 133 ISSN 0065-9746s) Includes index.IBibliography: p. 274-286. [Q11.P612 vol. 133] [E203.W38] 973.3'092'4 B 78-73168 ISBN 0-87169-133-7 pbk. : 10.00
1. Weedon, George, 1734-1793. 2. United States. Army. Continental Army—Biography. 3. United States—History—Revolution, 1775-1783—Campaigns and battles. 4. Generals—United States—Biography. I. Title. II. Series: American Philosophical Society, Philadelphia. Memoirs ; v. 133.
Publisher's Address : 104 s. Fifth St., Philadelphia, PA 19106 **BIP**

Weekley, Montague.

WEEKLEY, Montague. 927.6
Thomas Bewick. London, New York, Oxford University Press, 1953. x, 224p. illus. 23cm. 'Bewickiana: a supplementary note on manuscripts. personal relics. etc.':p. [218]-219. [NE1217.B4W4] 53-2758
I. Bewick, Thomas, 1753-1828. II. Title.

Weeks, John Elmer,

WEEKS, John Elmer, 1853-1949. 926.1
Autobiography. [Portland Or., 1954] 115p. illus. 23cm. [RE36.W4A3] 55-388
I. Title.

Weelkes, Thomas, 1575 (ca.)-1623.

BROWN, David, 1929- 780'.92'4
Thomas Weelkes : a biographical and critical study / by David Brown. New York : Da Capo Press, 1979 [c1979] 223 p. ; 24 cmm. (Da Capo Press music reprint series) Reprint of the ed. published by F. A. Praeger, New York. Includes indexes. Bibliography: p. 209-210. [ML410.W36B8 1979] 79-10068 ISBN 0-306-79523-X : 19.50
1. Weelkes, Thomas, 1575 (ca.)-1623. 2. Composers—England—Biography.

BROWN, David, 1929- 783'.0924
Thomas Weelkes; a biographical and critical study. New York, F. A. Praeger [1969] 223 p. music. 26 cm. Bibliography: p. 209-210. [ML410.W36B8] 69-20021 13.50
1. Weelkes, Thomas, 1575 (ca.)-1623.

Weems, Mason Locke, 1759-1825.

KELLOCK, Harold, 1879- 283'.0924 B
Parson Weems of the cherry-tree; being a short account of the eventful life of the Reverend M. L. Weems. Ann Arbor, Mich., Gryphon Books, 1971. ix, 212 p. illus. 22 cm. "Facsimile reprint of the 1928 edition." [E302.6.W4K4 1928a] 75-107137
1. Weems, Mason Locke, 1759-1825. I. Title.

Weigel, Gustave, 1906-1964.

ONE of a kind; 271'.5'0924
essays in tribute to Gustave Weigel. With an introd. by John Courtney Murray. Wilkes-Barre, Pa., Dimension Books [1967] 111 p. 21 cm. Contents.Contents.—A memorable man, by J. C. Murray.—The gringo, by J. Ochagavia.—An uncommon ecumenist, by A. C. Outler.—A living epistle of Christ, by D. Horton.—One of a kind, by J. B. Sheerin.—Unstucknes, by H. M. Jenkins.—A figure in transition, by E. Burke.—An ocumenical pioneer, by M. Brown.—Liquidator of prejudices, by R. Balkam. [BX4705.W415O5] 67-27131
1. Weigel, Gustave, 1906-1964. I. Murray, John Courtney.

Weight lifting.

TODD, Terry. 796.4'1
Inside powerlifting / Terry Todd. Chicago : Contemporary Books, c1978. xiii, 111 p. : ill. ; 29 cm. Includes index. [GV511.T63 1978] 77-23710 ISBN 0-8092-7858-8 : 7.95 ISBN 0-8092-7854-5 pbk. : 4.95
1. Weight lifting. 2. Weight lifters—Biography. 3. Weight lifting—Rules. I. Title. **BIP**

Weil, Joseph R.

WEIL, Joseph R. 364.1'63'0924 B
The con game and "Yellow Kid" Weil : the autobiography of the famous con artist as told to W. T. Brannon. New York : Dover Publications, 1974, c1948. 297 p., [7] leaves of plates : ill. ; 22 cm. Reprint of the ed. published by Ziff-Davis Pub. Co., Chicago, under title: "Yellow Kid" Weil. [HV6248.W474A3 1974] 74-12575 ISBN 0-486-23127-5 pbk. : 3.50
1. Weil, Joseph R. I. Brannon, William T. II. Title.

Weil, Simone, 1909-1943.

CABAUD, Jacques 921.4
Simone Weil; a fellowship in love [Tr. from French] New York, Channel [dist. Meredith, 1965, c.1964] 392p. illus., ports. 22cm. Bibl. [B2430.W474C2] 65-17167 5.95
1. Weil, Simone, 1909-1943. I. Title.

PETREMENT, Simone. 194 B
Simone Weil : a life / Simone Petrement ; translated from the French by Raymond Rosenthal. 1st American ed. New York : Pantheon Books, c1976. xiv, 576 p., [12] leaves of plates : ill. ; 24 cm. Translation of La vie de Simone Weil. Includes bibliographical references and index. [B2430.W474P4613] 76-9576 ISBN 0-394-49815-1 : 15.00
1. Weil, Simone, 1909-1943. 2. Philosophers—France—Biography. **BIP**

REES, Richard, Sir, bart. 194
Simone Weil : a sketch for a portrait / Richard Rees ; with a pref. by Harry T. Moore. Carbondale : Southern Illinois University Press, [1977, c1966] p. cm. (Arcturus books ; AB 142) Bibliography: p. [B2430.W474R4 1977] 77-24990 ISBN 0-8093-0852-5 : 6.95
1. Weil, Simone, 1909-1943. 2. Philosophers—France—Biography. **BIP**

TOMLIN, Eric Walter Frederick, 1913- 921.4
Simone Weil. New Haven, Yale University Press, 1954. 64p. 23cm. (Studies in modern European literature and thought) 'The works of Simone Well': p. 64. Bibliographical footnotes. [B2430.W474T6] A54
1. Weil, Simone, 1909-1943. I. Title. II. Series.

Weingarten, Violet—Diaries.

WEINGARTEN, Violet. 818'.5'403
Intimations of mortality / Violet Weingarten. 1st ed. New York : Knopf, 1978. vi, 242 p. ; 22 cm. [PS3573.E396Z52] 77-75004 ISBN 0-394-41290-7 : 8.95
1. Weingarten, Violet—Diaries. 2. Authors, American—20th century—Biography. 3. Cancer—Biography. I. Title. **BIP**

Weingartner, Felix, 1863-1942.

FELIX Weingartner 785'.092'4 B
: recollections & recordings / [edited by] Christopher Dyment. Rickmansworth : Triad Press, 1976. 5-116 p. : ill., facsims., music, ports. ; 30 cm. (Triad Press bibliographical series ; no. 5) "The recorded legacy of Felix Weingartner": p. [61]-92. Includes bibliographical references and index. [ML422.W325F4] 76-369869 ISBN 0-902070-17-7 : £5.95
1. Weingartner, Felix, 1863-1942. 2. Weingartner, Felix, 1863-1942—Discography. I. Weingartner, Felix, 1863-1942. II. Dyment, Christopher.

Weintraub, Julie.

LINN, Edward. 301.5'7
Big Julie of Vegas. Greenwich, Conn., Fawcett [1975, c1974] 271 p. 18 cm. (A Fawcett crest book) [HV6721.L3L55 1975] 74-78690 1.75 (pbk.)
1. Weintraub, Julie. I. Title.

Weir, Charles O.

WEIR, Charles O. 629.13'092'4 B
Vertical ascent : my 16 years as a helicopter pilot / by Charles O. Weir, with Leonard Taylor. Seattle : Hancock House Publishers, c1977. p. cm. [TL540.W38A38 1977] 77-3516 ISBN 0-919654-76-2 : 8.95
1. Weir, Charles O. 2. Helicopter pilots—Biography. I. Title.

Weir, Julian Alden, 1852-1919.

YOUNG, Dorothy (Weir) 927.5
The life & letters of J. Alden Weir. Edited with an introd. by Lawrence W. Chisolm. New Haven, Yale University Press [c.] 1960. xxxii, 227p. col. front., plates, ports. 26cm. 60-13128 10.00
1. Weir, Julian Alden, 1852-1919. I. Title.

YOUNG, Dorothy (Weir) 927.5
The life & letters of J. Alden Weir. Edited with an introd.by Lawrence W. Chisholm. New Haven, Yale University Press, 1960. xxxii, 277 p. col. front., plates, ports. 26 cm. [ND237.W4Y6] 60-13128
1. Weir, Julian Alden, 1852-1919. I. Title. **BIP**

YOUNG, Dorothy (Weir) 769'.924 B
The life and letters of J. Alden Weir. Edited with an introd. by Lawrence W. Chisolm. New York, Kennedy Graphics, 1971 [c1960] xxxii, 277 p. illus., ports. 24 cm. (Library of American art) Includes bibliographical references. [ND237.W4Y6 1971] 76-146157 ISBN 0-306-70097-2
1. Weir, Julian Alden, 1852-1919.

Weisbord, Vera Buch, 1895-

WEISBORD, Vera 335.43'092'4 B
Buch, 1895-
A radical life / Vera Buch Weisbord. Bloomington : Indiana University Press, c1977. xviii, 330 p. : ill. ; 25 cm. Includes bibliographical references and index. [HX84.W42A37 1977] 76-28276 15.00
1. Weisbord, Vera Buch, 1895- 2. Communists—United States—Biography. 3. Communism—United States—History. 4. Trade-unions and communism—United States—History. I. Title. BIP

Weiser, Conrad, 1696-1760.

WALLACE, Paul A. W. 970.5
Conrad Weiser, 1696-1760, friend of colonist and Mohawk, by Paul A. W. Wallace New York, Russell & Russell [1971, c1945] xiv, 648 p. geneal. table, maps. 25 cm. Includes bibliographical references. [F152.W4286 1971] 73-102553
1. Weiser, Conrad, 1696-1760. 2. Pennsylvania—History—Colonial period, ca. 1600-1775. 3. Indians of North America—Pennsylvania. 4. Iroquois Indians.

WALTON, Joseph 970.5'0924 B
Solomon, d.1912.
Conrad Weiser and the Indian policy of colonial Pennsylvania. [New York] Arno Press [1971, c1900] 420 p. illus. 23 cm. (The First American frontier) Includes bibliographical references. [E78.P4W2 1971] 71-146425 ISBN 0-405-02895-4
1. Weiser, Conrad, 1696-1760. 2. Pennsylvania—History—Colonial period, ca. 1600-1775. 3. Indians of North America—Pennsylvania. I. Title. II. Series. BIP

Weiser family.

WEISER, Jacob. 929'.2'0973
Letters from the Mahantongo Valley; correspondence from Jacob Weiser in the Mahantongo Valley, Northumberland County, Pennsylvania, to Frederick Weiser, his brother, in Delaware County, Ohio. Translated and edited by Frederick S. Weiser. Manheim, Pa., John Conrad Weiser Family Association, 1967. 12 p. 23 cm. Includes some sentences and paragraphs in the original Pennsylvania German. [CS71.W428 1967] 73-171409
1. Weiser family. 2. Wesier, Jacob. I. Weiser, Frederick, 1776-1855. II. Title.

Weisgal, Meyer Wolfe, 1894-

THE Odyssey of an 956.94'05'0924
optimist. Meyer W. Weisgal; an anthology by his contemporaries. [1st ed.] New York, Atheneum, 1967. xi, 268 p. ports. 22 cm. "Portions of this book were previously published in Meyer Weisgal at seventy: an anthology, edited by Edward Victor." [DS151.W37O3] 67-14333
1. Weisgal, Meyer Wolfe, 1894-

WEISGAL, Meyer 956.94'001'0924 B
Wolfe, 1894-
Meyer Weisgal ... so far; an autobiography. [1st American ed.] New York, Random House [1972, c1971] 404 p. illus. 24 cm. [DS151.W37A3 1972] 70-171983 ISBN 0-394-47594-1 10.00
1. Zionists—Correspondence, reminiscences, etc. I. Title.

Weiss, Carl Austin, 1905-1935.

DEUTSCH, Hermann Bacher, FIC
1889-
The Huey Long murder case. [1st ed.] Garden City, N.Y., Doubleday, 1963. 180 p. illus. 22cm. [KF224.W4D4] 923.273 62-15869
1. Weiss, Carl Austin, 1905-1935. 2. Long, Huey Pierce, 1893-1935.

Weissmuller, John.

ONYX, Narda. 927.9
Water, world & Weissmuller, a biography. Los Angeles, VION Pub. Co. [1964] 330 p. illus., ports. 22 cm. [GV697.W4O5] 64-6555
1. Weissmuller, John. I. Title.

Weit, Erwin.

WEIT, Erwin. 320.9'438'05
At the Red summit; interpreter behind the Iron Curtain. Translated by Mary Schofield. With a pref. by Harry Schwartz. [1st American ed.] New York, Macmillan [1973] 226 p. illus. 21 cm. Translation of Ostblock intern. [DK443.W413 1973] 72-88151 6.95
1. Weit, Erwin. 2. Poland—Politics and government—1945- I. Title. BIP

Weitling, Wilhelm Christian, 1808-1871.

WITTKE, Carl Frederick, 923.343
1892-
The Utopian communist; a biography of Wilhelm Weitling, nineteenth-century reformer. Baton Rouge, Louisiana State University Press [1950] vii, 327 p. illus., ports. 24 cm. [HX708.W6W5] 50-7564
1. Weitling, Wilhelm Christian, 1808-1871. I. Title.

Weitzel, Lawrence M., 1915—

LEIPOLD, L. 658'.92'190924 B
Edmond, 1902-
Lawrence M. Weitzel; mechanical specialist, by L. Edmond Leipold. Minneapolis, Denison [1968] 212 p. illus., ports. 22 cm. (Men of achievement series) [TJ140.W4L4] 68-21248
1. Weitzel, Lawrence M., 1915-

Weizman, Ezer, 1924—

WEIZMAN, Ezer, 358.4'13'310924 B
1924-
On eagles' wings : the personal story of the leading commander of the Israel Air Force / Ezer Weizman. New York : Berkley Pub. Corp., 1979, c1976. ix, 291p. ; 18 cm. (A Berkley book) Includes index. [UG626.2W46A36 1977] ISBN 0-425-04022-4 pbk. : 2.50
1. Weizman, Ezer, 1924- 2. Israel, Hel ha-avir — Biography. 3. Generals — Israel — Biography. 4. Air pilots — Israel — Biography. I. Title.
L.C. card no. for 1976 Macmillan ed. : 76-27290.

Weizmann, Chaim, Pres. Israel, 1874-1952.

BAKER, Rachel (Mininberg), 922.96
1903-
Chaim Weizmann, builder of a nation. New York, Messner [1950] 180 p. port. 22 cm. Bibliography: p. 171-172. [DS151.W4B3] 50-10151
1. Weizmann, Chaim, Pres. Israel, 1874- I. Title.

BERLIN, Isaiah, Sir v. 12
Chaim Weizmann. New York, Farrar, Straus and Cudahy [1958] 60p. 19cm. (Herbert Samuel lecture, 2) A60
1. Weizmann, Chaim, Pres. Israel, 1874-1932. I. Title. II. Series.

BLUMBERG, Harold 956.94'05'0924 B
M.
Weizmann, his life and times / H. M. Blumberg. New York : St. Martin's Press, 1975. 273 p. : ill. ; 25 cm. Includes excerpts from papers, letters, and the autobiography of C. Weizmann. [DS125.3.W45B58 1975] 75-9465 ISBN 0-903895-34-X : 25.00
1. Weizmann, Chaim, Pres. Israel, 1874-1952. 2. Zionism—History. I. Title.

CHAIM Weizmann. v. 12
New York, 1958. 60p. 17cm. (Herzl Institute pamphlet no. 8)
1. Weizmann, Chaim, Pres. Israel, 1874-1952. I. Berlin, Isaiah, Sir II. Series.

CHAIM Weizmann; 923.15694
a biography by several hands. Pref. by David Ben-Gurion. Ed. by Meyer W. Weisgal, Joel Carmichael. New York, Atheneum, 1963 [c.1962] 364p. illus. 22cm. 63-7797 6.95
1. Weizmann, Chaim Pres. Israel, 1874-1952. I. Weisgal, Meyer Wolfe; 1894- ed. II. Carmichael, Joel, ed.

LITVINOFF, 956.94'05'0924 B
Barnet.
Weizmann : last of the patriarchs / by Barnet Litvinoff. 1st American ed. New York : Putnam, 1976. 288 p., [8] leaves of plates : ill. ; 24 cm. Includes index. Bibliography: p. [269]-270. [DS125.3.W45L58 1976] 76-22549 ISBN 0-399-11718-0 : 25.00
1. Weizmann, Chaim, Pres. Israel, 1874-1952. BIP

SHIHOR, Schmuel, 1910- 923.15694
Hollow glory; the last days of Chaim Weizmann, first President of Israel. Translated from the Hebrew by Julian L. Meltzer. New York, T. Yoseloff [1960] 256 p. illus. 22 cm. Translation of Hineh hem ba'lm (transliterated) [DS151.W4S353] 60-6837
1. Weizmann, Chaim, Pres. Israel, 1874-1952. I. Title.

WEIZMANN, Chaim, 956.94'05'0924
Pres. Israel, 1874-1952.
The letters and papers of Chaim Weizmann. English ed. London, Oxford U.P., 1968- v. illus., facsims., ports. 25 cm. Contents.Contents.—Series A: Letters. v. 1. Summer 1885-29 October 1902, edited by Leonard Stein in collaboration with Gedalia Yogev.—v. 2. November 1902-August 1903; editorial direction: Gedalia Yogev.—v. 3. September 1903-December 1904, general editor: Meyer W. Weisgal. —v. 5. January 1907-February 1913; edited by Hanna Weiner and Barnet Litvinoff. [DS125.3.W45A43] 74-354485 ISBN 0-19-711216-1 (v. 1) 63/- (v. 1) varies
1. Weizmann, Chaim, Pres. Israel, 1874-1952 2. Zionists Correspondence, reminiscences, etc. I. Stein, Leonard, ed. II. Title. BIP

WEIZMANN, Chaim, 956.94050924 (B)
Pres. Israel, 1874-1952.
Trial and error; the autobiography of Chaim Weizmann. New York, Schocken Books [1966] xviii, 493 p. illus., maps, ports. 21 cm. (Schocken paperbacks, SB116) [DS125.3.W45A3] 66-14878
I. Title.

WEIZMANN, Chaim, 956.94'05'0924 B
Pres. Israel, 1874-1952.
Trial and error; the autobiography of Chaim Weizmann. Westport, Conn., Greenwood Press [1972, c1949] vii, 498 p. port., map. 24 cm. [DS125.3.W45A3 1972] 70-156215 ISBN 0-8371-6166-5
1. Zionists—Correspondence, reminiscences, etc. I. Title.

WEIZMANN, Chaim, 956.94050924
Pres. Israel, 1874-1952
Trial and error; the autobiography of Chaim Weizmann. New York, Schocken [c.1949, 1966] xviii, 493p. illus., maps, ports. 21cm. (SB116) [DS125.3.W45A3 1966] 66-14878 2.95 pap.,
I. Title.

WEIZMANN, Vera, 956.94'05'0924 B
1881-1966.
The impossible takes longer; the memoirs of Vera Weizmann, wife of Israel's first President, as told to David Tutaev. [1st U.S. ed.] New York, Harper & Row [1967] xii, 308 p. illus., ports. 22 cm. [DS125.3.W45W4 1967b] 67-22510
1. Weizmann, Chaim, Pres. Israel, 1874-1952. I. Tutaeff, David. II. Title.

Weizmann, Chaim, Pres. Israel, 1874-1952—Juvenile literature.

ZAGOREN, Ruby. 956.94'05'0924 B
Chaim Weizmann, first president of Israel. Champaign, Ill., Garrard Pub. Co. [1972] 176 p. illus. 22 cm. (A Century book) A biography of the scientist and Zionist leader who became the first President of the newly-formed state of Israel in 1948. [DS125.3.W45Z3] 92 74-177893 ISBN 0-8116-4755-2
1. Weizmann, Chaim, Pres. Israel, 1874-1952—Juvenile literature. I. Title.

Weizmann, Ezer, 1924-

WEIZMANN, Ezer, 358.4'13'310924 B
1924-
On eagles' wings : the personal story of the leading commander of the Israeli Air Force / Ezer Weizman. New York : MacMillan, [1977] p. cm. Includes index. [UG626.2.W46A36 1977] 76-27290 ISBN 0-02-625790-4 : 8.95
1. Weizmann, Ezer, 1924- 2. Israel. Hel ha-avir—Biography. 3. Generals—Israel—Biography. 4. Air pilots—Israel—Biography. I. Title. BIP

Welch, Ashbel, 1809-1882.

HOWELL, J. Roscoe, 624'.092'4 B
1881-1972.
Ashbel Welch, civil engineer. Lambertville, N.J., Lambertville Historical Society, 1972?] iv, 25 p. illus. 24 cm. Originally published in the Proceedings of the New Jersey Historical Society, Oct., 1961, and Jan., 1972. [TA140.W4H68] 73-80333
1. Welch, Ashbel, 1809-1882. I. Title.

Welch, Herbert, Bp.

WELCH, Herbert, Bp. 1862- 922.773
As I recall my past century. Nashville, Abingdon [c.1962] 144p. illus. 21cm. 62-20456 3.00
I. Title.

Welch, Lew—Friends and associates.

SAROYAN, Aram. 811'.5'4 B
Genesis angels : the saga of Lew Welch and the beat generation / by Aram Saroyan. 1st ed. New York : Morrow, 1979. 128 p. : ill. ; 22 c . [PS3573.E457Z87] 78-31172 ISBN 0-688-03436-5 : 7.95
1. Welch, Lew—Friends and associates. 2. Authors, American—20th century—Biography. 3. Bohemianism—United States. I. Title. II. Title: Beat generation. BIP

Welch, Robert Alonzo. 1872-1952.

CLARK, James Anthony, 923.873
1907-
A biography of Robert Alonzo Welch. With Nathan Broch. [Houston, Clark Book Co., 1963] ix. 153 p. illus., ports (1 col.) 24 cm. [CT275.W377C55] 63-21980
1. Welch, Robert Alonzo. 1872-1952. I. Title.

Welch, Robert Henry Winborne, 1899-

GRIFFIN, G. 322.4'4'0924 B
Edward.
The life and words of Robert Welch, founder of the John Birch Society / by G. Edward Griffin ; with an introd. by E. Merrill Root. Thousand Oaks, Calif. : American Media, [1975]. xix, 330 p., [16] leaves of plates : ill. ; 22 cm. Includes bibliographical references and index. [E748.W436G74] 74-33111 ISBN 0-912986-07-7 : 12.50
1. Welch, Robert Henry Winborne, 1899- 2. John Birch Society. I. Title. BIP

Welch, William Henry, 1850-1934.

FLEMING, Donald Harnish, 1923- 926.1
William H. Welch and the rise of modern medicine. [1st ed.] Boston, Little, Brown [1954] 216p. 21cm. (The Library of American biography) [R154.W32F5] 54-6867
1. Welch, William Henry, 1830-1934. I. Title.

FLEXNER, Simon, 1863-1946 610/.924
William Henry Welch and the heroic age of American medicine, by Simon Flexner, James Thomas Flexner [Magnolia, Mass., P. Smith 1968] x. 539p. ports. 22cm. (Dover bk. rebound) Unabridged, corrected repubn. of the work first pub. in 1941. Bibl. [R154.W32F6 1966] (B) 5.50
1. Welch, William Henry, 1850-1934. I. Flexner, James Thomas, 1908- joint author II. Title.

FLEXNER, Simon, 1863-1946. 610'.924 (B)
William Henry Welch and the heroic age of American medicine, by Simon Flexner and James Thomas Flexner. New York, Dover Publications [1966, c1941] x, 539 p. ports. 22 cm. "An unabridged and corrected republication of the work first published ... in 1941." Bibliographical references included in "Notes to the text" (p. 466-524) [R154.W32F6 1966] 66-28492
1. Welch, William Henry, 1850-1934. I. Flexner, James Thomas, 1908- joint author. II. Title. BIP

FLEXNER, Simon, 1863-1946. 610'.924 B
William Henry Welch and the heroic age of American medicine, by Simon Flexner and James Thomas Flexner. New York, Dover Publications [1966, c1941] x, 539 p. ports. 22 cm. "An unabridged and corrected republication of the work first published ... in 1941." Bibliographical references included in "Notes to the text" (p. 466-524) [R154.W32F6 1966] 66-28492
1. Welch, William Henry, 1850-1934. I. Flexner, James Thomas, 1908- joint author.

Weld, Theodore Dwight, 1803-1895.

THOMAS, Benjamin Platt, 1902- 923.673
Theodore Weld, crusader for freedom. New Brunswick, Rutgers University Press, 1950. xii, 307 p. port. 22 cm. Bibliography: p. [289]-300. [E449.W46] 50-9667
1. Weld, Theodore Dwight, 1803-1895. I. Title. BIP

THOMAS, Benjamin Platt, 1902-1956. 326'.092'4 B
Theodore Weld, crusader for freedom. New York, Octagon Books, 1973 [c1950] xii, 307 p. port. 23 cm. Reprint of the ed. published by Rutgers University Press, New Brunswick, N.J. Bibliography: p. 291-300. [E449.W46T48 1973] 73-4479 ISBN 0-374-97857-3
1. Weld, Theodore Dwight, 1803-1895. I. Title.

Welk, Lawrence, 1904-

COAKLEY, Mary Lewis, 1907- 927.8
Mister Music Maker, Lawrence Welk. With a foreword by Lawrence Welk. [1st ed.] Garden City, N.Y., Doubleday, 1958. 280 p. illus. 22 cm. [ML422.W33C6] 58-6634
1. Welk, Lawrence, 1904- I. Title.

GOVONI, Albert. 785'.0924 B
The Lawrence Welk story. New York [Pocket Books] 1966. 122 p. 22 cm. (A PB special) [ML422.W33G7] 67-1425
1. Welk, Lawrence, 1904- I. Title.

WELK, Lawrence, 1904- 785.4'1'0924 B
Ah-one, ah-two! Life with my musical family [by] Lawrence Welk with Bernice McGeehan. Englewood Cliffs, N.J., Prentice-Hall [1974] 215 p. illus. 24 cm. [ML422.W33A27] 74-8086 ISBN 0-13-020990-2 7.95
1. Welk, Lawrence, 1904- 2. Musicians—Correspondence, reminiscences, etc. I. McGeehan, Bernice. II. Title.

WELK, Lawrence, 1904- 785.4'1'0924 B
Ah-one, ah-two! : Life with my musical family / Lawrence Welk, with Bernice McGeehan. Boston : G. K. Hall, 1975, c1974. 352 p. ; 25 cm. Large print ed. [ML422.W33A27 1975] 75-8558 ISBN 0-8161-6293-X lib.bdg. : 10.95
1. Welk, Lawrence, 1904- 2. Musicians—Correspondence, reminiscences, etc. I. McGeehan, Bernice. II. Title.

WELK, Lawrence, 1904- v. 12 B
Ah-one, ah-two! Life with my musical family [by] Lawrence Welk with Bernice McGeehan New York, Ballantine Books [1975 c1974] 256 p. illus. 18 cm. [ML422.W33A27] 785.410924 1.75 (pbk.)
1. Welk, Lawrence, 1904- 2. Musicians—Correspondence, reminiscences, etc. I. McGeehan, Bernice II. Title.
L.C. card no. for original edition: 74-8086. BIP

WELK, Lawrence, 1904- 785.4'1'0924 B
My America, your America / Lawrence Welk, with Bernice McGeehan. Englewood Cliffs, N.J. : Prentice-Hall, c1976. vi, 182 p., [17] leaves of plates (1 fold.) : ill. ; 24 cm. [ML422.W33A28] 76-20456 ISBN 0-13-608414-1 : 7.95
1. Welk, Lawrence, 1904- 2. Musicians—Correspondence, reminiscences, etc. I. McGeehan, Bernice, joint author. II. Title.

WELK, Lawrence, 1904- 785.4'1'0924 B
My America, your America / Lawrence Welk, with Bernice McGeehan. Boston : G. K. Hall, 1977, c1976. 296 p. ; 25 cm. "Published in large print." [ML422.W33A28 1977] 77-698 ISBN 0-8161-6466-5 lib.bdg. : 10.95
1. Welk, Lawrence, 1904- 2. Conductors (Music)—United States—Biography. I. McGeehan, Bernice, joint author. II. Title. BIP

WELK, Lawrence, 1904- 785.4'1'0924 [B]
Wunnerful, wunnerful! The autobiography of Lawrence Welk, by Lawrence Welk with Bernice McGeehan. New York, Bantam [1973, c.1971] 404 p. illus. 18 cm. [ML422.W33A3] pap., 1.95
1. Musicians—Correspondence, reminiscences, etc. I. McGeehan, Bernice.

WELK, Lawrence, 1904- 785.4'1'0924 B
Wunnerful, wunnerful; the autobiography of Lawrence Welk, by Lawrence Welk with Bernice McGeehan. Englewood Cliffs, N.J., Prentice-Hall [1971] 294 p. illus. 24 cm. [ML422.W33A3] 70-155983 ISBN 0-13-971515-0 7.95
1. Musicians—Correspondence, reminiscences, etc. I. McGeehan, Bernice. II. Title.

ZEHNPFENNIG, Gladys. 785'.0924
Lawrence Welk, champagne music man. Minneapolis, T. S. Denison [1968] 390 p. illus., ports. 22 cm. [ML422.W33Z4] 67-31411
1. Welk, Lawrence, 1904- I. Title.

Wellborn, Maximillian Bethune, 1862-1957.

BIOGRAPHY of Maximilian Bethune Wellborn. v. 12 Pub. by his children. [Atlanta] Darby Print. Co., 1960. 273p. illus. 22cm.
1. Wellborn, Maximillian Bethune, 1862-1957. I. Hopkins, Linton C 1872-

Weller, Robert E., 1914-

WELLER, Robert E., 1914- 248'.86'0924 B
Blind-and I see! / Robert E. Weller. St. Louis : Concordia Pub. House, c1978. 145 p. ; 21 cm. [HV1792.W44A32] 77-13241 pbk. : 3.95
1. Weller, Robert E., 1914- 2. Lutheran Church—Clergy—Biography. 3. Blind—Michigan—Biography. I. Title. BIP

Welles, Gideon, 1802-1878.

NIVEN, John. 973.7'092'4 B
Gideon Welles; Lincoln's Secretary of the Navy. New York, Oxford University Press, 1973. xii, 676 p. illus. 24 cm. Bibliography: p. [639]-654. [E467.1.W46N58] 73-82671 ISBN 0-19-501693-9 17.50
1. Welles, Gideon, 1802-1878.

WELLES, Gideon, 1802-1878. 923.273
Diary. Edited by Howard K. Beale, assisted by Alan W. Brownsword. With an introd. by Howard K. Beale and appendices drawn from Welles's correspondence. New York, W.W. Norton [1960] 3 v. ports. 25 cm. Contents.v. 1. 1861-March 30, 1864. -- v. 2. April 1, 1864-December 31, 1866. -- v. 3. January 1, 1867-June 6, 1869. [E468.W444] 60-6275
1. U.S. — Pol. & govt. — Civil War. 2. U.S. — Pol. & govt. — 1865-1869. 3. U.S. — Hist. — Civil War — Sources. 4. Reconstruction. I. Title.

Welles, Orson, 1915-

MCBRIDE, Joseph. 791.43'028'0924 B
Orson Welles, actor and director / by Joseph McBride. New York : Harvest/HBJ Books, [1977] p. cm. (An illustrated history of the movies) Includes index. "The films of Orson Welles": p. [PN2287.W456M3] 77-76450 pbk. : 2.50
1. Welles, Orson, 1915- I. Title.

MCBRIDGE, Joseph D 791.43'0233'0924
Orson Welles. New York, Viking Press [1972] 192 p. illus. 20 cm. (Cinema one, 19) Bibliography: p. 188-190. [PN1998.A3W45 1972b] 70-178854 ISBN 0-670-52893-5 2.95 (pbk)
1. Welles, Orson, 1915-

Welleser, Richard Coller Wellesler Marquis, 1760-1842.

HUTTON, William Holden, 1860-1930. 301.24'2'0924
The Marquess Wellesler, KG Delhi, S. Chand. [Mystic conn., verry, 1966. ii, 155p. 19 cm (Rulers of India) Fist pub. under title: The Marquess Wellesler KG, and the development of the company into the supreme power in India. Bibl. [DS475.3H98 1961] [SA66-5827] 2.50
1. Welleser, Richard Coller Wellesler Marquis, 1760-1842. I. Title. II. Series.

Wellington, Arthur Wellesley, 1st Duke of, 1769-1852.

BRYANT, Arthur, Sir, 1899- 942.07'092'4 B
The Great Duke; or, The invincible general. New York, Morrow, 1972 [c1971] 492 p. illus. 25 cm. Bibliography: p. 457-464. [DA68.12.W4B96 1972] 74-189273 8.95
1. Wellington, Arthur Wellesley, 1st Duke of, 1769-1852. I. Title.

COOPER, Leonard. 923.242
The age of Wellington; the life and times of the Duke of Wellington, 1769-1852. New York, Dodd, Mead [1963] xi, 308 p. maps. 25 cm. [DA68.12.W4C66] 63-17130
1. Wellington, Arthur Wellesley, 1st duke of, 1769-1852. I. Title.

DAVIES, Godfrey, 1892- 923.242
Wellington and his army Oxford, Blackwell, 1954. x, 154p. illus., ports. 23cm. Bibliographical footnotes. [DA68.12.W4D3] 54-4438
1. Wellington, Arthur Wellesley, 1st duke of, 1769-1852. 2. Gt. Brit. Army-Milltary life. I. Title. BIP

DAVIES, Godfrey, 1892-1957. 942.07'092'4 B
Wellington and his army. Westport, Conn., Greenwood Press [1974] x, 154 p. illus. 22 cm. Reprint of the 1954 ed. published by B. Blackwell, Oxford. Includes bibliographical references. [DA68.12.W4D3 1974] 74-8376 ISBN 0-8371-7566-6 9.50
1. Wellington, Arthur Wellesley, 1st Duke of, 1769-1852. 2. Great Britain. Army—Military life. I. Title.

GLOVER, Michael. 940.2'7'0924
Wellington as military commander. London, Batsford; Princeton, N. J., Van Nostrand, 1968. 288p. 26 plates, illus. 13 maps (3 col.), ports. 25cm. Bibl. [DA68.12.W4G57] 68-103553 8.95
1. Wellington, Arthur Wellesley, 1st Duke of, 1769-1852. I. Title.

GUEDALLA, Philip, 1889-1944. 941.07'092'4 B
The Duke / by Philip Guedalla. Westport, Conn. : Greenwood Press, 1976, c1931. xx, 523 p. ; 23 cm. Reprint of the 1974 ed. published by Hodder and Stoughton, London. Includes bibliographical references and index. [DA68.12.W4G84 1976] 75-38381 ISBN 0-8371-8670-6 lib.bdg. : 26.00
1. Wellington, Arthur Wellesley, 1st Duke of, 1769-1852. I. Title. BIP

LONGFORD, Elizabeth (Harman) Pakenham, Countess of, 1906- 942.07'092'4 B
Wellington [by] Elizabeth Longford. [1st U.S. ed.] New York, Harper & Row [1970-73, c1969-72] 2 v. illus., facsim., maps, ports. 25 cm. Contents.—[1] The years of the sword.—[2] Pillar of state. Bibliography: v. 1, p. 493-501; v. 2, p. 419-427. [DA68.12.W4L62] 75-95973 ISBN 0-06-012669-8 (v. 1) 10.00 per vol.
1. Wellington, Arthur Wellesley, 1st Duke of, 1769-1852.

PHILIPS, Cyril Henry, 1912- 954.03'1'0924
The young Wellington in India [by] C. H. Philips. London, Athlone Press, 1973. [2], 38 p. maps. 22 cm. (The Creighton lecture in history, 1972) Distributed by Humanities Press, Inc., New York. [DS475.2.W28P46] 74-157189 ISBN 0-485-14120-5 1.50
1. Wellington, Arthur Wellesley, 1st Duke of, 1796-1852. 2. India—History—Mysore War, 1799. 3. Maratha War, 1803. I. Title. II. Series: Creighton memorial lecture on history, 1972. BIP

WARD, Stephen George Peregrine 923.242
Wellington. New York, Arco [1964, c.1963] 152p. illus., maps, ports. 23cm. (Makers of world hist.) Bibl. 64-17015 3.95
1. Wellington, Arthur Wellesley, 1st duke of, 1769-1852. I. Title.

WELLINGTON: a summary of the career of the 1st Duke of Wellington and an account of Apsley House and its contents; 942.07'0924 written by Viscount Montgomery [& others] foreword by the 7th Duke of Wellington. Derby, English Life Publications, 1970. [1], 29 p. illus. (some col.), coat of arms, ports. 28 cm. [DA68.12.W4W49] 70-523427 4/-
1. Wellington, Arthur Wellesley, 1st Duke of, 1769-1852. 2. Apsley House, London. I. Montgomery of Alamein, Bernard Law Montgomery, 1st Viscount, 1887-

WELLINGTON, Arthur Wellesley, 1st Duke of, 1769-1852 942.07'092'4
Despatches, correspondence, and memoranda of Field Marshall Arthur,

Duke of Wellington, K. G., edited by his son, the Duke of Wellington, K. G. (In continuation of the former series) London, J. Murray, 1867-80. Milwood, N.Y., Kraus Reprint Co., 1973 8 v. 24 cm. [DA68.12.W4A32] 72-13736 270.00
1. Wellington, Arthur Wellesley, 1st Duke of, 1769-1852 2. Great Britain—History, Military. I. Title.
Contents omitted.

WELLINGTON, Arthur 923.242
Wellesley, 1st duke of, 1769-1852.
Wellington and his friends; letters of the first Duke of Wellington to the Rt. Hon. Charles and Mrs. Arbuthnot, the Earl and Countess of Wilton, Princess Lieven, and Miss Burdett-Coutts. Selected and edited by the seventh Duke of Wellington. London, Macmillan; New York, St. Martin's Press, 1965. viii, 317 p. illus., facsims., ports. 23 cm. [DA68.12.W4A42] 65-12617
I. Wellington, Gerald Wellesley, 7th duke of, 1885- ed. II. Title.

Wellington, Gerald Wellesley, 7th duke of, 1885-

WELLINGTON, Arthur 923.242
Wellesley 1st duke of, 1769-1852
Wellington and his friends; letters of the first Duke of Wellington to the Rt. Hon. Charles and Mrs. Arbuthnot, the Earl and Countess of Wilton, Princess Lieven, and Miss Burdett-Coutts. Sel., ed. by the seventh Duke of Wellington. London, Macmillan; New York, St Martin's [c.] 1965. viii, 317p. illus. facsims., ports. 23cm. [DA68.12.W4A45] 65-12617 7.50
1. Wellington, Gerald Wellesley, 7th duke of, 1885- I. Title.

Wellman, William Augustus, 1896-

WELLMAN, 791.43'0233'0924 B
William Augustus, 1896-
A short time for insanity, an autobiography [by] William A. Wellman. New York, Hawthorn Books [1974] ix, 276 p. illus. 25 cm. "Filmography:" p. 263-271. [PN1998.A3W46 1974] 73-11743 10.00
1. Wellman, William Augustus, 1896- I. Title.

Wells, Charles Knox Polk,

WELLS, Charles 364.15'5'0924 B
Knox Polk, b.1851.
Life and adventures of Polk Wells (Charles Knox Polk Wells) the notorious outlaw ... Written by himself. Freeport, N.Y., Books for Libraries Press [1971] 259 p. illus., ports. 23 cm. Reprint of the 1907 ed. [HV6448.W4 1971] 77-164635 ISBN 0-8369-5919-1
I. Title.

Wells, David Ames, 1828-1898.

FERLEGER, Herbert 336'.092'4 B
Ronald, 1914-
David A. Wells and the American revenue system, 1865-1870 / by Herbert Ronald Ferleger. Philadelphia : Porcupine Press, 1977. p. cm. (Perspectives in American history ; no. 32) Reprint of the ed. originally presented as the author's thesis, Columbia, 1942. Includes index. Bibliography: p. [HJ2373.W44F47 1977] 77-7106 ISBN 0-87991-356-8 lib.bdg. : 17.50
1. Wells, David Ames, 1828-1898. 2. United States—Officials and employees—Biography. 3. Internal revenue—United States—History. I. Title. II. Series: Perspectives in American history (Philadelphia) ; no. 32. **BIP**

Wells, Fargo and Company.

DODGE, Fred, 1854- 364.12'0924 B
1938.
Under cover for Wells Fargo; the unvarnished recollections of Fred Dodge. Edited by Carolyn Lake. Foreword by Neil Morgan. Boston, Houghton Mifflin, 1969. xx, 280 p. illus., maps (on lining papers), ports. 22 cm. [HE5903.W5D6] 69-15018 6.95
1. Wells, Fargo and Company. I. Lake, Carolyn, ed. II. Title.

Wells, Herbert George, 1866-1946.

BROME, Vincent, 1910- 823'.9'12 B
H. G. Wells; a biography. Westport, Conn., Greenwood Press [1970, c1951] 255 p. ports. 23 cm. Bibliography: p. 241-245. [PR5776.B67 1970b] 70-109284 ISBN 0-8371-3827-2
1. Wells, Herbert George, 1866-1946. I. Title.

BROME, Vincent, 1910- 823'.9'12 B
H. G. Wells; a biography. Freeport, N.Y., Books for Libraries Press [1970] 255 p. illus., ports. 23 cm. Bibliography: p. 241-245. [PR5776.B67 1970] 78-133515
1. Wells, Herbert George, 1866-1946. **BIP**

BROME, Vincent, 1910- 928.2
H. G. Wells, a biography. London, New York, Longmans, Green [1951] 255 p. ports. 23 cm. Bibliography: p. 241-245. [PR5776.B67 1951] 51-10774
1. Wells, Herbert George, 1866-1946. I. Title. **BIP**

DICKSON, Lovat, 1902- 823'.9'12 B
H. G. Wells; his turbulent life and times. [1st ed.] New York, Atheneum, 1969. x, 330 p. ports. 25 cm. Bibliography: p. [319]-322. [PR5776.D5] 68-12534 10.00
1. Wells, Herbert George, 1866-1946.

HOPKINS, Robert 823'.9'12
Thurston, 1884-
H. G. Wells: personality, character, topography, by R. Thurston Hopkins. With illus. by E. Harries. [Folcroft, Pa.] Folcroft Library Editions, 1972 [c1922] xvi, 256 p. illus. 24 cm. [PR5776.H6 1972] 72-10657 ISBN 0-8414-0737-1 (lib. bdg.)
1. Wells, Herbert George, 1866-1946.

KAGARLITSKII, IUlii 823.912
Iosifovich, 1926-
The life and thought of H. G. Wells [by] J. Kagarlitski. Translated from the Russian by Moura Budberg. New York, Barnes & Noble [1966] xiv, 210 p. illus., ports. 23 cm. [PR5776.K313] 66-31548
1. Wells, Herbert George, 1866-1946. I. Title.

MACKENZIE, Norman 823'.9'12 B
Ian.
H. G. Wells; a biography, by Norman and Jeanne MacKenzie. New York, Simon and Schuster [1973] xvi, 487 p. illus. 25 cm. Bibliography: p. 469-474. [PR5776.M3 1973b] 73-1184 ISBN 0-671-21520-5 10.00
1. Wells, Herbert George, 1866-1946. I. MacKenzie, Jeanne Daisy, 1922- joint author.

MEYER, Mathilde Marie, 928.2
1883-
H. G. Wells and his family, as I have known them, with a pref. by F. R. Wells. Edinburgh, International Pub. Co. [1956] 143p. illus. 23cm. [PR5776.M4 1956] 56-36277
1. Wells, Herbert George, 1866-1946. I. Title.

NICHOLSON, Norman, 1914- 231
H. G. Wells. Denver, A. Swallow [1950] 98 p. 19 cm (The English novelists) [[PR5776.N]] A52
1. Wells, Herbert George, 1866-1946. I. Title. II. Series: The English novelists (Denver) **BIP**

Wells, Herbert George, 1866-1946—Criticism and interpretation.

NICHOLSON, Norman, 823'.9'12 B
1914-
H. G. Wells / by Norman Nicholson. Norwood, Pa. : Norwood Editions, 1976. p. cm. Reprint of the 1950 ed. published by A. Barker, London, in series: The English novelists. Includes index. Bibliography: p. [PR5776.N5 1976] 76-10200 ISBN 0-8482-1913-9 : 10.00
1. Wells, Herbert George, 1866-1946—Criticism and interpretation. I. Series: The English novelists (London)

Wells, Herbert George, 1866-1946—Friends and associates.

JAMES, Henry, 1843-1916. 813'.4 B
Henry James and H. G. Wells : a record of their friendship, their debate on the art of fiction, and their quarrel / edited with an introd. by Leon Edel & Gordon N. Ray. Westport, Conn. : Greenwood Press, 1979, c1958. 272 p. : ports. ; 23 cm. Reprint of the ed. published by University of Illinois Press, Urbana. Includes index. [PS2123.A47 1979] 78-25756 lib. bdg. : 22.50
1. James, Henry, 1843-1916—Friends and associates. 2. James, Henry, 1843-1916—Correspondence. 3. Wells, Herbert George, 1866-1946—Friends and associates. 4. Wells, Herbert George, 1866-1946—Correspondence. 5. Fiction—Technique. 6. Novelists—Biography. I. Wells, Herbert George, 1866-1946. II. Edel, Leon, 1927- III. Ray, Gordon Norton, 1915- IV. Title. **BIP**

Wells, Herbert George, 1866-1946—Juvenile literature.

PALEY, Alan L. 823'.9'12 B
H. G. Wells, author of famous science fiction stories, by Alan L. Paley. Charlotteville, N.Y., SamHar Press, 1973. 32 p. 22 cm. (Outstanding personalities, no. 51) Bibliography: p. 31-32. A biography of the English novelist best known for his science fiction. [PR5776.P28] 92 72-91098 ISBN 0-87157-554-X 1.98 (lib. bdg.)
1. Wells, Herbert George, 1866-1946—Juvenile literature. I. Title.
Pbk. 0.98; ISBN 0-87157-054-8

WOOD, James Playsted, 823'.9'12 B
1905-
I told you so! A life of H. G. Wells. [New York] Pantheon Books [1969] 182 p. illus,. ports. 22 cm. (A Pantheon portrait) A biography of the English author whose interest in science and social reform greatly influenced the basic themes of his work. [PR5776.W63] 92 68-24566
1. Wells, Herbert George, 1866-1946—Juvenile literature. I. Title.

Wells, Herbert George, 1866-1946—Relationship with women.

RAY, Gordon 820'.9'00912 B
Norton, 1915-
H. G. Wells & Rebecca West [by] Gordon N. Ray. New Haven, Yale University Press, 1974. xxvi, 215 p. illus. 22 cm. Includes bibliographical references. [PR5776.R38] 74-77990 ISBN 0-300-01753-7 7.95
1. Wells, Herbert George, 1866-1946—Relationship with women. 2. West, Rebecca, pseud.—Relationship with men. I. Title. **BIP**

Wells, Ida B., 1862-1931.

STERLING, Dorothy, 973'.0992
1913-
Black foremothers : three lives / Dorothy Sterling ; introd. by Margaret Walker ; ill. by Judith Eloise Hooper. Old Westbury, N.Y. : Feminist Press, c1979. xxiii, 167 p. : ill.; 23 cm. (Women's lives/women's work) Includes index. Bibliography: p. 160-162. [E185.96.S75] 78-8094 ISBN 0-07-020434-9 teacher's ed. : 3.69 ISBN 0-07-020433-0 pbk. : 4.25
1. Craft, Ellen. 2. Wells, Ida B., 1862-1931. 3. Terrell, Mary Church, 1863-1954. 4. Afro-American women—Biography. I. Title. II. Series. **BIP**

Welsh, Edward.

WELSH, Edward. 629.132'52'07
We grew wings : the story of the civilian flight instructors / Edward Welsh. 1st ed. Hicksville, N.Y. : Exposition Press, c1975. 176 p., [8] leaves of plates : ill. ; 22 cm. [TL540.W42A38] 75-330983 ISBN 0-682-48378-8 : 7.50
1. Welsh, Edward. 2. Air pilots—Correspondence, reminiscences, etc. I. Title.

Welty, Eudora, 1909-

BRYANT, Joseph Allen, 813'.5'2
1919-
Eudora Welty, by J. A. Bryant, Jr. Minneapolis, University of Minnesota Press [1968] 48 p. 21 cm. (University of Minnesota pamphlets on American writers, no. 66) Bibliography: p. 47-48. [PS3545.E6Z6] 68-63651
1. Welty, Eudora, 1909- I. Series: Minnesota. University. Pamphlets on American writers, no. 66 **BIP**

Welty, Eudora, 1909-—Addresses, essays, lectures.

EUDORA Welty : 813'.5'2
a form of thanks / essays by Cleanth Brooks .. [et al.] ; edited by Louis D. Dollarhide annd Ann J. Abodie. Jackson : University Press of Mississippi, c1979. xiii, 138 p. : port. ; 22 cm. Includes bibliographical references. [PS3545.E6Z66] 78-13285 ISBN 0-87805-089-2 : 8.95. ISBN 0-87805-090-6 pbk. : 3.95
1. Welty, Eudora, 1909-—Addresses, essays, lectures. 2. Novelists, American—20th century—Biography—Addresses, essays, lectures. I. Brooks, Cleanth, 1906- II. Abadie, Ann J. III. Dollarhide, Lois D.

Welty, Susan Elizabeth (Fulton)

WELTY, Susan Elizabeth 922.89
(Fulton) 1905-
Look up and hope! the motto of the Volunteer Prison League; the life of Maud Ballington Booth. New York, T. Nelson [1961] 284 p. Illus. 24 cm. Includes bibliography. [BX9975.Z8B6] 61-12423
I. Title.

Welz, Justinian Ernst von, Baron von Eberstein, 1621-1668.

WELZ, Justinian 266.4'1'0924 B
Ernst von, Baron von Eberstein, 1621-1668.
Justinian Welz: essays by an early prophet of mission. Translated, annotated, and with an historical introd., by James A. Scherer. Grand Rapids, Mich., Eerdmans [1969] 111 p. 20 cm. (A Christian world mission book) Bibliography: p. 109-111. [BV2853.D9W4] 68-54103 2.45
1. Welz, Justinian Ernst von, Baron von Eberstein, 1621-1668. 2. Lutheran Church—Missions—Collected works. I. Scherer, James A., tr.

Wendel, Natalja—Biography.

WENDEL, Natalja. 811'.5'4 B
Born in April : the story of Natascha and Pierre / by Natalja Wendel. New York : F. Fell Publishers, [1975] 489 p. : ill. ; 24 cm. [PS3573.E5Z515 1975] 74-31096 ISBN 0-8119-0245-5 : 6.95
1. Wendel, Natalja—Biography. I. Title.

Weniger, Charles Elliott, 1896-1964.

UTT, Richard H. 378.1'2'0924 B
Uncle Charlie : a biography of Charles Elliott Weniger / by Richard H. Utt. Mountain View, Calif. : Pacific Press Pub. Association, c1978. 176 p. : ill. ; 22 cm. Bibliography: p. 152. [LA2317.W38U77] 77-85499 6.95 pbk. : 4.50
1. Weniger, Charles Elliott, 1896-1964. 2. College teachers—United States—Biography. I. Title.

Wenning, Pieter, 1873-1921.

WENNING, Harco, 1899- 759.968 B
My father / by Harco Wenning. Cape Town : H. Timmins, 1976. 163 p. : ill. ; 25 cm. [ND1096.W46W46] 76-369918 ISBN 0-86978-131-6 : R9.50
1. Wenning, Pieter, 1873-1921. I. Title.

Wentworth, John, Sir, 1737-1820.

ABBOTT, Wilbur Cortez, 420.042
1869-1947.
Conflicts with oblivion. Port Washington, N.Y., Kennikat Press [1969] xxii, 404 p. illus., ports. 22 cm. (Essay and general literature index reprint series) First published in 1924. [DA28.4.A3 1969] 68-8193
1. Wentworth, John, Sir, 1737-1820. 2. Scott, John, 1632-1704. 3. Great Britain—Biography. I. Title. **BIP**

Wentworth, John W., 1858-1954.

HAYES, Jess G., 1901- 979.1'55'040924 B
Boots and bullets; the life and times of John W. Wentworth, by Jess G. Hayes. [Tucson] University of Arizona Press [1966, c1967] xv, 139 p. illus., port. 20 cm. [F817.G5H3] 66-20659
1. Wentworth, John W., 1858-1954. 2. Frontier and pioneer life—Arizona—Gila Co. I. Title.

Wentworth, John, 1815-1888.

FEHRENBACHER, Don Edward, 1920- 923.273
Chicago giant; a biography of 'Long John' Wentworth. Madison, Wis., American History Research Center, 1957. viii, 278p. illus., ports., map. 24cm. 'Bibliographical note': p.233-236. Bibliographical references included in 'Notes' (p.237-266) [F548.4.W5F4] 57-43906
1. Wentworth, John, 1815-1888. I. Title. BIP

Wentworth, William Charles, 1793-1872—Juvenile literature.

PERSSE, Michael D. de B. Collins, 1931- 994.02'092'4 B
W. C. Wentworth [by] Michael D. de B. Collins Persse. Melbourne, New York, Oxford University Press, 1972. 30 p. ill., ports. 18 cm. (Great Australians) A brief biography of a statesman who greatly influenced Australia's national life by such acts as starting a newspaper, agitating for colonial self-government, and founding Sydney University. [DU172.W4P47 1972] 92 73-180622 ISBN 0-19-550425-9 0.70
1. Wentworth, William Charles, 1793-1872—Juvenile literature. I. Title.

Werfel, Alma Schindler Mahler.

SORELL, Walter, 1905- 920.72
Three women : lives of sex and genius / Walter Sorell. Indianapolis : Bobbs-Merrill, [1975] p. cm. [HQ1123.S67] 74-17644 ISBN 0-672-51750-7 : 7.95
1. Andreas-Salome, Lou, 1861-1937. 2. Werfel, Alma Schindler Mahler. 3. Stein, Gertrude, 1874-1946. I. Title.

Werkman, Hendrik Nicolaas,

WERKMAN, Hendrik Nicolaas, 1882-1945. 769'.924
H. N. Werkman. Herausgeber/Editor: Fridolin Muller. Einfuhrung/Introd: Peter F. Althaus. Biographie/Biography: Jan Martinet. New York, Hastings House [1967] 104 p. (chiefly illus. (part col.), port.) 25 cm. (Dokumente visueller Gestaltung, Bd. 2) Visual communication books. English, French, and German. [ND653.W43M8 1967b] 67-66203
I. Muller, Fridolin, ed.

Werner, Alfred, 1866-1919.

KAUFFMAN, George B., 1930- 540.924
Alfred Werner, founder of coordination chemistry [by] George B. Kauffman.Berlin. Berlin, New York, Springer Verlag, 1966. xv, 127p. illus., facsims., ports. 24cm. Bibl [QD22.W38K3] 66-20634 6.00 pap.,
1. Werner, Alfred, 1866-1919. 2. Coordination compounds. I. Title.

Werner, Alfred, 1911-

MODIGLIANI, Amedeo, 1884-1920 760'.0924
Amedeo Modigliani. Text by Alfred Werner. [1st ed.] New York, Abrams [1966, i.e., 1967] 158, [2] p. illus. (pt. col.) 33cm. (Lib. of great painters) Bibl. [ND623. 67W4] 66-10990 15.00
1. Werner, Alfred, 1911- I. Title.

Werner, Buddy, 1936-1964.

BURROUGHS, John Rolfe. 796.9'3
"I never look back"; the story of Buddy Werner. Boulder, Colo., Johnson Pub. Co. [1967] viii, 200 p. illus., ports. 24 cm. [GV854.2.W4B8] 67-17922
1. Werner, Buddy, 1936-1964. 2. Skis and skiing. I. Title.

Wernle, William F

WERNLE, William F 1915-1944. 920
To the one I lost, by Rose Marshall Wernle. [Geneva! N. Y., 1955] 259p. illus. 23cm. Chiefly letters of the author to his family. [CT275.W388A4] 56-253350
I. Wernle, Rose Marshall. II. Title.

Wertheimer, Samson, 1658-1724.

APSLER, Alfred. 923.3
The court factor; the story of Samson Wertheimer. Illustrated by Albert Gold. Philadelphia, Jewish Publication Society of America [1964] vi, 150 p. illus. 22 cm. (Covenant books, 17) [HG186.A8A7] 64-16755
1. Wertheimer, Samson, 1658-1724. 2. Capitalists and financiers — Austria. I. Title.

Wescott, Glenway, 1901-

RUECKERT, William Howe, 1926- v. 12
Glenway Wescott, by William H. Rueckert. New Haven, Conn., College & University Press [c1965] 174 p. 21 cm. Bibliography: p. 165-171. 67-55709
1. Wescott, Glenway, 1901- I. Title. BIP

Wesendonck, Mathilde (Luckemyer) 1828-1902.

HARDING, Bertita (Leonarz) 927.8
Magic fire; scenes around Richard Wagner. [1st ed.] Indianapolis, Bobbs-Merrill [1953] 451p. illus. 23cm. [ML410.W19H3] 53-9860
1. Wagner, Richard, 1813-1883. 2. Wagner, Minna (Planer) 1809-1866. 3. Wesendonck, Mathilde (Luckemyer) 1828-1902. 4. Wagner, Cosima (Liszt) 1837-1930. I. Title.

Wesker, Arnold, 1932-

HAYMAN, Ronald, 1932- 822'.9'14
Arnold Wesker. New York, Ungar [1973] 144 p. illus. 20 cm. (World dramatists) Bibliography: p. 139-140. [PR6073.E75Z7 1973] 78-153120 ISBN 0-8044-2387-3 6.50
1. Wesker, Arnold, 1932- BIP

Wesley, Charles, 1707-1788.

FLINT, Charles Wesley, Bp. 922.742
Charles Wesley and his colleagues. With introductory notes by Gerald Kennedy, G. Bromley Oxnam, and Norman Vincent Peale. Washington, Public Affairs Press [1957] 221 p. 24 cm. Includes bibliography. [BX8495.W4F57] 57-9822
1. Wesley, Charles, 1707-1788.

GILL, Frederick Cyril, 1898- 922.742
Charles Wesley, the first Methodist [by] Frederick C. Gill. New York, Abingdon Press [1964] 238 p. illus., facsims., ports. 23 cm. [BX8495.W4G5] 65-3307
1. Wesley, Charles, 1707-1788.

MYERS, Elisabeth P. 287.0924
Singer of six thousand songs; a life of Charles Wesley, Drawings by Leonard Vosburgh. New York, Nelson [c.1965] 160p. illus. 21cm. Bibl [BX8495.W4M9] 65-20772 2.95; 2.92 lib. ed.
1. Wesley, Charles, 1707-1788. I. Title.

MYERS, Elisabeth P 287.0924
Singer of six thousand songs; a life of Charles Wesley, by Elisabeth P. Myers. Drawings by Leonard Vosburgh. London, New York, T. Nelson [1965] 160 p. illus. 21 cm. Bibliography: p. 159. [BX8495.W4M9] 65-20772
1. Wesley, Charles, 1707-1788. I. Title.

Wesley family.

ROUTLEY, Erik. 780'.922
The musical Wesleys. New York, Oxford University Press, 1968. xi, 272 p. music. 23 cm. (Studies in church music) Bibliography: p. 264-265. [ML410.W51R7] 68-55307 7.50
1. Wesley family. I. Title. II. Series BIP

ROUTLEY, Erik. 786'.026'0922 B
The musical Wesleys / by Erik Routley. Westport, Conn. : Greenwood Press, 1976. xi, 272 p. : music ; 23 cm. Reprint of the 1968 ed. published by Oxford University Press, New York, in series: Studies in church music. Includes indexes. Bibliography: p. 264-265. [ML410.W51R7 1976] 75-36511 ISBN 0-8371-8644-7 : 15.25
1. Wesley family. I. Title. II. Series: Studies in church music.

Wesley, John, 1703-1791.

BAKER, Frank, 1910- 287'.0924 B
John Wesley and the Church of England. Nashville, Abingdon Press [1970] viii, 422 p. 26 cm. Bibliography: p. 407-412. [BX8495.W5B33 1970b] 73-23809 ISBN 0-687-20445-3 14.50
1. Wesley, John, 1703-1791. 2. Church of England. I. Title.

BREADY, John Wesley, 1887-1953. 274.2
England: before and after Wesley; the evangelical revival and social reform. New York, Russell & Russell [1971] 463 p. illus., ports. 22 cm. Reprint of the 1938 ed. [BR755.B7 1971] 72-139906
1. Wesley, John, 1703-1791. 2. Great Britain—Church history—Modern period, 1485- 3. Great Britain—Social conditions. 4. Evangelical revival. I. Title.

CLARK, Elmer Talmage, 1886- 922.742
The warm heart of Wesley, by Elmer T. Clark. With the Aldersgate story, by John Wesley. New York, Association of Methodist Historical Societies [1950] 78 p. illus., port. 20 cm. The Aldersgate story is reprinted from Wesley's Journal. [BX8495.W5C549] 50-3500
1. Wesley, John, 1703-1791. I. Wesley, John, 1708-1791. II. Title.

DOBREE, Bonamy, 1891- 287'.092'4 B
John Wesley. [Folcroft, Pa.] Folcroft Library Editions, 1974. p. cm. Reprint of the 1933 ed. published by Duckworth, London, which was issued as no. 4 of Great lives. Bibliography: p. [BX8495.W5D57 1974] 74-7428 10.00 (lib. bdg.).
1. Wesley, John, 1703-1791.

DOBREE, Bonamy, 1891- 920.02
Three eighteenth century figures: Sarah Churchill, John Wealy, Giacomo Casanova New York, Oxford, 1962[ ] 248p. Bibl. 62-1635 4.80
1. Marlborough, Sarah (Jennings) duchess of, 1660-1744. 2. Wesley, Hohn, 1703-1791. 3. Casanova de Seingalt, Giacomo Girolamo, 1725-1798. I. Title.

EDWARDS, Maldwyn Lloyd, 1903- 922.742
John Wesley and the eighteenth century; a study of his social and political influence [Rev. ed.] London, Epworth Pr. [dist. Mystic, Conn., Verry, 1964] 207p. 19cm. Bibl. 55-12751 3.00
1. Wesley, John, 1703-1791. I. Title.

ENSLEY, Francis Gerald, Bp. 922.742
John Wesley, evangelist. Nashville, Tidings [1955] 64 p. 19 cm. [BX8495.W5E5] 56-18679
1. Wesley, John, 1708-1791. I. Title.

ETHRIDGE, Willie (Snow) 287'.0924 B
Strange fires; the true story of John Wesley's love affair in Georgia. New York, Vanguard Press [1971] 254 p. 24 cm. Bibliography: p. 249-254. [BX8495.W5E84 1971] 77-170902 ISBN 0-8149-0693-1 6.95
1. Wesley, John, 1703-1791. 2. Hopkey, Sophy. I. Title. BIP

GREEN, Vivian Hubert Howard. 922.742
The young Mr. Wesley; a study of John Wesley and Oxford. New York, St. Martin's Press [1961] 342p. illus. 23cm. Includes bibliography. [BX8495.W5G74] 61-10197
1. Wesley, John, 1703-1791. I. Title.

HADDAL, Ingvar. 922.742
John Wesley, a biography. Translated from the original Norwegian. New York, Abingdon Press [1961] 175p. illus. 23cm. [BX8495.W5H233] 61-66826
1. Wesley, John, 1703-1791. I. Title.

HIGGINS, Paul Lambourne 922.742
John Wesley: spiritual witness. Minneapolis, T.S. Denison [c.1960] 134p. Bibl.: p.134. 22cm. 60-16801 3.00
1. Wesley, John, 1703-1791. I. Title.

HIGGINS, Paul Lambourne. 922.742
John Wesley: spiritual witness. Minneapolis, T. S. Denison [1960] 134p. 22cm. Includes bibliography. [BX8495.W5H48] 60-16801
1. Wesley, John. 1703-1791. I. Title.

JEFFERY, Thomas Reed. 922.742
John Wesley's religious quest. [1st ed.] New York, Vantage Press [1960] 439p. 21cm. Includes bibliography. [BX8495.W5J4] 59-11127
1. Wesley, John, 1703-1791. I. Title.

KROLL, Harry Harrison, 1888- 922.742
The long quest; the story of John Wesley. Philadelphia, Westminster Press [1954] 192p. 22cm. [BX8495.W5K7] 53-8356
1. Wesley, John, 1703-1791. I. Title.

LEE, Umphrey, 1893- 922.742
The Lord's horseman; John Wesley the man. Nashville, Abingdon Press [1954] 220 p. 22 cm. [BX8495.W5L35 1954] 54-11235
1. Wesley, John, 1703-1791. I. Title.

LIPSKY, Abram, 1872-1946. 287'.0924 B
John Wesley; a portrait. New York, AMS Press [1971, c1928] ix, 305 p. facsim., ports. 19 cm. Bibliography: p. 297-300. [BX8495.W5L47 1971] 76-155619 ISBN 0-404-03994-4
1. Wesley, John, 1703-1791. BIP

MCCONNELL, Francis John, bp. 922.742
John Wesley. Nashville, Abingdon Press [1961, c.1939] 355p. (Apex Bks. E-4) 1.75pap.,
1. Wesley, John 1703-1791. I. Title.

MCNEER, May Yonge, 1902- 922.742
John Wesley, by May McNeer and Lynd Ward. New York, Abingdon-Cokesbury Press [1951] 95 p. illus. (part col.) 25 cm. [BX8495.W5M28] 51-10148
1. Wesley, John, 1703-1791. I. Ward, Lynd Kendall, 1905- illus.

MARSHALL, Dorothy 922.742
John Wesley. [New York] Oxford [c.]1965. 64p. illus., ports. 21cm. (Clarendon biographies) Bibl. [BX8495.W5M29] 65-3896 1.40 bds.,
1. Wesley, John, 1703-1791. I. Title.

•MILLER, Basil 287.0924(B)
John Wesley; 'I look upon the world as my parish.' Introd. by Stephen W. Paine. Minneapolis, Bethany Fellowship [1966, c.1943] 140p. 19cm. (BF150) 1.50 pap.,
1. Wesley, John, 1703-1791. I. Title.

MITCHELL, T Crichton. 922.742
Mr. Wesley; an intimate sketch of John Wesley. Kansas City, Mo., Beacon Hill Press [1957] 96p. 19cm. Includes bibliography. [BX8495.W5M55] 57-3716
1. Wesley, John, 1703- 1791. I. Title.

MONK, Robert C. 287.0924
John Wesley; his puritan heritage; a study of the Christian life [by] Robert C. Monk. Nashville, Abingdon [1966] 286p. 24cm. Based on thesis. Priceton Univ. Bibl. [BX8495.W5M6] 66-15494 5.50
1. Wesley, John, 1703-1791. 2. Puritans. I. Title.

PUDNEY, John, 1909- 1977. 287'.092'4 B
John Wesley and his world / John Pudney. New York : Scribner, c1978. 128 p. : ill. ; 24 cm. Includes index. Bibliography: p. 119. [BX8495.W5P77 1978] 78-59110 ISBN 0-684-15922-8 : 10.95
1. Wesley, John, 1703-1791. 2. Methodist Church—Clergy—Biography. 3. Clergy—England—Biography. I. Title. **BIP**

SCHMIDT, Martin, 1909- 922.742
John Wesley: a theological biography. Translated by Norman P. Goldhawk. New York, Abingdon Press [1963, c1962- v. 23 cm. Contents.v. 1. From 17th June 1706 until 24th May 1738. Includes bibliography. [BX8495.W5S283] 63-3396
1. Wesley, John, 1703-1791. I. Title. **BIP**

SHERWIN, Oscar, 1902- 922.742
John Wesley, friend of the people. New York, Twayne [c.1961] 234p. Bibl. 61-150943 5.00 bds.,
1. Wesley, John, 1703-1791. I. Title.

SHERWIN, Oscar, 1902- 922.742
John Wesley, friend of the people. New York, Twayne Publishers [1961] 284 p. 21 cm. Includes bibliography. [BX8495.W5S43] 61-15094
1. Wesley, John, 1703-1791. I. Title.

TUTTLE, Robert G., 1941- 287'.092'4 B
John Wesley : his life and theology / Robert G. Tuttle, Jr. Grand Rapids : Zondervan Pub. House, c1978. 368 p., [4] leaves of plates : ill. ; 23 cm. Includes bibliographies and index. [BX8495.W5T73] 77-27583 ISBN 0-310-36660-7 : 9.95
1. Wesley, John, 1703-1791. 2. Methodists—England—Biography. 3. Evangelists—England—Biography. **BIP**

TYERMAN, Luke, 1819or20-1889. 287'.092'4 B
The life and times of the Rev. John Wesley, M.A., founder of the Methodists. New York, B. Franklin [1973] 3 v. ports. 23 cm. (Burt Franklin research & source works series. Philosophy & religious history monographs 132) Reprint of the 1872 ed. published by Harper & Brothers, New York. Includes bibliographical references. [BX8495.W5T8 1973] 73-14910 ISBN 0-8337-4710-X 72.50
1. Wesley, John, 1703-1791.

WESLEY, John, 1703-1791. 922.742
By John Wesley; a modern reader's introduction to the man and his message through selections from his own writings -- sermons, tracts, letters, diaries -- in his lucid prose. Selected by T. Otto Nall. New York, Association Press [1961] 127 p. 15 cm. (An Association Press reflection book, 542) [BX8495.W5A17] 61-7113
I. Nall, Torney Otto 1900- ed. II. Title.

WESLEY, John, 1703-1791. 287'.092'4 B
The heart of John Wesley's Journal / with an introd. by Hugh Price Hughes, and an appreciation of the Journal by Augustine Birrell ; edited by Percy Livingstone Parker. New Canaan, Conn. : Keats Pub., 1979. xxxviii, 512 p., [12] leaves of plates : ill. ; 22 cm. (A Shepherd illustrated classic) Condensed ed. Reprint of the 1903 ed. published by Revell, New York. Includes index. [BX8495.W5A342 1979] 79-64828 ISBN 0-87983-207-X : 5.95
1. Wesley, John, 1703-1797. 2. Methodist Church—Clergy—Biography. 3. Clergy—England—Biography. I. Parker, Percy Livingstone, 1867-1925. II. Title.

WESLEY, John, 1703-1791. 922.742
Journal, as abridged by Nehemiah Curnock. With an introd. by Gerald Kennedy. New York, Capricorn Books [1963] xxii, 433 p. port. (on cover) 19 cm. (A Capricorn book, Cap89) [BX8495.W5A224 1963] 63-4586

WESLEY, John, 1703-1791 922.742
The journal of John Wesley. Abridged by Nehemiah Curnock. Introd. by Bishop Gerald Kennedy. New York [Putnam, 1963] 433p. 19cm. (Capricorn bk., 89) 1.85 pap.,
I. Title.

WOOD, Arthur Skevington. 287'.0924
The burning heart; John Wesley, evangelist, by A. Skevington Wood. Grand Rapids, Eerdmans [c.1967] 302p. 23cm. Bibl. [BX8495.W5W7 1967b] 68-20489 4.95
1. Wesley, John, 1703-1791. I. Title.

Wesley, John, 1703-1791—Homes and haunts.

GILL, Frederick Cyril, 1898- 922.742
In the steps of John Wesley. London. Lutterworth Pr. [dist. Nashville, Abingdon 1963, c.1962] 239-. illus., port., map, plan. 23cm. 63-25950 5.00
1. Wesley, John, 1703-1791—Homes and haunts. I. Title.

Wesley, Martha, 1707-1791.

WILDER, Franklin. 287'.1'0924 B
Martha Wesley / by Franklin Wilder. 1st ed. Hicksville, N.Y. : Exposition Press, c1976. 136 p. ; 21 cm. Bibliography: p. 135-136. [BX8495.W53W54] 76-360632 ISBN 0-682-48488-1 : 6.50
1. Wesley, Martha, 1707-1791. **BIP**

Wesley, Samuel, 1662-1735.

WILDER, Franklin. 287'.1'0924 B
Father of the Wesleys; a biography. [1st ed.] New York, Exposition Press [1971] 220 p. port. 22 cm. Bibliography: p. 219-220. [BX5199.W396W5] 72-146917 ISBN 0-682-47238-7 6.00
1. Wesley, Samuel, 1662-1735. I. Title.

Wesley, Samuel, 1766-1837.

LIGHTWOOD, James Thomas, 1856-1944. 786.5'092'4 B
Samuel Wesley, musician; the story of his life. New York, B. Blom, 1972. 238 p. ports. 18 cm. Reprint of the 1937 ed. [ML410.W515L72 1972] 72-83745 12.50
1. Wesley, Samuel, 1766-1837. **BIP**

Wesley, Susanna (Annesley) 1670-1742.

HARMON, Rebecca Lamar. 287'.1'0924
Susanna, mother of the Wesleys. Nashville, Abingdon Press [1968] 175 p. illus., ports. 22 cm. Bibliography: p. 170-172. [BX8495.W55H3] 68-11463
1. Wesley, Susanna (Annesley) 1670-1742. I. Title.

Wesson, Laurence Goddard, 1888-1963.

WESSON, Elizabeth M. 547'.00924 B
Laurence Goddard Wesson; a biographical sketch, by Elizabeth M. Wesson. [Boston] 1969. 107 p. illus., ports. 24 cm. [QD22.W39W4] 73-7537
1. Wesson, Laurence Goddard, 1888-1963.

West, Benjamin, 1738-1820.

ALBERTS, Robert C. 759.13 B
Benjamin West : a biography / Robert C. Alberts. Boston : Houghton Mifflin, 1978. xvi, 525 p., [24] leaves of plates : ill. ; 24 cm. Includes index. Bibliography: p. [477]-507. [ND237.W45A86] 78-17241 ISBN 0-395-26289-5 : 20.00
1. West, Benjamin, 1738-1830. 2. Painters—United States—Biography. **BIP**

GALT. JOHN, 1779-1839. 759.2
The life of Benjamin West (1816-1820) a facsimile reproduction with an introd. by Nathalia Wright. Gainesville, Fla., Scholars' Facsimiles & Reprints, 1960. ix p., facsim.: iv, 160, 251p. plates, ports. 23cm. (Scholars' facsimilies & reprints) Reproduction of copies in Ohio State University and Yale University Library, with title pages reading: [pt.] 1, The life, studies, and works of Benjamin West, Esq., composed from materials furnished by Himself. London, Printed for T. Cadell and W. Davies, 1820; pt. 2, The life and works of Benjamin West, Esq., subsequent to his arrival in this country. London, Printed for T. Cadell and W. Davies, 1820. 60-5041 8.50
1. West, Benjamin, 1738-1820. I. Title.

SNOW, Dorothea J., 1909- 92
Benjamin West, gifted young painter, by Dorothea J. Snow. Illustrated by George Buctel. Indianapolis, Bobbs-Merrill [1967] 200 p. col. illus. 20 cm. (Childhood of famous Americans) Biography of the "Father of American painting" who, as a Quaker, had to secure special permission from his townsmen to engage in his chosen profession of "making images." [ND237.W45S6] AC 67
1. West, Benjamin, 1738-1820. I. Buctel, George, illus. II. Title.

West, Benjamin, 1738-1820—Juvenile literature.

SNOW, Dorothea J., 1909- 92
Benjamin West, gifted young painter, by Dorothea J. Snow. Illus. by George Buctel. Indianapolis, Bobbs [1967] 200p. col. illus. 20cm. (Childhood of famous Americans) [ND237.W45S6] 67-17738 2.50
1. West, Benjamin, 1738-1820—Juvenile literature. I. Title.

SNOW, Dorothea J., 1909- 759.13
Benjamin West, gifted young painter, by Dorothea J. Snow. Illustrated by George Buctel. Indianapolis, Bobbs-Merrill [1967] 200 p. col. illus. 20 cm. (Childhood of famous Americans) [ND237.W45S6] 67-17773
1. West, Benjamin, 1738-1820 — Juvenile literature. I. Title. **BIP**

West, Daniel, 1893-1971.

YODER, Glee. 286'.5 B
Passing on the gift : the story of Dan West / by Glee Yoder. Elgin, Ill. : Brethren Press, c1978. 168 p. : ill. ; 21 cm. (Brethren biographies.) [BX7843.W46Y62] 78-6291 ISBN 0-87178-689-3 pbk. : 3.95
1. West, Daniel, 1893-1971. 2. Church of the Brethren—Biography. I. Title. II. Series.

West Indian Americans—Biography.

HALL, Herman. 973'.04'969729
200 years of West Indian-American contributions / [written by H. Hall [Brooklyn, N.Y. : Herman Hall Associates, c1976] 59 p. : ill. ; 28 cm. Cover title. [E184.W54H34] 76-370601
1. West Indian Americans—Biography. I. Title.

West Indies—History.

LANSING, Marion Florence, 1883- 972.9
Liberators and heroes of the West Indian islands. Jacket and end leaves by George Eisenberg. Boston, L.C. Page [1953] 294 p. illus. 23 cm. Bibliography: p. 287-288. [F1621.L3 1953] 53-6893
1. West Indies—History. 2. West Indies—Biography. I. Title.

West Indies—Social life and customs.

MACPHERSON, Charles, fl.1773-1790. 917.29'04'30924 B
Memoirs of the life and travels of the late Charles Macpherson, esq., in Asia, Africa, and America ... Freeport, N.Y., Books for Libraries Press, 1973. p. (The Black heritage library collection) This vol., the only one published, relates chiefly to the West Indies. Reprint of the 1800 ed. [F1609.5.M32 1973] 72-12925 ISBN 0-8369-9229-6
1. West Indies—Social life and customs. 2. Slavery in the West Indies. I. Title. II. Series.

West, Jerry,

WEST, Jerry, 1938- 796.32'3'0924 B
Mr. Clutch; the Jerry West story [by] Jerry West with Bill Libby. Englewood Cliffs, N.J., Prentice-Hall [1969] 241 p. illus., ports. 22 cm. "An Associated Features book." [GV884.W4A3] 73-82904 ISBN 0-13-604710-6 5.95
I. Libby, Bill, joint author. II. Title.

West, Jerry, 1938- —Juvenile literature.

DEEGAN, Paul J., 1937- 796.32'3'0924 B
Jerry West, by Paul J. Deegan. Illustrated by Harold Henriksen. Mankato, Minn., Creative Education distributed by Childrens Press, Chicago [1973] c1974. 29 p. illus. (part col.) 25 cm. (Creative's superstars) "Prepared for the publisher by Amecus Street." A brief biography of the star of the Los Angeles Lakers basketball team who holds many scoring records. [GB884.W4D43] 92 73-19525 ISBN 0-87191-311-9 4.95
1. West, Jerry, 1938- —Juvenile literature. I. Henriksen, Harold, illus. II. Amecus Street, inc. III. Title.

ETTER, Les. 796.32'3'0922
Basketball superstars: three great pros. Champaign, Ill., Garrard Pub. Co. [1974] 96 p. illus. 24 cm. Brief biographies stressing the careers of basketball stars Wilt Chamberlain, Jerry West, and Oscar Robertson. [GV884.A1E87] 920 73-9659 ISBN 0-8116-6667-0 2.98 (lib. bdg.)
1. Chamberlain, Wilton Norman, 1936- —Juvenile literature. 2. West, Jerry, 1938- —Juvenile literature. 3. Robertson, Oscar, 1938- —Juvenile literature. I. Title.

WEST, Jerry, 1938- 796.32'3'0924 B
Mr. Clutch; the Jerry West story [by] Jerry West with Bill Libby. Englewood Cliffs, N.J., Prentice-Hall [1969] 241 p. illus., ports. 22 cm. "An Associated Features book." [GV884.W4A3] 73-82904 ISBN 0-13-604710-6 5.95
I. Libby, Bill, joint author. II. Title.

West, Jessamyn.

WEST, Jessamyn. 928.1
To see the dream. [1st ed.] New York. Harcourt, Brace [1957] 314 p. 21 cm. An outgrowth of the author's journal kept when she was spending part of her time at home in Napa, Calif., and part of it in Hollywood as a script writer and technical adviser to William Wyler, who was converting her book, The Friendly persuasion, into a movie. [PS3545.E8315Z52] 56-11961
I. Title. **BIP**

West, Jessamyn—Biography.

WEST, Jessamyn. 928.1
To see the dream. [1st ed.] New York. Harcourt, Brace [1957] 314 p. 21 cm. An outgrowth of the author's journal kept when she was spending part of her time at home in Napa, Calif., and part of it in Hollywood as a script writer and technical adviser to William Wyler, who was converting her book, The Friendly persuasion, into a movie. [PS3545.E8315Z52] 56-11961
I. Title. **BIP**

WEST, Jessamyn. 813'.5'4 B
The woman said yes : encounters with life and death : memoirs / Jessamyn West. Boston : G. K. Hall, c1976. p. cm. Large print ed. [PS3545.E8315Z518 1976] 76-41710 ISBN 0-8161-6440-1 : 9.95
1. West, Jessamyn—Biography. 2. Authors, American—20th century—Biography. 3. Sight-saving books. I. Title.

WEST, Jessamyn. 813'.5'4 B
The woman said yes : encounters with life and death : memoirs / Jessamyn West. 1st ed. New York : Harcourt Brace Jovanovich, c1976. 180 p. ; 22 cm. Contents.Contents.—Grace.—Carmen. [PS3545.E8315Z518] 75-40368 ISBN 0-15-198400-X : 7.95
1. West, Jessamyn—Biography. 2. Authors, American—20th century—Biography. I. Title.

West, Lucy (Brewer)

WEST, Lucy (Brewer) 818.203
The female marine; or, Adventures of Miss Lucy Brewer. Introd. to the Da Capo ed. by Alexander Medlicott, Jr. New York, Da Capo [dist. Plenum, c.]1966. x1, 101p. front. 20cm. This ed. follows the fifth ed., printed in Boston in 1817. [CT275.W3896A3] 65-23390 5.95 bds.,
I. Title.

West, Mae

*BAVAR, Michael 791.43'028'0924 B
Mae West. New York, Pyramid, [1975] 157 p. ill. 20 cm. (Pyramid illustrated history of the movies.) Includes index. "Films of Mae West" p. 153-154. Bibliography: p. 151. [PN2287] 75-18545 ISBN 0-515-03868-7 1.75 (pbk.)
1. West, Mae 2. Moving-pictures—Biography. 3. Moving picture actors and actresses. I. Sennett, Ted. ed. II. Title. **BIP**

HANNA, David. 791.43'028'0924 B
"Come up and see me sometime"; an uncensored biography of Mae West. New York, Belmont Tower Books [1976] 206 p. illus. 18 cm. [PN2287.W4566] 1.50 (pbk.)
1. West, Mae. I. Title.

WEST, Mae 927.92
Goodness had nothing to do with it. Complete and unabridged. New York, Avon [1960, c.1959] 223p. illus. 17cm. (G1047) .50 pap.,
I. Title.

WEST, Mae. 927.92
Goodness had nothing to do with it; autobiography. Englewood Cliffs, N. J., Prentice-Hall [1959] 271 p. illus. 22 cm. [PN2287.W4566A3] 59-12962
I. Title.

West, Marion B.

WEST, Marion B. 248'.2 B
Out of my bondage / Marion B. West. Nashville, Tenn. : Broadman Press, 1977, c1976. 128 p. ; 20 cm. [HQ759.W45A36] 76-5297 ISBN 0-8054-5144-7 : 2.50
1. West, Marion B. 2. Mothers—Biography. 3. Housewives—Biography. 4. Family. I. Title.

West, Nathanael, 1902-1940.

COMERCHERO, Victor. 813.52
Nathanael West, the ironic prophet. Seattle, Univ. of Wash. Pr. [1967,c.1964] xii, 189p. 21cm. (WP-30) Bibl. [PS3545.E8334Z6] 2.95 pap.,
1. West, Nathanael, 1902-1940. I. Title. **BIP**

COMERCHERO, Victor. 813.52
Nathanael West, the ironic prophet. [Syracuse, N. Y.] Syracuse University Press, 1964. xii, 189 p. 22 cm. Bibliographical references included in "Notes to chapters" (p. 173-184) [PS3545.E8334Z6] 64-23342
1. West, Nathanael, 1902-1940.

West, Rebecca, pseud.

WOLFE, Peter. 828'.9'1209
Rebecca West: artist and thinker. With a pref. by Harry T. Moore. Carbondale, Southern Illinois University Press [1971] xi, 166 p. 22 cm. (Crosscurrents/modern critiques) Bibliography: p. 159. [PR6045.E8Z9] 73-132486 ISBN 0-8093-0483-X 5.95
1. West, Rebecca, pseud. I. Title.

West Virginia—Politics and government.

PERRY, Lester. 320.9'754 B
Forty years mountain politics, 1930-1970, by Lester "Bus" Perry. Parsons, W. Va., McClain Print. Co., 1971. xv, 113 p. illus. 23 cm. [F241.P413] 71-154283 ISBN 0-87012-101-4
1. West Virginia—Politics and government. 2. West Virginia—Biography. I. Title. **BIP**

West, Walter Richard, 1912-

WAUGAMAN, Charles A. 759.11 B
Cheyenne artist: the story of Richard West, by Charles A. Waugaman. New York, Friendship Press [1970] 95 p. 18 cm. (Bold believers series) [E99.C53W3] 70-130779 ISBN 0-377-84211-7 1.50
1. West, Walter Richard, 1912- I. Title. **BIP**

West, William,

WEST, William, 1890- 922.773
Personality in retrospection-introspection; My God and I. [Denver? 1962] 182 p. illus. 20 cm. Autobigraphical. [BX8495.W56A3] 63-38377
I. Title.

West, Winifred Mary, 1881-1971.

KENNEDY, Priscilla 371.1'0092'4 B
Winifred Hume, 1920-
Portrait of Winifred West / [by] Priscilla Kennedy. Gordon, N.S.W. : Fine Arts Press, 1976. xiv, 225 p. : ill. ; 23 cm. Includes index. [LA2394.W47K46] 77-363912 ISBN 0-86917-001-5
1. West, Winifred Mary, 1881-1971. 2. Teachers—New South Wales—Biography. 3. Education—New South Wales—History. I. Title.

Westermann, Horace Clifford, 1922-

WESTERMANN, Horace 709'.2'4
Clifford, 1922-
H. C. W., Whitney Museum of American Art / Barbara Haskell. New York : Whitney Museum of American Art, c1978. 111 p. : ill. (some col.) ; 23 cm. Cover title: H. C. Westermann. Bibliography: p. 111. [N6537.W38A4 1978] 78-3527 ISBN 0-87427-016-2 pbk. : 8.00
1. Westermann, Horace Clifford, 1922- Exhibitions. 2. Artists—United States—Biography. I. Haskell, Barbara. II. Whitney Museum of American Art, New York. III. Title.

WESTERMANN, Horace 730'.924
Clifford, 1922-
H. C. Westermann. [Exhibition] Los Angeles County Museum of Art, November 26, 1968-January 12, 1968 [i.e., 1969. Los Angeles, Los Angeles County Museum of Art, 1968] 48 p. illus. 26 cm. "Sponsored by the Contemporary Art Council, Lytton Hall." Bibliography: p. 47. [NB237.W44A45] 68-59033
I. Los Angeles Co., Calif. Museum of Art, Los Angeles. Contemporary Art Council.

Western Australia—Biography.

STOKES, John 994'.1'00992 B
Philip.
The Western State : some of its people and ports / by John Stokes. Facsim. 3d ed. Nedlands, W.A. : University of Western Australia Press, 1976. 176 p. : ill. ; 22 cm. Distributed in North America by International Scholarly Book Services, Forest Grove, Or. [DU372.A2S8 1976] 76-375777 ISBN 0-85564-119-3
1. Western Australia—Biography. 2. Western Australia—History. I. Title. **BIP**

WESTRALIAN portraits 920'.0941 B
/ editor, Lyall Hunt. Nedlands, W.A. : University of Western Australia Press for the Education Committee of the 150th Anniversary Celebrations, 1979. xviii, 318 p. : ports., map on endpapers ; 26 cm. (Sesquicentenary celebrations series) Includes bibliographies. [CT2807.W47W47] 79-670403 ISBN 0-85564-157-6 : 15.00
1. Western Australia—Biography. I. Hunt, Lyall J. II. Title. III. Series. **BIP**

Western Australia—Disc. & explor.

TROTMAN, Hubert 994.030924
Stanslake, 1874-1965
The beckoning west; the story of H. S. Trotman and the Canning Stock Route [by] Eleanor Smith. [Sydney] Angus & Robertson [1966] vii, 220p. map. 23cm. The 5 expeditions of H. S. Trotman as told to E. Smith. [DU360.T75] 66-17964 5.95
1. Western Australia—Disc. & explor. 2. Canning Stock Route, Western Australia. I. Smith, Eleanor Page. II. Title.
Available from Tri-Ocean, San Francisco.

Western films.

LAHUE, Kalton 791.43'028'0922 B
C.
Winners of the West: the sagebrush heroes of the silent screen, by Kalton C. Lahue. South Brunswick, A. S. Barnes [1971, c1970] 353 p. illus., ports. 26 cm. [PN1995.9.W4L3] 72-107120 ISBN 0-498-07396-3 10.00
1. Western films. 2. Moving-picture actors and actresses—United States—Biography. I. Title.

WHO'S who in western 927.92
stars. [New York, Dell Pub. Co.] v. illus. 27cm. annual. [PN1993.W46] 54-36895
1. Western films—Period. 2. Moving-pictures—Biog.

Western films—History and criticism.

CARY, Diana Serra, 791.43'0909'32
1918-
The Hollywood posse : the story of a gallant band of horsemen who made movie history / Diana Serra Cary. Boston : Houghton Mifflin, 1975. xv, 268 p., [8] leaves of plates : ill. ; 24 cm. [PN1995.9.W4C35] 75-17531 ISBN 0-395-20437-2 : 8.95
1. Western films—History and criticism. 2. Cowboys—Biography. I. Title.

ROTHEL, David, 791.43'0909'32
1936-
The singing cowboys / David Rothel. South Brunswick, [N.J.] : A. S. Barnes, c1978. p. cm. Bibliography: p. [PN1995.9.W4R67] 77-89646 ISBN 0-498-02163-7 : 19.95
1. Western films—History and criticism. 2. Cowboys—Songs and music. 3. Moving-picture actors and actresses—United States—Biography. 4. Country musicians—United States—Biography. I. Title. **BIP**

Western Reserve—History—Miscellanea.

HOOVER, Earl R. 977.1'04 B
Cradle of greatness : national and world achievements of Ohio's Western Reserve / by Earl R. Hoover. Cleveland : Shaker Savings Association, c1977. [88] p. : ill. ; 23 cm. Cover title. Bibliography: p. [82]-[88] [F497.W5H66] 76-52585 3.75
1. Western Reserve—History—Miscellanea. 2. Western Reserve—Biography. I. Title.

Westfeldt, Lulie.

WESTFELDT, Lulie. 926.1
F. Matthias Alexander; the man and his work. Westport, Conn., Associated Booksellers [1964] 163 p. illus., ports. 22 cm. [RM699.7.A5W4] 64-6273
1. Alexander, Frederick Matthias, 1869-1955. II. Title.

Westinghouse, George, 1846-1914.

PROUT, Henry 620'.0092'4 B
Goslee.
A life of George Westinghouse, by Henry G. Prout. New York, Arno Press, 1972 [c1921] xii, 375 p. illus. 23 cm. (Technology and society) [T40.W4P7 1972] 72-5068 ISBN 0-405-04719-3
1. Westinghouse, George, 1846-1914. I. Title. II. Series. **BIP**

THOMAS, Henry 926.2
George Westinghouse. Illustrated by Charles Beck. New York, Putnam [c.1960] 128p. illus. 21cm. (Lives to rember) 60-12539 2.50
1. Westinghouse, George, 1846-1914. I. Title.

THOMAS, Henry, 1886- 926.2
George Westinghouse. Illustrated by Charles Back. New York, Putnam [1960] 128 p. illus. 21 cm. (Lives to remember) [T40.W4T5] 60-12539
1. Westinghouse, George, 1846-1944. I. Title.

Westinghouse, George, 1846-1914—Juvenile literature.

LEVINE, Israel E. 920
Inventive wizard: George Westinghouse. New York, Messner [c.1962] 190p. Bibl. 62-10192 2.95; 2.99 lib. ed.,
1. Westinghouse, George, 1846-1914—Juvenile literature. I. Title. **BIP**

Westmacott, Spencer, 1885-1960.

WESTMACOTT, Spencer, 993.1'1
1885-1960.
The after-breakfast cigar : selected memoirs of a King Country settler / by Spencer Westmacott ; edited by H. F. Westmacott. Wellington : Reed, 1977. 206 p. : ill., port. ; 26 cm. Includes index. [DU430.K5W47 1977] 78-322070 ISBN 0-589-01011-5 : 18.75

1. Westmacott, Spencer, 1885-1960. 2. King Country, N.Z.—Biography. 3. Frontier and pioneer life—New Zealand—King Country. 4. Pioneers—New Zealand—King Country—Biography. I. Westmacott, Honor F., 1926- II. Title.
Distributed by C.E.Tuttle **BIP**

Westminister, Elizabeth Mary (Levenson-Gower) Grosvenor, 2d marchloness of, 1797-1891.

HUXLEY, Gervas. 914.203740924
Lady Elizabeth and the Grosvenors; life in a Whig family, 1822-1839. London, New York, Oxford University Press, 1965. 187 p. illus., ports. 23 cm. Bibliography: p. 178-179. [DA538.W4H89] 65-29639
1. Westminister, Elizabeth Mary (Levenson-Gower) Grosvenor, 2d marchloness of, 1797-1891. 2. Grosvenor family. 3. Gt. Brit. — Soc. life & cust. — 19th cent. 4. Gt. Brit. — Nobility. I. Title.

Westminster Abbey—History.

SCOTT, Carolyn. 942.1'32
Westminster Abbey : its links with the famous / [by] Carolyn Scott ; drawings by Frank Hoar. London : Sheldon Press, 1976. ix, 182 p. : ill., map, ports. ; 21 cm. [DA687.W5S36 1976] 77-351991 ISBN 0-85969-055-5 : £5.50. ISBN 0-85969-056-3 pbk.
1. Westminster Abbey—History. 2. Great Britain—Biography. I. Title. **BIP**

Westminster, Hugh Lupus Grosvenor, 1st Duke of, 1825-1899.

HUXLEY, Gervas. 942.081'0924 B
Victorian duke: the life of Hugh Lupus Grosvenor, first Duke of Westminster. London, New York [etc.] Oxford U.P., 1967. xiii, 214 p. front., 16 plates (incl. ports., diagrs.). 22 1/2 cm. Bibliographical footnotes. [DA565.W54H89] 67-85915
1. Westminster, Hugh Lupus Grosvenor, 1st Duke of, 1825-1899. I. Title.

Westminster, Loelia (Ponsonby) Grosvenor,

WESTMINSTER, Loelia 920.7
(Ponsonby) Grosvenor, duchess of
Grace and favour; the memoirs of Loelia, duchess of Westminster. New York, Reynal [dist. Morrow, 1962, c.1961] 244p. illus. 23cm. 62-13230 5.75
I. Title.

Westmoreland, William Childs, 1914-

FURGURSON, Ernest 973.92'0924 B
B., 1929-
Westmoreland; the inevitable general, by Ernest B. Furgurson. [1st ed.] Boston, Little, Brown [1968] 347 p. ports. 22 cm. Bibliographical references included in "Sources" (p. 339-342) [E840.5.W4F8] 68-24097
1. Westmoreland, William Childs, 1914- I. Title.

WESTMORELAND, 959.704'34'0924
William Childs, 1914-
A soldier reports / William C. Westmoreland. 1st ed. Garden City, N.Y. : Doubleday, 1976. x, 446 p., [16] leaves of plates : ill. ; 25 cm. Includes index. [DS559.5.W47] 74-27593 ISBN 0-385-00434-6 : 12.95
1. Westmoreland, William Childs, 1914- 2. Vietnamese Conflict, 1961-1975—Personal narratives, American. 3. Vietnamese Conflict, 1961-1975. 4. Generals—United States—Biography. I. Title. **BIP**

Weston, Edward, 1886-1958.

WESTON, Edward, 1886- 770'.92'4 B
1958.
Edward Weston, his life and photographs : the definitive volume of his photographic work / illustrated biography by Ben Maddow ; afterword by Cole Weston. Rev. ed. Millerton, N.Y. : Aperture, c1979. 299 p. : ill. ; 32 x 35 cm. Edition for 1973 published under title: Edward Weston, fifty years. Bibliography: p. 282-285. [TR653.W457 1979] 79-7058 ISBN 0-89381-043-6 : 75.00 ISBN 0-89381-045-2 ltd. ed. : 300.00
1. Weston, Edward, 1886-1958. 2. Photography, Artistic. 3. Photographers—United States—Biography. I. Maddow, Ben, 1909- II. Title.

Weston, Richard, Sir, Earl of Portland, 1577-1635.

ALEXANDER, 941.06'2'0924 B
Michael Van Cleave, 1937-
Charles I's Lord Treasurer, Sir Richard Weston, Earl of Portland (1577-1635) / Michael Van Cleave Alexander ; foreword by A. L. Rowse. Chapel Hill : University of North Carolina Press, [1975] xvi, 261 p., [1] leaf of plates : port. ; 23 cm. Includes bibliographical references and index. [DA396.W47A63 1975b] 74-34370 ISBN 0-8078-1248-X : 18.95
1. Weston, Richard, Sir, Earl of Portland, 1577-1635. 2. Great Britain—Politics and government—1603-1649. I. Title.

Weston, William,

WESTON, William, 1550- 922.242
1615.
The autobiography of an Elizabethan. Translated from the Latin by Philip Caraman; with a foreword by Evelyn Waugh. London, New York, Longmans, Green [1955] xxxi. 259p. illus., ports. 23cm. American ed. (New York, Farrar, Straus and Cudahy) has title: An autobiography from the Jesuit underground. Includes bibliographical references. [BX4705.W465A3 1955a] 56-1209
I. Title.

Wetherill, Benjamin Alfred, 1861-1950.

WETHERILL, Benjamin 978.8'27 B
Alfred, 1861-1950.
The Wetherills of the Mesa Verde : autobiography of Benjamin Alfred Wetherill / edited and annotated by Maurice S. Fletcher. Cranbury, N.J. : Associated University Presses, c1976 p. cm. Includes index. Bibliography: p. [E78.C6W47] 75-10144 ISBN 0-8386-1757-3 : 16.50
1. Wetherill, Benjamin Alfred, 1861-1950. 2. Mesa Verde National Park. 3. Pueblo Indians—Antiquities. 4. Colorado—Biography. I. Title.
Distributed by FairleighDickenson

Wetzel, Lewis, 1763-1808.

ALLMAN, Clarence Brent, 923.973
1895-
Lewis Wetzel, Indian fighter; the life and times of a frontier hero. New York, Devin-Adair Co., 1961. 237 p. illus. 21 cm. "Originally published under the title, The life and times of Lewis Wetzel." Includes bibliography. [F517.W512 1961] 61-15210
1. Wetzel, Lewis, 1763-1808. 2. Frontier and pioneer life—Ohio Valley. 3. Indians of North America—Wars—1750-1815.

Weyand, Clint.

†WEYAND, Clint. 811'.5'4
Thank you for being / by Clint Weyand. Encino, Calif. : Weyand/Shaw Publications, c1977. [99] p. : ill. ; 23 cm. [PS3573.E98T5] 78-101834 pbk. : 5.95
I. Title.
Publisher's address: Whiteoak, Suite B-203, Encino, CA 91316

Weyandt, Steve, 1905-

WEYANDT, Dorothy E. 799.1'2
I was a guide for three U.S. Presidents : as taken from the log of a famous Brule guide, Steve Weyandt I / by Dorothy E. Weyandt. [Brule, Wis.] : Weyandt, c1976. 298 p., [4] leaves of plates : ill. ; 24 cm. [SH415.W47] 75-25219
1. Weyandt, Steve, 1905- 2. Coolidge, Calvin, Pres. U.S., 1872-1933. 3. Hoover, Herbert Clark, Pres. U.S., 1874-1964. 4. Eisenhower, Dwight David, Pres. U.S., 1890-1969. 5. Trout fishing—Wisconsin—Brule River. 6. Guides for hunters, fishermen, etc.—Biography. I. Weyandt, Steve, 1905- II. Title.

Weybright, Victor.

WEYBRIGHT, Victor. 655.4'24
The making of publisher; a life in the 20th century book revolution. New York, Reynal [distributed by] W. Morrow [1967] viii, 360 p. port. 22 cm. Autobiographical. [Z473.W57A3] 67-20750
I. Title.

Weyl, Alfred Richard.

WEYL, Alfred 629.13'00924(B)
Richard.
Fokker: the creative years [by] A. R. Weyl. Edited by J. M. Bruce. London, Putnam; [Fallbrook, Calif.] Aero Publishers [1965] 420 p. illus., ports. 23 cm. [TL540.F6W4 1965b] 65-17636
I. Fokker, Anthony Herman Gerard, 1890-1939. II. Title.

Whalemen—New England—Biography.

AMARAL, Pat. 639'.28'0922 B
They ploughed the seas : profiles of Azorean master mariners / Pat Amaral. 1st ed. St. Petersburg, Fla. : Valkyrie Press, c1978. xix, 171 p. : ill. ; 24 cm. Bibliography: p. 169-170. [SH383.2.A45] 78-56813 ISBN 0-912760-74-5 : 12.95
1. Whalemen—New England—Biography. 2. Whalemen—Azores—Biography. 3. Shipmasters—New England—Biography. 4. Shipmasters Azores—Biography. 5. Azorians in New England. I. Title.

Wharton, Edith Newbold Jones, 1862-1937—Biography.

AUCHINCLOSS, Louis. 813'.5'2 B
Edith Wharton; a woman in her time. New York, Viking Press [1971] 191 p. 25 cm. (A Studio book) [PS3545.H16Z56] 77-146606 ISBN 0-670-28911-6 10.00
1. Wharton, Edith Newbold (Jones) 1862-1937.

AUCHINCLOSS, Louis. 813.52
Edith Wharton. Minneapolis, University of Minnesota Press [1961] 46 p. 21 cm. (University of Minnesota pamphlets on American writers, no. 12) Includes bibliography. [PS3545.H16Z55 1961] 61-63841
1. Wharton, Edith Newbold (Jones) 1862-1937.

COOLIDGE, Olivia E. 813'.5'2 B
Edith Wharton, 1862-1937. New York, Scribner [1964] 221 p. port. 21 cm. A biography of the novelist, a contemporary of Henry James, who wrote about New York society life in such noted works as The House of Mirth and The Age of Innocence. [PS3545.H16Z64] 92 AC 68
1. Wharton, Edith Newbold (Jones) 1862-1937. I. Title.

GRIFFITH, Grace 813.52 (B)
(Kellogg)
The two lives of Edith Wharton; the woman and her work, by Grace Kellogg. [1st ed.] New York, Appleton-Century [1965] xiv, 332 p. col. port. 24 cm. Bibliography: p. 325-327. [PS3545.H16Z66] 65-5135
1. Wharton, Edith Newbold (Jones) 1862-1937. I. Title.

LEWIS, Richard 813'.5'2 B
Warrington Baldwin.
Edith Wharton : a biography / R. W. B. Lewis. 1st ed. New York : Harper & Row, [1975] xiv, 592 p. : port. ; 25 cm. Includes index. Bibliography: p. [549]-573. [PS3545.H16Z696] 74-1833 ISBN 0-06-012603-5 : 15.00
1. Wharton, Edith Newbold Jones, 1862-1937—Biography. **BIP**

QUINN, Arthur Hobson, 813'.5'2
1875-1960.
Edith Wharton. [Folcroft, Pa.] Folcroft Library Editions, 1973. 11 p. port. 26 cm. Reprint of the 1938 ed. [PS3545.H16Z8 1973] 73-1923 4.00
1. Wharton, Edith Newbold (Jones) 1862-1937. **BIP**

WHARTON, Edith Newbold 928.1
(Jones) 1862-1937.
A backward glance. New York, Scribner [1964] xxvii, 385 p. illus., ports. 21 cm. [PS3545.H16Z5 1964] 64-3270
1. Authors — Correspondence, reminiscences, etc. I. Title.

Wharton, May (Cravath)

WHARTON, May (Cravath) 926.1
1873-
Doctor woman of the Cumberlands; the autobiography of May Cravath Wharton, M. D. Pleasant Hill, Tenn., Uplands [1953] 208p. illus. 21cm. [R154.W356A3] 53-4504
I. Title.

Whatman, James, 1702-1759.

BALSTON, Thomas. 676'.2'0922 B
James Whatman, father & son / by Thomas Balston. New York : Garland Pub., 1979. xi, 170 p., [8] leaves of plates : ill. ; 23 cm. (Nineteenth-century book arts & printing history) Reprint of the 1957 ed. published by Methuen, London. Includes bibliographical references and index. [TS1098.W53B34 1979] 78-74386 ISBN 0-8240-3875-4 : 20.00
1. Whatman, James, 1702-1759. 2. Whatman, James, 1741-1798. 3. Paper making and trade—Great Britain—History. 4. Paper making and trade—Great Britain—Biography. I. Title. II. Series. **BIP**

Wheatley, Phillis,

WHEATLEY, Phillis, 811'.1 B
afterwards Phillis Peters, 1753?-1784.
Life and works of Phillis Wheatley, containing her complete poetical works, numerous letters, and a complete biography of this famous poet of a century and a half ago, by G. Herbert Renfro. Also, a sketch of the life of Mr. Renfro, by Leila Amos Pendleton. Washington, 1916. Miami, Fla., Mnemosyne Pub. Co. [1969] 112 p. port. 23 cm. [PS866.W5 1969c] 70-83899
I. Renfro, G. Herbert, 1867-1894. II. Title.

Wheatley, Phillis, afterwards Phillis Peters, 1753-1784—Juvenile literature.

ALLEN, William G., comp. 811'.008
Wheatley, Banneker, and Horton; with selections from the poetical works of Wheatley and Horton, by William G. Allen. Freeport, N.Y., 1970. 48 p. 23 cm. (The Black heritage library collection) Reprint of the 1849 ed. [E185.96.A53 1970] 77-133145 ISBN 0-8369-8657-1
1. Wheatley, Phillis, afterwards Phillis Peters, 1753?-1784. 2. Banneker, Benjamin, 1731-1806. 3. Horton, George Moses, 1798?-ca. 1880. I. Title.

FULLER, Miriam Morris, 811'.1 B
1933-
Phillis Wheatley, America's first Black poetess. Illustrated by Victor Mays. Champaign, Ill., Garrard Pub. Co. [1971] 94 p. illus. (part col.) 24 cm. (Americans all) Follows the life of one of America's first black poets from her sale as a child slave on the Boston auction block to her death as an impoverished freedwoman in 1784. [PS866.W5Z59] 92 77-154858 ISBN 0-8116-4569-X 2.79
1. Wheatley, Phillis, afterwards Phillis Peters, 1753-1784—Juvenile literature. I. Mays, Victor, 1927- illus. II. Title. **BIP**

WHEATLEY, Phillis, 811'.1 B
afterwards Phillis Peters, 1753?-1784.
Life and works of Phillis Wheatley, containing her complete poetical works, numerous letters, and a complete biography of this famous poet of a century and a half ago, by G. Herbert Renfro. Also, a sketch of the life of Mr. Renfro, by Leila Amos Pendleton. Washington, 1916. Miami, Fla., Mnemosyne Pub. Co. [1969] 112 p. port. 23 cm. [PS866.W5 1969c] 70-83899
I. Renfro, G. Herbert, 1867-1894. II. Title.

Wheeler-Bennett, John Wheeler, Sir, 1902-1975.

WHEELER-BENNETT, 941.082'092'4
John Wheeler, Sir, 1902-1975
Friends, enemies, and sovereigns / by Sir John Wheeler-Bennett ; with a foreword by Harold Macmillan. New York : St. Martin's Press, 1976. 176 p. ; 23 cm. Includes index. [D15.W45A33 1976] 76-23198 8.95
1. Wheeler-Bennett, John Wheeler, Sir, 1902-1975. 2. Historians—Great Britain—Biography. I. Title. **BIP**

Wheeler, Burton Kendall, 1882-

WHEELER, Burton Kendall, 923.273
1882-
Yankee from the West; the candid, turbulent life story of the Yankee-born U.S. Senator from Montana [by] Burton K. Wheeler with Paul F. Healy. [1st ed.] Garden City, N.Y., Doubleday, 1962. 436 p. illus. 22 cm. [E748.W5A3] 62-15909
I. Healy, Paul F. II. Title.

WHEELER, Burton 328.73'092'4 B
Kendall, 1882-
Yankee from the West : the candid, turbulent life story of the Yankee-born U.S. Senator from Montana / Burton K. Wheeler, with Paul F. Healy. New York : Octagon Books, 1977, c1962. p. cm. Reprint of the ed. published by Doubleday, Garden City, N.Y. [E748.W5A3 1977] 77-11011 ISBN 0-374-98405-0 lib.bdg. : 20.00
1. Wheeler, Burton Kendall, 1882- 2. United States. Congress. Senate—Biography. 3. Legislators—United States—Biography. 4. United States—Politics and government—1901-1953. I. Healy, Paul F., joint author. II. Title.

Wheeler, Charles Stearns, 1816-1843.

EIDSON, John Olin, 1908- 920
Charles Stearns Wheeler, friend of Emerson. Athens, University of Georgia Press [1951] xii, 117 p. illus., port. 22 cm. "The published writings of Wheeler": p. 93-95. Bibliographical references included in "Notes" (p. 101-112) [CT275.W524E4] 51-8464
1. Wheeler, Charles Stearns, 1816-1843. I. Title.

Wheeler, Joseph, 1836-1906.

DYER, John Percy, 1902- 923.573
From Shiloh to San Juan; the life of 'Fightin' Joe' Wheeler. [Rev. ed.] Baton Rouge, La. State Univ. Pr. [c.1941, 1961] 275p. illus. First published in 1941 under title: Fightin' Joe Wheeler. Bibl. 61-10832 5.00
1. Wheeler, Joseph, 1836-1906. I. Title.

Wheeler, Lynde Phelps

WHEELER, Lynde Phelps 925
Josiah Willard Gibbs, the history of a great mind. Foreword by A. Whitney Griswold. New Haven, [conn.] Yale [c-1951-1962] 270p. illus. 21cm. (Yale paperbound, Y-70) (Bibl.) 62-6570 1.75 pap.,
I. Title.

Wheeler, Robert Eric Mortimer Sir 1890-

CLARK, Ronald William. 925.71
Sir Mortimer Wheeler. New York, Roy Publishers [1960] 106p. illus. 19cm. (The Living biographies series) [CC115.W58C55] 60-13054
1. Wheeler, Robert Eric Mortimer Sir 1890- I. Title.

WHEELER, Robert Eric 925.71
Mortimer, Sir 1890-
Still digging. [1st American ed.] New York, Dutton, 1956 [c1955] 236 p. illus. 21 cm. [CC115.W58A3 1956] 56-5269
1. Archaeologists — Correspondence, reminiscences, etc. I. Title.

Wheeler, Wayne Bidwell, 1869-1927.

STEUART, Justin. 363.4'1'0924 B
Wayne Wheeler, dry boss; an uncensored biography of Wayne B. Wheeler. Westport, Conn., Greenwood Press [1970] 304 p. ports. 23 cm. Reprint of the 1928 ed. [HV5293.W4S8 1970] 75-100207 ISBN 0-8371-4033-1
1. Wheeler, Wayne Bidwell, 1869-1927. 2. Prohibition—U.S. I. Title.

Wheeler, William Almon, 1819-1887.

†HOWELLS, William 973.8'3'0924 B
Dean, 1837-1920.
Sketch of the life and character of Rutherford B. Hayes : also a biographical sketch of William A. Wheeler / by Wm. D. Howells. Folcroft, Pa. : Folcroft Library Editions, 1977 [c1876] p. cm. Reprint of the ed. published by Hurd and Houghton, New York. [E682.H85 1977] 77-19043 ISBN 0-8414-4786-1 lib. bdg. : 25.00
1. Hayes, Rutherford Birchard, Pres. U.S., 1822-1893. 2. Wheeler, William Almon, 1819-1887. 3. United States. Congress. House—Biography. 4. Presidents—United States—Biography. 5. Legislators—United States—Biography. 6. United States—Politics and government—1865-1883. I. Title.

Wheeler, William Morton, 1865-1937.

EVANS, Mary Alice. 574'.0924 B
William Morton Wheeler, biologist [by] Mary Alice Evans and Howard Ensign Evans. Cambridge, Mass., Harvard University Press, 1970. xi, 363 p. illus., ports. 25 cm. Includes bibliographical references. [QH31.W54E8] 76-129117 ISBN 0-674-95330-4 11.00
1. Wheeler, William Morton, 1865-1937. I. Evans, Howard Ensign, joint author. **BIP**

Wheelock, Edwin Miller, 1829-1901.

FRAZEE, Jerry D. 973.8'092'4 B
The magnificent carpetbagger : the life, the times, and the literature of Edwin M. Wheelock (1829-1901) / by Jerry D. Frazee. Austin, Texas : Frazee, 1976. 105, 38, [37] leaves : ill. ; 28 cm. "Selected writings of Edwin Wheelock": leaves [1]-[36] (3d group) Includes bibliographical references. [CT275.W5278F7] 77-351959
1. Wheelock, Edwin Miller, 1829-1901. 2. United States—Biography. I. Title.

Wheelock, Eleazar, 1711-1779.

MCCALLUM, James Dow, 378.742'3 B
1892-
Eleazar Wheelock. New York, Arno Press, 1969. ix, 236 p. port. 23 cm. (American education: its men, ideas, and institutions) Reprint of the 1939 ed., originally published as no. 4 of the Dartmouth College manuscript series. Bibliography: p. 217-219. [LD1436 1769.M212] 78-89200
1. Wheelock, Eleazar, 1711-1779. 2. Dartmouth College—History. I. Title. II. Series. **BIP**

MCCLURE, David, 378.1'12'0924 B
1748-1820.
Memoirs of the Rev. Eleazar Wheelock, D.D., by David M'Clure and Elijah Parish. New York, Arno Press, 1972. 336 p. port. 23 cm. (Religion in America, series II) Reprint of the 1811 ed. [LD1436 1769.M32] 75-38454 ISBN 0-405-04074-1
1. Wheelock, Eleazar, 1711-1779. 2. Dartmouth College. I. Parish, Elijah, 1762-1825, joint author. **BIP**

Wheelwright, Charles Henry,

WHEELWRIGHT, Charles Henry, 926.1
1813-1862.
Correspondence of Dr. Charles H. Wheelwright, surgeon of the United States Navy. Edited by Hildegarde B. Forbes. [Boston?] 1958. xiv, 350 p. ports., 3 geneal. tables. 24 cm. [VG227.W4A4] 58-33071
I. Title.

Wheelwright, James B.,

WHEELWRIGHT, James B., v. 12 B
1911-
All is not butter, by Robert Banning [pseud.] [1st ed.] Boston, Little, Brown [1954] 284 p. 21 cm. Autobiographical. [PZ4.W566Al] [W] fic 54-6875
I. Title.

Wherry, Kenneth Spicer, 1892-1951.

STROMER, Marvin E., 973.918'0924
1933-
The making of a political leader; Kenneth S. Wherry and the United States Senate, by Marvin E. Stromer. Lincoln, University of Nebraska Press [1969] xiii, 202 p. illus., facsims., ports. 24 cm. Bibliography: p. 193-196. [E748.W54S7] 69-10405 7.95
1. Wherry, Kenneth Spicer, 1892-1951. I. Title.

Whillans, Don, 1933-

WHILLANS, Don, 796.5'22'0924 B
1933-
Don Whillans : portrait of a mountaineer / [by] Don Whillans and Alick Ormerod. Harmondsworth ; Baltimore : Penguin, 1976. 301 p., [12] p. of plates : ill., ports. ; 18 cm. Includes index. [GV199.92.W46A33 1976] 77-360378 ISBN 0-14-003627-X pbk. : 2.50
1. Whillans, Don, 1933- 2. Mountaineers—Great Britain—Biography. 3. Mountaineering. I. Ormerod, Alick, joint author.

Whipple, George Hoyt, 1878-

CORNER, George Washington, 926.1
1889-
George Hoyt Whipple and his friends; the life-story of a Nobel prize pathologist. Philadelphia, Lippincott [c.1963] vii, 335p. illus., ports. 23cm. Bibl. 63-20828 5.50
1. Whipple, George Hoyt, 1878- I. Title.

Whipple, Henry Benjamin, Bp., 1822-1901.

OSGOOD, Phillips 922.373
Endecott, 1882-
Straight tongue; a story of Henry Benjamin Whipple, first Episcopal bishop of Minnesota. Minneapolis, T. S. Denison [1958] 288p. 23cm. [BX5995.W48O8] 58-14164
1. Whipple, Henry Benjamin, Bp., 1822-1901. I. Title.

Whistler, Anna Mathilda (McNeill) 1804-1881.

MUMFORD, Elizabeth, pseud. 759.13
Whistler's mother; the life of Anna McNeill Whistler. Ann Arbor, Mich., Plutarch Press, 1971. 256 p. 22 cm. Reprint of the 1940 ed. [ND237.W612M8 1971] 75-141655
1. Whistler, Anna Mathilda (McNeill) 1804-1881. I. Title.

Whistler, James Abbott McNeill, 1834-1903.

FLEMING, Gordon H., 760'.092'4 B
1920-
The young Whistler, 1834-66 / by Gordon Fleming. London ; Boston : Allen & Unwin, 1978. 264 p., [8] leaves of plates : ill. ; 24 cm. Includes index. Bibliography: p. [247]-255. [ND237.W6F56] 77-30588 ISBN 0-04-927009-5 : 30.95
1. Whistler, James Abbott McNeill, 1834-1903. 2. Painters—United States—Biography. I. Title. **BIP**

GREGORY, Horace, 1898- 759.13 B
The world of James McNeill Whistler. Freeport, N.Y., Books for Libraries Press [1969, c1959] 255 p. illus., ports. 23 cm. (Select bibliographies reprint series) [ND237.W6G7 1969] 70-80621
1. Whistler, James Abbott McNeill, 1834-1903. I. Title. **BIP**

MCMULLEN, Roy. 759.13 B
Victorian outsider; a biography of J. A. M. Whistler. [1st ed.] New York, E. P. Dutton, 1973. 307 p. illus. 25 cm. Bibliography: p. 283-288. [ND237.W6M33] 72-94702 ISBN 0-525-22853-5 10.00
1. Whistler, James Abbott McNeill, 1834-1903. I. Title.

PEARSON, Hesketh, 1887- 927.5
The man Whistler. [1st American ed.] New York, Harper [1953, c1952] 276p. illus. 22cm. [ND237.W6P25 1953] 52-11694
1. Whistler, James Abbott McNeill, 1834-1903. I. Title.

PEARSON, Hesketh, 760'.092'4 B
1887-1964.
The man Whistler / Hesketh Pearson ; introd. by Benny Green. New York : Taplinger Pub. Co., 1978. xviii, 198 p., [4] leaves of plates : ill. ; 23 cm. Includes index. Bibliography: p. 191-193. [ND237.W6P25 1978] 78-52949 ISBN 0-8008-5097-1 : 9.95
1. Whistler, James Abbott McNeill, 1834-1903. 2. Painters—United States—Biography. I. Title. **BIP**

PENNELL, Elizabeth 759.13
(Robins) 1855-1936.
The life of James McNeill Whistler, by E. R. and J. Pennell. Philadelphia, Lippincott, 1908. [New York, AMS Press, 1973] 2 v. illus. 24 cm. [ND237.W6P4 1973] 70-148285 ISBN 0-404-04988-5 47.50 per vol.
1. Whistler, James Abbott McNeill, 1834-1903. I. Pennell, Joseph, 1857-1926, joint author.
Set 95.00 **BIP**

SPALDING, Frances. 760'.092'4 B
Whistler / [by] Frances Spalding. Oxford : Phaidon, 1979. 80 p. : ill. (some col.), ports. (some col.) ; 29 cm. Bibliography: p. 6. [ND237.W6S69 1979] 78-73433 ISBN 0-7148-1972-7 : 14.95
1. Whistler, James Abbott McNeill, 1834-1903. I. Title.
Dist. by Dutton, N.Y.

TAYLOR, Hilary. 760'.092'4 B
James McNeill Whistler / Hilary Taylor. New York : Putnam, c1978. 192 p. : ill. (some col.) ; 29 cm. Includes index. Bibliography: p. 186-187. [ND237.W6T35 1978] 78-50983 ISBN 0-399-12238-9 : 22.50
1. Whistler, James Abbott McNeill, 1834-1903. 2. Painters—United States—Biography. **BIP**

WEINTRAUB, Stanley, 759.13 B
1929-
Whistler; a biography. New York, Weybright and Talley [1974] x, 498 p. illus. 25 cm. Bibliography: p. 469-481. [ND237.W6W44] 73-76570 ISBN 0-679-40099-0 12.50
1. Whistler, James Abbott McNeill, 1834-1903.

Whitaker, William, 1776-1840.

WHITAKER, William, 942.3'15 B
1776-1840.
William Whitaker, his book, 1776-1840 / edited and introduced by Jean Morrison [Westbury] : West Wiltshire Branch of the Historical Association, [1974] 3-71 p., [4] p. of plates : ill., facsim., map ; 23 cm.

[CT788.W577A33] 75-325635 ISBN 0-902026-01-1 : £0.75
1. Whitaker, William, 1776-1840. I. Title.

Whitbread Round the World Race.

RIDGWAY, John M. 797.1'4
Around the world with Ridgway / by John and Marie-Christine Ridgway. 1st American ed New York : Holt, Rinehart, and Winston, c1979. 317 p., [9] leaves of plates : ill. ; 25 cm. Includes index. [GV832.R5 1979] 78-11848 ISBN 0-03-043751-2 : 15.95
1. Whitbread Round the World Race. 2. Ridgway, John M. 3. Ridgway, Marie-Christine. 4. Seamen—Great Britain—Biography. I. Ridway, Marie-Christine, joint author. II. Title.

Whitby, Jonathan

WHITBY, Jonathan 926.1
Bundu doctor. New York, Roy [1962, c.1961] 191p. illus. 23cm. 62-15485 4.00
I. Title.

Whitde, Oscar, 1854-1900.

HARRIS, Frank, 1855-1931 928.2
Oscar Wilde, including My Memories of Oscar Wilde, by George Bernard Shaw and Oscar's Last Days (A letter from Robert Ross). And an introductory note by Lyle Blair. [New York, Dell, 1963, c.1916-1959] 381p. 17cm. (Laurel Edition LX130) .75 pap.,
1. Whitde, Oscar, 1854-1900. I. Shaw, George Bernbard, 1856-1950. II. Title.

White, Andrew Dickson, 1832-1918.

ALTSCHULER, Glenn C. 973.8'092'4 B
Andrew D. White, educator, historian, diplomat / by Glenn C. Altschuler. Ithaca, N.Y. : Cornell University Press, 1979. 300 p. ; 27 cm. Includes index. Bibliography: p. [286]-294. [E664.W58A57] 78-58065 ISBN 0-8014-1156-4 : 15.00
1. White, Andrew Dickson, 1832-1918. 2. Diplomats—United States—Biography. 3. Historians—United States—Biography. 4. College teachers—United States—Biography. I. Title.

White, Christopher, 1949-

WHITE, Robin, 1928- 362.7'8'30924 B
Be not afraid; the story of a tragically afflicted child and his stubbornly courageous family. New York, Dial Press, 1972. 235 p. 22 cm. [RJ506.M4W5] 77-37444 5.95
1. White, Christopher, 1949- 2. Brain-damaged children—Personal narratives. I. Title.

White, Clarence H., 1871-1925.

WHITE, Clarence H., 1871-1925. 770'.92'4 B
Clarence H. White. Millerton, N.Y. : Aperture, c1979. 95 p. : ill. ; 22 cm. (The Aperture history of photography series ; 11) Bibliography: p. 93-95. [TR653.W5 1979] 77-80019 ISBN 0-89381-019-3 : 7.95
1. White, Clarence H., 1871-1925. 2. Photography, Artistic. 3. Photographers—United States—Biography.

White, Edwin Lee.

WHITE, Edwin Lee. 940.54'25
Ten thousand tons by Christmas / [Edwin Lee White] ; illustrated with photos. 2d ed. St. Petersburg, Fla. : Valkyrie Press, c1975. 256 p. : ill. ; 22 cm. [D810.T8W53 1975] 76-356972 ISBN 0-912760-05-2 : 7.95
1. White, Edwin Lee. 2. World War, 1939-1945—Transportation. 3. World War, 1939-1945—Aerial operations, American. 4. World War, 1939-1945—India. 5. World War, 1939-1945—China. I. Title.

White, Ellen Gould Harmon, 1827-1915.

GRAYBILL, Ronald D. 261.8'3
E. G. White and church race relations [by] Ronald D. Graybill. Washington, Review and Herald Pub. Association [1970] 128 p. 22 cm. On spine: Church race relations. Bibliography: p. 124-128. [BX6193.W5G7] 76-122392
1. White, Ellen Gould (Harmon) 1827-1915. 2. Church and race relations—U.S. I. Title. II. Title: Church race relations.

JOHNSON, Helen M. 922.673
Stories of little Ellen and the message, by Helen M. Johnson and Evelyn Roose Dinsmore. Drawings by Peter J. Rennings. Mountain View, Calif., Pacific Press Pub. Association [1950] 95 p. illus., ports. 21 cm. [BX6193.W5J6] 50-3148
1. White, Ellen Gould (Harmon) 1827-1915. I. Dinsmore, Evelyn Roose. joint author. II. Title.

NOORBERGEN, Rene. 286'.73 B
Ellen G. White, prophet of destiny. New Canaan, Conn., Keats Pub. [1972] xiv, 241 p. illus. 22 cm. Bibliography: p. 229-231. [BX6193.W5N66] 70-190456 ISBN 0-87983-014-X 6.95
1. White, Ellen Gould (Harmon) 1827-1915. I. Title. BIP

RICCHIUTI, Paul B. 286'.73 B
Ellen : [trial and triumph on the American frontier] / Paul B. Ricchiuti. Mountain View, Calif. : Pacific Press Pub. Association, 1976c1977 159 p. ; 22 cm. (Destiny book ; D-160) Includes bibliographical references. [BX6193.W5R5] 76-44051 pbk. : 3.50
1. White, Ellen Gould Harmon, 1827-1915. 2. Adventists—United States—Biography. I. Title.

ROBINSON, Ella May (White) j92
Stories of my grandmother, by Ella M. Robinson. Illustrated by Jim Padgett. Nashville, Southern Pub. Association [1967] 200 p. illus. 21 cm. Autobiographical. [BX6193.W5R6] 67-6562
1. White, Ellen Gould (Harmon) 1827-1915. I. Title.

ROBINSON, Ella May (White) 92
Stories of my grandmother; by Ella M. Robinson. Illustrated by Jim Padgett. Nashville, Southern Pub. Association [1967] 200 p. illus. 21 cm. A granddaughter's reminiscences of life with her grandmother, a Seventh Day Adventist missionary. [BX6193.W5R6] AC 67
1. White, Ellen Gould (Harmon) 1827-1915. 2. Christian life. I. Padgett, James, illus. II. Title.

SPALDING, Arthur Whitefield, 1877- 922.673
Sister White, a life of Ellen G. White for primary children; illustrated by Kreigh Collins. Washington, Review and Herald Pub. Association [1950] 128 p. col. illus. 24 cm. [BX6193.W5S7] 51-792
1. White, Ellen Gould (Harmon) 1827-1915. I. Title.

White, Elliott Pendleton,

WHITE, Elliott Pendleton, 1903- 920
The beautiful Ohio; a pageant of yesterday. With illus. by George Joseph. New York, Exposition Press [1950] 196p. illus. 23cm. Autobiographical. [CT275.W5328A3] 50-58015
I. Title.

White, Elwyn Brooks, 1899- — Correspondence.

WHITE, Elwyn Brooks, 1899- 818'.5'209 B
Letters of E. B. White / collected and edited by Dorothy Lobrano Guth. 1st ed. New York : Harper & Row, c1976. p. cm. Includes index. [PS3545.H5187Z53 1976] 73-18660 ISBN 0-06-014601-X : 15.00
1. White, Elwyn Brooks, 1899- — Correspondence. I. Guth, Dorothy Lobrano. II. Title. BIP

White Fathers—Missions.

LINDEN, Ian. 266'.00967'571
Church and revolution in Rwanda / Ian Linden, with Jane Linden. Manchester : Manchester University Press ; New York : Africana Pub. Co., c1977. xvi, 304 p. : ill. ; 23 cm. Includes index. Bibliography: p. 290-296. [BR1443.R95L56 1977] 76-58329 ISBN 0-8419-0305-0 : 24.50
1. White Fathers—Missions. 2. Catholic Church in Rwanda. 3. Christianity—Rwanda. 4. Missions—Rwanda. 5. Social classes—Rwanda. 6. Rwanda—Politics and government. 7. Rwanda—Social conditions. I. Linden, Jane, joint author. II. Title. BIP

White, Harry Dexter, 1892-1948.

REES, David, 1928- 330.9'2'4 B
Harry Dexter White: a study in paradox. New York, Coward, McCann & Geoghegan [1973] 506 p. 24 cm. Bibliography: p. 488-494. [HJ257.R43] 72-94121 ISBN 0-698-10524-9 12.50
1. White, Harry Dexter, 1892-1948. I. Title.

REES, David, 1928- 330.9'2'4 B
Harry Dexter White: a study in paradox. New York, Coward, McCann & Geoghegan [1973] 506 p. 24 cm. Bibliography: p. 488-494. [HJ257.R43] 72-94121 ISBN 0-698-10524-9 12.50
1. White, Harry Dexter, 1892-1948. I. Title.

WHITE, Nathan I 364.13
Harry Dexter White, loyal American. Waban, Mass., B. W. Bloom [1956] 415p. illus. 24cm. [HJ257.W6] 351.74 56-40027
1. White, Harry Dexter, 1892-1948. I. Title.

WHITE, Nathan I 364.13
Harry Dexter White, loyal American. Waban, Mass., B. W. Bloom [1956] 415p. illus. 24cm. [HJ257.W6] 351.74 56-40027
1. White, Harry Dexter, 1892-1948. I. Title.

White, Horace, 1834-1916.

LOGSDON, Joseph. 973.8'0924 B
Horace White, nineteenth century liberal. Westport, Conn., Greenwood Pub. Corp. [1971] xiii, 418 p. 22 cm. (Contributions in American history, no. 10) Bibliography: p. 395-409. [E415.9.W395L6] 77-105982 ISBN 0-8371-3309-2
1. White, Horace, 1834-1916. BIP

White, James, 1821-1881.

†ROBINSON, Virgil E. 286'.73 B
James White / Virgil Robinson. Washington : Review and Herald Pub. Association, c1976. 316 p. : ill. ; 22 cm. Includes bibliographical references. [BX6193.W54R6] 75-16921 7.50
1. White, James, 1821-1881. 2. Seventh-Day Adventists—United States—Biography. BIP

THIELE, Margaret Rossiter 65-18670
By saddle and sleigh; a story of James White's youth. Washington, D.C., Review & Hearld [1965] 128p. illus., ports. 22cm. [BX6193.W54T50286.73] price unreported
1. White, James, 1821-1881. I. Title.

White, Jim, 1882-1946.

CAIAR, Ruth. 978.9
One man's dream; the story of Jim White, discoverer and explorer of the Carlsbad Caverns. a biography by Ruth Caiar with Jim White, Jr. [1st ed.] New York, Pageant Press [1957] 111p. illus. 21cm. [F802.C28C25] 57-9925
1. White, Jim, 1882-1946. 2. Carlsbad Caverns, N. M. I. White, Jim, 1919- joint author. II. Title.

White, John Alexander, 1909-

WHITE, John Alexander, 1909- 940.54'72'52
The United States Marines in north China / John A. White. Millbrae, Calif. : White, 1974. ix, 217 p. : ill. ; 23 cm. [D805.J3W44] 74-80832 6.95
1. White, John Alexander, 1909- 2. World War, 1939-1945—Prisoners and prisons, Japanese. 3. World War, 1939-1945—Personal narratives, American. I. Title. BIP

White, John, 1866 (Jan. 6)-1933.

ANDREWS, Charles Freer, 1871-1940. 266'.7'0924 B
John White of Mashonaland. New York, Negro Universities Press [1969] 316 p. 23 cm. Reprint of the 1935 ed. [BV3625.M3A6 1969] 79-91660 ISBN 0-8371-2070-5
1. White, John, 1866 (Jan. 6)-1933. BIP

White, Jon Ewbank Manchip, 1924-

WHITE, Jon Ewbank Manchip, 1924- 979'.03
A world elsewhere : one man's fascination with the American Southwest / Jon Manchip White. New York : Crowell, [1975] 320 p., [2] leaves of plates : ill. ; 24 cm. Includes index. [F787.W48 1975] 74-32338 ISBN 0-690-00720-5 : 8.95
1. White, Jon Ewbank Manchip, 1924- 2. Southwest, New—Description and travel—1951- 3. Southwest, New—History. I. Title.

White, Minor.

WHITE, Minor. 770'.92'4 B
Minor White : rites & passages : his photographs accompanied by excerpts from his diaries and letters / biographical essays by James Baker Hall. Millerton, N.Y. : Aperture, 1978. 141 p., [1] leaf of plates : ill. ; 30 cm. Bibliography: p. 137-141. [TR650.W48] 77-80023 ISBN 0-89381-022-3 : 25.00
1. White, Minor. 2. Photography, Artistic. 3. Photographers—United States—Biography.

White Oaks, N.M.—History.

PARKER, Morris B., 1871-1957. 917.89'64 B
Morris B. Parker's White Oaks; life in a New Mexico gold camp, 1880-1900. Edited with an introd. by C. L. Sonnichsen. Tucson, University of Arizona Press [1971] xxiii, 151 p. illus., maps, ports. 20 cm. (Southwest chronicle series) Bibliography: p. 145-146. [F804.W55P3] 75-143274 ISBN 0-8165-0261-7 3.95
1. White Oaks, N.M.—History. 2. Gold mines and mining—New Mexico—White Oaks.

White, Paul Dudley, 1886-

DIMOND, Edmunds Grey, 1918- ed. 926.1
Paul Dudley White; a portrait. E. Grey Dimond: editor. [New York] American Journal of Cardiology [1965] xvi, 167 p. illus., ports. 28 cm. "Originally appeared as a special issue of the American journal of cardiology." "Bibliography of Paul Dudley

White, 1913-1964": p. 145-166. [R154.W45D5] 65-3812
1. White, Paul Dudley, 1886- 2. Heart — Diseases — Bibl. I. White, Paul Dudley, 1886- II. Title.

DIMOND, Edmunds Grey, M.D. 926.1
1918- ed.
Paul Dudley White; a portrait. [New York] Amer. Journal of Cardiology, 466 Lexington Ave. [c.1965] xvi, 167p. illus., ports. 28cm. Orig. appeared as a special issue of the American journal of cardiology. Bibl. [R154.W45D5] 65-3812 6.00
1. White, Paul Dudley, 1886- 2. Heart—Diseases—Bibl. I. White, Paul Dudley, 1886- II. Title.

WHITE, Paul Dudley, 610'.924 B
1886-
My life and medicine; an autobiographical memoir, by Paul Dudley White, with the assistance of Margaret Parton. Boston, Gambit, 1971. xiii, 269 p. illus., group ports. 24 cm. [R154.W45A3] 70-137020 6.95
I. Title.

White, Pearl, 1889-1938.

WELTMANN, 791.43'028'0924 B
Manuel, 1931-
Pearl White: the peerless fearless girl, by Manuel Weltman and Raymond Lee. South Brunswick, A. S. Barnes [1969] 266 p. illus., facsims., ports. 26 cm. [PN2287.W458W4 1969] 69-15769 8.50
1. White, Pearl, 1889-1938. I. Lee, Raymond, joint author. II. Title.

White, Peter, 1830-1908.

BRINKS, Herbert, 1935- 332.1'0924
Peter White. [Grand Rapids, Mich.] W. B. Eerdmans [1970] 63 p. port. 22 cm. (A Great men of Michigan book) Includes bibliographical references. [F566.W58B7] 77-125031 1.95
1. White, Peter, 1830-1908. 2. Marquette, Mich.—History.

White, Robert,

WHITE, Robert, 914.2'03'750924 B
1802-1874.
Autobiographical notes. Newcastle upon Tyne, University (Library), 1966. [3], 25 p. plate (port.). 19 cm. "90 copies impressed." [CT788.W58A32] 67-85932

White Seal (Ketch)

TROBRIDGE, Gerry. 910'.41 B
Conversation with a world voyager, by Gerry Trobridge as told to Steve Doherty. 2d ed. [New York, Seven Seas Press, 1974] 50 p. illus. 28 cm. Cover title. [G440.W623T76 1974] 74-165230 4.00
1. White Seal (Ketch) 2. Voyages around the world—1951- I. Doherty, Steve. II. Title. BIP

White, Stanford, 1853-1906.

BALDWIN, Charles 720'.924 B
Crittenton, 1888-
Stanford White, by Charles C. Baldwin. New York, Da Capo Press, 1971 [c1931] xii, 399 p. illus., ports. 24 cm. (Da Capo Press series in architecture and decorative art, v. 39) [NA737.W5B3 1971] 78-150512 ISBN 0-306-70138-3
1. White, Stanford, 1853-1906. BIP

MOONEY, Michael 364.1'523'0922
Macdonald, 1930-
Evelyn Nesbit and Stanford White : love and death in the gilded age / by Michael Macdonald Mooney. New York : Morrow, 1976. p. cm. Includes index. [HV6534.N5M66] 76-18111 ISBN 0-688-03079-3 : 10.95
1. Nesbit, Evelyn. 2. White, Stanford, 1853-1906. 3. Thaw, Harry Kendall, 1871-1947. I. Title. BIP

White, Stephen Mallory, 1853-1901.

DOBIE, Edith, 1891- .328.73'0924 B
The political career of Stephen Mallory White; a study of party activities under the convention system. New York, AMS Press [1971, c1927] 266 p. illus. 23 cm. (Stanford University publications. University series. History, economics, and political science, v. 2, no. 1) Originally presented as the author's thesis, Stanford, 1925. Bibliography: p. [255]-260. [E664.W61D6 1971] 74-155605 ISBN 0-404-50963-0 11.00
1. White, Stephen Mallory, 1853-1901. 2. California—Politics and government—1850-1950. 3. U.S.—Politics and government—1865-1900. I. Title. II. Series: Stanford studies in history, economics, and political science, v. 2, no. 1.

White, Terence Hanbury, 1906-1964.

WARNER, Sylvia 828'.9'1209 B
Townsend, 1893-
T. H. White; a biography. New York, Viking Press [1968, c1967] 352 p. illus., ports. 22 cm. Bibliography: p. [346]-348. [PR6045.H2Z9 1968] 68-16633
1. White, Terence Hanbury, 1906-1964.

White, Theodore Harold, 1915-

WHITE, Theodore 070'.92'4 B
Harold, 1915-
In search of history : a personal expedition / by Theodore H. White. 1st ed. New York : Harper & Row, c1978. p. cm. [PN4874.W517A34] 78-2177 ISBN 0-06-014599-4 : 12.50
1. White, Theodore Harold, 1915- 2. Journalists—United States—Biography. I. Title.

WHITE, Theodore 070'.92'4 B
Harold, 1915-
In search of history : a personal adventure / Theodore H. White. New York : Warner Books, [1979] c1978. 561 p. ; 21 cm. Reprint of the ed. published by Harper & Row, New York. Includes index. [PN4874.W517A34 1978b] 79-11601 ISBN 0-446-97146-4 : 5.95
1. White, Theodore Harold, 1915- 2. Journalists—United States—Biography. I. Title. BIP

White, Thomas Bruce, 1881-1971.

ADAMS, Verdon R. 363.2'092'4 B
Tom White; the life of a lawman, by Verdon R. Adams. [El Paso] Texas Western Press, 1972. ix, 153 p. illus. 25 cm. [HV7911.W45A64] 73-190576 ISBN 0-87404-035-3 8.00
1. White, Thomas Bruce, 1881-1971. BIP

White, Walter Francis, 1893-1955.

CANNON, Poppy 920.932526
A gentle knight: my husband, Walter White. New York, Popular Lib. [1965, c.1956] 237p. 18cm. (SP337) [E185.97.W6C3] .50 pap.,
1. White, Walter Francis, 1893-1955. I. Title.

CANNON, Poppy. 920.932526
A gentle knight: my husband, Walter White. New York, Rinehart [1956] 309 p. illus. 22 cm. [E185.97.W6C3] 56-11833
1. White, Walter Francis, 1893-1955. I. Title.

WALDRON, Edward E. 813'.5'2 B
Walter White and the Harlem Renaissance / Edward E. Waldron. Port Washington, N.Y. : Kennikat Press, 1978. x, 185 p. ; 22 cm. (Literary criticism series) (National university publications) Includes index. Bibliography: p. 179-182. [PS3545.H6165Z95] 77-6241 ISBN 0-8046-9197-5 : 12.50
1. White, Walter Francis, 1893-1955. 2. Novelists, American—20th century—Biography. I. Title. II. Title: Harlem Renaissance. BIP

WHITE, Walter 323.4'0924 B
Francis, 1893-1955.
A man called White. New York, Arno Press, 1969. viii, 382 p. port. 23 cm. (The American Negro, his history and literature) Reprint of the 1948 ed. [E185.97.W6A3 1969] 69-18561
1. Negroes. I. Title. II. Series. BIP

WHITE, Walter 323.4'0924 B
Francis, 1893-1955.
A man called White. New York, Arno Press, 1969. viii, 382 p. port. 23 cm. (The American Negro, his history and literature) Reprint of the 1948 ed. [E185.97.W6A3 1969] 69-18561
1. Negroes. I. Title. II. Series. BIP

WHITE, Walter 323'.4'0924 B
Francis, 1893-1955.
A man called White; the autobiography of Walter White. Bloomington, Indiana University Press [1970, c1948] viii, 382 p. port. 20 cm. (A Midland book, MB135) [E185.97.W6A3 1970] 76-108216 3.25
1. Negroes. I. Title. BIP

White, William Allen, 1868-1944.

CLOUGH, Frank C. 070'.924 B
William Allen White of Emporia, by Frank C. Clough. Westport, Conn., Greenwood Press [1970, c1941] xiv, 265 p. illus., ports. 23 cm. [PN4874.W52C5 1970] 73-100149
1. White, William Allen, 1868-1944. I. Title. BIP

HOFF, John Seabury. v. 12
William Allen White: a progressive attempts to adjust to the twenties. [n.p.] 1962. 1 v. Honors thesis -- Harvard.
1. White, William Allen, 1868-1944. I. Title.

RICH, Everett, comp. 813'.5'2
William Allen White, 1868-1968; a memorial to a great American. 2d ed. Emporia, Kan., Published for the William Allen White Memorial Library by the Teachers College Press, Kansas State Teachers College of Emporia [1968] [31] p. illus., ports. 23 cm. First ed. published under title: A memorial to a great American, by Kansas State Teachers College, Emporia. [PN4874.W52R48 1968] 68-66214
1. White, William Allen, 1868-1944. I. Kansas. State Teachers College, Emporia. Allen White Memorial Library. II. Kansas. State Teachers College, Emporia. A memorial to a great American. III. Title: A memorial to a great American.

WHITE, William Allen, 070.9'24
1868-1944.
Selected letters of William Allen White, 1899-1943. Edited with an introd. by Walter Johnson New York, Greenwood Press, 1968 [c1947] viii, 460 p. port. 24 cm. [PN4874.W52A4 1968] 68-54442
I. Johnson, Walter, 1915- ed.

White, William Bayard,

WHITE, William Bayard, 1893- 920
When fond recollection ...; the boyhood memories of W. B. White. [1st ed.] New York, Exposition Press [1957] 72 p. 21 cm. [CT275.W5515A3] 56-9571
I. Title.

White, William Charles, Bp., 1873-1960.

WALMSLEY, Lewis 266'.3'0924 B
Calvin, 1897-
Bishop in Honan : mission and museum in the life of William C. White / Lewis C. Walmsley. Toronto ; Buffalo : University of Toronto Press, [1974] xi, 230 p. : ill. ; 23 cm. "Publications of the Right Reverend W. C. White": p. [217]-220. Includes index. [BV3427.W48W34] 74-82288 ISBN 0-8020-3324-5 : 10.00
1. White, William Charles, Bp., 1873-1960. I. Title.

White, William Hale, 1831-1913.

STONE, Wilfred Healey, 928.2
1917-
Religion and art of William Hale White (Mark Rutherford) Stanford, Stanford University Press [1954] 240p. 23cm. (Stanford University publications. University series. Language and literature, v.12) Includes bibliography. [PR5795.W7Z8] 54-6171
1. White, William Hale, 1831-1913. I. Title.

Whitechapel murders, 1888.

KNIGHT, Stephen. 364.1'523'0922
Jack the Ripper : the final solution / [by] Stephen Knight. London : Harrap, 1976. 284 p., [16] p. of plates : ill., facsims., geneal. table, map, ports. ; 23 cm. Errata slip inserted. Includes index. Bibliography: p. [265]-268. [HV6535.G6L637] 76-380246 ISBN 0-245-52724-9 : £4.50
1. Whitechapel murders, 1888. 2. Murder—England—London. I. Title. BIP

RUMBELOW, Donald. 364.1'523'0924
The complete Jack the Ripper / Donald Rumbelow. Introd. by Colin Wilson. Boston : New York Graphic Society, [1975] 288 p., [16] leaves of plates : ill. ; 26 cm. Includes index. Bibliography: p. 276-278. [HV6535.G6L658 1975] 74-24831 ISBN 0-8212-0661-3 : 9.95
1. Whitechapel murders, 1888. I. Title. BIP

Whitefield, George, 1714-1770.

BELDEN, Albert David, 922.542
1883-
George Whitefield, the awakener; a modern study of the Evangelical Revival. New York, Macmillan, 1953. 302p. illus. 23cm. [BX9225.W4B45 1953a] 53-4496
1. Whitefield, George, 1714-1770. 2. Evangelical Revival. I. Title.

HENRY, Stuart Clark. 922.542
George Whitefield: wayfaring witness. New York Abingdon Press [1957] 224p. 24cm. Includes bibliography. [BX9225.W4H4] 57-10273
1. Whitefield, George, 1714-1770. I. Title.

POLLOCK, John 287'.1'0924 B
Charles.
George Whitefield and the Great Awakening [by] John Pollock. [1st ed.] Garden City, N.Y., Doubleday, 1972. x, 272 p. 22 cm. [BX9225.W4P65] 72-76198 ISBN 0-385-03466-0 6.95
1. Whitefield, George, 1714-1770. I. Title.

SHORT, Ruth Gordon. 269'.2'0924 B
George Whitefield, trumpet of the Lord / Ruth Gordon Short. Washington : Review and Herald Pub. Association, [1979] p. cm. [BX9225.W4S54] 79-15420 pbk. : 4.95
1. Whitefield, George, 1714-1770. 2. Evangelists—England—Biography. 3. Evangelists—United States—Biography. I. Title.

Whitehead, Alfred North, 1861-1947.

PITTENGER, William Norman, 192 B
1905-
Alfred North Whitehead, by Norman Pittenger. Richmond, John Knox Press [1969] xiv, 54, [1] p. 19 cm. (Makers of contemporary theology) Bibliography: p. [55] [B1674.W354P5 1969] 69-14338 1.25
1. Whitehead, Alfred North, 1861-1947. I. Title.

Whitehead, Alfred North, 1861-1947—Addresses, essays, lectures.

WHITEHEAD, Alfred North, 192
1861-1947.
Dialogues of Alfred North Whitehead / as recorded by Lucien Price. Westport, Conn. : Greenwood Press, 1977, c1954. 396 p. ; 23 cm. Reprint of the ed. published by Little, Brown, Boston. Includes index. [B1674.W353D5 1977] 76-49903 ISBN 0-8371-9341-9 lib. bdg. : 24.00
1. Whitehead, Alfred North, 1861-1947—

Addresses, essays, lectures. 2. Philosophy—Addresses, essays, lectures. 3. Philosophers—England—Biography—Addresses, essays, lectures. I. Price, Lucien, 1883-1964. II. Title. **BIP**

Whitehead, Thomas North.

WHITEHEAD, Thomas North. 818.5403
Now I am an American: habit and change. Corr. to February 1963. [By] T. North Whitehead. [Cambridge? Mass., 1966] iii p., 169 l. 28 cm. Cover title. [CT275.W5517A3] 66-6042
I. Title.

Whitehill, Walter Muir,

WALTER Muir Whitehill: 920.2
a record compiled by his friends, 13 September 1958. Minot, Mass. [1958] xv, 92 p. illus., ports., map (on lining papers) 24 cm. "Five hundred copies." [Z720.W39W3] 59-17189
1. Whitehill, Walter Muir,
Contents omitted.

Whiteley, Bruce.

WHITELEY, Bruce. 910'.45'0924 B
Tina / Bruce Whiteley. New York : D. McKay Co., c1979. v, 184 p. : ill. ; 22 cm. [G475.W47] 79-1004 ISBN 0-679-51378-7 : 9.95
1. Whiteley, Bruce. 2. Tina (Ship) 3. Voyages and travels—1951- 4. Travelers—South Africa—Biography.

Whiteley, Opal Stanley.

BEDE, Elbert, 1881- 928.1
Fabulous Opal Whiteley; from Oregon logging camp to princess in India. Portland, Or., Binfords & Mort [1954] 181 p. illus. 22 cm. [PS3545.H625Z65] 54-3679
1. Whiteley, Opal Stanley. I. Title.

Whiteley, Opal Stanley, in fiction drama, poetry, etc.

BOULTON, Jane. 813'.5'2 B
Opal / Opal Whiteley ; arranged and adapted by Jane Boulton. New York : Macmillan, c1976. 183 p. ; 22 cm. Adaptation of a work by O. Whiteley which originally appeared in the Atlantic monthly under title: The story of Opal. [PS3545.H625Z68] 76-12591 ISBN 0-02-513970-3 : 6.95
1. Whiteley, Opal Stanley, in fiction drama, poetry, etc. I. Whiteley, Opal Stanley. The story of Opal. II. Title. **BIP**

Whitfield, Henry Lewis, 1868-1927.

BAKER, Bill R. 976.2'062'0924 B
Catch the vision : the life of Henry L. Whitfield of Mississippi / Bill R. Baker. Jackson : University Press of Mississippi, [1974] x, 173 p. : ill. ; 24 cm. Includes index. Bibliography: p. 155-170. [F341.W48B34] 74-82918 ISBN 0-87805-062-0 : 7.95
1. Whitfield, Henry Lewis, 1868-1927. I. Title. **BIP**

Whitfield, Joseph.

WHITFIELD, Joseph. 133.9'3
The treasure of El Dorado : featuring "the Dawn Breakers" / by Joseph Whitfield. Washington : Occidental Press, 1977. 213 p. : ill. ; 22 cm. [BF1283.W543A37] 77-89125 ISBN 0-911050-44-2 : 8.95
1. Whitfield, Joseph. 2. Spiritualists—United States—Biography. I. Title.

Whitlam, Edward Gough, 1916-

OAKES, Laurie. 329.9'94
The making of an Australian Prime Minister [by] Laurie Oakes [and] David Solomon. Melbourne, Cheshire, 1973. 318 p. plates, table. 22 cm. [DU117.2.W47O24] 73-165053 ISBN 0-7015-1711-5 3.50
1. Whitlam, Edward Gough, 1916- 2. Australia—Politics and government—1945- I. Solomon, David, joint author. II. Title.

Whitlock, Brand, 1869-1934.

TAGER, Jack. 301.15'3'0924 B
The intellectual as urban reformer; Brand Whitlock and the Progressive movement. Cleveland, Press of Case Western Reserve University, 1968. 198 p. 22 cm. Bibliography: p. 183-192. [HN57.T3] 67-27798 6.50
1. Whitlock, Brand, 1869-1934. 2. Progressivism (U.S. politics) 3. United States—Social conditions. I. Title.

Whitman, Marcus, 1802-1847.

DRURY, Clifford Merrill, 1897- 917.95'03'30924
Marcus and Narcissa Whitman, and the opening of old Oregon, by Clifford M. Drury. Glendale, Calif., A. H. Clark Co., 1973. 2 v. illus. 25 cm. (Northwest historical series, 10-11) Bibliography: v. 2, p. [405]-406. [F880.W5922] 72-97550 ISBN 0-87062-104-1
1. Whitman, Marcus, 1802-1847. 2. Whitman, Narcissa (Prentiss) 1808-1847. 3. Oregon—History—To 1859. I. Title. II. Series.

DRURY, Clifford Merrill, 1897- 917.95'03'30924
Marcus and Narcissa Whitman, and the opening of old Oregon, by Clifford M. Drury. Glendale, Calif., A. H. Clark Co., 1973. 2 v. illus. 25 cm. (Northwest historical series, 10-11) Bibliography: v. 2, p. [405]-406. [F880.W5922] 72-97550 ISBN 0-87062-104-1 38.50 (2 vols.)
1. Whitman, Marcus, 1802-1847. 2. Whitman, Narcissa (Prentiss) 1808-1847. 3. Oregon—History—To 1859. I. Title. II. Series.

Whitman, Narcissa (Prentiss) 1808-1847.

ALLEN, Opal (Sweazea) 920.7
Narcissa Whitman; an historical biography. Portland, Or., Binfords & Mort [1959] 325p. illus. 23cm. Includes bibliography. [F880.W613] 59-16918
1. Whitman, Narcissa (Prentiss) 1808-1847. 2. Whitman, Marcus 1802-1847. I. Title.

Whitman, Sarah Helen Power, 1803-1878—Biography.

TICKNOR, Caroline, 1866-1937. 818'.3'09 B
Poe's Helen / by Caroline Ticknor. Norwood, Pa. : Norwood Editions, 1975, [c1916] ix, 292 p., [12] leaves of plates : ill. ; 23 cm. Reprint of the 1917 ed. published by J. Lane, London. [PS3189.W4Z9 1975] 75-15585 ISBN 0-88305-676-3 lib. bdg. : 16.75
1. Whitman, Sarah Helen Power, 1803-1878—Biography. 2. Poe, Edgar Allan, 1809-1849—Relationship with women. I. Title. **BIP**

Whitman, Sarah Helen Power, 1803-1878—Correspondence.

WHITMAN, Sarah Helen Power, 1803-1878. 818'.3'09 B
Poe's Helen remembers / edited by John Carl Miller. Charlottesville : University Press of Virginia, 1979. p. cm. "Correspondence that passed between John Ingram and Sarah Helen Whitman from late 1873 through mid-1878." Includes index. [PS2630.5.W5 1979] 79-742 ISBN 0-8139-0771-3 : 24.95
1. Poe, Edgar Allan, 1809-1849—Biography—Sources. 2. Whitman, Sarah Helen Power, 1803-1878—Correspondence. 3. Ingram, John Henry, 1842-1916. 4. Authors, American—19th century—Biography. I. Ingram, John Henry, 1842-1916, joint author. II. Miller, John Carl. III. Title.

Whitman, Walt, 1819-1892.

ALLEN, Gay Wilson, 1903- 928.1
The solitary singer; a critical biography of Walt Whitman. New York, Macmillan, 1955. xii, 616 p. illus., ports., mpas. 24 cm. Bibliographical references included in "Notes" (p. 545-594) [PS3231.A69] 55-114
1. Whitman, Walt, 1819-1892. I. Title.

ALLEN, Gay Wilson, 1903- 811'.3
The solitary singer: a critical biography of Walt Whitman. reissue with revisions New York] New York University Press, 1967. xii, 616 p. illus., geneal. table, maps, ports. 24 cm. Bibliographical references included in "Notes" (p. 545-594) [PS3231.A69 1967] 67-23414
1. Whitman, Walt, I. Title.

ALLEN, Gay Wilson, 1903- 928.1
Walt Whitman [Gloucester, Mass., Peter Smith, 1961] 192p. illus. (Evergreen profile bk. 19 rebound) Bibl. 3.35
1. Whitman, Walt,, 1819-1892. I. Title.

ALLEN, Gay Wilson, 1903- 928.1
Walt Whitman. New York, Grove Press [1961] 192p. illus., ports (Evergreen profile book 19) Bibl. 60-7191 1.35 pap.,
1. Whitman, Walt, 1819-1892. I. Title.

BINNS, Henry Bryan, 1873- 811'.3
Walt Whitman & his poetry. London, G. G. Harrap, 1915. [New York, AMS Press, 1972] 167, [1] p. port. 19 cm. (Poetry and life series) Bibliography: p. [168] [PS3231.B55 1972] 75-120971 ISBN 0-404-52502-4 8.00
1. Whitman, Walt, 1819-1892. I. Title. II. Series. **BIP**

BRIGGS, Arthur E. 928.1
Walt Whitman: thinker and artist New York, Philosophical Library [1952] 489 p. 23 cm. [PS3231.B7] 52-13025
1. Whiltman, Walt, 1819-1892. I. Title.

BUCKE, Richard Maurice, 1837-1902. 811'.3
Walt Whitman. New York, Johnson Reprint Corp., 1970. xviii, 236 p. illus., facsim., geneal. tables, port. 21 cm. (Belles lettres in English) Reprint of the 1883 ed., with a new introd. by Harold Jaffe. [PS3231.B8 1970] 79-108596
1. Whitman, Walt, 1819-1892.

BURROUGHS, John, 1837-1921. 811'.3
Notes on Walt Whitman, as poet and person. New York, Haskell House, 1971. 108 p. 23 cm. Reprint of the 1867 ed. [PS3231.B85 1971] 68-24932 ISBN 0-8383-0922-4
1. Whitman, Walt, 1819-1892 I Title. **BIP**

CLARKE, William, 1852-1901. 811'.3
Walt Whitman. New York, Haskell House, 1970. 132 p. port. 23 cm. Reprint of the 1906 ed. Includes bibliographical references. [PS3238.C5 1970] 77-130249 ISBN 0-8383-1139-3
1. Whitman, Walt, 1819-1892.

DONALDSON, Thomas Corwin, 1843-1898. 811'.3 B
Walt Whitman the man. [Folcroft, Pa.] Folcroft Library Editions, 1973 [c1896] p. Reprint of the ed. published by F. P. Harper, New York. [PS3231.D6 1973] 73-9633 ISBN 0-8414-1883-7 (lib. bdg.)
1. Whitman, Walt, 1819-1892. I. Title.

ELLIOT, Charles Nathan, 1873- comp. 811'.3 B
Walt Whitman as man, poet, and friend, being autograph pages from many pens, collected by Charles N. Elliot. [Folcroft, Pa.] Folcroft Library Editions, 1973 [c1915] 257 p. facsims., ports. 26 cm. Reprint of the ed. published by R. G. Badger, Boston. [PS3231.E4 1973] 73-8682 25.00
1. Whitman, Walt, 1819-1892. I. Title.

HAMBLEN, Emily S., 1864- 811'.3
Walt Whitman: bard of the West. Girard, Kan., Haldeman-Julius Co. [Folcroft, Pa.] Folcroft Library Editions, 1973 [c1924] p. Original ed. issued as no. 529 of the Little blue book. [PS3231.H4 1973] 73-3176 6.50
1. Whitman, Walt, 1819-1892. I. Title. II. Series: Little blue book no. 529.

HARNED, Thomas Biggs, 1851- 340'.0924 B
Memoirs of Thomas B. Harned, Walt Whitman's friend and literary executor. Edited, with a detailed index, by Peter Van Egmond. Hartford, Transcendental Books [1972] 58 l. illus. 29 cm. [KF368.H27A3] 72-170119
1. Whitman, Walt, 1819-1892. 2. Lawyers—United States—Correspondence, reminiscences, etc.

MASTERS, Edgar Lee, 1869-1950. 811'.3 B
Whitman. New York, Biblo and Tannen, 1968 [c1937] 342 p. port. 24 cm. [PS3231.M25 1968] 68-22695
1. Whitman, Walt, 1819-1892. **BIP**

MILLER, James Edwin, 1920- v. 12
Walt Whitman. New Haven, College and University Press, Paperback Division [1962] 188 p. (Twayne's United States authors series, T-20) Includes bibliography. 65-78033
1. Whitman, Walter, 1819-1892. I. Title.

PERRY, Bliss, 1860-1954. 811'.3
Walt Whitman; his life and work. New York, AMS Press [1969] vii, 318 p. illus., facsims., ports. 23 cm. Reprint of the 1906 ed. Bibliographical footnotes. [PS3231.P4 1969] 79-86165
1. Whitman, Walt, 1819-1892.

SCHYBERG, Frederik, 1905-1950. 928.1
Walt Whitman; translated from the Danish by Evie Allison Allen. With an introd. by Gay Wilson Allen, New York, Columbia University Press, 1951. xv, 387 p. 24 cm. Bibliography: p. [361]-365. [PS3231.S43] 51-10116
1. Whitman, Walt, 1819-1802. I. Title

THE solitary singer; v. 12
a critical biography of Walt Whitman. New York, Grove Press [1959] xii, 616p. illus., ports. 21cm. (Evergreen book E-136) Bibliographical references included in 'Notes' (p. 545-594)
1. Whitman, Walt, 1819-1892. I. Allen, Gay Wilson, 1903- **BIP**

STOUTENBURG, Adrien. 811'.3 B
Listen, America; a life of Walt Whitman [by] Adrien Stoutenburg and Laura Nelson Baker. New York, Scribner [1968] 182 p. port. 22 cm. Bibliography: p. [175] [PS3231.S7] 68-12520
1. Whitman, Walt, 1819-1892. I. Baker, Laura Nelson, 1911- joint author. II. Title.

THOMSON, James, 1834-1882. 811'.3 B
Walt Whitman, the man and the poet, by James Thomson ("B. V.") With an introd. by Bertram Dobell. New York, Haskell House, 1971. xxxv, 106 p. 23 cm. Reprint of the 1910 ed. [PS3231.T5 1971] 71-163457 ISBN 0-8383-1319-1
1. Whitman, Walt, 1819-1892. I. Title.

TRIMBLE, W. H. 811'.3
Walt Whitman and Leaves of grass : an introduction / by W. H. Trimble. Norwood, Pa. : Norwood Editions, 1975.

100 p. ; 23 cm. Reprint of the 1905 ed. published by Watts, London. Bibliography: p. 92-100. [PS3231.T7 1975] 75-34349 ISBN 0-88305-671-2 : 15.00
1. Whitman, Walt, 1819-1892. I. Title.

WHITMAN, Walt, 1819- 811'.3 B 1892.
Autobiographia; or, The story of a life, by Walt Whitman. Selected from his prose writings. [Folcroft, Pa.] Folcroft Library Editions, 1972 [c1892] 205 p. front. 24 cm. Original ed. issued in series: Fiction, fact, and fancy series. [PS3231.A2 1972] 72-6245 ISBN 0-8414-0083-0 (lib. bdg.)
I. Title. **BIP**

WHITMAN, Walt, 1819- 811'.3 B 1892.
Calamus: a series of letters written during the years 1868-1880 by Walt Whitman to a young friend (Peter Doyle). Edited with an introd. by Richard Maurice Bucke. London, G. P. Putnam's Sons; Boston, Small, Maynard, 1898. [Folcroft, Pa.] Folcroft Library Editions, 1972. viii, 173 p. 24 cm. Reprint of the 1898 issue first published in 1897. [PS3231.A2 1972b] 72-190680
I. Doyle, Peter, 1847- II. Title.

WHITMAN, Walt, 1819- 818'.3'03 B 1892.
Walt Whitman's diary in Canada, with extracts from other of his diaries and literary note-books. Edited by William Sloane Kennedy. [Folcroft, Pa.] Folcroft Press [1970] vi, 73 p. port. 21 cm. Reprint of the 1904 ed. [PS3232.K4 1970] 72-190708
I. Title.

Whitman, Walt, 1819-1892— Addresses, essays, lectures.

O'HIGGINS, Harvey 811'.3 B Jerrold, 1876-1929.
Alias Walt Whitman / by Harvey O'Higgins. Folcroft, Pa. : Folcroft Library Editions, 1976, [c1929] 49 p. ; 23 cm. Reprint of the 1930 ed. published by the Carteret Book Club, Newark, N.J. [PS3231.O5 1976] 76-47445 ISBN 0-8414-6539-8 lib. bdg. : 10.00
1. Whitman, Walt, 1819-1892—Addresses, essays, lectures. 2. Poets, American—19th century—Biography—Addresses, essays, lectures. I. Title. **BIP**

Whitman, Walt, 1819-1892— Biography.

ALLEN, Gay Wilson, 1903- 811'.3 B
Aspects of Walt Whitman / by Gay Wilson Allen. Folcroft, Pa. : Folcroft Library Editions, 1977. ix, 317 p. ; 23 cm. Reprint of the 1961 ed. published by Southern Illinois Univeristy Press, Carbondale, under title: Walt Whitman as man, poet, and legend; with 3 supplementary essays. "A check list of Whitman publications, 1945-1960": p. [PS3231.A698 1977] 77-751 ISBN 0-8414-2882-4 lib. bdg. : 30.00
1. Whitman, Walt, 1819-1892—Biography. 2. Whitman, Walt, 1819-1892—Bibliography. 3. Poets, American—19th century—Biography. I. Title. **BIP**

ALLEN, Gay Wilson, 1903- 811'.3
The solitary singer; a critical biography of Walt Whitman. [Reissue with revisions. New York] New York University Press, 1967. xii, 616 p. illus., geneal. table, maps, ports. 24 cm. Bibliographical references included in "Notes" (p. 545-594) [PS3231.A69 1967] 67-23414
1. Whitman, Walt, 1819-1892—Biography. I. Title.

ALLEN, Gay Wilson, 1903- 811'.3
Walt Whitman. Rev. ed. Detroit, Wayne State University Press, 1969. 251 p. illus., facsims., ports. 22 cm. (Waynebook no. 31) Bibliography: p. 237-243. [PS3231.A697 1969] 68-30926 ISBN 0-8143-1406-6 7.50
1. Whitman, Walt, 1819-1892—Biography.

ALLEN, Gay Wilson, 1903- 811.3
Walt Whitman as man, poet, and legend. With a check list of Whitman publications, 1945-1960, by Evie Allison Allen. Carbondale, Southern Illinois University Press [1961] xii, 260 p. 22 cm. [PS3231.A698] 61-10924
1. Whitman, Walt, 1819-1892—Biography. 2. Whitman, Walt, 1819-1892—Bibliography. I. Allen, Evie Allison.

ARVIN, Newton, 1900-1963. 811'.4
Whitman. New York, Russell & Russell [1969, c1938] viii, 320 p. 23 cm. Bibliography: p. 299-312. [PS3231.A8 1969] 68-27047
1. Whitman, Walt, 1819-1892—Biography. **BIP**

BAILEY, John Cann, 1864- 811'.3 1931.
Walt Whitman. New York, Macmillan, 1926. St. Clair Shores, Mich., Scholarly Press, 1970. 220 p. 21 cm. (English men of letters) [PS3231.B25 1970] 74-131615 ISBN 0-403-00502-7
1. Whitman, Walt, 1819-1892—Biography.

BAZALGETTE, Leon, 1873- 811'.3 B 1928.
Walt Whitman, the man and his work. Translated from the French by Ellen FitzGerald. New York, Cooper Square Publishers, 1970 [i.e. 1971] xviii, 355 p. 22 cm. Reprint of the 1920 ed. Translation of Walt Whitman, l'homme et son ouvre. Includes bibliographical references. [PS3231.B32 1970] 72-128770 ISBN 0-8154-0352-6 9.00
1. Whitman, Walt, 1819-1892—Biography. I. Title.

BINNS, Henry Bryan, 811'.3 B 1873-
A life of Walt Whitman. New York, Haskell House, 1969. xxviii, 369 p. illus., facsims., ports. 23 cm. Reprint of the 1905 ed. [PS3231.B5 1969] 78-92937 ISBN 0-8383-1001-X
1. Whitman, Walt, 1819-1892—Biography. I. Title. **BIP**

BRASHER, Thomas L. 818'.3'08
Whitman as editor of the Brooklyn daily eagle [by] Thomas L. Brasher. Detroit, Wayne State University Press, 1970. 264 p. 24 cm. Includes bibliographical references. [PS3231.B66 1970] 70-91872 ISBN 0-8143-1408-2 9.50
1. Whitman, Walt, 1819-1892—Biography. I. Title. **BIP**

BRIGGS, Arthur E. 811'.3
Walt Whitman: thinker and artist, by Arthur E. Briggs. New York, Greenwood Press, 1968 [c1952] 489 p. 23 cm. [PS3231.B7 1968] 68-8052
1. Whitman, Walt, 1819-1892—Biography.

CANBY, Henry Seidel, 811'.3 B 1878-1961.
Walt Whitman, an American; a study in biography. Westport, Conn., Greenwood Press [1970, c1943] viii, 381 p. illus., ports. 23 cm. Bibliography: p. [371]-375. [PS3231.C27 1970] 72-106663 ISBN 0-8371-3421-8
1. Whitman, Walt, 1819-1892—Biography.

CARPENTER, George Rice, 811'.3 B 1863-1909.
Walt Whitman. Introd. by William White. New York, Macmillan Co. [1909] Detroit, Gale Research Co., 1967. v, 175 p. 23 cm. (The Gale Library of lives and letters. American writers series) [PS3231.C3 1967] 67-23891
1. Whitman, Walt, 1819-1892—Biography.

FAUSSET, Hugh I'Anson, 811'.3 B 1895-
Walt Whitman, poet of democracy. New York, Haskell House, 1966. 320 p. ports. 22 cm. Reprint of the 1942 ed. Bibliography: p. 309-310. [PS3231.F3 1966] 68-1196
1. Whitman, Walt, 1819-1892—Biography.

FAUSSET, Hugh I'Anson, 811.3 B 1895-
Walt Whitman: poet of democracy. New York, Russell & Russell [1969] 320 p. ports. 23 cm. Reprint of the 1942 ed. Bibliography: p. 309-310. [PS3231.F3 1969] 67-28777
1. Whitman, Walt, 1819-1892—Biography.

HARTMANN, Sadakichi, 811'.3 B 1867-1944.
Conversations with Walt Whitman, by Sadakichi. [Folcroft, Pa.] Folcroft Library Editions, 1973 [c1895] 51 l. 33 cm. Reprint of the ed. published by E. P. Coby, New York. [PS3233.H3 1973] 73-3183 ISBN 0-8414-2637-6 (lib. bdg.)
1. Whitman, Walt, 1819-1892—Biography. I. Title. **BIP**

HOLLOWAY, Emory, 1885- 811'.3
Whitman; an interpretation in narrative. Illustrated with ports. and facsims. of Whitman's letters and diaries. New York, Biblo and Tannen, 1969. xxiii, 330 p. illus., facsims., ports. 24 cm. Reprint of the 1926 ed., with a new, 2d pref. by the author. "List of Whitman's more important volumes": p. 317-318. [PS3231.H55 1969] 70-79953
1. Whitman, Walt, 1819-1892—Biography.

JOHNSTON, John, fl.1890- 811'.3 1918.
Visits to Walt Whitman in 1890-1891 by two Lancashire friends, J. Johnston, M.D. and J. W. Wallace. New York, Haskell House, 1970. 279 p. illus., ports. 23 cm. "First published in 1917." [PS3232.J6 1970] 77-129195 ISBN 0-8383-1159-8
1. Whitman, Walt, 1819-1892—Biography. I. Wallace, J. W., joint author. II. Title. **BIP**

KENNEDY, William Sloane, 811'.3 1850-1929.
Reminiscences of Walt Whitman, with extracts from his letters and remarks on his writings. New York, Haskell House Publishers, 1973. ix, 190 p. 23 cm. Reprint of the 1896 ed. [PS3231.K4 1972] 72-4113 ISBN 0-8383-1605-0 9.95
1. Whitman, Walt, 1819-1892—Biography. I. Title.

KOMROFF, Manuel, 1890- 811'.3
Walt Whitman: the singer and the chains. [Folcroft, Pa.] Folcroft Library Editions, 1973 [c1966] 19 p. front. 26 cm. [PS3238.K6 1973] 73-4600 ISBN 0-8414-2215-X (lib. bdg.)
1. Whitman, Walt, 1819-1892—Biography. I. Title.

MARINACCI, Barbara. 811'.3 B
O wondrous singer! An introduction to Walt Whitman. New York, Dodd, Mead [1970] 371 p. illus., ports. 24 cm. Bibliography: p. 351-353. [PS3231.M18] 77-105292 7.50
1. Whitman, Walt, 1819-1892—Biography. I. Title. **BIP**

MENDEL'SON, Moris 811'.3 B Osipovich.
Life and work of Walt Whitman : a Soviet view / Maurice Mendelson ; [translated from the Russian by Andrew Bromfield ; illustrated by G. Dauman]. Moscow : Progress Publishers, 1976. 347 p. : port. ; 21 cm. Translation of Zhizn' i tvorchestvo Uitmena. Includes bibliographies and index. [PS3231.M4E5] 77-355158
1. Whitman, Walt, 1819-1892—Biography. 2. Poets, American—19th century—Biography. I. Title. **BIP**

MORRIS, Harrison Smith, 811'.3 B 1856-1948.
Walt Whitman : a brief biography with reminiscences / by Harrison S. Morris. Folcroft, Pa. : Folcroft Library Editions, 1976. p. cm. Reprint of the 1929 ed. published by Harvard University Press, Cambridge, Mass. [PS3231.M58 1976] 76-40430 ISBN 0-8414-6067-1 lib. bdg. : 20.00
1. Whitman, Walt, 1819-1892—Biography. 2. Poets, American—19th century—Biography. **BIP**

PERRY, Bliss, 1860-1954. 811'.3 B
Walt Whitman. Boston, Houghton Mifflin. St. Clair Shores, Mich., Scholarly Press, 1971 [c1906] viii, 334 p. 20 cm. (American men of letters) Includes bibliographical references. [PS3231.P4 1971] 77-145231 ISBN 0-403-01147-7
1. Whitman, Walt, 1819-1892—Biography.

†PLATT, Isaac Hull, 811'.3 B 1853-1912.
Walt Whitman / by Isaac Hull Platt. Folcroft, Pa. : Folcroft Library Editions, 1977 [c1904] xxii, 147 p. ; 18 cm. Reprint of the ed. published by Small, Maynard, Boston, in series: The Beacon biographies of eminent Americans. Bibliography: p. [141]-147. [PS3231.P5 1977] 77-22294 ISBN 0-8414-6835-4 lib. bdg. : 15.00
1. Whitman, Walt, 1819-1892—Biography. 2. Poets, American—19th century—Biography. I. Series: The Beacon biographies of eminent Americans.

SYMONDS, John Addington, 811'.3 1840-1893.
Walt Whitman; a study. [New York] B. Blom [1967] xxxv, 160 p. illus., facsim., port. 20 cm. Reprint of the 1893 ed. Bibliographical footnotes. [PS3231.S8 1967] 67-29559
1. Whitman, Walt, 1819-1892—Biography.

Whitman, Walt, 1819-1892— Correspondence.

BUCKE, Richard Maurice, 811'.3 1837-1902.
Richard Maurice Bucke, medical mystic : letters of Dr. Bucke to Walt Whitman and his friends / selected and edited by Artem Lozynsky ; with a foreword by Gay Wilson Allen. Detroit : Wayne State University Press, 1977. p. cm. Includes index. [PS3231.A34 1977b] 77-6818 ISBN 0-8143-1576-3 : 12.95
1. Whitman, Walt, 1819-1892—Correspondence. 2. Bucke, Richard Maurice, 1837-1902. 3. Poets, American—19th century—Correspondence. 4. Physicians—Canada—Correspondence. I. Whitman, Walt, 1819-1892. II. Lozynsky, Artem, 1941- III. Title. **BIP**

WHITMAN, Walt, 1819-1892. 811'.3
Calamus : a series of letters written during the years, 1868-1880, by Walt Whitman to a young friend (Peter Doyle) / edited, with an introd., by Richard Maurice Bucke. Norwood, Pa. : Norwood Editions, 1974. viii, 173 p., [2] leaves of plates : ill. ; 23 cm. Reprint of the 1898 issue first published in 1897 by Putnam, London. [PS3231.A3 1974] 74-36065 ISBN 0-88305-755-7 lib. bdg. : 20.00
1. Whitman, Walt, 1819-1892—Correspondence. 2. Doyle, Peter, 1847- I. Doyle, Peter, 1847- II. Title. **BIP**

WHITMAN, Walt, 1819- 811'.3 B 1892.
Letters written by Walt Whitman to his mother, 1866-1872 / with an introductory note by Rollo G. Silver. Folcroft, Pa. : Folcroft Library Editions, 1977 [c1936] 71 p., [1] leaf of plates : ill. ; 25 cm. Reprint of the ed. published by A. F. Goldsmith, New York. [PS3231.A46 1977] 77-7610 ISBN 0-8414-7571-7 lib. bdg. : 17.50
1. Whitman, Walt, 1819-1892—Correspondence. 2. Whitman, Louise (Van Velsor), Mrs., 1795-1873. 3. Poets, American—19th century—Correspondence. 4. Mothers—Correspondence. I. Title. **BIP**

WHITMAN, Walt, 1819- 811'.3 B 1892.
Walt Whitman, The correspondence : supplement / edited by Edwin Haviland Miller. New York : New York University Press, 1977. p. cm. Includes an index as well as corrections and additions to vols. 1-5 of The correspondence. [PS3231.A3 1977] 76-25786 ISBN 0-8147-5415-5 : 20.00
1. Whitman, Walt, 1819-1892—Correspondence. 2. Poets, American—19th century—Correspondence. I. Whitman, Walt, 1819-1892. The correspondence. II. Miller, Edwin Haviland. III. Title.

WHITMAN, Walt, 1819-1892. 811'.3
The wound dresser : a series of letters written from the hospitals in Washington during the war of the rebellion / by Walt Whitman ; edited by Richard Maurice Bucke. Folcroft, Pa. : Folcroft Library Editions, 1975. p. cm. Reprint of the 1898 ed. published by Small, Maynard, Boston. [PS3221.A1 1975] 75-29496 ISBN 0-8414-9447-9 lib. bdg. : 35.00
1. Whitman, Walt, 1819-1892—Correspondence. 2. United States—History—Civil War, 1861-1865—Hospitals, charities, etc. I. Title.

Whitman, Walt, 1819-1892—Diaries.

WHITMAN, Walt, 1819-1892. 811'.5
Daybooks and notebooks / Walt Whitman ; edited by William White. [New York] : New York University Press, 1978, c1977. 3 v. (xxvii, 869 p.) : facsims. ; 27 cm. (The Collected writings of Walt Whitman) Contents.Contents.—v. 1. Daybooks, 1876-November 1881.—v. 2. Daybooks,

December 1881-1891.—v. 3. Diary in Canada, notebooks, index. Includes bibliographical references. [PS3231.A23 1978] 75.00
1. Whitman, Walt, 1819-1892—Diaries. 2. Poets, American—19th century—Biography. I. Title.
Available only as part of a 3 vol set. **BIP**

Whitman, Walt, 1819-1892—Friends and associates.

BARRUS, Clara, 1864-1931. 811'.3
Whitman and Burroughs, comrades. Port Washington, N.Y., Kennikat Press [1968, c1931] xxx, 392 p. map, ports. 23 cm. "Bibliography of Burroughs and Whitman": p. [375]-379. Bibliographical footnotes. [PS3233.B25 1968] 67-27575
1. Whitman, Walt, 1819-1892—Friends and associates. 2. Burroughs, John, 1837-1921. I. Title.

Whitman, Walt, 1819-1892—Homes and haunts—New Jersey.

WALT Whitman at home / 811'.3 B
by himself. Folcroft, Pa. : Folcroft Library Editions, 1976. p. cm. Selections which originally appeared in the Critic, edited by J. L. and J. B. Gilder. Reprint of the 1898 ed. published by the Critic Co., New York, as Critic pamphlet, no. 2. [PS3234.W25 1976] 76-13619 lib. bdg. : 6.50
1. Whitman, Walt, 1819-1892—Homes and haunts—New Jersey. 2. Camden, N.J.—Description. I. Gilder, Joseph Benson, 1858-1936. II. Gilder, Jeannette Leonard, 1849-1916. III. Series: Critic pamphlet ; no. 2.

Whitman, Walt, 1819-1892—Knowledge and learning.

STOVALL, Floyd, 1896- 811'.3
The foreground of Leaves of grass. Charlottesville, University Press of Virginia [1974] x, 320 p. 25 cm. Includes bibliographical references. [PS3236.S8] 73-87861 ISBN 0-8139-0523-0 15.00
1. Whitman, Walt, 1819-1892—Knowledge and learning. 2. Whitman, Walt, 1819-1892—Biography. I. Title. **BIP**

Whitman, Walt, 1819-1892—Relationship with men.

RIVERS, Walter Courtenay. 811'.3
Walt Whitman's anomaly / by W. C. Rivers ; with an introd. by Gay Wilson Allen. Folcroft, Pa. : Folcroft Library Editions, 1977. p. cm. Reprint of the 1976 ed. published by Norwood Editions, Norwood, Pa. Includes bibliographical references. [PS3232.R55 1977] 77-12520 ISBN 0-8414-7357-9 lib. bdg. : 15.00
1. Whitman, Walt, 1819-1892—Relationship with men. 2. Poets, American—19th century—Biography. 3. Homosexuals, Male—Biography. I. Title. **BIP**

Whitney, Albert Wurts, 1870-1943.

STACK, Herbert James, 1892- ed. 923.673
Safety for greater adventures, the contributions of Albert Wurts Whitney. New York Center for Safety Education, Division of General Education, New York University 1953 98p. illus. 24cm. [HG9956.S8] 53-24746
1. Whitney, Albert Wurts, 1870-1943. 2. Insurance, Casualty—U.S. I. Title.

Whitney, Clara, A.

WHITNEY, Clara A. 952.03'1
Clara's diary : an American girl in Meiji, Japan / Clara A. N. Whitney ; edited by M. William Steele and Tamiko Ichimata. 1st ed. Tokyo ; New York : Kodansha International, 1979. 353 p. : ill. ; 22 cm. Includes index. [DS822.25.W45] 78-60970 ISBN 0-87011-341-0 : 15.00
1. Whitney, Clara, A. 2. Japan—Social life and customs—1868-1912. 3. Japan—Politics and government—1868-1912. 4. Americans in Japan—Biography. 5. Japan—Biography. I. Steele, M. William, 1942- II. Ichimata, Tamiko, 1912- III. Title. **BIP**

Whitney, Eleanor Searle.

WHITNEY, Eleanor Searle. 248'.0924 B
Invitation to joy; a personal story. [1st ed.] New York, Harper & Row [1971] ix, 195 p. ports. 22 cm. [CT275.W5543A3 1971] 70-148435 5.95
I. Title.

Whitney, Eli, 1765-1825.

GILBERT, Miriam. 926
Eli Whitney; master craftsman. Illustrated by Leonard Vosburgh. New York, Abingdon Press [1956] 128 p. illus. 21 cm. (Makers of America) [TS1570.W4G5] 56-3745
1. Whitney, Eli, 1765-1825.

GREEN, Constance (McLaughlin) 1897- 926
Eli Whitney and the birth of American technology. [1st ed.] Boston, Little, Brown [1956] 215 p. 21 cm. (THe library of American biography) [TS1570.W4G7] 56-5930
1. Whitney, Eli, 1765-1825. **BIP**

HAYS, Wilma Pitchford. 926
Eli Whitney and the machine age. Pictures by Alfred Petersen. New York, F. Watts [1959] 58p. illus. 22cm. (A First biography) [TS1570.W4H3] 59-10957
1. Whitney, Eli, 1765-1825. I. Title.

HAYS, Wilma Pitchford. 681'.7631'0924 B
Eli Whitney and the machine age. Pictures by Alfred Petersen. New York, F. Watts [1959] 58 p. illus. 22 cm. (A First biography) A biography of Eli Whitney who invented the cotton gin and other useful machines. His greatest contribution, interchangeable parts for machines, was a major influence in the development of industry. [TS1570.W4H3] 92 AC 68
1. Whitney, Eli, 1765-1825. I. Petersen, Alfred, illus. II. Title.

LATHAM, Jean Lee. 681'.7631'0924 B
Eli Whitney, great inventor. Illustrated by Cary. Champaign, Ill., Garrard Pub. Co. [1963] 80 p. illus. 23 cm. (A Discovery book) A brief biography of the inventor of a gin to seed upland cotton and of a way to mass produce musket locks. [TS1570.W4L28] 92 AC 68
1. Whitney, Eli, 1765-1825. I. Cary, illus. II. Title.

LATHAM, Jean Lee. 926
The story of Eli Whitney; invention and progress in the young Nation. Illustrated by Fritz Kredel. [1st ed.] New York, Aladdin Books, 1953. 192 p. illus. 21 cm. (American heritage) [TS1570.W4L3] 53-12188
1. Whitney, Eli, 1765-1825.

LATHAM, Jean Lee. 681'.7631'0924 B
The story of Eli Whitney. Illustrated by Fritz Kredel. New York, Harper & Row [1962, c1953] 192 p. illus. 21 cm. A biography of Eli Whitney tracing his long legal journey to win rights over his pirated cotton gin and to fulfill his Government contract for ten thousand muskets with interchangable parts. [TS1570.W4L3 1962] 92 AC 68
1. Whitney, Eli, 1765-1825. I. Kredel, Fritz, 1900- illus. II. Title.

MIRSKY, Jeannette, 1903- 926
The world of Eli Whitney, by Jeannette Mirsky, Allan Nevins. New York, Collier [1962, c.1952] 350p. (AS168) Bibl. .95 pap.,
1. Whitney, Eli, 1765-1825. I. Nevins, Allan, 1890- joint author. II. Title.

MIRSKY, Jeannette, 1903- 926
The world of Eli Whitney, by Jeannette Mirsky & Allan Nevins. New York, Macmillan, 1952. xvi, 346 p. illus., port. 22 cm. Bibliography: p. 317-337. [TS1570.W4M5] 52-4520
1. Whitney, Eli, 1765-1825. I. Nevins, Allan, 1890-1971, joint author. II. Title.

OLMSTED, Denison, 1791-1859. 681'.7631'0924 B
Memoir of Eli Whitney, Esq. New York, Arno Press, 1972. 80 p. illus. 23 cm. (Technology and society) Reprint of the 1846 ed. [TS1570.W4O4 1972] 72-5065 ISBN 0-405-04716-9
1. Whitney, Eli, 1765-1825. I. Title. II. Series. **BIP**

Whitney, Eli, 1765-1825—Juvenile literature.

HAYS, Wilma Pitchford 92
Eli Whitney, founder of modern industry. New York, Watts [c.1965] 94p. 22cm. (Immortals of engin.) [TS1570.W4H4] 65-23816 2.95; 2.21 lib. ed.,
1. Whitney, Eli, 1765-1825—Juvenile literature. I. Title.

LATHAM, Jean Lee. 92 (J)
Eli Whitney, great inventor. Illustrated by Cary. Champaign, Ill., Garrard Pub. Co. [1963] 80 p. illus. 23 cm. (A Discovery book) [TS1570.W4L28] 63-7110
1. Whitney, Eli, 1765-1825—Juvenile literature.

LATHAM, Jean Lee. j 92
The story of Eli Whitney. Illustrated by Fritz Kredel. New York, Harper & Row [1962, c1953] 192 p. illus. 21 cm. [TS1570.W4L3 1962] 62-16413
1. Whitney, Eli, 1765-1825 — Juvenile literature. I. Title. **BIP**

Whitney, Gertrude Vanderbilt, 1877-1942.

FRIEDMAN, Bernard Harper, 1926- 704'.7 B
Gertrude Vanderbilt Whitney : a biography / by B. H. Friedman, with the research collaboration of Flora Miller Irving. 1st ed. Garden City, N.Y. : Doubleday, 1978. xi, 684 p., [32] leaves of plates : ill. ; 24 cm. Includes index. [N5220.W65F74] 77-26524 ISBN 0-385-12994-7 : 14.95
1. Whitney, Gertrude Vanderbilt, 1877-1942. 2. Art patrons United States—Biography. I. Title.

Whitney, Hugh,

WHITNEY, Hugh, 1903-1967. 917.3'03'90924 B
The letters of Hugh Whitney. Boston, Boston Athenaeum, 1970 xvi, 315 p. ports. 24 cm. [CT275.W555A3 1970] 73-19193

Whitney, Joel Parker, 1835-1913.

MILLER, Richard A., 1934- 650'.0924 B
Fortune built by gun; the Joel Parker Whitney story, by Richard A. (Bob) Miller. [1st ed.] Walnut Grove, Calif., Mansion Pub. Co. [1969] xxiii, 225 p. illus., maps, port. 24 cm. Includes bibliographies. [HD9506.U62W45] 70-10958
1. Whitney, Joel Parker, 1835-1913. I. Title.

Whitney, Steven.

*WHITNEY, Steven. 791.43'028'0922
Charles Bronson: superstar. [New York] Dell [1975] 284 p. illus. 18 cm. [PN2287] 1.50 (pbk.)
I. Title.

Whitney, William Collins, 1841-1904.

HIRSCH, Mark David, 1910- 973.8'0924 B
William C. Whitney: modern Warwick, by Mark D. Hirsch. [Unaltered and unabridged ed. Hamden, Conn.] Archon Books, 1969 [c1948] xiii, 622 p. illus., ports. 23 cm. Includes bibliographical references. [E664.W613H5 1969] 69-19214
1. Whitney, William Collins, 1841-1904. **BIP**

Whitney, Willis Rodney, 1868-1958.

WESTERVELT, Virginia Veeder. 925.4
The world was his laboratory; the story of Dr. Willis R. Whitney. New York, J. Messner [1964] 191 p. 22 cm. Bibliography: p. 181-183. [QD22.W47W4] 64-20163
1. Whitney, Willis Rodney, 1868-1958. I. Title.

Whitsett, William Paul, 1875-

ARMITAGE, Merle, 1893- 926.5
Success is no accident; the biography of William Paul Whitsett. [Yucca Valley. Calif.] Manzanita Press [1959] 326p. illus. 24cm. [HC102.5.W5A75] 59-14885
1. Whitsett, William Paul, 1875- I. Title.

Whittaker, James, 1751-1787.

EVANS, Frederick William, 1808-1893. 289.8
Shakers : compendium of the origin, history, principles, rules and regulations, government, and doctrines of the United Society of Believers in Christ's Second Appearing ... / by F. W. Evans. 4th ed. New York : AMS Press, 1975. 190 p. ; 19 cm. (Communal societies in America) Reprint of the 1867 ed. published in New Lebanon, N.Y. Bibliography: p. [188]-190. [BX9771.E85 1975] 72-2985 ISBN 0-404-10747-8
1. Shakers. 2. Shakers—Biography. 3. Lee, Ann, 1736-1784. 4. Lee, William, 1740-1784. 5. Whittaker, James, 1751-1787. 6. Hocknell, John, 1723?-1799. 7. Meacham, Joseph, 1742-1796. 8. Wright, Lucy, 1760-1821. I. Title: Compendium of the origin, history, principles, rules and regulations, government, and doctrines of the United Society of Believers in Christ's Second Appearing. **BIP**

SHAKERS. 289.8'092'2 B
Testimonies of the life, character, revelations, and doctrines of Mother Ann Lee, and the elders with her, through whom the word of eternal life was opened in this day, of Christ's second appearing, collected from living witnesses, in union with the church. 2d ed. New York : AMS Press, 1975. 302 p. ; 19 cm. (Communal societies in America) Reprint of the 1888 ed. printed by Weed, Parsons, Albany, N.Y. [BX9793.L4S5 1975] 72-2994 ISBN 0-404-10756-7 : 16.00
1. Lee, Ann, 1736-1784. 2. Lee, William, 1740-1784. 3. Whittaker, James, 1751-1787. 4. Shakers. I. Title: Testimonies of the life, character, revelations, and doctrines of Mother Ann Lee ... **BIP**

Whittier, Frank L., b. 1870.

WHITTIER, Charles L. 792.7
Dear Dad; our life in the theater around the turn of the century, by Charles Leroy Whittier. Freeport, Me., Bond Wheelwright Co. [1972] ix, 188 p. illus. 22 cm. [PN2287.W4585W5] 72-83013 ISBN 0-87027-124-5 5.95
1. Whittier, Frank L., b. 1870. I. Title. **BIP**

Whittier, John Greenleaf, 1807-1892.

FIELDS, Annie (Adams) 1834-1915. 811'.3 B
Whittier: notes of his life and of his friendships, by Mrs. James T. Fields. [Folcroft, Pa.] Folcroft Library Editions, 1973. p. Reprint of the 1893 ed. published by Harper, New York, in series: Harper's black and white series. [PS3281.F5 1973] 73-13954 12.50
1. Whittier, John Greenleaf, 1807-1892. I. Title. II. Series: Harper's black and white series.

HOLBERG, Ruth (Langland) 1891- 928.1
John Greenleaf Whittier: fighting Quaker.

Illustrated by Aldren A. Watson. New York, Crowell [1958] 151p. illus. 21cm. [PS3281.H6] 58-7307
1. Whittier, John Greenleaf, 1807-1892. I. Title.

HUDSON, William Henry, 1862-1918. 811'.3
Whittier & his poetry. London, G. G. Harrap, 1917. [New York, AMS Press, 1972] 142, [1] p. 19 cm. (Poetry & life series) Includes selections from the poems. Bibliography: p. [143] [PS3281.H8 1972] 77-120993 ISBN 0-404-52523-7 8.00
1. Whittier, John Greenleaf, 1807-1892. I. Title. II. Series. **BIP**

HUDSON, William Henry, 1862-1918. 811'.3 B
Whittier & his poetry / by William Henry Hudson. Norwood, Pa. : Norwood Editions, 1976. 142, [1] p. : port. ; 22 cm. Reprint of the 1921 issue of the ed. first published in 1917 by G. G. Harrap, London, which was issued as no. 29 of Poetry & life series. Bibliography: p. 143. [PS3281.H8 1976] 76-8890 ISBN 0-8482-1028-X : 7.00
1. Whittier, John Greenleaf, 1807-1892. I. Title. II. Series: Poetry & life series ; no. 29.

KENNEDY, William Sloane, 1850-1929. 811'.3 B
John Greenleaf Whittier; his life, genius, and writings, by W. Sloane Kennedy. Introd. by S. F. Smith. Rev. and enl. New York, Haskell House Publishers, 1973. 373 p. illus. 23 cm. [PS3281.K35 1973] 72-2002 ISBN 0-8383-1452-X 14.95
1. Whittier, John Greenleaf, 1807-1892.

KENNEDY, William Sloane, 1850-1929. 811'.3 B
John Greenleaf Whittier; his life, genius, and writings. Introd. by S. F. Smith. Rev. and enl. [Folcroft, Pa.] Folcroft Library Editions, 1973. 373 p. illus. 20 cm. Reprint of the 1903 ed. published by Saalfield Pub. Co., Akron, Ohio. [PS3281.K35 1973b] 73-13653 ISBN 0-8414-5464-7 (lib. bdg.)
1. Whittier, John Greenleaf, 1807-1892.

LEWIS, Georgina King (Stoughton) d.1924. 811'.3 B
John Greenleaf Whittier; his life and work. Port Washington, N.Y., Kennikat Press [1972] 221 p. illus. 23 cm. Reprint of the 1913 ed. Includes bibliographical references. [PS3281.L4 1972] 70-160767 ISBN 0-8046-1589-6
*1. Whittier, John Greenleaf, 1807-1892.***BIP**

LINTON, William James, 1812-1897. 811'.3 B
Life of John Greenleaf Whittier. Port Washington, N.Y., Kennikat Press [1972] 202, viii p. 21 cm. Reprint of the 1893 ed. "Bibliography by John P. Anderson": p. [i]-viii. [PS3281.L5 1972] 74-160768 ISBN 0-8046-1596-9
1. Whittier, John Greenleaf, 1807-1892. I. Title.

LINTON, William James, 1812-1897. 811'.3 B
Life of John Greenleaf Whittier. [Folcroft, Pa.] Folcroft Library Editions, 1973. p. Reprint of the 1893 ed. published by W. Scott, London, in series: Great writers. Bibliography: p. [PS3281.L5 1973] 73-13676 9.00
*1. Whittier, John Greenleaf, 1807-1892.***BIP**

MORDELL, Albert, 1885- 811'.3 B
Quaker militant, John Greenleaf Whittier. Port Washington, N.Y., Kennikat Press [1969, c1933] xxi, 354 p. illus. 22 cm. Bibliography: p. [333]-343. [PS3281.M6 1969] 68-8239
1. Whittier, John Greenleaf, 1807-1892. I. Title.

PICKARD, Samuel Thomas, 1828-1915. 811'.3 B
Life and letters of John Greenleaf Whittier. New York, Haskell House, 1969. 2 v. (vi, 802 p.) illus. 23 cm. Reprint of the 1907 ed. Bibliography: p. 787-790. [PS3281.P5 1969] 68-24941 ISBN 0-8383-0191-6 28.95
1. Whittier, John Greenleaf, 1807-1892. I. Title. **BIP**

POLLARD, John Albert, 1901-1968. 811'.3 B
John Greenleaf Whittier, friend of man. [Hamden, Conn.] Archon Books, 1969 [c1949] xviii, 615 p. map (on lining papers) 22 cm. Bibliography: p. 571-582. [PS3281.P6 1969] 69-11556
*1. Whittier, John Greenleaf, 1807-1892.***BIP**

ROWNTREE, Arthur, 1861-1949. 811'.3
Whittier, crusader and prophet. [Folcroft, Pa.] Folcroft Library Editions, 1973. viii, 108 p. port. 24 cm. Reprint of the 1946 ed. published by Headley Bros., London, in series: The Firbank series. Includes bibliographical references. [PS3281.R6 1973] 73-13660 15.00
1. Whittier, John Greenleaf, 1807-1892. I. Title. II. Series: The Firbank series.

WAGENKNECHT, Edward Charles, 1900- 811'.3
John Greenleaf Whittier; a portrait in paradox [by] Edward Wagenknecht. New York, Oxford University Press, 1967. vii, 262 p. port. 21 cm. Bibliography: p. 241-249. [PS3281.W3] 67-20407
*1. Whittier, John Greenleaf, 1807-1892.***BIP**

Whittier, John Greenleaf, 1807-1892—Addresses, essays, lectures.

PORTER, Maria S. 811'.3 B
Recollections of Louisa May Alcott, John Greenleaf Whittier, and Robert Browning, together with several memorial poems / by Maria S. Porter. Folcroft, Pa. : Folcroft Library Editions, 1976, c1892. p. cm. Reprint of the 1893 ed. published for the author by the New England Magazine Corp., Boston. [PS121.P64 1976] 76-13453 ISBN 0-8414-6701-3 lib. bdg. : 10.00
1. Alcott, Louisa May, 1832-1888—Addresses, essays, lectures. 2. Whittier, John Greenleaf, 1807-1892—Addresses, essays, lectures. 3. Browning, Robert, 1812-1889—Addresses, essays, lectures. I. Title: Recollections of Louisa May Alcott, John Greenleaf Whittier, and Robert Browning ... **BIP**

Whittier, John Greenleaf, 1807-1892—Biography.

BURTON, Richard, 1861-1940. 811'.3 B
John Greenleaf Whittier / by Richard Burton. Norwood, Pa. : Norwood Editions, 1975 [c1901] p. cm. Reprint of the ed. published by Small, Maynard, Boston, in series: The Beacon biographies of eminent Americans. Bibliography: p. [PS3281.B6 1975] 75-25941 ISBN 0-88305-066-8 : 12.50
1. Whittier, John Greenleaf, 1807-1892—Biography. I. Series: The Beacon biographies of eminent Americans (Boston)

WHITTEN, Wilfred, 1864-1942. 811'.3 B
John G. Whittier; a biographical sketch. London, E. Hicks, Jr., 1892. New York, Haskel House Pubishers, 1972. 151 p. 23 cm. [PS3281.W5 1972] 72-3171 ISBN 0-8383-1505-4
1. Whittier, John Greenleaf, 1807-1892—Biography.

Whittier, John Greenleaf, 1807-1892—Biography—Juvenile literature.

CODY, Sherwin, 1868-1959. 811'.3'09
Four American poets : William Cullen Bryant, Henry Wadsworth Longfellow, John Greenleaf Whittier, Oliver Wendell Holmes : a book for young Americans / by Sherwin Cody. Folcroft, Pa. : Folcroft Library Editions, 1977. p. cm. Reprint of the 1899 ed. published by American Book Co., New York, which was issued as v. 4 of The Four great Americans series. Essays discussing the life and work of four major American poets of the nineteenth century. [PS96.C57 1977] 920 77-24729 ISBN 0-8414-1811-X lib. bdg. : 25.00
1. Bryant, William Cullen, 1794-1878—Biography—Juvenile literature. 2. Longfellow, Henry Wadsworth, 1807-1882—Biography—Juvenile literature. 3. Whittier, John Greenleaf, 1807-1892—Biography—Juvenile literature. 4. Holmes, Oliver Wendell, 1809-1894—Biography—Juvenile literature. 5. Poets, American—19th century—Biography—Juvenile literature. I. Title. II. Series: The Four great Americans series ; v. 4.

VINING, Elizabeth Gray, 1902- 811'.3 B
Mr. Whittier. [1st ed.] New York, The Viking Press [1974] 169 p. illus. 24 cm. Bibliography: p. 163. A biography of the nineteenth-century Quaker poet stressing his deep involvement in abolition, women's suffrage, and other human rights, with emphasis on the articles and poems he wrote in defense of his beliefs. [PS3281.V5] 92 74-8162 ISBN 0-670-49431-3
1. Whittier, John Greenleaf, 1807-1892—Biography—Juvenile literature. I. Title. **BIP**

Whittier, John Greenleaf, 1807-1892—Correspondence.

WHITTIER, John Greenleaf, 1807-1892. 811'.3 B
The letters of John Greenleaf Whittier / edited by John B. Pickard. Cambridge, Mass. : Belknap Press of Harvard University Press, 1975. 3 v. : ill. ; 25 cm. Contents.Contents.—v. 1. 1828-1845.—v. 2. 1846-1860.—v. 3. 1861-1892. Includes bibliographical references and index. [PS3281.A3 1975] 73-88055 ISBN 0-674-52830-1 : 75.00(set)
1. Whittier, John Greenleaf, 1807-1892—Correspondence. I. Title. **BIP**

Whittier, John Greenleaf, 1807-1892—Homes and haunts—Essex Co., Mass.

PICKARD, Samuel Thomas, 1828-1915. 811'.3
Whittier-land; a handbook of North Essex, containing many anecdotes of and poems by John Greenleaf Whittier never before collected. [Folcroft, Pa.] Folcroft Library Editions, 1973 [c1904] p. Reprint of the ed. published by the trustees of the John Greenleaf Whittier Homestead, printed at the Riverside Press, Cambridge, Mass. [PS3284.P5 1973b] 73-12226 ISBN 0-8414-2483-7 (lib. bdg.)
1. Whittier, John Greenleaf, 1807-1892—Homes and haunts—Essex Co., Mass. I. Title. **BIP**

Whittinghill, Dick.

WHITTINGHILL, Dick. 791.44'5 B
Did you Whittinghill this morning? The madcap adventures of a Hollywood disc jockey / Dick Whittinghill, with Don Page ; foreword by Bob Hope. Chicago : H. Regnery, c1976. xv, 153 p., [8] leaves of plates : ill. ; 22 cm. Includes index. [ML429.W44A3] 76-6294 ISBN 0-8092-8064-7 : 7.95
1. Whittinghill, Dick. 2. Disc jockeys—Correspondence, reminiscences, etc. I. Page, Don, joint author. II. Title.

WHITTINGHILL, Dick. 789.9'1 B
Let's Whittinghill again (like we did last summer) / Dick Whittinghill, with Don Page. Chicago : Contemporary Books, c1977. p. cm. Autobiographical. Includes index. [ML429.W44A33] 77-75842 ISBN 0-8092-7742-5 : 7.95
1. Whittinghill, Dick. 2. Disc jockeys—United States—Biography. I. Page, Don, joint author. II. Title.

Whittle, Frank, Sir, 1907-

ROWLAND, John, 1907- 629.133'349'0924 B
The jet man; the story of Sir Frank Whittle. New York, Roy Publishers [1967] 139 p. 21 cm. [TL540.W48R6] 67-25638
1. Whittle, Frank, Sir, 1907- Juvenile literature. I. Title.

Whittredge, Worthington,

WHITTREDGE, Worthington, 1820-1910. 759.13
The autobiography of Worthington Whittredge, 1820-1910. Edited by John I. H. Baur. New York, Arno Press, 1969 [c1942] 68 p. illus., port. 27 cm. Originally published in 1942 in the Journal of the Brooklyn Museum. [ND237.W624A3] 74-85661 10.00 202 •

Whitworth, Joseph, Sir, 1803-1887.

JEANS, William T. 669'.142'0922 B
The creators of the age of steel, by W. T. Jeans. Freeport, New York, Books for Libraries Press [1973] p. (Essay index reprint series) "First published 1854." Contents.Contents.—Introduction.—Sir Henry Bessemer.—Sir William Siemens.—Sir Joseph Whitworth.—Sir John Brown.—Mr. S. G. Thomas.—Mr. G. J. Snelus. [TN139.J45 1973] 73-1583 ISBN 0-518-10054-5
1. Bessemer, Henry, Sir, 1813-1898. 2. Siemens, William, Sir, 1816-1896. 3. Whitworth, Joseph, Sir, 1803-1887. 4. Brown, John, Sir, 1816-1896. 5. Thomas, Sidney Gilchrist, 1850-1885. 6. Snelus, George James, 1837-1906. 7. Steel—History. 8. Inventors. I. Title.

Who (Musical quartet)

HERMAN, Gary. 784'.092'2 B
The Who. New York, Macmillan [1972, c1971] 159 p. illus. 22 cm. Discography: p. 152-159. [ML421.W5H5 1972] 70-186439 5.95
1. Who (Musical quartet) **BIP**

TREMLETT, George. 784'.092'2 B
The Who / George Tremlett. New York : Warner Books, 1975. 142 p. : ports. ; 18 cm. [ML421.W5T73 1975b] 75-325521 ISBN 0-446-76791-3 pbk. : 1.25
1. Who (Musical quartet)

TREMLETT, George. 784'.092'2 B
The Who / George Tremlett. New York : Warner Books, 1975. 142 p. : ports. ; 18 cm. [ML421.W5T73 1975b] 75-325521 ISBN 0-446-76791-3 pbk. : 1.25
1. Who (Musical quartet)

Whyte, Don, 1926-

WHYTE, Don, 1926- 070'.92'4 B
On the lonely shore : an autobiography / [by] Don Whyte ; foreword by Hugh MacDiarmid. London : Hutchinson, 1977. 192 p., [8] p. of plates : ill., ports. ; 23 cm. Includes index. [RC180.2.W45] 78-312289 ISBN 0-09-128800-2 : 8.95
1. Whyte, Don, 1926- 2. Poliomyelitis—Scotland—Biography. 3. Journalists—Scotland—Biography. I. Title.
Distributed by Hutchinson, Salem, NH

Whyte, John,

WHYTE, John, 1887-1952. 923.773
John Whyte; his life and thought, as shown in a selection of his unpublished writings. Edited by William R. Gaede and Daniel Coogan: with a foreword by Harry D. Gideonse, [1st ed.] Brooklyn, Brooklyn College Press, 1954. 183p. illus. 23cm. [CT275.W5572A3] 54-3537
I. Gaede, William Richard, ed. II. Title.

Wibaux Co., Mont.—History.

JONES, Irene James. 978.6'34'03 B
Trails along Beaver Creek : a chronicle of Wibaux County, Montana / by Irene James Jones. Wibaux, Mont. : Wibaux Pioneer Gazette, c1976. 229 p. : ill. ; 28 cm. [F737.W5J66] 76-381522
1. Wibaux Co., Mont.—History. 2. Wibaux Co., Mont.—Biography. 3. Wibaux Co., Mont.—Genealogy. I. Title.

Wibberley, Leonard Patrick O'Connor,

WIBBERLEY, Leonard Patrick O'Connor, 1915- 920
Zebulon Pike, soldier and explorer. New York, Funk & Wagnalls [c.1961] 179p. 61-6817 2.95
I. Pike, Zebulon Montgomery, 1779-1813—Juvenile literature. II. Title.

Wicclair, Walter.

FIFTY years in the theater; 792'.028'0924 a publication celebrating Walter Wicclair's 70th birthday. Editor: Marta Mierendorff. Los Angeles, 1971. 19 p. illus. 22 cm. Cover title. [PN2287.W4587F5] 74-185008
1. Wicclair, Walter. I. Wicclair, Walter. II. Mierendorff, Marta, ed.

Wickard, Claude Raymond, 1893-1967.

ALBERTSON, Dean, 1920- 923.273
Roosevelt's farmer: Claude R. Wickard in the New Deal. New York, Columbia University Press, 1961 [c1955] ix, 424p. illus., ports. 23cm. Issued also in microfilm form as thesis, Columbia University. Bibliographical footnotes. [S417.W48A7 1961] 58-8804
1. Wickard, Claude Raymond, 1893- I. Title. BIP

ALBERTSON, Dean, 1920- 973.917'092'4 B
Roosevelt's farmer : Claude R. Wickard in the New Deal / by Dean Albertson. New York : Da Capo Press, 1975, c1955. ix, 424 p., [4] leaves of plates : ill. ; 22 cm. (Franklin D. Roosevelt and the era of the New Deal) Reprint of the 1961 ed. published by Columbia University Press, New York, which was originally issued on microfilm as the author's thesis, Columbia University, 1955. Includes bibliographical references and index. [S417.W48A7 1975] 74-23430 ISBN 0-306-70702-0 : 26.50
1. Wickard, Claude Raymond, 1893-1967. 2. Agriculture—United States—History. I. Title. II. Series.

Wicker, Tom.

WICKER, Tom. 071'.3
On press / Tom Wicker. New York : Viking, 1978. ix, 271 p. ; 25 cm. Includes index. [PN4888.P6W5] 77-25929 ISBN 0-670-52456-5 : 10.00
1. Wicker, Tom. 2. Press and politics—United States. 3. Journalism—United States. 4. Journalists—United States—Biography. I. Title. BIP

Wickersham, James, 1857-1939.

ATWOOD, Evangeline. 328.73'092'4 B
Frontier politics : Alaska's James Wickersham / by Evangeline Atwood. 1st ed. Portland, Or. : Binford & Mort, 1979. x, 449 p. : ill. ; 24 cm. Includes bibliographical references and index. [E664.W628A88] 79-71140 ISBN 0-8323-0317-8 : 14.95
1. Wickersham, James, 1857-1939. 2. United States. Congress. House—Biography. 3. Alaska—Politics and government—1889-1950. 4. Legislators—United States—Biography. 5. Judges—Alaska—Biography. I. Title. BIP

Wicks, Robert Russell, 1882-

GILLESPIE, Janet. 974'.04'0924 B
With a merry heart / Janet Gillespie. 1st ed. New York : Harper & Row, c1976. 231 p. ; 22 cm. [BX9225.G49A34 1976] 76-5125 ISBN 0-06-011537-8 : 8.95
1. Gillespie, Janet. 2. Wicks, Robert Russell, 1882- 3. Wickes family. 4. Presbyterians—United States—Biography. I. Title. BIP

GILLESPIE, Janet. 974'.04'0924 B
With a merry heart / Janet Gillespie. Boston : G. K. Hall, 1977, c1976. 467 p. ; 24 cm. Large print ed. [BX9225.G49A34 1977] 77-5585 lib.bdg. : 12.95
1. Gillespie, Janet. 2. Wicks, Robert Russell, 1882- 3. Wickes family. 4. Presbyterians—United States—Biography. 5. Large type books. I. Title.

Wicks, Walter, 1891-

WICKS, Walter, 1891- 971.1'32
Memories of the Skeena / by Walter Wicks. Saanichton, B.C. ; Seattle : Hancock House, 1977, c1976 215 p., [16] leaves of plates : ill. ; 23 cm. [F1089.S5W52] 77-367406 ISBN 0-919654-62-2 : 9.95
1. Wicks, Walter, 1891- 2. Skeena River Valley—Biography. 3. Pioneers—British Columbia—Skeena River Valley—Biography. I. Title. BIP

Widforss, Gunnar.

BELKNAP, Bill, 1920- 759.13
Gunnar Widforss: painter of the Grand Canyon [by] Bill Belknap and Frances Spencer Belknap. Flagstaff, Published for the Museum of Northern Arizona by the Northland Press, 1969. xx, 86 p. col. plates, port. 28 cm. [ND1998.W5B4] 79 94654 14.50
1. Widforss, Gunnar. I. Belknap, Frances Spencer, 1913- joint author. II. Flagstaff, Ariz. Museum of Northern Arizona.

Widtsoe, Anna Karine (Gaarden) 1849-1919.

WIDTSOE, John Andreas, 1872-1952. 289.3'0924 B
In the gospel net; the story of Anna Karine Gaarden Widtsoe, by John A. Widtsoe. [3d ed.] Salt Lake City, Bookcraft [1966] 140 p. illus., maps, ports. 24 cm. [BX8695.W54W5 1966] 67-2680
1. Widtsoe, Anna Karine (Gaarden) 1849-1919. I. Title.

Wieand, Albert Cassel, 1871-1954.

SCHWALM, Vernon Franklin 922.673
Albert Cassel Wieand. Elgin, Ill., Brethren Press [c.1960] 155p. illus. 21cm. 60-16194 2.75
1. Wieand, Albert Cassel, 1871-1954. I. Title.

SCHWALM, Vernon Franklin, 1887- 922.673
Albert Cassel Wieand. Elgin, Ill., Brethren Press [1960] 155p. illus. 21cm. [BX7843.W55S3] 60-16194
1. Wieand, Albert Cassel, 1871-1954. I. Title.

Wieland, Christoph Martin, 1733-1813.

MCCARTHY, John Aloysius, 1942- 838'.6'09 B
Christoph Martin Wieland / by John A. McCarthy. Boston : Twayne Publishers, 1979. 192 p. : port. ; 21 cm. (Twayne's world authors series ; TWAS 528 : Germany) Includes index. Bibliography: p. 180-188. [PT2569.M3] 78-14338 ISBN 0-8057-6369-4 : 12.50
1. Wieland, Christoph Martin, 1733-1813. 2. Authors, German—18th century—Biography. BIP

Wieland family.

SKILLINGS, Helen Wieland. 917.74'9'0330922 B
We're standing on iron; the story of the five Wieland brothers, 1856-1883. Illustrated by Harold A. Wieland. Duluth, Minn., St. Louis County Historical Society, 1972. 69 p. illus. 25 cm. Bibliography: p. 69. [CS71.W64 1972] 72-86659 4.95
1. Wieland family. I. Title.

Wien, Noel.

HARKEY, Ira B. 629.13'092'4 B
Pioneer bush pilot: the story of Noel Wien [by] Ira Harkey. Seattle, University of Washington Press [1974] xviii, 307 p. illus. 24 cm. Includes bibliographical references. [TL540.W513H37] 74-13213 ISBN 0 295-95339-X 12.95
1. Wien, Noel. 2. Aeronautics—Alaska—History. 3. Alaska—History. I. Title. BIP

Wiener, Norbert,

WIENER, Norbert, 1894-1964. 925.1
Ex-prodigy: my childhood and youth. New York, Simon and Schuster, 1953. 309 p. illus. 22 cm. [QA29.W497A3] 53-7583
I. Title.

WIENER, Norbert, 1894-1964. 925.1
I am a mathematician, the later life of a prodigy; an autobiographical account of the mature years and career of Norbert Wiener and a continuation of the account of his childhood in Ex-prodigy. [1st ed.] Garden City, N.Y., Doubleday, 1956. 380 p. 22 cm. [QA29.W497A35] 56-5598
I. Title.

Wiens, Helena.

KROEKER, Nettie, 1900- 289.7'092'4 B
Far above rubies : the story of Helena Wiens / by Nettie Kroeker. Winnipeg : Christian Press, c1976. 368 p. : ill., facsims., maps, ports. ; 24 cm. Bibliography: p. 368. [BX8143.W45K76] 77-368212 10.00
1. Wiens, Helena. 2. Mennonites—Manitoba—Biography. I. Title.

Wier, Delight Bobilya.

WIER, Delight Bobilya. 977'.03'0924 B
Diary of the farmer's wife / by Delight Bobilya Wier. Des Moines, Iowa : Wallace-Homestead Book Co., c1976. 195 p. : ill. ; 22 cm. [CT275.W5576A32] 76-43200 ISBN 0-87069-187-2
1. Wier, Delight Bobilya. 2. Farmers' wives—United States—Biography. I. Title. BIP

Wier, Johann, 1515-1588.

COBBEN, J. J., 1926- 610'.92'4 B
Jan Wier, devils, witches, and magic / J. J. Cobben ; translated by Sal A. Prins. Philadelphia : Dorrance, c1976 viii, 218 p. : ill. ; 22 cm. Translation of Johannes Wier, zijn opvattingen over bezetenheid, hekserij en magic. Includes bibliographical references. [R147.W5C613] 76-372709 ISBN 0-8059-2277-6 : 8.95
1. Wier, Johann, 1515-1588. 2. Physicians—Netherlands—Biography. 3. Witchcraft. I. Title. BIP

Wier, Robert, 1886-1974.

WIER, Sadye H. 646.7'4'0924 B
A Black businessman in white Mississippi, 1886-1974 / by Sadye H. Wier with John F. Marszalek. Jackson : University Press of Mississippi, 1977. p. cm. Includes bibliographical references and index. [HD8039.B32U68] 77-13358 ISBN 0-87805-042-6 : 4.95
1. Wier, Robert, 1886-1974. 2. Barbers—Mississippi—Starkville—Biography. 3. Starkville, Miss.—Biography. 4. Afro-Americans in business—Biography. I. Marszalek, John F., joint author. II. Title. BIP

Wiesel, Elie, 1928- —Biography.

WIESEL, Elie, 1928- 813'.5'4 B
A Jew today / Elie Wiesel ; translated from the French by Marion Wiesel. 1st ed. New York : Random House, c1978. xii, 208 p. ; 22 cm. Translation of Un Juif aujourd'hui. [PQ2683.I32Z51713] 77-90261 ISBN 0-394-42054-3 : 10.00
1. Wiesel, Elie, 1928- —Biography. 2. Authors, French—20th century—Biography. 3. Judaism—Addresses, essays, lectures. I. Title.

WIESEL, Elie, 1928- 813'.5'4 B
A Jew today / Elie Wiesel ; translated from the French by Marion Wiesel. 1st Vintage books ed. New York : Vintage Books, 1979, c1978. x, 247 p. ; 18 cm. Translation of Un Juif aujourd'hui. [PQ2683.I32Z51713 1979] 79-11251 ISBN 0-394-74057-2 pbk. : 2.50
1. Wiesel, Elie, 1928- —Biography. 2. Authors, French—20th century—Biography. 3. Judaism—Addresses, essays, lectures. I. Title. BIP

Wiesenthal, Simon.

WIESENTHAL, Simon. 179'.7
The sunflower / Simon Wiesenthal ; with a symposium. New York : Schocken Books, 1976. 216 p. ; 21 cm. Translation of Die Sonnenblume. [D810.J4W5313 1976] 75-35446 ISBN 0-8052-3612-0 : 7.50
1. Wiesenthal, Simon. 2. Wiesenthal, Simon. Die Sonnenblume. 3. World War, 1939-1945—Personal narratives, Jewish. I. Title.

Wiggin, Kate Douglas Smith, 1856-1923.

MASON, Miriam Evangeline, 1899- 928.1
Yours with love, Kate. Illus. by Barbara Cooney. Boston, Houghton Mifflin, 1952. 277 p. illus. 22 cm. [PS3303.M3] 52-5907
1. Wiggin, Kate Douglas Smith, 1856-1923. I. Title. BIP

Wiggins, Florence Roe.

WIGGINS, Florence Roe. 301.41'2'0924 B
Where the heart is / Florence Roe Wiggins. 1st ed. Chappaqua, N.Y. : Christian Herald House, c1976. ix, 131 p. ; 21 cm. [HQ759.6.W53A38] 75-45857 ISBN 0-915684-03-9 : 5.95
1. Wiggins, Florence Roe. 2. Executives' wives—United States—Biography. 3. Mothers—United States—Biography. I. Title. BIP

Wiggins, Oliver Perry, 1823?-1913.

ENGLERT, Lorene. 978'.02'0924 B
Oliver Perry Wiggins; fantastic, bombastic frontiersman, by Lorene and Kenneth Englert. Palmer Lake, Colo., Filter Press, 1968. iv, 60 p. illus., port. 20 cm. (Wild & woolly West series, 6) "Limited to 500 copies." Bibliographical references included in "Footnotes" (p. 32-58) [F780.W55E5] 68-6669
1. Wiggins, Oliver Perry, 1823?-1913. I. Englert, Kenneth, joint author. II. Title.

Wigglesworth, Michael, 1631-1705.

CROWDER, Richard 922.573
No featherbed to heaven; a biography of Michael Wigglesworth, 1631-1705. [East Lansing] Mich. State Univ. Pr. [c.1962] 299p. 22cm. Bibl. 61-16933 7.00
1. Wigglesworth, Michael, 1631-1705. I. Title. BIP

Wigglesworth, Richard Bowditch, 1891-1960.

WEEKS, Sinclair, 1893- 923.273
Richard Bowditch Wigglesworth; way-stations of a fruitful life. [n.p., 1964] 78 p. ports. 21 cm. [E748.W66W4] 65-42173
1. Wigglesworth, Richard Bowditch, 1891-1960. I. Title.

Wight, Levi Lamoni,

WIGHT, Levi Lamoni, 1836-1918. 289.3'0924 B
The reminiscences and Civil War letters of Levi Lamoni Wight; life in a Mormon splinter colony on the Texas frontier. Davis Bitton, editor. Salt Lake City, University of Utah Press [1970] 191 p. facsim., geneal. table, map, ports. 24 cm.

(University of Utah publications in the American West, v. 4) Includes bibliographical references. [BX8678.W5A3 1970] 74-120412 ISBN 0-87480-060-9
I. Title. II. Series: Utah. University. Publications in the American West, v. 4

Wigmore, John Henry, 1863-1943.

ROALFE, William R. 340'.07'1173 B
John Henry Wigmore, : scholar and reformed / William R. Roalfe. Evanston : Northwestern University Press, 1977. xvi, 340 p., [1] leaf of plates : ill. ; 24 cm. Includes bibliographical references and index. [KF373.W458R6] 77-73200 ISBN 0-8101-0465-2 : 17.00
1. Wigmore, John Henry, 1863-1943. 2. Law teachers—Illinois—Biography. I. Title.

Wigton, Eng. (Cumberland)—Social life and customs.

SPEAK for England : 942.7'87
an oral history of England from 1900-1975, based on interviews with inhabitants of Wigton, Cumberland / Melvyn Bragg. New York : Knopf; New York : distributed by Random House, 1976. 498 p., [16] leaves of plates : ill. ; 25 cm. [DA690.W599S7 1976b] 76-48172 ISBN 0-394-40855-1 : 15.00
1. Wigton, Eng. (Cumberland)—Social life and customs. 2. Wigton, Eng. (Cumberland)—Biography. I. Bragg, Melvyn, 1939-

Wikoff, Henry, 1813-1884.

WIKOFF, Henry, 1813-1884. 327'.2'0924 B
The reminiscences of an idler. Freeport, N.Y., Books for Libraries Press [1973] p. (Essay index reprint series) Reprint of the 1880 ed. published by Fords, Howard & Hulbert, New York. [PS3308.W5R4 1973] 73-5850 ISBN 0-518-10139-8
1. Wikoff, Henry, 1813-1884. 2. Europe—Description and travel—1800-1918. I. Title.

Wilberforce, Samuel, Bp. of Winchester, 1805-1873.

COLSON, Percy, 1873-1952. 920.042
Victorian portraits. Freeport, N.Y., Books for Libraries Press [1968] 256 p. ports. 22 cm. (Essay index reprint series) Reprint of the 1932 ed. Contents.Contents.—The unhappy prince and Baron Stockmar.—The best of both worlds [Bishop Samuel Wilberforce]—Virtue is its own reward [Harriet Martineau]—A fallen idol [Felix Mendelssohn-Bartholdy] Bibliography: p. 255-256. [DA562.C7 1968] 68-16921
1. Albert, Consort of Queen Victoria, 1819-1861. 2. Wilberforce, Samuel, Bp. of Winchester, 1805-1873. 3. Martineau, Harriet, 1802-1876. 4. Mendelssohn-Bartholdy, Felix, 1809-1847. I. Title. **BIP**

MEACHAM, Standish. 283'.0924 B
Lord Bishop; the life of Samuel Wilberforce, 1805-1873. Cambridge, Mass., Harvard University Press, 1970. x, 328 p. port. 25 cm. Bibliography: p. [ix]-x. [BX5199.W6M4] 70-102669 13.50
1. Wilberforce, Samuel, Bp. of Winchester, 1805-1873. I. Title. **BIP**

Wilberforce University, Wilberforce, Ohio.

SMITH, David, 1784- 287'.83'0924 B
Biography of Rev. David Smith of the A.M.E. Church. Freeport, N.Y., Books for Libraries Press, 1971. vii, 135 p. illus. 23 cm. (The Black heritage library collection) Reprint of the 1881 ed. Includes The history of the origin and development of Wilberforce University, by Bishop D. A. Payne (p. [99]-132). [BX8449.S6A3 1971] 77-168520 ISBN 0-8369-8872-8
1. Wilberforce University, Wilberforce, Ohio. I. Payne, Daniel Alexander, Bp., 1811-1893. II. Title. III. Series.

Wilberforce, William, 1759-1833.

CLARKSON, Thomas, 1760-1846. 326'.0924
Strictures on a Life of William Wilberforce, by the Rev. W. [i.e. Robert Isaac] Wilberforce, and the Rev. S. Wilberforce. With a correspondence between Lord Brougham and Mr. Clarkson; also a supplement, containing Remarks on the Edinburgh review of Mr. Wilberforce's Life, etc. Freeport, N.Y., Books for Libraries Press, 1971. xv, 136 p. 23 cm. (The Black heritage library collection) Reprint of the 1838 ed. [HT1029.W5C48 1971] 77-164398 ISBN 0-8369-8857-4
1. Wilberforce, William, 1759-1833. 2. Wilberforce, Robert Isaac, 1802-1857. The life of William Wilberforce. I. Title. II. Series.

COUPLAND, Reginald, Sir, 1884-1952. 326'.0924 B
Wilberforce, a narrative. New York, Negro Universities Press [1968] vi, 528 p. port. 24 cm. Reprint of the 1923 ed. Bibliographical footnotes. [HT1029.W5C65 1968] 68-55879
1. Wilberforce, William, 1759-1833. **BIP**

HUGHES, Benjamin F. 326'.0924 B
Eulogium on the life and character of William Wilberforce, Esq., by Benjamin F. Hughes. Delivered and published at the request of the people of color of the City of New York, 22d of October, 1833. [Philadelphia, Rhistoric Publications, 1969] 16 p. 21 cm. (Afro-American history series) (Rhistoric publications, no. 221.) Cover title. Reprint of the 1833 ed., with "Benjamin F. Hughes on William Wilberforce; a bibliographical note, by Maxwell Whiteman" added. [HT1029.W5H9 1969] 73-77058
1. Wilberforce, William, 1759-1833. I. Title.

LAWSON, Audrey 301.4522
The man who freed the slaves; the story of William Wilberforce, by Audrey & Herbert Lawson. London, Faber & Faber [dist. Levittown, N.Y., Transatlantic, 1966. c.1962] 141p. illus., ports., map. 19cm. (Men & events) Bibl. [HT1029.W5L3] 64-39321 2.50 bds.,
1. Wilberforce, William, 1759-1833. I. Lawson, Herbert, joint author. II. Title.

LUDWIG, Charles, 1918- 326'.092'4 B
He freed Britain's slaves / Charles Ludwig. Scottdale, Pa. : Herald Press, 1977. 206 p. : port. ; 21 cm. Bibliography: p. 205-206. [HT1029.W5L8] 77-9521 ISBN 0-8361-1822-7 : 5.95
1. Wilberforce, William, 1759-1833. 2. Abolitionists—Biography. I. Title. **BIP**

WARNER, Oliver Martin Wilson, 1903- 923.642
William Wilberforce and his times. New York, Arco [1963, c.1962] 174p illus. 23cm. 63-17092 3.95
1. Wilberforce, William, 1759-1833. I. Title.

WILBERFORCE, Robert Isaac, 1802-1857. 326'.092'4 B
The life of William Wilberforce, by his sons, Robert Isaac Wilberforce and Samuel Wilberforce. Freeport, N.Y., Books for Libraries Press, 1972. 5 v. illus. 22 cm. (The Black heritage library collection) Reprint of the 1838 ed. [HT1029.W5W5 1972] 72-5506 ISBN 0-8369-9151-6
1. Wilberforce, William, 1759-1833. I. Wilberforce, Samuel, Bp. of Winchester, 1805-1873, joint author. II. Title. III. Series.

WILBERFORCE, William, 1759-1833. 326'.092'4 B
The correspondence of William Wilberforce. Edited by his sons, Robert Isaac Wilberforce and Samuel Wilberforce. London, 1840. Miami, Fla., Mnemosyne Pub. Co. [1969] 2 v. 23 cm. Reprint of the ed. published by J. Murray, London. [DA522.W6A3 1969] 71-83894
1. Wilberforce, William, 1759-1833. I. Wilberforce, Robert Isaac, 1802-1857, ed. II. Wilberforce, Samuel, Bp. of Winchester, 1805-1873, ed. III. Title. **BIP**

WILBERFORCE, William, 1759-1833. 361'.02
Private papers of William Wilberforce. Collected and edited, with a pref., by A. M. Wilberforce. New York, B. Franklin [1968] vii, 285 p. illus., ports. 24 cm. (Burt Franklin: Research source works series, no. 174) Reprint of the 1897 ed. [DA522.W6A4 1968] 68-4278
1. Wilberforce, Anna Maria, Mrs., ed. II. Title. **BIP**

Wilbourn, Carole, 1940-

WILBOURN, Carole, 1940- 636.8'08'96
Cats prefer it this way / Carole Wilbourn ; introd. by Paul Rowan. New York : Coward, McCann & Geoghegan, c1976. 224 p. : ill. ; 22 cm. [SF447.W65 1976] 76-49 ISBN 0-698-10744-6 : 8.95
1. Wilbourn, Carole, 1940- 2. Rowan, Paul. 3. Cats. 4. Cats—Diseases. 5. Cats—Behavior. 6. Veterinarians—New York (City)—Biography. I. Title. **BIP**

Wilbur, Ray Lyman,

WILBUR, Ray Lyman, 1875-1949. 923.773
Memoirs. Edgar Eugene Robinson and Paul Carroll Edwards, editors. Stanford, Calif., Stanford University Press, 1960. 687 p. illus. 24 cm. Includes bibliography. [E748.W68A3] 60-9051
I. Title.

Wilbur, Richard, 1921-

HILL, Donald Louis, 1914- 811'.5'2
Richard Wilbur, by Donald L. Hill. New York, Twayne Publishers [1967] 192 p. 21 cm. (Twayne's United States authors series, TUSAS 117) Bibliography: p. 183-186. [PS3545.I32165Z69] 67-13182
1. Wilbur, Richard, 1921- **BIP**

Wilcox, Brad.

WILCOX, Brad. 248'.48'933
The super baruba success book for under-achievers, over-expecters, and other ordinary people / Brad Wilcox. Salt Lake City : Bookcraft, c1979. xi, 116 p. ; 24 cm. [BX8695.W544A37] 79-53050 ISBN 0-88494-372-0 pbk. : 4.50
1. Wilcox, Brad. 2. Mormons and Mormonism—United States—Biography. I. Title.

Wilcox, Herbert Sydney,

WILCOX, Herbert Sydney, 1892- 791.43'023'0924 B
Twenty-five thousand sunsets; the autobiography of Herbert Wilcox. [1st American ed.] South Brunswick [N.J.] A. S. Barnes [1969, c1967] xiii, 233 p. 62 illus. (incl. facsims., ports.) 22 cm. [PN1998.A3W48 1969] 69-14890 5.95
I. Title.

Wilcox, Lorena

*WILCOX, Lorena 920
My Oklahoma childhood by Lorena Wilcox with the assistance of Benton H. Wilcox Madison, Wisc., Benton H. Wilcox [1974] v, 195 p. 29 cm. Autobiography Order from publisher 332 South Hamilton St., Madison, Wisc., 53703 [CT104] 25.00
I. Wilcox, Benton H, joint author II. Title.

Wilcox, Morris R., 1893-

WILCOX, Morris R., 1893- 974.3'04'0924 B
Keep your mind off the puddin' : an autobiography / Morris R. Wilcox. [Burlington? Vt.] : Wilcox, c1975. 216 p., [5] leaves of plates : ill. ; 22 cm. [CT275.W5584A34] 75-21588
1. Wilcox, Morris R., 1893- I. Title.

Wild flowers—Texas—Pictorial works.

JOHNSTON, Eliza Griffin, 1821-1896. 582'.13'09764
Texas wild flowers. With a biography of Mrs. Johnston by Mildred Pickle Mayhall. Austin, Shoal Creek Publishers, 1972. xl, 205 p. illus. (part col.) 32 cm. Bibliography: p. xxxix-xl. [QK188.J58] 72-77252 25.00
1. Wild flowers—Texas—Pictorial works. I. Title.
Deluxe ed. 100.00 **BIP**

Wild, Jonathan, 1682?-1725.

HOWSON, Gerald. 364.1'0924 B
Thief-Taker General: the rise and fall of Jonathan Wild. New York, St. Martin's Press [1971, c1970] xii, 338 p. illus., facsims., ports. 24 cm. Bibliography: p. [317]-327. [HV6248.W48H65 1971] 76-136972 8.95
1. Wild, Jonathan, 1682?-1725. 2. Gangs—London—History. I. Title.

SMITH, Alexander, fl.1714-1726. 364.1'092'4 B
Memoirs of the life and times of the famous Jonathan Wild. With a new introd. for the Garland ed. by Malcolm J. Bosse. New York, Garland, 1973. 8, xii, 287 p. illus. 22 cm. (Foundations of the novel) Facsim. reprint. Original t.p. has imprint: London, Printed for S. Briscoe at the Bell-Savage, and sold by J. Jackson, 1726. [HV6248.W48S54 1726a] 76-170567 ISBN 0-8240-0560-0 22.00 ea.
1. Wild, Jonathan, 1682?-1725. I. Title. II. Series.
Part of a 71 volume series selling for 1400.00 a set.

Wild, Reginald L

WILD, Reginald L 1912- 920
Wild oats. Edinburgh, Blackwood, 1959. 242 p. 23 cm. Autobiographical. [CT788.W68A3] 59-35455
I. Title.

Wilde, Jane Francesca (Elgee) lady, 1826-1896.

WYNDHAM, Horace, 1875- 928.2
Speranza; a biography of Lady Wilde. London, New York T. V. Boardman [1951] 247 p. illus., ports. 23 cm. [PR5809.Z5W9] 52-326
1. Wilde, Jane Francesca (Elgee) lady, 1826-1896. I. Title.

Wilde, Oscar Fingall O'Flahertie Wills,

WILDE, Oscar Fingall 928.2
O'Flahertie Wills, 1854-1900
Letters. Ed. by Rupert Hart-Davis. New York, Harcourt [c.1962] xxv, 958p. illus. 24cm. Bibl. 60-10942 15.00
I. Hart-Davis, Rupert, ed. II. Title.

Wilde, Oscar, 1854-1900.

BRASOL, Boris Leo, 828'.8'09
1885-
Oscar Wilde : the man, the artist, the martyr / Boris Brasol. New York : Octagon Books, 1975, c1938. p. cm. Reprint of the ed. published by Scribner, New York. Includes index. "Works by Oscar Wilde": p. [PR5823.B68 1975] 75-23335 ISBN 0-374-90940-7 lib.bdg. : 15.00
1. Wilde, Oscar, 1854-1900. BIP

BRAYBROOKE, Patrick, 828'.8'09
1894-
Oscar Wilde; a study. [Folcroft, Pa.] Folcroft Press, 1970. 150 p. illus. 23 cm. Reprint of the 1930 ed., which was issued as no. 2 of The "Studies" library. "Limited to 150 copies." Bibliography: p. 147. [PR5823.B7 1970] 72-194984
1. Wilde, Oscar, 1854-1900. I. Series: The "Studies" library, 2.

BREMONT, Anna 828'.8'09 B
(Dunphy) comtesse de.
Oscar Wilde and his mother; a memoir, by Anna, comtesse de Bremont. London, Everett, 1911. New York, Haskell House Publishers [1972] 199 p. port. 23 cm. Reprint of the 1911 ed. [PR5823.D73 1972] 72-2155 ISBN 0-8383-1457-0 9.95
1. Wilde, Oscar, 1854-1900. 2. Wilde, Jane Francesca (Elgee) Lady, 1826-1896. I. Title.

CROFT-COOKE, Rupert, 828'.8'09 B
1903-
The unrecorded life of Oscar Wilde. [1st American ed.] New York, D. McKay Co. [1972] x, 289 p. illus. 22 cm. [PR5823.C7 1972] 72-85843 6.95
1. Wilde, Oscar, 1854-1900. I. Title.

DOUGLAS, Lord Alfred Bruce, 928.2
1870-1945
Oscar Wilde; a summing-up. London, Duckworth [Mystic, Conn., Verry, 1965] xiv, 140p. Facsim. port. 23cm. First pub. in 1940 [PR5823.D58] 40 31761 5.00 bds.,
1. Wilde, Oscar Fingal O'Flahertie Wills, 1854-1900 I. Title. BIP

ERVINE, St. John Greer, 928.2
1883-
Oscar Wilde; a present time appraisal. New York, Morrow, 1952 [c1951] 336 p. 23 cm. [PR5823.E7 1952] 52-9699
1 Wilde, Oscar, 1854-1900. I. Title.

GIDE, Andre Paul 828'.8
Guillaume, 1869-1951.
Oscar Wilde : a study / by Andre Gide ; translated from the French by Lucy Gordon. New York : Gordon Press, 1975 p. cm. Contents.Contents.—In memoriam.—The "De profundis" of Oscar Wilde. [PR5823.G514 1975] 75-13357 lib.bdg. : 34.95
1. Wilde, Oscar, 1854-1900. BIP

GULL, Cyril Arthur 828'.8'09 B
Edward Ranger, 1876-1923.
Oscar Wilde; some reminiscences, by Leonard Cresswell Ingleby. London, T. W. Laurie. [Folcroft, Pa.] Folcroft Library Editions, 1973. p. Reprint of the 1907 ed. [PR5823.G8 1973] 72-13766 ISBN 0-8414-1309-6 (lib. bdg.)
1. Wilde, Oscar, 1854-1900.

HARRIS, Frank, 1855-1931. 928.2
Oscar Wilde, including My memories of Oscar Wilde, by George Bernard Shaw. And an introductory note by Lyle Blair. [East Lansing] MichiganState University Press, 1959. ix, 358p. 24cm. [PR5823.H3 1959] 59-6709
1. Wilde, Oscar, 1854- 1900. I. Shaw, George Bernard, 1856-1950. II. Title.

HOLLAND, Vyvyan Beresford, 928.2
1886-
Oscar Wilde, a pictorial biography. New York, Viking Press [1960] 144 p. illus. 24 cm. (A Studio book) [PR5823.H58] 61-2371
1. Wilde, Oscar, 1854-1900.

HOLLAND, Vyvyan 828'.9'1209 B
Beresford, 1886-1967.
Son of Oscar Wilde. Westport, Conn., Greenwood Press [1973, c1954] xv, 237 p. illus. 22 cm. Reprint of the ed. published by Dutton, New York. [PR6015.O4115S6 1973] 73-5267 ISBN 0-8371-6884-8
1. Holland, Vyvyan Beresford, 1886-1967. 2. Wilde, Oscar, 1854-1900. 3. Wild family. I. Title.

HOLLAND, Vyvyan Beresford, 928.2
1886-
Son of Oscar Wilde. [1st American ed.] New York, Dutton, 1954. 237 p. illus. 21 cm. [PR5823.H6 1954] 54-10920
1. Wilde, Oscar, 1854-1900. I. Title. BIP

HYDE, Harford Montgomery, 928.2
1907-.
Oscar Wilde: the aftermath. New York, Farrar, Straus [1963] xxi, 221 p. facsim. 22 cm. Bibliographical footnotes. [PR5823.H9] 63-20020
1. Wilde, Oscar, 1854-1900. I. Title. BIP

HYDE, Harford Montgomery, 928.2
1907-
Oscar Wilde: the aftermath. New York, Farrar [c.1963] xxi, 221p. facsim. 22cm. Bibl. 63-20020 4.50 bds.,
1. Wilde, Oscar, 1854-1900. I. Title.

JULLIAN, Philippe. 821'.8 B
Oscar Wilde. Translated by Violet Wyndham. New York, Viking Press [1969] 420 p. illus., facsims. (on lining papers), ports. 23 cm. Bibliography: p. 411-414. [PR5823.J813 1969b] 69-15653 7.95
1. Wilde, Oscar, 1854-1900.

KENILWORTH, Walter 828'.8'09
Winston.
A study of Oscar Wilde. New York, R. F. Fenno. New York, Haskell House Publishers, 1972. 139 p. 23 cm. [PR5823.K6 1972] 72-3091 ISBN 0-8383-1524-0
1. Wilde, Oscar, 1854-1900. I. Title.

THE life of Oscar Wilde. v. 12
[Harmondsworth, Middlesex] Penguin Books [1960] 399p. illus., ports. 19cm. American edition (New York and London, Harper) has title: Oscar Wilde, his life and wit. Bibliography: p. [384]-387.
1. Wilde, Oscar, 1854-1900. I. Pearson, Hesketh, 1887- BIP

OSCAR Wilde, including an v. 12
introductory note by Lyle Blair; My memories of Oscar Wilde, by George Bernard Shaw; and Oscar's last days (a letter from Robert Ross) [New York, Dell Pub. Co., 1960] 381p 17cm. (Laurel edition LX130)
1. Wilde, Oscar, 1854-1900. I. Harris, Frank, 1855-1931. II. Shaw, George Bernard, 1856-1950.

O'SULLIVAN, Vincent, 828'.8'09
1872-1940.
Aspects of Wilde / by Vincent O'Sullivan. Folcroft, Pa. : Folcroft Library Editions, 1976 [c1936] p. cm. Reprint of the ed. published by H. Holt and Co., New York. [PR5823.O7 1976] 76-41406 ISBN 0-8414-6537-1 lib. bdg. : 25.00
1. Wilde, Oscar, 1854-1900. 2. Authors, English—19th century—Biography. I. Title. BIP

RICKETTS, Charles S., 828'.8'09 B
1866-1931.
Oscar Wilde; recollections, by Jean Paul Raymond & Charles Ricketts. [Folcroft, Pa.] Folcroft Press [1969] 59 p. 26 cm. Reprint of the 1932 ed. Jean Paul Raymond is an imaginary author introduced by Ricketts into his own recollections of Oscar Wilde. [PR5823.R5 1969] 72-194424
1. Wilde, Oscar, 1854-1900.

SHERARD, Robert 828'.8'09 B
Harborough, 1861-1943.
Oscar Wilde: the story of an unhappy friendship. [Folcroft, Pa.] Folcroft Library Editions, 1973. p. Reprint of the 1908 ed. published by Greening, London. [PR5823.S525 1973] 73-13674 10.75
1. Wilde, Oscar, 1854-1900.

SYMONS, Arthur, 1865- 828'.8'09
1945.
A study of Oscar Wilde. [Folcroft, Pa.] Folcroft Library Editions, 1974. 87 p. port. 23 cm. Reprint of the 1930 ed. published by C. J. Sawyer, London. [PR5823.S8 1974] 74-13194 ISBN 0-8414-7796-5 (lib. bdg.)
1. Wilde, Oscar, 1854-1900. I. Title. BIP

WILDE, Oscar, 1854-1900, 928.2
defendant.
The three trials of Oscar Wilde, Edited, with an introd. by H. Montgomery Hyde. With a foreword by Sir Travers Humphreys. New York, University Books [1956] 384 p. ports., facsims. 22 cm. Account of the trial in a libel action brought against Lord Queensberry and the trials of Oscar Wilde and Alfred Taylor, which were held in the Central Criminal Court of London. First published in 1948 under title: The trials of Oscar Wilde. 56-13694
I. Queensberry, John Sholto Douglas, 8th marquis 1844-1900, defendant. II. Taylor, Alfred 1862 or 3- defendant. III. Hyde, Harford Montgomery, 1907- ed. IV. London. Central Criminal Court. V. Title.

WILDE, Oscar Fingall 928.2
O'Flahertie Wills, 1854-1900
Letters. Ed. by Rupert Hart-Davis. New York, Harcourt [c.1962] xxv, 958p. illus. 24cm. Bibl. 60-10942 15.00
I. Hart-Davis, Rupert, ed. II. Title.

WINWAR, Frances, pseud. 928.2
Oscar Wilde and the yellow nineties. New York, Harper [1958] 375 p. illus. 22 cm. [PR5823.W5 1958] 57-11789
1. Wilde, Oscar, 1854-1900. I. Title.

WOODCOCK, George, 828'.8'09 B
1912-
The paradox of Oscar Wilde. [Folcroft, Pa.] Folcroft Library Editions, 1973. p. Reprint of the 1949 ed. published by T. V. Boardman, London, New York. [PR5823.W6 1973] 73-7643 ISBN 0-8414-9358-8
1. Wilde, Oscar, 1854-1900. I. Title. BIP

WOODCOCK, George, 1912- 928.2
The paradox of Oscar Wilde. New York, Macmillan, 1950 [c1949] 250 p. 22 cm. [PR5823.W6 1950] 50-5446
1. Wilde, Oscar, 1854-1900.

Wilde, Oscar, 1854-1900—Addresses, essays, lectures.

ELLMANN, Richard, 1918- 828'.8'09
Oscar Wilde : two approaches : papers read at a Clark Library seminar, April 17, 1976 / by Richard Ellmann, John Espey. Los Angeles : William Andrews Clark Memorial Library, 1977. vii, 56 p. ; 23 cm. [PR5823.E4] 77-378720
1. Wilde, Oscar, 1854-1900—Addresses, essays, lectures. 2. Authors, Irish—19th century—Biography—Addresses, essays, lectures. I. Espey, John Jenkins, 1913- joint author.

Wilde, Oscar, 1854-1900—Biography.

DOUGLAS, Alfred 828'.8'09 B
Bruce, Lord, 1870-1945.
Oscar Wilde : a summing-up / Lord Alfred Douglas ; with an introduction by Derek Hudson. Folcroft, Pa. : Folcroft Library Editions, 1977. xiv, 140 p., [1] leaf of plates : port. ; 23 cm. Reprint of the 1950 ed. published by Richards Press, London. [PR5823.D58 1977] 77-1324 ISBN 0-8414-3815-3 lib. bdg. : 25.00
1. Wilde, Oscar, 1854-1900—Biography. 2. Authors, English—19th century—Biography.

FIDO, Martin. 828'.8'09 B
Oscar Wilde. New York, Viking Press [1973] 144 p. illus. 31 cm. (A Studio book) Bibliography: p. 142. [PR5823.F47] 73-993 ISBN 0-670-52907-9 12.00
1. Wilde, Oscar, 1854-1900—Biography. 2. Great Britain—Intellectual life—19th century.

FIDO, Martin. 828'.8'09 B
Oscar Wilde. London, New York, Hamlyn, 1973. 144 p. illus. (some col.), facsims., ports. (some col.) 31 cm. Illus. on lining papers. Includes index. Bibliography: p. 142. [PR5823.F47 1973b] 74-165106 ISBN 0-600-36714-2 £1.95
1. Wilde, Oscar, 1854-1900—Biography.

HARRIS, Frank, 1855- 828'.8'09 B
1931.
Oscar Wilde, his life and confessions / Frank Harris. Memories of Wilde / by Bernard Shaw ; introd. by Frank MacShane. New York : Horizon Press, [1974] xxii, 612, 32 p., [4] leaves of plates : ill. ; 22 cm. Caption title of Shaw's work: My memories of Oscar Wilde. [PR5823.H3 1974] 74-19884 ISBN 0-8180-0225-5 : 10.00
1. Wilde, Oscar, 1854-1900—Biography. I. Shaw, George Bernard, 1856-1950. My memories of Oscar Wilde. 1974. II. Title.

HYDE, Harford 828'.8'09 B
Montgomery, 1907-
Oscar Wilde : a biography / by H. Montgomery Hyde. New York : Farrar, Straus, and Giroux, 1975. p. cm. Includes index. Bibliography: p. [PR5823.H88] 75-22439 ISBN 0-374-22474-9 : 15.00
1. Wilde, Oscar, 1854-1900—Biography. I. Title. BIP

KRONENBERGER, Louis, 828'.8'09 B
1904-
Oscar Wilde / Louis Kronenberger. 1st ed. Boston : Little, Brown, c1976. x, 236 p. ; 21 cm. (Library of World biography) Includes index. Bibliography: p. [227]-228. [PR5823.K7] 76-4939 ISBN 0-316-50458-0 : 8.95
1. Wilde, Oscar, 1854-1900—Biography.

MORLEY, Sheridan, 828'.8'09 B
1941-
Oscar Wilde / Sheridan Morley. New York : Holt, Rinehart and Winston, c1976. 160 p., [24] leaves of plates : ill. ; 26 cm. Includes index. Bibliography: p. [151]-152. [PR5823.M6] 76-4727 ISBN 0-03-017586-0 : 14.95
1. Wilde, Oscar, 1854-1900—Biography.

PEARSON, Hesketh, 1887- 828'.8'09
1964.
The life of Oscar Wilde : a biography / by Hesketh Pearson ; introd. by Peter Quennell. Westport, Conn. : Greenwood Press, 1978. xvi, 399 p., [4] leaves of plates : ill. ; 22 cm. Reprint of the Rev. ed. published in 1975 by Macdonald and Jane's, London. Includes index. Bibliography: p. 388-391. [PR5823.P4 1978] 78-6898 ISBN 0-313-20491-8 lib.bdg. . 25.00
1. Wilde, Oscar, 1854-1900—Biography. 2. Authors, Irish—19th century—Biography. I. Title.

SHERARD, Robert 828'.8'09 B
Harborough, 1861-1943.
The real Oscar Wilde : to be used as a supplement to, and in illustration of The life of Oscar Wilde : with numerous unpublished letters, facsimiles, portraits and illustrations / by Robert Harborough Sherard. Norwood, Pa. : Norwood Editions, 1975. xvi, 431 p., [4] leaves of plates ; 23 cm. Reprint of the 1916 ed. published by T. W. Laurie, London. Includes index. [PR5823.S52 1975] 75-33087 ISBN 0-88305-632-1 lib. bdg. : 40.00
1. Wilde, Oscar, 1854-1900—Biography. I. Title.

Wilde, Oscar, 1854-1900—Juvenile literature.

CEVASCO, George A. 828'.8'09 B
Oscar Wilde; British author, poet, and wit, by G. A. Cevasco. Compiled with the assistance of the research staff of SamHar Press. Charlotteville, N.Y., SamHar Press, 1972. 31 p. 22 cm. (Outstanding personalities, no. 45) A biography of the British author whose flamboyant career was brought to an end by a damaging lawsuit. [PR5823.C4] 92 72-89209
1. Wilde, Oscar, 1854-1900—Juvenile literature. I. Title. BIP

Wilde, Oscar, 1854-1900—Relationship with men—Alfred Douglas.

DOUGLAS, Alfred Bruce, Lord, 1870-1945. 828'.8'09 B
Oscar Wilde and myself / by Lord Alfred Douglas. New York : AMS Press, 1977. xiii, 306 p., [13] leaves of plates : ill. ; 23 cm. Reprint of the 1914 ed. published by Duffield, New York. Includes index. [PR5823.D6 1977] 75-30021 ISBN 0-404-14026-2 : 19.50
1. Wilde, Oscar, 1854-1900—Relationship with men—Alfred Douglas. 2. Douglas, Alfred Bruce, Lord, 1870-1945—Biography. 3. Authors, Irish—19th century—Biography. 4. Poets, English—20th century—Biography. I. Title. BIP

QUEENSBERRY, Francis Archibald Kelhead Douglas, 10th Marquis, 1896- 828'.8'09 B
Oscar Wilde and the Black Douglas / by the Marquess of Queensberry, in collaboration with Percy Colson. Folcroft, Pa. : Folcroft Library Editions, 1977. p. cm. Reprint of the 1949 ed. published by Hutchinson, London. Includes index. Bibliography: p. [PR5823.Q4 1977] 77-10990 ISBN 0-8414-6227-5 lib. bdg. : 25.00
1. Wilde, Oscar, 1854-1900—Relationship with men—Alfred Douglas. 2. Douglas, Alfred Bruce, Lord, 1870-1945—Biography. 3. Authors, Irish—19th century—Biography. 4. Poets, English—20th century—Biography. I. Title. BIP

Wilder, Alec.

WILDER, Alec. 780'.92'4 B
Letters I never mailed / Alec Wilder. 1st ed. Boston : Little, Brown, 1975. 243 p. ; 22 cm. [ML410.W6975A3] 74-34033 7.95
1. Wilder, Alec. 2. Composers—Correspondence, reminiscences, etc. I. Title.

Wilder, Almanzo.

WILDER, Laura Ingalls, 1867-1957. 813'.5'2
West from home : letters of Laura Ingalls Wilder to Almanzo Wilder, San Francisco, 1915 / edited by Roger Lea MacBride ; historical setting by Margot Patterson Doss. 1st ed. New York : Harper & Row, [1974] xviii, 124 p., [12] leaves of plates : ill. ; 21 cm. A selection of letters by Laura Ingalls Wilder to her husband in which she describes the highlights of her visit to the west coast in 1915. [PS3545.I342Z55 1974] 73-14342 ISBN 0-06-024110-1 : 4.95. ISBN 0-06-024111-X lib.bdg. : 4.79
1. Wilder, Laura Ingalls, 1867-1957—Correspondence. 2. Wilder, Almanzo. 3. San Francisco. Panama Pacific International Exposition, 1915. 4. The West—Description and travel—1880-1950. I. Wilder, Almanzo. II. Title.

Wilder, Billy, 1906-

MADSEN, Axel. 791.43'0233'0924
Billy Wilder. Bloomington, Indiana University Press [1969] 167 p. illus., ports. 20 cm. (Cinema one, 8) [PN1998.A3W53 1969] 68-66392 5.95
1. Wilder, Billy, 1906-

ZOLOTOW, Maurice, 1913- 791.43'0233'0924 B
Billy Wilder in Hollywood / Maurice Zolotow. New York : Putnam, c1977. 364 p., [8] leaves of plates : ill. ; 23 cm. Includes index. [PN1998.A3W59 1977] 77-75684 ISBN 0-399-11789-X : 8.95
1. Wilder, Billy, 1906- 2. Moving-picture producers and directors—United States—Biography. I. Title. BIP

Wilder, Laura Ingalls, 1867-1957—Biography.

EDDINS, Doris Kerns, 1917- 813'.6'2
A teacher's tribute to Laura Ingalls Wilder [by] Doris K. Eddins. [Washington, Dept. of Elementary School Principals, National Education Association, 1967] 23 p. illus. 23 cm. [PS3545.I342Z63] 67-18641
1. Wilder, Laura (Ingalls), 1867-1957. I. Title.

ZOCHERT, Donald. 813'.5'2 B
Laura : the life of Laura Ingalls Wilder / Donald Zochert. Chicago : H. Regnery Co., c1976. xii, 260 p., [4] leaves of plates : ill. ; 24 cm. Includes index. [PS3545.I342Z98 1976] 75-35002 ISBN 0-8092-8174-0 : 8.95
1. Wilder, Laura Ingalls, 1867-1957—Biography. I. Title. BIP

Wilder, Laura Ingalls, 1867-1957—Correspondence.

WILDER, Laura Ingalls, 1867-1957. 813'.5'2
West from home : letters of Laura Ingalls Wilder to Almanzo Wilder, San Francisco, 1915 / edited by Roger Lea MacBride ; historical setting by Margot Patterson Doss. 1st ed. New York : Harper & Row, [1974] xviii, 124 p., [12] leaves of plates : ill. ; 21 cm. A selection of letters by Laura Ingalls Wilder to her husband in which she describes the highlights of her visit to the west coast in 1915. [PS3545.I342Z55 1974] 73-14342 ISBN 0-06-024110-1 : 4.95. ISBN 0-06-024111-X lib.bdg. : 4.79
1. Wilder, Laura Ingalls, 1867-1957—Correspondence. 2. Wilder, Almanzo. 3. San Francisco. Panama Pacific International Exposition, 1915. 4. The West—Description and travel—1880-1950. I. Wilder, Almanzo. II. Title.

Wilder, Thornton Niven, 1897-1975.

BURBANK, Rex J. 813.52
Thornton Wilder. New York, Twayne Publishers [1961] 156 p. 21 cm. (Twayne's United States authors series, 5) Includes bibliography. [PS3545.I345Z57] 61-9854
1. Wilder, Thornton Niven, 1897- BIP

GOLDSTONE, Richard Henry. 813'.5'2 B
Thornton Wilder, an intimate portrait / Richard H. Goldstone. 1st ed. New York : Saturday Review Press, c1975. xvii, 299 p., [4] leaves of plates : ill. ; 24 cm. Includes index. Bibliography: p. 281-284. [PS3545.I345Z664] 75-12990 ISBN 0-8415-0392-3 : 12.95
1. Wilder, Thornton Niven, 1897- I. Title.

GREBANIER, Bernard D. N., 1903- 813'.5'2
Thornton Wilder. Minneapolis, University of Minnesota Press [1964] 48 p. 21 cm. (University of Minnesota pamphlets on American writers, no. 34) Bibliography: p. 45-48. [PS3545Z67] 64-63339
1. Wilder, Thornton Niven, 1897- I. Series: Minnesota. University. Pamphlets on American writers, no. 34

KUNER, Mildred Christophe, 1922- 813'.5'2
Thornton Wilder: the bright and the dark, by M. C. Kuner. New York, Crowell [1972] 226 p. 22 cm. (Twentieth-century American writers) Bibliography: p. [216]-219. [PS3545.I345Z75] 76-158696 ISBN 0-690-82002-X 4.50 4.50
1. Wilder, Thornton Niven, 1897- I. Title.

SIMON, Linda, 1946- 813'.5'2 B
Thornton Wilder, his world / Linda Simon. 1st ed. Garden City, N.Y. : Doubleday, 1979. p. cm. Includes index. Bibliography: p. [PS3545.I345Z89] 78-73193 ISBN 0-385-12840-1 : 10.95
1. Wilder, Thornton Niven, 1897-1975. 2. Authors, American—20th century—Biography.

Wildman family.

BREY, Jane W. T. 929.2
A Quaker saga; the Watsons of Strawberryhowe, the Wildmans, and other allied families from England's north counties and Lower Bucks County in Pennsylvania, by Jane W. T. Brey. Philadelphia, Dorrance [1967] xxvi, 646 p. illus., maps. 25 cm. Bibliographical footnotes. [CS71.W34 1967] 66-11051
1. Watson family. 2. Wildman family. 3. Friends, Society of. I. Title.

Wiles, Ralph William.

WILES, Ralph William. 923.573
Pipe-dreams and memories, an autobiography. New York, William-Frederick Press, 1953. 312p. illus. 23cm. [CT275.W55863A3] 53-5667
I. Title.

Wiley, George Alvin, 1931-1973.

KOTZ, Nick. 361'.0092'4 B
A passion for equality : George A. Wiley and the movement / Nick Kotz & Mary Lynn Kotz. 1st ed. New York : Norton, c1977. 372 p.,[6] leaves of plates : ill. ; 24 cm. Includes index. Bibliography: p. 349-359. [HV28.W47K67 1977] 77-8015 ISBN 0-393-07517-6 : 8.95
1. Wiley, George Alvin, 1931-1973. 2. Social reformers—United States—Biography. 3. Civil rights—United States. 4. Welfare rights movement—United States. 5. Afro-Americans—Biography. I. Kotz, Mary Lynn, joint author. II. Title. BIP

Wiley, Harvey Washington, 1844-1930.

NATENBERG, Maurice. 926.143
The legacy of Doctor Wiley. Chicago, Regent House [1957] 166p. illus. 23cm. [TX518.W5N3] 57-8422
1. Wiley, Harvey Washington, 1844-1930. 2. Food adulteration and inspection. I. Title.

Wiley, Jennie (Sellards), d. 1831.

CONNELLEY, William Elsey, 1855-1930. 973'.04'97 S
Eastern Kentucky papers / William Elsey Connelley. New York : Garland Pub., 1977. 177 p., [27] p. : ill. ; 23 cm. (The Garland library of narratives of North American Indian captivities ; v. 106) Reprint of the ed. published by Torch Press, New York. Issued with the reprint of the 1907 ed. of Carrigan, W. B. Captured by the Indians. New York, 1977. [E85.G2 vol. 106] [E87.W66] 976.9'2'030924 B 75-7134 ISBN 0-8240-1730-7 : 25.00
1. Wiley, Jennie (Sellards), d. 1831. 2. Connelly family. 3. Indians of North America—Captivities. 4. Kentucky—History—To 1792. 5. Harmon's Station, Ky.—History. 6. Kentucky—Biography. I. Title. II. Series.

WHEELER, Arville, 1900- v. 12
White Squaw: the true story of Jennie Wiley. Illustrated by Ture Bengtz. Paintville, Ky., Eastern Kentucky Pub. [1958] 163 p. illus. 24 cm. 67-26283
1. Wiley, Jennie (Sellards) d. 1831 — Fiction. 2. Indians of North America — Captivities. I. Title.

Wilfred, Saint, Bp. of York, 634-709.

DUCKETT, Eleanor Shipley. 274.2
Anglo-Saxon saints and scholars Hamden, Conn., Archon Books, 1967 [c1947] x, 484 p. 22 cm. Contents.Contents. -- Aldheim of Malmesbury. -- Wilfrid of York. -- Bede of Jarrow. -- Boniface of Devon. -- Bibliogrpahy and abbreviations (p. 456-473) [BR754.A1D8] 67-11473
1. Aldhcim, Saint, Bp. of Sherborne, 640?-709. 2. Wilfrid, Saint, Bp. of York, 634-709. 3. Beda Venerabilis, 673-735. 4. Boniface, originally Winfrid, Saint, Bp. of Mainz, 680-755. I. Title. BIP

SAINT Wilfrid at Hexham / D. P. Kirby, editor. 270.2'092'4 B
Newcastle upon Tyne [Eng.] : Oriel Press, 1974. xi, 196, 31 p. : ill. ; 24 cm. Includes bibliographical references and index. [BX4700.W5S24] 75-308585 ISBN 0-85362-155-1 : £5.50
1. Wilfred, Saint, Bp. of York, 634-709. 2. Art—Hexham, Eng. 3. Art, Anglo-Saxon—Hexham, Eng. 4. Hexham, Eng.—History. I. Kirby, D. P.

Wilhelm, Crown Prince of the German Empire and of Prussia, 1882-1951.

JONAS, Klaus W 923.243
The life of Crown Prince William. Translated from the German by Charles W. Bangert. Pittsburgh, University of Pittsburgh Press [1961] 252p. illus. 23cm. Includes bibliography. [DD229.8.W5J613] 61-9990
1. Wilhelm, Crown Prince of the German Empire and of Prussia, 1882-1951. I. Title.

Wilhelm I, German Emperor, 1797-1888.

ARONSON, Theo. 943.08'3'0922
The kaisers. Indianapolis, Bobbs-Merrill [1971] xii, 276 p. illus., ports. 22 cm. Bibliography: p. [261]-269. [DD370.A7 1971b] 74-142483 8.95
1. Wilhelm I, German Emperor, 1797-1888. 2. Friedrich III, German Emperor, 1831-1888. 3. Wilhelm II, German Emperor, 1859-1941. I. Title.

Wilhelm II, German Emperor, 1859-1941.

BALFOUR, Michael Leonard Graham, 1908- 923.143
The Kaiser and his times, by Micahel Balfour. Boston, Houghton Mifflin, 1964. xi, 524 p. illus., geneal, table, ports. 22 cm. "Notes on sources": p. [448]-487. [DD229.B26 1964a] 64-22678
1. Wilhelm II, German Emperor, 1859-1941. I. Title. BIP

BALFOUR, Michael Leonard Graham, 1908- 943.08'4'0924 B
The Kaiser and his times, by Michael Balfour. With an afterword. New York, Norton [1972] xi, 531 p. illus. 20 cm. (The Norton library, N661) Bibliography: p. 487-517. [DD229.B26 1972] 72-6600 ISBN 0-393-00661-1 3.95
1. Wilhelm II, German Emperor, 1859-1941. I. Title.

COWLES, Virginia Spencer 923.143
The Kaiser. New York, Harper [1964, c.1963] 445p. illus., ports., geneal. table. 25cm. Bibl. 63-20288 6.95
1. Wilhelm II, German Emperor, 1859-1941. I. Title.

KURENBERG, Joachim von, 1892- 923.143
The Kaiser; a life of Wilhelm II, last Emperor of Germany. Translated by H. T. Russell and Herta Hagen. With a foreword, notes, and appendix by Quincy Howe. New York, Simon and Schuster, 1955. 461p. illus. 22cm. Translation of War alies faisch? [DD228.K812 1955] 55-8807
1. Wilhelm II, German Emperor, 1859-1941. 2. Germany—Hist.—William II, 1888-1918. I. Title.

LUDWIG, Emil, 1881-1948. 943.084'0924 B
Wilhelm Hohenzollern, the last of the Kaisers. Translated from the German, by Ethel Colburn Mayne. New York, AMS Press [1970] xviii, 528 p. illus., facsim., ports. 23 cm. Reprint of the 1927 ed. Translation of Wilhelm der Zweite. [DD229.L95 1970] 74-100815
1. Wilhelm II, German Emperor, 1859-1941.

PALMER, Alan Warwick. 943.08'4'0924 B
The Kaiser : warlord of the Second Reich / Alan Palmer. New York : Scribner, c1978. 276 p., [4] leaves of plates : ill. ; 25 cm. Includes index. Bibliography: p. 254-262. [DD229.P33] 77-92797 ISBN 0-684-15637-7 : 14.95
1. Wilhelm II, German Emperor, 1859-1941. 2. Germany—Kings and rulers—Biography. 3. Germany—History—William II, 1888-1918. I. Title. BIP

WILHELM II, German Emperor, 1859-1941. 943.08'4'0924 B
The Kaiser's memoirs / Wilhelm II ; English translation by Thomas R. Ybarra. New York : H. Fertig, 1975, c1922. p. cm. Translation of Ereignisse und Gestalten aus den Jahren 1878-1918. Reprint of the ed. published by Harper,

New York. [DD229.A45 1975] 74-22349 15.00
1. Wilhelm II, German Emperor, 1859-1941. 2. Germany—Politics and government—1888-1918. 3. European War, 1914-1918. I. Title.

WILHELM II, 943'.08'4'0924 B
German Emperor, 1859-1941.
My early life. Translated from the German. New York, G. H. Doran Co. [1971] xii, 353 p. illus., facsim., ports. 23 cm. Reprint of the 1926 ed. Translation of Aus meinem Leben. [DD229.A5 1971] 71-137306 ISBN 0-404-06947-9
1. Germany—Court and courtiers. I. Title. BIP

Wilhelm, Maria.

WILHELM, Maria. 923.2
The fighting Irishman; the story of "Wild Bill" Donovan. Illustrated by Al Fiorentino. New York, Hawthorn Books [c1964] 185 p. illus., port. 22 cm. (Credo books) Bibliography: p. [179] 64-19492
I. Donovan, William Joseph, 1883-1959. II. Title.

Wilhelmina,

WILHELMINA, Queen of 923.1492
the Netherlands, 1880-
Lonely but not alone. Translated from the Dutch by John Peereboom. New York, McGraw-Hill [1960] 247p. illus. 24cm. 60-14966 5.95
I. Title.

Wilk, Max.

WILK, Max. 791'.092'4 B
Every day's a matinee : memoirs scribbled on a dressing room door / by Max Wilk. 1st ed. New York : Norton, [1975] 288 p. : ill. ; 21 cm. Includes index. [PN2287.W459A33] 74-30082 ISBN 0-393-07491-9 : 8.50
1. Wilk, Max. I. Title. BIP

Wilkens, Lenny, 1937-

WILKENS, Lenny, 796.34'2'0924 B
1937-
The Lenny Wilkens story. Introd. by Thomas Mannion. New York, P. S. Eriksson [1974] xiv, 174 p. ports. 22 cm. [GV884.W54A34 1974] 73-92647 ISBN 0-8397-5032-3 6.95
1. Wilkens, Lenny, 1937- 2. Basketball. I. Title. BIP

Wilkerson, David R.

WILKERSON, David R. 259
Beyond the cross and the switchblade [by] David Wilkerson. Special introd. by John and Elizabeth Sherrill. Old Tappan, N.J., Chosen Books; distributed by F. H. Revell [1974] 191 p. 21 cm. [BV4470.W48] 74-12155 ISBN 0-912376-08-2
1. Wilkerson, David R. 2. Church work with narcotic addicts. I. Title. BIP

Wilkes, Charles, 1798-1877.

HENDERSON, Daniel 923.573
MacIntyre, 1880-1955.
The hidden coasts; a biography of Admiral Charles Wilkes. New York, Sloane, 1953. 306 p. port., map (on lining papers) 22 cm. Bibliography: p. 287-293. [E340.W6H4] 52-13837
1. Wilkes, Charles, 1798-1877. I. Title. BIP

HENDERSON, Daniel 973'.099 B
MacIntyre, 1880-1955.
The hidden coasts; a biography of Admiral Charles Wilkes [by] Daniel Henderson. Westport, Conn., Greenwood Press [1971, c1953] 306 p. illus. 23 cm. Bibliography: p. 287-293. [E340.W6H4 1971] 78-138589 ISBN 0-8371-5789-7
1. Wilkes, Charles, 1798-1877. I. Title.

Wilkes, John, 1727-1797.

CHENEVIX Trench, 942.07'3'0924
Charles Pocklington, 1914-
Portrait of a patriot; a biography of John Wilkes. Edinburgh, W. Blackwood [1962] 412 p. illus. 23 cm. Includes bibliography. [DA512.W6C5] 62-68109
1. Wilkes, John. 1727-1797. 2. Gt. Brit. — Pol. & govt. — 1760-1789. I. Title.

KRONENBERGER, 328.42'092'4 B
Louis, 1904-
The extraordinary Mr. Wilkes: his life and times. [1st ed.] Garden City, N.Y., Doubleday, 1974. xv, 269 p. illus. 22 cm. Bibliography: p. [253]-255. [DA512.W6K76] 73-79686 ISBN 0-385-05131-X 10.00
1. Wilkes, John, 1727-1797. 2. Great Britain—Politics and government—1760-1789. I. Title.

SHERRARD, Owen 328.42'092'4 B
Aubrey, 1887-1962.
A life of John Wilkes. New York, B. Blom, 1971. 319 p. ports. 22 cm. Reprint of the 1930 ed. Bibliography: p. [313]-314. [DA512.W6S5 1971b] 72-177508
1. Wilkes, John, 1727-1797. 2. Great Britain—Politics and government—1760-1789. I. Title. BIP

SHERRARD, Owen 328.42'092'4 B
Aubrey 1887-1962.
A life of John Wilkes. Freeport, N.Y., Books for Libraries Press [1971] 319 p. ports. 23 cm. Reprint of the 1930 ed. Bibliography: p. [313]-314. [DA512.W6S5 1971] 77-164627 ISBN 0-8369-5910-8
1. Wilkes, John, 1727-1797. 2. Great Britain—Politics and government—1760-1789.

WILKES, John, 1727-1797. 923.242
The correspondence of John Wilkes and Charles Churchill; edited with an introd. by Edward H. Weatherly. New York, Columbia University Press, 1954. xxvii, 114p. 21cm. 'British Museum Add. MS 30.878 . . . contains all but two of the letters . . . Numbers 13 and 49 come from Guildhall Library MS 214. vol. I. Bibliography: p. [101]- 105. [PR3765.W531Z52] 53-10939
I. Churchill, Charles, 1731-1764. II. Weatherly, Edward Howell, 1905- ed. III. Title.

WILKES, John, 1727- 942.07'2'0924
1797.
The correspondence of the late John Wilkes, with his friends; printed from the original manuscripts in which are introduced memoirs of his life, by John Almon. New York, B. Franklin [1970] 5 v. port. 19 cm. (Burt Franklin research and source works series, 436. Selected essays in history, economics, & social science, 116) "Originally published 1804-05." [DA512.W6A2 1970] 70-114823
I. Almon, John, 1737-1805, ed.

WILLIAMSON, 941.07'3'0924 B
Audrey, 1913-
Wilkes, a friend to liberty / by Audrey Williamson. 1st ed. New York : Reader's Digest Press : [distributed by] Dutton, 1974. 250 p., [6] leaves of plates : ill. ; 22 cm. Includes index. Bibliography: p. 236-238. [DA512.W6W54 1974b] 74-21005 ISBN 0-88349-031-5 : 10.00
1. Wilkes, John, 1727-1797. I. Title.

Wilkin, Marijohn.

HICKS, Darryl. 783.7'092'4 B
Marijohn: Lord, let me leave a song / Darryl E. Hicks. Waco, Tex. : Word Books, c1978. 159 p. : ill. ; 22 cm. [ML410.W699H5] 77-92466 ISBN 0-8499-0019-0 : 6.95
1. Wilkin, Marijohn. 2. Gospel musicians—United States—Biography. I. Title.

Wilkins, George Hubert, Sir, 1888-1958.

THOMAS, Lowell Jackson, 923.942
1892-
Sir Hubert Wilkins: his world of adventure; a biography. New York, McGraw-Hill [1961] 296 p. illus. 22 cm. [G246.W56T5] 61-16533
1. Wilkins, George Hubert, Sir, 1888-1958.

Wilkins, John, Bp. of Chester, 1614-1672.

SHAPIRO, Barbara J. 283'.0924 B
John Wilkins, 1614-1672; an intellectual biography [by] Barbara J. Shapiro. Berkeley, University of California Press, 1969. 333 p. port. 24 cm. Bibliographical references included in "Notes" (p. 251-320) [LF724.W5S5] 73-84042 9.50
1. Wilkins, John, Bp. of Chester, 1614-1672. 2. Religion and science—History of controversy. BIP

Wilkins, John, gamekeeper.

WILKINS, John, 639'.9'0924 B
gamekeeper.
The autobiography of an English gamekeeper / by John Wilkins ; illustrated by Sidney Starr. Facsim. ed. Chesham, Eng. : Sporting & Leisure Press, 1976. 441 p. : ill., ports. ; 20 cm. (Country classic) Photoreprint of the 1892 ed., edited by A. H. Byng and S. Starr, and published by J. F. Unwin, London. [SK185.W5 1976] 77-359749 ISBN 0-86023-025-2 : £6.95
1. Wilkins, John, gamekeeper. 2. Gamekeepers—England—Biography. I. Title. BIP

Wilkins, Sir George Hubert, 1888-1958.

THOMAS, Lowell Jackson, 923.942
1892-
Sir Hubert Wilkins: his world of adventure; a biography. New York, McGraw-Hill [1961] 296 p. illus. 22 cm. [G246.W56T5] 61-16533
1. Wilkins, Sir George Hubert, 1888-1958. I. Title.

Wilkinson, Asbury, 1818-1909.

CLINE, Rodney. 922.773
Asbury Wilkinson: pioneer preacher. [1st ed.] New York, Vantage Press [1956] 116p. illus. 21cm. [BX8495.W635C55] 56-9032
1. Wilkinson, Asbury, 1818-1909. I. Title.

CLINE, Rodney. 922.773
Asbury Wilkinson: pioneer preacher. [1st ed.] New York, Vantage Press [1956] 116p. illus. 21cm. [BX8495.W635C55] 56-9032
1. Wilkinson, Asbury, 1818-1909. I. Title.

Wilkinson, James, 1757-1825.

JACOBS, James 973.4'8'0924 B
Ripley, 1886-
Tarnished warrior. Major General James Wilkinson. Freeport, N.Y., Books for Libraries Press [1972] p. Reprint of the 1938 ed. Bibliography: p. [E353.1.W6J3 1972] 72-7032 ISBN 0-8369-6943-X
1. Wilkinson, James, 1757-1825. I. Title.

WEEMS, John Edward. 976
Men without countries; three adventurers of the early Southwest. Illustrated by Rick Duiker. Boston, Houghton Mifflin, 1969. 272 p. illus., map (on lining papers) 22 cm. Bibliography: p. [267]-272. [F396.W38] 69-19567 5.95
1. Wilkinson, James, 1757-1825. 2. Nolan, Philip, d. 1801. 3. Bean, Ellis Peter, 1783-1846. 4. Southwest, Old—History. I. Title.

Wilkinson, Jemima, 1752-1819.

HUDSON, David. 289.9 B
Memoir of Jemima Wilkinson. New York, AMS Press [1972] 288 p. port. 22 cm. First published in 1821 under title: History of Jemima Wilkinson. Reprint of the 1844 ed. [BR1719.W5H8 1972] 78-134417 ISBN 0-404-08475-3 12.50
1. Wilkinson, Jemima, 1752-1819. I. Title.

JACOBS, James 973.4'8'0924 B
Ripley, 1886-
Tarnished warrior, Major-General James Wilkinson. Freeport, N.Y., Books for Libraries Press [1972] p. Reprint of the 1938 ed. Bibliography: p. [E353.1.W6J3 1972] 72-7032 ISBN 0-8369-6943-X
1. Wilkinson, James, 1757-1825. I. Title.

WEEMS, John Edward. 976
Men without countries; three adventurers of the early Southwest. Illustrated by Rick Duiker. Boston, Houghton Mifflin, 1969. 272 p. illus., map (on lining papers) 22 cm. Bibliography: p. [267]-272. [F396.W38] 69-19567 5.95
1. Wilkinson, James, 1757-1825. 2. Nolan, Philip, d. 1801. 3. Bean, Ellis Peter, 1783-1846. 4. Southwest, Old—History. I. Title.

WISBEY, Herbert Andrew, 922.89
Jr. 1919-
Pioneer prophetess: Jemima Wilkinson, the Publick Universal Friend. Ithaca, N.Y., Cornell [c.1964] xiv, 232p. illus., facsim., ports. 23cm. Bibl. [BR1719.W5W5] 64-7875 4.95
1. Wilkinson, Jemima, 1752-1819. I. Title.

Wilkinson, Thomas, 1751-1836.

DALGLISH, Doris N. 289.6'0922
People called Quakers, by Doris N. Dalglish. Freeport, N.Y., Books for Libraries Press [1969] 169 p. 23 cm. (Essay index reprint series) Reprint of the 1938 ed. Contents.Contents.—The first Quaker poet.—An American saint.—A digression on women and the eighteenth century.—A neighbour of Wordsworth.—A friend from France.—Convert and critic. [BX7791.D3 1969] 78-90628
1. Story, Thomas, 1662-1742. 2. Woolman, John, 1720-1772. 3. Wilkinson, Thomas, 1751-1836. 4. Grellet, Stephen, 1773-1855. 5. Stephen, Caroline Emelia, 1834-1909. 6. Friends, Society of—Biography. I. Title.

Willams family (Roger Williams, 1604?-1683)

ANTHONY, Bertha E v. 12
(Willams)1892-
Roger Williams of Providence, R.I. Por. [Cranston, R.I., 196- v. illus. 26 cm. 68-51007
1 Willams family (Roger Williams, 1604?-1683) I. Title.

Willard, Daniel, 1861-1942.

HUNGERFORD, Edward, 385'.092'4 B
1875-1948.
Daniel Willard rides the line; the story of a great railroad man. Freeport, N.Y., Books for Libraries Press [1972] ix, 301 p. illus. 22 cm. Reprint of the 1938 ed. Bibliography: p. 295. [HE2754.W55H8 1972] 72-1281 ISBN 0-8369-6828-X 17.75
1. Willard, Daniel, 1861-1942. 2. Baltimore and Ohio Railroad. I. Title

Willard, Emma (Hart) 1787-1870.

LUTZ, Alma. 923.773
Emma Willard, pioneer educator of American women. Boston. Beacon Press [1964] viii. 143 p. 21 cm. [LA2317.W5L82] 64-15364
1. Willard, Emma (Hart) 1787-1870 2. Emma Willard School, Troy, N.Y. I. Title.

LUTZ, Alma. 370'.92'4 B
Emma Willard : daughter of democracy / by Alma Lutz. Washington : Zenger Pub. Co., 1975, c1929. p. cm. Reprint of the ed. published by Houghton Mifflin, Boston. Includes index. Bibliography: p. [LA2317.W5L82 1975] 75-37635 ISBN 0-89201-018-5 : 12.50
1. Willard, Emma (Hart) 1787-1870. 2. Emma Willard School, Troy, N.Y. BIP

Willard, Frances Elizabeth, 1839-1898.

STRACHEY, Rachel 322.4'4'0924 B
Conn (Costelloe) 1887-1940.
Frances Willard, her life and work. With an introd. by Lady Henry Somerset. Freeport, N.Y., Books for Libraries Press [1973] p. Reprint of the 1913 ed. [HV5232.W6S8 1973] 72-10608 ISBN 0-8369-7125-6
1. Willard, Frances Elizabeth, 1839-1898. I. Title.

Willard, Samuel, 1640-1707.

VAN DYKEN, Seymour. 285'.9'0924 B
Samuel Willard, 1640-1707; preacher of

orthodoxy in an era of change Grand Rapids, Eerdmans [1972] 224 p. 23 cm. Bibliography: p. 195-211. [BX7260.W5V3] 75-168438 ISBN 0-8028-3408-6 5.95
1. Willard, Samuel, 1640-1707.

Willard, Theodore Arthur, 1862-1943.

WEBSTER, Edna Robb. 621.35'4'0924 B
T. A. Willard : wizard of the storage battery : the biography of a famous inventor / by Edna Robb Webster. Sherman Oaks, Calif. : Wilmar Publishers, c1976. 180 p. : ill. ; 23 cm. [TK140.W62W4] 76-372550
1. Willard, Theodore Arthur, 1862-1943. 2. Inventors—United States—Biography. 3. Storage battery—History.

Willcox, Joseph Morgan, 1791?-1814.

A Narrative of the life and death of Lieut. J. M. Willcox. 973'.04'97 S New York : Garland Pub., 1978. p. cm. (The Garland library of narratives of North American Indian captivities ; v. 33) Issued with the reprint of the 1813 ed. of U.S. War Dept. Message from the President relative to murders committed by the Indians. New York, 1978. Reprint of the 1816 ed. printed by R. Prentiss, Marietta, Ohio, under title: A narrative of the life and death of Lieut. Joseph Morgan Willcox. [E85.G2 vol. 33] [E83.813] 973.5'238 75-7055 ISBN 0-8240-1657-2 lib.bdg. : 29.50
1. Willcox, Joseph Morgan, 1791?-1814. 2. Creek War, 1813-1814. 3. United States—Biography. I. Series.

Willeford, Charles Ray, 1919- —Biography.

WILLEFORD, Charles Ray, 1919- 813'.5'4 B
A guide for the undehemorrhoided / Charles Willeford. Miami : Willeford, c1977. 32 p. ; 23 cm. "From ... [Willeford's] autobiography ... I was looking for a street."—Book jacket. [PS3545.I464Z516] 77-78973
1. Willeford, Charles Ray, 1919- —Biography. 2. Authors, American—20th century—Biography. 3. Hemorrhoids—Biography. I. Title.

Willem I, Prince of Orange, 1533-1584.

HARRISON, Frederic, 1831-1923. 949'.203'0924 B
William the Silent. Port Washington, N.Y., Kennikat Press [1970] vi, 260 p. 21 cm. Reprint of the 1897 ed. Bibliography: p. 258-260. [DH188.W7H3 1970] 70-112805
1. Willem I, Prince of Orange, 1533-1584. BIP

SIMMONS, Dawn Langley. 949.2'03'0924 B
William, Father of The Netherlands, by Gordon Langley Hall. Chicago, Rand McNally [1969] 240 p. illus., maps, ports. 22 cm. Bibliography: p. 228. The public and private life of William of Orange who in the sixteenth century ruled England, Scotland, and Ireland. [DH188.W7S54] 92 71-80072 4.95
1. Willem I, Prince of Orange, 1533-1584. 2. Netherlands—History—Wars of Independence, 1556-1648. I. Title.

Willert, Arthur,

WILLERT, Arthur, Sir, 1882- 327'.2'0924 B
Washington and other memories. Boston, Houghton Mifflin, 1972 [c1971] vi, 248 p. 22 cm. [DA566.9.W46A3 1972] 74-162013 ISBN 0-395-12727-0 6.95
I. Title.

Willett, Anne Anne (Coddington) 1653-1751.

WHITE, Elizabeth (Nicholson) 1877- 974.5
Anne of Kings Towne. Illus. by Mary Elmore. [East Providence R. I., 1955] 51p. illus. 21cm. [F82.W5W4] 55-32217
1. Willett, Anne Anne (Coddington) 1653-1751. I. Title.

Willett, Marinus,

THOMAS, Howard, 1898- 923.573
Marinus Willett, soldier-patriot, 1740-1830. [Limited 1st ed.] Prospect, N. Y., Prospect Books, 1954. ix. 242p. port., map (on lining papers) 21cm. Bibliography: p. 235-236. [E207.W65T5] 54-8876
1. Willett, Marinus, I. Title.

Willey, Waltman Thomas, 1811-1900.

AMBLER, Charles Henry, 1876- 923.273
Waitman Thomas Willey, orator, churchman, humanitarian; together with a history of Wesley Methodist Church, Morgantown, West Virginia. Huntington, W. Va., Standard Print. & Pub. Co. [c1954] 282p. illus. 22cm. Includes bibliography. [E415.9.W44A6] 55-30538
1. Willey, Waltman Thomas, 1811-1900. 2. Morgantown, W. Va. Wesley Methodist Church. I. Title.

Willey, Willis R., 1884-1956.

YATES, Keith L. 920
The life of Willie Willey: nature boy, traveler, ambassador of good will. New York, Exposition [c.1966] 76p. illus., ports. 22cm. Bibl. [F899.S7Y3] 66-2320 3.50
1. Willey, Willis R., 1884-1956. I. Title.

YATES, Keith L 920
The life of Willie Willey; nature boy, traveler, ambassador of good will, by Keith L. Yates [1st ed.] New York, Exposition Press [1966] 76 p. illus., ports. 22 cm. Bibliography: p. [71]-76. [F899.S7Y3] 66-2820
1. Willey, Willie R., 1884-1956. I. Title.

William D. Lawrence (Ship)

STEPHENS, David E., 1946- 387.2'2'0924
W. D. Lawrence : the man and the ship / by David E. Stephens. Windsor, N.S. : Lancelot Press, 1975. 68 p., [2] leaves of plates : ill. ; 21 cm. Bibliography: p. 67-68. [VM395.W54S74] 76-351513
1. William D. Lawrence (Ship) 2. Lawrence, William David, 1817-1886. 3. Voyages around the world.

William Dodge, 1867-1957.

FROST, Russell E. 925.8
Beloved professor, life and times of William Dodge Frost. New York, Vantage Press. [c.1961] 350 p. illus. ports. 60-15570 3.75
1. William Dodge, 1867-1957. I. Title.

William I, the Conqueror, King of England, 1027?-1087.

BAKER, George Edward, 1902- 923.142
Hawk of Normandy; the story of William the Conqueror. New York, Roy Publishers [1957] 174p. illus. 21cm. [DA197.B3] 57-10700
1. William I, the Conqueror, King of England, 1027?-1087. I. Title.

SLOCOMBE, George Edward, 1894- 923.142
William, the Conqueror. New York, Putnam [1961, c.1959] 271p. illus. Bibl. 61-8350 4.50
1. William I, the Conqueror, King of England, 1027?-1087. I. Title.

STENTON, Frank Merry, Sir, 1880-1967. 942.021
William the Conqueror and the rule of the Normans. [Rev.] New York, Barnes & Noble [1967] xi, 518 p. illus., facsims., geneal. tables, maps, port. 20 cm. Bibliographical footnotes. [DA197.S7 1967] 66-28853
1. William I, the Conqueror, King of England, 1027?-1087. 2. Great Britain—History—Norman period, 1066-1154. I. Title.

William I, the Conqueror, King of England, 1027?-1087—Juvenile literature.

COSTAIN, Thomas Bertram, 1885-1965. 923.142
William the Conqueror. Illustrated by Jack Coggins. New York, Random House [1959] 180 p. illus. 22 cm. (World landmark books, W-41) [DA197.C62] 59-5523
1. William I, the Conqueror, King of England, 1027?-1087—Juvenile literature.

LUCKOCK, Elizabeth 92
William the Conqueror. Illus. with segments of the Bayeux Tapestry. [1st Amer. ed.] New York, Putnam [1966, c.1964] 127p. illus. 23cm. [DA197.L8] 66-6184 2.86 lib. ed.,
1. William the conqueror, King of England, 1027-1087—Juvenile Literature I. Title.

WALKER, David, 1923- 942.02'1'0924 B
William the Conqueror. London, Oxford U.P., 1968. [4], 60 p. 8 plates, illus., facsims., map. 21 cm. (The Clarendon biographies, 22) Bibliography: p. [58] [DA197.W3] 75-353318 9/6
1. William I, the Conqueror, King of England, 1027?-1087—Juvenile literature. I. Title.

William III, King of Great Britain, 1650-1702.

ROBB, Nesca Adeline. 923.142
William of Orange, a personal portrait. New York, St. Martin's Press [1963, c1962-1966] 2 v. geneal. tables, maps, ports. 22 cm. Contents.Contents.—v. 1. 1650-1673.—v. 2. 1674-1702. Includes bibliographical references. [DA462.A2R62] 63-18762
1. William III, King of Great Britain, 1650-1702. BIP

THOMSON, Mark Almeras. 327'.42'044
William III and Louis XIV: essays 1680-1720, by and for Mark A. Thomson. Edited by Ragnhild Hatton and J S Bromley Toronto, University of Toronto Press, 1968. 332 p. port. 24 cm. Bibliography: p. [306]-317. [DA47.1.T48 1968] 68-98219 7.25 Can.
1. William III, King of Great Britain, 1650-1702. 2. Louis XIV, King of France, 1638-1715. 3. Great Britain—Foreign relations—France. 4. France—Foreign relations—Great Britain. I. Hatton, Ragnhild Marie, ed. II. Bromley, John Selwyn, ed. III. Title.

VAN DER ZEE, Henri 942.06'8'0924 B
William and Mary [by] Henri and Barbara van der Zee. [1st American ed.] New York, Knopf, 1973. xv, 526, x p. illus. 25 cm. Bibliography: p. [515]-526. [DA462.A2V36 1973b] 72-11033 ISBN 0-394-48092-9 12.50
1. William III, King of Great Britain, 1650-1702. 2. Mary II, Queen of Great Britain, 1662-1694. 3. Great Britain—History—William and Mary, 1689-1702. I. Van der Zee, Barbara, joint author. II. Title.

William (Name)—Juvenile literature.

GLAZER, Tom. 929.4
All about your name, William (Will, Bill, Willie, Billy, Willy) / Tom Glazer ; illustrated by Demi. 1st ed. Garden City, N.Y. : Doubleday, c1978. 43 p. ill. ; 22 cm. Discusses the name William and the many interesting people throughout history who have held that name. [CS2391.W5G57] 76-23763 ISBN 0-385-06419-5 : 4.95. ISBN 0-385-06420-9 lib.bdg. : 5.90
1. William (Name)—Juvenile literature. 2. Biography—Miscellanea—Juvenile literature. I. Hitz, Demi. II. Title.

William, Roger, 1604?-1683.

MILLER, Perry, 1905- v. 12
Roger Williams; his contribution to the American tradition. [1st Atheneum ed.] New York, Atheneum, 1962. 264 p. (Atheneum paperbacks, 6) 63-51648
1. William, Roger, 1604?-1683. I. Title. BIP

Williams, Alfred, 1877-1930.

CLARK, Leonard. 821'.9'12 B
Alfred Williams, his life and work. A reprint with a new introd. by the author. New York, A. M. Kelley, 1969. xv, 206 p. illus., ports. 23 cm. Reprint of the 1945 ed. "Published works by Alfred Williams": p. 194. "Unpublished works by Alfred Williams": p. 195. [PR6045.I45Z6 1969] 69-13754
1. Williams, Alfred, 1877-1930.

Williams, Alice Cary—Biography.

WILLIAMS, Alice Cary. 813'.5'4 B
Thru the turnstile : tales of my two centuries / Alice Cary Williams ; illustrated by Samuel H. Bryant. Boston : Houghton Mifflin, 1976. viii, 150 p. : ill. ; 22 cm. [PS3573.I4474Z52] 76-15977 ISBN 0-395-20621-9 : 6.95
1. Williams, Alice Cary—Biography. 2. Boston—Social life and customs. 3. Nantucket, Mass.—Social life and customs. I. Title. BIP

Williams, Allan.

WILLIAMS, Allan. 380.1'45'784 B
The man who gave the Beatles away / by Allan Williams and William Marshall. New York : Macmillan, 1975. vi, 216 p. : ill. ; 24 cm. [ML429.W54] 74-28067 ISBN 0-02-629050-2 : 9.95
1. Williams, Allan. 2. The Beatles. 3. Concert agents—Correspondence, reminiscences, etc. I. Marshall, William, joint author. II. Title. BIP

Williams, Billy.

WILLIAMS, Billy. 796.357'092'4 B
Billy: the classic hitter, by Billy Williams and Irv Haag. Chicago, Rand McNally [1974] 205 p. illus. 24 cm. [GV865.W49A29] 74-8753 ISBN 0-528-81980-1 7.95
1. Williams, Billy. 2. Baseball. I. Haag, Irv. II. Title.

WILLIAMS, Billy. 796.357'0924 B
Iron man, by Billy Williams, with Rick Simon. [Chicago, Childrens Press, 1970] 64 p. illus., ports. 18 cm. (Open door books) A record-breaking pro baseball player tells about his childhood as a black boy in Alabama. [GV865.W49A3] 92 74-124087
I. Simon, Richard Edward, 1945- joint author. II. Title.

WILLIAMS, Billy. 796.357'0924 B
Iron man, by Billy Williams, with Rick Simon. [Chicago, Childrens Press, 1970] 64 p. illus., ports. 18 cm. (Open door books) A record-breaking pro baseball player tells about his childhood as a black boy in Alabama. [GV865.W49A3] 92 74-124087
I. Simon, Richard Edward, 1945- joint author. II. Title.

Williams, Daniel Hale, 1856-1931.

BUCKLER, Helen. 926.1
Daniel Hale Williams, Negro surgeon. New York, Pitman [1968] xvi, 381p., port., 22cm. Orig. pub. in 1954 as: Doctor Dan: Pioneer in American Surgery. Bibl. refs. in notes. [p.271-361] [R154.W5225B8] 6.95
1. Williams, Daniel Hale, 1856-1931. I. Title.

BUCKLER, Helen. 610'.924 B
Daniel Hale Williams, Negro surgeon. [2d ed.] New York, Pitman Pub. Corp. [1968] xvi, 381 p. geneal. table, ports. 22 cm. First ed. published in 1954 under title: Doctor Dan, pioneer in American surgery. [R154.W5225 1968] 72-288 6.95
1. Williams, Daniel Hale, 1856-1931. I. Title.

BUCKLER, Helen. 926.1
Doctor Dan, pioneer in American surgery. [1st ed.] Boston, Little, Brown [1954] 381 p. illus. 21 cm. Second ed. published in 1968 under title: Daniel Hale Williams, Negro surgeon. [R154.W5225B8] 54-6881

1. Williams, Daniel Hale, 1856-1931. I. Title.

Williams, Daniel Hale, 1856-1931—Juvenile literature.

MERIWETHER, Louise. 617'.092'4 B
The heart man: Dr. Daniel Hale Williams. Illus. by Floyd Sowell. Englewood Cliffs, N.J., Prentice-Hall [1972] [32] p. illus. 25 cm. A brief biography of the black surgeon who performed the first successful heart operation in 1893. [R154.W5225M4] 92 72-883 ISBN 0-13-385229-6 4.95
1. Williams, Daniel Hale, 1856-1931—Juvenile literature. I. Sowell, Floyd, illus. II. Title.

Williams, Daniel Jenkins, 1874-1952.

WILLIAMS, Robert Hugh, 1907- 922.573
Young minister of Wisconsin, the story of Daniel Jenkins Williams and his brothers. New York, Exposition [c.1963] 75p. illus. 21cm. 63-5225 2.75
1. Williams, Daniel Jenkins, 1874-1952. I. Title.

WILLIAMS, Robert Hugh, 1907- 922.573
Young minister of Wisconsin, the story of Daniel Jenkins Williams and his brothers. [1st ed.] New York, Exposition Press [1963] 75 p. illus. 21 cm. [BX9225,W452W5] 63-5225
1. Williams, Daniel Jenkins, 1874-1952. I. Title.

Williams, Edward D., 1921-

WILLIAMS, Edward D., 1921- 363.2'092'4 B
The first Black captain / Edward D. Williams. 1st ed. New York : Vantage Press, [1974] 110 p., [2] leaves of plates : ill. ; 22 cm. Autobiographical. [HV7911.W48A34] 74-194425 ISBN 0-533-01271-6 : 4.95
1. Williams, Edward D., 1921- 2. Negro policemen. 3. Police—New Jersey—Correspondence, reminiscences, etc. I. Title.

Williams, Edward, 1750-1813.

OWEN, William Thomas. 922.5
Edward Williams, D.D., 1750-1813; his life, thought, and influence. Cardiff, Univ. of Wales [Mystic, Conn., Verry, 1966] xii, 171p. facsim., ports. 22cm. Bibl. [BX5207.W53O9] 66-4704 4.00
1. Williams, Edward, 1750-1813. I. Title.

Williams, Egbert Austin, 1875-1922.

CHARTERS, Ann. 792'.028'0924 B
Nobody: the story of Bert Williams. [New York] Macmillan [1970] 157 p. illus., ports. 26 cm. Includes songs. [PN2287.W46C5] 69-20215
1. Williams, Egbert Austin, 1875-1922. I. Title.

ROWLAND, Mabel, ed. 792'.028'0924 B
Bert Williams, son of laughter; a symposium of tribute to the man and to his work, by his friends and associates, with a pref. by David Belasco. New York, Negro Universities Press [1969] xvii, 218 p. illus., facsims, ports. 23 cm. Reprint of the 1923 ed. [PN2287.W46R6 1969] 72-84693
1. Williams, Egbert Austin, 1875-1922. I. Williams, Egbert Austin, 1875-1922.

Williams, Elisha, 1694-1775.

PARSONS, Francis, 1871-1937. 378.746'8 B
Six men of Yale. Foreword by Charles Seymour. Freeport, N.Y., Books for Libraries Press [1971, c1939] xii, 145 p. ports. 23 cm. (Essay index reprint series) Contents.Contents.—Elisha Williams, 1694-1755.—Ezra Stiles, 1727-1795.—The young Silliman in Nelson's England, 1805-1806.—Edward J. Phelps, 1822-1900.—The second President Dwight, 1828-1916.—Henry Augustin Beer, 1847-1926. [LD6319.P3 1971] 72-156702 ISBN 0-8369-2329-4
1. Williams, Elisha, 1694-1775. 2. Stiles, Ezra, 1727-1795. 3. Silliman, Benjamin, 1779-1864. 4. Phelps, Edward John, 1822-1900. 5. Dwight, Timothy, 1828-1916. 6. Beers, Henry Augustin, 1847-1926. I. Title.
BIP

Williams, Emlyn, 1905-

EMLYN Williams, v. 12
by Richard Findlater [pseud.] New York, The Macmillan Company [c1956] 112p. illus. 23cm. (Theatre world monograph no. 8)
1. Williams, Emlyn, 1905- I. Bain, Kenneth Bruce Findlater, 1921-

Williams, Emlyn, 1905-—Biography.

WILLIAMS, Emlyn, 1905- 791'.092'4 B
Emlyn, an early autobiography, 1927-1933. New York, Viking Press [1974, c1973] viii, 424 p. 22 cm. A sequel to his George, an early autobiography. [PR6045.I52Z498 1974] 73-19324 ISBN 0-670-29295-8 10.00
1. Williams, Emlyn, 1905-—Biography. I. Title.

WILLIAMS, Emlyn, 1905- 791'.092'4 B
George; an early autobiography. New York, Random House [1962, c1961] 437 p. illus. 24 cm. Sequel: Emlyn; an early autobiography. [PR6045.I52Z5 1962] 61-13840
1. Williams, Emlyn, 1905- —Biography. I. Title.

Williams, Ephraim, 1715-1755.

WRIGHT, Wyllis Eaton, 1903- 378.744'1'0924 B
Colonel Ephraim Williams, a documentary life, by Wyllis E. Wright. Pittsfield, Mass., Berkshire County Historical Society, 1970. xvi, 180 p illus., geneal. table, maps. 24 cm. Bibliography: p. 165-166. [E199.W69W7] 73-137841 7.50
1. Williams, Ephraim, 1715-1755. 2. George, Lake, Battle of, 1755. I. Williams, Ephraim, 1715-1755. II. Title.

Williams, Evelyn (Lewis)

WILLIAMS, Evelyn (Lewis) 818.5
In the afterglow. Sketches by Anna Lewis Morton. New York, Vantage Press [1950] iv, 164 p. illus. 22 cm. Autobiographical. [CT275.W5655A3] 51-9046
I. Title.

Williams family.

WILLIAMS, Franklin Hubbard, 1834-1891. 929'.2'0973
Diary from 1852 to 1891 ... and certain pertinent addenda / Franklin H. Williams. Sunderland, Mass. : Williams Family, 1975. 95 p. : ill. ; 28 cm. Edited by J. L. Williams. [CS71.W72 1975] 75-325683
1. Williams family. 2. Williams, Franklin Hubbard, 1834-1891. I. Title.

Williams, G. Mennen, 1911-

MCNAUGHTON, Frank 923.273
Mennen Williams of Michigan, fighter for progress. Pref. by John D. Voelker. New York, Oceana Publications [c.1960] viii, 246p. front. 22cm. 60-7354 3.50
1. Williams, G. Mennen, 1911— I. Title.

MCNAUGHTON, Frank. 923.273
Mennen Williams of Michigan, fighter for progress. Pref. by John D. Voelker. New York, Oceana Publications [1960] 246p. illus. 22cm. [F570.W5M25] 60-7354
1. Williams, G. Mennen, 1911- I. Title.

Williams, George H., 1890-

WILLIAMS, George H., 1919- 625.1'00924 B
Life on a locomotive; the story of Buddy Williams, C & NW engineer, by George H. Williams. Berkeley, Calif., Howell-North Books [1971] 219 p. illus., maps, ports. 24 cm. [TF140.W47W5] 79-165591 ISBN 0-8310-7084-6 5.95
1. Williams, George H., 1890- I. Title.

Williams, George Walton, 1820-1903.

COULTER, Ellis Merton, 1890- 338'.092'4 B
George Walton Williams : the life of a Southern merchant and banker, 1820-1903 / by E. Merton Coulter. Athens, Ga. : Hibriten Press, 1976. ix, 320 p., [7] leaves of plates : ill. ; 25 cm. Includes index. Bibliography: p. [302]-311. [HC102.5.W54C68] 76-13734
1. Williams, George Walton, 1820-1903. 2. Businessmen—Southern states—Biography.

Williams, Gordon M

WILLIAMS, Gordon M 1934- FIC
The camp, by Gordon M. Williams. New York, Stein and Day [1966] 345 p. 22 cm. [PZ4.W7253Cam2] fic 66-22344
I. Title. BIP

Williams, Hank, 1923-1953.

CARESS, Jay. 784'.092'4 B
Hank Williams, country music's tragic king / Jay Caress. New York : Stein and Day, 1979. p. cm. Includes index. Bibliography: p. [ML420.W55C4] 78-23942 ISBN 0-8128-2583-7 : 9.95
1. Williams, Hank, 1923-1953. 2. Country musicians—United States—Biography.

MOORE, Thurston, comp. 784'.0924 B
Hank Williams, the legend. [Denver, Heather Enterprises, 1972] 63 p. illus. 28 cm. Bibliography: p. 63. [ML420.W55M7] 78-185425
1. Williams, Hank, 1923-1953. I. Title.

WILLIAMS, Hank. 784'.092'4 B
Living proof : an autobiography / Hank Williams, Jr., with Michael Bane. New York : Putnam, c1979. 222 p., [8] leaves of plates : ill. ; 24 cm. Includes index. [ML420.W55A3] 79-11741 ISBN 0-399-12369-5 : 10.95
1. Williams, Hank. 2. Country musicians—United States—Biography. I. Bane, Michael, joint author. II. Title. BIP

WILLIAMS, Roger M., 1934- 784'.0924 B
Sing a sad song; the life of Hank Williams [by] Roger M. Williams. [1st ed.] Garden City, N.Y., Doubleday, 1970. x, 275 p. illus., ports. 22 cm. [ML420.W55W5] 76-94944 5.95
1. Williams, Hank, 1923-1953. I. Title.

Williams, Hank, 1923-1953—Juvenile literature.

KRISHEF, Robert K. 784'.092'4' B
Hank Williams / Robert K. Krishef. Minneapolis : Lerner Publications Co., 1977,c1978. p. cm. (Country music library) Includes index. Discography: p. A biography of the country music perfomer who composed over 125 songs during his brief career. [ML3930.W54K7] 92 77-90157 ISBN 0-8225-1402-8 lib.bdg. : 4.95
1. Williams, Hank, 1923-1953—Juvenile literature. 2. Country musicians—United States—Biography—Juvenile literature. I. Title. BIP

Williams, James, b. 1790?

PROCTOR, Charles Hayden, 1848?-1890. 647'.2'0924 B
The life of James Williams, better known as Professor Jim, for half a century janitor of Trinity College. Hartford, Case, Lockwood & Brainard, 1873. [Tacoma, Wash., R. F. Crase, 1971] 79 p. illus. 17 cm. Title on cover: Professor Jim. Running title: Biography of Prof. Jim. [E185.97.W7P7 1971] 72-177924
1. Williams, James, b. 1790? 2. Trinity College, Hartford. I. Title. II. Title: Professor Jim.

Williams, James, 1834 (Jan. 8)-1887.

CALLAWAY, Llewellyn Link, 1868-1951. 364'.9786 B
Two true tales of the wild West. Oakland, Calif., Maud Gonne Press [1973] 130 p. illus. 22 cm. On spine: Vigilantes: two true tales of the wild West. Contents.Contents.—The life and death of Captain James Williams.—The life and death of Joseph Alfred Slade. [F731.C33 1973] 74-157017 3.95
1. Williams, James, 1834 (Jan. 8)-1887. 2. Slade, Joseph Alfred, 1829-1864. 3. Vigilance committees—Montana. 4. Montana—History. I. Callaway, Llewellyn Link, 1868-1951. The life and death of Joseph Alfred Slade. 1973. II. Title. III. Title: Vigilantes: two true tales of the wild West.

Williams, Jane, 1798-1884.

HOGG, Thomas Jefferson, 1792-1862. 821'.7 B
After Shelley; the letters of Thomas Jefferson Hogg to Jane Williams. Edited with a biographical introduction by Sylva Norman. [Folcroft, Pa.] Folcroft Library Editions [1973] p. Reprint of the 1934 ed. published by Oxford University Press, London, New York. [PR4793.H4A8 1973] 72-14369 ISBN 0-8414-1359-2 (lib. bdg.)
1. Hogg, Thomas Jefferson, 1792-1862. 2. Williams, Jane, 1798-1884. 3. Shelley, Percy Bysshe, 1792-1822. I. Williams, Jane, 1798-1884. II. Title.

HOGG, Thomas Jefferson, 1792-1862. 821'.7 B
After Shelley : the letters of Thomas Jefferson Hogg to Jane Williams / edited, with a biographical introd., by Sylva Norman. Folcroft, Pa. : Folcroft Library Editions, 1975. xlvi, 94 p. : port. ; 26 cm. Reprint of the 1934 ed. published by Oxford University Press, London. [PR4793.H4A8 1975] 75-11764 ISBN 0-8414-6286-0 lib. bdg. : 17.50
1. Hogg, Thomas Jefferson, 1792-1862. 2. Williams, Jane, 1798-1884. 3. Shelley, Percy Bysshe, 1792-1822. I. Norman, Sylva, 1901- II. Title.

Williams, John Alfred,

WILLIAMS, John Alfred, 1925- 813'.5'2 B
The most native of sons; a biography of Richard Wright, by John A. Williams. Dorothy Sterling, editorial consultant. [1st ed.] Garden City, N.Y., Doubleday, 1970. 141 p. port. 22 cm. "A perspective book." A biography of the black American author whose novels dealt with the social problems of the American Negro. [PS3545.R815Z93] 92 77-94947 3.95
I. Title.

Williams, John Howard, 1894-1958.

BROWN, Henry Clifton, Jr., ed. 922.673
J. Howard Williams, prophet of God and friend of man. Comp., ed. by H. C. Brown, Jr., Charles P. Johnson. San Antonio, Tex., Naylor [c.1963] xv, 147p. 22cm. Bibl. 63-23376 1.95
1. Williams, John Howard, 1894-1958. I. Johnson, Charles P., joint ed. II. Title.

BROWN, Henry Clifton, ed. 922.673
J. Howard Williams, prophet of God and friend of man. Compiled and edited by H. C. Brown, Jr. and Charles P. Johnson. San Antonio, Naylor Co. [c1963] xv, 147 p. 22 cm. Bibliographical footnotes. [BX6495.W49B7] 63-23376
1. Williams, John Howard, 1894-1958. I. Johnson, Charles P., joint ed. II. Title.

Williams, Joseph, 1780-1818

HOLT, Basil Fenelon, 1902- 922
Joseph Williams and the pioneer mission to the southeastern Bantu. [Lovedale, C. P.] Lovedale Press, 1954. vii, 186p. illus., ports., facsim. 20cm. [The Lovedale Historical series, no. 1] Bibliography: p.167-172. [BV3557.W53H6] 56-22641
1. Williams, Joseph, 1780-1818 2. Missions—Africa, South. I. Title.

Williams, Kate Barnwell,

WILLIAMS, Kate Barnwell, 1861-1950. 917.5'959'0380924 B
A post bellum autobiography of south west Florida. [1970?] 18 l. 29 cm. Typescript (carbon copy) Copy of the autobiography written in 1927 and given to Ianthe Bond Hebel, Daytona Beach, Fla. [CT275.W5663A3] 76-289468
I. Title.

Williams, Lacey Kirk, 1871-1940.

HORACE, Lillian B. 286'.133 B
"Crowned with glory and honor" : the life of Rev. Lacey Kirk Williams / by Lillian B. Horace ; edited by L. Venchael Booth. 1st ed. Hicksville, N.Y. : Exposition Press, c1978. 246 p. : port. ; 22 cm. [BX6455.W54H67] 78-100358 ISBN 0-682-48939-5 : 8.00
1. Williams, Lacey Kirk, 1871-1940. 2. Baptists—Clergy—Biography. 3. Clergy—United States—Biography. I. Booth, L. Venchael. II. Title.

Williams, Leila.

JENSEN, Margaret Adelia (Rounds) 1889- 917.8665033
Looking back, by Margaret Jensen, assisted by Leila Williams. Denver. Big Mountain Pr. [1966] 59p. illus., ports. 21cm. Autobiographical [CT275.J566A3] 66-8168 2.00 pap.,
1. Williams, Leila. I. Title.

Williams, Mark.

WILLIAMS, Laura Wineburg, 1928- 362.8'2'0926
Our runaway / L. Weinberg Williams. Valley Forge, PA : Judson Press, c1978. 64 p. ; 22 cm. [HV9105.T44W54] 78-15132 ISBN 0-8170-0813-6 : 2.95
1. Williams, Mark. 2. Juvenile delinquents—Texas—Biography. 3. Runaway youth—Texas—Biography. 4. Christian life—1960- I. Title. BIP

Williams, Mike, 1926-

WILLIAMS, Mike, 1926- 355.3'5 B
Major Mike / by Major Mike Williams, as told to Robin Moore. Westport, Conn. : Condor, 1978. 373 p. : ill. ; 18 cm. [DT962.76.W54A35] 78-71536 ISBN 0-89516-057-9 pbk. : 2.50
1. Williams, Mike, 1926- 2. Rhodesia, Southern. Army. Grey's Scouts—Biography. 3. Rhodesia, Southern—Politics and government—1965-1979. 4. National liberation movements—Rhodesia, Southern. 5. Soldiers of fortune—Rhodesia, Southern—Biography. 6. Soldiers of fortune—United States—Biography. I. Moore, Robin. II. Title. BIP

***Williams, Norman Lloyd**

*WILLIAMS, Norman Lloyd 942.0550924
Sir Walter Raleigh. Baltimore. Penguin [1965, c.1962] 275p. 18cm. (2147) 1.25 pap.,
I. Title.

Williams, Roger, 1604?-1683.

CARPENTER, Edmund James, 1845-1924. 974.5'02'0924 B
Roger Williams; a study of the life, times and character of a political pioneer. Freeport, N.Y., Books for Libraries Press [1972] xxxiv, 246 p. illus. 23 cm. Reprint of the 1909 ed., issued in the series: The Grafton historical series. [F82.W72 1972] 72-13 ISBN 0-8369-9955-X
1. Williams, Roger, 1604?-1683. I. Series: The Grafton historical series

EASTON, Emily. 974.5'02'0924 B
Roger Williams; prophet and pioneer. New York, AMS Press [1969] ix, 399 p. port. 22 cm. Reprint of the 1930 ed. Bibliography: p. [379]-380. [F82.W737 1969b] 76-101266
1. Williams, Roger, 1604?-1683.

EASTON, Emily. 974.5'02'0924 B
Roger Williams, prophet and pioneer. Boston, Houghton Mifflin, 1930. St. Clair Shores, Mich., Scholarly Press, 1972. ix, 399 p. port. 21 cm. Bibliography: p. [379]-380. [F82.W737 1972] 78-144994 ISBN 0-403-00793-3
1. Williams, Roger, 1604?-1683. BIP

EASTON, Emily. 974.5*092*4
Roger Williams; prophet and pioneer. Freeport, N.Y., Books for Libraries Press [1969] ix, 399 p. maps (on lining papers), port. 23 cm. (Select bibliographies reprint series) Reprint of the 1930 ed. Bibliography: p. [377]-380. [F82.W737 1969] 71-102235
1. Williams, Roger, 1604?-1683.

EATON, Jeanette 923.273
Lone journey; the life of Roger Williams. by Jeanette Eaton, illus. by Woodi Ishmael. New York, Harcourt, [1966, c.1944] 266p. illus. 18cm. (Voyager bk., AVB 40) [F82.W72] .75 pap.,
1. Williams, Roger, 1604?-1683. I. Title.

ERNST, James Emanuel. 320.10924
The political thought of Roger Williams, by James E. Ernst. Port Washington, N.Y., Kennikat Press [1966] iii, 229 p. 22 cm. Reprint of the 1929 ed., which was first issued as thesis, University of Washington, 1926. Bibliography: p. 211-229. [JC153.E7 1966] 66-25909
1. Williams, Roger, 1604?-1683. 2. State, The. I. Title.

ERNST, James Emanuel. 974.5'02'0924 B
Roger Williams, New England firebrand, by James Ernst. New York, AMS Press [1969] xiv, 538 p. port. 23 cm. Reprint of the 1932 ed. Bibliographical footnotes. [F82.W757 1969] 76-90097
1. Williams, Roger, 1604?-1683. 2. Rhode Island—History—Colonial period, ca. 1600-1775. I. Title.

GARRETT, John, 1920- 974.5'02'0924
Roger Williams, witness beyond Christendom, 1603-1683. [New York] Macmillan [1970] x, 306 p. map. 21 cm. Bibliography: p. 279-289. [F82.W7732] 76-109449
1. Williams, Roger, 1604?-1683. I. Title.

MILLER, Perry, 1905- 923.273
Roger Williams: his contribution to the American tradition. [1st ed.] Indianapolis, Lobbs-Merrill [1953] 273p. 23cm. (Makers of the American tradition series) [F82.W788] 53-8874
1. Williams, Roger, 1604?-1683. I. Title.

PETERSON, Helen Stone. 974.5'02'0924 B
A colony leader: Roger Williams. Illustrated by Ray Burns. Champaign, Ill., Garrard Pub. Co. [1968] 64 p. illus., map, ports. 24 cm. (Colony leaders) Part of the illustrative matter is colored. A biography of the Englishman whose belief in religious freedom and separation of church and state led him to establish the colony of Rhode Island and Providence Plantations. [F82.W7914] 92 AC 68
1. Williams, Roger, 1604?-1683. I. Burns, Ray, illus. II. Title.

STRAUS, Oscar Solomon, 1850-1926. 322'.1'0924 B
Roger Williams; the pioneer of religious liberty. With an interpretation by R. E. E. Harkness and an address by Charles Evans Hughes. Freeport, N.Y., Books for Libraries Press [1970] lx, 257 p. 23 cm. Includes bibliographical references. [F82.W797 1970] 76-137385 ISBN 0-8369-5586-2
1. Williams, Roger, 1604?-1683. 2. Rhode Island—History—Colonial period, ca. 1600-1775. I. Harkness, Reuben Elmore Ernest, 1884- II. Hughes, Charles Evans, 1862-1948. BIP

WINSLOW, Ola Elizabeth. 923.273
Master Roger Williams, a biography. New York, Macmillan, 1957. 328 p. illus. 22 cm. Includes bibliography. [F82.W692] 57-10016
1. Williams, Roger, 1604?-1683.

WINSLOW, Ola Elizabeth. 974.5'02'0924 B
Master Roger Williams, a biography. New York, Octagon Books, 1973 [c1957] xi, 328 p. illus. 23 cm. Original ed. published by Macmillan, New York. Bibliography: p. 313-316. [F82.W855 1973] 73-8608 ISBN 0-374-98682-7 12.50 (lib. bdg.)
1. Williams, Roger, 1604?-1683.

Williams, Roger, 1604?-1683—Juvenile literature.

COVEY, Cyclone 974.5020924
The gentle radical; a biography of Roger Williams. New York, Macmillan [c.1966] 273p. 21cm. Bibl. p5.95 [F82.W727] 66-19094
1. Williams, Roger, 1604-1683. I. Title.

JACOBS, William Jay. 974.5'02'0924 B
Roger Williams [by] W. J. Jacobs. New York, F. Watts, 1975. 55 p. illus. 26 cm. (A Visual biography) Bibliography: p. 51. A biography of the founder of Rhode Island, often called the "father of religious liberty in America." [F82.W779] 92 74-12280 ISBN 0-531-02784-8 4.90 (lib. bdg.)
1. Williams, Roger, 1604?-1683—Juvenile literature. I. Title. BIP

Williams, Rose Berthenia Clay

WILLIAMS, Rose Berthenia Clay 920.7
Black and white orange. New York, Vantage [1962, c.1961] 135p. 2.75 bds.,
I. Title.

WILLIAMS, Rose Berthenia Clay, 1910- 920.7
Black and white Orange: an autobiography. [1st ed.] New York, Vantage Press [c1961] 135 p. 21 cm. [LA2317] A62
I. Title.

Williams, Sally, American slave.

AUNT Sally; 301.45'22'0924 B
or, The cross the way of freedom. A narrative of the slave-life and purchase of the mother of Rev. Isaac Williams, of Detroit, Michigan. Cincinnati, American Reform Tract and Book Society, 1858. Miami, Fla., Mnemosyne Pub. Co. [1969] 216 p. illus. 23 cm. [E444.W79 1969] 75-89438
1. Williams, Sally, American slave. 2. Slavery in the United States—North Carolina. 3. Slavery in the United States—Alabama.

Williams, Samuel May, 1795-1858.

HENSON, Margaret Swett, 1924- 976.4'05'0924 B
Samuel May Williams, early Texas entrepreneur / by Margaret Swett Henson. 1st ed. College Station : Texas A & M University Press, c1976. xvi, 190 p., [7] leaves of plates : ill. ; 24 cm. Includes index. Bibliography: p. [173]-181. [F390.W73H46] 75-40894 ISBN 0-89096-009-7 : 10.00
1. Williams, Samuel May, 1795-1858.

ROSENBERG Library, Galveston. 923.373
Samuel May Williams, 1795-1858; biography. Calendar to Samuel May Williams papers compiled by Ruth G. Nichols and S. W. Lifflander. Galveston, Tex., Rosenberg Library Press [1956] xxx, 331p. port. 24cm. Bibliographical footnotes. [CD3539.G3R6] 57-16726
1. Williams, Samuel May, 1795-1858. 2. Texas —Hist.—Sources. I. Nichols, Ruth Gencvieve, 1882- II. Title.

Williams, Samuel Wells, 1812-1884.

WILLIAMS, Frederick Wells, 1857-1928. 327.51'073
The life and letters of Samuel Wells Williams, LL.D., missionary, diplomatist, sinologue. Wilmington, Del., Scholarly Resources [1972] vi, 490 p. port. 23 cm. Reprint of the 1889 ed. published by G. P. Putnam's Sons, New York. [DS763.W5W5 1972] 72-79841 ISBN 0-8420-1355-5
1. Williams, Samuel Wells, 1812-1884. 2. Missions—China. 3. Taiping Rebellion, 1850-1864. I. Title.

WILLIAMS, Frederick Wells, 1857-1928. 327.51'073
The life and letters of Samuel Wells Williams, LL.D., missionary, diplomatist, sinologue. Wilmington, Del., Scholarly Resources [1972] vi, 490 p. port. 23 cm. Reprint of the 1889 ed. published by G. P. Putnam's Sons, New York. [DS763.W5W5 1972] 72-79841 ISBN 0-8420-1355-5
1. Williams, Samuel Wells, 1812-1884. 2. Missions—China. 3. Taiping Rebellion, 1850-1864. I. Title.

Williams, Slim, 1881 or 2-

MORENUS, Richard. 917.98
Alaska sourdough, the story of Slim Williams. Chicago, Rand McNally [1956] 278 p. 21 cm. [F909.W694M6] 56-11019
1. Williams, Slim, 1881 or 2- 2. Frontier and pioneer life—Alaska. 3. Alaska—Description and travel—1896-1959. I. Title.

Williams, Tennessee, 1911-

LEAVITT, Richard F. 812'.5'4 B
The world of Tennessee Williams / by Richard Freeman Leavitt ; with an introd. by Tennessee Williams. New York : Putnam, c1977. 168 p. : ill. ; 31 cm. Includes index. Bibliography: p. 163-164. [PS3545.I5365Z735 1977] 76-28473 ISBN 0-399-11773-3 : 20.00
1. Williams, Tennessee, 1911- 2. Dramatists, American—20th century—Biography. I. Williams, Tennessee, 1911- II. Title. BIP

TISCHLER, Nancy Marie (Patterson) 928.1
Tennessee Williams: rebellious Puritan. New York, Citadel [1965, c.1961] 319p. 21cm. Bibl. (C-178) [PS3545.I5365Z85] 1.95 pap.,
1. Williams, Tennessee, 1911- I. Title.

TISCHLER, Nancy Marie Patterson. 928.1
Tennessee Williams: rebellious Puritan. New York, Citadel Press [1961] 319 p. 22 cm. [PS3545.I5365Z85] 61-16975
1. Williams, Tennessee, 1911-

Williams, Tennessee, 1911- —Biography.

WILLIAMS, Tennessee, 1911- 812'.5'4 B
Memoirs / Tennessee Williams. 1st ed. Garden City, N.Y. : Doubleday, 1975. xix, 264 p., [32] leaves of plates : ill. ; 24 cm. Includes index. [PS3545.I5365Z52] 74-1523 ISBN 0-385-00573-3 : 8.95
1. Williams, Tennessee, 1911- —Biography.

Williams, Tennessee, 1911- —Correspondence.

WILLIAMS, Tennessee, 1911- 812'.5'4 B
Tennessee William's Letters to Donald Windham, 1940-1965 / edited and with comments by Donald Windham. New York : Holt, Rinehart and Winston, 1977. xi, 333 p., [3] leaves of plates : facsims ; 24 cm. Includes bibliographical references and index. [PS3545.I5365Z548 1977] 77-73863 ISBN 0-03-022636-8 : 10.00
1. Williams, Tennessee, 1911- —Correspondence. 2. Windham, Donald—Correspondence. 3. Authors, American—20th century—Correspondence. I. Windham, Donald. II. Title. III. Title: Letters to Donald Windham, 1940-1965. BIP

Williams, Tennessee, 1911- —Journeys—Morocco—Tangier.

CHOUKRI, Mohamed, 1935- 812'.5'4 B
Tennessee Williams in Tangier / Mohamed Choukri ; translated from the Arabic by Paul Bowles ; foreword by Gavin Lambert ; note by Tennessee Williams. 1st ed. Santa Barbara, : Cadmus Editions, 1979. 85 p. ; port. ; 18 cm. [PS3545.I5365Z613] 78-60367 ISBN 0-932274-00-5 : 15.00 ISBN 0-932274-01-3 pbk. : 6.00
1. Williams, Tennessee, 1911- —Journeys—Morocco—Tangier. 2.

Dramatists, American—20th century—Biography. 3. Tangier—Social life and customs. I. Title. BIP

TISCHLER, Nancy Marie (Patterson) 928.1
Tennessee Williams: rebellious Puritan. New York, Citadel Press [1961] 319 p. 22 cm. [PS3545.I5365Z85] 61-16975
1. Williams, Tennessee, 1914- I. Title.

Williams, Theodore Samuel, 1918-

LINN, Ed 927.96357
Ted Williams, The eternal kid. New York, Bartholomew House [c.1961] 175p. (Sport magazine lib. no. 3) 61-4116 .50 pap.,
1. Williams, Theodore Samuel, 1918- I. Title. II. Series.

LINN, Ed. 927.96357
Ted Williams, The Eternal Kid. New York, Bartholomew House [1961] 175p. 18cm. (Sport magazine library no. 3) [GV865.W5L5] 61-4116
1. Williams, Theodore Samuel, 1918- I. Title. II. Series.

POPE, Edwin. 796.357'0924 B
Ted Williams. Englewood Cliffs, N.J., Prentice-Hall, [1970] vi, 167 p. illus., ports. 22 cm. (The Golden year, 1957) [GV865.W5P6] 70-93101 5.95
1. Williams, Theodore Samuel, 1918-

ROBINSON, Ray, 1920- 927.96357
Ted Williams. New York, Putnam [1962] 191p. illus. 21cm. [GV865.W5R6] 62-10981
1. Williams, Theodore Samuel, 1918- I. Title.

SCHOOR, Gene. 927.96357
The Ted Williams story, by Gene Schoor, with Henry Gilfond. New York, J. Messner [1954] 188 p. illus. 22 cm. [GV865.W5S35] 54-10594
1. Williams, Theodore Samuel, 1918-

WILLIAMS, Theodore Samuel, 1918- 796.357'0924 B
My turn at Bat: the story of my life, by Ted Williams with John Underwood. New York, Simon and Schuster [1969] 288 p. illus., ports. 23 cm. [GV865.W5A3] 78-75869 5.95
I. Underwood, John, 1934- II. Title.

Williams, Thomas E., 1894-

CURTISS, Richard D. 686.2'092'4 B
Thomas E. Williams & the Fine Arts Press, by Richard D. Curtiss. Los Angeles, Dawson's Book Shop, 1973. xv, 119 p. ports., facsims. 25 cm. [Z232.W69C87] 73-85053 ISBN 0-87093-091-5
1. Williams, Thomas E., 1894- 2. Fine Arts Press. I. Title. BIP

Williams, Thomas, 1737-1802.

HARRIS, John Raymond 338.4767330942
The copper king; a biography of Thomas Williams of Llandan [Toronto] Univ. of Toronto Pr., 1964. xviii, 194p. illus., port. 24cm. Bibl. 64-55416 price unreported
1. Williams, Thomas, 1737-1802. 2. Copper industry and trade—Gt. Brit. I. Title.

Williams, Walter, 1864-1935.

RUCKER, Frank Warren. 920.5
Walter Williams, by Frank W. Rucker. Columbia, Missourian Pub. Association, 1964. xiv, 221 p. illus., facsims., ports. 24 cm. Bibliography: p. [216]-221. [PN4874.W634R8] 64-20657
1. Williams, Walter, 1864-1935. 2. Journalism — Missouri. I. Title.

Williams, William Carlos, 1883-1963.

BRINNIN, John Malcolm, 1916- 811.52
William Carlos Williams. Minneapolis, University of Minnesota Press [1963] 48 p. 21 cm. (University of Minnesota. Pamphlets on American writers, no. 24) Includes bibliography. [PS3545.I544Z58 1963] 63-62710
1. Williams, William Carlos, 1883-1963.

WILLIAMS, William Carlos, 1883- 928.1
The autobiography of William Carlos Williams [New York] New Directions [1967, c.1951] 402p. 21cm. (NDP223) [PS3545.I544Z5] 6.50; 1.95 pap.,
I. Title.
Distributed by Lippincott, Philadelphia. BIP

WILLIAMS, William Carlos, 1883- 928.1
Selected letters. Edited with an introd. by John C. Thirlwall. New York, McDowell, Obolensky [1957] 347p. 22cm. [PS3545.I544Z53] 57-12112
1. Authors— Correspondence, Reminiscences, etc. I. Title.

Williams, William Carlos, 1883-1963—Biography.

WHITTEMORE, Reed, 1919- 811'.5'2
William Carlos Williams, poet from Jersey / Reed Whittemore. Boston : Houghton-Mifflin, 1975. xii, 404 p., [8] leaves of plates : ill. ; 24 cm. Includes index. Bibliography: p. [389]-393. [PS3545.I544Z95] 75-20274 ISBN 0-395-20735-5 : 10.95
1. Williams, William Carlos, 1883-1963—Biography. I. Title.

Williams, William Carlos, 1883-1963—Interviews.

WILLIAMS, William Carlos, 1883-1963. 818'.5'209 B
Interviews with William Carlos Williams : "speaking straight head" / edited with an introduction by Linda Welshimer Wagner. New York : New Directions, 1976. xix, 108 p. ; 21 cm. (A New Directions book) Includes bibliographical references and index. [PS3545.I544Z526 1976] 76-14797 ISBN 0-8112-0620-3 : 8.50 ISBN 0-8112-0621-1 pbk. : 2.95
1. Williams, William Carlos, 1883-1963—Interviews. I. Wagner, Linda Welshimer. II Title.

Williams, William Frank, 1877-1963.

BRITTS, Maurice W., 1928- 977.6'05'0924 B
Billy Williams : Minnesota's Assistant Governor / by Maurice W. Britts. Saint Cloud, Minn. : North Star Press, c1977. xii, 198 p., [5] leaves of plates : ill. ; 23 cm. [F606.W54B74] 78-104826 ISBN 0-87839-025-1 : 7.95
1. Williams, William Frank, 1877-1963. 2. Minnesota—Governors—Staff—Biography. 3. Minnesota—Politics and government—1858-1950. I. Title. BIP

Williams, William Sherley, 1787-1849.

FAVOUR, Alpheus Hoyt, 1880-1939. 923.973
Old Bill Williams, mountain man. With an introd. by Willian Brandon. [New ed.] Norman, University of Oklahoma Press [1962] 234 p. illus. 24 cm. Includes bibliography. [F592.W672 1962] 62-10767
1. Williams, William Sherley, 1787-1849. I. Title. BIP

JOHNSON, Enid, 1892- 923.973
Bill Williams: mountain man. Decorations by Richard Bennett. New York, Messner [1952] 174 p. illus. 22 cm. Includes bibliography. [F592.W674] 52-12729
1. Williams, William Sherley, 1787-1849.

Williams, William, 1727-1791.

WILLIAMS, John Francis, 1894- 759.13
The ancestor; the world of William Williams. Philadelphia, Dorrance [1971] xv, 184 p. illus., geneal. table, ports. 22 cm. Bibliography: p. 180-184. [ND237.W717W5] 79-137848 ISBN 0-8059-1517-6 5.00
1. Williams, William, 1727-1791. I. Title.

Williams, William, 1731-1811.

STARK, Bruce P. 973.3'13'0924 B
Connecticut signer, William Williams / Bruce P. Stark. Chester, Conn. : Pequot Press, 1975. 87 p. ; 23 cm. (Connecticut bicentennial series ; 12) "A Publication of the American Revolution Bicentennial Commission of Connecticut." Includes bibliographical references. [E302.6.W55S7] 75-27801 ISBN 0-87106-061-2 pbk. : 2.50
1. Williams, William, 1731-1811. I. Title. II. Series.

Williamsburg, Va.—Biography.

DAVIS, Burke. 975.5'4252'020922
A Williamsburg galaxy. Williamsburg, Va., Colonial Williamsburg; distributed by Holt, Rinehart and Winston, New York, [1968] 232 p. ports. 24 cm. (Williamsburg in America series, 6) "A note on sources": p. 229-232. [F234.W7W7 vol. 6] 68-12135 4.95
1. Williamsburg, Va.—Biography. I. Title. II. Series. BIP

Williamson, Charles, 1757-1808.

COWAN, Helen I. 974.7'92'03 B
Charles Williamson, Genesee promoter; friend of Anglo-American rapprochement [by] Helen I. Cowan. With a new foreword by Blake McKelvey. [1st ed.] Clifton [N.J.] A. M. Kelley, 1973 [c1941] 327, [22], 24, [22] p. 22 cm. (Library of early American business and industry, 45) Reprint of the ed. published by the Rochester Historical Society, Rochester, N.Y., which was issued as v. 19 of the society's Publication fund series. Includes bibliographical references. [F127.G2C72 1973] 68-55516 ISBN 0-678-00862-0 16.50
1. Williamson, Charles, 1757-1808. 2. Genesee region, N.Y. I. Title. II. Series: Rochester Historical Society, Rochester, N.Y. Publications. Publication fund series, v. 19.

Williamson, Ellen.

WILLIAMSON, Ellen. 917.3'04'91
When we went first class / Ellen Williamson. 1st ed. Garden City, N.Y. : Doubleday, 1977. xii, 250 p. ; 22 cm. [E169.W64] 77-72417 ISBN 0-385-12374-4 : 8.95
1. Williamson, Ellen. 2. United States—Description and travel—1920-1940. 3. United States—Social life and customs—1918-1945. I. Title. BIP

Williamson, John,

WILLIAMSON, John, 1902- 335.43'0924 B
Dangerous Scot; the life and work of an American "undesirable". [1st ed.] New York, International Publishers [1969] 221 p. port. 21 cm. [HX84.W53A3] 74-86082 5.95
I. Title.

Williamson. John Gustavus Adolphus, 1793-1840.

DE GRUMMOND, Jane Lucas, 1905- 923.287
Envoy to Caracas; the story of John G. A. Williamson, nineteenth-century diplomat. Baton Rouge, Louisiana State University Press [1951] xx, 228 p. illus., map (on lining papers) 23 cm. "Essays on authorities": p. [211]-217. [E183.7.W73D4] 51-11504
1. Williamson. John Gustavus Adolphus, 1793-1840. 2. Venezuela—Soc. life & cust. I. Title.

Williamson, Joseph,

WILLIAMSON, Joseph, 1895- 922.342
Father Joe, the autobiography of Joseph Williamson. Nashville, Abingdon [c.1963] 207p. illus., ports. 21cm. 64-14621 3.95
I. Title.

WILLIAMSON, Joseph, 1895- 922.342
Father Joe, the autobiography of Joseph Williamson. New York, Abingdon Press [c1963] 207 p. illus., ports. 21 cm. [BX5199.W66A3] 64-14621
I. Title.

Williamson, Peter, 1730-1799.

WILLIAMSON, Peter, 1730-1799. 973'.04'97 S
French and Indian cruelty / Peter Williamson. New York : Garland Pub., 1978. iv, 103 p. ; 23 cm. (The Garland library of narratives of North American Indian captivities ; v. 9) Reprint of the 1757 ed. printed for the author by N. Nickson, York. Issued with the reprint of the 1758 ed. of the author's French and Indian cruelty. New York, 1978. The reprint of the 1796 ed. of the author's Sufferings of Peter Williamson. New York, 1978. The reprint of the 1761 ed. of Thomson, J. The travels and surprising adventures of John Thomson. New York, 1978. The reprint of the 1784 ed. of Gatenby, W. A full and particular account of the sufferings of William Gatenby. New York, 1978. [E85.G2 vol. 9] [E199] 973'.04'97 78-16987 ISBN 0-8240-1633-5 : 29.50
1. Williamson, Peter, 1730-1799. 2. United States—History—French and Indian War, 1755-1763—Personal narratives. 3. Indians of North America—Captivities. 4. Oswego, Fort, Capture of, 1756. 5. Pennsylvania—Biography. I. Title. II. Series.

Willig, George

WILLIG, George. 796.5'22'0924 B
Going it alone / by George Willig and Drew Bergman. 1st ed. Garden City, N.Y. : Doubleday, 1979. 158 p. : ill. ; 27 cm. [GV199.92.W54A33] 78-24839 ISBN 0-385-14725-2 : 12.95
1. Willig, George. 2. New York (City). World Trade Center. 3. Mountaineers—United States—Biography. I. Bergman, Drew, joint author. II. Title. BIP

Willis, Nathaniel Parker, 1806-1867.

BEERS, Henry Augustin, 1847-1926. 818'.3'09 B
Nathaniel Parker Willis. New York, AMS Press [1969] viii, 365 p. port. 23 cm. Reprint of the 1885 ed. Bibliography: p. [353]-356. [PS3326.B4 1969] 70-89458
1. Willis, Nathaniel Parker, 1806-1867. I. Title. BIP

SYMONDS, Emily Morse, d.1936. 920.042
Little memoirs of the nineteenth century. Freeport, N.Y., Books for Libraries Press [1969] ix, 375 p. ports. 23 cm. (Essay index reprint series) Reprint of the 1902 ed. Contents.Contents.—Benjamin Robert Haydon.—Lady Morgan (Sydney Owenson)—Nathaniel Parker Willis.—Lady Hester Stanhope.—Prince Puckler-Muskau in England.—William and Mary Howitt. [DA531.1.S9 1969] 70-86787 ISBN 8-369-11970-
1. Puckler-Muskau, Hermann Ludwig Heinrich, furst von, 1785-1871. 2. Morgan, Sydney (Owenson) lady, 1783?-1859. 3. Haydon, Benjamin Robert, 1786-1846. 4.

Willis, Nathaniel Parker, 1806-1867. 5. Stanhope, Hester Lucy, Lady, 1776-1839. 6. Howitt, William, 1792-1879. 7. Howitt, Mary (Botham) 1799-1888. I. Title. **BIP**

Willis, Thomas, 1621-1675.

ISLER, Hansruedi. 610'.924 (B)
Thomas Willis, 1621-1675: doctor and scientist. [Translated by the author] New York, Hafner Pub. Co., 1968. xiii, 235 p. illus., ports. 22 cm. Translation of Thomas Willis; ein Wegbereiter der modernen Medizin. "Willis' works": p. 199-200. Bibliography: p. 201-217. [R489.W72I83] 67-25769
1. Willis, Thomas, 1621-1675. I. Title. **BIP**

Willison, Marilyn Murray.

WILLISON, Marilyn Murray. 301.42'84'0924 B
Diary of a divorced mother / Marilyn Murray Willison. 1st ed. New York : Wyden Books, c1980. p. cm. [HQ834.W6253] 79-66071 ISBN 0-87223-577-7 : 9.95
1. Willison, Marilyn Murray. 2. Divorcees—United States—Biography. 3. Single parents—United States—Biography. I. Title. **BIP**

Williston, Samuel Wendell, 1851-1918.

SHOR, Elizabeth Noble. 560.9 B
Fossils and flies; the life of a compleat scientist Samuel Wendell Williston (1851-1918). [1st ed.] Norman, University of Oklahoma Press [1971] xiv, 285 p. illus., ports. 23 cm. Bibliography: p. 277-279. [QE707.W55S5] 77-145503 ISBN 0-8061-0949-1
1. Williston, Samuel Wendell, 1851-1918. I. Title. **BIP**

Willkie, Wendell Lewis, 1892-1944.

BARNARD, Ellsworth, 1907- 973.9170924 B
Wendell Willkie, fighter for freedom. Marquette, Northern Michigan University Press [1966] xi, 611 p. ports. 24 cm. Bibliographical references included in "Notes" (p. 505-596) [E748.W7B3] 66-19668
1. Willkie, Wendell Lewis, 1892-1944.

DILLON, Mary Earhart. 973.917'0924 B
Wendell Willkie, 1892-1944. New York, Da Capo Press, 1972 [c1952] 378 p. 22 cm. (Franklin D. Roosevelt and the era of the New Deal) Bibliography: p. 357-370. [E748.W7D5 1972] 71-39040 ISBN 0-306-70456-0
1. Willkie, Wendell Lewis, 1892-1944. I. Title. II. Series.

DILLON, Mary Earhart. 923.373
Wendell Willkie, 1892-1944. [1st ed.] Philadelphia, Lippincott [1952] 378 p. illus. 22 cm. [E748.W7D5] 52-5091
1. Willkie, Wendell Lewis, 1892-1944.

RUKEYSER, Muriel, 1913- 923.373
One life. New York, Simon and Schuster, 1957. 330 p. 24 cm. [E748.W7R8] 57-5680
1. Willkie, Wendell Lewis, 1892-1944. I. Title.

SEVERN, William. 973.917'0924 B
Toward one world; the life of Wendell Willkie, by Bill Severn. New York, I. Washburn [1967] 230 p. 21 cm. Bibliography: p. 223-224. [E748.W7S4] 67-22010
1. Willkie, Wendell Lewis, 1892-1944. I. Title.

STAHL, Edward M. 329'.023'730917
We want Willkie; a pictorial guide to the campaign memorabilia of Wendell L. Willkie, by Edward M. Stahl. With a foreword by Philip H. Willkie. Trenton, N.J., Independence Pub. Co. [1972] 83 p. illus. 24 cm. [E748.W7S72] 72-95282
1. Willkie, Wendell Lewis, 1892-1944. 2. Presidents—United States—Election—1940. 3. Campaign paraphernalia—United States. I. Title.

Wills, Bob, 1905-1975.

LATHAM, Jimmy. 785'.092'4 B
The life of Bob Wills : the king of western swing / by Jimmy Latham. Odessa, Tex. : Latham Pub., [1974] 129 p. : ill. ; 22 cm. Includes discographies. [ML410.W7138L4] 74-182864
1. Wills, Bob, 1905-

TOWNSEND, Charles R. 785'.092'4 B
San Antonio Rose : the life and music of Bob Wills / Charles R. Townsend ; with a discography and filmusicography by Bob Pinson. Urbana : University of Illinois Press, c1976. xv, 395 p. [44] leaves of plates : ill. ; 26 cm. (Music in American life) Includes index. Bibliography: p. 325-335. [ML410.W7138T7] 75-45431 ISBN 0-252-00470-1 : 12.50
1. Wills, Bob, 1905-1975. I. Title. **BIP**

Wills—Maine.

SARGENT, William Mitchell, 1848-1891, comp. 929'.3741
Maine wills, 1640-1760. Compiled and edited with notes by William M. Sargent. Baltimore, Genealogical Pub. Co., 1972. xii, 953 p. 22 cm. "The Maine Historical Society designated ... [W. M. Sargent] to compile, copy and edit the work." Reprint of the 1887 ed. [F18.S24 1972] 72-5681 ISBN 0-8063-0516-9
1. Wills—Maine. I. Maine Historical Society. II. Title.

Wills, Maury, 1932-

WILLS, Maury, 1932- 796.357'092'4 B
How to steal a pennant / by Maury Willis, with Don Freeman. New York : Putnam, c1976. 252 p. ; 22 cm. Autobiographical. [GV865.W55A28 1976] 75-34442 8.95
1. Wills, Maury, 1932- 2. Baseball. I. Freeman, Don, 1922- joint author. II. Title. **BIP**

Wills—New Castle Co., Del.

NATIONAL Society of the Colonial Dames of America. Delaware. Historical Research Committee. 929.3
A calendar of Delaware wills, New Castle County, 1682-1800. Abstracted and compiled by the Historical Research Committee of the Colonial Dames of Delaware. Baltimore, Genealogical Pub. Co., 1969. 218 p. 23 cm. Reprint of the 1911 ed. [F172.N5N2 1969] 71-76816
1. Wills—New Castle Co., Del. I. Title.

Wills—New York (State)

FERNOW, Berthold, 1837-1908, comp. 929.3
Calendar of wills on file and recorded in the offices of the Clerk of the Court of Appeals, of the County Clerk at Albany, and of the Secretary of State, 1626-1836. Baltimore, Genealogical Pub. Co., 1967. xv, 657 p. 24 cm. Cover title: New York calendar of wills, 1626-1836. Reprint of the 1896 ed. "Under the auspices of the Colonial Dames of the State of New York." [F118.F36] 67-28621
1. Wills—New York (State) 2. New York (State)—Geneal. I. New York (State) Court of Appeals. II. Albany County. N.Y. III. New York (State) Secretary of State. IV. Title. V. Title: New York calendar of wills. 1626-1836.

Wills—North Carolina—Indexes.

JOHNSON, William Perry, 1918- 929.3'756
Index to North Carolina wills, 1663-1900, compiled and edited by William Perry Johnson Raleigh, N.C. [1963]- v. map. 28 cm. Cover title. Compiled from records in the office of the Secretary of State, North Carolina, and in the North Carolina State Dept. of Archives. Contents.Contents.—v. 1. Alamance, Alexander, Alleghany, Anson, Ashe, and Beaufort Counties.—v. 2. Bertie, Bladen, Brunswick, Buncombe, and Burke Counties.—v. 3. Cabarrus, Caldwell, Camden, Carteret, Caswell, Catawba, Chatham, and Cherokee Counties. [F262.A15J6] 72-21599 10.00 per vol.
1. Wills—North Carolina—Indexes. I. North Carolina. Secretary of State. II. North Carolina. State Dept. of Archives and History. III. Title.

Willson, Meredith, 1902-

WILLSON, Meredith, 1902- 780'.92'4 B
And there I stood with my piccolo / Meredith Willson. Westport, Conn. : Greenwood Press, 1975, c1948. 255 p. : music ; 23 cm. Reprint of the ed. published by Doubleday, Garden City, N.Y. [ML422.W63A3 1975] 75-26870 ISBN 0-8371-8486-X lib.bdg. : 13.50
1. Willson, Meredith, 1902- 2. Musicians—Correspondence, reminiscences, etc. I. Title. **BIP**

WILLSON, Meredith, 1902- 782.81
"But he doesn't know the territory." New York, Putnam [1959] 190 p. 21 cm. Autobiographical. [ML410.W714A3] 59-13376
I. Title.

WILLSON, Meredith, 1902- 927.8
Eggs I have laid. [1st ed.] New York, Holt [1955] 185 p. 21 cm. [ML422.W63A32] 55-9878
1. Musicians—Correspondence, reminiscences, etc. I. Title.

Willstatter, Richard Martin,

WILLSTATTER, Richard Martin, 1872-1942 925.4
From my life; the memoirs of Richard Willstatter. Tr. from German ed. by Lilli S. Hornig. Ed. in the orig. German by Arthur Stoll. New York, W. A. Benjamin, 1965[c.1958] xiii, 461p. illus., ports. 24cm. First pub. in 1949. Bibl. [QD22.W49A313] 65-12063 8.75
I. Title.

Wilmot, David, 1814-1868.

GOING, Charles Buxton, 1863- 973.60924 B
David Wilmot, free-soiler; a biography of the great advocate of the Wilmot proviso. Gloucester, Mass., P. Smith, 1966. xvii, 787 p. port. 22 cm. Bibliographical footnotes. [E340.W65G6 1966] 66-9507
1. Wilmot, David, 1814-1868. **BIP**

Wilsingham, Francis,Sir 1530?1590.

READ, Conyers, 1881-1959 942.05'5'0924(B)
Mr. Secretary Walsingham and the policy of Queen Elizabeth. [Hamden, Conn.] Archon 1967 3v. illus. 22cm. Reprint of the 1925 ed. Bibl. [DA358.W2R42] 67-19513 30.00 set
1. Wilsingham, Francis,Sir 1530?1590. 2. Elizabeth, Queen of England, 1533-1603. 3. Gt. Brit.—Pol. & govt.—1558-1603. I. Title. **BIP**

Wilson, Alexander, 1766-1813.

PLATE, Robert. 598.20924 B
Alexander Wilson, wanderer in the wilderness. Illus. from Wilson's American ornithology. New York, D. McKay Co., 1966. viii, 216 p. plates, port. 21 cm. Bibliography: p. 209-211. [QL31.W7P5] 66-11348
1. Wilson, Alexander, 1766-1813.

Wilson, Amy V.

WILSON, Amy V. 610.730924
A nurse in the Yukon [by] Amy V. Wilson. New York, Dodd, Mead [1966] 209 p. illus., map. 21 cm. First published in 1965 under title: No man stands alone. [RT37.W53A3 1966] 66-27940
I. Title. **BIP**

Wilson, Angus, 1913-

HALIO, Jay L v. 12
Angus Wilson. Edinburgh, Oliver & Boyd [1964] 120 p. (Writers and critics, 037) 65-36827
1. Wilson, Angus, 1913- I. Title.

Wilson, Arthur

WILSON, Arthur 922.373
Thy will be done; the autobiography of an Episcopal minister. New York, Dial Press, [c.]1960. 213p. 21cm. 59-15487 3.95
I. Title.

WILSON, Arthur, 1888- 922.373
Thy will be done; the autobiography of an Episcopal minister. New York, Dial Press, 1960. 213 p. 21 cm. [BX5-95.W68A3] 59-15487
I. Title.

Wilson, Augusta Jane (Evans) 1835-1909.

FIDLER, William Perry. 928.1
Augusta Evans Wilson, 1835-1909, a biography. University, Ala., University of Alabama Press, 1951. 251 p. illus., ports. 23 cm. Bibliographical references included in "Notes" (p. [228]-239) [PS3333.F5] 52-102
1. Wilson, Augusta Jane (Evans) 1835-1909. I. Title.

Wilson, Donald, 1892-

WILSON, Donald, 1892- 358.4'13'310924 B
Wooing peponi : my odyssey thru many years / Donald Wilson. [Carmel, Calif.] : D. Wilson, c1973. 342 p. : ill. ; 28 cm. Includes bibliographical references. [U53.W62A38] 73-93072
1. Wilson, Donald, 1892- I. Title.

Wilson, Edith Bolling Galt, 1872-1961.

HATCH, Alden, 1898- 920.7
Edith Bolling Wilson, First Lady extraordinary. New York, Dodd, Mead, 1961. 285p. 22cm. [E767.3.W57] 61-15995
1. Wilson, Edith (Bolling) Galt, 1872- I. Title.

ROSS, Ishbel, 1897- 973.91'3'0924 B
Power with grace : the life story of Mrs. Woodrow Wilson / Ishbel Ross. New York : Putnam, [1975] 374 p., [4] leaves of plates : ill. ; 22 cm. Includes index. Bibliography: p. 353-359. [E767.3.W59] 74-16615 ISBN 0-399-11459-9 : 9.95
1. Wilson, Edith Bolling Galt, 1872-1961. I. Title.

Wilson, Edmund, 1895-1972—Biography.

BERTHOFF, Warner. 818'.5'209
Edmund Wilson. Minneapolis, University of Minnesota Press [1968] 47 p. 21 cm. (University of Minnesota. Pamphlets on American writers, no. 67) Bibliography: p. 46-47. [PS3545.I6245Z58] 68-64750 0.95
1. Wilson, Edmund, 1895- I. Series: Minnesota. University. Pamphlets on American writers, no. 67 **BIP**

WILSON, Edmund, 1895-1972. 818'.5'209 B
The Twenties : from notebooks and diaries of the period / Edmund Wilson ; edited with an introd. by Leon Edel. New York : Farrar, Straus and Giroux, 1975. xlviii, 557 p. : ill. ; 20 cm. Includes index. [PS3545.I6245Z536 1975] 74-34339 ISBN 0-374-27963-2 : 10.00
1. Wilson, Edmund, 1895-1972—Biography. I. Title.

Wilson, Edmund, 1895-1972—Criticism and interpretation.

EDMUND Wilson : 818'.5'209 B
the man and his work / edited by John Wain. New York : New York University Press, 1978. x, 182 p. ; 23 cm. Includes index. "Edmund Wilson's books": p. 174-176. [PS3545.I6245Z62] 78-53094 ISBN 0-8147-9183-2 : 12.00
1. Wilson, Edmund, 1895-1972—Criticism and interpretation. I. Wain, John. **BIP**

Wilson, Edmund, 1895-1972—Journeys—Israel.

WILSON, Edmund, 1895- 221.4'4
1972.
Israel and The Dead Sea scrolls / Edmund Wilson. New York : Farrar, Straus, Giroux, 1978. xii, 420 p. ; 19 cm. Includes index. [BM487.W498 1978] 78-7365 ISBN 0-374-51438-0 : pbk. : 4.95
1. Wilson, Edmund, 1895-1972—Journeys—Israel. 2. Dead Sea scrolls. 3. Bible. O.T. Genesis—Criticism, interpretation, etc. 4. Israel—Description and travel. 5. Authors, American—20th century—Biography. I. Wilson, Edmund, 1895-1972. The Dead Sea scrolls, 1947-1969. 1978. II. Title: Israel. III. Title: The Dead Sea scrolls. **BIP**

Wilson, Edward Adrian, 1872-1912.

SEAVER, George Fenn 923.942
Edward Wilson of the Antarctic; naturalist and friend; together with a memoir of Oriana Wilson. Introd. by Apsley Cherry-Garrard. London, Murray [Mystic, Conn., Verry, 1965] 310p. front., plates, maps, facsims. 22cm. First pub. 1933. [G875.W5S4] 4.50 bds.,
1. Wilson, Edward Adrian, 1872-1912. 2. Antarctic regions. 3. Scientific expeditions. I. Title.

Wilson, Edward Raymond, 1896-

WILSON, Edward 327'.172'0924 B
Raymond, 1896-
Thus far on my journey / by E. Raymond Wilson. Richmond, Ind. : Friends United Press, c1976. xviii, 308 p., [8] leaves of plates : ill. ; 24 cm. Includes bibliographical references. [JX1962.W54A37] 76-42308 ISBN 0-913408-26-3 : 5.95
1. Wilson, Edward Raymond, 1896- 2. Pacifists—United States—Biography. I. Title. **BIP**

Wilson, Eleanor, 1891-

CORMACK, Maribelle, 1902- 922
The lady was a skipper; the story of Eleanor Wilson, missionary extraordinary to the Marshall and Caroline Islands. Foreword by Eleanor Wilson. New York, Hill and Wang, 1956. 224 p. 21 cm. [BV3678.W5C6] 56-10675
1. Wilson, Eleanor, 1891- I. Title.

Wilson, Ellen Louis (Axson)

WILSON, Woodrow, Pres. 923.173
of U.S. 1856-1924.
The priceless gift; the love letters of Woodrow Wilson and Ellen Axson Wilson. Edited by Eleanor Wilson McAdoo. With a foreword by Raymond B. Fosdick. [1st ed.] New York, McGraw-Hill [1962] 324 p. illus. 24 cm. [E767.W838] 62-18529
1. Wilson, Ellen Louis (Axson) I. McAdoo, Eleanor Randolph (Wilson) 1800- ed. II. Title.

Wilson, Evelyn.

WILSON, Evelyn. 920
He wore a red tam. [1st ed.] New York, Pageant Press [1953] 238p. 21cm. [CT275.W5816A3] 53-81099
I. Title.

Wilson, Frank John, 1888-

SPIERING, Frank. 364.1'092'4 B
The man who got Capone / by Frank Spiering. Indianapolis : Bobbs-Merrill, c1976. 231 p., [8] leaves of plates : ill. ; 24 cm. Includes index. Bibliography: p. 224-226. [HV6248.C17S64] 76-11626 ISBN 0-672-52231-4 : 10.00
1. Capone, Alphonse, 1899-1947. 2. Wilson, Frank John, 1888- 3. United States. Office of Internal Revenue.—Officials and employees—Biography. 4. Crime and criminals—United States—Biography. I. Title.

Wilson, Harold, 1916-

FOOT, Michael, 1913- 923.242
Harold Wilson, a pictorial biography. [Comp., ed. by John Parker, Eugene Prager] [Long Island City, N.Y.] Pergamon [1965, c.1964] 100p. illus., ports. 23cm. [DA591.W5F6] 64-7678 2.95
1. Wilson, Harold, 1916- I. Title.

SMITH, Leslie. 923.242
Harold Wilson, the authentic portrait. New York, Scribner [1965, c1964] viii, 231 p. ports. 22 cm. [DA591.W5S6 1965] 65-11522
1. Wilson, Harold, 1916-

WILSON, Harold 928.2
The private life of Mr. Pepys [New York] Dell [1961, c.1959] 287p. (F141) Bibl. .50 pap.,
1. Pepys, Samuel, 1633-1703. II. Title.

Wilson, Henry, 1812-1875.

ABBOTT, Richard H. 973.8'2'0924 B
Cobbler in Congress; the life of Henry Wilson, 1812-1875 [by] Richard H. Abbott. [Lexington] University Press of Kentucky [1972] xii, 289 p. ports. 23 cm. Bibliography: p. [267]-280. [E415.9.W6A64] 70-147856 ISBN 0-8131-1249-4 13.50
1. Wilson, Henry, 1812-1875. I. Title. **BIP**

NASON, Elias, 973.8'2'0924 B
1811-1887.
The life and public services of Henry Wilson, late Vice-President of the United States, by Elias Nason and Thomas Russell. New York, Negro Universities Press [1969] 452 p. illus. 23 cm. Title on spine: Life of Henry Wilson. Reprint of the 1876 ed. [E415.9.W6N18 1969] 69-19358
1. Wilson, Henry, 1812-1875. I. Russell, Thomas, 1825-1887, joint author. II. Title.

Wilson, James Harrison, 1837-1925.

LONGACRE, Edward 355.3'31'0924 B
G., 1946-
From Union stars to top hat; a biography of the extraordinary General James Harrison Wilson, by Edward G. Longacre. [Harrisburg, Pa.] Stackpole Books [1972] 320 p. illus. 24 cm. Bibliography: p. 301-311 p. [E467.1.W74L6] 72-7401 ISBN 0-8117-0697-4 10.00
1. Wilson, James Harrison, 1837-1925. I. Title.

Wilson, James, 1742-1798.

SEED, Geoffrey. 973.3'092'4 B
James Wilson / Geoffrey Seed. Millwood, N.Y. : KTO Press, c1978. viii, 229 p. : port. ; 24 cm. (KTO studies in American history) Includes index. Bibliography: p. [217]-221. [E302.6.W64S44] 78-2034 ISBN 0-527-81050-9 : 15.00
1. Wilson, James, 1742-1798. 2. Statesmen—United States—Biography. 3. United States—Politics and government—Revolution, 1775-1783. 4. United States—Politics and government—1783-1809. 5. Pennsylvania—Politics and government—1775-1865. I. Title. II. Series. **BIP**

SMITH, Charles Page. v. 12
James Wilson, founding father, 1742-1798. Chapel Hill, N.C., University of North Carolina Press for the Institute of Early American History and Culture [c1956] xii, 426 p. port. 24 cm. A56
1. Wilson, James, 1742-1798. I. Title.

SMITH, Charles 973.3'092'4 B
Page.
James Wilson, founding father, 1742-1798. Westport, Conn., Greenwood Press [1973, c1956] xii, 426 p. port. 24 cm. Reprint of the ed. published by University of North Carolina Press, Chapel Hill. Includes bibliographical references. [E302.6.W64S6 1973] 73-7077 ISBN 0-8371-6908-9
1. Wilson, James, 1742-1798. **BIP**

SMITH, Charles 973.3'092'4 B
Page.
James Wilson, founding father, 1742-1798. Westport, Conn., Greenwood Press [1973, c1956] xii, 426 p. port. 24 cm. Reprint of the ed. published by University of North Carolina Press, Chapel Hill. Includes bibliographical references. [E302.6.W64S6 1973] 73-7077 ISBN 0-8371-6908-9 18.00
1. Wilson, James, 1742-1798.

Wilson, John Albert,

WILSON, John 913'.031'0924 B
Albert, 1899-
Thousands of years; an archaeologist's search for ancient Egypt [by] John A. Wilson. New York, Scribner [1972] 218 p. illus. 25 cm. (Scribners scientific memoirs) [PJ1063.W5] 73-179442 ISBN 0-684-12728-8 9.95
I. Title.

Wilson, John Edward.

WILSON, John Edward. 818'.5'409 B
Soul salutes, by John E. Wilson. Fort Worth, Tex., Branch-Smith, 1970. ix, 157 p. illus. 23 cm. Autobiographical. [PS3573.I45697A6 1970] 71-141149 5.45
I. Title.

Wilson, John Minnich.

WILSON, John Minnich. 928.1
The dark and the damp; an autobiography of Jock Wilson, with pen sketches by the author. [1st ed.] New York, Dutton, 1951. 256 p. illus. 21 cm. [PS3545.I6347Z53] 51-11796
I. Title.

Wilson, Lawrence Patrick Roy

WILSON, Lawrence 943.0840924
Patrick Roy
The incredible Kaiser; a portrait of William II. New York, A. S. Barnes [1965, c.1963] 196p. illus., geneal. table ports. 22cm. Bibl. [DD229.W55] 65-24580 5.00
I. Title.

Wilson, Louis Round, 1876-

TAUBER, Maurice 027.7'0924 (B)
Falcolm, 1908-
Louis Round Wilson, librarian and administrator, by Maurice F. Tauber. Foreword by Robert Maynard Hutchins. New York, Columbia, 1967. xv, 290p. illus., ports. 23cm. (Columbia Univ. studies in lib. serv., no. 14) 'Chronological list of works and editorial activities of Louis Round Wilson': p. 245-[267] Bibl. [Z720.W47T32] 67-14603 8.50
1. Wilson, Louis Round, 1876- I. Title.

Wilson, Margery,

I found my way; 927.92
an autobiography. [1st ed.] Philadelphia, Lippincott [1956] 296p. illus. 21cm. [P2287.] [49A3] 56-11678
I. Wilson, Margery, 1898-

Wilson, Orlando Winfield, 1900-1972.

BOPP, William J. 363.2'092'4 B
"O. W." : a biography of Orlando W. Wilson / by William J. Bopp. Port Washington, N.Y. : Kennikat Press, 1977. p. cm. (National university publications) (Interdisciplinary urban series) Includes index. Bibliography: p. [HV7911.W54B66] 77-329 ISBN 0-8046-9179-7 : 9.95 ISBN 0-8046-9201-7 pbk. : 5.95
1. Wilson, Orlando Winfield, 1900-1972. 2. Police—United States—Biography. 3. Police administration—United States—History. I. Title.

Wilson, Patty.

GRAGG, Sheila. 796.4'26 B
Run Patty run : the story of a very special long-distance runner who lights the way for others / Sheila Gragg, with Jim, Dotty, and Patty Wilson. 1st ed. San Francisco : Harper & Row, c1980. p. cm. [GV697.W5G7] 78-20583 ISBN 0-06-250160-7 : 7.95
1. Wilson, Patty. 2. Runners (Sports)—United States—Biography. 3. Epileptics—Biography. I. Title.

Wilson, Robert Anton, 1932-

WILSON, Robert Anton, 1932- 133
Cosmic trigger : final secret of the illuminati / by Robert Anton Wilson ; illustrated by John Thompson. Berkeley, Calif. : And/Or Press, c1977. p. cm. Includes bibliographical references and index. [BF1408.2.W54A33] 77-89429 ISBN 0-915904-29-2 pbk. : 5.95
1. Wilson, Robert Anton, 1932- 2. Occult sciences—Biography. 3. Occult sciences. I. Title. **BIP**

WILSON, Robert Anton, 1932- 133
Cosmic trigger : the final secret of the illuminati / Robert Anton Wilson ; illustrated by John Thompson. New York : Pocket Books, 1978,c1977. xxx, 288p. : ill. ; 18 cm. (A Kangaroo Book) Includes bibliographical references and index. [BF1408.2W54A33] ISBN 0-671-81669-1 pbk. : 1.95
1. Wilson, Robert Anton, 1932- 2. Occult sciences — Biography. 3. Occult sciences. I. Title.
L.C. card no. for 1977and / Or Press ed.: 77-89429.

Wilson, Robert Thomas, Sir, 1777-1849.

CLOVER, Michael, 355.3'31'0924 B
1922-
A very slippery fellow : the life of Sir Robert Wilson, 1777-1849 / Michael Glover. Oxford [Eng.] ; New York : Oxford University Press, c1978. xiii, 224 p., [4] leaves of plates : ill. ; 23 cm. Includes index. Bibliography: p. 197-201. [DA68.12.W75G58] 77-30189 ISBN 0-19-211745-9 : 14.50
1. Wilson, Robert Thomas, Sir, 1777-1849. 2. Great Britain. Army—Biography. 3. Generals—Great Britain Biography. I. Title.

Wilson, Samuel, 1766-1854.

KETCHUM, Alton. 398.22
Uncle Sam: the man and the legend. New York, Hill and Wang [1959] 143p. illus. 25cm. Includes bibliography. [E179.K35] 59-12601
1. Wilson, Samuel, 1766-1854. 2. Uncle Sam (Nickname) I. Title.

Wilson, Samuel 1766-1854—Juvenile literature.

GERSON, Thomas Isadore, 1905- 920
Uncle Sam, by Thomas I. Gerson, Flora M. Hood. Illus. by James Alexander. Indianapolis, Bobbs [c.1963] 158p. illus., port. 22cm. 63-19019 2.95
1. Wilson, Samuel 1766-1854—Juvenile literature. 2. Uncle Sam (Nickname) — Juvenile literature. I. Hood, Flora Mae, joint author. II. Title.

GERSON, Thomas Isadore, 1905- 92
Uncle Sam, by Thomas I. Gerson and Flora M. Hood. Illustrated by James Alexander. Indianapolis, Bobbs-Merrill [1963] 158 p. illus., port. 22 cm. [E179.G38] 63-19019
1. Wilson, Samuel, 1766-1854 — Juvenile literature. 2. Uncle Sam (Nickname) — Juvenile literature. I. Hood, Flora Mae, joint author. II. Title.

Wilson, Sandy, 1924-

WILSON, Sandy, 1924- 782.8'1'0924 B
I could be happy : an autobiography / Sandy Wilson. New York : Stein and Day, 1975. p. cm. Includes index. [ML410.W716A3] 75-12729 ISBN 0-8128-1843-1 : 10.00
1. Wilson, Sandy, 1924- 2. Musical revue, comedy, etc. I. Title.

Wilson, Sloan, 1920- —Biography.

WILSON, Sloan, 1920- 813'.5'4 B
What shall we wear to this party? : The man in the gray flannel suit / twenty years before & after / Sloan Wilson. New York : Arbor House, c1976. 442 p. ; 24 cm. [PS3573.I475Z518] 75-11152 ISBN 0-87795-119-5 : 12.95
1. Wilson, Sloan, 1920- —Biography. 2. Authors, American—20th century—Biography. I. Title.

Wilson, William Lyne, 1843-1900.

SUMMERS, Festus Paul, 1895- 923.273
William L. Wilson and tariff reform, a biography. New Brunswick, Rutgers University Press, 1953. xi. 288p. port. 24cm. Bibliography: p. 269-280. [HF1755.S912] 53-8214
1. Wilson, William Lyne, 1843-1900. 2. Tariff—U. S. I. Title. BIP

SUMMERS, Festus Paul, 1895- 320.9'2'4 B
William L. Wilson and tariff reform, a biography by Festus P. Summers. Westport, Conn., Greenwood Press [1974, c1953] xi, 288 p. port. 23 cm. Reprint of the ed. published by Rutgers University Press, New Brunswick, N.J. Bibliography: p. 269-280. [HF1755.S912 1974] 74-3627 ISBN 0-8371-7447-3 15.50
1. Wilson, William Lyne, 1843-1900. 2. Tariff—United States. I. Title.

Wilson, Woodrow, Pres. U.S., 1856-1924.

ANDERSON, David D. 973.91'3'0924 B
Woodrow Wilson / by David D. Anderson. Boston : Twayne Publishers, 1978. p. cm. (Twayne's world leaders series ; TWLS 76) Includes index. Bibliography: p. [E767.A53] 78-17169 ISBN 0-8057-7705-9 lib. bdg. : 9.95
1. Wilson, Woodrow, Pres. U.S., 1856-1924. 2. Presidents—United States—Biography.

ARCHER, Jules. 973.91'3'0924 B
World citizen: Woodrow Wilson. New York, J. Messner [1967] 191 p. 22 cm. Bibliography: p. 183-184. [E767.A64] 67-21614
1. Wilson, Woodrow, Pres. U.S., 1859-1924. I. Title.

BAKER, Ray Stannard, 1870-1946. 937.8'0924 (B)
Woodrow Wilson; life and letters. [1st ed.] New York, Greenwood Press, 1968 [1927] 8 v. facsims., ports. 24 cm. Contents.CONTENTS--v. 1. Youth, 1856-1890--v. 2. Princeton, 1890-1910.--v. 3. Governor, 1910-1913.--v. 4. President, 1913-1914.--v. 5. Neutrality, 1914-1915.--v. 6. Facing war, 1915-1917.--v. 7. War leader, 1917-1918.--v. 8. Armistice. Bibliographical footnotes. [E767.B16 1968] 68-8332
1. Wilson, Woodrow, Pres. U. S. 1856-1924. I. Title. BIP

BAKER, Ray Stannard, 1870-1946 937.8'0924
Woodrow Wilson; life and letters. [1st ed.] New York, Greenwood Pr., 1968[c.1927] 8v. facsims., ports. 24cm. Contents.v.1. Youth, 1856-1890.--v.2. Princeton, 1890-1910.--v.3. Governor, 1910-1913.--v.4. President, 1913-1914.--v.5. Neutrality, 1914-1915.--v.6. Facing war, 1915-1917.--v.7. War leader, 1917-1918.--v.8. Armistice. Bibl. footnotes. [E767.B16 1968] (B) 68-8332 175.00 set
1. Wilson, Woodrow, Pres. U.S., 1856-1924. I. Title.

BAKER, Ray Stannard, 1870-1946. 973.91'30924 B
Woodrow Wilson; life and letters. [1st ed.] New York, Greenwood Press, 1968 [c1927] 8 v. facsims., ports. 24 cm. Contents.Contents.—v. 1. Youth, 1856-1890.—v. 2. Princeton, 1890-1910.—v. 3. Governor, 1910-1913.—v. 4. President, 1913-1914.—v. 5. Neutrality, 1914-1915.—v. 6. Facing war, 1915-1917.—v. 7. War leader, 1917-1918.—v. 8. Armistice. Bibliographical footnotes. [E767.B16 1968] 68-8332
1. Wilson, Woodrow, Pres. U.S., 1856-1924.

BRADFORD, Gamaliel, 1863-1932. 920.02
The quick and the dead. Port Washington, N.Y., Kennikat Press [1969, c1931] x, 282 p. ports. 22 cm. (Essay and general literature index reprint series) Contents.Contents.—Theodore Roosevelt.—Woodrow Wilson.—Thomas Alva Edison.—Henry Ford.—Nikolai Lenin.—Benito Mussolini.—Calvin Coolidge. Bibliographical references included in "Notes" (p. [259]-[274]) [CT120.B65 1969] 70-85991
1. Roosevelt, Theodore, Pres. U.S., 1858-1919. 2. Wilson, Woodrow, Pres. U.S., 1856-1924. 3. Edison, Thomas Alva, 1847-1931. 4. Ford, Henry, 1863-1947. 5. Lenin, Vladimir Il'ich, 1870-1924. 6. Mussolini, Benito, 1883-1945. 7. Coolidge, Calvin, Pres. U.S., 1872-1933. I. Title.

BRAEMAN, John, 1932- 973.91'3'0924 B
Wilson. Edited by John Braeman. Englewood Cliffs, N.J., Prentice-Hall [1972] vi, 186 p. 21 cm. (Great lives observed) (A Spectrum book) Bibliography: p. 172-183. [E767.B73] 72-7442 ISBN 0-13-960260-7 5.95
1. Wilson, Woodrow, Pres. U.S., 1856-1924.

BRAGDON, Henry Wilkinson. 973.8'0924
Woodrow Wilson: the academic years. Cambridge, Mass., Belknap Press of Harvard University Press, 1967. xiii, 519 p. illus. ports. 24 cm. Bibliographical references included in "Notes" (p. 413-494) [E767.B75] 67-27081
1. Wilson, Woodrow, Pres. U.S., 1856-1924. I. Title.

DANIELS, Josephus, 1862-1948. 973.91'3'0924
The life of Woodrow Wilson, 1856-1924. Westport, Conn., Greenwood Press [1971] 381 p. illus., ports. 23 cm. Reprint of the 1924 ed. [E767.D18 1971] 72-114509 ISBN 0-8371-4729-8
1. Wilson, Woodrow, Pres. U.S., 1856-1924. BIP

DANIELS, Josephus, 1862-1948. 973.91'3'0924 B
The life of Woodrow Wilson, 1856-1924. Philadelphia, Winston. St. Clair Shores, Mich., Scholarly Press, 1971 [c1924] 381 p. illus., ports. 22 cm. [E767.D18 1970] 70-144965 ISBN 0-403-00934-0
1. Wilson, Woodrow, Pres. U.S., 1856-1924. I. Title.

DANIELS, Josephus, 1862-1948. 973.91'3
The Wilson era: years of peace, 1910-1917. Westport, Conn., Greenwood Press [1974, c1944] xvi, 615 p. illus. 22 cm. Reprint of the ed. published by The University of North Carolina Press, Chapel Hill. [E766.D3 1974] 74-9269 ISBN 0-8371-7634-4 27.00
1. Wilson, Woodrow, Pres. U.S., 1856-1924. 2. United States—Politics and government—1913-1921. I. Title.

DANIELS, Josephus, 1862-1948. 940.3'73
The Wilson years of war and after 1917-1923 Westport, Conn., Greenwood Press [1974, c1946] xviii, 654 p. illus. 22 cm. Reprint of the ed. published by The University of North Carolina Press, Chapel Hill. [E766.D33 1974] 74-9271 ISBN 0-8371-7635-2
1. Wilson, Woodrow, Pres. U.S., 1856-1924. 2. League of Nations. 3. United States—Politics and government—1913-1921. 4. European War, 1914-1918—United States. I. Title.

DEVLIN, Patrick, Baron, 1905- 940.3'22'73
Too proud to fight : Woodrow Wilson's neutrality / Patrick Devlin. London ; New York : Oxford University Press, 1974. xviii, 731 p., [16] p. of plates, leaf of plate : 1 ill., ports. ; 24 cm. Includes index. Bibliography: p. [691]-693. [D619.D49 1974] 75-309769 ISBN 0-19-215807-4 : 19.50
1. Wilson, Woodrow, Pres. U.S., 1856-1924. 2. European War, 1914-1918—United States. 3. United States—Neutrality. I. Title. BIP

GARRATY, John Arthur, 1920- 923.173
Woodrow Wilson; a great life in brief. [1st ed.] New York, Knopf, 1956. 206 p. 19 cm. (Great lives in brief; a new series of biographies) [E767.G26] 56-5802
1. Wilson, Woodrow, Pres. U.S., 1856-1924. BIP

GARRATY, John Arthur, 1920- 973.91'3'0924 B
Woodrow Wilson : a great life in brief / by John A. Garraty. Westport, Conn. : Greenwood Press, 1977, c1956. 206, vi p. ; 23 cm. Reprint of the 1966 issue of the 1956 ed. published by Knopf, New York, in series: Great lives in brief. Includes index. [E767.G26 1977] 76-54860 ISBN 0-8371-9371-0 lib.bdg. : 15.00
1. Wilson, Woodrow, Pres. U.S., 1856-1924. 2. Presidents—United States—Biography.

GEORGE, Alexander L. 923.173
Woodrow Wilson and Colonel House, a personality study [by] Alexander L. George, Juliette L. George. New York, Dover [c.1956, 1964] xxii, 361p. group port. 22cm. Bibl. 64-18850 2.00 pap.,
1. Wilson, Woodrow, Pres. U.S., 1856-1924. 2. House, Edward Mandell, 1858-1938. I. George, Juliette L., joint author. II. Title.

GEORGE, Alexander L 923.173
Woodrow Wilson and Colonel House; a personality study [by] Alexander L. George and Juliette L. George. New York, J. Day Co. [1956] 362p. illus. 22cm. Includes bibliography. [E767.G4] 56-13372
1. Wilson, Woodrow, Pres. U. S., 1856-1924. 2. House, Edward Mandell, 1853-1933. I. George, Jullette L., joint author. II. Title.

GEORGE, Alexander L. 923.173
Woodrow Wilson and Colonel House, a personality study [by] Alexander L. George, Juliette L. George [Gloucester, Mass., P. Smith, 1966, c.1956, 1964] xxii, 361p. group port. 22cm. (Dover bk. rebound) First pub. in 1956 by John Day. Bibl. [E767.G4] 4.00
1. Wilson, Woodrow, Pres. U.S., 1856-1924. 2. House, Edward Mandell, 1858-1938. I. George, Juliette L., joint author. II. Title.

GEORGE, Alexander L 923.173
Woodrow Wilson and Colonel House, a personality study [by] Alexander L. George and Juliette L. George. New York, Dover Publications [1964] xxii, 361 p. group port. 22 cm. Bibliographical references included in "Notes and bibliography" (p. 323-353) [E767.G4 1964] 64-18850
1. Wilson, Woodrow, Pres. U.S., 1856-1924. 2. House, Edward Mandell, 1858-1938. I. George, Juliette L., joint author. II. Title. BIP

GRAYSON, Cary Travers 923.173
Woodrow Wilson, an intimate memoir. New York, Holt, Rinehart and Winston [c.1959, 1960] xi, 143p. illus. 21cm. 60-10998
1. Wilson, Woodrow, Pres U.S., 1856-1924. I. Title.

GRAYSON, Cary Travers, 1878-1938. 923.173
Woodrow Wilson, an intimate memoir. [1st ed.] New York, Holt, Rinehart and Winston [1960] 143 p. illus. 21 cm. [E767.G85] 60-10998
1. Wilson, Woodrow, Pres. U.S., 1856-1924. BIP

GRAYSON, Cary Travers, 1878-1938. 973.91'3'0924
Woodrow Wilson : an intimate memoir / by Cary T. Grayson. 2nd ed. Washington : Potomac Books, c1977. xi, 143 p., [1] leaf of plates : port. ; 22 cm. [E767.G85 1977] 77-153699 ISBN 0-87107-038-3 : 7.50
1. Wilson, Woodrow, Pres. U.S., 1856-1924. 2. Presidents—United States—Biography.

GRAYSON, Cary Travers, 1878-1938. 973.91'3'0924
Woodrow Wilson : an intimate memoir / by Cary T. Grayson. 2nd ed. Washington : Potomac Books, c1977. xi, 143 p., [1] leaf of plates : port. ; 22 cm. [E767.G85 1977] 77-153699 ISBN 0-87107-038-3 : 7.50
1. Wilson, Woodrow, Pres. U.S., 1856-1924. 2. Presidents—United States—Biography.

HANDY, Edward Smith Craighill, 1892- 929.2
Woodrow Wilson's heritage and environment; ethnic and cyclic patterns in time, place, and circumstance, by Craighill and Elizabeth Handy. Drawings by Lorna Edwards Freeman. Philadelphia, Dorrance [1969] xvii, 263 p. illus. 22 cm. Bibliography: p. 259-263. [E767.H22] 68-57734 5.95
1. Wilson, Woodrow, Pres., U.S., 1856-1924. 2. Wilson family. I. Handy, Elizabeth Green, 1921- joint author.

LEWIS, McMillan, 1903- 923.173
Woodrow Wilson of Princeton. Narberth, Pa., Livingston Pub. Co., 1952. 118 p. illus. 24 cm. [E767.L58] 52-11943
1. Wilson, Woodrow, Pres. U. S. 1856-1924. I. Title.

LINK, Arthur Stanley 923.173
Wilson [v.4] Princeton, N.J. Princeton [c.] 1964. 386p. illus., plates, ports. 24cm. Bibl. Contents.[v.4.] Confusion and crises, 1915-1916. [E767.L65] 47-3554 8.50
1. Wilson, Woodrow, Pres. U.S., 1856-1924. I. Title.

LINK, Arthur Stanley. 923.173
Wilson. Princeton, Princeton Univ. Pr., [1968,c.1947] v. illus., plates. ports. 24cm. Contents.[1] The road to the White House. Bibl. [E767.L65] 47-3554 3.95 pap.,
1. Wilson, Woodrow, Pres. U. S., 1856-1924. I. Title.

LINK, Arthur Stanley 923.173
Wilson [v.3]. Princeton, Princeton University Press [c.]1960. 736p. illus., plates. Contents.v[1] The road to the White House. --[2] The new freedom.--[3] The struggle for neutrality, 1914- new freedom.--[3] The struggle for neutrality, 1914-1915. Bibl.: p.[696]-711. 47-3554 10.00
1. Wilson, Woodrow, Pres. U.S., 1856-1924. I. Title.

*LINK, Arthur Stanley 923.173
Wilson, the new freedom. Princeton, N.J., Princeton [1967, c.1956] ix, 504p. 21cm. (Princeton paperback 71) Bibl. 2.95 pap.,
1. Wilson, Woodrow, Pres. U.S., 1856-1924. I. Title.

LINK, Arthur Stanley. 923.173
Woodrow Wilson, a brief biography. [1st ed.] Cleveland, World Pub. Co. [1963] 191 p. illus. 22 cm. Includes bibliography. [E767.L666] 63-8980
1. Wilson, Woodrow, Pres. U.S., 1856-1924. BIP

LOTH, David Goldsmith, 1899- 923.173
The story of Woodrow Wilson. Rev. 1957 to include program suggestions. New York, Woodrow Wilson Foundation [1957] 56p. illus. 22cm. Includes bibliography. [E767.L84 1957] 57-59202
1. Wilson, Woodrow, Pres. U. S., 1856-1924. I. Title.

MCKINLEY, Silas Bent, 1893- 923.173
Woodrow Wilson, a biography. New York, Praeger [1957] 284p. illus. 22cm. Includes bibliography. [E767.M14] 57-5962
1. Wilson, Woodrow, Pres. U. S., 1856-1924. I. Title.

MOONEY, Booth, 1912- 973.91'3'0924 B
Woodrow Wilson. Illustrated with photos.

Chicago, Follett Pub. Co. [1968] 157, [3] p. illus., ports. 23 cm. (Library of American heroes) Bibliography: p. [158] A biography of Woodrow Wilson, America's twenty-eighth President, whose unsuccessful plans for the League of Nations paved the way for the United Nations. [E767.M6] 92 78-1770 1.95
1. Wilson, Woodrow, Pres. U.S., 1856-1924—Juvenile literature. I. Title.

MOTHNER, Ira. 973.91'3'0924 B
Woodrow Wilson, champion of peace. New York, F. Watts [1968, c1969] 152 p. ports. 22 cm. (Immortals of history) A biography of the twenty-eighth President of the United States who, while still in office, won the Nobel Peace Prize for founding the League of Nations. [E767.M62] 92 69-10888
1. Wilson, Woodrow, Pres., U.S., 1856-1924—Juvenile literature. I. Title. **BIP**

MULDER, John M., 973.91'3'0924 B 1946-
Woodrow Wilson : the years of preparation / John M. Mulder. Princeton, N.J. : Princeton University Press, c1978. xv, 304 p., [5] leaves of plates : ill. ; 25 cm. (Supplementary volumes to The papers of Woodrow Wilson) (Series: Wilson, Woodrow, Pres. U.S., 1856-1924. Papers : Supplementary volume.) Includes index. Bibliography: p. [278]-289. [E767.M75] 77-72128 ISBN 0-691-04647-6 : 16.50
1. Wilson, Woodrow, Pres. U.S., 1856-1924. 2. Princeton University—Presidents—Biography. 3. Presidents—United States—Biography. 4. Historians—United States—Biography. I. Series. **BIP**

OSBORN, George 973.91'3'0924 Coleman, 1904-
Woodrow Wilson; the early years, by George C. Osborn. Baton Rouge, La. State Univ. Pr. [1968] ix, 345p. facsim., ports. 24cm. Bibl. [E767.O8] (B) 68-13451 10.00
1. Wilson, Woodrow, Pres. U.S., 1856-1924. I. Title.

OSBORN, George 973.91'3'0924 B Coleman, 1904-
Woodrow Wilson; the early years, by George C. Osborn. Baton Rouge, Louisiana State University Press [1968] ix, 345 p. facsim., ports. 24 cm. Bibliography: p. 329-338. [E767.O9] 68-13451
1. Wilson, Woodrow, Pres. U.S., 1856-1924.

SMITH, Gene. v. 12
When the cheering stopped; the last years of Woodrow Wilson. With an introd. by Allan Nevins. New York, Bantam Books [1965] xiii, 305 p. 18 cm. "N2931." 67-59580
1. Wilson, Woodrow, Pres. U.S., 1856-1924. 2. Wilson, Edith (Bolling) Galt, 1872-1961. I. Title. **BIP**

SMITH, Gene 923.173
When the cheering stopped; the last years of Woodrow Wilson. Introd. by Allan Nevins. New York, Bantam [1965, c.1964] xiii, 305p. 18cm. (N2931) Bibl. [E767.S65] .95 pap.,
1. Wilson, Woodrow, Pres. U.S.—1856-1924. 2. Wilson, Edith (Bolling) Galt, 1872-1961. I. Title.

SMITH, Gene. 923.173
When the cheering stopped; the last years of Woodrow Wilson. With an introd. by Allan Nevins. New York, Morrow, 1964. xi, 307 p. illus., ports. 24 cm. Bibliography: p. [266]-271. Includes bibliographical references. [E767.S65] 64-12044
1. Wilson, Woodrow, Pres. U.S., 1856-1924. 2. Wilson, Edith (Bolling) Galt, 1872-1961. I. Title.

STEINBERG, Alfred, 1917- 923.173
Woodrow Wilson. New York, Putnam [1961] 194 p. 21 cm. (Lives to remember) Includes bibliography. [E767.S82] 61-13422
1. Wilson, Woodrow, Pres. U.S., 1856-1924—Juvenile literature.

THOMPSON, Charles 973.9'0922 Willis, 1871-1946.
Presidents I've known and two near Presidents. Freeport, N.Y., Books for Libraries Press [1970, c1956] 386 p. 23 cm. (Essay index reprint series) Contents.Contents.—Hanna-McKinley.—Bryan.—Roosevelt.—Taft.—Wilson.—Harding.—Coolidge. [E176.1.T45 1970] 71-93383
1. Hanna, Marcus Alonzo, 1837-1904. 2. McKinley, William, Pres. U.S., 1843-1901. 3. Bryan, William Jennings, 1860-1925. 4. Roosevelt, Theodore, Pres. U.S., 1858-1919. 5. Taft, William Howard, Pres. U.S., 1857-1930. 6. Wilson, Woodrow, Pres. U.S., 1856-1924. 7. Harding, Warren Gamaliel, Pres. U.S., 1865-1923. 8. Coolidge, Calvin, Pres. U.S., 1872-1933. I. Title. **BIP**

TUMULTY, Joseph 973.91'3'0924 Patrick, 1879-1954.
Woodrow Wilson as I know him. New York, AMS Press [1970] xvi, 553 p. facsims., port. 24 cm. Reprint of the 1921 ed. [E767.T9 1970] 71-127912 ISBN 0-404-06527-9
1. Wilson, Woodrow, Pres. U.S., 1856-1924. I. Title. **BIP**

VIERECK, George 973.91'3'0924 Sylvester, 1884-1962.
The strangest friendship in history : Woodrow Wilson and Colonel House / George Sylvester Viereck. Westport, Conn. : Greenwood Press, 1976, c1932. xiv, 375 p. ; 23 cm. Reprint of the ed. published by Liveright, New York. Includes index. [E767.V52 1976] 75-26222 ISBN 0-8371-8413-4 lib.bdg. : 21.00
1. Wilson, Woodrow, Pres. U.S., 1856-1924. 2. House, Edward Mandell, 1858- 3. United States—Politics and government—1913-1921. 4. European War, 1914-1918—United States. I. Title.

WALWORTH, Arthur 923.173 Clarence, 1903-
Woodrow Wilson. 2d ed. rev. Boston, Houghton, 1965[c.1958, 1965] xiv, 436, 439p. port. 24cm. Bibl. [E767.W34] 64-21740 12.50
1. Wilson, Woodrow, Pres. U.S., 1856-1924. I. Title.

WALWORTH, Arthur 923.173 Clarence, 1903-
Woodrow Wilson. [1st ed] New York, Longman's Green, 1958. 2 v. ports. 24 cm. Issued in a case. "A note on sources": v. 2, p. 423-425. Contents.Contents. - [1] American prophet. - [2] World prophet. Bibliographical footnotes. [E767.W34] 56-12569
1. Wilson, Woodrow, Pres. U.S., 1856-1924. **BIP**

WALWORTH, Arthur 973.91'3'0924 B Clarence, 1903-
Woodrow Wilson / Arthur Walworth. 3d ed. New York : Norton, c1978. p. cm. Includes index. Bibliography: p. [E767.W34 1978] 78-8706 ISBN 0-393-07533-8 : 19.95 ISBN 0-393-09012-4 pbk. 19.95
1. Wilson, Woodrow, Pres. U.S., 1856-1924. 2. Presidents—United States—Biography. 3. United States—Politics and government—1913-1921-

WILSON, Woodrow, 973.91'3'0924 B Pres. U.S., 1856-1924.
The priceless gift : the love letters of Woodrow Wilson and Ellen Axson Wilson / edited by Eleanor Wilson McAdoo ; with a foreword by Raymond B. Fosdick. Westport, Conn. : Greenwood Press, 1975, c1962. x, 324 p., [4] leaves of plates : ill. ; 23 cm. Reprint of the ed. published by McGraw-Hill, New York. Includes bibliographical references and index. [E767.W838 1975] 75-3874 ISBN 0-8371-8095-3 : 18.75
1. Wilson, Woodrow, Pres. U.S., 1856-1924. 2. Wison, Ellen Louise (Axson) I. Wilson, Ellen Louise Axson. II. Title.

WILSON, Woodrow, Pres. 923.173 U.S., 1856-1924
The priceless gift; the love letters of Woodrow Wilson, Ellen Axson Wilson. Ed. by Eleanor Wilson McAdoo. Foreword by Raymond B. Fosdick. New York, McGraw [c.1962] 324p. illus. 24cm. 62-18529 6.95 bds.,
I. Wilson, Ellen Louise (Axson). II. McAdoo, Eleanor Randolph (Wilson) 1890- ed. III. Title.

WILSON, Woodrow, Pres. 923.173 U.S., 1856-1924.
Woodrow Wilson's own story, selected and edited by Donald Day. [1st ed.] Boston, Little, Brown [1952] 371 p. 23 cm. "Sources and acknowledgments": p. [359]-360. [E767.W833] 52-9078
1. U.S.—Pol. & govt.—1913-1921. I. Day, Donald, 1899- ed. II. Title.

Wilson, Woodrow, Pres. U. S., 1856-1924—Juvenile literature.

PEARE, Catherine Owens 920
The Woodrow Wilson story; an idealist in politics. New York, Crowell [c.1963] 277p. illus. 21cm. Bibl. 63-9211 4.50
1. Wilson, Woodrow, Pres. U. S., 1856-1924—Juvenile literature. I. Title.

Wilson, Woodrow, Pres. U.S., 1856-1924—Addresses, essays, lectures.

ALSOP, Em Bowles, ed. 923.173
The greatness of Woodrow Wilson, 1856-1956. Introd. by Dwight D. Eisenhower New York, Rinehart [1956] 268 p. illus. 22 cm. Includes bibliography. [E767.A45] 56-11640
1. Wilson, Woodrow, Pres. U.S., 1856-1924—Addresses, essays, lectures. I. Title. **BIP**

ALSOP, Em Bowles, 973.9'3'0924 ed.
The greatness of Woodrow Wilson, 1856-1956. Introd. by Dwight D. Eisenhower. Port Washington, N.Y., Kennikat Press [1971, c1956] xiv, 268 p. 22 cm. (Essay and general literature index reprint series) Includes bibliographical references. [E767.A45 1971] 70-95331 ISBN 8-04-613958-
1. Wilson, Woodrow, Pres. U.S., 1856-1924—Addresses, essays, lectures. I. Title.

WILSON'S diplomacy: 327.73
an international symposium. Contributors: Arthur S. Link [and others] Cambridge, Mass., Schenkman Pub. Co. [1973] xiv, 120 p. 23 cm. (The American forum series) Includes bibliographical references. [E766.W835] 72-92265 4.50 (pbk.)
1. Wilson, Woodrow, Pres. U.S., 1856-1924—Addresses, essays, lectures. 2. United States—Foreign relations—1913-1921—Addresses, essays, lectures. I. Link, Arthur Stanley.

†WOODROW Wilson 973.91'3'0924 B
: idealism and reality / edited by Raymond F. Pisney. Verona, Va. : McClure Press, c1977. 83 p. ; 24 cm. [E767.W883] 77-73304 7.50
1. Wilson, Woodrow, Pres. U.S., 1856-1924 Addresses, essays, lectures. 2. Presidents—United States—Biography—Addresses, essays, lectures. 3. United States—Politics and government—1913-1921—Addresses, essays, lectures. I. Pisney, Raymond F.

WOODROW Wilson in 973.91'3'0924
retrospect / edited by Raymond F. Pisney ; with an introductory essay by Robert G. Hartje. Verona, Va. : McClure Press, c1978. 144 p. ; 23 cm. [E767.W94] 78-51213 9.50
1. Wilson, Woodrow, Pres. U.S., 1856-1924—Addresses, essays, lectures. 2. Presidents—United States—Biography—Addresses, essays, lectures. I. Pisney, Raymond F.

Wilson, Woodrow, Pres. U.S., 1856-1924—Juvenile literature.

MOONEY, Booth, 973.91'3'0924 B 1912-
Woodrow Wilson. Illustrated with photos. Chicago, Follett Pub. Co. [1968] 157, [3] p. illus., ports. 23 cm. (Library of American heroes) Bibliography: p. [158] A biography of Woodrow Wilson, America's twenty-eighth President, whose unsuccessful plans for the League of Nations paved the way for the United Nations. [E767.M6] 92 78-1770 1.95
1. Wilson, Woodrow, Pres. U.S., 1856-1924—Juvenile literature. I. Title.

STEINBERG, Alfred, 1917- 923.173
Woodrow Wilson. New York, Putnam [1961] 194 p. 21 cm. (Lives to remember) Includes bibliography. [E767.S82] 61-13422
1. Wilson, Woodrow, Pres. U.S., 1856-1924—Juvenile literature.

Wilson, Woodrow, Pres. U.S., 1856-1924—Personality.

FREUD, Sigmund, 1856- 973.91309 1939.
Thomas Woodrow Wilson, twenty-eighth President of the United States; a psychological study, by Sigmund Freud and William C. Bullitt. Boston, Houghton Mifflin, 1967 [c1966] xxii, 307 p. port. 24 cm. [E767.F7] 65-19312
1. Wilson, Woodrow, Pres. U.S., 1856-1924—Personality. I. Bullitt, William Christian, 1891- joint author.

Wilt, Christian, 1790-1819.

JENNINGS, Marietta, 380'.0924 B 1875-
A pioneer merchant of St. Louis, 1810-1820; the business career of Christian Wilt. New York, AMS Press [1968] 219 p. 23 cm. (Studies in history, economics and public law, no. 462) Series statement also appears as: Columbia University studies in the social sciences, 462. Reprint of the 1939 ed.; also issued as the author's thesis, Columbia University, 1939. Bibliography: p. 203-210. [CT275.W584525J4 1968] 68-58594
1. Wilt, Christian, 1790-1819. 2. St. Louis—Commerce. 3. Frontier and pioneer life—Missouri. I. Title. II. Series: Columbia studies in the social sciences, 462.

Winans, William, 1788-1857.

HOLDER, Ray. 286'.6'0924 B
William Winans : Methodist leader in antebellum Mississippi / by Ray Holder. Jackson : University Press of Mississippi, 1976. p. cm. Includes index. Bibliography: p. [BX8495.W657H64] 76-26967 ISBN 0-87805-027-2 :7.95
1. Winans, William, 1788-1857. 2. Methodist Church—Clergy—Biography. 3. Clergy—Mississippi—Biography. 4. Mississippi—Biography. **BIP**

Winchell, Florance (Sylvester)

WINCHELL, Florance 926.1 (Sylvester)
Three incarnations,; part of the story of a woman's life. Boston, Christopher Pub. House [1954] 268p. illus. 21cm. Autobiographical. [R154.W5267A3] 54-10039
I. Title.

Winchell, Mary Edna,

WINCHELL, Mary Edna, 917.77'023 1878-
A time to keep. Ecclesiastes 3.6, by Mary E. Winchell. Pasadena, Calif., 1968. 219 p. 24cm. Autobiographical. [CT275.W584529A3] 68-3499 price unreported
I. Title.

WINCHELL, Mary Edna, 917.77'03'2 1878-
A time to keep: Ecclesiastes 3:6, by Mary E. Winchell Pasadena, Calif., 1968. 219 p. 24 cm. Autobiographical. [CT275.W584529A3] 68-3499
I. Title.

Winchell, Oscar.

WACHEL, Pat. v. 12
Oscar Winchell, Alaska's flying cowboy, by Pat Wachel. Minneapolis, T.S. Denison [c1967] 210 p. 22 cm. (Men of achievement) NUC68
1. Winchell, Oscar. I. Title.

Winchell, Walter, 1897-1972.

KLURFELD, Herman. 070'.92'4 B
Winchell, his life and times / Herman Klurfeld. New York : Praeger, 1976. ix, 211 p. [4] leaves of plates : ill. ; 24 cm.

Includes index. [PN4874.W67K4] 74-29358 ISBN 0-275-33720-0 : 8.95
1. Winchell, Walter, 1897-1972. I. Title.

THOMAS, Bob, 1922- 070.924 B
Winchell. [1st ed.] Garden City, N.Y., Doubleday, 1971. 288 p. ports. 22 cm. [PN4874.W67T5] 71-154705 7.95
1. Winchell, Walter, 1897-

WEINER, Edward Horace. 920.5
Let's go to press; a biography of Walter Winchell. New York, Putnam [1955] 270p. illus. 21cm. [PN4874.W67W4] 55-12041
1. Winchell, Walter, 1897- I. Title.

WINCHELL, Walter, 1897-1972. 070'.92'4 B
Winchell exclusive : "things that happened to me—and me to them / by Walter Winchell ; introduction by Ernest Cuneo. Englewood, N.J. : Prentice-Hall, [1975] xx, 332 p., [12] leaves of plates : ill. ; 24 cm. Autobiography. Includes index. [PN4874.W67A38 1975] 75-16316 ISBN 0-13-960286-0 : 8.95
1. Winchell, Walter, 1897-1972. I. Title.

Winchester, Elhanan, 1751-1797.

REVEREND Elhanan 289.1'0924 B
Winchester: biography and letters. New York, Arno Press, 1972. 252, 100 p. port. 23 cm. (Religion in America, series II) Reprint of Biography of Rev. Elhanan Winchester, by E. M. Stone, first published 1836; and of Ten letters addressed to Mr. Paine, in answer to his pamphlet, entitled The age of reason, by E. Winchester, first published 1795. [BX9969.W7R48] 72-38464 ISBN 0-405-04090-3
1. Winchester, Elhanan, 1751-1797. 2. Paine, Thomas, 1737-1809. The age of reason. I. Stone, Edwin Martin, 1805-1883. Biography of Rev. Elhanan Winchester. 1972. II. Winchester, Elhanan, 1751-1797. Ten letters addressed to Mr. Paine, in answer to his pamphlet, entitled The age of reason. 1972.

Winckelmann, Johann Joachim, 1717-1768.

LEPPMANN, Wolfgang. 913.03'1'0924 B
Winckelmann. [1st ed.] New York, Knopf, 1970. xx, 312, xii p. illus., ports. 22 cm. Bibliography: p. [309]-312. [N7483.W5L4] 70-118711 10.00
1. Winckelmann, Johann Joachim, 1717-1768.

Windsor Castle.

HIBBERT, Christopher, 1924- 923.142
The court at Windsor; a domestic history [1st Amer. ed.] New York, Harper [1965, c.1964] xx, 347p. illus., ports. 25cm. Bibl. [DA690.W76H46] 64-25115 6.50
1. Windsor Castle. 2. Gt. Brit.—Kings & rulers. 3. Gt. Brit.—Court & courtiers. I. Title.

Windsor, House of.

BERTON, Pierre, 1920- 929.7201
The royal family; the story of the British monarchy from Victoria to Elizabeth. [1st American ed.] New York, Knopf, 1954. 273 p. illus. 22 cm. Includes bibliography. [DA28.1.B45 1954] 53-9456
1. Windsor, House of. 2. Gt. Brit.—Kings and rulers. I. Title.

LONGFORD, Elizabeth Harman Pakenham, Countess of, 1906- 942.082'092'2 B
The Royal House of Windsor / Elizabeth Longford. 1st American ed. New York : Knopf, 1974. 288 p. : ill. (some col.) ; 26 cm. Includes index. Bibliography: p. 276-278. [DA28.1.L64 1974] 74-3737 ISBN 0-394-47906-8 : 15.00
1. Windsor, House of. 2. Great Britain—Kings and rulers—Biography. I. Title. BIP

Windsor, Wallis Warfield, Duchess of, 1896-

BOCCA, Geoffrey. 920.7
The woman who would be queen, a biography of the Duchess of Windsor. New York, Rinehart [1954] 309 p. illus. 21 cm. Includes bibliography. [DA581.W5B68 1954] 54-9123
1. Windsor, Wallis Warfield, Duchess of, 1896- I. Title.

GARRETT, Richard. 941.084'092'4 B
Mrs. Simpson / by Richard Garrett. New York : St. Martin's Press, [1980] p. cm. [DA581.W5G37] 79-22979 ISBN 0-312-55138-X : 10.95
1. Windsor, Wallis Warfield, Duchess of, 1896- 2. Edward VIII, King of Great Britain, 1894-1972. 3. Great Britain—Nobility—Biography. I. Title. BIP

MARTIN, Ralph G., 1920- 942.084'092'4 B
The woman he loved [by] Ralph G. Martin. New York, Simon and Schuster [1974, c1973] 543 p. illus. 24 cm. Bibliography: p. 505-509. [DA581.W5M37 1974] 74-4405 ISBN 0-671-21810-7 9.95
1. Windsor, Wallis Warfield, Duchess of, 1896- 2. Edward VIII, King of Great Britain, 1894-1972. I. Title. BIP

WINDSOR, Wallis (Warfield) duchess of, 1896- 920.7
The heart has its reasons; the memoirs of the Duchess of Windsor. New York, D. McKay Co. [1956] 372 p. illus. 22 cm. [DA581.W5A3] 56-14107
I. Title.

Winebrenner, John, 1797-1860.

KERN, Richard, 1932- 289.9 B
John Winebrenner: nineteenth century reformer. Harrisburg, Pa., Central Pub. House, 1974. xi, 226 p. illus. 23 cm. Bibliography: p. 215-226. [BX7096.W5K47] 74-84501
1. Winebrenner, John, 1797-1860.

Wineburgh, H. Harold.

WINEBURGH, H. Harold. 901.9'4
A boy, a man, and an era [by] H. Harold Wineburgh. [Dallas, Printed by the Southern Methodist University Print. Dept., 1968] xi, 287 p. illus., ports. 24 cm. Autobiographical. [CT275.W58455A3] 68-5590
I. Title.

Winfield, Roland, 1910-1970.

WINFIELD, Roland, 1910-1970. 940.54'49'410924 B
The sky belongs to them / Roland Winfield ; with an introduction by H. L. Roxburgh. London : Kimber, 1976. 188 p., [16] p. of plates : ill., ports. ; 24 cm. [D811.W4913 1976] 77-355577 ISBN 0-7183-0414-4 : £4.75
1. Winfield, Roland, 1910-1970. 2. Great Britain. Royal Air Force. Bomber Command—Biography. 3. World War, 1939-1945—Personal narratives, English. 4. Air pilots—Great Britain—Biography. I. Title.

Winfrey, Carey.

WINFREY, Carey. 917.3'03'920924 B
Starts and finishes : coming of age in the fifties / Carey Winfrey. 1st ed. New York : Saturday Review Press, [1975] 183 p. ; 22 cm. Autobiographical. [CT275.W58458A34] 74-28086 ISBN 0-8415-0371-0
1. Winfrey, Carey. I. Title.

Wingate, Francis Reginald, Sir, bart., 1861-1953.

WINGATE, Ronald, Sir, bart., 1889- 962.4'03'0924 B
Wingate of the Sudan : the life and times of General Sir Reginald Wingate, maker of the Anglo-Egyptian Sudan / by Sir Ronald Wingate. Westport, Conn. : Greenwood Press, 1975. ix, 274 p., [4] leaves of plates : ill. ; 22 cm. Reprint of the 1955 ed. published by Murray, London. Includes index. [DT108.05.W5W5 1975] 74-22507 ISBN 0-8371-7862-2 : 16.00
1. Wingate, Francis Reginald, Sir, bart., 1861-1953. I. Title.

Wingate, Orde Charles, 1903-1944.

SYKES, Christopher, 1907- 923.542
Orde Wingate, a biography. [1st ed.] Cleveland, World Pub. Co. [1959] 575 p. illus. 23 cm. [DA585.W6S9 1959a] 59-11533
1. Wingate, Orde Charles, 1903-1944. I. Title.

Wingate, William, 1808-1899.

CARLYLE, Gavin. 266'.023'0924
Life and work of the Rev. William Wingate, missionary to the Jews. London, A. Holness [19 --] 299 p. illus. 20 cm. [BV2622.W5C3] 63-45578
1. Wingate, William, 1808-1899. 2. Missions — Jews. 3. Missions — Hungary. I. Title.

Wingblade, Henry,

WINGBLADE, Henry, 1883- 922.673
Windows of memory; memoirs that warm the heart. Chicago, Harvest [1961] 226 p. illus. 22 cm. [BX6495.W62A3] 61-14299
I. Title.

Winifred, Saint.

ROBERTUS, Prior of Shrewsbury. 230'.2 S
The admirable life of Saint Wenefride / Robert, Prior of Shrewsbury. Ilkley [Eng.] : Scolar Press, 1976. 5, 5, 275 p. : ill. ; 20 cm. (English recusant literature, 1558-1640 ; v. 319) (Series: Rogers, David Morrison, comp. English recusant literature, 1558-1640 ; v. 319.) "STC 21102." Reprint of the 1635 ed. [BX1750.A1E5 vol. 319] [BX4700.W58] 270.2'092'4 B 77-351171 ISBN 0-85967-333-2
1. Winifred, Saint. 2. Christian saints—Wales—Biography. I. Title. II. Series.

Winkler, Henry, 1945-

*MUNSHOWER, Suzanne. 791.45028092
Hollywood's newest superstar-Henry Winkler Suzanne Munshower. New York : Berkley ,1976. 144 p. : ill. ; 18 cm. (Berkley Medallion Book) [PN1992.4] ISBN 0-425-03231-0 pbk. : 1.25
1. Winkler, Henry. I. Title.

PIKE, Charles E. 791.450280924
The Fonz : the Henry Winkler story Charles E. Pike. New York : Pocket Books ,1976. 124 p. : ill. ; 18 cm. [PN1992.4] ISBN 0-671-80746-3 pbk. : 1.50
1. Winkler, Henry. I. Title. BIP

WINKLER, Henry, 1945- 792'.028'0924 B
The other side of Henry Winkler : my story / by Henry Winkler. New York : Warner Books, c1976. 151 p. : ill. ; 28 cm. [PN2287.W497A35] 77-362391 ISBN 0-446-87340-3 : 3.95
1. Winkler, Henry, 1945- 2. Actors—United States—Biography. I. Title.

Winkler, Henry, 1945- —Juvenile literature.

JACOBS, Linda. 792'.028'0924 B
Henry Winkler, born actor / by Linda Jacobs. St. Paul : EMC Corp., 1978. 39 p. : ill. ; 23 cm. (Headliners I) A biography of Henry Winkler whose rise to television stardom fulfilled a childhood dream to become an actor. [PN2287.W497J3] 92 77-27991 ISBN 0-88436-426-7 lib. bdg. : 4.95. ISBN 0-88436-427-5 pbk. : 2.95
1. Winkler, Henry, 1945- —Juvenile literature. 2. Actors—United States—Biography—Juvenile literature. I. Title. II. Series.

Winkler, Max,

WINKLER, Max, 1888- 926.555
From A to X: reminiscences. New York, Crown Publishers [1957] 178 p. 22 cm. [CT275.W58465A3] 57-8701
I. Title.

WINKLER, Max, 1888- 926.555
From A to X: reminiscences. New York, Crown Publishers [1957] 178p. 22cm. [CT275.W58465A3] 57-8701
I. Title.

Winn, Viola Schuldt.

WINN, Viola Schuldt. 940.53'161'0924 B
The escape / Viola S. Winn. Wheaton, Ill. : Tyndale House Publishers, 1975. 213 p. ; 18 cm. Autobiographical. [BV3382.W56A33] 74-19645 ISBN 0-8423-0699-4 pbk. : 1.95
1. Winn, Viola Schuldt. I. Title. BIP

Winnebago Indians—Social life and customs.

[BLOWSNAKE, Sam] 970.2
The autobiography of a Winnebago Indian [edited and translated] by Paul Radin. New York, Dover Publications [1963] 91 p. 22 cm. "The writer is referred to throughout the notes as S. B." Cf. Introd. "Unabridged and unaltered republication of the work first published ... in the University of California publications in American archaeology and ethnology, volume 16, no. 7, April 15, 1920." [E90.B55A3 1963] 63-17914
1. Winnebago Indians—Social life and customs. I. Radin, Paul, 1883-1959, ed. and tr. II. Title. BIP

MOUNTAIN WOLF WOMAN, 1884-1960. 970.2
Mountain Wolf Woman, sister of Crashing Thunder; the autobiography of a Winnebago Indian. Ed. by Nancy Oestreich Lurie; foreword by Ruth Underhill. Ann Arbor, Univ. of Mich. Pr. [1966, c.1961] 142p. illus. 21cm. (Ann Arbor paperbacks, AA109) [E90.M6A3] 61-5019 1.75 pap.,
1. Winnebago Indians—Soc. life & cust. I. Lurie, Nancy (Oestreich), ed. II. Title.

MOUNTAIN Wolf Woman, 1884-1960. 970.2
Mountain Wolf Woman, sister of Crashing Thunder; the autobiography of a Winnebago Indian. Ed. by Nancy Oestreich Lurie; forward by Ruth Underhill. Ann Arbor, Univ. of Michigan Press [c.1961] 142p. illus. 61-5019 4.95
1. Winnebago Indians—Soc. life & cust. I. Lurie, Nancy (Oestreich), ed. II. Title.

MOUNTAIN WOLF WOMAN, 1884-1960. 970.2
Mountain Wolf Woman, sister of Crashing Thunder; the autobiography of a Winnebago Indian. Edited by Nancy Oestreich Lurie; foreword by Ruth Underhill. Ann Arbor, University of Michigan Press [1961] 142p. illus. 23cm. [E90.M6A3] 61-5019
1. Winnebago Indians—Soc. life & cust. I. Lurie, Nancy (Oestreich) ed. II. Title. BIP

Winogradsky, Serge, 1856-1953.

WAKSMAN, Selman Abraham, 1888- 925.8
Sergei N. Winogradsky: his life and work the story of a great bacteriologist. New Brunswick, N. J., Rutgers University Press, 1953. 150p. illus. 22cm. [QR31.W55W3] 53-12648
1. Winogradsky, Serge, 1856-1953. I. Title.

Winslow, Edith (Black)

WINSLOW, Edith (Black) 920.7
In those days; memoirs of Edwards Plateau. San Antonio, Naylor [1950] ix, 184 p. illus., ports. 22 cm. [CT275.W58472A3] 50-13493
I. Title.

Winslow, Edward, 1595-1655.

WOLKINS, George G 923.273
Edward Winslow (o. v. 1606-11) King's scholar and printer. Worcester, Mass., The Society, 1951. 238-266 p. 25 cm. At head of title: American Antiquarian Society. "Reprinted from the Proceedings of the American Antiquarian Society for October 1950." Bibliographical footnotes. [F68.W55W6] 52-3324
1. Winslow, Edward, 1595-1655. I. Title.

Winslow, Mary Nelson.

ANDERSON, Mary, 1872- 923.373
Woman at work; the autobiography of Mary Anderson as told to Mary N. Winslow. Minneapolis, University of Minnesota Press, 1951. 266 p. illus. 23 cm. [HD6095.A668] 51-14305
1. Winslow, Mary Nelson. 2. Women—Employment—U.S. I. Title. BIP

Winter, Colin O'Brien.

WINTER, Colin 261.8'34'5109688
O'Brien.
Namibia / by Colin O'Brien Winter. Grand Rapids, MI : Eerdmans, c1977. v, 234 p. ; 22 cm. [DT709.W56] 76-56830 pbk. : 3.95
1. Winter, Colin O'Brien. 2. Church of England—Bishops—Biography. 3. Africa, Southwest—Race relations. 4. Church and race problems—Africa, Southwest. 5. Bishops—Africa, Southwest—Biography. I. Title. BIP

Winter, Elmer L.

HODGSON, Louise. 331.1'12'0924 B
Elmer L. Winter, the Manpower man. Minneapolis, Denison [1969] 184 p. illus., ports. 22 cm. (Men of achievement series) Bibliography: p. 183-184. [HD5875.W54H6] 76-91358
1. Winter, Elmer L. 2. Manpower, inc.

Winterbotham, Frederick William.

WINTERBOTHAM, 940.54'86'41
Frederick William.
The Nazi connection / F. W. Winterbotham. 1st ed. New York : Harper & Row, c1978. 222 p. ; 22 cm. Includes index. [D810.S8W538 1978] 77-11540 ISBN 0-06-014686-9 : 8.95
1. Winterbotham, Frederick William. 2. World War, 1939-1945—Secret service—Great Britain. 3. World War, 1939-1945—Personal narratives, English. 4. Spies—Great Britain—Biography. 5. World War, 1939-1945—Germany. I. Title.

WINTERBOTHAM, 940.54'86'41
Frederick William.
The Nazi Connection / F.W. Winterbotham. New York : Dell Pub. Co., 1979. 270p. / 18 cm. Includes index. [D810.S8W538 1978] ISBN 0-440-16197-5 pbk. : 2.50
1. Winterbotham, Frederick William. 2. World War, 1939-1945 — Secret Service — Great Britain. 3. World War, 1939-1945 — Personal narratives, English. 4. Spies, Great Britain —Biography. 5. World War, 1939-1945 — Germany. I. Title.
L.C. card no. for c1978 Harper & Row ed.: 77-11540

Winters, Lee Lowell, 1889-

WINTERS, Lee 917.3'03'90924 B
Lowell, 1889-
True hard scrabble / by Lee Lowell Winters. Philadelphia : Dorrance, [1974] 212 p. ; 22 cm. Autobiography. [CT275.W584743A34] 74-80397 ISBN 0-8059-2037-4 : 8.95
1. Winters, Lee Lowell, 1889- I. Title. BIP

Winthrop, John, 1588-1649.

BANKS, Charles Edward, 974.4'02
1854-1931.
The Winthrop fleet of 1630; an account of the vessels, the voyage, the Passengers, and their English home from original authorities Baltimore, Genealogical Pub. Co., 1968. ix, 118 p. illus., map. 23 cm. Reprint of the 1930 ed. Bibliographical footnotes. [F67.B21 1968] 68-57951
1. Winthrop, John, 1588-1649. 2. Arbella (Ship) 3. Puritans—Massachusetts. I. Title.

MORGAN, Edmund Sears. 923.273
The Puritan dilemma; the story of John Winthrop. Edited by Oscar Handlin. [1st ed.] Boston, Little, Brown [1958] 224 p. 21 cm. (The Library of American biography) Includes bibliography. [F67.W798] 58-6029
1. Winthrop, John, 1588-1649. I. Title. BIP

RAYMER, Robert George 923.273
John Winthrop. Governor of the Company of Massachusetts Bay in New England. New York, Vantage [1964, c.1963] 182p. 21cm. Bibl. 64-2331 3.75
1. Winthrop, John, I. Title.

RAYMER, Robert George. 923.273
John Winthrop, Governor of the Company of Massachusetts Bay in New England. [1st ed.] New York, Vantage Press [1963] 182 p. 21 cm. Bibliographical references included in "Notes" (p. 170-182) [F67.W799] 64-2331
1. Winthrop, John, 1588-1649. I. Title.

WHEELWRIGHT, John, 974'.02'0924 B
1592?-1679.
John Wheelwright; his writings, including his fast-day sermon, 1637 and his Mercurius americanus, 1645; and a memoir, by Charles H. Bell. New York, B. Franklin [1971?] 3, viii, 253 p. illus. 23 cm. (Burt Franklin research and source works series, #131. American classics in history and social science, #2) On spine: Writings and Mercurius Americanus, 1645. First published in 1876 as v. 9 of the Publications of the Prince Society. Bibliography: p. [149]-151. [F67.W547 1971] 72-184811
1. Winthrop, John, 1588-1649. A short story. 2. Massachusetts—History—Colonial period, ca. 1600-1775—Sources. 3. New Hampshire—History—Colonial period, ca. 1600-1775—Sources. 4. Antinomianism. I. Title: Writings and Mercurius Americanus, 1645. II. Series: Prince Society, Boston. Publications, v. 9 BIP

WINTHROP, Robert 974.4'01'0924
Charles, 1809-1894.
Life and letters of John Winthrop. New York, Da Capo Press, 1971. 2 v. facsims., ports. 24 cm. Reprint of the 1864-1867 ed. [F67.W8172] 72-152833 ISBN 0-306-70147-2
1. Winthrop, John, 1588-1649. BIP

Winthrop, Margaret (Tyndal) 1591-1647.

EARLE, Alice 974.4'02'0924
(Morse), 1851-1911
Margaret Winthrop. New York, Scribners, 1896. [Spartanburg, S.C., Reprint Co., 1968] xiii, 341p. facsim. 22cm. (Women of colonial & Revolutionary times) Series: Massachusetts heritage series, no. 2) Massachusetts heritage ser., no. 2. [F67.W84 1968] (B) 67-30156 12.50
1. Winthrop, Margaret (Tyndal) 1591-1647. I. Title. II. Series. BIP

Winthrop, Theodore, 1828-1861.

COLBY, Elbridge, 1891- 928.1
Theodore Winthrop. New York, Twayne Publishers [1965] 192 p. 21 cm. (Twayne's United States authors series, 84) "Notes and references": p. 153-182. Bibliography: p. 183-188. [PS3343.W2Z58] 65-18903
1. Winthrop, Theodore, 1828-1861. BIP

Winton, A. H., 1838-1896.

FREEMAN, Aileen 974.8'36'00994
Sallom.
A. H. Winton : being a description of the warp and woof of the Great Wyoming Valley in Pennsylvania / by Aileen Sallom Freeman. 1st ed. New York : Vantage Press, c1979. 521 p. : ill. ; 21 cm. [F157.W9W583] 78-63078 ISBN 0-533-03964-9 : 9.95
1. Winton, A. H., 1838-1896. 2. Wyoming Valley, Pa.—History. 3. Wyoming Valley, Pa.—Biography. I. Title.

***Winwar, Frances.**

*WINWAR, Frances. 920.042
Elizabeth, the romantic story of Elizabeth Barrett Browning [by] Frances Winwar. Illus. by Enrico Arno. New York, Avon [1968, c. 1957] 157p. 18cm. (ZS 131) .60 pap.,
I. Title.

Wirt, Loyal Lincoln,

WIRT, Loyal Lincoln, 922.573
1863-
The world is my parish; an autobiographical odyssey. Introd. by Albert Wentworth Palmer. Los Angeles, W. F. Lewis [1951] 272 p. 22 cm. [BX7260.W563A3] 51-8683
I. Title.

Wirt, William, 1772-1834.

KENNEDY, John 973.5'092'4 B
Pendleton, 1795-1870.
Memoirs of the life of William Wirt, Attorney-General of the United States. A new and rev. ed. Freeport, N.Y., Books for Libraries Press [1973] p. Reprint of the 1850 ed. published by Lea and Blanchard, Philadelphia. [E340.W79K3 1973] 73-5958 ISBN 0-518-19053-6
1. Wirt, William, 1772-1834. I. Title.

Wisconsin—Biog.

PLUMP, Ralph Gordon, 920.0775
1881-
Wisconsin diplomats. [Manitowoc, Wis, 1963] 79 p. 22 cm. [F580.P55] 64-28431
1. Wisconsin—Biog. 2. Diplomats, American. I. Title.

WISCONSIN. State 920.0775
Historical Society.
Dictionary of Wisconsin biography. Madison, 1960. xiv, 385 p. 28 cm. [F580.W825] 60-63043
1. Wisconsin — Biog. I. Title.

Wise, Isaac Mayer, 1819-1900.

HELLER, James Gutheim, 922.96
1892-
Isaac M. Wise: his life, work, and thought [New York] Union of Amer. Hebrew Cong. [c.1965] xxi, 819p. 21cm. Bibl [BM755.W5H4] 64-24340 10.00
1. Wise, Isaac Mayer, 1819-1900. I. Title.

HELLER, James Gutheim, 922.96
1892-
Isaac M. Wise: his life, work, and thought, by James G. Heller. [New York] Union of American Hebrew Congregations [1965] xxi, 819 p. 21 cm. Bibliography, including works of and about Rabbi Wise: p. 677-692. [BM755.W5H4] 64-24340
1. Wise, Isaac Mayer, 1819-1900. I. Title.

KNOX, Israel, 1904- 922.96
Rabbi in America: the story of Isaac M. Wise. [1st ed.] Boston, Little, Brown [1957] x. 173p. 22cm. (The Library of American biography) 'A notes on the sources':p. [165]-168. [BM755.W5K6] 57-11995
1. Wise, Isaac Mayer, 1819-1900. I. Title. II. Series.

KNOX, Israel, 1904- 922.96
Rabbi in America: the story of Issac M. Wise. [1st ed.] Boston, Little, Brown [1957] x, 173 p. 22 cm. (The Library of American biography) "A note on the sources": p. [165]-168. [BM755.W5K6] 57-11995
1. Wise, Isaac Mayer, 1819-1900. I. Title. II. Series.

WISE, Isaac 301.45'19'24073 B
Mayer, 1819-1900.
Reminiscences. [Translated from the German and] edited by David Philipson. New York, Arno Press, 1973 [c1901] 367 p. illus. 21 cm. (The Jewish people: history, religion, literature) Translated from the German. Reprint of the ed. published by L. Wise, Cincinnati. [BM755.W5A33 1973] 73-2233 ISBN 0-405-05294-4 20.00
1. Wise, Isaac Mayer, 1819-1900. 2. Jews in the United States. 3. Reform Judaism—United States. I. Philipson, David, 1862-1949, ed. II. Title. III. Series. BIP

Wise, Isaac Mayer, 1819-1900—Juvenile literature.

GUMBINER, Joseph Henry, 922.96
1906-
Iscc Mayer Wise, pioneer of American Judaism. New York, Union of American Hebrew Congregations [1959] 187p. illus. 21cm. [BM755.W5G8] 59-9711
1. Wise, Isaac Mayer, 1819-1900—Juvenile literature. I. Title.

Wise, John, 1652-1725.

COOK, George Allan. 922.573
John Wise, early American democrat. New York, King's Crown Press, 1952. 246p. 21cm. [BX7260.W565C6] 52-14615
1. Wise, John, 1652-1725. I. Title.

COOK, George Allan 285'.80924(B)
John Wise, early American democrat. New York, Octagon, 1966. ix, 246p. 21cm. Bibl. [BX7260.W565C6 1966] 66-28373 7.50
1. Wise, John, 1652-1725. I. Title. BIP

Wise, Jonah Bondi, 1881-1959.

CAUMAN, Samuel. 296'.0924
Jonah Bondi Wise; a biography, by Sam Cauman. New York, Crown Publishers [1966?] ix, 214 p. illus., ports. 23 cm. [BM755.W52C3] 66-29745
1. Wise, Jonah Bondi, 1881-1959.

Wise, Louise (Waterman)

WISE, James Waterman, 922.76
1901-
Legend of Louise; the life story of Mrs. Stephen S. Wise. New York, Jewish Opinion Pub. Corp., 1949. 96 p. port. 21 cm. [CT275.W58476W5] 49-9185
1. Wise, Louise (Waterman) I. Title.

Wise, Stephen Samuel, 1874-1949.

VOSS, Carl Hermann. 922
Rabbi and minister; the friendship of Stephen S. Wise and John Haynes Holmes. New York Association Pr. [1968,C1964] 383p. ports., facsim. 22cm. Bibl. [BM755.W43V6] 2.75 pap.,
1. Wise, Stephen Samuel, 1874-1949. 2. Holmes, John Haynes, 1879- I. Title. BIP

WISE, Stephen Samuel, 922.96
1874-1949.
Personal letters, edited by Justine Wise Polier and James Waterman Wise. With an introd. by John Haynes Holmes. Boston, Beacon Press [1956] 289 p. illus. 22 cm. [BM755.W53A4] 56-7399
I. Title.

WISE, Stephen 296.6'1'0924
Samuel, 1874-1949.
Stephen S. Wise: Servant of the people. Selected letters edited by Carl Hermann Voss. Foreword, by Justine Wise Polier and James Waterman Wise. [1st ed.] Philadelphia, Jewish Publication Society of America, 1969. xxi, 332 p. ports. 22 cm. [BM755.W53A42] 69-13549 5.50
I. Voss, Carl Hermann, ed. II. Title.

Wise, Thomas James, 1859-1937.

PARTINGTON, Wilfred George, 1888- 010'.92'4
Forging ahead; the true story of the upward progress of Thomas James Wise, prince of book collectors, bibliographer extraordinary, and otherwise, by Wilfred Partington. New York, Cooper Square Publishers, 1973. xv, 315 p. illus. 24 cm. Reprint of the 1939 ed. A rev. ed. was published in London, in 1947, under title: Thomas J. Wise in the original cloth. "The bibliography of the bibliographer; a record of his compilations, privately printed publications, edited works, forgeries, piracies, etc.": p. [283]-304. [Z989.W8P3 1973] 72-89409 ISBN 0-8154-0442-5 10.00
1. Wise, Thomas James, 1859-1937. 2. Literary forgeries and mystifications. I. Title.

PARTINGTON, Wilfred George, 1888- 364.1'63 B
Thomas J. Wise in the original cloth; the life and record of the forger of the nineteenth-century pamphlets, by Wilfred Partington. With an appendix by George Bernard Shaw. Folkestone [Eng.] Dawsons of Pall Mall, 1974. 372 p. illus. 24 cm. Reprint of the 1947 ed. published by R. Hale, London which was an enl. ed., with alterations, of the author's Forging ahead, published in New York, 1939. "The bibliography of the bibliographer": p. 323-346. [Z989.W8P3 1974] 74-173588 ISBN 0-7129-0617-7
1. Wise, Thomas James, 1859-1937. 2. Literary forgeries and mystifications. I. Shaw, George Bernard, 1856-1950. II. Title.
Distributed by Rowman & Littlefield; 21.50

Wiseman, Nicholas Patrick Stephen, Cardinal, 1802-1865.

FOTHERGILL, Brian. 922.242
Nicholas Wiseman, [1st ed. in the U.S.A.] Garden City, N.Y., Doubleday, 1963. 303 p. 22 cm. [BX4705.W6F6] 63-17155
1. Wiseman, Nicholas Patrick Stephen, Cardinal, 1802-1865. I. Title.

GWYNN, Dennis Rolleston, 1893- 922.242
Cardinal Wiseman. Dublin, Browne & Nolan [dist. Mystic, Conn., Lawrence Verry, River Rd., 1964] x,197p. illus., ports. 23cm. 51-5142 3.25 bds.,
1. Wiseman, Nicholas Patrick Stephen, Cardinal, 1802-1865. I. Title.

JACKMAN, Sydney Wayne, 1925- 282'.092'4 B
Nicholas Cardinal Wiseman : a Victorian prelate and his writings / [by] S. W. Jackman. [Dublin] : Five Lamps Press ; Charlottesville, Va. : [Distributed by] University of Virginia, c1977. 143 p. : port. ; 23 cm. Includes index. [BX4705.W6J33] 77-380003 ISBN 0-901072-70-2 : 7.95
1. Wiseman, Nicholas Patrick Stephen, Cardinal, 1802-1865. 2. Cardinals—England—Biography.

REYNOLDS, Ernest Edwin, 1894- 922.242
Three cardinals: Newman, Wiseman, Manning. New York, Kenedy [1958] 278p. illus. 22cm. Includes bibliography. [BX4665.G7R4] 58-10991
1. Newman, John Henry, Cardinal, 1801-1890. 2. Wiseman, Nicholas Patrick Stephen, Cardinal, 1802-1895. 3. Manning, Henry Edward, Cardinal, 1808-1892. 4. Cardinals—Gt. Brit. I. Title.

REYNOLDS, Ernest Edwin, 1894- 922.242
Three cardinals: Newman, Wiseman, Manning. New York, Kenedy [1958] 278p. illus. 22cm. Includes bibliography. [BX4665.G7R4] 58-10991
1. Newman, John Henry, Cardinal, 1801-1890. 2. Wiseman, Nicholas Patrick Stephen, Cardinal, 1802-1895. 3. Manning, Henry Edward, Cardinal, 1808-1892. 4. Cardinals—Gt. Brit. I. Title.

Wiseman, William Henderson. 1829-1911.

PARKS, Louise (Wiseman) 1876- 929.2
Captain Wiseman; a bit of family history. [McAllen, Tex., 1950] 65, 17 p. port. (on cover) 28 cm. "Life as I found it, memoirs of eighty years of living, by William Henderson Wiseman, Jr., as told to Louise Wiseman Parks": 17 p. at end. [CT275.W58478P3] 50-22788
1. Wiseman, William Henderson. 1829-1911. 2. Wiseman family (Jacob Wiseman, b. ca. 1730) I. Wiseman, William Henderson, 1869- II. Title.

Wishes.

BARRETT, Ethel. 222'.09'505
If I had a wish ... / by Ethel Barrett. Glendale, Calif. : G/L Regal Books, c1974. 140 p. : ill. ; 20 cm. (A Regal venture book) Includes bibliographical references. [BJ1500.W55B37] 74-83139 ISBN 0-8307-0314-4 pbk. : 1.25
1. Bible. O.T.—Biography. 2. Wishes. I. Title. BIP

Wister, Owen, 1860-1938.

STOKES, Frances K (Wister) 928.1
My father, Owen Wister, and ten letter. written by Owen Wister to his mother during his first trip to Wyoming in 1885. Laramie, Wyo., 1952. 54p. 18cm. [PS3346.S7] 53-3075
1. Wister, Owen, 1860-1938. I. Title.

VORPAHL, Ben Merchant. 813'.5'2
My dear Wister: the Frederic Remington-Owen Wister letters. By Ben Merchant Vorpahl. With a foreword by Wallace Stegner. Palo Alto, Calif., American West Pub. Co. [1972] xix, 343 p. illus. 24 cm. Includes bibliographical references. [PS3346.V6] 76-187022 ISBN 0-910118-24-8 9.95
1. Wister, Owen, 1860-1938. 2. Remington, Frederic, 1861-1909. I. Remington, Frederic, 1861-1909. II. Wister, Owen, 1860-1938. III. Title.

Withers family.

WITHERS, Walter Spencer, 1902-1966. v. 12
The story of Walter Samuel Withers, 1833-1907; also, early days in Atlanta as lovingly told by his grandson Walter Spencer Withers. Edited and published by Julia Harriet Shealy, a great granddaughter. Wilmington, Del., 1967. 76 p. illus., diagrams, ports. 23 cm. 68-88538
1. Withers family. I. Shealy, Harriet, ed. II. Title.

Witherspoon, John, 1723-1794.

COLLINS, Varnum Lansing, 1870-1936. 973.31'0924 B
President Witherspoon. New York, Arno Press, 1969. 2 v. in 1. illus., facsims., ports. 24 cm. (Religion in America) Reprint of the 1925 ed. Bibliography: v. 2, p. 273-[275] [E302.6.W7C7 1969] 78-83416
1. Witherspoon, John, 1723-1794. 2. Princeton University—History. 3. United States—Politics and government—Revolution, 1775-1783. I. Title. BIP

STOHLMAN, Martha Lou Lemmon. 973.3'092'4 B
John Witherspoon : parson, politician, patriot / Martha Lou Lemmon Stohlman. Philadelphia : Westminster Press, c1976. 176 p. : ill. ; 21 cm. Bibliography: p. [175]-176. [E302.6.W7S76] 75-43679 ISBN 0-664-20812-6 : 5.95 ISBN 0-664-24795-4 pbk. :
1. Witherspoon, John, 1723-1794. BIP

Witt, Johan de, 1625-1672.

ROWEN, Herbert Harvey. 949.2'04'0924 B
John de Witt, grand pensionary of Holland, 1625-1672 / Herbert H. Rowen. Princeton, N.J. : Princeton University Press, c1978. xiii, 949 p. ; 25 cm. Includes index. Bibliography: p. 895-928. [DJ173.W7R68] 76-45909 ISBN 0-691-05247-6 : 40.00
1. Witt, Johan de, 1625-1672. 2. Statesmen—Netherlands—Biography. I. Title.

Witte, Sergei IUl'evich, graf, 1849-1915.

BRENNER, Wladimir, 1895- 947.08'092'4 B
Count Witte : scenes from his life and times, 1902-1915 / Vladimir Brenner ; [translation by Anna Brenner]. 1st ed. Hicksville, N.Y. : Exposition Press, c1979. xvii, 186 p., [1] leaf of plates : port. ; 21 cm. Bibliography: p. 185-186. [DK254.W5B73] 79-114343 ISBN 0-682-49293-0 : 7.50
1. Witte, Sergei IUl'evich, graf, 1849-1915. 2. Statesmen—Russia—Biography. 3. Russia—History—Nicholas II, 1894-1917. BIP

BRENNER, Wladimir, 1895- 947.08'092'4 B
Count Witte : scenes from his life and times, 1902-1915 / Vladimir Brenner ; [translation by Anna Brenner]. 1st ed. Hicksville, N.Y. : Exposition Press, c1979. xvii, 186 p., [1] leaf of plates : port. ; 21 cm. Bibliography: p. 185-186. [DK254.W5B73] 79-114343 ISBN 0-682-49293-0 : 7.50
1. Witte, Sergei IUl'evich, graf, 1849-1915. 2. Statesmen—Russia—Biography. 3. Russia—History—Nicholas II, 1894-1917. BIP

LAUE, Theodore H von. v. 12
Sergei Witte and the industrialization of Russia. New York, Columbia UP, 1963. x, 360 p. illus. (Studies of the Russian Institute, Columbia University) 65-70275
1. Witte, Sergei Iulevich, graf, 1849-1915. 2. Russia — Econ. policy. I. Title. BIP

Wittenmyer, Annie (Turner) 1827-1900.

SILLANPA, Tom. 973.7'76'0924 B
Annie Wittenmyer, God's angel: one of America's "first" ladies from Keokuk, Iowa; historical biography of a Christian heroine. [Keokuk? Iowa; printed by Hamilton Press, Hamilton, Ill., 1972] 42 p. illus. 22 cm. (His "Lest we forget" series) [E601.W83S5] 72-85592
1. Wittenmyer, Annie (Turner) 1827-1900.

Wittfogel, Karl August, 1896-

ULMEN, G. L. 300'.92'4 B
The science of society : toward an understanding of the life and work of Karl August Wittfogel / G. L. Ulmen. The Hague ; New York : Mouton, c1978. xxviii, 747 p. : port. ; 24 cm. Includes index. "Chronological bibliography of the published writings of Karl August Wittfogel, 1917-1977": p. [509]-523. [H59.W54U45] 78-324306 ISBN 9-02-797766-6 : 103.00
1. Wittfogel, Karl August, 1896- 2. Social scientists—United States—Biography. 3. Historians—United States—Biography. I. Title. BIP

Wittgenstein, Ludwig, 1889-1951.

ENGELMANN, Paul. 193
Letters from Ludwig Wittgenstein, with a memoir. [Translated by L. Furtmuller. Edited by B. F. McGuinness] New York, Horizon Press [1968, c1967] xv, 150 p. 19 cm. Translation of Ludwig Wittgenstein: Briefe und Begegnungen. Bibliographical footnotes. [B3376.W564E53] 68-14711
1. Wittgenstein, Ludwig, 1889-1951. I. Wittgenstein, Ludwig, 1889-1951. II. Title.

JANIK, Allan. 914.36'13'034
Wittgenstein's Vienna [by] Allan Janik and Stephen Toulmin. New York, Simon and Schuster [1973] 314 p. illus. 25 cm. Bibliography: p. 289-301. [B3376.W564J36] 72-83932 ISBN 0-671-21360-1 8.95
1. Wittgenstein, Ludwig, 1889-1951. 2. Vienna—Intellectual life. 3. Logical positivism. I. Toulmin, Stephen Edelston, joint author. II. Title. BIP

KENNY, Anthony John Patrick. 192
Wittgenstein [by] Anthony Kenny. Cambridge, Mass., Harvard University Press, 1973. ix, 240 p. 22 cm. Bibliography: p. [233] [B3376.W564K4 1973b] 73-81671 ISBN 0-674-95390-8 7.50
1. Wittgenstein, Ludwig, 1889-1951. BIP

MALCOLM, Norman, 1911- 921.3
Ludwig Wittgenstein, a memoir. With a biographical sketch by George Henrik von Wright. London, New York, Oxford University Press, 1958. 99p. illus. 23cm. [B3376.W564M2 1958] 58-4281
1. Wittgenstein, Ludwig, 1889-1951. I. Title.

MALCOLM, Norman Adrian, 1911- 921.3
Ludwig Wittgenstein, a memoir.Biographical sketch by Georg Henrik von Wright. [New York] Oxford [1962, c.1958] 99p. front. port. 20cm. (46) 1.25 pap.,
1. Wittgenstein, Ludwig, 1889-1951. I. Title.

Wittgenstein, Ludwig, 1889-1951—Addresses, essays, lectures.

LUDWIG Wittgenstein, personal recollections / edited by Rush Rhees. Totowa, N.J. : Rowman and Littlefield, [1980] p. cm. Includes index. [B3376.W564L82] 79-28474 ISBN 0-8476-6253-5 : 18.00 192
1. Wittgenstein, Ludwig, 1889-1951—Addresses, essays, lectures. 2. Philosophers—Germany—Biography—Addresses, essays, lectures. I. Rhees, Rush.

Wives—Biography.

MOORE, Katharine. 920.72
Victorian wives. New York, St. Martin's Press [1974] xxviii, 207 p. illus. 23 cm. [HQ1150.M65 1974b] 73-89048 8.50
1. Wives—Biography. 2. Women—Great Britain. 3. Women—United States. I. Title.

Wives—Conduct of life.

WE became wives of happy husbands : true stories of personal transformation / compiled by Darien B. Cooper, with her own comments and questions for contemplation, in collaboration with Anne Kristin Carroll. Wheaton, Ill. : Victor Books, c1976. 165 p. ; 21 cm. Bibliography: p. 165. [BJ1610.W5] 76-4314 ISBN 0-88207-731-7 pbk. : 2.50 248'.843'0922 B
1. Wives—Conduct of life. 2. Women—United States—Biography. I. Cooper, Darien B. II. Carroll, Anne Kristin.

Wives—Religious life.

NELSON, Martha. 253'.2'0922
On being a deacon's wife. Nashville, Broadman Press [1973] 96 p. 21 cm. Includes bibliographical references. [BV4527.N382] 72-96150 ISBN 0-8054-3505-0 2.95
1. Wives—Religious life. 2. Deacons. I. Title. BIP

Woburn Abbey.

BEDFORD, John Robert Russell, 13th duke of, 1917- 923.242
A silver-plated spoon. [1st American ed.] Garden City, N. Y., Doubleday, 1959. 235 p. illus. 22 cm. Autobiographical. [DA690.W84B4 1959] 59-10672
1. Woburn Abbey. I. Title.

I. Title.

Wodehouse, Pelham Grenville, 1881-

WIND, Herbert Warren, 1918- 823'.9'12 B
The world of P. G. Wodehouse. New York, Praeger [1972, c1971] 102 p. illus. 22 cm. [PR6045.O53Z97 1972] 78-176401 5.95
1. Wodehouse, Pelham Grenville, 1881- I. Title.

WODEHOUSE, Pelham Grenville, 1881-1975. 928.2
Author! Author! New York, Simon and Schuster, 1962. 191 p. 24 cm. Comprises a selection of the letters Wodehouse wrote to Townend over a period of more than thirty years. First published in 1953 under title: Performing flea. [PR6045.O53Z52 1962] 62-12415
I. Title.

Wodehouse, Pelham Grenville, 1881- —Biography.

JASEN, David A. 823'.9'12 B
P. G. Wodehouse: a portrait of a master, [by] David A. Jasen. New York, Mason & Lipscomb [1974] 294 p. illus. 24 cm. Bibliography: p. 254-285. [PR6045.O53Z72] 73-84879 ISBN 0-88405-010-6 12.50
1. Wodehouse, Pelham Grenville, 1881- —Biography.

Woerishoffer, Carola, d. 1911.

BRYN Mawr College. Class of 1907. 361'.92'4 B
Carola Woerishoffer, her life and work. New York, Arno Press, 1974. 137 p. port. 21 cm. (Women in America: from colonial times to the 20th century) Reprint of the 1912 ed. published by the Class of 1907 of Bryn Mawr College, Philadelphia. [HV28.W6B7 1974] 74-3979 ISBN 0-405-06081-5
1. Woerishoffer, Carola, d. 1911. I. Title. II. Series.

Woffington, Margaret, d. 1760.

DALY, Augustin, 1838-1899. 792'.028'0924 B
Woffington; a tribute to the actress and the woman. 2d ed. New York, B. Blom, 1972. 182 p. illus. 25 cm. Reprint of the 1891 ed. Includes bibliographical references. [PN2598.W6D3 1972] 70-91489 15.75
1. Woffington, Margaret, d. 1760.

DUNBAR, Janet. 792'.028'0924 B
Peg Woffington and her world. Boston, Houghton Mifflin, 1968. 245 p. illus., ports. 23 cm. Bibliography: p. [239]-241. [PN2598.W6D8] 68-22385
1. Woffington, Margaret, d. 1760. I. Title.

Wojciechowska, Maia, 1927- —Juvenile literature.

WOJCIECHOWSKA, Maia, 1927- 813'.5'4 B
Till the break of day. [1st ed.] New York, Harcourt Brace Jovanovich [1972] 156 p. 21 cm. Memoirs of the author's adolescence during World War II, when her family escaped from Poland to temporary haven in France, Portugal, England, and finally, the United States. [PS3573.O43Z52] 92 72-79145 ISBN 0-15-287800-9 4.50
1. Wojciechowska, Maia, 1927- —Juvenile literature. I. Title. BIP

Wold, Erling.

WOLD, Erling. 248
What do I have to do - break my neck? [By] Erling and Marge Wold. Minneapolis, Minn., Augsburg Pub. House [1973, c1974] 112 p. 20 cm. [BR1725.W59A37] 73-88604 ISBN 0-8066-1407-2 2.95
1. Wold, Erling. 2. Wold, Marge. I. Wold, Marge, joint author. II. Title. BIP

Wolf, Howard R., 1936-

WOLF, Howard R., 1936- 973.92'092'4 B
Forgive the father : a memoir of changing generations / by Howard Wolf. Washington : New Republic Books, [1978] p. cm. [CT275.W6217A3] 78-14396 8.95
1. Wolf, Howard R., 1936- 2. United States—Biography. I. Title. BIP

Wolf, Hugo, 1860-1903.

NEWMAN, Ernest, 1868-1959 784/.0924
Hugo Wolf. New introd. by Walter Legge [Magnolia, Mass., P. Smith, 1967] xxv, 279p. illus., facsims., music, ports. 22cm. (Dover bk. rebound) Unabridged, corrected repubn. of the work first pub. in 1907 [ML410.W8N5] (B) 4.25
1. Wolf, Hugo, 1860-1903. I. Title.

NEWMAN, Ernest, 1868-1959. 784'.0924 B
Hugo Wolf. With a new introd. by Walter Legge. New York, Dover Publications [1966] xxv, 279 p. illus., facsims., music, ports. 22 cm. "This Dover edition is an unabridged and corrected republication of the work first published in 1907." [ML410.W8N5 1966] 66-23973
1. Wolf, Hugo, 1860-1903.

WALKER, Frank, 1907- 927.8
Hugo Wolf, a biography. New York, Knopf, 1952. x, 502 p. ports., facsim, music. 22 cm. Bibliography: p. 448-461. "Wolf's compositions": p. 462-492. [ML410.W8W25] 51-13230
1. Wolf, Hugo, 1800-1903. I. Title.

WALKER, Frank, 1907-1962. 784'.0924 B
Hugo Wolf; a biography. 2d enl. ed. New York, A. A. Knopf, 1968. x, 522 p. facsim., music, ports. 26 cm. Bibliography: p. 468-481. [ML410.W8W25 1968b] 68-10870
1. Wolf, Hugo, 1860-1903.

Wolf, Marguerite Hurrey.

WOLF, Marguerite Hurrey. 974.3
I'll take the back road / Marguerite Hurrey Wolf ; drawings by Robert MacLean. Brattleboro, Vt. : S. Greene Press, [1975] xii, 171 p. : ill. ; 24 cm. Published in 1965 under title: Anything can happen in Vermont. Essays. [F55.W6 1975] 74-27458 ISBN 0-8289-0244-5 : 7.95
1. Vermont—Social life and customs. 2. Vermont—Description and travel—1951- 3. Country life—Vermont. 4. Wolf, Marguerite Hurrey. I. Title. BIP

WOLF, Marguerite Hurrey. 974.3'17 B
The sheep's in the meadow, raccoon's in the corn : or, Life in the country / Marguerite Hurrey Wolf ; ill. by Adelaide Murphy. Shelbourne, Vt. : New England Press, c1979. 127 p. : ill. ; 21 cm. [F59.J5W64] 79-91349 ISBN 0-933050-03-8 : 6.95
1. Wolf, Marguerite Hurrey. 2. Wolfe family. 3. Country life—Vermont—Jericho. 4. Jericho, Vt.—Biography. I. Title.
Publisher's address: PO Box 525, Shelbourne, VT 05482

Wolfe, Bertram David, 1896-1977.

WOLFE, Bertram David, 1896-1977. 335'.0092'4 B
A life in two centuries / Bertram D. Wolfe. New York : Stein and Day, 1979 p. cm. Autobiographical. [HX84.W64A35] 78-7420 ISBN 0-8128-2520-9 : 17.95
1. Wolfe, Bertram David, 1896-1977. 2. Socialists—United States—Biography. I. Title. BIP

Wolfe, Harold,

WOLFE, Harold, 1907- 923.173
Herbert Hoover: public servant and leader of the loyal opposition, a study of his life and career. [1st ed.] New York, Exposition Press [1956] 507p. 21cm. (A Banner book) Includes bibliography. [E802.W74] 56-8724
I. Hoover, Herbert Clark, Pres U. S., 1874- II. Title.

Wolfe, James, 1727-1759.

MAY, Robin. 973.2'6
Wolfe's army / text by Robin May ; colour plates by G. A. Embleton. Reading : Osprey Publishing, 1974. 40 p., [8] p. of plates : ill. (some col.), 2 maps, port. ; 25 cm. (Men-at-arms series) Bibliography: p. 32. [E199.M458] 74-195332 ISBN 0-85045-193-0 : £1.25
1. Wolfe, James, 1727-1759. 2. United States—History—French and Indian War, 1755-1763. 3. Quebec Campaign, 1759. I. Title.

REILLY, Robin 923.542
The rest to fortune; the life of Major-General James Wolfe. London. Cassell [dist. Chester Springs. Pa., Dufour. 1964, c.1960] xiv. 366p. illus., maps, ports, (1 col.) 23cm. ibl 64-7326 6.00
1. Wolfe, James, 1727-1759. I. Title.

Wolfe, Karl, 1904-

WOLFE, Karl, 1904- 759.13 B
Karl Wolfe, Mississippi artist : a memoir / by Karl Wolfe. Jackson : University Press of Mississippi, 1979. p. cm. [ND237.W784A2 1979] 79-18098 ISBN 0-87805-106-6 pbk. : 10.00
1. Wolfe, Karl, 1904- 2. Painters—Mississippi—Biography. I. Title.

Wolfe, Leslie E.,

ALLISON, Edith Wolfe, 1904- v. 12
Prisoner of Christ; the life story of Leslie and Carrie Wolfe. Joplin, Mo., College Press [c1960] vii, 104 p.illus., ports. 68-23226
1. Wolfe, Leslie E., 2. Wolfe, Carrie Austin, I. Title.

Wolfe, Thomas, 1900-1938.

ADAMS, Agatha Boyd. 928.1
Thomas Wolfe, Carolina student, a brief biography. Chapel Hill, University of North Carolina Library, 1950. 91, [1] p. 22 cm. (The University of North Carolina. Library publication, v. 15, no. 2) Bibliography: p. [92] [PS3545.O337Z6] 50-63183
1. Wolfe, Thomas, 1900-1938. I. Title. II. Series: North Carolina. University.Library. Extension Dept. Library extension publication, v. 15, no. 2

AUSTIN, Neal F. 813'.5'2 B
A biography of Thomas Wolfe, by Neal F. Austin. [Austin, Tex.] R. Beacham [1968] 212 p. illus., ports. 24 cm. Bibliography: p. 207-208. [PS3545.O337Z62] 68-14890
1. Wolfe, Thomas, 1900-1938. I. Title. BIP

COCKE, William J. 813'.5'2
Johnny Park talks of Thomas Wolfe, by William J. Cocke. Asheville, N.C., 1973. 34 p. illus. 23 cm. Includes bibliographical references. [PS3545.O337Z65] 73-86254
1. Wolfe, Thomas, 1900-1938. I. Title.

DANIELS, Jonathan [Worth] 1902- 928.1
Thomas Wolfe: October recollections. Columbia, S. C., Bostwick & Thornley [c.1961] 26p. p5.00 lim. ed., 61-10158
1. Wolfe, Thomas, 1900-1938. I. Title.

NOWELL, Elizabeth. 813'.5'2 B
Thomas Wolfe; a biography. Westport, Conn., Greenwood Press [1972, c1960] 456 p. port. 24 cm. Includes bibliographical references. [PS3545.O337Z82 1972] 72-7507 ISBN 0-8371-6519-9 18.50
1. Wolfe, Thomas, 1900-1938.

RAYNOLDS, Robert, 1902- 928.1
Thomas Wolfe and Robert Raynolds; memoir of a friendship. Newton, Conn. [1964] 76 p. 28 cm. [PS3545.O337Z835] 65-1267
1. Wolfe, Thomas, 1900-1938. 2. Raynolds, Robert, 1902- I. Title.

RUBIN, Louis Decimus, 1923- 813.5
Thomas Wolfe; the weather of his youth. Baton Rouge, Louisiana State University Press [1955] 183p. illus. 23cm. [PS3545.O337Z85] 55-7364
1. Wolfe, Thomas, 1900-1938. I. Title.

WALSER, Richard Gaither, 1908- ed. 928.1
The enigma of Thomas Wolfe; boigraphical and critical selections. Cambridge. Harvard University Press, 1953. vi, 313p. 22cm. [PS3345.O337Z9] 52-13698
1. Wolfe, Thomas, 1900-1938. I. Title.

WHEATON, Mabel (Wolfe) 928.1
Thomas Wolfe and his family, by Mable Wolfe Wheaton, with LeGette Blythe. [1st ed.] Garden City, N.Y., Doubleday, 1961. 336 p. illus. 22 cm. [PS3545.O337Z96] 61-5987
1. Wolfe, Thomas, 1900-1968. 2. Wolfe family. I. Title.

WOLFE, Thomas, 1900-1938. 928.1
The correspondence of Thomas Wolfe and Homer Andrew Watt; edited by Oscar Cargill and Thomas Clark Pollock. New York, New York University Press, 1954. xi, 53p. port., facsim. 24cm. [PS3545.O337Z546] 54-5274
I. Watt, Homer Andrew, 1884-1948. II. Cargill, Oscar, 1898- ed. III. Pollock, Thomas Clark, 1902- ed. IV. Title.

WOLFE, Thomas, 1900-1938. 928.1
Letters. Collected and edited, with an introd. and explanatory text, by Elizabeth Nowell. New York, Scribner [1956] xviii, 797 p. port. 25 cm. Bibliographical footnotes. [PS3545.O337Z54] 56-9880
I. Title.

WOLFE, Thomas, 1900-1938. 816'.5'2
The letters of Thomas Wolfe to his mother. Newly edited from the original manuscripts by C. Hugh Holman and Sue Fields Ross. [Chapel Hill, University of North Carolina Press, 1968] xxxi, 320 p. group port. 24 cm. [PS3545.O337Z552] 68-14361
I. Wolfe, Julia Elizabeth (Westall) 1860-1945. II. Holman, Clarence Hugh, 1914- ed. III. Ross, Sue Fields, ed. IV. Title. BIP

Wolfe, Thomas, 1900-1938—Biography.

GOULD, Elaine Westall. 813'.5'2 B
Look behind you, Thomas Wolfe : ghosts of a common tribal heritage / Elaine Westall Gould. 1st ed. Hicksville, N.Y. : Exposition Press, c1976. 157 p., [2] leaves of plates : ill. ; 22 cm. (An Exposition-university book) Includes bibliographical references. [PS3545.O337Z714] 76-362041 ISBN 0-682-48431-8 : 7.00
1. Wolfe, Thomas, 1900-1938—Biography. 2. Wolfe, Thomas, 1900-1938—Biography—Ancestry. I. Title.

NOWELL, Elizabeth. 928.1
Thomas Wolfe, a biography. [1st ed.] Garden City, N.Y., Doubleday, 1960. 456 p. illus. 24 cm. [PS3545.O337Z74] 60-8689
1. Wolfe, Thomas, 1900-1938—Biography. BIP

Wolfe, Thomas, 1900-1938—Biography—Youth.

WALSER, Richard Gaither, 1908- 813'.5'2 B
Thomas Wolfe undergraduate / Richard Walser. Durham, N.C. : Duke University Press, 1977. 166 p., [4] leaves of plates : ill. ; 23 cm. Includes bibliographical references and index. [PS3545.O337Z93] 77-74768 ISBN 0-8223-0387-6 : 8.75
1. Wolfe, Thomas, 1900-1938—Biography—Youth. 2. North Carolina. University. 3. Novelists, American—20th century—Biography. I. Title. BIP

Wolfe, Thomas, 1900-1938—Juvenile literature.

GURKO, Leo, 1914- 813'.5'2
Thomas Wolfe : beyond the romantic ego / by Leo Gurko. New York : Crowell, [1975] 183 p. ; 21 cm. (Twentieth-century American writers) Includes index. Bibliography: p. 177-179. A brief biography of the author, Thomas Wolfe, and an analysis of his works including Look Homeward, Angel and You Can't Go Home Again. [PS3545.O337Z715 1975] 92 74-34204 ISBN 0-690-00751-5 : 5.95
1. Wolfe, Thomas, 1900-1938—Juvenile literature. I. Title. BIP

Wolfe, Willy, 1951-1974.

KINNEY, Jean Brown. 322.4'2'0924 B
Death to Willy Wolfe / by Jean Kinney. New York: Simon and Schuster, c1979. p. cm. [F866.4.W64K56] 79-16577 ISBN 0-671-22857-9 : 10.95
1. Wolfe, Willy, 1951-1974. 2. Symbionese Liberation Army—Biography. 3. California—Biography. I. Title.

Wolfenden, John Frederick, Baron Wolfenden of Westcott.

WOLFENDEN, John Frederick, Baron Wolfenden of Westcott. 370'.92'4 B
Turning points : the memoirs of Lord Wolfenden. London : Bodley Head, 1976. 184 p., [4] leaves of plates : ill. ; 23 cm. [LA2375.G72W648] 76-367609 ISBN 0-370-10442-0 : £4.00
1. Wolfenden, John Frederick, Baron Wolfenden of Westcott. I. Title. BIP

Wolff, Geoffrey, 1937- —Biography—Youth.

WOLFF, Geoffrey, 1937- 813'.5'4 B
The Duke of deception : memories of my father / Geoffrey Wolff. 1st ed. New York : Random House, c1979. 275 p., [8] leaves of plates : ill. ; 24 cm. [PS3573.O53Z463] 79-4782 ISBN 0-394-41052-1 : 12.95
1. Wolff, Geoffrey, 1937- —Biography—Youth. 2. Wolff, Arthur Samuels, 1907- 3. Authors, American—20th century—Biography. 4. Fathers—United States—Biography. 5. Impostors and imposture—United States—Biography. I. Title. BIP

Wolff, Rick, 1951-

WOLFF, Rick, 1951- 796.357'092'4 B
What's a nice Harvard boy like you doing in the bushes? / By Rick Wolff ; edited by Phil Pepe. Englewood Cliffs, N.J. : Prentice-Hall, [1975] viii, 216 p. : ill. ; 22 cm. "An Associated Features book." Autobiographical. [GV865.W64A38] 75-2499 ISBN 0-13-951814-2 : 7.95
1. Wolff, Rick, 1951- 2. Baseball. I. Title.

Wolfit, Donald, Sir, 1902-1968.

HARWOOD, Ronald, 1934- 792'.028'0924 B
Sir Donald Wolfit, C.B.E.; his life and work in the unfashionable theatre. New York, St. Martin's Press [1971] xviii, 302 p. illus. 24 cm. Bibliography: p. [291]-292. [PN2598.W63H3 1971b] 74-173563 10.00
1. Wolfit, Donald, Sir, 1902-1968.

Wolfskill, William, 1798-1866.

WILSON, Iris (Higbie) 979.40924
William Wolfskill, 1798-1866; frontier trapper to California ranchero. Glendale, Calif., A. H. Clark [c.] 1965. 268p. illus., facisms., maps, ports. 25cm. (Western frontiersmen ser., 12) Bibl. [F864.W87W5] 65-21331 9.00
1. Wolfskill, William, 1798-1866. I. Title.

WILSON, Iris (Higbie) 979.40924 (B)
William Wolfskill, 1788-1866 frontier trapper to California rachero. Glendale, Calif., A. H. Clark Co., 1965. 268 p. illus., facsims, maps, ports. 25 cm. (Western frontiersmen series, 12) Bibliography: p. [239]-251. [F864.W87W5] 65-21331
1. Wolfskill, William, 1798-1866. I. Title.

Wollaston, John Ramsden,

WOLLASTON, John Ramsden, 1791-1856 922.394
Journals and diaries, 1841-1856; v.1. Coll. by Canon A. Burton. Ed., introd., notes by Canon Burton, Percy U. Henn [Perth, Australia, Paterson Brokensha; New Rochelle, N. Y., Australian Bk. Ctr., 1965] xxvi, 289p. illus., port. maps. 23cm. Contents.v.1. Picton journal, 1841-1844 [BX5700.W6A3] 50-19665 5.50
I. Title.

Wollstonecraft, Mary, 1759-1797.

BOWEN, Marjorie, pseud. 301.41'2'0924 B
This shining woman, Mary Wollstonecraft Godwin, 1759-1797, by George R. Preedy. [Folcroft, Pa.] Folcroft Library Editions, 1973. p. Reprint of the 1937 ed. published by Collins, London. Bibliography: p. [PR5841.W8Z6 1973] 73-14889 ISBN 0-8414-6738-2 (lib. bdg.)
1. Wollstonecraft, Mary, 1759-1797. I. Title.

GEORGE, Margaret. 301.41'2'0924 B
One woman's "situation"; a study of Mary Wollstonecraft. Urbana, University of Illinois Press [1970] viii, 174 p. ports. 21 cm. Includes bibliographical references. [PR5841.W8Z68] 70-100381 ISBN 0-252-00090-0 6.50
1. Wollstonecraft, Mary, 1759-1797. I. Title. BIP

GODWIN, William, 1756-1836. 301.41'2'0924 B
Memoirs of Mary Wollstonecraft. Edited with a pref., a supplement chronologically arranged and containing hitherto unpublished or uncollected material and a bibliographical note, by W. Clark Durant. New York, Haskell House, 1969. xlvi, 351 p. illus., port. 23 cm. Reprint of the 1927 ed. [PR5841.W8Z7 1969] 72-92965 ISBN 0-8383-0975-5
1. Wollstonecraft, Mary, 1759-1797. I. Durant, W. Clark, ed. II. Title.

GODWIN, William, 1756-1836. 301.41'2'0924 B
Memoirs of Mary Wollstonecraft. Edited, with a pref., a suppl., chronologically arranged and containing hitherto unpublished or uncollected material, and a bibliographical note by W. Clark Durant. New York, Gordon Press, 1972. xlvi, 351 p. illus. 21 cm. Reprint of the 1927 ed. published by Constable, London, and Greenberg, New York. "A supplement to Memoirs of Mary Wollstonecraft": p. 135-334. [PR5841.W8Z7 1972] 72-88303 ISBN 0-87968-022-9 14.95
1. Wollstonecraft, Mary, 1759-1797. I. Durant, W. Clark, ed. BIP

JAMES, Henry Rosher, 1862-1931. 301.41'2'0924 B
Mary Wollstonecraft, a sketch, by H. R. James. New York, Haskell House, 1971. xiv, 180 p. ports. 23 cm. Reprint of the 1932 ed. Includes bibliographies. [PR5841.W8Z75 1971] 73-181004 ISBN 0-8383-1373-6
1. Wollstonecraft, Mary, 1759-1797.

JAMES, Henry Rosher, 1862-1931. 828'.6'09 B
Mary Wollstonecraft; a sketch. [Folcroft, Pa.] Folcroft Library Editions, 1973. p. Reprint of the 1932 ed. published by Oxford University Press, London. Bibliography: p. [PR5841.W8Z75 1973] 73-12600 10.75
1. Wollstonecraft, Mary, 1759-1797. BIP

JAMES, Henry Rosher, 1862-1931. 301.41'2'0924 B
Mary Wollstonecraft; a sketch. [Folcroft, Pa.] Folcroft Library Editions, 1973. xiv, 180 p. ports. 23 cm. Reprint of the 1932 ed. published by Oxford University Press, London. Bibliography: p. [165]-171. [PR5841.W8Z75 1973] 73-12600 ISBN 0-8414-5254-7 (lib. bdg.)
1. Wollstonecraft, Mary, 1759-1797.

LINFORD, Madeline. 828'.6'09 B
Mary Wollstonecraft (1759-1797). [Folcroft, Pa.] Folcroft Library Editions, 1973. p. Reprint of the 1924 ed. published by Small, Maynard, Boston, in series: The Roadmaker series. Bibliography: p. [PR5841.W8Z755 1973] 73-14526 17.50
1. Wollstonecraft, Mary, 1750-1797. I. Series: The Roadmaker series. BIP

PENNELL, Elizabeth Robins, 1855-1936. 301.41'2'0924 B
Mary Wollstonecraft Godwin. [Folcroft, Pa.] Folcroft Library Editions, 1974. p. cm. Reprint of the 1885 ed. published by W. A. Allen, London, in the Eminent women series. [PR5841.W8Z77 1974] 74-10773 17.50
1. Wollstonecraft, Mary, 1759-1797. I. Series: Eminent women series. BIP

TIMS, Margaret, 1919- 301.41'2'0924 B
Mary Wollstonecraft : a social pioneer / [by] Margaret Tims. London : Millington, 1976. xii, 3-374 p. : port. ; 23 cm. Includes index. Bibliography: p. 370-371. [HQ1595.W64T55 1976] 77-354677 ISBN 0-86000-034-6 : £5.00
1. Wollstonecraft, Mary, 1759-1797. 2. Feminists—England—Biography. 3. Authors, English—19th century—Biography.

WARDLE, Ralph Martin, 1909- 828.608 B
Mary Wollstonecraft, a critical biography, by Ralph M. Wardle. Lincoln, University of Nebraska Press [1966, c1951] 366 p. 21 cm. (A Bison book, BB340) Bibliographical references included in "Notes" (p. [342]-359) [PR4719.G5Z9 1966] 66-8869
1. Wollstonecraft, Mary, 1759-1797.

Wollstonecraft, Mary, 1759-1797—Biography.

FLEXNER, Eleanor, 1908- 301.41'2'0924 [B]
Mary Wollstonecraft: a biography. Baltimore, Penguin Books [1973, c1972] 307 p. illus., ports. 20 cm. Bibliography: p. 281 [HQ1595.W64F5] ISBN 0-14-003773-X 2.50 (pbk.)
1. Wollstonecraft, Mary. 1759-1797. I. Title.
L.C. card no. for the hardbound edition: 72-76664.

FLEXNER, Eleanor, 1908- 301.41'2'0924 B
Mary Wollstonecraft; a biography. New York, Coward, McCann & Geoghegan [1972] 307 p. illus. 24 cm. Bibliography: p. 285-286. [HQ1595.W64F5] 72-76664 ISBN 0-698-10447-1 8.95
1. Wollstonecraft, Mary, 1759-1797—Biography.

GODWIN, William, 1756-1836. 828'.6'09 B
Memoirs of the author of A vindication of the rights of woman. With an introd. for the Garland ed. by Gina Luria. New York, Garland Pub., 1974. 10, 199 p. port. 18 cm. (The Feminist controversy in England, 1788-1810) Reprint of the 1798 ed. printed for J. Johnson, London. Bibliography: p. 10. [PR5841.W8Z714 1974] 74-8123 ISBN 0-8240-0861-8 22.00
1. Wollstonecraft, Mary, 1759-1797—Biography. I. Title. II. Series. BIP

JAMES, Henry Rosher, 1862-1931. 301.41'2'0924 B
Mary Wollstonecraft, a sketch. [Folcroft, Pa.] Folcroft Press [1970] xiv, 180 p. ports. 23 cm. Reprint of the 1932 ed. Bibliography: p. [153]-171. [PR5841.W8Z75 1970] 72-191680
1. Wollstonecraft, Mary, 1759-1797—Biography.

SUNSTEIN, Emily W. 828'.6'09 B
A different face : the life of Mary Wollstonecraft / by Emily W. Sunstein. Boston : Little, Brown, c1975. xiv, 383 p., [4] leaves of plates : ill. ; 20 cm. "Works by Mary Wollstonecraft": p. [xiii]-xiv. [PR5841.W8Z79 1975] 76-5468 ISBN 0-316-82245-0 : 4.95
1. Wollstonecraft, Mary, 1759-1797—Biography. I. Title.

SUNSTEIN, Emily W. 828'.6'09 B
A different face : the life of Mary Wollstonecraft / Emily W. Sunstein. 1st ed. New York : Harper & Row, [1975] xiv, 383 p., [4] leaves of plates : ill. ; 25 cm. Includes index. Includes bibliographical references. [PR5841.W8Z79] 74-15856 ISBN 0-06-014201-4 : 15.00
1. Wollstonecraft, Mary, 1759-1797—Biography. I. Title. BIP

TOMALIN, Claire. 301.41'2'0924 B
The life and death of Mary Wollstonecraft. 1st American ed. New York, Harcourt Brace Jovanovich [1975] c 1974. 316 p. illus. 22 cm. Bibliography: p. 293-300. [PR5841.W8Z84 1975] 74-14816 1.95 (pbk.)
1. Wollstonecraft, Mary, 1759-1797—Biography. I. Title. BIP

Wollstonecraft, Mary, 1759-1797—Biography—Last years and death.

DETRE, Jean. 828'.6'09 B
A most extraordinary pair : Mary Wollstonecraft and William Godwin / by Jean Detre. 1st ed. Garden City, N.Y. : Doubleday, 1975. 328 p., [8] leaves of plates : ill. ; 22 cm. [PR5841.W8Z66] 74-25101 ISBN 0-385-07334-8 : 8.95
1. Wollstonecraft, Mary, 1759-1797—Biography—Last years and death. 2. Godwin, William, 1756-1836—Relationship with women—Mary Wollstonecraft. 3. Authors, English—Correspondence, reminiscences, etc. I. Wollstonecraft, Mary, 1759-1797. II. Godwin, William, 1756-1836. III. Title.

Wollstonecraft, Mary, 1759-1797—Correspondence.

WOLLSTONECRAFT, Mary, 1759-1797. 828'.6'09 B
Letters written during a short residence in Sweden, Norway, and Denmark / Mary Wollstonecraft ; edited with an introd. by Carol H. Poston. Lincoln : University of Nebraska Press, c1976. xxiv, 200 p. : ill. ; 21 cm. Bibliography: p. [xxiii]-xxiv. [PR5841.W8Z53 1976] 75-38056 ISBN 0-8032-0862-6 : 11.50 pbk. :
1. Wollstonecraft, Mary, 1759-1797—Correspondence. 2. Imlay, Gilbert, 1754?-1828? 3. Scandinavia—Description and travel. I. Title. BIP

WOLLSTONECRAFT, Mary, 1759-1797. 301.41'2'0924 B
The love letters of Mary Wollstonecraft to Gilbert Imlay. With a prefatory memoir by Roger Ingpen. [Folcroft, Pa.] Folcroft Library Editions, 1974. xxxii, 177 p. ports. 22 cm. Reprint of the 1908 ed. published by Hutchinson, London. [PR5841.W8Z54 1974] 74-14529 ISBN 0-8414-5062-5 (lib. bdg.)
1. Wollstonecraft, Mary, 1759-1797—Correspondence. 2. Imlay, Gilbert, 1754?-1828? I. Imlay, Gilbert, 1754?-1828? II. Title. BIP

WOLLSTONECRAFT, Mary, 1759-1797. 828'.6'09 B

Mary Wollstonecraft; letters to Imlay, with prefatory memoir by C. Kegan Paul. New York, Haskell House Publishers, 1971. lxiii, 207 p. ports. 23 cm. Reprint of the 1897 ed. [PR5841.W8Z545 1971] 77-158203 ISBN 0-8383-1269-1
1. Wollstonecraft, Mary, 1759-1797—Correspondence. 2. Imlay, Gilbert, 1754?-1828? I. Imlay, Gilbert, 1754?-1828?

Wolseley, Garnet Joseph Wolseley, viscount, 1833-1913.

LEHMANN, Joseph H., 1921- 923.542
The model major-general; a biography of FieldMarshal Lord Wolseley. Boston, Houghton [c.]1964. 414p. maps, port. 23cm. London ed. (J. Cape) has title: All Sir Garnet. Bibl. 64-55057 5.95
1. Wolseley, Garnet Joseph Wolseley, viscount, 1833-1913. I. Title.

LEHMANN, Joseph H 1921- 923.542
The model major-general; a biography of Field-Marshal Lord Wolseley, by Joseph H. Lehmann. Boston, Houghton Mifflin, 1964. 414 p. maps, port. 23 cm. London ed. (J. Cape) has title: All Sir Garnet. Bibliographical references included in "Notes" (p. 396-403) [DA68.32.W7L4 1964a] 64-55057
1. Wolseley, Garnet Joseph Wolseley, viscount 1833-1913. I. Title.

Wolsey, Thomas, Cardinal, 1475?-1530.

CAVENDISH, George, 1500-1561 923.242
The life and death of Cardinal Wolsey. Edited by Richard S. Sylvester. London, New York, Published for the Early English Text Society by the Oxford University Press, 1959. xii, 304p. facsim. 23cm. (Early English Text Society. [Publications] no. 243) Formerly ascribed to the author's brother, Sir William Cavendish. First ed. published in 1641 under title: The negotiations of Thomas Wolsey. Includes bibliographical references. [PR1119.A2 no. 243] 59-1732
1. Wolsey, Thomas, Cardinal, 1475?-1530. I. Sylvester, Richard Standish, ed. II. Title. III. Series.

CAVENDISH, George, 1500-1561? 942.05'2'0924 B
Thomas Wolsey, late Cardinal, his life and death. Edited with an introd. by Roger Lockyer. London, Folio Press; [Distributed by] J. M. Dent, 1973, [i.e.1974 c1972] scholaryly 242 p. illus. 22 cm. First ed. published in 1641 under title: The negotiations of Thomas Wolsey. "Folio Society first edition of 1962 ... reprinted ... in 1973." [DA334.W8C37 1973] 74-170928 ISBN 0-460-04143-6
1. Wolsey, Thomas, Cardinal, 1475?-1530. I. Title.
Distributed by Rowman & Littlefield; 7.50.

FERGUSON, Charles Wright, 1901- 923.242
Naked to mine enemies; the life of Cardinal Wolsey. Boston, Little [1963, c.1958] 543p. 20cm. (24) Bibl. 2.45 pap.,
1. Wolsey, Thomas, Cardinal, 1475?-1530. 2. Gt. Brit.—Pol. & govt.—1509-1547. I. Title.

FERGUSON, Charles Wright, 1901- 923.242
Naked to mine enemies; the life of Cardinal Wolsey. [1st ed.] Boston, Little, Brown [1958] 543 p. illus. 22 cm. [DA334.W8F38] 922.242 57-9320
1. Wolsey, Thomas, Cardinal, 1475?-1530. 2. Great Britain—Politics and government—1509-1547. I. Title.

LAW, Ernest Philip Alphonse, 1854-1930. 942.05'2'0924
England's first great war minister: how Wolsey made a new army and navy and organized the English expedition to Artois and Flanders in 1513. Port Washington, N.Y., Kennikat Press [1971] xxvi, 273 p. facsims., ports. 22 cm. Reprint of the 1916 ed. [DA334.W8L3 1971] 77-118481
1. Wolsey, Thomas, Cardinal, 1475?-1530. 2. Anglo-French War, 1512-1513. I. Title.

POLLARD, Albert Frederick, 1869- 922.242
Wolsey. [Illustrated ed., with additional notes and corrections] London, New York, Longmans, Green [1953] xvi, 393p. ports. 22cm. Bibliographical footnotes. [DA334.W8P6 1953] [DA334.W8P6 1953] 923.242 53-10735 53-10735
1. Wolsey, Thomas, Cardinal, 1475?-1530. I. Title.

POLLARD, Albert Frederick, 1869-1948 923.242
Wolsey; church and state in sixteenth-century England. Introd. to the Torchbk. ed. by A. G. Dickens. New York, Harper [c.1966] xxxv, 393p. illus., ports., 21cm. (Torchbk., Acad. lib., TB1248Q) First pub. in 1929 Bibl. [DA334.W8P6] 2.95 pap.,
1. Wolsey, Thomas, Cardinal, 1475?-1530. I. Title.

POLLARD, Albert Frederick, 1869-1948. 942.0520924
Wolsey; church and state in sixteenth-century England. Introd. to the Torchbook ed. by A. G. Dickens. New York, Harper & Row [1966] xxxv, 393 p. ports. 21 cm. (Harper torchbooks. The Academy library, TB1248Q) "Originally published in 1929." Bibliography: p. xxx-xxxi. [DA334.W8P6] 66-4726
1. Wolsey, Thomas, Cardinal 1475?-1530. I. Title.

POLLARD, Albert Frederick, 1869-1948. 942.05'2'0924 B
Wolsey / by A. F. Pollard. Westport, Conn. : Greenwood Press, 1978. xvi, 393 p., [3] leaves of plates : ill. ; 23 cm. Reprint of the 1953 ed. published by Longmans, Green, London. Includes bibliographical references and index. [DA334.W8P6 1978] 74-33897 ISBN 0-8371-7997-1 lib.bdg. : 24.75
1. Wolsey, Thomas, Cardinal, 1475?-1530. 2. Great Britain—Politics and government—1509-1547. 3. Cardinals—Great Britain—Biography. BIP

SYLVESTER, Richard Standish, ed. 923.242
Two early Tudor lives: The life and death of Cardinal Wolsey, by George Cavendish [and] The life of Sir Thomas More, by William Roper. Ed. by Richard S. Sylester, Davis P. Harding. New Haven, Conn., Yale [1963, c.]1962. xxi, 260p. 21cm. (Yale paper-bound, Y81) 1.65 pap.,
1. Wolsey, Thomas, Cardinal, 1475?-1530. 2. More, Thomas, Saint, Sir 1478-1535. I. Harding, Davis Philoon, 1914- joint ed. II. Cavendish, George, 1500-1561?The life and death of Cardinal Wolsey. III. Roper, William, 1496-1578. The life of Sir Thomas, Saint, 1478-1535. IV. Title.

TAUNTON, Ethelred Luke, 1857-1907. 942.05'2'0924
Thomas Wolsey, legate and reformer. Port Washington, N.Y., Kennikat Press [1970] xviii, 274 p. ports. 22 cm. Reprint of the 1902 ed. [DA334.W812 1970] 72-112819
1. Wolsey, Thomas, Cardinal, 1475?-1530.

WILLIAMS, Neville, 1924- 942.05'2'0922 B
The Cardinal and the Secretary : Thomas Wolsey and Thomas Cromwell / Neville Williams. 1st American ed. New York : Macmillan, 1976, c1975. ix, 278 p., [4] leaves of plates : ill. ; 22 cm. Includes index. Bibliography: p. 265-269. [DA334.W8W54 1976] 75-37559 ISBN 0-02-629070-7 : 9.95
1. Wolsey, Thomas, Cardinal, 1475?-1530. 2. Cromwell, Thomas, Earl of Essex, 1485?-1540. I. Title. BIP

Wolveridge, Jim, 1920-

WOLVERIDGE, Jim, 1920- 942.1'5 B
Ain't it grand : (or, This was Stepney) / [by] Jim Wolveridge ; drawings by Alan Gilbey ; cover photographs by David Lonsdale. London : Stepney Books, 1976. 93 p. : ill. ; 21 cm. [DA690.S825W648] 77-375213 ISBN 0-9505241-0-7 : £0.75
1. Wolveridge, Jim, 1920- 2. Stepney, Eng. (Middlesex)—Biography. I. Title.

Woman—Biography.

ARMOUR, Richard Willard, 1906- 920.7
It all started with Eve, being a brief acount of certain famous women, each of them richly endowed with some quality that drives men mad, omitting no impertinent and unbelievable fact, and based upon a stupendous amount of firsthand and secondhand research, some of it in books. Suitably illus. by Campbell Grant. New York, Mcgraw [1963,c1956] 136p. illus. 21 cm. (02242) pap., 1.25
1. Woman—Biog. I. Title.

BIGLAND, Eileen. 920.7
The true book about heroines of the sea. Illustrated by Gerald Facey. London, Muller stamped: distributed by Sportshelf, New Rochelle, N. Y. [c1958] 143p. illus. 20cm. [CT3205.B5] 59-3237
1. Woman—Biog. I. Title.

BOCCACCIO, Giovanni, 1313-1375 920.7
Concerning famous women. Tr., introd., notes, by Guido A. Guarino. New Brunswick, N.J., Rutgers [c.1963] xxxviii, 257p. illus. 24cm. Bibl. 63-18945 7.50
1. Woman—Biog. I. Guarino, Guido Aldo, 1925- ed. and tr. II. Title.

BOCCACCIO, Giovanni, 1313-1375. 920.7
Concerning famous women. Translated, with an introd. and notes. By Guido A. Guarino. New Brunswick, N. J., Rutgers University Press [1963] xxxviii, 257 p. illus. 24 cm. Includes bibliographical references. [PQ274.D5E5] 62-18945
1. Woman — Biog. I. Guarino, Guido Aldo, 1925- ed. and tr. II. Title.

BOLTON, Sarah Knowles, 1841-1916. 920.72
Famous leaders among women. Freeport, N.Y., Books for Libraries Press [1972] vi, 356 p. ports. 23 cm. (Essay index reprint series) Reprint of the 1895 ed. Contents.Contents.—Madame de Maintenon.—Catharine II. of Russia.—Madame le Brun.—Dolly Madison.—Catherine Booth.—Lucy Stone.—Lady Henry Somerset.—Julia Ward Howe.—Queen Victoria. [CT3202.B6 1972] 76-38745 ISBN 0-8369-2639-0
1. Woman—Biography. I. Title. BIP

BORER, Mary Irene Cathcart. 920.7
Women who made history. With drawings by Moira Hoddell. London, New York, F. Warne [1963] 192 p. illus., ports., facsims. 22 cm. [CT3202.B66 1963] 63-19180
1. Woman—Biography. I. Title.

BOWIE, Walter Russell, 1882- 920.7
Women of light. New York, Harper [1964, c.1963] xi, 205p. 22cm. Bibl. 63-20285 3.95
1. Woman—Biog. I. Title.

BRADFORD, Gamaliel, 1863-1932. 920.044
Daughters of Eve. Port Washington, N.Y., Kennikat Press [1969, c1930] 303 p. ports. 22 cm. (Essay and general literature index reprint series) Contents.Contents.—Eve in the apple-orchard: Ninon de Lenclos.—Eve as dove and serpent: Madame de Maintenon.—Eve and Almighty God: Madame Guyon.—Eve and Adam: Mademoiselle de Lespinasse.—Eve enthroned: Catherine the Great.—Eve and the pen: George Sand.—Eve in the spotlight: Sarah Bernhardt.—Notes (p. 285-[296]) [CT3202.B68 1969] 72-85989 ISBN 8-04-605424-
1. Woman—Biography. 2. Women in France—Biography. I. Title. BIP

CLYMER, Eleanor (Lowenton) 1906- 920.7
Modern American career women [by] Eleanor Clymer and Lillian Erlich. New York, Dodd, Mead, 1959. 178p. illus. 21cm. [CT3260.C65] 59-6873
1. Woemen in the U. S.—Biog. I. Erlich, Lillian, joint author. II. Title.

CROWTHER, Duane S. 301.41'2'0922
The joy of being a woman; [guidance for meaningful living by outstanding LDS women] Compiled and edited by Duane S. Crowther and Jean D. Crowther. [Bountiful, Utah, Horizon, c1972] x, 326 p. ports. 24 cm. Includes bibliographical references. [HQ1412.C73] 72-88910 ISBN 0-88290-015-3 4.95
1. Woman—Biography. 2. Mormons and mormonism. 3. Conduct of life. I. Crowther, Jean Decker, joint author. II. Title. BIP

DARK, Sidney, 1874-1947. 920.02
Twelve more ladies; good, bad, and indifferent. Freeport, N.Y., Books for Libraries Press [1969] xii, 285 p. 23 cm. (Essay index reprint series) Reprint of 1932 ed. Contents.Contents.—Cleopatra—Philippa of Hainault.—St. Joan of Arc.—St. Teresa.—Queen Elizabeth.—Mme. de Maintenon.—Nell Gwynne.—Madame de Pompadour.—Mme. Mere.—Mme. de Stael.—Florence Nightingale.—Catherine Booth. [D109.D3 1969] 70-86744
1. Woman—Biography. I. Title.

DEEN, Edith 922
Great women of the Christian faith Edith Deen. New York : Harper & Row, 1976 c1959. xix, 410 ; 21 cm. Includes index. Bibliography: pp. 393-397. [BR1713.D4] ISBN 0-06-061849-3 pbk. : 4.95
1. Woman—Biography. 2. Christian Biography. I. Title.
L.C. card no. for 1959 ed.: 59-12821.

D'HUMY, Fernand Emile, 1873- 920.7
Women who influenced the world. New York, Library Publishers [c1955] 342p. 23cm. [CT3203.D48] 55-14025
1. Woman—Biog. I. Title.

EDWARDS, Matilda Barbara Betham-, 1836-1919. 920.72
Six life studies of famous women. Freeport, N.Y., Books for Libraries Press [1972] xiv, 303 p. ports. 23 cm. (Essay index reprint series) Reprint of the 1880 ed. Contents.Contents.—Fernan Caballero (Spanish novelist).—Alexandrine Tinne (African explorer).—Caroline Herschel (astronomer and mathematician).—Marie Pape-Carpantier (educational reformer).—Elizabeth Carter (scholar).—Matilda Betham (litterateur and artist) [CT3234.E3 1972] 73-39701 ISBN 0-8369-2746-X
1. Woman—Biography. I. Title. BIP

EWART, Andrew 920.02
The world's wickedest women; intriguing studies of Eve and evil through the ages. New York, Taplinger [1965, c.1964] 288p. 22cm. [CT3203.E9] 65-19254 4.50 bds.,
1. Woman—Biog. I. Title.

FORSEE, Aylesa 920.7
Women who reached for tomorrow. With decorations by Ruth Macrae. Philadelphia, Macrae Smith Co. [c.1960] 203p. illus. 22cm. 60-14034 2.95
1. Woman—Biog. I. Title.

FOSTER, Warren Dunham, 1886- ed. 209'.22 B
Heroines of modern religion. Freeport, N.Y., Books for Libraries Press [1970]. iv, 275 p. ports. 23 cm. (Essay index reprint series) Reprint of the 1913 ed. Contents.Contents.—Anne Hutchinson, by A. E. Jenkins.—Susannah Wesley, by W. H. Foster.—Elizabeth Ann Seton, by R. V. Trevel.—Lucretia Mott, by A. E. Jenkins.—Fanny Crosby, by W. Bradbury.—Sister Dora, by G. L. Mumford.—Hannah Whitall Smith, by W. H. Foster.—Frances Ridley Havergal, by W. Bradbury.—Ramabai Dongre Medhavi, by J. C. Minot.—Maud Ballington Booth, by R. V. Trevel. Bibliography: p. 258-261. [CT3203.F75 1970] 77-107700
1. Woman—Biography. I. Title. BIP

FREDERICK, Pauline. 920.02
Ten first ladies of the world. [1st ed.] New York, Meredith Press [1967] xiii, 174 p. ports. 21 cm. Contents.Contents.—Bibliography (p. v-vii)—Indira Gandhi, India.—Lady Bird Johnson, United States.—Mary Wilson, United Kingdom.—Yvonne de Gaulle, France.—Carmen Polo de Franco, Spain.—Jovanka Broz Tito, Yugoslavia.—Tahia Nasser, United Arab Republic.—Fathia Nkrumah, Ghana.—Daw Thein Tin (Mme. Thant), United Nations.—Imelda Romualdez Marcos, Republic of the Philippines. [CT3235.F7]

67-14745
1. Woman—Biography. I. Title.

GERLINGER, Irene (Hazard). 920.7
Mistresses of the White House; narrator's tale of a pageant of First Ladies. New York, French [1950] xx, 125 p. ports. 21 cm. Bibliography: p. 109-116. [E176.2.G4 1950] 50-8016
1. Woman—Biog. 2. U. S.—Biog. 3. Presidents—U. S.—Biog. I. Title.

HALE, Sarah Josepha Buell, 1788-1879. 920.72
Woman's record; or, Sketches of all distinguished women, from the creation to A.D. 1868, arranged in four eras, with selections from authoresses of each era. Illustrated by two hundred and thirty portraits, engraved on wood by Lossing and Barritt. 3d ed., rev., with additions. New York, Harper & Bros., 1870. Detroit, Gale Research Co., 1974. p. cm. Bibliography: p. [CT3202.H3 1974] 74-19149 ISBN 0-8103-4081-X
1. Woman—Biography. I. Title.

HOROWITZ, Caroline, 1909- 920.7
A treasury of the world's great heroines, by Joanna Strong [pseud.] and Tom B. Leonard [pseud.] with illus. by Hubert Whatley. New York, Hart Pub. Co. [1951] 190 p. illus. 23 cm. [CT3205.H73] 52-6677
1. Woman—Biography. I. Title.

JAMES, George Payne Rainsford, 1801?-1860. 920.72
Memoirs of celebrated women. Edited by G. P. R. James. Plainview, N.Y., Books for Libraries Press [1974] p. cm. (Essay index reprint series) Reprint· of the 1876 ed. published by G. Routledge, London, New York. [D109.J2 1974] 74-4311 ISBN 0-518-10180-0 19.50
1. Woman—Biography. I. Title.
Contents omitted.

KOOIMAN, Helen W. 209'.22
Cameos, women fashioned by God [by] Helen W. Kooiman. Wheaton, Ill., Tyndale House [1969, c1968] 163 p. ports. 22 cm. [BR1713.K66] 68-56393 3.50
1. Woman—Biography. 2. Christian biography. I. Title.

KOOIMAN, Helen W. 920.72
Silhouettes; women behind great men, by Helen Kooiman. Waco, Tex., Word Books [1972] 170 p. illus. 21 cm. [CT3235.K66] 72-76440 4.95
1. Woman—Biography. I. Title.

MADDEN, Bill. 920.72
Mistresses of mayhem. South Brunswick, A. S. Barnes [1972] 137 p. 21 cm. [CT3203.M25] 78-39346 ISBN 0-498-01139-9 5.95
1. Woman—Biography. I. Title.

MATHEWS, Winifred, 1894- 266'.023'0922 B
Dauntless women; stories of pioneer wives. Illus. by Rafael Palacios. Freeport, N.Y., Books for Libraries Press [1970, c1947] 164 p. illus. 23 cm. (Biography index reprint series) Contents.Contents.—Ann Judson, comrade of an ambassador in chains.—Mary Moffat, mother of the tribe.—Mary Livingstone, "the main spoke in my wheel."—Christina Coillard, home-maker in the wagon.—Mary Williams, friend of the island women.—Agnes Watt, no ordinary woman.—Lillias Underwood, she followed "a red-maned star." [BV3703.M3 1970] 70-126325
1. Woman—Biography. 2. Missionaries. I. Title. **BIP**

MOFFAT, Mary Jane, comp. 920.72
Revelations: diaries of women, edited by Mary Jane Moffat & Charlotte Painter. [1st ed.] New York, Random House [1974] x, 411 p. 22 cm. Bibliography: p. 405-411. [CT3202.M618] 74-8040 ISBN 0-394-49128-9 10.00
1. Woman—Biography. I. Painter, Charlotte, joint comp. II. Title.

MUIR, Charles Stothard, 1873- 920.7
Women, the makers of history. [1st ed.] New York, Vantage Press [1956] 234p. 21cm. [CT3203.M8] 56-12187
1. Woman—Biog. I. Title.

*MUNSHOWER, Suzanne. 920
Margaret, the imperfect princess / by Suzanne Munshower. New York : Berkley Pub. Corp., 1977. 200p. ; 18 cm. (A Berkley Medallion Book) [DA228.3] ISBN 0-425-03341-4 pbk. : 1.25
1. Woman — Biography. 2. Great Britain — Princess and princesses. I. Title.

MYRON, Nancy, 1943- comp. 301.41'2'0922 B
Women remembered; a collection of biographies from the Furies, edited by Nancy Myron and Charlotte Bunch. [Baltimore, Diana Press Publications, 1974] p. cm. [HQ1123.M95] 74-4080 ISBN 0-88447-003-2 1.50
1. Woman—Biography. I. Bunch, Charlotte, 1944- joint comp. II. Title.

PRINGLE, Patrick. 920.7
When they were girls; girlhood stories of fourteen famous women. New York, Roy Publishers [1956?] 208p. illus. 21cm. [CT3205] 56-7071
1. Woman—Biog. I. Title.

PRINGLE, Patrick. 920.7
When they were girls; girlhood stories of fourteen famous women. New York, Roy Publishers [1956?] 208p. illus. 21cm. [CT3205] 56-7071
1. Woman—Biog. I. Title.

*RITTER, Lucy Elizabeth. 920[B]
Lucy's twentieth century 1st ed. New York Vantage [1974] 142 p. illus., (part. col.) 22 cm. [E749] ISBN 0-533-00964-2 6.95
1. Woman—Biography. I. Title.

SCHNITTKIND, Henry Thomas, 1888- 920.7
Living biographies of famous women, by Henry Thomas [pseud.] and Dana Lee Thomas [pseud.] Garden City, N.Y., Perma Giants [1950, c1912] viii, 313 p. 22 cm. [CT3202.S32 1950] 51-21341
1. Woman — Biog. I. Schmittkind, Dana Arnold, 1918- joint author. II. Title.

SERGEANT, Philip Walsingham, 1872- 909'.00922 B
Dominant women. Freeport, N.Y., Books for Libraries Press [1969] 288 p. ports. 23 cm. (Essay index reprint series) Reprint of the 1929 ed. Contents.Contents.—Cleopatra the Magnificent.—Zenobia, Queen of the East.—Theodora of Byzantium.—England's royal enigma.—Tarabai Rani.—"The Beastly Brace"—Duchess Sarah.—Woman-rule in Russia.—The dancer-politician.—"The Old Buddha". Bibliographical footnotes. [D109.S4 1969] 75-86783
1. Woman—Biography. I. Title. **BIP**

SMITH, George Barnett, 1841-1909. 920.72
Women of renown; nineteenth century studies. Freeport, N.Y., Books for Libraries Press [1972] x, 478 p. 22 cm. (Essay index reprint series) Reprint of the 1893 ed. Contents.Contents.—Fredrika Bremer.—Marguerite Countess of Blessington.—George Eliot.—Jenny Lind.—Mary Somerville.—George Sand.—Mary Carpenter.—Sydney Lady Morgan.—Rachel.—Lady Hester Stanhope. [CT3234.S64 1972] 72-5659 ISBN 0-8369-7288-0
1. Woman—Biography. I. Title. **BIP**

SNOW, Edward Rowe. 920.7
Women of the sea; New York, Dodd [c.1962] 272p. illus. 21cm. 62-17924 4.00
1. Woman—Biog. I. Title.

STEVENS, William Oliver, 1878- 920.7
Famous women of America. New York, Dodd, Mead, 1950. ix, 174 p. illus., ports. 23 cm. [Famous biographies for young people] Contents.Contents.—Pocahontas.—Mad Ann Bailey.—Margaret Lewis.—Betsy Ross.—Molly Pitcher.—Sally Townsend.—Martha Dandridge Washington.—Dolly Madison.—Sacajawea.—Harriet Lane.—Clara H. Barton.—Four crusaders: Lucretia Coffin Mott, Harriet Beecher Stowe, Susan B. Anthony, Dr. Mary Walker.—Maria Mitchell.—Louisa May Alcott.—Two actresses: Charlotte Cushman, Clara Morris.—Mary Cassatt.—Carrie Jacobs Bond.—Anne Sullivan Macy.—Mary Mapes Dodge.—Jane Addams. [CT3260.S75] 50-10179
1. Woman—Biography. 2. U.S.—Biography. I. Title.

STONE, Elizabeth. 909
Political women, by Sutherland Menzies. Port Washington, N.Y., Kennikat Press [1970] 2 v. 22 cm. Reprint of the 1873 ed. Includes bibliographical references. [D109.S7 1970] 78-112815
1. Woman—Biography.

THOMAS, Henry, 1886- 920.7
Living biographies of famous women, by Henry Thomas and Dana Lee Thomas. Garden City, N. Y., Perma Giants [1950, c1942] viii. 313p. 22cm. [CT3202.T53 1950] 51-21341
1. Woman—Biog. I. Thomas, Dana Lee, 1918- joint author. II. Title.

Woman—Employment—U.S.

NESTOR, Agnes. 923.373
Woman's labor leader, an autobiography. Rockford, Ill., Bellevne Books Pub. Co. [1954] 307p. illus. 22cm. [HD6095.N37A3] 54-9372
1. Woman—Employment—U.S. I. Title.

Woman—Religious life.

GREELEY, Andrew M., 1928- 248.8'3
Letters to Nancy, from Andrew M. Greeley. [New and rev.] Garden City, N.Y., Image Books [1967] 160 p. 19 cm. (Image D226) [BX2365.G7 1967] 67-8684
1. Woman—Religious life. I. Title.

Woman—Sexual behavior.

ZOLTAN, Anne. 301.41'76'33
Annie: the female experience. [1st ed. in U.S.A.] New York, Julian Press [1973] 153 p. 22 cm. Autobiographical. [HQ29.Z64 1973] 72-97451 6.00
1. Woman—Sexual behavior. 2. Woman—Psychology. I. Title.

Woman—Suffrage—Oregon.

DUNIWAY, Abigail (Scott), 1834-1915. 324'.3'0924 B
Path breaking; an autobiographical history of the equal suffrage movement in Pacific Coast states. With a new introd. by Eleanor Flexner. 2d ed. New York, Schocken Books [1971] xviii, 297 p. illus. 21 cm. (Studies in the life of women) (A Schocken paperback series) [JK1896.D8 1971] 79-162285 ISBN 0-8052-0322-2 3.45
1. Woman—Suffrage—Oregon. 2. Woman—Suffrage—U.S. 3. Prohibition. I. Title. **BIP**

Womelsdorf, Pa.—History.

IBACH, Earl W. 974.8'16 B
The hub of the Tulpehocken / Earl W. Ibach, author. [s.l. : s.n.], c1976 (Lebanon, Pa. : Boyer Print. Co.) 653, [11] p. : ill. ; 29 cm. Bibliography: p. [664] [F159.W82I2] 76-380585
1. Womelsdorf, Pa.—History. 2. Womelsdorf, Pa.—Biography. 3. Womelsdorf, Pa.—Genealogy. 4. Registers of births, etc.—Womelsdorf, Pa. I. Title.

Women air pilots—Juvenile literature.

CROWLEY, Kitty A., 1942- 629.1'092'2 B
First women of the skies / by Kitty A. Crowley ; illustrated by Russell Charpentier. New York : C.P.I., c1978. 48 p. : ill. (some col.) ; 24 cm. Brief biographies of five women pioneers of the air: Harriet Quimby, Mathilde Moissant, Bessie Coleman, Valentina Tereshkova, and Emily Warner. [TL539.C76] 920 78-21907 ISBN 0-89547-063-2 : 5.58
1. Women air pilots—Juvenile literature. 2. Women astronauts—Juvenile literature. I. Charpentier, Russell. II. Title.
Distributed by Silver Burdell, Morristown, NJ 07960 **BIP**

Women—Alaska—History.

JONES, Helen Wendy, 1906. 920.72'09798
Women who braved the far North : 200 years of Alaskan women / H. Wendy Jones. 1st ed. San Diego, Calif. : Grossmont Press, c1976- v. : ill. ; 22 cm. Bibliography: v. 1, p. 199-206. [HQ1438.A4J66] 76-18601 ISBN 0-913182-63-X pbk. : 6.95
1. Women—Alaska—History. 2. Women—Alaska—Bibliography. I. Title.

Women, American.

NATHAN, Dorothy 920.7
Women of courage. Illus. by Carolyn Cather. New York, Random [c.1964] 188p. illus. 22cm. (U. S. landmark bks., 107) 63-7827 1.95; 2.28 lib. ed.,
1. Women, American. I. Title.
Contents omitted.

NATHAN, Dorthy. 920.7
Women of courage. Illustrated by Carolyn Cather. New York, Random House [1964] 188 p. illus. 22 cm. (U.S. Landmark books, 107) CONTENTS. -- Susan B. Anthony. -- Jane Addams. -- Mary McLeod Bethune. -- Amelia Earhart. -- Margaret Mead. Bibliography: p. 178-181. [CT3260.N3] 63-7827
1. Women. American. I. Title.

Women artists—Australia—South Australia—Biography.

BIVEN, Rachel. 709'.2'2 B
Some forgotten, some remembered : women artists of South Australia / written and compiled by Rachel Biven. Norwood, S.A. : Sydenham Gallery, 1976. [76] p. : ill. (part col.) ; 28 cm. [N7402.S6B58] 77-355746 ISBN 0-9597105-0-7
1. Women artists—Australia—South Australia—Biography. I. Title.

Women artists—Biography.

FINE, Elsa Honig. 709'.2'2 B
Women and art : the fifteenth to the eighteenth century / by Elsa Honig Fine. Montclair, N.J. : Allanheld & Schram, [1978] p. cm. Includes index. Bibliography: p. [N43.F56] 77-15897 ISBN 0-8390-0187-8 : 38.50 ISBN 0-8390-0212-2 pbk. : 8.95
1. Women artists—Biography. 2. Art, Renaissance. 3. Art, Modern. I. Title.

PETERSEN, Karen, 1943- 709'.2'2 B
Women artists : recognition and reappraisal from the early Middle Ages to the twentieth century / Karen Petersen & J. J. Wilson. 1st ed. New York : Harper & Row, 1976. 212 p. : ill. ; 24 cm. (Harper colophon books ; CN 387) Includes index. Bibliography: p. 179-189. [N40.P45 1976] 75-39543 ISBN 0-06-090387-2 : 5.95
1. Women artists—Biography. I. Wilson, J. J., 1936- joint author. II. Title. **BIP**

TUFTS, Eleanor. 709'.2'2 B
Our hidden heritage: five centuries of women artists. [New York] Paddington Press [1974] 256 p. illus. 29 cm. Bibliography: p. 247-251. [N43.T83] 73-20955 ISBN 0-8467-0026-3 12.95
1. Women artists—Biography. I. Title.

WORKING it out : 301.41'2'0922 B
23 women writers, artists, scientists, and scholars talk about their lives and work / edited by Sara Ruddick and Pamela Daniels ; with a foreword by Adrienne Rich. 1st ed. New York : Pantheon Books, c1977. xxxii, 349 p. : ill. ; 25 cm. Includes bibliographical references. [HQ1123.W64] 76-54624 ISBN 0-394-40936-1 : 10.00
1. Women artists—Biography. 2. Women authors—Biography. 3. Women scientists—Biography. 4. Women college teachers—

Biography. I. Ruddick, Sara, 1935- II. Daniels, Pamela, 1937-
Contents omitted. BIP

Women artists—Directories.

WOMEN'S History Research Center. 709'.2'2
Female artists, past and present. Berkeley, Calif., c1972. 42 p. 28 cm. [N43.W65 1972] 74-184169 4.00
1. Women artists—Directories. 2. Women artists—Bibliography. I. Title.

Women artists—United States—Biography—Juvenile literature.

DAVIS, Mary Lee, 1935- 700'.92'2 B
Women in entertainment and the arts / by Mary L. Davis. Minneapolis : T. S. Denison, c1976. 12 p. ; 22 cm. (Her Women in American life series ; book 3) Brief sketches of the careers of women who have made significant contributions to the arts and the field of entertainment. [NX504.D38] 920 76-150795 ISBN 0-513-01499-3
1. Women artists—United States—Biography—Juvenile literature. 2. Arts, Modern—20th century—United States—Juvenile literature. I. Title. II. Series.

FOWLER, Carol. 709'.2'2 B
Art / by Carol Fowler. Minneapolis : Dillon Press, c1976. p. cm. (Contributions of women) Bibliography: p. Brief biographies of six prominent American women artists: Mary Cassatt, Grandma Moses, Georgia O'Keefe, Louise Nevelson, Helen Frankenthaler, and Suzanne Jackson. [N6536.F64] 920 76-3479 ISBN 0-87518-115-5
1. Women artists—United States—Biography—Juvenile literature. I. Title.

Women artists—United States—Juvenile literature.

BOWMAN, Kathleen. 700'.92'2 B
New women in art & dance / by Kathleen Bowman ; designed by Larry Soule. Mankato, Minn. : Creative Education, [1976] p. cm. Brief biographies of a sculptor, weaver photographer, artist, and dancers, including Louise Nevelson, Charlene Burningham, Cynthia Gregory, Barbara Morgan, Martha Graham, Judith Jamison, and Marie Burton. [NX504.B6] 920 76-5457 ISBN 0-87191-510-3
1. Women artists—United States—Juvenile literature. 2. Arts, Modern—20th century—United States—Juvenile literature. I. Title. BIP

Women as economists.

THOMSON, Dorothy Lampen. 330'.092'2 B
Adam Smith's daughters. [1st ed.] New York, Exposition Press [1973] vii, 140 p. ports. 22 cm. (An Exposition-university book) Contents.Contents.—Jane Haldimand Marcet.—Harriet Martineau.—Millicent Garrett Fawcett.—Rosa Luxemburg.—Beatrice Potter Webb.—Joan Robinson. Includes bibliographical references. [HB76.T46 1973] 72-97724 ISBN 0-682-47675-7 6.00
1. Women as economists. I. Title. BIP

Women as teachers.

SWANSONK, Nellie R ed. 371.100922
Pioneer women teachers of North Dakota, edited and compiled by Nellie R. Swanson and Eleanor C. Bryson. Minot, N.D., Ward County Independent [1965] vi, 178 p. illus., port. 23 cm. "Published in recognition of the silver anniversary of Alpha Omicron State, and the diamond anniversary of North Dakota." [LA2315.N9S8] 65-6019
1. Women as teachers. 2. Teachers — North Dakota — Biog. I. Bryson, Eleanor C., 1879- joint ed. II. Delta Kappa Gamma Society. Alpha Omicron State. III. North Dakota. IV. Title.

Women as teachers—Oregon.

LAMPLIGHTERS: leaders in learning. 370'.922 B [Prineville, Or.] Alpha Rho State, Oregon, Delta Kappa Gamma Society, 1959-66. 2 v. illus. 23 cm. v. 1 compiled by Neva Dallas, and others; vol. 2, by Pearl Clements Gischler, Ruth Ellsworth Richardson [and] Minnie Kjelde. [LB2837.L3] 79-6997
1. Women as teachers—Oregon. I. Dallas, Neva, comp. II. Gischler, Pearl Clements, 1903- comp. III. Richardson, Ruth Ellsworth, comp. IV. Kjelde, Minnie, comp. V. Delta Kappa Gamma Society. Alpha Rho State (Or.)

Women—Australia—Biography.

LARKINS, John. 301.41'2'0994
Sheilas : a tribute to Australian women / [text] John Larkins ; [photographer] Bruce Howard. Adelaide : Rigby, 1976. 280 p. : ill. (some col.) ; 26 cm. Aus [HQ1822.A3L37] 77-369755 ISBN 0-7270-0207-4 : 9.95
1. Women—Australia—Biography. I. Howard, Bruce. II. Title.

Women authors—Biography.

KIRKLAND, Winifred Margaretta, 1872-1943. 809
Girls who became writers, by Winifred and Frances Kirkland. Freeport, N.Y., Books for Libraries Press [1971, c1933] 121 p. 23 cm. (Essay index reprint series) Contents.—Fanny Burney, a long-ago lady of letters.—Selma Lagerlof, who listened and remembers.—Edna St. Vincent Millay, how a poet is made.—Pearl Buck, who opened a door into China.—Mary Roberts Rinehart, an adventurer and her adventures.—Sarah Josepha Hale, a lady and her book.—Anne Shannon Monroe, who sees and hears the out-of-doors.—Louisa Alcott, the girl who wrote for girls.—Willa Cather, a transplanted writer.—Dorothy Canfield Fisher, at home and abroad. [PN471.K5 1971] 78-152182 ISBN 0-8369-2234-4
1. Women authors—Biography. 2. Girls—Biography. I. Kirkland, Frances, joint author. II. Title. BIP

Women authors, English—Biography.

HUFSTADER, Alice Anderson. 828'.009 B
Sisters of the quill / by Alice Anderson Hufstader. New York : Dodd, Mead, c1978. viii, 329 p., [4] leaves of plates : ill. ; 24 cm. Includes index. Bibliography: p. 313-315. [PR113.H78] 78-2642 ISBN 0-396-07544-4 : 15.00
1. Women authors, English—Biography. 2. Authors, English—18th century—Biography. I. Title. BIP

Women authors—France—Biography.

CROSLAND, Margaret, 1920- 840'.9'9287 B
Women of iron and velvet : French women writers after George Sand / Margaret Crosland. New York : Taplinger Pub. Co., 1976. 255 p., [5] leaves of plates : ill. ; 23 cm. Includes index. Bibliography: p. 241-248. [PC149.C7] 75-8202 ISBN 0-8008-8436-1 : 10.95
1. Women authors—France—Biography. I. Title. BIP

CROSLAND, Margaret, 1920- 840'.9'9287 B
Women of iron and velvet, and the books they wrote in France / [by] Margaret Crosland. London : Constable, 1976. 255 p., leaf of plate, [8] p. of plates : ill., plan, ports. ; 23 cm. Includes index. Bibliography: p. 241-248. [PQ149.C7 1976b] 77-359824 ISBN 0-09-461500-4 : £4.95
1. Women authors—France—Biography. I. Title.

Women authors—Great Britain.

WILSON, Mona, 1872- 820'.9'9287 B
Jane Austen and some contemporaries. With an introduction by G. M. Young. [Folcroft, Pa.] Folcroft Library Editions, 1973. p. Reprint of the 1938 ed. published by Cresset Press, London. Contents.Contents.—Jane Austen, 1775-1817.—Eliza Fletcher, 1770-1858.—Anne Woodrooffe, 1766-1830.—Mary Martha Butt, 1775-1795.—Mary Anne Schimmelpenninck, 1778-1856.—Charlotte Elizabeth Tonna, 1790-1846.—Mary Somerville, 1780-1872.—Harriet Grote, 1792-1878. [PR111.W54 1973b] 73-12809 11.50
1. Women authors—Great Britain. 2. Authors, English—Biography. 3. Great Britain—Social life and customs—19th century. I. Title.

Women authors—Great Britain—Biography.

BLACK, Helen C. 820'.9'9287 B
Notable women authors of the day, by Helen C. Black. London, Maclaren, 1906. Detroit, Gale Research Co., 1974. p. [PR115.B6 1974] 74-4267 ISBN 0-8103-3991-9
1. Women authors—Great Britain—Biography. 2. Authors, English—19th century—Biography. I. Title. BIP

ELWOOD, Anne Katharine (Curteis) 820'.9'9287 B
Memoirs of the literary ladies of England, from the commencement of the last century. London, H. Colburn, 1843. [New York, AMS Press, 1973] 2 v. ports. 19 cm. On spine: WOL. [PR111.E5 1973] 72-37692 ISBN 0-404-56749-5 35.00 (2 vols.)
1. Women authors—Great Britain—Biography. 2. Authors, English. I. Title.

Women—Biography.

ARMOUR, Richard Willard, 1906- 920.72'02'07
It all started with Eve / Richard Armour ; suitably illustrated by Campbell Grant. Boston : G. K. Hall, 1976, c1956. xiv, 235 p. : ill. ; 24 cm. Large print ed. [CT3203.A67 1976] 76-9028 ISBN 0-8161-6373-1 lib.bdg. : 8.95
1. Women—Biography. 2. Sight-saving books. I. Title. BIP

ARMOUR, Richard Willard, 1906- 920.7
It all started with Eve, being a brief account of certain famous women, each of them richly endowed with some quality that drives men mad, omitting no impertinent and unbelievable fact, and based upon a stupendous amount of firsthand and secondhand research, some of it in books. Suitably illustrated by Campbell Grant. New York, McGraw-Hill [1956] 136 p. illus. 20 cm. [CT3203.A67] 56-10304
1. Women—Biography. I. Title.

BEACH, Seth Curtis, 1837-1932. 920.074
Daughters of the Puritans; a group of brief biographies. Freeport, N.Y., Books for Libraries Press [1967] 286 p. 19 cm. (Essay index reprint series) Reprint of the 1905 ed. Contents.Contents.—Catharine Maria Sedgwick, 1789 867.—Mary Lovell Ware, 1798 849.—Lydia Maria Child, 1802 880.—Dorothea Lynde Dix, 1802 887.—Sarah Margaret Fuller Ossoli, 1810 850.—Harriet Beecher Stowe, 1811 896.—Louisa May Alcott, 1832 888. [CT3260.B4 1967] 67-22054
I. Sedgwick, Catharine Maria, 1787-1867. II. Ware, Mary Lovell (Pickard) 1798-1849. III. Child, Lydia Maria (Francis) 1802-1880. IV. Dix, Dorothea Lynde, 1802-1887. V. Ossoli, Sarah Margaret (Fuller) marchesa d', 1810-1850. VI. Stowe, Harriet Elizabeth (Beecher) 1811-1896. VII. Alcott, Louisa May, 1832-1888. VIII. Title.

BRADFORD, Gamaliel, 1863-1932. 920.02
Portraits of women. Freeport, N.Y., Books for Libraries Press [1969] xi, 201 p. ports. 23 cm. (Essay index reprint series) Reprint of the 1916 ed. Contents.Contents.—Lady Mary Wortley Montagu.—Lady Holland.—Miss Austen.—Madame d'Arblay.—Mrs. Pepys.—Madame de Sevigne.—Madame du Deffand.—Madame de Choiseul.—Eugenie de Guerin. [CT3230.B7 1969] 75-90611 ISBN 0-8369-1247-0
1. Women—Biography. 2. Women—France—Biography. I. Title. BIP

DEEN, Edith. 922
Great women of the Christian faith. [1st ed.] New York, Harper [1959] 428 p. 25 cm. [BR1713.D4] 59-12821
1. Women—Biography. 2. Christian biography. I. Title. BIP

DIAGRAM Group. 920.72
Mothers : 100 mothers of the famous and the infamous / by the Diagram Group. New York : Paddington Press, c1976. 267 p. : ill. ; 28 cm. Includes index. [CT3203.D54 1976] 75-22962 ISBN 0-8467-0114-6 pbk. : 6.95
1. Women—Biography. 2. Mothers—Biography. I. Title.

EMINENT women of the age 920.72
[by] James Parton [and others] New York, Arno Press, 1974 [c1868] 628 p. ports. 23 cm. (Women in America: from colonial times to the 20th century) Reprint of the 1869 ed. published by S. M. Betts, Hartford, Conn. [CT3234.E5 1974] 74-3968 ISBN 0-405-06116-1
1. Women—Biography. I. Parton, James, 1822-1891. II. Title. III. Series.

GOLDSMITH, Margaret Leland, 1894- 920.72
Seven women against the world / by Margaret Goldsmith. [Westport, Conn. : Hyperion Press, 1976. ix, 236 p., [1] leaf of plates : port. ; 23 cm. (Pioneers of the woman's movement) Reprint of the 1935 ed. published by Methuen, London. Contents.Contents.—Charlotte Corday.—Theroigne de Mericourt.—Flora Tristan.—Louise Michel.—Vera Figner.—Emma Goldman.—Rosa Luxemburg.—Is there a revolutionary type? Bibliography: p. 235-236. [HQ1123.G64 1976] 75-21989 ISBN 0-88355-316-3 : 17.50
1. Women—Biography. 2. Revolutionists—Psychology. I. Title. BIP

GRAHAM, Sheilah. 920.72
How to marry super rich : or, Love, money, and the morning after / Sheilah Graham. New York : Grosset & Dunlap, [1974] viii, 246 p., [8] leaves of plates : ports. ; 22 cm. [CT3203.G69] 73-18532 ISBN 0-448-01304-5 : 7.95
1. Women—Biography. I. Title.

KLOCK, Frank. 301.41'2'0922 B
The predators; tales of legendary liberated ladies. New York, Drake Publishers [1974] viii, 304 p. 24 cm. Bibliography: p. 297-304. [HQ1123.K58] 74-4524 ISBN 0-87749-664-1
1. Women—Biography. I. Title.

KOSTMAN, Samuel. 920.72
Twentieth century women of achievement / Samuel Kostman. 1st ed. New York : R. Rosen Press, 1976. xiv, 178 p. ; 22 cm. & workbook. Contents.Contents.—Mary Baker Eddy.—Mary McLeod Bethune.—Margaret Sanger.—Pearl S. Buck.—Marie Curie.—Golda Meir.—Margaret Mead.—Marian Anderson.—Gloria Steinem.—Billie Jean King. Includes bibliographies. [HQ1154.K665] 920 75-31557 ISBN 0-8239-0333-8 : 4.80
1. Women—Biography. I. Title. BIP

MARLOW, Joan. 920.72
The great women / Joan Marlow. New York : A & W Publishers, c1979. 383 p. : ill. ; 27 cm. "A Hart book." Includes index. [HQ1123.M37] 79-65342 ISBN 0-89479-056-0 : 14.95
1. Women—Biography. I. Title. BIP

MAY, Antoinette. 920.72
Different drummers : they did what they wanted / Antoinette May. Millbrae, Calif. : Les Femmes Pub., c1976. iii, 156 p. : ports. ; 22 cm. Includes index. Bibliography: 153-154. [CT3234.M37] 76-11373 ISBN 0-89087-907-9 pbk. : 4.95
1. Women—Biography. I. Title. BIP

MOFFAT, Mary Jane, comp. 920.72
Revelations—diaries of women / edited by Mary Jane Moffat & Charlotte Painter. New York : Vintage Books, 1975, c1974. x, 411 p. ; 19 cm. Bibliography: p. 409-411. [CT3202.M618 1975] 75-6602 ISBN 0-394-71151-3 pbk. : 2.95
1. Women—Biography. I. Painter, Charlotte, joint comp. II. Title.

THOMAS, Henry, 1886- 920.7
Living biographies of famous women, by Henry Thomas and Dana Lee Thomas. Garden City, N.Y., Garden City Books [1959] 313 p. 22 cm. [CT3202.T53 1959] 59-2810
1. Women — Biog. I. Thomas, Dana Lee, 1918- joint author. II. Title. **BIP**

THE Women's book of world records and achievements / edited by Lois Decker O'Neill. 1st ed. Garden City, N.Y. : Anchor Press/Doubleday, 1979. xiii, 798 p., [36] leaves of plates : ill. ; 25 cm. "An Information House book." Includes index. [CT3234.W65] 77-82961 ISBN 0-385-12732-4 : 19.95 920.72
1. Women—Biography. 2. Biography—19th century. 3. Biography—20th century. I. O'Neill, Lois Decker. **BIP**

**WORLD Who's who of women* 920 B *vol. 2 1974-1975.* Cambridge, England, Melrose Press, 1975 1390 p. illus. 26 cm. [E749] 0-900332-30-1
1. Women—Biography.
Distributed by Rowman and Littlefield, for 30.00.

Women—Biography—Juvenile literature.

FERRIS, Helen Josephina, 1890-1969, ed. 920.72
Five girls who dared; the girlhood stories of five courageous girls as told by themselves. Collected by Helen Ferris. Illustrated by Allan McNab. Freeport, N.Y., Books for Libraries Press [1971] 270 p. illus., ports. 23 cm. (Essay index reprint series) Reprint of the 1931 ed. Extracts from the autobiographies of five women who accepted and met unusual challenges in their lives: Amelia Earhart, Louise de Koven Bowen, Josephine De Mott Robinson, Elisabeth Marbury, and Marie, Grand Duchess of Russia. [CT3205.F38 1971] 920 77-107699 ISBN 0-8369-2313-8
1. Women—Biography—Juvenile literature. 2. Autobiographies—Juvenile literature. I. McNab, Allan, illus. II. Title.

KULKIN, Mary-Ellen, 1932- 920.72
Her way : biographies of women for young people / Mary-Ellen Kulkin ; [illustrated by Tim Basaldua]. Chicago : American Library Association, 1976. xxv, 449 p. : ill. ; 25 cm. Includes bibliographical references and index. A collection of 260 short profiles and bibliographies of notable women throughout history and an additional bibliography of over 300 collective biographies of women. [HQ1123.K75] 920 76-25861 ISBN 0-8389-0221-9 : 25.00
1. Women—Biography—Juvenile literature. 2. Women—Juvenile literature—Bio-Bibliography. I. Basaldua, Tim. II. Title. **BIP**

LISTON, Robert A. 920.72
Women who ruled : Cleopatra to Elizabeth II / Robert A. Liston. New York : J. Messner, c1978. 192 p. ; 22 cm. Includes index. Bibliography: p.186-187. Biographies of 17 women rulers, including Cleopatra, Elizabeth I of England, and Golda Meir, focus on how they came to power, their accomplishments, methods of ruling, and impact on history. [HQ1123.L57] 920 78-15629 ISBN 0-671-32919-7. : 7.79
1. Women—Biography—Juvenile literature. 2. Women in politics—Juvenile literature. I. Title. **BIP**

WOMEN with a cause / 920.72
edited, with commentary, by Bennett Wayne. Champaign, Ill. : Garrard Pub. Co., [1975] 168 p. : ill. ; 22 cm. (A Target book) Includes index. Biographies of four outstanding women in United States history: Anne Hutchinson, Lucretia Mott, Susan B. Anthony, and Eleanor Roosevelt. [HQ1123.W63] 920 75-4971 ISBN 0-8116-4914-8 lib.bdg. : 3.98
1. Women—Biography—Juvenile literature. I. Wayne, Bennett. **BIP**

Women—Canada—Biography.

INNIS, Mary (Quayle) 920.72'0971
The clear spirit : twenty Canadian women and their times / edited by Mary Quayle Innis. Toronto : Published for the Canadian Federation of University Women by the University of Toronto Press, 1973, c1966. xvi, 304 p., [6] leaves of plates : ports. ; 23 cm. (Canadian university paperbooks ; 135) Includes some text in French. Includes bibliographies. [CT3270.I5 1973] 75-318917 ISBN 0-8020-1418-6 : 4.95
1. Women—Canada—Biography. I. Title. **BIP**

JOHNSTON, Jean. 920.72'0971
Wilderness women : Canada's forgotten history / Jean Johnston ; drawings by Patricia Wilson Johnston. Paperback ed. Toronto : P. Martin Associates, 1976. viii, 242 p. : ill. ; 21 cm. Bibliography: p. 242. [HQ1455.A3J63 1976] 77-362100 ISBN 0-88778-127-6 : 4.95
1. Women—Canada—Biography. I. Title.

Women clergy—United States—Biography.

SMITH, Betsy Covington. 291.6'1'0924 B
Women in religion / by Betsy Covington Smith. New York : Walker, 1978. xix, 139 p. : ill. ; 24 cm. (Breakthrough) Describes the efforts of five women to break through the traditional male dominance of the clergy in churches and synagogues. [BV676.S64] 920 78-3016 ISBN 0-8027-6286-7 : 8.95
1. Women clergy—United States—Biography. I. Title. II. Series: Breakthrough (New York)

Women composers—Biography.

ELSON, Louis Charles, 1848-1920. 780'.92'2 B
Woman in music / by Louis C. Elson. New York : Gordon Press, 1976. p. cm. Reprint of the 1918 ed. published by The University Society, New York. [ML82.E5 1976] 76-20469 ISBN 0-87968-459-3 lib.bdg. : 34.95
1. Women composers—Biography. 2. Women musicians. I. Title. **BIP**

LAURENCE, Anya. 780'.92'2 B
Women of notes : 1,000 women composers born before 1900 / by Anya Laurence. 1st ed. New York : R. Rosen Press, 1978. xix, 101 p. : ports ; 29 cm. (The Theatre student) Discography: p. 96-100. [ML105.L28] 78-7862 ISBN 0-8239-0463-6 : 12.50 12.50
1. Women composers—Biography. I. Title.

STERN, Susan, 1953- 780'.92'2 B
Women composers : a handbook / by Susan Stern. Metuchen, N.J. : Scarecrow Press, 1978. p. cm. Contents.Contents.—Introduction.—List of sources.—The handbook.—Supplementary list of composers.—Supplementary bibliography. [ML105.S7] 78-5505 ISBN 0-8108-1138-3 : 8.00
1. Women composers—Biography. 2. Music—Bio-bibliography—Indexes. I. Title. **BIP**

Women—Employment—Massachusetts—Lowell—Personal narratives.

ROBINSON, Harriet Jane Hanson, 1825-1911. 331.4'87'7210924 B
Loom and spindle : or, Life among the early mill girls : with a sketch of "The Lowell offering" and some of its contributors / by Harriet H. Robinson ; introd. by Jane Wilkins Pultz. Rev. ed. Kailua, Hawaii : Press Pacifica, 1976. xii, 128 p. : ill. ; 23 cm. [HD6096.L9R7 1976] 75-46389 ISBN 0-916630-01-3 : 7.95. ISBN 0-916630-02-1 pbk. : 4.50
1. Women—Employment—Massachusetts—Lowell—Personal narratives. 2. Women—Employment—Massachusetts—Lowell—Biography. 3. Factory system. 4. Lowell, Mass.—Social conditions. 5. Lowell offering. I. Title.

Women—Employment—United States—Juvenile literature.

DAVIS, Mary Lee, 1935- 331.4'0973
Women in the traditional role and unusual occupations / by Mary L. Davis. Minneapolis : T. S. Denison, c1976. 16 p. : ports. ; 22 cm. (Her Women in American life series ; book 8) Brief biographies of women in the traditional role of homemaker, women who have turned homemaking skills into commercial ventures, and women employed in nontraditional occupations. [HD6095.D38] 920 77-354352 ISBN 0-513-01504-3
1. Women—Employment—United States—Juvenile literature. I. Title. II. Series.

Women—England—Biography.

BOYD, Elizabeth French, 1905- 700'.92'2 B
Bloomsbury heritage : their mothers and their aunts / [by] Elizabeth French Boyd. London : Hamilton, 1976. xii, 161 p., [8] p. of plates : ill., geneal. tables, ports. ; 23 cm. Includes index. Bibliography: p. [148]-154. [CT3320.B68 1976] 76-379709 ISBN 0-241-89406-9 : £4.95
1. Women—England—Biography. 2. England—Biography. 3. England—Intellectual life—19th century. I. Title. **BIP**

BOYD, Elizabeth French, 1905- 920.72'0942
Bloomsbury heritage, their mothers and their aunts / Elizabeth French Boyd. New York : Taplinger Pub. Co., 1976. xii, 161 p., [4] leaves of plates : ill. ; 23 cm. Includes index. Bibliography: p. [148]-154. [CT3320.B68 1976b] 76-422 ISBN 0-8008-0821-5 : 10.50
1. Women—England—Biography. 2. England—Biography. 3. England—Intellectual life—19th century. I. Title.

HOGREFE, Pearl. 920.72'0942
Women of action in Tudor England / by Pearl Hogrefe. 1st ed. Ames : Iowa State University Press, 1976. p. cm. Includes bibliographies. [HQ1595.A3H63] 76-28496 ISBN 0-8138-0910-X : 9.95
1. Women—England—Biography. I. Title. **BIP**

JENKINS, Elizabeth, 1907- 920.042
Ten fascinating women. [1st American ed.] New York, Coward-McCann [1968] 207 p. ports. 23 cm. Contents.Contents.—Martha Ray.—Elizabeth Tudor.—Sarah Churchill, Duchess of Marlborough.—Fair Rosamond.—Elizabeth Inchbald.—Becky Wells.—Harriette Wilson.—Lady Blessington.—The Duchess of Lauderdale.—Mary Fitton.—Bibliography (p. 201-202) [CT3320.J4 1968] 68-23368
1. Women—England—Biography. I. Title.

Women entertainers—United States—Biography—Juvenile literature.

BOWMAN, Kathleen. 790.2'092'2 B
New women in entertainment / by Kathleen Bowman ; design by Larry Soule. Mankato, Minn. : Creative Education, [1976] p. cm. Brief biographies of seven women who have been highly successful in various fields of entertainment: Lily Tomlin, Diana Ross, Melvina Reynolds, Cicely Tyson, Buffy Sainte-Marie, Valerie Harper, and Judy Collins. [PN2285.B66] 920 76-4940 ISBN 0-87191-512-X
1. Women entertainers—United States—Biography—Juvenile literature. 2. Entertainers. I. Title. **BIP**

Women ethologists—Biography—Juvenile literature.

FACKLAM, Margery. 591.5 B
Wild animals, gentle women / Margery Facklam ; illustrated with line drawings by Paul Facklam and with photos. 1st ed. New York : Harcourt Brace Jovanovich, c1978. 139 p. : ill. ; 24 cm. Includes index. Bibliography: p. [129]-131. Describes the experiences of eleven women who study animal behavior: Belle Benchley, Ruth Harkness, Jane Goodall, Kay McKeever, Hope Buyukmihci, Karen Pryor, Eugenie Clark, Dian Fossey, Birute Galdikas, Leone Pippard, and Heather Malcolm. [QL26.F3] 920 77-88961 5.95
1. Women ethologists—Biography—Juvenile literature. I. Facklam, Paul. II. Title. **BIP**

Women—France—Biography.

BROOKS, Geraldine, 1875- 920.044
Dames and daughters of the French Court. Freeport, N.Y., Books for Libraries Press [1968] vii, 290 p. ports. 23 cm. (Essay index reprint series) Reprint of the 1904 ed. Contents.Contents.—Madame de Sevigne (1626-1696)—Madame de LaFayette (1634-1693)—Madame Geoffrin (1699-1777)—Mademoiselle de Lespinasse (1732-1776)—Madame Roland (1754-1792)—Madame Le Brun (1755-1842)—Madame de Stael (1766-1817)—Madame Recamier (1777-1849)—Madame Valmore (1789-1859)—Madame de Remusat (1780-1821) [DC36.2.B7 1968] 68-8443
1. Women—France—Biography. 2. France—Court and courtiers. I. Title. **BIP**

BUTLER, Pierce, 1873- 920.72'0944
Women of mediaeval France / by Pierce Butler. New York : Gordon Press, 1978. p. cm. Reprint of the 1907-08 ed. published by Rittenhouse Press, Philadelphia, which was issued as v. 5 of Woman in all ages and in all countries. [HQ1147.F7B87 1978] 78-2946 ISBN 0-87968-269-8 lib.bdg. : 49.95
1. Women—France—Biography. I. Title. II. Series: Woman in all ages and in all countries ; v. 5.

WILSON, Robert McNair, 1882- 944.04'0922
Women of the French Revolution, by R. McNair Wilson. Port Washington, N.Y., Kennikat Press [1970] 287 p. ports. 23 cm. [DC145.W59 1970] 72-110928 ISBN 0-8046-0910-1
1. Women—France—Biography. 2. France—History—Revolution, 1789-1799—Biography. I. Title. **BIP**

Women—Georgia—Biography.

GEORGIA women : 920.72'09764
a celebration / Barbara B. Reitt, editor. Atlanta : Atlanta Branch, American Association of University Women, 1976. 90 p. ; 23 cm. Includes bibliographical references and index. [HQ1438.G4G5] 76-29185
1. Women—Georgia—Biography. I. Reitt, Barbara B. II. American Association of University Women. Atlanta Branch.

Women—Germany—Social conditions.

QUATAERT, Jean H. 301.41'2'0943
Reluctant feminists : Socialist women in Imperial Germany, 1885-1917 / Jean H. Quataert. Princeton, N.J. : Princeton University Press, c1979. p. cm. Includes index. Bibliography: p. [HQ1627.Q37] 79-84011 ISBN 0-691-05276-X : 18.50
1. Women—Germany—Social conditions. 2. Feminism—Germany—History. 3. Women and socialism—Germany—History. 4. Women in politics—Germany—History. 5. Women—Germany—Biography. I. Title.

VETTER, Hal 920.7
Women of the swastika. Evanston, Ill., Regency [c.1963] 156p. 18cm. (RB 312) .50 pap.,
I. Title.

Women—Great Britain—Biography.

ADAMS, William Henry Davenport, 1828-1891. 301.41'2'0942 B
Stories of the lives of noble women. Plainview, N.Y., Books for Libraries Press [1974] p. cm. (Essay index reprint series) Reprint of the 1891 ed. published by T. Nelson, London; originally published under title: The sunshine of domestic life. Contents.Contents.—Steadfastness to the truth: the story of Anne Askew.—Matronly excellence: the story of Lady Vere.—Hospitality: the story of Lady Alicia Lisle.—The Charity that endureth all things: the story of Elizabeth Gaunt.—Mental energy and self-reliance: the story of Elizabeth Inchbald.—Faithful to the end: the story of Lady Arabella Stuart.—Womanly virtues in an exalted station: the story of Lady Jane Grey.—A noble English mother: the story of Mary, Countess of Pembroke.—A heroic life: the story of Queen Jeanne D'Albret.—Woman the enthusiast: the story of Madame Roland.—The patience of genius: the story of Charlette Bronte. [HQ1595.A3A32 1974] 920 74-5072 ISBN 0-518-10174-6
1. Women—Great Britain—Biography. 2. Women—Conduct of life. I. Title.

COLE, Margaret Isabel (Postgate) 1893- 920.042
Women of to-day, by Margaret Cole. Freeport, N.Y., Books for Libraries Press [1968] vii, 311 p. ports. 22 cm. (Essay index reprint series) Reprint of the 1938 ed. Contents.Contents.—Ethel Smyth.—Lady Henry Somerset.—Edith Cavell. —Mary Macarthur.—Elizabeth Garrett Anderson.—Laura Knight. —Annie Besant.—Clare Sheridan.—Beatrice Webb.—Rosita Forbes. [CT3320.C57 1968] 68-16920
1. Women—Great Britain—Biography. I. Title. BIP

DUTIFUL daughters : 920.72'0941
women talk about their lives / edited by Jean McCrindle and Sheila Rowbotham. Austin : University of Texas Press, c1977. 411 p. ; 23 cm. [HQ1595.A3D87 1977] 78-68308 ISBN 0-292-71518-8 : 14.95
1. Women—Great Britain—Biography. 2. Women—Great Britain—Social conditions—Addresses, essays, lectures. 3. Labor and laboring classes—Great Britain—Addresses, essays, lectures. I. McCrindle, Jean, 1937- II. Rowbotham, Sheila. BIP

FAWCETT, Millicent (Garrett), Dame, 1847-1929. 920.72
Some eminent women of our times; short biographical sketches, by Mrs. Henry Fawcett. Freeport, N.Y., Books for Libraries Press [1973] p. (Essay index reprint series) Reprint of the 1889 ed. published by Macmillan, London. Contents.Contents.—Elizabeth Fry.—Mary Carpenter.—Caroline Herschel.—Sarah Martin.—Mary Somerville.—Queen Victoria.—Harriet Martineau.—Florence Nightingale.—Mary Lamb.—Agnes Elizabeth Jones.—Charlotte and Emily Bronte.—Elizabeth Barrett Browning.—Lady Sale and her fellow-hostages in Afghanistan.—Elizabeth Gilbert.—Jane Austen.—Maria Edgeworth.—Queen Louisa of Prussia.—Dorothy Wordsworth.—Sister Dora.—Mrs. Barbauld.—Joanna Baillie.—Hannah More.—The American abolitionists - Prudence Crandall and Lucretia Mott. [CT3320.F3 1973] 73-4529 ISBN 0-518-10080-4
1. Women—Great Britain—Biography. I. Title.

VINCENT, Arthur, ed. 920.72
Lives of twelve bad women; illustrations and reviews of feminine turpitude set forth by impartial hands. Freeport, N.Y., Books for Libraries Press [1973] p. (Essay index reprint series) Reprint of the 1897 ed. published by L. C. Page, Boston. Contents.Contents.—Vincent, A. Alice Perrers, favourite of King Edward III (d. 1400).—Coppinger, A. H. Alice Arden, murderess (ex. 1551).—Andrews, C. Moll Cutpurse, thief and receiver (?1584-1659).—Martin, G. Frances Howard, Countess of Somerset (1593-1632).—Kalisch, A. Barbara Villiers, Duchess of Cleveland (1640-1709).—Andrews, C. Jenny Diver, pickpocket (ex. 1741).—Burgess, G. Teresia Constantia Phillips (1709-1765).—Stubbs, E. Elizabeth Brownrigg, cruelty personified (?1720-1767).—Waters, W. G. Elizabeth Canning, imposter (1734-1773).—Waters, W. G. Elizabeth Chudleigh, Duchess of Kingston (1720-1788).—Vincent, A. Mary Bateman, "The Yorkshire Witch" (1768-1809).—Waters, W. G. Mary Anne Clarke (1776-1852). [CT3320.V6 1973] 73-5597 OLives of twelve bad
1. Women—Great Britain—Biography. 2. Female offenders—Great Britain—Biography. I. Title.

WALLAS, Ada Radford, 1859- 920.72'0941
Before the bluestockings / by Ada Wallas (Mrs. Graham Wallas). Folcroft, Pa. : Folcroft Library Editions, 1977. p. cm. Reprint of the 1929 ed. published by G. Allen & Unwin, London. Includes index. [CT3320.We 1977] 77-20229 ISBN 0-8414-9637-4 lib. bdg. : 25.00
1. Women—Great Britain—Biography. 2. Women—History. 3. Great Britain—Biography. I. Title. BIP

Women—History—Middle Ages, 500-1500.

GIES, Frances. 301.41'2'0902
Women in the Middle Ages / Frances and Joseph Gies. 1st ed. New York : Crowell, c1978. 264 p. : ill. ; 21 cm. Includes index. Bibliography: p. [246]-259. [HQ1143.G53 1978] 77-25832 ISBN 0-690-01724-3 : 10.95
1. Women—History—Middle Ages, 500-1500. 2. Women—Europe—Biography. 3. Women—Europe—Social conditions. I. Gies, Joseph, joint author. II. Title. BIP

Women in aeronautics.

ADAMS, Jean. 629.13'0922 B
Heroines of the sky, by Jean Adams & Margaret Kimball in collaboration with Jeanette Eaton. Freeport, N.Y., Books for Libraries Press [1970, c1942] xxiv, 295 p. 22 cm. (Essay index reprint series) [TL539.A3 1970] 78-99615
1. Women in aeronautics. 2. Women in the United States—Biography. I. Kimball, Margaret, joint author. II. Eaton, Jeanette, joint author. III. Title. BIP

Women in aeronautics—Juvenile literature.

GENETT, Ann. 629.13'092'2 B
Aviation. Minneapolis, Dillon Press [1975] 113, [3] p. illus. 23 cm. (Contributions of women) Bibliography: p. [114] Brief biographies of six famous female aviators—Amelia Earhart, Anne Morrow Lindberg, Jacqueline Cochran, Jerrie Mock, Geraldyn Cobb, and Emily Howell—as well as a chapter on other outstanding women in that field. [TL539.G46] 920 74-19004 ISBN 0-87518-089-2 6.95 (lib. bdg.)
1. Women in aeronautics—Juvenile literature. I. Title.

JABLONSKI, Edward. 629.13'00922
Ladybirds: women in aviation. Illustrated by Haris Petie. [1st ed.] New York, Hawthorn Books [1968] 160 p. illus. 22 cm. Bibliography: p. 156. Traces the place of women in the history of aviation from the first ladies to go up in balloons in the eighteenth century to the well-known twentieth-century pioneers such as Jacqueline Cochran and Amelia Earhart. [TL547.J28] 68-27652 3.95
1. Women in aeronautics—Juvenile literature. I. Petie, Haris, illus. II. Title.

Women in Africa—Biography—Juvenile literature.

CRANE, Louise, 1917- 920.72'096
Ms. Africa: profiles of modern African women. [1st ed.] Philadelphia, Lippincott [1973] 159 p. illus. 21 cm. Includes bibliographical references. Brief biographies of thirteen prominent African women emphasizing their achievements in their chosen careers. Included are Angie Brooks, Margaret Kenyatta, and Miriam Makeba. [CT3750.C73] 920 72-11767 ISBN 0-397-31446-9 4.95
1. Women in Africa—Biography—Juvenile literature. I. Title.

Women in astronautics—Juvenile literature.

HOYT, Mary Finch 629.40922
American women of the space age. New York, Atheneum [c.]1966. 88p. ports. 22cm. [TL850.H67] 64-19556 3.50
1. Women in astronautics—Juvenile literature. I. Title.

Women in business—Juvenile literature.

FRENCH, Laura, 1949- 331.4'092'2
Women in business / Laura French and Diana Stewart ; ill. by Jon Zalesak]. Milwaukee : Raintree Publishers, c1979. p. cm. Bibliography: p. Presents brief career biographies of women prominent in business, including Coco Chanel, Barbara Proctor, Irma Wyman, and Mercedes Bates. [HF5500.2.F73] 920 79-13694 ISBN 0-8172-1377-5 lib. bdg. : 7.49
1. Women in business—Juvenile literature. 2. Women in business—Biography—Juvenile literature. I. Stewart, Diana, joint author. II. Zalesak, Jon. III. Title. BIP

Women in California—Biog.

RICE, Bertha Marguerite. 920.7
The women of our valley. [San Jose ? Calif.] c1955- v. illus. 24cm. [CT3260.R5] 56-22625
1. Women in California—Biog. I. Title.

Women in Canada — Biog.

INNIS, Mary (Quayle) 920.071
The clear spirit; twenty Canadian women and their times, edited by Mary Quayle Innis. [Toronto] Published for the Canadian Federation of University Women by University of Toronto Press [1966] xvi, 304 p. ports. 24 cm. "Published on the occasion of the Centennial of Canadian Federation." Includes bibliographies. [CT3270.I 5] 66-31236
1. Women in Canada — Biog. I. Canadian Federaion of University Women. II. Title.

INNIS, Mary (Quayle) 920'.071
The clear spirit; twenty Canadian women and their times, edited by Mary Quayle Innis. [Toronto] Published for the Canadian Federation of University Women by University of Toronto Press [1973, c.1966] xvi, 304 p. ports. 23 cm. ([Canadian University paperbacks] 15) [CT3270.] 66-31236 ISBN 0-8020-6209-1 4.95 (pbk.)
1. Women in Canada—Biography. I. Canadian Federation of University Women. II. Title.
First published on the occasion of the Centennial of Canadian Federation of University Women. Available from the publisher's Buffalo, N.Y., office.

Women in church work—Seventh-Day Adventists.

BEACH, John G. 286'.73' B
Notable women of spirit : the historical role of women in the Seventh-day Adventist Church / by John G. Beach. Nashville, Tenn. : Southern Pub. Association, c1976. 125 p. ; 21 cm. Bibliography: p. 123-125. [BV4415.B42] 76-6620 ISBN 0-8127-0115-1
1. Women in church work—Seventh-Day Adventists. I. Title.

Women in England —Biog.

NORTHCROFT, Dorothea Mary 920.042
Famous girls of the past. by Dora Northcroft. London. Epworth Pr. 1966. 144p. 21cm. [CT3320.N59] 66-76841 3.00 bds.,
1. Women in England —Biog. I. Title.
Contents omitted. American distributor: Verry in Mystic, Conn.

Women in Florida—Biog.

COZENS, Eloise N 920.0759
Florida women of distinction. [Daytona Beach, Fla.] College Pub. Co. [1956- v. illus. 23cm. [F310.C6] 56-41966
1. Women in Florida—Biog. I. Title.

Women in France—Biography.

HALL, Evelyn Beatrice, 1868-1919. 944'.03'0922 B
The women of the salons, and other French portraits, by Evelyn Beatrice Hall (S. G. Tallentyre, pseud.) Freeport, N.Y., Books for Libraries Press [1969] vii, 235 p. ports. 22 cm. (Essay index reprint series) Reprint of the 1926 ed. Contents.Contents.—Madame du Deffand.—Mademoiselle de Lespinasse.—Madame Geoffrin.—Madame d'Epinay.—Madame Necker.—Madame de Stael.—Madame Recamier.—Tronchin: a great doctor.—The mother of Napoleon.—Madame de Sevigne.—Madame Vigee Le Brun. [DC36.2.H25 1969] 73-90640
1. Women in France—Biography. 2. Salons. 3. Paris—Intellectual life. I. Title.

WATSON, Paul Barron, 1861-1948. 920.044
Some women of France. Freeport, N.Y., Books for Libraries Press [1969] vi, 269 p. ports. 23 cm. (Essay index reprint series) Reprint of the 1936 ed. Contents.Contents.—Heloise.—Isabeau de Baviere.—Madame du Deffand.—Madame de Stael.—Delphine Gay.—Marie d'Agoult.—Juliette Lamber. [CT3420.W3 1969] 73-90691
1. Women in France—Biography. I. Title. BIP

Women in France—History.

COLLINS, Marie, comp. 301.41'2'0944
Les femmes en France. Edited by Marie Collins and Sylvie Weil Sayre. New York, C. Scribner's Sons [1974] xiv, 330 p. illus. 23 cm. (The Scribner French series) Bibliography: [329]-330. [HQ1613.C73] 73-5170 ISBN 0-684-13803-4
1. Women in France—History. 2. Women in France—Biography. 3. French language—Readers—Women—History and conditions. I. Sayre, Sylvie Weil, joint comp. II. Title. BIP

WRIGHT, Constance. 920.7
Madame de Lafayette. [1st ed.] New York, Holt [1959] 280 p. illus. 22 cm. Lafayette, Marie Adrienne (de Noailles) marguise de, 1750-1807. Includes bibliography. [DC146.L21W7] 59-6675
I. Title.

Women in Great Britain—Biography.

GUEDALLA, Philip, 1889-1944. 920
Bonnet and shawl; an album. Freeport, N.Y., Books for Libraries Press [1970] 204 p. ports. 23 cm. (Essay index reprint series) Reprint of the 1928 ed. [CT3320.G8 1970] 70-121475
1. Women in Great Britain—Biography. I. Title. BIP

HASTED, Jane Eliza. 920.72
Unsuccessful ladies; an intimate account of the aunts (official and unofficial) of the late Queen Victoria. Freeport, N.Y., Books for Libraries Press [1971, c1950] xx, 260 p. illus., geneal. table, ports. 23 cm. (Biography index reprint series) [DA531.1.H37 1971] 73-148216 ISBN 0-8369-8063-8
1. Women in Great Britain—Biography. I. Title.

WELTY, Susan Elizabeth (Fulton) 1905- 922.89
Look up and hope! the motto of the Volunteer Prison League; the life of Maud Ballington Booth. New York, T. Nelson [1961] 284 p. Illus. 24 cm. Includes bibliography. [BX9975.Z8B6] 61-12423
I. Title.

Women in Israel—Biog.

STERN, Geraldine 920.7
Daughters from afar; profiles of Israeli women. New York, Bloch [1963, c.1958] 190p. 24cm. 63-2629 3.95
1. Women in Israel—Biog. I. Title.

STERN, Geraldine. 920.7
Daughters from afar; profiles of Israeli women. London, New York, Abelard-Schuman [1958] 190 p. 22 cm. [CT3725.S8] 57-11493
1. Women in Israel — Biog. I. Title.

Women in journalism—United States.

BEASLEY, Maurine Hoffman. 070.4'092'2 B
Women in media : a documentary source book / by Maurine Beasley and Sheila Silver. Washington : Women's Institute for Freedom of the Press, c1977. viii, 198 p. ; 23 cm. Includes bibliographical references. [PN4872.B43] 77-82376 ISBN 0-930470-00-1 : 5.95
1. Women in journalism—United States. 2. Women journalists—United States—Biography. I. Silver, Sheila, joint author. II. Title.

Women in literature.

JAMESON, Anna 809.1'9'352
Brownell (Murphy) 1794-1860.
Memoirs of the loves of the poets; biographical sketches of women celebrated in ancient and modern poetry. Freeport, N.Y., Books for Libraries Press [1972] 517 p. 22 cm. (Essay index reprint series) Reprint of the 1857 ed. First published in 1829 under title: Loves of the poets. [PN481.J3 1972] 72-4605 ISBN 0-8369-2953-5 13.00
1. Women in literature. 2. Woman—Biography. I. Title. BIP

Women in medicine—Biography—Juvenile literature.

BOWMAN, Kathleen. 610'.92'2 B
New women in medicine / by Kathleen Bowman ; design by Larry Soule. Mankato, Minn. : Creative Education, [1976] p. cm. Brief biographies of seven notable women in the medical field: Elisabeth Kubler-Ross, Kathryn Nichol, Anna Ellington, Estelle Ramey, Mary Louise Robbins, Margaret Hewitt, and Mary Calderone. [R692.B68] 76-4873 ISBN 0-87191-508-1
1. Women in medicine—Biography—Juvenile literature. I. Title. BIP

Women in medicine—United States—Biography—Juvenile literature.

DAVIS, Mary Lee, 1935- 610'.92'2
Women in science and medicine / by Mary L. Davis. Minneapolis : T. S. Denison, c1976. 16 p. : ports. ; 22 cm. (Her Women in American life series ; book 7) Brief description of the role women have traditionally played in science and medicine, and biographical notes of women who have achieved distinction in the field in the twentieth century. [R692.D37] 920 77-354618 ISBN 0-513-01503-5
1. Women in medicine—United States—Biography—Juvenile literature. 2. Medicine—United States—Biography—Juvenile literature. 3. Women scientists—United States—Biography—Juvenile literature. 4. Scientists—United States—Biography—Juvenile literature. I. Title. II. Series.

Women in Montana—Biog.

TOWLE, Virginia Rowe 978.6010922
Vigilante woman. South Brunswick [N. J.] A. S. Barnes [1966] 182p. illus., facsims., ports. 22cm. Bibl. [F731.T68] 66-21603 6.00
1. Women in Montana—Biog. 2. Vigilance committees—Montana. 3. Frontier and pioneer life—Montana. I. Title.

Women in Northwest, Old—Biography.

ELLET, Elizabeth 301.41'2'0922 B
Fries (Lummis), 1818-1877.
The pioneer women of the West. Freeport, N.Y., Books for Libraries Press [1973] 434 p. front. 23 cm. (Essay index reprint series) Reprint of the 1852 ed. [HQ1418.E43 1973] 72-13219 ISBN 0-8369-8157-X
1. Women in Northwest, Old—Biography. 2. Frontier and pioneer life—Ohio Valley. I. Title.

Women in politics—Biography—Juvenile literature.

CONTA, Marica Maher. 323.4'092'2
Women for human rights / Marcia Maher Conta. Milwaukee : Raintree Publishers, c1979. p. cm. Bibliography: p. Brief descriptions of the lives, accomplishments, and goals of various women prominent in the field of human rights. Includes Shirley Chisholm, Dorothy Day, Margaret Kuhn, and Eleanor Roosevelt. [HQ1390.C66] 920 79-13331 ISBN 0-8172-1378-3 lib. bdg. : 7.49
1. Women in politics—Biography—Juvenile literature. 2. Civil rights—Juvenile literature. I. Title. BIP

MCREYNOLDS, Ginny. 329
Women in power / Ginny McReynolds ; [ill. by Jane Palecek]. Milwaukee : Raintree Publishers, c1979. p. cm. Bibliography: p. Brief descriptions of the lives, accomplishments, and goals of various women prominent in the field of politics. Includes Ella Grasso, Barbara Jordan, Golda Meir, and Jeannette Rankin. [HQ1390.M32] 920 79-13301 ISBN 0-8172-1376-7 lib. bdg. : 7.49
1. Women in politics—Biography—Juvenile literature. I. Palecek, Jane. II. Title. BIP

Women in politics—United States.

KELLY, Rita Mae. 301.41'2'0973
The making of political women : a study of socialization and role conflict / Rita Mae Kelly & Mary Boutilier. Chicago : Nelson-Hall, c1978. x, 368 p. ; 23 cm. Includes bibliographical references and index. [HQ1236.K45] 77-17081 ISBN 0-88229-290-0 : 16.95
1. Women in politics—United States. 2. Sex role. 3. Women—Political activity. 4. Statesmen's wives—Biography. I. Boutilier, Mary, joint author. II. Title. BIP

LAMSON, Peggy. 301.41'29'0973
Few are chosen; American women in political life today. With a foreword by Maurine B. Neuberger. Boston, Houghton Mifflin, 1968. xxxii, 240 p. ports. 22 cm. Bibliographical footnotes. [HQ1412.L35] 68-30801 5.95
1. Women in politics—United States. I. Title.

Women in politics—United States—Biography.

LAMSON, Peggy. 320.9'2'2 B
In the vanguard : six American women in public life / Peggy Lamson. Boston : Houghton Mifflin, 1979. xiv, 233 p., [4] leaves of plates : ill. ; 22 cm. Includes index. [HQ1255.L35] 79-4264 ISBN 0-395-27608-X : 19.95
1. Women in politics—United States—Biography. I. Title. BIP

Women in politics—United States—Biography—Juvenile literature.

BOWMAN, Kathleen. 329'.0092'2 B
New women in politics / by Kathleen Bowman ; design by Larry Soule. Mankato, Minn. : Creative Education, [1976] p. cm. Brief biographies of Bess Myerson, Patsy Mink, Dolores Huerta, Yvonne Brathwaite Burke, Elizabeth Holtzman, Barbara Jordan, and Ella Grosso—all women involved in politics who are sincerely dedicated to solving human problems. [HQ1412.B68] 920 76-5513 ISBN 0-87191-507-3
1. Women in politics—United States—Biography—Juvenile literature. I. Title. BIP

GREENEBAUM, Louise G. 320.9'2'2 B
Politics and government / by Louise G. Greenebaum. Minneapolis : Dillon Press, [1977] p. cm. (Contributions of women) Bibliography: p. Biographies of American women who have been involved in politics and government at various levels. [HQ1391.U5G73] 920 77-9593 ISBN 0-87518-144-9 : 6.95
1. Women in politics—United States—Biography—Juvenile literature. I. Title.

Women in public life—Nova Scotia—Biography.

STIRLING, Lilla. 920.72'09716
In the vanguard : Nova Scotia women, mid-twentieth century / by Lilla Stirling. Windsor, N.S. : Lancelot Press, 1976. 71 p. : ports. ; 21 cm. [HQ1391.C3S75] 76-382837 ISBN 0-88999-062-X
1. Women in public life—Nova Scotia—Biography. I. Title.

Women in public life—United States—Biography.

BAILEY, Janice. 920.72'0973
Those meddling women / Janice Bailey. Valley Forge, PA. : Judson Press, c1977. 95 p. ; 22 cm. Includes bibliographical references. [HQ1412.B34] 77-3891 ISBN 0-8170-0757-1 pbk. : 3.25
1. Women in public life—United States—Biography. I. Title. BIP

Women in rodeos—Biography—Juvenile literature.

HANEY, Lynn. 791.8
Ride 'em cowgirl! / by Lynn Haney ; with photos. by Peter Burchard. New York : Putnam, c1975. 128 p. : ill. ; 21 cm. Documents the colorful, arduous life of the women's rodeo circuit. Includes personal accounts of some of the rising stars of the sport. [GV1833.5.H36 1975] 74-21085 ISBN 0-399-60974-1 lib. bdg. : 6.95
1. Women in rodeos—Biography—Juvenile literature. I. Burchard, Peter. II. Title. BIP

Women in science—Juvenile literature.

MCLENIGHAN, Valjean. 509'.2'2 B
Women and science / Valjean McLenighan ; [ill. by Jane Palecek]. Milwaukee : Raintree Publishers, c1979. p. cm. Bibliography: p. Presents brief career biographies of women prominent in the field of science, including Florence Sabin, Chien Shiung Wu, Margaret Mead, and Alice Hamilton. [Q130.M32] 920 79-13659 ISBN 0-8172-1379-1 lib. bdg. : 5.96
1. Women in science—Juvenile literature. I. Palecek, Jane. II. Title. BIP

Women in Texas—Biography.

HILL, Kate Adele, 1900- 920.0764
Home builders of west Texas. San Antonio, Naylor Co. [1970] xx, 108 p. illus., ports. 20 cm. Reprint of the 1937 ed. [F385.H55 1970] 79-127129 3.95
1. Women in Texas—Biography. I. Title.

MCADAMS, Ina May 920.0764
(Ogletree) 1906-
Texas women of distinction; a biographical history. Austin, Tex., McAdams Publishers, 1962. 332 p. 28 cm. [F385.M19] 63-1214
1. Women in Texas — Biog. I. Title.

Women in the Bible.

AGUILAR, Grace, 1816- 221.9'22 B
1847.
The women of Israel; or, Characters and sketches from the Holy Scriptures and Jewish history illustrative of the past history, present duties, and future destiny of the Hebrew females, as based on the Word of God. Plainview, N.Y., Books for Libraries Press [1974] p. cm. (Essay index reprint series) Reprint of the 1879 ed. published by G. Routledge, London, and E. P. Dutton, New York. [BS575.A3 1974] 74-4358 ISBN 0-518-10174-6
1. Bible. O.T.—Biography. 2. Women in the Bible. 3. Women, Jewish. I. Title. II. Title: Characters and sketches from the Holy Scriptures and Jewish history.

CHAPPELL, Clovis Gillham, 220.92
1882-
Feminine faces. Nashville, Abingdon [1966, c.1942] 219p. 20cm. (Apex bks., X3-125) [BS575.C53] 42-5030 1.25 pap.,
1. Women in the Bible. 2. Bible — Biog. I. Title. BIP

DAUGHTERS of St. Paul. 220.9'2 B
Women of the Gospel / written by the Daughters of St. Paul ; ill. by Gregori. Boston : St. Paul Editions, 1975. 134 p. : ill. ; 25 cm. [BS2445.D38] 74-32122
1. Bible. N.T.—Biography. 2. Women in the Bible. I. Titlc. BIP

DEEN, Edith. 220.92
All of the women of the Bible. [1st ed.] New York, Harper [1955] xxii, 410p. 25cm. Bibliography: p.381-385. [BS575.D4] 55-8521
1. Women in the Bible. 2. Bible—Biog. I. Title.

DRIMMER, Frederick. 220.8'30141'2
Daughters of Eve : women in the Bible / by Frederick Drimmer ; ill. by Hal Frenck. Norwalk, Conn. : C. R. Gibson Co., [1975] 88 p. : ill. ; 21 cm. [BS575.D7] 74-83776 ISBN 0-8378-1765-X
1. Women in the Bible. I. Frenck, Hal. II. Title.

GILLILAND, Dolores 220.9'505
Scott.
Selected women of the Scriptures of stamina and courage / by Dolores Scott Gilliland ; illustrated by Gael Scott. Spearfish, SD : Honor Books, c1978. 101 p. : ill. ; 22 cm. [BS575.G47] 78-50069 ISBN 0-931446-02-3 pbk. : 3.95
1. Bible—Biography. 2. Women in the Bible. I. Title. BIP

KULOW, Nelle Wahler. 220.92
Even as you and I; sketches of human women from the Divine Book. Columbus, Ohio, Wartburg Press [1955] 72p. 20cm. [BS575.K76] 55-4428
1. Women in the Bible. 2. Bible—Biog. I. Title.

MCALLISTER, Grace Edna. 221.92
God portrays more women. Chicago, Moody Press [1956] 188p. 22cm. [BS575.M24] 56-1610
1. Women in the Bible. 2. Bible. O.T.—Biog. I. Title.

MARSHALL, Zona Bays. 220.92
Certain women; a study of Biblical women. With a foreword by James Gordon Lott, and an introd. by Robert G. Lee. [1st ed.] New York, Exposition Press [1960] 141p. 21cm. (An Exposition-Testament Book) [BS575.M337] 60-2131
1. Women in the Bible. I. Title.

MORTON, Henry Canova 220.92
Vollam, 1892-
Women of the Bible. Illustrated with a full-color front. and 18 ports. by famous old masters. [Illustrated ed.] New York, Dodd, Mead, 1956 [c1941] 204p. illus. 21cm. [BS575] 57-817
1. Women in the Bible. 2. Bible—Biog. I. Title.

MULLIKEN, Frances 220.9'2 B
Hartman, 1924-
Women of destiny in the Bible / by Frances Hartman Mulliken and Margaret Salts. Independence, Mo. : Herald Pub. House, c1978. 187 p. ; 18 cm. Bibliography: p. 186-187. Introduces seventeen women who play a significant role in the Bible including Sarah, Esther, Mary Magdalene, and Lydia. [BS575.M83] 78-5132 ISBN 0-8309-0211-2 pbk. : 4.00
1. Bible—Biography. 2. Women in the Bible. I. Salts, Margaret, 1918- joint author. II. Title.
Publisher's address : Drawer HH, Independence, MO 64055 BIP

NEAL, Hazel G 220.92
Bible women of faith. Anderson, Ind., Warner Press [1955] 158p. 20cm. [BS575.N4] 55-3206
1. Women in the Bible. 2. Bible—Biog. I. Title.

PRICE, Eugenia. 220.8'30141'2
The unique world of women, in Bible times and now. Grand Rapids, Zondervan Pub. House [1969] 245 p. 25 cm. Bibliography: p. 245. [BS575.P7] 79-91644 3.95
1. Women in the Bible. I. Title.

PRICE, Eugenia. 220.8'30141'2
The unique world of women ... in Bible times and now. Boston, G. K. Hall, 1974 [c1969] 287 p. 25 cm. Large print ed. Bibliography: p. 287. [BS575.P7 1974] 74-5126 ISBN 0-8161-6218-2 9.95 (lib. bdg.)
1. Women in the Bible. 2. Sight-saving books. I. Title.

RUSCHE, Helga. 220.92
They lived by faith; women in the Bible. Translated by Elizabeth Williams. Baltimore, Helicon [1963] vi, 124 p. 22 cm. [BS575.R813] 63-19402
1. Women in the Bible. I. Title.

SPURGEON, Charles Haddon, 221.92
1834-1892.
Sermons on women of the Old Testament; sel. and ed. by Chas. T. Cook. Grand Rapids, Zondervan Pub. House [c.1960] 256p. (Library of Spurgeon's sermons, v. 11) 61-706 2.95
1. Women in the Bible. 2. Bible. O. T.—Biog. I. Title.

SUDLOW, Elizabeth 220.92
(Williams) 1878-
Career women of the Bible. [1st ed] New York, Pageant Press [1951] 79 p. 21 cm. [BS575.S8] 51-14985

1. Women in the Bible. 2. Bible — Biog. I. Title.

THOMAS, Metta Newman. 220.92
Women of the Bible; a study in their life and character. Nashville, 20th Century Christian, 1956. 131 p. 21 cm. [BS575.T48] 57-20949
1. Women in the Bible. 2. Bible — Giog. I. Title.

THOMSON, Lucy Gertsch. 220.92
Women of the Bible: a book telling the life stories of twenty prominent women of the Old and New Testament. Salt Lake City, Deseret Book Co. [1957] 96 p. 16 cm. [BS575.T53] 57-59113
1. Women in the Bible. 2. Women in the Bible. I. Title.

VANDER VELDE, Frances. 220.92
She shall be called woman; a gallery of character sketches. With illus. by Dick Gringhuis. Grand Rapids, Grand Rapids International Publications; distributed by Kregel's [1957] 258 p. illus. 23 cm. (Women of the Bible) Includes bibliography. [BS575.V3] 57-13178
1. Women in the Bible. 2. Bible — Biog. I. Title.

Women in the Bible—Juvenile literature.

COAKLEY, Mary Lewis, 1907- 225.92
Famous women of the New Testament. Sponsored by the Benedicitine monks of Belmont Abbey. Garden City, N. Y. [N. Doubleday, 1960] 64p. illus. 21cm. (The Catholic know-Your-Bible program) [BS2445.C6] 60-3653
1. Women in the Bible—Juvenile literature. 2. Bible. N. T.—Biog.—Juvenile literature. I. Title.

MOSLEY, Jean (Bell) 1913- 225.92
Famous women of the New Testament. Garden City, N. Y. [N. Doubleday, 1960] 64p. illus. 21cm. (Know your Bible program) [BS2445.M6] 60-3654
1. Women in the Bible—Juvenile literature. 2. Bible. N. T.—Biog.—Juvenile literature. I. Title.

Women in the mass media industry—Biography—Juvenile literature.

BOWMAN, Kathleen. 301.16'1'0922
New women in media / by Kathleen Bowman ; design by Larry Soule. Mankato, Minn. : Creative Education, [1976] p. cm. Brief biographies of seven women involved in various aspects of mass media: Katharine Graham, Judith Viorst, Loretta Long, Barbara Walters, Annie Leibovitz, Ann Chevalier, and Connie Goldman. [P96.W6B6] 920 76-6061 ISBN 0-87191-511-1
1. Women in the mass media industry—Biography—Juvenile literature. 2. Mass media—United States—Biography—Juvenile literature. I. Soule, Larry. II. Title. **BIP**

Women in the professions—Biography.

CROVITZ, Elaine. 301.41'2'0922
Courage knows no sex / by Elaine Crovitz and Elizabeth Buford. North Quincy, Mass. : Christopher Pub. House, c1978. 186 p. ; 24 cm. Contents.Contents.—Teresa of Avila.—Mercy Otis Warren.—Florence Nightingale.—Elizabeth Blackwell.—Jane Addams.—Marie Curie. Bibliography: p. 179-186. [HQ1123.C76] 77-99235 ISBN 0-8158-0363-X : 8.95
1. Women in the professions—Biography. 2. Women—Psychology—Case studies. 3. Courage—Case studies. I. Buford, Elizabeth, joint author. II. Title. **BIP**

Women in the United States.

D'ARUSMONT, 301.24'2'0924 B
Frances Wright, 1795-1852.
Life, letters, and lectures, 1834/1844. New York, Arno Press, 1972. xi, 220, 47, 47 p. 23 cm. (American women: images and realities) Contents.Contents.—Course of popular lectures; with three addresses, on various public occasions, and a reply to the charges against the French reformers of 1789.—Supplement course of lectures, containing the last four lectures delivered in the United States.—Biography, notes, and political letters of Frances Wright D'Arusmont. [HQ1615.D37A3] 72-2598 ISBN 0-405-04454-2 23.00
I. Title. II. Series. **BIP**

HORAN, James David, 1914- 920.7
Desperate women. New York, Putnam [1952] 336 p. illus. 23 cm. Includes bibliography. [E176.H8] 52-9838
1. Women in the United States. 2. United States—Biography. I. Title.

Women in the United States—Biography.

BOYNICK, David King, 1911- 920.7
Pioneers in petticoats. New York, Crowell [1959] 245p. 21cm. Includes bibliography. [CT3260.B73] 59-7763
1. Women in the U. S.—Biog. I. Title.

BOYNICK, David King, 1911- 920.72
Women who led the way; eight pioneers for equal rights, by David K. Boynick. New York, Crowell [1972, c1959] ix, 245 p. 22 cm. First ed. published under title: Pioneers in petticoats. Contents.Contents.—Mary Lyon, founder of a college.—Susan B. Anthony, exponent of woman's rights.—Belva Ann Lockwood, pioneering attorney.—Antoinette Brown, ordained minister.—Alice Hamilton, doctor in industry.—Lillian M. Gilbreth, efficiency engineer.—Amelia Earhart, first lady of aviation.—Dorothy Shaver, department store president.—Bibliography (p. 237-240) [CT3260.B73 1972] 72-186406 ISBN 0-690-89741-3
1. Women in the United States—Biography. I. Title. **BIP**

BRADFORD, Gamaliel, 1863- 920.7'2
1932.
Wives. New York, Arno Press, 1972 [c1925] xiii, 298 p. ports. 23 cm. (American women: images and realities) Includes bibliographical references. [CT3260.B743 1972] 72-2591 ISBN 0-405-04448-8 14.00
1. Women in the United States—Biography. I. Title. II. Series. **BIP**

BRANNUM, Mary, 1938- 920.073
When I was 16, by Mary Brannum and the editors. Photos. by Camilla Smith. New York, Platt & Munk [1967] 318 p. ports. 23 cm. [CT3260.B75] 67-22933
1. Women in the U.S.—Biography. I. Title.

BRENNEMAN, Helen 920.72'0973
Good.
Ring a dozen doorbells; twelve women tell it like it is. Photos. by David Hiebert. Scottdale, Pa., Herald Press, 1973. 190 p. illus. 21 cm. [CT3260.B77] 72-6601 ISBN 0-8361-1702-6 4.95
1. Women in the United States—Biography. I. Title.

BUCKMASTER, Henrietta, 920.073
pseud.
Women who shaped history. New York, Collier Books [1974, c1966] 181 p. 18 cm. Contents.Contents: Dorothea Dix.—Prudence Crandall.—Elizabeth Cady Stanton.—Elizabeth Blackwell.—Harriet Tubman.—Mary Baker Eddy. [CT3260.B8] 65-23073 0.95 (pbk.)
1. Women in the United States—Biography. I. Title. **BIP**

DAUGHERTY, Sonia 920.7
Medviedeva, 1893-
Ten brave women: Anne Hutchinson, Abigail Adams, Dolly Madison, Narcissa Whitman, Julia Ward Howe, Susan B. Anthony, Dorothea Lynde Dix, Mary Lyon, Ida M. Tarbell [and] Eleanor Roosevelt. With drawings by James Daugherty. [1st ed.] Philadelphia, Lippincott [1953] 147 p. illus. 22 cm. [CT3260.D38] 53-10216
1. Women in the U.S.—Biography. I. Title.

DOUGLAS, Emily (Taft) 973.0922
1899-
Remember the ladies; the story of great women who helped shape America. New York, Putnam [1966] 254 p. illus., ports. 22 cm. Bibliography: p. 241-246. [HQ1412.D6] 66-10467
1. Women in the U.S. — Biog. I. Title.

FORSEE, Aylesa. 920.7
American women who scored firsts. Philadelphia, Macrae Smith Co. [1958] 253 p. 22 cm. Contents.Contents.—Grace before greatness: Marian Anderson.—Angel of Henry Street: Lillian Wald.—Rebel in ballet slippers: Agnes de Mille.—A modern Portia: Florence Ellinwood Allen.—A migrant Juliet: Katharine Cornell.—Blazer of skyway trails: Amelia Earhart.—Citizen of the world: Eleanor Roosevelt.—Pioneer of the air waves: Kate Smith.—Queen of trench and typewriter: Marguerite Higgins.—A friend to all: Juliette Gordon Low. [CT3260.F67] 58-12064
1. Women in the U.S.—Biography. I. Title.

FOWLER, William 917.3'03
Worthington, 1833-1881.
Woman on the American frontier; a valuable and authentic history of the heroism, adventures, privations, captivities, trials, and noble lives and deaths of the "pioneer mothers of the Republic." Ann Arbor, Mich., Plutarch Press, 1971. 527 p. illus. 22 cm. "Facsimile reprint of the 1878 edition." [E176.F69 1878a] 73-152915
1. Women in the United States—Biography. 2. Frontier and pioneer life—U.S. I. Title.

FOWLER, William 920.72
Worthington, 1833-1881.
Woman on the American frontier; a valuable and authentic history of the heroism, adventures, privations, captivities, trials, and noble lives and deaths of the "pioneer mothers of the Republic." Hartford, S. S. Scranton, 1878. Detroit, Gale Research Co., 1974. 527 p. illus. 18 cm. [E176.F69 1974] 73-12867 16.50
1. Women in the United States—Biography. 2. Frontier and pioneer life—United States. I. Title.

GURKO, Miriam. 301.41'2'0973
The ladies of Seneca Falls; the birth of the woman's rights movement. New York, Macmillan [1974] vi, 328 p. illus. 24 cm. Bibliography: p. 316-320. An account of the feminist movements of the eighteenth and nineteenth centuries focusing on Elizabeth Cady Stanton and Susan B. Anthony. [HQ1412.G85] 73-6049 ISBN 0-02-737770-9 6.95
1. Women in the United States—Biography. 2. Women—Suffrage—United States. 3. Woman—Rights of women. I. Title.

KELLEY, Joseph J. 301.41'2'0973
Courage & candlelight; the feminine Spirit of '76, by Joseph J. Kelley, Jr. and Sol Feinstone. [Harrisburg, Pa.] Stackpole Books [1974] 240 p. port. 24 cm. Bibliography: p. 232-236. [HQ1418.K45] 73-23105 ISBN 0-8117-0452-1 8.95
1. Women in the United States—Biography. I. Feinstone, Sol, 1890- joint author. II. Title.

LEIPOLD, L. Edmond, 1902- 920
Famous American women, by L. Edmond Leipold. Minneapolis, T. S. Denison [1967] 77 p. 25 cm. (Famous American heroes and leaders series) Profiles of eleven women who distinguished themselves in major or minor ways in America's history: Willa Cather, Molly Pitcher, Susan B. Anthony, Sacajawea, Martha Washington, Elizabeth Palmer Peabody, Emily Dickinson, Clara Barton, Emma Lazarus, Amelia Earhart, and Dolly Madison. [CT3260.L4] AC 68
1. Women in the United States—Biography. I. Title.

LOGAN, Mary Simmerson 920.72
(Cunningham) 1838-1923.
The part taken by women in American history. New York, Arno Press, 1972 [c1912] xii, 927 p. illus. 24 cm. (American women: images and realities) [CT3260.L57 1972] 72-2613 ISBN 0-405-04467-4 41.00
1. Women in the United States—Biography. I. Title. II. Series. **BIP**

LONGWELL, Marjorie R 920.7
America and women; fictionized biography. Philadelphia, Dorrance [1962] 205p. 21cm. [CT3260.L6] 62-11978
1. Women in the U. S.—Biog. I. Title.

MERRIAM, Eve, 1916- 920.72'0973
comp.
Growing up female in America; ten lives. Edited and introduced by Eve Merriam [New York, Dell, 1973, c.1972] 352 p. illus. 19 cm. (Laurel ed., 3269) [HQ1412.M45] Pap., 1.50
1. Women in the U.S.—Biography. 2. Woman—History and conditions of women. I. Title.

MONTGOMERY, Ala. Junior 920.073
Chamber of Commerce.
Outstanding young women of America. 1965- Montgomery, Ala., Junior Chamber of Commerce. v. 27 cm. annual. [CT3260.O75] 66-3374
1. Women in the U.S. — Biog. I. Title.

NOTABLE American 920.72'0973
women, 1607-1950; a biographical dictionary. Edward T. James, editor. Janet Wilson James, associate editor. Paul S. Boyer, assistant editor. Cambridge, Mass., Belknap Press of Harvard University Press, 1971. 3 v. 27 cm. "Prepared under the auspices of Radcliffe College." [CT3260.N57] 76-152274 ISBN 0-674-62731-8
1. Women in the United States—Biography. I. James, Edward T., ed. II. James, Janet Wilson, 1918- ed. III. Boyer, Paul S., ed. IV. Radcliffe College.

NOTABLE American 920.72'0973
women, 1607-1950; a biographical dictionary. Edward T. James, ed. Janet Wilson James, assoc. ed. Paul S. Boyer, assist. ed. Cambridge, Mass., Belknap Press of Harvard University Press [1974, c1971] 3 v. 26 cm. "Prepared under the auspices of Radcliffe College." [CT3260.N57 1974] ISBN 0-674-62734-2 19.50 (pbk.)
1. Women in the United States—Biography. I. James, Edward T., comp. II. James, Janet Wilson, 1918-, joint comp. III. Boyer, Paul S., joint comp. IV. Radcliffe College.
L.C. card no. for original ed.: 76-152274 **BIP**

PARKMAN, Mary Rosetta, 920.073
1875-1941.
Heroines of service. Freeport, N.Y., Books for Libraries Press [1969, c1917] ix, 322 p. illus., ports. 23 cm. (Essay index reprint series) Contents.Contents.—Mary Lyon.—Alice Freeman Palmer.—Clara Barton.—Frances Willard.—Julia Ward Howe.—Anna Shaw.—Mary Antin.—Alice C. Fletcher.—Mary Slessor of Calabar.—Madame Curie.—Jane Addams. [CT3234.P3 1969] 68-58808
1. Women in the United States—Biography. I. Title. **BIP**

PARSHALLE, Eve. 920.073
The Kashmir bridge-women. Los Angeles, Oxford Press, 1965. viii, 231 p. ports. 21 cm. [HQ1412.P3] 65-22253
1. Women in the U.S.—Biog. I. Title.

PEACOCK, Virginia 920.72'0973
Tatnall, 1873-1918.
Famous American belles of the nineteenth century. Freeport, N.Y., Books for Libraries Press [1970] xv, 297 p. ports. 23 cm. (Essay index reprint series) Reprint of the 1900 ed. Contents.Contents.—Marcia Burns (Mrs. John Peter Van Ness)—Theodosia Burr (Mrs. Joseph Alston)—Elizabeth Patterson (Madame Jerome Bonaparte)—The Caton sisters.—Margaret O'Neill (Mrs. John H. Eaton)—Cora Livingston (Mrs. Thomas Pennant Barton)—Emily Marshall (Mrs. William Foster Otis)—Octavia Walton (Madame Le Vert)—Fanny Taylor (Mrs. Thomas Harding Ellis)—Jessie Benton (Mrs. John C. Fremont)—Sallie Ward (Mrs. George F. Downs)—Harriet Lane (Mrs. Henry Elliott Johnston)—Adele Cutts (Mrs. Robert Williams)—Emilie Schaumburg (Mrs. Hughes-Hallett)—Kate Chase (Mrs. William Sprague)—Mattie Ould (Mrs. Oliver Schoolcraft)—Jennie Jerome (Lady Randolph Churchill)—Nellie Hazeltine (Mrs. Frederick W. Paramore)—Mary Victoria Leiter (Baroness Curzon of Kedleston)—New York as a social centre. [CT3260.P4 1970] 73-1OFamous American belles of
1. Women in the United States—Biography. I. Title. **BIP**

PEARSON, Hesketh, 1887- 920.02
The marrying Americans. New York,

Coward McCann [1961] 313p. illus. 22cm. [CT3260.P43] 61-5427
1. Women in the U. S.—Biog. 2. Marriages, International. 3. Marriages of royalty and nobility. I. Title.

PEARSON, Hesketh [Edward Hesketh Gibbons Pearson] 1887- 920.02
The marrying Americans. New York, Coward McCann [c.1961] 313p. ports. Bibl. 61-5427 5.00
1. Women in the U.S.— Biog. 2. Marriages, International. 3. Marriages of royalty and nobility. I. Title.

ROSS, Ishbel, 1897- 920.7
Charmers and cranks; twelve famous American women who defied the conventions. New York, Harper [c.1965] xii, 306p. illus., facsims., ports. 22cm. Bibl. [CT3260.R6] 65-14657 5.95
1. Women in the U.S.—Biog. I. Title.
Contents omitted.

ROSS, Ishbel, 1897- 301.41'2'0922
Sons of Adam, daughters of Eve. [1st ed.] New York, Harper & Row [1969] viii, 340 p. illus., ports. 22 cm. Bibliography: p. 313-327. [HQ1412.R6] 67-13691 7.95
1. Women in the United States—Biography. I. Title.

SMITH, Margaret (Chase) 1898- 920
Gallant women, by Margaret Chase Smith and H. Paul Jeffers. Illustrated by Paul Giovanopoulos. New York, McGraw-Hill [1968] 124, [1] p. ports. 24 cm. Bibliography (p. 124-[125]) Brief biographies of twelve American women who proved their courage in fighting prejudice, adversity, and poverty. Included are Anne Hutchinson, Dolly Madison, Harriet Tubman, Harriet Beecher Stowe, Clara Barton, Elizabeth Blackwell, Susan B. Anthony, Annie Sullivan, Amelia Earhart, Althea Gibson, Frances Perkins, Eleanor Roosevelt. [CT3260.S6] AC 68
1. Women in the United States—Biography. I. Jeffers, Harry Paul, 1934- joint author. II. Giovanopoulos, Paul, illus. III. Title.

STERN, Madeleine Bettina, 1912- 920.7
We the women; career first of nineteenth-century America. Wood engravings by John De Pol. New York, Schulte Pub. Co., 1963 [i.e. 1962] 403 p. illus. 22 cm. Includes bibliography. [CT3260.S73] 62-19366
1. Women in the U.S.—Biography. I. Title.

STODDARD, Hope. 920'.073
Famous American women. New York, Crowell [1970] viii, 461 p. ports. 23 cm. Includes bibliographies. [CT3260.S83 1970] 73-87158 7.50
1. Women in the United States—Biography. I. Title. BIP

THORP, Margaret (Farrand) 1891- 920.72
Female persuasion; six strong-minded women. [Hamden, Conn.] Archon Books, 1971 [c1949] x, 253, [1] p. illus., ports. 21 cm. Contents.Contents.—Strong-minded women.—Woman's profession, Catharine E. Beecher.—Beware of Sister Jane, Jane G. Swisshelm.—The Lily and the Bloomer, Amelia Bloomer.—Greenwood leaves, "Grace Greenwood" (Sara J. C. Lippincott)—Altogether Doric, Louisa S. McCord.—Dusting mirrors, L. Maria Child.—Bibliography (p. [254]) [CT3260.T5 1971] 74-150771 ISBN 0-208-00999-X
1. Women in the United States—Biography. I. Title. BIP

VANCE, Marguerite. 920.7
The lamp lighters; women in the Hall of Fame. Foreword by Sarah Gibson Blanding. Illustrated by J. Luis Pellicer. [1st ed.] New York, Dutton, 1960. 254 p. illus. 21 cm. [E176.6.V3] 60-11869
1. Women in the U.S. — Biog. 2. New York University. Hall of Fame. I. Title.

WHITTON, Mary Ormsbee. 920.7
These were the women; U. S. A. 1776-1860. New York, Hastings House [1954] 288 p. 21 cm. Includes bibliography. [E176.W62] 54-7597
1. Women in the U.S.—Biography. I. Title.

WHO'S who of American women, and women of Canada; 920.7 a biographical dictionary of notable living women of the United States of America, and other countries. 4th ed., 1966-1967. Chicago, Marquis [c.1958-1965] 1298p. 29cm. biennial [CT3260.W5] 58-13264 26.50
1. Women in the U.S.—Biog.

WILLARD, Frances Elizabeth, 1839-1898, ed. 920.073
A woman of the century, fourteen hundred-seventy biographical sketches accompanied by portraits of leading American women in all walks of life. Edited by Frances E. Willard and Mary A. Livermore, assisted by a corps of able contributors. With a new introd. by Leslie Shepard. Detroit, Gale Research Co., 1967. 812 p. ports. 26 cm. Title page includes originial imprint: Buffalo, C. W. Moulton, 1893. [E176.W691 1967] 67-21361
1. Women in the U. S.—Biography. 2. U. S.—Biography. I. Livermore, Mary Ashton (Rice), 1820-1905, joint ed. II. Title.

WOODWARD, Helen Beal. 920.7
The bold women. New York, Farrar, Straus and Young [1953] 373 p. 22 cm. [CT3260.W6] 53-7084
1. Women in the U.S.—Biography. I. Title. BIP

WOODWARD, Helen Beal. 920.72
The bold women. Freeport, N.Y., Books for Libraries Press [1971, c1953] 373 p. 23 cm. (Biography index reprint series) Contents.Contents.—Lafayette slept here.—She saw America first: Anne Royall.—A love affair with the U.S.A.: Frances Wright.—The lady and the magnificent beast: Jane Grey Swisshelm.—Miss Anti-Marriage: Lucina Umphreville.—Ill angels only.—The woman who hated Shakespeare: Delia Bacon.—Brown bread, cold water, and sex: Mary Gove-Nichols.—The oblique editor: Sarah Josepha Hale.—The woman in the footnote: Kate Field.—The Redpath story.—Aren't I a woman? Sojourner Truth and Harriet Tubman.—The body: Adah Isaacs Menken.—The right to wear pants: Dr. Mary Walker.—Mrs. Tom Thumb: Lavinia Warren.—Brigham's other wife: Ann Eliza Young.—Biology triumphant: Eliza Woodson Farnham.—Bibliography (p. 357-373) [CT3260.W67 1971] 71-160928 ISBN 0-8369-8091-3
1. Women in the United States—Biography. I. Title.

WORTHY women of our first century. 301.41'2'0922 B Edited by Mrs. O. J. Wister and Agnes Irwin. Plainview, N.Y., Books for Libraries Press [1975] 328 p. 22 cm. (Essay index reprint series) Reprint of the 1877 ed. [HQ1418.W67 1975] 72-13216 ISBN 0-8369-8182-0
1. Women in the United States—Biography. I. Wister, Sarah (Butler), "Mrs. O. J. Wister," 1835-1908, ed. II. Irwin, Agnes, 1841-1914, ed. BIP

Women in the United States—Biography—Juvenile literature.

DOLIN, Arnold, 1928- 920.7
Great American heroines. Illus. by Rafaello Busoni. New York, Hart [1962, c.1960] 189p. illus. 20cm. (World-famous ser., 203) 60-6577 1.95
1. Women in the U.S.—Biog.—Juvenile literature I. Title.

GERSH, Harry 920
Women who made America great. Stone lithographs by Mel Silverman. Philadelphia, Lippincott [c.1962] 224p. illus. 21cm. 62-18009 4.50
1. Women in the U.S.—Biog.—Juvenile literature. I. Title.

JOHNSTON, Johanna. 301.41'2'0922 B
Women themselves. Illustrated by Deanne Hollinger. New York, Dodd, Mead [1973] 126 p. illus. 24 cm. Portraits of fourteen American women determined to use their talents despite the difficulties encountered in getting into careers reserved exclusively for men. [HQ1412.J64] 920 73-1657 ISBN 0-396-06802-2 4.50
1. Women in the United States—Biography—Juvenile literature. I. Hollinger, Deanne, illus. II. Title. BIP

ROSS, Pat, comp. 920.72'0973
Young and female; turning points in the lives of eight American women. Personal accounts compiled with introductory notes by Pat Ross. New York, Random House [1972] 107 p. ports. 21 cm. (A Vintage sundial book, VS-8) Contents.Contents.—Shirley MacLaine.—Shirley Chisholm.—Dorothy Day.—Emily Hahn.—Margaret Sanger.—Althea Gibson.—Edna Ferber.—Margaret Bourke-White. Bibliography: p. 107. [CT3260.R63 1972b] 920 72-3250 ISBN 0-394-70808-3 1.50
1. Women in the United States—Biography—Juvenile literature. 2. Women in the United States—Biography. I. Title.

YOST, Edna, 1889- 920
Famous American pioneering women. New York, Dodd, Mead, 1961. 158 p. illus. 22 cm. (Famous biographies for young people) [CT3260.Y6] 61-15993
1. Women in the U.S. — Biog. — Juvenile literature. I. Title.

Women in the United States—History.

BLANC, Marie Therese (de Solms) 1840-1907. 301.41'2'0973
The condition of woman in the United States; a traveller's notes. New York, Arno Press [1972, c1895] 285 p. 23 cm. (American women: images and realities) [HQ1419.B65 1972] 72-2590 ISBN 0-405-04447-X 13.00
1. Women in the United States—History. 2. United States—Social life and customs—1865-1918. I. Title. II. Series.

Women in the West—Biography.

DRAGO, Harry Sinclair, 1888- 917.8'03'20922 B
Notorious ladies of the frontier. New York, Dodd, Mead [1969] x, 270 p. illus., ports. 24 cm. Bibliography: p. 257-259. [F591.D714] 78-80710 6.00
1. Women in the West—Biography. 2. Frontier and pioneer life—The West. I. Title.

Women in the West—Juvenile literature.

JOHNSON, Dorothy M. 920
Some went West [by] Dorothy M. Johnson. New York, Dodd, Mead [1965] xii, 180 p. illus., ports. 21 cm. Bibliography: p. 175-177. [F591.J613] 65-20911
1. Women in the West — Biog. — Juvenile literature. I. Title.

LEVENSON, Dorothy. 920.72'0978
Women of the West. New York, Watts, 1973. 88 p. illus. 22 cm. (A First book) Bibliography: p. 86. Discusses the life of women—black, white, and Indian—in western United States since 1818. [F591.L48] 72-10441 ISBN 0-531-00793-6 3.75
1. Women in the West—Juvenile literature. 2. Frontier and pioneer life—The West—Juvenile literature. I. Title. BIP

Women in trade-unions—United States—History—Exhibitions—Catalogs.

O'SULLIVAN, Judith. 331.4
Workers and allies : female participation in the American Trade Union Movement, 1824-1976 : exhibition organized by Judith O'Sullivan : catalog / by Judith O'Sullivan and Rosemary Gallick. Washington : Published for the Smithsonian Institution Traveling Exhibition Service by the Smithsonian Institution Press, 1975. 96 p. : ill. ; 26 cm. Bibliography: p. 91-96. [HD6079.2.U5O85] 75-619279
1. Women in trade-unions—United States—History—Exhibitions—Catalogs. 2. Women in trade-unions—United States—Biography—Exhibitions—Catalogs. I. Gallick, Rosemary, joint author. II. Smithsonian Institution. Traveling Exhibition Service. III. Title.

Women in Washington, D.C.—Biog.

COOKE, Helen H. 920.7
Distinguished women of Washington, D.C., 1964, by Helen Cooke, Evelyn Dent Boyer [Arlington, Va., Cooke and Bover Co., P.O. Box 95, c.1964] 86p. ports. 25cm. [F193.C6] 63-16346 15.00 pap.,
1. Women in Washington, D.C.—Biog. I. Boyer, Evelyn Dent, joint author. II. Title.

Women—Ireland—Biography.

GERARD, Frances A. 920.72'09415
Some celebrated Irish beauties of the last century. Plainview, N.Y., Books for Libraries Press [1974] p. cm. (Essay index reprint series) Reprint of the 1895 ed. published by Ward and Downey, London. [DA916.7.G3 1974] 74-4332 ISBN 0-518-10178-9
1. Women—Ireland—Biography. 2. Ireland—Biography. I. Title.

Women, Jewish.

LEBESON, Anita (Libman) 1896- 920.073
Recall to life—the Jewish woman in America. South Brunswick, T. Yoseloff [1970] 351 p. 22 cm. Includes bibliographical references. [DS115.2.L36 1970] 77-88278 7.50
1. Women, Jewish. 2. Jews in the United States. I. Title.

Women, Jewish—Biography.

HENRY, Sondra. 920'.0092'924
Written out of history : a hidden legacy of Jewish women revealed through their writings and letters / by Sondra Henry and Emily Taitz. New York : Bloch Pub. Co., c1978. xi, 293 p. : ill. ; 22 cm. Includes index. Bibliography: p. 284-289. [DS115.2.H46] 77-99195 ISBN 0-8197-0454-7 : 12.50
1. Women, Jewish—Biography. I. Taitz, Emily, joint author. II. Title.

Women jockeys.

HANEY, Lynn. 798'.4'00922
The lady is a jock. New York, Dodd, Mead [1973] 180 p. illus. 22 cm. [SF336.A2H36] 73-11548 5.95
1. Women jockeys. I. Title. BIP

Women journalists—United States.

MARZOLF, Marion. 070.4'092'2 B
Up from the footnote : a history of women journalists / by Marion Marzolf. New York : Hastings House, c1977. p. cm. (Communication arts books) Includes bibliographies and index. [PN4872.M37] 77-5398 ISBN 0-8038-7502-9 : 12.95
1. Women journalists—United States. 2. Women journalists—Europe. I. Title. BIP

ROSS, Ishbel, 1897- 070.4'092'2
Ladies of the press. New York, Arno Press, 1974 [c1936] xii, 622 p. ports. 24 cm. (Women in America: from colonial times to the 20th century) Reprint of the ed. published by Harper, New York. [PN4872.R7 1974] 74-3972 ISBN 0-405-06120-X
1. Women journalists—United States. 2. Journalism—United States. I. Title. II. Series. BIP

Women judges—United States.

ALPHA Kappa Alpha. 347'.73'14 B
Negro women in the judiciary. [Chicago, 1968] 24 p. ports. 22 cm. (Heritage series no. 1) [KF372.A43] 74-184160
1. Women judges—United States. 2. Negro judges—United States. I. Title. II. Series: Heritage series (Chicago) no. 1.

Women kindergarten teachers—United States—Biography.

SNYDER, Agnes, 1885- 372.1'1'00922 B
Dauntless women in childhood education, 1856-1931, by Agnes Snyder for Early Leaders in Childhood Education Committee of Association for Childhood Education International. Editor, Margaret Rasmussen. Washington, Association for Childhood Education International, 1972.

Includes index. Bibliography: p. 264-269. [F591.R48] 75-26293 ISBN 0-8310-7110-9 : 7.95
1. Women—The West—Biography. 2. The West—Biography. I. Title. **BIP**

Women—The West—Biography—Juvenile literature.

WILLIAMS, Brad. 978'.02'0922
Legendary women of the West / Brad Williams ; ill. by Paul Blaine Henrie. New York : D. McKay Co., c1978. xi, 142 p. : ill. ; 24 cm. Includes index. Contents.Contents.—Juana Maria.—Gertrudes Barcelo (Dona Tula).—Julia Bulette and Eilley Orrum Bowers.—Pearl Hart.—Ella Watson (Cattle Kate).—Mary Ellen Smith (Mammy Pleasant).—Baby Doe Tabor.—Aimee Semple McPherson. [F591.W7173] 920 78-296 ISBN 0-679-20411-3 : 7.95
1. Women—The West—Biography—Juvenile literature. 2. The West—Biography—Juvenile literature. 3. The West—History—Juvenile literature. I. Henrie, Paul Blaine, 1932- II. Title. **BIP**

Women—United States.

GINZBERG, Eli, 1911- 301.41'2
Educated American women: life styles and self-portraits [by] Eli Ginzberg and associates. New York, Columbia University Press [1971, c1966] vii, vii, 220, x, 198 p. forms. 21 cm. (A Columbia paperback, 119) "First one-volume printing of the two books published ... under the titles: Life styles of educated women and Educated American women: self portraits." Bibliography: p. [209]-212 (3d group) [HQ1420.G5 1971] 73-31186 ISBN 0-231-03604-3 3.95
1. Women—United States. 2. Women college graduates—Employment—United States. 3. United States—Social conditions. I. Ginzberg, Eli, 1911- Educated American women: self portraits. 1971. II. Title.

Women—United States—Biography.

AMERICAN Mothers Committee. 920.72'0973
Mothers of achievement in American history, 1776-1976 : Bi-centennial project, 1974-1976 / compiled by the American Mothers Committee Inc. Rutland, Vt. : C. E. Tuttle Co., c1976. xi, 636 p. : ill. ; 29 cm. Includes index. Bibliography: p. 627-629. [CT3260.A47 1976] 76-461 ISBN 0-8048-1201 2 : 14.50
1. Women—United States—Biography. 2. United States Biography. I. Title

ANTICAGLIA, Elizabeth, 1939- 920.72
12 American women / Elizabeth Anticaglia. Chicago : Nelson-Hall, [1975] xiv, 256 p. : ports. ; 23 cm. Bibliography: p. 245-256. [HQ1412.A57] 74-23229 ISBN 0-88229-102-5 : 12.00
1. Women—United States—Biography. I. Title.
Contents omitted.

BROOKS, Geraldine, 1875- 920.72
Dames and daughters of colonial days. New York, Arno Press, 1974 [c1900] 284 p. illus. 21 cm. (Women in America: from colonial times to the 20th century) Reprint of the ed. published by Crowell, New York. [E187.5.B87 1974] 74-3934 ISBN 0-405-06080-7
1. Women—United States—Biography. 2. United States—History—Colonial period, ca. 1600-1775. I. Title. II. Series. **BIP**

CLARK, Electa. 920.72'0973
Leading ladies : an affectionate look at American women of the twentieth century / by Electa Clark. New York : Stein and Day, [1976] p. cm. Includes index. [CT3260.C57] 75-34263 ISBN 0-8128-1909-8
1. Women—United States—Biography. I. Title. **BIP**

CLEMENT, Jesse, ed. 920.72'0973
Noble deeds of American women. New York, Arno Press, 1974 [c1851] 480 p. port. 23 cm. (Women in America from colonial times to the 20th century) Reprint of the ed. published by G. H. Derby, Buffalo. [CT3260.C6 1974] 74-3935 ISBN 0-405-06082-3
1. Women—United States—Biography. I. Title. II. Series.

CONRAD, Susan Phinney. 301.41'2'0973
Perish the thought : intellectual women in romantic America, 1830-1860 / Susan Phinney Conrad. New York : Oxford University Press, 1976. vi, 292 p. : ports. ; 22 cm. Includes index. Bibliography: p. [276]-283. [HQ1423.C74] 75-25463 ISBN 0-19-501995-4 : 12.95
1. Women—United States—Biography. 2. Feminism—United States—History. 3. United States—Intellectual life—1783-1865. 4. Women authors, American—Biography. I. Title. **BIP**

ELLET, Elizabeth Fries Lummis, 1818-1877. 920.72'0973
The eminent and heroic women of America. New York, Arno Press, 1974 [c1873] 763 p. illus. 21 cm. (Women in America: from colonial times to the 20th century) Reprint of the ed. published by McMenamy, Hess, New York which was a reprint from the original plates of the author's 3-volume The women of the American Revolution, published by Baker and Scribner, New York, 1848-50, with omissions and changes. [CT3260.E42 1974] 74-3945 ISBN 0-405-06091-2
1. Women—United States—Biography. I. Title. II. Series. **BIP**

ELLET, Elizabeth Fries (Lummis), 1818-1877 920.72
The queens of American society, by Mrs. Ellet. Freeport, N.Y., Books for Libraries Press [1973] p. (Essay index reprint series) Reprint of the 1867 ed. [CT3260.E44 1973] 72-13173 ISBN 0-8369-8158-8
1. Women—United States—Biography. I. Title.

FOWLER, William Worthington, 1833-1881. 917.3'03
Woman on the American frontier. [New York] Source Book Press [1970, c1876] 527 p. illus. 23 cm. Reprint of the ed. published by S. S. Scranton, Hartford. [E176.F69 1970] 77-134185 ISBN 0-87681-072-5
1. Women—United States—Biography. 2. Frontier and pioneer life—United States. I. Title. **BIP**

GURKO, Miriam. 301.41'2'0973
The ladies of Seneca Falls : the birth of the woman's rights movement / Miriam Gurko. New York : Schocken Books, 1976, c1974. p. cm. (Studies in the life of women) Reprint of the ed. published by Macmillan, New York. Includes index. Bibliography: p. [HQ1412.G85 1976] 76-9144 ISBN 0-8052-0545-4 pbk. : 4.95
*1. Women—United States—Biography. 2. Women—Suffrage—United States. 3. Women's rights—United States. I. Title.***BIP**

HANAFORD, Phebe Ann Coffin, 1829-1921. 920.72'0973
Daughters of America, or, Women of the century. Plainview, N.Y., Books for Libraries Press [1974] p. cm. (Essay index reprint series) Reprint of the 1882 ed. published by B. B. Russell, Boston. [E176.H25 1974] 74-4331 ISBN 0-518-10179-7
1. Women—United States—Biography. 2. United States—Biography. I. Title. II. Title: Women of the century.

HOSIER, Helen Kooiman. 280'.092'2 B
Cameos, women fashioned by God / Helen Kooiman Hosier. Irvine, Calif. : Harvest House Publishers, c1979. 173 p. : ports. ; 18 cm. [BR1713.H63] 79-128734 0890810954 : 2.25
1. Women—United States—Biography. 2. Christian biography—United States. I. Title.

HUMPHREY, Grace, 1882- 973
Women in American history. Freeport, N.Y., Books for Libraries Press [1968, c1919] 222 p. illus. 23 cm. (Essay index reprint series) Contents.Contents.—Pocahontas.—Anne Hutchinson.—Betsy Ross.—Mary Lindley Murray.—Molly Pitcher.—Martha Washington.—Jemima Johnson.—Sacajawea.—Dolly Madison.—Lucretia Mott.—Harriet Beecher Stowe.—Julia Ward Howe.—Mary A. Livermore.—Barbara Fritchie.—Clara Barton.—Epilogue.—Bibliography (p. 211-[215]) [E176.H94 1968] 68-57323
1. Women—United States—Biography. I. Title. **BIP**

LONGSTREET, Stephen, 1907- 301.41'2'0922
The queen bees : the women who shaped America / Stephen Longstreet. Indianapolis : Bobbs-Merrill, c1979. p. cm. Includes index. Bibliography: p. [HQ1412.L66] 79-1128 10.95
1. Women—United States—Biography. I. Title. **BIP**

NEIDLE, Cecyle S. 920.72
America's immigrant women / by Cecyle S. Neidle. Boston : Twayne Publishers, [1975] p. cm. (The immigrant heritage of America series) Includes index. Bibliography: p. [HQ1412.N44] 75-12738 ISBN 0-8057-8400-4 lib.bdg. : 9.95
1. Women—United States—Biography. 2. United States—Emmigration and immigration—Biography. I. Title. **BIP**

NIES, Judith. 301.41'2'0922
Seven women : portraits from the American radical tradition / Judith Nies. New York : Penguin Books, 1978, c1977. xvi, 235 p. ; 20 cm. Includes bibliographies and index. Brief biographies of seven women whose philosophies and actions have had great impact on American society. Included are Sarah Moore Grimke, Harriet Tubman, Elizabeth Cady Stanton, Mother Jones, Charlotte Perkins Gilman, Anna Louise Strong, and Dorothy Day. [HQ1412.N53 1978] 920 78-3399 ISBN 0-14-004792-1 pbk. : 2.95
1. Women—United States—Biography 2. Radicalism—United States. I. Title.

NIES, Judith. 301.41'2'0922 B
Seven women : portraits from the American radical tradition / Judith Nies. 1st ed. New York : Viking Press, c1977. xvi, 236 p. ; 24 cm. Includes index. Bibliography: p. 209-227. Brief biographies of seven women whose philosophies and actions have had great impact on American society. Included are Sarah Moore Grimke, Harriet Tubman, Elizabeth Cady Stanton, Mother Jones, Anna Louise Strong, and Dorothy Day. [HQ1412.N53 1977] 920 76-49942 ISBN 0-670-63599-5 : 10.00
1. Women—United States—Biography. 2. Radicalism—United States. I. Title. **BIP**

OUR famous women: 920.72
an authorized record of the lives and deeds of distinguished American women of our times ... by the following twenty eminent authors: Elizabeth Stuart Phelps [and others] Freeport, N.Y., Books for Libraries Press [1975] 715 p. illus. 23 cm. (Essay index reprint series) "First published 1883." [CT3260.O7 1975] 73-1192 ISBN 0-518-10060-X
1. Women—United States—Biography. I. Ward, Elizabeth Stuart (Phelps), 1844-1911.

REMARKABLE American women, 920.72
1776-1976. [New York : Time, inc., c1976] 116 p. : ill. ; 34 cm. (Life special report) [HQ1412.R45] 76-379193 2.00
1. Women—United States—Biography. I. Time, inc.

ROOSEVELT, Felicia Warburg. 920.72
Doers & dowagers / Felicia Warburg Roosevelt. 1st ed. Garden City, N.Y. : Doubleday, 1975. ix, 228 p. : ill. ; 22 cm. [CT3260.R58] 74-12708 ISBN 0-385-06527-2 : 8.95
1. Women—United States—Biography. I. Title.

ST. Johns, Adela Rogers. 301.41'2'0922
Some are born great. [1st ed.] Garden City, N.Y., Doubleday, 1974. vi, 297 p. 24 cm. [HQ1412.S25] 74-7636 ISBN 0-385-08769-1
1. Women—United States—Biography. I. Title.

SEIFER, Nancy. 301.41'2'0973
Nobody speaks for me! : Self-portraits of American working class women / Nancy Seifer. New York : Simon and Schuster, c1976. 477 p. : ill. ; 22 cm. [HQ1412.S44] 76-11836 ISBN 0-671-22308-9 : 7.95
1. Women—United States—Biography. 2. Labor and laboring classes—United States. I. Title.

SICKELS, Eleanor Maria, 1894- 973'.0099
In calico and crinoline; true stories of American women, 1608-1865. By Eleanor Sickels, with 19 drawings by Ilse Bischoff. Freeport, N.Y., Books for Libraries Press [1971, c1935] 274 p. illus. 23 cm. (Essay index reprint series) Contents.Contents.—Adventures in a new world.—Running up the stars and stripes.—Aboard the covered wagon.—Cotton fields and factories. [CT3260.S5 1971] 70-167418 ISBN 0-8369-2474-6
1. Women—United States—Biography. I. Title. **BIP**

SICKELS, Eleanor Maria, 1894- 920.073
Twelve daughters of democracy; true stories of American women, 1865-1930, by Eleanor Sickels. Illustrated by Dorothy Bayley. Freeport, N.Y., Books for Libraries Press [1968, c1941] 256 p. illus. 23 cm. (Essay index reprint series) Bibliography: p. 251-256. [CT3260.S53 1968] 68-55858
1. Women—United States—Biography. I. Title.

STEIN, Leon, 1912- comp. 301.41'2'0973 B
Fragments of autobiography. New York, Arno Press, 1974. 1 v. (various pagings) illus. 26 cm. (Women in America: from colonial times to the 20th century) Reprint of autobiographical pieces published 1832-1938. [HQ1412.S73] 74-3982 ISBN 0-405-06096-3
1. Women—United States—Biography. I. Title. II. Series.

STEIN, Leon, 1912- comp. 301.41'2'0973 B
Lives to remember. New York, Arno Press, 1974. 1 v. (various pagings) illus. 24 cm. (Women in America: from colonial times to the 20th century) Contents.Contents.—Gundy, H. P. Molly Brant loyalist.—Oldham, E. M. Early women printers of America.—Small, E. W. and M. R. Prudence Crandall: champion of Negro education.—Shippee, L. B. Jane Grey Swisshelm: agitator.—Van Rensselaer, G. The original of Rebecca in Ivanhoe.—Mabbott, T. O. "Maria del Occidente."—Fleischer, N. Reckless lady: the life story of Adah Isaacs Menken.—Fatout, P. Amelia Bloomer and bloomerism.—Green, N. K. Four sisters: daughters of Joseph La Flesche.—Hogan, W. R. Pamella Mann: Texas frontierswoman.—Haddock, E. Women as land-owners in the West.—Diggs, A. L. The women in the alliance movement.—McKelway, A. J. "Kate," the "good angel" of Oklahoma.—Altman, A. R. Julia Richman.—Cantwell, R. "The awakening," by Kate Chopin.—Wolcott, R. W. A woman in steel—Rebecca Lukens.—Dwyer, J. L. Lady with the hatchet.—De FordOLives to remember. New York, Arno Press, 1974. 1 v. (various pagings) illus. 24 cm. (Women in America: from colonial times to the 20th cent
1. Women—United States—Biography. I. Title. II. Series.

TRUMAN, Margaret, 1924- 920.72
Women of courage / by Margaret Truman. New York : Morrow, 1976. p. cm. Includes index. Brief biographies emphasizing the courage of twelve women both famous and little-known in United States history. [CT3260.T79] 920 75-45456 ISBN 0-688-03038-6 : 7.95
1. Women—United States—Biography. I. Title. **BIP**

TRUMAN, Margaret, 1924- 920.72
Women of courage / Margaret Truman. South Yarmouth, Ma. : J. Curley & Associates, 1978, c1976. 397 p. ; 22 cm. Large print ed. Brief biographies emphasizing the courage of 12 women both famous and little-known in United States history. [CT3260.T79 1978] 77-13658 ISBN 0-89340-124-2 pbk. : 9.95
1. Women—United States—Biography. 2. Large type books. I. Title.

WHO'S who of American women; 920.7
a biographical dictionary of

notable living American women. v. 1- Chicago, Marquis-Who's Who. 1958-59- v. 28 cm. Bienniel. Accompanied by Geographical-vocational index. [CT3260.W5] 58-13264
1. Women—U.S.—Biography.

WILLARD, Frances 920.72'0973
Elizabeth, 1839-1898, ed.
A woman of the century : fourteen hundred-seventy biographical sketches accompanied by portraits of leading American women in all walks of life / edited by Frances E. Willard and Mary A. Livermore ; assisted by a corps of able contributors. New York : Gordon Press, 1975,i.e.1976 2 v. (812 p.) : ports. ; 27 cm. Published in 1893 and 1967 under title: A woman of the century; in 1897 and 1973 under title: American women; and in 1901 under title: Portraits and biographies of prominent American women. Reprint of the 1893 ed. published by C. W. Moulton, Buffalo. [HQ1412.W54 1975] 74-27501 ISBN 0-87968-183-7 lib.bdg. : 200.00
1. Women—United States—Biography. 2. United States—Biography. I. Livermore, Mary Ashton Rice, 1820-1905. II. Title.

WOMAN'S who's who of 920.72'0973
America; a biographical dictionary of contemporary women of the United States and Canada. John William Leonard, editor-in-chief. New York, American Commonwealth Co. Detroit, Gale Research Co., 1974 [c1914] p. cm. [CT3260.W65 1974] 74-6280 ISBN 0-8103-4018-6
1. Women—United States—Biography. 2. Women—Canada—Biography. I. Leonard, John William, 1849-1932, ed.

Women—United States—Biography—Juvenile literature.

AS I saw it : 973
women who lived the American adventure / [compiled] by Cheryl G. Hoople. New York : Dial Press, c1978. p. cm. Bibliography: p. Presents excerpts from the diaries, letters, and journals of American women which provide glimpses of United States history and social conditions from 1600 to 1900. [HQ1412.A78] 78-51324 7.95
1. Women—United States—Biography—Juvenile literature. 2. Women—United States—History—Juvenile literature. 3. United States—Social conditions—Addresses, essays, lectures—Juvenile literature. I. Hoople, Cheryl G. BIP

MCLENIGHAM, 301.41'2'0922 B
Valjean.
Women who dared / Valjean McLenigham ; [illustrated by Jackie Denison]. Milwaukee : Raintree Publishers, c1979. p. cm. Bibliography: p. Presents brief biographies of prominent women, including Margaret Bourke-White, Diana Nyad, Janet Guthrie, and Kitty O'Neill. [HQ1412.M27] 79-13718 ISBN 0-8172-1375-9 (lib. bdg.) : 7.49
1. Women—United States—Biography—Juvenile literature. I. Denison, Jackie. II. Title.

OLSON, Nathanael. 920.72'0973
Women to remember : portraits of women who helped shape America / Nathanael Olson. Westchester, Ill. : Good News Publishers, c1976. 123 p. : ports. ; 21 cm. Brief biographies of nineteen women emphasizing their contributions to the literature, education, social reform, and spiritual life of the United States. [HQ1412.O5] 76-17668 ISBN 0-89107-144-X : 3.95
1. Women—United States—Biography—Juvenile literature. I. Title.

ROSS, Pat, comp. 920.72'0973
Young and female; turning points in the lives of eight American women, personal accounts. New York, Random House [1972] 107 p. illus. 22 cm. Contents.Contents.—Shirley MacLaine.—Shirley Chisholm.—Dorothy Day.—Emily Hahn.—Margaret Sanger.—Althea Gibson.—Edna Ferber.—Margaret Bourke-White. Bibliography: p. 107. [CT3260.R63] 920 76-37417 ISBN 0-394-82392-3 4.39
1. Women—United States—Biography—Juvenile literature. I. Title.

SIGNIFICANT American 920.72'0973
women. Chicago : Childrens Press, [1976] p. cm. Includes index. Brief biographies of 159 notable women arranged in chronological-alphabetical order. [CT3260.S55] 920 75-20686 ISBN 0-516-05312-4 : 9.25
1. Women—United States—Biography—Juvenile literature. I. Title: Women.

SMITH, Margaret (Chase) 920.073
1898-
Gallant women, by Margaret Chase Smith and H. Paul Jeffers. Illustrated by Paul Giovanopoulos. New York, McGraw-Hill [1968] 124, [1] p. ports. 24 cm. Contents.Contents.—Anne Hutchinson, an impudent dame.—Dolly Madison, I must leave this house.—They wanted to help.—Harriet Tubman, the slaves called her Moses; Harriet Beecher Stowe, the book that started a great war; Clara Barton, angel of the battlefield.—Elizabeth Blackwell, either mad or bad.—Susan B. Anthony, we intend to vote.—Annie Sullivan, all the best of me.—Amelia Earhart, adventure is worthwhile.—Althea Gibson, to be somebody.—Frances Perkins, a good Democrat.—Eleanor Roosevelt, honor to all of us.—Bibliography (p. 124-[125]) [CT3260.S6] 68-31666 4.75
1. Women—United States—Biography—Juvenile literature. I. Jeffers, Harry Paul, 1934- II. Giovanopoulos, Paul, illus. III. Title.

WALKER, Greta. 920.72
Women today : ten profiles / Greta Walker. New York : Hawthorn Books, [1975] 174 p. : ports. ; 22 cm. Includes index. Bibliography: p. 167-168. Biographical sketches of ten women engaged in a variety of professions stressing their approach to their work and its place in their lives. [HQ1412.W34] 920 74-22925 ISBN 0-8015-7760-8 : 6.95
1. Women—United States—Biography—Juvenile literature. 2. Women—Employment—United States—Biography—Juvenile literature. 3. Success—Biography—Juvenile literature. I. Title.

WILLIAMS, Selma R. 920.72'0973
Demeter's daughters : the women who founded America (1587-1792) / by Selma R. Williams. New York : Atheneum, 1976. p. cm. Details the varied activities of colonial women, the extensive legal rights they enjoyed, and the difficulties they faced in a new land. Includes bibliographical sketches of representative women of that period. [HQ1416.W54] 920 75-13773 ISBN 0-689-30494-3 : 9.95
1. Women—United States—Biography—Juvenile literature. 2. United States—History—Colonial period, ca. 1600-1775—Juvenile literature. I. Title. BIP

Women—United States—History.

EARNEST, Ernest 301.41'2'0973
Penney, 1901-
The American Eve in fact and fiction, 1775-1914 [by Ernest Earnest Urbana, University of Illinois Press [1974] 280 p. 24 cm. Includes bibliographical references. [HQ1410.E17] 74-19339 ISBN 0-252-00448-5 9.50
1. Women—United States—History. 2. Women—United States—Biography. 3. Women in literature. I. Title. BIP

REIFERT, Gail. 301.41'2'0973
Women who fought : an American history / Gail Reifert, Eugene M. Dermody. Norwalk, Calif. : Dermody, c1978. ii, 227, [6] p. ; 22 cm. Bibliography: p. [229]-[233] [HQ1412.R43] 78-106358 4.95
1. Women—United States—History. 2. Women—United States—Biography. 3. Feminists—United States—Biography. I. Dermody, Eugene M., joint author. II. Title. BIP

Women—United States—History—Addresses, essays, lectures.

WOMEN'S experience 301.41'2'0973
in America : an historical anthology / edited by Esther Katz and Anita Rapone. New Brunswick, N.J. : Transaction Books, [1979] p. cm. Includes index. Bibliography: p. [HQ1410.W67] 79-64179 ISBN 0-87855-668-0 : 5.95
1. Women—United States—History—Addresses, essays, lectures. 2. Women—United States—Social conditions—Addresses, essays, lectures. 3. Women—United States—Biography—Addresses, essays, lectures. I. Katz, Esther. II. Rapone, Anita.

Women—United States—History—Biography.

MERRIAM, Eve, 1916- 920.72'0973
comp.
Growing up female in America; ten lives. Edited and introduced by Eve Merriam. [1st ed.] Garden City, N.Y., Doubleday, 1971. 308 p. illus. 22 cm. Contents.Contents.—Eliza Southgate (1783-1809): schoolgirl.—Elizabeth Cady Stanton (1815-1902): founder of the women's suffrage movement.—Maria Mitchell (1818-1889): astronomer.—Mary Ann Webster Loughborough (1836-1887): wife of a Confederate officer.—Arvazine Angeline Cooper (1845-1929): pioneer across the plains.—Dr. Anna Howard Shaw (1847-1919): minister and doctor.—Susie King Taylor (1848-1912): born a slave.—"Mother" Mary Jones (1830-1930): labor organizer.—Elizabeth Gertrude Stern (1890-1954): in the Jewish ghetto.—Mountain Wolf Woman (1884-1960): Winnebago Indian.—Attic.—Bibliography (p. 23) [HQ1412.M45] 79-157611 7.95
1. Women—United States—History—Biography. I. Title.

Women—United States—History—Biography—Juvenile literature.

CLYNE, Patricia 973.3'092'2 B
Edwards.
Patriots in petticoats / Patricia Edwards Clyne ; illustrated by Richard Lebenson. New York : Dodd, Mead, c1976. xi, 144 p. : ill. ; 21 cm. Includes index. More than twenty brief biographies of women who fought for their country's independence. Includes information on related historic sites and markers that can be visited today. [HQ1416.C57] 920 75-38361 ISBN 0-396-07292-5 : 4.95
1. Women—United States—History—Biography—Juvenile literature. 2. United States—History—Revolution, 1775-1783—Juvenile literature. I. Lebenson, Richard. II. Title. BIP

Women—United States—History—Juvenile literature.

LENNON, Janice. 301.41'2'0973
Women in America : the illustrated story of their interests and achievements from colonial days to the present / written and designed by Janice Lennon, Steven Hill ; editor Maryjane Hooper Tonn. Milwaukee : Ideals Pub. Corp., [1975] 79 p. : ill. (some col.) ; 29 cm. Includes index. [HQ1410.L35] 75-309487
1. Women—United States—History—Juvenile literature. 2. Women—United States—Bibliography—Juvenile literature. I. Hill, Steven, joint author. II. Title.

Women—United States—Juvenile literature.

LANDAU, Elaine. 301.41'2'0973
Woman, woman! Feminism in America. New York, J. Messner [1974] 189 p. 21 cm. Bibliography: p. 181-183. Discusses the role of women in American history, stereotypes and discrimination that have kept them from realizing their potential, and the move for equality in the 1960s and '70s. [HQ1426.L33] 74-7590 ISBN 0-671-32689-9
1. Women—United States—Juvenile literature. 2. Women's rights—United States—Juvenile literature. I. Title. BIP

Women—United States—Social conditions.

CAMPBELL, Barbara 301.41'2'0973
Kuhn, 1946-
The "liberated" woman of 1914 : prominent women in the progressive era / by Barbara Kuhn Campbell. Ann Arbor, Mich. : UMI Research Press, c1979. xviii, 220 p. : ill. ; 24 cm. (Studies in American history and culture ; no. 6) Includes index. Bibliography: p. [183]-195. [HQ1412.C35 1979] 78-27703 ISBN 0-8357-0980-9 : 23.95. ISBN 0-8357-0981-7 pbk. : 20.95
1. Women—United States—Social conditions. 2. Feminists—United States—Biography. I. Title. II. Series.

Women—United States—Social conditions—Biography.

WESTIN, Jeane. 301.41'2'0973
Making do : how women survived the '30s / by Jeane Westin. Chicago : Follett, c1976. xi, 329 p. ; 24 cm. Includes index. [HQ1412.W48] 75-170 ISBN 0-695-80593-2 : 9.95
1. Women—United States—Social conditions—Biography. 2. Depressions—1929—United States. I. Title.

Women—Washington (State)—Biography.

AMERICAN Association 920.72'09797
of University Women. Washington State Division.
Women of Washington : women's involvement in community concern : a Washington State history / compiled by American Association of University Women, Washington State Division ; executive editor, Jean Wheeler Schuddakopf. Gig Harbor, WA : Available from J. Schuddakopf, [1977] 24 p. ; 28 cm. Includes index. Bibliography: p. 22. [HQ1438.W2A48 1977] 77-670136 3.25
1. Women—Washington (State)—Biography. I. Schuddakopf, Jean Wheeler. II. Title.

GALLAGHER, Dorothy. 301.41'2'0922
Hannah's daughters : six generations of an American family, 1876-1976 / Dorothy Gallagher. New York : Crowell, c1976. 343 p. : ill. ; 16 x 24 cm. [HQ1412.G34 1976] 75-38557 ISBN 0-690-01103-2 : 10.95
1. Women—Washington (State)—Biography. I. Title. BIP

Women—Wisconsin—Biography.

BROWN, Victoria 920.72'09775
Bissell.
Uncommon lives of common women : the missing half of Wisconsin history : a project of the Wisconsin Feminists Project Fund, inc., in cooperation with the Commission on the Status of Women, the Kohler Foundation, the Oscar Mayer Foundation, the Cudahy Foundation / by Victoria Brown. [Madison] : The Fund, c1975. v, 94 p. : ill., ports. ; 22 cm. Includes bibliographical references. [HQ1438.W5B76] 76-356034
1. Women—Wisconsin—Biography. 2. Women—Wisconsin—History. 3. Indians of North America—Wisconsin—Women. I. Wisconsin Feminists Project Fund. II. Title.

Women—Yosemite Valley—Biography.

SARGENT, 917.94'47'0340922
Shirley.
Pioneers in petticoats; Yosemite's early women, 1856-1900. Book design by Hank Johnston. [1st ed.] Los Angeles, Trans-Anglo Books [1966] 80 p. illus., ports. 28 cm. Bibliographical footnotes. [F868.Y6S25] 66-22382
1. Women—Yosemite Valley—Biography. 2. Yosemite Valley. I. Title.

Womunafu, Mukama, 1830?-1906.

COHEN, David 967.6'101'0924 B
William.
Womunafu's Bunafu : a study of authority in a nineteenth-century African community / David William Cohen. Princeton : Princeton University Press, c1977. p. cm. Includes index. Bibliography: p. [DT433.242.W65C64] 77-71976 ISBN 0-691-03093-6 : 15.00
1. Womunafu, Mukama, 1830?-1906. 2. Soga (Bantu tribe)—Politics and government. 3. Soga (Bantu tribe)—Kings and rulers—Biography. I. Title. BIP

Wonder, Stevie.

DRAGONWAGON, Crescent. 784'.092'4 B
Stevie Wonder / by C. Dragonwagon. New York : Flash Books, c1977. 94, [1] p. : ill. ; 26 cm. Discography: p. 93-[95] A biography of the blind black musician who has become one of America's most popular performers. [ML410.W836D7] 92 77-78535 ISBN 0-8256-3908-5 : 3.95
1. Wonder, Stevie. 2. Rock musicians—United States—Biography. I. Title.

HASKINS, James, 1941- 784'.092'4 B
The Stevie Wonder scrapbook / by Jim Haskins, with Kathleen Benson. New York : Grosset & Dunlop, c1978. 159 p. : ill. ; 28 cm. Bibliography: p. 158-159. [ML410.W836H4] 78-53021 ISBN 0-448-14464-6 : 12.95 ISBN 0-448-14465-4 pbk. : 5.95
1. Wonder, Stevie. 2. Rock musicians—United States—Biography. I. Benson, Kathleen, joint author. II. Title. BIP

Wonder, Stevie - Juvenile literature.

EDWARDS, Audrey. 784'.092'4 B
The picture life of Stevie Wonder / by Audrey Edwards and Gary Wohl. New York : Watts, 1977. p. cm. (Picture life books) A biography of a young, blind musician who had his first hit record at the age of thirteen. [ML3930.W65E4] 92 76-47566 ISBN 0-531-012271-9 lib.bdg. . 4.47
1. Wonder, Stevie—Juvenile literature. 2. Rock musicians—United States—Biography—Juvenile literature. I. Wohl, Gary, joint author. II. Title. BIP

HASEGAWA, Sam. 784'.092'4 B
Stevie Wonder. Illus.: Dick Brude. Mankato, Minn., Creative Education; [distributed by Childrens Press, Chicago, 1974, c1975] 31 p. illus. (part col.) 25 cm. (Rock 'n pop stars) A biography of the blind black musician who from early childhood showed signs of the talent that has made him one of America's most popular performers. [ML3930.W65H4] 92 74-14746 ISBN 0-87191-395-X
1. Wonder, Stevie—Juvenile literature. I. Brude, Dick, illus. II. Title.

HASKINS, James. 784'.092'4 B
The story of Stevie Wonder / James Haskins. New York : Dell Publishing Company, 1979, c1976 112p. : ill. ; 18 cm. (Laurel-Leaf Library) [ML3930.W65H4] 92 ISBN 0-440-98259-6 pbk. : 1.25
1. Wonder, Stevie — Juvenile literature. I. Title.
L.C. card no. for 1976 Lothrop, Lee & Shepard Co., ed: 75-37517

HASKINS, James, 1941- 784'.092'4 B
The story of Stevie Wonder / by James Haskins. New York : Lothrop, Lee & Shepard Co., c1976. p. cm. A biography of the blind composer, pianist, and singer who was a child prodigy and went on to win nine Grammy awards. [ML3930.W65H4] 92 75-37517 ISBN 0-688-41740-X : 5.50 ISBN 0-688-51740-4 lib.bdg. : 4.81
1. Wonder, Stevie—Juvenile literature. I. Title.

HASKINS, James, 1941- 784'.092'4 B
The story of Stevie Wonder / James Haskins ; illustrated with photos. New York : Dell Pub. Co., 1979, c1976. 112p. : photos ; 18 cm. (Laurel-Leaf library) Includes index. Discography: p. 108-109. A biography of the blind composer, pianist, and singer who was a child prodigy and went on to win nine Grammy awards. [ML3930.W65H4] 92 ISBN 0-440-98259-6 pbk. : 1.25
1. Wonder, Stevie — Juvenile literature. I. Title.
L.C. card no. for 1976 Lothrop, Lee & Shepard ed.: 75-37517. BIP

JACOBS, Linda. 784'.092'4 B
Stevie Wonder : sunshine in the shadow / by Linda Jacobs. St. Paul : EMC Corp., [1975] p. cm. A biography tracing the rise to stardom of a black musician who was blind from birth. [ML3930.W65J3] 92 75-33012 ISBN 0-88436-258-2 pbk. : 2.95
1. Wonder, Stevie—Juvenile literature. 2. Wonder, Stevie. I. Title.

WILSON, Beth P. 784'.092'4 B
Stevie Wonder / by Beth P. Wilson ; illustrated by James Calvin. New York : Putnam, 1978. p. cm. (A See and read biography) A biography of the blind composer, pianist, and singer whose musical ability, apparent since childhood, has earned him many awards. [ML3930.W65W54] 92 78-6054 ISBN 0-399-61106-1 : 4.49
1. Wonder, Stevie—Juvenile literature. 2. Rock musicians—United States—Biography—Juvenile literature. I. Calvin, James. II. Title. BIP

Wong, Sai Hee, 1857-1927.

LAI, Bessie C. 299'.514'0924 B
Ah Ya, I still remember / by Bessie C. Lai. Taipei : Meadea Enterprise Co., c1976. 173 p. ; 20 cm. Added title in Chinese romanized: Chi nien fu ch'in Huang Shih-hsi. [BL1940.W66L34] 77-358819
1. Wong, Sai Hee, 1857-1927. 2. Taoists—Hawaii—Biography. I. Title.

Wood, Benjamin DeKalbe, 1894—

DOWNEY, Matthew T. 923.773
Ben D. Wood, educational reformer, by Matthew T. Downey. [Princeton, N. J.] [Educational Testing Serivce] [1965] 106 p. illus., ports. 23 cm. Bibliographical references included in "Notes" (p. 93-100) "Bibliography of Ben D. Wood": p. 101-106. [LB885.W65D6] 65-23014
1. Wood, Benjamin DeKalbe, 1894- I. Title.

Wood-carving.

PARDEE, Caroline Julia, 1911- 927.364
The little boy who found a knife; the story of Ernest Warther, master carver. With a foreword by Henry C. Hagloch. Modern photography by Paul S. Somogy. [1st ed.] Dover, Ohio, Printed by Dover Daily Reporter, 1951. 65 p. illus. 23 cm. [TT188.P3] 51-7872
1. Wood-carving. 2. Models and model making. I. Warther, Ernest, 1885- II. Title.

Wood, Christine.

WOOD, Christine. 283'.092'4 B
Exclusive by-path : the autobiography of a pilgrim / by Christine Wood. Evesham : James, 1976. 141 p. ; 19 cm. [BX5179.W74A33] 76-373348 ISBN 0-85305-183-6 : £2.80
1. Wood, Christine. 2. Church of England—Biography. 3. Plymouth Brethren—Biography. I. Title.

Wood, David, 1851-1944.

WOOD, Frances Elizabeth. 388.3'24'0924 B
I hauled these mountains in here / by Frances and Dorothy Wood. Caldwell, Idaho : Caxton Printers, 1977. xviii, 337 p. : ill. ; 24 cm. Includes index. [HE5633.C6W66] 76-187948 ISBN 0-87004-233-5 : 9.95
1. Wood, David, 1851-1944. 2. David Wood Transportation Lines. 3. Freight forwarders—Colorado—Biography. I. Wood, Florence Dorothy, joint author. II. Title. BIP

Wood, Fernando, 1812-1881.

PLEASANTS, Samuel Augustus, 1918- 973.5'0924 B
Fernando Wood of New York. New York, AMS Press, 1966 [c1948] 216 p. 24 cm. (Studies in history, economics, and public law, no. 536) Originally presented as the author's thesis, Columbia. Bibliography: p. 207-214. [F128.44.W872 1966] 79-29912
1. Wood, Fernando, 1812-1881. I. Series: Columbia studies in the social sciences, no. 536. BIP

Wood, George Arnold, 1865-1928.

CRAWFORD, Raymond Maxwell, 1906- 994'.04'0924 B
A bit of a rebel : the life and work of George Arnold Wood / by R. M. Crawford. Sydney : Sydney University Press, 1975. xiv, 386 p., [4] leaves of plates : ill. ; 24 cm. Includes bibliographical references and index. [DU109.W66C72] 76-351110 ISBN 0-424-00005-9 : 26.50
1. Wood, George Arnold, 1865-1928. I. Title.
Distributed by International Scholarly Book Service BIP

Wood, Henry Joseph, Sir, 1869-1944.

BROOK, Donald. 785'.0922 B
Conductor's gallery; biographical sketches of well-known orchestral conductors, including notes on the leading symphony orchestras, and a short biography of the late Sir Henry Wood. Freeport, N.Y., Books for Libraries Press [1971] xii, 188 p. ports. 23 cm. (Biography index reprint series) Reprint of the 1947 ed. "This is a book about conductors, chiefly those who are directing Britain's music at the present time." [ML402.B76 1971] 70-136642 ISBN 0-8369-8037-9
1. Wood, Henry Joseph, Sir, 1869-1944. 2. Conductors (Music)—Biography. 3. Symphony orchestras—Great Britain. I. Title.

Wood, Horatio C., 1841-1920.

HORATIO C. Wood, Jr., 1841-1920; a biographical memoir. v. 12
New York, Pub. for the National Academy of Sciences [by] Columbia Univ. Press, 1959. [462]-484p. port. Reprinted from the National Academy of Sciences' Biographical memoirs, v. 33.
1. Wood, Horatio C., 1841-1920. I. Roth, George Byron, 1879-

*Wood, James Playsted

*WOOD, James Playsted 973.9220924(B)
The life and words of John F. Kennedy by James Playsted Wood and the eds. of Country Beautiful magazine. New York, Scholastic [1966,c.1964] 79p. illus. 23cm. .60 pap.,
I. Title.

Wood, Joan, 1945-

WOOD, Joan, 1945- 792'.028'0924 B
The casting couch and me; the uninhibited memoirs of a young actress. New York, Pocket Books [1976 c1975] 222 p. 18 cm. [PN2287.W5BA33] 1.75 (pbk.)
1. Wood, Joan, 1945- I. Title.
L.C. card no. of 1974 Walker edition: 73-90386.

WOOD, Joan, 1945- 792'.028'0924 B
The casting couch and me : the uninhibited memoirs of a young actress / by Joan Wood. New York : Walker, 1974, c1975. 216 p. : ill. ; 22 cm. "A Sam Post book." [PN2287.W5BA33 1975] 73-90386 ISBN 0-8027-0452-2 : 7.95
1. Wood, Joan, 1945- I. Title.

Wood, John Taylor.

SHINGLETON, Royce. 973.7'5'0924
John Taylor Wood, Sea Ghost of the Confederacy / Royce Gordon Shingleton. Athens : University of Georgia Press, c1979. p. cm. Includes index. Bibliography: p. [E467.1.W86S47] 78-13934 ISBN 0-8203-0466-2 : 15.00
1. Wood, John Taylor. 2. United States—History—Civil War, 1861-1865—Naval operations. 3. Shipmasters—Southern States—Biography. I. Title.

Wood, Miriam.

WOOD, Miriam. 286'.73 B
Reluctant saint, reluctant sinner / Miriam Wood. Washington : Review and Herald Pub. Association, c1975. 127 p. ; 21 cm. [BX6193.W64A29] 74-25818 2.95
1. Wood, Miriam. I. Title.

Wood, Stella Louise, 1865-1949.

BELL, Marguerite N 923.773
With banners, a biography of Stella L. Wood. [St. Paul, Macalester College Press [c1954] 163p. illus. 23cm. [LB1238.M5W62] 55-14052
1. Wood, Stella Louise, 1865-1949. 2. Kindergarten—Hist. I. Title.

Wood, Violet.

WOOD, Violet. 926.1
So sure of life. Illustrated by Oliver Grimley. New York, Friendship Press [1950] 185 p. illus. 22 cm. [R154.T52W6] 50-12344
I. Thomas, Robert Follet, 1891- II. Title.

Woodard, Arvle,

WOODARD, Arvle, 1908- 269'.2'0924 B
The Mexico Kid: from an outlaw to a preacher; the life story of evangelist Arvle Woodard. New York, Carlton Press [1968] 77 p. 21 cm. (A Hearthstone book) [BV3785.W62A3] 71-226 2.50
I. Title.

Woodbury, David Oakes,

WOODBURY, David Oakes, 1896- 926.2
Elihu Thomson, beloved scientist, 1853-1937; inventive genius, engineer, educator, pioneer of the electrical age. With appreciations by James R. Killian, Jr., and Owen D. Young. Boston, Museum of Science, 1960. 358 p. illus. 24 cm. First published in 1944 under title: Beloved scientist; Elihu Thomson, a guiding spirit of the electrical age. Includes bibliography. [TK140.T5W6 1960] 60-11802
I. Thomson, Elihu, 1853-1937. II. Title.

Woodcock, Ronald—Juvenile literature.

CLARK, James I. 613.6'9'09711
Shortcut to peril / James I. Clark ; ill., Jan Palmer. Milwaukee : Raintree Publishers, c1980. p. cm. Relates the adventure of a beaver trapper who survived for 57 days after becoming lost in the wilderness of British Columbia. [GV200.5.C56] 79-22151 ISBN 0-8172-1570-0 (lib. bdg.) : 7.99
1. Woodcock, Ronald—Juvenile literature. 2. Wilderness survival—British Columbia—Juvenile literature. 3. Fur traders—Canada—Biography—Juvenile literature. I. Glessner, Marc. II. Title. BIP

Woodforde, James, 1740-1803.

WOODFORDE, James, 1740-1803. 942.07'3'0924 B
The diary of a country parson, 1758-1802 / by James Woodforde ; passages selected and edited by John Beresford. Oxford [Eng.] ; New York : Oxford University Press, 1978. xviii, 622 p. ; 20 cm. (Oxford paperbacks) The present selection was published in 1935 under title: Woodforde; passages from the five volumes of The diary of a country parson, 1758-1802. Includes bibliographical references. [BX5199.W755A332 1978] 77-30569 ISBN 0-19-281241-6 pbk. : 7.50
1. Woodforde, James, 1740-1803. 2. Church of England—Clergy—Biography. 3. Clergy—England—Biography. I. Beresford, John, 1888-1940. II. Title. BIP

Woodhull, Nathaniel, 1722-1776.

SABINE, William Henry Waldo, 1903- 923.573
Suppressed history of General Nathaniel Woodhull, president of the New York Congress and Convention in 1776. New York, [Colburn & Tegg] 1954. 225p. illus. 29cm. Includes bibliography. [E207.W8S3] 54-1510
1. Woodhull, Nathaniel, 1722-1776. I. Title.

Woodis, Clark, 1888-1971.

WOODIS, Clark, 1888-1971. 978.8'03 B
Diaries of Clark and Ruth Woodis : the story of a Colorado homestead 1913-1928. [s.l.] : Woodis Enterprise, c1976. ca. 150 p. : ill. ; 29 cm. [F781.W85] 76-5996
1. Woodis, Clark, 1888-1971. 2. Woodis, Ruth, 1889-1931. 3. Ranch life—Colorado. 4. Colorado—Biography. I. Woodis, Ruth, 1889-1931, joint author. II. Title.

Woodman, Cyrus, 1814-1889.

GARA, Larry. 923.373
Westernized Yankee; the story of Cyrus Woodman. Madison, State Historical Society of Wisconsin, 1956. 254p. illus. 24cm. Includes bibliography. [CT275.W665G3] 56-14602
1. Woodman, Cyrus, 1814-1889. I. Title.
BIP

Woodring, Harry Hines, 1887-1967.

MCFARLAND, Keith D., 1940- 353.6'092'4 B
Harry H. Woodring : a political biography of FDR's controversial Secretary of War / by Keith D. McFarland. Lawrence : University Press of Kansas, [1975] x, 346 p., [4] leaves of plates : ill. ; 23 cm. Includes index. Bibliography: p. 318-334. [E748.W79M32] 75-2336 ISBN 0-7006-0130-9 : 12.50
1. Woodring, Harry Hines, 1887-1967. BIP

Woods, Charles, 1921-

DEWS, Robert P., 1915- 976.1'06'0924 B
Survival at 25000 (Enduring Phoenix) : the Charles Woods story / Robert P. Dews. Chicago : Adams Press, 1975. 279 p. ; 23 cm. Running title: Enduring Phoenix. [F330.W66D48] 75-13052 pbk. : 5.00
1. Woods, Charles, 1921- I. Title. II. Title: Enduring Phoenix.

Woods, Robert Archey, 1865-1925.

WOODS, Eleanor Howard (Bush) 361.8 B
Robert A. Woods, champion of democracy, by Eleanor H. Woods. Freeport, N.Y., Books for Libraries Press [1971] x, 376 p. illus., ports. 23 cm. Reprint of the 1929 ed. [HV28.W65W6 1971] 70-150206 ISBN 0-8369-5719-9
1. Woods, Robert Archey, 1865-1925. BIP

Woodsworth, James Shaver, 1874-1942.

MCNAUGHT, Kenneth. 923.271
A prophet in politics; a biography of J. S. Woodsworth. [Toronto] University of Toronto Press [1959] 339p. illus. 24cm. [F1034.W6M23] 59-4879
1. Woodswroth, James Shaver, 1874-1942. I. Title.
BIP

MCNAUGHT, Kenneth William Kirkpatrick, 1918- 923.271
A prophet in politics; a biography of J. S. Woodsworth. [Toronto] University of Toronto Press [1959] 339 p. illus. 24 cm. [F1034.W6M23] 59-4879
1. Woodsworth, James Shaver, 1874-1942. I. Title.

Woodward, Augustus Brevoort, d. 1827.

WOODFORD, Frank Bury, 1903- 923.473
Mr. Jefferson's disciple; a life of Justice Woodward. East Lansing, Michigan State [1953] 212p. 23cm. 53-12008
1. Woodward, Augustus Brevoort, d. 1827. I. Title.

Woodward, Calvin Milton, 1837-1914.

DYE, Charles M., 1938- 370'.92'4 b
Calvin Milton Woodward and American urban education : biography of a reformer / Charles M. Dye. Ann Arbor, Mich. : Xerox University Microfilms, 1976. ix, 309 leaves ; 27 cm. (Monograph publishing on demand, sponsor series) "Published under the aegis of the University of Akron Chapter, Phi Delta Kappa." Bibliography: leaf 267-309. [LA2317.W66D93] 75-37477 ISBN 0-8357-0158-1 : 16.50
1. Woodward, Calvin Milton, 1837-1914. 2. Education, Urban—United States. I. Title.

Woodward, Henry, 1646?-ca. 1688—Juvenile literature.

STEELE, William O., 1917- 973.2'4'0924 B
Henry Woodward of Carolina, surgeon, trader, Indian chief, by William O. Steele. Illustrated by Hoyt Simmons. [1st ed. Columbia, S.C.] Sandlapper Press [1972] 96 p. illus. 23 cm. Biography of a surgeon and Indian trader who assisted in the English colonization of the Carolinas. [F272.W78S8] 92 72-76381 ISBN 0-87844-008-9 4.50
1. Woodward, Henry, 1646?-ca. 1688—Juvenile literature. I. Simmons, Hoyt, illus. II. Title.

Woodward, John, 1665-1728.

LEVINE, Joseph M. 941.07'092'4 B
Dr. Woodward's shield : history, science, and satire in Augustan England / Joseph M. Levine. Berkeley : University of California Press, c1977. x, 362 p., [4] leaves of plates : ill. ; 25 cm. Includes bibliographical references and index. [CT788.W854L48] 75-27927 ISBN 0-520-03132-6 : 19.75
1. Woodward, John, 1665-1728. 2. England—Biography. 3. Shields. I. Title.
BIP

Woodward, Walter Carleton,

EMERSON, Elizabeth (Holaday). 922.8673
Walter C. Woodward; Friend on the frontier, a biography. With a pref. by Errol T. Elliott. [Richmond? Ind., 1952] 316 p. illus. 20 cm. [BX7795.W67E5] 52-29135
1. Woodward, Walter Carleton, I. Title.

Woody, Regina Llewellyn (Jones)

WOODY, Regina Llewellyn (Jones) 927.933
Dancing for joy. Illustrated with photos. Drawings by Arline K. Thomson. [1st ed.] New York, Dutton, 1959. 223 p. illus. 21 cm. Autobiographical. [GV1785.W6A3] 59-11504
I. Title.

Woolf, Bob.

WOOLF, Bob. 344'.73'099
Behind closed doors / Bob Woolf ; with the editorial assistance of Mickey Herskowitz ; introd. by Roger Kahn. 1st ed. New York : Atheneum, 1976. xx, 300 p. [8] leaves of plates : ill. ; 22 cm. [KF373.W6A32] 75-41851 ISBN 0-689-10712-9 : 9.95
1. Woolf, Bob. 2. Lawyers—United States—Correspondence, reminiscences, etc. 3. Professional sports—United States. I. Title.
BIP

Woolf, Leonard Sidney, 1880-1969.

WILSON, Duncan, Sir. 320'.092'4 B
Leonard Woolf : a political biography / Duncan Wilson. New York : St. Martin's Press, 1978. p. cm. Includes index. Bibliography: p. [JA94.W6W54 1978] 78-16778 ISBN 0-312-48001-6 : 18.50
1. Woolf, Leonard Sidney, 1880-1969. 2. Political scientists—Great Britain—Biography.
BIP

WOOLF, Leonard Sidney, 1880- v. 12
[An autobiography of the years 1880-1911] New York, Harcourt, Brace [1960-1964] 3 v. Contents.-- [v. 1] Sowing, an autobiography of the years 1880-1904. -- [v. 2] Growing; an autobiography of the years 1904-1911. -- [v. 3] Beginning again; an autobiography of the years 1911 to 1918. 67-17019
1. Woolf, Leonard Sidney, 1880- 2. Ceylon — Descr. & trav. 3. Authors — Correspondence, reminiscences, etc. I. Title.

WOOLF, Leonard Sidney, 1880-1969. 928.2
Beginning again; an autobiography of the years 1911 to 1918 [by] Leonard Woolf. 1st American ed. New York, Harcourt, Brace & World 1964 263 p. illus., ports. 22 cm. Continuation of Growing; an autobiography of the years, 1904-1911. [JA94.W6A26 1964] 64-11545
I. Title.
BIP

WOOLF, Leonard Sidney, 1880-1969. 320'.092'4 B
Beginning again : an autobiography of the years 1911 to 1918 / Leonard Woolf. New York : Harcourt Brace Jovanovich, 1972 [i.e. 1975] 263 p., [12] leaves of plates : ill. ; 21 cm. (A Harvest book ; HB 321) Continuation of Growing; an autobiography of the years 1904-1911. Continued by Downhill all the way; an autobiography of the years 1919-1939. Includes index. [JA94.W6A26 1975] 75-9848 ISBN 0-15-611680-4 pbk. : 3.45
1. Woolf, Leonard Sidney, 1880-1969. I. Title.

WOOLF, Leonard Sidney, 1880-1969. 655.5'92'0924
Downhill all the way: an autobiography of the years 1919-1939 [by] Leonard Woolf. [1st American ed.] New York, Harcourt, Brace & World [1967] 259 p. illus., ports. 21 cm. Continuation of Beginning again; an autobiography of the years 1911-1918. Continued by The journey not the arrival matters: an autobiography of the years 1939-1969. [JA94.W6A27 1967b] 67-20326
I. Title.
BIP

WOOLF, Leonard Sidney, 1880-1969. 320'.092'4 B
Downhill all the way : an autobiography of the years 1919 to 1939 / Leonard Woolf. New York : Harcourt Brace Jovanovich, [1975] c1967. p. cm. (A Harvest book ; HB 322) Continues Beginning again; an autobiography of the years 1911 to 1918. Continued by The journey not the arrival matters; an autobiography of the years 1939 to 1969. Includes index. [JA94.W6A27 1975] 75-9821 ISBN 0-15-626145-6 pbk. : 3.45
1. Woolf, Leonard Sidney, 1880-1969. I. Title.

WOOLF, Leonard Sidney, 1880-1969. 320'.092'4 B
Growing : an autobiography of the years 1904 to 1911 / Leonard Woolf. New York : Harcourt Brace Jovanovich, 1975, c1961. 256 p., [4] leaves of plates : ill. ; 21 cm. (A Harvest book ; HB 320) Continuation of Sowing: an autobiography of the years 1880 to 1904. Continued by Beginning again; an autobiography of the years 1911 to 1918. Includes index. [JA94.W6A28 1975] 75-9832 ISBN 0-15-637215-0 pbk. : 3.45
1. Woolf, Leonard Sidney, 1880-1969. 2. Ceylon—Description and travel. I. Title.
BIP

WOOLF, Leonard Sidney, 1880-1969. 655.5'92'0924
The journey, not the arrival matters; an autobiography of the years, 1939-1969 [by] Leonard Woolf. [1st American ed.] New York, Harcourt, Brace & World [1970, c1969] 217 p. illus., ports. 21 cm. Continuation of Downhill all the way; an autobiography of the years 1919-1939. Includes bibliographical references. [JA94.W6A29 1970] 71-100502
I. Title.
BIP

WOOLF, Leonard Sidney, 1880-1969. 320'.092'4 B
The journey not the arrival matters : an autobiography of the years 1939 to 1969 / Leonard Woolf. New York : Harcourt Brace Jovanovich, 1975, c1969. 217 p., [8] leaves of plates : ill. ; 21 cm. (A Harvest book ; HB 323) Continuation of Downhill all the way; an autobiography of the years 1919-1939. Includes bibliographical references and index. [JA94.W6A29 1975] 75-9822 ISBN 0-15-646523-X
1. Woolf, Leonard Sidney, 1880-1969. I. Title.

WOOLF, Leonard Sidney, 1880-1969. 320'.092'4 B
Sowing, an autobiography of the years 1880 to 1904 / by Leonard Woolf. New York : Harcourt Brace Jovanovich, 1975, c1960. 206 p., [6] leaves of plates : ill. ; 21 cm. (A Harvest book ; HB 319) Continued by Growing, an autobiography of the years 1904-1911. Includes index. [JA94.W6A3 1975] 75-12870 ISBN 0-15-683945-8 pbk. : 2.95
1. Woolf, Leonard Sidney, 1880-1969. I. Title.

WOOLF, Leonard Sidney, 1880- 928.2
Sowing, an autobiography of the years 1880 to 1904. [1st American ed.] New York, Harcourt, Brace [1960] 224 p. illus. 22 cm. [PR6045.O68Z5] 60-12726
1. Authors — Correspondence, reminiscences, etc. I. Title.

WOOLF, Leonard Sidney 928.2
Sowing, an autobiography of the years 1880 to 1904. New York, Harcourt, Brace [c.1960] 224p. illus. 21cm. 60-12726 4.50 half cloth,
1. Authors—Correspondence, reminiscences, etc. I. Title.
BIP

Woolf, Leonard Sidney, 1880-1969—Friends and associates.

LEHMANN, John, 1907- 821'.9'12 B
Thrown to the Woolfs / John Lehmann. 1st American ed. New York : Holt, Rinehart, and Winston, 1979, c1978. xx, 164 p., [4] leaves of plates : ill. ; 22 cm. Includes index. [PR6023.E4Z519 1979] 79-1925 ISBN 0-03-052191-2 : 10.95
1. Lehmann, John, 1907- —Biography. 2. Woolf, Leonard Sidney, 1880-1969—Friends and associates. 3. Woolf, Virginia Stephen, 1882-1941—Friends and associates. 4. Hogarth Press. 5. Authors, English—20th century—Biography. I. Title.
BIP

Woolf, Virginia Stephen, 1882-1941.

BELL, Quentin. 823'.9'12 B
Virginia Woolf; a biography. New York, Harcourt Brace Jovanovich [1974, c1972] xvii, 314 p. illus. 21 cm. (A Harvest book, HB 269) Bibliography: p. 282-284. [PR6045.O72Z545 1974] 73-12870 ISBN 0-15-193765-6
1. Woolf, Virginia (Stephen) 1882-1941. BIP

BLACKSTONE, Bernard, 1911- v. 12
Virginia Woolf, by Bernard Blackstone. E. M. Foster, by Rex Warner. Katherine Mansfield, by Ian A. Gordon. Lincoln, University of Nebraska Press [1964] 126 p. illus. 21 cm. (British writers and their work, no. 3) NUC65
1. Woolf, Virginia (Stephen) 1882-1941. 2. Forster, Edward Morgan, 1879- 3. Mansfield, Katherine, 1888-1923. I. Warner Rex, 1905- II. Gordon, Ian Alistair, 1908- III. Title.

BREWSTER, Dorothy, 1883- 823.912
Virginia Woolf. [New York] N.Y. Univ. Pr. [c.]1962. 184p. 22cm. Bibl. 62-19050 3.50; 1.75 pap.,
1. Woolf, Virginia (Stephen) 1882-1941. I. Title.

DAICHES, David, 1912- 828.912
Virginia Woolf. [Rev. ed. New York, New Directions, 1963] 169 p. 19 cm. (A New Directions paperbook, 96) [PR6045.O72Z58 1963] 62-16926
1. Woolf, Virginia (Stephen) 1882-1941.

DAICHES, David, 1912- 823'9'12
Virginia Woolf / by David Daiches. Westport, Conn. : Greenwood Press, 1979, c1963. xix, 169 p. ; 23 cm. Reprint of the ed. published by New Directions, New York, which was issued as no. 96 of A New Directions paperbook. Includes index. Bibliography: p. [159]-163. [PR6045.O72Z58 1979] 78-12655 ISBN 0-313-21187-6 lib.bdg. : 15.95
1. Woolf, Virginia Stephen, 1882-1941. 2. Novelists, English—20th century—Biography.

GUIGUET, Jean. 823'.9'12 B
Virginia Woolf and her works / by Jean Guiguet ; translated by Jean Stewart. New York : Harcourt Brace Jovanovich, [1976] c1965. p. cm. (A Harvest book ; HB 342) Includes index. Bibliography: p. [PR6045.O72Z673 1976] 76-14812 ISBN 0-15-693630-5 pbk. : 4.95
1. Woolf, Virginia Stephen, 1882-1941. I. Title. BIP

HOLTBY, Winifred, 1898-1935. 823'.9'12
Virginia Woolf. Folcroft, Pa., Folcroft Press [1969] 203 p. port. 23 cm. Reprint of the 1932 ed. [PR6045.O72Z7 1969] 72-193724
1. Woolf, Virginia (Stephen) 1882-1941.

MOODY, Anthony David 823.912
Virginia Woolf. New York, Grove [1963] 119p. 18cm. (Evergreen pilot bks., EP25) Bibl. 63-9404 .95 pap.,
1. Woolf, Virginia (Stephen) 1882-1941. I. Title.

NEWTON, Deborah. 823'.9'12 B
Virginia Woolf / Deborah Newton. Norwood, Pa. : Norwood Editions, 1976. 79 p. ; 24 cm. Reprint of the 1946 ed. published by Melbourne University Press, Melbourne. Bibliography: p. 78-79. [PR6045.O72Z83 1976] 76-10193 ISBN 0-8482-1911-2 : 7.50
1. Woolf, Virginia Stephen, 1882-1941.

NOBLE, Joan Russell. 823'.9'12 B
Recollections of Virginia Woolf. Edited and with an introd. by Joan Russell Noble. New York, W. Morrow, 1972. 207 p. 22 cm. "Bibliography: Principal works of Virginia Woolf": p. 205-207. [PR6045.O72Z833] 72-5595 ISBN 0-688-00007-X 6.95
1. Woolf, Virginia (Stephen) 1882-1941. I. Title. BIP

PIPPETT, Aileen. 928.2
The moth and the star; a biography of Virginia Woolf. [1st ed.] Boston, Little, Brown [1955] 368p. illus. 23cm. [PR6045.O72Z86] 55-7465
1. Woolf, Virginia (Stephen) 1882-1941. I. Title.

POOLE, Roger. 823'.9'12 B
The unknown Virginia Woolf / Roger Poole. Cambridge [Eng.] ; New York : Cambridge University Press, 1978. 285 p. ; 22 cm. Includes index. Bibliography: p. [280]-282. [PR6045.O72Z862] 78-3458 ISBN 0-521-21987-6 : 11.95
1. Woolf, Virginia Stephen, 1882-1941. 2. Authors, English—20th century—Biography. I. Title. BIP

RANTAVAARA, Irma Irene. 823'.9'12
Virginia Woolf and Bloomsbury, by Irma Rantavaara. [Folcroft, Pa.] Folcroft Press, 1970. 171 p. 26 cm. "Limited to 150 copies." Reprint of the 1953 ed., which was issued as nide 82 of Suomalainen Tiediakatemia toimituksia, annales, sarja B. Bibliography: p. [161]-167. [PR6045.O72Z864 1970] 72-195893
1. Woolf, Virginia (Stephen) 1882-1941. 2. English literature—20th century—History and criticism. 3. London—Intellectual life. I. Title. II. Series: Suomalainen Tiedeakatemia. Toimituksia. Annales. Sarja B, nide 82. BIP

ROSE, Phyllis, 1942- 823'.9'12
Woman of letters : a life of Virginia Woolf / Phyllis Rose. New York : Oxford University Press, 1978. xxii, 298 p. : ill. ; 22 cm. Includes bibliographical references and index. [PR6045.O72Z867] 77-16489 ISBN 0-19-502370-6 : 11.95
1. Woolf, Virginia Stephen, 1882-1941. 2. Authors, English—20th century—Biography. I. Title. BIP

WOODRING, Carl Ray, 1919- 823.912
Virginia Woolf, by Carl Woodring. New York, Columbia University Press, 1966. 47 p. 21 cm. (Columbia essays on modern writers, no. 18) Bibliography: p. 45-47. [PR6045.O72Z93] 66-19554
1. Woolf, Virginia (Stephen) 1882-1941. I. Title. II. Series. BIP

WOOLF, Virginia (Stephen) 1882-1911. 928.2
Letters: Virginia Woolf & Lytton Strachey. Edited by Leonard Woolf & James Strachey. [1st American ed.] New York, Harcourt, Brace [c1956] vii, 166 p. 21 cm. "Chronological bibliography of the books of Virginia Woolf": p. [viii] "Chronological bibliography of the books of Lytton Strachey": p. [ix] [PR6045.072Z53 1956a] 56-11962
I. Strachey, Giles Lytton, 1880-1932. II. Title.

WOOLF, Virginia Stephen, 1882-1941. 928.2
A writer's diary: being extracts from the diary of Virginia Woolf, edited by Leonard Woolf. [1st American ed.] New York, Harcourt, Brace [1954] x, 356 p. 22 cm. "Chronological bibliography of the books of Virginia Woolf": p. 352. [PR6045.O72Z5 1954] 54-5257
I. Title. BIP

WOOLF, Virginia (Stephen) 1882-1941. 828'.9'1203 B
A writer's diary, being extracts from the diary of Virginia Woolf. Edited by Leonard Woolf. New York, Harcourt Brace Jovanovich [1973, c1954] x, 355 p. 21 cm. (A Harvest book, HB 264) [PR6045.O72Z5 1973] 73-5737 ISBN 0-15-698380-X 2.95
1. Woolf, Virginia (Stephen) 1882-1941. I. Title.

Woolf, Virginia Stephen, 1882-1941—Biography.

BELL, Quentin. 823'.9'12 B
Virginia Woolf; a biography. [1st American ed.] New York, Harcourt Brace Jovanovich [1972] xv, 216, 314 p. illus. 23 cm. Bibliography: p. 282-284. [PR6045.O72Z545 1972] 72-79926 ISBN 0-15-193765-6 12.50
1. Woolf, Virginia (Stephen) 1882-1941—Biography. BIP

KENNEDY, Richard, 1910- 338.7'61'0705092 B
A boy at the Hogarth Press / [by] Richard Kennedy ; illustrated by the author ; with an introduction by Bevis Hillier. Harmondsworth ; New York [etc.] : Penguin, 1978. 104 p. : ill. ; 20 cm. [PR6021.E712Z463 1978] 79-306749 ISBN 0-14-004862-6 pbk. : 1.95
1. Kennedy, Richard, 1910- 2. Hogarth Press. 3. Woolf, Virginia Stephen, 1882-1941—Biography. 4. Woolf, Leonard Sidney, 1880-1969—Biography. 5. Authors, English—20th century—Biography. I. Title. BIP

LOVE, Jean O., 1920- 823'.9'12 B
Virginia Woolf : sources of madness and art / Jean O. Love. Berkeley : University of California Press, c1977- v. ; 23 cm. Includes index. Bibliography: v. [1] p. 365-370. [PR6045.O72Z812] 76-48004 ISBN 0-520-03358-2 : 12.50
1. Woolf, Virginia Stephen, 1882-1941—Biography. 2. Authors, English—20th century—Biography. BIP

SPATER, George. 823'.9'1209 B
A marriage of true minds : an intimate portrait of Leonard and Virginia Woolf / George Spater and Ian Parsons. 1st American ed. New York : Harcourt Brace Jovanovich, 1977. xiii, 210 p. : ill. ; 25 cm. Includes bibliographical references and index. [PR6045.O72Z877 1977] 77-73062 ISBN 0-15-157449-9 : 12.95
1. Woolf, Virginia Stephen, 1882-1941—Biography. 2. Woolf, Leonard Sidney, 1880-1969—Biography. 3. Authors, English—20th century—Biography. I. Parsons, Ian Macnaghten, joint author. II. Title.

SPATER, George. 823'.9'1209 B
A marriage of true minds : an intimate portrait of Leonard and Virginia Woolf / George Spater and Ian Parsons. New York : Harcourt, Brace, Jovanovich, 1979, c1977. p. cm. (A Harvest/HBJ book) Includes bibliographical references and index. [PR6045.O72Z877 1979] 78-14914 ISBN 0-15-657299 pbk. : 5.95
1. Woolf, Virginia Stephen, 1882-1941—Biography. 2. Woolf, Leonard Sidney, 1880-1969—Biography. 3. Authors, English—20th century—Biography. I. Parsons, Ian Macnaghten, joint author. II. Title. BIP

WOOLF, Virginia Stephen, 1882-1941. 823'.9'12 B
Moments of being : unpublished autobiographical writings / Virginia Woolf ; edited and with an introd. and notes by Jeanne Schulkind. 1st American ed. New York : Harcourt Brace Jovanovich, 1977,c1976 207 p. ; 22 cm. Includes bibliographical references and index. [PR6045.O72Z496 1976b] 76-27410 ISBN 0-15-162034-2 : 8.95
1. Woolf, Virginia Stephen, 1882-1941—Biography. 2. Authors, English—20th century—Biography. I. Title. BIP

WOOLF, Virginia Stephen, 1882-1941. 823'.9'12 B
Moments of being : unpublished autobiographical writings / Virginia Woolf ; edited and with an introd. and notes by Jeanne Schulkind. 1st Harvest/HBJ ed. New York : Harcourt Brace Jovanovich, 1978, c1976. p. cm. (A Harvest/HBJ book) Includes bibliographical references and index. [PR6045.O72Z496 1978] 78-6666 ISBN 0-15-661917-2 : 8.95
1. Woolf, Virginia Stephen, 1882-1941—Biography. 2. Authors, English—20th century—Biography. I. Title.

Woolf, Virginia Stephen, 1882-1941—Correspondence.

WOOLF, Virginia Stephen, 1882-1941. 823'.9'12 B
The letters of Virginia Woolf / editor, Nigel Nicolson, assistant editor, Joanne Trautmann. New York : Harcourt Brace Jovanovich, [1976 i.e.1975] p. cm. First published under title: The flight of the mind. Contents.Contents.—v. 1. 1888-1912. Includes bibliographical references and index. [PR6045.O72Z525 1976] 75-25538 ISBN 0-15-150924-7 : 14.95
1. Woolf, Virginia Stephen, 1882-1941—Correspondence. BIP

WOOLF, Virginia Stephen, 1882-1941. 823'.9'12
The letters of Virginia Woolf / editor, Nigel Nicolson, assistant editor, Joanne Trautmann. New York : Harcourt Brace Jovanovich, 1977- v. : ill. ; 21 cm. (A Harvest book ; HB 358) First published under title: The flight of the mind. Contents.Contents.—v. 1. 1888-1912 (Virginia Stephen) Includes bibliographical references and index. [PR6045.O72Z525 1977] 76-40422 ISBN 0-15-650881-8 pbk. : 5.95
1. Woolf, Virginia Stephen, 1882-1941—Correspondence. 2. Authors, English—20th century—Correspondence. BIP

WOOLF, Virginia Stephen, 1882-1941. 823'.9'12 S
The question of things happening / editor, Nigel Nicolson ; assistant editor, Joanne Trautmann. London : Hogarth Press, 1976. 627 p., [4] leaves of plates : ill. ; 25 cm. (The Letters of Virginia Woolf ; v. 2, 1912-1922) Includes index. [PR6045.O72Z525 1975b vol. 2] 823'.9'12 77-364468 ISBN 0-7012-0420-6 : £9.50
1. Woolf, Virginia Stephen, 1882-1941—Correspondence. 2. Authors, English—20th century—Correspondence. I. Nicolson, Nigel. II. Trautmann, Joanne. III. Title.

Woolf, Virginia Stephen, 1882-1941—Diaries.

WOOLF, Virginia Stephen, 1882-1941. 823'.9'12 B
The diary of Virginia Woolf / edited by Anne Oliver Bell ; introd. by Quentin Bell. 1st American ed. New York : Harcourt Brace Jovanovich, 1977- v. ; 25 cm. Includes index. Contents.Contents.—v. 1. 1915-1919. [PR6045.O72Z494 1977] 77-73111 ISBN 0-15-125597-0 : 12.95
1. Woolf, Virginia Stephen, 1882-1941—Diaries. 2. Authors, English—20th century—Biography.

WOOLF, Virginia Stephen, 1882-1941. 823'.9'12 B
The diary of Virginia Woolf / edited by Anne Olivier Bell ; introd. by Quentin Bell. New York : Harcourt, Brace, Jovanovich, 1979- c1977- p. cm. (A Harvest/HBJ book) Includes index. Contents.Contents.—v. 1. 1915-1919. [PR6045.O72Z494 1978] 78-23882 ISBN 0-15-626036-0 pbk. . 3.95
1. Woolf, Virginia Stephen, 1882-1941—Diaries. 2. Authors, English—20th century—Biography. I. Bell, Anne Olivier. II. Title.

Woolf, Virginia Stephen, 1882-1941—Friends and associates.

LEHMANN, John, 1907- 821'.9'12 B
Thrown to the Woolfs / John Lehmann. 1st American ed. New York : Holt, Rinehart, and Winston, 1979, c1978. xx, 164 p., [4] leaves of plates : ill. ; 22 cm. Includes index. [PR6023.E4Z519 1979] 79-1925 ISBN 0-03-052191-2 : 10.95
1. Lehmann, John, 1907- —Biography. 2. Woolf, Leonard Sidney, 1880-1969—Friends and associates. 3. Woolf, Virginia Stephen, 1882-1941—Friends and associates. 4. Hogarth Press. 5. Authors, English—20th century—Biography. I. Title. BIP

TRAUTMANN, Joanne. 823'.9'12
The Jessamy brides : the friendship of Virginia Woolf and V. Sackville-West / by Joanne Trautmann ; [edited by the Institute for the Arts and Humanistic Studies]. University Park : Administrative Committee on Research, Pennsylvania State University, c1973. 57 p. ; 23 cm. (The Pennsylvania State University studies ; no. 36) [PR6045.O72Z884] 74-621569 3.00
1. Woolf, Virginia Stephen, 1882-1941—Friends and associates. 2. Sackville-West, Victoria Mary, Hon., 1892-1962—Friends and associates. I. Title. II. Series: Pennsylvania. State University.

Pennsylvania State University studies ; no. 36. BIP

Woolfolk, Josiah Pitts,

WOOLFOLK, Josiah Pitts, 1894- 818.52
The autobiography of Jack Woodford [pseud.] [1st ed.] Garden City, N.Y., Doubleday, 1962. 349 p. 22 cm. [PS3545.O765Z52] 62-17697

Woollcott. Alexander, 1887-1943.

ADAMS, Samuel Hopkins, 1871-1958. 818'.5'209 B
Alexander Woollcott, his life and his world. Freeport, N.Y., Books for Libraries Press [1970] 388 p. illus., ports. 23 cm. Reprint of the 1946 ed., published under title: A Woollcott, his life and his world. [PS3545.O77Z6 1970] 77-130545
1. Woollcott, Alexander, 1887-1943. I. Title.

HOYT, Edwin Palmer. 818'.5'209
Alexander Woollcott: the man who came to dinner; a biography by Edwin P. Hoyt. London, New York Abelard 1968. 357p. ports. 22cm. [PS3545.O77Z7] 67-13458 6.50
1. Woollcott. Alexander, 1887-1943. I. Title.

HOYT, Edwin Palmer. 818'.5'209 B
Alexander Woollcott: the man who came to dinner; a biography by Edwin P. Hoyt. New ed. Radnor, Pa., Chilton Book Co. [1973] 357 p. illus. 22 cm. Includes bibliographical references. [PS3545.O77Z7 1973] 73-11009 ISBN 0-8019-5928-4 7.50
1. Woollcott, Alexander, 1887-1943. I. Title.

WOOLLCOTT, Alexander, 1887-1943. 818'.5'209 B
The letters of Alexander Woollcott. Edited by Beatrice Kaufman and Joseph Hennessey. Westport, Conn., Greenwood Press [1972, c1944] xxiv, 410 p. illus. 22 cm. [PS3545.O77Z53 1972] 74-163542 ISBN 0-8371-6199-1 16.00
I. Kaufman, Beatrice (Bakrow) 1895-1945, ed. II. Hennessey, Joseph, ed. BIP

Woollcott, Alexander, 1887-1943—Biography.

TEICHMANN, Howard. 818'.5'209 B
Smart Aleck : the wit, world, and life of Alexander Woollcott / by Howard Teichmann. New York : Morrow, 1976. 334 p., [97] leaves of plates : ill. ; 24 cm. Includes index. Bibliography: p. 319-324. [PS3545.O77Z9] 75-40129 ISBN 0-688-03034-3 : 9.95
1. Woollcott, Alexander, 1887-1943—Biography. I. Title.

Woolley, Edwin Dilworth, 1897-1881.

ARRINGTON, Leonard J. 288.3'3 B
From Quaker to Latter-Day Saint : Bishop Edwin D. Woolley / Leonard J. Arrington. Salt Lake City : Deseret Book Co., 1976. xiii, 592 p. ; 24 cm. Includes index. Bibliography: p. 497-500. [BX8695.W57A77] 76-43171 ISBN 0-87747-591-1 : 6.95
1. Woolley, Edwin Dilworth, 1897-1881. 2. Mormons and Mormonism—Biography. I. Title. BIP

Woolley, Mary Emma, 1863-1947.

MARKS, Jeannette Augustus, 1875- 923.773
Life and letters of Mary Emma Woolley. Washington, Public Affairs Press [1955] 300p. illus. 24cm. [LD7092.7 1901.M3] 55-9780
1. Woolley, Mary Emma, 1863-1947. I. Title.

WELLS, Anna Mary. 378.1'12'0974423
Miss Marks and Miss Woolley / by Anna Mary Wells. Boston : Houghton Mifflin, 1978. xviii, 268 p., [8] leaves of plates : ill. ; 24 cm. Bibliography: p. [267]-268. [LD7092.7 1901.W44] 78-1391 ISBN 0-395-25724-7 : 10.95
1. Woolley, Mary Emma, 1863-1947. 2. Mount Holyoke College. 3. Marks, Jeannette Augustus, 1875-1964. 4. Wellesley College. 5. Lesbians—United States—Biography. I. Title.

Woolman, John, 1720-1772.

BENTON, Josephine Moffett. 289.6'0924
John woolman, most modern of ancient Friends. Philadelphia, Friends Central Bureau [195-?] 62p. 21cm. 'Publication of Religious Education Committee of Friends GeneralConference.' [BX7795.W7B4] 62-1975
1. Woolman, John, 1720-1772. I. Title.

CADY, Edwin Harrison. 922.8673
John Woolman. Author of this volume: Edwin H. Cady. New York, Washington Square Press [1965] ix, 182 p. 18 cm. (The Great American thinkers series) "W-882." Bibliography: p. 173-178. [BX7795.W7C3] 65-1754
1. Woolman, John, 1720-1772.

DALGLISH, Doris N. 289.6'0922
People called Quakers, by Doris N. Dalglish. Freeport, N.Y., Books for Libraries Press [1969] 169 p. 23 cm. (Essay index reprint series) Reprint of the 1938 ed. Contents.Contents.—The first Quaker poet.—An American saint.—A digression on women and the eighteenth century.—A neighbour of Wordsworth.—A friend from France.—Convert and critic. [BX7791.D3 1969] 78-90628
1. Story, Thomas, 1662-1742. 2. Woolman, John, 1720-1772. 3. Wilkinson, Thomas, 1751-1836. 4. Grellet, Stephen, 1773-1855. 5. Stephen, Caroline Emelia, 1834-1909. 6. Friends, Society of—Biography. I. Title.

PEARE, Catherine Owens. 922.8673
John Woolman: child of light; the story of John Woolman and the Friends. New York, Vanguard Press [1954] 254p. illus. 22cm. [BX7795.W7P4] 54-6990
1. Woolman. John, 1720-1772. I. Title.

WOOLMAN, John, 1720-1772. 922.8673
Journal; edited by Janet Whitney. Chicago, H. Regnery Co., 1950. xv, 233 p. 22 cm. [BX7795.W7A3 1950] 50-10962

WOOLMAN, John, 1720-1772. 922.8673
Journal; edited and with an introd. by Thomas S. Kepler. Cleveland, World Pub. Co. [1954] xx, 235p. 17cm. (World devotional classics) [BX7795.W7A3 1954] 54-5339
I. Title.

WOOLMAN, John, 1720-1772. 289.6'0924 B
The journal and major essays of John Woolman. Edited by Phillips P. Moulton. New York, Oxford University Press, 1971. xviii, 336 p. 24 cm. (A Library of Protestant thought) Contents.—The journal of John Woolman.—Major essays of John Woolman: Introduction to the essays. Some considerations on the keeping of Negroes. Considerations on keeping Negroes, part second. A plea for the poor. Bibliography: p. 315-318. [BX7795.W7A3 1971b] 71-171970 10.50
1. Slavery in the United States—Controversial literature. 2. Poor. I. Title. II. Series.

WOOLMAN, John, 1720-1772. 922.8673
The journal of John Woolman, and A plea for the poor. The John Greenleaf Whittier ed. text. Introd. by Frederick B. Tolles. New York, Corinth Books [1961] xii, 249 p. facsim. 19 cm. (The American experience series, AE2) "For further reading": p. xii. [BX7795.W7A3 1961] 61-8147
I. Woolman, John, 1720-1772. II. Title. III. Title: A plea for the poor.

WOOLMAN, John, 1720-1772. 289.6'0924 B
The journal of John Woolman, and A plea for the poor. The John Greenleaf Whittier ed. text. Introd. by Frederick B. Tolles. Gloucester, Mass., P. Smith, 1971 [c1961] xii, 249 p. 21 cm. Reprint of two works published in 1774 and 1793 respectively; the first work originally had title: A journal of the life, gospel labours, and Christian experiences of that faithful minister of Jesus Christ, John Woolman. Includes bibliographical references. [BX7795.W7A3 1971] 72-27383
I. Woolman, John, 1720-1772. A plea for the poor. 1971.

WOOLMAN, John, 1720-1772. 922.8673
The journal of John Woolman, and A plea for the poor. John Greenleaf Whittier ed. text. Introd. by Frederick B. Tolles. New York, [Citadel Press, c.1961] xii, 249p. (Corinth bks. AE2; American experience series) Bibl. 61-8147 1.75 pap.,
I. Woolman, John, 1720-1772. A plea for the poor. II. Title.

Woolrich, Willis Raymond,

WOOLRICH, Willis Raymond, 1889- 620'.00924 B
Odyssey of a professional engineer, by W. R. Woolrich. San Antonio, Tex., Naylor Co. [1971] xii, 74 p. 22 cm. Autobiographical. [TA140.W3A3] 79-176167 ISBN 0-8111-0433-8 4.95
I. Title.

Woolsey, Elmo Murray,

WOOLSEY, Elmo Murray, 1877- 920
Moving on. [Bristol? Tenn.] 1954. 220p. illus. 24cm. Autobiographical. [CT275.W685A3] 54-24356
I. Title.

Woolsey, Theodore Dwight, 1801-1889.

KING, George A 923.773
Theodore Dwight Woolsey, his political and social ideas. Chicago, Loyola University Press, 1956. xiii, 305p. 24cm. (Jesuit studies; contributions to the arts and sciences by members of the Society of Jesus) Bibliography: p. 273-288. [LD6330 1846.K5] 56-12108
1. Woolsey, Theodore Dwight, 1801-1889. I. Title.

Woolsey, Vernor Gens, 1899-

WOOLSEY, Vernor Gens, 1899- 976.4'06'0924 B
The gospel truth / by Vernor Gens Woolsey. San Antonio : Naylor Co., c1976. p. cm. Autobiography. [CT275.W687A33] 76-28780 ISBN 0-8111-0635-7 : 7.95
1. Woolsey, Vernor Gens, 1899- 2. Texas—Biography. I. Title.

Woolson, Constance Fenimore, 1840-1894.

MOORE, Rayburn S 1920- v. 12
Constance F. Woolson. New Haven, Conn., College & University Press, 1963. 173 p. 21 cm. (Twayne's United States authors series, T-34) 68-75617
1. Woolson, Constance Fenimore, 1840-1894. I. Title. BIP

Woolworth (F. W.) Company.

NICHOLS, John Peter, 1906- 381'.45'0006573
Skyline queen and the merchant prince; the Woolworth story, by John P. Nichols. New York, Trident Press [1973] 144 p. illus. 21 cm. [HF5465.U6W86] 72-92496 ISBN 0-671-27098-2 7.95
1. Woolworth (F. W.) Company. 2. Woolworth, Frank Winfield, 1852-1919. I. Title. BIP

Woolworth, Frank Winfield, 1852-1919.

BAKER, Nina (Brown) 1888- 923.873
Nickels and dimes; the story of F. W. Woolworth. Illustrated by Douglas Gorsline. [1st ed.] New York, Harcourt, Brace [1954] 134p. illus. 21cm. [HF5465.U6W825] 54-9621
1. Woolworth, Frank Winfield, 1852-1919. I. Title.

WINKLER, John Kennedy, 1891-1958. 338.7'6'6588730924 B
Five and ten; the fabulous life of F. W. Woolworth. Freeport, N.Y., Books for Libraries Press [1970] 256 p. illus., ports. 23 cm. Reprint of the 1940 ed. [HF5465.U6W89 1970] 79-130567 ISBN 8-369-55404-
1. Woolworth, Frank Winfield, 1852-1919. I. Title. BIP

Wootten, Morgan.

WOOTTEN, Morgan. 796.32'3'0924 B
From orphans to champions : the story of DeMatha's Morgan Wootten / Morgan Wootten and Bill Gilbert. 1st ed. New York : Atheneum, 1979. xvii, 172 p. : ill. ; 22 cm. [GV884.W67A33 1979] 79-63847 ISBN 0-689-11011-1 : 8.95
1. Wootten, Morgan. 2. DeMatha Catholic High School. 3. Basketball coaches—United States—Biography. I. Gilbert, Bill, 1931- joint author. II. Title. BIP

Wootton, Bailey Peyton, 1870-1949.

WOOTTON, Clara. 923.473
They have topped the mountain. Introd. by Thomas D. Clark. Frankfort, Ky., Blue

Grass Press, 1960. 159 p. illus. 22 cm. [F456.W65W6] 60-12022
1. Wootton, Bailey Peyton, 1870-1949. I. Title.

Wootton, Barbara,

WOOTTON, Barbara, 300'.924 B
Baroness Wootton of Abinger, 1897-
In a world I never made; autobiographical reflections, by Barbara Wootton. Toronto, University of Toronto Press [1967] 283 p. illus., ports. 22 cm. Bibliographical footnotes. [H59.W58A3 1967a] 67-3841
I. Title.

Worcester, Noah, 1758-1837.

WARE, Henry, 1794- 288'.092'4 B
1843.
Memoirs of the Rev. Noah Worcester, D.D., by Henry Ware, Jr. With a pref., notes, and a concluding chapter, by Samuel Worcester. Boston, J. Munroe, 1844. [New York, J. S. Ozer, 1972] xii, 155 p. front. 22 cm. (The Peace movement in America) A facsim. reprint. [BX9869.W8W3 1844a] 78-137557 8.95
1. Worcester, Noah, 1758-1837. I. Worcester, Samuel, 1793-1844, ed. II. Title. III. Series.

Word portraits.

UDEN, Grant, comp. 920.042
They looked like this, an assembly of authentic word-portraits of men and women in English history and literature over 1900 years. New York, Barnes & Noble [1966] viii, 306p. 23cm. Bibl. [CT775.U3] 66-7971 6.00 bds.,
1. Word portraits. 2. Gt. Brit.—Biog. I. Title.

Worde, Wynkyn de, d. 1534?

MORAN, James. 686.2'092'4 B
Wynkyn de Worde, father of Fleet Street / James Moran. 2d ed. London : Wynkyn de Worde Society, 1976. 52, [8] p., [1] fold. leaf of plates : ill. ; 20 cm. Originally published in 1960. Includes index. Bibliography: p. [53] [Z232.W87M6 1976] 77-357537 ISBN 0-85331-388-1 : £2.95
1. Worde, Wynkyn de, d. 1534? 2. Printing—England—London—History. I. Wynkyn de Worde Society. II. Title.

Wordsworth, Anne Caroline, b. 1792.

HARPER, George McLean, 929/.2
1863-1947
Wordsworth's French daughter; the story of her birth, with the certificates of her baptism and marriage. New York, Russell & Russell [1967,c.1921] 41p. 20cm. [PR5882.H3 1967] 66-27094 5.00
1. Wordsworth, Anne Caroline, b. 1792. 2. Wordsworth, William, 1770-1850. I. Title.

HARPER, George McLean, 808.1'0924
1863-1947.
Wordsworth's French daughter; the story of her birth, with the certificates of her baptism and marriage. New York, Russell & Russell [1967, c1921] 41 p. 20 cm. [PR5882.H3 1967] 66-27094
1. Wordsworth, Anne Caroline, b. 1792. 2. Wordsworth, William, 1770-1850.—Biography. I. Title.

Wordsworth, Dorothy, 1771-1855.

ELLIS, Amanda Mae, 1898- 821'.7
Rebels and conservatives; Dorothy and William Wordsworth and their circle, by Amanda M. Ellis. Bloomington, Indiana University Press [1967] xiv, 367 p. illus., ports. 24 cm. Bibliography: p. 340-357. [PR5849.E5] 67-13021
1. Wordsworth, Dorothy, 1771-1855. 2. Wordsworth, William, 1770-1850. I. Title.

MACLEAN, Catherine 828'.7'03 B
Macdonald.
Dorothy Wordsworth: the early years. Freeport, N.Y., Books for Libraries Press [1970] xiii, 439 p. illus., ports. 22 cm. Reprint of the 1932 ed. Bibliography: p. 393-429. [PR5849.M3 1970] 77-124243
1. Wordsworth, Dorothy, 1771-1855. 2. Wordsworth family.

MACLEAN, Catherine 828'.7'03 B
Macdonald.
Dorothy Wordsworth: the early years. London, Chatto & Windus, 1932. St. Clair Shores, Mich., Scholarly Press, 1971. xiii, 439 p. illus., ports. 22 cm. Bibliography: p. 393-429. [PR5849.M3 1971] 79-145158 ISBN 0-403-01086-1
1. Wordsworth, Dorothy, 1771-1855. 2. Wordsworth family.

MACLEAN, Catherine 828'.7'03 B
Macdonald.
Dorothy Wordsworth, the early years. [Folcroft, Pa.] Folcroft Library Editions, 1973. xiii, 439 p. illus. 23 cm. Reprint of the 1932 ed. published by Viking Press, New York. Bibliography: p. 393-429. [PR5849.M3 1973] 73-11390 13.50
1. Wordsworth, Dorothy, 1771-1855. 2. Wordsworth family.

MACLEAN, Catherine 828'.7'03 B
Macdonald.
Dorothy Wordsworth, the early years. [Folcroft, Pa.] Folcroft Library Editions, 1973. xiii, 439 p. illus. 23 cm. Reprint of the 1932 ed. published by Viking Press, New York. Bibliography: p. 393-429. [PR5849.M3 1973] 73-11390 ISBN 0-8414-5960-6 (lib. bdg.)
1. Wordsworth, Dorothy, 1771-1855. 2. Wordsworth family.

WORDSWORTH, Dorothy 928.1
Home at Grasmere; extracts from the Journal of Dorothy Wordsworth, written between 1800 and 1803, and from the poems of William Wordsworth. Edited by Colette Clark. [Baltimore], Penguin Books [1960] 325p. 18cm. (Pelican books, A466) 60-3032 1.25 pap.,
1. Wrodsworth, William, 1770-1850. II. Clark, Colette, ed. III. Title.

Wordsworth, William, 1770-1850.

BATHO, Edith Clara, 1895- 928.2
The later Wordsworth. New York, Russell & Russell, 1963. x, 417 p. port. 22 cm. Bibliography: p. [397]-404. [PR5882.B3 1963] 64-10381
1. Wordsworth, William, 1770-1850. I. Title.

BURRA, Peter, 1909-1937. 821'.7 B
Wordsworth. [Folcroft, Pa.] Folcroft Library Editions, 1973. p. Reprint of the 1936 ed. published by Duckworth, London, which was issued as no. 63 of Great lives. Bibliography: p. [PR5881.B8 1973] 73-10495 8.75
1. Wordsworth, William, 1770-1850.

BURRA, Peter, 1909-1937. 821'.7 B
Wordsworth. London, Duckworth. New York, Haskell House Publishers, 1972. 160 p. 23 cm. Reprint of the 1936 ed., issued in series: Great lives. Bibliography: p. 159-160. [PR5881.B8 1972] 72-2096 ISBN 0-8383-1486-4 8.95
1. Wordsworth, William, 1770-1850.

BURRA, Peter James Salkeld, 928.2
1909-
Wordsworth. New York, Collier [1962] 160p. 18cm. (AS58Y) Bibl. .95 pap.,
1. Wordsworth, William, 1770-1850. I. Title.

BYATT, Antonia Susan 821'.7'09
(Drabble) 1936-
Wordsworth and Coleridge in their time [by] A. S. Byatt. [1st American ed.] New York, Crane, Russak [1973, c1970] 287 p. illus. 23 cm. Includes bibliographical references. [PR5883.B9 1973] 73-82999 ISBN 0-8448-0040-6 5.95
1. Wordsworth, William, 1770-1850. 2. Coleridge, Samuel Taylor, 1772-1834. I. Title. **BIP**

CALVERT, George Henry, 821'.7
1803-1889.
Wordsworth; a biographic aesthetic study. [Folcroft, Pa.] Folcroft Press [1970, c1878] 232 p. 23 cm. [PR5881.C3 1970] 72-193661
1. Wordsworth, William, 1770-1850. **BIP**

CALVERT, George Henry, 821'.7 B
1803-1889.
Wordsworth : a biographic aesthetic study / by George H. Calvert. Norwood, Pa. : Folcroft Press, 1975 [c1878] 232 p., [1] leaf of plates : port. ; 23 cm. Reprint of the ed. published by Lee and Shepard, Boston. [PR5881.C3 1975] 75-28394 ISBN 0-88305-127-3 : 20.00
1. Wordworth, William, 1770-1850.

DOUGLAS, Wallace W. 821.7
Wordsworth; the construction of a personality [by] Wallace W. Douglas. [1st ed. Kent? Ohio] Kent State University Press [1968] v, 212 p. 22 cm. (Kent studies in English, 7 [i.e. 6]) Bibliography: p. 179-204. [PR5881.D6] 67-64957
1. Wordsworth, William, 1770-1850. I. Series: Ohio. State University, Kent. Kent studies in English, 6.

HARPER, George McLean, 928.2
1863-1947.
William Wordsworth, his life, works, and influence [2v.] New York, Russell & Russell, 1960. 2v. (621p.) illus. 25cm. 60-11020 15.00 set,
1. Wordsworth, William, 1770-1850. I. Title.

HAVENS, Raymond Dexter, 821'.7
1880-1954.
The mind of a poet / by Raymond Dexter Havens. 1st AMS ed. New York : AMS Press, 1979, c1941. 2 v. in 1 ; 23 cm. Reprint of the ed. published by Johns Hopkins Press, Baltimore. Includes bibliographical references and index. [PR5881.H35 1978] 75-33514 ISBN 0-404-14090-4 : 57.50
1. Wordsworth, William, 1770-1850. 2. Wordsworth, William, 1770-1850. The prelude. 3. Poets, English—19th century—Biography. I. Title.

HERFORD, Charles Harold, 821'.7 B
1853-1931.
Wordsworth / by C. H. Herford. Norwood, Pa. : Norwood Editions, 1975. 255 p., [1] leaf of plates : port. ; 23 cm. Reprint of the 1930 ed. published by G. Routledge, London, in series: The Republic of letters. Includes index. Bibliography: p. 243-249. [PR5881.H4 1975] 75-30515 ISBN 0-88305-259-8 : 20.00
1. Wordsworth, William, 1770-1850. 2. Poets, English—19th century—Biography. I. Title. II. Series: The Republic of letters.

HUDSON, William Henry, 821'.7
1862-1918.
Wordsworth & his poetry. Port Washington, N.Y., Kennikat Press [1970] 198 p. 18 cm. Bibliography: p. 197-[199] [PR5881.H85 1970] 70-103193
1. Wordsworth, William, 1770-1850. I. Title. **BIP**

HUDSON, William Henry, 821'.7
1862-1918.
Wordsworth & his poetry. London, G. G. Harrap, 1914. [New York, AMS Press, 1972] 198, [1] p. port. 19 cm. (Poetry and life series) Bibliography: p. 197-[199] [PR5881.H85 1972] 73-120984 ISBN 0-404-52520-2 8.00
1. Wordsworth, William, 1770-1850. I. Title. II. Series.

LEGOUIS, Emile Hyacinthe. 821.7
1861-1937
The early life of William Wordsworth, 1770-1798; a study of 'The prelude.' Tr. [from French] by J. W. Matthews; prefatory note by Leslie Stephen. New York, Russell & Russell. 1965. xvi, 480p. port. 23cm. Orig. pub. in 1897. This is a reprint of the 2d rev. ed., 1921. [PR5882.L5] 65-18815 8.50
1. Wordsworth, William, 1770-1850. I. Title.

MARGOLIOUTH, Herschel 928.2
Maurice, 1887-
Wordsworth and Coleridge, 1795-1834 London, New York, Oxford University Press, 1953. 206 p. illus. 18 cm. (The Home university library of modern knowledge, 223) Includes bibliography. [PR5883.M3] 53-3001
1. Wordsworth, William, 1770-1850. 2. Coleridge, Samuel Taylor, 1772-1834. **BIP**

MOORMAN, Mary (Trevelyan) 928.2
1905-
William Wordsworth, a biography [v.2. New York, Oxford, c.]1965. 632p. illus. 23cm. Contents.[v.2.] The later years, 1803-1850 [PR5881.M6] 57-2574 11.20
1. Wordsworth, William, 1770-1850. I. Title.

MOORMAN, Mary Trevelyan, 928.2
1905-
William Wordsworth, a biography. Oxford, Clarendon Press, 1957- v. illus. 23 cm. Contents.Contents.—[1] The early years, 1770-1803. [PR5881.M6] 57-2574
1. Wordsworth, William, 1770-1850. **BIP**

NOYES, Russell. 821'.7
William Wordsworth. New York, Twayne [1971] 194 p. 21 cm. (Twayne's English authors series, TEAS 118) Bibliography: p. 185-190. [PR5881.N6] 77-125819
1. Wordsworth, William, 1770-1850. **BIP**

PHILLIPS, George Searle, 821'.7 B
1815-1889.
Memoirs of William Wordsworth, compiled from authentic sources, with numerous quotations from his poems, illustrative of his life and character, by January Searle. [Folcroft, Pa.] Folcroft Press [1970] 312 p. port. 24 cm. Reprint of the 1852 ed. [PR5881.P5 1970] 72-191651
1. Wordsworth, William, 1770-1850. **BIP**

RALEIGH, Walter Alexander, 821'.7
Sir, 1861-1922.
Wordsworth. London, E. Arnold, 1903. St. Clair Shores, Mich., Scholarly Press, 1970. 232 p. 21 cm. [PR5881.R27 1970] 76-131811
1. Wordsworth, William, 1770-1850.

RALEIGH, Walter Alexander, 821'.7
Sir, 1861-1922.
Wordsworth. [Folcroft, Pa.] Folcroft Library Editions, 1973. p. Reprint of the 1918 ed. published by E. Arnold, London. [PR5881.R27 1973] 73-16468 ISBN 0-8414-7275-0 (lib. bdg.)
1. Wordsworth, William, 1770-1850.

SUTHERLAND, James 821'.7 B
Middleton.
William Wordsworth; the story of his life, with critical remarks on his writings. 2d ed., rev. and enl. London, E. Stock, 1892. [Folcroft, Pa.] Folcroft Library Editions, 1973. [PR5881.S95 1973] 72-13472 ISBN 0-8414-1181-6 (lib. bdg.)
1. Wordsworth, William, 1770-1850.

SYMINGTON, Andrew James, 821'.7 B
b.1825.
William Wordsworth, a biographical sketch, with selections from his writings in poetry and prose / by Andrew James Symington. Folcroft, Pa. : Folcroft Library Editions, 1977- v. ; 23 cm. Reprint of the 1881 ed. published by Roberts Brothers, Boston. Includes bibliographical references. [PR5881.S97 1977] 77-14115 ISBN 0-8414-7877-5 lib. bdg. : 60.00
1. Wordsworth, William, 1770-1850. 2. Poets, English—19th century—Biography. I. Wordsworth, William, 1770-1850. II. Title.

WORDSWORTH, v. 12 by Peter Burra ... New York, Macmillan [1957] 160p. 19cm. (Great lives. [63]) 'First published 1936.' Bibliography: p.159-160.
1. Wordsworth, William, 1770-1850. I. Burra, Peter, 1909-1937.

WORDSWORTH, Dorothy, 1771- 928.2 1855.
Journals; The Alfoxden journal, 1798 [and] The Grasmere journals, 1800-1803; with an appendix of Wordsworth's shorter poems referred to in the journals. Edited with an introd. by Helen Darbishire. London, New York, Oxford University Press, 1958. xviii, 264 p. 16 cm. (The World's classics, 568) [PR5849.A8 1958] 58-59419
1. Wordsworth, William, 1770-1850. I. Title.

WORDSWORTH, Mary 928.2 (Hutchinson) 1770-1859.
The letters of Mary Wordsworth, 1800-1855, selected and edited by Mary E. Burton. Oxford, Clarendon Press, 1958. xxix, 363 p. illus., port. fold. geneal. table. 28 cm. [PR5881.A43] 58-4681
1. Wordsworth, William, 1770-1850. I. Burton, Mary Elizabeth, 1900- ed. II. Title.

WORDSWORTH, William, 1770- 826'.7 1850.
The letters of William and Dorothy Wordsworth; arranged and edited by the late Ernest de Selincourt. 2nd ed. Oxford, Clarendon P., 1967- v. fronts (facsims.), maps, diagrs. 22 1/2 cm. Contents.Contents.—1. The early years, 1787-1805, revised by Chester L. Shaver.—2. The middle years: pt. 1: 1806-1811, revised by Mary Moorman.—3. The middle years: pt. II: 1812-1820, revised by Mary Moorman and Alan G. Hill. [PR5881.A316] 67-89058
I. Wordsworth, Dorothy, 1771-1855. II. De Selincourt, Ernest, 1870-1943, ed. III. Shaver, Chester L. IV. Title. **BIP**

Wordsworth, William, 1770-1850—Addresses, essays, lectures.

GARROD, Heathcote William, 821'.7 1878-1960.
Wordsworth : lectures and essays / by H. W. Garrod. 1st AMS ed. New York : AMS Press, 1978. 211 p. ; 19 cm. Reprint of the 1923 ed. published by the Clarendon Press, Oxford. Includes bibliographical references. [PR5881.G3 1978] 75-28997 ISBN 0-404-14008-4 : 12.50
1. Wordsworth, William, 1770-1850—Addresses, essays, lectures. 2. Poets, English—19th century—Biography—Addresses, essays, lectures. I. Title. **BIP**

†TUCKWELL, William, 1829- 821'.7 1919.
The poet Wordsworth : a lecture delivered at the House of Education, Ambleside, on Thursday, June 20th, 1901 / by W. Tuckwell. Folcroft, Pa. : Folcroft Library Editions, 1976. 21 p. ; 23 cm. Reprint of the 1901 ed., by S. Read, bookseller and stationer, Grasmere, Eng. [PR5881.T8 1976] 76-26103 ISBN 0-8414-8617-4 lib. bdg. : 7.50
1. Wordsworth, William, 1770-1850—Addresses, essays, lectures. 2. Poets, English—19th century—Biography—Addresses, essays, lectures. I. Title.

Wordsworth, William, 1770-1850—Anniversaries, etc.

THE Eagle (Cambridge, 928.2 Eng.).
Wordsworth at Cambridge; a record of the commemoration held at St. John's College, Cambridge, in April 1950. Cambridge, University Press [1950?] 71 p. illus., ports., facsim. 22 cm. Cover title. Corrigenda slip inserted. "A reprint of p. 73-143 of vol. liv. no. 237 of the Eagle." [PR5885.E2] 52-19529
1. Wordsworth, William, 1770-1850—Anniversaries, etc. 2. Wordsworth. William, 1770-1850—Portraits. 3. Cambridge. University. I. Title.

Wordsworth, William, 1770-1850—Biography.

MACLEAN, Catherine 821'.7 B Macdonald.
Dorothy and William Wordsworth. New York, Haskell House Publishers, 1972. 129 p. 23 cm. Reprint of the 1927 ed. [PR5881.M3 1972] 71-39678 ISBN 0-8383-1403-1
1. Wordsworth, William, 1770-1850—Biography. 2. Wordsworth, Dorothy, 1771-1885.

MACLEAN, Catherine 821'.7 B Macdonald.
Dorothy and William Wordsworth. New York, Octagon Books, 1972. 129 p. 20 cm. Reprint of the 1927 ed. [PR5881.M3 1972b] 72-5164 ISBN 0-374-95250-7
1. Wordsworth, William, 1770-1850—Biography. 2. Wordsworth, Dorothy, 1771-1855. I. Title. **BIP**

MANLEY, Seon. 821'.7 B
Dorothy and William Wordsworth : the heart of a circle of friends / by Seon Manley. New York : Vanguard Press, [1974] xi, 241 p. : ill. ; 24 cm. Bibliography: p. 235-239. [PR5881.M36] 70-188693 ISBN 0-8149-0710-5 : 6.95
1. Wordsworth, William, 1770-1850—Biography. 2. Wordsworth, Dorothy, 1771-1855—Biography. I. Title. **BIP**

MOORMAN, Mary 821'.7 B (Trevelyan) 1905-
William Wordsworth: a biography, by Mary Moorman. London, New York [etc.] Oxford U.P., 1968- v. plates, illus., map, ports. 21 cm. (Oxford paperback no. 145) Contents.Contents.—[1] The early years: 1770-1803. Bibliographical footnotes. [PR5881.M6 1968] 73-357082 ISBN 0-19-881145-4 (v. 1) 18/6 per vol.
1. Wordsworth, William, 1770-1850—Biography. I. Title.

NESBITT, George Lyman, 821'.7 B 1903-
Wordsworth: the biographical background of his poetry [by] George L. Nesbitt. New York, Pegasus [1970] ix, 197 p. port. 22 cm. [PR5881.N4] 77-110440 6.95
1. Wordsworth, William, 1770-1850—Biography. I. Title.

PHILLIPS, George Searle, 821'.7 1815-1889.
Memoirs of William Wordsworth : compiled from authentic sources, with numerous quotations from his poems, illustrative of his life and character / by January Searle [i.e. G. S. Phillips]. Folcroft, Pa. : Folcroft Library Editions, 1977. 312 p. ; 24 cm. Reprint of the 1852 ed. published by Partridge & Oakey, London. [PR5881.P5 1977] 77-6717 ISBN 0-8414-7657-8 lib. bdg. : 45.00
1. Wordsworth, William, 1770-1850—Biography. 2. Authors, English—19th century—Biography.

WORDSWORTH, Dorothy, 828'.7'03 B 1771-1855.
Journals of Dorothy Wordsworth: the Alfoxden journal, 1798; the Grasmere journals, 1800-1803, with an introduction by Helen Darbishire. New ed. edited by Mary Moorman. London, New York, Oxford University Press, 1971. xxi, 231 p. map. 21 cm. (Oxford paperbacks, 248) [PR5849.A8 1971] 74-27074 ISBN 0-19-281103-7 £0.75 2.95 U.S.
1. Wordsworth, William, 1770-1850—Biography. I. Moorman, Mary (Trevelyan), 1905- ed.

WORDSWORTH, Elizabeth, 821'.7 B Dame, 1840-1932.
William Wordsworth. New York, Haskell House Publishers, 1974. x, 232 p. 21 cm. Reprint of the 1891 ed. published by Percival, London. [PR5881.W7 1974] 74-16289 ISBN 0-8383-1800-2
1. Wordsworth, William, 1770-1850—Biography. **BIP**

Wordsworth, William, 1770-1850—Biography—Juvenile literature.

BOBER, Natalie. 821'.7 B
William Wordsworth, the wandering poet / by Natalie Bober. 1st ed. Nashville : T. Nelson, [1975] 191 p. : ill. ; 21 cm. Includes indexes. Bibliography: p. 181-183. A biography of the English romantic poet whose relationship with Samuel Taylor Coleridge was a source of great inspiration to him. [PR5881.B6] 92 74-32392 ISBN 0-8407-6431-6 : 6.95
1. Wordsworth, William, 1770-1850—Biography—Juvenile literature. I. Title.

Wordsworth, William, 1770-1850—Biography—Marriage.

WORDSWORTH, Mary 821'.7 B Hutchinson, 1770-1859.
The letters of Mary Wordsworth, 1800-1855 / selected and edited by Mary E. Burton. Westport, Conn. : Greenwood Press, 1978, c1958. p. cm. Reprint of the ed. published at the Clarendon Press, Oxford, Eng. Includes bibliographical references and index. [PR5882.W6 1978] 78-14345 ISBN 0-313-20632-5 lib. bdg. : 25.00
1. Wordsworth, William, 1770-1850—Biography—Marriage. 2. Wordsworth, Mary Hutchinson, 1770-1859. 3. Poets, English—19th century—Biography. I. Burton, Mary Elizabeth, 1900-

Wordsworth, William, 1770-1850—Biography—Youth.

LEGOUIS, Emile 821'.7 B Hyacinthe, 1861-1937.
The early life of William Wordsworth, 1770-1798; a study of "The prelude". Translated by J. W. Matthews. With a prefatory note by Leslie Stephen. London, Dent; New York, Dutton. St. Clair Shores, Mich., Scholarly Press, 1971. xvi, 481 p. 21 cm. Translation of La jeunesse de William Wordsworth. Reprint of the 1932 ed. Includes bibliographical references. [PR5882.L413 1971] 74-145138 ISBN 0-403-01070-5
1. Wordsworth, William, 1770-1850—Biography—Youth. 2. Wordsworth, William, 1770-1950. The prelude. I. Title. **BIP**

MEYER, George Wilbur. 821'.7 B
Wordsworth's formative years. [Folcroft, Pa.] Folcroft Library Editions, 1974 [c1943] vii, 265 p. 26 cm. Reprint of the ed. published by the University of Michigan Press, Ann Arbor, which was issued as v. 20 of University of Michigan publications, Language and literature. Bibliography: p. 255-257. [PR5882.M4 1974] 74-3373 ISBN 0-8414-6119-8 30.00 (lib. bdg.)
1. Wordsworth, William, 1770-1850—Biography—Youth. I. Title. II. Series: Michigan. University. University of Michigan publications. Language and literature, v. 20.

ROSE, Stanley Charles. 821'.7 B
The boy Wordsworth. Dubuque, Iowa, Kendall/Hunt Pub. Co. [1973] xiv, 90 p. 23 cm. Bibliography: p. 89-90. [PR5882.R6] 73-84130 ISBN 0-8403-0778-0 3.75 (pbk.)
1. Wordsworth, William, 1770-1850—Biography—Youth. I. Title.

Wordsworth, William, 1770-1850—Chronology.

REED, Mark L. 821'.7
Wordsworth : the chronology of the middle years, 1800-1815 / Mark L. Reed. Cambridge, Mass. : Harvard University Press, 1975. xiii, 782 p. ; 24 cm. Includes bibliographical references and index. [PR5882.R43] 74-77179 ISBN 0-674-95777-6 : 25.00
1. Wordsworth, William, 1770-1850—Chronology. **BIP**

Wordsworth, William, 1770-1850.—Criticism and interpretation.

SNEATH, Elias Hershey, 821'.7 1857-1935.
Wordsworth, poet of nature and poet of man. Port Washington, N.Y., Kennikat Press [1967] viii, 320 p. 22 cm. Reprint of the 1912 ed. Bibliographical footnotes. [PR5888.S6 1967] 67-27653
1. Wordsworth, William, 1770-1850.—Criticism and interpretation. I. Title. **BIP**

Wordsworth, William, 1770-1850—Homes and haunts.

BENSUSAN, Samuel Levy, 821'.7 B 1872-1958.
William Wordsworth : his homes and haunts / by S. L. Bensusan ; with twelve drawings in crayon by A. Forestier and four portraits. Folcroft, Pa. : Folcroft Library Editions, 1977. p. cm. Reprint of the 1910 ed. published by T. C. & E. C. Jack, London, in series: The Pilgrim books. Includes index. [PR5884.B4 1977] 77-10639 ISBN 0-8414-0502-6 lib. bdg. : 12.50
1. Wordsworth, William, 1770-1850—Homes and haunts. 2. Poets, English—19th century—Biography. **BIP**

THOMPSON, Thomas William, 821'.7 1888-1968.
Wordsworth's Hawkshead [by] T. W. Thompson; edited, with introduction, notes and appendices, by Robert Woof. London, New York, Oxford U.P., 1970. xx, 403 p., 17 plates. illus., facsims., fold. map (on lining paper). 23 cm. Bibliography: p. [380]-382. [PR5884.T5 1970] 78-554880 ISBN 0-19-212186-3 £6/-/-
1. Wordsworth, William, 1770-1850—Homes and haunts. 2. Hawkshead, Eng. (Parish) I. Woof, Robert, ed. II. Title. **BIP**

Wordsworth, William, 1770-1850—Homes and haunts—England—Lake district.

KNIGHT, William Angus, 821'.7 1836-1916.
The English Lake District as interpreted in the poems of Wordsworth / by William Knight. 2d ed., rev. and enl. Folcroft, Pa. : Folcroft Library Editions, 1977. xvi, 270 p., [1] leaf of plates : port. ; 23 cm. Reprint of the 1891 ed. published by D. Douglas, Edinburgh. Includes bibliographical references. [PR5884.K6 1977] 77-10463 ISBN 0-8414-5453-1 lib. bdg. : 27.50
1. Wordsworth, William, 1770-1850—Homes and haunts—England—Lake district. 2. Lake district, Eng.—History. 3. Authors, English—19th century—Biography. 4. Lake district, Eng., in literature. I. Wordsworth, William, 1770-1850. II. Title. **BIP**

Wordsworth, William, 1770-1850—Juvenile literature.

WEST, Trudy 92
The young Wordsworth. Illus. by Michael Godfrey. New York, Roy [1966, c.1965] 136p. illus. 21cm. [PR5881.W43] 66-13354 3.25 bds.,
1. Wordsworth, William, 1770-1850—Juvenile literature. I. Title.

Wordsworth, William, 1770-1850—Knowledge and learning.

SCHNEIDER, Ben Ross, 1920- 928.2
Wordsworth's Cambridge education. Cambridge [Eng.] University Press, 1957. 208p. illus. 23cm. Issued in 1955 in microfilm form as thesis, Columbia University. [PR5888.S36 1957] 58-693
1. Wordsworth, William, 1770-1850—Knowledge and learning. I. Title.

Worker, Dwight, 1946-

WORKER, Dwight, 1946- 365'.641 B
Escape! / Dwight and Barbara Worker. San Francisco : San Francisco Book Co., 1977. p. cm. [HV8657.W67] 77-78676 ISBN 0-913374-76-8 :·8.95
1. Worker, Dwight, 1946- 2. Worker, Barbara, 1954- 3. Escapes. 4. Fugitives from justice—Biography. I. Worker, Barbara, 1954- joint author. II. Title. **BIP**

Workman, Gladys.

WORKMAN, Gladys. 920.7
Only when I laugh. Englewood Cliffs, N.J., Prentice-Hall [1959] 236 p. 22 cm. [CT275.W7A3] 59-8378
I. Title.

Workman, Willie Mae Cartwright.

KYTLE, Elizabeth 325.2609758 Larisey.
Willie Mae. [1st ed.] New York, Knopf,

1958. 243 p. 21 cm. [E185.97.W62K9] 58-7560
1. Workman, Willie Mae Cartwright. 2. Negroes—Georgia. I. Title.

Workswick, David Jay, 1958-

WORSWICK, Marilyn E. 362.7'8'3
Thank you Davey ; thank you God / Marilyn E. Worswick with Robert Selle. Minneapolis : Augsburg Pub. House, c1978. 151 p. ; 20 cm. [RJ506.M4W67] 77-84089 ISBN 0-8066-1614-8 pbk. : 3.50
1. Workswick, David Jay, 1958- 2. Mentally handicapped children—United States—Biography. 3. Family—Religious life. I. Selle, Robert, joint author. II. Title. BIP

World history.

BEST, Allena (Champlin) 1892- 920
Men who changed the map, A.D. 400 to 1914 [by] Erick Berry & Herbert Best. New York, Funk & Wagnalls [1968, c1967] 170 p. illus., maps, ports. 28 cm. Brief biographies of great leaders whose actions changed the course of world history: Attila the Hun, Justinian the Great, Mohammed, Charlemagne, William the Conqueror, Genghis Khan, Frederick II, the Ottoman Empire, Hernando Cortes, Catherine the Great, and Napoleon Bonaparte. [D21.B525] AC 68
1. World history. 2. Biography. I. Best, Herbert, 1894- joint author. II. Berry, Erick, pseud. III. Title.

World history—Juvenile literature.

BEST, Allena (Champlin) 920.02
1892-
Men who changed the map, A. D. 400 to 1914 New York, Funk & Wagnalls [1968, c1967] 170 p. illus., maps, ports. 28 cm. Bibliography: p. [165]-166. [D21.B525] 67-26044
1. World history—Juvenile literature. I. Best, Herbert. 1894- joint author. II. Title. III. Title: ..[by]Erick Berry & Herbert Best.

World politics.

SHOTWELL, James Thomson, 928.1
1874--
Autobiography. Indianapolis, bobbs [c.1961] 347p. illus. 61-15139 6.00 bds.,
1. World politics. I. Title.

World politics—1945-

CROCKER, Walter 994'.04'0924
Russell, 1902-
Australian ambassador; international relations at first hand [by] W. R. Crocker. [Melbourne] Melbourne University Press [1971] vii, 211 p. 22 cm. [D413.C76A3 1971] 71-24346 ISBN 0-522-83993-2 6.60
1. World politics—1945- 2. Australia—Diplomatic and consular service. I. Title.

World politics—20th century.

BARMAN, Thomas. 327'.1
Diplomatic correspondent. [1st American ed.] New York, Macmillan [1969, c1968] xiv, 273 p. 22 cm. Bibliography: p. 265-266. [D443.B348 1969] 69-11208 6.95
1. World politics—20th century. I. Title.

MENZIES, Robert 994'.040924
Gordon, Sir, 1894-
Afternoon light; some memories of men and events. [1st American ed.] New York, Coward-McCann [1968] 384 p. group port. 22 cm. [DU114.M4A3 1968] 68-19223
1. World politics—20th century. I. Title.

World War, 1939-1945—Aerial operations.

FIGHTERS in the 940.54'4'0922 B
sky / compiled by Aidan Chambers. Basingstoke : Macmillan, 1976. 125 p. : ill. ; 18 cm. (Topliners) [D785.F53] 77-352306 ISBN 0-333-19451-9 : £0.35
1. World War, 1939-1945—Aerial operations. 2. World War, 1939-1945—Personal narratives. 3. Air pilots—Biography. I. Chambers, Aidan.

JACKSON, Robert, 940.54'4'0922 B
1941-
Air heroes of World War II : Sixteen stories of heroism in thhe air / Robert Jackson. New York : St. Martins Press, 1978. 175 p., [2] leaves of plates : ill. ; 23 cm. [D785.J318 1978] 77-18382 ISBN 0-312-01516-X : 7.95
1. World War, 1939-1945—Aerial operations. 2. World War, 1939-1945—Biography. I. Title.

JACKSON, Robert, 940.54'4'0922 B
1941-
Fighter pilots of World War II / Robert Jackson. London : A. Barker, c1976. 176 p. ; 23 cm. [D785.J32] 76-364823 ISBN 0-213-16578-3 : £3.50
1. World War, 1939-1945—Aerial operations. 2. World War, 1939-1945—Biography. I. Title. BIP

JACKSON, Robert, 940.54'4'0922 B
1941-
Fighter pilots of World War II / Robert Jackson New York : St. Martin's Press, 1976. 176 p. ; 23 cm. [D785.J32 1976b] 76-11691 8.95
1. World War, 1939-1945—Aerial operations. 2. World War, 1939-1945—Biography. 3. Air pilots—Biography.

World War, 1939-1945—Aerial operations, American.

BOYINGTON, Gregory. 940.54'49'73
Baa baa, black sheep, by "Pappy" Boyington (Gregory Boyington) [New York] Arno Press [1972, c1958] 384 p. illus. 23 cm. (Literature and history of aviation) Autobiographical. [D790.B63 1972] 77-169406 ISBN 0-405-03752-X
1. World War, 1939-1945—Aerial operations, American. 2. World War, 1939-1945—Prisoners and prisons, Japanese. I. Title. II. Series. BIP

World War, 1939-1945—Biography.

HIRSCH, Phi, ed. 923.573
The Kennedy war heroes. New York, Pyramid [c.1960-1962] 159p. 19cm. (F-748) 62-5781 .40 pap.,
1. World War, 1939-1945—Biog. I. Title.

KEEGAN, John, 1934- 940.53'092'2
Who was who in World War II / edited by John Keegan. New York : T. Y. Crowell, 1978. 224 p. : ill. ; 31 cm. "A Bison book." [D736.K43 1978] 77-95149 ISBN 0-690-01753-7 : 14.95
1. World War, 1939-1945—Biography. I. Title. BIP

THOMAS, Lowell 940.54'0922 B
Jackson, 1892-
These men shall never die, by Lowell Thomas. Illustrated with official photos. by U.S. Army Air Corps [and others] Freeport, N.Y., Books for Libraries Press [1971, c1943] xii, 308 p. illus. 24 cm. (Essay index reprint series) [D736.T455 1971] 73-152217 ISBN 0-8369-2379-0
1. World War, 1939-1945—Biography. 2. World War, 1939-1945—U.S. I. Title. BIP

World War, 1939-1945—Biography—Addresses, essays, lectures.

TAYLOR, Alan John 940.54 B
Percivale, 1906-
The war lords / A. J. P. Taylor. 1st American ed. New York : Atheneum, 1978, c1977. 189 p. : ill. ; 24 cm. Transcripts of 6 lectures delivered on BBC television in Aug. 1976. Includes index. [D736.T35 1978] 77-13962 ISBN 0-689-10840-0 : 10.00
1. World War, 1939-1945—Biography—Addresses, essays, lectures. 2. World War, 1939-1945—Diplomatic history—Addresses, essays, lectures. 3. Heads of states—Biography—Addresses, essays, lectures. I. Title. BIP

World War, 1939-1945 — Campaigns.

MONTGOMERY of Alamein, 923.542
Bernard Law Montgomery, 1st viscount, 1887-
The memoirs of Field-Marshal the Viscount Montgomery of Alamein. [1st ed.] Cleveland, World Pub. Co. [1958] 508 p. illus., facsims., plans, ports. 25 cm. [DA69.3.M56A3] 58-9414
1. World War, 1939-1945 — Campaigns. I. Title.

SMYTH, John George, 940.54'01
Sir, bart., 1893-
Leadership in war, 1939-1945 : the generals in victory and defeat / Sir John Smyth. New York : St. Martin's Press, 1974. 247 p., [4] leaves of plates : ill. ; 22 cm. Includes index. Bibliography: p. 234-235. [D744.S586 1974b] 74-80213 8.95
1. World War, 1939-1945—Campaigns. 2. Generals. I. Title.

World War, 1939-1945—Diplomatic history.

MAISKII, Ivan 940.532'0924
Mikhailovich, 1884-
Memoirs of a Soviet ambassador; the War, 1939-43 [by] Ivan Maisky. Translated from the Russian by Andrew Rothstein. New York, Scribner [1968, c1967] viii, 408 p. 24 cm. Translation of Vospominaniia sovetskogo posla (romanized form) Bibliographical footnotes. [D754.R9M313 1968] 68-12501
1. World War, 1939-1945—Diplomatic history. 2. Russia—Foreign relations—1917-1945. I. Title.

World War, 1939-1945—Jews.

FRANK, Anne, 1929-1945. 940.53492
The diary of a young girl; translated from the Dutch by B. M. Mooyaart-Doubleday, with an introd. by Eleanor Roosevelt. [1st ed.] Garden City, N.Y., Doubleday, 1952. 285 p. illus. 20 cm. Translation of Het achterhuis. [D810.J4F715] 949.2 52-6355
1. World War, 1939-1945—Jews. 2. Netherlands—History—German occupations, 1940-1945. I. Title.

FRANK, Anne, 1929-1945. 940.531'5
The diary of a young girl. Translated from the Dutch by B. M. Mooyaart-Doubleday. With an introd. by Eleanor Roosevelt. Garden City, N.Y., Doubleday [1967] 308 p. illus., port. (on lining papers) 22 cm. Translation of Het achterhuis. [D810.J4F715 1967] 67-66285
1. World War, 1939-1945—Jews. 2. Netherlands—History—German occupation, 1940-1945. I. Title.

World War, 1939-1945—Naval operations, American.

SCHOFIELD, William 940.545973
Greenough, 1909-
Eastward the convoys [by] William G. Schofield. Chicago, Rand McNally [1965] 239 p. 22 cm. Autobiographical. [D773.S4] 65-14459
1. World War, 1939-1945—Naval operations, American. 2. Merchant marine—U.S. I. Title.

World War, 1939-1945—Naval operations, British.

CUNNINGHAM, Andrew Browne 923.542
Cunningham, 1st viscount, 1883-
A sailor's odyssey; the autobiography of Admiral of the Fleet, Viscount Cunningham of Hyndhope. [1st ed.] New York, Dutton, 1951. 715 p. illus. 24 cm. [DA89.1.C8A3 1951a] 51-14146
1. World War, 1939-1945—Naval operations, British. 2. World War, 1939-1945—Mediterranean Sea. I. Title.

World War, 1939-1945 — Near East.

STARK, Freya. 828.912
Dust in the lion's paw; autobiography, 1939-1946. [1st American ed.] New York, Harcourt, Brace & World [1962, c1961] 296 p. illus. 23 cm. [D766.S77 1962] 62-7374
1. World War, 1939-1945 — Near East. I. Title.

World War, 1939-1945—Persona narratives, American.

MINARIK, William 940.554 9 730924
H.
Sailors, subs, and senoritas, tby Winiam H. Minarik. Boston, Branden Pr. [1968] 349p. 23cm. [D811.M528] 67-27327 6.95
1. World War, 1939-1945—Personai narratives, American. I. Title.

World War, 1939-1945—Personal narratives, Austrian.

PAULI, Hertha 940.53'159 B
Ernestine, 1909-
Break of time, by Hertha Pauli. New York, Hawthorn Books [1972] vii, 239 p. 24 cm. "A Martin Dale book." Translation of Der Riss der Zeit geht durch mein Herz. [D811.5.P3513 1972] 70-179113 5.95
1. World War, 1939-1945—Personal narratives, Austrian. 2. World War, 1939-1945—Refugees. I. Title.

WATSON, Ann. 940.54'82'436
"They came in peace." Palos Verdes Estates, Calif., T. W. Pub. [1972] 382 p. 18 cm. [D811.5.W384] 77-190577 2.00 (pbk)
1. World War, 1939-1945—Personal narratives, Austrian. I. Title.

World War, 1939-1945—Personal narratives, Dutch.

BLOKZIJL, Jan. 940.548'1'492
Captain Blokzijl and the Nazis. Philadelphia, Dorrance [1971] 308 p. 22 cm. Autobiographical. [D811.5.B55] 76-148920 ISBN 0-8059-1551-6 5.95
1. World War, 1939-1945—Personal narratives, Dutch. I. Title.

World War, 1939-1945—Personal narratives, English.

BEATON, Cecil Walter 940.548142
Hardy, 1904-
The years between, diaries 1939-44 [by] Cecil Beaton. [1st ed.] New York, Holt, Rinehart and Winston [1965] 352 p. illus., ports. 22 cm. [D811.5.B32 1965a] 65-22457
1. World War, 1939-1945—Personal narratives, English. I. Title.

HORROCKS, Brian, Sir 923.542
1895-
Escape to action. New York, St. Martin's Press [1961, c1960] 320p. illus. 22cm. Autobiographical. First published in 1960 under title: A full life. [DA69.3.H63A3 1961] 62-7130
1. World War, 1939-1945—Personal narratives, English. I. Title.

World War, 1939-1945—Personal narratives, Filipino.

PANLILIO, Yay. 940.5481914
The crucible, an autobiography by "Colonel Yay." New York, Macmillan, 1950. xi, 348 p. 21 cm. [D811.5.P28] 50-5373
1. World War, 1939-1945—Personal narratives, Filipino. 2. World War, 1939-1945—Philippine Islands. I. Title.

World War, 1939-1945—Personal narratives, French.

TEISSIER du Cros, 940.548144
Janet.
Divided loyalties. With a pref. by D. W. Brogan. [1st American ed.] New York, Knopf, 1964. xxvii, 350 p. map. 22 cm. Autobiographical. [D811.5.T42 1964] 63-22140
1. World War, 1939-1945—Personal narratives, French. I. Title.

World War, 1939-1945—Personal narratives, German.

CHESNEY, Inga L. 940.54'82'43
A time of rape [by] Inga L. Chesney. Englewood Cliffs, N.J., Prentice-Hall [1972] vi, 255 p. 24 cm. Autobiographical. [D811.5.C4453] 70-168757 ISBN 0-13-922013-5 6.95

1. World War, 1939-1945—Personal narratives, German. I. Title.

KONRAT, Georg von. 940.542'1
Assault from within. London, New York, Wingate, 1970. 286 p., plate. port. 21 cm. [D811.5.K657 1970b] 73-561804 ISBN 0-85523-018-5 £1.50
1. World War, 1939-1945—Personal narratives, German. I. Title.

World War, 1939-1945—Personal narratives, Jewish—Juvenile literature.

REISS, Johanna. 940.53'15'03924
The upstairs room. New York, Crowell [1972] ix, 196 p. 22 cm. Autobiographical. A Dutch Jewish girl describes the two-and-one-half years she spent in hiding in the upstairs bedroom of a farmer's house during World War II. [D810.J4R42] 77-187940 ISBN 0-690-85127-8 4.50
1. World War, 1939-1945—Personal narratives, Jewish—Juvenile literature. I. Title. BIP

World War, 1939-1945 — Prisoners and prisons, German.

CALNAN, T. D., 1914- 940.547'2'43
Free as a running fox [by] T. D. Calnan. New York, Dial Press, 1970. 323 p. 24 cm. Autobiographical. [D805.G3C28 1970] 70-131168 6.95
1. World War, 1939-1945—Prisoners and prisons, German. 2. World War, 1939-1945—Personal narratives, English. 3. Escapes. I. Title. BIP

MOEN, Petter, 1901-1944. 940.547243
Diary; translated from the Norwegian by Bjorn Koefoed. New York, Creative Age Press, 1951. xii, 176 p. illus. (on lining papers) 21 cm. [CT1308.M58A32] 51-2579
1. World War, 1939-1945 — Prisoners and prisons, German. 2. World War, 1939-1945 — Personal narratives, Norwegian. I. Title.

World War, 1939-1945—Prisoners and prisons, Japanese.

BOYLE, Martin. 940.547252
Yanks don't cry. [New York] B. Geis Associates; distributed by Random House [1963] 249 p. 22 cm. Autobiographical. [D805.J3B617] 63-14217
1. World War, 1939-1945—Prisoners and prisons, Japanese. I. Title.

World War, 1939-1945—Propaganda.

LOCKHART, Robert Hamilton Bruce, Sir, 1887-1970. 940.54'81'42
Comes the reckoning. New York, Arno Press, 1972. 384 p. 23 cm. (International propaganda and communications) Reprint of the 1947 ed. [D810.P7G758 1972] 72-4672 ISBN 0-405-04756-8 19.00
1. World War, 1939-1945—Propaganda. 2. World War, 1939-1945—Diplomatic history. 3. World War, 1939-1945—Personal narratives, English. I. Title. II. Series. BIP

World War, 1939-1945—Russia.

ZHUKOV, Georgii Konstantinovich, 1896- 940.542'1'0924
The memoirs of Marshal Zhukov. [1st American ed.] New York, Delacorte Press [1971] 703, viii p. illus., plans (part col.), ports. 23 cm. Translation of Vospominaniia i razmyshleniia (romanized form) "A Seymour Lawrence book." [DK268.Z52A313 1971] 73-120846 15.00
1. World War, 1939-1945—Russia. I. Title.

World War, 1939-1945—Secret Service.

GEHLEN, Reinhard. 327'.12'0924 [B]
The Service; the memoirs of General Reinhard Gehlen. Translated by David Irving. Introd. by George Bailey. New York, Popular Lib. [1972] xxvii, 386 p. illus. 18 cm. Translation of Der Dienst. [DD247.G37A313 1972] pap., 1.50
1. World War, 1939-1945—Secret Service. 2. Organisation Gehlen. I. Title.

WHITING, Charles, 1926- 940.54'85
The war in the shadows. New York, Ballantine Books [1973] xvi, 268 p. illus. 18 cm. (A Ballantine original) Bibliography: p. 267-268. [D810.S7W46] 73-171117 1.50 (pbk.)
1. World War, 1939-1945—Secret service. 2. Spies. I. Title.

World War, 1939-1945—South Carolina.

SOUTH Carolina. Adjutant-General's Office. 940.54'12'73
The official roster of South Carolina servicemen and servicewomen in World War II, 1941-46. Compiled under the direction of Robert E. McNair, Governor [and] Frank D. Pinckney, the Adjutant General. [Columbia? 1972?] 5 v. (lxxxv, 4624 p.) 29 cm. [D769.85.S6A5] 73-620852
1. World War, 1939-1945—South Carolina. 2. World War, 1939-1945—Registers, lists, etc. 3. South Carolina—Biography. I. Title.

Worldwide Church of God.

HOPKINS, Joseph Martin, 1919- 289.9
The Armstrong empire; a look at the Worldwide Church of God. [Grand Rapids] Eerdmans [1974] 304 p. map. 21 cm. Bibliography: p. 286-291. [BR1725.A77H66] 74-8255 3.95
1. Worldwide Church of God. 2. Armstrong, Herbert W. 3. Armstrong, Garner Ted. I. Title.

Worrall, Olga Nathalie Ripich, 1906-

CERUTTI, Edwina. 133.9'092'4 B
Olga Worrall : mystic with the healing hands / Edwina Cerutti. 1st ed. New York : Harper & Row, [1975] 169 p. ; 21 cm. [BF1027.W65C47 1975] 75-9317 ISBN 0-06-061358-0 : 7.95
*1. Worrall, Olga Nathalie Ripich, 1906-*BIP

Worrell, Eric—Juvenile literature.

NORRY, Roy. 92 (J)
Australian snake man; the story of Eric Worrell. Illustrations by Michael Hutchards. [Melbourne, Nelson (Australia) 1966. 27 p. col. illus., col. maps. 18 x 20 cm. (Lyrebird books) [QL644.N6] 67-89808
1. Worrell, Eric—Juvenile literature. 2. Snakes—Australia—Juvenile literature. I. Title.

Worsley, Gump.

WORSLEY, Gump. 796.9'62'0924 B
They call me Gump / by Lorne "Gump" Worsley, with Tim Moriarty. New York : Dodd, Mead, [1975] xii, 176 p., [8] leaves of plates : ill. ; 22 cm. "An Associated Features book." Autobiographical. [GV848.5.W67A37] 74-30414 ISBN 0-396-07029-9 : 6.95
1. Worsley, Gump. 2. Hockey. I. Moriarty, Tim, joint author. II. Title. BIP

Worth, Charles Frederick, 1825-1895.

SAUNDERS, Edith. 926.46
The age of Worth, Counturier to the Empress Eugenie. London, New York, Longmans, Green [1954] 218p. illus. 23cm. [TT505.W58S3] 55-1216
1. Worth, Charles Frederick, 1825-1895. 2. France—Court and courtiers. I. Title.

SAUNDERS, Edith. 926.46
The age of Worth, couturier to the Empress Eugenie. Bloomington, Indiana University Press, 1955. 218p. illus. 23cm. [TT505] 55-8084
1. Worth, Charles Frederick, 1825-1895. 2. France—Court and courtiers. I. Title.

Worth, Jennifer.

WORTH, Jennifer. 362.1'8'0973
Emergency room / by Jennifer Worth. 1st ed. New York : Elsevier/Nelson Books, [1980] c1979. p. cm. [RA975.5.E5W67 1980] 79-28314 ISBN 0-525-66675-3 : 7.95
1. Worth, Jennifer. 2. Hospitals—Emergency service. 3. Hospitals—Admission and discharge. 4. Hospital ward clerks—United States—Biography. I. Title. BIP

Worth, Jonathan, 1802-1869.

ZUBER, Richard L. 923.2
Jonathan Worth; a biography of a Southern Unionist. Chapel Hill, Univ. of N.C. Pr. [c.1965] 351p. port. 24cm. [F259.W94Z8] 65-12061 7.50
1. Worth, Jonathan, 1802-1869. 2. North Carolina—Pol. & govt. I. Title.

ZUBER, Richard L. 923.273
Jonathan Worth; a biography of a Southern Unionist, by Richard L. Zuber. Chapel Hill, University of North Carolina Press [1965] 351 p. port. 24 cm. Bibliography: p. [333]-342. [F259.W94Z8] 65-12061
1. Worth, Jonathan, 1802-1869. 2. North Carolina—Politics and government.

Worth, Patience.

LITVAG, Irving. 133.9'3'0924 B
Singer in the shadows; the strange story of Patience Worth. New York, Macmillan [1972] xiii, 293 p. 21 cm. Includes bibliographical references. [BF1301.W865L58] 70-165570 7.95
1. Worth, Patience. 2. Spirit writings. I. Title.

LITVAG, Irving. 133.9'3'0924 [B]
Singer in the shadows; the strange story of Patience Worth. New York, Popular Lib. [1973, c.1972] 319 p. 18 cm. Includes bibliographical references. [BF1301.W865L58] 0.95 (pbk.)
1. Worth, Patience. 2. Spirit writing. I. Title.
L.C. card no. for the hardbound edition: 70-165570.

Worth, William Jenkins, 1794-1849.

WALLACE, Edward Seccomb, 1897- 923.573
General William Jenkins Worth, Monterey's forgotten hero. Dallas, Southern Methodist University Press, 1953. viii, 242p. illus., ports., maps. 23cm. 'In somewhat different form, this biography ... served to satisfy one of the requirements for the PH. D. degree at Boston University.' Bibliography: p. 225-233. [E403.1.W9W3] 53-12918
1. Worth, William Jenkins, 1794-1849. I. Title.

Worthington, Frederic Franklin.

WORTHINGTON, Larry, 1902- 923.571
Worthy a biography of Major-General F. F. Worthington, C. B., M. C., M. M. [dist. New York, St. Martin's, c.1961] 236p. front port. 61-66203 6.00
1. Worthington, Frederic Franklin. I. Title.

Worthington, Thomas, 1773-1827.

SEARS, Alfred Byron, 1900- 923.273
Thomas Worthington, father of Ohio statehood. Columbus, Ohio State University Press for the Ohio Historical Society [1958] viii, 260p. 24cm. Bibliography: p. [243]-250. [F495.W73] 58-63517
1. Worthington, Thomas, 1773-1827. I. Title.

Wotton, Henry, Sir, 1568-1639.

WARD, Adolphus William, Sir, 1837-1924. 327'.2'0924 B
Sir Henry Wotton; a biographical sketch. Westminster, A. Constable, 1898. [Folcroft, Pa.] Folcroft Library Editions, 1973. p. [DA391.1.W9W2 1973] 73-1247 ISBN 0-8414-2806-9
1. Wotton, Henry, Sir, 1568-1639. BIP

Woytinsky, Wladimir S., 1885-1960.

WOYTINSKY, Emma (Shadkhan) 1893- 308.2
So much alive; the life and work of Wladimir S. Woytinsky, edited by Emma S. Woytinsky. New York, Vanguard Press [1962] xx, 272 p. illus., port. 25 cm. "Bibliography of Woytinsky's writings": p. [229]-272. [H59.W6W6] 62-19858
1. Woytinsky, Wladimir S., 1885-1960. 2. Social sciences — Addresses, essays, lectures. I. Title.

Wren, Christopher, Sir, 1632-1723.

HUTCHINSON, Harold Frederick. 720'.92'4 B
Sir Christopher Wren : a biography / by Harold F. Hutchinson. New York : Stein and Day, [1976] c1975. p. cm. Includes index. Bibliography: p. [NA997.W8H87 1976] 75-34324 10.00
1. Wren, Christopher, Sir, 1632-1723.

HUTCHISON, Harold Frederick. 720'.92'4 B
Sir Christopher Wren : a biography / by Harold F. Hutchison. London : Gollancz, 1976. 191 p., leaf of plate, [16] p. of plates : ill., plan, ports. ; 23 cm. Includes index. Bibliography: p. [177]-181. [NA997.W8H87 1976b] 76-367374 ISBN 0-575-01876-3 : £5.00
1. Wren, Christopher, Sir, 1632-1723.

SUMMERSON, John Newenham, 1904- 927.2
Sir Christopher Wren. New York, Macmillan [1953] 159p. illus. 19cm. (Brieg lives, no. 9) [NA997.W8S8] 53-12511
1. Wren, Christopher, Sir 1632-1723. I. Title.

SUMMERSON, John Newenham, Sir 1904- 927.2
Sir Christopher Wren. Hamden, Conn., Archon [dist. Shoe String] 1965[c.1953, 1965] 159p. illus., plans. port. 21cm. (Makers of hist.) [NA997.W8S8] 65-4284 4.00
1. Wren, Sir Christopher, 1632-1723. I. Title.

WEIR, Rosemary. 720.924 B
The man who built a city; a life of Sir Christopher Wren. [1st ed.] New York, Farrar, Straus & Giroux [1971] viii, 208 p. illus. 21 cm. (An Ariel book) Bibliography: p. 201. A biography of the seventeenth-century inventor, astronomer, and mathematician principally known for his architectural achievements such as the rebuilding of London's St. Paul's Cathedral. [NA997.W8W44] 92 74-161371 ISBN 0-374-35008-6 4.95
1. Wren, Christopher, Sir, 1632-1723. I. Title. BIP

WHINNEY, Margaret Dickens. 720.924 B
Christopher Wren [by] Margaret Whinney. New York, Praeger [1971] 216 p. illus., plans, ports. 22 cm. Bibliography: p. 206-208. [NA997.W8W48 1971b] 78-155448 8.95
1. Wren, Christopher, Sir, 1632-1723. I. Title.

Wren, Christopher, Sir, 1632-1723—Bibliography.

GROPIUS, Wren, Latrobe, Wright. 016.72 S
Charlottesville, Published for the American Association of Architectural Bibliographers [by the] University Press of Virginia [1972] 132 p. 24 cm. (American Association of Architectural Bibliographers. Papers, v. 9) [Z5941.A5 vol. 9] [Z8369.43] 016.72'092'2 72-195645 ISBN 0-8139-0391-2 7.50
1. Gropius, Walter, 1883-1969—Bibliography. 2. Wren, Christopher, Sir, 1632-1723—Bibliography. 3. Latrobe, Benjamin Henry, 1764-1820—Bibliography. 4. Wright, Frank Lloyd, 1867-1959—Bibliography. I. American Association of Architectural Bibliographers. II. Title. III. Series.

Wren, Christopher, Sir, 1632-1723— Juvenile literature.

GOULD, Heywood. 720'.92'4
Sir Christopher Wren: Renaissance architect, philosopher and scientist. London, New York, Franklin Watts Ltd, 1970, [i.e. 1972] x, 3-216 p. illus., plans, ports. 23 cm. Bibliography: p. [208] [NA997.W8G6 1972] 73-154615 ISBN 0-85166-316-8 £1.25
1. Wren, Christopher, Sir, 1632-1723— Juvenile literature.

GOULD, Heywood. 720'.924 B
Sir Christopher Wren; Renaissance architect, philosopher, and scientist. New York, Watts [1970] x, 216 p. illus., ports. 22 cm. (Immortals of history) Bibliography: p. [208] A biography of the architect who helped rebuild London after the fire of 1666 and who redesigned St. Paul's Cathedral. [NA997.W8G6] 92 75-101752
1. Wren, Christopher, Sir, 1632-1723— Juvenile literature. I. Title.

Wren, John, 1871-1953.

BRENNAN, Niall. 364.1'72'0924 B
John Wren: gambler, his life and times. [Melbourne] Hill of Content [1971] xii, 259 p. illus. 24 cm. [CT2808.W74B73] 72-175372 ISBN 0-85572-041-7 6.95
1. Wren, John, 1871-1953.

Wrestling.

MORGAN, Roberta, 1953- 796.8'12
Main event : the world for professional wrestling / Roberta Morgan. New York : Dial Press, c1979. xiii, 226 p., [8] leaves of plates : ill. ; 28 cm. Includes index. [GV1195.M67] 79-362 ISBN 0-8037-5631-3 : 12.95. pbk. : 7.95
1. Wrestling. 2. Wrestlers—Biography. I. Title. BIP

Wrestling—History.

JARES, Joseph Frank, 1937- 796.8'123'0973
Whatever happened to Gorgeous George? By Joe Jares. Englewood Cliffs, N.J., Prentice-Hall [1974] viii, 198 p. illus. 24 cm. [GV1195.J37] 74-13312 ISBN 0-13-951830-4
1. Wrestling—History. 2. Wrestling— Biography. I. Title. BIP

Wright, Anna Maria Rose,

WRIGHT, Anna Maria Rose, 1890- 818.5
Room for one more [by] Anna Perrott Rose. Illustrated by John V. Morris. Boston, Houghton Mifflin [1950] 272 p. illus. 22 cm. Autobiographical. [CT275.W74A3] 50-6866
I. Title.

Wright, Billie.

WRIGHT, Billie. 917.98'7'045
Four seasons north. [1st ed.] New York, Harper & Row [1973] x, 278 p. illus. 22 cm. [F912.B75W74 1973] 79-138774 ISBN 0-06-014756-3 7.95
1. Wright, Billie. 2. Brooks Range, Alaska. 3. Alaska—Description and travel—1959- I. Title.

Wright, Catharine (Morris)

THE color of life. 759.13
Boston, Houghton Mifflin, 1957. 203p. 21cm. Autobiographical. [ND237.W87A25] 927.5 57-12076
I. Wright, Catharine (Morris) 1899-

Wright, Chauncey,

WRIGHT, Chauncey, 1830-1875. 191 B
Letters of Chauncey Wright, with some account of his life, by James Bradley Thayer. New York, B. Franklin [1971] 392 p. 19 cm. (Burt Franklin research & source works series 775. Philosophy monograph series 67) Reprint of the 1878 ed. Includes bibliographical references. [B945.W74A4 1971] 79-156125 ISBN 0-8337-3892-5
I. Thayer, James Bradley, 1831-1902, ed.

Wright, Christopher Norton,

WRIGHT, Christopher Norton, 1790-ca.1871. 658.8'09'6555730924 B
No hero, I confess: a nineteenth-century autobiography. Edited by Margaret P. Medlicott. New York, Taplinger [1970, c1969] 161 p. 23 cm. [CT788.W88A3 1970] 75-103016 4.95
I. Medlicott, Margaret P., ed. II. Title. BIP

Wright, Cobina.

WRIGHT, Cobina. 920.7
I never grew up. New York, Prentice-Hall [1952] 316 p. 24 cm. [CT275.W755A3] 52-7067
I. Title.

Wright, Constance.

WRIGHT, Constance. 920.7
Madame de Lafayette. [1st ed.] New York, Holt [1959] 280 p. illus. 22 cm. Lafayette, Marie Adrienne (de Noailles) marguise de, 1750-1807. Includes bibliography. [DC146.L21W7] 59-6675
I. Title.

Wright, Ellen,

WRIGHT, Ellen, b,1839or40. 920
Daughter of abolitionists [edited] by Nancy Hale. Northampton, Mass., Smith College, 1964. 15 p. group port. 23 cm. At head of title: The Sophia Smith Collection. Letter from Ellen Wright to her brother, William Wright. [CT275.W7554A48] 67-7625
I. Wright, William, b. ca. 1842. II. Hale, Nancy, 1908- ed. III. Title.

Wright, Elsie (McColl)

LINDSAY, Cynthia (Hobart) 927.92
Mother climbed trees. New York, Simon and Schuster, 1958. 236p. illus. 21cm. [PN1998.A3L5] 58-7516
1. Wright, Elsie (McColl) 2. Stunt men— Correspondence, reminiscences, etc. I. Title.

Wright family.

RITCHIE, Anne Reed, 1905- 929'.2'0973
Major Francis Wright and Ann Washington, with allied families. [Firestone? Colo., 1973] 336 p. illus. 28 cm. "Limited to two hundred copies, of which this is number 13." Includes bibliographical references. [CS71.W95 1973] 73-159361
1. Wright family. 2. Washington family. I. Title.

Wright, Frank Lloyd, 1867-1959.

COWLES, Linn Ann. 720'.92'4 B
An index and guide to An autobiography, the 1943 edition, by Frank Lloyd Wright / prepared by Linn Ann Cowles. [Hopkins, Minn.] : Greenwich Design, c1976. 113 leaves ; 22 x 23 cm. [NA737.W7A323] 77-150602
1. Wright, Frank Lloyd, 1867-1959. An autobiography—Indexes. I. Title.

EATON, Leonard K. 720'.922
Two Chicago architects and their clients: Frank Lloyd Wright and Howard Van Doren Shaw [by] Leonard K. Eaton, with an appendix by Elizabeth M. Douvan. Cambridge, Mass., MIT Press [1969] ix, 259 p. illus., plans, ports. 27 cm. Bibliography: p. 239-242. [NA736.E15] 69-12752 ISBN 0-262-05007-2 10.00
1. Wright, Frank Lloyd, 1867-1959. 2. Shaw, Howard Van Doren, 1869-1926. I. Title.

FARR, Finis 927.2
Frank Lloyd Wright, a biography. New York, Scribners [c.1961] 293p. illus. 61-13363 5.95
1. Wright, Frank Lloyd, 1869-1959. I. Title.

FRANK Lloyd Wright. v. 12
[New York] 1959. 264p. illus. (part col.) plans. 31cm. Cover title. Regular issue of the Architectural forum, June, 1959, vol. 110, no. 6.
1. Wright, Frank Lloyd, 1869-1959. I. The Architectural forum.

JACOBS, Herbert Austin. 724.90924 B
Frank Lloyd Wright; America's greatest architect [by] Herbert Jacobs. [1st ed.] New York, Harcourt, Brace & World [1965] 223 p. illus., ports. 22 cm. Bibliographical references included in "Notes" (p. [214]-217) [NA737.W7J3] 65-25306
1. Wright, Frank Lloyd, 1867-1959.

JACOBS. HERBERT AUSTIN 724.90924
Frank Lloyd Wright: America's greatest architect. New York, Harcourt [c.1965] 223p. illus., ports. 22cm. Bibl. [NA737.W7J3] 65-25306 3.95
1. Wright. Frank Lloyd, 1869-1959. I. Title.

NADEN, Corinne J. 730'.924 B
Frank Lloyd Wright, the rebel architect, by Corinne J. Naden. Illustrated with photos. New York, F. Watts [1968] 147 p. illus., ports. 22 cm. (Immortals of engineering) Bibliography: p. 143-144. [NA737.W7N3] 68-10349
1. Wright, Frank Lloyd, 1867-1959.

NADEN, Corinne J. 720'.924 B
Frank Lloyd Wright, the rebel architect, by Corinne J. Naden. Illustrated with photos. New York, F. Watts [1968] 147 p. illus., ports. 22 cm. (Immortals of engineering) Bibliography: p. 143-144. During a professional career of sixty-six years Wright designed 600 buildings. His designs were uncluttered, his life chaotic. This is the story of the conflict. [NZ737.W7N3] 92 AC 68
1. Wright, Frank Lloyd, 1869 1959. I. Title.

NORRIS, Geoffrey 920
The Wright brothers. Illus. by John Norbury. New York, Roy [1963,c.1961] 159p. illus. 21cm. (People, places and things) 62-21659 2.95 bds.,
1. Aeronautics—Juvenile literature. I. Title.

TAFEL, Edgar. 720'.92'4 B
Apprentice to genius : years with Frank Lloyd Wright / Edgar Tafel. New York : McGraw-Hill, c1979. 228 p. : ill. (some col.) ; 29 cm. Includes index. [NA737.W7T33] 78-18504 ISBN 0-07-062815-7 : 19.50
1. Wright, Frank Lloyd, 1867-1959. 2. Tafel, Edgar. 3. Architects—United States—Biography. I. Title. BIP

TWOMBLY, Robert C. 720'.92'4 B
Frank Lloyd Wright; an interpretive biography, by Robert C. Twombly. [1st ed.] New York, Harper & Row [1973] x, 373 p. illus. 22 cm. Bibliography: p. 343-362. [NA737.W7T94 1973] 72-9248 ISBN 0-06-014467-X 10.00
1. Wright, Frank Lloyd, 1867-1959. BIP

TWOMBLY, Robert C. 720'.92'4
Frank Lloyd Wright; an interpretive biography by Robert C. Twombly. New York, Harper & Row [1974, c1973] x, 373 p. illus. 20 cm. (A Harper colophon book) Bibliography: p. 343-362. [NA737.W7T94 1974] ISBN 0-06-090359-7 3.95 (pbk.)
1. Wright, Frank Lloyd, 1867-1959. I. Title.
L.C. card number for hardbound ed.: 72-9248

TWOMBLY, Robert C. 720'.92'4 B
Frank Lloyd Wright, his life and his architecture / Robert C. Twombly. New York : Wiley, c1979. x, 444 p. : ill. ; 24 cm. "A Wiley-Interscience publication." Includes index. Bibliography: p. 423-434. [NA737.W7T95] 78-9466 19.95
1. Wright, Frank Lloyd, 1867-1959. 2. Wright, Frank Lloyd, 1867-1959— Influence. 3. Architects—United States— Biography. I. Title.

WRIGHT, Frank Lloyd, 1867-1959. 720'.92'4 B
An autobiography / Frank Lloyd Wright. New York : Horizon Press, c1977. 620 p., [20] leaves of plates : ill. ; 24 cm. Includes index. [NA737.W7A3 1977] 72-86739 ISBN 0-8180-0222-0 : 17.50
1. Wright, Frank Lloyd, 1867-1959. 2. Architects—United States—Biography.

WRIGHT, Olgivanna Lloyd. 720.924 B
Frank Lloyd Wright: his life, his work, his words. New York, Horizon Press [1966] 224 p. illus., ports. 26 cm. Bibliography: p. 223-224. [NA737.W7W725] 66-26703
1. Wright, Frank Lloyd, 1867-1959.

WRIGHT, Olgivanna Lloyd 927.2
The roots of life. New York, Horizon [c.] 1963. 256p. 23cm. 63-21570 5.50
1. Wright, Frank Lloyd, 1869-1959. I. Title. BIP

WRIGHT, Olgivanna Lloyd. 927.2
The roots of life. New York, Horizon Press, 1963. 256 p. 23 cm. [NA737.W7W736] 63-21570
1. Wright, Frank Lloyd, 1869-1959. I. Title.

WRIGHT, Olgivanna Lloyd. 720.973
The shining brow; Frank Lloyd Wright. New York, Horizon Press, 1960. 300 p. illus., ports. 23 cm. [NA737.W7W74] 60-1926
1. Wright, Frank Lloyd, 1869-1959. I. Title. BIP

WRIGHT, Olgivanna Lloyd 927.2
When past is future [v.] New York, Horizon[1964, c.1959-1963] 3v. (308;300;256p.) illus. 23cm. Contents.[1] Our house.--[2] The shining brows.--[3] The roots of life. 9.95, set, bxd.
1. Wright, Frank Lloyd, 1869-1959. I. Title.

Wright, Frank Lloyd, 1867-1959— Juvenile literature.

HOAG, Edwin. 720'.922 B
Masters of modern architecture : Frank Lloyd Wright, Le Corbusier, Mies van der Rohe, and Walter Gropius / by Edwin and Joy Hoag. Indianapolis : Bobbs-Merrill, c1977. xiii, 209 p., [8] leaves of plates : ill. ; 23 cm. Includes index. Bibliography: p. 193-197. Discusses the founding of modern architecture through the lives and works of four important architects. [NA680.H54] 920 77-76888 ISBN 0-672-52365-5 pbk. : 10.00
1. Wright, Frank Lloyd, 1867-1959— Juvenile literature. 2. Le Corbusier-Galerie Heidi Weber—Juvenile literature. 3. Mies van der Rohe, Ludwig, 1886-1969— Juvenile literature. 4. Gropius, Walter, 1883-1969—Juvenile literature. 5. Architecture, Modern—20th century— Juvenile literature. 6. Architects— Biography—Juvenile literature. I. Hoag, Joy, joint author. II. Title.

WILLARD, Charlotte. 720'.9'24 B
Frank Lloyd Wright, American architect. New York, Macmillan [1972] xiv, 183 p. illus. 21 cm. A biography of the man whose new concept of design revolutionized the development of American architecture in the twentieth century. [NA737.W7W54] 92 71-188775 5.95
1. Wright, Frank Lloyd, 1867-1959— Juvenile literature. I. Title.

Wright, Jacqueline

WRIGHT, Jacqueline 927.92
The life and loves of Lana Turner. New York 36, Wisdom House, 520 Fifth Ave. [c.1961] 160p. (Timely bks., W104) .50 pap.,
I. Title.

Wright, Melton.

WRIGHT, Melton. 922
Giant for God; a biography of the life of William Ashley ("Billy") Sunday. Boyce, Va., Distributed by Carr Pub. Co. [c1951] 168 p. illus. 24 cm. [BV3785.S8W7] 52-378
I. U. Sunday, William Ashley, 1862-1935. II. Title.

Wright, Nellie (Morse)

ZIEGLER, Inas. 920.7
Nellie's prairie; the life story of Nellie Morse Wright. Illus. by Harry Baerg. Washington, Review and Herald Pub. Association [1959] 222 p. illus. 22 cm. [CT275.W7565Z5] 59-43212
1. Wright, Nellie (Morse) I. Title.

Wright, Orville, 1871-1948.

COMBS, Harry. 629.13'0092'4 B
Kill Devil Hill : the epic of the Wright Brothers, 1900-1909 / Harry Combs, with Martin Caidin ; foreword by Neil Armstrong. Boston : Houghton Mifflin, 1979. p. cm. Includes index. Bibliography: p. [TL540.W7C65] 79-9362 ISBN 0-395-28216-0 : 12.50
1. Wright, Orville, 1871-1948. 2. Wright, Wilbur, 1867-1912. 3. Aeronautics—United States—Biography. I. Caidin, Martin, 1927- joint author. II. Title.

GLINES, Carroll V., 1920- 929.13'0922 B
The Wright brothers, pioneers of power flight, by Carroll V. Glines. New York, F. Watts [1968] 112 p. illus., port. 22 cm. (Immortals of science) Bibliography: p. 109. A biography of the two brothers, unknown bicycle repairmen, who built and flew the first powered airplane in 1903, which concentrates on the contributions to the history of flight. [TL540.W7G55] 92 AC 68
1. Wright, Orville, 1871-1948. 2. Wright, Wilbur, 1867-1912. I. Title.

KELLY, Fred Charters, 1882- v. 12
The Wright brothers; a biography authorized by Orville Wright. New York, Ballantine Books [1966] 214 p. (A Ballantine Bal-hi book, U2836) 68-50149
1. Wright, Orville, 1871-1948. 2. Wright, Wilbur, 1867-1912. I. Title.

KELLY, Fred Charters, 1882- 926.2913
The Wright brothers; a biography authorized by Orville Wright. New York, Ballantine [1966, c.1950] 214p. diagrs. 18cm. (Bal-hi bk. U2836) [TL540.W7K4 1951] .50 pap.,
1. Wright, Orville, 1871-1948. 2. Wright, Wilbur, 1867-1912. I. Title.

KELLY, Fred Charters, 1882- 926.2913
The Wright brothers; a biography authorized by Orville Wright. New York, Farrar, Straus, and Young [1951] 340 p. illus., group ports., facsims. 22 cm. [TL540.W7K4 1951] 51-11660
1. Wright, Orville, 1871-1948. 2. Wright, Wilibur, 1867-1912. I. Title.

MILLS, Lois, 1892- 926.29
Three together; the story of the Wright brothers and their sister. Illustrated by William Moyers. New York, Follett Pub. Co. [1955] 160 p. illus. 25 cm. [TL540.W7M5] 55-7496
1. Wright, Orville, 1871-1948. 2. Wright, Wilbur, 1867-1912. 3. Wright, Katharine, 1874- I. Title.

NORRIS, Geoffrey 920
The Wright brothers. Illus. by John Norbury. New York, Roy [1963,c.1961] 159p. illus. 21cm. (People, places and things) 62-21659 2.95 bds.,
1. Aeronautics—Juvenile literature. I. Title.

REYNOLDS, Quentin James, 1902-1965. 926.29
The Wright brothers, pioneers of American aviation; illustrated by Jacob Landau. New York, Random House [1950] 183 p. col. illus. 22 cm. (Landmark books [10]) [TL540.W7R48 1950] 50-11766
1. Wright, Orville, 1871-1948. 2. Wright, Wilbur, 1867-1912.

STEVENSON, Augusta. 926.2913
Wilbur and Orville Wright, boys with wings; illustrated by Paul Laune. [1st ed.] Indianapolis, Bobbs-Merrill [1951] 192 p. illus. 20 cm. (The Childhood of famous Americans series) [TL540.W7S75] 51-12392
1. Wright, Orville, 1871-1948. 2. Wright, Wilbur, 1867-1912. I. Title.

STEVENSON, Augusta. 629.13'0924 B
Wilbur and Orville Wright, boys with wings. Illustrated by Robert Doremus. Indianapolis, Bobbs-Merrill [1959] 200 p. illus. 20 cm. (Childhood of famous Americans) The boyhood of the brothers who flew the first airplane in 1903. [PZ7.S8467Wi2] 92 AC 68
1. Wright, Orville, 1871-1948. 2. Wright, Wilbur, 1867-1912. I. Doremus, Robert, illus. II. Title.

THOMAS, Henry 926.2913
The Wright brothers. Illustrated by Charles Beck. New York, Putnam [c.1960] 126p. illus. 21cm. (Lives to remember) 60-6915 2.50
1. Wright, Orville, 1871-1918. 2. Wright, Wilbur, 1867-1912. I. Title.

THOMAS, Henry, 1886- 926.2913
The Wright brothers. Illustrated by Charles Beck. New York, Putnam [1960] 126 p. illus. 21 cm. (Lives to remember) [TL540.W7T45] 60-6915
1. Wright, Orville, 1871-1948. 2. Wright, Wilbur, 1867-1912. I. Title.

Wright, Orville, 1874-1948 — Juvenile literature.

FRANCHERE, Ruth. 629.13'092'2 B
The Wright brothers. Illustrated by Louis Glanzman. New York, Crowell [1972] 41 p. illus. 24 cm. (A Crowell biography) An easy-to-read biography of the two brothers who built and flew the first powered airplane in 1903. [TL540.W7F68 1972] 920 70-158689 ISBN 0-690-90700-1 3.75
1. Wright, Orville, 1871-1948—Juvenile literature. 2. Wright, Wilbur, 1867-1912—Juvenile literature. I. Title.

GARDNER, Jeanne (LeMonnier) 629.13'0924
Sky pioneers, the story of Wilbur and Orville Wright. Illustrated by Douglas Gorsline. [1st ed.] New York, Harcourt, Brace & World [1963] 62 p. illus. 22 cm. Bibliography: p. 61-62. [TL540.W7G3] 920 63-16033
1. Wright, Orville, 1874-1948 — Juvenile literature. 2. Wright, Wilbur, 1867-1942 — Juvenile literature. I. Title.

GLINES, Carroll V., 1920- 629.13'00922
The Wright brothers, pioneers of power flight, by Carroll V. Glines. New York, F. Watts [1968] 112 p. illus., port. 22 cm. (Immortals of science) Bibliography: p. 109. [TL540.W7G55] 68-10635
1. Wright, Orville, 1871-1948—Juvenile literature. 2. Wright, Wilbur, 1867-1912—Juvenile literature. I. Title.

GLINES, Carroll V., 1920- 629.13'0922 B
The Wright brothers: pioneers of power flight, by Carroll V. Glines. London, New York, Franklin Watts Ltd., 1968. [7], 112 p., 8 plates; illus., facsims. 23 cm. (Immortals of science) Bibliography: p. 109. A biography of the two brothers, unknown bicycle repairmen, who built and flew the first powered airplane in 1903. [TL540.W7G55 1968b] 920 70-859289 ISBN 0-85166-300-1 £1.25
1. Wright, Orville, 1871-1948—Juvenile literature. 2. Wright, Wilbur, 1867-1912—Juvenile literature. I. Title.

JOHNSON, Spencer. 629.13'092'2 B
The value of patience : the story of the Wright brothers / by Spencer Johnson ; illustrated by Steve Pileggi. 2d ed. La Jolla, Calif. : Value Communications, c1976. 62 p. : col. ill. ; 29 cm. (A ValueTale) First ed. published in 1975 under title: The ValueTale of the Wright brothers. Describes the patient efforts of the Wright brothers to build a flying machine. [TL540.W7J63 1976] 920 76-55022 ISBN 0-916392-08-2 : 4.95
1. Wright, Orville, 1871-1948—Juvenile literature. 2. Wright, Wilbur, 1867-1912—Juvenile literature. 3. Aeronautics—United States—Biography—Juvenile literature. 4. Patience—Juvenile literature. I. Pileggi, Steve. II. Title. BIP

KAUFMAN, Mervyn D. 920 (J)
The Wright brothers; kings of the air, by Mervyn D. Kaufman. Illustrated by Gray Morrow. Champaign, Ill., Garrard Pub. Co. [1964] 80 p. col. illus. 23 cm. (A Discovery book) [TL540.W7K3] 64-12629
1. Wright, Orville, 1871-1948—Juvenile literature. 2. Wright, Wilbur, 1867-1912—Juvenile literature. I. Title.

Wright, Patience.

SELLERS, Charles Coleman, 1903- 736'.93'0924 B
Patience Wright, American artist and spy in George III's London / by Charles Coleman Sellers. 1st ed. Middletown, Conn. : Wesleyan University Press, c1976. x, 281 p., [12] leaves of plates : ill. ; 24 cm. Includes bibliographical references and index. [NK9582.W74S44] 76-7193 ISBN 0-8195-5001-9 : 14.95
1. Wright, Patience. 2. Wax-modeling—United States. I. Title.

Wright, Richard Robert, 1855-1947.

HAYNES, Elizabeth (Ross). 923.273
The black boy of Atlanta. Boston, House of Edinboro [1952] 237 p. illus. 21 cm. [E185.97.W87H3] 52-7005
1. Wright, Richard Robert, 1855-1947. I. Title.

Wright, Richard, 1908-1960— Biography.

FABRE, Michel. 813'.5'2 B
The unfinished quest of Richard Wright. Translated from the French by Isabel Barzun. New York, Morrow, 1973. xx, 652 p. illus. 24 cm. Bibliography: p. 625-638. [PS3545.R815Z6513] 73-4227 ISBN 0-688-00163-7 15.00
1. Wright, Richard, 1908-1960—Biography. I. Title. BIP

WEBB, Constance. 813'.5'2 B
Richard Wright; a biography. New York, Putnam [1968] 443 p. illus. 24 cm. Bibliography: p. 423-429. [PS3545.R815Z9] 68-12115
1. Wright, Richard, 1908-1960—Biography.

WRIGHT, Richard 920.9
Black boy; a record of childhood and youth. [New York] New Lib. [1963, c.1937-1945] 285p. 18cm. (Signet bk. T2341) .75 pap.,
I. Title. BIP

*WRIGHT, Richard 928.1
Black boy: a record of childhood and youth [Reissue. New York] New Amer. Lib. [1964, c.1937-1945] 285p. 18cm. (Signet bk., T2341) .75 pap.,
I. Title.

WRIGHT, Richard, 1908- 928.1
Black boy: a record of childhood and youth. Illustrated by Ashley Bryan. Introductory note by Dorothy Canfield Fisher. Cleveland, World Pub. Co. [1950] 296p. illus. 20cm. (The Living library [L22]) [PS3545.R815Z5 1950] 50-11959
I. Title.

WRIGHT, Richard, 1909- 928.1
Black boy; a record of childhood and youth. Illustrated by Ashley Bryan. Introductory note by Dorothy Canfield Fisher. Cleveland, World Pub. Co. [1950] 298 p. illus. 20 cm. (The Living library [L22]) Full name: Richard Nathaniel Wright [PS3545.R815Z5] 50-11959
I. Title.

Wright, Silas, 1795-1847.

GARRATY, John Arthur, 1920- 973.4'0924 B
Silas Wright. New York, AMS Press [1970] 426 p. 23 cm. (Studies in history, economics, and public law, 552) Bibliography: p. 411-417. [E340.W95G37 1970] 73-120199
1. Wright, Silas, 1795-1847. I. Series: Columbia studies in the social sciences, 552 BIP

Wright, Wilbur, 1867-1912.

MILLS, Lois, 1892- 926.29
Three together; the story of the Wright brothers and their sister. Illustrated by William Moyers. New York, Follett Pub. Co. [1955] 160 p. illus. 25 cm. [TL540.W7M5] 55-7496
1. Wright, Orville, 1871-1948. 2. Wright, Wilbur, 1867-1912. 3. Wright, Katharine, 1874- I. Title.

RENSTROM, Arthur George, 1905- 629.13'092'2 B
Wilbur & Orville Wright: a chronology commemorating the hundredth anniversary of the birth of Orville Wright, August 19, 1871, by Arthur G. Renstrom, Science and Technology Division. Washington, Library of Congress, 1975. ix, 234 p. port. 23 cm. [TL540.W7R46] 74-11244 ISBN 0-8444-0131-5
1. Wright, Wilbur, 1867-1912. 2. Wright, Orville, 1871-1948. I. United States. Library of Congress. Science and Technology Division. II. Title.

Wright, Wilbur, 1867-1912—Juvenile literature.

GRAVES, Charles Parlin, 1911-1972. 629.13'092'2 B
The Wright brothers, by Charles P. Graves. Illustrated by Fermin Rocker. New York, Putnam [1973] 62 p. illus. 23 cm. (A See and read beginning to read biography) A biography of the mechanically-inclined Wright brothers, tracing their determined efforts to build the first self-propelled flying machine. [TL540.W7G7 1973] 920 72-81589 ISBN 0-399-60790-0 3.39 (lib. bdg.)
1. Wright, Wilbur, 1867-1912—Juvenile literature. 2. Wright, Orville, 1871-1948—Juvenile literature. I. Rocker, Fermin, illus. II. Title.

Wrigley, Philip Knight, 1894-

ANGLE, Paul McClelland, 1900- 796.357'092'4 B
Philip K. Wrigley : a memoir of a modest man / Paul M. Angle. Chicago : Rand McNally, 1975. 192 p. : ill. ; 24 cm. Includes index. [CT275.W78A53] 75-2339 ISBN 0-528-81015-4 : 8.95
1. Wrigley, Philip Knight, 1894-

Wu, Hsien, 1803-1950.

WU, Daisy (Yen) 926.1
Hsien Wu, 1893-1959; in loving memory. Boston, 1959, c1960. 75 p. illus. 22 cm. [QD22.W828] 60-32788
1. Wu, Hsien, 1803-1950. I. Title.

Wulf, Christa—Biography.

WULF, Christa. 823.914
Wir machen alles selbst : Geschichten aus d. Alltag e. Hausfrau / Christa Wulf ; [Textzeichnungen, Kurt Schmischke]. Hamburg : Agentur des Rauhen Hauses, 1975. 79 p. : ill. ; 20 cm. [PT2685.U42Z52] 75-508580 ISBN 3-7600-0120-3 : DM9.80
1. Wulf, Christa—Biography. I. Title.

Wurmbrand, Richard.

MOISE, Anutza. 230'.4'10924 B
A ransom for Wurmbrand. Edited by Myrtle Powley. Grand Rapids, Mich., Zondervan Pub. House [1972] 126 p. 18 cm. (Zondervan books) [BR1725.W88M6] 72-83869 0.95
1. Wurmbrand, Richard. 2. Wurmbrand, Sabina. I. Title.

Wyatt, John Riley,

WYATT, John Riley, 1919- 920
Journey through the springtime. [1st ed.] New York, Vantage Press [1957] 151 p. 21 cm. Autobiographical. [CT275.W88A3] 56-12920
I. Title.

Wycherley, William, 1640-1716.

CONNELY, Willard, 1888- 822'.4
Brawny Wycherley, first master in English modern comedy. Port Washington, N.Y., Kennikat Press [1969] x, 352 p. facsims., port. 22 cm. Reprint of the 1930 ed. Bibliography: p. 337-344. [PR3776.C6 1969] 71-93060
1. Wycherley, William, 1640?-1716. I. Title.

MCCARTHY, B. Eugene, 822'.4 B 1934-
William Wycherley : a biography / by B. Eugene McCarthy. Athens : Ohio University Press, c1979. p. cm. Includes bibliographical references. [PR3776.M3] 79-9210 ISBN 0-8214-0410-5 : 12.00
1. Wycherley, William, 1640-1716. 2. Dramatists, English Early modern, 1500-1700—Biography.

Wycliffe Bible Translators.

HEFLEY, James C. 266'.023'0924 B
Uncle Cam : the story of William Cameron Townsend, founder of the Wycliffe Bible Translators and the Summer Institute of Linguistics / James & Marti Hefley ; photo editor, Cornell Capa. Waco, Tex. : Word Books, [1974] 272 p. : ports. ; 23 cm. [BV2372.T68H43] 73-91556 6.95
1. Townsend, William Cameron, 1896- 2. Wycliffe Bible Translators. 3. Summer Institute of Linguistics. I. Hefley, Marti, joint author. II. Title.

Wycliffe, John, d. 1384.

LEWIS, John, 1675- 270.5'092'4 B 1747.
The history of the life and sufferings of the Reverend and learned John Wiclif, D.D. ... Together with a collection of papers and records relating to the said history. A new ed., corr. and enl. by the author. Oxford, Clarendon Press, 1820. [New York, AMS Press, 1973] xxxii, 389 p. port. 23 cm. [BX4905.L45 1973] 74-178543 ISBN 0-404-56625-1 21.00
1. Wycliffe, John, d. 1384. I. Title.

MCFARLANE, Kenneth 270.5'0924 Bruce.
John Wycliffe and the beginnings of English noncomformity [by] K. B. McFarlane [London] English Universities Pr. [1972, c.1952] xiii, 188 p. maps. 23 cm. ([Men & their times]) Bibliography: p. [174]-175 [BX4905.M3] A53 ISBN 0-340-16648-7
1. Wycliffe, John, d. 1384. 2. Reformation—Early movements. 3. Reformation—England. I. Title. II. Title: English nonconformity. III. Series.
Available from Verry, Mystic, Conn., for 5.00.

MCFARLANE, Kenneth Bruce. 922.342
John Wycliffe and the beginnings of English nonconformity. New York, Macmillan, 1953. 197 p. illus. 19 cm. (Teach yourself history library) [BX4905.M2] 53-4122
1. Wycliffe, John, d. 1384. BIP

SERGEANT, Lewis, 270.5'092'4 B d.1902.
John Wyclif, last of the schoolmen and first of the English reformers. Freeport, N.Y., Books for Libraries Press [1973] p. (Essay index reprint series) Reprint of the 1893 ed., issued in series: Heroes of the nations. [BX4905.S4 1973] 72-14162 ISBN 0-518-10022-7
1. Wycliffe, John, d. 1384. I. Series: Heroes of the nations.

VAUGHAN, Robert, 270.5'092'4 B 1795-1868.
The life and opinions of John de Wycliffe, D. D. Illustrated principally from his unpublished manuscripts; with a preliminary view of the papal system, and of the state of the Protestant doctrine in Europe, to the commencement of the fourteenth century. 2d ed. much improved. London, Holdsworth and Ball, 1831. [New York, AMS Press, 1973] 2 v. port. 23 cm. Includes bibliographical references. [BX4905.V36 1973] 71-178561 ISBN 0-404-56678-2
1. Wycliffe, John, d. 1384. I. Title. BIP

Wyer, Malcolm Glenn, 1877-1965.

GRIPTON, Judith. 027.7'0924
Dr. Malcolm Glenn Wyer; a biobibliography. Biographical material prepared by Judith Gripton; bibliography compiled by Lorraine Bangoura. Edited by Bohdan S. Wynar with the assistance of Kathleen Kirk. Denver, Graduate School of Librarianship, University of Denver, 1966. v, 93 p. 28 cm. (Studies in librarianship, no. 6) The biographical study was based on the author's thesis (M.A. in Librarianship), University of Denver, 1965. Bibliographical footnotes. [Z720.W9G7] 67-2685
1. Wyer, Malcolm Glenn, 1877-1965. I. Bangoura, Lorraine. II. Wynar, Bohdan S., ed. III. Title. IV. Series.

Wyeth, Andrew, 1917-

LOGSDON, Gene. 759.13 B
Wyeth people, a portrait of Andrew Wyeth as he is seen by his friends and neighbors. Illustrated with photos. by the author. Garden City, N.Y., Doubleday, 1971. 159 p. illus., ports. 22 cm. [ND237.W93L6] 75-147360 5.95
1. Wyeth, Andrew, 1917- I. Title.

WYETH, Andrew, 1917- 760'.0924
Andrew Wyeth [by] Richard Meryman. Boston, Houghton Mifflin, 1968. 174 p. illus. (part col.) 34 x 44 cm. [ND237.W93M4] 67-18254 75.00
I. Meryman, Richard, 1926-

Wyeth, Andrew, 1917- —Juvenile literature.

BAKER, Donna. 759.13 B
Andrew Wyeth / by Donna and Eugene Baker. Chicago : Childrens Press, [1976] p. cm. (Artists in America) Includes bibliographical references. Biography of painter Andrew Wyeth, who maintains his family's artistic tradition yet has developed his own unique style. [ND237.W93B34] 92 76-8440 ISBN 0-516-03681-5
1. Wyeth, Andrew, 1917- —Juvenile literature. I. Baker., Eugene H., joint author. II. Title.

Wyler, William, 1902-

MADSEN, Axel. 791.43'0233'0924 B
William Wyler: the authorized biography. New York, Crowell [1973] 456 p. illus. 24 cm. Bibliography: p. 439-441. [PN1998.A3W92] 73-10450 ISBN 0-690-00083-9 9.95
1. Wyler, William, 1902-

Wylie, Elinor Hoyt, 1885-1928—Biography.

HOYT, Nancy, 1902- 811'.5'2 B
Elinor Wylie : the portrait of an unknown lady / by Nancy Hoyt. Westport, Conn. : Greenwood Press, 1977, c1935. 203 p., [15] leaves of plates (1 fold.) : ill. ; 23 cm. Reprint of the 1st ed. published by Bobbs-Merrill, Indianapolis. [PS3545.Y45Z7 1977] 76-56441 ISBN 0-8371-9413-X lib. bdg. : 16.75
1. Wylie, Elinor Hoyt, 1885-1928—Biography. 2. Authors, American—20th century—Biography. BIP

Wylie, Janice.

LEFKOWITZ, 364.15'2'3'0922 Bernard.
The victims; the Wylie-Hoffert murder case and its strange aftermath, by Bernard Lefkowitz and Kenneth G. Gross. New York, Putnam [1969] 510 p. 22 cm. [HV6534.N5L38] 68-15511 6.95
1. Wylie, Janice. 2. Hoffert, Emily. 3. Murder—New York (City) I. Gross, Kenneth G., joint author. II. Title.

Wyman, Bruce, 1944-

WYMAN, Dorothy, 362.4'3'0926 B 1918-
Bruce / by Dorothy Wyman. Nashville : Southern Pub. Association, c1979. 126 p. ; 17 cm. [RC406.F7W95] 78-23504 ISBN 0-8127-0217-4 pbk. : 1.95
1. Wyman, Bruce, 1944- 2. Friedreich's ataxia—Biography. BIP

Wyndham, George, 1863-1913.

LESLIE, Shane, Sir 920.042 bart., 1885
Men were different; five studies in late Victorian biography. Freeport, N. Y., Books for Libraries Press [1967] 288 p. 22 cm. (Essay index reprint series) Reprint of the 1937 ed. Contents.CONTENTS.--Randolph Churchill, 1849-1895.--Augustus Hare, 1834-1903.--Arthur Dunn, 1860-1902.--George Wyndham, 1863-1913.--Wilfrid Blunt, 1840-1922. Includes bibliographies. [DA562.L46] 67-26754
1. Churchill, Lord Randolph Henry Spencer, 1849-1895. 2. Hare, Augustus John Cuthbert, 1834-1903. 3. Dunn, Arthur Tempest Blakiston, 1860-1902. 4. Wyndham, George, 1863-1913. 5. Blunt, Wilfrid Scawen, 1840-1922. I. Title. BIP

LESLIE, Shane, Sir, 920.042 bart., 1885-1971.
Men were different; five studies in late Victorian biography. Freeport, N.Y., Books for Libraries Press [1967] 288 p. 22 cm. (Essay index reprint series) Reprint of the 1937 ed. Contents.Contents.—Randolph Churchill, 1849-1895.—Augustus Hare, 1834-1903.—Arthur Dunn, 1860-1902.—George Wyndham, 1863-1913.—Wilfrid Blunt, 1840-1922. Includes bibliographies. [DA562.L46 1967] 67-26754
1. Churchill, Randolph Henry Spencer, Lord, 1849-1895. 2. Hare, Augustus John Cuthbert, 1834-1903. 3. Dunn, Arthur Tempest Blakiston, 1860-1902. 4. Wyndham, George, 1863-1913. 5. Blunt, Wilfrid Scawen, 1840-1922. I. Title.

Wynette, Tammy.

WYNETTE, Tammy. 784'.092'4 B
Stand by your man / Tammy Wynette, with Joan Dew. New York : Simon and Schuster, c1979. 349 p., [16] leaves of plates : ill. ; 25 cm. Includes index. [ML420.W9A3] 79-13765 10.95
1. Wynette, Tammy. 2. Country musicians—United States—Biography. I. Dew, Joan, joint author. II. Title. BIP

Wynn, Ed.

WYNN, Keenan, 1916- 927.92
Ed Wynn's son, by Keenan Wynn as told to James Brough. [1st ed.] Garden City, N.Y., Doubleday, 1959. 236 p. illus. 22 cm. Autobiographical. [PN2287.W9A3] 59-12663
1. Wynn, Ed. I. Brough, James, 1918- II. Title.

Wynn, Samuel, 1892-

WYNN, Allan. 663'.2'00924 B
The fortunes of Samuel Wynn; winemaker, humanist, Zionist; a biography. [Melbourne] Cassell Australia [1968] x, 236 p. illus., ports. 25 cm. [TP547.W9W9] 79-381586 4.50
1. Wynn, Samuel, 1892-

Wynne, David.

JONES, Richard Elfyn. 780'.92'4 B
David Wynne / Richard Elfyn Jones. Cardiff : University of Wales Press for the Welsh Arts Council, 1979. 73 p. : music ; 24 cm. (Composers of Wales ; 3) "List of works and recordings": p. 65-73. [ML410.W98J6] 79-310846 ISBN 0-7083-0714-0 : 5.00
1. Wynne, David. 2. Composers—Wales—Biography. I. Title. II. Series.
Dist. by Verry, Mystic CT 06355 BIP

Wyrtzen, Jack, 1913-

SWEETING, George, 1924- 922
The Jack Wyrtzen story; the personal story of the man, his message and his ministry. Grand Rapids, Zondervan Pub. House [1960] 151 p. illus. 21 cm. [BV3785.W9S8] 60-4404
1. Wyrtzen, Jack, 1913- 2. Word of life hour (Radio program) I. Title.

Wythe, George, 1726-1806.

BLACKBURN, Joyce. 347.73'2234 B
George Wythe of Williamsburg / Joyce Blackburn. 1st ed. New York : Harper & Row, [1975] xvi, 156 p. : ill. ; 21 cm. Includes index. Bibliography: p. 149-152. [KF363.W9B55] 75-9327 ISBN 0-06-060791-2 : 7.95
1. Wythe, George, 1726-1806. I. Title. BIP

CLARKIN, William. 347.99'24 B
Serene patriot: a life of George Wythe. Albany, Alan Publications, 1970. x, 235 p. port. 24 cm. Bibliography: p. [222]-230. [KF363.W9C5] 74-102990
1. Wythe, George, 1726-1806. I. Title.

Xantus, Janos, 1825-1894.

XANTUS, Janos, 917.94'9'044 1825-1894.
Travels in southern California / by John Xantus. Detroit : Wayne State University Press, 1976. p. cm. Translation of Utazas Kalifornia deli reszeiben. Includes index. Bibliography: p. [F867.X213] 76-23224 ISBN 0-8143-1570-4 : 13.95
1. Xantus, Janos, 1825-1894. 2. California, Southern—Description and travel. 3. Baja California—Description and travel. I. Title. BIP

X, Mr.

DOUBLE eagle : 327'.12'0924 B
the autobiography of a Polish spy who defected to the West / Mr. X, with Bruce E. Henderson and C. C. Cyr. Indianapolis : Bobbs-Merrill, c1979. x, 227 p. ; 24 cm. Includes index. [UB271.P72X153] 78-55651 ISBN 0-672-52526-7 : 10.00
1. X, Mr. 2. Spies—Poland—Biography. 3. Espionage. I. X, Mr. II. Henderson, Bruce E., 1929- III. Cyr, C. C.

Xainctonge, Anne de, 1567-1621.

BRESLIN, Mary Thomas. 922.244
Anne de Xainctonge, her life and spirituality. Kingston, N. Y., Society of St. Ursula of the Blessed Virgin, 1957. 273p. illus. 24cm. Includes bibliography. [BX4705.X3B7] 57-9169
1. Xainctonge, Anne de, 1567-1621. 2. Ursulines. I. Title.

Xenophon.

STRAUSS, Leo. 183'.2
Xenophon's Socrates. Ithaca [N.Y.] Cornell University Press [1972] 181 p. 21 cm. [PA4497.S8] 71-38122 ISBN 0-8014-0712-5 8.50
1. Xenophon. Memorabilia. 2. Xenophon. Apologia Socratis. 3. Xenophon. Symposium. 4. Socrates. I. Title. BIP

STRAUSS, Leo. 183'.2
Xenophon's Socrates. Ithaca [N.Y.] Cornell University Press [1972] 181 p. 21 cm. [PA4497.S8] 71-38122 ISBN 0-8014-0712-5 8.50
1. Xenophon. Memorabilia. 2. Xenophon. Apologia Socratis. 3. Xenophon. Symposium. 4. Socrates. I. Title. BIP

STRAUSS, Leo. 183'.2
Xenophon's Socrates. Ithaca [N.Y.] Cornell University Press [1972] 181 p. 21 cm. [PA4497.S8] 71-38122 ISBN 0-8014-0712-5 8.50
1. Xenophon. Memorabilia. 2. Xenophon. Apologia Socratis. 3. Xenophon. Symposium. 4. Socrates. I. Title. BIP

Yablonski, Joseph.

ARMBRISTER, Trevor. 364.1'523'0924 B
Act of vengeance : the true story behind the Yablonski murders / Trevor Armbrister. 1st ed. New York : Saturday Review Press, 1975. p. cm. [HD6509.Y3A74 1975] 75-14113 ISBN 0-8415-0375-3 : 12.95
1. Yablonski, Joseph. 2. United Mine Workers of America. 3. Murder—Pennsylvania. I. Title.

Yacht-building.

ROBINSON, William Wheeler, 1918- 623.82'02'0922 B
The great American yacht designers [by] Bill Robinson. [1st ed.] New York, Knopf; [distributed by Random House] 1974. 195, xii p. illus. 29 cm. Contents.Contents.—The lonely profession.—Nathanael Herreshoff.—Clinton H. Crane.—John Alden.—Philip L. Rhodes.—Bill Tripp.—Ray Hunt.—Bill Lapworth.—Olin Stephens. [VM139.R6 1974] 74-7746 ISBN 0-394-42721-1
1. Yacht-building. 2. Yachts and yachting—United States. I. Title. BIP

Yadin, Yigael, 1917-

MILLER, Shane. 92
Desert fighter; the story of General Yigael Yadin and the Dead Sea scrolls. Illustrated with drawings and maps by the author and photos. [1st ed.] New York, Hawthorn Books [1967] 178 p. illus., maps, ports. 22 cm. Bibliography: p. 171. Biography of General Yadin, who helped to establish and defend the new nation of Israel, and whose interest in archaeology led to important discoveries in the texts of the Dead Sea scrolls and to the uncovering of the Biblical city, Hazor. [DS126.6.Y3M5] AC 67
1. Yadin, Yigael, 1917- 2. Dead Sea scrolls. 3. Israel—Antiquities. I. Title.

Yale, Elihu, 1649-1721.

BINGHAM, Hiram, 1875- 942.06'0924 B
Elihu Yale, the American nabob of Queen Square. [Hamden, Conn.] Archon Books, 1968 [c1939] xiii, 362 p. illus., facsims., map, ports. 23 cm. Bibliography: p. 345-350. [LD6331.Y3B5 1968] 68-2829
1. Yale, Elihu, 1649-1721.

Yale University — Biog.

YALE University. 378.746'8
Men of Yale series. v. 1- [New Haven?] Yale University, 1962- v. illus. 24 cm. [LD6319.M4] 63-1067
1. Yale University — Biog. I. Title.

Yale University. Divinity School.

LATOURETTE, Kenneth Scott, 1884- 286/.0924
Beyond the ranges; an autobiography. Grand Rapids, Eerdmans [1967] 161p. 23 cm. [BR139.L3A3] (B) 67-13980 3.95
1. Yale University. Divinity School. I. Title.

Yale University. Sheffield Scientific School.

HAVEMEYER, Loomis, 1886- v. 12
My student days on Wall Street. [New Haven? Priv. print,] 1963] 82 p. 23 cm. The story of the author's three undergraduate years in Sheffield Scientific School, Yale University, and his five years in the Graduate School as a Ph.D. candidate (1907-1915) 67-32376
1. Yale University. Sheffield Scientific School. 2. Yale University — Students. I. Title.

KIRBY, Richard Shelton, 1874- ed. 609'.22 B
Inventors and engineers of Old New Haven; a series of six lectures given in 1938 under the auspices of the School of Engineering, Yale University. Freeport, N.Y., Books for Libraries Press [1969] 111 p. illus., ports. 23 cm. (Essay index reprint series.) (New Haven tercentenary publications) Reprint of the 1939 ed. Contents.Contents.—Eli Whitney, by J. W. Roe.—Early New Haven inventors, by J. W. Roe.—Early Yale inventors, by R. H. Gabriel.—Early Yale engineers, by R. S. Kirby.—The formative years of New Haven's public utilities, by H. H. Townshend.—The story of the founding of the Sheffield Scientific School, by R. H. Chittenden. [T39.K5 1969] 78-86765 ISBN 0-8369-1144-X
1. Yale University. Sheffield Scientific School. 2. Inventors—New Haven. 3. Engineers—New Haven. 4. Public utilities—New Haven. I. Yale University. School of Engineering. II. Title. III. Series.

Yamamoto, Isoroku, 1884-1943.

POTTER, John Deane. 940.5459520924
Yamamoto; the man who menaced America. New York, Viking Press [1965] xvii, 332 p. illus., map (on lining paper) ports. 22 cm. "First published in Great Britain as Admiral of the Pacific: the life of Yamamoto." Bibliography: p. [321]-323. [DS890.Y25P6 1965] 65-19274
1. Yamamoto, Isoroku, 1884-1943. 2. World War, 1939-1945—Naval operations, Japanese.

Yamasaki, Minoru, 1912-

YAMASAKI, Minoru, 1912- 720'.92'4 B
A life in architecture / by Minoru Yamasaki. 1st ed. New York : Weatherhill, 1979. p. cm. [NA737.Y3A2 1979] 79-11561 ISBN 0-8348-0136-1 : 50.00
1. Yamasaki, Minoru, 1912- 2. Architects—United States—Biography. I. Title. BIP

Yamashita, Tomoyuki, 1885-1946.

BARKER, A. J. 940.54'26'0924 B
Yamashita [by] A. J. Barker. [New York, Ballantine Books, 1973] 159 p. illus. 21 cm. (Ballantine's illustrated history of the violent century. War leader book, no. 24) [DS890.Y3B37] 74-156974 ISBN 0-345-23671-8 1.50 (pbk.)
1. Yamashita, Tomoyuki, 1885-1946.

REEL, Adolf Frank. 341'.69
The case of General Yamashita [by] A. Frank Reel. New York, Octagon Books, 1971 [c1949] vi, 323 p. 22 cm. Includes bibliographical references. [D804.J33Y36 1971] 71-154015 ISBN 0-374-96766-0
1. Yamashita, Tomoyuki, 1885-1946. 2. War crime trials—Manila, 1946. I. Title. BIP

Yamassee Indians—Biography.

TODD, Helen, 1908- 970'.004'97 B
Tomochichi Indian friend of the Georgia Colony / by Helen Todd. Atlanta : Cherokee Pub. Co., 1977. xiii, 182 p. : ill. ; 19 cm. Includes index. Bibliography: p. 167-176. [E99.Y22T657] 77-75268 ISBN 0-87797-040-8 : 7.95
1. Tomo-chi-chi, d. 1739. 2. Yamassee Indians—Biography. 3. Greek Indians—History. 4. Oglethorpe, James Edward, 1696-1785. 5. Georgia—History—Colonial period, ca. 1600-1775. I. Title.

Yandell, David Wendell, 1826-1898.

BAIRD, Nancy Disher. 610'.92'4 B
David Wendel Yandell : physician of old Louisville / Nancy Disher Baird. Lexington, Ky. : University Press of Kentucky, c1978. x, 115, [1] p., [2] leaves of plates: ill. ; 22 cm. (The Kentucky Bicentennial bookshelf) Bibliography: p. 115-[116] [R154.Y25B34] 77-80461 ISBN 0-8131-0245-6 : 4.95
1. Yandell, David Wendell, 1826-1898. 2. Louisville, Ky. University. School of Medicine—History. 3. Physicians—Kentucky—Louisville—Biography. 4. Louisville, Ky.—Biography. I. Title. II. Series. BIP

Yang, Wan-li, 1127-1206.

SCHMIDT, J. D., 1946- 895.114
Yang Wan-li / by J. D. Schmidt. Boston : Twayne, c1976. p. cm. (Twayne's world authors series ; TWAS 413 : China) Includes index. Bibliography: p. [PL2687.Y3Z87] 76-18839 ISBN 0-8057-6255-8 lib.bdg. : 8.95
1. Yang, Wan-li, 1127-1206. BIP

Yani.

POWELL, Virgil S. 301.44'93'0924 B
From the slave cabin of Yani / Virgil S. Powell. 1st ed. Hicksville, N.Y. : Exposition Press, c1977. 301 p. ; 22 cm. (An Exposition-banner book) [E444.Y3P68] 77-74872 ISBN 0-682-48781-3 : 11.50
1. Yani. 2. Slaves—South Carolina—Biography. 3. South Carolina—Biography. 4. Slavery in the United States—South Carolina. I. Title. BIP

Yankovic, Frank.

YANKOVIC, Frank. 786.9'7'0924 B
The Polka King : the life of Frankie Yankovic, as told to Robert Dolgan. Cleveland, Ohio : Dillon/Liederbach, c1977. 226 p. : ill. ; 23 cm. [ML419.Y36A3] 77-72539 ISBN 0-913228-23-0 : 8.95
1. Yankovic, Frank. 2. Accordonists—United States—Biography. I. Dolgan, Robert, joint author. II. Title.

Yaqui Indians.

MOISES, Rosalio, 1896-1969. 970.3
The tall candle; the personal chronicle of Yaqui Indian, by Rosalio Moises, Jane Holden Kelley, and William Curry Holden. Introd. by Jane Holden Kelley. Lincoln, University of Nebraska Press [1971] lviii, 251 p. illus., geneal. table, map. 24 cm. Bibliography: p. lvii-lviii. [E99.Y3M6] 71-100809 ISBN 0-8032-0747-6 7.50
1. Yaqui Indians. I. Kelley, Jane Holden, 1928- II. Holden, William Curry, 1896- III. Title.

Yaqui Indians—Women—Biography.

KELLEY, Jane Holden, 1928- 970'.004'97
Yaqui women : contemporary life histories / by Jane Holden Kelley. Lincoln : University of Nebraska Press, c1978. 265 p. : ill. ; 23 cm. Bibliography: p. 70. [E99.Y3K44] 77-14063 ISBN 0-8032-0912-6 : 12.50
1. Yaqui Indians—Women—Biography. 2. Indians of North America—Arizona—Women—Biography. 3. Yaqui Indians—Social life and customs. I. Title. BIP

Yastrzemski, Carl.

JACKSON, Robert B. 796.357
Let's go, Yaz; the story of Carl Yastrzemski, by Robert B. Jackson. New York, H. Z. Walck [1968] 54 p. illus., ports. 21 cm. Traces the career of the Red Sox's successor to Ted Williams, from his high school days and brief minor league experience, with emphasis on the 1967 season and World Series. [GV865.Y35J3] AC 68
1. Yastrzemski, Carl. I. Title.

Yastrzemski, Carl—Juvenile literature.

JACKSON, Robert B. 796.3576 (J)
Let's go, Yaz; the story of Carl Yastrzemski, by Robert B. Jackson. New York, H. Z. Walck [1968] 54 p. illus., ports. 21 cm. [GV865.Y35J3] 68-17106
1. Yastrzemski, Carl—Juvenile literature. I. Title.

Yates, Brock W.

YATES, Brock W. 796.7'2
Sunday driver, by Brock Yates. New York, Farrar, Straus and Giroux [1972] 257 p. illus. 22 cm. [GV1032.Y37A37 1972] 72-84773 ISBN 0-374-27183-6 6.95
I. Title. BIP

Yates, Hube—Anecdotes.

YATES, Hube. 979.1'05
From thunder to breakfast / by Hube Yates, with Gene K. Garrison. Rev. and enl. Flagstaff, Ariz. : Northland Press, c1978. xii, 187 p. : ill. ; 23 cm. Edition statement also appears as: Revised second

edition. [F811.6.Y37 1978] 79-104738 ISBN 0-87358-175-X : 10.50 ISBN 0-87358-178-4 pbk. : 7.50
1. Yates, Hube—Anecdotes. 2. Arizona—Social life and customs—Anecdotes, facetiae, satire, etc. 3. Arizona—Biography—Anecdotes, facetiae, satire, etc. I. Garrison, Gene K., joint author. II. Title. **BIP**

Yates, Richard,

YATES, Richard, 977.3'04'0924 B 1860-1936.
Serving the Republic: Richard Yates, Illinois Governor and Congressman, son of Richard Yates, Civil War Governor; an autobiography. Edited by John H. Krenkel. Danville, Ill., Interstate Printers & Publishers [1968] 268 p. illus., ports. 24 cm. Bibliography: p. 253-257. [E748.Y3A3] 67-29640
1. Krenkel, John Henry, 1906- ed. II. Title.

Yava, Albert, 1888-

YAVA, Albert, 1888- 970'.004'97 B
Big Falling Snow : a Tewa-Hopi Indian's life and times and the history and traditions of his people / by Albert Yava ; edited and annotated by Harold Courlander. New York : Crown Publishers, c1978. xiii, 178 p., [8] leaves of plates : ill. ; 24 cm. Includes index. Bibliography: p. 174. [E99.H7Y38 1978] 78-658 ISBN 0-517-53244-1 : 10.00
1. Yava, Albert, 1888- 2. Hopi Indians. 3. Tewa Indians. 4. Tewa Indians—Biography. 5. Hopi Indians—Biography. I. Courlander, Harold, 1908- II. Title.

Yeager, Charles E.

LUNDGREN, William R 926.2913
Across the high frontier; the story of test pilot, Major Charles E. Yeager, USAF. Foreword by J. H. Doolittle. New York, Morrow, 1955. 288p. illus. 23cm. [TL540.Y4L8] 55-10263
1. Yeager, Charles E. I. Title.

Yeardley, George, Sir 1587-1627.

TRUMAN, Nora (Miller) 923.273
George Yeardley, Governor of Virginia and organizer of the General Assembly in 1619. Richmond, Va., Garrett and Massie, [c.] 1959 192p. (bibl.) illus. 21cm. 59-13020 3.20
1. Yeardley, George, Sir 1587-1627. I. Title.

Yeats, John Butler, 1839-1922.

MURPHY, William 759.9415 B Michael, 1916-
Prodigal father : the life of John Butler Yeats, 1839-122 / William M. Murphy. Ithaca : Cornell University Press, 1978. 680 p. : ill. ; 25 cm. Includes index. Bibliography: p. [543]-547. [ND1329.Y43M86] 77-3122 ISBN 0-8014-1047-9 : 27.50
1. Yeats, John Butler, 1839-1922. 2. Portrait painters—Ireland—Biography. I. Title. **BIP**

Yeats, John Butler, 1839-1922—Biography.

ARCHIBALD, Douglas N. 821'.8 B
John Butler Yeats [by] Douglas N. Archibald. Lewisburg [Pa.] Bucknell University Press [1974] 103 p. 21 cm. (The Irish writers series) Bibliography: p. 100-103. [PR5899.Y6Z62] 71-125792 ISBN 0-8387-7759-7 4.50
1. Yeats, John Butler, 1839-1922—Biography. **BIP**

Yeats, William Butler, 1865-1939.

BARKER, Dudley. 942.082'0922 B
Prominent Edwardians. [1st American ed.] New York, Atheneum, 1969. 254 p. ports. 22 cm. Contents.Contents.—Fisher of Kilverstone.—An episode in the life of William Butler Yeats.—The Marquess of Lansdowne.—Mrs. Emmeline Pankhurst. Bibliography: p. 247-248. [DA568.A1B34 1969] 68-27658 6.50
1. Fisher, John Arbuthnot Fisher, baron, 1841-1920. 2. Yeats, William Butler, 1865-1939. 3. Lansdowne, Henry Charles Keith Petty-Fitzmaurice, 5th marquis of, 1845-1927. 4. Pankhurst, Emmeline (Goulden) 1858-1928. I. Title.

BLOOM, Harold. 821'.8
Yeats. London, New York, Oxford University Press, 1972. xii, 500 p. port. 21 cm. (A Galaxy book 378) Includes bibliographical references. [PR5907.B55 1972] 73-331117 ISBN 0-19-501603-3 £1.60 ($3.50 U.S.)
1. Yeats, William Butler, 1865-1939. **BIP**

DONOGHUE, Denis. 821'.8
William Butler Yeats. New York, Viking Press [1971] xiii, 160 p. 19 cm. (Modern masters, M13) Bibliography: p. [149]-152. [PR5907.D6] 70-146595 ISBN 0-670-76956-8 2.50
1. Yeats, William Butler, 1865-1939.

ELLMANN, Richard, 1918- 821'.8 B
Yeats : the man and the masks / by Richard Ellmann. New York : Norton, 1978, c1948. vi, 336 p. ; 20 cm. Includes bibliographical references and index. [PR5906.E4 1978] 78-2271 ISBN 0-393-00859-2 pbk. : 4.95
1. Yeats, William Butler, 1865-1939. 2. Poets, Irish—20th century—Biography. **BIP**

ELLMANN, Richard, 1918- 821'.8 B
Yeats, the man and the masks / Richard Ellmann ; with a new pref. New York : Norton, c1979. p. cm. Reprint of the 1949 ed. published by Macmillan, London. Includes bibliographical references and index. [PR5906.E4 1979] 79-18876 ISBN 0-393-00859-2 pbk. : 4.95
1. Yeats, William Butler, 1865-1939. 2. Poets, Irish—20th century—Biography. I. Title.

GIBBON, Monk 928.2
The masterpiece and the man; Yeats as I knew him. New York, Macmillan, 1959 [i.e. 1960] 226p. illus. 23cm. 60-795 4.50 bds.,
1. Yeats, William Butler, 1865-1939. I. Title.

GOGARTY, Oliver St. John, 928.2 1878-1957
William Butler Yeats: a memoir. Pref. by MylesDillon. Dublin, Dolmen Pr. [dist. New York, Oxford, 1964, c.]1963. 27p. port. 19cm. 64-2461 1.20 bds.,
1. Yeats, William Butler, 1865-1939. I. Title.

HONE, Joseph Maunsell, 928.2 1882-1959.
W. B. Yeats, 1865-1939. [2d ed.]W B Yeats eighteen sixty-five--nineteen thirty-nine New York, St. Martin's Press, 1962. 503 p. illus. 23 cm. Includes bibliography. [PR5906.H6 1962] 62-51057
1. Yeats, William Butler, 1865-1939.

HONE, Joseph Maunsell, 821'.8 B 1882-1959.
William Butler Yeats; the poet in contemporary Ireland. [Folcroft, Pa.] Folcroft Library Editions, 1973. 134 p. 24 cm. Reprint of the 1916 ed. published by Maunsel & Co., Dublin, in series: Irishmen of today. Includes bibliographical references. [PR5906.H62 1973] 73-21999 ISBN 0-8414-4803-5 (lib. bdg.)
1. Yeats, William Butler, 1865-1939. I. Series: Irishmen of today (London, Dublin, 1916-)

HONE, Joseph Maunsell, 821'.8 B 1882-1959.
William Butler Yeats : the poet in contemporary Ireland / by J. M. Hone. Norwood, Pa. : Norwood Editions, 1976. p. cm. Reprint of the 1916 ed. published by Maunsel, Dublin, in series: Irishmen of to-day. Includes bibliographical references. [PR5906.H62 1976] 76-16522 ISBN 0-8482-1035-2 lib. bdg. : 20.00
1. Yeats, William Butler, 1865-1939. I. Series: Irishmen of today (London, Dublin, 1916-) **BIP**

JEFFARES, Alexander Norman. 821
W. B. Yeats, man and poet, by A. Norman Jeffares. New York, Barnes & Noble [1966] ix, 365 p. illus., ports. 23 cm. Bibliography: p. 339-350. [PR5906.J42 1966] 66-31815
1. Yeats, William Butler, 1865-1939.

LYNCH, David, 1943- 821'.8 B
Yeats, the poetics of the self / David Lynch. Chicago : University of Chicago Press, 1979. ix, 240 p. ; 24 cm. Includes index. Bibliography: p. 229-234. [PR5906.L9] 78-13242 ISBN 0-226-49816-6 : 19.50
1. Yeats, William Butler, 1865-1939. 2. Authors, Irish—20th century—Biography. 3. Creation (Literary, artistic, etc.) 4. Narcissism. I. Title.

MACLIAMMHOIR, 821'.8 B Micheal, 1899-
W. B. Yeats and his world / Micheal Mac Liammoir and Eavan Boland. New York : Scribner, 1978, c1971. 144 p. : ill. ; 24 cm. Includes index. Bibliography: p. 130. [PR5906.M27 1978] 77-90492 ISBN 0-684-15573-7 : 10.95
1. Yeats, William Butler, 1865-1939. 2. Authors, Irish—20th century—Biography. I. Boland, Eavan, joint author. II. Title.

MOORE, Virginia, 1903- 928.2
The unicorn; William Butler Yeats' search for reality. New York, Macmillan, 1954. xix, 519p. port. 22cm. Bibliography: p. 476-488. [PR5906.M6] 54-9962
1. Yeats, William Butler, 1865-1939. I. Title. **BIP**

TINDALL, William York, 1903- 821
W. B. Yeats. New York, Columbia University Press, 1966. 48 p. 21 cm. (Columbia essays on modern writers, no. 15) Bibliography: p. 46-48. [PR5906.T5] 66-19551
1. Yeats, William Butler, 1865-1939. I. Title. II. Series.

URE, Peter 821.912
W. B. Yeats. New York, Grove [1964, c.1963] 129p. 19cm. (Evergreen pilot bks., EP27) Bibl. 64-10096 .95 pap.,
1. Yeats, William Butler, 1865-1939. I. Title.

USSHER, Arland. v. 12
Three great Irishmen; Shaw, Yeats, Joyce, with portraits by Augustus John. [New York] The New American Library [1957] 127 p. ports. 18 cm. (A Mentor book, MD 205)
1. Shaw, George Bernard, 1856-1950. 2. Yeats, William Butler, 1865-1939. 3. Joyce, James, 1882-1941. I. Title. **BIP**

YEATS, William Butler, 821'.8 B 1865-1939.
Ah, sweet dancer: W. B. Yeats, Margot Ruddock: a correspondence. Edited by Roger McHugh. [1st American ed.] New York, Macmillan [1971, c1970] 144 p. facsims., ports. 22 cm. Bibliography: p. 138-139. [PR5906.A66 1971] 70-134881
I. Ruddock, Margot, 1907- II. McHugh, Roger Joseph, ed. III. Title.

YEATS, William Butler, 928.2 1865-1939.
Autobiography: consisting of Reveries over childhood and youth. The trembling of the veil, and Dramatis personae. New York, Macmillan, 1953 [c1944] 344 p. illus. 22 cm. [PR5906] 53-12858
I. Title: Reveries over childhood and youth. II. Title: The trembling of the veil. III. Title: Dramatis personae.

YEATS, William Butler, 928.2 1865-1939
The autobiography of William Butler Yeats, consisting of Reveries over childhood and youth, The trembling of the veil, and Dramatis personae. New York, Collier [c.1916-1965] 404p. 18cm. (05559) [PR5906.A538] 1.95 pap.,
I. Title. II. Title: Reveries over childhood and youth. III. Title: The trembling of the veil. IV. Title: Dramatis personae.

YEATS, William Butler, 928.2 1865-1939.
Letters: edited by Allan Wade. New York, Macmillan, 1955 [c1954] 938p. ports., facsims. 24cm. Bibliographical footnotes. [PR5906.A63 1955] 55-732
I. Title.

YEATS, William Butler, 928.2 1865-1939.
Letters to Katharine Tynan, edited by Roger McHugh. New York, McMullen Books [1953] 190p. ports., facsim. 23cm. Bibliography: p. [185]-186. [PR5906.A67] 53-11146
I. McHugh, Roger Joseph, ed. II. Hinkson, Katharine (Tynan) 1861-1931. III. Title.

YEATS, William Butler, 821'.8 B 1865-1939.
Memoirs. Transcribed and edited by Denis Donoghue. [1st American ed.] New York, Macmillan [1973, c1972] 318 p. 22 cm. Consists of the 1st draft of the Autobiography written in 1915 and 1916, and the Journal written from 1908-1930. [PR5906.A552 1973] 72-11279 7.95
1. Yeats, William Bulter, 1865-1939. I. Yeats, William Butler, 1865-1939. Journal. 1973.

YEATS, William Butler, 1865- 821 1939.
Yeats and Patrick McCartan, a Fenian friendship: letters with a commentary by John Unterecker & an address on Yeats, the Fenian, by Patrick McCartan. [Dublin, Dolmen Press; U.S. distributors: Dufour Editions, Chester Springs, Pa., 1967] 335-443 p. 5 plates (incl. facsim., 3 ports.) 23 cm. (The Dolmen Press Yeats centenary papers MCMLXV, no. 10) [PR5906.A64 1967] 70-253760
1. Yeats, William Butler, 1865-1939. I. McCartan, Patrick, 1889-1963. II. Unterecker, John Eugene, 1922- III. Title. IV. Series: Yeats centenary papers, no. 10

Yeats, William Butler, 1865-1939—Biography.

MASEFIELD, John, 1878- 821'.8 B 1967.
Some memories of W. B. Yeats / by John Masefield. Folcroft, Pa. : Folcroft Library Editions, 1977. 35 p. ; 23 cm. Reprint of the 1940 ed. published by Macmillan, New York. [PR5906.M33 1977] 77-7607 ISBN 0-8414-6204-6 lib. bdg. : 10.00
1. Yeats, William Butler, 1865-1939—Biography. 2. Authors, Irish—19th century—Biography. I. Title. **BIP**

TUOHY, Frank, 1925- 821'.8 B
Yeats / Frank Tuohy. 1st American ed. New York : Macmillan, 1976. 232 p., [8] leaves of plates : ill. ; 26 cm. Includes index. Bibliography: p. 224-225. [PR5906.T8 1976] 76-12608 ISBN 0-02-620450-9 : 19.95
1. Yeats, William Butler, 1865-1939—Biography. 2. Authors, Irish—19th century—Biography. I. Title.

TUOHY, Frank, 1925- 821'.8
Yeats / [by] Frank Tuohy. London : Macmillan, 1976. 232 p., [16] p. of plates : ill. (some col.), facsims. (1 col.), ports. (some col.) ; 26 cm. Includes index. Bibliography: p. 224-225. [PR5906.T8 1976b] 77-355098 ISBN 0-333-18723-7 : £6.95
1. Yeats, William Butler, 1865-1939—Biography. 2. Authors, Irish—19th century—Biography.

W. B. Yeats : 821'.8 B
interviews and recollections / edited by E. H. Mikhail ; with a foreword by A. Norman Jeffares. New York : Barnes & Noble Books, 1977. p. cm. Includes indexes. Bibliography: v. 2, p. [PR5906.W2 1977] 75-41581 ISBN 0-06-494820-X(v.2) 19.75 ISBN 0-06-494820-X (v. 2) : 19.75
1. Yeats, William Butler, 1865-1939—Biography. 2. Authors, Irish—20th century—Biography. I. Yeats, William Butler, 1865-1939. II. Mikhail, E. H.

Yeats, William Butler, 1865-1939—Correspondence.

LETTERS to W. B. Yeats 821'.8 B
/ edited by Richard J. Finneran, George Mills Harper, William M. Murphy, with the assistance of Alan B. Himber. New York : Columbia University Press, 1977. 2 v. (xvii, 628 p.) ; 24 cm. Includes indexes. [PR5906.A63 1977] 77-5645 ISBN 0-231-04424-0 : 37.50
1. Yeats, William Butler, 1865-1939—Correspondence. 2. Poets, Irish—20th century—Correspondence. I. Yeats, William Butler, 1865-1939. II. Finneran, Richard J. III. Harper, George Mills. IV. Murphy, William Michael, 1916- BIP

YEATS, William Butler, 821'.8' B
1865-1939.
W. B. Yeats and T. Sturge Moore : their correspondence, 1901-1937 / edited by Ursula Bridge. Westport, Conn. : Greenwood Press, 1978, c1953. xix, 213 p., [2] leaves of plates : ill. ; 22 cm. Reprint of the ed. published by Oxford University Press, New York. Includes index. [PR5906.A65 1978] 78-6910 ISBN 0-313-20489-6 lib bdg : 18.25
1. Yeats, William Butler, 1865-1939—Correspondence. 2. Moore, Thomas Sturge, 1870-1944—Correspondence. 3. Poets, Irish—20th century—Correspondence. I. Moore, Thomas Sturge, 1870-1944. II. Bridge, Ursula. BIP

Yeats, William Butler, 1865-1939—Criticism and interpretation.

HARRIS, Daniel A., 1942- 821'.8
Yeats: Coole Park & Ballylee [by] Daniel A. Harris. Baltimore, Johns Hopkins University Press [1974] viii, 262 p. illus. 23 cm. Includes bibliographical references. [PR5907.H33] 74-5185 ISBN 0-8018-1576-2 10.00 (lib. bdg.)
1. Yeats, William Butler, 1865-1939—Criticism and interpretation. 2. Yeats, William Butler, 1865-1939 Homes and haunts. I. Title.

Yeats, William Butler, 1865-1939—Friends and associates.

ELLMANN, Richard, 1918- 821
Eminent domain; Yeats among Wilde, Joyce, Pound, Eliot and Auden. London, New York, Oxford University Press [1970, c1967] vii, 161 p. 21 cm. (A Galaxy book, 305) Includes bibliographical references. [PR5906.E38 1970] 71-462589 1.75
1. Yeats, William Butler, 1865-1939—Friends and associates. I. Title.

ELLMANN, Richard, 1918- 821
Eminent domain; Yeats among Wilde, Joyce, Pound, Eliot, and Auden. New York, Oxford University Press, 1967. vii, 159 p. 21 cm. Bibliographical references included in "Notes" (p. 127-150) [PR5906.E38] 67-25458
1. Yeats, William Butler, 1865-1939—Friends and associates. I. Title.

Yeats, William Butler, 1865-1939—Friends and associates—Addresses, essays, lectures.

FINNERAN, Richard J. 821'.8 B
The olympian & the leprechaun : W. B. Yeats and James Stephens / [by] Richard J. Finneran. Dublin : Dolmen Press ; Atlantic Highlands, N.J. : distributed by Humanities Press, 1978. 36 p. : 2 ports. ; 25 cm. (New Yeats papers ; 16) Includes bibliographical references. [PR5906.F5] 79-313109 ISBN 0-85105-338-6 pbk. : 7.50
1. Yeats, William Butler, 1865-1939—Friends and associates—Addresses, essays, lectures. 2. Stephens, James, 1882-1950—Friends and associates—Addresses, essays, lectures. 3. Authors, Irish—20th century—Biography—Addresses, essays, lectures. I. Title. II. Series.
Distributed by Humanities Press, Atlantic Highlands, NJ

Yeats, William Butler, 1865-1939—Homes and haunts—Ireland—Ballylee (Castle)

HANLEY, Mary. 821'.7 B
Thoor Ballylee : home of William Butler Yeats / [by] Mary Hanley & Liam Miller ; with a foreword by T. R. Henn. 2nd ed., revised. Dublin : Dolmen Press, 1977. 32 p. : ill., facsim., map, plans, ports. ; 25 cm. Distributed in the U.S.A. by Humanities Press, Atlantic Highlands, N.J. A development of a lecture delivered by M. Hanley to the Kiltartan Society, June 1961, rearranged with additional matter by L. Miller. [PR5906.H3 1977] 78-309339 ISBN 0-85105-300-9 : 3.25
1. Yeats, William Butler, 1865-1939—Homes and haunts—Ireland—Ballylee (Castle) 2. Authors, Irish—20th century—Biography. 3. Ballylee (Castle), Ireland. I. Miller, Liam, joint author. II. Title. BIP

Yeats, William Butler, 1865-1939—Juvenile literature.

SPIVAK, Gayatri 821'.8 B
Chakravorty.
Myself must I remake: the life and poetry of W. B. Yeats. New York, Crowell [1974] vii, 201 p. illus. 20 cm. Bibliography: p. 189-191. A biography of the Irish poet, dramatist, and essayist generally considered the most important poet in English of his time. [PR5906.S6 1974] 73-16343 ISBN 0-690-00114-2 4.50
1. Yeats, William Butler, 1865-1939—Juvenile literature. I. Title. BIP

Yeats, William Butler, 1865-1939—Supernatural element.

RAINE, Kathleen Jessie, 821'.8
1908-
Yeats, the tarot, and the Golden Dawn, by Kathleen Raine. [Dublin] Dolmen Press [1972] 60, [31] p. illus. 25 cm. (New Yeats papers, 2) Imprint covered by label: Distributed in the U.S.A. by Humanities Press, New York. Includes bibliographical references. [PR5908.O25R3] 73-166426 ISBN 0-85105-195-2 £2
1. Yeats, William Butler, 1865-1939—Supernatural element. 2. Hermetic Order of the Golden Dawn. 3. Tarot. I. Title. II. Series. BIP

Yeh, Ming-ch'en, 1807-1859.

WONG, J. Y. 951'.03'0924 B
Yeh Ming-ch'en : Viceroy of Liang Kuang 1852-8 / J. Y. Wong. Cambridge [Eng.] ; New York : Cambridge University Press, 1976. xviii, 260 p. : ill. ; 24 cm. (Cambridge studies in Chinese history, literature, and institutions) Includes index. Bibliography: p. [242]-253. [DS760.9.Y43W66] 75-18119 ISBN 0-521-21023-2 : 30.00
1. Yeh, Ming-ch'en, 1807-1859.

Yeh, Shih, 1150-1223.

LO, Winston Wan. 895.1'3'5
The life and thought of Yeh Shih / Winston Wan Lo. Gainesville : University Presses of Florida, c1974. 206 p. ; 24 cm. Based on the author's thesis, Harvard University, 1970. Includes index. Bibliography: p. [195]-201. [PL2687.Y42Z7] 73-92410 10.00
1. Yeh, Shih, 1150-1223. I. Title. BIP

Yellowstone National Park.

LANGFORD, Nathaniel 917.87'52'042
Pitt, 1832-1911.
The discovery of Yellowstone Park; journal of the Washburn Expedition to the Yellowstone and Firehole Rivers in the year 1870. Foreword by Aubrey L. Haines. Lincoln, University of Nebraska Press [1972] lxi, 125 p. illus. 22 cm. Reprint of the 1905 ed., which has title: Diary of the Washburn expedition to the Yellowstone and Firehole Rivers in the year 1870. [F722.L28 1972] 78-93106 ISBN 0-8032-0710-7 4.95
1. Yellowstone National Park. I. Title. BIP

Yen, Chih-t'ui, 531-591—Biography.

DIEN, Albert E. 895.1'1'2
Pei Ch'i shu 45 : biography of Yen Chih-t'ui / Albert E. Dien. Bern : Herbert Lang, 1976. viii, 184 p. ; 21 cm. (Wurzburger Sino-Japonica ; Bd. 6) [PL2668.Y4Z62] 76-487986 ISBN 3-261-01756-2 : 38.00F
1. Yen, Chih-t'ui, 531-591—Biography. 2. Authors, Chinese—Biography. I. Title. II. Series.

Yen, Hsi-shan, 1883-1960.

GILLIN, Donald G. 951.040924 B
Warlord: Yen Hsi-shan in Shansi Province, 1911-1949, by Donald G. Gillin. Princeton, N.J., Princeton University Press, 1967. xiv, 334 p. maps, ports. 22 cm. Bibliography: p. [299]-321. [DS778.Y4G6] 66-14308
1. Yen, Hsi-shan, 1883-1960. I. Title.

Yen, Hui-ch'ing, 1877-1950.

YEN, Hui-ch'ing, 951.04'092'4 B
1877-1950.
East-West kaleidoscope, 1877-1946 : an autobiography / by W. W. Yen. N.Y. : St. John's University Press, [1974] xvi, 302 p. : port. ; 22 cm. (Asia in the modern world series ; no. 14) [DS778.Y43A33] 74-20791 ISBN 0-87075-074-7 pbk. : 3.95
1. Yen, Hui-ch'ing, 1877-1950. I. Title. II. Series: Asia in the modern world ; no. 14.

Yerkes, Robert Mearns, 1876-1956—Congresses.

PROGRESS in ape research 599'.88
/ edited by Geoffrey H. Bourne. New York : Academic Press, 1977. xiii, 300 p. : ill. ; 24 cm. Papers presented at a conference to observe the centenary of the birth of Robert Mearns Yerkes, held at the Yerkes Primate Research Center, Emory University, Oct. 26-27, 1976. Includes bibliographies and index. [QL737.P96P76] 77-24746 ISBN 0-12-119350-0 : 16.00
1. Yerkes, Robert Mearns, 1876-1956—Congresses. 2. Apes—Congresses. 3. Zoologists—United States—Biography—Congresses. I. Bourne, Geoffrey Howard, 1909-

Yezierska, Anzia,

YEZIERSKA, Anzia, 1885- 928.1
Red ribbon on a white horse. [Autobiography] with an introd. by W. H. Auden. New York, Scribner, 1950. 220 p. 21 cm. [PS3547.E95Z53] 50-9574
I. Title.

Yin, Old Madam.

PRUITT, Ida. 951'.1704'0924 B
Old Madam Yin : a memoir of Peking life, 1926-1938 / Ida Pruitt. Stanford, Calif. : Stanford University Press, 1979. ix, 129 p. : port. ; 23 cm. [CT1828.Y47P78] 78-68782 ISBN 0-8047-1038-4 : 8.95
1. Yin, Old Madam. 2. Peking—Biography. 3. China—Social life and customs. 4. Women—China—Social conditions. I. Title. BIP

YMCA of Los Angeles.

WAGNER, Harold A. 267'.39794'93
As I lived it : an autobiographical history of the YMCA of Los Angeles, 1925-1966 / by Harold A. Wagner. Glendale, Calif. : A. H. Clark Co., 1979. 332 p. : ill. ; 25 cm. Includes index. [BV1050.L67W33] 79-50564 ISBN 0-87062-129-7 : 10.00
1. YMCA of Los Angeles. 2. Wagner, Harold A. 3. Young Men's Christian Associations—Biography. I. Title. BIP

Yoder, Sanford Calvin,

YODER, Sanford Calvin, 922.8773
Bp., 1879-
The days of my years. Scottdale, Pa., Herald Press [1959] 247 p. 21 cm. [BX8143.Y63A3] 59-11041
I. Title. BIP

Yogananda,

YOGANANDA, Paramhansa, 921.9
1893-1952.
Autobiography of a yogi, With a pref. by W. Y. Evans-Wentz. London, New York, Rider [1950] 403 p. plates, ports., map. 22 cm. [B133.Y63A3 1950] 58-18867
I. Title.

YOGANANDA, Paramhansa, 181'.45 B
1893-1952.
Autobiography of a Yogi. With a pref. by W. Y. Evans-Wentz. [10th ed.] Los Angeles, Self-Realization Fellowship, 1969 [c1946] xvi, 514 p. illus., map, ports. 22 cm. [BP605.S43Y6 1969b] 69-11377 5.00
I. Title.

YOGANANDA, Paramhanse, 181'.45 B
1893-1952.
Autobiography of a Yogi. With a pref. by W. Y. Evans-Wentz. [9th ed.] Los Angeles, Self-Realization Fellowship, 1968 [c1946] xvi, 514 p. illus., map, ports. 22 cm. [BP605.S43Y6 1968] 68-17564
I. Title. BIP

YOGANANDA, Paramhansa, 181'.45
1893-1952.
Autobiography of a Yogi. With a pref. by W. Y. Evans-Wentz. [11th ed.] Los Angeles, Self-Realization Fellowship, 1971 [c1946] xv, 516 p. illus., map. 23 cm. [BP605.S43Y6 1971] 78-151319 ISBN 0-87612-075-3 5.00
I. Title.

Yokoi, Shoichi, 1915—

ASAHI Shimbun Tokuha 940.54'82'52
Kishadan.
28 years in the Guam jungle; Sergeant Yokoi home from World War II, compiled by a special group of correspondents of the Asahi Shimbun Tokyo, San Francisco, Japan Publications [1972] vii, 135 p. illus. (part col.) 21 cm. Translation of Guamu ni ikita nijuhachinen. [D811.Y55A813] 72-186022 Y800 ($3.95 U.S.)
1. Yokoi, Shoichi, 1915- 2. World War, 1939-1945—Guam. I. Title.

Yokoyama, Talkan, 1868-

YOKOYAMA Taikan 759.952
(1868-) Text by Seiroku Noma English adaptation by Meredith Weatherby. [1st English ed.] Tokyo, Rutland, Vt., C. E. Tuttle Co. [1956] 1v. (unpaged) illus. (part col.) port. 18cm. (Kodansha library of Japanese art, no. 4) Title also in Japanese on t. p. Bibliography: [1] p. at end. [ND1059.Y6N6] 927.5 56-8489
1. Yokoyama, Talkan, 1868- I. Noma, Seiroku. II. Weatherby, Meredith, ed. and tr. III. Series.

Yonge, Charlotte Mary, 1823-1901.

COLERIDGE, Christabel 813'.3
Rose, 1843-1921.
Charlotte Mary Yonge, her life and letters. London, New York, Macmillan, 1903. Detroit, Gale Research Co., 1969. xiii, 391 p. illus., geneal. tables, ports. 22 cm. Bibliography: p. 355-368. [PR5913.C6 1969] 77-75961
1. Yonge, Charlotte Mary, 1823-1901. **BIP**

MARE, Margaret Laura. 823'.8 B
Victorian best-seller; the world of Charlotte M. Yonge, by Margaret Mare and Alicia C. Percival. Port Washington, N.Y., Kennikat Press [1970] 292 p. illus., facsims., ports. 22 cm. Reprint of the 1947 ed. [PR5913.M3 1970] 70-103202
1. Yonge, Charlotte Mary, 1823-1901. I. Percival, Alicia Constance, joint author. II. Title.

Yonge, James,

YONGE, James, 1647-1721. 926.1
The journal of James Yonge, 1647-1721, Plymouth surgeon. Edited by F. N. L. Poynter. Hamden, Conn., Archon Books, 1963. 247 p. illus. 22 cm. [R489.Y6A3 1963] 63-554

Yoni, 1946-1976.

HASTINGS, Max. 356'.166'0924 B
Yoni, hero of Entebbe / by Max Hastings. New York : Dial Press/J. Wade, c1979. 248 p., [4] leaves of plates : ill. ; 24 cm. Includes index. [U55.Y665H37 1979] 79-51479 ISBN 0-8037-4263-0 : 11.95
1. Yoni, 1946-1976. 2. Israel—Armed Forces—Biography. 3. Entebbe Airport Raid, 1976. I. Title.

Yoors, Jan.

YOORS, Jan. 940.54'85
Crossing. New York, Simon and Schuster [1971] 224 p. 25 cm. Autobiographical. [D810.G5Y66] 78-156165 ISBN 0-671-20988-4 6.95
1. Yoors, Jan. 2. World War, 1939-1945—Gipsies. 3. World War, 1939-1945—Personal narratives. I. Title. **BIP**

Yorgason, James, 1847-1917.

YORGASON, Blaine M., 289.3'3 B
1942
Tall timber : the struggles of James Yorgason, a Mormon polygamist / by Blaine M. Yorgason. [Rexburg, Idaho] : Ricks College Press, 1976. xx, 315 p. : ill. ; 29 cm. Includes index. Bibliography: p. 224-228. [BX8695.Y67Y67] 76-28588 25.00
1. Yorgason, James, 1847-1917. 2. Mormons and Mormonism—Biography. I. Title.

York, Alvin Cullum, 1887-1964.

WEDDLE, Ethel 940.4'34 B
Harshbarger.
Alvin C. York, young marksman, by Ethel H. Weddle. Illustrated by Nathan Goldstein. Indianapolis, Bobbs-Merrill [1967] 200 p. illus. 20 cm. (Childhood of famous Americans) Bibliography: p. 198. The life story of a Tennessee Mountain man and expert marksman who received a Medal of Honor for his capture of 132 German prisoners in World War I. Concentrates on his boyhood and youth. [PZ7.W4126Al] 92 AC 68
1. York, Alvin Cullum, 1887-1964. I. Goldstein, Nathan, illus. II. Title.

York, Alvin Cullum, 1887-1964—Juvenile fiction.

ANDREWS, Peter. 9404.34 B
Sergeant York: reluctant hero. Illustrated by Charles Brey. New York, Putnam [1969] 95 p. illus. 24 cm. (An American pioneer biography) After turning from brawling and drinking to religion, a Tennessee mountain boy then had to reconcile religious and patriotic convictions before going to fight in World War I where he captured an entire German machine gun batallion almost single-handedly and became one of the war's great heroes. [D570.9.Y7A65] 92 68-57757 3.29
1. York, Alvin Cullum, 1887-1964—Juvenile literature. I. Brey, Charles, illus. II. Title.

WEDDLE, Ethel Harshbarger. JUV
Alvin C. York, young marksman, by Ethel H. Weddle. Illustrated by Nathan Goldstein. Indianapolis. Bobbs [1967] 200p. illus. 20cm. (Childhood of famous Americans) Bibl. [PZ7.W4126A1] 92 67-26334 2.50
1. York, Alvin Cullum, 1887-1964—Juvenile fiction. I. Title.

York, Charlie, 1887-1962.

YORK, Charlie, 639'.22'0924 B
1887-1962.
Charlie York, Maine coast fisherman / by Harold B. Clifford. Camden, Maine : International Marine Pub. Co., 1974. ix, 155 p. : ill., maps (on lining papers) ; 24 cm. [SH20.Y67A33 1974] 74-81712 ISBN 0-87742-043-2 : 7.95
1. York, Charlie, 1887-1962. 2. Fisheries—Maine, Gulf of. 3. Fishermen—Maine—Correspondence, reminiscences, etc. I. Clifford, Harold Burton, 1893- II. Title.

York Co., Pa.—Biography.

GIBSON, John, ed. 929'.3748'41
A biographical history of York County, Pennsylvania / edited by John Gibson. Baltimore : Genealogical Pub. Co., 1975. 207 p., [7] leaves of plates : ill. ; 23 cm. "Originally published as part 2 of History of York County, Pennsylvania, edited by John Gibson, Chicago 1886." [F157.Y6G42 1975] 75-7834 ISBN 0-8063-0675-0 : 12.50
1. York Co., Pa.—Biography. I. Title. **BIP**

York, Edward Palmer, 1865-1928.

SAWYER, Philip, 1868-1950. 927.2
Edward Palmer York; personal reminiscences by his friend and partner, Philip Sawyer, and a biographical sketch by Royal Cortissoz. Stonington [Conn.] Priv. print., 1951. 68 p. port. 25 cm. "One hundred copies printed." [NA737.Y6S3] 51-27372
1. York, Edward Palmer, 1865-1928. I. Title.

York, Raymond.

YORK, Raymond. 282'.0924 B
Pentecost comes to Central Park. [New York] Herder and Herder [1969] 160 p. 22 cm. Autobiographical. [BX4705.Y56A3] 69-11391 4.95
1. Title.

York, Thomas Lee.

YORK, Thomas Lee. 248'.2'0924 B
And sleep in the woods : the story of one man's spiritual quest / Thomas York. 1st ed. Toronto : Doubleday Canada Ltd. ; Garden City, N.Y. : Doubleday, 1978. x, 221 p. ; 22 cm. [BV4935.Y67A32] 77-82775 ISBN 0-385-13236-0 : 7.95
1. York, Thomas Lee. 2. Converts—Canada—Biography. 3. Vietnamese Conflict, 1961-1975—Draft resisters—Arkansas. I. Title.

Yorkshire, Eng.—Biography.

COLERIDGE, Hartley, 920'.0427'2
1796-1849.
Lives of northern worthies. Edited by his brother. A new ed., with the corrections of the author, and the marginal observations of S. T. Coleridge. Freeport, N.Y., Books for Libraries Press [1973] p. (Essay index reprint series) Published in 1833 under title: Biographica borealis. Reprint of the 1852 ed. published by E. Moxon, London. Contents.Contents.—v. 1. Andrew Marvell. Dr. Richard Bentley. Thomas Lord Fairfax. James Earl of Derby.—v. 2. Lady Anne Clifford. Roger Ascham. John Fisher. Rev. William Mason. Sir Richard Arkwright.—v. 3. William Roscoe. Captain James Cook. William Congreve. Dr. John Fothergill. [DA670.Y6C68 1973] 73-4629 ISBN 0-518-10075-8
1. Yorkshire, Eng.—Biography. 2. Lancashire, Eng.—Biography. I. Title.

HESELTINE, George 920.042'74
Coulehan, 1895-
Great Yorkshiremen, by George C. Heseltine. Freeport, N.Y., Books for Libraries Press [1971] viii, 302 p. ports. 23 cm. (Essay index reprint series) Reprint of the 1932 ed. Contents.Contents.—A sailor (Captain James Cook, R.N.).—A poet (Andrew Marvell).—A plotter (Guy Fawkes).—A philanthropist (William Wilberforce).—A marvel (Blind Jack Metcalf).—A soldier (Thomas, third Lord Fairfax).—A hermit (Richard Rolle of Hampole).—A chemist (Dr. Joseph Priestley).—A reformer (Dr. John Wycliffe).—A scholar (Dr. Richard Bentley).—A bishop (John, Cardinal Fisher).—An ancient (Henry Jenkins) [CT785.Y6H4 1971] 71-142643 ISBN 0-8369-2054-6
1. Yorkshire, Eng.—Biography. I. Title. **BIP**

Yorty, Samuel William, 1909-

AINSWORTH, Edward 352.079494 (B)
Maddin, 1902-
Maverick mayor, a biography of Sam Yorty of Los Angeles, by Ed Ainsworth. [1st ed.] Garden City, N.Y., Doubledays, 1966. viii, 256 p. illus., ports. 22 cm. Bibliography: p. 254-256 [F869.L8Y63] 66-19531
1. Yorty, Samuel William, 1909- 2. Los Angelies—Pol. 7 govt. I. Title.

Yoseloff, Thomas, 1913-

YOSELOFF, Thomas, 977.7'03'0924 B
1913-
The time of my life / Thomas Yoseloff. South Brunswick : A. S. Barnes, c1976 p. cm. Autobiographical. [CT275.Y46A34] 75-5174 ISBN 0-498-01761-3 : 7.95
1. Yoseloff, Thomas, 1913- I. Title. **BIP**

Yoshida, Shigeru, 1878-1967.

YOSHIDA, Shigeru, 1878- 952.04
1967.
The Yoshida memoirs; the story of Japan in crisis. Translated by Kenichi Yoshida. Westport, Conn., Greenwood Press [1973, c1961] 305 p. 22 cm. Translation of Kaiso junen. [DS889.Y583 1973] 72-12336 ISBN 0-8371-6733-7 13.00
1. Yoshida, Shigeru, 1878-1967. 2. Japan—History Allied occupation, 1945-1952. **BIP**

Youmans, Edward Livingston, 1821-1887.

FISKE, John, 1842- 509'.2'4 B
1901.
Edward Livingston Youmans, interpreter of science for the people; a sketch of his life with selections from his published writings and extracts from his correspondence with Spencer, Huxley, Tyndall, and others. Freeport, N.Y., Books for Libraries Press [1972] vi, 597 p. illus. 22 cm. Reprint of the 1894 ed. "List of writings": p. 590-591. [Q143.Y6F5 1972] 72-4171 ISBN 0-8369-6879-4
1. Youmans, Edward Livingston, 1821-1887.

Young, Amy Ross.

YOUNG, Amy Ross. 301.42'8'0924
By death or divorce ... it hurts to lose / Amy Ross Young. Denver : Accent Books, c1976. 151 p. ; 21 cm. [HQ1058.5.U5Y68] 76-8737 ISBN 0-916406-32-6 pbk. : 2.95
1. Young, Amy Ross. 2. Widows—Colorado—Denver—Biography. 3. Divorcees—Colorado—Denver—Biography. I. Title. **BIP**

Young, Andrew J., 1932-

GARDNER, Carl, 341.23'3'0924 B
1931-
Andrew Young : a biography / by Carl Gardner. New York : Drake, [1978] p. cm. [E840.8.Y64G37] 77-88945 ISBN 0-8473-1700-5 : 9.95
1. Young, Andrew J., 1932- 2. United Church of Christ—Clergy—Biography. 3. United States. Congress. House—Biography. 4. Clergy—United States—Biography. 5. Legislators—United States—Biography. 6. Ambassadors—United States—Biography. **BIP**

SIMPSON, Janice 341.23'3'0924 B
Claire.
Andrew Young : a matter of choice / by Janice C. Simpson. St. Paul : EMC Corp., 1978. p. cm. (Headlines I) A biography of the black congressman who was appointed United States ambassador to the United Nations in 1977. [E840.8.Y64S55] 77-29229 ISBN 0-88436-472-0 lib. bdg. : 4.95. ISBN 0-88436-473-9 pbk. : 2.95
1. Young, Andrew J., 1932- 2. United States. Congress. House—Biography—Juvenile literature. 3. Civil rights workers—United States—Biography—Juvenile literature. 4. Ambassadors—United States—Biography—Juvenile literature. 5. Legislators—United States—Biography—Juvenile literature. I. Title. II. Series. **BIP**

Young, Andrew J., 1932- —Juvenile literature.

HASKINS, James, 973.92'092'4 B
1941-
Andrew Young, man with a mission / James Haskins. 1st ed. New York : Lothrop, Lee & Shepard Co., c1979. 192 p. : ill. ; 24 cm. Includes index. An account of the life of Andrew Young, including his activities as a clergyman, civil rights worker, legislator, and United States Ambassador to the United Nations. [E840.8.Y64H37] 79-1046 ISBN 0-688-41896-1 : 6.25 ISBN 0-688-51896-6 lib.bdg. : 6.00
1. Young, Andrew J., 1932- —Juvenile literature. 2. United States. Congress. House—Biography—Juvenile literature. 3. United Church of Christ—Clergy—Biography—Juvenile literature. 4. Ambassadors—United States—Biography—Juvenile literature. 5. Legislators—United States—Biography—Juvenile literature. 6. Clergy—United States—Biography—Juvenile literature.

Young, Ann Eliza (Webb) b.1844.

WALLACE, Irving 922.8373
The twenty-seventh wife. New York, New Amer. Lib. [1962, c.1961] 400p. 18cm. (Signet Bk. T2133) Bibl. .75 pap.,
1. Young, Ann Eliza (Webb) b.1844. 2. Mormons and Mormonism. 3. Polygamy. I. Title. **BIP**

Young, Arthur Henry, 1866-1943.

YOUNG, Arthur Henry, 741.5'973 B
1866-1943.
Art Young : his life and times / by Art Young ; edited by John Nicholas Beffel. Westport, Conn. : Hyperion Press, 1975, c1939. p. cm. Reprint of the ed. published by Sheridan House, New York. Includes index. [NC1429.Y57B43 1975] 75-352 ISBN 0-88355-255-8
1. Young, Arthur Henry, 1866-1943. **BIP**

YOUNG, Arthur Henry, 741.5'973 B
1866-1943.
Art Young : his life and times / by Art Young ; edited by John Nicholas Beffel. Westport, Conn. : Hyperion Press, 1975, c1939. p. cm. Reprint of the ed. published by Sheridan House, New York. Includes index. [NC1429.Y57B43 1975] 75-352 ISBN 0-88355-255-8 : 28.50
1. Young, Arthur Henry, 1866-1943.

Young, Arthur, 1741-1820.

GAZLEY, John Gerow, 1895- 081 S
The life of Arthur Young, 1741-1820 [by] John G. Gazley. Philadelphia, American Philosophical Society, 1973. xvi, 727 p. illus. 25 cm. (Memoirs of the American Philosophical Society, v. 97) Bibliography: p. 704-713. [Q11.P612 vol. 97] [S417.Y6] 630'.92'4 B 72-89402 ISBN 0-87169-097-7 10.00
1. Young, Arthur, 1741-1820. 2. Agriculture—Great Britain—History. I. Title. II. Series: American Philosophical Society, Philadelphia. Memoirs, v. 97. BIP

YOUNG, Arthur, 1741-1820 630/.924
The autobiography of Arthur Young. Ed. by M. Betham-Edwards. New York, Kelley, 1967. x, 480p. illus., facsims., port. 22cm. (Reprints of econ. classics) Reprint of the 1898 ed. [S417.Y6A3 1967] 67-29463 12.50
I. Edwards, Matilda Barbara Betham, 1836- 1919. ed. II. Title.

Young, Bernice Elizabeth.

YOUNG, Bernice Elizabeth. 796.357'092'4 B
The picture story of Frank Robinson / byB.E. Young ; illustrated with photos. New York : Pocket Books, 1977,c1975 77p. ; 18 cm. (An Archway Paperback) A brief biography of the baseball star who in 1974 became major league baseball's first black manager. [GV865.R59Y68] ISBN 0-671-29806-2 pbk. : 1.25
I. Title.
LC. card no. for Messner ed.:75-2236 BIP

Young, Brigham, 1801-1877.

BURT, Olive (Woolley) 1894- 922.8373
Brigham Young. New York, J. Messner [1956] 192p. 22cm. [BX8695.Y7B8] 56-10445
1. Young, Brigham, 1801-1877. I. Title.

BURT, Olive (Woolley) 1894- 922.8373
Brigham Young. New York, J. Messner [1956] 192p. 22cm. [BX8695.Y7B8] 56-10445
1. Young, Brigham, 1801-1877. I. Title.

BURT, Olive (Woolley) 1894- 289.3'0924 B
Brigham Young [by] Olive Burt. New York, J. Messner [1956] 192 p. 22 cm. Bibliography p. 188. A biography of the Mormon convert who later became the President of his church and led his people to the Great Salt Lake Valley to establish a large Mormon colony. [BX8695.Y7B8] 92 AC 68
1. Young, Brigham, 1801-1877. I. Title.

GATES, Susa (Young) 1856-1933. 289.3'0924 B
The life story of Brigham Young: Mormon leader, founder of Salt Lake City, and builder of an empire in the uncharted wastes of Western America, by Susa Young Gates, in collaboration with Leah D. Widtsoe. Freeport, N.Y., Books for Libraries Press [1971] 287 p. illus., map, ports. 24 cm. Reprint of the 1930 ed. [BX8695.Y7G3 1971] 74-164602 ISBN 0-8369-5886-1
1. Young, Brigham, 1801-1877. 2. Mormons and Mormonism. I. Widtsoe, Leah Eudora (Dunford) 1874- joint author. II. Title.

HIRSHSON, Stanley P., 1928- 289.3'0924 B
The lion of the Lord; a biography of Brigham Young [by] Stanley P. Hirshson. [1st ed.] New York, Knopf, 1969. xx, 391, xxvi p. illus. 25 cm. Bibliography: p. 377-391. [BX8695.Y7H55] 70-79334 8.95
1. Young, Brigham, 1801-1877. I. Title.

HUNTER, Milton Reed, 1902- 289.3'092'4 B
Brigham Young the colonizer, by Milton R. Hunter. [4th ed., rev.] Santa Barbara, Calif., Peregrine Smith, 1973. xviii, 399 p. illus. 23 cm. A revision of the author's thesis, University of California, Berkeley, 1935. Bibliography: p. [384]-389. [BX8695.Y7H8 1973] 73-85421 ISBN 0-87905-017-9 8.95
1. Young, Brigham, 1801-1877. 2. Mormons and Mormonism. I. Title.

SEMINAR on Brigham Young, Provo, Utah, 1962. v. 12
Seminar on Brigham Young, Provo, Utah, 1962. Truman G. Madsen, conference director. Provo, Utah, 1963. 100 p. 28 cm. Bibliographical footnotes. 67-70368
1. Young, Brigham, 1808-1887. I. Madsen, Truman G. II. Brigham Young University, Provo, Utah. III. Title.

SPENCER, Clarissa (Young) 1860- 922.8373
Brigham Young at home, by Clarissa Young Spencer with Mabel Harmer. Salt Lake City, Deseret Book Co., 1961 [e1940] 301 p. illus. 24 cm. [BX8695.Y7S58 1961] 61-3053
1. Young, Brigham, 1801-1877. 2. Mormons and Mormonism. I. Title.

STEWART, John J v. 12
Brigham Young and his wives, and the true story of plural marriage. Salt Lake City, Mercury Pub. Co. [c1961] 99, [14] p. illus. 20 cm. Includes bibliography. 65-60295
1. Young, Brigham, 1801-1877. I. Title.

WAIT, Mary (Van Sickle) 922.8373
Brigham Young in Cayuga County, 1813-1829. Ithaca, N. Y., DeWitt Historical Soc. of Tompkins County, 1964. 66p. 23cm. Bibl. 64-55148 price unreported
1. Young, Brigham, 1801-1877. 2. Cayuga Co., N.Y.—Hist. I. Title.

WERNER, Morris Robert, 1897- 289.3'092'4 B
Brigham Young / by M. R. Werner. Westport, Conn. : Hyperion Press, 1975, c1925. p. cm. Reprint of the ed. published by Harcourt, Brace, New York. Includes index. Bibliography: p. [BX8695.Y7W4 1975] 75-351 ISBN 0-88355-254-X : 26.50
1. Young, Brigham, 1801-1877. 2. Mormons and Mormonism. BIP

WEST, Ray Benedict, 1908- 289.309
Kingdom of the saints; the story of Brigham Young and the Mormons. New York, Viking Press, 1957. 389 p. illus. 22 cm. [BX8611.W4] 57-6437
1. Young, Brigham, 1801-1877. 2. Mormons and Mormonism — Hist. I. Title.

WEST, Ray Benedict, 1908- 289.309
Kingdom of the saints; the story of Brigham Young and the Mormons. New York, Viking Press, 1957. 389 p. illus. 22 cm. [BX8611.W4] 57-6437
1. Young, Brigham, 1801-1877. 2. Mormons and Mormonism—History. I. Title.

YOUNG, Brigham, 1801-1877. 289.3'092'4 B
Letters of Brigham Young to his sons / edited and introduced by Dean C. Jessee ; with a foreword by J. H. Adamson. Salt Lake City : Deseret Book Co., 1974. xliv, 375 p. : ports. ; 25 cm. (The Mormon heritage series ; v. 1) Includes bibliographical references and index. [BX8695.Y7A4 1974] 74-80041 ISBN 0-87747-522-9 : 9.95
1. Young, Brigham, 1801-1877. 2. Mormons and Mormonism—Biography. I. Jessee, Dean C., ed. II. Title. BIP

YOUNG, Brigham, 1801-1877. 289.3'0924
Manuscript history of Brigham Young, 1801-1844. Elden Jay Watson. [Salt Lake City, Smith Secretarial Service, c1968] xxxv, 274 p. illus., facsims., port. 26 cm. "From volumes 25 and 26 of Millennial Star." [BX8695.Y7A3] 75-15709
I. Watson, Elden Jay. II. Title.

YOUNG, Brigham, 1801-1877. 289.3'0924
Manuscript history of Brigham Young, 1846-1847. [Edited by] Elden J. Watson. [Salt Lake City, Utah, J. Watson, 1971] 672 p. illus. 23 cm. [BX8695.Y7A3 1971] 77-27431
I. Watson, Elden Jay. II. Title.

YOUNG, Seymour Dilworth, 1897- 922.8373
Here is Brigham; Brigham Young, the years to 1844, by S. Dilworth Young. Salt Lake City, Bookcraft [c1964] 370 p. illus., facsims., maps, ports. 24 cm. Bibliography: p. [6] [BX8695.Y7Y7] 65-1650
1. Young, Brigham, 1801-1877. I. Title.

Young, Brigham, 1801-1877—Biography.

NIBLEY, Preston. v. 12
Brigham Young, the man and his work. [5th ed.] Salt Lake City Deseret Book Co., 1965 [c1936] 553 p. illus., front., ports. 24 cm. 68-61479
1. Young, Brigham, 1801-1877—Biography. 2. Young, Brigham, 1801-1877—Teachings. I. Title.

Young, Brigham, 1801-1877—Juvenile literature.

NEELEY, Deta Petersen. 922.8373
A child's story of the prophet Brigham Young, by Deta Petersen Nelley and Nathan Glen Neeley. Salt Lake City, Deseret News Press, 1959. 171p. illus. 20cm. [BX8695.Y7N4] 60-457
1. Young, Brigham, 1801-1877—Juvenile literature. I. Neeley, Nathan Glen, joint author. II. Title.

Young, Charles, 1864-1922.

GREENE, Robert Ewell, 1931- 355.3'32'0924 B
The early life of Colonel Charles Young: 1864-1889, by Robert E. Greene. [Washington] Dept. of History, Howard University [1973] 18 p. 23 cm. Thesis (M.A.)—Howard University. Includes bibliographical references. [E185.97.Y63G73] 73-165467
1. Young, Charles, 1864-1922. I. Title.

Young, Denton True, 1867-1955.

ROMIG, Ralph H. 927.96357
Cy Young, baseball's legendary giant. Philadelphia, Dorrance [c.1964] 127p. illus., ports. 21cm. 64-25332 3.50
1. Young, Denton True, 1867-1955. I. Title.

ROMIG, Ralph H 927.96357
Cy Young, baseball's legendary giant [by] Ralph H. Romig. Philadelphia, Dorrance [1964] 127 p. illus., ports. 21 cm. [GV865.Y6R6] 64-25332
1. Young, Denton True, 1867-1955. I. Title.

Young, Denton True, 1867-1955—Juvenile literature.

EPSTEIN, Samuel, 1909- 796.357'092'2
More stories of baseball champions: in the Hall of Fame, by Sam and Beryl Epstein. Illustrated by Victor Mays. Champaign, Ill., Garrard Pub. Co. [1973] 96 p. illus. (part col.) 24 cm. Traces the careers of three baseball stars elected to the Baseball Hall of Fame in 1937. [GV865.A1E59] 920 73-2941 2.98
1. Young, Denton True, 1867-1955—Juvenile literature. 2. Lajoie, Napoleon, 1875-1959—Juvenile literature. 3. Speaker, Tris—Juvenile literature. 4. Cooperstown, N.Y. National Baseball Hall of Fame and Museum—Juvenile literature. 5. Baseball—Biography—Juvenile literature. I. Epstein, Beryl (Williams) 1910- joint author. II. Mays, Victor, 1927- illus. III. Title.

Young, Desmond

YOUNG, Desmond 923.543
Rommel, the desert fox. New ed. [New York] Berkley [1961, c.1950] 250p. maps (Berkley Medallion BG522) .50 pap.,
I. Title.

Young, Edward, 1683-1765.

BLISS, Isabel St. John, 1895- 821'.5 B
Edward Young. New York, Twayne Publishers [1969] 173 p. 22 cm. (Twayne's English authors series, 80) Bibliography: p. 160-167. [PR3783.B5] 68-28488
1. Young, Edward, 1683-1765.

SHELLEY, Henry Charles. 821'.5 B
The life and letters of Edward Young, by Henry C. Shelley. Boston, Little, Brown, 1914. St. Clair Shores, Mich., Scholarly Press, 1970. xi, 289 p. illus., ports. 22 cm. [PR3783.S5 1970] 70-131831 ISBN 0-403-00718-6
1. Young, Edward, 1683-1765. I. Title. BIP

YOUNG, Edward, 1683-1765. 821'.5 B
The correspondence of Edward Young, 1683-1765; edited by Henry Pettit Oxford, Clarendon Press, 1971. xl, 624, [4] p. 1 illus., facsim., ports. 23 cm. Includes bibliographical references. [PR3783.A44 1971] 72-179679 ISBN 0-19-812426-0 £10.00
I. Pettit, Henry, 1906- ed.

Young, Erma Thurston,

YOUNG, Erma Thurston, 1892- 920.7
Yesterday and today. Manchester, Me. [1953] 103p. illus. 21cm. 'A Dirigo edition.' Autobiographical. [CT275.Y57A3] 54-21224
I. Title.

Young, Ewing, d. 1841.

HOLMES, Kenneth L 978'.02
Ewing Young, master trapper, by Kenneth L. Holmes. [1st ed.] Portland, Or., Published by Binfords & Mort, for the Peter Binford Foundation [1967] vii, 180 p. illus., map (on lining papers), ports. 23 cm. Bibliography: p. 151-169. [F786.Y57H6] [917.8'04'20924 (B)] 67-19751
1. Young, Ewing, d. 1841. I. Title.

Young family.

WALLACE, Mildred (Young) 920.7
We three: papa's ladies. San Antonio, Naylor Co. [1957] 192 p. 22 cm. [CT275.W2527A3] 57-59432
1. Young family. I. Title.

Young, Francis Brett, 1884-1954.

YOUNG, Jessica (Hankinson) Brett 928.2
Francis Brett Young; a biography. Pref. by C. P. Snow. London, Heinemann [New York, Hillary House, 1966, c.1962] 360p. illus., ports., map. 23cm. [PR6047.O47Z9] 63-6384 6.00
1. Young, Francis Brett, 1884-1954. I. Title.

Young-Hunter, John,

YOUNG-HUNTER, John, 1874- 1955. 927.5
Reviewing the years. New York, Crown Publishers, [1963] 173 p. illus. 24 cm. Autobiographical. [ND497.Y6A2] 63-14861
I. Title.

Young, Jimmy, 1948- —Juvenile literature.

DOLAN, Edward F., 1924- 796.5'36924 B
Jimmy Young, heavyweight challenger / Edward F. Dolan, Jr., and Richard B. Lyttle. 1st ed. Garden City, N.Y. : Doubleday, c1979. 83 p., [8] leaves of plates : ill. ; 22 cm. Includes index. A biography of the young prizefighter who has already fought Ron Lyle, Muhammad Ali, and George Foreman, and hopes to become the heavyweight champion. [GV1132.Y66D64] 92 78-18560 ISBN 0-385-14097-5 : 5.95
1. Young, Jimmy, 1948- —Juvenile literature. 2. Boxers (Sports)—United States—Biography—Juvenile literature. I. Lyttle, Richard B., joint author. II. Title.

YOUNG, Jimmy. 791.44'7 B
J. Y.; the autobiography of Jimmy Young. London, New York, W. H. Allen, 1973. 176 p. illus. 22 cm. [PN1991.4.Y6A34] 73-177735 ISBN 0-491-01371-X £1.95
1. Young, Jimmy. I. Title.

Young, Neil.

DUFRECHOU, Carole. 784'.092'4 B
Neil Young / Carole Dufrechou. New York : Quick Fox, c1978. 126 p. : ill. ; 26 cm. Discography: p. 123-126. [ML420.Y75D8] 77-88754 ISBN 0-8256-3917-4 pbk. : 3.95
1. Young, Neil. 2. Rock musicians—Biography. BIP

Young, Owen D., 1874-

TARBELL, Ida Minerva, 1857-1944. 338.7'62'130924 B
Owen D. Young, a new type of industrial leader. Freeport, N.Y., Books for Libraries Press [1973] p. Reprint of the 1932 ed., published by Macmillan, New York. Bibliography: p. [E748.Y74T3 1973] 73-6511 ISBN 0-518-19069-2
1. Young, Owen D., 1874-

Young, Percy Marshall,

YOUNG, Percy Marshall, 1912- 780.924
Tchaikovsky [by] Percy M. Young; [illustrated by Richard Shirley Smith] London, Benn; New York, D. White, 1968. 76 p. illus., music, ports. 23 cm. (Masters of music) [ML410.C4Y7] 68-9037 15/- ($3.50)

Young, Perry Deane.

YOUNG, Perry Deane. 959.704'38
Two of the missing : a reminiscence of some friends in the war / by Perry Deane Young. New York : Coward, McCann & Geoghegan, [1975] 254 p. ; 22 cm. [DS559.5.Y68] 74-79685 ISBN 0-698-10602-4 : 8.95
1. Young, Perry Deane. 2. Vietnamese Conflict, 1961-1975—Personal narratives, American. 3. Vietnamese Conflict, 1961-1975—Journalists. I. Title.

Young, Pierce Manning Butler, 1836-1896.

HOLLAND, Lynwood Mathis, 1905- 923.273
Pierce M. B. Young; the Warwick of the South [by] Lynwood M. Holland. Athens, Univ. of Ga. Pr. [c.1964] viii, 259p. port. 25cm. Bibl. 64-17062 6.00
1. Young, Pierce Manning Butler, 1836-1896. I. Title.

Young, Robert R., 1897-1958.

BORKIN, Joseph. 332.6
Robert R. Young, the populist of Wall Street. [1st ed.] New York, Harper & Row [1969] xi, 236 p. illus., facsims., ports. 22 cm. Bibliographical footnotes. [HG172.Y67B6] 69-15300 6.95
1. Young, Robert R., 1897-1958. 2. Railroads—U.S.—Finance—Case studies.

Young, Rosamond McPherson—Biography—Addresses, essays, lectures.

YOUNG, Rosamond McPherson. 070.4'4
Queen of the north parlor : a light-hearted collection of columns / by Roz Young. 1st ed. Dayton, Ohio : Landfall Press, c1976. 198 p. ; 21 cm. [PS3575.O85Z52] 75-41655 ISBN 0-913428-23-X : 4.95
1. Young, Rosamond McPherson—Biography—Addresses, essays, lectures. I. Title.

Young, Sheila, 1950- Juvenile literature.

SOUCHERAY, Joe. 796.9'1'0924 B
Sheila Young / by Joe Soucheray ; illustrated by John Keely. Mankato, Minn. : Creative Education, 1977. 31 p. : col. ill. ; 25 cm. (Creative Education sports superstars) A brief biography of the speed skater whose victories in 1976 made her the first American to win three medals in Winter Olympics competition. [GV850.Y68S65] 92 76-48165 ISBN 0-87191-541-3 lib.bdg. : 6.60
1. Young, Sheila, 1950- Juvenile literature. 2. Skaters—Biography—Juvenile literature. I. Keely, John. II. Title. BIP

Young, Stark, 1881-1963—Correspondence.

YOUNG, Stark, 1881-1963. 818'.5'209 B
Stark Young : a life in the arts : letters, 1900-1962 / edited by John Pilkington. Baton Rouge : Louisiana State University Press, c1975. 2 v. (xxix, 1454 p.) ; 25 cm. Includes bibliographical references and index. [PS3547.O6Z53 1975] 73-90874 ISBN 0-8071-0100-1 : 50.00 set
1. Young, Stark, 1881-1963—Correspondence. I. Pilkington, John, 1918- II. Title: A life in the arts.

Young, Thomas, 1773-1829.

WOOD, Alexander, 1879-1950. 925
Thomas Young, natural philosopher, 1773-1829, by Alexander Wood, completed by Frank Oldham. With a memoir of Alexander Wood by Charles E. Raven. Cambridge [Eng.] University Press, 1954. 355p. illus. 23cm. [Q143.Y7W6] 54-2548
1. Young, Thomas, 1773-1829. I. Oldham, Frank. II. Title.

Young, Valton Joseph.

YOUNG, Valton Joseph. 923.273
The Speaker's agent. [1st ed.] New York, Vantage Press [1956] 83p. illus. 22cm. [E748.R24Y6] 55-11654
I. Rayburn. Sam Taliaferro, 1882- II. Title.

Young, Whitney M.—Juvenile literature.

BRUNER, Richard. 323.4'092'4 B
Whitney M. Young, Jr.; the story of a pragmatic humanist. New York, D. McKay Co. [1972] 73 p. 22 cm. A biography of the black social worker who used his many positions, including that of Executive Secretary of the National Urban League, to unite blacks and whites. [E185.97.Y635B7] 92 77-165080 4.25
1. Young, Whitney M.—Juvenile literature. I. Title.

MANN, Peggy. 323.4'092'4 B
Whitney Young, Jr., crusader for equality. Illustrated by Victor Mays. Champaign, Ill., Garrard Pub. Co. [1972] 96 p. illus. (part col.) 24 cm. (Americans all) A brief biography of the black crusader for civil rights who for many years was head of the National Urban League. [E185.97.Y635M36] 92 72-75423 ISBN 0-8116-4577-0 3.50
1. Young, Whitney M.—Juvenile literature. I. Mays, Victor, 1927- illus. II. Title.

Young, William Stewart, 1859-1937.

YOUNG, Nellie May. 917.94'94'0340924
William Stewart Young, 1859-1937: builder of California institutions; an intimate biography Glendale, Calif., A. H. Clark, 1967. 196 p. illus., ports. 25 cm. [F869.L8Y68] 67-18217
1. Young, William Stewart, 1859-1937. 2. Presbyterian Church in Los Angeles. 3. Los Angeles. Hollenbeck Home for the Aged. 4. Los Angeles. Occidental College. I. Title: Builder of California institutions.

Young Women's Christian Associations—Biog.

ROBINSON, Marion O. 267.50922
Eight women of the YWCA, by Marion O. Robinson. Pref. by Mary French Rockefeller. New York, Natl. Bd. of the Young Women's Christian Assn. of the U.S.A. 1966. 118p. ports. 25cm. Bibl. [BV1365.R6] 66-27675 3.50
1. Young Women's Christian Associations—Biog. I. Title.
Contents omitted. Publisher's address: 600 lexington Ave., New York, N.Y. 10022.

Youngblood, Rufus W.

YOUNGBLOOD, Rufus W. 364.4'6 B
20 years in the Secret Service; my life with five Presidents [by] Rufus W. Youngblood New York, Simon and Schuster, [1973] 256 p. 22 cm. Includes bibliographical references. [HV7911.Y68A3] 73-10049 7.95
1. Youngblood, Rufus W. I. Title.

Younge, Sammy, 1944-1966.

FORMAN, James, 1928- 322'.4 B
Sammy Younge, Jr.: the first black college student to die in the black liberation movement. New York, Grove Press [1968] 282 p. illus., map, ports. 21 cm. [E185.97.Y64F6] 68-58143 5.95
1. Younge, Sammy, 1944-1966. 2. Tuskegee, Ala.—Race question.

Younger, Cole, 1844-1916.

CROY, Homer, 1883- 923.4173
Last of the great outlaws; the story of Cole Younger. [1st ed.] New York, Duell, Sloan and Pearce [1956] 242 p. illus. 21 cm. Includes bibliography. [F594.Y76C7] 56-9583
1. Younger, Cole, 1844-1916. I. Title.

Youngman, Henny.

YOUNGMAN, Henny. 790.2'092'4 B
Take my wife ... please! My life and laughs by Henny Youngman as confessed to Carroll Carroll. New York, Putnam [1973] 255 p. illus. 22 cm. [PN2287.Y62A38] 72-87633 ISBN 0-399-11066-6 6.95
1. Youngman, Henny. I. Carroll, Carroll. II. Title.

Youth—Biography.

FREEDMAN, Russell. 920.'02
Teenagers who made history. Portraits by Arthur Shilstone. New York, Holiday House [1961] 272 p. illus. 22 cm. [CT105.F7] 61-16062
1 Youth—Biography. I. Title.

Youth—U.S.

SELIGSON, Tom. 322'.42
To be young in Babylon; a dramatic, personal account of teen-age radicals. New York, Paperback Library [1971] 237 p. 18 cm. [HQ769.S45] 72-32294 1.25
1. Youth—U.S. 2. Radicalism—U.S. 3. U.S.—Social conditions—1960- I. Title.

Youville, Marie Marguerite (Dufrost de La Jemmerais) d', 1701-1771.

FITTS, Mary Pauline. 271'.979 B
Hands to the needy; Blessed Marguerite d'Youville, apostle to the poor. Garden City, N.Y., Doubleday, 1971. xiii, 332 p. 21 cm. Bibliography: p. 323-326. [BX4705.Y6F5 1971] 79-182572
1. Youville, Marie Marguerite (Dufrost de La Jemmerais) d', 1701-1771. 2. Grey nuns. I. Title.

Yoxall, Harold Waldo.

YOXALL, Harold Waldo. 659.1'9'39100924
A fashion of life [by] H. W. Yoxall. [1st American ed.] New York, Taplinger Pub. Co. [1967] viii, 269 p. illus., ports. 23 cm. Autobiographical. [TT505.Y6A3 1967] 67-12613
1. Yoxall, Harold Waldo. 2. Vogue. I. Title.

Ysaye, Eugene, 1858-1931.

YSAYE, Antoine, 1894- 787'.1'0924 B
Ysaye, his life, work, and influence / by Antoine Ysaye and Bertram Ratcliffe ; with a preface by Yehudi Menuhin. St. Clair Shores, Mich. : Scholarly Press, 1978. xi, 250 p., [8] leaves of plates : ill. ; 22 cm. Reprint of the 1947 ed. published by W. Heinemann, London. Includes index. "The published works of Ysaye": p. 244-245. [ML418.Y8Y8 1978] 70-181298 ISBN 0-403-01723-8 : 25.00
1. Ysaye, Eugene, 1858-1931. 2. Violinists, violoncellists, etc.—Belgium—Biography. I. Ratcliffe, Bertram, joint author. II. Title.

Yu-wen, Hu, 513?-572.

LING-HU, Te-fen, 583-666. 923.251
Biography of Yu-wen Hu. [Chou shu, chuan 11] Translated and annotated by Albert E. Dien. Berkeley, University of California Press, 1962. 165 p. fold. map, geneal. table. 24 cm. (Chinese dynastic histories translations, no. 9) At head of title: Insitute of International Studies, University of California. Illustrative matter in pocket. Text in English and Chinese: notes in English. The translation was originally A. E. Dien's thesis (M.A.) Bibliography: p. 116-120. [DS741.C5] 63-62677
1. Yu-wen, Hu, 513?-572. I. Dien, Albert E. tr. II. Title. III. Series.

Yuan, Chen, 779-831.

PALANDRI, Angela C. Y. Jung, 1926- 895.1'1'3 B
Yuan Chen / by Angela C. Y. Jung Palandri. Boston : Twayne Publishers, c1977. 202 p. : port. ; 21 cm. (Twayne's world authors series ; TWAS 442 : China) Includes index. Bibliography: p. 191-196. [PL2677.Y8Z8 1977] 77-3453 ISBN 0-8057-6279-5 lib.bdg. : 9.95
1. Yuan, Chen, 779-831. 2. Authors, Chinese—Biography. BIP

Yuan, Shih-k'ai, 1859-1916.

CH'EN, Jerome, 1919- 951'.03'0924 B
Yuan Shih-k'ai. 2d ed. Stanford, Calif., Stanford University Press, 1972. 258 p. map. 23 cm. Bibliography: p. [235]-247. [DS777.2.C48 1972] 76-153815 8.95
1. Yuan, Shih-k'ai, 1859-1916.

CH'EN, Jerome, 1919- 923.151
Yuan Shih-k'ai, 1859-1916; Brutus assumes the purple. Stanford, Calif., Stanford University Press, 1961. 290 p. illus. 23 cm. [DS763.Y73C5] 61-14066
1. Yuan, Shih-k'ai, 1859-1916. I. Title: Brutus assumes the purple.

YOUNG, Ernest P. 951'.03'0924
The presidency of Yuan Shih-k'ai : liberalism and dictatorship in early republican China / Ernest P. Young. Ann Arbor : University of Michigan Press, c1977. viii, 347 p., [4] leaves of plates : ill. ; 24 cm. (Michigan studies on China) Includes index. Bibliography: p. 323-338. [DS777.2.Y68 1977] 75-31057 ISBN 0-472-08995-1 : 17.50
1. Yuan, Shih-k'ai, 1859-1916. 2. China—History—1912-1937. I. Title. II. Series. BIP

Yugoslavia—History.

PETER II King of Yugoslavia, 1923- 923.1497
A King's heritage. New York, Putnam [1954] 304 p. illus. 22 cm. [DR369.P4] 54-10501
1. Yugoslavia—History. I. Title.

Yugoslavian Americans—History—Juvenile literature.

IFKOVIC, Edward, 1943- 973'.04'9182
The Yugoslavs in America / Edward Ifkovic. Minneapolis : Lerner Publications Co., c1977. p. cm. (The In America series) Includes index. Surveys Yugoslav

immigration to the United States and discusses the contributions made by Yugoslavs to various areas of American life. [E184.Y7I35] 77-73742 ISBN 0-8225-0231-3 lib.bdg. : 4.95
1. Yugoslova Americans—History—Juvenile literature. 2. United States—Emigration and immigration—Juvenile literature. 3. Yugoslav Americans—Biography—Juvenile literature. I. Title. BIP

Yurka, Blanche.

YURKA, Blanche. 792'.028'0924 B
Bohemian girl; Blanche Yurka's theatrical life. Athens, Ohio University Press [1970] xii, 306 p. illus., ports. (1 col.) 25 cm. [PN2287.Y8A3] 79-81449 7.95
I. Title. BIP

Zacchaeus (Biblical character) — Juvenile literature.

ELLINGBOE, Betty. 209'.22
The little man from Jericho. Written and illustrated by Betty Ellingboe. Minneapolis, Augsburg Pub. House [1963] unpaged. illus. 22 x 28 cm. [BS2520.Z3E4] 63-16596
1. Zacchaeus (Biblical character) — Juvenile literature. I. Title.

Zachariah, Father, 1850-1936.

AN Early Soviet 281.9'092'4 B
saint : the life of Father Zachariah / translated [from the Russian MS.] by Jane Ellis ; and with an introduction by Sir John Lawrence. London : Mowbrays, 1976. xiv, 111 p. ; 23 cm. (Modern Russian spirituality series) (Keston books ; no. 6) [BX597.Z3E17] 77-361317 ISBN 0-264-66334-9 : £4.25
1. Zachariah, Father, 1850-1936. 2. Orthodox (Orthodox Eastern Church)—Biography. I. Ellis, Jane, 1951- II. Series: Modern Russian spirituality series. BIP

Zacharias, Ellis M.

WILHELM, Maria. 940.548'6'730924
The man who watched the rising sun; the story of Admiral Ellis M. Zacharias. New York, F. Watts [1967] 238 p. 22 cm. (Hidden heroes series) "A Giniger book." Bibliography: p. 223-224. [D810.S8Z39] 67-16024
1. Zacharias, Ellis M. 2. World War, 1939-1945—Secret service. I. Title.

WILHELM, Maria. 92
The man who watched the rising sun; the story of Admiral Ellis M. Zacharias. New York, F. Watts [1967] 238 p. 22 cm. (Hidden heroes series) "A Giniger book." Bibliography: p. 223-224. A biography of the U.S. Naval officer who gained a thorough knowledge of Japan and whose World War II broadcasts in Japanese were significant in breaking down Japanese morale. [D810.S8Z39] AC 67
1. Zacharias, Ellis M. 2. World War, 1939-1945—Secret Service. I. Title.

Zaharias, Mildred Babe (Didrikson) 1913-1956.

JOHNSON, William O., 796'.092'4 B
1931-
Whatta-gal! : The Babe Didrikson Story / William Oscar Johnson and Nancy P. Williamson. 1st ed. Boston : Little, Brown, c1977. 224 p., [8] leaves of plates : ill. ; 22 cm. "A Sports illustrated book." [GV697.Z26J63 1977] 76-56812 ISBN 0-316-46943-2 : 8.95
1. Zaharias, Babe Didrikson, 1911-1956. 2. Athletes—United States—Biography. I. Williamson, Nancy P., joint author. II. Title.

MILLER, Helen Markley 927.96352
Babe Didrikson Zaharias; striving to be a champion. Illus. by Richard Mlodock. Chicago, Britannica Bks., div. of Ency. Britannica [1963, c.1961] 191p. col. illus. 22cm. (Britannica bkshelf: Great lives for young Amers.) 2.36 lib. ed.,
1. Zaharias, Mildred Babe (Didrikson) 1913-1956. I. Title.

SCHOOR, Gene. 796.352'092'4 B
Babe Didrikson, the world's greatest woman athlete / Gene Schoor. 1st ed. Garden City, N.Y. : Doubleday, c1978. 185 p., [8] leaves of plates : ill. ; 22 cm. Includes index. A biography of the American considered by many to be the greatest woman athlete of all time. [GV697.Z26S33] 92 77-16944 ISBN 0-385-13031-7 : 6.95. ISBN 0-385-13032-5 lib.bdg. : 7.90
1. Zaharias, Babe Didrikson, 1911-1956—Juvenile literature. 2. Athletes—United States—Biography—Juvenile literature. I. Title.

ZAHARIAS, Mildred Babe 927.96352
(Didrikson) 1913-
This life I've led: an autobiography, [by] Babe Didrikson Zaharias, as told to Harry Paxton, with an introduction by Joanna Lee. [New York] Dell [1975 c1955] 217 p. 18 cm. [GV964Z3A3] 1.50 (pbk.)
I. Title.
L.C. card no. for original edition: 55-10217

Zaharoff, Basil, Sir 1850-1936.

MCCORMICK, Donald, 382.4562340924
1911-
Peddler of death; the life and time of Sir Basil Zaharoff. New York, Holt [c.1965] 255p. illus., facsim., ports. 22cm. Bibl. [D400.Z3M3] 65-22456 5.95
1. Zaharoff, Basil, Sir 1850-1936. I. Title.

Zahm, John Augustine, 1851-1921.

WEBER, Ralph Edward 922.273
Notre Dame's John Zahm; American Catholic apologist and educator. [Notre Dame, Ind.] Univ. of Notre Dame Press [c.] 1961. 214p. Front port. Bibl. 61-10175 5.00
1. Zahm, John Augustine, 1851-1921. I. Title.

WEBER, Ralph Edward. 922.273
Notre Dame's John Zahm; American Catholic apologist and educator. [Notre Dame, Ind.] University of Notre Dame Press, 1961. 214 p. illus. 22 cm. "Stems from ... [the author's] doctoral dissertation at the University of Notre Dame." Includes bibliography. [BX4705.Z25W4] 61-10175
1. Zahm, John Augustine, 1851-1921. I. Title.

Zalon, Jean.

ZALON, Jean. 618.1'9
I am whole again : the case for breast reconstruction after mastectomy / Jean Zalon with Jean Libman Block. 1st ed. New York : Random House, c1978. vii, 151 p., [4] leaves of plates : ill. ; 22 cm. [RD539.8.Z34] 77-90305 ISBN 0-394-42532-4 : 8.95
1. Zalon, Jean. 2. Mammaplasty—Biography. 3. Mastectomy—Psychological aspects. I. Block, Jean Libman, joint author. II. Title.

Zamenhof, Ludwik Lazar, 1859-1917.

BOULTON, Marjorie 924.0892
Zamenhof, creator of Esperanto. [dist. New York, Humanities Press, 1961, c.1960] 223p. illus. 60-4379 6.00
1. Zamenhof, Ludwik Lazar, 1859-1917. 2. Esperanto—Hist. I. Title.

Zamiatin, Evgenii Ivanovich, 1884-1937.

SHANE, Alex M. 891.7'3'42 B
The life and works of Evgenij Zamjatin [by] Alex M. Shane. Berkeley, University of California Press, 1968. 302 p. port. 23 cm. (Russian and East European studies) Bibliographical references included in "Notes" (p. [211]-228) "A bibliography of Zamjatiana": p. [232]-293. [PG3476.Z34Z84] 68-19643 7.95
1. Zamiatin, Evgenii Ivanovich, 1884-1937. I. Title. II. Series.

Zangwill, Israel, 1864-1926.

LEFTWICH, Joseph, 1892- 928.2
Israel Zangwill. New York, T. Yoseloff [1957] 306 p. illus. 24 cm. [PR5923.L4] 57-7644
1. Zangwill, Israel, 1864-1926.

Zanta, Leontine.

TEILHARD de Chardin, 271'.5'0924
Pierre.
Letters to Leontine Zanta. Introd. by Robert Garric and Henri de Lubac. Translated by Bernard Wall. [1st U.S. ed.] New York, Harper & Row [1969] 127 p. 21 cm. Bibliographical footnotes. [B2430.T374A493 1969b] 69-17020 4.00
1. Zanta, Leontine. I. Title.

Zanuck, Darryl Francis, 1902-

GUILD, Leo, 791.43'0232'0924 B
1911-
Zanuck, Hollywood's last tycoon. Los Angeles, Holloway House Pub. Co.; [distributed by All America Distributors Corp., 1970] 255 p. illus., ports. 18 cm. [PN1998.A3Z423] 74-18479 ISBN 0-87067-409-9 1.50
1. Zanuck, Darryl Francis, 1902-

GUSSOW, Mel. 791.43'0232'0924 B
Don't say yes until I finish talking; a biography of Darryl F. Zanuck. [1st ed.] Garden City, N.Y., Doubleday, 1971. xvi, 318 p. illus., ports. 22 cm. "Filmography": p. 285-301. [PN1998.A3Z424] 74-132509 7.95
1. Zanuck, Darryl Francis, 1902- I. Title. BIP

Zapata, Emiliano, 1879-1919.

PARKINSON, Roger. 972.08'1'0924 B
Zapata : a biography / by Roger Parkinson. New York : Stein and Day, [1975] p. cm. [F1234.Z327] 74-28202 ISBN 0-8128-1776-1 : 10.00
1. Zapata, Emiliano, 1879-1919. BIP

Zapata, Emiliano, 1879-1919— Juvenile literature.

SYME, Ronald, 972'.08'10924 B
1910-
Zapata, Mexican rebel. New York, Morrow [1971] 96 p. illus., map. 22 cm. Bibliography: p. 96. An easy-to-read biography of the Indian who became one of the primary leaders in the Mexican Revolution. [F1234.Z365] 92 79-128118 3.75
1. Zapata, Emiliano, 1879-1919—Juvenile literature. I. Title. BIP

Zarcillos Largos (Navaho Indian)

BRUGGE, David M. 970.3'05 S
Zarcillos Largos—courageous advocate of peace, by David M. Brugge. [Window Rock, Ariz.] Research Section, Navajo Parks and Recreation, The Navajo Tribe, 1970. 42 p. 22 cm. (Navajo historical publications. Biographical series, no. 2) Includes bibliographical references. [E99.N3N32 no. 2] 970.3 B 73-174266
1. Zarcillos Largos (Navaho Indian) I. Title. II. Series.

Zassenhaus, Hiltgunt.

ZASSENHAUS, 943.086'092'4
Hiltgunt.
Walls: resisting the Third Reich—one woman's story. Boston, Beacon Press [1974] 248 p. 21 cm. [DD256.3.Z34] 73-16443 7.95
1. Zassenhaus, Hiltgunt. 2. Anti-Nazi movement. I. Title.

Zehme, Friedrich Wilhelm Heinrich, 1840-1895.

ZEHME, Friedrich 917.3'04'840924
Wilhelm Heinrich, 1840-1895.
The diary of Friedrich Wilhelm Heinrich Zehme, May-July, 1882 : a perspective of America / by Friedrich Wilhelm Heinrich Zehme ; translation and preparation by David Dustin Clement and Associated Zehme family genealogy / prepared by David Dustin Clement. Eureka, Calif. : Clement, 1976. 98 p. : ill. ; 29 cm. Includes index. [E168.Z44 1976] 76-42065
1. Zehme, Friedrich Wilhelm Heinrich, 1840-1895. 2. Zehme family. 3. United States—Description and travel—1865-1900. I. Clement, David Dustin, 1946- II. Title. BIP

Zeisberger, David, 1721-1808.

DE SCHWEINITZ, 266'.46'0924 B
Edmund Alexander, 1825-1887.
The life and times of David Zeisberger. [New York] Arno Press [1971] 747 p. 23 cm. (The First America frontier) Reprint of the 1870 ed. "Published works of David Zeisberger": p. 687-692. [E99.M9Z44 1971] 70-146391 ISBN 0-405-02844-X
1. Zeisberger, David, 1721-1808. I. Title. II. Series.

DE SCHWEINITZ, 266'.46'0924 B
Edmund Alexander, 1825-1887.
The life and times of David Zeisberger, the Western pioneer and apostle of the Indians. Philadelphia, Lippincott, 1871. New York, Johnson Reprint Corp., 1971. xii, 747 p. 23 cm. (Series in American studies) Includes bibliographical references. [E98.M6Z4 1971] 71-155745
1. Zeisberger, David, 1721-1808. I. Title.

Zelle, Margaretha Geertruida, 1876-1917.

OSTROVSKY, 940.4'87'430924 B
Erika.
Eye of dawn : the rise and fall of Mata Hari / Erika Ostrovsky. New York : Macmillan, 1978. viii, 273 p., [4] leaves of plates : ill. ; 24 cm. Includes index. Bibliography: p. 261-266. [D639.S8Z466] 77-17391 ISBN 0-02-594030-9 : 8.95
1. Zelle, Margaretha Geertruida, 1876-1917. 2. Spies—Europe—Biography. 3. European War, 1914-1918—Secret service—Germany. I. Title.

OSTROVSKY, 940.4'87'430924 B
Erika.
Eye of dawn : the rise and fall of Mata Hari / Erika Ostrovsky. Boston : G. K. Hall, 1978. 493 p. ; 25 cm. "Published in large print." Bibliography: p. 485-493. [D639.S8Z466 1978b] 78-15920 ISBN 0-8161-6612-9 lib. bdg. : 12.95
1. Zelle, Margaretha Geertruide, 1876-1917. 2. Spies—Europe—Biography. 3. European War, 1914-1918—Secret service—Germany. 4. Large type books. I. Title. BIP

SINGER, Kurt D., 940.4'87'430924
1911-
Mata Hari [by] Kurt Singer. New York, Award Books [1967] 191 p. 18 cm. [D639.S8Z478] 67-9491
1. Zelle, Margaretha Geertruida, 1876-1917. I. Title.

WAAGENAAR, Sam. 940.487430924
Mata Hari. [1st U.S. ed.] New York, Appleton-Century [1965] xiii, 305 p. illus., facsims., ports. 21 cm. Published in London in 1964 under title: The murder of Mata Hari. [D639.S8Z485 1965] 65-21678
1. Zelle, Margaretha Geertruida, 1876-1917.

ZELLE, Margaretha 940.3
Geertruida, 1876-1917.
The diary of Mata Hari. Translated, and with a preface, by Mark Alexander. Introd. by Hilary E. Holt. North Hollywood, Calif. [Brandon House, 1967] xxi, 248 p. 17 cm. (A Brandon House book) [D639.S8Z413] 261.7'0941 67-66264
I. Title.

Zemach, Margot—Juvenile literature.

ZEMACH, Margot. 741'.092'4 B
Self protrait : Margot Zemach. Reading, Mass. : Addison-Wesley, c1978. p. cm. A well-known illustrator of children's books talks about herself, her life, and her work. [NC975.5.Z45A4 1978] 92 78-17140 ISBN 0-201-09096-1 : 7.95
1. Zemach, Margot—Juvenile literature. 2. Illustrators—United States—Biography—Juvenile literature. I. Title.

Zenobia, Queen of Palmyra.

VAUGHAN, Agnes Carr. 939'.4
Zenobia of Palmyra. [1st ed.] Garden City, N.Y., Doubleday, 1967. xiv, 250 p. plates. 25 cm. [DS99.P17V3] 67-10424
1. Zenobia, Queen of Palmyra. 2. Palmyra—History.

Zeppelin, Ferdinand Adolf August Heinrich, Graf von, 1838-1917.

NITSKE, W. 629.133'24'0924 B
Robert.
The Zeppelin story / W. Robert Nitske. South Brunswick, [N.J.] : A. S. Barnes, c1977. 191 p. : ill. ; 29 cm. Includes index. Bibliography: p. 185-187. [TL540.Z4N5 1977] 76-10875 ISBN 0-498-01805-9 : 20.00
1. Zeppelin, Ferdinand Adolf August Heinrich, Graf von, 1838-1917. 2. Airships—History. 3. Aeronautics—Germany—Biography. I. Title. BIP

Zerbe, Jerome, 1904-

GILL, Brendan, 1914- 779'.2'0924
Happy times. Text by Brendan Gill. Photos. by Jerome Zerbe. [1st ed.] New York, Harcourt Brace Jovanovich [1973] 288 p. illus. 32 cm. [TR140.Z47G54] 74-157920 ISBN 0-15-138480-0 25.00
1. Zerbe, Jerome, 1904- 2. United States—Biography—Portraits. I. Zerbe, Jerome, 1904- illus. II. Title.

Zervas, Annella, 1900-1926.

KRITZECK, James. 922.273
Ticket for eternity; a life of Sister Annella Zervas, O. S. B. Collegeville, Minn., St. John's Abbey Press, 1957. 107p. illus. 19cm. [BX4705.Z37K7] 57-49204
1. Zervas, Annella, 1900-1926. I. Title.

Zeta Phi Beta Sorority.

ZETA Phi Beta 378.1'98'560973
Sorority.
Biographical directory of Zeta women : a pictorial biographical directory / edited by a committee from Xi Zeta Chapter, St. Louis, Mo. ; foreword by Janice Gantt Kissner. 1st ed. [Washington : Zeta Phi Beta Sorority], 1976. xxxiii, 123 p. : ill. ; 30 cm. [LJ145.Z373Z47 1976] 76-376702
1. Zeta Phi Beta Sorority. I. Zeta Phi Beta Sorority. Xi Zeta Chapter, St. Louis. II. Title.

Zhabotinskii, Vladimir Evgen'evich, 1880-1940.

SCHECHTMAN, Joseph B., 922.96
1891-
Fighter and prophet; the Vladimir Jabotinsky story. New York, T.Yoseloff [c.1961] 643p. illus. Contents.[v.2,54 The last Years. Bibl. 55-11785 7.50
1. Zhabotinskii, Vladimir Evgen'evich, 1880-1940. I. Title.

SCHECHTMAN, Joseph B 1891- 922.96
Rebel and statesman; the Vladmir Jabotinsky story. New York, T. Yoseloff [c1956- v. illus. 24cm. [DS151.Z5S23] 55-11785
1. Zhabotinskil, Vladimir Evagen'evich, 1880-1940. I. Title.
Contents omitted.

SCHECHTMAN, Joseph B 923.25693
1891-
The Vladimir Jabotinsky story. New York, T. Yoseloff [c1956-61] 2v. illus. 24cm.
Contents.[1] Rebel and statesman: the early years.--2. Fighter and prophet: the last years. [DS151.Z5S23] 58-12145
1. Zhabotinskif, Vladimir Evgen'evich, 1880-1940. I. Title.

Zheliabov, Andrei Ivanovich, 1851-1881.

FOOTMAN, David, 947.08'092'4 B
1895-
The Alexander conspiracy; a life of A. I. Zhelyabov. LaSalle, Ill., Open Court [1974, c1968] xvi, 354 p. illus. 21 cm. Previous editions published in London under title: Red prelude. "A library press book." Bibliography: p. [343]-348. [DK219.6.Z5F6 1974] 74-57 ISBN 0-912050-47-0 8.95
1. Zheliabov, Andrei Ivanovich, 1851-1881. 2. Narodnaia volia (Political party) 3. Alexander II, Emperor of Russia, 1818-1881. I. Title.

FOOTMAN, David, 322.4'2'0924 B
1895-
Red prelude : the life of the Russian terrorist Zhelyabov / by David Footman. Westport, Conn. : Hyperion Press, [1979] p. cm. Reprint of the 1945 ed. published by Yale University Press, New Haven. Includes index. Bibliography: p. [DK219.6.Z5F6 1979] 78-14119 22.00
1. Zheliabov, Andrei Ivanovich, 1851-1881. 2. Narodnaia volia (Political party) 3. Alexander II, Emperor of Russia, 1818-1881. 4. Revolutionist—Russia—Biography. 5. Terrorism—Russia. I. Title. BIP

Zhukov, Georgii Konstantinovich, 1896-1974.

CHANEY, Otto 355.3'32'0924 B
Preston.
Zhukov. Foreword by Malcolm Mackintosh. [1st ed.] Norman, University of Oklahoma Press [1971] xxiii, 512 p. illus., col. maps, ports. 23 cm. Bibliography: p. 463-490. [DK268.Z52C48] 74-145505 ISBN 0 8061 0951 3
1. Zhukov, Georgii Konstantinovich, 1896- BIP

CHANEY, Otto 355.3'32'0924 B
Preston.
Zhukov, Marshal of the Soviet Union / Otto Preston Chaney, Jr. New York : Ballantine Books, 1974. 159 p. : ill. ; 22 cm. (War leader book ; no. 28) (Ballantine's illustrated history of the violent century) Includes bibliographical references. [DK268.Z52C49] 75-301295 ISBN 0-345-24018-9 pbk. : 2.00
1. Zhukov, Georgii Konstantinovich, 1896-1974.

ZHUKOV, Georgii 940.542'1'0924
Konstantinovich, 1896-
The memoirs of Marshal Zhukov. [1st American ed.] New York, Delacorte Press [1971] 703, viii p. illus., plans (part col.), ports. 23 cm. Translation of Vospominaniia i razmyshleniia (romanized form) "A Seymour Lawrence book." [DK268.Z52A313 1971] 73-120846 15.00
1. World War, 1939-1945—Russia. I. Title.

Zizka, Jan, 1360 (ca.)-1424.

HEYMANN, 943.7'02'0924 B
Frederick Gotthold, 1900-
John Zizka and the Hussite revolution, by Frederick G. Heymann. New York, Russell & Russell [1969, c1955] 521 p. illus., maps. 25 cm. Bibliography: p. 499-507. [DB208.H4 1969] 71-77671
1. Zizka, Jan, 1360 (ca.)-1424. I. Title. BIP

Ziegfeld, Florenz, 1869-1932.

CARTER, 792'.0232'0924 B
Randolph.
The world of Flo Ziegfeld. New York, Praeger [1974] 176 p. illus. 25 cm. Bibliography: p. 173-174. [PN2287.Z5C34] 74-3065
1. Ziegfeld, Florenz, 1869-1932. I. Title. BIP

HIGHAM, Charles, 792'.0232'0924
1931-
Ziegfeld. Chicago, Regnery [1972] 245 p. illus. 24 cm. [PN2287.Z5H5] 72-80928
1. Ziegfeld, Florenz, 1869-1932.

ZIEGFELD, Patricia, 1916- 927.92
The Ziegfelds' girl; confessions of an abnormally happy childhood. [1st ed.] Boston, Little, Brown [1964] 210 p. illus., ports. 22 cm. [PN2287.Z5Z5] 64-23289
1. Ziegfeld, Florenz, 1869-1932. I. Title.

Ziegfeld, Florenz, 1869-1932—Juvenile literature.

BADRIG, Robert 792'.0232'0924 B
H.
Florenz Ziegfeld, twentieth-century showman, by Robert H. Badrig. Charlotteville, N.Y., SamHar Press, 1972. 27 p. 22 cm. (Outstanding personalities, no. 37) Bibliography: p. 27. A biography of the early twentieth-century showman whose productions featuring some of the best performers of the day were renowned for beautiful girls and sumptuous sets. [PN2287.Z5B3] 92 73-165423
1. Ziegfeld, Florenz, 1869-1932—Juvenile literature. I. Title. BIP

PHILLIPS, Julien. 790.2'0922 B
Stars of the Ziegfeld Follies. Minneapolis, Lerner Publications Co. [1972] 79 p. illus. 22 cm. (A Pull ahead book) A brief biography of Ziegfeld, creator of the famous musical reviews, and profiles of some of the performers who starred in his productions. [PN2287.Z5P5] 920 72-165324 ISBN 0-8225-0464-2 3.95
1. Ziegfeld, Florenz, 1869-1932—Juvenile literature. 2. Actors—United States—Biography—Juvenile literature. I. Title. BIP

Ziemian, Joseph.

ZIEMIAN, Joseph. 940.53'1503'924
The cigarette sellers of Three Crosses Square / by Joseph Ziemian ; translated from the Polish by Janina David. Minneapolis : Lerner Publications Co., 1975, c1970. 166 p., [7] leaves of plates : ill. ; 23 cm. [DS135.P62W42 1975] 75-315465 ISBN 0-8225-0757-9 : 6.95
1. Ziemian, Joseph. 2. Jews in Warsaw—Persecutions. 3. World War, 1939-1945—Personal narratives, Jewish. I. Title. BIP

Zigas, Vincent.

ZIGAS, Vincent. 362.1'092'4 B
Auscultation of two worlds / Vincent Zigas. 1st ed. New York : Vantage Press, c1978. 229 p. ; 24 cm. Autobiographical. [RA424.5.Z53A3] 77-156055 ISBN 0-533-03118-4 : 9.50
1. Zigas, Vincent. 2. Health-officers—Papua New Guinea—Biography. 3. Ethnology—Papua New Guinea. I. Title. BIP

Zilberts, Zavel.

FLIEGEL, Hyman J. 784'.0924 B
Zavel Zilberts, his life and works, by Hyman J. Fliegel. [New York, Printed by Shulsinger] 1971. 159 p. illus. 24 cm. Bibliography: p. 76. [ML410.Z545F6] 70-30992
1. Zilberts, Zavel.

Zimmer, Norma.

†ZIMMER, Norma. 783.7'092'4 B
Norma / Norma Zimmer. Wheaton, Ill. : Tyndale House Publishers, 1976. xii, 368 p., [18] leaves of plates : ill. ; 22 cm. Autobiographical. [ML420.Z55A3] 76-42117 ISBN 0-8423-4716-X : 7.95
1. Zimmer, Norma. 2. Gospel musicians—United States—Biography. I. Title. BIP

Zinsser, Hans,

ZINSSER, Hans, 1878-1940 926.1
As I remember him; the biography of R. S. Boston, Atlantic-Little [c.1939-1964] 443p., 20cm. (39) 2.45 pap.,
I. Title.

ZINSSER, Hans, 1878-1940 926.1
As I remember him; the biography of R. S. Introd. by Edward Weeks [Gloucester, Mass., P. Smith, 1965, c.1939-1964] ix, 443p. 21cm. (Atlantic-Little bk. rebound) [R154.S15Z5] 4.50
I. Title.

Zinsser, William Knowlton.

LEVIN, Martin, ed. 818.082
Five boyhoods: Howard Lindsay, Harry Golden, Walt Kelly, William K. Zinsser and John Updike. [1st ed.] New York, Doubleday, 1962. 198 p. illus. 22 cm. [PS221.L4] 61-9527
1. Lindsay, Howard, 1889- 2. Golden, Harry Lewis, 1902- 3. Kelly, Walt. 4. Zinsser, William Knowlton. 5. Updike, John. I. Title.

Zinzendorf, Nicolaus Ludwig, Graf von, 1700-1760.

WEINLICK, John Rudolf. 922.443
Count Zinzendorf. Illus. drawn by Fred Bees. Nashville, Abingdon Press [1956] 240 p. illus. 24 cm. [DX8593.Z6W4] 56-5375
1. Zinzendorf, Nicolaus Ludwig, Graf von, 1700-1760. I. Title.

Zionism— Addresses, essays, lectures.

HERZL, Theodor, 1860-1904. 922.96
Theodor Herzl: a portrait for this age, edited and with an introd. by Ludwig Lewisohn. Pref. by David Ber. Gurion. [1st ed.] Cleveland, World Pub. Co. [1955] 345p. illus. 22cm. [DS149.H523] 55-6226
1. Zionism— Addresses, essays, lectures. I. Lewisohn, Ludwig, 1882- A portrait for this age. II. Title.
Contents omitted.

Zionism—Biog.

LIPSKY, Louis, 1876- 922.96
A gallery of Zionist profiles. New York, Farrar, Straus and Cudahy [1956] 226p. illus. 22cm. [DS151.A2L5] 56 13175
1. Zionism—Biog. I. Title.

Zionists

COHEN, Max, 1895- 956.94'001
They wanted a state. New York, House of Hillel Press [1970] xi, 209 p. 24 cm. [DS151.C63A3] 75-16355
1. Zionists—Correspondence, reminiscences, etc. I. Title.

GOLDMANN, 956.94'001'0924 B
Nachum, 1894-
The autobiography of Nahum Goldmann; sixty years of Jewish life. Translated by Helen Sebba. [1st ed.] New York, Holt, Rinehart and Winston [1969] viii, 358 p. illus., ports. 22 cm. [DS151.G585A313] 77-80340 7.95
1. Zionists—Correspondence, reminiscences, etc. I. Title.

ROSENBLUTH, Martin 923.25693
Michael, 1886-
Go forth and serve: early years and public life. New York, Herzl Press [c.]1961. 318p. 60-53237 5.00
1. Zionists—Correspondence, reminiscences, etc. I. Title.

WEISGAL, Meyer 956.94'001'0924 B
Wolfe, 1894-
Meyer Weisgal ... so far; an autobiography. [1st American ed.] New York, Random House [1972, c1971] 404 p. illus. 24 cm. [DS151.W37A3 1972] 70-171983 ISBN 0-394-47594-1 10.00
1. Zionists—Correspondence, reminiscences, etc. I. Title.

WEIZMANN, Chaim, 956.94'05'0924 B
Pres. Israel, 1874-1952.
Trial and error; the autobiography of Chaim Weizmann. Westport, Conn., Greenwood Press [1972, c1949] vii, 498 p. port., map. 24 cm. [DS125.3.W45A3 1972] 70-156215 ISBN 0-8371-6166-5
1. Zionists—Correspondence, reminiscences, etc. I. Title.

Zionists—Biography.

BEIN, Alex, 1903- 922.96
Theodore Herzl, a biography. Tr. from German by Maurice Samuel. Cleveland, World [c.1941, 1962] 557p. 21cm. (Meridian bks., JP30) Bibl. 62-20753 2.25 pap.,
I. Herzl, Theodor, 1860-1904. II. Title.

HOME at last 956.94'001'0922 B
/ edited by Azriel Eisenberg and Leah Ain-Globe. New York : Bloch Pub. Co., c1977. ii, 181 p. ; 22 cm. [DS151.A2H6] 920 75-4126 ISBN 0-8197-0386-9 : 7.95
1. Zionists—Biography. 2. Zionism—Literary collections. I. Eisenberg, Azriel Louis, 1903- II. Globe, Leah Ain. Contents omitted BIP

WINER, Gershon. 956.94'001'0922
The founding fathers of Israel. New York, Bloch Pub. Co. [1971] xi, 289 p. ports. 22 cm. Bibliography: p. [273]-280. [DS151.A2W5] 79-136422 ISBN 0-8197-0264-1 7.95
1. Zionists—Biography. I. Title. BIP

Zita, Saint, 1218-1278.

REGGIO, Edwin, 1933- 922.245
A saint in the kitchen; a story of Saint Zita. Illus. by Mary Agnes Majewski. Notre Dame, Ind., Dukarie Press [1955] 96p. illus. 24cm. [BX4700.Z5R4] 55-336914
1. Zita, Saint, 1218-1278. I. Title.

Zitkala-Sa, 1976-1938.

ZITKALA-SA, 1876-1938. 813'.5'2
American Indian stories / Gertrude (Zitkala-Sa) Bonnin. Glorieta, N.M. : Rio Grande Press, [1976] p. cm. (A Rio Grande classic) Reprint of the 1921 ed., published by Hayworth Pub. House, WAshington; with a new pref. Contents.Contents.—Impressions of an Indian childhood.—The school days of an Indian girl.—An Indian teacher among Indians.—Why I am a pagan.—The soft-hearted Sioux.—The trial path.—A Warrior's daughter.—A dream of her grandfather.—The widespread enigma of Blue-Star Woman.—America's Indian problem. [E99.Y25Z57 1976] 76-47687 ISBN 0-87380-116-4 lib.bdg. : 8.00
1. Zitkala-Sa, 1976-1938. 2. Yankton Indians—Biography. 3. Indians of North America—Social conditions. I. Title.

Zola, Emile, 1840-1902.

HEMMINGS, Frederick William 928.4
John.
Emile Zola. Oxford, Clarendon Press, 1953. 308p. 23cm. Bibliography: p. [292]-303. [PQ2528.H4] 53-2535
1. Zola, Emile, 1840-1902. I. Title. BIP

HEMMINGS, Frederick William 843.8
John.
Emile Zola. 2nd ed. Oxford [Eng.] Clarendon Pr. [New York] Oxford 1966[c.1953] [7], 330p. 22cm. Bibl. [PQ2528.H4 1966] 66-72002 8.80
1. Zola, Emile, 1840-1902. I. Title.

HEMMINGS, Frederick William 843.8
John.
Emile Zola [by] F. W. J. Hemmings. 2nd ed. Oxford, Clarendon P. 1966. [7], 330 p. 22 1/2 cm. 55/- Bibliography: p. [307]-324. [PQ2528.H4 1966] 66-72002
1. Zola, Emile, 1840-1902. I. Title.

KING, Graham, 1930- 843'.8 B
Garden of Zola : Emile Zola and his novels for English readers / Graham King. New York : Barnes & Noble Books, 1978. xxiv, 432 p., [8] leaves of plates : ill. ; 25 cm. Includes index. Bibliography: p. 424-426. [PQ2528.K5 1978] 78-107938 ISBN 0-06-493711-9 : 25.00
1. Zola, Emile, 1840-1902. 2. Novelists, French—19th century—Biography. I. Title. BIP

RICHARDSON, Joanna. 843'.8
Zola / Joanna Richardson. New York : St. Martin's Press, 1978. xiii, 283 p., [4] leaves of plates : ill. ; 23 cm. Includes index. Bibliography: p. [254]-276. [PQ2528.R5 1978b] 78-19433 ISBN 0-312-89902-5 : 14.95
1. Zola, Emile, 1840-1902. 2. Novelists, French—19th century—Biography.

VIZETELLY, Ernest 843'.8 B
Alfred, 1853-1922.
Emile Zola, novelist and reformer; an account of his life & work. Freeport, N.Y., Books for Libraries Press [1971] x, 560 p. illus., facsim., ports. 23 cm. Reprint of the 1904 ed. Includes bibliographical references. [PQ2528.V6 1971] 79-148902 ISBN 0-8369-5665-6
1. Zola, Emile, 1840-1902.

ZOLA, Emile, 1840-1902. 928.4
Zola [edited by] Marc Bernard. Translated [from the French] by Jean M. Leblon. New York, Grove Press [1960] 189p. illus. 18cm. (Evergreen profile book 16) Bibls.: p.183-189. 60-7122 1.35 pap.,
1. Zola, Emile, 1840-1902. I. Bernard, Marc, 1900- ed. II. Title.

Zola, Emile, 1840-1902—Biography.

HEMMINGS, Frederick 843'.8
William John.
The life and times of Emile Zola / F. W. J. Hemmings. New York : Scribner, c1977. 192 p. : ill. ; 25 cm. Includes bibliographical references and index. [PQ2528.H44 1977b] 77-73899 ISBN 0-684-15227-4 : 10.00.
1. Zola, Emile, 1840-1902—Biography. 2. Authors, French—19th century—Biography. I. Title. BIP

ZOLA, Emile, 1840-1902. 843'.8 B
Zola / [edited by] Marc Bernard ; translated by Jean M. Leblon. Westport, Conn. : Greenwood Press, 1977. p. cm. Translation of Zola par lui-meme. Reprint of the 1960 ed. published by Grove Press, New York, which was issued as no. 16 of Evergreen profile book. Bibliography: p. [PQ2493.L4 1972] 77-10959 ISBN 0-8371-9820-8 lib.bdg. : 16.75
1. Zola, Emile, 1840-1902—Biography. 2. Authors, French—19th century—Biography. BIP

Zolotow, Maurice,

ZOLOTOW, Maurice, 1913- 927.92
Marilyn Monroe. New York, Bantam Bks. [1961, c.1960] xxi, 338p. illus. (S2282) .75 pap.,
I. Title.

Zoological gardens.

ILES, Gerald. 590.744
My home in the zoo. [1st ed.] Garden City, N. Y., Doubleday, 1961 [c1960] 239 p. illus. 22 cm. Autobiographical. First published in 1960 under title: At home in the zoo. [QL76.I45 1961] 61-9519
1. Zoological gardens. I. Title.

Zoologists—Austria—Biography.

NISBETT, Alec. 591.5'092'4 B
Konrad Lorenz / Alec Nisbett. 1st American ed. New York : Harcourt Brace Jovanovich, 1977, c1976. xii, 240 p., [8] leaves of plates : ill. ; 24 cm. "A Helen and Kurt Wolff book." Includes index. Bibliography: p. 225-230. [QL31.L76N57 1977] 76-29116 ISBN 0-15-147286-6 : 10.00
1. Zoologists—Austria—Biography.

Zoologists—Biography.

MACGILLIVRAY, 591'.092'2 B
William, 1796-1852.
Lives of eminent zoologists, from Aristotle to Linnaeus. With introductory remarks on the study of natural history, and occasional observations on the progress of zoology. Freeport, N.Y., Books for Libraries Press [1973] p. (Essay index reprint series) Reprint of the 1834 ed. published by Oliver & Boyd, Edinburgh. Contents.Contents.—Aristotle.—Pliny, the Elder.—Gesner, Belon, Salviani, Rondelet, and Aldrovandi.—Jonston, Goedart, Redi, and Swammerdam.—Ray.—Reaumur.—Linnaeus. [QL26.M2 1973] 73-4536 ISBN 0-518-10091-X
1. Zoologists—Biography. I. Title.

Zoology—U.S.

BAIRD, Spencer Fullerton, 925.9
1823-1887.
Correspondence between Spencer Fullerton Baird and Louis Agassiz--two pioneer American naturalists. Collected and edited by Elmer Charles Herber. Washington, Smithsonian Institution, 1963. 237 p. illus., ports., facsims. 24 cm. (Smithsonian Institution. Publication 4515) [QL21.U6B3 1963] 63-61889
1. Zoology—U.S. 2. Science—Hist.—U.S. I. Agassiz, Louis, 1807-1873. II. Herber, Elmer Charles, ed. III. Title.

Zoology—Guyana.

BROCK, Stanley E. 591'.092'4 B
Jungle cowboy [by] Stanley E. Brock. New York, Taplinger Pub. Co. [1972] 190 p. illus. 23 cm. [QL246.B75 1972] 79-163885 ISBN 0-8008-4444-0 7.95
1. Zoology—Guyana. 2. Guyana—Description and travel. 3. Ranch life—Guyana. 4. Wild animal collecting—Guyana. I. Title. BIP

Zorach, William, 1887-

BAUR, John Ireland Howe 730.973
William Zorach. New York, Published for the Whitney Museum of American Art by Praeger. [c.] 1959. 116p. (bibl..: p.112-114.) illus., plates (part col.) port. 30cm. 59-10500 7.50
1. Zorach, William, 1887- I. Whitney Museum of American Art, New York. II. Title.

BAUR, John Ireland Howe, 730.973
1909-
William Zorach. New York, Published for the Whitney Museum of American Art of Praeger, 1959. 116p. illus., plates (part col.) 30cm. (Books that matter) Bbibliography: p. 112-114. [NB237.Z6B3] 59-10500
1. Zorach, William, 1887- I. Whitney Museum of American Art, New York. II. Title.

ZORACH, William, 1887- 730'.924
1966.
Art is my life; the autobiography of William Zorach. Cleveland, World Pub. Co. [1967] ix, 205 p. illus., ports. 26 cm. [NB237.Z6A2] 67-12900
1. Artists—Correspondence, reminiscences, etc. 2. Art—United States. I. Title.

Zoroaster.

HERZFELD, Ernst Emil, 295'.63 B
1879-1948.
Zoroaster and his world. New York, Octagon Books, 1974 [c1947] 2 v. (xvii, 851 p.) 24 cm. Reprint of the ed. published by Princeton University Press, Princeton, N.J. Includes bibliographical references. [BL1555.H4 1974] 74-6219 ISBN 0-374-93877-6
1. Zoroaster. 2. Zoroastrianism. I. Title. BIP

Zorzano, Isidoro,

SARGENT, Daniel, 1890- 922.246
God's engineer; with a pref. by William P. O'Connor. Chicago, Scepter, 1954. 191p. 21cm. [BX4705.Z64S3] 54-20983
1. Zorzano, Isidoro, I. Title.

Zoshchenko, Mikhail Mikhailovich, 1895-1958—Biography.

ZOSHCHENKO, Mikhail 891.7'3'42
Mikhailovich, 1895-1958.
Before sunrise : a novella / Mikhail Zoshchenko ; the first complete text, translated, with an afterword by Gary Kern. Ann Arbor, Mich. : Ardis, c1974. 377 p. : ill. ; 24 cm. Translation of Pered voskhodom solntsa. [PG3476.Z7P413] 74-195241 ISBN 0-88233-060-8 : 12.95. ISBN 0-88233-061-6 pbk. : 3.25
1. Zoshchenko, Mikhail Mikhailovich, 1895-1958—Biography. I. Title.

Zucchi, Virginia, 1849-1930.

GUEST, Ivor Forbes. 792.8'092'4 B
The divine Virginia : a biography of Virginia Zucchi / Ivor Guest. New York : M. Dekker, c1977. xv, 187 p., [10] leaves of plates : ill. ; 24 cm. ([The Dance program ; v. 1]) Includes index. Bibliography: p. 177-180. [GV1785.Z82G83] 76-20006 ISBN 0-8247-6492-7 : 19.50
1. Zucchi, Virginia, 1849-1930. 2. Dancers—Biography. I. Title. II. Series. BIP

Zuck, Barb.

†ZUCK, Roy B. 248'.86'0926
"Barb, please wake up!" : How God helped a couple through their daughter's accident and long recovery from a nearly fatal auto accident / Roy B. Zuck. Wheaton, Ill. : Victor Books, c1976. 127 p. ; 18 cm. [RD594.Z8] 77-371325 ISBN 0-88207-653-1 pbk. : 1.75
1. Zuck, Barb. 2. Brain—Wounds and injuries—Biography. 3. Crash injuries—Biography. I. Title.

Zuckmayer, Carl, 1896-

BAUER, Arnold. 832'.9'12 B
Carl Zuckmayer / Arnold Bauer ; translated by Edith Simmons. New York : Ungar, c1976. xi, 100 p. ; 21 cm. (Modern literature monographs) Includes index. Bibliography: p. [93] [PT2653.U33Z5813] 75-29600 ISBN 0-8044-2026-2 : 7.00
1. Zuckmayer, Carl, 1896- BIP

ZUCKMAYER, Carl, 832'.9'12 B
1896-
A part of myself. Translated from the German by Richard and Clara Winston. [1st American ed.] New York, Harcourt, Brace, Jovanovich [1970] 425 p. 22 cm. "A Helen and Kurt Wolff book." Translation of Als war's ein Stuck von mir. [PT2653.U33A7513] 70-126526 7.95
I. Title.

Zumwalt, Elmo R., 1920-

ZUMWALT, Elmo R., 1920- 359.009'2
On watch : a memoir / Elmo R. Zumwalt, Jr. New York : Quadrangle/New York Times Book Co., c1976. xv, 568 p., [8] leaves of plates : ill. ; 24 cm. Includes index. [V63.Z85A33 1976] 75-8301 ISBN 0-8129-0520-2 : 12.50
1. Zumwalt, Elmo R., 1920- 2. United States. Navy. 3. United States—Military policy. I. Title. BIP

Zuni Indians—Pictorial works.

WHITESIDE, Frank Reed, 759.13
1866-1929.
Frank Reed Whiteside, 1866-1929; the Zuni and the Indian country (The Zuni Indians—their life and tradition) [Phoenix, Ariz., 1971] [32] p. illus. 25 cm. Catalogue of an exhibition held at the Phoenix Art Museum, in cooperation with Western Art Associates, Jan.-Mar., 1971. [ND237.W623A45] 70-23555
1. Zuni Indians—Pictorial works. I. Phoenix, Ariz. Art Museum. II. Western Art Associates. III. Title: The Zuni and the Indian country.

Zurbaran, Francisco, 1598-1664.

ZURBARAN, Francisco, 1598- 1664. 759.6
Zurbaran, 1598-1664 / biography and critical analysis by Julian Gallego ; catalogue of the works by Jose Gudiol. New York : Rizzoli, 1977. 415 p. : ill. (some col.) ; 30 cm. Includes indexes. Bibliography: p. 411-415. [ND813.Z85A4 1977] 77-77657 ISBN 0-8478-0118-7 : 60.00
1. Zurbaran, Francisco, 1598-1664. 2. Painters—Spain—Biography. I. Gallego, Julian. II. Gudiol i Ricart, Josep.

Zweig, Paul—Biography.

ZWEIG, Paul. 818'.5'409 B
Three journeys : an automythology / Paul Zweig. New York : Basic Books, c1976. x, 182 p. ; 22 cm. [PS3576.W4Z52] 75-36386 ISBN 0-465-08610-1 : 8.95
1. Zweig, Paul—Biography. I. Title. BIP

Zweig, Stefan, 1881-1942.

ALLDAY, Elizabeth. 838'.9'1209
Stefan Zweig; a critical biography. Chicago, J. P. O'Hara [1972] 248 p. front. 23 cm. "A Howard Greenfeld book" Bibliography: p. 240-243. [PT2653.W42Z58 1972] 74-190753 ISBN 0-87955-301-4 12.50
1. Zweig, Stefan, 1881-1942. BIP

PRATER, D. A. 838'.9'1209 B
European of yesterday: a biography of Stefan Zweig [by] D. A. Prater. Oxford, Clarendon Press, 1972. xix, 390, [8] p. illus., facsims., ports. 23 cm. Bibliography: p. [359]-370. [PT2653.W42Z67] 72-183844 ISBN 0-19-815707-X £4.00
1. Zweig, Stefan, 1881-1942. I. Title. BIP

Zwemer, Samuel Marinus, 1867-1952.

WILSON, J Christy, 1891- 922
Apostle to Islam; a biography of Samuel M. Zwemer. Grand Rapids, Baker Book House, [1952] 261p. illus. 24cm. [BV2626.Z8W5] 52-131901
1. Zwemer, Samuel Marinus, 1867-1952. I. Title.

Zwingli, Ulrich, 1484-1531.

FARNER, Oskar, 1884- 922.4494
Zwingli the reformer; his life and work. Translated by D. G. Sear. New York, Philosophical Library [1952] 135 p. illus. 19 cm. Translation of Huldrych Zwingli, der schweizerische Reformator. [BR345.F295] 52-11584
1. Zwingli, Ulrich, 1484-1531. I. Title.

FARNER, Oskar, 1884- 270.6'0924 B
Zwingli the reformer; his life and work. Translated by D. G. Sear. [Hamden, Conn.] Archon Books, 1968. 135 p. facsims., ports. 18 cm. Reprint of the 1952 ed. Translation of Huldrych Zwingli, der schweizerische Reformator. [BR345.F295 1968] 68-8017 ISBN 0-208-00694-X
1. Zwingli, Ulrich, 1484-1531. I. Title. BIP

JACKSON, Samuel Macauley, 1851-1912. 270.6'0924 B
Huldreich Zwingli, 1484-1531, the reformer of German Switzerland. Together with an historical survey of Switzerland before the Reformation, by Prof. John Martin Vincent ... and a chapter on Zwingli's theology, by Prof. Frank Hugh Foster. New York, Putnam, 1901. St. Clair Shores, Mich., Scholarly Press [1969] xxvi, 519 p. illus., facsims., plan, ports. 22 cm. (Heroes of the Reformation [v. 5]) Bibliography: p. xxi-xxvi. [BR345.J3 1969] 70-8883
1. Zwingli, Ulrich, 1484-1531. 2. Reformation—Switzerland. I. Vincent, John Martin, 1857-1939. II. Foster, Frank Hugh, 1851-1935.

POTTER, George Richard, 1900- 270.6'092'4 B
Zwingli / G. R. Potter. Cambridge ; New York : Cambridge University Press, 1976. p. cm. Includes index. [BR345.P68] 75-46136 ISBN 0-521-20939-0 ; 43.50
1. Zwingli, Ulrich, 1484-1531. BIP

RILLIET, Jean Horace 922.4494
Zwingli, third man of the Reformation, by Jean Rilliet. Tr. [from French] by Harold Knight. Philadelphia, Westminster [c.1959, 1964] 320p. 23cm. Bibl. 64-19150 6.00
1. Zwingli, Ulrich, 1484-1531. I. Title.

RILLIET, Jean Horace. 922.4494
Zwingli, third man of the Reformation, by Jean Rilliet. Translated by Harold Knight. Philadelphia, Westminster Press [1964] 320 p. 23 cm. Bibliography: p. 313-314. [BR345.R554] 64-19150
1. Zwingli, Ulrich, 1484-1531. I. Title.

Zygmanik, Lester.

MITCHELL, Paige. 364.1'523'0924 B
Act of love : the killing of George Zygmanik / by Paige Mitchell. 1st ed. New York : Knopf, 1976. 274 p. ; 22 cm. [HV6248.Z93M58 1976] 75-36785 ISBN 0-394-49197-1 : 8.95
1. Zygmanik, Lester. I. Title.

AUTHOR INDEX

A

C

E

I

J

L

M

N

Paine, Lauran. 45, 200, 547, 1088
Painter, George Duncan. 216, 226, 450, 956
Painter, Nell Irvin. 555
Painter, Sidney. 607, 908
Painter, Sidney. 607, 925
Painting, Norman. 39, 1023
Pak, In-dok. 891
Pakenham, Simona. 891, 1214
Palandri, Angela C. Y. Jung. 1307
Palau, Luis. 915
Pale Moon. 892
Paleologue, Georges Maurice. 24, 215
Palermo, Louie. 892
Palermo, Patrick F. 1112
Paley, Alan L. 342, 608, 646, 756, 839, 934, 1105, 1249
Paley, Morton D. 130
Paley, William Samuel. 892
Palffy, Eleanor. 435
Palgrave, Francis Turner. 892, 1049
Palij, Michael. 739
Pallandt, Nina. 892
Pallenberg, Corrado. 904
Palley, Reese. 134
Pallister, George. 13
Pallister, John. 727
Palmer, Alan Warwick. 24, 126, 475, 786, 1264
Palmer, Benjamin Morgan. 1166
Palmer, Bernard Alvin. 247
Palmer, Christopher. 132, 319
Palmer, Christopher Harold. 413
Palmer, Colin A. 16
Palmer, David John. 1152
Palmer, Frederick. 132, 913
Palmer, George Herbert. 893
Palmer, Jim. 329
Palmer, John Leslie. 618, 802, 1064
Palmer, John McAuley. 1116
Palmer, Kenyon T. 893
Palmer, Lilli. 893
Palmer, Patricia J. 1111
Palmer, Samuel. 893
Palmer, Thomas Waverly. 893
Palmer, William Preston. 893
Paloczi Horvath, Gyorgy. 268, 744
Paloczi Horvath, Gyorgy. 646
Paloczi Horvath, Gyorgy [George Paloczi-Horvath]. 646
Palou, Francisco. 1054
Pambrun, Andrew Dominique. 893
Pan American Union. 778
Pan, Ku. 233, 1233
Panassie, Hugues. 832
Pancake, John S. 589
Pancoast, Chalmers Lowell. 622
Pandit, Vijaya Lakshmi Nehru. 893
Panel on Science and Technology. 52
Panella, Vincent. 893
Panikkar, Kavalam Madhava. 489
Panikkar, Kavalam Madhava. 893
Panjabi, Kewal Lalchand. 944
Pankey, Joe. 893
Pankey, William Russell. 893
Panko, Stephen M. 170
Panlilio, Benjamin L. 737
Panlilio, Yay. 1297
Pannain, Guido. 270
Pannell, Anne Gary. 1186
Panofsky, Walter. 1227
Panos, Chris. 894
Panov, Valery. 894
Panta, Ilona. 951
Panzeri, Louis. 269
Paolozzi, Eduardo. 894
Paolucci, Henry. 653
Papashvily, Helen (Waite) 23
Papasogli, Giorgio. 722, 1153
Paper, Lewis J. 640
Papich, Stephen. 73
Papini, Giovanni. 174
Papini, Giovanni. 306, 894
Pappenheim, Bertha. 894
Paradis, Adrian A. 393, 403
Paradis, James G. 565
Pardee, Alice DeWolf. 895
Pardee, Caroline Julia. 1291
Pare, Ambroise. 895, 1134
Paredi, Angelo. 30
Parent, Bernie. 895
Parente, Pascal P. 91
Paret, Peter. 249, 422
Paris, Leonard Allen. 269
Paris, William Francklyn. 858
Parish, Helen Rand. 206
Parish, James Robert. 7, 731, 786, 796, 820, 821, 823, 895, 951, 952, 963, 987, 1186
Parish, John Edward. 898
Parish, Lawrence Charles. 345
Parish, Robert. 898
Park, Brad. 895
Park, Clara (Horne) 547
Park, Clyde William. 471
Park, Etta Wolcott. 895
Park, Julian. 195
Park, Ruth. 192
Parker, Alfred Eustace. 1223
Parker, Arthur Caswell. 971
Parker, Audrey. 896
Parker, Derek. 184, 335
Parker, Douglas Charles. 127
Parker, Edmund K. 951
Parker, Elinor Milnor. 367
*Parker, Emma. 896
Parker, Emma (Krause) 82
Parker, Franklin. 905
Parker, George Frederick. 255
Parker, J. A. 311
Parker, Joan H. 896
Parker, John R. 838
Parker, Morris B. 896, 1255
Parker, Noel Geoffrey. 388
Parker, Richard Alexander. 662
Parker, Robert. 518
Parker, Robert Allerton. 871
Parker, Sarah W. 865
Parker, Scudder M. 896
Parker, Theodore. 897
Parker, Thomas Henry Louis. 83, 190
Parker, Tony. 697
Parker, William Belmont. 814
Parker, William Mathie. 64
Parker, William Riley. 794
Parker, William Robert. 124
Parker, Willie J. 897
Parkes, Henry Bamford. 360
Parkhill, Forbes. 321, 691, 735
Parkinson, Cyril Northcote. 124
Parkinson, Roger. 249, 662, 723, 809, 1308
Parkinson, Thomas Francis. 289
Parkman, Ebenezer. 897, 980
Parkman, Francis. 664, 897
Parkman, Mary Rosetta. 119, 120, 1285
Parks, Edd Winfield. 731, 1004
Parks, Edd Winfield. 830
Parks, Gordon. 897
Parks, Gordon. 851, 897
Parks, Joseph Howard. 99, 163, 652, 937
Parks, Lillian (Rogers) 948
Parks, Louise (Wiseman) 1276
*Parlin, John. 351, 352
Parmelee, Alice. 114
Parmeley, June. 265
Parmelin, Helene. 923
Parmenter, Mary Fisher. 393
Parmet, Herbert S. 178
Parmiter, Geoffrey de Clinton. 310
Parmiter, Geoffrey Vincent de Clinton. 310
Parr, Adolph Henry. 689
Parr, Charles McKew. 706, 736
Parr, Jeanne. 55
Parriott, Virginia Patterson. 765
Parris, John. 436
Parrish, Jasper. 898
Parrish, Jasper. 898
Parrish, Margaret Ware. 55
Parrish, Robert. 898
Parrish, William Earl. 53
Parrott, Cecil. 898
Parrott, Thomas Marc. 1059
Parry, Albert. 1046
Parry, Charles Hubert Hastings. 69
Parry, Hugh. 22
Pars, Edd Winfield. 1168
Parshalle, Eve. 1285
Parsons, Florence Mary (Wilson) 438, 1074
Parsons, Francis. 350, 917, 1075, 1121, 1267
Parsons, Fredric Hundy. 976
Parsons, Geneve Shaffer. 898
Parsons, Louella (Oettinger) 822
Parsons, Peter. 455
Parsons, Schuyler Livingston. 898
Parsons, Theophilus. 898
Parsons, Thomas W. 898
Parsons, William Barclay. 428
Partington, Paul G. 379
Partington, Wilfred George. 1276
Parton, James. 178
Parton, James. 123, 178, 415, 477, 570, 577, 589
Parton, Margaret. 404
Partridge, Bellamy, 1877. 899
Partridge, Eric. 670
Parvate, Trimbak Vishnu. 966
Pascal, John. 504
Pascall, Jeremy. 1157
Paschal, George Washington. 899
Paschal, Joel Francis. 1134
Paschasius Radbertus, d. ca. 860. 8
Pasek, Jan Chryzostom. 899
Pashko, Stanley. 592
Pasley, Fred D. 195
Pasquier, Etienne Denis. 409, 899
Passavant, Johann David. 967
Pastene, Jerome. 1126
Pasternak, Boris Leonidovich. 899
Pasternak, Boris Leonidovich. 899
Pasternak, Joseph. 899
Pastor, Paul. 22
Patai, Irene. 706
Patch, Blanche Eliza. 1064
Pater, Walter Horatio. 900
Patmore, Katherine Alexandra. 358, 359
Patnode, Genevieve Carroll. 994, 1108
Paton, Alan. 250, 538
Paton, Graham. 120
Paton, Lucy Allen. 17
Paton, Tam. 992
Patricia, Jean. 945
Patrick, 373?-463? 901
Patrick, Alison. 409
Patrick, Lucille Nichols. 862
Patrick, William J. 901
Patsouras, Louis. 33
Patten, George Zeboim. 901
Patten, Gilbert. 901
Patten, Robert L. 327
Patterson, Ada. 11
Patterson, Alfred Temple. 64
Patterson, Becky Crouch. 296
Patterson, Bob E. 863
Patterson, Caleb Perry. 590
Patterson, Elizabeth C. 304
Patterson, Emma Lillie. 848
Patterson, Floyd. 901
Patterson, Grove. 622
Patterson, James T. 1140
Patterson, John Alvin. 901
Patterson, Katheryn. 565
Patterson, Lillie. 77, 339, 648, 649, 1054
Patterson, Paul. 901
Patterson, Rebecca. 328
Patterson, Robert. 1194
Patterson, Samuel White. 683, 808
Patterson, Webster T. 860
Patterson, William L. 901
Pattison, Mark. 794
Pattison, Walter Thomas. 887
Patton, Elda Clayton. 1031
Pauck, Wilhelm. 505, 1168
Paul, fl. 1654-1666. 729
Paul, Charles Kegan. 902
Paul, Frances Lackey. 628
Paul, Harry Gilbert. 321
Paul, Harry Gilbert. 321
Paul, Herbert Woodfield. 45
Paul, John E. 210
Paul, Justus F. 181
Paul, Leslie Allen. 810, 811
Paul, Leslie Allen. 594, 595, 811
Paul, Ronald C. 469
Paul, Sherman. 288, 1132
Paul Wilhelm, 1797-1860. 904
Paul, William Henry. 400
Paulding, James Kirke. 904, 1239
Pauli, Hertha Ernestine. 417, 491, 1095, 1135, 1182, 1297
Pauli, Reinhold. 26
Paullin, Charles Oscar. 994
Paulson, Ronald. 539
Paulus. 1218
Paustovskii, Konstantin Georgievich. 904
Paustovskii, Konstantin Georgievich. 904
Pauwels, Louis. 489
Paval, Philip. 48
Paxton, Elisha Franklin. 905
Paxton, M. W. 157
Paylin, Jolie. 905
Payne, Alma Smith. 686, 1044
Payne, Anthony. 1038
Payne, Ben Iden. 905
Payne, Cril. 905, 1189
Payne, Daniel Alexander. 16
Payne, Darwin. 27
Payne, David John. 746
Payne, Doris (Palmer) 577
Payne, Edward F. 327
Payne, George Andrew. 439
Payne, Pierre Stephen Robert. 447
Payne, Pierre Stephen Robert. 223, 231, 237, 244, 337, 433, 435, 447, 535, 689, 690, 740, 744, 751, 756, 1037, 1042, 1060, 1105, 1179
Payne, Robert. 678
Payne, Walter A. 791
*Payton, Barbara. 905
Payton, Everett J. 905
Payton, Walter. 905
Peabody, Francis Greenwood. 237
Peabody, Marian Lawrence. 142
Peace, Judy Boppell. 905
Peacock, Carlos. 893
Peacock, Thomas Love. 1068, 1069
Peacock, Virginia Tatnall. 1285
Peacocke, Marguerite D. 917
Peake, Charles. 624
Peake, Richard Brinsley. 261, 264
Peaker, Ora. 340
Peale, Norman Vincent. 595, 598
Pearce, Catherine Owens. 545
Pearce, Charles E. 1217
Pearce, Haywood Jefferson. 531
Pearce, T. S. 365
Pearce, Thomas Matthews. 22
Peare, Catherine Owens. 17, 22, 57, 110, 137, 152, 185, 252, 281, 327, 406, 433, 434, 544, 573, 574, 635, 715, 906, 909, 1002, 1119, 1216, 1273, 1294
Pearl, Cyril. 320, 816
Pearl, Jack. 496, 902
Pearl, Ralph. 906
Pears, Edwin. 2, 1184
Pearsall, Robert Brainard. 160
Pearsall, Ronald. 340
Pearse, Cecilia Maria de Candia. 748
Pearson, Alan. 561
Pearson, Benjamin Harold. 287, 805
Pearson, Billy. 606
Pearson, Carol Lynn. 814
Pearson, Charles T. 1183
Pearson, Daniel Merle. 1136
Pearson, Drew. 906
Pearson, Haydn Sanborn. 906
Pearson, Hesketh [Edward Hesketh Gibbons Pearson]. 6, 63, 90, 91, 225, 309, 340, 450, 451, 485, 521, 613, 1049, 1059, 1064, 1090, 1176, 1254, 1263, 1285, 1286
Pearson, Irving Frederick. 906
*Pearson, James R. 947
Pearson, John. 191, 359, 1079, 1080
Pearson, John George. 191
Pearson, Lester B. 193, 906
Pearson, Lon. 491
Pearson, Michael. 689
Pease, Jane H. 1082
Pease, Mae (Townsend) 907
Peat, Wilbur David. 567
Peate, Iorwerth Cyfeiliog. 398
Peattie, Donald Culross. 119
Pecher, Erich. 606
Peck, Anne Merriman. 174
Peck, Clara Temple (Boardman) 907
Peck, Harry Thurston. 945, 946
Peck, John Mason. 797
Peck, Louis F. 694
Peck, Mary Gray. 214
Peck, Walter Edwin. 1067
Peckham, Harry Houston. 169
Peckham, Howard Henry. 507, 938
Peckman, Harry Houston. 169
Peden, Rachel. 385
Pederson, Kern O. 1198
Pedley, Avril J. M. 379
Pedrotti, Louis. 1052
Peebles, Robert Whitney. 286
Peel, John Hugh Brignall. 907
Peel, Robert. 355
Peele, George. 907
Peele, Herbert. 622
Peerce, Jan. 907
Peerman, Frank. 907
Peers, Edgar Allison. 625, 724, 1153
Peery, Paul Denver. 207
Peirce, Charles Santiago Sanders. 1053
Peirce, Ebenezer Weaver. 760
Peladeau, Marius B. 372
Pelgrin, Mark. 193, 194
Pelikan, Jaroslav Jan. 726
Pell, John. 27
Pellegreno, Ann Holtgren. 351
Peller, Sigismund. 908
Pellet, Elizabeth (Eyre) 908
Pelletier, Wilfred. 908
Pellew, George. 585
Pellico, Silvio. 908
Pelling, Henry. 244
Pellowe, William Charles Smithson. 252
Pelotte, Donald E. 831
Pelzel, Thomas. 783
Pemberton, Thomas Edgar. 508
Pendar, Kenneth Whittemore. 908
Pendered, Norman C. 1147
Penders, C. L. M. 1131
Pendleton, Everett Hall. 908
Pendrigh, Ernest. 920
Penfield, Marc. 547
Penfield, Thomas. 905
Penfield, Wilder. 909
Peng, Ming-min. 1141
Penn, Irvine Garland. 849
Penn, Jack. 909
Penn, William. 909, 937
Pennell, Elizabeth (Robins) 688, 1254, 1278
Pennewell, Almer. 1229
Penney, Annette Culler. 331
Penney, James Cash. 909
Penney, Sherry. 80
Penning de Vries, Piet. 722
Penning, Louwrens. 190
Pennington, James W. C. 1083

R

S

T

U

V

Z

TITLE INDEX

A

C

D

E

F

G

H

K

L

N

O

P

Q

R

T

U

W

X

Y

Z

BIOGRAPHICAL BOOKS IN PRINT INDEX

A

Adventures of a Mathematician. pap. 4.95 (ISBN 0-684-15064-6, SL728). Scribner.
Adventures of a White-Collar Man. facs. ed. 14.50 (ISBN 0-8369-5485-8). Arno.
Adventures of a Zoologist. 10.00 (ISBN 0-684-16439-6). Scribner.
Adventures of Captain Bonneville. 10.00 (ISBN 0-8323-0100-0). Binford.
Adventures of Captain Bonneville. lib. bdg. 25.00 (ISBN 0-8057-8508-6). Twayne.
Adventures of Captain Bonneville, U.S.A. in the Rocky Mountains & the Far West. 18.95 (ISBN 0-8061-0502-X). U of Okla Pr.
Adventures of Conan Doyle: The Life of the Creator of Sherlock Holmes. 9.95 (ISBN 0-393-07507-9). Norton.
Adventures of George Washington. PLB 3.27 (ISBN 0-590-07002-9). Schol Bk Serv.
Adventures of George Washington. pap. 0.95 (ISBN 0-590-01316-5). Schol Bk Serv.
Adventures of Mark Twain. 6.75 (ISBN 0-8446-0453-4). Peter Smith.
Adventures of Peter & Paul: Acts of the Apostles for the Young. pap. 2.95 (ISBN 0-89243-094-X). Liguori Pubns.
Adventures with Bernard Shaw. lib. bdg. 7.50 (ISBN 0-8414-7266-1). Folcroft.
Adventures with Bernard Shaw. lib. bdg. 10.95 (ISBN 0-8383-2023-6). Haskell.
Adventures with D. W. Griffith. 10.00 (ISBN 0-374-10093-4). FS&G.
Adventures with D. W. Griffith. pap. 4.95 (ISBN 0-306-80032-2). Da Capo.
Adventurous Americans. facsimile ed. 18.75 (ISBN 0-8369-2264-6). Arno.
Advertisements for Myself. pap. 3.95 (ISBN 0-425-03282-5). Berkley Pub.
Advocate for God. pap. 2.50 (ISBN 0-8170-0723-7). Judson.
Aesthetics of Freud: A Study in Psychoanalysis & Art. pap. 3.95 (ISBN 0-07-060015-5). McGraw.
Aesthetics of Robert Schumann. 5.95 (ISBN 0-8022-0185-7). Philos Lib.
Aesthetics of Robert Schumann. lib. bdg. 13.00x (ISBN 0-8371-7184-9, BRAS). Greenwood.
Affair. 7.95 (ISBN 0-399-12106-4). Putnam.
Affecting History of Mrs. Howe see Essay on the Life of the Honorable Major-General Israel Putnam.
Africa As I Have Known It: Nyasaland, East Africa, Liberia, Senegal. 19.50x (ISBN 0-8371-2762-9). Negro U Pr.
African Apostles: Ritual & Conversion in the Church of John Maranke. 19.50x (ISBN 0-8014-0846-6). Cornell U Pr.
African Apprenticeship: An Autobiographical Journey in Southern Africa, 1929. 17.50x (ISBN 0-8419-0169-4). Holmes & Meier.
African Dream: Martin R. Delany & the Emergence of Pan-African Thought. 11.75x (ISBN 0-271-01181-5). Pa St U Pr.
African Heroes. 3.95 (ISBN 0-374-30165-4). FS&G.
African Profiles. 6.75 (ISBN 0-8446-0904-8). Peter Smith.
African Tightrope: My Two Years As Nkrumah's Chief of Staff. 7.50. Univ Place.
Afro-American Artists: A Bio-Bibliographical Directory. 10.00 (ISBN 0-89073-007-5). Boston Public Lib.
Afro-American Press & Its Editors. 21.00 (ISBN 0-405-01887-8). Arno.
Afro-American Writing: An Anthology of Prose & Poetry. 20.00x set (ISBN 0-8147-4954-2); pap. 10.00x set (ISBN 0-8147-4955-0). NYU Pr.
After-Breakfast Cigar: Selected Memoirs of a King Country Settler. 18.75 (ISBN 0-589-01011-5). Reed.
After Great Pain: The Inner Life of Emily Dickinson. 15.00x (ISBN 0-674-00878-2). Harvard U Pr.
After Kilvert. 16.95x (ISBN 0-19-211748-3). Oxford U Pr.
After Many Days. 7.50 (ISBN 0-8283-1664-3). Branden.
After Olympic Glory: The Lives of Ten Outstanding Medalists. 7.95 (ISBN 0-7232-6135-0). Warne.
After Shelley: The Letters of Thomas Jefferson Hogg to Jane Williams. lib. bdg. 17.50. Folcroft.
After the Revolution: Profiles of Early American Culture. 16.95 (ISBN 0-393-01253-0). Norton.
After the Sundown. 8.95 (ISBN 0-396-07773-0). Dodd.
Aftermath. pap. 1.95 (ISBN 0-380-00407-0, 25387). Avon.
Aftermath. 10.25x (ISBN 0-19-211195-7). Oxford U Pr.
Afternoons in Montana. 5.95 (ISBN 0-87970-123-4). North Plains.
Again Calls the Owl. 7.95 (ISBN 0-399-12453-5). Putnam.
Against All Odds. 9.95 (ISBN 0-690-01763-4). T Y Crowell.
Against All Odds. pap. 2.50 (ISBN 0-446-81546-2). Warner Bks.
Agam. 55.00 (ISBN 0-8109-0294-X). Abrams.
Agam. rev., enl. ed. 65.00 (0693-7). Abrams.
Age of Jackson. 14.95x (ISBN 0-87249-274-5). U of SC Pr.
Age of Jewett: Charles Coffin Jewett & American Librarianship, 1841-1868. lib. bdg. 17.50x (ISBN 0-87287-113-4). Libs Unl.
Age of Kipling. 12.95 (ISBN 0-671-21405-5). S&S.
Agnes Moorehead: A Very Private Person. 5.95 (ISBN 0-8059-2317-9). Dorrance.
Agnes Repplier, Lady of Letters. lib. bdg. 13.50x (ISBN 0-8371-3823-X, STAG). Greenwood.
Agnew the Unexamined Man: A Political Profile. 5.95 (ISBN 0-87131-032-5). M Evans.
Ah-One, Ah-Two: Life with My Musical Family. 7.95 (ISBN 0-13-020990-2). P-H.
Ah-One, Ah-Two! Life with My Musical Family. pap. 1.75 (ISBN 0-345-24576-8). Ballantine.
Ahaz. 7.95 (ISBN 0-8054-7309-2). Broadman.
Aiming for the Jugular in New Orleans. 8.95 (ISBN 0-87949-035-7). Ashley Bks.
Ain't Misbehavin: The Story of Fats Waller. lib. bdg. 16.50 (ISBN 0-306-70683-0); pap. 4.95 (ISBN 0-306-80015-2). Da Capo.
Air. 7.00 (ISBN 0-89366-089-2). Ultramarine Pub.
Airborne: A Sentimental Journey. 5.95 (ISBN 0-02-097340-3). Macmillan.
Airborne: A Sentimental Journey. 12.95 (ISBN 0-02-518040-1, 51804). Macmillan.
Al Capone: The Biography of a Self-Made Man. facsimile ed. 18.50 (ISBN 0-8369-5709-1). Arno.
Al Packer: A Colorado Cannibal. 3.50; limited signed ed 50.00; pap. 2.00. F&J Mazzulla.
Al Smith & His America. 5.00 (ISBN 0-316-34304-8); pap. 4.95 (ISBN 0-316-34305-6, 1965). Little.
Alan Page. PLB 5.50 (ISBN 0-87191-381-X). Creative Ed.
Alan Shepard: First American in Space. PLB 6.95 (ISBN 0-87518-184-8). Dillon.
Alaska Adventures of a Norwegian Cheechako: Greenhorn with a Gold Pan. pap. 3.95 (ISBN 0-88240-063-0). Alaska Northwest.
Alaskan Voyage, 1881-1883: An Expedition to the Northwest Coast of America. 17.50 (ISBN 0-226-39032-2). U of Chicago Pr.
Alaskans All. facs. ed. 15.00 (ISBN 0-8369-2091-0). Arno.
Alban Berg. 15.00 (ISBN 0-395-27762-0). HM.
Alban Berg: The Man & the Work. text ed. 26.00x (ISBN 0-8419-0301-8). Holmes & Meier.
Albert Einstein, Creator & Rebel. pap. 3.95 (ISBN 0-452-25152-4, Z5152). NAL.
Albert Einstein, the Human Side: New Glimpses from His Archives. 8.95 (ISBN 0-691-08231-6). Princeton U Pr.
Albert Einstein's Theory of General Relativity. 14.95 (ISBN 0-517-53661-7). Crown.
Albert Gallatin. 15.00 (ISBN 0-404-50863-4). AMS Pr.
Albert Gallatin: Jeffersonian Financier & Diplomat. pap. 5.95 (ISBN 0-8229-5210-6). U of Pittsburgh Pr.
Albert J. Beveridge: American Nationalist. 13.50x (ISBN 0-226-07060-3). U of Chicago Pr.
Albert Roussel: A Study. 16.00 (ISBN 0-88355-736-3). Hyperion Conn.
Albert Schweitzer: A Biography. 12.95 (ISBN 0-399-11421-1). Putnam.
Albert Schweitzer: Genius in the Jungle. 5.95 (ISBN 0-8149-0308-8). Vanguard.
Albert Shaw of the Review of Reviews: An Intellectual Biography. 12.50 (ISBN 0-8131-1300-8). U Pr of Ky.
Alberta Homestead: Chronicle of a Pioneer Family. 12.50 (ISBN 0-292-70143-8). U of Tex Pr.
Alberto Moravia. 9.95 (ISBN 0-8044-2131-5). Ungar.
Albion W. Small. lib. bdg. 10.95 (ISBN 0-8057-7718-0). Twayne.
Alcuin & the Rise of the Christian Schools. 10.00 (ISBN 0-404-06908-8). AMS Pr.
Alcuin & the Rise of the Christian Schools. 19.00 (ISBN 0-403-00031-9). Scholarly.
Alcuin & the Rise of the Christian Schools. lib. bdg. 11.75x (ISBN 0-8371-1635-X, WEAS). Greenwood.
Aldous Huxley. lib. bdg. 7.95 (ISBN 0-8057-1284-4). Twayne.
Aleksandr Solzhenitsyn, Beleaguered Literary Giant of the U. S. S. R. lib. bdg. 2.45 incl catalog cards (ISBN 0-87157-560-4); pap. 1.25 vinyl laminated covers (ISBN 0-87157-060-2). SamHar Pr.
Alex J. Groesbeck: Portrait of a Public Man. 8.95x (ISBN 0-8143-1212-8). Wayne St U Pr.
Alex Karras: My Life in Football, Television, & Movies. 5.95 (ISBN 0-385-12529-1); PLB (ISBN 0-385-12530-5). Doubleday.
Alex Katz. 55.00 (ISBN 0-8109-1202-3). Abrams.
Alexander Bryan Johnson: Philosophical Banker. 16.00x (ISBN 0-8156-2188-4). Syracuse U Pr.
Alexander Dolgun's Story: An American in the Gulag. 10.00 (ISBN 0-394-49497-0). Knopf.
Alexander Graham Bell: the Man Who Contracted Space. facsimile ed. 22.00 (ISBN 0-8369-5706-7). Arno.
Alexander Gumberg & Soviet-American Relations, 1917-1933. 15.00 (ISBN 0-8131-1361-X). U Pr of Ky.
Alexander Hamilton. pap. 3.95 (ISBN 0-498-04027-5). A S Barnes.
Alexander Hamilton: A Biography. 17.50 (ISBN 0-393-01218-2). Norton.
Alexander Hamilton: A Biography in His Own Words. 15.00 (ISBN 0-06-012417-2). Har-Row.
Alexander Hamilton: A Concise Biography. 15.95 (ISBN 0-19-501979-2). Oxford U Pr.
Alexander Hamilton & the Idea of Republican Government. 12.50x (ISBN 0-8047-0724-3). Stanford U Pr.
Alexander Hamilton in the American Tradition. lib. bdg. 15.50x (ISBN 0-8371-7878-9, HAAL). Greenwood.
Alexander Hamilton: Selections Representing His Life, His Thought, & His Style. 5.00 (ISBN 0-672-61272-0, AHS20). Bobbs.
Alexander Herzen & the Role of the Intellectual Revolutionary. 18.95 (ISBN 0-521-22166-8). Cambridge U Pr.
Alexander James Dallas, Lawyer-Politician-Financier. lib. bdg. 22.50 (ISBN 0-306-71814-6). Da Capo.
Alexander Kuprin. lib. bdg. 10.95 (ISBN 0-8057-6322-8). Twayne.
Alexander Mackenzie, Canadian Explorer. PLB 6.48 (ISBN 0-688-31010-9). Morrow.
Alexander of Yugoslavia: The Story of the King Who Was Murdered at Marseilles. 15.00 (ISBN 0-208-01082-3). Shoe String.
Alexander Phimister Proctor, Sculptor in Buckskin: An Autobiography. 17.50 (ISBN 0-8061-0912-2). U of Okla Pr.
Alexander Pope. lib. bdg. 7.75x (ISBN 0-8371-2459-X, DOAP). Greenwood.
Alexander Pope. 9.00 (ISBN 0-8274-0621-5). R West.
Alexander Porter, Whig Planter of Old Louisiana. lib. bdg. 15.00 (ISBN 0-306-71254-7). Da Capo.
Alexander the Great. pap. 3.95x (ISBN 0-8070-5797-5, BP26). Beacon Pr.
Alexander the Great. 18.50 (ISBN 0-521-22584-1); pap. 4.95 (ISBN 0-521-29563-7); 39.50 (ISBN 0-521-22585-X). Cambridge U Pr.
Alexandre-Gabriel Decamps (1803-1860) lib. bdg. 105.00 (ISBN 0-8240-2714-0). Garland Pub.
Alexandre Millerand: The Socialist Years. text ed. 26.75x. Mouton.
Alexis Carrel Visionary Surgeon. text ed. 5.75 (ISBN 0-398-03130-4). C C Thomas.
Alexis de Tocqueville: A Biographical Study in Political Science. 6.50 (ISBN 0-8446-1307-X). Peter Smith.
Alfonso Ossorio. 55.00 (ISBN 0-8109-0352-0). Abrams.
Alfonso Reyes & Spain: His Dialogue with Unamuno, Valle-Inclan, Ortega y Gasset, Jimenez & Gomez De la Serna. 10.00x (ISBN 0-292-70300-7). U of Tex Pr.
Alfred Binet. 13.75x (ISBN 0-226-90498-9). U of Chicago Pr.
Alfred De Musset (1810-1857) lib. bdg. 30.00 (ISBN 0-8414-7890-2). Folcroft.
Alfred Deakin: A Biography. 32.00x (ISBN 0-522-83884-7). Intl Schol Bk Serv.
Alfred E. Smith: A Critical Study. 9.00 (ISBN 0-404-00627-2). AMS Pr.
Alfred E. Smith: A Critical Study. 8.50 (ISBN 0-403-01164-7). Scholarly.
Alfred Henry Lewis. pap. 2.00 (ISBN 0-88430-056-0). Boise St Univ.
Alfred Hugenberg: The Radical Nationalist Campaign Against the Weimar Republic. 18.50x (ISBN 0-300-02068-6). Yale U Pr.
Alfred Kroeber. 12.50x (ISBN 0-231-03489-X); pap. 4.00x (ISBN 0-231-03490-3). Columbia U Pr.
Alfred Lord Tennyson. 64.50 (ISBN 0-8274-1838-8). R West.
Alfred Russel Wallace: Letters & Reminiscences. 29.00x (ISBN 0-405-06601-5). Arno.
Alfred Tennyson. lib. bdg. 11.75x (ISBN 0-8371-1071-8, BENA). Greenwood.
Alfred Tennyson. 2nd ed. 10.00 (ISBN 0-404-03856-5). AMS Pr.
Alfred Tennyson. lib. bdg. 9.95 (ISBN 0-8414-5668-2). Folcroft.
Alfred Tennyson. lib. bdg. 17.50 (ISBN 0-8495-3233-7). Arden Lib.
Alfred Tennyson. 22.50 (ISBN 0-208-00716-4). Shoe String.
Alfred Tennyson: A Saintly Life. lib. bdg. 25.00 (ISBN 0-8492-5228-8). R West.
Alfred Tennyson: A Saintly Life. lib. bdg. 26.95 (ISBN 0-8383-1687-5). Haskell.
Alfred Thayer Mahan: The Man & His Letters. 24.95x (ISBN 0-87021-359-8). Naval Inst Pr.
Alfred the Great: The Truth Teller Maker of England 848-899. text ed. 25.00x (ISBN 0-87696-029-8). Humanities.
Alfred: The Passionate Life of Alfred de Musset. lib. bdg. 30.00 (ISBN 0-8492-5207-5). R West.
Alfred V. Kidder. 12.50x (ISBN 0-231-03484-9); pap. 4.00x (ISBN 0-231-03485-7). Columbia U Pr.
Alger Hiss: The True Story. pap. 2.95 (ISBN 0-14-004427-2). Penguin.
Algernon C. Swinburne. lib. bdg. 7.95 (ISBN 0-8057-1524-X). Twayne.
Alias Simon Suggs: The Life & Times of Johnson Jones Hooper. lib. bdg. 13.75x (ISBN 0-8371-3367-X, HOAS). Greenwood.
Alias Walt Whitman. lib. bdg. 10.00 (ISBN 0-8414-6539-8). Folcroft.
Alice's World: The Life & Photography of an American Original: Alice Austen, 1866-1952. 22.50 (ISBN 0-85699-128-7). Chatham Pr.
Aline. 12.95 (ISBN 0-06-012423-7). Har-Row.
All Aboard with E. M. Frimbo: World's Greatest Railroad Buff. pap. 2.95 (ISBN 0-14-004918-5). Penguin.
All About Your Name James, Jim, Jamie, Jimmy. 4.95 (ISBN 0-385-06436-5); PLB (ISBN 0-385-06449-7). Doubleday.
All About Your Name John, Johnny, Jack, Jackie. 4.95 (ISBN 0-385-06424-1); PLB (ISBN 0-385-06428-4). Doubleday.
All About Your Name Joseph, Joe, Joey, Jo-Jo. 4.95 (ISBN 0-385-06554-X); PLB (ISBN 0-385-06558-2). Doubleday.
All-Americans. 20.00 (ISBN 0-87000-363-1). Arlington Hse.
All-Americans. pap. 12.95 (ISBN 0-89508-011-7). Rainbow Bks.
All & Sundry: An Oblique Autobiography. 4.75 (ISBN 0-15-104550-X). HarBraceJ.
All Creatures Great & Small. 10.00 (ISBN 0-312-01960-2, A20000). St Martin.
All Creatures Great & Small. lib. bdg. 10.95 (ISBN 0-8161-6095-3). G K Hall.
All Creatures Great & Small. pap. 2.75 (ISBN 0-553-10759-3, B13270-9). Bantam.
All God's Dangers: The Life of Nate Shaw. 12.50 (ISBN 0-394-49084-3). Knopf.
All God's Dangers: The Life of Nate Shaw. pap. 2.95 (ISBN 0-380-00508-5, 46573). Avon.
All Is Well. 9.95 (ISBN 0-688-03045-9). Morrow.
All Our Hearts Are Trump. 8.95 (ISBN 0-87716-066-X). Moore Pub Co.
All Said & Done. pap. 2.50 (ISBN 0-446-81191-2). Warner Bks.
All-Stars of the NFL. PLB 3.69 (ISBN 0-394-83258-2). Random.
All Summer in a Day: An Autobiographical Fantasia. 24.50 (ISBN 0-403-01214-7). Scholarly.
All the Home Run Kings. 6.95 (ISBN 0-399-20249-8). Putnam.
All the Strange Hours: The Excavation of a Life. pap. 4.95 (ISBN 0-684-14868-4, SL690); encore edition 3.95 (ISBN 0-684-15405-6). Scribner.
All These. 25.00 (ISBN 0-8274-1739-X). R West.
All These. facs. ed. 14.50 (ISBN 0-8369-1182-2). Arno.
All Things Bright & Beautiful. 10.00 (ISBN 0-312-02030-9). St Martin.
All Things Bright & Beautiful. lib. bdg. 17.50 (ISBN 0-8161-6269-7). G K Hall.
All Things Bright & Beautiful. pap. 2.75 (ISBN 0-553-11000-4, A13287-3). Bantam.
All Things Wise & Wonderful. 10.00 (ISBN 0-312-02031-7). St Martin.
All Things Wise & Wonderful. pap. 2.75 (ISBN 0-553-11746-7). Bantam.
All Things Wise & Wonderful. lib. bdg. 17.95 (ISBN 0-8161-6525-4). G K Hall.
All Things Wise & Wonderful. pap. 3.95. Pasadena Art.
Allan Ramsay. lib. bdg. 15.00. Folcroft.
Allan Ramsay. 12.00 (ISBN 0-404-08599-7). AMS Pr.
Allan Ramsay: A Study of His Life & Works. lib. bdg. 11.00x (ISBN 0-8371-5830-3, MAR). Greenwood.
Allan Shivers: The Pied Piper of Texas Politics. 6.95 (ISBN 0-88319-017-6). Shoal Creek Pub.
Allart van Everdingen. lib. bdg. 52.50 (ISBN 0-8240-3223-3). Garland Pub.
Allen Tate. pap. 3.45 (ISBN 0-8084-0050-9, T124). Coll & U Pr.
Allies for Freedom: Blacks & John Brown. 11.95 (ISBN 0-19-501770-6). Oxford U Pr.
Almost a Famous Person. 9.95. HarBraceJ.
Almost World. pap. 2.95 (ISBN 0-85345-362-4, PB3624). Monthly Rev.
Alone. PLB 5.95 (ISBN 0-87966-108-9). Dexter & Westbrook.
Alone Around the World. 9.95 (ISBN 0-698-10986-4). Coward.
Alone on a Desert Island. PLB 7.99 (ISBN 0-8172-1571-9). Raintree Pubs.
Along Came the Model T! How Henry Ford Put the World on Wheels. 6.50 (ISBN 0-8193-0952-4); PLB 6.19 (ISBN 0-8193-0953-2). Parents.
Along Came the Witch: A Journal of the 1960's. 8.95 (ISBN 0-15-105080-5). HarBraceJ.
Along This Way: The Autobiography of James Weldon Johnson. lib. bdg. 35.00 (ISBN 0-306-70539-7). Da Capo.
Alphonse Bertillon, Father of Scientific Detection. lib. bdg. 17.00x (ISBN 0-8371-0636-2, RHAB). Greenwood.

Alphonse Daudet. lib. bdg. 25.00 (ISBN 0-8414-3712-2). Folcroft.
Alphonse in Austin. 6.95 (ISBN 0-88426-005-4). Encino Pr.
Also Rans: Great Men Who Missed Making the Presidential Goal. facs. ed. 16.75 (ISBN 0-8369-0863-5). Arno.
Alvarez on Alvarez. pap. 5.95 (ISBN 0-89407-005-3). Strawberry Hill.
Alvin Langdon Coburn, Photographer: An Autobiography. pap. 6.00 (ISBN 0-486-23685-4). Dover.
Always Another Dawn: The Story of a Rocket Test Pilot. 25.00 (ISBN 0-405-03758-9). Arno.
Always Becoming. 4.95 (ISBN 0-914850-32-6); pap. 2.50 (ISBN 0-914850-36-9). Impact Tenn.
Always Merry & Bright: The Life of Henry Miller. 15.00 (ISBN 0-88496-082-X). Capra Pr.
Always Merry & Bright: The Life of Henry Miller. pap. 8.95 (ISBN 0-14-005548-7). Penguin.
Always Movin' on: The Life of Langston Hughes. PLB 6.90 (ISBN 0-531-01211-5). Watts.
Always the Young Strangers. 12.95 (ISBN 0-15-105459-2). HarBraceJ.
Always Young for Liberty: Biography of William Ellery Channing. 7.00x (ISBN 0-8156-0004-6). Syracuse U Pr.
Alwin Schockemohle. 7.95 (ISBN 0-8120-5186-6). Barron.
Amazing Grace. 5.95 (ISBN 0-8007-0468-1). Revell.
Amazing Grace. pap. 1.50 (ISBN 0-8007-8148-1). Revell.
Amazing Grace. lib. bdg. 6.95 (ISBN 0-8161-6136-4). G K Hall.
Amazing Mr. Doolittle: A Biography of Lieutenant General James H. Doolittle. 14.00 (ISBN 0-405-03778-3). Arno.
Amazing Mr. Noel Coward. lib. bdg. 15.00 (ISBN 0-8414-3250-3). Folcroft.
Amazing Nellie Bly. facs. ed. 15.56 (ISBN 0-8369-8074-3). Arno.
Amazing Uri Geller. pap. 1.50 (ISBN 0-451-06475-5, W6475). NAL.
Amazing World of Kreskin. pap. 1.50 (ISBN 0-380-00121-7, 19034). Avon.
Amazon of Letters: The Life & Loves of Natalie Barney. 10.00 (ISBN 0-399-11864-0). Putnam.
Amberley Papers: Bertrand Russell's Family Background. 12.50 (ISBN 0-671-01895-7). S&S.
Ambrose Bierce: A Biography. 18.50 (ISBN 0-208-00370-3). Shoe String.
Ambrose Bierce, F. A. Mitchell-Hedges & the Crystal Skull. pap. 3.95 (ISBN 0-9600310-3-0). Cadleon Pr.
Ambush: The Real Story of Bonnie & Clyde. 12.50 (ISBN 0-88319-041-9). Shoal Creek Pub.
Amelia Earhart: First Lady of Flight. PLB 4.99 (ISBN 0-698-30008-4). Coward.
Amelia Earhart: The Myth & the Reality. 6.00 (ISBN 0-682-47447-9). Exposition.
Amelia Gayle Gorgas: A Biography. 11.50 (ISBN 0-8173-5235-X). U of Ala Pr.
Amelia's Flying Machine. 6.95 (ISBN 0-385-07945-1); PLB (ISBN 0-385-08139-1). Doubleday.
America: Ideals & Men. text ed. 4.48; tchr's ed. 4.48. Benson.
America, Their America. pap. 4.50x (ISBN 0-8419-0012-4). Holmes & Meier.
American Anarchist: The Life of Voltairine De Cleyre. text ed. 16.50 (ISBN 0-691-04657-3). Princeton U Pr.
American & British Theatrical Biography: A Directory. 37.50 (ISBN 0-8108-1201-0). Scarecrow.
American Apostles to the Philippines. 16.00 (ISBN 0-8369-8089-1). Arno.
American Architects from the Civil War to the First World War: A Guide to Information Sources. 24.00 (ISBN 0-8103-1269-7). Gale.
American Aristocracy: The Lives & Times of James Russell, Amy, & Robert Lowell. 17.95 (ISBN 0-396-07608-4). Dodd.
American Artists. 9.50 (ISBN 0-404-01736-3). AMS Pr.
American Association of Public Accountants: Its First Twenty Years, 1886-1906. lib. bdg. 25.00x (ISBN 0-405-10919-9). Arno.
American Autobiography: The Prophetic Mode. lib. bdg. 15.00x (ISBN 0-87023-263-0). U of Mass Pr.
American Bard: The Story of Henry Wadsworth Longfellow. 6.95 (ISBN 0-690-05923-X). T Y Crowell.
American Biographical Notes, Being Short Notices of Deceased Persons. 15.00 (ISBN 0-916346-06-4). Harbor Hill Bks.
American Biographies. 34.00 (ISBN 0-8103-4054-2). Gale.
American Book Collectors & Collecting from Colonial Times to the Present. lib. bdg. 26.00x (ISBN 0-8371-8841-5, CAAB). Greenwood.
American Chemists & Chemical Engineers. 30.00 (ISBN 0-8412-0278-8). Am Chemical.
American Composers. 3.95 (ISBN 0-395-07035-X). HM.
American Diary 1857-8. 10.75 (ISBN 0-7100-7330-5). Routledge & Kegan.
American Dissenter: The Life of Algie Martin Simons, 1870-1950. 9.25 (ISBN 0-8131-1177-3). U Pr of Ky.
American Entomologists. 30.00 (ISBN 0-8135-0686-7). Rutgers U Pr.
American Eve in Fact & Fiction, 1775-1914. 9.50 (ISBN 0-252-00448-5). U of Ill Pr.
American Film Directors: The World As They See It. PLB 4.95 (ISBN 0-531-05595-7). Watts.
American Genesis: Captain John Smith & the Founding of Virginia. 6.95 (ISBN 0-316-89808-2); pap. text ed. 4.95 (ISBN 0-316-89807-4). Little.
American Heroes of the 20th Century. 4.95 (ISBN 0-394-80296-9); PLB 5.99 (ISBN 0-394-90296-3). Random.
American Inventors. 5.75g (ISBN 0-02-745890-3). Macmillan.
American Judge: Marmaduke Dent of West Virginia. 10.00x (ISBN 0-8147-0359-3). NYU Pr.
American Leonardo: A Life of Samuel F. B. Morse. lib. bdg. 22.50 (ISBN 0-374-95225-6). Octagon.
American Literary Pioneer: A Biographical Study of James A. Hillhouse. lib. bdg. 30.00 (ISBN 0-8495-2228-5). Arden Lib.
American Memoir. lib. bdg. 18.75x (ISBN 0-8371-0339-8, CAAM). Greenwood.
American Notebooks. 17.50 (ISBN 0-8142-0159-8); pap. 5.75x (ISBN 0-8142-0186-5). Ohio St U Pr.
American Olympic Stars. new ed. PLB 5.29 (ISBN 0-399-61005-7). Putnam.
American Orchestra & Theodore Thomas. lib. bdg. 20.25x (ISBN 0-8371-5762-5, RUAO). Greenwood.
American People on the Western Frontier. new ed. PLB 7.95 (ISBN 0-88301-089-5); pap. 2.50 (ISBN 0-88301-073-9). Pendulum Pr.
American Political Bosses & Machines. PLB 5.90 (ISBN 0-531-02646-9). Watts.
American Preachers of to-Day: Intimate Appraisals of Thirty-Two Leaders. facsimile ed. 14.50 (ISBN 0-8369-2279-4). Arno.
American Renaissance in New England. 42.00. Bruccoli.
American Renaissance in New England. 42.00 (ISBN 0-8103-0913-0). Gale.
American Revolutionary: A Biography of General Alexander McDougall. lib. bdg. 13.95x (ISBN 0-8371-9035-5, MAR/). Greenwood.
American Singers. 10.00 (ISBN 0-19-502524-5). Oxford U Pr.
American Slave: A Composite Autobiography, Supplement Series 1. lib. bdg. 325.00x set (ISBN 0-8371-9756-2, RAA/). Greenwood.
American Statesmen: An Interpretation of Our History & Heritage. 16.50 (ISBN 0-8369-1810-X). Arno.
American Talleyrand: The Career & Contemporaries of Martin Van Buren. 13.50 (ISBN 0-8462-1043-6). Russell.
American Teacher in Early Meiji Japan. pap. text ed. 4.75x (ISBN 0-8248-0404-X). U Pr of Hawaii.
American Voyageur: The Journal of David Bates Douglass. 4.25 (ISBN 0-918616-08-5). Northern Mich.
American Writers & Compilers of Sacred Music. 10.00 (ISBN 0-8462-0876-8). Russell.
American Writers of the Present Day. 20.00 (ISBN 0-8274-0975-3). R West.
American Writers of the Present Day: 1890-1920. lib. bdg. 20.00 (ISBN 0-8414-7362-5). Folcroft.
America's Dizzy Dean. 9.95 (ISBN 0-8272-0014-5). Bethany Pr.
America's Eleven Greatest Presidents. 2nd ed. pap. text ed. 7.95 (ISBN 0-528-66103-5). Rand.
America's Ethan Allen. reinforced bdg. 8.95 (ISBN 0-395-24449-8); pap. 3.95 (ISBN 0-395-24908-2). HM.
America's First Hamlet. lib. bdg. 23.75x (ISBN 0-8371-8446-0, OVAH). Greenwood.
America's Immigrant Women. lib. bdg. 9.95 (ISBN 0-8057-8400-4). Twayne.
America's Immigrant Women. pap. 4.95x (ISBN 0-88254-369-5). Hippocrene Bks.
America's Journeys into Space: The Astronauts of the United States. PLB 8.29 (ISBN 0-671-33020-9). Messner.
America's Master of Bee Culture: The Life of L. L. Langstroth. 9.95 (ISBN 0-8014-1053-3). Cornell U Pr.
America's Robert E. Lee. 8.95 (ISBN 0-395-06707-3). HM.
America's Thousand Bishops: From 1513 to 1974, from Abramowicz to Zuroweste. pap. 3.50 (ISBN 0-913228-09-5). R J Liederbach.
AMIRIA: The Life Story of a Maori Woman. 22.50 (ISBN 0-589-00978-8). Reed.
Among Men & Beasts. 9.95 (ISBN 0-498-02168-8). A S Barnes.
Among My Klediments. 6.95 (ISBN 0-310-38170-3). Zondervan.
Among the Shoshones. 9.00 (ISBN 0-912720-01-8). Pine Cone Pubs.
Amos Fortune, Free Man. 6.95 (ISBN 0-525-25570-2). Dutton.
Amos the Prophet: The Man & His Background. pap. 2.95 (ISBN 0-8006-0012-6). Fortress.
Amy: The World of Amy Lowell & the Imagist Movement. 12.50 (ISBN 0-396-07022-1). Dodd.
Anatoly Karpov: Chess Is My Life. text ed. 30.00 (ISBN 0-08-023118-7); pap. text ed. 14.00 (ISBN 0-08-023119-5). Pergamon.
Anatomy of an Illness As Perceived by the Patient: Reflections on Healing & Regeneration. 9.95 (ISBN 0-393-01252-2). Norton.
Ancestral Voices. 10.95 (ISBN 0-684-15647-4). Scribner.
Anchored in Love: The Carter Family Story. 5.95 (ISBN 0-8007-0735-4). Revell.
Anchor's Aweigh: The Story of David Glasgow Farragut. PLB 7.87 (ISBN 0-06-023703-1). Har-Row.
Anchors in the Sky: Spuds Ellyson, the First Naval Aviator. 12.95 (ISBN 0-89141-034-1). Presidio Pr.
And a Time to Die. pap. 2.95 (ISBN 0-8356-0305-9). Theos Pub Hse.
And I Remember Spain: A Spanish Civil War Anthology. 7.95 (ISBN 0-02-612960-4). Macmillan.
And I Worked at the Writer's Trade: Chapters of Literary History, 1918-1978. pap. 3.95 (ISBN 0-14-005075-2). Penguin.
And No Birds Sang. 10.95 (ISBN 0-316-58695-1). Little.
And Now New Zealand. 3rd ed. pap. 5.00x (ISBN 0-908565-07-0). Intl Pubns Serv.
And Perhaps: The Story of Ruth Dayan. 6.95 (ISBN 0-15-106845-3). HarBraceJ.
And Say What He Is: The Life of a Special Child. 10.00x (ISBN 0-262-13115-3); pap. 4.95 (ISBN 0-262-63069-9). MIT Pr.
And Then What Happened, Paul Revere? 6.95 (ISBN 0-698-20274-0). Coward.
And There I Stood with My Piccolo. lib. bdg. 14.75x (ISBN 0-8371-8486-X, WIMP). Greenwood.
And Tyler Too. 7.95 (ISBN 0-8407-6585-1). Elsevier-Nelson.
Andre Bazin. 17.95 (ISBN 0-19-502165-7). Oxford U Pr.
Andre Chenier: His Life, Death & Glory. 12.00 (ISBN 0-8214-0009-6). Ohio U Pr.
Andre Gide. pap. 2.95 (ISBN 0-8044-6283-6). Ungar.
Andre Gide & the Crisis of Modern Thought. lib. bdg. 15.00 (ISBN 0-374-95266-3). Octagon.
Andre Malraux. 9.95 (ISBN 0-8044-2379-2). Ungar.
Andre Malraux. 12.95 (ISBN 0-394-48367-7). Pantheon.
Andre Masson. 20.00 (ISBN 0-87070-465-6); pap. 8.95 (ISBN 0-87070-464-8). Museum Mod Art.
Andrea Palladio. 47.50 (ISBN 0-8212-0643-1). NYGS.
Andrew Bradford, Colonial Journalist. lib. bdg. 12.50x (ISBN 0-8371-2429-8, DEBR). Greenwood.
Andrew Carnegie. 25.00 (ISBN 0-19-501282-8). Oxford U Pr.
Andrew Dasburg. 24.95 (ISBN 0-8263-0516-4). U of NM Pr.
Andrew Furuseth, Emancipator of the Seamen. 14.50x (ISBN 0-520-01322-0). U of Cal Pr.
Andrew Jackson. lib. bdg. 7.50 (ISBN 0-8057-3048-6). Twayne.
Andrew Jackson & the Search for Vindication. 7.50 (ISBN 0-316-16554-9); pap. text ed. 4.95 (ISBN 0-316-16553-0). Little.
Andrew Jackson As a Public Man: What He Was, What Chances He Had, & What He Did with Them. lib. bdg. 15.50x (ISBN 0-8371-4104-4, SUAJ). Greenwood.
Andrew Jackson, Hero. 7.95 (ISBN 0-8407-6514-2). Elsevier-Nelson.
Andrew Jackson: The Border Captain. 10.00 (ISBN 0-8446-2309-1). Peter Smith.
Andrew Johnson: A Study in Courage. 44.00 (ISBN 0-403-01231-7). Scholarly.
Andrew Marvell. 13.50 (ISBN 0-8369-9929-0). Arno.
Andrew Marvell. 8.50 (ISBN 0-8462-1526-8). Russell.
Andrew Marvell. lib. bdg. 10.00 (ISBN 0-8495-5036-X). Arden Lib.
Andrew Marvell. lib. bdg. 7.50 (ISBN 0-8414-9537-8). Folcroft.
Andrew Marvell: His Life & Writings. 17.50x (ISBN 0-8014-1202-1). Cornell U Pr.
Andrew Young: A Biography. 10.95 (ISBN 0-8069-8118-0, 002700). Sterling.
Andrew Young: A Matter of Choice. 5.95 (ISBN 0-88436-472-0); pap. 3.50 (ISBN 0-88436-473-9). EMC.
Anecdotes of Public Men. lib. bdg. 49.50 (ISBN 0-306-71456-6). Da Capo.
Anecdotes of Samuel Johnson. 14.75 (ISBN 0-8369-5097-6). Arno.
Anecdotes of the Late Samuel Johnson, LL.D During the Last Twenty Years of His Life see Memoirs of the Life & Writings of the Late Dr. Samuel Johnson.
Angel Dusted: A Family's Nightmare. 8.95 (ISBN 0-02-536600-9). Macmillan.
Angel Face: The Making of a Criminal. 13.50 (ISBN 0-04-923070-0). Allen Unwin.
Angel Face: The Making of a Criminal. pap. 9.50 (ISBN 0-04-923071-9). Allen Unwin.
Angel Mo' & Her Son, Roland Hayes. lib. bdg. 13.00x (ISBN 0-8371-2449-2, HEAM). Greenwood.
Angel of the Prison: A Story About Elizabeth Fry. pap. 1.50 (ISBN 0-03-022121-8). Winston Pr.
Angela Ambrosia. 7.95 (ISBN 0-394-50096-2). Knopf.
Angela Ambrosia. pap. price not set (ISBN 0-671-83324-3). PB.
Anglican Church in New Zealand: A History. 7.50x (ISBN 0-8002-0487-5). Intl Pubns Serv.
Anglo-Saxon Saints & Scholars. 18.50 (ISBN 0-208-00200-6). Shoe String.
Animal Doctor. pap. 1.95 (ISBN 0-515-04440-7). BJ Pub Group.
Animal Doctor. 8.95 (ISBN 0-8415-0466-0). Dutton.
Animals Come First. 8.95 (ISBN 0-671-22440-9). S&S.
Ann Griffiths. pap. text ed. 4.50x (ISBN 0-7083-0628-4). Verry.
Ann the Word: The Life of Mother Ann Lee, Founder of the Shakers. PLB 7.95 (ISBN 0-316-12767-1). Little.
Anna Pavlova in Art & Life. 28.00 (ISBN 0-405-08428-5). Arno.
Annals of an Abiding Liberal. 12.95 (ISBN 0-395-27617-9). HM.
Annals of an Abiding Liberal. pap. 5.95 (ISBN 0-452-00544-2, F544). NAL.
Annals of Labour: Autobiographies of British Working Class People, 1820-1920. 12.50x (ISBN 0-253-30745-7). Ind U Pr.
Annals of Tacitus. 52.00 (ISBN 0-521-08584-5). Cambridge U Pr.
Annals of Tacitus. 2nd ed. 26.00x (ISBN 0-19-814421-0); 19.95x (ISBN 0-19-814422-9). Oxford U Pr.
Annals of the Irish Harpers. 17.50 (ISBN 0-87696-044-1). Lemma.
Anne & the Princesses Royal. 2nd ed. 7.75 (ISBN 0-491-01321-3). Transatlantic.
Anne Boleyn: A Chapter of English History, 1527-1536. 35.00 (ISBN 0-404-09050-8); 18.00 ea. (ISBN 0-404-09051-6) (ISBN 0-404-09052-4). AMS Pr.
Anne Bradstreet: Young Puritan Poet. 5.95 (ISBN 0-672-50013-2). Bobbs.
Anne Bronte. 16.50x (ISBN 0-87471-797-3). Rowman.
Anne Bronte: Her Life & Writings. lib. bdg. 10.00 (ISBN 0-8414-4758-6). Folcroft.
Anne Bronte: Her Life & Writings. lib. bdg. 10.00 (ISBN 0-8495-2304-4). Arden Lib.
Anne Carroll Moore: A Biography. 8.95 (ISBN 0-689-10523-1). Atheneum.
Anne Royall's U. S. A. 25.00 (ISBN 0-8135-0732-4). Rutgers U Pr.
Anne Sexton: A Self-Portrait in Letters. 15.00 (ISBN 0-395-25727-1). HM.
Anne Sexton: A Self-Portrait in Letters. pap. 6.95 (ISBN 0-395-27763-9). HM.
Annie: A Theatre Memoir. 14.95 (ISBN 0-525-05550-9); pap. 7.95 (ISBN 0-525-03010-7). Dutton.
Annie Oakley & the World of Her Time. 8.95 (ISBN 0-02-700270-5, 70027). Macmillan.
Annie Wauneka. PLB 6.95 (ISBN 0-87518-053-1). Dillon.
Anonymous Was a Woman. 19.95 (ISBN 0-312-04185-3); pap. 9.95 (ISBN 0-312-04186-1). St Martin.
Another Part of the Wood: A Self-Portrait. 12.95 (ISBN 0-06-010783-9). Har-Row.
Another Part of the Wood: A Self Portrait. pap. 2.25 (ISBN 0-345-24919-4). Ballantine.
Another World. 7.95 (ISBN 0-385-12719-7). Doubleday.
Anson Jones: The Last President of Texas. 17.50 (ISBN 0-292-73164-7). U of Tex Pr.
Antebellum Writers in New York & the South. 48.00 (ISBN 0-8103-0915-7). Gale.
Anthony Burns: A History. 9.50 (ISBN 0-87928-027-1). Corner Hse.
Anthony Eden. 8.95 (ISBN 0-312-04235-3). St Martin.
Anthony Trollope, His Public Services, Private Friends & Literary Originals. 11.00 (ISBN 0-8046-0137-2). Kennikat.
Anthony Wayne, Trouble Shooter of the American Revolution. lib. bdg. 20.50x (ISBN 0-8371-3383-1, WIAW). Greenwood.
Anthony Wayne, Washington's General. 5.50 (ISBN 0-664-32547-5). Westminster.

Anthropologist at Work: Writings of Ruth Benedict. lib. bdg. 31.50x (ISBN 0-8371-9576-4, BEAW). Greenwood.
Anti-Slavery Leaders of North Carolina. 11.50 (ISBN 0-404-61120-6). AMS Pr.
Anti-Slavery Leaders of North Carolina. 12.50 (ISBN 0-87152-061-3). Reprint.
Anti-Slavery Leaders of North Carolina. pap. 7.00 (ISBN 0-384-03526-4). Johnson Repr.
Anton Raphael Mengs & Neoclassicism. lib. bdg. 25.00 (ISBN 0-8240-3962-9). Garland Pub.
Antonin Artaud. pap. 2.95 (ISBN 0-14-004368-3). Penguin.
Antonin Dvorak. lib. bdg. 10.50x (ISBN 0-8371-3946-5, HOAD). Greenwood.
Antonin Raymond: An Autobiography. 27.50 (ISBN 0-8048-1044-3). C E Tuttle.
Antonio & Francesco Guardi: Their Life & Milieu: With a Catalogue of Their Figure Drawings. lib. bdg. 40.00 (ISBN 0-8240-1979-2). Garland Pub.
Antonio De Mendoza, First Viceroy of New Spain. 8.50 (ISBN 0-8462-0783-4). Russell.
Antonio Gramsci. pap. 3.95 (ISBN 0-14-004934-7). Penguin.
Antonio Gramsci & the Origins of Italian Communism. 15.00x (ISBN 0-8047-0141-5); pap. 5.95 (ISBN 0-8047-0142-3, SP91). Stanford U Pr.
Antonio Gramsci: Towards an Intellectual Biography. pap. 7.95. Carrier Pigeon.
Antonio Maceo: The "Bronze Titan" of Cuba's Struggle for Independence. 15.00 (ISBN 0-85345-423-X). Monthly Rev.
Antonio Stradivari, His Life & Work (1644-1739) 2nd. ed. pap. 5.00 (ISBN 0-486-20425-1). Dover.
Anwar el Sadat: Man with a Mission. 10.50x (ISBN 0-7069-0490-7). Intl Pubns Serv.
A.P. Hill: Lee's Forgotten General. 7.00 (ISBN 0-8078-0973-X). U of NC Pr.
Apache Agent: The Story of John P. Clum. lib. bdg. 34.95 (ISBN 0-8490-1441-7). Gordon Pr.
Apache Agent: The Story of John P. Clum. 13.95x (ISBN 0-8032-0967-3); pap. 4.25 (ISBN 0-8032-5886-0, 654). U of Nebr Pr.
Aphra Behn. lib. bdg. 6.95x (ISBN 0-8057-1040-X). Irvington.
Aphra Behn, the Incomparable Astrea. lib. bdg. 15.00. Folcroft.
Apocalyptic Vision: The Art of Franz Marc As German Expressionism. 17.50 (ISBN 0-06-435275-7). Har-Row.
Apologia Pro Vita Sua. pap. 8.95. Chr Classics.
Apologia Pro Vita Sua. pap. 3.95 (FA2912). Collins Pubs.
Apologia Pro Vita Sua. pap. 3.95 (ISBN 0-395-05109-6, B10, 3-47644). HM.
Apologia Pro Vita Sua. pap. text ed. 4.95x (ISBN 0-393-09766-8, 9766). Norton.
Apologia Pro Vita Sua. 3.50 (ISBN 0-385-12646-8). Doubleday.
Apologia Pro Vita Sua: Being a History of His Religious Opinions. 44.00x (ISBN 0-19-811840-6). Oxford U Pr.
Apologie & Treatise of Ambroise Pare: Containing the Voyages Made into Divers Places with Many of His Writings Upon Surgery. pap. 3.00 (ISBN 0-486-21902-X). Dover.
Apology for the Life of James Fennell. 20.00 (ISBN 0-405-08499-4). Arno.
Apostles & Prophets: Medicine for Society's Ills. 6.00 (ISBN 0-682-48694-9). Exposition.
Appalachian Odyssey: Walking the Trail from Georgia to Maine. o.p. 10.50 (ISBN 0-8289-0294-1); pap. 7.95 (ISBN 0-8289-0295-X). Greene.
Appleton's Cyclopaedia of American Biography. 168.00 (ISBN 0-8103-3155-1). Gale.
Apprentice to Genius: Years with Frank Lloyd Wright. 19.95. McGraw.
Apprenticeship of Abraham Lincoln. 6.95 (ISBN 0-684-14003-9). Scribner.
Approach to Christian Ethics: The Life Contribution, & Thought of T. B. Maston. 5.95 (ISBN 0-8054-6120-5). Broadman.
Approaches to Victorian Autobiography. 18.00x (ISBN 0-8214-0400-8). Ohio U Pr.
Arab Contemporaries: The Role of Personalities in Politics. 17.00x (ISBN 0-8018-1453-7). Johns Hopkins.
Arabian Diary. 13.95x (ISBN 0-520-01386-7). U of Cal Pr.
Arabian Highlands. lib. bdg. 39.50 (ISBN 0-306-70765-9). Da Capo.
Archaeology Beneath the Sea. pap. 3.45 (ISBN 0-06-090515-8, CN 515). Har-Row.
Archer Fullingim: A Country Editor's View of Life. new ed. 12.00 (ISBN 0-913206-07-5). Heidelberg Pubs.
Archer Milton Huntington. 1.25 (ISBN 0-87535-098-4). Hispanic Soc.
Archie Griffin. 5.95 (ISBN 0-385-12524-0). Doubleday.
Archie Griffin. pap. 1.25 (ISBN 0-671-29904-2). Archway.
Archilochus of Paros. 15.00 (ISBN 0-8155-5053-7). Noyes.
Architect As Developer. 27.50 (ISBN 0-07-050536-5). McGraw.
Architects of Aviation. facs. ed. 16.75 (ISBN 0-8369-8065-4). Arno.
Architecture of Joy. 14.95 (ISBN 0-912458-96-8). E A Seemann.
Arctic Diary of Russell Williams Porter. 20.00x (ISBN 0-8139-0649-0). U Pr of Va.
Aretha Franklin. PLB 5.95 (ISBN 0-87191-390-9); pap. 2.75 (ISBN 0-89812-100-0). Creative Ed.
Arid Acres: A History of the Kimama Minidoka Homesteaders. pap. 6.00 (ISBN 0-8466-0291-1, SJS291). Shorey.
Aristotle, New Light on His Life & Some of His Lost Works. Incl. Some Novel Interpretations of the Man & His Life (ISBN 0-268-00517-6); Observations on Some of Aristotle's Lost Works (ISBN 0-268-00518-4). text ed. 45.00x (ISBN 0-268-00522-2); text ed. 24.00x ea. U of Notre Dame Pr.
Aristotle Onassis. pap. 2.50 (ISBN 0-345-27470-9). Ballantine.
Aristotle Onassis. 12.50 (ISBN 0-397-01218-7). Lippincott.
Arkansas Rockefeller. 14.95 (ISBN 0-8071-0253-9). La State U Pr.
Arlene Francis: A Memoir. 9.95 (ISBN 0-671-22808-0). S&S.
Armed with Love: Stories of the Disciples. 6.95 (ISBN 0-687-01741-6). Abingdon.
Armenia & the Near East. lib. bdg. 20.00 (ISBN 0-306-70760-8). Da Capo.
Arms of Krupp, 1587-1968. 14.95 (ISBN 0-316-54490-6). Little.
Arms of Krupp: 1587-1968. pap. 3.95 (ISBN 0-553-06470-3, J13149-4). Bantam.
Armstrongism: The Worldwide Church of God Examined in the Searching Light of Scripture. 7.95 (ISBN 0-914012-15-0). Bibl Evang Pr.
Arnold Bennett: A Biography. 14.50 (ISBN 0-8274-1551-6). R West.
Arnold Bennett: A Biography. 14.50 (ISBN 0-8046-1549-7). Kennikat.
Arnold Bennett: A Last Word. 7.95 (ISBN 0-385-14545-4). Doubleday.
Arnold of Brescia. 23.50 (ISBN 0-404-16116-2). AMS Pr.
Arnold Schoenberg. 20.00 (ISBN 0-02-872480-1). Schirmer Bks.
Arnold Schoenberg. lib. bdg. 15.75x (ISBN 0-313-20762-3, STAS). Greenwood.
Arnold: The Education of a Body Builder. 9.95 (ISBN 0-671-22879-X). S&S.
Arnold: The Education of a Bodybuilder. pap. 5.95 (ISBN 0-671-79041-2). PB.
Arnold Wesker. 10.50 (ISBN 0-8044-2387-3). Ungar.
Arrow in the Blue. 10.95 (ISBN 0-02-565020-3). Macmillan.
Art & Science of Grand Prix Driving. 14.95 (ISBN 0-87938-049-7). Motorbooks Intl.
Art-Life of William Morris Hunt. 15.00 (ISBN 0-405-08714-4). Arno.
Art of Biography. lib. bdg. 17.50 (ISBN 0-8414-8450-3). Folcroft.
Art of Emily Carr. 39.95 (ISBN 0-295-95687-9). U of Wash Pr.
Art of Living Long. lib. bdg. 14.00x (ISBN 0-405-11812-0). Arno.
Art Young: His Life & Times. 28.50 (ISBN 0-88355-255-8). Hyperion Conn.
Artemus Ward (Charles Farrar Browne) A Biography & Bibliography. 20.00x (ISBN 0-8464-0009-X). Beekman Pubs.
Arthur Ashe. 5.50 (ISBN 0-87191-340-2). Creative Ed.
Arthur Ashe: Alone in the Crowd. PLB 5.95 (ISBN 0-88436-263-9); pap. 3.50 (ISBN 0-88436-264-7). EMC.
Arthur Ashe: Tennis Champion. pap. 1.25 (ISBN 0-671-29552-7). Archway.
Arthur Ashe, Tennis Champion. 5.95 (ISBN 0-385-06284-2). Doubleday.
Arthur Dux Bellorum. lib. bdg. 7.50 (ISBN 0-8414-9864-4). Folcroft.
Arthur E. Stilwell: Promoter with a Hunch. 10.00 (ISBN 0-8265-1173-2). Vanderbilt U Pr.
Arthur Hugh Clough: A Descriptive Catalogue, Poetry, Prose, Biography & Criticism. 10.00 (ISBN 0-87104-016-6). NY Pub Lib.
Arthur Hugh Clough: A Monograph. 12.45 (ISBN 0-8274-1313-0). R West.
Arthur Machen: A Bibliography. 10.00 (ISBN 0-8103-3682-0). Gale.
Arthur Machen: A Bibliography. lib. bdg. 15.00 (ISBN 0-8414-3683-5). Folcroft.
Arthur Mitchell. PLB 6.79 (ISBN 0-690-00662-4). T Y Crowell.
Arthur Rimbaud. lib. bdg. 31.75x (ISBN 0-313-21024-1, STRI). Greenwood.
Arthur Rimbaud. rev. ed. pap. 6.95 (ISBN 0-8112-0197-X, NDP254). New Directions.
Artist in America. 3rd rev. ed. 15.00 (ISBN 0-8262-0071-0). U of Mo Pr.
Artist in Chrysalis: A Biographical Study of Goethe in Italy. 7.95 (ISBN 0-252-00326-8). U of Ill Pr.
Artists & Their Friends in England 1700-1799. 36.00. Arno.
Artists in Their Own Words. 12.95 (ISBN 0-312-05512-9). St Martin.
Artists of Early Michigan: A Biographical Dictionary of Artists Native to or Active in Michigan 1701-1900. text ed. 9.95x (ISBN 0-8143-1528-3). Wayne St U Pr.
Artists of the American West: A Biographical Dictionary. 15.00x (ISBN 0-8040-0607-5). Swallow.
Artists of the Renaissance. 17.95 (ISBN 0-670-43445-0). Viking Pr.
Artist's Reminiscences. 14.50 (ISBN 0-8103-3522-0). Gale.
As Bees in Honey Drown: Elbert Hubbard & the Roycrofters. 10.00 (ISBN 0-498-01052-X). A S Barnes.
As Far As I Can Step. pap. 2.50 (ISBN 0-87680-961-1, 98016). Word Bks.
As Far As Yesterday: Memories & Reflections. 10.95x (ISBN 0-8061-0805-3). U of Okla Pr.
As I Lived It: An Autobiographical History of the YMCA of Los Angeles, 1925-1966. 10.00 (ISBN 0-87062-129-7). A H Clark.
As I Remember Him: The Biography of R. S. 7.50 (ISBN 0-8446-0975-7). Peter Smith.
As I Saw It: Women Who Lived the American Adventure. 8.95 (ISBN 0-8037-0339-2). Dial.
As It Happened. 10.00 (ISBN 0-7710-3195-5). McClelland.
As It Happened: A Memoir. 14.95 (ISBN 0-385-14639-6). Doubleday.
As It Was. 12.00x (ISBN 0-7022-1278-4); pap. 5.50x (ISBN 0-7022-1279-2). U of Queensland Pr.
As Their Friends Saw Them. facs. ed. 10.25 (ISBN 0-8369-0375-7). Arno.
As Up They Grew: Autobiographical Essays. pap. 6.95x (ISBN 0-673-05890-5). Scott F.
Asimov's Biographical Encyclopedia of Science & Technology: The Lives & Achievements of 1195 Great Scientists from Ancient Times to the Present Chronologically Arranged. rev ed. 14.95 (ISBN 0-385-04693-6). Doubleday.
Ask Me Lord, I Want to Say Yes. pap. 1.95 (ISBN 0-88270-381-1). Logos.
Asoka the Great: India's Royal Missionary. PLB 5.90 (ISBN 0-531-00947-5). Watts.
Aspects of Doctor Johnson. lib. bdg. 15.00. Folcroft.
Aspects of Walt Whitman. lib. bdg. 30.00 (ISBN 0-8414-2882-4). Folcroft.
Aspects of Walt Whitman. lib. bdg. 40.00 (ISBN 0-8495-0101-6). Arden Lib.
Aspects of Wilde. lib. bdg. 25.00 (ISBN 0-8414-6537-1). Folcroft.
Aspects of Wilde. lib. bdg. 34.95 (ISBN 0-8490-1460-3). Gordon Pr.
Asquith. text ed. 15.95 (ISBN 0-312-05740-7). St Martin.
Assassination of Malcolm X. 9.00 (ISBN 0-87348-472-X); pap. 2.45 (ISBN 0-87348-473-8). Path Pr NY.
Assassination of Martin Luther King, Jr. lib. bdg. 4.90 s&l (ISBN 0-531-02465-2). Watts.
Assault with a Deadly Weapon: The Autobiography of a Street Criminal. pap. 3.95 (ISBN 0-07-001073-0). McGraw.
Assignment in Utopia. lib. bdg. 27.00x (ISBN 0-8371-4497-3, LYAU). Greenwood.
Astaire & Rogers. pap. 1.50 (ISBN 0-8439-0380-5, LB380DK). Nordon Pubns.
Astonish Us in the Morning: Tyrone Guthrie Remembered. 16.95 (ISBN 0-09-128860-6). Merrimack Bk Serv.
Astors: An American Legend. 4.95 (ISBN 0-396-05830-2). Dodd.
Astrological Who's Who. 10.00 (ISBN 0-912240-08-3). Arcane Pubns.
At Random: The Reminiscences of Bennett Cerf. 12.95 (ISBN 0-394-47877-0). Random.
At the Feet of Mahatma Gandhi. lib. bdg. 16.75x (ISBN 0-8371-6154-1, PRMG). Greenwood.
At the Red Summit: Interpreter Behind the Iron Curtain. 6.95 (ISBN 0-02-625780-7). Macmillan.
Athanasius Kircher: A Renaissance Man & the Quest for Lost Knowledge. pap. 8.95 (ISBN 0-500-81020-6). Thames Hudson.
Athenae Oxonienses: An Exact History of All the Writers & Bishops Who Have Had Their Education in the University of Oxford. 3rd ed. 185.00 (ISBN 0-8337-3863-1). B Franklin.
Atlantic Brief Lives: A Biographical Companion to the Arts. 15.00 (ISBN 0-316-50451-3); pap. 4.95 (ISBN 0-316-50457-2). Little.
Atlantic Merchant - Apothecary: Letters of Joseph Cruttenden 1710-1717. 12.50x (ISBN 0-8020-5364-5). U of Toronto Pr.
Atlantic World of Robert G. Albion. 15.00x (ISBN 0-8195-4085-4). Columbia U Pr.
Atlas of the Presidents. rev. ed. 4.50 (ISBN 0-8437-1045-4). Hammond Inc.
Atonement of George Fox. pap. 0.70x (ISBN 0-87574-166-5). Pendle Hill.
Aubrey Beardsley: The Man & His Work. lib. bdg. 13.95 (ISBN 0-8414-5904-5). Folcroft.
Audacity to Believe. 8.95 (ISBN 0-529-05464-7, A1161). Collins Pubs.
Audie Murphy, American Soldier. new ed. 12.50 (ISBN 0-912172-20-7). Hill Jr Coll.
Audubon: The Kentucky Years. 4.95 (ISBN 0-8131-0215-4). U Pr of Ky.
August Strindberg. 25.00 (ISBN 0-405-08724-1). Arno.
August Strindberg: A Psychoanalytic Study with Special Reference to the Oedipus Complex. lib. bdg. 14.95 (ISBN 0-8383-1026-5). Haskell.
Auguste Comte: The Foundation of Sociology. 17.95 (ISBN 0-470-85988-1). Halsted Pr.
Augustine Laure, S.J., Missionary to the Yakimas. 6.95 (ISBN 0-87770-176-8); pap. 4.95. Ye Galleon.
Augustine of Hippo: A Biography. 18.50x (ISBN 0-520-00186-9); pap. 4.95 (ISBN 0-520-01411-1, CAL179). U of Cal Pr.
Augustus. pap. 3.95 (ISBN 0-393-00584-4). Norton.
Augustus Baldwin Longstreet: A Study of the Development of Culture in the South. 12.00x (ISBN 0-8203-0002-0). U of Ga Pr.
Augustus John. 34.50 (ISBN 0-404-14560-4). AMS Pr.
Auscultation of Two Worlds. 9.50 (ISBN 0-533-03118-4). Vantage.
Australian Adventure: Letters from an Ambassador's Wife. 10.00 (ISBN 0-292-70001-6). U of Tex Pr.
Australian Alternative. 7.95 (ISBN 0-87000-251-1). Arlington Hse.
Australian Dictionary of Biography. Incl. 1788-1850, A-H (ISBN 0-522-83516-3); 1788-1850, I-Z (ISBN 0-522-83705-0); 1851-1890, A-C (ISBN 0-522-83909-6); 1851-1890, D-J (ISBN 0-522-84034-5). 32.50 ea. Intl Schol Bk Serv.
Australian Primitive Painters. 24.25x (ISBN 0-7022-1039-0). U of Queensland Pr.
Authentic Life of Billy, the Kid. 6.95 (ISBN 0-8061-0297-7); pap. 3.95 (ISBN 0-8061-1195-X). U of Okla Pr.
Author in His Work: Essays on a Problem in Criticism. 22.50x (ISBN 0-300-02179-8). Yale U Pr.
Authors & Friends. 8.00 (ISBN 0-403-00092-0). Scholarly.
Authors & Friends. 9.00 (ISBN 0-404-00596-9). AMS Pr.
Authors & Friends. lib. bdg. 20.00 (ISBN 0-8414-4251-7). Folcroft.
Authors of Books for Young People. 2nd ed. 19.00 (ISBN 0-8108-0404-2). Scarecrow.
Auto Racing's Young Lions. 6.50 (ISBN 0-399-20579-9). Putnam.
Autobiographia: Or, The Story of a Life. lib. bdg. 30.00 (ISBN 0-8495-5738-0). Arden Lib.
Autobiographic Memoirs. 42.50 (ISBN 0-404-13990-6). AMS Pr.
Autobiographic Memoirs. 50.00 set (ISBN 0-8274-0183-3). R West.
Autobiographical Notes of Charles Evans Hughes. 15.00x (ISBN 0-674-05325-7). Harvard U Pr.
Autobiographical Reminiscences: With Family Letters & Notes on Music. lib. bdg. 20.00 (ISBN 0-306-71081-1). Da Capo.
Autobiographical Sketches. 14.95 (ISBN 0-236-40010-X). Merrimack Bk Serv.
Autobiographical Study. pap. 2.95 (ISBN 0-393-00146-6). Norton.
Autobiographical Writings. pap. 3.95 (ISBN 0-374-50964-6, N417). FS&G.
Autobiographical Writings. 8.95 (ISBN 0-374-10733-5); pap. 3.95 (ISBN 0-374-50964-6). FS&G.
Autobiographical Writings see Booker T. Washington Papers.
Autobiographies. 14.95x (ISBN 0-19-255410-7). Oxford U Pr.
Autobiographies of the Hay Market Martyrs. text ed. 6.50x (ISBN 0-391-00449-2). Humanities.
Autobiographies of the Haymarket Martyrs. 7.50. Am Inst Marxist.
Autobiographies of the Haymarket Martyrs. pap. 4.45 (ISBN 0-913460-58-3). Monad Pr.
Autobiography: A Critical & Comparative Study. lib. bdg. 30.00 (ISBN 0-8414-1468-8). Folcroft.
Autobiography & Correspondence of Mary Granville, Mrs. Delany. 180.00 (ISBN 0-404-02080-1). AMS Pr.
Autobiography & Other Poems. pap. 2.95 (ISBN 0-915342-18-9). SUN.
Autobiography & Selected Letters. pap. 5.00 (ISBN 0-486-20479-0). Dover.
Autobiography & Selected Letters. 8.50 (ISBN 0-8446-1947-7). Peter Smith.
Autobiography, Letters, & Literary Remains of Mrs. Piozzi (Thrale) 68.50 set (ISBN 0-404-56776-2). AMS Pr.
Autobiography of a Female Slave. 13.00x (ISBN 0-8371-2194-9). Negro U Pr.
Autobiography of a Female Slave. pap. 3.50 (N109P). Mnemosyne.
Autobiography of a Female Slave. 14.00 (ISBN 0-403-00163-3). Scholarly.
Autobiography of a Female Slave. facs. ed. 15.50 (ISBN 0-8369-8584-2). Arno.
Autobiography of a Fugitive Negro. 19.00 (ISBN 0-405-01842-8). Arno.

Autobiography of a Fugitive Negro. 4.95 (ISBN 0-87485-032-0). Johnson Chi.
Autobiography of a Happy Woman. 23.00x (ISBN 0-405-06073-4). Arno.
Autobiography of a Philosopher. 10.00 (ISBN 0-384-44675-2). Johnson Repr.
Autobiography of a Philosopher. lib. bdg. 8.25x (ISBN 0-8371-0605-2, PAAP). Greenwood.
Autobiography of a Shaker, & Revelation of the Apocalypse. new & enl. ed. 10.00 (ISBN 0-404-10748-6). AMS Pr.
Autobiography of a Shaker & Revelation of the Apocalypse. lib. bdg. 15.00x (ISBN 0-87991-002-X). Porcupine Pr.
Autobiography of a Thief. 31.00 (ISBN 0-384-21350-2, R165). Johnson Repr.
Autobiography of a Winnebago Indian. pap. 1.75 (ISBN 0-486-20096-5). Dover.
Autobiography of a Winnebago Indian. 5.50 (ISBN 0-8446-2774-7). Peter Smith.
Autobiography of a Yaqui Poet. 18.50x (ISBN 0-8165-0698-1); pap. 8.95 (ISBN 0-8165-0628-0). U of Ariz Pr.
Autobiography of a Yogi. 6.95. Wehman.
Autobiography of a Yogi. Marathi ed. 4.00 (ISBN 0-87612-078-8). Self Realization.
Autobiography of a Yogi. 6.95 (ISBN 0-87612-075-3); Bengali ed. 14.00 (ISBN 0-87612-071-0); Dutch ed. 20.00 (ISBN 90-202-4016-1); German ed. 16.00 (ISBN 3-87041-015-9); Gujarati ed. 4.00 (ISBN 0-87612-072-9); Japanese ed. 8.75 (ISBN 0-87612-073-7); pap. 2.50 (ISBN 0-87612-079-6). Self Realization.
Autobiography of a Yogi. pap. 5.00 British ed. (ISBN 0-09-021051-4); pap. 12.00 Danish ed. (ISBN 87-418-7082-4); pap. 11.00 French ed. (ISBN 0-87612-066-4); pap. 12.00 Greek ed. (ISBN 0-87612-069-9); pap. 10.00 Italian ed. (ISBN 0-87612-067-2); pap. 9.00 Spanish ed. (ISBN 0-87612-068-0); pap. 4.00 Hindu ed. (ISBN 0-87612-077-X). Self Realization.
Autobiography of Alfred Austin, Poet Laureate. 30.00 (ISBN 0-527-03880-6). Kraus Repr.
Autobiography of Alfred Austin, Poet Laureate, 1835-1910. 34.50 (ISBN 0-404-08717-5). AMS Pr.
Autobiography of Alice B. Toklas. pap. 2.45 (ISBN 0-394-70133-X). Random.
Autobiography of Alice B. Toklas. 6.50 (ISBN 0-8446-3003-9). Peter Smith.
Autobiography of American Business: The Story Told by Those Who Made It. pap. 3.95 (ISBN 0-385-06972-3). Doubleday.
Autobiography of an Androgyne. 15.00x (ISBN 0-405-07400-X). Arno.
Autobiography of an Elderly Woman. 15.00x (ISBN 0-405-06125-0). Arno.
Autobiography of an English Gamekeeper. 20.00 (ISBN 0-86023-025-2). State Mutual Bk.
Autobiography of an Ex-Coloured Man. 7.95 (ISBN 0-394-41582-5). Knopf.
Autobiography of an Ex-Coloured Man. pap. 4.95 (ISBN 0-8090-0032-6). Hill & Wang.
Autobiography of an Ex-Coloured Man. lib. bdg. 25.00 (ISBN 0-8495-2713-9). Arden Lib.
Autobiography of an Unknown Indian. 14.50x (ISBN 0-520-00224-5). U of Cal Pr.
Autobiography of an Unknown South African. 14.95x (ISBN 0-520-01845-1); pap. 3.95 (ISBN 0-520-02903-8). U of Cal Pr.
Autobiography of Anton Rubinstein, 1829-1889 14.00 (ISBN 0-403-00707-0). Scholarly.
Autobiography of Benjamin Franklin. pap. text ed. 3.33 (ISBN 0-87720-721-6). AMSCO Sch.
Autobiography of Benjamin Franklin. PLB 7.95 (ISBN 0-531-00159-8). Watts.
Autobiography of Benjamin Franklin. pap. 1.95 (ISBN 0-02-002910-1). Macmillan.
Autobiography of Benjamin Franklin. pap. 1.25 (ISBN 0-8049-0071-X, CL-71). Airmont.
Autobiography of Benjamin Franklin. 22.50x (ISBN 0-300-00648-9); pap. 4.45x (ISBN 0-300-00147-9, Y117). Yale U Pr.
Autobiography of Bertrand Russell. pap. 7.95 (ISBN 0-04-921022-X). Allen Unwin.
Autobiography of Bertrand Russell: 1872-1914. 17.95 (ISBN 0-04-921003-3). Allen Unwin.
Autobiography of Bertrand Russell: 1914-1944. 14.95 (ISBN 0-04-921009-2). Allen Unwin.
Autobiography of Charles Caldwell, M. D. 39.50 (ISBN 0-306-70978-3). Da Capo.
Autobiography of Charles G. Finney. pap. 3.95 (ISBN 0-87123-010-0). Bethany Fell.
Autobiography of Clara Fisher Maeder. 16.50 (ISBN 0-8337-2180-1). B Franklin.
Autobiography of Dying. 8.95 (ISBN 0-385-14481-4). Doubleday.
Autobiography of Edward Gibbon. lib. bdg. 15.00 (ISBN 0-89760-312-5). Dynamic Learn Corp.
Autobiography of Edward, Lord Herbert of Cherbury. 2nd ed. lib. bdg. 17.75x (ISBN 0-8371-4235-0, HEAU). Greenwood.
Autobiography of Federico Sanchez & the Communist Underground in Spain. text ed. 14.95 (ISBN 0-918294-05-3); pap. cancelled (ISBN 0-918294-10-X). Karz Pub.
Autobiography of Francis Place 1771-1854. 38.00 (ISBN 0-521-08539-0). Cambridge U Pr.
Autobiography of George Dewey: Admiral of the Navy. 11.50 (ISBN 0-403-00942-1). Scholarly.
Autobiography of Giuseppe Garibaldi. 45.00. Fertig.
Autobiography of James Gallier, Architect. lib. bdg. 20.00 (ISBN 0-306-71247-4). Da Capo.
Autobiography of Johann Wolfgang Von Goethe. 10.00 ea. (ISBN 0-226-30055-2) (ISBN 0-226-30056-0). U of Chicago Pr.
Autobiography of John Fitch. pap. 7.00 (ISBN 0-87169-113-2). Am Philos.
Autobiography of John Hays Hammond. 44.00x (ISBN 0-405-05913-2). Arno.
Autobiography of John Milton: Milton's Life in His Own Words. lib. bdg. 20.00 (ISBN 0-8414-0287-6). Folcroft.
Autobiography of Karl Von Dittersdorf. lib. bdg. 17.50 (ISBN 0-306-71864-2). Da Capo.
Autobiography of Lincoln Steffens. 17.50 (ISBN 0-15-110283-X). HarBraceJ.
Autobiography of Lincoln Steffens. pap. 3.75 (ISBN 0-15-609395-2, HB149); pap. 4.95 (ISBN 0-15-609396-0, HB150). HarBraceJ.
Autobiography of Lord Alfred Douglas. 25.00 (ISBN 0-8274-1903-1). R West.
Autobiography of Lord Alfred Douglas. 20.00 (ISBN 0-403-00796-8). Scholarly.
Autobiography of Lord Alfred Douglas. facs. ed. 14.50 (ISBN 0-8369-5421-1). Arno.
Autobiography of Martin Van Buren. lib. bdg. 55.00 (ISBN 0-306-71275-X). Da Capo.
Autobiography of Mother Jones. 14.00 (ISBN 0-405-02130-5). Arno.
Autobiography of Mother Jones. 3rd rev. ed. lib. bdg. 10.00 (ISBN 0-88286-023-2); pap. 4.50 (ISBN 0-88286-013-5). C H Kerr.
Autobiography of Mrs. Tom Thumb: Some of My Life Experiences. 15.00 (ISBN 0-208-01760-7). Shoe String.
Autobiography of Peter Cartwright: The Backwoods Preacher. 20.50 (ISBN 0-8369-6761-5). Arno.
Autobiography of Rev. E. Mathews, the Father Dickson of Mrs. Stowe's 'Dred' facs. ed. 16.50 (ISBN 0-8369-8629-6). Arno.
Autobiography of Samuel Bamford. Incl. Early Days; Passages in the Life of a Radical. 37.50x (ISBN 0-678-05025-2). Kelley.
Autobiography of Sir John Martin Harvey. 35.50 (ISBN 0-384-21695-1). Johnson Repr.
Autobiography of Sir John Martin-Harvey. 24.00 (ISBN 0-403-01015-2). Scholarly.
Autobiography of Sir Walter Besant. 14.45 (ISBN 0-8274-1721-7). R West.
Autobiography of Sir Walter Besant. 13.50 (ISBN 0-403-00864-6). Scholarly.
Autobiography of the Reverend Josiah Henson. pap. 4.25 (ISBN 0-201-08712-X). A-W.
Autobiography of the Supreme Court: Off-the-Bench Commentary by the Justices. lib. bdg. 31.75x (ISBN 0-313-20385-7, WESU). Greenwood.
Autobiography of Thomas Collier Platt. 30.00x (ISBN 0-405-05894-2). Arno.
Autobiography of Thurlow Weed see Life of Thurlow Weed.
Autobiography of W. E. B. Du Bois: A Soliloquy on Viewing My Life from the Last Decade of Its First Century. 12.00 (ISBN 0-527-25262-X). Kraus Repr.
Autobiography of Will Rogers. pap. 1.95 (ISBN 0-380-00213-2, 34397). Avon.
Autobiography of William Carlos Williams. pap. 5.75 (ISBN 0-8112-0226-7, NDP223). New Directions.
Autobiography of William Plomer. rev. new ed. 20.00 (ISBN 0-8008-0543-7). Taplinger.
Autobiography of Worthington Whittredge. 10.00 (ISBN 0-405-00874-0). Arno.
Autobiography: The Story of My Experiments with Truth. pap. 6.95 (ISBN 0-8070-5981-1, BP35). Beacon Pr.
Automotive Career of Ransom E. Olds. 7.50 (ISBN 0-87744-008-5). Mich St U Busn.
Automotive Giants of America: Men Who Are Making Our Motor Industry. 16.00 (ISBN 0-8369-2989-6). Arno.
Autopsy: The Memoirs of a Medical Detective. 10.00 (ISBN 0-312-06211-7). St Martin.
Aventures De L'esprit. 15.00x (ISBN 0-405-07394-1). Arno.
Aviation's Mr. Sam. 9.95 (ISBN 0-8168-3100-9). Aero.
Avicenna on Theology. 11.00 (ISBN 0-88355-676-6). Hyperion Conn.
Away From It All. 7.95 (ISBN 0-498-06827-7). A S Barnes.
Away with All Pests: An English Surgeon in People's China, 1954-1969. pap. 3.95 (ISBN 0-85345-199-0, PB1990). Monthly Rev.
Aycock Brown's Outer Banks. 14.95 (ISBN 0-915442-18-3). Donning Co.
Az Ismeretlen Illyes. 2nd ed. 4.50 (ISBN 0-911050-34-5). Occidental.

B

Baa Baa Black Sheep. pap. 2.25 (ISBN 0-553-13510-4, B13510-4). Bantam.
Baa Baa Black Sheep. 15.00. J B Wilson.
Bab: The Herald of the Day of Days. 8.95 (ISBN 0-85398-048-9, 7-31-50); pap. 4.50 (ISBN 0-85398-054-3, 7-31-51). Baha'i.
Baba. pap. 1.25 (ISBN 0-671-78260-6). PB.
Babe Ruth - Jackie Robinson. text ed. 4.50 (ISBN 0-88301-371-1); pap. text ed. 1.45 (ISBN 0-88301-359-2); wkbk 0.95 (ISBN 0-88301-383-5). Pendulum Pr.
Babe Ruth & Hank Aaron: The Home Run Kings. PLB 6.48 (ISBN 0-688-51654-8). Lothrop.
Babe Ruth & Hank Aaron: The Home Run Kings. pap. 1.75 (ISBN 0-688-46654-0). Lothrop.
Babeuf Plot: The Making of a Republican Legend. lib. bdg. 11.00x (ISBN 0-8371-8466-5, THBP). Greenwood.
Bach. PLB 8.79 (ISBN 0-690-11391-9). T Y Crowell.
Bach: A Biography. 24.00 (ISBN 0-403-01699-1). Scholarly.
Bach Family: Seven Generations of Creative Genius. lib. bdg. 29.50 (ISBN 0-306-79596-5). Da Capo.
Bach: The Conflict Between the Sacred & the Secular. lib. bdg. 12.50 (ISBN 0-306-70581-8). Da Capo.
Back in the Saddle Again. 8.95 (ISBN 0-385-03234-X). Doubleday.
Back to Kant: The Revival of Kantianism in German Social & Historical Thought, 1860-1914. text ed. 17.95x (ISBN 0-8143-1590-9). Wayne St U Pr.
Background for Domenico Scarlatti, 1685-1757. lib. bdg. 9.25x (ISBN 0-8371-4335-7, SIDS). Greenwood.
Background for Queen Anne. lib. bdg. 25.00 (ISBN 0-8414-7600-4). Folcroft.
Backstairs Dragon: A Life of Robert Harley, Earl of Oxford. 10.00 (ISBN 0-8008-0587-9). Taplinger.
Bacon. 5.00 (ISBN 0-404-51704-8). AMS Pr.
Bacon. lib. bdg. 15.00 (ISBN 0-8414-3404-2). Folcroft.
Bacon. lib. bdg. 20.00 (ISBN 0-8414-2825-5). Folcroft.
Bad Company: The Story of California's Legendary & Actual Stage-Robbers, Bandits, Highwaymen & Outlaws from the Fifties to the Eighties. 15.00x (ISBN 0-8032-0930-4); pap. 5.95 (ISBN 0-8032-5866-6, 649). U of Nebr Pr.
Bad Nigger! The National Impact of Jack Johnson. 9.95 (ISBN 0-8046-9061-8). Kennikat.
Baden-Powell. 10.00 (ISBN 0-87266-045-1). Argosy.
Baker James Cauthen: A Man for All Nations. 6.95 (ISBN 0-8054-7219-3). Broadman.
Baker's Biographical Dictionary of Musicians. 6th ed. 75.00 (ISBN 0-02-870240-9). Schirmer Bks.
Baker's Dozen: Thirteen Unusual Americans. lib. bdg. 15.75x (ISBN 0-8371-7495-3, NYBD). Greenwood.
Bakunin. lib. bdg. 13.95 (ISBN 0-8383-1259-1). Haskell.
Balboa: Discoverer of the Pacific. PLB 7.89 (ISBN 0-06-024316-3). Har-Row.
Balfour: A Political Biography. 23.95 (ISBN 0-521-08536-5). Cambridge U Pr.
Ball of Fire: An Autobiography. 8.95x (ISBN 0-460-04304-8). Biblio Dist.
Ballantyne the Brave: A Victorian Writer & His Family. 8.95 (ISBN 0-8023-1240-3). Dufour.
Ballantyne the Brave: A Victorian Writer & His Family. 15.00 (ISBN 0-89366-023-X). Ultramarine Pub.
Balloon Tytler. 12.00 (ISBN 0-571-09986-6). Transatlantic.
Ballyhoo Bonanza: Charles Sweeny & the Idaho Mines. 12.50 (ISBN 0-295-95129-X). U of Wash Pr.
Balthasar Hubmaier: Anabaptist Theologian & Martyr. 19.95 (ISBN 0-8170-0793-8). Judson.
Balzac. 20.00 (ISBN 0-8274-0710-6). R West.
Balzac. lib. bdg. 21.95 (ISBN 0-8383-1778-2). Haskell.
Balzac. 10.00 (ISBN 0-404-01959-5). AMS Pr.
Banda. 16.75 (ISBN 0-7100-7631-2). Routledge & Kegan.
Bandit King: Lampiao of Brazil. 15.00 (ISBN 0-89096-050-X). Tex A&M Univ Pr.
Baptist Relations with Other Christians. 12.00 (ISBN 0-8170-0602-8). Judson.
Baptists in America. pap. 6.95 (ISBN 0-385-14655-8). Doubleday.
Baptists Who Dared. pap. 3.95 (ISBN 0-8170-0855-1). Judson.
Baptists Who Shaped a Nation. 2.50 (ISBN 0-8054-6517-0). Broadman.
Barbara Jordan. 7.95 (ISBN 0-8037-0452-6). Dial.
Barbara Jordan: Keeping Faith. text ed. 5.95 (ISBN 0-88436-432-1). EMC.
Barbara Stanwyck. pap. 1.75 (ISBN 0-515-03641-2, M3641). HarBraceJ.
Barclay Fox's Journal. 23.50x (ISBN 0-8476-6187-3). Rowman.
Bard of Savagery: Thorstein Veblen & Modern Social Theory. 14.95 (ISBN 0-8164-9323-5). Continuum.
Barefoot Abe. pap. 0.95 (ISBN 0-440-40639-0). Dell.
Barefoot in the Grass: The Story of Grandma Moses. 4.95 (ISBN 0-385-06032-7); PLB (ISBN 0-385-00454-0). Doubleday.
Barely Audible: A History of the Denver Broncos. 15.95 (ISBN 0-914628-01-1). Graphic Impress.
Barnett Newman. 55.00 (ISBN 0-8109-1360-7). Abrams.
Barney Ford, Black Baron. 4.50 (ISBN 0-396-06751-4). Dodd.
Baron Dominique Vivant Denon, 1747-1825: Hedonist & Scholar in a Period of Transition. 12.00 (ISBN 0-8386-7470-4). Fairleigh Dickinson.
Baron of Beacon Hill: A Biography of John Hancock. 12.95 (ISBN 0-395-27619-5). HM.
Barrett: A Street Cop Who Cared. 7.95 (ISBN 0-8007-0918-7). Revell.
Barrington-Bernard Correspondence, & Illustrative Matter, 1760-1770. lib. bdg. 29.50 (ISBN 0-306-71909-6). Da Capo.
Barrio Boy. 8.95x (ISBN 0-268-00440-4); pap. 3.95 (ISBN 0-268-00441-2). U of Notre Dame Pr.
Barry Manilow. pap. 1.95 (ISBN 0-448-17035-3). G&D.
Barry Manilow. PLB 5.95 (ISBN 0-87191-617-7); pap. 2.75 (ISBN 0-89812-122-1). Creative Ed.
Barry Richards Story. 10.95 (ISBN 0-571-11187-4). Merrimack Bk Serv.
Bart Markel Story. 5.95 (ISBN 0-87880-010-7). Norton.
Bart Starr: A Biography. 6.95 (ISBN 0-385-11694-2); PLB (ISBN 0-385-11695-0). Doubleday.
Bartholomew De Las Casas: His Life, His Apostolate, & His Writings. 11.00 (ISBN 0-404-07146-5). AMS Pr.
Bartok. 7.95x (ISBN 0-460-03136-8). Biblio Dist.
Bartolome de Las Casas in History: Toward an Understanding of the Man & His Work. 20.00x (ISBN 0-87580-025-4); boxed set of 3 vols., with Hanke & Poole 50.00 (HPFK-3). N Ill U Pr.
Baseball As I Have Known It. pap. 1.95 (ISBN 0-448-17345-X). G&D.
Baseball [illegible] 10815-9). [illegible]
Baseball: Records, Stars, [illegible] (ISBN 0-15-205718-8). HarBraceJ.
Baseball's Best: The Hall of Fame Gallery. 24.95 (ISBN 0-07-002144-9). McGraw.
Baseball's Champion Pitchers: The Cy Young Award Winners. PLB 6.64 (ISBN 0-671-32698-8). Messner.
Baseball's Golden Dozen. 8.50 (ISBN 0-682-48564-0). Exposition.
Baseball's Great Moments. 2.50 (ISBN 0-394-83030-X); PLB 3.69 (ISBN 0-394-93030-4). Random.
Baseball's Greatest Sluggers. 2.50 (ISBN 0-394-82538-1); PLB 3.69 (ISBN 0-394-92538-6) Random.
Baseball's Home-Run Hitters. PLB 5.95g (ISBN 0-8225-1055-3). Lerner Pubns.
Baseball's Most Colorful Managers. PLB 4.97 (ISBN 0-399-60044-2). Putnam.
Baseball's Zaniest Stars. 2.50 (ISBN 0-394-82142-4); PLB 3.69 (ISBN 0-394-92142-9). Random.
Basil Henriques: A Portrait. 16.95 (ISBN 0-7100-8439-0). Routledge & Kegan.
Basil Rathbone: His Life & His Films. 12.00 (ISBN 0-498-01471-1). A S Barnes.
Basketball's Big Men. PLB 5.95 (ISBN 0-8225-1054-5). Lerner Pubns.
Basketball's Greatest Stars. PLB 4.97 (ISBN 0-399-60045-0). Putnam.
Basketball's High Flyers. PLB 5.95g (ISBN 0-8225-1058-8). Lerner Pubns.
Battle Drums & Geysers: The Life & Journals of Lt. Gustavus Cheyney Doane. 15.00. Bonney.
Battle for Burma. text ed. 19.50x (ISBN 0-8419-0468-5). Holmes & Meier.
Baudelaire. pap. 3.95x (ISBN 0-8147-0369-0). NYU Pr.
Baudelaire. 12.50 (ISBN 0-8112-0387-5). New Directions.
Baudelaire: A Collection of Critical Essays. 9.95 (ISBN 0-13-072496-3). P-H.
Baudelaire & the Symbolists. 8.50 (ISBN 0-8046-0935-7). Kennikat.
Baudelaire & the Symbolists. facsimile ed. 13.50 (ISBN 0-8369-2423-1). Arno.
Baudelaire: Flesh & Spirit. lib. bdg. 23.95 (ISBN 0-8383-2058-9). Haskell.
Baudelaire: Flesh & Spirit. lib. bdg. 27.50 (ISBN 0-8495-4930-2). Arden Lib.

Baudelaire: Paradox of Redemptive Satanism. 9.00 (ISBN 0-8173-7602-X). U of Ala Pr.

Bay City Rollers. pap. 0.95 (ISBN 0-425-03044-X). Berkley Pub.

Bayard Taylor. 12.25 (ISBN 0-8274-1915-5). R West.

Be My Son. pap. 2.95 (ISBN 0-87793-121-6). Ave Maria.

Beach Boys & the California Myth. 14.95 (ISBN 0-448-14625-8); pap. 7.95 (ISBN 0-448-14626-6). G&D.

Beach Boys: Southern California Pastoral. lib. bdg. 7.95 (ISBN 0-89370-102-5); pap. 1.95 (ISBN 0-89370-202-1). Borgo Pr.

Bear & I: The Story of the World's Most Famous Caddie. 7.95 (ISBN 0-689-10983-0). Atheneum.

Bearings: A Foreign Correspondent's Life Behind the Lines. 12.50 (ISBN 0-670-15149-1). Viking Pr.

Bear's Heart: Scenes from the Life of a Cheyenne Artist of One Hundred Years Ago with Pictures by Himself. 8.95 (ISBN 0-397-31746-8). Lippincott.

Beasts Go West. 10.00 (ISBN 0-312-07049-7). St Martin.

Beasts of My Field. 8.95 (ISBN 0-312-07052-7). St Martin.

Beat Book. 10.00 (ISBN 0-934660-00-X). TUVOTI.

Beatles: An Illustrated Record. 15.00 (ISBN 0-517-52010-9); pap. 7.95 (ISBN 0-517-52045-1). Crown.

Beatles: An Illustrated Record. rev. ed. 15.00 (ISBN 0-517-53366-9); pap. 7.95 (ISBN 0-517-53367-7). Crown.

Beatles Forever. pap. 8.95 (ISBN 0-07-055087-5). McGraw.

Beau Brummell. 28.50. Porter.

Beau Brummell. lib. bdg. 12.50 (ISBN 0-8414-9616-1). Folcroft.

Beaumont the Dramatist: A Portrait with Some Account of His Circle, Elizabethan & Jacobean & His Association with John Fletcher. 11.50 (ISBN 0-8462-1257-9). Russell.

Beauty & the Traitor: The Story of Mrs Benedict Arnold. 6.25 (ISBN 0-8255-5400-4). Macrae.

Beaversprite: My Years Building an Animal Sanctuary. 7.95 (ISBN 0-87701-104-4). Chronicle Bks.

Because He Lives. 6.95 (ISBN 0-8007-0881-4). Revell.

Because He Lives. pap. 4.95 (ISBN 0-8007-5037-3). Revell.

Beckford. lib. bdg. 25.00 (ISBN 0-8414-3448-4). [illegible]

[illegible] 571-10794- [illegible]

[illegible] aphy of James [illegible] Laurie. 10.00 (ISBN 0-911536-61-2). Trinity U Pr.

Bed & the Throne: The Life of Isabella D'Este. 12.50 (ISBN 0-06-012810-0). Har-Row.

Bed-Time-Story. 7.95 (ISBN 0-394-48803-2). Random.

Bed-Time-Story. pap. 1.95 (ISBN 0-449-24064-9, X2540). Fawcett.

Bee Gees: A Photo-Bio. pap. 1.95 (ISBN 0-515-05158-6). BJ Pub Group.

Beecham Remembered. 28.00x (ISBN 0-7156-1117-8). Biblio Dist.

Been There & Back. 8.95 (ISBN 0-910244-91-X); pap. 3.95 (ISBN 0-910244-92-8). Blair.

Beerbohm Tree, His Life & Laughter. lib. bdg. 14.00x (ISBN 0-8371-5699-8, PEBT). Greenwood.

Beethoven. pap. 0.95 (ISBN 0-02-061460-8). Macmillan.

Beethoven. 3.50 (ISBN 0-87250-200-7); PLB 3.27 (ISBN 0-87250-400-X). D White.

Beethoven & the Age of Revolution. pap. 2.75 (ISBN 0-7178-0422-6). Intl Pub Co.

Beethoven & the World of Music. lib. bdg. 10.25x (ISBN 0-8371-6845-7, KOBE). Greenwood.

Beethoven As I Knew Him. pap. 6.95 (ISBN 0-393-00638-7). Norton.

Beethoven: Biography of a Genius. 17.50 (ISBN 0-308-70104-6). T Y Crowell.

Beethoven: Biography of a Genius. pap. 8.95 (ISBN 0-8152-0331-4, A331). T Y Crowell.

Beethoven Handbook. lib. bdg. 19.25x (ISBN 0-8371-8540-8, NEBH). Greenwood.

Beethoven: His Spiritual Development. pap. 1.95 (ISBN 0-394-70100-3). Random.

Beethoven the Creator: The Great Creative Epochs: From Eroica to the Appassionata. pap. 4.50 (ISBN 0-486-21182-7). Dover.

Beethoven: The Search for Reality. facsimile ed. 16.00 (ISBN 0-8369-5818-7). Arno.

Before Honor. 7.95 (ISBN 0-87981-046-7). Holman.

Before the Bluestockings. lib. bdg. 25.00 (ISBN 0-8414-9637-4). Folcroft.

Before the Colors Fade: Portrait of a Soldier, George S. Patton Jr. lib. bdg. 14.00 (ISBN 0-910220-61-1). Larlin Corp.

Before the Supreme Court: The Story of Belva Ann Lockwood. 4.95 (ISBN 0-395-18520-3). HM.

Beggar on Horseback: The Autobiography of Thomas D. Cabot. 12.50 (ISBN 0-87923-268-4). Godine.

Beginning Again: An Autobiography of the Years 1911 to 1918. pap. 3.45 (ISBN 0-15-611680-4, HB321). HarBraceJ.

Beginnings. PLB 5.95 (ISBN 0-689-20653-4). Atheneum.

Beginnings in the Life of Christ. rev. ed. pap. 3.50 (ISBN 0-8024-0608-4). Moody.

Beginnings of Telephony. 19.00x (ISBN 0-405-06057-2). Arno.

Behind Closed Doors. 9.95 (ISBN 0-689-10712-9). Atheneum.

Behind Closed Doors. pap. 1.95 (ISBN 0-451-07423-8, J7423). NAL.

Behind the Ballots: The Personal History of a Politician. lib. bdg. 17.25x (ISBN 0-8371-4738-7, FABB). Greenwood.

Behind the Scenes at the Zoo. o.p. 5.95 (ISBN 0-385-09515-5); PLB (ISBN 0-385-09514-7). Doubleday.

Behind the Scenes or Thirty Years a Slave, & Four Years in the White House. 11.00 (ISBN 0-405-01824-X). Arno.

Behind the Wheel: Great Road Racing Drivers. 5.95g (ISBN 0-8098-2076-5). Walck.

Behind the White Screen. 10.95 (ISBN 0-87376-022-0). Red Dust.

Behold the Sun. 6.95 (ISBN 0-918464-08-0); pap. 3.95 (ISBN 0-918464-06-4). D Armstrong.

Being Busted. pap. 1.95 (ISBN 0-8128-1341-3). Stein & Day.

Being Seventy: The Measure of a Year. 10.00 (ISBN 0-670-15539-X). Viking Pr.

Bela Bartok. pap. 7.50x (ISBN 0-8443-0105-1). Vienna Hse.

Bela Bartok. 10.00 (ISBN 0-8008-0720-0). Taplinger.

Bell Rings at Four: A Black Teacher's Chronicle of Change. 11.00 (ISBN 0-89052-024-0). Madrona Pr.

Belles on Their Toes. 7.95 (ISBN 0-690-13023-6). T Y Crowell.

Belonging: Conversations in Israel. 9.95 (ISBN 0-03-046796-9). HR&W.

Beloved Friend: The Story of Tchaikowsky & Nadejda Von Meck. lib. bdg. 22.25x (ISBN 0-8371-6861-9, BOBF). Greenwood.

Below Stairs. 4.95 (ISBN 0-396-06076-5). Dodd.

Ben Butler: The South Called Him Beast. lib. bdg. 17.50 (ISBN 0-374-97977-4). Octagon.

Ben Dowell El Paso's First Mayor. 3.00 (ISBN 0-87404-107-4). Tex Western.

Ben-Gurion & the Birth of Israel. PLB 4.39 (ISBN 0-394-90562-8). Random.

Ben Gurion Looks Back: In Talks with Moshe Pearlman. pap. 2.25 (ISBN 0-8052-0274-9). Schocken.

Ben Jonson. lib. bdg. 9.95. Folcroft.

Ben Jonson. 10.00 (ISBN 0-404-06320-9). AMS Pr.

Ben Jonson & King James. 12.50 (ISBN 0-8046-1689-2). Kennikat.

Ben K. Green: A Descriptive Bibliography of Writings by & About Him. 10.50 (ISBN 0-87358-160-1). Northland.

Ben Lilly Legend. 7.95 (ISBN 0-316-18792-5). Little.

Ben Snipes: Northwest Cattle King. 4th ed. pap. 4.95 (ISBN 0-8323-0250-3). Binford.

Bench & Bar of the Commonwealth of Massachusetts. lib. bdg. 85.00 (ISBN 0-306-70612-1). Da Capo.

Benchmark & Blaze: The Emergence of William Everson. lib. bdg. 12.50 (ISBN 0-8108-1198-7). Scarecrow.

Bending Cross: A Biography of Eugene Victor Debs. 20.00 (ISBN 0-8462-1401-6). Russell.

Benedict Arnold: The Dark Eagle. 7.95 (ISBN 0-393-07471-4). Norton.

Benedict De Spinoza. lib. bdg. 9.50 (ISBN 0-8057-2853-8). Twayne.

Benedict Kiely. lib. bdg. 7.95 (ISBN 0-8057-1304-2). Twayne.

Benevolent Man: A Life of Ralph Allen of Bath. 15.00x (ISBN 0-674-06650-2). Harvard U Pr.

Benito Mussolini, Fascist Dictator of Italy. new ed. lib. bdg. 2.45; pap. 1.25. SamHar Pr.

Benito Perez Galdos. lib. bdg. 8.95 (ISBN 0-8057-2689-6). Twayne.

Benjamin Constant: His Private Life & His Contribution to the Cause of Liberal Government in France, 1767-1830. lib. bdg. 34.95 (ISBN 0-8383-1199-7). Haskell.

Benjamin Franklin. PLB 3.86 (ISBN 0-399-60053-1). Putnam.

Benjamin Franklin: A Biography in His Own Words. 15.00 (ISBN 0-06-011286-7). Har-Row.

Benjamin Franklin: A Collection of Critical Essays. text ed. 9.95 (ISBN 0-13-074856-0); pap. 3.95 (ISBN 0-13-074849-8). P-H.

Benjamin Franklin & American Foreign Policy. 2nd ed. 12.50x (ISBN 0-226-77634-4); pap. 3.25 (ISBN 0-226-77635-2). U of Chicago Pr.

Benjamin Franklin & the Zealous Presbyterians. 15.00x (ISBN 0-271-01176-9). Pa St U Pr.

Benjamin Franklin As a Man of Letters. 19.00 (ISBN 0-405-01687-5). Arno.

Benjamin Franklin As a Man of Letters. 11.95 (ISBN 0-8274-1381-5). R West.

Benjamin Franklin As Man of Letters. 35.00 (ISBN 0-87968-722-3). Gordon Pr.

Benjamin Franklin: His Wit, Wisdom & Women. 12.95 (ISBN 0-8038-0767-8). Hastings.

Benjamin Franklin, Printer. 12.50 (ISBN 0-8103-3642-1). Gale.

Benjamin Franklin Wade: Radical Republican from Ohio. 10.95. Cyrco Pr.

Benjamin Jarnes. lib. bdg. 12.95x (ISBN 0-8057-2464-8). Irvington.

Benjamin Lundy & the Struggle for Negro Freedom. 6.75 (ISBN 0-252-72748-7). U of Ill Pr.

Benjamin N. Cardozo, American Judge. 12.50 (ISBN 0-8462-1343-5). Russell.

Benjamin Thompson, Count Rumford. 19.95 (ISBN 0-262-02138-2). MIT Pr.

Benjamin West: A Biography. 20.00 (ISBN 0-395-26289-5). HM.

Benjamin West: Gifted Young Painter. 5.95 (ISBN 0-672-50021-3). Bobbs.

Benserade & His Ballets de Cour. 30.00 (ISBN 0-404-60195-2). AMS Pr.

Bentley. lib. bdg. 17.50 (ISBN 0-89984-250-X). Century Bookbindery.

Bentley. lib. bdg. 12.00. Folcroft.

Bentley. lib. bdg 12.50 (ISBN 0-404-51716-1). AMS Pr.

Bergson. 5.95 (ISBN 0-8274-1750-0). R West.

Bergson. 6.00 (ISBN 0-8046-0743-5). Kennikat.

Bergson & the Evolution of Physics. 17.50x (ISBN 0-87049-092-3). U of Tenn Pr.

Bering's Voyages: Whither & Why. 17.95 (ISBN 0-295-95562-7). U of Wash Pr.

Berlin Diary: The Journal of a Foreign Correspondent, 1934-1941. pap. 5.95 (ISBN 0-14-005182-1). Penguin.

Berlioz & His Century: An Introduction to the Age of Romanticism. 5.50 (ISBN 0-8446-1602-8). Peter Smith.

Berlioz & the Romantic Century. 3rd ed. 40.00x (ISBN 0-231-03135-1). Columbia U Pr.

Berlioz in London. 22.50 (ISBN 0-88355-740-1). Hyperion Conn.

Bernard Baruch, Portrait of a Citizen. lib. bdg. 10.50x (ISBN 0-8371-3348-3, WHBB). Greenwood.

Bernard Berenson: The Making of a Connoisseur. 15.00 (ISBN 0-674-06775-4). Harvard U Pr.

Bernard DeVoto. lib. bdg. 8.95x (ISBN 0-89197-675-2); pap. text ed. 4.95x (ISBN 0-8290-0011-9). Irvington.

Bernard Maybeck: Artisan, Architect, Artist. 24.95 (ISBN 0-87905-022-5). Peregrine Smith.

Bernard Shaw. lib. bdg. 9.75 (ISBN 0-8414-7513-X). Folcroft.

Bernard Shaw. lib. bdg. 16.95 (ISBN 0-8383-1955-6). Haskell.

Bernard Shaw: A Chronicle. lib. bdg. 26.95 (ISBN 0-8383-1892-4). Haskell.

Bernard Shaw: A Psychological Study. 15.00 (ISBN 0-8387-1418-8). Bucknell U Pr.

Bernard Shaw: An Epitaph. lib. bdg. 10.00 (ISBN 0-8414-1012-7). Folcroft.

Bernard Shaw's Postscript to Fame. lib. bdg. 7.50 (ISBN 0-8414-3955-9). Folcroft.

Bernardo De Galvez in Louisiana: 1776-1783. 2nd ed. 15.00 (ISBN 0-911116-78-8). Pelican.

Bernhard Eduard Fernow: A Story of North American Forestry. 11.95 (ISBN 0-02-851090-9). Hafner.

Bernini. pap. 4.95 (ISBN 0-14-020701-5). Penguin.

Bert Jones & the Battling Colts. 7.95 (ISBN 0-396-07503-7). Dodd.

Bert Jones: Born to Play Football. PLB 5.29 (ISBN 0-399-61103-7). Putnam.

Bertrand Barere: A Reluctant Terrorist. 21.00 (ISBN 0-691-05105-4). Princeton U Pr.

Bertrand Russell: A Life. pap. 2.95 (ISBN 0-04-921001-7). Allen Unwin.

Bessie. 7.95 (ISBN 0-8128-1406-1); pap. 2.95 (ISBN 0-8128-1700-1). Stein & Day.

Bessie Smith. pap. 1.95 (ISBN 0-498-04031-3). A S Barnes.

Bessie Smith: Empress of the Blues. 12.95 (ISBN 0-02-870020-1); pap. 7.95 (ISBN 0-02-870030-9). Schirmer Bks.

Best Defense. 8.95 (ISBN 0-02-585590-5). Macmillan.

Best in Baseball. 3rd ed. 6.95 (ISBN 0-690-00314-5). T Y Crowell.

Best of the Music Makers. 17.50 (ISBN 0-385-14380-X). Doubleday.

Bethlehem Star: Children's Newspaper Reports of the Life of Jesus. 4.95 (ISBN 0-8027-6097-X). Walker & Co.

Bethune. 15.00 (ISBN 0-208-01776-3). Shoe String.

Bette Davis. 5.95 (ISBN 0-88365-167-X). Brown Bk.

Bette Davis. pap. 1.75 (ISBN 0-515-02932-7, M2932). HarBraceJ.

Better Known As Johnny Appleseed. 8.95 (ISBN 0-397-30163-4). Lippincott.

Better Than I Was. pap. 3.95 (ISBN 0-8407-5671-2). Nelson.

Bettina: Portraying Life in Art. 35.00 (ISBN 0-87358-169-5). Northland.

Betty Ford: Woman of Courage. pap. 1.95 (ISBN 0-89559-116-2). Dale Books Inc.

Between a Rock & a Hard Place. pap. 1.75 (ISBN 0-671-81056-1). PB.

Between a Rock & a Hard Place. pap. 1.75 (ISBN 0-8499-4101-6, 4101-6). Word Bks.

Between Actor & Critic: Selected Letters of Edwin Booth & William Winter. 15.00 (ISBN 0-691-06193-9). Princeton U Pr.

Between Paris & St. Petersburg: Selected Diaries of Zinaida Hippius. 12.50 (ISBN 0-252-00307-1). U of Ill Pr.

Between the Devil & the Sea: The Life of James Forten. 6.75 (ISBN 0-15-206965-8). HarBraceJ.

Beyond Defeat. 7.95 (ISBN 0-385-13486-X). Doubleday.

Beyond Defeat. pap. 2.25 (ISBN 0-553-12651-2). Bantam.

Beyond Divorce: A Personal Journey. 6.95 (ISBN 0-8007-0903-9); pap. 3.95 (ISBN 0-8007-5021-7). Revell.

Beyond Reason. pap. 2.50 (ISBN 0-671-82778-2). PB.

Beyond Reason. 10.00 (ISBN 0-448-23037-2). Paddington.

Beyond the Cross & the Switchblade. 1.75 (ISBN 0-8007-8236-4). Revell.

Beyond the Cross & the Switchblade. 5.95 (ISBN 0-912376-08-2). Chosen Bks Pub.

Beyond the Goal. pap. 1.25 (ISBN 0-425-03261-2). Berkley Pub.

B.F. Skinner. lib. bdg. 7.50 (ISBN 0-8057-7713-X). Twayne.

Bhartrhari. lib. bdg. 9.95 (ISBN 0-8057-6243-4). Twayne.

Bi-Centenary Memorial of John Bunyan Who Died A.D. 1688. lib. bdg. 17.50 (ISBN 0-8414-9510-6). Folcroft.

Bibliography of the Works of Dante Gabriel Rossetti. 5.00 (ISBN 0-404-05439-0). AMS Pr.

Bibliography of the Works of Dante Gabriel Rossetti. lib. bdg. 4.95 (ISBN 0-8414-7379-X). Folcroft.

Big Bill Haywood & the Radical Union Movement. 8.95x (ISBN 0-8156-2140-X). Syracuse U Pr.

Big Black Fire. pap. 0.95 (ISBN 0-87067-166-9, BH166). Holloway.

Big Four, & Others of the Peace Conference. facsimile ed. 14.50 (ISBN 0-8369-2556-4). Arno.

Big Jim Thompson of Illinois. 9.95 (ISBN 0-528-81824-4). Rand.

Big League Pitchers & Catchers. PLB 5.54 (ISBN 0-8116-4907-5). Garrard.

Big-Little World of Doc Pritham. pap. 4.95. Juniper Maine.

Big Red: The Story of the Football Cardinals. new ed. lib. bdg. 4.95 (ISBN 0-913656-05-4). Forum Pr MO.

Big Star Fallin' Mama: Five Women in Black Music. 5.95 (ISBN 0-670-16408-9). Viking Pr.

Big Thicket Legacy. 12.95 (ISBN 0-292-70716-9). U of Tex Pr.

Biggs: The World's Most Wanted Man. 8.95 (ISBN 0-688-02959-0). Morrow.

Biggs: The World's Most Wanted Man. pap. 1.95 (ISBN 0-380-01823-3, 36137). Avon.

Biko. 10.95 (ISBN 0-448-23169-7). Paddington.

Biko. pap. 2.50 (ISBN 0-394-72654-5). Random.

Bill Cosby, Coming at You. PLB 5.50 (ISBN 0-89565-031-2). Childs World.

Bill Nye, His Own Life Story. facsimile ed. 18.75 (ISBN 0-8369-5434-3). Arno.

Bill Pickett, Bulldogger: The Biography of a Black Cowboy. 8.95 (ISBN 0-8061-1391-X). U of Okla Pr.

Bill Pickett: First Black Rodeo Star. pap. 1.95 (ISBN 0-15-207393-0). HarBraceJ.

Bill Pickett: First Black Rodeo Star. 5.95 (ISBN 0-15-207392-2). HarBraceJ.

Bill Russell. PLB 5.50 (ISBN 0-87191-281-3). Creative Ed.

Bill Sublette, Mountain Man. 12.50 (ISBN 0-8061-0429-5); pap. 5.95 (ISBN 0-8061-1111-9). U of Okla Pr.

Bill W. 11.95 (ISBN 0-06-014267-7). Har-Row.

Bill W. pap. 2.50 (ISBN 0-445-04492-6). Popular Lib.

Bill Wallace of China. pap. 1.25 (ISBN 0-8054-7204-5). Broadman.

Bill Walton. PLB 5.50 (ISBN 0-87191-379-8). Creative Ed.

Bill Walton: Maverick Cager. text ed. 5.95 (ISBN 0-88436-443-7). EMC.

Bill Walton: On the Road with the Portland Trail Blazers. 10.95 (ISBN 0-690-01694-8). T Y Crowell.

Billie Jean. 8.95 (ISBN 0-06-012392-3). Har-Row.

Billie Jean. pap. 1.95 (ISBN 0-671-78938-4). PB.

Billy Bitzer, His Story. 10.00 (ISBN 0-374-11294-0). FS&G.

Billy Graham: His Life & Faith. pap. 1.95 (ISBN 0-671-81890-2). PB.

Billy Mitchell: Crusader for Air Power. new ed. 10.00x (ISBN 0-253-31203-5); pap. 2.95x (ISBN 0-253-20180-2). Ind U Pr.

Billy Wilder in Hollywood. 10.00 (ISBN 0-399-11789-X). Putnam.

Billy Williams: Minnesota's Assistant Governor. 7.95 (ISBN 0-87839-025-1); pap. 5.95 (ISBN 0-87839-026-X). North Star.

Bing Crosby. pap. 1.95 (ISBN 0-515-04331-1). HarBraceJ.

Bing Crosby: A Lifetime of Music. pap. 7.95. Palm Tree Lib.

Bio-Bibliographical Index of Musicians in the United States of America Since Colonial Times. 2nd ed. 20.00 (ISBN 0-404-08075-8). AMS Pr.

Bio-Bibliography of Countee P. Cullen, 1903-1946. 12.50x (ISBN 0-8371-3325-4). Negro U Pr.

Bio-Bibliography of Franciscan Authors in Colonial Central America. 6.00 (ISBN 0-88382-101-X). AAFH.

Bio-Bibliography of Langston Hughes, 1902-1967. 2nd ed. 17.50 (ISBN 0-208-01269-9). Shoe String.

Biograph Bulletins, 1896-1908. 20.00 (ISBN 0-913986-03-8). Locare.

Biographia Nigeriana: A Biographical Dictionary of Eminent Nigerians. lib. bdg. 40.00 (ISBN 0-8161-8049-0). G K Hall.

Biographical & Bibliographical Dictionary of the Italian Printers & of Foreign Printers in Italy from the Introduction of the Art of Printing into Italy to 1800. lib. bdg. 75.00 (ISBN 0-8161-0766-1). G K Hall.

Biographical & Critical Studies. lib. bdg. 16.25. Folcroft.

Biographical & Critical Studies. facsimile ed. 20.50 (ISBN 0-8369-2630-7). Arno.

Biographical & Historical Index of American Indians & Persons Involved in Indian Affairs. 760.00 (ISBN 0-8161-0716-5). G K Hall.

Biographical & Historical Sketches of Early Indiana. facsimile ed. 32.00x (ISBN 0-405-06896-4). Arno.

Biographical Dictionaries & Related Works: An International Bibliography. 40.00 (ISBN 0-8103-0972-6); supplement no. 1 40.00 (ISBN 0-8103-0973-4); supplement no. 2 40.00 (ISBN 0-8103-0974-2). Gale.

Biographical Dictionary of Actors, Actresses, Musicians, Dancers, Managers, & Other Stage Personnel in London, 1660-1800: Vol. 2: Belfort to Byzand. 25.00x (ISBN 0-8093-0518-6). S Ill U Pr.

Biographical Dictionary of Actors, Actresses, Musicians, Dancers, Managers, & Other Stage Personnel in London, 1660-1800: Vol. 1: Abaco to Belfille. 25.00x (ISBN 0-8093-0517-8). S Ill U Pr.

Biographical Dictionary of Actors, Actresses, Musicians, Dancers, Managers, & Other Stage Personnel in London, 1660-1800: Vol. 5: Eagan to Garrett. 25.00x (ISBN 0-8093-0832-0). S Ill U Pr.

Biographical Dictionary of Actors, Actresses, Musicians, Dancers, Managers, & Other Stage Personnel in London, 1660-1800: Vol. 6: Garrick to Gyngell. 25.00x (ISBN 0-8093-0833-9). S Ill U Pr.

Biographical Dictionary of Actors, Actresses, Musicians, Dancers, Managers, & Other Stage Personnel in London, 1660-1800: Vol. 4: Corye to Dynion. 25.00x (ISBN 0-8093-0693-X). S Ill U Pr.

Biographical Dictionary of Actors, Actresses, Musicians, Dancers, Managers, & Other Stage Personnel in London, 1660-1800: Vol. 3: Cabanel to Cory. 25.00x (ISBN 0-8093-0692-1). S Ill U Pr.

Biographical Dictionary of American Civil Engineers. pap. text ed. 5.00 (ISBN 0-87262-034-4). Am Soc Civil Eng.

Biographical Dictionary of American Educators. lib. bdg. 95.00x (ISBN 0-8371-9893-3, OHB/). Greenwood.

Biographical Dictionary of American Labor Leaders. lib. bdg. 25.00x (ISBN 0-8371-7643-3, FAL). Greenwood.

Biographical Dictionary of American Music. 13.95 (ISBN 0-13-076331-4). P-H.

Biographical Dictionary of American Science: The Seventeenth Through the Nineteenth Centuries. lib. bdg. 45.00x (ISBN 0-313-20419-5, EAS/). Greenwood.

Biographical Dictionary of Fiddlers Including Performers on the Violon Cello & Double Bass. 25.00 (ISBN 0-403-01352-6). Scholarly.

Biographical Dictionary of Film. pap. 9.95 (ISBN 0-688-07974-1). Morrow.

Biographical Dictionary of Japanese Literature. 29.50x (ISBN 0-87011-253-8). Kodansha.

Biographical Dictionary of Musicians. 18.00 (ISBN 0-403-01364-X). Scholarly.

Biographical Dictionary of Parapsychology. 9.00x (ISBN 0-912326-09-3). Garrett-Helix.

Biographical Dictionary of Railway Engineers. 28.95 (ISBN 0-7153-7489-3). David & Charles.

Biographical Dictionary of Republican China. Incl. Ai-Ch'u. 32.50x (ISBN 0-231-08955-4); Dalai-Ma. 32.50x (ISBN 0-231-08956-2); Mao-Wu. 32.50x (ISBN 0-231-08957-0); Yang-Bibliography. 37.50x (ISBN 0-231-08958-9). Columbia U Pr.

Biographical Dictionary of Scottish Graduates to A. D. 1410. 66.00x (ISBN 0-19-822447-8). Oxford U Pr.

Biographical Dictionary of Southern Authors. 28.00 (ISBN 0-8103-4269-3). Gale.

Biographical Dictionary of the Confederacy. lib. bdg. 29.95x (ISBN 0-8371-6124-X, WCL). Greenwood.

Biographical Dictionary of the Federal Judiciary. 42.00 (ISBN 0-8103-1125-9). Gale.

Biographical Dictionary of the Left. pap. 2.00 (ISBN 0-88279-108-7). Western Islands.

Biographical Dictionary of the Left. Incl. 8.00 (ISBN 0-88279-216-4); 9.00 (ISBN 0-88279-223-7); 9.00 (ISBN 0-88279-224-5); 11.95 (ISBN 0-88279-226-1). Western Islands.

Biographical Dictionary of the Living Authors of Great Britain & Ireland. 20.00 (ISBN 0-8103-3019-9). Gale.

Biographical Directory of Librarians in the United States & Canada. 5th ed. 45.00 (ISBN 0-8389-0084-4). ALA.

Biographical Directory of Negro Ministers. 3rd ed. lib. bdg. 28.00 (ISBN 0-8161-1183-9). G K Hall.

Biographical Directory of Scholars, Artists & Professionals of Croatian Descent in the United States & Canada. 10.00. R & E Res Assoc.

Biographical Directory of the American College of Physicians 1979. 52.50 (ISBN 0-8352-1145-2). Bowker.

Biographical Directory of the Governors of the United States, 1789-1978. 225.00 (ISBN 0-930466-00-4). Meckler Bks.

Biographical Directory of the South Carolina House of Representatives, Vol. 2: The Commons House of Assembly, 1692-1775. 14.95x (ISBN 0-87249-350-4). U of SC Pr.

Biographical Directory of the United States Executive Branch, 1774-1977. 2nd ed. lib. bdg. 29.95x (ISBN 0-8371-9527-6, SBU/). Greenwood.

Biographical Essays. pap. 2.45 (ISBN 0-15-612616-8, HB163). HarBraceJ.

Biographical History of Greene County, Pennsylvania. 15.00 (ISBN 0-8063-0676-9). Genealog Pub.

Biographical History of Medicine: Excerpts & Essays on the Men & Their Work. 99.00 (ISBN 0-8089-0657-7). Grune.

Biographical History of York County, Pennsylvania. 12.50 (ISBN 0-8063-0675-0). Genealog Pub.

Biographical Index of American Artists. 13.00 (ISBN 0-8103-4251-0). Gale.

Biographical Index of American Artists. 35.00 (ISBN 0-87968-751-7). Gordon Pr

Biographical Index of British Engineers in the 19th Century. lib. bdg. 31.00 (ISBN 0-8240-1078-7). Garland Pub.

Biographical Memoir of Adam Smith. 17.50x (ISBN 0-678-00141-3). Kelley

Biographical Memoirs of Saint John Bosco. Incl. lib. bdg. 8.00 (ISBN 0-89944-001-0); lib. bdg. 9.00 (ISBN 0-89944-002-9); lib. bdg. 9.95 (ISBN 0-89944-003-7); lib. bdg. 10.95 (ISBN 0-89944-004-5); lib. bdg. 10.95 (ISBN 0-89944-005-3); lib. bdg. 10.95 (ISBN 0-89944-006-1); lib. bdg. 10.95 (ISBN 0-89944-007-X); lib. bdg. 10.95 (ISBN 0-89944-008-8); lib. bdg. 10.95 (ISBN 0-89944-009-6); lib. bdg. 13.95 (ISBN 0-89944-010-X); lib. bdg. 10.95 (ISBN 0-89944-011-8). lib. bdg. price not set (ISBN 0-89944-000-2). D Bosco Pubns.

Biographical Notes Upon Botanists. 295.00 (ISBN 0-8161-0695-9). G K Hall.

Biographical Process: Studies in the History & Psychology of Religion. text ed. 49.50x (ISBN 90-2797-522-1). Mouton.

Biographical Register of the Confederate Congress. 17.50x (ISBN 0-8071-0092-7). La State U Pr.

Biographical Register of the University of Cambridge to 1500. 90.00 (ISBN 0-521-05994-1). Cambridge U Pr.

Biographical Sketch of the Life of the Late Captain Michael Cresap. 7.00 (ISBN 0-87012-077-8). McClain.

Biographical Sketches. 21.50 (ISBN 0-8369-2824-5). Arno.

Biographical Sketches of Distinguished American Naval Heroes in the War of the Revolution Between the American Republic & the Kingdom of Great Britain. 13.25 (ISBN 0-8046-1290-0). Kennikat.

Biographical Sketches of Our Pulpit. lib. bdg. 12.00 (ISBN 0-8411-0026-8). Metro Bks.

Biographical Sketches of the Bench & Bar of South Carolina. Incl. 21.00 (ISBN 0-87152-198-9); 24.00 (ISBN 0-87152-199-7). Reprint.

Biographical Sketches of the Delegates from Georgia to the Continental Congress. 15.00 (ISBN 0-87152-085-0). Reprint.

Biographical Sketches of the Veterans of the Battalion of Orleans, 1814 - 1815. 12.50 (ISBN 0-918784-51-4). Legacy Pub Co.

Biographical Studies. 15.00 (ISBN 0-8274-1486-2). R West.

Biographical Studies. 12.50 (ISBN 0-404-00445-8). AMS Pr.

Biographical Studies. 11.50 (ISBN 0-403-00850-6). Scholarly.

Biographical Studies. 14.50 (ISBN 0-8274-1943-0). R West.

Biographical Studies in Modern Indian Education. facs. ed. 15.00 (ISBN 0-8369-8042-5). Arno.

Biographie Friedrich Hebbel's. 57.50 (ISBN 0-404-03784-4). AMS Pr.

Biographies of Distinguished Scientific Men. 40.75 (ISBN 0-8369-2737-0). Arno.

Biographies of Judges of Louisiana. 12.50. Claitors.

Biography. text ed. 7.50x (ISBN 0-416-83680-1); pap. 4.75 (ISBN 0-416-83690-9). Methuen Inc.

Biography: A Reader's Guide. lib. bdg. 6.50 (ISBN 0-8414-8565-8). Folcroft.

Biography & Bibliography of Shakespeare. 12.50 (ISBN 0-404-00920-4). AMS Pr.

Biography & Bibliography of Shakespeare. 12.45 (ISBN 0-8274-1465-X). R West.

Biography & the Human Heart. 14.50 (ISBN 0-8369-1023-0). Arno.

Biography of a Businessman: Henry W. Sage, 1814-1897. 17.50x (ISBN 0-8014-0156-9). Cornell U Pr.

Biography of Alice B. Toklas. pap. 2.95 (ISBN 0-380-39073-6, 39073). Avon.

Biography of Edward Marsh. 6.75 (ISBN 0-15-112215-6). HarBraceJ.

Biography of Eld. Barton Warren Stone, Written by Himself: With Additions & Reflections. 19.00 (ISBN 0-405-04089-X). Arno.

Biography of Gospel Song & Hymn Writers. 18.00 (ISBN 0-404-07226-7). AMS Pr.

Biography of the Brothers Davenport. 20.00x (ISBN 0-405-07969-9). Arno.

Biography of Thomas Wolfe. 12.75 (ISBN 0-911796-00-2). Beacham.

Biography: The Craft & the Calling. lib. bdg. 15.50x (ISBN 0-313-20219-2, BOBI). Greenwood.

Bird Lives! The High Life & Hard Times of Charlie (Yardbird) Parker. 10.95 (ISBN 0-88327-007-2). McKay.

Bird: The Legend of Charlie Parker. lib. bdg. 16.50 (ISBN 0-306-70677-6); pap. 6.95 (ISBN 0-306-80069-1). Da Capo.

Birds, Beasts, & Relatives. pap. 2.95 (ISBN 0-14-004385-3). Penguin.

Birth of Ballets-Russes. pap. 3.50 (ISBN 0-486-22962-9). Dover.

Birth of the Ballets-Russes. 6.75 (ISBN 0-8446-4775-6). Peter Smith.

Birthmark. 8.95 (ISBN 0-87131-299-9). M Evans.

Bishop J. G. Strossmayer: New Light on Vatican I. 7.95 (ISBN 0-8199-0491-0). Franciscan Herald.

Bishop Joseph Hall (1574-1656) A Biographical & Critical Study. 21.50x (ISBN 0-8476-2376-9). Rowman.

Bishop to All Peoples. 5.95 (ISBN 0-687-03571-6). Abingdon.

Bismarck. pap. 1.50 (ISBN 0-02-005390-8). Macmillan.

Bismarck. 16.50 (ISBN 0-86527-008-2). Fertig.

Bismarck & His Times. 12.50x (ISBN 0-8093-0858-4); pap. 4.95 (ISBN 0-8093-0859-2). S Ill U Pr.

Bismarck & the German Empire. pap. 4.95 (ISBN 0-393-00235-7, N235). Norton.

Bismarck at the Crossroads: The Reorientation of German Foreign Policy After the Congress of Berlin 1878-1880. text ed. 20.75x (ISBN 0-485-13135-8). Humanities.

Bismarck, Some Secret Pages of His History. 42.50 (ISBN 0-404-01242-6). AMS Pr.

Bismarck: The Man & the Statesman. pap. 2.95 (ISBN 0-394-70387-1). Random.

Bismarck's Rival: A Political Biography of General & Admiral Albrecht Von Stosch. lib. bdg. 18.25x (ISBN 0-8371-8686-2, HOBR). Greenwood.

Bit of a Rebel: The Life & Work of George Arnold Wood (1865-1928) 25.00 (ISBN 0-424-00005-9). Intl Schol Bk Serv.

Bittersweet Triumph. 5.95 (ISBN 0-385-12456-2). Doubleday.

Bix: Man & Legend. pap. 4.95 (ISBN 0-02-872500-X). Schirmer Bks.

Bizet. 23.50 (ISBN 0-88355-735-5). Hyperion Conn.

Bizet. pap. 6.50 (ISBN 0-8226-0706-9). Littlefield.

Bizet. rev. ed. 9.95x (ISBN 0-460-03163-5). Biblio Dist.

Bizet & His World. pap. 15.00x (ISBN 0-8443-0085-3). Vienna Hse.

Bizet & His World. lib. bdg. 29.50x (ISBN 0-8371-9427-X, CUBI). Greenwood.

Bjorn Borg. pap. 3.95 (ISBN 0-8256-3931-X). Music Sales.

Bjorn Borg. PLB 5.95 (ISBN 0-87191-721-1); pap. 2.75 (ISBN 0-89812-161-2). Creative Ed.

Bjorn Borg: The Coolest Ace. text ed. 5.95 (ISBN 0-88436-478-X); pap. text ed. 3.50 (ISBN 0-88436-479-8). EMC.

Black Abolitionists. pap. 3.95 (ISBN 0-19-500804-9). Oxford U Pr.

Black Americans in Autobiography: An Annotated Bibliography of Autobiographies & Autobiographical Books Written Since the Civil War. 8.75 (ISBN 0-8223-0317-5). Duke.

Black Americans in Congress. rev. ed. 12.95 (ISBN 0-690-01102-4). T Y Crowell.

Black & Trying. 5.95 (ISBN 0-89221-023-0). New Leaf.

Black & White: A Portrait of Aubrey Beardsley. pap. 1.95 (ISBN 0-8128-1295-6). Stein & Day.

Black Apostles: Afro-American Clergy Confront the Twentieth Century. lib. bdg. 22.00 (ISBN 0-8161-8137-3). G K Hall.

Black Artists of the New Generation. 9.95 (ISBN 0-396-07434-0). Dodd.

Black As I Am. pap. 5.95 (ISBN 0-89615-001-1). Guild of Tutors.

Black Boy: A Record of Childhood & Youth. 10.95 (ISBN 0-06-014761-X). Har-Row.

Black Champions of the Gridiron: O. J. Simpson & Leroy Keyes. 5.50 (ISBN 0-15-208399-5). HarBraceJ.

Black Coach. 5.95 (ISBN 0-396-06430-2). Dodd.

Black College Sport. 10.95 (ISBN 0-396-07023-X). Dodd.

Black Courage. PLB 5.97 (ISBN 0-8255-7801-9). Macrae.

Black Crusaders for Freedom. PLB 5.54 (ISBN 0-8116-4910-5). Garrard.

Black Douglas. 11.50 (ISBN 0-7100-7753-X). Routledge & Kegan.

Black Foremothers: Three Lives. pap. 4.25 (ISBN 0-912670-60-6). Feminist Pr.

Black Frontiersmen: Adventures of Negroes Among American Indians, 1528-1918. 7.95 (ISBN 0-381-99799-5, A09050). John Day.

Black Hawk. PLB 6.95 (ISBN 0-87518-172-4). Dillon.

Black Heart: Gore-Browne & the Politics of Multiracial Zambia. 16.75x (ISBN 0-520-03164-4). U of Cal Pr.

Black Jack, John A. Logan & Southern Illinois in the Civil War Era. 8.95 (ISBN 0-8130-0485-3). U Presses Fla.

Black Jack: The Life & Times of John J. Pershing. 35.00 (ISBN 0-89096-024-0). Tex A&M Univ Pr.

Black Like Me. 2nd ed. 7.95 (ISBN 0-395-07756-7). HM.

Black Like Me. pap. 1.95 (ISBN 0-451-09099-3, J9099). NAL.

Black Man, His Antecedents, His Genius and His Achievements. 14.00 (ISBN 0-527-12100-2). Kraus Repr.

Black Man, His Antecedents, His Genius, & His Achievements. pap. 2.95 (N189P). Mnemosyne.

Black Man, His Antecedents, His Genius, & His Achievements. 11.50 (ISBN 0-405-00618-7). Arno.

Black Man, His Antecedents, His Genius, & His Achievements. facs. ed. 12.25 (ISBN 0-8369-8516-8). Arno.

Black Man: His Antecedents, His Genius & His Achievements. 2nd ed. 13.00 (ISBN 0-384-05075-9). Johnson Repr.

Black Man's Burden. 12.00x (ISBN 0-8371-2932-X). Negro U Pr.

Black Man's Burden. lib. bdg. 24.95 (ISBN 0-8383-1277-2). Haskell.

Black Men in Chains: Narratives by Escaped Slaves. o. p. 8.95 (ISBN 0-88208-003-2); pap. 4.95 (ISBN 0-88208-004-0). Lawrence Hill.

Black Moses: The Story of Marcus Garvey & the Universal Negro Improvement Association. 2nd ed. pap. 5.95 (ISBN 0-299-01214-X). U of Wis Pr.

Black People Who Made the Old West. 8.95 (ISBN 0-690-01253-5). T Y Crowell.

Black Pilgrimage. PLB 7.44 (ISBN 0-688-51630-0). Lothrop.

Black Pioneers of Science & Invention. 6.75 (ISBN 0-15-208565-3). HarBraceJ.

Black Power & the Garvey Movement. lib. bdg. 7.95 (ISBN 0-87867-007-6, 20727); pap. 4.95 (ISBN 0-87867-037-8). Ramparts.

Black Presence in the Era of the American Revolution. 18.50 (ISBN 0-8212-0541-2). NYGS.

Black Presence in the Era of the American Revolution, 1770-1800. pap. 9.95 (ISBN 0-87474-576-4). Smithsonian.

Black Prince & His Age. 16.00x (ISBN 0-87471-818-X). Rowman.

Black Redemption: Churchmen Speak for the Garvey Movement. 12.50x (ISBN 0-87722-116-2). Temple U Pr.

Black Sheep: Adventures in West Africa. 13.00x (ISBN 0-8371-1761-5). Negro U Pr.

Black Side. facsimile ed. 30.75 (ISBN 0-8369-8882-5). Arno.

Black Society. 25.00 (ISBN 0-87485-054-1). Johnson Chi.

Black Sociologists: Historical & Contemporary Perspectives. pap. 4.95 (ISBN 0-226-05566-3, P593). U of Chicago Pr.

Black Stars. 3.95 (ISBN 0-396-06914-2). Dodd.

Black Sun: The Brief Transit & Violent Eclipse of Harry Crosby. 12.95 (ISBN 0-394-47450-3). Random.

Black Sun: The Brief Transit & Violent Eclipse of Harry Crosby. pap. 4.95 (ISBN 0-394-72472-0). Random.

Black Women in Nineteenth-Century American Life: Their Words, Their Thoughts, Their Feelings. 16.95 (ISBN 0-271-01207-2); pap. 7.95 (ISBN 0-271-00507-6). Pa St U Pr.

Black Women of Valor. PLB 6.29 (ISBN 0-671-32700-3). Messner.

Blackbeard the Pirate: A Reappraisal of His Life & Times. 8.95 (ISBN 0-910244-77-4). Blair.

Blacks in Black & White: A Source Book on Black Films. 14.50 (ISBN 0-8108-1023-9). Scarecrow.

Blacks in Classical Music: A Personal History. 8.95 (ISBN 0-396-07394-8). Dodd.

Blacks in Science: Astrophysicist to Zoologist. 6.00 (ISBN 0-682-48911-5). Exposition.

Blacks on John Brown. 6.95 (ISBN 0-252-00245-8). U of Ill Pr.

Blaise Cendrars: Discovery & Re-Creation. 25.00x (ISBN 0-8020-5352-1). U of Toronto Pr.

Blaise Pascal: The Life & Work of a Realist. lib. bdg. 25.00 (ISBN 0-8414-6341-7). Folcroft.

Blaise Pascal: The Life & Work of a Realist. lib. bdg. 16.00x (ISBN 0-8371-8747-8, MOBP). Greenwood.

Blake. lib. bdg. 10.75. Folcroft.

Blake. lib. bdg. 15.95 (ISBN 0-8383-1055-9). Haskell.

Blake. 8.75 (ISBN 0-8274-1740-3). R West.

Blake. lib. bdg. 18.95 (ISBN 0-8383-1057-5). Haskell.

Blake: A Psychological Study. 35.00 (ISBN 0-87968-753-3). Gordon Pr.

Blake: A Psychological Study. lib. bdg. 20.00 (ISBN 0-8414-9574-2). Folcroft.

Blake & Rossetti. 18.50. Porter.

Blake & Rossetti. lib. bdg. 23.95 (ISBN 0-8383-1054-0). Haskell.

Blake & Rossetti. lib. bdg. 17.50 (ISBN 0-8414-6782-X). Folcroft.

Blake's Hayley: The Life, Works, & Friendships of William Hayley. 27.75 (ISBN 0-8369-8133-2). Arno.

Blazing the Gospel Trail. pap. 3.50 (ISBN 0-88270-165-7). Logos.

Blessed Assurance: The Life & Hymns of Fanny J. Crosby. pap. 3.95 (ISBN 0-8054-7220-7). Broadman.

Blind--& I See. pap. 3.95 (ISBN 0-570-03772-7, 12-2708). Concordia.

Bliss, Peacemaker: The Life & Letters of General Tasker Howard Bliss. facsimile ed. 18.75 (ISBN 0-8369-5535-8). Arno.

Blood & Money. pap. 2.50 (ISBN 0-440-10679-6). Dell.

Blood & Money. 10.95 (ISBN 0-385-09685-2). Doubleday.

Blood, Brains & Beer: An Autobiography. 7.95 (ISBN 0-689-10809-5). Atheneum.

Blood in My Eye. 8.95 (ISBN 0-394-47981-5). Random.

Blood of My Blood: The Dilemma of the Italian Americans. 3.50 (ISBN 0-385-07564-2). Doubleday.

Bloodletters & Badmen: A Narrative Encyclopedia of American Criminals from the Pilgrims to the Present. 16.95 (ISBN 0-87131-113-5); pap. 7.95 (ISBN 0-87131-200-X). M Evans.

Bloom Where You Are. pap. 2.95 (ISBN 0-88449-024-6). Vision Hse.

Bloomers & Ballots: Elizabeth Cady Stanton & Women's Rights. PLB 6.50 (ISBN 0-670-17437-8). Viking Pr.

Bloomsbury: A House of Lions. pap. 2.75. Avon.

Bloomsbury: A House of Lions. 12.95 (ISBN 0-397-01043-5). Lippincott.

Bloomsbury Heritage: Their Mothers & Their Aunts. 10.50 (ISBN 0-8008-0821-5). Taplinger.

Blow Away. 9.95 (ISBN 0-670-17447-5). Viking Pr.

Blucher's Army 1813-1815. pap. 6.95 (ISBN 0-88254-159-5). Hippocrene Bks.

Blue Jolts: True Stories from the Cuckoo's Nest. 8.95 (ISBN 0-915220-30-X, 22969). New Republic.

Blue Thirst. pap. 3.95 (ISBN 0-88496-017-X). Capra Pr.

Bluebird of Happiness: The Memoirs of Jan Peerce. 12.50 (ISBN 0-06-013311-2). Har-Row.

Blye, Private Eye. pap. 1.75 (ISBN 0-87216-414-4). Playboy Pr Pbks.

Bob Cousy. PLB 4.97 (ISBN 0-399-60061-2). Putnam.

Bob Crosby: World Champion Cowboy. 6.00. Nortex Pr.

Bob Dylan. pap. 2.25 (ISBN 0-451-08609-0, E8609). NAL.

Bob Dylan: A Retrospective. 10.95 (ISBN 0-688-01175-6); pap. 4.50 (ISBN 0-688-06025-0). Morrow.

Bob Dylan in His Own Words. pap. 4.95 (ISBN 0-8256-3924-7). Music Sales.

Bob Dylan: The Illustrated Record. 15.00 (ISBN 0-517-53354-5); pap. 8.95 (ISBN 0-517-53355-3). Crown.

Bob Griese. 5.50 (ISBN 0-87191-345-3). Creative Ed.

Bob McAdoo. PLB 5.50 (ISBN 0-87191-497-2). Creative Ed.

Bob Newhart. PLB 5.50 (ISBN 0-87191-561-8). Creative Ed.

Bobby Clarke. 5.95 (ISBN 0-385-12523-2). Doubleday.

Bobby Clarke: Pride of the Team. PLB 5.29 (ISBN 0-399-61067-7). Putnam.

Bobby Fischer Vs. the Rest of the World. 25.00x (ISBN 0-8128-1618-8). Stein & Day.

Bobby Fischer Vs. the Rest of the World. pap. 2.95 (ISBN 0-8128-1850-4). Stein & Day.

Bobby Orr. PLB 5.50 (ISBN 0-87191-368-2). Creative Ed.

Bobby Orr: Fire on Ice. new ed. PLB 5.79 (ISBN 0-399-60954-7). Putnam.

Bobby Orr Story. 2.50 (ISBN 0-394-82612-4); PLB 3.69 (ISBN 0-394-92612-9). Random.

Bobby Unser Story. 10.00 (ISBN 0-385-13436-3). Doubleday.

Boccaccio: The Man & His Works. 19.50x, UKE (ISBN 0-8147-0953-2). NYU Pr.

Body Has Its Reasons: Anti-Exercises & Self-Awareness. 7.95 (ISBN 0-394-41134-X). Pantheon.

Bogey's Baby. 8.95 (ISBN 0-312-08740-3). St Martin.

Bogey's Baby. pap. 2.95 (ISBN 0-346-12433-6). Cornerstone.

Bohemian Girl: Blanche Yurka's Theatrical Life. 10.50 (ISBN 0-8214-0071-1). Ohio U Pr.

Bohemians to Hippies: Waves of Rebellion. ltd. ed. 20.00. Rather Pr.

Boileau & the French Classical Critics in England, 1660-1830. lib. bdg. 29.00 (ISBN 0-8337-4046-6). B Franklin.

Boileau & the French Classical Critics in England, 1660-1830. 11.50 (ISBN 0-8462-0637-4). Russell.

Bokhara Burnes. 4.95 (ISBN 0-571-08935-6). Merrimack Bk Serv.

Bokotola. pap. 3.95 (ISBN 0-8096-1924-5). Follett.

Bold Leaders of the American Revolution. 6.95 (ISBN 0-316-73670-8). Little.

Bold Women. 19.50 (ISBN 0-8369-8091-3). Arno.

Boldest Dream: The Story of Twelve Who Climbed Mount Everest. 10.95 (ISBN 0-15-113432-4). HarBraceJ.

Bolingbroke & Harley. 10.00 (ISBN 0-394-46974-7). Knopf.

Bolingbroke & His Times. lib. bdg. 49.95 (ISBN 0-8383-0170-3). Haskell.

Bolingbroke & His Times. lib. bdg. 50.00x (ISBN 0-8371-0225-1, SIBO). Greenwood.

Bolivar. lib. bdg. 39.75x (ISBN 0-313-22029-8, MABO). Greenwood.

Bolivar. 8.95 (ISBN 0-316-95390-3). Little.

Bolshevik Feminist: The Life of Aleksandra Kollontai. 15.00x (ISBN 0-253-31209-4). Ind U Pr.

Bonanza Theater. ltd. ed. 20.00. Rather Pr.

Bonaparte. 19.95 (ISBN 0-8090-3049-7). Hill & Wang.

Bonnet & Shawl: An Album. 13.50 (ISBN 0-8369-1753-7). Arno.

Boogie Lightning. 6.95 (ISBN 0-8037-2061-0). Dial.

Book. 8.95 (ISBN 0-688-00342-7). Morrow.

Book. pap. 2.50 (ISBN 0-446-91148-8). Warner Bks.

Book Illustrators in Eighteenth-Century England. 29.00x (ISBN 0-300-01895-9). Yale U Pr.

Book of American Presidents. 18.25 (ISBN 0-8369-1576-3). Arno.

Book of Daniel Drew. 20.00 (ISBN 0-405-05118-2). Arno.

Book of Jesus. pap. 1.25 (ISBN 0-451-06217-5, Y6217). NAL.

Book of Remarkable Criminals. 15.00 (ISBN 0-88355-194-2). Hyperion Conn.

Book of Saints & Wonders. 11.00x (ISBN 0-7165-1334-X). Biblio Dist.

Book of Scoundrels. lib. bdg. 12.45. Folcroft.

Book of Scoundrels. 15.00 (ISBN 0-405-09066-8). Arno.

Book of the Lord: Reflections on the Life of Christ. 11.95 (ISBN 0-87973-852-9). Our Sunday Visitor.

Book of the Presidents. 6th ed. 2.50 (ISBN 0-910086-02-8). Am Hist Res.

Book of Unlikely Saints. 14.50 (ISBN 0-8369-1528-3). Arno.

Book of Women's Achievements. 12.95 (ISBN 0-8128-1933-0). Stein & Day.

Book of Women's Achievements. pap. 6.95 (ISBN 0-8128-2238-2). Stein & Day.

Book Parade. 9.00 (ISBN 0-8046-0980-2). Kennikat.

Book Traveller. 4.95 (ISBN 0-396-06951-7). Dodd.

Booker T. Washington. 8.95 (ISBN 0-13-945311-3); pap. 1.95 (ISBN 0-13-945303-2, S712). P-H.

Booker T. Washington. pap. 1.25 (ISBN 0-451-61171-3, MY1171). NAL.

Booker T. Washington. PLB 4.49 (ISBN 0-399-60066-3). Putnam.

Booker T. Washington & the Negro's Place in American Life. pap. 4.95 (ISBN 0-316-80621-8). Little.

Booker T. Washington Papers. text ed. 20.00 (ISBN 0-252-00771-9). U of Ill Pr.

Booker T. Washington Papers. Incl. Autobiographical Writings. 17.50 (ISBN 0-252-00242-3); Eighteen Sixty to Eighteen Eighty-Nine. 17.50 (ISBN 0-252-00243-1). U of Ill Pr.

Booker T. Washington Papers: 1895-98. 20.00 (ISBN 0-252-00529-5). U of Ill Pr.

Booker T. Washington Papers: 1899 to 1900. 20.00 (ISBN 0-252-00627-5). U of Ill Pr.

Booker T. Washington Papers: 1901-2. 20.00 (ISBN 0-252-00650-X). U of Ill Pr.

Booker T. Washington Papers, 1903-4. 20.00 (ISBN 0-252-00666-6). U of Ill Pr.

Booker T. Washington: The Making of a Black Leader, 1856-1901. 14.95 (ISBN 0-19-501596-7). Oxford U Pr.

Booker T. Washington: The Making of a Black Leader, 1856-1901. pap. 4.95 (ISBN 0-19-501915-6, GB428). Oxford U Pr.

Boomtown Lawyer in the Osage. 6.00 (ISBN 0-89015-101-6). Nortex Pr.

Booth Tarkington. lib. bdg. 8.50 (ISBN 0-8057-0715-8). Twayne.

Booth Tarkington, Gentleman from Indiana. lib. bdg. 18.25x (ISBN 0-8371-0757-1, WOBT). Greenwood.

Boots & Forceps. facsimile ed. pap. 7.45x (ISBN 0-8138-2255-6). Iowa St U Pr.

Boris Godunof. 16.50 (ISBN 0-208-00969-8). Shoe String.

Boris Karloff & His Films. 10.00 (ISBN 0-498-01324-3). A S Barnes.

Boris Pil'niak: A Soviet Writer in Conflict with the State. 12.50x (ISBN 0-7735-0237-8); pap. 6.00 (ISBN 0-7735-0248-3). McGill-Queens U Pr.

Born Again. pap. 2.25 (ISBN 0-8007-8290-9). Revell.

Born Again. 8.95 (ISBN 0-912376-13-9). Chosen Bks Pub.

Born Again. lib. bdg. 18.95 (ISBN 0-8161-6428-2). G K Hall.

Born Again. pap. 2.50 (ISBN 0-553-10405-5, C12444-7). Bantam.

Born Again but Still Wet Behind the Ears. 6.95 (ISBN 0-915684-43-8). Christian Herald.

Born Black. 10.00 (ISBN 0-397-00690-X). Lippincott.

Born Exile: George Gissing. 10.00 (ISBN 0-15-113594-0). HarBraceJ.

Born on the Circus. 7.95 (ISBN 0-15-209970-0). HarBraceJ.

Born on the Fourth of July. 7.95 (ISBN 0-07-035359-X). McGraw.

Born Primitive in the Philippines. 8.95x (ISBN 0-8093-0746-4). S Ill U Pr.

Born Remembering. pap. 0.95x (ISBN 0-87574-200-9). Pendle Hill.

Born to Be. pap. 4.95 (ISBN 0-295-95428-0). U of Wash Pr.

Born to Play Ball. PLB 4.97 (ISBN 0-399-10900-5). Putnam.

Born to Run: The Bruce Springsteen Story. pap. 7.95 (ISBN 0-385-15443-7). Doubleday.

Born to Struggle. pap. 3.50 (ISBN 0-913780-35-9). Daughters.

Borodin & Liszt. 17.50 (ISBN 0-404-12938-2). AMS Pr.

Borromini. text ed. 15.00 (ISBN 0-674-07925-6). Harvard U Pr.

Borrowing Time: Growing up with Juvenile Diabetes. 8.95 (ISBN 0-690-01841-X). T Y Crowell.

Boss Cowman: The Recollections of Ed Lemmon, 1857-1946. 14.50x (ISBN 0-8032-0102-8); pap. 4.25 (ISBN 0-8032-5810-0, 595). U of Nebr Pr.

Boss Lady: An Executive Woman Talks About Making It. 9.95 (ISBN 0-690-01398-1). T Y Crowell.

Boswell. 28.50. Porter.

Boswell. lib. bdg. 6.00 (ISBN 0-8414-2860-3). Folcroft.

Boswell. lib. bdg. 6.50 (ISBN 0-8495-0123-7). Arden Lib.

Boswell in Extremes: 1776-1778. 18.95 (ISBN 0-07-069059-6). McGraw.

Boswell the Biographer. 15.00 (ISBN 0-8103-3675-8). Gale.

Boswell the Biographer. 14.95 (ISBN 0-8274-1562-1). R West.

Boswell the Biographer. 35.00 (ISBN 0-87968-778-9). Gordon Pr.

Boswellian Hero. 15.00 (ISBN 0-8203-0461-1). U of Ga Pr.

Boswell's Clap & Other Essays: Medical Analyses of Literary Men's Afflictions. 17.50 (ISBN 0-8093-0889-4). S Ill U Pr.

Boswell's Johnson: A Preface to the "Life". 17.50 (ISBN 0-299-07630-X). U of Wis Pr.

Boswell's Journal of a Tour to the Hebrides see Life of Johnson.

Botanists of the Eucalypts. pap. 10.00 (ISBN 0-643-00271-5). Intl Schol Bk Serv.

Both Feet in the Water. 7.95 (ISBN 0-915684-31-4). Christian Herald.

Both Sides of the Circle: The Autobiography of Christmas Humphreys. 18.95 (ISBN 0-04-921023-8). Allen Unwin.

Botolph of Boston. 10.00 (ISBN 0-8158-0252-8). Chris Mass.

Botticelli. 15.95 (ISBN 0-8467-0376-9); pap. 9.95 (ISBN 0-8467-0379-3). Two Continents.

Bougainville. 24.95 (ISBN 0-86033-059-1). Gordon-Cremonesi.

Boulez. 12.95 (ISBN 0-02-871700-7). Schirmer Bks.

Boulez. pap. 5.95 (ISBN 0-02-871810-0). Schirmer Bks.

Bound with Them in Chains: A Biographical History of the Antislavery Movement. lib. bdg. 15.95 (ISBN 0-8371-6265-3, PEB/). Greenwood.

Bounder from Wales: Lloyd George's Career Before the First World War. 17.50x (ISBN 0-8262-0203-9). U of Mo Pr.

Boundless Privilege. 8.50 (ISBN 0-89052-007-0). Madrona Pr.

Bourbon Kings of France. text ed. 16.50x (ISBN 0-06-496185-0). B&N.

Bourke Cockran: A Free Lance in American Politics. 19.00 (ISBN 0-405-00428-1). Arno.

Boxing's Heavyweight Champions. PLB 5.95 (ISBN 0-8225-1053-7). Lerner Pubns.

Boxing's Heavyweight Championship. PLB 8.95 (ISBN 0-87191-503-0). Creative Ed.

Boy at the Commercial. 11.95 (ISBN 0-571-10977-2). Merrimack Bk Serv.

Boy at the Hogarth Press. pap. 1.95 (ISBN 0-14-004862-6). Penguin.

Boy in That Situation: An Autobiography. 7.95 (ISBN 0-06-022218-2). Har-Row.

Boy of Old Shenandoah. 7.50 (ISBN 0-87012-265-7). McClain.

Boy Who Dared to Rock: The Definitive Elvis. 7.95 (ISBN 0-385-12636-0). Doubleday.

Boy Who Drew Sheep. 4.50 (ISBN 0-689-30097-2). Atheneum.

Boy Who Sailed Around the World Alone. 6.95 (ISBN 0-307-16510-8); PLB 12.23 (ISBN 0-307-66510-0). Western Pub.

Boyd H. Bode (1873-1953) & the Reform of American Education: Recollections & Correspondence. pap. 4.00. H C Sun.

Boyhood of Algernon Charles Swinburne. lib. bdg. 22.50. Folcroft.

Boyhood of Living Authors. 17.50 (ISBN 0-8274-0949-4). R West.

Boyhood on the Upper Mississippi: A Reminiscent Letter. 4.50 (ISBN 0-87351-069-0). Minn Hist.

Boyhoods of Great Composers. 4.95g (ISBN 0-8098-2012-9). Walck.

Boys of Indy. 8.95 (ISBN 0-89474-002-4). Corwin.

Boys of Indy. pap. 1.95 (ISBN 0-523-40327-5). Pinnacle Bks.

Brahms. lib. bdg. 15.00x (ISBN 0-8154-0310-0). Cooper Sq.

Brahms: A Biography, with a Survey of Books, Editions & Recordings. 8.50 (ISBN 0-208-01056-4). Shoe String.

Brahms, the Man & His Music. 14.00 (ISBN 0-404-13001-1). AMS Pr.

Brain Child: A Mother's Diary. 10.00 (ISBN 0-06-013156-X). Har-Row.

Bramante. 22.50 (ISBN 0-500-34065-X). Thames Hudson.

Brancusi. 15.00 (ISBN 0-8283-1362-8). Branden.

Brando for Breakfast. 10.00 (ISBN 0-517-53686-2). Crown.

Brasspounder. 8.95 (ISBN 0-8015-0881-9). Hawthorn.

Brave Coward Zack. rev. ed. pap. 6.95 (ISBN 0-912760-30-3). Valkyrie Pr.

Brave Men. lib. bdg. 25.00x (ISBN 0-8371-7368-X, PYBM). Greenwood.

Brave New World: A Different Projection. pap. 2.00 (ISBN 0-914752-08-1). Sovereign Pr.

Bravo Baryshnikov. 12.95 (ISBN 0-448-16386-1); pap. 5.95 (ISBN 0-448-16388-8). G&D.

Breach of Faith: Fall of Richard Nixon. 10.95 (ISBN 0-689-10658-0). Atheneum.

Breakdown. 10.00 (ISBN 0-8128-1941-1). Stein & Day.

Breakdown. pap. 1.95 (ISBN 0-451-07912-4, J7912). NAL.

Brecht Chronicle. 9.50 (ISBN 0-8164-9231-X); pap. 3.95 (ISBN 0-8164-9232-8). Continuum.

Brecht: The Man & His Work. pap. 4.95 (ISBN 0-393-00754-5). Norton.

Breckinridge: Statesman, Soldier & Symbol. 34.95x (ISBN 0-8071-0068-4). La State U Pr.

Breeze of the Spirit: Sam Shoemaker & the Story of Faith-at-Work. 8.95 (ISBN 0-8164-0399-6). Seabury.
Bret Harte. 8.75 (ISBN 0-8369-5545-5). Arno.
Bret Harte: Bibliography & Biographical Data. 23.50 (ISBN 0-8337-1254-3). B Franklin.
Brian Piccolo: A Short Season. pap. 1.75 (ISBN 0-440-10889-6). Dell.
Bribe. 8.95 (ISBN 0-06-013658-8). Har-Row.
Brick Agent: Inside the Mafia for the FBI. 10.00 (ISBN 0-8129-0687-X). Times Bks.
Bride of the Revolution: Krupskaya & Lenin. 10.00 (ISBN 0-472-61600-5). U of Mich Pr.
Bridge at the Top. 9.95 (ISBN 0-571-11123-8). Merrimack Bk Serv.
Bridge Bum: My Life & Play. pap. 2.95 (ISBN 0-688-08197-5). Morrow.
Bridge for Passing. pap. 1.75 (ISBN 0-671-80320-4). PB.
Bridge: My Own Story. 34.50 (ISBN 0-384-41780-3). Johnson Repr.
Brief American Lives: Four Studies in Collective Biography. 11.00 (ISBN 0-8108-1114-6). Scarecrow.
Brief Chronicles. 33.50. B Franklin.
Brief Handbook of American Authors. 15.00 (ISBN 0-8274-1976-7). R West.
Brief Handbook of American Authors. lib. bdg. 15.00 (ISBN 0-89341-450-6). Longwood Pr.
Brief Memoir of Christina G. Rossetti. lib. bdg. 6.50 (ISBN 0-8414-6780-3). Folcroft.
Brigham Young. 28.50 (ISBN 0-88355-254-X). Hyperion Conn.
Brigham Young. lib. bdg. 20.00 (ISBN 0-8492-2907-3). R West.
Bright Eyes: The Story of Susette la Flesche, an Omaha Indian. 9.95 (ISBN 0-07-070752-9). McGraw.
Bright Light of Death. pap. 3.95 (ISBN 0-87516-230-4). De Vorss.
Bright Lights: A Theatre Life. 9.95 (ISBN 0-395-26481-2). HM.
Bright Particular Star: The Life & Times of Charlotte Cushman. 27.50x (ISBN 0-300-01205-5). Yale U Pr.
Brigitte Bardot & the Lolita Syndrome. 9.00 (ISBN 0-405-03912-3). Arno.
Brik & Mayakovsky. pap. text ed. 26.75 (ISBN 90-279-7826-3). Mouton.
Bring Me a Unicorn: Diaries & Letters of Anne Morrow Lindbergh, 1922-1928. 7.95 (ISBN 0-15-114180-0). HarBraceJ.
Bring on the Empty Horses. 9.95 (ISBN 0-399-11542-0). Putnam.
Bring on the Empty Horses. pap. 2.50 (ISBN 0-440-10824-1). Dell.
Bring on the Empty Horses. lib. bdg. 18.95 (ISBN 0-8161-6369-3). G K Hall.
Brissot De Warville: A Study in the History of the French Revolution. 12.50 (ISBN 0-404-02279-0). AMS Pr.
Brissot De Warville: A Study in the History of the French Revolution. 20.50 (ISBN 0-8337-1032-X). B Franklin.
Britannica Encyclopedia of American Art. 35.00 (ISBN 0-87827-160-0). Ency Brit Ed.
British Autobiographies: An Annotated Bibliography of British Autobiographies Published or Written Before 1951. 18.50 (ISBN 0-208-00623-0). Shoe String.
British Diaries: An Annotated Bibliography of British Diaries Written Between 1442-1942. 7.50 (ISBN 0-8446-1304-5). Peter Smith.
British Diarists. lib. bdg. 10.00 (ISBN 0-8414-6703-X). Folcroft.
British Eccentric. 12.50 (ISBN 0-517-52499-6). Potter.
British Masters of Medicine. facsimile ed. 18.25 (ISBN 0-8369-1375-2). Arno.
British Musical Biography: A Dictionary of Musical Artists, Authors & Composers, Born in Britain & Its Colonies. lib. bdg. 35.00 (ISBN 0-306-70076-X). Da Capo.
British Prime Ministers in the Twentieth Century. 16.95x (ISBN 0-312-10517-7). St Martin.
British Prime Ministers in the Twentieth Century. 16.95x (ISBN 0-312-10518-5). St Martin.
British Ranchero in Old California: The Life & Times of Henry Dalton & the Rancho Azusa. 15.50 (ISBN 0-87062-122-X). A H Clark.
British Settlement of Penang. 16.75x (ISBN 0-19-638216-5). Oxford U Pr.
British Winners of the Nobel Literary Prize. 11.95 (ISBN 0-8061-1075-9). U of Okla Pr.
British Writers. 52.50 (ISBN 0-684-16407-8). Scribner.
British Writers. lib. bdg. 52.50 (ISBN 0-684-16408-6). Scribner.
Britten. 3.50 (ISBN 0-87250-201-5); PLB 3.27 (ISBN 0-87250-401-8). D White.
Broad Street Bullies: The Incredible Story of the Philadelphia Flyers. pap. 5.95 (ISBN 0-02-028180-3). Macmillan.
Broken Hand: The Life of Thomas Fitzpatrick, Mountain Man, Guide & Indian Agent. rev. ed. 15.00 (ISBN 0-912094-17-6). Old West.
Brokenburn: The Journal of Kate Stone, 1861-1868. 14.95 (ISBN 0-8071-0231-8). La State U Pr.
Bronson Alcott, Teacher. 17.00 (ISBN 0-405-01440-6). Arno.
Brontes. lib. bdg. 4.95. Folcroft.
Brontes. pap. 2.25 (ISBN 0-7156-0042-7). Dufour.
Brontes. lib. bdg. 8.50 (ISBN 0-8414-9435-5). Folcroft.
Brontes. lib. bdg. 17.95 (ISBN 0-8383-2141-0). Haskell.
Brontes & Their World. 10.95 (ISBN 0-684-16023-4). Scribner.
Bronx Cheer: A Memoir. pap. 3.45 (ISBN 0-912526-16-5). Lib Res.
Brook. 10.00 (ISBN 0-914916-10-6); pap. 3.50 (ISBN 0-914916-15-7). Topgallant.
Brooke Book. pap. 3.95 (ISBN 0-671-79018-8). PB.
Brooklands & Beyond. text ed. 17.50x (ISBN 0-8277-2812-3). British Bk Ctr.
Brooks Adams: A Biography. lib. bdg. 20.00 (ISBN 0-374-90611-4). Octagon.
Brooks Adams: Constructive Conservative. 14.50x (ISBN 0-8014-0013-9). Cornell U Pr.
Brother Billy. 8.95 (ISBN 0-06-014063-1). Har-Row.
Brother Dante. 3.00 (ISBN 0-8199-0357-4, L38051). Franciscan Herald.
Brother Francis: A Story About Saint Francis of Assisi. pap. 1.50 (ISBN 0-03-022131-5). Winston Pr.
Brother to a Dragonfly. pap. 5.95 (ISBN 0-8164-9002-3). Seabury.
Brother to a Dragonfly. 9.95 (ISBN 0-8164-9321-9); pap. 5.95 (ISBN 0-8164-9002-3). Continuum.
Brother Wolf. 6.95 (ISBN 0-916820-13-0). Center Pubns.
Brotherhood of Pirates. PLB 7.29 (ISBN 0-671-32965-0). Messner.
Brothers Duchamp: Jacques Villon, Raymond Duchamp-Villon, Marcel Duchamp. 49.50 (ISBN 0-8212-0666-4). NYGS.
Brothers Reuther & the Story of the UAW: A Memoir. 16.95 (ISBN 0-395-24304-1). HM.
Brown. 8.95 (ISBN 0-394-41043-2). Random.
Browning & His Century. lib. bdg. 29.95 (ISBN 0-8383-1734-0). Haskell.
Browning & His Century. 25.00 (ISBN 0-8274-1494-3). R West.
Browning & His Poetry. 7.25 (ISBN 0-404-52529-6). AMS Pr.
Browning & His Poetry. lib. bdg. 7.50 (ISBN 0-8414-7280-7). Folcroft.
Browning Love-Story. lib. bdg. 25.00 (ISBN 0-8414-5509-0). Folcroft.
Browning, Poet & Man: A Survey. 30.00 (ISBN 0-8274-1501-X). R West.
Browning, Poet & Man: A Survey. 29.00 (ISBN 0-403-07267-0). Scholarly.
Brownings. 17.00 (ISBN 0-403-00882-4). Scholarly.
Browning's Youth. 20.00x (ISBN 0-674-08441-1). Harvard U Pr.
Bruce. pap. 1.95 (ISBN 0-8127-0217-4). Southern Pub.
Bruce Jenner. PLB 5.95 (ISBN 0-87191-723-8); pap. 2.75 (ISBN 0-89812-158-2). Creative Ed.
Bruce Lee Farewell, My Friend. 3.95 (ISBN 0-89750-054-7). Ohara Pubns.
Bruce Lee: The Man Only I Knew. pap. 1.95 (ISBN 0-446-89407-9). Warner Bks.
Bruce Springsteen. pap. 4.95 (ISBN 0-8256-3935-2). Music Sales.
Bruchko. pap. 1.95 (ISBN 0-88419-133-8). Creation Hse.
Bruckner. rev ed. pap. 6.95 (ISBN 0-7145-0145-X). Merrimack Bk Serv.
Bruckner. 15.00x (ISBN 0-670-19260-0); pap. 3.95 (ISBN 0-670-19261-9). Vienna Hse.
Brunel & His World. 8.75 (ISBN 0-500-13047-7). Transatlantic.
Bubbles: A Self-Portrait. 13.95. Bobbs.
Buckminster Fuller: An Autobiographical Monologue Scenario. 15.95 (ISBN 0-312-10678-5). St Martin.
Bucky: A Guided Tour of Buckminster Fuller. pap. 3.25 (ISBN 0-688-05141-3). Morrow.
Bud and Lou: The Abbott & Costello Story. 10.00 (ISBN 0-397-01195-4). Lippincott.
Bud Harrelson: Super Shortstop. PLB 5.49 (ISBN 0-399-60901-6). Putnam.
Buddha. 4.95 (ISBN 0-440-00832-8). Delacorte.
Buddha. pap. 3.50 (ISBN 0-521-20368-6). Cambridge U Pr.
Buddhist Leader in Ming China: The Life & Thought of Han-shan Te-ch'ing, 1546-1623. text ed. 16.95 (ISBN 0-271-00542-4). Pa St U Pr.
Bufano, an Intimate Biography. 6.50 (ISBN 0-8310-7089-7). Howell-North.
Bufano & the U. S. A. ltd. ed. 20.00. Rather Pr.
Buffalo Bill. PLB 4.79 (ISBN 0-399-60983-0). Putnam.
Buffalo Wallow: A Prairie Boyhood. 5.00 (ISBN 0-8446-2296-6). Peter Smith.
Buffalo Wallow: A Prairie Boyhood. pap. 3.25 (ISBN 0-8032-5099-1, 373). U of Nebr Pr.
Buffon. lib. bdg. 7.95 (ISBN 0-8057-2184-3). Twayne.
Buggies, Blizzards, & Babies. facsimile ed. pap. 7.45x (ISBN 0-8138-2245-9). Iowa St U Pr.
Builders & Pioneers of Australia. 13.50 (ISBN 0-8369-1522-4). Arno.
Builders of Latin America. 28.25 (ISBN 0-8369-2724-9). Arno.
Builders of the American Dream. 9.95 (ISBN 0-87000-381-X). Arlington Hse.
Builders of the Bay Colony. 23.50 (ISBN 0-404-14741-0). AMS Pr.
Builders of the Bay Colony. rev. ed. pap. 5.95 (ISBN 0-395-08381-8, 32). HM.
Builders of the Bridge: The Story of John Roebling & His Son. 22.00 (ISBN 0-405-04724-X). Arno.
Builders of the Canadian Commonwealth. facs. ed. 14.25 (ISBN 0-8369-0621-7). Arno.
Building of a Department: Chemistry at Southern Illinois University, 1927-1967. 12.95x (ISBN 0-8093-0901-7). S Ill U Pr.
Building Poe Biography. 20.00x (ISBN 0-8071-0195-8). La State U Pr.
Bukharin & the Bolshevik Revolution: A Political Biography, 1888-1938. pap. 3.95 (ISBN 0-394-71261-7, V-261). Random.
Bukharin & the Bolshevik Revolution: A Political Biography, 1888-1938. pap. 6.95 (ISBN 0-19-502697-7, GB 593). Oxford U Pr.
Bulwer-Lytton. lib. bdg. 10.00. Folcroft.
Bum Ticker: A Hearty Traveler's Tale. 9.95 (ISBN 0-917112-01-6); pap. 4.95 (ISBN 0-917112-62-8). Multinational Media.
Bunyan. lib. bdg 12.50 (ISBN 0-404-51711-0). AMS Pr.
Bunyan. lib. bdg. 12.00 (ISBN 0-8414-1985-X). Folcroft.
Bunyan Calling: A Voice from the Seventeenth Century. 17.50 (ISBN 0-8274-1984-8). R West.
Bunyan Calling: A Voice from the Seventeenth Century. lib. bdg. 25.00 (ISBN 0-8414-9718-4). Folcroft.
Burgoyne of Saratoga: A Biography. 17.50 (ISBN 0-8129-0770-1). Times Bks.
Buried Alive: The Biography of Janis Joplin. pap. 2.50 (ISBN 0-553-08422-4, C13442-6). Bantam.
Buried Alive: The Biography of Janis Joplin. 7.95 (ISBN 0-688-00160-2); pap. 4.50 (ISBN 0-688-05160-X). Morrow.
Buried Life: A Study of the Relation Between Thackeray's Fiction & His Personal History. lib. bdg. 15.00 (ISBN 0-8414-7323-4). Folcroft.
Buried Life: Personal Recollections of A. E. Housman. lib. bdg. 12.50. Folcroft.
Buried Life: Personal Recollections of A. E. Housman. 35.00 (ISBN 0-87968-805-X). Gordon Pr.
Burke. lib. bdg. 15.00 (ISBN 0-8495-3831-9). Arden Lib.
Burmese Family. 22.50 (ISBN 0-404-15291-0). AMS Pr.
Burmese Journey. 6.00x (ISBN 0-87338-061-4). Kent St U Pr.
Burned to Life. pap. 1.95 (ISBN 0-87123-044-5). Bethany Fell.
Burning to Speak: The Life & Art of Henri Gaudier-Brzeska. 30.00 (ISBN 0-7148-1805-4). Dutton.
Burns. facsimile ed. 13.50 (ISBN 0-8369-5909-4). Arno.
Burns. lib. bdg. 15.00 (ISBN 0-8495-4941-8). Arden Lib.
Burns. lib. bdg. 12.50. Folcroft.
Burns & His Poetry. lib. bdg. 7.50. Folcroft.
Burns & His Poetry. 6.00 (ISBN 0-8046-1024-X). Kennikat.
Burns & His Poetry. 7.25 (ISBN 0-404-52525-3). AMS Pr.
Burns in His Youth, & How He Grew to Be a Poet; Burns in His Maturity, & How He Spent It. lib. bdg. 10.00 (ISBN 0-8414-5344-6). Folcroft.
Burro Bill & Me. pap. 4.95 (ISBN 0-913612-00-6). Strawberry Valley.
Burt Reynolds. pap. 4.95 (ISBN 0-8256-3942-5). Music Sales.
Burton: A Biography of Sir Richard Francis Burton. lib. bdg. 21.25x (ISBN 0-8371-8056-2, FABU). Greenwood.
Business & Politics in America from the Age of Jackson to the Civil War: The Career Biography of W. W. Corcoran. lib. bdg. 19.00 (ISBN 0-8371-3300-9, CBP/). Greenwood.
Business & Politics Under James I: Lionel Cranfield As Merchant & Minister. 20.00 (ISBN 0-8462-1790-2). Russell.
Business Career of Moses Taylor: Merchant, Finance Capitalist, & Industrialist. 17.50x (ISBN 0-8147-3374-3). NYU Pr.
Business of Crime. lib. bdg. 14.75x (ISBN 0-8371-7317-5, RIBU). Greenwood.
Buster Keaton. 6.95x (ISBN 0-253-10950-7); pap. 1.95x (ISBN 0-253-10951-5). Ind U Pr.
But God Has Promised. pap. 2.95 (ISBN 0-88419-002-1). Creation Hse.
But What's He Really Like. 5.95; pap. 3.95. Pacific Coast.
But You Look So Well! 10.95 (ISBN 0-88229-399-0). Nelson-Hall.
Butch Cassidy, My Brother. 9.95 (ISBN 0-8425-1222-5). Brigham.
Butch Cassidy, My Brother. pap. 2.50 (ISBN 0-14-004187-7). Penguin.
Buttercups & Daisy. 7.95 (ISBN 0-312-11007-3). St Martin.
By Death or Divorce...It Hurts to Lose. pap. 1.95 (ISBN 0-89636-004-0). Accent Bks.
By Death or Divorce...It Hurts to Lose. pap. 2.95 (ISBN 0-916406-32-6). Accent Bks.
By Force of Will: The Life & Art of Ernest Hemingway. 13.95 (ISBN 0-670-19824-2). Viking Pr.
By Force of Will: The Life & Art of Ernest Hemingway. pap. 3.95 (ISBN 0-14-004689-5). Penguin.
By Me, William Shakespeare. 15.95 (ISBN 0-89696-064-1). Everest Hse.
By Post to the Apostles. facs. ed. 15.25 (ISBN 0-8369-8066-2). Arno.
Byrd. 7.95 (ISBN 0-571-09813-4). Merrimack Bk Serv.
Byron. 100.00 (ISBN 0-87968-807-6). Gordon Pr.
Byron. lib. bdg. 17.95 (ISBN 0-8383-1784-7). Haskell.
Byron. 16.95 (ISBN 0-370-00506-6). Merrimack Bk Serv.
Byron & His Poetry. 7.25 (ISBN 0-404-52508-3). AMS Pr.
Byron & His Poetry. lib. bdg. 7.50 (ISBN 0-8414-3783-1). Folcroft.
Byron & His Poetry. lib. bdg. 18.95 (ISBN 0-8383-2142-9). Haskell.
Byron & Shelley. lib. bdg. 6.00 (ISBN 0-8414-5347-0). Folcroft.
Byron & the Honourable Augusta Leigh. 15.00x (ISBN 0-300-01876-2). Yale U Pr.
Byron & the Need of Fatality. lib. bdg. 19.95 (ISBN 0-8383-0971-2). Haskell.
Byron & the Ruins of Paradise. lib. bdg. 29.50x (ISBN 0-313-22421-8, GLBR). Greenwood.
Byron & Where He Is Buried. lib. bdg. 20.00 (ISBN 0-8414-3203-1). Folcroft.
Byron, the Last Phase. lib. bdg. 24.95 (ISBN 0-8383-1441-4). Haskell.
Byron the Man. 35.00 (ISBN 0-87968-808-4). Gordon Pr.
Byron the Man. lib. bdg. 25.00 (ISBN 0-8414-3326-7). Folcroft.
Byron: The Years of Fame. rev ed. 17.50 (ISBN 0-208-01256-7). Shoe String.

C

s Have Known It. 9.95 (IS
Coward.
& Facts

C. G. Jung: The Haunted Prophet. 8.95 (ISBN 0-8076-0811-4). Braziller.
C. K. Ogden: A Collective Memoir. 12.95 (ISBN 0-301-76061-6); pap. 5.95 (ISBN 0-301-76062-4). Merrimack Bk Serv.
C. S. Lewis: A Biography. 6.95 (ISBN 0-15-123190-7). HarBraceJ.
C. S. Lewis: A Biography. pap. 3.95 (ISBN 0-15-623205-7, HB331). HarBraceJ.
C. Wright Mills. lib. bdg. 9.95 (ISBN 0-8057-7708-3). Twayne.
Cadenza: A Musical Career. 10.95 (ISBN 0-395-24401-3). HM.
Caesars of the Wilderness: Medard Chouart, Sieur des Groseilliers & Pierre Esprit Radisson, 1618-1710. 12.50 (ISBN 0-87351-127-1); pap. 5.95 (ISBN 0-87351-128-X). Minn Hist.
Caesars of the Wilderness: Medard Chouart, Sieurdes Groseilliers & Pierre Espirt Radisson, 1618-1710. lib. bdg. 24.00x (ISBN 0-405-09766-2). Arno.
Cagney by Cagney. pap. 1.95 (ISBN 0-671-80889-3). PB.
Cagney: The Actor As Auteur. 12.00 (ISBN 0-498-01462-2). A S Barnes.
Cagney: The Actor As Auteur. pap. 6.95 (ISBN 0-306-80120-5). Da Capo.
Calamus: A Series of Letters Written During the Years 1868-1880 by Walt Whitman to a Young Friend. lib. bdg. 20.00 (ISBN 0-8414-0837-8). Folcroft.
Calder. pap. 14.95 (ISBN 0-8109-2198-7). Abrams.
Calder: An Autobiography with Pictures. 15.95 (ISBN 0-394-42142-6); pap. 7.95 (ISBN 0-394-73408-4). Pantheon.
Calder: Mobilist, Ringmaster, Innovator. 12.95 (ISBN 0-02-711780-4). Macmillan.
Calder's Universe. 28.50 (ISBN 0-670-19966-4). Viking Pr.
Calendar of the Correspondence of George Washington, Commander in Chief of the Continental Army with the Continental Congress. lib. bdg. 40.50 (ISBN 0-8337-1143-1). B Franklin.
Calendar of the Correspondence of James Madison. 51.50 (ISBN 0-8337-2179-8). B Franklin.

Calendar of the Correspondence of Thomas Jefferson. lib. bdg. 88.50 (ISBN 0-8337-1833-9). B Franklin.

Calhoun County, Alabama, Boy in the 1860s. 5.00 (ISBN 0-87805-081-7). U Pr of Miss.

California Gold Rush Diary of a German Sailor. 7.50 (ISBN 0-8310-7074-9). Howell-North.

California Gold Rush Merchant: The Journal of Stephen Chapin Davis. lib. bdg. 10.25x (ISBN 0-8371-6408-7, DAGR). Greenwood.

California Gold Rush Overland Diary of Byron N. McKinstry. 15.00 (ISBN 0-87062-114-9). A H Clark.

California Historymakers. pap. text ed. 4.95 (ISBN 0-8403-1416-7). Kendall-Hunt.

Call Him a Man: The Story of Hazzard Parks. pap. 0.95 (ISBN 0-377-84191-9). Friend Pr.

Call Me Counselor. 8.95 (ISBN 0-397-01239-X). Lippincott.

Call of the Cricket. pap. 4.95 (ISBN 0-89087-216-3). Celestial Arts.

Call of the Sea. 12.95 (ISBN 0-06-011631-5). Har-Row.

Call Them Irreplaceable. 14.95 (ISBN 0-8128-1927-6). Stein & Day.

Call to Revolution: The Mystical Anarchism of Gustav Landauer. text ed. 9.50x (ISBN 0-8143-1441-4). Wayne St U Pr.

Callahan. pap. 19.50 (ISBN 0-912334-76-2). Aperture.

Callahan. 35.00 (ISBN 0-912334-75-4); ltd. ed. o.p 400.00 (ISBN 0-89381-010-X). Aperture.

Callas Legacy. encore ed. 3.95 (ISBN 0-684-16343-8). Scribner.

Callas: Portrait of a Prima Donna. 28.25 (ISBN 0-8369-8096-4). Arno.

Calling Dr. Horowitz. 8.95 (ISBN 0-688-03140-4). Morrow.

Calling Dr. Horowitz. pap. 1.95 (ISBN 0-515-04509-8). BJ Pub Group.

Calverley & Some Cambridge Wits of the Nineteenth Century. lib. bdg. 17.50 (ISBN 0-8414-0887-4). Folcroft.

Cambridge Sketches. facs. ed. 15.25 (ISBN 0-8369-0903-8). Arno.

Camera at the Ballet: Pioneer Dancers of the Royal Ballet. 11.95 (ISBN 0-7153-6717-X). David & Charles.

Camera of My Family. 20.00 (ISBN 0-394-48838-5). Knopf.

Camille Saint-Saens, His Life & Art. lib. bdg. 13.75x (ISBN 0-8371-4266-0, LYCS). Greenwood.

Camp. 13.95 (ISBN 0-85031-306-6); pap. 5.95 (ISBN 0-85031-307-4). Schocken.

Campaigns of the British Army at Washington & New Orleans. 11.50x (ISBN 0-87471-023-5). Rowman.

[illegible] a Woman Over Forty? 8.95 (ISBN 0-933380-41-0); pap. 5.95 (ISBN 0-933380-47-X). Olive Pr Pubns.

Can You Survive Your Escape? Life on California's North Coast. pap. 6.95 (ISBN 0-89141-066-X). Presidio Pr.

Canaan Valley & the Black Bear. 2nd ed. 5.00 (ISBN 0-87012-220-7). McClain.

Canada's Past & Present: A Dialogue. pap. 3.50 (ISBN 0-8020-6044-7). U of Toronto Pr.

Canal Boatman: My Life on Upstate Waterways. 11.95 (ISBN 0-8156-0139-5). Syracuse U Pr.

Canal Boy. pap. 1.95 (ISBN 0-89191-106-5). Cook.

Cancan & Barcarolle: The Life & Times of Jacques Offenbach. lib. bdg. 15.75x (ISBN 0-8371-8045-7, MOCB). Greenwood.

Candidates for Sainthood. 8.95 (ISBN 0-89310-035-8); pap. 3.95 (ISBN 0-89310-036-6). Carillon Bks.

Candles & Carnival Lights: The Catholic Sensibility of F. Scott Fitzgerald. 15.00x (ISBN 0-8147-0563-4); pap. 4.95x (ISBN 0-8147-0564-2). NYU Pr.

Can't You Make Them Behave, King George? 6.95 (ISBN 0-698-20315-1). Coward.

Canterbury Pilgrims & Their Ways. lib. bdg. 25.00 (ISBN 0-8414-9353-7). Folcroft.

Canyon Summer. 6.95 (ISBN 0-399-20585-3). Putnam.

Capability Brown. 35.00 (ISBN 0-571-10267-0). Merrimack Bk Serv.

Capability Brown & Humphry Repton. 12.95 (ISBN 0-912158-83-2). Hennessey.

Cape Cod Fisherman. 9.95 (ISBN 0-87742-045-9). Intl Marine.

Capitol Names: Individuals Woven into Oregon's History. 4.95; pap. 2.95 (ISBN 0-87595-054-X). Oreg Hist Soc.

Captain & Tennille. PLB 5.95 (ISBN 0-87191-615-0); pap. 2.75 (ISBN 0-89812-119-1). Creative Ed.

Captain Blossom in Civvy Street. 16.95 (ISBN 0-86033-052-4). Gordon-Cremonesi.

Captain General & Rebel Chief: The Life of James, Duke of Monmouth. text ed. 22.50x (ISBN 0-04-920058-5). Allen Unwin.

Captain Jack, Modoc Renegade. pap. 4.95 (ISBN 0-8323-0295-3). Binford.

Captain James Cook. lib. rep. ed. 15.00x (ISBN 0-684-15553-2); pap. 4.95 (ISBN 0-684-71918-5, SL198). Scribner.

Captain John Ericsson: Father of the Monitor. 5.95 (ISBN 0-8149-0284-7). Vanguard.

Captain John Smith. PLB 4.90 (ISBN 0-531-01105-4). Watts.

Captain Luckless: James First Duke of Hamilton, 1606-1649. 16.50x (ISBN 0-87471-806-6). Rowman.

Captain Marryat: A Rediscovery. 19.50 (ISBN 0-88355-721-5). Hyperion Conn.

Captain of the Planter: The Story of Robert Smalls. pap. 1.75 (ISBN 0-671-29550-0). Archway.

Captain Sam Grant. 10.95 (ISBN 0-316-52332-1). Little.

Captain Steele: The Early Career of Richard Steele. 15.00x (ISBN 0-8018-0686-0). Johns Hopkins.

Captains. 7.95 (ISBN 0-689-10871-0). Atheneum.

Captain's Daughters of Martha's Vineyard. 10.00 (ISBN 0-85699-141-4). Chatham Pr.

Captain's Daughters of Martha's Vineyard. pap. 5.95 (ISBN 0-85699-142-2). Chatham Pr.

Captains of Industry: Or, Men of Business Who Did Something Besides Making Money; a Book for Young Americans. 20.50 (ISBN 0-8369-2853-9). Arno.

Captive of Time. 12.50 (ISBN 0-385-12731-6). Doubleday.

Captive of Time. pap. 2.95 (ISBN 0-446-83968-X). Warner Bks.

Captive Spirit: Selected Prose. 22.50 (ISBN 0-88233-352-6). Ardis Pubs.

Captivity of the Oatman Girls. lib. bdg. 18.75x (ISBN 0-8398-1877-7). Irvington.

Captured! o.p. 6.95 (ISBN 0-915684-17-9); pap. 3.95 (ISBN 0-915684-24-1). Christian Herald.

Car Racing Against the Clock: The Story of the World Land Speed Record. 6.75 (ISBN 0-688-41743-4); PLB 6.48 (ISBN 0-688-51743-9). Lothrop.

Caravaggio Studies. pap. 7.95 (ISBN 0-691-00308-4). Princeton U Pr.

Caravaggio Studies. 15.00x (ISBN 0-8052-3028-9). Schocken.

Cardinal & the Secretary: Thomas Wolsey & Thomas Cromwell. 9.95 (ISBN 0-02-629070-7). Macmillan.

Cardinal Newman. lib. bdg. 20.00. Folcroft.

Cardinal Newman in His Age: His Place in English Theology & Literature. 11.50 (ISBN 0-8265-1182-1). Vanderbilt U Pr.

Cardinal Richelieu and the Development of Absolutism. text ed. 17.95 (ISBN 0-312-12040-0). St Martin.

Career of a Tsarist Officer: Memoirs, 1872-1916. 20.00x (ISBN 0-8166-0698-6). U of Minn Pr.

Career of Dion Boucicault. 15.00 (ISBN 0-405-09052-8). Arno.

Career of Lujo Brentano: A Study of Liberalism & Social Reform in Imperial Germany. 10.00x (ISBN 0-226-75209-7). U of Chicago Pr.

Carew. 9.95 (ISBN 0-671-24236-9). S&S.

Caricatures of Americans on the English Stage Prior to 1870. 7.50 (ISBN 0-8046-0134-8). Kennikat.

Caril. 10.00 (ISBN 0-397-00997-6). Lippincott.

Carl Becker: A Biographical Study in American Intellectual History. pap. 4.95 (ISBN 0-262-73016-2). MIT Pr.

Carl H. Milam & the American Library Association. 17.50 (ISBN 0-8242-0592-8). Wilson.

Carl Jonas Love Almqvist. lib. bdg. 9.95 (ISBN 0-8057-6241-8). Twayne.

Carl Maria Von Weber. 2nd ed. 35.00 (ISBN 0-521-21354-1); pap. 9.95 (ISBN 0-521-29121-6). Cambridge U Pr.

Carl Maria Von Weber, the Life of an Artist. lib. bdg. 33.00x (ISBN 0-8371-1931-6, WECW). Greenwood.

Carl Rogers: The Man & His Ideas. pap. 3.95 (ISBN 0-525-47396-3). Dutton.

Carl Sandburg Remembered. 12.50 (ISBN 0-8108-1202-9). Scarecrow.

Carl Van Vechten. pap. 3.45 (ISBN 0-8084-0070-3, T74). Coll & U Pr.

Carl Zuckmayer. 9.95 (ISBN 0-8044-2026-2). Ungar.

Carlo Gesualdo, Prince of Venosa, Musician & Murderer. lib. bdg. 13.00x (ISBN 0-8371-3934-1, GRCG). Greenwood.

Carlo Maderno & Roman Architecture, 1580-1630. 39.50x (ISBN 0-271-01112-2). Pa St U Pr.

Carlos Complex: A Study in Terror. 8.95 (ISBN 0-399-11903-5). Putnam.

Carlos de Alvear, Man of Revolution: The Diplomatic Career of Argentina's First Minister to the United States. lib. bdg. 15.75x (ISBN 0-8371-0373-8, DACA). Greenwood.

Carlos Pellicer. 9.50 (ISBN 0-8057-6288-4). Twayne.

Carlota Joaquina, Queen of Portugal. facsimile ed. 14.75 (ISBN 0-8369-5040-2). Arno.

Carly Simon. PLB 5.95 (ISBN 0-87191-393-3); pap. 2.75 (ISBN 0-89812-101-9). Creative Ed.

Carly Simon Complete. 15.00 (ISBN 0-394-48753-2); pap. 9.95 (ISBN 0 394-70625-0). Knopf.

Carlyle. lib. bdg. 10.00 (ISBN 0-8414-1509-9). Folcroft.

Carlyle. 10.00 (ISBN 0-8462-1081-9). Russell.

Carlyle & the Open Secret of His Life. 14.75 (ISBN 0-8274-0488-3). R West.

Carlyle & the Open Secret of His Life. lib. bdg. 22.95 (ISBN 0-8383-0905-4). Haskell.

Carlyle at His Zenith, 1848-53. 35.00 (ISBN 0-87968-813-0). Gordon Pr.

Carlyle till Marriage, 1795-1826. lib. bdg. 29.95 (ISBN 0-8383-1557-7). Haskell.

Carnival of Speed: True Adventures in Motor Racing. PLB 5.49 (ISBN 0-399-60807-9). Putnam.

Carol Burnett. PLB 5.50 (ISBN 0-87191-555-3). Creative Ed.

Carole King. PLB 5.95 (ISBN 0-87191-465-4); pap. 2.75 (ISBN 0-89812-111-6). Creative Ed.

Carole Lombard. pap. 1.75 (ISBN 0-515-04085-1). HarBraceJ.

Caroline Courtier: The Life of Lord Cottington. 14.95x (ISBN 0-87249-284-2). U of SC Pr.

Carpetbagger's Crusade: The Life of Albion Winegar Tourgee. 22.00x (ISBN 0-8018-0499-X). Johns Hopkins.

Carry Nation. 6.95 (ISBN 0-525-66540-4). Elsevier-Nelson.

Carson McCullers. pap. 1.25x (ISBN 0-8166-0546-7, MPAW84). U of Minn Pr.

Carter Glass, a Biography. facs. ed. 18.75 (ISBN 0-8369-5446-7). Arno.

Carters of Plains. 8.95 (ISBN 0-87397-117-5). Strode.

Carving the Path to the Summit. 12.00x (ISBN 0-8214-0397-4); pap. 5.50 (ISBN 0-8214-0409-1). Ohio U Pr.

Cary Grant. 5.95 (ISBN 0-88365-291-9). Brown Bk.

Cary Grant. pap. 1.75 (ISBN 0-515-03246-8, M3246). HarBraceJ.

Case of Ezra Pound. pap. 6.50 (ISBN 0-89366-106-6). Ultramarine Pub.

Case of Frank L. Smith: Study of Representative Government. 21.00x (ISBN 0-405-05907-8). Arno.

Case of General Yamashita. lib. bdg. 13.00 (ISBN 0-374-96766-0). Octagon.

Case of Joe Hill. pap. 1.95 (ISBN 0-7178-0022-9). Intl Pub Co.

Case of Tyler Kent. lib. bdg. 42.95. Revisionist Pr.

Case of Walter Pater. 14.95 (ISBN 0-500-01193-1). Thames Hudson.

Caspar David Friedrich. 17.50 (ISBN 0-8478-0033-4). Rizzoli Intl.

Cassiodorus. 17.50x (ISBN 0-520-03646-8). U of Cal Pr.

Cast a Giant Shadow: The Story of Mickey Marcus, a Soldier for All Humanity. 3.50 (ISBN 0-8276-0034-8, 269). Jewish Pubn.

Cast of Thousands. 8.95 (ISBN 0-448-12264-2). G&D.

Castaneda's Journey: The Power & the Allegory. pap. 4.95 (ISBN 0-88496-068-4). Capra Pr.

Castello Branco: The Making of a Brazilian President. 17.50 (ISBN 0-89096-043-7). Tex A&M Univ Pr.

Castlereagh. text ed. 11.00x (ISBN 0-333-00556-2). Humanities.

Castlereagh. 17.95 (ISBN 0-312-12355-8). St Martin.

Catalogue of Canadian Composers. 21.00 (ISBN 0-403-01375-5). Scholarly.

Catalogue of Renaissance Philosophers. 19.95 (ISBN 0-87462-433-9). Marquette.

Catch Me a Colobus. pap. 1.95 (ISBN 0-14-004337-3). Penguin.

Catch the Vision: The Life of Henry L. Whitfield of Mississippi. 7.95 (ISBN 0-87805-062-0). U Pr of Miss.

Catch You Later: The Autobiography of Johnny Bench. 8.95 (ISBN 0-06-010324-8). Har-Row.

Catchers. PLB 7.50 (ISBN 0-87191-519-7). Creative Ed.

Caterina Sforza: A Renaissance Virago. 10.00x (ISBN 0-226-07271-1). U of Chicago Pr.

Catfish Hunter: The Three-Million Dollar Arm. PLB 5.49 (ISBN 0-399-61023-5). Putnam.

Catharine Beecher: A Study in American Domesticity. 20.00x (ISBN 0-300-01580-1). Yale U Pr.

Catharine Beecher: A Study in American Domesticity. pap. 4.95 (ISBN 0-393-00812-6, N812). Norton.

Catherine the Great. 8.95 (ISBN 0-13-121160-9). P-H.

Catherine the Great: A Profile. 7.95 (ISBN 0-8090-3367-4); pap. 5.95 (ISBN 0-8090-1400-9). Hill & Wang.

Catherine the Great: Autocrat & Empress of All Russia. lib. bdg. 16.25x (ISBN 0-8371-8219-0, GRCTG). Greenwood.

Catholic Colonization on the Western Frontier. 20.00 (ISBN 0-405-09357-8). Arno.

Cathy Rigby: On the Beam. lib. bdg. 5.95 (ISBN 0-88436-168-3); pap. 3.50 (ISBN 0-88436-169-1). EMC.

Cato the Censor. text ed. 43.50x (ISBN 0-19-814809-7). Oxford U Pr.

Cato the Censor. lib. bdg. 8.50 (ISBN 0-8057-3017-6). Twayne.

Cats Prefer It This Way. 8.95 (ISBN 0-698-10744-6). Coward.

Cats Prefer It This Way. pap. 1.50 (ISBN 0-425-03555-7). Berkley Pub.

Catskill Flytier: My Life, Times, & Techniques. 8.95 (ISBN 0-397-01214-4). Lippincott.

Cattle Kings. 12.50x (ISBN 0-253-11080-7). Ind U Pr.

Cattle Kings. pap. 3.50 (ISBN 0-8032-5759-7, 552). U of Nebr Pr.

Cattle Kings of Texas. 2nd ed. 5.95 (ISBN 0-87706-005-3). Branch-Smith.

Catullus. 9.00x (ISBN 0-674-10350-5). Harvard U Pr.

Cavalier in the Wilderness: The Story of the Explorer & Trader Louis Juchereau De St. Denis. 7.00 (ISBN 0-8446-0846-7). Peter Smith.

Cavalli. 17.95x (ISBN 0-312-12546-1). St Martin.

Cavour. 8.25 (ISBN 0-8046-1065-7). Kennikat.

Cavour. 17.50. Norwood Edns.

Caxton: England's First Publisher. text ed. 22.50x (ISBN 0-06-490450-4). B&N.

Cecil Rhodes. 8.95 (ISBN 0-316-28630-3). Little.

Cecil Rhodes. lib. bdg. 22.50x (ISBN 0-8371-0754-7, WICR). Greenwood.

Celebrated Comedians of Light Opera & Musical Comedy in America. 17.00 (ISBN 0-403-04001-9). Somerset Pub.

Celebrated Mrs. Centlivre. 12.50. SBD.

Celebrated Mrs. Centlivre. lib. bdg. 14.75x (ISBN 0-8371-0026-7, BOCC). Greenwood.

Celebrities of the Century: Being a Dictionary of Men & Women of the Nineteenth Century. 39.00 (ISBN 0-8103-3774-6). Gale.

Celebrities of the Italian Renaissance in Florence & in the Louvre. facsimile ed. 18.25 (ISBN 0-8369-1302-7). Arno.

Centers. PLB 7.50 (ISBN 0-87191-565-0). Creative Ed.

Century of Darwin. facs. ed. 18.25 (ISBN 0-8369-1019-2). Arno.

Century of Great Actors 1750-1850. 15.00. Norwood Edns.

Century of Music-Making: The Lives of Josef & Rosina Lhevinne. 17.50x (ISBN 0-253-31330-9). Ind U Pr.

Cervantes. 9.95x (ISBN 0-19-815367-8). Oxford U Pr.

Cervantes. 25.00 (ISBN 0-8274-2019-6). R West.

Cervantes in Russia. 10.00 (ISBN 0-87752-175-1). Gordian.

Cesar. 55.00 (ISBN 0-8109-0358-X). Abrams.

Cesar Chavez. PLB 6.89 (ISBN 0-690-18384-4). T Y Crowell.

Cesar Chavez. pap. 2.95 (ISBN 0-690-18385-2). T Y Crowell.

Cesar Chavez: Autobiography of La Causa. 12.95 (ISBN 0-393-07494-3). Norton.

Cesar Chavez: The Rhetoric of Nonviolence. text ed. 6.50 (ISBN 0-682-48274-9). Exposition.

Cesar Franck. lib. bdg. 16.50x (ISBN 0-8371-6873-2, VACF). Greenwood.

Cesar Franck & His Circle. lib. bdg. 19.50 (ISBN 0-306-77410-0). Da Capo.

Chaadayev & His Friends: An Intellectual History of Peter Chaadayev & His Russian Contemporaries. 15.00 (ISBN 0-910512-11-6). Diplomatic Fla.

Chain of Friendship: Selected Letters of Dr. John Fothergill of London, 1735-1780. 22.50x (ISBN 0-674-10660-1). Harvard U Pr.

Chaliapin: An Autobiography As Told to Maxim Gorky. pap. 5.95 (ISBN 0-8128-1257-3). Stein & Day.

Chalk Dust on My Shoulder. text ed. 11.95 (ISBN 0-675-09543-3). Merrill.

Challenge & Crisis in Missionary Medicine. pap. 3.95 (ISBN 0-87808-172-0). William Carey Lib.

Challenge of Anne Boleyn. 7.95 (ISBN 0-698-10612-1). Coward.

Chambers Biographical Dictionary. 25.00 (ISBN 0-8467-0510-9). Two Continents.

Chambers Biographical Dictionary. rev. ed. pap. 7.95 set (ISBN 0-8226-0498-1). Littlefield.

Champion of Southern Federalism: Robert Goodloe Harper of South Carolina. 12.50 (ISBN 0-8046-9025-1). Kennikat.

Champion of the Cross. 15.00 (ISBN 0-404-07202-X). AMS Pr.

Champions at Bat: Three Power Hitters. PLB 3.84 (ISBN 0-8116-6661-1). Garrard.

Champions at Speed. 5.95 (ISBN 0-396-07656-4). Dodd.

Champions of Democracy. facs. ed. 14.50 (ISBN 0-8369-1826-6). Arno.

Champions of Labor. 7.95 (ISBN 0-200-71723-5, B13020). Abelard.

Champions of Peace: The Story of Alfred Nobel, the Peace Prize, & the Laureates. 10.95 (ISBN 0-448-23316-9). Paddington.

Chance Meetings. 8.95 (ISBN 0-393-08809-X). Norton.

Chance Meetings. pap. 3.50 (ISBN 0-393-00969-6). Norton.

Chanel: Her Life, Her World-& the Woman Behind the Legend She Herself Created. 15.00 (ISBN 0-394-47613-1). Knopf.
Chang Tso-Lin in Northeast China, 1911-1928: China, Japan, & the Manchurian Idea. 16.50x (ISBN 0-8047-0945-9). Stanford U Pr.
Changing. 8.95 (ISBN 0-394-41148-X). Knopf.
Changing. pap. 2.75 (ISBN 0-553-13592-9, A13592-9). Bantam.
Changing of the Guard: The New Breed of Black Politicians. 4.00 (ISBN 0-698-20171-X). Coward.
Chansonetta: The Life & Photographs of Chansonetta Stanley Emmons. pap. 8.95 (ISBN 0-917312-01-5). Maine Antique.
Chaplin. 8.95 (ISBN 0-316-54550-3); pap. 3.95 (ISBN 0-316-54551-1). Little.
Chaplin, the Movies & Charlie. 6.95 (ISBN 0-06-022782-6); PLB 7.89 (ISBN 0-06-022783-4). Har-Row.
Chapter in the Early Life of Shakespeare: Polesworth in Arden. 6.50 (ISBN 0-404-02892-6). AMS Pr.
Chapters in My Life. 10.95 (ISBN 0-02-911350-4). Free Pr.
Character of John Adams. 13.50 (ISBN 0-8078-1254-4). U of NC Pr.
Character of John Adams. pap. 3.95 (ISBN 0-393-00856-8, N856). Norton.
Character of Shakespeare. lib. bdg. 5.50 (ISBN 0-8414-3263-5). Folcroft.
Character of Shakespeare. lib. bdg. 6.00 (ISBN 0-8492-3579-0). R West.
Character People. 17.50 (ISBN 0-498-01697-8). A S Barnes.
Characters of the Reformation. facs. ed. 19.50 (ISBN 0-8369-1696-4). Arno.
Charcoal's World. 11.95 (ISBN 0-8032-1651-3); pap. 3.95 (ISBN 0-8032-6552-2, BB 717). U of Nebr Pr.
Charismatic Bureaucrat: A Political Biography of Matsudaira Sadanobu, 1758-1829. 10.50x (ISBN 0-226-63031-5). U of Chicago Pr.
Charlemagne (Charles the Great) The Hero of Two Nations. 24.00 (ISBN 0-8369-9957-6). Arno.
Charlemagne: The Legend and the Man. 4.95 (ISBN 0-385-04066-0). Doubleday.
Charles A. Beard & American Foreign Policy. 8.50 (ISBN 0-8130-0354-7). U Presses Fla.
Charles Albert Fechter. 18.00 (ISBN 0-405-08502-8). Arno.
Charles Alexander Eastman (Ohiyesa) pap. 2.00 (ISBN 0-88430-057-9). Boise St Univ.
Charles-Augustin Sainte-Beuve. facs. ed. 16.00 (ISBN 0-8369-5425-4). Arno.
Charles Baudelaire. lib. bdg. 17.50 (ISBN 0-8414-6789-7). Folcroft.
Charles Brockden Brown. pap. 3.45 (ISBN 0-8084-0071-1, T98). Coll & U Pr.
Charles Brockden Brown, American Gothic Novelist. lib. bdg. 14.00 (ISBN 0-374-98244-9). Octagon.
Charles Brockden Brown: Pioneer Voice of America. 22.50 (ISBN 0-404-01548-4). AMS Pr.
Charles Burchfield. 35.00 (ISBN 0-8230-0533-X). Watson-Guptill.
Charles Carroll of Carrollton. 17.50 (ISBN 0-8462-1545-4). Russell.
Charles Chevillet De Champmesle, Actor & Dramatist. 14.00 (ISBN 0-384-47973-1). Johnson Repr.
Charles Churchill: Poet, Rake & Rebel. lib. bdg. 13.00x (ISBN 0-8371-0328-2, BRCC). Greenwood.
Charles Darwin. 8.95 (ISBN 0-8057-6718-5). Twayne.
Charles Darwin & Natural Selection. PLB 5.90 (ISBN 0-531-00865-7). Watts.
Charles De Gaulle. lib. bdg. 7.50 (ISBN 0-8057-3663-8). Twayne.
Charles De Sainte-Marthe. 15.00 (ISBN 0-404-50610-0). AMS Pr.
Charles Demuth: Behind a Laughing Mask. 12.95 (ISBN 0-8061-0913-0). U of Okla Pr.
Charles Dickens. text ed. 3.00x (ISBN 0-7100-2953-5). Humanities.
Charles Dickens: A Biographical-Critical Study. 22.00 (ISBN 0-527-57200-4). Kraus Repr.
Charles Dickens: A Sketch of His Life & Works. lib. bdg. 20.00 (ISBN 0-8414-6760-9). Folcroft.
Charles Dickens & His Publishers. 39.00 (ISBN 0-19-812076-1). Oxford U Pr.
Charles Dickens & His World. 10.95 (ISBN 0-684-15574-5). Scribner.
Charles Dickens & the Begging-Letter Writer. lib. bdg. 10.95 (ISBN 0-8383-1532-1). Haskell.
Charles Dickens As a Reader. 11.75 (ISBN 0-8274-1270-3). R West.
Charles Dickens As a Reader. lib. bdg. 21.95 (ISBN 0-8383-1608-5). Haskell.
Charles Dickens Encyclopedia. 20.00 (ISBN 0-684-13562-0). Scribner.
Charles Dickens: His Life. PLB 3.07 (ISBN 0-03-035140-5). HR&W.
Charles Dickens in America. lib. bdg. 23.95 (ISBN 0-8383-1092-3). Haskell.
Charles Dickens Originals. 18.00 (ISBN 0-404-08895-3). AMS Pr.
Charles Drew. PLB 7.89 (ISBN 0-690-18598-7). T Y Crowell.
Charles Dudley Warner. 13.50 (ISBN 0-8369-6878-6). Arno.
Charles Eastman. PLB 5.95 (ISBN 0-87518-175-9). Dillon.
Charles Eliot Norton: Apostle of Culture in a Democracy. 12.50x (ISBN 0-674-11025-0). Harvard U Pr.
Charles Ellet Jr.: the Engineer As Individualist, 1810-1862. 7.50 (ISBN 0-252-72525-5). U of Ill Pr.
Charles Evans Hughes & American Democratic Statesmanship. lib. bdg. 18.00x (ISBN 0-313-20463-2, PECH). Greenwood.
Charles Evans Hughes & the Illusions of Innocence: A Study in American Diplomacy. 10.00 (ISBN 0-252-72749-5). U of Ill Pr.
Charles Evans Hughes & the Supreme Court. 11.50 (ISBN 0-8462-1092-4). Russell.
Charles Evans Hughes: Politics & Reform in New York, 1905-1910. 20.00x (ISBN 0-8014-0446-0). Cornell U Pr.
Charles Ezra Sprague. lib. bdg. 12.00x (ISBN 0-405-10905-9). Arno.
Charles F. A. Voysey, Architect. 12.95 (ISBN 0-912158-54-9). Hennessey.
Charles F. Lummis: Editor of the Southwest. lib. bdg. 12.25x (ISBN 0-8371-7149-0, BICL). Greenwood.
Charles Fenno Hoffman. 18.50 (ISBN 0-404-00656-6). AMS Pr.
Charles Follen McKim: A Study of His Life & Work. 15.00 (ISBN 0-405-08570-2). Arno.
Charles Follen McKim: A Study of His Life & Work. 12.00 (ISBN 0-404-02890-X). AMS Pr.
Charles Francis Adams, Jr., 1835-1915: The Patrician at Bay. 8.50x (ISBN 0-674-11050-1). Harvard U Pr.
Charles Francis Adams, 1807-1886. 18.50x (ISBN 0-8047-0625-5); pap. 4.95 (ISBN 0-8047-0626-3, SP84). Stanford U Pr.
Charles Francis Adams, 1835-1915: An Autobiography. lib. bdg. 14.00x (ISBN 0-8371-7037-0, ADAU). Greenwood.
Charles Godfrey Leland: A Biography. 38.00 set (ISBN 0-8274-1583-4). R West.
Charles Godfrey Leland: A Biography. facsimile ed. 47.00 (ISBN 0-8369-5613-3). Arno.
Charles-Guillaume Etienne, Dramatist & Publicist. 11.50 (ISBN 0-384-68273-1). Johnson Repr.
Charles I: A Biography. 12.50 (ISBN 0-316-10404-3). Little.
Charles I: A Study. lib. bdg. 30.00 (ISBN 0-8414-4951-1). Folcroft.
Charles Ives and His America. 15.00 (ISBN 0-87140-610-1). Liveright.
Charles Ives Remembered: An Oral History. pap. 3.95 (ISBN 0-393-00825-8). Norton.
Charles Ives Remembered: An Oral History. 16.00x (ISBN 0-300-01758-8). Yale U Pr.
Charles James Fox & the Disintegration of the Whig Party, 1782-1794. 13.75x (ISBN 0-19-821838-9). Oxford U Pr.
Charles, King of England, 1600-1637. lib. bdg. 21.75x (ISBN 0-8371-7949-1, WICK). Greenwood.
Charles Kingsley. 11.95 (ISBN 0-8057-6752-5). Twayne.
Charles Kingsley & His Ideas. lib. bdg. 19.95 (ISBN 0-8383-1639-5). Haskell.
Charles Kingsley & the Christian Social Movement. 10.00 (ISBN 0-404-08914-3). AMS Pr.
Charles Kingsley, His Letters & Memories of His Life. 30.00 (ISBN 0-932062-97-0). Sharon Hill.
Charles Kingsley, 1819-1875. lib. bdg. 13.00 (ISBN 0-374-97942-1). Octagon.
Charles Lamb. 9.95 (ISBN 0-8274-2038-2). R West.
Charles Lamb. 15.00 (ISBN 0-403-00492-6). Scholarly.
Charles Lamb. lib. bdg 10.00 (ISBN 0-404-51701-3). AMS Pr.
Charles Lamb. lib. bdg. 15.00 (ISBN 0-8495-0175-X). Arden Lib.
Charles Lamb: A Memoir. lib. bdg. 25.00 (ISBN 0-8414-3429-8). Folcroft.
Charles Lamb & His Contemporaries. 14.50 (ISBN 0-208-00461-0). Shoe String.
Charles Lamb & His Friends. lib. bdg. 18.00x (ISBN 0-8371-6454-0, HOCL). Greenwood.
Charles Lamb & His Hertfordshire. 40.00 (ISBN 0-8274-2040-4). R West.
Charles Lamb & His Hertfordshire. lib. bdg. 18.50x (ISBN 0-8371-7111-3, HICL). Greenwood.
Charles Lamb: His Friends, His Haunts & His Books. lib. bdg. 30.00 (ISBN 0-8414-4359-9). Folcroft.
Charles Lamb: His Friends, His Haunts & His Books. lib. bdg. 30.00 (ISBN 0-8482-0849-8). Norwood Edns.
Charles Lamb: His Life Recorded by His Contemporaries. 25.00 (ISBN 0-8274-2039-0). R West.
Charles Middleton: The Life & Times of a Restoration Politician. 12.75x (ISBN 0-226-40947-3). U of Chicago Pr.
Charles Nodier: His Life & Works: A Critical Bibliography. pap. 6.50x (ISBN 0-8078-9095-2). U of NC Pr.
Charles Olson in Connecticut. 7.95 (ISBN 0-8040-0649-0). Swallow.
Charles Peguy: A Study in Integrity. lib. bdg. 21.75x (ISBN 0-8371-7190-3, VICP). Greenwood.
Charles Porterfield Krauth. 37.00 (ISBN 0-405-00265-3). Arno.
Charles Reade. 10.50 (ISBN 0-8462-1276-5). Russell.
Charles Rennie Mackintosh & the Modern Movement. 44.95 (ISBN 0-7100-8538-9). Routledge & Kegan.
Charles Rennie Mackintosh & the Modern Movement. lib. bdg. 40.00 (ISBN 0-8240-2487-7). Garland Pub.
Charles Richard Drew: Pioneer in Blood Research. 5.95 (ISBN 0-684-92299-1). Scribner.
Charles Simeon of Cambridge. 7.95 (ISBN 0-8028-3498-1). Eerdmans.
Charles Stewart Parnell. 22.50 (ISBN 0-19-519949-9). Oxford U Pr.
Charles Sumner. 12.50 (ISBN 0-404-50880-4). AMS Pr.
Charles Sumner. 13.50 (ISBN 0-8462-1387-7). Russell.
Charles Sumner: An Essay. lib. bdg. 9.75x (ISBN 0-8371-5233-X, SCSU). Greenwood.
Charles Sumner & the Coming of the Civil War. 15.00 (ISBN 0-394-41900-6). Knopf.
Charles Sumner & the Rights of Man. 15.00 (ISBN 0-394-41899-9). Knopf.
Charles Sumner Slichter: The Golden Vector. 17.50 (ISBN 0-299-06060-8). U of Wis Pr.
Charles the Great. 8.25 (ISBN 0-8046-1075-4). Kennikat.
Charles Thomson & the Making of a New Nation, 1729-1824. 15.00 (ISBN 0-8386-2072-8). Fairleigh Dickinson.
Charles V: Elected Emperor & Hereditary Ruler. 16.95 (ISBN 0-500-87001-2). Thames Hudson.
Charles W. Chesnutt: America's First Great Black Novelist. 15.00 (ISBN 0-208-01380-6). Shoe String.
Charles W. Eliot, President of Harvard University. 35.00 (ISBN 0-404-03545-0); 18.00 ea. (ISBN 0-404-04998-2) (ISBN 0-404-04999-0). AMS Pr.
Charleston in the Age of the Pinckney's. pap. 4.95 (ISBN 0-87249-297-4). U of SC Pr.
Charley Pride. PLB 5.95 (ISBN 0-87191-397-6); pap. 2.75 (ISBN 0-89812-108-6). Creative Ed.
Charlie Chaplin. 22.00 (ISBN 0-405-03920-4). Arno.
Charlie Chaplin. pap. 1.75 (ISBN 0-515-03640-4, M3640). HarBraceJ.
Charlie Chaplin, Famous Silent Movie Actor & Comic. lib. bdg. 2.45 incl. catalog cards (ISBN 0-87157-539-6); pap. 1.25 vinyl laminated covers (ISBN 0-87157-039-4). SamHar Pr.
Charlie Hustle. pap. 4.95 (ISBN 0-13-448217-4). P-H.
Charlie Hustle. 7.95 (ISBN 0-13-448209-3); pap. 4.95 (ISBN 0-13-448217-4). P-H.
Charlie Rich. PLB 5.95 (ISBN 0-87191-463-8); pap. 2.75 (ISBN 0-89812-116-7). Creative Ed.
Charlotte Bronte. lib. bdg. 25.00. Folcroft.
Charlotte Bronte. 17.00 (ISBN 0-405-08262-2). Arno.
Charlotte Bronte. facsimile ed. 17.25 (ISBN 0-8369-6602-3). Arno.
Charlotte Bronte & Her Sisters. 12.50 (ISBN 0-404-08911-9). AMS Pr.
Charlotte Bronte & Her Sisters. 12.45 (ISBN 0-8274-1742-X). R West.
Charlotte Bronte at Home. lib. bdg. 30.00 (ISBN 0-8414-4820-5). Folcroft.
Charlotte Bronte: The Evolution of Genius. pap. 10.50x (ISBN 0-19-881152-7, OPB 152). Oxford U Pr.
Charlotte Bronte: The Self Conceived. 11.95x (ISBN 0-393-07505-2); pap. 3.95 (ISBN 0-393-00888-6). Norton.
Charlotte Bronte's World of Death. text ed. 11.95x (ISBN 0-292-75043-9). U of Tex Pr.
Charlotte Corday & Certain Men of the Revolutionary Torment. 10.00 (ISBN 0-404-05588-5). AMS Pr.
Charlotte Mary Yonge, Her Life & Letters. 16.00 (ISBN 0-8103-3891-2). Gale.
Charlotte Perkins Gilman: The Making of a Radical Feminist, 1860-1896. 14.95x (ISBN 0-87722-160-X). Temple U Pr.
Charlton Heston. pap. 1.75 (ISBN 0-515-04189-0). HarBraceJ.
Charmed Lives: A Family Romance. 15.00 (ISBN 0-394-41954-5). Random.
Chase the Game. 8.95 (ISBN 0-396-07632-7). Dodd.
Chat with Robert Frost. lib. bdg. 6.50 (ISBN 0-8414-3567-7). Folcroft.
Chateaubriand et le Tasse. pap. 11.50 (ISBN 0-384-03675-9). Johnson Repr.
Chaucer. lib. bdg. 30.00. Folcroft.
Chaucer. lib. bdg. 30.00 (ISBN 0-8482-2139-7). Norwood Edns.
Chaucer. lib. bdg. 18.00x (ISBN 0-8371-1478-0, PRCH). Greenwood.
Chaucer. lib. bdg. 10.00 (ISBN 0-8492-2645-7). R West.
Chaucer - the Consolation of Philosophy of Boethius. lib. bdg. 18.95 (ISBN 0-8383-0574-1). Haskell.
Chaucer Among the Gods: The Poetics of Classical Myth. text ed. 10.95x (ISBN 0-271-00201-8). Pa St U Pr.
Chaucer & His Poetry. lib. bdg. 7.50 (ISBN 0-8414-3932-X). Folcroft.
Chaucer & His Poetry. 7.25 (ISBN 0-404-52509-1). AMS Pr.
Chaucer & His Times. lib. bdg. 17.50 (ISBN 0-8414-8608-5). Folcroft.
Chaucer & His Times. lib. bdg. 20.00 (ISBN 0-8495-5129-3). Arden Lib.
Chaucer & Some of His Friends. 6.00 (ISBN 0-8414-2201-X). Folcroft.
Chaucer & Some of His Friends. 35.00 (ISBN 0-87968-844-0). Gordon Pr.
Chaucer & the Consolation of Philosophy of Boethius. 7.50 (ISBN 0-87752-055-0). Gordian.
Chaucer's Official Life. 6.00 (ISBN 0-87753-022-X). Phaeton.
Chautauqua to Opera: An Autobiography of a Voice Teacher & Daughter of a Chautauqua Pioneer. 8.00 (ISBN 0-682-49112-8). Exposition.
Cheaper by the Dozen. rev. ed. 9.95 (ISBN 0-690-18632-0). T Y Crowell.
Cheaper by the Dozen. pap. 1.95 (ISBN 0-553-13533-3, Y13533-3). Bantam.
Checklist of the Letters of Richard Aldington. 9.85x (ISBN 0-8093-0781-2). S Ill U Pr.
Checklist of Writings About John Dewey, 1887-1977. 2nd, enl. ed. 15.00x (ISBN 0-8093-0842-8). S Ill U Pr.
Checkmate in Prague: The Memoirs of a Grand Master. 8.95 (ISBN 0-02-594300-6). Macmillan.
Cheechakoes. 8.95 (ISBN 0-394-41901-4). Random.
Cheer the Lonesome Traveler: The Life of W. E. B. Du Bois. 5.95 (ISBN 0-8037-1186-7). Dial.
Chekhov: A Biography. pap. 3.95 (ISBN 0-226-75805-2, P372). U of Chicago Pr.
Chekhov, a Life. lib. bdg. 12.00x (ISBN 0-8371-4095-1, MACH). Greenwood.
Chekhov in My Life. lib. bdg. 9.50x (ISBN 0-8371-5551-7, AVCH). Greenwood.
Chekhov, the Man. lib. bdg. 13.95 (ISBN 0-8383-1867-3). Haskell.
Cher: Simply Cher. PLB 5.95 (ISBN 0-88436-186-1); pap. 3.50 (ISBN 0-88436-187-X). EMC.
Cherokee Crown of Tannassy. 7.95 (ISBN 0-910244-99-5). Blair.
Cherubini: Memorials Illustrative of His Life & Work. lib. bdg. 22.50 (ISBN 0-306-70071-9). Da Capo.
Che's Guerrilla War. pap. 2.50 (ISBN 0-14-021884-X). Penguin.
Chess Is My Life: Autobiography & Games. 8.95 (ISBN 0-668-04528-0). Arco.
Chess Panorama. pap. 3.95 (ISBN 0-8128-2316-8). Stein & Day.
Chester, N.Y. Presbyterian Church: A History. 9.45 (ISBN 0-912526-11-4). Lib Res.
Chesterfield & His Critics. lib. bdg. 40.00 (ISBN 0-8414-3461-1). Folcroft.
Chesterton As Seen by His Contemporaries. 49.95 (ISBN 0-87968-027-X). Gordon Pr.
Chesterton As Seen by His Contemporaries. lib. bdg. 18.95 (ISBN 0-8383-0968-2). Haskell.
Chevalier: The Films & Career of Maurice Chevalier. 12.00 (ISBN 0-8065-0354-8). Citadel Pr.
Chevalier: The Films & Career of Maurice Chevalier. pap. 6.95 (ISBN 0-8065-0483-8). Citadel Pr.
Cheyenne Artist: The Story of Richard West. pap. 0.95 (ISBN 0-377-84211-7). Friend Pr.
Chicago. PLB 5.95 (ISBN 0-87191-458-1); pap. 2.75 (ISBN 0-89812-114-0). Creative Ed.
Chicago Giant: A Biography of Long John Wentworth. 10.00 (ISBN 0-87057-042-0). Brown U Pr.
Chicano Scholars & Writers: A Bio-Bibliographical Directory. 26.50 (ISBN 0-8108-1205-3). Scarecrow.
Chicorel Index to Biographies. 132.00. Am Lib Pub Co.
Chief Dogho of Warri. pap. text ed. 1.95x (ISBN 0-435-94473-8). Heinemann Ed.
Chief Joseph. PLB 6.95 (ISBN 0-87518-062-0). Dillon.
Chief Ministers of England, 920-1720. facs. ed. 18.75 (ISBN 0-8369-0703-5). Arno.
Child in Prison Camp. 8.75 (ISBN 0-688-20113-X); PLB 8.40 (ISBN 0-688-30113-4). Morrow.
Child of Satan, Child of God. pap. 1.95 (ISBN 0-553-11472-7). Bantam.
Child of Satan, Child of God. 7.95 (ISBN 0-88270-229-7); pap. 2.95 (ISBN 0-88270-276-9). Logos.

Childbirth, Cooperative Style: Family Experience with Prepared Childbirth & Prenatal Classes. 6.00 (ISBN 0-682-48785-6). Exposition.
Childe Hassam. 20.00 (ISBN 0-8230-0622-0). Watson-Guptill.
Childhood Revisited. pap. 7.50. Macmillan.
Childhood, the Biography of a Place. lib. bdg. 12.95 (ISBN 0-8161-6752-4). G K Hall.
Children of Fantasy: The First Rebels of Greenwich Village. 17.95 (ISBN 0-471-42100-6). Wiley.
Children of the Conestoga. pap. 3.95 (ISBN 0-87178-133-6). Brethren.
Children of the Incas. 8.95 (ISBN 0-590-07500-4). Schol Bk Serv.
Children of Theatre Street. 15.95 (ISBN 0-670-21769-7). Viking Pr.
China Childhood. 7.05x (ISBN 0-89644-523-2). Chinese Materials.
China Diary: Crisis Diplomacy in Dairen. 7.50 (ISBN 0-8138-0240-7). Iowa St U Pr.
China to Me: A Partial Autobiography. lib. bdg. 29.50 (ISBN 0-306-70695-4). Da Capo.
China's Red Masters: Political Biographies of the Chinese Communist Leaders. lib. bdg. 13.00x (ISBN 0-8371-5215-1, ELCR). Greenwood.
Chinese Warlord: The Career of Feng Yu-hsiang. 17.50x (ISBN 0-8047-0145-8); pap. 4.95 (ISBN 0-8047-0146-6, SP111). Stanford U Pr.
Chitlangou, Son of a Chief. text ed. 11.75x (ISBN 0-8371-5839-7). Negro U Pr.
Choice of Weapons. 9.95 (ISBN 0-06-013281-7). Har-Row.
Choice of Weapons. pap. 1.95 (ISBN 0-06-080305-3, P305). Har-Row.
Choice of Weapons. pap. 37.50 set (ISBN 0-8372-9561-0). Bowmar-Noble.
Chopin. rev. ed. 7.95x (ISBN 0-460-03154-6). Biblio Dist.
Chopin. rev. ed. pap. 5.95 (ISBN 0-8226-0709-3). Littlefield.
Chopin: A Biography, with a Survey of Books, Editions, & Recordings. 8.50 (ISBN 0-208-01542-6). Shoe String.
Chopin & George Sand in Majorca. lib. bdg. 18.95 (ISBN 0-8383-1807-X). Haskell.
Chopin: His Life & Times. 9.95 (ISBN 0-8467-0415-3); pap. 5.95 (ISBN 0-8467-0416-1). Two Continents.
Chopin: Man & His Music. pap. 3.00 (ISBN 0-486-21687-X). Dover.
Chopin, the Composer: His Structural Art & Its Influence on Contemporaneous Music. 9.00x (ISBN 0-8154-0306-2). Cooper Sq.
Chopin: The Man & His Music. 5.50 (ISBN 0-8446-2284-2). Peter Smith.
Chopin: The Man & His Music. 27.00 (ISBN 0-403-01587-1). Scholarly.
Chris Evert, Tennis Pro. 5.95 (ISBN 0-88436-128-4); pap. 3.50 (ISBN 0-88436-129-2). EMC.
Christ, Hope of the World. 8.00 (ISBN 0-8198-0020-1); pap. 7.00 (ISBN 0-8198-0021-X); deluxe ed. 10.00 (ISBN 0-8198-0022-8). Dghtrs St Paul.
Christ in the Country Club. pap. 1.75 (ISBN 0-8361-1315-2). Herald Pr.
Christ of the New Testament. lib. bdg. 12.50x (ISBN 0-8371-2323-2, MOCN). Greenwood.
Christ the Lord. 0.95 (ISBN 0-385-00620-9, E6). Doubleday.
Christian A. Herter. 12.50x (ISBN 0-8154-0341-0). Cooper Sq.
Christian Singers of Germany. 17.75 (ISBN 0-8369-2878-4). Arno.
Christian Social Reformers of the Nineteenth Century. facsimile ed. 14.00 (ISBN 0-8369-1526-7). Arno.
Christiana Tsai. pap. 3.50 (ISBN 0-8024-1422-2). Moody.
Christianity for Pious Skeptics. pap. 4.95 (ISBN 0-687-07646-3). Abingdon.
Christianity Rubs Holes in My Religion. pap. 1.95 (ISBN 0-917726-03-0). Hunter Bks.
Christina Georgina Rossetti. 12.00 (ISBN 0-404-06385-3). AMS Pr.
Christina of Denmark, Duchess of Milan & Lorraine, 1522-1590. 25.00 (ISBN 0-404-09205-5). AMS Pr.
Christina Rossetti. 22.50x (ISBN 0-520-00980-0). U of Cal Pr.
Christina Rossetti. lib. bdg. 18.95 (ISBN 0-8383-1299-3). Haskell.
Christina Rossetti: A Biographical & Critical Study. lib. bdg. 26.95 (ISBN 0-8383-1292-6). Haskell.
Christina Rossetti: A Study. lib. bdg. 12.00 (ISBN 0-374-97410-1). Octagon.
Christina Rossetti: A Study. lib. bdg. 7.75 (ISBN 0-8414-7536-9). Folcroft.
Christina Rossetti & Her Poetry. 7.25 (ISBN 0-404-52503-2). AMS Pr.
Christina Rossetti & Her Poetry. lib. bdg. 7.50 (ISBN 0-8495-0426-0). Arden Lib.
Christina Rossetti: Her Life & Religion. lib. bdg. 20.00 (ISBN 0-8414-7616-0). Folcroft.
Christology at the Crossroads: A Latin American Approach. pap. 12.95 (ISBN 0-88344-076-8). Orbis Bks.
Christoph Martin Wieland. lib. bdg. 12.50 (ISBN 0-8057-6369-4). Twayne.
Christoph Martin Wieland. lib. bdg. 12.50 (ISBN 0-8057-6369-4). G K Hall.
Christopher & His Kind. 10.00 (ISBN 0-374-12330-6). FS&G.
Christopher & His Kind. pap. 2.75 (ISBN 0-380-01795-4, 35394). Avon.
Christopher Columbus & the Participation of the Jews in the Spanish & Portuguese Discoveries. 6.75 (ISBN 0-87203-005-9). Hermon.
Christopher Columbus: Being the Life of the Very Magnificent Lord Don Cristobal Colon. lib. bdg. 33.50x (ISBN 0-313-22031-X, MACB). Greenwood.
Christopher Columbus, Mariner. 8.95 (ISBN 0-316-58356-1). Little.
Christopher Columbus, Mariner. pap. 1.50 (ISBN 0-451-61662-6, MW1662). NAL.
Christopher Columbus, Who Sailed on! PLB 5.50 (ISBN 0-89565-032-0). Childs World.
Christopher Isherwood: A Critical Biography. 13.95 (ISBN 0-19-520134-5). Oxford U Pr.
Christopher Isherwood: A Reference Guide. lib. bdg. 24.00 (ISBN 0-8161-8072-5). G K Hall.
Christopher Isherwood: Myth & Anti-Myth. 12.50x (ISBN 0-231-04118-7). Columbia U Pr.
Christopher Marlowe. 13.50 (ISBN 0-208-00715-6). Shoe String.
Christopher Marlowe & His Associates. 10.95 (ISBN 0-8274-1335-1). R West.
Christopher Marlowe & His Associates. lib. bdg. 13.00x (ISBN 0-8154-0326-7). Cooper Sq.
Christopher Marlowe in London. lib. bdg. 12.50 (ISBN 0-374-92470-8). Octagon.
Christopher Marlowe: The Muse's Darling. 7.50 (ISBN 0-672-51406-0). Bobbs.
Christopher Smart. lib. bdg. 8.50 (ISBN 0-8057-1502-9). Twayne.
Christ's Life, Our Life. 6.95 (ISBN 0-8164-0384-8). Seabury.
Chromatography: An Adventure in Graduate School. o.p. 7.50 (ISBN 0-8412-0277-X); pap. 4.50 (ISBN 0-8412-0277-X). Am Chemical.
Chronicler of European Chivalry. lib. bdg. 35.00 (ISBN 0-8492-4010-7). R West.
Chronicles of the Pilgrim Fathers of the Colony of Plymouth, 1602-1625. lib. bdg. 37.50 (ISBN 0-306-71760-3). Da Capo.
Chronicles of the Pilgrim Fathers of the Colony of Plymouth, from 1602-1625. 20.00 (ISBN 0-8063-0611-4). Genealog Pub.
Chronology & Documentary Handbook of the State of Arkansas. PLB 7.50 (ISBN 0-379-16129-X). Oceana.
Chronology & Documentary Handbook of the State of California. PLB 7.50 (ISBN 0-379-16130-3). Oceana.
Chronology of Paul's Life. 11.95 (ISBN 0-8006-0522-5). Fortress.
Chrysalis of Religion: A Guide to the Jewishness of Buber's I & Thou. pap. 5.95 (ISBN 0-687-08040-1). Abingdon.
Chuck Foreman. pap. 5.95 (ISBN 0-87191-543-X); pap. 2.75 (ISBN 0-89812-168-X). Creative Ed.
Church & Revolution in Rwanda. text ed. 26.00 (ISBN 0-8419-0305-0). Holmes & Meier.
Churchill: A Profile. 7.95 (ISBN 0-8090-3447-6). Hill & Wang.
Churchill & Beaverbrook: A Study in Friendship & Politics. 6.50. Heineman.
Churchill As War Lord. 25.00 (ISBN 0-8128-1560-2). Stein & Day.
Churchill in America: An Affectionate Portrait. 10.00 (ISBN 0-15-117880-1). HarBraceJ.
Cicero: A Biography. 12.50 (ISBN 0-8196-0119-5). Biblo.
Cicero & His Friends: A Study of Roman Society in the Time of Caesar. lib. bdg. 15.00x (ISBN 0-8154-0318-6). Cooper Sq.
Cicero & the End of the Roman Republic. text ed. 16.50x (ISBN 0-06-494013-6). B&N.
Cicero & the Fall of the Roman Republic. 25.25 (ISBN 0-8369-6866-2). Arno.
Cicero & the Fall of the Roman Republic. 30.00 (ISBN 0-404-58287-7). AMS Pr.
Cicero, the Secrets of His Correspondence. lib. bdg. 20.50x (ISBN 0-8371-2505-7, CACI). Greenwood.
Ciceron y el Imperio. pap. 1.85 (ISBN 0-8477-0050-X). U of PR Pr.
Cicero's Letters to Atticus. 43.00 (ISBN 0-521-04643-2); 26.50 (ISBN 0-521-04644-0); 37.50 (ISBN 0-521-06927-0); 49.00 (ISBN 0-521-06928-9); 45.00 (ISBN 0-521-04645-9); 37.50 (ISBN 0-521-04646-7); 16.95 (ISBN 0-521-07840-7); 220.00 (ISBN 0-521-08773-2). Cambridge U Pr.
Cigarette Sellers of Three Crosses Square. new ed. 6.95 (ISBN 0-8225-0757-9). Lerner Pubns.
Cinema Eye, Cinema Ear: Some Key Film-Makers of the Sixties. 3.95 (ISBN 0-8090-1328-2); pap. 3.95. Hill & Wang.
Circle of Quiet. 8.95 (ISBN 0-374-12374-8). FS&G.
Citizen: An American Boy's Early Manhood Aboard a Sag Harbor Whale-Ship Chasing Delirium & Death Around the World, 1843-1849. 10.00 (ISBN 0-930766-01-6); pap. 4.95 (ISBN 0-930766-02-4). O W Frost.
Citizen Hoover: A Critical Study of the Life & Times of J. Edgar Hoover & His FBI. 10.95 (ISBN 0-911012-60-5). Nelson-Hall.
Citizen of New Salem. 3.75 (ISBN 0-374-31320-2). FS&G.
Citizen Paul: A Story of Father & Son. 8.95 (ISBN 0-374-12385-3). FS&G.
Citizen Toussaint. pap. 2.95 (ISBN 0-8090-1326-6). Hill & Wang.
Citizen Toussaint. lib. bdg. 22.50x (ISBN 0-313-20794-1, KOCT). Greenwood.
City Cop. 5.95 (ISBN 0-385-13460-6). Doubleday.
City Lives. 12.95 (ISBN 0-03-015131-7); pap. 7.95 (ISBN 0-03-015126-0). HR&W.
City of Discontent: An Interpretive Biography of Vachel Lindsay, Being Also the Story of Springfield, Illinois, USA. lib. bdg. 17.50 (ISBN 0-374-93676-5). Octagon.
Clara Barton, Founder of American Red Cross. PLB 4.99 (ISBN 0-394-90358-7). Random.
Clara's Diary: An American Girl in Meiji Japan. 15.00 (ISBN 0-87011-341-0). Kodansha.
Clare Sheridan. 10.00 (ISBN 0-385-06745-3). Doubleday.
Clarence Luther Herrick, Pioneer Naturalist, Teacher & Psychobiologist. pap. 1.50 (ISBN 0-87169-451-4). Am Philos.
Clarke of St. Vith: The Sergeants' General. 10.00 (ISBN 0-913228-08-7). Dillon-Liederbach.
Clarke of the Kindur: Convict, Bushranger, Explorer. 12.50x (ISBN 0-522-83952-5). Intl Schol Bk Serv.
Claros Varones De Castilla. 9.50x (ISBN 0-19-815702-9). Oxford U Pr.
Classic Stories from the Lives of Our Prophets. 7.50 (ISBN 0-87747-438-9). Deseret Bk.
Classical Moment: Studies of Corneille, Moliere, & Racine. lib. bdg. 15.00x (ISBN 0-8371-5803-6, TUCM). Greenwood.
Classified Directory of Artists' Signatures, Symbols, & Monograms. 75.00 (ISBN 0-8103-0985-8). Gale.
Claude De l' Estoille, Poet & Dramatist, 1597-1652. pap. 11.50 (ISBN 0-384-44862-3). Johnson Repr.
Claude Debussy & the Poets. 26.75x (ISBN 0-520-02827-9). U of Cal Pr.
Claude Debussy, His Life & Works. 6.50 (ISBN 0-8446-4829-9). Peter Smith.
Claude Kitchin & the Wilson War Policies. 16.00 (ISBN 0-8462-1549-7). Russell.
Claude Levi-Strauss. rev. ed. 7.50 (ISBN 0-670-22515-0). Viking Pr.
Claude Levi-Strauss. rev. ed. pap. 2.50 (ISBN 0-14-004300-4). Penguin.
Claude Levi-Strauss: Social Psychotherapy & the Collective Unconscious. lib. bdg. 12.50x (ISBN 0-87023-260-6). U of Mass Pr.
Claude Lorrain. 7.95 (ISBN 0-8076-0594-8). Braziller.
Clausewitz & the State. 22.50x (ISBN 0-19-501988-1). Oxford U Pr.
Clear Spirit: Twenty Canadian Women & Their Times. pap. 6.00 (ISBN 0-8020-6209-1). U of Toronto Pr.
Clear the Bridge! The War Patrols of the U.S.S. Tang. 12.50 (ISBN 0-528-81058-8). Rand.
Clearing the Air. pap. 2.75 (ISBN 0-425-03903-X). Berkley Pub.
Clemenceau. 13.50 (ISBN 0-208-00152-2). Shoe String.
Clement Greenberg, Art Critic. 15.00 (ISBN 0-299-07900-7). U of Wis Pr.
Clement of Alexandria: A Study in Christian Platonism & Gnosticism. 19.95x (ISBN 0-19-826706-1). Oxford U Pr.
Clemente! pap. 1.45 (ISBN 0-671-48355-2). WSP.
Clemente Guillen, Explorer of the South: Diaries of the Overland Expeditions to Bahia Magdalena & La Paz, 1719, 1720-1721. 18.00 (ISBN 0-87093-242-X). Dawsons.
Clementi: His Life & Music. 44.00x (ISBN 0-19-315227-4). Oxford U Pr.
Clementine Churchill: The Biography of a Marriage. 16.95 (ISBN 0-395-27597-0). HM.
Cleon. 5.95 (ISBN 0-698-10057-3). Coward.
Cleopatra of Egypt. PLB 4.39 (ISBN 0-394-90550-4). Random.
Cleopatra's Children. 5.00 (ISBN 0-396-06376-4). Dodd.
Clint: Biography of a Labor Intellectual Clinton S. Golden. 14.95 (ISBN 0-689-10923-7). Atheneum.
Clockmakers of Lancaster County & Their Clocks: 1750-1850. 17.95 (ISBN 0-442-29531-6). Van Nos Reinhold.
Clocks of Columbus: The Literary Career of James Thurber. 10.00 (ISBN 0-689-10516-9, 242); pap. 6.95 (ISBN 0-689-70574-3). Atheneum.
Close up: The Contract Director. 19.50 (ISBN 0-8108-0961-3). Scarecrow.
Close-up: The Hollywood Director. 19.50 (ISBN 0-8108-1085-9). Scarecrow.
Closed World of Love. 6.95 (ISBN 0-671-22845-5). S&S.
Closed World of Love. pap. 1.75 (ISBN 0-380-39917-2, 39917). Avon.
Clovis Chappell: Preacher of the Word. 3.95 (ISBN 0-8054-7223-1). Broadman.
C'nelia. 7.95 (ISBN 0-87981-047-5). Holman.
Coach: A Season with Lombardi. 7.50 (ISBN 0-393-08622-4). Norton.
Coach: A Season with Lombardi. pap. 1.75 (ISBN 0-445-04056-4). Popular Lib.
Coach's Art. 9.95 (ISBN 0-917304-36-5); pap. 6.95 (ISBN 0-917304-55-1). Intl Schol Bk Serv.
Cobbler in Congress: The Life of Henry Wilson, 1812-1875. 15.25 (ISBN 0-8131-1249-4). U Pr of Ky.
Code of Honor. 7.95 (ISBN 0-393-05533-7). Norton.
Codline's Child: The Autobiography of Wilbert Snow. 17.50x (ISBN 0-8195-4069-2). Columbia U Pr.
Coed Killer. 8.95 (ISBN 0-8027-0514-6). Walker & Co.
Coffee, Martinis & San Francisco. pap. 7.95 (ISBN 0-89141-039-2). Presidio Pr.
Cohographs. 15.00 (ISBN 0-87706-071-1); pap. 12.50 (ISBN 0-87706-072-X). Branch-Smith.
Coils, Magnets & Rings: Michael Faraday's World. 5.95 (ISBN 0-698-20384-4). Coward.
Colditz Story. lib. bdg. 21.00x (ISBN 0-313-20245-1, RECS). Greenwood.
Cole Porter: A Biography. 9.95 (ISBN 0-8037-1464-5). Dial.
Cole Porter: A Biography. pap. 6.95 (ISBN 0-306-80097-7). Da Capo.
Cole Porter, Twentieth Century Composer of Popular Songs. lib. bdg. 2.45 incl. catalog cards; pap. 1.25 vinyl laminated covers (ISBN 0-87157-038-6). SamHar Pr.
Coleridge & Christian Doctrine. text ed. 8.50x (ISBN 0-674-13691-8). Harvard U Pr.
Coleridge at Highgate. lib. bdg. 20.00. Folcroft.
Coleridge Fille: A Biography of Sara Coleridge. lib. bdg. 25.00 (ISBN 0-8414-2015-7). Folcroft.
Coleridge: Studies by Several Hands on the Hundredth Anniversary of His Death. 11.00 (ISBN 0-8462-1075-4). Russell.
Coleridge, the Damaged Archangel. 12.50 (ISBN 0-8076-0607-3). Braziller.
Coleridge's American Disciples: Selected Correspondence of James Marsh. 15.00x (ISBN 0-87023-121-9). U of Mass Pr.
Colette. 12.95 (ISBN 0-688-03601-5). Morrow.
Colette: A Taste of Life. pap. 5.95 (ISBN 0-15-618550-4). HarBraceJ.
Colgate Darden: Conversations with Guy Friddell. 12.95 (ISBN 0-8139-0744-6). U Pr of Va.
Colin Archer & the Seaworthy Double-Ender. 17.50 (ISBN 0-87742-086-6). Intl Marine.
Collapse of Orthodoxy: The Intellectual Ordeal of George Frederick Holmes. 9.50x (ISBN 0-8139-0345-9). U Pr of Va.
Collected Letters of Oliver Goldsmith. lib. bdg. 15.00 (ISBN 0-8414-3334-8). Folcroft.
Collected Letters of Oliver Goldsmith. lib. bdg. 20.00 (ISBN 0-8492-3757-2). R West.
Collected Letters of Sir Arthur Pinero. 15.00x (ISBN 0-8166-0717-6). U of Minn Pr.
Collected Letters of Thomas Hardy, 1840-1842. 39.00x (ISBN 0-19-812470-8). Oxford U Pr.
Collection of Letters of W. M. Thackeray. lib. bdg. 27.50. Folcroft.
Collection of the Facts & Documents Relative to the Death of Major General Alexander Hamilton. 5.95 (ISBN 0-88319-012-5). Shoal Creek Pub.
Collection of the Facts & Documents, Relative to the Death of Major-General Alexander Hamilton. 20.00 (ISBN 0-8369-5025-9). Arno.
Collector's Progress. lib. bdg. 16.50x (ISBN 0-8371-7219-5, LECP). Greenwood.
Collins. lib. bdg. 11.00 (ISBN 0-374-93011-2). Octagon.
Collins. 9.00. Somerset Pub.
Collins. lib. bdg. 7.45 (ISBN 0-8414-2018-1). Folcroft.
Collis Potter Huntington. 12.50x (ISBN 0-8139-0376-9). U Pr of Va.
Collision Course. pap. 2.95 (ISBN 0-88270-230-0). Logos.
Collura: Actor with a Gun. pap. 1.95 (ISBN 0-671-81539-3). PB.
Colombo's Canadian References. 18.95 (ISBN 0-19-540253-7). Oxford U Pr.
Colonel Alexander K. McClure's Recollections of Half a Century. 31.50 (ISBN 0-404-00086-X). AMS Pr.
Colonel Gordon in Central Africa, 1874-1879. 21.00 (ISBN 0-527-34600-4). Kraus Repr.
Colonel Grenfell's Wars: The Life of a Soldier of Fortune. 17.50x (ISBN 0-8071-0921-5). La State U Pr.
Colonel Joe, the Last of the Rough Riders: Recollections of a Centenarian. 8.00 (ISBN 0-682-48988-3). Exposition.
Colonel John Pelham: Lee's Boy Artillerist. 6.00 (ISBN 0-8078-0974-8). U of NC Pr.

Colonel of Chicago. 12.95 (ISBN 0-525-08267-0). Dutton.
Colonial Clergy of Virginia, North Carolina & South Carolina. 10.00 (ISBN 0-8063-0731-5). Genealog Pub.
Colonial Officer & His Times, 1754-1773: A Biographical Sketch of Gen. Hugh Waddell of North Carolina. 12.00 (ISBN 0-87152-142-3). Reprint.
Colonial Riflemen in the American Revolution. 18.00 (ISBN 0-87387-074-3). Shumway.
Coltrane: A Biography. 8.95 (ISBN 0-915542-82-X). Herndon Hse.
Coltrane: A Biography. pap. 4.95 (ISBN 0-915542-83-8). Herndon Hse.
Columbus & His Discovery of America. 11.50 (ISBN 0-404-00287-0). AMS Pr.
Columbus & His Discovery of America. pap. 8.00 (ISBN 0-384-00326-5). Johnson Repr.
Columbus Story. reinforced bdg. 7.95 (ISBN 0-684-13179-X). Scribner.
Come & See. 5.95 (ISBN 0-87680-438-5, 80438). Word Bks.
Come into My Parlor: A Biography of the Aristocratic Everleigh Sisters of Chicago. facsimile ed. 18.00x (ISBN 0-405-06126-9). Arno.
Come, Meet My Friend. pap. 0.95 (ISBN 0-8007-9001-4). Revell.
Come See the Place: The Holy Land Jesus Knew. 12.95 (ISBN 0-13-152538-7). P-H.
Come Tell Me How You Live. pap. write for info. (ISBN 0-671-83438-X). PB.
Comeback. 5.95 (ISBN 0-02-563040-7). Macmillan.
Comeback. 9.95 (ISBN 0-912376-45-7). Chosen Bks Pub.
Comedians of Country Music. PLB 5.95 (ISBN 0-8225-1409-5). Lerner Pubns.
Comes the Reckoning. 19.00 (ISBN 0-405-04756-8). Arno.
Coming Home. 14.95 (ISBN 0-04-920047-X). Allen Unwin.
Coming of Age in Mississippi. pap. 1.75 (ISBN 0-440-31488-7). Dell.
Coming to My Senses. pap. 1.75 (ISBN 0-345-24815-5). Ballantine.
Command and Leadership in the German Air Force. 20.00 (ISBN 0-405-00051-0). Arno.
Command at Sea: Great Fighting Admirals from Hawke to Nimitz. 8.95 (ISBN 0-312-15120-9). St Martin.
Commanders of the Army of the Potomac. 14.00x (ISBN 0-8071-0527-9). La State U Pr.
Commanders of the Army of the Potomac. lib. bdg. 24.50x (ISBN 0-313-21976-1, HACR). Greenwood.
Commitment Total. 7.95 (ISBN 0-8027-0449-2). Walker & Co.
Commodore James Biddle & His Sketch Book. 1.50. Pa Hist Soc.
Commodore Vanderbilt: An Epic of the Steam Age. 26.00 (ISBN 0-384-31275-6). Johnson Repr.
Common Sense About Shaw. lib. bdg. 17.50 (ISBN 0-8414-2409-8). Folcroft.
Common Sense About the Shaw. lib. bdg. 25.00 (ISBN 0-8495-4217-0). Arden Lib.
Commune on the Frontier: The Story of Frances Wright. 6.95 (ISBN 0-690-20401-9). T Y Crowell.
Communication to My Friends. lib. bdg. 16.95 (ISBN 0-8383-1910-6). Haskell.
Communication to My Friends. lib. bdg. 10.00 (ISBN 0-8414-6162-7). Folcroft.
Communists of Poland: An Historical Outline. pap. text ed. 7.95. Hoover Inst Pr.
Compassionate Landscape. 17.50 (ISBN 0-8020-2186-7); pap. 6.00 (ISBN 0-8020-6269-5). U of Toronto Pr.
Compendium of Irish Biography: Comprising Sketches of Distinguished Irishmen & of Eminent Persons Connected with Ireland by Office or by Their Writings. text ed. 22.50x (ISBN 0-87696-007-7). Humanities.
Competition Wallah. 2nd corr. ed. 21.50 (ISBN 0-404-14782-8). AMS Pr.
Complete Jack the Ripper. 9.95 (ISBN 0-8212-0661-3). NYGS.
Complete Jack the Ripper. pap. 1.95 (ISBN 0-451-07148-4, J7148). NAL.
Composers, Conductors, & Critics. 8.50 (ISBN 0-911772-63-4). Info Coord.
Composers Eleven. facsimile ed. 16.50 (ISBN 0-8369-1554-2). Arno.
Composer's Gallery: Biographical Sketches of Contemporary Composers. facs. ed. 18.25 (ISBN 0-8369-8036-0). Arno.
Composers of Operetta. lib. bdg. 17.00x (ISBN 0-8371-7612-3, HUCO). Greenwood.
Composers of Tomorrow's Music: A Non-Technical Introduction to the Musical Avant-Garde Movement. lib. bdg. 17.75x (ISBN 0-313-22107-3, EWCT). Greenwood.
Comprehension & Composition: An Introduction to the Essay. pap. text ed. 7.95 (ISBN 0-02-329920-7). Macmillan.
Comte De Chambord: The Third Republic's Uncompromising King. 9.75 (ISBN 0-8223-0029-X). Duke.
Comte: The Founder of Sociology. 7.50 (ISBN 0-8462-0595-5). Russell.
Concise Dictionary of American Biography. thub-indexed 44.00 (ISBN 0-684-15178-2); 40.00 (ISBN 0-684-14654-1). Scribner.
Concise Dictionary of American Literature. lib. bdg. 12.50x (ISBN 0-8371-2106-X, RIDA). Greenwood.
Concise Dictionary of Literature. 6.00 (ISBN 0-8022-0924-6). Philos Lib.
Conditioning for Baseball. pap. 3.95 (ISBN 0-89305-020-2). Anna Pub.
Confederate Leaders in the New South. lib. bdg. 9.25x (ISBN 0-8371-3686-5, HECL). Greenwood.
Confederate Portraits. facs. ed. 19.75 (ISBN 0-8369-0241-6). Arno.
Confederate Spy Stories. 8.95 (ISBN 0-397-31230-X). Lippincott.
Confederate Women. lib. bdg. 12.75x (ISBN 0-8371-7534-8, WCW/); pap. 3.95 (ISBN 0-8371-8357-X, WCW). Greenwood.
Confession. 7.95 (ISBN 0-688-01352-X). Morrow.
Confession of a Fool. 15.95 (ISBN 0-8383-1397-3). Haskell.
Confession of a Jew. 12.00x (ISBN 0-405-06717-8). Arno.
Confession, Trial & Execution of Nat Turner, the Negro Insurrectionist. 5.00 (ISBN 0-404-00120-3). AMS Pr.
Confessions of a Conservative Evangelical. pap. 2.65 (ISBN 0-664-24996-5). Westminster.
Confessions of a Divorce Lawyer. pap. 1.75 (ISBN 0-345-25119-9). Ballantine.
Confessions of a Hollywood Columnist. 5.95 (ISBN 0-688-05017-4). Morrow.
Confessions of a Poet. 18.50 (ISBN 0-404-16352-1). AMS Pr.
Confessions of a Poet. 18.00 (ISBN 0-88355-875-0). Hyperion Conn.
Confessions of a Promiscuous Counterfeiter. 9.95 (ISBN 0-15-121853-6). HarBraceJ.
Confessions of a Psychic. 7.95 (ISBN 0-02-612120-4). Macmillan.
Confessions of a School Master. 15.00 (ISBN 0-405-01381-7). Arno.
Confessions of a White Racist. pap. 2.95 (ISBN 0-670-00351-4). Penguin.
Confessions of an Actor. 12.00 (ISBN 0-405-08240-1). Arno.
Confessions of an Advertising Man. 10.00 (ISBN 0-689-10215-1). Atheneum.
Confessions of an Advertising Man. pap. 5.95 (ISBN 0-689-70601-4, 260). Atheneum.
Confessions of Edward Dahlberg. 6.50 (ISBN 0-8076-0589-1). Braziller.
Confessions of Two Brothers. 25.00 (ISBN 0-403-00691-0). Scholarly.
Conflict & Crisis: The Presidency of Harry S Truman, 1945-1948. 12.95 (ISBN 0-393-05636-8). Norton.
Conflict & Crisis: The Presidency of Harry S. Truman, 1945-1948. pap. 5.95 (ISBN 0-393-00924-6). Norton.
Conflicts with Oblivion. 12.50 (ISBN 0-8046-0000-7). Kennikat.
Confucius. 3.95 (ISBN 0-684-15706-3). Scribner.
Confucius & the Chinese Way. 6.00 (ISBN 0-8446-1918-3). Peter Smith.
Confucius in Life & Legend. 5.95 (ISBN 0-8407-6152-X). Elsevier-Nelson.
Confucius, the Man & the Myth. lib. bdg. 20.00x (ISBN 0-8371-6531-8, CRCO). Greenwood.
Congress of Nations: Addresses at the International Peace Congresses at Brussels (1848), Paris (1849), & Frankfort (1850; see Learned Blacksmith: The Letters & Journals of Elihu Burritt.
Congressman Abraham Lincoln. lib. bdg. 21.00x (ISBN 0-8371-9307-9, RIAL). Greenwood.
Congreve Gallery. lib. bdg. 12.00 (ISBN 0-374-95188-8). Octagon.
Connecticut Clockmakers of the Eighteenth Century. pap. 3.00 (ISBN 0-486-22922-X). Dover.
Connecticut Clockmakers of the Eighteenth Century. 12.50 (ISBN 0-8048-1152-0). C E Tuttle.
Connecticut Clockmakers of the Eighteenth Century. 2nd ed. 7.50 (ISBN 0-8446-5046-3). Peter Smith.
Connecticut Clockmakers of the Eighteenth Century. lib. bdg. 9.95 (ISBN 0-932268-00-5). New Eng Pub.
Connie's New Eyes. 8.95 (ISBN 0-397-31697-6). Lippincott.
Connie's New Eyes. pap. 1.25 (ISBN 0-671-29897-6). Archway.
Conquest of Fear. 2.95 (ISBN 0-8054-8228-8). Broadman.
Conquest of Florida Under Hernando De Soto. 10.00 ea.; (ISBN 0-87208-017-X); (ISBN 0-87208-018-8); 17.50 (ISBN 0-87208-036-6). Island Pr.
Conquest of New Granada: Being the Life of Gonzalo Jimenez De Quesada. 12.00x (ISBN 0-8154-0086-1). Cooper Sq.
Conquest of New Mexico & California. 20.00. Sullivan Bks Intl.
Conquest of New Mexico & California. lib. bdg. 15.00. Sullivan Bks Intl.
Conquest: The Story of a Negro Pioneer. pap. 2.95 (N288P). Mnemosyne.
Conquest: The Story of a Negro Pioneer. facs. ed. 14.00 (ISBN 0-8369-8632-6). Arno.
Conrad & the Reporters. lib. bdg. 10.00 (ISBN 0-8414-6094-9). Folcroft.
Conrad: The Moral World of the Novelist. text ed. 19.50x (ISBN 0-06-492348-7). B&N.
Conrad Weiser & the Indian Policy of Colonial Pennsylvania. 19.00 (ISBN 0-405-02895-4). Arno.
Conrade Webb of Hampstead. 5.00x (ISBN 0-87057-050-1). Brown U Pr.
Conscience in Conflict: The Life of St. George Jackson Mivart. lib. bdg. 23.75x (ISBN 0-313-22041-7, GRCC). Greenwood.
Conservationists. new ed. pap. text ed. 4.24 (ISBN 0-201-07303-X). A-W.
Constance F. Woolson. pap. 3.45 (ISBN 0-8084-0092-4, T34). Coll & U Pr.
Constantine. 7.95 (ISBN 0 8037-1486-6). Dial.
Constantine the Great & the Christian Church. lib. bdg. 9.95 (ISBN 0-8383-0131-2). Haskell.
Constantine the Great & the Christian Church. lib. bdg. 34.95 (ISBN 0-87968-934-X). Gordon Pr.
Constitutional Principles of Thomas Jefferson. 7.50 (ISBN 0-8446-1340-1). Peter Smith.
Constitutional Principles of Thomas Jefferson. facsimile ed. 14.00 (ISBN 0-8369-5813-6). Arno.
Constructive Revolutionary: John Calvin & His Socio-Economic Impact. 9.95 (ISBN 0-8042-0880-8). John Knox.
Constructive Revolutionary: John Calvin & His Socio-Economic Impact. pap. 4.95 (ISBN 0-8042-0881-6). John Knox.
Contemporaries. 15.00 (ISBN 0-8274-0239-2). R West.
Contemporaries of Shakespeare. lib. bdg. 20.00. Folcroft.
Contemporary American Authors: A Critical Survey & 219 Bio-Bibliographies. 29.50 (ISBN 0-404-04342-9). AMS Pr.
Contemporary American Biography. facsimile ed. 17.25 (ISBN 0-8369-2483-5). Arno.
Contemporary American Composers: A Biographical Dictionary. lib. bdg. 50.00 (ISBN 0-8161-1117-0). G K Hall.
Contemporary American Indian Leaders. 4.95g (ISBN 0-396-06633-X). Dodd.
Contemporary Black Leaders. 4.95 (ISBN 0-396-06231-8); pap. 1.95 (ISBN 0-396-06765-4). Dodd.
Contemporary Canadian Composers. 14.95x (ISBN 0-19-540244-8). Oxford U Pr.
Contemporary Composers. 13.00 (ISBN 0-404-08327-7). AMS Pr.
Contemporary Dramatists. 30.00x (ISBN 0-312-16660-5). St Martin.
Contemporary Immortals. facs. ed. 13.00 (ISBN 0-8369-0533-4). Arno.
Contemporary Musicians in Photographs. pap. 6.00 (ISBN 0-486-23859-8). Dover.
Contemporary Personalities. facsimile ed. 14.25 (ISBN 0-8369-0061-8). Arno.
Contemporary Poets of the English Language. 30.00x (ISBN 0-312-16800-4). St Martin.
Contemporary Russian Composers. 15.00 (ISBN 0-403-01623-1). Scholarly.
Contemporary Russian Composers. lib. bdg. 16.00x (ISBN 0-8371-4285-7, MORC). Greenwood.
Contemporary Women Scientists of America. PLB 7.29 (ISBN 0-671-32920-0). Messner.
Contentious Consul: A Biography of John Coffin Jones First United States Counselor Agent at Hawai. 10.00 (ISBN 0-87093-175-X). Dawsons.
Continuum: An Autobiography at Thirty. pap. 9.95 (ISBN 0-917960-03-3). Padma.
Controversial Mark Hopkins. 2nd rev ed. 5.00 (ISBN 0-910740-23-2). Holmes.
Conundrum. 6.95 (ISBN 0-15-122563-X). HarBraceJ.
Conundrum. pap. 1.50 (ISBN 0-451-06413-5, W6413). NAL.
Conversation with a World Voyager. 3.00. Seven Seas.
Conversation with a World Voyager. pap. 4.00 (ISBN 0-915160-13-7). McKay.
Conversations: The Diary of a Worried Journalist's Trek Across a Divided & Threatened Canada. pap. 7.95 (ISBN 0-13-172056-2). P-H.
Conversations with Einstein. 8.50 (ISBN 0-8180-0215-8). Horizon.
Conversations with Eric Sevareid. 7.00 (ISBN 0-8183-0258-5). Pub Aff Pr.
Conversations with Eric Sevareid. 6.00 (ISBN 0-8183-0248-8). Pub Aff Pr.
Conversations with Frederick Manfred. pap. 7.00 (ISBN 0-87480-091-9). U of Utah Pr.
Conversations with Husserl & Fink. 31.60 (ISBN 90-247-1793-0). Kluwer Boston.
Conversations with Jean Piaget. 12.95 (ISBN 0-226-07503-6). U of Chicago Pr.
Conversations with Joan Crawford. 9.95 (ISBN 0-8065-0720-9). Citadel Pr.
Conversations with Kafka. rev. ed. 8.50 (ISBN 0-8112-0295-X). New Directions.
Conversations with Kennedy. pap. 1.95 (ISBN 0-671-80432-4). PB.
Conversations with Kennedy. 7.95 (ISBN 0-393-08722-0). Norton.
Conversations with Marilyn. pap. 1.75 (ISBN 0-345-25568-2). Ballantine.
Conversations with Menuhin. 14.95 (ISBN 0-312-16943-4). St Martin.
Conversations with Walt Whitman. 49.95 (ISBN 0-87968-011-3). Gordon Pr.
Conversations with Walt Whitman. lib. bdg. 10.95 (ISBN 0-8383-1627-1). Haskell.
Conversations with Willie: Recollections of W. Somerset Maugham. 8.95 (ISBN 0-671-24046-3). S&S.
Conversion of a Klansman: The Story of a Former Ku Klux Klan Terrorist. 7.95 (ISBN 0-385-14926-3). Doubleday.
Conversion of a Psychic. 5.95 (ISBN 0-385-12638-7). Doubleday.
Conversion of Constantine. 6.00 (ISBN 0-8446-0084-9). Peter Smith.
Conversion of Constantine. pap. text ed. 4.95 (ISBN 0-88275-453-X). Krieger.
Convict. 10.00 (ISBN 0-312-16948-5). St Martin.
Coole. 11.00x (ISBN 0-7165-1372-2). Biblio Dist.
Coop. 10.95 (ISBN 0-312-16955-8). St Martin.
Cope: Master Naturalist: Life & Letters of Edward Drinker Cope, with a Bibliography of His Writings. lib. bdg. 45.00x (ISBN 0-405-10735-8). Arno.
Copey of Harvard: A Biography of Charles Townsend Copeland. lib. bdg. 15.50x (ISBN 0-8371-6465-6, ADCO). Greenwood.
Coping with Cancer. pap. 2.95 (ISBN 0-8054-5245-1, 4252-45). Broadman.
Coppin the Great: Father of the Australian Theatre. 16.00x (ISBN 0-522-83520-1). Intl Schol Bk Serv.
Corbitt: The Story of Ted Corbitt, Long Distance Runner. 4.00 (ISBN 0-911520-45-7). Tafnews.
Coretta Scott King. lib. bdg. 4.78 (ISBN 0-8116-4585-1). Garrard.
Coretta Scott King. PLB 5.75 (ISBN 0-87191-410-7). Creative Ed.
Cornish Childhood: Autobiography of a Cornishman. 10.00 (ISBN 0-517-53845-8). Potter.
Coronary Event. pap. 1.95 (ISBN 0-445-04213-3). Popular Lib.
Corps Commander. 14.95 (ISBN 0-684-15324-6). Scribner.
Correspondence & Conversations of Alexis De Tocqueville with Nassau W. Senior. 2nd ed. 17.50x (ISBN 0-678-00444-7). Kelley.
Correspondence & Papers of Edmond Halley. 18.00x (ISBN 0-405-06596-5). Arno.
Correspondence & Public Papers of John Jay, 1763-1781. 91.00 (ISBN 0-8337-1847-9). B Franklin.
Correspondence Between Thomas Jefferson & Pierre Samuel Du Pont De Nemours, 1798-1817. lib. bdg. 32.50 (ISBN 0-306-71301-2). Da Capo.
Correspondence of Andre Gide & Edmund Gosse: 1904-1928. lib. bdg. 17.50x (ISBN 0-8371-9736-8, GICO). Greenwood.
Correspondence of Henrik Ibsen. lib. bdg. 27.95 (ISBN 0-8383-1098 2). Haskell.
Correspondence of Henry David Thoreau. lib. bdg. 35.00x (ISBN 0-8371-7247-0, THCO). Greenwood.
Correspondence of James Fenimore Cooper. lib. bdg. 47.95 (ISBN 0-8383-1295-0). Haskell.
Correspondence of James Fenimore Cooper. facsimile ed. 40.25 (ISBN 0-8369-5881-0). Arno.
Correspondence of Jefferson & Du Pont de Nemours. lib. bdg. 29.00 (ISBN 0-8337-4186-1). B Franklin.
Correspondence of John Locke. Incl. Letters 1-461, Covering the Years 1650-1679 (ISBN 0-19-824396-0); Letters - 462-848 Covering the Years 1679-1686 (ISBN 0-19-824559-9). 69.00 ea. Oxford U Pr.
Correspondence of John Ray. 29.00x (ISBN 0-405-06613-9). Arno.
Correspondence of Sir Thomas More. facsimile ed. 25.00 (ISBN 0-8369-5404-1). Arno.
Correspondence of the Van Cortlandt Family of Cortlandt Manor, 1748-1800. 19.00 (ISBN 0-912882-29-8). Sleepy Hollow.
Correspondence of the Van Cortlandt Family of Cortlandt Manor, 1800-1814. 22.00 (ISBN 0-912882-34-4). Sleepy Hollow.
Correspondence of Thomas Gray. 85.00x (ISBN 0-19-811335-8). Oxford U Pr.
Correspondence of Wagner & Liszt. lib. bdg. 17.75x (ISBN 0-8371-2743-2, WAWL). Greenwood.
Correspondence of Wagner & Liszt. rev. ed. lib. bdg. 34.95 (ISBN 0-8383-0316-1). Haskell.
Correspondence of William Hickling Prescott, 1833-1847. lib. bdg. 39.50 (ISBN 0-306-71912-6). Da Capo.

Correspondence of William Wilberforce. facs. ed. 32.25 (ISBN 0-8369-8690-3). Arno.
Cortes. 8.95 (ISBN 0-316-46754-5). Little.
Cortes the Conqueror: The Exploits of the Earliest & Greatest of the Gentlemen Adventures in the New World. lib. bdg. 25.00 (ISBN 0-8492-8243-8). R West.
Cortisone. 7.95 (ISBN 0-684-31062-7). Scribner.
Cosell. pap. 1.75 (ISBN 0-671-78671-7). PB.
Cosima Wagner's Diaries: 1869-1877. 29.95 (ISBN 0-15-122635-0). HarBraceJ.
Cosmic Trigger: Final Secret of the Illuminati. pap. 4.95 (ISBN 0-915904-29-2). And-or Pr.
Cosmic Trigger: The Final Secret of the Illuminati. pap. 2.25 (ISBN 0-671-81669-1). PB.
Cotton Mather: The Young Life of the Lord's Remembrancer, 1663-1703. 16.50x (ISBN 0-674-17507-7). Harvard U Pr.
Coulomb & the Evolution of Physics & Engineering in Eighteenth-Century France. 21.00x (ISBN 0-691-08095-X). Princeton U Pr.
Count Rumford, Physicist Extraordinary. lib. bdg. 18.25x (ISBN 0-313-20772-0, BRCR). Greenwood.
Count the Cats in Zanzibar. pap. 5.95 (ISBN 0-87033-216-3). Cornell Maritime.
Count Witte: Scenes from His Life and Times, 1902-1915. 7.50 (ISBN 0-682-49293-0). Exposition.
Counterfeit Spy. 10.00 (ISBN 0-06-011019-8). Har-Row.
Counterpoint. pap. 2.95 (ISBN 0-671-16541-0). S&S.
Country & Calling. lib. bdg. 19.25x (ISBN 0-313-20447-0, HACAC). Greenwood.
Country Doctor. 9.50x (ISBN 0-8476-1058-6). Rowman.
Country Journal. 7.95 (ISBN 0-396-06872-3). Dodd.
Country Life in America As Lived by Ten Presidents of the United States. lib. bdg. 15.00x (ISBN 0-8371-7018-4, BOCL). Greenwood.
Country Music Encyclopedia. 15.95 (ISBN 0-690-00442-7); pap. 7.95 (ISBN 0-690-01220-9). T Y Crowell.
Country Squire in the White House. lib. bdg. 15.00 (ISBN 0-306-70324-6). Da Capo.
Country Vet. 6.95 (ISBN 0-8008-1950-0). Taplinger.
Courage Knows No Sex. 8.95 (ISBN 0-8158-0363-X). Chris Mass.
Courage to Change: An Introduction to the Life & Thought of Reinhold Niebuhr. lib. bdg. 15.00x (ISBN 0-678-02766-8). Kelley.
Courage to Choose: An American Nun's Story. 7.95 (ISBN 0-316-32864-2). Little.
Court & Times of James the First. 30.00 (ISBN 0-404-00906-9). AMS Pr.
Court of the Medici. 13.50x (ISBN 0-8476-6024-9). Rowman.
Courtesans of the Italian Renaissance. 10.00 (ISBN 0-312-17045-9). St Martin.
Courts & Cabinets. 19.75 (ISBN 0-8369-2901-2). Arno.
Cousin Beedie & Cousin Hot: My Life with the Carter Family of Plains, Georgia. 12.50 (ISBN 0-13-185470-4). P-H.
Cousin Mercedes & the White Russian. 5.00 (ISBN 0-88279-231-8). Western Islands.
Cousinhood. 10.95 (ISBN 0-02-510080-7). Macmillan.
Coventry Patmore. 11.95 (ISBN 0-8274-0648-7). R West.
Coventry Patmore. 10.00 (ISBN 0-403-00607-4). Scholarly.
Coventry Patmore. lib. bdg. 12.00x (ISBN 0-8371-1980-4, GOPA). Greenwood.
Coventry Patmore. lib. bdg. 20.00 (ISBN 0-8492-2008-4). R West.
Cowboy & Indian Trader. pap. 5.95 (ISBN 0-8263-0319-6). U of NM Pr.
Cowboy Artist: The Joe Beeler Story. 22.50 (ISBN 0-87358-196-2); pap. 10.00 (ISBN 0-87358-195-4). Northland.
Cowboys Under the Mogollon Rim. pap. 6.50 (ISBN 0-8165-0642-6). U of Ariz Pr.
Cowden Clarkes. lib. bdg. 14.00x (ISBN 0-8371-5338-7, ALCC). Greenwood.
Cowper. lib. bdg. 12.00. Folcroft.
Cowper. lib. bdg. 12.50 (ISBN 0-404-51728-5). AMS Pr.
Cowper & His Poetry. 7.25 (ISBN 0-404-52530-X). AMS Pr.
Cowper & His Poetry. lib. bdg. 7.50 (ISBN 0-8414-7340-4). Folcroft.
Crabbe. lib. bdg. 20.00 (ISBN 0-89987-001-5). Darby Bks.
Crazy Horse. PLB 6.95 (ISBN 0-87518-063-9). Dillon.
Crazy Horse, the Strange Man of the Oglalas: A Biography. pap. 4.50 (ISBN 0-8032-5171-8, 110). U of Nebr Pr.
Crazy Love: An Autobiographical Account of Marriage & Madness. 7.95 (ISBN 0-688-03178-1). Morrow.
Crazy Women in the Rafters: Memories of a Texas Boyhood. 10.95 (ISBN 0-8061-1280-8). U of Okla Pr.
Created Equal: A Biography of Elizabeth Cady Stanton, 1815-1902. lib. bdg. 15.00 (ISBN 0-374-95167-5). Octagon.
Creative Tension: The Life & Thought of Kenneth Boulding. 12.50 (ISBN 0-472-51500-4). U of Mich Pr.
Cricket in the Thorn Tree: Helen Suzman & the Progressive Party of South Africa. 12.50x (ISBN 0-253-31483-6). Ind U Pr.
Crime of Claudius Ptolemy. text ed. 22.50x (ISBN 0-8018-1990-3). Johns Hopkins.
Crime of Galileo. pap. 10.00x (ISBN 0-226-73481-1). U of Chicago Pr.
Crimes That Shook the World. facs. ed. 15.75 (ISBN 0-8369-8064-6). Arno.
Crisis, Charisma & British Political Leadership: Winston Churchill As the Outsider. 3.00x (ISBN 0-8039-9904-6). Sage.
Cristofano & the Plague: A Study in the History of Public Health in the Age of Galileo. 11.95x (ISBN 0-520-02341-2). U of Cal Pr.
Croker Papers. rev. ed. 2nd ed. 52.50 (ISBN 0-404-01880-7); 17.50 ea. (ISBN 0-404-01881-5) (ISBN 0-404-01882-3) (ISBN 0-404-01883-1). AMS Pr.
Cromwell's Captains. facsimile ed. 21.00 (ISBN 0-8369-6746-1). Arno.
Crooked Shall Be Made Straight. 10.00 (ISBN 0-8042-1101-9). John Knox.
Cross Fire. pap. 2.95 (ISBN 0-88270-157-6). Logos.
Crossing. 6.95 (ISBN 0-671-20988-4). S&S.
Crow Killer: The Saga of Liver-Eating Johnson. rev. ed. 10.95x (ISBN 0-253-11425-X). Ind U Pr.
Crucial Experiences in the Life D. L. Moody. pap. 1.50 (ISBN 0-914520-12-1). Insight Pr.
Cruise of the Essex: An Incident from the War of 1812. 6.25 (ISBN 0-8255-9201-1). Macrae.
Crunch. 7.95 (ISBN 0-393-08726-3). Norton.
Crusader & Feminist: Letters of Jane Grey Swisshelm, 1858-1865. 25.00 (ISBN 0-88355-276-0). Hyperion Conn.
Crusader in Crinoline: The Life of Harriet Beecher Stowe. lib. bdg. 35.25x (ISBN 0-8371-6191-6, WIHS). Greenwood.
Crusoe of Lonesome Lake. 8.95 (ISBN 0-394-42092-6). Random.
Crying Wind. 6.95 (ISBN 0-8024-1676-4). Moody.
Cuarenta Anos De Legislador: Biografia Del Senador Casimiro Barela. 29.00x (ISBN 0-405-09501-5). Arno.
Cuba, Castro, & the United States. 12.95 (ISBN 0-8229-3225-3). U of Pittsburgh Pr.
Cudjoe of Jamaica: Pioneer for Black Freedom in the New World. 8.95x (ISBN 0-89490-001-3). Enslow Pubs.
Cult of Elizabeth: Elizabethan Portraiture & Pageantry. 24.95 (ISBN 0-500-23263-6). Thames Hudson.
Cultism to Charisma: My Seven Years with Jeane Dixon. 4.00 (ISBN 0-682-48755-4). Exposition.
Curtain Calls: Travels in Albania, Romania & Bulgaria. 20.00 (ISBN 0-7156-1026-0). Biblio Dist.
Curzon in India. Incl. Achievement (ISBN 0-8008-2106-8); Frustration (ISBN 0-8008-2107-6). 10.00 ea. Taplinger.
Cushing of Boston: A Candid Portrait. 5.95 (ISBN 0-8283-1382-2). Branden.
Cutover Country: Jolie's Story. 5.95 (ISBN 0-8138-0015-3). Iowa St U Pr.
Cutting Edge. 10.95 (ISBN 0-07-055019-0). McGraw.
Cutting Edge: The Life of John Rogers. 9.75 (ISBN 0-8061-1329-4). U of Okla Pr.
Cutting Loose. 10.00 (ISBN 0-316-52733-5). Little.
Cycle Cop: The True Story of Jack Muller, the Chicago Giant-Killer Who Feared No Evil. 5.95 (ISBN 0-399-20534-9). Putnam.
Cycle of Power: The Career of Jersey City Mayor Frank Hague. 8.50 (ISBN 0-8108-0435-2). Scarecrow.
Cyclopedia of World Authors. lib. bdg. 16.29 (ISBN 0-06-003960-4). Har-Row.
Cynewulf & His Poetry. lib. bdg. 5.00 (ISBN 0-8414-7838-4). Folcroft.
Cynthia Ann Parker, the Sto see Two Months in the Camp of Big Bear: The Life & Adventures of Theresa Gowanlock & Theresa Delaney.
Cyprian. 7.50. Greeno Hadden.
Cyprian. pap. 8.95 (ISBN 0-915646-00-5). Phila Patristic.
Cyrus the Great. pap. 1.50 (ISBN 0-523 00908-9). Pinnacle Bks.

D

D. Gwenallt Jones (1899-1968) pap. text ed. 4.50x (ISBN 0-8426-0430-8). Verry.
D. H. Lawrence. lib. bdg. 12.50 (ISBN 0-8414-1422-X). Folcroft.
D. H. Lawrence: A Bibliography 1911-1976. 15.00x (ISBN 0-87875-042-8). Whitston Pub.
D. H. Lawrence & Susan His Cow. 9.00x (ISBN 0-8154-0436-0). Cooper Sq.
D. H. Lawrence Companion: Life, Thought & Works. text ed. 23.50x (ISBN 0-06-495574-5). B&N.
D. H. Lawrence: Portrait of a Genius But-- pap. 1.50 (ISBN 0-02-001070-2). Macmillan.
D. H. Lawrence: The Novels. 19.95 (ISBN 0-521-21744-X); pap. 6.95 (ISBN 0-521-29272-7). Cambridge U Pr.
D. H. Lawrence's Nightmare: The Writer & His Circle in the Years of the Great War. 15.95 (ISBN 0-465-01641-3). Basic.
Daddyji. 6.95 (ISBN 0-374-13438-3). FS&G.
Daddyji. pap. 3.95 (ISBN 0-19-502619-5). Oxford U Pr.
Daddy's Girl, Mama's Boy. pap. 2.25 (ISBN 0-451-08822-0, E8822). NAL.
Daddy's Girl, Mama's Boy. 8.95 (ISBN 0-672-52348-5). Bobbs.
Daily Life of Early Christians. lib. bdg. 12.00x (ISBN 0-8371-2413-1, DAEC). Greenwood.
Daisy Hooee Nampeyo. PLB 6.95 (ISBN 0-87518-141-4). Dillon.
D'Alembert & Frederick the Great: A Study of Their Relationship. 12.50 (ISBN 0-912116-11-0). Learned Pubns.
Dali. 12.95 (ISBN 0-517-53675-7). Crown.
Dallas Cowboys. 8.95 (ISBN 0-02-588970-2). Macmillan.
Dalton Gang Days. 17.65. Bear State.
Dames & Daughters of Colonial Days. 20.00x (ISBN 0-405-06080-7). Arno.
Dames & Daughters of the French Court. facs. ed. 14.25 (ISBN 0-8369-0256-4). Arno.
Dames of the Theatre. 8.95 (ISBN 0-87000-310-0). Arlington Hse.
Damien. 3.50 (ISBN 0-8248-0693-X). U Pr of Hawaii.
Damien the Leper. 2.45 (ISBN 0-385-02918-7, D3). Doubleday.
Damn Yankee: The First Career of Frederick A. P. Barnard. 12.50 (ISBN 0-8046-9177-0). Kennikat.
Damned Englishman: A Study of Erskine Childers (1870-1922) 10.00 (ISBN 0-682-47821-0). Exposition.
Damned in Paradise: A Life of John Barrymore. 12.95 (ISBN 0-689-10814-1). Atheneum.
Damned Old Crank: A Self-Portrait of E. W. Scripps Drawn from His Unpublished Writings. lib. bdg. 13.75x (ISBN 0-8371-6159-2, SCDO). Greenwood.
Dance Around the Sun: The Life of Mary Little Bear Inkanish: Cheyenne. 12.95 (ISBN 0-690-01450-3). T Y Crowell.
Dance Autobiography. 30.00 (ISBN 0-394-50141-1). Knopf.
Dance to the Piper. lib. bdg. 19.50 (ISBN 0-306-79613-9). Da Capo.
Dangerous Life. 22.00x (ISBN 0-405-05400-9). Arno.
Daniel Boone. facsimile ed. 16.75 (ISBN 0-8369-5966-3). Arno.
Daniel Boone: Taming the Wilds. PLB 4.48 (ISBN 0-8116-6251-9). Garrard.
Daniel Carl Solander, Naturalist on the "Endeavour". pap. 1.00 (ISBN 0-87169-588-X). Am Philos.
Daniel De Leon: Social Architect. 2.50 (ISBN 0-935534-12-1). NY Labor News.
Daniel Defoe. lib. bdg. 20.00 (ISBN 0-8414-1983-3). Folcroft.
Daniel Defoe. 8.00 (ISBN 0-8274-1113-8). R West.
Daniel Defoe. lib. bdg. 17.95 (ISBN 0-8383-1806-1). Haskell.
Daniel Defoe. lib. bdg. 10.00. Folcroft.
Daniel Defoe: A Study in Conflict. 21.00 (ISBN 0-403-08922-0). Somerset Pub.
Daniel Defoe: A Study in Conflict. lib. bdg. 25.00 (ISBN 0-8414-4231-2). Folcroft.
Daniel Defoe: A Study in Conflict. lib. bdg. 25.00 (ISBN 0-8495-1615-3). Arden Lib.
Daniel E. Morgan, 1877-1949: The Good Citizen in Politics. 10.00 (ISBN 0-8295-0054-5). UPBS.
Daniel Inouye. PLB 6.49 (ISBN 0-690-01358-2). T Y Crowell.
Daniel Lee, Agriculturist: His Life North & South. 7.00 (ISBN 0-8203-0285-6). U of Ga Pr.
Daniel Webster & the Rise of National Conservatism. pap. text ed. 4.95 (ISBN 0-316-16515-8). Little.
Daniel Webster & the Supreme Court. 12.50x (ISBN 0-87023-008-5). U of Mass Pr.
D'Annunzio: The Poet As Superman. 10.00 (ISBN 0-8392-1022-1). Astor-Honor.
Danseur: The Male in Ballet. 19.95 (ISBN 0-07-049811-3). McGraw.
Danseur: The Male in Ballet. pap. 8.95 (ISBN 0-07-049812-1). McGraw.
Dante. 4.95 (ISBN 0-02-537300-5). Macmillan.
Dante. pap. 3.95 (ISBN 0-02-069350-8, 06935). Macmillan.
Dante Alighieri. lib. bdg. 30.00 (ISBN 0-8482-0938-9). Norwood Edns.
Dante & His Early Biographers. lib. bdg. 15.95 (ISBN 0-8383-1002-8). Haskell.
Dante & His Time. 9.75 (ISBN 0-8274-1187-1). R West.
Dante & His Time. 10.50 (ISBN 0-8046-0693-5). Kennikat.
Dante & His Time. lib. bdg. 24.95 (ISBN 0-8383-1192-X). Haskell.
Dante Gabriel Rossetti: Painter, Poet of Heaven in Earth. lib. bdg. 26.95 (ISBN 0-8383-1336-1). Haskell.
Dante, Poet of the Desert: History & Allegory in the Divine Comedy. 20.00x (ISBN 0-691-06399-0). Princeton U Pr.
Dante the Maker. 45.00 (ISBN 0-7100-0322-6). Routledge & Kegan.
Dante Vivo. 10.95 (ISBN 0-8274-1183-9). R West.
Dante Vivo. 11.00 (ISBN 0-8046-0697-8). Kennikat.
Danton. text ed. 19.75x (ISBN 0-8419-0408-1). Holmes & Meier.
Danton: A Study. 24.50 (ISBN 0-404-00737-6). AMS Pr.
Dare to Be Brave. casebd. 10.00 (ISBN 0-912404-06-X). Alpha Pubns.
Dare to Be Great. 8.95 (ISBN 0-688-03101-3). Morrow.
Daredevils Do Amazing Things. 3.95 (ISBN 0-394-83623-5); 3.99g (ISBN 0-394-93623-X). Random.
Daredevils of the Speedway. pap. 1.50 (ISBN 0-448-14016-0). G&D.
Daring Sea Captains. PLB 3.95 (ISBN 0-8225-0465-0). Lerner Pubns.
Dark Child. 5.95 (ISBN 0-374-13472-3); pap. 3.95 (ISBN 0-374-50768-6, N365). FS&G.
Dark Eagle: The Story of Benedict Arnold. 6.95 (ISBN 0-02-700210-1, 70021). Macmillan.
Dark Quartet: The Story of the Brontes. 10.95 (ISBN 0-440-01657-6). Delacorte.
Darling, You Were Wonderful. 8.95 (ISBN 0-8092-7872-3). Contemp Bks.
Darrell Royal Story. 5.95 (ISBN 0-88319-016-8). Shoal Creek Pub.
Darwin. pap. text ed. 5.95x (ISBN 0-393-09901-6). Norton.
Darwin. 2nd ed. 24.95 (ISBN 0-393-01192-5); pap. 5.95x (ISBN 0-393-95009-3). Norton.
Darwin & His Flowers: The Key to Natural Selection. 14.50 (ISBN 0-8008-2113-0). Taplinger.
Darwin & His Great Discovery. 6.95g (ISBN 0-02-726450-5). Macmillan.
Darwin & the Darwinian Revolution. pap. 6.95 (ISBN 0-393-00455-4). Norton.
Darwin & the Darwinian Revolution. 8.50 (ISBN 0-8446-1240-5). Peter Smith.
Darwin & the Enchanted Isles. PLB 4.99 (ISBN 0-698-30679-1). Coward.
Dasher: The Roots & the Rising of Jimmy Carter. 11.95 (ISBN 0-671-40004-5). Summit Bks.
Dashiell Hammett: A Casebook. 6.95; pap. 4.95 (ISBN 0-87461-017-6). McNally.
Daughter: A Novel Based on the Life of Eleanor Marx. 9.95 (ISBN 0-06-010757-X). Har-Row.
Daughter of Peter the Great. 14.50 (ISBN 0-404-00447-4). AMS Pr.
Daughter of Peter the Great. 19.00 (ISBN 0-403-00002-5). Scholarly.
Daughter of the Middle Border. 6.50 (ISBN 0-8446-0105-5). Peter Smith.
Daughter of the Pacific. lib. bdg. 13.00x (ISBN 0-8371-6683-7, MADP). Greenwood.
Daughter of Zion. 7.95 (ISBN 0-394-47032-X). Knopf.
Daughters of Eve. 11.00 (ISBN 0-8046-0542-4). Kennikat.
Daughters of the Puritans: A Group of Brief Biographies. facs. ed. 13.75 (ISBN 0-8369-0180-0). Arno.
Daumier & His World. 15.75x (ISBN 0-8101-0019-3). Northwestern U Pr.
Dauntless in Mississippi: The Life of Sarah A. Dickey. 11.95 (ISBN 0-89201-006-1). Zenger Pub.
Dauntless Women in Childhood Education, 1856-1931. pap. 9.50x (ISBN 0-87173-021-9). ACEI.
Dauntless Women: Stories of Pioneer Wives. 12.75 (ISBN 0-8369-8031-X). Arno.
Dave Beck. 9.95 (ISBN 0-916076-27-X). Writing.
Dave Cowens. PLB 5.95 (ISBN 0-87191-668-1); pap. 2.75 (ISBN 0-89812-182-5). Creative Ed.
Dave Cowens: A Biography. 5.95 (ISBN 0-385-11523-7); PLB (ISBN 0-385-11524-5). Doubleday.
David. pap. 3.95 (ISBN 0-8042-2031-X). John Knox.

David: A Mother's Story of Her Son's Recovery from Coma & Brain Damage. pap. 1.50 (ISBN 0-671-81793-0). PB.
David A. Wells & the American Revenue System 1865-1870. lib. bdg. 17.50x (ISBN 0-87991-356-8). Porcupine Pr.
David & His Mighty Men. facs. ed. 12.50 (ISBN 0-8369-8041-7). Arno.
David Curtis De Forest & the Revolution of Buenos Aires. lib. bdg. 11.50x (ISBN 0-8371-3970-8, KEDF). Greenwood.
David Curtis Deforest & the Revolution of Buenos Aires. 10.00x. Elliots Bks.
David Dubinsky: A Life with Labor. 9.95. S&S.
David French Boyd: Founder of Louisiana State University. 20.00x (ISBN 0-8071-0266-0). La State U Pr.
David Friedrich Strauss & His Place in Modern Thought. 12.50 (ISBN 0-913638-05-6). Intl Schol Bk Serv.
David Garrick. 17.00 (ISBN 0-405-08711-X). Arno.
David Garrick, Dramatist. 18.00 (ISBN 0-405-08994-5). Arno.
David Garrick, Dramatist. pap. 20.00 (ISBN 0-527-86100-6). Kraus Repr.
David Hockney. 30.00 (ISBN 0-8109-1058-6). Abrams.
David Hume. 8.00 (ISBN 0-8462-1237-4). Russell.
David Hume. lib. bdg. 7.95 (ISBN 0-8057-1280-1). Twayne.
David Hume & the Miraculous. lib. bdg. 6.50 (ISBN 0-8414-0845-9). Folcroft.
David Jones Letters to Vernon Watkins. text ed. 8.50x (ISBN 0-7083-0616-0). Verry.
David Lavender's Colorado. 12.95 (ISBN 0-385-06337-7). Doubleday.
David Lloyd, Colonial Lawmaker. 8.50 (ISBN 0-295-73762-X). U of Wash Pr.
David Lloyd George: A Biography. 20.00 (ISBN 0-02-605590-2). Macmillan.
David Ricardo. 10.00x (ISBN 0-231-03524-1); pap. 3.50x (ISBN 0-231-03916-6). Columbia U Pr.
David Rittenhouse. lib. bdg. 30.00x (ISBN 0-405-12569-0). Arno.
David Snedden & Education for Social Efficiency. 17.00x (ISBN 0-299-04460-2). U of Wis Pr.
David Teniers the Younger. lib. bdg. 25.00x (ISBN 0-89158-564-8). Westview.
David Urquhart: Some Chapters in the Life of a Victorian Knight Errant of Justice & Liberty. 15.00x (ISBN 0-678-00609-1). Kelley.
David Wendel Yandell: Physician of Old Louisville. 4.95 (ISBN 0-8131-0245-6). U Pr of Ky.
David Wilmot, Free Soiler: A Biography of the Great Advocate of the Wilmot Proviso. 10.00 (ISBN 0-8446-1200-6). Peter Smith.
David Wynne. pap. text ed. 5.50 (ISBN 0-7083-0714-0). Verry.
Davy Crockett. PLB 4.49 (ISBN 0-399-60120-1). Putnam.
Davy Crockett. 5.50 (ISBN 0-15-222517-X). HarBraceJ.
Dawns & Dusks: Taped Conversations with Diana MacKown. 12.95 (ISBN 0-684-14781-5); pap. 7.95 (ISBN 0-684-15895-7, SL 810). Scribner.
Day I Died. 10.00x (ISBN 0-85614-035-X). Intl Pubns Serv.
Day Is Born of Darkness. 10.95 (ISBN 0-394-49166-1). Knopf.
Day of Pleasure: Stories of a Boy Growing up in Warsaw. 8.95 (ISBN 0-374-31749-6); pap. 5.95 (ISBN 0-374-51367-8). FS&G.
Day the Red Baron Died. pap. 1.95 (ISBN 0-345-24923-2). Ballantine.
Day They Shook the Plum Tree. pap. 1.50 (ISBN 0-671-78492-7). PB.
Day with Charlotte Bronte. lib. bdg. 8.50 (ISBN 0-8414-1653-2). Folcroft.
Day with Samuel Taylor Coleridge. lib. bdg. 8.50 (ISBN 0-8414-1745-8). Folcroft.
Daybooks & Notebooks. Incl. Daybooks, 1876-November, 1881 (ISBN 0-8147-9167-0); Daybooks, December 1881--1891 (ISBN 0-8147-9176-X); Diary in Canada, Notebooks, Index (ISBN 0-8147-9177-8). 75.00x set (ISBN 0-8147-9191-3). NYU Pr.
Daybooks, December 1881--1891 see Daybooks & Notebooks.
Daybooks, 1876--November, 1881 see Daybooks & Notebooks.
Days & Nights in Calcutta. 8.95 (ISBN 0-385-02895-4). Doubleday.
Days of My Years. 4.00 (ISBN 0-8361-1356-X). Herald Pr.
Days of Sorrow & Pain: Leo Baeck & the Berlin Jews. 14.95 (ISBN 0-02-506340-5). Macmillan.
Days with Albert Schweitzer: A Lambarene Landscape. lib. bdg. 10.75x (ISBN 0-8371-7341-8, FRAS). Greenwood.
Days with Ulanova. pap. 6.95 (ISBN 0-671-24294-6). S&S.
De Quincey at Work. lib. bdg. 15.00 (ISBN 0-8414-3162-0). Folcroft.
De Sade: A Critical Biography. 12.95 (ISBN 0-690-01416-3). T Y Crowell.
De Soto & the Conquistadores. 17.50 (ISBN 0-404-04279-1). AMS Pr.
Deadline. 6.95. (ISBN 0-399-20611-6). Putnam.
Deadline. pap. 1.50 (ISBN 0-440-91718-2). Dell.
Deadly Magic. 9.95 (ISBN 0-684-15873-6). Scribner.
Dean Acheson: The State Department Years. 17.50 (ISBN 0-396-07313-1). Dodd.
Dean Swift. lib. bdg. 25.00. Folcroft.
Dear Alben: Mr. Barkley of Kentucky. 4.95 (ISBN 0-8131-0238-3). U Pr of Ky.
Dear Dad, Our Life in the Theater Around the Turn of the Century. pap. 3.95 (ISBN 0-87027-125-3). Wheelwright.
Dear Josephine: The Theatrical Career of Josephine Hull. 14.95 (ISBN 0-8061-0558-5). U of Okla Pr.
Dear Mamma, Please Don't Die. pap. 3.95 (ISBN 0-8407-5689-5). Nelson.
Dear Me. 9.95 (ISBN 0-316-89051-0). Little.
Dear Me. pap. 2.95 (ISBN 0-14-004940-1). Penguin.
Dear Shipmates. pap. 3.95 (ISBN 0-913182-94-X). Grossmont Pr.
Dear Teddy Robinson. pap. 1.50 (ISBN 0-14-030272-7). Penguin.
Death & Life of Malcolm X. 10.95 (ISBN 0-06-011582-3). Har-Row.
Death & Life of Malcolm X. 2nd ed. pap. 7.95 (ISBN 0-252-00774-3). U of Ill Pr.
Death Be Not Proud. 3.95 (ISBN 0-394-60286-2, M286). Modern Lib.
Death Be Not Proud. new ed. 10.00 (ISBN 0-06-011634-X); PLB 7.89 (ISBN 0-06-011633-1). Har-Row.
Death Be Not Proud: A Memoir. pap. 1.95 (ISBN 0-06-080111-5, P111). Har-Row.
Death Camp Treblinka: A Documentary. 9.95 (ISBN 0-89604-008-9); pap. 4.95 (ISBN 0-89604-009-7). Schocken.
Death of a Guru. pap. 3.95 (ISBN 0-87981-083-1). Holman.
Death of Captain Cook. 20.00 (ISBN 0-7156-0956-4). Biblio Dist.
Death of Christopher Marlowe. 6.75 (ISBN 0-8274-2159-1). R West.
Death of Christopher Marlowe. 7.50 (ISBN 0-8462-0938-1). Russell.
Deathroads: The Story of the Donut Shop Murders. 14.95 (ISBN 0-87108-538-0). Pruett.
Deborah Kerr. 8.95 (ISBN 0-312-18895-1). St Martin.
Deborah Sampson, Soldier of the Revolution. 4.95 (ISBN 0-396-07343-3). Dodd.
Debussy. rev 5th ed. 17.50x (ISBN 0-460-03173-2). Biblio Dist.
Debussy. 14.50 (ISBN 0-88355-752-5). Hyperion Conn.
Debussy. pap. 4.50x (ISBN 0-19-315426-9). Oxford U Pr.
Debussy: His Life & Mind. 33.00 (ISBN 0-521-22053-X); pap. 8.95 (ISBN 0-521-29341-3). Cambridge U Pr.
Debussy: His Life & Mind. 39.50 (ISBN 0-521-22054-8); pap. 10.95 (ISBN 0-521-29342-1). Cambridge U Pr.
Debussy, His Life & Mind. 8.00 ea. Macmillan.
Debussy: Man & Artist. pap. 4.00 (ISBN 0-486-21783-3). Dover.
Debussy: Musician of France. 18.75 (ISBN 0-8369-8032-8). Arno.
Decade of Still Life. 35.00 (ISBN 0-299-04121-2). U of Wis Pr.
Decathlon Challenge: Bruce Jenner's Story. 8.95 (ISBN 0-13-197699-0). P-H.
Decathlon Men: Greatest Athletes in the World. PLB 3.84 (ISBN 0-8116-6654-9). Garrard.
Decline & Rebirth: 1933-1962 see Ford.
Dedicated Life & Rainer Maria Rilke. lib. bdg. 10.95 (ISBN 0-8383-1920-3). Haskell.
Deeds of John & Manuel Comnenus. 20.00x (ISBN 0-231-04080-6). Columbia U Pr.
Defeat of Baudelaire: A Psycho-Analytical Study of the Neurosis of Charles Baudelaire. lib. bdg. 20.00 (ISBN 0-8414-5812-X). Folcroft.
Defoe. lib. bdg. 25.00 (ISBN 0-8414-7887-2). Folcroft.
Defoe. pap. 1.95 (ISBN 0-8277-6051-5, WTW51). British Bk Ctr.
Degas. 6.95 (ISBN 0-517-00502-6). Crown.
Delegate from New Jersey: The Journal of John Fell. 9.50 (ISBN 0-8046-9041-3). Kennikat.
DeLesseps S. Morrison & the Image of Reform: New Orleans Politics, 1946-1961. 19.95x (ISBN 0-8071-0073-0). La State U Pr.
Delightful Discipline: Humorous Stories of Woodshed Wisdom & Biblical Principles. pap. 2.75 (ISBN 0-915134-43-8). Mott Media.
Delius. lib. bdg. 11.25x (ISBN 0-8371-3958-9, HUDE). Greenwood.
Delius: A Life in Pictures. 19.95x (ISBN 0-19-315437-4). Oxford U Pr.
Delius As I Knew Him. lib. bdg. 15.50x (ISBN 0-8371-8394-4, FEDE). Greenwood.
Delius: Portrait of a Cosmopolitan. text ed. 22.50x (ISBN 0-8419-0274-7). Holmes & Meier.
Delmore Schwartz: The Life of an American Poet. 15.00 (ISBN 0-374-13761-7). FS&G.
Delmore Schwartz: The Life of an American Poet. pap. 2.95 (ISBN 0-380-41038-9, 41038). Avon.
Demeter's Daughters: The Women Who Founded America (1587-1792) 9.95 (ISBN 0-689-30494-3). Atheneum.
Democracy's Norris: The Biography of a Lonely Crusade. lib. bdg. 25.00 (ISBN 0-374-94998-0). Octagon.
Democratic Despot: A Life a Napoleon III. lib. bdg. 20.75x (ISBN 0-8371-7587-9, CODC). Greenwood.
Dempsey. 12.50 (ISBN 0-06-011054-6). Har-Row.
Denison Family of Toronto. 6.50x (ISBN 0-8020-3296-6); pap. 2.95 (ISBN 0-8020-3297-4). U of Toronto Pr.
Denison's Ice Road. 8.95 (ISBN 0-525-09006-1). Dutton.
Dennis Brain: A Biography. 10.00 (ISBN 0-8008-2160-2). Taplinger.
Derain. 6.95 (ISBN 0-517-03720-3). Crown.
Descartes. lib. bdg. 13.00x (ISBN 0-8371-4249-0, KEDE). Greenwood.
Descartes. 8.50x (ISBN 0-87663-717-9). Universe.
Desert Journal: A Naturalist Reflects on Arid California. 12.50 (ISBN 0-520-02879-1); pap. 4.95 (ISBN 0-520-03636-0). U of Cal Pr.
Desert People & Mountain Men: Exploration of the Great Basin 1824-1865. 6.50 (ISBN 0-912494-24-7); pap. 3.95 (ISBN 0-912494-25-5). Chalfant Pr.
DeSoto Didn't Land at Tampa. 3.95 (ISBN 0-87208-011-0); pap. 1.95 (ISBN 0-87208-048-X). Island Pr.
Desperado. 8.95 (ISBN 0-8037-1898-5). Dial.
Destiny of Isabelle Eberhardt. 7.95 (ISBN 0-912946-22-9). Ecco Pr.
Destiny of Isabelle Eberhardt. pap. 1.75 (ISBN 0-380-00886-6, 31542). Avon.
Devil Drives: A Life of Sir Richard Burton. 15.95 (ISBN 0-393-07374-2). Norton.
Devils' Coach. 6.95 (ISBN 0-89191-103-0). Cook.
Devil's Disciple: Ben Jonson's Debt to Machiavelli. lib. bdg. 14.50x (ISBN 0-8371-7183-0, BODD). Greenwood.
Dialogue with Photography. 12.95 (ISBN 0-374-13893-1); pap. 7.95 (ISBN 0-374-51544-1). FS&G.
Dialogues of Alfred North Whitehead. lib. bdg. 24.00x (ISBN 0-8371-9341-9, WHDI). Greenwood.
Diamond Jim: The Life & Times of James Buchanan Brady. 12.50 (ISBN 0-404-04418-7). AMS Pr.
Diana: A Strange Autobiography. 15.00x (ISBN 0-405-07359-3). Arno.
Diane Keaton Scrapbook. 5.95 (ISBN 0-448-16380-2). G&D.
Diaries of Court Ladies of Old Japan. 14.50 (ISBN 0-404-04819-6). AMS Pr.
Diaries of Donald Macdonald. lib. bdg. 12.50x (ISBN 0-678-00914-7). Kelley.
Diaries of George Washington. Incl. Vol. V, July 1786 December 1789. 30.00x (ISBN 0-8139-0801-9); Vol. VI, January 1790-December 1799. 30.00 (ISBN 0-8139-0807-8). U Pr of Va.
Diaries of George Washington: 1771-75, 1780-81. Incl. Vol I: 1748-65. 20.00x (ISBN 0-8139-0643-1), Vol. II: 1766-70. 20.00x (ISBN 0-8139-0688-1); Vol. III: 1976. 20.00x (ISBN 0-8139-0721-7). U Pr of Va.
Diaries of Lewis Carroll. lib. bdg. 27.50x (ISBN 0-8371-4494-9, DOLC). Greenwood.
Diaries of Paul Klee, 1898-1918. pap. 6.95 (ISBN 0-520-00653-4). U of Cal Pr.
Diaries of Tchaikovsky. lib. bdg. 22.50x (ISBN 0-8371-5680-7, CHDI). Greenwood.
Diaries of William Charles Macready. 32.00 (ISBN 0-405-08772-1). Arno.
Diary & Correspondence of Salmon P. Chase. lib. bdg. 39.50 (ISBN 0-306-71264-4). Da Capo.
Diary & Letters of Gouverneur Morris. lib. bdg. 75.00 (ISBN 0-306-71835-9). Da Capo.
Diary & Sundry Observations of Thomas Alva Edison. lib. bdg. 11.50x (ISBN 0-8371-0067-4, EDTE). Greenwood.
Diary in Canada, Notebooks, Index see Daybooks & Notebooks.
Diary of a Century. pap. 9.95 (ISBN 0-14-004840-5). Penguin.
Diary of a Country Parson, 1758-1802. 7.95x (ISBN 0-19-281241-6). Oxford U Pr.
Diary of a Delinquent Episode. pap. 4.50 (ISBN 0-7100-8340-8). Routledge & Kegan.
Diary of a Divorced Mother. 9.95 (ISBN 0-87223-577-7). Wyden.
Diary of a Dying Empire. 17.50 (ISBN 0-8046-1726-0). Kennikat.
Diary of a Lover of Marilyn Monroe. 8.95 (ISBN 0-87795-216-7). Arbor Hse.
Diary of a Lover of Marilyn Monroe. pap. 2.25 (ISBN 0-553-13123-0). Bantam.
Diary of a Man in Despair. 6.95 (ISBN 0-02-601400-9). Macmillan.
Diary of a Paper Boy. new ed. 5.50 (ISBN 0-399-20255-2). Putnam.
Diary of a Pigeon Watcher. 8.95 (ISBN 0-688-03019-X). Morrow.
Diary of a Pigeon Watcher. pap. 1.75 (ISBN 0-380-01638-9, 32953). Avon.
Diary of a Russian Schoolteacher. lib. bdg. 13.00x (ISBN 0-8371-6909-7, VIRS). Greenwood.
Diary of a Student Social Worker. 11.50 (ISBN 0-7100-8857-4). Routledge & Kegan.
Diary of a Westward Voyage. lib. bdg. 11.00x (ISBN 0-8371-7904-1, TAWV). Greenwood.
Diary of an Artist. 15.95 (ISBN 0-915220-29-6, 22965); deluxe ed. 200.00 (ISBN 0-915220-33-4, 22966). New Republic.
Diary of Anais Nin. pap. 21.75 (ISBN 0-15-626034-4). HarBraceJ.
Diary of Anais Nin. Incl. 1931-34 (ISBN 0-15-125588-1); 1934-39 (ISBN 0-15-125589-X); 1939-44 (ISBN 0-15-125591-1); 1944-47 (ISBN 0-15-125592-X). 9.50 ea. HarBraceJ.
Diary of Anais Nin, 1947-1955. 7.95 (ISBN 0-15-125593-8). HarBraceJ.
Diary of Anais Nin, 1947-1955. pap. 2.95 (ISBN 0-15-626030-1, HB309). HarBraceJ.
Diary of Anais Nin: 1955-1966. 12.95 (ISBN 0-15-125594-6). HarBraceJ.
Diary of Anais Nin: 1955-1966. pap. 3.95 (ISBN 0-15-626032-8). HarBraceJ.
Diary of Anna Green Winslow: A Boston School Girl of 1771. 7.50 (ISBN 0-87928-050-6). Corner Hse.
Diary of Elisabeth Koren: 1853-1855. lib. bdg. 26.00x (ISBN 0-405-11653-5). Arno.
Diary of Erasmus Smit. 13.50x (ISBN 0-86977-013-6). Verry.
Diary of Friedrich Wilhelm Heinrich Zehme, May-July, 1882: A Perspective of America. 20.00 (ISBN 0-9601618-0-5). D Clement.
Diary of George Washington: From 1789 to 1791; Embracing the Opening of the First Congress, His Tours Through New England, Long Island & Southern States, Together with His Journal of a Tour to the Ohio, in 1753. 13.50 (ISBN 0-8369-6791-7). Arno.
Diary of Isaac Backus. 120.00x (ISBN 0-87057-148-6). Brown U Pr.
Diary of Miss Emma Holmes, 1861-1866. 35.00x (ISBN 0-8071-0386-1). La State U Pr.
Diary of Philip Hone, 1828-1851. 48.00 (ISBN 0-527-42100-6). Kraus Repr.
Diary of Pierre Laval. 16.50 (ISBN 0-404-10644-7). AMS Pr.
Diary of Ralph Josselin, 1616-1683. 69.00x (ISBN 0-19-725955-3). Oxford U Pr.
Diary of Samuel Pepys. Incl. 1660. 20.00 (ISBN 0-520-01575-4); 1661. 16.50 (ISBN 0-520-01576-2); 1662. 16.50 (ISBN 0-520-01577-0); 1663. 18.50 (ISBN 0-520-01857-5); 1664. 16.50 (ISBN 0-520-01858-3); 1665. 16.50 (ISBN 0-520-01859-1); 1666. 18.50 (ISBN 0-520-02094-4); 1667. 20.00 (ISBN 0-520-02095-2); 1668-1669. 20.00 (ISBN 0-520-02096-0). U of Cal Pr.
Diary of Samuel Sewall, 1674-1729. 100.00 (ISBN 0-405-03311-7). Arno.
Diary of Simeon Perkins, 1766-1780. lib. bdg. 18.25x (ISBN 0-8371-5067-1, PEDI). Greenwood.
Diary of Simeon Perkins, 1780-1789. lib. bdg. 33.50x (ISBN 0-8371-5068-X, PEDJ). Greenwood.
Diary of Ten Years Eventful Life of an Early Settler in Western Australia. 35.00x (ISBN 0-85564-137-1). Intl Schol Bk Serv.
Diary of the Farmer's Wife. pap. 4.00 (ISBN 0-87069-187-2). Wallace-Homestead.
Diary of the Sinai Campaign. pap. 1.95 (ISBN 0-8052-0140-8). Schocken.
Diary of the Sinai Campaign. lib. bdg. 20.75x (ISBN 0-313-20928-6, DADO). Greenwood.
Diary of the "Terra Nova" Expedition to the Antarctic: 1910-1912. text ed. 21.50x (ISBN 0-391-00242-2). Humanities.
Diary of Vaslav Nijinsky. pap. 3.45 (ISBN 0-520-00945-2, CAL152). U of Cal Pr.
Diaz. 11.00 (ISBN 0-8046-1071-1). Kennikat.
Dickens. lib. bdg. 12.50. Folcroft.
Dickens. lib. bdg. 17.95 (ISBN 0-8383-1710-3). Haskell.
Dickens. lib. bdg. 10.00. Arden Lib.
Dickens & Charity. 15.00x (ISBN 0-231-04478-X). Columbia U Pr.
Dickens & Daughter. lib. bdg. 22.95 (ISBN 0-8383-1321-3). Haskell.
Dickens & Phiz. 12.50x (ISBN 0-253-31705-3). Ind U Pr.
Dickens & the Invisible World: Fairy Tales, Fantasy, & Novel-Making. 17.50x (ISBN 0-253-18366-9). Ind U Pr.
Dickens Country. lib. bdg. 25.00 (ISBN 0-8482-1444-7). Norwood Edns.
Dickens Landmarks in London. 35.00 (ISBN 0-8490-0028-9). Gordon Pr.
Dickens Landmarks in London. lib. bdg. 21.95 (ISBN 0-8383-1625-5). Haskell.
Dickens of London. 5.98 (ISBN 0-02-579410-8, 57941). Macmillan.
Dickens, the Immortal. lib. bdg. 10.00 (ISBN 0-8414-5723-9). Folcroft.

Dickens the Novelist. 19.95x (ISBN 0-8061-0768-5). U of Okla Pr.
Dickens: The Story of the Life of the World's Favourite Author. lib. bdg. 12.50 (ISBN 0-8414-3653-3). Folcroft.
Dictator of Portugal: A Life of the Marquis of Pombal, 1699-1782. facsimile ed. 21.75 (ISBN 0-8369-5041-0). Arno.
Dictators Face to Face. lib. bdg. 21.75x (ISBN 0-313-20285-0, ALDF). Greenwood.
Dictators of Latin America. PLB 5.29 (ISBN 0-399-60720-X). Putnam.
Dictators of the Baton. 28.50x (ISBN 0-8486-3002-5). CORE Collection.
Dictionary Johnson: The Middle Years of Samuel Johnson. 17.95 (ISBN 0-07-011378-5). McGraw.
Dictionary of American Authors. 35.00 (ISBN 0-8490-0031-9). Gordon Pr.
Dictionary of American Authors. 5th ed. 18.00 (ISBN 0-8103-3148-9). Gale.
Dictionary of American Authors. lib. bdg. 25.00 (ISBN 0-89341-456-5). Longwood Pr.
Dictionary of American Biography. text ed. 680.00 (ISBN 0-684-15226-6). Scribner.
Dictionary of American Painters, Sculptors & Engravers. 17.50. Wallace-Homestead.
Dictionary of American Philosophy. 10.00 (ISBN 0-8022-2093-2). Philos Lib.
Dictionary of American Philosophy. pap. 2.95 (ISBN 0-8226-0275-X). Littlefield.
Dictionary of American Religious Biography. lib. bdg. 29.95x (ISBN 0-8371-8906-3, BAR/). Greenwood.
Dictionary of Art & Artists. lib. bdg. 10.50x (ISBN 0-88307-415-X). Gannon.
Dictionary of Art & Artists. rev. ed. pap. 3.95 (ISBN 0-14-051014-1). Penguin.
Dictionary of Biographies of Authors Represented in the Authors Digest Series: With a Supplemental List of Later Titles & a Supplementary Biographical Section. 19.50 (ISBN 0-8103-3876-9). Gale.
Dictionary of Biography. 5.00 (ISBN 0-8446-2818-2). Peter Smith.
Dictionary of Biography. 11.50x (ISBN 0-87471-647-0). Rowman.
Dictionary of Biography. pap. 4.95 (ISBN 0-8226-0281-4). Littlefield.
Dictionary of Black Culture. 15.00 (ISBN 0-8022-2090-8). Philos Lib.
Dictionary of British Miniature Painters. 145.00; (ISBN 0-571-08295-5); (ISBN 0-571-09746-4). Merrimack Bk Serv.
Dictionary of Chivalry. 25.00 (ISBN 0-690-23815-0). T Y Crowell.
Dictionary of Composers. 14.95 (ISBN 0-8008-2194-7). Taplinger.
Dictionary of Composers & Their Music: Every Listener's Companion Arranged Chronologically & Alphabetically. 12.95 (ISBN 0-448-22364-3). Paddington.
Dictionary of Contemporaries. 10.00 (ISBN 0-8283-1513-2). Branden.
Dictionary of Contemporaries. text ed. 15.00x (ISBN 0-8277-1945-0). British Bk Ctr.
Dictionary of Contemporaries. 15.00 (ISBN 0-8022-0935-1). Philos Lib.
Dictionary of Contemporary American Artists. 3rd ed. 35.00 (ISBN 0-312-20090-0). St Martin.
Dictionary of English Authors. lib. bdg. 30.00. Folcroft.
Dictionary of English Authors. lib. bdg. 20.00 (ISBN 0-89341-199-X). Longwood Pr.
Dictionary of Indian Biography. 28.50 (ISBN 0-8103-3156-X). Gale.
Dictionary of Indian Biography. lib. bdg. 29.95 (ISBN 0-8383-0277-7). Haskell.
Dictionary of Indian Biography. lib. bdg. 21.00x (ISBN 0-8371-0331-2, BUIB). Greenwood.
Dictionary of Irish Biography. text ed. 25.00x (ISBN 0-06-490620-5). B&N.
Dictionary of Irish Literature. lib. bdg. 39.95 (ISBN 0-313-20718-6, HDI/). Greenwood.
Dictionary of Japanese Artists: Painting, Sculpture, Ceramics, Prints, Lacquer. 25.00 (ISBN 0-8348-0113-2). Weatherhill.
Dictionary of Labour Biography. lib. bdg. 37.50x (ISBN 0-678-07008-3); lib. bdg. 47.50x (ISBN 0-678-07018-0); lib. bdg. 37.50x (ISBN 0-333-14415-5); lib. bdg. write for info. (ISBN 0-333-19704-6). Kelley.
Dictionary of Scientific Biography. 55.00 (ISBN 0-684-15144-8). Scribner.
Dictionary of Scientific Biography. text ed. 695.00 (ISBN 0-684-15144-8). Scribner.
Dictionary of Victorian Painters. 2nd ed. 88.00 (ISBN 0-902028-72-3). Gale.
Dictionary of Violin Makers. lib. bdg. 12.50 (ISBN 0-89341-070-5). Longwood Pr.
Did the FBI Kill Martin Luther King? pap. 3.95 (ISBN 0-8407-4062-X). Nelson.
Diderot. 37.50 (ISBN 0-19-501506-1). Oxford U Pr.
Diderot & Sterne. lib. bdg. 14.00 (ISBN 0-374-92884-3). Octagon.
Diderot's Letters to Sophie Volland: A Selection. 12.00x (ISBN 0-19-212551-6). Oxford U Pr.
Die Song: A Journey into the Mind of a Mass Murderer. 11.95 (ISBN 0-393-01315-4). Norton.
Diego De Saavedra Fajardo. lib. bdg. 8.95 (ISBN 0-8057-6200-0). Twayne.
Diesel, the Man & the Engine. 8.95 (ISBN 0-689-30652-0). Atheneum.
Dietrich Bonhoeffer. pap. 2.25 (ISBN 0-8042-0535-3). John Knox.
Different Drummers: They Did What They Wanted. pap. 4.95 (ISBN 0-89087-907-9). Les Femmes Pub.
Different Face: The Life of Mary Wollstonecraft. 15.00 (ISBN 0-06-014201-4). Har-Row.
Different Valor, the Story of General Joseph E. Johnston, C.S.A. lib. bdg. 21.50x (ISBN 0-8371-7012-5, GOVD). Greenwood.
Difficult Individual: Ezra Pound. 31.00 (ISBN 0-404-17081-1). AMS Pr.
Difficulty of Being Christian. 22.50x (ISBN 0-89197-730-9). Irvington.
Digging in the Southwest. rev. ed. pap. 5.95 (ISBN 0-87905-045-4). Peregrine Smith.
Dillinger Days. 15.00 (ISBN 0-394-42221-X). Random.
Dim Memories of a Polish Jew Born in France. 12.50 (ISBN 0-670-27273-6). Viking Pr.
Dinah! A Biography. 10.95 (ISBN 0-531-09915-6). Watts.
Ding: The Life of Jay Norwood Darling. 10.95 (ISBN 0-8138-0010-2). Iowa St U Pr.
Dino Story. 4.95 (ISBN 0-8007-0733-8). Revell.
Diogenes Discovers Us. facs. ed. 15.00 (ISBN 0-8369-0647-0). Arno.
Dionne Years: A Thirties Melodrama. 10.95 (ISBN 0-393-07529-X). Norton.
Disastrous Marriage: A Study of George IV & Caroline of Brunswick. lib. bdg. 16.50x (ISBN 0-8371-8439-8, RIDM). Greenwood.
Disciple in Blue Suede Shoes. 6.95 (ISBN 0-310-36730-1). Zondervan.
Discoverers. 6.95 (ISBN 0-668-04784-4, 4784-4). Arco.
Discoverers: An Encyclopedia of Explorers & Exploration. 29.95 (ISBN 0-07-016264-6). McGraw.
Discoveries of Esteban the Black. 4.50 (ISBN 0-396-06195-8). Dodd.
Discovery: Being the Second Book of an Autobiography. lib. bdg. 14.00. Folcroft.
Discovery: Being the Second Book of an Autobiography, 1897-1913. 13.00 (ISBN 0-403-00578-7). Scholarly.
Discovery of Yellowstone Park: Journal of the Washburn Expedition to the Yellowstone & Firehole Rivers in the Year 1870. 9.75x (ISBN 0-8032-0710-7); pap. 2.75 (ISBN 0-8032-5705-8, 508). U of Nebr Pr.
Disease in a Minor Chord: Being a Semihistorical & Semibiographical Account of a Period in Science When One Could Be Happily Yet Seriously Concerned with the Diseases of Lowly Animals Without Backbones, Especially the Insects. 20.00x (ISBN 0-8142-0218-7). Ohio St U Pr.
Dispatches. 8.95 (ISBN 0-394-41788-7). Knopf.
Dispatches. pap. 3.95 (ISBN 0-380-40196-7, 40196). Avon.
Disraeli & His World. 10.95 (ISBN 0-684-15915-5). Scribner.
Dissipations at Uffington House: The Letters of Emmy Hughes, Rugby, Tennessee, 1881-1887. rev ed. pap. 5.95 (ISBN 0-87870-039-0). Memphis St Univ.
Distant Grief. pap. 3.95 (ISBN 0-8307-0684-4, 5411807). Regal.
Distinguished American Jews. 10.25 (ISBN 0-8369-1671-9). Arno.
District Nurse. 7.95 (ISBN 0-312-21358-1). St Martin.
Diversity in Holiness. facs. ed. 12.75 (ISBN 0-8369-0906-2). Arno.
Divided People. lib. bdg. 11.95x (ISBN 0-8371-9271-4, LYD/). Greenwood.
Divine Garbo. 17.95 (ISBN 0-448-16245-8). G&D.
Divine Virginia: A Biography of Virginia Zucchi. 21.50 (ISBN 0-8247-6492-7). Dekker.
Divus Julius. 42.00x (ISBN 0-19-814287-0). Oxford U Pr.
Dizzy Dean: His Story in Baseball. PLB 5.49 (ISBN 0-399-60128-7). Putnam.
Dizzy: The Life & Nature of Benjamin Disraeli, Earl of Beaconsfield. lib. bdg. 17.75x (ISBN 0-8371-7729-4, PEDIZ). Greenwood.
Dmitri Shostakovich: The Life & Background of a Soviet Composer. 16.00 (ISBN 0-403-01678-9). Scholarly.
Dmitri Shostakovich, the Man & His Work. lib. bdg. 13.25x (ISBN 0-8371-2100-0, MAS). Greenwood.
Doc Holliday. pap. 2.45 (ISBN 0-8032-5781-3, 570). U of Nebr Pr.
Dr. Beaumont & the Man with the Hole in His Stomach. PLB 5.49 (ISBN 0-698-30680-5). Coward.
Doctor Darwin. lib. bdg. 20.00. Folcroft.
Dr. Ed: The Story of General Edward Hand. 5.75 (ISBN 0-915010-24-0). Sutter House.
Dr. Elizabeth: The Story of the First Woman Doctor. PLB 6.48 (ISBN 0-688-51581-9). Lothrop.
Doctor Freud. pap. 1.25 (ISBN 0-532-12154-6). Manor Bks.
Doctor from Cordova: A Biographical Novel About the Great Philosopher Maimonides. 8.95 (ISBN 0-385-11472-9). Doubleday.
Doctor from Lhasa. pap. 1.95. Weiser.
Dr. George Washington Carver: Scientist. PLB 8.29 (ISBN 0-671-32510-8). Messner.
Dr. George Washington Carver: Scientist. pap. 1.25 (ISBN 0-671-22979-6). Archway.
Doctor in Belle Starr Country. write for info. Century Pr.
Doctor in the Zoo. pap. 3.95 (ISBN 0-14-004238-5). Penguin.
Doctor in the Zoo. 12.95 (ISBN 0-670-27527-1). Viking Pr.
Dr. Johnson. lib. bdg. 35.00 (ISBN 0-8492-5249-0). R West.
Dr. Johnson & His Circle. 15.00 (ISBN 0-8274-2198-2). R West.
Dr. Johnson & His Circle. lib. bdg. 15.00 (ISBN 0-8414-3338-0). Folcroft.
Dr. Johnson & Mr. Boswell. lib. bdg. 30.00 (ISBN 0-8414-7669-1). Folcroft.
Doctor Johnson & the Fair Sex: A Study of Contrasts. 35.00 (ISBN 0-8490-0053-X). Gordon Pr.
Doctor Johnson & the Fair Sex: A Study of Contrasts. lib. bdg. 30.00 (ISBN 0-8414-1836-5). Folcroft.
Doctor Johnson: His Life, Works & Table Talk. lib. bdg. 17.50 (ISBN 0-8414-6215-1). Folcroft.
Dr. Nina & the Panther. 8.95 (ISBN 0-396-07348-4). Dodd.
Doctor of Revolution: The Life & Genius of Erasmus Darwin. 29.00 (ISBN 0-571-10781-8). Merrimack Bk Serv.
Dr. Quicksilver: The Life of Charles Lever. 11.00 (ISBN 0-8462-1216-1). Russell.
Doctor Reminisces. 9.95 (ISBN 0-87397-133-7). Strode.
Dr. Schweitzer of Lambarene. lib. bdg. 15.25x (ISBN 0-8371-6902-X, CODS). Greenwood.
Dr. Woodward's Shield: History, Science, & Satire in Augustan England. 23.75x (ISBN 0-520-03132-6). U of Cal Pr.
Doctors, Devils & the Woman: Fort Scott, Kansas 1870-1890. 8.50x (ISBN 0-87291-074-1). Coronado Pr.
Doctors Herff: A Three-Generation Memoir. text ed. 18.00 boxed set (ISBN 0-911536-40-X). Trinity U Pr.
Doctor's Life. 12.95 (ISBN 0-15-126161-X). HarBraceJ.
Doctors Mayo. pap. 2.95 (ISBN 0-671-81212-2). PB.
Doctors Mayo. 2nd ed. 17.50x (ISBN 0-8166-0029-5); pap. 4.95 (ISBN 0-8166-0465-7). U of Minn Pr.
Dog Days at the White House: The Outrageous Memoirs of the Presidential Kennel-Keeper Truman to Nixon. 9.95 (ISBN 0-02-517990-X). Macmillan.
Dollfuss. lib. bdg. 22.00x (ISBN 0-313-20527-2, SHDO). Greenwood.
Dolly Parton. pap. 3.95 (ISBN 0-8256-3922-0). Music Sales.
Dolly Parton. PLB 5.95g (ISBN 0-8225-1411-7). Lerner Pubns.
Dolmetsch: The Man & His Work. 17.50 (ISBN 0-295-95416-7). U of Wash Pr.
Dom Helder Camara: The Violence of a Peacemaker. 6.95x (ISBN 0-88344-099-7). Orbis Bks.
Domenico Scarlatti. rev. ed. 22.00x (ISBN 0-691-09101-3). Princeton U Pr.
Domenico Scarlatti. 385.00 set (ISBN 0-384-29519-3); per volume 23.00. Johnson Repr.
Domestic & Artistic Life of John Singleton Copley, R.A. facs. ed. 20.50 (ISBN 0-8369-5368-1). Arno.
Domestic Life of Thomas Jefferson. 12.50 (ISBN 0-8044-1759-8). Ungar.
Domestic Life of Thomas Jefferson. 7.50 (ISBN 0-8139-0718-7). U Pr of Va.
Domestic Manners of Sir Walter Scott. lib. bdg. 20.00 (ISBN 0-8495-2301-X). Arden Lib.
Dominant Women. facs. ed. 14.00 (ISBN 0-8369-1155-5). Arno.
Domingo Faustino Sarmiento. lib. bdg. 7.95 (ISBN 0-8057-2798-1). Twayne.
Don Coryell Win with Honor. 8.95 (ISBN 0-89325-003-1). Joyce Pr.
Don: The Life & Death of Sam Giancana. 10.95 (ISBN 0-06-010447-3). Har-Row.
Donald Francis Tovey: A Biography Based on Letters. lib. bdg. 15.25x (ISBN 0-8371-3935-X, GRDT). Greenwood.
Donizetti & the World of Opera in Italy, Paris & Vienna in the First Half of the Nineteenth Century. lib. bdg. 24.00x (ISBN 0-374-98337-2). Octagon.
Donkeys Galore. 11.50 (ISBN 0-7153-7150-9). David & Charles.
Donny & Marie. PLB 5.95 (ISBN 0-87191-618-5); pap. 2.75 (ISBN 0-89812-121-3). Creative Ed.
Donny & Marie Osmond: Breaking All the Rules. PLB 5.95 (ISBN 0-88436-408-9); pap. 3.50 (ISBN 0-88436-409-7). EMC.
Don't Bury Me 'til I'm Dead. pap. 2.95 (ISBN 0-916406-61-X). Accent Bks.
Don't Call Me Ma. 7.95 (ISBN 0-385-08481-1). Doubleday.
Don't Make No Waves - Don't Back No Losers: An Insider's Analysis of the Daley Machine. 10.00x (ISBN 0-253-11725-9); pap. 4.95x (ISBN 0-253-20202-7). Ind U Pr.
Don't Ride the Bus on Monday: The Rosa Parks Story. 5.95 (ISBN 0-13-218750-7). P-H.
Don't Say Yes Until I Finish Talking: A Biography of Darryl F. Zanuck. pap. 1.25 (ISBN 0-671-78129-4). PB.
Doris Day. pap. 1.75 (ISBN 0-515-03959-4). HarBraceJ.
Doris Day Scrapbook. 2.95 (ISBN 0-448-12868-3). G&D.
Dorothea Lange: A Photographer's Life. 15.00 (ISBN 0-374-14323-4). FS&G.
Dorothy & William Wordsworth. lib. bdg. 18.95 (ISBN 0-8383-1403-1). Haskell.
Dorothy & William Wordsworth. lib. bdg. 11.00 (ISBN 0-374-95250-7). Octagon.
Dorothy & William Wordsworth: The Heart of a Circle of Friends. 6.95 (ISBN 0-8149-0710-5). Vanguard.
Dorothy Hamill. PLB 5.95 (ISBN 0-87191-546-4); pap. 2.75 (ISBN 0-89812-194-9). Creative Ed.
Dorothy Hamill: Olympic Champion. PLB 5.39 (ISBN 0-8178-5522-X). Harvey.
Dorothy L. Sayers: A Literary Biography. 15.00x (ISBN 0-87338-228-5). Kent St U Pr.
Dorothy Parker. 8.95 (ISBN 0-8057-7241-3). Twayne.
Dorothy Parker. lib. bdg. 8.95 (ISBN 0-8057-7241-3). G K Hall.
Dorothy Richardson: A Biography. 15.00 (ISBN 0-252-00631-3). U of Ill Pr.
Dorothy Thompson: A Legend in Her Time. pap. 1.95 (ISBN 0-380-00019-9, 18911). Avon.
Dos Passos Path to U.S.A. A Political Biography, 1912-1936. text ed. 12.95 (ISBN 0-87081-018-9). Colo Assoc.
Dostoevsky: A Self Portrait. lib. bdg. 17.25x (ISBN 0-8371-8405-3, CODO). Greenwood.
Dostoevsky: His Life & Work. 22.00x (ISBN 0-691-06027-4); pap. 6.95 (ISBN 0-691-01299-7). Princeton U Pr.
Dostoevsky: Reminiscences. pap. 5.95 (ISBN 0-87140-117-7). Liveright.
Dostoevsky, the Man & His Work. lib. bdg. 29.95 (ISBN 0-8383-1390-6). Haskell.
Dostoevsky (1821-1881) A New Biography. lib. bdg. 30.00 (ISBN 0-8414-1104-2). Folcroft.
Double Lives: An Autobiography. 16.00 (ISBN 0-8369-8105-7). Arno.
Doug & Mary: A Biography of Douglas Fairbanks & Mary Pickford. 8.95 (ISBN 0-525-09512-8). Dutton.
Douglas Diary: Student Days at Franklin & Marshall College 1856-1858. 7.95 (ISBN 0-910626-00-6). Franklin & Marsh.
Douglas Hyde. 4.50 (ISBN 0-8387-7883-6); pap. 1.95 (ISBN 0-8387-7975-1). Bucknell U Pr.
Douglas Jerrold. lib. bdg. 7.95 (ISBN 0-8057-1292-5). Twayne.
Douglas of the Supreme Court: A Selection of His Opinions. lib. bdg. 21.00x (ISBN 0-8371-6790-6, DODS). Greenwood.
Douglas Sirk. lib. bdg. 9.95 (ISBN 0-8057-9269-4). Twayne.
Downfall of a King: Dom Manuel II of Portugal. pap. text ed. 9.00x (ISBN 0-8191-0168-0). U Pr of Amer.
Downhill All the Way: An Autobiography of the Years 1919 to 1939. pap. 3.45 (ISBN 0-15-626145-6, HB322). HarBraceJ.
Dozen & One. 12.75 (ISBN 0-8369-2980-2). Arno.
Dozen Doctors: Autobiographic Sketches. 11.50x (ISBN 0-226-38331-8). U of Chicago Pr.
Drawn from Memory: A Self-Portrait. 4.95x (ISBN 0-87015-129-0). Pacific Bks.
Dreadful Man. 9.95 (ISBN 0-671-24797-2). S&S.
Dream of Lhasa: The Life of Nikolay Przhevalsky (1839-88), Explorer of Central Asia. 14.00 (ISBN 0-8214-0369-9). Ohio U Pr.
Dream Quest of H. P. Lovecraft. lib. bdg. 8.95x (ISBN 0-89370-117-3); pap. 2.95 (ISBN 0-89370-217-X). Borgo Pr.
Dreamer's Journey: The Autobiography of Morris Raphael Cohen. facsimile ed. 22.00x (ISBN 0-405-06702-X). Arno.
Dreamers of Empire. facs. ed. 13.50 (ISBN 0-8369-0099-5). Arno.
Dreamers of the American Dream. 6.95 (ISBN 0-385-04889-0). Doubleday.
Dreemz. pap. 2.25 (ISBN 0-345-28156-X). Ballantine.
Dreiser. lib.rep.ed. 17.50x (ISBN 0-684-14552-9). Scribner.

Drummond of Hawthornden: The Story of His Life & Writings. 10.75 (ISBN 0-8274-2204-0). R West.

Drummond of Hawthornden: The Story of His Life & Writings. lib. bdg. 23.95 (ISBN 0-8383-0282-3). Haskell.

Drummond of Hawthornden: The Story of His Life & Writings. lib. bdg. 13.50x (ISBN 0-8371-1110-2, MADR). Greenwood.

Dry Messiah: The Life of Bishop Cannon. lib. bdg. 16.00x (ISBN 0-8371-3225-8, DADM). Greenwood.

Dryden. lib. bdg. 19.95 (ISBN 0-8383-1753-7). Haskell.

Dryden. lib. bdg. 20.00 (ISBN 0-8414-4828-0). Folcroft.

Dryden. lib. bdg. 15.00 (ISBN 0-8495-4811-X). Arden Lib.

Dryden. lib. bdg. 7.75. Folcroft.

Dryden. 11.00 (ISBN 0-8103-3053-9). Gale.

Dryden. lib. bdg. 7.80 (ISBN 0-404-51726-9). AMS Pr.

Dryden & His Poetry. lib. bdg. 6.45 (ISBN 0-8414-6263-1). Folcroft.

Du Bose Heyward: A Critical & Biographical Sketch. lib. bdg. 8.50 (ISBN 0-8495-0043-5). Arden Lib.

Du Bose Heyward: Critical & Biographical Sketch. lib. bdg. 8.50 (ISBN 0-8414-1731-8). Folcroft.

Dual Autobiography. 12.95 (ISBN 0-671-22925-7). S&S.

Dublin's Joyce. 6.75 (ISBN 0-8446-0735-5). Peter Smith.

Duccio Di Buoninsegna & His School. 55.00x (ISBN 0-691-03944-5). Princeton U Pr.

Duchess of Bloomsbury Street. 5.95 (ISBN 0-397-00976-3). Lippincott.

Duchess of Bloomsbury Street. pap. 2.95 (ISBN 0-380-00634-0, 41988). Avon.

Duchess of Jermyn Street: The Life & Good Times of Rosa Lewis of the Cavendish Hotel. pap. 1.95 (ISBN 0-14-004909-6). Penguin.

Duel with Destiny. 6.95 (ISBN 0-89227-001-2). Commonwealth Pr.

Duke. lib. bdg. 28.25x (ISBN 0-8371-8670-6, GUTD). Greenwood.

Duke: A Portrait of Duke Ellington. 9.95 (ISBN 0-393-07512-5). Norton.

Duke: A Portrait of Duke Ellington. pap. 4.95 (ISBN 0-393-00973-4). Norton.

Duke Ellington. pap. 1.95 (ISBN 0-498-04029-1). A S Barnes.

Duke Ellington. lib. bdg. 17.50 (ISBN 0-306-70727-6). Da Capo.

Duke Ellington: His Life & Music. lib. bdg. 17.50 (ISBN 0-306-70874-4). Da Capo.

Duke Ellington in Person: An Intimate Memoir. 10.95 (ISBN 0-395-25711-5). HM

Duke Ellington: King of Jazz. PLB 4.78 (ISBN 0-8116-4573-8). Garrard.

Duke of Deception: Memories of My Father. 12.95 (ISBN 0-394-41052-1). Random.

Duke of Newcastle. 25.00x (ISBN 0-300-01746-4). Yale U Pr.

Duke: The Musical Life of Duke Ellington. 6.95 (ISBN 0-394-83097-0). Random.

Dulles: A Biography of Eleanor, Allen, & John Foster Dulles & Their Family Network. 12.95 (ISBN 0-8037-1744-X). Dial.

Duncan Upshaw Fletcher: Dixie's Reluctant Progressive. 10.00 (ISBN 0-8130-0426-8). U Presses Fla.

Durham Company. 14.25 (ISBN 0-8369-2714-1). Arno.

Dust Tracks on a Road: An Autobiography. 14.00 (ISBN 0-405-01927-0). Arno.

Dutiful Daughters: Women Talk About Their Lives. text ed. 14.95 (ISBN 0-292-71518-8). U of Tex Pr.

Duty, Honor or Country: General George Weedon & the American Revolution. pap. 10.00 (ISBN 0-87169-133-7). Am Philos.

Dvorak. pap. 6.50 (ISBN 0-8226-0710-7). Littlefield.

Dvorak. rev. ed. 7.95x (ISBN 0-460-03116-3). Biblio Dist.

Dwight D. Eisenhower. PLB 5.75 (ISBN 0-87191-409-3). Creative Ed.

Dwight D. Eisenhower: Young Military Leader. 5.95 (ISBN 0-672-51235-1). Bobbs.

Dwight Eisenhower. PLB 6.79 (ISBN 0-200-00172-8). Abelard.

Dwight L. Moody, American Evangelist: 1837-1899. 12.00x (ISBN 0-226-24925-5). U of Chicago Pr.

Dwight Morrow. facsimile ed. 26.00x (ISBN 0-405-06982-0). Arno.

Dylan Thomas, "Dog Among the Fairies". lib. bdg. 17.50 (ISBN 0-8414-8600-X). Folcroft.

E

E. E. Cummings: The Growth of a Writer. pap. price not set (ISBN 0-8093-0978-5). S Ill U Pr.

E. E. Cummings: The Magic-Maker. pap. 3.45 (ISBN 0-316-61184-0). Little.

E. L. Godkin: A Biography. 35.00 (ISBN 0-87395-371-1). State U NY Pr.

E. M. Forster. 7.95 (ISBN 0-8093-0265-9). S Ill U Pr.

E. M. Forster: A Life. 19.95 (ISBN 0-15-128759-7). HarBraceJ.

E. W. Scripps. lib. bdg. 17.50x (ISBN 0-8371-6326-9, COSP). Greenwood.

Earliest Diary of John Adams: June 1753-April 1754, September 1758-January 1759. 5.00x (ISBN 0-674-22000-5). Harvard U Pr.

Early American Craftsmen. pap. cancelled (ISBN 0-89102-132-9). B Franklin.

Early American Craftsmen. lib. bdg. 25.50 (ISBN 0-8337-0986-0). B Franklin.

Early American Portraiture. lib. bdg. 18.00 (ISBN 0-405-08966-X). Arno.

Early American Women Printers & Publishers, 1639-1820. 32.50 (ISBN 0-8108-1119-7). Scarecrow.

Early Biographies of Samuel Johnson. text ed. 15.00x (ISBN 0-87745-038-2). U of Iowa Pr.

Early Career of Alexander Pope. 18.95x (ISBN 0-19-811675-6). Oxford U Pr.

Early Career of Alexander Pope. 11.00 (ISBN 0-8462-0376-6). Russell.

Early Career of Lord North the Prime Minister, 1754-1770. 18.00 (ISBN 0-8386-1899-5). Fairleigh Dickinson.

Early Chiang Kai-Shek: A Study of His Personality & Politics, 1887-1924. 12.50x (ISBN 0-231-03596-9). Columbia U Pr.

Early Diary of Frances Burney, 1768-1778. 39.50 (ISBN 0-8274-2210-5). R West.

Early Doors: My Life & the Theatre. 5.95 (ISBN 0-8037-2199-4). Dial.

Early History of Charles James Fox. lib. bdg 13.75. Folcroft.

Early History of Charles James Fox. 14.00 (ISBN 0-404-06524-4). AMS Pr.

Early Letters of Robert Schumann. 25.00 (ISBN 0-403-00249-4). Scholarly.

Early Life & Letters of Cavour, 1810-1848. 32.50 (ISBN 0-404-15356-9). AMS Pr.

Early Life & Letters of Cavour, 1810-1848. lib. bdg. 26.00x (ISBN 0-8371-8504-1, WHLC). Greenwood.

Early Life of George Eliot. 30.00 (ISBN 0-8492-0681-2). R West.

Early Life of James McBey: An Autobiography 1883-1911. 12.00x (ISBN 0-19-211738-6). Oxford U Pr.

Early Life of Robert Southey. lib. bdg. 16.50 (ISBN 0-374-93382-0). Octagon.

Early Life of Robert Southey: 1774-1803. 10.00. Norwood Edns.

Early Life of Thomas Hardy 1840-1891. 19.00 (ISBN 0-8274-2215-6). R West.

Early Life of Thomas Hardy: 1840-1891. 14.00 (ISBN 0-403 00772-0) Scholarly.

Early Life of William Wordsworth 1770-1798: A Study of the Prelude. lib. bdg. 9.45. Folcroft.

Early Life of William Wordsworth, 1770-1798: A Study of the Prelude. 12.00 (ISBN 0-403-01070-5). Scholarly.

Early Lives of Melville: Nineteenth-Century Biographical Sketches & Their Authors. 17.50x (ISBN 0-299-06570-7). U of Wis Pr.

Early Lives of Milton. 29.00 (ISBN 0-403-00935-9). Scholarly.

Early Memories. facsimile ed. 22.00x (ISBN 0-405-06919-7). Arno.

Early Negro American Writers: Selections with Biographical & Critical Introductions. 6.50 (ISBN 0-8446-0509-3). Peter Smith.

Early Recollections & Life of Dr. James Still. facsimile ed. 16.75 (ISBN 0-8369-8853-1). Arno.

Early Recollections & Life of Dr. James Still, 1812-1885. 17.50 (ISBN 0-8135-0769-3). Rutgers U Pr.

Early Reminiscences, 1834-1864. 11.00 (ISBN 0-8103-3049-0). Gale.

Early Soviet Saint: The Life of Father Zachariah. 6.95 (ISBN 0-87243-069-3). Templegate.

Early Stages. 8.95 (ISBN 0-316-45501-6). Little.

Early Tudor Composers: Biographical Sketches of Thirty-Two Musicians & Composers of the Period 1485-1555. facs. ed. 9.75 (ISBN 0-8369-0447-8). Arno.

Early Women Directors. 9.95 (ISBN 0-498-01701-X). A S Barnes.

Early Years of Alec Waugh. 6.00 (ISBN 0-374-14593-8). FS&G.

Early Years of Isaac Thomas Hecker (1819-1844) 18.00 (ISBN 0-404-57779-2). AMS Pr.

Earp Brothers of Tombstone: The Story of Mrs. Virgil Earp. 14.95 (ISBN 0-8032-0873-1); pap. 3.75 (ISBN 0-8032-5838-0, 618). U of Nebr Pr.

Eban. pap. 3.45 (ISBN 0-440-52347-8). Dell.

Eban. 10.00 (ISBN 0-385-08944-9). Doubleday.

Ebenezer Cooke: The Sot-Weed Canon. 10.00x (ISBN 0-8203-0346-1). U of Ga Pr.

Ebony Book of Black Achievement. rev. ed. 5.50 (ISBN 0-87485-040-1). Johnson Chi.

Ecce Homo (Nietzsche's Autobiography) 100.00 (ISBN 0-87968-211-6). Gordon Pr.

Eccentrics & Other American Visionary Painters. pap. 9.95 (ISBN 0-525-47500-1). Dutton.

Echoes from the Sandhills. 10.00 (ISBN 0-918626-00-5). Word Serv.

Eclectic First Reader see Life of Washington the Great.

Economists. 12.50 (ISBN 0-465-01810-6). Basic.

Economists. pap. 2.75 (ISBN 0-380-01835-7, 47761). Avon.

Eddie. 8.95 (ISBN 0-689-10715-3). Atheneum.

Eden: The Making of a Statesman. lib. bdg. 19.00x (ISBN 0-8371-8813-X, CAED). Greenwood.

Edgar Allan Poe: A Critical Biography. lib. bdg. 24.00x (ISBN 0-8154-0313-5). Cooper Sq.

Edgar Allan Poe, American Poet & Mystery Writer. new ed. lib. bdg. 2.45 incl. catalog cards; pap. 1.25 vinyl laminated covers. SamHar Pr.

Edgar Allan Poe: The Man, the Master, the Martyr. lib. bdg. 12.50 (ISBN 0-8414-0360-0). Folcroft.

Edgar Allan Poe: The Man, The Master, The Martyr. lib. bdg. 12.50 (ISBN 0-8495-3311-2). Arden Lib.

Edgar Rice Burroughs: The Man Who Created Tarzan. 19.95 (ISBN 0-8425-0079-0). Brigham.

Edgar Rice Burroughs: The Man Who Created Tarzan. pap. 10.00 (ISBN 0-345-25131-8); (ISBN 0-345-25947-5); Ballantine.

Edge of Paradise: Fifty Years in the Pulpit. 7.00 (ISBN 0-87012-111-1). McClain.

Edison: The Man Who Made the Future. 12.95 (ISBN 0-399-11952-3). Putnam.

Edith Pechey-Phipson, M.D. The Story of England's Foremost Pioneering Woman Doctor. 7.50 (ISBN 0-682-47597-1). Exposition.

Edith Simcox & George Eliot. lib. bdg. 14.75x (ISBN 0-313-20269-9, MCES). Greenwood.

Edith Wharton. lib. bdg. 7.50 (ISBN 0-8414-2500-0). Folcroft.

Edith Wharton: A Biography. 15.00 (ISBN 0-06-012603-5). Har-Row.

Edith Wharton: A Biography. pap. 6.95 (ISBN 0-06-090554-9, CN 554). Har-Row.

Editor in Politics. lib. bdg. 38.50x (ISBN 0-8371-7439-2, DAEI). Greenwood.

Edmond Jaloux: The Evolution of a Novelist. 7.50 (ISBN 0-8022-2064-9). Philos Lib.

Edmund Burke: A Life. 20.00 (ISBN 0-8462-1723-6). Russell.

Edmund Burke & His World. 12.95 (ISBN 0-8159-5404-2). Devin.

Edmund Burke: The Practical Imagination. 14.00x (ISBN 0-674-23750-1). Harvard U Pr.

Edmund Dulac. 10.95 (ISBN 0-684-15470-6). Scribner.

Edmund Kean. 21.00 (ISBN 0-404-03269-9). AMS Pr.

Edmund Kean: Fire from Heaven. 8.95 (ISBN 0-8037-4533 8). Dial

Edmund Spenser & the Faerie Queene. 8.50x (ISBN 0-226-07051-4). U of Chicago Pr.

Edmund Wilson. pap. 1.25 (ISBN 0-8166-0481-9, MPAW67). U of Minn Pr.

Edmund Wilson: The Man & His Work. 12.00x, USA (ISBN 0-8147-9183-2). NYU Pr.

Edna O'Brien. 4.50 (ISBN 0-8387-7838-0); pap. 1.95 (ISBN 0-8387-7976-X). Bucknell U Pr.

Edna St. Vincent Millay. pap. 1.25x (ISBN 0-8166-0437-1, MPAW64). U of Minn Pr.

Edouard Rod (1857-1910) A Portrait of the Novelist & His Times. pap. text ed. 32.75x (ISBN 90-2793-027-9). Mouton.

Eduard Morike: The Man & the Poet. lib. bdg. 14.00x (ISBN 0-8371-6538-5, MEMO). Greenwood.

Eduardo Mallea. lib. bdg. 9.50 (ISBN 0-8057-6273-6). Twayne.

Eduardo Mallea, Novelista. 6.25 (ISBN 0-8477-0524-2); pap. text ed. 5.00 (ISBN 0-8477-0525-0). U of PR Pr.

Eduardo Santos & the Good Neighbor, 1938-1942. pap. 3.75 (ISBN 0-8130-0038-6). U Presses Fla.

Education of a Prejudiced Man. text ed. 18.50x (ISBN 0-8290-0168-9). Irvington.

Education of a Public Man: My Life & Politics. 5.95 (ISBN 0-385-05603-6). Doubleday.

Education of a Woman Golfer. pap. 4.95 (ISBN 0-346-12492-1). Cornerstone.

Education of a Woman Golfer. 9.95 (ISBN 0-671-24756-5). S&S.

Education of Abraham Cahan. 7.50 (ISBN 0-8276-0138-7, 221). Jewish Pubn.

Education of Abraham Lincoln. PLB 4.64 (ISBN 0-698-30525-6). Coward.

Education of an American. 23.00 (ISBN 0-384-58770-4). Johnson Repr.

Education of an American Soccer Player. 8.95 (ISBN 0-396-07568-1). Dodd.

Education of an American Soccer Player. pap. 2.25 (ISBN 0-553-12619-9). Bantam.

Education of an Editor. 8.95 (ISBN 0-385-15032-6). Doubleday.

Education of Carey McWilliams. 11.95 (ISBN 0-671-22876-5). S&S.

Education of Edward Kennedy: A Family Biography. 10.95 (ISBN 0-688-00075-4). Morrow.

Education of Henry Adams. pap. 5.95 (ISBN 0-395-08352-4, 3). HM.

Education of Henry Adams. pap. text ed. 5.75 (ISBN 0-395-16620-9). HM.

Education of Henry Adams. lib. bdg. 18.00 (ISBN 0-910220-74-3). Larlin Corp.

Education of John Randolph. 18.95 (ISBN 0-393-01242-5). Norton.

Education of Little Tree. 8.95 (ISBN 0-440-02319-X). Delacorte.

Edvard Munch. pap. text ed. 7.95 (ISBN 0-19-519936-7). Oxford U Pr.

Edward Atkinson: The Biography of an American Liberal 1827-1905. 14.00 (ISBN 0-405-00448-6). Arno.

Edward Bellamy. lib. bdg. 19.50x (ISBN 0-87991-346-0). Porcupine Pr.

Edward Benlowes (1602-1676) Biography of a Minor Poet. 30.00 (ISBN 0-8274-2224-5). R West.

Edward Bulwer: First Baron Lytton of Knebworth: A Social, Personal, & Political Monograph. lib. bdg. 30.00 (ISBN 0-8495-1305-7). Arden Lib.

Edward Charles Elliott, Educator. 5.50 (ISBN 0-911198-19-9). Purdue.

Edward Dowden. lib. bdg. 8.50 (ISBN 0-8057-1164-3). Twayne.

Edward Eggleston. pap. 3.45 (ISBN 0-8084-0116-5, T45). Coll & U Pr.

Edward Eggleston. 6.00 (ISBN 0-8446-1377-0). Peter Smith.

Edward Elgar, His Life & Music. 23.50 (ISBN 0-88355-750-9). Hyperion Conn.

Edward F. Ricketts. pap. 2.00 (ISBN 0-88430-020-X). Boise St Univ.

Edward G. Robinson. pap. 1.75 (ISBN 0-515-03642-0, M3642). HarBraceJ.

Edward G. Ryan: Lion of the Law. pap 7.50 (ISBN 0-87020-002-X). State Hist Soc Wis.

Edward Garnett. lib. bdg. 12.50 (ISBN 0-8414-4505-2). Folcroft.

Edward Gibbon. 17.50 (ISBN 0-8274-3804-4). R West.

Edward Gibbon & His Age. lib. bdg. 7.50 (ISBN 0-8495-0448-1). Arden Lib.

Edward Gibbon & His Age. lib. bdg. 7.50 (ISBN 0-8414-3287-2). Folcroft.

Edward Gordon Craig. 7.75 (ISBN 0-87830-042-2). Theatre Arts.

Edward Johnston. pap. 6.95 (ISBN 0-8008-2367-2). Taplinger.

Edward Lear & His World. 9.95 (ISBN 0-684-15173-1). Scribner.

Edward Palmer, Plant Explorer of the American West. 15.00 (ISBN 0-913728-26-8). Theophrastus.

Edward Prince of Wales & Aquitaine: A Biography of the Black Prince. 17.50 (ISBN 0-684-15864-7). Scribner.

Edward Rose, Negro Trail Blazer. 4.50 (ISBN 0-396-05597-4). Dodd.

Edward Taylor. lib. bdg. 7.95 (ISBN 0-8057-0720-4). Twayne.

Edward Taylor. pap. 3.45 (ISBN 0-8084-0117-3, T8). Coll & U Pr.

Edward the Confessor. 15.95x (ISBN 0-520-01671-8). U of Cal Pr.

Edward Thomas: A Biography & a Bibliography. 30.00 (ISBN 0-8414-4040-9). Folcroft.

Edward Thomas: A Biography & a Bibliography. lib. bdg. 30.00 (ISBN 0-8482-0718-1). Norwood Edns.

Edward VIII: The Road to Abdication. 12.95 (ISBN 0-397-01319-1). Lippincott.

Edward Wilmot Blyden: Pan-Negro Patriot, 1832-1912. pap. 3.50 (ISBN 0-19-501268-2). Oxford U Pr.

Edwin Arlington Robinson. 35.00 (ISBN 0-8490-0098-X). Gordon Pr.

Edwin Arlington Robinson. lib. bdg. 16.95 (ISBN 0-8383-2045-7). Haskell.

Edwin Arlington Robinson. lib. bdg. 8.50 (ISBN 0-8414-7321-8). Folcroft.

Edwin Arlington Robinson. lib. bdg. 15.00 (ISBN 0-8495-4522-6). Arden Lib.

Edwin Arlington Robinson. lib. bdg. 10.00. Folcroft.

Edwin Arlington Robinson. lib. bdg. 16.95 (ISBN 0-8383-2103-8). Haskell.

Edwin D. Morgan, 1811-1833: Merchant in Politics. 22.50 (ISBN 0-404-51582-7). AMS Pr.

Edwin Forrest. 12.00 (ISBN 0-405-08238-X). Arno.

Edwin Forrest. 8.00 (ISBN 0-403-00242-7). Scholarly.

Edwin Muir: A Critical Study. 8.95 (ISBN 0-533-02270-3). Vantage.

Eggert Olafsson: A Biographical Sketch. pap. 6.00 (ISBN 0-527-00346-8). Kraus Repr.

Egypt Under Nasir: A Study in Political Dynamics. 24.50 (ISBN 0-87395-080-1); microfiche 24.50 (ISBN 0-87395-180-8). State U NY Pr.
Eight American Women Painters. lib. bdg. 47.95 (ISBN 0-87968-457-7). Gordon Pr.
Eight Friends of the Great. lib. bdg. 20.00 (ISBN 0-8414-3546-4). Folcroft.
Eight Is Enough. 7.95 (ISBN 0-394-49583-7). Random.
Eight Is Enough. pap. 1.95 (ISBN 0-449-23002-3). Fawcett.
Eight Soviet Composers. lib. bdg. 10.00x (ISBN 0-8371-3350-5, ABSC). Greenwood.
Eighteen Sixty to Eighteen Eighty-Nine see Booker T. Washington Papers.
Eighteenth Century Shopkeeper, Abraham Dent of Kirkby Stephen. lib. bdg. 11.50x (ISBN 0-678-06778-3). Kelley.
Eighty Years & More: Reminiscences, 1815-1897. pap. 6.50 (ISBN 0-8052-0324-9). Schocken.
Eileen. 8.95 (ISBN 0-312-24080-5). St Martin.
Eileen Garrett & the World Beyond the Senses. 6.95 (ISBN 0-688-00250-1). Morrow.
Eisenhower Declassified. 12.95 (ISBN 0-8007-1063-0). Revell.
Eisenhowers: Reluctant Dynasty. 10.95 (ISBN 0-385-12447-3). Doubleday.
Eisenstein. 15.00x (ISBN 0-253-12135-3). Ind U Pr.
Eisenstein: A Documentary Portrait. pap. 3.50 (ISBN 0-525-47443-9). Dutton.
Either Is Love. 9.00x (ISBN 0-405-07379-8). Arno.
Either Way, I Win: A Guide for Growth in the Power of Prayer. pap. 2.50 (ISBN 0-8066-1706-3, 10-2040). Augsburg.
Eleanor - Franklin: The Story of Their Relationship Based on Eleanor Roosevelt's Private Papers. 15.95 (ISBN 0-393-07459-5). Norton.
Eleanor Marx. 10.00 (ISBN 0-394-42143-4); 17.95 (ISBN 0-394-42151-5); pap. 4.95 (ISBN 0-394-73456-4); pap. 6.95 (ISBN 0-394-73457-2). Pantheon.
Eleanor of Aquitaine: A Biography. 13.95 (ISBN 0-8015-2231-5). Hawthorn.
Eleanor of Aquitaine & the Four Kings. 16.50x (ISBN 0-674-24250-5); pap. 4.50 (ISBN 0-674-24254-8). Harvard U Pr.
Eleanor Roosevelt: An American Conscience. lib. bdg. 22.50 (ISBN 0-306-70705-5). Da Capo.
Eleanor: The Years Alone. 14.95 (ISBN 0-393-07361-0). Norton.
Eleanor: The Years Alone. pap. 2.25 (ISBN 0-451-07419-X, E7419). NAL.
Eleazar Wheelock. 17.00 (ISBN 0-405-01439-2). Arno.
Eleonora Duse. 2nd ed. 15.00 (ISBN 0-405-09021-8). Arno.
Elephant Man: A Study in Human Dignity. rev. ed. pap. 4.95 (ISBN 0-525-47617-2). Dutton.
Elephant's Ballet. 6.95 (ISBN 0-8164-0373-2). Seabury.
Elgar. 3rd ed. 14.50 (ISBN 0-404-13058-5). AMS Pr.
Elgar. 14.00 (ISBN 0-403-01656-8). Scholarly.
Eli Whitney & the Birth of American Technology. 5.00 (ISBN 0-316-32620-8); pap. 4.95 (ISBN 0-316-32621-6, 1965). Little.
Elihu Root & the Conservative Tradition. pap. text ed. 4.95 (ISBN 0-316-52114-0). Little.
Elinor Wylie: The Portrait of an Unknown Lady. lib. bdg. 17.75x (ISBN 0-8371-9413-X, HOEW). Greenwood.
Eliot's Early Years. 10.95 (ISBN 0-19-812078-8). Oxford U Pr.
Eliot's Early Years. pap. 2.95 (ISBN 0-19-520086-1, GB 561). Oxford U Pr.
Elisha Kent Kane & the Seafaring Frontier. lib. bdg. 11.25x (ISBN 0-8371-6004-9, MIEK). Greenwood.
Eliza Pinckney. PLB 7.35 (ISBN 0-516-04658-6). Childrens.
Eliza Pinckney. 15.00 (ISBN 0-87152-037-0). Reprint.
Elizabeth. 4.95 (ISBN 0-472-93000-1). U of Mich Pr.
Elizabeth Barrett Browning. 12.50 (ISBN 0-8274-0701-7). R West.
Elizabeth Barrett Browning. lib. bdg. 21.95 (ISBN 0-8383-1722-7). Haskell.
Elizabeth Barrett Browning. lib. bdg. 7.00. Folcroft.
Elizabeth Barrett Browning. lib. bdg. 16.95 (ISBN 0-8383-1622-0). Haskell.
Elizabeth Barrett Browning & Her Poetry. 7.25 (ISBN 0-404-52531-8). AMS Pr.
Elizabeth Barrett Browning & Her Poetry. lib. bdg. 7.50 (ISBN 0-8414-7331-5). Folcroft.
Elizabeth Barrett Browning in Her Letters. 12.50 (ISBN 0-404-08879-1). AMS Pr.
Elizabeth Barrett Browning in Her Letters. lib. bdg. 25.00 (ISBN 0-8414-5693-3). Folcroft.
Elizabeth Bayley Seton. pap. 2.25 (ISBN 0-89129-218-7). Pillar Bks.
Elizabeth Bayley Seton. pap. 2.25 (ISBN 0-89310-005-6). Carillon Bks.
Elizabeth Bayley Seton. lib. rep. ed. 17.50x (ISBN 0-684-14735-1). Scribner.
Elizabeth Blackwell. PLB 4.95 (ISBN 0-87191-307-0). Creative Ed.
Elizabeth Bowen. 12.50 (ISBN 0-394-40533-1). Knopf.
Elizabeth Bowen. pap. 3.50 (ISBN 0-380-44354-6, 44354). Avon.
Elizabeth Bowen. 4.50 (ISBN 0-8387-7939-5); pap. 1.95 (ISBN 0-8387-7978-6). Bucknell U Pr.
Elizabeth Cady Stanton. 2nd ed. pap. 2.95 (ISBN 0-912670-03-7). Feminist Pr.
Elizabeth Cary Agassiz: A Biography. 24.00x (ISBN 0-405-06117-X). Arno.
Elizabeth Fry. 10.00. Norwood Edns.
Elizabeth Fry. lib. bdg. 13.50x (ISBN 0-8371-1005-X, PIEF). Greenwood.
Elizabeth Gaskell. 13.00 (ISBN 0-8462-1544-6). Russell.
Elizabeth Gaskell. 12.00 (ISBN 0-403-00711-9). Scholarly.
Elizabeth Gaskell: A Biography. 18.50x (ISBN 0-19-812070-2). Oxford U Pr.
Elizabeth Our Queen. lib. bdg. 20.00x (ISBN 0-313-21096-9, DIEQ). Greenwood.
Elizabeth the Great. 8.95 (ISBN 0-698-10110-3). Coward.
Elizabethan Garland. 9.50 (ISBN 0-404-07965-2). AMS Pr.
Elizabethan Lyrists & Their Poetry. lib. bdg. 7.50. Folcroft.
Elizabethan Lyrists & Their Poetry. 7.25 (ISBN 0-404-52507-5). AMS Pr.
Elizabethan: Sir Horatio Palavicino. 12.00x (ISBN 0-19-821256-9). Oxford U Pr.
Ellen G. White Prophet of Destiny. pap. 1.75 (ISBN 0-87983-077-8). Keats.
Ellen G. White, Prophet of Destiny. pap. 1.75 (ISBN 0-8163-0120-4, 05359-5). Pacific Pr Pub Assn.
Ellen Glasgow & the Woman Within. 15.95x (ISBN 0-8071-0040-4). La State U Pr.
Ellen Knauff Story. lib. bdg. 27.50 (ISBN 0-306-70238-X). Da Capo.
Ellen Swallow: The Woman Who Founded Ecology. 7.95 (ISBN 0-695-80388-3). Follett.
Ellen Terry's Memoirs. 17.50 (ISBN 0-405-09024-2). Arno.
Ellen Terry's Memoirs. lib. bdg. 16.00x (ISBN 0-8371-4039-0, TEME). Greenwood.
Elton John. pap. 1.50 (ISBN 0-445-03052-6). Popular Lib.
Elton John. PLB 5.95 (ISBN 0-87191-457-3); pap. 2.75. Creative Ed.
Elvis Presley. PLB 5.95 (ISBN 0-87191-394-1); pap. 2.75 (ISBN 0-89812-103-5). Creative Ed.
Elvis Presley Scrapbook. pap. 7.95 (ISBN 0-345-27594-2). Ballantine.
Elvis: The Films and Career of Elvis Presley. 14.00 (ISBN 0-8065-0511-7). Citadel Pr.
Elvis: The Films & Career of Elvis Presley. pap. 6.95 (ISBN 0-8065-0655-5). Citadel Pr.
Elvis We Love You Tender. 14.95 (ISBN 0-440-02323-8). Delacorte.
Elvis: What Happened? pap. 1.95 (ISBN 0-345-27215-3). Ballantine.
Emancipation of Angelina Grimke. 14.50 (ISBN 0-8078-1232-3). U of NC Pr.
Emancipation of Robert Sadler. 6.95 (ISBN 0-87123-132-8). Bethany Fell.
Emanuel Swedenborg, Scientist & Mystic. 25.00 (ISBN 0-8369-8140-5). Arno.
Embattled Justice: The Story of Louis Dembitz Brandeis. 4.25 (ISBN 0-8276-0139-5, 269). Jewish Pubn.
Emergency Room. 7.95 (ISBN 0-525-66675-3). Elsevier-Nelson.
Emerson & Asia. lib. bdg. 19.95 (ISBN 0-8383-0710-8). Haskell.
Emerson & the Orphic Poet in America. 13.50x (ISBN 0-520-03317-5). U of Cal Pr.
Emerson, Our Contemporary. 4.95 (ISBN 0-02-729000-X). Macmillan.
Emerson Today. 11.50 (ISBN 0-208-00798-9). Shoe String.
Emil Brunner. 6.95 (ISBN 0-87680-453-9). Word Bks.
Emile Durkheim. pap. 3.95 (ISBN 0-14-005002-7). Penguin.
Emile Zola. 2nd ed. 18.95x (ISBN 0-19-815369-4). Oxford U Pr.
Emily & Anne Bronte. text ed. 2.75x (ISBN 0-7100-6224-9). Humanities.
Emily Bronte. lib. bdg. 30.00 (ISBN 0-8414-7785-X). Folcroft.
Emily Bronte: A Biography. pap. 6.95 (ISBN 0-19-281251-3, OPB). Oxford U Pr.
Emily Bronte, a Psychological Portrait. 10.00 (ISBN 0-527-20400-5). Kraus Repr.
Emily Carr: The Untold Story. 24.95 (ISBN 0-88839-003-3). Hancock Hse.
Emily Dickinson. lib. bdg. 17.50x (ISBN 0-8371-5208-9, CHD). Greenwood.
Emily Dickinson: An Interpretive Biography. pap. text ed. 4.95x (ISBN 0-689-70113-6, 102). Atheneum.
Emily Dickinson Face to Face: Unpublished Letters, with Notes & Reminiscences by Her Niece. 15.00 (ISBN 0-208-00905-1). Shoe String.
Emily Dickinson: The Mind of the Poet. pap. 2.95 (ISBN 0-393-00555-0). Norton.
Emin Pasha & the Rebellion at the Equator: A Story of Nine Months' Experiences in the Last of the Soudan Provinces. 3rd ed. 22.50x (ISBN 0-8371-1949-9). Negro U Pr.
Emin Pasha, His Life & Work. 27.50x (ISBN 0-8371-5090-6). Negro U Pr.
Eminent American Jews: 1776 to the Present. text ed. 12.50 (ISBN 0-8044-1576-5). Ungar.
Eminent & Heroic Women of America. 45.00x (ISBN 0-405-06091-2). Arno.
Eminent English Liberals in & Out of Parliament. facsimile ed. 15.00 (ISBN 0-8369-2542-4). Arno.
Eminent Women of the West. 7.95 (ISBN 0-8310-7110-9). Howell-North.
Emissary: A Life of Enzo Sereni. 9.95 (ISBN 0-316-10130-3). Little.
Emma Hamilton. 14.95 (ISBN 0-698-10912-0). Coward.
Emma Willard: Daughter of Democracy. 15.00 (ISBN 0-89201-018-5). Zenger Pub.
Emmeline & Her Daughters: The Pankhurst Suffragettes. PLB 5.29 (ISBN 0-671-32438-1). Messner.
Emperor Charles V. lib. bdg. 105.00 (ISBN 0-8490-1762-9). Gordon Pr.
Emperor Gaius (Caligula) 16.50 (ISBN 0-404-14503-5). AMS Pr.
Emperor Gaius (Caligula) lib. bdg. 19.75x (ISBN 0-8371-9074-6, BAEG). Greenwood.
Emperor Julian. 15.00 (ISBN 0-520-03034-6); pap. 4.95 (ISBN 0-520-03731-6). U of Cal Pr.
Emperor Julian. lib. bdg. 8.95 (ISBN 0-8057-7650-8). Twayne.
Emperors & Biography: Studies in the Historia Augusta. 19.95x (ISBN 0-19-814357-5). Oxford U Pr.
Empire of Howard Hughes. pap. 2.95 (ISBN 0-914024-22-1). SF Arts & Letters.
Empire: The Life, Legend & Madness of Howard Hughes. 15.95 (ISBN 0-393-07513-3). Norton.
Empire: The Life, Legend, & Madness of Howard Hughes. pap. 6.95 (ISBN 0-393-00025-7). Norton.
Enchanted Places. 8.25 (ISBN 0-525-29293-4). Dutton.
Enchanted Places. pap. 1.95 (ISBN 0-14-003449-8). Penguin.
Encore: The Private & Professional Triumph of Emily Frankel. 10.00 (ISBN 0-13-275032-5). P-H.
Encounter with an Angry God: Recollections of My Life with John Peabody Harrington. 10.00. Malki Mus Pr.
Encyclopedia of American Biography. 25.00 (ISBN 0-06-011438-X). Har-Row.
Encyclopedia of Jazz in the Seventies. 20.00 (ISBN 0-8180-1215-3). Horizon.
Encyclopedia of Jazz in the Sixties. 17.50 (ISBN 0-8180-1205-6). Horizon.
Encyclopedia of Pop, Rock & Soul. 19.95 (ISBN 0-312-24990-X). St Martin.
Encyclopedia of Pop, Rock & Soul. pap. 6.95 (ISBN 0-312-25025-8). St Martin.
Encyclopedia of Psychoanalysis. 29.50 (ISBN 0-02-909340-6). Free Pr.
End of Innocence. 25.00 (ISBN 0-306-70423-4). Da Capo.
End of the Line: Alexander J. Cassatt & Pennsylvania Railroad. 16.95 (ISBN 0-88202-181-8). N Watson.
Endings: Death, Glorious & Otherwise, As Faced by Ten Outstanding Figures of Our Time. 9.95 (ISBN 0-517-53405-3). Crown.
Endless Steppe: Growing up in Siberia. 8.95 (ISBN 0-690-26371-6). T Y Crowell.
Energy & Conflict: The Life & Times of Edward Teller. 12.95 (ISBN 0-399-11551-X). Putnam.
Energy Merchant. PLB 10.00 (ISBN 0-8239-0366-4). Rosen Pr.
England, Before & After Wesley: The Evangelical Revival & Social Reform. 17.00 (ISBN 0-8462-1533-0). Russell.
England in the Age of Hogarth. 14.95 (ISBN 0-8464-0101-0). Beekman Pubs.
England in the Age of Hogarth. pap. 5.95 (ISBN 0-586-08251-4). Academy Chi Ltd.
English Blake. 18.50 (ISBN 0-208-00114-X). Shoe String.
English Climate: An Excursion into a Biography of John Galsworthy. lib. bdg. 12.00x (ISBN 0-472-08349-X, 08349). U of Mich Pr.
English Eccentrics. 10.00 (ISBN 0-8149-0204-9). Vanguard.
English Lake District As Interpreted in the Poems of Wordsworth. lib. bdg. 27.50 (ISBN 0-8414-5453-1). Folcroft.
English Messiahs: Studies of Six English Religious Pretenders, 1656-1927. 12.75 (ISBN 0-405-08783-7). Arno.
English Mystics of the Fourteenth Century. lib. bdg. 9.50x (ISBN 0-8371-4213-X, COEM). Greenwood.
Enid Starkie. 7.95 (ISBN 0-02-602910-3). Macmillan.
Enigma of Rabelais: An Essay in Interpretation. lib. bdg. 15.00 (ISBN 0-8414-3412-3). Folcroft.
Enigmatic Chancellor: Bethmann Hollweg & the Hubris of Imperial Germany. 35.00x (ISBN 0-300-01295-0). Yale U Pr.
Enigmatic Czar: The Life of Alexander I of Russia. 17.50 (ISBN 0-208-00748-2). Shoe String.
Enoch Powell & the Powellites. 19.95 (ISBN 0-312-25672-8). St Martin.
Enormous Room. rev. ed. 12.95 (ISBN 0-87140-630-6); pap. 4.95 (ISBN 0-87140-119-3). Liveright.
Enormous Room. new ed. 5.95 (ISBN 0-87140-956-9); pap. 3.25 (ISBN 0-87140-001-4, L-001). Liveright.
Enrico Caruso: A Biography. 40.00x (ISBN 0-8443-0074-8). Vienna Hse.
Enrico Fermi, Physicist. 8.50x (ISBN 0-226-74472-8). U of Chicago Pr.
Enrico Fermi, Physicist. pap. 2.95 (ISBN 0-226-74473-6, P468). U of Chicago Pr.
Enrique Jardiel Poncela. lib. bdg. 7.95 (ISBN 0-8057-2462-1). Twayne.
Ensor. 24.95 (ISBN 0-8212-0649-4). NYGS.
Enterprising Admiral: The Personal Fortune of Admiral Sir Peter Warren. 16.00x (ISBN 0-7735-0170-3). McGill-Queens U Pr.
Entrepreneurs: Explorations Within the American Business Tradition. pap. 6.95x (ISBN 0-679-40066-4). Longman.
Envoy to Africa: The Interior Life of Edel Quinn. pap. 2.25 (ISBN 0-8199-0560-7). Franciscan Herald.
Epicurus: An Introduction. 26.50 (ISBN 0-521-08426-1); pap. 6.95 (ISBN 0-521-29200-X). Cambridge U Pr.
Epoch & a Man: Martin Van Buren & His Times. 22.50 (ISBN 0-8046-1485-7). Kennikat.
Epoch of Napoleon. pap. text ed. 5.50 (ISBN 0-88275-622-2). Krieger.
Epoch: The Life of Steele MacKaye Genius of the Theatre, in Relation to His Time & Contemporaries, a Memoir. 43.00 (ISBN 0-403-00077-7). Scholarly.
Equivocal Men: Tales of the Establishment. 4.00 (ISBN 0-88279-205-9). Western Islands.
Erasmus. pap. 5.95 (ISBN 0-8128-1444-4). Stein & Day.
Erasmus: A Study of His Life, Ideals & Place in History. 6.00 (ISBN 0-8446-2959-6). Peter Smith.
Erasmus of Christendom. 17.50 (ISBN 0-684-15380-7). Scribner.
Erastus Corning, Merchant & Financier: 1794-1872. lib. bdg. 17.50x (ISBN 0-8371-9791-0, NEEC). Greenwood.
Eric Dolphy: A Musical Biography & Discography. 12.50 (ISBN 0-87474-142-4). Smithsonian.
Erik H. Erikson: The Power & Limits of a Vision. 8.95 (ISBN 0-02-926450-2). Free Pr.
Erik Satie. 18.50 (ISBN 0-306-76039-8). Da Capo.
Erle Stanley Gardner: The Case of the Real Perry Mason. 15.00 (ISBN 0-688-03282-6). Morrow.
Ernest. 17.50 (ISBN 0-8037-2392-X). Dial.
Ernest Chausson: The Composer's Life & Works. lib. bdg. 15.00x (ISBN 0-8371-6915-1, BAEC). Greenwood.
Ernest Hemingway: American Literary Giant. new ed. lib. bdg. 2.45 incl. catalog cards; pap. 1.25 vinyl laminated covers. SamHar Pr.
Ernest Hemingway & His World. 10.95 (ISBN 0-684-15661-X). Scribner.
Ernest Thompson Seton: Man in Nature & the Progressive Era, 1880-1915. lib. bdg. 32.00x (ISBN 0-405-10736-6). Arno.
Ernst Lubitsch: A Guide to References & Resources. lib. bdg. 20.00 (ISBN 0-8161-7895-X). G K Hall.
Ernst Ludwig Kirchner. 40.00x (ISBN 0-674-26100-3). Harvard U Pr.
Errol Flynn: A Memoir. 8.95 (ISBN 0-396-07502-9). Dodd.
Erskine Caldwell. pap. 1.25x (ISBN 0-8166-0528-9, MPAW78). U of Minn Pr.
Escapades of Frank & Jesse James. 7.95 (ISBN 0-8119-0228-5). Fell.
Escape. pap. 1.95 (ISBN 0-8423-0699-4). Tyndale.
Escape! 8.95 (ISBN 0-913374-76-8). SF Bk Co.
Escape. pap. 2.25 (ISBN 0-345-27742-2). Ballantine.
Escape King: The Story of Harry Houdini. 5.95 (ISBN 0-13-283416-2); pap. 1.50 (ISBN 0-13-283424-3). P-H.
Escape: The Life of Harry Houdini. PLB 7.79 (ISBN 0-671-32937-5). Messner.
Escape to the Mountain: A Family's Adventures in the Wilderness. 9.95 (ISBN 0-498-02365-6). A S Barnes.
Escoffier, Master Chef. 6.95 (ISBN 0-374-32227-9). FS&G.
Esenin: A Life. 15.00 (ISBN 0-88233-182-5). Ardis Pubs.
Essay on Frederic the Great. 8.50 (ISBN 0-404-04100-0). AMS Pr.

Essay on the Life of the Honorable Major-General Israel Putnam. Bd. with Genuine & Correct Account of the Captivity, Sufferings & Deliverance of Mrs. Jemima Howe; Affecting History of Mrs. Howe. lib. bdg. 40.00 (ISBN 0-8240-1643-2). Garland Pub.

Essays in Biography. lib. bdg. 9.95. Folcroft.

Essays in Biography. facs. ed. 13.75 (ISBN 0-8369-0987-9). Arno.

Essays of E.B. White see Letters of E.B. White.

Essays on Educational Reformers. pap. 4.95 (ISBN 0-8226-0244-X). Littlefield.

Essays on Educational Reformers. 15.50 (ISBN 0-404-05179-0). AMS Pr.

Essays on Educational Reformers. 14.00 (ISBN 0-403-00485-3). Scholarly.

Essays on Educational Reformers. lib. bdg. 35.00 (ISBN 0-8495-4428-9). Arden Lib.

Essays on Educational Reformers. lib. bdg. 25.00 (ISBN 0-8482-2225-3). Norwood Edns.

Essays on Schubert. lib. bdg. 19.50 (ISBN 0-306-77439-9). Da Capo.

Essential Articles for the Study of Thomas More. 20.00 (ISBN 0-208-01554-X). Shoe String.

Essential Documents Never Yet Presented in the Shakespeare Case. lib. bdg. 8.50. Folcroft.

Etched in Sunlight: Fifty Years in the Graphic Arts. 20.00 (ISBN 0-89073-036-9). Boston Public Lib.

Eternal Male. 7.95 (ISBN 0-385-12541-0). Doubleday.

Ethan Allen. 7.50 (ISBN 0-8323-0060-8); pap. 4.50 (ISBN 0-8323-0266-X). Binford.

Ethan Allen. 25.00 (ISBN 0-8369-6919-7). Arno.

Ethnic at Large: A Memoir of America in the Thirties & Forties. 12.50 (ISBN 0-399-11774-1). Putnam.

Ettrick Shepherd. lib. bdg. 12.50x (ISBN 0-8371-0298-7, BAET). Greenwood.

Eubie Blake. 10.00 (ISBN 0-02-872170-5). Schirmer Bks.

Eudora Welty. pap. 1.25x (ISBN 0-8166-0470-3, MPAW66). U of Minn Pr.

Eugen von Bohm-Bawerk. pap. 1.45 (ISBN 0-231-03021-5). Columbia U Pr.

Eugene Field: A Study in Heredity & Contradictions. 34.50 (ISBN 0-8274-2316-0). R West.

Eugene Field: A Study in Heredity & Contradictions. 37.50x (ISBN 0-8464-0005-7). Beekman Pubs.

Eugene Field's Creative Years. 25.00 (ISBN 0-8274-2318-7). R West.

Eugene Field's Creative Years. 21.00 (ISBN 0-403-00939-1). Scholarly.

Eugene Ionesco. pap. 11.50 (ST00049). Grove.

Eugene Meyer. 15.00 (ISBN 0-394-47897-5). Knopf.

Eugene O'Neill. 9.95 (ISBN 0-8044-2211-7); pap. 3.45 (ISBN 0-8044-6159-7). Ungar.

Eugene Scribe & the French Theatre, 1815-1860. 18.00 (ISBN 0-405-08216-9). Arno.

Eugene V. Debs. lib. bdg. 8.95 (ISBN 0-8057-7167-0). Twayne.

Eugene V. Debs: Socialist for President. lib. bdg. 13.75x (ISBN 0-8371-6885-6, MOED). Greenwood.

Eugene V. Debs Speaks. cancelled (ISBN 0-87348-131-3); pap. 5.45 (ISBN 0-87348-132-1). Path Pr NY.

Euripides. 10.50 (ISBN 0-8044-2612-0). Ungar.

Euripides & His Age. lib. bdg. 15.50x (ISBN 0-313-20989-8, MUEA). Greenwood.

European Dramatists. facs. ed. 19.75 (ISBN 0-8369-2163-1). Arno.

European of Yesterday: A Biography of Stefan Zweig. 14.50x (ISBN 0-19-815707-X). Oxford U Pr.

Eustratios Argenti: Study of the Greek Church Under Turkish Rule. 7.50x. Eastern Orthodox.

Evelyn Nesbit & Stanford White: Love & Death in the Gilded Age. 10.00 (ISBN 0-688-03079-3). Morrow.

Evelyn Waugh: A Biography. 12.50 (ISBN 0-316-82600-6). Little.

Evelyn Waugh & His World. 12.95 (ISBN 0-316-72040-2). Little.

Evelyn Waugh's Officers, Gentlemen & Rogues: The Fact Behind His Fiction. 9.95 (ISBN 0-88229-172-6); pap. 5.95 (ISBN 0-88229-495-4). Nelson Hall.

Even Big Guys Cry. pap. 2.25 (ISBN 0-451-08283-4, E8283). NAL.

Ever Thine Truly: Love Letters from Sam Houston to Anna Raguet. 19.50 (ISBN 0-89063-002-X); limited ed. 75.00. Jenkins.

Every Day's a Matinee: Memoirs Scribbled on a Dressing Room Door. 8.50 (ISBN 0-393-07491-9). Norton.

Every Man My Brother. 4.00 (ISBN 0-8198-0410-X); pap. 3.00 (ISBN 0-8198-0411-8). Dghtrs St Paul.

Everybody Who Was Anybody: A Biography of Gertrude Stein. 17.50 (ISBN 0-399-11605-2). Putnam.

Everybody's Autobiography. pap. 1.95 (ISBN 0-394-71826-7). Random.

Everybody's Autobiography. lib. bdg. 12.50x (ISBN 0-8154-0386-0). Cooper Sq.

Everyone in the Bible. 8.95 (ISBN 0-8007-0084-8). Revell.

Everything but Money. pap. 1.75 (ISBN 0-671-81143-6). PB.

Everything but Money. pap. 3.95 (ISBN 0-671-24216-4). S&S.

Evita--First Lady: A Biography of Eva Peron. 8.95 (ISBN 0-394-50289-2, GP816). Grove.

Evita--First Lady: A Biography of Eva Peron. pap. 2.25 (ISBN 0-394-17087-3, B425). Grove.

Evonne Goolagong. 5.50 (ISBN 0-87191-339-9). Creative Ed.

Evonne Goolagong: Smiles & Smashes. lib. bdg. 5.95 (ISBN 0-88436-158-6); pap. 3.50 (ISBN 0-88436-159-4). EMC.

Example of Edward Taylor. 17.50x (ISBN 0-87023-174-X). U of Mass Pr.

Excellent Becomes the Permanent. facsimile ed. 12.50 (ISBN 0-8369-1488-0). Arno.

Exceptional Stories from the Lives of Our Apostles. 5.95 (ISBN 0-87747-486-9). Deseret Bk.

Exclusive! The Inside Story of Patricia Hearst & the SLA. 8.95 (ISBN 0-02-506400-2). Macmillan.

Execution of Isaac Hayne. new ed. 9.95 (ISBN 0-87844-037-2); ltd signed ed 12.95. Sandlapper Store.

Exiles. 6.95 (ISBN 0-374-15096-6). FS&G.

Exiles. pap. 1.75 (ISBN 0-345-25196-2). Ballantine.

Exile's Odyssey: The Memoirs of an American Deserter. 12.00 (ISBN 0-498-02387-7). A S Barnes.

Exile's Return: A Literary Odyssey of the 1920's. pap. 3.95 (ISBN 0-14-004392-6). Penguin.

Exit Laughing. 18.50 (ISBN 0-8103-3687-1). Gale.

Exon, Biography of a Governor. 5.95 (ISBN 0-934988-01-3); pap. 2.95 (ISBN 0-934988-02-1). Foun Bks.

Expansion & Challenge, 1915-1933 see Ford.

Expedition of Pedro De Ursua & Lope De Aguirre in Search of El Dorado & Omagua in 1560. lib. bdg. 25.50 (ISBN 0-8337-3271-4). B Franklin.

Experiences & Impressions: The Autobiography of Colonel A.A. Anderson. facs. ed. 15.50 (ISBN 0-8369-5411-4). Arno.

Experiences of a Forty-Niner. 19.00 (ISBN 0-405-04982-X). Arno.

Exploding Star: A Young Austrian Against Hitler. 10.00 (ISBN 0-688-03381-4). Morrow.

Expressman & the Detective. 16.00x (ISBN 0-405-07894-3). Arno.

Eye of Dawn: The Rise & Fall of Mata Hari. 9.95 (ISBN 0-02-594030-9). Macmillan.

Eye of Dawn: The Rise & Fall of Mata Hari. lib. bdg. 12.95 (ISBN 0-8161-6612-9). G K Hall.

Eye-Witnesses to Wagon Trains West. o.p. 7.95 (ISBN 0-684-13864-6); pap. text ed. 4.95 (ISBN 0-684-15042-5, SSP 39). Scribner.

Eyes, Etc. A Memoir. 7.95 (ISBN 0-394-41550-7). Pantheon.

Eyes of Eternity: A Spiritual Autobiography. 10.95 (ISBN 0-15-129627-8). HarBraceJ.

Eyvind Johnson. lib. bdg. 7.95 (ISBN 0-8057-2468-0). Twayne.

Ezekiel Holmes, Father of Maine Agriculture. pap. 2.50 (ISBN 0-89101-016-5). U Maine Orono.

Ezio Pinza: An Autobiography. lib. bdg. 21.00x (ISBN 0-405-09702-6). Arno.

Ezra Pound, Father & Teacher: Discretions. pap. 4.75 (ISBN 0-8112-0589-4, NDP405). New Directions.

F

F-F-F-Frank Polk: An Uncommonly Frank Autobiography. 10.50 (ISBN 0-87358-174-1). Northland.

F. Scott Fitzgerald: A Descriptive Bibliography. 25.00x (ISBN 0-8229-3239-3). U of Pittsburgh Pr.

F. Scott Fitzgerald & the American Dream. 6.95 (ISBN 0-690-00078-2). T Y Crowell.

F. Scott Fitzgerald & the Craft of Fiction. 7.95 (ISBN 0-8093-0216-0). S Ill U Pr.

F. Scott Fitzgerald in Minnesota: His Homes & Haunts. pap. 3.75 (ISBN 0-87351-134-4). Minn Hist.

Fabulous Dr. J: All-Time All-Star. PLB 5.29 (ISBN 0-399-61042-1). Putnam.

Fabulous Ego: Absolute Power in History. 15.00 (ISBN 0-8129-0490-7). Times Bks.

Fabulous Life of Diego Rivera. pap. 6.95 (ISBN 0-8128-1259-X). Stein & Day.

Fabulous Life of Sarah Bernhardt. lib. bdg. 16.00x (ISBN 0-8371-5707-2, VESB). Greenwood.

Face for Me. 7.95 (ISBN 0-88326-156-1). Wyden.

Face of Liberty: Founders of the United States. 15.95. Potter.

Face of the Saints. 24.00 (ISBN 0-8369-8128-6). Arno.

Face of the Third Reich: Portraits of the Nazi Leadership. pap. 5.95 (ISBN 0-394-73407-6). Pantheon.

Face of War: Reflections on Men & Combat. 13.95 (ISBN 0-672-52350-7). Bobbs.

Face to Face. pap. 3.95 (ISBN 0-19-520014-4, GB537). Oxford U Pr.

Faces Among the Faithful. 2.75 (ISBN 0-87178-273-1). Brethren.

Faces That Won't Sit Still: Celebrated Subjects by a Prominent Portrait Artist & How They Were Captured. 18.00 (ISBN 0-87491-261-X); ltd. ed. 35.00 (ISBN 0-87491-260-1); pap. 9.95 (ISBN 0-87491-262-8). Acropolis.

Facing the Chair: Story of the Americanization of Two Foreign-Born Workmen. 12.50 (ISBN 0-306-71871-5). Da Capo.

Facts of Life. 8.95 (ISBN 0-316-37469-5). Little.

Facts of Life. pap. 2.95 (ISBN 0-14-005500-2). Penguin.

Facts of Life. pap. 1.95 (ISBN 0-345-25761-8). Ballantine.

Facts of Life: An Essay in Feelings, Facts & Fantasy. 7.95 (ISBN 0-394-49666-3). Pantheon.

Fair Winds & Foul: A Narrative of Daily Life Aboard an American Clipper Ship. text ed. 17.50 (ISBN 0-930576-25-X). E M Coleman Ent.

Faith Is Not a Feeling. pap. 2.95 (ISBN 0-918956-45-5). Campus Crusade.

Faith of the Presidents. 4.95 (ISBN 0-570-07877-6, 39-1202); pap. 2.95 (ISBN 0-570-07882-2, 39-1212). Concordia.

Faithful Unto Death: Fifteen Young People Who Were Not Afraid to Die for Their Faith. 5.95 (ISBN 0-8499-0067-0). Word Bks.

Falcon & the Snowman: A True Story of Friendship & Espionage. pap. price not set (ISBN 0-671-41160-8). PB.

Fall of Stein. 10.00x (ISBN 0-674-29200-6). Harvard U Pr.

False Spring. 7.95 (ISBN 0-396-07078-7). Dodd.

False Starts: A Memoir of San Quentin & Other Prisons. pap. 1.95 (ISBN 0-14-004454-X). Penguin.

Family. 7.95 (ISBN 0-89310-029-3); pap. 3.95 (ISBN 0-89310-030-7). Carillon Bks.

Famous American Admirals. 18.95 (ISBN 0-442-26068-7). Van Nos Reinhold.

Famous American Architects. 5.95 (ISBN 0-396-05517-6). Dodd.

Famous American Belles of the Nineteenth Century. 17.00 (ISBN 0-8369-1893-2). Arno.

Famous American Cowboys. 5.95 (ISBN 0-528-82250-0); PLB 5.97 (ISBN 0-528-80250-X). Rand.

Famous American Naval Officers. rev. facs. ed. 21.50 (ISBN 0-8369-2170-4). Arno.

Famous American Negro Poets. 5.95 (ISBN 0-396-05129-4). Dodd.

Famous American Statesmen. 5.95 (ISBN 0-396-03449-7). Dodd.

Famous American Women. 10.00 (ISBN 0-690-28751-8). T Y Crowell.

Famous Baseball Stars. 5.95 (ISBN 0-396-06776-X). Dodd.

Famous Black Americans. pap. 0.95 (ISBN 0-8170-0591-9). Judson.

Famous Black Entertainers of Today. 5.95 (ISBN 0-396-06849-9). Dodd.

Famous British Women Novelists. 5.95 (ISBN 0-396-05612-1). Dodd.

Famous Characters of the Wild West. 7.95 (ISBN 0-312-28157-9). St Martin.

Famous Chess Players. PLB 3.95 (ISBN 0-8225-0466-9). Lerner Pubns.

Famous Coaches. 5.95 (ISBN 0-396-05717-9). Dodd.

Famous Couples of the Bible. pap. 2.25 (ISBN 0-8054-5630-9). Broadman.

Famous Crimefighters. PLB 3.95 (ISBN 0-8225-0459-6). Lerner Pubns.

Famous European Artists. 19.75 (ISBN 0-8369-2750-8). Arno.

Famous European Artists. lib. bdg. 48.75 (ISBN 0-8490-1801-3). Gordon Pr.

Famous Ex-Priests. 4.95 (ISBN 0-8184-0030-7). Lyle Stuart.

Famous Firsts in Tennis. PLB 4.49 (ISBN 0-399-61111-8). Putnam.

Famous Flaws. 9.95 (ISBN 0-02-575101-8, 57510). Macmillan.

Famous Frontiersmen. 6.95 (ISBN 0-528-82807-X). Rand.

Famous Generals. PLB 5.90 s&l (ISBN 0-531-09120-1). Watts.

Famous Givers & Their Gifts. facsimile ed. 20.75 (ISBN 0-8369-2484-3). Arno.

Famous Gunfighters of the Western Frontier. pap. 2.95 (ISBN 0-89646-051-7). Outbooks.

Famous Hebrew Christians. pap. 5.95 (ISBN 0-8010-3733-6). Baker Bk.

Famous Hockey Players. 5.95 (ISBN 0-396-06848-0). Dodd.

Famous Horses & Their People. 7.95 (ISBN 0-8289-0231-3). Greene.

Famous in Their Twenties. 12.75 (ISBN 0-8369-1659-X). Arno.

Famous Indian Chiefs. 6.95 (ISBN 0-528-82808-8). Rand.

Famous Labor Leaders. 5.95 (ISBN 0-396-06168-0). Dodd.

Famous Leaders Among Women. facsimile ed. 19.75 (ISBN 0-8369-2639-0). Arno.

Famous Literary Teams for Young People. 5.95 (ISBN 0-396-07407-3). Dodd.

Famous Mather Byles: Noted Boston Tory Preacher, Poet, & Wit 1707-1788. facsimile ed. 16.75 (ISBN 0-8369-5933-7). Arno.

Famous Merchants. 5.95 (ISBN 0-396-05140-5). Dodd.

Famous Mexican-Americans. 5.95 (ISBN 0-396-06489-2). Dodd.

Famous Modern American Women Athletes. 5.95g (ISBN 0-396-07195-3). Dodd.

Famous Modern Negro Musicians. lib. bdg. 13.50 (ISBN 0-306-77523-9). Da Capo.

Famous Modern Storytellers for Young People. 3.95 (ISBN 0-396-05998-8). Dodd.

Famous Negro Entertainers of Stage, Screen & TV. 5.95 (ISBN 0-396-05503-6). Dodd.

Famous Negro Heroes of America. 3.95 (ISBN 0-396-04072-1). Dodd.

Famous New England Authors. 5.95 (ISBN 0-396-06196-6). Dodd.

Famous Old-World Sea Fighters. 21.25 (ISBN 0-8369-1419-8). Arno.

Famous People on Film. 15.00 (ISBN 0-8108-1051-4). Scarecrow.

Famous Pianists & Their Technique. 3rd. ed. 17.95 (ISBN 0-88331-066-X). Luce.

Famous Pro Basketball Stars. 5.95 (ISBN 0-396-06046-3). Dodd.

Famous Pro Football Stars. 5.95 (ISBN 0-396-05490-0). Dodd.

Famous Puerto Ricans. 5.95 (ISBN 0-396-07149-X). Dodd.

Famous Sculptors of America. facs. ed. 18.00 (ISBN 0-8369-0086-3). Arno.

Famous Singers of Today & Yesterday. lib. bdg. 35.00 (ISBN 0-89341-438-7). Longwood Pr.

Famous Spies. PLB 3.95 (ISBN 0-8225-0454-5). Lerner Pubns.

Famous Tennis Players. 5.95 (ISBN 0-396-07470-7). Dodd.

Famous Violinists for Young People. 18.75 (ISBN 0-8369-8118-9). Arno.

Famous Violinists of Today & Yesterday. lib. bdg. 40.00 (ISBN 0-89341-118-3). Longwood Pr.

Famous Voyagers & Explorers. 25.00 (ISBN 0-8369-2751-6). Arno.

Famous Women Tennis Players. 6.95 (ISBN 0-396-07681-5). Dodd.

Fannie Lou Hamer. 6.95 (ISBN 0-690-28893-X); PLB 6.89 (ISBN 0-690-28894-8). T Y Crowell.

Fanny Burney. lib. bdg. 12.95x (ISBN 0-8057-1072-8). Irvington.

Fanny Burney & the Burneys. lib. bdg. 16.50. Folcroft.

Fanny Crosby. 8.00 (ISBN 0-8298-0290-8). Pilgrim NY.

Fanny Elssler. 17.50x (ISBN 0-8195-4022-6). Columbia U Pr.

Fanny Kemble. 8.00x (ISBN 0-8371-2697-5). Negro U Pr.

Fanny Kemble. 8.95 (ISBN 0-312-28162-5). St Martin.

Fanny Kemble's America. pap. 0.95 (ISBN 0-440-93398-6). Dell.

Fanny Kemble's America. 6.95 (ISBN 0-690-28911-1). T Y Crowell.

Fantastic Flight to Freedom. PLB 7.99 (ISBN 0-8172-1551-4). Raintree Pubs.

Fantin-Latour. pap. 6.95 (ISBN 0-517-53414-2). Crown.

Far Side of Paradise: A Biography of F. Scott Fitzgerald. rev. & enl. ed. pap. 4.95 (ISBN 0-395-08395-8, 46). HM.

Faraday As a Natural Philosopher. 15.00x (ISBN 0-226-01046-5). U of Chicago Pr.

Farther off from Heaven. 8.95 (ISBN 0-394-41188-9). Knopf.

Fashion Is Our Business. facs. ed. 14.75 (ISBN 0-8369-1920-3). Arno.

Fassbinder. pap. 3.50 (ISBN 0-85170-052-7). NY Zoetrope.

Fassbinder. 2nd, rev. ed. 17.50 (ISBN 0-85170-095-0); pap. 8.25 (ISBN 0-85170-096-9). NY Zoetrope.

Fast Company. 7.95 (ISBN 0-06-120455-2). Harper Mag Pr.

Faster Than Sound. 15.00 (ISBN 0-498-01507-6). A S Barnes.

Fastest Man Alive. lib. bdg. 20.00x (ISBN 0-405-12163-6). Arno.

Fastest Woman on Earth. PLB 7.99 (ISBN 0-8172-1566-2). Raintree Pubs.

Fate of the Griffon. 8.95 (ISBN 0-8040-0674-1). Swallow.

Father Divine. pap. 1.95 (ISBN 0-02-033070-7). Macmillan.

Father Feelings. 7.95 (ISBN 0-688-03251-6). Morrow.

Father Feelings. pap. 2.25 (ISBN 0-671-82271-3). PB.

Father Goose. pap. 1.95 (ISBN 0-380-01179-4, 15966). Avon.

Father Henson's Story. lib. bdg. 16.00x (ISBN 0-8398-0776-7). Irvington.
Father Henson's Story of His Own Life. 9.00 (ISBN 0-87928-037-9). Corner Hse.
Father Henson's Story of His Own Life. pap. 1.50 (ISBN 0-87091-017-5). Corinth Bks.
Father Henson's Story of His Own Life. lib. bdg. 12.50 (ISBN 0-8411-0052-7). Metro Bks.
Father of the Brontes. lib. bdg. 11.50x (ISBN 0-8371-0483-1, HOFB). Greenwood.
Father Struck It Rich. facsimile ed. 22.00x (ISBN 0-405-06922-7). Arno.
Father Was a Tenor. 5.00 (ISBN 0-682-48956-5). Exposition.
Fathers of Classical Music. facs. ed. 12.50 (ISBN 0-8369-1119-9). Arno.
Fats Waller. 12.95 (ISBN 0-02-872730-4). Schirmer Bks.
Fats Waller. pap. 5.95 (ISBN 0-02-872710-X). Schirmer Bks.
Faulkner: A Biography. 30.00 (ISBN 0-394-47452-X). Random.
Faulkner-Cowley File: Letters & Memories, 1944-1962. pap. 2.50 (ISBN 0-14-004684-4). Penguin.
Faulkner: The Transfiguration of Biography. 17.50x (ISBN 0-8032-4707-9). U of Nebr Pr.
Faure. 22.00 (ISBN 0-88355-745-2). Hyperion Conn.
Faure. lib. bdg. 19.75x (ISBN 0-313-20667-8, SUFA). Greenwood.
FDR Story. 8.95 (ISBN 0-690-29355-0). T Y Crowell.
Fearful Void. 10.00 (ISBN 0-397-01019-2). Lippincott.
Federal Street Pastor: The Life of William Ellery Channing. 8.50x (ISBN 0-8084-0372-9). Coll & U Pr.
Federico Fellini: The Search for a New Mythology. pap. 3.95 (ISBN 0-8091-1957-9). Paulist Pr.
Feet Was I to the Lame. 14.95 (ISBN 0-285-64836-5). Intl Schol Bk Serv.
Felisa Rincon de Gautier: The Mayor of San Juan. pap. 0.95 (ISBN 0-440-94609-3). Dell.
Felix Adler. lib. bdg. 9.50 (ISBN 0-8057-3650-6). Twayne.
Felix Frankfurter Reminisces. lib. bdg. 23.50x (ISBN 0-313-20466-7, FRFF). Greenwood.
Felix Mendelssohn & His Times. lib. bdg. 19.75x (ISBN 0-8371-6823-6, JAFM). Greenwood.
Fellini on Fellini. pap. 2.95 (ISBN 0-440-52531-4). Dell.
Fellini on Fellini. 7.95 (ISBN 0-440-02528-1). Delacorte.
Felton & Fowler's Famous Americans You Never Knew Existed. 12.95 (ISBN 0-8128-2511-X). Stein & Day.
Female Persuasion: Six Strong-Minded Women. 15.00 (ISBN 0-208-00999-X). Shoe String.
Female Poets of America: With Portraits, Biographical Notices, & Specimens of Their Writings. 32.00 (ISBN 0-8103-4290-1). Gale.
Feminine Faces. pap. 2.95 (ISBN 0-8010-2355-6). Baker Bk.
Femmes En France. pap. 5.95x (ISBN 0-684-13803-4). Scribner.
Fenian Chief: A Biography of James Stephens. 19.95x (ISBN 0-87024-100-1). U of Miami Pr.
Fenimore Cooper: A Study of His Life & Imagination. 16.00 (ISBN 0-691-06358-3). Princeton U Pr.
Feodor Dostoevsky. pap. 1.50 (ISBN 0-231-03205-6, MW40). Columbia U Pr.
Ferdinand De Saussure. pap. 2.95 (ISBN 0-14-004369-1). Penguin.
Ferdinand Lassalle. lib. bdg. 12.50x (ISBN 0-8371-2800-5, BRFL). Greenwood.
Ferdinand Lassalle As a Social Reformer. lib. bdg. 11.75x (ISBN 0-8371-0971-X, BEFL). Greenwood.
Ferdinand Lassalle As a Social Reformer. 11.00 (ISBN 0-403-00518-3). Scholarly.
Ferdinand Lassalle, Romantic Revolutionary. lib. bdg. 12.00x (ISBN 0-8371-2202-3, FOFL). Greenwood.
Ferdinand Magellan: Noble Captain. pap. 2.44 (ISBN 0-395-01751-3). HM.
Ferenc Deak. lib. bdg. 9.50 (ISBN 0-8057-3030-3). Twayne.
Ferencz (Francois) Liszt. 18.50 (ISBN 0-404-12888-2). AMS Pr.
Ferguson Jenkins: The Quiet Winner. PLB 5.29 (ISBN 0-399-60936-9). Putnam.
Fermin Francisco De Lasuen: A Biography. 17.50 (ISBN 0-88382-059-5). AAFH.
Fernando Wood of New York. 15.00 (ISBN 0-404-51536-3). AMS Pr.
Fertile Fields: Recollections & Reflections of a Busy Life. 8.95 (ISBN 0-498-01545-9). A S Barnes.
Fessenden of Maine, Civil War Senator. 8.00x (ISBN 0-8156-0023-2). Syracuse U Pr.
Festschrift for B. F. Skinner. 28.00x (ISBN 0-89197-497-0). Irvington.
Fever at the Core: The Idealist in Politics. text ed. 13.50x (ISBN 0-06-494791-2). B&N.
Few Comforts or Surprises: The Arkansas Delta. 15.00 (ISBN 0-262-18062-6). MIT Pr.
Few Comforts or Surprises: The Arkansas Delta. pap. 4.95 (ISBN 0-262-68024-6). MIT Pr.
Fiddledust. 2.95 (ISBN 0-8040-0109-X). Swallow.
Field Days: The Life, Times, & Reputation of Eugene Field. 12.50. Ultramarine Pub.
Field Days: The Life, Times & Reputation of Eugene Field. 12.50 (ISBN 0-684-13780-1). Ultramarine Pub.
Field-Marshal in the Family: A Personal Biography of Montgomery of Alamein. 14.95 (ISBN 0-8008-2635-3). Taplinger.
Field-Marshal's Memoirs: From the Diary, Correspondence, & Reminiscences of Alfred Count Von Waldersee. lib. bdg. 20.25x (ISBN 0-8371-5326-3, WAFM). Greenwood.
Fielding. lib. bdg. 15.00 (ISBN 0-8482-9951-5). Norwood Edns.
Fiery Tennis Star: Jimmy Connors. PLB 5.45 (ISBN 0-87191-587-1). Creative Ed.
Fiery Trial: A Life of Lincoln. 7.95 (ISBN 0-670-31182-0). Viking Pr.
Fifteen Famous Latin Americans. text ed. 6.64 (ISBN 0-13-314609-X). P-H.
Fifty Days: Napoleon in England. 7.95x (ISBN 0-87024-139-7). U of Miami Pr.
Fifty Famous Americans. 17.00 (ISBN 0-8369-8017-4). Arno.
Fifty Lives for God. 4.95 (ISBN 0-8170-0629-X). Judson.
Fifty Major Film-Makers. 20.00 (ISBN 0-498-01255-7). A S Barnes.
Fifty-Two Years a Newsman. 10.00 (ISBN 0-87404-047-7). Tex Western.
Fifty Voices of the Twentieth Century. PLB 5.71 (ISBN 0-688-51152-X). Lothrop.
Fifty Years a Journalist. facs. ed. 17.25 (ISBN 0-8369-5447-5). Arno.
Fifty Years a Journalist. lib. bdg. 20.50x (ISBN 0-8371-0240-5, STFJ). Greenwood.
Fifty Years in Chains. pap. 3.75 (ISBN 0-486-22462-7). Dover.
Fifty Years in Chains. 5.75 (ISBN 0-8446-0021-0). Peter Smith.
Fifty Years in Chains: Or the Life of an American Slave. 9.00 (ISBN 0-403-00149-8). Scholarly.
Fifty Years in Chains: Or, the Life of an American Slave. facs. ed. 15.50 (ISBN 0-8369-8507-9). Arno.
Fifty Years in Neurology & Psychiatry. 9.75 (ISBN 0-913258-03-2). Stratton Intercon.
Fifty Years of Accountancy. lib. bdg. 40.00x (ISBN 0-405-10908-3). Arno.
Fifty Years of Public Service: Personal Recollections of Shelby M. Cullom. lib. bdg. 39.50 (ISBN 0-306-71410-8). Da Capo.
Fight Doctor. 8.95 (ISBN 0-671-22894-3). S&S.
Fighter Aces of the U. S. A. 24.95 (ISBN 0-8168-5792-X). Aero.
Fighter Pilots of World War I. 8.95 (ISBN 0-312-28874-3). St Martin.
Fighter Pilots of World War II. 8.95 (ISBN 0-312-28875-1). St Martin.
Fighter Pilots of World War II. pap. 1.50 (ISBN 0-505-51192-4). Belmont-Tower.
Fighters. pap. 7.95 (ISBN 0-385-13524-6). Doubleday.
Fighters for Independence: A Guide to Sources of Biographical Information on Soldiers & Sailors of the American Revolution. lib. bdg. 8.00x (ISBN 0-226-89498-3). U of Chicago Pr.
Fighting Back. 8.95 (ISBN 0-8128-1845-8). Stein & Day.
Fighting Back. pap. 1.95 (ISBN 0-446-89037-5). Warner Bks.
Fighting Back: One Woman's Struggle Against Cancer. 10.95 (ISBN 0-06-012958-1). Har-Row.
Fighting Bob Evans. 24.25 (ISBN 0-8369-5151-4). Arno.
Fighting Douglas MacArthur. 4.50 (ISBN 0-396-05141-3). Dodd.
Fighting Editor; or, Warren & the Appeal. 14.50x (ISBN 0-8464-0030-8). Beekman Pubs.
Fighting Men of the West. facs. ed. 17.50 (ISBN 0-8369-0334-X). Arno.
Fighting Sail. new ed. 10.95 (ISBN 0-8094-2654-4). Time-Life.
Fighting Sail. lib. bdg. 11.49. Silver.
Fighting Tuscarora: The Autobiography of Chief Clinton Rickard. 10.50 (ISBN 0-8156-0092-5). Syracuse U Pr.
Figure of Arthur. 9.00x (ISBN 0-87471-129-0). Rowman.
Filibusters & Financiers: The Story of William Walker & His Associates. 13.00 (ISBN 0-8462-1419-9). Russell.
Fillets of Plaice. pap. 1.95 (ISBN 0-14-004338-1). Penguin.
Film Archetypes: Sisters, Mistresses, Mothers & Daughters. lib. bdg. 22.00x (ISBN 0-405-10757-9). Arno.
Film Directors: A Guide to Their American Films. 17.00 (ISBN 0-8108-0752-1). Scarecrow.
Films of Montgomery Clift. 14.95 (ISBN 0-8065-0717-9). Citadel Pr.
Films of Shirley Temple. 14.95 (ISBN 0-8065-0615-6). Citadel Pr.
Films of Shirley Temple. pap. 6.95 (ISBN 0-8065-0725-X). Citadel Pr.
Films of Susan Hayward. 14.95 (ISBN 0-8065-0682-2). Citadel Pr.
Films of Tyrone Power. 14.95 (ISBN 0-8065-0477-3). Citadel Pr.
Finale. 19.00 (ISBN 0-403-01539-1). Scholarly.
Finally Home. 5.95 (ISBN 0-8007-0934-9). Revell.
Financial Phenomenon: An Investigation of the Rise & Fall of the Slater Walker Empire. 12.95 (ISBN 0-06-013506-9). Har-Row.
Finding a Way Out: An Autobiography. 12.75x (ISBN 0-8371-1897-2). Negro U Pr.
Finding My Father: One Man's Search for Identity. pap. 1.95 (ISBN 0-425-03456-9). Berkley Pub.
Fine Old Conflict. 10.00 (ISBN 0-394-49995-6). Knopf.
Finest Kind: The Fishermen of Gloucester. pap. 2.95 (ISBN 0-380-44339-2, 44339). Avon.
Finger Game Miracle. PLB 6.65 (ISBN 0-8172-0452-0). Raintree Pubs.
Finishing Touch. 8.95 (ISBN 0-396-07534-7). Dodd.
Fire & Ice: The Art & Thought of Robert Frost. 13.00 (ISBN 0-8462-0283-2). Russell.
Fire & Ice: The Charles Revson-Revlon Story. 10.00 (ISBN 0-688-03023-8). Morrow.
Fire & the Glory: Lafayette & America's Fight for Freedom. 8.95 (ISBN 0-664-32592-0). Westminster.
Fire That Will Not Die. 10.00 (ISBN 0-88280-066-3). ETC Pubns.
First & Last Love. lib. bdg. 21.00x (ISBN 0-313-20549-3, SHFL). Greenwood.
First Bolshevik: A Political Biography of Peter Tkachev. 10.00x (ISBN 0-8147-0427-1). NYU Pr.
First Book of Presidents. rev. ed. PLB 4.90 (ISBN 0-531-00615-8); pap. 1.25 (ISBN 0-531-02316-8). Watts.
First Encounter with Francis of Assisi. pap. 6.95 (ISBN 0-8199-0698-0). Franciscan Herald.
First Five Lives of Annie Besant. 11.50x (ISBN 0-226-57316-8). U of Chicago Pr.
First Four Georges. pap. 2.25 (ISBN 0-531-06007-1). Watts.
First Four Georges. 17.50 (ISBN 0-316-71126-8); pap. 3.95 (ISBN 0-316-71127-6). Little.
First Henry Ford: A Study in Personality & Business Leadership. 12.00x (ISBN 0-262-10008-8); pap. 4.95 (ISBN 0-262-60005-6). MIT Pr.
First in the Field: America's Pioneering Naturalists. pap. 5.95 (ISBN 0-442-21565-7). Van Nos Reinhold.
First Lady of the South: The Life of Mrs. Jefferson Davis. lib. bdg. 24.00x (ISBN 0-8371-6927-5, ROFL). Greenwood.
First Lady: Rosalynn Carter. PLB 7.95 (ISBN 0-516-03459-6); pap. 1.95 (ISBN 0-516-43459-4). Childrens.
First Lady's Lady: With the Fords at the White House. 11.95 (ISBN 0-399-12292-3). Putnam.
First Mrs. Thomas Hardy. 18.50x (ISBN 0-312-29246-5). St Martin.
First One Hundred Justices: Statistical Studies on the Supreme Court of the United States. 15.00 (ISBN 0-208-01290-7). Shoe String.
First Person Plural. lib. bdg. 22.50 (ISBN 0-306-77594-8). Da Capo.
First Person Rural. lib. bdg. 18.00x (ISBN 0-8371-9727-9, CAFI). Greenwood.
First Stunt Stars of Hollywood. lib. bdg. 6.33. Silver.
First Textbooks in American History & Their Compiler John M'culloch. 17.50 (ISBN 0-404-55744-9). AMS Pr.
First to the Top of the World: Admiral Peary at the North Pole. lib. bdg. 6.33. Silver.
First Women of the Skies. lib. bdg. 6.33. Silver.
First, You Cry. 7.95 (ISBN 0-397-01167-9). Lippincott.
First You Cry. pap. 1.95 (ISBN 0-451-08534-5, J8534). NAL.
Fishbait: The Memoirs of the Congressional Doorkeeper. pap. 2.50 (ISBN 0-446-81637-X). Warner Bks.
Five & Ten: Fabulous Life of F. W. Woolworth. facs. ed. 14.50 (ISBN 0-8369-5540-4). Arno.
Five for Freedom: Lucretia Mott, Elizabeth Cady Stanton, Lucy Stone, Susan B. Anthony, Carrie Chapman Catt. lib. bdg. 14.75x (ISBN 0-8371-0034-8, BUFF). Greenwood.
Five George Masons: Patriots & Planters of Virginia & Maryland. 17.50x (ISBN 0-8139-0590-7). U Pr of Va.
Five Jewish Lawyers of the Common Law. facs. ed. 10.25 (ISBN 0-8369-8059-X). Arno.
Five Letters. lib. bdg. 34.95 (ISBN 0-8490-1841-2). Gordon Pr.
Five Men: Character Studies from the Roman Empire. facsimile ed. 10.25 (ISBN 0-8369-0292-0). Arno.
Five Mexican-American Women in Transition: A Case Study of Migrants in the Midwest. soft bdg. 8.00 (ISBN 0-88247-444-8). R & E Res Assoc.
Five of Me: The Autobiography of a Multiple Personality. 1.95 (ISBN 0-671-81880-5). PB.
Five of Me: The Autobiography of a Multiple Personality. 9.95 (ISBN 0-8092-7869-3). Contemp Bks.
Flame in Sunlight: The Life & Work of Thomas de Quincey. 15.00x (ISBN 0-87471-712-4). Rowman.
Flashback: Nora Johnson on Nunnally Johnson. 11.95 (ISBN 0-385-13406-1). Doubleday.
Flaubert. 16.00 (ISBN 0-8156-0057-7); pap. 5.95 (ISBN 0-8156-0087-9). Syracuse U Pr.
Flaubert & Madame Bovary: A Double Portrait. pap. 5.95 (ISBN 0-226-77137-7, P709). U of Chicago Pr.
Fleet Admiral: The Story of William F. Halsey. 3.95 (ISBN 0-664-32343-X). Westminster.
Fleischer Story. 12.50 (ISBN 0-517-52580-1). Crown.
Fleming: Discoverer of Penicillin. lib. bdg. 10.00 (ISBN 0-8482-1632-6). Norwood Edns.
Flight of an Empress. 18.50 (ISBN 0-88355-098-9). Hyperion Conn.
Flight of Marie Antoinette. 12.50 (ISBN 0-404-07128-7). AMS Pr.
Flight of the Lone Eagle: Charles Lindbergh Flies Nonstop from New York to Paris. PLB 4.47 (ISBN 0-531-02723-6). Watts.
Flight of the Swan: A Memory of Anna Pavlova. 19.50 (ISBN 0-306-79580-9). Da Capo.
Flora: A Biography. 4.95 (ISBN 0-397-00427-3). Lippincott.
Florence & the Medici: The Pattern of Control. 14.95 (ISBN 0-500-25059-6). Thames Hudson.
Florence Farr: Bernard Shaw's "New Woman". 13.75x (ISBN 0-87471-707-8). Rowman.
Florence Kelley: The Making of a Social Pioneer. 10.00x (ISBN 0-678-00185-5). Kelley.
Florencio Sanchez & the Argentine Theatre. 59.95 (ISBN 0-87968-227-2). Gordon Pr.
Florenz Ziegfeld, Twentieth Century Showman. 1st ed. lib. bdg. 2.45 incl. catalog cards; pap. 1.25 vinyl laminated covers (ISBN 0-87157-037-8). SamHar Pr.
Florid Victorian Ornament. pap. 3.50 (ISBN 0-486-23490-8). Dover.
Flower of Evil: Life of Charles Baudelaire. 14.50 (ISBN 0-8369-5293-6). Arno.
Flower of Evil: Life of Charles Baudelaire. 12.00 (ISBN 0-8274-1558-3). R West.
Flower of Light: A Biography of Mary Webb. 28.00x (ISBN 0-7156-1120-8). Biblio Dist.
Flush: A Biography. pap. 2.45 (ISBN 0-15-631952-7, HPL12). HarBraceJ.
Flushed with Pride: The Story of Thomas Crapper. 3.95 (ISBN 0-13-322560-7). P-H.
Flute Solo: Reflections of a Trappist Hermit. pap. 3.50 (ISBN 0-385-17173-0). Doubleday.
Flute Solo: Reflections of a Trappist Hermit. 7.95 (ISBN 0-8362-3912-1). Andrews & McMeel.
Fly the Biggest Piece Back. 14.95 (ISBN 0-87842-108-4). Mountain Pr.
Fly the Biggest Piece Back. limited ed. 49.50 (ISBN 0-87842-118-1). Mountain Pr.
Flying. pap. 2.95 (ISBN 0-345-27608-6). Ballantine.
Flying Dutchman: The Life of Anthony Fokker. 15.00 (ISBN 0-405-03760-0). Arno.
Flying Nurse. 8.95 (ISBN 0-8008-2892-5). Taplinger.
Flying Tiger: Chennault of China. lib. bdg. 16.75x (ISBN 0-8371-6774-4, SCFT). Greenwood.
Flying to Be Free. softcover 7.95 (ISBN 0-930294-13-0). World Wide OR.
Flying to the Moon & Other Strange Places. 6.95g (ISBN 0-374-32412-3). FS&G.
Foch, the Man of Orleans. lib. bdg. 35.00x (ISBN 0-313-22171-5, LHFO). Greenwood.
Fonteyn & Nureyev: The Story of a Partnership. 22.50 (ISBN 0-8129-0860-0). Times Bks.
Fonteyn: The Making of a Legend. 25.00 (ISBN 0-688-61163-X). Morrow.
Fonz: The Henry Winkler Story. pap. 1.50 (ISBN 0-671-80746-3). PB.
Fool of Love: The Life of Ramon Lull. lib. bdg. 20.00. Folcroft.
Football Immortals. 6.95 (ISBN 0-02-626200-2). Macmillan.
Football Running Backs: Three Ground Gainers. PLB 4.78 (ISBN 0-8116-6677-8). Garrard.
Football Superstars of the '70s. PLB 7.29 (ISBN 0-671-32751-8). Messner.
Football's Clever Quarterbacks. PLB 5.95 (ISBN 0-8225-1051-0). Lerner Pubns.
Football's Fierce Defenses. PLB 5.95g (ISBN 0-8225-1057-X). Lerner Pubns.
Football's Greatest Coach, Vince Lombardi. 4.95. Doubleday.
Football's Rugged Running Backs. PLB 5.95 (ISBN 0-8225-1052-9). Lerner Pubns.
Footprints of Robert Burns. lib. bdg. 22.50 (ISBN 0-8414-4303-3). Folcroft.
Footsteps of Dr. Johnson - Scotland. lib. bdg. 50.00 (ISBN 0-8414-4855-8). Folcroft.
For Once in My Life. pap. 1.50 (ISBN 0-446-78799-X). Warner Bks.
For the Love of My Daughter. pap. 2.95 (ISBN 0-89191-104-9). Cook.

Friendship's Bright Shinings. kivar 4.95 (ISBN 0-310-20037-7). Zondervan.
Froissart, Chronicler & Poet. lib. bdg. 20.00. Folcroft.
Frolic & the Gentle: A Centenary Study of Charles Lamb. lib. bdg. 8.45. Folcroft.
Frolic & the Gentle: A Centenary Study of Charles Lamb. 8.50 (ISBN 0-8046-0852-0). Kennikat.
From Anne to Victoria: Essays by Various Hands. facs. ed. 20.00 (ISBN 0-8369-0378-1). Arno.
From Anne to Victoria: Fourteen Biographical Studies Between 1702 & 1901. 8.50 (ISBN 0-8046-0478-9). Kennikat.
From Canton to California: The Epic of Chinese Immigration. 8.95g (ISBN 0-590-07344-3). Schol Bk Serv.
From Clerk to Cleric. pap. 3.75 (ISBN 0-227-67825-7). Attic Pr.
From Eminently Disadvantaged to Eminence. 8.50 (ISBN 0-87527-104-9). Green.
From Football to Finance: The Story of Brady Keys Jr. 4.75 (ISBN 0-15-230265-4). HarBraceJ.
From Goethe to Hauptmann: Studies in a Changing Culture. 8.50 (ISBN 0-8196-0178-0). Biblo.
From Grieg to Brahms. new & enl. ed. 17.00 (ISBN 0-404-04199-X). AMS Pr.
From Lady Washington to Mrs. Cleveland. 19.50 (ISBN 0-8369-2990-X). Arno.
From Lew Alcindor to Kareem Abdul-Jabbar. rev. ed. pap. 2.95 (ISBN 0-688-46821-7). Lothrop.
From Lew Alcindor to Kareem Abdul-Jabbar. rev. ed. 6.50 (ISBN 0-688-41821-X); PLB 6.24 (ISBN 0-688-51821-4). Lothrop.
From Loyalist to Founding Father: The Political Odyssey of William Samuel Johnson. 22.50x (ISBN 0-231-04506-9). Columbia U Pr.
From Medicine to Miracles. pap. 1.50 (ISBN 0-87123-383-5). Bethany Fell.
From Orphans to Champions: The Story of Dematha's Morgan Wootten. 8.95 (ISBN 0-689-11011-1). Atheneum.
From Peanuts to President. PLB 6.65 (ISBN 0-8172-0428-8). Raintree Pubs.
From Place to Place: Travels with Paul Tillich, Travels Without Paul Tillich. 10.00 (ISBN 0-8128-1902-0). Stein & Day.
From Power to Peace. 7.95 (ISBN 0-8499-0074-3, 0074-3). Word Bks.
From Quaker to Latter-Day Saint: Bishop Edwin D. Woolley. 6.95. Deseret Bk.
From Reason to Romanticism. lib. bdg. 17.95 (ISBN 0-8383-1595-X). Haskell.
From Reform Judaism to Ethical Culture: The Religious Evolution of Felix Adler. 15.00 (ISBN 0-87820-404-0). Ktav.
From Sepoy to Subedar: Being the Life & Adventures of Subedar Sita Ram, a Native Officer of the Bengal Army. 12.50 (ISBN 0-208-01152-8). Shoe String.
From Slave to Abolitionist: The Life of William Wells Brown. 7.95 (ISBN 0-8037-2743-7). Dial.
From Slavery to Wealth: The Life of Scott Bond. facsimile ed. 30.50 (ISBN 0-8369-8907-4). Arno.
From Stolnoy to Spartanburg: The Two Worlds of a Former Russian Princess. 3.95 (ISBN 0-87844-001-1). Sandlapper Store.
From the Deep Woods to Civilization: Chapters in the Autobiography of an Indian. 11.95x (ISBN 0-8032-0936-3); pap. 3.75 (ISBN 0-8032-5873-9, 651). U of Nebr Pr.
From the Heartland: Profiles of People & Places of the Southwest & Beyond. 9.50 (ISBN 0-87358-155-5). Northland.
From the Life. 6.75 (ISBN 0-8274-1718-7). R West.
From the Life. facsimile ed. 9.25 (ISBN 0-8369-2215-8). Arno.
From the Nolichucky to Memphis: Reminiscences of a Tennessee Doctor. 12.95 (ISBN 0-87870-064-1). Memphis St Univ.
From the Slave Cabin of Yani. 10.00 (ISBN 0-682-48781-3). Exposition.
From the Steeples & Mountains: A Study of Charles Ives. 10.00 (ISBN 0-394-48110-0). Knopf.
From the Virginia Plantation to the National Capitol. 21.00 (ISBN 0-405-01877-0). Arno.
From These Beginnings: A Biographical Approach to American History. 2nd ed. pap. text ed. 9.50x (ISBN 0-06-044717-6). Har-Row.
From These Beginnings: A Biographical Approach to American History. 2nd ed. pap. text ed. 9.50x (ISBN 0-06-044718-4). Har-Row.
From Thunder to Breakfast. 10.50 (ISBN 0-87358-175-X); pap. 7.50 (ISBN 0-87358-178-4). Northland.
From Time to Time. 7.95 (ISBN 0-8128-1626-9). Stein & Day.
From Time to Time. pap. 1.95 (ISBN 0 8128-1742-7). Stein & Day.
Front & Center. 15.00 (ISBN 0-671-24328-4). S&S.
Frontenac of New France. 6.50 (ISBN 0-688-21318-9). Morrow.
Frontier Bishop: The Life of Bishop Simon Brute. pap. 1.95 (ISBN 0-87973-804-9). Our Sunday Visitor.
Frontier Crusader-William F. M. Arny. pap. 5.95 (ISBN 0-8165-0390-7). U of Ariz Pr.
Frontier Lady: Recollections of the Gold Rush & Early California. 8.95x (ISBN 0-8032-0909-6); pap. 2.45 (ISBN 0-8032-5856-9, 634). U of Nebr Pr.
Frontier Politics: Alaska's James Wickersham. 14.95 (ISBN 0-8323-0317-8). Binford.
Frontier Tales of Tennessee. 10.00 (ISBN 0-88289-084-0). Pelican.
Frontier World of Doc Holliday: Faro Dealer from Dallas to Deadwood. pap. 4.95 (ISBN 0-8032-7550-1, BB697). U of Nebr Pr.
Frontiers of Dance: The Life of Martha Graham. 8.95 (ISBN 0-690-00920-8). T Y Crowell.
Frontiersman: A Biography of George Elphinstone Dalrymple. 6.75x (ISBN 0-19-550077-6). Oxford U Pr.
Froude's Life of Carlyle. 30.00x (ISBN 0-8142-0274-8). Ohio St U Pr.
Full Circle: Stories of Mennonite Women. pap. 5.25 (ISBN 0-87303-014-1). Faith & Life.
Full History of the Wonderful Career of Moody & Sankey, in Great Britain & America. 25.00 (ISBN 0-404-07227-5). AMS Pr.
Full Moon to France. 8.95 (ISBN 0-06-013586-7). Har-Row.
Fulton Oursler's Greatest: The Greatest Book Ever Written, The Greatest Story Ever Told, The Greatest Faith Ever Known. Softbound 8.95 (ISBN 0-385-14659-0). Doubleday.
Fun of It: Random Records of My Own Flying & of Women in Aviation. 14.00 (ISBN 0-8103-4078-X). Gale.
Funk of Funk's Grove. 5.50 (ISBN 0-912226-10-2). Ill St Hist Soc.
Funky. pap. 3.95 (ISBN 0-8163-0001-1, 06829-6). Pacific Pr Pub Assn.
Fur Trader of the North: The Story of Pierre de la Verendrye. 6.50 (ISBN 0-688-20076-1). Morrow.
Fyodor Dostoevsky. lib. bdg. 20.00 (ISBN 0-8495-3228-0). Arden Lib.

G

G. D. H. Cole: An Intellectual Biography. 28.50 (ISBN 0-521-08702-3). Cambridge U Pr.
G. Howard Ferguson: Ontario Tory. 14.95 (ISBN 0-8020-3346-6). U of Toronto Pr.
G. K. Chesterton. pap. 1.95 (ISBN 0-8277-6003-5, WTW3). British Bk Ctr.
G. K. Chesterton: A Bibliography. lib. bdg. 12.00x (ISBN 0-8371-7422-8, SUGC). Greenwood.
G. K. Chesterton: A Portrait. lib. bdg. 19.95 (ISBN 0-8383-1679-4). Haskell.
G. Stanley Hall: The Psychologist As Prophet. 17.50x (ISBN 0-226-72821-8). U of Chicago Pr.
G. Washington; Master Mason. 8.50 (M-323). Macoy Pub.
Gabby, Ernie & Me: A Vancouver Boyhood. 8.95 (ISBN 0-88894-059-9). Intl Schol Bk Serv.
Gabriel Faure, 1845-1924. 8.50 (ISBN 0-404-14679-1). AMS Pr.
Gabriel Naude, 1600-1653. 12.50 (ISBN 0-208-00971-X). Shoe String.
Gabriela Mistral: The Poet & Her Work. pap. 3.95x (ISBN 0-8147-0011-X). NYU Pr.
Gaetano Filangieri & His Science of Legislation. pap. 6.00 (ISBN 0-87169-666-5). Am Philos.
Gaitan of Colombia: A Political Biography. 12.95 (ISBN 0-8229-3354-3). U of Pittsburgh Pr.
Galileo. 14.95 (ISBN 0-399-11364-9). Putnam.
Galileo at Work: His Scientific Biography. 25.00 (ISBN 0-226-16226-5). U of Chicago Pr.
Galileo's Intellectual Revolution: Middle Period, 1610-1632. pap. 6.95x. N Watson.
Galla Monarchy: Jimma Abba Jifar, Ethiopia, 1830-1932. 14.00x (ISBN 0-299-03690-1). U of Wis Pr.
Galla Placidia Augusta: A Biographical Essay. 16.50x (ISBN 0-226-63050-1). U of Chicago Pr.
Gallery of Champions. facs. ed. 15.00 (ISBN 0-8369-8043-3). Arno.
Gallery of Irish Writers: The Irish Writers of the Seventeenth Century. Bd. with Poets & Dramatists of Ireland. 39.50 (ISBN 0-404-13815-2). AMS Pr.
Galli-Curci's Life of Song. 14.95 (ISBN 0-917734-00-9). Monitor.
Galloping Swede. 8.50 (ISBN 0-87842-013-4). Mountain Pr.
Game of Their Lives. 7.95 (ISBN 0-394-40923-X). Random.
Game of Their Lives. pap. 1.95 (ISBN 0-451-07532-3, J7532). NAL.
Gamebreakers of the NFL. 2.50 (ISBN 0-394-82501-2); PLB 3.69 (ISBN 0-394-92501-7). Random.
Gandhi. 5.95 (ISBN 0-395-12573-1). HM.
Gandhi in South Africa: British Imperialism & the Indian Question, 1860-1914. 19.50x (ISBN 0-8014-0586-6). Cornell U Pr.
Gandhi My Refrain: Controversial Essays, 1950-1972. 11.25x (ISBN 0-8002-1445-5). Intl Pubns Serv.
Gandhi Reader: A Source Book of His Life & Writings. 27.50 (ISBN 0-404-03540-X). AMS Pr.
Gandhi the Man. 10.50 (ISBN 0-915132-13-3); pap. 6.95 (ISBN 0-915132-14-1). Nilgiri Pr.
Garcia the Centenarian & His Times. lib. bdg. 22.50 (ISBN 0-306-70671-7). Da Capo.
Garden of Zola: Emile Zola & His Novels for English Readers. 25.00x (ISBN 0-06-493711-9). B&N.
Gardener Touched with Genius: The Life of Luther Burbank. 10.00 (ISBN 0-698-10691-1). Coward.
Garibaldi: The Legend & the Man. lib. bdg. 15.75x (ISBN 0-8371-8361-8, DEGA). Greenwood.
Garrick. lib. bdg. 23.00x (ISBN 0-313-20270-2, BAGAR). Greenwood.
Garrick & His Circle. lib. bdg. 50.00 (ISBN 0-8495-4367-3). Arden Lib.
Garrick & His Circle. 20.00 (ISBN 0-405-08836-1). Arno.
Garry Unger & the Battling Blues. 7.95 (ISBN 0-396-07388-3). Dodd.
Garvey & Garveyism. pap. 2.95 (ISBN 0-02-032670-X). Macmillan.
Garvey & Garveyism. lib. bdg. 15.50 (ISBN 0-374-93015-5). Octagon.
Gather Together in My Name. 5.95 (ISBN 0-394-48692-7). Random.
Gather Together in My Name. pap. 2.25 (ISBN 0-553-11251-1, 13092-7). Bantam.
Gaudier-Brzeska: A Memoir. pap. 3.95 (ISBN 0-8112-0527-4, NDP372). New Directions.
Gauguin. 28.50 (ISBN 0-8109-0137-4). Abrams.
Gauguin. pap. 2.95 (ISBN 0-448-00460-7). G&D.
Gay Diary 1933-1946. 14.95 (ISBN 0-9602270-0-8); pap. 9.95 (ISBN 0-9602270-1-6). Pepys Pr.
Gay Genius: The Life & Times of Su Tungpo. lib. bdg. 18.00x (ISBN 0-8371-4715-8, LIGG). Greenwood.
Gay Theology. pap. 2.50 (ISBN 0-88270-241-6). Logos.
Gayoso: The Life of a Spanish Governor in the Mississippi Valley 1789-1799. 7.50 (ISBN 0-8446-0704-5). Peter Smith.
Gemini: An Extended Autobiographical Statement on My First Twenty-Five Years of Being a Black Poet. pap. 1.95 (ISBN 0-14-004264-4). Penguin.
General Billy Mitchell: Champion of Air Defense. lib. bdg. 18.75x (ISBN 0-313-20170-6, BUGM). Greenwood.
General Custer's Libbie. 19.95 (ISBN 0-87564-806-1). Superior Pub.
General De Kalb, Lafayette's Mentor. 13.00x (ISBN 0-8078-8053-1). U of NC Pr.
General Dean's Story. lib. bdg. 18.00x (ISBN 0-8371-6690-X, DEDS). Greenwood.
General George B. McClellan, Shield of the Union. lib. bdg. 19.50x (ISBN 0-8371-7606-9, HAGG). Greenwood.
General Grant's Letters to a Friend, 1861-1880. 6.00 (ISBN 0-404-04598-7). AMS Pr.
General Greene. 12.75 (ISBN 0-8046-1271-4). Kennikat.
General Henry Atkinson: A Western Military Career. pap. 4.95 (ISBN 0-8061-1087-2). U of Okla Pr.
General Monck. 18.50x (ISBN 0-87471-934-8). Rowman.
General Robert E. Lee After Appomattox. facsimile ed. 16.00 (ISBN 0-8369-6700-3). Arno.
General Sterling Price & the Civil War in the West. 14.95 (ISBN 0-8071-0342-X). La State U Pr.
General Sullivan: New Hampshire Patriot. 9.00 (ISBN 0-533-02684-9). Vantage.
General Tom Thumb & His Lady. 5.95x (ISBN 0-88492-018-6); pap. 2.95x (ISBN 0-88492-019-4). W S Sullwold.
General Von Steuben. 12.50 (ISBN 0-8046-0346-4). Kennikat.
General Washington's Son of Israel & Other Forgotten Heroes of History. 14.50 (ISBN 0-8369-1296-9). Arno.
General Wauchope. 17.00 (ISBN 0-8369-9094-3). Arno.
Generals in Blue: Lives of the Union Commanders. 25.00 (ISBN 0-8071-0822-7). La State U Pr.
Generals in Gray: Lives of the Confederate Commanders. 20.00 (ISBN 0-8071-0823-5). La State U Pr.
Generals in the White House. facsimile ed 15.50 (ISBN 0-8369-2501-7). Arno.
Generation of Women: Education in the Lives of Progressive Reformers. 12.50x (ISBN 0-674-34471-5). Harvard U Pr.
Generous Years: Remembrances of a Frontier Boyhood. 5.50 (ISBN 0-394-42618-5). Random.
Genesis Angels: The Saga of Lew Welch & the Beat Generation. 7.95 (ISBN 0-688-03436-5). Morrow.
Genius: A Memoir of Max Reinhardt. 16.95 (ISBN 0-394-49085-1). Knopf.
Genji Days. 15.00 (ISBN 0-87011-296-1). Kodansha.
Gentle Barbarian: The Life & Work of Turgenev. pap. 3.95 (ISBN 0-394-72526-3). Random.
Gentleman in a Dustcoat: A Biography of John Crowe Ransom. 32.50x (ISBN 0-8071-0190-7); pap. 8.95 (ISBN 0-8071-0255-5). La State U Pr.
Gentleman Jim & the Great John L. PLB 4.69 (ISBN 0-698-30669-4). Coward.
Gentleman Joe: The Story of Harness Driver Joe O'Brien. 7.95 (ISBN 0-668-03624-9). Arco.
Gentleman of the Old Natchez Region, Benjamin L. C. Wailes. 15.00x (ISBN 0-8371-4989-4). Negro U Pr.
Genuine & Correct Account of the Captivity, Sufferings & Deliverance of Mrs. Jemima Howe see Essay on the Life of the Honorable Major-General Israel Putnam.
Geoffrey Chaucer. Bd. with Sir Thomas Malory. pap. 1.60x (ISBN 0-8032-5650-7, 450). U of Nebr Pr.
Georg Brandes. lib. bdg. 10.95 (ISBN 0-8057-6232-9). Twayne.
George & Mary Schlosser: Ambassadors for Christ in China. pap. 1.00. Light & Life.
George & Robert Stephenson: The Railway Revolution. lib. bdg. 24.50x (ISBN 0-8371-9747-3, RORR). Greenwood.
George Bancroft. lib. bdg. 15.00 (ISBN 0-374-96133-6). Octagon.
George Bentham. 12.00 (ISBN 0-404-07895-8). AMS Pr.
George Berkeley in America. text ed. 15.00x (ISBN 0-300-02394-4). Yale U Pr.
George Bernard Shaw: His Life & Personality. pap. 1.95 (ISBN 0-689-70149-7, 36). Atheneum.
George Cabot Lodge. lib. bdg. 8.50 (ISBN 0-8057-7165-4). Twayne.
George Caleb Bingham: River Portraitist. 29.95 (ISBN 0-8061-0446-5). U of Okla Pr.
George Croghan: Wilderness Diplomat. 15.50x (ISBN 0-8078-0759-1). U of NC Pr.
George Eastman. lib. bdg. 22.50x (ISBN 0-678-03556-3). Kelley.
George Elbert Burr, 1859-1939: Catalogue Raisonne & Guide to the Etched Works. 15.00 (ISBN 0-87358-067-2). Northland.
George Eliot. lib. bdg. 17.95 (ISBN 0-8383-1503-8). Haskell.
George Eliot. lib. bdg. 12.50 (ISBN 0-8414-8538-0). Folcroft.
George Eliot & Her World. 9.95 (ISBN 0-684-15511-7). Scribner.
George Eliot: Her Mind & Her Art. 23.95 (ISBN 0-521-04158-9); pap. 6.95 (ISBN 0-521-09174-8, 174). Cambridge U Pr.
George Eliot: The Emergent Self. 15.00 (ISBN 0-394-49010-X). Knopf.
George Eliot: Thoughts Upon Her Life, Her Books, & Herself. lib. bdg. 10.00 (ISBN 0-8414-5816-2). Folcroft.
George Eliot's Life As Related in Her Letters & Journals. 59.00 (ISBN 0-403-00093-9). Scholarly.
George Fitzhugh: Propagandist of the Old South. 7.50 (ISBN 0-8446-1481-5). Peter Smith.
George Foster Story. rev. ed. 7.95. Holiday.
George Foster Story. 6.95 (ISBN 0-8234-0351-3). Holiday.
George Frederick Watts, Sandro Botticelli, Matthew Arnold. lib. bdg. 15.00 (ISBN 0-8414-1910-8). Folcroft.
George Frideric Handel. 20.00 (ISBN 0-393-02131-9); pap. 7.95 (ISBN 0-393-00815-0). Norton.
George Gershwin: His Journey to Greatness. lib. bdg. 21.00x (ISBN 0-8371-9663-9, EWGG). Greenwood.
George Gissing: A Biography. 15.00 (ISBN 0-208-01700-3). Shoe String.
George Gissing: A Biography. 17.50x (ISBN 0-8020-5330-0). U of Toronto Pr.
George Gissing: A Critical Biography. pap. 6.95 (ISBN 0-295-95679-8). U of Wash Pr.
George Gissing, Classicist. lib. bdg. 15.00 (ISBN 0-8414-1109-3). Folcroft.
George Henry Boker, Poet & Patriot. 9.95 (ISBN 0-8274-2401-9). R West.
George Henry Boker, Poet & Patriot. 12.50 (ISBN 0-404-00928-X). AMS Pr.
George Henry Boker, Poet & Patriot. 9.50 (ISBN 0-403-00832-8). Scholarly.
George Henry Lewes: A Victorian Mind. 10.00x (ISBN 0-674-34874-5). Harvard U Pr.
George Jacob Holyoake: A Study in the Evolution of a Victorian Radical. lib. bdg. 15.00x (ISBN 0-87991-619-2). Porcupine Pr.
George Joachim Goschen: The Transformation of a Victorian Liberal. 33.00 (ISBN 0-521-20210-8). Cambridge U Pr.

George Keller, Architect. pap. 9.95 (ISBN 0-917482-14-X). Stowe-Day.

George Lewis: A Jazzman from New Orleans. 12.50 (ISBN 0-520-03212-8). U of Cal Pr.

George Logan of Philadelphia. 17.00 (ISBN 0-405-00444-3). Arno.

George M. Cohan: Boy Theater Genius. 5.95 (ISBN 0-672-50066-3). Bobbs.

George M. Cohan, Prince of the American Theater. lib. bdg. 13.75x (ISBN 0-8371-6225-4, MOGC). Greenwood.

George M. Cohan: The Man Who Owned Broadway. pap. 6.95 (ISBN 0-306-80118-3). Da Capo.

George Macdonald & His Wife. 38.50 (ISBN 0-384-34777-0, E240). Johnson Repr.

George Mason, Gentleman Revolutionary. 19.00 (ISBN 0-8078-1250-1). U of NC Pr.

George Mason of Virginia. 4.50 (ISBN 0-02-743560-1). Macmillan.

George Meredith, His Life & Work. 34.00 (ISBN 0-527-57230-6). Kraus Repr.

George Mifflin Dallas: Jacksonian Patrician. 13.75x (ISBN 0-271-00510-6). Pa St U Pr.

George Morrison. PLB 6.95 (ISBN 0-87518-110-4). Dillon.

George Peabody, Merchant & Financier: 1829-1854. lib. bdg. 27.00x (ISBN 0-405-11228-9). Arno.

George Pierce Baker & the American Theatre. lib. bdg. 18.00x (ISBN 0-8371-0129-8, KIGB). Greenwood.

George Ripley. 17.50 (ISBN 0-404-02625-7). AMS Pr.

George Ripley. lib. bdg. 8.95 (ISBN 0-8057-7181-6). Twayne.

George Rogers Clark & the War in the West. 4.95 (ISBN 0-8131-0224-3). U Pr of Ky.

George Romney. facsimile ed. 29.50 (ISBN 0-8369-5789-X). Arno.

George S. Kaufman: His Life, His Theater. 20.00 (ISBN 0-19-502623-3). Oxford U Pr.

George Saintsbury. lib. bdg. 5.50 (ISBN 0-8414-9618-8). Folcroft.

George Sand. 7.45 (ISBN 0-8274-1507-9). R West.

George Sand. 7.50 (ISBN 0-8046-0810-5). Kennikat.

George Sand. lib. bdg. 25.00 (ISBN 0-8414-8633-6). Folcroft.

George Sand: A Biographical Portrait. 12.50 (ISBN 0-8008-3199-3). Taplinger.

George Sand: A Biography. 17.50 (ISBN 0-395-19954-9). HM.

George Sand: A Biography. pap. 3.50 (ISBN 0-380-00700-2, 43778). Avon.

George Sand & Her Lovers. lib. bdg. 30.00 (ISBN 0-8414-4504-4). Folcroft.

George Santayana. 12.50 (ISBN 0-8462-1518-7). Russell.

George Sessions Perry: His Life & Works. 8.95 (ISBN 0-8363-0119-6). Jenkins.

George Smith's Money: A Scottish Investor in America. 6.50 (ISBN 0-87020 093-3). State Hist Soc Wis.

George W. Cable: A Biography. 7.50 (ISBN 0-8446-3091 2). Peter Smith.

George W. Cable: A Biography. pap. 5.95x (ISBN 0-8071-0106-0). La State U Pr.

George W. Norris: Gentle Knight of American Democracy. 8.95 (ISBN 0-252-72735-5). U of Ill Pr.

George W. Norris: The Making of a Progressive, 1861 to 1912. lib. bdg. 29.00x (ISBN 0-313-22103-0, LOGN). Greenwood.

George W. Norris: The Triumph of a Progressive, 1933-1944. 20.00 (ISBN 0-252-00223-7). U of Ill Pr.

George W. P. Hunt & His Arizona. 10.00 (ISBN 0-87026-038-3). Westernlore.

George Washington. PLB 4.49 (ISBN 0-399-60195-3). Putnam.

George Washington. 7.50x (ISBN 0-8052-3279-6). Schocken.

George Washington: A Biography. lib. bdg. 150.00x set (ISBN 0-678-02834-6); lib. bdg. 25.00 ea. Kelley.

George Washington: A Biography in His Own Words. 15.00 (ISBN 0-06-010127-X). Har-Row.

George Washington & American Independence. lib. bdg. 21.75x (ISBN 0-8371-9325-7, NEGW). Greenwood.

George Washington Carver: An American Biography. 6.95 (ISBN 0-385-03045-2). Doubleday.

George Washington: Father of Freedom. PLB 4.48 (ISBN 0-8116-6280-2). Garrard.

George Washington: The Virginia Period 1732-1775. pap. 6.75 (ISBN 0-8223-0367-1). Duke.

George Washington's Generals. lib. bdg. 25.00x (ISBN 0-313-22280-0, BIGW). Greenwood.

George Wythe of Williamsburg. 7.95 (ISBN 0-06-060791-2). Har-Row.

Georges Bizet. lib. bdg. 10.50x (ISBN 0-8371-5571-1, COGB). Greenwood.

Georges Guynemer, Knight of the Air. 13.00 (ISBN 0-405-03751-1). Arno.

Georges Mandel & the Third Republic. 18.50x (ISBN 0-8047-0731-6). Stanford U Pr.

Georges Rouault. 28.50 (ISBN 0-8109-0459-4). Abrams.

Georgian Satirists. lib. bdg. 15.00 (ISBN 0-8414-9183-6). Folcroft.

Georgina Hogarth & the Dickens Circle. 19.00 (ISBN 0-527-01050-2). Kraus Repr.

Gerald Ford. PLB 4.49 (ISBN 0-399-60944-X). Putnam.

Gerald Griffin: A Critical Biography 1803-1840. 19.95 (ISBN 0-521-21800-4). Cambridge U Pr.

Gerard Manley Hopkins. lib. bdg. 16.95 (ISBN 0-8383-0986-0). Haskell.

Gerard Manley Hopkins. lib. bdg. 12.00 (ISBN 0-374-94709-0). Octagon.

Gerard Manley Hopkins. lib. bdg. 49.95 (ISBN 0-87968-030-X). Gordon Pr.

Gerard Manley Hopkins: Priest & Poet. lib. bdg. 16.75x (ISBN 0-313-20589-2, PIGH). Greenwood.

Gerard Manley Hopkins: The Man & the Poet. lib. bdg. 20.00 (ISBN 0-8414-5061-7). Folcroft.

Geronimo. PLB 6.95 (ISBN 0-87518-059-0). Dillon.

Geronimo: The Man, His Time, His Place. 14.95 (ISBN 0-8061-1333-2). U of Okla Pr.

Gerrit Smith: A Biography. 16.50x (ISBN 0-8371-2767-X). Negro U Pr.

Gershom Scholem: Kabbalah & Counter-History. text ed. 15.00x (ISBN 0-674-36330-2). Harvard U Pr.

Gershwin, His Life & Music. pap. 7.95 (ISBN 0-306-80096-9). Da Capo.

Gershwin Years. rev. ed. 6.95 (ISBN 0-385-02847-4). Doubleday.

Gertrude Lawrence As Mrs. A: An Intimate Biography of the Great Star. lib. bdg. 18.75x (ISBN 0-8371-2469-7, ALGL). Greenwood.

Gertrude Stein: A Composite Portrait. pap. 1.65 (ISBN 0-380-00169-1, 20115). Avon.

Gertrude Stein & the Present. 7.50x (ISBN 0-674-35400-1). Harvard U Pr.

Gervasutti's Climbs. pap. 6.95 (ISBN 0-916890-67-8). Mountaineers.

Gesualdo: The Man & His Music. 17.50x (ISBN 0-8078-1201-3). U of NC Pr.

Getting It Together: Black Businessmen in America. 6.95 (ISBN 0-15-135275-5). HarBraceJ.

Getting to Know Him: A Biography of Oscar Hammerstein II. 15.00 (ISBN 0-394-49441-5). Random.

Ghana: The Autobiography of Kwame Nkrumah. 7.50 (ISBN 0-7178-0293-0); pap. 3.25 (ISBN 0-7178-0294-9). Intl Pub Co.

Ghost in My Life. 5.95 (ISBN 0-912376-00-7). Chosen Bks Pub.

Giambattista Della Porta: Dramatist. 16.50 (ISBN 0-691-06051-7). Princeton U Pr.

Giant of the Atom: Ernest Rutherford. PLB 3.34 (ISBN 0-671-18620-5). Messner.

Giants for Justice: Bethune, Randolph & King. 6.95 (ISBN 0-15-230781-8). HarBraceJ.

Giants of Jazz. rev. ed. 8.95 (ISBN 0-690-00998-4). T Y Crowell.

Giants of the Old West. facs. ed. 14.50 (ISBN 0-8369-1020-6). Arno.

Giants, Pigmies & Other Advertising People. 9.95 (ISBN 0-87251-013-1). Crain Bks.

Gibbon. 12.00 (ISBN 0-8274-1373-4). R West.

Gibbon. lib. bdg. 12.50 (ISBN 0-404-51719 6). AMS Pr.

Gibbon. lib. bdg. 15.00 (ISBN 0-8492-1754-7). R West.

Gibbon. lib. bdg. 15.00 (ISBN 0-8495-3842-4). Arden Lib.

Gibbon. 35.00 (ISBN 0-8490-0234-6). Gordon Pr.

Gibbon. lib. bdg. 25.00 (ISBN 0-8495-6125-6). Arden Lib.

Gibboniana. Incl (ISBN 0-8240-1338-7) (ISBN 0-8240-1339-5) (ISBN 0-8240-1340-9) (ISBN 0-8240-1341-7) (ISBN 0-8240-1342-5) (ISBN 0-8240-1343-3) (ISBN 0-8240-1344-1) (ISBN 0-8240-1345-X) (ISBN 0-8240-1346-8); lib. bdg. 76.00 (ISBN 0-8240-1347-6) (ISBN 0-8240-1348-4) (ISBN 0-8240-1349-2) (ISBN 0-8240-1350-6) (ISBN 0-8240-1351-4) (ISBN 0-8240-1352-2) (ISBN 0-8240-1353-0). lib. bdg. 43.00 ea. Garland Pub.

Gifford Pinchot, Bull Moose Progressive. lib. bdg. 14.00x (ISBN 0-8371-6943-7, FAGP). Greenwood.

Gift for People. 8.95 (ISBN 0-87131-244-1). M Evans.

Gilbert: His Life & Strife. lib. bdg. 21.50x (ISBN 0-313-20364-4, PEGI). Greenwood.

Ginger, Loretta & Irene Who? 9.95 (ISBN 0-399-11822-5). Putnam.

Giovanni Boccaccio As Man & Author. 10.00 (ISBN 0-404-06329-2). AMS Pr.

Giovanni Pierluigi Da Palestrina, His Life & Times. facsimile ed. 16.50 (ISBN 0-8369-5159-X). Arno.

Giovanni Pierluigi Da Palestrina, His Life & Times. lib. bdg. 12.75x (ISBN 0-8371-4002-1, PYPA). Greenwood.

Girl Rebel: The Autobiography of Hsieh Pingying with Extracts from Her "New War Diaries". lib. bdg. 22.50 (ISBN 0-306-70691-1). Da Capo.

Girls Who Became Writers. facsimile ed. 10.00 (ISBN 0-8369-2234-4). Arno.

Girls Who Made Good. facsimile ed. 9.50 (ISBN 0-8369-2235-2). Arno.

Giuseppe Ferrari & the Italian Revolution. 15.00x (ISBN 0-8078-1354-0). U of NC Pr.

Giuseppe Garibaldi: A Biography. 12.00 (ISBN 0-8046-1078-9). Kennikat.

Give Joy to My Youth: A Memoir of Dr. Tom Dooley. 5.95 (ISBN 0-374-16300-6). FS&G.

Give Me That Old Time Religion. pap. 2.95 (ISBN 0-88270-227-0). Logos.

Gladstone. 17.95 (ISBN 0-312-32760-9). St Martin.

Glamour Girls. pap. 7.95 (ISBN 0-89508-002-8). Rainbow Bks.

Glass Eyes Can See. 3.50. Valkyrie Pr.

Glenway Wescott. pap. 3.45 (ISBN 0-8084-0146-7, T87). Coll & U Pr.

Glimpses of Authors. facsimile ed. 18.75 (ISBN 0-8369-2674-9). Arno.

Glorious Scoundrel: A Biography of Captain John Smith. 7.95 (ISBN 0-396-07518-5). Dodd.

Glorious Triumphs: Athletes Who Conquered Adversity. rev. ed. 6.95g (ISBN 0-396-07793-5). Dodd.

Gluck & the Opera: A Study in Musical History. 18.00 (ISBN 0-404-60176-6). AMS Pr.

Gluck & the Opera: A Study in Musical History. lib. bdg. 20.00x (ISBN 0-8371-8849-0, NEGO). Greenwood.

Go Out in Joy. 7.95 (ISBN 0-8042-2073-5). John Knox.

Go up for Glory. pap. 2.25 (ISBN 0-425-04676-1). Berkley Pub.

Go Up for Glory. pap. 37.50 set (ISBN 0-8107-0001-8); teachers' notes incl. Bowmar-Noble.

God, Church, & Flag: Senator Joseph R. McCarthy & the Catholic Church, 1950-1957. 16.95 (ISBN 0-8078-1312-5). U of NC Pr.

God Demands Doctrinal Preaching. 9.95; pap. 7.95. Natl Christian Pr.

God, Woman, & Ministry. 6.95 (ISBN 0-912760-61-3). Valkyrie Pr.

Godfather Papers & Other Confessions. 6.95 (ISBN 0-399-10935-8). Putnam.

God's Englishman: Oliver Cromwell & the English Revolution. pap. 6.95x (ISBN 0-06-131666-0, TB1666). Har-Row.

God's Gold: The Story of Rockefeller & His Times. lib. bdg. 22.50x (ISBN 0-8371-5588-6, FLGG). Greenwood.

God's Man: The Story of Pastor Niemoeller. lib. bdg. 19.75x (ISBN 0-313-21065-9, DAGM). Greenwood.

God's Spy. o.p. 6.95 (ISBN 0-88270-213-0, H213-9); pap. 3.95 (ISBN 0-88270-214-9, P214-7). Logos.

God's Super Salesman. 4.95 (ISBN 0-8054-5529-9); pap. 2.50 (ISBN 0-8054-5529-9). Broadman.

God's Young Church. pap. 2.65 (ISBN 0-664-24884-5). Westminster.

Godwin & the Age of Transition. lib. bdg. 18.95 (ISBN 0-8383-2146-1). Haskell.

Godwin & the Age of Transition. lib. bdg. 25.00 (ISBN 0-8414-7249-1). Folcroft.

Goethe. 8.00 (ISBN 0-8046-0816-4). Kennikat.

Goethe & the Weimar Theatre. 15.00x (ISBN 0-8014-1118-1). Cornell U Pr.

Going Home. 6.95 (ISBN 0 06 066768-0). Har-Row.

Going Home. 12.50 (ISBN 0-8129-0701-9). Times Bks.

Going It Alone. pap. 6.95 (ISBN 0-385-14726-0). Doubleday.

Going It Alone. 12.95 (ISBN 0-385-14725-2); pap. 6.95 (ISBN 0-385-14726-0). Doubleday.

Gokhale, Gandhi & the Nehrus: Studies in Indian Nationalism. 19.95 (ISBN 0-312-33145-2). St Martin.

Gokhale: The Indian Moderates & the British Raj. text ed. 27.50 (ISBN 0-691-03115-0). Princeton U Pr.

Gold & Iron: Bismarck, Bleichroder & the Building of the German Empire. 17.95 (ISBN 0-394-49545-4). Knopf.

Gold Hunter: The Adventures of Marshall Bond. 8.50 (ISBN 0-8263-0140-1). U of NM Pr.

Gold Hustlers. pap. 7.95 (ISBN 0-88240-088-6). Alaska Northwest.

Gold... No Gold. 8.95 (ISBN 0-89127-021-3). Omni Pubs.

Gold Record. pap. 4.95 (ISBN 0-916184-04-8). Fountain Pub Co NY.

Golda Meir Story. reinforced bdg. 6.95 (ISBN 0-684-14610-X). Scribner.

Golda: The Life of Israel's Prime Minister. pap. 1.25 (ISBN 0-671-48132-0). WSP.

Golden Days of San Simeon. 12.95 (ISBN 0-385-04632-4). Doubleday.

Golden Lands of Thomas Hobbes. text ed. 15.95x (ISBN 0-8143-1574-7). Wayne St U Pr.

Golden Visit. 10.00x (ISBN 0-460-04433-8). Biblio Dist.

Goldsmith & His Booksellers. lib. bdg. 8.45 (ISBN 0-8414-5545-7). Folcroft.

Goldsmith & His Booksellers. lib. bdg. 8.00x (ISBN 0-678-00725-X). Kelley.

Goldsmith & His Booksellers. lib. bdg. 12.50 (ISBN 0-8495-3017-2). Arden Lib.

Goldsmiths and Silversmiths of England. pap. text ed. 15.00x (ISBN 0-09-121220-0). Humanities.

Goldwyn: A Biography of the Man Behind the Myth. 9.95 (ISBN 0-393-07497-8). Norton.

Goliath: The Wilt Chamberlain Story. 8.95 (ISBN 0-396-07392-1). Dodd.

Gomez, Tyrant of the Andes. lib. bdg. 14.75x (ISBN 0-8371-2698-3, CLG). Greenwood.

Goncourt Journals, 1851-1870. lib. bdg. 19.75x (ISBN 0-8371-0448-3, GOJ). Greenwood.

Gone the Golden Dream. pap. 3.95 (ISBN 0-87123-049-6, 210049). Bethany Fell.

Gonzalo De Tapia, 1561-1594: Founder of the First Permanent Jesuit Mission in North America. lib. bdg. 17.50x (ISBN 0-8371-7758-8, SHGT). Greenwood.

Good Christian Men. facsimile ed. 14.50 (ISBN 0-8369-2390-1). Arno.

Good Cops - Bad Cops: Memoirs of a Police Psychiatrist. 8.95 (ISBN 0 913374-69-5). SF Bk Co.

Good Evening Everybody: From Cripple Creek to Samarkand. 12.50 (ISBN 0-688-03068-8). Morrow.

Good Fight: The Life & Times of Ben B. Lindsey. 10.00 (ISBN 0-8129-0237-8). Times Bks.

Good Morning Judy! pap. 3.50 (ISBN 0-8066-1673-3, 10-2801). Augsburg.

Good Morning, Lord. pap. 2.95 (ISBN 0-8423-1120-3). Tyndale.

Good Old Boy. pap. 0.95 (ISBN 0-380-01229-4, 18077). Avon.

Good Old Boys. 7.95 (ISBN 0-671-21771-2). S&S.

Goodbye Lizzie Borden. 8.95 (ISBN 0-8289-0203-8). Greene.

Goon for Lunch. 7.95 (ISBN 0-312-34020-6). St Martin.

Gordon Lightfoot. pap. 4.95 (ISBN 0-8256-3148 3). Music Sales.

Gordon, the Sudan & Slavery. 13.75x (ISBN 0-8371-1764-X). Negro U Pr.

Gospel According to Billy. 8.95 (ISBN 0-8184-0251-2). Lyle Stuart.

Gospel Characters: The Personalities Around Jesus. pap. 3.95 (ISBN 0-8028-1646-0). Eerdmans.

Gotama Buddha. 7.95x (ISBN 0-914910-05-1); pap. 5.95x (ISBN 0-914910-06-X). Buddhist Bks.

Gotham Yankee: A Biography of William Cullen Bryant. 12.50 (ISBN 0-8462-1564-0). Russell.

Gottfried Wilhelm Leibniz. pap. 5.00. N Watson.

Gould's Millions. lib. bdg. 16.50x (ISBN 0-8371-6875-9, OCGM). Greenwood.

Gouverneur Morris. 15.00 (ISBN 0-404-50858-8). AMS Pr.

Gouverneur Morris. 14.00 (ISBN 0-403-00313-X). Scholarly.

Gouverneur Morris. lib. bdg. 22.95 (ISBN 0-8383-0274-2). Haskell.

Gouverneur Morris & the American Revolution. 14.50x (ISBN 0-8061-0900-9). U of Okla Pr.

Governor Charles Robinson of Kansas. 11.00x (ISBN 0-7006-0133-3). Regents Pr Ks.

Governor O. Max Gardner: A Power in North Carolina & New Deal Washington. 12.50 (ISBN 0-8078-1153-X). U of NC Pr.

Governor Takes a Bride: The Celebrated Marriage of Cora English & John R. Tanner, Governor of Illinois, 1897-1901. pap. 3.95x (ISBN 0-8093-0825-8). S Ill U Pr.

Governor Versus the Anaconda 1917-1934 see **Joseph M. Dixon of Montana.**

Governors of Alabama. 12.95 (ISBN 0-88289-067-0). Pelican.

Governors of Mississippi. 12.95 (ISBN 0-88289-237-1). Pelican.

Governors of Tennessee. 12.95 (ISBN 0-88289-169-3). Pelican.

Governors of Texas. 12.95 (ISBN 0-88289-078-6). Pelican.

Goya. 7.95 (ISBN 0-7148-1587-X). Dutton.

Gracchus Babeuf: The First Revolutionary Communist. 18.50x (ISBN 0-8047-0949-1). Stanford U Pr.

Graham Greene. lib. bdg. 8.50 (ISBN 0-8057-1240-2). Twayne.

Graham Taylor: Pioneer for Social Justice, 1851-1938. 10.50x (ISBN 0-226-86886-9). U of Chicago Pr.

Grand Prix Champions. 7.95 (ISBN 0-87880-014-X). Norton.

Grandmasters of Chess. 15.95. Norton.

Granny Brand, Her Story. 6.95 (ISBN 0-915684-11-X); pap. 3.50 (ISBN 0-915684-27-6). Christian Herald.

Grant & His Generals. facs. ed. 17.25 (ISBN 0-8369-2171-2). Arno.

Grant the Soldier. 7.95 (ISBN 0-87491-112-5). Acropolis.

Granville Sharp & the Freedom of Slaves in England. 8.50x (ISBN 0-8371-2420-4). Negro U Pr.

Grassroots: The Autobiography of George McGovern. 12.50 (ISBN 0-394-41941-3). Random.

Great Abnormals. 30.00 (ISBN 0-8495-6251-1). Arden Lib.
Great Abnormals. 16.50 (ISBN 0-8103-3797-5). Gale.
Great American Athletes of the Twentieth Century. 4.95 (ISBN 0-394-81554-8). Random.
Great American Catholics. pap. 3.50 (ISBN 0-87793-111-9). Ave Maria.
Great American Families. 15.95 (ISBN 0-393-08752-2). Norton.
Great American Foundresses. facs. ed. 17.50 (ISBN 0-8369-0319-6). Arno.
Great American Liberals. facsimile ed. 12.75 (ISBN 0-8369-2413-4). Arno.
Great American Naturalists. PLB 3.95 (ISBN 0-8225-0467-7). Lerner Pubns.
Great American Popular Singers. 9.95 (ISBN 0-671-21681-3). S&S.
Great American Yacht Designers. 15.00 (ISBN 0-394-42721-1). Knopf.
Great & the Near Great: A Century of Sports in Virginia. 14.95 (ISBN 0-915442-07-8). Donning Co.
Great Artists & Great Anatomists: A Biographical & Philosophical Study. 18.00 (ISBN 0-404-13291-X). AMS Pr.
Great Astronomers. 17.50. Ridgeway Bks.
Great Astronomers. 20.50 (ISBN 0-518-10142-8). Arno.
Great Astronomers. lib. bdg. 35.00 (ISBN 0-8414-9837-7). Folcroft.
Great Auto Racing Champions. PLB 4.78 (ISBN 0-8116-6666-2). Garrard.
Great Baseball Pitchers. 2.50 (ISBN 0-394-80183-0); PLB 3.69 (ISBN 0-394-90183-5). Random.
Great Baseball Stories. pap. 1.95 (ISBN 0-448-17018-3). G&D.
Great Biographers. facs. ed. 13.50 (ISBN 0-8369-1077-X). Arno.
Great Biologists. facs. ed. 12.75 (ISBN 0-8369-0935-6). Arno.
Great Black Americans. new ed. pap. 0.75 (ISBN 0-88301-107-7). Pendulum Pr.
Great Book Collectors. lib. bdg. 44.75 (ISBN 0-8490-1898-6). Gordon Pr.
Great Book-Collectors. 12.50 (ISBN 0-8274-2439-6). R West.
Great Composers & Their Work. facsimile ed. 16.75 (ISBN 0-8369-2545-9). Arno.
Great Composers & Their Work. lib. bdg. 30.00 (ISBN 0-89341-423-9). Longwood Pr.
Great Conductors. pap. 3.95 (ISBN 0-671-20735-0). S&S.
Great Conductors. 2nd ed. 9.95 (ISBN 0-671-20834-9). S&S.
Great Contemporaries. 7.95x (ISBN 0-226-10630-6). U of Chicago Pr.
Great Contemporaries. facsimile ed. 18.50 (ISBN 0-8369-2309-X). Arno.
Great Contemporaries. pap. 4.95 (ISBN 0-226-10631-4, P692). U of Chicago Pr.
Great Days in the Rockies: The Photographs of Byron Harmon 1906-1934. 15.95 (ISBN 0-19-540288-X). Oxford U Pr.
Great Democrats. facs. ed. 26.25 (ISBN 0-8369-1942-4). Arno.
Great Dissenters. pap. 3.95 (ISBN 0-393-00529-1). Norton.
Great Dr. Burney: His Life, His Travels, His Works, His Family & His Friends. 29.95 (ISBN 0-8274-1098-0). R West.
Great Dr. Burney: His Life, His Travels, His Works, His Family & His Friends. lib. bdg. 35.50x (ISBN 0-8371-4017-X, SCDB). Greenwood.
Great Doctors: A Biographical History of Medicine. facsimile ed. 27.25 (ISBN 0-8369-2297-2). Arno.
Great Doctors of the Nineteenth Century. 14.75 (ISBN 0-8369-1575-5). Arno.
Great Economists in Their Times. pap. 1.75 (ISBN 0-8226-0056-0). Littlefield.
Great Educators of Three Centuries: Their Work & Its Influence on Modern Education. 17.50 (ISBN 0-404-02891-8). AMS Pr.
Great Educators: Readings for Leaders in Education. 16.95x (ISBN 0-911012-48-6). Nelson-Hall.
Great Engineers. facs. ed. 10.50 (ISBN 0-8369-0515-6). Arno.
Great Engineers. 20.50 (ISBN 0-8369-1837-1). Arno.
Great Englishmen of the Sixteenth Century. 17.25 (ISBN 0-8369-1885-1). Arno.
Great Englishmen of the Sixteenth Century. 14.50 (ISBN 0-8274-2442-6). R West.
Great Englishmen of the Sixteenth Century. 13.50 (ISBN 0-8046-1655-8). Kennikat.
Great Englishmen of the Sixteenth Century. lib. bdg. 25.00 (ISBN 0-8495-3213-2). Arden Lib.
Great Escaper. PLB 7.32 (ISBN 0-8393-0152-9). Raintree Child.
Great Explorers. lib. bdg. 19.95 (ISBN 0-87196-411-2). Facts on File.
Great Film Directors: A Critical Anthology. pap. text ed. 7.95x (ISBN 0-19-502312-9). Oxford U Pr.
Great Flower Painters: Four Centuries of Floral Art. 35.00 (ISBN 0-87951-008-0). Overlook Pr.
Great Fortunes & How They Were Made: Or, the Struggles & Triumphs of Our Selfmade Men. facsimile ed. 31.00 (ISBN 0-8369-6732-1). Arno.
Great Gamble. 12.50 (ISBN 0-671-21404-7). S&S.
Great Games by Chess Prodigies. 5.95 (ISBN 0-02-601970-1). Macmillan.
Great Games by Chess Prodigies. pap. 2.95 (ISBN 0-02-029710-6). Macmillan.
Great Goalies. PLB 7.50 (ISBN 0-87191-491-3). Creative Ed.
Great Goalies of Pro Hockey. 2.50 (ISBN 0-394-82539-X); PLB 3.69 (ISBN 0-394-92539-4). Random.
Great Goldwyn. lib. bdg. 15.00x (ISBN 0-405-11133-9). Arno.
Great Golfers. PLB 4.97 (ISBN 0-399-60211-9). Putnam.
Great Governing Families of England. facsimile ed. 37.00 (ISBN 0-8369-2623-4). Arno.
Great Gunfighters of the Kansas Cowtowns, 1867-1886. 16.95x (ISBN 0-8032-0123-0); pap. 4.50 (ISBN 0-8032-5137-8, 333). U of Nebr Pr.
Great Gunfighters of the West. pap. 1.50 (ISBN 0-451-07434-3, W7434). NAL.
Great Hitters of the Major Leagues. 2.50 (ISBN 0-394-80180-6). Random.
Great Hitters of the Major Leagues. PLB 3.69 (ISBN 0-394-90180-0). Random.
Great Hoaxes & Famous Imposters. 9.95 (ISBN 0-8246-0200-5). Jonathan David.
Great Houdini. new ed. PLB 4.29 (ISBN 0-399-61020-0). Putnam.
Great Immigrants. lib. bdg. 8.95 (ISBN 0-8057-3222-5). Twayne.
Great Indian Chiefs. 5.95g (ISBN 0-02-777650-6). Macmillan.
Great Infielders of the Major Leagues. PLB 3.69 (ISBN 0-394-92383-9). Random.
Great Italian & French Composers. lib. bdg. 37.95 (ISBN 0-8490-1899-4). Gordon Pr.
Great Jazz Artists. 7.95g (ISBN 0-590-07493-8). Schol Bk Serv.
Great Jewish Personalities in Ancient & Medieval Times. pap. 4.95. B'nai B'rith.
Great Jurists of the World. 22.50x (ISBN 0-678-04503-8). Kelley.
Great Kids of the Movies. 6.95 (ISBN 0-385-14127-0); PLB (ISBN 0-385-14128-9). Doubleday.
Great Latin Sports Figures: The Proud People. 5.95 (ISBN 0-385-11117-7); PLB (ISBN 0-385-12060-5). Doubleday.
Great Leaders in Human Progress. facs. ed. 10.50 (ISBN 0-8369-1135-0). Arno.
Great Leaders of the Book of Mormon. 8.95. Promised Land.
Great Linebackers of the NFL. 2.50 (ISBN 0-394-80152-0); PLB 3.69 (ISBN 0-394-90152-5). Random.
Great Mathematicians. 7.95x (ISBN 0-8147-0419-0). NYU Pr.
Great Men As Prophets of a New Era. 12.50 (ISBN 0-8274-2445-0). R West.
Great Men As Prophets of a New Era. facs. ed. 10.50 (ISBN 0-8369-0541-5). Arno.
Great Men: Being Short Impressions of X, H. H. Almond, W. A. Smith, A. H. Stanton, Kingsley Fairbridge, Alexander Paterson. 8.00 (ISBN 0-8369-8035-2). Arno.
Great Men of Modern Agriculture. 5.50g (ISBN 0-02-716460-8). Macmillan.
Great Men of Science. PLB 6.90 s&l (ISBN 0-531-09150-3). Watts.
Great Men of Science: A History of Scientific Progress. lib. bdg. 40.00 (ISBN 0-89987-500-9). Darby Bks.
Great Men of the Christian Church. facs. ed. 18.25 (ISBN 0-8369-0966-6). Arno.
Great Missionaries of the Church. facsimile ed. 18.75 (ISBN 0-8369-2541-6). Arno.
Great Missionaries to China. 12.75 (ISBN 0-8369-8124-3). Arno.
Great Missionaries to the Orient. 12.75 (ISBN 0-8369-8125-1). Arno.
Great Morning. lib. bdg. 17.50x (ISBN 0-8371-6162-2, SIGM). Greenwood.
Great Movie Heroes. pap. 1.95 (ISBN 0-06-465039-1). B&N.
Great Negroes, Past & Present. 3rd rev. ed. 11.95 (ISBN 0-910030-07-3); pap. text ed. 7.95 (ISBN 0-910030-08-1); 9 portfolios of display prints 9.95 ea. Afro-Am.
Great North American Indians: Profiles in Life & Leadership. 17.95 (ISBN 0-442-02148-8). Van Nos Reinhold.
Great Pass Receivers of the NFL. 2.50 (ISBN 0-394-80196-2). Random.
Great Physicists. 10.25 (ISBN 0-8369-1656-5). Arno.
Great Pianists. pap. 4.45 (ISBN 0-671-28999-3). S&S.
Great Piano Virtuosos of Our Time. lib. bdg. 11.50 (ISBN 0-306-70528-1). Da Capo.
Great Plains Command: William B. Hazen in the Frontier West. 9.95 (ISBN 0-8061-1318-9). U of Okla Pr.
Great Quarterbacks of the NFL. PLB 3.69 (ISBN 0-394-90192-4). Random.
Great Road: The Life & Times of Chu Teh. pap. 6.95 (ISBN 0-85345-206-7, PB-2067). Monthly Rev.
Great Running Backs of the NFL. 2.50 (ISBN 0-394-80195-4). Random.
Great Singers of Today. lib. bdg. 16.00x (ISBN 0-405-09704-2). Arno.
Great Slave Narratives. pap. 4.95x (ISBN 0-8070-5473-9, BP331). Beacon Pr.
Great Soldiers of the Two World Wars. facs. ed. 18.25 (ISBN 0-8369-1032-X). Arno.
Great South African Christians. lib. bdg. 11.00x (ISBN 0-8371-3916-3, DAGC). Greenwood.
Great South Carolinians. 21.25 (ISBN 0-8369-1658-1). Arno.
Great Sports Feats of the 70's. PLB 7.79 (ISBN 0-671-32954-5). Messner.
Great Tone-Poets: Being Short Memoirs of the Greater Musical Composers. facsimile ed. 18.25 (ISBN 0-8369-2641-2). Arno.
Great Tudors. lib. bdg. 50.00. Arden Lib.
Great Tudors. lib. bdg. 40.00 (ISBN 0-8414-4503-6). Folcroft.
Great Upon the Mountain: The Story of Crazy Horse, Legendary Mystic & Warrior. 5.95 (ISBN 0-02-517350-2, 51735). Macmillan.
Great Victorians. 9.95 (ISBN 0-8274-0596-0). R West.
Great Victorians. facsimile ed. 13.75 (ISBN 0-8369-2284-0). Arno.
Great Victorians: Memories & Personalities. lib. bdg. 30.00. Folcroft.
Great Violinists & Pianists. 16.75 (ISBN 0-8369-7257-0). Arno.
Great Women. 14.95 (ISBN 0-89479-056-0). A & W Pubs.
Great Women of the Christian Faith. pap. text ed. 4.95 (ISBN 0-06-061849-3, RD 163). Har-Row.
Great Women-Singers of My Time. facs. ed. 13.50 (ISBN 0-8369-0601-2). Arno.
Great Yorkshiremen. facs. ed. 15.25 (ISBN 0-8369-2054-6). Arno.
Greatest American Leaguers. PLB 5.29 (ISBN 0-399-60205-4). Putnam.
Greatest American Woman, Lucretia Mott. lib. bdg. 13.25x (ISBN 0-8371-3593-1, HLM&). Greenwood.
Greatest: My Own Story. 10.95 (ISBN 0-394-46268-8). Random.
Greatest: My Own Story. pap. 2.25 (ISBN 0-345-27585-3). Ballantine.
Greatest Thinkers. 15.95 (ISBN 0-399-11762-8). Putnam.
Greatness of Woodrow Wilson 1856-1956. 10.50 (ISBN 0-8046-1395-8). Kennikat.
Greek Fathers. 5.95x (ISBN 0-8154-0046-2). Cooper Sq.
Greek Leaders. facs. ed. 13.75 (ISBN 0-8369-0017-0). Arno.
Green Memories: The Story of Geddes Mumford. lib. bdg. 17.50x (ISBN 0-8371-6892-9, MUGM). Greenwood.
Green Mount After the War: The Correspondence of Maria Louisa Wacker Fleet & Her Family, 1865-1900. 12.50x (ISBN 0-8139-0730-6). U Pr of Va.
Greenhorn: A Twentieth-Century Childhood. 7.00 (ISBN 0-7100-7570-7). Routledge & Kegan.
Gregor Mendel. 3.95 (ISBN 0-8037-3243-0); PLB 3.69 (ISBN 0-8037-3244-9). Dial.
Gregor Mendel: Father of the Science of Genetics. 5.95 (ISBN 0-8149-0409-2). Vanguard.
Gregory Peck. pap. 1.75 (ISBN 0-515-04239-0). HarBraceJ.
Grey Eminence. lib. bdg. 19.00x (ISBN 0-8371-7508-9, HUGE). Greenwood.
Grey Wolf: Mustafa Kemal: An Intimate Study of a Dictator. 18.00 (ISBN 0-8369-6962-6). Arno.
Griffith & the Rise of Hollywood. pap. 3.50 (ISBN 0-498-07718-7). A S Barnes.
Grinding It Out: The Making of McDonald's. 9.95 (ISBN 0-8092-8259-3). Contemp Bks.
Grinding It Out: The Making of McDonald's. pap. 1.95 (ISBN 0-425-03842-4). Berkley Pub.
Gringo Lawyer. 5.00 (ISBN 0-8130-0175-7). U Presses Fla.
Groat: I Hit & Ran. 7.95 (ISBN 0-87716-094-5). Moore Pub Co.
Groucho & Me. pap. 1.95 (ISBN 0-532-19165-X). Manor Bks.
Ground Under Our Feet: An Autobiography. lib. bdg. 20.00x (ISBN 0-405-10011-6). Arno.
Group of Comedians. lib. bdg. 16.50 (ISBN 0-8337-1903-3). B Franklin.
Grover Cleveland. 6.95 (ISBN 0-02-620330-8). Macmillan.
Growing a Soul: The Story of A. Frank Smith. 15.00 (ISBN 0-87074-171-3). SMU Press.
Growing: An Autobiography of the Years 1904 to 1911. pap. 3.45 (ISBN 0-15-637215-0, HB320). HarBraceJ.
Growing Older. 7.95 (ISBN 0-525-31050-9). Dutton.
Growing up at Grossinger's. 8.95 (ISBN 0-679-50570-9). McKay.
Growing up Black. pap. 1.50 (ISBN 0-671-80177-5). PB.
Growing up Black. pap. 2.45 (ISBN 0-671-20521-8). S&S.
Growing up in Hollywood. 10.00 (ISBN 0-15-137473-2). HarBraceJ.
Growing up in Hollywood. pap. 3.95 (ISBN 0-15-637315-7). HarBraceJ.
Growing up Is a Family Affair. pap. 6.95 (ISBN 0-8024-3357-X). Moody.
Growing up on Bald Hill Creek. 6.95 (ISBN 0-8138-0080-3, 0080-3). Iowa St U Pr.
Growing up Puerto Rican. 6.95 (ISBN 0-87795-033-4, A4319). Arbor Hse.
Growing up Puerto Rican. pap. 1.25 (ISBN 0-451-61233-7, MY1233). NAL.
Growing Up Yanqui. 6.95 (ISBN 0-670-35597-6). Viking Pr.
Guardians of the Hearth: Utah's Pioneer Midwives & Women Doctors. 4.95 (ISBN 0-88290-030-7). Horizon Utah.
Guardians of Tomorrow: Pioneers in Ecology. 4.95 (ISBN 0-670-35646-8). Viking Pr.
Guards. PLB 7.50 (ISBN 0-87191-564-2). Creative Ed.
Guessing at Truth: The Life of Julius Charles Hare 1795-1855. 19.95 (ISBN 0-915762-07-2). Patmos Pr.
Guests of My Life. 9.00 (ISBN 0-914064-12-6); pap. 6.50 (ISBN 0-914064-13-4). Celo Pr.
Guggenheims: An American Epic. 14.95 (ISBN 0-688-03273-7). Morrow.
Guggenheims: An American Epic. pap. 6.95 (ISBN 0-688-08273-4). Morrow.
Guggenheims: The Making of an American Dynasty. 30.00x (ISBN 0-405-09292-X). Arno.
Guide to American Biography. lib. bdg. 21.50x (ISBN 0-8371-7134-2, DAAB). Greenwood.
Guide to Jazz. lib. bdg. 18.50x (ISBN 0-8371-6766-3, PAGJ). Greenwood.
Guideposts Treasury of Hope. 8.95 (ISBN 0-385-14975-1). Doubleday.
Guides, Philosophers & Friends: Studies of College Men. facsimile ed. 20.50 (ISBN 0-8369-2445-2). Arno.
Guillaume De Machaut. lib. bdg. 12.50 (ISBN 0-306-71831-6). Da Capo.
Guillaume De Machaut. pap. 8.95x (ISBN 0-19-315218-5). Oxford U Pr.
Guitar & Mandolin: Biographies of Celebrated Players & Composers. 39.00 (ISBN 0-403-01349-6). Scholarly.
Guitar Heroes. 8.95 (ISBN 0-312-35320-0). St Martin.
Gulf of Years: Letters from John Ruskin to Kathleen Olander. lib. bdg. 12.25x (ISBN 0-313-20188-9, RUGY). Greenwood.
Gulliveriana. 34.95 (ISBN 0-8490-0274-5). Gordon Pr.
Gunfighters. 12.95 (ISBN 0-87004-207-6). Caxton.
Gurdjieff. pap. 5.95 (ISBN 0-87728-178-5). Weiser.
Gurdjieff: His Work on Myself... with Others... for the Work. rev ed. pap. 5.95 (ISBN 0-87728-417-2). Weiser.
Gurdjieff: Making a New World. pap. 4.95 (ISBN 0-06-090474-7, CN474). Har-Row.
Guru Tegh Bahadur: A Biography. 11.50x (ISBN 0-88386-725-7). South Asia Bks.
Gustav Holst, a Biography. 2nd ed. 23.50x (ISBN 0-19-315417-X). Oxford U Pr.
Gustav Holst,1874-1934: A Centenary Documentation. 45.00x (ISBN 0-8476-1219-8). Rowman.
Gustav Klimt. 37.50 (ISBN 0-8212-0452-1). NYGS.
Gustav Mahler. pap. 15.00x (ISBN 0-8443-0035-7). Vienna Hse.
Gustav Mahler. lib. bdg. 12.50 (ISBN 0-306-71701-8). Da Capo.
Gustave Courbet. lib. bdg. 24.00x (ISBN 0-8371-2588-X, MAGC). Greenwood.
Gustave Flaubert. pap. 8.50 (ISBN 0-8057-2312-9). Twayne.
Gustave Flaubert As Seen in His Works & Correspondence. 25.00 (ISBN 0-8274-2456-6). R West.
Gustave Moreau. 5.95 (ISBN 0-517-53449-5). Crown.
Gymnastics Guide. pap. 6.95 (ISBN 0-89037-139-3). World Pubns.
Gypsy in My Soul: The Autobiography of Jose Greco. 10.00 (ISBN 0-385-11504-0). Doubleday.
Gyro! The Life & Times of Lawrence Sperry. 12.95 (ISBN 0-684-15793-4). Scribner.

H

H. G. J. Moseley: The Life & Letters of an English Physicist, 1887-1915. 20.00x (ISBN 0-520-02375-7). U of Cal Pr.

H. G. Wells. lib. bdg. 12.50 (ISBN 0-8414-1434-3). Folcroft.

H. G. Wells: A Biography. 13.50 (ISBN 0-8369-5547-1). Arno.

H. G. Wells: A Biography. lib. bdg. 20.00 (ISBN 0-8492-3743-2). R West.

H. G. Wells, a Biography. lib. bdg. 12.25x (ISBN 0-8371-3827-2, BRHW). Greenwood.

H. G. Wells & Rebecca West. 12.50x (ISBN 0-300-01753-7). Yale U Pr.

H. H. Stevens. 9.50x (ISBN 0-8020-3339-3). U of Toronto Pr.

H. L. Mencken. 10.00 (ISBN 0-8414-9860-1). Folcroft.

H. L. Mencken. lib. bdg. 7.50 (ISBN 0-8414-2585-X). Folcroft.

H. M. Daugherty & the Politics of Expediency. 15.00x (ISBN 0-87338-215-3). Kent St U Pr.

H. Richard Niebuhr. 7.95 (ISBN 0-8499-0078-6, 0078-6). Word Bks.

H. Rider Haggard: A Voice from the Infinite. 19.50 (ISBN 0-7100-0026-X). Routledge & Kegan.

Habit of Being: Letters. 15.00 (ISBN 0-374-16769-9). FS&G.

Hadrian. lib. bdg. 15.75x (ISBN 0-8371-8723-0, PEHAD). Greenwood.

Haile Selassie I: Ethiopia's Lion of Judah. 13.95 (ISBN 0-88229-342-7). Nelson-Hall.

Hall Jackson & the Purple Foxglove: Medical Practice & Research in Revolutionary America, 1760-1820. text ed. 15.00x (ISBN 0-87451-173-9). U Pr of New Eng.

Halldor Hermannsson. 20.00x (ISBN 0-8014-1085-1). Cornell U Pr.

Hallelujah Hole: The Story of a Frontier Preacher. 6.95 (ISBN 0-8170-0709-1); pap. 3.95 (ISBN 0-8170-0750-4). Judson.

Hallowed Flame. 5.75 (ISBN 0-911536-31-0). Trinity U Pr.

Hamada, Potter. 55.00 (ISBN 0-87011-252-X). Kodansha.

Hamilton Holt: Journalist, Internationalist, Educator. 9.00 (ISBN 0-8130-0137-4). U Presses Fla.

Hamlin Garland: A Biography. facsimile ed. 19.50 (ISBN 0-8369-5802-0). Arno.

Hammarskjold. 12.50 (ISBN 0-394-47960-2). Knopf.

Hancock the Superb. 15.00. Pr of Morningside.

Hand Upon the Time: A Life of Charles Dickens. PLB 5.99 (ISBN 0-394-91258-6). Pantheon.

Handbook of Audubon Prints. pap. 9.95 (ISBN 0-88289-202-9). Pelican.

Handbook of Austrian Literature. 13.50 (ISBN 0-8044-2929-4). Ungar.

Handbook of Soviet Musicians. lib. bdg. 9.25x (ISBN 0-8371-4764-6, BOSM). Greenwood.

Handbook of Soviet Musicians. 12.00 (ISBN 0 403-01348-8). Scholarly.

Handel. lib. bdg. 10.95 (ISBN 0-8383-1250-0). Haskell.

Handel. rev. ed. pap. 1.50 (ISBN 0-02-061980-4). Macmillan.

Handel. 9.95x (ISBN 0-460-03161-9). Biblio Dist.

Handel. rev. ed. pap. 4.95 (ISBN 0-8226-0712-3). Littlefield.

Handel. 3.50 (ISBN 0-87250-213-9); PLB 3.27 (ISBN 0-87250-413-1). D White.

Handel: A Biography, with a Survey of Books, Editions & Recordings. 8.50 (ISBN 0-208-01068-8). Shoe String.

Handel: A Documentary Biography. lib. bdg. 42.50 (ISBN 0-306-70624-5). Da Capo.

Handel & the Opera Seria. 22.75x (ISBN 0-520-01438-3). U of Cal Pr.

Handicaps: Six Studies. facs. ed. 12.75 (ISBN 0-8369-0642-X). Arno.

Hank Aaron. PLB 4.49 (ISBN 0-399-60904-0). Putnam.

Hank Williams. PLB 5.95 (ISBN 0-8225-1402-8). Lerner Pubns.

Hanna. lib. bdg. 16.50 (ISBN 0-374-90518-5). Octagon.

Hannah More. lib. bdg. 25.00 (ISBN 0-8414-9751-6). Folcroft.

Hannah Senesh - Her Life & Diary. pap. 6.95x (ISBN 0-8052-3443-8); pap. 4.95 (ISBN 0-8052-0410-5). Schocken.

Hannah's Daughters: Six Generations of an American Family. 10.95 (ISBN 0-690-01103-2). T Y Crowell.

Hannis Taylor: The New Southerner As an American. 11.75. U of Ala Pr.

Hans Andersen the Man. 12.00 (ISBN 0-8103-3902-1). Gale.

Hans Andersen the Man. 9.50 (ISBN 0-8274-2465-5). R West.

Hans Christian Andersen & His World. 6.95 (ISBN 0-399-11070-4). Putnam.

Hans Rookmaaker: A Biography. pap. 4.95 (ISBN 0-87784-725-8). Inter-Varsity.

Hanya Holm: The Biography of an Artist. pap. 7.50 (ISBN 0-8195-6060-X). Columbia U Pr.

Happily Ever After: A Portrait of Frances Hodgson Burnett. 5.95 (ISBN 0-8149-0283-9). Vanguard.

Happy Profession. lib. bdg. 16.00x (ISBN 0-8371-6039-1, SEHP). Greenwood.

Happy Times in Norway. lib. bdg. 18.75x (ISBN 0-313-21267-8, UNHT). Greenwood.

Harley Granville Barker: Man of the Theatre, Dramatist & Scholar. 17.00 (ISBN 0-8274-4025-1). R West.

Harley Granville Barker Man of the Theatre, Dramatist & Scholar. lib. bdg. 17.25x (ISBN 0-8371-6155-X, PUGB). Greenwood.

Harmony from Discords: A Life of Sir John Denham. 16.00x (ISBN 0-520-00953-3). U of Cal Pr.

Harold Adams Innis: Portrait of a Scholar. pap. 4.95 (ISBN 0-8020-6329-2). U of Toronto Pr.

Harold Lloyd: The King of Daredevil Comedy. 14.95 (ISBN 0-02-601940-X). Macmillan.

Harold Lloyd: The King of Daredevil Comedy. pap. 9.95 (ISBN 0-02-036350-8). Macmillan.

Harold Martin Remembers a Place in the Mountains. 10.95 (ISBN 0-931948-03-7). Peachtree Pubs.

Harold Monro & the Poetry Bookshop. 15.00x (ISBN 0-520-00512-0). U of Cal Pr.

Harp That Once: A Chronicle of the Life of Thomas Moore. 15.00 (ISBN 0-8462-1498-9). Russell.

Harriet & the Runaway Book: The Story of Harriet Beecher Stowe & Uncle Tom's Cabin. PLB 5.79 (ISBN 0-06-022840-7). Har-Row.

Harriet Beecher Stowe & American Literature. pap. text ed. 4.00 (ISBN 0-917482-15-8). Stowe-Day.

Harriet Martineau. 9.00 (ISBN 0-8274-1333-5). R West.

Harriet Martineau. 9.25 (ISBN 0-8046-1604-3). Kennikat.

Harriet Martineau. lib. bdg. 25.00 (ISBN 0-8495-3840-8). Arden Lib.

Harriet Monroe & the Poetry Renaissance: The First Ten Years of Poetry, 1912-22. 10.95 (ISBN 0-252-00478-7). U of Ill Pr.

Harriet Shelley: Five Long Years. lib. bdg. 20.00x (ISBN 0-313-21143-4, BOHF). Greenwood.

Harriet Tubman. pap. 2.45 (ISBN 0-8065-0415-3). Citadel Pr.

Harry Anderson: The Man Behind the Paintings. 5.95. Review & Herald.

Harry Bertoia, Sculptor. 15.95x (ISBN 0-8143-1402-3). Wayne St U Pr.

Harry Elmer Barnes, Learned Crusader: The New History in Action. 10.00 (ISBN 0-87926 002-5). R Myles

Harry Four Eyes. PLB 6.65 (ISBN 0-8172-0453-9). Raintree Pubs.

Harry H. Woodring: A Political Biography of FDR's Controversial Secretary of War. 12.50x (ISBN 0-7006-0130-9). Regents Pr Ks.

Harry Hopkins: A Biography. 15.00 (ISBN 0-399-11833-0). Putnam.

Harry Houdini, Master of Magic. pap. 0.95 (ISBN 0-590-05374-4). Schol Bk Serv.

Harry S. Truman. 10.95 (ISBN 0-688-00005-3). Morrow.

Harry S. Truman. pap. 1.95 (ISBN 0-671-81216-5). PB.

Harry S. Truman: People's President. PLB 4.48 (ISBN 0-8116-6318-3). Garrard.

Harry Somers. 17.50x (ISBN 0-8020-5325-4). U of Toronto Pr.

Harry Stack Sullivan: His Life & His Work. 8.95 (ISBN 0-399-11734-2). Putnam.

Harry Truman. 6.79 (ISBN 0-200-71906-8, B32230). Abelard.

Harry Warren & the Hollywood Musical. 17.95 (ISBN 0-8065-0468-4). Citadel Pr.

Harry Woodburn Chase. 3.00x (ISBN 0-8078-0785-0). U of NC Pr.

Harsh & Dreadful Love: Dorothy Day & the Catholic Worker Movement. 9.95 (ISBN 0-87140-558-X). Liveright.

Hart Crane: A Biographical & Critical Study. 18.00 (ISBN 0-8462-1223-4). Russell.

Hart Crane & Yvor Winters: Their Literary Correspondence. 11.95 (ISBN 0-520-03538-0). U of Cal Pr.

Hart Crane: The Life of an American Poet. lib. bdg. 16.00 (ISBN 0-374-93958-6). Octagon.

Hartley Coleridge Letters: A Calendar & Index. 18.50 (ISBN 0-87959-078-5). U of Tex Hum Res.

Hart's Bridge. 12.50 (ISBN 0-252-00257-1). U of Ill Pr.

Harvest of Salmon: Adventures in Fishing the B.C. Coast. 9.95 (ISBN 0-919654-75-4). Hancock Hse.

Harvest of Yesterdays. 7.95 (ISBN 0-397-01133-4). Lippincott.

Harvesters. facsimile ed. 15.75 (ISBN 0-8369-2295-6). Arno.

Hasty Pudding & Barbary Pirates: A Life of Joel Barlow. 5.95 (ISBN 0-664-32559-9, *F11VS). Westminster.

Hawthorne. 18.00 (ISBN 0-8462-0110-0). Russell.

Hawthorne. pap. 4.95. British Am Bks.

Hawthorne. lib. bdg. 15.00. Folcroft.

Hawthorne. 12.50 (ISBN 0-404-51715-3). AMS Pr.

Hawthorne. pap. 11.50x (ISBN 0-8014-0203-4). Cornell U Pr.

Hawthorne. 29.95 (ISBN 0-8490-1935-4). Gordon Pr.

Hawthorne's Son: The Life & Literary Career of Julian Hawthorne. 10.00 (ISBN 0-8142-0003-6). Ohio St U Pr.

Haydn. rev. ed. 7.95x (ISBN 0-460-03160-0). Biblio Dist.

Haydn. rev. ed. pap. 7.50 (ISBN 0-8226-0713-1). Littlefield.

Haydn: A Biography, with a Survey of Books, Editions & Recordings. 8.50 (ISBN 0-208-00886-1). Shoe String.

Haydn: A Creative Life in Music. 17.75x (ISBN 0-520-00460-4); pap. 4.95x (ISBN 0-520-00461-2, CAL143). U of Cal Pr.

Haydn: Chronicle & Works. Incl. Hayden at Eszterhaza 1766-1790. 57.50x (ISBN 0-253-37002-7); Hayden in England 1791-1795. 45.00x (ISBN 0-253-37003-5); "The Years of Creation" 1796-1800. 45.00x (ISBN 0-253-37004-3); The Late Years 1800-1809. 45.00x (ISBN 0-253-37005-1). Ind U Pr.

Haywire. 10.00 (ISBN 0-394-49325-7). Knopf.

Haywire. pap. 2.50 (ISBN 0-553-11256-2). Bantam.

He Freed Britains Slaves. 5.95 (ISBN 0-8361-1822-7). Herald Pr.

He Gave Himself to the Sea. PLB 7.99 (ISBN 0-8172-1561-1). Raintree Pubs.

He Saw a Hummingbird. 8.95 (ISBN 0-525-12225-7). Dutton.

He Saw a Hummingbird. lib. bdg. 9.95 (ISBN 0-8161-6726-5). G K Hall.

He Sets the Captive Free. 4.95 (ISBN 0-8007-0929-2). Revell.

Headman & I: Ambiguity & Ambivalence in the Fieldworking Experience. text ed. 12.95x (ISBN 0-292-73007-1). U of Tex Pr.

Heads of Religious Houses, England & Wales, 940-1216. 33.95 (ISBN 0-521-08367-2). Cambridge U Pr.

Healed of Cancer. pap. 2.50 (ISBN 0-88270-251-3). Logos.

Healing Power of the Bible. 6.95 (ISBN 0-397-10103-1). Lippincott.

Healing Power of the Bible. pap. 1.95 (ISBN 0-87981-059-9). Holman.

Healing Power of the Bible. pap. 1.75 (ISBN 0-89129-192-X). Pillar Bks.

Healing Touch. 5.95 (ISBN 0-8008-3818-1). Taplinger.

Hear My Confession. rev. ed. pap. 3.95 (ISBN 0-88270-231-9). Logos.

Hearing His Voice. pap. 3.50 (ISBN 0-87793-187-9). Ave Maria.

Heart Beat: My Life with Jack & Neal. pap. 4.00 (ISBN 0-916870-03-0). Creative Arts Bk.

Heart Is Like Heaven: The Life of Lydia Maria Child. 10.00x (ISBN 0-8122-7442-3). U of Pa Pr.

Heart That Would Not Hold: A Biography of Washington Irving. 7.95 (ISBN 0-87131-057-0). M Evans.

Heartsounds. 9.95 (ISBN 0-671-24329-2). S&S.

Heaven's Hall of Heroes. pap. 3.95 (ISBN 0-87227-062-9). Reg Baptist.

Hector Berlioz. 4.95g (ISBN 0-02-781910-8). Macmillan.

Hector Berlioz. 18.50 (ISBN 0-384-69310-5). Johnson Repr.

Hector Berlioz. facsimile ed. 14.00 (ISBN 0-8369-5306-1). Arno.

Hector Berlioz: Selections from His Letters, and Aesthetic, Humorous & Satirical Writings. lib. bdg. 40.00 (ISBN 0-89341-018-7). Longwood Pr.

Hefner. 8.95 (ISBN 0-02-514600-9). Macmillan.

Hegel. 14.50 (ISBN 0-404-01362-7). AMS Pr.

Hegel. 47.50 (ISBN 0-521-20679-0); pap. 11.95 (ISBN 0-521-29199-2). Cambridge U Pr.

Hegel: A Re-Examination. pap. 3.95 (ISBN 0-19-519879-4, 473). Oxford U Pr.

Hegel: A Re-Examination. text ed. 16.50x (ISBN 0-391-00893-5). Humanities.

Hegel As Educator. 7.50 (ISBN 0-404-04068-3). AMS Pr.

Heinrich Heine: The Artist in Revolt. lib. bdg. 21.50x (ISBN 0-8371-8992-6, BRHA). Greenwood.

Heinrich Von Treitschke. 16.00 (ISBN 0-8046-1693-0). Kennikat.

Heiress: The Rich Life of Marjorie Merriweather Post. 12.50 (ISBN 0-915220-36-9, 24152). New Republic.

Helen Hunt Jackson. 5.95 (ISBN 0-8149-0735-0). Vanguard.

Helen Keller Story. 8.95 (ISBN 0-690-37520-4). T Y Crowell.

Hellenistic Queens: A Study of Woman-Power in Macedonia, Seleucid Syria, & Ptolemaic Egypt. 17.50 (ISBN 0-404-14683-X). AMS Pr.

Hello, I Must Be Going: Groucho & His Friends. pap. 4.95 (ISBN 0-14-005222-4). Penguin.

Helmet of Navarre. 4.95 (ISBN 0-02-792990-6). Macmillan.

Helter Shelter. 8.95 (ISBN 0-397-01334-5). Lippincott.

Hemingway: High on the Wild. 5.95 (ISBN 0-448-14290-2). G&D.

Henri Bergson. 12.50 (ISBN 0-404-01488-7). AMS Pr.

Henri Bergson. facsimile ed. 18.75 (ISBN 0-8369-5179-4). Arno.

Henri De Toulouse-Lautrec. 6.95 (ISBN 0-385-04942-0); PLB (ISBN 0-385-07206-6). Doubleday.

Henri Rousseau. 6.95 (ISBN 0-385-04932-3); PLB (ISBN 0-385-07182-5). Doubleday.

Henrietta Maria, Queen of the Cavaliers. 12.00 (ISBN 0-252-00198-2). U of Ill Pr.

Henrik Ibsen. 10.50 (ISBN 0-8044-2616-3). Ungar.

Henrik Ibsen: A Critical Biography. lib. bdg. 23.95 (ISBN 0-8383-1414-7). Haskell.

Henrik Ibsen: A Critical Biography. 15.00 (ISBN 0-405-08664-4). Arno.

Henrik Ibsen: A Critical Biography. 11.75 (ISBN 0-8274-0016-0). R West.

Henrik Ibsen: A Study in Art and Personality. lib. bdg. 31.75x (ISBN 0-313-20209-5, JOHE). Greenwood.

Henrik Pontoppidan. lib. bdg. 13.95 (ISBN 0-8057-6366-X). Twayne.

Henrik Pontoppidan. lib. bdg. 13.95 (ISBN 0-8057-6366-X). G K Hall.

Henry Aaron: Quiet Superstar. rev. ed. PLB 5.29 (ISBN 0-399-60915-6). Putnam.

Henry Adams: A Biography. lib. bdg. 20.00 (ISBN 0-374-97624-4). Octagon.

Henry Adams: Scientific Historian. 17.50 (ISBN 0-208-00828-4). Shoe String.

Henry Alline (1748-1784) 4.50x (ISBN 0-8020-3247-8). U of Toronto Pr.

Henry Barnard. 7.50 (ISBN 0-8057-7710-5). Twayne.

Henry Burney: A Political Biography. 16.00x (ISBN 0-19-713583-8). Oxford U Pr.

Henry Cabot Lodge: A Biography. 8.50. Heineman.

Henry Clay. 29.50 (ISBN 0-404-50891-X); 15.00 ea. (ISBN 0-404-50869-3) (ISBN 0-404-50870-7). AMS Pr.

Henry Clay & the Art of American Politics. pap. 3.95 (ISBN 0-316-20412-9). Little.

Henry Clay: Leader in Congress. PLB 3.40 (ISBN 0-8116-6284-5). Garrard.

Henry David Thoreau. pap. 3.95 (ISBN 0-688-06774-3). Morrow.

Henry David Thoreau. lib. bdg. 17.50x (ISBN 0-8371-6587-3, KRHT). Greenwood.

Henry De Montherlant: A Critical Biography. 6.95 (ISBN 0-8093-0411-2). S Ill U Pr.

Henry Edward Manning, His Life & Labours. lib. bdg. 21.25x (ISBN 0-8371-4257-1, LEHM). Greenwood.

Henry Fielding. lib. bdg. 10.00 (ISBN 0-8414-5295-4). Folcroft.

Henry Fielding, Novelist & Magistrate. lib. bdg. 30.00 (ISBN 0-8492-1265-0). R West.

Henry Fielding: Playwright, Journalist & Master of the Art of Fiction, His Life & Works. 9.50 (ISBN 0-8462-0116-X). Russell.

Henry Ford. pap. 3.95 (ISBN 0-8129-6123-4, QP76). Times Bks.

Henry Ford. pap. 1.95 (ISBN 0-13-386599-1, S715). P-H.

Henry Ford & Grass-Roots America. 10.00 (ISBN 0-472-97200-6). U of Mich Pr.

Henry Ford & Grass-Roots America. pap. 3.95 (ISBN 0-472-06193-3). U of Mich Pr.

Henry George. lib. bdg. 33.00x (ISBN 0-8371-7775-8, BAHG). Greenwood.

Henry George. pap. 3.45 (ISBN 0-8084-0003-7, T128). Coll & U Pr.

Henry George, Citizen of the World. lib. bdg. 22.75x (ISBN 0-8371-5575-4, DEHG). Greenwood.

Henry George: Dreamer or Realist? 5.00. Schalkenbach.

Henry George in the British Isles. 5.00. Schalkenbach.

Henry George in the British Isles. 5.00 (ISBN 0-87013-029-3). Mich St U Pr.

Henry Grattan & His Times. facsimile ed. 20.00 (ISBN 0-8369-6614-7). Arno.

Henry Grattan & His Times. lib. bdg. 17.25x (ISBN 0-8371-4828-6, GWHG). Greenwood.

Henry Hudson. PLB 4.90 (ISBN 0-531-01276-X). Watts.

Henry Hudson: Captain of Ice-Bound Seas. PLB 3.40 (ISBN 0-8116-6257-8). Garrard.

Henry Irving. 15.00 (ISBN 0-405-08380-7). Arno.

Henry James & H. G. Wells: A Record of Their Friendship, Their Debate on the Art of Fiction, & Their Quarrel. lib. bdg. 22.50x (ISBN 0-313-20810-7, JAHJ). Greenwood.

Henry James & Robert Louis Stevenson: A Record of Friendship & Criticism. text ed. 22.50 (ISBN 0-88355-850-5). Hyperion Conn.

Henry James at Home. 6.95 (ISBN 0-374-16944-6). FS&G.

Henry Knox, a Soldier of the Revolution. lib. bdg. 17.50 (ISBN 0-306-70617-2). Da Capo.
Henry of Navarre: The King Who Dared. lib. bdg. 18.75x (ISBN 0-8371-9015-0, PEHN). Greenwood.
Henry P. Davison: The Record of a Useful Life. facsimile ed. 26.00x (ISBN 0-405-06969-3). Arno.
Henry Plantagenet: A Biography. 11.50x (ISBN 0-87471-062-6). Rowman.
Henry the Navigator: The Story of a Great Prince & His Times. 17.50 (ISBN 0-208-00681-8). Shoe String.
Henry the Seventh. 11.50 (ISBN 0-404-02667-2). AMS Pr.
Henry the Seventh. 19.00 (ISBN 0-403-00020-3). Scholarly.
Henry Thoreau: A Cosmic Yankee. lib. bdg. 25.00 (ISBN 0-8495-0051-6). Arden Lib.
Henry Thoreau As Remembered by a Young Friend. pap. 3.00 (ISBN 0-912130-00-8). Thoreau Found.
Henry Timrod, Laureate of the Confederacy. 11.50 (ISBN 0-404-06421-3). AMS Pr.
Henry VIII & His Court. 6th ed. lib. bdg. 17.50 (ISBN 0-8414-8545-3). Folcroft.
Henry W. Grady, Spokesman of the New South. 12.00 (ISBN 0-8462-1289-7). Russell.
Henry W. Longfellow & Montecassino, His Rhode Island Friendship, His Birthplace. lib. bdg. 8.75 (ISBN 0-8414-5060-9). Folcroft.
Henry Wadsworth Longfellow. lib. bdg. 7.95 (ISBN 0-8057-0456-6). Twayne.
Henry Wadsworth Longfellow. pap. 3.45 (ISBN 0-8084-0155-6, T68). Coll & U Pr.
Henry Wadsworth Longfellow: A Biographical Sketch. lib. bdg. 25.00 (ISBN 0-8495-5400-4). Arden Lib.
Henry Ward Beecher. facs. ed. 18.25 (ISBN 0-8369-8500-1). Arno.
Henry Ward Beecher: An American Portrait. 12.50 (ISBN 0-8274-2481-7). R West.
Henry Ward Beecher: An American Portrait. 17.50x (ISBN 0-8464-0019-7). Beekman Pubs.
Henry Ward Beecher: Spokesman for a Middle-Class America. 12.95 (ISBN 0-252-00608-9). U of Ill Pr.
Her Name Was Sojourner Truth. pap. 1.50 (ISBN 0-380-00719-3, 29074). Avon.
Her Way: Biographies of Women for Young People. 25.00 (ISBN 0-8389-0221-9). ALA.
Heraclitean Fire: Sketches from a Life Before Nature. 13.00 (ISBN 0-87470-029-9). Rockefeller.
Heralds of the King. 12.75 (ISBN 0-8369-1516-X). Arno.
Herbert Eugene Bolton: The Historian & the Man, 1870-1953. text ed. 15.00x o.p. (ISBN 0-8165-0557-8); pap. 8.95x (ISBN 0-8165-0644-2). U of Ariz Pr.
Herbert Hoover Story. 8.95 (ISBN 0-690-37733-9). T Y Crowell.
Herbert Spencer. 17.50 (ISBN 0-404-07891-5). AMS Pr.
Hercules Seghers. lib. bdg. 40.00 (ISBN 0-87817-209-2). Hacker.
Herder: His Life & Thought. 18.50x (ISBN 0-520-01514-2). U of Cal Pr.
Here at the New Yorker. 12.95 (ISBN 0-394-48989-6). Random.
Here at the New Yorker. pap. 1.95 (ISBN 0-425-03043-1). Berkley Pub.
Here Come the Clowns: A Cavalcade of Comedy from Antiquity to the Present. 10.00 (ISBN 0-670-36874-1). Viking Pr.
Here I Am, Take My Hand. 8.95 (ISBN 0-06-010531-3). Har-Row.
Here I Stand. pap. 3.95 (ISBN 0-8070-6407-6, BP410). Beacon Pr.
Here I Stand: A Life of Martin Luther. pap. 1.75 (ISBN 0-687-16894-5). Abingdon.
Here I Stand: A Life of Martin Luther. pap. 1.95 (ISBN 0-451-61756-8, MJ1756). NAL.
Here Lies Richard Brinsley Sheridan. lib. bdg. 20.00 (ISBN 0-8414-1250-2). Folcroft.
Here Lies the Heart. 16.00x (ISBN 0-405-07360-7). Arno.
Here's Ed: Or How to Be a Second Banana from Midway to Midnight. 8.95 (ISBN 0-399-11691-5). Putnam.
Herman Melville. lib. bdg. 15.50x (ISBN 0-8371-6524-5, ARHM); pap. 5.95 (ISBN 0-8371-8952-7, ARH:). Greenwood.
Herman Melville, Mariner & Mystic. 9.50x (ISBN 0-8154-0244-9). Cooper Sq.
Hermann Hesse: Life & Art. 14.95 (ISBN 0-520-03351-5). U of Cal Pr.
Hermann Hesse: The Man Who Sought & Found Himself. text ed. 8.75x (ISBN 0-85496-049-X). Humanities.
Hermann Von Helmholtz. pap. 4.00 (ISBN 0-486-21517-2). Dover.
Hermit of Peking: The Hidden Life of Sir Edmund Backhouse. pap. 2.95 (ISBN 0-14-004776-X). Penguin.
Hernan Cortes: Conquistador in Mexico. PLB 4.95 (ISBN 0-8225-1205-X). Lerner Pubns.
Hernando Cortes. PLB 4.90 (ISBN 0-531-00974-2). Watts.
Heroes & Gods: Spiritual Biographies in Antiquity. facsimile ed. 14.75 (ISBN 0-8369-1880-0). Arno.
Heroes, Heroines & Holidays. facs. ed. 18.75 (ISBN 0-8369-8075-1). Arno.
Heroes I Have Known: Twelve Who Lived Great Lives. 20.50 (ISBN 0-8369-7215-5). Arno.
Heroes of Civilization. rev. ed. 7.50 (ISBN 0-316-15790-2). Little.
Heroes of Conservation. 6.95 (ISBN 0-8303-0103-8). Fleet.
Heroes of Journalism. 6.95 (ISBN 0-8303-0114-3). Fleet.
Heroes of Modern Europe. facs. ed. 10.50 (ISBN 0-8369-0213-0). Arno.
Heroes of Pro Basketball. 2.50 (ISBN 0-394-80871-1); PLB 3.69 (ISBN 0-394-90871-6). Random.
Heroes of Pro Hockey. 2.50 (ISBN 0-394-82146-7). Random.
Heroes of Stock Car Racing. PLB 3.69 (ISBN 0-394-92994-2). Random.
Heroes of the American Indian. 6.95 (ISBN 0-8303-0090-2). Fleet.
Heroes of the American Revolution. PLB 6.99 (ISBN 0-394-92152-6). Random.
Heroes of the Home Run. PLB 5.54 (ISBN 0-8116-4903-2). Garrard.
Heroes of Thought. facsimile ed. 19.25 (ISBN 0-8369-2436-3). Arno.
Heroine or the Horse: Leading Ladies in Republic's Films. 17.50 (ISBN 0-498-01962-4). A S Barnes.
Heroines of Modern Religion. 14.75 (ISBN 0-8369-1572-0). Arno.
Heroines of Service. facs. ed. 16.50 (ISBN 0-8369-1152-0). Arno.
Heroines of the Sky. facsimile ed. 20.50 (ISBN 0-8369-1539-9). Arno.
Herself. 10.00 (ISBN 0-87795-042-3). Arbor Hse.
Heyday: An Autobiography. 14.95 (ISBN 0-316-77270-4). Little.
Heywood Broun: A Biography. 8.95. Chr Classics.
Hidden Coasts: A Biography of Admiral Charles Wilkes. lib. bdg. 16.00x (ISBN 0-8371-5789-7, HEHI). Greenwood.
Hidden Durer. 19.95 (ISBN 0-528-81041-3). Rand.
Hidden Terrors. 10.00 (ISBN 0-394-40674-5). Pantheon.
Hidden Terrors. pap. 3.95 (ISBN 0-394-73802-0). Pantheon.
Hiding Place. pap. 8.95 (ISBN 0-8161-6735-4). G K Hall.
Hiding Place. pap. 1.95 (ISBN 0-8007-8156-2). Revell.
Hiding Place. lib. bdg. 10.95 (ISBN 0-8161-6138-0). G K Hall.
Hiding Place. pap. 2.50 (ISBN 0-553-13844-8, C13844-8). Bantam.
High Adventurers. facs. ed. 18.50 (ISBN 0-8369-0770-1). Arno.
High Ministry of Government: The Political Career of Frank Murphy. 9.95x (ISBN 0-8143-1250-0). Wayne St U Pr.
High Priest of Rebirth: The Life, Times & Thought of Abraham Isaac Kuk. 2nd ed. 6.95x (ISBN 0-8197-0281-1). Bloch.
Highly Ramified Tree. 8.95 (ISBN 0-670-37205-6). Viking Pr.
Highstick. 5.95 (ISBN 0-396-06427-2). Dodd.
Hilaire Belloc: A Memoir. lib. bdg. 15.00 (ISBN 0-8414-6149-X). Folcroft.
Hindemith. pap. 7.95x (ISBN 0-19-314118-3). Oxford U Pr.
Hinsdale of Hiram: The Life of Burke Aaron Hinsdale, Pioneer Educator 1837-1900. student ed. 5.50 (ISBN 0-87419-041-X); lib. bdg. 8.00 (ISBN 0-87419-028-2). U Pr of Wash.
Hiram Martin Chittenden: His Public Career. 13.25 (ISBN 0-8131-1283-4). U Pr of Ky.
His Darling Wife, Evelyn: The Autobiography of Mrs. Oral Roberts. lib. bdg. 11.95 (ISBN 0-8161-6469-X). G K Hall.
His Eye Is on the Sparrow. pap. 2.25 (ISBN 0-89129-067-2). BJ Pub Group.
His Eye Is on the Sparrow: An Autobiography. lib. bdg. 18.50x (ISBN 0-313-20201-X, WAEY). Greenwood.
His Messengers Went Forth. facs. ed. 9.50 (ISBN 0-8369-8056-5). Arno.
His Story: The Life of Christ. pap. text ed. 3.25 (ISBN 0-87148-406-4). Pathway Pr.
His Touch Is Love. pap. 4.50 (ISBN 0-8127-0189-5). Southern Pub.
His Was the Voice: The Life of W. E. B. Dubois. 4.95g (ISBN 0-02-788140-7). Macmillan.
Historian Ephorus. 18.50 (ISBN 0-404-15343-7). AMS Pr.
Historians & Historiography in Modern India. 25.00x (ISBN 0-8002-1495-1). Intl Pubns Serv.
Historical Briefs: With a Biography. 15.25 (ISBN 0-8369-2974-8). Arno.
History of Alabama & Dictionary of Alabama Biography. 150.00 (ISBN 0-87152-259-4); 37.50 ea. (ISBN 0-87152-260-8) (ISBN 0-87152-261-6) (ISBN 0-87152-262-4) (ISBN 0-87152-263-2). Reprint.
History of Alexander the Great. 36.00 (ISBN 0-527-76000-5). Kraus Repr.
History of Bacteriology. pap. 6.50 (ISBN 0-486-23761-3). Dover.
History of Baldwin County Georgia. 22.50 (ISBN 0-87152-279-9). Reprint.
History of Edward the Third: 1327-1377. 21.50x (ISBN 0-87471-465-6). Rowman.
History of Fanny Burney. 29.00x (ISBN 0-19-811549-0). Oxford U Pr.
History of Hungary in Biographical Sketches. facs. ed. 13.00 (ISBN 0-8369-0635-7). Arno.
History of Mehmed the Conqueror. lib. bdg. 11.00x (ISBN 0-8371-3119-7, KRHM). Greenwood.
History of Montgomery County, Maryland, from Its Earliest Settlement in 1650-1879. 12.50 (ISBN 0-8063-7954-5). Regional.
History of Napoleon First. 2nd ed. 75.00 (ISBN 0-404-07340-9); 19.00 ea. (ISBN 0-404-07341-7) (ISBN 0-404-07342-5) (ISBN 0-404-07343-3) (ISBN 0-404-07344-1). AMS Pr.
History of Nevada. 50.00 (ISBN 0-405-04956-0). Arno.
History of Religious Educators. 8.95 (ISBN 0-8010-8829-1). Baker Bk.
History of Russian Music. 10.00 (ISBN 0-8196-0251-5). Biblo.
History of Russian Music. lib. bdg. 25.00 (ISBN 0-89341-129-9). Longwood Pr.
History of Scott County, Virginia. 17.50 (ISBN 0-8063-0771-4). Regional.
History of the Life & Adventures of Mr. Duncan Campbell. 11.00 (ISBN 0-404-07914-8). AMS Pr.
History of the Life & Times of Edward Third. 40.50 (ISBN 0-8337-2141-0). B Franklin.
History of the Life & Times of James Madison. facs. ed. 80.00 (ISBN 0-8369-5480-7). Arno.
History of the Most Renowned & Victorious Princess Elizabeth, Late Queen of England. text ed. 12.50x (ISBN 0-226-09218-6). U of Chicago Pr.
History of the Most Renowned & Victorious Princess Elizabeth Late Queen of England: Selected Chapters. pap. 3.45 (ISBN 0-226-09219-4, P399). U of Chicago Pr.
History of the Underground Railroad in Chester & the Neighboring Counties of Pennsylvania. 16.00 (ISBN 0-405-01895-9). Arno.
History of the Underground Railroad in Chester & the Neighboring Counties of Pennsylvania. 14.00x (ISBN 0-8371-0660-5). Negro U Pr.
History's Carnival: A Dissident's Autobiography. 14.95 (ISBN 0-15-141614-1). HarBraceJ.
Hitch: The Life & Times of Alfred Hitchcock. 10.00 (ISBN 0-394-49996-4). Pantheon.
Hitchhiking on Hope Street. 6.95 (ISBN 0-385-14540-3). Doubleday.
Hitler: A Biography. 24.50 (ISBN 0-404-56401-1). AMS Pr.
Hitler: A Study in Personality & Politics. 18.50x (ISBN 0-312-38818-7). St Martin.
Hitler, a Study in Tyranny. rev. ed. 15.00x (ISBN 0-06-010580-1). Har-Row.
Hitler, a Study in Tyranny. abr. ed. pap. 2.95 (ISBN 0-06-080216-2, P216). Har-Row.
Hitler, a Study in Tyranny. rev. ed. pap. 7.95 (ISBN 0-06-131123-5, TB 1123). Har-Row.
Hitler & the Nazis. PLB 5.49 (ISBN 0-399-60261-5). Putnam.
Hitler's Generals. 18.75 (ISBN 0-518-10165-7). Arno.
Hitler's War. 17.50 (ISBN 0-670-37412-1). Viking Pr.
Hitler's Youth. lib. bdg. 15.50x (ISBN 0-8371-8617-X, JEHY). Greenwood.
Hitters. PLB 7.50 (ISBN 0-87191-515-4). Creative Ed.
Ho. 6.95 (ISBN 0-394-46275-0). Random.
Hobbes. 7.45 (ISBN 0-8274-1355-6). R West.
Hobbes. 7.50 (ISBN 0-404-05359-9). AMS Pr.
Hobbes. 7.00 (ISBN 0-403-00251-6). Scholarly.
Hockey Hotshots. lib. bdg. 5.54 (ISBN 0-8116-4917-2). Garrard.
Hockey I Love. 7.50 (ISBN 0-88208-080-6). Lawrence Hill.
Hockey Stars of the '70's. new ed. PLB 4.97 (ISBN 0-399-60831-1). Putnam.
Hockey's Greatest Stars. PLB 4.97 (ISBN 0-399-60262-3). Putnam.
Hockey's Masked Men: Three Great Goalies. lib. bdg. 4.78 (ISBN 0-8116-6676-X). Garrard.
Hockey's Top Scorers. PLB 5.95 (ISBN 0-8225-1056-1). Lerner Pubns.
Hog Wild: The Autobiography of Frank Broyles. 12.95 (ISBN 0-87870-065-X). Memphis St Univ.
Hogan: The Man Who Played for Glory. 8.95 (ISBN 0-13-392464-5). P-H.
Hogarth: His Art & His World. 14.95 (ISBN 0-8008-3916-1). Taplinger.
Hogarth, His Life, Art, & Times. abr ed. 30.00x (ISBN 0-300-01766-9). Yale U Pr.
Hoke Smith & the Politics of the New South. pap. text ed. 5.95x (ISBN 0-8071-0118-4). La State U Pr.
Hokusai, the Old Man Mad with Painting. lib. bdg. 10.00 (ISBN 0-8414-7753-1). Folcroft.
Hollywood Beauties. 25.00 (ISBN 0-87000-412-3). Arlington Hse.
Hollywood Character Actors. 30.00 (ISBN 0-87000-384-4). Arlington Hse.
Hollywood Directors: 1914-1940. 16.95 (ISBN 0-19-502085-5). Oxford U Pr.
Hollywood Directors, 1914-1940. pap. 4.50 (ISBN 0-19-502086-3). Oxford U Pr.
Hollywood Directors, 1941-1976. 16.95 (ISBN 0-19-502217-3). Oxford U Pr.
Hollywood Directors, 1941-1976. pap. 5.95 (ISBN 0-19-502218-1, GB 509). Oxford U Pr.
Hollywood Posse: The Story of a Gallant Band of Horsemen Who Made Movie History. 8.95 (ISBN 0-395-20437-2). HM.
Hollywood Renaissance. pap. 6.95 (ISBN 0-440-53382-1). Dell.
Hollywood Renaissance. 12.00 (ISBN 0-498-01785-0). A S Barnes.
Hollywood Scapegoat: The Biography of Erich Von Stroheim. 12.00 (ISBN 0-405-03922-0). Arno.
Hollywood's Children: An Inside Account of the Child Star Era. 11.95 (ISBN 0-395-27095-2). HM.
Holocaust Kingdom: A Memoir. pap. 4.95 (ISBN 0-89604-001-1). Schocken.
Holy Johnson, Pioneer of African Nationalism: 1836-1917. 24.00x (ISBN 0-7146-1743-1). Biblio Dist.
Home at Last. 7.95 (ISBN 0-8197-0386-9). Bloch.
Home Below Hell's Canyon. 11.95x (ISBN 0-8032-0946-0); pap. 2.95 (ISBN 0-8032-5107-6, 143). U of Nebr Pr.
Home in the Wilds. 9.95 (ISBN 0-8008-3922-6). Taplinger.
Home in the Woods: Pioneer Life in Indiana. 8.95x (ISBN 0-253-32842-X). Ind U Pr.
Home Is Over the Mountains: The Journey of Five Black Children. PLB 4.48 (ISBN 0-8116-4256-9). Garrard.
Home Life of Poe. lib. bdg. 30.00 (ISBN 0-8495-5617-1). Arden Lib.
Home Life of Poe. lib. bdg. 30.00 (ISBN 0-8414-9513-0). Folcroft.
Homecoming: An Autobiography. 12.50 (ISBN 0-8046-0674-9). Kennikat.
Homer. pap. 4.95 (ISBN 0-312-38885-3). St Martin.
Homer. lib. bdg. 8.95 (ISBN 0-8057-2432-X). Twayne.
Homer Folks: Pioneer in Social Welfare. 20.00x (ISBN 0-231-03057-6). Columbia U Pr.
Honda: The Man & His Machines. 7.95 (ISBN 0-316-77007-8). Little.
Honest John Adams. 7.50 (ISBN 0-8446-1854-3). Peter Smith.
Honeycomb. 8.95 (ISBN 0-385-02094-5). Doubleday.
Honeymoon Is Over. 6.95 (ISBN 0-88419-130-3). Creation Hse.
Honeymoon Is Over. pap. 4.95 (ISBN 0-8407-5721-2). Nelson.
Honolulu Madam. pap. 1.95 (ISBN 0-87067-620-2, BH620). Holloway.
Honorable Men: My Life in the CIA. 12.95 (ISBN 0-671-22875-7). S&S.
Honore De Balzac. lib. bdg. 25.95 (ISBN 0-8383-2040-6). Haskell.
Hoover off the Record. facsimile ed. 17.25 (ISBN 0-8369-5953-1). Arno.
Hopkins of the Mayflower: Portrait of a Dissenter. 5.95 (ISBN 0-374-33324-6). FS&G.
Horace. 24.95x (ISBN 0-19-814310-9). Oxford U Pr.
Horace: A Biography. 7.50 (ISBN 0-8462-0950-0). Russell.
Horace Greeley: The Editor. 19.50x (ISBN 0-8464-0000-6). Beekman Pubs.
Horace Walpole. 13.00 (ISBN 0-691-09790-9). Natl Gallery Art.
Horace Walpole's Memoirs. pap. 1.25 (ISBN 0-8084-0161-0, L1). Coll & U Pr.
Horace White, Nineteenth Century Liberal. lib. bdg. 16.95 (ISBN 0-8371-3309-2, LHW/). Greenwood.
Horatia Nelson. 11.50x (ISBN 0-19-822331-5). Oxford U Pr.
Horatio Greenough: The First American Sculptor. 9.50x (ISBN 0-8122-7324-9). U of Pa Pr.
Horatio Nelson: A Short Biography. lib. bdg. 21.00x (ISBN 0-313-20481-0, GRHN). Greenwood.
Horatio Parker. 5.00 (ISBN 0-404-08304-8). AMS Pr.
Horatio Parker: A Memoir for His Grandchildren, Compiled from Letters & Papers. 15.00 (ISBN 0-404-08333-1). AMS Pr.
Horatio's Boys: The Life & Works of Horatio Alger, Jr. 8.95 (ISBN 0-8019-5966-7). Chilton.
Horizonte Humano: Vida De Jose Eustasio Rivera. 17.50 (ISBN 0-299-02000-2). U of Wis Pr.
Horn of Plenty: The Story of Louis Armstrong. lib. bdg. 17.50 (ISBN 0-306-77430-5). Da Capo.

Horner of Illinois. 11.75x (ISBN 0-8101-0250-1). Northwestern U Pr.

Horns of the Moon: A Short Biography of Adolf Hitler. 7.95 (ISBN 0-88327-027-7). McKay.

Horror People. pap. 3.95 (ISBN 0-452-25160-5, Z5160). NAL.

Horse on Course. 15.00 (ISBN 0-498-02034-7); pap. 7.95 (ISBN 0-498-02301-X). A S Barnes.

Horse Tradin' 10.00 (ISBN 0-394-42929-X). Knopf.

Horsecars & Cobblestones. 4.95 (ISBN 0-498-01301-4). A S Barnes.

Hosteen Klah: Navaho Medicine Man & Sand Painter. 11.95 (ISBN 0-8061-0622-0); pap. 4.95 (ISBN 0-8061-1008-2). U of Okla Pr.

Hot Shots of Pro Basketball. 2.50 (ISBN 0-394-82901-8); PLB 3.69 (ISBN 0-394-92901-2). Random.

Hot Shots of Pro Hockey. 2.50 (ISBN 0-394-83104-7); PLB 3.69 (ISBN 0-394-93104-1). Random.

Houdini: A Pictorial Life. 14.95 (ISBN 0-690-01152-0). T Y Crowell.

Houdini & Conan Doyle: The Story of a Strange Friendship. 15.00 (ISBN 0-405-08490-0). Arno.

Houdini & Other Masters of Magic. PLB 7.95 (ISBN 0-8172-1032-6). Raintree Pubs.

Houdini: His Legend & His Magic. 14.95 (ISBN 0-8129-0686-1). Times Bks.

Houdini: His Legend & His Magic. pap. 8.95 (ISBN 0-446-87328-4). Warner Bks.

Houdini: the Untold Story. pap. 1.75 (ISBN 0-671-80730-7). PB.

Hound of Heaven. 2.95 (ISBN 0-442-82255-3). Peter Pauper.

Hound of Heaven. pap. 0.95 (ISBN 0-8192-1205-9). Morehouse.

Hours & the Ages: Sequence of Americans. 10.00 (ISBN 0-8046-0580-7). Kennikat.

House by the Sea: A Journal. 10.95 (ISBN 0-393-07518-4). Norton.

House in Bali. 26.50 (ISBN 0-404-16766-7). AMS Pr.

House of Krupp. pap. 4.95 (ISBN 0-8128-1232-8). Stein & Day.

House of Tudor. 35.00. Stein & Day.

Housman the Poet. lib. bdg. 7.50 (ISBN 0-8414-2062-9). Folcroft.

How Am I Doing God? pap. 2.25 (ISBN 0-570-03150-8, 12-2535). Concordia.

How Did They Die? 12.95 (ISBN 0-312-39488-8). St Martin.

How Green Is My Mountain. pap. 3.95 (ISBN 0-87784-561-1). Inter-Varsity.

How I Came to Be a Writer. 6.95 (ISBN 0-689-30625-3). Atheneum.

How I Found Livingstone. 23.00x (ISBN 0-8371-1995-2). Negro U Pr.

How I Learned to Meditate. pap. 3.95 (ISBN 0-88270-253-X). Logos.

How It Was. pap. 2.50 (ISBN 0-345-25432-5). Ballantine.

How It Was. 12.50 (ISBN 0-394-40109-3). Knopf.

How Jimmy Won: The Victory Campaign from Plains to the White House. 10.95 (ISBN 0-688-03153-6). Morrow.

How Many Mountains? 4.95 (ISBN 0-8054-5272-9). Broadman.

How My World Turns. 5.95 (ISBN 0-8008-3970-6). Taplinger.

How Shall They Hear Without a Preacher: The Life of Ernest Fremont Tittle. 19.00x (ISBN 0-8078-1173-4). U of NC Pr.

How to Be a Jewish Grandmother. 6.95 (ISBN 0-385-15205-1). Doubleday.

How to Be a Winner. o.p. 5.95 (ISBN 0-88270-178-9); pap. 3.95 (ISBN 0-88270-179-7). Logos.

How to Become a Christian & Stay One. pap. 1.25 (ISBN 0-8127-0221-2). Southern Pub.

How to Live Above & Beyond Your Circumstances. pap. 3.95 (ISBN 0-912582-20-0). Kirban.

How to Live Above and Beyond Your Circumstances. pap. 3.95 (ISBN 0-8423-1514-4). Tyndale.

How to Sell Anything to Anybody. pap. 2.75 (ISBN 0-446-95810-7). Warner Bks.

How to Sell Anything to Anybody. 8.95 (ISBN 0-671-22651-7). S&S.

How to Sell Anything to Anybody. pap. 2.25 (ISBN 0-446-82957-9). Warner Bks.

How to Steal a Pennant. 8.95 (ISBN 0-399-11699-0). Putnam.

How We Lost the Vietnam War. pap. 3.95 (ISBN 0-8128-6016-0). Stein & Day.

Howard Hughes: The Hidden Years. 7.95 (ISBN 0-394-41042-4). Random.

Howard Hughes: The Hidden Years. pap. 2.50 (ISBN 0-446-91223-9). Warner Bks.

Howard Mumford Jones: An Autobiography. 17.50 (ISBN 0-299-07770-5). U of Wis Pr.

Howard Nemerov. pap. 1.25x (ISBN 0-8166-0484-3, MPAW70). U of Minn Pr.

Howard Phillips Lovecraft: Dreamer on the Nightside. 8.50 (ISBN 0-87054-068-8). Arkham.

Hsiang-Ya Journal. 10.00 (ISBN 0-208-01614-7). Shoe String.

Hsiao Hung. lib. bdg. 9.95 (ISBN 0-8057-6228-0). Twayne.

Hubert H. Humphrey: The Happy Warrior. PLB 5.95g (ISBN 0-8225-0476-6). Lerner Pubns.

Hubert Howe Bancroft, Historian of the West. 15.00 (ISBN 0-8462-1472-5). Russell.

Hubert Murray: Australian Pro-Consul. 15.00x (ISBN 0-19-550288-4). Oxford U Pr.

Hubert: The Triumph & Tragedy of the Humphrey I Knew. 10.95 (ISBN 0-399-12314-8). Putnam.

Hubert Walter, Lord of Canterbury & Lord of England. 9.75 (ISBN 0-8223-0203-9). Duke.

Huey Long. pap. 8.95 (ISBN 0-13-444612-7). P-H.

Huey Long. 20.00 (ISBN 0-394-42954-0). Knopf.

Hugh Latimer, Apostle to the English. lib. bdg. 13.50 (ISBN 0-374-91492-3). Octagon.

Hugo Black & the Judicial Revolution. 12.50 (ISBN 0-671-22341-0). S&S.

Hugo Black & the Judicial Revolution. pap. 5.95 (ISBN 0-671-24406-X). S&S.

Human Side of Science. 20.50 (ISBN 0-8369-2877-6). Arno.

Human Story of Long Island. 6.50 (ISBN 0-87198-078-9). Friedman.

Human Story of Long Island. 6.50 (ISBN 0-8046-8078-7). Kennikat.

Humanist As Hero: The Life of Sir Thomas More. 14.75 (ISBN 0-02-849040-1). Hafner.

Humboldt Years: 1930-39. pap. 4.50. B W Brace.

Hume. 8.25 (ISBN 0-8274-1353-X). R West.

Humiliations Follow'd with Deliverances...with a Narrative, of a Notable Delivarance Lately Recieved by Some English Captives, from the Hands of Cruel Indians see True History of the Captivity & Restoration of Mrs. Mary Rowlandson.

Hunted Heretic: The Life & Death of Michael Servetus. 7.50 (ISBN 0-8446-1580-3). Peter Smith.

Hussite King: Bohemia in European Affairs, 1440-1471. 20.00 (ISBN 0-8135-0497-X). Rutgers U Pr.

Hustler for the Lord. pap. 1.95 (ISBN 0-88270-309-9). Logos.

Huxley: A Biographical Introduction. 5.95 (ISBN 0-684-13053-X). Scribner.

Huxley, Prophet of Science. 21.50 (ISBN 0-404-14040-8). AMS Pr.

Hyrum Smith, Patriarch. 6.95 (ISBN 0-87747-118-5). Deseret Bk.

I

I Always Wanted to Be Somebody. PLB 8.79 (ISBN 0-06-011516-5). Har-Row.

I Always Wanted to Be Somebody. pap. 37.50 set (ISBN 0-8107-0002-6); tchrs' notes incl. Bowmar-Noble.

I Am a Memory Come Alive: Autobiographical Writings. 10.00 (ISBN 0-8052-3556-6); pap. 5.95 (ISBN 0-8052-0428-8). Schocken.

I Am a Stranger on the Earth: The Story of Vincent Van Gogh. PLB 7.95 (ISBN 0-7232-6121-0). Warne.

I Am Chrystie. pap. 4.95 (ISBN 0-89087-925-7). Les Femmes Pub.

I Am Joseph. 9.95 (ISBN 0-688-41933-X); PLB 9.55 (ISBN 0-688-51933-4). Lothrop.

I Am Not an Island: An Experiment in Autobiography. 12.50x (ISBN 0-88386-941-1). South Asia Bks.

I Am Third. 6.95 (ISBN 0-670-38977-3). Viking Pr.

I Am Third. pap. 1.95 (ISBN 0-553-12865-5). Bantam.

I Beat Cancer. 8.95 (ISBN 0-8092-7736-0). Contemp Bks.

I Believe in Justice & Hope. pap. 5.95 (ISBN 0-8190-0628-9). Fides Claretian.

I Called Him Babe: Elvis Presley's Nurse Remembers. 10.00 (ISBN 0-87870-053-6); deluxe ed. 25.00 (ISBN 0-87870-056-0). Memphis St Univ.

I Cannot Go Back. o.p. 5.95 (ISBN 0-88270-193-2); pap. 2.95 (ISBN 0-88270-194-0). Logos.

I, Charlotte Forten, Black & Free. 6.95 (ISBN 0-690-42869-3). T Y Crowell.

I Dared to Call Him Father. 7.95 (ISBN 0-912376-22-8, 76-22-8). Chosen Bks Pub.

I Don't Want to Be Brave Anymore. 10.95 (ISBN 0-915220-42-3, 24153). New Republic.

I Hauled These Mountains in Here. 9.95 (ISBN 0-87004-233-5). Caxton.

I Have a Dream. PLB 5.99 (ISBN 0-394-91234-9). Knopf.

I Have a Dream: The Life & Times of Martin Luther King, Jr. lib. bdg. 14.75x (ISBN 0-8371-5977-6, DHD&). Greenwood.

I Have Kept the Faith: The Life of the Apostle Paul. pap. 4.95 (ISBN 0-528-88015-2). Rand.

I Knew a Phoenix: Sketches for an Autobiography. pap. 2.95 (ISBN 0-393-00916-5). Norton.

I Knew Dietrich Bonhoeffer. pap. 1.95 (ISBN 0-00-623314-7, FA3314). Collins Pubs.

I Know Why the Caged Bird Sings. 8.95 (ISBN 0-394-42986-9). Random.

I Know Why the Caged Bird Sings. pap. 2.25 (ISBN 0-553-10842-5, 13184-2). Bantam.

I Learn About Jesus. 5.00 (ISBN 0-8198-0246-8); pap. 3.50x (ISBN 0-8198-0247-6). Dghtrs St Paul.

I Live on an Island. pap. 2.75 (ISBN 0-87793-171-2). Ave Maria.

I Love Being Married to a Grandma. 6.95 (ISBN 0-8407-5132-X). Nelson.

I Love: The Story of Vladimir Mayakovsky & Lili Brik. price not set. FS&G.

I Married a Best Seller. 8.95 (ISBN 0-385-12337-X). Doubleday.

I Married a Bestseller. pap. 2.25 (ISBN 0-553-12267-3). Bantam.

I Married a Prince: A Cinderella Story from Hawaii. 10.00 (ISBN 0-682-48649-3). Exposition.

I Married Wyatt Earp: The Recollections of Josephine Sarah Marcus Earp. 10.50 (ISBN 0-8165-0484-9); pap. 4.95 (ISBN 0-8165-0583-7). U of Ariz Pr.

I Meet My Contemporaries. facs. ed. 13.50 (ISBN 0-8369-0509-1). Arno.

I Must Not Rock. pap. 5.00 (ISBN 0-913780-19-7). Daughters.

I Never Had It Made. 7.95 (ISBN 0-399-11021-6). Putnam.

I Never Walked Alone. 6.95 (ISBN 0-312-40250-3). St Martin.

I Passed This Way. 15.95 (ISBN 0-394-42612-6). Knopf.

I Pick up Hitchhikers. pap. 2.95 (ISBN 0-8170-0774-1). Judson.

I Remember It Well. pap. 1.75 (ISBN 0-425-02907-7). Berkley Pub.

I Remember Lindbergh. 8.95 (ISBN 0-15-238895-8). HarBraceJ.

I Seek the Miraculous. 8.95 (ISBN 0-525-13081-0). Dutton.

I Send a Voice. 10.95 (ISBN 0-8356-0513-2); pap. 4.95 (ISBN 0-8356-0511-6). Theos Pub Hse.

I Should Care: The Sammy Cahn Story. 8.95 (ISBN 0-87795-090-3). Arbor Hse.

I Should Have Seen It Coming When the Rabbit Died. 8.95 (ISBN 0-385-14057-6). Doubleday.

I Should Have Seen It Coming When the Rabbit Died. pap. 2.25 (ISBN 0-553-13744-1). Bantam.

I Sing the Song of Myself: An Anthology of Autobiographical Poems. 8.50 (ISBN 0-688-80172-2); PLB 8.16 (ISBN 0-688-84172-4). Greenwillow.

I Skate! 8.95g (ISBN 0-316-26002-9). Little.

I Thunk Me a Thaut. 4.20 (ISBN 0-8077-2488-2). Tchrs Coll.

I, Tut: The Boy Who Became Pharaoh. 8.95g (ISBN 0-590-07571-3). Schol Bk Serv.

I Want Somebody to Know My Name. pap. 3.95 (ISBN 0-8407-5642-9). Nelson.

I Was Raised a Jehovah's Witness. pap. 3.95 (ISBN 0-89636-018-0). Accent Bks.

I Will Be Heard: The Life of William Lloyd Garrison. 6.50 (ISBN 0-688-41106-1); PLB 6.24 (ISBN 0-688-51106-6). Lothrop.

I, William Shakespeare Do Appoint Thomas Russell, Esquire. 16.00 (ISBN 0-8369-5260-X). Arno.

I, William Shakespeare Do Appoint Thomas Russell, Esquire. 12.25 (ISBN 0-8274-0288-0). R West.

I Wonder As I Wander: An Autobiographical Journey. pap. 5.95 (ISBN 0-8090-0068-7). Hill & Wang.

I Won't Be Crippled When I See Jesus. pap. 3.95 (ISBN 0-8066-1716-0, 10-3188). Augsburg.

Ibsen: The Master Builder. lib. bdg. 15.00 (ISBN 0-374-98910-9). Octagon.

Icarie et Son Fondateur, Etienne Cabet: Contribution a L'etude Du Socialisme Experimental. lib. bdg. 32.50x (ISBN 0-87991-005-4). Porcupine Pr.

Icart. 19.95 (ISBN 0-517-52498-8). Potter.

Icelandic Jaunt: A Study of the Expeditions Made by Morris to Iceland in 1871 & 1873. lib. bdg. 10.00 (ISBN 0-8414-6792-7). Folcroft.

I'd Do It Again: A Record of All My Uproarious Years. 24.00 (ISBN 0-405-09329-2). Arno.

Ida Lupino. pap. 1.95 (ISBN 0-515-04306-0). HarBraceJ.

Ida M'Toy. 25.00 (ISBN 0-252-00760-3). U of Ill Pr.

Idi Amin Dada: Hitler in Africa. 7.95 (ISBN 0-8362-0783-1). Andrews & McMeel.

Idle Passion: Chess & the Dance of Death. pap. 2.95 (ISBN 0-452-25109-5, Z5109). NAL.

Idols of Silence. 15.00 (ISBN 0-498-01611-0). A S Barnes.

If at First... 8.95 (ISBN 0-8128-2145-9). Stein & Day.

If I Had a Wish. pap. 1.85 (ISBN 0-8307-0314-4, 57-001-08). Regal.

If Only They Could Talk. lib. bdg. 10.95 (ISBN 0-8161-6415-0). G K Hall.

If You Don't Weaken: The Autobiography of Oscar Ameringer. lib. bdg. 20.50x (ISBN 0-8371-2499-9, AMDW). Greenwood.

Ignacio de Luzan. lib. bdg. 7.95 (ISBN 0-8057-2552-0). Twayne.

Ignacio Manuel Altamirano. lib. bdg. 7.95 (ISBN 0-8057-2040-5). Twayne.

Ignacio Manuel Altamirano. lib. bdg. 12.95x (ISBN 0-8057-2040-5). Irvington.

Igor Sikorsky, His Three Careers in Aviation. rev. ed. 5.25 (ISBN 0-396-07282-8). Dodd.

Igor Stravinsky: An Autobiography. 4.95 (ISBN 0-8079-0066-4). October.

I'll Cry Tomorrow. pap. 3.95 (ISBN 0-88391-074-8). Fell.

I'll See You in Court. 9.95 (ISBN 0-8092-7399-3). Contemp Bks.

I'll Take the Back Road. 7.95 (ISBN 0-8289-0244-5). Greene.

Illustrated Biographical Encyclopedia of Artists of the American West. 30.00 (ISBN 0 385-01730-8). Doubleday.

Illustrated Elvis. pap. 1.95 (ISBN 0-441-36514-0). Ace Bks.

Illustrated Pepys: Extracts from the Diary. 15.95 (ISBN 0-520-03633-6). U of Cal Pr.

I'm an Endangered Species: The Autobiography of a Free Enterpriser. 6.95 (ISBN 0-88415-258-8). Pacesetter Pr.

I'm Dancing As Fast As I Can. 9.95 (ISBN 0-06-011499-1). Har-Row.

I'm Dancing As Fast As I Can. pap. 2.75 (ISBN 0-553-13410-8). Bantam.

I'm Deborah Sampson: A Soldier in the War of the Revolution. PLB 6.96 (ISBN 0-688-51799-4). Lothrop.

I'm Eve. pap. 2.25 (ISBN 0-515-04656-6). BJ Pub Group.

I'm Eve. 10.00 (ISBN 0-385-12062-1). Doubleday.

I'm Frank Hamer: The Life of a Texas Peace Officer. 8.95 (ISBN 0-8363-0051-3); limited ed. 45.00. Jenkins.

I'm Mad As Hell. 9.95 (ISBN 0-8129-0858-9). Times Bks.

I'm No Hero. new ed. pap. 1.95 (ISBN 0-8307-0254-7, 54-068-03). Regal.

I'm Nobody, Who Are You: The Story of Emily Dickinson. 6.95 (ISBN 0-8164-3029-2). HM.

I'm Thirsty Too. 6.95 (ISBN 0-498-06730-0). A S Barnes.

Image Makers: A Bibliography of American Presidential Campaign Biographies. 12.50 (ISBN 0-8108-1252-5). Scarecrow.

Image of the King: A Biography of Charles I & Charles II. 12.95 (ISBN 0-689-11006-5). Atheneum.

Images & Shadows: Part of a Life. 8.50 (ISBN 0-15-144101-4). HarBraceJ.

Images of Yesterday. 12.95 (ISBN 0-517-52700-6). Crown.

Immigrant Saint: Life of Mother Cabrini. 4.95. Chr Classics.

Immigrant's American Odyssey: A Biography of Ernst Skarstedt. 5.95 (ISBN 0-910184-24-0). Augustana.

Immigrant's Two Worlds: A Biography of Hjalmar Edgren. 4.95 (ISBN 0-910184-23-2). Augustana.

Immortal Henry: The Story of a Lipizzaner Stallion. 9.95 (ISBN 0-236-40096-7). Merrimack Bk Serv.

Immortals at First Hand. lib. bdg. 20.00. Folcroft.

Impatient Crusader: Florence Kelley's Life Story. lib. bdg. 16.25x (ISBN 0-8371-9011-8, GOIM). Greenwood.

Imperial Charade: A Biography of Emperor Napoleon III & Empress Eugenie. 12.95 (ISBN 0-672-52346-9). Bobbs.

Imperial Orgy: An Account of the Tsars from the First to the Last. 10.00 (ISBN 0-404-05544-3). AMS Pr.

Impossible Friendship: Boswell & Mrs. Thrale. 7.50x (ISBN 0-674-44541-4). Harvard U Pr.

Impossible Major Rogers. 5.95 (ISBN 0-399-20593-4). Putnam.

Improbable Fiction: The Life of Mary Roberts Rinehart. 16.95 (ISBN 0-8229-3401-9). U of Pittsburgh Pr.

Improper Bostonian: Dr. Oliver Wendell Holmes. 12.95 (ISBN 0-688-03429-2). Morrow.

Improvising: Sixteen Jazz Musicians & Their Art. 11.95 (ISBN 0-19-502149-5). Oxford U Pr.

In a Year of Our Lord: A Memoir of American Innocence. 8.95 (ISBN 0-87795-160-8). Arbor Hse.

In & Out of Doors with Charles Dickens. 9.50 (ISBN 0-404-08749-3). AMS Pr.

In & Out of the Ivory Tower: The Autobiography of William L. Langer. 17.00 (ISBN 0-88202-177-X). N Watson.

In at the Beginnings: A Physicist's Life. text ed. 14.95x (ISBN 0-262-13124-2). MIT Pr.

In Brief Authority. lib. bdg. 14.50x (ISBN 0-8371-8807-5, BIIB). Greenwood.

Jesse Owens Story. PLB 5.29 (ISBN 0-399-60315-8). Putnam.

Jesse Stuart. lib. bdg. 8.50 (ISBN 0-8057-0704-2). Twayne.

Jessie Tarbox Beals, First Woman News Photographer. 25.00 (ISBN 0-918696-08-9). Camera Graphic.

Jessie Willcox Smith. 22.95 (ISBN 0-690-01493-7). T Y Crowell.

Jesus. pap. 2.95 (ISBN 0-13-509646-4, S704). P-H.

Jesus, a New Biography. 17.50 (ISBN 0-404-01406-2). AMS Pr.

Jesus, a New Biography. 30.00 (ISBN 0-932062-36-9). Sharon Hill.

Jesus: A New Biography. lib. bdg. 18.50x (ISBN 0-8371-0342-8, CAJE). Greenwood.

Jesus: An Historian's Review of the Gospels. 12.50 (ISBN 0-684-14889-7); pap. 4.95 (ISBN 0-684-15891-4). Scribner.

Jesus & His Contemporaries. pap. 1.45 (ISBN 0-8091-1606-5). Paulist Pr.

Jesus Confronts Life's Issues. pap. 1.95 (ISBN 0-8170-0547-1). Judson.

Jesus, His Life & Times. 22.95 (ISBN 0-688-03577-9). Morrow.

Jesus, Our Friend. Incl. Friends in the Bible. pap. 1.50 ea.; pap. (ISBN 0-8170-0713-X); pap. (ISBN 0-8170-0714-8). Judson.

Jesus Scroll. 5.95 (ISBN 0-8037-4300-9). Dial.

Jesus, Teacher & Lord. pap. 2.95 (ISBN 0-8170-0318-5). Judson.

Jesus: The Man, the Mission, & the Message. 2nd ed. 16.95 (ISBN 0-13-509521-2). P-H.

Jesus the Pagan. 6.00 (ISBN 0-8022-2097-5). Philos Lib.

Jesus: the Story of His Life: A Modern Retelling Based on the Gospels. 10.95 (ISBN 0-88229-308-7). Nelson Hall.

Jesus Years: A Chronological Study of the Life of Christ. pap. 5.95 (ISBN 0-87239-136-1, 40061). Standard Pub.

Jew Today. 10.00 (ISBN 0-394-42054-3). Random.

Jew Today. pap. 2.50 (ISBN 0-394-74057-2). Random.

Jewel-Hinged Jaw: Notes on the Language of Science Fiction. 13.95. Dragon Pr.

Jewish Grandmothers. pap. 4.95 (ISBN 0-8070-5421-6, BP553). Beacon Pr.

Jewish Paradox. 4.95 (ISBN 0-448-15166-9). G&D.

Jewish Portraits. 13.50 (ISBN 0-8369-2912-8). Arno.

Jewish Radicals 1875-1914: From Czarist Stetl to London Ghetto. 12.95 (ISBN 0-394-49764-3). Pantheon.

Jews Are Like That. facs. ed. 12.75 (ISBN 0-8369-1114-8). Arno.

Jews in American Life. 5.95 (ISBN 0-88482-891-3). Hebrew Pub.

Jews in Music: From the Age of Enlightenment to the Mid-Twentieth Century. rev. ed. 7.95 (ISBN 0-8197-0372-9). Bloch.

J.F.K. The Man & the Myth. pap. 2.75 (ISBN 0-440-14407-8). Dell.

Jim Bridger. 14.95 (ISBN 0-8061-0546-1). U of Okla Pr.

Jim Bridger. pap. 6.95 (ISBN 0-8061-1509-2). U of Okla Pr.

Jim Bridger, Mountain Man: A Biography. pap. 3.95 (ISBN 0-8032-5720-1, 519). U of Nebr Pr.

Jim Croce: The Feeling Lives on. PLB 5.95 (ISBN 0-88436-215-9); pap. 3.50 (ISBN 0-88436-216-7). EMC.

Jim Hart Story. 9.95 (ISBN 0-8272-1705-6); pap. 6.95 (ISBN 0-8272-1704-8). Bethany Pr.

Jim Palmer: Great Comeback Competitor. PLB 5.69 (ISBN 0-399-61114-2). Putnam.

Jim Thorpe. PLB 6.95 (ISBN 0-87518-076-0). Dillon.

Jimi Hendrix: Voodoo Child of the Aquarian Age. 12.95 (ISBN 0-385-07357-7). Doubleday.

Jimmie Rodgers. PLB 5.95 (ISBN 0-8225-1404-4). Lerner Pubns.

Jimmie Rodgers: The Life & Times of America's Blue Yodeler. 15.00 (ISBN 0-252-00750-6). U of Ill Pr.

Jimmie Walker: Funny Is Where It's at. PLB 5.95 (ISBN 0-88436-416-X); pap. 3.50 (ISBN 0-88436-417-8). EMC.

Jimmy Carter. PLB 4.29 (ISBN 0-399-61094-4). Putnam.

Jimmy Carter-Jimmy Carter. pap. 1.00 (ISBN 0-89245-006-1). Seventy Six.

Jo Siffert. 8.95 (ISBN 0-7183-0402-0). Motorbooks Intl.

Joachim of Flora. lib. bdg. 13.50 (ISBN 0-915172-24-0). Richwood Pub.

Joan Moore Rice: The Olympic Dream. lib. bdg. 5.95 (ISBN 0-88436-164-0); pap. 3.50 (ISBN 0-88436-165-9). EMC.

Joan of Arc. pap. 1.95 (ISBN 0-472-06122-4, 122). U of Mich Pr.

Job's Illness: Loss, Grief & Integration; a Psychological Interpretation. text ed. 23.00 (ISBN 0-08-018087-6). Pergamon.

Jody. 6.95 (ISBN 0-07-031147-1). McGraw.

Jody. pap. 1.95 (ISBN 0-446-89324-2). Warner Bks.

Jody: An Autobiography. 13.50 (ISBN 0-949997-23-4). Motorbooks Intl.

Joe Bailey, the Last Democrat. facs. ed. 17.25 (ISBN 0-8369-5199-9). Arno.

Joe Namath: A Football Legend. PLB 5.29 (ISBN 0-399-60317-4). Putnam.

Joe Namath, Superstar. rev. ed. 5.95g (ISBN 0-8098-2102-8). Walck.

Joe Petrosino. 5.95 (ISBN 0-02-595160-2). Macmillan.

Joe Scott, the Woodsman-Songmaker. 22.50 (ISBN 0-252-00683-6); cassette 6.95 (ISBN 0-252-00727-1). U of Ill Pr.

Joel Chandler Harris: A Biography. 11.95x (ISBN 0-8071-0411-6). La State U Pr.

Joey: A Loving Portrait of Alfred Perles Together with Some Bizarre Episodes Relating to the Other Sex. 8.95 (ISBN 0-88496-136-2); pap. 3.95 (ISBN 0-88496-137-0). Capra Pr.

Joey Kills. pap. 1.75 (ISBN 0-671-80193-7). PB.

Johan Bojer, the Man & His Works. lib. bdg. 30.00 (ISBN 0-8495-2001-0). Arden Lib.

Johan Bojer, the Man & His Works. lib. bdg. 14.25x (ISBN 0-8371-7263-2, GAJB). Greenwood.

Johann Christian Edelmann: From Orthodoxy to Enlightenment. text ed. 24.00x (ISBN 90-2797-691-0). Mouton.

Johann Conrad Beissel, Mystic & Martinet: 1690-1768. lib. bdg. 12.50x (ISBN 0-87991-012-7). Porcupine Pr.

Johann Ludwig Eberhardt & His Salem Clocks. 12.95 (ISBN 0-8078-1324-9). U of NC Pr.

Johann Sebastian Bach: Revolutionary of Music. PLB 5.90 (ISBN 0-531-00956-4). Watts.

Johann Sebastian Bach, the Organist & His Works for the Organ. 11.50 (ISBN 0-404-13089-5). AMS Pr.

Johann Sebastian Bach: The Story of the Development of a Great Personality. 19.00 (ISBN 0-403-01643-6). Scholarly.

Johann Strauss: The End of an Era. 13.75 (ISBN 0-271-01131-9). Pa St U Pr.

Johannes Amos Comenius. 6.00 (ISBN 0-405-02753-2). Arno.

Johannes Brahms: His Work & Personality. lib. bdg. 17.50x (ISBN 0-8371-9367-2, GABR). Greenwood.

Johannes Brahms: The Herzogenberg Correspondence. 50.00x (ISBN 0-8443-0011-X). Vienna Hse.

John A. Lee. 20.00x (ISBN 0-908569-04-1). Intl Pubns Serv.

John Adams. lib. bdg. 39.00x (ISBN 0-8371-2515-4, SMKA). Greenwood.

John Adams: A Biography in His Own Words. 15.00 (ISBN 0-06-013308-2). Har-Row.

John Adams, 1735-1826: Chronology, Documents, Bibliographical Aids. 6.00 (ISBN 0-379-12052-6). Oceana.

John Addington Symonds: A Biography. 20.00x (ISBN 0-405-07356-9). Arno.

John Amos Comenius, Bishop of the Moravians, His Life & Educational Works. 21.00 (ISBN 0-8337-2028-7). B Franklin.

John & Sebastian Cabot. PLB 5.90 (ISBN 0-531-00970-X). Watts.

John Arbuthnot: Mathematician & Satirist. 12.50 (ISBN 0-8462-0915-2). Russell.

John Bach McMaster, American Historian. lib. bdg. 12.00 (ISBN 0-374-93179-8). Octagon.

John Barrett, Progressive Era Diplomat: A Study of a Commercial Expansionist, 1887-1920. 8.50 (ISBN 0-8173-5162-0). U of Ala Pr.

John Beckley, Zealous Partisan in a Nation Divided. 7.50 (ISBN 0-87169-100-0). Am Philos.

John Book. 18.50 (ISBN 0-8369-8107-3). Arno.

John Bracken: A Political Biography. 17.50 (ISBN 0-8020-5439-0). U of Toronto Pr.

John Breckinridge, Jeffersonian Republican. 9.50 (ISBN 0-9601072-2-3). Filson Club.

John Bright. 18.50 (ISBN 0-7100-8992-9). Routledge & Kegan.

John Brown. PLB 4.29 (ISBN 0-671-23150-2). Messner.

John Brown & the Jim Lane Trail. 10.00 (ISBN 0-931068-11-8). Purcells.

John Brown's Journey: Notes & Reflections on His America & Mine. 10.00 (ISBN 0-385-05511-0). Doubleday.

John Buchan & His World. 10.95 (ISBN 0-684-16278-4). Scribner.

John Bunyan. lib. bdg. 15.00 (ISBN 0-8414-1804-7). Folcroft.

John Bunyan. 5.95 (ISBN 0-02-630280-2). Macmillan.

John Bunyan, His Life & Times. lib. bdg. 20.00 (ISBN 0-8414-4933-3). Folcroft.

John Bunyan, Pilgrim & Dreamer. 25.00 (ISBN 0-8414-4782-9). Folcroft.

John Bunyan: The Man & His Work. lib. bdg. 20.00 (ISBN 0-8414-3319-4). Folcroft.

John Bunyan, the Man & His Works. lib. bdg. 27.50 (ISBN 0-8414-8611-5). Folcroft.

John Burgoyne of Saratoga. 14.95 (ISBN 0-15-146402-2). HarBraceJ.

John Burroughs, the Famous Naturalist. lib. bdg. 2.45 incl. catalog cards (ISBN 0-87157-543-4); pap. 1.25 vinyl laminated covers (ISBN 0-87157-043-2). SamHar Pr.

John Butler Yeats. 4.50 (ISBN 0-8387-7759-7); pap. 1.95 (ISBN 0-8387-7733-3). Bucknell U Pr.

John C. Calhoun. lib. bdg. 20.00 (ISBN 0-910220-85-9). Larlin Corp.

John C. Calhoun. pap. 1.95 (ISBN 0-13-112391-2, S719). P-H.

John C. Calhoun. Incl. Nationalist, 1782-1828; Nullifier, 1829-1839; Sectionalist, 1840-1850. 55.00 (ISBN 0-8462-1041-X). Russell.

John C. Calhoun, Opportunist: A Reappraisal. pap. 3.45 (ISBN 0-8129-6076-9, QP70). Times Bks.

John Cabot & His Son Sebastian. PLB 6.48 (ISBN 0-688-31816-9). Morrow.

John Calvin: A Biography. 10.95 (ISBN 0-664-20810-X). Westminster.

John Calvin: The Man & His Ethics. lib. bdg. 39.95 (ISBN 0-8490-2106-5). Gordon Pr.

John Caples: Adman. 11.95 (ISBN 0-87251-030-1). Crain Bks.

John Cartwright. 29.95 (ISBN 0-521-08537-3). Cambridge U Pr.

John Coltrane. 12.95 (ISBN 0-02-870660-9). Schirmer Bks.

John Coltrane. pap. 5.95 (ISBN 0-02-870500-9). Schirmer Bks.

John Courtney Murray: Theologian in Conflict. 9.95 (ISBN 0-8091-0212-9). Paulist Pr.

John Curry. 17.50 (ISBN 0-394-50134-9). Knopf.

John Dalton. 14.50 (ISBN 0-404-07896-6). AMS Pr.

John Dalton & the Atom. 13.50x (ISBN 0-8014-0160-7). Cornell U Pr.

John Denver. pap. 3.95 (ISBN 0-8256-3909-3). Music Sales.

John Denver. PLB 5.95 (ISBN 0-87191-392-5); pap. 2.75 (ISBN 0-89812-104-3). Creative Ed.

John Denver: A Natural High. PLB 5.95 (ISBN 0-88436-211-6); pap. 3.50 (ISBN 0-88436-212-4). EMC.

John Dewey, an Intellectual Portrait. lib. bdg. 15.25x (ISBN 0-8371-3951-1, HOJD). Greenwood.

John Dewey: The Reconstruction of the Democratic Life. text ed. 5.50 (ISBN 0-8044-5721-2); pap. 2.45 (ISBN 0-8044-6580-0). Ungar.

John Dickinson, American Revolutionary Statesman. new ed. lib. bdg. 2.45 incl. catalog cards; pap. 1.25 vinyl laminated covers. SamHar Pr.

John Donne: A Life. 19.95x (ISBN 0-19-500130-3). Oxford U Pr.

John Donne & His World. 10.95 (ISBN 0-684-15301-7). Scribner.

John Endecott: A Biography. 25.00 (ISBN 0-403-01099-3). Scholarly.

John F. Kennedy. lib. bdg. 7.50 (ISBN 0-8057-3696-4). Twayne.

John F. Kennedy American. 5.00 (ISBN 0-8198-0068-6); pap. 4.00 (ISBN 0-8198-0069-4). Dghtrs St Paul.

John F. Kennedy: Man of the Sea. 15.95 (ISBN 0-87294-018-7). Country Beautiful.

John F. Kennedy: New Frontiersman. PLB 4.48 (ISBN 0-8116-6287-X). Garrard.

John Fitzgerald Kennedy. PLB 4.49 (ISBN 0-399-60319-0). Putnam.

John Ford. expanded rev. ed. pap. 4.95 (ISBN 0-520-03498-8). U of Cal Pr.

John Ford. 11.95 (ISBN 0-8037-4826-4). Dial.

John Foster Dulles: A Statesman & His Times. 20.00x (ISBN 0-231-03664-7). Columbia U Pr.

John G. Neihardt: A Critical Biography. pap. text ed. 23.50x (ISBN 90-6203-109-9). Humanities.

John Galsworthy: A Biography. 12.50 (ISBN 0-698-10715-2). Coward.

John Galt: The Life of a Writer. 12.50x (ISBN 0-8020-1941-2). U of Toronto Pr.

John Garfield. pap. 2.50 (ISBN 0-15-646250-8). HarBraceJ.

John George Jackson. 18.50 (ISBN 0-87012-241-X). McClain.

John Greenleaf Whittier. lib. bdg. 10.00. Folcroft.

John Greenleaf Whittier: A Portrait in Paradox. 11.95 (ISBN 0-19-500650-X). Oxford U Pr.

John Greenleaf Whittier, Friend of Man. 22.50 (ISBN 0-208-00684-2). Shoe String.

John Greenleaf Whittier: His Life & Work. 10.00 (ISBN 0-8046-1589-6). Kennikat.

John Hancock. PLB 7.35 (ISBN 0-516-04653-5). Childrens.

John Hancock, the Picturesque Patriot. lib. bdg. 25.00x (ISBN 0-8398-1880-7). Irvington.

John Hart: The Biography of a Signer of the Declaration of Independence. 15.95x. Pioneer VT.

John Havlicek. PLB 5.50 (ISBN 0-87191-498-0). Creative Ed.

John Hay. lib. bdg. 9.50 (ISBN 0-8057-7199-9). Twayne.

John Hay: The Gentleman As Diplomat. 15.00 (ISBN 0-472-23400-5). U of Mich Pr.

John Henry Cardinal Newman. lib. bdg. 15.00 (ISBN 0-8414-9379-0). Folcroft.

John Hunt Morgan & His Raiders. 4.95 (ISBN 0-8131-0214-6). U Pr of Ky.

John Hus: A Biography. lib. bdg. 22.25x (ISBN 0-313-21050-0, SPJH). Greenwood.

John Huston. 10.00 (ISBN 0-385-11070-7). Doubleday.

John Is Easy to Please: Encounters with the Written & Spoken Word. 7.50 (ISBN 0-374-17986-7). FS&G.

John James Audubon: Bird Artist. PLB 3.58 (ISBN 0-8116-6291-8). Garrard.

John Jay. 12.50 (ISBN 0-404-50859-6). AMS Pr.

John Jay: Founder of a State & Nation. text ed. 7.90x (ISBN 0-8077-2177-8). Tchrs Coll.

John Jones Pettus, Mississippi Fire-Eater: His Life & Times, 1813-1867. 12.50 (ISBN 0-87805-066-3). U Pr of Miss.

John Kenneth Galbraith. pap. 4.95 (ISBN 0-312-44380-3). St Martin.

John Kenneth Galbraith. lib. bdg. 6.95 (ISBN 0-8057-3681-6). Twayne.

John Knox: Portrait of a Calvinist. facsimile ed. 16.00 (ISBN 0-8369-5656-7). Arno.

John Lackland. 15.00 (ISBN 0-404-00614-0). AMS Pr.

John Lackland. 65.00 (ISBN 0-8490-0455-1). Gordon Pr.

John Lackland. 14.00 (ISBN 0-403-01129-9). Scholarly.

John Langdon of New Hampshire. 12.50 (ISBN 0-8046-1277-3). Kennikat.

John Lennon: One Day at a Time. A Personal Biography of the Seventies. 2nd ed. pap. 7.95 (ISBN 0-394-17754-1, E772). Grove.

John Letcher of Virginia: The Story of Virginia's Civil War Governor. 15.00 (ISBN 0-8173-5216-3). U of Ala Pr.

John Lind of Minnesota. 14.00 (ISBN 0-8046-1389-3). Kennikat.

John Locke. 3rd ed. 22.50x (ISBN 0-19-824355-3). Oxford U Pr.

John Locke: A Biography. lib. bdg. 30.00x (ISBN 0-405-11690-X). Arno.

John Lothrop Motley: A Memoir. 14.00 (ISBN 0-8369-6775-5). Arno.

John Lothrop Motley: A Memoir. lib. bdg. 20.00 (ISBN 0-8495-2213-7). Arden Lib.

John Lothrop Motley: A Memoir. lib. bdg. 25.00 (ISBN 0-8495-2265-X). Arden Lib.

John Lyly. lib. bdg. 14.95 (ISBN 0-8383-0261-0). Haskell.

John M. Synge: A Few Personal Recollections with Biographical Notes. lib. bdg. 10.00 (ISBN 0-8414-1726-1). Folcroft.

John McIntosh Kell of the Raider Alabama. 15.00 (ISBN 0-8173-5106-X). U of Ala Pr.

John Mackenzie, South African Missionary & Statesman. 22.50x (ISBN 0-8371-2443-3). Negro U Pr.

John McLoughlin: Father of Oregon. pap. 4.95 (ISBN 0-8323-0257-0). Binford.

John Maher of Delancey Street: A Guide for Peaceful Revolution in America. 7.95 (ISBN 0-393-07499-4). Norton.

John Marshall. lib. bdg. 16.50 (ISBN 0-306-70287-8). Da Capo.

John Marshall. pap. 1.95 (ISBN 0-226-79408-3, P260). U of Chicago Pr.

John Marshall - Judicial Statesman. PLB 5.72 (ISBN 0-07-014903-8). McGraw.

John Maynard Keynes. pap. 2.95 (ISBN 0-14-004319-5). Penguin.

John Millington Synge. lib. bdg. 7.95 (ISBN 0-8057-1532-0). Twayne.

John Mill's Boyhood Visit to France: Being a Journal & Notebook Written by John Stuart Mill in France, 1820-21. 7.50x (ISBN 0-8020-5088-3). U of Toronto Pr.

John Milton. lib. bdg. 16.95 (ISBN 0-8383-2097-X). Haskell.

John Milton. lib. bdg. 10.00 (ISBN 0-8414-9389-8). Folcroft.

John Milton: A Short Study of His Life & Works. 12.00 (ISBN 0-404-06523-6). AMS Pr.

John Milton Gregory & the University of Illinois. 10.00 (ISBN 0-252-72563-8). U of Ill Pr.

John Milton Hay. lib. bdg. 9.95 (ISBN 0-8057-7719-9). Twayne.

John Milton the Elder & His Music. lib. bdg. 13.00 (ISBN 0-374-90980-6). Octagon.

John Mitchell, Miner: Labor's Bargain with the Gilded Age. 14.50 (ISBN 0-404-02829-2). AMS Pr.

John Mitchell, Miner: Labor's Bargain with the Gilded Age. lib. bdg. 15.50x (ISBN 0-8371-2170-1, GLJM). Greenwood.

John Morgan: Continental Doctor. 5.00. N Watson.

John Morgan: Continental Doctor. 10.00x (ISBN 0-8122-7479-2). U of Pa Pr.

John Muir. new ed. PLB 4.49 (ISBN 0-399-60880-X). Putnam.

John Neal. lib. bdg. 9.95 (ISBN 0-8057-7230-8). Twayne.

John of Salisbury. 13.00 (ISBN 0-8462-1614-0). Russell.

John Osborne. 10.50 (ISBN 0-8044-2386-5). Ungar.

John Paul II: A Pictorial Biography. 14.95x (ISBN 0-07-033327-0); pap. 7.95x (ISBN 0-07-033328-9). McGraw.

John Paul Jones: A Sailor's Biography. 12.95 (ISBN 0-316-58358-8). Little.

John Paul Jones, America's First Naval Hero. lib. bdg. 2.45 incl. catalog cards; pap. 1.25 vinyl laminated covers. SamHar Pr.

John Pendleton Kennedy: Gentleman from Baltimore. 18.50x (ISBN 0-8018-0083-8). Johns Hopkins.

John Pory, 1572-1636: The Life & Letters of a Man of Many Parts. incl. microfiche 17.00x (ISBN 0-8078-1270-6). U of NC Pr.

John Pym. lib. bdg. 15.25x (ISBN 0-8371-4561-9, WAJP). Greenwood.

John Quincy Adams. 12.50 (ISBN 0-404-50866-9). AMS Pr.

John Quincy Adams: His Theory & Ideas. pap. 1.95 (ISBN 0-8152-0100-1, A100). T Y Crowell.

John Randolph. 12.50 (ISBN 0-404-50865-0). AMS Pr.

John Randolph. 5.25 (ISBN 0-8446-0451-8). Peter Smith.

John Ross. PLB 6.95 (ISBN 0-87518-173-2). Dillon.

John Ross & the Cherokee Indians. 18.00 (ISBN 0-404-15526-X). AMS Pr.

John Ruskin. lib. bdg. 29.95 (ISBN 0-8383-1053-2). Haskell.

John Ruskin. lib. bdg. 12.50. Folcroft.

John Ruskin: A Sketch of His Life, His Work & His Opinions with Personal Reminiscences. lib. bdg. 22.50 (ISBN 0-8495-4893-4). Arden Lib.

John Ruskin: A Study. lib. bdg. 17.50 (ISBN 0-8414-1872-1). Folcroft.

John Ruskin: An Introduction to Further Study of His Life & Work. 28.50 (ISBN 0-404-14046-7). AMS Pr.

John Ruskin, Economist. lib. bdg. 8.50 (ISBN 0-8492-4930-9). R West.

John Ruskin: The Argument of the Eye. 16.50 (ISBN 0-691-03890-2). Princeton U Pr.

John Ruskin's Letters to William Ward. lib. bdg. 22.50 (ISBN 0-8414-3219-8). Folcroft.

John Sandfield Macdonald, 1812-1872. 4.50 (ISBN 0-8020-3248-6). U of Toronto Pr.

John Sharp Williams: Planter-Statesman of the Deep South. 7.50 (ISBN 0-8446-1331-2). Peter Smith.

John Shaw Neilson. text ed. 10.00x (ISBN 0-85179-357-6). Verry.

John Sherman. 16.00 (ISBN 0-404-50883-9). AMS Pr.

John Sherman Cooper: The Global Kentuckian. 4.95 (ISBN 0-8131-0220-0). U Pr of Ky.

John Skelton: A Sketch of His Life & Writings. 8.00 (ISBN 0-8462-1365-6). Russell.

John Smart: The Man & His Miniatures. 7.50 (ISBN 0-8079-0071-0). October.

John Smith of Virginia. 6.50 (ISBN 0-688-21597-1). Morrow.

John Stark Freedom Fighter. 5.95; pap. 2.95. Dale Bks.

John Strachan: 1778-1867. 6.50 (ISBN 0-8020-3225-7). U of Toronto Pr.

John Strachan, 1778-1867. pap. 4.50x (ISBN 0-7746-6433-9). Intl Schol Bk Serv.

John Stuart Mill. lib. bdg. 7.95 (ISBN 0-8057-1392-1). Twayne.

John Stuart Mill. text ed. 21.00x (ISBN 0-04-320113-X); pap. text ed. 9.95x (ISBN 0-04-320114-8). Allen Unwin.

John Stuart Mill in Love. 14.95 (ISBN 0-86033-020-6). Gordon-Cremonesi.

John Trumbull, Connecticut Wit. lib. bdg. 12.75x (ISBN 0-8371-6094-4, COJT). Greenwood.

John Wanamaker. 35.00x (ISBN 0-8046-1479-2). Kennikat.

John Wayne. PLB 5.50 (ISBN 0-87191-551-0). Creative Ed.

John Wayne Story. 8.95 (ISBN 0-87000-171-X). Arlington Hse.

John Wesley: A Portrait. 10.00 (ISBN 0-404-03994-4). AMS Pr.

John Wesley: A Theological Biography. 6.50 (ISBN 0-687-20480-1). Abingdon.

John Wesley: A Theological Biography. 12.95 (ISBN 0-687-20481-X). Abingdon.

John Wesley & His World. 10.95 (ISBN 0-684-15922-8). Scribner.

John Wesley: His Life & Theology. 9.95 (ISBN 0-310-36660-7). Zondervan.

John Wheelwright: His Writings, Including His Fast-Day Sermon, 1637. 24.00 (ISBN 0-8337-3763-5). B Franklin.

John White of Mashonaland. 13.50x (ISBN 0-8371-2070-5). Negro U Pr.

John Wilkes Booth Himself. 17.50 (ISBN 0-9602256-0-9). Hired Hand.

John Wilkins, 1614-1672: An Intellectual Biography. 18.50x (ISBN 0-520-01396-4). U of Cal Pr.

John William De Forest. pap. 3.45 (ISBN 0-8084-0192-0, T82). Coll & U Pr.

John William Draper & the Religion of Science. lib. bdg. 11.00 (ISBN 0-374-92750-2). Octagon.

John Wise, Early American Democrat. lib. bdg. 13.00 (ISBN 0-374-91919-4). Octagon.

John Witherspoon: Parson, Politician, Patriot. 5.95 (ISBN 0-664-20812-6); pap. 2.95 (ISBN 0-664-24795-4). Westminster.

John Wycliffe & the Beginnings of English Nonconformity. 5.50x (ISBN 0-340-16648-7). Verry.

John Zizka & the Hussite Revolution. 17.50 (ISBN 0-8462-1344-3). Russell.

Johnny. pap. 3.95 (ISBN 0-498-02400-8). A S Barnes.

Johnny. 7.95 (ISBN 0-498-06766-1); pap. 3.95 (ISBN 0-498-02400-8). A S Barnes.

Johnny Appleseed: Man & Myth. 6.75 (ISBN 0-8446-1366-5). Peter Smith.

Johnny Bench. 5.95g (ISBN 0-8098-2077-3). Walck.

Johnny Carson. PLB 5.50 (ISBN 0-87191-560-X). Creative Ed.

Johnny Cash. PLB 5.95 (ISBN 0-87191-391-7); pap. 2.75 (ISBN 0-89812-102-7). Creative Ed.

Johnny Dodds. pap. 1.95 (ISBN 0-498-04053-4). A S Barnes.

Johnny Miller. PLB 5.50 (ISBN 0-87191-455-7). Creative Ed.

Johnny Unitas. 5.50 (ISBN 0-87191-346-1). Creative Ed.

Johnny Unitas Story. PLB 4.97 (ISBN 0-399-60325-5). Putnam.

Johnny, We Hardly Knew Ye: Memories of John Fitzgerald Kennedy. 10.00 (ISBN 0-316-71625-1). Little.

Johnson & Goldsmith & Their Poetry. lib. bdg. 7.50. Folcroft.

Johnson & Goldsmith & Their Poetry. 7.25 (ISBN 0-404-52515-6). AMS Pr.

Johnson & Goldsmith & Their Poetry. lib. bdg. 8.00 (ISBN 0-8495-2308-7). Arden Lib.

Johnson: His Characteristics & Aphorisms. lib. bdg. 25.00 (ISBN 0-8414-4806-X). Folcroft.

Johnson's Diary of a Journey into North Wales see **Life of Johnson.**

Jomo Kenyatta: Towards Truth About "the Light of Kenya". lib. bdg. 14.50x (ISBN 0-8371-8307-3, DEJK). Greenwood.

Jonah & the Great Fish. 7.95 (ISBN 0-690-46430-4). T Y Crowell.

Jonathan Edwards, the Fiery Puritan. 24.50 (ISBN 0-404-59144-2). AMS Pr.

Jonathan Edwards, 1703-1758. lib. bdg. 20.00 (ISBN 0-374-98684-3). Octagon.

Jonathan Swift. 27.50 (ISBN 0-8414-0687-1). Folcroft.

Jonathan Swift: A Biographical & Critical Study. 34.95 (ISBN 0-8490-0461-6). Gordon Pr.

Jonathan Swift: A Biographical & Critical Study. lib. bdg. 30.00 (ISBN 0-8414-3605-3). Folcroft.

Jones Very, Emerson's Brave Saint. lib. bdg. 16.75x (ISBN 0-8371-0296-0, BAJV). Greenwood.

Jones Very: The Effective Years, 1833-1840. 20.00x (ISBN 0-231-03043-6). Columbia U Pr.

Joni. pap. 2.95 (ISBN 0-310-23982-6). Zondervan.

Joni. pap. 2.25 (ISBN 0-553-11572-3, 13154-0). Bantam.

Joni. pap. 3.95 (ISBN 0-89066-002-6). World Wide Pubs.

Joni. 6.95 (ISBN 0-310-23960-5); kivar, large print 4.95 (ISBN 0-310-23967-2); pap. 3.95 (ISBN 0-310-23961-3); pap. 2.25 mass mkt. (ISBN 0-310-23962-1). Zondervan.

Joni Mitchell. pap. 3.95 (ISBN 0-8256-3907-7). Music Sales.

Jorge Isaacs. lib. bdg. 7.95 (ISBN 0-8057-2460-5). Twayne.

Jorge Luis Borges: A Literary Biography. 19.95 (ISBN 0-525-13748-3). Dutton.

Jose Antonio Paez. facsimile ed. 18.50 (ISBN 0-8369-5624-9). Arno.

Jose Antonio Paez. 12.50 (ISBN 0-8046-1069-X). Kennikat.

Jose Antonio Paez. lib. bdg. 12.00x (ISBN 0-8154-0329-1). Cooper Sq.

Jose Carlos Mariategui & the Rise of Modern Peru, 1890-1930. 14.95x (ISBN 0-8263-0507-5). U of NM Pr.

Jose Del Valle of Central America. 14.75 (ISBN 0-8223-0031-1). Duke.

Jose Ortega y Gasset. 9.95 (ISBN 0-8044-2659-7). Ungar.

Joseph B. Eastman, Servant of the People. lib. bdg. 21.25x (ISBN 0-8371-7769-3, FUJE). Greenwood.

Joseph Brant, Iroquois Ally of the British. new ed. lib. bdg. 2.45 incl. catalog cards; pap. 1.25 vinyl laminated covers. SamHar Pr.

Joseph Chamberlain & English Social Politics. lib. bdg. 16.50 (ISBN 0-374-93322-7). Octagon.

Joseph Chamberlain & Liberal Reunion: The Round Table Conference 1887. 15.00x (ISBN 0-8020-1438-0). U of Toronto Pr.

Joseph, Chief of the Nez Perce. 4.50 (ISBN 0-8323-0172-8). Binford.

Joseph Conrad. 6.00 (ISBN 0-396-05711-X). Dodd.

Joseph Conrad. pap. 1.95 (ISBN 0-8277-6002-7, WTW2). British Bk Ctr.

Joseph Conrad: A Critical Biography. lib. bdg. 25.25x (ISBN 0-8371-8304-9, BAJOC). Greenwood.

Joseph Conrad: A Psychoanalytic Biography. 17.50x (ISBN 0-691-06065-7); pap. 5.45 (ISBN 0-691-01296-2). Princeton U Pr.

Joseph Conrad As I Knew Him. 8.50 (ISBN 0-8274-1277-0). R West.

Joseph Conrad As I Knew Him. 11.00 (ISBN 0-403-00560-4). Scholarly.

Joseph Conrad As I Knew Him. facs. ed. 12.50 (ISBN 0-8369-5497-1). Arno.

Joseph Conrad in the Congo. lib. bdg. 10.00 (ISBN 0-8414-2197-8). Folcroft.

Joseph Conrad in the Congo. lib. bdg. 10.95 (ISBN 0-8383-1638-7). Haskell.

Joseph Conrad: The Man. lib. bdg. 15.95 (ISBN 0-8383-1487-2). Haskell.

Joseph Conrad: The Man. lib. bdg. 15.00 (ISBN 0-8495-0136-9). Arden Lib.

Joseph Conrad: The Three Lives. 25.00 (ISBN 0-374-18014-8). FS&G.

Joseph Conrad: The Three Lives. pap. 14.95 (ISBN 0-374-51547-6). FS&G.

Joseph de Maistre. lib. bdg. 9.50 (ISBN 0-8057-6247-7). Twayne.

Joseph Dennie & His Circle: A Study in American Literature from 1792-1812. pap. 11.00 (ISBN 0-384-14195-1). Johnson Repr.

Joseph E. Brown & the Confederacy. lib. bdg. 18.75x (ISBN 0-8371-5722-6, HIJB). Greenwood.

Joseph E. Brown of Georgia. 35.00x (ISBN 0-8071-0189-3). La State U Pr.

Joseph Fels & the Single - Tax Movement. 18.00x (ISBN 0-87722-010-7). Temple U Pr.

Joseph Fourier: The Man & the Physicist. 39.00x (ISBN 0-19-858149-1). Oxford U Pr.

Joseph Hawley: Colonial Radical. 8.50 (ISBN 0-404-01128-4). AMS Pr.

Joseph Haydn: His Art, Times & Glory. lib. bdg. 17.25x (ISBN 0-8371-5792-7, JAJH). Greenwood.

Joseph Haydn: His Life in Contemporary Pictures. 12.95 (ISBN 0-8008-4425-4). Taplinger.

Joseph Hopkins Twichell: Mark Twain's Friend & Pastor. 8.00x (ISBN 0-8203-0104-3). U of Ga Pr.

Joseph Jones, M.D. Scientist of the Old South. 15.50 (ISBN 0-8131-1296-6). U Pr of Ky.

Joseph Lister. 35.00 (ISBN 0-8128-2156-4). Stein & Day.

Joseph M. Dixon of Montana. Incl. Senator & Bull Moose Manager 1867-1917; Governor Versus the Anaconda 1917-1934. 14.95 set; 7.95 ea. U of MT Pubns Hist.

Joseph Neef: The Americanization of Pestalozzianism 1800-1840. 10.75 (ISBN 0-8173-9110-X). U of Ala Pr.

Joseph Pulitzer & the New York World. 19.50x (ISBN 0-691-04521-6). Princeton U Pr.

Joseph Pulitzer, Giant of Journalism. lib. bdg. 2.45 incl. catalog cards (ISBN 0-87157-558-2); pap. 1.25 vinyl laminated covers (ISBN 0-87157-058-0). SamHar Pr.

Joseph Pulitzer, His Life & Letters. 17.50 (ISBN 0-404-05699-7). AMS Pr.

Joseph R. McCarthy. 8.95 (ISBN 0-13-566729-1); pap. 2.95 (ISBN 0-13-566711-9, S720). P-H.

Joseph Reed: A Moderate in the American Revolution. 22.50 (ISBN 0-404-51595-9). AMS Pr.

Joseph Sadoc Alemany: Harbinger of a New Era. 9.50 (ISBN 0-87093-094-X). Dawsons.

Joseph Schillinger: A Memoir. lib. bdg. 17.50 (ISBN 0-306-70780-2). Da Capo.

Joseph Smith Chronology. 6.95 (ISBN 0-87747-734-5). Deseret Bk.

Joseph Smith, the Man & the Seer. 4.95 (ISBN 0-87747-131-2). Deseret Bk.

Joseph Stalin. lib. bdg. 7.95 (ISBN 0-8057-3080-X). Twayne.

Joseph Stalin & Communist Russia. PLB 4.28 (ISBN 0-8116-4753-6). Garrard.

Joseph Stephen Cullinan: A Study of Leadership in the Texas Petroleum Industry, 1897-1937. 10.95 (ISBN 0-8265-1155-4). Vanderbilt U Pr.

Joseph Warren: Physician, Politician, Patriot. 8.00 (ISBN 0-252-72503-4). U of Ill Pr.

Josephine. pap. 1.95 (ISBN 0-505-51351-X). Belmont-Tower.

Josephine: The Empress & Her Children. 10.95 (ISBN 0-393-07500-1). Norton.

Josephus. lib. bdg. 30.00 (ISBN 0-8495-0369-8). Arden Lib.

Josh Gibson: A Life in the Negro Leagues. 9.95 (ISBN 0-06-010446-5). Har-Row.

Joshua Coit: American Federalist, 1758-1798. 12.50x (ISBN 0-8195-3023-9). Columbia U Pr.

Joshua James. PLB 5.95 (ISBN 0-87966-104-6). Dexter & Westbrook.

Joshua Slocum. 14.50 (ISBN 0-8135-0700-6). Rutgers U Pr.

Josiah Quincy, 1772-1864: The Last Federalist. text ed. 12.00 (ISBN 0-674-48375-8). Harvard U Pr.

Josiah Walls: Florida's Black Congressman of Reconstruction. 7.50 (ISBN 0-8130-0399-7). U Presses Fla.

Josiah Warren, the First American Anarchist: A Sociological Study. 18.50 (ISBN 0-404-60977-5). AMS Pr.

Josiah Wedgwood. 35.00 (ISBN 0-8128-1907-1). Stein & Day.

Josiah Willard Gibbs, the History of a Great Mind. 16.50 (ISBN 0-208-00826-8). Shoe String.

Josie Pearl. 2.95. Nevada Pubns.

Journal in Jail. 16.00 (ISBN 0-405-01690-5). Arno.

Journal of a Neurosurgeon. 10.25 (ISBN 0-398-02325-5). C C Thomas.

Journal of a Solitude. lib. bdg. 13.95 (ISBN 0-8161-6777-X). G K Hall.

Journal of a Solitude. pap. 2.95 (ISBN 0-393-00853-3, N853). Norton.

Journal of a Solitude, 1970-1971. 11.95 (ISBN 0-393-07474-9). Norton.

Journal of a Tour to Corsica & Memoirs of Pascal Paoli. lib. bdg. 17.50 (ISBN 0-8414-3155-8). Folcroft.

Journal of an Itinerant Artist. 9.95 (ISBN 0-87973-887-1, 887). Our Sunday Visitor.

Journal of Arnold Bennett. 20.75 (ISBN 0-518-19119-2). Arno.

Journal of Edward Ellerker Williams, Companion of Shelley & Byron in 1821 & 1822. lib. bdg. 12.50 (ISBN 0-8414-4552-4). Folcroft.

Journal of George Fox. lib. bdg. 47.50 (ISBN 0-374-92826-6). Octagon.

Journal of Katherine Mansfield. 17.00 (ISBN 0-86527-265-4). Fertig.

Journal of Madam Knight. 6.00 (ISBN 0-8446-1268-5). Peter Smith.

Journal of Madam Knight. 6.00 (ISBN 0-403-00650-3). Scholarly.

Journal of Madam Knight. 6.95 (ISBN 0-87923-044-4). Godine.

Journal of Madame Royale. 7.50 (ISBN 0-8027-6251-4); PLB 7.39 (ISBN 0-8027-6252-2). Walker & Co.

Journal of Mule Train Packing in Eastern Washington in the 1860's. 9.95 (ISBN 0-87770-205-5). Ye Galleon.

Journal of Rehearsals: A Memoir. 12.75 (ISBN 0-8223-0401-5). Duke.

Journal of Samuel Curwen, Loyalist. text ed. 35.00x (ISBN 0-674-48380-4). Harvard U Pr.

Journal of Sir Walter Scott. lib. bdg. 45.25x (ISBN 0-313-20305 9, SCJO). Greenwood.

Journal of Sir Walter Scott. 44.00x (ISBN 0-19-812438-4). Oxford U Pr.

Journal of the Adventures of Matthew Bunn. facsimile ed. pap. 1.75. Newberry.

Journal to Stella. text ed. 28.50x (ISBN 0-06-496664-X). B&N.

Journals & Correspondence of Lady Eastlake. 38.50 (ISBN 0-404-56746-0); 19.50 ea. AMS Pr.

Journals: Early Fifties Early Sixties. pap. 6.95 (ISBN 0-394-17034-2, E704). Grove.

Journals of David E. Lilienthal. Incl. The TVA Years, 1939-45 (ISBN 0-06-012610-8); The Atomic Energy Years, 1945-50 (ISBN 0-06-012611-6); Venturesome Years, 1950-55 (ISBN 0-06-012612-4); The Road to Change, 1955-59 (ISBN 0-06-012613-2); The Harvest Years, 1959-63 (ISBN 0-06-012614-0), Creativity & Conflict, 1964-1967 (ISBN 0-06-012619-1). 20.00 ea. Har-Row.

Journals of Jim Elliot. 12.95 (ISBN 0-8007-0922-5). Revell.

Journey into Light. pap. 7.95 (ISBN 0-916438-06-6). Univ of Trees.

Journey Not the Arrival Matters: An Autobiography of the Years 1939 to 1969. pap. 3.25 (ISBN 0-15-646523-X, HB323). HarBraceJ.

Journey to Armenia. 32.00. G F Ritchie.

Journey to the Trenches: The Life of Isaac Rosenberg, 1890-1918. 13.95x (ISBN 0-465-03676-7). Basic.

Journey with Genius: Recollections & Reflections Concerning D. H. Lawrence. lib. bdg. 20.00 (ISBN 0-374-91137-1). Octagon.

Journey with the Saints. facs. ed. 12.75 (ISBN 0-8369-8070-0). Arno.

Journeys Out of the Body. pap. 4.95 (ISBN 0-385-00861-9). Doubleday.

Journeys with the Senator. 12.95 (ISBN 0-87397-129-9). Strode.

Joy of Bach. pap. 4.95 (ISBN 0-8066-1776-4, 10-3598). Augsburg.

Joy of Being a Woman: Guidance for Meaningful Living by Outstanding LDS Women. 6.95 (ISBN 0-88290-015-3). Horizon Utah.

Joy of Discovery. bds. 3.95 (ISBN 0-8054-7217-7). Broadman.

Joy of the Snow. 8.95 (ISBN 0-698-10605-9). Coward.

Joyce Country. new ed. pap. 3.95 (ISBN 0-8052-0347-8). Schocken.

Joyce Grenfell Requests the Pleasure. 10.95 (ISBN 0-312-44528-8). St Martin.

Joyce in Nighttown: A Psychoanalytic Inquiry into Ulysses. 12.50x (ISBN 0-520-02398-6). U of Cal Pr.
Jozef-Julian Sekowski: The Genesis of a Literary Alien. pap. 7.00x (ISBN 0-520-09267-8). U of Cal Pr.
J.P. Marquand,Esquire: A Portrait in the Form of a Novel. 11.00 (ISBN 0-8369-8144-8). Arno.
Juan Martinez Montanes, Sevillian Sculptor. 35.00 (ISBN 0-87535-107-7). Hispanic Soc.
Juarez, Man of Law. 5.95 (ISBN 0-374-33950-3). FS&G.
Juarez, the Founder of Modern Mexico. 5.95 (ISBN 0-688-21769-9). Morrow.
Jubilee!! The Autobiography of Hermon Pettit. pap. 3.95 (ISBN 0-933082-00-2). Bookmates Intl.
Judah P. Benjamin: Confederate Statesman. facsimile ed. 27.00x (ISBN 0-405-06733-X). Arno.
Judge Frank M. Johnson Jr. A Biography. 10.95 (ISBN 0-399-12123-4). Putnam.
Judge Legett of Abilene: A Texas Frontier Profile. 12.95 (ISBN 0-89096-041-0). Tex A&M Univ Pr.
Judge: The Life of Robert A. Hefner. 9.75 (ISBN 0-8061-1307-3). U of Okla Pr.
Judgment of Jonah. pap. 1.95 (ISBN 0-8028-1373-9). Eerdmans.
Judicial Murder of Mary E. Surratt. 25.00 (ISBN 0-403-00423-3). Scholarly.
Judy. 12.50 (ISBN 0-06-011337-5). Har-Row.
Judy. pap. 2.50 (ISBN 0-440-15107-4). Dell.
Judy Collins. pap. 3.95 (ISBN 0-8256-3914-X). Music Sales.
Judy Garland. pap. 2.50 (ISBN 0-15-646558-2, M3482). HarBraceJ.
Juggernaut: The Path of Dictatorship. 18.50 (ISBN 0-404-56109-8). AMS Pr.
Juggernaut, the Path of Dictatorship. facs. ed. 21.25 (ISBN 0-8369-1280-2). Arno.
Juice: Football's Superstar O.J. Simpson. 6.95 (ISBN 0-8098-0005-5). Walck.
Jule: The Story of Composer Jule Styne. 10.95 (ISBN 0-394-41296-6). Random.
Jules Laforgue. text ed. 14.50x (ISBN 0-485-14606-1); pap. text ed. 6.25x (ISBN 0-485-12206-5). Humanities.
Jules Verne, & His Work. lib. bdg. 9.60 (ISBN 0-88411-906-8, 906). Amereon Ltd.
Julia Margaret Cameron: Her Life & Photographic Work. 25.00 (ISBN 0-912334-50-9); pap. 14.50 (ISBN 0-912334-51-7). Aperture.
Julia Ward Howe. lib. bdg. 20.00x (ISBN 0-910220-24-7). Larlin Corp.
Julian the Apostate. 12.50x (ISBN 0-674-48881-4). Harvard U Pr.
Julio Gonzalez: Sculpture in Iron. 40.00x (ISBN 0-8147-9171-9). NYU Pr.
Julius Caesar. PLB 4.79 (ISBN 0-671-32286-9). Messner.
Julius Caesar & the Foundation of the Roman Imperial System. 30.00 (ISBN 0-404-58261-3). AMS Pr.
Julius Erving. PLB 5.95 (ISBN 0-87191-499-9); pap. 2.75 (ISBN 0-89812-181-7). Creative Ed.
Julius Erving: Doctor J & Julius W. PLB 5.95 (ISBN 0-88436-265-5); pap. 3.50 (ISBN 0-88436-266-3). EMC.
Julius K Nyerere: Teacher of Africa. PLB 5.29 (ISBN 0-671-32717-8). Messner.
Jungle Cowboy. 8.95 (ISBN 0-8008-4444-0). Taplinger.
Junior Book of Authors. 2nd rev. ed. 10.00 (ISBN 0-8242-0028-4). Wilson.
Junius Smith: Biography of the Father of the Atlantic Liner. facsimile ed. 15.50 (ISBN 0-8369-6664-3). Arno.
Just a Country Lawyer: A Biography of Senator Sam Ervin. 8.50x (ISBN 0-253-14540-6). Ind U Pr.
Just Like Abraham Lincoln. reinforced bdg. 6.95 (ISBN 0-395-20107-1). HM.
Justice William Johnson, the First Dissenter: The Career & Constitutional Philosophy of a Jeffersonian Judge. lib. bdg. 14.95x (ISBN 0-87249-060-2). U of SC Pr.

K

Kafka's Prayer. 9.95 (ISBN 0-88373-051-0); pap. 3.95 (ISBN 0-88373-047-2). Stonehill Pub Co.
Kafu the Scribbler: The Life & Writings of Nagai Kafu, 1879-1959. 15.00x (ISBN 0-8047-0267-5). Stanford U Pr.
Kahlil Gibran: A Self-Portrait. pap. 2.45 (ISBN 0-8065-0108-1, 241). Citadel Pr.
Kahtahah. pap. 5.95 (ISBN 0-88240-058-4). Alaska Northwest.
Kaiser & His Times. pap. 6.95 (ISBN 0-393-00661-1). Norton.
Kaiser: Warlord of the Second Reich. 14.95 (ISBN 0-684-15637-7). Scribner.
Kamala Nehru: An Intimate Biography. 7.50x. Intl Bk Dist.
Kamaladevi Chattopadhyaya: Portrait of a Rebel. 11.00x (ISBN 0-88386-784-2). South Asia Bks.
Kandinsky. 6.95 (ISBN 0-517-53708-7). Crown.
K'ang-Hsi & the Consolidation of Ch'ing Rule, 1661-1684. lib. bdg. 22.00x (ISBN 0-226-43203-3). U of Chicago Pr.
K'ang Yu-Wei: A Biography & a Symposium. 14.50x (ISBN 0-8165-0152-1). U of Ariz Pr.
Kano Eitoku. 14.95 (ISBN 0-87011-295-3). Kodansha.
Kant. pap. 2.50 (ISBN 0-14-020338-9). Penguin.
Kant. lib. bdg. 22.50 (ISBN 0-89984-503-7). Century Bookbindery.
Kant. 14.25 (ISBN 0-8369-6894-8). Arno.
Kant. 17.50 (ISBN 0-8274-2642-9). R West.
Kapellmeister Hummel in England & France. 10.50 (ISBN 0-911772-82-0). Info Coord.
Kareem Abdul Jabbar. 5.50 (ISBN 0-87191-350-X). Creative Ed.
Karen Horney: Gentle Rebel of Psychoanalysis. 9.95 (ISBN 0-8037-4425-0). Dial.
Karl Barth: His Life from Letters & Autobiographical Texts. 19.95 (ISBN 0-8006-0485-7). Fortress.
Karl Marx. pap. 0.95 (ISBN 0-02-007140-X). Macmillan.
Karl Marx: A Political Biography. 16.95 (ISBN 0-316-73210-9). Little.
Karl Marx, Biographical Memoirs. 12.00 (ISBN 0-403-00200-1). Scholarly.
Karl Marx: His Life & Environment. 4th ed. pap. 4.50 (ISBN 0-19-520052-7, GB 25). Oxford U Pr.
Karl Marx: His Life and Environment. 4th ed. 11.95 (ISBN 0-19-219122-5). Oxford U Pr.
Karl Marx: His Life & Thought. 15.00 (ISBN 0-06-012829-1). Har-Row.
Karl Marx: His Life & Thought. pap. 5.95 (ISBN 0-06-090585-9, CN585). Har-Row.
Karl Marx: Man & Fighter. pap. 4.95 (ISBN 0-14-021594-8). Penguin.
Karl Philipp Moritz: At the Fringe of Genius. 20.00x (ISBN 0-8020-5414-5). U of Toronto Pr.
Kate Greenaway. 18.00 (ISBN 0-405-08990-2). Arno.
Kate Greenaway. lib. bdg. 150.95 (ISBN 0-8490-2113-8). Gordon Pr.
Kate Jackson: Special Kind of Angel. text ed. 5.95 (ISBN 0-88436-430-5). EMC.
Kate: The Life of Katharine Hepburn. 7.95 (ISBN 0-393-07486-2). Norton.
Kate: The Life of Katherine Hepburn. pap. 2.25 (ISBN 0-451-09088-8, E9088). NAL.
Katharine Hepburn. pap. 1.75 (ISBN 0-515-02931-9, M2931). HarBraceJ.
Katherine Mansfield: A Biography. 17.50 (ISBN 0-8112-0751-X). New Directions.
Katherine Mansfield: The Memories of LM. 7.95 (ISBN 0-8008-4447-5). Taplinger.
Kathleen & Frank. 10.00 (ISBN 0-671-20991-4). S&S.
Kazan on Kazan. 7.50 (ISBN 0-670-41187-6). Viking Pr.
Kean. lib. bdg. 18.50x (ISBN 0-8371-7047-8, PLKE). Greenwood.
Keaton. 8.95 (ISBN 0-02-511570-7). Macmillan.
Keaton. pap. 3.95 (ISBN 0-02-012090-7). Macmillan.
Keaton: The Silent Features Close up. 12.95 (ISBN 0-520-03126-1); pap. 4.50 (ISBN 0-520-03155-5, CAL 338). U of Cal Pr.
Keats. lib. bdg. 15.00 (ISBN 0-8495-1952-7). Arden Lib.
Keats & Shakespeare: A Study of Keats Poetic Life from 1816-1820. lib. bdg. 20.00x (ISBN 0-313-20581-7, MUKS). Greenwood.
Keats As Doctor & Patient. lib. bdg. 9.50 (ISBN 0-374-93376-6). Octagon.
Keats As Doctor & Patient. lib. bdg. 6.45 (ISBN 0-8414-4868-X). Folcroft.
Keeping Your Personal Journal. 7.95 (ISBN 0-8091-0236-6); pap. 4.95 (ISBN 0-8091-2092-5). Paulist Pr.
Kelly Blue. 14.95 (ISBN 0-89096-073-9). Tex A&M Univ Pr.
Kelly Blue. pap. 2.95 (ISBN 0-8032-5795-3, 583). U of Nebr Pr.
Ken Stabler. PLB 5.95 (ISBN 0-87191-670-3); pap. 2.75 (ISBN 0-89812-170-1). Creative Ed.
Ken Stabler: Southpaw Passer. new ed. PLB 5.29 (ISBN 0-399-61056-1). Putnam.
Kennedy. 17.50 (ISBN 0-06-013950-1). Har-Row.
Kennedy Brothers. PLB 5.49 (ISBN 0-399-60335-2). Putnam.
Kennedy Case. pap. 1.75 (ISBN 0-445-08259-3). Popular Lib.
Kennedy Without Tears: The Man Beneath the Myth. 2.95 (ISBN 0-688-01934-X). Morrow.
Kenneth Kaunda of Zambia: The Times & the Man. 11.95x (ISBN 0-19-572338-4). Oxford U Pr.
Kenneth Patchen: A Collection of Essays. lib. bdg. 19.50 (ISBN 0-404-16005-0). AMS Pr.
Kenneth Slessor. lib. bdg. 7.95 (ISBN 0-8057-2838-4). Twayne.
Kenyatta. 12.50 (ISBN 0-525-13855-2). Dutton.
Kenyatta. 2nd ed. 17.95 (ISBN 0-04-920059-3). Allen Unwin.
Kepler's Dream: With the Full Text & Notes of Somnium Sive Astronomia Lunaris, Joannis Kepleri. 12.50x (ISBN 0-520-00716-6). U of Cal Pr.
Kerouac West Coast: A Bohemian Pilot, Detailed Navigational Instructions. bds. 5.95 (ISBN 0-918704-02-2); pap. 1.50. Fels & Firn.
Kerouac's Town. rev. ed. pap. 2.50 (ISBN 0-916870-07-3). Creative Arts Bk.
Keshub Chunder Sen. rev. ed. 6.00x (ISBN 0-88386-862-8). South Asia Bks.
Key of See: Travel Journals of a Composer. 4.00 (ISBN 0-87368-061-8). Plowshare.
Khrushchev: A Career. pap. 3.95 (ISBN 0-670-00330-1). Penguin.
Khrushchev: The Years in Power. pap. 2.95 (ISBN 0-393-00879-7). Norton.
Khrushchev: The Years in Power. 13.00x (ISBN 0-231-03939-5). Columbia U Pr.
Kid. 2.50 (ISBN 0-553-12000-X). Bantam.
Kid. 10.00 (ISBN 0-670-41296-1). Viking Pr.
Kidnapped. 5.95 (ISBN 0-06-061975-9). Har-Row.
Kierkegaard. 10.00 (ISBN 0-394-47092-3). Knopf.
Kilgallen. 12.95 (ISBN 0-440-04522-3). Delacorte.
Kindly Light: The Spiritual Vision of John Henry Newman. pap. 2.95 (ISBN 0-87793-185-2). Ave Maria.
King: A Biography. 2nd ed. 17.50 (ISBN 0-252-00679-8); pap. 5.95 (ISBN 0-252-00680-1). U of Ill Pr.
King Arthur, King of Kings. 24.95 (ISBN 0-86033-044-3). Gordon-Cremonesi.
King Charles the Martyr, 1643-1649. lib. bdg. 26.00x (ISBN 0-8371-7922-X, WIKCM). Greenwood.
King Danced in the Marketplace. pap. 10.00 (ISBN 0-87480-148-6). U of Utah Pr.
King Edward the Seventh. pap. 3.95 (ISBN 0-14-002658-4). Penguin.
King George III. pap. 4.95 (ISBN 0-586-03944-9). Academy Chi Ltd.
King George VI & Queen Elizabeth. 12.95 (ISBN 0-397-01229-2). Lippincott.
King in Haiti: The Story of Henri Christophe. 4.50 (ISBN 0-374-34140-0). FS&G.
King John. rev. ed. 15.00x (ISBN 0-520-03610-7); pap. 4.95x (ISBN 0-520-03643-3). U of Cal Pr.
King of Court Poets: A Study of the Work, Life & Times of Lodovico Ariosto. lib. bdg. 15.75x (ISBN 0-8371-0440-8, GALA). Greenwood.
King of the Court Poets: A Study of the Work, Life & Times of Lodovico Ariosto. lib. bdg. 24.95 (ISBN 0-8383-0944-5). Haskell.
King of the Gypsies. pap. 2.25 (ISBN 0-553-12584-2). Bantam.
King of the Mountains. 4.50. Holt Atherton.
King of the Road. 9.95 (ISBN 0-02-596030-X, 59603). Macmillan.
King of Two Worlds: Philip II of Spain. 12.95 (ISBN 0-399-11384-3). Putnam.
King Oliver. pap. 1.95 (ISBN 0-498-04036-4). A S Barnes.
King Stephen. pap. text ed. 6.50x (ISBN 0-582-48727-7). Longman.
King Stephen, 1135-1154. 12.50x (ISBN 0-520-00298-9). U of Cal Pr.
King Twist: A Portrait of Frank Randle. 14.25 (ISBN 0-7100-8977-5). Routledge & Kegan.
King Without a Crown: Albert, Prince Consort of England 1819-1861. 12.95 (ISBN 0-397-01143-1). Lippincott.
Kingdom Within: A Spiritual Autobiography. 9.95 (ISBN 0-07-062224-8). McGraw.
Kings & Kingship in Early Scotland. 16.50x (ISBN 0-87471-204-1). Rowman.
Kings & Queens of England. 5.95 (ISBN 0-88254-313-X). Hippocrene Bks.
Kings & Queens of England & Scotland. 14.95 (ISBN 0-8148-0654-6). L Amicl Pub.
Kings & Queens of Scotland. 9.95 (ISBN 0-8008-4477-7). Taplinger.
Kings & Queens: The Plantagenets of England. 7.95 (ISBN 0-8407-6438-3). Elsevier-Nelson.
King's Ballet Master: A Biography of Denmark's August Bournonville. 8.95 (ISBN 0-396-07722-6). Dodd.
Kings in the Making: The Princes of Wales. facs. ed. 16.50 (ISBN 0-8369-0937-2). Arno.
Kings of Commerce. facs. ed. 13.50 (ISBN 0-8369-0102-9). Arno.
Kings of Jazz. 20.00 (ISBN 0-498-01724-9). A S Barnes.
Kings of Motor Speed. PLB 5.29 (ISBN 0-399-60338-7). Putnam.
Kings of the Drag Strip. PLB 4.97 (ISBN 0-399-60336-0). Putnam.
Kings, Rulers & Statesmen. 20.00 (ISBN 0-8069-0050-4); lib. bdg. 17.59 (ISBN 0-8069-0051-2). Sterling.
Kinta Years. 7.95 (ISBN 0-395-14011-0). HM.
Kipling: The Glass, the Shadow & the Fire. 10.00 (ISBN 0-06-012833-X). Har-Row.
Kirk Douglas. pap. 1.75 (ISBN 0-515-04084-3). HarBraceJ.
Kirpal Singh: The Story of a Saint. pap. 3.95 (ISBN 0-918224-05-5). Sawan Kirpal Pubns.
Kiss Hollywood Good-by. lib. bdg. 10.95 (ISBN 0-8161-6263-8). G K Hall.
Kissinger. 12.50 (ISBN 0-316-48221-8). Little.
Kissinger & the Meaning of History. 15.95 (ISBN 0-521-22113-7). Cambridge U Pr.
Kissinger: Portrait of a Mind. new ed. text ed. 9.95 (ISBN 0-393-05481-0); pap. text ed. 3.45x (ISBN 0-393-09278-X). Norton.
Kissinger: The Adventures of Super-Kraut. 7.95 (ISBN 0-8184-0047-1). Lyle Stuart.
Kissinger: The European Mind in American Policy. 13.50 (ISBN 0-465-03727-5). Basic.
Kissinger: The Uses of Power. 5.95 (ISBN 0-395-14366-7). HM.
Kit Carson: A Portrait in Courage. 15.95 (ISBN 0-8061-0541-0). U of Okla Pr.
Kit Carson: A Portrait in Courage. pap. 7.95 (ISBN 0-8061-1601-3). U of Okla Pr.
Kit Carson's Autobiography. pap. 2.95 (ISBN 0-8032-5031-2, 325). U of Nebr Pr.
Kitty, My Rib. pap. 4.50 (ISBN 0-570-03113-3, 12-2347). Concordia.
Klaus Mann. lib. bdg. 9.50 (ISBN 0-8057-6309-0). Twayne.
Knife Is Not Enough. 5.95 (ISBN 0-393-07416-1). Norton.
Knight of El Dorado: The Tale of Don Gonzalo Jimenez De Quesada & His Conquest of New Granada. lib. bdg. 15.00x (ISBN 0-8371-0007-0, AREL). Greenwood.
Knight Prisoner: The Tale of Sir Thomas Malory & His King Arthur. 7.95 (ISBN 0-374-34269-5). FS&G.
Knights of Malta. 10.95 (ISBN 0-87599-087-8). S G Phillips.
Knot in the Thread: The Life & Work of Jacques Roumain. 12.95 (ISBN 0-88258-057-4). Howard U Pr.
Knot of Love. pap. 1.95x. Dothard.
Knowing Christ. pap. 4.95 (ISBN 0-8024-3502-5). Moody.
Known Violin Makers. 13.00 (ISBN 0-403-01552-9). Scholarly.
Known Violin Makers. text ed. 14.00x (ISBN 0-918624-00-2). Virtuoso.
Knox Brothers. 10.95 (ISBN 0-698-10860-4). Coward.
Knute Rockne: Notre Dame's Football Great. PLB 3.84 (ISBN 0-8116-4561-4). Garrard.
Korean Pentecost & the Sufferings Which Followed. pap. 1.95. Banner of Truth.
Kosciuszko in the American Revolution. text ed. 7.50 (ISBN 0-917004-09-4). Kosciuszko.
Kossuth. 10.00 (ISBN 0-8046-1090-8). Kennikat.
Koufax. 6.95 (ISBN 0-670-41508-1). Viking Pr.
Koxinga & Chinese Nationalism: History, Myth & the Hero. pap. 6.00x (ISBN 0-674-50566-2). Harvard U Pr.
Krieghoff. 29.95 (ISBN 0-8020-2348-7). U of Toronto Pr.
Krinkle Nose: A Prayer of Thanks. 4.95 (ISBN 0-8159-6002-6). Devin.
Kris Kristofferson. pap. 4.95 (ISBN 0-8256-3932-8). Music Sales.
Krishnamurti: The Years of Awakening. 8.95 (ISBN 0-374-18222-1). FS&G.
Krishnamurti's Notebook. pap. 1.95 (ISBN 0-06-080435-1, P 435). Har-Row.
Kristofer Janson in America. lib. bdg. 10.95 (ISBN 0-8057-9000-4). Twayne.
Kropotkin. pap. 5.95 (ISBN 0-226-52594-5, P818). U of Chicago Pr.
Kuo Mo-Jo: The Early Years. 7.50x (ISBN 0-674-50570-0). Harvard U Pr.
Kurt Schumacher: A Study in Personality & Political Behavior. 17.50x (ISBN 0-8047-0247-0). Stanford U Pr.
Kwame Nkrumah: The Anatomy of an African Dictatorship. 17.50x (ISBN 0-8419-0036-1). Holmes & Meier.

L

L. Emmett Holt: Pioneer of a Children's Century. 19.00x (ISBN 0-405-05960-4). Arno.
L. J. M. Daguerre: The History of the Diorama & the Daguerreotype. 2nd rev. ed. 7.50 (ISBN 0-8446-2120-X). Peter Smith.
L. T. Hobhouse, Sociologist. 11.00 (ISBN 0-8142-0235-7). Ohio St U Pr.
La Fayette: A Bibliography. 21.50 (ISBN 0-8337-1813-4). B Franklin.
La Follette. pap. 1.95 (ISBN 0-13-522433-0, S713). P-H.
La Follette & the Rise of the Progressives in Wisconsin. 18.00 (ISBN 0-8462-1696-5). Russell.
La Follette's Autobiography: A Personal Narrative of Political Experiences. pap. 5.25 (ISBN 0-299-02194-7). U of Wis Pr.
La Guardia: A Fighter Against His Times, 1882-1933. pap. 2.95 (ISBN 0-226-50330-5, P330). U of Chicago Pr.
La Guardia in Congress. lib. bdg. 15.25x (ISBN 0-8371-6434-6, 2ILG). Greenwood.
La Salle & the Discovery of the Great West. 12.50 (ISBN 0-87928-004-2). Corner Hse.
Labourers in the Vineyard. 8.75 (ISBN 0-8046-0933-0). Kennikat.

Lachlan McIntosh & the Politics of Revolutionary Georgia. 16.00 (ISBN 0-8203-0459-X). U of Ga Pr.
Ladd: The Life, the Legend, the Legacy of Alan Ladd. 10.95 (ISBN 0-87795-203-5). Arbor Hse.
Ladd: The Life, the Legend, the Legacy of Alan Ladd. pap. 2.75 (ISBN 0-425-04531-5). Berkley Pub.
Ladies & Gentlemen... Lenny Bruce. pap. 2.25 (ISBN 0-345-24269-6). Ballantine.
Ladies & Gentlemen, Lenny Bruce!!! 10.00 (ISBN 0-394-46274-2). Random.
Ladies of Seneca Falls: The Birth of the Woman's Rights Movement. 7.95 (ISBN 0-02-737770-9). Macmillan.
Ladies of Seneca Falls: The Birth of the Woman's Rights Movement. pap. 5.95 (ISBN 0-8052-0545-4). Schocken.
Ladies of the Press. lib. bdg. 15.00. Havertown Bks.
Lady & Her Tiger. pap. 1.95 (ISBN 0-345-25711-1). Ballantine.
Lady & the President: The Letters of Dorothea Dix & Millard Fillmore. 12.50 (ISBN 0-8131-1332-6). U Pr of Ky.
Lady from Vermont: Dorothy Canfield Fisher's Life & World. rev. ed. pap. 3.95 (ISBN 0-8289-0127-9). Greene.
Lady Gregory: A Literary Portrait. rev. ed. text ed. 3.75x (ISBN 0-900675-74-8). Humanities.
Lady Gregory: Interviews & Recollections. 13.50x (ISBN 0-87471-961-5). Rowman.
Lady Is a Jock. 5.95 (ISBN 0-396-06870-7). Dodd.
Lady Isabella Persse Gregory. lib. bdg. 8.95 (ISBN 0-8057-6658-8). Twayne.
Lady Laureates: Women Who Have Won the Nobel Prize. 13.00 (ISBN 0-8108-1161-8). Scarecrow.
Lady Lawyer. 8.95 (ISBN 0-8315-0141-3). Speller.
Lady Morgan in France. 19.95 (ISBN 0-85362-103-9). Routledge & Kegan.
Lady of the Tboli. 7.95 (ISBN 0-915684-28-4). Christian Herald.
Lady Sackville: A Biography. 10.00 (ISBN 0-385-11379-X). Doubleday.
Lady Sings the Blues. pap. 2.25 (ISBN 0-380-42374-X, 42374). Avon.
Lady Unknown: The Life of Angela Burdett-Coutts. 12.50 (ISBN 0-698-10939-2). Coward.
Lafayette: A Guide to the Letters, Documents, & Manuscripts in the United States. 40.00x (ISBN 0-8014-0953-5). Cornell U Pr.
Lafayette Between the American & French Revolution: 1783-1789. pap. 17.50x (ISBN 0-226-30536-8). U of Chicago Pr.
Lafayette Comes to America. pap. 9.50x (ISBN 0-226-30540-6). U of Chicago Pr.
Lafayette in Brooklyn. lib. bdg. 15.00 (ISBN 0-8414-2840-9). Folcroft.
Lafcadio Hearn. lib. bdg. 10.00 (ISBN 0-8414-8630-1). Folcroft.
Lafcadio Hearn in Japan. 34.95 (ISBN 0-8490-0480-2). Gordon Pr.
LaGuardia in Congress. pap. 2.35 (ISBN 0-393-00488-0). Norton.
Lamb Before Elia. lib. bdg. 27.50 (ISBN 0-8414-5995-9). Folcroft.
Lambs: A Study of Pre-Victorian England. lib. bdg. 20.00 (ISBN 0-8495-0299-3). Arden Lib.
Lambs: A Study of Pre-Victorian England. lib. bdg. 14.50x (ISBN 0-8371-6523-7, ANLA). Greenwood.
Lambs, Their Lives, Their Friends & Their Correspondence: New Particulars & New Materials. 10.00 (ISBN 0-404-07369-7). AMS Pr.
Lana Turner. pap. 1.75 (ISBN 0-515-04194-7). HarBraceJ.
Lancastrian Kings & Lollard Knights. 22.00x (ISBN 0-19-822344-7). Oxford U Pr.
Lancia. 24.50 (ISBN 0-901564-22-2). Motorbooks Intl.
Land & Cattle: Conversations with Joe Pankey, A New Mexico Rancher. 15.00 (ISBN 0-8263-0491-5). U of NM Pr.
Land of Eternal Darkness: Memories of Siberian Labor Camps. 10.00 (ISBN 0-533-03149-4). Vantage.
Land of Milk & Honey. 5.95 (ISBN 0-932260-00-4). Rock Harbor.
Land Unknown. 6.95 (ISBN 0-8076-0800-9). Braziller.
Landlord William Scully. 15.00x (ISBN 0-7006-0189-9). Regents Pr KS.
Landon of Kansas. 34.50x (ISBN 0-8032-0116-8). U of Nebr Pr.
Landor. 12.00 (ISBN 0-8274-2797-2). R West.
Landor. lib. bdg. 15.00 (ISBN 0-89987-100-3). Darby Bks.
Landscape Artist in America: The Life & Work of Jens Jensen. 15.00x (ISBN 0-226-18053-0). U of Chicago Pr.
Landseer: The Victorian Paragon. 19.95 (ISBN 0-241-89432-8). David & Charles.
Lanfranc of Bec. 28.50x (ISBN 0-19-822462-1). Oxford U Pr.
Langston Hughes. lib. bdg. 8.50 (ISBN 0-8057-0388-8). Twayne.
Langston Hughes. pap. 3.45 (ISBN 0-8084-0004-5, T123). Coll & U Pr.
Langston Hughes, American Poet. PLB 6.79 (ISBN 0-690-00219-X). T Y Crowell.
Lao She & the Chinese Revolution. 8.50x (ISBN 0-674-51075-5). Harvard U Pr.
Larry Csonka. PLB 5.50 (ISBN 0-87191-382-8). Creative Ed.
Larry Gorman: The Man Who Made the Songs. lib. bdg. 14.00x (ISBN 0-405-10100-7). Arno.
Lars Gyllensten. lib. bdg. 9.50 (ISBN 0-8057-6314-7). Twayne.
Las Vegas Is My Beat. 6.00 (ISBN 0-8184-0149-4). Lyle Stuart.
Las Vegas Is My Beat. pap. 2.95 (ISBN 0-8065-0618-0). Citadel Pr.
Last Actor-Managers. facs. ed. 16.00 (ISBN 0-8369-8072-7). Arno.
Last Barrier. pap. 3.95 (ISBN 0-06-062586-4, RD 202). Har-Row.
Last Captive. 8.95 (ISBN 0-88426-004-6). Encino Pr.
Last Confucian: Liang Shu-Ming & the Chinese Dilemma of Modernity. 17.50x (ISBN 0-520-03123-7). U of Cal Pr.
Last Cowboy. pap. 1.95 (ISBN 0-671-82425-2). PB.
Last Cowboy. 9.95 (ISBN 0-06-012454-7). Har-Row.
Last Crusade: A Negotiator's Middle East Handbook. text ed. 22.95x (ISBN 0-88229-554-3); pap. 11.95 (ISBN 0-88229-738-4). Nelson-Hall.
Last Days of Dietrich Bonhoeffer. 10.95 (ISBN 0-06-011564-5). Har-Row.
Last Days of Hitler. lib. bdg. 25.00 (ISBN 0-8495-5146-3). Arden Lib.
Last Days of Hitler. 3rd ed. pap. 1.95 (ISBN 0-02-038000-3). Macmillan.
Last Days of Marie Antoinette: An Historical Sketch. 6.50 (ISBN 0-404-07129-5). AMS Pr.
Last Days of Tolstoy. 17.00 (ISBN 0-527-16500-X). Kraus Repr.
Last Earls of Barrymore, 1769-1824. 15.00 (ISBN 0-405-08895-7). Arno.
Last Four Lives of Annie Besant. 11.50x (ISBN 0-226-57317-6). U of Chicago Pr.
Last Hours of Jesus. 4.50 (ISBN 0-8362-0221-X). Guild Bks.
Last Journals of David Livingstone in Central Africa, from 1865 to His Death. lib. bdg. 35.00x (ISBN 0-8371-3899-X, LILJ). Greenwood.
Last King of Paradise. 18.25 (ISBN 0-8369-7102-7). Arno.
Last Laugh: The World of the Stand-up Comics. 8.95 (ISBN 0-688-02888-8). Morrow.
Last Letters of Aubrey Beardsley. lib. bdg. 20.00 (ISBN 0-8414-4426-9). Folcroft.
Last Links with Byron, Shelley & Keats. lib. bdg. 15.00. Folcroft.
Last Months of Chaucer's Earliest Patron. 6.50 (ISBN 0-404-01698-7). AMS Pr.
Last of the Bohemians: Twenty Years with Leon-Paul Fargue. lib. bdg. 12.25x (ISBN 0-8371-3729-2, BEBO). Greenwood.
Last of the Conquistadors, Junipero Serra, 1713-1784. lib. bdg. 21.25x (ISBN 0-8371-7523-2, ENJS). Greenwood.
Last of the Fathers: Saint Bernard of Clairvaux & the Encyclical Letter, Doctor Mellifluus. lib. bdg. 10.00x (ISBN 0-8371-4434-5, MELF). Greenwood.
Last of the Scottsboro Boys: An Autobiography. 10.95 (ISBN 0-399-12018-1). Putnam.
Last Season of Weeb Ewbank. 10.00 (ISBN 0-374-18462-3). FS&G.
Last Stuart: The Life & Times of Bonnie Prince Charlie. 10.00 (ISBN 0-399-11109-3). Putnam.
Last Testament of Lucky Luciano. 10.00 (ISBN 0-316-32140-0). Little.
Last Twelve Years of Joseph Conrad. 9.45 (ISBN 0-8274-1278-9). R West.
Last Twelve Years of Joseph Conrad. 9.50 (ISBN 0-8462-1062-2). Russell.
Last Victorians. 20.00. Norwood Edns.
Last Victorians. facsimile ed. 17.00 (ISBN 0-8369-1445-7). Arno.
Last Witness for Robert Louis Stevenson. 15.95 (ISBN 0-8061-0453-8). U of Okla Pr.
Last Year of Leo Tolstoy. 7.95 (ISBN 0-8037-4662-8). Dial.
Last Years of Nijinsky. 16.00 (ISBN 0-404-04775-0). AMS Pr.
Last Years of Rodin. lib. bdg. 19.95 (ISBN 0-8383-1945-9). Haskell.
Last Years of Thomas Jefferson, 1809-1826. 5.50 (ISBN 0-682-48168-8). Exposition.
Late Seventeenth Century Scientists. 16.75 (ISBN 0-08-013359-2); pap. 9.00 (ISBN 0-08-013358-4). Pergamon.
Later Years of the Saturday Club, 1870-1920. facs. ed. 18.75 (ISBN 0-8369-0548-2). Arno.
Latin American Government Leaders. 8.00x (ISBN 0-87918-021-8); pap. 5.50x. ASU Lat Am St.
Laugh, Clown, Cry: The Story of Charlie Chaplin. 6.60 (ISBN 0-8172-0427-X); PLB 6.60 (ISBN 0-8172-0426-1). Raintree Pubs.
Laughing Last: Alger Hiss. 8.95 (ISBN 0-395-24899-X). HM.
Laughter in the Next Room. lib. bdg. 18.50x (ISBN 0-8371-6042-1, SILA). Greenwood.
Laura Baugh. PLB 5.50 (ISBN 0-87191-501-4). Creative Ed.
Laura Baugh: Golf's Golden Girl. lib. bdg. 5.95 (ISBN 0-88436-160-8); pap. 3.50 (ISBN 0-88436-161-6). EMC.
Laura: The Life of Laura Ingalls Wilder. 8.95 (ISBN 0-8092-8174-0). Contemp Bks.
Laura: The Life of Laura Ingalls Wilder. pap. 1.95 (ISBN 0-380-01636-2, 40865). Avon.
Lauren Bacall by Myself. pap. 2.75. Ballantine.
Lauren Bacall by Myself. 10.95 (ISBN 0-394-41308-3). Knopf.
Laurence Olivier. lib. bdg. 10.95 (ISBN 0-8057-9260-0). Twayne.
Laurence Stallings. lib. bdg. 7.95 (ISBN 0-8057-0686-0). Twayne.
Laurence Sterne As Yorick. lib. bdg. 19.00x (ISBN 0-313-22000-X, COLS). Greenwood.
Lawrence. 18.50 (ISBN 0-404-00385-0). AMS Pr.
Lawrence - the Story of His Life. 20.00 (ISBN 0-8274-2810-3). R West.
Lawrence & Oppenheimer. 7.50 (ISBN 0-671-41068-7). S&S.
Lawrence M. Judd & Hawaii: An Autobiography. 8.00 (ISBN 0-8048-0910-0). C E Tuttle.
Lawrence of Arabia & His World. 8.95 (ISBN 0-684-14726-2). Scribner.
Lawrence, the Story of His Life. lib. bdg. 25.00 (ISBN 0-8482-5877-0). Norwood Edns.
Lawyering. pap. 3.95 (ISBN 0-374-51394-5). FS&G.
Lawyering. 10.00 (ISBN 0-374-18422-4); pap. 3.95 (ISBN 0-374-51394-5). FS&G.
Lawyers for the People: A New Breed of Defenders & Their Work. PLB 5.99 (ISBN 0-394-92659-5). Knopf.
Lawyer's Lawyer: The Life of John W. Davis. 22.50 (ISBN 0-19-501699-8). Oxford U Pr.
Lawyer's Lawyer: The Life of John W. Davis. pap. 7.95 (ISBN 0-19-502354-4, GB526). Oxford U Pr.
Lay up Your Treasures in Heaven. pap. 3.95 (ISBN 0-88270-257-2). Logos.
Layman Shares Jesus. pap. 3.95 (ISBN 0-8054-5558-7). Broadman.
Lazarus. 7.95 (ISBN 0-03-015351-4). HR&W.
Lazarus. pap. 2.95 (ISBN 0-394-17068-7, E719). Grove.
Lazarus Spengler: A Lay Leader of the Reformation. 15.00x (ISBN 0-8142-0290-X). Ohio St U Pr.
LBJ: An Irreverent Chronicle. 9.95 (ISBN 0-690-01089-3). T Y Crowell.
L.B.J. the Man from Johnson City. rev. ed. 5.95 (ISBN 0-396-06199-0). Dodd.
Le Corbusier. 10.00 (ISBN 0-88208-002-4). Lawrence Hill.
Le Corbusier & the Tragic View of Architecture. 13.95x (ISBN 0-674-51860-8). Harvard U Pr.
Le Corbusier & the Tragic View of Architecture. pap. 4.95 (ISBN 0-674-51861-6). Harvard U Pr.
Le Corbusier. The Machine & the Grand Design. 7.95 (ISBN 0-8076-0514-X); pap. 3.95 (ISBN 0-8076-0518-2). Braziller.
Lead, Kindly Light. 13.50 (ISBN 0-8369-1529-1). Arno.
Lead Me to the Exit. 6.95 (ISBN 0-918056-01-2). Ariadne Pr.
Leaders in Education. 5th ed. 52.50 (ISBN 0-8352-0699-8). Bowker.
Leaders in Israel: Thumb-Nail Sketches of the Officers of the First Provisional Government. 10.00 (ISBN 0-8369-8111-1). Arno.
Leaders of American Conservation. 15.50 (ISBN 0-8260-2045-3, 16263). Wiley.
Leaders of Our People. text ed. 4.50 (122921); text ed. 5.00 (123921); tchrs'. guide 3.25 (202922). UAHC.
Leaders of Public Opinion in Ireland. lib. bdg. 47.50 (ISBN 0-306-70574-5). Da Capo.
Leaders of Socialism: Past & Present. facs. ed. 10.50 (ISBN 0-8369-0928-3). Arno.
Leaders of the American Revolution. 5.95g (ISBN 0-590-07130-0). Schol Bk Serv.
Leaders of the Church of England, 1828-1944. 14.50x (ISBN 0-19-213110-9). Oxford U Pr.
Leaders of the Communist World. 17.95 (ISBN 0-02-932380-0). Free Pr.
Leaders of Thought in the Modern Church. 14.00 (ISBN 0-8369-7333-X). Arno.
Leadership in Eastern Africa: Six Political Biographies. 15.00x (ISBN 0-87270-011-9). Holmes & Meier.
Leadership of Abraham Lincoln. pap. text ed. 6.95x (ISBN 0-471-25689-7). Wiley.
Leadership of Abraham Lincoln. text ed. 7.75 (ISBN 0-471-25688-9). Krieger.
Leadership Through the Ages. facs. ed. 15.00 (ISBN 0-8369-0657-8). Arno.
Leading American Inventors. facs. ed. 19.50 (ISBN 0-8369-0557-1). Arno.
Leading Ladies. 25.00 (ISBN 0-87000-388-7). Arlington Hse.
Leading Ladies. pap. 12.95 (ISBN 0-89508-016-8). Rainbow Bks.
Leading Ladies: An Affectionate Look at American Women of the Twentieth Century. 10.00 (ISBN 0-8128-1909-8). Stein & Day.
Leah. 3.95 (ISBN 0-8007-0595-5). Revell.
Leakey's Luck: The Life of Louis Seymour Bazett Leakey. 15.95 (ISBN 0-15-149456-8). HarBraceJ.
Learned Blacksmith: The Letters & Journals of Elihu Burritt. lib. bdg. 12.95x (ISBN 0-89198-063-6). Ozer.
Learned Blacksmith: The Letters & Journals of Elihu Burritt. Bd. with Congress of Nations: Addresses at the International Peace Congresses at Brussels (1848), Paris (1849), & Frankfort (1850. lib. bdg. 38.00 (ISBN 0-8240-0248-2). Garland Pub.
Learned Doctor William Ames: Dutch Backgrounds of English & American Puritanism. 12.50 (ISBN 0-252-00233-4). U of Ill Pr.
Leaves from the Journals of Sir George Smart. lib. bdg. 29.50 (ISBN 0-306-70164-2). Da Capo.
Leaves from the Notebook of a Tamed Cynic. pap. 4.95 (ISBN 0-06-066231-X). Har-Row.
Leavis. 11.50x (ISBN 0-87471-917-8). Rowman.
Lectures & Discourses of Earthquakes & Subterraneous Eruptions. lib. bdg. 15.00x (ISBN 0-405-10443-X). Arno.
Lectures on Shakespeare. lib. bdg. 15.00 (ISBN 0-8414-5075-7). Folcroft.
Lectures on the Historians of Bohemia. 12.50 (ISBN 0-405-08756-X). Arno.
Lee After the War. lib. bdg. 14.75x (ISBN 0-8371-6911-9, FILW). Greenwood.
Lee Elder: The Daring Dream. PLB 5.95 (ISBN 0-88436-267-1); pap. 3.50 (ISBN 0-88436-268-X). EMC.
Lee of Virginia: A Biography. lib. bdg. 20.00x (ISBN 0-8371-8270-0, BRLV). Greenwood.
Lee Trevino. 5.50 (ISBN 0-87191-342-9). Creative Ed.
Left Hand, Right Hand. 6.25 (ISBN 0-8446-2949-9). Peter Smith.
Legacy. 9.95 (ISBN 0-308-10351-3). T Y Crowell.
Legacy of Albion Small. 15.00x (ISBN 0-226-14520-4). U of Chicago Pr.
Legacy of Mark Rothko. 14.95 (ISBN 0-03-014751-4). HR&W.
Legacy of Mark Rothko. pap. 4.95 (ISBN 0-14-005205-4). Penguin.
Legend of Henry Ford. 10.00 (ISBN 0-8462-1084-3). Russell.
Legend of Henry Ford. pap. text ed. 5.95x (ISBN 0-689-70191-8, 129). Atheneum.
Legend of John Brown: A Biography & a History. 15.00 (ISBN 0-394-46124-X). Knopf.
Legendary Outlaws of the West. 9.95 (ISBN 0-8098-5006-0). Walck.
Legendary Women of the West. 7.95 (ISBN 0-679-20776-7). McKay.
Legends of the Patriarchs & Prophets & Other Old Testament Characters. lib. bdg. 30.00 (ISBN 0-8414-3205-8). Folcroft.
Leif Erikson the Lucky. PLB 5.45 sL (ISBN 0-531-02297-8). Watts.
Leigh Hunt. 8.75 (ISBN 0-8274-1350-5). R West.
Leigh Hunt. lib. bdg. 15.95 (ISBN 0-8383-1010-9). Haskell.
Lelia: The Life of George Sand. pap. 3.95 (ISBN 0-14-004354-3). Penguin.
Lella Secor: A Diary in Letters, 1915-1922. pap. 5.95 (ISBN 0-89102-114-0). B Franklin.
Lella Secor: A Diary in Letters, 1915-1922. lib. bdg. 14.95 (ISBN 0-89102-071-3). B Franklin.
Lelooska. pap. 7.95 (ISBN 0-89087-126-4). Celestial Arts.
Lemieux. 39.50 (ISBN 0-7715-9352-X). Vanguard.
Lend Me an Eye. 9.95 (ISBN 0-236-31058-5). Merrimack Bk Serv.
Lenin. lib. bdg. 17.25x (ISBN 0-8371-8191-7, GOLE). Greenwood.
Lenin. 12.95 (ISBN 0-8214-0094-0). Lib Soc Sci.
Lenin. 12.95 (ISBN 0-8128-2519-5). Stein & Day.
Lenin: A Biography. pap. 3.95 (ISBN 0-14-020809-7). Penguin.
Lenin & Gandhi. 18.50 (ISBN 0-8369-6932-4). Arno.
Lenin & World Revolution. 6.50 (ISBN 0-8446-1338-X). Peter Smith.
Lenin, Red Dictator. 18.50 (ISBN 0-404-06758-1). AMS Pr.
Lenin's Childhood. 7.95 (ISBN 0-19-211704-1). Oxford U Pr.
Lennon Remembers. pap. 1.25 (ISBN 0-445-08191-0). Popular Lib.
Lenny Bruce: The Comedian As Social Critic & Secular Moralist. 10.00 (ISBN 0-913460-31-1); pap. 2.95 (ISBN 0-913460-32-X). Monad Pr.
Lenny, Janis & Jimi. pap. 1.75 (ISBN 0-671-78969-4). PB.
Lenny Wilkens Story. 6.95 (ISBN 0-8397-5032-3). Eriksson.

Leo Ornstein: The Man, His Ideas, His Work. facsimile ed. 9.00x (ISBN 0-405-06732-1). Arno.

Leo Tolstoy. 15.00 (ISBN 0-8274-2822-7). R West.

Leo Tolstoy & His Works. lib. bdg. 5.50 (ISBN 0-8414-2303-2). Folcroft.

Leo Tolstoy & His Works. lib. bdg. 13.95 (ISBN 0-8383-2009-0). Haskell.

Leo Tolstoy & His Works. lib. bdg. 10.00 (ISBN 0-8495-3791-6). Arden Lib.

Leon Blum: The Formative Years 1872-1914. 15.00x (ISBN 0-87580-030-0). N Ill U Pr.

Leon Trotsky. 10.00 (ISBN 0-670-42372-6). Viking Pr.

Leon Trotsky. pap. 2.95 (ISBN 0-14-005067-1). Penguin.

Leon Trotsky. lib. bdg. 8.95 (ISBN 0-8057-7720-2). Twayne.

Leonard Covello: A Study of an Immigrants Contribution to New York City. lib. bdg. 28.00x (ISBN 0-405-11090-1). Arno.

Leonard of Pisa & the New Mathematics of the Middle Ages. 7.95 (ISBN 0-690-48809-2). T Y Crowell.

Leonard Woolf: A Political Biography. 18.50x (ISBN 0-312-48001-6). St Martin.

Leonardo. 12.95 (ISBN 0-385-04154-3). Doubleday.

Leonardo Da Vinci. 15.00x (ISBN 0-674-52450-0). Harvard U Pr.

Leonhard Rauwolf: Sixteenth-Century Physician, Botanist, & Traveler. 15.00x (ISBN 0-674-52500-0). Harvard U Pr.

Leonid Andreyev. 9.95 (ISBN 0-8044-2657-0). Ungar.

Leonid I. Brezhnev: Pages from His Life. 11.95 (ISBN 0-671-24111-7). S&S.

Leontiev. lib. bdg. 25.00 (ISBN 0-8495-0405-8). Arden Lib.

Lermontov: Tragedy in the Caucasus. 12.50 (ISBN 0-8076-0874-2). Braziller.

Leslie Stephen, His Thought & Character in Relation to His Time. 23.00 (ISBN 0-404-14021-1). AMS Pr.

Leslie Weatherhead: A Personal Portrait. 7.95 (ISBN 0-687-21375-4). Abingdon.

Lester Frank Ward. lib. bdg. 9.50 (ISBN 0-8057-7175-1). Twayne.

Lester Pearson & the Dream of Unity. 17.95 (ISBN 0-385-13478-9). Doubleday.

Lester Roloff: Living by Faith. pap. 3.95 (ISBN 0-8407-9506-8). Nelson.

Let Me Live. 15.00 (ISBN 0-405-01869-X). Arno.

Let Me Speak! Testimony of Domitila, a Woman of the Bolivian Mines. 12.50 (ISBN 0-85345-445-0, CL-4450); pap. 5.95 (ISBN 0-85345-485-X, PB485X). Monthly Rev.

Let Me Speak: Testimony of Domitila, a Woman of the Bolivian Mines. pap. 5.95 (ISBN 0-85345-485-X, PB485X). Monthly Rev.

Let the Hammer Down. pap. 1.95 (ISBN 0-671-82626-3). PB.

Let the Hammer Down. 6.95 (ISBN 0-8499-0062-X, 0062-X). Word Bks.

Let the Record Show: Memoirs of a Parole Board Member. 5.50 (ISBN 0-682-48991-3). Exposition.

Let Them Speak for Themselves: Women in the American West,1849-1900. 15.00 (ISBN 0-208-01645-7). Shoe String.

Let Them Speak for Themselves: Women in the American West 1849-1900. pap. 5.95 (ISBN 0-525-47521-4) Dutton.

Let's Be Frank About It. 10.95 (ISBN 0-385-11493-1). Doubleday.

Let's Find Out About Daniel Boone. PLB 4.47 (ISBN 0-531-00008-7). Watts.

Letter from Reachfar. 7.95 (ISBN 0-312-48230-2). St Martin.

Letterbook of Eliza Lucas Pinckney, 1739-1762. 11.00 (ISBN 0-8078-1182-3). U of NC Pr.

Letters About Shelley. lib. bdg. 12.45. Folcroft.

Letters About Shelley Interchanged by Three Friends-Edward Dowden, Richard Garnett & William Michael Rossetti. 12.50 (ISBN 0-404-05444-7). AMS Pr.

Letters About Shelley Interchanged by Three Friends-Edward Dowden, Richard Garnett & William Michael. lib. bdg. 12.00 (ISBN 0-8414-0579-4). Folcroft.

Letters & Diaries of Oskar Schlemmer. 25.00x (ISBN 0-8195-4047-1). Columbia U Pr.

Letters & Diary of Laura M. Towne: Written from the Sea Islands of South Carolina, 1862-1884. 14.25x (ISBN 0-8371-2654-1). Negro U Pr.

Letters & Friendships of Sir Cecil Spring Rice: A Record. facsimile ed. 42.50 (ISBN 0-8369-6750-X). Arno.

Letters & Journals of Samuel Gridley Howe. 45.00 (ISBN 0-404-03357-1). AMS Pr.

Letters & Journals of Thomas Wentworth Higginson: 1846-1906. 15.50x (ISBN 0-8371-1843-3). Negro U Pr.

Letters & Journals of Thomas Wentworth Higginson, 1846-1906. lib. bdg. 32.50 (ISBN 0-306-71495-7). Da Capo.

Letters & Literary Memorials of Samuel J. Tilden. 27.50x (ISBN 0-8046-1491-1). Kennikat.

Letters & Literary Memorials of Samuel J. Tilden. facsimile ed. 36.00 (ISBN 0-8369-5913-2). Arno.

Letters & Literary Remains of Edward Fitzgerald. lib. bdg. 65.00. Folcroft.

Letters & Literary Remains of Edward Fitzgerald. 175.00 (ISBN 0-404-02440-8). AMS Pr.

Letters & Memorials of Jane Welsh Carlyle. 32.50 (ISBN 0-404-56709-6). AMS Pr.

Letters & Memorials of State, in the Reigns of Queen Mary, Queen Elizabeth, King James, King Charles the First, Part of the Reign of King Charles the Second, & Oliver's Usurpation. lib. bdg. 185.00 (ISBN 0-404-01631-6). AMS Pr.

Letters & Papers from Prison. enl. ed. 7.95 (ISBN 0-02-513110-9). Macmillan.

Letters & Papers from Prison. rev. ed. 9.95 (ISBN 0-02-513100-1). Macmillan.

Letters & Papers of Alfred Thayer Mahan. 95.00x (ISBN 0-87021-339-3). Naval Inst Pr.

Letters & Papers of Cadwallader Colden, 1711-1775. 247.50 (ISBN 0-404-01690-1). AMS Pr.

Letters & Papers of Chaim Weizmann. Incl (ISBN 0-87855-194-8) (ISBN 0-87855-195-6) (ISBN 0-87855-196-4) (ISBN 0-87855-197-2) (ISBN 0-87855-198-0) (ISBN 0-87855-199-9) (ISBN 0-87855-200-6) (ISBN 0-87855-224-3) (ISBN 0-87855-249-9) (ISBN 0-87855-250-2) (ISBN 0-87855-251-0) (ISBN 0-87855-252-9) (ISBN 0-87855-253-7). casebound 400.00; 24.95 ea. Transaction Bks.

Letters & Papers of John Singleton Copley & Henry Pelham, 1739-1776. lib. bdg. 29.50 (ISBN 0-306-71406-X). Da Capo.

Letters & Poems of Fulbert of Chartres. 29.95x (ISBN 0-19-822233-5). Oxford U Pr.

Letters & Times of the Tylers. lib. bdg. 95.00 (ISBN 0-306-71316-0). Da Capo.

Letters from & to Joseph Joachim. 45.00x (ISBN 0-8443-0043-8). Vienna Hse.

Letters from Attica. pap. 1.95 (ISBN 0-688-06031-5). Morrow.

Letters from England, 1813-1844. 22.50x (ISBN 0-19-812430-9). Oxford U Pr.

Letters from George Moore to Ed Dujardin. lib. bdg. 12.50. Folcroft.

Letters from George W. Eveleth to Edgar Allan Poe. lib. bdg. 10.00 (ISBN 0-8414-5915-0). Folcroft.

Letters from Italy & Switzerland. 18.25 (ISBN 0-8369-5271-5). Arno.

Letters from Mrs. Elizabeth Carter to Mrs. Montagu Between the Years 1755-1800. 82.50 (ISBN 0-404-56720-7); 27.50 ea. AMS Pr.

Letters from Percy Bysshe Shelley to Jane Clairmont. lib. bdg. 20.00 (ISBN 0-8414-7682-9). Folcroft.

Letters from Prison. pap. 3.95 (ISBN 0-06-090452-6, CN452). Har-Row.

Letters from Rupert Brooke to His Publisher, 1911-1914. lib. bdg. 25.00 (ISBN 0-374-90997-0). Octagon.

Letters from Russia, 1919. pap. 3.50 (ISBN 0-7100-0077-4). Routledge & Kegan.

Letters from Sunnyside & Spain. 14.50x. Elliots Bks.

Letters from Sunnyside & Spain. lib. bdg. 15.00 (ISBN 0-8414-5056-0). Folcroft.

Letters from Sunnyside & Spain. lib. bdg. 14.00 (ISBN 0-8495-2615-9). Arden Lib.

Letters from the Grand Tour. 25.00x (ISBN 0-7735-0090-1). McGill-Queens U Pr.

Letters from the Lake Poets. (Samuel Taylor Coleridge, William Wordsworth, Robert Southey) lib. bdg. 50.00 (ISBN 0-8414-7749-3). Folcroft.

Letters from William Blake to Thomas Butts. lib. bdg. 10.00. Folcroft.

Letters Hitherto Unpublished, Written by Members of Sir Walter Scott's Family to Their Old Governess. lib. bdg. 22.50 (ISBN 0-8414-2662-7). Folcroft.

Letters Home: Correspondence 1950-1963. 15.00 (ISBN 0-06-013372-4). Har-Row.

Letters of A. Bronson Alcott. 19.50x (ISBN 0-8138-0087-0). Iowa St U Pr.

Letters of A. E. Housman. 15.95 (ISBN 0-8464-0090-1). Beekman Pubs.

Letters of A. E. Housman. text ed. 13.75x (ISBN 0-246-64007-3). Humanities.

Letters of Abelard & Heloise. lib. bdg. 9.00x (ISBN 0-8154-0486-7). Cooper Sq.

Letters of Abelard & Heloise. pap. 2.50 (ISBN 0-14-044297-9). Penguin.

Letters of Alexander Woollcott. lib. bdg. 18.50x (ISBN 0-8371-6199-1, WOLW). Greenwood.

Letters of Anne Gilchrist & Walt Whitman. lib. bdg. 21.95 (ISBN 0-8383-1630-1). Haskell.

Letters of Anthony Trollope. lib. bdg. 31.00x (ISBN 0-313-21156-6, TRLE). Greenwood.

Letters of Anton Chekhov. 12.50 (ISBN 0-670-42596-6) Viking Pr.

Letters of Arthur Henry Hallam. write for info. (ISBN 0-8142-0300-0). Ohio St U Pr.

Letters of Asa Gray. lib. bdg. 47.00 (ISBN 0-8337-1430-9). B Franklin.

Letters of Aubrey Beardsley. 25.00 (ISBN 0-8386-6884-4). Fairleigh Dickinson.

Letters of Bret Harte. 27.50 (ISBN 0-404-09024-9). AMS Pr.

Letters of Bret Harte. 40.00 (ISBN 0-932062-78-4). Sharon Hill.

Letters of Brigham Young to His Sons. 9.95 (ISBN 0-87747-522-9). Deseret Bk.

Letters of C. S. Lewis. pap. 4.95 (ISBN 0-15-650870-2, HB300). HarBraceJ.

Letters of Carl Sandburg. 12.50 (ISBN 0-15-150695-7). HarBraceJ.

Letters of Caroline Norton to Lord Melbourne. 10.75 (ISBN 0-8142-0208-X). Ohio St U Pr.

Letters of Charles & Mary Anne Lamb: 1809-1817. 35.00x (ISBN 0-8014-1129-7). Cornell U Pr.

Letters of Charles Baudelaire to His Mother, 1833-1866. 16.00 (ISBN 0-405-08242-8). Arno.

Letters of Charles Dickens to Wilkie Collins 1851-1870. 12.75 (ISBN 0-8274-2834-0). R West.

Letters of Clara Schumann & Johannes Brahms. 50.00x (ISBN 0-8443-0116-7). Vienna Hse.

Letters of Clara Schumann & Johannes Brahms. pap. 15.00x (ISBN 0-8443-0056-X). Vienna Hse.

Letters of Composers: An Anthology 1603-1945. lib. bdg. 27.75x (ISBN 0-313-20664-3, NOLC). Greenwood.

Letters of Dennys De Berdt, 1757-70. facsimile ed. 12.75 (ISBN 0-8369-5931-0). Arno.

Letters of E. B. White. 15.00 (ISBN 0-06-014601-X). Har-Row.

Letters of E. B. White. pap. 7.50 (ISBN 0-06-090606-5, CN 606). Har-Row.

Letters of E.B. White. Incl. Essays of E.B. White. pap. 12.95 (ISBN 0-06-090736-3, CN 736). Har-Row.

Letters of Edward Fitzgerald. lib. bdg. 30.00. Folcroft.

Letters of Edward Fitzgerald. lib. bdg. 45.00 (ISBN 0-8495-1607-2). Arden Lib.

Letters of Edward John Trelawny. lib. bdg. 25.00. Folcroft.

Letters of Elizabeth Hitchener to Percy Bysshe Shelley. lib. bdg. 10.00 (ISBN 0-8414-7787-6). Folcroft.

Letters of Emily Lady Tennyson. 15.00x (ISBN 0-271-01123-8). Pa St U Pr.

Letters of Ernest Dowson. 25.00 (ISBN 0-8386-6747-3). Fairleigh Dickinson.

Letters of Ezra Pound. lib. bdg. 29.95 (ISBN 0-8383-1991-2). Haskell.

Letters of Felix Mendelssohn Bartholdy from Italy & Switzerland. lib. bdg. 30.00 (ISBN 0-89341-429-8). Longwood Pr.

Letters of Felix Mendelssohn Bartholdy from 1833 to 1847. lib. bdg. 30.00. Longwood Pr.

Letters of Felix Mendelssohn-Bartholdy from 1833-1847. 19.50 (ISBN 0-8369-5272-3). Arno.

Letters of Felix Mendelssohn to Ignaz & Charlotte Moscheles. 22.00 (ISBN 0-405-08786-1). Arno.

Letters of Felix Mendelssohn to Ignaz & Charlotte Moscheles. 22.00 (ISBN 0-8369-5217-0). Arno.

Letters of Franz Liszt. lib. bdg. 44.95 (ISBN 0-8383-0307-2). Haskell.

Letters of Franz Liszt to Marie Zu Sayn-Wittgenstein. lib. bdg. 17.00x (ISBN 0-8371-5933-4, LILM). Greenwood.

Letters of Franz Liszt to Olga von Meyendorff, 1871-1886, in the Mildred Bliss Collection at Dumbarton Oaks. text ed. 30.00 (ISBN 0-88402-078-9). Dumbarton Oaks.

Letters of Frederick Philip Grove. 27.50x (ISBN 0-8020-5311-4). U of Toronto Pr.

Letters of George Ade. 9.75 (ISBN 0-911198-34-2). Purdue.

Letters of George Gissing to Members of His Family. lib. bdg. 28.95 (ISBN 0-8383-1158-X). Haskell.

Letters of George Gissing to Members of His Family. 21.00 (ISBN 0-403-00480-2). Scholarly.

Letters of George Moore. lib. bdg. 17.50 (ISBN 0-8414-3980-X). Folcroft.

Letters of George Sand. 85.00 (ISBN 0-404-15230-9). AMS Pr.

Letters of George Sand. lib. bdg. 75.00 (ISBN 0-87968-451-8). Gordon Pr.

Letters of Grover Cleveland. lib. bdg. 49.50 (ISBN 0-306-71982-7). Da Capo.

Letters of Hart Crane & His Family. 25.00 (ISBN 0-231-03740-6). Columbia U Pr.

Letters of Hartley Coleridge. 21.50 (ISBN 0-404-14524-8). AMS Pr.

Letters of Hawthorne to William D Ticknor. 17.00 (ISBN 0-910972-19-2). IHS-PDS.

Letters of Hawthorne to William D. Ticknor. 17.00. Bruccoli.

Letters of Henry Wadsworth Longfellow. Incl. 1814-36; 1837-43. 37.50x (ISBN 0-674-52725-9); 1844-1856; 1857-1865. 40.00x (ISBN 0-674-52728-3). Harvard U Pr.

Letters of Horatio Greenough. lib. bdg. 20.00 (ISBN 0-306-71828-6). Da Capo.

Letters of Horatio Greenough, American Sculptor. 27.50x (ISBN 0-299-06070-5). U of Wis Pr.

Letters of James Agee to Father Flye. 2nd ed. 15.00 (ISBN 0-910220-91-3). Larlin Corp.

Letters of James Branch Cabell. 15.00x (ISBN 0-8061-1220-4). U of Okla Pr.

Letters of James Whitcomb Riley. 15.00 (ISBN 0-404-05336-X). AMS Pr.

Letters of John Addington Symonds. 19.95x ea. (ISBN 0-8143-1310-8) (ISBN 0-8143-1311-6) (ISBN 0-8143-1312-4). Wayne St U Pr.

Letters of John Chamberlain. lib. bdg. 72.50x (ISBN 0-313-20710-0, CHLE). Greenwood.

Letters of John Greenleaf Whittier. text ed. 75.00x (ISBN 0-674-52830-1). Harvard U Pr.

Letters of John Hamilton Reynolds. 8.50x (ISBN 0-8032-0827-8). U of Nebr Pr.

Letters of John Marin. lib. bdg. 9.00x (ISBN 0-8371-4270-9, MALE). Greenwood.

Letters of John Masefield to Florence Lamont. 20.00x (ISBN 0-231-04706-1). Columbia U Pr.

Letters of John Ruskin to Bernard Quaritch. lib. bdg. 20.00 (ISBN 0-8414-9539-4). Folcroft.

Letters of Jonathan Swift to Charles Ford. 23.50 (ISBN 0-404-15325-9). AMS Pr.

Letters of Jonathan Swift to Charles Ford. lib. bdg. 30.00 (ISBN 0-8495-4878-0). Arden Lib.

Letters of Joseph Conrad to Marguerite Poradowska 1890-1920. 9.50 (ISBN 0-8046-1747-3). Kennikat.

Letters of Joseph Conrad to Richard Curle. lib. bdg. 20.00 (ISBN 0-8414-3470-0). Folcroft.

Letters of Karl Marx. 19.95 (ISBN 0-13-531533-6). P-H.

Letters of Katherine Mansfield. 23.00 (ISBN 0-86527-271-9). Fertig.

Letters of Lenin. 25.00 (ISBN 0-88355-045-8). Hyperion Conn.

Letters of Letitia Hargrave. lib. bdg. 24.50x (ISBN 0-8371-5065-5, HALE). Greenwood.

Letters of Lincoln Steffens. lib. bdg. 60.00x (ISBN 0-8371-7710-3, STLLS). Greenwood.

Letters of Louis D. Brandeis. Incl. 1870-1907; Urban Reformer. 36.00 (ISBN 0-87395-078-X); microfiche 36.00 (ISBN 0-87395-178-6); 1907-1912; People's Attorney. 40.00 (ISBN 0-87395-091-7); microfiche 40.00 (ISBN 0-87395-191-3); 1913-1915; Progressive & Zionist. 36.00 (ISBN 0-87395-231-6); microfiche 36.00 (ISBN 0-87395-232-4); 1916-1921: Mr. Justice Brandeis. 36.00 (ISBN 0-87395-297-9). State U NY Pr.

Letters of Ludwig Tieck, Hitherto Unpublished, 1792-1853. 28.00 (ISBN 0-527-90100-8). Kraus Repr.

Letters of Lydia Maria Child. 12.00 (ISBN 0-405-00622-5). Arno.

Letters of Lydia Maria Child. 10.00 (ISBN 0-404-00141-6). AMS Pr.

Letters of Lydia Maria Child. 13.25x (ISBN 0-8371-2189-2). Negro U Pr.

Letters of Mary Russell Mitford. 10.00 (ISBN 0-8046-1583-7). Kennikat.

Letters of Mary Russell Mitford. lib. bdg. 25.00 (ISBN 0-8414-5403-5). Folcroft.

Letters of Mary W. Shelley (Mostly Unpublished) lib. bdg. 25.00 (ISBN 0-8414-0425-9). Folcroft.

Letters of Matthew Arnold to Arthur Hugh Clough. 8.00 (ISBN 0-8462-1220-X). Russell.

Letters of Matthew Arnold to Arthur Hugh Clough. 17.50x (ISBN 0-19-812401-5). Oxford U Pr.

Letters of Matthew Arnold to Arthur Hugh Clough. lib. bdg. 20.00. Folcroft.

Letters of Mrs. Gaskell. 35.00x (ISBN 0-674-52675-9). Harvard U Pr.

Letters of Olive Schreiner 1876-1920. 26.50 (ISBN 0-88355-259-0). Hyperion Conn.

Letters of Rebecca Gratz. facsimile ed. 29.00x (ISBN 0-405-06714-3). Arno.

Letters of Richard Wagner: The Burrell Collection. 50.00x (ISBN 0-8443-0031-4). Vienna Hse.

Letters of Richard Wagner to Anton Pusinelli. 40.00x. Vienna Hse.

Letters of Robert Browning. 17.50 (ISBN 0-8046-1735-X). Kennikat.

Letters of Robert Burns. lib. bdg. 20.00 (ISBN 0-8414-5287-3). Folcroft.

Letters of Robert Schumann. 16.00 (ISBN 0-405-08939-2). Arno.

Letters of Robert Southey to John May, 1797-1838. 14.95 (ISBN 0-8363-0137-4). Jenkins.

Letters of Sacco & Vanzetti. lib. bdg. 20.00 (ISBN 0-374-97003-3). Octagon.

Letters of Saint Boniface. lib. bdg. 15.00 (ISBN 0-374-92584-4). Octagon.

Letters of Saint Evremond. 20.00 (ISBN 0-405-08908-2). Arno.

Letters of Saint Evremond. facsimile ed. 22.00 (ISBN 0-8369-5907-8). Arno.

Letters of Samuel Palmer. 80.00x (ISBN 0-19-817309-1). Oxford U Pr.

Letters of Samuel Pepys & His Family Circle. lib. bdg. 23.75x (ISBN 0-313-20656-2, HELE). Greenwood.

Letters of Sarah, Duchess of Marlborough. 12.00 (ISBN 0-404-56766-5). AMS Pr.
Letters of Sarah, Duchess of Marlborough. 15.00 (ISBN 0-527-61750-4). Kraus Repr.
Letters of Sean O'Casey: 1910-1941. 35.00 (ISBN 0-02-566660-6). Macmillan.
Letters of Sigmund Freud. 15.00x (ISBN 0-465-03911-1). Basic.
Letters of Sir George Etherege. 21.00x (ISBN 0-520-02218-1). U of Cal Pr.
Letters of Sir Walter Scott. 300.00 (ISBN 0-404-05650-4); 25.00 ea. AMS Pr.
Letters of Sir Walter Scott & Charles Kirkpatrick Sharpe to Robert Chambers. lib. bdg. 15.00. Folcroft.
Letters of Sir William Jones. 45.00x (ISBN 0-19-812404-X). Oxford U Pr.
Letters of the Late Ignatius Sancho, an African. facs. ed. 17.75 (ISBN 0-8369-8791-8). Arno.
Letters of the Lewis & Clark Expedition with Related Documents, 1783-1854. 35.00 (ISBN 0-252-00697-6). U of Ill Pr.
Letters of the Tsar to the Tsaritsa, (1914-1917) 8.95 (ISBN 0-8179-4121-5). Hoover Inst Pr.
Letters of Thomas Carlyle. 19.45 (ISBN 0-8274-1149-9). R West.
Letters of Thomas Carlyle. 18.00 (ISBN 0-403-00897-2). Scholarly.
Letters of Thomas Carlyle: 1826-1936. 45.00 set (ISBN 0-8274-2847-2). R West.
Letters of Thomas Gorges, Deputy Governor of the Province of Maine: 1640-1643. 20.00 (ISBN 0-915592-30-4). Maine Hist.
Letters of Thomas Hood. 20.00x (ISBN 0-8020-5222-3). U of Toronto Pr.
Letters of Thomas Hood. lib. bdg. 10.50 (ISBN 0-374-93936-5). Octagon.
Letters of Thomas Jefferson. 8.95 (ISBN 0-89142-022-3). Sant Bani Ash.
Letters of Thomas Lovell Beddoes. 18.00 (ISBN 0-405-08261-4). Arno.
Letters of Thomas Wolfe to His Mother. 10.50 (ISBN 0-8078-1072-X). U of NC Pr.
Letters of Virginia Woolf. 14.95 (ISBN 0-15-150928-X). HarBraceJ.
Letters of Virginia Woolf, 1929-1931. 14.95 (ISBN 0-15-150927-1). HarBraceJ.
Letters of W. B. Yeats. lib. bdg. 52.50x (ISBN 0-374-98833-1). Octagon.
Letters of Walter Pater. 11.25x (ISBN 0-19-812406-6). Oxford U Pr.
Letters of Warwick Greene, 1915-28. facsimile ed. 17.75 (ISBN 0-8369-6651-1). Arno.
Letters of William & Dorothy Wordsworth. Incl. The Early Years 1787-1805. 2nd ed. 39.95x (ISBN 0-19-811464-8); The Middle Years, Pt. 1: 1806-1811. 2nd ed. 39.00x (ISBN 0-19-811491-5); The Middle Years, Pt. 1: 1812-1820. 2nd ed. 33.00x (ISBN 0-19-812403-1). Oxford U Pr.
Letters of William Cowper. facsimile ed. 42.50 (ISBN 0-8369-5147-6). Arno.
Letters of William Cullen Bryant: 1836-1849. 35.00 (ISBN 0-8232-0992-X). Fordham.
Letters of William Hazlitt. cOB*e 22.50x (ISBN 0-8147-4986-0); pap. 8.50x cODE (ISBN 0-8147-4987-9). NYU Pr.
Letters of William Morris to His Family & Friends. 24.50 (ISBN 0-404-14711-9). AMS Pr.
Letters of William Shenstone. 49.50 (ISBN 0-404-14601-5). AMS Pr.
Letters of William Shenstone. 65.00 (ISBN 0-8274-2849-9). R West.
Letters on Scottish Ballads from Professor Francis J. Child to W. W. Aberdeen. lib. bdg. 8.50 (ISBN 0-8414-1808-X). Folcroft.
Letters to an American Jewish Friend: A Zionist's Polemic. 7.50 (ISBN 0-8276-0093-3, 402). Jewish Pubn.
Letters to Felice. 6.95 (ISBN 0-8052-3500-0). Schocken.
Letters to Ibbotson. 12.95 (ISBN 0-915032-10-4). Natl-Poet Univ ME.
Letters to Ibbotson. 12.95 (ISBN 0-915032-10-4). Natl Poet-Univ Me.
Letters to Laura: Letters from Josiah Pierce, Jr. to Laura Dunham, 1884-1889. 7.50 (ISBN 0-87923-156-4). Godine.
Letters to Mamie. 8.95 (ISBN 0-385-12931-9). Doubleday.
Letters to Milena. 7.50x (ISBN 0-8052-3145-5); pap. 2.75 (ISBN 0-8052-0427-X). Schocken.
Letters to Molly: John Millington Synge to Maire O'Neill. 15.00x (ISBN 0-674-52834-4). Harvard U Pr.
Letters to Mrs. Gaskell & Charles Eliot Norton. lib. bdg. 20.00 (ISBN 0-8414-9450-9). Folcroft.
Letters to the Future: An Approach to Sinyavsky-Tertz. 10.00x (ISBN 0-8014-0890-3). Cornell U Pr.
Letters to Thomas & Adele Seltzer. 14.00 (ISBN 0-87685-225-8); pap. 5.00 (ISBN 0-87685-224-X). Black Sparrow.
Letters to Various Persons. lib. bdg. 20.00 (ISBN 0-8414-8591-7). Folcroft.
Letters to Various Persons. lib. bdg. 20.00 (ISBN 0-8495-5141-2). Arden Lib.
Letters to Vernon Watkins. 3.75 (ISBN 0-8112-0396-4). New Directions.
Letters Written by Walt Whitman to His Mother. lib. bdg. 10.00 (ISBN 0-8414-7571-7). Folcroft.
Letters Written During a Short Residence in Sweden, Norway, & Denmark. 11.50x (ISBN 0-8032-0862-6); pap. 4.95 (ISBN 0-8032-5832-1, 613). U of Nebr Pr.
Levi Parsons Morton: Banker, Diplomat & Statesman. facsimile ed. 22.00x (ISBN 0-405-06971-5). Arno.
Levi Yitzhak of Berditchev: Portrait of a Hasidic Master. 10.00. Hartmore.
Levine the Spartacist. pap. 6.95 (ISBN 0-86033-062-1). Gordon-Cremonesi.
Lewis Carroll. 18.50. Porter.
Lewis Carroll. lib. bdg. 10.95 (ISBN 0-8383-1489-9). Haskell.
Lewis Carroll. lib. bdg. 10.00 (ISBN 0-8414-3662-2). Folcroft.
Lewis Carroll. 15.00 (ISBN 0-8274-2858-8). R West.
Lewis Carroll: An Illustrated Biography. 12.95 (ISBN 0-517-53078-3). Potter.
Lewis Carroll: An Illustrated Biography. pap. 7.95 (ISBN 0-452-00486-1, F486). NAL.
Lewis Carroll & His World. 8.95 (ISBN 0-684-14728-9). Scribner.
Lewis Carroll As I Knew Him. pap. 2.00 (ISBN 0-486-20560-6). Dover.
Lewis Cass. 14.25 (ISBN 0-404-50874-X). AMS Pr.
Lewis Cass, the Last Jeffersonian. lib. bdg. 18.50 (ISBN 0-374-98718-1). Octagon.
Lewis Henry Morgan, Social Evolutionist. 7.50 (ISBN 0-8462-0855-5). Russell.
Li Hung-Chang. facsimile ed. 16.00 (ISBN 0-8369-6603-1). Arno.
Liberators & Heroes of Mexico & Central America. facsimile ed. 18.25 (ISBN 0-8369-2237-9). Arno.
Liberators & Heroes of South America. facsimile ed. 21.00 (ISBN 0-8369-2321-9). Arno.
Liberators of Latin America. PLB 5.52 (ISBN 0-688-51030-2). Lothrop.
Liberators of the Female Mind: The Shirreff Sisters, Educational Reform, & the Women's Movement. lib. bdg. 25.00 (ISBN 0-313-20644-9, ELL/). Greenwood.
Liberty Hyde Bailey: A Story of American Plant Sciences. 11.95 (ISBN 0-02-851100-X). Hafner.
Life & Accomplishments of Herbert Hoover. 7.95 (ISBN 0-87716-024-4). Moore Pub Co.
Life & Activities of Sir John Hawkins: Musician, Magistrate & Friend of Johnson. lib. bdg. 22.50 (ISBN 0-306-77571-9). Da Capo.
Life & Administration of Sir Robert Eden. 11.50 (ISBN 0-404-61121-4). AMS Pr.
Life & Administration of Sir Robert Eden. pap. 11.50 (ISBN 0-384-57827-6). Johnson Repr.
Life & Adventures of a Quaker Among the Indians. 12.50 (ISBN 0-87928-025-5). Corner Hse.
Life & Adventures of Carl Laemmle. lib. bdg. 28.00x (ISBN 0-405-11130-4). Arno.
Life & Adventures of Daniel Boone. 4.95 (ISBN 0-8131-0244-8). U Pr of Ky.
Life & Adventures of Frank Grouard. 12.50 (ISBN 0-8061-0407-4). U of Okla Pr.
Life & Adventures of James P. Beckwourth. 17.50 (ISBN 0-8032-0724-7). U of Nebr Pr.
Life & Adventures of James P. Beckwourth. 12.50 (ISBN 0-87018-003-7). Ross.
Life & Art of Edwin Booth. 10.50 (ISBN 0-8274-1756-X). R West.
Life & Art of Edwin Booth. rev. & enl. ed. 12.00 (ISBN 0-405-09090-0). Arno.
Life & Art of Edwin Booth. lib. bdg. 15.50x (ISBN 0-8371-0275-8, WIEB). Greenwood.
Life & Art of George Jamesone. 41.00x (ISBN 0-19-817337-7). Oxford U Pr.
Life & Art of Henry Fuseli. 29.95 (ISBN 0-912158-35-2). Hennessey.
Life & Art of William Merritt Chase. lib. bdg. 25.00 (ISBN 0-87817-156-8). Hacker.
Life & Character of the Rev. Sylvester Judd. 17.50 (ISBN 0-8046-1303-6). Kennikat.
Life & Character of the Reverend Benjamin Colman, D. D. 23.00x (ISBN 0-8201-1104-X). Schol Facsimiles.
Life & Confessions of a Psychologist. lib. bdg. 37.00x (ISBN 0-405-10008-6). Arno.
Life & Correspondence of David Hume. 39.50 (ISBN 0-8337-0433-8). B Franklin.
Life & Correspondence of David Hume. 65.00x (ISBN 0-8002-1296-7). Intl Pubns Serv.
Life & Correspondence of Henry Ingersoll Bowditch. 34.75 (ISBN 0-8369-5459-9). Arno.
Life & Correspondence of Major Cartwright. 30.00x (ISBN 0-678-00449-8). Kelley.
Life & Correspondence of Major Cartwright. 33.50 (ISBN 0-8337-0489-3). B Franklin.
Life & Correspondence of the Late Admiral Lord Rodney. lib. bdg. 54.00x (ISBN 0-8398-1271-X). Irvington.
Life & Correspondence of the Rev. William Smith, D.D. 55.00 (ISBN 0-405-04084-9). Arno.
Life & Correspondence of Theodore Parker. 39.00 (ISBN 0-405-00279-3). Arno.
Life & Correspondence of Theodore Parker. 65.00 (ISBN 0-306-71874-X). Da Capo.
Life & Correspondence of Theodore Parker. 40.00 (ISBN 0-403-02096-4). Somerset Pub.
Life & Correspondence of Theodore Parker. facs. ed. 37.00 (ISBN 0-8369-5018-6). Arno.
Life & Correspondence of Theodore Parker. text ed. 42.50 (ISBN 0-87503-021-1). Humanities.
Life & Crimes of Errol Flynn. 7.95 (ISBN 0-312-48385-6). St Martin.
Life & Curious Death of Marilyn Monroe. pap. 2.25 (ISBN 0-523-40090-X). Pinnacle Bks.
Life & Death in Rebel Prisons. facsimile ed. 20.75 (ISBN 0-8369-8869-8). Arno.
Life & Death of Adolf Hitler. pap. 2.95 (ISBN 0-445-08254-2). Popular Lib.
Life & Death of Colonel Albert Jennings Fountain. 14.95 (ISBN 0-8061-0647-6); pap. 5.95 (ISBN 0-8061-1231-X). U of Okla Pr.
Life & Death of John Henry Tunstall: The Letters, Diaries & Adventures of an Itinerant Englishman, Supplemented with Other Documents & Annotations. 8.95 (ISBN 0-8263-0078-2). U of NM Pr.
Life & Death of King James the First of Scotland. 7.50 (ISBN 0-404-53019-2). AMS Pr.
Life & Death of Louis XVI. 7.50 (ISBN 0-8008-4776-8). Taplinger.
Life & Death of Martin Luther King, Jr. 6.25 (ISBN 0-688-41802-3); PLB 6.48 (ISBN 0-688-51802-8). Lothrop.
Life & Death of Mary Wollstonecraft. 8.95 (ISBN 0-15-151539-5). HarBraceJ.
Life & Death of Mary Wollstonecraft. pap. 1.95 (ISBN 0-451-61450-X, MJ1450). NAL.
Life & Death of Mozart. pap. 3.95 (ISBN 0-8128-1530-0). Stein & Day.
Life & Death of Robert Devereux, Earl of Essex. lib. bdg. 30.00 (ISBN 0-8414-4774-8). Folcroft.
Life & Death of Trotsky. 14.95 (ISBN 0-07-048940-8). McGraw.
Life & Death of Yukio Mishima. 10.00 (ISBN 0-374-18620-0). FS&G.
Life & Destiny of Isak Dinesen. pap. 8.95 (ISBN 0-226-46916-6, P686). U of Chicago Pr.
Life & Genius of Lord Byron. lib. bdg. 12.50 (ISBN 0-8414-4401-3). Folcroft.
Life & Genius of Nathaniel Hawthorne. lib. bdg. 25.00 (ISBN 0-8414-7710-8). Folcroft.
Life & Genius of Shakespeare. 17.45 (ISBN 0-8274-0377-1). R West.
Life & Genius of Shakespeare. 17.50 (ISBN 0-404-03657-0). AMS Pr.
Life & History of the Rev. Elijah P. Marrs. facs. ed. 12.25 (ISBN 0-8369-8625-3). Arno.
Life & Ideas of Robert Owen. pap. 1.95 (ISBN 0-7178-0115-2). Intl Pub Co.
Life & Ideas of the Marquis de Sade. lib. bdg. 18.50x (ISBN 0-313-20023-8, GOMDS). Greenwood.
Life & Journeys of Paul. pap. 4.95 (ISBN 0-8024-4720-1). Moody.
Life & Land of Burns. 24.00 (ISBN 0-404-08512-1). AMS Pr
Life & Legal Writings of Hugo Grotius. 7.95x (ISBN 0-8061-0848-7). U of Okla Pr.
Life & Legend of Gene Fowler. 10.00 (ISBN 0-688-03188-9). Morrow.
Life & Legend of George McJunkin: Black Cowboy. 6.95 (ISBN 0-8407-6326-3). Elsevier-Nelson.
Life & Letters in the Fourth Century. 11.00 (ISBN 0-8462-1065-7). Russell.
Life & Letters of Christopher Pearse Cranch. 23.00 (ISBN 0-404-05641-5). AMS Pr.
Life & Letters of Christopher Pearse Cranch. 10.00. Ridgeway Bks.
Life & Letters of Edward Young. 21.00 (ISBN 0-403-00718-6). Scholarly.
Life & Letters of Edwin Lawrence Godkin. lib. bdg. 27.00x (ISBN 0-8371-5516-9, GOLL). Greenwood.
Life & Letters of Emily Dickinson. 12.50 (ISBN 0-8196-0276-0). Biblo.
Life & Letters of Erasmus. 12.45 (ISBN 0-8274-3878-8). R West.
Life & Letters of Erasmus. 12.50 (ISBN 0-404-02627-3). AMS Pr.
Life & Letters of Frederic Shields. 16.50 (ISBN 0-404-04344-5). AMS Pr.
Life & Letters of George Bancroft. lib. bdg. 55.00 (ISBN 0-306-71877-4). Da Capo.
Life & Letters of George Bancroft. 26.50x (ISBN 0-8046-1483-0). Kennikat.
Life & Letters of George Cabot. lib. bdg. 52.50 (ISBN 0-306-71001-3). Da Capo.
Life & Letters of George Darley, Poet & Critic. 9.00x (ISBN 0-19-811470-2). Oxford U Pr.
Life & Letters of Harriet Beecher Stowe. 12.50 (ISBN 0-8103-3602-2). Gale.
Life & Letters of Harriet Beecher Stowe. lib. bdg. 27.50 (ISBN 0-8495-1606-4). Arden Lib.
Life & Letters of Henry Lee Higginson. 19.50 (ISBN 0-8274-1550-8). R West.
Life & Letters of Henry Lee Higginson. facsimile ed. 25.25 (ISBN 0-8369-6743-7). Arno.
Life & Letters of Horace Bushnell. 17.00 (ISBN 0-405-00236-X). Arno.
Life & Letters of J. Alden Weir. lib. bdg. 22.50 (ISBN 0-306-70097-2). Da Capo.
Life & Letters of James Abram Garfield. 37.50 (ISBN 0-208-00667-2). Shoe String.
Life & Letters of Joel Chandler Harris. 20.00 (ISBN 0-8274-2906-1). R West.
Life & Letters of Joel Chandler Harris. 21.00 (ISBN 0-404-00059-2). AMS Pr.
Life & Letters of John Burroughs. 27.50 (ISBN 0-8462-1097-5). Russell.
Life & Letters of John Galsworthy. 27.50x (ISBN 0-678-02759-5). Kelley.
Life & Letters of John Gibson Lockhart. 32.50 (ISBN 0-404-03849-2). AMS Pr.
Life & Letters of John Greenleaf Whittier. 32.75 (ISBN 0-8274-0471-9). R West.
Life & Letters of John Greenleaf Whittier. lib. bdg. 49.95 (ISBN 0-8383-0191-6). Haskell.
Life & Letters of John Keats. 5.00x (ISBN 0-460-00801-3, E801). Dutton.
Life & Letters of John Muir. 45.00 (ISBN 0-404-00444-X); 23.50 ea. (ISBN 0-404-08001-4) (ISBN 0-404-08002-2). AMS Pr.
Life & Letters of John Winthrop. lib. bdg. 59.50 (ISBN 0-306-70147-2). Da Capo.
Life & Letters of Joseph Severn. lib. bdg. 14.50. Folcroft.
Life & Letters of Joseph Severn. 15.00 (ISBN 0-404-07438-3). AMS Pr.
Life & Letters of Leslie Stephen. 11.00 (ISBN 0-8103-3058-X). Gale.
Life & Letters of Lord Macaulay. pap. 10.50 (ISBN 0-19-822487-7). Oxford U Pr.
Life & Letters of Maria Edgeworth. facsimile ed. 31.00 (ISBN 0-8369-5734-2). Arno.
Life & Letters of Maria Edgeworth. 24.50 (ISBN 0-8274-0394-1). R West.
Life & Letters of Mary Wollstonecraft Shelley. lib. bdg. 44.95 (ISBN 0-8383-1011-7). Haskell.
Life & Letters of Peter Ilich Tchaikovsky. lib. bdg. 39.95 (ISBN 0-8383-0997-6). Haskell.
Life & Letters of Robert Browning. 16.45 (ISBN 0-8274-1106-5). R West.
Life & Letters of Robert Browning. lib. bdg. 21.00x (ISBN 0-8371-5416-2, ORRB). Greenwood.
Life & Letters of Sir Edmund Gosse. lib. bdg. 36.95 (ISBN 0-8383-1456-2). Haskell.
Life & Letters of Sir George Grove. lib. bdg. 50.00 (ISBN 0-89341-059-4). Longwood Pr.
Life & Letters of Sir John Everett Millais, President of the Royal Academy. 95.00 (ISBN 0-404-04326-7); 47.50 ea. AMS Pr.
Life & Letters of Stuart P. Sherman. facsimile ed. 40.25 (ISBN 0-8369-5720-2). Arno.
Life & Letters of Theodore Watts-Dunton. 42.50 (ISBN 0-384-20920-3, F425). Johnson Repr.
Life & Letters of Thomas Henry Huxley. 67.50 set (ISBN 0-404-14980-4). AMS Pr.
Life & Letters of Thomas Henry Huxley. lib. bdg. 75.00 (ISBN 0-8492-5317-9). R West.
Life & Letters of Walter H. Page. 71.00 (ISBN 0-403-00769-0). Scholarly.
Life & Letters of Washington Allston. 25.00 (ISBN 0-405-08521-4). Arno.
Life & Letters of Washington Allston. lib. bdg. 32.50 (ISBN 0-306-71168-0). Da Capo.
Life & Letters of Washington Irving. 38.00 set (ISBN 0-8103-3044-X). Gale.
Life & Liberation of Padmasambhava. 50.00 set (ISBN 0-913546-18-6) (ISBN 0-913546-20-8). Dharma Pub.
Life & Loves of Cary Grant. 9.95 (ISBN 0-8473-1613-0). Sterling.
Life & Loves of Gable. 12.95 (ISBN 0-8246-0205-6). Jonathan David.
Life & Mind of Emily Dickinson. 12.00x (ISBN 0-8154-0229-5). Cooper Sq.
Life & Mind of John Dewey. 15.00x (ISBN 0-8093-0616-6). S Ill U Pr.
Life & Mind of John Dewey. pap. 5.95 (ISBN 0-8093-0869-X). S Ill U Pr.
Life & Minor Works of George Peele. lib. bdg. 23.50x (ISBN 0-8371-9071-1, HOGP). Greenwood.
Life & Music of Bela Bartok. rev. ed. pap. 5.95 (ISBN 0-19-500754-9). Oxford U Pr.
Life & Opinions of John de Wycliffe, D. D. 2nd ed. 45.00 set (ISBN 0-404-56678-2) (ISBN 0-404-56679-0) (ISBN 0-404-56680-4). AMS Pr.
Life & Opinions of T. E. Hulme. 20.00 (ISBN 0-404-17117-6). AMS Pr.
Life & Papers of Frederick Bates. facsimile ed. 39.00x (ISBN 0-405-06876-X). Arno.
Life & Pontificate of Leo the Tenth. 100.00. Ridgeway Bks.
Life & Public Services of George Luther Stearns. 21.00 (ISBN 0-527-85920-6). Kraus Repr.
Life & Public Services of Justin Smith Morrill. lib. bdg. 37.50 (ISBN 0-306-71595-3). Da Capo.
Life and Public Services of Martin R. Delany. 18.00 (ISBN 0-527-76400-0). Kraus Repr.
Life & Public Services of Millard Fillmore. 25.50 (ISBN 0-8337-4634-0). B Franklin.
Life & Public Services of Salmon Portland Chase. facs. ed. 22.00 (ISBN 0-8369-8649-0). Arno.

Life of Robert Toombs. 21.00 (ISBN 0-8337-2738-9). B Franklin.
Life of Roger Brooke Taney, Chief Justice of the United States Supreme Court. lib. bdg. 21.50x (ISBN 0-8371-4344-6, STRT). Greenwood.
Life of S. T. Coleridge: The Early Years. 18.00 (ISBN 0-8462-0192-5). Russell.
Life of St. Paul. 5.95 (ISBN 0-8007-0178-X). Revell.
Life of Samuel Johnson. pap. 3.25x (ISBN 0-394-30962-6, T62). Modern Lib.
Life of Samuel Johnson. abr. ed. pap. 2.50 (ISBN 0-451-51150-6, CE1150). NAL.
Life of Samuel Johnson. 8.45 (ISBN 0-8274-1341-6). R West.
Life of Samuel Johnson. 8.50 (ISBN 0-8046-1574-8). Kennikat.
Life of Samuel Johnson. lib. bdg. 17.50 (ISBN 0-8492-4934-1). R West.
Life of Samuel Johnson. lib. bdg. 20.00 (ISBN 0-8495-1904-7). Arden Lib.
Life of Sarmiento. lib. bdg. 20.00x (ISBN 0-8371-2392-5, BULS). Greenwood.
Life of Sebastian Lerdo De Tejada, 1823-1889: A Study of Influence & Obscurity. lib. bdg. 17.75x (ISBN 0-8371-0132-8, KNLT). Greenwood.
Life of Sir Humphrey Gilbert, England's First Empire Builder. lib. bdg. 15.25x (ISBN 0-8371-4227-X, GOHG). Greenwood.
Life of Sir Joseph Banks. 22.00x (ISBN 0-405-06618-X). Arno.
Life of Sir Philip Sidney. 25.00 (0-8414-5733). Folcroft.
Life of Sir Philip Sidney. lib. bdg. 20.00 (ISBN 0-374-98189-2). Octagon.
Life of Sir Richard Burton. 35.50 (ISBN 0-8337-3893-3). B Franklin.
Life of Sir Walter Scott. lib. bdg. 33.95 (ISBN 0-8383-1927-0). Haskell.
Life of Sir Walter Scott. lib. bdg. 20.00. Folcroft.
Life of Sir William Phips. 12.00 (ISBN 0-404-04249-X). AMS Pr.
Life of Sir William Phips. 13.00 (ISBN 0-403-04150-3). Somerset Pub.
Life of Sir William Rowan Hamilton. 2nd ed. price not set. Chelsea Pub.
Life of Sir William Rowan Hamilton. 120.00x (ISBN 0-405-06594-9). Arno.
Life of Stephen F. Austin, Founder of Texas, 1793-1836: A Chapter in the Westward Movement of the Anglo-American People. 10.00 (ISBN 0-87611-002-2). Tex St Hist Assn.
Life of the Black Prince. 18.50 (ISBN 0-404-56532-8). AMS Pr.
Life of the Drama. pap. text ed. 5.95x (ISBN 0-689-70011-3, 112). Atheneum.
Life of the Emperor Frederick. 32.00 (ISBN 0-403-01157-4). Scholarly.
Life of the Honorable Henry Cavendish. 28.00x (ISBN 0-405-06631-7). Arno.
Life of the Reverend Mr. George Trosse. 9.75x (ISBN 0-7735-0153-3). McGill-Queens U Pr.
Life of the Right Honourable Stratford Canning, Viscount Stratford de Redcliffe. 70.00 set (ISBN 0-404-07387-5). AMS Pr.
Life of the Right Honourable William Pitt. 75.00 (ISBN 0-404-06250-4); 19.00 ea. (ISBN 0-404-06251-2) (ISBN 0-404-06252-0) (ISBN 0-404-06253-9) (ISBN 0-404-06254-7). AMS Pr.
Life of Themistocles: A Critical Survey of the Literary & Archaeological Evidence. 19.95x (ISBN 0-7735-0185-1). McGill-Queens U Pr.
Life of Thomas Bailey Aldrich. 9.00 (ISBN 0-8274-2941-X). R West.
Life of Thomas Bailey Aldrich. 9.50 (ISBN 0-8046-0181-X). Kennikat.
Life of Thomas Carlyle. 21.50 (ISBN 0-404-14028-9). AMS Pr.
Life of Thomas Carlyle. lib. bdg. 15.00 (ISBN 0-8495-1903-9). Arden Lib.
Life of Thomas Chatterton. 24.50 (ISBN 0-8274-2900-2). R West.
Life of Thomas Chatterton. 25.00 (ISBN 0-8462-1658-2). Russell.
Life of Thomas Cooper. 33.00 (ISBN 0-403-07695-1). Scholarly.
Life of Thomas Cooper. text ed. 12.50x (ISBN 0-391-00159-0). Humanities.
Life of Thomas Hardy. lib. bdg. 26.95 (ISBN 0-8383-1672-7). Haskell.
Life of Thomas Hart Benton. lib. bdg. 39.50 (ISBN 0-306-70043-3). Da Capo.
Life of Thomas Jefferson. facs. ed. 80.00 (ISBN 0-8369-5343-6). Arno.
Life of Thomas Jefferson. lib. bdg. 65.00 ea.; lib. bdg. 160.00 set (ISBN 0-306-70250-9). Da Capo.
Life of Thomas Lodge. lib. bdg. 5.00 (ISBN 0-8414-9552-1). Folcroft.
Life of Thomas Love Peacock. 8.50 (ISBN 0-8462-0675-7). Russell.
Life of Thomas Paine. 20.00. Norwood Edns.
Life of Thurlow Weed. 66.00 (ISBN 0-404-04639-8); 33.50 ea. (ISBN 0-404-04640-1) (ISBN 0-404-04641-X). AMS Pr.
Life of Thurlow Weed. Incl. Autobiography of Thurlow Weed; Memoir of Thurlow Weed. lib. bdg. 75.00 (ISBN 0-306-71706-9). Da Capo.
Life of Tobias George Smollett. lib. bdg. 15.00. Folcroft.
Life of Tobias George Smollett. 8.00 (ISBN 0-8046-1576-4). Kennikat.
Life of Tom Horn, Government Scout & Interpreter. lib. bdg. 15.00 (ISBN 0-87380-144-X). Rio Grande.
Life of Voltaire. 29.25 (ISBN 0-8274-0370-4). R West.
Life of W. M. Thackeray. lib. bdg. 15.00. Folcroft.
Life of W. T. Stead. lib. bdg. 66.00 (ISBN 0-8240-0320-9); lib. bdg. 38.00 ea. Garland Pub.
Life of Wallenstein, Duke of Friedland. lib. bdg. 14.75x (ISBN 0-8371-0569-2, MILW). Greenwood.
Life of Walt Whitman. lib. bdg. 24.95 (ISBN 0-8383-1001-X). Haskell.
Life of Walter Pater. lib. bdg. 49.95 (ISBN 0-8383-0178-9). Haskell.
Life of Walter Quintin Gresham 1832-1895. facs. ed. 40.25 (ISBN 0-8369-5579-X). Arno.
Life of Washington. 19.50 (ISBN 0-8046-1283-8). Kennikat.
Life of Washington. 8.50x (ISBN 0-674-53250-3); pap. 3.25 (ISBN 0-674-53251-1). Harvard U Pr.
Life of Washington Irving. lib. bdg. 12.50 (ISBN 0-8414-7816-3). Folcroft.
Life of Washington Irving. lib. bdg. 47.50 (ISBN 0-374-98630-4). Octagon.
Life of Washington the Great. 5th, rev. ed. Bd. with Eclectic First Reader. PLB 30.00 (ISBN 0-8240-2270-X). Garland Pub.
Life of Wild Bill Hickok. pap. 1.25 (LB422ZK). Nordon Pubns.
Life of William Barnes, Poet & Philologist. 25.00 (ISBN 0-403-00855-7). Scholarly.
Life of William Beckford. lib. bdg. 25.00 (ISBN 0-8414-6530-4). Folcroft.
Life of William Blake. 15.00x (ISBN 0-8154-0309-7). Cooper Sq.
Life of William Blake. 3rd ed. 15.75 (ISBN 0-19-211297-X). Oxford U Pr.
Life of William Blake. 25.95 (ISBN 0-8337-3894-1). B Franklin.
Life of William Cobbett. lib. bdg. 18.75x (ISBN 0-8371-4781-6, COLC). Greenwood.
Life of William Congreve. 7.75 (ISBN 0-8046-1525-X). Kennikat.
Life of William Congreve. lib. bdg. 15.00 (ISBN 0-8414-1428-9). Folcroft.
Life of William Congreve. 19.00 (ISBN 0-403-03070-6). Somerset Pub.
Life of William Cowper. 11.00 (ISBN 0-8046-1602-7). Kennikat.
Life of William Cowper. lib. bdg. 49.95 (ISBN 0-8383-1251-9). Haskell.
Life of William Ewart Gladstone. 50.00 (ISBN 0-8274-3864-8). R West.
Life of William Ewart Gladstone. 108.00 (ISBN 0-403-01117-5). Scholarly.
Life of William Ewart Gladstone. lib. bdg. 64.50x (ISBN 0-8371-0576-5, MOWG). Greenwood.
Life of William Godwin. lib. bdg. 25.00 (ISBN 0-8414-0641-3). Folcroft.
Life of William H. Seward. 16.00 (ISBN 0-8446-1053-4). Peter Smith.
Life of William Hazlitt. lib. bdg. 19.75x (ISBN 0-8371-6512-1, HOWH). Greenwood.
Life of William Hickling Prescott. 25.00 (ISBN 0-8274-2946-0). R West.
Life of William J. Brown, of Providence, R. I. With Personal Recollections of Incidents in Rhode Island. facsimile ed. 15.50 (ISBN 0-8369-8841-8). Arno.
Life of William Morris. 30.00 (ISBN 0-405-08767-5). Arno.
Life of William Morris. lib. bdg. 28.95 (ISBN 0-8383-1070-2). Haskell.
Life of William Penn: With Selections from His Correspondence & Autobiography. facsimile ed. 20.00 (ISBN 0-8369-5528-5). Arno.
Life of William Pinkney. lib. bdg. 32.50 (ISBN 0-306-71307-1). Da Capo.
Life of William Pitt, Earl of Chatham. lib. bdg. 42.50 (ISBN 0-374-98626-6). Octagon.
Life of William Plumer. lib. bdg. 49.50 (ISBN 0-306-71608-9). Da Capo.
Life of William Shakespeare. 17.50 (ISBN 0-404-03065-3). AMS Pr.
Life of William Shakespeare. 19.45 (ISBN 0-8274-0099-3). R West.
Life of William Shakespeare. 7.50 (ISBN 0-8446-0770-3). Peter Smith.
Life of William Shakespeare. 19.95 (ISBN 0-8274-1064-6). R West.
Life of William Shakespeare. 20.00 (ISBN 0-404-05387-4). AMS Pr.
Life of William T. Porter. 15.00 (ISBN 0-405-01655-7). Arno.
Life of Woodrow Wilson, 1856-1924. 16.00 (ISBN 0-403-00934-0). Scholarly.
Life of Woodrow Wilson, 1856-1924. lib. bdg. 17.00x (ISBN 0-8371-4729-8, DAWW). Greenwood.
Life on the Run. 8.95 (ISBN 0-8129-0623-3). Times Bks.
Life on the Run. pap. 2.25 (ISBN 0-553-12880-9). Bantam.
Life on the Upper Michigan Frontier. 8.95 (ISBN 0-8283-1544-2). Branden.
Life on Two Levels: An Autobiography. 12.50 (ISBN 0-913232-56-4). W Kaufmann.
Life on Wheels. pap. 3.25 (ISBN 0-89144-001-1). Crescent Pubns.
Life Sentence. 9.95 (ISBN 0-912376-41-4). Chosen Bks Pub.
Life Story of an Old Rebel. 12.00x (ISBN 0-7165-0012-4). Biblio Dist.
Life Story of Lala Lajpat Rai. 9.00x (ISBN 0-88386-312-X). South Asia Bks.
Life Styles: Diversity in American Society. 2nd ed. pap. text ed. 7.95 (ISBN 0-316-27756-8). Little.
Life That Ruth Built: A Biography. 12.50 (ISBN 0-8129-0540-7). Times Bks.
Life, Times & Labours of Robert Owen. 17.00 (ISBN 0-404-08449-4). AMS Pr.
Life, Times, & Treacherous Death of Jesse James. pap. 1.25 (ISBN 0-8439-0432-1, LB432ZK). Nordon Pubns.
Life, Times & Treacherous Death of Jesse James. 16.95 (ISBN 0-8040-0187-1); limited ed. 30.00 (ISBN 0-8040-0188-X). Swallow.
Life Travels & Opinions of Benjamin Lundy: Including His Journeys to Texas. Bd. with War in Texas (1836. lib. bdg. 13.50x (ISBN 0-678-00809-4). Kelley.
Life, Travels & Opinions of Benjamin Lundy. 13.75x (ISBN 0-8371-2179-5). Negro U Pr.
Life with Grandma. 7.95 (ISBN 0-236-31146-8). Merrimack Bk Serv.
Life with Lindsay & Crouse. 10.00 (ISBN 0-395-24511-7). HM.
Life with Mother Superior. 5.95 (ISBN 0-374-18680-4). FS&G.
Life with the Painters of la Ruche. 6.95 (ISBN 0-02-579450-7). Macmillan.
Life, Writings & Character of Edward Robinson. lib. bdg. 12.00x (ISBN 0-405-10290-9). Arno.
Lifelines. 8.50 (ISBN 0-385-11644-6). Doubleday.
Lifelines: The Stacey Letters, 1836-1858. 8.95 (ISBN 0-8008-4841-1). Taplinger.
Lifetime on Deadline. 12.50 (ISBN 0-88289-076-X). Pelican.
Light in the Far East: Archbishop Harold Henry's Forty-Two Years in Korea. 8.95 (ISBN 0-8164-0307-4). Seabury.
Light on the Horizon: The Quaker Pilgrimage of Tom Jones. new ed. 3.95 (ISBN 0-913408-13-1). Friends United.
Lighthouse. 8.95 (ISBN 0-8008-4853-5). Taplinger.
Like Normal People. 9.95 (ISBN 0-07-041761-X). McGraw.
Like Normal People. pap. 2.25 (ISBN 0-451-09112-4, E9112). NAL.
Limbo. pap. 5.95 (ISBN 0-88316-536-8). Chandler & Sharp.
Lincoln. pap. 1.25 (ISBN 0-02-038300-2). Macmillan.
Lincoln: His Words & His World. 9.95 (ISBN 0-87294-088-8). Country Beautiful.
Lincoln Library of Sports Champions. 2nd ed. 239.95 (ISBN 0-912168-01-3). Frontier Pr Co.
Lincoln-Lore: Lincoln in the Popular Mind. 20.00 (ISBN 0-87972-035-2). Bowling Green Univ.
Lincoln Names & Epithets. pap. 3.00 (ISBN 0-8283-1389-X). Branden.
Lincoln Nobody Knows. pap. 4.95 (ISBN 0-8090-0059-8). Hill & Wang.
Lincoln Nobody Knows. lib. bdg. 25.00x (ISBN 0-313-22450-1, CULN). Greenwood.
Lincoln Steffens. 9.50 (ISBN 0-8057-7253-7). Twayne.
Lincoln Steffens. lib. bdg. 9.95 (ISBN 0-8057-7253-7). G K Hall.
Lincoln Steffens. 9.95 (ISBN 0-8044-2829-8). Ungar.
Lincoln's Attorney General: Edward Bates of Missouri. 9.00x (ISBN 0-8262-0038-9). U of Mo Pr.
Lincoln's Religion. pap. 2.25 (ISBN 0-8298-0181-2). Pilgrim NY.
Lincoln's Secretary: A Biography of John G. Nicolay. lib. bdg. 17.50x (ISBN 0-8371-5626-2, NILS). Greenwood.
Lincoln's Youth: Indiana Years, Seven to Twenty-One, 1816-1830. lib. bdg. 22.75x (ISBN 0-8371-8408-8, WALY). Greenwood.
Linda Ronstadt. pap. 3.95 (ISBN 0-8256-3918-2). Music Sales.
Lindbergh: A Biography. pap. 2.25 (440-15057-4-225). Dell.
Lindbergh: A Biography. 12.95 (ISBN 0-385-09578-3). Doubleday.
Lindbergh Alone. 11.95 (ISBN 0-15-152401-7). HarBraceJ.
Lindbergh Flies the Atlantic. new ed. lib. bdg. 2.45 incl. catalog cards; pap. 1.25 vinyl laminated covers. SamHar Pr.
Lindbergh of Minnesota: A Political Biography. 14.50 (ISBN 0-15-152400-9). HarBraceJ.
Lindberghs: Three Generations. pap. 1.50 (ISBN 0-87351-094-1) Minn Hist.
Linotte: The Early Diary of Anais Nin 1914-1920. 14.95 (ISBN 0-15-152488-2). HarBraceJ.
Lion & the Throne: The Life & Times of Sir Edward Coke. pap. 5.95 (ISBN 0-316-10386-1); pap. 4.95 (ISBN 0-316-10393-4, LB29). Little.
Lion of Judah Hath Prevailed: Being the Biography of His Imperial Majesty Haile Selassie I. lib. bdg. 10.00x (ISBN 0-8371-5198-8, SLJ&). Greenwood.
Lion of White Hall: The Life of Cassius M. Clay (1810-1903) 7.50. Peter Smith.
Lionhead Lodge. 9.95 (ISBN 0-87770-167-9); pap. 5.95. Ye Galleon.
Lion's Mouth. 7.95 (ISBN 0-8076-0877-7). Braziller.
Lippmann, Liberty & the Press. 11.00 (ISBN 0-8173-4722-4). U of Ala Pr.
Liszt. 35.00 (ISBN 0-8490-0543-4). Gordon Pr.
Liszt. 6.00 (ISBN 0-8446-2950-2). Peter Smith.
Liszt. pap. 5.00 (ISBN 0-486-21702-7). Dover.
Literary Criticism & Authors' Biographies: An Annotated Index. 10.00 (ISBN 0-8108-1172-3). Scarecrow.
Lito the Shoeshine Boy. 6.95g (ISBN 0-590-07382-6). Schol Bk Serv.
Little Boy in Search of God: Mysticism in a Personal Light. 17.95 (ISBN 0-385-06653-8); Limited Edition 50.00 (ISBN 0-385-11668-3). Doubleday.
Little Flowers of St. Francis. pap. 2.95 (ISBN 0-385-07544-8). Doubleday.
Little Giants of Pro Sports. PLB 5.95g (ISBN 0-8225-1059-6). Lerner Pubns.
Little League to Big League. 2.50 (ISBN 0-394-80190-3). Random.
Little Lion of the Southwest: A Life of Manuel Antonio Chaves. 9.95 (ISBN 0-8040-0632-6). Swallow.
Little Love & Good Company. 8.95 (ISBN 0-916144-10-0). Stemmer Hse.
Little Memoirs of the Nineteenth Century. facs. ed. 16.00 (ISBN 0-8369-1197-0). Arno.
Little Men of the NFL. 2.50 (ISBN 0-394-92807-5). Random.
Little Men of the NFL. 2.50 (ISBN 0-394-82807-0). Random.
Little Schubert. 5.95 (ISBN 0-06-022026-0); recordings of 5 Noble Waltzes avail. Har-Row.
Little Things in the Hands of a Big God. 4.95 (ISBN 0-8499-2855-9). Word Bks.
Little Turtle. PLB 6.95 (ISBN 0-87518-158-9). Dillon.
Liu Shao-Ch'i & the Chinese Cultural Revolution: The Politics of Mass Criticism. 16.50x (ISBN 0-520-02574-1); pap. 4.95 (ISBN 0-520-02957-7). U of Cal Pr.
Lives & Legends of Buffalo Bill. 18.50 (ISBN 0-8061-0474-0). U of Okla Pr.
Lives & Legends of Buffalo Bill. pap. 8.95 (ISBN 0-8061-1537-8). U of Okla Pr.
Lives & Letters: A. R. Orage-Beatrice Hastings-Katherine Mansfield-John Middleton Murray-S. S. Koteliansky. 15.00 (ISBN 0-8112-0681-5). New Directions.
Lives He Touched: The Relationships of Jesus. 5.95 (ISBN 0-06-066815-6). Har-Row.
Lives in Science. 1.95 (ISBN 0-671-42702-4). S&S.
Lives of Eminent Africans. 11.75x (ISBN 0-8371-2062-4). Negro U Pr.
Lives of Eminent Korean Monks: The Haedong Kosung Chon. text ed. 7.00x (ISBN 0-674-53662-2). Harvard U Pr.
Lives of English Poets. 8.00x (ISBN 0-460-00770-X); pap. 4.95 (ISBN 0-460-01770-5). Dutton.
Lives of Famous Poets. 14.00 (ISBN 0-404-05425-0). AMS Pr.
Lives of Famous Poets. lib. bdg. 13.95 (ISBN 0-8414-0579-4). Folcroft.
Lives of Famous Poets. lib. bdg. 35.00 (ISBN 0-8495-4626-5). Arden Lib.
Lives of Famous Romans. 3.50 (ISBN 0-395-06730-8). HM.
Lives of Labor-Lives of Love: Fragments of Friendly Autobiographies. 8.50 (ISBN 0-682-48632-9). Exposition.
Lives of Pearl Buck: A Tale of China & America. 8.95 (ISBN 0-690-00165-7). T Y Crowell.
Lives of Philip & Matthew Henry. 11.95. Banner of Truth.
Lives of Roger Casement. 30.00x (ISBN 0-300-01801-0). Yale U Pr.
Lives of Talleyrand. pap. 4.95 (ISBN 0-393-00188-1). Norton.
Lives of the Chief Justices of England: From the Norman Conquest till the Death of Lord Tenterden. facsimile ed. 85.00 (ISBN 0-8369-5728-8). Arno.
Lives of the English Poets. 152.00 (ISBN 3-4870-1955-8). Adler.
Lives of the English Poets. lib. bdg. 80.00 (ISBN 0-374-94237-4). Octagon.
Lives of the English Poets. 8.95 (ISBN 0-19-250083-X); 8.95 (ISBN 0-19-250084-8). Oxford U Pr.
Lives of the Georgian Age. 25.00x (ISBN 0-06-494332-1). B&N.
Lives of the Great Composers. 25.25 (ISBN 0-8369-2783-4). Arno.

Lives of the Great Composers. 19.95 (ISBN 0-393-02146-7). Norton.
Lives of the Kings & Queens of France. 20.00 (ISBN 0-394-50734-7). Knopf.
Lives of the Painters. 24.95x (ISBN 0-393-04231-6). Norton.
Lives of the Saints. 59.50 (ISBN 0-87061-045-7) (ISBN 0-87061-046-5) (ISBN 0-87061-047-3) (ISBN 0-87061-048-1) (ISBN 0-87061-049-X). Chr Classics.
Lives of the Stuart Age. text ed. 25.00x (ISBN 0-06-494330-5). B&N.
Lives of the Tudor Age. text ed. 25.00x (ISBN 0-06-494331-3). B&N.
Lives of the Warriors of the Civil Wars of France & England: Warriors of the Seventeenth Century. facsimile ed. 34.75 (ISBN 0-8369-2642-0). Arno.
Lives of the Warriors of the Thirty Years' War: Warriors of the Seventeenth Century. facsimile ed. 31.00 (ISBN 0-8369-2643-9). Arno.
Lives of William Benton. 10.00x (ISBN 0-226-36548-4). U of Chicago Pr.
Living Beyond Depression. pap. 1.95 (ISBN 0-87123-339-8). Bethany Fell.
Living Biographies of Famous Women. 15.00 (ISBN 0-8274-4300-5). R West.
Living Black American Authors: A Biographical Directory. 15.95 (ISBN 0-8352-0662-9). Bowker.
Living Black in White America. pap. 2.95 (ISBN 0-688-06044-7). Morrow.
Living Buddha: An Interpretive Biography. 7.95 (ISBN 0-8348-0117-5). Weatherhill.
Living Christian Science: Fourteen Lives. 7.95 (ISBN 0-13-538884-8). P-H.
Living in Sin: The Victorian Sexual Revolution. 13.95x (ISBN 0-88229-445-8); pap. 6.95 (ISBN 0-88229-649-3). Nelson-Hall.
Living Longer & Loving It. 7.95 (ISBN 0-8437-3409-4). Hammond Inc.
Living Priesthood. pap. 3.95 (ISBN 0-87973-708-5). Our Sunday Visitor.
Living Proof: An Autobiography. 10.95 (ISBN 0-399-12369-5). Putnam.
Living Saints Witness at Work. 6.00 (ISBN 0-8309-0153-1). Herald Hse.
Living Socrates: The Man Who Dared to Question, As Plato Knew Him. 11.95 (ISBN 0-916144-00-3). Stemmer Hse.
Living Tradition of Maria Martinez. 39.95 (ISBN 0-87011-319-4). Kodansha.
Living with the Bible. 14.95 (ISBN 0-688-03361-X). Morrow.
Liza Minnelli. PLB 5.50 (ISBN 0-87191-558-8). Creative Ed.
Locke. 10.00 (ISBN 0-8046-0825-3). Kennikat.
Loftier Flight: The Life & Accomplishments of Charles Louis Didelot, Balletmaster. 15.00x (ISBN 0-8195-4070-6). Columbia U Pr.
Log of a Cowboy. pap. 1.25 (LB344ZK). Nordon Pubns.
Log of a Cowboy. pap. 1.95 (ISBN 0-8049-0201-1, CL-201). Airmont.
Log of Rubin the Sailor. pap. 2.25 (ISBN 0-7178-0387-2). Intl Pub Co.
Lola Montes: The Tragic Story of a Liberated Woman. 9.50 (ISBN 0-914418-03-3). Brooks-Sterling.
London & the Life of Literature in Late Victorian England: The Diary of George Gissing, Novelist. 30.00 (ISBN 0-8387-2145-1). Bucknell U Pr.
London Diary, 1717-1721 & Other Writings. 24.00 (ISBN 0-405-03305-2). Arno.
London Yankees: Portraits of American Writers & Artists in England, 1894-1914. 14.95 (ISBN 0-15-152978-7). HarBraceJ.
Lone Woman: The Story of Elizabeth Blackwell - The First Woman Doctor. 10.00 (ISBN 0-316-94488-2). Little.
Loneliest Campaign: The Truman Victory of 1948. lib. bdg. 18.50x (ISBN 0-8371-8353-7, ROLCT). Greenwood.
Lonely Americans. facs. ed. 16.00 (ISBN 0-8369-1699-9). Arno.
Lonely Hunter: A Biography of Carson McCullers. 5.95 (ISBN 0-385-12289-6). Doubleday.
Lonely Lady of San Clemente: The Story of Pat Nixon. 9.95 (ISBN 0-690-01688-3). T Y Crowell.
Lonely Walk: The Life of Senator Mark Hatfield. 8.95 (ISBN 0-915684-49-7). Christian Herald.
Long Ago in Florence: The Story of Della Robbia Sculpture. 5.95 (ISBN 0-688-41205-X); PLB 5.71 (ISBN 0-688-51205-4). Lothrop.
Long Journey: The Autobiography of Pitirim A. Sorokin. 6.00 (ISBN 0-8084-0203-X). Coll & U Pr.
Long Live the King: A Biography of Clark Gable. 10.95 (ISBN 0-399-11863-2). Putnam.
Long Return. pap. 2.25 (ISBN 0-345-24803-1). Ballantine.
Long Road Home: An Autobiography. facsimile ed. 17.00x (ISBN 0-405-06975-8). Arno.
Long Suffering. 3.95 (ISBN 0-8091-0206-4). Paulist Pr.
Long Way, Baby: Behind-the-Scenes in Women's Pro Tennis. 7.25 (ISBN 0-688-00263-3). Morrow.
Long Way from Home. 12.00 (ISBN 0-405-01880-0). Arno.
Long Way from Home. pap. 2.85 (ISBN 0-15-653145-3, HB172). HarBraceJ.
Longden Legend. 9.95 (ISBN 0-498-01242-5); pap. 2.95 (ISBN 0-498-01950-0). A S Barnes.
Longfellow & His Poetry. lib. bdg. 7.50. Folcroft.
Longfellow & His Poetry. 7.25 (ISBN 0-404-52533-4). AMS Pr.
Look & Move on. 10.00 (ISBN 0-87685-255-X). Black Sparrow.
Look Behind You, Thomas Wolfe: Ghosts of a Common Tribal Heritage. 7.00 (ISBN 0-682-48431-8). Exposition.
Look-It-Up Book of Presidents. PLB 5.99 (ISBN 0-394-90748-5). Random.
Looking Back: A Chronicle of Growing up Old in the Sixties. pap. 1.25 (ISBN 0-380-01402-5, 18747). Avon.
Looking Backwards. 8.95x (ISBN 0-253-14900-2). Ind U Pr.
Looking for a Bluebird. lib. bdg. 12.25x (ISBN 0-8371-7234-9, WELO). Greenwood.
Loose Change: Three Women of the Sixties. 9.50 (ISBN 0-385-03630-2). Doubleday.
Loose Herd of Texans. 10.50 (ISBN 0-89096-044-5). Tex A&M Univ Pr.
Lopez of Newport: Colonial American Merchant Prince. 9.95x (ISBN 0-8143-1407-4). Wayne St U Pr.
Lord Acton & His Times. 17.50 (ISBN 0-8173-5700-9). U of Ala Pr.
Lord Acton: Historian of Liberty. 12.50 (ISBN 0-87548-294-5). Open Court.
Lord Beaconsfield. 10.50 (ISBN 0-8274-1735-7). R West.
Lord Beaconsfield. facsimile ed. 14.25 (ISBN 0-8369-5793-8). Arno.
Lord Bishop: The Life of Samuel Wilberforce, 1805-1873. 15.00x (ISBN 0-674-53913-3). Harvard U Pr.
Lord Brougham & the Whig Party. 16.50 (ISBN 0-208-01240-0). Shoe String.
Lord Byron. 2nd ed. lib. bdg. 7.95 (ISBN 0-8057-6694-4). Twayne.
Lord Byron's Wife. text ed. 18.75x (ISBN 0-7195-3010-5). Humanities.
Lord Chesterfield & His Letters to His Sons. lib. bdg. 12.50 (ISBN 0-8414-7551-2). Folcroft.
Lord Chesterfield & His World. 13.50 (ISBN 0-8196-0271-X). Biblo.
Lord Derby & Victorian Conservatism. 13.00x (ISBN 0-8203-0121-3). U of Ga Pr.
Lord Hervey, Eighteenth Century Courtier. 16.95 (ISBN 0-19-501731-5). Oxford U Pr.
Lord John Russell. 19.50x (ISBN 0-87249-269-9). U of SC Pr.
Lord Liverpool & Liberal Toryism 1820-1827. 15.00 (ISBN 0-208-00428-9). Shoe String.
Lord Liverpool & Liberal Toryism: 1820-27. 2nd ed. 22.50x (ISBN 0-7146-1457-2). Biblio Dist.
Lord Macaulay, Victorian Liberal. 17.50 (ISBN 0-208-01037-8). Shoe String.
Lord Norman. lib. bdg. 32.00x (ISBN 0-405-11211-4). Arno.
Lord North. 17.95 (ISBN 0-312-49840-3). St Martin.
Lord of Beasts: The Saga of Buffalo Jones. pap. 2.95 (ISBN 0-8032-5727-9, 522). U of Nebr Pr.
Lord of the Mohawks: A Biography of Sir William Johnson. rev. ed. 16.95 (ISBN 0-316-28609-5). Little.
Lord Salisbury. 17.95 (ISBN 0-312-49875-6). St Martin.
Lord Selkirk of Red River. 6.50 (ISBN 0-87013-082-X). Mich St U Pr.
Lord Shaftesbury. 10.00. Folcroft.
Lord Shaftesbury. 4th ed. 17.50 (ISBN 0-208-00215-4). Shoe String.
Lord Shaftesbury. facsimile ed. 16.50 (ISBN 0-8369-5982-5). Arno.
Lord Strafford. facs. ed. 12.25 (ISBN 0-8369-5587-0). Arno.
Lord William Russell & His Wife - 1815-1846. 19.00 (ISBN 0-8420-1681-3). Scholarly Res Inc.
Lorenzo: D. H. Lawrence & the Women Who Loved Him. 12.95 (ISBN 0-397-00772-8). Lippincott.
Lorenzo in Search of the Sun: D. H. Lawrence in Italy, Mexico & the American Southwest. 11.50 (ISBN 0-404-02373-8). AMS Pr.
Loretta Lynn. 4.95 (ISBN 0-8225-1401-X). Lerner Pubns.
Loretta Lynn: Coal Miner's Daughter. pap. 2.50. Warner Bks.
Loretta Lynn: Coal Miner's Daughter. pap. 2.50 (ISBN 0-446-91150-X). Warner Bks.
Lorie: A Story of Hope. pap. 3.95 (ISBN 0-8407-5677-1). Nelson.
Lost Boundaries. 5.95 (ISBN 0-15-153477-2). HarBraceJ.
Lost Boundaries. pap. 0.50 (ISBN 0-15-653610-2, HPL24). HarBraceJ.
Lost Illusions: Paul Leautaud & His World. 10.00 (ISBN 0-8386-1744-1). Fairleigh Dickinson.
Lost Paradise: A Boyhood on a Maine Coast Farm. 21.00 (ISBN 0-403-00904-9). Scholarly.
Lost Paradise: Early Reminiscences. facsimile ed. 23.00x (ISBN 0-405-06700-3). Arno.
Lost Tales of Appalachia. 8.00 (ISBN 0-87012-193-6). McClain.
Lost World of Thomas Jefferson. 8.50 (ISBN 0-8446-1701-6). Peter Smith.
Lost World of Thomas Jefferson. pap. 4.95 (ISBN 0-8070-5491-7, BP106). Beacon Pr.
Lott Carey: First Black Missionary to Africa. pap. 5.95 (ISBN 0-8170-0820-9). Judson.
Lou Henry Hoover, Gallant First Lady. 4.50 (ISBN 0-396-05992-9). Dodd.
Louis & Antoinette. 12.50 (ISBN 0-688-00331-1). Morrow.
Louis & the King of Siam. 8.95 (ISBN 0-915806-03-7). Thai-Am Pubs.
Louis Armstrong. pap. 1.95 (ISBN 0-498-04033-X). A S Barnes.
Louis "David" Riel: "Prophet of the New World". 15.00 (ISBN 0-8020-5430-7). U of Toronto Pr.
Louis Houck: Missouri Historian & Entrepreneur. 10.00x (ISBN 0-8262-0542-9). U of Mo Pr.
Louis I. Kahn: Complete Works, 1935-1974. lib. bdg. 82.75x (ISBN 0-89158-648-2). Westview.
Louis Kossuth & Young America: A Study of Sectionalism & Foreign Policy, 1848-1852. 12.50x (ISBN 0-8262-0223-3). U of Mo Pr.
Louis Napoleon & the Second Empire. pap. 2.95 (ISBN 0-393-00403-1). Norton.
Louis Pasteur. 4.79 (ISBN 0-671-32604-X). Messner.
Louis Sullivan: Prophet of Modern Architecture. 8.50 (ISBN 0-8446-1317-7). Peter Smith.
Louis Sullivan: Prophet of Modern Architecture. pap. 5.95 (ISBN 0-393-00116-4). Norton.
Louis Sullivan: Prophet of Modern Architecture. lib. bdg. 21.75x (ISBN 0-8371-5757-9, MOLS). Greenwood.
Louisa May: A Modern Biography of Louisa May Alcott. 14.95 (ISBN 0-395-25720-4). HM.
Louisa May Alcott. lib. bdg. 21.00x (ISBN 0-8371-9552-7, ANLMA). Greenwood.
Louisa May Alcott. 14.95x (ISBN 0-8061-0206-3); pap. 4.95 (ISBN 0-8061-0938-6). U of Okla Pr.
Louisa May Alcott: Her Life Letters & Journals. 13.50 (ISBN 0-8274-2996-7). R West.
Louise Imogen Guiney: Laureate of the Lost. 12.95 (ISBN 0-87343-039-5). Magi Bks.
Louise Nevelson. pap. 13.95 (ISBN 0-525-47439-0). Dutton.
Love Affairs of Some Famous Men. 17.50 (ISBN 0-8369-2948-9). Arno.
Love Has a Price Tag. 6.95 (ISBN 0-915684-50-0). Christian Herald.
Love Is Not for Cowards: The Autobiography of Shirley Dyckes Kelley. 9.95 (ISBN 0-13-541029-0). P-H.
Love Letters of Herb & Sandy McCabe. pap. 0.95 (ISBN 0-570-03159-1, 12-2544). Concordia.
Love Letters of Mark Twain. lib. bdg. 21.50x (ISBN 0-8371-8995-0, WELL). Greenwood.
Love Letters of Mary Wollstonecraft to Gilbert Imlay. lib. bdg. 20.00 (ISBN 0-8414-5062-5). Folcroft.
Love Letters of Nathaniel Hawthorne. 17.00 (ISBN 0-910972-18-4). IHS-PDS.
Love Letters of Thomas Carlyle & Jane Welsh. 60.00 set (ISBN 0-404-14050-5). AMS Pr.
Love-Lives of Charles Dickens. lib. bdg. 17.00x (ISBN 0-8371-6464-8, DULL). Greenwood.
Love Scene: The Story of Laurence Olivier & Vivien Leigh. 10.95 (ISBN 0-690-01413-9). T Y Crowell.
Lovecraft: A Biography. pap. 1.95 (ISBN 0-345-25115-6). Ballantine.
Loves of the Poets. lib. bdg. 20.00 (ISBN 0-8414-1003-8). Folcroft.
Lowell & His Poetry. lib. bdg. 7.50. Folcroft.
Lowell & His Poetry. 7.25 (ISBN 0-404-52517-2). AMS Pr.
Loyalist Mind: Joseph Galloway & the American Revolution. 11.75 (ISBN 0-271-00514-9). Pa St U Pr.
Luchino Visconti. 6.95 (ISBN 0-670-44426-X). Viking Pr.
Lucille Ball. PLB 5.50 (ISBN 0-87191-557-X). Creative Ed.
Lucius Polk Brown & Progressive Food & Drug Control: Tennessee & New York City,1908-1920. 12.50x (ISBN 0-7006-0163-5). Regents Pr KS.
Lucretia Mott. 14.00 (ISBN 0-8462-1579-9). Russell.
Lucretius, Poet & Philosopher. 12.00 (ISBN 0-8462-1410-5). Russell.
Lucrezia Borgia: A Biography. pap. 6.95 (ISBN 0-8015-4724-5). Dutton.
Lucy Larcom: Life, Letters & Diary. 12.50 (ISBN 0-8103-3611-1). Gale.
Lucy Larcom: Life, Letters & Diary. facsimile ed. 15.00 (ISBN 0-8369-5759-8). Arno.
Ludwig Bamberger: German Liberal Politician & Social Critic,1823-1899. 16.95x (ISBN 0-8229-3298-9). U of Pittsburgh Pr.
Ludwig Thoma. lib. bdg. 13.50 (ISBN 0-8057-6335-X). Twayne.
Ludwig Tieck & America. 18.50 (ISBN 0-404-50912-6). AMS Pr.
Lugard. Incl. Years of Adventure 1858-1898; Years of Authority 1898-1945. 39.50 (ISBN 0-208-00235-9); 22.50 ea. Shoe String.
Luigi Capuana & His Times. 7.00 (ISBN 0-913298-37-9). S F Vanni.
Luis Bunuel. expanded rev. ed. pap. 4.95 (ISBN 0-520-03424-4). U of Cal Pr.
Luis Bunuel. lib. bdg. 10.95 (ISBN 0-8057-9261-9). Twayne.
Luis Bunuel: A Critical Biography. 15.00 (ISBN 0-306-70754-3); pap. 4.95 (ISBN 0-306-80028-4). Da Capo.
Luis de Leon. lib. bdg. 12.95x (ISBN 0-8057-2524-5). Irvington.
Lulu. 6.95 (ISBN 0-8007-0956-X). Revell.
Lumbercamp Life in Michigan: An Autobiographical Account. 5.00 (ISBN 0-682-48102-5). Exposition.
Lumberjack Sky Pilot. 3rd ed. 7.95 (ISBN 0-932052-07-X). North Country.
Lunatic Fringe. lib. bdg. 13.00x (ISBN 0-8371-6680-2, JOLF). Greenwood.
Lunsford Lane: Or, Another Helper from North Carolina. 12.75x (ISBN 0-8371-2059-4). Negro U Pr.
Lunsford Lane: Or, Another Helper from North Carolina. facs. ed. 13.75 (ISBN 0-8369-8591-5). Arno.
Lusty Scripps: The Life of E. W. Scripps, 1854-1926. 19.00 (ISBN 0-403-00981-2). Scholarly.
Luther: An Introduction to His Thought. pap. 4.50 (ISBN 0-8006-1162-4). Fortress.
Luther & His Times: The Reformation from a New Perspective. 19.95 (ISBN 0-570-03246-6, 15-1164). Concordia.
Luther & Music. 7.50 (ISBN 0-8462-1008-8). Russell.
Luther and the False Brethren. 10.00x (ISBN 0-8047-0883-5). Stanford U Pr.
Luther & the German Reformation. 20.00. Folcroft.
Luther & the Mystics: A Re-Examination of Luther's Spiritual Experience & His Relationship to the Mystics. 9.95 (ISBN 0-8066-1514-1, 10-4140). Augsburg.
Luther Halsey Gulick: 1865-1918. 17.50 (ISBN 0-404-55635-3). AMS Pr.
Luther Martin of Maryland. 20.00x (ISBN 0-8018-1067-1). Johns Hopkins.
Lyndon Baines Johnson. PLB 4.49 (ISBN 0-399-60433-2). Putnam.
Lyndon Johnson & the American Dream. 12.50 (ISBN 0-06-012284-6). Har-Row.
Lyndon Johnson & the American Dream. pap. 2.50 (ISBN 0-451-07609-5, E7609). NAL.
Lytton Strachey. 10.00 (ISBN 0-8274-1213-4). R West.
Lytton Strachey. lib. bdg. 10.95 (ISBN 0-8383-1936-X). Haskell.
Lytton Strachey. lib. bdg. 6.00 (ISBN 0-8414-1781-4). Folcroft.
Lytton Strachey. lib. bdg. 6.50 (ISBN 0-8414-3476-X). Folcroft.
Lytton Strachey: His Mind & Art. 17.50 (ISBN 0-8046-1717-1). Kennikat.

M

M. Cornelii Frontonis Epistulae, Adnotatione Critica Instructae. 20.00x (ISBN 0-405-07070-5). Arno.
M. S. Lunin: Catholic Decembrist. pap. text ed. 25.00x (ISBN 90-2793-444-4). Mouton.
M. Stambuloff. 12.00 (ISBN 0-405-02733-8). Arno.
Maalesh: A Theatrical Tour in the Middle-East. lib. bdg. 13.50x (ISBN 0-313-20054-8, COMT). Greenwood.
Mabel: A Biography of Mabel Dodge Luhan. 10.00 (ISBN 0-395-25349-7). HM.
MacArthur: His Rendezvous with History. lib. bdg. 31.75x (ISBN 0-8371-9564-0, WHMA). Greenwood.
Macaulay. 15.00 (ISBN 0-8274-2655-0). R West.
McCarthy & the Communists. lib. bdg. 10.50x (ISBN 0-8371-5636-X, ROCO). Greenwood.
McCarthyism. pap. text ed. 5.50 (ISBN 0-88275-674-5). Krieger.
McClellan, Sherman, & Grant. lib. bdg. 11.75x (ISBN 0-8371-9280-3, WIMS). Greenwood.
Machiavelli & His Times. lib. bdg. 19.75x (ISBN 0-8371-7889-4, MUMA). Greenwood.
Machiavelli & the Art of Renaissance History. text ed. 12.95x (ISBN 0-8143-1499-6). Wayne St U Pr.
Mackenzie King of Canada: A Biography. lib. bdg. 17.75x (ISBN 0-8371-5164-3, HAMK). Greenwood.
McLaren - the Man, the Cars & the Team. 7.95 (ISBN 0-87880-007-7). Norton.

McMan: The Lives of Robert M. McFarlin & James A. Chapman. 9.75 (ISBN 0-8061-1446-0). U of Okla Pr.
Macmillan: A Study in Ambiguity. 6.50 (ISBN 0-671-43840-9). S&S.
Mad Men of Hockey. 8.95 (ISBN 0-396-07060-4). Dodd.
Mad Shelley. 7.50 (ISBN 0-87752-178-6). Gordian.
Madam As Entrepreneur: Career Management in House Prostitution. 14.95 (ISBN 0-87855-211-1). Transaction Bks.
Madam Prime Minister: Margaret Thatcher & Her Rise to Power. 8.95 (ISBN 0-88225-285-2). Newsweek.
Madame De Pompadour. rev. ed. 20.00 (ISBN 0-06-012989-1). Har-Row.
Madame De Sevigne. 10.50 (ISBN 0-8369-6794-1). Arno.
Madame De Sevigne. 20.00 (ISBN 0-8274-0068-3). R West.
Madame De Sevigne. 10.00 (ISBN 0-404-56809-2). AMS Pr.
Madame de Sevigne: A Portrait in Letters. lib. bdg. 19.25x (ISBN 0-313-20537-X, ALMS). Greenwood.
Madame De Sevigne, Her Letters & Her World. lib. bdg. 27.50 (ISBN 0-8414-7727-2). Folcroft.
Madame Prime Minister: The Story of Indira Gandhi. 4.50 (ISBN 0-374-34686-0). FS&G.
Madame Vestris & Her Times. 17.00 (ISBN 0-405-08845-0). Arno.
Made in Hollywood. 8.95 (ISBN 0-8092-7870-7). Contemp Bks.
Made in Hollywood. pap. 2.25 (ISBN 0-446-82913-7). Warner Bks.
Madeleine De Scudery: Her Romantic Life & Death. 17.00 (ISBN 0-405-08764-0). Arno.
Madeleine De Scudery: Her Romantic Life & Death. 13.45 (ISBN 0-8274-1039-5). R West.
Madeline Manning Jackson: Running on Faith. PLB 5.95 (ISBN 0-88436-261-2); pap. 3.50 (ISBN 0-88436-262-0). EMC.
Mademoiselle De Scudery. 9.95 (ISBN 0-8057-6278-7). Twayne.
Madmen of History. 9.95 (ISBN 0-8246-0202-1). Jonathan David.
Mae West. pap. 1.75 (ISBN 0-515-03868-7). HarBraceJ.
Maestro: The Life of Arturo Toscanini. lib. bdg. 19.75x (ISBN 0-8371-9434-2, TAMA). Greenwood.
Magic City Doctor. pap. 7.50 (ISBN 0-8283-1685-6). Branden.
Magic Image: The Genius of Photography from 1839 to the Present Day. 19.95 (ISBN 0-316-08597-9). Little.
Magic Makers: Magic & the Men Who Made It. 6.95 (ISBN 0-8407-6476-6). Elsevier-Nelson.
Magic Man: The Life of Robert Houdin. 6.95 (ISBN 0-8407-6146-5). Elsevier-Nelson.
Magic of Light: The Craft & Career of Jean Rosenthal, Pioneer in Lighting for the Modern Stage. 15.00 (ISBN 0-316-93120-9). Little.
Magic of Maeterlinck. 14.00 (ISBN 0-527-60750-9). Kraus Repr.
Magic Years of Beatrix Potter. 25.00 (ISBN 0-7232-2108-1). Warne.
Magical World of Aleister Crowley. 8.95 (ISBN 0-698-10884-1). Coward.
Magician of the Golden Dawn: The Story of Aleister Crowley. 10.00 (ISBN 0-8092-7802-2). Contemp Bks.
Magician of the Golden Dawn: The Story of Aleister Crowley. pap. 5.95 (ISBN 0-8092-7221-0). Contemp Bks.
Magnalia Christi Americana: Or the Ecclesiastical History of New England. 6.75 (ISBN 0-8044-5668-2); pap. 2.95 (ISBN 0-8044-6478-2). Ungar.
Magnificent Matriarch: Kaahumanu, Queen of Hawaii, 1772-1838. new ed. pap. 7.95 (ISBN 0-8038-4732-7). Hastings.
Magnificent Missourian: The Life of Thomas Hart Benton. lib. bdg. 17.00x (ISBN 0-8371-6933-X, SMMM). Greenwood.
Mahalia, Gospel Singer. 4.50 (ISBN 0-396-07280-1). Dodd.
Mahalia Jackson: Young Gospel Singer. 5.95 (ISBN 0-672-51931-3). Bobbs.
Maharishi: The Founder of Transcendental Meditation. pap. 1.50 (ISBN 0-451-07012-7, W7012). NAL.
Mahatma Gandhi. pap. 4.50 (ISBN 0-210-22542-4). Asia.
Mahatma Gandhi & His Apostles. 14.95 (ISBN 0-670-45087-1). Viking Pr.
Mahatma Gandhi & His Apostles. pap. 3.95 (ISBN 0-14-004571-6). Penguin.
Mahatma Gandhi at Work: His Own Story Continued. facsimile ed. 18.25 (ISBN 0-8369-6690-2). Arno.
Mahatma Gandhi: The Man Who Became One with the Universal Being. 20.00 (ISBN 0-8274-4303-X). R West.
Mahler. 17.50 (ISBN 0-385-00524-5). Doubleday.
Mahler: The Man & His Music. 14.95 (ISBN 0-02-870840-7). Schirmer Bks.
Mahler: The Man & His Music. pap. 6.95 (ISBN 0-02-871540-3). Schirmer Bks.
Main Event: The World of Professional Wrestling. 12.95 (ISBN 0-8037-5540-6); pap. 7.95 (ISBN 0-8037-5633-X). Dial.
Main Spark: Sparky Anderson & the Cincinnati Reds. 7.95 (ISBN 0-385-12464-3). Doubleday.
Maine Doings. lib. bdg. 11.50 (ISBN 0-89621-025-1); pap. 4.95 (ISBN 0-89621-024-3). Thorndike Pr.
Mainstream. facsimile ed. 14.75 (ISBN 0-8369-1444-9). Arno.
Maitland: A Critical Examination & Assessment. 5.00x (ISBN 0-678-04545-3). Kelley.
Majesty: Elizabeth II & the House of Windsor. 12.95 (ISBN 0-15-155684-9). HarBraceJ.
Major Andre's Journal. 8.00 (ISBN 0-405-01103-2). Arno.
Major-General Anthony Wayne & the Pennsylvania Line of the Continental Army. 15.00. Friedman.
Major Mike. pap. 2.50 (ISBN 0-89516-057-9). Condor Pub Co.
Major Prophets of To-Day. facs. ed. 15.25 (ISBN 0-8369-0882-1). Arno.
Majority of One: Tom Aikens & Independent Politics in Townsville. 18.00x (ISBN 0-7022-1285-7). U of Queensland Pr.
Makarios: Pragmatism V. Idealism. 8.25 (ISBN 0-200-72207-7). Transatlantic.
Make a Joyful Noise Unto the Lord: The Life of Mahalia Jackson, Queen of Gospel Singers. 8.95 (ISBN 0-690-43344-1). T Y Crowell.
Make 'em Laugh: Famous Comedians & Their Worlds. 13.50 (ISBN 0-04-792011-4). Allen Unwin.
Make 'em Laugh: Life Studies of Comedy Writers. 8.95 (ISBN 0-8314-0041-2). Sci & Behavior.
Make Today Count. 7.95 (ISBN 0-440-05256-4); pap. 3.95 (ISBN 0-440-05257-2). Delacorte.
Maker of Modern Japan: The Life of Tokugawa Ieyasu. 27.50 (ISBN 0-404-14595-7). AMS Pr.
Makers of Arab History. pap. text ed. 4.50x (ISBN 0-06-131548-6, TB1548). Har-Row.
Makers of Democracy in Latin America. 7.00x (ISBN 0-8154-0272-4). Cooper Sq.
Makers of History. 14.25 (ISBN 0-8369-8121-9). Arno.
Makers of India. facsimile ed. 8.75 (ISBN 0-8369-2251-4). Arno.
Makers of Modern Medicine. 17.00 (ISBN 0-8369-1538-0). Arno.
Makers of Naval Tradition. 21.25 (ISBN 0-8369-2733-8). Arno.
Makers of North American Botany. 10.50 (ISBN 0-8260-4520-0). Wiley.
Makers of Opera. 11.00 (ISBN 0-8046-1412-1). Kennikat.
Makers of the Russian Revolution: Biographies of Bolshevik Leaders. 20.00x (ISBN 0-8014-0809-1). Cornell U Pr.
Makers of Venice: Doges, Conquerors, Painters & Men of Letters. 14.50 (ISBN 0-404-04815-3). AMS Pr.
Making of a Genius. 10.95 (ISBN 0-916560-02-3). Renaissance Pubs.
Making of a History: Walter Prescott Webb & the Great Plains. 10.95x (ISBN 0-292-75029-3). U of Tex Pr.
Making of a Missionary. pap. 2.95 (ISBN 0-8010-5358-7). Baker Bk.
Making of a Psychiatrist. 8.95 (ISBN 0-87795-049-0). Arbor Hse.
Making of a Psychiatrist. pap. 5.95 (ISBN 0-87795-240-X). Arbor Hse.
Making of a Rookie. PLB 3.69 (ISBN 0-394-90199-1). Random.
Making of a Southerner. lib. bdg. 12.25x (ISBN 0-8371-5194-5, LUMS). Greenwood.
Making of a Stockbroker. facsimile ed. 19.00x (ISBN 0-405-06970-7). Arno.
Making of a Surgeon. 8.95 (ISBN 0-394-43447-1). Random.
Making of a Surgeon. pap. 1.95 (ISBN 0-671-80062-0). PB.
Making of a Surgeon. pap. 2.50 (ISBN 0-440-15455-3). Dell.
Making of a Woman Cop. new ed. 8.95 (ISBN 0-688-02982-5). Morrow.
Making of an American. 6.95 (ISBN 0-02-603430-1). Macmillan.
Making of an Arab Nationalist: Ottomanism & Arabism in the Life & Thought of Sati' Al-Husri. 12.50 (ISBN 0-691-03088-X). Princeton U Pr.
Making of an Assassin: The Life of James Earl Ray. 8.95 (ISBN 0-316-56241-6). Little.
Making of Frederick the Great. lib. bdg. 20.25x (ISBN 0-8371-9440-7, SIMF). Greenwood.
Making of George Washington. 2nd ed. pap. 1.50 (ISBN 0-912530-02-2). Patriotic Educ.
Making of Lloyd George. 15.00 (ISBN 0-208-01627-9). Shoe String.
Making of Nicholas Longworth: Annals of an American Family. facsimile ed. 19.75 (ISBN 0-8369-5882-9). Arno.
Making of Political Women: A Study of Socialization & Role Conflict. text ed. 17.95x (ISBN 0-88229-290-0). Nelson-Hall.
Making of Walton's Lives. 22.50x (ISBN 0-8014-0319-7). Cornell U Pr.
Making of William Penn. facs. ed. 16.50 (ISBN 0-8369-5416-5). Arno.
Maksim Gorki. 9.95 (ISBN 0-8044-2326-1); pap. 3.45 (ISBN 0-8044-6239-9). Ungar.
Maladies of Marcel Proust. text ed. 19.50x (ISBN 0-8419-0546-0). Holmes & Meier.
Malcolm Forbes: Peripatetic Millionaire. 10.00 (ISBN 0-06-012204-8). Har-Row.
Malcolm Lowry: A Biography. 16.95 (ISBN 0-19-501711-0). Oxford U Pr.
Malcolm Sargent: A Biography. 12.00 (ISBN 0-8008-5080-7). Taplinger.
Malcolm X. pap. 1.95 (ISBN 0-690-51415-8). T Y Crowell.
Malcolm X. bds. 6.95 (ISBN 0-690-51413-1). T Y Crowell.
Malinki of Malawi. pap. 3.95 (ISBN 0-8163-0089-5, 13054-2). Pacific Pr Pub Assn.
Mallarme. 10.00x (ISBN 0-8147-0304-6); pap. 3.95 (ISBN 0-8147-0305-4). NYU Pr.
Mallory of Everest. 4.95 (ISBN 0-02-788540-2). Macmillan.
Mallowan's Memoirs. 10.95 (ISBN 0-396-07467-7). Dodd.
Malpractice: Autobiography of a Victim. 9.95 (ISBN 0-498-02185-8). A S Barnes.
Malraux: Life & Work. 12.95 (ISBN 0-15-156280-6). HarBraceJ.
Malthus. text ed. 17.50x (ISBN 0-674-54425-0). Harvard U Pr.
Mamaji. 12.95 (ISBN 0-19-502640-3). Oxford U Pr.
Man About Paris: The Confessions of Arsene Houssaye. 15.00 (ISBN 0-688-02029-1). Morrow.
Man Against the Elements: Adolphus W. Greely. pap. price not set (ISBN 0-671-29600-0). Archway.
Man Against the Mountain. pap. 1.95 (ISBN 0-89191-143-X). Cook.
Man & His Mountain: A Biography of Paul Cezanne. 9.95 (ISBN 0-02-583670-6). Macmillan.
Man & Mask: Forty Years in the Life of a Singer. 16.00 (ISBN 0-403-01679-7). Scholarly.
Man & Mask: Forty Years in the Life of a Singer. lib. bdg. 17.25x (ISBN 0-8371-4332-2, SHMM). Greenwood.
Man Bilbo. lib. bdg. 13.25x (ISBN 0-8371-9103-3, GRTM). Greenwood.
Man Called Intrepid: The Secret War. 14.95 (ISBN 0-15-156795-6). HarBraceJ.
Man Called White. 17.00 (ISBN 0-405-01906-8). Arno.
Man Called White: The Autobiography of Walter White. pap. 3.25x (ISBN 0-253-20135-7). Ind U Pr.
Man Charles Dickens: A Victorian Portrait. rev. ed. 10.95 (ISBN 0-8061-0685-9). U of Okla Pr.
Man for All Time. pap. 2.50 (ISBN 0-8192-1127-3); leaders' guide 2.50 (ISBN 0-8192-4035-4). Morehouse.
Man from Monticello: An Intimate Life of Thomas Jefferson. 12.50 (ISBN 0-688-02030-5). Morrow.
Man from Nazareth: As His Contemporaries Saw Him. lib. bdg. 21.00x (ISBN 0-313-20603-1, FOMN). Greenwood.
Man from Plains: The Mind & Spirit of Jimmy Carter. pap. 1.95 (ISBN 0-06-080417-3, P417). Har-Row.
Man in Black. pap. 2.25 (ISBN 0-446-92222-6). Warner Bks.
Man in the Mirror: William Marion Reedy & His Magazine. lib. bdg. 16.75x (ISBN 0-8371-6453-2, PUMM). Greenwood.
Man Mencken: A Biographical & Critical Survey. 21.50 (ISBN 0-404-02857-8). AMS Pr.
Man of Aran. pap. 4.95 (ISBN 0-262-63027-3). MIT Pr.
Man of Independence. 12.75 (ISBN 0-8046-1427-X). Kennikat.
Man of Liberty: A Life of Thomas Jefferson. rev. ed. 6.95g (ISBN 0-374-34752-2). FS&G.
Man of Mayflower Hill: A Biography of Franklin W. Johnson. 5.00 (ISBN 0-910394-05-9). Colby.
Man of Principle: A Biography of John Galsworthy. pap. 4.95 (ISBN 0-8128-1297-2). Stein & Day.
Man of the Monitor: Story of John Ericsson. PLB 7.89 (ISBN 0-06-023711-2). Har-Row.
Man of the Renaissance: Four Law Givers - Savonarola, Machiavelli, Castiglione, Aretino. 22.50x (ISBN 0-678-03171-1). Kelley.
Man of the Woods. pap. 4.95 (ISBN 0-8156-0126-3). Syracuse U Pr.
Man on the Flying Trapeze: The Circus Life of Emmett Kelly Sr. Told with Pictures & Song! 8.95 (ISBN 0-397-31643-7). Lippincott.
Man Possessed: The Case History of Sigmund Freud. 7.95 (ISBN 0-911238-53-0); pap. 2.45 (ISBN 0-911238-57-3). Regent House.
Man Sent by God: The Life of Patriarch Athenagoras of Constantinople. pap. 3.95 (ISBN 0-916586-07-3). Holy Cross Orthodox.
Man Verdi. 15.00 (ISBN 0-394-40833-0). Knopf.
Man Whistler. 9.95 (ISBN 0-8008-5097-1). Taplinger.
Man Who Beat Clout City. 10.00 (ISBN 0-8040-0777-2). Swallow.
Man Who Bought Himself: The Story of Peter Still. 7.95 (ISBN 0-02-762220-7, 76222). Macmillan.
Man Who Built a City: A Life of Sir Christopher Wren. 4.95 (ISBN 0-374-34779-4). FS&G.
Man Who Changed China: The Story of Sun Yat-Sen. PLB 4.39 (ISBN 0-394-90509-1). Random.
Man Who Elected Lincoln. lib. bdg. 15.75x (ISBN 0-8371-6920-8, MOMW). Greenwood.
Man Who Gave the Beatles Away. 9.95 (ISBN 0-02-629050-2). Macmillan.
Man Who Gave the Beatles Away. pap. 1.95 (ISBN 0-345-27074-6). Ballantine.
Man Who Keeps Going to Jail. 6.95 (ISBN 0-89191-107-3). Cook.
Man Who Killed Boys. 8.95 (ISBN 0-312-51157-4). St Martin.
Man Who Loved Laughter: The Story of Sholom Aleichem. 4.25 (ISBN 0-8276-0033-X, 265). Jewish Pubn.
Man Who Presumed: A Biography of Henry M. Stanley. lib. bdg. 17.50x (ISBN 0-8371-7160-1, FAMW). Greenwood.
Man Who Rode the Thunder. bds. 5.35 (ISBN 0-13-548271-2). P-H.
Man Who Said No. 4.95 (ISBN 0-698-20086-1). Coward.
Man Who Saw Through Time. pap. 2.95 (ISBN 0-684-13285-0, SL 429). Scribner.
Man Who Shot Jesse James. 12.00 (ISBN 0-498-02068-1). A S Barnes.
Man Who Walked in His Head. 9.95 (ISBN 0-688-03529-9). Morrow.
Man Who Was Left for Dead. PLB 7.99 (ISBN 0-8172-1556-5). Raintree Pubs.
Man Who Would Be Perfect: John Humphrey Noyes & the Utopian Impulse. 12.95x (ISBN 0-8122-7724-4). U of Pa Pr.
Man with a Million Ideas: Fred Jones, Genius Inventor. PLB 6.95 (ISBN 0-8225-0761-7). Lerner Pubns.
Man with the Noisy Heart. 6.95 (ISBN 0-8024-5171-3). Moody.
Managers. PLB 7.50 (ISBN 0-87191-516-2). Creative Ed.
Manchild in the Promised Land. 9.95 (ISBN 0-02-517320-0). Macmillan.
Manchild in the Promised Land. pap. 1.75 (ISBN 0-451-08206-0, E8206). NAL.
Manet-Olympia. 14.95 (ISBN 0-670-45408-7). Viking Pr.
Mank: The Wit, World, & Life of Herman Mankiewicz. 12.95 (ISBN 0-688-03356-3). Morrow.
Manny: A Criminal-Addict's Story. pap. text ed. 7.75 (ISBN 0-395-24838-8). HM.
Manuel De Falla, His Life & Works. 17.50 (ISBN 0-88355-756-8). Hyperion Conn.
Manuel Ii Palaeologus, 1391-1425: A Study in Late Byzantine Statesmanship. 37.50 (ISBN 0-8135-0582-8). Rutgers U Pr.
Manuel Lisa. 12.50 (ISBN 0-87266-006-0). Argosy.
Many Lives of Benjamin Franklin. PLB 6.95 (ISBN 0-13-556019-5). P-H.
Many-Sided Franklin. 29.50 (ISBN 0-8369-6770-4). Arno.
Many Sided Franklin. 22.50 (ISBN 0-8274-2671-2). R West.
Manya's Story. PLB 7.95 (ISBN 0-8225-0762-5). Lerner Pubns.
Manzoni & His Times: A Biography of the Author of The Betrothed (I Promessi Sposi) 25.00 (ISBN 0-88355-688-X). Hyperion Conn.
Mao: A Biography. 17.95 (ISBN 0-06-014243-X). Har-Row.
Mao for Beginners. 8.95 (ISBN 0-394-50589-1); pap. 2.95 (ISBN 0-394-73886-1). Pantheon.
Mao Tse-Tung. pap. 0.95 (ISBN 0-671-47910-5). WSP.
Mao Tse-Tung. pap. 4.95 (ISBN 0-14-020840-2). Penguin.
Mao Tse-Tung. 9.95 (ISBN 0-671-44874-9). S&S.
Mao Tse-Tung: A Guide to His Thought. 10.00 (ISBN 0-312-51397-6). St Martin.
Mao Tse-Tung & China. pap. 2.50 (ISBN 0-14-021947-1). Penguin.
Mao Tse-Tung & China. text ed. 12.50x (ISBN 0-8419-0268-2). Holmes & Meier.
Mao Tse-Tung & I Were Beggars. pap. 1.95 (ISBN 0-02-037000-8). Macmillan.
Mao Tse-Tung & I Were Beggars. deluxe ed. 10.00 (ISBN 0-8156-0015-1). Syracuse U Pr.
Mao Tse Tung & the Chinese People. 16.50 (ISBN 0-85345-413-2, CL4132). Monthly Rev.
Mao Tse-Tung, Emperor of the Blue Ants. lib. bdg. 19.25x (ISBN 0-8371-6775-2, PAMT). Greenwood.
Marble Man: Robert E Lee & His Image in American Society. 10.00 (ISBN 0-394-47179-2). Knopf.

Marble Man: Robert E. Lee & His Image in American Society. pap. 5.95 (ISBN 0-8071-0474-4). La State U Pr.

Marc Chagall. 6.95 (ISBN 0-385-04917-X); PLB (ISBN 0-385-05125-5). Doubleday.

Marc Connelly. lib. bdg. 7.95 (ISBN 0-8057-0152-4). Twayne.

Marcel Proust: A Biography. pap. 4.95 ea.; (ISBN 0-394-72561-1); (ISBN 0-394-72562-X). Random.

Marcel Proust: Letters to His Mother. lib. bdg. 12.50x (ISBN 0-8371-6760-4, PRLM). Greenwood.

Marchesi & Music: Passages from the Life of a Famous Singing-Teacher. lib. bdg. 22.50 (ISBN 0-306-77577-8). Da Capo.

Marching to Freedom: The Life of Martin Luther King Jr. pap. 1.25 (ISBN 0-451-07314-2, Y7314). NAL.

Marco Polo. pap. 0.75 (ISBN 0-671-29602-7). Archway.

Marco Polo: A Story of the Middle Ages. 3.50g (ISBN 0-02-775140-6). Macmillan.

Marcus Aurelius Antoninus. facsimile ed. 16.00 (ISBN 0-8369-5667-2). Arno.

Marcus Crassus & the Late Roman Republic. 15.50x (ISBN 0-8262-0216-0). U of Mo Pr.

Marcus Garvey. 6.95 (ISBN 0-13-556068-3). Brown Bk.

Marcus Garvey. PLB 5.88 (ISBN 0-531-02577-2). Watts.

Margaret Fell Speaking. pap. 0.95x (ISBN 0-87574-206-8). Pendle Hill.

Margaret Fuller. pap. 3.45 (ISBN 0-8084-0209-9, T48). Coll & U Pr.

Margaret Fuller - Marchesa Ossoli. lib. bdg. 11.25x (ISBN 0-8371-4089-7, HOMF). Greenwood.

Margaret Fuller: A Psychological Biography. lib. bdg. 25.00 (ISBN 0-8495-0020-6). Arden Lib.

Margaret Fuller: From Transcendentalism to Revolution. pap. 5.95 (ISBN 0-440-56242-2). Dell.

Margaret Mitchell of Atlanta. pap. 1.75 (ISBN 0-380-00810-6, 20594). Avon.

Margaret Mitchell's "Gone with the Wind" Letters: 1936-1949. 12.95 (ISBN 0-02-548650-0). Macmillan.

Margaret Ogilvy. 14.00 (ISBN 0-403-00243-5). Scholarly.

Margaret Sanger: A Biography of the Champion of Birth Control. 15.00 (ISBN 0-399-90019-5). R Marek.

Margaret Sanger: An Autobiography. pap. 5.50 (ISBN 0-486-20470-7). Dover.

Margaret Sanger: Pioneer of Birth Control. pap 0.95 (ISBN 0-440-95395-2). Dell.

Margaret Sanger Story, & the Fight for Birth Control. lib. bdg. 15.75x (ISBN 0-8371-7076-1, LAMS). Greenwood.

Margaret Winthrop. 15.00 (ISBN 0-87152-041-9) Reprint.

Margery Kempe, Genius & Mystic. lib. bdg. 17.50 (ISBN 0-8414-0296-5). Folcroft.

Margot Fonteyn: Autobiography. 12.50 (ISBN 0-394-48570-X). Knopf.

Margot Fonteyn: Autobiography. pap. 2.50 (ISBN 0-446-01380 X) Warner Bks.

Marguerite of Navarre. 10.00 (ISBN 0-8037-5207-5). Dial.

Maria. pap. 1.95 (ISBN 0-380-00783-5, 41111). Avon.

Maria Callas. 12.95 (ISBN 0-312-51448-4). St Martin.

Maria Edgeworth. lib. bdg. 10.00 (ISBN 0-8414-2364-4). Folcroft.

Maria Edgeworth: A Literary Biography. 24.95x (ISBN 0-19-812017-6). Oxford U Pr.

Maria Edgeworth: Her Family & Friends. lib. bdg. 15.00 (ISBN 0-8414-0691-X). Folcroft.

Maria Edgeworth: Her Family & Friends. lib. bdg. 25.00 (ISBN 0-8495-0905-X). Arden Lib.

Maria Malibran: A Biography of the Singer. 17.95 (ISBN 0-271-00222-0). Pa St U Pr.

Maria Martinez. 2nd ed. lib. bdg. 6.95 (ISBN 0-87518-098-1). Dillon.

Maria Mitchell, First Lady of American Astronomy. 7.95 (ISBN 0-664-32614-5). Westminster.

Maria Sanford, Pioneer Professor. PLB 5.95 (ISBN 0-87518-134-1). Dillon.

Maria Tallchief. PLB 6.95 (ISBN 0-87518-060-4). Dillon.

Maria Tallchief. PLB 6.89 (ISBN 0-690-51829-3). T Y Crowell.

Maria Tallchief. pap. 1.95 (ISBN 0-690-51830-7). T Y Crowell.

Maria Theresa. facsimile ed. 13.50 (ISBN 0-8369-5761-X). Arno.

Maria Theresa. pap. 2.45 (ISBN 0-13-556183-3, S-471). P-H.

Marian Anderson. PLB 6.89 (ISBN 0-690-51847-1). T Y Crowell.

Marian Anderson, a Portrait. lib. bdg. 13.50x (ISBN 0-8371-4051-X, VEMA). Greenwood.

Marian Anderson: Lady from Philadelphia. 5.50 (ISBN 0-664-32370-7). Westminster.

Marian: The Life of George Eliot. lib. bdg. 15.00 (ISBN 0-8414-3766-1). Folcroft.

Mariano De Larra & Spanish Political Rhetoric. 25.00 (ISBN 0-299-05750-X). U of Wis Pr.

Marie Antoinette's Daughter. 4.50 (ISBN 0-396-05641-5). Dodd.

Marie Curie. PLB 4.29 (ISBN 0-399-60447-2). Putnam.

Marie Curie. pap. 2.25 (ISBN 0-451-08370-9, E8370). NAL.

Marilyn Chambers: My Story. pap. 1.95 (ISBN 0-446-79827-4). Warner Bks.

Marina & Lee. 15.00 (ISBN 0-06-012953-0). Har-Row.

Mariners, Renegades & Castaways: The Story of Herman Melville & the World We Live in. lib. bdg. 20.00 (ISBN 0-8482-1297-5). Norwood Edns.

Mario Lanza. pap. 1.25 (ISBN 0-532-12113-9). Manor Bks.

Marjoe. 10.95 (ISBN 0-06-011401-0). Har-Row.

Mark Akenside: A Biographical & Critical Study. 10.00 (ISBN 0-8462-1497-0). Russell.

Mark & the Knowledge: Social Stigma in Classic American Fiction. 15.00 (ISBN 0-8142-0296-9). Ohio St U Pr.

Mark Twain: A Portrait. 8.50 (ISBN 0-8196-0171-3). Biblo.

Mark Twain & Bret Harte. 15.95 (ISBN 0-8061-0634-4). U of Okla Pr.

Mark Twain: As Others Saw Him. PLB 5.89 (ISBN 0-698-30686-4). Coward.

Mark Twain, Dean of American Humorists. new ed. lib. bdg. 2.45 incl. catalog cards; pap. 1.25 vinyl laminated covers. SamHar Pr.

Mark Twain: God's Fool. 10.95 (ISBN 0-06-011893-8). Har-Row.

Mark Twain: God's Fool. pap. 3.95 (ISBN 0-06-090391-0, CN391). Har-Row.

Mark Twain in England. text ed. 20.00x (ISBN 0-391-00553-7). Humanities.

Mark Twain in the Movies: A Meditation with Pictures. 12.95 (ISBN 0-670-45830-9). Viking Pr.

Mark Twain, Pilgrim from Hannibal. lib. bdg. 30.00 (ISBN 0-8414-6743-9). Folcroft.

Mark Twain: Social Critic. pap. 2.25 (ISBN 0-7178-0356-2). Intl Pub Co.

Mark Twain, Son of Missouri. 18.00 (ISBN 0-8462-0412-6). Russell.

Mark Twain: The Man & His Work. 3rd ed. 13.95 (ISBN 0-8061-0737-5). U of Okla Pr.

Mark Twain's America. lib. bdg. 21.00x (ISBN 0-313-20368-7, DEVMT). Greenwood.

Mark Twain's Last Years As a Writer. text ed. 16.50x (ISBN 0-8262-0264-0). U of Mo Pr.

Mark Twain's Notebook. 35.00 (ISBN 0-8274-1403-X). R West.

Mark Twain's Notebook. 11.00 (ISBN 0-403-01411-5). Scholarly.

Mark Twain's Notebook. lib. bdg. 14.00x (ISBN 0-8154-0418-2). Cooper Sq.

Marks of American Potters. 11.50 (ISBN 0-89344-001-9). Ars Ceramica.

Marlborough. lib. bdg. 25.00 (ISBN 0-8414-7733-7). Folcroft.

Marlborough As Military Commander. 14.95 (ISBN 0-684-13314-8). Hippocrene Bks.

Marlborough, His Life & Times. lib. bdg. 135.00x (ISBN 0-678-02769-2). Kelley.

Marlene. pap. 2.50 (ISBN 0-671-82182-2). PB.

Marlene Dietrich. 6.95 (ISBN 0-07-043117 7). McGraw.

Marlene: The Life of Marlene Dietrich. 9.95 (ISBN 0-393-07515-X). Norton.

Marlin Compound: Letters of a Singular Family. 14.50x (ISBN 0-292-78380-9). U of Tex Pr.

Marlon Brando. PLB 5.50 (ISBN 0-87191-552-9). Creative Ed.

Marlowe & His Circle: A Biographical Survey. 10.00 (ISBN 0-8462-1192-0). Russell.

Marlowe & His Poetry. lib. bdg. 7.50. Folcroft.

Marlowe & His Poetry. 7.25 (ISBN 0-404-52522-9). AMS Pr.

Marlowe & His Poetry. lib. bdg. 8.50 (ISBN 0-8495-2608-6). Arden Lib.

Marquand: An American Life. 17.95 (ISBN 0-316-08828-5). Little.

Marquis: A Study of Lord Rockingham, 1730-1782. 20.00 (ISBN 0-8232-0970-9). Fordham.

Marquis De Sade. 12.95 (ISBN 0-8212-0653-2). NYGS.

Marrano. pap. 5.95 (ISBN 0-8283-1666-X). Branden.

Marriage of True Minds: An Intimate Portrait of Leonard & Virginia Woolf. 12.95 (ISBN 0-15-157449-9). HarBraceJ.

Marriage of True Minds: An Intimate Portrait of Leonard & Virginia Woolf. pap. 5.95 (ISBN 0-15-657299-0). HarBraceJ.

Marriage to a Difficult Man: The Uncommon Union of Jonathan & Sarah Edwards. 6.95 (ISBN 0-664-20900-9). Westminster.

Married Saints. facs. ed. 13.75 (ISBN 0-8369-0071-5). Arno.

Married to Genius. text ed. 20.00x (ISBN 0-06-494790-4). B&N.

Married to Tolstoy. 7.95 (ISBN 0-251-15039-9). Dufour.

Married to Tolstoy. lib. bdg. 15.00x (ISBN 0-8371-0288-X, ASMT). Greenwood.

Martha & the Doctor: A Frontier Family in Central Nevada. pap. 5.00 (ISBN 0-87417-049-4). U of Nev Pr.

Martha Berry. PLB 6.89 (ISBN 0-690-52113-8). T Y Crowell.

Martha Berry, the Sunday Lady of Possum Trot. 13.50 (ISBN 0-8103-3783-5). Gale.

Martha Washington. 15.00 (ISBN 0-87152-038-9). Reprint.

Martha's Vineyard Decoys. 25.00 (ISBN 0-87923-260-9). Godine.

Marti, Martyr of Cuban Independence. lib. bdg. 13.75x (ISBN 0-8371-7329-9, LIMA). Greenwood.

Martin A. Hansen. lib. bdg. 10.50 (ISBN 0-8057-6259-0). Twayne.

Martin Behrman of New Orleans: Memoirs of a City Boss. 20.00x (ISBN 0-8071-0275-X). La State U Pr.

Martin Buber. 6.95 (ISBN 0-87680-470-9, 80470). Word Bks.

Martin Buber: The Life of Dialogue. 3rd, rev. ed. 12.50x (ISBN 0-226-26354-1). U of Chicago Pr.

Martin Buber: The Life of Dialogue. 3rd, rev. ed. pap. 4.95 (ISBN 0-226-26356-8, P653). U of Chicago Pr.

Martin Bucer. 20.00 (ISBN 0-8462-1604-3). Russell.

Martin Dies. lib. bdg. 27.50 (ISBN 0-306-70200-2). Da Capo.

Martin Lopez. Conquistador Citizen of Mexico. lib. bdg. 11.50x (ISBN 0-8371-7322-1, GAML). Greenwood.

Martin Luther. 17.50 (ISBN 0-404-02577-3). AMS Pr.

Martin Luther--Reformer or Revolutionary? 3rd ed. pap. text ed. 1.50x. Random.

Martin Luther King, Jr. 9.95 (ISBN 0-87294-028-4). Country Beautiful.

Martin Luther King, Jr. PLB 4.49 (ISBN 0-399-60452-9). Putnam.

Martin Luther King, Jr. A Documentary...Montgomery to Memphis. 15.00 (ISBN 0-393-07487-0); limited ed. o.p. 100.00; pap. 8.95 (ISBN 0-393-07492-7). Norton.

Martin Luther King, Jr: A Profile. pap. 4.95 (ISBN 0-8090-0209-4). Hill & Wang.

Martin Luther King, Jr: Man of Peace. PLB 4.78 (ISBN 0-8116-4555-X). Garrard.

Martin Luther, the Hero of the Reformation. 18.00 (ISBN 0-404-03544-2). AMS Pr.

Martin Van Buren. 18.50 (ISBN 0-404-50868-5). AMS Pr.

Martin Van Buren, 1782-1862: Chronology, Documents, Bibliographical Aids. 7.00 (ISBN 0-379-12057-7). Oceana.

Martina Navratilova. 5.95 (ISBN 0-385-12525-9). Doubleday.

Martinu. text ed. 22.50x (ISBN 0-8419-0256-9). Holmes & Meier.

Martov: Political Biography of a Russian Social Democrat. 37.50 (ISBN 0-521-05073-1). Cambridge U Pr.

Martyr: The Story of a Secret Jew & the Mexican Inquisition in the Sixteenth Century. 7.95 (ISBN 0 8276-0011-9, 327). Jewish Pubn.

Martyrdom of Lovejoy: An Account of the Life, Trials, & Perils of Rev. Elijah P. Lovejoy. lib. bdg. 12.50x (ISBN 0-678 00744-6) Kelley.

Marx & Marxism. 12.50 (ISBN 0-8164-9127-5). Continuum.

Marx Brothers. pap. 1.75 (ISBN 0-515-03754-0). HarBraceJ.

Marx, Engels & the Workers of the World. 7.95g (ISBN 0-590-07407-5). Schol Bk Serv.

Marx for Beginners. pap. 2.95 (ISBN 0-394-73716-4). Pantheon.

Marx's Daughters: Eleanor Marx, Rosa Luxemburg, Angelica Balabanoff. 10.00 (ISBN 0-8037-5432-9). Dial.

Marx's Fate: The Shape of a Life. 16.50 (ISBN 0-691-05259-X). Princeton U Pr.

Mary & I: Forty Years with the Sioux. 12.00 (ISBN 0-87928-019-0). Corner Hse.

Mary Ann Cotton: Her Story & Trial. 9.50 (ISBN 0-7181-1184-2). Transatlantic.

Mary Astell. 7.50 (ISBN 0-404-06120-6). AMS Pr.

Mary Baker Eddy: The Years of Authority. new ed. 16.95. HR&W.

Mary Baker Eddy: The Years of Authority. pap. 7.95 (ISBN 0-03-056709-2). HR&W.

Mary Baker Eddy: The Years of Discovery. 7.50 (ISBN 0-87510-085-6). Chr Science.

Mary Baker Eddy: The Years of Trial. 8.95 (ISBN 0-87510-118-6). Chr Science.

Mary Barnes: Two Accounts of a Journey Through Madness. pap. 2.50 (ISBN 0-345-27527-6). Ballantine.

Mary Barnes: Two Accounts of Journey Through Madness. pap. 1.95 (ISBN 0-345-23221-6). Ballantine.

Mary Brown: From Harper's Ferry to California. pap. 1.50. Am Inst Marxist.

Mary Carpenter & the Children of the Streets. text ed. 29.95x (ISBN 0-435-32569-8). Heinemann Ed.

Mary Cassatt. 6.95 (ISBN 0-517-53740-0). Crown.

Mary Cassatt. PLB 7.95 (ISBN 0-516-01852-3). Childrens.

Mary Decker: Speed Records & Spaghetti. lib. bdg. 5.95 (ISBN 0-88436-162-4); pap. 3.50 (ISBN 0-88436-163-2). EMC.

Mary E. Wilkins Freeman. 7.50 (ISBN 0-87532-058-9). Hendricks House.

Mary Fran & Mo. 8.95 (ISBN 0-312-51864-1). St Martin.

Mary Howitt: An Autobiography. 50.00 (ISBN 0-8274-2680-1). R West.

Mary Howitt: An Autobiography. 27.25 ea.; 54.50 (ISBN 0-404-56754-1). AMS Pr.

Mary I: The History of an Unhappy Tudor Queen. 8.95g (ISBN 0-13-559096-5). P-H.

Mary Lamb. 13.50 (ISBN 0-404-07348-4). AMS Pr.

Mary Lamb. 25.00 (ISBN 0-932062-63-6). Sharon Hill.

Mary Lincoln: Biography of a Marriage. 12.50 (ISBN 0-316-73359-8). Little.

Mary Lyon & Mount Holyoke: Opening the Gates. text ed. 17.50x (ISBN 0-87451-172-0). U Pr of New Eng.

Mary McCarthy: A Bibliography. 4.50 (ISBN 0-15-157775-7). HarBraceJ.

Mary McLeod Bethune. 5.95 (ISBN 0-8149-0375-4). Vanguard.

Mary McLeod Bethune. PLB 5.39 (ISBN 0-394-91397-3). Knopf.

Mary McLeod Bethune: Girl Devoted to Her People. 5.95 (ISBN 0-672-51236-X). Bobbs.

Mary of Nazareth. 6.00 (ISBN 0-8198-0092-9); pap. 5.00 (ISBN 0-8198-0093-7). Dghtrs St Paul.

Mary Pickford & Douglas Fairbanks: The Most Popular Couple the World Has Known. 9.95 (ISBN 0-393-07508-7). Norton.

Mary Shelley. 20.00 (ISBN 0-8274-2687-9). R West.

Mary Shelley. lib. bdg. 10.00. Folcroft.

Mary Shelley. lib. bdg. 15.00 (ISBN 0-8495-0743-X). Arden Lib.

Mary Shelley: A Biography. lib. bdg. 25.00 (ISBN 0-8414-4535-4). Folcroft.

Mary Shelley: A Biography. lib. bdg. 23.95 (ISBN 0-8383-0978-X). Haskell.

Mary Tudor, the White Queen. 10.00 (ISBN 0-295-95006-4). U of Wash Pr.

Mary Tyler Moore. PLB 5.50 (ISBN 0-87191-559-6). Creative Ed.

Mary Wollstonecraft. lib. bdg. 35.00 (ISBN 0-8490-0588-4). Gordon Pr

Mary Wollstonecraft. lib. bdg. 17.50 (ISBN 0-8414-5674-7). Folcroft.

Mary Wollstonecraft: A Critical Biography. pap. 3.75x (ISBN 0-8032-5211-0, 340). U of Nebr Pr.

Mary Wollstonecraft: A Sketch. lib. bdg. 20.00 (ISBN 0-8414-5292-X). Folcroft.

Mary Wollstonecraft Godwin. lib. bdg. 34.95 (ISBN 0-8490-0590-6). Gordon Pr.

Mary Wollstonecraft Godwin. lib. bdg. 25.00 (ISBN 0-8414-6711-0). Folcroft.

Masamune Hakucho. lib. bdg. 13.95 (ISBN 0-8057-6375-9). Twayne.

Masks in a Pageant. 17.00 (ISBN 0-403-01272-4). Scholarly.

Masks in a Pageant. lib. bdg. 18.75x (ISBN 0-8371-4568-6, WHMP). Greenwood.

Masks of Jonathan Swift. 21.00 (ISBN 0-8462-0923-3). Russell.

Massenet. 8.95 (ISBN 0-312-51940-0, M18100). St Martin.

Massenet & His Operas. 18.50 (ISBN 0-404-12912-9). AMS Pr.

Master Builders of Opera. 14.50 (ISBN 0-8369-1964-5). Arno.

Master John Milton of the Citie of London. lib. bdg. 6.50 (ISBN 0-8414-0725-8). Folcroft.

Master Minds of Modern Science. facs. ed. 13.75 (ISBN 0-8369-0064-2). Arno.

Master Minds: Portraits of Contemporary American Artists & Intellectuals. 7.95 (ISBN 0-02-566510-3). Macmillan.

Master of Light: A Biography of Albert A. Michelson. pap. 6.95 (ISBN 0-226-48711-3, P813). U of Chicago Pr.

Master of Precision: Henry M. Leland. lib. bdg. 17.75x (ISBN 0-8371-7192-X, LEMP). Greenwood.

Master of the Russian Ballet: The Memoirs of Cav. Enrico Cecchetti. lib. bdg. 19.50 (ISBN 0-306-77589-1). Da Capo.

Master of Villainy: A Biography of Sax Rohmer. 10.00 (ISBN 0-87972-032-8). Bowling Green Univ.

Master Spy. 4.95 (ISBN 0-07-025548-2). McGraw.

Masters of English Journalism: A Study of Personal Forces. lib. bdg. 16.00x (ISBN 0-8371-3020-4, ESME). Greenwood.

Masters of English Music. 21.25 (ISBN 0-8369-7280-5). Arno.

Masters of English Music. lib. bdg. 30.00 (ISBN 0-89341-132-9). Longwood Pr.

Masters of French Music. 24.00 (ISBN 0-518-10014-6). Arno.

Masters of French Music. lib. bdg. 25.00 (ISBN 0-89341-114-0). Longwood Pr.
Masters of German Music. lib. bdg. 25.00 (ISBN 0-89341-133-7). Longwood Pr.
Masters of Italian Music. 20.50 (ISBN 0-8369-2929-2). Arno.
Masters of Music. facsimile ed. 14.75 (ISBN 0-8369-8012-3). Arno.
Masters of Russian Music. 31.00 (ISBN 0-384-07218-6). Johnson Repr.
Masters of Social Psychology: Freud, Mead, Lewin, & Skinner. pap. 2.95 (ISBN 0-19-502622-5, GB 590). Oxford U Pr.
Masters of Social Psychology: Freud, Mead, Lewin & Skinner. 10.95 (ISBN 0-19-502278-5); pap. 2.50x o.p. (ISBN 0-19-502279-3). Oxford U Pr.
Masters of the Keyboard. facsimile 2nd ed. 16.00 (ISBN 0-8369-8053-0). Arno.
Masters of the Keyboard. lib. bdg. 10.75x (ISBN 0-8371-4768-9, BRMK). Greenwood.
Masters of the Occult. 5.95 (ISBN 0-396-06407-8). Dodd.
Masters of the Orchestra from Bach to Prokofieff. lib. bdg. 17.75x (ISBN 0-8371-2545-6, BIMO). Greenwood.
Masters or Servants? A Study of Selected English Painters & Their Patrons of the Late 18th & Early 19th Centuries. lib. bdg. 51.00 (ISBN 0-8240-2690-X). Garland Pub.
Masters Way to Beauty. pap. 2.25 (ISBN 0-451-08044-0, E8044). NAL.
Matabele Journals of Robert Moffat, 1829-1860. 75.00 (ISBN 0-404-12111-X). AMS Pr.
Materials for the Life of Shakespeare. 8.50 (ISBN 0-404-01248-5). AMS Pr.
Mathieu. 6.95 (ISBN 0-517-53086-4). Crown.
Mathu of Kenya: A Political Study. 8.95 (ISBN 0-8179-6571-8). Hoover Inst Pr.
Matinee Idols. 10.00 (ISBN 0-87795-031-8, A4320); pap. 4.95 (ISBN 0-87795-060-1, A4320P). Arbor Hse.
Matisse. 6.95 (ISBN 0-517-03723-8). Crown.
Matter of Life & Death: Vital Biographical Facts About Selected American Artists. lib. bdg. 15.00 (ISBN 0-8240-9883-8). Garland Pub.
Matthew Arnold. 7.50 (ISBN 0-8462-1009-6). Russell.
Matthew Arnold. pap. 6.95 (ISBN 0-15-657734-8). HarBraceJ.
Matthew Arnold: A Study. 5.50 (ISBN 0-8462-0459-2). Russell.
Matthew Arnold & His Poetry. 7.00 (ISBN 0-8274-2690-9). R West.
Matthew Arnold & His Poetry. 7.25 (ISBN 0-404-52501-6). AMS Pr.
Matthew Arnold, John Ruskin, & the Modern Temper. 11.00 (ISBN 0-8142-0188-1). Ohio St U Pr.
Matthew Fontaine Maury, the Pathfinder of the Seas. 16.00 (ISBN 0-404-03984-7). AMS Pr.
Matthew Henson. PLB 4.49 (ISBN 0-399-60456-1). Putnam.
Matthew Henson, Black Explorer. 7.95 (ISBN 0-396-07728-5). Dodd.
Matthew Paris. 29.50 (ISBN 0-521-22612-0); pap. 10.95 (ISBN 0-521-29575-0). Cambridge U Pr.
Matthew Prior: A Study of His Public Career & Correspondence. lib. bdg. 16.00 (ISBN 0-374-94890-9). Octagon.
Matthias Grunewald: Personality & Accomplishment. lib. bdg. 40.00 (ISBN 0-87817-186-X). Hacker.
Maugham. 16.95 (ISBN 0-671-24077-3). S&S.
Maupassant. 12.50 (ISBN 0-8076-0803-3). Braziller.
Maurice Maeterlinck: A Study of His Life & Thought. lib. bdg. 17.50x (ISBN 0-313-20574-4, HAMM). Greenwood.
Maurice Ravel. 17.25 (ISBN 0-8369-8033-6). Arno.
Maverick Republican in the Old North State: A Political Biography of Daniel L. Russell. 14.95x (ISBN 0-8071-0291-1). La State U Pr.
Maverick with a Paintbrush: Thomas Hart Benton. 6.95a (ISBN 0-385-00421-4); PLB (ISBN 0-385-08017-4). Doubleday.
Mawson's Will: The Greatest Survival Story Ever Written. 10.00 (ISBN 0-8128-2177-7). Stein & Day.
Max Beckmann. 28.50 (ISBN 0-8109-0269-9). Abrams.
Max Beckmann: Memories of a Friendship. 7.95x (ISBN 0-87024-120-6). U of Miami Pr.
Max Ernst. pap. 7.95 (ISBN 0-19-520004-7). Oxford U Pr.
Max Weber: A Biography. 29.95 (ISBN 0-471-92333-8). Wiley.
Max Weber: An Intellectual Portrait. 21.50x (ISBN 0-520-03194-6); pap. 6.95x. U of Cal Pr.
Maximilian & Charlotte of Mexico. lib. bdg. 150.00 (ISBN 0-8490-0595-7). Gordon Pr.
Maxine Cheshire, Reporter. 10.95 (ISBN 0-395-26303-4). HM.
Maxine Cheshire Reporter. pap. 2.25 (ISBN 0-440-15788-9). Dell.
Maxwell Anderson. lib. bdg. 8.50 (ISBN 0-8057-7179-4). Twayne.
Maxwell Anderson: The Man & His Plays. lib. bdg. 12.50 (ISBN 0-8414-3585-5). Folcroft.
Maxwell Street: Survival in a Bazaar. 14.50 (ISBN 0-385-06723-2). Doubleday.
Maxwell's Ghost: An Epilogue to Gavin Maxwell's Camusfearna. text ed. 16.00x (ISBN 0-575-02044-X). Verry.
May I Speak? The Diary of a Crossover Teacher. 6.95 (ISBN 0-911116-59-1). Pelican.
Maybe You Should Write a Book. 8.95 (ISBN 0-13-566380-6). P-H.
Maybe You Should Write a Book. pap. 3.95 (ISBN 0-13-566372-5). P-H.
Mayo Brothers. PLB 6.49 (ISBN 0-690-52751-9). T Y Crowell.
Mayo Brothers. pap. 1.45 (ISBN 0-690-00639-X). T Y Crowell.
Mayor Watching & Other Pleasures. 15.50 (ISBN 0-8369-7221-X). Arno.
Mazarin. facs. ed. 12.25 (ISBN 0-8369-5580-3). Arno.
Mazzini: Portrait of an Exile. lib. bdg. 15.00 (ISBN 0-374-90415-4). Octagon.
Mazzini: The Story of a Great Italian. 16.50 (ISBN 0-8369-5287-1). Arno.
Me & My Russian Wife. lib. bdg. 16.25x (ISBN 0-8371-0085-2, GIRW). Greenwood.
Meade of Gettysburg. 15.00. Pr of Morningside.
Measure of My Days. 6.95 (ISBN 0-394-43565-6). Knopf.
Measure of My Days. pap. 2.95 (ISBN 0-14-005164-3). Penguin.
Medardo Rosso. 13.00 (ISBN 0-405-01558-5). Arno.
Medical Detective. 10.95 (ISBN 0-399-90058-6). R Marek.
Medical Encounters: The Experience of Illness & Treatment. text ed. 18.95x (ISBN 0-312-52605-9). St Martin.
Medical Heroes & Heretics. 10.00 (ISBN 0-8159-6214-2). Devin.
Medical Sociologists at Work. text ed. 14.95 (ISBN 0-87855-139-5). Transaction Bks.
Medora Leigh: A History & an Autobiography. 14.00 (ISBN 0-404-56759-2). AMS Pr.
Meet Abraham Lincoln. 3.95 (ISBN 0-394-80057-5); PLB 3.99 (ISBN 0-394-90057-X). Random.
Meet Andrew Jackson. 2.95 (ISBN 0-394-80066-4). Random.
Meet Andrew Jackson. PLB 3.99 (ISBN 0-394-90066-9). Random.
Meet Benjamin Franklin. 2.95 (ISBN 0-394-80070-2). Random.
Meet Benjamin Franklin. PLB 3.99 (ISBN 0-394-90070-7). Random.
Meet Christopher Columbus. 3.95 (ISBN 0-394-80071-0); PLB 3.99 (ISBN 0-394-90071-5). Random.
Meet John F. Kennedy. 3.95 (ISBN 0-394-80059-1); PLB 3.99 (ISBN 0-394-90059-6). Random.
Meet Martin Luther King Jr. 3.95 (ISBN 0-394-80055-9); PLB 3.99 (ISBN 0-394-90055-3). Random.
Meet Robert E. Lee. 3.95 (ISBN 0-394-80073-7). Random.
Meet Robert E. Lee. PLB 3.99 (ISBN 0-394-90073-1). Random.
Meet the Catchers. PLB 4.95 (ISBN 0-87191-575-8). Creative Ed.
Meet the Centers. PLB 5.45 (ISBN 0-87191-534-0). Creative Ed.
Meet the Coaches. PLB 5.95 (ISBN 0-87191-600-2); pap. 2.75 (ISBN 0-89812-206-6). Creative Ed.
Meet the Defensive Linemen. PLB 5.45 (ISBN 0-87191-467-0). Creative Ed.
Meet the Forwards. PLB 5.95 (ISBN 0-87191-603-7); pap. 2.75 (ISBN 0-89812-205-8). Creative Ed.
Meet the Goalies. PLB 5.45 (ISBN 0-87191-533-2). Creative Ed.
Meet the Guards. PLB 5.95 (ISBN 0-87191-602-9); pap. 2.75 (ISBN 0-89812-204-X). Creative Ed.
Meet the Hitters. PLB 5.45 (ISBN 0-87191-579-0). Creative Ed.
Meet the Infielders. PLB 5.45 (ISBN 0-87191-578-2). Creative Ed.
Meet the Managers. PLB 5.45 (ISBN 0-87191-577-4). Creative Ed.
Meet the Masters: Eight Great Chess Players & Their Most Characteristic Games. pap. 4.00 (ISBN 0-486-23207-7). Dover.
Meet the Pitchers. PLB 4.95 (ISBN 0-87191-576-6). Creative Ed.
Meet the Prophets. 4.95 (ISBN 0-8054-1510-6). Broadman.
Meet the Receivers. PLB 5.45 (ISBN 0-87191-468-9). Creative Ed.
Meet the Stars of Country Music. 4.95 (ISBN 0-87695-212-0). Aurora Pubs.
Meet the Twelve. rev. ed. pap. 3.50 (ISBN 0-8066-0604-5, 10-4311). Augsburg.
Meet Theodore Roosevelt. 2.95 (ISBN 0-394-80065-6); PLB 3.99 (ISBN 0-394-90065-0). Random.
Meet These Men. pap. 2.50 (ISBN 0-8010-2354-8). Baker Bk.
Meet Thomas Jefferson. 3.95 (ISBN 0-394-80067-2); PLB 3.99 (ISBN 0-394-90067-7). Random.
Meeting Him in the Wilderness: A True Story of Adventure & Faith. 9.95 (ISBN 0-385-15132-2). Doubleday.
Meeting Jesus: A New Way to Christ. 7.95 (ISBN 0-8164-1065-8). Seabury.
Meetings with Pasternak: A Memoir. 8.95 (ISBN 0-15-158590-3). HarBraceJ.
Mehdi: Nothing Is Impossible. 8.95 (ISBN 0-87863-131-3). Farnswth Pub.
Mehmed the Conqueror & His Time. 30.00x (ISBN 0-691-09900-6). Princeton U Pr.
Meir Goldschmidt. lib. bdg. 8.95 (ISBN 0-8057-6253-1). Twayne.
Melba: A Biography. lib. bdg. 25.00 (ISBN 0-306-77428-3). Da Capo.
Melba: A Biography. 22.50 (ISBN 0-404-13057-7). AMS Pr.
Melbourne. 8.95 (ISBN 0-672-52038-9). Bobbs.
Melbourne. pap. 6.95 (ISBN 0-517-53782-6). Crown.
Melbourne. lib. bdg. 19.25x (ISBN 0-8371-5782-X, CEME). Greenwood.
Melnikov: Solo Architect in a Mass Society. text ed. 25.00 (ISBN 0-691-03931-3). Princeton U Pr.
Melodeon. pap. 1.75 (ISBN 0-671-82210-1). PB.
Melodeon. 6.95 (ISBN 0-385-06163-3). Doubleday.
Melodeon. lib. bdg. 8.95 (ISBN 0-8161-6549-1). G K Hall.
Melodies & Memories. 19.50 (ISBN 0-8369-5192-1). Arno.
Melodies & Memories. 17.00 (ISBN 0-404-04287-2). AMS Pr.
Melville. pap. 7.95 (ISBN 0-89255-008-2). Persea Bks.
Melville. lib. bdg. 15.50 (ISBN 0-374-97632-5). Octagon.
Melville's Early Life & Redburn. 23.00 (ISBN 0-8462-1632-9). Russell.
Melvin Belli: My Life on Trial. 9.95 (ISBN 0-688-03085-8). Morrow.
Members of Congress Since 1789. pap. 6.95 (ISBN 0-87187-105-X). Congr Quarterly.
Members of Parliament, 1734-1832. 17.50 (ISBN 0-208-01230-3). Shoe String.
Memoir & Letters of Charles Sumner. 79.00 (ISBN 0-405-00650-0). Arno.
Memoir & Letters of Charles Sumner. facs. ed. 80.00 (ISBN 0-8369-8641-5). Arno.
Memoir & Letters of Sara Coleridge. 24.00 (ISBN 0-8274-2701-8). R West.
Memoir & Letters of Sara Coleridge. 25.00 (ISBN 0-404-56736-3). AMS Pr.
Memoir of Eli Whitney, Esq. 9.00 (ISBN 0-405-04716-9). Arno.
Memoir of George Edmund Street, R. A. 1824-1881. 20.00 (ISBN 0-405-09007-2). Arno.
Memoir of Henry Jacob Bigelow. lib. bdg. 35.00 (ISBN 0-89341-138-8). Longwood Pr.
Memoir of Madame Jenny Lind-Goldschmidt: Her Early Art-Life & Dramatic Career 1820-1851. lib. bdg. 60.00 (ISBN 0-89341-416-6). Longwood Pr.
Memoir of Michael William Balfe. lib. bdg. 19.50 (ISBN 0-306-77528-X). Da Capo.
Memoir of Mrs. Barbauld, Including Letters & Notices of Her Family & Friends. 10.00 (ISBN 0-404-07397-2). AMS Pr.
Memoir of Pierre Toussaint, Born a Slave in St. Domingo. 8.50x (ISBN 0-8371-5036-1). Negro U Pr.
Memoir of Ralph Waldo Emerson. 25.00 (ISBN 0-404-01357-0); 12.50 ea. (ISBN 0-404-01358-9) (ISBN 0-404-01359-7). AMS Pr.
Memoir of Shelley. 5.00 (ISBN 0-404-05427-7). AMS Pr.
Memoir of Shelley. lib. bdg. 4.95 (ISBN 0-8414-7237-8). Folcroft.
Memoir of Shelley. lib. bdg. 20.00 (ISBN 0-8495-4630-3). Arden Lib.
Memoir of the Hon. Nathan Appleton, LL.D. lib. bdg. 9.00x (ISBN 0-8371-1124-2, WINA). Greenwood.
Memoir of the Life & Character of the Rev. Samuel Bacon. facs. ed. 18.25 (ISBN 0-8369-8781-0). Arno.
Memoir of the Life of Josiah Quincy. lib. bdg. 39.50 (ISBN 0-306-70098-0). Da Capo.
Memoir of the Life of Laurence Oliphant & of Alice Oliphant, His Wife. 24.00x (ISBN 0-405-07970-2). Arno.
Memoir of the Public Services of William Henry Harrison, of Ohio. facs. ed. 17.00 (ISBN 0-8369-5332-0). Arno.
Memoir of the Warsaw Uprising. 15.00 (ISBN 0-88233-275-9). Ardis Pubs.
Memoir of Theophilus Parsons. lib. bdg. 35.00 (ISBN 0-306-71939-8). Da Capo.
Memoir of Thurlow Weed see Life of Thurlow Weed.
Memoirs & Correspondence of Madame Recamier. 27.50 (ISBN 0-404-56808-4). AMS Pr.
Memoirs & Letters of James Kent. lib. bdg. 32.50 (ISBN 0-306-71847-2). Da Capo.
Memoirs & Recollections of Count Louis Philippe De Segur. 45.00 (ISBN 0-405-03061-4). Arno.
Memoirs, Journal & Correspondence of Thomas Moore. 195.00 (ISBN 0-403-00346-6). Scholarly.
Memoirs of a Dissident Publisher. 12.95 (ISBN 0-15-173752-5). HarBraceJ.
Memoirs of a Ghillie. 15.95 (ISBN 0-7153-7584-9). David & Charles.
Memoirs of a Janissary. pap. 7.00 (ISBN 0-930042-16-6). Mich Slavic Pubns.
Memoirs of a Late Eminent Bookseller. 15.00x (ISBN 0-678-00972-4). Kelley.
Memoirs of a Literary Veteran: Including Sketches & Anecdotes of the Most Distinguished Literary Characters from 1794-1849. 40.00 (ISBN 0-404-07650-5); 13.50 ea. (ISBN 0-404-07651-3) (ISBN 0-404-07652-1) (ISBN 0-404-07653-X). AMS Pr.
Memoirs of a Maverick Publisher. 5.00 (46235). S&S.
Memoirs of a Naturalist. 14.95 (ISBN 0-8061-0857-6); pap. 5.95 (ISBN 0-8061-1167-4). U of Okla Pr.
Memoirs of a Revolutionary, 1901-1944. pap. 6.95x (ISBN 0-19-281037-5). Oxford U Pr.
Memoirs of a Revolutionist. lib. bdg. 15.25x (ISBN 0-8371-0418-1, FIRE). Greenwood.
Memoirs of a Revolutionist. pap. 6.00 (ISBN 0-486-22485-6). Dover.
Memoirs of a Revolutionist. 6.50 (ISBN 0-8446-0172-1). Peter Smith.
Memoirs of a Revolutionist. 6.75 (ISBN 0-8446-1274-X). Peter Smith.
Memoirs of a Russian Diplomat: Outposts of the Empire, 1893-1917. 20.00x (ISBN 0-300-01201-2). Yale U Pr.
Memoirs of a Soviet Diplomat: Twenty Years in the Service of the U. S. S. R. 21.50 (ISBN 0-88355-040-7). Hyperion Conn.
Memoirs of a Speleologist: The Adventurous Life of a Famous French Cave Explorer. 9.00 (ISBN 0-914264-08-7); pap. 5.00 (ISBN 0-914264-09-5). Zephyrus Pr.
Memoirs of a Terrorist. 22.00 (ISBN 0-527-79050-8). Kraus Repr.
Memoirs of a World War II Pilot. new ed. pap. 25.00 (ISBN 0-89126-064-1). Military Aff Aero.
Memoirs of American Jews: 1775-1865. 35.00 (ISBN 0-87068-232-6). Ktav.
Memoirs of an American Lady: With Sketches of Manners & Scenes in America As They Existed Previous to the Revolution; with Unpublished Letters & a Memoir of Mrs. Grant, by James Grant Wilson. 25.00 (ISBN 0-8369-6771-2). Arno.
Memoirs of an American Prima Donna. lib. bdg. 25.00 (ISBN 0-306-77527-1). Da Capo.
Memoirs of Andrew Sherburne: A Pensioner of the Navy of the Revolution. facs. ed. 13.50 (ISBN 0-8369-5564-1). Arno.
Memoirs of Babikr Bedri. 11.00x (ISBN 0-19-211194-9). Oxford U Pr.
Memoirs of Beniamino Gigli. lib. bdg. 22.00x (ISBN 0-405-09679-8). Arno.
Memoirs of Carl Flesch. 25.00 (ISBN 0-306-77574-3). Da Capo.
Memoirs of Carlo Goldoni. 35.00 (ISBN 0-932062-64-4). Sharon Hill.
Memoirs of Carlo Goldoni. lib. bdg. 27.75x (ISBN 0-8371-8871-7, GOME). Greenwood.
Memoirs of Chancellor Pasquier 1767-1815. 10.00 (ISBN 0-8386-6981-6). Fairleigh Dickinson.
Memoirs of Dr. Joseph Priestley, to the Year 1795, Written by Himself, with a Continuation,... lib. bdg. 50.00 (ISBN 0-527-72730-X). Kraus Repr.
Memoirs of Eighty Years. 13.00 (ISBN 0-404-03025-4). AMS Pr.
Memoirs of Elleanor Eldridge. facs. ed. 12.25 (ISBN 0-8369-8748-9). Arno.
Memoirs of Eugenie Schumann. 23.50 (ISBN 0-88355-762-2). Hyperion Conn.
Memoirs of Friedrich Ferdinand, Count Von Beust. 39.00 (ISBN 0-403-00812-3). Scholarly.
Memoirs of General Lord Ismay. lib. bdg. 21.75x (ISBN 0-8371-6280-7, ISMF). Greenwood.
Memoirs of General Miller, in the Service of the Republic of Peru. 2nd ed. 47.50 (ISBN 0-404-04339-9). AMS Pr.
Memoirs of Giorgio De Chirico. 13.95x (ISBN 0-87024-125-7). U of Miami Pr.
Memoirs of Gluckel of Hameln. pap. 6.95 (ISBN 0-8052-0572-1). Schocken.
Memoirs of Henry Heth. lib. bdg. 17.00x (ISBN 0-8371-6389-7, MHH/). Greenwood.
Memoirs of John Quincy Adams, Comprising Portions of His Diary from 1795 to 1848. facs. ed. 375.00 (ISBN 0-8369-5021-6). Arno.
Memoirs of Li Tsung-Jen. lib. bdg. 25.00x (ISBN 0-89158-343-2). Westview.
Memoirs of Lieut. Henry Timberlake. 13.00 (ISBN 0-405-02903-9). Arno.
Memoirs of Lorenzo Da Ponte. 7.50 (ISBN 0-8446-1945-0). Peter Smith.
Memoirs of Mary Wollstonecraft. lib. bdg. 23.95 (ISBN 0-8383-0975-5). Haskell.

Memoirs of Mary Wollstonecraft. lib. bdg. 59.95 (ISBN 0-87968-022-9). Gordon Pr.

Memoirs of My Life. 16.50 (ISBN 0-86527-127-5). Fertig.

Memoirs of Pancho Villa. 22.50x (ISBN 0-292-73301-1); pap. 8.95 (ISBN 0-292-75028-5). U of Tex Pr.

Memoirs of Philippe De Commynes. 19.50x (ISBN 0-87249-130-7); 19.50x; 37.50x (ISBN 0-87249-199-4). U of SC Pr.

Memoirs of Prince Chlodwig of Hohenlohe-Schillingsfuerst. 47.50 (ISBN 0-404-03305-9). AMS Pr.

Memoirs of Prince Metternich, 1773-1835. 75.00 (ISBN 0-86527-128-3). Fertig.

Memoirs of Prota Matija Nenadovic. 10.25x (ISBN 0-19-821476-6). Oxford U Pr.

Memoirs of Raymond Poincare. 110.00 (ISBN 0-404-09090-7); 27.50 ea. (ISBN 0-404-09091-5) (ISBN 0-404-09092-3) (ISBN 0-404-09093-1) (ISBN 0-404-09094-X). AMS Pr.

Memoirs of Rev. Charles G. Finney. 19.50 (ISBN 0-404-00047-9). AMS Pr.

Memoirs of Robert William Elliston. 40.00 (ISBN 0-405-08875-2). Arno.

Memoirs of Sir Edward Blount. lib. bdg. 19.00x (ISBN 0-405-09717-4). Arno.

Memoirs of Sir Ronald Storrs. 28.00 (ISBN 0-405-04593-X). Arno.

Memoirs of Sir Ronald Storrs. 32.50 (ISBN 0-404-56337-6). AMS Pr.

Memoirs of the Author of a Vindication of the Rights of Woman. lib. bdg. 45.00 (ISBN 0-8240-0861-8). Garland Pub.

Memoirs of the Devil. 7.95 (ISBN 0-15-111906-6). HarBraceJ.

Memoirs of the Forty Five First Years of the Life of James Lackington. 7th ed. lib. bdg. 15.00x (ISBN 0-678-00843-4). Kelley.

Memoirs of the Life & Peregrinations of the Florentine, Philip Mazzei 1730-1816. 28.00 (ISBN 0-527-62470-5). Kraus Repr.

Memoirs of the Life & Writings of Lord Byron. lib. bdg. 85.00 (ISBN 0-8414-3379-8). Folcroft.

Memoirs of the Life & Writings of the Late Dr. Samuel Johnson. Bd. with Anecdotes of the Late Samuel Johnson, LL.D During the Last Twenty Years of His Life. 13.00x (ISBN 0-19-255416-6). Oxford U Pr.

Memoirs of the Life of Anthony Benezet. 20.50 (ISBN 0-8337-3621-3). B Franklin.

Memoirs of the Life of Colonel Hutchinson. 5.00x (ISBN 0-460-00317-8). Dutton.

Memoirs of the Life of Daniel Mendoza. facsimile ed. 10.00x (ISBN 0-405-06734-8). Arno.

Memoirs of the Life of David Garrick. 40.00 (ISBN 0-405-08438-2). Arno.

Memoirs of the Life of John Philip Kemble. 40.00 (ISBN 0-405-08276-2). Arno.

Memoirs of the Life of the Right Honourable Richard Brinsley Sheridan. 65.00 (ISBN 0-8274-1021-2). R West.

Memoirs of the Life of the Right Honourable Richard Brinsley Sheridan. 100.00 (ISBN 0-8492-6748-X). R West.

Memoirs of the Life of the Rt. Hon. Richard Brinsley Sheridan. facsimile ed. 31.00 (ISBN 0-8369-5749-0). Arno.

Memoirs of the Loves of the Poets: Biographical Sketches of Women Celebrated in Ancient & Modern Poetry. 16.75 (ISBN 0-8369-2953-5). Arno.

Memoirs of the Polish Baroque: The Writings of Jan Chryzostom Pasek, a Squire of the Commonwealth of Poland & Lithuania. 26.50x (ISBN 0-520-02752-3). U of Cal Pr.

Memoirs of the Prince De Talleyrand. 100.00 (ISBN 0-404-07510-X). AMS Pr.

Memoirs of the Rev. Eleazar Wheelock, D. D. 16.00 (ISBN 0-405-04074-1). Arno.

Memoirs of Theodore Thomas. facsimile ed. 28.25 (ISBN 0-8369-6703-8). Arno.

Memoirs of Waldo Frank. 15.00x (ISBN 0-87023-081-6). U of Mass Pr.

Memoirs of William Hickey. 19.95 (ISBN 0-7100-8129-4). Routledge & Kegan.

Memoirs of William Jennings Bryan. lib. bdg. 29.95 (ISBN 0-8383-1165-2). Haskell.

Memoirs of William Jennings Bryan. 22.50 (ISBN 0-8046-1472-5). Kennikat.

Memoirs of William Smith. lib. bdg. 12.00x (ISBN 0-405-10455-3). Arno.

Memoirs of William Wordsworth. lib. bdg. 12.50. Folcroft.

Memoirs: Ten Years & Twenty Days. pap. 1.95 (ISBN 0-8439-0493-3). Nordon Pubns.

Memoirs: Ten Years & Twenty Days. lib. bdg. 30.50x (ISBN 0-8371-7867-3, DOME). Greenwood.

Memorials of the Faithful. 9.75 (ISBN 0-87743-041-1, 7-06-12). Baha'i.

Memorials of the Life of Amelia Opie. 30.00 (ISBN 0-404-56774-6). AMS Pr.

Memories & Adventures. lib. bdg. 22.50 (ISBN 0-306-77515-8). Da Capo.

Memories Beyond Bloomers. 15.00 (240-26218). AAHPER.

Memories of a Bloomer Girl. text ed. 12.50x (240-25974). AAHPER.

Memories of a Country Childhood. 8.50x (ISBN 0-7022-1067-6). U of Queensland Pr.

Memories of a Former Kid. pap. 6.95 (ISBN 0-8138-1070-1). Iowa St U Pr.

Memories of a Musical Life. 12.00 (ISBN 0-404-07216-X). AMS Pr.

Memories of a Musical Life. lib. bdg. 27.50 (ISBN 0-306-70021-2). Da Capo.

Memories of a Singer. lib. bdg. 20.00x (ISBN 0-405-09680-1). Arno.

Memories of a Southern Woman of Letters. facsimile ed. 17.25 (ISBN 0-8369-5630-3). Arno.

Memories of an Old Actor. 16.00 (ISBN 0-403-00199-4). Scholarly.

Memories of Concord. lib. bdg. 15.00 (ISBN 0-8414-0633-2). Folcroft.

Memories of Evil Days. 12.50x (ISBN 0-8139-0553-2). U Pr of Va.

Memories of Fifty Years. 40.00 (ISBN 0-403-02027-1). Somerset Pub.

Memories of Fifty Years. 15.00 (ISBN 0-405-09051-X). Arno.

Memories of George Meredith. 6.50 (ISBN 0-8274-1329-7). R West.

Memories of My Childhood: Further Years at Marbacka. 17.00 (ISBN 0-527-54010-2). Kraus Repr.

Memories of My Father. lib. bdg. 10.95 (ISBN 0-8383-1509-7). Haskell.

Memories of My Life. 21.50 (ISBN 0-404-08128-2). AMS Pr.

Memories of My Life, Being My Personal Professional, Social Recollections As a Woman & Artist. 17.00 (ISBN 0-403-00111-0). Scholarly.

Memories of North Carver Village. pap. text ed. 6.50 (ISBN 0-9600496-6-5). Channing Bks.

Memories of the Opera. 25.00 (ISBN 0-8443-0022-5). Vienna Hse.

Memories of the Skeena. 9.95 (ISBN 0-919654-62-2). Hancock Hse.

Men & Discoveries in Mathematics. 8.75 (ISBN 0-7195-2587-X). Transatlantic.

Men & Forces of Our Time. facs. ed. 12.75 (ISBN 0-8369-0678-0). Arno.

Men & Ideas in Economics: A Dictionary of World Economists Past & Present. 9.50x (ISBN 0-87471-867-8). Rowman.

Men & Ideas in Economics: A Dictionary of World Economists Past & Present. pap. 3.95 (ISBN 0-8226-0284-9). Littlefield.

Men & Policies: Addresses. facs. ed. 17.50 (ISBN 0-8369-0832-5). Arno.

Men & Politics: An Autobiography. lib. bdg. 25.75x (ISBN 0-8371-4641-0, FIMP). Greenwood.

Men & Women Behind the Atom. 7.95 (ISBN 0-200-00086-1, B55230). Abelard.

Men & Women in John's Gospel. 2.95 (ISBN 0-8054-8123-0). Broadman.

Men & Women of the French Revolution. facs. ed. 15.50 (ISBN 0-8369-0990-9). Arno.

Men & Work: An Autobiography. lib. bdg. 24.00x (ISBN 0-8371-8613-7, CIMW). Greenwood.

Men Around Churchill. facs. ed. 16.00 (ISBN 0-8369-2056-2). Arno.

Men Behind the Music. 6.50 (ISBN 0-8046-0766-4). Kennikat.

Men for the Mountains. 12.95 (ISBN 0-8149-0812-8). Vanguard.

Men in Business: Essays on the Historical Role of the Entrepreneur. lib. bdg. 25.00x (ISBN 0-313-20867-0, MIME). Greenwood.

Men in Dark Times. 6.50 (ISBN 0-15-159147-4). HarBraceJ.

Men in Dark Times. pap. 3.95 (ISBN 0-15-658890-0, HB167). HarBraceJ.

Men, Money & Magic: The Story of Dorothy Schiff. 9.95 (ISBN 0-698-10666-0). Coward.

Men, Money & Magic: The Story of Dorothy Schiff. pap. 2.25 (ISBN 0-451-07691-5, E7691). NAL.

Men of Business. 22.00 (ISBN 0-8369-2927-6). Arno.

Men of Cajamarca: A Social & Biographical Study of the First Conquerors of Peru. 12.00x (ISBN 0-292-75001-3). U of Tex Pr.

Men of Conviction. facs. ed. 14.00 (ISBN 0-8369-2081-3). Arno.

Men of Destiny. pap. 2.95 (ISBN 0-295-95097-8). U of Wash Pr.

Men of Good Hope: A Story of American Progressives. 14.95 (ISBN 0-19-501232-1). Oxford U Pr.

Men of Mark in Georgia: A Complete & Elaborate History of the State from Its Settlement to the Present Time. Incl. 21.00 (ISBN 0-87152-176-8); 21.00 (ISBN 0-87152-177-6); 24.00 (ISBN 0-87152-178-4); 21.00 (ISBN 0-87152-179-2); 21.00 (ISBN 0-87152-180-6); 21.00 (ISBN 0-87152-181-4); 21.00 (ISBN 0-87152-182-2). Reprint.

Men of Maryknoll. 13.50 (ISBN 0-8369-2775-3). Arno.

Men of Mexico. facs. ed. 35.25 (ISBN 0-8369-0666-7). Arno.

Men of Popular Music. 16.25 (ISBN 0-8369-7263-5). Arno.

Men of the First French Republic: Political Alignments in the National Convention of 1792. 27.50x (ISBN 0-8018-1305-0). Johns Hopkins.

Men of the Supreme Court: Profiles of the Justices. lib. bdg. 22.50x (ISBN 0-87196-459-7). Facts on File.

Men of the Wild Frontier. PLB 5.54 (ISBN 0-8116-4905-9). Garrard.

Men That Count. pap. 2.95 (ISBN 0-8010-2304-1). Baker Bk.

Men Were Different: Five Studies in Late Victorian Biography. facs. ed. 13.50 (ISBN 0-8369-0615-2). Arno.

Men Who Are Making the West. 18.25 (ISBN 0-8369-2793-1). Arno.

Men Who Conquered. facs. ed. 10.25 (ISBN 0-8369-0438-9). Arno.

Men Who Govern: A Biographical Profile of Federal Political Executives. 9.95 (ISBN 0-8157-8108-3). Brookings.

Men Who Knew Christ. pap. 1.95 (ISBN 0-8307-0086-2, S252-1-04). Regal.

Men Who Lead Labor. 14.50 (ISBN 0-8369-1309-4). Arno.

Men Who Made Mexico. 4.95 (ISBN 0-396-06778-6). Dodd.

Men Who Shaped America. pap. 1.25 (ISBN 0-8024-5242-6). Moody.

Men, Women & Issues in American History. pap. text ed. 7.95x ea.; pap. text ed. 6.95x (ISBN 0-256-01686-0). Dorsey.

Men, Women & Tenors. 16.50 (ISBN 0-404-00306-0). AMS Pr.

Men, Women & Tenors. facsimile ed. 19.50 (ISBN 0-8369-5174-3). Arno.

Menachem Begin: The Legend & the Man. pap. 2.25 (ISBN 0-440-16107-X). Dell.

Menagerie in F Sharp. lib. bdg. 19.75x (ISBN 0-313-21004-7, HEME). Greenwood.

Menahem Begin: The Legend & the Man. 9.95 (ISBN 0-440-05553-9). Delacorte.

Mencken. 12.50x (ISBN 0-8093-0376-0). S Ill U Pr.

Mencken: A Study of His Thought. 15.00 (ISBN 0-394-41354-7). Knopf.

Mendelssohn. rev ed. 8.95x (ISBN 0-460-03123-6). Biblio Dist.

Mendelssohn. rev. ed. pap. 6.50 (ISBN 0-8226-0715-8). Littlefield.

Mendelssohn: A New Image of the Composer & His Age. lib. bdg. 31.75x (ISBN 0-313-20302-4, WEMN). Greenwood.

Mendelssohn: Letters & Recollections. 35.00x (ISBN 0-8443-0003-9). Vienna Hse.

Mental Healers: Franz Anton Mesmer, Mary Baker Eddy, Sigmund Freud. 11.50 (ISBN 0-8044-2995-2); pap. 4.95 (ISBN 0-8044-6996-2). Ungar.

Menuhins: A Family Odyssey. 11.95 (ISBN 0-915572-22-2). Panjandrum.

MERC: American Soldiers of Fortune. 14.95 (ISBN 0-02-579330-6). Macmillan.

Merchant Congressman in the Young Republic: Samuel Smith of Maryland, 1752-1839. 20.00 (ISBN 0-299-06000-4). U of Wis Pr.

Merchant of Manchac: The Letterbooks of John Fitzpatrick, 1768-1790. 30.00x (ISBN 0-8071-0268-7). La State U Pr.

Merchant Princes: An Intimate History of Jewish Families Who Built Great Department Stores. 12.95 (ISBN 0-06-011797-4). Har-Row.

Mercy Warren. 15.00 (ISBN 0-87152-042-7). Reprint.

Meredith. 9.00 (ISBN 0-8046-0404-5). Kennikat.

Meredith. lib. bdg. 25.00 (ISBN 0-8492-8089-3). R West.

Merman. 9.95 (ISBN 0-671-22712-2). S&S.

Mervyn Peake. 10.95 (ISBN 0-312-53025-0). St Martin.

Mervyn Wall. 4.50 (ISBN 0-8387-1065-4); pap. 1.95 (ISBN 0-8387-1064-6). Bucknell U Pr.

Meshumed! pap. 3.95 (ISBN 0-8024-5253-1). Moody.

Message of the Prophets. pap. 4.95 (ISBN 0-06-068929-3, RD45). Har-Row.

Messenger: The Life of Mohammed. lib. bdg. 14.75x (ISBN 0-8371-2423-9, BOTM). Greenwood.

Metaphors of Self: The Meaning of Autobiography. 17.00x (ISBN 0-691-06221-8). Princeton U Pr.

Mexican Political Biographies: 1935-1975. 27.50x (ISBN 0-8165-0581-0); pap. 8.95x (ISBN 0-8165-0496-2). U of Ariz Pr.

Mexico's Miguel Caldera: The Taming of America's First Frontier, 1548-1597. 14.95x (ISBN 0-8165-0638-8); pap. 7.95x (ISBN 0-8165-0569-1). U of Ariz Pr.

Meyer Lansky: Mogul of the Mob. 11.95 (ISBN 0-448-22206-X). Paddington.

MG Experience. 11.95 (ISBN 0-85184-013-2). Motorbooks Intl.

M.I.A. (Missing in Action) 7.95 (ISBN 0-918442-00-1). Phipps Pub.

Michael Bakunin. lib. bdg. 27.50 (ISBN 0-374-91296-3). Octagon.

Michael Faraday. pap. 4.95 (ISBN 0-671-20929-9). S&S.

Michael Faraday, Father of Electronics. 6.95 (ISBN 0-8361-1864-2). Herald Pr.

Michael Foster & the Cambridge School of Physiology: The Scientific Enterprise in Late Victorian Society. text ed. 27.50 (ISBN 0-691-08197-2). Princeton U Pr.

Michael Naranjo. PLB 6.95 (ISBN 0-87518-111-2). Dillon.

Michel de Montaigne. lib. bdg. 20.00. Folcroft.

Michel De Montaigne. lib. bdg. 25.00 (ISBN 0-8495-1002-3). Arden Lib.

Michel De Montaigne: A Biographical Study. lib. bdg. 27.50 (ISBN 0-8414-5738-7). Folcroft.

Michelangelo. 2nd ed. text ed. 38.50x (ISBN 0-416-15140-X); pap. text ed. 17.50 (ISBN 0-416-18050-7). Methuen Inc.

Michelangelo. PLB 5.88 (ISBN 0-531-00944-0). Watts.

Michelangelo: His Life, His Times, His Era. 15.00 (ISBN 0-8044-2071-8). Ungar.

Michelangelo: Painter, Sculptor, Architect. 40.00 (ISBN 0-670-47397-9). Viking Pr.

Michelson & the Speed of Light. lib. bdg. 16.75x (ISBN 0-313-20777-1, JAMI). Greenwood.

Michigan & the Cleveland Era: Sketches of University of Michigan Staff Members & Alumni Who Served the Cleveland Administrations, 1885-89,1893-97. facsimile ed. 25.00 (ISBN 0-8369-8092-1). Arno.

Mickey Mantle. 5.50 (ISBN 0-87191-375-5). Creative Ed.

Microbes & Men. 8.95 (ISBN 0-8415-0348-6). Dutton.

Mid-Channel. facsimile ed. 19.00x (ISBN 0-405-06729-1). Arno.

Middle Five: Indian Schoolboys of the Omaha Tribe. 10.95x (ISBN 0-8032-2852-X); pap. 2.95 (ISBN 0-8032-7901-9, BB682). U of Nebr Pr.

Middle Ground. 15.00 (ISBN 0-262-13073-4). MIT Pr.

Middle Man: The Adventures of a Literary Agent. 6.95 (ISBN 0-688-00119-X). Morrow.

Midnight Baby: An Autobiography. 8.95 (ISBN 0-02-599000-4). Macmillan.

Mighty Atom: The Life & Times of Joseph L. Greenstein. 10.95 (ISBN 0-670-47564-5). Viking Pr.

Mighty Macs: Three Famous Baseball Managers. PLB 3.84 (ISBN 0-8116-6663-8). Garrard.

Mighty Stonewall. lib. bdg. 27.50x (ISBN 0-8371-7331-0, VAMS). Greenwood.

Migrant with Hope. 4.95 (ISBN 0-8054-7218-5). Broadman.

Migueis--to the Seventh Decade. 13.50x (ISBN 84-399-7900-2). Romance.

Mike Fink, King of Mississippi Keelboatmen. lib. bdg. 15.25x (ISBN 0-8371-5600-9, BLMF). Greenwood.

Mike: The Memoirs of the Right Honourable Lester B. Pearson, 1957-1968. 12.50 (ISBN 0-8129-0601-2). Times Bks.

Mikhail Bulgakov: Life & Interpretations. 25.00x (ISBN 0-8020-5402-1). U of Toronto Pr.

Mild Murderer: The True Story of the Dr. Crippen Case. 8.95 (ISBN 0-395-25776-X). HM.

Miles Davis. pap. 1.95 (ISBN 0-498-04054-2). A S Barnes.

Miles Davis: A Musical Biography. 7.95 (ISBN 0-688-00203-X); pap. 3.95 (ISBN 0-688-05203-7). Morrow.

Military Journal of the American Revolution. 25.00 (ISBN 0-405-01184-9). Arno.

Military Life of George Washington, American Soldier. PLB 4.90 (ISBN 0-531-01871-7). Watts.

Military Life of Napoleon, Emperor of the French. PLB 4.90 (ISBN 0-531-01870-9). Watts.

Military Life of Winston Churchill of Britain. PLB 4.90 (ISBN 0-531-01881-4). Watts.

Military Lives of Hindenburg & Ludendorff of Imperial Germany. PLB 4.90 (ISBN 0-531-01882-2). Watts.

Millard Fillmore: Biography of a President. 15.00. Stewart.

Millay in Greenwich Village. 8.75 (ISBN 0-8173-7161-3). U of Ala Pr.

Million Dollar Studs. 8.95 (ISBN 0-440-05683-7). Delacorte.

Millionaires & Grub Street: Comrades - Contacts in the Last Half Century. facs. ed. 15.25 (ISBN 0-8369-0253-X). Arno.

Millionairess: Self-Made Women in America. 8.95 (ISBN 0-06-012852-6). Har-Row.

Millionairess: Self-Made Women of America. pap. 2.25 (ISBN 0-06-080509-9, P 509). Har-Row.

Milton. lib. bdg. 16.95 (ISBN 0-8383-1911-4). Haskell.

Milton. lib. bdg. 9.75x (ISBN 0-8371-4094-3, MAM). Greenwood.

Milton. 12.00 (ISBN 0-8274-2735-2). R West.

Milton. lib. bdg. 15.00 (ISBN 0-88305-757-3). Norwood Edns.

Milton & Sex. 12.50x (ISBN 0-231-04340-6). Columbia U Pr.

Milton & the English Mind. lib. bdg. 21.95 (ISBN 0-8383-1906-8). Haskell.
Milton & the English Mind. lib. bdg. 17.50 (ISBN 0-8414-4897-3). Folcroft.
Milton Cross New Encyclopedia of the Great Composers & Their Music. two-volume, boxed set 19.95 (ISBN 0-385-03635-3). Doubleday.
Milton in Chancery: New Chapters in the Lives of the Poet & His Father. 29.00 (ISBN 0-403-04175-9). Somerset Pub.
Milton Steinberg: Portrait of a Rabbi. 15.00x (ISBN 0-87068-444-2). Ktav.
Milton's Blindness. lib. bdg. 12.50 (ISBN 0-374-91007-3). Octagon.
Milton's Blindness. lib. bdg. 20.00 (ISBN 0-8414-3197-3). Folcroft.
Mind & Art of Henry Adams. 17.50x (ISBN 0-8047-0623-9). Stanford U Pr.
Mind of a Monarch. 18.95 (ISBN 0-04-923069-7). Allen Unwin.
Mind of Her Own: A Life of the Writer George Sand. 7.95 (ISBN 0-06-022616-1); PLB 7.89 (ISBN 0-06-022617-X). Har-Row.
Mind of Poe, & Other Studies. 13.00 (ISBN 0-8462-0146-1). Russell.
Mind on Harlem. soft cover 12.00 (ISBN 0-88247-537-1). R & E Res Assoc.
Mindanao Mission: Archbishop Patrick Cronin's Forty Years in the Phillipines. 8.95 (ISBN 0-8164-0412-7). Seabury.
Minds in Many Pieces: The Making of a Very Special Doctor. 10.95 (ISBN 0-89256-097-5). Rawson Wade.
Mindszenty the Man. 2.00. Pere Marquette.
Mine Enemy Grows Older. 4.50 (47430). S&S.
Mine Eyes Have Seen the Glory. lib. bdg. 9.95 (ISBN 0-8161-6426-6). G K Hall.
Mine Eyes Have Seen the Glory. 5.95 (ISBN 0-8007-0375-8); pap. 1.50 (ISBN 0-8007-8098-1). Revell.
Mine Eyes Have Seen the Glory: A/Biography of Julia Ward Howe. 15.00 (ISBN 0-316-14747-8). Little.
Mingled Chime: An Autobiography. 18.50 (ISBN 0-306-70791-8). Da Capo.
Mingled Chime: An Autobiography. lib. bdg. 20.50x (ISBN 0-8371-9274-9, BEMCH). Greenwood.
Mingled Yarn: Autobiographical Sketches. facsimile ed. 12.25 (ISBN 0-8369-2254-9). Arno.
Minister's Wife. 14.95 (ISBN 0-7100-8846-9). Routledge & Kegan.
Ministry & Message of Paul. kivar 2.95 (ISBN 0-310-28341-8). Zondervan.
Mira De Amescua. lib. bdg. 9.50 (ISBN 0-8057-6285-X). Twayne.
Mirabeau. 19.50 (ISBN 0-8369-6923-5). Arno.
Mirabeau. 8.25 (ISBN 0-8046-1089-4). Kennikat.
Miracle in Darien. 4.95 (ISBN 0-88270-355-2). Logos.
Miracles in Pinafores & Bluejeans. 4.95 (ISBN 0-87747-644-6). Deseret Bk.
Mirambo of Tanzania. pap. text ed. 1.95x (ISBN 0-435-94374-X). Heinemann Ed.
Miranda: World Citizen. 9.00 (ISBN 0-8130-0226-5). U Presses Fla.
Mirror Image. 8.95 (ISBN 0-03-040646-3). HR&W.
Mirrors of Moscow. 14.00 (ISBN 0-88355-030-X). Hyperion Conn.
Misbehavin' with Fats: A Toby Bradley Adventure. PLB 5.95 (ISBN 0-201-07159-2). A-W.
Mischling, Second Degree: My Childhood in Nazi Germany. 8.50 (ISBN 0-688-80110-2); PLB 8.16 (ISBN 0-688-84110-4). Greenwillow.
Misia. 16.95 (ISBN 0-394-48710-9). Knopf.
Miss Lillian & Friends: The Plains, Georgia, Family Philosophy & Recipe Book. pap. 1.75 (ISBN 0-451-07852-7, E7852). NAL.
Miss Ruth: The More Living Life of Ruth St. Denis. 6.95 (ISBN 0-396-06027-7). Dodd.
Miss Strong Arm: The Story of Annie Armstrong. 3.95 (ISBN 0-8054-4308-8). Broadman.
Miss Tallulah Bankhead. pap. 2.75 (ISBN 0-425-04574-9). Berkley Pub.
Missing Persons: An Autobiography. 14.95x (ISBN 0-19-812086-9). Oxford U Pr.
Mission a - Go - Go. 9.95 (ISBN 0-9602122-2-1). Apple-Gems.
Missionary Heroes of Africa. 12.00x (ISBN 0-8371-1738-0). Negro U Pr.
Mississippi Black History Makers. 15.00 (ISBN 0-87805-034-5); pap. 4.95 (ISBN 0-87805-040-X). U Pr of Miss.
Mississippians All. 4.95 (ISBN 0-911116-22-2). Pelican.
Mr. & Mrs. Charles Dickens: His Letters to Her. lib. bdg. 22.95 (ISBN 0-8383-1429-5). Haskell.
Mr. Baruch. lib. bdg. 36.75x (ISBN 0-8371-8251-4, COMRB). Greenwood.
Mr. Carlyle My Patient: A Psychosomatic Biography. 12.50 (ISBN 0-8274-0634-7). R West.
Mr. Creator's Borrowed Brown Hands. pap. 3.95 (ISBN 0-8163-0263-4, 13698-6). Pacific Pr Pub Assn.
Mr. Justice Brandeis. 19.50x. Elliots Bks.
Mr. Justice Brandeis. lib. bdg. 20.00 (ISBN 0-306-70430-7). Da Capo.
Mr. Justice Frankfurter & the Constitution. 11.50x (ISBN 0-226-46405-9). U of Chicago Pr.
Mr. Laurel & Mr. Hardy. pap. 1.50 (ISBN 0-451-07313-4, W7313). NAL.
Mr. Lincoln. 5.00 (ISBN 0-8446-0865-3). Peter Smith.
Mr. Lincoln's Inaugural Journey. 7.95. T Y Crowell.
Mister Maloga: Daniel Matthews & His Mission, Murray River, 1864-1902. 19.25x (ISBN 0-7022-1110-9). U of Queensland Pr.
Mr. Pepys & Mr. Evelyn. lib. bdg. 12.50 (ISBN 0-8414-5976-2). Folcroft.
Mr. Piper & His Cubs. 8.50 (ISBN 0-8138-1250-X). Iowa St U Pr.
Mr. Pops. pap. 4.95 (ISBN 0-517-51738-8). Barre.
Mr. President: An Introduction to American History. 21.00 (ISBN 0-8369-8115-4). Arno.
Mr. Rutledge of South Carolina. facsimile ed. 21.00 (ISBN 0-8369-5618-4). Arno.
Mr. Samuel McIntire, Carver: The Architect of Salem. 15.00 (ISBN 0-8446-1263-4). Peter Smith.
Mr. Secretary Walsingham & the Policy of Queen Elizabeth. 84.50 (ISBN 0-404-13490-4). AMS Pr.
Mr. Whittier. 7.95 (ISBN 0-670-49431-3). Viking Pr.
Mistral. 22.50x. Elliots Bks.
Mistress of the Mansion. pap. 2.50 (ISBN 0-87015-087-1). Pacific Bks.
Mistress to an Age: A Life of Madame De Stael. pap. 6.95 (ISBN 0-517-53783-4). Crown.
Mistress to an Age: A Life of Madame de Stael. lib. bdg. 25.25x (ISBN 0-8371-8339-1, HEMTA). Greenwood.
Mitchell, Pioneer of Air Power. 18.00 (ISBN 0-405-03777-5). Arno.
Modern Agitators: Or, Pen Portraits of Living American Reformers. 48.00 (ISBN 0-403-06360-4). Scholarly.
Modern American Profiles. pap. text ed. 6.50 (ISBN 0-15-559866-X). HarBraceJ.
Modern Baseball Superstars. 4.50 (ISBN 0-396-06805-7). Dodd.
Modern Basketball Superstars. PLB 4.95 (ISBN 0-396-07192-9). Dodd.
Modern British Plutarch: Or, Lives of Men Distinguished in the Recent History of England for Their Talents, Virtues, or Achievements. 17.25 (ISBN 0-8369-2866-0). Arno.
Modern Composers. 17.25 (ISBN 0-8369-1715-4). Arno.
Modern Composers of Europe. lib. bdg. 35.00 (ISBN 0-89341-419-0). Longwood Pr.
Modern Danish Authors. lib. bdg. 22.50 (ISBN 0-8414-4879-5). Folcroft.
Modern English Painters. 11.95 ea. (ISBN 0-312-53830-8) (ISBN 0-312-53865-0). St Martin.
Modern Frenchmen: Five Biographies. 18.25 (ISBN 0-8369-2947-0). Arno.
Modern Hockey Superstars. 4.95 (ISBN 0-396-07368-9). Dodd.
Modern Mexican Painters. pap. 6.00 (ISBN 0-486-22889-4). Dover.
Modern Mexican Painters. facs. ed. 20.50 (ISBN 0-8369-0532-6). Arno.
Modern Motorcycle Superstars. 5.95g (ISBN 0-396-07786-2). Dodd.
Modern Music-Makers: Contemporary American Composers. lib. bdg. 22.50x (ISBN 0-8371-2957-5, GOMM). Greenwood.
Modern Olympic Superstars. 5.95 (ISBN 0-396-07651-3). Dodd.
Modern Painters. lib. bdg. 17.50x (ISBN 0-8154-0458-1). Cooper Sq.
Modern Pathfinders of Christianity: The Lives & Deeds of Seven Centuries of Christian Leaders. facs. ed. 12.75 (ISBN 0-8369-0839-2). Arno.
Modern Plays, Short & Long. 23.75 (ISBN 0-8369-8250-9). Arno.
Modern Priestess of Isis. 20.00x (ISBN 0-405-07976-1). Arno.
Modern Russian Composers. facs. ed. 14.00 (ISBN 0-8369-0847-3). Arno.
Modern Scottish Writers. facs. ed. 13.25 (ISBN 0-8369-0769-8). Arno.
Modern Soccer Superstars. 5.95 (ISBN 0-396-07731-5). Dodd.
Modern Women Superstars. 5.25g (ISBN 0-396-07489-8). Dodd.
Modigliani. 6.95 (ISBN 0-517-50798-6). Crown.
Moe Berg: Athlete, Scholar, Spy. 7.95 (ISBN 0-316-48348-6). Little.
Moe Berg: Athlete, Scholar...Spy. pap. 1.75 (ISBN 0-345-24811-2). Ballantine.
Mohammed & the Rise of Islam. 29.50 (ISBN 0-8369-6778-X). Arno.
Mohammed & the Rise of Islam. 30.00 (ISBN 0-404-58273-7). AMS Pr.
Mohammed: The Man & His Faith. facsimile ed. 15.50 (ISBN 0-8369-5821-7). Arno.
Mohammed: The Man & His Faith. pap. text ed. 3.95x (ISBN 0-06-130062-4, TB 62). Har-Row.
Moliere. 12.45 (ISBN 0-8274-1314-9). R West.
Moliere. 11.00 (ISBN 0-8462-1086-X). Russell.
Moliere: The Man Seen Through the Plays. lib. bdg. 14.00x (ISBN 0-374-92739-1). Octagon.
Mollie: Journal of Mollie Dorsey Sanford in Nebraska & Colorado Territories, 1857-1866. 8.50 (ISBN 0-8032-0162-1). U of Nebr Pr.
Mollie: The Journal of Mollie Dorsey Sanford in Nebraska & Colorado Territories, 1857-1866. pap. 3.95 (ISBN 0-8032-5826-7, 607). U of Nebr Pr.
Moltke: A Biographical & Critical Study. lib. bdg. 22.95 (ISBN 0-8383-0222-X). Haskell.
Moment. 8.95 (ISBN 0-934168-00-8). Progeny Pr.
Moments of Being: Unpublished Autobiographical Writings. 8.95 (ISBN 0-15-162034-2). HarBraceJ.
Moments of Being: Unpublished Autobiographical Writings. pap. 2.95 (ISBN 0-15-661917-2). HarBraceJ.
Moments of Decision. 5.00 (ISBN 0-8198-0445-2); pap. 4.00 (ISBN 0-8198-0446-0). Dghtrs St Paul.
Moments of Decision. 5.95 (ISBN 0-8007-1091-6). Revell.
Mon Cher Papa: Franklin & the Ladies of Paris. 20.00x (ISBN 0-300-00725-6). Yale U Pr.
Mondale: Portrait of an American Politician. 10.95 (ISBN 0-06-012599-3). Har-Row.
Monet at Giverny. pap. 8.95 (ISBN 0-8317-6100-8). Mayflower Bks.
Money Isn't Important: The Life of Maurice Gusman. 9.95 (ISBN 0-912458-76-3). E A Seemann.
Money Player: The Confessions of America's Greatest Table Tennis Champion & Hustler. 7.25 (ISBN 0-688-00273-0). Morrow.
Mongkut, the King of Siam. o.p. 12.50x (ISBN 0-8014-0301-4); pap. 2.95 (ISBN 0-8014-9069-3, CP69). Cornell U Pr.
Monk. facsimile ed. 13.50 (ISBN 0-8369-5764-4). Arno.
Monsarrat at Sea. 10.00 (ISBN 0-688-03103-X). Morrow.
Monsarrat at Sea. pap. 1.95 (ISBN 0-445-04152-8). Popular Lib.
Montaigne: A Biography. 10.00 (ISBN 0-15-162099-7). HarBraceJ.
Montaigne in France, 1812-1852. lib. bdg. 15.50 (ISBN 0-374-92845-2). Octagon.
Montauk. 7.95 (ISBN 0-15-162100-4). HarBraceJ.
Montesquieu. 7.50 (ISBN 0-8046-0434-7). Kennikat.
Montesquieu: A Critical Biography. 24.50x (ISBN 0-19-815339-2). Oxford U Pr.
Montesquieu & Burke. lib. bdg. 13.25x (ISBN 0-8371-7406-6, COMB). Greenwood.
Monteverdi. 9.95x (ISBN 0-460-03155-4). Biblio Dist.
Monteverdi. pap. 5.95 (ISBN 0-8226-0716-6). Littlefield.
Monteverdi: His Life & Work. lib. bdg. 14.00x (ISBN 0-8371-3996-1, PRMO). Greenwood.
Montgomery. pap. 2.00 (ISBN 0-345-24294-7). Ballantine.
Montgomery of Alamein. 12.95 (ISBN 0-689-10744-7). Atheneum.
Monty: A Biography of Montgomery Clift. 12.95 (ISBN 0-87795-155-1). Arbor Hse.
Monument Maker: A Biography of Frederick Ernst Triebel. 5.95 (ISBN 0-682-49051-2). Exposition.
Moon in Eclipse: A Life of Mary Shelley. 15.95 (ISBN 0-312-54692-0). St Martin.
Moon Is Not Enough. 6.95 (ISBN 0-310-37050-7); pap. 3.95 (ISBN 0-310-37051-5). Zondervan.
Moons a Balloon. pap. 2.25 (ISBN 0-440-15806-0). Dell.
Moral Choices: Memory, Desire, & Imagination in Nineteenth-Century American Abolition. 24.95x (ISBN 0-8071-0262-8). La State U Pr.
More Fun Than Heaven. pap. 3.95 (ISBN 0-912760-86-9). Valkyrie Pr.
More Heroes of Modern Adventure. facsimile ed. 17.00 (ISBN 0-8369-1343-4). Arno.
More Junior Authors. 10.00 (ISBN 0-8242-0036-5). Wilson.
More Lives Than a Cat. pap. 3.95 (ISBN 0-8127-0243-3). Southern Pub.
More Modern Baseball Superstars. 5.95 (ISBN 0-396-07616-5). Dodd.
More Modern Women Superstars. 5.95 (ISBN 0-396-07680-7). Dodd.
More New Breed Stars. PLB 5.95g (ISBN 0-8225-1410-9). Lerner Pubns.
More Than a Run. 10.00 (ISBN 0-312-90719-2). St Martin.
More Than a Run. new ed. 10.00 (ISBN 0-312-90719-2). J P Tarcher.
More Than Conquerors. facs. ed. 18.25 (ISBN 0-8369-1036-2). Arno.
More Than Land: Stories of New England Country Life & Surveying. pap. 4.95 (ISBN 0-87233-045-1). Bauhan.
More Travels in a Donkey Trap. 9.95 (ISBN 0-285-62217-X). Intl Schol Bk Serv.
Morley Marvels. 8.95 (ISBN 0-498-02397-4). A S Barnes.
Morning After Death. 5.95 (ISBN 0-8054-2412-1). Broadman.
Morning Deluge: Mao Tsetung & the Chinese Revolution, 1893-1954. 12.50 (ISBN 0-316-34289-0). Little.
Morris Hillquit: A Political History of an American Jewish Socialist. lib. bdg. 18.50x (ISBN 0-313-20526-4, PMH/). Greenwood.
Moscow Was My Parish. lib. bdg. 20.75x (ISBN 0-313-20594-9, BIMM). Greenwood.
Moses. text ed. 13.95x (ISBN 0-8143-1491-0). Wayne St U Pr.
Moses - Born to Be a Slave, but God... 5.50 (ISBN 0-682-48843-7). Exposition.
Moses Brown: Reluctant Reformer. 15.50x (ISBN 0-8078-0859-8). U of NC Pr.
Moses: God's Helper. 3.95 (ISBN 0-8054-4225-1). Broadman.
Moses Mendelssohn: A Biographical Study. 25.00 (ISBN 0-8173-6860-4). U of Ala Pr.
Moses, the Servant of Yahweh. pap. text ed. 5.95 (ISBN 0-933462-03-4). Pryor Pettengill.
Moshe Dayan: Story of My Life. 15.00 (ISBN 0-688-03076-9). Morrow.
Moshe Dayan: Story of My Life. pap. 2.95 (ISBN 0-446-83425-4). Warner Bks.
Most Beautiful Women in Imperial Rome. deluxe ed. 37.50 (ISBN 0-930582-05-5). Gloucester Art.
Most Exciting Years of Show Business. 5.95 (ISBN 0-8059-1939-2). Dorrance.
Most Powerful Man in the World: The Life of Sir Henri Deterding. 23.50 (ISBN 0-88355-301-5). Hyperion Conn.
Most Wanted Man in America. 25.00x (ISBN 0-8128-1771-0); pap. 1.95. Stein & Day.
Mostly in the Line of Duty: Thirty Years with Books. lib. bdg. 28.95 (ISBN 90-247-2228-4). Kluwer Boston.
Mother Cabrini. 3.50 (ISBN 0-8198-0440-1); pap. 2.50 (ISBN 0-8198-0441-X). Dghtrs St Paul.
Mother Ireland. 12.95 (ISBN 0-15-162587-5). HarBraceJ.
Mother Jones, the Miners' Angel: A Portrait. 11.85x (ISBN 0-8093-0643-3). S Ill U Pr.
Mother Jones, the Miners' Angel: A Portrait. pap. 4.95 (ISBN 0-8093-0896-7). S Ill U Pr.
Mother R: Eleanor Roosevelt's Untold Story. 8.95 (ISBN 0-399-11998-1). Putnam.
Mother Seton: First American-Born Saint. pap. 1.25 (ISBN 0-671-29785-6). Archway.
Motion Picture Directors: A Bibliography of Magazine & Periodical Articles, 1900-1972. 15.00 (ISBN 0-8108-0590-1). Scarecrow.
Motion Picture Performers: A Bibliography of Magazine & Periodical Articles. 30.00 (ISBN 0-8108-0879-X). Scarecrow.
Mount Vernon Family. 3.95g (ISBN 0-02-789190-9). Macmillan.
Mountain Charley: Or the Adventures of Mrs. E. J. Guerin, Who Was Thirteen Years in Male Attire. 4.95 (ISBN 0-8061-0790-1). U of Okla Pr.
Mountain Never Too High: The Story of J. E. O'Neill. 15.00 (ISBN 0-913548-46-4). Valley Calif.
Mountain to Climb. pap. 3.95 (ISBN 0-8163-0223-5, 13685-3). Pacific Pr Pub Assn.
Mountain Wolf Woman, Sister of Crashing Thunder: Autobiography of a Winnebago Indian. 5.00 (ISBN 0-472-09109-3). U of Mich Pr.
Mountain Wolf Woman, Sister of Crashing Thunder: The Autobiography of a Winnebago Indian. pap. 2.95 (ISBN 0-472-06109-7, 109). U of Mich Pr.
Moussorgsky. 7.00 (ISBN 0-8446-4802-7). Peter Smith.
Moussorgsky. 14.00 (ISBN 0-404-05334-3). AMS Pr.
Moussorgsky. lib. bdg. 18.00x (ISBN 0-8371-4007-2, RIMO). Greenwood.
Movable Type: Biography of Legh R. Freeman. text ed. 11.50x (ISBN 0-8138-0890-1). Iowa St U Pr.
Move That Mountain! o.p. 5.95 (ISBN 0-88270-182-7); pap. 1.95 (ISBN 0-88270-212-2). Logos.
Mover of Men & Mountains: The Autobiography of R. G. LeTourneau. pap. 2.95 (ISBN 0-8024-3818-0). Moody.
Movers & Shakers in Georgia. 12.95 (ISBN 0-671-24043-9). S&S.
Movie Comedy Teams. pap. 1.75 (ISBN 0-451-06480-1, E6480). NAL.
Movie Stars, Real People, & Me. 9.95 (ISBN 0-440-06258-6). Delacorte.
Movies in the Age of Innocence. 12.50x (ISBN 0-8061-0539-9); pap. 4.95 (ISBN 0-8061-1297-2). U of Okla Pr.
Mozart. 13.75x (ISBN 0-460-03157-0). Biblio Dist.
Mozart. rev. ed. pap. 5.95 (ISBN 0-8226-0717-4). Littlefield.
Mozart. rev. ed. pap. 5.95 (ISBN 0-8226-0700-X). Littlefield.
Mozart. facsimile ed. 12.75 (ISBN 0-8369-5300-2). Arno.

My Son Eric. 8.95 (ISBN 0-8298-0372-6). Pilgrim NY.

My Son Johnny. pap. 4.95 (ISBN 0-8423-4647-3). Tyndale.

My Stephen Crane. 6.00x (ISBN 0-8156-0012-7). Syracuse U Pr.

My Theatre Life. 37.50 (ISBN 0-8195-5035-3). Columbia U Pr.

My Thirty Years in Baseball. 17.00x (ISBN 0-405-06381-4). Arno.

My Truth. 8.95 (ISBN 0-688-03099-8). Morrow.

My Twenty-Five Years in China. lib. bdg. 27.50 (ISBN 0-306-70761-6). Da Capo.

My Two Roads. 2nd ed. 7.95 (ISBN 0-88415-570-6). Pacesetter Pr.

My Universities. pap. 2.95 (ISBN 0-14-044302-9). Penguin.

My War Memoirs. lib. bdg. 20.00x (ISBN 0-8371-4763-8, BEMW). Greenwood.

My Way of Life. pap. 1.50 (ISBN 0-671-78568-0). PB.

My Wayward Parent: A Book About Irvin S. Cobb. lib. bdg. 13.00x (ISBN 0-8371-6125-8, CHWP). Greenwood.

My Wicked, Wicked Ways. lib. bdg. 16.35. Buccaneer Bks.

My Wicked, Wicked Ways. pap. 1.95 (ISBN 0-425-03213-2). Berkley Pub.

My Wicked, Wicked Ways. pap. 2.50 (ISBN 0-425-04118-2). Berkley Pub.

My Wife & I: The Story of Louise & Sidney Homer. lib. bdg. 22.50 (ISBN 0-306-77526-3). Da Capo.

My Wild Life. 8.95 (ISBN 0-399-11616-8). Putnam.

My Works & Days: A Personal Chronicle, 1895-1975. 19.95 (ISBN 0-15-164087-4). HarBraceJ.

My World. 4.95 (ISBN 0-8131-0211-1). U Pr of Ky.

My Years with Corrie. 5.95 (ISBN 0-8007-0957-8). Revell.

My Years with Corrie. lib. bdg. 11.95 (ISBN 0-8161-6773-7). G K Hall.

My Years with Ferrari. 12.95 (ISBN 0-87938-059-4). Motorbooks Intl.

My Years with General Motors. 3.50 (ISBN 0-385-04235-3). Doubleday.

My Years with Louis St. Laurent: A Political Memoir. 20.00 (ISBN 0-8020-2215-4). U of Toronto Pr.

My Years with Ludwig Von Mises. 9.95 (ISBN 0-87000-368-2). Arlington Hse.

My Young Years. 10.00 (ISBN 0-394-46890-2). Knopf.

My Young Years. pap. 2.50 (ISBN 0-445-08296-8). Popular Lib.

Myaskovsky: His Life & Work. lib. bdg. 11.00x (ISBN 0-8371-2158-2, IKM). Greenwood.

Myrna Loy. pap. 1.95. HarBraceJ.

Myrtilla Miner: A Memoir. Bd. with School for Colored Girls in Washington, D. C. 8.75 (ISBN 0-405-01933-5). Arno.

Myself Must I Remake: The Life & Poetry of W. B. Yeats. 5.50 (ISBN 0-690-00114-2). T Y Crowell.

Myself: The Autobiography of John R. Commons. pap. 4.75x (ISBN 0-299-02924-7). U of Wis Pr.

Myself When Young: The Shaping of a Writer. 7.95 (ISBN 0-385-13016-3). Doubleday.

Myself When Young: The Shaping of a Writer. pap. 1.95 (ISBN 0-380-40485-0, 40485). Avon.

Myself When Young: The Shaping of a Writer. lib. bdg. 9.95 (ISBN 0-8161-6611-0). G K Hall.

Myselves When Young. 10.00x (ISBN 0-19-212184-7). Oxford U Pr.

Mysterious Rays: Marie Curie's World. PLB 4.99 (ISBN 0-698-30681-3). Coward.

Mysterious World of Agatha Christie. pap. 1.95 (ISBN 0-441-55190-4). Charter Bks.

Mystery of Agatha Christie. 8.95 (ISBN 0-385-12623-9). Doubleday.

Mystery of Agatha Christie. pap. 2.95 (ISBN 0-14-005228-3). Penguin.

Mystery of B. Traven. 6.95 (ISBN 0-913232-32-7). W Kaufmann.

Mystery of Mary Stuart. 12.50 (ISBN 0-404-03858-1). AMS Pr.

Mystery of the Princes: An Investigation into a Supposed Murder. 16.00x (ISBN 0-8476-6103-2). Rowman.

Mystery Train: Images of America in Rock 'n' Roll Music. pap. 4.50 (ISBN 0-525-47422-6). Dutton.

Mystic in the Theatre: Eleonora Duse. pap. 2.45 (ISBN 0-8093-0631-X). S Ill U Pr.

Mysticism & Dissent: Religious Ideology & Social Protest in the Sixteenth Century. 17.50x (ISBN 0-300-01576-3). Yale U Pr.

Mystics of Our Times. pap. 2.45 (ISBN 0-8091-1641-3). Paulist Pr.

Myth of the Conqueror: Prince Henry Stuart, a Study of 17th Century Personation. 21.00 (ISBN 0-404-16004-2). AMS Pr.

Mzilikazi of the Ndebele. pap. text ed. 1.95x (ISBN 0-435-94475-4). Heinemann Ed.

N

N. S. Trubetzkoy's Letters & Notes. 105.50 (ISBN 90-2793-181-X). Mouton.

Nadia Comaneci. PLB 5.95 (ISBN 0-87191-592-8); pap. 2.75 (ISBN 0-89812-195-7). Creative Ed.

Nadia Comaneci. pap. text ed. 1.50 (ISBN 0-448-12973-6). G&D.

Nadia Comaneci: Enchanted Sparrow. PLB 5.95 (ISBN 0-88436-402-X); pap. 3.50 (ISBN 0-88436-403-8). EMC.

Nadia of Romania. 13.50; pap. 8.95 (ISBN 0-7156-1241-7). Biblio Dist.

Nadia: The Success Secrets of the Amazing Romanian Gymnast. pap. 3.95 (ISBN 0-8015-5296-6). Hawthorn.

Nahum Tate. lib. bdg. 7.95 (ISBN 0-8057-1536-3). Twayne.

Naimbana of Sierra Leone. pap. text ed. 1.95x (ISBN 0-435-94474-6). Heinemann Ed.

Naked Civil Servant. 7.95 (ISBN 0-03-022451-9). HR&W.

Naked Civil Servant. pap. 2.25 (ISBN 0-451-08292-3, E8292). NAL.

Naked Soul of Iceberg Slim. pap. 1.95 (ISBN 0-87067-645-8, BH645). Holloway.

Names: A Memoir. 10.00 (ISBN 0-06-012981-6). Har-Row.

Namibia. pap. 4.95 (ISBN 0-8028-1664-9). Eerdmans.

Namkwa: Life Among the Bushmen. 10.95 (ISBN 0-395-27611-X). HM.

Nancy. 9.95 (ISBN 0-688-03533-7). Morrow.

Nancy Lopez. PLB 5.95 (ISBN 0-87191-694-0); pap. 2.75 (ISBN 0-89812-164-7). Creative Ed.

Nancy Lopez: Golfing Pioneer. text ed. 5.95 (ISBN 0-88436-480-1); pap. text ed. 3.50 (ISBN 0-88436-481-X). EMC.

Nancy Lopez: Wonder Woman of Golf. PLB 6.60 (ISBN 0-516-04302-1). Childrens.

Nancy Mitford: A Memoir. 10.00 (ISBN 0-06-010018-4). Har-Row.

Nancy: The Life of Lady Astor. pap. 5.95 (ISBN 0-586-08257-3). Academy Chi Ltd.

Nancy Ward, Cherokee. 4.95 (ISBN 0-396-07072-8). Dodd.

Naples '44. 8.95 (ISBN 0-394-50354-6). Pantheon.

Napoleon. pap. 1.25 (ISBN 0-02-001870-3). Macmillan.

Napoleon: An Outline. facsimile ed. 16.75 (ISBN 0-8369-6632-5). Arno.

Napoleon III - Man of Destiny: Enlightened Statesman or Proto-Fascist? pap. 4.95 (ISBN 0-88275-323-1). Krieger.

Napoleon III: The Modern Emperor. 18.75 (ISBN 0-8369-6783-6). Arno.

Napoleon in Captivity: Reports of Count Balmain Russian Commissioner on the Island of St. Helena 1816-1820. facsimile ed. 17.50 (ISBN 0-8369-5822-5). Arno.

Napoleon in Love. 10.95 (ISBN 0-671-24041-2). S&S.

Napoleon: The Last Campaigns, 1813-15. 17.95 (ISBN 0-517-52634-4). Crown.

Napoleonists: A Study in Political Disaffection, 1760-1960. 17.00x (ISBN 0-19-215184-3). Oxford U Pr.

Napoleon's Marshal: The Life of Michel Ney. 7.75 (ISBN 0-688-21606-4). Morrow.

Napoleon's Marshals. pap. 6.95 (ISBN 0-8128-6055-1). Stein & Day.

Napoleon's Second Empress. pap. 1.95 (ISBN 0-532-19152-8). Manor Bks.

Napper Tandy. 14.95 (ISBN 0-900068-34-5). Irish Bk Ctr.

Narrative of the Adventures of Zenas Leonard. 14.25x (ISBN 0-8032-2853-8); pap. 3.95 (ISBN 0-8032-7903-5, BB684). U of Nebr Pr.

Narrative of the Captivity & Adventures of John Tanner (U.S. Interpreter at the Saut de Ste. Marie) During 30 Years Residence Among the Indians in the Interior of North America. lib. bdg. 40.00 (ISBN 0-8240-1670-X). Garland Pub.

Narrative of the Life & Adventures of Henry Bibb, an American Slave. 9.50x (ISBN 0-8371-1267-2). Negro U Pr.

Narrative of the Life & Adventures of Henry Bibb, an American Slave. facs. ed. 12.25 (ISBN 0-8369-8511-7). Arno.

Narrative of the Life of David Crockett. 28.00 (ISBN 0-403-07781-8). Scholarly.

Narrative of the Life of David Crockett. 6.00x (ISBN 0-8084-0020-7); pap. 3.45x (ISBN 0-8084-0021-5, M38). Coll & U Pr.

Narrative of the Life of David Crockett of the State of Tennessee. 9.95 (ISBN 0-87049-119-9). U of Tenn Pr.

Narrative of the Life of Mrs. Mary Jemison. 6.00 (ISBN 0-8446-2899-9). Peter Smith.

Narrative of the Shipwreck, Captivity & Sufferings of Horace Holden & Benj. H. Nute: Who Were Cast Away in the American Ship Mentor, on the Pelew Islands, in the Year 1832 Etc. 7.50 (ISBN 0-87770-147-4). Ye Galleon.

Nat Turner. 8.95 (ISBN 0-13-933143-3). P-H.

Nat Turner. PLB 3.99 (ISBN 0-698-30249-4). Coward.

Natalia Makarova. pap. 1.50 (ISBN 0-87127-057-9). Dance Horiz.

Natalia Makarova, Ballerina. 15.95 (ISBN 0-87127-103-6). Dance Horiz.

Natalie Cole: Star Child. PLB 5.95 (ISBN 0-88436-410-0); pap. 3.50 (ISBN 0-88436-411-9). EMC.

Nathan Hale. 3.50 (ISBN 0-89799-128-1); pap. 1.50 (ISBN 0-89799-035-8). Dandelion Pr.

Nathan Hale. PLB 4.49 (ISBN 0-399-60484-7). Putnam.

Nathan Trotter: Philadelphia Merchant, 1787-1853. 14.00 (ISBN 0-405-04729-0). Arno.

Nathanael Greene, Commander of the American Continental Army in the South. lib. bdg. 2.45 incl. catalog cards; pap. 1.25 vinyl laminated covers. SamHar Pr.

Nathanael West: The Ironic Prophet. pap. 2.95 (ISBN 0-295-97876-7, WP30). U of Wash Pr.

Nathaniel Hawthorne. lib. bdg. 15.50x (ISBN 0-8371-6552-0, VANH). Greenwood.

Nathaniel Hawthorne. 11.00 (ISBN 0-8103-3043-1). Gale.

Nathaniel Hawthorne, a Biography. 17.50 (ISBN 0-208-00829-2). Shoe String.

Nathaniel Hawthorne, a Modest Man. lib. bdg. 21.00x (ISBN 0-8371-2594-4, MANH). Greenwood.

Nathaniel Hawthorne & His Wife: A Biography. 27.50 (ISBN 0-208-00672-9). Shoe String.

Nathaniel Parker Willis. lib. bdg. 9.00. Folcroft.

Nathaniel Parker Willis. 9.50 (ISBN 0-404-00726-0). AMS Pr.

Nathaniel Parker Willis. write for info. (ISBN 0-403-00859-X). Scholarly.

Native Daughter. 6.95 (ISBN 0-02-567220-7). Macmillan.

Natural Man Observed: A Study of Catlin's Indian Gallery. 40.00 (ISBN 0-87474-918-2). Smithsonian.

Natural Man: The Life of William Beebe. 11.50x (ISBN 0-253-33975-8). Ind U Pr.

Nature of Alexander. 17.95 (ISBN 0-394-49113-0). Pantheon.

Nature of Alexander. pap. 2.95 (ISBN 0-394-73825-X). Pantheon.

Nature of Alexander. pap. 7.95 (ISBN 0-394-73254-5). Pantheon.

Nature of Biography. 7.95 (ISBN 0-295-95604-6). U of Wash Pr.

Naught to Thirty-Three. 22.50 (ISBN 0-522-84101-5). Intl Schol Bk Serv.

Navajo Biographies. new ed. 9.50. Navajo Curr.

Navajo Biographies. new ed. 9.50 (ISBN 0-89019-003-8). Navajo Curr.

Navajo Blessingway Singer: The Autobiography of Frank Mitchell, 1881-1967. pap. text ed. 8.50x (ISBN 0-8165-0568-3). U of Ariz Pr.

Naval Biography of Great Britain: Consisting of Historical Memoirs of Those Officers of the British Navy Who Distinguished Themselves During the Reign of His Majesty George III. lib. bdg. 140.00x (ISBN 0-8398-1773-8). Irvington.

Nazi Hunter: Simon Wiesenthal. PLB 7.29 (ISBN 0-671-32964-2). Messner.

Necessary Evil: The Life of Jane Welsh Carlyle. 27.50 (ISBN 0-374-93652-8). Octagon.

Ned. 7.95 (ISBN 0-689-30650-4). Atheneum.

Neglected Brother: A Study of Henry Kingsley. 10.00 (ISBN 0-8130-0436-5). U Presses Fla.

Negotiator Out of Season: The Career of Wilhelm Egon von Furstenberg (1629-1704) 20.00 (ISBN 0-8203-0436-0). U of Ga Pr.

Negro Authors & Composers of the United States. 9.00 (ISBN 0-404-12953-6). AMS Pr.

Negro Explorer at the North Pole. 9.00 (ISBN 0-405-01868-1). Arno.

Negro Firsts in Sports. 4.95 (ISBN 0-87485-006-1). Johnson Chi.

Negro Lawmakers in the South Carolina Legislature, 1868-1902. pap. 10.00. L C Bryant.

Negro Senators & Representatives in the South Carolina Legislature. 15.00; pap. 10.00. L C Bryant.

Negro Vanguard. text ed. 19.25x (ISBN 0-8371-5183-X). Negro U Pr.

Negroes in the Early West. PLB 6.64 (ISBN 0-671-32146-3). Messner.

Nehemiah: God's Builder. pap. 2.95 (ISBN 0-8024-5868-8). Moody.

Nehru. 25.00 (ISBN 0-8128-1931-4). Stein & Day.

Nehru: A Study in Colonial Liberalism. text ed. 15.00x (ISBN 0-8426-0925-3). Verry.

Nehrus: Motilal & Jawaharlal. pap. 3.95 (ISBN 0-226-56806-7, P582). U of Chicago Pr.

Nehrus of India: Three Generations of Leadership. 5.95 (ISBN 0-02-751320-3). Macmillan.

Neil Diamond. PLB 5.95 (ISBN 0-87191-464-6); pap. 2.75 (ISBN 0-89812-115-9). Creative Ed.

Neil Young. pap. 3.95 (ISBN 0-8256-3917-4). Music Sales.

Neither Fire nor Steel: Sir Christopher Hatton. 13.95x (ISBN 0-88229-372-9). Nelson-Hall.

Nelson & Sea Power. 5.50x (ISBN 0-340-12413-X). Verry.

Nelson & the Hamiltons. 10.00 (ISBN 0-671-20324-X). S&S.

Nero. lib. bdg. 20.50x (ISBN 0-8371-9302-8, WANER). Greenwood.

Nestorius & His Place in the History of the Christian Doctrine. 18.50 (ISBN 0-8337-4903-X). B Franklin.

Never Too Old for God. pap. 1.50 (ISBN 0-8007-8348-4). Revell.

Nevil Shute (Nevil Shute Norway) lib. bdg. 8.50 (ISBN 0-8057-6664-2). Twayne.

New Brahmans: Five Maharashtrian Families. 17.50x (ISBN 0-520-00635-6). U of Cal Pr.

New Breed. PLB 5.95 (ISBN 0-8225-1406-0). Lerner Pubns.

New Breed Heroes in Pro Baseball. PLB 5.79 (ISBN 0-671-32668-6). Messner.

New Breed of Athlete. pap. 1.25 (ISBN 0-671-48150-9). WSP.

New Breed of Performer. pap. 1.95 (ISBN 0-671-48767-1). WSP.

New Century Handbook of Leaders of the Classical World. 8.95 (ISBN 0-13-612002-4). P-H.

New Century Italian Renaissance Encyclopedia. 42.95 (ISBN 0-13-612051-2). P-H.

New Dictionary of Modern Sculpture. 12.50 (ISBN 0-8148-0479-9). L Amiel Pub.

New England Boyhood. 24.25 (ISBN 0-8422-8067-7). Mss Info.

New England Boyhood. 10.00 (ISBN 0-403-00618-X). Scholarly.

New England Boyhood. lib. bdg. 13.50x (ISBN 0-8398-0750-3). Irvington.

New England Girlhood. 6.25 (ISBN 0-8446-2431-4). Peter Smith.

New England Men of Letters. 6.95 (ISBN 0-02-788680-8). Macmillan.

New Johnny Cash. pap. 1.25 (ISBN 0-8007-8141-4). Revell.

New Kind of Country. 6.95 (ISBN 0-385-13628-5). Doubleday.

New Kind of Country. lib. bdg. 9.50 (ISBN 0-8161-6694-3). G K Hall.

New Letters of Abigail Adams, 1788-1801. lib. bdg. 18.25x (ISBN 0-8371-7055-9, ADNL). Greenwood.

New Letters of Berlioz, 1830-1868. lib. bdg. 16.75x (ISBN 0-8371-3251-7, BENL). Greenwood.

New Links with Shakespeare. 9.95 (ISBN 0-8274-1679-2). R West.

New Links with Shakespeare. 10.00 (ISBN 0-404-00655-8). AMS Pr.

New Lives: Survivors of the Holocaust Living in America. 8.95 (ISBN 0-394-48573-4). Knopf.

New Lives: Survivors of the Holocaust Living in America. pap. 2.25 (ISBN 0-380-01790-3, 35345). Avon.

New Shelley Letters. 17.00 (ISBN 0-88355-713-4). Hyperion Conn.

New Trail Blazers of Technology. 7.95 (ISBN 0-684-14718-1). Scribner.

New Women in Art & Dance. PLB 5.95 (ISBN 0-87191-512-X). Creative Ed.

New Women in Entertainment. PLB 5.95 (ISBN 0-87191-510-3). Creative Ed.

New Women in Media. PLB 5.95 (ISBN 0-87191-511-1). Creative Ed.

New Women in Medicine. PLB 5.95 (ISBN 0-87191-508-1). Creative Ed.

New Women in Politics. PLB 5.95 (ISBN 0-87191-507-3). Creative Ed.

New York Abolitionists: A Case Study of Political Radicalism. lib. bdg. 11.75x (ISBN 0-8371-3308-4, SNY/). Greenwood.

New York Jew. 10.95 (ISBN 0-394-49567-5). Knopf.

New York Jew. pap. 2.95 (ISBN 0-394-72867-X). Random.

Newcomers: Ten Tales of American Immigrants. 7.25 (ISBN 0-688-41590-3); PLB 6.96 (ISBN 0-688-51590-8). Lothrop.

Newman. lib. bdg. 10.00 (ISBN 0-8414-1870-5). Folcroft.

Newman & Bloxam: An Oxford Friendship. lib. bdg. 13.75x (ISBN 0-8371-3986-4, MINB). Greenwood.

Newman Brothers: An Essay in Comparative Intellectual Biography. 7.50x (ISBN 0-674-62200-6). Harvard U Pr.

Newman's Way. 7.50 (ISBN 0-8159-6303-3). Devin.

Newspaper Days. 21.50x (ISBN 0-8464-0023-5). Beekman Pubs.

Newton, the Man. 19.50. Johnson Repr.

Next-Year Country: One Woman's View. 9.95 (ISBN 0-917624-09-2); pap. 7.95 (ISBN 0-917624-07-6). Lame Johnny.

Next Year in Jerusalem. 9.95 (ISBN 0-688-03552-3). Morrow.

Nice Guys Finish Last. 10.95 (ISBN 0-671-22057-8). S&S.

Nice Guys Finish Last. pap. 1.95 (ISBN 0-671-80446-4). PB.

Nichiren: The Buddhist Prophet. 6.50 (ISBN 0-8446-1029-1). Peter Smith.

Nicholas & Alexandra. 17.50 (ISBN 0-689-10177-5). Atheneum.

Nicholas & Alexandra. pap. 2.50 (ISBN 0-440-16358-7). Dell.

Nicholas Bacon: The Making of a Tudor Statesman. 15.00 (ISBN 0-8214-0225-0). Ohio U Pr.

Nicholas of Cusa. lib. bdg. 17.50 (ISBN 0-915172-05-4). Richwood Pub.

Nicholas Ridley: A Biography. lib. bdg. 35.00 (ISBN 0-8492-2273-7). R West.

Nicholas Roerich. 6.00 (ISBN 0-911794-34-4). Aqua Educ.

Nickels Worth of Skim Milk: A Boy's View of Great Depression. 4.95. Univ Graphics.

Nietzsche. lib. bdg. 19.95 (ISBN 0-8383-1791-X). Haskell.

Nietzsche: The Story of a Human Philosopher. lib. bdg. 24.50x (ISBN 0-8371-6674-8, RENI). Greenwood.

Nigger. pap. 1.95 (ISBN 0-671-81214-9). PB.

Nigger: An Autobiography. 7.95 (ISBN 0-525-16697-1). Dutton.

Nigger in the Window. 7.95 (ISBN 0-385-07142-6). Doubleday.

Night Cometh: Two Wealthy Evangelicals Face the Nation. pap. 2.95 (ISBN 0-87808-429-0). William Carey Lib.

Night Duty Social Worker. 8.95 (ISBN 0-525-66630-3). Elsevier-Nelson.

Night of the Mist. lib. bdg. 16.25x (ISBN 0-313-20229-X, HENM). Greenwood.

Night Watch. 9.95 (ISBN 0-689-10754-4). Atheneum.

Nijinsky. 15.00 (ISBN 0-02-871870-4). Schirmer Bks.

Nijinsky. 23.00 (ISBN 0-404-04776-9). AMS Pr.

Nijinsky, Pavlova, Duncan: Three Lives in Dance. lib. bdg. 22.50 (ISBN 0-306-70845-0); pap. 6.95 (ISBN 0-306-80035-7). Da Capo.

Nikolai Gogol. pap. 4.50 (ISBN 0-8112-0120-1, NDP78). New Directions.

Nikolai Leskov: The Man & His Art. 30.00x (ISBN 0-674-62471-8). Harvard U Pr.

Nikolai Strakhov. 8.50x (ISBN 0-674-62475-0). Harvard U Pr.

Nimitz. 17.95 (ISBN 0-87021-492-6). Naval Inst Pr.

Nine Black American Doctors. PLB 6.95 (ISBN 0-201-02842-5, 2842). A-W.

Nine Men of Power. 17.95 (ISBN 0-8277-4465-X). British Bk Ctr.

Nineteenth Century Painters & Painting: A Dictionary. 38.50 (ISBN 0-520-03328-0). U of Cal Pr.

Ninety-Four Years - Agnes Paschal. 16.50 (ISBN 0-87152-184-9). Reprint.

Nisei Daughter. pap. 5.95 (ISBN 0-295-95688-7). U of Wash Pr.

Nixon Agonistes: The Crisis of the Self Made Man. rev ed. pap. 2.50 (ISBN 0-451-61750-9, ME1750). NAL.

Nixon Vs. Nixon: An Emotional Tragedy. 10.95 (ISBN 0-374-22275-4). FS&G.

Nixon Vs Nixon: An Emotional Tragedy. pap. 2.25 (ISBN 0-451-07902-7, E7902). NAL.

No Bed of Roses. 9.95 (ISBN 0-688-03344-X). Morrow.

No Bed of Roses. pap. 2.50 (ISBN 0-425-04241-3). Berkley Pub.

No Castles on Main Street. American Authors & Their Homes. 9.95 (ISBN 0-528-81828-7). Rand.

No Castles on Main Street: American Authors & Their Homes. pap. 5.95 (ISBN 0-14-005729-3). Penguin.

No Day Without a Line. 15.00 (ISBN 0-88233-211-2); pap. 7.00 (ISBN 0-88233-212-0). Ardis Pubs.

No Echo in the Sky. 24.00 (ISBN 0-405-03776-7). Arno.

No Featherbed to Heaven: A Biography of Michael Wigglesworth 1631-1705. 7.00 (ISBN 0-87013-071-4). Mich St U Pr.

No Hero, I Confess: A Nineteenth-Century Autobiography. 4.95 (ISBN 0-8008-5590-6). Taplinger.

No Laughing Matter: The Autobiography of a WASP. 8.95 (ISBN 0-397-01240-3). Lippincott.

No Longer Alone. 5.95 (ISBN 0-8007-0749-4). Revell.

No Longer Alone. pap. 1.50 (ISBN 0-912692-60-X). Cook.

No More for the Road: One Man's Journey from Chemical Dependency to Freedom. pap. 3.50 (ISBN 0-8066-1515-X, 10-4665). Augsburg.

No Pickle, No Performance: An Irreverent Theatrical Excursion from Tallulah to Travolta. 8.95 (ISBN 0-385-13241-7). Doubleday.

No Souvenirs: Journal, 1957-1969. 15.00 (ISBN 0-06-062141-9). Har-Row.

No Time for Tears. 3.95 (ISBN 0-87485-016-9). Johnson Chi.

No Valley Too Deep. pap. 2.95 (ISBN 0-8024-5947-1). Moody.

Noa Noa. 20.00 (ISBN 0-8492-4913-9). R West.

NOA-NOA. 17.50 (ISBN 0-89097-006-8). Archer Edns.

Noa Noa. pap. 2.95 (ISBN 0-374-50040-1, N110). FS&G.

Noah & the Great Flood. 7.95 (ISBN 0-689-50098-X). Atheneum.

Noah Webster. lib. bdg. 12.45. Folcroft.

Noah Webster. lib. bdg. 20.00 (ISBN 0-8495-4842-X). Arden Lib.

Noam Chomsky. rev ed. pap. 2.95 (ISBN 0-14-004370-5). Penguin.

Noam Chomsky: A Philosophic Overview. lib. bdg. 8.50 (ISBN 0-8057-3661-1). Twayne.

Nobel Prize Winners in Physics, 1901-1950. facsimile ed. 31.00 (ISBN 0-8369-2455-X). Arno.

Nobody Asked Me, but... The World of Jimmy Cannon. 10.95 (ISBN 0-03-015381-6). HR&W.

Nobody's Perfect. pap. 1.75 (ISBN 0-88207-577-2). Victor Bks.

Nocturne: A Life of Chopin. 12.50 (ISBN 0-8008-5593-0). Taplinger.

Noel Coward & His Friends. 20.00 (ISBN 0-688-03510-8). Morrow.

Nolan Ryan: Fireballer. PLB 5.29 (ISBN 0-399-60951-2). Putnam.

Nonsense & Wonder: The Poems & Cartoons of Edward Lear. 12.95 (ISBN 0-525-16835-4). Dutton.

Nook Farm: Mark Twain's Hartford Circle. pap. 2.95 (ISBN 0-295-78576-4, WP49). U of Wash Pr.

Norma. pap. 1.95 (ISBN 0-553-11375-5). Bantam.

Norma. pap. 2.95 (ISBN 0-89066-001-8). World Wide Pubs.

Norma. 7.95 (ISBN 0-8423-4717-8); with cassette 8.95; pap. 2.95. Tyndale.

Norman Douglas. lib. bdg. 13.95 (ISBN 0-8383-1804-5). Haskell.

Norman Douglas. lib. bdg. 8.50 (ISBN 0-8414-8572-0). Folcroft.

Norman Lindsay: The Embattled Olympian. 14.00x (ISBN 0-19-550388-0). Oxford U Pr.

Norman Thomas. lib. bdg. 8.95 (ISBN 0-8057-0727-1). Twayne.

Norman Thomas: Respectable Rebel. 2nd ed. 9.00x (ISBN 0-8156-0056-9). Syracuse U Pr.

North Africa Story: An Anthropologist As OSS Agent. 11.95 (ISBN 0-87645-108-3). Gambit.

North Carolina Governors,1585-1975: Brief Sketches. rev. ed. pap. 3.00 (ISBN 0-86526-033-8). NC Archives.

North Country Bishop: A Biography of William Nicolson. 37.50x. Elliots Bks.

North Ships: The Life of a Trawlerman. 5.50 (ISBN 0-7153-6483-9). David & Charles.

North Toward Home. 15.00 (ISBN 0-910220-86-7). Larlin Corp.

Northern Daughter & a Southern Wife: The Civil War Reminiscences & Letters of Katharine H. Cumming, 1860-1865. 12.00; pap. 6.00. Richmond Cty Hist Soc.

Northern Expeditions of Stephen H. Long: The Journals of 1817 & 1823 & Related Documents. 17.50 (ISBN 0-87351-129-8). Minn Hist.

Northumberland: The Political Career of John Dudley, Earl of Warwick & Duke of Northumberland. 10.00x (ISBN 0-87338-140-8). Kent St U Pr.

Nostalgia: A Psychoanalytic Study of Marcel Proust. 11.00 (ISBN 0-8046-0627-7). Kennikat.

Nostalgia Isn't What It Used to Be. 12.95 (ISBN 0-06-013986-2). Har Row.

Nostalgia Isn't What It Used to Be. pap. 2.95 (ISBN 0-14-005181-3). Penguin.

Not by Politics Alone: The Other Lenin. pap. 4.95 (ISBN 0-88208-063-6). Lawrence Hill.

Not in My Time: The Story of a Doctor. 15.00 (ISBN 0-8022-2239-0). Philos Lib.

Not Ready to Walk Alone. 5.95 (ISBN 0-310-37070-1). Zondervan.

Not So Wild a Dream. 12.50 (ISBN 0-689-10741-2, 235); pap. 8.95 (ISBN 0-689-70578-6). Atheneum.

Not Without Honor: The Life of John H. Reagan. 9.50 (ISBN 0-292-73318-6); pap. 3.95 (ISBN 0-292-70099-7). U of Tex Pr.

Notable American Women, 1607-1950: A Biographical Dictionary. 75.00x (ISBN 0-674-62731-8). Harvard U Pr.

Notable Maryland Women. 12.50 (ISBN 0-87033-236-8); pap. 8.00. Cornell Maritime.

Notable Men of Alabama: Personal & Genealogical with Portraits. 22.50 ea.; (ISBN 0-87152-225-X) (ISBN 0-87152-226-8). Reprint.

Notable New Zealand Statesmen: Twelve Prime Ministers. 19.00 (ISBN 0-8369-8139-1). Arno.

Notable Southern Families. 15.00 (ISBN 0-87152-147-4). Reprint.

Notable Southern Families. 12.00 (ISBN 0-87152-146-6). Reprint.

Notable Southern Families. 15.00 (ISBN 0-87152-148-2). Reprint.

Notable Southern Families. 70.00 (ISBN 0-8063-0508-8). Genealog Pub.

Notable Southern Families. lib. bdg. 34.95 (ISBN 0-8490-2355-6). Gordon Pr.

Notable Women Authors of the Day. 17.50 (ISBN 0-8274-1786-1). R West.

Notable Women Authors of the Day. facsimile ed. 25.75 (ISBN 0-8369-2637-4). Arno.

Notes & Anecdotes of Many Years. facs. ed. 13.50 (ISBN 0-8369-1904-1). Arno.

Notes from the Other Side of Night. 8.95 (ISBN 0-89526-685-7). Regnery-Gateway.

Notes of a Lost Pilot. 15.00 (ISBN 0-208-01437-3). Shoe String.

Notes of a Pianist. 27.50 (ISBN 0-306-79508-6). Da Capo.

Notes of a Processed Brother. pap. 1.95 (ISBN 0-380-01360-6, 14175). Avon.

Notes on Chopin. lib. bdg. 13.75x (ISBN 0-313-20371-7, GINC). Greenwood.

Notes on the Life & Works of Bernard Romans. 12.50 (ISBN 0-8130-0413-6). U Presses Fla.

Notes on the Life of Noah Webster. lib. bdg. 53.00 (ISBN 0-8337-1196-2). B Franklin.

Notes on Walt Whitman As Poet & Person. lib. bdg. 14.95 (ISBN 0-8383-0922-4). Haskell.

Nothing Could Be Finer. 12.00 (ISBN 0-7178-0553-0); pap. 3.95 (ISBN 0-7178-0498-4). Intl Pub Co.

Nothing Is Impossible. 6.95 (ISBN 0-8024-5963-3). Moody.

Nothing Is Impossible: The Story of Beatrix Potter. PLB 6.95 (ISBN 0-689-20618-6). Atheneum.

Nothing to Kick About: The Autobiography of a Modern Immigrant. 6.95 (ISBN 0-396-06820-0). Dodd.

Nothing Too Daring: A Biography of Commodore David Porter, 1780-1843. 17.50 (ISBN 0-87021-494-2). Naval Inst Pr.

Nothing Venture, Nothing Win. 12.95 (ISBN 0-698-10649-0). Coward.

Novelist to a Generation: Life & Thought of Winston Churchill. 12.95 (ISBN 0-87972-116-2); pap. 4.95 (ISBN 0-87972-117-0). Bowling Green.

Novels of R. K. Narayan. 15.00 (ISBN 0-88253-584-6); pap. text ed. 8.00 (ISBN 0-88253-583-8). InterCulture.

Nun of Monza. 4.95 (ISBN 0-671-53052-6). S&S.

Nurse. 10.95 (ISBN 0-312-58021-5). St Martin.

Nurse. pap. 2.50 (ISBN 0-425-04220-0). Berkley Pub.

Nurse in the Yukon. 4.50 (ISBN 0-396-05443-9). Dodd.

O

O. C. Marsh: Pioneer in Paleontology. lib. bdg. 35.00x (ISBN 0-405-10733-1). Arno.

O. J. Simpson. PLB 5.95 (ISBN 0-87191-312-7); pap. 2.75 (ISBN 0-89812-166-3). Creative Ed.

O. J. Simpson. PLB 3.69 (ISBN 0-394-93061-4). Random

O. J. Simpson Story: Born to Run. 6.95 (ISBN 0-396-07009-4). Dodd.

O. J. Simpson's Most Memorable Games. 8.95 (ISBN 0-399-12108-0). Putnam.

O. J. The Education of a Rich Rookie. 5.95 (ISBN 0-02-611300-7). Macmillan.

O. P. McMains & the Maxwell Land Grant Conflict. 16.50x (ISBN 0-8165-0652-3); pap. 9.50x (ISBN 0-8165-0575-6). U of Ariz Pr.

O Rugged Land of Gold. 4.95 (ISBN 0-02-580460-X). Macmillan

O Wondrous Singer: An Introduction to Walt Whitman. 7.50 (ISBN 0-396-06078-1). Dodd.

Oblomov & His Creator: The Life & Art of Ivan Goncharov. 17.50x (ISBN 0-691-06245-5). Princeton U Pr.

Occultist's Travels. lib. bdg. 9.80 (ISBN 0-914294-09-1); pap. 3.95 (ISBN 0-914294-10-5). Running Pr.

Ocean on a Plank. 7.50 (ISBN 0-533-03450-7). Vantage.

Odd World: A Photo-Reporter's Story. 4.50 (53060). S&S.

Odilon Redon. lib. bdg. 45.00 (ISBN 0-306-70975-9). Da Capo.

Odyssey of a Desert Prospector. pap. 4.95 (ISBN 0-8061-1180-1). U of Okla Pr.

Odyssey of a Film-Maker: Robert Flaherty's Story. 8.00 (ISBN 0-405-03918-2). Arno.

Odyssey of Cabeza De Vaca. lib. bdg. 18.00x (ISBN 0-8371-5739-0, BICV). Greenwood.

Of Battles Long Ago: Memoirs of an American Ambulance Driver in World War I. 15.00 (ISBN 0-682-49396-1). Exposition.

Of Life & Love & Things. 4.95 (ISBN 0-87012-075-1). McClain.

Of Men, Matter & Me. 4.50x (ISBN 0-210-34006-1). Asia.

Of Music & Music-Making. pap. 3.95 (ISBN 0-393-00242-X). Norton.

Of Time & an Island. 7.95 (ISBN 0-88327-033-1). McKay.

Off at Sunrise: The Overland Journal of Charles Glass Gray. 12.00 (ISBN 0-87328-069-5). Huntington Lib.

Off-Hand Portraits of Prominent New Yorkers. facsimile ed. 21.00x (ISBN 0-405-06914-6). Arno.

Office Without Power: Secretary-General Sir Eric Drummond 1919-1933. 41.00x (ISBN 0-19-822551-2). Oxford U Pr.

Oglethorpe in America. lib. bdg. 12.50 (ISBN 0-226-76846-5). U of Chicago Pr.

Oglethorpe Ladies & the Jacobite Conspiracies. bds. 7.95 (ISBN 0-87797-039-4). Cherokee.

Oh, Lizzie: Life of Elizabeth Cady Stanton. pap. 0.75 (ISBN 0-671-29617-5). Archway.

Oh, Lizzie: The Life of Elizabeth Cady Stanton. PLB 6.96 (ISBN 0-688-51405-7). Lothrop.

O'Hara Concern: A Biography of John O'Hara. 15.00 (ISBN 0-394-48446-0). Random.

Oil, Land & Politics: The California Career of Thomas Robert Bard. 30.00 (ISBN 0-8061-0641-7). U of Okla Pr.

Old Acquaintance: Barry Cornwall & Some of His Friends. 15.00 (ISBN 0-8414-4197-9). Folcroft.

Old Acquaintance: Barry Cornwall & Some of His Friends. lib. bdg. 17.50 (ISBN 0-8492-0890-4). R West.

Old Bill Williams, Mountain Man. 11.95 (ISBN 0-8061-0515-1). U of Okla Pr.

Old Burnside. 4.95 (ISBN 0-8131-0208-1). U Pr of Ky.

Old Friends & New Music. lib. bdg. 15.75x (ISBN 0-8371-7594-1, NAOF). Greenwood.

Old Guy Who Feels Good. pap. 4.50 (ISBN 0-914476-68-8). Thorp Springs.

Old Hickory: A Life of Andrew Jackson. 12.95 (ISBN 0-8037-6548-7). Dial.

Old Madam Yin: A Memoir of Peking Life. 8.95x (ISBN 0-8047-1038-4). Stanford U Pr.

Old Merchants of New York City. lib. bdg. 105.00x (ISBN 0-8371-0214-6, SCOM). Greenwood.

Old Rail Fence Corners: Frontier Tales Told by Minnesota Pioneers. 8.50 (ISBN 0-87351-108-5); pap. 4.50 (ISBN 0-87351-109-3). Minn Hist.

Oldenbarnevelt. 120.00 (ISBN 0-521-08429-6). Cambridge U Pr.

Oldest Biography of Spinoza. 8.00 (ISBN 0-8046-0854-7). Kennikat.

Ole Bull: A Memoir. 45.00 (ISBN 0-89341-112-4). Longwood Pr.

Ole Bull Returns to Pennsylvania: The Biography of a Norwegian Violin Virtuoso and Pioneer in the Keystone State. 5.00. Exposition.

Olga. pap. 2.95 (ISBN 0-448-23312-6). Paddington.

Olga Korbut. PLB 5.95 (ISBN 0-87191-384-4); pap. 2.75 (ISBN 0-89812-190-6). Creative Ed.

Olga Korbut: A Biographical Portrait. 6.95 (ISBN 0-385-09498-1). Doubleday.

Olga Worrall: Mystic with the Healing Hands. 7.95 (ISBN 0-06-061358-0). Har-Row.

Oliver Cromwell & the English People. facsimile ed. 10.00 (ISBN 0-8369-6674-0). Arno.

Oliver Cromwell & the Rule of the Puritans in England. 9.95 (ISBN 0-19-250536-X). Oxford U Pr.

Oliver Cromwell: Pretender, Puritan, Statesman, Paradox? pap. text ed. 5.50 (ISBN 0-88275-457-2). Krieger.

Oliver Evans: A Chronicle of Early American Engineering. 37.00 (ISBN 0-405-04684-7). Arno.

Oliver Goldsmith. lib. bdg. 20.00 (ISBN 0-8414-4185-5). Folcroft.

Oliver Goldsmith: Essays Towards an Interpretation. 9.25 (ISBN 0-8369-8199-5). Arno.

Oliver Wendell Holmes. lib. bdg. 15.00 (ISBN 0-8414-8612-3). Folcroft.

Oliver Wendell Holmes: An Appreciation. lib. bdg. 17.50 (ISBN 0-8414-7640-3). Folcroft.

Oliver Wendell Holmes: Poet, Litterateur, Scientist. lib. bdg. 35.00 (ISBN 0-8414-5514-7). Folcroft.

Olivia Newton-John. PLB 5.95 (ISBN -087191-475-1); pap. 2.75 (ISBN 0-89812-117-5). Creative Ed.

Olivia Newton-John. pap. 4.95 (ISBN 0-8256-3934-4). Music Sales.

Olivier. pap. 4.95 (ISBN 0-8128-1859-8). Stein & Day.

Olympics & Me. 6.95a (ISBN 0-385-14928-X); PLB (ISBN 0-385-14929-8). Doubleday.

Omar Khayyam As a Mystic. 6.50 (ISBN 0-8414-7503-2). Folcroft.

Omarr: Astrology & the Man. 8.95 (ISBN 0-385-04443-7). Doubleday.

Omarr: Astrology & the Man. pap. 1.95 (ISBN 0-451-07897-7, J7897). NAL.

Omar's Interpreter: A New Life of Edward Fitzgerald. lib. bdg. 25.00. Folcroft.

On Active Service in Peace & War. lib. bdg. 25.00 (ISBN 0-374-97627-9). Octagon.

On Alexander's Track in the Indus: Personal Narrative of the Explorations on the North-West Frontier of India. 22.00 (ISBN 0-405-08995-3). Arno.

On & Off the Fairway: A Pictorial Autobiography. 12.95 (ISBN 0-671-22568-5). S&S.

On Becoming American. 10.95 (ISBN 0-395-26283-6). HM.

On Becoming Carl Rogers. 12.95 (ISBN 0-440-06707-3). Delacorte.
On Being a Deacon's Wife. 4.50 (ISBN 0-8054-3505-0). Broadman.
On Being Funny: Woody Allen & Comedy. 8.95 (ISBN 0-88327-042-0). McKay.
On Eagles' Wings: The Personal Story of the Leading Commander of the Israeli Air Force. 8.95 (ISBN 0-02-625790-4, 62579). Macmillan.
On High Steel: The Education of an Ironworker. 7.95 (ISBN 0-8129-0470-2). Times Bks.
On High Steel: The Education of an Ironworker. pap. 1.50 (ISBN 0-345-24580-6). Ballantine.
On Press. 10.95 (ISBN 0-670-52456-5). Viking Pr.
On Press. pap. 2.75 (ISBN 0-425-04068-2). Berkley Pub.
On Sigmund Freud's Dreams. 19.95x (ISBN 0-8143-1351-5). Wayne St U Pr.
On Stage with John Denver. PLB 5.95 (ISBN 0-87191-483-2); pap. 2.95 (ISBN 0-89812-104-3). Creative Ed.
On the Air in World War II. 12.95 (ISBN 0-688-03558-2). Morrow.
On the Edges of the Time. lib. bdg. 18.75x (ISBN 0-313-20760-7, TAET). Greenwood.
On the Frontier with Mr. Audubon. 6.95 (ISBN 0-698-20385-2). Coward.
On the Other Side of Anger. pap. 2.95 (ISBN 0-8042-1047-0). John Knox.
On the Run from Dogs & People. pap. 6.95 (ISBN 0-914090-59-3). Chicago Review.
On the Run: In Search of the Perfect Race. 9.95 (ISBN 0-688-03405-5). Morrow.
On the Shoulders of Giants: Notable Names in Hand Surgery. 20.00 (ISBN 0-397-50357-1). Lippincott.
On the Track of the Mystery Animal: The Story of the Discovery of the Okapi. 6.95g (ISBN 0-590-07488-1). Schol Bk Serv.
On Watch: A Memoir. 12.95 (ISBN 0-8129-0520-2). Times Bks.
Once a Marine, Always a Marine. 6.95 (ISBN 0-517-53275-1). Crown.
Once a Pony Time. 5.95 (ISBN 0-8059-2148-6). Dorrance.
Once a Thief. pap. 0.95 (ISBN 0-8007-9007-3). Revell.
Once They Heard the Cheers. 12.95 (ISBN 0-385-12609-3). Doubleday.
Once Upon a Time & Today. 21.00 (ISBN 0-405-06113-7). Arno.
Once-Upon-a-Time Saints: Faith-Tales for Children. pap. 1.95 (ISBN 0-912228-37-7). St Anthony Mess Pr.
One & Only Bing. pap. 1.95 (ISBN 0-441-06233-4). Ace Bks.
One for the Record: The Inside Story of Hank Aaron's Chase for the Home-Run Record. 8.95 (ISBN 0-06-013373-2). Har-Row.
One Hundred Famous Americans. 32.25 (ISBN 0-8369-7286-4). Arno.
One "L". 8.95 (ISBN 0-399-11932-9). Putnam.
One Man & His Sea. 6.95 (ISBN 0-8038-5391-2). Hastings.
One Man's West. 14.95x (ISBN 0-8032-0908-8); pap. 3.95 (ISBN 0-8032-5855-0, 633). U of Nebr Pr.
One Special Summer. 7.95 (ISBN 0-440-06037-0). Delacorte.
One Way to Play Basketball. pap. 3.95 (ISBN 0-89293-080-2). Beta Bk.
One Woman's Liberation. o.p. 4.95 (ISBN 0-88419-113-3); pap. 1.75 (ISBN 0-88419-113-3). Creation Hse.
One Woman's Liberation. pap. 4.95 (ISBN 0-8407-5722-0). Nelson.
One Woman's "Situation" A Study of Mary Wollstonecraft. 6.50 (ISBN 0-252-00090-0). U of Ill Pr.
O'Neill. enl. ed. 25.00 (ISBN 0-06-011487-8); pap. 7.95 (ISBN 0-06-011484-3, TD-202). Har-Row.
O'Neill, Son & Playwright. 15.00 (ISBN 0-316-78335-8); pap. 5.25 (ISBN 0-316-78338-2). Little.
Only One Year. 12.50 (ISBN 0-06-010102-4). Har-Row.
Ooti. pap. 6.95 (ISBN 0-89087-213-9). Celestial Arts.
Opal. 6.95 (ISBN 0-02-513970-3). Macmillan.
Open Door Diplomat: The Life of W. W. Rockhill. lib. bdg. 12.25x (ISBN 0-8371-7858-4, VAOD). Greenwood.
Open Field. 7.95 (ISBN 0-395-19882-8). HM.
Open Hand: Essays on le Corbusier. text ed. 25.00x (ISBN 0-262-23074-7). MIT Pr.
Open Spaces: The Life of American Cities. pap. 9.95 (ISBN 0-06-090619-7, CN 619). Har-Row.
Open Spirit. pap. 3.95 (ISBN 0-8091-1856-4). Paulist Pr.
Ordeal of the Presidency. 6.00. Pub Aff Pr.
Ordeal of the Presidency. lib. bdg. 21.00x (ISBN 0-8371-6612-8, COOP). Greenwood.
Ordeal of Thomas Hutchinson. 15.00x (ISBN 0-674-64160-4); pap. 3.95 (ISBN 0-674-64161-2). Harvard U Pr.
Order of the Rose: The Life & Ideas of Christine de Pizan. 15.00x (ISBN 0-87471-810-4). Rowman.
Orestes A. Brownson. pap. 3.45 (ISBN 0-8084-0238-2, T88). Coll & U Pr.
Organs for America: The Life & Work of David Tannenberg. 9.95x (ISBN 0-8122-7000-2). U of Pa Pr.
Orie O. Miller: The Story of a Man & an Era. 7.95 (ISBN 0-8361-1613-5). Herald Pr.
Oscar Howe. 2nd ed. PLB 6.95 (ISBN 0-87518-043-4). Dillon.
Oscar Wilde: A Biography. 15.00 (ISBN 0-374-22747-0). FS&G.
Oscar Wilde: A Study. lib. bdg. 12.50. Folcroft.
Oscar Wilde: A Study. 65.00 (ISBN 0-87968-229-9). Gordon Pr.
Oscar Wilde: A Summing-up. lib. bdg. 25.00 (ISBN 0-8414-3815-3). Folcroft.
Oscar Wilde & Myself. 19.50 (ISBN 0-404-14026-2). AMS Pr.
Oscar Wilde & the Black Douglas. lib. bdg. 25.00 (ISBN 0-8414-6227-5). Folcroft.
Oscar Wilde, British Author, Poet & Wit. lib. bdg. 2.45 incl. catalog cards (ISBN 0-87157-541-8); pap. 1.25 vinyl laminated covers. SamHar Pr.
Oscar Wilde: The Aftermath. lib. bdg. 18.50x (ISBN 0-313-20084-X, HYOW). Greenwood.
Oscar Wilde: The Man, the Artist, the Martyr. lib. bdg. 20.00 (ISBN 0-374-90940-7). Octagon.
Osceola. PLB 6.95 (ISBN 0-87518-055-8). Dillon.
Osceola, Seminole Leader. 6.25 (ISBN 0-688-22054-1); PLB 6.00 (ISBN 0-688-32054-6). Morrow.
Osei Tutu & the Asante. pap. text ed. 1.95x (ISBN 0-435-94470-3). Heinemann Ed.
Osmonds: The Official Story of the Osmond Family. pap. 1.75 (ISBN 0-380-01717-2, 34066). Avon.
Oswald Garrison Villard, Liberal of the 1920's. lib. bdg. 20.25x (ISBN 0-8371-9752-X, HUOGV). Greenwood.
Other Edens: The Sketchbook of an Artist-Naturalist. 19.95 (ISBN 0-8159-6412-9). Devin.
Other Half: A Self-Portrait. 13.95 (ISBN 0-06-010774-X). Har-Row.
Other People's Children. 8.95 (ISBN 0-236-40117-3). Merrimack Bk Serv.
Other People's Letters: A Memoir. 9.95 (ISBN 0-395-26291-7). HM.
Other Samuel Johnson: A Psychohistory of Early New England. 16.50 (ISBN 0-8386-2059-0). Fairleigh Dickinson.
Other Shores. 8.95 (ISBN 0-394-50175-6). Random.
Other Side: Growing up Italian in America. 12.95 (ISBN 0-385-14733-3). Doubleday.
Otis Redding Story. 5.95 (ISBN 0-385-02335-9). Doubleday.
Otto Von Bismarck: A Historical Assessment. 2nd, new ed. pap. text ed. 4.25x (ISBN 0-669-82008-3). Heath.
Ottoline at Garsington: Memoirs of Lady Ottoline Morrell, 1915-1918. 12.95 (ISBN 0-394-49636-1). Knopf.
Our Appalachia: An Oral History. 12.95 (ISBN 0-8090-7462-1); pap. 6.95 (ISBN 0-8090-0126-8). Hill & Wang.
Our Basketball Lives. PLB 4.97 (ISBN 0-399-60792-7). Putnam.
Our Blood & Tears: Black Freedom Fighters. PLB 4.99 (ISBN 0-399-60717-X). Putnam.
Our Country's Presidents. 5th ed. 5.75, avail. only from Natl. Geog. (ISBN 0-87044-024-1). Natl Geog.
Our Foreign-Born Citizens. 6th ed. 9.95 (ISBN 0-690-60525-0). T Y Crowell.
Our Four Boys: Foster Parenting Retarded Teenagers. 11.95x (ISBN 0-8156-0146-8); pap. 6.95 (ISBN 0-8156-0155-7). Syracuse U Pr.
Our Friend James Joyce. 6.50 (ISBN 0-8446-1122-0). Peter Smith.
Our Friend, John Burroughs. 17.75 (ISBN 0-8274-1162-6). R West.
Our Friend, John Burroughs. lib. bdg. 23.95 (ISBN 0-8383-1169-5). Haskell.
Our Hearts Are Restless: The Prayer of St. Augustine. pap. 4.95 (ISBN 0-8164-2127-7). Seabury.
Our Heritage. pap. 5.95. Hope Farm.
Our Kate. 5.95 (ISBN 0-672-51618-7). Bobbs.
Our Miracle Called Louise: A Parent's Story. 8.95 (ISBN 0-448-22073-3). Paddington.
Our Runaway. pap. 2.95 (ISBN 0-8170-0813-6). Judson.
Out of My Bondage. 3.50 (ISBN 0-8054-5144-7). Broadman.
Out of My Later Years. pap. 4.95 (ISBN 0-8065-0357-2). Citadel Pr.
Out of My Later Years. lib. bdg. 15.50x (ISBN 0-8371-2086-1, EILY). Greenwood.
Out of This Century: Confessions of an Art Addict. 17.50 (ISBN 0-87663-337-8). Universe.
Out of This Century: Confessions of an Art Addict. pap. 7.95 (ISBN 0-385-17109-9). Doubleday.
Outer You...the Inner You. 5.95 (ISBN 0-8499-0055-7). Word Bks.
Outlaw: Bill Mitchell, Alias Baldy Russell: His Life & Times. 4.95 (ISBN 0-8040-0238-X). Swallow.
Outline of Lay Sanctity. pap. 2.95 (ISBN 0-87973-737-9). Our Sunday Visitor.
Outstanding Stories by General Authorities. 4.95 ea.; (ISBN 0-87747-369-2); (ISBN 0-87747-461-3); (ISBN 0-87747-492-3). Deseret Bk.
Outward Journey. new ed. text ed. 23.45 (ISBN 0-7081-0830-X). Bks Australia.
Over Forty: Feeling Great & Looking Good! pap. 2.95 (ISBN 0-671-25189-9). S&S.
Overcomers. 6.95 (ISBN 0-8007-0944-6). Revell.
Owl & the Rossettis: Letters of Charles A. Howell & Dante Gabriel, Christina, & William Michael Rossetti. 12.50 (ISBN 0-271-00530-0). Pa St U Pr.
Oxford Dictionary of Saints. 17.50 (ISBN 0-19-869120-3). Oxford U Pr.

P

P. G. T. Beauregard: Napoleon in Gray. 14.95 (ISBN 0-8071-0831-6). La State U Pr.
P. H. Emerson: The Fight for Photography As a Fine Art. 22.50 (ISBN 0-912334-58-4); pap. 15.00 (ISBN 0-912334-59-2). Aperture.
P. T. Barnum. new ed. PLB 4.29 (ISBN 0-399-61083-9). Putnam.
Pablita Velarde. PLB 6.95 (ISBN 0-87518-037-X). Dillon.
Pablo Casals. rev. ed. lib. bdg. 11.75x (ISBN 0-8371-3010-7, LIPC). Greenwood.
Pablo Morillo & Venezuela, 1815-1820. 13.00 (ISBN 0-8142-0219-5). Ohio St U Pr.
Pablo Picasso. 6.95 (ISBN 0-385-04924-2); PLB (ISBN 0-385-05115-8). Doubleday.
Pacifying the Plains: General Alfred Terry & the Decline of the Sioux, 1866-1890. lib. bdg. 18.95 (ISBN 0-313-20625-2, BAT/). Greenwood.
Paderewski. 4.95 (ISBN 0-670-53416-1). Viking Pr.
Padre Martinez & Bishop Lamy. 9.95 (ISBN 0-932906-01-X); pap. 6.95 (ISBN 0-932906-00-1). Pan-Am Publishing Co.
Padre on Horseback. 3.00 (ISBN 0-8294-0003-6). Loyola.
Padre Pio. 9.500 (ISBN 0-227-67557-6). Attic Pr.
Padre Pio. pap. 4.95 (ISBN 0-87973-856-1). Our Sunday Visitor.
Paganini. lib. bdg. 15.00x (ISBN 0-8371-4013-7, SAPA). Greenwood.
Page by Page. 14.95 (ISBN 0-87127-102-8). Dance Horiz.
Pageant of English Actors. 20.00. Norwood Edns.
Pageant of English Actors. 18.25 (ISBN 0-8369-8116-2). Arno.
Pageant of English Actors. 14.00 (ISBN 0-8274-3095-7). R West.
Pages from a Journal. 7.95 (ISBN 0-89080-006-5). Mercer Hse.
Pages from a Musician's Life. 11.00 (ISBN 0-403-01519-7). Scholarly.
Pages from a Musician's Life. lib. bdg. 11.75x (ISBN 0-8371-3445-5, BUML). Greenwood.
Pages from an Oxford Diary. 7.00 (ISBN 0-8046-1638-8). Kennikat.
Paine. 15.00 (ISBN 0-06-011784-2). Har-Row.
Painful Labour of Mr. Elsyng. pap. 1.00 (ISBN 0-87169-628-2). Am Philos.
Palaces & Prisons. 7.95 (ISBN 0-395-24671-7). HM.
Palestrina. 32.00 (ISBN 0-404-12878-5). AMS Pr.
Palestrina. 22.50 (ISBN 0-88355-732-0). Hyperion Conn.
Pan Bread 'n Jerky. pap. 3.95 (ISBN 0-87004-150-9). Caxton.
Pancho Gonzales. 5.50 (ISBN 0-87191-341-0). Creative Ed.
Pancho Villa: Intimate Recollections by People Who Knew Him. 12.95 (ISBN 0-8038-5819-1). Hastings.
Panhandle Pioneer: Henry C. Hitch, His Ranch, & His Family. 9.75 (ISBN 0-8061-1529-7). U of Okla Pr.
Pantarch: A Biography of Stephen Pearl Andrews. 9.95 (ISBN 0-292-73210-4). U of Tex Pr.
Papa: A Personal Memoir. 7.95 (ISBN 0-395-24348-3). HM.
Papa Hemingway in Key West. pap. 0.95 (ISBN 0-445-00520-3). Popular Lib.
Paper House. 6.95 (ISBN 0-374-22978-3). FS&G.
Paper Lion. pap. 1.95 (ISBN 0-451-07668-0, J7668). NAL.
Papers & Addresses. facs. ed. 15.25 (ISBN 0-8369-0439-7). Arno.
Papillon. 9.95 (ISBN 0-688-02269-3). Morrow.
Papillon. pap. 2.75 (ISBN 0-671-78528-1). PB.
Pappy: The Life of John Ford. 12.95 (ISBN 0-13-648493-X). P-H.
Papua New Guinea Portraits: The Expatriate Experience. text ed. 24.95 (ISBN 0-7081-0232-8, 0410); pap. text ed. 13.95 (ISBN 0-7081-1149-1). Bks Australia.
Paradox of George Orwell. pap. 1.95 (ISBN 0-911198-00-8). Purdue.
Paradox of Oscar Wilde. 20.00 (ISBN 0-8274-3100-7). R West.
Paradox of Pancho Villa. 10.00 (ISBN 0-87404-059-0). Tex Western.
Parson Pettigrew of the "Old Church" 1744-1807. pap. 4.50x (ISBN 0-8078-5052-7). U of NC Pr.
Part of My Life. pap. 5.95 (ISBN 0-19-281245-9, BG558). Oxford U Pr.
Part of My Life: The Memoirs of a Philosopher. 14.95 (ISBN 0-15-170973-4). HarBraceJ.
Part of the Solution: Portrait of a Revolutionary. pap. 2.95 (ISBN 0-8112-0471-5, NDP350). New Directions.
Part Taken by Women in American History. 41.00 (ISBN 0-405-04467-4). Arno.
Particularly Cats. pap. 3.95. S&S.
Particularly Cats. pap. 0.95 (ISBN 0-451-04842-3, Q4842). NAL.
Particulars of My Life. 10.00 (ISBN 0-394-40071-2). Knopf.
Partners in Progress. facs. ed. 13.50 (ISBN 0-8369-0518-0). Arno.
Pascal, the Life of Genius. lib. bdg. 24.00x (ISBN 0-8371-0021-6, BILG). Greenwood.
Pascin. 6.95 (ISBN 0-517-09890-3). Crown.
Passage to Power: K'ang-Hsi & His Heir Apparent, 1661-1722. text ed. 22.50x (ISBN 0-674-65625-3). Harvard U Pr.
Passion for Cars. 2.95 (ISBN 0-684-14974-5). Scribner.
Passion for Equality: George Wiley & the Movement. 8.95 (ISBN 0-393-07517-6). Norton.
Passion of Fulton Sheen. 6.95 (ISBN 0-396-06438-8). Dodd.
Passionate Crusader: The Life of Marie Stopes. 14.95 (ISBN 0-15-171288-3). HarBraceJ.
Passionate Exiles: Madame de Stael & Madame Recamier. 19.75 (ISBN 0-8369-8086-7). Arno.
Passionate Eye: The Life of William R. Valentiner. 19.95x (ISBN 0-8143-1631-X). Wayne St U Pr.
Passionate Prodigality: Letters to Alan Bird from Richard Aldington, 1949-1962. 15.00 (ISBN 0-87104-259-2). NY Pub Lib.
Passionate Years. pap. 6.95 (ISBN 0-912946-66-0). Ecco Pr.
Passion's Child: The Extraordinary Life of Jane Digby. 12.50 (ISBN 0-06-013807-6). Har-Row.
Past Masters: Politics & Politicians 1906-1939. 15.00 (ISBN 0-06-012814-3). Har-Row.
Pastmasters: Some Essays on American Historians. 6.50 (ISBN 0-8446-5174-5). Peter Smith.
Pastmasters: Some Essays on American Historians. lib. bdg. 29.75x (ISBN 0-313-20938-3, CUPA). Greenwood.
Pat Haden: My Rookie Season with Los Angeles Rams. 8.95 (ISBN 0-688-03224-9). Morrow.
Pat Harrison: The New Deal Years. 15.00 (ISBN 0-87805-076-0). U Pr of Miss.
Pat Nixon of Texas: Autobiography of a Doctor. 13.50 (ISBN 0-89096-072-0). Tex A&M Univ Pr.
Paterna: The Autobiography of Cotton Mather. lib. bdg. 50.00x (ISBN 0-8201-1273-9). Schol Facsimiles.
Path: Autobiography of a Western Yogi. 12.50 (ISBN 0-916124-11-8). Ananda.
Path Breaking: An Autobiographical History of the Equal Suffrage Movement in the Pacific Coast States. 2nd ed. pap. 4.50 (ISBN 0-8052-0322-2). Schocken.
Path Through the Trees. 10.95 (ISBN 0-525-17630-6). Dutton.
Patients Are People Like Us: The Experiences of Half a Century in Neuropsychiatry. 10.95 (ISBN 0-688-03271-0). Morrow.
Patrician Democrat: The Political Life of Charles Cowper 1843-1870. 17.00 (ISBN 0-522-84132-5). Intl Schol Bk Serv.
Patrick Ford & His Search for America: A Case Study of Irish-American Journalism, 1870-1913. 20.00 (ISBN 0-405-09354-3). Arno.
Patrick Henry. 34.95 (ISBN 0-8490-0806-9). Gordon Pr.
Patrick Henry. 13.95. Norwood Edns.
Patrick Henry. 14.00 (ISBN 0-404-50853-7). AMS Pr.
Patrick Henry. text ed. 29.00 (ISBN 0-8337-3587-X). B Franklin.
Patrick Henry. pap. 3.95 (ISBN 0-8014-9094-4, CP94). Cornell U Pr.
Patrick Henry: A Biography. 13.50 (ISBN 0-07-004280-2). McGraw.
Patrick Henry, Life Correspondence & Speeches. lib. bdg. 87.00 (ISBN 0-8337-1662-X). B Franklin.
Patrick Pearse: The Triumph of Failure. 14.95 (ISBN 0-8008-6267-8). Taplinger.
Patriots in Petticoats. 4.95 (ISBN 0-396-07292-5). Dodd.

Patriots off Their Pedestals. 14.50 (ISBN 0-8369-1738-3). Arno.

Patriots: The American Revolution, Generation of Genius. 14.95 (ISBN 0-689-10690-4). Atheneum.

Patterns & Coincidences: A Sequel to "All Is But a Beginning". 9.50x (ISBN 0-8262-0233-0). U of Mo Pr.

Patton. pap. 2.50 (ISBN 0-345-24986-0). Ballantine.

Patton: A Study in Command. 8.95 (ISBN 0-684-13671-6); pap. text ed. 3.95 (ISBN 0-684-14692-4, SL660). Scribner.

Patton: Ordeal & Triumph. pap. 2.50 (ISBN 0-440-16853-8). Dell.

Patton: Ordeal & Triumph. 19.95 (ISBN 0-8392-1084-1). Astor-Honor.

Paul. pap. 4.50 (ISBN 0-664-24234-0). Westminster.

Paul: A Study in Social & Religious History. 8.50 (ISBN 0-8446-1965-5). Peter Smith.

Paul Claudel: The Man & the Mystic. lib. bdg. 21.00x (ISBN 0-313-20465-9, CHCL). Greenwood.

Paul Cuffe & the African Promised Land. 6.95 (ISBN 0-8407-6521-5). Elsevier-Nelson.

Paul Green. lib. bdg. 10.95 (ISBN 0-8383-2016-3). Haskell.

Paul Hamilton Hayne. lib. bdg. 7.95 (ISBN 0-8057-0352-7). Twayne.

Paul Klee. 6.95 (ISBN 0-385-04916-1); PLB (ISBN 0-385-05113-1). Doubleday.

Paul Martin: Victorian Photographer. 24.95 (ISBN 0-292-76436-7). U of Tex Pr.

Paul Revere & the World He Lived In. 12.95 (ISBN 0-395-07695-1). HM.

Paul Revere & the World He Lived In. pap. 4.95 (ISBN 0-395-08370-2, 21). HM.

Paul Robeson. PLB 6.89 (ISBN 0-690-00660-8). T Y Crowell.

Paul Robeson Rediscovered. 1.00. Am Inst Marxist.

Paul Robeson: The Life & Times of a Free Black Man. pap. 1.50 (ISBN 0-440-96806-2). Dell.

Paul Robeson: The Life & Times of a Free Black Man. 7.95 (ISBN 0-06-022188-7); PLB 7.89 (ISBN 0-06-022189-5). Har-Row.

Paul Rosenfeld, Voyager in the Arts. lib. bdg. 14.50 (ISBN 0-374-95561-1). Octagon.

Paul the Traveller. 9.95 (ISBN 0-02-514390-5, 51439). Macmillan.

Pauline Johnson. PLB 6.95 (ISBN 0-87518-156-2). Dillon.

Pavlov: A Biography. 12.50x (ISBN 0-226-03372-4). U of Chicago Pr.

Pavlov: A Biography. pap. 4.25 (ISBN 0-226-03373-2, P621). U of Chicago Pr.

Pawnee Bill: A Biography of Major Gordon W. Lillie. pap. 2.95 (ISBN 0-8032-5185-8, 331). U of Nebr Pr.

Payday Everyday. 4.95 (ISBN 0-8054-5548-5). Broadman.

Payne Hollow: Life on the Fringe of Society. 6.95 (ISBN 0-690-01023-0); pap. 3.95 (ISBN 0-690-01024-9). T Y Crowell.

Peace Chiefs of the Cheyennes. 14.95 (ISBN 0-8061-1573-4). U of Okla Pr.

Peculiar Treasures: A Biblical Who's Who. 7.95 (ISBN 0-06-061157-X). Har-Row.

Pedro De Valdivia, Conqueror of Chile. lib. bdg. 14.25x (ISBN 0-8371-7454-6, GRPV). Greenwood.

Pedro De Valdivia, Conqueror of Chile. lib. bdg. 25.00 (ISBN 0-89341-281-3). Longwood Pr.

Pedro Menendez de Aviles & the Founding of St. Augustine. 4.95 (ISBN 0-02-837740-0, 83774). Kenedy.

Peel. 17.50x (ISBN 0-582-48083-3). Longman.

Peel. pap. text ed. 11.95 (ISBN 0-582-48599-1). Longman.

Peel. 13.50 (ISBN 0-8369-6815-8). Arno.

Peerless Leader, William Jennings Bryan. 10.00 (ISBN 0-8462-0983-7). Russell.

Peggy Fleming. PLB 5.95 (ISBN 0-87191-380-1); pap. 2.75 (ISBN 0-89812-192-2). Creative Ed.

Pegler, Angry Man of the Press. lib. bdg. 16.75x (ISBN 0-8371-6838-4, PIPE). Greenwood.

PEIG: The Autobiography of Peig Sayers of the Great Blasket Island. 7.95 (ISBN 0-8156-0106-9). Syracuse U Pr.

Pele. 6.95 (ISBN 0-689-10713-7). Atheneum.

Pele' PLB 5.95 (ISBN 0-87191-513-8); pap. 2.75 (ISBN 0-89812-193-0). Creative Ed.

Pele. 10.00 (ISBN 0-06-014254-5). Har-Row.

Pele: A Biography. 6.95 (ISBN 0-385-11565-2). Doubleday.

Pele, the King of Soccer. pap. 0.95 (ISBN 0-440-96944-1). Dell.

Pele's New World. 8.95 (ISBN 0-393-08758-1). Norton.

Pen & Politics: The Autobiography of a Working Writer. 5.00. McClain.

Pend Oreille Profiles. 14.95 (ISBN 0-87770-185-7). Ye Galleon.

Penguin Dictionary of Saints. pap. 3.95 (ISBN 0-14-051030-3, R30). Penguin.

Penitent. 3.95. Chr Classics.

People & Places in the Texas Past. new ed. 13.95 (ISBN 0-912854-05-7). GLA Pr.

People Called Quakers. facsimile ed. 12.75 (ISBN 0-8369-1254-3). Arno.

People Just Like Us. pap. 4.95 (ISBN 0-8024-6459-9). Moody.

People of Plains, Ga. pap. 7.95 (ISBN 0-07-006535-7). McGraw.

People's Pope: The Story of Karol Wojtyla of Poland. pap. 7.95 (ISBN 0-87701-159-1). Chronicle Bks.

Percy Bysshe Shelley. pap. 4.95 (ISBN 0-312-60060-7). St Martin.

Percy Bysshe Shelley. lib. bdg. 8.50 (ISBN 0-8057-1488-X). Twayne.

Percy Grainger. 21.95 (ISBN 0-236-40004-5). Merrimack Bk Serv.

Percy Grainger: The Inveterate Innovator. 8.95. Instrumental Co.

Peretz. 21.25 (ISBN 0-8369-8137-5). Arno.

Perfect Balance: The Story of an Elite Gymnast. 8.95 (ISBN 0-399-20661-2). Putnam.

Perfect Joy of St. Francis. 2.50 (ISBN 0-385-02378-2). Doubleday.

Perils & Prospects of Southern Black Leadership: Gordon Blaine Hancock, 1884-1970. 11.75 (ISBN 0-8223-0381-7). Duke.

Period Piece. pap. 3.95 (ISBN 0-393-00822-3). Norton.

Period Piece. 10.95 (ISBN 0-571-03501-9). Merrimack Bk Serv.

Period Piece. pap. 4.95 (ISBN 0-571-06742-5). Merrimack Bk Serv.

Perish the Thought: Intellectual Women in Romantic America, 1830-1860. 13.95 (ISBN 0-19-501995-4). Oxford U Pr.

Perish the Thought: Intellectual Women in Romantic America 1830-1860. pap. 5.95 (ISBN 0-8065-0650-4). Citadel Pr.

Peroff: The Man Who Knew Too Much. 8.95 (ISBN 0-688-02934-5). Morrow.

Peroff: The Man Who Knew Too Much. pap. 1.95 (ISBN 0-345-25104-0). Ballantine.

Persecution of Peter Olivi. pap. 6.00 (ISBN 0-87169-665-7). Am Philos.

Persecutor. pap. 1.50. Chr Classics.

Persecutor. pap. 1.95 spire bk. (ISBN 0-8007-8177-5). Revell.

Persian Corridor: The Little-Known Story of the Signal Corps in the Middle East During World War II. 9.50 (ISBN 0-682-49337-6). Exposition.

Personal & Controversial: An Autobiography. 7.95 (ISBN 0-8070-0514-2). Beacon Pr.

Personal & Professional Recollections. lib. bdg. 27.50 (ISBN 0-306-70873-6). Da Capo.

Personal Aspects of Jane Austen. lib. bdg. 20.00 (ISBN 0-8414-2972-3). Folcroft.

Personal Aspects of Jane Austen. lib. bdg. 20.00 (ISBN 0-8495-0057-5). Arden Lib.

Personal Book. 8.95 (ISBN 0 06-013588-3). Har-Row.

Personal Country. 12.95 (ISBN 0-89096-077-1). Tex A&M Univ Pr.

Personal Memoirs & Recollections of Editorial Life. 20.00 (ISBN 0-405-01657-3). Arno.

Personal Memoirs of a Residence of Thirty Years with the Indian Tribes on the American Frontiers. 1812-1842. facsimile ed. 41.00x (ISBN 0-405-06885-9). Arno.

Personal Memoirs of a Residence of Thirty Years with the Indian Tribes on the American Frontiers: With Brief Notices of Passing Events, Facts & Opinions, A.D. 1812 to A.D. 1842. 37.50 (ISBN 0-404-11899-2). AMS Pr.

Personal Memories, Social, Political & Literary. 24.00 (ISBN 0-405-01688-3). Arno.

Personal Recollections & Observations of General Nelson A. Miles. rev. ed. 42.50 (ISBN 0-306-71020-X). Da Capo.

Personal Recollections, from Early Life to Old Age, of Mary Somerville. 19.00 (ISBN 0-404-56837-8). AMS Pr.

Personal Recollections of Lamb, Hazlitt, & Others. lib. bdg. 30.00 (ISBN 0-8492-2584-1). R West.

Personal Recollections of Nathaniel Hawthorne. 10.75 (ISBN 0-8274-1362-9). R West.

Personal Recollections of Nathaniel Hawthorne. lib. bdg. 19.95 (ISBN 0-8383-0916-X). Haskell.

Personal Recollections of Thomas De Quincey. lib. bdg. 15.00 (ISBN 0-8414-4155-3). Folcroft.

Personal Reminiscences of a Great Crusade. 18.00 (ISBN 0-88355-257-4). Hyperion Conn.

Personal Reminiscences of Henry Irving. lib. bdg. 32.25x (ISBN 0-8371-2845-5, STHI). Greenwood.

Personal Sketches of Recent Authors. 19.00 (ISBN 0-8274-0031-4). R West.

Personal Vision of Ingmar Bergman. 18.25 (ISBN 0-8369-8119-7). Arno.

Personalities in American Art. 10.00 (ISBN 0-8369-1582-8). Arno.

Personalities of the Eighteenth Century. lib. bdg. 22.50 (ISBN 0-8414-0316-3). Folcroft.

Personality of Chaucer. 7.95x (ISBN 0-8061-0775-8). U of Okla Pr.

Personality of Emerson. lib. bdg. 9.75 (ISBN 0-8414-7590-3). Folcroft.

Personality of Emerson. lib. bdg. 18.95 (ISBN 0-8383-1290-X). Haskell.

Personality of Milton. 8.95x (ISBN 0-8061-0916-5). U of Okla Pr.

Personality of Shakespeare. 8.95x (ISBN 0-8061-1028-7). U of Okla Pr.

Personality of Shakespeare. pap. 4.95 (ISBN 0-8061-1597-1). U of Okla Pr.

Personality of Shakespeare: A Venture in Psychological Method. 11.00 (ISBN 0-8046-1700-7). Kennikat.

Persons of Consequence: Queen Victoria & Her Circle. 17.95 (ISBN 0-394-50427-5). Random.

Perspectives in Quantum Theory. pap. 5.00 (ISBN 0-486-63778-6). Dover.

Pestalozzi: The Man & His Work. 11.50x (ISBN 0-8052-3521-3). Schocken.

Pete Maravich. PLB 5.95 (ISBN 0-87191-669-X); pap. 2.75 (ISBN 0-89812-183-3). Creative Ed.

Pete Rose. PLB 3.69 (ISBN 0-394-93026-6). Random.

Pete Rose: My Life in Baseball. 6.95 (ISBN 0-385-13639-0); PLB (ISBN 0-385-13640-4). Doubleday.

Pete: The Story of Peter V. Cacchione, New York's First Communist Councilman. 10.00 (ISBN 0-7178-0482-8); pap. 3.50 (ISBN 0-7178-0473-9). Intl Pub Co.

Peter Abelard. facsimile ed. 16.50 (ISBN 0-8369-5655-9). Arno.

Peter Cooper. 10.00 (ISBN 0-8369-6835-2). Arno.

Peter Frampton. pap. 4.95 (ISBN 0-8256-3933-6). Music Sales.

Peter Frampton. pap. 1.95 (ISBN 0-448-17026-4). G&D.

Peter Pitseolak's Escape from Death. 7.95 (ISBN 0-440-06894-0); PLB 7.45 (ISBN 0-440-06896-7). Delacorte.

Peter Porcupine in America: Career of William Cobbett 1792-1800. lib. bdg. 10.00 (ISBN 0-8414-3512-X). Folcroft.

Peter Porcupine in America: The Career of William Cobbett. 11.00x (ISBN 0-8464-0026-X). Beekman Pubs

Peter Porcupine in America: The Career of William Cobbett, 1792-1800. lib. bdg. 25.00 (ISBN 0-8495-0830-4). Arden Lib.

Peter Skene Ogden & the Hudson's Bay Company. 12.50 (ISBN 0-8061-1073-2). U of Okla Pr.

Peter Skene Ogden & the Hudson's Bay Company. pap. 6.95 (ISBN 0-8061-1595-5). U of Okla Pr.

Peter Skene Ogden, Fur Trader. 7.95 (ISBN 0-8323-0054-3). Binford.

Peter the Great. 29.00 (ISBN 0-403-01258-9). Scholarly.

Peter the Great. lib. bdg. 31.95 (ISBN 0-8383-0265-3). Haskell.

Peter the Great. lib. bdg. 18.00x (ISBN 0-8371-0734-2, WAPG). Greenwood.

Peter the Great Changes Russia. 2nd ed. pap. text ed. 4.25x (ISBN 0-669-82701-0). Heath.

Peter, the Revolutionary Tsar. PLB 8.79 (ISBN 0-06-024780-0). Har-Row.

Peter Voulkos: A Dialogue with Clay. 27.50 (ISBN 0-8212-0712-1). NYGS.

Peter's People. lib. bdg. 8.95 (ISBN 0-688-03488-8). Morrow.

Petr Thaohev, the Critic As Jacobin. 12.50 (ISBN 0-295-95547-3). U of Wash Pr.

Petrarch & His World. 15.00 (ISBN 0-8046-1730-9). Kennikat.

Petrarch's Eight Years in Milan. 12.00 (ISBN 0-910956-43-X). Mediaeval Acad.

Phaidon Encyclopedia of Art & Artists. 35.00 (ISBN 0-7148-1513-6). Dutton.

Phaidon Encyclopedia of Impressionism. 14.95 (ISBN 0-7148-1897-6); pap. 8.95 (ISBN 0-7148-1911-5). Dutton.

Pharisee Among Philistines: The Diary of Judge Matthew P. Deady, 1871-1892. 27.95 (ISBN 0-87595-046-9); deluxe ed. 30.00 (ISBN 0-87595-046-9); pap. 21.95 (ISBN 0-87595-080-9). Oreg Hist Soc.

Philadelphia Merchant: The Diary of Thomas P. Cope, 1800-1851. 19.95 (ISBN 0-89526-689-X). Regnery-Gateway.

Philadelphia's First Fuel Crisis: Jacob Cist & the Developing Market for Pennsylvania Anthracite. 10.00x (ISBN 0-271-00533-5). Pa St U Pr.

Philanthropic Work of Josephine Shaw Lowell, Containing a Biographical Sketch of Her Life Together with a Selection of Her Public Papers & Private Letters. 17.50 (ISBN 0-87585-163-0). Patterson Smith.

Philip Barry. pap. 3.45 (ISBN 0-8084-0243-9, T78). Coll & U Pr.

Philip Freneau. lib. bdg. 8.95 (ISBN 0-8057-7161-1). Twayne.

Philip Mironov & the Russian Civil War. 15.00 (ISBN 0-394-40681-8). Knopf.

Philip of Macedon. 19.95. Merrimack Bk Serv.

Philip: Traveling Preacher. 3.95 (ISBN 0-8054-4241-3). Broadman.

Philippe, Duke of Orleans: Regent of France, 1715-1723. 16.95 (ISBN 0-500-87009-8). Thames Hudson.

Philippe Pinel et Son Oeuvre Au Point De Vue De la Medecine Mentale. 10.00x (ISBN 0-405-07454-9). Arno.

Philippe Pinel, Unchainer of the Insane. PLB 5.90 (ISBN 0-531-00915-7). Watts.

Philippine Pagans: The Autobiographies of Three Ifugaos. 24.50 (ISBN 0-404-15903-6). AMS Pr.

Phillis Wheatley: America's First Black Poetess. PLB 4.78 (ISBN 0-8116-4569-X). Garrard.

Philosopher at Large: An Intellectual Autobiography. 12.95 (ISBN 0-02-500490-5, 50049). Macmillan.

Philosophers in Action. text ed. 10.95 (ISBN 0-675-08490-3). Merrill.

Photographer of a Frontier: The Photographs of Peter Britt. 20.95 (ISBN 0-915580-05-5). Interface Calif.

Photographer of the World: A Biography of Herbert Ponting. 10.00 (ISBN 0-8386-7959-5). Fairleigh Dickinson.

Photographing History: The Career of Mathew Brady. 8.95 (ISBN 0-399-20602-7). Putnam.

Photographing the Frontier. 9.95 (ISBN 0-399-20694-9). Putnam.

Photojournalist: The Career of Jimmy Hare. 12.95 (ISBN 0-292-74004-2). U of Tex Pr.

Physician Signers of the Declaration of Independence. 14.95 (ISBN 0-88202-159-1). N Watson.

Physics, Patents & Politics: A Biography of Charles Grafton Page. 18.00 (ISBN 0-88202-046-3). N Watson.

P'I Jih-Hsiu. lib. bdg. 13.95 (ISBN 0-8057-6372-4). Twayne.

Pianist's Progress. 8.95 (ISBN 0-690-01761-8). T Y Crowell.

Picasso: Artist of the Century. 50.00 (ISBN 0-8478-0090-3). Rizzoli Intl.

Picasso: His Life & Work. rev ed. pap 6.95 (ISBN 0-06-430016-1, IN-16). Har-Row.

Pictorial Autobiography. rev. ed. text ed. 10.00x (ISBN 0-239-00179-6). Humanities.

Pictorial History of American Presidents. 17.50 (ISBN 0 498-02011-8). A S Barnes.

Pictorial Life of Jack London. 14.95 (ISBN 0-517-53163-1). Crown.

Picture Life of Bobby Orr. PLB 4.90 (ISBN 0-531-01208-5). Watts.

Picture Life of Herman Badillo. PLB 4.90 (ISBN 0-531-00985-8). Watts.

Picture Life of Jesse Jackson. PLB 4.90 (ISBN 0-531-00986-6). Watts.

Picture Life of Malcolm X. PLB 4.90 (ISBN 0-531-02771-6). Watts.

Picture Life of Muhammad Ali. PLB 4.90 (ISBN 0-531-00327-2). Watts.

Picture Life of O. J. Simpson. PLB 4.90 s&l (ISBN 0-531-01270-0). Watts.

Picture Life of Reggie Jackson. pap. 1.25 (ISBN 0-380-40345-5, 40345). Avon.

Picture Life of Stevie Wonder. PLB 4.90 s&l (ISBN 0-531-01271-9). Watts.

Picture Life of Thurgood Marshall. PLB 4.90 (ISBN 0-531-00984-X). Watts.

Picture of Persia. 15.00 (ISBN 0-682-48410-5). Exposition.

Picture Story of Frank Robinson. pap. 1.25 (ISBN 0-671-29806-2). Archway.

Picture Story of Hank Aaron. PLB 5.79 (ISBN 0-671-32672-4). Messner.

Picture Story of Jockey Steve Cauthen. PLB 6.97 (ISBN 0-671-32990-1). Messner.

Picture Story of Nadia Comaneci. PLB 6.97 (ISBN 0-671-32925-1). Messner.

Picture Story of Reggie Jackson. 6.97 (ISBN 0-671-32913-8). Messner.

Picture Story of Terry Bradshaw. PLB 6.97 (ISBN 0-671-32867-0). Messner.

Picture Story of Walt Frazier. PLB 5.79 (ISBN 0-671-32773-9). Messner.

Pictures Will Talk: The Life & Films of Joseph L. Mankiewicz. 12.95 (ISBN 0-684-15500-1). Scribner.

Piece of the Power: Four Black Mayors. 5.95 (ISBN 0-8037-6973-3). Dial.

Pierre-Gibault, Missionary, 1737-1802. 8.00 (ISBN 0-8294-0203-9). Loyola.

Pierre Leroux & the Birth of Democratic Socialism. lib. bdg. 39.95. Revisionist Pr.

Pierre Loti. lib. bdg. 8.95 (ISBN 0-8057-2546-6). Twayne.

Piet Mondrian's Early Career: The Naturalistic Periods. lib. bdg. 51.00x (ISBN 0-8240-2738-8). Garland Pub.

Pike in Colorado. 10.95 (ISBN 0-88342-058-9); pap. 3.95 (ISBN 0-88342-241-7). Old Army.

Pilgrimage: Adventures of a Wandering Jew. 12.95 (ISBN 0-395-27620-9). HM.

Pilgrimage of Passion: The Life of Wilfrid Scawen Blunt. 15.95 (ISBN 0-394-50944-7). Knopf.

Pilgrimage to the Holy Land. 40.00x (ISBN 0-8201-1323-9). Schol Facsimiles.

Pilgrim's Way: An Essay in Recollection. 32.50 (ISBN 0-404-15278-3). AMS Pr.

Pillars of the Church. 14.75 (ISBN 0-8369-1940-8). Arno.

Pills, Pen & Politics: The Story of General Leon Jastremski. 6.95 (ISBN 0-9600814-1-0). Cptn Stanislaus.
Pilot for Spaceship Earth: R. Buckminster Fuller, Architect, Inventor & Poet. 7.95 (ISBN 0-02-761420-4, 76142). Macmillan.
Pioneer Bush Pilot: The Story of Noel Wien. 12.95 (ISBN 0-295-95339-X). U of Wash Pr.
Pioneer Decoy Carvers: A Biography of Lemuel & Stephen Ward. 17.50 (ISBN 0-87033-243-0). Cornell Maritime.
Pioneer in Modern Medicine: David Linn Edsall of Harvard. 15.00x (ISBN 0-674-66875-8). Harvard U Pr.
Pioneer in the Florida Keys: The Life & Times of Del Layton. 9.95 (ISBN 0-912458-79-8). E A Seemann.
Pioneer Leaders & Early Institutions in Louisiana Education. 7.95x. Claitors.
Pioneer of Sociology: The Life & Letters of Patrick Geddes. 21.00 (ISBN 0-88355-859-9). Hyperion Conn.
Pioneer Prophetess: Jemima Wilkinson, the Publick Universal Friend. 11.50x (ISBN 0-8014-0459-2). Cornell U Pr.
Pioneer Women of the West. 20.50 (ISBN 0-8369-8157-X). Arno.
Pioneer Women of the West. lib. bdg. 45.00 (ISBN 0-89341-325-9). Longwood Pr.
Pioneering in Montana: The Making of a State 1864-1887. 12.50x (ISBN 0-8032-0933-9); pap. 3.50 (ISBN 0-8032-5870-4, 648). U of Nebr Pr.
Pioneering Role of Clarence Luther Herrick in American Neuroscience. 7.50 (ISBN 0-682-49340-6). Exposition.
Pioneers in Policing. 15.00x (ISBN 0-87585-213-0); pap. 6.75x (ISBN 0-87585-803-1). Patterson Smith.
Pioneers in Protest. 5.95 (ISBN 0-87485-026-6). Johnson Chi.
Pioneers in the Arab World. pap. 3.95 (ISBN 0-8028-1585-5). Eerdmans.
Pioneer's Mission: The Story of Lyman Copeland Draper. 15.25x (ISBN 0-8371-2881-1, HEPM). Greenwood.
Pioneers of Baseball. 7.95 (ISBN 0-316-80156-9). Little.
Pioneers of Criminology. 2nd, enl. ed. 16.50 (ISBN 0-87585-121-5); pap. 9.50 (ISBN 0-87585-902-X). Patterson Smith.
Pioneers of Electrical Communication. facs. ed. 18.50 (ISBN 0-8369-0156-8). Arno.
Pioneers of Freedom. facs. ed. 12.75 (ISBN 0-8369-0326-9). Arno.
Pioneers of Plant Study. facs. ed. 14.50 (ISBN 0-8369-1139-3). Arno.
Pioneers of Public Health: The Story of Some Benefactors of the Human Race. facs. ed. 15.00 (ISBN 0-8369-0965-8). Arno.
Pioneers of the Unseen. 6.50 (ISBN 0-8008-6310-0). Taplinger.
Pirate Lafitte & the Battle of New Orleans. PLB 4.39 (ISBN 0-394-90319-6). Random.
Pistol Pete - Veteran of the Old West. text ed. 14.95 (ISBN 0-934188-01-7). Evans Pubns.
Pistol Pete Maravich: The Louisiana Purchase. 5.95 (ISBN 0-87397-056-X). Strode.
Pitchers. PLB 7.50 (ISBN 0-87191-518-9). Creative Ed.
Pitcher's Story. 5.95 (ISBN 0-385-08502-8). Doubleday.
Pitt. lib. bdg. 16.95 (ISBN 0-8383-0236-X). Haskell.
Pitt. 12.00 (ISBN 0-404-05405-6). AMS Pr.
Pitt. lib. bdg. 12.50x (ISBN 0-8371-1968-5, ROPI). Greenwood.
Pittsburgh Steelers. 8.95 (ISBN 0-02-589000-X). Macmillan.
Pity the Poor Rich. 9.95 (ISBN 0-8092-8198-8). Contemp Bks.
Place for Noah. 10.00 (ISBN 0-03-089896-X). HR&W.
Place in the Country: A Narrative on the Imperfect Art of Homesteading & the Value of Ignorance. pap. 3.95 (ISBN 0-15-672008-6). HarBraceJ.
Place of Springs. 10.95 (ISBN 0-8173-5318-6). U of Ala Pr.
Place, Profit, & Power: A Study of the Servants of William Cecil, Elizabethan Statesman. pap. text ed. 4.50x (ISBN 0-8078-5051-9). U of NC Pr.
Places Where I've Done Time. pap. 2.25 (ISBN 0-440-57125-1). Dell.
Plain Speaking: An Oral Biography of Harry S. Truman. 8.95 (ISBN 0-399-11261-8). Berkley Pub.
Plain Speaking: On Oral Biography of Harry S. Truman. pap. 2.95 (ISBN 0-425-04592-7). Berkley Pub.
Plant Hunting on the Edge of the World. 12.50 (ISBN 0-913728-21-7). Theophrastus.
Plant-Magic Man. new ed. pap. 2.50 (ISBN 0-912264-51-9). Capra Pr.
Plant Wizard: The Life of Lue Gim Gong. 3.95g (ISBN 0-02-767750-8). Macmillan.
Plantagenets. pap. 2.25 (ISBN 0-531-06017-9). Watts.
Plants That Changed Our Gardens. 13.95 (ISBN 0-7153-6721-8). David & Charles.
Platon: Sein Leben, Seine Schriften, Seine Lehre. facsimile ed. 84.00x set (ISBN 0-405-07333-X). Arno.
Play the Game. Incl. Climb Any Mountain (ISBN 0-8372-2268-0); The Skillful Rider (ISBN 0-8372-2269-9); Holdup at the Crossover (ISBN 0-8372-2270-2); More Than Speedy Wheels (ISBN 0-8372-2271-0). pap. text ed. 2.52 ea.; cassette for ea. title 8.10 ea.; 6 ea. of 8 titles, spiritmasters 102.12. Bowmar-Noble.
Play the Game. Incl. Forty for Sixty (ISBN 0-8372-2264-8); Viva Gonzales (ISBN 0-8372-2265-6); Chief Cloud of Dust (ISBN 0-8372-2267-2); Bull on Ice (ISBN 0-8372-2266-4). pap. text ed. 2.52 ea.; tchrs' guide 2.10 (ISBN 0-8372-0728-2). cassettes 8.10 ea.; 48 bks, 6 ea. of 8 titles with 8 cassettes & spiritmasters avail. (ISBN 0-8372-2262-1). 4 titles 18.40 (ISBN 0-8372-0606-5). Bowmar-Noble.
Play to Win: A Profile of Princeton Basketball Coach Pete Carril. 8.95 (ISBN 0-13-683904-5). P-H.
Playboy to Priest. pap. 1.50 (ISBN 0-87973-782-4). Our Sunday Visitor.
Player Queens. 10.95 (ISBN 0-8008-6324-0). Taplinger.
Player Under Three Reigns. 18.00 (ISBN 0-405-08525-7). Arno.
Players of the Present. lib. bdg. 34.00 (ISBN 0-8337-0577-6). B Franklin.
Players of the Present. 15.00 (ISBN 0-405-08360-2). Arno.
Playing for Time. 8.95 (ISBN 0-689-10796-X). Atheneum.
Playing for Time. pap. 2.50 (ISBN 0-425-04199-9). Berkley Pub.
Please, God, Help Me Get Well in Your Spare Time. pap. 3.50 (ISBN 0-87123-027-5, 210027). Bethany Fell.
Plutarch & His Times. 19.00 (ISBN 0-404-15276-7). AMS Pr.
Plutarch & Rome. 11.25x (ISBN 0-19-814363-X). Oxford U Pr.
Plutarch's Lives. 19.95 (ISBN 0-236-17622-6). Merrimack Bk Serv.
Plutarch's Lives of the Noble Grecians & Romans. anno ed. 147.00 (ISBN 0-404-51870-2); 24.50 ea. AMS Pr.
Pocahontas. PLB 4.49 (ISBN 0-399-60515-0). Putnam.
Pocahontas. 11.95 (ISBN 0-8061-0835-5). U of Okla Pr.
Pocahontas. pap. 5.95 (ISBN 0-8061-1642-0). U of Okla Pr.
Poe: A Biography. pap. 2.75 (ISBN 0-316-09686-5). Little.
Poe: A Biography. lib. bdg. 10.00 (ISBN 0-8495-0362-0). Arden Lib.
Poe & His Poetry. lib. bdg. 7.50 (ISBN 0-8414-3453-0). Folcroft.
Poe & His Poetry. lib. bdg. 16.95 (ISBN 0-8383-2112-7). Haskell.
Poe & His Poetry. 7.25 (ISBN 0-404-52506-7). AMS Pr.
Poe's Helen. lib. bdg. 25.95 (ISBN 0-8383-1632-8). Haskell.
Poet Chaucer. 2nd ed. pap. 3.50x (ISBN 0-19-888023-5). Oxford U Pr.
Poet Errant: A Biography of Ruben Dario. 4.50 (ISBN 0-8022-1817-2). Philos Lib.
Poet Toilers in Many Fields. 16.00 (ISBN 0-8369-7336-4). Arno.
Poet Under Saturn: The Tragedy of Verlaine. 7.50 (ISBN 0-8046-0813-X). Kennikat.
Poetical Career of Alexander Pope. 6.75 (ISBN 0-8446-1392-4). Peter Smith.
Poetry & Politics: The Life & Works of Juan Chi (A.D. 210-263) 34.95 (ISBN 0-521-20855-6). Cambridge U Pr.
Poetry of Robert Graves. text ed. 10.75x (ISBN 0-485-11103-9). Humanities.
Poets & Dramatists of Ireland see Gallery of Irish Writers: The Irish Writers of the Seventeenth Century.
Poets Chantry. 8.25 (ISBN 0-8046-1043-6). Kennikat.
Poets in Their Letters. 16.00 (ISBN 0-403-01300-3). Scholarly.
Poets of Ireland: A Biographical & Bibliographical Dictionary of Irish Writers of English Verse. 34.50 (ISBN 0-384-42975-0). Johnson Repr.
Poets of the Church: A Series of Biographical Sketches of Hymn-Writers, with Notes on Their Hymns. 48.00 (ISBN 0-8103-4291-X). Gale.
Point of View. 22.45 (ISBN 0-8195-5019-1); ltd. ed. o.p. 150.00 (ISBN 0-8195-8037-6). Columbia U Pr.
Polish Memoirs of William John Rose. 17.50x (ISBN 0-8020-5306-8). U of Toronto Pr.
Polish Prince. 8.95 (ISBN 0-87131-270-0). M Evans.
Polish Prince. pap. 2.25 (ISBN 0-553-13041-2). Bantam.
Polish Shades & Ghosts of Joseph Conrad. lib. bdg. 12.95 (ISBN 0-8057-9004-7). G K Hall.
Polish Shades & Ghosts of Joseph Conrad. 12.95 (ISBN 0-913994-20-0); pap. 8.95 (ISBN 0-913994-26-X). Hippocrene Bks.
Political Activities of Philip Freneau. 10.00 (ISBN 0-405-01670-0). Arno.
Political Career of Lord Byron. 19.00 (ISBN 0-8462-1663-9). Russell.
Political Career of Peter Paul Rubens. 9.25 (ISBN 0-500-55007-7). Transatlantic.
Political Career of Richard Brinsley Sheridan: The Stanhope Essay for 1912. lib. bdg. 15.00 (ISBN 0-8414-7512-1). Folcroft.
Political Ideas of Harold J. Laski. 18.50 (ISBN 0-208-01234-6). Shoe String.
Political Ideas of Richard Hooker. lib. bdg. 10.50 (ISBN 0-374-92073-7). Octagon.
Political Leaders of Provincial Pennsylvania. facsimile ed. 14.50 (ISBN 0-8369-5994-9). Arno.
Political Leaders of Upper Canada. facs. ed. 15.00 (ISBN 0-8369-0886-4). Arno.
Political Life & Letters of Cavour, 1848-1861. lib. bdg. 25.50x (ISBN 0-8371-7939-4, WHPL). Greenwood.
Political Memoir, 1880-92. lib. bdg. 20.75x (ISBN 0-8371-8101-1, CHPOM). Greenwood.
Political Portraits. lib. bdg. 9.25. Folcroft.
Political Portraits. 10.00 (ISBN 0-8046-1088-6). Kennikat.
Political Portraits, Second Series. 14.50 (ISBN 0-8369-1734-0). Arno.
Political Principles of Robert A. Taft. 7.50 (ISBN 0-8303-0033-3). Fleet.
Political Thought of John Henry Newman. lib. bdg. 11.50x (ISBN 0-8371-7226-8, KEJU). Greenwood.
Political Thought of Max Weber: In Quest of Statesmanship. 24.00x (ISBN 0-89197-349-4); pap. text ed. 8.95x (ISBN 0-89197-350-8). Irvington.
Politics of Friendship: Pompey & Cicero. pap. 9.00 (ISBN 0-424-06800-1). Intl Schol Bk Serv.
Politics of God & the Politics of Man. new ed. pap. 3.45 (ISBN 0-8028-1442-5). Eerdmans.
Polk & the Presidency. lib. bdg. 21.95 (ISBN 0-8383-1686-7). Haskell.
Polybius. 14.50x (ISBN 0-520-02190-8). U of Cal Pr.
Polygamist's Wife. pap. 1.75 (ISBN 0-671-81053-7). PB.
Polygamist's Wife. 5.95 (ISBN 0-913420-52-2). Olympus Pub Co.
Pompey the Great. 15.00x (ISBN 0-8476-6035-4). Rowman.
Pontiac. PLB 4.49 (ISBN 0-399-60516-9). Putnam.
Pontiac & the Indian Uprising. 2nd ed. 17.00 (ISBN 0-8462-1502-0). Russell.
Pontiac, King of the Great Lakes. 5.95g (ISBN 0-8038-5716-0). Hastings.
Pope Alexander III & the Council of Tours (1163) A Study of Ecclesiastical Politics & Institutions in the Twelfth Century. 10.00x (ISBN 0-520-03184-9). U of Cal Pr.
Pope & His Poetry. lib. bdg. 17.95 (ISBN 0-8383-1735-9). Haskell.
Pope & His Poetry. lib. bdg. 7.50 (ISBN 0-8414-3934-6). Folcroft.
Pope & His Poetry. 7.25 (ISBN 0-404-52510-5). AMS Pr.
Porcelain Art of Edward Marshall Boehm. 40.00 (ISBN 0-8109-0701-1). Abrams.
Porfirio Diaz, Dictator of Mexico. lib. bdg. 22.75x (ISBN 0-8371-5159-7, BEPD). Greenwood.
Porsche, the Man & His Cars. 10.95 (ISBN 0-8376-0329-3). Bentley.
Portal of Hungerford: The Life of Marshal of the Royal Air Force Viscount Portal of Hungerford KG, GCB, OM, DSO, MC. text ed. 24.50x (ISBN 0-8419-6103-4). Holmes & Meier.
Portrait of a Marriage. 10.00 (ISBN 0-689-10574-6). Atheneum.
Portrait of a Primitive: The Art of Henri Rousseau. 12.95 (ISBN 0-7148-1825-9); pap. 6.95 (ISBN 0-7148-1908-5). Dutton.
Portrait of Ambrose Bierce. 18.50x (ISBN 0-8464-0737-X). Beekman Pubs.
Portrait of Aristotle. pap. text ed. 10.00x (ISBN 0-226-30822-7). U of Chicago Pr.
Portrait of Barrie. 10.00 (ISBN 0-8274-1702-0). R West.
Portrait of Barrie. lib. bdg. 11.75x (ISBN 0-8371-6115-0, ASPB). Greenwood.
Portrait of Isaac Newton. 19.95 (ISBN 0-915220-52-0, 24925); pap. 7.95 (ISBN 0-915220-53-9, 24931). New Republic.
Portrait of Jane Austen. 19.95 (ISBN 0-8090-7811-2). Hill & Wang.
Portrait of T. E. Lawrence. lib. bdg. 17.95 (ISBN 0-8383-2093-7). Haskell.
Portraits. 16.00 (ISBN 0-8369-7299-6). Arno.
Portraits. lib. bdg. 25.00 (ISBN 0-8492-1753-9). R West.
Portraits. lib. bdg. 30.00 (ISBN 0-8495-3511-5). Arden Lib.
Portraits & Personalities. facs. ed. 13.75 (ISBN 0-8369-0242-4). Arno.
Portraits & Portents. 12.50 (ISBN 0-8274-3191-0). R West.
Portraits & Portents. facsimile ed. 17.25 (ISBN 0-8369-2499-1). Arno.
Portraits in British History. pap. text ed. 8.25x (ISBN 0-256-01679-8). Dorsey.
Portraits in Color. facsimile ed. 15.75 (ISBN 0-8369-2516-5). Arno.
Portraits in Prose: A Collection of Characters. 9.50x. Elliots Bks.
Portraits in Words: An Introduction to the Study of Biography. 4.60 (ISBN 0-672-73251-3); pap. 3.50 o.p. (ISBN 0-672-73229-7). Odyssey Pr.
Portraits of American Women. facs. ed. 14.75 (ISBN 0-8369-0004-9). Arno.
Portraits of Crime. pap. 2.25 (ISBN 0-89516-010-2). Condor Pub Co.
Portraits of Faith. pap. 2.50 (ISBN 0-87973-764-6). Our Sunday Visitor.
Portraits of Genius. 8.95 (ISBN 0-7195-1215-8). Transatlantic.
Portraits of Ideas. facsimile ed. 19.50 (ISBN 0-8369-8014-X). Arno.
Portraits of Men. 14.50 (ISBN 0-8369-2972-1). Arno.
Portraits of Power. 14.95 (ISBN 0-8129-0846-5). Times Bks.
Portraits of Russian Personalities Between Reform & Revolution. lib. bdg. 20.50x (ISBN 0-8371-8063-5, HAPR). Greenwood.
Portraits of the Artist in Exile: Recollections of James Joyce by Europeans. 12.95 (ISBN 0-295-95614-3). U of Wash Pr.
Portraits of the Eighties. lib. bdg. 30.00 (ISBN 0-8414-4854-X). Folcroft.
Portraits of the Eighties. 18.25 (ISBN 0-8369-1441-4). Arno.
Portraits of the Nineties. 17.00 (ISBN 0-8369-1686-7). Arno.
Portraits of the Seventies. 25.00 (ISBN 0-8369-1717-0). Arno.
Portraits of the Sixties. 25.00 (ISBN 0-8274-0752-1). R West.
Portraits of the Sixties. facsimile ed. 18.75 (ISBN 0-8369-2061-9). Arno.
Portraits of Women. facsimile ed. 13.75 (ISBN 0-8369-1247-0). Arno.
Portraits, Political & Personal. 17.00 (ISBN 0-87348-503-3); pap. 4.95 (ISBN 0-87348-504-1). Path Pr NY.
Portraiture of Shakerism. 17.50 (ISBN 0-404-08461-3). AMS Pr.
Portuguese Explorers. PLB 5.29 (ISBN 0-399-60518-5). Putnam.
Positively Main Street: An Unorthodox View of Bob Dylan. 5.95 (ISBN 0-698-10305-X). Coward.
Post Victorians. lib. bdg. 21.45. Folcroft.
Post Victorians. lib. bdg. 40.00 (ISBN 0-89987-401-0). Darby Bks.
Post Victorians. facsimile ed. 27.25 (ISBN 0-8369-2618-8). Arno.
Postillion Struck by Lightning. 8.95 (ISBN 0-03-021511-0). HR&W.
Potomac Fever. 8.95 (ISBN 0-393-05610-4). Norton.
Potter's Mexico. 17.50 (ISBN 0-8263-0472-9). U of NM Pr.
Potters on Pottery. 11.95 (ISBN 0-312-63280-0). St Martin.
Power & Glory, the Life of Boies Penrose. 11.50 (ISBN 0-404-01938-2). AMS Pr.
Power & Glory: The Life of Boies Penrose. 11.00 (ISBN 0-403-00570-1). Scholarly.
Power & Responsibility: The Life & Times of Theodore Roosevelt. lib. bdg. 26.00 (ISBN 0-374-93660-9). Octagon.
Power Broker: Robert Moses & the Fall of New York. 9.95 (ISBN 0-394-72024-5). Random.
Power Broker: Robert Moses & the Fall of the New York. 20.00 (ISBN 0-394-48076-7). Knopf.
Power Lovers: An Intimate Look at Politics & Marriage. 10.00 (ISBN 0-399-11495-5). Putnam.
Power of Biblical Thinking. 5.95 (ISBN 0-8007-0862-8). Revell.
Powerful Stories from the Lives of Latter-Day Saint Men. 5.95 (ISBN 0-87747-521-0). Deseret Bk.
Powhatan. PLB 6.95 (ISBN 0-87518-036-1). Dillon.
Practical Theorist: The Life & Work of Kurt Lewin. pap. text ed. 6.85 (ISBN 0-8077-2525-0). Tchrs Coll.
Practice Makes Perfect. 8.95 (ISBN 0-312-63535-4). St Martin.
Practice What You Preach. 8.95 (ISBN 0-312-63542-7). St Martin.
Pragmatic Illusions: The Presidential Politics of John F. Kennedy. 9.95x (ISBN 0-679-30298-0); pap. 6.95x (ISBN 0-582-28130-X). Longman.
Pragmatic Revolt in American History: Carl Becker & Charles Beard. pap. 1.95 (ISBN 0-8014-9034-0, CP34). Cornell U Pr.
Pragmatic Revolt in American History: Carl Becker & Charles Beard. lib. bdg. 17.25x (ISBN 0-313-22203-7, STPG). Greenwood.

Prairie Stationmaster: The Story of One Man's Railroading Career in Nebraska 1917-1963. 6.50 (ISBN 0-8187-0034-3). Harlo Pr.

Pre! pap. 4.50 (ISBN 0-911520-79-1). Tafnews.

Pre-Eminent Victorian: A Study of Tennyson. lib. bdg. 18.00x (ISBN 0-8371-6596-2, RIPV). Greenwood.

Pre-Raphaelite Circle. 19.50x (ISBN 0-8476-6025-7). Rowman.

Pre-War Biographies of Romain Rolland & Their Place in His Work & the Period. 9.95 (ISBN 0-8274-0558-8). R West.

Pre-War Biographies of Romain Rolland & Their Place in His Work & the Period. 10.00 (ISBN 0-8046-1618-3). Kennikat.

Preface to Dryden. text ed. 9.00x (ISBN 0-582-35101-4); pap. text ed. 5.95x (ISBN 0-582-35102-2). Longman.

Preface to Spenser. text ed. 10.95x (ISBN 0-582-31511-5); pap. text ed. 6.95x (ISBN 0-582-31512-3). Longman.

Prelude to Fame: Crawford Long's Discovery of Anaesthesia. 4.95 (ISBN 0-87672-104-8). Geron-X.

Prelude to Greatness: Lincoln in the 1850's. 10.00x (ISBN 0-8047-0119-9); pap. 3.75 (ISBN 0-8047-0120-2, SP109). Stanford U Pr.

Presence of the Actor. pap. text ed. 3.95x (ISBN 0-689-70338-4, 194). Atheneum.

Presidency of Andrew Johnson. 15.00x (ISBN 0-7006-0190-2). Regents Pr KS.

Presidency of Dwight D. Eisenhower. 12.00x (ISBN 0-7006-0183-X). Regents Pr KS.

Presidency of George Washington. pap. 3.95 (ISBN 0-393-00773-1). Norton.

Presidency of George Washington. 12.00x (ISBN 0-7006-0110-4). Regents Pr KS.

Presidency of John Adams. 12.00x (ISBN 0-7006-0134-1). Regents Pr Ks.

Presidency of Rutherford B. Hayes. lib. bdg. 16.00 (ISBN 0-8371-6275-0, DPH/); pap. 4.95 (ISBN 0-8371-7564-X, DPH). Greenwood.

Presidency of Warren G. Harding. 12.00x (ISBN 0-7006-0152-X). Regents Pr KS.

Presidency of William Howard Taft. 12.00x (ISBN 0-7006-0096-5). Regents Pr KS.

Presidency of Yuan Shih-K'ai: Liberalism & Dictatorship in Early Republican China. text ed. 17.50x (ISBN 0-472-08995-1). U of Mich Pr.

Presidency on Trial: Robert Kennedy's 1968 Campaign & Afterwards. 7.50 (ISBN 0-8248-0202-0). U Pr of Hawaii.

President Charles Bradlaugh, MP. 18.50 (ISBN 0-208-01155-2). Shoe String.

President James Buchanan: A Biography. 13.95 (ISBN 0-271-73093-5). Pa St U Pr.

President Masaryk. facs. ed. 14.75 (ISBN 0-8369-5388-6). Arno.

President Witherspoon. 22.00 (ISBN 0-405-00242-4). Arno.

President Wore Spats: A Biography of Glenn Frank. 4.50 (ISBN 0-87020-056-9). State Hist Soc Wis.

Presidential Losers. PLB 3.95 (ISBN 0-8225-0457-X). Lerner Pubns.

Presidents in American History. rev. ed. PLB 7.79 (ISBN 0-671-32838-7). Messner.

Presidents in Uniform. PLB 5.58 (ISBN 0-8038-5746-2). Hastings.

Presidents I've Known & Two Near Presidents. 18.25 (ISBN 0-8369-1728-6). Arno.

Presidents' Mothers. 10.00 (ISBN 0-312-64132-X). St Martin.

President's Odyssey. lib. bdg. 16.50x (ISBN 0-8371-7921-1, SMPR). Greenwood.

Presidents of the United States. 5.95 (ISBN 0-307-17863-3); PLB 12.23 (ISBN 0-307-67863-6). Western Pub.

Presidents of the United States & Their Administrations from Washington to Ford. 6th ed. 10.00 (ISBN 0-8180-0815-6). Horizon.

Presidents' Sons: The Prestige of Name in a Democracy. facs. ed. 20.50 (ISBN 0-8369-8073-5). Arno.

Presidents: Tidbits & Trivia. rev. ed. pap. 6.95 (ISBN 0-8437-3350-0). Hammond Inc.

Presidents: Tidbits & Trivia. rev. ed. pap. 2.95 (ISBN 0-8437-3232-6). Hammond Inc.

Presley Speaks. 10.00 (ISBN 0-918544-10-6). Wimmer Bks.

Preston Smith: The Making of a Texas Governor. 6.95 (ISBN 0-8363-0078-5). Jenkins.

Presumptuous Dreamers: A Sociological History of the Life & Times of Abigail Scott Duniway, 1834-1871. lib. bdg. 9.95 (ISBN 0-913626-11-2); pap. 6.95 (ISBN 0-913626-12-0). S S S Pub Co.

Presumptuous Dreamers: A Sociological History of the Life & Times of Abigail Scott Duniway, 1872-1886. lib. bdg. price not set (ISBN 0-913626-26-0); pap. price not set (ISBN 0-913626-27-9). S S S Pub Co.

Pretty-shield, Medicine Woman of the Crows. pap. 2.45 (ISBN 0-8032-5791-0, 580). U of Nebr Pr.

Pretty Witty Nell: An Account of Nell Gwyn & Her Environment. 17.00 (ISBN 0-405-08243-6). Arno.

Price of Free Land. 6.95 (ISBN 0-397-31836-7). Lippincott.

Prick up Your Ears: The Biography of Joe Orton. 15.00 (ISBN 0-394-50153-5). Knopf.

Pride of Our People: The Stories of One Hundred Outstanding Jewish Men & Women. 14.95 (ISBN 0-385-13573-4). Doubleday.

Pride of the Terrys: Family Saga. lib. bdg. 29.25x (ISBN 0-313-20221-4, STPT). Greenwood.

Priest Forever. 6.95 (ISBN 0-06-063893-1). Har-Row.

Priest Named Horse. pap. 4.95 (ISBN 0-87973-748-4). Our Sunday Visitor.

Priest of Love: A Life of D. H. Lawrence. rev. ed. 15.00 (ISBN 0-374-23718-2). FS&G.

Priest of Love: A Life of D. H. Lawrence. rev ed. pap. 5.95 (ISBN 0-8093-0839-8). S Ill U Pr.

Prime Minister on Prime Ministers. 15.00 (ISBN 0-671-40029-0). Summit Bks.

Prime Ministers. 35.00 (ISBN 0-8128-1738-9). Stein & Day.

Prime Ministers of Britain. 14.50 (ISBN 0-7153-7486-9). David & Charles.

Primer, Presses, & Composing Sticks: Women Printers of the Colonial Period. 7.50 (ISBN 0-682-49195-0). Exposition.

Prince Among Slaves. 12.95 (ISBN 0-15-174250-2). HarBraceJ.

Prince Bishop: A Life of St. Francis De Sales. text ed. write for info. (ISBN 0-8277-4121-9). British Bk Ctr.

Prince Charles, Growing up in Buckingham Palace. PLB 5.50 (ISBN 0-89565-029-0). Childs World.

Prince Consort. 15.95 (ISBN 0-8467-0321-1); pap. 9.95 (ISBN 0-8467-0322-X). Two Continents.

Prince Eugene of Savoy. 16.95 (ISBN 0-500-87007-1). Thames Hudson.

Prince Felix Zu Schwarzenberg: Prime Minister of Austria, 1848-1852. 8.00 (ISBN 0-404-05628-8). AMS Pr.

Prince Henry of Prussia, Brother of Frederick the Great. lib. bdg. 19.50x (ISBN 0-8371-4697-6, EAPH). Greenwood.

Prince Henry the Navigator. PLB 4.90 (ISBN 0-531-00972-6). Watts.

Prince Jack. pap. 2.25. BJ Pub Group.

Prince Lichnowsky & the Great War. 12.00x (ISBN 0-8203-0385-2). U of Ga Pr.

Prince Napoleon in America, 1861: Letters from His Aide-De-Camp. 12.50 (ISBN 0-8046-1695-7). Kennikat.

Prince of Carpetbaggers. lib. bdg. 16.00x (ISBN 0-8371-7466-X, DAPO). Greenwood.

Prince of Librarians: The Life & Times of Antonio Panizzi of the British Museum. 12.00 (ISBN 0-8214-0030-4). Ohio U Pr.

Prince of Our Disorder: The Life of T. E. Lawrence. 15.00 (ISBN 0-316 54232-6). Little.

Prince of Our Disorder: The Life of T. E. Lawrence. 15.00 (ISBN 0-316-54232-6); pap. 6.95 (ISBN 0-316-54229-6). Little.

Prince of the City: The True Story of the Cop Who Knew Too Much. 10.95 (ISBN 0-395-27096-0). HM.

Prince of the Ghetto. pap. 2.45 (ISBN 0-8052-0401-6). Schocken.

Prince of Thieves: Memoirs of the World's Greatest Forger. 8.95 (ISBN 0-8037-5387-X). Dial.

Princes in the Tower. 10.95 (ISBN 0-698-10842-6). Coward.

Princes of Wales. 5.00 (ISBN 0-8048-0896-1). C E Tuttle.

Princess Grace. 8.95 (ISBN 0-679-50612-8). McKay.

Princess of Wales. 15.95 (ISBN 0-684-16153-2). Scribner.

Princess Remembers: The Memoirs of the Maharani of Jaipur. 12.50 (ISBN 0-397-01103-2). Lippincott.

Principles of Biography. lib. bdg. 5.00 (ISBN 0-8414-0356-2). Folcroft.

Prison Diary. 8.95 (ISBN 0-295-95613-5). U of Wash Pr.

Prison Memoirs of an Anarchist. 8.50; pap. 3.50. Frontier Press Calif.

Prison Memoirs of an Anarchist. pap. 4.95 (ISBN 0-8052-0267-6). Schocken.

Prisoner at War: The Survival of Commander Richard A. Stratton. pap. 2.95 (ISBN 0-14-005225-9). Penguin.

Private Battle. 12.95 (ISBN 0-671-22594-4). S&S.

Private Battle. pap. 2.95 (ISBN 0-445-04564-7). Popular Lib.

Private Correspondence of Henry Clay. facsimile ed. 26.50 (ISBN 0-8369-5976-0). Arno.

Private Diary of Dr. John Dee & the Catalogue of His Library of Manuscripts. 10.00 (ISBN 0-404-50119-2). AMS Pr.

Private Diary of Dr. John Dee & the Catalogue of His Library of Manuscripts. 15.50 (ISBN 0-384-11180-7). Johnson Repr.

Private Franklin: The Man & His Family. 11.95 (ISBN 0-393-07496-X). Norton.

Private Journal of Louis McLane, U.S.N. 1844-1848. 10.00 (ISBN 0-87093-155-5). Dawsons.

Private Lives of Public Servants. 10.95x (ISBN 0-253-34606-1). Ind U Pr.

Private Memoirs of Madame Roland. 2nd ed. 24.50 (ISBN 0-404-56829-7). AMS Pr.

Private Papers of Senator Vandenberg. lib. bdg. 32.50x (ISBN 0-8371-7829-0, VAPR). Greenwood.

Private Papers of William Wilberforce. 20.50 (ISBN 0-8337-3797-X). B Franklin.

Private Placements & Restricted Securities. rev. ed. looseleaf with 1976 rev. pages 90.00 (ISBN 0-87632-078-7). Boardman.

Private Road. 14.00 (ISBN 0-404-14587-6). AMS Pr.

Private View of a Public Life. 9.95 (ISBN 0-88327-047-1). McKay.

Private World of Ballet. 15.00 (ISBN 0-670-57851-7). Viking Pr.

Private World of Ballet. pap. 4.95 (ISBN 0-14-004343-8). Penguin.

Private World of Jean Giono. 9.75 (ISBN 0-8223-0144-X). Duke.

Private World of William Faulkner. lib. bdg. 6.50x (ISBN 0-8154-0424-7). Cooper Sq.

Privileged Ones: The Well-off & the Rich in America. 15.00 (ISBN 0-316-15149-1). Little.

Privileged Persons: Four Seventeenth-Century Studies. 6.00 (ISBN 0-688-61082-X). Reynal.

Pro Basketball's Greatest: Selected All-Star Offensive & Defensive Teams. PLB 5.29 (ISBN 0-399-60999-7). Putnam.

Pro Basketball's Little Men. PLB 3.69 (ISBN 0-394-92768-0). Random.

Pro Football A to Z: A Fully Illustrated Guide to America's Favorite Sport. 10.00 (ISBN 0-87691-202-1). Winchester Pr.

Pro Football Heroes of Today. 4.95 (ISBN 0-394-82629-9); PLB 5.99 (ISBN 0-394-92629-3). Random.

Pro Quarterback: My Own Story. 6.95 (ISBN 0-671-60145-8). S&S.

Pro Quarterbacks. PLB 4.64 (ISBN 0 671-32306-7). Messner.

Pro Sports Trivia. 5.88 (ISBN 0-531-01091-0). Watts.

Probing the Unknown. pap. 1.25 (ISBN 0-440-97156-X). Dell.

Procession of Saints. 18.50 (ISBN 0-8369-8134-0). Arno.

Prodigal Father: The Life of John Butler Yeats, 1839-1922. 27.50x (ISBN 0-8014-1047-9); pap. 9.95 (ISBN 0-8014-9179-7). Cornell U Pr.

Professing History. 10.50 (ISBN 0-424-00024-5). Intl Schol Bk Serv.

Professional Amateur: The Biography of Charles Franklin Kettering. 13.00 (ISBN 0-405-04689-8). Arno.

Professional Fence. 8.95 (ISBN 0-02-917560-7). Free Pr.

Professional Fence. pap. text ed. 5.95 (ISBN 0-02-917820-7). Free Pr.

Profile of Vachel Lindsay. pap. text ed. 2.50x (ISBN 0-675-09287-6). Merrill.

Profiles & Portraits of American Presidents. 5.98. McKay.

Profiles & Portraits of American Presidents. 12.50 (ISBN 0-679-50618-7). McKay.

Profiles in Courage. pap. 1.95 (ISBN 0-06-080001-1, P1). Har-Row.

Profiles in Courage. memorial ed. 12.50 (ISBN 0-06-012315-X). Har-Row.

Profiles in Russian Resistance. 10.95 (ISBN 0-8129-0484-2). Times Bks.

Profiles of Christian Athletes Who Became...the Overcomers. pap. 4.95 (ISBN 0-8499-2837-0). Word Bks.

Profiles of Maine. pap. 6.95 (ISBN 0-917312-00-7). Maine Antique.

Profiles of Protestant Saints. 7.50 (ISBN 0-8303-0037-6). Fleet.

Profiles of Revival Leaders. bds. 2.95 (ISBN 0-8054-7213-4). Broadman.

Profiles of the Presidents. 6.95 (ISBN 0-87747-800-7). Deseret Bk.

Profiles of the Presidents. 5.95 (ISBN 0-87747-489-3). Deseret Bk.

Prokofiev. 15.00x (ISBN 0-670-57955-6); pap. 3.95x (ISBN 0-670-57956-4). Vienna Hse.

Prokofiev by Prokofiev: A Composer's Memoir. 14.00 (ISBN 0-385-09960-6). Doubleday.

Proletarian Science? The Case of Lysenko. 14.00 (ISBN 0-902308-69-6). Schocken.

Promise of Bultmann. pap. 3.95 (ISBN 0-8006-1357-0). Fortress.

Promised Land. lib. bdg. 15.00 (ISBN 0-89760-001-0). Dynamic Learn Corp.

Promoter Ain't a Dirty Word. new ed. 9.95 (ISBN 0-917304-35-7); pap. 6.95 (ISBN 0-917304-54-3). Intl Schol Bk Serv.

Proof of Eminence: The Life of Sir John Hawkins. 15.00x (ISBN 0-253-34617-7). Ind U Pr.

Prophet from Nazareth. o.p. 6.00x (ISBN 0-8052-3210-9); pap. 1.95 (ISBN 0-8052-0184-X). Schocken.

Prophet in His Own Country: The Story of the Young Edgar Cayce. pap. 1.75 (ISBN 0-345-24464-8). Ballantine.

Prophet in His Own Country: The Story of the Young Edgar Cayce. lib. bdg. 13.95 (ISBN 0-8161-6239-5). G K Hall.

Prophet in Politics: A Biography of J. S. Woodsworth. pap. 6.50 (ISBN 0-8020-6018-8). U of Toronto Pr.

Prophet of Community: The Romantic Socialism of Gustav Landauer. 20.00x (ISBN 0-520-02207-6). U of Cal Pr.

Prophet of Liberty: The Life & Times of Wendell Phillips. lib. bdg. 39.00x (ISBN 0-8371-7553-4, SHPL). Greenwood.

Prophet of Plenty: The First Ninety Years of W. D. Weatherford. 9.50x (ISBN 0-87049-068-0). U of Tenn Pr.

Prophet of Prohibition: Neal Dow & His Crusade. 7.50 (ISBN 0-8446-0533-6). Peter Smith.

Prophet of the People: A Biography of Padre Pio. pap. 3.95 (ISBN 0-8189-0351-1). Alba.

Prophet of Wheat Street: The Story of William Holmes Borders - a Man Who Refused to Fail. pap. 1.25 (ISBN 0-912692-19-7). Cook.

Prophets in the Church. 6.95 (ISBN 0-8091-0120-3). Paulist Pr.

Prophets of the Soul. facsimile ed. 14.00 (ISBN 0-8369-2277-8). Arno.

Prophets True & False. 20.25 (ISBN 0-8369-1386-8). Arno.

Proskauer, His Life & Times. 16.25 (ISBN 0-8173-9361-7). U of Ala Pr.

Prosopography of the Later Roman Empire. 140.00 (ISBN 0-521-07233-6). Cambridge U Pr.

Proud Shoes: The Story of an American Family. 12.95 (ISBN 0-06-013109-8). Har-Row.

Proud Shoes: The Story of an American Family. 15.00 (ISBN 0-87152-136-9). Reprint.

Proud Shoes: The Story of an American Family. pap. 4.95 (ISBN 0-06-090617-0, CN 617). Har-Row.

Provoked Wife: The Life & Times of Susannah Cibber. 12.50 (ISBN 0-316-59831-3). Little.

Psychic Adventures & the Unseen World. pap. 3.50 (ISBN 0-912760-33-8). Valkyrie Pr.

Psychic Healers. pap. 1.95 (ISBN 0-553-02056-0). Bantam.

Psychic Summer. pap. 1.95. Dell.

Psychologist of Sorts: The Autobiography & Publications of the Inventor of the Porteus Maze Tests. 10.00 (ISBN 0-87015-174-6). Pacific Bks.

Psychologists on Psychology. 12.95 (ISBN 0-8008-6557-X); pap. 6.50 (ISBN 0-8008-6558-8). Taplinger.

Psychology of a Musical Prodigy. 12.75 (ISBN 0-405-08879-5). Arno.

Psychology of a Musical Prodigy. 15.50 (ISBN 0-384-50360-8). Johnson Repr.

Psychology of a Musical Prodigy. facs. ed. 12.75 (ISBN 0-8369-5294-4). Arno.

Psychology of a Musical Prodigy. lib. bdg. 9.00x (ISBN 0-8371-4004-8, REMP). Greenwood.

Psychology of the Poet Shelley. lib. bdg. 7.75 (ISBN 0-8414-3590-1). Folcroft.

Psychopathic God: Adolf Hitler. pap. 2.95 (ISBN 0-451-08078-5, E8078). NAL.

Psychopathic God: Adolf Hitler. 13.50 (ISBN 0-465-06743-3). Basic.

Public & the Private Lincoln: Contemporary Perspectives. 18.95x (ISBN 0-8093-0921-1). S Ill U Pr.

Public Career of Sir James Graham. lib. bdg. 20.00x (ISBN 0-8371-7383-3, ERJG). Greenwood.

Public Enemies: The Mayor, the Mob, & the Crime That Was. 12.95 (ISBN 0 393-01306-5). Norton.

Public Finance & Private Wealth: The Career of Sir Stephen Fox, 1627-1716. 32.50 (ISBN 0-19-822467-2). Oxford U Pr.

Public Life of Thomas Cooper, 1783-1839. 37.50 (ISBN 0-404-59117-5). AMS Pr.

Public Men in & Out of Office. lib. bdg. 37.50 (ISBN 0-306-70457-9). Da Capo.

Public Nuisances. 11.95 (ISBN 0-465-06772-7). Basic.

Public Persons. 7.95 (ISBN 0-87140-620-9). Liveright.

Puccini: A Critical Biography. 2nd ed. text ed. 27.50x (ISBN 0-8419-0302-6). Holmes & Meier.

Puccini: The Man & His Music. 8.95 (ISBN 0-525-18610-7). Dutton.

Puerto Rican Patriot: The Life of Luis Munoz Rivera. 3.95g (ISBN 0-02-776160-6). Macmillan.

Pulitzer's Prize Editor: A Biography of John A. Cockerill, 1845-1896. 14.75 (ISBN 0-8223-0097-4). Duke.

Purcell. pap. 5.50 (ISBN 0-8226-0720-4). Littlefield.

Purcell. rev. ed. 8.95x (ISBN 0-460-03150-3). Biblio Dist.

Puritan Dilemma: The Story of John Winthrop. 5.00 (ISBN 0-316-58285-9); pap. 4.95 (ISBN 0-316-58286-7, 1962). Little.

Puritan Experience: Studies in Spiritual Autobiography. 12.00x (ISBN 0-8052-3425-X). Schocken.

Puritan in Babylon: The Story of Calvin Coolidge. 8.00 (ISBN 0-8446-3173-6). Peter Smith.

Puritan Protagonist: President Thomas Clap of Yale College. 15.00x (ISBN 0-8078-0841-5). U of NC Pr.

Purple Passage: Life of Mrs Frank Leslie. 10.95 (ISBN 0-8061-0271-3); pap. 4.95 (ISBN 0-8061-0939-4). U of Okla Pr.

Pursuit in the Wilderness. 8.75x (ISBN 0-8002-1889-2). Intl Pubns Serv.

Pursuit of Perfection: A Life of Maggie Teyte. 15.95 (ISBN 0-689-10964-4). Atheneum.

Pursuit of the Ancient Maya: Some Archaeologists of Yesterday. 8.95 (ISBN 0-8263-0363-3). U of NM Pr.

Pushkin. lib. bdg. 21.95 (ISBN 0-8383-1998-X). Haskell.

Putting Life in Your Life Story. pap. 2.95 (ISBN 0-87747-679-9). Deseret Bk.

Q

Quaker Profiles from the American West. pap. 3.95 (ISBN 0-913408-05-0). Friends United.

Quaker Singer's Recollections. lib. bdg. 21.00x (ISBN 0-405-09669-0). Arno.

Quality of Hurt: The Autobiography of Chester Himes. 7.95 (ISBN 0-385-01442-2). Doubleday.

Quartet in Heaven. facs. ed. 14.25 (ISBN 0-8369-8044-1). Arno.

Queen Bees: The Women Who Shaped America. 10.95 (ISBN 0-672-52394-9). Bobbs.

Queen Elizabeth & Her Subjects. 10.50 (ISBN 0-8369-1895-9). Arno.

Queen Elizabeth II: The Silver Jubilee Book. 10.00 (ISBN 0-312-65975-X). St Martin.

Queen of Hearts: The Passionate Pilgrimage of Lola Montez. 18.00. Arno.

Queen of Navarre, Jeanne D'Albret, 1528-1572. 16.50x (ISBN 0-674-74150-1). Harvard U Pr.

Queen of Populists: The Story of Mary Elizabeth Lease. 6.95 (ISBN 0-690-66252-1). T Y Crowell.

Queen of the Ritz. 10.00 (ISBN 0-672-52316-7). Bobbs.

Queen Victoria. 3.95 (ISBN 0-15-175695-3). HarBraceJ.

Queen Victoria. pap. 4.95 (ISBN 0-15-675696-X). HarBraceJ.

Queen Victoria Was Amused. 8.95 (ISBN 0-8008-6566-9). Taplinger.

Queen Victoria's Jubilees: 1887 & 1897. 15.95 (ISBN 0-668-04402-0, 4402). Arco.

Queens of England. 12.50 (ISBN 0-385-12780-4). Doubleday.

Queens of England. o.p. 6.95 (ISBN 0-8128-2096-7); pap. 1.95. Stein & Day.

Queens of Song: Being Memoirs of Some of the Most Celebrated Female Vocalists. facsimile ed. 25.25 (ISBN 0-8369-2640-4). Arno.

Queens of the Court. 5.95 (ISBN 0-396-06973-8). Dodd.

Quest for Arthur's Britain. pap. 6.50 (ISBN 0-586-08044-9). Academy Chi Ltd.

Quest for Corvo: An Experiment in Biography. pap. 3.95 (ISBN 0-14-000291-X). Penguin.

Quest for the Best. 12.95 (ISBN 0-670-58470-3). Viking Pr.

Question of Madness. pap. 3.95 (ISBN 0-393-00921-1). Norton.

Quests for the Historical Jesus. pap. 3.95 (ISBN 0-8010-5378-1). Baker Bk.

Quick & the Dead. 11.00 (ISBN 0-8046-0544-0). Kennikat.

Quiet Riot. 5.95 (ISBN 0-8007-0789-3). Revell.

R

R. C. Gorman: The Lithographs. 35.00 (ISBN 0-87358-179-2). Northland.

R. D. Blackmore: The Author of "Lorna Doone"; a Biography. lib. bdg. 16.00x (ISBN 0-8371-7286-1, DUBL). Greenwood.

R. D. Laing. 5.95 (ISBN 0-670-58984-5). Viking Pr.

R. D. Laing & Anti-Psychiatry. pap. 1.95 (ISBN 0-06-080229-4, P229). Har-Row.

R. D. Laing & Anti-Psychiatry. lib. bdg. 14.00 (ISBN 0-374-90906-7). Octagon.

R. G. Collingwood. pap. 1.95 (ISBN 0-8277-6042-6, WTW42). British Bk Ctr.

R. H. Tawney & His Times: Socialism As Fellowship. 15.00x (ISBN 0-674-81480-0). Harvard U Pr.

R. H. Tawney & His Times: Socialism As Fellowship. new ed. pap. 4.95 (ISBN 0-674-74377-6). Harvard U Pr.

R. L. Stevenson. lib. bdg. 10.00. Folcroft.

R. V. W. A Biography of Ralph Vaughan Williams. 14.50x (ISBN 0-19-315411-0). Oxford U Pr.

Rabad of Posquieres: A Twelfth-Century Talmudist. 15.00x (ISBN 0-674-74550-7). Harvard U Pr.

Rabad of Posquieres: A Twelfth-Century Talmudist. pap. 5.95 (ISBN 0-8276-0123-9, 444). Jewish Pubn.

Rabbi & Minister: The Friendship of Stephen S. Wise & John Haynes Holmes. pap. 6.95 (ISBN 0-87975-130-4). Prometheus Bks.

Rabin Memoirs. 12.95 (ISBN 0-316-73002-5). Little.

Rabindranath Tagore: Poet & Dramatist. 15.00 (ISBN 0-8274-3235-6). R West.

Rabindranath Tagore: Poet & Dramatist. lib. bdg. 25.95 (ISBN 0-8383-1982-3). Haskell.

Rabindranath Tagore: Poet & Dramatist. lib. bdg. 19.00x (ISBN 0-8371-8065-1, THRT). Greenwood.

Rabindranath Tagore, the Man & His Poetry. lib. bdg. 25.00 (ISBN 0-8492-7700-0). R West.

Rabindranath Tagore's Visit to Canada. lib. bdg. 16.95 (ISBN 0-8383-2130-5). Haskell.

Rachel. 9.00 (ISBN 0-405-08192-8). Arno.

Rachel of Old Louisiana. 6.95 (ISBN 0-8071-0095-1). La State U Pr.

Rachmaninoff. 16.50 (ISBN 0-8369-8034-4). Arno.

Rachmaninoff's Recollections Told to Oskar Von Riesemann. 20.50 (ISBN 0-8369-5232-4). Arno.

Radical Life. 15.00x (ISBN 0-253-34773-4). Ind U Pr.

Radical Lord Radnor: The Public Life of Viscount Folkestone, Third Earl of Radnor, 1779-1869. 18.50x (ISBN 0-8166-0809-1). U of Minn Pr.

Radical Spinoza. 12.50x (ISBN 0-8147-9186-7). NYU Pr.

Radie's World. 8.95 (ISBN 0-399-11667-2). Putnam.

Rafinesque: Autobiography & Lives. original Anthology ed. lib. bdg. 39.00x (ISBN 0-405-10723-4). Arno.

Rage of Edmund Burke: Portrait of an Ambivalent Conservative. 12.95x (ISBN 0-465-06829-4). Basic.

Rahel Varnhagen: The Life of a Jewish Woman. rev ed. 7.95 (ISBN 0-15-175850-6). HarBraceJ.

Rahel Varnhagen: The Life of a Jewish Woman. pap. 3.95 (ISBN 0-15-676100-9, HB287). HarBraceJ.

Rails That Climb: A Narrative History of the Moffat Road. 24.95 (ISBN 0-918654-29-7). CO RR Mus.

Rainbow Bridge. lib. bdg. 22.00x (ISBN 0-405-09674-7). Arno.

Rainbow Bridge. pap. 1.00x. Samisdat.

Rainbow: The Stormy Life of Judy Garland. pap. 1.95 (ISBN 0-345-28113-6). Ballantine.

Rainbow: The Stormy Life of Judy Garland. pap. 4.95 (ISBN 0-448-11731-2); pap. 7.95 (ISBN 0-448-12142-5). G&D.

Rainer Maria Rilke. lib. bdg. 20.00 (ISBN 0-374-91129-0). Octagon.

Rainer Maria Rilke: Creative Anguish of a Modern Poet. lib. bdg. 23.50x (ISBN 0-8371-1807-7, GRRR). Greenwood.

Rainer Maria Rilke: Masks & the Man. 9.50 (ISBN 0-87752-198-0). Gordian.

Rainey of Illinois: A Political Biography, 1903-34. 12.50 (ISBN 0-252-00647-X). U of Ill Pr.

Raissa's Journal. 12.95 (ISBN 0-87343-041-7). Magi Bks.

Rakhmaninov. 8.95x (ISBN 0-460-03145-7). Biblio Dist.

Rakhmaninov. pap. 6.50 (ISBN 0-8226-0701-8). Littlefield.

Raleigh. lib. bdg. 17.50 (ISBN 0-8414-4532-X). Folcroft.

Ralph Adams Cram, American Medievalist. 8.00 (ISBN 0-89073-038-5). Boston Public Lib.

Ralph Linton. 12.50x (ISBN 0-231-03355-9); pap. 4.00x (ISBN 0-231-03398-2). Columbia U Pr.

Ralph Vaughan Williams: A Pictorial Biography. 10.75x (ISBN 0-19-315420-X). Oxford U Pr.

Ralph Vaughan Williams: A Study. lib. bdg. 14.00x (ISBN 0-8371-7610-7, FORW). Greenwood.

Ralph Waldo Emerson. lib. bdg. 12.75. Folcroft.

Ralph Waldo Emerson. lib. bdg. 16.95 (ISBN 0-8383-0262-9). Haskell.

Ralph Waldo Emerson: Portrait of a Balanced Soul. 13.95 (ISBN 0-19-501766-8). Oxford U Pr.

Ramakrishna & His Disciples. pap. 4.95 (ISBN 0-671-20740-7). S&S.

Ramakrishna, His Life & Sayings. 14.50 (ISBN 0-404-11452-0). AMS Pr.

Ramana Maharshi & the Path of Self-Knowledge. pap. 3.95 (ISBN 0-87728-071-1). Weiser.

Ramban: His Life & Teachings. pap. 3.95 (ISBN 0-87306-037-7). Feldheim.

Rambles & Recollections of an Indian Official. 2nd ed. 10.00x (ISBN 0-19-636096-X). Oxford U Pr.

Ramblings. 6.50 (ISBN 0-87012-161-8). McClain.

Ramiro De Maeztu. lib. bdg. 10.95 (ISBN 0-8057-6325-2). Twayne.

Ramon Lull: A Biography. 29.50 (ISBN 0-8337-2706-0). B Franklin.

Ranade & the Roots of Indian Nationalism. pap. 11.00x (ISBN 0-226-81532-3). U of Chicago Pr.

Random Reminiscences of Men & Events. 10.00 (ISBN 0-405-05111-5). Arno.

Randy & Janet Jackson: Ready & Right! PLB 5.95 (ISBN 0-88436-404-6); pap. 3.50 (ISBN 0-88436-405-4). EMC.

Randy Matson Story. 4.00 (ISBN 0-911520-30-9). Tafnews.

Ranke: The Meaning of History. lib. bdg. 23.00x (ISBN 0-226-45349-9). U of Chicago Pr.

Raphael of Urbino & His Father Giovanni Santi. lib. bdg. 35.00 (ISBN 0-8240-3275-6). Garland Pub.

Raquela: A Woman of Israel. 10.95 (ISBN 0-698-10895-7). Coward.

Raquela: A Woman of Israel. pap. 2.50 (ISBN 0-451-08950-2, E8950). NAL.

Rare Book Saga: The Autobiography of H. P. Kraus. 15.00 (ISBN 0-399-12064-5). Putnam.

Rasputin the Holy Devil. lib. bdg. 20.00 (ISBN 0-8414-4308-4). Folcroft.

Rauschenberg. pap. 3.95 (ISBN 0-452-00356-3, FM356). NAL.

Ravel. lib. bdg. 19.00x (ISBN 0-8371-8473-8, JARA). Greenwood.

Ravel. 9.95x (ISBN 0-460-03146-5). Biblio Dist.

Raven: A Biography of Sam Houston. lib. bdg. 15.00 (ISBN 0-910220-15-8). Larlin Corp.

Ravenstein: Portrait of a German General. 14.95 (ISBN 0-241-89957-5). Hippocrene Bks.

Raw Pearl. pap. 1.50 (ISBN 0-671-78830-2). PB.

Raw Pearl. 9.50 (ISBN 0-15-175930-8). HarBraceJ.

Ray Charles. 6.95 (ISBN 0-690-67065-6); PLB 6.89 (ISBN 0-690-67066-4). T Y Crowell.

Ray Kroc: Big Mac Man. text ed. 5.95 (ISBN 0-88436-434-8). EMC.

Ray Kroc: Mayor of McDonaldland. PLB 6.95 (ISBN 0-87518-185-6). Dillon.

Raymond III of Tripolis & the the Fall of Jerusalem: 1140-1187. 22.50 (ISBN 0-404-15411-5). AMS Pr.

Raymond of the Times. lib. bdg. 16.25x (ISBN 0-8371-3256-8, BRRT). Greenwood.

Raymond Poincare & the French Presidency. lib. bdg. 15.00 (ISBN 0-374-98797-1). Octagon.

R.D. Laing: The Philosophy & Politics of Psychotherapy. 10.00 (ISBN 0-394-41130-7); pap. 3.95 (ISBN 0-394-73353-3). Pantheon.

Reaching for God. 6.95 (ISBN 0-915684-33-0). Christian Herald.

Readings in Vedic Literature for Children. 4.95 (ISBN 0-89647-001-6). Bala Bks.

Real Conversations. lib. bdg. 20.00 (ISBN 0-8414-1199-9). Folcroft.

Real Isadora. pap. 1.50 (ISBN 0-380-01382-7, 11742). Avon.

Real Jesus. pap. 2.25 (ISBN 0-380-40055-3, 40055). Avon.

Real Jesus. 8.95 (ISBN 0-8362-0727-0). Andrews & McMeel.

Real Mary Tyler Moore. pap. 1.50 (ISBN 0-523-24098-8). Pinnacle Bks.

Real Men. pap. 8.95 (ISBN 0-385-14421-0). Doubleday.

Real Tinsel. pap. 3.95 (ISBN 0-02-012550-X). Macmillan.

Reason Why. pap. 4.50 (ISBN 0-525-47053-0). Dutton.

Rebel Coach: My Football Family. 8.95 (ISBN 0-87870-008-0). Memphis St Univ.

Rebel on the Bridge: A Life of the Decembrist Baron Andrey Rozen (1800-84) 19.00 (ISBN 0-8214-0217-X). Ohio U Pr.

Rebel, Priest & Prophet: A Biography of Dr. Edward McGlynn. 18.00 (ISBN 0-88355-206-X). Hyperion Conn.

Rebel Raider: A Biography of Admiral Semmes. 4.95 (ISBN 0-397-30910-4). Lippincott.

Rebel Saints. facs. ed. 14.25 (ISBN 0-8369-0205-X). Arno.

Rebel Saints. lib. bdg. 17.50 (ISBN 0-89984-053-1). Century Bookbindery.

Rebel Slave. PLB 6.65 (ISBN 0-8172-0450-4). Raintree Pubs.

Rebirth: The Story of Eliezer Ben-Yehudah & the Modern Hebrew Language. 3.50 (ISBN 0-8276-0156-5). Jewish Pubn.

Recital. 19.00 (ISBN 0-403-01564-2). Scholarly.

Recollections & Experiences of an Abolitionist, from 1855 to 1865. lib. bdg. 13.50 (ISBN 0-8411-0074-8). Metro Bks.

Recollections & Reflections. lib. bdg. 12.75x (ISBN 0-8371-7366-3, STRF). Greenwood.

Recollections & Reflections. 27.00x (ISBN 0-405-06622-8). Arno.

Recollections of a Busy Life. 21.00 (ISBN 0-405-01674-3). Arno.

Recollections of a Busy Life. 27.50x (ISBN 0-8046-1481-4). Kennikat.

Recollections of a Busy Life. facs. ed. 20.50 (ISBN 0-8369-8582-6). Arno.

Recollections of a Georgia Loyalist. 15.00 (ISBN 0-87152-083-4). Reprint.

Recollections of a Newspaperman: A Record of Life & Events in California. 20.00x (ISBN 0-8464-0016-2). Beekman Pubs.

Recollections of a Picture Dealer. pap. 4.50 (ISBN 0-486-23582-3). Dover.

Recollections of a Picture Dealer. lib. bdg. 30.00 (ISBN 0-87817-218-1). Hacker.

Recollections of a Texas Educator. 10.00. A Jones.

Recollections of Alexis De Tocqueville. lib. bdg. 20.50x (ISBN 0-313-21052-7, TRRE). Greenwood.

Recollections of an Indonesian Diplomat in the Sukarno Era. 20.00x (ISBN 0-7022-1440-X). U of Queensland Pr.

Recollections of an Old Musician. 25.00 (ISBN 0-306-79521-3). Da Capo.

Recollections of Charley Russell. 9.95 (ISBN 0-8061-0582-8). U of Okla Pr.

Recollections of Country Joe. 5.95 (ISBN 0-88289-040-9). Pelican.

Recollections of Early Texas: Memoirs of John Holland Jenkins. 12.95 (ISBN 0-292-73347-X). U of Tex Pr.

Recollections of Fenians & Fenianism. 18.00x (ISBN 0-7165-0606-8). Biblio Dist.

Recollections of Grover Cleveland. facsimile ed. 25.00 (ISBN 0-8369-5958-2). Arno.

Recollections of James Lenox & the Formation of His Library. rev. ed. 6.00 (ISBN 0-87104-155-3). NY Pub Lib.

Recollections of Louisa May Alcott, John Greenleaf Whittier, & Robert Browning, Together with Several Memorial Poems. lib. bdg. 12.50 (ISBN 0-8492-2088-2). R West.

Recollections of Louisa May Alcott, John Greenleaf Whittier, & Robt. Browning, Together with Several Memorial Poems. lib. bdg. 10.00 (ISBN 0-8414-6701-3). Folcroft.

Recollections of Richard Dewey: Pioneer in American Psychiatry. 12.00 (ISBN 0-405-05203-0). Arno.

Recollections of Robert Louis Stevenson in the Pacific. lib. bdg. 25.00 (ISBN 0-8414-5324-1). Folcroft.

Recollections of Rossetti. 35.00 (ISBN 0-8490-0935-9). Gordon Pr.

Recollections of Rossetti. lib. bdg. 21.95 (ISBN 0-8383-1634-4). Haskell.

Recollections of Seventy Years. 12.00 (ISBN 0-405-01834-7). Arno.

Recollections of Sir Walter Scott, Bart. lib. bdg. 25.00 (ISBN 0-8414-2040-8). Folcroft.

Recollections of the Last Days of Shelley & Byron. 10.95 (ISBN 0-8274-1155-3). R West.

Recollections of the Last Days of Shelley & Byron. facsimile ed. 14.50 (ISBN 0-8369-5866-7). Arno.

Recollections of Thirteen Presidents. facs. ed. 15.00 (ISBN 0-8369-1005-2). Arno.

Recollections of Virginia Woolf. 6.95 (ISBN 0-688-00007-X); pap. 2.50 (ISBN 0-688-05007-7). Morrow.

Record Breakers. 5.95 (ISBN 0-13-767426-0). P-H.

Record-Breakers of the Major Leagues. PLB 3.69 (ISBN 0-394-92769-9). Random.

Record Makers & Record Breakers. 9.95 (ISBN 0-8246-0208-0). Jonathan David.

Red Auerbach: An Autobiography. 9.95 (ISBN 0-399-11893-4). Putnam.

Red Baron. PLB 6.95 (ISBN 0-07-072040-1). McGraw.

Red Cloud. 2nd ed. PLB 6.95 (ISBN 0-87518-151-1). Dillon.

Red Cloud & the Sioux Problem. 15.00x (ISBN 0-8032-0136-2); pap. 5.50 (ISBN 0-8032-5817-8, 602). U of Nebr Pr.

Red Guard: The Political Biography of Dai Hsiao-Ai. 4.50 (ISBN 0-8446-4710-1). Peter Smith.

Red Monarch: Scenes from the Life of Stalin. 10.95 (ISBN 0-393-08836-7). Norton.

Red Prelude: The Life of the Russian Terrorist Zhelyabov. 22.00 (ISBN 0-88355-792-4). Hyperion Conn.

Red Rose. 16.95 (ISBN 0-7153-7440-0). David & Charles.

Red Skelton. 12.95 (ISBN 0-525-18953-X). Dutton.

Red Son Rising. 5.95 (ISBN 0-87518-077-9). Dillon.

Red Wine of Youth: A Life of Rupert Brooke. lib. bdg. 14.50x (ISBN 0-8371-6456-7, STRW). Greenwood.

Red World & White: Memories of a Chippewa Boyhood. 5.95 (ISBN 0-8061-1069-4). U of Okla Pr.

Redlands & Certain Old-Timers. pap. 3.00. Creative Pr.

Reflections. 50.00 (ISBN 0-87359-020-1). Northwood Inst.

Reflections of a Clyde-Built Man. pap. 4.95 (ISBN 0-285-64825-X). Intl Schol Bk Serv.

Reflections on the Theatre. 19.75 (ISBN 0-88355-679-0). Hyperion Conn.

Reformer in the Marketplace: Edward W. Bok & the Ladies' Home Journal. 12.95x (ISBN 0-8071-0398-5). La State U Pr.

Regency Rogue: Dan Donnelly, His Life & Legends. 2nd ed. 11.50 (ISBN 0-905140-06 0). Irish Bk Ctr.

Reggie Jackson. PLB 5.95 (ISBN 0-87191-724-6); pap. 2.75 (ISBN 0-89812-162-0). Creative Ed.
Reggie Jackson: Slugger Supreme. text ed. 5.95 (ISBN 0-88436-449-6); pap. text ed. 3.50 (ISBN 0-88436-475-5). EMC.
Reggie Jackson Story. 7.50 (ISBN 0-688-41889-9); PLB 7.20 (ISBN 0-688-51889-3). Lothrop.
Reggie: Portrait of Reginald Turner. 6.00 (ISBN 0-8076-0306-6). Braziller.
Register of Polish American Scholars, Scientists, Writers & Artists. pap. 3.00. Polish Inst Arts.
Reich Marshal: A Biography of Hermann Goering. 12.50 (ISBN 0-385-04961-7). Doubleday.
Reign of Patti. lib. bdg. 32.00x (ISBN 0-405-09686-0). Arno.
Reign of Patti. lib. bdg. 25.00 (ISBN 0-306-77530-1). Da Capo.
Reinhold Niebuhr. 6.95 (ISBN 0-87680-508-X). Word Bks.
Reinhold Niebuhr: A Political Account. 13.95x (ISBN 0-7735-0216-5). McGill-Queens U Pr.
Reinhold Niebuhr: A Prophetic Voice in Our Time. 11.00 (ISBN 0-518-10150-9). Arno.
Reinhold Niebuhr: Prophet from America. facs. ed. 10.75 (ISBN 0-8369-5324-X). Arno.
Relatives. 8.95 (ISBN 0-8037-7733-7). Dial.
Relief Pitcher: Baseball's New Hero. 10.95 (ISBN 0-525-19048-1). Dutton.
Religion of George Fox: As Revealed in His Epistles. pap. 0.70x (ISBN 0-87574-161-4). Pendle Hill.
Religion of Thomas Jefferson. 5.25 (ISBN 0-8446-2073-4). Peter Smith.
Religious Faith of Great Men. facs. ed. 12.75 (ISBN 0-8369-0968-2). Arno.
Remarkable Life of Dr. Armand Hammer. 12.50 (ISBN 0-06-010836-3). Har-Row.
Remarkable Stories from the Lives of Latter-Day Saint Women. 5.95 (ISBN 0-87747-504-0). Deseret Bk.
Remarkable Stories from the Lives of Latter-Day Saint Women. 5.95 (ISBN 0-87747-569-5). Deseret Bk.
Rembrandt's House. 13.95 (ISBN 0-395-25706-9). HM.
Remember the Good Times. 2.95 (ISBN 0-8054-5704-6). Broadman.
Remembering E. G. Peterson His Life & Our Story. 4.50 (ISBN 0-87421-069-0). Utah St U Pr.
Remembering How We Stood: Bohemian Dublin at the Mid-Century. 8.95 (ISBN 0-8008-6770-X). Taplinger.
Remembering James Agee. 8.95 (ISBN 0-8071-0086-2). La State U Pr.
Remembering John Masefield. 6.00 (ISBN 0-8386-7836-X). Fairleigh Dickinson.
Remembrances of Emerson. lib. bdg. 12.50 (ISBN 0-8414-2877-8). Folcroft.
Reminiscences. 22.00 (ISBN 0-405-05294-4). Arno.
Reminiscences & Reflexions of a Mid & Late Victorian. 13.50x (ISBN 0-678-00313-0). Kelley.
Reminiscences of a Newburyport Nonagenarian. 20.50 (ISBN 0-917890-09-4). Heritage Bk.
Reminiscences of a Ranchman. 5.00 (ISBN 0-8446-1749-0) Peter Smith.
Reminiscences of a Ranchman. 15.00x (ISBN 0-8032-0886-3); pap. 4.50 (ISBN 0-8032-5023-1, 127). U of Nebr Pr.
Reminiscences of a Trip Across the Plains in 1846 & Early Days in California. 12.00 (ISBN 0-87770-180-6). Ye Galleon.
Reminiscences of Alexander Dyce. 11.00 (ISBN 0-8142-0160-1). Ohio St U Pr.
Reminiscences of an Active Life: The Autobiography of John Roy Lynch. 15.00x (ISBN 0-226-49818-2). U of Chicago Pr.
Reminiscences of Augustus Saint-Gaudens. lib. bdg. 66.00 (ISBN 0-8240-2247-5). Garland Pub.
Reminiscences of D. H. Lawrence. facsimile ed. 14.25 (ISBN 0-8369-5810-1). Arno.
Reminiscences of Edgar Allan Poe. lib. bdg. 10.95 (ISBN 0-8383-2068-6). Haskell.
Reminiscences of Edgar Allan Poe. lib. bdg. 6.00 (ISBN 0-8414-2350-4). Folcroft.
Reminiscences of James Burrill Angell. facsimile ed. 14.00 (ISBN 0-8369-5722-9). Arno.
Reminiscences of Lafcadio Hearn. lib. bdg. 17.50 (ISBN 0-8482-1225-8). Norwood Edns.
Reminiscences of Levi Coffin, the Reputed President of the Underground Railroad. 19.00 (ISBN 0-405-01810-X). Arno.
Reminiscences of My Childhood & Youth. facsimile ed. 25.00x (ISBN 0-405-06697-X). Arno.
Reminiscences of Peace & War. facs. ed. 18.25 (ISBN 0-8369-5475-0). Arno.
Reminiscences of Present-Day Saints. facsimile ed. 18.25 (ISBN 0-8369-2576-9). Arno.
Reminiscences of Robert Louis Stevenson. lib. bdg. 7.50 (ISBN 0-8414-1552-8). Folcroft.
Reminiscences of Robert Louis Stevenson. lib. bdg. 6.50 (ISBN 0-8495-0910-6). Arden Lib.
Reminiscences of Rosa Bonheur. 30.00 (ISBN 0-87817-096-0). Hacker.
Reminiscences of Sixty Years in Public Affairs. lib. bdg. 37.50x (ISBN 0-8371-0322-3, BORS). Greenwood.
Reminiscences of the Civil War & Reconstruction. pap. 3.45 (ISBN 0-8093-0791-X). S Ill U Pr.
Reminiscences of the Last Sixty-Five Years. 21.00 (ISBN 0-405-01700-6). Arno.
Reminiscences of the Russian Ballet. lib. bdg. 29.50 (ISBN 0-306-77426-7). Da Capo.
Reminiscences of Thomas Dibdin. 49.50 (ISBN 0-404-02124-7); 24.75 ea. AMS Pr.
Reminiscences: Story of an Emigrant. lib. bdg. 22.00x (ISBN 0-405-11651-9). Arno.
Reminiscing with Sissle & Blake. 12.95 (ISBN 0-670-59388-5). Viking Pr.
Renaissance of Canadian History: A Biography of A. L. Burt. 17.50x (ISBN 0-8020-5304-1). U of Toronto Pr.
Renata Tebaldi: The Woman & the Diva. 15.00 (ISBN 0-8369-8048-4). Arno.
Rendezvous with Destiny: The Roosevelts of the White House. 10.00 (ISBN 0-399-11545-5). Putnam.
Renoir, My Father. pap. 3.95 (ISBN 0-316-74010-1). Little.
Republican Roosevelt. 2nd ed. 8.95x (ISBN 0-674-76300-9); pap. 2.95 (ISBN 0-674-76302-5). Harvard U Pr.
Reputations Ten Years After. facs. ed. 15.00 (ISBN 0-8369-0619-5). Arno.
Requiem: The Decline & Demise of Mayor Daley & His Era. 8.95 (ISBN 0-8092-7920-7). Contemp Bks.
Requiem: The Decline & Demise of Mayor Daley & His Era. pap. 3.95 (ISBN 0-8092-7409-4). Contemp Bks.
Rescue! True Stories of Heroism. pap. 1.50 (ISBN 0-671-29989-1). Archway.
Rescue: True Stories of Heroism. PLB 5.90 s&l (ISBN 0-531-02223-4). Watts.
Rescuing Horace Walpole. 20.00x (ISBN 0-300-02278-6). Yale U Pr.
Respectable Radical: George Howell & Victorian Working Class Politics. 12.50x (ISBN 0-674-76540-0). Harvard U Pr.
Restless Journey of James Agee. 10.95 (ISBN 0-688-03141-2); pap. 4.95 (ISBN 0-688-08141-X). Morrow.
Restless Spirit: Journal of a Gemini. pap. 4.95 (ISBN 0-89087-917-6). Les Femmes Pub.
Restoration Radical: Robert Blum & the Challenge of German Democracy, 1807-1848. text ed. 8.00 (ISBN 0-8283-1530-2). Branden.
Resurrection in Cannes: The Making of the Picasso Summer. 14.50 (ISBN 0-498-01942-X). A S Barnes.
Retainer from the Lord. 4.95 (ISBN 0-89279-004-0); pap. 2.95 (ISBN 0-89279-003-2). Graphic Pub.
Retreat to Glory: The Story of Sam Houston. PLB 7.89 (ISBN 0-06-023726-0). Har-Row.
Return from Tomorrow. 5.95 (ISBN 0-912376-23-6). Chosen Bks Pub.
Return of Billy the Kid. 8.95 (ISBN 0-698-10834-5). Coward.
Return of the Black Ships. 11.95 (ISBN 0-533-03368-3). Vantage.
Return to Albion: Americans in England 1760-1940. 16.95 (ISBN 0-03-042861-0). HR&W.
Revaluations: Studies in Biography. lib. bdg. 19.95 (ISBN 0-8383-2106-2). Haskell.
Revelations of a Russian Diplomat: The Memoirs of Dmitrii I. Abrikossow. 10.50 (ISBN 0-295-73911-8); pap. 2.95 (ISBN 0-295-97896-1, WPRA5). U of Wash Pr.
Revelations of a Soviet Diplomat. 18.50 (ISBN 0-88355-424-0). Hyperion-Conn.
Revelliere-Lepeaux, Citizen Director, 1753-1824. lib. bdg. 15.00 (ISBN 0-374-96893-4). Octagon.
Revell's Dictionary of Bible People. 7.95 (ISBN 0-8007-1038-X). Revell.
Revolt Against Chivalry: Jessie Daniel Ames & the Women's Campaign Against Lynching. 14.95 (ISBN 0-231-04040-7). Columbia U Pr.
Revolutionaries, Traditionalists & Dictators in Latin America. lib. bdg. 9.50x (ISBN 0-8154-0420-4). Cooper Sq.
Revolutionaries Without Revolution. 15.95 (ISBN 0-02-617400-6, 61740). Macmillan.
Revolutionary Jews from Marx to Trotsky. text ed. 17.50x (ISBN 0-06-497806-0). B&N.
Revolutionists. pap. 0.95 (ISBN 0-671-47855-9). WSP.
Rex Brasher--Painter of Birds: A Biography. 7.50x (ISBN 0-87471-298-X). Rowman.
Rex Stout: A Biography. 17.50 (ISBN 0-316-55340-9). Little.
Ricasoli & the Risorgimento in Tuscany. 13.50 (ISBN 0-86527-171-2). Fertig.
Rich Rich: The Story of the Big Spenders. 12.50 (ISBN 0-399-12062-9). Putnam.
Rich Who Own Sports. 8.95 (ISBN 0-394-49561-6). Random.
Richard & Elizabeth. pap. 1.95 (ISBN 0-345-25652-2). Ballantine.
Richard Bennett Hubbard: An American Life. 15.00 (ISBN 0-88319-032-X). Shoal Creek Pub.
Richard Bourke. 16.50x (ISBN 0-19-550349-X). Oxford U Pr.
Richard Brinsley Sheridan. lib. bdg. 8.95 (ISBN 0-8057-6650-2). Twayne.
Richard Coeur De Lion: A Biography. lib. bdg. 16.25x (ISBN 0-8371-8724-9, HERI). Greenwood.
Richard E. Byrd. PLB 4.29 (ISBN 0-399-60532-0). Putnam.
Richard Florsheim. 15.00 (ISBN 0-498-01636-6); 100.00 (ISBN 0-498-01760-5). A S Barnes.
Richard Henry Dana, Jr. 5.00 (ISBN 0-87013-062-5). Mich St U Pr.
Richard Hovey, Man & Craftsman. lib. bdg. 14.50x (ISBN 0-8371-0157-3, MARH). Greenwood.
Richard III: The Making of a Legend. 8.00 (ISBN 0-8108-1034-4). Scarecrow.
Richard Jefferies. 11.95 (ISBN 0-571-11236-6); pap. 5.95 (ISBN 0-571-11237-4). Merrimack Bk Serv.
Richard Lion Heart. 10.00 (ISBN 0-684-13802-6). Scribner.
Richard Malcolm Johnston. 9.95 (ISBN 0-8057-7238-3). Twayne.
Richard Malcolm Johnston. lib. bdg. 9.95 (ISBN 0-8057-7238-3). G K Hall.
Richard Mather of Dorchester. 15.95 (ISBN 0-8131-1343-1). U Pr of Ky.
Richard Maurice Bucke, Medical Mystic: Letters of Dr. Bucke to Walt Whitman & Friends. 12.95 (ISBN 0-8143-1576-3). Wayne St U Pr.
Richard Middleton's Letters to Henry Savage. 45.00. Lib Serv Inc.
Richard Middleton's Letters to Henry Savage. 10.75 (ISBN 0-8274-3280-1). R West.
Richard Nixon. PLB 4.29 (ISBN 0-399-60533-9). Putnam.
Richard Payne Knight: The Twilight of Virtuosity. text ed. 24.00x. Mouton.
Richard Porson: A Biographical Essay. lib. bdg. 20.00 (ISBN 0-8495-0828-2). Arden Lib.
Richard Savage: A Mystery in Biography. 11.95 (ISBN 0-8274-1567-2). R West.
Richard Savage: A Mystery in Biography. 12.00 (ISBN 0-8046-1597-7). Kennikat.
Richard Steere: Colonial Merchant Poet. pap. text ed. 3.95 (ISBN 0-271-00207-7). Pa St U Pr.
Richard Strauss. 8.95x (ISBN 0-460-03148-1). Biblio Dist.
Richard Strauss. 14.75 (ISBN 0-8369-5053-4). Arno.
Richard Strauss. lib. bdg. 10.75x (ISBN 0-8371-4297-0, NERS). Greenwood.
Richard the Lion Heart. 12.00 (ISBN 0-8462-1326-5). Russell.
Richard the Third. pap. 6.95 (ISBN 0-393-00785-5, N785). Norton.
Richard the Third. text ed. 25.00x (ISBN 0-04-942048-8). Allen Unwin.
Richard Wagner & the Synthesis of the Arts. lib. bdg. 15.00x (ISBN 0-8371-6806-6, STRX). Greenwood.
Richard Wagner: His Life, Art & Thought. 14.95 (ISBN 0-8008-4792-X). Taplinger.
Richard Wagner: His Life in His Work. facsimile ed. 24.00 (ISBN 0-8369-5176 X). Arno
Richard Wagner: His Life in His Work. lib. bdg. 20.25x (ISBN 0-8371-3443-9, BERW). Greenwood.
Richard Wagner: The Man, His Mind, & His Music. pap. 4.50 (ISBN 0-15-677610-3, HB272). HarBraceJ.
Richard Wagner: The Story of an Artist. lib. bdg. 25.25x (ISBN 0-8371-5630-0, PORW). Greenwood.
Richard Wagner: The Story of an Artist. 27.00 (ISBN 0-403-01558-8). Scholarly.
Richard Wilbur. pap. 3.45 (ISBN 0-8084-0259-5, T117). Coll & U Pr.
Richelieu: A Study. lib. bdg. 20.00 (ISBN 0-8495-0383-3). Arden Lib.
Richelieu & Reason of State. 25.00x (ISBN 0-691-05199-2). Princeton U Pr.
Richelieu & the French Monarchy. pap. 1.95 (ISBN 0-02-038240-5). Macmillan.
Richelieu & the Growth of French Power. facsimile ed. 24.00 (ISBN 0-8369-5814-4). Arno.
Rick Barry. PLB 5.95 (ISBN 0-87191-539-1); pap. 2.75 (ISBN 0-89812-185-X). Creative Ed.
Rick Barry: Basketball Ace. PLB 5.29 (ISBN 0-399-61060-X). Putnam.
Riddle of Emily Dickinson. lib. bdg. 15.00x (ISBN 0-8154-0451-4). Cooper Sq.
Riddle of Erskine Childers. 15.95 (ISBN 0-09-128490-2). Merrimack Bk Serv.
Riddle of MacArthur: Japan, Korea, & the Far East. lib. bdg. 15.25x (ISBN 0-8371-7701-4, GURM). Greenwood.
Ride 'em Cowgirl! 6.95 (ISBN 0-399-20484-9). Putnam.
Riding & Roping: The Memoirs of J. Will Harris. 20.00 (ISBN 0-913480-23-1); pap. 6.00 (ISBN 0-913480-34-7). Inter Am U Pr.
Riding to Win. 10.00x (ISBN 0-392-04411-0). Soccer.
Right-Hand Man: The Life of George W. Perkins. lib. bdg. 27.75x (ISBN 0-313-20186-2, GARH). Greenwood.
Ring: A Biography of Ring Lardner. 12.95 (ISBN 0-394-49811-9). Random.
Ringling Brothers. 6.95 (ISBN 0-690-70287-6); PLB 6.89 (ISBN 0-690-70288-4). T Y Crowell.
Ripe Mangoes: Miracle Missionary Stories from Bangladesh. pap. 2.95 (ISBN 0-87227-060-2). Reg Baptist.
Rise & Decline of Fidel Castro: An Essay in Contemporary History. pap. 3.95 (ISBN 0-520-02767-1). U of Cal Pr.
Rise & Fall of a Proper Negro: An Autobiography. 5.95 (ISBN 0-02-567200-2). Macmillan.
Rise & Fall of Adolf Hitler. PLB 4.99 (ISBN 0-394-90547-4). Random.
Rise & Fall of the Romanovs. pap. 4.95x (ISBN 0-442-00050-2, 50). Van Nos Reinhold.
Rise of Chingis Khan & His Conquest of North China. lib. bdg. 17.00 (ISBN 0-374-95287-6). Octagon.
Rise of Gladstone to the Leadership of the Liberal Party, 1859-1868. lib. bdg. 12.00 (ISBN 0-374-98614-2). Octagon.
Rise of Rawlins Lowndes, 1721-1800. lib. bdg. 14.95x (ISBN 0-87249-259-1). U of SC Pr.
Rise of the House of Rothschild. 75.00 (ISBN 0-87968-170-5). Gordon Pr.
Rise of the House of Rothschild. pap. 2.00 (ISBN 0-88279-112-5). Western Islands.
Rise of U. S. Grant. facs. ed. 17.25 (ISBN 0-8369-5572-2). Arno.
Rise to Follow: An Autobiography. lib. bdg. 19.50 (ISBN 0-306-77421-6). Da Capo.
Rise to Follow: An Autobiography. 25.00 (ISBN 0-403-01755-6). Scholarly.
Rise up & Remember. Softbound 2.95 (ISBN 0-385-12955-6). Doubleday.
Rising Above Color. facsimile ed. 10.00 (ISBN 0-8369-2605-6). Arno.
Rising Son: The Antecedents & Advancement of the Colored Race. facs. ed. 20.50 (ISBN 0-8369-8519-2). Arno.
Rita Hayworth: The Time, the Place, the Woman. 12.95 (ISBN 0-393-07526-5). Norton.
Rivers. pap. 3.95 (ISBN 0-452-00357-1, FM357). NAL.
Riza Shah Pahlavi: The Resurrection & Reconstruction of Iran 1878-1944. 15.00 (ISBN 0-682-48206-4). Exposition.
RKO Gals. pap. 7.95 (ISBN 0-89508-005-2). Rainbow Bks.
Road to Gundagai. 5.95 (ISBN 0-8277-0476-3). British Bk Ctr.
Road to Hollywood: My 40 Year Love Affair with the Movies. 12.50 (ISBN 0-385-02292-1). Doubleday.
Road to Winesburg: A Mosaic of the Imaginative Life of Sherwood Anderson. 19.00 (ISBN 0-8108-0312-7). Scarecrow.
Robber Rocks: Letters & Memories of Hart Crane, 1923-1932. 10.00x (ISBN 0-8195-4007-2). Columbia U Pr.
Robbers Roost Recollections. 7.95 (ISBN 0-87421-083-6). Utah St U Pr.
Robert A. Woods: Champion of Democracy. facsimile ed. 17.50 (ISBN 0-8369-5719-9). Arno.
Robert Alexander, Maryland Loyalist. text ed. 18.00x (ISBN 0-8398-0960-3). Irvington.
Robert & Elizabeth Barrett Browning: An Annotated Bibliography, 1951-1970. 26.50x. Browning Inst.
Robert Bacon: Life & Letters. lib. bdg. 25.00 (ISBN 0-8495-5015-7). Arden Lib.
Robert Bacon: Life & Letters. facsimile ed. 31.00x (ISBN 0-405-07232-5). Arno.
Robert Barnwell Rhett: Father of Secession. 7.50 (ISBN 0-8446-1477-7). Peter Smith.
Robert Bennett. PLB 6.95 (ISBN 0-87518-108-2). Dillon.
Robert Boyle & the English Revolution: A Study in Social & Intellectual Change. pap. cancelled (ISBN 0-89102-106-X). B Franklin.
Robert Boyle & the English Revolution: A Study in Social & Intellectual Change. lib. bdg. 18.95 (ISBN 0-89102-072-1). B Franklin.
Robert Browning. 10.00 (ISBN 0-8274-1497-8). R West.
Robert Browning. 4.95 (ISBN 0-312-10675-0). St Martin.
Robert Browning. lib. bdg. 8.50 (ISBN 0-8414-7593-8). Folcroft.
Robert Browning. lib. bdg. 15.00 (ISBN 0-8414-9396-0). Folcroft.
Robert Browning Personalia. lib. bdg. 16.95 (ISBN 0-8383-1728-6). Haskell.
Robert Browning, Personalia. lib. bdg. 12.50 (ISBN 0-8414-0050-4). Folcroft.
Robert Browning: The Poet & the Man. lib. bdg. 19.95 (ISBN 0-8383-1538-0). Haskell.
Robert Bruce & the Community of the Realm of Scotland. 19.50x (ISBN 0-520-00083-8). U of Cal Pr.
Robert Bruce, King of Scots. facsimile ed. 18.75 (ISBN 0-8369-5500-5). Arno.
Robert Burns. 8.95 (ISBN 0-02-529390-7). Macmillan.

Robert Burns & His World. 8.95 (ISBN 0-500-13034-5). Thames Hudson.
Robert Burns & the Common People. lib. bdg. 8.75. Folcroft.
Robert Burns & the Common People. lib. bdg. 15.95 (ISBN 0-8383-1333-7). Haskell.
Robert Burns & the Riddell Family. lib. bdg. 22.95 (ISBN 0-8383-1802-9). Haskell.
Robert Burns & the Riddell Family. 14.75. Folcroft.
Robert Cavelier De la Salle. PLB 4.90 (ISBN 0-531-02843-7). Watts.
Robert Creeley: An Inventory. 7.50x (ISBN 0-87338-139-4). Kent St U Pr.
Robert Creeley: An Inventory 1945-1970. 6.00x (ISBN 0-7735-0191-6). McGill-Queens U Pr.
Robert E. Lee. lib. bdg. 18.50x (ISBN 0-8371-1864-6, WHRL). Greenwood.
Robert E. Park: Biography of a Sociologist. 12.75 (ISBN 0-8223-0402-3). Duke.
Robert F. Kennedy Apostle of Change. 7.95 (ISBN 0-671-27013-3). Trident.
Robert F. Kennedy: Man Who Dared to Dream. PLB 4.78 (ISBN 0-8116-4557-6). Garrard.
Robert Frost. rev. ed. pap. 1.25x (ISBN 0-8166-0192-5, MPAW2). U of Minn Pr.
Robert Frost, a Tribute to the Source. 20.00 (ISBN 0-03-046326-2). HR&W.
Robert Frost & the Lawrence Massachusetts, "High School Bulletin.". 20.00x (ISBN 0-8139-0460-9). Grolier Club.
Robert Frost & the Lawrence Massachusetts, "High School Bulletin" The Beginning of a Literary Career. 20.00x (ISBN 0-8139-0460-9). U Pr of Va.
Robert Frost: Life & Talks-Walking. 17.95 (ISBN 0-8061-0653-0). U of Okla Pr.
Robert Frost, Teacher. 7.95, o.s.i. (ISBN 0-87367-758-7); pap. 3.95 (ISBN 0-87367-759-5). Phi Delta Kappa.
Robert Fulton. PLB 4.49 (ISBN 0-399-60537-1). Putnam.
Robert Fulton & the Submarine. 8.00 (ISBN 0-404-04888-9). AMS Pr.
Robert Grosseteste & the Origins of Experimental Science, 1100-1700. 34.50x (ISBN 0-19-824189-5). Oxford U Pr.
Robert Grosseteste, Bishop of Lincoln: A Contribution to the Religious, Political & Intellectual History of the Thirteenth Century. lib. bdg. 28.50x (ISBN 0-697-00018-4). Irvington.
Robert H. Goddard: Space Pioneer. PLB 3.40 (ISBN 0-8116-6308-6). Garrard.
Robert H. Lowie, Ethnologist: A Personal Record. 18.00x (ISBN 0-520-00775-1). U of Cal Pr.
Robert Henryson. 12.00 (ISBN 0-404-06225-3). AMS Pr.
Robert Herrick. 10.00 (ISBN 0-312-68740-0). St Martin.
Robert Hooke. pap. 1.95 (ISBN 0-520-00391-8, CAL65). U of Cal Pr.
Robert Kennedy & His Times. pap. 3.50 (ISBN 0-345-28344-9). Ballantine.
Robert Kennedy & His Times. 19.95 (ISBN 0-395-24897-3); ltd. ed. 100.00 (ISBN 0-395-27394-3). HM.
Robert Louis Stevenson. lib. bdg. 20.00. Folcroft.
Robert Louis Stevenson. lib. bdg. 10.00 (ISBN 0-8414-6004-3). Folcroft.
Robert Louis Stevenson. lib. bdg. 10.00 (ISBN 0-8414-7875-9). Folcroft.
Robert Louis Stevenson, a Teller of Tales. 13.00 (ISBN 0-8103-4080-1). Gale.
Robert Louis Stevenson & His World. 9.95 (ISBN 0-684-15299-1). Scribner.
Robert Lowe. 20.00x (ISBN 0-8020-5323-8). U of Toronto Pr.
Robert Lowell: Life of Art. text ed. 14.50 (ISBN 0-691-06363-X); pap. 5.95 (ISBN 0-691-01364-0). Princeton U Pr.
Robert McAlmon: Expatriate Publisher & Writer. pap. 1.50x (ISBN 0-8032-5226-9). U of Nebr Pr.
Robert Mills: Architect of the Washington Monument, 1781-1855. 21.00 (ISBN 0-404-02668-0). AMS Pr.
Robert Morley: A Reluctant Autobiography. 6.95 (62657). S&S.
Robert Oliver: Merchant of Baltimore, 1783-1819. 31.00 (ISBN 0-404-61327-6). AMS Pr.
Robert Oliver, Merchant of Baltimore, 1783-1819. lib. bdg. 28.00x (ISBN 0-405-11458-3). Arno.
Robert Owen, Aspects of His Life & Work. text ed. 12.75x (ISBN 0-391-00154-X). Humanities.
Robert Owen of New Lanark. 12.50x (ISBN 0-678-00565-6). Kelley.
Robert Redford. PLB 5.50 (ISBN 0-87191-554-5). Creative Ed.
Robert S. Kerr: The Senate Years. 14.50 (ISBN 0-8061-1402-9). U of Okla Pr.
Robert S. Kerr: The Senate Years. pap. 8.95 (ISBN 0-8061-1635-8). U of Okla Pr.
Robert Schumann: The Man & His Music. pap. 11.95 (ISBN 0-214-20340-9, 8027). Barrie & Jenkins.
Robert Schumann, 1810-1856. 6.50 (ISBN 0-8046-0760-5). Kennikat.
Robert Smith Surtees: A Critical Study. lib. bdg. 30.00 (ISBN 0-8495-5622-8). Arden Lib.
Robert Southwell, the Writer: A Study in Religious Inspiration. 20.00 (ISBN 0-403-04241-0). Somerset Pub.
Robert Spencer, Earl of Sunderland, 1641-1702. lib. bdg. 21.50x (ISBN 0-8371-8150-X, KERS). Greenwood.
Robert Y. Hayne & His Times. lib. bdg. 39.50 (ISBN 0-306-71870-7). Da Capo.
Roberta Flack. PLB 5.95 (ISBN 0-87191-396-8); pap. 2.75 (ISBN 0-89812-105-1). Creative Ed.
Roberto Clemente. PLB 6.89 (ISBN 0-690-00322-6). T Y Crowell.
Roberto Clemente: Batting King. rev. ed. PLB 5.29 (ISBN 0-399-60865-6). Putnam.
Robespierre. 30.00 (ISBN 0-86527-174-7). Fertig.
Robespierre: A Study. 19.50 (ISBN 0-8369-6964-2). Arno.
Robespierre: A Study. 14.75 (ISBN 0-8274-3296-8). R West.
Robespierre & the French Revolution. 5.50x (ISBN 0-340-08369-7). Verry.
Robespierre: Portrait of a Revolutionary Democrat. 10.95 (ISBN 0-670-60128-4). Viking Pr.
Robin Campbell: Joy in the Morning. PLB 5.95 (ISBN 0-88436-238-8); pap. 3.50 (ISBN 0-88436-239-6). EMC.
Robinson Jeffers. lib. bdg. 7.95 (ISBN 0-8057-0412-4). Twayne.
Robinson Jeffers. pap. 3.45 (ISBN 0-8084-0269-2, T22). Coll & U Pr.
Robinson Jeffers: A Portrait. lib. bdg. 8.50 (ISBN 0-8414-2881-6). Folcroft.
Robinson Jeffers: A Portrait. lib. bdg. 8.50 (ISBN 0-8495-0048-6). Arden Lib.
Robyn Smith: In Silks. PLB 5.95 (ISBN 0-88436-234-5); pap. 3.50 (ISBN 0-88436-235-3). EMC.
Rochambeau. 6.95 (ISBN 0-02-627780-8). Macmillan.
Rochambeau. pap. 3.95 (ISBN 0-02-007900-1). Macmillan.
Rock of Chickamauga, the Life of General George H. Thomas. lib. bdg. 18.50x (ISBN 0-8371-6973-9, CLRC). Greenwood.
Rock on: The Illustrated Encyclopedia of Rock 'n Roll: the Solid Gold Years. 14.95 (ISBN 0-690-00583-0). T Y Crowell.
Rockefeller Power. 7.95 (ISBN 0-671-21718-6). S&S.
Rockefeller Power. rev. ed. pap. 1.75 (ISBN 0-523-00665-9). Pinnacle Bks.
Rockwell Portrait: An Intimate Biography. 12.95 (ISBN 0-8362-6602-1). Andrews & McMeel.
Rod Carew: A Promise & a Dream. text ed. 5.95 (ISBN 0-88436-441-0). EMC.
Rod Carew: Master Hitter. new ed. PLB 5.29 (ISBN 0-399-60996-2). Putnam.
Rodeo Road: My Life As a Pioneer Cowgirl. 7.95 (ISBN 0-8038-2670-2). Hastings.
Rodin. pap. 9.95 (ISBN 0-19-520191-4). Oxford U Pr.
Rodney. lib. bdg. 18.00x (ISBN 0-8398-0805-4). Irvington.
Roeblings: A Century of Engineers, Bridge-Builders & Industrialists. 24.50 (ISBN 0-404-05625-3). AMS Pr.
Roentgen's Revolution: The Discovery of the X-Ray. 5.95 (ISBN 0-316-32821-9). Little.
Roger Ascham. 15.00x (ISBN 0-8047-0149-0). Stanford U Pr.
Roger Bacon & His Search for a Universal Science: A Reconsideration of the Life & Work of Roger Bacon in the Light of His Own Stated Purposes. 13.50 (ISBN 0-8462-1537-3). Russell.
Roger Bacon in Life & Legend. lib. bdg. 17.50 (ISBN 0-8414-9547-5). Folcroft.
Roger Boyle: First Earl of Orrery. 12.00x (ISBN 0-87049-060-5). U of Tenn Pr.
Roger Casement. 8.95 (ISBN 0-15-178327-6). HarBraceJ.
Roger Fry: A Biography. pap. 4.50 (ISBN 0-15-678520-X, HB338). HarBraceJ.
Roger of Salisbury, Viceroy of England. 18.50x (ISBN 0-520-01985-7). U of Cal Pr.
Roger of Sicily & the Normans in Lower Italy, 1016-1154. 30.00 (ISBN 0-404-56536-0). AMS Pr.
Roger Sherman & the Independent Oil Men. 17.50x (ISBN 0-8014-0105-4). Cornell U Pr.
Roger Staubach. PLB 5.50 (ISBN 0-87191-378-X). Creative Ed.
Roger Williams. PLB 4.90 (ISBN 0-531-02784-8). Watts.
Roger Williams: His Contribution to the American Tradition. 6.75 (ISBN 0-8446-2594-9). Peter Smith.
Roger Williams: His Contribution to the American Tradition. pap. text ed. 2.65x (ISBN 0-689-70145-4, 6). Atheneum.
Roger Williams, Prophet & Pioneer. 23.50 (ISBN 0-8369-5120-4). Arno.
Roger Williams, Prophet & Pioneer. 19.50 (ISBN 0-404-02236-7). AMS Pr.
Roger Williams, the Pioneer of Religious Liberty. facs. ed. 14.50 (ISBN 0-8369-5586-2). Arno.
Rogue I Remember. pap. 6.95 (ISBN 0-916890-94-5). Mountaineers.
Rogues & Heroes from Iowa's Amazing Past. facsimile ed. pap. 8.70x (ISBN 0-8138-2415-X). Iowa St U Pr.
Roland De La Platiere: A Public Servant in the Eighteenth Century. pap. 1.00 (ISBN 0-87169-566-9). Am Philos.
Role of Joseph McGarrity in the Struggle for Irish Independence. 22.00 (ISBN 0-405-09360-8). Arno.
Rolling Stones: An Illustrated Record. pap. 6.95 (ISBN 0-517-52641-7). Crown.
Romain Rolland & a World at War. 15.00 (ISBN 0-404-50731-X). AMS Pr.
Roman Portraits: The Flavian-Trajanic Period. text ed. 16.50 (ISBN 0-8262-0275-6). U of Mo Pr.
Romance of a Great Singer: Memoir of Mario. lib. bdg. 19.00x (ISBN 0-405-09701-8). Arno.
Romance of Forgotten Men. facs. ed. 18.25 (ISBN 0-8369-1033-8). Arno.
Romance of History. 17.00 (ISBN 0-8369-7285-6). Arno.
Romance of Ruth. pap. 1.95 (ISBN 0-8254-2718-5). Kregel.
Romantic Biography of the Age of Elizabeth: Or, Sketches of Life from the Bye-Ways of History. 46.50 (ISBN 0-518-10027-8). Arno.
Romantic Composers. 14.00 (ISBN 0-404-04223-6). AMS Pr.
Romantic Composers. lib. bdg. 15.75x (ISBN 0-8371-4096-X, MARC). Greenwood.
Romantic Decatur. facsimile ed. 16.00 (ISBN 0-8369-5898-5). Arno.
Romantic Life of Shelley & the Sequel. 15.75 (ISBN 0-8274-3916-4). R West.
Romantic Life of Shelley & the Sequel. lib. bdg. 35.00 (ISBN 0-8492-1018-6). R West.
Romantic Life of Shelley & the Sequel. lib. bdg. 28.95 (ISBN 0-8383-1566-6). Haskell.
Romantic Rebels: Essays on Shelley & His Circle. 10.00 (ISBN 0-674-77937-1). Harvard U Pr.
Romantic Recollections. lib. bdg. 19.50 (ISBN 0-306-77572-7). Da Capo.
Romantic Revolutionary: A Biography of John Reed. 15.00 (ISBN 0-394-46103-7). Knopf.
Romantic Triangle: Schleiermacher & Early German Romanticism. pap. 6.00x (ISBN 0-89130-124-0, 010013). Scholars Pr MT.
Rome Was My Beat. 8.95 (ISBN 0-8184-0216-4). Lyle Stuart.
Rommel, the Desert Fox. lib. bdg. 9.87 (ISBN 0-06-014776-8). Har-Row.
Ron's Story: A Legacy of Love. pap. 3.50 (ISBN 0-89107-155-5). Good News.
Roomful of Hovings & Other Profiles. 9.95 (ISBN 0-374-25208-4); pap. 4.95 (ISBN 0-374-51501-8). FS&G.
Roosevelt & Churchill - 1939-1941: The Partnership That Saved the West. 12.95 (ISBN 0-393-05594-9). Norton.
Roosevelt Family of Sagamore Hill. 7.50 (ISBN 0-02-547350-6). Macmillan.
Roosevelt: The Lion & the Fox. 15.00 (ISBN 0-15-178869-3). HarBraceJ.
Roosevelt: The Lion & the Fox. pap. 4.95 (ISBN 0-15-678870-5, HB57). HarBraceJ.
Roosevelt: The Lion & the Fox. Bd. with Roosevelt: The Soldier of Freedom. boxed set 30.00 (ISBN 0-15-178872-3). HarBraceJ.
Roosevelt: The Soldier of Freedom. 15.00 (ISBN 0-15-178871-5). HarBraceJ.
Roosevelt: The Soldier of Freedom. pap. 6.95 (ISBN 0-15-678875-6, HB247). HarBraceJ.
Roosevelt: The Soldier of Freedom see Roosevelt: The Lion & the Fox.
Roosevelt's Farmer: Claude R. Wickard in the New Deal. lib. bdg. 27.50 (ISBN 0-306-70702-0). Da Capo.
Roots. pap. 2.75 (ISBN 0-440-17464-3). Dell.
Roots of Life. 5.50 (ISBN 0-8180-0013-9). Horizon.
Rosa Luxemburg Speaks. 25.00 (ISBN 0-87348-147-X); pap. 6.95 (ISBN 0-87348-146-1). Path Pr NY.
Rosa Parks. 6.95 (ISBN 0-690-71210-3); PLB 6.89 (ISBN 0-690-71211-1). T Y Crowell.
Rosalind Franklin & DNA. 8.95 (ISBN 0-393-07493-5). Norton.
Rosalynn. pap. 2.95 (ISBN 0-88270-260-2). Logos.
Rose Hill. 9.95 (ISBN 0-399-11622-2). Putnam.
Rose Kennedy. PLB 4.49 (ISBN 0-399-60921-0). Putnam.
Rosemary Casals: The Rebel Rosebud. lib. bdg. 5.95 (ISBN 0-88436-166-7); pap. 3.50 (ISBN 0-88436-167-5). EMC.
Rosi Mittermaier. PLB 5.50 (ISBN 0-87191-544-8). Creative Ed.
Rossetti Family, 1824-1854. 18.00 (ISBN 0-403-01261-9). Scholarly.
Rossetti-Macmillan Letters: Some 125 Unpublished Letters Written to Alexander Macmillan, F. S. Ellis, & Others, by Dante Gabriel, William Michael, & Christina Rossetti, 1861-1889. 14.75x (ISBN 0-520-00979-7). U of Cal Pr.
Rossetti Papers, 1862-1870. 17.50 (ISBN 0-404-05438-2). AMS Pr.
Rossetti: A Biographical & Critical Study. 12.50 (ISBN 0-404-08724-8). AMS Pr.
Rossini: A Biography. 12.50 (ISBN 0-394-44447-7). Knopf.
Roster of Revolutionary Soldiers & Patriots in Alabama. 25.00. Parchment Pr.
Rothschilds: A Family Portrait. 10.95 (ISBN 0-689-10204-6). Atheneum.
Rothschilds: Family of Fortune. 17.50 (ISBN 0-394-48773-7). Knopf.
Rothschilds: Financial Rulers of Nations. 75.00 (ISBN 0-87968-193-4). Gordon Pr.
Rounds with a Country Vet. 6.95 (ISBN 0-396-07482-0). Dodd.
Rousseau. 9.75 (ISBN 0-8274-0495-6). R West.
Rousseau. 10.00 (ISBN 0-8046-1590-X). Kennikat.
Rousseau & Education According to Nature. 15.00 (ISBN 0-8274-3308-5). R West.
Rousseau & Education According to Nature. 34.95 (ISBN 0-8490-0976-6). Gordon Pr.
Rousseau & Education According to Nature. 15.00 (ISBN 0-404-01977-3). AMS Pr.
Rousseau & Education According to Nature. 19.00 (ISBN 0-403-00427-6). Scholarly.
Rousseau & the French Revolution 1762-91. text ed. 15.75x (ISBN 0-485-13117-X). Humanities.
Roy Bean: Law West of the Pecos. 5.95 (ISBN 0-8159-6715-2). Devin.
Royal Charles: Charles II & the Restoration. 16.95 (ISBN 0-394-49721-X). Knopf.
Royal Duke: Augustus Frederick, Duke of Sussex. 18.95x (ISBN 0-8464-0804-X). Beekman Pubs.
Royal Government in Colonial Brazil: With Special Reference to the Administration of the Marquis of Lavradio, Viceroy, 1769-1779. 27.50x (ISBN 0-520-00008-0). U of Cal Pr.
Royal House of Windsor. 15.00 (ISBN 0-394-47906-8). Knopf.
Royal Victorians: King Edward VII His Family & Friends. 12.95 (ISBN 0-397-01111-3). Lippincott.
Royal Victorians: King Edward VII, His Family & Friends. pap. 2.25 (ISBN 0-425-03462-3). Berkley Pub.
Royall Tyler. 12.50x (ISBN 0-674-78000-0). Harvard U Pr.
Rubens & Italy. 55.00 (ISBN 0-8014-1064-9). Cornell U Pr.
Ruby in the Rough. 8.95 (ISBN 0-88289-099-9). Pelican.
Rudolf Bultmann. 5.95 (ISBN 0-87680-252-8, 80252). Word Bks.
Rudolf Bultmann. pap. 2.25 (ISBN 0-8042-0698-8). John Knox.
Rudolph Valentino. 8.95 (ISBN 0-8128-2098-3). Stein & Day.
Rudolph Valentino. pap. 2.95 (ISBN 0-14-003615-6). Penguin.
Rudyard Kipling: Creative Adventurer. 6.95 (ISBN 0-8149-0360-6). Vanguard.
Rudyard Kipling, His Life & Works. lib. bdg. 12.50 (ISBN 0-8495-0838-X). Arden Lib.
Rudyard Kipling: The Story of a Genius. lib. bdg. 250.00 (ISBN 0-8414-4956-2). Folcroft.
Rudyard Kipling's Vermont Feud. lib. bdg. 16.95 (ISBN 0-8383-2024-4). Haskell.
Ruffled Feathers. 8.95 (ISBN 0-312-69561-6). St Martin.
Rufus Choate, the Wizard of the Law. 15.00 (ISBN 0-208-00938-8). Shoe String.
Rufus Jones, Master Quaker. facsimile ed. 16.00 (ISBN 0-8369-5554-4). Arno.
Rufus King: American Federalist. 19.50x (ISBN 0-8078-1070-3). U of NC Pr.
Rugged Heart. pap. 4.50 (ISBN 0-8127-0241-7). Southern Pub.
Ruggles of New York: A Life of Samuel B. Ruggles. 15.00 (ISBN 0-404-51524-X). AMS Pr.
Rulers of New Testament Times. pap. 2.25 (ISBN 0-916406-15-6). Accent Bks.
Ruling Passions. 11.95 (ISBN 0-8128-2176-9); pap. 4.95 (ISBN 0-8128-6027-6). Stein & Day.
Rumor of War. 10.00 (ISBN 0-03-017631-X). HR&W.
Rumor of War. pap. 2.25 (ISBN 0-345-27298-6). Ballantine.
Run Baby Run. pap. 1.50. BJ Pub Group.
Run with the Vision. pap. 3.95 (ISBN 0-88270-261-0). Logos.
Runner of the Mountain Tops: The Life of Louis Agassiz. 14.00 (ISBN 0-8103-3806-8). Gale.
Runners & Races: 1500m.-Mile. 5.00 (ISBN 0-911520-40-6). Tafnews.
Running Back. 11.95 (ISBN 0-8015-6494-8). Hawthorn.
Running for Jesus. 6.95 (ISBN 0-87680-460-1, 80460). Word Bks.

Running Saga of Walter Stack. pap. 4.95 (ISBN 0-89087-226-0). Celestial Arts.

Running Start: An Athlete, a Woman. 8.95 (ISBN 0-8129-0523-7). Times Bks.

Rupert Brooke: A Biography. pap. 5.95 (ISBN 0-571-10196-8). Merrimack Bk Serv.

Rupert Brooke: The Man & Poet. pap. text ed. 10.00x (ISBN 90-6203-437-3). Humanities.

Ruskin. lib. bdg. 12.50 (ISBN 0-8414-3530-8). Folcroft.

Ruskin: A Study in Personality. 15.00 (ISBN 0-403-01757-2). Scholarly.

Ruskin: A Study in Personality. lib. bdg. 20.00 (ISBN 0-8414-3293-7). Folcroft.

Ruskin: A Study of Personality. 35.00 (ISBN 0-8490-0981-2). Gordon Pr.

Ruskin & His Circle. 15.00 (ISBN 0-404-02232-4). AMS Pr.

Ruskin & His Circle. 15.00 (ISBN 0-8274-1690-3). R West.

Ruskin and His Circle. lib. bdg. 17.50 (ISBN 0-8495-1308-1). Arden Lib.

Ruskin & His Circle. lib. bdg. 25.00 (ISBN 0-8482-0734-3). Norwood Edns.

Ruskin, the Great Victorian. 19.50 (ISBN 0-208-00815-2). Shoe String.

Russell Grimwade. 18.50x (ISBN 0-522-83827-8). Intl Schol Bk Serv.

Russell W. Porter, Arctic Explorer, Artist, Telescope Maker. 12.50 (ISBN 0-87027-168-7). Wheelwright.

Russian Childhood. 14.80 (ISBN 0-387-90348-8). Springer-Verlag.

Russian Composers. 3.50 (ISBN 0-395-07034-1). HM.

Russian Composers & Musicians: A Biographical Dictionary. lib. bdg. 15.00 (ISBN 0-306 71321-7). Da Capo.

Russian Mystics. 13.95 (ISBN 0-87907-826-X). Cistercian Pubns.

Russian Rockefellers: The Saga of the Nobel Family & the Russian Oil Industry. text ed. 14.95 (ISBN 0-8179-6581-5). Hoover Inst Pr.

Russian Schoolboy. 10.95 (ISBN 0-19-274526-3). Oxford U Pr.

Russian Scientist. 5.95 (ISBN 0-02-594820-2). Macmillan.

Russia's Lomonosov: Chemist, Courtier, Physicist, Poet. lib. bdg. 11.00x (ISBN 0-8371-3688-1, MELO). Greenwood.

Ruth Benedict. 12.00x (ISBN 0-231-03519-5); pap. 4.50x (ISBN 0-231-03520-9). Columbia U Pr.

Ruth Page: An Intimate Biography. 17.50 (ISBN 0-8247-6490-0). Dekker.

Ruth Suckow. lib. bdg. 12.95x (ISBN 0-8057-0712-3). Irvington.

Ruth V. Hemenway, M.D. A Memoir of Revolutionary China, 1924-1941. 12.50 (ISBN 0-87023-230-4). U of Mass Pr.

Rutherford - Recollections of the Cambridge Days. 17.00 (ISBN 0-444-40968-8). Elsevier.

Rutherford & the Nature of the Atom. 7.50 (ISBN 0-8446-2053-X). Peter Smith.

Rutherford B. Hayes & His America. 17.50 (ISBN 0-8462-0863-6). Russell.

Rutherford B. Hayes, 1822-1893: Chronology, Documents, Bibliographical Aids. 6.00 (ISBN 0-379-12062-3). Oceana.

S

S. N. Behrman. lib. bdg. 7.95 (ISBN 0-8057-7154-9). Twayne.

S. T. P. A Journey Through America with the Rolling Stones. pap. 3.95 (ISBN 0-8415-0323-0). Dutton.

Sabbatai Sevi: The Mystical Messiah. 33.00x (ISBN 0-691-09916-2); pap. 12.50 (ISBN 0-691-01809-X). Princeton U Pr.

Sacagawea. PLB 6.95 (ISBN 0-87518-095-7). Dillon.

Sacajawea. pap. 5.95 (ISBN 0-8061-1578-5). U of Okla Pr.

Sacco-Vanzetti Case: A Transcript of the Record of the Trial of Nicola Sacco & Bartolomeo Vanzetti in the Courts of Massachusetts & Subsequent Proceedings, 1920-27. 2nd ed. 200.00 (ISBN 0-911858-01-6). Appel.

Sacred Circle: The Dilemma of the Intellectual in the Old South, 1840-1860. text ed. 11.00x (ISBN 0-8018-1967-9). Johns Hopkins.

Sacred Stories from Byzantium. 5.95 (ISBN 0-916586-15-4); pap. 3.95 (ISBN 0-916586-16-2). Holy Cross Orthodox.

Sad Nun at Synanon. 5.95 (ISBN 0-03-084493-2). HR&W.

Sad Swashbuckler: The Life of William Walker. 6.95 (ISBN 0-8407-6483-9). Elsevier-Nelson.

Safe at Home. pap. 3.95 (ISBN 0-570-03619-4, 39-1061). Concordia.

Saga & Myth of Sir Thomas More. lib. bdg. 8.50 (ISBN 0-8414-3642-8). Folcroft.

Saga & the Myth of Sir Thomas More. lib. bdg. 10.00 (ISBN 0-8495-0744-8). Arden Lib.

Saga of an American Jewish Family Since the Revolution: A History of the Family of Jonas Phillips. text ed. 16.75 (ISBN 0-8191-0939-8); pap. text ed. 9.25 (ISBN 0-8191-0940-1). U Pr of Amer.

Saga of Billy the Kid. 20.00. Ridgeway Bks.

Saga of Chief Joseph. pap. 5.95 (ISBN 0-8032-7202-2, BB699). U of Nebr Pr.

Saga of Hugh Glass: Pirate, Pawnee, & Mountain Man. 10.95x (ISBN 0-8032-0867-7); pap. 3.25 (ISBN 0-8032-5834-8, 614). U of Nebr Pr.

Saga of Saints. facs. ed. 15.25 (ISBN 0-8369-0959-3). Arno.

Saga of Themistocles. 19.95 (ISBN 0-500-40036-9). Thames Hudson.

Sage & Society: The Life & Thought of Ho Hsin-yin. pap. text ed. 4.75x (ISBN 0-8248-0347-7). U Pr of Hawaii.

Sage of Kanchi. lib. bdg. 6.25 (ISBN 0-89253-018-9). InterCulture.

Sailor's Admiral: A Biography of William F. Halsey. 9.95 (ISBN 0-690-01163-6). T Y Crowell.

Sails to Atoms: From Seaman to Admiral. 5.95 (ISBN 0-8059-2141-9). Dorrance.

Saint & Thought for Every Day. 3.95 (ISBN 0-8198-0471-1). Dghtrs St Paul.

Saint Augustine. 11.00 (ISBN 0-404-03155-2). AMS Pr.

Saint Benedict & the Sixth Century. lib. bdg. 11.50x (ISBN 0-8371-4209-1, CHSB). Greenwood.

St. Bernard of Clairvaux. 3.95 (ISBN 0-8198-0463-0); pap. 2.95 (ISBN 0-8198-0464-9). Dghtrs St Paul.

Saint-Exupery in America, 1942-1943: A Memoir. 8.00 (ISBN 0-8386-7610-3). Fairleigh Dickinson.

Saint Francis & His Four Ladies. 6.95 (ISBN 0-393-05427-6). Norton.

St. Francis of Assisi. lib. bdg. 17.50 (ISBN 0-8495-0933-5). Arden Lib.

Saint Francis of Assisi. lib. bdg. 8.95 (ISBN 0-8057-6249-3). Twayne.

Saint Francis of Assisi. PLB 5.90 (ISBN 0-531-00922-X). Watts.

St. Joan of Arc, Virgin-Soldier. 3.95 (ISBN 0-8198-0465-7); pap. 2.95 (ISBN 0-8198-0466-5). Dghtrs St Paul.

St. John of the Cross: His Life & Poetry. 32.50 (ISBN 0-521-20006-7); pap. 7.95 (ISBN 0-521-09953 6). Cambridge U Pr.

Saint-Just: Apostle of the Terror. 11.50 (ISBN 0-208-00531-5). Shoe String.

St. Louis Woman. lib. bdg. 19.00x (ISBN 0-405-09712-3). Arno.

Saint Nicholas of Myra, Bari & Manhattan: Biography of a Legend. lib. bdg. 28.00x (ISBN 0-226-40699-7). U of Chicago Pr.

Saint Paul. 14.95 (ISBN 0-684-14682-7). Scribner.

Saint Peter Canisius. 10.00 (ISBN 0-8294-0008-7). Loyola.

St. Pius V - A Brief Account of His Life, Times, Virtues & Miracles. pap. 2.00 (ISBN 0-89555-068-7, 964). TAN Bks Pubs.

Saint-Saens. 15.00 (ISBN 0-8369-5045-3). Arno.

Saint-Saens. lib. bdg. 10.00x (ISBN 0-8371-4236-9, HECS). Greenwood.

St. Seraphim of Sarov. pap. 5.50 (ISBN 0-913836-28-1, BX597 S3772). St Vladimirs.

St. Simons Memoir: The Personal Story of Finding the Island & Writing the St. Simons Trilogy of Novels. 10.00 (ISBN 0-397-01216-0). Lippincott.

St. Thomas Aquinas. lib. bdg. 8.95 (ISBN 0-8057-6248-5). Twayne.

Sainte-Beuve. lib. bdg. 20.75x (ISBN 0-313-20013-0, NISB). Greenwood.

Saints Alive. facsimile ed. 13.75 (ISBN 0-8369-8011-5). Arno.

Saints Alive: The Humble Heroes of the New Testament. 2.95 (ISBN 0-8054-8116-8). Broadman.

Saints Alive! The Lives of Thirteen Heroic Saints. 7.95 (ISBN 0-385-12441-4). Doubleday.

Saints & Heroes Since the Middle Ages. 17.25 (ISBN 0-8369-1515-1). Arno.

Saints & Heroes Speak. pap. 7.95 (ISBN 0-87973-640-2). Our Sunday Visitor.

Saints & Heroes to the End of the Middle Ages. facs. ed. 15.50 (ISBN 0-8369-0544-X). Arno.

Saints & Rebels. facsimile ed. 17.25 (ISBN 0-8369-2322-7). Arno.

Saints Beyond the White Cliffs: Stories of English Saints. facs. ed. 15.00 (ISBN 0-8369-8058-1). Arno.

Saints for All Seasons. pap. 2.95 (ISBN 0-385-12909-2). Doubleday.

Saints for All Seasons. 7.95 (ISBN 0-385-12908-4); pap. 2.95 (ISBN 0-385-12909-2). Doubleday.

Saints for Our Time. pap. 1.95. Arena Lettres.

Saints for Sinners. 13.75 (ISBN 0-8369-1504-6). Arno.

Saints in Times of Turmoil. pap. 2.45 (ISBN 0-8091-2005-4). Paulist Pr.

Saints of Chaos. facs. ed. 12.25 (ISBN 0-8369-0752-3). Arno.

Saints of the Americas. 9.95 (ISBN 0-87973-880-4). Our Sunday Visitor.

Saints That Moved the World: Anthony, Augustine, Francis, Ignatius, Theresa. 24.50 (ISBN 0-8369-8159-6). Arno.

Saints Who Changed Things. 6.95 (ISBN 0-89310-022-6); pap. 3.95 (ISBN 0-89310-023-4). Carillon Bks.

Saints Who Spoke English. 8.95 (ISBN 0-89310-045-5); pap. 4.95 (ISBN 0-89310-046-3). Carillon Bks.

Sakharov Speaks. 6.95 (ISBN 0-394-49209-9). Knopf.

Saladin. 19.50 (ISBN 0-87395-095-X); microfiche 19.50 (ISBN 0-87395-195-6). State U NY Pr.

Saladin. text ed. 16.00x (ISBN 0-06-492877-2). B&N.

Saladin & the Fall of the Kingdom of Jerusalem. 30.00 (ISBN 0-404-58270-2). AMS Pr.

Salmon Portland Chase. 13.00 (ISBN 0-403-00216 8). Scholarly.

Salmon Portland Chase. lib. bdg. 29.95 (ISBN 0-8383-0952-6). Haskell.

Salmon Portland Chase. lib. bdg. 15.00x (ISBN 0-8371-0465-3, HAX&). Greenwood.

Salmon Portland Chase. 10.00 (ISBN 0-404-50878-2). AMS Pr.

Saltonstall Papers: 1607-1815. 25.00. Mass Hist Soc.

Salvado Memoirs: Historical Memoirs of Australia & Particularly of the Benedictine Mission of New Norcia & of the Habits & Customs of the Australian Natives. pap. 10.95 (ISBN 0-85564-114-2). Intl Schol Bk Serv.

Salvador De Sa & the Struggle for Brazil & Angola: 1602-1686. lib. bdg. 24.00x (ISBN 0-8371-7411-2, BOSS). Greenwood.

Sam Clemens of Hannibal. 27.00 (ISBN 0-404-15328-3). AMS Pr.

Sam Foote, Comedian, 1720-1777. 12.00x (ISBN 0-8147-8153-5). NYU Pr.

Sam Francis. 55.00 (ISBN 0-8109-0265-6). Abrams.

Sam Houston & the Senate. 9.50 (ISBN 0-8363-0087-4). Jenkins.

Sam Houston: Boy Chieftain. 5.95 (ISBN 0-672-50163-5). Bobbs.

Sam Houston: Hero of Texas. PLB 3.58 (ISBN 0-8116-6286-1). Garrard.

Sam Houston: The Great Designer. pap. 3.95x (ISBN 0-292-78422-8). U of Tex Pr.

Sam Houston with the Cherokees, 1829-1833. pap. 4.95 (ISBN 0-292-77526-1). U of Tex Pr.

Sam Houston's Navy. lib. bdg. 5.95; pap. 2.25. Grossmont Pr.

Sam Houston's Wife: A Biography of Margaret Lea Houston. 12.50 (ISBN 0-8061-0926-2). U of Okla Pr.

Samson & Delilah. 6.25 (ISBN 0-688-41238-6). Lothrop.

Samuel Adams. 14.50 (ISBN 0-8274-3319-0). R West.

Samuel Adams. 14.75 (ISBN 0-404-50852-9). AMS Pr.

Samuel Beckett. pap. 1.50 (ISBN 0-231-02659-5, MW4). Columbia U Pr.

Samuel Beckett. A Biography. pap. 7.95 (ISBN 0-15-679241-9). HarBraceJ.

Samuel Bell Maxey: A Biography. 11.50 (ISBN 0-292-77509-1). U of Tex Pr.

Samuel Butler: A Sketch. lib. bdg. 8.50 (ISBN 0-8414-2195-1). Folcroft.

Samuel Butler & His Family Relations. lib. bdg. 25.00 (ISBN 0-8414-4586-9). Folcroft.

Samuel Butler, Author of Erewhon: The Man & His Work. lib. bdg. 20.00 (ISBN 0-8414-0962-5). Folcroft.

Samuel Coleridge-Taylor: Anglo-Black Composer, 1875-1912. 9.50 (ISBN 0-8108-1010-7). Scarecrow.

Samuel De Champlain. PLB 4.90 (ISBN 0-531-01275-1). Watts.

Samuel F. B. Morse: His Letters & Journals. 52.00 (ISBN 0-527-65250-4). Kraus Repr.

Samuel F. B. Morse: His Letters & Journals. lib. bdg. 55.00 (ISBN 0-306-71304-7). Da Capo.

Samuel Foote: A Biography. 18.00 (ISBN 0-405-08519-2). Arno.

Samuel Goldwyn Presents. 19.95 (ISBN 0-498-01658-7). A S Barnes.

Samuel Gompers, American Statesman. lib. bdg. 10.50x (ISBN 0-8371-2293-7, THSG). Greenwood.

Samuel Gompers and the Origins of the American Federation of Labor, 1848-1896. lib. bdg. 14.95 (ISBN 0-8371-6277-7, KAP/). Greenwood.

Samuel Greenberg, Hart Crane & the Lost Manuscripts. text ed. 7.50 (ISBN 0-391-00558-8). Humanities.

Samuel H. Walker's Account of the Mier Expedition. 10.00 (ISBN 0-87611-040-5); special collector's edition 40.00 (ISBN 0-87611-038-3). Tex St Hist Assn.

Samuel Johnson. pap. 4.95 (ISBN 0-07-067715-8). McGraw.

Samuel Johnson: A Biography. 12.50 (ISBN 0-670-61671-0). Viking Pr.

Samuel Johnson Als Kritiker Im Lichte Von Pseudoklassizismus und Romantik. pap. 9.50 (ISBN 0-384-08955-0). Johnson Repr.

Samuel Johnson & the Age of Travel. 14.00x (ISBN 0-8203-0380-1). U of Ga Pr.

Samuel Johnson & the New Science. 17.50x (ISBN 0-299-06010-1). U of Wis Pr.

Samuel Johnson, Biographer. 12.50x (ISBN 0-8014-0968-3). Cornell U Pr.

Samuel Johnson's Early Biographers. 6.95x (ISBN 0-87745-021-8). U of Iowa Pr.

Samuel Jones Tilden: A Study in Political Sagacity. lib. bdg. 31.00x (ISBN 0-8371-6912-7, FLST). Greenwood.

Samuel Marsden: The Great Survivor. 26.00x (ISBN 0-522-84120-1). Intl Schol Bk Serv.

Samuel Pepys. lib. bdg. 22.95 (ISBN 0-8383-2061-9). Haskell.

Samuel Pepys. lib. bdg. 20.00. Folcroft.

Samuel Pepys. 7.75 (ISBN 0-8046-1548-9). Kennikat.

Samuel Pepys. facsimile ed. 12.75 (ISBN 0-8369-5855-1). Arno.

Samuel Pepys & His World. 9.95 (ISBN 0-684-15512-5). Scribner.

Samuel Pepys & the Royal Navy. lib. bdg. 9.75 (ISBN 0-8414-8532-1). Folcroft.

Samuel Pepys & the Royal Navy. lib. bdg. 14.95 (ISBN 0-8383-1314-0). Haskell.

Samuel Pepys & the World He Lived in. 25.00 (ISBN 0-8274-0575-8). R West.

Samuel Pepys in the Diary. lib. bdg. 16.25x (ISBN 0-313-20363-6, HUSD). Greenwood.

Samuel Peter Heintzelman & the Sonora Exploring & Mining Company. 12.50x (ISBN 0-8165-0679-5); pap. text ed. 7.95x (ISBN 0-8165-0574-8). U of Ariz Pr.

Samuel Phelps & Sadler's Wells Theatre. 20.00x (ISBN 0-8195-4029-3). Columbia U Pr.

Samuel Richardson. 11.00 (ISBN 0-8103-3055-5). Gale.

Samuel Richardson. 7.50 (ISBN 0-8274-1778-0). R West.

Samuel Richardson. 15.00 (ISBN 0-403-00018-1). Scholarly.

Samuel Richardson: A Biographical & Critical Study. lib. bdg. 10.95. Folcroft.

Samuel Richardson: A Biographical & Critical Study. 11.00 (ISBN 0-8046-0851-2). Kennikat.

Samuel Richardson: A Biographical & Critical Study. lib. bdg. 30.00 (ISBN 0-8495-5109-9). Arden Lib.

Samuel Richardson: A Biography. 29.00x (ISBN 0-19-812431-7) Oxford U Pr.

Samuel Richardson: Master Printer. lib. bdg. 23.25x (ISBN 0-8371-9732-5, SASR). Greenwood.

Samuel S. Stratton: A Story of Political Gumption. 3.95 Heineman.

Samuel Seabury: Priest & Physician, Bishop of Connecticut. 12.50 (ISBN 0-208-00532-3). Shoe String.

Samuel Seabury, 1729-1796: A Study in the High Church Tradition. 15.00 (ISBN 0-8214-0098-3). Ohio U Pr.

Samuel Sewall & the World He Lived In. 9.00 (ISBN 0-8462-0987-X). Russell.

Samuel Sewall of Boston. 5.95 (ISBN 0-02-630310-8) Macmillan.

Samuel Taylor Coleridge. 21.00 (ISBN 0-403-00792-5). Scholarly.

Samuel Taylor Coleridge: A Biographical Study. lib. bdg. 24.00x (ISBN 0-313-20539-6, CHST). Greenwood.

Samuel Taylor Coleridge: A Bondage of Opium. 15.00 (ISBN 0-8128-1711-7). Stein & Day.

Samuel Taylor Coleridge: A Bondage of Opium. pap. 7.95 (ISBN 0-8128-1852-0). Stein & Day.

Samuel Wesley, Musician: The Story of His Life. 12.50 (ISBN 0-405-08751-9). Arno.

San Antonio Rose: The Life & Music of Bob Wills. 12.50 (ISBN 0-252-00470-1). U of Ill Pr.

San Martin the Liberator. lib. bdg. 9.50x (ISBN 0-8371-3012-3, MESM). Greenwood.

Sand in My Eyes. 7.50 (ISBN 0-87358-130-X). Northland.

Sandhills Beckon. 10.00 (ISBN 0-931068-08-8). Purcells.

Sandro Botticelli. Incl. Life & Work (ISBN 0-520-03372-8); Complete Catalogue (ISBN 0-520-03574-7). boxed set 120.00x. U of Cal Pr.

Sandy: The Autobiography of a Star. pap. 3.95 (ISBN 0-671-33046-2). Wanderer Bks.

Sane Positivist: A Biography of Edward L. Thorndike. 30.00x (ISBN 0-8195-3093-X). Columbia U Pr.

Sanford Robinson Gifford (1823-1880) lib. bdg. 73.00 (ISBN 0-8240-2737-X). Garland Pub.

Sanity of William Blake. pap. 7.95 (ISBN 0-8383-0097-9). Haskell.

Sanity of William Blake. lib. bdg. 5.50 (ISBN 0-8414-6156-2). Folcroft.

Santa Anna: The Story of an Enigma Who Once Was Mexico. 17.50 (ISBN 0-208-00533-1). Shoe String.

Santos-Dumont: A Study in Obsession. lib. bdg. 22.00x (ISBN 0-405-12210-1). Arno.

Santos-Dumont: Study in Obsession. 12.50. Beachcomber Bks.

Sanz, Promotor De la Conciencia Separatista En Puerto Rico. pap. 1.85 (ISBN 0-8477-0035-6). U of PR Pr.
Sara Teasdale: A Biography. 14.95 (ISBN 0-913110-03-5). Pentelic Pr.
Sarah & Abe in Indiana. 7.95 (ISBN 0-87716-016-3). Moore Pub Co.
Sarah Bernhardt. 12.00 (ISBN 0-405-08237-1). Arno.
Sarah Bernhardt. lib. bdg. 9.50x (ISBN 0-8371-3018-2, BASB). Greenwood.
Sarah Bernhardt. 12.95 (ISBN 0-02-535470-1). Macmillan.
Sarah Bernhardt & Her World. 15.95 (ISBN 0-399-11887-X). Putnam.
Sarah Orne Jewett. 7.50 (ISBN 0-8446-1305-3). Peter Smith.
Sarah Tyson Rorer: The Nation's Instructress in Dietetics & Cookery. 6.00 (ISBN 0-87169-119-1). Am Philos.
Sarnoff, an American Success. 12.50 (ISBN 0-8129-0672-1). Times Bks.
Sartre. 6.95 (ISBN 0-397-00750-7). Lippincott.
Satire & the Correspondence of Swift. pap. 2.50 (ISBN 0-674-78976-8). Harvard U Pr.
Satyendra Nath Bose. pap. 2.25 (ISBN 0-89744-196-6). Auromere.
Savage Messiah. pap. 2.95 (ISBN 0-380-01394-0, 12831). Avon.
Savage Pilgrimage: A Narrative by D. H. Lawrence. 18.00 (ISBN 0-403-01760-2). Scholarly.
Savage Pilgrimage: A Narrative by D. H. Lawrence. 19.00 (ISBN 0-8274-3325-5). R West.
Savage Ruskin. 14.95x (ISBN 0-8143-1619-0). Wayne St U Pr.
Savage Scene: The Life & Times of James Kirker, Frontier King. 8.95 (ISBN 0-8038-6712-3). Hastings.
Saviors of Mankind. 24.50 (ISBN 0-8369-1432-5). Arno.
Savonarola & Florence: Prophecy & Patriotism in the Renaissance. 13.50x (ISBN 0-691-05184-4). Princeton U Pr.
Say It Ain't So, Joe! The Story of Shoeless Joe Jackson. 9.95 (ISBN 0-316-32925-8). Little.
Scandinavian Kings in the British Isles, 850-880. 29.00x (ISBN 0-19-821865-6). Oxford U Pr.
Scapegoat: The Lonesome Death of Bruno Richard Hauptmann. 12.50 (ISBN 0-399-11660-5). Putnam.
Scarlett O'Hara's Younger Sister: My Lively Life in & Out of Hollywood. 10.00 (ISBN 0-8184-0243-1). Lyle Stuart.
Scavullo on Men. 15.00 (ISBN 0-394-41934-0). Random.
Scenes from Childhood. 7.95 (ISBN 0-525-38820-6). Dutton.
Scenes from Country Life. 8.95 (ISBN 0-13-791632-9). P-H.
Scenes from Surgical Life. 14.95x (ISBN 0-8464-0813-9). Beekman Pubs.
Scenes from the Life of an Actor. lib. bdg. 15.00x (ISBN 0-405-08617-2). Arno.
Scenes in the Life of Harriet Tubman. facs. ed. 13.25 (ISBN 0-8369-8782-9). Arno.
Schoenberg. pap. 6.95x (ISBN 0-19-314116-7). Oxford U Pr.
Scholar-Friends: Letters of Francis James Child & James Russell Lowell. lib. bdg. 8.50x (ISBN 0-8371-3333-5, CHSF). Greenwood.
Scholar in Action, Edwin F. Gay. lib. bdg. 13.50x (ISBN 0-8371-0101-8, HEEG). Greenwood.
Scholar in the Wilderness: Francis Adrian Van der Kemp. 6.95x (ISBN 0-8156-0034-8). Syracuse U Pr.
School for Colored Girls in Washington, D. C; see Myrtilla Miner: A Memoir.
School in Uganda. text ed. 13.00x (ISBN 0-575-02050-4). Verry.
Schoolmaker: Sawney Webb & the Bell Buckle Story. 10.00x (ISBN 0-8078-1163-7); pap. 6.00 (ISBN 0-8078-1395-8). U of NC Pr.
Schoolmasters of the Tenth Century. 13.50 (ISBN 0-208-01628-7). Shoe String.
Schopenhauer As Educator. pap. 3.95x (ISBN 0-89526-950-3). Regnery-Gateway.
Schubert. lib. bdg. 16.25x (ISBN 0-8371-8472-X, SCSCH). Greenwood.
Schubert: A Critical Biography. lib. bdg. 19.50 (ISBN 0-306-77409-7). Da Capo.
Schubert, the Man. facsimile ed. 18.25 (ISBN 0-8369-5177-8). Arno.
Schubert, the Man. lib. bdg. 13.25x (ISBN 0-8371-4201-6, BISM). Greenwood.
Schubert's Songs: A Biographical Study. 12.50 (ISBN 0-394-48048-1). Knopf.
Schumann. rev. ed. 12.50x (ISBN 0-460-03170-8). Biblio Dist.
Schumann, a Life of Suffering. facsimile ed. 14.75 (ISBN 0-8369-5175-1). Arno.
Schumann: A Symposium. lib. bdg. 20.25x (ISBN 0-8371-9050-9, SCSY). Greenwood.
Schumpeter, Social Scientist. facs. ed. 18.25 (ISBN 0-8369-1138-5). Arno.
Schwiering & the West. new ed. 25.00 (ISBN 0-87970-128-5). North Plains.
Science of Society: Toward an Understanding of the Life & Work of Karl August Wittfogel. 103.00 (ISBN 90-279-7766-6). Mouton.
Scientific Autobiography of Joseph Priestley, 1733-1804: Selected Scientific Correspondence, with Commentary. 19.95x (ISBN 0-262-19035-4). MIT Pr.
Scientific Blacksmith. 15.00 (ISBN 0-405-04693-6). Arno.
Scientists & Inventors. 17.50 (ISBN 0-87196-410-4). Facts on File.
Scientists Who Work Outdoors. 3.50 (ISBN 0-396-04804-8). Dodd.
Scoop: The Life & Politics of Henry M. Jackson. 25.00x (ISBN 0-8128-1884-9). Stein & Day.
Scope of Happiness: A Personal Memoir. 12.95 (ISBN 0-517-53688-9). Crown.
Scotland Yard Scientist: My Thirty Years in Forensic Science. 6.95 (ISBN 0-8008-7010-7). Taplinger.
Scott & Ernest: The Authority of Failure & the Authority of Success. pap. price not set (ISBN 0-8093-0977-7). S Ill U Pr.
Scott & His Circle. facsimile ed. 16.00 (ISBN 0-8369-6607-4). Arno.
Scott & His Poetry. lib. bdg. 7.50. Folcroft.
Scott & His Poetry. 7.25 (ISBN 0-404-52526-1). AMS Pr.
Scott Fitzgerald. 4.95 (ISBN 0-684-14661-4). Scribner.
Scott Joplin. 8.95 (ISBN 0-385-11155-X). Doubleday.
Scott Joplin & the Ragtime Years. 4.95 (ISBN 0-396-07308-5). Dodd.
Scott of the Antarctic. 12.95 (ISBN 0-689-10861-3). Atheneum.
Scott Was Here. 8.95 (ISBN 0-440-07665-X). Delacorte.
Scoundrel Time. 8.95 (ISBN 0-316-35515-1). Little.
Scoundrel Time. pap. 1.95 (ISBN 0-553-10282-6). Bantam.
Scoundrel Time. lib. bdg. 8.95 (ISBN 0-8161-6446-0). G K Hall.
Scourge of the Clergy: Peter of Dreux, Duke of Brittany. lib. bdg. 12.00 (ISBN 0-374-96175-1). Octagon.
Scream Queens: Heroines of the Horrors. 15.95 (ISBN 0-02-508170-5). Macmillan.
Scream Queens: Heroines of the Horrors. pap. 7.95 (ISBN 0-02-012140-7). Macmillan.
Screen of Time: A Study of Luchino Visconti. 14.95 (ISBN 0-15-179684-X). HarBraceJ.
Screwball. pap. 1.25 (ISBN 0-451-06421-6, Y6421). NAL.
Scriabin. lib. bdg. 12.50 (ISBN 0-306-71322-5). Da Capo.
Scriabin. lib. bdg. 9.25x (ISBN 0-8371-4350-0, SWSC). Greenwood.
Sculptor France Gorse. 10.00. Studia Slovenica.
Sculptor Giovanni Bologna. lib. bdg. 51.00x (ISBN 0-8240-2696-9). Garland Pub.
Sculptor Jules Dalou: Studies in His Style & Imagery. lib. bdg. 54.00 (ISBN 0-8240-2699-3). Garland Pub.
Se-Quo-Yah, the American Cadmus & Modern Moses. 23.50. AMS Pr.
Sea & Earth: The Life of Rachel Carson. pap. 0.95 (ISBN 0-440-98134-4). Dell.
Sea & Earth: The Life of Rachel Carson. 7.95 (ISBN 0-690-72288-5). T Y Crowell.
Sea-Dragon: Journals of Francis Drake's Voyage Around the World. PLB 8.79 (ISBN 0-06-025186-7). Har-Row.
Sea Fighters from Drake to Farragut. facs. ed. 14.50 (ISBN 0-8369-0461-3). Arno.
Sea Road to the Indies: An Account of the Voyages & Exploits of the Portuguese Navigators, Together with the Life & Times of Dom Vasco De Gama, Capitao-Mor, Viceroy of India & Count of Vidigueira. lib. bdg. 14.00x (ISBN 0-8371-5165-1, HARO). Greenwood.
Sealth. PLB 6.95 (ISBN 0-87518-155-4). Dillon.
Sean O'Casey. pap. text ed. 2.50 (ISBN 0-87695-097-7). Aurora Pubs.
Sean O'Casey & His World. 8.95 (ISBN 0-684-14727-0). Scribner.
Sean O'Casey: The Man & His Plays. pap. 1.75 (ISBN 0-8065-0061-1, 227). Citadel Pr.
Search for Adele Parker. 6.95 (ISBN 0-87212-046-5). Libra.
Search for Harry Price. 28.00 (ISBN 0-7156-1143-7). Biblio Dist.
Search for JFK. pap. 2.25 (ISBN 0-425-03354-6). Berkley Pub.
Search for JFK. 12.95 (ISBN 0-399-11418-1). Berkley Pub.
Search for Me. pap. 3.25 (ISBN 0-8054-5252-4). Broadman.
Searching Spirit: Joy Adamson's Autobiography. 14.95 (ISBN 0-15-179919-9). HarBraceJ.
Season in Hell: The Life of Arthur Rimbaud. 27.50 (ISBN 0-404-16309-2). AMS Pr.
Second Empire. lib. bdg. 19.75x (ISBN 0-8371-7985-8, GOSE). Greenwood.
Second Fatherland: The Life & Fortunes of a German Immigrant. 11.95 (ISBN 0-89096-017-8). Tex A&M Univ Pr.
Second Flowering: Works & Days of the Lost Generation. 7.95 (ISBN 0-670-62826-3). Viking Pr.
Second Flowering: Works & Days of the Lost Generation. pap. 4.95 (ISBN 0-14-005498-7). Penguin.
Second Ring of Power. 9.95 (ISBN 0-671-22942-7). S&S.
Second Ring of Power. pap. write for info. (ISBN 0-671-81650-0). PB.
Second Sight: A Miraculous Story of Vision Regained. 7.95 (ISBN 0-87131-287-5). M Evans.
Second Time Is Better. pap. 1.95 (ISBN 0-87216-515-9). Playboy Pr Pbks.
Second Wind: The Memoirs of an Opinionated Man. 9.95 (ISBN 0-394-50385-6). Random.
Secret Country of C. S. Lewis. 4.95 (ISBN 0-8028-3468-X). Eerdmans.
Secret Diary of Harold L. Ickes. lib. bdg. 125.00 (ISBN 0-306-70626-1); lib. bdg. 47.50 ea. (ISBN 0-306-70627-X) (ISBN 0-306-70628-8) (ISBN 0-306-70629-6). Da Capo.
Secret Diary of William Byrd of Westover 1709-1712. 29.00 (ISBN 0-405-03304-4). Arno.
Secret Journal & Other Writings. 10.50 (ISBN 0-86527-300-6). Fertig.
Secret Life of Henry Ford. 10.95 (ISBN 0-672-52377-9). Bobbs.
Secret Life of Tyrone Power. 9.95 (ISBN 0-688-03484-5). Morrow.
Secret Love Affairs. 9.95 (ISBN 0-8246-0201-3). Jonathan David.
Secret of Paul the Apostle. pap. 6.95 (ISBN 0-88344-454-2). Orbis Bks.
Secret of Samson. pap. 1.95 (ISBN 0-8362-4302-1). Andrews & McMeel.
Secret Orchard of Roger Ackerley. 6.95 (ISBN 0-8076-0799-1). Braziller.
Secret Places of Trout Fishermen. 8.95 (ISBN 0-02-584300-1). Macmillan.
Secret Soldier: The Story of Deborah Sampson. 5.95g (ISBN 0-590-07432-6). Schol Bk Serv.
Secret Soldier: The Story of Deborah Sampson. pap. 1.25 (ISBN 0-590-10150-1). Schol Bk Serv.
Secretary: Martin Bormann, the Man Who Manipulated Hitler. 15.95 (ISBN 0-394-50321-X). Random.
Secretary of Europe: The Life of Friedrich Gentz, Enemy of Napoleon. 16.50 (ISBN 0-208-00957-4). Shoe String.
Secretary Stimson: A Study in Statecraft. 17.50 (ISBN 0-208-00966-3). Shoe String.
Secrets of Grownups. 14.95 (ISBN 0-07-010223-6). McGraw.
Secrets of Houdini. 2.50. Wehman.
Secrets of Houdini. 16.00 (ISBN 0-8103-3725-8). Gale.
Secrets of Houdini. pap. 3.00 (ISBN 0-486-22913-0). Dover.
Secrets of Houdini. 6.50 (ISBN 0-8446-4719-5). Peter Smith.
See You in the Morning. 4.50 (ISBN 0-8054-5237-0). Broadman.
Seeds of Southern Change: The Life of Will Alexander. pap. 4.95 (ISBN 0-393-00813-4). Norton.
Seeds of Southern Change: The Life of Will Alexander. 12.50x (ISBN 0-226-17665-7). U of Chicago Pr.
Seeing Fingers: The Story of Louis Braille. 5.95 (ISBN 0-679-25133-2). McKay.
Seeing Stars. lib. bdg. 24.00x (ISBN 0-405-09714-X). Arno.
Sego. pap. 2.95 (ISBN 0-88270-247-5). Logos.
Seizure. pap. 2.25. Putnam.
Seizure. pap. 1.95 (04875-5). BJ Pub Group.
Seizure. 8.95 (ISBN 0-87131-254-9). M Evans.
Selected Black American Authors: An Illustrated Bio-Bibliography. lib. bdg. 30.00 (ISBN 0-8161-8065-2). G K Hall.
Selected Correspondence of Fryderyk Chopin. 29.50 (ISBN 0-306-79579-5). Da Capo.
Selected Letters of Cotton Mather. 22.50x (ISBN 0-8071-0920-7). La State U Pr.
Selected Letters of Ezra Pound, 1907-1941. pap. 6.95 (ISBN 0-8112-0161-9, NDP317). New Directions.
Selected Letters of Horace Walpole. 19.50x (ISBN 0-300-01643-3); pap. 5.45x (ISBN 0-300-01669-7, Y258). Yale U Pr.
Selected Letters of Hubert Murray. 9.95x (ISBN 0-19-550313-9). Oxford U Pr.
Selected Letters of Voltaire. 15.00x (ISBN 0-8147-0972-9). NYU Pr.
Selected Women of the Scriptures of Stamina & Courage. pap. 3.95 (ISBN 0-931446-02-3). Honor Bks.
Selections from Bayle's Dictionary. lib. bdg. 15.25x (ISBN 0-8371-1068-8, BABD). Greenwood.
Selections from the Correspondence of Theodore Roosevelt & Henry Cabot Lodge, 1884-1918. lib. bdg. 75.00 (ISBN 0-306-70129-4). Da Capo.
Selections from "The History of the Rebellion" & "The Life by Himself". 12.95x (ISBN 0-19-215852-X). Oxford U Pr.
Selections from the Letters of Thomas Sergeant Perry. 19.00 (ISBN 0-403-00684-8). Scholarly.
Selections from the Letters of Thomas Sergeant Perry. 15.00 (ISBN 0-8274-3360-3). R West.
Self-Made Woman: Biography of Nobel-Prize-Winner Grazia Deledda. 6.95 (ISBN 0-395-21914-0). HM.
Self Portrait. pap. 8.00. SBD.
Self-Portrait. pap. 2.50 (ISBN 0-425-04485-8). Berkley Pub.
Self-Portrait. 10.95 (ISBN 0-88326-152-9). Wyden.
Self-Portrait of a Family: Letters by Jessie, Dorothy Lee, Claude, & David Bernard. 12.95 (ISBN 0-8070-3798-2); pap. 6.95 (ISBN 0-8070-3799-0, BP597). Beacon Pr.
Self-Portrait with Donors: Confessions of an Art Collector. 12.95 (ISBN 0-316-91803-2). Little.
Self-Portrait with Friends: The Selected Diaries of Cecil Beaton, 1926-1974. 14.95 (ISBN 0-8129-0859-7). Times Bks.
Selma Lagerlof, Her Life & Work. 6.00 (ISBN 0-8046-0027-9). Kennikat.
Selznick. pap. 1.25 (ISBN 0-671-78207-X). PB.
Selznick Players. 17.50 (ISBN 0-498-01375-8). A S Barnes.
Senator & Bull Moose Manager 1867-1917 see Joseph M. Dixon of Montana.
Senator from Maine - Margaret Chase Smith. pap. 1.25 (ISBN 0-440-98223-5). Dell.
Senator Hugh Butler & Nebraska Republicanism. 15.50 (ISBN 0-8357-0185-9, IS-00014). Univ Microfilms.
Senator Joe McCarthy. pap. 3.95 (ISBN 0-06-090345-7, CN345). Har-Row.
Senator Joseph McCarthy & the American Labor Movement. 12.50x (ISBN 0-8262-0188-1). U of Mo Pr.
Senator Josiah William Bailey of North Carolina: A Political Biography. 13.75 (ISBN 0-8223-0117-2). Duke.
Senator William J. Stone & the Politics of Compromise. 12.50 (ISBN 0-8046-9232-7). Kennikat.
Senators from Georgia. 12.95 (ISBN 0-87397-082-9). Strode.
Seneca Ray Stoddard, Versatile Camera Artist. 10.50 (ISBN 0-9601158-1-1). Adirondack Yes.
Sense of Place. text ed. 13.50x (ISBN 0-8419-7100-5). Holmes & Meier.
Sentenced to Die: The People, the Crimes & the Controversy. 9.95 (ISBN 0-02-543070-X). Macmillan.
Sequoyah. PLB 6.95 (ISBN 0-87518-057-4). Dillon.
Sequoyah. pap. 2.95 (ISBN 0-8061-1056-2). U of Okla Pr.
Sequoyah: The Cherokee Who Captured Words. PLB 4.48 (ISBN 0-8116-6612-3). Garrard.
Serengeti Home. 9.95 (ISBN 0-8037-8173-3). Dial.
Sergei Eisenstein. pap. 2.95 (L00257). Crown.
Sergei Koussevitzky & His Epoch. 18.25 (ISBN 0-8369-5050-X). Arno.
Sergei Nechaev. 18.00 (ISBN 0-8135-0867-3). Rutgers U Pr.
Sergei Rachmaninoff: A Lifetime in Music. 15.00x (ISBN 0-8147-0044-6). NYU Pr.
Sergei Witte & the Industrialization of Russia. pap. text ed. 4.95x (ISBN 0-689-70196-9, 141). Atheneum.
Series of Letters Between Mrs. Elizabeth Carter & Miss Catherine Talbot from the Year 1741 to 1770. 98.00 (ISBN 0-404-56730-4); 24.50 ea. AMS Pr.
Serpent & the Nightingale. 19.50 (ISBN 0-571-10869-5). Merrimack Bk Serv.
Serpico. 7.95 (ISBN 0-670-63498-0). Viking Pr.
Serpico. pap. 2.25 (ISBN 0-553-10265-6, 13424-8). Bantam.
Servant of the Cecils: The Life of Sir Michael Hickes, 1543-1612. 17.50x (ISBN 0-87471-933-X). Rowman.
Set Point: The Story of Chris Evert. PLB 5.29 (ISBN 0-399-61073-1). Putnam.
Seth Low. 11.50 (ISBN 0-404-04037-3). AMS Pr.
Seumas O'Kelly. 4.50 (ISBN 0-8387-7765-1); pap. 1.95 (ISBN 0-8387-7661-2). Bucknell U Pr.
Seurat. pap. 7.95 (ISBN 0-19-519954-5). Oxford U Pr.
Seven Edwards of England. 12.75 (ISBN 0-8046-1241-2). Kennikat.
Seven Founders of American Literature. 8.95 (ISBN 0-910244-87-1). Blair.
Seven Houses: A Memoir of Time & Places. 5.95 (ISBN 0-671-21454-3). S&S.
Seven Houses: My Life with Books. 7.95 (ISBN 0-690-01353-1). T Y Crowell.
Seven Queens of England. 5.95 (ISBN 0-8149-0430-0). Vanguard.
Seven Sovereign Queens. 5.95 (ISBN 0-8149-0660-5). Vanguard.
Seven Stages. 5.95 (ISBN 0-8149-0425-4). Vanguard.
Seven Stairs. pap. 3.50 (ISBN 0-87955-307-3). O'Hara.
Seven Steeples. lib. bdg. 11.50x (ISBN 0-89621-023-5); pap. 4.95x (ISBN 0-89621-022-7). Thorndike Pr.

Seven Storey Mountain. pap. 4.95 (ISBN 0-15-680679-7). HarBraceJ.
Seven Storey Mountain. pap. 1.95 (ISBN 0-451-61393-7, MJ1393). NAL.
Seven Who Shaped Our Destiny: The Founding Fathers As Revolutionaries. 11.95 (ISBN 0-06-013078-4). Har-Row.
Seven Who Shaped Our Destiny: The Founding Fathers As Revolutionaries. pap. 5.50x (ISBN 0-06-131939-2, TB 1939). Har-Row.
Seven Wise Men of Colonial America. 5.00x (ISBN 0-674-80250-0). Harvard U Pr.
Seven Women Against the World. 17.50 (ISBN 0-88355-316-3). Hyperion-Conn.
Seven Women: Portraits from the American Radical Tradition. 8.95 (ISBN 0-670-63599-5). Viking Pr.
Seven Women: Portraits from the American Radical Tradition. pap. 2.95 (ISBN 0-14-004792-1). Penguin.
Seven Years of My Life. lib. bdg. 7.95 (ISBN 0-8057-5740-6). Twayne.
Seventeen Black Artists. 7.95 (ISBN 0-396-06391-8). Dodd.
Seventeen Letters of George Noel Gordon, Lord Byron, to an Unknown Lady. lib. bdg. 12.50 (ISBN 0-8414-6765-X). Folcroft.
Seventeenth-Century Biographies. lib. bdg. 6.50 (ISBN 0-8492-2189-7). R West.
Seventeenth Century Biographies. lib. bdg. 6.00 (ISBN 0-8414-6798-6). Folcroft.
Seventy Years of It: An Autobiography. lib. bdg. 20.00x (ISBN 0-405-10010-8). Arno.
Severe Mercy. 6.95 (ISBN 0-06-068821-1). Har-Row.
Severe Mercy. pap. 2.50 (ISBN 0-553-12963-5). Bantam.
Sex & Spirit: God, Woman, & the Ministry. 6.95 (ISBN 0-912760-38-9); pap. 4.95 (ISBN 0-912760-29-X). Valkyrie Pr.
Shadow & Light: An Autobiography. 14.00 (ISBN 0-405-01817-7). Arno.
Shadow of Henry Irving. 10.00 (ISBN 0-405-08674-1). Arno.
Shadow of the Almighty: The Life & Testament of Jim Elliot. pap. 3.95 (ISBN 0-06-062211-3, RD 305). Har-Row.
Shadowland. 9.95 (ISBN 0-07-002311-5). McGraw.
Shadowland. pap. 2.25 (ISBN 0-515-05124-1). BJ Pub Group.
Shadows of the Sun: The Diaries of Harry Crosby. 14.00 (ISBN 0-87685-304-1); pap. 5.00 (ISBN 0-87685-303-3). Black Sparrow.
Shaft of Sunlight. 12.50 (ISBN 0-684-15920-1). Scribner.
Shaftesbury: The Great Reformer 1801-1885. 15.00 (ISBN 0-395-19953-0). HM.
Shah of Iran: The Man & His Land. 6.95 (ISBN 0-03-015561-4). HR&W.
Shakers: Compendium of the Origin, History, Principles, Rules & Regulations, Government & Doctrines of the United Society of Believers in Christ's Second Appearing. 4th ed. 14.00 (ISBN 0-404-10747-8). AMS Pr.
Shakers: Compendium of the Origin, History, Principles, Rules, & Regulations, Government, & Doctrines, of the United Society of Believers in Christ's Second Appearing. lib. bdg. 17.50 (ISBN 0-8337-4091-1). B Franklin.
Shakespeare: A Biographical Handbook. pap. 4.95x (ISBN 0-300-00021-9, Y63). Yale U Pr.
Shakespeare: A Portrait Restored. 17.00 (ISBN 0-8274-3368-9). R West.
Shakespeare: A Portrait Restored. facsimile ed. 21.25 (ISBN 0-8369-5251-0). Arno.
Shakespeare & Ibsen. lib. bdg. 12.95 (ISBN 0-8383-1019-2). Haskell.
Shakespeare & Music. lib. bdg. 14.95 (ISBN 0-306-70868-X). Da Capo.
Shakespeare & Spenser. 15.50x (ISBN 0-691-06274-9, 60); pap. 4.95 (ISBN 0-691-01282-2). Princeton U Pr.
Shakespeare & the Englishman. lib. bdg. 19.95 (ISBN 0-8383-1288-8). Haskell.
Shakespeare Biography & Other Papers, Chiefly Elizabethan. facs. ed. 10.50 (ISBN 0-8369-0853-8). Arno.
Shakespeare Documents: Facsimiles, Transliterations, Translations & Commentary. lib. bdg. 170.00x (ISBN 0-8371-4622-4, LESH). Greenwood.
Shakespeare in America. 15.00 (ISBN 0-405-08475-7). Arno.
Shakespeare in Warwickshire. 11.50x (ISBN 0-299-02330-3); pap. 4.25 (ISBN 0-299-02334-6). U of Wis Pr.
Shakespeare of London. 8.95 (ISBN 0-525-20182-3); pap. 3.95 (ISBN 0-525-47001-8). Dutton.
Shakespeare Once a Printer & Bookman. 10.95 (ISBN 0-8383-1372-8). Haskell.
Shakespeare Once a Printer & Bookman. lib. bdg. 10.00 (ISBN 0-8414-2191-9). Folcroft.
Shakespeare Personally. lib. bdg. 22.50 (ISBN 0-8414-6164-3). Folcroft.
Shakespeare the Man: An Essay. lib. bdg. 7.45 (ISBN 0-8414-1765-2). Folcroft.
Shakespeare the Man: An Essay. lib. bdg. 8.50 (ISBN 0-8495-0396-5). Arden Lib.
Shakespeare: The Poet in His World. 15.00x (ISBN 0-231-04648-0). Columbia U Pr.
Shakespeare: The Writer & His Work. 8.95 (ISBN 0-684-15983-X); pap. 3.95 (ISBN 0-684-15984-8). Scribner.
Shakespeare's Life & Art. pap. 3.95x (ISBN 0-8147-0005-5). NYU Pr.
Shakespeare's Life & Art. lib. bdg. 19.25x (ISBN 0-313-20666-X, ALSA). Greenwood.
Shakespeare's Life & Times: A Pictorial Record. 16.00x (ISBN 0-691-06119-X); pap. 6.95 (ISBN 0-691-01318-7). Princeton U Pr.
Shakespeare's Magic Circle. facs. ed. 12.25 (ISBN 0-8369-5504-8). Arno.
Shakespeare's Self. 9.75 (ISBN 0-8274-3383-2). R West.
Shakespeare's Self. lib. bdg. 19.95 (ISBN 0-8383-1366-3). Haskell.
Shakspere Coat-of-Arms. 5.00 (ISBN 0-404-06336-5). AMS Pr.
Shakspere, His Birthplace & Its Neighbourhood. 7.50 (ISBN 0-404-07003-5). AMS Pr.
Shane Gould, Olympic Swimmer. 5.95 (ISBN 0-88436-126-8); pap. 3.50 (ISBN 0-88436-127-6). EMC.
Shapers of Baptist Thought. 10.00 (ISBN 0-8170-0503-X). Judson.
Shaping of a Man of Faith. pap. 1.75 (ISBN 0-88207-516-0). Victor Bks.
Shaping Vision of Gerard Manley Hopkins. 11.00 (ISBN 0-208-00296-0). Shoe String.
Sharing of My Love. new ed. 5.95 (ISBN 0-910812-20-9); pap. 2.95 (ISBN 0-910812-23-3). Johnny Reads.
Sharing Society. 12.00 (ISBN 0-8184-0284-9). Lyle Stuart.
Shaun Cassidy. PLB 5.95 (ISBN 0-87191-717-3); pap. 2.75 (ISBN 0-89812-097-7). Creative Ed.
Shaw. lib. bdg. 15.00 (ISBN 0-8414-2340-7). Folcroft.
Shaw, Books & Libraries. 5.95 (ISBN 0-87959-022-X). U of Tex Hum Res.
Shaw, George Versus Bernard. lib. bdg. 12.50 (ISBN 0-8414-4872-8). Folcroft.
Shaw in His Time. lib. bdg. 19.75x (ISBN 0-313-21999-0, BRSW). Greenwood.
She Stands Accused: Being a Series of Accounts of the Lives & Deeds of Notorious Women Murderesses. 14.00 (ISBN 0-88355-196-9). Hyperion Conn.
She Wanted to Read: The Story of Mary McLeod Bethune. pap. 1.25 (ISBN 0-671-29861-5). Archway.
Shedding. pap. 5.00 (ISBN 0-913780-22-7). Daughters.
Sheila Young. PLB 5.50 (ISBN 0-87191-545-6). Creative Ed.
Shelley. lib. bdg. 7.50 (ISBN 0-8414-8554-2). Folcroft.
Shelley. 18.50. Porter.
Shelley. lib. bdg. 67.50 (ISBN 0-374-98426-3). Octagon.
Shelley: A Critical Biography. lib. bdg. 19.95 (ISBN 0-8383-1727-8). Haskell.
Shelley: A Critical Biography. lib. bdg. 12.75 (ISBN 0-8414-7768-X). Folcroft.
Shelley: A Life Story. lib. bdg. 20.00. Folcroft.
Shelley & His Friends in Italy. 15.75 (ISBN 0-8274-3391-3). R West.
Shelley & His Friends in Italy. lib. bdg. 29.95 (ISBN 0-8383-1539-9). Haskell.
Shelley & His Poetry. lib. bdg. 17.95 (ISBN 0-8383-2124-0). Haskell.
Shelley & His Poetry. lib. bdg. 7.50 (ISBN 0-8414-3953-2). Folcroft.
Shelley & His Poetry. 7.25 (ISBN 0-404-52511-3). AMS Pr.
Shelley at Oxford. lib. bdg. 20.00 (ISBN 0-8414-4881-7). Folcroft.
Shelley: The Last Phase. lib. bdg. 7.45. Folcroft.
Shelley: The Last Phase. lib. bdg. 10.00x (ISBN 0-8154-0464-6). Cooper Sq.
Shelley: The Man & the Poet. 20.00 (ISBN 0-8274-0055-1). R West.
Shelley's Early Life from Original Sources, with Curious Incidents, Letters, & Writings, Now First Published or Collected. lib. bdg. 40.00 (ISBN 0-8414-6076-0). Folcroft.
Shelley's Eccentricities. lib. bdg. 10.00 (ISBN 0-8414-2030-0). Folcroft.
Shelley's Lost Letters to Harriet. lib. bdg. 16.95 (ISBN 0-8383-1925-4). Haskell.
Shelley's Mary: A Life of Mary Godwin Shelley. 5.95 (ISBN 0-374-36779-5). FS&G.
Shepherd of an Immigrant People: The Story of Erland Carlsson. 7.50 (ISBN 0-910184-26-7). Augustana.
Shepherd Watches, a Shepherd Sings. 8.95 (ISBN 0-385-11652-7). Doubleday.
Sheridan. lib. bdg. 12.50 (ISBN 0-8495-1106-2). Arden Lib.
Sheridans Troopers on the Borders: A Winter Campaign on the Plains. lib. bdg. 15.00 (ISBN 0-87380-124-5). Rio Grande.
Sheridan's Troopers on the Borders: A Winter Campaign on the Plains. facsimile ed. 15.00 (ISBN 0-8369-5555-2). Arno.
Sherman's March. 11.95 (ISBN 0-690-01746-4). T Y Crowell.
Sherwood Anderson. 10.00x (ISBN 0-8047-0236-5); pap. 3.95 (ISBN 0-8047-0237-3, SP34). Stanford U Pr.
Shining Brow: Frank Lloyd Wright. 5.95 (ISBN 0-8180-0014-7). Horizon.
Shining Season. 8.95 (ISBN 0-698-10888-4). Coward.
Shining Season. pap. 2.25 (ISBN 0-553-12804-3). Bantam.
Ship's Doctor. 6.50 (ISBN 0-8008-7179-0). Taplinger.
Shirley Chisholm: A Biography. 5.95 (ISBN 0-385-02309-X). Doubleday.
Shirley Temple Scrapbook. 12.95 (ISBN 0-8246-0195-5). Jonathan David.
Shirt-Sleeve Diplomat. lib. bdg. 27.50x (ISBN 0-8371-7082-6, DASD). Greenwood.
Shooter. 9.95 (ISBN 0-88225-265-8). Newsweek.
Shooting Star: A Biography of John Wayne. 9.95 (ISBN 0-671-21686-4). S&S.
Short Biography of William Lloyd Garrison. 9.50x (ISBN 0-8371-4590-2). Negro U Pr.
Short Life of Christ. pap. 5.95 (ISBN 0-8028-1824-2). Eerdmans.
Short Life of Kierkegaard. 12.00x (ISBN 0-691-07163-2); pap. 4.25 (ISBN 0-691-01957-6). Princeton U Pr.
Shortchanged by History: America's Neglected Innovators. 8.95 (ISBN 0-399-20665-5). Putnam.
Shortcut to Peril. PLB 7.99 (ISBN 0-8172-1570-0). Raintree Pubs.
Shorter Life of Christ. kivar 3.95 (ISBN 0-310-25441-8). Zondervan.
Shotgun for Hire: The Story of Deacon Jim Miller, Killer of Pat Garrett. 5.95 (ISBN 0-8061-0902-5). U of Okla Pr.
Shotgun for Hire: The Story of "Deacon" Jim Miller, Killer of Pat Garrett. pap. 3.95 (ISBN 0-8061-1646-3). U of Okla Pr.
Showdown at Daytona. new ed. 5.95 (ISBN 0-399-20507-1). Putnam.
Showman of Vanity Fair: The Life of William Makepeace Thackeray. 15.00 (ISBN 0-8462-1181-5). Russell.
Sibelius. rev. ed. 10.00x (ISBN 0-460-03169-4). Biblio Dist.
Sibelius. 32.50x (ISBN 0-520-03014-1). U of Cal Pr.
Sidney Lanier. 11.00 (ISBN 0-8046-0314-6). Kennikat.
Sidney Lanier. 35.00 (ISBN 0-8490-1052-7). Gordon Pr.
Sidney Lanier: A Paper. lib. bdg. 8.50 (ISBN 0-8414-2001-7). Folcroft.
Sidney Poitier. PLB 5.50 (ISBN 0-87191-556-1). Creative Ed.
Sigmund Freud: A New Appraisal. lib. bdg. 9.50x (ISBN 0-8371-6593-8, CLSF). Greenwood.
Sigmund Freud: His Life in Pictures & Words. 39.95 (ISBN 0-15-182546-7). HarBraceJ.
Sigmund Freud: The World Within. 6.95 (ISBN 0-15-274164-X). HarBraceJ.
Sigmund Freud's Dreams. text ed. 22.50x (ISBN 0-8236-6074-5). Intl Univs Pr.
Sign of Jonas. 2.95 (ISBN 0-385-07898-6). Doubleday.
Sign of Jonas. pap. 4.95 (ISBN 0-15-682529-5). HarBraceJ.
Signers of the Declaration. 6.95 (ISBN 0-395-06581-X). HM.
Significant American Artists & Architects. PLB 9.25 (ISBN 0-516-05303-5). Childrens.
Significant American Blacks. PLB 9.25 (ISBN 0-516-05304-3). Childrens.
Significant American Colonial Leaders. PLB 9.25 (ISBN 0-516-05315-9). Childrens.
Significant American Entertainers. PLB 9.25 (ISBN 0-516-05309-4). Childrens.
Significant American Government Leaders. PLB 9.25 (ISBN 0-516-05314-0). Childrens.
Significant American Historians & Educators. PLB 9.25 (ISBN 0-516-05301-9). Childrens.
Significant American Indians. PLB 9.25 (ISBN 0-516-05305-1). Childrens.
Significant American Inventors. PLB 9.25 (ISBN 0-516-05313-2). Childrens.
Significant American Military Leaders. PLB 9.25 (ISBN 0-516-05316-7). Childrens.
Significant American Musicians, Composers & Singers. PLB 9.25 (ISBN 0-516-05306-X). Childrens.
Significant American Scientists. PLB 9.25 (ISBN 0-516-05310-8). Childrens.
Significant American Social Reformers & Humanitarians. PLB 9.25 (ISBN 0-516-05307-8). Childrens.
Significant American Sport Champions. PLB 9.25 (ISBN 0-516-05308-6). Childrens.
Significant American Women. PLB 9.25 (ISBN 0-516-05312-4). Childrens.
Signs of Spring. 7.95 (ISBN 0-525-20428-8). Dutton.
Sigrid Undset: A Study in Christian Realism. lib. bdg. 12.75x (ISBN 0-8371-4502-3, WISU). Greenwood.
Silas Deane, Patriot or Traitor. 8.50x (ISBN 0-87013-194-X). Mich St U Pr.
Silas Downer - Forgotten Patriot: His Life & Writings. 8.95 (ISBN 0-917012-01-1). Ri Pubns Soc.
Silas Wright. 22.50 (ISBN 0-404-51552-5). AMS Pr.
Silence Will Speak: A Study of the Life of Denys Finch Hatton & His Relationship with Karen Blixen. 15.00 (ISBN 0-226-81286-3). U of Chicago Pr.
Silent Missions. 12.95 (ISBN 0-385-13500-9). Doubleday.
Silent Years: An Autobiography with Memoirs of James Joyce & Our Ireland. lib. bdg. 15.00 (ISBN 0-374-91144-4). Octagon.
Silver Queen: The Fabulous Story of Baby Doe Tabor. pap. 2.50 (ISBN 0-933472-21-8). Johnson Colo.
Silver Spade: The Conrad Hilton Story. 19.50 (ISBN 0-8369-8142-1). Arno.
Simon De Montfort. lib. bdg. 17.50x (ISBN 0-8371-8359-6, LASM). Greenwood.
Simon De Montfort, Earl of Leicester, 1208-1265. lib. bdg. 20.50x (ISBN 0-8371-7625-5, BESM). Greenwood.
Simon Kenton, His Life & Period, 1755-1836. 18.00 (ISBN 0-405-02865-2). Arno.
Simone De Beauvoir. 9.95 (ISBN 0-8044-2132-3). Ungar.
Simone Weil: A Life. 15.00 (ISBN 0-394-49815-1). Pantheon.
Simone Weil: A Life. pap. 5.95 (ISBN 0-394-73462-9). Pantheon.
Simone Weil: A Sketch for a Portrait. 7.95 (ISBN 0-8093-0191-1). S Ill U Pr.
Sinai: The Great & Terrible Wilderness. 13.95 (ISBN 0-670-34837-6). Viking Pr.
Sinatra: The Unauthorized Biography. pap. 2.25 (ISBN 0-451-07487-4, E7487). NAL.
Sinclair Lewis. lib. bdg. 7.95 (ISBN 0-8057-0448-5). Twayne.
Singer & Her Songs: Almeda Riddle's Book of Ballads. 10.00 (ISBN 0-8071-0021-8). La State U Pr.
Singers of the Blues. PLB 3.95 (ISBN 0-8225-0453-7). Lerner Pubns.
Singers of Today. 19.75 (ISBN 0-8369-8080-8). Arno.
Singer's Pilgrimage. lib. bdg. 20.00x (ISBN 0-405-09692-5). Arno.
Singer's Pilgrimage. lib. bdg. 22.50 (ISBN 0-306-70878-7). Da Capo.
Singin' & Swingin' & Gettin' Merry Like Christmas. 8.95 (ISBN 0-394-40545-5). Random.
Singin' & Swingin' & Gettin' Merry Like Christmas. pap. 2.25 (ISBN 0-553-13520-1, B13520-1). Bantam
Singing Cowboys. 19.95 (ISBN 0-498-02163-7). A S Barnes.
Singing Swan: An Account of Anna Seward & Her Acquaintance with Dr. Johnson, Etc. 20.00 (ISBN 0-8274-3417-0). R West.
Sinners & Showoffs. 5.95 (ISBN 0-915442-01-9). Donning Co.
Sir Arthur Sullivan: Composer & Personage. pap. 15.00 (ISBN 0-87598-049-X). Pierpont Morgan.
Sir Arthur Sullivan: Composer & Personage. 25.00 (ISBN 0-87923-145-9). Godine.
Sir Charles Sedley, 1639-1701: A Study in the Life & Literature of the Restoration. 21.00 (ISBN 0-404-05056-5). AMS Pr.
Sir Charles V Stanford. lib. bdg. 15.00 (ISBN 0-306-70790-X). Da Capo.
Sir Cornelius Vermuyden: The Lifework of a Great Anglo-Dutchman in Land-Reclamation & Drainage, with Some Notes by the Author on the Present Condition of Drainage in England & a Resume of the Drainage Legislation in Holland. lib. bdg. 17.00 (ISBN 0-405-09767-0). Arno.
Sir Edward Elgar. 8.00 (ISBN 0-8046-0763-X). Kennikat.
Sir Edward Elgar. facsimile ed. 14.50 (ISBN 0-8369-5194-8). Arno.
Sir Francis Drake. 10.00 (ISBN 0-688-00057-6). Morrow.
Sir Francis Drake. lib. bdg. 11.50x (ISBN 0-8371-7886-X, WIFD). Greenwood.
Sir Henry Wotton: A Biographical Sketch. lib. bdg. 22.50 (ISBN 0-8414-2806-9). Folcroft.
Sir John Berkenhead 1617-1679: A Royalist Career in Politics & Polemics. 11.25x (ISBN 0-19-811678-0). Oxford U Pr.
Sir John Richardson: Arctic Explorer, Natural Historian, Naval Surgeon. 32.50x (ISBN 0-8448-1030-4). Crane-Russak Co.
Sir John Vanbrugh. lib. bdg. 8.95 (ISBN 0-8057-6665-0). Twayne.
Sir Joshua Reynolds. lib. bdg. 12.50 (ISBN 0-8414-7867-8). Folcroft.
Sir Matthew Nathan: British Colonial Governor & Civil Servant. 22.00x (ISBN 0-7022-0965-1). U of Queensland Pr.
Sir Oliver Mowat: A Biographical Sketch. 24.00 (ISBN 0-404-00858-5); 12.50 ea. (ISBN 0-404-08021-9) (ISBN 0-404-08022-7). AMS Pr.
Sir Philip Sidney. 12.45 (ISBN 0-8274-1207-X). R West.

Sir Philip Sidney. 12.50 (ISBN 0-8046-1005-3). Kennikat.
Sir Philip Sidney. lib. bdg. 20.00 (ISBN 0-8414-0525-5). Folcroft.
Sir Philip Sidney: A Study in Conflict. 10.75 (ISBN 0-8274-0435-2). R West.
Sir Philip Sidney, Representative Elizabethan: His Life & Writings. 11.00 (ISBN 0-8462-1221-8). Russell.
Sir Randal Cremer: His Life & Work. lib. bdg. 33.00 (ISBN 0-8240-0250-4). Garland Pub.
Sir Richard Steele. 12.00 (ISBN 0-8274-0053-5). R West.
Sir Richard Steele. 12.50 (ISBN 0-8046-0086-4). Kennikat.
Sir Robert Howard, 1626-1698: A Critical Biography. 14.75 (ISBN 0-8223-0124-5). Duke.
Sir Robert Peel. facsimile ed. 20.50 (ISBN 0-8369-5076-3). Arno.
Sir Robert Peel: The Life of Sir Robert Peel After 1830. 25.00x (ISBN 0-87471-132-0). Rowman.
Sir Robert Walpole. Incl. Making of a Statesman; King's Minister. lib. bdg. 30.00x (ISBN 0-678-03550-4). Kelley.
Sir Thomas Elyot, Tudor Humanist. lib. bdg. 14.00x (ISBN 0-8371-2123-X, LETE). Greenwood.
Sir Thomas Malory see Geoffrey Chaucer.
Sir Thomas More. facsimile ed. 13.50 (ISBN 0-8369-5502-1). Arno.
Sir Thomas Urquhart & Rabelais. lib. bdg. 7.50 (ISBN 0-8414-2570-1). Folcroft.
Sir Walter Mildmay & Tudor Government. 14.50x (ISBN 0-292-73377-1). U of Tex Pr.
Sir Walter Ralegh. pap. 6.95 (ISBN 0-689-70585-9, 248). Atheneum.
Sir Walter Raleigh: Captain & Adventurer. 5.95 (ISBN 0-8149-0435-1). Vanguard.
Sir Walter Scott. lib. bdg. 12.45. Folcroft.
Sir Walter Scott. lib. bdg 12.50 (ISBN 0-404-51713-7). AMS Pr.
Sir Walter Scott. lib. bdg. 15.00 (ISBN 0-89987-358-8). Darby Bks.
Sir Walter Scott. lib. bdg. 17.50 (ISBN 0-8495-2233-1). Arden Lib.
Sir Walter Scott. lib. bdg. 15.00 (ISBN 0-89760-331-1). Telegraph Bks.
Sir Walter Scott & the Aberdonians. lib. bdg. 8.50 (ISBN 0-8414-4182-0). Folcroft.
Sir Walter Scott, Bart. lib. bdg. 15.00. Folcroft.
Sir William Johnson, Colonial American, 1715-1763. 17.50 (ISBN 0-8046-9134-7). Kennikat.
Sir William Macgregor. 22.50x (ISBN 0-19-550367-8). Oxford U Pr.
Sir William Preece F. R. S. Victorian Engineer Extraordinary. 19.75x (ISBN 0-8476-1369-0). Rowman.
Sister Kenny: The Woman Who Challenged the Doctors. 16.50 (ISBN 0-8166-0755-9). U of Minn Pr.
Sister Saints. pap. 7.95 (ISBN 0-8425-1235-7). Brigham.
Sister to the Sioux: The Memoirs of Elaine Goodale Eastman, 1885-91. 10.95 (ISBN 0-8032-0971-1). U of Nebr Pr.
Sisters of the Quill. 15.00 (ISBN 0-396-07544-4). Dodd.
Sita. 10.00 (ISBN 0-374-26546-1). FS&G.
Sita. pap. 2.25 (ISBN 0-345-27362-1). Ballantine.
Sitting Bull. PLB 6.95 (ISBN 0-87518-065-5). Dillon.
Sitting Bull, Champion of the Sioux: A Biography. rev.ed ed. 15.95 (ISBN 0-8061-0363-9). U of Okla Pr.
Sitting Bull: Great Sioux Chief. PLB 4.48 (ISBN 0-8116-6608-5). Garrard.
Sitwells: A Family's Biography. 15.00 (ISBN 0-15-182703-6). HarBraceJ.
Six Architects. facs. ed. 14.00 (ISBN 0-8369-1340-X). Arno.
Six Criminal Women. facs. ed. 15.00 (ISBN 0-8369-8069-7). Arno.
Six Crises. pap. 2.95 (ISBN 0-446-93101-2). Warner Bks.
Six-Day Warriors: An Introduction to Those Who Gave Israel Its Vigor and Its Victories. 4.95 (ISBN 0-8197-0199-8). Bloch.
Six Great Advocates. 12.25 (ISBN 0-8369-8132-4). Arno.
Six Korean Women: The Socialization of Shamans. text ed. 10.95 (ISBN 0-8299-0243-0). West Pub.
Six Life Studies of Famous Women. 16.75 (ISBN 0-8369-2746-X). Arno.
Six Lives, Six Deaths: Portraits from Modern Japan. pap. 7.95 (ISBN 0-300-02600-5). Yale U Pr.
Six Medieval Men & Women. pap. text ed. 2.95x (ISBN 0-689-70009-1, 3). Atheneum.
Six Men. 8.95 (ISBN 0-394-48434-7). Knopf.
Six Men. pap. 2.75 (ISBN 0-425-04689-3). Berkley Pub.
Six Men. lib. bdg. 11.95 (ISBN 0-8161-6547-5). G K Hall.
Six Men. pap. 2.25 (ISBN 0-425-03885-8). Berkley Pub.
Six Men of Yale. facsimile ed. 13.25 (ISBN 0-8369-2329-4). Arno.
Six Presidents from the Empire State. buckram bnd. 8.95 (ISBN 0-912882-07-7). Sleepy Hollow.
Six Weeks in the Sioux Tepees. price not set (ISBN 0-87770-215-2). Ye Galleon.
Sixteen Authors to One: Intimate Sketches of Leading American Storytellers. facs. ed. 13.50 (ISBN 0-8369-0584-9). Arno.
Sixteenth Round. pap. 2.50 (ISBN 0-446-91020-1). Warner Bks.
Sixty Years a Builder: The Autobiography of Henry Ericsson. 19.00 (ISBN 0-405-04698-7). Arno.
Sixty Years on the Frontier in the Pacific Northwest. 14.95 (ISBN 0-87770-183-0). Ye Galleon.
Skelton, the Life & Times of an Early Tudor Poet. 26.00 (ISBN 0-403-04284-4). Somerset Pub.
Sketch for a Portrait of Rimbaud. 15.00 (ISBN 0-8274-3439-1). R West.
Sketch for a Portrait of Rimbaud. lib. bdg. 16.95 (ISBN 0-8383-1922-X). Haskell.
Sketches in Nineteenth Century Biography. 12.50 (ISBN 0-8369-1501-1). Arno.
Sketches of Great Painters. facs. ed. 15.00 (ISBN 0-8369-0304-8). Arno.
Sketches of Reforms & Reformers of Great Britain & Ireland. facs. ed. 15.25 (ISBN 0-8369-8654-7). Arno.
Sketches of the Life & Character of Patrick Henry. facs. ed. 17.50 (ISBN 0-8369-5541-2). Arno.
Skiing to Win. 5.95 (ISBN 0-15-275400-8). HarBraceJ.
Skin Deep: The Making of a Plastic Surgeon. 9.95 (ISBN 0-316-58700-1). Little.
Skippy & Percy Crosby. 16.95 (ISBN 0-03-018491-6). HR&W.
Skyline Queen & the Merchant Prince: The Woolworth Story. 7.95 (ISBN 0-671-27098-2). Trident.
Skymen: Heroes of Fifty Years of Flying. 7.95 (ISBN 0-312-72782-8). St Martin.
Slave Who Bought His Freedom: Equiano's Story. rev. & abr. ed. 6.95 (ISBN 0-525-39455-9). Dutton.
Slave Who Freed Haiti: The Story of Toussaint Louverture. PLB 4.99 (ISBN 0-394-90515-6). Random.
Smuts. Incl. The Sanguine Years, 1870-1919. (ISBN 0-521-05187-8); The Fields of Force, 1919-1950. (ISBN 0-521-05188-6). 38.50 ea. Cambridge U Pr.
Snakes & Ladders. 12.95 (ISBN 0-03-047161-3). HR&W.
Snatched from Oblivion: A Cambridge Memoir. 9.95 (ISBN 0-316-77348-4). Little.
Snowbound with Mr. Lincoln. 6.95 (ISBN 0-533-03859-6). Vantage.
So Great a Lover. 2.50 (ISBN 0-8199-0132-6, L38815). Franciscan Herald.
So Long As There Are Women. 10.95 (ISBN 0-688-03596-5). Morrow.
So Noble a Captain: The Life & Times of Ferdinand Magellan. lib. bdg. 25.75x (ISBN 0-8371-8521-1, PASN). Greenwood.
Soccer: The World Game. 15.00 (ISBN 0-312-73134-5). St Martin.
Social & Political Ideas of the Muckrakers. facs. ed. 11.00 (ISBN 0-8369-1745-6). Arno.
Socrates. 10.00 (ISBN 0-8274-3448-0). R West.
Socrates. lib. bdg. 13.25x (ISBN 0-8371-6793-0, TASO). Greenwood.
Socrates. 17.00 (ISBN 0-88355-718-5). Hyperion Conn.
Socrates & Aristophanes. pap. text ed. 11.00x (ISBN 0-226-77691-3). U of Chicago Pr.
Socrates in the Agora. 1.50x (ISBN 0-87661-617-1). Am Sch Athens.
Sod & Stubble: The Story of a Kansas Homestead. 13.50x (ISBN 0-8032-0207-5); pap. 3.50 (ISBN 0-8032-5098-3, 372). U of Nebr Pr.
Soldier from Texas. 12.50 (ISBN 0-87706-104-1). Branch-Smith.
Soldier Girl. 5.95 (ISBN 0-87966-110-0). Dexter & Westbrook.
Soldier in White: The Life of General George Miller Sternberg. 12.75 (ISBN 0-8223-0065-6). Duke.
Soldier of Fortune: The Story of a Nineteenth Century Adventurer. 5.95 (ISBN 0-87645-050-8). Gambit.
Soldier of the Church: The Life of Ignatius Loyola. 12.50 (ISBN 0-404-04187-6). AMS Pr.
Soldier Reports. pap. 2.95 (ISBN 0-440-10025-9). Dell.
Soldiers As Statesmen. text ed. 16.50x (ISBN 0-06-491669-3). B&N.
Solitary in the Ranks: Lawrence of Arabia As Airman & Private Soldier. 11.95 (ISBN 0-689-10848-6). Atheneum.
Solitary Singer: A Critical Biography of Walt Whitman. 16.00x (ISBN 0-8147-0006-3). NYU Pr.
Solzhenitsyn. pap. 6.95 (ISBN 0-8128-1582-3). Stein & Day.
Solzhenitsyn: A Documentary Record. 10.95 (ISBN 0-06-012487-3). Har-Row.
Solzhenitsyn & the Secret Circle. 8.95 (ISBN 0-03-040696-X). HR&W.
Some Are Born Great. pap. 1.95 (ISBN 0-451-06707-X, J6707). NAL.
Some British Pioneers of Social Medicine. 8.75 (ISBN 0-8369-8026-3). Arno.
Some Composers of Opera. facsimile ed. 11.25 (ISBN 0-8369-2654-4). Arno.
Some Early Australian Bookmen. new ed. text ed. 28.95 (ISBN 0-7081-0225-5). Bks Australia.
Some English Dictators. 10.00 (ISBN 0-8046-1087-8). Kennikat.
Some Famous Singers of the 19th Century. lib. bdg. 11.00x (ISBN 0-405-09703-4). Arno.
Some Great Leaders in the World Movement. facs. ed. 13.25 (ISBN 0-8369-0895-3). Arno.
Some Great Men of Queen's. facs. ed. 10.00 (ISBN 0-8369-1200-4). Arno.
Some Living Masters of the Pulpit: Studies in Religious Personality. facsimile ed. 13.75 (ISBN 0-8369-2287-5). Arno.
Some Memories & Reflections. lib. bdg. 24.00x (ISBN 0-405-09676-3). Arno.
Some Memories of W. B. Yeats. 11.00x (ISBN 0-7165-1392-7). Biblio Dist.
Some Memories of W. B. Yeats. lib. bdg. 10.00 (ISBN 0-8414-6204-6). Folcroft.
Some Minor Characters in the New Testament. pap. 2.95 (ISBN 0-8054-1514-9). Broadman.
Some Minor Characters in the New Testament. pap. 2.95 (ISBN 0-8010-7637-4). Baker Bk.
Some Musical Recollections of Fifty Years. 9.50 (ISBN 0-911772-79-0). Info Coord.
Some Musicians of Former Days. 16.00 (ISBN 0-405-08897-3). Arno.
Some Musicians of Former Days. facs. ed. 18.00 (ISBN 0-8369-0831-7). Arno.
Some Nineteenth Century Composers. facs. ed. 12.25 (ISBN 0-8369-8068-9). Arno.
Some of My Best Friends Are Animals. 10.00 (ISBN 0-448-22683-9). Paddington.
Some Passages in the Life & Death of John Earl of Rochester. lib. bdg. 25.00 (ISBN 0-8414-3202-3). Folcroft.
Some Pictures from My Life: A Diary. pap. 1.35 (ISBN 0-87810-022-9). Times Change.
Some Portraits of the Lake Poets & Their Homes. lib. bdg. 20.00 (ISBN 0-8495-0129-6). Arden Lib.
Some Portraits of the Lake Poets, & Their Homes. lib. bdg. 20.00 (ISBN 0-8414-2874-3). Folcroft.
Some Queer People. lib. bdg. 30.00 (ISBN 0-8414-9842-3). Folcroft.
Some Run with Feet of Clay. 5.95 (ISBN 0-8007-0901-2). Revell.
Some Sense About Wilhelm Reich. 6.00 (ISBN 0-8022-2212-9). Philos Lib.
Some Tennessee Heroes of the Revolution. 10.00 (ISBN 0-8063-0684-X). Genealog Pub.
Some Victorian Portraits & Others. 10.00 (ISBN 0-8369-8030-1). Arno.
Some Victorian Portraits & Others. lib. bdg. 20.00 (ISBN 0-8414-6224-0). Folcroft.
Some Women of France. 17.00 (ISBN 0-8369-1433-3). Arno.
Somebody Knows I'm Alive. 4.95 (ISBN 0-8042-2206-1). John Knox.
Somebody's Angel Child: The Story of Bessie Smith. pap. 0.95 (ISBN 0-440-97778-9). Dell.
Someone Had to Hold the Lantern. pap. 3.95 (ISBN 0-8127-0238-7). Southern Pub.
Somerset & All the Maughams. lib. bdg. 18.75x (ISBN 0-8371-8236-0, MASOM). Greenwood.
Somerset Maugham. 6.98 (ISBN 0-02-529280-3). Macmillan.
Something Beautiful for God: Mother Teresa of Calcutta. 1.95 (ISBN 0-385-12639-5). Doubleday.
Son Is Given. pap. 3.50 (ISBN 0-8042-9457-7). John Knox.
Son of Guyana. 9.75x (ISBN 0-19-911059-X); pap. 3.00x (ISBN 0-19-911060-3). Oxford U Pr.
Son of Heaven: A Biography of Li Shih-Min, Founder of the T'ang Dynasty. 7.00x (ISBN 0-89644-176-8). Chinese Materials.
Son of Heaven: A Biography of Li Shih-Min, Founder of the T'ang Dynasty. 14.50 (ISBN 0-404-02404-1). AMS Pr.
Son of Oscar Wilde. lib. bdg. 22.50 (ISBN 0-8495-2280-3). Arden Lib.
Son of Oscar Wilde. lib. bdg. 22.50 (ISBN 0-8482-4411-7). Norwood Edns.
Son of Oscar Wilde. lib. bdg. 15.50x (ISBN 0-8371-6884-8, HOOW). Greenwood.
Son of Sam: The .44 Caliber Killer. pap. 2.25 (ISBN 0-532-22112-5). Manor Bks.
Son of the Bowery: The Life Story of an East Side American. facsimile ed. 16.50 (ISBN 0-8369-6669-4). Arno.
Son of the Middle Border. 5.95 (ISBN 0-02-542720-2). Macmillan.
Son of the Middle Border. 19.50x (ISBN 0-8032-2102-9); pap. 6.95 (ISBN 0-8032-7000-3, BB694). U of Nebr Pr.
Son of the Wilderness: The Life of John Muir. 20.00 (ISBN 0-299-07730-6); pap. 6.95 (ISBN 0-299-07734-9). U of Wis Pr.
Song of Ascents: A Spiritual Autobiography. pap. 2.25 (ISBN 0-687-39100-8). Abingdon.
Songs & Song Writers. 35.00 (ISBN 0-8490-1083-7). Gordon Pr.
Songs & Song Writers. lib. bdg. 25.00 (ISBN 0-89341-439-5). Longwood Pr.
Sonia Delaunay. 55.00 (ISBN 0-8109-0292-3). Abrams.
Sonny & Cher. PLB 5.95 (ISBN 0-87191-620-7); pap. 2.75. Creative Ed.
Sons of Africa. 11.50x (ISBN 0-8371-1746-1). Negro U Pr.
Sons of Liberty. PLB 4.79 (ISBN 0-671-32124-2). Messner.
Sons of the Prophets: Leaders in Protestantism from Princeton Seminary. 12.00x (ISBN 0-691-07136-5). Princeton U Pr.
Sons of the Wild Jackass. 10.50 (ISBN 0-295-95092-7, AL17). U of Wash Pr.
Sons of the Wild Jackass. 19.75 (ISBN 0-8369-1385-X). Arno.
Soong Sisters. PLB 5.90 (ISBN 0-531-02835-6). Watts.
Soong Sisters. lib. bdg. 14.75x (ISBN 0-8371-4429-9, HASI). Greenwood.
Sophia Living & Loving: Her Own Story. 9.95 (ISBN 0-688-03428-4). Morrow.
Sophie Dorothea. 7.95 (ISBN 0-8076-0626-X). Braziller.
Sopwith Camel Fighter Ace. softcover 6.95. Ajay Ent.
Sor Juana Ines de la Cruz. lib. bdg. 12.95x (ISBN 0-8057-2256-4). Irvington.
Sorcerer of Bolinas Reef. 8.95 (ISBN 0-394-49192-0). Random.
Soren Kierkegaard. lib. bdg. 16.00 (ISBN 0-374-93923-3). Octagon.
Sort of Life. 7.95 (ISBN 0-671-21010-6). S&S.
Sort of Life. pap. 3.95 (ISBN 0-671-24082-X). S&S.
Soul of Samuel Pepys. 9.95 (ISBN 0-8274-3474-X). R West.
Soul of Samuel Pepys. 10.00 (ISBN 0-8046-0603-X). Kennikat.
Soul on Fire. 8.95 (ISBN 0-8499-0046-8, 0046-8). Word Bks.
Soul Rush: The Odyssey of a Young Woman of the '70s. 8.95 (ISBN 0-688-03276-1). Morrow.
South of the Cottonwood Tree. 10.00 (ISBN 0-931068-09-6). Purcells.
Southern Baptist in the White House. pap. 3.95 (ISBN 0-664-24144-1). Westminster.
Southern Part of Heaven. 6.95 (ISBN 0-8078-1112-2). U of NC Pr.
Southern Pioneers in Social Interpretation. facs. ed. 12.75 (ISBN 0-8369-0750-7). Arno.
Southern Writers: A Biographical Dictionary. 30.00x (ISBN 0-8071-0354-3); pap. 7.95x (ISBN 0-8071-0390-X). La State U Pr.
Southey. lib. bdg. 12.00. Folcroft.
Southey. lib. bdg. 12.50 (ISBN 0-404-51709-9). AMS Pr.
Southey. 8.00 (ISBN 0-8274-1395-5). R West.
Southey. 8.25 (ISBN 0-8046-0421-5). Kennikat.
Souvenirs & Prophecies: The Young Wallace Stevens. 12.50 (ISBN 0-394-49138-6). Knopf.
Soviet Art in Exile. 17.50 (ISBN 0-394-41644-9). Random.
Soviet Chess. pap. 3.00 (ISBN 0-87980-311-8). Wilshire.
Soviet Cinema: Directors & Films. 17.50 (ISBN 0-208-01581-7). Shoe String.
Sowing: An Autobiography of the Years 1880 to 1904. pap. 2.95 (ISBN 0-15-683945-8, HB319). HarBraceJ.
Space Below My Feet. pap. 2.95 (ISBN 0-14-003991-0). Penguin.
Spaced Out & Gathered in: A Sort of an Autobiography of a Jesus Freak. pap. 0.95 (ISBN 0-8007-0511-4). Revell.
Spain Again. pap. 5.95 (ISBN 0-88316-516-3). Chandler & Sharp.
Spanish-Speaking Heroes. pap. 5.50 (ISBN 0-87812-041-6). Pendell Pub.
Spanish Tudor: The Life of Bloody Mary. 21.50 (ISBN 0-404-05133-2). AMS Pr.
Spare Chancellor: The Life of Walter Bagehot. 5.00 (ISBN 0-87013-051-X). Mich St U Pr.
Spartans: A Story of Michigan State Football. 7.95 (ISBN 0-87397-067-5). Strode.
Speak to Me, Dance with Me. pap. 1.50 (ISBN 0-445-03023-2). Popular Lib.
Speaking of Cardinals. facs. ed. 13.75 (ISBN 0-8369-2002-3). Arno.
Spearless Leader: Senator Borah & the Progressive Movement in the 1920s. 10.00 (ISBN 0-252-00220-2). U of Ill Pr.
Special Bravery. 4.50 (ISBN 0-396-06728-X). Dodd.
Special People. 8.95. S&S.
Special People. pap. 1.95 (ISBN 0-345-27530-6). Ballantine.
Species of Eternity. 15.00 (ISBN 0-394-49033-9). Knopf.
Species of Eternity. pap. 8.95 (ISBN 0-525-47531-1). Dutton.

Streak of Luck. pap. 3.95 (ISBN 0-553-13141-9). Bantam.

Stream of Music. new & rev. ed. 8.00 (ISBN 0-8446-1281-2). Peter Smith.

Street. pap. 1.95 (ISBN 0-14-004418-3). Penguin.

Streetcar Man: Tom Lowry & the Twin City Rapid Transit Company. 7.95 (ISBN 0-8225-0764-1). Lerner Pubns.

Streets. 11.95 (ISBN 0-87973-754-9). Our Sunday Visitor.

Streisand. pap. 1.50 (LB298DK). Nordon Pubns.

Strength of the Hills. new ed. 6.95 (ISBN 0-915684-06-3). Christian Herald.

Stresemann & the Politics of the Weimar Republic. lib. bdg. 22.50x (ISBN 0-313-20900-6, TUST). Greenwood.

Stress of My Life: A Scientist's Memoirs. 2nd ed. text ed. 12.95 (ISBN 0-442-27659-1). Van Nos Reinhold.

Strictly Personal. 15.00x (ISBN 0-405-07829-3). Arno.

Strindberg. lib. bdg. 18.95 (ISBN 0-8383-1320-5). Haskell.

Strindberg the Man. lib. bdg. 18.95 (ISBN 0-8383-1401-5). Haskell.

Stroheim. movie ed. pap. 2.45 (ISBN 0-520-00413-2, CAL155). U of Cal Pr.

Stroke: A Doctor's Personal Story of His Recovery. 11.95 (ISBN 0-393-08720-4). Norton.

Studied Madness. 12.50 (ISBN 0-531-07308-4); pap. 5.95 (ISBN 0-531-07326-2). Watts.

Studied Madness. 12.50 (ISBN 0-933256-00-0); pap. 5.95 (ISBN 0-933256-03-5). Second Chance.

Studies in Milton. lib. bdg. 6.75 (ISBN 0-8414-5707-7). Folcroft.

Studies in Music History: Essays for Oliver Strunk. lib. bdg. 39.75x (ISBN 0-313-22501-X, POSM). Greenwood.

Studies in Nietzsche & the Classical Tradition. 14.95x (ISBN 0-8078-8085-X). U of NC Pr.

Studies in Pre-Vesalian Anatomy: Biography, Translations, Documents. 18.00 (ISBN 0-87169-104-3). Am Philos.

Studies in Regional Consciousness & Environment: Essays Presented to H. J. Fleure. facs. ed. 15.25 (ISBN 0-8369-0917-8). Arno.

Studies in Tennyson. 9.45 (ISBN 0-8274-0585-5). R West.

Studies in Tennyson. 9.50 (ISBN 0-8046-0476-2). Kennikat.

Studies in the Life & Works of Petrarch. 12.00 (ISBN 0-910956-37-5). Mediaeval Acad.

Studies in the Life of Christ. 24.95 (ISBN 0-8010-3452-3). Baker Bk.

Studies of Contemporary Poets. 12.45 (ISBN 0-8274-1614-8). R West.

Studies of Contemporary Poets. 12.50 (ISBN 0-8046-1055-X). Kennikat.

Studies of Paris. 14.25 (ISBN 0-8369-2888-1). Arno.

Studies of Paris. 25.00 (ISBN 0-8274-3545-2). R West.

Studies on the "Cancionero de Baena". pap. 6.50x (ISBN 0-8078-9061-8). U of NC Pr.

Study of Elizabeth Barrett Browning. lib. bdg. 9.25. Folcroft.

Study of Elizabeth Barrett Browning. 9.50 (ISBN 0-404-08924-0). AMS Pr.

Study of Goethe. lib. bdg. 17.00x (ISBN 0-8371-9330-3, FASG). Greenwood.

Study of Greatness in Men. facsimile ed. 15.50 (ISBN 0-8369-2557-2). Arno.

Study of Hawthorne. 17.50 (ISBN 0-404-03884-0). AMS Pr.

Study of Hawthorne. 15.00 (ISBN 0-403-00237-0). Scholarly.

Study of Naima. 12.50x (ISBN 0-8147-8150-0). NYU Pr.

Study of Oscar Wilde. lib. bdg. 17.95 (ISBN 0-8383-1524-0). Haskell.

Study of Oscar Wilde. lib. bdg. 15.00 (ISBN 0-8414-7796-5). Folcroft.

Study of Vasyl' Stefanyk: The Pain at the Heart of Existence. lib. bdg. 9.50x (ISBN 0-87287-056-1). Ukrainian Acad.

Sturge Moore & the Life of Art. lib. bdg. 20.00. Folcroft.

Style in History. pap. 3.95 (ISBN 0-07-023063-3). McGraw.

Style of Sophocles. 12.00 (ISBN 0-8462-1618-3). Russell.

Su Man-Shu. lib. bdg. 7.95 (ISBN 0-8057-2870-8). Twayne.

Success & Failure of Picasso. pap. 4.95 (ISBN 0-394-73900-0). Pantheon.

Such a Life. 8.95 (ISBN 0-688-03280-X). Morrow.

Such a Life. pap. 2.50 (ISBN 0-671-82282-9). PB.

Such a Life. lib. bdg. 13.95 (ISBN 0-8161-6662-5). G K Hall.

Such a Strange Lady: A Biography of Dorothy L. Sayers. 10.00 (ISBN 0-06-011903-9). Har-Row.

Suddenly Rich. 8.95 (ISBN 0-13-875609-0). P-H.

Suitors of Spring. 6.95 (ISBN 0-396-06711-5). Dodd.

Suitors to the Queen: The Men in the Life of Elizabeth I of England. 8.95 (ISBN 0-698-10698-9). Coward.

Sukarno & the Struggle for Indonesian Independence. 25.00x (ISBN 0-8014-0488-6). Cornell U Pr.

Suleiman the Magnificent, 1520-1566. 9.50x (ISBN 0-8154-0152-3). Cooper Sq.

Sulla the Fortunate: The Great Dictator, Being an Essay on Politics in the Form of a Historical Biography. 11.50x (ISBN 0-87471-215-7). Rowman.

Summer of My Content. 3.95 (ISBN 0-87747-585-7). Deseret Bk.

Summer of the Great Grandmother. 7.95 (ISBN 0-374-27174-7). FS&G.

Summer of Triumph. 8.95 (ISBN 0-399-11911-6). Putnam.

Summing up. 15.00x (ISBN 0-405-07830-7). Arno.

Summing Up. pap. 2.95 (ISBN 0-14-001852-2). Penguin.

Summoned to Jerusalem: The Life of Henrietta Szold. 15.00 (ISBN 0-06-010963-7). Har-Row.

Sun Is My Enemy. pap. 4.95 (ISBN 0-8070-2171-7, BP537). Beacon Pr.

Sun Valley: A Biography. 12.95 (ISBN 0-916238-04-0); pap. 7.95 (ISBN 0-916238-02-4). R O Beatty Assocs.

Sun Yat-Sen & Communism. lib. bdg. 16.75x (ISBN 0-8371-8455-X, LESY). Greenwood.

Sun Yat Sen & the Chinese Republic. 19.50 (ISBN 0-404-03989-8). AMS Pr.

Sun Yat-sen & the Origins of the Chinese Revolution. 14.50x (ISBN 0-520-01142-2). U of Cal Pr.

Sun Yat-sen, His Life & Its Meaning: A Critical Biography. 15.00x (ISBN 0-8047-0609-3); pap. 4.95 (ISBN 0-8047-0610-7, SP75). Stanford U Pr.

Sunday Driver. 7.95 (ISBN 0-374-27183-6). FS&G.

Sunlight & Song: A Singer's Life. lib. bdg. 21.00x (ISBN 0-405-09684-4). Arno.

Sunset Over Dartmoor. 10.95 (ISBN 0-09-128010-9). Merrimack Bk Serv.

Super Showmen. PLB 5.54 (ISBN 0-8116-4909-1). Garrard.

Superdrivers: Three Auto Racing Champions. lib. bdg. 4.78 (ISBN 0-8116-6681-6). Garrard.

Superiority & Social Interest: A Collection of Later Writings. pap. 5.95 (ISBN 0-393-00910-6). Norton.

Superiority & Social Interest: A Collection of Later Writings. 2nd. rev ed. 12.95x (ISBN 0-8101-0037-1). Northwestern U Pr.

Supernatural Superpowers. pap. 3.95 (ISBN 0-88270-244-0). Logos.

Superstars of Auto-Racing. PLB 6.29 (ISBN 0-399-60959-8). Putnam.

Superstars of Golf. 10.95 (ISBN 0-914178-13-X, 22975). Golf Digest Bks.

Superstars of the Sports World. PLB 7.29 (ISBN 0-671-32827-1). Messner.

Superwives. 8.95 (ISBN 0-698-10716-0). Coward.

Superwives. pap. 1.75 (ISBN 0-380-01641-9, 32995). Avon.

Superwomen of Rock. pap. 1.50 (ISBN 0-448-16254-7). G&D.

Suppressed Truth About the Assassination of Abraham Lincoln. 7.50. Chedney.

Supreme Court & Its Great Justices. lib. bdg. 5.95 (ISBN 0-668-02372-4). Arco.

Surgeon to Soldiers: Diary & Records of the Surgical Consultant, Allied Force Headquarters, World War 2. text ed. 12.00 (ISBN 0-397-59053-9). Lippincott.

Surgeon's World. 10.00 (ISBN 0-394-46745-0). Random.

Survival in Two Worlds: Moshoeshoe of Lesotho 1786-1870. pap. 8.95x (ISBN 0-19-822702-7). Oxford U Pr.

Survival in Two Worlds: Moshoeshoe of Lesotho, 1786-1870. text ed. 27.50x (ISBN 0-19-821693-9). Oxford U Pr.

Surviving. 7.95 (ISBN 0-8090-9028-7). Hill & Wang.

Surviving. pap. 1.95 (ISBN 0-441-79105-0). Ace Bks.

Surviving the Long Night: An Autobiographical Account of a Political Kidnapping. 7.95 (ISBN 0-8149-0756-3). Vanguard.

Survivors. 8.95 (ISBN 0-393-08727-1). Norton.

Susan B. Anthony. PLB 5.29 (ISBN 0-671-32715-1). Messner.

Susan B. Anthony, a Crusader for Women's Rights. lib. bdg. 2.45 incl. catalog cards (ISBN 0-87157-544-2); pap. 1.25 vinyl laminated covers (ISBN 0-87157-044-0). SamHar Pr.

Susan B. Anthony: Her Personal History & Her Era. 25.00 (ISBN 0-8462-1742-2). Russell.

Susan B. Anthony: Rebel, Crusader, Humanitarian. 15.00. Zenger Pub.

Susan B. Anthony, the Woman Who Changed the Mind of a Nation. 22.50 (ISBN 0-404-00626-4). AMS Pr.

Suspension of Henry Adams: A Study of Manner & Matter. 12.95x (ISBN 0-8143-1359-0). Wayne St U Pr.

Sutter of California: A Biography. lib. bdg. 24.00x (ISBN 0-8371-7644-1, DASC). Greenwood.

Suzuki Changed My Life. pap. text ed. 8.00 (ISBN 0-87487-084-4). Summy.

Swami. pap. 1.95 (ISBN 0-671-81407-9). PB.

Swami. 10.00 (ISBN 0-394-49603-5). Random.

Swami. pap. 1.95 (ISBN 0-671-81407-9). PB.

Swami Ramakrishnananda: The Apostle of Sri Ramakrishna to the South. 1.95 (ISBN 0-87481-453-7). Vedanta Pr.

Swan's Wide Waters: Ramakrishna & Western Culture. new ed. 11.95 (ISBN 0-8046-9055-3). Kennikat.

Swashbucklers. 19.95 (ISBN 0-87000-326-7). Arlington Hse.

Swashbucklers. pap. 7.95 (ISBN 0-89508-006-0). Rainbow Bks.

Swedes in America, 1638-1938. lib. bdg. 34.95 (ISBN 0-8383-0326-9). Haskell.

Sweet As the Showers of Rain. pap. 5.95 (ISBN 0-8256-0178-9). Music Sales.

Sweet Promised Land. 10.00 (ISBN 0-06-012540-3). Har-Row.

Sweet Spirits. 10.95 (ISBN 0-8092-7625-9). Contemp Bks.

Sweetheart: The Story of Mary Pickford. lib. bdg. 10.95 (ISBN 0-8161-6234-4). G K Hall.

Sweetness. 7.95 (ISBN 0-8092-7544-9). Contemp Bks.

Swift. 26.50 (ISBN 0-404-15239-2). AMS Pr.

Swift: An Introduction. lib. bdg. 16.75x (ISBN 0-313-22052-2, QUST). Greenwood.

Swift & Carroll: A Psychoanalytic Study of Two Lives. text ed. 15.00 (ISBN 0-8236-6280-2). Intl Univs Pr.

Swift & the Church of Ireland. 12.00x (ISBN 0-19-811559-8). Oxford U Pr.

Swift in Ireland. lib. bdg. 10.75 (ISBN 0-8414-5511-2). Folcroft.

Swift in Ireland. lib. bdg. 19.95 (ISBN 0-8383-1338-8). Haskell.

Swift: The Mystery of His Life & Love. lib. bdg. 20.00 (ISBN 0-8414-0075-X). Folcroft.

Swinburne: A Biography. 8.00x (ISBN 0-8052-3388-1). Schocken.

Swinburne: A Literary Biography. lib. bdg. 35.00 (ISBN 0-8414-5843-X). Folcroft.

Swinburne: A Literary Biography. lib. bdg. 30.00 (ISBN 0-8482-1617-2). Norwood Edns.

Swinburne: An Essay Written in 1875 & Now First Printed. lib. bdg. 10.00 (ISBN 0-8414-2036-X). Folcroft.

Swinburne: Portrait of a Poet. 10.95 (ISBN 0-02-550960-8). Macmillan.

Sydney Smith. lib. bdg. 17.50 (ISBN 0-8495-4556-0). Arden Lib.

Sydney Smith. lib. bdg. 20.00. Folcroft.

Sydney Smith. 11.00 (ISBN 0-8103-3720-7). Gale.

Sydney Smith. lib. bdg. 17.50 (ISBN 0-8495-4511-0). Arden Lib.

Sylvester Stallone: Going the Distance. text ed. 5.95 (ISBN 0-88436-436-4). EMC.

Sylvia Plath. 5.75x (ISBN 0-06-490038-X). B&N.

Sylvia Plath: Her Life & Work. pap. 1.25 (ISBN 0-06-080341-X, P341). Har-Row.

Sylvia Plath: Poetry & Existence. text ed. 17.25x (ISBN 0-391-01022-0). Humanities.

Sylvia Plath: The Woman & the Work. 8.95 (ISBN 0-396-07497-9). Dodd.

Symphony Writers Since Beethoven. lib. bdg. 10.00 (ISBN 0-403-03756-5). Scholarly.

Symphony Writers Since Beethoven. lib. bdg. 11.00x (ISBN 0-8371-4369-1, WESW). Greenwood.

Syrie Maugham. 22.00 (ISBN 0-7156-1307-3). Biblio Dist.

T

T. Butler King of Georgia. 10.00 (ISBN 0-8203-0174-4). U of Ga Pr.

T. E. Hulme. lib. bdg. 22.95 (ISBN 0-8383-1342-6). Haskell.

T. E. Lawrence. 12.95 (ISBN 0-399-11584-6). Putnam.

T. E. Lawrence: A Bibliography. lib. bdg. 13.95 (ISBN 0-8383-1385-X). Haskell.

T. H. Huxley: Man's Place in Nature. 13.50x (ISBN 0-8032-0917-7). U of Nebr Pr.

T. H. Jones. pap. 4.50 (ISBN 0-8426-0880-X). Verry.

T. H. Parry-Williams. pap. text ed. 6.00 (ISBN 0-7083-0670-5). Verry.

T. J. Ryan: A Political Biography. 22.50x (ISBN 0-7022-1300-4). U of Queensland Pr.

T. S. Eliot's Intellectual Development, 1922-1939. 10.50x (ISBN 0-226-50518-9). U of Chicago Pr.

T. S. Stribling. lib. bdg. 7.95 (ISBN 0-8057-7151-4). Twayne.

T. Thomas Fortune: Militant Journalist. 12.50x (ISBN 0-226-79832-1). U of Chicago Pr.

Tadeo Ortiz, Mexican Colonizer & Reformer. 3.00 (ISBN 0-87404-101-5). Tex Western.

Tails' of a Dog Psychoanalyst. 10.95 (ISBN 0-9601292-2-7). M R K.

Take Heart. 2.95 (ISBN 0-8054-5534-5). Broadman.

Take It All off. pap. 2.95 (ISBN 0-89293-074-8). Beta Bk.

Take off the Masks. 7.95 (ISBN 0-385-13219-0). Doubleday.

Take Them up Tenderly: A Collection of Profiles. 18.25 (ISBN 0-8369-2991-8). Arno.

Take This House. pap. 1.95 (ISBN 0-8361-1817-0). Herald Pr.

Take Time for Sunsets. 6.95 (ISBN 0-8199-0565-8). Franciscan Herald.

Taking Out My Bucketful. pap. 2.95 (ISBN 0-89636-009-1). Accent Bks.

Tale of Beatrix Potter: A Biography. 2nd ed. 20.00 (ISBN 0-7232-0138-2). Warne.

Tales of a Western Mountaineer. pap. 6.95 (ISBN 0-916890-62-7). Mountaineers.

Tales of an All-Night Town. 9.95 (ISBN 0-15-184993-5). HarBraceJ.

Talking to Myself. pap. 1.50 (ISBN 0-671-78829-9). PB.

Talking to Myself: A Memoir of My Times. 10.00 (ISBN 0-394-41102-1). Pantheon.

Talking Woman. 8.95 (ISBN 0-440-08595-0). Delacorte.

Talks with Lady Shelley. lib. bdg. 20.00 (ISBN 0-8414-7306-4). Folcroft.

Tall Trees & Far Horizons: Adventures & Discoveries of Early Botanists in America. 20.50 (ISBN 0-8369-2686-2). Arno.

Talleyrand: A Biography. 12.95 (ISBN 0-399-11022-4). Putnam.

Talleyrand: The Art of Survival. 12.95 (ISBN 0-394-47299-3). Knopf.

Tallis. 2nd ed. pap. 6.95x (ISBN 0-19-314122-1). Oxford U Pr.

Tallulah, Darling: A Biography of Tallulah Bankhead. 11.95 (ISBN 0-02-515200-9). Macmillan.

Tamate - a King: James Chalmers in New Guinea, 1877-1901. 17.50x (ISBN 0-522-84079-5). Intl Schol Bk Serv.

Tame the Restless Wind: The Life & Legends of Sam Bass. 4.95. Jenkins.

Tantalizing Disclosures of a Welsh Girl. 8.50 (ISBN 0-8022-2218-8). Philos Lib.

Tantrums, Toads, & Teddy Bears. 8.95 (ISBN 0-8361-1891-X). Herald Pr.

Tanzanian Doctor. 10.95 (ISBN 0-7735-0305-6). McGill-Queens U Pr.

Tapadero: The Making of a Cowboy. 8.95 (ISBN 0-292-78001-X). U of Tex Pr.

Tar Heel Editor. lib. bdg. 34.00x (ISBN 0-8371-7440-6, DATH). Greenwood.

Tarkenton. 8.95 (ISBN 0-06-012412-1). Har-Row.

Tarkenton. pap. 1.95 (ISBN 0-06-080425-4, P 425). Har-Row.

Tasso & His Times. 13.75 (ISBN 0-8274-3570-3). R West.

Tasso & His Times. lib. bdg. 24.95 (ISBN 0-8383-0915-1). Haskell.

Taste of Hope. 8.95 (ISBN 0-09-130230-7). Merrimack Bk Serv.

Tchaikovsky. 3.50 (ISBN 0-87250-236-8). D

Tchaikovsky. [illegible] 8008-7552-4). Taplinger.

Teacher. pap. 2.25 (ISBN 0-553-12988-0). Bantam.

Teachers of Gurdjieff. pap. 2.45 (ISBN 0-87728-213-7). Weiser.

Teaching of Charles Fourier. 16.50x (ISBN 0-520-01405-7). U of Cal Pr.

Teagle of Jersey Standard. 12.00. Tulane Univ.

Tecumseh & the Indian Confederation: The Indian Nations East of the Mississippi Are Defeated. PLB 4.90 (ISBN 0-531-02780-5). Watts.

Tecumseh: Vision of Glory. 25.00 (ISBN 0-8462-1698-1). Russell.

Teilhard. 10.00 (ISBN 0-385-02444-4). Doubleday.

Teilhard De Chardin. pap. 2.25 (ISBN 0-8042-0723-2). John Knox.

Tell Him That I Heard. 7.95 (ISBN 0-06-011788-5). Har-Row.

Tell It on the Mountain. pap. 1.95 (ISBN 0-671-81265-3). PB.

Tell It on the Mountain. pap. 1.95 (ISBN 0-8007-8311-5). Revell.

Tell It to the Dead: Memories of a War. 9.95 (ISBN 0-88229-287-0); pap. 5.95 (ISBN 0-88229-354-0). Nelson Hall.

Tell It to the Mafia. pap. 2.50 (ISBN 0-88270-322-6). Logos.

Tell Me About Jesus. rev. ed. pap. 2.50 (ISBN 0-528-87657-0). Rand.

Tell Me, Rabbi. 7.95 (ISBN 0-8197-0395-8). Bloch.

Tell Me, Rabbi. pap. 2.95 (ISBN 0-02-086340-3). Macmillan.

Tell Me Who I Am Before I Die. 8.95 (ISBN 0-89256-063-0). Rawson Wade.

Tell-Tale Heart: The Life & Works of Edgar Allan Poe. 10.95 (ISBN 0-06-014208-1). Har-Row.

Ten Africans. 5.95 (ISBN 0-571-05525-7). Merrimack Bk Serv.

Ten Against Napoleon. 11.95 (ISBN 0-88229-253-6). Nelson Hall.

Ten Christians: By Their Deeds You Shall Know Them. pap. 5.95 (ISBN 0-87793-183-6). Ave Maria.

Ten New England Leaders. 18.00 (ISBN 0-405-00278-5). Arno.

Ten Personal Studies. 16.00 (ISBN 0-8369-1584-4). Arno.

Ten Thousand Working Days. 12.50 (ISBN 0-262-19169-5); pap. 4.95 (ISBN 0-262-69064-0). MIT Pr.

Ten Tudor Statesmen. 11.00 (ISBN 0-8046-1228-5). Kennikat.

Ten Years After Ivan Denisovich. pap. 1.95 (ISBN 0-394-71112-2). Random.

Ten Years in Japan: A Contemporary Record Drawn from the Diaries & Private & Official Papers of Joseph C. Grew, United States Ambassador to Japan, 1932-1942. lib. bdg. 23.50x (ISBN 0-8371-6723-X, GRTY). Greenwood.

Ten Years on a Georgia Plantation Since the War. 14.00x (ISBN 0-8371-1177-3). Negro U Pr.

Ten Years to Live. 7.95 (ISBN 0-8010-8127-0). Baker Bk.

Tench Coxe & the Early Republic. 25.00 (ISBN 0-8078-1308-7). U of NC Pr.

Tender Tyrant: The Legend of Pete Cawthon. 12.50. Staked Plains.

Tendoy, Chief of the Lemhis. pap. 2.75 (ISBN 0-87004-129-0). Caxton.

Tennessee Williams in Tangier. pap. 6.00 (ISBN 0-932274-00-5); signed limited 15.00 (ISBN 0-932274-01-3). Cadmus Eds.

Tennessee Williams' Letters to Donald Windham: 1940-1965. 10.00 (ISBN 0-03-022636-8). HR&W.

Tennis: Great Stars, Great Moments. PLB 5.49 (ISBN 0-399-61029-4). Putnam.

Tennyson. lib. bdg. 10.00 (ISBN 0-8414-9406-1). Folcroft.

Tennyson: A Modern Portrait. 11.00 (ISBN 0-8462-1121-1). Russell.

Tennyson & His Poetry. lib. bdg. 7.50. Folcroft.

Tennyson & His Poetry. 7.25 (ISBN 0-404-52524-5). AMS Pr.

Tennyson & His Poetry. 6.00 (ISBN 0-8046-0833-4). Kennikat.

Tennyson & His Poetry. lib. bdg. 8.00 (ISBN 0-8492-5604-6). R West.

Tennyson: Aspects of His Life, Character & Poetry. 15.25 (ISBN 0-8369-9967-3). Arno.

Tennyson: Aspects of His Life, Character & Poetry. lib. bdg. 23.95 (ISBN 0-8383-1458-9). Haskell.

Tennyson: The Growth of a Poet. pap. 5.50 (ISBN 0-395-04244-5, 3-07630). HM.

Tennyson: The Growth of a Poet. pap. 3.95 (ISBN 0-674-87408-0). Harvard U Pr.

Tennyson: The Story of His Life. lib. bdg. 20.00 (ISBN 0-8495-0745-6). Arden Lib.

Tennyson's Two Brothers. lib. bdg. 6.50. Folcroft.

Teresita. 14.95 (ISBN 0-916144-24-0); pap. 8.95 (ISBN 0-916144-25-9). Stemmer Hse.

Term to Remember. 9.95 (ISBN 0-698-10751-9). Coward.

Terry Bradshaw. PLB 5.50 (ISBN 0-87191-542-1). Creative Ed.

Testimonies in the Life, Character, Revelations, & Doctrines of Mother Ann Lee. 2nd ed. 20.00 (ISBN 0-404-10756-7). AMS Pr.

Testimony: The Memoirs of Dmitri Shostakovich. 15.00 (ISBN 0-06-014476-9). Har-Row.

Texas Governor. 13.95 (ISBN 0-912854-09-X). GLA Pr.

Texas Riverman: The Life & Times of Captain Andrew Smyth. 8.95 (ISBN 0-292-73625-8). U of Tex Pr.

Texas Senator. 13.95. GLA Pr.

Texas Wild Flowers. collectors ed. 100.00 (ISBN 0-88319-006-0); deluxe ed. 35.00. Shoal Creek Pub.

Texas Writers of Today. cancelled. Gale.

Thackeray. lib. bdg. 47.50 (ISBN 0-374-96722-9). Octagon.

Thackeray. lib. bdg. 4.95 (ISBN 0-668-01952-2). Arco.

Thackeray: A Reconsideration. 13.50 (ISBN 0-208-00476-9). Shoe String.

Thackeray's Haunts & Homes. lib. bdg. 15.00 (ISBN 0-8414-3542-1). Folcroft.

Thaddeus Stevens. 15.00. Folcroft.

Thaddeus Stevens. 12.50 (ISBN 0-404-50881-2). AMS Pr.

Thaddeus Stevens, Commoner. 10.00 (ISBN 0-404-00011-8). AMS Pr.

Thaddeus Stevens, Scourge of the [illegible]th. pap. 4.95 (ISBN 0-393-00331-0). [illegible]

Thaddeus Stevens, Scourge of t[illegible] 7.75 (ISBN 0-8446-0329-5). Pet[illegible]

Thank You Davey; Thank Yo[illegible] [illegible]50 (ISBN 0-8066-1614-8, 10[illegible]

Thank You for Being. pap. [illegible] 9601922-0-4). Weyand[illegible]

Thanks Lord, I Needed [illegible] 88270-248-3). Logos[illegible]

Thanks Lord, I Needed That. pocket size 2.50 (ISBN 0-88270-411-7). Logos.

Thanksgiving Visitor. 9.95 (ISBN 0-394-44824-3). Random.

That Grand Whig Milton. 14.00 (ISBN 0-405-08948-1). Arno.

That Grand Whig, Milton. 14.50 (ISBN 0-404-51821-4). AMS Pr.

That Man Haupt: A Biography of Herman Haupt. 14.95x (ISBN 0-8071-0225-3). La State U Pr.

That Summer in Paris: Memories of Tangled Friendships with Hemingway, Fitzgerald & Some Others. pap. 3.95 (ISBN 0-14-005074-4). Penguin.

That Tent by the Sawdust Pile. pap. 3.95 (ISBN 0-8163-0267-7, 20249-9). Pacific Pr Pub Assn.

That Wild Fellow John Neal & the American Literary Revolution. 10.00x (ISBN 0-226-46969-7). U of Chicago Pr.

Theatre of Erwin Piscator: Half a Century of Politics in the Theatre. text ed. 24.75x (ISBN 0-8419-0501-0). Holmes & Meier.

Theatre of Meyerhold: Revolution on the Modern Stage. text ed. 13.95x (ISBN 0-89676-003-0); pap. text ed. 10.00x (ISBN 0-89676-004-9). Drama Bk.

Theatre Through Its Stage Door. 15.00 (ISBN 0-405-08261-4). Arno.

Their Finest Hour. pap. 1.95 (ISBN 0-912692-45-6). Cook.

Their Name Is Pius: Portraits of Five Great Modern Popes. 12.50. Folcroft.

Their Religion. facs. ed. 15.50 (ISBN 0-8369-2131-3). Arno.

Their Ruling Passions. facs. ed. 15.50 (ISBN 0-8369-8040-9). Arno.

Theobald Archbishop of Canterbury. lib. bdg. 23.00x (ISBN 0-8371-0643-5, SATH). Greenwood.

Theodor Boveri: The Life & Work of a Great Biologist, 1862-1915. 15.75x (ISBN 0-520-00074-9). U of Cal Pr.

Theodor Fontane: An Introduction to the Man & His Work. text ed. 17.50x (ISBN 0-7083-0617-9). Verry.

Theodore Dreiser. lib. bdg. 22.50 (ISBN 0-8492-6823-0). R West.

Theodore Dreiser. lib. bdg. 16.75x (ISBN 0-8371-6550-4, MATD). Greenwood.

Theodore Hook & His Novels. 25.00 (ISBN 0-403-00814-X). Scholarly.

Theodore Roethke. pap. 1.25x (ISBN 0-8166-0304-9, MPAW30). U of Minn Pr.

Theodore Roosevelt & the Philippines, 1897-1909. 12.50 (ISBN 0-88211-052-7). Oriole Edns.

Theodore Roosevelt & the Politics of Power. 5.00 (ISBN 0-316-13871-1); pap. 4.95 (ISBN 0-316-13870-3). Little.

Theodore Roosevelt, the Citizen. 17.50 (ISBN 0-404-05335-1). AMS Pr.

Theodore Roosevelt, the Citizen. 17.00 (ISBN 0-403-00224-9). Scholarly.

Theodore Roosevelt, 1858-1919: Chronology, Documents, Bibliographical Aids. 7.00 (ISBN 0-379-12058-5). Oceana.

Theodore Roosevelt's Boys. PLB 3.68 (ISBN 0-8116-6254-3). Garrard.

Theodore Roosevelt's Letters to His Children. 12.50. Norwood Edns.

Theodore Weld, Crusader for Freedom. lib. bdg. 15.00 (ISBN 0-374-97857-3). Octagon.

Theodore Winthrop. pap. 3.45 (ISBN 0-8084-0296-X, T84). Coll & U Pr.

Theophile Gautier. 13.50 (ISBN 0-8369-5732-6). Arno.

Theophile Gautier. 8.50 (ISBN 0-8274-3592-4). R West.

Theophile Gautier. 8.75 (ISBN 0-8046-1564-0). Kennikat.

Theophile Gautier. 30.00 (ISBN 0-8495-6280-5). Arden Lib.

Theophile Gautier. text ed. 13.50x (ISBN 0-485-14604-5); pap. text ed. 5.50x (ISBN 0-485-12204-9). Humanities.

There Is a Fountain: The Autobiography of a Civil Rights Lawyer. 12.00 (ISBN 0-88208-098-9). Lawrence Hill.

There's a Raccoon in My Parka. 8.95 (ISBN 0-385-12755-3). Doubleday.

There's an Iguana in My Plumbing. 7.95 (ISBN 0-87949-050-0). Ashley Bks.

These Men Shall Never Die. facsimile ed. 29.50 (ISBN 0-8369-2379-0). Arno.

These Modern Women: Autobiographies of Women in the Twenties. pap. 4.95 (ISBN 0-912670-46-0). Feminist Pr.

These Splendid Priests. facs. ed. 12.25 (ISBN 0-8369-0973-9). Arno.

These Splendid Sisters. 13.50 (ISBN 0-8369-1856-8). Arno.

These Strange Ashes. 7.95 (ISBN 0-06-062233-4). Har-Row.

These Strange Ashes. pap. 3.95 (ISBN 0-06-062234-2, RD 306). Har-Row.

These Were Actors: Extracts from a Newspaper Cutting Book, 1811-1833. 12.00 (ISBN 0-405-08195-2). Arno.

They Also Ran. pap. 2.25 (ISBN 0-451-07110-7, E7110). NAL.

They Also Ran. rev. ed. 6.95 (ISBN 0-385-07409-3). Doubleday.

They Also Speak. pap. 2.95 (ISBN 0-8054-1133-X). Broadman.

They Call Me Gump. 6.95 (ISBN 0-396-07029-9). Dodd.

They Call Me Mister 500. 6.95 (ISBN 0-8092-9635-7). Contemp Bks.

They Call Me Mother Graham. pap. 1.95 (ISBN 0-8007-9000-6). Revell.

They Call Me the Big E. 8.95 (ISBN 0-13-917054-5). P-H.

They Call Me the Show Biz Priest. pap. 1.25 (ISBN 0-671-78452-8). PB.

They Called Me Cassandra. lib. bdg. 32.50 (ISBN 0-306-70298-3). Da Capo.

They Called Me Mama. pap. 4.25 (ISBN 0-8024-8683-5). Moody.

They Dared to Live. facsimile ed. 11.00 (ISBN 0-8369-1273-X). Arno.

They Did Something About It. facsimile ed. 12.50 (ISBN 0-8369-1243-8). Arno.

They Looked for a City. pap. 1.95 (ISBN 0-87508-041-3). Chr Lit.

They Named Me Gertrude Stein. 5.50g (ISBN 0-374-37467-8). FS&G.

They Played the Game: The Story of Baseball Greats. 20.50 (ISBN 0-8369-2692-7). Arno.

They Showed the Way: Forty American Negro Leaders. 7.95 (ISBN 0-690-81612-X). T Y Crowell.

They Were Giants. facs. ed. 13.75 (ISBN 0-8369-0257-2). Arno.

They Were San Franciscans. facs. ed. 17.50 (ISBN 0-8369-1914-9). Arno.

They Won the War. facs. ed. 9.50 (ISBN 0-8369-0126-6). Arno.

They Wouldn't Let Us Die: The Prisoners of War Tell Their Story. 8.95 (ISBN 0-8246-0157-2). Jonathan David.

Thiers & the French Monarchy. 17.50 (ISBN 0-208-00017-8). Shoe String.

Things I Love. 1.95 (ISBN 0-448-12718-0). G&D.

Things I Remember. facsimile ed. 17.00x (ISBN 0-405-06925-1). Arno.

Thinking Like a Mountain: Aldo Leopold & the Evolution of an Ecological Attitude Toward Deer, Wolves, & Forests. 15.00x (ISBN 0-8262-0167-9). U of Mo Pr.

Thinking Like a Mountain: Aldo Leopold & the Evolution of an Ecological Attitude Toward Deer, Wolves & Forests. pap. 4.50 (ISBN 0-8032-6850-5, BB668). U of Nebr Pr.

Third Force: The Psychology of Abraham Maslow. pap. 1.95 (ISBN 0-671-80216-X). PB.

Third Rose: Gertrude Stein & Her World. 8.00 (ISBN 0-8446-0328-7). Peter Smith.

Thirteen Worthies. facs. ed. 10.25 (ISBN 0-8369-0799-X). Arno.

Thirteen Years of Travel & Exploration in Alaska: 1877-1889. pap. 3.95 (ISBN 0-88240-076-2). Alaska Northwest.

Thirty-Five Years in Russia. 16.00 (ISBN 0-405-03082-7). Arno.

Thirty-Five Years of Luther Research. 5.00 (ISBN 0-404-05284-3). AMS Pr.

Thirty-One Banana Leaves. 3.95 (ISBN 0-8042-2582-6). John Knox.

Thirty Years of Billiards. pap. 3.00 (ISBN 0-486-23126-7). Dover.

Thirty Years with G. B. S. 12.50 (ISBN 0-8274-0990-7). R West.

This for Remembrance. pap. 1.95 (ISBN 0-87216-542-6). Playboy Pr Pbks.

This House Is Haunted! PLB 7.95 (ISBN 0-8172-1033-4). Raintree Pubs.

This House of Sky: Landscapes of a Western Mind. 9.95 (ISBN 0-15-190054-X). HarBraceJ.

This House of Sky: Landscapes of a Western Mind. pap. 4.95 (ISBN 0-15-689982-5). HarBraceJ.

This I Remember. lib. bdg. 25.50x (ISBN 0-8371-7702-2, ROTI). Greenwood.

This I Saw: The Life & Times of Goya. lib. bdg. 17.75x (ISBN 0-8371-6047-2, VATI). Greenwood.

This Is My Story, This Is My Song. 4.95 (ISBN 0-8007-0313-8). Revell.

This Land, These Voices: A Different View of Arizona History in Words of Those Who Lived It. 12.50 (ISBN 0-87358-166-0). Northland.

This Stubborn Soil. 6.95 (ISBN 0-684-10444-X). Scribner.

This Timeless Moment: A Personal View of Aldous Huxley. pap. 4.95 (ISBN 0-89087-022-5). Celestial Arts.

This Too Shall Pass. 7.95 (ISBN 0-915684-30-6). Christian Herald.

This Was Toscanini. 19.50 (ISBN 0-8149-0018-6). Vanguard.

Thomas A. R. Nelson of East Tennessee. 11.00x (ISBN 0-87402-007-7). U of Tenn Pr.

Thomas B. Reed. 12.50 (ISBN 0-404-50885-5). AMS Pr.

Thomas Benton Catron & His Era. 12.50 (ISBN 0-8165-0341-9); pap. 6.95 (ISBN 0-8165-0454-7). U of Ariz Pr.

Thomas Betterton. lib. bdg. 7.25. Folcroft.

Thomas Betterton. 7.00 (ISBN 0-404-04038-1). AMS Pr.

Thomas Bewick & His Pupils. 7.80 (ISBN 0-8103-3523-9). Gale.

Thomas Carlyle. lib. bdg. 12.50 (ISBN 0-404-51723-4). AMS Pr.

Thomas Carlyle. lib. bdg. 12.50 (ISBN 0-8482-1958-9). Norwood Edns.

Thomas Carlyle. lib. bdg. 17.50 (ISBN 0-8414-0058-X). Folcroft.

Thomas Carlyle. lib. bdg. 8.50 (ISBN 0-8414-9634-X). Folcroft.

Thomas Carlyle: A History of His Life in London. 40.00 (ISBN 0-403-00191-9). Scholarly.

Thomas Carlyle: A History of His Life in London 1834-1881. 50.00 (ISBN 0-8274-3602-5). R West.

Thomas Carlyle & the Art of History. 20.00 (ISBN 0-8414-9768-0). Folcroft.

Thomas Carlyle & the Art of History. lib. bdg. 12.50 (ISBN 0-374-98841-2). Octagon.

Thomas Carlyle & the Art of History. lib. bdg. 30.00 (ISBN 0-8495-6137-X). Arden Lib.

Thomas Chatterton. 9.00 (ISBN 0-8046-0845-8). Kennikat.

Thomas Chaucer. 11.50 (ISBN 0-404-05469-2). AMS Pr.

Thomas Clarkson: The Friend of Slaves. 11.00x (ISBN 0-8371-3754-3). Negro U Pr.

Thomas Cranmer, Theologian. text ed. 4.50x (ISBN 0-8401-0242-9). Allenson.

Thomas Dekker: A Study. lib. bdg. 27.50 (ISBN 0-8495-2305-2). Arden Lib.

Thomas Dongan, Governor of New York (1682-1688) 11.50 (ISBN 0-404-57759-8). AMS Pr.

Thomas E. Williams & the Fine Arts Press. 12.50 (ISBN 0-87093-091-5). Dawsons.

Thomas Edison, Chemist. 8.50 (ISBN 0-8412-0129-3); pap. 6.00 (ISBN 0-8412-0534-5). Am Chemical.

Thomas Edison, Father of Electricity & Master Inventor of Our Modern Age. lib. bdg. 2.45 incl. catalog cards (ISBN 0-87157-542-6); pap. 1.25 vinyl laminated covers. SamHar Pr.

Thomas Francis Meagher: An Irish Revolutionary in America. 12.00 (ISBN 0-405-09318-7). Arno.

Thomas Gray of Pembroke. lib. bdg. 8.50 (ISBN 0-8414-2593-0). Folcroft.

Thomas H. Benton. 15.00 (ISBN 0-404-50873-1). AMS Pr.

Thomas H. Huxley. 11.50 (ISBN 0-404-07892-3) AMS Pr.

Thomas Hardy. pap. 2.25 (ISBN 0-312-80080-0). St Martin.

Thomas Hardy: A Critical Biography. 20.00 (ISBN 0-8462-1411-3). Russell.

Thomas Hardy: A Critical Biography. 6.95 (ISBN 0-396-06338-1). Dodd.

Thomas Hardy's Later Years. 12.50 (ISBN 0-316-31454-4). Little.

Thomas Hardy's Wessex Scene. 11.75 (ISBN 0-8274-0043-8). R West.

Thomas Hart Benton. 14.00 (ISBN 0-403-00310-5). Scholarly.

Thomas Hart Benton. lib. bdg. 22.95 (ISBN 0-8383-0275-0). Haskell.

Thomas Henry Huxley. lib. bdg. 15.00. Folcroft.

Thomas Henry Huxley. 14.50 (ISBN 0-404-14023-8). AMS Pr.

Thomas Heywood. 7.50 (ISBN 0-87753-056-4). Phaeton.

Thomas Heywood. 19.00 (ISBN 0-403-02292-4). Somerset Pub.

Thomas Heywood. lib. bdg. 15.00 (ISBN 0-8414-9938-1). Folcroft.

Thomas Hobbes. 6.00 (ISBN 0-8046-0746-X). Kennikat.

Thomas Hobbes in His Time. 10.00x (ISBN 0-8166-0727-3). U of Minn Pr.

Thomas Hooker: Writings in England & Holland, 1626-1633. pap. text ed. 10.00x (ISBN 0-674-88520-1). Harvard U Pr.

Thomas Hooker, 1586-1647. text ed. 19.00 (ISBN 0-691-05249-2). Princeton U Pr.

Thomas Hunt Morgan: Pioneer of Genetics. 7.50 (ISBN 0-8131-0095-X). U Pr of Ky.

Thomas Hunt Morgan: Pioneer of Genetics. 4.95 (ISBN 0-8131-0219-7). U Pr of Ky.

Thomas J. Comber, Missionary Pioneer to the Congo. 9.00x (ISBN 0-8371-2769-6). Negro U Pr.

Thomas Jefferson: A Biography in His Own Words. 15.00 (ISBN 0-06-011148-8). Har-Row.

Thomas Jefferson: An Intimate History. 15.95 (ISBN 0-393-07480-3). Norton.

Thomas Jefferson: An Intimate History. pap. 3.50 (ISBN 0-553-13709-3, V13709-3). Bantam.

Thomas Jefferson & American Democracy. 4.00x (ISBN 0-8426-1152-5). Verry.

Thomas Jefferson & American Democracy. pap. 1.25 (ISBN 0-02-030620-2). Macmillan.

Thomas Jefferson & His World. 6.95 (ISBN 0-8281-0386-0, J00301-08). Am Heritage.

Thomas Jefferson & the Development of American Public Education. 7.50x (ISBN 0-520-00262-8). U of Cal Pr.
Thomas Jefferson & the Law. 25.00 (ISBN 0-8061-1441-X). U of Okla Pr.
Thomas Jefferson & the New Nation: A Biography. 35.00 (ISBN 0-19-500054-4). Oxford U Pr.
Thomas Jefferson & the New Nation: A Biography. pap. 8.95 (ISBN 0-19-501909-1, GB436). Oxford U Pr.
Thomas Jefferson As Political Leader. lib. bdg. 13.50x (ISBN 0-313-20730-5, MATJ). Greenwood.
Thomas Jefferson: The Apostle of Americanism. pap. 5.95 (ISBN 0-472-06013-9, 13). U of Mich Pr.
Thomas Jefferson: The Apostle of Liberty. 6.95 (ISBN 0-87140-809-0). Liveright.
Thomas Jefferson: The Complete Man. PLB 4.90 (ISBN 0-531-00886-X). Watts.
Thomas Killigrew, Cavalier Dramatist. 14.00 (ISBN 0-405-08597-4). Arno.
Thomas Lodge. 8.00 (ISBN 0-8462-1182-3). Russell.
Thomas Lodge & Other Elizabethans. lib. bdg. 25.00 (ISBN 0-374-97467-5). Octagon.
Thomas Love Peacock. 10.00 (ISBN 0-8369-5787-3). Arno.
Thomas Love Peacock. lib. bdg. 15.00 (ISBN 0-8482-3531-2). Norwood Edns.
Thomas Lovell Beddoes: Eccentric & Poet. lib. bdg. 15.00. Folcroft.
Thomas McKean: The Shaping of an American Republicanism. text ed. 15.00x (ISBN 0-87081-100-2). Colo Assoc.
Thomas Mann. 9.95 (ISBN 0-8044-2023-8); pap. 3.45 (ISBN 0-8044-6018-3). Ungar.
Thomas Mann: A Study. 7.50 (ISBN 0-8462-1038-X). Russell.
Thomas Merton. pap. 3.95 (ISBN 0-385-17172-2). Doubleday.
Thomas Merton: The Daring Young Man on the Flying Belltower. 6.95 (ISBN 0-02-788630-1, 78863). Macmillan.
Thomas Merton's Shared Contemplation: A Protestant Perspective. 17.95 (ISBN 0-87907-862-6). Cistercian Pubns.
Thomas Moore. lib. bdg. 15.00 (ISBN 0-8414-4448-X). Folcroft.
Thomas More. pap. 4.95 (ISBN 0-472-06018-X, 18). U of Mich Pr.
Thomas More. facs. ed. 14.75 (ISBN 0-8369-5406-8). Arno.
Thomas More & Erasmus. 15.00 (ISBN 0-8232-0670-X). Fordham.
Thomas More: The King's Good Servant. 14.95 (ISBN 0-529-05494-9, RB5494). Collins Pubs.
Thomas Paine. lib. bdg. 17.50 (ISBN 0-8414-7910-0). Folcroft.
Thomas Paine. lib. bdg. 8.95 (ISBN 0-8057-7206-5). Twayne.
Thomas Paine, American Revolutionary Writer. lib. bdg. 2.45 incl. catalog cards; pap. 1.25 vinyl laminated covers. SamHar Pr.
Thomas Shadwell: His Life & Comedies. 15.00 (ISBN 0-405-08289-4). Arno.
Thomas Southerne Dramatist. lib. bdg. 30.00 (ISBN 0-89984-154-6). Century Bookbindery.
Thomas Tomkins 1572-1656. 5.50 (ISBN 0-8446-3010-1). Peter Smith.
Thomas Willis, 1621-1675: Doctor & Scientist. 13.75 (ISBN 0-02-846980-1). Hafner.
Thomas Wolfe: A Biography. lib. bdg. 25.00x (ISBN 0-8371-6519-9, NOTW). Greenwood.
Thomas Wolfe: Beyond the Romantic Ego. 7.95 (ISBN 0-690-00751-5). T Y Crowell.
Thomas Wolfe Undergraduate. 9.75 (ISBN 0-8223-0387-6). Duke.
Thomas Woolner, R. A., Sculptor & Poet: His Life & Letters. 17.50 (ISBN 0-404-07030-2). AMS Pr.
Thoor Ballylee: Home of William Butler Yeats. 2nd rev. ed. text ed. 3.75x (ISBN 0-85105-300-9). Humanities.
Thoreau. 6.50 (ISBN 0-85493-042-6). Dufour.
Thoreau: His Life & Aims. lib. bdg. 30.00 (ISBN 0-8414-6778-1). Folcroft.
Thoreau of Walden: The Man & His Eventful Life. 15.00 (ISBN 0-208-00929-9). Shoe String.
Thoreau Profile. pap. 4.00 sewn (ISBN 0-912130-01-6). Thoreau Found.
Thoreau Profile. 7.50 (ISBN 0-8446-0797-5). Peter Smith.
Thornton Wilder. pap. 3.45 (ISBN 0-8084-0300-1, T5). Coll & U Pr.
Thornton Wilder. 2nd ed. lib. bdg. 7.95 (ISBN 0-8057-7223-5). Twayne.
Thornton Wilder. pap. 1.25x (ISBN 0-8166-0318-9, MPAW34). U of Minn Pr.
Thornton Wilder--His World. 10.95 (ISBN 0-385-12840-1). Doubleday.
Those Inventive Americans. 5.75, avail. only from Natl. Geog. (ISBN 0-87044-089-6). Natl Geog.
Those Meddling Women. pap. 3.25 (ISBN 0-8170-0757-1). Judson.
Those Philadelphia Kellys--with a Touch of Grace. 8.95 (ISBN 0-688-03226-5). Morrow.
Those Radio Commentators. 14.95 (ISBN 0-8138-1500-2); 2 records incl. Iowa St U Pr.
Those Wild, Wild Kennedy Boys. pap. 1.75 (ISBN 0-523-00968-2). Pinnacle Bks.
Thou Swell, Thou Witty: The Life & Lyrics of Lorenz Hart. 25.00 (ISBN 0-06-011776-1). Har-Row.
Thought of C. S. Peirce. pap. 3.50 (ISBN 0-486-22216-0). Dover.
Thousand Days with Rajaji. 6.50x (ISBN 0-8002-2084-6). Intl Pubns Serv.
Thread That Runs So True. lib.rep.ed. 15.00x (ISBN 0-684-15160-X); pap. 4.95 (ISBN 0-684-71904-5, SL44). Scribner.
Three Alexander Calders: A Family Memoir. 15.00 (ISBN 0-8397-8017-6). Eriksson.
Three & Two! pap. 2.25 (ISBN 0-425-04642-7). Berkley Pub.
Three Aspects of the Late Alfred Lord Tennyson. lib. bdg. 15.95 (ISBN 0-8383-1387-6). Haskell.
Three Brontes. lib. bdg. 15.00 (ISBN 0-8482-6185-2). Norwood Edns.
Three Catholic Reformers of the Fifteenth Century. facsimile ed. 14.50 (ISBN 0-8369-2633-1). Arno.
Three Centuries: Family Chronicles of Turkey & Egypt. lib. bdg. 22.50x (ISBN 0-8371-7117-2, TUTC). Greenwood.
Three Criminal Law Reformers: Beccaria, Bentham, Romilly. 14.00 (ISBN 0-87585-113-4); pap. 4.50 (ISBN 0-87585-904-6). Patterson Smith.
Three Dimensional Poe. 10.00 (ISBN 0-87404-045-0). Tex Western.
Three English Statesmen: A Course of Lectures on the Political History of England. 16.00 (ISBN 0-8369-2979-9). Arno.
Three Essays. 10.95 (ISBN 0-8006-0224-2). Fortress.
Three for Revolution. PLB 6.25 (ISBN 0-15-286653-1). HarBraceJ.
Three Great Irishmen: Shaw, Yeats, Joyce. 6.75 (ISBN 0-8196-0222-1). Biblo.
Three Journeys: An Automythology. 10.00 (ISBN 0-465-08610-1). Basic.
Three Literary Men: A Memoir of Sinclair Lewis, Sherwood Anderson & Edgar Lee Masters. lib. bdg. 10.00 (ISBN 0-8414-3686-X). Folcroft.
Three Lives of Joseph Conrad. 5.95 (ISBN 0-395-13890-6). HM.
Three Master Builders, & Another: Studies in Modern Revolutionary & Liberal Statesmanship. facs. ed. 15.00 (ISBN 0-8369-0234-3). Arno.
Three Men of Boston. 10.00 (ISBN 0-690-01018-4). T Y Crowell.
Three on the Tower: The Lives & Works of Ezra Pound, T. S. Eliot & William Carlos Williams. 12.50 (ISBN 0-688-02899-3); pap. 5.95 (ISBN 0-688-07899-0). Morrow.
Three Popes & the Cardinal. pap. 1.50 (ISBN 0-445-08221-6). Popular Lib.
Three-Quarter Time: The Life & Music of the Strauss Family of Vienna. lib. bdg. 18.00x (ISBN 0-8371-3991-0, PATQ). Greenwood.
Three Sitwells: A Biographical & Critical Study. 10.00 (ISBN 0-8046-0305-7). Kennikat.
Three Sitwells: A Biographical & Critical Study. 22.50 (ISBN 0-403-01102-7). Scholarly.
Three Ways of Love. 6.00 (ISBN 0-8198-0477-0); pap. 5.00 (ISBN 0-8198-0478-9). Dghtrs St Paul.
Three Weeks in Spring. 7.95 (ISBN 0-395-26282-8). HM.
Three Weeks in Spring. pap. 2.25 (ISBN 0-425-04018-6). Berkley Pub.
Three Who Dared. 5.95 (ISBN 0-385-08898-1). Doubleday.
Three Worlds. lib. bdg. 20.75x (ISBN 0-8371-9831-3, VATH). Greenwood.
Three Years in California. 26.00x (ISBN 0-405-09496-5). Arno.
Threescore & Ten. 4.95 (ISBN 0-8007-0578-5). Revell.
Through Ferrengi Eyes: The Diary of a Peace Corps Volunteer in Ethiopia, 1974-1976. 9.00 (ISBN 0-682-49303-1). Exposition.
Through Poverty's Vale: A Hardscrabble Boyhood in Upstate New York, 1832-1862. 8.50 (ISBN 0-8156-0098-4); pap. 4.50 (ISBN 0-8156-0117-4). Syracuse U Pr.
Through Some Eventful Years. 11.50 (ISBN 0-8130-0074-2). U Presses Fla.
Through the Brazilian Wilderness. lib. bdg. 25.75x (ISBN 0-8371-1492-6, ROBW). Greenwood.
Through the Great City. 5.95 (ISBN 0-02-505540-2). Macmillan.
Through the Russian Revolution. 27.50 (ISBN 0-88355-446-1). Hyperion Conn.
Through the Valley. pap. 4.95 (ISBN 0-8096-1917-2). Follett.
Through the Valley. pap. 1.25 (ISBN 0-380-01759-8, 34827). Avon.
Through Troubled Waters. pap. 1.25 (ISBN 0-451-06466-6, Y6466). NAL.
Thrown to the Woolfs. 10.95 (ISBN 0-03-052191-2). HR&W.
Thru' the Turnstile: Tales of My Two Centuries. 6.95 (ISBN 0-395-24404-8). HM.
Thumbnail Sketches of Famous Arizona Desert Riders, 1538-1946. facs. ed. 8.75 (ISBN 0-8369-8071-9). Arno.
Thurber & Company. 10.95 (ISBN 0-06-014305-3). Har-Row.
Thurman Munson. 8.95 (ISBN 0-698-10917-1). Coward.
Thurman Munson. pap. 2.50 (ISBN 0-448-17191-0). G&D.
Thurman Munson: Pressure Player. PLB 6.96 (ISBN 0-399-61124-X). Putnam.
Thursday's Child. 10.95 (ISBN 0-316-71334-1). Little.
Thus Far on My Journey. new ed. 5.95 (ISBN 0-913408-26-3). Friends United.
Tiberius. 17.50x (ISBN 0-520-02212-2). U of Cal Pr.
Tiberius Caesar. 11.50x (ISBN 0-87471-216-5). Rowman.
Tiger Is My Brother. pap. 10.95 (ISBN 0-688-03575-2). Morrow.
Tiger, Tiger. pap. 1.95 (ISBN 0-87216-376-8). Playboy Pr Pbks.
Till Death Us Do Part: A True Murder Mystery. pap. 2.75 (ISBN 0-553-12500-1). Bantam.
Till Death Us Do Part: A True Murder Mystery. 10.95 (ISBN 0-393-08821-9). Norton.
Till the Break of Day. 5.95 (ISBN 0-15-287800-9). HarBraceJ.
Tillamook Light. 8.95 (ISBN 0-8323-0339-9); pap. 4.95 (ISBN 0-8323-0334-8). Binford.
Time & Again: Memoirs & Letters. 11.95 (ISBN 0-85635-243-8). Persea Bks.
Time Enough: Essays in Autobiography. lib. bdg. 13.00x (ISBN 0-8371-6445-1, MOTE). Greenwood.
Time of Gifts. 10.95 (ISBN 0-06-011224-7). Har-Row.
Time of My Life. 8.95 (ISBN 0-498-01761-3). A S Barnes.
Time of Our Lives: The Story of My Father & Myself. lib. bdg. 15.00 (ISBN 0-374-94215-3). Octagon.
Time of Their Dying. 7.95 (ISBN 0-393-08771-9). Norton.
Time to Be Human. 6.95 (ISBN 0-02-737200-6). Macmillan.
Time to Heal: The Autobiography of Gerald R. Ford. 12.95 (ISBN 0-06-011297-2). Har-Row.
Time to Remember. 3.95 (ISBN 0-8315-0005-0). Speller.
Time to Speak. 9.95 (ISBN 0-03-050576-3); pap. 4.95 (ISBN 0-03-013956-2). HR&W.
Timeless Affair: The Life of Anita McCormick Blaine. 15.00 (ISBN 0-226-31804-4). U of Chicago Pr.
Times of My Life. 10.95 (ISBN 0-06-011298-0). Har-Row.
Times of My Life. pap. 2.50 (ISBN 0-345-28079-2). Ballantine.
Times, the Man, the Company see Ford.
Times to Remember. 12.50 (ISBN 0-385-01625-5). Doubleday.
Time's Unfading Garden: Anne Spencer's Life and Poetry. 11.95x (ISBN 0-8071-0294-6). La State U Pr.
Timothy Dwight, 1752-1817: A Biography. 21.50 (ISBN 0-404-14746-1). AMS Pr.
Timothy Pickering As the Leader of New England Federalism, 1800-1815. lib. bdg. 15.00 (ISBN 0-306-71052-8). Da Capo.
Tiny: The Story of Nate Archibald. PLB 5.29 (ISBN 0-399-61098-7). Putnam.
Titans of the Soil: Great Builders of Agriculture. lib. bdg. 19.00x (ISBN 0-8371-9329-X, DITS). Greenwood.
Titian. 17.50 (ISBN 0-8369-8143-X). Arno.
Titian's Assistants During the Later Years. lib. bdg. 46.00x (ISBN 0-8240-2689-6). Garland Pub.
Titled Elizabethans: A Directory of Elizabethan State & Church Officers & Knights, with Peers of England, Scotland, & Ireland, 1558-1603. 10.00 (ISBN 0-208-01334-2). Shoe String.
Tito. 21.00 (ISBN 0-405-04565-4). Arno.
Tito of Yugoslavia. 4.95 (ISBN 0-02-735680-9). Macmillan.
Titus of Rome. 5.95 (ISBN 0-396-07299-2). Dodd.
To Alaska for Gold. 4.95 (ISBN 0-87770-096-6). Ye Galleon.
To Build a Castle: My Life As a Dissenter. 17.50 (ISBN 0-670-71640-5). Viking Pr.
To Catch an Angel: Adventures in the World I Cannot See. 7.95 (ISBN 0-8149-0194-8). Vanguard.
To Dance. pap. 3.95 (ISBN 0-380-47233-3). Avon.
To Do Justly. 6.00. Intl Schol Bk Serv.
To Drop a Dime. pap. 1.95 (ISBN 0-515-04424-5). BJ Pub Group.
To Hell with the Kids! 4.95. Chr Classics.
To Jerusalem. 19.00 (ISBN 0-88355-311-2). Hyperion Conn.
To Jerusalem & Back: A Personal Account. 8.95 (ISBN 0-670-71729-0). Viking Pr.
To Jerusalem & Back: A Personal Account. lib. bdg. 10.95 (ISBN 0-8161-6480-0). G K Hall.
To Know Christ Jesus. pap. 3.50 (ISBN 0-89283-080-8). Servant.
To Live Again. pap. 2.25 (ISBN 0-8007-8042-6). Revell.
To Live Long Enough: The Memoirs of Naum Jasny, Scientific Analyst. 11.00x (ISBN 0-7006-0140-6). Regents Pr Ks.
To Meet Will Shakespeare. 25.25 (ISBN 0-8369-5259-6). Arno.
To Purge This Land with Blood: A Biography of John Brown. 12.50 (ISBN 0-06-013231-0). Har-Row.
To Purge This Land with Blood: A Biography of John Brown. pap. 5.95x (ISBN 0-06-131655-5, TB1655). Har-Row.
To Rule the Night: The Discovery Voyage of Astronaut Jim Irwin. 6.95 (ISBN 0-87981-024-6). Holman.
To Sea in Haste. 12.50 (ISBN 0-87491-204-0); pap. 5.95 (ISBN 0-87491-020-X). Acropolis.
To See the Dream. pap. 1.25 (ISBN 0-380-00008-3, 19174). Avon.
To See the Wind. 4.95 (ISBN 0-8170-0622-2). Judson.
To Teach, to Love. pap. 1.50 (ISBN 0-14-003763-2). Penguin.
To the Barricades: The Anarchist Life of Emma Goldman. 8.95 (ISBN 0-690-83280-X). T Y Crowell.
To the Golden Shore: The Life of Adoniram Judson. pap. 5.95 (ISBN 0-310-36131-1). Zondervan.
To the Harbor Light. 8.95 (ISBN 0-395-24774-8). HM.
To the Harbor Light. lib. bdg. 9.95 (ISBN 0-8161-6435-5). G K Hall.
To the Top of the Mountain: The Life of Father Umberto Olivieri, "Padre of the Otomis". 8.00 (ISBN 0-682-48558-6). Exposition.
Tobias Smollett. lib. bdg. 15.00. Folcroft.
Toby: A Real-Life Ripping Yarn. 16.95 (ISBN 0-86033-069-9). Gordon-Cremonesi.
Today's Young Stars of Stage & Screen. s&l 6.90 (ISBN 0-531-02885-2). Watts.
Tojo & the Coming of the War. 20.00x (ISBN 0-8047-0690-5); pap. 7.50x (I[illegible] 0-8047-0691-3). Stanford U Pr.
Tolkien: A Biography. 10.00 (ISB[illegible]-25360-8). HM.
Tolkien: A Biography. pap. 2.50 (ISBN 0-345-27256-0). Ballantine.
Tolkien Scrapbook. lib. bdg. 19.80 (ISBN 0-89471-083-4); pap. 7.95 (ISBN 0-89471-082-6). Running Pr.
Tolstoy. 9.95 (ISBN 0-8274-1062-X). R West.
Tolstoy. 10.00 (ISBN 0-8046-1608-6). Kennikat.
Tolstoy. lib. bdg. 33.00 (ISBN 0-8240-0316-0). Garland Pub.
Tolstoy: A Life of My Father. pap. 8.95 (ISBN 0-913124-15-X). Nordland Pub.
Tolstoy: A Life of My Father. lib. bdg. 20.00 (ISBN 0-374-97956-1). Octagon.
Tolstoy the Rebel. lib. bdg. 60.00 (ISBN 0-87700-222-3). Revisionist Pr.
Tom Boyle, Master Privateer. pap. 4.00 (ISBN 0-87033-218-X). Cornell Maritime.
Tom Edison Finds Out. pap. 0.95 (ISBN 0-440-48384-0). Dell.
Tom Jones. pap. 0.75 (ISBN 0-380-02397-0, 03848). Avon.
Tom Moore's Diary. 23.00 (ISBN 0-403-00670-8). Scholarly.
Tom Paine, Revolutionary. lib. rep. ed. 10.00x (ISBN 0-684-15152-9). Scribner.
Tom Seaver. PLB 5.50 (ISBN 0-87191-280-5). Creative Ed.
Tom Seaver. pap. 1.50 (ISBN 0-445-03027-5). Popular Lib.
Tom Seaver: Portrait of a Pitcher. 7.95 (ISBN 0-8234-0322-X). Holiday.
Tom Sullivan's Adventures in Darkness. 7.95 (ISBN 0-679-20377-X). McKay.
Tom Sullivan's Adventures in Darkness. pap. 1.50 (ISBN 0-451-07698-2, W7698). NAL.
Tom Watson: Agrarian Rebel. pap. 6.95 (ISBN 0-19-500707-7). Oxford U Pr.
Tom White: The Life of a Lawman. 8.00 (ISBN 0-87404-035-3). Tex Western.
Tommy & Jimmy: The Dorsey Years. pap. 6.95 (ISBN 0-306-80117-5). Da Capo.
Tommy John Story. 6.95 (ISBN 0-8007-0923-3). Revell.
Tomo-Chi-Chi. PLB 6.95 (ISBN 0-87518-146-5). Dillon.
Tongue of Flame: The Life of Lydia Maria Child. pap. 0.95 (ISBN 0-440-97814-9). Dell.
Tongue of [illegible] of Lydia Maria Child. 8.95 [illegible] Crowell.
Tongu[illegible] [illegible]
T[illegible]

Two Months in the Camp of Big Bear: The Life & Adventures of Theresa Gowanlock & Theresa Delaney. Bd. with Cynthia Ann Parker, the Story of Her Capture at the Massacre of the Inmates of Parker's Fort: Of Her Quarter of a Century Spent Among the Comanches As the Wife of the War Chief Peta Nocona: and of Her Recapture at the Battle of Pease River by Captain L. S. Ross of the Texian Rangers. lib. bdg. 33.00 (ISBN 0-8240-1719-6). Garland Pub.

Two Reminiscences of Thomas Carlyle. 8.75 (ISBN 0-8223-0307-8). Duke.

Two Roads to Ignorance: A QuasiBiography. 15.00 (ISBN 0-8093-0916-5). S Ill U Pr.

Two Rothschilds & the Land of Israel. 15.95 (ISBN 0-394-50137-3). Knopf.

Two Tickets to Freedom: The True Story of Ellen & William Craft, Fugitive Slaves. 5.95 (ISBN 0-671-65169-2). S&S.

Tycho Brahe: A Picture of Scientific Life & Work in the Sixteenth Century. 10.00 (ISBN 0-8446-1996-5). Peter Smith.

Tyrants & Conquerors. 8.95 (ISBN 0-8098-0010-1). Walck.

Tyrone Power: The Last Idol. 15.95 (ISBN 0-385-14383-4). Doubleday.

Tyrone Power: The Last Idol. pap. 2.75 (ISBN 0-425-04619-2). Berkley Pub.

U

U-Boat Killer. 10.95 (ISBN 0-87021-964-2). Naval Inst Pr.

U Nu of Burma. rev. ed. 12.50x (ISBN 0-8047-0155-5). Stanford U Pr.

UAW & Walter Reuther. lib. bdg. 27.50 (ISBN 0-306-70485-4). Da Capo.

Uganda's Katikiro in England. facs. ed. 18.25 (ISBN 0-8369-8770-5). Arno.

Ulrich Von Hutten & the German Reformation. lib. bdg. 17.50x (ISBN 0-313-20125-0, HOUV). Greenwood.

Ulysses S. Grant: Politician. 16.00 (ISBN 0-8044-1385-1). Ungar.

Umano & the Price of Lasting Peace. 6.00 (ISBN 0-8022-2103-3). Philos Lib.

Unattended Moment: Excerpts from Autobiographies with Hints & Guesses. pap. text ed. 2.25x (ISBN 0-8401-1803-1). Allenson.

Uncensored Celebrities. 13.75 (ISBN 0-8369-1687-5). Arno.

Uncertain Greatness: Henry Kissinger & American Foreign Policy. 10.95 (ISBN 0-06-013097-0). Har-Row.

Uncertain Tradition: American Secretaries of State in the Twentieth Century. lib. bdg. 25.00x (ISBN 0-313-22317-3, GRUT). Greenwood.

Uncle Frank: The Biography of Frank Costello. pap. 1.75 (ISBN 0-671-78876-0). PB.

Uncle Joe Cannon: The Story of a Pioneer American. 26.00 (ISBN 0-403-00887-5). Scholarly.

Uncle of Europe: The Social & Diplomatic Life of Edward Vii. 12.95 (ISBN 0-15-192697-2). HarBraceJ.

Uncle Sam Ward & His Circle. facsimile ed. 43.00x (ISBN 0-405-06912-X). Arno.

Uncle Will of Wildwood: Nineteenth-Century Life in the Bluegrass. 4.95 (ISBN 0-8131-0206-5). U Pr of Ky.

Undefeated: The Life of Hubert H. Humphrey. 25.00 (ISBN 0-8225-9953-8). Lerner Pubns.

Under Eleven Governors. 5.50 (ISBN 0-8323-0296-1); pap. 3.95 (ISBN 0-8323-0297-X). Binford.

Under the Rainbow: Growing up Gay. 8.95 (ISBN 0-688-03191-9). Morrow.

Under the Rainbow: Growing up Gay. pap. 2.25 (ISBN 0-671-81965-8). PB.

Under the SS Shadow. 6.95 (ISBN 0-8054-7216-9). Broadman.

Underground Church of Jerusalem. pap. 3.95 (ISBN 0-8407-5629-1). Nelson.

Unfinished Journey. 12.50 (ISBN 0-394-41051-3). Knopf.

Unfinished Odyssey of Robert Kennedy. 4.95 (ISBN 0-394-45025-6). Random.

Unfinished Quest of Richard Wright. 15.00 (ISBN 0-688-02857-8). Morrow.

Unfinished Quest of Richard Wright. pap. 7.95 (ISBN 0-688-07857-5). Morrow.

Unforgettable Men of the West. 10.00; pap. 8.00. Wallis Pubns.

Unicorn: William Butler Yeats' Search for Reality. lib. bdg. 22.50 (ISBN 0-374-95856-4). Octagon.

Union Portraits. facs. ed. 15.25 (ISBN 0-8369-0243-2). Arno.

Union Portraits. lib. bdg. 25.00 (ISBN 0-8492-3524-3). R West.

United States Against Bergdoll: How the Government Spent Twenty Years & Millions of Dollars to Capture & Punish America's Most Notorious Draft Dodger. 9.95 (ISBN 0-498-02070-3). A S Barnes.

United States Marines in North China. 6.95. J A White.

Universal Experience of Adolescence. text ed. 27.50 (ISBN 0-8236-6720-0). Intl Univs Pr.

Universal Pronouncing Dictionary of Biography & Mythology. 95.00 (ISBN 0-8103-4221-9). Gale.

Universal Pronouncing Dictionary of Biography & Mythology. 5th ed. 225.00 (ISBN 0-404-06386-1). AMS Pr.

Universe of G. B. S. 13.00 (ISBN 0-8462-1125-4). Russell.

Universes of E. E. Smith. pap. 5.00 (ISBN 0-911682-03-1). Advent.

Unknown Life of Jesus Christ. 49.95 (ISBN 0-87968-073-3). Gordon Pr.

Unknown Orwell. 8.95 (ISBN 0-394-47393-0). Knopf.

Unknown Virginia Woolf. 12.95 (ISBN 0-521-21987-6). Cambridge U Pr.

Unknown Witnesses. 6.00 (ISBN 0-8309-0107-8). Herald Hse.

Unless They Kill Me First. pap. 1.95 (ISBN 0-441-84669-6). Charter Bks.

Unpardonable Sin: A Life of Nathaniel Hawthorne. PLB 5.99 (ISBN 0-394-90443-5). Pantheon.

Unpublished Letters of Matthew Arnold. lib. bdg. 10.00 (ISBN 0-8414-9490-8). Folcroft.

Unquiet Soul: A Biography of Charlotte Bronte. pap. 2.75 (ISBN 0-671-80712-9). PB.

Unsung Heroes of Pro Basketball. 2.50 (ISBN 0-394-82415-6); PLB 3.69 (ISBN 0-394-92415-0). Random.

Unsung Heroes of the Major Leagues. 2.50 (ISBN 0-394-83096-2); PLB 3.69 (ISBN 0-394-93096-7). Random.

Unsuspected Revolution: The Birth & Rise of Castroism. 12.50x (ISBN 0-8014-1094-0). Cornell U Pr.

Untersuchungen Zur Geschichte Des Kaisers Septimius Severus. 12.00x (ISBN 0-405-07085-3). Arno.

Until Tomorrow Comes. 8.95 (ISBN 0-89696-031-5). Everest Hse.

Until Victory: Horace Mann & Mary Peabody. lib. bdg. 24.50x (ISBN 0-8371-9653-1, THUV). Greenwood.

Untold Story of Douglas MacArthur. pap. 2.25 (ISBN 0-532-22107-9). Manor Bks.

Untold Story: The Roosevelts of Hyde Park. 7.95 (ISBN 0-399-11127-1). Putnam.

Untouchable: An Indian Life History. 18.95x (ISBN 0-8047-1001-5). Stanford U Pr.

Untriangulated Stars: Letters of Edwin Arlington Robinson to Harry de Forest Smith, 1890-1905. lib. bdg. 16.25x (ISBN 0-8371-4704-2, ROUS). Greenwood.

Unwanted Boy: The Autobiography of Governor Ben W. Hooper. 11.00x (ISBN 0-87049-044-3). U of Tenn Pr.

Up & Down & Around: A Publisher Recollects the Time of His Life. 10.00 (ISBN 0-06-121540-6). Harper Mag Pr.

Up & Down with the Rolling Stones. pap. 2.95 (E9448). NAL.

Up & Down with the Rolling Stones. 17.95 (ISBN 0-688-03515-9); pap. 8.95 (ISBN 0-688-08515-6). Morrow.

Up from Nigger. 8.95 (ISBN 0-8128-1832-6). Stein & Day.

Up from Nigger. pap. 1.95 (ISBN 0-449-23416-9). Fawcett.

Up from Slavery. pap. 0.95 (ISBN 0-440-99224-9). Dell.

Up from Slavery. 5.95 (ISBN 0-385-00003-0). Doubleday.

Up from Slavery. 9.50 (ISBN 0-87928-021-2). Corner Hse.

Up from Slavery. pap. 1.50 (ISBN 0-553-11520-0). Bantam.

Up from Slavery. pap. 0.95 (ISBN 0-8049-0157-0, CL-157). Airmont.

Up from the Cellar. 9.95 (ISBN 0-917266-17-X). Vanilla.

Up from the Footnote: A History of Women Journalists. 12.95 (ISBN 0-8038-7502-9). Hastings.

Up from the Ghetto. 5.95 (ISBN 0-8092-9224-6). Contemp Bks.

Up from the Ghetto. pap. 0.95 (ISBN 0-671-47838-9). WSP.

Up the Staircase Backwards. pap. 2.95 (ISBN 0-916406-96-2). Accent Bks.

Up to Now. 8.95 (ISBN 0-393-07525-7). Norton.

Upstairs Room. 8.95 (ISBN 0-690-85127-8). T Y Crowell.

Upstairs Room. pap. 1.75 (ISBN 0-553-12754-3). Bantam.

Upstairs to a Mine. 7.95 (ISBN 0-87421-085-2). Utah St U Pr.

Upton Sinclair: A Study in Social Protest. 14.00 (ISBN 0-404-02076-3). AMS Pr.

Urban Builder: The Life & Times of Stanley Draper. 9.75 (ISBN 0-8061-1447-9). U of Okla Pr.

Uriah Phillips Levy. 5.25 (ISBN 0-396-07604-1). Dodd.

Ursa Major: A Study of Dr. Johnson & His Friends. lib. bdg. 20.00. Folcroft.

Ushant: An Essay. 15.95 (ISBN 0-19-501452-9). Oxford U Pr.

V

Vagabond Newsman. bds. 5.95 (ISBN 0-87797-028-9). Cherokee.

Valentines & Vitriol. pap. 1.95 (ISBN 0-440-19359-1). Dell.

Valentino. pap. 1.95 (ISBN 0-671-81394-3). PB.

Valentino. 2nd ed. pap. 1.50 (ISBN 0-532-15143-7). Manor Bks.

Valentino: The Love God. pap. 1.95 (ISBN 0-441-85906-2). Ace Bks.

Valentino: The Love God. 12.50x (ISBN 0-903925-49-4). Intl Pubns Serv.

Valery Briusov & the Rise of Russian Symbolism. 12.00 (ISBN 0-88233-064-0). Ardis Pubs.

Valiant Pilgrim: The Story of John Bunyan & Puritan England. 20.00 (ISBN 0-8274-3665-3). R West.

Valiant Vagabonds. facs. ed. 15.00 (ISBN 0-8369-0112-6). Arno.

Valley of the Shadow. pap. 2.95 (ISBN 0-8006-1699-5). Fortress.

Value of Believing in Yourself: The Story of Louis Pasteur. 2nd ed. 5.95 (ISBN 0-916392-06-6). Value Comm.

Value of Caring: The Story of Eleanor Roosevelt. 5.95 (ISBN 0-916392-11-2). Value Comm.

Value of Courage: The Story of Jackie Robinson. 5.95 (ISBN 0-916392-12-0). Value Comm.

Value of Curiosity: The Story of Christopher Columbus. 5.95 (ISBN 0-916392-13-9). Value Comm.

Value of Dedication: The Story of Albert Schweitzer. 6.95g (ISBN 0-916392-44-9). Value Comm.

Value of Determination: The Story of Helen Keller. 2nd ed. 5.95 (ISBN 0-916392-07-4). Value Comm.

Value of Fairness: The Story of Nellie Bly. 5.95 (ISBN 0-916392-16-3). Value Comm.

Value of Fantasy: The Story of Hans Christian Andersen. 6.95 (ISBN 0-916392-43-0). Value Comm.

Value of Friendship: The Story of Jane Addams. 6.95g (ISBN 0-916392-45-7). Value Comm.

Value of Helping: The Story of Harriet Tubman. PLB 6.95g (ISBN 0-916392-41-4). Value Comm.

Value of Honesty: The Story of Confucius. 5.95g (ISBN 0-916392-36-8). Value Comm.

Value of Humor: The Story of Will Rogers. 5.95 (ISBN 0-916392-05-8). Value Comm.

Value of Imagination: The Story of Charles Dickens. 5.95 (ISBN 0-916392-15-5). Value Comm.

Value of Kindness: The Story of Elizabeth Fry. 2nd ed. 5.95 (ISBN 0-916392-09-0). Value Comm.

Value of Love: The Story of Johnny Appleseed. 5.95g (ISBN 0-916392-35-X). Value Comm.

Value of Patience: The Story of the Wright Brothers. 2nd ed. 5.95 (ISBN 0-916392-08-2). Value Comm.

Value of Respect: The Story of Abraham Lincoln. 5.95 (ISBN 0-916392-14-7). Value Comm.

Value of Responsibility: The Story of Ralph Bunche. 5.95 (ISBN 0-916392-29-5). Value Comm.

Value of Saving: The Story of Benjamin Franklin. 5.95 (ISBN 0-916392-17-1). Value Comm.

Value of Sharing: The Story of the Mayo Brothers. PLB 5.95 (ISBN 0-916392-28-7). Value Comm.

Value of the Individual: Self & Circumstance in Autobiography. 24.00x (ISBN 0-226-88621-2). U of Chicago Pr.

Value of Truth & Trust: The Story of Cochise. 5.95 (ISBN 0-916392-10-4). Value Comm.

Value of Understanding: The Story of Margaret Mead. 5.95g (ISBN 0-916392-37-6). Value Comm.

Van Dyke & the Mythical City Hollywood. lib. bdg. 22.00 (ISBN 0-8240-2870-8). Garland Pub.

Van Gogh. 6.95 (ISBN 0-517-00500-X). Crown.

Van Gogh Assignment. 7.95 (ISBN 0-448-23167-0). Paddington.

Van Til. pap. 1.25 (ISBN 0-87552-591-1). Presby & Reformed.

Vanessa & Her Correspondence with Jonathan Swift. 15.00 (ISBN 0-8414-4206-1). Folcroft.

Vanished Arizona: Recollections of an Army Life of a New England Woman. lib. bdg. 12.00 (ISBN 0-87380-120-2). Rio Grande.

Vanished Arizona: Recollections of the Army Life of a New England Woman. 15.00x (ISBN 0-8032-4106-2); pap. 4.95 (ISBN 0-8032-9105-1, BB683). U of Nebr Pr.

Vanya. pap. 2.50 (ISBN 0-88419-009-9). Creation Hse.

Vargas of Brazil: A Political Biography. 17.50x (ISBN 0-292-73655-X). U of Tex Pr.

Variety of Catholic Modernists. 28.50 (ISBN 0-521-07649-8). Cambridge U Pr.

Vaslav Nijinsky. lib. bdg. 10.95 (ISBN 0-8383-1752-9). Haskell.

Vaughan Williams. rev. ed. 8.95x (ISBN 0-460-03162-7). Biblio Dist.

Vaughan Williams. rev. ed. pap. 4.95 (ISBN 0-8226-0722-0). Littlefield.

Veblen. 11.50x (ISBN 0-678-00019-0). Kelley.

Velazquez: The Art of Painting. 17.50 (ISBN 0-06-433575-5); pap. 7.95 (ISBN 0-06-430079-X, IN-79). Har-Row.

Velvet Glove: A Life of Dolly Madison. 6.95 (ISBN 0-8407-6472-3). Elsevier-Nelson.

Velvet on Iron: The Diplomacy of Theodore Roosevelt. 15.00x (ISBN 0-8032-3057-5). U of Nebr Pr.

Venerable Ancestor: The Life & Times of Tz'u Hsi, 1835-1908, Empress of China. lib. bdg. 17.00x (ISBN 0-8371-4430-2, HUVA). Greenwood.

Venture in Remembrance. lib. bdg. 14.25x (ISBN 0-8371-3582-6, HORE). Greenwood.

Venture to the Interior. pap. 3.95 (ISBN 0-15-693529-5). HarBraceJ.

Venture to the Interior. lib. bdg. 13.00x (ISBN 0-8371-7058-3, VAVI). Greenwood.

Venus in Hollywood: The Continental Enchantress from Garbo to Loren. 6.95 (ISBN 0-8184-0091-9). Lyle Stuart.

Verdi. pap. 6.50 (ISBN 0-8226-0723-9). Littlefield.

Verdi: A Documentary Study. 37.50 (ISBN 0-500-01184-2). Thames Hudson.

Vermont Afternoons with Robert Frost. pap. 4.50 (ISBN 0-911570-17-9). Vermont Bks.

Vernon Lee: Violet Paget, 1856-1935. 12.00x (ISBN 0-405-07357-7). Arno.

Verrazano, Explorer of the Atlantic Coast. 6.75 (ISBN 0-688-21771-0); PLB 6.00 (ISBN 0-688-31771-5). Morrow.

Verrier Elwin: A Pioneer Indian Anthropologist. lib. bdg. 7.95 (ISBN 0-210-40556-2). Asia.

Very Different Love Story: Burt & Linda Pugach's Intimate Account of Their Triumph Over Tragedy. 8.95 (ISBN 0-688-03089-0). Morrow.

Very Human President. 9.95 (ISBN 0-393-05552-3). Norton.

Very Human President. pap. 1.95 (ISBN 0-671-80834-6). PB.

Very Slippery Fellow: The Life of Sir Robert Wilson 1777-1849. 15.95x (ISBN 0-19-211745-9). Oxford U Pr.

Very, Very Rich & How They Got That Way. pap. 2.50 (ISBN 0-87216-645-7). Playboy Pr Pbks.

Very Young Circus Flyer. 9.95 (ISBN 0-394-50574-3). Knopf.

Very Young Skater. 9.95 (ISBN 0-394-50833-5). Knopf.

Vesco. pap. 1.95 (ISBN 0-380-00526-3, 27474). Avon.

Veterinary Odyssey. 7.50 (ISBN 0-682-49115-2). Exposition.

Vibrations: The Adventures & Musical Times of David Amram. lib. bdg. 29.50x (ISBN 0-313-22230-4, AMVI). Greenwood.

Vice-Presidents of Destiny. PLB 5.89 (ISBN 0-399-60653-X). Putnam.

Vice-Presidents of the United States. PLB 4.90 s&l (ISBN 0-531-02907-7). Watts.

Victor & the Spoils: A Life of William L. Marcy. 15.00x (ISBN 0-87057-056-0). Brown U Pr.

Victor Berger & the Promise of Constructive Socialism, 1910-1920. lib. bdg. 14.50 (ISBN 0-8371-6264-5, MVB/). Greenwood.

Victor Considerant, 1808-1893: sa vie, ses idees. lib. bdg. 16.50 (ISBN 0-8337-0625-X). B Franklin.

Victor Cousin As a Comparative Educator. text ed. 7.60x (ISBN 0-8077-1117-9). Tchrs Coll.

Victor Herbert: A Life in Music. lib. bdg. 35.00 (ISBN 0-306-79502-7). Da Capo.

Victor Hugo. 9.25 (ISBN 0-8274-1351-3). R West.

Victor Hugo. 9.50 (ISBN 0-8046-1594-2). Kennikat.

Victor Hugo. 14.95 (ISBN 0-312-84035-7). St Martin.

Victor Hugo & His Poetry. 7.25 (ISBN 0-404-52514-8). AMS Pr.

Victor: The Victor Landero Story. 3.95 (ISBN 0-8007-0974-8). Revell.

Victoria & Albert. 12.95 (ISBN 0-8129-0692-6). Times Bks.

Victoria & Disraeli: The Making of a Romantic Partnership. 9.95 (ISBN 0-02-503490-1). Macmillan.

Victoria Travels: Journeys of Queen Victoria Between 1830 & 1900 with Extracts from Her Journal. 14.95 (ISBN 0-8008-7972-4). Taplinger.
Victorian Album: Julia Margaret Cameron and Her Circle. lib. bdg. 350.00 (ISBN 0-306-70749-7); deluxe ed. 200.00. Da Capo.
Victorian Cabinet Maker: The Memoirs of James Hopkinson, 1819-1894. 10.00x (ISBN 0-678-06526-8). Kelley.
Victorian Country Parsons. 11.95x (ISBN 0-8032-0981-9). U of Nebr Pr.
Victorian Courtship: The Story of Beatrice Potter & Sidney Webb. 10.95 (ISBN 0-19-520166-3). Oxford U Pr.
Victorian Eminence: Life & Works of Henry Thomas Buckle. 6.95. Dufour.
Victorian Engagement: Letters & Journals of Walter Hume & Anna Kate Fowler During the 1860s. 11.50x (ISBN 0-7022-0998-8). U of Queensland Pr.
Victorian Forerunner: The Later Career of Thomas Hood. 12.75 (ISBN 0-8223-0038-9). Duke.
Victorian Gentlewoman in the Far West: The Reminiscences of Mary Hallock Foote. 12.50 (ISBN 0-87328-057-1). Huntington Lib.
Victorian in the Modern World. 12.50 (ISBN 0-295-95183-4, AL24). U of Wash Pr.
Victorian Knight-Errant: A Study of the Early Literary Career of James Russell Lowell. lib. bdg. 17.25x (ISBN 0-8371-5222-4, HOVK). Greenwood.
Victorian Murderesses: A True History of Thirteen Respectable French & English Women Accused of Unspeakable Crimes. 15.00x (ISBN 0-8052-3608-2). Schocken.
Victorian Murderesses: A True History of Thirteen Respectable French & English Women Accused of Unspeakable Crimes. pap. 6.95 (ISBN 0-8052-0627-2). Schocken.
Victorian People: A Reassessment of Persons & Themes, 1851-67. rev. ed. 12.00x (ISBN 0-226-07487-0). U of Chicago Pr.
Victorian People: A Reassessment of Persons & Themes, 1851-67. new rev. ed. pap. 4.95 (ISBN 0-226-07488-9, P365). U of Chicago Pr.
Victorian Photographs of Famous Men & Fair Women. new ed. 25.00 (ISBN 0-87923-076-2). Godine.
Victorian Portraits. facs. ed. 12.75 (ISBN 0-8369-0328-5). Arno.
Victorian Rebel: The Life of William Morris. lib. bdg. 17.50 (ISBN 0-374-92627-1). Octagon.
Victorians All. lib. bdg. 6.45. Folcroft.
Victorians All. 6.50 (ISBN 0-8046-0962-4). Kennikat.
Victorio & the Mimbres Apaches. 15.95 (ISBN 0-8061-1076-7). U of Okla Pr.
Victorio & the Mimbres Apaches. pap. 9.95 (ISBN 0-8061-1645-5). U of Okla Pr.
Victory on Praise Mountain. pap. 2.95 (ISBN 0-88270-378-1). Logos.
Vienna & the Young Hitler. lib. bdg. 14.50 (ISBN 0-374-94206-4). Octagon.
Viet Journal. 7.95 (ISBN 0-440-08764-3). Delacorte.
View from a Broad. 12.50 (24780). S&S.
View from Morningside: One Family's New York. 8.95 (ISBN 0-397-01257-8). Lippincott.
View from Serendip. pap. 1.95 (ISBN 0-345-27108-4). Ballantine.
View from the Vue. 8.95 (ISBN 0-8246-0215-3). Jonathan David.
Villiers De L'isle - Adam. 11.50 (ISBN 0-8057-6332-5). Twayne.
Vince Lombardi Story. 6.95 (ISBN 0-87460-256-4); lib. bdg. 6.39 (ISBN 0-87460-257-2). Lion.
Vincent Van Gogh: A Biographical Study. lib. bdg. 21.25x (ISBN 0-8371-4278-4, MEVG). Greenwood.
Vincent Van Gogh: A Psychological Study. text ed. 12.50 (ISBN 0-8236-6740-5). Intl Univs Pr.
Vincent Van Gogh: Artist of His Time. 12.95 (ISBN 0-7148-1883-6); pap. 6.95 (ISBN 0-7148-1906-9). Dutton.
Vincenzo Bellini: His Life & His Operas. 15.00 (ISBN 0-394-41656-2). Knopf.
Vindication of Ruskin. lib. bdg. 12.50 (ISBN 0-8414-9638-2). Folcroft.
Violet Dots. 7.95 (ISBN 0-8076-0887-4). Braziller.
Virgil. lib. bdg. 7.75. Folcroft.
Virgil. lib. bdg. 10.95 (ISBN 0-8383-1564-X). Haskell.
Virgil, Father of the West. 11.50 (ISBN 0-384-20705-7). Johnson Repr.
Virgil Thomson. pap. 6.95 (ISBN 0-306-80081-0). Da Capo.
Virginia Convention of 1776. lib. bdg. 19.50 (ISBN 0-306-71281-4). Da Capo.
Virginia Journals of Benjamin Henry Latrobe, 1795-1798. 60.00x (ISBN 0-300-02198-4); 30.00x (ISBN 0-300-02160-7); 30.00x (ISBN 0-300-02176-3). Yale U Pr.
Virginia Law Reporters Before 1880. 9.75x (ISBN 0-8139-0747-0). U Pr of Va.
Virginia Plutarch. 32.50 (ISBN 0-8462-1215-3). Russell.
Virginia Woolf. pap. 1.50 (ISBN 0-231-02829-6, MW18). Columbia U Pr.
Virginia Woolf: A Biography. pap. 4.50 (ISBN 0-15-693580-5, HB269). HarBraceJ.
Virginia Woolf & Bloomsbury. lib. bdg. 15.00 (ISBN 0-8414-7358-7). Folcroft.
Virginia Woolf & Her Works. 4.95 (ISBN 0-15-693630-5, HB342). HarBraceJ.
Virginia Woolf: Sources of Madness & Art. 14.95 (ISBN 0-520-03358-2). U of Cal Pr.
Viscount Maua & the Empire of Brazil: A Biography of Irineu Evangelista De Sousa. 18.00x (ISBN 0-520-00807-3). U of Cal Pr.
Visible College: The Collective Biography of British Scientific Socialists in the 1930's. 12.95 (ISBN 0-03-012261-9). HR&W.
Vision Accomplished: The Enigma of Ho Chi Minh. pap. 2.95 (ISBN 0-02-073590-1). Macmillan.
Visionary & Dreamer: Two Poetic Painters, Samuel Palmer & Edward Burne-Jones. 22.50x (ISBN 0-691-09853-0). Princeton U Pr.
Visionary Hand: Essays for the Study of William Blake's Art & Aesthetics. 18.50 (ISBN 0-912158-22-0); pap. 9.95 (ISBN 0-912158-41-7). Hennessey.
Visionary Poetics of Allen Ginsberg. lib. bdg. 11.95 (ISBN 0-915520-17-6); pap. 4.95 (ISBN 0-915520-12-5). Ross-Erikson.
Visions & Profits: Studies in the Business Career of Thomas Sutcliffe Mort. 12.50x (ISBN 0-522-83523-6). Intl Schol Bk Serv.
Visions of the Great Rememberer. pap. 2.50 (ISBN 0-913142-03-4). SBD.
Visit to Abyssinia: An Account of Travel in Modern Ethiopia. 25.00x (ISBN 0-8371-3872-8). Negro U Pr.
Visit to Haldeman & Other States of Mind. 8.95 (ISBN 0-87131-229-8). M Evans.
Visits to Walt Whitman. lib. bdg. 23.95 (ISBN 0-8383-1159-8). Haskell.
Vissarion Belinski, 1811-1848: A Study in the Origins of Social Criticism in Russia. 8.50 (ISBN 0-8462-1273-0). Russell.
Visual Dictionary of Art. 30.00 (ISBN 0-8212-0424-6). NYGS.
Visual Dictionary of Art. pap. 14.95 (ISBN 0-8212-1094-7, 903825PB). NYGS.
Vita Karoli Magni: The Life of Charlemagne. 8.95x (ISBN 0-87024-212-1). U of Miami Pr.
Vita Quorundum Anglo-Saxonum: Original Lives of Anglo-Saxons Who Lived Before the Conquest. 24.00 (ISBN 0-8337-1349-3). B Franklin.
Vital Few: American Economic Progress & Its Protagonists. pap. 5.95 (ISBN 0-19-519743-7, GB393). Oxford U Pr.
Vito Marcantonio, Radical in Congress. 8.50x (ISBN 0-8156-0053-4). Syracuse U Pr.
Viva Juarez! A Biography. lib. bdg. 24.50x (ISBN 0-8371-6145-2, SMVJ). Greenwood.
Viva Villa: A Recovery of the Real Pancho Villa, Peon, Bandit, Soldier. Patriot. 18.00 (ISBN 0-405-02045-7). Arno.
Vivaldi. 11.50x (ISBN 0-460-03164-3). Biblio Dist.
Vivekananda: A Biography. 4.95 (ISBN 0-911206-08-6). Ramakrishna.
Vivien Leigh: A Biography. 9.95. S&S.
Vladimir Nabokov. pap. 1.25x (ISBN 0-8166-0600-5, MPAW96). U of Minn Pr.
Voice Crying in the Wilderness: The Memoirs of Jacob L. Reddix. 10.95 (ISBN 0-87805-024-8). U Pr of Miss.
Voice of the Lord: A Biography of George Fox. 11.50x (ISBN 0-8122-7431-8). U of Pa Pr.
Voices from the Countryside. 6.95 (ISBN 0-916224-13-9). Banyan Bks.
Voices from the Great Black Baseball Leagues. 9.95 (ISBN 0-396-07124-4). Dodd.
Voices in Exile: The Decembrist Memoirs. 18.50x (ISBN 0-7735-0183-5). McGill-Queens U Pr.
Voices of American Fundamentalism: Seven Biographical Studies. 15.00 (ISBN 0-664-20814-2). Westminster.
Voltaire. 3rd ed. lib. bdg. 25.00x (ISBN 0-226-04430-0). U of Chicago Pr.
Voltaire. 11.25 (ISBN 0-8274-3683-1). R West.
Voltaire. 11.50 (ISBN 0-8046-1004-5). Kennikat.
Voltaire & Jean Meslier. 11.00 (ISBN 0-404-53209-8). AMS Pr.
Voltaire & the Century of Light. 25.00 (ISBN 0-691-06287-0). Princeton U Pr.
Voltaire in Love. lib. bdg. 15.00x (ISBN 0-8371-2307-0, MIVL). Greenwood.
Von Stroheim. 10.00 (ISBN 0-374-28520-9). FS&G.
Voyage of Charles Darwin. 12.50 (ISBN 0-8317-9212-4). Mayflower Bks.
Voyage to America: The Journals of Thomas Cather. lib. bdg. 10.75x (ISBN 0-8371-6650-0, CAVA). Greenwood.
Voyage to Greenland: A Personal Initiation into Anthropology. 9.95 (ISBN 0-393-06413-1). Norton.
Voyager: A Life of Hart Crane. 15.00 (ISBN 0-374-28568-3). FS&G.
Voyages & Adventures of La Perouse. 8.00x (ISBN 0-87022-445-X). U Pr of Hawaii.
Voyages from Montreal, on the River St. Laurence, Through the Continent of North America, to the Frozen & Pacific Oceans. 19.25 (ISBN 0-8048-1006-0). C E Tuttle.
Voyages of Abel Janszoon Tasman. 17.00x (ISBN 0-19-821536-3). Oxford U Pr.
Voyages of Mohamed Ibrahim Munshi. 20.50x (ISBN 0-19-580267-5). Oxford U Pr.
Voyages of Peter Esprit Radisson, Being an Account of His Travels & Experiences Among the North American Indians, from 1652 to 1684. 26.50 (ISBN 0-8337-3285-4). B Franklin.
Voyages of Samuel De Champlain. 62.00 (ISBN 0-8337-3287-0). B Franklin.
Vuillard, His Life & Work. 25.00 (ISBN 0-404-14718-6). AMS Pr.

W

W. A. P Martin: Pioneer of Progress in China. pap. 6.95x (ISBN 0-8028-1715-7). Eerdmans.
W. B. Yeats & His World. 10.95 (ISBN 0-684-15573-7). Scribner.
W. B. Yeats & T. Sturge Moore: Their Correspondence, 1901-1937. lib. bdg. 19.50x (ISBN 0-313-20489-6, YEYM). Greenwood.
W. E. B. Du Bois. 8.95 (ISBN 0-13-220905-5); pap. 2.45 (ISBN 0-13-220889-X, S744). P-H.
W. E. B. Du Bois: Propagandist of the Negro Protest. pap. text ed. 6.95x (ISBN 0-689-70169-1, NL6). Atheneum.
W. E. B. Dubois: A Biography. 8.95 (ISBN 0-690-87256-9). T Y Crowell.
W. H. Auden: The Life of a Poet. 15.95 (ISBN 0-15-194286-2). HarBraceJ.
W. H. Hudson. lib. bdg. 9.00x (ISBN 0-8371-2097-7, TOWH). Greenwood.
W. H. R. Rivers. 20.00x (ISBN 0-231-03582-9). Columbia U Pr.
W. L. Garrison & His Times. facs. ed. 17.00 (ISBN 0-8369-8613-X). Arno.
W. R. Rodgers. 4.50 (ISBN 0-8387-7750-3); pap. 1.95 (ISBN 0-8387-7630-2). Bucknell U Pr.
W. S. Gilbert: His Life & Letters. 14.00 (ISBN 0-405-08430-7). Arno.
W. Somerset Maugham & His World. 8.95 (ISBN 0-684-14839-0). Scribner.
Wagner. pap. 6.95 (ISBN 0-8226-0724-7). Littlefield.
Wagner. rev ed. 7.95x (ISBN 0-460-03153-8). Biblio Dist.
Wagner. lib. bdg. 13.75x (ISBN 0-313-21084-5, TUWG). Greenwood.
Wagner the Dramatist. 11.00x (ISBN 0-8476-6058-3). Rowman.
Wake up, Wake up, to Do the Work of the Creator. 8.95 (ISBN 0-06-011823-7). Har-Row.
Walk Across America. 12.95 (ISBN 0-688-03427-6). Morrow.
Walk Across America. pap. 2.75 (ISBN 0-449-24277-3). Fawcett.
Walk on the North Side: Memoirs of a Violist. 15.95x (ISBN 0-8425-1264-0); pap. 9.95x (ISBN 0-8425-1313-2). Brigham.
Walk on Water, Pete! pap. 1.95 (ISBN 0-930014-34-0). Multnomah.
Walk on Water, Pete! pap. 1.75 (ISBN 0-8307-0286-5, 50-119-06). Regal.
Walk Quietly Through the Night and Cry Softly. new ed. 7.00 (ISBN 0-913642-08-8). Balamp Pub.
Walk the Distant Hills: The Story of Longri Ao. pap. 0.95 (ISBN 0-377-84171-4). Friend Pr.
Walk with the Cross. o.p. 6.95 (ISBN 0-88270-302-1, H302-0); pap. 4.95 (ISBN 0-88270-374-9). Logos.
Walking Through the Fire: A Hospital Journal. 6.95 (ISBN 0-525-22955-8). Dutton.
Walking Through the Fire: A Hospital Journal. pap. 1.95 (ISBN 0-553-11430-1). Bantam.
Walking with the Giants: A Minister's Guide to Good Reading & Great Preaching. 8.95 (ISBN 0-8010-9578-6). Baker Bk.
Wallace. rev. ed. pap. 3.95 (ISBN 0-452-00442-X, F442). NAL.
Wallace Stevens. 17.50. Chips.
Wallace Stevens: A Celebration. 22.50x (ISBN 0-691-06414-8). Princeton U Pr.
Wallaces of Iowa. lib. bdg. 42.50 (ISBN 0-306-70325-4). Da Capo.
Wallenda: A Biography of Karl Wallenda. 9.95 (ISBN 0-915298-04-X). Sagarin Pr.
Walls of Windy Troy: A Biography of Heinrich Schliemann. pap. 1.45 (ISBN 0-15-694201-1, AVB20). HarBraceJ.
Walpole. lib. bdg. 10.00. Folcroft.
Walpole. lib. bdg. 10.25x (ISBN 0-8371-4527-9, MOHW). Greenwood.
Walpole & the Whig Supremacy. 5.50x (ISBN 0-340-11515-7). Verry.
Walt Disney. PLB 5.75 (ISBN 0-87191-407-7). Creative Ed.
Walt Disney. PLB 4.29 (ISBN 0-399-61021-9). Putnam.
Walt Disney's America. 25.00 (ISBN 0-89659-000-3). Abbeville Pr.
Walt Frazier. PLB 5.95 (ISBN 0-87191-348-8); pap. 2.75 (ISBN 0-89812-179-5). Creative Ed.
Walt Kuhn, Painter: His Life & Work. 35.00 (ISBN 0-8142-0258-6). Ohio St U Pr.
Walt Whitman. 21.00 (ISBN 0-404-05629-6). AMS Pr.
Walt Whitman: A Brief Biography with Reminiscences. lib. bdg. 17.50 (ISBN 0-8495-3758-4). Arden Lib.
Walt Whitman & His Poetry. lib. bdg. 7.50. Folcroft.
Walt Whitman & His Poetry. 7.25 (ISBN 0-404-52502-4). AMS Pr.
Walt Whitman: Thinker & Artist. lib. bdg. 19.50x (ISBN 0-8371-0028-3, BRWW). Greenwood.
Walt Whitman's Anomaly. lib. bdg. 15.00 (ISBN 0-8414-7357-9). Folcroft.
Walt Whitman's Champion: William Douglas O'Connor. 13.50 (ISBN 0-89096-039-9). Tex A&M Univ Pr.
Walter Bagehot. 17.50 (ISBN 0-208-00900-0). Shoe String.
Walter Crane. 25.00 (ISBN 0-02-612930-2). Macmillan.
Walter De la Mare: An Exploration. lib. bdg. 16.95 (ISBN 0-8383-2105-4). Haskell.
Walter De la Mare: An Exploration. lib. bdg. 7.50 (ISBN 0-8482-0059-4). Norwood Edns.
Walter Frye & the Contenance Angloise. 22.50 (ISBN 0-306-76011-8). Da Capo.
Walter George Smith. 13.95 (ISBN 0-8132-0539-5). Cath U Pr.
Walter Hines Page: The Southerner As American, 1855-1918. 16.00 (ISBN 0-8078-1298-6). U of NC Pr.
Walter Knott - Keeper of the Flame. 7.95x (ISBN 0-916434-07-9). Plycon Pr.
Walter Murdoch: A Biographical Memoir. 18.00 (ISBN 0-522-84119-8). Intl Schol Bk Serv.
Walter Pater. lib. bdg. 15.00. Folcroft.
Walter Payton. PLB 5.95 (ISBN 0-87191-722-X); pap. 2.75 (ISBN 0-89812-160-4). Creative Ed.
Walter Prescott Webb: His Life & Impact. 12.00 (ISBN 0-8263-0412-5). U of NM Pr.
Walter Raleigh. PLB 5.32 (ISBN 0-688-31595-X). Morrow.
Walter Raleigh: Man of Two Worlds. PLB 4.39 (ISBN 0-394-90558-X). Random.
Walter Savage Landor: A Biography. 45.00 (ISBN 0-8274-3688-2). R West.
Walter Savage Landor: A Biography. 42.00 (ISBN 0-403-00407-1). Scholarly.
Walter Savage Landor: A Biography. lib. bdg. 125.00 (ISBN 0-8492-4612-1). R West.
Walter Savage Landor: A Biography. lib. bdg. 37.25x (ISBN 0-8371-9783-X, SUWL). Greenwood.
Walter Sickert. A Biography. 20.00x. Intl Pubns Serv.
Walter White & the Harlem Renaissance. 12.50 (ISBN 0-8046-9197-5). Kennikat.
Walther Rathenau: His Life & Work. 9.00 (ISBN 0-86527-203-4). Fertig.
Walther Rathenau, His Life & Work. 9.00 (ISBN 0-404-03665-1). AMS Pr.
Walton Experience. pap. 1.95 (ISBN 0-425-03675-8). Berkley Pub.
Walton Gang. 8.95 (ISBN 0-698-10565-6). Coward.
Wanda Gag, Author & Illustrator of Childrens Books. lib. bdg. 2.45 incl. catalog cards (ISBN 0-87157-546-9); pap. 1.25 vinyl laminated covers (ISBN 0-87157-046-7). SamHar Pr.
Wanderer. pap. 2.50 (ISBN 0-380-39834-6, 39834). Avon.
Wanderers All: An American Pilgrimage. 6.95 (ISBN 0-06-010139-3). Har-Row.
Wandering Thoughts of a Dying Man: The Life & Times of Haji Abdul Majid bin Zainuddin. 19.95x (ISBN 0-19-580349-3). Oxford U Pr.
Wanderings of a Biochemist. 14.50 (ISBN 0-471-54080-3). Krieger.
Wanted. rev. ed. pap. 2.95 (ISBN 0-89293-016-0). Beta Bk.
Wanted! The Search for Nazis in America. 8.95 (ISBN 0-8129-0607-1). Times Bks.
Wanted: The Search for Nazis in America. pap. 1.95 (ISBN 0-449-23409-6). Fawcett.
War Criminal: The Life and Death of Hirota Koki. 10.00 (ISBN 0-87011-275-9). Kodansha.
War Criminal: The Life & Death of Hirota Koki. pap. 4.95 (ISBN 0-87011-368-2). Kodansha.
War Eagle: A Life of General Eugene A. Carr. 14.95x (ISBN 0-8032-0092-7). U of Nebr Pr.
War in Texas (1836; see Life Travels & Opinions of Benjamin Lundy: Including His Journeys to Texas.
War Lords. 10.00 (ISBN 0-689-10840-0). Atheneum.
War Ministry of Winston Churchill. 9.95 (ISBN 0-8138-0260-1). Iowa St U Pr.
Warner Brothers Directors: The Hard-Boiled, the Comic, & the Weepers. 20.00 (ISBN 0-87000-397-6). Arlington Hse.

Warren G. Harding, 1865-1923: Chronology, Documents, Bibliographical Aids. 7.00 (ISBN 0-379-12064-X). Oceana.
Warren Harding: President Betrayed by Friends. lib. bdg. 2.45 incl. catalog cards (ISBN 0-87157-506-X); pap. 1.25 vinyl laminated covers (ISBN 0-87157-006-8). SamHar Pr.
Warren Hastings. 18.50 (ISBN 0-208-00287-1). Shoe String.
Warren Hastings. 3.50x (ISBN 0-8426-1572-5). Verry.
Warrior Bard: The Life of William Morris. 7.00 (ISBN 0-8046-0827-X). Kennikat.
Warrior Diplomats: Guardians of the National Security & Modernization of Turkey. 15.00x (ISBN 0-87480-115-X). U of Utah Pr.
Warrior in Two Camps: Ely S. Parker, Union General & Seneca Chief. 11.95 (ISBN 0-8156-0143-3). Syracuse U Pr.
Wartime. 14.95 (ISBN 0-15-194609-4). HarBraceJ.
Wartime Journals of Charles A. Lindbergh. 12.95 (ISBN 0-15-194625-6). HarBraceJ.
Wartime Mission in Spain. lib. bdg. 22.50 (ISBN 0-306-70771-3). Da Capo.
Was Jesus a Revolutionist? pap. 1.50 (ISBN 0-8006-3066-1). Fortress.
Washington: A Biography. 12.95 (ISBN 0-399-11617-6). Putnam.
Washington & the Theatre. 9.00. Arno.
Washington Irving: A Sketch. lib. bdg. 20.00 (ISBN 0-8414-3489-1). Folcroft.
Washington Irving: As Others Saw Him. 5.95 (ISBN 0-698-20296-1). Coward.
Washington: The Indispensable Man. pap. 2.95 (ISBN 0-451-61742-8, ME1742). NAL.
Washington: The Indispensable Man. 12.50 (ISBN 0-316-28605-2); pap. 6.95 (ISBN 0-316-28607-9). Little.
Washington's Lady. lib. bdg. 14.80 (ISBN 0-88411-957-2, 957). Amereon Ltd.
Waterspout. pap. 3.95 (ISBN 0-89144-021-6). Crescent Pubns.
Watteau. 7.95 (ISBN 0-8076-0545-X). Braziller.
Way Down South, Up North. 4.95 (ISBN 0-8298-0246-0). Pilgrim NY.
Way It Was with Me. 15.00 (ISBN 0-8184-0288-1). Lyle Stuart.
Way Out West: Recollections & Tales. 14.95 (ISBN 0-8061-0833-9). U of Okla Pr.
Way the Future Was: A Memoir. pap. 1.95 (ISBN 0-345-26059-7). Ballantine.
Wayward Child: A Personal Odyssey. 7.95 (ISBN 0-385-08873-6). Doubleday.
We Barrymores. lib. bdg. 18.00x (ISBN 0-8371-7550-X, BAB). Greenwood.
We Called It Music: A Generation of Jazz. lib. bdg. 19.25x (ISBN 0-8371-3223-1, CWCI). Greenwood.
We Came to Help. 8.95 (ISBN 0-15-195595-6). HarBraceJ.
We Knew Stonewall Jackson. 8.95 (ISBN 0-690-01289-6). T Y Crowell.
We Knew William Tecumseh Sherman. 8.95 (ISBN 0-690-01426-0). T Y Crowell.
We Live in the Alaskan Bush. pap. 7.95 (ISBN 0-88240-101-7). Alaska Northwest.
We Saw Stars. pap. 3.95 (ISBN 0-8272-4211-5). Bethany Pr.
We Still Love You, Bob. 7.95 (ISBN 0-915684-34-9). Christian Herald.
We Wore Jump Boots & Baggy Pants. pap. 7.95 (ISBN 0-912450-15-0). Willow Hse.
Wealthy Citizens of New York. 8.00 (ISBN 0-405-05117-4). Arno.
Weathering the Storm: Women of the American Revolution. 4.95 (ISBN 0-684-15673-3). Scribner.
Webfoot Volunteer: The Diary of William M. Hilleary, 1864-1866. 7.50 (ISBN 0-87071-075-3). Oreg St U Pr.
Webster's American Biographies. 15.00 (ISBN 0-87779-253-4). Merriam.
Webster's American Military Biographies. 12.95 (ISBN 0-87779-063-9). Merriam.
Webster's Biographical Dictionary. 15.00 (ISBN 0-87779-343-3). Merriam.
Wedding Cake House: The World of George W. Bourne. pap. 5.25 (ISBN 0-932006-07-8). Durrell.
Week on the Concord & Merrimack Rivers. 25.00x (ISBN 0-691-06376-1). Princeton U Pr.
Week on the Concord & Merrimack Rivers. pap. 4.95 (ISBN 0-8152-0118-4, A118). T Y Crowell.
Weetman Pearson, First Viscount Cowdray, 1856-1927. lib. bdg. 21.00 (ISBN 0-405-09801-4). Arno.
Weizmann: Last of the Patriarchs. 10.00 (ISBN 0-399-11718-0). Putnam.
Welfare Mother. 6.95 (ISBN 0-395-24505-2). HM.
Welfare Mother. pap. 1.50 (ISBN 0-451-61563-8, MW1563). NAL.
Well Do I Remember. 7.00 (ISBN 0-916536-01-7). Berwyn-London.
Wellington & His Army. lib. bdg. 10.75x (ISBN 0-8371-7566-6, DAWA). Greenwood.
Wendell Phillips, Brahmin Radical. lib. bdg. 18.75x (ISBN 0-8371-7071-0, BAWP). Greenwood.
Wendell Phillips: The Agitator. lib. bdg. 25.00. Norwood Edns.
Wendell Phillips: The Agitator. 22.00x (ISBN 0-8371-2181-7). Negro U Pr.
Wendell Phillips: The Agitator. lib. bdg. 15.00 (ISBN 0-8495-3756-8). Arden Lib.
Wendell Phillips: The Agitator. lib. bdg. 18.50 (ISBN 0-8411-0064-0). Metro Bks.
Werner Erhard: The Transformation of a Man, the Founding of EST. 10.00 (ISBN 0-517-53502-5). Potter.
Wesley Paul, Marathon Runner. 7.95 (ISBN 0-397-31845-6); PLB 7.89 (ISBN 0-397-31861-8). Lippincott.
West to the Sunrise. 12.50x (ISBN 0-8138-0895-2). Iowa St U Pr.
Western Lawmen. PLB 3.95 (ISBN 0-8225-0451-0). Lerner Pubns.
Western Outlaws. PLB 3.95 (ISBN 0-8225-0452-9, 8225-0452-9). Lerner Pubns.
Western State: Some of Its People & Ports. facsim. 3d ed. pap. text ed. 7.00 (ISBN 0-85564-119-3). Intl Schol Bk Serv.
Western Wind, Eastern Shore: A Sailing Cruise around the Eastern Shore of Maryland, Delaware & Virginia. 14.95 (ISBN 0-8018-1767-6). Johns Hopkins.
Westerners. pap. cancelled (ISBN 0-553-02503-1). Bantam.
Westernized Yankee: The Story of Cyrus Woodman. 7.50 (ISBN 0-87020-032-1). State Hist Soc Wis.
Westminster Abbey: Its Links with the Famous. pap. 12.50 (ISBN 0-8277-5535-X). British Bk Ctr.
Westralian Portraits. 22.50x (ISBN 0-85564-157-6). Intl Schol Bk Serv.
Westward to Paradise. 5.95 (ISBN 0-89301-054-5). U Pr of Idaho.
Wha' Hae Wi' (Pender) Bled. 7.50 (ISBN 0-533-03517-1). Vantage.
What Are Saints: Fifteen Chapters in Sanctity. facs. ed. 9.75 (ISBN 0-8369-0681-0). Arno.
What Do I Have to Do---Break My Neck? pap. 3.50 (ISBN 0-8066-1407-2, 10-7045). Augsburg.
What Happened in Between: A Doctor's Story. 6.95 (ISBN 0-8076-0660-X). Braziller.
What I Have Lived by: An Autobiography. 5.95 (ISBN 0-8007-0805-9); lmtd gift ed 9.95 (ISBN 0-8007-0806-7). Revell.
What I Owe to My Father. facsimile ed. 13.50 (ISBN 0-8369-2672-2). Arno.
What I Remember. 18.50 (ISBN 0-88355-261-2). Hyperion-Conn.
What Is an Editor? Saxe Commins at Work. 10.00 (ISBN 0-226-11427-9). U of Chicago Pr.
What Jesus Began: The Life & Ministry of Christ. 4.95 (ISBN 0-8054-1356-1). Broadman.
What Little I Remember. 14.95 (ISBN 0-521-22297-4). Cambridge U Pr.
What Manner of Man: A Biography of Martin Luther King Jr, 1929-1968. 9.95 (ISBN 0-87485-027-4). Johnson Chi.
What My Heart Wants to Tell. 8.95 (ISBN 0-915220-47-4, 24872). New Republic.
What the Woman Lived: Selected Letters of Louise Bogan 1920-1970. 14.50 (ISBN 0-15-195878-5). HarBraceJ.
Whatever Happened to Gorgeous George. pap. 1.95 (ISBN 0-448-14595-2). G&D.
What's It Like Out There. 5.95 (ISBN 0-8092-9672-1). Contemp Bks.
What's the Big Idea, Ben Franklin? 6.95 (ISBN 0-698-20365-8). Coward.
Wheat Flour Messiah: Eric Jansson of Bishop Hill. 7.95x (ISBN 0-8093-0787-1). S Ill U Pr.
Wheel of Life: The Autobiography of a Western Buddhist. pap. 5.95 (ISBN 0-394-73548-X). Shambhala Pubns.
When All the Bridges Are Down. pap. 2.75 (ISBN 0-8054-5416-0). Broadman.
When Being Jewish Was a Crime. pap. 3.95 (ISBN 0-8407-5659-3). Nelson.
When Boys Were Men. 6.75x (ISBN 0-19-637100-7). Oxford U Pr.
When France Was De Gaulle. PLB 5.88 (ISBN 0-531-02005-3). Watts.
When I Was a Boy. pap. 1.95 (ISBN 0-8220-1625-7). Centennial.
When I Was a Boy. pap. text ed. 1.95 (ISBN 0-8220-1624-9). Centennial.
When I Was Old. 8.50 (ISBN 0-15-195950-1). HarBraceJ.
When I Was Young. 10.00 (ISBN 0-316-54977-0). Little.
When King Was Carpenter. pap. 1.95 (ISBN 0-89221-018-4). New Leaf.
When Memory Comes. 9.95 (ISBN 0-374-28898-4). FS&G.
When the Angels Laughed. pap. 3.95 (ISBN 0-88270-264-5). Logos.
When the Cheering Stopped: The Last Years of Woodrow Wilson. pap. 4.95 (ISBN 0-688-06011-0). Morrow.
When the Queen Was Crowned. 10.95 (ISBN 0-679-50693-4). McKay.
When the Smoke Hit the Fan. 10.95 (ISBN 0-385-14860-7). Doubleday.
When This You See Remember Me: Gertrude Stein in Person. lib. bdg. 12.75x (ISBN 0-8371-5761-7, ROWT). Greenwood.
When We Went First Class. 7.95 (ISBN 0-385-12374-4). Doubleday.
When We Were Young: An Album of Stars. lib. bdg. 8.95 (ISBN 0-13-956482-9). P-H.
When William Rose, Stephen Vincent & I Were Young. 5.95 (ISBN 0-396-07289-5). Dodd.
Where Does a Mother Go to Resign? pap. 3.50 (ISBN 0-87123-606-0). Bethany Fell.
Where Have You Gone, Joe DiMaggio? The Story of America's Last Hero. pap. 1.50 (ISBN 0-451-06986-2, W6986). NAL.
Where Is He Now? Sports Heroes of Yesterday Revisited. 7.95 (ISBN 0-8246-0145-9). Jonathan David.
Where the Heart Is. 5.95 (ISBN 0-915684-03-9). Christian Herald.
Where the Wings Grow. 8.95 (ISBN 0-385-12106-7). Doubleday.
Where the Word Ends: The Life of Louis Moreau Gottschalk. 14.95x (ISBN 0-8071-0607-0); pap. 4.95 (ISBN 0-8071-0373-X). La State U Pr.
Where Time Becomes Space. 7.95 (ISBN 0-8199-0699-9). Franciscan Herald.
Where Was Patrick Henry on the 29th of May? 6.95 (ISBN 0-698-20307-0). Coward.
Where We Came Out. lib. bdg. 13.00x (ISBN 0-8371-6970-4, HIWW). Greenwood.
Where Your Heart Is: The Story of Harvey Dunn, Artist. 15.00 (ISBN 0-87970-118-8). North Plains.
Whispers from Old Genesee & Echoes of the Salmon River. 10.00 (ISBN 0-87770-143-1). Ye Galleon.
Whistling Girl. 6.95 (ISBN 0-385-11573-3). Doubleday.
White African: An Early Autobiography. 8.95 (ISBN 0-87073-720-1, Sk16). Schenkman.
White & Black Under the Old Regime. facs. ed. 13.75 (ISBN 0-8369-5371-1). Arno.
White Fire: The Life & Works of Jessie Sampter. lib. bdg. 15.00x (ISBN 0-405-10224-0). Arno.
White House. 12.95 (ISBN 0-88225-020-5). Newsweek.
White House Children. 3.95 (ISBN 0-394-84094-1); PLB 3.99 (ISBN 0-394-94094-6). Random.
White House Years. 22.50 (ISBN 0-316-49661-8). Little.
White Minority: Pioneers for Racial Equality. 6.95. HarBraceJ.
White Niggers of America: The Precocious Autobiography of a Quebec Terrorist. pap. 4.50 (ISBN 0-85345-198-2, PB-1982). Monthly Rev.
White Nights: The Story of a Prisoner in Russia. 8.95 (ISBN 0-06-010289-6). Har-Row.
White Pagoda. pap. 3.95 (ISBN 0-8423-8213-5). Tyndale.
White Savage: The Case of John Dunn Hunter. 12.50x (ISBN 0-8052-3461-6). Schocken.
Whitelaw Reid: Journalist, Politician, Diplomat. 13.00x (ISBN 0-8203-0353-4). U of Ga Pr.
Whitey & Mickey: A Joint Autobiography of the Yankee Years. new ed. 8.95 (ISBN 0-670-76394-2). Viking Pr.
Whitman. 13.00 (ISBN 0-8462-1191-2). Russell.
Whitman. 12.50 (ISBN 0-8196-0210-8). Biblo.
Whitman As Editor of the Brooklyn Daily Eagle. 12.95x (ISBN 0-8143-1408-2). Wayne St U Pr.
Whittier & His Poetry. lib. bdg. 7.50. Folcroft.
Whittier & His Poetry. 7.25 (ISBN 0-404-52523-7). AMS Pr.
Whittier & His Poetry. lib. bdg. 8.00 (ISBN 0-8495-2302-8). Arden Lib.
Whittier-Land: A Handbook of North Essex. lib. bdg. 22.95 (ISBN 0-8383-1698-0). Haskell.
Whittier's Unknown Romance: Letters to Elizabeth Lloyd. lib. bdg. 16.95 (ISBN 0-8383-1707-3). Haskell.
Who. 5.95 (ISBN 0-02-551180-7). Macmillan.
Who. pap. 1.95 (ISBN 0-02-060730-X). Macmillan.
Who Are You, Lord? pap. 2.95 (ISBN 0-8042-9702-9). John Knox.
Who Is Chauncey Spencer? 7.95. Broadside.
Who Is Sylvia? 9.95 (ISBN 0-87795-197-7). Arbor Hse.
Who, Me? 15.75 (ISBN 0-8369-8099-9). Arno.
Who the Hell Is William Loeb? 8.95; pap. 5.95. Amoskeag Pr.
Who Was Jack Ruby? 10.95 (ISBN 0-89696-004-8). Everest Hse.
Who Was Roberto: A Biography of Roberto Clemente. 7.95 (ISBN 0-385-08421-8). Doubleday.
Who Was Who in Alabama. 12.95 (ISBN 0-87397-017-9). Strode.
Who Was Who in Church History. pap. 2.25 (ISBN 0-87983-100-6). Keats.
Who Was Who in Florida. 14.95 (ISBN 0-87397-039-X). Strode.
Who Was Who in World War II. 14.95 (ISBN 0-690-01753-7). T Y Crowell.
Who Was Who on Screen. 2nd ed. 32.50 (ISBN 0-8352-0914-8). Bowker.
Whole of Their Lives: Communism in America - a Personal History & Intimate Portrayal of Its Leaders. 20.50 (ISBN 0-8369-8094-8). Arno.
Whom the Gods Love: The Story of Evariste Galois. 11.00 (ISBN 0-87353-125-6). NCTM.
Who's Calling My Name. pap. 3.50 (ISBN 0-8054-5418-7). Broadman.
Who's Who in Alaskan Politics: A Biographical Dictionary of Alaskan Political Personalities, 1884-1974. 10.00 (ISBN 0-8323-0287-2). Binford.
Who's Who in Basketball. 7.95 (ISBN 0-87000-222-8). Arlington Hse.
Who's Who in Boswell? 15.00 (ISBN 0-8462-1471-7). Russell.
Who's Who in Boxing. 7.95 (ISBN 0-87000-232-5). Arlington Hse.
Who's Who in Burns. 18.00 (ISBN 0-404-08547-4). AMS Pr.
Who's Who in Canadian Sport. pap. 10.00 (ISBN 0-13-958421-8). P-H.
Who's Who in Church History. pap. 2.95 (ISBN 0-8010-0705-4). Baker Bk.
Who's Who in Church History. pap. 0.95 (ISBN 0-687-45340-2). Abingdon.
Who's Who in Football. 11.95 (ISBN 0-87000-237-6). Arlington Hse.
Who's Who in Hockey. 7.95 (ISBN 0-87000-221-X). Arlington Hse.
Who's Who in Hollywood, 1900-1976. 30.00 (ISBN 0-87000-349-6). Arlington Hse.
Who's Who in Labor. 65.00 (ISBN 0-405-06651-1). Arno.
Who's Who in Librarianship & Information Science. 2nd ed. 17.50x (ISBN 0-200-71871-1). Intl Pubns Serv.
Who's Who in Library Service: A Biographical Directory of Professional Librarians in the United States & Canada. 4th ed. 25.00 (ISBN 0-208-00598-6). Shoe String.
Who's Who in Malaysia: 1978-79. 12th ed. 50.00x (ISBN 0-8002-0411-5). Intl Pubns Serv.
Who's Who in Modern Japanese Prints. 12.50 (ISBN 0-8348-0101-9). Weatherhill.
Who's Who in Philosophy. lib. bdg. 13.75x (ISBN 0-8371-2095-0, WWIP). Greenwood.
Who's Who in Romanian America. 35.00 (ISBN 0-917944-01-1). Am Inst Writing Res.
Who's Who in Science Fiction. 8.95 (ISBN 0-8008-8274-1). Taplinger.
Who's Who in Science Fiction. pap. 4.95 (ISBN 0-8008-8279-2). Taplinger.
Who's Who in Scottish History. 18.00x (ISBN 0-06-491739-8). B&N.
Who's Who in Shakespeare. 6.50 (ISBN 0-8008-8269-5). Taplinger.
Who's Who in Shaw. 8.95 (ISBN 0-8008-8270-9). Taplinger.
Who's Who in the Ancient World. pap. 4.95 (ISBN 0-14-051055-9). Penguin.
Who's Who in the Bible. 8.95. Jonathan David.
Who's Who in the Book of Mormon. pap. 1.95 (ISBN 0-87747-609-8). Deseret Bk.
Who's Who in the Jewelry Industry. 54.95 (ISBN 0-931744-02-4). Jewelers Circular.
Who's Who in the Midwest. 17th ed. 57.50 (ISBN 0-8379-0717-9, 030234). Marquis.
Who's Who in the Midwest: 1978-79. 16th ed. 52.50 (ISBN 0-8379-0716-0). Marquis.
Who's Who in the New Testament. 18.95 (ISBN 0-03-086262-0). HR&W.
Who's Who in the New Testament. pap. 2.45 (ISBN 0-687-45352-6). Abingdon.
Who's Who in the Old Testament: Together with the Apocrypha. pap. 2.45 (ISBN 0-687-45357-7). Abingdon.
Who's Who in the United Nations & Related Agencies. 65.00 (ISBN 0-405-06490-X). Arno.
Who's Who in Track & Field. 6.95 (ISBN 0-87000-219-8). Arlington Hse.
Who's Who in Twentieth Century Literature. 12.95 (ISBN 0-03-013926-0). HR&W.
Who's Who in Twentieth-Century Literature. pap. 4.95 (ISBN 0-07-056350-0). McGraw.
Who's Who of Southern Africa 1979: Including Mauritius & Incorporating South African Who's Who & the Central African Who's Who. 62nd ed. 50.00x (ISBN 0-8002-1324-6). Intl Pubns Serv.
Who's Who on the Postage Stamps of Eastern Europe. lib. bdg. 29.50 (ISBN 0-8108-1266-5). Scarecrow.
Who's Who on the Screen. 95.00 (ISBN 0-87968-277-9). Gordon Pr.
Who's Who 1976-1977: An Annual Biographical Dictionary. 62.50 (ISBN 0-312-87465-0). St Martin.
Why Be a Headmaster? 16.50 (ISBN 0-522-84117-1). Intl Schol Bk Serv.
Why Billy Graham? 6.95 (ISBN 0-310-36350-0). Zondervan.
Why Catholic. 7.95 (ISBN 0-385-14184-X). Doubleday.
Why Catholic. pap. 3.50 (ISBN 0-385-14185-8). Doubleday.
Why Don't You Get a Horse, Sam Adams? 6.95 (ISBN 0-698-20292-9). Coward.
Why I Am a Jew. pap. 2.95 (ISBN 0-8197-0009-6). Bloch.

Why I Am a Jew. 2nd facsimile ed. 9.00x (ISBN 0-405-06711-9). Arno.
Why I Left Canada: Reflections on Science & Politics. lib. bdg. 16.95 (ISBN 0-7735-0272-6). McGill-Queens U Pr.
Why Not the Best. pap. 1.95 (ISBN 0-553-10198-6). Bantam.
Why Not the Best? 5.95 (ISBN 0-8054-5561-2); pap. 1.95 (ISBN 0-8054-5564-7); presidential ed. 8.95 (ISBN 0-8054-5582-5). Broadman.
Wicked Uncles: The Father of Queen Victoria - His Brothers. facs. ed. 14.25 (ISBN 0-8369-0466-4). Arno.
Wickford Memories. 6.95 (ISBN 0-8283-1360-1). Branden.
Wide-Eyed in Babylon. 7.95 (ISBN 0-688-00257-9). Morrow.
Wide World of Aaron Burr. 4.95 (ISBN 0-664-32416-9). Westminster.
Widow's Pilgrimage. 7.95 (ISBN 0-8164-9118-6). Continuum.
Wifredo Lam. 50.00 (ISBN 0-8478-0032-6). Rizzoli Intl.
Wilberforce, a Narrative. 20.75x (ISBN 0-8371-0362-2). Negro U Pr.
Wild Animals, Gentle Women. 5.95 (ISBN 0-15-296987-X). HarBraceJ.
Wild Bill & His Era: The Life & Adventures of James Butler Hickok. 10.00x (ISBN 0-8154-0413-1). Cooper Sq.
Wild Irish Girl: The Life of Sydney Owenson, Lady Morgan, 1776-1859. 11.00 (ISBN 0-8462-1217-X). Russell.
Wild Irish Girl: The Life of Sydney Owenson, Lady Morgan 1776-1859. lib. bdg. 30.00 (ISBN 0-8492-8050-8). R West.
Wild Man from Sugar Creek: The Political Career of Eugene Talmadge. 11.95 (ISBN 0-8071-0088-9). La State U Pr.
Wild Man from Sugar Creek: The Political Career of Eugene Talmadge. pap. 4.95x (ISBN 0-8071-0170-2). La State U Pr.
Wilderness Manhunt: The Spanish Search for La Salle. 10.00 (ISBN 0-292-79000-7). U of Tex Pr.
Wilderness Neighbors. 9.95 (ISBN 0-8128-2578-0). Stein & Day.
Wilderness Tattoo: A Narrative of Juan Ortiz. 5.95 (ISBN 0-15-297325-7). HarBraceJ.
Wilfred Grenfell, His Life & Work. lib. bdg. 19.50x (ISBN 0-8371-6068-5, KEWG). Greenwood.
Wilfred Owen. 18.50 (ISBN 0-19-211719-X). Oxford U Pr.
Wilfred Pickles Invites You to Have Another Go. 12.95 (ISBN 0-7153-7393-5). David & Charles.
Wilhelm Von Humboldt: A Biography. write for info. (ISBN 0-8142-0279-9). Ohio St U Pr.
Wilkie Collins. lib. bdg. 17.95 (ISBN 0-8383-2095-3). Haskell.
Wilkie Collins. lib. bdg. 12.50 (ISBN 0-8414-2975-8). Folcroft.
Will Rogers. lib. bdg. 8.50 (ISBN 0-8057-0634-8). Twayne.
Will Rogers, America's Cowboy Philosopher. new ed. lib. bdg. 2.45 incl. catalog cards; pap. 1.25 vinyl laminated covers. SamHar Pr.
Will You Sign Here, John Hancock? 6.95 (ISBN 0-698-20308-9). Coward.
Willa Cather. lib. bdg. 10.00 (ISBN 0-8414-1598-6). Folcroft.
Willa Cather: A Critical Biography. pap. 2.95 (ISBN 0-380-49676-3, 49676). Avon.
Willa Cather: A Critical Introduction. lib. bdg. 13.25x (ISBN 0-8371-5211-9, DAWC). Greenwood.
Willa Cather: A Memoir. pap. 1.95 (ISBN 0-8032-5179-3, 159). U of Nebr Pr.
Willa Cather: Her Life & Art. pap. 3.50 (ISBN 0-8032-5815-1, 600). U of Nebr Pr.
Willa Cather Living: A Personal Record. pap. 2.95 (ISBN 0-8032-5849-6, 623). U of Nebr Pr.
William Allen White of Emporia. lib. bdg. 13.75x (ISBN 0-8371-3910-4, CLWA). Greenwood.
William Balston, Paper Maker, 1759-1849. lib. bdg. 20.00 (ISBN 0-8240-3876-2). Garland Pub.
William Barclay: A Spiritual Autobiography. pap. 1.50 (ISBN 0-8028-1667-3). Eerdmans.
William Beebe (1877-1962) An Annotated Bibliography. 15.00 (ISBN 0-208-01608-2). Shoe String.
William Beltz. PLB 6.95 (ISBN 0-87518-044-2). Dillon.
William Berry Hartsfield, Mayor of Atlanta. 7.50 (ISBN 0-8203-0445-X). U of Ga Pr.
William Beveridge: A Biography. 22.00x (ISBN 0-19-822459-1). Oxford U Pr.
William Blake. 12.50 (ISBN 0-208-00177-8). Shoe String.
William Blake. lib. bdg. 12.00. Folcroft.
William Blake. lib. bdg. 15.00x (ISBN 0-8154-0325-9). Cooper Sq.
William Blake: A Critical Essay. lib. bdg. 12.00 (ISBN 0-8414-7741-8). Folcroft.
William Blake: A Critical Essay. pap. 4.75x (ISBN 0-8032-5707-4, 504). U of Nebr Pr.
William Blake: A New Kind of Man. 12.95 (ISBN 0-520-03443-0); pap. 6.95 (ISBN 0-520-03456-2). U of Cal Pr.
William Blake: The Man. lib. bdg. 8.95. Folcroft.
William Blake: The Man. 9.00 (ISBN 0-404-07906-7). AMS Pr.
William Blake: the Seer & His Visions. 12.95 (ISBN 0-517-52939-4); pap. 7.95 (ISBN 0-517-52940-8). Crown.
William Blount. lib. bdg. 15.25x (ISBN 0-8371-2308-9, MABL). Greenwood.
William Booth & His Army. pap. 3.95 (ISBN 0-8163-0272-3, 23685-1). Pacific Pr Pub Assn.
William Bradford of Plymouth Colony. PLB 4.90 (ISBN 0-531-02724-4). Watts.
William Butler Yeats: The Poet in Contemporary Ireland. lib. bdg. 8.75 (ISBN 0-8414-4803-5). Folcroft.
William Byrd. lib. bdg. 20.25x (ISBN 0-313-20182-X, HOWI). Greenwood.
William Byrd of Westover. 2nd ed. 15.00 (ISBN 0-208-00944-2). Shoe String.
William Byrd of Westover, 1674-1744. 15.00x (ISBN 0-8139-0346-7). U Pr of Va.
William C. Handy: Father of the Blues. PLB 4.78 (ISBN 0-8116-4551-7). Garrard.
William C. Whitney, Modern Warwick. 25.00 (ISBN 0-208-00722-9). Shoe String.
William Carlos Williams. pap. 1.25x (ISBN 0-8166-0287-5, MPAW24). U of Minn Pr.
William Caxton. 13.45 (ISBN 0-8274-0486-7). R West.
William Caxton. 19.50 (ISBN 0-8337-2788-5). B Franklin.
William Caxton: A Biography. 14.95 (ISBN 0-399-11888-8). Putnam.
William Caxton: A Portrait in a Background. 8.95 (ISBN 0-312-88068-5). St Martin.
William Caxton 1422-1491. lib. bdg. 22.50 (ISBN 0-8337-0948-8). B Franklin.
William Clark: Jeffersonian Man on the Frontier. 9.95 (ISBN 0-8061-1373-1). U of Okla Pr.
William Clark: Jeffersonian Man on the Frontier. pap. 5.95 (ISBN 0-8061-1593-9). U of Okla Pr.
William Cobbett. 12.95 (ISBN 0-7100-7560-X); pap. 5.95 (ISBN 0-7100-7561-8). Routledge & Kegan.
William Conant Church & the Army & Navy Journal. 21.00 (ISBN 0-404-51576-2). AMS Pr.
William Congreve. lib. bdg. 20.00 (ISBN 0-8414-8566-6). Folcroft.
William Cowper. lib. bdg. 7.50 (ISBN 0-8414-6301-8). Folcroft.
William Cowper: A Critical Life. lib. bdg. 12.25x (ISBN 0-8371-3425-0, QUWC). Greenwood.
William Cullen Bryant. 9.50 (ISBN 0-8103-3369-4). Gale.
William Cullen Bryant. 17.00 (ISBN 0-405-01653-0). Arno.
William Cullen Bryant. lib. bdg. 20.00 (ISBN 0-8495-0447-3). Arden Lib.
William Cullen Bryant. 12.50 (ISBN 0-684-12370-3). Scribner.
William D. Howells. pap. 1.25 (ISBN 0-8166-0436-3, MPAW63). U of Minn Pr.
William Dampier. 13.50 (ISBN 0-208-00187-5). Shoe String.
William Dunbar. lib. bdg. 15.00. Folcroft.
William Dunbar. lib. bdg. 17.50 (ISBN 0-8495-4917-5). Arden Lib.
William Dunbar. 14.50 (ISBN 0-404-08604-7). AMS Pr.
William Dunbar: A Biographical Study. 15.50 (ISBN 0-8369-5672-9). Arno.
William Dunlap: A Study of His Life & Works & of His Place in Contemporary Culture. 8.50 (ISBN 0-8462-0159-3). Russell.
William E. Borah & American Foreign Policy. 12.95x (ISBN 0-8071-0907-X). La State U Pr.
William Ellery Channing. 4.75 (ISBN 0-8274-3706-4). R West.
William Ellery Channing. pap. 3.45 (ISBN 0-8084-0325-7, T7). Coll & U Pr.
William Empson. pap. 1.50 (ISBN 0-231-03131-9, MW39). Columbia U Pr.
William Faulkner. lib. bdg. 8.50 (ISBN 0-8057-0244-X). Twayne.
William Faulkner. pap. 3.45 (ISBN 0-8084-0326-5, T1). Coll & U Pr.
William Faulkner of Oxford. pap. 4.95x (ISBN 0-8071-0143-5). La State U Pr.
William Faulkner of Yoknapatawpha County. 6.50 (ISBN 0-690-89173-3). T Y Crowell.
William Faulkner: The Yoknapatawpha Country. 30.00x (ISBN 0-300-00329-3); pap. 5.45x (ISBN 0-300-00028-6, Y170). Yale U Pr.
William G. Brownlow: Fighting Parson of the Southern Highlands. 10.50x (ISBN 0-87049-118-0). U of Tenn Pr.
William George Ward & the Catholic Revival. 31.50 (ISBN 0-404-14042-4). AMS Pr.
William George Ward & the Oxford Movement. 31.50 (ISBN 0-404-14043-2). AMS Pr.
William Gibbs McAdoo: A Passion for Change, 1863-1917. 15.00 (ISBN 0-8046-9043-X). Kennikat.
William Gilmore Simms. lib. bdg. 11.75. Folcroft.
William Gilmore Simms. lib. bdg. 18.95 (ISBN 0-8383-0249-1). Haskell.
William Gilmore Simms. lib. bdg. 14.75x (ISBN 0-8371-1171-4, TRWS). Greenwood.
William Goddard, Newspaperman. 12.95 (ISBN 0-8223-0115-6). Duke.
William Godwin: A Biographical Study. 17.50 (ISBN 0-8492-3028-4). R West.
William Godwin: A Study in Liberalism. lib. bdg. 9.50x (ISBN 0-8371-6807-4, FLWG). Greenwood.
William Godwin & His World. lib. bdg. 30.00 (ISBN 0-8495-1930-6). Arden Lib.
William Godwin & Mary Wollstonecraft. 44.95 (ISBN 0-8490-1304-6). Gordon Pr.
William Goebel: The Politics of Wrath. 4.95 (ISBN 0-8131-0240-5). U Pr of Ky.
William H. Ashley: Enterprise & Politics in the Trans-Mississippi West. 18.95 (ISBN 0-8061-1525-4). U of Okla Pr.
William H. Crawford, 1772-1834. 16.50 (ISBN 0-8131-1246-X). U Pr of Ky.
William H. Jackson. 14.00 (ISBN 0-87100-045-8). Morgan.
William Hazlitt, Critic of Power. 22.50x (ISBN 0-231-04600-6). Columbia U Pr.
William Henry Bartlett 1809-1854: Artist, Author, & Traveller. 17.50 (ISBN 0-8020-1986-2). U of Toronto Pr.
William Henry Fox Talbot: Pioneer of Photography & Man of Science. 31.95 (ISBN 0-09-129600-5). Merrimack Bk Serv.
William Henry Harrison: A Political Biography. lib. bdg. 19.50x (ISBN 0-87991-326-6). Porcupine Pr.
William Henry Harrison: Young Tippecanoe. 5.95 (ISBN 0-672-50189-9). Bobbs.
William Henry Welch & the Heroic Age of American Medicine. 7.50 (ISBN 0-8446-2068-8). Peter Smith.
William Hickling Prescott. 5.00 (ISBN 0-404-04966-4). AMS Pr.
William Hickling Prescott. lib. bdg. 11.50x (ISBN 0-8371-0614-1, PEWP). Greenwood.
William Hickling Prescott: A Biography. 15.00x (ISBN 0-292-70005-9). U of Tex Pr.
William Howard Taft. PLB 5.95 (ISBN 0-8092-8630-0). Contemp Bks.
William Howard Taft & United States Foreign Policy: The Apprenticeship Years 1900-1908. 9.50 (ISBN 0-252-00427-2). U of Ill Pr.
William Howard Taft, 1857-1930: Chronology, Documents, Bibliographical Aids. 6.00 (ISBN 0-379-12080-1). Oceana.
William Inge. pap. 3.45 (ISBN 0-8084-0328-1, T95). Coll & U Pr.
William Jay & the Constitutional Movement for the Abolition of Slavery. 11.00x (ISBN 0-8371-4592-9). Negro U Pr.
William Jay & the Constitutional Movement for the Abolition of Slavery. lib. bdg. 17.50 (ISBN 0-8337-4709-6). B Franklin.
William Jennings Bryan. Incl. Political Evangelist, 1860-1908. 14.95x (ISBN 0-8032-0022-6); Progressive Politician & Moral Statesman, 1909-1915. 13.95x (ISBN 0-8032-0023-4); Political Puritan, 1915-1925. 13.50x (ISBN 0-8032-0024-2). 38.50x (ISBN 0-8032-4050-3). U of Nebr Pr.
William King, Friend & Champion of Slaves. 11.50x (ISBN 0-8371-2074-8). Negro U Pr.
William Knox: The Life & Thought of an Eighteenth-Century Imperialist. text ed. 14.95x (ISBN 0-292-79007-4). U of Tex Pr.
William L. Wilson & Tariff Reform: A Biography. lib. bdg. 17.75x (ISBN 0-8371-7447-3, SUWW). Greenwood.
William Lloyd Garrison & the Humanitarian Reformers. pap. 4.95 (ISBN 0-316-61736-9). Little.
William Lloyd Garrison, the Abolitionist. 12.50 (ISBN 0-404-00057-6). AMS Pr.
William Lloyd Garrison, the Abolitionist. 13.50x (ISBN 0-8371-2190-6). Negro U Pr.
William Makepeace Thackeray. lib. bdg. 20.00. Folcroft.
William Makepeace Thackeray: A Biography Including Hitherto Uncollected Letters & Speeches & a Bibliography of 1300 Items. 39.00 (ISBN 0-403-00112-9). Scholarly.
William Marsh Rice & His Institute: A Biographical Study. pap. 3.25x (ISBN 0-89263-212-7). Rice Univ.
William Montague Browne, 1823-1883: Versatile Anglo-Irish American. 11.00 (ISBN 0-8203-0205-8). U of Ga Pr.
William Morris. lib. bdg. 12.50. Folcroft.
William Morris. 14.00 (ISBN 0-8369-6803-4). Arno.
William Morris. 12.75 (ISBN 0-405-08822-1). Arno.
William Morris. lib. bdg. 12.50 (ISBN 0-8414-2800-X). Folcroft.
William Morris & His Circle. lib. bdg. 6.75. Folcroft.
William Morris & His Circle. lib. bdg. 10.95 (ISBN 0-8383-1018-4). Haskell.
William Morris & His Poetry. lib. bdg. 7.50 (ISBN 0-8414-3947-8). Folcroft.
William Morris & His Poetry. 7.25 (ISBN 0-404-52512-1). AMS Pr.
William Morris & His World. 10.95 (ISBN 0-684-15867-1). Scribner.
William Morris As Designer. 22.50 (ISBN 0-289-70673-4). Eastview.
William Morris: His Life & Work. 14.95 (ISBN 0-8008-8339-X). Taplinger.
William Morris, Medievalist & Revolutionary. 10.00 (ISBN 0-8462-1459-8). Russell.
William Morris, Poet, Craftsman, Socialist. 29.00 (ISBN 0-403-07268-9). Scholarly.
William Morris: Romantic to Revolutionary. pap. 7.95 (ISBN 0-394-73320-7). Pantheon.
William Morton Wheeler, Biologist. 15.00x (ISBN 0-674-95330-4). Harvard U Pr.
William of Orange: Personal Portrait. Incl. Early Years, 1650-1673. o.p. (ISBN 0-312-88165-7); Later Years, 1674-1702. o.p.. St Martin.
William of St. Thierry: The Man & His Work. 10.95 (ISBN 0-87907-810-3). Cistercian Pubns.
William Penn. 14.95 (ISBN 0-02-628570-3). Macmillan.
William Penn, Quaker & Pioneer. lib. bdg. 35.00. Folcroft.
William Pickering, Publisher: A Memoir & Checklist of His Publications. 22.50 (ISBN 0-8337-1917-3). B Franklin.
William Pitt the Younger. 19.95 (ISBN 0-399-12130-7). Putnam.
William Plumer of New Hampshire. 16.50x (ISBN 0-8078-0845-8). U of NC Pr.
William Samuel Johnson: A Maker of the Constitution. 10.00 (ISBN 0-404-02936-1). AMS Pr.
William Shakespeare: A Compact Documentary Life. 14.95 (ISBN 0-19-502211-4). Oxford U Pr.
William Shakespeare: A Compact Documentary Life. pap. 4.95 (ISBN 0-19-502433-8, GB 551). Oxford U Pr.
William Shakespeare: A Documentary Life. 65.00 (ISBN 0-19-812046-X). Oxford U Pr.
William Shakespeare, His Family & Friends. 22.50 (ISBN 0-404-02324-X). AMS Pr.
William Shenstone: An Eighteenth-Century Portrait. 8.50 (ISBN 0-404-14673-2). AMS Pr.
William Shirley: King's Governor of Massachusetts. 15.00x (ISBN 0-8078-0830-X). U of NC Pr.
William Stevenson: Riding Preacher. pap. 1.45 (ISBN 0-87074-118-7). SMU Press.
William Strickland-Architect & Engineer 1788-1854. enl. ed. lib. bdg. 25.00 (ISBN 0-306-71235-0). Da Capo.
William Swaim, Fighting Editor: The Story of O. Henry's Grandfather. 6.95. Straughan.
William the Silent. lib. bdg. 8.00. Folcroft.
William Vans Murray, Federalist Diplomat: The Shaping of Peace with France, 1797-1801. 8.50x (ISBN 0-8156-0078-X). Syracuse U Pr.
William Warren. PLB 6.95 (ISBN 0-87518-056-6). Dillon.
William Winans: Methodist Leader in Antebellum Mississippi. 7.95 (ISBN 0-87805-027-2). U Pr of Miss.
William Winston Seaton on the National Intelligencer. 18.00 (ISBN 0-405-01695-6). Arno.
William Wordsworth. lib. bdg. 8.50 (ISBN 0-8057-1580-0). Twayne.
William Wordsworth. 12.45 (ISBN 0-8414-9600-5). Folcroft.
William Wordsworth. lib. bdg. 19.95 (ISBN 0-8383-1800-2). Haskell.
William Wordsworth: A Biography. 29.00x (ISBN 0-19-811565-2); o.p. (ISBN 0-19-811617-9); pap. o.p. (ISBN 0-19-881145-8); pap. 5.95x (ISBN 0-19-881146-2, OPB). Oxford U Pr.
William Wordsworth: His Homes & Haunts. lib. bdg. 12.50 (ISBN 0-8414-0502-6). Folcroft.
Williamsburg Galaxy. 4.95 (ISBN 0-03-068690-3). HR&W.
Willie Geary "Bunk" Johnson: The New Iberia Years. pap. 5.00 (ISBN 0-8008-1122-4). Taplinger.
Willie Mays. PLB 4.49 (ISBN 0-399-60824-9). Putnam.
Willie Mays: Baseball Superstar. PLB 4.78 (ISBN 0-8116-6671-9). Garrard.
Willie Mays: Coast to Coast Giant. PLB 4.97 (ISBN 0-399-60673-4). Putnam.
Willy Brandt: A Biography. 6.95 (ISBN 0-8407-6391-3). Elsevier-Nelson.
Wilma Rudolph: Run for Glory. lib. bdg. 5.95 (ISBN 0-88436-172-1); pap. 3.50 (ISBN 0-88436-173-X). EMC.
Wimbledon. PLB 8.95 (ISBN 0-87191-444-1). Creative Ed.
Wind & the Book: Memoirs of a Country Doctor. 16.50 (ISBN 0-522-84099-X). Intl Schol Bk Serv.
Wind Is Howling. pap. 3.95 (ISBN 0-87784-782-7). Inter-Varsity.
Winding Stair. pap. 2.25 (ISBN 0-380-01848-9, 36459). Avon.
Windows of Westminster. facsimile ed. 14.50 (ISBN 0-8369-1447-3). Arno.

Windows to His World: The Story of Trevor Kincaid. 9.95 (ISBN 0-87015-210-6). Pacific Bks.
Winds in the Woods: The Story of John Muir. 7.95 (ISBN 0-664-32556-4). Westminster.
Winds of Change, 1914-1939. 20.00 (ISBN 0-06-012753-8). Har-Row.
Winds Over Lake Huron: Chronicles in the Life of a Great Lakes Mariner. 7.50 (ISBN 0-682-48709-0). Exposition.
Wings Are Gone. 6.95 (ISBN 0-688-03037-8). Morrow.
Wings for Words: The Story of Johann Gutenberg & His Invention of Printing. 13.00 (ISBN 0-8103-3936-6). Gale.
Wings of Adventure. 6.95 (ISBN 0-396-06469-8). Dodd.
Wings of the North. 10.95 (ISBN 0-919654-61-4). Hancock Hse.
Winners in Gymnastics. PLB 4.90 s&l (ISBN 0-531-02887-9). Watts.
Winners in Gymnastics. pap. 1.25 (ISBN 0-380-43299-4, 43299). Avon.
Winners on Ice. PLB 5.45 s&l (ISBN 0-531-02291-9). Watts.
Winners on the Ski Slopes. PLB 5.45 s&l (ISBN 0-531-02292-7). Watts.
Winners on the Tennis Court. PLB 4.90 s&l (ISBN 0-531-02912-3). Watts.
Winners on the Tennis Court. pap. 1.25 (ISBN 0-380-43307-9, 43307). Avon.
Winning Tennis Star: Chris Evert. PLB 5.95 (ISBN 0-87191-588-X); pap. 2.95 (ISBN 0-89812-199-X). Creative Ed.
Winston Churchill: A Biography. lib. bdg. 47.00x (ISBN 0-8371-5558-4, BRWC). Greenwood.
Winston S. Churchill. Incl. Youth, 1874-1900. 10.00 (ISBN 0-395-07530-0); companion vol. I, pt. 1. 1874-1896 15.00 (ISBN 0-395-07529-7); companion vol. I, pt. 2. 1896-1900 15.00 (ISBN 0-395-07528-9); Young Statesman, 1901-1914. 10.00 (ISBN 0-395-07526-2); companion vol. II, pt. 1. 1901-1907 15.00 (ISBN 0-395-07525-4); companion vol. II, pt. 2.1907-1911 15.00 (ISBN 0-395-07524-6); companion vol. II, pt. 3. 1911-1914 15.00 (ISBN 0-395-07523-8). HM.
Winston S. Churchill. Incl. January 1917-June 1919 (ISBN 0-395-24585-0); July 1919-March 1921 (ISBN 0-395-24584-2); April 1921-November 1922 (ISBN 0-395-24587-7). 65.00 (ISBN 0-395-26055-8). HM.
Winter Olympics. PLB 5.90 s&l (ISBN 0-531-02946-8). Watts.
Wit & Wisdom of Idi Amin. pap. 2.75 (ISBN 0-930830-01-6). Great Basin.
With a Merry Heart. 8.95 (ISBN 0-06-011537-8). Har-Row.
With a Merry Heart. lib. bdg. 12.95 (ISBN 0-8161-6486-X). G K Hall.
With a Quiet Heart: An Autobiography. lib. bdg. 17.25x (ISBN 0-8371-7470-8, LEQH). Greenwood.
With an Holy Calling. pap. 3.95 (ISBN 0-8163-0250-2). Pacific Pr Pub Assn.
With Love from Karen. 6.95 (ISBN 0-13-961524-5). P-H.
With Love from Karen. pap. 1.75 (ISBN 0-440-19615-9). Dell.
With Malice Toward None: The Life of Abraham Lincoln. 15.95 (ISBN 0-06-013283-3). Har-Row.
With Malice Toward None: The Life of Abraham Lincoln. pap. 2.95 (ISBN 0-451-61627-8, ME1627). NAL.
With My Shoes Off. 10.00 (ISBN 0-533-02950-3). Vantage.
With Nixon. 12.95 (ISBN 0-670-77672-6). Viking Pr.
With No Apologies: The Personal & Political Memoirs of United States Senator Barry M. Goldwater. 12.95 (ISBN 0-688-03547-7). Morrow.
With One Sky Above Us: Life on an Indian Reservation at the Turn of the Century. 14.95 (ISBN 0-399-12420-9). Putnam.
With Pen & Pencil on the Frontier in 1851: The Diary & Sketches of Frank Blackwell Mayer. facsimile ed. 13.00x (ISBN 0-405-06871-9). Arno.
With Strings Attached: Reminiscences & Reflections. 22.50 (ISBN 0-306-79567-1). Da Capo.
With This Gift: The Story of Edgar Cayce. 7.50 (ISBN 0-688-22147-5); PLB 7.20 (ISBN 0-688-32147-X). Morrow.
With Two Wheels & a Camera. 12.50 (ISBN 0-682-49352-X). Exposition.
Within the Sound of These Waves: The Story of the Kings of Hawaii Island, Containing a Full Account of the Death of Captain Cook, Together with the Hawaiian Adventures of George Vancouver & Sundry Other Mariners. lib. bdg. 16.75x (ISBN 0-8371-5783-8, CHSW). Greenwood.
Without a Doubt. pap. 0.85 (ISBN 0-8163-0181-6, 23773-5). Pacific Pr Pub Assn.
Witness. 15.00 (ISBN 0-394-45233-X). Random.
Witness. pap. 9.95 (ISBN 0-89526 915 5). Regnery-Gateway.
Witness & I. 15.00x (ISBN 0-231-03859-3). Columbia U Pr.
Witness in Israel: The Story of Paul Rowden. pap. 0.75 (ISBN 0-8054-4314-2). Broadman.
Witnesses. pap. 3.95 (ISBN 0-87709-221-4). Boyd & Fraser.
Witnesses of the Light. facs. ed. 13.75 (ISBN 0-8369-1081-8). Arno.
Wit's End: Days & Nights of the Algonquin Round Table. 12.95 (ISBN 0-15-197521-3). HarBraceJ.
Wit's End: Days & Nights of the Algonquin Round Table. pap. 6.95 (ISBN 0-15-697651-X). HarBraceJ.
Wittgenstein. pap. 2.95 (ISBN 0-674-95393-2). Harvard U Pr.
Wittgenstein's Vienna. pap. 4.95 (ISBN 0-671-21725-9). S&S.
Wives. 16.00 (ISBN 0-405-04448-8). Arno.
Wizard from Vienna: Franz Anton Mesmer. 8.95 (ISBN 0-698-10697-0). Coward.
Wizard of the Winds. 12.00 (ISBN 0-87839-032-4). North Star.
Wolf by the Ears: Thomas Jefferson & Slavery. 12.95 (ISBN 0-02-921500-5). Free Pr.
Wolf by the Ears: Thomas Jefferson & Slavery. pap. 5.95 (ISBN 0-452-00530-2, F530). NAL.
Wolf Children. 10.00 (ISBN 0-8090-9776-1). Hill & Wang.
Wolf Children. pap. 3.95 (ISBN 0-14-005053-1). Penguin.
Wolfgang Amade Mozart. 19.50 (ISBN 0-8369-5046-1). Arno.
Wolfgang Amade Mozart. lib. bdg. 16.00x (ISBN 0-8371-3957-0, HUWM). Greenwood.
Wolfgang Amadeus Mozart. 4.95g (ISBN 0-02-781870-5). Macmillan.
Wolfhart Pannenberg. 5.95 (ISBN 0-87680-251-X). Word Bks.
Wolsey. lib. bdg. 26.25x (ISBN 0-8371-7997-1, POWO). Greenwood.
Woman & the Myth: Margaret Fuller's Life & Writings. pap. 6.95 (ISBN 0-912670-43-6). Feminist Pr.
Woman at Work. lib. bdg. 18.00x (ISBN 0-8371-7133-4, ANWW). Greenwood.
Woman for Peace: The Life of Bertha Von Suttner. 8.95 (ISBN 0-8155-5013-8). Noyes.
Woman He Loved. 9.95 (ISBN 0-671-21810-7). S&S.
Woman He Loved. pap. 1.95 (ISBN 0-451-06640-5, J6640). NAL.
Woman in Levi's. 4.95 (ISBN 0-8165-0645-0). U of Ariz Pr.
Woman in Music. 49.95 (ISBN 0-87968-459-3). Gordon Pr.
Woman of Letters: A Life of Virginia Woolf. 12.95 (ISBN 0-19-502370-6). Oxford U Pr.
Woman of Letters: A Life of Virginia Woolf. pap. 4.95 (ISBN 0-19-502621-7, GB 589). Oxford U Pr.
Woman of Tekoah & Other Sermons on Bible Characters. pap. 2.95 (ISBN 0-8010-6020-6). Baker Bk.
Woman of the American Frontier. 35.00 (ISBN 0-8490-1316-X). Gordon Pr.
Woman on the American Frontier. 19.50 (ISBN 0-8103-3702-9). Gale.
Woman Overboard. PLB 7.99 (ISBN 0-8172-1569-7). Raintree Pubs.
Woman Question in Mrs. Gaskell's Life & Works. 22.00 (ISBN 0-8462-1717-1). Russell.
Woman to Woman. 14.95 (ISBN 0-385-13645-5). Doubleday.
Woman Warrior. 7.95 (ISBN 0-394-40067-4). Knopf.
Woman Warrior: Memoirs of a Girlhood Among Ghosts. pap. 2.45 (ISBN 0-394-72392-9). Random.
Woman Who Created Frankenstein: A Portrait of Mary Shelley. 7.95 (ISBN 0-06-022228-X); PLB 7.89 (ISBN 0-06-022229-8). Har-Row.
Woman Within. 14.95 (ISBN 0-8090-9783-4); pap. 6.95 (ISBN 0-8090-0147-0). FS&G.
Woman, Woman! Feminism in America. PLB 5.29 (ISBN 0-671-32690-2). Messner.
Womanpriest: A Personal Odyssey. 9.95 (ISBN 0-8091-0243-9). Paulist Pr.
Womanpriest: A Personal Odyssey. 5.00x (ISBN 0-8091-0243-9). Wisdom House.
Woman's Way to God. 7.95 (ISBN 0-312-88690-X). St Martin.
Woman's Who's Who of America: A Biographical Dictionary of Contemporary Women of the United States & Canada, 1914-1915. 45.00 (ISBN 0-8103-4018-6). Gale.
Woman's Work in Music. 15.00 (ISBN 0-89201-009-6). Zenger Pub.
Woman's Work in Music. lib. bdg. 30.00 (ISBN 0-89341-013-6). Longwood Pr.
Women & Men of the French Renaissance. 12.50 (ISBN 0-8046-0905-5). Kennikat.
Women & Science. PLB 7.95 (ISBN 0-8172-1379-1). Raintree Pubs.
Women Artists: Recognition & Reappraisal From the Early Middle Ages to the Twentieth Century. 12.50x (ISBN 0-8147-6567-X). NYU Pr.
Women Artists: Recognition & Reappraisal from the Early Middle Ages to the Twentieth Century. pap. 5.95 (ISBN 0-06-090387-2, CN387). Har-Row.
Women As World Builders: Studies in Modern Feminism. 12.00 (ISBN 0-88355-258-2). Hyperion-Conn.
Women Composers: A Handbook. 9.00 (ISBN 0-8108-1138-3). Scarecrow.
Women for Human Rights. PLB 7.95 (ISBN 0-8172-1378-3). Raintree Pubs.
Women in American History. facs. ed. 17.00 (ISBN 0-8369-0555-5). Arno.
Women in Business. PLB 7.95 (ISBN 0-8172-1377-5). Raintree Pubs.
Women in Congress. PLB 8.29 (ISBN 0-671-32896-4). Messner.
Women in Iberian Expansion Overseas, 1415-1815: Some Facts, Fancies & Personalities. 12.75x (ISBN 0-19-519817-4). Oxford U Pr.
Women in Mathematics. 12.50x (ISBN 0-262-15014-X); pap. 4.95 (ISBN 0-262-65009-6). MIT Pr.
Women in Music: A Biobibliography. 14.00 (ISBN 0-8108-0869-2). Scarecrow.
Women in Power. PLB 7.95 (ISBN 0-8172-1376-7). Raintree Pubs.
Women in Sports. PLB 4.95 (ISBN 0-385-07426-3). Doubleday.
Women in Sports: Records, Stars, Feats, & Facts. 2.95 (ISBN 0-15-299186-7). HarBraceJ.
Women in the Middle Ages. 10.95 (ISBN 0-690-01724-3). T Y Crowell.
Women in the White House: Four First Ladies. PLB 5.54 (ISBN 0-8116-4915-6). Garrard.
Women of Action in Tudor England. 10.50 (ISBN 0-8138-0910-X). Iowa St U Pr.
Women of Courage. PLB 4.39 (ISBN 0-394-90407-9); pap. 0.75 (ISBN 0-394-82186-6). Random.
Women of Courage. 7.95 (ISBN 0-688-03038-6). Morrow.
Women of Courage. pap. 1.95 (ISBN 0-553-10939-1). Bantam.
Women of Destiny in the Bible. pap. 6.00 (ISBN 0-8309-0211-2). Herald Hse.
Women of Iron & Velvet: French Women Writers After George Sand. 10.95 (ISBN 0-8008-8436-1). Taplinger.
Women of Letters. 44.25 (ISBN 0-518-10059-6). Arno.
Women of Minnesota: Selected Biographical Essays. 12.00 (ISBN 0-87351-112-3). Minn Hist.
Women of Power: The Life & Times of Catherine De Medici. 12.95 (ISBN 0-15-198370-4). HarBraceJ.
Women of Renown: Nineteenth Century Studies. 21.25 (ISBN 0-8369-7288-0). Arno.
Women of the French Revolution. 10.00 (ISBN 0-8046-0910-1). Kennikat.
Women of the French Revolution. 59.95 (ISBN 0-8490-1324-0). Gordon Pr.
Women of the Gospel. 5.95 (ISBN 0-8198-0495-9); pap. 4.95 (ISBN 0-8198-0496-7). Dghtrs St Paul.
Women of the West. pap. 5.95 (ISBN 0-89087-911-7). Les Femmes Pub.
Women of the West. PLB 4.90 (ISBN 0-531-00793-6). Watts.
Women of To-Day. facs. ed. 15.00 (ISBN 0-8369-0325-0). Arno.
Women Physicians of the World: Autobiographies of Medical Pioneers. text ed. 26.50 (ISBN 0-07-027954-3). McGraw.
Women Prefer Women. 8.95 (ISBN 0-688-03407-1). Morrow.
Women Prefer Women. pap. 2.95 (ISBN 0-553-13025-0). Bantam.
Women Shaping History. PLB 7.95 (ISBN 0-8172-1380-5). Raintree Pubs.
Women Themselves. 4.50g (ISBN 0-396-06802-2). Dodd.
Women We Wanted to Look Like. 14.95 (ISBN 0-312-88783-3). St Martin.
Women Who Carried the Good News. pap. 2.95 (ISBN 0-8170-0651-6). Judson.
Women Who Dared. PLB 7.95 (ISBN 0-8172-1375-9). Raintree Pubs.
Women Who Dared to Be Different. PLB 5.54 (ISBN 0-8116-4902-4). Garrard.
Women Who Fought: An American History. pap. 4.95 (ISBN 0-9603636-0-2). Dermody.
Women Who Led the Way: Eight Pioneers for Equal Rights. 8.95 (ISBN 0-690-89741-3). T Y Crowell.
Women Who Ruled: Cleopatra to Elizabeth II. PLB 7.79 (ISBN 0-671-32919-7). Messner.
Women Who Shaped History. 6.95 (ISBN 0-02-715210-3). Macmillan.
Women Who Shaped History. pap. 1.95 (ISBN 0-02-042050-1, 04205). Macmillan.
Women Who Win. pap. 1.25 (ISBN 0-440-99643-0). Dell.
Women Who Win. 3.95 (ISBN 0-394-82832-1); PLB 4.99 (ISBN 0-394 92832-6). Random.
Women with a Cause. PLB 5.54 (ISBN 0-8116-4914-8). Garrard.
Women's Book of World Records & Achievements. 19.95 (ISBN 0-385-12732-4); pap. 9.95 (ISBN 0-385-12733-2). Doubleday.
Womunafu's Bunafu: A Study of Authority in a Nineteenth-Century African Community. text ed. 15.00 (ISBN 0-691-03093-6). Princeton U Pr.
Wonder of It All. 8.95 (ISBN 0-06-012654-X). Har-Row.
Wood Carver of Salem: Samuel McIntire, His Life & Work. 20.00 (ISBN 0-404-01786-X). AMS Pr.
Woodrow Wilson. PLB 4.97 (ISBN 0-399-60683-1). Putnam.
Woodrow Wilson. 3rd ed. 19.95 (ISBN 0-393-07533-8); pap. 8.95x (ISBN 0-393-09012-4). Norton.
Woodrow Wilson: A Brief Biography. pap. 2.45 (ISBN 0-531-06462-X). New Viewpoints.
Woodrow Wilson: A Great Life in Brief. lib. bdg. 15.00x (ISBN 0-8371-9371-0, GAWW). Greenwood.
Woodrow Wilson: An Intimate Memoir. new ed. 7.50 (ISBN 0-87107-038-3). Potomac.
Woodrow Wilson & Colonel House: A Personality Study. 6.75 (ISBN 0-8446-2118-8). Peter Smith.
Woodrow Wilson & Colonel House: A Personality Study. pap. 4.00 (ISBN 0-486-21144-4). Dover.
Woodrow Wilson & the Paris Peace Conference. 2nd ed. pap. text ed. 3.95x (ISBN 0-669-83915-9). Heath.
Woodrow Wilson As I Know Him. 29.50 (ISBN 0-404-06527-9). AMS Pr.
Woodrow Wilson As I Know Him. 27.00 (ISBN 0-403-01243-0). Scholarly.
Woodrow Wilson, Champion of Peace. PLB 5.90 (ISBN 0-531-00932-7). Watts.
Woodrow Wilson: Life & Letters. lib. bdg. 222.00x (ISBN 0-8371-0010-0, BAWW). Greenwood.
Woodrow Wilson: The Years of Preparation. text ed. 16.50 (ISBN 0-691-04647-6). Princeton U Pr.
Woodswoman. 10.95 (ISBN 0-525-23715-1); pap. 3.95 (ISBN 0-525-47504-4). Dutton.
Woody. pap. 4.95 (ISBN 0-915684-52-7). Christian Herald.
Woody Allen: Clown Prince of American Humor. pap. 1.75 (ISBN 0-523-00786-8). Pinnacle Bks.
Word Portraits of Famous Writers. lib. bdg. 20.00. Folcroft.
Words. pap. 1.50 (ISBN 0-449-30803-0). Fawcett.
Words & Faces. 8.95 (ISBN 0-15-198460-3). HarBraceJ.
Wordsworth. lib. bdg. 17.95 (ISBN 0-8383-1486-4). Haskell.
Wordsworth. lib. bdg. 10.75 (ISBN 0-8414-3191-4). Folcroft.
Wordsworth: A Biographic Aesthetic Study. lib. bdg. 20.00. Folcroft.
Wordsworth & Coleridge in Their Time. 14.50x (ISBN 0-8448-0040-6). Crane-Russak Co.
Wordsworth & Coleridge 1795-1834. 12.50 (ISBN 0-208-00604-4). Shoe String.
Wordsworth & His Poetry. lib. bdg. 7.50. Folcroft.
Wordsworth & His Poetry. 7.25 (ISBN 0-404-52520-2). AMS Pr.
Wordsworth & His Poetry. 7.50 (ISBN 0-8046-0830-X). Kennikat.
Wordsworth: Lectures & Essays. lib. bdg. 12.50 (ISBN 0-8495-1917-9). Arden Lib.
Wordsworth, Poet of Nature & Poet of Man. 9.50 (ISBN 0-8046-0432-0). Kennikat.
Wordsworth: The Chronology of the Middle Years, 1800-1815. text ed. 25.00x (ISBN 0-674-95777-6). Harvard U Pr.
Wordsworth's Hawkshead. 19.25x (ISBN 0-19-212186-3). Oxford U Pr.
Work & Life of Solon, with a Translation of His Poems. facsimile ed. 15.00x (ISBN 0-405-07307-0). Arno.
Work & Words of Jesus. rev. ed. pap. 4.25 (ISBN 0-664-24976-0). Westminster.
Working It Out: 23 Women Writers, Artists, Scientists & Scholars Talk About Their Lives & Work. 11.95 (ISBN 0-394-40936-1). Pantheon.
Working It Out: 23 Women Writers, Artists, Scientists, & Scholars Talk About Their Lives & Work. pap. 4.95 (ISBN 0-394-73557-9). Pantheon.
Working with Roosevelt. lib. bdg. 37.50 (ISBN 0-306-70328-9). Da Capo.
Works of Anne Frank. lib. bdg. 16.75x (ISBN 0-8371-7206-3, FRWO). Greenwood.
Works of John Woolman. facs. ed. 17.75 (ISBN 0-8369-8694-6). Arno.
World & Art of Shakespeare. 8.50 (ISBN 0-8088-2602-6). Davey.
World & Ideas of Ernst Freund: The Search for General Principles of Legistlation & Administrative Law. 10.00 (ISBN 0-8173-4819-0); pap. 3.50 (ISBN 0-8173-4822-0). U of Ala Pr.
World & William Walker. lib. bdg. 18.75x (ISBN 0-8371-8328-6, CAWWW). Greenwood.

World Does Move. lib. bdg. 17.50x (ISBN 0-8371-8876-8, TAWD). Greenwood.
World Heavyweight Boxing Championship: A History. 15.00 (ISBN 0-8019-5951-9). Chilton.
World in My Mirror. 7.95 (ISBN 0-687-46270-3). Abingdon.
World Leaders I Have Known. pap. 1.75 (ISBN 0-8065-0019-0, 149). Citadel Pr.
World Military Leaders. 32.50 (ISBN 0-8352-0785-4). Bowker.
World of Aldus Manutius: Business & Scholarship in Renaissance Venice. 34.50 (ISBN 0-8014-1214-5). Cornell U Pr.
World of Bede. 12.95 (ISBN 0-312-89215-2, W59000). St Martin.
World of C. A. Stephens. pap. 9.95 (ISBN 0-917070-01-1). Waynor.
World of Defoe. 12.50 (ISBN 0-689-10772-2). Atheneum.
World of Diaghilev. 10.00 (ISBN 0-517-53902-0); pap. 5.95 (ISBN 0-517-53903-9). Crown.
World of Earl Hines. encore ed. 5.95 (ISBN 0-684-16351-9); pap. 7.95 (ISBN 0-684-15030-1). Scribner.
World of Flannery O'Connor. pap. 2.50x (ISBN 0-253-20150-0). Ind U Pr.
World of Flo Ziegfeld. 9.95 (ISBN 0-236-31053-4). Merrimack Bk Serv.
World of George Orwell. 14.95 (ISBN 0-671-21124-2). S&S.
World of George Washington. 35.00 (22998). S&S.
World of Goya. 12.93 (ISBN 0-8094-0276-9). Silver.
World of Goya. 13.95 (ISBN 0-8094-0247-5). Time-Life.
World of Great Composers. 17.50 (ISBN 0-13-968073-X). P-H.
World of James McNeill Whistler. facs. ed. 18.25 (ISBN 0-8369-5033-X). Arno.
World of Jimmy Connors. pap. 1.50 (LB330DK). Nordon Pubns.
World of M. C. Escher. 20.00 (ISBN 0-8109-0107-2). Abrams.
World of Marcel Duchamp. 12.93 (ISBN 0-8094-0265-3). Silver.
World of Marcel Duchamp. 13.95 (ISBN 0-8094-0236-X). Time-Life.
World of Marcel Proust. pap. text ed. 5.50 (ISBN 0-395-04229-1, 3-05950). HM.
World of Mary Cassatt. pap. 1.25 (ISBN 0-440-99432-2). Dell.
World of Mary Cassatt. 8.95 (ISBN 0-690-90274-3). T Y Crowell.
World of Michelangelo. 13.95 (ISBN 0-8094-0232-7). Time-Life.
World of Philip Potter. pap. 2.95 (ISBN 0-377-00006-X). Friend Pr.
World of Rembrandt. 12.93 (ISBN 0-8094-0273-4). Silver.
World of Rembrandt. 13.95 (ISBN 0-8094-0244-0). Time-Life.
World of Robert Flaherty. lib. bdg. 17.50 (ISBN 0-306-70296-7). Da Capo.
World of Robert Flaherty. lib. bdg. 14.00x (ISBN 0-8371-3400-5, GRRF). Greenwood.
World of Roger Tory Peterson: An Authorized Biography. 14.95 (ISBN 0-8129-0694-2). Times Bks.
World of Samuel Adams. 7.95 (ISBN 0-8407-6383-2). Elsevier-Nelson.
World of Tennessee Williams. 20.00 (ISBN 0-399-11773-3). Putnam.
World of the Economist. pap. 3.95x (ISBN 0-87249-332-6). U of SC Pr.
World of Van Gogh. 12.93 (ISBN 0-8094-0280-7). Silver.
World of Van Gogh. 13.95 (ISBN 0-8094-0251-3). Time-Life.
World of Watteau. 12.93 (ISBN 0-8094-0267-X). Silver.
World of Watteau. 13.95 (ISBN 0-8094-0238-6). Time-Life.
World of Willa Cather. 13.95x (ISBN 0-8032-1151-1); pap. 3.95 (ISBN 0-8032-5013-4, 112). U of Nebr Pr.
World of William Penn. lib. rep. ed. 15.00 (ISBN 0-684-15725-X). Scribner.
World, the Work, & the West of W. H. D. Koerner. 35.00 (ISBN 0-8061-1471-1). U of Okla Pr.
World's Great Men of Color. o.p. 9.95 (60437); 9.95 (ISBN 0-02-604380-7, 60437). Macmillan.
World's Great Race Drivers. PLB 3.69 (ISBN 0-394-92416-9). Random.
Worlds of Ernest Thompson Seton. 25.00 (ISBN 0-394-49547-0). Knopf.
Worlds of Patrick Geddes: Biologist, Town Planner, Re-Educator, Peace-Warrior. 31.50 (ISBN 0-7100-8548-6). Routledge & Kegan.
Worthy Dr. Fuller. 13.50 (ISBN 0-8274-3772-2). R West.
Worthy Women of Our First Century. 17.50 (ISBN 0-8369-8182-0). Arno.
Wrecked on the Feejees. 5.50 (ISBN 0-87770-085-0). Ye Galleon.
Wright Morris. pap. 1.25x (ISBN 0-8166-0483-5, MPAW69). U of Minn Pr.
Writer's Capital. pap. 4.95 (ISBN 0-395-28518-6). HM.
Writer's Capital. 8.95x (ISBN 0-8166-0707-9). U of Minn Pr.
Writer's Diary: Being Extracts from the Diary of Virginia Woolf. pap. 3.65 (ISBN 0-15-698380-X, HB264). HarBraceJ.
Writers for Young Adults: Biographies Master Index. 32.00 (ISBN 0-8103-1083-X). Gale.
Writings of a Savage. 17.95 (ISBN 0-670-79173-3). Viking Pr.
Writings on Lev Ivanov. unbound 4.50 (ISBN 0-384-55980-8). Johnson Repr.
Wyndham Lewis. text ed. 5.50x (ISBN 0-391-00212-0). Humanities.
Wyndham Lewis: A Portrait of the Artist As the Enemy. lib. bdg. 17.00x (ISBN 0-8371-6692-6, WAWK). Greenwood.

X

Xenophon's Socrates. 13.50x (ISBN 0-8014-0712-5); pap. 3.45 (ISBN 0-8014-9133-9, CP133). Cornell U Pr.

Y

Yang Wan-Li. lib. bdg. 9.95 (ISBN 0-8057-6255-8). Twayne.
Yank in Bomber Command. 8.95 (ISBN 0-88254-428-4). Hippocrene Bks.
Yankee from Georgia: The Emergence of Jimmy Carter. 10.95 (ISBN 0-8129-0753-1). Times Bks.
Yankee Quaker Confederate General: The Curious Career of Bushrod Rust Johnson. 18.00 (ISBN 0-8386-7706-1). Fairleigh Dickinson.
Yankee Revenooer. 7.95 (ISBN 0-87716-007-4). Moore Pub Co.
Yankee Saint: John Humphrey Noyes & the Oneida Community. 17.50 (ISBN 0-208-01319-9). Shoe String.
Yankee Saint: John Humphrey Noyes & the Oneida Community. lib. bdg. 12.50x (ISBN 0-87991-009-7). Porcupine Pr.
Yankee's Odyssey: Life of Joel Barlow. lib. bdg. 16.25x (ISBN 0-8371-0758-X, WOYO). Greenwood.
Yannis Manglis. lib. bdg. 8.50 (ISBN 0-8057-2578-4). Twayne.
Yaqui Life: The Personal Chronicle of a Yaqui Indian. 13.95x (ISBN 0-8032-0944-4), pap. 3.95 (ISBN 0-8032-5857-7, 637). U of Nebr Pr.
Yaqui Women: Contemporary Life Histories. 12.50 (ISBN 0-8032-0912-6). U of Nebr Pr.
Yea, Coach! Three Great Football Coaches. PLB 3.84 (ISBN 0-8116-6652-2). Garrard.
Year at the Catholic Worker. pap. 1.95 (ISBN 0-8091-2140-9). Paulist Pr.
Year in a Coal-Mine. lib. bdg. 12.00x (ISBN 0-405-10178-3). Arno.
Year of the Longley. pap. 4.75. Penobscot Bay.
Year of Three Popes. 8.95 (ISBN 0-529-05652-6, RB5652). Collins Pubs.
Yearbook Book. pap. 5.95 (ISBN 0-345-24732-9). Ballantine.
Years of Adventure 1858-1898 see Lugard.
Years of Authority 1898-1945 see Lugard.
Years of Grace. 12.00 (ISBN 0-931980-02-X); pap. 5.95 (ISBN 0-931980-01-1). Iroquois Hse.
Years of MacArthur 1941-1945. 15.00 (ISBN 0-395-20446-1). HM.
Years of My Youth. lib. bdg. 20.00. Folcroft.
Years of My Youth. facsimile ed. 14.00 (ISBN 0-8369-5626-5). Arno.
Years of My Youth & Three Essays. 20.00x (ISBN 0-253-36850-2). Ind U Pr.
Years of the Locust. pap. text ed. 11.00x (ISBN 0-8277-5561-9). British Bk Ctr.
Yeats. 16.95 (ISBN 0-19-500489-2). Oxford U Pr.
Yeats. pap. 5.95 (ISBN 0-19-501603-3, 378). Oxford U Pr.
Yeats: The Man & the Masks. pap. 4.95 (ISBN 0-393-00859-2). Norton.
Yeats: The Man & the Masks. 12.95 (ISBN 0-393-07522-2); pap. 4.95 (ISBN 0-393-00859-2). Norton.
Yeats, the Tarot & the Golden Dawn. 2nd rev. ed. pap. text ed. 7.50x (ISBN 0-85105-195-2). Humanities.
Yenan Way. lib. bdg. 14.75x (ISBN 0-8371-5959-8, RAYW). Greenwood.
Yes. 5.95 (ISBN 0-8423-4653-8). Tyndale.
Yes I Can: The Story of Sammy Davis Jr. 12.95 (ISBN 0-374-29353-8). FS&G.
Yesterday: A Memoir of a Russian-Jewish Family. 11.95 (ISBN 0-06-014810-1). Har-Row.
Yesterday in the Texas Hill Country. 12.95 (ISBN 0-89096-067-4). Tex A&M Univ Pr.
Yoshida Memoirs: The Story of Japan in Crisis. lib. bdg. 16.00x (ISBN 0-8371-6733-7, YOYM). Greenwood.
You Could Look It up: The Life of Casey Stengel. 10.95 (ISBN 0-8129-0830-9). Times Bks.
You Might As Well Live: The Life & Times of Dorothy Parker. 8.95 (ISBN 0-671-20660-5). S&S.
You, Too, Can Stop Drinking. 8.50 (ISBN 0-682-48733-3). Exposition.
Young & Black in Africa. 3.95 (ISBN 0-394-82304-4). Random.
Young & Black in America. 3.95 (ISBN 0-394-80482-1); PLB 4.99 (ISBN 0-394-90482-6). Random.
Young & Black in America. pap. 1.95 (ISBN 0-394-70804-0, VS4). Random.
Young Ardizzone: An Autobiographical Fragment. 7.95 (ISBN 0-02-503000-0). Macmillan.
Young Bear: The Legend of Bear Bryant's Boyhood. 5.95 (ISBN 0-87397-127-2). Strode.
Young Chemists & Great Discoveries. facs. ed. 14.75 (ISBN 0-8369-0023-5). Arno.
Young Duke: A Moral Tale, Though Gay. lib. bdg. 12.50. Folcroft.
Young Gemini. 7.95 (ISBN 0-689-11004-9). Atheneum.
Young George Du Maurier: A Selection of His Letters, 1860-67. lib. bdg. 13.75x (ISBN 0-8371-2830-7, DUDU). Greenwood.
Young Hamilton: A Biography. 15.00 (ISBN 0-316-28594-3). Little.
Young Henry James 1813-1876. 20.00 (ISBN 0-404-03897-2). AMS Pr.
Young Hitler I Knew. lib. bdg. 22.75x (ISBN 0-8371-8664-1, KUYH). Greenwood.
Young Jim: The Early Years of James Weldon Johnson. 4.50 (ISBN 0-396-05398-2). Dodd.
Young John Kennedy. 6.95 (ISBN 0-15-299876-4). HarBraceJ.
Young Lions of Judah. pap. 1.95 (ISBN 0-88270-059-6). Logos.
Young Longfellow, 1807-1843. lib. bdg. 17.50 (ISBN 0-374-97885-9). Octagon.
Young Man in a Hurry: The Story of Cyrus W. Field. PLB 7.89 (ISBN 0-06-023756-2). Har-Row.
Young Man in Search of Love. 12.95 (ISBN 0-385-12357-4); limited ed. 50.00 (ISBN 0-385-13492-4). Doubleday.
Young Man Thoreau. 15.00 (ISBN 0-87023-231-2). U of Mass Pr.
Young Man Thoreau. pap. 3.95 (ISBN 0-06-090614-6, CN 614). Har-Row.
Young Mark Twain & the Mississippi. PLB 4.39 (ISBN 0-394-90413-3). Random.
Young Maude Adams. 4.00 (ISBN 0-8338-0058-2). M Jones.
Young Mazarin. 16.95 (ISBN 0-500-87004-7). Thames Hudson.
Young Nietzsche & the Wagnerian Experience. 18.50 (ISBN 0-404-50939-8). AMS Pr.
Young Nixon: An Oral Inquiry. 13.95 (ISBN 0-930046-02-1); pap. 7.95 (ISBN 0-930046-01-3). CSU Oral Hist.
Young Philip Sidney, 1572-1577. 37.50x (ISBN 0-300-01443-0). Yale U Pr.
Young Readers' Picturebook of Tar Heel Authors. rev. ed. pap. 1.00 (ISBN 0-86526-107-5). NC Archives.
Young Sam Clemens. lib. bdg. 30.00 (ISBN 0-8414-3473-5). Folcroft.
Young Shelley: Genesis of a Radical. lib. bdg. 22.50 (ISBN 0-374-91255-6). Octagon.
Young Thomas Edison. 2.95 (ISBN 0-395-07252-2). HM.
Young Thomas Hardy. 10.95 (ISBN 0-316-31453-6). Little.
Young Voltaire. facsimile ed. 16.75 (ISBN 0-8369-5830-6). Arno.
Young Wellington in India. pap. text ed. 1.50x (ISBN 0-485-14120-5). Humanities.
Young Whistler. 32.50 (ISBN 0-04-927009-5). Allen Unwin.
Your Daughter Is Brain Damaged: A Mother's Story. 10.95 (ISBN 0-525-93152-X). Dutton.
Your Daughter Is Brain Damaged: A Mother's Story. 10.00 (ISBN 0-448-22126-8). Paddington.
Your Desert & Mine. 10.00 (ISBN 0-88280-072-8). ETC Pubns.
Your Favorite Country Music Stars. pap. 1.50 (ISBN 0-445-03076-3). Popular Lib.
Your Loving Anna: Letters from the Ontario Frontier. 10.00 (ISBN 0-8020-1927-7); pap. 3.50 (ISBN 0-8020-6166-4). U of Toronto Pr.
You're on Open Line: Inside the Wacky World of Late-Night Talk Radio. 8.95 (ISBN 0-8289-0335-2). Greene.
You're Only Human Once. lib. bdg. 17.00 (ISBN 0-405-09698-4). Arno.
Yours, with Love Kate. 3.75 (ISBN 0-395-06901-7). HM.
Youth of Erasmus. 2nd ed. 16.00 (ISBN 0-8462-1080-0). Russell.
Youth of Frederick the Great. 18.50 (ISBN 0-404-03891-3). AMS Pr.
Youth of Goethe. 25.00 (ISBN 0-8274-0078-0). R West.
Youth of Goethe. lib. bdg. 24.95 (ISBN 0-8383-1182-2). Haskell.
Yuan Chen. lib. bdg. 9.95 (ISBN 0-8057-6279-5). Twayne.
Yuan Shih-k'ai. 2nd ed. 12.50x (ISBN 0-8047-0789-8). Stanford U Pr.
Yugoslavs in America. PLB 5.95 (ISBN 0-8225-0231-3). Lerner Pubns.
Yuri Gagarin: First Man in Space. 3.95 (ISBN 0-87397-203-1). Strode.

Z

Zachariah Chandler: A Political Biography. 8.50 (ISBN 0-87013-139-7). Mich St U Pr.
Zachary Taylor. Incl. Soldier of the Republic; Soldier in the White House. 27.50 (ISBN 0-208-00608-7). Shoe String.
Zachary Taylor. PLB 4.49 (ISBN 0-399-60696-3). Putnam.
Zachary Taylor, 1784-1850 & Millard Fillmore, 1800-1874: Chronology, Documents, Bibliographical Aids. 7.00 (ISBN 0-379-12078-X). Oceana.
Zane Grey. pap. text ed. 2.00 (ISBN 0-88430-016-1). Boise St Univ.
Zapata: A Biography. 35.00x (ISBN 0-8128-1776-1). Stein & Day.
Zapata, Mexican Rebel. 6.75 (ISBN 0-688-21604-8); PLB 6.48 (ISBN 0-688-31604-2). Morrow.
Zelda: A Biography. 13.95 (ISBN 0-06-012991-3). Har-Row.
Zen Master Dogen: An Introduction with Selected Writings. 9.75 (ISBN 0-8348-0116-7); pap. 4.75 (ISBN 0-8348-0116-7). Weatherhill.
Zeppelin Story. 17.50 (ISBN 0-498-01805-9). A S Barnes.
Zhukov. 19.95 (ISBN 0-8061-0951-3). U of Okla Pr.
Zola. 14.95 (ISBN 0-312-89902-5). St Martin.
Zola. lib. bdg. 17.75x (ISBN 0-8371-9820-8, BEZO). Greenwood.
Zoo Vet: Adventures of a Wild Animal Doctor. 8.95 (ISBN 0-397-01207-1). Lippincott.
Zora Neale Hurston: A Literary Biography. 15.00 (ISBN 0-252-00652-6). U of Ill Pr.
Zoroaster & His World. lib. bdg. 45.00 (ISBN 0-374-93877-6). Octagon.
Zubin: The Zubin Mehta Story. 10.00 (ISBN 0-06-120400-5). Har-Row.
Zwingli. 47.00 (ISBN 0-521-20939-0). Cambridge U Pr.
Zwingli the Reformer: His Life & Work. 10.00 (ISBN 0-208-00694-X). Shoe String.

KEY TO PUBLISHERS' AND DISTRIBUTORS' DIRECTORY

A & W Pubs, *(A & W Pubs., Inc.; 0-89479),* 95 Madison Ave., New York, NY 10016 Tel 212-725-4970; Do Not Confuse with A-W, Addison-Wesley Publishing Co., Inc.
A & W Visual Library *See* A & W Pubs
A H Clark, *(Clark, Arthur H., Co.; 0-87062),* P.O. Box 230, Glendale, CA 91209 Tel 213-245-9119.
A Jones, *(Jones, Anson, Press; 0-912432),* P.O. Box 65, Salado, TX 76571 Tel 817-947-5414.
A R Liss, *(Liss, Alan R., Inc.; 0-8451),* 150 Fifth Ave., New York, NY 10011 Tel 212-741-2515.
A S Barnes, *(Barnes, A. S., & Co., Inc.; 0-498),* 11175 Flintkote Ave., Suite C, San Diego, CA 92121 Tel 714-452-5515.
A-W, *(Addison-Wesley Publishing Co., Inc.; 0-201),* Jacob Way, Reading, MA 01867 Tel 617-944-3700. *Imprints:* A-W Childrens (Addison-Wesley Children's Books).
A-W Childrens *Imprint of* **A-W**
AA *Imprint of* **U of Mich Pr**
AAFH, *(Academy of American Franciscan History; 0-88382),* P.O. Box 34440, Washington, DC 20034 Tel 301-365-1763.
AAHPER, *(American Alliance for Health, Physical Education & Recreation; 0-88314),* Affiliate of National Education Assn., 1201 16th St., N. W., Washington, DC 20036 Tel 202-833-5555.
Abbeville Pr, *(Abbeville Press Inc.; 0-89659),* 505 Park Ave., New York, NY 10022 Tel 212-888-1969.
Abelard, *(Abelard-Schuman Ltd.; 0-200),* 10 E. 53rd St., New York, NY 10022 Tel 212-593-7000; c/o Harper & Row Pubs., Keystone Industrial Park, Scranton, PA 18512.
Abingdon, *(Abingdon Press; 0-687),* 201 Eighth Ave. S., Nashville, TN 37202 Tel 615-749-6403; Orders to: Customer Service Dept., 201 Eighth Ave. S., Nashville, TN 37202 Tel 615-749-6347.
Abrams, *(Abrams, Harry N., Inc.; 0-8109),* Subs. of Times Mirror Co., 110 E. 59th St., New York, NY 10022 Tel 212-758-8600.
Accent Bks, *(Accent Books; 0-89636; 0-916406),* P.O. Box 15337, Lakewood Sta., Denver, CO 80215 Tel 303-988-5300; 12100 W. Sixth Ave., Denver, CO 80215.
Ace Bks, *(Ace Books; 0-441),* Div. of Charter Communications Inc., 51 Madison Ave., New York, NY 10010 Tel 212-689-9200; c/o Grosset & Dunlap, 51 Madison Ave., New York, NY 10010 Tel 212-689-9200.
ACEI, *(Assn. for Childhood Education International; 0-87173),* 3615 Wisconsin Ave., N.W., Washington, DC 20016 Tel 202-363-6963.
Acropolis, *(Acropolis Books; 0-87491),* 2400 17th St. N.W., Washington, DC 20009 Tel 202-387-6805.
Adirondack Yes, *(Adirondack Yesteryears, Inc.; 0-9601158),* Lake St Extension-Drawer 209, Saranac Lake, NY 12983 Tel 518-891-3206.
Adler, *(Adler's Foreign Books, Inc.; 0-8417),* 162 Fifth Ave., New York, NY 10010 Tel 212-691-5151.
Advent, *(Advent Pubs., Inc.; 0-911682),* P.O. Box A3228, Chicago, IL 60690.
Aeonian Pr *See* Amereon Ltd
Aero, *(Aero Pubs., Inc.; 0-8168),* 329 W. Aviation Rd., Fallbrook, CA 92028 Tel 714-728-8456.
Africana *Imprint of* **Holmes & Meier**
Afro-Am, *(Afro-Am Publishing Co., Inc.; 0-910030),* 910 S. Michigan Ave., Rm. 556, Chicago, IL 60605 Tel 312-922-1147.
Airmont, *(Airmont Publishing Co., Inc.; 0-8049),* 22 E. 60th St., New York, NY 10022.
AJAY Ent, *(AJAY Enterprises),* P.O. Box 2018, Mosby Branch, Falls Church, VA 22042 Tel 703-573-8220.
Akers, *(Akers, Mona J. Coole; 0-912706),* 219 S. Williams St., Denver, CO 80209 Tel 303-722-1917.
ALA, *(American Library Assn.; 0-8389),* 50 E. Huron St., Chicago, IL 60611 Tel 312-944-6780.
Alaska Northwest, *(Alaska Northwest Publishing Co.; 0-88240),* 130 Second Ave. S., Edmonds, WA 98020 Tel 206-774-4111.
Alba, *(Alba House; 0-8189),* Div. of the Society of St. Paul, 2187 Victory Blvd., Staten Island, NY 10314 Tel 212-761-0047.
Allen Unwin, *(Allen & Unwin, Inc.; 0-04; 0-86861),* 9 Winchester Terrace, Winchester, MA 01890 Tel 617-729-0830; Orders to: P.O. Box 978, Edison, NJ 08817 Tel 201-225-1900.
Allenson, *(Allenson, Alec R., Inc.; 0-8401),* 635 E. Ogden Ave., Box 31, Naperville, IL 60540 Tel 312-355-2595.
Alpha Pubns, *(Alpha Pubns., Inc.; 0-912404),* 1079 De Kalb Pike, Blue Bell, PA 19422 Tel 215-277-6342.
Am Chemical, *(American Chemical Society; 0-8412),* 1155 16th St., N.W., Washington, DC 20036 Tel 202-872-4600.
Am Heritage, *(American Heritage Publishing Co.; 0-8281),* Ten Rockefeller Plaza, New York, NY 10020 Tel 212-399-8900.
Am Hist Res, *(American History Research Associates; 0-910086),* P.O. Box 140, Brookeville, MD 20729 Tel 301-774-3573.
Am Inst Marxist, *(American Institute for Marxist Studies; 0-89977),* 20 E. 30th St., New York, NY 10016 Tel 212-689-4530.
Am Inst Writing Res, *(American Institute for Writing Research, Corp.; 0-917944),* Box 2129, Grand Central Sta., New York, NY 10017 Tel 212-449-2372.
Am Lib Pub Co, *(American Library Publishing Co., Inc.; 0-87729),* 275 Central Park, W., New York, NY 10024 Tel 212-787-0766.
Am Media, *(American Media; 0-912986),* 790 Hampshire Rd., Suite H, Westlake Village, CA 91361 Tel 213-889-1231.
Am Philos, *(American Philosophical Society; 0-87169),* 104 S. Fifth St., Philadelphia, PA 19106 Tel 215-627-0706.
Am Sch Athens, *(American School of Classical Studies at Athens; 0-87661),* c/o Institute for Advanced Study, Princeton, NJ 08540 Tel 609-924-4400.
Am Soc Civil Eng, *(American Society of Civil Engineers; 0-87262),* 345 E. 47th St., New York, NY 10017 Tel 212-752-6800.
AmCen *Imprint of* **Hill & Wang**
Amereon Ltd, *(Amereon Ltd.; 0-88411),* P.O. Box 1200, Mattituck, NY 11952 Tel 516-298-5100.
AMI Pr, *(AMI International Press; 0-911988),* Mountain View Rd., Washington, NJ 07822 Tel 201-689-1700.
Amoskeag Pr, *(Amoskeag Press, Inc.),* P.O. Box 666, Hooksett, NH 03106 Tel 603-622-6626.
AMS Pr, *(AMS Press, Inc.; 0-404),* 56 E. 13th St., New York, NY 10003 Tel 212-777-4700.
AMSCO Sch, *(AMSCO School Pubns., Inc.; 0-87720),* 315 Hudson St., New York, NY 10013 Tel 212-675-7005.
Ananda, *(Ananda Pubns.; 0-916124),* 900 Alleghany Star Rte., Nevada City, CA 95959 Tel 916-265-5877.
Anch *Imprint of* **Doubleday**
Anchor Pr *Imprint of* **Doubleday**
And-Or Pr, *(And-or Press, Inc.; 0-915904),* P.O. Box 2246, Berkeley, CA 94702 Tel 415-849-2665.
Andrews & McMeel, *(Andrews & McMeel, Inc.; 0-8362),* 6700 Squibb Rd., Mission, KS 66202 Tel 913-362-1523.
Anna Pub, *(Anna Publishing, Inc.; 0-89305),* 2469 Aloma Ave., Winter Park, FL 32792 Tel 305-671-5995.
Anv *Imprint of* **Van Nos Reinhold**

Aperture, *(Aperture, Inc.; 0-89381; 0-912334),* Elm St., Millerton, NY 12546 Tel 518-789-4491.
Appel, *(Appel, Paul P., Pub.; 0-911858),* 119 Library Lane, Mamaroneck, NY 10543 Tel 914-698-8115.
Apple-Gems, *(Apple-Gems; 0-9602122),* P.O. Box 16292, San Francisco, CA 94116 Tel 415-587-9752.
Aqua Educ, *(Aquarian Educational Group; 0-911794),* 30188 Mulholland Hwy., Agoura, CA 91301 Tel 213-889-9678.
Arbor Hse, *(Arbor House Publishing Co.; 0-87795),* 235 E. 45th St., New York, NY 10017 Tel 212-599-3131; Dist. by: E. P. Dutton & Co., 2 Park Ave., New York, NY 10016.
Arcane Bks
See Arcane Pubns
Arcane Pubns, *(Arcane Pubns.; 0-912240),* Box 36, York Harbor, ME 03911 Tel 207-363-3333.
Archer Edns, *(Archer Editions Press; 0-89097),* P.O. Box 562, Danbury, CT 06810 Tel 203-438-0282.
Archway, *(Archway Paperbacks; 0-671),* c/o Pocket Books, 1230 Avenue of the Americas, New York, NY 10020 Tel 212-246-2121.
Arco, *(Arco Publishing, Inc.; 0-668),* Div. of Prentice-Hall, Inc., 219 Park Ave., S., New York, NY 10003 Tel 212-777-6300.
Arden Lib, *(Arden Library; 0-8495),* Mill & Main Sts., Darby, PA 19023 Tel 215-726-5505.
Ardis Pubs, *(Ardis Pubs.; 0-88233),* 2901 Heatherway, Ann Arbor, MI 48104 Tel 313-971-2367.
Arena Lettres, *(Arena Lettres; 0-88479),* 432 Park Ave., S., New York, NY 10016 Tel 212-889-6626; 8 Lincoln Place, Waldwick, NJ 07463 Tel 201-445-7154.
Argosy, *(Argosy-Antiquarian, Ltd.; 0-87266),* 116 E. 59th St., New York, NY 10022.
Ariadne Pr, *(Ariadne Press; 0-918056),* 4400 P St., N.W., Washington, DC 20007 Tel 202-337-2514.
Arkham, *(Arkham House Pubs.; 0-87054),* Sauk City, WI 53583 Tel 608-643-4500.
Arlington Hse, *(Arlington House Pubs.; 0-87000),* 333 Post Rd. W., Westport, CT 06880 Tel 914-636-3850.
Arno, *(Arno Press; 0-405),* 3 Park Ave., New York, NY 10016 Tel 212-725-2050.
Ars Ceramica, *(Ars Ceramica, Ltd.; 0-89344),* P.O. Box 7366, Ann Arbor, MI 48107 Tel 313-429-7864; Dist. by: Keramos, P.O. Box 7500, Ann Arbor, MI 48107.
Ashley Bks, *(Ashley Books, Inc.; 0-87949),* 223 Main St., Port Washington, NY 11050 Tel 516-883-2221; Orders to: P.O. Box 768, Port Washington, NY 11050 Tel 516-883-2221.
Asia, *(Asia Publishing House; 0-210),* 141 E. 44th St., New York, NY 10017 Tel 212-697-0887; Dist. by: APT Books, Inc., 141 E. 44th St., Suite 511, New York, NY 10017.
Astor-Honor, *(Astor-Honor, Inc.; 0-8392),* 48 E. 43rd St., New York, NY 10017.
ASU Lat Am St, *(Arizona State Univ., Center for Latin American Studies; 0-87918),* Tempe, AZ 85281 Tel 602-965-5127.
Atheneum, *(Atheneum Pubs.; 0-689),* 597 Fifth Ave., New York, NY 10017 Tel 212-486-2700; Dist. by: Book Warehouse, Inc., Vreeland Ave., Boro of Totowa, Paterson, NJ 07512. *Imprints:* McElderry Bk (McElderry Book).
Athlone Pr *Imprint of* **Humanities**
Attic Pr, *(Attic Press; 0-87921),* Stony Point, Rte. 2, Greenwood, SC 29646 Tel 803-374-3013.
Augsburg, *(Augsburg Publishing House; 0-8066),* 426 S. Fifth St., Minneapolis, MN 55415 Tel 612-330-3300.
Augustana, *(Augustana Historical Society; 0-910184),* Augustana College Library, Rock Island, IL 61201 Tel 309-794-7266; Orders to: Denkmann Memorial Library, Augustana College, Rock Island, IL 61201.
Auromere, *(Auromere; 0-89744),* 1291 Weber St., Pomona, CA 91768 Tel 714-629-8255.
Aurora Pubs, *(Aurora Pubs.; 0-87695),* 1503 Laurel St., Nashville, TN 37203 Tel 615-254-5842.
Ave Maria, *(Ave Maria Press; 0-87793),* Notre Dame, IN 46556 Tel 219-287-2831.
Avon, *(Avon Books; 0-380),* 959 Eighth Ave., New York, NY 10019 Tel 212-262-5700. *Imprints:* Bard (Avon Bard Books); Camelot (Avon Camelot Books); Discus (Avon Discus Books).
B Franklin, *(Franklin, Burt, Pub.; 0-89102),* Dist. by: Lenox Hill Publishing & Distributing Corp., 235 E. 44th St., New York, NY 10017.
B W Brace, *(Brace, Beverly W.),* 455 Crescent Dr., No. 27, Sunnyvale, CA 94087 Tel 408-738-5404.
Baha'i, *(Baha'i Publishing Trust; 0-87743),* 415 Linden Ave., Wilmette, IL 60091 Tel 312-251-1854.
Baker Bk, *(Baker Book House; 0-8010),* P.O. Box 6287, 1019 Wealthy St. S.E., Grand Rapids, MI 49506 Tel 616-676-9186.
Bala Bks, *(Bala Books; 0-89647),* 51 West Allens Lane, Philadelphia, PA 19119 Tel 215-247-4602.
Balamp Pub, *(Balamp Publishing; 0-913642),* 7430 Second Blvd., Detroit, MI 48202 Tel 313-873-6320; Orders to: P.O. Box 02367, North End, Detroit, MI 48202.
Ballantine, *(Ballantine Books, Inc.; 0-345),* Div. of Random House, Inc., 201 E. 50th St., New York, NY 10022 Tel 212-751-2600; Orders to: 400 Hahn Rd., Westminster, MD 21157.
B&N, *(Barnes & Noble Books; 0-389),* Div of Harper & Row Pubs., Inc., 10 E. 53rd St., New York, NY 10022 Tel 212-593-7141; Orders to: Harper & Row Pubs., Inc., Keystone Industrial Park, Scranton, PA 18512.
Banner *Imprint of* **Exposition**
Banner of Truth, *(Banner of Truth, The),* P.O. Box 621, Carlisle, PA 17013.
Bantam, *(Bantam Books, Inc.; 0-553),* 666 Fifth Ave., New York, NY 10019 Tel 212-765-6500; Orders to: 414 E. Golf Rd., Des Plaines, IL 60016.
Banyan Bks, *(Banyan Books; 0-916224),* P.O. Box 431160, Miami, FL 33143 Tel 305-665-6011.
Bard *Imprint of* **Avon**
Barre, *(Barre Publishing Co.),* Valley Rd., Barre, MA 01005 Tel 617-355-2914; Dist. by: Crown Publishers, Inc., 1 Park Ave., New York, NY 10016.
Barrie & Jenkins, *(Barrie & Jenkins; 0-214),* Dist. by: Arco, 219 Park Ave. S., New York, NY 10003 Tel 212-777-6300.
Barron, *(Barron's Educational Series, Inc.; 0-8120),* 113 Crossways Park Dr., Woodbury, NY 11797 Tel 516-921-8750.
Basic, *(Basic Books, Inc.; 0-465),* 10 E. 53rd St., New York, NY 10022 Tel 212-593-7057.
Bauhan, *(Bauhan, William L., Inc.; 0-87233),* Old County Rd., Dublin, NH 03444 Tel 603-563-8020.
BC *Imprint of* **Grove**
Beacham, *(Beacham, Roger, Pub.; 0-911796),* P.O. Box 8254, Austin, TX 78712 Tel 512-451-4572.
Beachcomber Bks, *(Beachcomber Books; 0-913076),* 714 N. Euclid, Tucson, AZ 85719.
Beacon Pr, *(Beacon Press, Inc.; 0-8070),* 25 Beacon St., Boston, MA 02108 Tel 617-742-2110; Orders to: Harper & Row Pubs., Inc., Keystone Industrial Park, Scranton, PA 18512.
Bear State, *(Bear State Books),* 304 High St., Santa Cruz, CA 95060 Tel 408-426-3272.
Beekman Pubs, *(Beekman Pubs., Inc.; 0-8464),* 38 Hicks St., Brooklyn Heights, NY 11201 Tel 212-624-4514.
Belmont-Tower, *(Belmont-Tower Books, Inc.; 0-505),* 2 Park Ave., Suite 910, New York, NY 10016 Tel 212-679-7707; Orders to: Increased Sales Co., Inc., 327 Main Ave., Norwalk, CT 06852 Tel 203-846-2027.
Benson, *(Benson, W. S., & Co., Inc.; 0-87443),* P.O. Box 1866, Austin, TX 78767 Tel 512-476-5050.
Bentley, *(Bentley, Robert, Inc.; 0-8376),* 872 Massachusetts Ave., Cambridge, MA 02139 Tel 617-547-4170.
Berg
See Larlin Corp
Berkley Pub, *(Berkley Publishing Corp.; 0-425),* Affiliate of G. P. Putnam's Sons, 200 Madison Ave., New York, NY 10016 Tel 212-686-9820. *Imprints:* Medallion (Medallion Books); Windhover (Windhover).
Berwyn-London, *(Berwin-London Pubs.; 0-916536),* 2401 Calumet St., Flint, MI 48503 Tel 313-785-2316.
Beta Bk, *(Beta Book Co.; 0-89293);* 10857 Valiente Court, San Diego, CA 92124 Tel 714-293-3832.
Bethany Fell, *(Bethany Fellowship, Inc.; 0-87123),* 6820 Auto Club Rd., Minneapolis, MN 55438 Tel 612-944-2121.
Bethany Pr, *(Bethany Press; 0-8272),* 2640 Pine Blvd., Box 179, St. Louis, MO 63166 Tel 314-371-6900.
Bibl Evang Pr, *(Biblical Evangelism Press; 0-914012),* 11 Blvd. Motif, Brownsburg, IN 46112 Tel 317-852-3535; Orders to: P.O. Box 157, Brownsburg, IN 46112.
Biblo, *(Biblo & Tannen Booksellers & Pubs., Inc.; 0-8196),* 63 Fourth Ave., New York, NY 10003 Tel 212-475-1257.
Binford, *(Binford & Mort Pubs.; 0-8323),* 2536 S.E. 11th Ave., Portland, OR 97202 Tel 503-238-9666.
Biobooks
See Sullivan Bks Intl
Jove Jove C
Black Sparrow, *(Black Sparrow Press; 0-87685),* P.O. Box 3993, Santa Barbara, CA 93105 Tel 805-687-5014.
Blair, *(Blair, John F., Pub.; 0-910244; 0-89587),* 1406 Plaza Dr., Winston-Salem, NC 27103 Tel 919-768-1374.
Bloch, *(Bloch Publishing Co.; 0-8197),* 915 Broadway, New York, NY 10010 Tel 212-673-7910.
B'nai B'rith, *(B'nai B'rith, Dept. of Adult Jewish Education; 0-910250),* 1640 Rhode Island Ave., N.W., Washington, DC 20036 Tel 202-857-6588; Orders to: Bloch Publishing Co., 915 Broadway, New York, NY 10010.
Boardman, *(Boardman, Clark, Co., Ltd.; 0-87632),* 435 Hudson St., New York, NY 10014 Tel 212-929-7500.
Bobbs, *(Bobbs-Merrill Co., Inc.; 0-672),* A Thomas Audel Co., 4300 W. 62nd St., Indianapolis, IN 46468 Tel 317-298-5400.
Boise St Univ, *(Boise State Univ.; 0-88430),* Dept. of English, Boise, ID 83725 Tel 208-385-1246.
Bonney, *(Bonney, Orrin H.; 0-931620),* 625 E. 14th St., Houston, TX 77008 Tel 713-864-8697.
Bookmates Intl, *(Bookmates International, Inc.; 0-933082),* P.O. Box 9883, Fresno, CA 93795 Tel 209-298-3308.
Borgo Pr, *(Borgo Press; 0-89370),* P.O. Box 2845, San Bernardino, CA 92406 Tel 714-884-5813; Orders to: Newcastle Publishing Co. (trade orders only), P.O. Box 7589, Van Nuys, CA 91409; Orders to: P.O. Box 2845 (library and individual orders only), San Bernardino, CA 92406.
Boston Public Lib, *(Boston Public Library; 0-89073),* P.O. Box 286, Boston, MA 02117 Tel 617-536-5400.
Bowker, *(Bowker, R. R., Co.; 0-8352),* A Xerox Publishing Co., 1180 Ave. of the Americas, New York, NY 10036 Tel 212-764-5100; Orders to: P.O. Box 1807, Ann Arbor, MI 48106.
Bowling Green Univ, *(Bowling Green Univ., Popular Press; 0-87972),* Bowling Green State Univ., Popular Culture Ctr., Bowling Green, OH 43403 Tel 419-372-2981.
Bowmar
See Bowmar-Noble
Bowmar-Noble, *(Bowmar/Noble Publishers, Inc.; 0-8372; 0-8107),* 4563 Colorado Blvd., Los Angeles, CA 90039 Tel 213-247-8995.
Boyd & Fraser, *(Boyd & Fraser Publishing Co.; 0-87835),* 3627 Sacramento St., San Francisco, CA 94118 Tel 415-346-0686.
Branch-Smith, *(Branch-Smith, Inc.; 0-87706),* P.O. Box 1868, Fort Worth, TX 76101 Tel 817-332-6377; 120 St. Louis Ave., Fort Worth, TX 76101.
Branden, *(Branden Press, Inc.; 0-8283),* P.O. Box 843, 21 Station St., Brookline, MA 02147 Tel 617-734-2045.
Braziller, *(Braziller, George, Inc.; 0-8076),* One Park Ave., New York, NY 10016 Tel 212-889-0909.
Brethren, *(Brethren Press; 0-87178),* 1451 Dundee Ave., Elgin, IL 60120 Tel 312-742-5100.

Brigham, *(Brigham Young Univ. Press; 0-8425),* 218 University Press Bldg., Provo, UT 84602 Tel 801-374-1211; Orders to: 205 University Press Bldg., Provo, UT 84602.
British Am Bks, *(British American Books; 0-89979),* P. O. Box 302, Willits, CA 95490.
British Bk Ctr, *(British Book Center; 0-8277),* Fairview Park, Elmsford, NY 10523 Tel 914-592-7700.
Broadman, *(Broadman Press; 0-8054),* 127 Ninth Ave., N., Nashville, TN 37234 Tel 615-251-2544.
Broadside, *(Broadside Press Pubns.; 0-910296),* 74 Glendale Ave., Highland Park, MI 48203 Tel 313-868-1585.
Brookings, *(Brookings Institution; 0-8157),* 1775 Massachusetts Ave., N.W., Washington, DC 20036 Tel 202-797-6254.
Brooks-Cole, *(Brooks/Cole Publishing Co.; 0-8185),* Div. of Wadsworth, Inc., 555 Abrego St., Monterey, CA 93940 Tel 408-373-0728; Orders to: Wadsworth, Inc., 10 Davis Dr., Belmont, CA 94002 Tel 415-595-2350.
Brooks-Sterling, *(Brooks-Sterling Co.; 0-914418),* P.O. Box 265, Danville, CA 94526 Tel 415-837-1318.
Brown Bk, *(Brown Book Co.; 0-910294),* 120 Secatogue Ave., Farmingdale, NY 11735 Tel 516-293-6969.
Brown U Pr, *(Brown Univ. Press; 0-87057),* 194 Meeting St., Box 1881, Providence, RI 02912 Tel 401-863-2455.
Browning Inst, *(Browning Institute, Inc.; 0-930252),* P.O. Box 2983, Grand Central Sta., New York, NY 10017.
Bruccoli, *(Bruccoli Clark Books; 0-89723),* 1700 Lone Pine, Bloomfield Hills, MI 48013.
Buccaneer Bks, *(Buccaneer Books; 0-89966),* P.O. Box 168, Cutchogue, NY 11935.
Bucknell U Pr, *(Bucknell Univ. Press; 0-8387),* Div. of Associated University Presses, P.O. Box 421, Cranbury, NJ 08512 Tel 609-655-0190.
Buddhist Bks, *(Buddhist Books Intl; 0-914910),* Orders to: P.O. Box 665, Chatsworth, CA 91311 Tel 213-998-8485.
C C Thomas, *(Thomas, Charles C., Pub.; 0-398),* 301-327 E. Lawrence Ave., Springfield, IL 62717 Tel 217-789-8980.
C E Tuttle, *(Tuttle, Charles E., Co., Inc.; 0-8048),* P.O. Drawer F, Rutland, VT 05701 Tel 802-773-8930.
C H Kerr, *(Kerr, Charles H., Publishing Co.; 0-88286),* 600 W. Jackson, Suite 413, Chicago, IL 60606 Tel 312-454-0363; Orders to: P.O. Box 914, Chicago, IL 60690.
C N Aronson, *(Aronson, Charles N., Writer-Publisher; 0-915736),* 11520 Bixby Hill Road, Arcade, NY 14009 Tel 716-496-6002.
Cadillac, *(Cadillac Publishing Co., Inc.; 0-87445),* 709 S. Skinker Blvd., St. Louis, MO 63105 Tel 314-862-7560; 6611 Clayton Rd., St. Louis, MO 63117.
Cadleon Pr, *(Cadleon Press; 0-9600310),* P.O. Box 24, San Francisco, CA 94101.
Cadmus Eds, *(Cadmus Editions; 0-932274),* P.O. Box 4725, Santa Barbara, CA 93103.
Cambridge U Pr, *(Cambridge Univ. Press; 0-521),* 32 E. 57th St., New York, NY 10022 Tel 212-688-8885; Orders to: 510 North Ave., New Rochelle, NY 10801.
Camelot *Imprint of* **Avon**
Camera Graphic, *(Camera/Graphic Press Ltd.; 0-918696),* P.O. Box 1702, F.D.R. Sta., New York, NY 10022 Tel 212-832-0760.
Campus Crusade, *(Campus Crusade for Christ, Inc.; 0-918956),* P.O. Box 1576, 2700 Little Mountain Dr., Bldg. "B", San Bernardino, CA 92402 Tel 714-886-7981.
Capra Pr, *(Capra Press; 0-912264; 0-88496),* P.O. Box 2068, Santa Barbara, CA 93120 Tel 805-966-4590.
Carcanet
See Dufour
Carillon Bks, *(Carillon Books; 0-89310),* Div. of Catholic Digest, 405 Lexington Ave., New York, NY 10017 Tel 212-867-9766; Orders to: 2115 Summit Ave., St. Paul, MN 55105 Tel 612-647-5251.
Carolina Acad Pr, *(Carolina Academic Press; 0-89089),* P.O. Box 8795, Durham, NC 27707 Tel 919-688-5155.
Carrier Pigeon, *(Carrier Pigeon; 0-932870),* 75 Kneeland St. Rm. 309, Boston, MA 02111 Tel 617-542-5679.
Cath U Pr, *(Catholic Univ. of America Press; 0-8132),* 620 Michigan Ave., N.E., Washington, DC 20064 Tel 202-635-5052; Dist. by: International Scholarly Book Services, Inc., P.O. Box 555, Forest Grove, OR 97116 Tel 503-357-7192; All Titles Dist. by Intl Schol Bk Serv, Except Fathers of the Church Series.
Caxton, *(Caxton Printers, Ltd.; 0-87004),* P.O. Box 700, Caldwell, ID 83605 Tel 208-459-7421.
CCPr *Imprint of* **Macmillan**
Celestial Arts, *(Celestial Arts Publishing Co.; 0-912310; 0-89087),* 231 Adrian Rd., Millbrae, CA 94030 Tel 415-692-4500.
Celo Pr, *(Celo Press; 0-914064),* Rte. 5, Burnsville, NC 28714 Tel 704-675-4925.
Centennial, *(Centennial Press; 0-8220),* Div. of Cliff's Notes, Inc., P.O. Box 80728, Lincoln, NE 68501 Tel 402-477-6971.
Center Pubns, *(Center Pubns.; 0-916820),* 905 S. Normandie Ave., Los Angeles, CA 90006 Tel 213-387-2356.
Century Bookbindery, *(Century Bookbindery; 0-89984),* P.O. Box 6471, Philadelphia, PA 19145.
Century Pr, *(Century Press; 0-915680),* 412 N. Hudson, Oklahoma City, OK 73102.
Chalfant Pr, *(Chalfant Press, Inc.; 0-912494),* P.O. Box 787, Bishop, CA 93514 Tel 714-873-3535.
Chandler & Sharp, *(Chandler & Sharp Pubs., Inc.; 0-88316),* 11A Commercial Blvd., Novato, CA 94947 Tel 415-883-2353.
Channing Bks, *(Channing Books; 0-9600496),* P.O. Box 552, 35 Main St., Marion, MA 02738 Tel 617-748-0087.
Channings
See Channing Bks
Charter Bks, *(Charter Books; 0-441),* Div. of Ace Books, 360 Park Ave. S., New York, NY 10010 Tel 212-889-9800.
Charterhouse *Imprint of* **McKay**
Chatham Pr, *(Chatham Press; 0-85699),* 143 Sound Beach, Old Greenwich, CT 06870 Tel 203-637-4531; Dist. by: The Devin-Adair Co., Old Greenwich, CT 06870.
Chedney, *(Chedney Press; 0-910358),* Claridge House One, Claridge Dr., Apt. 911, Verona, NJ 07044 Tel 516-294-8408.
Chelsea Pub, *(Chelsea Publishing Co.; 0-8284),* 432 Park Avenue S., Rm. 503, New York, NY 10016 Tel 212-889-8095.
Cherokee, *(Cherokee Publishing Co.; 0-87797),* P.O. Box 1081, Covington, GA 30209 Tel 404-786-0565.
Chicago Review, *(Chicago Review Press, Inc.; 0-914090),* 215 W. Ohio St., Chicago, IL 60610 Tel 312-644-5457.
Chicorel Lib
See Am Lib Pub Co
Childrens, *(Childrens Press; 0-516),* 1224 W. Van Buren St., Chicago, IL 60607 Tel 312-666-4200. *Imprints:* Golden Gate (Golden Gate).
Childs World, *(Child's World, Inc., The; 0-89565; 0-913778),* 980 N. McLean, Elgin, IL 60120 Tel 312-741-7591; Orders to: P.O. Box 681, Elgin, IL 60120.
Chilton, *(Chilton Book Co.; 0-8019),* Orders to: School, Library Services, Chilton Way, Radnor, PA 19089 Tel 215-687-8200.
Chinese Materials, *(Chinese Materials Center, Inc.; 0-89644),* 809 Taraval Street, San Francisco, CA 94116.
Chips, *(Chip's Bookshop, Inc.; 0-912378),* Box 639, Cooper Sta., New York, NY 10003 Tel 212-362-9336.
Chosen Bks Pub, *(Chosen Books Publishing Co., Ltd.; 0-912376),* Lincoln, VA 22078 Tel 703-338-4131; Dist. by: Word, Inc., 4800 W. Waco Dr., Waco, TX 76703 Tel 817-772-7650.
Chr Classics, *(Christian Classics, Inc.; 0-87061),* P.O. Box 30, Westminster, MD 21157 Tel 301-848-3065.
Chr Lit, *(Christian Literature Crusade, Inc.; 0-87508),* Pennsylvania Ave., Fort Washington, PA 19034.
Chr Science, *(Christian Science Publishing Society; 0-87510),* General Pubns. Dept., 1 Norway St., Boston, MA 02115 Tel 617-262-2300; Orders to: P.O. Box 1875, Boston, MA 02117.
Chris Mass, *(Christopher Publishing House (Mass); 0-8158),* 53 Billings Rd., North Quincy, MA 02171 Tel 617-328-3880.
Christian Herald, *(Christian Herald Books; 0-915684),* 40 Overlook Dr., Chappaqua, NY 10514 Tel 914-769-9000.
Chronicle Bks, *(Chronicle Books/Prism Editions; 0-87701),* Div. of Chronicle Publishing Co., 870 Market St., Suite 915, San Francisco, CA 94102 Tel 415-777-7240.
Cistercian Pubns, *(Cistercian Pubns., Inc.; 0-87907),* WMU Sta., Kalamazoo, MI 49008 Tel 616-383-4985.
Citadel Pr, *(Citadel Press; 0-8065),* Subs. of Lyle Stuart, Inc., 120 Enterprise Ave., Secaucus, NJ 07094 Tel 201-866-0490.
Claitors, *(Claitors Publishing Division; 0-87511),* 3165 S. Acadian at Interstate 10, Box 239, Baton Rouge, LA 70821.
Clarion *Imprint of* **HM**
CN *Imprint of* **Har-Row**
CO RR Mus, *(Colorado Railroad Museum; 0-918654),* P.O. Box 10, Golden, CO 80401 Tel 303-279-4591.
Colby, *(Colby College Press; 0-910394),* Library, Waterville, ME 04901 Tel 207-873-0311.
Coll & U Pr, *(College & Univ. Press; 0-8084),* 267 Chapel St., New Haven, CT 06513 Tel 203-562-3101. *Imprints:* Twayne (Twayne's U.S. Author Series).
Collier *Imprint of* **Macmillan**
Collins Pubs, *(Collins, William, Pubs., Inc.),* 2080 W. 117th St., Cleveland, OH 44111 Tel 216-941-6930; 200 Madison Ave., Suite 1405, New York, NY 10016.
Collins-World
See Collins Pubs
Colo Assoc, *(Colorado Associated Univ. Press, Univ. of Colorado; 0-87081),* 1424 15th St. Univ. of Colorado, Boulder, CO 80309 Tel 303-492-7191.
Columbia U Pr, *(Columbia Univ. Press; 0-231),* 562 W. 113th St., New York, NY 10025 Tel 212-678-6777; Orders to: 136 S. Broadway, Irvington-on-Hudson, NY 10533 Tel 914-591-9111.
Commonwealth Pr, *(Commonwealth Press, Inc.; 0-89227),* 415 First St., Radford, VA 24141 Tel 703-639-2475.
Concordia, *(Concordia Publishing House; 0-570),* 3558 S. Jefferson Ave., St. Louis, MO 63118 Tel 314-664-7000.
Condor Pub Co, *(Condor Pub. Co., Inc.; 0-89516),* 29 E. Main St., Westport, CT 06880 Tel 203-226-9591.
Congr Quarterly, *(Congressional Quarterly, Inc.; 0-87187),* 1414 22nd St., N.W., Washington, DC 20037 Tel 202-296-6800.
Connect Pr, *(Connections Press; 0-930474),* P.O. Box 454, Bolinas, CA 94924.
Contemp Bks, *(Contemporary Books, Inc.; 0-8092),* 180 N. Michigan Ave., Chicago, IL 60601 Tel 312-782-9181; Formerly Named Henry Regnery .o.
Continuum, *(Continuum Publishing Corp.; 0-8264),* 815 Second Ave., New York, NY 10017 Tel 212-557-0500; Dist. by: The Seabury Press, 815 Second Ave., New York, NY 10017 Tel 212-557-0500.
Cook, *(Cook, David C., Publishing Co.; 0-89191; 0-912692),* 850 N. Grove Ave., Elgin, IL 60120 Tel 312-741-2400.
Coole
See Akers
Cooper Sq, *(Cooper Square Pubs., Inc.; 0-8154),* Dist. by: Biblio Distribution Centre, 81 Adams Dr., Totowa, NJ 07512 Tel 201-256-8600.
CORE Collection, *(Core Collection Books, Inc.; 0-8486),* 11 Middle Neck Rd., Great Neck, NY 11021 Tel 516-466-3676.
Corinth Bks, *(Corinth Books; 0-87091),* 228 Everit St., New Haven, CT 06511 Tel 203-789-1935.
Cornell Maritime, *(Cornell Maritime, Press, Inc.; 0-87033),* P.O. Box 456, Centerville, MD 21617 Tel 301-758-1075.
Cornell U Pr, *(Cornell Univ. Press; 0-8014),* 124 Roberts Place, P.O. Box 250, Ithaca, NY 14850 Tel 607-257-7000.
Corner Hse, *(Corner House Pubs.; 0-87928),* 1321 Green River Rd., Williamstown, MA 01267 Tel 413-458-8561.
Cornerstone, *(Cornerstone Library, Inc.; 0-346),* Div. of Simon & Schuster, Inc., 1230 Avenue of the Americas, New York, NY 10020 Tel 212-246-1350; Orders to: Simon & Schuster, Inc., 1230 Avenue of the Americas, New York, NY 10020 Tel 212-245-6400.

Coronado Pr, *(Coronado Press, Inc.; 0-87291),* P.O. Box 3232, Lawrence, KS 66044 Tel 913-843-5988.
Corwin, *(Corwin Books; 0-89474),* One Century Plaza, 2029 Century Park, E., Los Angeles, CA 90067 Tel 213-552-9111; Dist. by: Independent News, 75 Rockefeller Plaza, New York, NY 10019.
Country Beautiful, *(Country Beautiful Corp.; 0-87294),* 24198 W. Bluemound Rd., Waukesha, WI 53186 Tel 414-542-9361.
Coward, *(Coward, McCann & Geoghegan, Inc.; 0-698),* A Member of the Putnam Publishing Group, 200 Madison Ave., New York, NY 10016 Tel 212-576-8900; Orders to: 1050 W. Wall St., Lyndhurst, NJ 07071 Tel 201-933-9292.
Cptn Stanislaus, *(Captain Stanislaus Mlotkowski Memorial Brigade Society; 0-9600814),* 247 Philadelphia Pike, Wilmington, DE 19809.
Crain Bks, *(Crain Books; 0-87251),* Div. of Crain Communications, Inc., 740 Rush St., Chicago, IL 60611 Tel 312-649-5250.
Crane-Russak Co, *(Crane, Russak & Co., Inc.; 0-8448),* 3 E. 44th St, New York, NY 10017 Tel 212-867-1490.
Creation Hse, *(Creation House; 0-88419),* 396 E. St. Charles Rd., Carol Stream, IL 60187 Tel 312-653-1472.
Creative Arts Bk, *(Creative Arts Book Co.; 0-916870),* 833 Bancroft Way, Berkeley, CA 94710 Tel 415-848-4777.
Creative Ed, *(Creative Education, Inc.; 0-87191),* 3137 Holmes Ave., Minneapolis, MN 55408 Tel 612-825-3678.
Creative Pr, *(Creative Press; 0-912512),* P.O. Box 1058, Claremont, CA 91711 Tel 714-593-5060.
Crescent Pubns, *(Crescent Pubns., Inc.; 0-914184),* 5410 Wilshire Blvd., Suite 400, Los Angeles, CA 90036.
Crest *Imprint of* **Avon**
Crossroads Bks *Imprint of* **Seabury**
Crown, *(Crown Pubs., Inc.; 0-517),* 1 Park Ave., New York, NY 10016 Tel 212-532-9200.
CSU Oral Hist, *(California State Univ., Oral History Program; 0-930046),* Fullerton, CA 92634 Tel 714-870-3580.
Cyrco Pr, *(Cyrco Press, Inc.; 0-915326),* 342 Madison Ave., New York, NY 10017 Tel 212-682-8410.
D Armstrong, *(Armstrong, D., Co., Inc.; 0-918464),* 2000-B Governor's Circle, Houston, TX 77092 Tel 713-688-1441.
D Bosco Pubns, *(Don Bosco Pubns.; 0-89944),* Div. of Salsian Society, Inc., Box T, 148 Main St., New Rochelle, NY 10802 Tel 914-632-6562.
D Clement, *(Clement, David D. & Dorothy Z., ; 0-9601618),* 3931 Villa Ct., Fair Oaks, CA 95628 Tel 916-966-1666.
D White, *(White, David, Co.; 0-87250),* 14 Vanderventer Ave., Port Washington, NY 11050 Tel 516-944-9325.
Da Capo, *(Da Capo Press, Inc.; 0-306),* 227 W. 17th St., New York, NY 10011 Tel 212-255-0713.
Dale Bks, *(Dale Books),* 51 Springdale Ave., Waterbury, CT 06708 Tel 203-753-0255.
Dale Books Inc, *(Dale Books, Inc.; 0-89559),* Subs. of Davis Pubns. Inc., 380 Lexington Ave., New York, NY 10017 Tel 212-949-9190.
Dance Horiz, *(Dance Horizons; 0-87127),* 1801 E. 26th St., Brooklyn, NY 11229 Tel 212-645-9607.
Dandelion Pr, *(Dandelion Press; 0-89799),* RFD No. 2, Box 118, Bedford, NY 10506 Tel 914-764-8172; Orders to: 10 W. 66th St., New York, NY 10023 Tel 212-787-3793.
Darby Bks, *(Darby Books; 0-89987),* P.O. Box 148, Darby, PA 19023.
Daughters, *(Daughters Publishing Co, Inc.; 0-913780),* MS 590, P.O. Box 42999, Houston, TX 77042.
Davey, *(Davey, Daniel, & Co., Inc., Pubs.; 0-8088),* P. O. Box 6088, Hartford, CT 06106 Tel 203-525-0997.
David & Charles, *(David & Charles, Inc.; 0-7153),* P.O. Box 57, North Pomfret, VT 05053 Tel 802-457-1911.
Dawsons, *(Dawson's Book Shop; 0-87093),* 535 N. Larchmont Blvd., Los Angeles, CA 90004 Tel 213-469-2186.
De Vorss, *(De Vorss & Co.; 0-87516),* P.O. Box 550, Marina Del Rey, CA 90291 Tel 213-870-7478.
Dekker, *(Dekker, Marcel, Inc.; 0-8247),* 270 Madison Ave., New York, NY 10016 Tel 212-889-9595.
Delacorte, *(Delacorte Press),* c/o Dell Publishing Co., 1 Dag Hammarskjold Plaza, 245 E. 47th St., New York, NY 10017 Tel 212-832-7300. *Imprints:* E Friede (Eleanor Friede); Sey Lawr (Seymour Lawrence).
Dell, *(Dell Publishing Co., Inc.; 0-440),* 1 Dag Hammarskjold Plaza, 245 E. 47th St., New York, NY 10017 Tel 212-832-7300. *Imprints:* Delta (Delta Books); LE (Laurel Editions); LFL (Laurel Leaf Library); YB (Yearling Books).
Delta *Imprint of* **Dell**
Dermody, *(Dermody, Gail R. & Eugene M.),* P.O. Box 324, Lakewood, CA 90714.
Deseret Bk, *(Deseret Book Co.; 0-87747),* 40 E. South Temple, P.O. Box 30178, Salt Lake City, UT 84130 Tel 801-534-1515.
Devin, *(Devin-Adair Co., Inc.; 0-8159),* 143 Sound Beach Ave., Old Greenwich, CT 06870 Tel 203-637-4531.
Dexter & Westbrook, *(Dexter & Westbrook, Ltd.; 0-87966),* 958 Church St., Baldwin, NY 11510 Tel 516-868-6064.
Dghtrs St Paul, *(Daughters of St. Paul; 0-8198),* 50 St. Paul's Ave., Boston, MA 02130 Tel 617-522-8911.
Dharma Pub, *(Dharma Publishing; 0-913546; 0-89800),* 2425 Hillside Ave., Berkeley, CA 94704 Tel 415-548-5407.
Dial, *(Dial Press; 0-8037),* 1 Dag Hammarskjold Plaza, 245 E. 47th St., New York, NY 10017 Tel 212-832-7300.
Dillon, *(Dillon Press, Inc.; 0-87518),* 500 S. Third St., Minneapolis, MN 55415 Tel 612-336-2691.
Dillon-Liederbach, *(Dillon/Liederbach, Inc.; 0-913228),* 601 Grand Ave. - M, Ojai, CA 93023 Tel 805-646-6144; Orders to: 2720 East Blvd., Cleveland, OH 44104 Tel 216-231-8896.
Diplomatic Fla, *(Diplomatic Press, Inc.; 0-910512),* 1001 Lasswade Dr., Tallahassee, FL 32312 Tel 904-386-8487.
Discus *Imprint of* **Avon**
Dodd, *(Dodd, Mead & Co.; 0-396),* 79 Madison Ave., New York, NY 10016 Tel 212-685-6464.
Dolmen Pr *Imprint of* **Humanities**
Dolp *Imprint of* **Doubleday**
Donning Co, *(Donning Co. Pubs.; 0-915442; 0-89865),* 5041 Admiral Wright Rd., Virginia Beach, VA 23462 Tel 804-499-0589.
Dorrance, *(Dorrance & Co.; 0-8059),* 35 Cricket Terrace, Ardmore, PA 19003 Tel 215-642-8303.
Dorsey, *(Dorsey Press; 0-256),* Div. of Richard D. Irwin, Inc., 1818 Ridge Rd., Homewood, IL 60430 Tel 312-798-6000.
Dothard, *(Dothard, R. L., Associates; 0-912668),* RD 2, Brattleboro, VT 05301 Tel 802-254-9009.
Doubleday, *(Doubleday & Co., Inc.; 0-385),* 501 Franklin Ave., Garden City, NY 11530 Tel 516-294-4561. *Imprints:* Anch (Anchor Books); Anchor Pr (Anchor Press); Dolp (Dolphin Books); Echo (Echo Books); Galilee (Galilee); Im (Image Books).
Dover, *(Dover Pubns., Inc.; 0-486),* 180 Varick St., New York, NY 10014 Tel 212-255-3755.
Dragon Pr, *(Dragon Press),* Church St., Elizabethtown, NY 12932 Tel 518-873-2680.
Drama Bk, *(Drama Book Specialists (Pubs.); 0-910482; 0-89676),* 150 W. 52nd St., New York, NY 10019 Tel 212-582-1475.
Dufour, *(Dufour Editions, Inc.; 0-8023),* Chester Springs, PA 19425 Tel 215-458-5005.
Duke, *(Duke Univ. Press; 0-8223),* 6697 College Sta., Durham, NC 27708 Tel 919-684-2173.
Dumbarton Oaks, *(Dumbarton Oaks; 0-88402),* Orders to: Ctr Byzantine Only: J.J. Augustin, Inc., Locust Valley, NY 11560.
Durrell, *(Durrell Pubns., Inc.; 0-911764),* P.O. Box 743, Mast Cove Lane, Kennebunkport, ME 04046 Tel 207-985-3904.
Dutton, *(Dutton, E. P.; 0-525),* 2 Park Ave., New York, NY 10016 Tel 212-725-1818. *Imprints:* Evman (Everyman); Phaidon (Phaidon).
Telegraph Telegraph Books
E A Seemann, *(Seemann, E. A., Publishing, Inc.; 0-912458; 0-89530),* P.O. Box K, Miami, FL 33156 Tel 305-233-5852.
E Friede *Imprint of* **Delacorte**
E M Coleman Ent, *(Coleman, Earl M., Enterprises, Inc.; 0-930576),* P.O. Box 143, Pine Plains, NY 12567 Tel 518-398-7193.
Eastern Orthodox, *(Eastern Orthodox Books; 0-89981),* P.O. Box 302, Willits, CA 95490.
Eastview, *(Eastview Editions, Inc.; 0-89860),* P.O. Box 783, Westfield, NJ 07091 Tel 201-233-0474.
Ecco Pr, *(Ecco Press; 0-912946),* 1 W. 30th St., New York, NY 10001 Tel 212-736-2599; Orders to: Vikeship, 299 Murray Hill Pkwy., East Rutherford, NJ 07073.
Echo *Imprint of* **Doubleday**
Eerdmans, *(Eerdmans, Wm. B., Publishing Co.; 0-8028),* 255 Jefferson Ave., S.E., Grand Rapids, MI 49503 Tel 616-459-4591.
Elliots Bks, *(Elliot's Books; 0-911830),* P.O. Box 6, Northford, CT 06472 Tel 203-484-2184.
Elsevier, *(Elsevier-North Holland Pub. Co.; 0-444; 0-7204),* 52 Vanderbilt Ave., New York, NY 10017 Tel 212-867-9040.
Elsevier-Nelson, *(Elsevier/Nelson Books; 0-525),* 2 Park Ave., New York, NY 10016 Tel 212-725-1818.
Elsevier Sci
See Elsevier
EMC, *(EMC Corp.; 0-88436; 0-912022),* 180 E. Sixth St., St. Paul, MN 55101 Tel 612-227-7366.
Encino Pr, *(Encino Press; 0-88426),* 510 Baylor St., Austin, TX 78703 Tel 512-476-6821.
Ency Brit Ed, *(Encyclopaedia Britannica Educational Corp.; 0-87827),* Affiliate of Encyclopaedia Britannica, Inc., 425 N. Michigan Ave., Chicago, IL 60611 Tel 312-321-6800.
Enslow Pubs, *(Enslow Pubs. Inc.; 0-89490),* 60 Crescent Place, Box 301, Short Hills, NJ 07078 Tel 201-379-6308.
Eriksson, *(Eriksson, Paul S., Pubs.; 0-8397),* Battell Bldg., Middlebury, VT 05753 Tel 802-388-7303; Dist. by: Independent Publishers Group, 14 Vanderventer Ave., Port Washington, NY 11050 Tel 516-944-9325.
ETC Pubns, *(ETC Pubns.; 0-88280),* 700 E. Vereda del Sur, Palm Springs, CA 92263 Tel 714-325-5352; Orders to: Pubns. Dept., P.O. Drawer 1627-A, Palm Springs, CA 92263.
Evang & Ref, *(Evangelical & Reformed Historical Society; 0-910564),* c/o Philip Schaff Library, 555 W. James St., Lancaster Theological Seminary, Lancaster, PA 17603.
Evans
See M Evans
Evans Pubns, *(Evans Pubns.),* P.O. Box 520, Perkins, OK 74059 Tel 405-547-2882.
Ever *Imprint of* **Grove**
Everest Hse, *(Everest House Pubs.; 0-89696),* 1133 Ave. of the Americas, New York, NY 10036 Tel 212-764-3400; Orders to: Box 978, Edison, NJ 08817.
Evman *Imprint of* **Dutton**
Exposition, *(Exposition Press, Inc.; 0-682),* 900 S. Oyster Bay Rd., Hicksville, NY 11801 Tel 516-822-5700. *Imprints:* Banner (Banner); Lochinvar (Lochinvar); University (University).
Facts on File, *(Facts on File, Inc.; 0-87196),* 119 W. 57th St., New York, NY 10019 Tel 212-265-2011.
Fairleigh Dickinson, *(Fairleigh Dickinson Univ. Press; 0-8386),* Div. of Associated University Presses, P.O. Box 421, Cranbury, NJ 08512 Tel 609-655-0190.
Faith & Life, *(Faith & Life Press; 0-87303),* 718B Main St., Box 347, Newton, KS 67114 Tel 316-283-5100.
Family Serv, *(Family Service Assn. of America; 0-87304),* 44 E. 23rd St., New York, NY 10010 Tel 212-674-6100.
F&J Mazzulla, *(Mazzulla, Fred & Jo),* 1930 E. Eighth Ave., Denver, CO 80206 Tel 303-322-9119; Orders to: Mazfoto, 1130 Western Federal Savings Bldg., Denver, CO 80202.
Farnswth Pub, *(Farnsworth Publishing Co., Inc.; 0-910580; 0-87863),* 78 Randall Ave., Rockville Ctr., NY 11570 Tel 516-536-8400.

Farnum Films, *(Farnum Films; 0-915790),* Executive House, 225 E. 46th St., New York, NY 10017 Tel 212-371-8679; Orders to: P.O. Box 1094, New York, NY 10017.
Crest Crest Books C
Prem Premier Books TF
Feldheim, *(Feldheim, Philipp, Inc.; 0-87306),* 96 E. Broadway, New York, NY 10002 Tel 212-925-3180.
Fell, *(Fell, Frederick, Publishers, Inc.; 0-8119),* 386 Park Ave., S., New York, NY 10016 Tel 212-685-9017.
Fels & Firn, *(Fels & Firn Press; 0-918704),* 1843 Vassar Ave., Mountain View, CA 94043 Tel 415-965-4291.
Feminist Pr, *(Feminist Press; 0-912670; 0-935312),* SUNY/College at Old Westbury, Box 334, Old Westbury, NY 11568 Tel 516-997-7660.
Ferry Pr
See SBD
Fertig, *(Fertig, Howard, Inc.; 0-86527),* 80 E. 11th St., New York, NY 10003 Tel 212-982-7922.
Fides
See Fides Claretian
Fides Claretian, *(Fides/Claretian; 0-8190),* P.O. Box F, Notre Dame, IN 46556 Tel 219-288-4479.
Filson Club, *(Filson Club, Inc.; 0-9601072),* 118 W. Breckinridge St., Louisville, KY 40203 Tel 502-582-3727.
Fireside *Imprint of* **S&S**
Flash Bks *Imprint of* **Music Sales**
Fleet, *(Fleet Press Corp.; 0-8303),* 160 Fifth Ave., New York, NY 10010 Tel 212-243-6100.
Folcroft, *(Folcroft Library Editions; 0-8414),* P.O. Box 182, Folcroft, PA 19032.
Follett, *(Follett Publishing Co.; 0-695),* Div. of Follett Corp., 1010 W. Washington Blvd., Chicago, IL 60607 Tel 312-666-5858.
Fontana Pap *Imprint of* **Watts**
Fordham, *(Fordham Univ. Press; 0-8232),* University Box L, Bronx, NY 10458 Tel 212-933-2233.
Fortress, *(Fortress Press; 0-8006),* 2900 Queen Lane, Philadelphia, PA 19129 Tel 800-523-3824.
Piraeus Piraeus Publishers
Foun Bks, *(Foundation Books; 0-934988),* P.O. Box 29229, Lincoln, NE 68529 Tel 402-466-4988.
Fountain Pub Co NY, *(Fountain Publishing Co., Inc.; 0-916184),* 509 Madison Ave., Rm. 712, New York, NY 10022 Tel 212-838-9215; Dist. by: Harper & Row, Scranton, PA 18512.
Four Winds *Imprint of* **Scribner**
Franciscan Herald, *(Franciscan Herald Press; 0-8199),* 1434 W. 51st St., Chicago, IL 60609 Tel 312-254-4455.
Franklin & Marsh, *(Franklin & Marshall College; 0-910626),* Lancaster, PA 17604 Tel 717-291-3981.
Free Pr, *(Free Press; 0-02),* Div. of Macmillan Publishing Co., Inc., 866 Third Ave., New York, NY 10022 Tel 212-935-2000; Dist. by: Macmillan Co., Riverside, NJ 08370.
Friedman, *(Friedman, Ira J., Inc.; 0-87198),* Div. of Kennikat Press, Inc., 90 S. Bayles Ave., Port Washington, NY 11050 Tel 516-883-0570.
Friend Pr, *(Friendship Press; 0-377),* 475 Riverside Dr., Rm. 772, New York, NY 10027 Tel 212-870-2497; Orders to: Friendship Press Distribution, P.O. Box 37844, Cincinnati, OH 45237 Tel 513-761-2100.
Friends United, *(Friends United Press; 0-913408),* 101 Quaker Hill Dr., Richmond, IN 47374 Tel 317-962-7573.
Frontier Pr Co, *(Frontier Press Co.; 0-912168),* P.O. Box 1098, Columbus, OH 43216 Tel 614-864-3737.
Frontier Press Calif, *(Frontier Press),* P.O. Box 5023, Santa Rosa, CA 95402 Tel 707-544-5174.
FS&G, *(Farrar, Straus & Giroux, Inc.; 0-374),* 19 Union Square, W., New York, NY 10003 Tel 212-741-6900.
G F Ritchie, *(Ritchie, George F.),* 665 Pine St., No. 503, San Francisco, CA 94108 Tel 415-433-6115.
G K Hall, *(Hall, G. K., & Co.; 0-8161),* 70 Lincoln St., Boston, MA 02111 Tel 617-423-3990. *Imprints:* Large Print Bks (Large Print Books Series).
Gale, *(Gale Research Co.; 0-8103),* Book Tower, Detroit, MI 48226 Tel 313-961-2242.
Galilee *Imprint of* **Doubleday**
Gambit, *(Gambit; 0-87645),* 27 North Main St., Meeting House Green, Ipswich, MA 01938 Tel 617-356-2956.
G&D, *(Grosset & Dunlap, Inc.; 0-448),* 51 Madison Ave., New York, NY 10010 Tel 212-689-9200. *Imprints:* MSP (Madison Square Press); Tempo (Tempo Books).
Gannon, *(Gannon, William; 0-88307),* P.O. Box 2610, Santa Fe, NM 87501 Tel 505-983-1579.
Garland Pub, *(Garland Publishing, Inc.; 0-8240),* 136 Madison Ave., 2nd Floor, New York, NY 10016 Tel 212-686-7492.
Garrard, *(Garrard Publishing Co.; 0-8116),* 107 Cherry St., New Canaan, CT 06840 Tel 203-966-4581; Orders to: 1607 N. Market St., Champaign, IL 61820.
Garrett-Helix, *(Garrett Pubns.-Helix Press; 0-912326),* Orders to: Taplinger Publishing Co., 200 Park Ave, S., New York, NY 10003.
Gateway Ed Ltd
See Regnery-Gateway
GB *Imprint of* **Oxford U Pr**
Genealog Pub, *(Genealogical Publishing Co., Inc.; 0-8063),* 111 Water St., Baltimore, MD 21202 Tel 301-837-8271.
Geron-X, *(Geron-X, Inc.; 0-87672),* P.O. Box 1108, Los Altos, CA 94022.
GLA Pr, *(G. L. A. Press; 0-912854),* P. O. Box 5312, Irving, TX 75062 Tel 214-438-1123.
Gloucester Art, *(Gloucester Art Press; 0-930582),* P.O. Box 4526, Albuquerque, NM 87196 Tel 505-843-7749.
Godine, *(Godine, David R., Pub., Inc.; 0-87923),* 306 Dartmouth St., Boston, MA 02116 Tel 617-536-0761.
Golden Gate *Imprint of* **Childrens**
Golden Pr *Imprint of* **Wayne St U Pr**
Golf Digest Bks, *(Golf Digest Books; 0-914178),* Div. of Golf Digest, Inc., 495 Westport Ave., Norwalk, CT 06856 Tel 203-847-5811.
Good News, *(Good News Pubs.; 0-89107),* 9825 W. Roosevelt Rd., Westchester, IL 60153 Tel 312-345-7474.
Gordian, *(Gordian Press, Inc.; 0-87752),* 85 Tompkins St., Staten Island, NY 10304 Tel 212-273-4700.
Gordon-Cremonesi, *(Gordon-Cremonesi Book),* Dist. by: Atheneum Pubs., 597 Fifth Ave., New York, NY 10017 Tel 212-486-2700.
Gordon Pr, *(Gordon Press Pubs.; 0-87968),* P.O. Box 459, Bowling Green Sta., New York, NY 10004.
Graphic Impress, *(Graphic Impressions; 0-914628),* 1939 W. 32nd Ave., Denver, CO 80211 Tel 303-458-7475.
Graphic Pub, *(Graphic Publishing Co.; 0-89279),* 204 N. Second Ave., W., Lake Mills, IA 50450 Tel 515-592-0031.
Great Basin, *(Great Basin Press; 0-930830),* Box 11162, Reno, NV 89510 Tel 702-826-7729.
Great Eastern, *(Great Eastern Book Co.; 0-87773),* P.O. Box 271, Boulder, CO 80306 Tel 303-449-6113.
Green, *(Green, Warren H., Inc.; 0-87527),* 8356 Olive Blvd., St. Louis, MO 63132 Tel 314-991-1335.
Greene, *(Greene, Stephen, Press; 0-8289),* Fessenden Rd. at Indian Flat, P.O. Box 1000, Brattleboro, VT 05301 Tel 802-257-7757.
Greeno Hadden, *(Greeno, Hadden & Co., Ltd.; 0-913550),* 518 Central St., Winchendon, MA 01475 Tel 617-354-4691; Tel 617-297-1006; Orders to: Box 305, Winchedon, MA 01475.
Greenwillow, *(Greenwillow Books; 0-688),* Div. of William Morrow & Co., Inc., 105 Madison Ave., New York, NY 10016 Tel 212-889-3050; Orders to: William Morrow & Co., Inc., Wilmor Warehouse, 6 Henderson Dr., West Caldwell, NJ 07006.
Greenwood, *(Greenwood Press, Inc.; 0-8371; 0-313),* 88 Post Rd. W., Westport, CT 06881 Tel 203-226-3571.
Grossmont Pr, *(Grossmont Press, Inc.; 0-913182; 0-89543),* 7071 Convoy Court, Suite 310, San Diego, CA 92111 Tel 714-299-2205.
Grove, *(Grove Press, Inc.; 0-8021; 0-394),* 196 W. Houston St., New York, NY 10014 Tel 212-242-4900; Orders to: Grove Press Order Dept., 196 W. Houston St., New York, NY 10014. *Imprints:* BC (Black Cat Books); Ever (Evergreen Books).
Grune, *(Grune & Stratton; 0-8089),* c/o Academic Press, 111 Fifth Ave., 12th Fl., New York, NY 10003 Tel 212-741-6800.
Guild Bks, *(Guild Books; 0-912080),* 86 Riverside Dr., New York, NY 10024 Tel 212-799-2600.
Guild of Tutors, *(Guild of Tutors; 0-89615),* 1019 Gavley Ave., Los Angeles, CA 90024.
H C Sun, *(Sun, H. C.),* Box 391, Sterling, VA 22170 Tel 703-430-7040.
H J Schneider
See World Wide OR
Hacker, *(Hacker Art Books; 0-87817),* 54 W. 57th St., New York, NY 10019 Tel 212-757-1450.
Hafner, *(Hafner Press; 0-02),* Div. of Macmillan Publishing Co., Inc., 866 Third Ave., New York, NY 10022 Tel 212-935-2000; Dist. by: Collier-Macmillan Distribution Ctr., Riverside, NJ 08075.
Halsted Pr, *(Halsted Press),* Div. of John Wiley & Sons, Inc., 605 Third Ave., New York, NY 10016 Tel 212-867-9800.
Hammond Inc, *(Hammond, Inc.; 0-8437),* 515 Valley St., Maplewood, NJ 07040 Tel 201-763-6000.
Hancock Hse, *(Hancock House Pubs., Ltd.; 0-88839),* 12008 First Ave., S., Seattle, WA 98168 Tel 206-243-1500; Dist. by: Universe Books, 183 Munroe St., Passaic, NJ 07055.
Handy *Imprint of* **HarBraceJ**
Har-Row, *(Harper & Row Pubs., Inc.; 0-06),* 10 E. 53rd St., New York, NY 10022 Tel 212-593-7000; Orders to: Keystone Industrial Park, Scranton, PA 18512. *Imprints:* CN (Colophon Books); HarpC (Harper's College East); HarpJ (Juvenile Books); HarpR (Harper Religious Books); HarpT (Harper Trade Books); PL (Perennial Library); Torch Lib (Torchbooks Library Binding).
Harbor Hill Bks, *(Harbor Hill Books; 0-916346),* P.O. Box 407, Harrison, NY 10528 Tel 914-698-3495.
HarBraceJ, *(Harcourt Brace Jovanovich, Inc.; 0-15),* 757 Third Ave., New York, NY 10017 Tel 212-888-4444. *Imprints:* Handy (Handy Books); Harv (Harvest Books); HC (Harcourt Brace Jovanovich, Inc., College Dept.); HPL (Harbrace Paperback Library); VoyB (Voyager Books).
Harlo Pr, *(Harlo Press; 0-8187),* 50 Victor Ave., Detroit, MI 48203 Tel 313-883-3600.
HarpC *Imprint of* **Har-Row**
Harper Mag Pr, *(Harper's Magazine Press),* 10 E. 53rd St., New York, NY 10022 Tel 212-593-7000.
HarpJ *Imprint of* **Har-Row**
HarpR *Imprint of* **Har-Row**
HarpT *Imprint of* **Har-Row**
Hartmore, *(Hartmore House),* Dist. by: Associated Booksellers, 147 McKinley Ave., Bridgeport, CT 06606.
Harv *Imprint of* **HarBraceJ**
Harvard U Pr, *(Harvard Univ. Press; 0-674),* 79 Garden St., Cambridge, MA 02138 Tel 617-495-2600; Orders to: Customer Service, Harvard Univ. Press, 79 Garden St., Cambridge, MA 02138.
Harvey, *(Harvey House, Pubs.; 0-8178),* 20 Waterside Plaza, New York, NY 10010 Tel 212-889-9520; Orders to: 128 W. River St., Chippewa Falls, WI 54729 Tel 715-723-2814.
Haskell, *(Haskell House Pubs., Inc.; 0-8383),* P.O. Box FF, Blythebourne Sta., Brooklyn, NY 11219 Tel 212-435-0500.
Hastings, *(Hastings House Pubs., Inc.; 0-8038),* 10 E. 40th St., New York, NY 10016 Tel 212-689-5400.
Havertown Bks, *(Havertown Books),* P.O. Box 711, Havertown, PA 19083.
Hawthorn, *(Hawthorn Books, Inc.; 0-8015),* 260 Madison Ave., New York, NY 10016 Tel 212-725-7740; Orders to: E. P. Dutton, 2 Park Ave., New York, NY 10016 Tel 212-725-1818.
HC *Imprint of* **HarBraceJ**
Heath, *(Heath, D. C., Co., Elhi Dept.; 0-669),* Div. of Raytheon Co., 125 Spring St., Lexington, MA 02173 Tel 617-862-6650; Orders to: D. C. Heath & Co., Distribution Center, 2700 Richardt Ave., Indianapolis, IN 46219 Tel 317-359-5585.
Hebrew Pub, *(Hebrew Publishing Co.; 0-88482),* 80 Fifth Ave., New York, NY 10011 Tel 212-675-3878.

Heidelberg Pubs, *(Heidelberg Pubs., Inc.; 0-913206),* 1003 Brown Bldg., Austin, TX 78701.
Heineman, *(Heineman, James H., Inc., Pub.; 0-87008),* 475 Park Ave., New York, NY 10022 Tel 212-688-2028.
Heinemann Ed, *(Heinemann Educational Books Inc.; 0-435),* 4 Front St., Exeter, NH 03833 Tel 603-778-0534.
Hendricks House, *(Hendricks House, Inc.; 0-87532),* 488 Greenwich St., New York, NY 10013 Tel 212-966-1765.
Hennessey, *(Hennessey & Ingalls, Inc.; 0-912158),* 10814 W. Pico Blvd., Los Angeles, CA 90064 Tel 213-474-2541.
Herald Hse, *(Herald House; 0-8309),* Drawer HH, 3225 S. Noland Rd., Independence, MO 64055 Tel 816-252-5010.
Herald Pr, *(Herald Press; 0-8361),* 616 Walnut Ave., Scottdale, PA 15683 Tel 412-887-8500.
Heritage Bk, *(Heritage Books, Inc.; 0-917890),* 3602 Maureen Lane, Bowie, MD 20715 Tel 301-464-1159.
Hermon, *(Sepher-Hermon Press, Inc.; 0-87203),* 175 Fifth Ave., New York, NY 10010 Tel 212-777-4530.
Herndon Hse, *(Herndon House; 0-915542),* P.O. Box 353, Brooklyn, NY 11230.
Herzl Pr, *(Herzl Press; 0-930832),* 515 Park Ave., New York, NY 10022 Tel 212-752-0600.
Highlander, *(Highlander Research & Education Center; 0-9602226),* Box 32313, Washington, DC 20007.
Hill & Wang, *(Hill & Wang, Inc.; 0-8090),* Div. of Farrar, Straus & Giroux, Inc., 19 Union Square, New York, NY 10003 Tel 212-741-6900. *Imprints:* AmCen (American Century Series).
Hill Jr Coll, *(Hill Junior College Press; 0-912172),* P.O. Box 619, Hillsboro, TX 76645 Tel 817-582-2555.
Hill Pubns, *(Hill Pubns.; 0-9602704),* 4974 Cedar Ridge N.E., Grand Rapids, MI 49505.
Hippocrene Bks, *(Hippocrene Books, Inc.; 0-88254),* 171 Madison Ave., New York, NY 10016 Tel 212-685-4372.
Hired Hand, *(Hired Hand Press; 0-9602256),* P.O. Box 426, Dover, MA 02030 Tel 617-325-8155.
Hispanic Soc, *(Hispanic Society of America; 0-87535),* 613 W. 155th St., New York, NY 10032 Tel 212-926-2234.
HM, *(Houghton Mifflin Co.; 0-395),* 2 Park St., Boston, MA 02107 Tel 617-725-5000; Orders to: Wayside Road, Burlington, MA 01803 Tel 617-272-1500. *Imprints:* Clarion (Clarion Books); Piper (Piper Books); RivEd (Riverside Editions); RivSL (Riverside Studies in Literature); SenEd (Sentry Editions).
Holiday, *(Holiday House, Inc.; 0-8234),* 18 E. 53rd St., New York, NY 10022 Tel 212-688-0085.
Holloway, *(Holloway House Publishing Co.; 0-87067),* 8060 Melrose Ave., Los Angeles, CA 90046 Tel 213-653-8060.
Holman, *(Holman, A.J., Co.; 0-87981),* 127 Ninth Ave., N., Nashville, TN 37234 Tel 615-251-2611.
Holmes, *(Holmes Book Co.; 0-910740),* 274 14th St., Oakland, CA 94612 Tel 415-893-6860.
Holmes & Meier, *(Holmes & Meier Pubs., Inc.; 0-8419),* IUB Bldg., 30 Irving Place, New York, NY 10003 Tel 212-254-4100. *Imprints:* Africana (Africana Pub.).
Holt-Atherton, *(Holt-Atherton Pacific Center for Western Studies; 0-931156),* Univ. of the Pacific, Stockton, CA 95211.
HoltC *Imprint of* **HR&W**
Holy Cross Orthodox, *(Holy Cross Orthodox Press; 0-916586),* 50 Goddard Ave., Brookline, MA 02146 Tel 617-232-4544.
Honor Bks, *(Honor Books; 0-931446),* P.O. Box 94, Spearfish, SD 57783 Tel 605-642-3516.
Hoover Inst Pr, *(Hoover Institution Press; 0-8179),* Stanford University, Stanford, CA 94305 Tel 415-497-3373.
Hope Farm, *(Hope Farm Press & Bookshop; 0-910746),* Strong Rd., Cornwallville, NY 12418 Tel 518-239-4745.
Horizon, *(Horizon Press Pubs.; 0-8180),* 156 Fifth Ave., New York, NY 10010 Tel 212-924-9225.
Horizon Utah, *(Horizon Publishers & Distributors; 0-88290),* P.O. Box 490, 50 S. 500 West, Bountiful, UT 84010 Tel 801-295-9451.
Howard U Pr, *(Howard Univ. Press; 0-88258),* 2900 Van Ness St., N.W., Washington, DC 20008 Tel 202-686-6696.
Howell-North
See Howell North
Howell North, *(Howell North Pubs., Inc.; 0-8310),* Subs. of Leisure Dynamics, Inc., 11175 Flintkote Ave., Suite C, San Diego, CA 92121 Tel 714-452-8676.
HPL *Imprint of* **HarBraceJ**
HR&W, *(Holt, Rinehart & Winston, Inc.; 0-03),* 383 Madison Ave., New York, NY 10017 Tel 212-688-9100. *Imprints:* HoltC (Holt College Department).
Humanities, *(Humanities Press, Inc.; 0-391),* Atlantic Highlands, NJ 07716 Tel 201-872-1441. *Imprints:* Athlone Pr (Athlone Press); Dolmen Pr (Dolmen Press); Leicester (Leicester Univ. Press).
Hunt Inst Botanical, *(Hunt Institute for Botanical Documentation; 0-913196),* Carnegie-Mellon Univ., Pittsburgh, PA 15213 Tel 412-578-2434.
Hunter Bks, *(Hunter Books; 0-917726),* 1602 Townhurst, Houston, TX 77043 Tel 713-461-6800.
Hunter Ministries
See Hunter Bks
Huntington Lib, *(Huntington Library Pubns.; 0-87328),* 1151 Oxford Rd., San Marino, CA 91108 Tel 213-792-6141.
Hyperion Conn, *(Hyperion Press, Inc.; 0-88355; 0-8305),* 45 Riverside Ave., Westport, CT 06880 Tel 203-226-1091.
IHS-Library & Educ Div
See IHS-PDS
IHS-PDS, *(Information Handling Services/PDS Hard Copy Publishing; 0-910972; 0-89847),* 15 Inverness Way E., P.O. Box 1154, Englewood, CO 80150 Tel 303-779-0600.
Ill St Hist Soc, *(Illinois State Historical Society; 0-912226),* Old State Capitol, Springfield, IL 62706 Tel 217-782-4836.
Im *Imprint of* **Doubleday**
Impact Tenn, *(Impact Books; 0-914850),* Div. of the Benson Co., 365 Great Circle Rd., Nashville, TN 37228 Tel 615-259-9111.
Ind U Pr, *(Indiana Univ. Press; 0-253),* Tenth & Morton Sts., Bloomington, IN 47405 Tel 812-337-6804.
Info Coord, *(Information Coordinators, Inc.; 0-911772; 0-89990),* 1435-37 Randolph St., Detroit, MI 48226.
Insight Pr, *(Insight Press, Inc.; 0-914520),* P.O. Box 8369, New Orleans, LA 70182.
Instrumental Co, *(Instrumentalist Co.),* 1418 Lake St., Evanston, IL 60204 Tel 312-328-6000.
Inter Am U Pr, *(Inter American Univ. Press; 0-913480),* G.P.O. Box 3255, San Juan, PR 00936 Tel 809-763-9622.
Inter-Varsity, *(Inter-Varsity Press; 0-87784; 0-8308),* P.O. Box F, Downers Grove, IL 60515 Tel 312-964-5700.
InterCulture, *(InterCulture Associates; 0-88253; 0-89253),* Quaddick Rd., P.O. Box 277, Thompson, CT 06277 Tel 203-923-9494.
Interface Calif, *(Interface California Corp.; 0-915580),* 106 T St., P.O. Box 3611, Eureka, CA 95501 Tel 707-442-8112; Dist. by: Stein & Day Pubs., Scarborough House, Briarcliff Manor, NY 10510 Tel 914-762-2151.
Intl Bk Dist, *(International Book Distributors),* P.O. Box 180, Murray Hill Sta., New York, NY 10016.
Intl Marine, *(International Marine Publishing Co.; 0-87742),* 21 Elm St., Camden, ME 04843 Tel 207-236-4342.
Intl Pub Co, *(International Pubs. Co.; 0-7178),* 381 Park Ave., S., Suite 1301, New York, NY 10016 Tel 212-685-2864.
Intl Pubns Serv, *(International Pubns. Service; 0-8002),* 114 E. 32nd St., New York, NY 10016 Tel 212-685-9351.
Intl Univs Pr, *(International Universities Press, Inc.; 0-8236),* 315 Fifth Ave., New York, NY 10016 Tel 212-684-7900.
Iowa St U Pr, *(Iowa State Univ. Press; 0-8138),* South State Ave., 112 C Press Office, Ames, IA 50010 Tel 515-294-5280.
Irish Bk Ctr, *(Irish Book Center),* 245 W. 104th St., New York, NY 10025 Tel 212-866-0309.
Iroquois Hse, *(Iroquois House, Pubs.; 0-931980),* Box 15, Sunspot, NM 88349 Tel 505-437-2807.
Irvington, *(Irvington Pubs.; 0-89197),* 551 Fifth Ave., New York, NY 10017 Tel 212-697-8100.
Irwinton, *(Irwinton Pubs.),* 9685 Anderson Rd., Mercersburg, PA 17236.
Island Pr, *(Island Press; 0-87208),* 175 Bahia Via, Fort Myers Beach, FL 33931 Tel 813-463-9482.
J A White, *(White, John A.; 0-9603242),* 1200 Toyon Dr, Millbrae, CA 94030 Tel 415-697-1187.
J B Wilson, *(Wilson, J.B., Press, Inc.; 0-933458),* 1730 Columbia Dr. E., Fresno, CA 93727 Tel 209-251-8751.
J P Tarcher, *(Tarcher, J. P., Inc.; 0-87477),* 9110 Sunset Blvd., Suite 250, Los Angeles, CA 90069 Tel 213-273-3274; Dist. by: St. Martin's Press, Inc., 175 5th Ave, New York, NY 10010 Tel 212-674-5151.
JD-J *Imprint of* **Elsevier**
Jenkins, *(Jenkins Publishing Co.; 0-8363),* P.O. Box 2085, Austin, TX 78767 Tel 512-444-6616.
Jesuit Hist, *(Jesuit Historical Institute),* c/o Loyola Univ. Press, 3441 N. Ashland Ave., Chicago, IL 60657.
Jewelers Circular, *(Jewelers' Circular Keystone; 0-931744),* Chilton Way, Radnor, PA 19089 Tel 215-687-8200.
Jewish Pubn, *(Jewish Publication Society of America; 0-8276),* 117 S. 17th St., Philadelphia, PA 19103 Tel 215-564-5925.
JD-J John Day Juvenile **Books**
John Knox, *(John Knox Press; 0-8042),* 341 Ponce De Leon Ave., N.E., Rm. 416, Atlanta, GA 30308 Tel 404-873-1531.
Johnny Reads, *(Johnny Reads, Inc.; 0-910812),* P.O. Box 12834, St. Petersburg, FL 33733 Tel 813-867-7647.
Johns Hopkins, *(Johns Hopkins Univ. Press; 0-8018),* Baltimore, MD 21218 Tel 301-338-7832.
Johnson Chi, *(Johnson Publishing Co., Inc.; 0-87485),* 820 S. Michigan Ave., Chicago, IL 60605 Tel 312-786-7657.
Johnson Colo, *(Johnson Publishing Co.; 0-933472),* P.O. Box 990, 1880 S. 57th Court, Boulder, CO 80301 Tel 303-443-1576.
Johnson Repr, *(Johnson Reprint Corp.; 0-384),* Subs. of Harcourt, Brace & Jovanovich, Inc., 111 Fifth Ave., New York, NY 10003 Tel 212-741-6800.
Jonathan David, *(Jonathan David Pubs., Inc.; 0-8246),* 68-22 Eliot Ave., Middle Village, NY 11379 Tel 212-456-8611.
Jove *Imprint of* **Shoe String**
Joyce Pr, *(Joyce Press Inc.; 0-89325),* 7341 Clairemont Mesa Blvd., San Diego, CA 92111 Tel 714-565-6133.
Judson, *(Judson Press; 0-8170),* Valley Forge, PA 19481 Tel 215-768-2111.
Juniper Maine, *(Juniper Press),* c/o Betts Bookstore, Sunbury Mall, Bangor, ME 04401.
Juveniles *Imprint of* **S&S**
Karz Howard
See Karz Pub
Karz Pub, *(Karz Pubs.; 0-918294),* 320 W. 105th St., New York, NY 10025 Tel 212-663-9059.
Keats, *(Keats Publishing, Inc.; 0-87983),* 36 Grove St., P.O. Box 876, New Canaan, CT 06840 Tel 203-966-8721.
Kelley, *(Kelley, Augustus M., Pubs.; 0-678),* 1140 Broadway, Room 901, New York, NY 10001; Orders to: 300 Fairfield Rd., P.O. Box 1308, Fairfield, NJ 07006 Tel 201-575-7338.
Kendall-Hunt, *(Kendall/Hunt Publishing Co.; 0-8403),* 2460 Kerper Blvd., Dubuque, IA 52001 Tel 319-588-1451.
Kenedy, *(Kenedy, P. J., & Sons),* Subs. of Macmillan Publishing Co., 866 Third Ave., New York, NY 10022 Tel 212-935-2000; Orders to: Macmillan Co., Riverside, NJ 08075.
Kennikat, *(Kennikat Press, Corp.; 0-8046),* 90 S. Bayles Ave., Port Washington, NY 11050 Tel 516-883-0570.
Kent St U Pr, *(Kent State Univ. Press; 0-87338),* Kent, OH 44242 Tel 216-672-7913.
Kirban, *(Kirban, Salem, Inc.; 0-912582),* 2117 Kent Rd., Huntingdon Valley, PA 19000 Tel 215-947-1330.

Kluwer Boston, *(Kluwer Boston, Inc.),* 160 Old Derby St., Hingham, MA 02043 Tel 617-749-5262.
Knopf, *(Knopf, Alfred A., Inc.; 0-394),* Subs. of Random House, Inc., 201 E. 50th St., New York, NY 10022 Tel 212-757-2600; Orders to: 400 Hahn Rd., Westminster, MD 21157.
Kodansha, *(Kodansha International, Ltd.; 0-87011),* 10 E. 53rd St., New York, NY 10022; Dist. by: Harper & Row Pubs., Inc., Keystone Industrial Park, Scranton, PA 18512.
Kosciuszko, *(Kosciuszko Foundation, Inc.; 0-917004),* 15 E. 65th St., New York, NY 10021 Tel 212-734-2130.
Kraus Intl, *(Kraus International; 0-527),* Div. of Kraus-Thomson Organization Ltd., Rte. 100, Millwood, NY 10546 Tel 914-762-2200.
Kraus Repr, *(Kraus Reprint; 0-527),* U.S. Div. of Kraus-Thomson Organization, Ltd., Rte. 100, Millwood, NY 10546 Tel 914-762-2200.
Kregel, *(Kregel Pubns.; 0-8254),* P.O. Box 2607, Grand Rapids, MI 49501 Tel 616-459-9444.
Krieger, *(Krieger, Robert E., Pub. Co., Inc.; 0-88275; 0-89874),* 645 New York Ave., Huntington, NY 11743 Tel 516-271-5252.
Krohn & Assocs, *(Krohn, Barbara, & Assocs.),* 835 Securities Bldg., Seattle, WA 98101 Tel 206-622-3538.
Ktav, *(Ktav Publishing House, Inc.; 0-87068),* 75 Varick St., New York, NY 10013 Tel 212-966-6980.
KTO Pr
See Kraus Intl
L Amiel Pub, *(Amiel, Leon, Pub.; 0-8148),* 31 W. 46th St., New York, NY 10036 Tel 212-575-0010.
L C Bryant, *(Bryant, Lawrence C.),* Rte. 1, Box 1069-C, Orangeburg, SC 29115 Tel 803-536-1305.
La State U Pr, *(Louisiana State Univ. Press; 0-8071),* Baton Rouge, LA 70803 Tel 504-388-2071.
Lame Johnny, *(Lame Johnny Press; 0-917624),* P.O. Box 66, Hermosa, SD 57744 Tel 605-255-4228.
Landfall Pr, *(Landfall Press, Inc.; 0-913428),* 20 W. Stroop Rd., Dayton, OH 45429 Tel 513-298-9123.
Large Print Bks *Imprint of* **G K Hall**
Larlin Corp, *(Larlin Corp.; 0-910220; 0-89783),* P.O. Box 1523, Marietta, GA 30061 Tel 404-424-6210.
Lawrence Hill, *(Hill, Lawrence, & Co., Inc.; 0-88208),* 520 Riverside Ave., Westport, CT 06880 Tel 203-226-9392.
LE *Imprint of* **Dell**
Lea & Febiger, *(Lea & Febiger; 0-8121),* 600 S. Washington Square, Philadelphia, PA 19106 Tel 215-922-1330.
Learned Pubns, *(Learned Pubns., Inc.; 0-912116),* 83-53 Manton St., Jamaica, NY 11435 Tel 212-441-8084.
Legacy Pub Co, *(Legacy Pub. Co.; 0-918784),* 2008 Perkins Rd., Baton Rouge, LA 70808 Tel 504-343-0366.
Leicester *Imprint of* **Humanities**
Lemma, *(Lemma Publishing Corp.; 0-87696),* 509 Fifth Ave., New York, NY 10017.
Lerner Bks
See Lerner Pubns
Lerner Pubns, *(Lerner Publications Co.; 0-8225),* 241 First Ave., N., Minneapolis, MN 55401 Tel 612-332-3344.
Les Femmes Pub, *(Les Femmes Publishing; 0-89087),* 231 Adrian Rd., Millbrae, CA 94030 Tel 415-692-4500.
LFL *Imprint of* **Dell**
Lib Res, *(Library Research Associates; 0-912526),* Dunderberg Rd., R.D. 5, Box 41, Monroe, NY 10950 Tel 914-783-1144.
Lib Serv Inc, *(Library Services Inc.),* Box 711, Havertown, PA 19083.
Lib Soc Sci, *(Library of Social Science; 0-915042),* 475 Amsterdam Ave., New York, NY 10024 Tel 212-874-6718.
Liberty Fund, *(Liberty Fund, Inc.; 0-913966),* 7440 North Shadeland Ave., Indianapolis, IN 46250 Tel 317-842-0880.
Libra, *(Libra Pubs., Inc.; 0-87212),* 391 Willets Rd., Roslyn Heights, L. I., NY 11577 Tel 516-484-4950.
Libs Unl, *(Libraries Unlimited, Inc.; 0-87287),* P.O. Box 263, Littleton, CO 80160 Tel 303-770-1220.
Light & Life, *(Light & Life Press; 0-89367),* 999 College Ave., Winona Lake, IN 46590.
Liguori Pubns, *(Liguori Pubns.; 0-89243),* 1 Liguori Dr., Liguori, MO 63057 Tel 314-464-2500.
Lion, *(Lion Press; 0-87460),* Dist. by: Sayre Publishing, Inc., 111 E. 39th St., New York, NY 10016.
Lippincott, *(Lippincott, J. B., Co.; 0-397),* 10 E. 53rd St., New York, NY 10022 Tel 212-593-7213; Orders to: Harper & Row, Publishers, Inc., Keystone Industrial Park, Scranton, PA 18512 Tel 717-343-4761.
Little, *(Little, Brown & Co.; 0-316),* 34 Beacon St., Boston, MA 02106 Tel 617-227-0730; Orders to: 200 West St., Waltham, MA 02154.
Little Brick Hse, *(Little Brick House, The; 0-9601648),* 621 Saint Clair St., Vandalia, IL 62471 Tel 618-283-0024.
Littlefield, *(Littlefield, Adams & Co.; 0-8226),* 81 Adams Dr., Box 327, Totowa, NJ 07511 Tel 201-256-8600.
Liveright, *(Liveright Publishing Corp.; 0-87140),* Subs. of W. W. Norton Co., Inc., 500 Fifth Ave., New York, NY 10036 Tel 212-354-5500.
Locare, *(Locare Research Group; 0-913986),* 910 N. Fairfax Ave., Los Angeles, CA 90046 Tel 213-656-4420.
Lochinvar *Imprint of* **Exposition**
Logos, *(Logos International; 0-912106; 0-88270),* 201 Church St., Plainfield, NJ 07060.
Longman, *(Longman Inc.),* 19 W. 44th St., Suite 1012, New York, NY 10036 Tel 212-764-3950.
Longwood Pr, *(Longwood Press, Ltd.; 0-89341),* P.O. Box 101, Kennebunkport, ME 04046 Tel 207-646-5913.
Lothrop, *(Lothrop, Lee & Shepard Books; 0-688),* Div. of William Morrow & Co., Inc., 105 Madison Ave., New York, NY 10016 Tel 212-889-3050; Orders to: William Morrow & Co., Inc., Wilmor Warehouse, 6 Henderson Dr., West Caldwell, NJ 07006.
Lowell Pr, *(Lowell Press; 0-913504),* 115 E. 31st St., Box 1877, Kansas City, MO 64141 Tel 816-753-4545.
Loyola, *(Loyola Univ. Press; 0-8294),* 3441 N. Ashland Ave., Chicago, IL 60657 Tel 312-281-1818.
Luce, *(Luce, Robert B., Inc.; 0-88331),* 6919 Radnor Rd., Bethesda, MD 20034 Tel 301-320-3327; Dist. by: David McKay Co., Inc, 2 Park Ave., New York, NY 10016 Tel 212-340-9800.
Lyle Stuart, *(Stuart, Lyle, Inc.; 0-8184),* 120 Enterprise Ave., Secaucus, NJ 07094 Tel 201-866-0490.
M Evans, *(Evans, M., & Co., Inc.; 0-87131),* 216 E. 49th St., New York, NY 10017 Tel 212-688-2810; Dist. by: E. P. Dutton, 2 Park Ave., New York, NY 10016.
M Jones, *(Jones,, Marshall,, Co.; 0-8338),* Div. of Golden Quill Press, Francestown, NH 03043.
M R K, *(M-R-K Publishing; 0-9601292),* 448 Seavey Lane, Petaluma, CA 94952 Tel 707-763-0056.
McClain, *(McClain Printing Co.; 0-87012),* 212 Main St., Parsons, WV 26287 Tel 304-478-2881.
McClelland, *(McClelland & Stewart, Ltd.),* 25 Hollinger Rd., Toronto, Ontario, M4B 3G2, Tel 416-751-4520.
McElderry Bk *Imprint of* **Atheneum**
McGill-Queens U Pr, *(McGill-Queens Univ. Press; 0-7735),* 1020 Pine Ave., W., Montreal, Canada H3A 1A2, Tel 514-392-4421; Orders to: University of Toronto Press, 33 E. Tupper St., Buffalo, NY 14203.
McGraw, *(McGraw-Hill Book Co.; 0-07),* 1221 Ave. of the Americas, New York, NY 10020 Tel 212-997-1221.
McKay, *(McKay, David, Co., Inc.; 0-679),* 2 Park Ave., New York, NY 10016 Tel 212-340-9800. *Imprints:* Charterhouse (Charterhouse Books, Inc.).
Macmillan, *(Macmillan Publishing Co., Inc.; 0-02),* 866 Third Ave., New York, NY 10022 Tel 212-935-2000; Orders to: Front & Brown Sts., Riverside, NJ 08370. *Imprints:* CCPr (Crowell-Collier Press); Collier (Collier Books).
McNally, *(McNally & Loftin, Pubs.; 0-87461),* P.O. Box 1316, Santa Barbara, CA 93102 Tel 805-964-5117.
Macoy Pub, *(Macoy Publishing & Masonic Supply Co., Inc.; 0-910928),* P.O. Box 9759, Richmond, VA 23228 Tel 804-262-6551.
Macrae, *(Macrae Smith Co.; 0-8255),* Rtes. 54 & Old 147, Turbotville, PA 17772.
Madrona Pr, *(Madrona Press, Inc.; 0-89052),* P.O. Box 3750, Austin, TX 78764 Tel 512-327-2683.
Magi Bks, *(Magi Books, Inc.; 0-87343),* 33 Buckingham Dr., Albany, NY 12208 Tel 518-482-7781.
Maine Antique, *(Maine Antique Digest, Inc.; 0-917312),* P.O. Box 358, Waldoboro, ME 04572 Tel 207-832-7534.
Maine Hist, *(Maine Historical Society; 0-915592),* 485 Congress St., Portland, ME 04111 Tel 207-774-1822.
Malki Mus Pr, *(Malki Museum Press),* c/o Malki Museum, Inc., 11-795 Fields Rd., Morongo Indian Reservation, Banning, CA 92220 Tel 714-849-7289.
Manor Bks, *(Manor Books, Inc.; 0-532),* 45 E. 30th St., New York, NY 10016 Tel 212-686-9100.
Marquette, *(Marquette Univ. Press; 0-87462),* 1324 W. Wisconsin Ave., Rm. 409, Milwaukee, WI 53233 Tel 414-224-1564.
Marquis, *(Marquis Who's Who, Inc.; 0-8379),* 200 E. Ohio St., Chicago, IL 60611 Tel 312-787-2008; Orders to: 4300 W. 62nd St., Indianapolis, IN 46206 Tel 317-298-5400.
Mason Charter
See Van Nos Reinhold
Mass Hist Soc, *(Massachusetts Historical Society),* 1154 Boylston St., Boston, MA 02215 Tel 617-536-1608.
Mayflower Bks, *(Mayflower Books, Inc.; 0-8317),* 575 Lexington Ave., New York, NY 10022 Tel 212-888-9200.
Meckler Bks, *(Meckler Books; 0-930466),* 520 Riverside Ave., P.O. Box 405, Saugatuck Sta., Westport, CT 06880 Tel 203-226-6967.
Medallion *Imprint of* **Berkley Pub**
Mediaeval Acad, *(Mediaeval Academy of America; 0-910956),* 1430 Massachusetts Ave., Cambridge, MA 02138 Tel 617-491-1622.
Memphis St Univ, *(Memphis State Univ. Press; 0-87870),* Memphis State Univ., Memphis, TN 38152 Tel 901-454-2752.
Ment *Imprint of* **NAL**
Mer *Imprint of* **NAL**
Mercer Hse, *(Mercer House Press; 0-89080),* Clover Leaf Farm, Old Rte. 9, Kennebunkport, ME 04046 Tel 207-282-7116; Orders to: P.O. Box 681, Kennebunkport, ME 04046.
Merriam, *(Merriam, G. & C., Co.; 0-87779),* Subs. of Encyclopaedia Britannica, Inc., 47 Federal St., Springfield, MA 01101 Tel 413-734-3134.
Merrill, *(Merrill, Charles E., Publishing Co.; 0-675),* Div. of Bell & Howell Co., 1300 Alum Creek Dr., Columbus, OH 43216 Tel 614-258-8441.
Messner, *(Messner, Julian; 0-671),* A Simon & Schuster Div. of Gulf & Western Corp., 1230 Ave. of the Americas, New York, NY 10020 Tel 212-245-6400.
Meth U Pr
See SMU Press
Methuen Inc, *(Methuen Inc.; 0-416),* 733 Third Ave, New York, NY 10017 Tel 212-922-3550; Dist. by: Transworld Distribution Services, Inc., 80 Northfield Ave., Raritan Center, Edison, NJ 08817.
Metro Bks, *(Metro Books, Inc.; 0-8411),* 3110 N. Arlington Heights Rd., Arlington Heights, IL 60004 Tel 312-253-9720.
Mich Slavic Pubns, *(Michigan Slavic Pubns; 0-930042),* Dept. of Slavic Languages & Literatures, Univ. of Michigan, Ann Arbor, MI 48109 Tel 313-763-4496.
Mich St U Busn, *(Michigan State Univ., Div. of Research, Grad. School of Business Administration; 0-87744),* 5J Berkey Hall, East Lansing, MI 48824 Tel 517-355-7560.
Mich St U Pr, *(Michigan State Univ. Press; 0-87013),* 1405 S. Harrison Rd., 25 Manly Miles Bldg., East Lansing, MI 48824 Tel 517-355-9543.
Military Aff Aero, *(Military Affairs/Aerospace Historian; 0-89126),* Eisenhower Hall, Kansas State University, Manhattan, KS 66506 Tel 913-532-6733.

Minn Hist, *(Minnesota Historical Society; 0-87351),* 690 Cedar St., St. Paul, MN 55101 Tel 612-296-2264; Orders to: 1500 Mississippi St., St. Paul, MN 55101.
MIT Pr, *(MIT Press; 0-262),* 28 Carleton St., Cambridge, MA 02142 Tel 617-253-2884.
Mnemosyne, *(Mnemosyne Publishing Co., Inc.),* 410 Alcazar Ave., Coral Gables, FL 33134 Tel 305-444-8908.
Mod LibC *Imprint of* **Modern Lib**
Modern Lib, *(Modern Library, Inc.),* 201 E. 50th St., New York, NY 10022 Tel 212-751-2600; Orders to: Order Dept., 400 Hahn Rd., Westminster, MD 21157. *Imprints:* Mod LibC (Modern Library College Department).
Monad Pr, *(Monad Press; 0-913460),* 410 West St., New York, NY 10014 Tel 212-989-3212; Dist. by: Pathfinder Press, 410 West St., New York, NY 10014 Tel 212-741-0690.
Monitor, *(Monitor Book Co., Inc.; 0-9600252),* 195 S. Beverly Dr., Beverly Hills, CA 90212 Tel 213-271-5558.
Monthly Rev, *(Monthly Review Press; 0-85345),* 62 W. 14th St., New York, NY 10011 Tel 212-691-2555.
Moody, *(Moody Press; 0-8024),* 2101 Howard St., Evanston, IL 60645 Tel 312-329-4343; Orders to: 1777 Shermer Rd., Northbrook, IL 60062.
Moore Pub Co, *(Moore Publishing Co.; 0-87716),* P.O. Box 3036, W. Durham Sta., Durham, NC 27705 Tel 919-286-2250.
Morehouse, *(Morehouse-Barlow Co.; 0-8192),* 78 Danbury Rd., Wilton, CT 06897 Tel 203-762-0721.
Morgan, *(Morgan & Morgan, Inc.; 0-87100),* 145 Palisades St., Dobbs Ferry, NY 10522 Tel 914-693-9303.
Morrow, *(Morrow, William, & Co., Inc.; 0-688),* 105 Madison Ave., New York, NY 10016 Tel 212-889-3050; Orders to: Wilmor Warehouse, 6 Henderson Dr., West Caldwell, NJ 07006.
Mosby, *(Mosby, C. V., Co.; 0-8016),* 11830 Westline Industrial Dr., St. Louis, MO 63141 Tel 314-872-8370.
Motorbooks Intl, *(Motorbooks International, Pubs. & Wholesalers, Inc.; 0-87938),* P.O. Box 2, 729 Prospect Ave, Osceola, WI 54020 Tel 800-826-6600.
Mott Media, *(Mott Media; 0-915134),* 305 Caroline, Milford, MI 48042 Tel 313-685-8773.
Mountain Pr, *(Mountain Press Publishing Co., Inc.; 0-87842),* P.O. Box 2399, Missoula, MT 59806 Tel 406-728-1900.
Mountaineers, *(Mountaineers-Books; 0-916890; 0-89886),* 719-B Pike St., Seattle, WA 98101 Tel 206-682-4636.
Mouton, *(Mouton Pubs.),* Div. of Walter De Gruyter, Inc., 200 Saw Mill River Rd., Hawthorne, NY 10532 Tel 914-747-0111.
MSP *Imprint of* **G&D**
Mss Info, *(Mss Information Corp.; 0-8422),* P.O. Box 985, Edison, NJ 08817 Tel 201-225-1900.
Multinational Media, *(Multinational Media; 0-917112),* 228 Burlwood Dr., Scotts Valley, CA 95066 Tel 408-438-0253.
Multnomah, *(Multnomah Press; 0-930014),* 10209 S.E. Division St., Portland, OR 97266 Tel 503-257-0526.
Museum Mod Art, *(Museum of Modern Art; 0-87070),* 11 W. 53rd St., New York, NY 10019 Tel 212-956-7216; Orders to: Customer Sales Service, 11 W. 53rd St., New York, NY 10019 Tel 212-956-7264.
Music Sales, *(Music Sales Corp.; 0-8256),* Dist. by: Quick Fox, Inc., 33 W. 60th St., New York, NY 10023 Tel 212-246-0325. *Imprints:* Flash Bks (Flash Books); Quick Fox (Quick Fox).
N Ill U Pr, *(Northern Illinois Univ. Press; 0-87580),* 515 Garden Rd., DeKalb, IL 60115 Tel 815-753-1826.
N Watson, *(Neale Watson Academic Pubns. Inc.; 0-88202),* 156 Fifth Ave., Suite 1100, New York, NY 10010 Tel 212-675-7480.
NAL, *(New American Library; 0-451; 0-452; 0-453),* 1633 Broadway, New York, NY 10019 Tel 212-397-8000; Orders to: 120 Woodbine St., Bergenfield, NJ 07621 Tel 201-387-0600. *Imprints:* Ment (Mentor Books); Mer (Meridian Books); Plume (Plume Books); Sig (Signet Books); Sig Classics (Signet Classics).
Natl Christian Pr, *(National Christian Press, Inc.; 0-934916),* P.O. Box 280, Algood, TN 38501 Tel 615-537-9434.
Natl Gallery Art, *(National Gallery of Art; 0-89468),* Sixth St. & Constitution Ave., N.W., Washington, DC 20565 Tel 202-737-4215.
Natl Geog, *(National Geographic Society; 0-87044),* 17th & "M" Sts., N.W., Washington, DC 20036 Tel 202-857-7000.
Natl Poet-Univ Me, *(National Poetry Foundation, Inc. & Univ. of Maine Press; 0-915032),* Univ. of Maine, 303 English/Math Bldg, Orono, ME 04473; c/o C. F. Terrell, Natl Poetry, 305 EM UMO, Orano, ME 04469.
Natural Sci Youth, *(Natural Science for Youth Foundation; 0-916544),* 763 Silvermine Rd., New Canaan, CT 06840 Tel 203-966-5643.
Navajo Coll Pr, *(Navajo Community College Press; 0-912586),* 408 E. Loma Vista Dr., Tempe, AZ 85282 Tel 602-967-2333.
Navajo Curr, *(Navajo Curriculum Center Press; 0-936008),* Rough Rock Demonstration School, Star Rte. 1, Rough Rock, AZ 86503.
Naval Inst Pr, *(Naval Institute Press; 0-87021),* Annapolis, MD 21402 Tel 301-268-6110.
NC Archives, *(North Carolina Division of Archives & History; 0-86526),* 109 E. Jones St., Raleigh, NC 27611 Tel 919-733-7442.
NCTM, *(National Council of Teachers of Mathematics; 0-87353),* 1906 Association Dr., Reston, VA 22091 Tel 703-620-9840.
NE Conf Teach Foreign, *(Northeast Conference on the Teaching of Foreign Languages; 0-915432),* P.O. Box 623, Middlebury, VT 05753 Tel 802-388-7973.
NE Outdoors, *(Northeast Outdoors, Inc.; 0-936216),* P.O. Box 2180, Waterbury, CT 06722.
Negro U Pr, *(Negro Universities Press; 0-8371),* Affiliate of Greenwood Press, Inc., 51 Riverside Ave., Westport, CT 06880 Tel 203-226-3571.
Nelson, *(Nelson, Thomas, Inc.; 0-8407),* P.O. Box 946, 407 Seventh Ave. S., Nashville, TN 37203 Tel 800-251-1236.
Nelson-Hall, *(Nelson-Hall Inc.; 0-911012; 0-88229; 0-8304),* 111 N. Canal St., Chicago, IL 60606 Tel 312-930-9446.
Nevada Pubns, *(Nevada Pubns.; 0-913814),* P.O. Box 15444, Las Vegas, NV 89114 Tel 702-870-5660.
New Directions, *(New Directions Publishing Corp.; 0-8112),* 80 Eighth Ave., New York, NY 10011 Tel 212-255-0230; Dist. by: W. W. Norton Co., 500 Fifth Ave., New York, NY 10036.
New Eng Pub, *(New England Pub. Co.; 0-932268),* 200 Glendale Rd., Stratford, CT 06497 Tel 203-375-3252.
New Leaf, *(New Leaf Press; 0-89221),* P.O. Box 1045, Harrison, AR 72601 Tel 501-741-2514.
New Republic, *(New Republic Books; 0-915220),* 1220 19th St. N.W., Suite 205, Washington, DC 20036 Tel 202-331-1250; Dist. by: Simon & Schuster, 1230 Ave. of the Americas, New York, NY 10020.
New Viewpoints, *(New Viewpoints),* Affiliate of Franklin Watts, Inc., 730 Fifth Ave., New York, NY 10019 Tel 212-757-4050.
Newberry, *(Newberry Library; 0-911028),* 60 W. Walton St., Chicago, IL 60610 Tel 312-943-9090.
Newsweek, *(Newsweek; 0-88225),* 444 Madison Ave., New York, NY 10022 Tel 212-350-2528.
Nilgiri Pr, *(Nilgiri Press; 0-915132),* P.O. Box 477, Petaluma, CA 94952 Tel 707-878-2369; Name Formerly Sadhana Pr.
Noble
See Bowmar-Noble
Nordland Pub, *(Nordland Publishing Co.; 0-913124),* 85 Evergreen Way, Belmont, MA 02178 Tel 617-484-8857.
Nordon Pubns, *(Nordon Pubns, Inc; 0-8439),* 2 Park Ave., Suite 910, New York, NY 10016 Tel 212-679-7707; Orders to: Increased Sales Co., Inc., 327 Main Ave., Norwalk, CT 06852 Tel 203-846-2027; Dist. by: Wholesale: Kable, P.O. Box 270, Norwalk, CT 06852.
Nortex Pr, *(Nortex Press; 0-89015),* Div. of Nortex Offset Pubns., Inc., P.O. Box 120, Quanah, TX 79252 Tel 817-663-4333.
North Country, *(North Country Books, Inc.; 0-932052),* P.O. Box 506, Sylvan Beach, NY 13157 Tel 315-762-5140.
North Plains, *(North Plains Press; 0-87970),* P.O. Box 1950, Aberdeen, SD 57401.
North Star, *(North Star Press; 0-87839),* P.O. Box 451, St. Cloud, MN 56301 Tel 612-253-1636.
Northern Mich, *(Northern Michigan Univ. Press; 0-918616),* 607 Cohodas Administrative Center, Marquette, MI 49855 Tel 906-227-2720; Orders to: NMU Bookstore, Don H. Bottum University Center, Marquette, MI 49855.
Northland, *(Northland Press; 0-87358),* P.O. Box N, Flagstaff, AZ 86002 Tel 602-774-5251.
Northwestern U Pr, *(Northwestern Univ. Press; 0-8101),* 1735 Benson Ave., Evanston, IL 60201 Tel 312-492-5313.
Northwood Inst, *(Northwood Institute Press; 0-87359),* 3225 Cook St., Midland, MI 48640 Tel 517-631-1600.
Norton, *(Norton, W. W., & Co., Inc.; 0-393),* 500 Fifth Ave., New York, NY 10036 Tel 212-354-5500. *Imprints:* NortonC (Norton College Division).
NortonC *Imprint of* **Norton**
Norwood
See Norwood Edns
Norwood Edns, *(Norwood Editions; 0-88305; 0-8482),* P.O. Box 38, Norwood, PA 19074 Tel 215-583-4550.
NP Noyes Press C
NP *Imprint of* **Music Sales**
NY Labor News, *(New York Labor News; 0-935534),* 914 Industrial Ave., Palo Alto, CA 94303 Tel 415-494-1532.
NY Pub Lib, *(New York Public Library; 0-87104),* Fifth Ave. & 42nd St., New York, NY 10018 Tel 212-790-6285; Orders to: Readex Books, 101 Fifth Ave., New York, NY 10003; Ordering Address for NYPL Branch Libraries Imprint Only: Eight E. 40th St., N.Y., N.Y. 10016.
NY Zoetrope, *(New York Zoetrope; 0-918432),* 31 E. 12th St., New York, NY 10003 Tel 212-473-2729.
NYGS, *(New York Graphic Society, Ltd.; 0-8212),* 34 Beacon St., Boston, MA 02106 Tel 617-227-0730; Dist. by: Little, Brown & Co., 200 West St., Waltham, MA 02154.
NYU Pr, *(New York Univ. Press; 0-8147),* 113-15 University Place, New York, NY 10003 Tel 212-598-2886.
O W Frost, *(Frost, O.W.; 0-930766),* 2141 Lord Baranof Dr., Anchorage, AK 99503.
Occidental, *(Occidental Press; 0-911050),* P.O. Box 1005, Washington, DC 20013.
Oceana, *(Oceana Pubns.; 0-379),* 75 Main St., Dobbs Ferry, NY 10522 Tel 914-693-1320.
Octagon, *(Octagon Books; 0-374),* 19 Union Square W., New York, NY 10003 Tel 212-741-6961.
October, *(October House; 0-8079),* P.O. Box 454, Stonington, CT 06378 Tel 203-535-3725.
Odyssey Pr, *(Odyssey Press; 0-8399),* Dist. by: Bobbs-Merrill Co., Inc., 4300 W. 62nd St., Indianapolis, IN 46206 Tel 317-291-3100.
O'Hara, *(O'Hara, J. Philip, Inc., Pubs.; 0-87955),* c/o Book Trading Ltd., 559 W. 26th St., New York, NY 10001 Tel 212-695-8222.
Ohara Pubns, *(O'Hara Pubns., Inc.; 0-89750),* 1847 W. Empire Ave., Burbank, CA 91504 Tel 213-843-4444.
Ohio St U Pr, *(Ohio State Univ. Press; 0-8142),* Hitchcock Hall, Rm. 316, 2070 Neil Ave., Columbus, OH 43210 Tel 614-422-6930.
Ohio U Pr, *(Ohio Univ. Press; 0-8214),* Scott Quadrangle, Athens, OH 45701 Tel 614-594-5852.
Old Army, *(Old Army Press; 0-88342),* P.O. Box 2243, Fort Collins, CO 80521 Tel 303-484-5535.
Old West, *(Old West Publishing Co.; 0-912094),* 1228 E. Colfax Ave., Denver, CO 80218 Tel 303-832-7190.
Olive Pr Pubns, *(Olive Press Pubns.; 0-933380),* 1161 Shelley St., Manhattan Beach, CA 90266.
Olympus Pub Co, *(Olympus Publishing Co.; 0-913420),* 1670 E. Thirteenth S., Salt Lake City, UT 84105 Tel 801-583-3666.
OMF Bks, *(OMF Books),* 404 S. Church St., Robesonia, PA 19551.

Omni Pubs, *(Omni Pubs.; 0-89127),* 218 E. Grand Ave., No. 201, Escondido, CA 92025 Tel 714-746-5833.
Open Court, *(Open Court Publishing Co.; 0-87548; 0-89688),* Div. of Carus Corp., P.O. Box 599, LaSalle, IL 61301 Tel 815-223-2520.
Orbis Bks, *(Orbis Books; 0-88344),* Maryknoll, NY 10545 Tel 914-941-7590.
Oreg Hist Soc, *(Oregon Historical Society; 0-87595),* 1230 S.W. Park Ave., Portland, OR 97205 Tel 503-222-1741.
Oreg St U Pr, *(Oregon State Univ. Press; 0-87071),* 101 Waldo Hall, Oregon State University, Corvallis, OR 97331 Tel 503-754-3166.
Oriel *Imprint of* **Routledge & Kegan**
Oriole Edns, *(Oriole Editions; 0-88211),* 120 E. 81st St., New York, NY 10028 Tel 212-861-3102.
Osterhus, *(Osterhus Publishing House),* 4500 W. Broadway, Minneapolis, MN 55422 Tel 612-537-9311.
Our Sunday Visitor, *(Our Sunday Visitor, Inc.; 0-87973),* 200 Noll Plaza, Huntington, IN 46750 Tel 219-356-8400.
Outbooks, *(Outbooks; 0-89646),* Box 10688, Edgemont, Golden, CO 80401.
Overlook Pr, *(Overlook Press; 0-87951),* 667 Madison Ave., Suite 401A, New York, NY 10021; c/o Viking Press, 625 Madison Ave, New York, NY 10022 Tel 212-755-4330.
Oxford U Pr, *(Oxford Univ. Press, Inc.; 0-19),* 200 Madison Ave., New York, NY 10016 Tel 212-679-7300; Orders to: 16-00 Pollitt Dr., Fair Lawn, NJ 07410 Tel 201-796-8000; New York Accounts Use 212-564-6680. *Imprints:* GB (Galaxy Books).
Ozer, *(Ozer, Jerome S., Pub., Inc.; 0-89198),* 340 Tenafly Rd., Englewood, NJ 07631 Tel 201-567-7040.
P-H, *(Prentice-Hall, Inc.; 0-13),* Englewood Cliffs, NJ 07632 Tel 201-592-2000. *Imprints:* Reward (Reward Books); Spec (Spectrum Books).
Pa Hist Soc, *(Historical Society of Pennsylvania; 0-910732),* 1300 Locust St., Philadelphia, PA 19107 Tel 215-732-6200.
Pa St U Pr, *(Pennsylvania State Univ. Press; 0-271),* 215 Wagner Bldg., University Park, PA 16802 Tel 814-865-1320.
Pacesetter Pr, *(Pacesetter Press; 0-88415),* Div. of Gulf Publishing Co., P.O. Box 2608, Houston, TX 77001 Tel 713-529-4301.
Pacific Bks, *(Pacific Books, Pubs.; 0-87015),* P.O. Box 558, Palo Alto, CA 94302 Tel 415-856-0550.
Pacific Coast, *(Pacific Coast Pubs.; 0-87465),* 4085 Campbell Ave., Menlo Park, CA 94025.
Pacific Pr Pub Assn, *(Pacific Press Publishing Assn.; 0-8163),* 1350 Villa St., Mountain View, CA 94042 Tel 415-961-2323.
Paddington, *(Paddington Press, Ltd.; 0-448),* 95 Madison Ave, New York, NY 10016 Tel 212-689-4801; Orders to: Grosset & Dunlap, 51 Madison Ave., New York, NY 10010.
Padma, *(Padma Press; 0-917960),* P.O. Box 56, Oatman, AZ 86433.
Palisades Pub, *(Palisades Pubs.; 0-913530),* P.O. Box 744, Pacific Palisades, CA 90272 Tel 213-454-0826.
Palm Tree Lib, *(Palm Tree Library; 0-933266),* 233 S. Barrington Ave., Los Angeles, CA 90049.
Pan-Am Publishing Co, *(Pan-American Publishing Co.; 0-932906),* P.O. Box 1505, Las Vegas, NM 87701.
Panjandrum, *(Panjandrum Books; 0-915572),* 11321 Iowa Ave., Suite 1, Los Angeles, CA 90025 Tel 213-477-8771; Dist. by: Publisher's Group West, 5855 Beaudry, Emeryville, CA 94608 Tel 415-549-3033; Dist. by: Robert Rainer Assocs, 318 Happ Rd., Northfield, IL 60093; Dist. by: Como Sales, Inc., 799 Broadway, New York, NY 10013; Dist. by: Ralph Woodward, New England Books & Arts, P.O. Drawer 1, Concord, MA 01742; Dist. by: Bookpeople, 2940 Seventh St., Berkeley, CA 94710; Dist. by: Book House Northwest, 2900 S.E. Stork St., Portland, OR 97214; Dist. by: Ingram Book Co., 347 Reedwood Dr., Nashville, TN 37217; Dist. by: WIP, P.O. Box 66285, Houston, TX 77006; Dist. by: Henry Walck, Jr., 731 E. Shore Dr., Ithaca, NY 14850; Dist. by: The Distributors, 702 S. Michigan, South Bend, IN 46618.
Panjandrum Pr
See Panjandrum
Pantheon, *(Pantheon Books),* Div. of Random House, Inc., 201 E. 50th St., New York, NY 10022 Tel 212-751-2600; Orders to: Random House, Inc., 400 Hahn Rd., Westminster, MD 21157.
Parchment Pr, *(Parchment Press; 0-88428),* P.O. Box 8534, Chattanooga, TN 37411 Tel 615-899-0351.
Parents, *(Parents Magazine Press; 0-8193),* 52 Vanderbilt Ave., New York, NY 10017 Tel 212-661-9080.
Pasadena Art, *(Pasadena Art Alliance),* 314 S. Mentor Ave., Pasadena, CA 91106 Tel 213-795-9276.
Path Pr NY, *(Pathfinder Press; 0-87348),* 410 West St., New York, NY 10014 Tel 212-741-0690.
Pathway Pr, *(Pathway Press; 0-87148),* 922-1080 Montgomery Ave., Cleveland, TN 37311 Tel 615-476-4512.
Patmos Pr, *(Patmos Press, The; 0-915762),* P.O. Box V, Shepherdstown, WV 25443 Tel 304-876-2086.
Patriotic Educ, *(Patriotic Education, Inc.; 0-912530),* P.O. Box 2121, Daytona Beach, FL 32015 Tel 904-252-3414.
Patterson Smith, *(Smith, Patterson, Publishing Corp.; 0-87585),* 23 Prospect Terrace, Montclair, NJ 07042 Tel 201-744-3291.
Paulist-Newman
See Paulist Pr
Paulist Pr, *(Paulist Press; 0-8091),* 1865 Broadway, New York, NY 10023 Tel 212-265-4028; Orders to: 545 Island Rd., Ramsey, NJ 07446 Tel 201-825-7300.
PB, *(Pocket Books, Inc.; 0-671),* Div. of Simon & Schuster, Inc., 1230 Ave. of the Americas, New York, NY 10020. *Imprints:* Wallaby (Wallaby).
Peace & Pieces
See SF Arts & Letters
Peachtree Pubs, *(Peachtree Pubs., Ltd.; 0-931948),* 494 Armour Circle, N.E., Atlanta, GA 30324 Tel 404-876-8761; Dist. by: Chicago Review Press, 215 W. Ohio St., Chicago, IL 60610 Tel 312-644-5457.
Pelican, *(Pelican Publishing Co., Inc.; 0-911116; 0-88289),* 630 Burmaster St., Gretna, LA 70053 Tel 504-368-1175. *Imprints:* Pelican (*Imprint of* Pengui).
Pendel Hill
See Pendle Hill
Pendell Pub, *(Pendell Publishing Co.; 0-87812),* 1700 James Savage Rd., P.O. Box 1666 PT, Midland, MI 48640 Tel 517-496-3337.
Pendle Hill, *(Pendle Hill Pubns.; 0-87574),* Pendle Hill, 338 Plush Mill Rd, Wallingford, PA 19086 Tel 215-566-4507.
Pendulum Pr, *(Pendulum Press, Inc.; 0-88301),* Academic Bldg., Saw Mill Rd., West Haven, CT 06516 Tel 203-933-2551.
Penguin, *(Penguin Books, Inc.; 0-14),* 625 Madison Ave., New York, NY 10022 Tel 212-755-4330. *Imprints:* Pelican (Pelican Books); Puffin (Puffin Books).
Penobscot Bay, *(Penobscot Bay Press, Inc.),* Box 36, Stonington, ME 04681.
Pentelic Pr, *(Pentelic Press; 0-913110),* 1032 Cambridge Crescent, Norfolk, VA 23508.
Pepys Pr, *(Pepys Press, The; 0-9602270),* 1270 Fifth Ave., New York, NY 10029 Tel 212-348-6847.
Pere Marquette, *(Pere Marquette Press; 0-934640),* P.O. Box 495, Alton, IL 62002.
Peregrine Smith, *(Peregrine Smith, Inc.; 0-87905),* P.O. Box 667, 1877 E. Gentile St., Layton, UT 84041 Tel 801-376-9800.
Pergamon, *(Pergamon Press, Inc.; 0-08),* Maxwell House, Fairview Park, Elmsford, NY 10523 Tel 914-592-7700.
Persea Bks, *(Persea Books, Inc.; 0-89255),* 225 Lafayette St., New York, NY 10012 Tel 212-431-5270.
Peter Pauper, *(Peter Pauper Press; 0-8342),* 135 W. 50th St., New York, NY 10020 Tel 212-247-3507.
Peter Smith, *(Smith, Peter, Publisher Inc.; 0-8446),* 6 Lexington Ave., Magnolia, MA 01930 Tel 617-525-3562.
Petrocelli-Charter
See Van Nos Reinhold
Phaeton, *(Phaeton Press, Inc.; 0-87753),* 85 Tompkins St., Staten Island, NY 10304 Tel 212-273-4700; Orders to: Gordian Press, 85 Tompkins St., Staten Island, NY 10304.
Phaidon
See Dutton
Phaidon *Imprint of* **Dutton**
Phi Delta Kappa, *(Phi Delta Kappa, Inc.; 0-87367),* 8th & Union, P.O. Box 789, Bloomington, IN 47402 Tel 812-339-1156.
Phila Patristic, *(Philadelphia Patristic Foundation, Ltd.; 0-915646),* 99 Brattle St., Cambridge, MA 02138 Tel 617-868-3450; Orders to: 518 Central St., Winchendon, MA 01475.
Philos Lib, *(Philosophical Library, Inc.; 0-8022),* 15 E. 40th St., New York, NY 10016 Tel 212-683-2945.
Phipps Pub, *(Phipps Pub. Co.; 0-918442),* Subs. of New England Mfgr. Co., 66 Bridge St., Norwell, MA 02061 Tel 617-659-7003.
Phoenix Pub, *(Phoenix Publishing; 0-914016),* Canaan, NH 03741 Tel 603-523-9902.
Pica Pr *Imprint of* **Universe**
Pierpont Morgan, *(Pierpont Morgan Library; 0-87598),* 29 E. 36th St., New York, NY 10016 Tel 212-685-0008.
Pilgrim NY, *(Pilgrim Press, The; 0-8298),* 132 W. 31st St., New York, NY 10001 Tel 212-239-8700; Orders to: Seabury Service Center, Somers, CT 06071.
Pillar Bks, *(Pillar Books; 0-89129),* c/o Harcourt Brace Jovanovich, Inc., 757 Third Ave., New York, NY 10017 Tel 212-754-3100.
Pine Cone Pubs, *(Pine Cone Pubs.; 0-912720),* 2251 Ross Lane, Medford, OR 97501 Tel 503-773-3892.
Pinnacle Bks, *(Pinnacle Books; 0-523),* 1 Century Plaza, 2029 Century Park E., Los Angeles, CA 90067 Tel 213-552-9111.
Pioneer VT, *(Pioneer Press, The; 0-9603426),* Newfane, VT 05345.
Piper *Imprint of* **HM**
Piraeus *Imprint of* **Fell**
PL *Imprint of* **Har-Row**
Playboy Pr Pbks, *(Playboy Press Paperbacks; 0-87216),* Div. of P.E.I. Books, Inc., 747 Third Ave., New York, NY 10017 Tel 212-688-3030.
Plowshare, *(Plowshare Press, Inc.; 0-87368),* P.O. Box 2252, Boston, MA 02107.
Plume *Imprint of* **NAL**
Plycon Pr, *(Plycon Press; 0-916434),* P.O. Box 220, Redondo Beach, CA 90277 Tel 213-530-1033; Dist. by: Burgess Publishing Co., 7108 Ohms Lane, Minneapolis, MN 55435.
Polish Inst Arts, *(Polish Institute of Arts & Sciences in America),* 59 E. 66th St., New York, NY 10021 Tel 212-988-4338.
Popular Lib, *(Popular Library, Inc.; 0-445),* Unit of CBS Pubns., 1515 Broadway, New York, NY 10036 Tel 212-975-4321.
Porcupine Pr, *(Porcupine Press, Inc.; 0-87991),* 1317 Filbert St., Philadelphia, PA 19107 Tel 215-563-2288.
Porter, *(Porter, Bern; 0-911156),* 22 Salmond Rd., Belfast, ME 04915 Tel 207-338-3763.
Potomac, *(Potomac Books, Inc., Pubs.; 0-87107),* 4418 MacArthur Blvd., N.W., Washington, DC 20007 Tel 202-338-5774; Orders to: P.O. Box 40604, Palisades Sta., Washington, DC 20016 Tel 202-333-6779.
Potter, *(Potter, Clarkson N., Inc.; 0-8247),* 1 Park Ave., New York, NY 10016 Tel 212-532-9200; Dist. by: Crown Pubs., 1 Park Ave., New York, NY 10016.
Pr of Morningside, *(Press of Morningside Bookshop; 0-89029),* P.O. Box 1087, Dayton, OH 45401 Tel 513-461-6736.

Prem *Imprint of* **Avon**
Presby & Reformed, *(Presbyterian & Reformed Publishing Co.; 0-87552),* Order Dept., Box 817, Phillipsburg, NJ 08865.
Presidio Pr, *(Presidio Press; 0-89141),* P.O. Box 3515, San Rafael, CA 94902 Tel 415-883-1373; Orders to: Presidio Press Distribution Center, P.O. Box 978, Edison, NJ 08817 Tel 201-225-1900.
Princeton U Pr, *(Princeton Univ. Press; 0-691),* 41 William St., Princeton, NJ 08540 Tel 609-452-4900.
Progeny Pr, *(Progeny Press, Inc.; 0-934168),* P.O. Box 206, Villanova, PA 19085 Tel 215-296-0595; Dist. by: Caroline House, 80 Northfield Ave., Raritan Center, Edison, NJ 08817.
Prometheus Bks, *(Prometheus Books; 0-87975),* 1203 Kensington Ave., Buffalo, NY 14215 Tel 716-837-2475.
Promised Land, *(Promised Land Publications, Inc.),* Div. of Community Press, 5600 N. University Ave., Provo, UT 84601 Tel 801-225-2293.
Pruett, *(Pruett Publishing Co.; 0-87108),* 3235 Prairie Ave., Boulder, CO 80301 Tel 303-449-4919.
Pryor Pettengill, *(Pryor Pettengill; 0-933462),* Box 7074, Ann Arbor, MI 48107.
Pub Aff Pr, *(Public Affairs Press; 0-8183),* 419 New Jersey Ave., Washington, DC 20003 Tel 202-544-3024.
Puffin *Imprint of* **Penguin**
Purcells, *(Purcells, Inc.; 0-931068),* 305 S. 10th, Box 190, Broken Bow, NE 68822 Tel 308-872-2471.
Purdue, *(Purdue Univ. Press; 0-911198),* S. Campus Courts-D, West Lafayette, IN 47907 Tel 317-749-6083.
Putnam, *(Putnam's, G. P., Sons; 0-399),* 200 Madison Ave., New York, NY 10016 Tel 212-576-8900; Orders to: 1050 Wall St. W., Lyndhurst, NJ 07071 Tel 201-933-9292.
Quadrangle
See Times Bks
Quest *Imprint of* **Swallow**
Quick Fox *Imprint of* **Music Sales**
R & E Res Assoc, *(R & E Research Associates, Inc.; 0-88247),* 936 Industrial Ave., Palo Alto, CA 94303 Tel 415-494-1112.
R Enslow
See Enslow Pubs
R J Liederbach, *(Liederbach, Robert J.; 0-934906),* 2720 East Boulevard, Cleveland, OH 44104 Tel 216-231-8896.
R Marek, *(Marek, Richard, Pubs., Inc.; 0-399),* Subs. of G.P. Putnam's Sons, 200 Madison Ave., New York, NY 10016 Tel 212-576-8900.
R Myles, *(Myles, Ralph, Pub., Inc.; 0-87926),* P.O. Box 1533, Colorado Springs, CO 80901 Tel 303-634-3206.
R Nicholson
See Barrie & Jenkins
R O Beatty Assocs, *(Beatty, R. O., & Assocs.; 0-916238),* P.O. Box 763, Boise, ID 83701 Tel 208-343-4949.
R West, *(West, Richard; 0-8492; 0-8274),* Box 6404, Philadelphia, PA 19145.
Rainbow Bks, *(Rainbow Books, Inc.; 0-89508),* 675 Dell Rd., Carlstadt, NJ 07072 Tel 201-935-3369.
Raintree Child, *(Raintree Childrens Books; 0-8172; 0-8393),* Div. of Raintree Publishers Group, 205 W. Highland Ave., Milwaukee, WI 53203 Tel 414-276-3430.
Raintree Pubs Ltd
See Raintree Pubs
Raintree Pubs, *(Raintree Pubs., Inc.; 0-8172),* 205 W. Highland Ave., Milwaukee, WI 53203 Tel 414-273-0873.
Ramakrishna, *(Ramakrishna-Vivekananda Center; 0-911206),* 17 E. 94th St., New York, NY 10028 Tel 212-534-9445.
Rampart Hse, *(Rampart House, Ltd.; 0-89773),* 1900 Bank of America Tower, One City Dr., West Orange, CA 92668.
Ramparts, *(Ramparts Press; 0-87867),* P.O. Box 50128, Palo Alto, CA 94303 Tel 415-325-7861.
Rand, *(Rand McNally & Co.; 0-528),* P.O. Box 7600, Chicago, IL 60680 Tel 312-673-9100.
Random, *(Random House, Inc.; 0-394),* Random House Publicity (11-6), 201 East 50th St., New York, NY 10022 Tel 212-751-2600; Orders to: 400 Hahn Rd., Westminster, MD 21157. *Imprints:* Vin (Vintage Trade Books).
Rather Pr, *(Rather Press),* 3200 Guido St., Oakland, CA 94602 Tel 415-531-2938.
Rawson Assocs
See Rawson Wade
Rawson Wade, *(Rawson, Wade Pubs., Inc.; 0-89256),* 630 Third Ave., New York, NY 10017 Tel 212-867-6610; Dist. by: Atheneum Pubs., 122 E. 42nd St., New York, NY 10017.
Red Dust, *(Red Dust Inc.; 0-87376),* P.O. Box 630, Gracie Sta., New York, NY 10028 Tel 212-348-4388.
Reed, *(Reed, A. H. & A. W., Books; 0-589),* Dist. by: Charles E. Tuttle, Inc., 28 S. Main St., Rutland, VT 05701 Tel 802-773-8930.
Reg Baptist, *(Regular Baptist Press; 0-87227),* 1300 N. Meacham Rd., P.O. Box 95500, Schaumburg, IL 60195 Tel 312-843-1600.
Regal, *(Regal Books),* Div. of G/L Pubns., P.O. Box 1591, 110 W. Broadway, Glendale, CA 91204 Tel 213-247-2330.
Regent House, *(Regent House; 0-911238),* 108 N. Roselake Ave., Los Angeles, CA 90026 Tel 213-413-5027.
Regents Pr KS, *(Regents Press of Kansas; 0-7006),* 303 Carruth-O'leary, Lawrence, KS 66045 Tel 913-864-4154.
Regional, *(Regional Publishing Co.),* Affiliate of Genealogical Publishing Co., 111 Water St., Baltimore, MD 21202 Tel 301-837-8271.
Regnery
See Contemp Bks
Regnery-Gateway, *(Regnery/Gateway, Inc.; 0-89526),* Box 207, South Bend, IN 46624 Tel 219-232-5911.
Reidel Pub
See Kluwer Boston
Reilly & Lee
See Contemp Bks
Renaissance Pubs, *(Renaissance Pubs.; 0-916560),* 2485 N.E 214th St., N. Miami Beach, FL 33180 Tel 305-931-3392.
Reprint, *(Reprint Co.; 0-87152),* P.O. Box 5401, 601 Hillcrest Offices, Spartanburg, SC 29304 Tel 803-582-0732.
Revell, *(Revell, Fleming H., Co.; 0-8007),* 184 Central Ave., Old Tappan, NJ 07675 Tel 201-768-8060.
Review & Herald, *(Review & Herald Publishing Assn.; 0-8280),* Takoma Park, Washington, DC 20012 Tel 202-723-7200.
Revisionist Pr, *(Revisionist Press; 0-87700),* P.O. Box 2009, Brooklyn, NY 11202.
Reward *Imprint of* **P-H**
Reynal, *(Reynal & Co.; 0-688),* 105 Madison Ave., New York, NY 10016 Tel 212-889-3050; Dist. by: William Morrow & Co., Order Dept., 6 Henderson Dr., West Caldwell, NJ 07006.
RI Bicentennial
See RI Pubns Soc
RI Pubns Soc, *(Rhode Island Pubns. Society; 0-917012),* Old State House, 150 Benefit St., Providence, RI 02903 Tel 401-272-1776.
Rice Univ, *(Rice University Studies; 0-89263),* History Dept., Houston, TX 77001 Tel 713-527-8101; Orders to: Rice Campus Store, P.O. Box 1892, Houston, TX 77001.
Richmond Cty Hist Soc, *(Richmond County Historical Society),* c/o Reese Library, Augusta College, 2500 Walton Way, Augusta, GA 30904 Tel 404-828-4566.
Richwood Pub, *(Richwood Pub., Co.; 0-915172),* P.O. Box 381, Scarsdale, NY 10583 Tel 914-723-1286.
Ridgeway Bks, *(Ridgeway Books),* P. O. Box 6431, Philadelphia, PA 19145.
Rio Grande, *(Rio Grande Press, Inc.; 0-87380),* P.O. Box 33, Glorieta, NM 87535 Tel 505-757-6275.
RivEd *Imprint of* **HM**
RivSL *Imprint of* **HM**
Rizzoli Intl, *(Rizzoli International Pubns., Inc.; 0-8478),* 712 Fifth Ave., New York, NY 10019 Tel 212-397-3740.
Rock Harbor, *(Rock Harbor Press; 0-932260),* P.O. Box 1206, Hyannis, MA 02601.
Rockefeller, *(Rockefeller Univ. Press; 0-87470),* 1230 York Ave., Box 291, New York, NY 10021 Tel 212-360-1217; Orders to: Box 269, 1230 York Ave., New York, NY 10021 Tel 212-360-1367.
Roller Coaster Pubns, *(Roller Coaster Pubns.),* P.O. Box 18058, Denver, CO 80218; Moved, Left No Forwarding Address.
Rolling Meadows, *(Rolling Meadows Library; 0-9602782),* 3110 Martin Lane, Rolling Meadows, IL 60008 Tel 612-259-6050.
Romance, *(Romance Monographs, Inc.),* P.O. Box 7553, University, MS 38677 Tel 601-234-0001.
Ronald Pr, *(Ronald Press),* 605 Third Ave., New York, NY 10016 Tel 212-867-9800.
Rook Pr, *(Rook Press; 0-916684),* P.O. Box 144, Ruffsdale, PA 15679.
Rookfield, *(Rookfield Press; 0-917610),* P.O. Box 45, Deer, AR 72628 Tel 904-477-5542.
Rose Hill, *(Rose Hill Press; 0-917264),* 12368 Old Pen Mar Rd., Waynesboro, PA 17268 Tel 717-762-7072.
Rosen Pr, *(Rosen, Richards, Press, Inc.; 0-8239),* 29 E. 21st St., New York, NY 10010 Tel 212-777-3017.
Ross, *(Ross & Haines Old Books Co.; 0-87018),* 639 E. Lake St., Wayzata, MN 55391 Tel 612-473-7551.
Ross-Erikson, *(Ross-Erikson, Inc.; 0-915520),* 629 State St., Suite 222, Santa Barbara, CA 93109 Tel 805-962-1175.
Routledge & Kegan, *(Routledge & Kegan Paul, Ltd.; 0-7100),* 9 Park St., Boston, MA 02108 Tel 617-742-5863. *Imprints:* Oriel (Oriel Press).
Rowman, *(Rowman & Littlefield, Inc.; 0-87471; 0-8476),* Div. of Littlefield, Adams, & Co., 81 Adams Dr., Box 327, Totowa, NJ 07511 Tel 201-256-8600.
Running Pr, *(Running Press; 0-89471),* 38 S. 19th St., Philadelphia, PA 19103 Tel 215-567-5080.
Russell, *(Russell & Russell, Pubs.; 0-8462),* Div. of Atheneum Pubs., 597 Fifth Ave., New York, NY 10017 Tel 212-486-2700; Do Not Confuse with Russell Pubns. in FL (Russell Pubns).
Rutgers U Pr, *(Rutgers Univ. Press; 0-8135),* 30 College Ave., New Brunswick, NJ 08903 Tel 201-932-7764.
S F Vanni, *(Vanni, S. F.; 0-913298),* 30 W. 12th St., New York, NY 10011 Tel 212-675-6336.
S G Phillips, *(Phillip's, S. G., Inc.; 0-87599),* 305 W. 86th St., New York, NY 10024 Tel 212-787-4405.
S Ill U Pr, *(Southern Illinois Univ. Press; 0-8093),* P.O. Box 3697, Carbondale, IL 62901 Tel 618-453-2281.
S Meth U Pr
See SMU Press
S S S Pub Co, *(Smith, Smith & Smith Publishing Co.; 0-913626),* 17515 S.W. Blue Heron Rd., Lake Oswego, OR 97034 Tel 503-636-2979.
Sagarin Pr, *(Sagarin Press; 0-915298),* Box 21, Sand Lake, NY 12153 Tel 518-674-2998.
Sage, *(Sage Pubns., Inc.; 0-8039),* 275 S. Beverly Dr., Beverly Hills, CA 90212 Tel 213-274-8003.
SamHar Pr, *(SamHar Press),* Div. of Story House Corp., Charlotteville, NY 12036 Tel 607-397-8725.
Samisdat, *(Samisdat),* Box 231, Richford, VT 05476.
Sandlapper Pr
See Sandlapper Store
Sandlapper Store, *(Sandlapper Store, Inc.; 0-87844),* Box 841, 101 W. Main, Lexington, SC 29072 Tel 803-359-6571; Formerly Sandlapper Press, Inc.
S&S, *(Simon & Schuster, Inc.; 0-671),* 1230 Ave. of the Americas, New York, NY 10020 Tel 212-245-6400. *Imprints:* Fireside (Fireside Paperbacks); Juveniles (Juvenile Books); Touchstone Bks (Touchstone Bks).
Sant Bani Ash, *(Sant Bani Ashram, Inc.),* Franklin, NH 03235 Tel 603-934-4209.
Sat Rev Pr
See Dutton
Sawan Kirpal Pubns, *(Sawan Kirpal Pubns.; 0-918224),* 115 S. "O" St., Lake Worth, FL 33460 Tel 305-588-1287; Orders to: Rt. 1, Box 24, Bowling Green, VA 22427 Tel 804-633-5789.
SBD, *(SBD: Small Press Distribution; 0-914068),* 1636 Ocean View Ave., Kensington, CA 94707 Tel 415-524-2107.
Scarecrow, *(Scarecrow Press, Inc.; 0-8108),* Subs. of Grolier Educational Corp., 52 Liberty St., Box 656, Metuchen, NJ 08840 Tel 201-548-8600.
Schalkenbach, *(Schalkenbach, Robert, Foundation; 0-911312),* 50 E. 69th St., New York, NY 10021 Tel 212-734-2468.
Schenkman, *(Schenkman Publishing Co., Inc.; 0-87073),* 3 Mt. Auburn Place, Cambridge, MA 02138.

Schirmer Bks, *(Schirmer Books; 0-02),* Div. of Macmillan Publishing Co., 866 Third Ave., New York, NY 10022 Tel 212-935-7642; Orders to: 100 Brown St., Riverside, NJ 08370.
Schocken, *(Schocken Books, Inc.; 0-8052),* 200 Madison Ave., New York, NY 10016 Tel 212-685-6500.
Four Winds Four Winds Press
Schol Pap Scholastic Paperbacks
Schol Facsimiles, *(Scholars' Facsimiles & Reprints; 0-8201),* P.O. Box 344, Delmar, NY 12054 Tel 518-439-6146.
Schol Pap *Imprint of* **Scribner**
Scholarly, *(Scholarly Press Inc.; 0-403),* 19722 E. Nine Mile Rd., Saint Clair Shores, MI 48080 Tel 313-773-4250.
Scholarly Res Inc, *(Scholarly Resources Inc.; 0-8420),* 104 Greenhill Ave., Wilmington, DE 19805 Tel 302-654-7713.
Scholars Pr
See Scholars Pr MT
Scholars Pr MT, *(Scholars Press; 0-89130),* 101 Salem St., Chico, CA 95926 Tel 916-343-1651.
Sci & Behavior, *(Science & Behavior Books, Inc.; 0-8314),* P.O. Box 11457, Palo Alto, CA 94306 Tel 415-326-6465.
Scott F, *(Scott, Foresman & Co.; 0-673),* 1900 E. Lake Ave., Glenview, IL 60025 Tel 312-729-3000.
Scribner, *(Scribner's, Charles, Sons; 0-684),* 597 Fifth Ave., New York, NY 10017 Tel 212-486-2700; Orders to: Shipping & Service Ctr., Vreeland Ave., Totowa, NJ 07512.
Scrip Pr
See Victor Bks
Seabury, *(Seabury Press, Inc.; 0-8164),* 815 Second Ave., New York, NY 10017 Tel 212-557-0500; Orders to: Seabury Service Center, Somers, CT 06071. *Imprints:* Crossroads Bks (Crossroads Books).
Second Chance, *(Second Chance Press; 0-933256),* Sagaponack, NY 11962.
Self Realization, *(Self Realization Fellowship; 0-87612),* 3880 San Rafael Ave., Los Angeles, CA 90065 Tel 213-225-2471.
SenEd *Imprint of* **HM**
Servant, *(Servant Publications; 0-89283),* P.O. Box 8617, 840 Airport Blvd., Ann Arbor, MI 48107 Tel 313-761-8505; Orders to: Customer Service Dept., Box 8617, Ann Arbor, MI 48107 Tel 313-761-8983; Formerly Named Word of Life.
Seven Seas, *(Seven-Seas Press; 0-915160),* 32 Union Square, New York, NY 10003 Tel 212-777-2525; Dist. by: David McKay Corp., Inc, 2 Park Ave., New York, NY 10016 Tel 212-340-9800.
Seventy-Six, *(Seventy-Six Press; 0-89245),* P.O. Box 2686, Seal Beach, CA 90740 Tel 213-596-3491.
Sey Lawr *Imprint of* **Delacorte**
SF Arts & Letters, *(San Francisco Arts & Letters Foundation; 0-914024),* P.O. Box 99394, San Francisco, CA 94109 Tel 415-771-3431.
SF Bk Co, *(San Francisco Book Co., Inc.; 0-913374),* 2311 Fillmore St., San Francisco, CA 94115 Tel 415-922-4570.
Shambala Pubns
See Shambhala Pubns
Shambhala Pubns, *(Shambhala Pubns., Inc.; 0-87773),* P.O. Box 271, Boulder, CO 80306 Tel 303-449-6111; Dist. by: Random House, Inc., 400 Hahn Rd., Westminster, MD 21157.
Sharon Hill, *(Sharon Hill Books; 0-932062),* P.O. Box 67, Sharon Hill, PA 19079.
Shelter Pubns
See Random
Shoal Creek Pub, *(Shoal Creek Pubs.; 0-88319),* P.O. Box 9737, Austin, TX 78766 Tel 512-451-7545.
Shoe String, *(Shoe String Press, Inc.; 0-208),* P.O. Box 4327, 995 Sherman Ave., Hamden, CT 06514 Tel 203-248-6307.
Shorey, *(Shorey Pubns.; 0-8466),* 110 Union St., Seattle, WA 98111 Tel 206-624-0221.
Shumway, *(Shumway, George; 0-87387),* R.D. 7, Box 388B, York, PA 17402 Tel 717-755-1196.
Sig *Imprint of* **NAL**
Sig Classics *Imprint of* **NAL**
Silver, *(Silver Burdett Co.; 0-382),* Div. of General Learning Co., 250 James St., Morristown, NJ 07960 Tel 201-285-8100.
Sleepy Hollow, *(Sleepy Hollow Restorations, Inc.; 0-912882),* 150 White Plains Rd., Tarrytown, NY 10591 Tel 914-631-8200; Dist. by: Independent Publishers Group, 14 Vanderventer Ave., Port Washington, NY 11050 Tel 516-944-9325.
Smithsonian, *(Smithsonian Institution Press; 0-87474),* Rm. 2280, Arts & Industries Bldg., Washington, DC 20560 Tel 202-381-5143; Orders to: P.O. Box 1579, Washington, DC 20013; Booksellers Order from: Publications Sales, 1111 North Capitol St., Washington, DC 20560.
SMU Press, *(Southern Methodist Univ. Press; 0-87074),* Dallas, TX 75275 Tel 214-692-2263.
Somerset Pub, *(Somerset Pubs.),* Div. of Scholarly Press, Inc., 19722 E. Nine Mile Rd, St. Clair Shores, MI 48080.
South Asia Bks, *(South Asia Books; 0-88386; 0-8364),* P.O. Box 502, Columbia, MO 65201 Tel 314-449-1359.
Southern Pub, *(Southern Publishing Assn.; 0-8127),* Box 59, 1900 Elm Hill Pike, Nashville, TN 37202 Tel 615-889-8000.
Sovereign Pr, *(Sovereign Press; 0-914752),* 326 Harris Rd., Rochester, WA 98579 Tel 206-273-5109.
Spec *Imprint of* **P-H**
Speller, *(Speller, Robert, & Sons, Pub., Inc.; 0-8315),* 10 E. 23rd St., New York, NY 10010 Tel 212-473-8788; Orders to: P.O. Box 461, Times Square Sta., New York, NY 10036.
Springer-Verlag, *(Springer-Verlag New York, Inc.; 0-387),* 175 Fifth Ave., New York, NY 10010 Tel 212-477-8200.
St Anthony Mess Pr, *(St. Anthony Messenger Press; 0-912228),* 1615 Republic St., Cincinnati, OH 45210 Tel 513-241-5616.
St Clair Pr
See Wiley
St Martin, *(St. Martin's Press, Inc.; 0-312),* 175 Fifth Ave., New York, NY 10010 Tel 212-674-5151.
St Vladimirs, *(St. Vladimir's Seminary Press; 0-913836),* 575 Scarsdale Rd., Crestwood, NY 10707 Tel 914-961-8313.
Staked Plains, *(Staked Plains Press; 0-918028),* P.O. Box 779, Canyon, TX 79015 Tel 806-655-7121.
Standard Pub, *(Standard Publishing Co.; 0-87239),* 8121 Hamilton Ave., Cincinnati, OH 45231 Tel 513-931-4050.
Stanford U Pr, *(Stanford Univ. Press; 0-8047),* Stanford, CA 94305 Tel 415-497-9434.
State Hist Soc Wis, *(State Historical Society of Wisconsin; 0-87020),* 816 State St., Madison, WI 53706 Tel 608-262-9604.
State Mutual Bk, *(State Mutual Book & Periodical Service, Ltd.; 0-89771),* 521 Fifth Ave., New York, NY 10017 Tel 212-682-5844.
State U NY Pr, *(State Univ. of New York Press; 0-87395),* State University Plaza, Albany, NY 12246 Tel 518-474-6050; P.O. Box 4830, Hampden Sta., Baltimore, MD 21211.
Stein & Day, *(Stein & Day; 0-8128),* Scarborough House, Briarcliff Manor, NY 10510 Tel 914-762-2151.
Stemmer Hse, *(Stemmer House Pubs., Inc.; 0-916144),* 2627 Caves Rd., Owings Mills, MD 21117 Tel 301-363-3690.
Sterling, *(Sterling Publishing Co., Inc.; 0-8069),* 2 Park Ave., New York, NY 10016 Tel 212-532-7160.
Stewart, *(Stewart, Henry, Inc.; 0-911444),* P.O. Box 177, 253 Main St., East Aurora, NY 14052 Tel 715-652-1770.
Stonehill Pub Co, *(Stonehill Publishing Co., Inc.; 0-88373),* 10 E. 40th St., Suite 2109, New York, NY 10016 Tel 212-658-5980; Dist. by: Farrar, Straus & Giroux, Inc., 19 Union Square, New York, NY 10003 Tel 212-741-6900.
Stowe-Day, *(Stowe-Day Foundation; 0-917482),* 77 Forest St., Hartford, CT 06105 Tel 203-522-9258.
Straughan, *(Straughan's Book Shop, Inc.; 0-911452),* 220 N. Elm St., Greensboro, NC 27401 Tel 919-274-5437.
Strawberry Hill, *(Strawberry Hill Press; 0-89407),* 2594 15th Ave., San Francisco, CA 94127 Tel 415-664-8112; Dist. by: Stackpole Books, Cameron & Kelker Sts., Harrisburg, PA 17105.
Strawberry Valley, *(Strawberry Valley Press; 0-913612),* P.O. Box 157, Idyllwild, CA 92349 Tel 714-659-2145.
Strode, *(Strode Pubs.; 0-87397),* 7917 Charlotte Dr., S.W., Huntsville, AL 35802 Tel 205-881-2357.
Studia Slovenica, *(Studia Slovenica, Inc.),* P.O. Box 232, New York, NY 10032.
Sullivan Bks Intl, *(Sullivan Books International; 0-913620),* 515 Weldon Ave., Oakland, CA 94610 Tel 415-893-5660.
Summit Bks, *(Summit Books),* Div. of Simon & Schuster, Inc., 1230 Ave. of the Americas, New York, NY 10020 Tel 212-246-2471.
Summy, *(Summy-Birchard Co.; 0-87487),* Box CN 27, Princeton, NJ 08540 Tel 609-896-1411.
SUN, *(SUN; 0-915342),* 456 Riverside Dr., New York, NY 10027 Tel 212-662-6121.
Superior Pub, *(Superior Publishing Co.; 0-87564),* 708 Sixth Ave., N., Box 1710, Seattle, WA 98111 Tel 206-282-4310.
Sutter House, *(Sutter House; 0-915010),* 77 Main St., P.O. Box 212, Lititz, PA 17543 Tel 717-626-0800.
Swallow, *(Swallow Press; 0-8040),* Scott Quadrangle, Athens, OH 45701 Tel 614-594-5852; Orders to: Publishers Marketing Group, P.O. Box 350, Momence, IL 60954 Tel 815-472-2661.
Sycamore Pr, *(Sycamore Press, Inc.; 0-916768),* P.O. Box 552, Terre Haute, IN 47808 Tel 812-299-2458.
Syracuse U Pr, *(Syracuse Univ. Press; 0-8156),* 1011 E. Water St., Syracuse, NY 13210 Tel 315-423-2596.
TYC-J Crowell, T Y, **Juvenile Books**
Tafnews, *(Tafnews Press; 0-911520; 0-911521),* Div. of Track & Field News, Inc., P.O. Box 296, Los Altos, CA 94022 Tel 415-948-8188.
TAN Bks Pubs, *(TAN Books & Pubs., Inc.; 0-89555),* P.O. Box 424, Rockford, IL 61105; 2135 N. Central Ave., Rockford, IL 61103 Tel 815-962-2662.
Taplinger, *(Taplinger Publishing Co., Inc.; 0-8008),* 200 Park Ave. S., New York, NY 10003 Tel 212-533-6110.
Tchrs Coll, *(Teachers College Press, Columbia Univ.; 0-8077),* 1234 Amsterdam Ave., New York, NY 10027 Tel 212-678-3931.
Telegraph *Imprint of* **Scholarly**
Telegraph Bks, *(Telegraph Books; 0-89760),* Box 38, Norwood, PA 19074 Tel 215-583-4550.
Temple U Pr, *(Temple Univ. Press; 0-87722),* Philadelphia, PA 19122 Tel 215-787-8787.
Templegate, *(Templegate Pubs.; 0-87243),* P.O. Box 963, Springfield, IL 62705 Tel 217-522-3361.
Tempo *Imprint of* **G&D**
Tex A&M Univ Pr, *(Texas A & M Univ. Press; 0-89096),* Drawer "C", College Station, TX 77843 Tel 713-845-1436.
Tex Christian, *(Texas Christian Univ. Press; 0-912646),* Box 30783, Fort Worth, TX 76129 Tel 817-921-7822.
Tex St Hist Assn, *(Texas State Historical Assn.; 0-87611),* 2-306 Richardson Hall, Univ. Sta., Austin, TX 78712 Tel 512-471-1525.
Tex Western, *(Texas Western Press, Univ. of Texas at El Paso; 0-87404),* El Paso, TX 79968 Tel 915-747-5688.
Texian, *(Texian Press; 0-87244),* P.O. Box 1684, Waco, TX 76703 Tel 817-754-5636.
Thai-Am Pubs, *(Thai-American Pubs.; 0-915806),* 101 Park Ave., Suite 1436N, New York, NY 10017 Tel 212-683-0501.
Thames Hudson, *(Thames & Hudson; 0-500),* Dist. by: W.W. Norton, & Co., Inc., 500 Fifth Ave., New York, NY 10036 Tel 212-354-3763.
Theatre Arts, *(Theatre Arts Books; 0-87830),* 153 Waverly Place, New York, NY 10014 Tel 212-675-1815.
Theophrastus, *(Theophrastus; 0-913728),* P.O. Box 458, Little Compton, RI 02837 Tel 401-635-4348.
Quest Quest Books C
Thomas More, *(More, Thomas, Press; 0-88347),* 225 W. Huron St., Chicago, IL 60610 Tel 312-951-2100.
Thoreau Found, *(Thoreau Foundation, Inc.; 0-912130),* Thoreau Lyceum, 156 Belknap St., Concord, MA 01742 Tel 617-369-5912.
Thorndike Pr, *(Thorndike Press, The; 0-89621),* Thorndike, ME 04986 Tel 207-948-2962.
Thorp Springs, *(Thorp Springs Press; 0-914476),* 803 Red River St., Austin, TX 78701.

Time Bks
See Times Bks
Time-Life, *(Time-Life Books; 0-8094),* Div. of Time, Inc., 777 Duke St., Alexandria, VA 22314 Tel 703-960-5000; Dist. by: Little, Brown & Co., 34 Beacon St., Boston, MA 02106; Dist. by: Morgan & Morgan Co., 400 Warburton Ave., Hastings on Hudson, NY 10706; Lib. & School Orders to: Silver Burdett Co., Morristown, NJ 13664.
Times Bks, *(Times Books; 0-8129),* Div. of The New York Times Co., 3 Park Ave., New York, NY 10016 Tel 212-725-2050; Dist. by: Harper & Row, Keystone Industrial Park, Scranton, PA 18512.
Times Change, *(Times Change Press; 0-87810),* P.O. Box 187, Albion, CA 95410 Tel 707-937-4266.
Topgallant, *(Topgallant Publishing Co., Ltd.; 0-914916),* Elizabeth Bldg. 845 Mission Lane, Honolulu, HI 96813 Tel 808-524-0884.
Torch Lib *Imprint of* **Har-Row**
Touchstone Bks *Imprint of* **S&S**
Tower
See Belmont-Tower
Transaction Bks, *(Transaction Books; 0-87855),* Bldg. 4051, Rutgers-State Univ., New Brunswick, NJ 08903 Tel 201-932-2280; Orders to: P.O. Box 978, Edison, NJ 08817.
Transatlantic, *(Transatlantic Arts, Inc.; 0-693),* 88 Bridge Rd., Central Islip, NY 11722 Tel 516-234-0055.
Trident, *(Trident Press; 0-671),* Div. of Simon & Schuster, Inc., 630 Fifth Ave., New York, NY 10020 Tel 212-245-6400.
Trinity U Pr, *(Trinity Univ. Press; 0-911536),* 715 Stadium Dr., San Antonio, TX 78284 Tel 512-736-7619.
Tulane U Ctr Busn
See Tulane Univ
Tulane Univ, *(Tulane Univ.),* Tulane University, New Orleans, LA 70118; Dist. by: Center for Business History Studies, History Bldg., Tulane Univ., New Orleans, LA 70118.
Tundra Bks, *(Tundra Books of Northern New York; 0-912776; 0-89541),* 51 Clinton St., Box 1030, Plattsburgh, NY 12901 Tel 518-561-1720; Dist. by: Charles Scribner's Sons, 597 5th Ave., New York, NY 10017.
TUVOTI, *(Unspeakable Visions of the Individual, The; 0-934660),* P. O. Box 439, California, PA 15419 Tel 412-938-8956.
Twayne, *(Twayne Pubs.; 0-8057),* Div. of G. K. Hall, Dist. by: G. K. Hall & Co., 70 Lincoln St., Boston, MA 02111. *Imprints:* Twayne (*Imprint of* Coll & U P).
Two Continents, *(Two Continents Publishing Group, Inc.; 0-8467),* 171 Madison Ave., New York, NY 10016 Tel 212-685-4371.
TYC-J *Imprint of* **Nelson**
Tyndale, *(Tyndale House Pubs.; 0-8423),* 336 Gundersen Dr., Wheaton, IL 60187 Tel 312-668-8300.
U Delaware Pr, *(Univ. of Delaware Press; 0-87413),* c/o Associated Univ. Presses, Inc., P.O. Box 421, Cranbury, NJ 08512 Tel 609-655-0190.
U Maine Orono, *(Univ. of Maine at Orono Press; 0-89101),* PICS Building, Univ. of Maine at Orono, Orono, ME 04469 Tel 207-581-7349.
U of Ala Pr, *(Univ. of Alabama Press; 0-8173),* Box 2877, University, AL 35486 Tel 205-348-5180.
U of Ariz Pr, *(Univ. of Arizona Press; 0-8165),* P.O. Box 3398, Tucson, AZ 85722 Tel 602-626-1441.
U of Cal Pr, *(Univ. of California Press; 0-520),* 2223 Fulton St., Berkeley, CA 94720 Tel 415-642-4562.
U of Chicago Pr, *(Univ. of Chicago Press; 0-226),* 5801 Ellis Ave., Chicago, IL 60637 Tel 312-753-2586; Orders to: 11030 S. Langley Ave., Chicago, IL 60628 Tel 312-568-1550.
U of Ga Pr, *(Univ. of Georgia Press; 0-8203),* Terrell Hall, Athens, GA 30602 Tel 404-542-2830.
U of Ill Pr, *(Univ. of Illinois Press; 0-252),* 54 E. Gregory Dr., P.O. Box 5081, Sta. A, Champaign, IL 61820 Tel 217-333-0950.
U of Iowa Pr, *(Univ. of Iowa Press; 0-87745),* 21 Graphic Services Bldg., Iowa City, IA 52242 Tel 319-353-3181.
U of Mass Pr, *(Univ. of Massachusetts Press; 0-87023),* P.O. Box 429, Amherst, MA 01002 Tel 413-545-2217.
U of Miami Pr, *(Univ. of Miami Press; 0-87024),* Dist. by: Texas Press Services, P.O. Box 7877, Austin, TX 78712.
U of Mich Pr, *(Univ. of Michigan Press; 0-472),* P.O. Box 1104, Ann Arbor, MI 48106 Tel 313-764-4391. *Imprints:* AA (Ann Arbor Books).
U of Minn Pr, *(Univ. of Minnesota Press; 0-8166),* 2037 University Ave. S.E., Minneapolis, MN 55414 Tel 612-373-3266.
U of Mo Pr, *(Univ. of Missouri Press; 0-8262),* 107 Swallow Hall, Columbia, MO 65211 Tel 314-882-7641.
U of MT Pubns Hist, *(Univ. of Montana Pubns. in History),* Missoula, MT 59812 Tel 406-243-5943.
U of NC Pr, *(Univ. of North Carolina Press; 0-8078),* P.O Box 2288, Chapel Hill, NC 27514 Tel 919-933-2105.
U of Nebr Pr, *(Univ. of Nebraska Press; 0-8032),* 901 N. 17th St., Lincoln, NE 68588 Tel 402-472-3581.
U of Nev Pr, *(Univ. of Nevada Press; 0-87417),* Reno, NV 89557 Tel 702-784-6573.
U of NM Pr, *(Univ. of New Mexico Press; 0-8263),* Albuquerque, NM 87131 Tel 505-277-2346.
U of Notre Dame Pr, *(Univ. of Notre Dame Press, 0-268),* P.O. Box L, Notre Dame, IN 46556 Tel 219-283-6346; Dist. by: Harper & Row Pubs., Keystone Industrial Park, Scranton, PA 18512.
U of Okla Pr, *(Univ. of Oklahoma Press; 0-8061),* 1005 Asp Ave., Norman, OK 73019 Tel 405-325-5111.
U of Pa Pr, *(Univ. of Pennsylvania Press; 0-8122),* 3933 Walnut St., Philadelphia, PA 19104 Tel 215-243-6261.
U of Pacific
See Holt-Atherton
U of Pittsburgh Pr, *(Univ. of Pittsburgh Press; 0-8229),* 127 N. Bellefield Ave., Pittsburgh, PA 15260 Tel 412-624-4110.
U of PR Pr, *(Univ. of Puerto Rico Press; 0-8477),* P.O. Box X, U.P.R. Sta., Rio Piedras, PR 00931 Tel 809-765-1924.
U of Queensland Pr, *(Univ. of Queensland Press),* 310 W. 85th St., New York, NY 10024 Tel 212-799-3854; Orders to: 5 S. Union St., Lawrence, MA 01843 Tel 617-685-3306.
U of SC Pr, *(Univ. of South Carolina Press; 0-87249),* Columbia, SC 29208 Tel 803-777-5243.
U of Tenn Pr, *(Univ. of Tennessee Press; 0-87049),* 293 Communications Bldg., Knoxville, TN 37916 Tel 615-974-3321.
U of Tex Hum Res, *(Univ. of Texas, Humanities Research Ctr.; 0-87959),* P.O. Box 7219, Austin, TX 78712 Tel 512-471-1833.
U of Tex Pr, *(Univ. of Texas Press; 0-292),* P.O. Box 7819, University Sta., Austin, TX 78712 Tel 512-471-7233.
U of Toronto Pr, *(Univ. of Toronto Press; 0-8020),* Orders to: 33 E. Tupper St., Buffalo, NY 14203 Tel 416-978-2052.
U of Utah Pr, *(Univ. of Utah Press; 0-87480),* Salt Lake City, UT 84112 Tel 801-581-6771.
U of Wash Pr, *(Univ. of Washington Press; 0-295),* Seattle, WA 98105 Tel 206-543-4050.
U of Wis Pr, *(Univ. of Wisconsin Press; 0-299),* 114 North Murray St., Madison, WI 53715 Tel 608-262-8782.
U Pr of Amer, *(University Press of America; 0-8191),* 4710 Auth Place, S.E., Washington, DC 20023 Tel 301-899-9600.
U Pr of Hawaii, *(Univ. Press of Hawaii; 0-8248),* 2840 Kolowalu St., Honolulu, HI 96822 Tel 808-948-8255.
U Pr of Idaho, *(Univ. Press of Idaho; 0-89301),* Div. of the Idaho Research Foundation, Inc., University Sta., Box 3368, Moscow, ID 83843 Tel 208-885-7925.
U Pr of Ky, *(Univ. Press of Kentucky; 0-8131),* Lexington, KY 40506 Tel 606-258-2951.
U Pr of Miss, *(Univ. Press of Mississippi; 0-87805),* 3825 Ridgewood Rd., Jackson, MS 39211 Tel 601-982-6205.
U Pr of New Eng, *(Univ. Press of New England; 0-87451),* P.O. Box 979, Hanover, NH 03755 Tel 603-646-3348.
U Pr of Va, *(Univ. Press of Virginia; 0-8139),* P.O. Box 3608, University Sta., Charlottesville, VA 22903 Tel 804-924-3468.
U Pr of Wash, *(Univ. Press of Washington, D.C.; 0-87419),* University Press Bldg., Delbrook Campus C.A.S., Riverton, VA 22651 Tel 703-635-9562.
U Presses Fla, *(Univ. Presses of Fla.; 0-8130),* 15 N.W. 15th St., Gainesville, FL 32603 Tel 904-392-1351.
UAHC, *(Union of American Hebrew Congregations; 0-8074),* 838 Fifth Ave., New York, NY 10021 Tel 212-249-0100.
Ukrainian Acad, *(Ukrainian Academic Press; 0-87287),* Div. of Libraries Unlimited, Inc., P.O. Box 263, Littleton, CO 80160 Tel 303-770-1220.
Ultramarine Pub, *(Ultramarine Publishing Co., Inc.; 0-89366),* P.O. Box 599, Midtown Sta., New York, NY 10018.
Ungar, *(Ungar, Frederick, Publishing Co., Inc.; 0-8044),* 250 Park Ave. S., New York, NY 10003 Tel 212-473-7885.
United Church Pr
See Pilgrim NY
Univ Graphics, *(University Graphics; 0-934932),* Southern Illinois University, Carbondale, IL 62901 Tel 618-536-3325.
Univ Microfilms, *(University Microfilms International; 0-8357),* A Xerox Publishing Co., 300 N. Zeeb Rd., Ann Arbor, MI 48106 Tel 313-761-4700; Any Book with Standard-Size Type Can Be Reproduced in Large Type Format with Permission from Author or Publish.r.
Univ of Trees, *(Univ. of the Trees Press; 0-916438),* P.O. Box 644, 13165 Pine St., Boulder Creek, CA 95006 Tel 408-338-3855.
Univ Place, *(University Place Book Shop; 0-911556),* 821 Broadway, New York, NY 10003 Tel 212-254-5998.
Universe, *(Universe Books, Inc.; 0-87663),* 381 Park Ave., S., New York, NY 10016 Tel 212-685-7400. *Imprints:* Pica Pr (Pica Press).
University *Imprint of* **Exposition**
UPBS, *(University Press Book Service; 0-8295),* 302 Fifth Ave., New York, NY 10001.
Utah St U Pr, *(Utah State Univ. Press; 0-87421),* UMC 95, Logan, UT 84322 Tel 801-750-1632.
Valkyrie Pr, *(Valkyrie Press, Inc.; 0-912760; 0-934616),* 2135 First Ave., S., St. Petersburg, FL 33712 Tel 813-822-6069.
Valley Calif, *(Valley Pubs.; 0-913548),* 8 East Olive Ave., Fresno, CA 93728 Tel 209-485-2690.
Value Comm, *(Value Communications, Inc.; 0-916392),* Subs. of Oak Tree Pubns., Inc., 11175 Flintkote Ave., Suite C, San Diego, CA 92121 Tel 714-452-8676.
Van Nos Reinhold, *(Van Nostrand Reinhold Co.; 0-442),* Div. of Litton Educational Publishing, Inc., 135 W. 50th St., New York, NY 10020 Tel 212-265-8700; Orders to: Lepi Order Processing, 7625 Empire Dr., Florence, KY 41042. *Imprints:* Anv (Anvil Books).
Vanderbilt U Pr, *(Vanderbilt Univ. Press; 0-8265),* 2505(Rear) West End Ave., Nashville, TN 37203 Tel 615-322-3585.
Vanguard, *(Vanguard Press, Inc.; 0-8149),* 424 Madison Ave., New York, NY 10017 Tel 212-753-3906.
Vanilla, *(Vanilla Press; 0-917266),* 2400 Colfax Ave. S., Minneapolis, MN 55405 Tel 612-374-4726.
Vantage, *(Vantage Press, Inc.; 0-533),* 516 W. 34th St., New York, NY 10001 Tel 212-736-1767.
Vedanta Pr, *(Vedanta Press; 0-87481),* 1946 Vedanta Place, Hollywood, CA 90068 Tel 213-465-7114; Orders to: P.O. Box 290, Hollywood, CA 90028.
Vermont Bks, *(Vermont Books, Inc.; 0-911570),* 38 Main St., Middlebury, VT 05753 Tel 802-388-2061.
Verry, *(Verry, Lawrence, Inc.; 0-8426),* Mystic, CT 06355 Tel 203-536-7373.
Vestal, *(Vestal Press Ltd.; 0-911572),* P.O. Box 97, 320 N. Jensen Rd., Vestal, NY 13850 Tel 607-797-4872.
Victor Bks, *(Victor Books; 0-88207),* P.O. Box 1825, Wheaton, IL 60187 Tel 312 668-6000, Orders to: 1825 College Ave., Wheaton, IL 60187.

Vienna Hse, *(Vienna House, Inc.; 0-8443),* 342 Madison Ave., New York, NY 10017 Tel 212-986-7724.
Vigo Pr, *(Vigo Press; 0-911574),* P.O. Box 2317, Dallas, TX 75221 Tel 214-521-6753.
Viking Pr, *(Viking Press, Inc.; 0-670),* 625 Madison Ave., New York, NY 10022 Tel 212-755-4330; Orders to: Viking/Penguin, Inc., 299 Murray Hill Pkwy., East Rutherford, NJ 07073.
Vin *Imprint of* **Random**
Virgo Pr, *(Virgo Press; 0-930558),* P.O. Box 402651, Miami Beach, FL 33140 Tel 305-538-6324.
Virtuoso, *(Virtuoso Pubns., Inc.; 0-918624),* 206 S.E. 46th Lane, Cape Coral, FL 33904 Tel 813-549-1802; Orders to: P.O. Box 56, Cape Coral, FL 33904.
Vision Hse, *(Vision House Pubs.; 0-88449),* 1651 E. Edinger, Suite 104, Santa Ana, CA 92705 Tel 714-558-0511.
VoyB *Imprint of* **HarBraceJ**
W A Benjamin
See A-W
W Kaufmann, *(Kaufmann, William, Inc.; 0-913232),* 1 First St., Los Altos, CA 94022 Tel 415-948-5810.
W S Sullwold, *(Sullwold, William S., Publishing, Inc.; 0-88492),* 18 Pearl St., Taunton, MA 02780 Tel 617-823-0924.
Walck, *(Walck, Henry Z., Inc.; 0-8098),* Div. of David McKay Co. Inc., c/o David McKay Co., Inc., 2 Park Ave., New York, NY 10016 Tel 212-340-9800.
Walker & Co, *(Walker & Co.; 0-8027),* 720 Fifth Ave., New York, NY 10019 Tel 212-265-3632.
Wallaby *Imprint of* **PB**
Wallace-Homestead, *(Wallace-Homestead Book Co.; 0-87069),* 1912 Grand Ave., Des Moines, IA 50305 Tel 515-243-6181.
Wallis Pubns, *(Wallis Pubns.; 0-930148),* 3485 Sylvan Lane, Melbourne, FL 32935 Tel 305-727-1270.
Wanderer Bks, *(Wanderer Books; 0-671),* Div. of Simon & Schuster, 1230 Ave. of the Americas, New York, NY 10020.
Warne, *(Warne, Frederick, & Co., Inc.; 0-7232),* 2 Park Ave., New York, NY 10016 Tel 212-686-9630.
Warner Bks, *(Warner Books, Inc.; 0-446),* 75 Rockefeller Plaza, New York, NY 10019 Tel 212-484-8000; Orders to: Independent News Co., 75 Rockefeller Plaza, New York, NY 10019; Name Formerly Paperback Lib
Watson-Guptill, *(Watson-Guptill Pubns., Inc.; 0-8230),* 1 Astor Plaza, 1515 Broadway, New York, NY 10036 Tel 212-764-7300; Orders to: 2160 Patterson St., Cincinnati, OH 45214.
Watts, *(Watts, Franklin, Inc.; 0-531),* Subs. of Grolier Inc., 730 Fifth Ave., New York, NY 10019 Tel 212-757-4050. *Imprints:* Fontana Pap (Fontana Paperbacks).
Wayne St U Pr, *(Wayne State Univ. Press; 0-8143),* The Leonard N. Simons Bldg., 5959 Woodward Ave., Detroit, MI 48202 Tel 313-577-4603.
Waynor, *(Waynor Publishing Co.; 0-917070),* 152 Sumner Ave., Springfield, MA 01108 Tel 413-733-2149.
Weatherhill, *(Weatherhill, John, Inc.; 0-8348),* Asia House, Derby Square, Salem, MA 01970 Tel 617-745-8257; Dist. by: Charles E. Tuttle, Co., Inc., 28 S. Main St., Rutland, VT 05701.
Wehman, *(Wehman Brothers, Inc.; 0-911604),* Ridgedale Ave., Morris County Mall, Cedar Knolls, NJ 07927 Tel 201-539-6300.
Weills
See Berkley Pub
Weiser, *(Weiser, Samuel, Inc.; 0-87728),* 625 Broadway, New York, NY 10012 Tel 212-777-6361.
West Pub, *(West Publishing Co.; 0-8299),* 50 W. Kellogg Blvd., P.O. Box 3526, St. Paul, MN 55165 Tel 612-228-2500; 170 Old Country Rd., Mineola, NY 11501 Tel 516-248-1900.
Western Islands, *(Western Islands; 0-88279),* 395 Concord Ave., Belmont, MA 02178 Tel 617-489-0600.
Golden Pr Golden Press C
Westernlore, *(Westernlore Pubns.; 0-87026),* 126 La Porte, Unit F, Arcadia, CA 91006 Tel 213-445-7119; Orders to: P.O. Box 4304, Pasadena, CA 91106.
Westminster, *(Westminster Press; 0-644),* 925 Chestnut St., Philadelphia, PA 19107 Tel 215-928-2700; Orders to: Order Dept., P.O. Box 718 Wm. Penn Annex, Philadelphia, PA 19105.
Westview, *(Westview Press; 0-89158),* 5500 Central Ave., Boulder, CO 80301 Tel 303-444-3541.
Weyand-Shaw, *(Weyand/Shaw Pubns.; 0-9601922),* 5460 Whiteoak, Suite B-203, Encino, CA 91316 Tel 213-783-1820.
Weybright
See McKay
Wheelwright, *(Bond Wheelwright Co.; 0-87027),* Box 296, Freeport, ME 04032 Tel 207-865-4951.
Whitston Pub, *(Whitston Publishing Co., Inc.; 0-87875),* P.O. Box 958, Troy, NY 12181 Tel 518-283-4363.
Wiley, *(Wiley, John, & Sons, Inc.; 0-471),* 605 Third Ave., New York, NY 10016 Tel 212-867-9800.
William Carey Lib, *(William Carey Library Pubs.; 0-87808),* 1705 N. Sierra Bonita Ave., Pasadena, CA 91104 Tel 213-798-0819.
William-F, *(William-Frederick Press, 0-87164),* 308 E. 79th St., New York, NY 10021 Tel 212-628-1995.
Willow Hse, *(Willow House Pubs., Inc.; 0-912450),* Box 155, Aptos, CA 95003 Tel 408-688-4128.
Wilshire, *(Wilshire Book Co.; 0-87980),* 12015 Sherman Rd., North Hollywood, CA 91605 Tel 213-875-1711.
Wilson, *(Wilson, H. W.; 0-8242),* 950 University Ave., Bronx, NY 10452 Tel 212-588-8400.
Wimmer Bks, *(Wimmer Brothers Books; 0-918544),* P.O. Box 18408, Memphis, TN 38118 Tel 901-362-8900.
Winchester Pr, *(Winchester Press; 0-87691),* P.O. Box 1260, Tulsa, OK 74101 Tel 918-836-0409.
Windhover *Imprint of* **Berkley Pub**
Winston Pr, *(Winston Press, Inc.; 0-03),* Subs. of CBS Educational Publishing, 430 Oak Grove, Suite 203, Minneapolis, MN 55403 Tel 612-871-7000.
Wisdom House, *(Wisdom House Press; 0-932560),* 4030 Raleigh Ave. S., Minneapolis, MN 55416 Tel 612-920-0510.
Word Bks, *(Word, Inc.; 0-87680; 0-8499),* P.O. Box 1790, Waco, TX 76703 Tel 817-772-7650.
Word of Life
See Servant
Word Serv, *(Word Services & Pied Pubns. Publishing Co.; 0-918626),* 1927 S. 26th St., Lincoln, NE 68502.
World Wide OR, *(World Wide Publishing Corp.; 0-930294),* P.O. Box 105, Ashland, OR 97520 Tel 503-482-3800; Formerly Named Hans World Wide Evangelism.
World Wide Pubs, *(World Wide Pubns.; 0-89066),* 1303 Hennepin Ave., Minneapolis, MN 55403 Tel 612-336-0940.
Writing, *(Writing Works Inc.; 0-916076),* 7438 S.E. 40th St., Mercer Island, WA 98040 Tel 206-232-2171.
WSP, *(Washington Square Press, Inc.),* Div. of Simon & Schuster, Inc., 1230 Ave. of the Americas, New York, NY 10020.
Wyden, *(Wyden Books; 0-87223),* Div. of P.E.I. Books, Inc., 747 Third Ave., New York, NY 10017 Tel 212-688-3030; P.O. Box 151, Ridgefield, CT 06877 Tel 203-438-9631; Dist. by: Harper & Row Pubs., Inc., Keystone Industrial Park, Scranton, PA 18512.
Wynnehaven, *(Wynnehaven Pub. Co.; 0-9601476),* 212 Ocean St., Beach Haven, NJ 08008 Tel 609-492-3601.
Yale U Pr, *(Yale Univ. Press; 0-300),* 302 Temple St., New Haven, CT 06520 Tel 203-432-4969; Orders to: 92A Yale Sta., New Haven, CT 06520.
Yankee Bookmen
See Heritage Bk
YB *Imprint of* **Dell**
Ye Galleon, *(Ye Galleon Press; 0-87770),* P.O. Box 25, Fairfield, WA 99012 Tel 509-283-2422.
Zen Ctr LA
See Center Pubns
Zenger Pub, *(Zenger Publishing Co., Inc.; 0-89201),* P.O. Box 9883, Washington, DC 20015 Tel 301-881-1470.
Zephyrus Pr, *(Zephyrus Press, Inc.; 0-914264),* 417 Maitland Ave., Teaneck, NJ 07666 Tel 201-833-0717.
Zondervan, *(Zondervan Publishing House; 0-310),* 1415 Lake Dr., S.E., Grand Rapids, MI 49506 Tel 616-459-6900.